1999

National Trade and Professional Associations

of the United States

Columbia Books, Inc.
Publishers
Washington, DC

Senior Editor: Buck Downs
Assistant Editor: Sarah E. White
Assistant Editor: Andrew G. Wood
Assistant Editor: Nkosi O. Yearwood

Thirty-fourth Edition – 1999
Copyright © by Columbia Books, Inc.

ISBN 1-880873-33-8
ISSN 0734-0734

Editorial Office

Suite 330
1212 New York Ave., N.W.
Washington, DC 20005
Phone: (202) 898-0662
E-mail: info@columbiabooks.com

Customer Service

P.O. Box 69
Spencerville, MD 20868-0069
Toll-free: (888) 265-0600

1999 National
Trade and
Professional
Associations

Table Of Contents

Introduction

The *National Trade and Professional Associations (NTPA)* directory lists over 7,600 trade associations, professional societies, labor unions, and similar national groups. It is unique in providing a comprehensive listing focused on the trade associations segment of the U.S. non-profit community.

The associations listed in *NTPA* are an important segment of the American business community. Each has been formed to advance knowledge and provide support for a particular occupation, industry, or field of study. These voluntary, cooperative organizations provide learning opportunities and a central resource for technical information, mentoring and networking. In this sense, they reflect a long history, dating back to the craft and merchant guilds of medieval Europe.

The individual listings and indexes of *NTPA* provide an overview of association activity in the U.S. *NTPA* is intended as a resource for people and businesses interested in the organizations which serve a specific profession or operate in a particular area, or for those who have an interest in the U.S. trade associations community as a whole.

Associations vary widely in the types of benefits and services conferred by membership, as well as in organizational structure and types of members. The concepts of professionalism and advancement that are at the heart of any association's mission find different ways of expression in almost every case. What follows is a brief description of the kinds of information found in *NTPA*.

Executives and Staff

Every association requires a coordinator or administrator to handle its affairs. In many cases, particularly among smaller or more specialized societies, the administrator is an elected officer from the ranks of the association's membership. Such an elected volunteer will serve as President, Chair, or Secretary for a term of 1-3 years. Other small associations are managed by volunteers on a permanent basis. There are some 2,000-2,500 of these member-administered associations listed in NTPA. Typically, the description of such an organization will include a statement to the effect that the association has no paid officers or full-time staff.

Even within the associations that employ a professional staff, there are may groups that provide a range of services and are leaders in their industry but do so with a minimal staff. There are only a few hundred associations listed in NTPA whose employees number in the dozens or hundreds. The majority of the associations found in NTPA have a staff of 1-10 people, with an Exec. Director (the most common designation) and a small support staff.

For each listing in the main body of the book (the "Association Index") we list at least one contact person, whether it is an elected volunteer, a permanent volunteer or single administrator, or an executive who serves as chief of staff. They are the primary contacts for their associations, serving as liaison to the Board of Directors and C.E.O. for the organization.

In addition, where applicable, we have included names and titles of staff members

who have been designated as contact in one of several administrative areas:

- Communications/Public Relations
- Government Relations
- Meetings & Conferences
- Education
- Administration
- Membership
- Publications
- Information Systems

Most of the organizations listed in NTPA do not have a specific contact for each of these administrative areas. But for those seeking more specific information about a larger organization's programs, the additional staff listings will serve to expedite an inquiry.

Association Size, History and Programs

As many as three statistical indicators of an association's size can be found in a typical NTPA listing. They are: number of members, number of full-time staff, and a budget size. Budget size is noted using one of fourteen budget categories in NTPA. A list of the organizations in each category can be found in the Budget Index.

Also included in each listing is a brief description of that association's history, purpose, membership, and programs. Again, these vary from association to association, depending on the age of the association and the type of membership it serves. Specific programs or subsidiaries are noted in the Historical Note, as well as any professional designations the association confers, political action committees and foundations, and alliances with other associations. Information on membership fees or dues is generally provided in this note.

Publications

Central to any association's role as a disseminator of information is the publication of newsletters, journals, and other periodicals for its membership. Any such serials published by the association and distributed to its members is included, along with a note on how frequently the publication appears (monthly, quarterly, etc.) and whether or not the publication regularly accepts advertising.

With the growth of digital communications, many associations now maintain an information presence on the World Wide Web in addition to or in place of traditional paper documents. The Web sites and e-mail addresses that provide access to these information resources are included in the contact information for each association, when available. As in many industries, the growth of association presence on the Web has been rapid. Since the 1996 edition, when we first began to include e-mail and Web addresses, the number of organizations with an Internet presence has grown, from a comparative handful to the majority of listed associations in this edition.

Meetings and Conventions

For many associations, the annual meeting or convention is the single most visible representation of the mission and goals of the association. Continuing education, professional networking, the exchange of ideas, and general fellowship combine to affirm an industry's continued vitality and the association's service to its members. NTPA lists approximately 11,000 conventions, meetings, trade shows, and similar functions sponsored by national associations for the benefit of their members. Also included are the names and titles of approximately 1,200 executive staff members with primary responsibility for meetings and conventions, and over 800 executive staff responsible for continuing education and training.

Using NTPA

The main body of the book, called the Association Index, contains the full listing for each association, along with cross-references for recent name changes, etc., in alphabetical order by organization name. Following the Association Index are five separate indexes:

1. Subject Index

For users interested in particular industries or occupations, the Subject Index provides about 200 different categories. Associations may be listed in as many as four categories.

2. Geographic Index

Associations are cross-referenced based on the city and state in which they are located.

3. Budget Index

An alphabetical list of associations in each of the fourteen budget categories.

4. Executive Index

Each executive listed in NTPA is listed here alphabetically, along with his or her association affiliation.

5. Acronym Index

Associations are often informally known by the abbreviations called Acronyms. The Acronym Index lists all such abbreviations, with the associations to which they refer.

The last section of NTPA is a roster of U.S. Association Management Firms. These are companies who provide professional and administrative services to a number of client associations on a contract basis. There are over 400 such firms listed, with contact information and a list of association clients.

DISTRIBUTION OF ASSOCIATION HEADQUARTERS BY STATE

Below is a listing of the twenty-four states that are home to at least 1% of the associations listed in NTPA. The actual number of associations in each state is also listed.

State	Number of Associations
District of Columbia	1,168
Virginia	839
Illinois	723
New York	692
California	459
Maryland	412
Texas	262
Pennsylvania	236
Ohio	235
Florida	229
New Jersey	204
Georgia	168
Missouri	168
Colorado	161
Massachusetts	131
North Carolina	124
Michigan	117
Indiana	110
Wisconsin	109
Minnesota	101
Kansas	87
Kentucky	86
Arizona	80
Tennessee	78

DISTRIBUTION BY BUDGET CATEGORY

Budgets included in each association's listing refer to the annual operating budget of the association. Listed below are the fourteen categories used in NTPA, along with the number of listees in each.

Budget Category	Number of Associations
under $10,000	575
$10-25,000	449
$25-50,000	462
$50-100,000	658
$100-250,000	996
$250-500,000	938
$500,000-1 Million	738
$1-2 Million	697
$2-5 Million	631
$5-10 Million	288
$10-25 Million	195
$25-50 Million	64
$50-100 Million	30
over $100 Million	22
No Budget Reported	1121

DISTRIBUTION BY SELECTED SUBJECTS

Each association listed in NTPA may be cross-referenced in as many as four subject categories. Below are twenty-four common industry categories, with the number of associations in each.

Category	Number of Associations
Agriculture	190
Automotive Industry	132
Apparel and Textiles	102
Banking and Finance	196
Broadcasting	95
Chemicals and Chemical Industry	110
Computers	183
Construction	187
Consultants	59
Electricity and Electronics	101
Food	163
Government	351
Health Care	203
Law	238
Manufacturing	664
Medicine	623
Mental Health	42
Nursing	100
Pharmaceutical Industry	60
Psychology and Psychiatry	148
Retailing	61
Transportation	94
Veterinary Medicine	62
Wholesalers	122

Association Index

The following listings include over 7,600 active national trade associations, professional societies, technical organizations, and labor unions. For each organization, the latest pertinent information has been compiled. Included among the current listings are references to organizations previously listed in NTPA that have since ceased operations, and cross-references to track association name changes.

AACE Internat'l (1956)

209 Prairie Ave., Suite 100
Morgantown, WV 26501
Tel: (304)296-8444 *Fax:* (304)291-5728
Toll Free: (800)858 - 2678
E-Mail: 76341.116@compuserve.com or info@aacei.org
Web Site: http://www.aacei.org
Members: 6,100 individuals
Staff: 14
Annual Budget: $1-2,000,000
Interim Exec. Director: Barry G. McMillan
Managing Editor: Kathy DeWeese
Meetings Manager: Charla Miller
Manager, Finance: Carol G. Rogers

Historical Note
Formerly (1993) American Ass'n of Cost Engineers. A professional society of individuals interested in applying scientific principles to the solution of problems of cost management, engineering estimating, cost control, planning and scheduling, project management, and profitability. Membership: $95/year.

Publications:
Cost Engineering. m. adv.
Cost Engineers Notebook. irreg.
Directory. a.
Transactions. a.

Meetings/Conferences:
Annual Meetings: July/1,000
1999 – Denver, CO(Sheraton Tech Center)/June 27-30
2000 – Calgary, Alberta(Palasier/Skyline Plaza)/June 25-28
2001 – Pittsburgh, PA(Hilton)/June 24-27
2002 – Portland, OR(Doubletree Hayden Island)

AACSB - the Internat'l Ass'n for Management Education (1916)

600 Emerson Rd., Suite 300
St. Louis, MO 63141-6762
Tel: (314)872-8481 *Fax:* (314)872-8495
Web Site: http://www.aacsb.edu
Members: 800 institutions
Staff: 30
Annual Budget: $2-5,000,000
Exec. V. President: William K. Laidlaw, Jr.
Director, Communications: Sharon Barber
Director, Public Policy: Janet Hall
Director, Conferences: Anita Craig
Director, Finance: Jane T. Rubin
Director, Projects and Services: Charles Hickman

Historical Note
Founded as American Ass'n of Collegiate Schools of Business; Became American Ass'n of Collegiate Schools of Business in 1973, and assumed its current name in 1997. Accrediting body for business administration and accounting education programs at the baccalaureate, master's degree, and doctoral levels.

Publications:
AACSB Newsline. q.

Meetings/Conferences:
1999 – Atlanta, GA/April 18-21

Abrasive Grain Ass'n (1933)

30200 Detroit Road
Cleveland, OH 44145-1967
Tel: (440)899-0010 *Fax:* (440)892-1404
Web Site: http://www.abrasivegrain.org
Members: 7 companies
Staff: 3
Annual Budget: $50-100,000
Manager: J. Jeffery Wherry

Historical Note
Members make natural and artificial grains used in grinding wheels, coated abrasives, etc.

Meetings/Conferences:
Semi-Annual Meetings: Spring and Fall
1999 – Ft. Lauderdale, FL(Marriott Harbor)/April 17-20
1999 – Cleveland, OH(Ritz-Carlton)/80

Abrasives Engineering Soc. (1956)

P.O. Box 3157
Butler, PA 16003
Tel: (724)282-6210
Members: 300 individuals
Staff: 1
Annual Budget: $25-50,000
Business Manager: Theodore L. Giese

Historical Note
Membership: $55/year (individual); $350/year (organization).

Publications:
Abrasive Users NewsFax. bi-w.
Proceedings, International Technical Conference. a.

Meetings/Conferences:
Annual Meetings: Spring/225

Academic Language Therapy Ass'n

4020 McEwen, Suite 105
Dallas, TX 75244-5019
Tel: (972)233-9107 *Fax:* (972)490-4219
Annual Budget: $25-50,000
Exec. Director: Madeleine Crouch

Historical Note
Membership: $40/year (individual); $25/year (student).

Publications:
ALTA Bulletin. q. adv.

Meetings/Conferences:
Annual Meetings: Spring

Academic Orthopaedic Soc. (1971)

6300 N. River Road, Suite 727
Rosemont, IL 60018-4226
Tel: (847)698-1694 *Fax:* (847)823-0536
Members: 500 individuals
Staff: 2
Ass'n Manager: Nancy Franzon

Historical Note
Formerly (1989) Ass'n of Orthopaedic Chairmen and (1991) American Orthopaedic Soc. AOS members are chairmen of orthopaedic departments and medical school divisions and faculty.

Publications:
Directory. a.
Presidential Newsletter. q.

Meetings/Conferences:
Annual Meetings: in conjunction with Ass'n of American Medical Colleges

Academy for Implants and Transplants (1972)

P.O. Box 223
Springfield, VA 22150
Tel: (703)451-0001 *Fax:* (703)451-0004
Members: 250 individuals
Annual Budget: $10-25,000
Secretary-Treasurer: Anthony J. Viscidio, D.D.S.

Historical Note
Dentists engaged in the field of implants and transplants. Has no paid staff. Membership: $150/year (individual).

Publications:
Implant Dentistry Journal. adv. adv.
Oral Implantologist. semi-a. adv.
Update Newsletter. irreg.

Meetings/Conferences:
Annual Meetings: Spring

Academy for Interscience Methodology (1961)

Historical Note
Organization defunct in 1997.

Academy for Sports Dentistry (1983)

Historical Note
Address unknown in 1998.

Academy of Accounting Historians (1973)

University of Alabama, Box 870220
Culverhouse School of Accountancy
Tuscaloosa, AL 35487-0220
Tel: (205)348-2903 *Fax:* (205)348-8453
Web Site: http://www.weatherhead.cwru.edu/accounting
Members: 850 individuals
Secretary: William D. Samson

Historical Note
AAH members are individuals and institutional affiliates with an interest in accounting/economic history. Membership: $40/year (individual); $48/year (organization/company), $90/year (institution).

Publications:
Accounting Historians Journal. semi-a.
Accounting Historians Notebook Newsletter. semi-a.
Membership Directory. a.
Mongraph Series. irreg.

Meetings/Conferences:
Annual Meetings: in conjunction with the American Accounting Ass'n
2000 – Barcelona, Spain

Academy of Ambulatory Foot Surgery (1972)

600 Lurleen Wallace Blvd. South
Tuscaloosa, AL 35401
Tel: (205)758-3678 *Fax:* (205)758-3688
Members: 1,500 individuals
Staff: 3
Annual Budget: $250-500,000
Exec. Director: Stanford Rosen, M.D.

Historical Note
Podiatric surgeons who specialize in surgical procedures that do not require hospitalization. Incorporated in the State of Pennsylvania. Membership: $345/year.

Publications:
Journal of the Academy of Ambulatory Foot Surgery. a. adv.
Newsletter. bi-m. adv.

Meetings/Conferences:

Academy of Aphasia (1962)

Dept. of Comm. Sciences & Disorders
Northwestern University
Evanston, IL 60208
Tel: (708)491-5073
Web Site: http://www.cortex.neurology.umab.edu/academy
Members: 200 individuals
Annual Budget: under $10,000
Board Secretary: Cynthia Thompson

Historical Note
Researchers specializing in the study of total or partial loss of speech due to brain damage. Has no paid staff. Membership: $50/year.

Publications:
Membership Directory. irreg.

Meetings/Conferences:
Annual Meetings: October (location determined by availability of volunteer coordinator)
1999 – Venice, Italy/October 23-26

Academy of Behavioral Medicine Research (1979)

Dept. of Biobehavioral Health
315 Health/Human Development East
University Park, PA 16802

Tel: (814)863-7256
Members: 275 individuals
Secretary: Lynn T. Kozlowski, Ph.D.
Historical Note
ABMR members are individuals actively pursuing research in more than one aspect of behavioral science.
Publications:
AMBR Membership Directory. a.
Perspectives on Behavioral Medicine. a.
Meetings/Conferences:
Annual Meetings: June
1999 – Wintergreen, VA

Academy of Clinical Laboratory Physicians and Scientists

Univ. of Utah, School of Medicine
500 Chipeta Way, Dept. of Pathology
Salt Lake City, UT 84108
Tel: (801)583-2787   *Fax:* (801)583-2712
Web Site: http://zapruder.path.med.umich.edu/users/aclps
Secretary-Treasurer: Ronald L. Weiss, M.D., M.B.
Historical Note
ACLPS members are physicians, scientists and educators primarily engaged in teaching, research and service in academic laboratory medicine, also known as clinical pathology. Membership: $75/year.
Meetings/Conferences:
Annual Meetings: June

Academy of Country Music *(1964)*

6255 Sunset Blvd., Suite 923
Hollywood, CA 90028-7410
Tel: (323)462-2351   *Fax:* (323)462-3253
E-Mail: acmoffice@value.net
Web Site: http://www.acmcountry.com
Members: 4,000 individuals
Staff: 4
Exec. Director: Fran Boyd
Historical Note
Formerly the Country and Western Music Academy, the Academy is involved in numerous activities and envents which promote country music, including an annual awards show. The Academy's members are individuals earning income from the country music industry. Membership: $60/year (individual).
Publications:
Academy of Country Music Newsletter. m. adv.
Meetings/Conferences:

Academy of Criminal Justice Sciences *(1963)*

1500 N. Beauregard St.
Suite 101
Alexandria, VA 22311
Tel: (703)379-2090   *Fax:* (703)379-8867
Toll Free: (800)757 - 2257
E-Mail: acjs@nku.edu
Web Site: http://www.nku.edu/~acjs
Members: 3,800 individuals
Staff: 3
Annual Budget: $250-500,000
Exec. Director: Patricia DeLancey
Historical Note
Professors and institutions who teach courses in criminology, law enforcement and corrections. Membership: $45/year (individual); $100/year (institution).
Publications:
ACJS Membership Directory. a. adv.
ACJS Program Book. a. adv.
ACJS Today. q. adv.
Employment Bulletin. 8/yr. adv.
Journal of Criminal Justice Education. semi-a. adv.
Justice Quarterly. q. adv.
Meetings/Conferences:
Annual Meetings: March
1999 – Orlando, FL(Coronado Springs)/March 10-14
2000 – New Orleans, LA(Sheraton)/March 21-25

Academy of Dental Materials *(1940)*

P.O. Box 660677
Dallas, TX 75266-0677
Tel: (214)828-8378   *Fax:* (214)874-4503
E-Mail: Dentmatr@airmail.net
Members: 340 individuals
Staff: 2
Annual Budget: $50-100,000
Editor: Victoria A. Marker, Ph.D.
Historical Note
Formerly (1983) American Academy for Plastics Research in Dentistry. Membership: $140/year.
Publications:
ADM Newsletter. 2-3/year.
Dental Materials Journal. bi-m. adv.
Meetings/Conferences:
Semi-Annual Meetings: late Winter and Fall

Academy of Dental Prosthetics

Historical Note
Address unknown in 1996.

Academy of Dentistry for Persons with Disabilities *(1952)*

211 E. Chicago Ave., Suite 948
Chicago, IL 60611
Tel: (312)440-2660   *Fax:* (312)440-2824
Members: 500 individuals
Staff: 3
Annual Budget: $250-500,000
Exec. Director: John S. Rutkauskas, D.D.S., MS

Historical Note
Established as the Academy for Oral Rehabilitation of Handicapped Persons by a group of dentists at a meeting of the American Dental Ass'n in September 1952. Incorporated in Delaware in 1953. In February 1957 the name was changed to the Academy of Dentistry for the Handicapped, changed to current name in 1994. Affiliated with the Federation of Special Care Organizations in Dentistry. Membership: $120/year (individual).
Publications:
Interface. q.
Special Care in Dentistry. bi-m. adv.
Meetings/Conferences:
1999 – Chicago, IL(Westin Hotel)/March 26-28

Academy of Dentistry Internat'l *(1974)*

5125 MacArthur Blvd., N.W.
Suite 50
Washington, DC 20016-3315
Tel: (202)364-8349   *Fax:* (202)364-8349
E-Mail: adintl@mindspring.com
Web Site: http://www.adint.org
Members: 2,400 individuals
Staff: 2
Annual Budget: $100-250,000
Exec. Director: Henry J. Sazima, D.D.S.
Historical Note
An honorary international dental society established and incorporated in California, ADI promotes and fosters continuing education and service projects world-wide for the dental profession. Membership: $80/year.
Publications:
International Communicator. semi-a.
Meetings/Conferences:
Annual Meetings: Fall with the American Dental Ass'n
1999 – Honolulu, HI

Academy of Dispensing Audiologists *(1977)*

3008 Millwood Ave.
Columbia, SC 29205
Tel: (803)252-5646   *Fax:* (803)765-0860
Toll Free: (800)445 - 8629
Web Site: www.audiologist.org
Members: 1000 individuals
Annual Budget: $50-100,000
Admin. Director: Carol H. Davis
Historical Note
Professional organization of audiologists dispensing hearing aids in rehabilitative practice. Membership: $120/year (fellow/associate), $25/year (student).
Publications:
ADA Feedback Newsletter. q. adv.
Membership Directory. a.
Meetings/Conferences:
Annual Meetings: Summer
1999 – Bermuda/Oct. 27-31

Academy of Family Mediators *(1981)*

5 Militia Drive
Lexington, MA 02421
Tel: (781)674-2663   *Fax:* (781)674-2690
Toll Free: (800)292 - 4236
Members: 3,700 individuals
Staff: 5
Annual Budget: $500-1,000,000
Exec. Director: Kathy Fazzalaro
Historical Note
Members are mediators who specialize in resolving family disputes. Membership: $145/year (practitioner); $105/year (general member).
Publications:
Mediation News. q.
Meetings/Conferences:
1999 – Chicago, IL

Academy of General Dentistry *(1952)*

211 East Chicago Ave., Suite 1200
Chicago, IL 60611-2670
Tel: (312)440-4300   *Fax:* (312)440-0559
E-Mail: AGDDENTED@aol.com
Web Site: http://www.agd.org
Members: 35,000 individuals
Staff: 66
Annual Budget: $5-10,000,000
Exec. Director: Harold E. Donnell, Jr., CAE
Director, Communications: Jo Ellyn Posselt
Director, Meeting Planning: Kathi Donovan
Director, Continuing Education: Betty A. Warner, CAE
Comptroller: Marcia Zitowsky
Director, Administrative Services: Barbara Emery
Director, Membership Services: Mary J. Jawgiel
Historical Note
Serves the needs and represents the interests of general dentists. AGD fosters continued proficiency through quality continuing dental education in order to better serve the public. Has an annual budget of approximately $8.0 million. Membership: $179/year.
Publications:
AGD Impact. 11/year. adv.
General Dentistry. bi-m. adv.
Meetings/Conferences:
Annual Meetings: Summer
1999 – Salt Lake City, UT(Marriott/Salt Palace C.C.)/July 22-25/6000
2000 – Toronto, Canada(Convention Center)/July 20-23/7000

Academy of Homiletics *(1967)*

c/o Lincoln Christian Seminary
100 Campus View Dr.
Lincoln, IL 62656

Tel: (217)732-3168   *Fax:* (217)732-1821
E-Mail: BBurwell@LCCS.EDU
Members: 200 individuals
Annual Budget: under $10,000
Exec. Officer: Wayne Shaw
Historical Note
Members are graduate schools of theology faculty teaching courses in homiletics.
Publications:
Homiletic Journal. semi-a.

Academy of Hospice Physicians *(1988)*

Historical Note
Name changed to American Academy of Hospice and Palliative Medicine in 1996.

Academy of Internat'l Business *(1959)*

Univ. of Hawaii at Manoa, CBA
2404 Maile Way
Honolulu, HI 96822-2223
Tel: (808)956-3665   *Fax:* (808)956-3261
E-Mail: aib@busadm.cba.hawaii.edu
Web Site: http://www.cba.hawaii.edu/aib
Members: 2,700 individuals
Staff: 2
Annual Budget: $100-250,000
Administrator: Laurel King
Historical Note
Formerly (1959) Ass'n for Education in Internat'l Business. Members are teachers and executives in the field of international business. Membership: $68/year (individual); $45/year (student).
Publications:
AIB Newsletter. 4/year.
Journal of International Business Studies. 4/year.
Membership Directory. bien.
Meetings/Conferences:
Annual Meetings: Fall
1999 – Charleston, SC

Academy of Laser Dentistry *(1993)*

10435 Vernon Ave.
Huntington Woods, MI 48070-1526
Tel: (248)548-7171   *Fax:* (248)548-7174
E-Mail: acohen@laserdentistry.org
Web Site: http://www.laserdentistry.org
Members: 500 individuals
Staff: 1
Annual Budget: $100-250,000
Exec. Director: Alison F. Cohen
Historical Note
A product of the merger of the American Academy of Laser Dentistry, the Internat'l Academy of Laser Dentistry and the North American Academy of Laser Dentistry in 1993. ALD promotes the advancement of research and education of laser applications in dentistry. Licensed dentists, auxiliaries, academic and research institutions, dental students, scientists and physicians are eligible for membership; suppliers are eligible for corporate memberships. Membership: $325/year (dentists); $500/year (corporate); $60/year (auxiliaries); $25/year (student).
Publications:
ALD Membership Directory. a.
Journal of Clinical Laser Medicine and Surgery.
Wavelengths. q. adv.
Meetings/Conferences:
Annual Meetings: Winter
1999 – Palm Springs, CA(Doubletree)/Feb. 3-6/250
2000 – Panama City, FL(Marriott Bay Point Resort)/March 1-4

Academy of Legal Studies in Business *(1924)*

Dept. of Finance, 120 Upham Hall
Miami University
Oxford, OH 45056
Tel: (513)529-2945   *Fax:* (513)529-6992
Toll Free: (800)831 - 8180
E-Mail: herrondj@muohio.edu
Members: 1000 individuals
Staff: 1
Annual Budget: $100-250,000
Exec. Secretary: Dr. Daniel J. Herron
Historical Note
Formerly (1991) American Business Law Ass'n. Members are teachers of business law, legal environment and other law-related courses in colleges and universities other than professional law schools. Membership: $50/year.
Publications:
ALSB Newsletter. 3x/year.
American Business Law Journal. q. adv.
Journal of Legal Studies Education. semi-a. adv.
Meetings/Conferences:
Annual Meetings: August
1999 – St. Louis, MO(Adams Mark Hotel)/Aug 3-7

Academy of Managed Care Pharmacy *(1989)*

100 N. Pitt St., #400
Alexandria, VA 22314-3134
Tel: (703)683-8416   *Fax:* (703)683-8417
Toll Free: (800)827 - 2627
Web Site: http://www.amcp.org
Members: 4,000 individuals
Staff: 6
Annual Budget: $2-5,000,000
Exec. Director: Judith A. Cahill
Manager, Communications: Julie MacDonald
Director, Pharmacy Affairs: Richard N. Fry
Director, Membership: Steve Jones
Historical Note
AMCP's mission is to promote the development and application of pharmaceutical care in order to ensure appropriate healthcare outcomes for all individuals. Represents approximately 200

healthcare organizations. Membership: $125/year (pharmacists); $225/year (non-pharmacists); $15/year (students).

Publications:
AMCP News. m.
Journal of Manged Care Pharmacy. bi-m.

Meetings/Conferences:
Annual Meetings: May
1999 – Minneapolis, MN(Hilton & Hyatt
    Regency)/April 29-May 2

Academy of Managed Care Providers (1993)
6285 Spring St., Suite 404
Long Beach, CA 90808-4000
Tel: (562)596-8660   *Fax:* (562)799-3355
Toll Free: (800)297 - 2627
E-Mail: 1)academymcp@aol.com
        2)membership@academymcp.org
Web Site: http://www.academymcp.org
Members: 1,500 individuals
President: Dr. John Russell

Historical Note
Members are companies and individuals interested in the provision of quality managed care. Sponsors education programs and other services. Membership: $75/year (individual); $250/year (company).

Academy of Management (1936)
P.O. Box 3020
Briarcliff Manor, NY 10510-8020
Tel: (914)923-2607   *Fax:* (914)923-2615
E-Mail: aom@academy.pace.edu
Web Site: http://www.aom.pace.edu
Members: 10,000 individuals
Staff: 5
Annual Budget: $1-2,000,000
Exec. Director: Nancy Urbanowicz

Historical Note
Members are professors who research and teach management, as well as doctoral students in management and business professionals interested in principles of management. Membership: $85/year (individual); $42.50/year (student).

Publications:
Academy of Management Executive. q. adv.
Academy of Management Journal. bi-m. adv.
Academy of Management Review. q. adv.
Proceedings. a.

Meetings/Conferences:
Annual Meetings: August/4,800
1999 – Chicago, IL
2000 – Toronto, ON
2001 – Washington, DC
2002 – Denver, CO
2003 – Seattle, WA

Academy of Marketing Science (1971)
P.O. Box 248012
Coral Gables, FL 33124
Tel: (305)284-6673   *Fax:* (305)284-3762
E-Mail: ssultan@miami.edu
Web Site: http://www.ams.web-org
Members: 1,700 individuals
Staff: 2
Annual Budget: $100-250,000
Exec. V. President & Director: Harold W. Berkman, Ph.D.
Coordinator: Sally Sultan

Historical Note
Professional (academicians and marketing executives) society concerned with fostering education in marketing, advancing the science of marketing and furthering professional standards in the discipline. Sponsors and supports the AMS Foundation which provides grants for both the advancement of the teaching of marketing and research in marketing. Membership: $55(U.S. residents); $65 (international).

Publications:
Developments in Marketing Science. a. adv.
Journal of the Academy of Marketing Science. q. adv.
Newsletter. q. adv.
Proceedings. a.

Meetings/Conferences:
Annual Meetings: May/300
1999 – Coral Gables, FL(Biltmore)/May 26-29/250
2000 – Montreal, Canada(Delta Montreal)/May 24-27/250

Academy of Medical-Surgical Nurses (1991)
East Holly Ave., P.O. Box 56
Pitman, NJ 08071-0056
Tel: (609)256-2323   *Fax:* (609)589-7463
Web Site: http://www.amsn.inurse.com
Members: 3,000 individuals
Annual Budget: $100-250,000
Exec. Director: Rick Grimes

Historical Note
AMSN seeks to represent members and promote the implementation of standards for the practice of adult/medical-surgical nursing. Also aims to support the use of guidelines for practice and enhance the image of the professional adult health/medical-surgical nurse. Membership: $75/year (individual).

Publications:
AMSN News. bi-m.
MEDSBURG Nursing. bi-m. adv.

Meetings/Conferences:
1999 – Phoenix, AZ(Hyatt Regency Phoenix)/Sept. 23-26

Academy of Motion Picture Arts and Sciences (1927)
8949 Wilshire Blvd.
Beverly Hills, CA 90211-1972
Tel: (310)247-3000   *Fax:* (310)859-9351
E-Mail: ampas@oscars.org
Web Site: http://www.lightside.com/ampas/

Members: 6,113 individuals
Staff: 100
Annual Budget: $10-25,000,000
Exec. Director: Bruce Davis
Director, Communications: John M. Pavlik
Exec. Administrator: Ric Robertson

Historical Note
A professional honorary organization of motion picture craftsmen and craftswomen founded to advance the arts and sciences of motion pictures; foster cooperation among the creative leadership of the industry for cultural, educational and technological progress; recognize outstanding achievements through annual awards of merit (Oscars); conduct cooperative technical research and stimulate improvement of methods and equipment. Has an annual budget of approximately $13.4 million.

Publications:
Academy Report. q.
Index to Motion Picture Credits. a.
Players Directory. 3/yr.

Meetings/Conferences:
Annual Meetings: Annual Academy Awards Ceremony in Spring

Academy of Operative Dentistry (1972)
P.O. Box 14996
Menomonie, WI 32604
Tel: (352)392-4341   *Fax:* (352)371-4882
E-Mail: gesaod@ufl.edu
Members: 1,050 individuals
Staff: 2
Annual Budget: $100-250,000
Secretary: Greg Smith, M.D.

Historical Note
Membership: $85/year (individual).

Publications:
Journal of Operative Dentistry. q.

Meetings/Conferences:
Annual Meetings: Chicago, IL/Winter
1999 – Chicago, IL/Feb. 17-19

Academy of Oral Diagnosis/Radiology/Medicine
Historical Note
Became American Ass'n of Stomatologists in 1995.

Academy of Oral Dynamics (1946)
8919 Sudley Road
Manassas, VA 22110
Tel: (703)365-2616   *Fax:* (703)331-0356
Members: 85 individuals
Annual Budget: $10-25,000
Exec. Secretary: Edward Paul Byrne, D.D.S., FA

Historical Note
Formerly (1950) Internat'l Academy of Oral Dynamics. Members are dentists interested in the application of biophysical priciples to diagnose, restore and maintain the health of the mouth and its supporting structures. Has no paid officers or full-time staff. Membership: $25/year (active); $15/year (associate).

Publications:
Academy of Oral Dynamics Membership Letters. q.

Meetings/Conferences:
Annual Meetings: Always Washington,
    DC(Sheraton/Hilton)/Spring/100

Academy of Organizational and Occupational Psychiatry
6728 Old McLean Village Drive
McLean, VA 22101
Tel: (703)556-9222   *Fax:* (703)556-8729
E-Mail: AOOP@degnon.org
Web Site: http://www.mcn.com/aoop.htm
Members: 100 individuals
Staff: 2
Exec. Director: George K. Degnon, CAE

Historical Note
AOOP members are psychiatrists with an interest in the relationship of work to general well-being and mental health. Organizational and occupational psychiatrists study the psychopathology brought to and resulting from work setting and utilize clinical, consultative, educational and preventive interventions and strategies to reduce symptoms and conflict, and facilitate health and well-being. Membership: $150/year (individual).

Publications:
OOP News Bulletin. semi-a. adv.

Meetings/Conferences:
Annual Meetings: January
1999 – Washington, DC/Jan. 15-17
2000 – San Diego, CA/Jan. 14-16

Academy of Osseointegration (1987)
401 N. Michigan Ave.
Chicago, IL 60611-4267
Tel: (312)321-5169   *Fax:* (312)527-6658
Toll Free: (800)656 - 7736
E-Mail: academy@osseo.org
Web Site: http://www.osseo.org
Members: 4,500 individuals
Staff: 7
Annual Budget: $1-2,000,000
Exec. Director: Tom Stautzenbach
Manager, Public Relations: Marianne Byrne
Manager, Convention Services: Peggy Sloyan
Director, Operations: Bret S. Beall, Ph.D.

Historical Note
The Academy was established to advance, promote and improve the art and science of rigid/living tissue interfaces (osseointegration). Members are dental specialists, general practitioners, materials scientists, dental technicians, laboratory personnel, and manufacturers' representatives. Membership: $205/year (individual).

Publications:
Academy News. Newsletter.
Annual Meeting Program/Abstract Book. a.
Internat'l Journal of Oral and Maxillofacial Implants. bi-m.
    adv.
Membership Roster. a.

Meetings/Conferences:
Annual Meetings: Spring
1999 – Palm Springs, CA/March 4-6
2000 – New Orleans, LA/March 9-11

Academy of Parish Clergy (1968)
P.O. Box 96
Wade, NC 28395-0096
Tel: (910)484-7867
E-Mail: apcoffice@apclergy.org
Web Site: www.apclergy.org
Members: 207 individuals
Staff: 10
Annual Budget: $10-25,000
Administrative V. President: Robert L. Yoder, Ph.D.

Historical Note
Formed in Indianapolis as a voluntary self-governing association of clergy who work together in an inter-faith, ecumenical parish setting. Affiliated with the Association of Theological Schools and the Society for the Advancement of Continuing Education for Ministry. Membership: $55/year (individual).

Publications:
Access. q.
Directory of Members. a.
Sharing the Practice. q. adv.

Meetings/Conferences:
Annual Meetings: Spring
1999 – Cleveland, OH(St. Joseph Christian Life
    Center)/April 27-29
2000 – Princeton, NJ(Princeton Theo. Ctr.)

Academy of Pharmaceutical Research and Science (1965)
c/o American Pharmaceutical Ass'n
2215 Constitution Ave., N.W.
Washington, DC 20037
Tel: (202)427-7507   *Fax:* (202)783-2351
Toll Free: (800)237 - 2742
E-Mail: ssa@mail.AphAnet.org
Web Site: http://www.AphAnet.org
Members: 3,000 individuals
Staff: 2
Annual Budget: $100-250,000
Senior V. President/Staff Liason: Lucinda L. Maine
Coordinator, Scientific Affairs: Scott Antall

Historical Note
Formerly (1987) the Academy of Pharmaceutical Sciences. The academy within the American Pharmaceutical Ass'n which promotes the professional growth of scientists and serves as a resource of scientific knowledge for the practitioner. Membership: $165/year (individual).

Publications:
Academy. q.
Journal of Pharmaceutical Sciences. m.

Meetings/Conferences:
Annual Meetings: Spring (with APhA)
1999 – San Antonio, TX/March 6-10
2000 – Washington, DC/March 11-15

Academy of Pharmacy Practice and Management (1965)
2215 Constitution Ave., N.W.
Washington, DC 20037
Tel: (202)628-4410   *Fax:* (202)783-2351
Members: 21,000 individuals
Staff: 3
Assoc. Dir., Practice Affairs: Janet Edwards

Historical Note
Originally the General Practice Section of the American Pharmaceutical Ass'n, became (1966) the Academy of General Practice of Pharmacy and (1975) the Academy of Pharmacy Practice; assumed its current name in 1987. Members are pharmacists concerned with providing professional services to the general public. APhA-APPM is an academy of the American Pharmaceutical Ass'n.

Publications:
Academy Reporter. q.

Meetings/Conferences:
Annual Meetings: March/5,000

Academy of Political Science (1880)
475 Riverside Drive, Suite 1274
New York, NY 10115-1274
Tel: (212)870-2500   *Fax:* (212)870-2202
E-Mail: aps321@aol.com
Web Site: http://www.epn.org/psq.html
Members: 4,000 individuals, 2,000 institutions
Staff: 8
Annual Budget: $500-1,000,000
President & Exec. Director: Demetrios Caraley
Business Manager: Loren Morales

Historical Note
Founded to promote political science and its application to the solution of political, social and economic problems. Membership: $39/year (individual); $159/year (company).

Publications:
Political Science Quarterly. q. adv.
Proceedings. irreg.

Meetings/Conferences:
Semi-Annual Meetings: usually New York, NY(Columbia
    Univ.)

Academy of Psychosomatic Medicine *(1953)*
5824 N. Magnolia
Chicago, IL   60660
Tel: (773)784-2025   *Fax:* (773)784-1304
Members: 1000 individuals
Staff: 2
Annual Budget: $250-500,000
Exec. Director: Evelyne A. Hallberg
Historical Note
Incorporated in New York in 1954. Attempts to advance medicine and allied health professions through interaction of mind, body and environment. Membership: $130/year (individual).
Publications:
APM Directory.
Directory of US Consultation-Liaison Training Programs. a.
Psychosomatics. bi-m. adv.
Meetings/Conferences:
Annual Meetings: October-November/400
1999 – New Orleans, LA(Hyatt Regency)/Nov. 19-21
2000 – Palm Springs, CA(Palm Springs Riviere Resort)/Nov. 16-19

Academy of Radiology Research *(1994)*
1112 16th St., N.W., Suite 500
Washington, DC   20036
Tel: (202)331-1201   *Fax:* (202)785-3948
E-Mail: acadrad@aol.com
Members: 19 organizational members
Staff: 2
Annual Budget: $250-500,000
Exec. Director: Edward C. Nagy
Historical Note
The Academy is intended to focus attention on radiology as a discipline committed to basic and clinical research and dedicated to the translation of research advances into higher quality and more cost-effective patient care.
Publications:
Washington Update. q.

Academy of Rehabilitative Audiology *(1966)*
P.O. Box 26532
Minneapolis, MN   55426
Tel: (612)920-0196   *Fax:* (612)920-6098
E-Mail: ara@mr.net
Members: 385 individuals
Annual Budget: $10-25,000
Association Executive: Frances J. Laven
Historical Note
Members hold graduate degrees in audiology, speech pathology, language or related fields and have had a minimum of two years post-degree experience. Membership: $40/year.
Publications:
Journal of the Academy of Rehabilitative Audiology. a.
Membership Directory. a.
Meetings/Conferences:
Annual Meetings: June
1999 – Howey-in-the-Hills, FL(Mission Inn)

Academy of Scientific Hypnotherapy *(1977)*
P.O. Box 12041
San Diego, CA   92112
Tel: (619)427-6225   *Fax:* (619)427-5650
Members: 232 individuals
Annual Budget: under $10,000
President: William E. Kemery, Ph.D.
Historical Note
Academy members are healthcare professionals employing hypnosis as a therapy.
Publications:
Hypnotherapy in Review Newsletter. irreg.

Academy of Security Educators and Trainers *(1980)*
P.O. Box 802
Berryville, VA   22611-0802
Tel: (540)955-1129   *Fax:* (540)554-2547
Web Site: http://www.suite2000.com/aset
Members: 400 individuals
Staff: 2
Annual Budget: $10-25,000
Director: Dr. Richard W. Kobetz
Historical Note
Awards the CST ("Certified Security Trainer") designation. Membership: $50/year.
Publications:
ASET Newsletter. q.
Meetings/Conferences:
Annual Meetings: Spring

Academy of Sport Psychology Internat'l *(1966)*
Historical Note
Address unknown in 1996.

Academy of Students of Pharmacy *(1954)*
c/o American Pharmaceutical Ass'n
2215 Constitution Ave., N.W.
Washington, DC   20037
Tel: (202)429-7595   *Fax:* (202)628-0443
Members: 17,800 individuals
Staff: 4
Annual Budget: $500-1,000,000
Assoc. Director: Eloise Thibault
Historical Note
Formerly (1987) the Student American Pharmaceutical Ass'n. A constituent section of the American Pharmaceutical Ass'n, ASP provides students in pharmacy school with a resource for networking, education, and other professional benefits prior to actual APhA membership. Membership: $25/year.

Publications:
Pharmacy Student Magazine. q. adv.
Meetings/Conferences:
Semi-Annual Meetings: March in conjunction with APhA and Oct-Nov

Academy of Veterinary Allergy and Clinical Immunology *(1960)*
330 Waukegan Road
Glenview, IL   60025
Tel: (847)729-5214   *Fax:* (847)729-5214
E-Mail: Richlge@aol.com
Members: 300 individuals
Staff: 1
Annual Budget: $25-50,000
President: Richard Rossman, D.V.M.
Historical Note
Formerly (1993) Academy of Veterinary Allergy. AVACI members are veterinarians, physicians and other professionals with an interest in animal and comparative allergy research. Membership: $50/year (individual).
Publications:
Journal of Veterinary Allergy & Clinical Immunology. q.
Membership List. q.
Meetings/Conferences:
Annual Meetings: in conjunction with American Animal Hospital Ass'n

Academy of Veterinary Cardiology *(1968)*
2100 Ronson Road
Iselin, NJ   08830
Tel: (908)855-3755   *Fax:* (908)855-3647
Members: 600 individuals
Staff: 1
Annual Budget: under $10,000
President: Frank Pipers, D.V.M.
Historical Note
Membership includes veterinarians and students interested in veterinary cardiology. Membership: $15/year.
Publications:
Newsletter. q.
Meetings/Conferences:
Annual Meetings: Spring, with American Animal Hospital Ass'n

ACCE Communications Council *(1947)*
Historical Note
Organization defunct in 1997.

Access Technology Ass'n *(1991)*
3612 Bent Branch Court
Falls Church, VA   22041
Tel: (703)942-4329
Members: 70 companies
Staff: 3
Annual Budget: $100-250,000
Exec. Director: William J. Tobin, Ph.D.
Historical Note
Members are companies supplying products and services which expand workplace access for disabled individuals and professionals concerned with improving access to the workplace for disabled persons.
Publications:
ATA Briefings Newsletter. m.
Directory of Access Technology Products & Services. a. adv.
Meetings/Conferences:

Accordion Federation of North America *(1955)*
11438 Elmcrest
El Monte, CA   91732
Tel: (323)686-1769
Members: 75 individuals
Annual Budget: $10-25,000
Exec. Secretary: Peggy Milne
Historical Note
AFNA members are primarily music teachers and music school owners. AFNA's primary purpose is to encourage young people to pursue their music study; to this end a four-day series of contests is held annually.
Meetings/Conferences:
Annual Meetings: August
1999 – Los Angeles, CA(Wyndham Hotel LAX)/Aug. 18-22

Accordionists and Teachers Guild Internat'l *(1940)*
813 W. Lakeshore Drive
O'Fallon, IL   62269-1216
Tel: (618)632-2859   *Fax:* (618)632-0599
E-Mail: amyjo@apci.net
Web Site: http://www.accordions.com/atg
Members: 100 individuals
Annual Budget: $10-25,000
President: Amy Jo Sawyer
Historical Note
Formerly the Accordion Teachers' Guild Internat'l (1998). ATGI members are accordion teachers, professional musicians, hobbyists, and students. Membership: $25/year (individual).
Publications:
ATG Bulletin. q. adv.
Meetings/Conferences:
Annual Meetings: Summer
1999 – Branson, MO(Lodge of the Ozarks)/July 16-18/500

Accountants for the Public Interest *(1975)*
1420 N. Charles St., Suite 153
Baltimore, MD   21201-0720
Tel: (410)837-6533   *Fax:* (410)837-6532
Web Site: http://www.accountingnet.com/index.html
Members: 1,650 individuals

Staff: 5
Annual Budget: $100-250,000
Exec. Director: Beverly A. Litsinger
Director, Communications: James Swan
Historical Note
Through its affiliates, API volunteer accountants provide pro bono accounting assistance to non-profit organizations, small businesses and individuals who need but cannot afford professional service. Membership: $35/year (individual); $275/year(company).
Publications:
Affiliate Newsbriefs.
API Account. q. adv.
National Directory of Volunteer Accounting Programs.
What a Difference Knowledge Makes: A Guide to Intermediate Sanctions.
What a Difference Nonprofits Make: A Guide to Accounting Procedures.
What a Difference Preparation Makes: A Guide to the Nonprofit Audit.
What a Difference Understanding Makes: A Guide to Nonprofit Management.
Meetings/Conferences:
1999 – Baltimore, MD(Marriott)

Accounting Firms Associated *(1978)*
2811 N.W. 41st St., Bldg. C-2
Gainesville, FL   32606
Tel: (352)375-2324   *Fax:* (352)375-4187
Web Site: http://www.afai.com
Members: 1,800 individuals, 143 companies
Staff: 12
Annual Budget: $1-2,000,000
President: Douglas H. Thompson, Jr.
Historical Note
Accounting Firms Associated, Inc. is an international network of independent public accounting firms founded to pursue and ensure excellence in accounting, financial and business consulting services.
Meetings/Conferences:
Annual Meetings: August

Accreditation Ass'n for Ambulatory Health Care *(1979)*
9933 Lawler Ave.
Skokie, IL   60077-3708
Tel: (847)676-9610   *Fax:* (847)676-9628
E-Mail: info@aahc.org
Web Site: http://www.aahc.org
Members: 1000 accredited facilities, 12 organ.
Staff: 10
Annual Budget: $2-5,000,000
Exec. Director: John E. Burke, Ph D.
Director, Communications and Development: Joan Riebock
Director, Operations: Cathy Holmgren
Historical Note
AAAHC is the leading accrediting body in the United States for a variety of ambulatory health care providers, including free-standing ambulatory surgery centers(ASCs), medical group practices and office-based surgical practices. Accreditation is conferred based upon in-depth initial and periodic site inspections of the practice to determine compliance with AAAHC quality standards.
Publications:
Accreditation Handbook for Ambulatory Health Care. a.
Update. q.
Meetings/Conferences:
Annual Meetings: AAAHC schedules separate and specialized meetings throughout the year.

Accredited Gemologists Ass'n *(1976)*
c/o Balzans Gem Lab, 21 Baywood Ct.
Fairfax, CA   94930-1705
Tel: (415)834-9209   *Fax:* (415)453-5340
Members: 250 individuals
Annual Budget: $25-50,000
President: Courtney Balzan
Historical Note
Members must hold a "gemologist" diploma from the Gemological Institute of America or the Gemological Ass'n of Great Britain and pass character, professional, and ethical investigation. Membership: $100/year.
Publications:
Cornerstone. a.
Update. bi-m.
Meetings/Conferences:
Annual Meetings: Tucson, AZ/February

Accredited Pet Cemetery Soc. *(1993)*
139 West Rush Road
West Rush, NY   14543
Tel: (716)533-1685   *Fax:* (716)533-9127
Members: 15 individuals
Annual Budget: under $10,000
President: Pally Hanna
Historical Note
A group of pet cemeterians who operate quality properties and adhere to high standards of operation and professionalism. Members must endorse and support deed restriction of pet cemetary property and meaningful pet cemetery legislation. Members must serve actively on committees and attend yearly conferences with the emphasis on continuing education and incentive for achievement. Educational programs for the APCS focus on the newest trends in the pet death care profession such as community involvement, pet bereavement and support groups, and professional business management.
Publications:
APCS Bulletin. q.
Meetings/Conferences:
1999 – Lafayette, NJ

Accredited Review Appraisers Council *(1987)*

P.O. Box 12528
San Antonio, TX   78212-0528
Tel: (210)225-2897   *Fax:* (210)225-8450
Toll Free: (800)486 - 3676
Members: 350 individuals
Staff: 2
Annual Budget: $50-100,000
President: Deborah J. Deane

Historical Note
Awards the designation AAR (Accredited in Appraisal Review), the fee for which is $150. Membership: $50/year (non-designated and candidate members).

Publications:
Review Appraiser. q.

Meetings/Conferences:
Annual Meetings: not held

Accrediting Ass'n of Bible Colleges *(1947)*
P.O. Box 780339
Orlando, FL   32878-0339
Tel: (407)207-0808   *Fax:* (407)207-0840
E-Mail: edir@aabc.org
Members: 111 colleges
Staff: 5
Annual Budget: $250-500,000
Exec. Director: Randall E. Bell, Ph.D.

Historical Note
Established as Accrediting Ass'n of Bible Institutes and Bible Colleges, it became (1957) Accrediting Ass'n of Bible Colleges, (1973) American Ass'n of Bible Colleges, and assumed its present name in 1994. Incorporated in the State of Illinois. A member of the Council for Higher Education Accreditation. Members are colleges providing curricula informed by the teachings of the Bible. Membership fee varies: $1,074 + $4/FTE student/year.

Publications:
Newsletter. 3/year.

Meetings/Conferences:
Annual Meetings: Winter/350
1999 – Virginia Beach, VA(Founders Inn)/Feb. 18-20

Accrediting Bureau of Health Education Schools
803 W. Broad St., #730
Falls Church, VA   22046-3108
Tel: (703)533-2082   *Fax:* (703)998-2550
E-Mail: abhes@erols.com
Exec. Director: Carol Moneymaker

Accrediting Commission for Career Schools and Colleges of Technology *(1993)*
2101 Wilson Blvd., Suite 302
Arlington, VA   22201
Tel: (703)247-4212   *Fax:* (703)247-4533
E-Mail: info@accsct.org
Web Site: http://www.accsct.org
Members: 13 individuals
Exec. Director: Thomas A. Kube
Director, Education/Inst, Development: Marie A. Bennett
Director, Finance and Administration: Thomas D. Fischetti

Meetings/Conferences:
1999 – Washington, DC/Jan. 30-Feb. 3
1999 – Santa Fe, NM/Apr. 30-May 5

Accrediting Council for Continuing Education and Training *(1974)*
1722 N. St.,NW
Washington, DC   20036
Tel: (703)525-3000   *Fax:* (703)525-3339
Members: 230 institutions and 700 branches
Staff: 10
Annual Budget: $1-2,000,000
Exec. Director: Roger J. Williams

Historical Note
Members are associations, private educational institutions, and companies who conduct continuing education and training programs. The Council's purpose is to provide accreditation to organizations that meet the quality standards established by ACCET. The Council has also attained registered status as an ISO 9001 quality system and is officially recognized by the U.S. Secretary of Education.

Publications:
Education: The Changing Scene. m.

Meetings/Conferences:
Annual Meetings: Fall
1999 – Dallas, TX(Hyatt)/Oct. 13-16/1000

Accrediting Council for Independent Colleges and Schools *(1953)*
750 1st St., N.E., Suite 980
Washington, DC   20002-4241
Tel: (202)336-6780   *Fax:* (202)842-2593
E-Mail: sparker1@acies.org
Web Site: http://www.acies.org
Annual Budget: $2-5,000,000
Exec. Director: Stephen D. Parker

Historical Note
ACIS is an independent accrediting agency and its members include different national and international education institutions.

Publications:
Criterion. 3/year

Meetings/Conferences:
1999 – Kansas City, MO(Marriott)/800
2000 – Dallas, TX(Hyatt)

Accrediting Council on Education in Journalism and Mass Communications *(1947)*
Univ. of Kansas School of Journalism
Stauffer-Flint Hall
Lawrence, KS   66045

Tel: (785)864-3973   *Fax:* (785)864-5225
Web Site: http://www.uk.ans.edu/~acejmc
Members: 23 associations
Staff: 4
Annual Budget: $100-250,000
Exec. Director: Susanne Shaw

Historical Note
ACEJMC members are journalism/media departments, education associations, and professional organizations concerned with journalism education. Membership: $650/year (accredited school); $1,000-6,000/year (company).

Publications:
Accredited Journalism and Mass Communications Education. a.
Benefits of Accreditation. bien.
Preparing for Journalism Accreditation. bien.

Meetings/Conferences:
1999 – Chicago, IL(Westin)/March 20-21/100
1999 – San Francisco, CA/April 30-May 1/100

ACIL *(1937)*
1629 K St., N.W., Suite 400
Washington, DC   20006
Tel: (202)887-5872   *Fax:* (202)887-0021
E-Mail: info@acil.org
Web Site: http://www.acil.org
Members: 325 companies
Staff: 7
Annual Budget: $500-1,000,000
Exec. Director: Joseph F. O'Neil
Director, Gov't. Relations: Anthony P. Pagliaro
Manager, Membership: Cheryl Dodds

Historical Note
Formerly (1954) the American Council of Commercial Laboratories, (1994) the American Council of Independent Laboratories, and (1995) ACIL: the Ass'n of Independent Scientific, Engineering and Testing Firms. Members are third-party commercial engineering and scientific testing laboratories offering analytical, testing, R&D, and consulting services to industry, commerce, and government. Promotes code of ethics among members, works with standards and accrediting bodies on programs to improve laboratory performance, publishes manuals and guidelines for quality control, risk management, human resource management and safety. Sponsors and supports the ACIL Education Institute.

Publications:
ACIL Buyers Guide. a.
ACIL Newsletter. m.
Financial Management Survey. a.
Wage and Salary Survey. a.

Meetings/Conferences:
Annual Meetings: Fall/230
1999 – Washington, DC(Wyndham Washington Hotel)/Feb. 9-10
1999 – St. Louis, MO(Adam's Mark)/April 8-10

ACL - Ass'n for Consortium Leadership *(1967)*
129 William Spong Hall
5215 Hampton Blvd.
Norfolk, VA   23529-0293
Tel: (757)683-3183   *Fax:* (757)683-4515
E-Mail: lgdotolo@aol.com
Web Site: http://www.acl.odu.adu
Members: 50 consortia of institutions
Staff: 1
Annual Budget: $25-50,000
Exec. Director: Lawrence G. Dotolo, Ph.D.

Historical Note
Encourages voluntary cooperation between colleges and universities. ACL members are organizations whose chief purpose is to help colleges and universities cooperate with one another to improve education and strengthen management. Formerly known as the Cooperative Program of the American Ass'n for Higher Education, and the Council for Interinstitutional Leadership (1994). Membership: $125/year (individual), $500/year (organization).

Publications:
ACL Newsletter. 4-6/year.
Consortium Directory. a.

Meetings/Conferences:
Annual Meetings: Fall
1999 – Washington, DC/Sept 30-Oct. 2

ACME - World Ass'n of Management Consulting Firms *(1929)*

Historical Note
See Ass'n of Management Consulting Firms.

Acoustical Soc. of America *(1929)*
500 Sunnyside Blvd.
Woodbury, NY   11797
Tel: (516)576-2360   *Fax:* (516)576-2377
E-Mail: asa@aip.org
Web Site: http://www.asa.aip.org
Members: 7,000 individuals
Staff: 7
Annual Budget: $250-500,000
Exec. Director: Charles Schmidt, Ph.D.

Historical Note
Incorporated in New York City in 1929, where its initial meeting was held May 10-11, 1929 with a charter membership of about 450. A member of the American Institute of Physics. Membership: $35/year (student); $100/year (associate); $120/year (member and fellows).

Publications:
Journal of the Acoustical Soc. of America. adv.

Meetings/Conferences:
Semi-Annual Meetings: Spring and Fall/1,000
1999 – Berlin, Germany/March 15-19
1999 – Columbus, OH/Nov. 1-5

ACPA Internat'l *(1978)*

Historical Note
See Affiliated Conference of Practicing Accountants Internat'l.

Acrylic Council *(1988)*

Historical Note
Address unknown in 1998

Acrylonitrile Group *(1981)*
1850 M St., N.W., Suite 700
Washington, DC   20036
Tel: (202)721-4162   *Fax:* (202)296-8120
Members: 10 companies
Staff: 2
Annual Budget: $250-500,000
Exec. Director: John F. Murray, CAE

Historical Note
Affiliated with the Synthetic Organic Chemical Manufacturers, AN represents producers and users of the industrial chemical used to make plastics, fibers and synthetic rubber products. Membership fee: pro rata share of annual budget.

Meetings/Conferences:

Actors' Equity Ass'n *(1913)*
165 W. 46th St.
New York, NY   10036
Tel: (212)869-8530   *Fax:* (212)719-9815
Members: 40,000 individuals
Staff: 120
Annual Budget: $10-25,000,000
Exec. Director: Alan Eisenberg

Historical Note
Organized in New York City May 26, 1913 by a group of members of the former Actors' Society of America. It is an autonomous component of Associated Actors and Artists of America and represents actors and stage managers on the legitimate stage.

Publications:
Equity News. 10/year.

Meetings/Conferences:
Annual Meetings: Always New York, NY

ADARA *(1966)*
PO Box 6956
San Mateo, CA   94403-6956
Tel: (650)372-0620   *Fax:* (650)372-0661
E-Mail: adarorgn@aol.com
Members: 600 individuals
Staff: 1
Annual Budget: $50-100,000
President: Michelle Berke
Nat'l Office Coordinator: Elizabeth Charlson, Ph.D.

Historical Note
Founded in St. Louis, Missouri in 1966 as Professional Rehabilitation Workers with the Adult Deaf and incorporated the following year. Became American Deafness and Rehabilitation Ass'n in 1976, and ADARA: Professionals Networking for Excellence in Service Delivery with Individuals Who Are Deaf or Hard of Hearing in 1994. Membership: $55/year.

Publications:
ADARA UPDATE q. adv. adv.
JADARA Journal. 3/year.

Meetings/Conferences:
1999 – Washington, DC/June 1-6
2001 – Monterey, CA/May 23-27

ADED - the Ass'n for Driver Rehabilitation Specialists *(1976)*
P.O. Box 49
Edgerton, WI   53534-0049
Tel: (608)884-8833   *Fax:* (608)884-4851
E-Mail: WEBMASTER@DRIVER-ED.ORG
Web Site: http://www.driver-ed.org
Members: 570 individuals, 125 vendors and corporations
Staff: 1
Annual Budget: $100-250,000
Exec. Secretary: Ricardo G. Cerna

Historical Note
Members are driver rehabilitation specialists who provide driver evaluation and training for persons with disabilities and manufacturers/distributors of equipment used by persons with disabilities. Membership: $50/year (individual); $25/year (associate/student); $100/year (vendor); $200/year (corporate).

Publications:
ADED Newsletter. q. adv.

Meetings/Conferences:
1999 – Louisville, KY(Hyatt Regency)/Aug. 28-31/300
2000 – San Jose, CA(Hyatt Regency)/Aug. 26-29

Adhesion Soc. *(1977)*
2 Davidson Hall-0201
Blacksburg, VA   24061
Tel: (540)231-7257   *Fax:* (540)231-3971
E-Mail: adhesoc@vt.edu
Web Site: http://www.mse.us.edu/adsoc.htm
Members: 514 individuals
Staff: 1
Manager: Kimberly A. Mills

Historical Note
Members are chemists, engineers, biologists, mathematicians, physicists, physicians, dentists, and other profesionals involved in adhesion science. Membership: $45/year (individual); $15/year (student/retiree).

Publications:
Adhesion Society Newsletter. q.
Proceedings of Adhesion Society. a.
Review of Adhesion Literature. q.

Meetings/Conferences:
Annual Meetings: February
1999 – Panama City Beach, FL/Feb. 21-24

Adhesive and Sealant Council *(1958)*
7979 Old Georgetown Rd., Suite 500
Bethesda, MD   20814-2429
Tel: (301)986-9700   *Fax:* (301)986-9795
E-Mail: kerry.lake@ascouncil.org
Web Site: http://www.ascouncil.org
Members: 156 companies
Staff: 10
Annual Budget: $1-2,000,000
President: Kerry L. Lake
Director, Government Relations: Mark Collatz
Manager, Meetings: Michelle Stevens
Director, Administration and Finance: Kate Zando

Historical Note
Formerly (1967) Rubber and Plastic Adhesive and Sealant Manufacturers Council. Members are makers of adhesives and sealants and their suppliers. Membership: $1,202-12,453/year, based on net sales (company).

Publications:
Government Relations: State & Federal Reports. every 6 wks.
Journal of The Adhesive and Sealant Council. semi-a.
Membership Directory. a.

Meetings/Conferences:
Semi-Annual Meetings: Spring and Fall
1999 – Toronto, Canada(Sheraton)/Apr. 11-14

Adhesives Manufacturers Ass'n *(1933)*
401 N. Michigan Ave.
Chicago, IL   60611-4267
Tel: (312)644-6610   *Fax:* (312)321-6869
E-Mail: AMA@sba.com
Web Site: http://www.adhesives.org/ama
Members: 200 individuals, 43 companies
Staff: 2
Annual Budget: $250-500,000
Exec. Director: Christine Norris

Historical Note
Members are makers of paper converting and packaging adhesives and hot melts or raw material suppliers. Known as Adhesives Manufacturers Ass'n of America until 1981.

Publications:
Adhesive Trends. q.

Meetings/Conferences:
Annual Meetings: Spring/120
1999 – Los Cabos, Mexico(Westib Regina)/March 24-27

Adjutants General Ass'n of the United States *(1912)*
One Massachusetts Ave., N.W.
Washington, DC   20001
Tel: (202)789-0031   *Fax:* (202)682-9358
Members: 55 individuals
Staff: 1
Annual Budget: under $10,000
President: Maj.Gen. E. Gordon Stump

Historical Note
Membership composed of the commander of the National Guard in each state, the District of Columbia, the Commonwealth of Puerto Rico, the Virgin Islands and Guam.

Meetings/Conferences:
Semi-Annual Meetings: early Feb./Washington, DC & Spring/various sites
1999 – Atlanta, GA

Administrators and Teachers in English as a Second Language *(1988)*
Historical Note
A section of NAFSA: Ass'n of Internat'l Educators.

ADSC: The Internat'l Ass'n of Foundation Drilling *(1971)*
9696 Skillman St., Suite 280
Dallas, TX   75243-8254
Tel: (214)343-2091   *Fax:* (214)343-2384
E-Mail: adsc@eaze.net
Web Site: www.adsc-iafd.com
Members: 750 companies
Staff: 7
Annual Budget: $500-1,000,000
Exec. Director: Scot Litke
Meeting Planner: Julie Roberts
Administrative Director: Ted Legard
Publications Editor: Susan King

Historical Note
Founded as Ass'n of Drilled Shaft Contractors; assumed its current name in 1995. ADSC seeks to advance technology in the foundation drilling and anchored earth retention industries. ADSC represents drilled shaft and anchored earth retention contractors, civil engineers, and foundation drilling and anchored earth retention equipment manufacturing firms world-wide. Provides scholarships and R&D support through its Industry Advancement Fund. Membership: $550-3,700/year, varies by contract limit; $325-650/year (associate); $75/year (technical affiliate).

Publications:
ASDC Membership Directory. a.
Foundation Drilling. 8/year.
Products and Services Guide. trien.
Technical Library Catalog. bien.

Meetings/Conferences:
1999 – Las Vegas, NV(Harrah's)/Jan. 20-24
2001 – San Antonio, TX(Hyatt Hill Country)/Jan. 17-21

Adult Video Ass'n *(1987)*
270 N. Canon Drive, Suite 1370
Beverly Hills, CA   90210
Tel: (213)650-7121

Members: 400 individuals
Annual Budget: under $10,000
Creative Coordinator: William Margold

Historical Note
Trade association primarily concerned with opposing legislative initiatives to restrict the sale of sexually explicit film and video.

Publications:
Newsletter. m.

Advanced Transit Ass'n *(1976)*
181 Littleton Rd., Unit 238
Chelmsford, MA   01824-2673
Tel: (978)250-9445
Web Site: http://advancedtransit.org
Members: 75 individuals, 5 companies
Annual Budget: $10-25,000
President: Thomas Richert

Historical Note
Members are tranportation professionals and others interested in applying advanced technology and planning concepts to urban transportation. Promotes low-cost and service-effective urban transit modes, with the goal of including underserved urban areas. Has no paid officers or full-time staff. Membership: $35/year.

Publications:
Journal of Advanced Transportation. 3/year.
Newsletter. q.

Meetings/Conferences:
Annual Meetings: always Washington, DC/January

Adventure Travel Trade Ass'n
6551 S. Revere Pkwy., Suite 160
Englewood, CO   80111-6410
Tel: (303)649-9016   *Fax:* (303)649-9017
E-Mail: atbta@adventuretravel.com
Web Site: http://www.adventuretravel.com
Members: 350 individuals
Staff: 2
Annual Budget: $250-500,000
Program Director: B.J. Hansen

Historical Note
Formerly (1997) Adventure Travel Soc. ATTA assists members in managing and marketing adventure travel and facilitates communication and business relationships within the adventure travel industry. Membership: $100-$150/year (individual); $150-$250/year (organization).

Meetings/Conferences:
Annual Meetings: Fall
1999 – Tucson, AZ/Sept. 19-22

Advertising and Marketing Internat'l Network *(1932)*
12323 Nantucket
Wichita, KS   67235
Tel: (316)722-2535   *Fax:* (316)722-8353
E-Mail: vaughn_sink@shscom.com
Web Site: http://www.commercepark.com/amin
Members: 61 agencies
Staff: 1
Annual Budget: $10-25,000
Exec. Director: Vaughn Sink

Historical Note
A world-wide network of cooperating, non-competitive advertising agencies in 60 cities which provides facilities and branch office services for its members. Formerly called the Continental Advertising Agency Network. Membership: $3,000/year (organization/company).

Publications:
AMIN News. q.

Meetings/Conferences:
Annual Meetings: June
1999 – Seatle, WA(Hotel Monaco)/June 27-30/150

Advertising Council *(1942)*
261 Madison Ave., 11th Floor
New York, NY   10016-2303
Tel: (212)922-1500   *Fax:* (212)922-1676
Toll Free: (800)933 - 7727
Web Site: http://www.adcouncil.org
Members: 500 companies
Staff: 40
Annual Budget: $2-5,000,000
President: Ruth A. Wooden
Senior V. President, Public Relations: Paula A. Veale

Historical Note
Founded in 1942 as the War Advertising Council. Reorganized after World War II and became the Advertising Council, Inc. Not a trade association in the accepted sense, the Ad Council is a private, non-profit organization of volunteers who conduct advertising campaigns in the public good.

Publications:
Annual Report.
Public Service Advertising Bulletin. bi-m.

Meetings/Conferences:
Biennial Meetings: Washington, DC/Spring

Advertising Mail Marketing Ass'n *(1947)*
1901 N. Fort Myer Dr.,
Arlington, VA   22209
Tel: (202)347-0055   *Fax:* (202)347-0789
E-Mail: genedp@amma.org
Web Site: http://amma.org
Members: 370 individuals, 500 companies
Staff: 5
Annual Budget: $1-2,000,000
President: Gene A. Del Polito, Ph.D.
Director, Public Affairs: Chad W. Robbins
Director, Public Affairs: Chad Robbins
V. President: Kathleen Siviter
Manager, Administrative: Donna M. Hoffman

Historical Note
Established as Associated Third Class Mail Users, it became the Third Class Mail Ass'n in 1981 and assumed its present name in 1991. Members are firms who use or support the use of mail for advertising, marketing, or fund raising purposes. Membership: $750-15,750/year (organization).

Publications:
AMMA Bulletin. w.
CEO Postal Update.
Membership Directory. a.
Postal Issues Summary. semi-a.
Postal Tech-Notes.

Meetings/Conferences:
Annual Meetings: Fall
1999 – Washington, DC
2000 – Washington, DC
2001 – Washington, DC
2002 – Washington, DC

Advertising Media Credit Executives Ass'n, Internat'l *(1953)*
8815 Centre Park Drive
Columbia, MD   21045-2117
Tel: (410)992-7609   *Fax:* (410)740-5574
Members: 300 individuals, 300 companies
Staff: 1
Annual Budget: $50-100,000
Administrative Assistant: Delores Richmond

Historical Note
Members are of the credit executives of newspapers, magazines, radio and television stations. Membership: $150-325/year.

Publications:
Between Edition.
News and Views Magazine. adv. adv.

Meetings/Conferences:
Annual Meetings: Fall
1999 – Cleveland, OH(Sheraton)
2000 – New York, NY

Advertising Photographers of America, Nat'l *(1985)*
333 S. Beverly Dr., Suite 216
Beverly Hills, CA   90212-4314
Tel: (310)201-0781   *Fax:* (310)201-9630
Toll Free: (800)272 - 6264
Staff: 2
Exec. Director: Dorie Ford

Historical Note
APA members are established, independent advertising and commercial photographers. Associate members are photographers who have been in business less than three years. APA was started with four regional chapters in 1981; in 1985 the original chapters formed APA Nat'l with the desire to coordinate and communicate on a national level. Only individuals located over 100 miles from the nearest regional chapter may join APA Nat'l directly as a member-at-large. Membership: $250/year (general, at large); $125/year (associate); $50/year (assistant/student); $3,000-$25,000/year (sustaining supplier).

Publications:
News-in-Focus Newsletter. q. adv.

Advertising Research Foundation *(1936)*
641 Lexington Ave., 11th Floor
New York, NY   10022
Tel: (212)751-5656   *Fax:* (212)319-5265
Web Site: http://www.arfsite.org
Members: 415 companies
Staff: 20
Annual Budget: $2-5,000,000
President: Jim Spaeth
Director, Conference Operations: Carol White
Manager, Publications: Kathryn K. Grubb
Director, Conference Content: Ajay Durani

Historical Note
Founded in 1936 by the Ass'n of Nat'l Advertisers and the American Ass'n of Advertising Agencies. The only industry-wide not-for-profit association dedicated to improving the practice of advertising, marketing and media research in pursuit of more effective marketing and advertising communications.

Publications:
Journal of Advertising Research. bi-m. adv.

Meetings/Conferences:
Annual Meetings: New York, NY(Hilton)
1999 – /March 15-17
2000 – /March 13-15
2001 – /March 5-7

AERA - Engine Rebuilders Ass'n *(1922)*
330 Lexington Drive
Buffalo Grove, IL   60089-6998
Tel: (847)541-6550   *Fax:* (847)541-5808
Web Site: http://www.aera.org
Members: 4,900 companies
Staff: 13
Annual Budget: $1-2,000,000
President and C.E.O.: Barry E. Soltz

Historical Note
Founded as Automotive Engine Rebuilders Ass'n; assumed its current name in 1995. Active members include: automotive jobber machine shops, custom automotive machine shops, heavy-duty, diesel and industrial shops, production engine rebuilders and high performance and marine shops. Associate membership is available for suppliers of automotive parts, tools, equipment and chemicals and services. Membership: $182-385/year (company, based on number of shop personnel).

Publications:
Directory. a. adv.
ID Guides. a. adv.
Shop Talk Newsletter. m.
Specifications Manuals. irreg.

Technical, Service, and News Bulletins. m.

Meetings/Conferences:
Annual Meetings: April
1999 – St. Louis, MO(Adam's Mark/Conv.
   Center)/April 30-May 2/5500
2001 – Orlando, FL(Clarion/Conv. Center)/April 6-8/5500

Aerial Firefighting Industry Ass'n (1988)
P.O. Box 523068
Springfield, VA   22152
Tel: (703)644-6454   Fax: (703)644-6454
E-Mail: broadwel@erols.com
Web Site: http://www.afia.com/
Members: 17 companies
Staff: 1
Annual Budget: $50-100,000
Exec. Director: William R. Broadwell

Historical Note
AFIA is a trade association composed of companies engaged in
forest and wildland firefighting utilizing air tankers. Membership:
$1,000/year, plus prorate by number of contracts (corporate).

Publications:
Internal Information Letter/Bulletin. w.

Meetings/Conferences:
Annual Meetings: Fall, usually in the western U.S.

Aerobics and Fitness Ass'n of America (1983)
15250 Ventura Blvd., Suite 200
Sherman Oaks, CA   91403
Tel: (818)905-0040   Fax: (818)990-5468
Toll Free: (800)225 - 2322
E-Mail: AFAA@pops.com
Web Site: http://www.AFAA.com
Members: 135,000 individuals
Staff: 50
President: Linda D. Pfeffer, RN
Executive V. President & Publisher: Roscoe K. Fawcett, Jr.
V. President, Marketing and Promotions: Petra Lansner
V. President, Educational Division: Robin Foss
V. President, Purchasing: Tony Eid
V. President/Controller: Phillip Longsworth
V. President, Sales: Michael Pesta

Historical Note
International professional association for the education, training
and certification of fitness professionals. Publishes standards and
guidelines in addition to providing educational materials,
continuing education programs, and home study courses.
Membership: $58/year (individual).

Publications:
A Guide to Personal Training.
An Emerging Profession: The Fitness Practitioner Manual.
Exercise Standards & Guidelines Reference Manual.
Fitness: Theory and Practice Textbook. 6/year. adv.

Meetings/Conferences:

Aeronautical Navigator Ass'n (1974)
Historical Note
Also known as the Navigator Association. Has no paid staff.

Aeronautical Repair Station Ass'n (1984)
121 N. Henry St.
Alexandria, VA   22314
Tel: (703)739-9543   Fax: (703)739-9488
Web Site: http://www.arsa.org
Members: 100 companies
Staff: 4
Annual Budget: $25-50,000
Exec. Director: Sarah MacLeod
Business Manager: Micheal L'Born

Historical Note
Established and incorporated in Washington, DC in June, 1984,
ARSA represents FAA certified repair stations. Absorbed the Airline
Services Ass'n in 1985. Membership: $250-1,000/year.

Publications:
The Hotline. m.

Meetings/Conferences:
1999 – Arlington, VA

Aerospace and Electronic Systems Soc.
Historical Note
A technical society of the Institute of Electrical and Electronics
Engineers (IEEE). Membership in the Society, open only to IEEE
members, includes a subscription to a technical periodical in the
field published by IEEE. All administrative support is provided by
IEEE.

Aerospace Department Chairmens' Ass'n (1968)
Sch. of Aeronautics and Astronautics
1282 Grissom Hall, Purdue Univ.
West Lafayette, IN   47907-1282
Tel: (765)494-5117   Fax: (765)494-0307
Web Site: http://www.ecn.purdue.edu/ENGR
Members: 80 individuals
Annual Budget: under $10,000
Chairman: Dave Dolling

Historical Note
Promotes aerospace engineering education and research to
stimulate the growth of the aerospace profession. Has no paid
officers or full-time staff. Membership: $3/year.

Publications:
Meeting Minutes. a. adv.

Meetings/Conferences:
Annual Meetings: January

Aerospace Electrical Soc. (1941)
18231 Fernando Circle
Villa Park, CA   92861
Tel: (714)538-1002

Members: 250 individuals
Annual Budget: under $10,000
President: Lloyd P. Appelman

Historical Note
Formerly (1960) Aircraft Electrical Soc. Members are engineers and
other professionals involved in the development and production of
electrical/electronic devices and systems.

Publications:
News & Views Newsletter. m.

Aerospace Industries Ass'n of America (1919)
1250 I St., N.W., Suite 1200
Washington, DC   20005-3924
Tel: (202)371-8400   Fax: (202)371-8470
E-Mail: aia@aia-aerospace.org
Web Site: http://www.aia-aerospace.org
Members: 56 companies
Staff: 42
Annual Budget: $5-10,000,000
President: John W. Douglass
Director, Communications: Alexis Allen
V. President, Legislative Affairs: Thomas N. Tate
V. President, International: Joel L. Johnson
Asst. V. President, Plans & Policy: Sandra Carney-Talley
V.P., Technical Operations: Stanley Siegel
Director, Research: David Vadas
V. President, Procurement & Finance: LeRoy J. Haugh
Secretary-Treasurer: George F. Copsey
V. President, Civil Aviation: Robert E. Robeson

Historical Note
Established in 1919 as the Aeronautical Chamber of Commerce of
America, Inc. Name changed to Aircraft Industries Ass'n of
America, Inc. in 1945 and to Aerospace Industries Ass'n of
America in 1959. The Nat'l Center for Advanced Technologies is its
non-profit affiliate. Membership fee based on percentage of sales.

Publications:
Aerospace Facts and Figures. a.
AIA Update. 10/year.
Annual Report, Aerospace Industries Ass'n. a.

Meetings/Conferences:
Semi-annual Meetings: Williamsburg, VA in May & Phoenix,
AZ in Nov.

Aerospace Medical Ass'n (1929)
320 S. Henry St.
Alexandria, VA   22314-3579
Tel: (703)739-2240   Fax: (703)739-9652
Members: 3,600 individuals, 65 companies
Staff: 7
Annual Budget: $500-1,000,000
Exec. Director: Russell B. Rayman, M.D.
Ass't Exec. Director: Richard B. Trumbo, Ph.D.

Historical Note
Founded in Detroit, MI as The Aero Medical Soc. of the United
States. Incorporated 1930 in Washington, DC. Name changed to
the Aero Medical Ass'n in 1947 and to the present name in 1959.
Membership: $150/year (individual), $400/year (company).

Publications:
Aviation, Space and Environmental Medicine. m. adv.

Meetings/Conferences:
Annual Meetings: Spring/2,000

Aestheticians Internat'l Ass'n (1972)
2611 N. Belt Line Rd., Suite 140
Sunnyvale, TX   75182-9357
Tel: (972)203-8530   Fax: (972)203-8754
Members: 1000 individuals
Annual Budget: $10-25,000
C.E.O.: William Strunk
: Mellony Cates

Historical Note
Individuals owning or working in a skin care salon, together with
manufacturers and distributors of skin care products. AIA produces
trade shows for both the specialized industry and full cosmetology
profession.

Meetings/Conferences:
Annual Meetings: Annual Meetings, Atlantic City, NJ

Affiliated Boards of Officials
1227 Lake Plaza Dr., Suite B
Colorado Springs, CO   80906
Tel: (316)773-1991   Fax: (316)773-1993
E-Mail: vbaboss@aol.com
Members: 1,900 individuals, 97 boards
Staff: 2
Annual Budget: $250-500,000
Exec. Director: Marsha Alterman
Program Assistant: Susie Senecaut

Historical Note
Rates and trains officials for girls' and women's sports programs
and promotes the involvement of women in the governing bodies of
other sport officiating groups. Formerly (1992) a sub-section of
Nat'l Ass'n for Girls and Women in Sport, administrative support
for ABO is now provided by American Volleyball Coaches Ass'n.
Membership: $35/year.

Publications:
ABO News. q.

Meetings/Conferences:
1999 – Honolulu, HI/Dec. 17-18
2000 – Richmond, VA/Dec. 15-16
2001 – San Diego, CA/Dec. 21-22

Affiliated Conference of Practicing Accountants Internat'l (1978)
30 Massachusetts Ave.
North Andover, MA   01845-3413
Tel: (978)689-9420   Fax: (978)689-9404
E-Mail: jeve@acpaintl.org or hlme@acpaintl.org
Web Site: http://www.acpaintl.org

Members: 80 firms
Staff: 3
Annual Budget: $250-500,000
Exec. Director: Heather Long Molinero

Historical Note
Founded as Atlantic Conference of CPAs; Assumed its current name
in 1985 to reflect its international constituency. ACPA Internat'l is a
worldwide network of individual accounting firms and business
consultants committed to quality standards, growth for its
members, and dedicated to personal services nationally and
internationally. Membership dues vary, based on net fees.

Publications:
ACPA Directory. a.
Perspective News Magazine. semi-a.
Update - Monthly Fax Newsletter. m.

Meetings/Conferences:
1999 – Boston, MA/October 4-9
2000 – Melbourne, Austriala/September 4-10

Affiliated Dress Manufacturers (1929)
500 Seventh Ave., 2nd Floor
New York, NY   10018
Tel: (212)819-1011
Members: 1 dress manufacturers
Exec. Director: Adam Harris

Historical Note
Members, primarily located in New York City, are manufacturers of
women's dresses.

Affiliated Inventors Foundation (1975)
1405 Potter Dr., Suite 107
Colorado Springs, CO   80909-3516
Tel: (719)380-1234   Fax: (719)380-1144
Toll Free: (800)525 - 5885
Members: 400 individuals
Staff: 6
Annual Budget: $250-500,000
President: John Farady

Historical Note
AIF members are independent inventors. Services include technical
information and legal/consultancy assistance, patent and
trademark searches and applications.

Affiliated Warehouse Companies (1953)
Box 295
Hazlet, NJ   07730-0295
Tel: (732)739-2323   Fax: (732)739-4154
E-Mail: sales@awco.com
Web Site: http://www.awco.com
Members: 85 companies
Staff: 9
Annual Budget: $250-500,000
President: James McBride, III

Historical Note
Affiliated Warehouse Companies, Inc. was organized in 1953 and
remains the first third party warehouse sales company owned and
operated by its employees. Through its offices in Hazlet, NJ,
Greensboro, NC, La Grange, IL, and Fresno, CA, AWC performs the
marketing and sales for third party warehouse companies in the
United States, Canada, Mexico, Europe and Southeast Asia. Of
equal importance, AWC assists the third party warehouse user by
being a resource for rates, data and information on warehousing
and distribution at no charge or obligation.

Publications:
Database of Public Warehouse Users.
Directory. a.
Newsletter. m.
Public Warehouse Selection Process.
Summary of Sales Work. w.

Meetings/Conferences:
Semi-annual Meetings: Spring and Fall

Affordable Housing Tax Credit Coalition (1988)
1255 23rd St., N.W., Suite 800
Washington, DC   20037
Tel: (202)973-7739   Fax: (202)973-7750
E-Mail: LIHTC@AOL.COM
Members: 110 companies
Staff: 1
Annual Budget: $100-250,000
Executive Director: Candace M. Kerman

Historical Note
AHTCC members include syndicators, investors, lenders,
developers, non-profit organizations and others with an interest in
the low-income housing tax credit. Founded as the Coalition to
Preserve the Low-Income Housing Tax Credit with the then-sole
purpose of achieving a permanent extension, its goals were
broadened after permanent extension was achieved in 1993.
Membership: Annual dues vary by membership category.

Publications:
Preserver. m.
Washington Alert. irreg.

Meetings/Conferences:

Afghanistan Studies Ass'n (1971)
Historical Note
Organization defunct in 1998.

Afram Films
Historical Note
A division of Motion Picture Ass'n, Which provides administrative
support.

Africa Travel Ass'n (1975)
347 5th Ave., Suite 610
New York, NY   10016
Tel: (212)447-1926   Fax: (212)725-8253
Members: 760 individuals
Staff: 3

Annual Budget: $50-100,000
Exec. Director: Mira Berman

Historical Note
Mission of ATA is to promote the tourist attractions of the continent of Africa to the travel industry in North America and educate all interested travel agents, planners and operators about the products and services offered by the travel and tourism industry in Africa. ATA works closely with individual African countries, tour and ground operators, incentive, meeting, and convention planners, travel agents, airline, hoteliers, and all other branches of the travel and leisure industry. ATA has broadened its programs to include business, economic and financial development in Africa.

Publications:
Africa Travel Magazine. q.
Membership Directory. a.

Meetings/Conferences:

African American Museums Ass'n

Historical Note
Became (1998) Ass'n of African American Museums.

African American Travel and Tourism Ass'n *(1993)*
P.O. Box 870712
New Orleans, LA   70187-0712
Tel: (504)242-0552   *Fax:* (504)242-0890
Members: 52 individuals
President: Caletha M. Powell
V. President: Gwendolyn M. Carter

Historical Note
ATTA members are African Americans in the hospitality, travel and tourism industry.

Meetings/Conferences:

African Heritage Studies Ass'n *(1969)*

Historical Note
Address unknown in 1996.

African Studies Ass'n *(1957)*
Rutgers, The State University of NJ
132 George St.
New Brunswick, NJ   08901-1400
Tel: (732)932-8173   *Fax:* (732)932-3394
E-Mail: callasa@rci.rutgers.edu
Web Site: see text
Members: 3,000 individuals, 550 institutions
Staff: 6
Annual Budget: $500-1,000,000
Exec. Director: Christopher P. Koch

Historical Note
Membership: $40-90/year (individual); $55-128/year (institutions). The African Studies Association has a web site located at http://www.sas.upenn.edu/African_Studies/Home _Page/ASA_Menu.html.

Publications:
African Studies Review. 3/year.
ASA NEWS. q.
History in Africa. a.
Issue: Journal of Opinion. 2/year.

Meetings/Conferences:
Annual Meetings: Fall
1999 – Philadelphia, PA(Marriott)/Nov. 19-22
2000 – Nashville, TN

African-American Library and Information Science Ass'n *(1993)*
UCLA Center for African-American Studies
Box 951545
Los Angeles, CA   90095-1545
Tel: (310)825-6060   *Fax:* (310)206-3421
E-Mail: aalisa-l@library.ucla.edu
Members: 100 individuals
Annual Budget: under $10,000
President: Itibari Zulu

Historical Note
Formed to address issues of under-representation within the library sciences profession and access to information resources for the African-American community at large. Has no paid officers or full-time staff. Membership: $20/year.

Meetings/Conferences:
Annual Meetings: March
1999 – New Orleans, LA

African-American Natural Foods Ass'n *(1990)*
P.O. Box 497336
Chicago, IL   60649-7336
Tel: (773)363-3939   *Fax:* (773)368-7101
Annual Budget: under $10,000
C.E.O.: Cheryl Simms

Historical Note
Members are health food retailers, manufacturers and others with interest in increasing the acceptance of natural foods in minority communities. Membership: $50-$75/year (individual); $100-$250/year (company).

African-American Women's Clergy Ass'n *(1969)*
214 P Street, N.W.
Washington, DC   20001
Tel: (202)518-8488   *Fax:* (202)518-1273
Members: 175 individuals
Chairperson: Rev. Imagene B. Stewart

Historical Note
Formerly (1990) American Women's Clergy Ass'n. AAWCA members are lay and ordained women clergy.

AFSM Internat'l *(1976)*
1342 Colonial Blvd., Suite 25
Fort Myers, FL   33907
Tel: (941)275-7887   *Fax:* (941)275-0794

E-Mail: dhenault@afsmi.org
Web Site: http://www.afsmi.org
Members: 5,000 individuals
Staff: 15
Annual Budget: $2-5,000,000
C.E.O.: David Henault
Editor: Suzannne Tissier

Historical Note
Members are executives and managers in the high technology services/support industry. Formerly (1985) Ass'n of Field Service Managers and (1989) Ass'n of Field Service Managers Internat'l. Membership: $200/year, first year; $175/year, renewal (individual).

Publications:
AFSM Internat'l, The Professional Journal. m. adv.
European Services Industry.
High Technology Services Management Magazine. m.

Meetings/Conferences:
Annual Meetings: Fall
1999 – Orlando, FL/Oct. 17-19
2000 – Nashville, TN/Oct. 15-17
2001 – Anaheim, CA/Oct. 28-30

Ag Electronics Ass'n
10 S. Riverside Plaza
Suite 1220
Chicago, IL   60606-3710
Tel: (312)321-1470   *Fax:* (312)321-1480
E-Mail: aea@agelectronicsassn.com
Web Site: http://www.agelectronicsassn.org
Members: 75 companies
Staff: 2
Annual Budget: $500-1,000,000
General Manager: Darrin Drollinger

Historical Note
Established in 1995 to bring together a wide diversity of interests related to the advancement of the use of electronics in agriculture. Maintains four councils: User, Equipment, Hardware and Software/Information Systems. Councils and work groups are establishing full liaison and working relationships with government agencies and universities related to the appropriate areas of mutual interest. Management services and headquarters operations are provided by the Equipment Manufactures Ass'n, one of the nation's oldest trade associations.

Publications:
Membership Directory. a.

Aggregate and Concrete Executives
c/o Texas Aggregates & Concrete Ass'n
6633 Hwy. 290 East, Suite 204
Austin, TX   78723
Tel: (512)451-5100   *Fax:* (512)451-4162
Chairman: Bob R. Beard

Historical Note
ACE is the result of a merger between the Internat'l Council of Executives and the State Aggregate Ass'n Executives. Works closely with the Nat'l Ready-Mixed Concrete Ass'n, the Nat'l Aggregates Ass'n and the Nat'l Stone Ass'n to serve concrete and aggregate associations nationwide.

Publications:
Directory. a.

Meetings/Conferences:
Annual Meetings: Summer

AGN Internat'l - North America *(1978)*
2851 S. Parker Road, Suite 850
Aurora, CO   80014-2729
Tel: (303)743-7880   *Fax:* (303)743-7660
E-Mail: rjhood@ix.netcom.com
Web Site: http://www.agn-na.org
Members: 25 firms
Staff: 4
Annual Budget: $1-2,000,000
Exec. Director: Rita J. Hood
Marketing Director: Nancy J. Williams
Meeting Planner: Patsy Bowen

Historical Note
Founded as Continental Ass'n of CPA Firms; assumed its current name in 1997. Membership fee varies, based on billings (company).

Publications:
Advantage for Health Care Professionals. q.
Client Newsletter. q.
Lawyer's Advantage Newsletter. q.
The Contractor Advantage. q.

Meetings/Conferences:
Semi-annual Meetings: Fall and Spring

Agribusiness Council *(1967)*
1312 18th St., N.W., Suite 300
Washington, DC   20036
Tel: (202)296-4563   *Fax:* (202)887-9178
E-Mail: agenergy@aol.com
Members: 400 companies and organizations
Staff: 3
President: Nicholas E. Hollis

Historical Note
ABC is a consortium of companies, universities, foundations and individuals. Its purpose is to stimulate and encourage agribusiness development both domestically and abroad. Identifies investment opportunities for agribusiness, supports research, and serves as an information and networking resource for its members. Agri-Energy Roundtable (AER) manages a series of overseas affiliates of ABC. AER is a UN accredited non-governmental organization.

Publications:
Newsletter.

Agricultural and Industrial Manufacturers' Representatives Ass'n *(1961)*
5800 Foxridge Dr., Suite 115

Mission, KS   66202-2333
Tel: (913)262-0317   *Fax:* (913)262-0174
Members: 130 companies & 23 associates
Staff: 3
Annual Budget: $100-250,000
Exec. Director: Frank A. Bistrom, CAE
Conference Manager: Betchie Bistrom, CAE

Historical Note
Formerly (1972) American Farm and Power Equipment Agents Ass'n. Membership: $400/year.

Publications:
AIMRA Newsline. 11/year.
Directory. a.

Meetings/Conferences:
Annual Meetings: Fall
1999 – Houston, TX/Nov. 7-10/150
2000 – Reno, NV(Reno Hilton)/Nov. 7-10
2001 – Denver, CO(Adam's Mark)/Nov. 3-7

Agricultural Communicators in Education *(1913)*
P.O. Box 11811
Gainesville, FL   32611
Tel: (352)392-9588   *Fax:* (352)392-7902
E-Mail: ace@gnv.ifas.ufl.edu
Web Site: http://www.aceweb.org
Members: 700 individuals
Staff: 4
Annual Budget: $50-100,000
Coordinator: Julia Graddy

Historical Note
Formerly (1978) the American Ass'n of Agricultural College Editors. Members are writers, editors, broadcasters, graphic designers, teachers and researchers who are involved in the dissemination of agricultural, food science and natural resource information. Membership: $75/year.

Publications:
Journal of Applied Communications. q.
Membership Directory. a.
SIGNALS Newsletter. bi-m.

Meetings/Conferences:
Annual Meetings: Summer/400
1999 – Knoxville, TN/June 12-15
2000 – Washington, DC

Agricultural History Soc. *(1919)*
1800 M St., N.W., Room 2103
Washington, DC   20036-5831
Tel: (202)694-5348   *Fax:* (202)694-5663
E-Mail: lkdyson@econ.ag.gov
Members: 1,400 individuals
Staff: 1
Annual Budget: $10-25,000
Exec. Secretary: Lowell K. Dyson

Historical Note
Organized to stimulate interest in, promote the study of and facilitate research and publication on the history of agriculture. The Secretariat is based in the Economic Research Service of the U.S. Department of Agriculture. Membership: $32/year (individual), $19/year (student), $69/year (organization/company).

Publications:
Agricultural History. q. adv.

Meetings/Conferences:
Annual Meetings: April, in conjunction with the Organization of American Historians.
1999 – Toronto, ON, Canada

Agricultural Publishers Ass'n *(1915)*
P.O. Box 410260
St. Louis, MO   63141
Tel: (314)576-7957   *Fax:* (314)576-7989
E-Mail: drake@drakeco.com
Web Site: http://www.Agpub.org
Members: 95 publishers of farm magazines
Staff: 2
Annual Budget: $100-250,000
Exec. Director: Steven Drake

Historical Note
Membership Fee: Varies according to size of circulation.

Meetings/Conferences:
Annual Meetings: October

Agricultural Relations Council *(1953)*

Historical Note
Merged with Agriculture Council of America in 1998.

Agricultural Research Institute *(1951)*
9650 Rockville Pike
Bethesda, MD   20814
Tel: (301)530-7122   *Fax:* (301)530-7007
Members: 125 organizations
Staff: 2
Annual Budget: $100-250,000
Exec. Director: Richard Herrett

Historical Note
Originally affiliated with the Nat'l Academy of Sciences, the ARI was separately incorporated in 1973, but still maintains close ties with the NAS Board on Agriculture. Membership: $600/year (organization), $1,200 (sustaining).

Publications:
Annual Meeting Proceedings. a.
ARI Newsletter. bi-m.
Directory. a.

Meetings/Conferences:
1999 – New Orleans, LA(Sheraton New Orleans)/Nov. 21-23

Agricultural Retailers Ass'n *(1955)*
11701 Borman Drive, Suite 110
St. Louis, MO   63146

Tel: (314)567-6655   *Fax:* (314)567-6808
Toll Free: (800)844 - 4900
E-Mail: ara@agretailerassn.org
Web Site: http://www.agretailerassn.org
Members: 1000 individuals
Staff: 15
Annual Budget: $1-2,000,000
President/C.E.O.: Paul E. Kindinger
Director, Communications: Amy L. Mills
Manager, Meeting and Planning: Kathy Witmeyer
Manager, Education and Professional Development: Sunny
    Wilkerson
V. President, Finance and Administration: Kevin M. Ryan
V. President, Member Services: Jeff Gabriel
V. President, Marketing and Member Services: Jim Stephens

Historical Note
*Formerly Nat'l Nitrogen Solutions Ass'n and (1992) Nat'l Fertilizer
Solutions Ass'n. Absorbed the Nat'l AgriChemical Retailers Ass'n
in 1992. Members are dealers; manufacturers and suppliers of
related products and services, nutrient materials, pesticides; and
fertilizer organizations.*

Publications:
Connections. q.

Meetings/Conferences:
1999 – St. Louis, MO(Convention Center)/Dec. 9-10/1000

Agricultural Transportation Conference (1994)
2200 Mill Road
Alexandria, VA   22314
Tel: (703)838-7990   *Fax:* (703)519-1866
Members: 100 companies
Staff: 3
Annual Budget: $100-250,000
Exec. Director: Fletcher R. Hall

Historical Note
*Represents transporters od agricultural products through lobbying,
educational programs, and communications. A conference of
American Trucking Ass'ns.*

Publications:
Horizons. m. adv.

Meetings/Conferences:
1999 – Orlando, FL(Marriott World Center)/Oct. 31-Nov. 3
2000 – San Diego, CA(Marriott)/Oct. 29-Nov. 1

Agriculture Council of America (1973)
11020 King Street, Suite 205
Overland Park, KS   66210
Tel: (913)491-1895   *Fax:* (913)491-6502
Toll Free: (800)676 - 3608
Web Site: http://www.nana.org
Members: 2,500 individuals, 300 individual & corporate
    members
Staff: 3
Annual Budget: $250-500,000
President and C.E.O.: Eldon White
Director, Communications: Jennifer Becket
Director of Programs: Dana Baith

Historical Note
*Members include producers, commodity groups/cooperatives,
general farm organizations, railroads, port authorities, market
development cooperators, private voluntary agencies, retailers and
financial institutions, and food and agricultural companies. Works
to promote and build public support on behalf of the industry.
Serves as coordinator for Nat'l Agriculture Day. Absorbed
Agricultural Relations Council in 1998. Membership fee varies
according to type of membership.*

Meetings/Conferences:

AIM USA (1972)
634 Alpha Drive
Pittsburgh, PA   15238-2802
Tel: (412)963-8588   *Fax:* (412)963-8753
E-Mail: aidc@aimusa.org
Web Site: http://www.aimusa.org
Members: 160 companies
Staff: 12
Annual Budget: $100-250,000
President and C.E.O.: Larry W. Roberts, CAE
V. President, Marketing: Lisa Dvorchak
V. President, Technology: Dan Mullen

Historical Note
*Formerly (1991) Automatic Indentification Manufacturers, AIM
USA is the trade association of the automatic data collection (ADC)
industry. Member companies are the creators, developers, and
suppliers of automatic data collection technologies, including bar
coding, optical character recognition (OCR), machine vision, radio
frequency identification and communications (RF), magnetic stripe,
smart cards, biometrics, optical cards, touch memory, voice data
entry and systems integration.*

Publications:
AIM USA Publications Guide. a.
Source Book Member Company Directory. a.

Meetings/Conferences:

Air and Expedited Motor Carriers Conference (1966)
2200 Mill Road
Alexandria, VA   22314
Tel: (703)838-7978   *Fax:* (703)519-1866
Members: 100 companies
Staff: 2
Annual Budget: $100-250,000
Exec. Director: David J. Osiecki

Historical Note
*Formerly (1986) Air Freight Motor Carriers Conference. An affiliate
of American Trucking Ass'ns. AEMCC members are truckers
moving freight that has previously been moved by air and handling
via expedited ground service. Membership: $400/year (company);
$550/year (associate).*

Publications:
Expedited Carriers Network Guide. a.
Expeditor. bi-m. adv.
Network Guide. a.

Meetings/Conferences:
Annual Meetings: Late Winter

Air and Waste Management Ass'n (1907)
1 Gateway Ctr., 3rd Fl
Pittsburgh, PA   15222
Tel: (412)232-3444   *Fax:* (412)232-3450
E-Mail: info@awma.org
Web Site: http://www.awma.org
Members: 16,000 organizations & individuals
Staff: 45
Annual Budget: $5-10,000,000
Exec. Director: John A. Thorner, CAE
Director, Meetings and Education: Steve Stasko
Finance Manager: Bill Braun
Director, Member and Product Marketing: Margaret L. Lazzari,
    CAE
Director, Publications: Bill Tony
Director, Staff Services: Jim Dougherty

Historical Note
*Formerly (1989) Air Pollution Control Ass'n. The Association
provides a neutral forum where environmental professionals share
technical and managerial information about air pollution control
and waste management. Members are drawn from a wide range of
disciplines and represent all viewpoints on environmental issues.
Has an annual budget over $7 million. Membership: $110/year
(individual); $1,000/year (contributing); $300/year
(organization).*

Publications:
A&WMA News. m.
EM. m.
Journal of the A&WMA. m. adv.
Resource Book & Membership Directory. a.

Meetings/Conferences:
Annual Meetings: June
1999 – St. Louis, MO
2000 – Salt Lake City, UT

Air Balance Consultants (1967)

Historical Note
Organization defunct in 1997.

Air Brake Ass'n (1891)
2009 Oriole Trail, LB
Michigan City, IN   46360
Tel: (219)874-3129   *Fax:* (219)874-3121
E-Mail: airbrake@niia.net
Members: 700 individuals
Staff: 1
Annual Budget: $10-25,000
Secretary-Treasurer: Henry E. Christie

Historical Note
*Members are engineers, manufacturers, distributors and suppliers of
railway air brakes, railroad personnel and associated foreign
affiliates. Membership: $35/year.*

Publications:
Proceedings. a. adv.

Meetings/Conferences:
Annual Meetings: September with Railway Supply Ass'n in
    Chicago, IL
1999 – (Hilton & Towers)/Spet. 19-22

Air Conditioning Contractors of America (1969)
1712 New Hampshire Ave., N.W.
Washington, DC   20009
Tel: (202)483-9370   *Fax:* (202)234-4721
E-Mail: admin@acca.org
Web Site: http://www.acca.org
Members: 4,030 companies
Staff: 23
Annual Budget: $5-10,000,000
Exec. V. President: Roger Jask, CAE
Director, Government Relations: John Herzog
Director, Education and Training: Michael Honeycutt
Director, Finance and Customer Service: Sondra Qualey
Exec. Director: Lisa Wolf, CAE
Dir., Membership Development/Marketing: Frances Shuping, CAE

Historical Note
*Consolidation of Air conditioning and Refrigeration Contractors of
America with the contractors of the Nat'l Warm Air Heating and
Air Conditioning Ass'n. From 1969 to 1978 known as the Nat'l
Environmental Systems Contractors Ass'n. Supports the Air
Conditioning Contractors of America Political Action Committee.
Membership: $325/year (company).*

Publications:
ACCA News. m.
Membership Directory. a. adv.

Meetings/Conferences:
Annual Meetings: February or March/600
1999 – Orlando, FL(Walt Disney Resort)/February 2-28
2000 – Albuquerque, NM

Air Courier Conference of America (1976)
1255 23rd St., N.W., Suite 850
Washington, DC   20037-1174
Tel: (202)452-0770   *Fax:* (202)833-3636
E-Mail: jmorris@ACCA.org
Web Site: http://www.aircour.org
Members: 100 companies
Staff: 2
Annual Budget: $250-500,000
Exec. Director: Joseph B. Morris

Historical Note
Members are air courier and air package delivery companies.

Publications:
ACCA Flash. m.
ACCA Issues Alert. m.
Member Handbook. a. adv.

Meetings/Conferences:
Annual Meetings: May/400
1999 – Tucson, AZ(Westin La Paloma)/May 16-18

Air Diffusion Council (1960)
104 South Michigan Ave., Suite 1500
Chicago, IL   60603
Tel: (312)201-0101   *Fax:* (312)201-0214
Members: 40 companies
Staff: 2
Annual Budget: $50-100,000
Account Executive: Jack L. Lagershausen

Historical Note
*Members are makers and suppliers of flexible ducts for air
distribution. Membership: $600-2,800/year (company).*

Publications:
Flexible Duct Performance & Installation Standards Manual
    and Videotape.

Meetings/Conferences:

Air Distributing Institute (1947)
4415 W. Harrison St., Suite 242-C
Hillside, IL   60162
Tel: (708)449-2933   *Fax:* (708)449-0837
Members: 27 companies
Staff: 2
Annual Budget: $25-50,000
General Manager: Patricia H. Keating

Historical Note
*Members are manufacturers of prefabricated ducts, pipes and
fittings used in residential housing.*

Publications:
Bulletin. m.

Meetings/Conferences:
1999 – Seattle, WA

Air Force Ass'n (1946)
1501 Lee Hwy.
Arlington, VA   22209-1198
Tel: (703)247-5800   *Fax:* (703)247-5853
Web Site: http://www.afa.org
Members: 170,000 individuals
Staff: 85
Annual Budget: $10-25,000,000
Exec. Director: Gen. John A. Shaud, USAF(Ret.)
Director, Communications: Stephen Aubin
Director, National Defense Issues: Kenneth A. Goss
Director, Meetings & Conference Services: Rosemary Pacenta
Dir., Aerospace Ed. Foundation: Darrell Hayes
Assistant Exec. Director: Ruth T. Fitzpatrick
Chief, Membership Division: Judy Galbreath

Historical Note
*Military and civilian members promoting public understanding of
aerospace power. Has an annual budget of approximately $11.5
million. Membership: $30/year.*

Publications:
Air Force Magazine. m. adv.

Meetings/Conferences:
Annual Meetings: Washington, DC/September/7,000-8,000
1999 – Washington, DC(Marriott Park Wardman)/Sept. 13-15

Air Force Sergeants Ass'n (1961)
P.O. Box 50
Temple Hills, MD   20757
Tel: (301)899-3500   *Fax:* (301)899-8136
Members: 165,000 individuals
Staff: 50
Annual Budget: $2-5,000,000
Director, Military/Gov't Relations: Herbert Wamsley
Dir., Military/Govt. Relations: Herbert C. Wamsley

Historical Note
*Formed May 3, 1961 by three noncommissioned Air Force officers,
and incorporated in the District of Columbia. Members are enlisted
personnel in the U.S. Air Force, Air National Guard and U.S. Air
Force Reserve. Street Address is 5211 Auth Road, Suitland, MD
20746. Membership: $18/year (individual).*

Publications:
AFSA Lobby Ledger. m.
The Sergeants Magazine. m. adv.

Meetings/Conferences:
1999 – Reno, NV(Silver Legacy)/Sept. 1-6

Air Freight Ass'n of America

Historical Note
Became Cargo Airline Ass'n in 1997.

Air Line Employees Ass'n, International (1951)
6500 65th St., Suite 201
Chicago, IL   60638
Tel: (708)563-9999   *Fax:* (708)563-9958
E-Mail: aleaintl@aol.com
Members: 300 individuals
Staff: 7
President: Victor J. Herbert
Director, Communications: Charlotte D. Buntin
Director, Education: David G. Nelson
Treasurer: Donald M. Krull

Historical Note
*Originally part of the Air Line Pilots Ass'n, ALEA became (1963)
an independent chartered affiliate of ALPA. Publishes an aviation
magazine with information covering all facets of the airline industry
and provides consulting work for aviation employee groups.*

Publications:
The Air Line Employee. 6/year.

Meetings/Conferences:
Annual Meetings: Quinquennial Meetings: (2000)

Air Line Pilots Ass'n, Internat'l *(1931)*
535 Herndon Pkwy.
Herndon, VA 20170
Tel: (703)689-2270   *Fax:* (202)689-4370
Members: 49,000 individuals
Staff: 400
Annual Budget: Over $100,000,000
President: J. Randolph Babbitt
Director, Communications: Don P. Skiados
Director, Government Affairs: Paul L. Hallisay
Asst. Director, Finance: Kevin Barnhurst
Director, Legal Department: Carole Thompson, CAE

Historical Note
Organized in Chicago in 1931 by pilot representatives of various air carriers under the leadership of David Behncke and chartered by the American Federation of Labor the same year. Once included the Air Line Employees Association and the Association of Flight Attendants which became independent chartered affiliates in 1963 and 1973, respectively. Absorbed Canadian Air Line Pilots Ass'n in 1997, and now represents pilots at 46 airlines. Supports the Air Line Pilots Political Action Committee. Has an annual budget of approximately $105.0 million.

Publications:
The Air Line Pilot. m. adv.

Meetings/Conferences:
Biennial meetings: Fall 1994

Air Movement and Control Ass'n Internat'l *(1955)*
30 W. University Drive
Arlington Heights, IL 60004-1893
Tel: (847)394-0150   *Fax:* (847)253-0088
E-Mail: amca@amca.org
Web Site: http://www.amca.org
Members: 260 companies
Staff: 21
Annual Budget: $2-5,000,000
Exec. V. President/C.E.O: Peter N. Hanly
Director, Marketing/Communications: Robert E. Davis

Historical Note
Formerly (1977) Air Moving and Conditioning Ass'n. Manufacturers of axial centrifugal fans, power roof ventilators, propeller fans, air curtains, ceiling fans, louvers, accoustic attenuates, dampers, shutters and other air system components. Administers a Certified Ratings Program to insure that products bearing the AMCA seal meet criteria established by the AMCA Certified Rating Program. The Home Ventilating Institute became a division of AMCA in 1984.

Publications:
Directory of Agricultural Products with Certified Ratings.
Home Ventilating Certified Products Directory. a.
Publications Catalog.
Techspecs. semi-a.

Meetings/Conferences:
Annual Meetings: Fall

Air Nat'l Guard Optometric Soc. *(1975)*
Historical Note
Address unknown in 1997.

Air Traffic Control Ass'n *(1956)*
2300 Clarendon Blvd., Suite 711
Arlington, VA 22201
Tel: (703)522-5717   *Fax:* (703)527-7251
E-Mail: atca@worldnet.att.net
Web Site: http://www.atca.org
Members: 4,000 individuals
Staff: 9
Annual Budget: $2-5,000,000
President: Col. Gabriel A. Hartl
Senior V. President: Carol Newmaster
General Counsel: Suzette Matthews

Historical Note
An independent, non-profit professional organization founded by air traffic controllers seeking professional recognition, it now includes all types of professionals working within the air traffic control system. Membership: $78/year (individual), $500-1,000/year (company).

Publications:
ATCA Bulletin. m.
Conference Proceedings. a.
Journal of Air Traffic Control. q. adv.
Quarterly of Air Traffic Control. q.

Meetings/Conferences:
Semi-Annual Meetings: one international, one U.S.
1999 – Vienna, Austria(Vienna Hilton Hotel)/June 8-12/400
1999 – San Diego, CA(Town and Country
    Resorts)/Sept. 26-30/4500

Air Transport Ass'n of America *(1936)*
1301 Pennsylvania Ave., N.W., Suite 1100
Washington, DC 20004-1707
Tel: (202)626-4000   *Fax:* (202)626-4181
Web Site: http://www.air-transport.org
Members: 25 airlines
Staff: 120
Annual Budget: $25-50,000,000
President and C.E.O.: Carol B. Hallett
Managing Director, Communications: David A. Fuscus
Senior V. President, Industry Policy: John M. Meenan
Senior V. President, Legislative and International Affairs: Edward A.
    Merlis
Managing Director, Administration: Karen V. Evans
C.F.O. and Treasurer: Richard T. Brandenburg
Senior V. President, Aviation Safety and Operations: Robert H.
    Franzel
Senior V. President, General Counsel and Secretary: Robert P.
    Warren

Historical Note
Organized January 5, 1936 at a meeting of airline representatives in Chicago, IL. Represents U.S. scheduled airlines in domestic and international passenger and cargo operations. Sponsors and supports the ATA Political Action Committee. Has an annual budget of approximately $27 million.

Publications:
Air Transport. a.

Meetings/Conferences:
Annual Meetings: Washington, DC/December

Air-Conditioning and Refrigeration Institute *(1953)*
4301 N. Fairfax Drive, Suite 425
Arlington, VA 22203
Tel: (703)524-8800   *Fax:* (703)528-3816
E-Mail: ari@ari.org
Web Site: http://www.ari.org
Members: 222 companies
Staff: 43
Annual Budget: $5-10,000,000
President: Clifford H. Rees, Jr.
V. President, Communications & Education: Edward Dooley
V. President, Government Affairs: W. Ted Leland
V. President, Administration & Statistics: Dave Martz
V. President, Engineering & Research: Mark Menzer

Historical Note
Formed in 1953 by a merger of the Refrigeration Equipment Manufacturers Ass'n and the Air Conditioning and Refrigerating Machinery Ass'n. Merged (1965) with the equipment manufacturers of the Nat'l Warm Air Heating and Air-Conditioning Ass'n and (1967) with the Air Filter Institute. Represents manufacturers of air conditioning, refrigeration and heating equipment; membership is divided into sections according to product type. Co-sponsors the Internat'l Air Conditioning, Heating, Refrigerating and Ventilating Trade Exposition. Has an annual budget of approximately $7.2 million. Membership fee based on sales volume.

Publications:
Directories of Certified Performance Ratings for Industry
    Products.
Koldfax. m.
Minuteman Bulletin. m.

Meetings/Conferences:
Annual Meetings: November/500

Air-Conditioning and Refrigeration Wholesalers Ass'n Internat'l *(1935)*
1650 S. Dixie Hwy., 5th Floor
Boca Raton, FL 33432
Tel: (561)338-3495   *Fax:* (561)795-8557
Members: 225 wholesalers, 300 suppliers
Staff: 6
Annual Budget: $500-1,000,000
Exec. Director: David L. Kellough

Historical Note
Formerly Nat'l Refrigeration Supply Jobbers Ass'n and Refrigeration Equipment Wholesalers Ass'n. Members do not service or install what they sell.

Publications:
Counterline. q.
National Directory. a.
Supplier News. 3/yr.
The Wholesaler News. bi-m.

Meetings/Conferences:
Annual Meetings: October

Airborne Law Enforcement Ass'n
P.O. Box 3683
Tulsa, OK 74101-3683
Tel: (918)599-0705   *Fax:* (918)583-2353
Web Site: www.alea.org
Members: 2,100 individuals
Staff: 2
Annual Budget: $100-250,000
Exec. Director: Sherry W. Hadley
President: Charles D. Perriguey

Historical Note
Law enforcement officers who use both fixed and rotary wing aircraft, and who are engaged or interested in the use of aircraft in law enforcement, plus equipment suppliers. Officers elected every 2 years. Membership: $30/year (individual); $360/year (organization/company).

Publications:
Air Beat Magazine. m.
Buyers Guide. a.
Conference Issue. a.

Meetings/Conferences:
Annual Meetings: Summer/800
1999 – Mobile, AL/July 21-24

Aircraft Electronics Ass'n *(1958)*
4217 South Hocker
Independence, MO 64055-7344
Tel: (816)373-6565   *Fax:* (816)478-3100
E-Mail: info@aea.net
Web Site: http://www.aeaavnews.org
Members: 1000 companies
Staff: 7
Annual Budget: $500-1,000,000
President: Paula Derks
V. President, Administration/Meeting Management: Debbie A.
    McFarland
Director, Membership Services: Mark Gibson

Historical Note
Companies engaged in the manufacture, installation, and servicing of aviation electronic equipment. Membership fee based on annual sales volume or size of personnel.

Publications:
Avionics News. m. adv.

Meetings/Conferences:
Annual Meetings: Spring
1999 – Atlanta, GA/(Hyatt)/May 12-15

Aircraft Locknut Manufacturers Ass'n
994 Old Eagle School Road, Suite 1019
Wayne, PA 19087-1802
Tel: (610)971-4850   *Fax:* (610)971-4859
E-Mail: JASHIFFERT@ALMANET.ORG
Members: 10 individuals, 50 companies
Staff: 2
Annual Budget: $25-50,000
Exec. Director: John A. Shiffert, CAE

Historical Note
ALMA established a code of practice to ensure the highest standards of quality and reliability are met by threaded fasteners produced by its members.

Meetings/Conferences:
Semi-Annual Meetings: usually in California

Aircraft Owners and Pilots Ass'n *(1939)*
421 Aviation Way
Frederick, MD 21701-4756
Tel: (301)695-2000   *Fax:* (301)695-2375
E-Mail: aopahq@aopa.org
Web Site: http://www.aopa.org
Members: 340,000 individuals
Staff: 180
Annual Budget: $5-10,000,000
President: Phil Boyer
Senior V. President, Communications: Drew Steketee
Director, Legislative Communications: Rick Hodges
Sr. V.P., Govt./Technical Affairs: Thomas B. Chapman
Director, Meetings and Conventions: Ann M. Kilian
Exec. V. President, Operations: Diana T. Roberts
General Counsel and Secretary: John S. Yodice
Sr. V.P., Membership Marketing: Karen Detert
Senior V. President, Publications: Thomas Haines
Sr. V. President, Products and Services: Andrew L. Horelick

Historical Note
AOPA is the world's largest aviation organization, representing more than 340,000 U.S. pilots. AOPA is a national advocate for operators of 96% of the 170,000 general aviation aircraft for personal and business transportation. AOPA Air Safety Foundation (ASF) conducts continuing pilot education and safety training. ASF's 35,000-record general aviation accident database is the most comprehensive outside of government. Membership: $39/year (individual).

Publications:
AOPA Pilot. m. adv.
AOPA's Aviation USA. a.

Meetings/Conferences:
Annual Meetings: October

Airforwarders Ass'n *(1990)*
P.O. Box 1602
2230 W. Chapman Ave., Suite 203
Orange, CA 92868
Tel: (714)634-9677   *Fax:* (714)634-9678
E-Mail: airfwdrasn@aol.com
Web Site: http://www.logcity.com/airfwdrasn
Members: 90 companies
Exec. Director: James Foster

Historical Note
Airforwarder Ass'n members are air freight forwarding companies holding valid FAA Security Agreement Numbers. Associate members are airlines, truckers and other non-forwarders with an interest in the industry.

Publications:
Forward Newsletter. bi-m. adv.

Meetings/Conferences:
1999 – Las Vegas, NV(Caeser's Palace)/March 7-10/300

Airline Industrial Relations Conference *(1971)*
1920 N St., N.W., Suite 250
Washington, DC 20036
Tel: (202)861-7550   *Fax:* (202)861-7557
Web Site: www.aircon.org
Members: 32 companies
Staff: 4
Annual Budget: $250-500,000
V. President and Treasurer: Robert J. DeLucia

Historical Note
Also known as the AIR Conference. Used by its members as an information exchange for such matters as industrial and personnel relations, equal employment opportunity, and related issues.

Airline Suppliers Ass'n *(1993)*
636 I St., NW, Suite 301
Washington, DC 20001-3736
Tel: (202)216-9140   *Fax:* (202)216-9227
E-Mail: airsup19@mail.idt.net
Web Site: http://www.airlinesuppliers.com
Members: 240 companies
Staff: 2
Annual Budget: $500-1,000,000
President: Michele L. Schweitzer

Historical Note
Members are companies providing materials and services to commercial airlines. Membership: $1,000-$2,500/year.

Publications:
The Update Report. m. adv.

Meetings/Conferences:
1999 – Marco Island, FL(Marriott Resorts)

Airlines Electronic Engineering Committee *(1949)*
2551 Riva Road
Annapolis, MD 21401
Tel: (410)266-4114   *Fax:* (410)266-2047

Members: 27 companies
Staff: 12
Chairman: Daniel A. Martinec

Historical Note
Develops voluntary standards for electronic systems used in aircraft, and serves as an advocate for the aircraft engineering community.

Airlines Medical Directors Ass'n *(1944)*
United Airlines Medical Dept. (DENMD)
Denver International Airport
Denver, CO 80249-6363
Tel: (303)348-4300 *Fax:* (303)348-4338
Members: 165 individuals
Staff: 2
Annual Budget: under $10,000
Secretary: Ralph G. Fennell, M.D.

Historical Note
An international organization founded in 1944 to improve the practice and standards of aviation and industrial medicine, particularly as pertaining to domestic and international airline operations, and to encourage research and study of medical problems in these fields. Membership: $25/year.

Publications:
Newsletter. 3/year.

Meetings/Conferences:
Annual Meetings: With the Aerospace Medical Association in May.

Airport Consultants Council *(1978)*
908 King St., Suite 100
Alexandria, VA 22314
Tel: (703)683-5900 *Fax:* (703)683-2564
E-Mail: info@acconline.org
Web Site: http://www.acconline.org
Members: 220 companies
Staff: 4
Annual Budget: $250-500,000
Exec. Director: Paula Bline
Director of Operations: Grice Whiteley

Historical Note
ACC represents the majority of airport consulting firms in the United States. Member firms include architectural, engineering, planning, management, construction, marketing, economic consultants as well as firms that manufacture or supply airport equipment, products or other services. Membership fee: $1,500/year.

Publications:
ACC News. m. adv.
Access Fax. w.
Guide to Selecting Airport Consultants & Membership Directory. a.

Meetings/Conferences:
1999 – Reno, NV(The Nugget)/March 17-19
1999 – Hilo, HI/Nov. 14-17

Airport Ground Transportation Ass'n *(1946)*
5320 Riverbriar Road
Knoxville, TN 37919-9335
Tel: (423)525-1108 *Fax:* (423)637-6419
Members: 350 individuals, 125 companies
Staff: 2
Annual Budget: $100-250,000
Administrator/Planner: Sandra Mundy

Historical Note
Members include airport authorities and operators and industry suppliers of ground transportation at airports and courtesy transportation providers. Membership: $330/year (organization/company).

Publications:
AGTA Newsletter. bi-m. adv.

Meetings/Conferences:
Semi-annual Meetings: February-March and September

Airport Security Council *(1968)*
Historical Note
Address unknown in 1996.

Airports Council Internat'l/North America *(1948)*
1775 K St., N.W., Suite 500
Washington, DC 20006
Tel: (202)293-8500 *Fax:* (202)331-1362
E-Mail: postmaster@aci-na.org
Web Site: http://www.aci-na.org
Members: 168 operating organizations
Staff: 28
Annual Budget: $2-5,000,000
President: David Z. Plavin
Senior V. President Technical and Environmental Affairs: Richard Marchi
Exec. V. President: Robert R. Wigington
V. President, Legal and Regulatory Affairs: Patricia A. Hahn
Director, Membership Services: Susan Black Olson

Historical Note
Founded in 1948 as the Airport Operators Council, the organization became (1965) Airport Operators Council Internat'l, and (1991) Airports Ass'n Cuncil Internat'l following its merger with Internat'l Civil Airports Ass'n; assumed its current name in 1993. Members are boards, commissions, local governmental entities operating public airport facilities. Membership: $500-93,000/year, according to size of airport.

Publications:
Airport Highlights. bi-w. adv.

Meetings/Conferences:
Annual Meetings: Fall/1,800
1999 – Las Vegas, NV/Oct. 24-27/2000
2000 – New York, NY/Oct. 1-4/2000

Alcohol and Drug Problems Ass'n of North America *(1949)*
Historical Note
Address unknown in 1996.

Alexander Graham Bell Ass'n for the Deaf *(1890)*
3417 Volta Place, N.W.
Washington, DC 20007
Tel: (202)337-5220 *Fax:* (202)337-8314
E-Mail: agbell2@aol.com
Web Site: http://www.agbell.org
Members: 5,200 individuals
Staff: 16
Annual Budget: $1-2,000,000
Dir., Membership/Marketing: Elizabeth Quigley

Historical Note
Founded by Alexander Graham Bell to promote the teaching of speech, speech-reading, and use of residual hearing. Has three sections: Parents Section; Internat'l Professional Section; Oral Hearing Impaired Section. The Bell Association is a member of the Council on Education of the Deaf. Membership: $50/year.

Publications:
The Volta Review. 5/year. adv.
Volta Voices. bi-m. adv.

Meetings/Conferences:
Biennial Meetings: usually June-July
2000 – Philadelphia, PA
2002 – St. Louis, MO(Adams Mark)

Alfalfa Council *(1953)*
23 Toyon Drive
Woodland, CA 95695
Tel: (530)662-6565 *Fax:* (530)669-2311
Web Site: http://www.alfalfa.org
Members: 800 individuals
Staff: 11
Annual Budget: $100-250,000
Exec. Director: Jerrold Johnson

Historical Note
Formerly (1998) Certified Alfalfa Seed Council. AC members are alfalfa seed growers, cleaners, conditioners and consumers.

Publications:
Alfalfa Talk. q.

Meetings/Conferences:
National Symposium: Feb.-March/300-550

Alkyl Amines Council *(1985)*
1850 M St., N.W., Suite 700
Washington, DC 20036
Tel: (202)721-4160 *Fax:* (202)296-8120
Members: 7 companies
Staff: 2
Exec. Director: Richard E. Opatick, CAE

Historical Note
Affiliated with the Synthetic Organic Chemical Manufacturers Ass'n.

All-America Rose Selections *(1938)*
221 N. LaSalle St., 35th Floor
Chicago, IL 60601
Tel: (312)372-7090 *Fax:* (312)372-6160
Web Site: http://www.rose.org
Members: 20 commercial rose growers
Staff: 3
Annual Budget: $250-500,000
Secretary-Treasurer: Paul Fullmer
Communications Director: Kathy Commings
Exec. Secretary: Paul Fullmer

Historical Note
A non-profit corporation formed by rose producers and introducers to test new varieties of roses and determine which, if any, could be recommended to the public as exceptional.

Publications:
Rose Report. 3/yr.

Meetings/Conferences:
Annual Meetings: July, with the American Ass'n of Nurserymen November Meetings.
1999 – Philadelphia, PA

Alliance for Children and Families *(1911)*
11700 W. Lake Park Drive
Milwaukee, WI 53224
Tel: (414)359-1040 *Fax:* (414)359-1074
Toll Free: (800)221 - 2681
Members: 280 agencies
Staff: 100
Annual Budget: $5-10,000,000
President & C.E.O.: Peter Goldberg
Director, National Info. Center: Susan Hornung

Historical Note
Merged with (1998) Nat'l Ass'n of Homes and Services for Children. Formerly (1998) Family Services America. FSA, founded in 1911, is an international nonprofit association dedicated to strengthening family life through services, education and advocacy. FSA's nearly 300 members in the United States, Canada and worldwide constitute the largest network of community-based, counseling and support organizations for families. In North America alone, FSA serves more than 4 million families annually in over 1,000 communities.

Publications:
Directory of Member Agencies. a.
Families in Society. 10/year. adv.

Meetings/Conferences:
Biennial Meetings: Odd years

Alliance for Community Media *(1976)*
666 11th St., N.W., Suite 806

Washington, DC 20001-4542
Tel: (202)393-2650 *Fax:* (202)393-2653
E-Mail: alliancecm@aol.com
Web Site: http://www.shadow.net/tapacm.html
Members: 900 individualsand organizations
Staff: 2
Annual Budget: $250-500,000
Exec. Director: Bunnie Riedel
Director, Member Services: Kelly M. Matthews

Historical Note
Formerly (1992) Nat'l Federation of Local Cable Programmers. Organized to foster citizen participation in community television programming. Membership: $85/year, professional (individual), $195-305/year (organization).

Publications:
Community Media Resource Directory. a.
Community Media Review. q. adv.

Meetings/Conferences:
Annual Meetings: July
1999 – Cinncinati, OH

Alliance for Competitive Transportation
Historical Note
Organization defunct in 1998.

Alliance for Continuing Medical Education *(1975)*
1025 Montgomery Hwy., Suite 208
Birmingham, AL 35216
Tel: (205)824-1355 *Fax:* (205)824-1357
E-Mail: acme@magicweb.net
Web Site: http://www.acme-assn.org
Members: 2,600 individuals
Staff: 5
Annual Budget: $500-1,000,000
Exec. Director: Bruce Bellande, Ph.D.
Director, Professional Development: Bernie Halbun

Historical Note
A professional association concerned exclusively with continuing medical education. Membership: $195/year (individual); $525/year (institution); $1,500/year (corporation).

Publications:
Almanac. m. adv.
Journal for Continuing Education in Health Professions. q.

Meetings/Conferences:
Annual Meetings: January
1999 – Atlanta, GA(Hilton Hotel)/Jan. 27-31/1100
2000 – New Orleans, LA(Hilton Hotel)/Jan. 18-23/1100
2001 – San Francisco, CA(Marriott)/Jan. 24-27/1400
2002 – Orlando, FL(Coronado Springs Resort)/Jan. 30-Feb. 3/1500

Alliance for Fire and Emergency Management
Historical Note
Became Internat'l Soc. of Fire Service Instructors in 1997.

Alliance for Healthcare Strategy and Marketing *(1984)*
11 S. LaSalle St., Suite 2300
Chicago, IL 60603-1303
Tel: (312)704-9700 *Fax:* (312)704-9709
Web Site: http://www.alliancehlth.org
Members: 2,700 individuals
Staff: 5
Annual Budget: $500-1,000,000
President: Carla Windhorst

Historical Note
Alliance members are marketing professionals working for health care institutions. Provides information on current strategies for business growth within the industry. Membership: $175/year.

Publications:
Alliance Report. m.
Membership Directory. a.
Resource Guide. adv. adv.
Trendwatch. q.

Meetings/Conferences:
Annual Meetings: March

Alliance for Nonprofit Management *(1998)*
1899 L St., N.W., Sixth Floor
Washington, DC 20036
Tel: (202)955-8406 *Fax:* (213)822-0669
E-Mail: alliance@allianceonline.org
Web Site: www.allianceonline.org
Members: 170 individuals
Staff: 3
Annual Budget: $100-250,000
President: Karen Simmons
Administrative Coordinator: Laura Pruteanu

Historical Note
Formerly (1998) Nonprofit Management Ass'n. The Alliance for Nonprofit Management is a professional association of member organizations and individuals devoted primarily to helping nonprofit organizations increase their effectiveness and impact. The alliance and its members work collectively and individually to develop, codify, and deliver practices in management and governance of nonprofit organizations.

Publications:
Alliance Member Directory. a.
PULSE! bi-m.

Meetings/Conferences:
Annual Meetings: Summer
1999 – Boston, MA/Dec. 2-5

Alliance for Responsible Atmospheric Policy *(1980)*
2111 Wilson Blvd., Suite 850
Arlington, VA 22201-3058
Tel: (703)243-0344 *Fax:* (703)243-2874
Members: 300 companies
Staff: 3

Annual Budget: $250-500,000
Exec. Director: David Stirpe

Historical Note
Formerly (1995) Alliance for Responsible CFC Policy. Members are companies that use or produce chlorofluorocarbons and their alternatives, a family of compounds containing carbon, chlorine, fluorine and sometimes hydrogen. Used primarily as refrigerants, specialty solvents, agents for foamed plastics, etc.

Publications:
Newsletter. m.

Alliance for Telecommunications Industry Solutions (1983)
1200 G St., N.W., Suite 500
Washington, DC 20005
Tel: (202)434-8847   *Fax:* (202)393-5453
Web Site: http://www.atis.org
Members: 125 companies
Staff: 34
Annual Budget: $2-5,000,000
President: George L. Edwards
Director, Public Relations: John Bernhards

Historical Note
ATIS, formerly (1993) known as Exchange Carriers Standards Ass'n, was created as part of the break-up of the Bell System. Membership open to North American and World Zone 1 Caribbean providers of telecommunications services with a plant investment in transport and/or switching, as well as resellers, manufacturers of telecommunications network equipment and/or software, and providers of enhanced services. Provides technical standards for telecommunications network interconnection and conducts open forums for resolving national telecommunications operational issues. Participation in forums open to local exchange interchange carriers, manufacturers, vendors, end users, cellular service providers, competitive access providers, cable t.v. Membership: Scaled by annual revenue.

Publications:
ATIS Annual Report. a.
ATIS News. m.
T1 Committee Annual Report. a.
Telecommunications Committee T1. semi-a.

Meetings/Conferences:
Annual Meetings: October

Alliance for Traffic Safety (1968)
c/o Missouri Safety Center
HUM Suite 201 CMSU
Warrensburg, MO 64093-5117
Tel: (816)543-4830   *Fax:* (816)543-4482
E-Mail: djones@cmsul.cmsu.edu
Members: 60 organizations
Annual Budget: under $10,000
Corresponding Secretary: Dennis W. Jones

Historical Note
Provides member organizations with a forum for the exchange of information, and acts as a liaison between members and state or federal safety officials.

Meetings/Conferences:

Alliance of American Insurers (1922)
3025 Highland Pkwy., Suite 800
Downers Grove, IL 60515
Tel: (847)330-8500   *Fax:* (847)330-8602
E-Mail: webmaster@allianceal.org
Web Site: http://www.allianceal.org
Members: 200 companies, 100 organizations
Staff: 80
Annual Budget: $5-10,000,000
President: Rodger S. Lawson
V. President, Public Affairs: Larry E. Kibbee
Senior V. President, State Government Affairs: Mike Stinziano, Ph.D.
Sr. V.P. and Secretary-Treasurer: Gregory W. Heidrich
V. President, Administration: JoAnn Stopka
V. President & General Counsel: Richard P. Hefferan
Associate V. President, Membership: Charles F. Stonehill
Senior V. President: Ann W. Spragens
V. President, Workers Compensation: John Lennes, Jr.

Historical Note
Founded as the American Mutual Alliance, it became the American Mutual Insurance Alliance in 1956. Broadened membership eligibility to include non-mutual as well as mutual insurers and assumed its present name in 1977. Maintains a Washington office. Supports the Alliance of American Insurers Federal Political Action Committee.

Meetings/Conferences:
Annual Meetings: Spring
1999 – New Orleans, LA/March 27-31

Alliance of Black Entertainment Technicians (1987)
1869 Buckingham Road
Los Angeles, CA 90019
Tel: (323)933-0746   *Fax:* (323)934-7643
E-Mail: SMabet@pacbell.net
Web Site: http://www.abetnetwork.com
Members: 1000 individuals
President: Shirley Moore

Historical Note
ABET members are African-American technicians employed in the entertainment industry.

Publications:
Newsletter. q.

Meetings/Conferences:
Annual Meetings: December

Alliance of Business Brokers and Intermediaries (1996)
1926 Waukegan Road, Suite #1
Glenview, IL 60025-1770

Tel: (847)657-6736   *Fax:* (847)657-6819
E-Mail: tcaghq@tcag.com
Members: 100 individuals
Staff: 1
Annual Budget: $10-25,000
Exec. V. President: Carl A. Wangman, CAE

Historical Note
Membership: $150/year.

Alliance of Cardiovascular Professionals (1957)
910 Charles St., Suite A
Fredericksburg, VA 22401-5810
Tel: (540)370-0102   *Fax:* (540)370-0015
Web Site: http://www.acp-online.org
Members: 3,500 individuals
Staff: 5
Annual Budget: $250-500,000
Exec. Director: Peggy McElgunn

Historical Note
Merger of the Nat'l Soc. of Cardiopulmonary Technologists, the American Cardiology Technology Ass'n, and the Nat'l Alliance of Cardiovascular Technologists. Formerly Nat'l Soc. for Cardiovascular and Pulmonary Technology, became Nat'l Soc. for Cardiovascular Technology/Nat'l Soc. for Pulmonary Technology in 1988. Absorbed American College of Cardiovascular Invasive Specialists in 1993, and Soc. for Cardiovascular Management 1995. Assumed its current name in 1998. Membership: $67-95/year (individual), $1,00/year (silver), $2,000/year (gold), $3,000/year (platinum).

Publications:
CP Digest. bi-m. adv.
Heart-to-Heart. q. adv.
Pulmonary News. q. adv.
Strategies. q.
The Beat Goes On. q. adv.
The Cardiovascular Professional. bi-m. adv.

Alliance of Claims Assistance Professionals
731 Naperville Road
Wheaton, IL 60187-6407
Tel: (630)588-1260   *Fax:* (630)690-0377
E-Mail: askus@claims.org
Web Site: http://www.claims.org

Alliance of Foam Packaging Recyclers (1991)
2128 Espey Ct., Suite 4
Crofton, MD 21114-2426
Tel: (410)451-8340   *Fax:* (410)451-8343
Toll Free: (800)944 - 8448
E-Mail: bdecampo@aol.com
Web Site: www.epspackaging.org
Members: 50 individuals
Staff: 2
Annual Budget: $250-500,000
Exec. Director: Betsy de Campos

Publications:
Molding the Future. q.

Meetings/Conferences:
1999 – Chicago, IL(Hotel Intercontinental)/April 27-29/180

Alliance of Information and Referral Systems (1973)
P.O. Box 31668
Seattle, WA 98103
Tel: (206)632-2477   *Fax:* (206)632-0855
E-Mail: PKAAIRS@aol.com
Web Site: www.airs.org
Members: 557 individuals, 420 agencies
Staff: 2
Annual Budget: $50-100,000
Exec. Director: Peter Aberg
Office Manager: Duane Gimbell

Historical Note
Organizations and individuals providing a contact point for those with various social problems so that they can be referred to others who can assist them. Membership: $50/yr. (volunteer/student); $70/yr. (professional); $90-220/yr. (agency).

Publications:
AIRS Newsletter. bi-m. adv.
Directory of Information & Referral Services. a.
Journal of Information and Referral. 5/yea.

Meetings/Conferences:
Annual Meetings: Spring
1999 – Portland, OR/May 1-5

Alliance of Metalworking Industries (1974)
Historical Note
Organization dissolved in 1995.

Alliance of Motion Picture and Television Producers (1924)
15503 Ventura Blvd
Encino, CA 91436
Tel: (818)995-3600   *Fax:* (818)382-1793
Members: 25 companies
Staff: 12
Annual Budget: $500-1,000,000
President: Nicholas Counter, III

Historical Note
Merger of Ass'n of Motion Picture Producers (1924) and Alliance of Television Film Producers (1951) and Soc. of Independent Producers. In 1964, the Ass'n of Motion Picture and Television Producers and the Alliance separated into two distinct organizations, but later merged in 1982 under the current title.

Alliance of Nonprofit Mailers (1980)
1211 Connecticut Ave., N.W., Suite 620
Washington, DC 20036-2701
Tel: (202)462-5132

E-Mail: NPMailers@Aol.com
Members: 200 nonprofit organizations
Staff: 3
Annual Budget: $500-1,000,000
Exec. Director: Neal Denton

Historical Note
A national association of nonprofit organizations and businesses interested in stabilizing nonprofit postal rates. Membership: sliding fee.

Publications:
Alliance Report. w.

Meetings/Conferences:
Annual Meetings: Spring/Early Summer

Alliance of State Car and Truck Renting and Leasing Ass'ns
1225 I St., N.W., Suite 500
Washington, DC 20005-3914
Tel: (202)682-4778   *Fax:* (202)789-4512
Members: 21 associations
Staff: 3
Annual Budget: under $10,000
Coordinator: Jan M. Armstrong
Operations Director: Melanie Fenoyar

Historical Note
The Alliance serves as a coordinating body for the state and regional CATRALAs (Car and Truck Leasing Ass'ns), serving the interests of motor vehicle renting/leasing organizations in the U.S.

Allied Artists of America (1914)
15 Gramercy Park South
New York, NY 10003
Tel: (212)582-6411
Members: 400 regular & 1,200 associates
Annual Budget: $10-25,000
President: Gary Erbe

Historical Note
Membership consists of painters and sculptors. Initiated at a meeting at the Grand Union Hotel in New York, January 24, 1914. Purpose is to promote American art and furnish exhibition space for American artists. Membership: $40/year (individual); $25/year (associate).

Publications:
Annual Exhibition Catalogue. a. adv.
Newsletter. a.

Meetings/Conferences:
Annual Meetings: Spring, third Wednesday in April in New York City
1999 – November

Allied Stone Industries (1958)
P.O. Box 273
Susquehanna, PA 18847
Tel: (717)465-7200   *Fax:* (800)672-3524
Members: 60 companies
Annual Budget: $25-50,000

Historical Note
Members are producers of natural stone. Has no paid officers or full-time staff; officers change biennially. Membership: $500/year.

Meetings/Conferences:

Allied Trades of the Baking Industry (1920)
4510 W. 89th St., Suite 110
Prairie Village, KS 66207-2282
Tel: (913)341-0765   *Fax:* (913)341-6912
Members: 500 individuals
Annual Budget: $10-25,000
Dir., Client Services: Wendi Rose

Historical Note
Members are salesmen working for companies servicing the baking industry. Membership: $25/year (individual); $250/year (corporate).

Publications:
The Allied Tradesman. 3/year. adv.

Meetings/Conferences:

Allied Underwear Ass'n (1913)
Historical Note
Organization defunct in 1995.

Alpha Chi Sigma (1902)
2141 North Franklin Road
Indianapolis, IN 46219
Tel: (317)357-5944
Toll Free: (800)252 - 4369
Members: 52,000 individuals
Staff: 4
Annual Budget: $100-250,000
Nat'l Secretary: Paul R. Jones

Historical Note
A professional fraternity of chemists and chemical engineers founded at the University of Wisconsin, December, 1902 and incorporated in Wisconsin.

Publications:
The Hexagon. q.

Meetings/Conferences:
Biennial Meetings: Even years, always held on a university campus

Alpha Gamma Rho (1904)
10101 N. Executive Hills Blvd.
Kansas City, MO 64153
Tel: (816)891-9200   *Fax:* (816)891-9401
Members: 54,000 individuals
Staff: 8
Annual Budget: $1-2,000,000
Exec. Director: Philip Josephson

Historical Note
Professional agricultural fraternity.
Publications:
Sickle & Sheaf. q.
Meetings/Conferences:
Biennial Meetings: even years
2000 – Savannah, GA August /400

Alpha Kappa Psi *(1904)*
9595 Angola Ct.
Indianapolis, IN   46268-1119
Tel: (317)872-1553   *Fax:* (317)872-1567
E-Mail: hqmail@akpsi.com
Web Site: http://www.akpsi.com
Members: 160,000 individuals
Staff: 8
Annual Budget: $500-1,000,000
Exec. Director: Gary L. Epperson, CAE
Manager, Finance: Patrich Gallagher

Historical Note
Professional fraternity, business administration. Founded at New York University October 5, 1904 and incorporated in the State of New York the following year. Membership: $60/year (student); $25/year (alumnus), plus initiation and pledge fee.
Publications:
Beacon Newsletter. q.
The Diary. q.
Meetings/Conferences:
Biennial Meetings: uneven years in August
1999 – Orlando, FL

Alpha Omega Internat'l Dental Fraternity *(1907)*
1314 Bedford Ave., Suite 206
Baltimore, MD   21208-3737
Tel: (410)602-3300   *Fax:* (410)602-3394
Toll Free: (800)677 - 8468
E-Mail: HQTRS@AOL.COM
Web Site: http://www.AO.ORG
Members: 15,000 individuals
Staff: 4
Annual Budget: $500-1,000,000
Exec. Director: Stephanie Block

Historical Note
A professional, international dental fraternity formed through the merger of the Ramach Fraternity (formed at the Pennsylvania College of Dental Surgery in 1906) and the Alpha Omega Dental Fraternity (formed at the University of Maryland in 1907). The fraternity remains dedicated to the same mission as its founding fathers: serving as the voice of the Jew in dentistry, aiding dental education and encouraging professional excellence. Membership: $115/year (international), plus chapter dues.
Publications:
AO Today. q. adv. adv.
The Alpha Omegan. q. adv.
Meetings/Conferences:
Annual Meetings: December
1999 – San Francisco, CA/Dec. 25-Jan. 1
2000 – Phoenix, AZ/Dec. 25-Jan. 1

Alpha Tau Delta *(1921)*
150 Cruickshank Dr.
Folsom, CA   95630
Tel: (916)984-9150
E-Mail: kerrik@atdnursing.org
Web Site: http://atdnursing.org
Members: 11,000 individuals
Annual Budget: $25-50,000
Corresponding Secretary: Kerri Kaye

Historical Note
ATD is a professional nursing fraternity affiliated with the Professional Fraternity Ass'n. It supports chapters which offer workshops, seminars, scholarships, grants, and loans. Membership: $35/year (individual).
Publications:
Cap'tions of Alpha Tau Delta. q.
President's Letter. q.
Meetings/Conferences:
Annual Meetings: Biennial Meetings: odd years.
1999 – Colorado Springs, CO

Alpha Zeta Omega *(1919)*
4422 Porpoise Drive
Tampa, FL   33617
Tel: (813)988-5338
Members: 11,000 individuals
Staff: 1
Annual Budget: $25-50,000
Director, Fraternal Affairs: Bruce Strell

Historical Note
Professional pharmacy fraternity founded at the Philadelphia College of Pharmacy in December 1919.
Publications:
Azoan. a. adv.
Meetings/Conferences:
Annual Meetings: Second week in July/350

Aluminum Anodizers Council *(1988)*
1000 N. Rand Road, Suite 214
Wauconda, IL   60084
Tel: (847)526-2010   *Fax:* (847)526-3993
E-Mail: mail@anodizing.org
Web Site: http://www.anodizing.org
Members: 60 companies
Staff: 5
Annual Budget: $100-250,000
President: Donn W. Sanford, CAE

Historical Note
Formerly (1992) Architectural Anodizers Council. Members are manufacturers of anodized aluminum products. AAC advances, supports, and promotes the anodizing aluminum industry. AAC released the Anodized Aluminum Color Standards for Architectural Applications to assure color consistency when specifying anodized aluminum. Membership: $1,500/year (firm); $1,875/year (supplier); $500/year (associate); $50/year (professional).
Publications:
AAC Reports Newsletter. bi-m.
Industry Guide. a. adv.
Meetings/Conferences:

Aluminum Ass'n *(1933)*
900 19th St., N.W. Suite 300
Washington, DC   20006
Tel: (202)862-5100   *Fax:* (202)862-5164
Web Site: http://www.aluminum.org
Members: 62 companies
Staff: 30
Annual Budget: $5-10,000,000
President: J. Stephen Larkin
Public Relations: Yvonne A. Folkerts
Director, Government Relations: Gordon Fry
V. President, Government Affairs: M. Barry Meyer
Director, Meetings and Member Services: Ysabel S. Korolevich
Director, Administration and Treasurer: Carol A. Williams

Historical Note
Members are manufacturers of aluminum mill products and producers of aluminum. Sponsors and supports the Aluminum Ass'n Political Action Committee.
Publications:
Aluminum Electrical Report. 2-3/year.
Aluminum Report. q.
Aluminum Situation. m.
Aluminum Standards and Data. every 3 years.
Aluminum Statistical Review. a.
Meetings/Conferences:
Semi-annual Meetings: Fall and early Spring/usually
          Washington, DC

Aluminum Extruders Council *(1951)*
1000 N. Rand Road, Suite 214
Wauconda, IL   60084
Tel: (847)526-2010   *Fax:* (847)526-3993
Web Site: http://www.aec.org
Members: 200 companies
Staff: 7
Annual Budget: $1-2,000,000
President: Donn W. Sanford, CAE
Director, Member Services: Greg Rajsky
Government Relations: Dick Penna
Director, Special Events: Joyce Sanford
Director of Administration: Gary Robinson
Administrative Assistant: Tina Shields
Publications:
The Executive Report. m.
Meetings/Conferences:
Annual Meetings: March

Aluminum Fenestration Products Ass'n *(1992)*
Historical Note
Defunct in 1996.

Aluminum Foil Container Manufacturers Ass'n *(1955)*
P.O. Box 531335
Mountain Brook, AL   35253
Tel: (205)802-7600   *Fax:* (205)802-7610
E-Mail: hrushing@usit.net
Web Site: http://www.afcma.org
Members: 14 companies
Staff: 2
Annual Budget: $50-100,000
Exec. Director: Hugh J. Rushing

Historical Note
Manufacturers of aluminum foil containers.
Meetings/Conferences:
Semi-Annual Meetings: late Winter-Spring and Fall/36

Aluminum Recycling Ass'n *(1929)*
Historical Note
Defunct in 1997.

Aluminum, Brick and Glass Workers Internat'l Union *(1953)*
Historical Note
Became a division of United Steelworkers of America in 1997.

AM/FM Internat'l
Historical Note
Became Geospatial Information and Technology Ass'n in 1998.

Amalgamated Clothing and Textile Workers Union *(1914)*
Historical Note
Merged with Internat'l Ladies Garment Workers Union to form Union of Needletrade Industrial and Textile Employees in 1995.

Amalgamated Printers' Ass'n *(1958)*
6906 Colony Loop Drive
Austin, TX   78724
Members: 150 individuals
Annual Budget: under $10,000
Archivist: David L. Kent

Historical Note
Voluntary ass'n of printers, typefounders, graphic artists, calligraphers, private presses, and type collectors interested in the
preservation of letterpress printing. Has no permanent address or paid staff. Membership limited to 150. Officers change biennially.
Publications:
"Treasure Gems". a.
Cooperative Calendar. a.
Membership List. a.
Meetings/Conferences:
1999 – Indianapolis, IN

Amalgamated Transit Union *(1892)*
5025 Wisconsin Ave., N.W.
3rd Floor
Washington, DC   20016
Tel: (202)537-1645   *Fax:* (202)244-7824
Web Site: http://www.atu.org
Members: 165,000 individuals
Staff: 25
Annual Budget: $5-10,000,000
Internat'l President: James La Sala

Historical Note
Established in Indianapolis on September 15, 1892 as the Amalgamated Ass'n of Street Railway Employees of America and affiliated with the American Federation of Labor in 1893. Became the Amalgamated Ass'n of Street and Electric Railway Employees of America in 1903, the Amalgamated Ass'n of Street, Electric Railway and Motor Coach Employees of America in 1934 and assumed its present name in 1964. The dominant union in the local transit and over the road bus industry with membership in the U.S. and Canada. Members are operating, maintenance and administrative employees. Sponsors and supports the Amalgamated Transit Union Political Contributions Committee.
Publications:
In Transit. bi-m.
Meetings/Conferences:
Triennial Meetings: (1998)

Ambulance Manufacturers Division
Historical Note
An affiliate of the Nat'l Truck Equipment Ass'n.

Ambulatory Pediatric Ass'n *(1960)*
6728 Old McLean Village Drive
McLean, VA   22101
Tel: (703)556-9222   *Fax:* (703)556-8729
E-Mail: info@ambpeds.org
Members: 1,800 individuals
Staff: 1
Annual Budget: $250-500,000
Exec. Secretary: Marge Degnon

Historical Note
Formerly (1969) Ass'n for Ambulatory Pediatric Services. An organization for those working in child health care programs, either in teaching and patient care or pediatrics research. Membership: $150/year (physicians); $60/year (non-physicians); $30/year (physicians-in-training).
Publications:
Newsletter.
Meetings/Conferences:
Annual Meetings: Spring
1999 – San Francisco, CA(Convention Center)/May 1-4
2000 – Boston, MA(Convention Center)/May 13-16/4500
2001 – Baltimore, MD(Convention Center)/Apr. 27-May
          1/4500
2002 – Baltimore, MD/May 3-7/4500

America Outdoors *(1991)*
P.O. Box 10847
Knoxville, TN   37939-0847
Tel: (423)558-3595   *Fax:* (423)558-3598
Toll Free: (800)524 - 4814
E-Mail: amoutdoors@aol.com
Web Site: http://www.americaoutdoors.org
Members: 450 companies
Staff: 4
Annual Budget: $250-500,000
Exec. Director: David L. Brown
Director, Communications: Robin D. Brown

Historical Note
AO members are professional outdoor recreation outfitters. Membership: $165-910/year, based on gross revenue from outfitting (corporate).
Publications:
America Outdoors Newsletter. q. adv.
America Outdoors Outfitter Directory & Vacation Guide. a.
          adv.
Meetings/Conferences:
Annual Meetings: December

America's Blood Centers *(1962)*
725 15th St., N.W., Folger Building, 700
Washington, DC   20005
Tel: (202)393-5725   *Fax:* (202)393-1282
E-Mail: ABC@americasblood.org
Web Site: http://www.americasblood.org
Members: 70 centers
Staff: 11
Annual Budget: $1-2,000,000
Exec. Director: Jim MacPherson
Associate Director, Research and Communications: Jane Starkey
Associate Director, Legislative and Public Affairs: Susan Parkinson
Group Conference Services: Trudy Thompson
Assoc. Director, Development: LaShonda Stewart-Tavares

Historical Note
Formerly (1962-1971) Community Blood Bank Council and (1971-1996) Council of Community Blood Centers. Members are non-profit regional and community centers that collect blood only from volunteer donors. Membership fee based on annual blood collection.

Publications:
ABC Newsletter. w. adv.
Meetings/Conferences:
Semi-Annual Meetings: February and July/75-150

America's Community Bankers (1992)
900 19th St., N.W., Suite 400
Washington, DC 20006-2105
Tel: (202)857-3100   *Fax:* (202)296-8716
E-Mail: info@acbankers.org
Web Site: http://www.acbankers.org
Members: 2,000 savings institutions/banks
Staff: 100
Annual Budget: $10-25,000,000
President: Paul A. Schosberg
Director, Communication: Robert Schmermund
Director, Government Relations: Robert Davis
PAC Manager: Matthew Smith
Sr. Meeting Planner: June Janny
Manager: Majorie Van Vort
Director, Finance and Administration: Frank Haas
General Counsel: C. Dawn Causey
Regulatory Counsel: Charlotte M. Bahin
Director, Membership: Roger Raber
Historical Note
*Established as the United States Savings and Loan League, it
became the United States League of Savings Ass'ns in 1975 and
the United States League of Savings Institutions in 1983. In 1992,
the United States League of Savings Institutions merged with the
Nat'l Council of Community Bankers to form Savings and
Community Bankers of America; assumed its current name in 1995.
Supports the Savings Ass'n Political Elections Committee. Has an
annual budget of approximately 22.3 million.*
Publications:
America's Community Bankers. m. adv.
Operations Alert. bi-w.
Perspective. w.
Regulatory Report. m.
Meetings/Conferences:
Annual Meetings: Fall

American Abstract Artists (1936)
470 West End Ave., Apt. 9-D
New York, NY 10024
Tel: (212)874-0747
Members: 88 individuals
Annual Budget: under $10,000
President: Beatrice Riese
Historical Note
*Members are abstract painters and sculptors. Has no paid officers
or full-time staff. Membership: $35/year.*

American Academy and Board of Neurological and Orthopaedic Surgery
Historical Note
See American Academy of Neurological and Orthopaedic Surgeons.

American Academy for Cerebral Palsy and Developmental Medicine (1948)
6300 N. River Road, Suite 727
Rosemont, IL 60018-4226
Tel: (847)698-1635   *Fax:* (847)823-0536
Members: 1,600 individuals
Staff: 3
Annual Budget: $250-500,000
Exec. Director: Sheril B. King
Historical Note
Mebership: $150-$210/year.
Publications:
Developmental Medicine & Child Neurology. m.
Membership Roster. a.
Newsletter. semi-a.
Meetings/Conferences:
Annual Meetings: Fall
1999 – Washington, DC(Omni Shoreham)/Sept. 16-19/700
2000 – Toronto, Canada(Sheraton Centre)/Sept. 21-23

American Academy for Physician and Patient
6728 Old McLean Village Dr.
McLean, VA 22101
Tel: (703)556-9222   *Fax:* (703)556-8729
E-Mail: AAPPatient@aol.com
Members: 481 individuals
Exec. Director: George K. Degnon, CAE
Historical Note
Membership: $120/year.
Publications:
Medical Encounter Newsletter. q.

American Academy of Actuaries (1965)
1100 17th St., N.W., Suite 700
Washington, DC 20036-4601
Tel: (202)223-8196   *Fax:* (202)296-2216
Web Site: http://www.actuary.org
Members: 13,000 individuals
Staff: 28
Annual Budget: $2-5,000,000
Exec. Director: Wilson W. Wyatt, Jr.
Director, Communications: Ken Krehbiel
Director, Public Policy: Christine M. Cassidy
Director, Standards: Christine Nickerson
Controller: Joanne B. Anderson
General Counsel: Lauren M. Bloom
Membership Manager: Jessica Johnson, CMP
Historical Note
*The American Academy of Actuaries is the public policy
organization for actuaries of all specialties within the United States.
In addition to setting qualification standards and standards of
actuarial practice, a major purpose of the Academy is to act as the*

public information organization for the profession. The Academy is
nonpartisan and assists the public policy process through the
presentation of clear, objective analysis. The Academy regularly
prepares testimony for Congress, provides information to senior
federal elected officials and congressional staff, comments on
proposed federal regulations, and works closely with state officials
on issues related to insurance. Has an annual budget of
approximately $4.9 million.
Publications:
Academy Alert. irreg.
Actuarial Update. m.
Contingencies. bi-m. adv.
Enrolled Actuaries Report. q.
Year Book. a.
Meetings/Conferences:

American Academy of Addiction Psychiatry (1985)
7301 Mission Road, Suite 252
Prairie Village, KS 66208-3005
Tel: (913)262-6161   *Fax:* (913)262-4311
E-Mail: addicpsych@aol.com
Web Site: http://www.aaap.org
Members: 1000 individuals
Staff: 4
Annual Budget: $250-500,000
Exec. Director: Jeanne Trumble
Administrative Director: Becky Stein
Historical Note
*Founded as American Academy of Psychiatrists in Alcoholism and
Addictions; assumed its current name in 1996. AAAP promotes
education, research, prevention, and treatment of addictions, as
well as improved training for psychiatrists and public information
about the psychiatrist's role in addiction treatment. Membership:
$185/year.*
Publications:
AAAP Newsletter. q. adv.
American Journal on Addictions. q. adv.
Membership Directory. a.
Meetings/Conferences:
1999 – Nassau, Bahamas(Nassau Marriott Resort)/Dec. 2-5
2000 – Phoenix, AZ(Hilton South Mountain)/Dec. 7-10

American Academy of Advertising (1958)
School of Business
Univ. of Richmond
Richmond, VA 23173
Tel: (804)289-8902   *Fax:* (804)289-8878
Members: 675 individuals
Staff: 1
Exec. Secretary: Dr. Robert L. King
Historical Note
*AAA members are primarily professors of advertising. Membership:
$35/year.*
Publications:
AAA Newsletter. q.
Contact. q.
Journal of Advertising. q.
Membership Directory. a.
Proceedings. a.
Meetings/Conferences:
Annual Meetings: Spring
1999 – Albuquerque, NM(Hyatt Regency)
2000 – Newport, RI(Marriott)

American Academy of Allergy and Immunology
Historical Note
*Became the American Academy of Allergy, Asthma and
Immunology in 1995.*

American Academy of Allergy, Asthma and Immunology (1943)
611 East Wells St.
Milwaukee, WI 53202
Tel: (414)272-6071   *Fax:* (414)272-6070
Web Site: http://www.aaaai.org
Members: 5,300 individuals
Staff: 40
Annual Budget: $10-25,000,000
Exec. V. President: Rick Iber
Historical Note
*Formed by a merger of the American Ass'n for the Study of Allergy
and the Ass'n for the Study of Asthma and Related Conditions as
the American Academy of Allergy; became the American Academy
of Allergy and Immunology in 1982; and assumed its present name
in 1982. Has an annual budget of over $10 million. Membership:
$275/year (fellows); $250/year (members).*
Publications:
Academy News. m
Journal of Allergy and Clinical Immunology. m. adv.
Meetings/Conferences:
1999 – Orlando, FL(Dolphin & Swan)/Feb. 26-March 3
2000 – San Diego, CA(Convention Center & Marriott)

American Academy of Ambulatory Care Nursing (1976)
East Holly Ave., P.O. Box 56
Pitman, NJ 08071-0056
Tel: (609)256-2350   *Fax:* (609)589-7463
Toll Free: (800)262 - 6877
E-Mail: AAACN@mail.ajj.com
Web Site: http://www.aaacn.inurse.com
Members: 2,100 individuals
Staff: 6
Annual Budget: $100-250,000
Exec. Director: Cynthia Nowicki, EdD, RN, C
Historical Note
*Formerly (1992) the American Academy of Ambulatory Nursing
Administration, and (1995) American Academy of Ambulatory*

Care Nursing Administration. Members are registered nurses
engaged in the care of ambulatory patients. Membership:
$120/year (full membership).
Publications:
Ambulatory Nursing Administration Newsletter. bi-m. adv.
Membership Directory.
Standards.
Viewpoint. bi-m. adv.
Meetings/Conferences:
Annual Meetings: Spring/400
2000 – Orlando, FL

American Academy of Appellate Lawyers (1990)
15245 Shady Grove Road, Suite 130
Rockville, MD 20850
Tel: (301)258-9210   *Fax:* (301)990-9771
E-Mail: msp@mgmtsol.com
Members: 200 individuals
Exec. Director: Sherri Mara
Historical Note
*AAAL promotes the improvement of appellate advocacy through
recognition of outstanding practitioners in the field. Membership, by
invitation only, consists of lawyers who have focused substantially
on appeals representation for at least 15 years.*
Meetings/Conferences:
Semi-Annual Meetings: held in conjunction with American
   Bar Ass'n

American Academy of Arts and Sciences (1780)
136 Irving St.
Cambridge, MA 02138
Tel: (617)576-5000   *Fax:* (617)576-5050
E-Mail: aas@amacad.org
Web Site: http://www.amacad.org
Members: 3,600 individuals, 600 internat'l
Staff: 34
Annual Budget: $2-5,000,000
Exec. Officer: Leslie Cohen Berlowitz
Historical Note
*Founded during the American Revolution by John Adams and other
individuals active in the nation's founding. Honors individual
achievement in science, scholarship, the arts, business, and public
affairs by election to membership, and conducts a wide-ranging
program of study projects and conferences on emerging issues of
intellectual inquiry and social concern. It maintains a Midwest and
a Western Center and holds monthly meetings in Cambridge as well
as occasional meetings in the Midwest, Far West, New York, and
Washington, D.C.*
Publications:
Bulletin of the American Academy of Arts and Sciences. m.
Daedalus. q.
Records. a.
Meetings/Conferences:
1999 – Cambridge, MA

American Academy of Audiology (1988)
8201 Greensboro Drive, Suite 300
McLean, VA 22102
Tel: (703)610-9022   *Fax:* (703)610-9005
Toll Free: (800)222 - 2336
Web Site: www.audiology.com
Members: 6,700 individuals
Staff: 7
Annual Budget: $2-5,000,000
Exec. Director: Carol Fraser Fisk
Director, Publications & Communications and Exhibits: Zane Kerby
Deputy Exec. Director: Judy Miller
Director, Meetings: Lisa Cebulash
Director, Education: Casey Goldberg
Director, Membership: Joan Taylor
Historical Note
*AAA fellows hold graduate degrees in audiology and are licensed by
a state to practice in the field. Students actively enrolled in graduate
programs in audiology qualify as candidate members. Individuals
holding Masters degrees in audiology and actively engaged in
research are affiliate members. Membership: $110/year.*
Publications:
Audiology Today. bi-m. adv.
Journal of the American Academy of Audiology. bi-m. adv.
Meetings/Conferences:
Annual Meetings: April/5,000
1999 – Miami Beach, FL/April 28-May 2
2000 – Chicago, IL/March 16-19
2001 – San Diego, CA/April 19-22
2002 – Philadelphia, PA/April 18-21

American Academy of Child and Adolescent Psychiatry (1953)
3615 Wisconsin Ave., N.W.
Washington, DC 20016-3007
Tel: (202)966-7300   *Fax:* (202)966-2891
Web Site: http://aacap.org
Members: 6,100 individuals, 28
Staff: 25
Annual Budget: $2-5,000,000
Exec. Director: Virginia Q. Anthony
Director, Development and Communications: Patricia Jutz
Dir., Govt. Affairs/Deputy Exec. Director: Mary Crosby
Director, Finance & Administration: Jack Flikeld
Manager, Membership Service: Katie Adair
Director, Meetings: Heidi Buttner
Historical Note
*Established in Feb., 1953 as American Academy of Child
Psychiatry and incorporated in Delaware in 1959; assumed its
present name in 1986. Encourages medical contributions to the
knowledge and treatment of psychiatric problems of children and
their families. Membership: $50/year (trainee); $160/year
(corresponding); $240/year (affiliate); $295/year (active/fellow).*

Publications:
AACAP Annual Meeting Magazine. a.
AACAP Journal. m.
AACP Newsletter. bi-m.
Membership Directory. bien.
Proceedings. a.
Research Notes. q.
Meetings/Conferences:
Annual Meetings: Fall/2,000-3,000
1999 – Chicago, IL

American Academy of Clinical Neurophysiology (1985)
104 13th St.
Hudson, WI 54016
Tel: (715)381-3440   *Fax:* (715)381-3442
Members: 800 individuals
Staff: 4
Exec. Director: Dan Tjornechoj
Historical Note
Membership: $25-95/year (individual); $100/year (company).
Publications:
AACN Newsletter. semi-a.
Meetings/Conferences:
1999 – Santa Fe, NM/Jan. 27-30

American Academy of Clinical Psychiatrists (1975)
1034 S. Brentwood, Suite 1180
St. Louis, MO 63117
Tel: (314)727-2392   *Fax:* (314)727-9415
E-Mail: aacp@aacp.com
Web Site: http://www.aacp.com
Members: 500 individuals
Staff: 1
Annual Budget: $100-250,000
Exec. Secretary: C. Joyce Hawkins
Historical Note
*Members are mainly private clinicians and academicians.
Disseminates scientific information relevant to clinical practice to its
members Membership: $100/year.*
Publications:
Annals of Clinical Psychiatry.
The Clinical Psychiatry Quarterly. q.
Meetings/Conferences:
Annual Meetings: October
1999 – Cincinnati, OH

American Academy of Clinical Sexologists (1979)
1929 18th St., N.W., Suite 1166
Washington, DC 20009
Tel: (202)462-2122
Members: 1000 individuals
Staff: 1
Annual Budget: $50-100,000
Exec. Director: W.B. Easterling
Historical Note
*Founded in 1979 in San Francisco as the American College of
Sexologists to serve professionals in the field of sexology. In 1989,
the College became the education division of the American Board of
Sexology. Assumed its present name in 1991 to clearly distiguish it
as a separate organization representing the practicing clinician/sex
therapist. Awards the designation Fellow of the AACS. Membership:
$75/year.*
Publications:
Journal of Sex and Marital Therapy. q.
The Bulletin. irreg.
Meetings/Conferences:

American Academy of Clinical Toxicology (1968)
777 East Park Drive
P.O. Box 8820
Harrisburg, PA 17105-8820
Tel: (717)558-7847   *Fax:* (717)558-7841
E-Mail: hmiller@pamedsoc.org
Web Site: www.clintox.org
Members: 600 individuals
Staff: 2
Annual Budget: $100-250,000
Exec. Director: Heather Miller
Historical Note
*ACCT members are physicians, research scientists, and analytical
chemists, veterinarians and pharmacists active in clinical
toxicology. Membership: $150/year.*
Publications:
AACT Update. q.
Journal Toxicology/Clinical Toxicology.
Meetings/Conferences:
Annual Meetings: Fall/650

American Academy of Cosmetic Dentistry (1984)
2810 Walton Commons West #200
Madison, WI 53718
Tel: (608)222-8583   *Fax:* (608)222-9540
Toll Free: (800)543 - 9220
Members: 4,000 individuals
Staff: 12
Annual Budget: $2-5,000,000
Exec. Director: Kenneth L. Zakariasen
Manager, Exhibits/Advertising: Renee Field
Manager, Meetings: Jeri Krohn
Historical Note
*AACD members are dental practitioners, educators and researchers
with an interest in the field of cosmetic dentistry. Has accreditation
and fellowship programs. Membership: $255/year (individual).*
Publications:
Academy New bi-m.
Journal of the AACD. q. adv.
Meetings/Conferences:
Annual Meetings: April-May

American Academy of Cosmetic Surgery (1985)
401 N. Michigan Ave.
Chicago, IL 60611-4267
Tel: (312)527-6713   *Fax:* (312)644-1815
Members: 1,500 individuals
Annual Budget: $1-2,000,000
Exec. Director: Jeffrey P. Knezovich
Manager,Exhibits: Mimi Ruffing
Historical Note
*Formed by a merger of the American Ass'n of Cosmetic Surgeons
(1969) and the American Soc. of Cosmetic Surgeons (1982).
Membership: $620/year (fellow), $475/year (associate),
$345/year (corresponding), $100/year (resident).*
Publications:
American Journal of Cosmetic Surgery. q. adv.
Cosmetic Surgery Newsline. q.
Membership Directory. a.
Meetings/Conferences:
Annual Meetings: Winter
1999 – Los Angeles, CA(Westin Century Plaza)/Jan. 28-31

American Academy of Crisis Interveners (1977)
9462 Brownsboro Road, Suite BX-184
Louisville, KY 40241-1118
Tel: (502)412-0200
E-Mail: dr_ed@bigfoot.com
Annual Budget: under $10,000
President: Edward S. Rosenbluh, Ph.D.
Historical Note
*AACI members are mental health workers, police and correctional
officers, social workers, psychologists, psychiatrists, nurses, clergy,
physicians, teachers and others involved in crisis intervention and
crisis management who provide training to agencies, companies
and organizations.*

American Academy of Dental Electrosurgery (1963)
Historical Note
Address unknown in 1997.

American Academy of Dental Group Practice (1973)
2525 E. Arizona Biltmore Cir.
Suite 127
Phoenix, AZ 85016-2129
Tel: (602)381-1185   *Fax:* (602)381-1093
E-Mail: aadgp@hibcc.org
Web Site: http://www.hibcc.org/aadgp/aadgp.htm
Members: 370 groups
Staff: 3
Annual Budget: $10-25,000
Exec. Director: Robert A. Hankin, Ph.D.
Director, Communications: Elyse Coffey
Historical Note
*AADGP was formed to address the unique needs of Dental Groups.
The Academy provides a national voice for the special interests of
dental group practices and a liaison to other nat'l dental
organizations. Members also receive public recognition along with
opportunities in professional improvement, peer contacts, and
networking. Membership: $125/year per group and $10 per dentist
within the group.*
Publications:
Contact. q. adv.
Meetings/Conferences:
1999 – Newport Beach, CA(Newport Beach
          Marriott)/Jan. 20-23

American Academy of Dental Practice Administration (1956)
1063 Whipoorwill Lane
Palatine, IL 60067
Tel: (847)934-4404
Members: 250 individuals
Staff: 1
Annual Budget: $50-100,000
Exec. Director: Kathleen Uebel
Historical Note
Membership: $450/year.
Publications:
The Communicator (newsletter). q.
Meetings/Conferences:
Annual Meetings: March
1999 – Amelia Island, FL(Ritz-Carlton)/500

American Academy of Dermatology (1938)
930 N. Meacham Road
Schaumburg, IL 60173-4965
Tel: (847)330-0230   *Fax:* (847)330-1123
Web Site: http://www.derm.infonet.com
Members: 12,000 individuals
Staff: 100
Annual Budget: $10-25,000,000
Exec. Director: Bradford W. Claxton, CAE
Director, Communications: Sandra R. Gordon
Director, Education: Thomas Pearson, Ed.D.
Director, Member Services: Thomas H. Stluka
Historical Note
*Representing virtually all practicing dermatologists, AAD is the
largest dermatologic organization in the United States and Canada.
The Academy promotes and advances the science and art of
medicine and surgery related to the skin; promotes the highest
possible standards in clinical practice, education and research in
dermatology and related disciplines; and supports and enhances
patient care and promotes the public interest relating to
dermatology. Has an annual budget of approximately $8 million.
Membership: $450/year (individual, US & Canada).*
Publications:
Dermatology World. adv. adv.

Directory of the American Academy of Dermatology. bien.
    adv.
Journal of the American Academy of Dermatology. m. adv.
Meetings/Conferences:

American Academy of Disability Evaluating Physicians (1987)
150 N. Wacker Dr., Suite 1420
Chicago, IL 60606
Tel: (312)658-1171   *Fax:* (312)658-1175
Members: 1,400 individuals
Staff: 5
Annual Budget: $1-2,000,000
Exec. Director: Sandra L. Yost
Historical Note
*AADEP members are physicians and osteopaths with an interest in
impairment and disability evaluation. Membership: $300/year
(individual).*
Publications:
Directory. a. adv.
Journal of Disability. q. adv.
Newsletter. q.
Meetings/Conferences:
1999 – Tucson, AZ/November 18-20/500

American Academy of Emergency Medicine
611 E. Wells St.
Milwaukee, WI 53202-3816
Tel: (414)276-7390   *Fax:* (414)276-3349
Toll Free: (800)884 - 2236
E-Mail: info@aaem.org
Web Site: http://www.aaem.org
Annual Budget: $500-1,000,000
Organizational Director: Kay Whalen
Assoc. Exec. Director: Eric Lanke
Membership Coordinator: David Feldner
Historical Note
Membership: $240/year (individual).
Publications:
Common Sense. bi-m.
Meetings/Conferences:
1999 – San Diego, CA

American Academy of Environmental Engineers (1955)
130 Holiday Court, Suite 100
Annapolis, MD 21401
Tel: (410)266-3311   *Fax:* (410)266-7653
E-Mail: aaee@ea.net
Web Site: http://www.enviro-engrs.org
Members: 2,600 individuals
Staff: 9
Annual Budget: $500-1,000,000
Exec. Director: William C. Anderson
Manager, Publications and Communications: John M. Buterbaugh
Manager, Admissions & Membership: Elizabeth W. Andrews
Historical Note
*Originally (1955) the American Sanitary Engineering Intersociety
Board; became the Environmental Engineering Intersociety Board in
1966 and assumed its present name in 1973. Members are board-
certified environmental engineers. Membership: $135/year
(individual).*
Publications:
Environmental Engineer. q. adv.
Environmental Engineering Selection Guide. a.
Who's Who in Environmental Engineering. a.
Meetings/Conferences:
Annual Meetings: late October

American Academy of Environmental Medicine (1965)
P.O. Box CN-1001-8001
New Hope, PA 18938
Tel: (215)862-4544
Members: 560 individuals
Staff: 3
Annual Budget: $250-500,000
Administrative Director: Peter Nakashian
Historical Note
*Originated as the Human Ecology Study Club. Formerly (1984) the
Soc. for Clinical Ecology. Members are interested in studying the
effects of the environment on human health. Membership:
$275/year (M.D.), $175/year (organization).*
Publications:
Directory. bien. adv.
Environmental Physician Newsletter. q. adv.
Meetings/Conferences:
Annual Meetings: Fall

American Academy of Equine Art (1980)
P.O. Box 1315
Middleburg, VA 20118
Tel: (540)687-6701
Web Site: http://www.imh.org/imh/aaea/exh.htm
Members: 60 individuals
Staff: 1
Annual Budget: under $10,000
Exec. Director: Elizabeth B. Dubenitz
Historical Note
*Members are professional artists who are willing and qualified to
exhibit works of equine art and to teach the subject. Membership:
$100/year (individual), initiation fee $150.*
Publications:
Exhibition Perspectives. a.
Newsletter. irreg.
Workshop Brochure. a.
Meetings/Conferences:
Annual Meetings: Lexington, KY(Kentucky Horse
          Park)/October-November/50

American Academy of Estate Planning Attorneys
4250 Executive Sq., Suite 900
La Jolla, CA 92037
Tel: (619)453-2128   *Fax:* (619)453-1147
Toll Free: (800)846 - 1555
Web Site: http://wwwaaepa.com
Members: 98 law firms
President: Robert G. Armstrong
Director, Education: Rod Goodwin
C.E.O.: Sanford M. Fisch
Director, Member Services: Jennifer Price

Historical Note
AAEPA provides continuing education, individualized consulting services, and other products and services to member firms. Members are lawyers and law firms specializing in estate planning practice.

Meetings/Conferences:
1999 – Orlando, FL

American Academy of Esthetic Dentistry *(1975)*
401 S. Michgigan Ave.
Chicago, IL 60611-4267
Tel: (312)644-6610   *Fax:* (312)321-6869
Members: 125 individuals
Staff: 2
Annual Budget: $250-500,000
Exec. Director: Laquita Cox

Historical Note
Dentists and other health professionals concerned with esthetics in dentistry, medicine and psychology. Affiliated with the Federation of Prosthodontic Organizations. Membership: $500/year.

Publications:
Newsletter. semi-a.

Meetings/Conferences:
Annual Meetings: August
1999 – Whistler, British Columbia(Chateau
    Whistler)/Aug. 3-6/225

American Academy of Facial Plastic and Reconstructive Surgery *(1964)*
310 S. Henry St.
Alexandria, VA 22314-3524
Tel: (703)299-9291   *Fax:* (703)299-8898
Members: 2,700 individuals
Staff: 14
Annual Budget: $1-2,000,000
Exec. V. President: Stephen Duffy
Meetings Manager: Madelaine Morgan
Director, Education(CME) & Training Programs: Caryl Herrington
Director of Finance and Administration: Lisa Sarrge
Director, Board, & Executive Services: Anne M. Biedscheid
Director, Membership Services: Michelle Spurlock
Assistant Manager, Membership Records: Maria Atkins
Director, Publications and Marketing: Rita Chua Magness
Director, Development, Research, & Humanitarian: Ann Holton
Manager, Fellowship Program & Credentialling: Fatima Porter

Historical Note
Merger (1964) of American Soc. of Facial Plastic Surgery and American Otorhinologic Soc. for Plastic Surgery Membership: $25-495/year.

Publications:
Facial Plastic Surgery Today. q.
Facial Plastic Times. m. adv.
Membership Directory. a. adv.

Meetings/Conferences:
Semi-annual Meetings: Spring and Fall
1999 – Palm Desert, CA/April 24-30
1999 – New Orleans, LA

American Academy of Family Physicians *(1947)*
8880 Ward Parkway
Kansas City, MO 64114
Tel: (816)333-9700   *Fax:* (816)822-0580
Toll Free: (800)274 - 2237
E-Mail: fp@aafp.org
Web Site: http://www.aafp.org
Members: 85,000 individuals
Staff: 280
Annual Budget: $25-50,000,000
Exec. V. President: Robert Graham, M.D., CAE
Director, Communications Division: William R. DeLay
V.P. of Communication and Publications: Clayton Hasser, Jr., CAE
V.P. of Administration, Membership, Meetings & Conventions: Mickey Schaefer
Director, Meetings and Conventions: Annette Hoel, CMP
V. President, Education/Science Affairs: Daniel J. Ostergaard
Controller: Robert I. Watchinski
Deputy Exec. V. President: R. Michael Miller
General Counsel: Todd C. Dicus
Manager, Membership/Mktg: Angela Broderick, CAE
Director, Chapter Affairs: Dona Flory, CAE
Editor: Paula H. Binder
Director, Research/Information Services: Gordon Schmittling

Historical Note
Founded in June 1947 in Atlantic City as the American Academy of General Practice. Name changed to the American Academy of Family Physicians in October 1971. Has an annual budget of approximately $40 million. Membership: $225/year (individual).

Publications:
AFP Report. m.
American Family Physician. m. adv.
Facts about Family Practice. a.
Family Practice Mangement.
Membership Directory. a. adv.
Transactions. a.

Meetings/Conferences:
1999 – Orlando, FL/Sept. 16-19
2000 – Dallas, TX/Sept. 21-24

American Academy of Fixed Prosthodontics *(1952)*
1930 Sea Way
P.O. Box 1409
Bodega Bay, CA 94923-1409
Tel: (707)875-3040   *Fax:* (707)875-2927
Toll Free: (800)880 - 5184
Members: 560 individuals
Annual Budget: $250-500,000
Secretary: Dr. Robert S. Staffanou

Historical Note
Organized under the leadership Dr. Stanley D. Tylman, Dr. Claude R. Baker and Dr. George H. Moulton at the Stevens Hotel, Chicago, February 5, 1951. Formerly (1991) American Academy of Crown and Bridge Prosthodontics. Has no paid staff. Membership: $275/year.

Publications:
Journal of Prosthetic Dentistry. m. adv.
Newsletter. 2/year.

Meetings/Conferences:
Annual Meetings: Chicago, IL in February/500-600
1999 – (Marriott)/Feb. 19-20
2000 – (Marriott)/Feb. 25-26
2001 – (Marriott)/Feb. 23-24/800
2002 – (Marriott)/Feb. 22-23/800

American Academy of Forensic Psychology *(1980)*
c/o American Bd. of Prof. Psychology
2100 E. Broadway, Suite 313
Columbia, MO 65201-6082
Tel: (573)875-1267   *Fax:* (573)443-1199
Members: 150 individuals
Staff: 4
Annual Budget: $100-250,000
Exec. Officer: Nicholas Palo

Historical Note
Members are psychologists who have passed the Diplomate Examination in Forensic Psychology of the American Board of Professional Psychology. Membership: $100/year (individual).

Publications:
Bulletin of the AAFP. a.
Directory of Diplomates. a.

American Academy of Forensic Sciences *(1948)*
P.O. Box 669
Colorado Springs, CO 80901-0669
Tel: (719)636-1100   *Fax:* (719)636-1993
E-Mail: membership@aafs.org
Web Site: http://www.aafs.org
Members: 5,000 individuals
Staff: 9
Annual Budget: $1-2,000,000
Exec. Director: Elizabeth Warren
Asst. Director: Brenda K. Papke

Historical Note
Formed in St. Louis in 1948 and incorporated in Illinois in 1964. Cooperates with the regional, national and international organizations dedicated to the use of science in the administration of justice. The Forensic Sciences Foundation is the Academy's educational, research and testing arm. Membership: $125/year.

Publications:
Journal of Forensic Sciences. bi-m.
Newsletter. bi-m. adv.

Meetings/Conferences:
Annual Meetings: February/2,200
1999 – Orlando, FL/Feb. 15-20
2000 – Reno, NV/Feb. 14-19

American Academy of Gnathologic Orthopedics *(1969)*
1400 Lamar Dr.
Richmond, TX 77469-4910
Tel: (281)341-5250
Members: 390 individuals
Staff: 1
Annual Budget: $50-100,000
Exec. Director: Larry M. Alderson, D.D.S.

Historical Note
Established in Portland, Oregon and incorporated in Wisconsin. Dentists specializing in treatment of malformations of the face and jaw. Officers are elected annually. Membership: $120/year.

Publications:
Membership Directory. bien. adv.
The Journal of A. A. adv.

Meetings/Conferences:
Annual Meetings: Fall/125
1999 – San Antonio, TX(St. Anthony)/Oct. 27-31
2000 – Anchorage, AK(Captain Cook)/Oct. 11-15

American Academy of Gold Foil Operators *(1952)*
17922 Tallgrass Court
Noblesville, IN 46060
Tel: (317)867-3011
E-Mail: pipron@aol.com
Members: 320 individuals
Staff: 1
Annual Budget: $25-50,000
Secretary-Treasurer: Ronald K. Harris

Historical Note
Members are dentists performing restorative procedures utilizing gold foil and the rubber dam. Membership: $60/year.

Publications:
Gold Leaf. (newsletter) q.
Journal of Operative Dentistry. bi-m. adv.

Meetings/Conferences:
Annual Meetings: Fall/150
1999 – Nashville, TN/Oct. 27-30

American Academy of Head, Neck and Facial Pain *(1985)*

520 W. Pipeline Road
Hurst, TX 76053
Tel: (817)282-1501   *Fax:* (817)282-8012
Toll Free: (800)322 - 6651
E-Mail: central@aahnfp.org
Web Site: http://www.aahnfp.org
Members: 500 individuals
Staff: 2
Exec. Secretary: Cordelia Mason

Historical Note
Members are dentists and other professionals concerned with disorders of the temporo-mandibular region. Membership: $250/year.

Publications:
Membership List. irreg.
TM Diary. semi-a. adv.

Meetings/Conferences:
Annual Meetings: Summer

American Academy of Health Care Providers in the Addictive Disorders
767 Concord Avenue
Cambridge, MA 02138
Tel: (617)661-6248   *Fax:* (617)492-3183
E-Mail: cas@Americanacademy.org
Web Site: http://www.americanacademy.org
Members: 2,000 individuals
Exec. Director: Richard Rogers

Publications:
Internat'l Register of Health Care Providers. semi-a.
Newsletter. Academy News.

Meetings/Conferences:
1999 – Boston, MA

American Academy of Health Physics
1313 Dolley Madison Blvd., Suite 402
McLean, VA 22101
Tel: (703)790-1745   *Fax:* (703)790-2672
E-Mail: aahp@burkinc.com
Web Site: http://phantom.ehs.uiuc.edu/~ aahp/
Exec. Director: Richard J. Burk, Jr.

American Academy of Healthcare Attorneys *(1968)*

Historical Note
Merged with the Nat'l Health Lawyers Ass'n to form the Nat'l Health Lawyers Ass'n/American Academy of Healthcare Attorneys in 1997.

American Academy of Home Care Physicians *(1989)*
P.O. Box 1037
Edgewood, MD 21040
Tel: (410)676-7966   *Fax:* (410)676-7980
E-Mail: hmecarephy@aol.com
Members: 1,300 individuals, 10 companies
Staff: 2
Annual Budget: $50-100,000
Exec. Director: Constance F. Rowe

Historical Note
AAHCP members are physicians and other home care professionals with an interest in the enhancement of quality home care. Membership: $100/year (individual); $150/year (agency); $2,000/year (corporate sponsor).

Publications:
Newsletter. q.

Meetings/Conferences:
Annual Meetings: Spring
1999 – Philadelphia, PA

American Academy of Hospice and Palliative Medicine *(1988)*
11250 Roger Bacon Dr., Suite 8
Reston, VA 20190-5202
Tel: (703)437-1377   *Fax:* (703)435-4390
E-Mail: aahpm@aahpm.org
Web Site: http://www.aahpm.org
Members: 1,400 individuals
Staff: 4
Annual Budget: $500-1,000,000
Exec. Director: William M. Drohan, CAE

Historical Note
Formerly the Academy of Hospice Physicians (1996). AAHPM members are physicians from many medical specialties interested in hospice and palliative care. Membership: $150/year.

Publications:
Hospice Update. q.

Meetings/Conferences:
Annual Meetings: Summer

American Academy of Implant Dentistry *(1952)*
211 E. Chicago Ave., Suite 750
Chicago, IL 60611
Tel: (312)335-1550   *Fax:* (312)335-9090
Web Site: http://www.aaid-implant.org
Members: 2,300 individuals
Staff: 6
Annual Budget: $500-1,000,000
Exec. Director: J. Vincent Shuck

Historical Note
Founded in Chicago in February 1952 as the American Academy of Implant Dentures and incorporated in Minnesota in October. Name changed to American Academy of Implant Dentistry in 1966. Membership: $300/year (fellow/assoc. fellow); $150/year (general member).

Publications:
AAID Newsletter. q. adv.
Journal of Oral Implantology. q. adv.

Meetings/Conferences:
Annual Meetings: October

1999 – Orlando, FL/Sept. 22-24

American Academy of Implant Prosthodontics *(1982)*
760 Whitehall Way
Roswell, GA 30076
Tel: (770)998-3223   *Fax:* (770)998-9924
Web Site: http://inca.net/aaip
Members: 350 individuals
Staff: 2
Annual Budget: $50-100,000
Chairman: Dr. Maurice J. Fagan, Jr.

Historical Note
AAIP supports and fosters fellowship among all members of the profession concerned with dental implants. Promotes cooperation among all members of the dental profession, with emphasis on prosthetics (artificial structures). Membership: $50-200/year.

Publications:
Directory. a.
Implant Dentistry - Journal. q.
Newsletter. q.

Meetings/Conferences:
Annual Meetings: Fall

American Academy of Industrial Hygiene *(1966)*
6015 W. St. Joseph Hwy., Suite 102
Lansing, MI 48917-3980
Tel: (517)321-5025   *Fax:* (517)321-4624
E-Mail: ambrdih@ibm.net
Web Site: http://www.abih.org
Members: 6,500 individuals
Staff: 5
Annual Budget: $100-250,000
Exec. Director: Lynn O'Donnell, CIH

Historical Note
AAIH members are practicing industrial hygienists who have participated successfully in a certification program administered by the American Board of Industrial Hygiene.

Publications:
AAIH Newsletter. q.
Roster of the AAIH. a.

Meetings/Conferences:
Annual Meetings: Fall
1999 – New Orleans, LA
2000 – Nashville, TN

American Academy of Insurance Medicine *(1889)*
P.O. Box 59811
Potomac, MD 20859-9811
Tel: (301)365-3572   *Fax:* (301)365-7705
Web Site: http://www.aaimedicine.org
Members: 600 individuals
Annual Budget: $50-100,000
Exec. Director: Russell E. Barker

Historical Note
Formerly (1991) Ass'n of Life Insurance Medical Directors. Membership: $350/year (individual).

Publications:
Journal of Insurance Medicine. q.
Newsletter.

Meetings/Conferences:
Annual Meetings: Fall/300
2000 – Indianapolis, IN

American Academy of Male Sexual Health
Historical Note
Organization defunct in 1998.

American Academy of Matrimonial Lawyers *(1963)*
150 North Michigan Ave., Suite 2040
Chicago, IL 60601
Tel: (312)263-6477   *Fax:* (312)263-7682
Members: 1,500 individuals
Staff: 2
Annual Budget: $250-500,000
Exec. Director: Lorraine J. West

Historical Note
Members are attorneys specializing in the field of marriage and family law. Membership: $325/year.

Publications:
Journal of the AAML. a.
Newsletter. q.
Proceedings. a.

Meetings/Conferences:
Semi-annual Meetings: March/250-300 and November
        1998-Chicago, IL/Nov. 11-15
1999 – Tuscon, AZ

American Academy of Maxillofacial Prosthetics *(1953)*
9360 Winchester Valley
Chesterland, OH 44026
Tel: (216)444-2084   *Fax:* (216)445-6360
E-Mail: cowpert@CESMTP.CCF.ORG
Members: 260 individuals
Annual Budget: $25-50,000
Exec. Secretary: Thomas Cowper, D.D.S.

Historical Note
The Academy provides a forum for discussion and presentation of new materials, procedures and techniques in the field of facial prosthetic reconstruction. Membership: $260/year (individual), $250/year (organization/ company).

Publications:
Journal of Prosthetic Dentistry. m. adv.

Meetings/Conferences:

American Academy of Mechanics *(1969)*
ESM Department-MC 0219
Virginia Tech
Blacksburg, VA 24061

Tel: (540)231-6841   *Fax:* (540)231-2290
E-Mail: sally@vt.edu
Web Site: htto://www.ecn.perdue.edu/aam
Members: 1,200 individuals
Staff: 1
Annual Budget: $25-50,000
Secretary: Dean T. Mook

Historical Note
AAM members are individuals who have made significant contributions in the field of mechanics. Membership: $50/year (individual).

Publications:
Directory. irreg.
Mechanics. m. adv.

American Academy of Medical Acupuncture *(1987)*
5820 Wilshire Blvd., Suite 500
Los Angeles, CA 90036
Tel: (213)937-5514   *Fax:* (213)937-0959
Members: 1,140 individuals
Annual Budget: $500-1,000,000
Exec. Director: C. James Dowden

Historical Note
Membership: $285/year (individual).

Publications:
AAMA Newsletter. bi-m.
AAMA Review Journal. semi-a. adv.

Meetings/Conferences:
Annual Meetings: Spring/340
1999 – Chicago, IL(The Drake)/April 8-11/350
2000 – Orlando, FL(Hyatt Regency)/April 27-30

American Academy of Medical Administrators *(1957)*
30555 Southfield Road, Suite 150
Southfield, MI 48076
Tel: (248)540-4310   *Fax:* (248)645-0590
E-Mail: INFO@AAMEDIA.ORG
Web Site: http://www.aameda.org
Members: 3,474 individuals
Staff: 8
Annual Budget: $1-2,000,000
President: Thomas R. O'Donovan, Ph.D.
Director of Education: Darlene Trudell
Director of Membership: Linda DiMichel

Historical Note
Founded in Boston in 1957. Hospital administrators, including department heads in such areas as nursing, food service management, housekeeping, purchasing. The American College of Cardiovascular Administrators, American College of Healthcare Information Administrators, American College of Home Healthcare Administrators, and the American College of Oncology Administrators are chapters of AAMA. Membership: $140/year (individual), $500/year (organization).

Publications:
AAMA Executive. bi-m. adv.
Journal of Cardiovascular Management. bi-m.
Journal of Oncology Management. bi-m.

Meetings/Conferences:
Annual Meetings: Fall
1999 – Atlanta, GA/Nov. 5-Nov 6/500
2000 – New Orleans, LA/Nov. 10-11/800

American Academy of Medical Hypnoanalysts *(1974)*
P.O. Box K
Ludlow, MA 01506
Members: 143 individuals
Annual Budget: $50-100,000
President: John A. Scott

Historical Note
Formerly the Soc. of Medical Hypnoanalysts. AAMH members include medical doctors, masters and Ph.D. level psychologists, social workers, counselors and nurses. Associate membership is open to any qualified mental health practitioner; clinical membership requires completion of a clinical training program. Membership: $175/year, clinical; $120/year, associate.

Publications:
Journal of the AAMH. q. adv.

Meetings/Conferences:
Semi-annual Meetings: Spring and Fall

American Academy of Microbiology *(1955)*
Historical Note
The professional services arm of the American Soc. for Microbiology.

American Academy of Ministry *(1992)*
P.O. Box 369
Jackson, TN 38302-0369
Tel: (901)668-9948   *Fax:* (901)668-9633
Toll Free: (800)288 - 9673
E-Mail: 74114.275@compuserve.com
Web Site: ministry.org
Members: 1000 individuals
Staff: 2
Annual Budget: $50-100,000
Exec. Director: Michael Duduit

Historical Note
An interdenominational professional and scholarly organization, AAM is organized to help ministers enhance their ministry gifts. Membership: $49/year.

Publications:
Academy News. q.
Journal of the AAM. q. adv.

Meetings/Conferences:
Annual Meetings: Summer

American Academy of Natural Family Planning *(1982)*

Historical Note
Address unknown in 1996.

American Academy of Neurological and Orthopaedic Surgeons *(1977)*
2300 S. Rancho Dr., Suite 202
Las Vegas, NV 89102-4508
Tel: (702)388-7390   *Fax:* (702)388-7395
Members: 269 individuals
Annual Budget: $100-250,000
Director: Kazem Fatie, M.D.

Historical Note
AANOS members are neurological and orthopaedic surgeons and other physicians. The Academy was formed to promote the combination of approaches from other disciplines (e.g., Neurosurgery, Orthopaedic Surgery, Physiatry) in the treatment of injury and disease in the neuromusculoskeletal system. The American Academy of Spinal Surgeons is a board under the auspices of AANOS. Also known as the American Academy and Board of Neurological and Orthopaedic Surgery. Membership: $600/year.

Publications:
FAANOS Directory. bien.
Journal of Neurological and Orthopaedic Medicine and
        Surgery. q. adv.

Meetings/Conferences:
Annual Meetings: always Las Vegas, NV
1999 – Cancun, Mexico/June 23-27

American Academy of Neurological Surgery *(1938)*
1501 N.W. 9th Ave., 2nd Floor
Miami, FL 33136
Tel: (305)243-6672   *Fax:* (305)243-5588
Members: 93 individuals, 70 senior members
Staff: 1
Annual Budget: under $10,000
Secretary: Dr. Roberto Heros

Historical Note
Founded in 1938 in Cincinnati. Affiliated with the American Ass'n of Neurological Surgery and the World Federation of Neurological Societies. Membership: $400/year.

Meetings/Conferences:
Annual Meetings: Fall

American Academy of Neurology *(1948)*
1080 Montreal Ave.
St. Paul, MN 55116-2325
Tel: (651)695-1940   *Fax:* (651)695-2491
E-Mail: aan@aan.com
Members: 15,000 individuals
Staff: 70
Annual Budget: $5-10,000,000
Exec. Director: Jan W. Kolehmainen
Director, Communications: Julie Emnett
Dir., Medical Services & Communications: Richard Hames
Director, Education: Glenna Case
Director, Div. of Administration/Finance: Thomas Cooper
Director, Management Services: Patricia Van Doren-Blake, CAE
Manager, Membership Project: Michael Bisping

Historical Note
Founded and incorporated in Minnesota in 1948. Members are medical doctors who specialize in nerve and nervous system diseases. Has an annual budget of approximately $10 million.

Publications:
AANews. bi-m.
Neurology. m. adv.

Meetings/Conferences:
Annual Meetings: April
1999 – Toronto, Canada/Apr. 17-24

American Academy of Nurse Practitioners *(1985)*
P.O. Box 12846
Austin, TX 78711
Tel: (512)442-4262   *Fax:* (512)442-6469
E-Mail: admin@aanp.org
Web Site: http://www.aanp.org
Members: 18,000 individuals, 45 organizations
Staff: 20
Annual Budget: $1-2,000,000
Exec. Director: Judith S. Dempster, DNSC
Director, Assn Services: Mari Z. DeMarchi
Coordinator, Membership: Jesse Gonzales

Historical Note
AANP promotes high standards of health care delivered by nurse practitioners and acts as a forum to enhance the identity and continuity of nurse practitioners. Maintains a Washington, DC office. Membership: $90/year (individual); $175/year (group); supporting memberships available.

Publications:
Academy Update. 10/year.
Journal of the AANP. m.

Meetings/Conferences:
Annual Meetings: June/1,700
1999 – Atlanta, GA(Hyatt/Marriott)/June 16-20
2000 – Washington, DC

American Academy of Nursing *(1973)*
600 Maryland Ave., N.W., Suite 100 West
Washington, DC 20024-2571
Tel: (202)651-7238   *Fax:* (202)554-2641
Web Site: htttp://www.nursingworld.org/aan
Members: 1000 individuals
Staff: 3
Annual Budget: $100-250,000
Director: Dr. Janet Heinrich

Historical Note
The American Academy of Nursing is a working body of nursing leaders and scholars in education, practice, administration and research. Fellows are elected to membership based on their

contributions to the profession. Following induction, members are designated Fellow of the American Academy of Nursing (FAAN). The Academy seeks to identify emerging nursing and health care issues, promote scholarly exploration, and propose solutions. Applicants must be sponsored by members and successfully complete the membership and selection process. Membership: $225/year (individual).

Publications:
Nursing Outlook. bi-m. adv.

Meetings/Conferences:
Annual Meetings: October
1999 - Arlington, VA(Marriott Crystal)/Nov. 18-21
2000 - San Diego, CA(Hotel del Coronado)/Nov. 2-5
2001 - Washington, DC

American Academy of Ophthalmology *(1896)*

P.O. Box 7424
San Francisco, CA 94120-7424
Tel: (415)561-8500 *Fax:* (415)561-8575
Web Site: http://www.eyenet.org
Members: 15,000 individuals
Staff: 165
Annual Budget: $10-25,000,000
Exec. V. President: Dr. H. Dunbar Hoskins, Jr.
V. President, Advocacy and Ophthalmic Relations: Steven D. Carter
V. President, Meetings/Exhibits: Debra Rosencrance, CMP
Director, Meetings and Management: William Jenkinson
V. President, Clinical Education: Kathryn Hecht, Ed.D.
V. President and C.F.O.: John McKinney
Director, Fin/Computer Services: Jill Boyett
Director, Administration: Orrin Carpenter, Jr.
V. President, Member Services: Ron Mattocks, CAE
Director, Assn. Management Services: Sue Brown
Manager, Member Service: Elaine C. Ireland

Historical Note
Founded as the Western Ophthalmological, Otolaryngological and Rhinological Ass'n. Name changed to Western Ophthalmologic and Otolaryngologic Ass'n in 1899. Became the American Academy of Ophthalmology and Otolaryngology in 1903. In 1979, the Academy split into the American Academy of Ophthalmology and the American Academy of Otolaryngology. Absorbed the American Association of Ophthalmology, July 1, 1981. Maintains a Washington office. Sponsors and supports the American Academy of Ophthalmology Political Action Committee (OPHTH PAC). Has an annual budget of approximately $21.3 million. Memberships: $675/year.

Publications:
Eyenet. m. adv.
Ophthalmology Journal. m.

Meetings/Conferences:
Annual Meetings: Fall/20,000

American Academy of Optometry *(1922)*

6110 Executive Blvd., Suite 506
Rockville, MD 20852
Tel: (301)984-1441 *Fax:* (301)984-4737
E-Mail: LoisS@aaoptom.org
Web Site: http://www.aaoptom.org
Members: 5,000 individuals
Staff: 10
Annual Budget: $2-5,000,000
Exec. Director: Lois Schoenbrun, CAE
Manager, Membership/Communications: Jonathan Mertz
Director, Meetings/Education: Susan Grimes
Director, Finance: Diane Bartkovich

Historical Note
Supports research, education and the dissemination of knowledge to foster and enhance excellence in basic and applied vision science. American Optometric Foundation and Ophthalmic Research Institute are affiliates of AAO. Membership: $215/year (full member); $25/year (student); $1,000/year (corporate sponsor).

Publications:
Directory. bien.
Newsletter. q. adv.
Optometry and Vision Science. m. adv.

Meetings/Conferences:
Annual Meetings: December/3,500
1999 - Seattle, WA
2000 - Orlando, FL
2001 - Philadelphia, PA

American Academy of Oral and Maxillofacial Pathology *(1946)*

710 E. Ogden Ave., Suite 600
Naperville, IL 60563-8614
Tel: (630)369-2406 *Fax:* (630)369-2488
Members: 700 individuals
Annual Budget: $100-250,000
Exec. Secretary: Ann E. Spehar, CAE

Historical Note
Formerly (1994) American Academy of Oral Pathology.

Publications:
Membership Directory. bien.
Newsletter. q.

Meetings/Conferences:

American Academy of Oral and Maxillofacial Radiology *(1949)*

P.O. Box 55722
Jackson, MS 39296
Tel: (601)984-6060 *Fax:* (601)984-6086
E-Mail: mocarroll@sod.umsmed.edu
Web Site: http://www.aaomr.org
Members: 500 individuals
Staff: 1
Annual Budget: $25-50,000
Exec. Secretary: Dr. M. Kevin O'Carroll

Historical Note
Formerly (1949) American Academy of Dental Roentgenologists, (1951) American Academy of Oral Roentgenology, (1989) American Academy of Dental Radiology. Membership: $85-$115 (individual); $500-$1500 (organization/company).

Publications:
AAOMR Newsletter. q.
Membership Roster. a.
Oral Surgery, Oral Med. , Oral Pathology, Or.

Meetings/Conferences:
Annual Meetings: Fall/125
1999 - Chicago, IL(Royal Knickerbocker)/Dec. 1-5/150
2000 - Nashville, TN(Doubletree Nashville)/Nov. 8-12/125

American Academy of Oral Medicine *(1946)*

159 W. 53rd St., Suite 12-B
New York, NY 10019-6050
Tel: (212)315-2899 *Fax:* (212)397-9875
E-Mail: aeinera@worldnet.att.com
Members: 775 individuals
Staff: 1
Annual Budget: $100-250,000
Exec. Coordinator: Abraham Reiner, D.D.S.

Historical Note
Founded and incorporated in New York as the American Academy of Dental Medicine, it assumed its present name in 1966. Its purpose is to promote the study and dissemination of knowledge of the cause, prevention and control of diseases of the teeth and oral tissues; and to foster increased scientific understanding and cooperation between the dental and medical professions. Membership: $150/year.

Publications:
Clinician's Guides for Treatment of Common Geriatic Oral Conditions.
Clinician's Guides for Treatment of Common Oral Conditions.
Clinician's Guides for Treatment of HIV Infected Patients.
Clinician's Guides for Treatment of Medically Compromised Patient.
Newsletter of Oral Medicine. 2/year.

Meetings/Conferences:
Annual Meetings: April-May
1999 - Seattle, WA
2000 - Las Vegas, NV(Alexis Park Hotel)

American Academy of Orofacial Pain *(1975)*

19 Mantua Rd.
Mount Royal, NJ 08061
Tel: (609)423-3629 *Fax:* (609)423-3420
E-Mail: dzeigle@tmg.smarthuo.com
Members: 280 individuals
Staff: 1
Annual Budget: $100-250,000
Exec. Director: Dale Zeigler

Historical Note
AAOP is dedicated to alleviating pain and suffering through the promotion of excellence in education, research and patient care in the field of orofacial pain and associated disorders.

Publications:
Journal of Orofacial Pain. q.

Meetings/Conferences:
1999 - Colorado Springs, CO(Broadmoor)/April 29-May 1/400
2000 - Korea

American Academy of Orthodontics for the General Practitioner *(1959)*

Historical Note
Address unknown in 1996.

American Academy of Orthopaedic Surgeons *(1933)*

6300 N. River Road
Rosemont, IL 60018-4262
Tel: (847)823-7186 *Fax:* (847)823-8125
Web Site: http://www.aaos.org
Members: 20,000 individuals
Annual Budget: $10-25,000,000
Exec. V. President: William W. Tipton, Jr., M.D.
Director, Communications: Al Nagelberg
Director, Convention & Meeting Services: Carole Murphy
V. President, Educational Programs: Mark Wieting
Dir., Electronic Media/Eval./Course Ops.: Howard Mevis
Director, Finance and Administration: Ron Kaye
General Counsel: Richard N. Peterson
Manager, Member Services: Pamela Winkler
Director, Information Services: James A. Ogle

Historical Note
Founded October 11, 1933 in Chicago. Incorporated in Illinois in 1948. AAOS fosters and assures the highest quality musculoskeletal health care through: education of orthopaedists, other health care providers, and the public; promotion of research; communication with other professionals and the public; and leadership in the development of health care policy. Has an annual budget of approximately $20 million. Membership: $500/year (active fellows), $250/year (candidate members), $300/year (international).

Publications:
AAOS Report. m.
Bulletin. q.
Emergency Services Newsletter. bi-m.
Journal of the AAOS: A Comprehensive Report. irreg.

Meetings/Conferences:
Annual Meetings: Winter
1999 - Anaheim, CA(Convention Center)/Feb. 4-8

American Academy of Orthotists and Prosthetists *(1970)*

1650 King St., Suite 500
Alexandria, VA 22314
Tel: (703)836-7118 *Fax:* (703)836-0838
E-Mail: aaopline@aol.com
Web Site: http://www.oandp.com/academy
Members: 2,000 individuals
Staff: 10
Annual Budget: $1-2,000,000
Exec. Director: Thomas A. Gorski, CAE
Director, Continuing Education: Kayte Lyons
Manager, Member Services: Catherine Hassinger

Historical Note
Members are individuals who have been certified for practice by the American Board for Certification in Orthotics and Prosthetics. Commonly referred to as the "Academy". Membership: $300/year.

Publications:
Academician Newsletter. q.
Journal of Prosthetics & Orthotics. q.

Meetings/Conferences:
1999 - New Orleans, LA(Grand Hyatt)/Mar. 3-6

American Academy of Osteopathy *(1937)*

3500 DePauw Blvd., Suite 1080
Indianapolis, IN 46268-1136
Tel: (317)879-1881 *Fax:* (317)879-0563
Members: 2,000 individuals
Staff: 6
Annual Budget: $500-1,000,000
Exec. Director: Stephen J. Noone, CAE

Historical Note
Founded July 6, 1937 in Chicago as The Section of Manipulative Therapeutics of the American Osteopathic Ass'n. Name changed in 1938 to Osteopathic Manipulative Therapeutic and Clinical Research Ass'n. Incorporated in 1944 as the Academy of Applied Osteopathy and became American Academy of Osteopathy in 1970. Affiliated with American Osteopathic Ass'n. Membership: $189/year (individual).

Publications:
AAO Journal. q. adv.
AAO Newsletter. 8/year. adv.
AAO Yearbook. a.

Meetings/Conferences:
Semi-Annual Meetings: Spring and Fall, with American Osteopathic Ass'n
1999 - St. Louis, MO(Adams Mark Hotel)/March 24-27/800
2000 - Cleveland, OH(Renaissance)/March 24-27/800
2001 - Colorado Springs, CO(Broadmoor)/March 22-25/800

American Academy of Otolaryngic Allergy *(1941)*

8455 Colesville Rd., Suite 745
Silver Spring, MD 20910-9998
Tel: (301)588-1800 *Fax:* (301)588-2454
Members: 2,100 individuals
Staff: 5
Annual Budget: $500-1,000,000
Exec. Director: Jami Lucas

Historical Note
Formerly (1982) the American Society of Ophthalmologic and Otolaryngologic Allergy. Membership: $100-350/year.

Publications:
Newsletter. q.

Meetings/Conferences:
Annual Meetings: Fall/600

American Academy of Otolaryngology-Head and Neck Surgery *(1896)*

One Prince St.
Alexandria, VA 22314-3357
Tel: (703)836-4444 *Fax:* (703)683-5100
Web Site: http://www.entnet.org
Members: 10,000 individuals
Staff: 60
Annual Budget: $5-10,000,000
Exec. V. President: Jerome Goldstein, CMP, FACS
Director, Communications: Moira DeWilde
Director, Health Policy and Government: Beverly Nissenbaum
Director, Meetings: Jack Harmon
Director, Continuing Education: Anne R. Kienzle
Asst. Director: Pat Carey
Assoc. V. President, Member Services: Lynn Kenney
Director, Publications: Jean McIntyre
Dep. Exec. V. President: Shirley Wester
Director, Marketing: Catherine R. Lincoln
Director, MIS: John C. Vickerman

Historical Note
Founded as the Western Ophthalmological, Otolaryngological and Rhinological Ass'n. Name changed to Western Ophthalmologic and Otolaryngologic Ass'n in 1899. Became the American Academy of Ophthalmology and Otolaryngology in 1903 and assumed its present name in 1979 when the ophthalomogists left the Academy and established the American Academy of Ophthalmology. Merged with the American Council of Otolaryngology-Head and Neck Surgery on January 1, 1982. Functions as a national information, liaison and promotional center of otolaryngological endeavors. Affiliated with the Internat'l Federation of Oto-Rhino-Laryngological Societies. Coordinates state and federal political action and organizes the Combined Otolaryngological Spring Meetings on behalf of six otolaryngologic societies. Has an annual budget of approximately $9.5 million. Membership: $400/year (individual).

Publications:
Otolaryngology-Head and Neck Surgery. m. adv.
The Bulletin. m. adv.

Meetings/Conferences:
Semi-Annual Meetings: Spring and Fall/8,500
1999 - New Orleans, LA/Sept. 26-29
2000 - Washington, DC/Sept. 24-27
2001 - Denver, CO/Sept. 9-12
2002 - San Diego, CA/Sept. 22-25

American Academy of Pain Management *(1988)*

13947 Mono Way, Suite A

Sonora, CA 95370-2807
Tel: (209)533-9744   *Fax:* (209)533-9750
E-Mail: aapm@aapainmanage.org
Web Site: http://www.aapainmanage.org
Members: 6,000 individuals
Staff: 8
Annual Budget: $1-2,000,000
Exec. Director: Richard S. Weiner, Ph.D.
Assoc. Director: Kathryn A. Weiner, Ph.D.

Historical Note
AAPM's primary function is to establish and monitor a national certification process in pain management, to identify individuals who have voluntarily sought and obtained certification in pain management, and to maintain a register of certified individuals. Membership: $140/year (individual).

Publications:
American Journal of Pain Management. q. adv.
Pain Practitioner. q. adv.

Meetings/Conferences:
1999 - Las Vegas, NV/Sept. 23-26

American Academy of Pain Medicine (1983)
4700 W. Lake Ave.
Glenview, IL 60025-1485
Tel: (847)375-4731   *Fax:* (847)375-4777
E-Mail: aapm@amctec.com
Web Site: http://www.Painmed.org
Members: 1000 individuals
Annual Budget: $250-500,000
Exec. Director: Jeffrey W. Engle, CMP, CAE

Historical Note
Formerly the American Academy of Algology, AAPM members physicians and surgeons who spend a significant portion of their practice in treating and studying pain disorders. Membership: $325/year.

Publications:
AAPM Newsletter. bi-m.
Clinical Journal of Pain. q. adv.
Membership Directory. a.

Meetings/Conferences:
Annual Meetings: always President's Day weekend
1999 - Palm Springs, CA/Feb. 10-14

American Academy of Pediatric Dentistry (1947)
211 East Chicago Ave., Suite 700
Chicago, IL 60611-2616
Tel: (312)337-2169   *Fax:* (312)337-6329
Web Site: http://www.aapd.org
Members: 4,200 individuals
Staff: 11
Annual Budget: $1-2,000,000
Exec. Director: John A. Bogert, D.D.S.
Coordinator, Comunications: Karen Fox
Director, Publications: John B. Ferguson
Publications: Crystal Beecher

Historical Note
Formerly (1984) the American Academy of Pedodontics. Membership: $400/year.

Publications:
Membership Directory. a. adv.
Pediatric Dental Impressions. q.
Pediatric Dentistry. bi-m. adv.
Pediatric Dentistry Today (Newsletter). bi-m. adv.

Meetings/Conferences:
Annual Meetings: Spring/800

American Academy of Pediatrics (1930)
141 Northwest Point Blvd.
Elk Grove Village, IL 60007-1098
Tel: (847)228-5005   *Fax:* (847)228-5097
Toll Free: (800)433 - 9016
E-Mail: KIDSDOCS@AAP.ORG
Web Site: http://www.aap.org
Members: 50,000 individuals
Staff: 260
Annual Budget: $25-50,000,000
Exec. Director: Joe M. Sanders, Jr., M.D.
Chief Information Officer: Antony Chan
Director, Division of Meeting Services: Donna Karl
Director, Education: Robert Perleman, M.D.
Director, Finance: Sharon Borowicz
Director, Human Resources: Roberta J. Bosak
C.F.O.: Keith Kampert, Jr.
Director, Membership: Kenneth M. Slaw, Ph.D.
Manager, Dist/Chpt Affairs: Nicole G. Blankenship

Historical Note
In 1922 the AMA's Section on Pediatrics dissented from the AMA in support of the Sheppard-Towner Act, a federal proposal to set up a small maternal and child health program. They were censured, causing the nation's pediatricians to realize that they needed a forum of their own. In 1930 35 charter members founded the AAP in Detroit and chartered it in the State of Illinois. Maintains a Washington office. Has an annual budget of approximately $40 million.

Publications:
AAP News. m. adv.
Pediatrics. m. adv.
Pediatrics-in-Review. m.

Meetings/Conferences:
Annual Meetings: Fall/6,000
1999 - Washington, DC/Oct. 6-13

American Academy of Periodontology (1914)
737 N. Michigan Ave., Suite 800
Chicago, IL 60611-2615
Tel: (312)787-5518   *Fax:* (312)787-3670
Web Site: http://www.perio.org
Members: 7,250 individuals
Staff: 35

Annual Budget: $5-10,000,000
Exec. Director: Alice DeForest, CAE
Director, Public/Practice Affairs: Shannon Wenninger
Director, Meetings and Membership: Barbara A. Connell, CMP, CAE
Dir., Scientific/Educational Affairs: Patricia Norfleet
Director, Business and Financial Affairs: Don Morin
C.I.O.: Steve Sieben
Director, Publications: Rita Shafer
Dep. Exec. Director: Nadine Seidman
Director, Information/Technology: Margo Pecoulas

Historical Note
Originated in Cleveland February 21, 1914 as the Academy of Oral Prophylaxis and Periodontology. Became the American Academy of Periodontology in 1919. Incorporated in Michigan in 1934 and merged with the American Soc. of Periodontists in 1967. Reincorporated in Illinois in 1988. Membership open to qualified periodontists in the U.S. and Canada. Has an annual budget of approximately $6 million. Membership: $540/year (active).

Publications:
AAP News. m.
Directory of Members. a.
Journal of Periodontology. m. adv.

Meetings/Conferences:
Annual Meetings: Winter/6,000
1999 - San Antonio, TX(Convention Center)/Sept. 25-29
2000 - Honolulu, HI(Convention Center)/Sept. 17-20

American Academy of Phalloplasty Surgeons (1995)

Historical Note
Members are surgeons specializing in cosmetic surgery on the penis.

American Academy of Physical Medicine and Rehabilitation (1938)
One IBM Plaza, Suite 2500
Chicago, IL 60611-3604
Tel: (312)464-9700   *Fax:* (312)464-0227
Web Site: http://www.aapmr.org
Members: 5,600 individuals
Staff: 26
Annual Budget: $2-5,000,000
Exec. Director: Ronald A. Henrichs, CAE
Director, Communications: John Wilson
Director, Meetings: Cathy Mason
Director, Education: Jack L. Nichols
Director, Administration & Finance: Sandran McDonald
Coordinator, Membership: Barbara A. Bogel
Deputy Exec. Director: Lynda M. Leedy

Historical Note
Founded in 1938 as the Soc. of Physical Therapy Physicians. Incorporated September 1939 in Chicago. Name changed to American Soc. of Physical Medicine in 1944 and American Academy of Physical Medicine and Rehabilitation in 1955. AAPM&R is a society of Physiatrists, physicians who are Board-certified in physical medicine and rehabilitation. Aprox. 87% of all physiatrists practicing in the US are members of AAPM&R. The mission of the AAPM&R is to maximize the quality of life, while minimizing the incidence, severity, and prevalence of impairments, disabilities, and handicaps. Membership: $520/year (individual).

Publications:
Archives of Physical Medicine and Rehabilitation. m. adv.
Membership Directory. January.
The Physiatrist (offical newsletter). 10/year. adv.

Meetings/Conferences:
Annual Meetings: October-November/2,000-2,300
1999 - Washington, DC(Hilton and Towers)/Nov. 11-14

American Academy of Physician Assistants (1968)
950 N. Washington St.
Alexandria, VA 22314
Tel: (703)836-2272   *Fax:* (703)684-1924
E-Mail: aapa@accessaapaalexandriavaus
Web Site: http://www.aapa.org
Members: 23,000 individuals
Staff: 60
Annual Budget: $5-10,000,000
Exec. V. President: Steven C. Crane
Director of Communications: Jane Howard
V.P., Government and Prof. Affairs: Nicole Gara
Asst. V.P., Education: Shelley L. Hicks
V. President, Clinical Affairs and Education: Greg Thomas, &1
V.P., Finance/Admin.: Robert A. Johnston
Director, Foundation and Development: Carolyn A. Blanco-Losada
Sr. V. President: Marilyn H. Fitzgerald

Historical Note
Formed by a group of physician assistants at Duke University in April 1968. Sponsors the American Academy of Physician Assistants Political Action Committee. Membership: $200/year.

Publications:
AAPA Journal. m. adv.
AAPA News. bi-monthly. adv.
PA Career. bi-monthly. adv.

Meetings/Conferences:
Annual Meetings: May
1999 - Atlanta, GA/May 29-June 3
2000 - Chicago, IL/May 27-June 1

American Academy of Physician Assistants in Occupational Medicine
950 N. Washington St.
Alexandria, VA 22314
Toll Free: (800)596 - 4398
Annual Budget: $25-50,000
Administrative Staff: Christina Largent

Historical Note
AAPA-OM is an educational organization representing physician assistants with an interest in the care of working people and the prevention of workplace illnesses and injuries. Administrtaive

support provided by the American Academy of Physician Assistants.
Membership: $75/year (individual).

American Academy of Physiologic Dentistry (1958)
567 S. Washington St.
Naperville, IL 60540
Tel: (708)355-2625
Members: 55 individuals
Annual Budget: under $10,000
Secretary: Dr. William Kopperud

Historical Note
Has no paid officers or full-time staff. Membership: $100/year.

American Academy of Podiatric Practice Management (1961)
10918 Kingston Pike
Knoxville, TN 39722
Tel: (423)966-5775   *Fax:* (423)966-5743
Members: 200 individuals
Annual Budget: under $10,000
President: Robert Purdy, M.D.
Treasurer: W. Steven Davis

Historical Note
Formerly (1993) the American Academy of Podiatric Administration, it was founded as American Academy of Practice Management in Podiatry and (1970) American Academy of Podiatric Management. AAPA members are doctors of podiatric medicine interested in practice administration.

Publications:
AAPPM Newsletter. q.
Directory of Membership. a.

American Academy of Podiatric Sports Medicine (1970)
1729 Glastonberry Road
Potomac, MD 20854
Tel: (301)424-7440   *Fax:* (301)424-1002
Toll Free: (800)438 - 3355
Members: 895 individuals
Staff: 3
Exec. Director: Larry I. Shane

Historical Note
Affiliated with the American Podiatric Medical Association. Membership: $175/year.

Publications:
Newsletter. q. adv.

Meetings/Conferences:

American Academy of Political and Social Science (1889)
3937 Chestnut St.
Philadelphia, PA 19104
Tel: (215)386-4594   *Fax:* (215)386-4630
Web Site: http://www.asc.upenn.edu/aapss
Members: 3 individuals
Staff: 5
President: Kathleen Hall Jamieson

Historical Note
AAPSS members are academics and others with an interest in the political and social sciences.

Publications:
Annals Journal. bi-m. adv.

Meetings/Conferences:
Annual Meetings: April

American Academy of Procedural Coders (1988)
145 West Crystal Ave.
Salt Lake City, UT 84115
Tel: (801)487-5590   *Fax:* (801)485-7803
Toll Free: (800)626 - 2633
Members: 5,000 individuals
Staff: 30
Exec. Director: Lan C. England

Historical Note
AAPC members are medical coding professionals. Membership: $75/year.

Publications:
AAPC News Newsletter. q.

American Academy of Psychiatrists in Alcoholism and Addictions

Historical Note
Became American Academy of Addiction Psychiatry in 1996.

American Academy of Psychiatry and the Law (1969)
One Regency Drive, P.O. Box 30
Bloomfield, CT 06002-0030
Tel: (860)242-5450   *Fax:* (860)286-0787
Toll Free: (800)331 - 1389
Web Site: http://www.aapl.org
Members: 2,000 individuals
Staff: 3
Annual Budget: $250-500,000
Exec. Director: Jacquelyn T. Coleman, CAE

Historical Note
AAPL members are forensic psychiatrists and general psychiatrists who have a professional interest in psychiatry and the law and are members of the American Psychiatric Ass'n, the American Academy of Child and Adolescent Psychiatry or an equivalent national organization to the APA. Membership: $175/year (individual); $55/year (trainee); $50/year (correspondent).

Publications:
Journal of the AAPL. q.
Newsletter of the AAPL. 3/year.

Meetings/Conferences:
Annual Meetings: October/650
1999 - Baltimore, MD(Reinaissance)/Oct. 21-24

2000 – Vancouver, British Columbia(Westin
        Bayshore)/Oct. 19-22

American Academy of Psychoanalysis (1956)
47 E. 19th St., 6th Floor
New York, NY 10003-1323
Tel: (212)475-7980   *Fax:* (212)479-8101
E-Mail: aapny@aol.com
Members: 800 individuals
Staff: 3
Annual Budget: $250-500,000
Exec. Director: Dianne Gabrielle

Historical Note
*Founded April 29, 1956 in Chicago as the Academy of
Psychoanalysis. Incorporated in New York in 1956. Became the
American Academy of Psychoanalysis in 1966. The Academy
advocates an acceptance of all relevant and responsible
psychoanalytic views of human behavior, rather than adherence to
one particular doctrine. It holds that divergent views should be
made available to psychoanalytic practitioners, candidates in
training, and related behavioral scientists. Membership: $475/year.*

Publications:
Academy News. semi-a.
Journal of American Academy of Psychoanalysis. q.
Membership Directory. bien.
The Academy Forum. semi-a.

Meetings/Conferences:
Semi-annual meetings: Spring and Winter
1999 – Washington, DC
2000 – New York, NY(The Plaza)/200
2001 – New Orleans, LA/200

American Academy of Psychotherapists (1955)
P.O. Box 1611
New Bern, NC 28563-1611
Tel: (919)634-3066
Members: 600 individuals
Staff: 1
Administrative Director: Nancy Hunt

Historical Note
AAP is a professional society of practicing psychotherapists.

Publications:
AAP Newsletter. m.
Directory. bien.
Voices. q.

Meetings/Conferences:

American Academy of Religion (1909)
825 Houston Mill Rd., N.E., #300
Atlanta, GA 30329-4211
Tel: (404)727-7920   *Fax:* (404)727-7959
E-Mail: aar@emory.edu
Web Site: http://www.aar-site.org
Members: 8,500 individuals
Staff: 7
Annual Budget: $1-2,000,000
Exec. Director: Barbara DeConcini

Historical Note
*Formerly (1964) Nat'l Ass'n of Biblical Instructors. A member of
the American Council of Learned Socs. and the Nat'l Humanities
Alliance. Members include students, persons who study religion
outside the field and members of the profession in colleges,
universities and seminaries. Membership: $35-$110/year, based on
income; $20/year (student).*

Publications:
Journal of The AAR. q. adv.
Religious Studies News. q. adv.
Spotlight on Teaching. semi-a. adv.

Meetings/Conferences:
Annual Meetings: Winter
1999 – Boston, MA/Nov. 20-23
2000 – Nashville, TN/Nov. 18-21
2001 – Denver, CO/Nov. 17-20
2002 – Toronto, ON/Nov. 23-26

American Academy of Research Historians of Medieval Spain (1974)
Department of History
University of Central Arkansas
Conway, AR 72035-4935
Tel: (501)450-5625   *Fax:* (501)450-5617
E-Mail: jimb@mail.uca.edu
Web Site: http://www.uca.edu/aarhms
Members: 200 individuals
President: James W. Brodman

Historical Note
*The Academy serves to promote and facilitate the study of the
history of the Iberian Peninsula during the Middle Ages.*

Publications:
Newsletter. bi-a.

Meetings/Conferences:

American Academy of Restorative Dentistry (1928)
Historical Note
Address unknown in 1997.

American Academy of Safety Education (1962)
Central Missouri State U., Safety Center
Humphreys Bldg.
Warrensburg, MO 64093
Tel: (660)543-4281
Members: 107 individuals
Secretary-Treasurer: Robert L. Baldwin

Publications:
AASE Newsletter. semi-a.

American Academy of Sanitarians (1966)
829 Brookside Drive

Miami, OK 74354-4924
Tel: (918)540-1437   *Fax:* (918)540-2025
Members: 300 individuals
Staff: 1
Annual Budget: under $10,000
Exec. Secretary-Treasurer: James W. Pees

Historical Note
*Members are licensed sanitarians with at least an M.A. in
environmental health sciences, environmental management or
public health. Membership: $50/year (individual).*

Publications:
Newsletter. semi-a.
Register of Professional Sanitarians. quinq.
Roster of Diplomates. a.

Meetings/Conferences:
Annual Meetings: June, in conjunction with Nat'l Environmental
        Health Ass'n
1999 – Nashville, TN(Stouffer Renaissance)/July 5-9
2000 – Denver, CO(Adam's Mark)/June 13-20

American Academy of Somnology (1986)
P.O. Box 29124
Las Vegas, NV 89126-3124
Toll Free: (800)649 - 0920
Members: 75 individuals
Staff: 6
Annual Budget: under $10,000
President: David L. Hopper, Ph.D.

Historical Note
*The Academy is an educational, scientific and professional
organization dedicated to advance the understanding of sleep and
sleep related processes. Certification of competence (diplomate
status) is provided to qualified individuals by the American Board of
Somnological Examiners. AAS bestows the title "fellow" and other
recognition on individuals who have made outstanding
contributions to the field of somnology. Membership: $35-95/year.*

Publications:
Journal of Somnology. a. adv.
The Somnologist. q. adv.

Meetings/Conferences:
Annual Meetings: July

American Academy of Spinal Surgeons (1982)
Historical Note
*AASS is a board functioning under the auspices of the American
Academy of Neurological and Orthopaedic Surgeons.*

American Academy of Sports Physicians (1979)
Historical Note
Address unknown in 1997.

American Academy of State Certified Appraisers
1438 W. Main St.
Ephrata, PA 17522-1345
Tel: (717)721-3500   *Fax:* (717)721-3515
Members: 1,200 individuals
Staff: 1
Annual Budget: $100-250,000
Exec. Director: John J. Matternas

Publications:
Peer Review. q. adv.

American Academy of Teachers of Singing (1922)
75 Bank St., Apt. 1-B
New York, NY 10014
Tel: (212)242-1836
Members: 35 individuals
Staff: 1
Annual Budget: $50-100,000
Secretary: William Gephart

Historical Note
Membership: $100/year (individual).

Meetings/Conferences:
Monthly Meetings: October through May

American Academy of the History of Dentistry (1951)
100 S. Vail Ave.
Arlington Heights, IL 60005-1866
Tel: (847)670-7561
Members: 450 individuals
Staff: 1
Annual Budget: $10-25,000
Secretary-Treasurer: Aletha A. Kowitz

Historical Note
*Seeks to stimulate interest, study, and research in the history of
dentistry. Membership: $35/year (professional), $20/year
(student); $45/year (organization/company).*

Publications:
Journal of the History of Dentistry. 3/yr. adv.

Meetings/Conferences:
Annual Meetings: Fall, prior to American Dental Ass'n Annual
        Session/ 50-100
1999 – Honolulu, HI
2000 – Chicago, IL

American Academy of Thermology (1968)
Office of the President, Suite 304
40 Medical Park
Wheeling, WV 26003
Tel: (304)242-2503   *Fax:* (304)242-2682
Web Site: aatusa.com
Members: 250 individuals
Staff: 1
Annual Budget: $50-100,000
President: Srini Govindan M.D.

Historical Note
*Membership composed of physicians (M.D. and D.O.) involved with
the use of infrared and liquid cholesteric imaging in medical*

---

*diagnosis. Formed as the American Thermographic Soc., it assumed
its present name in 1983. Membership: $200/year.*

Publications:
International Journal of Thermology. q.
Thermology Newsletter. q. adv.

Meetings/Conferences:
Annual Meetings: Spring
1999 – Pittsburg, PA(Allgheny General Hospital)

American Academy of Tropical Medicine (1984)
P.O. Box 24224
16126 E. Warren
Detroit, MI 48224-3202
Tel: (313)882-0641   *Fax:* (313)882-5110
Members: 1,500 individuals
Staff: 15
Annual Budget: $100-250,000
President: Ben Allie, M.D.

Historical Note
*AATM members are medical doctors and other health professionals
with an interest in tropical diseases.*

Publications:
Journal of the AATM. semi-a. adv.
Newsletter. irreg.

Meetings/Conferences:
Annual Meetings: Summer
2000 – Durban, South Africa(Downtown
        Hotel)/July 16-18/200
2001 – St. Paul, MN(Marriott)/July 16-18

American Academy of Veterinary and Comparative Toxicology (1958)
Coll. of Large Animal Clinical Science
P.O. Box 1071, Univ. of Tennessee
Knoxville, TN 37901-1071
Tel: (423)974-5702   *Fax:* (423)974-5773
Members: 220 individuals
Staff: 1
Annual Budget: $10-25,000
Secretary-Treasurer: Dr. Larry Kerr

Historical Note
*Organized in 1957, and incorporated Jan. 15, 1958 in Salt Lake
City. Formerly (1984) the American College of Veterinary
Toxicologists. Concerned with education, research and exchange of
proven methods and procedures in the field of veterinary toxicology.
Encourages the use of uniform toxicologic nomenclature.
Membership: $60/year.*

Publications:
Veterinary and Human Toxicology. bi-m. adv.

Meetings/Conferences:

American Academy of Veterinary Dermatology (1964)
c/o Cortez Travel
P.O. Box 77
Solana Beach, CA 92075-0077
Tel: (619)755-5136   *Fax:* (619)481-7474
Members: 500 individuals
Staff: 1
Annual Budget: $10-25,000
Exec. Secretary/Meeting Planner: Judy Schramm

Historical Note
*Founded in 1964 to foster interest in skin disease of animals.
Affiliated with American Animal Hospital Ass'n and American
Veterinary Medical Ass'n. Membership: $45/year.*

Publications:
Derm Dialogue Newsletter. semi-a.

Meetings/Conferences:
Annual Meetings: Spring
1999 – Wailea, Maui, HI(Aston Wailea)/Apr. 22-27/200

American Academy of Veterinary Nutrition (1956)
P.O. Box 189
Lewisburg, OH 45338-0189
Members: 310 individuals
Annual Budget: under $10,000
Secretary-Treasurer: Dan Carey

Historical Note
*Formerly (1978) the American Ass'n of Veterinary Nutritionists.
AAVN advances and expands information and interest in nutrition
for both well and diseased animals. Has no permanent address or
paid staff; officers change biennially. Membership: $25/year.*

Publications:
Directory.
Newsletter. irreg.

Meetings/Conferences:
Annual Meetings: With American Veterinary Medical Ass'n.

American Academy of Veterinary Pharmacology and Therapeutics (1977)
c/o Pfizer, Eastern Point Road
Groton, CT 06340
Tel: (860)441-7361   *Fax:* (860)441-5779
E-Mail: jernia@pfizer.com
Members: 200 individuals
Annual Budget: $10-25,000
Secretary-Treasurer: Dr. Ann D. Jernigan

Historical Note
*Formerly (1981) American College of Veterinary Pharmacology and
Therapeutics. Members are veterinary pharmacologists and
veterinarians. Has no paid officers or full-time staff. Membership:
$35/year (individual).*

Publications:
Journal of Veterinary Pharmacology and Therapeutics.
        8/year. adv.
Membership Directory. bien.
Newsletter. 3/year. adv.

Meetings/Conferences:
Annual Meetings: with ACVIM forum/odd years & Biennial
Symposium/even years

American Academy of Wound Management *(1995)*
1720 Kennedy Causeway, Suite 109
North Bay Village, FL   33141
Tel: (305)866-0250   *Fax:* (305)868-0905
E-Mail: Woundnet@aol.com
Web Site: http://members.aol.com/woundnet
Members: 200 individuals
Staff: 5
Annual Budget: $50-100,000
Administrative Manager: Mike Freedman

Historical Note
*AAWM provides board certification for physicians, nurses,
therapists and other healthcare professionals involved in wound
care. Awards the designation Certified Wound Specialist (CWS).
Membership: $75/year (U.S.); $95/year (international); $400
(certification fee); $150 (certification renewal).*

Publications:
AAWM News Briefings. q.
Nat'l Registry of Board Certified Wound Specialists.

American Academy on Mental Retardation *(1960)*
Historical Note
*The educational wing of the American Ass'n on Mental
Retardation.*

American Accordionists Ass'n *(1938)*
P.O. Box 616
Mineola, NY   11501
Tel: (516)746-3101   *Fax:* (516)746-7085
E-Mail: fdeffner@aol.com
Members: 17,000 individuals
Staff: 1
Annual Budget: $25-50,000
President: Faithe Deffner

Historical Note
*Members are teachers, manufacturers, importers, performers,
amateurs and suppliers united to promote the use of the accordion
and the development of accordion music. Membership: $50/year;
$25/Year (associate).*

Publications:
AAA Journal. a. adv.
AAA Newsletter. q.

American Accounting Ass'n *(1916)*
5717 Bessie Drive
Sarasota, FL   34233-2399
Tel: (941)921-7747   *Fax:* (941)923-4093
E-Mail: AAAhq@.aol.com
Web Site: http://aaa-edu.org
Members: 10,000 individuals
Staff: 10
Annual Budget: $2-5,000,000
Exec. Director: Craig Polhemus

Historical Note
*Founded as the American Ass'n of University Instructors in
Accounting, it assumed its present name in 1935. The American
Taxation Ass'n is one of its sections.*

Publications:
Accounting Education News. 6/year.
Accounting Horizons. q. adv.
Accounting Review. q. adv.
Issues in Accounting Education. semi-a. adv.

Meetings/Conferences:
Annual Meetings: August
1999 – San Diego, CA

American Acupuncture Ass'n *(1972)*
4262 Kissena Blvd.
Flushing, NY   11355
Tel: (718)886-4431   *Fax:* (718)463-0808
Members: 400 individuals
Chairman: Dr. David P.J. Hung

Historical Note
*AAA members are physicians and other health professionals with
an interest in acupuncture. Provides legislative support to the
profession.*

Publications:
Journal of Chinese Acupuncture. a.

Meetings/Conferences:
Annual Meetings: always New York, NY/December

American Advertising Federation *(1905)*
1101 Vermont Ave., N.W., Suite 500
Washington, DC   20005-6306
Tel: (202)898-0089   *Fax:* (202)898-0159
E-Mail: aaf@aaf.org
Web Site: http://www.aaf.org
Members: 37,000 individuals, 115 companies & 220 ad clubs
Staff: 26
Annual Budget: $2-5,000,000
President and C.E.O.: Wallace S. Snyder
Senior V. President, Marketing Communications: Julie A. Dolan
V. President, Public Affairs: Marjorie Valin
Senior V. President, Government Affairs: Jeffrey Perlman
Director, Conference Services: Karen Cohn
V. President, Diversity and Strategic Programs, AAF Foundation:
   Heide Gardner
Exec. Director, AAF Foundation: Mary Ellen Woolley
Controller: Laurel Penhale

Historical Note
*Formed by a merger of the Advertising Federation of America and
the Advertising Ass'n of the West (formerly Pacific Advertising
Ass'n). Supports the Advertising Political Action Committee and the
Advertising Hall of Fame. AAF represents all segments of the*

*advertising industry and its views and concerns on public issues
affecting advertising.*

Publications:
American Advertising. q. adv.
Government Report. m.
Newsline. m.
Report to the Membership. a.
The Communicator. 5 times/year. adv.
The Voice. m.

Meetings/Conferences:

American Agents Ass'n *(1980)*
P.O. Box 7079
Hilton Head Island, SC   29938
Tel: (803)785-2808   *Fax:* (803)785-9068
E-Mail: american@hargray.com
Members: 250 individuals
Staff: 2
Annual Budget: $10-25,000
President: James Fitzpatrick

Historical Note
*AAA members are licensed insurance agents. Membership:
$25/year.*

Publications:
American Eagle Newsletter. bi-m.

American Aging Ass'n *(1970)*
110 Chesley Dr.
Media, PA   19063-1755
Tel: (610)874-7550   *Fax:* (610)565-9747
E-Mail: ameraging@aol.com
Members: 500 individuals
Staff: 1
Annual Budget: $100-250,000
Exec. Director: Arthur K. Balin, M.D.

Historical Note
*Formed to promote biomedical aging research with the long-term
goal of increasing the span of healthy, productive life. Membership:
$110/year (scientific); $50/year (subscription); $50/year (student).*

Publications:
AGE News. q. adv.
AGE: The Journal of the American Aging Ass'n. q. adv.

Meetings/Conferences:
Annual Meetings: Fall/200
1999 – Seattle, WA/June 4-8

American Agricultural Economics Ass'n *(1910)*
415 S.Duff, Suite C
Ames, IA   50010-6600
Tel: (515)233-3202   *Fax:* (515)233-3101
Web Site: http://www.aaea.org
Members: 3,400 individuals
Staff: 8
Annual Budget: $1-2,000,000
Exec. Director: Donna F. Dunn
Manager, Meetings: Nancy Herselius
Assoc. Exec. Director: Lona Christoffers

Historical Note
*Originated in 1910 as the American Farm Management Ass'n.
Became the American Farm Economic Ass'n in 1918 and the
American Agricultural Economics Ass'n in 1968. Incorporated in
Iowa in 1968. Membership: $90/year (individual); $213/year
(organization).*

Publications:
AAEA Newsletter. bi-m. adv.
American Journal of Agricultural Economics. 5/year. adv.
Choices. q.
Review of Agricultural Economics. 2/yr. adv.

Meetings/Conferences:
Annual Meetings: Summer
1999 – Nashville, TN(Stouffer)/Aug. 8-11/1500
2000 – Philadelphia, PA(Marriott)/July 30-Aug. 2

American Agricultural Editors Ass'n *(1921)*
P.O. Box 162585
Austin, TX   78716-2585
Tel: (512)451-5000   *Fax:* (512)442-3239
Web Site: http://www.ageditors.com
Members: 500 individuals
Staff: 2
Annual Budget: $50-100,000
Exec. Secretary-Treasurer: Eddie Aldrete

Historical Note
*Established and incorporated in Illinois, AAEA members are
editors, writers and photographers associated with agricultural
publications. Membership: $100/year (individual).*

Publications:
Byline Newsletter. m.
Roster. a.

Meetings/Conferences:
Annual Meetings: Fall
1999 – Denver, CO(Hyatt)/July 28-31

American Agricultural Law Ass'n *(1980)*
LeFlar Law Center
Univ. of Arkansas
Fayetteville, AR   72701-5830
Tel: (501)575-7389   *Fax:* (501)575-5830
Web Site: http://www.aglaw-assn.org
Members: 900 individuals
Staff: 2
Annual Budget: $50-100,000
Exec. Director: William P. Babione

Historical Note
*Attorneys, law professors and others interested in agricultural law.
Membership: $75/year (individual), $125/year
(organization/company).*

Publications:
Agricultural Law Review. a. adv.
Agricultural Law Update. m.
Membership Directory. bi-a. adv.

Meetings/Conferences:
Annual Meetings: Fall
1999 – New Orleans, LA(Intercontinental)/200
2000 – St. Louis, MO(Regal Riverfront)/200

American Agricultural Marketing Ass'n *(1960)*
Historical Note
Affiliate of the American Farm Bureau Federation.

American Agriculture Movement *(1977)*
P.O. Box 399
Sunray, TX   79086-0399
Tel: (806)733-2203   *Fax:* (806)733-2965
Web Site: www.aaminc.org
Members: 35 state organizations
Staff: 2
Annual Budget: $250-500,000
National President: Bob Hemminger
: V.B. Morris
National Director: Tom Asbridge

Historical Note
*AAM is an umbrella organization composed of state organizations
representing family farm producers for all sectors of agriculture.
Membership: $100/year.*

Publications:
American Agriculture Movement Reporter. m. adv.

Meetings/Conferences:
Annual Meetings: Winter
1999 – Oklahoma City, OK(Radisson)/Jan 22-24

American Alfalfa Processors Ass'n *(1941)*
9948 W. 87th St., Suite E
Overland Park, KS   66212
Tel: (913)648-6800   *Fax:* (913)648-2648
E-Mail: aapa@aapausa.org
Web Site: http://www.aapausa.org
Members: 85 companies
Staff: 1
Annual Budget: $50-100,000
Exec. V. President: Wanda L. Cobb

Historical Note
*Formerly (1984) the American Dehydrators Ass'n. Suppliers to and
operators of alfalfa processing firms.*

Publications:
Bulletin. w. adv.

Meetings/Conferences:
Annual Meetings: February-March

American Alliance for Health, Physical Education, Recreation and Dance *(1885)*
1900 Association Drive
Reston, VA   20191
Tel: (703)476-3400   *Fax:* (703)476-9527
Members: 35,000 individuals
Staff: 71
Annual Budget: $2-5,000,000
Exec. V. President: Michael G. Davis
Director, Conventions: Anna Robinson
V. President, Finance: Donna Kates
Dir., Membership: Mary Ann Simpson

Historical Note
*The American Ass'n for Advancement of Physical Education was
founded at Adelphi Academy, Brooklyn, NY in 1885. In 1903 the
name was changed to the American Physical Education Ass'n and
in 1938 to the American Ass'n for Health, Physical Education and
Recreation. Incorporated in the District of Columbia in 1969.
Became the American Alliance for Health, Physical Education and
Recreation in 1974, and assumed its present name in 1979.
Composed of the American Ass'n for Leisure and Recreation,
American Ass'n for Health Education, American Ass'n for Active
Lifestyles and Fitness, Nat'l Ass'n for Girls and Women in Sports,
Nat'l Ass'n for Sport and Physical Education and the Nat'l Dance
Ass'n. Archival records available to researchers. Membership:
$100/year (individual).*

Publications:
Journal of Health Education. bi-m. adv.
Journal of Physical Education, Recreation, and Dance. m. adv.
Research Quarterly for Exercise and Sport. q. adv.
Strategies. 8/year. adv.
Update. 9/year. adv.

Meetings/Conferences:
Annual Meetings: Spring/8,000
1999 – Boston, MA
2000 – Orlando, FL/March 21-25
2001 – Cincinnati, OH/March 27-31
2002 – San Diego, CA/April 16-20

American Alliance for Theatre and Education *(1987)*
Box 872002
Dept. of Theatre, AZ State University
Tempe, AZ   85287-2002
Tel: (602)965-6064   *Fax:* (602)965-5351
E-Mail: aateinfo@asuvm.inre.asu.edu
Web Site: http://www.aate.com
Members: 1000 individuals, 240 organizations
Annual Budget: $100-250,000
Administrative Director: Christy M. Taylor

Historical Note
*Created by the merger of American Ass'n of Theatre for Youth with
American Ass'n of Theatre in Secondary Education in 1987. Both
organizations were orginally divisions of the American Theatre
Ass'n (Children's Theatre Ass'n and Secondary School Theatre
Ass'n) which were reorganized independently when ATA ceased
operations in 1986. Incorporated in Arizona, AATE members are
educators, artists, administrators and others serving young people*

in professional and community youth theatres and theatre educational programs. Membership: $90/year (individual); $120/year (organization); $55/year (students); $65/year (retired); add $20 outside U.S. and Canada.

Publications:
STAGE of the Art. q.
Youth Theatre Journal. a. adv.

Meetings/Conferences:
Annual Meetings: August
1999 - Chicago, IL(Holiday Inn Motel)July /500

American Ambulance Ass'n *(1977)*
1255 23rd St., N.W., Suite 200
Washington, DC 20037
Tel: (202)452-8888 *Fax:* (202)452-0008
Toll Free: (800)523 - 4447
Web Site: http://www.the-aaa.org
Members: 700 companies
Staff: 9
Annual Budget: $250-500,000
Exec. V. President: Steve Haracznak
Communications Coordinator: Johnna Crowe
Meetings Manager: Cathy Nevins
Director of Education: Brenda Staffan

Historical Note
A merger of the Ambulance Ass'n of America formed in 1962 and the Nat'l Ambulance and Medical Services Ass'n formed in 1963. Formerly (until 1979) known as the Ambulance and Medical Services Ass'n of America. Members are private ambulance services. Membership: annual dues vary by number ofamublances operated; $605/year (affiliate/vendor).

Publications:
Ambulance Industry Journal. bi-m. adv.
Ambulance Industry Update Newsletter. q.

Meetings/Conferences:
Annual Meetings: Fall/1,000
1999 - Nashville, TN/Nov. 16-20

American Amusement Machine Ass'n *(1981)*
450 E. Higgins Road, Suite 201
Elk Grove Village, IL 60007-1417
Tel: (847)290-9088 *Fax:* (847)290-9121
Web Site: http://www.coin-op.org
Members: 125 makers, distributors & suppliers
Staff: 4
Annual Budget: $500-1,000,000
Exec. Director: Robert C. Fay
Manager, Communication: Angela Orlando

Historical Note
Founded in Des Plaines, Illinois as the Amusement Device Manufacturers Ass'n, it became the Amusement Game Manufacturers Ass'n in 1982 and assumed its present name in 1985. Members are manufacturers, distributors and parts suppliers of coin-operated games and machines.

Publications:
Loose Change. m.

Meetings/Conferences:
Annual Meetings: Spring
1999 - Las Vegas, NV/March 10-12

American Anaplastology Ass'n *(1980)*
493 8th Ave.
San Francisco, CA 94118
Tel: (415)221-9775 *Fax:* (415)221-0755
Exec. Director: Toni Zappone

Historical Note
AAA is a noprofit educational organization dedicated to the art and science of rehabilitating patients with facial or somato disfigurements, thereby improving standards and advancing knowledge in prosthetic services and products. Founded to serve as an "information center" fostering communication among multidisciplined specialists involved in prosthetic rehabilitation. Membership is comprised of health care providers and researchers from the fields of medicine, dentistry, allied health, materials research and development, psychology, clinical cosmotology and others.

Publications:
AAA Newsletter. q.
Membership Directory.

American and Delaine-Merino Record Ass'n *(1906)*
1026 County Road 1175, Route 3
Ashland, OH 44805
Tel: (419)281-5786
Members: 200 flocks
Staff: 1
Annual Budget: under $10,000
Secretary-Treasurer: Elaine A. Clouser

Historical Note
Registry office for owners and breeders of Merino sheep. Membership: $10 (lifetime).

Publications:
Consider Merinos.

Meetings/Conferences:
Annual Meetings: always Harrisburg, PA(Keystone Int'l Livestock Expo)/ Sat. in October

American Angora Goat Breeder's Ass'n *(1900)*
Box 195
Rocksprings, TX 78880
Tel: (830)683-4483
Members: 900 individuals
Staff: 1
Annual Budget: under $10,000
Secretary-Treasurer: Patty C. Shanklin

Historical Note
Breeders and fanciers of Angora goats.

Meetings/Conferences:
Annual Meetings: Rocksprings, TX/3rd Tuesday in October

American Angus Ass'n *(1883)*
3201 Frederick Ave.
St. Joseph, MO 64506
Tel: (816)383-5100 *Fax:* (816)233-9703
E-Mail: angus@angus.org
Web Site: http://www.angus.org
Members: 21,548 individuals
Staff: 12
Annual Budget: $2-5,000,000
Exec. V. President: Richard L. Spader
Director, Communications: Susan Waters

Historical Note
Formerly (1956) American Aberdeen-Angus Breeder's Ass'n. The purpose of the ass'n is: 1) to register purebred calves, 2) to inform and educate people about the breed, 3) to work to improve the breed. Member of the Nat'l Pedigree Livestock Council, Nat'l Cattlemen's Beef Ass'n.

Publications:
Angus Beef Bulletin. 3/year.
Angus Journal. 11/year. adv.

Meetings/Conferences:
Annual Meetings: always Louisville, KY/November during North American International Livestock Exhibition

American Animal Hospital Ass'n *(1933)*
P.O. Box 150899
Denver, CO 80215-0899
Tel: (303)986-2800 *Fax:* (303)986-1700
Web Site: www.healthypet.com
Members: 18,000 individuals
Staff: 55
Annual Budget: $5-10,000,000
Exec. Director: John W. Albers, D.V.M.
Manager, Meetings: Chuck Potter
Director, Finance: Jim Parone

Historical Note
An association of animal hospitals and small animal practitioners. Founded in 1933 and incorporated in 1935 in Illinois. Has an annual budget of approximately $6 million. Membership: $260/year (practitioners).

Publications:
AAHA Trends. bi-m. adv.
Journal of the American Animal Hospital Association. bi-m. adv.

Meetings/Conferences:
Annual Meetings: Late March-Early April
1999 - Denver, CO/March 20-24

American Anthropological Ass'n *(1902)*
4350 N. Fairfax Drive, Suite 640
Arlington, VA 22203-1620
Tel: (703)528-1902 *Fax:* (703)528-3546
Web Site: http://www.ameranthassn.org
Members: 11,000 individuals, 4,500 institutional subscribers
Staff: 24
Annual Budget: $2-5,000,000
Exec. Director: Bill Davis
Director, Government Relations: Peggy Overbey
Director, Government Relations: Mary Margaret Overbey
Director, Meetings: Lucille Dinon Horn
Director, Academic Relations: Patsy Evans
Director, Finance and Administration: Frank Medina
Membership Supervisor: Rob Smariga

Historical Note
Established by members of the American Ethnological Soc. of New York, the Anthropological Soc. of Washington and Section H (Anthropology) of the American Ass'n for the Advancement of Science. Incorporated in the District of Columbia in May, 1902. Specialty sections of AAA include: American Ethnological Soc., Archeology Division, Ass'n for Africanist Anthropology, Ass'n for Feminist Anthropology, Ass'n for Political and Legal Anthropology, Ass'n of Black Anthropologists, Ass'n of Latina and Latino Anthropologists, Anthropology of Religion Section, Ass'n of Senior Anthropologists, Biological Anthropology Section, Central States Anthropological Soc., Council on Anthropology and Education, Council for Museum Anthropology, Council on Nutritional Anthropology, Culture and Agriculture, General Anthropology Section, Middle East Section, Nat'l Ass'n for the Practice of Anthropology, Nat'l Ass'n of Student Anthropologists, Soc. for Anthropology in Community Colleges, Soc. for the Anthropology in Consciousness, Soc. for the Anthropology of Europe, Soc. for the Anthropology of North America, Soc. for the Anthropology of Work, Soc. for Cultural Anthropology, Soc. for Humanistic Anthropology, Soc. for Latin American Anthropology, Soc. for Psychological Anthropology, Soc. for Linguistic Anthropology, Soc. for Medical Anthropology, Soc. for Urban Anthropology, and Soc. for Visual Anthropology. Membership: several categories; for information contact AAA.

Publications:
American Anthropologist. q. adv.
American Ethnologist. q. adv.
Anthropology and Education Quarterly. q. adv.
Anthropology and Humanism. semi-a. adv.
Anthropology Newsletter. m. adv.
Central Issues in Anthropology. semi-a.
Cultural Anthropology. q. adv.
Ethos. q. adv.
Guide to Departments of Anthropology. a.
Linguistic Anthropology. semi-a.
Medical Anthropology Quarterly. q. adv.
Museum Anthropology. 3/yr.
Visual Anthropology Review. semi-a.

Meetings/Conferences:
Annual Meetings: November-December/4,500

American Antiquarian Soc. *(1812)*
185 Salisbury St.
Worcester, MA 01609-1634
Tel: (508)755-5221 *Fax:* (508)753-3311
Members: 649 individuals
Staff: 50
Annual Budget: $2-5,000,000
President: Ellen S. Dunlap
Librarian: Nancy Burkett
V. Prsident, Academic and Public Programs: John B. Hench
V. President, Development: John M. Keenum

Historical Note
A learned society founded in 1812 by Isaiah Thomas and others to collect and preserve materials related to American history before 1877, it maintains an outstanding historical research library.

Publications:
Almanac: AAS Newsletter.
American Culture (trien).
Newsletter of the Program in the History of the Book in.
Proceedings. semi-a.

Meetings/Conferences:
Annual Meetings: third Wednesday in October, Worcester, MA (Antiquarian Soc.)

American Apitherapy Soc. *(1978)*
252 Broad St.
Red Bank, NJ 07701
Tel: (732)842-5700 *Fax:* (732)530-7220
Members: 3,500 individuals
Annual Budget: $100-250,000
President: Dr. Christopher Kim

Historical Note
AAS members are beekeepers, health professional and other with an interest in therpeutic applications of honey bee products, particularly Honey bee venom. Has no paid officers or full-time staff. Membership: $40/year (individual).

Publications:
Bee Inform. bi-m. adv.
BeeWell Newsletter. q. adv.
Directory. a.
Journal of AAS. a.
Proceedings. irreg.

Meetings/Conferences:

American Apparel Manufacturers Ass'n *(1933)*
2500 Wilson Blvd., Suite 301
Arlington, VA 22201
Tel: (703)524-1864 *Fax:* (703)522-6741
Toll Free: (800)520 - 2262
Web Site: http://www.americanapparel.org
Members: 650 companies
Staff: 20
Annual Budget: $2-5,000,000
President: Larry Martin
Director, Communications: Joan McNeal
Director, Marketing: H. Jack Carver
Director of Government Relations: Michael Gale
Director, Education & Conventions: Ann Lawrence Engels
Director, Technical Services: Richard Yardley
Director of Financial Services: Ralph Runecke

Historical Note
Formerly the Southern Garment Manufacturers Ass'n, the AAMA absorbed the Nat'l Ass'n of Shirt, Pajama and Sportswear Manufacturers in 1962, the Pacific Coast Garment Manufacturers Ass'n in 1965, the Textile Merchants and Associated Industries of Chicago in 1965, the Corset and Brassiere Ass'n in 1971, the Lingerie Industry Council in 1971, the New England Rainwear Manufacturers Ass'n in 1974, the Nat'l Outerwear and Sportswear Ass'n in 1983, the Headwear Institute of America in 1993, and the Nat'l Knitwear Manufacturers Ass'n in 1993. The Nat'l Knitwear Manufacturers Ass'n, Intimate Apparel Council and the Swimwear Industry Manufacturers Ass'n are divisions of AAMA.

Publications:
AAMA Newsletter. bi-m.
Apparel Research Notes. semi-a.
Membership Directory. a. adv.

Meetings/Conferences:
Annual Meetings: Spring/350
1999 - Washington, DC(Willard)/April 29-May 1
2000 - Atlanta, GA/Sept. 14-17
2001 - Atlanta, GA/Aug. 16-19

American Apparel Producers Network *(1980)*
P.O. Box 720693
Atlanta, GA 30358
Tel: (404)843-3171 *Fax:* (404)256-5380
E-Mail: sourcing@usawear.org
Web Site: http://www.usawear.org
Members: 340 companies
Staff: 3
Annual Budget: $100-250,000
Exec. Director: Sue Strickland

Historical Note
Formerly (1981) Southern Apparel Contractors and (1986) American Apparel Producers Ass'n. AACA was established for "the purpose of domestic apparel sourcing in direct competition with imports." Membership: $500/year.

Publications:
AAPN Directory for Sourcing American Apparel. m. adv.
AAPN News. m. adv.

Meetings/Conferences:
Semi-Annual Meetings: Spring and Fall
1999 - Pine Mountain, GA(Callaway Gardens)/April 22-24

American Arbitration Ass'n *(1926)*
335 Madison Ave., Tenth Floor
New York, NY 10017
Tel: (212)484-4000 *Fax:* (212)716-5901
Web Site: http://www.adr.org
Members: 8,000 individuals
Staff: 650

Annual Budget: $25-50,000,000
President and C.E.O.: William K. Slate, II
V. President, Government Programs: P. Jean Baker
Senior V. President, Educational Development: Richard M. Reilly, CAE
V. President, Program Development: Robert E. Meade
Senior V. President, Finance and C.F.O.: John C. Emmert, Jr.
Senior V. President, Business Development: Mark Appel
Senior V. President, Corporate: Richard Naimark
General Counsel: Michael F. Hoellering
V. President, Membership: Jennifer Jester
V. President, Publications: Susan E. Klein
Director, Public Relations: Toni Griffin

Historical Note
Formed by a merger of the Arbitration Society of America and the Arbitration Foundation. Members are individuals and organizations united to promote the use of arbitration, mediation, democratic elections and other non-judicial processes for the settlement of all types of disputes. Has an annual budget of approximately $45 million.

Publications:
ADR Currents. q.
Arbitration in the Schools. m.
Claims Forum. q.
Dispute Resolution Journal. q.
Dispute Resolution Times. q.
Labor Arbitration in Government. m.
New York State No-Fault/SUM Arbitration Reporter. q.
Punch List. q.
Summary of Labor Arbitrator Awards. m.

Meetings/Conferences:
1999 – San Francisco, CA

American Architectural Manufacturers Ass'n *(1936)*
1827 Walden Office Sq., Suite 104
Schaumburg, IL 60173-4268
Tel: (847)303-5664   *Fax:* (847)303-5774
Members: 270 companies
Staff: 12
Annual Budget: $1-2,000,000
Exec. Director: Stephen K. Sullivan
Mktg./Communications Manager: Steve Staub

Historical Note
Merger (1962) of Sliding Glass Door and Window Institute (1954) and Aluminum Window Manufacturers Ass'n (1936) to become the Architectural Aluminum Manufacturers Ass'n. Absorbed (1971) Aluminum Siding Ass'n. Assumed present name in 1984, after changing mission to include all framing materials. Manufacturers of storm windows, sliding glass doors, siding, skylights and curtain walls. Membership: $1,000/year minimum (company).

Publications:
AAMAScope.

Meetings/Conferences:
Annual Meetings: Fall/700
1999 – Marco Island, FL(Marco Island Hilton)/Feb. 7-10
2000 – Kamuela, HI(Hapuna Beach Prince Hotel)/Jan. 23-26

American Art Therapy Ass'n *(1969)*
1202 Allanson Road
Mundelein, IL 60060-3808
Tel: (847)949-6064   *Fax:* (847)566-4580
E-Mail: estygarIII@aol.com
Members: 4,500 individuals
Staff: 5
Annual Budget: $250-500,000
Exec. Director: Edward J. Stygar, Jr.
Manager, Conventions: Mary Buckley

Historical Note
AATA serves its members and the general public by providing standards of professional competence and disseminating knowledge relevant to the use of artistic processes and practices as tools for treatment, personal growth, and the reconciliation of emotional conflict. Membership: $35/year (student); $85/year (professional); $120/year (organization).

Publications:
Art Therapy Journal. q.
Directory. bien.
Newsletter. q.
Proceedings. a.

Meetings/Conferences:
Annual Meetings: November

American Artists Professional League *(1928)*
c/o Salmagundi Club
47 Fifth Ave.
New York, NY 10003
Tel: (212)645-1345   *Fax:* (212)645-1345
Members: 1000 individuals
Annual Budget: $25-50,000
President: Leo Yeni

Historical Note
Members are professional painters, sculptors and graphic artists working in style of traditional realism. Has no paid officers or full-time staff. Membership: $35/year.

Publications:
Catalog, Grand National Exhibition. a. adv.
Newsletter. semi.

Meetings/Conferences:
Annual Meetings: New York, NY(Salmagundi Club)/Nov.
1999 – New York, NY(Salmagundi Club)

American Arts Alliance *(1977)*
805 15th St., N.W., Suite 500
Washington, DC 20005-2207
Tel: (202)289-1776   *Fax:* (202)371-6601
Members: 2,600 Organizations
Staff: 5
Annual Budget: $250-500,000
Exec. Director: Jan Dento

Historical Note
Eastablished in 1977, and incorporated in the District of Columbia, the American Arts Alliance is the principle advocate for America's professional nonprofit arts organizations and their publics in representing arts interests and advancing arts support before Congress and other branches of the federal government. To achieve this mission, the Alliance will inform legislators and policy makers of the vital role of the arts in American society, and advocate the develpoment of national policies which recognize, enhance, and foster the contributions that the arts make to America.

Publications:
Grassroots Kit for Arts Advocates. irreg.
Legislative Update. m.

American Ass'n for Accreditation of Ambulatory Surgery Facilities *(1981)*
1202 Allanson Road
Mundelein, IL 60060-3808
Tel: (847)949-6058   *Fax:* (847)566-4580
Toll Free: (888)545 - 5222
E-Mail: aaaasf@sprynet.com
Web Site: http://www.aaaasf.org
Members: 550 individuals
Staff: 4
Annual Budget: $100-250,000
Exec. Director: Edward J. Stygar, Jr.

Historical Note
Formerly (1992) The American Ass'n for Accreditation of Ambulatory Plastic Surgery Facilities. Members are ambulatory surgical facilities operated by American Board of Medical Specialties board certified surgeons.

Publications:
AAAASF News Newsletter. semi-a. adv.

Meetings/Conferences:
Biennial Symposium: (odd years)

American Ass'n for Accreditation of Laboratory Animal Care *(1965)*

Historical Note
Became the Ass'n for Assessment and Acreditation of Laborataory Animal Care Internat'l in 1996.

American Ass'n for Active Lifestyles and Fitness *(1949)*
1900 Association Drive
Reston, VA 20191
Tel: (703)476-3430   *Fax:* (703)476-9527
Toll Free: (800)213 - 7193
E-Mail: aaalf@aahperd.org
Web Site: www.aahperd/aaalf/aaalf.html
Members: 65,000 individuals
Staff: 3
Annual Budget: $25-50,000
Exec. Director: Janet Seaman, Ph.D.

Historical Note
Formerly (1994) Ass'n for Research, Administration, Professional Councils and Societies. Established originally as a division of the American Ass'n for Health, Physical Education and Recreation. AAALF members are college and university fitness professionals, teachers and instructors in clubs and private businesses. AAALF became a semi-autonomous member of the American Alliance for Health, Physical Education, Recreation and Dance. Coordinates the work of special interest councils in health, physical education and recreation; including the School and Community Safety Soc. of America. Membership: $100/year.

Publications:
AAALF Newsletter. semi-a.
Measurement in Physical Education & Exercise Science. q.

Meetings/Conferences:
Annual Meetings: Spring, with AAHPERD/6,000
1999 – Boston, MA(Convention Center)/April 20-25

American Ass'n for Adult and Continuing Education *(1982)*
1200 19th St., N.W., Suite 300
Washington, DC 20036-2401
Tel: (202)857-1100   *Fax:* (202)223-4579
Members: 2,500 individuals
Staff: 2
Annual Budget: $500-1,000,000
Exec. Director: Drew W. Allbritten, Ph.D.

Historical Note
The product of a merger between the Adult Education Ass'n (founded in 1951) and the Nat'l Ass'n for Public and Continuing Adult Education (founded in 1952), AAACE coordinates local, state, regional and national adult education programs, publications and legislation. Absorbed Nat'l Council of Administrators of Adult Education in 1992. Membership: $115/year (professional).

Publications:
Adult Education Quarterly. q. adv.
Adult Learning. 6/year. adv.
OnLine (AAACE Newsletter). 6/year. adv.

Meetings/Conferences:
Annual Meetings: Fall

American Ass'n for Aerosol Research *(1981)*
1330 Kemper Meadow Dr., Suite 600
Cincinnati, OH 45240-1634
Tel: (513)742-2020   *Fax:* (513)742-3355
Members: 800 individuals, 600 individuals & organizations
Staff: 3
Annual Budget: $250-500,000
Exec. Director: Richard A. Strano, CAE

Historical Note
Promotes the research of small particles suspended in gases. Applications include air pollution research, production of fine powders and the study of atmospheric chemistry and nuclear safety. Has no paid staff. Managed by the American Conference of

Governmental Industrial Hygenists. Membership: $100/year (individual); $800/year (organization).*

Publications:
AAAR Newsletter. q.
Aerosol Science and Technology. semi-m. adv.
Membership Directory. a.

Meetings/Conferences:
1999 – Tacoma, WA(Sheraton)

American Ass'n for Agricultural Education *(1960)*
AgEd Program/Dept. of Occupation Studies
624 Alderhold Hall, Univ. of Georgia
Athens, GA 30602-7162
Tel: (706)542-1204
Members: 300 individuals
Staff: 1
Annual Budget: $10-25,000
President: Maynard Iverson

Historical Note
Formerly Teacher Trainers Section of the Agricultural Division of the American Vocational Ass'n, then American Ass'n of Teacher Educators in Agriculture; name changed, yet still part of AVA. Officers elected annually; has no permanent headquarters. Membership: $40/year (individual).

Publications:
Journal of Agricultural Education.

Meetings/Conferences:
Annual Meetings: With American Vocational Ass'n.

American Ass'n for Applied Linguistics *(1977)*
P.O. Box 21686
Eagan, MN 55121-0686
Tel: (612)953-0805   *Fax:* (612)431-8400
Web Site: http://igor.lis.wisc.edu/aaal/
Members: 1,300 individuals
Annual Budget: $50-100,000
Administrator: Matthew Howe

Historical Note
Individuals interested in multidisciplinary approaches to language issues and problems. Membership: $48/year (individual); $96/year (institution); $24/year (student).

Publications:
Newsletter. 3/year.

Meetings/Conferences:
Annual Meetings: Spring
1999 – New York, NY/March 6-9
2000 – Vancouver, British Columbia/March 11-14
2001 – St. Louis, MO/Feb. 24-27
2002 – Salt Lake City/April 6-9/1000

American Ass'n for Artificial Intelligence *(1980)*
445 Burgess Drive
Menlo Park, CA 94025-3496
Tel: (650)328-3123   *Fax:* (650)321-4457
Members: 7,000 individuals
Staff: 10
Annual Budget: $1-2,000,000
Exec. Director: Carol M. Hamilton

Historical Note
Members are individuals interested in attempting to approximate the human thinking process with computers in such fields as visual data interpretation, expert systems, natural language processing, common sense reasoning, automated problem solving and robotics. Membership: $50 (U.S./Canadian Institution), $75/year (foreign individual), $75/year (U.S./Canadian institution) $100/year (foreign company).

Publications:
AI Magazine. q. adv.
Conference Proceedings. a.

Meetings/Conferences:
Annual Meetings: July/August
1999 – Orlando, FL(Omni Rosen Hotel)/July 18-22/1200
2000 – Austin, TX/1200

American Ass'n for Budget and Program Analysis *(1976)*
P.O. Box 1157
Falls Church, VA 22041
Tel: (703)941-4300   *Fax:* (703)941-1535
Members: 600 individuals
Staff: 1
Annual Budget: $25-50,000
Nat'l Exec. Secretary: Christine LaChance

Historical Note
The result of a merger between the Budget Officers Conference and the American Public Policy Ass'n, AABPA was chartered as a non-profit educational corp. in Washington, DC in 1976. Members, largely in the DC area, have an interest in program management and budget analysis. Membership: $30/year (individual); $150/year (corporate), $15/year (student).

Publications:
Newsletter. bi-m.
Public Budgeting and Finance Journal. q. adv.

Meetings/Conferences:
Semi-Annual Symposia: Spring and Fall

American Ass'n for Cancer Education *(1947)*
P.O. Box 601
Snellville, GA 30078-0601
Tel: (404)329-7612   *Fax:* (404)321-4669
E-Mail: gkrawiec@cancer.org
Members: 500 individuals
Annual Budget: $25-50,000
Secretary: Virginia Krawiec

Historical Note
Formerly (1966) Coordinators of Cancer Teaching. Membership includes scientists, surgeons, internists, radiation oncologists, pediatricians, gynecologists, osteopathic physicians, dentists,

oncology nursing educators and professional educators. Concerned with cancer teaching in medical, dental and nursing schools, educational programs for the general public, for populations at special risk, and for cancer patients. Efforts involve developing and evaluating new educational strategies and methods, including the examination of objectives, courses, and evaluation instruments; expanding public education; fostering internat'l cooperative efforts in cancer education; and furthering education in cancer prevention. Has no paid staff. Membership: $95/year.

Publications:
American Ass'n for Cancer Education Newsletter q.
Journal of Cancer Education. q. adv.
Membership Directory.
President's Newsletter.

Meetings/Conferences:
Annual Meetings: Fall/200
1999 – Cleveland, OH/Oct. 7-10
2000 – Washington, DC/Nov. 2-5

American Ass'n for Cancer Research *(1907)*
Public Ledger Bldg., Suite 826
150 South Independence Mall West
Philadelphia, PA 19106-3483
Tel: (215)440-9300   *Fax:* (215)440-9313
E-Mail: webmaster@aacr.org
Web Site: http://www.aacr.org
Members: 13,000 individuals
Staff: 43
Annual Budget: $10–25,000,000
Exec. Director and Director, Publications: Margaret Foti
Public Information Coordinator: Jenny Anne Horst-Martz
Manager, Meetings and Exhibits: Jeffrey M. Ruben
Director, Administration: Adam D. Blistein
Controller: Joan D. Ritchie
Assoc. Director, Publications: Mary Anne Mennite

Historical Note
Founded 1907 in Washington, DC and incorporated in New York in 1940. An association of research workers for presentation and discussion of new or significant observations and problems in cancer, and to foster research on cancer. Membership: $175/year.

Publications:
Cancer Epidemiology, Biomarkers & Prevention. bi-m. adv.
Cancer Research. semi-m. adv.
Cell Growth and Differentiation. m. adv.
Clinical Cancer Research. m. adv.

Meetings/Conferences:
Annual Meetings: Spring/7,000
1999 – Philadelphia, PA(Convention Center)/April 10-14

American Ass'n for Career Education *(1980)*
2900 Amby Place
Hermosa Beach, CA 90254-2216
Tel: (310)376-7378   *Fax:* (310)376-2926
Members: 500 individuals, 10 companies
Annual Budget: under $10,000
President: Pat Nellor Wickwire, Ph.D.

Historical Note
Incorporated in the District of Columbia in 1981. AACE connects education, work, and careers through Career Education for all ages. AACE members are professional educators, community leaders, parents, business leaders, government leaders and other interested individuals. Membership: $15/year (individual); $100/year (sustaining).

Publications:
AACE Bonus Briefs. irreg.
AACE CareerGram. irreg.
AACE Careers Update. q.
AACE Distinguished Member Series. a.
AACE Forum. irreg.
AACE Registry of Member Products and Services.
Career Education That Works. a.

Meetings/Conferences:
Biennial Meeting: (odd years)

American Ass'n for Chinese Studies *(1958)*
CCNY North Academic Center, Room 5/144
Convent Ave.at 138th St.
New York, NY 10031
Tel: (212)650-8268   *Fax:* (212)650-8287
Members: 350 individuals
Staff: 2
Annual Budget: under $10,000
Exec. Secretary: Peter Chow

Historical Note
Formerly (1976) the American Ass'n of Teachers of Chinese Language and Culture, Inc.

Publications:
Journal of Chinese Studies. semi-a.
Newsletter. semi-a.

Meetings/Conferences:
Annual Meetings: Fall
1999 – Arlington, VA(Crystal Marriott Gateway)/April 16-17

American Ass'n for Clinical Chemistry *(1948)*
2101 L St., N.W., Suite 202
Washington, DC 20037-1526
Tel: (202)835-8739   *Fax:* (202)833-4576
Web Site: http://www.aacc.org
Members: 11,000 individuals
Staff: 42
Annual Budget: $5–10,000,000
Exec. V. President: Richard G. Flaherty
Director, Government Affairs: Pamela Nash
Director, Meetings: Christine Donnell
Director, Education: Penny Jones
Director, Finance and Administration: Eric Bellamy
Manager, Professional Affairs: Jean Rhame
Director, Marketing and Publications: John Gill
Editor: Nancy Sasavage

Historical Note
Incorporated in New York in 1949. Formerly (Jan. 1, 1976) American Ass'n of Clinical Chemists. Members are chemists, physicians and other scientists specializing in clinical chemistry. Provides educational and professional development services to its members in order to improve the level at which chemistry is practiced in chemical laboratories. Has an annual budget of approximately $8.6 million.

Publications:
ACC News. bi-m.
Clinical Chemistry Journal. m. adv.
Clinical Laboratory News. m. adv.
Endocrinology & Metabolism Continuing Education Program. m.
Forensic Urine Drug Testing Newsletter. q.
Therapeutic Drug Monitoring & Emergency Toxicology C. E.

Meetings/Conferences:
Annual Meetings: July/August
1999 – New Orleans, LA/July 25-29

American Ass'n for Continuity of Care *(1982)*
638 Prospect Ave.
Hartford, CT 06105
Tel: (860)586-7524   *Fax:* (860)586-7550
Members: 500 individuals
Staff: 1
Annual Budget: $100-250,000
Exec. Director: Cathy Hale

Historical Note
Incorporated in Washington, DC, AACC members are multi-disciplinary professionals involved in developing continuity of care, hospital discharge and home health care. Membership: $85/year (individual), $175-750/year (organization).

Publications:
Access. bi-m. adv.
Directory. a. adv.
Impaacct.

Meetings/Conferences:

American Ass'n for Correctional Psychology *(1953)*
Psych. Dept., Fordham University
Bronx, NY 10458
Tel: (718)817-3790   *Fax:* (718)817-3785
Members: 250 individuals
Annual Budget: $25-50,000
President-Elect and Program Chairperson: David Glenwick, Ph.D.

Historical Note
Affiliate of the American Correctional Association. Members of the AACP are involved in criminal justice in a variety of ways - through administration, practice, teaching and research. The purpose of the Ass'n is to bring together behavorial scientists interested in the psychology of crime, to promote the development of psychological practice in criminal justice and law enforcement settings, and to stimulate research into the nature of criminal behavior. Membership: $45/year; $30/year (student).

Publications:
Criminal Justice and Behavior Journal. q. adv.
The Correctional Psychologist. q. adv.

Meetings/Conferences:
Annual Meetings: Summer with American Correctional Ass'n

American Ass'n for Crystal Growth *(1966)*
P.O. Box 3233
Thousand Oaks, CA 91359-0233
Tel: (805)492-7047   *Fax:* (805)492-4062
E-Mail: aacg@lafn.org
Web Site: http://www.aml.arizona.edu/aacg
Members: 600 individuals, 10 corporate
Staff: 1
Annual Budget: $50-100,000
Exec. Administrator: Anthony L. Gentile, Ph.D.

Historical Note
Formerly (1970) American Committee for Crystal Growth. Members include engineers, scientists, educators, technologists, marketing representatives and students, all with a strong interest in one or more facets of the crystal growth field. Affiliated with the Internat'l Organization for Crystal Growth. Membership: $35/year (individual), $15/year (student), $500/year (corporate affiliation).

Publications:
AAGC Newsletter. 3/yr. adv.

Meetings/Conferences:
Annual Meetings: Triennial Meetings:
1999 – Tucson, AZ(Loew's Ventanan Canyon Resort)/Aug. 1-6/325

American Ass'n for Dental Research *(1952)*
1619 Duke St.
Alexandria, VA 22314-3406
Tel: (703)548-0066   *Fax:* (703)548-1883
E-Mail: research@iadr.com
Web Site: http://www.iadr.com
Members: 5,000 individuals
Staff: 16
Annual Budget: $1-2,000,000
Exec. Director: Dr. Eli Schwarz
Director, Meetings: Gwynn Breckenridge
Deputy Exec. Director: Robert J. Collins, D.M.D., MP

Historical Note
A division of Internat'l Ass'n for Dental Research. Membership: $145/year (individual), $500-4,000/year (company).

Publications:
Advances in Dental Research. q.
Critical Reviews in Oral Biology and Medicine.
Dental Research Newsletter. m. adv.
Journal of Dental Reseach. m. adv.
Special Care in Dentistry.

Meetings/Conferences:
Annual Meetings: Spring/6,000

1999 – Vancouver, British Columbia(Convention Center)/March 10-14
2000 – Washington, DC(Convention Center)/April 5-9

American Ass'n for Employment in Education *(1934)*
820 Davis St.
Suite 222
Evanston, IL 60201-4445
Tel: (847)864-1999   *Fax:* (847)864-8303
E-Mail: aaee@nwu.edu
Web Site: http://www.aaee.org
Members: 1000 institutions
Staff: 2
Annual Budget: $250-500,000
Exec. Director: Charles A. Marshall

Historical Note
Personnel in educational placement in colleges, universities and school districts. Formerly (1962) Nat'l Institutional Teacher Placement Ass'n and (1996) Ass'n for School, College and University Staffing. Membership: $160/year (institutional).

Publications:
AAEE Staffer. q.
Directory of Public School Systems in the U. S.
Guide to Services & Activities for Teacher Employment. a.
Nat'l Directory for Employment in Education. a.
National Directory of Job and Career Fairs for Educators. a.
Teacher Supply and Demand Report in the U. S.
The Higher Education Job Search.
The Job Search Handbook for Educators. a. adv.
The Journal of Employment in Education. semi-a.

Meetings/Conferences:
Annual Meetings: October
1999 – Ft. Worth, TX
2000 – Chicago, IL
2001 – Baltimore, MD

American Ass'n for Fuel Cells *(1992)*
50 San Miguel Ave.
Daly City, CA 94015
Tel: (415)992-3963
Members: 300 individuals
Annual Budget: under $10,000
Chairman: Thomas Dickerman

Historical Note
AAFC members are engineers, scientists and others with an interest in fuel cell technology and applications. Initially a project of Clean Air Revival Inc., AAFC became a project of the American Hydrogen Ass'n in 1992. Membership: $20/year.

Publications:
Our Energy Future Newsletter.

Meetings/Conferences:
Monthly Meeting: Palo Alto, CA(Penninsula Conservation Center)

American Ass'n for Functional Orthodontics *(1984)*
106 South Kent St.
Winchester, VA 22601
Tel: (540)662-2200   *Fax:* (540)665-8910
Toll Free: (800)441 - 3850
E-Mail: info@aafo.com
Web Site: http://www.aafo.com
Members: 2,100 individuals, 900 subscribers
Staff: 4
Annual Budget: $250-500,000
Exec. Officer: Mary Fuller

Historical Note
Formerly the American Ass'n of Functional Orthodontists. An independent association of orthodontists, pedodontists, and general dentists from throughout the U.S. and Canada with interests in functional appliance treatment and TMJ therapy. Membership: $155/year.

Publications:
AAFO Members' Directory. a.
The Functional Orthodontist. bi-m. adv.

Meetings/Conferences:
1999 – Washington, DC/April 9-11

American Ass'n for Geodetic Surveying *(1981)*

Historical Note
A member organization of the American Congress on Surveying and Mapping.

American Ass'n for Geriatric Psychiatry *(1978)*
7910 Woodmont Ave., Suite 1050
Bethesda, MD 20814-3004
Tel: (301)654-7850   *Fax:* (301)654-4137
Web Site: http://www.aagpgpa.org
Members: 1,400 individuals
Staff: 12
Annual Budget: $500-1,000,000
Exec. Director: Janet L. Pailet, JD
Director, Communications: Caroline O'Connell
Director, Government Relations: Betsy Beekwith
Director, Membership and Marketing: Zev Lewis
Director, Education: Jeannine Neloon
Director, Finance and Administration: Carol Segal
Coordinator, Membership: Clea English

Historical Note
An organization of psychiatrists interested in aging. Purpose is to promote better understanding and care of the mental health of the elderly. Membership: $160/year (general member); $65/year (member-in-training).

Publications:
AAGP Newsletter. bi-m.
American Journal of Geriatric Psychiatry. q. adv.
Membership Directory. a.

Meetings/Conferences:
Annual Meetings: February, over the George Washington Birthday Weekend

1999 – New Orleans, LA(Marriott)/March 14-17

American Ass'n for Hand Surgery (1970)
444 E. Algonquin Road
Arlington Heights, IL   60005
Tel: (847)228-9758   *Fax:* (847)228-6509
E-Mail: lmd@plasticsurgery.com
Members: 1,100 individuals
Staff: 2
Annual Budget: $500-1,000,000
Manager: Catherine Hay
Meetings Manager: Mary Jo Harrold

Historical Note
AAHS members are hand surgeons from the disciplines of plastic, orthopaedic and general surgery and hand therapists. AAHS evolved from the Joseph L. Posch Hand Soc. which originally met in 1967, an alumnus group of hand surgeons who trained under Dr. Posch in Detroit, Michigan. Membership: $275/year (physician); $75/year (therapist).

Publications:
Membership Roster. a.
Newsletter. q.

Meetings/Conferences:
1999 – Kamuela, HI(Hilton Waikoloa)/January 13-16

American Ass'n for Health Education (1937)
1900 Association Drive
Reston, VA   20191
Tel: (703)476-3437   *Fax:* (703)476-6638
Toll Free: (800)213 - 7193
E-Mail: aahe@aahperd.org
Members: 7,500 individuals
Staff: 6
Annual Budget: $25-50,000
Exec. Director: Becky J. Smith, Ph.D.

Historical Note
Formerly (1996) the Ass'n for the Advancement of Health Education. Until 1974 a division of the American Alliance for Health, Physical Education and Recreation. Now an independent member of the American Alliance for Health, Physical Education, Recreation and Dance. Membership: $100/year.

Publications:
HE-XTRA. 5/year.
Journal of Health Education. bi-m.

Meetings/Conferences:
Annual Meetings: With AAHPERD.
1999 – Boston, MA
2000 – Orlando, FL
2001 – Cincinnati, OH

American Ass'n for Higher Education (1870)
One Dupont Circle, N.W., Suite 360
Washington, DC   20036-1110
Tel: (202)293-6440   *Fax:* (202)293-0073
Web Site: http://www.aahe.org
Members: 9,000 individuals
Staff: 30
Annual Budget: $2-5,000,000
President: Margaret A. Miller
Director, Conferences/Meetings: Kendra LaDuca
Director, Membership/Marketing: C.J. Schwarz
Director, Publications: Bry Pollack

Historical Note
Established in 1870 as one of the four original departments of the Nat'l Education Ass'n, it became the Ass'n for Higher Education of NEA in 1952; assumed its present name in 1969 when it became independent from NEA. Members are educators and other professionals concerned with the purpose of educational institutions. Membership: $105/year.

Publications:
AAHE Bulletin. m.
Change Magazine. bi-m. adv.

Meetings/Conferences:
Annual Meetings: Nat'l Conference on Higher
       Education/Spring/1,500
1999 – Washington, DC(Sheraton)/March 20-24

American Ass'n for Holistic Health
One Scott Circle, N.W., Suite 108
Washington, DC   20036
Members: 100 individuals
Staff: 1
Exec. Director/V. P. Government Affairs: Jennifer L. Thomas

Historical Note
Supports professionals in holistic and alternative health care, and provides legislative advocacy on behalf of the industry. Membership: $20/year.

Publications:
Wellness for Life. q. adv.

American Ass'n for Laboratory Accreditation (1978)
5301 Buckeystown Pike, Suite 350
Frederick, MD   21704-8307
Tel: (301)644-3248   *Fax:* (301)662-2974
E-Mail: info@a2la.org
Web Site: http://www.a2la.org
Members: 961 laboratories & individuals
Staff: 22
Annual Budget: $5-10,000,000
President: Peter S. Unger
V. President: Roxanne M. Robinson
Financial Manager: Lisa C. Drake
Manager, Business Development: Percy S. Pan

Historical Note
Members are interested in establishing and maintaining quality laboratory testing by accrediting laboratories. A2LA also operates a program to certify environmental reference materials and to register the suppliers of such materials. Accreditation is available to all laboratories meeting the requirements of ISO/IEC Guide 25 (1990)

whether they are owned by private companies or government bodies. A2LA has 740 accreditations in 41 states, Guam and six foreign countries. Membership does not imply accreditation. Membership: $50/year (individual); $100/year (institution); $200-1,000/year (organization).

Publications:
A2LA Annual Report. a.
A2LA Directory of Accredited Laboratories. a.
A2LA News. bi-m.
General Requirments for Accreditation.
Requirements for the Reference Materials Program.

American Ass'n for Laboratory Animal Science (1950)
70 Timber Creek Drive
Cordova, TN   38018-4233
Tel: (901)754-8620   *Fax:* (901)753-0046
E-Mail: info@aalas.org
Web Site: http://www.aalas.org
Members: 8,000 individuals, 600 institutions
Staff: 19
Annual Budget: $1-2,000,000
Exec. Director: Michael Sondag
Director, Professional Development/Education: Jill C. Worley
Director, Membership Services: Judith S. Grisamore

Historical Note
Founded in 1950 and incorporated in Illinois in 1953 as the Animal Care Panel. Assumed its present name in 1966. Members are individuals professionally concerned with the production, care and study of laboratory animals.

Publications:
AALAS Contemporary Topics. bi-m. adv.
Laboratory Animal Science Journal. bi-m.

Meetings/Conferences:
Annual Meetings: October-November
1999 – Indianapolis, IN/Nov. 5-9
2000 – San Diego, CA(Convention Center)

American Ass'n for Leisure and Recreation (1938)
1900 Association Drive
Reston, VA   20191-1599
Tel: (703)476-3400   *Fax:* (703)476-9527
E-Mail: aalr@aahperd.org
Web Site: http://www.aahperd.org/aalr/aalr.html
Members: 2,800 individuals
Staff: 2
Annual Budget: $100-250,000

Historical Note
Until 1974 the Recreation Division of the American Ass'n for Health, Physical Education and Recreation. Now an independent member of the Alliance for Health, Physical Education, Recreation and Dance. Members are teachers of leisure studies, recreation, park administration; administrators in public and private park and recreation agencies. Membership: $100/year.

Publications:
AALReporter.
Leisure Today. m. adv.

Meetings/Conferences:
Annual Meetings: With the American Alliance for Health,
       Physical Education, Recreation and Dance
1999 – Boston, MA/April 20-24
2000 – Orlando, FL/March 21-25
2001 – Cincinnati, OH/March 27-31
2002 – San Diego, CA/April 16-20

American Ass'n for Marriage and Family Therapy (1942)
1133 15th St., N.W., Suite 300
Washington, DC   20005-2710
Tel: (202)467-5119   *Fax:* (202)223-2329
E-Mail: central@aamft.org
Web Site: http://www.aamft.org
Members: 23,000 individuals
Staff: 35
Annual Budget: $2-5,000,000
Exec. Director: Michael Bowers
Director, Marketing/Member Services: Stephanie Jester
Director, Legal/Government Affairs: John Ambrose
Deputy Director, Professional Affairs: Karen Gautney

Historical Note
Founded as American Ass'n of Marriage Counselors, it became American Ass'n of Marriage and Family Counselors in 1970 and assumed its present name in 1978. Members are clinical therapists specially trained to conduct marriage and family therapy with individuals, couples and families. Includes 55 regional divisions in the U.S. and Canada, with members around the world. Membership: $135/year, plus state division dues.

Publications:
Family Therapy News. bi-m. adv.
Journal of Marital and Family Therapy. q. adv.
Practice Strategies. m.

Meetings/Conferences:
Annual Meetings: Fall
1999 – Chicago, IL/Oct. 7-10

American Ass'n for Medical Transcription (1978)
P.O. Box 576187
Modesto, CA   95357-6187
Tel: (209)551-0883   *Fax:* (209)551-9317
E-Mail: aamt@sna.com
Web Site: http://www.aamt.org
Members: 9,500 individuals
Staff: 17
Annual Budget: $1-2,000,000
Exec. Director: Claudia Tessier, CAE
Director of Finance: Monika Knutson
Director of Marketing: Daryl Ochs
Director, Member Services: Melissa Flores
Director, Certification: Linda Byrne,

Director, Publications: Janel Heath
Assoc. Exec. Director, Professional Affairs: Pat Forbis,, CMT
Assoc. Exec. Director for Administrative Affairs: Kimberly Andosca
Director of Transcription Practices: Peggy Hughes,, CMT
Director, Data Services: Rathany Aellos

Historical Note
AAMT is a professional association for medical transcriptionists, supervisors, teachers, students and other interested health personnel. Awards the "CMT" (Certified Medical Transcriptionist) designation by voluntary examination. Membership: $100/year (individual); $200/year (institution). Street address is: 3460 Oakdale Rd., Suite M, Modesto, CA 95355.

Publications:
Journal of the American Ass'n for Medical Transcription. bi-m. adv.
The AAMT Desk Companion. a.
The Leading Edge. bi-m.

Meetings/Conferences:
Annual Meetings: August
1999 – Kansas City, MO(Hyatt Regency Crown Center)
2000 – Portland, OR(Portland Hilton)/Aug. 10-13/700
2001 – Arlington, VA(Crystal Gateway Marriott)/Aug. 2-5/700
2002 – Dallas, TX

American Ass'n for Music Therapy (1971)
Historical Note
Merged with Nat'l Ass'n for Music THerapy to form American Music Therapy Ass'n in 1997.

American Ass'n for Paralegal Education (1981)
88220 Santa Fe Dr.,
Overland Park, KS   66212
Tel: (913)381-4458   *Fax:* (913)381-9308
E-Mail: info@aafpe.org
Web Site: http://www.aafpe.org
Members: 390 institutions and individuals
Staff: 1
Annual Budget: $100-250,000
Exec. Director: Sandra L. Sabanske

Historical Note
Members are educational institutions and individuals. Membership: $75/year (individual); $225/year (institution/sustaining/associate).

Publications:
Journal of Paralegal Education and Practice. a.
Membership Directory. a.
Newsletter. q.

Meetings/Conferences:
Annual Meetings: October/350

American Ass'n for Partial Hospitalization (1965)
Historical Note
Name changed to Ass'n for Ambulatory Behavioral Healthcare (AABH) in 1996.

American Ass'n for Pediatric Ophthalmology and Strabismus (1974)
P.O. Box 193832
San Francisco, CA   94119
Tel: (415)561-8505   *Fax:* (415)561-8575
Web Site: http://med-aapos.bu.edu
Members: 893 individuals
Staff: 3
Annual Budget: $100-250,000
Exec. Administrator: Sue Brown

Historical Note
Has no paid staff. Membership: $300/year.

Publications:
Journal of the American Ass'n for Pediatric Ophthalmology and.
Strabismus. bi-m. adv.

Meetings/Conferences:
1999 – Toronto, ON, Canada(The Westin Harbor
       Castle)/April 15-18/500
2000 – San Diego, CA(Hotel del Coronado)/April 12-16/550
2001 – Orlando, FL(Walt Disney World
       Swan)/March 21-25/550

American Ass'n for Public Opinion Research (1947)
P.O. Box 1248
Ann Arbor, MI   48106-1248
Tel: (313)764-1555   *Fax:* (313)764-3341
E-Mail: aapor@umich.edu
Web Site: http://www.aapor.org
Members: 1,450 individuals
Staff: 2
Annual Budget: $100-250,000
Administrator: Marlene Bednarz

Historical Note
AAPOR members are individuals engaged or interested in the methods and applications of public opinion and social research. Founded at a meeting at the historic Opera House in Central City, Colorado, July 29-31, 1946. Membership: $15-90/year.

Publications:
AAPOR News. 3/year.
Public Opinion Quarterly. q.

Meetings/Conferences:
Annual Meetings: Spring/600

American Ass'n for Respiratory Care (1947)
11030 Ables Lane
Dallas, TX   75229
Tel: (972)243-2272   *Fax:* (972)484-2720
Members: 37,000 individuals
Staff: 42
Annual Budget: $5-10,000,000
Exec. Director: Sam P. Giordano

Historical Note
A professional organization of respiratory care personnel formed in Chicago and incorporated in the State of Illinois in 1947, it assumed the name, American Ass'n for Inhalation Therapists, in 1954; American Ass'n for Inhalation Therapy in 1967; American Ass'n for Repiratory Therapy in 1973; and its present name in 1986. Sponsored by the American College of Chest Physicians, the American Soc. of Anaesthesiologists and the American Thoracic Soc. In 1989, AARC conducted the nationwide survey of airplane passengers which led to a complete ban of smoking on commercial airline flights in the U.S. Sponsors and supports the AARC Political Action Committee. Has an annual budget of approximately $6 million. Membership: $60/year.

Publications:
AARC Report. m.
AARTimes. m. adv.
Respiratory Care. m. adv.

Meetings/Conferences:
Annual Meetings: Late Fall/6,000

American Ass'n for State and Local History (1940)
1717 Church St.
Nashville, TN   37203-2991
Tel: (615)320-3203   *Fax:* (615)327-9013
E-Mail: history@aaslh.org
Web Site: http://www.aaslh.org
Members: 5,000 individuals
Staff: 5
Annual Budget: $1-2,000,000
Exec. Director and C.E.O.: Terry Davis
Director, Special Events: Natalie Norris
Director, Programs: Deanna J. Kerrigan
Finance Officer: Risa Woodward

Historical Note
Formerly the Council of Historical Societies. Absorbed the Ass'n of Historic Sites Officials in 1963. An organization of individuals and groups interested in promoting the study of state and local history in the U.S. and Canada. Membership: $50-250/year (individual); $20/year (student); $75/year, minimum (institution).

Publications:
Directory of Historical Socs. & Agencies in the U.
History News. q.
History News Dispatch (newsletter). m.

Meetings/Conferences:
Annual Meetings: Fall/1,000
1999 – Baltimore, MD(Omni)/Sept. 29-Oct. 2

American Ass'n for Textile Technology (1934)
Historical Note
Organization defunct in 1997.

American Ass'n for the Advancement of Science (1848)
1200 New York Ave., N.W.
Washington, DC   20005
Tel: (202)326-6400   *Fax:* (202)371-9526
Web Site: http://www.aaas.org
Members: 139,000 individuals
Staff: 300
Annual Budget: $5-10,000,000
C.E.O.: Richard S. Nicholson
Chief Financial Officer: Phil Blair

Historical Note
Founded in September, 1848 in Philadelphia with 461 charter members. Incorporated in Massachusetts in 1874. An umbrella association, the AAAS has nearly 300 affiliates-societies, academies and other organizations which effectively comprise the whole spectrum of U.S. science and engineering. Membership: $92/year (individual), $50/year (student).

Publications:
AAAS Program.
Science. w. adv.
Science Books and Films - A Newsletter. 9/year.
Science Education News. q.

Meetings/Conferences:
Annual Meetings: Winter/3,000-4,000
1999 – Anaheim, CA(Hilton and Marriott)/Jan. 21-26

American Ass'n for the Advancement of Slavic Studies (1948)
8 Story St., Harvard University
Cambridge, MA   02138
Tel: (617)495-0677   *Fax:* (617)495-0680
E-Mail: aaass@hcs.harvard.edu
Members: 4,000 individuals
Staff: 5
Annual Budget: $500-1,000,000
Exec. Director: Carol R. Saivetz, Ph.D.
NewsNet Editor: Vicki Mills
Convention Coordinator: Wendy Walker
Comptroller: Galina Shaumyan
Membership Coordinator: Micheal Olson

Historical Note
Seeks to advance scholarly study, publication and teaching relating to the former Soviet Union and Eastern Europe. Membership: $25-85/year, based on annual income (individual); $25/year (affiliate).

Publications:
Membership Directory.
Newsnet Newsletter. 5/year. adv.
Slavic Review. q. adv.

Meetings/Conferences:
Annual Meetings: Fall
1999 – St. Louis, MI

American Ass'n for the History of Medicine (1925)
c/o Dept.of Medical Humanities
East Carolina Univ. School of Medicine
Greenville, NC   27858-4354
Tel: (252)816-2792   *Fax:* (252)816-2319
E-Mail: tsavitt@brody.med.edu.edu

Web Site: http://www.histmed.org
Members: 1,300 individuals
Annual Budget: $50-100,000
Secretary-Treasurer: J. Worth Estes, M.D.

Historical Note
AAHM members include physicians and practitioners of other health sciences, professional historians, laboratory scientists, librarians and individuals from other disciplines. Incorporated in New York in 1958. Membership: $50/year (individual); $60/year (organization/company).

Publications:
AAHM Newsletter. 3/year.
Bulletin of the History of Medicine. q. adv.
Membership Directory. bien.
Research in Progress. bien.

Meetings/Conferences:
Annual Meetings: Spring
1999 – New Brunswick, NJ
2000 – Bethesda, MD/May 6-9

American Ass'n for the History of Nursing (1980)
P.O. Box 175
Lanoka Harbor, NJ   08734-0175
Tel: (609)693-7250   *Fax:* (609)693-1037
E-Mail: NgsHistory@aol.com
Web Site: http://members.aol.com/NgsHistory/AAHN.html
Members: 450 individuals
Staff: 1
Annual Budget: $25-50,000
Exec. Secretary: Janet L. Fickeisson

Historical Note
Members are individuals with an interest in the history of nursing. Membership: $85/year (regular), $150/year (agency); $35/year (student); $45/year (retiree).

Publications:
Bulletin of AAHN. q. adv.
Nursing History Review. a. adv.

Meetings/Conferences:
Annual Meetings: Fall
1999 – Boston, MA
2000 – Villanova, PA

American Ass'n for the Study of Headache (1959)
19 Mantua Road
Mount Royal, NJ   08061
Tel: (609)423-0043   *Fax:* (609)423-0082
E-Mail: aashhq@aash.smarthub.org
Web Site: http://www.aash.org
Members: 1,200 individuals
Staff: 4
Annual Budget: $1-2,000,000
Exec. Director: Linda K. McGillicuddy

Historical Note
AASH are healthcare professionals with an interest in the illness of headache. Membership: $150/year (individual).

Publications:
Headache: The Journal of Head & Face Pain. 10/year. adv.

Meetings/Conferences:
Annual Meetings: June
1999 – Boston, MA(Marriott Copley Plaza)/June 11-13

American Ass'n for the Study of Liver Diseases (1949)
1729 King St., Suite 100
Alexandria, VA   22314-2720
Tel: (703)299-9766   *Fax:* (703)299-9622
E-Mail: AASLD@AASLD.org
Members: 2,500 individuals
Staff: 10
Annual Budget: $2-5,000,000
Exec. Director: Sharon A. Meehan, CAE

Historical Note
Membership: $145/year.

Publications:
Directory. a.
Hepatology. m. adv.
Liver Transplantation + Surgery. bi-m. adv.
Newsletter. semi-a.

Meetings/Conferences:
Annual Meetings: Fall
1999 – Dallas, TX(Wyndham Anatole)/Nov. 5-9/5

American Ass'n for the Surgery of Trauma (1938)
UCLA Medical Center, Room 71-178 CHS
10833 LeConte Avenue
Los Angeles, CA   90024
Tel: (310)794-4210   *Fax:* (310)206-2472
E-Mail: hcryer@surgery.medsch.ucla.edu
Web Site: http://www.aast.org
Members: 900 individuals
Staff: 1
Annual Budget: $250-500,000
Secretary-Treasurer: Ronald V. Maier, M.D.
Sec-Treasurer: H. Gill Cryer, MD, PhD

Historical Note
Organized June 14, 1938 in San Francisco. Promotes advancement of the surgical care of injured patients. Membership: $250/year.

Publications:
Journal of Trauma. m. adv.

Meetings/Conferences:
1999 – Boston, MA(Marriott Copley)/Sept. 16-18

American Ass'n for Therapeutic Humor (1987)
222 South Meramec Ave., Suite 303
St. Louis, MO   63105-3514
Tel: (314)863-6232   *Fax:* (314)863-6457
Web Site: http://www.aath.org
Members: 500 individuals
Staff: 1

Annual Budget: $10-25,000
Exec. Director: Cindy Lazzari

Historical Note
Members are healthcare providers and others interested in the therapeutic aspects of humor. Membership: $35/year (individual).

Publications:
Laugh It Up Newsletter. bi-m.

Meetings/Conferences:
1999 – Phoenix, AZ/Jan. 30-31

American Ass'n for Thoracic Surgery (1917)
13 Elm St.
Manchester, MA   01944
Tel: (978)526-8330   *Fax:* (978)526-4018
Members: 1,060 individuals
Annual Budget: $100-250,000

Historical Note
Organized in New York City in 1917.

Publications:
Journal of Thoracic and Cardiovascular Surgery. m. adv.

Meetings/Conferences:
Annual Meetings: Spring/2,500
1999 – New Orleans, LA(Hilton)/April 18-21/2500
2000 – Toronto, ON(Royal York Hotel)/April 30-May 3/2500
2001 – San Diego, CA(Marriott)/May 6-9/2500
2002 – Washington, DC(Sheraton)/April 28-May 1

American Ass'n for Vocational Instructional Materials (1949)
220 Smithonia Road
Winterville, GA   30683-9527
Tel: (706)742-5355   *Fax:* (706)742-7005
Toll Free: (800)228 - 4689
Web Site: http://www.aavim.com
Members: 6 U.S. states
Staff: 7
Annual Budget: $250-500,000
Director: George W. Smith, Jr.
Assistant Director: James E. Wren

Historical Note
Consortium, established in 1949, of states whose purpose is the development, publication and distribution of instructional materials (manuals, teacher keys, computer software, videos) in the areas of agriscience, technology education and consumer and life science education. Membership: $3,000/year (state).

Publications:
AAVIM Catalog. a.

Meetings/Conferences:
1999 – Athens, GA

American Ass'n for Women Podiatrists (1965)
5900 Princess Garden Pkwy., Suite 420
Lanham, MD   20706
Tel: (301)577-4464   *Fax:* (301)577-4702
Members: 800 individuals
Annual Budget: $25-50,000
President: Dr. Corinne Kauderer

Historical Note
Members must be members of the American Podiatric Medical Association. Maintains no paid staff. Membership: $60/year (individual); $150/year (organization/company); $100/year (friend of ass'n); $15/year (students).

Publications:
AAWP Newsletter. q. adv.

Meetings/Conferences:
Annual Meetings: August, in conjunction with the American Podiatric Medical Association

American Ass'n for Women Radiologists (1981)
1891 Preston White Drive
Reston, VA   20191
Tel: (703)648-8939   *Fax:* (703)391-1757
E-Mail: aawr@aacr.org
Web Site: http://www.aawr.org
Members: 1,730 individuals
Staff: 2
Annual Budget: $25-50,000
Exec. Director: Charleta Mason

Historical Note
AAWR addresses concerns of women radiologists. AAWR promotes participation of women in other radiological organization encourages scientific advancement and serves as a networking group. Formerly (1991) American Ass'n of Women Radiologists. Membership: $100/yr.

Publications:
AAWR Focus. q.
Membership Directory. a.

Meetings/Conferences:

American Ass'n of Acupuncture and Oriental Medicine (1983)
Historical Note
Became the American Ass'n of Oriental Medicine in 1996.

American Ass'n of Advertising Agencies (1917)
Chrysler Bldg., 405 Lexington Ave.
18th Fl.
New York, NY   10174-1801
Tel: (212)682-2500   *Fax:* (212)953-5665
Toll Free: (800)536 - 7346
Web Site: http://www.aaaa.org
Members: 1,200 companies
Staff: 80
Annual Budget: $10-25,000,000
President and C.E.O.: O. Burtch Drake
Senior V. President, Member Services: Marsha Appel

Senior V. President, Professional Development: Karen A. Proctor, CMP
Senior V. President, C.F.O.: James C. Martucci, Jr.
Senior V. President, Management Services: Jack Mennis
Exec. V. President, Member Services: Michael Donahue
Senior V. President, Membership: Bob Linden
Exec. V. President: Don Lewis
Exec. V. President: Jerry Gibbons

Historical Note
Maintains branch offices in San Francisco, CA, Charlotte, NC, and Washington, DC. Has an annual budget of approximately $15.0 million. Membership dues based on members gross income.

Publications:
Roster and Organization. a.

Meetings/Conferences:
Annual Meetings: Spring
1999 – Amelia Island, FL(Ritz Carlton)/April 21-23
2000 – Bermuda(South Hampton Princess)/May 11-14

American Ass'n of AIDS Executives *(1990)*
601 Pennsylvania Ave., N.W., Suite 900 South
Washington, DC   20004
Tel: (202)439-5285   *Fax:* (202)439-5279
E-Mail: amasnaids@aol.com
Members: 13,980 individuals
Staff: 12
Annual Budget: $25-50,000

Historical Note
Founded in New York, AAAE serves to coordinate and connect management personnel at the country's HIV/AIDS agencies. Membership: $150/year (individual); $150-450/year, based on budget (organization).

Publications:
AIDS Watch. q. adv.
Conference Proceedings. a.
Journal of AAAE. q. adv.
Meeting Directory. a. adv.
Membership Guide/Resource Directory. a. adv.

Meetings/Conferences:

American Ass'n of Airport Executives *(1928)*
4212 King St.
Alexandria, VA   22302
Tel: (703)824-0500   *Fax:* (703)820-1395
Web Site: http://www.airportnet.org
Members: 4,500 individuals
Staff: 25
Annual Budget: $2-5,000,000
President: Charles M. Barclay, AAE
Senior V. President, Communications: Joan Lowden
Director, Meetings: Sheila McManus
Staff V. President, Finance & Membership: James Workman

Historical Note
A professional organization of individuals concerned with the management, operation and construction of civil airports. Awards the "A.A.E." (Accredited Airport Executive) designation. Sponsors and supports the AAAE Good Government Committee. Membership: $225/year (individual), $475/year (company/organization).

Publications:
Airport Magazine. bi-m.
Airport Report. bi-w.
Airport Report Express. 2/week.

Meetings/Conferences:
Annual Meetings: May/1,400
1999 – Phoenix, AZ/May 16-19

American Ass'n of Ambulatory Surgery Centers *(1978)*
401 N. Michigan Ave.
Chicago, IL   60611-4267
Tel: (312)644-6610   *Fax:* (312)321-6869
Toll Free: (800)237 - 3768
E-Mail: aaasc@sba.com
Members: 400 individuals, 200 facilities
Staff: 2
Annual Budget: $100-250,000
Director, Administration: Kari Dabrowski

Historical Note
Founded as Soc. for Office Based Surgery; became American Soc. of Outpatient Surgeons in 1986, and assumed its current name in 1996). Promotes effective and reliable operation of the ambulatory surgery center as the best environment for outpatient surgery. Surgical specialists/board certified surgeons, nurses and administrators are admitted to membership. Membership: $350/year (individual); $350-750/year (facility).

Publications:
Monitor. semi-a.
Newsletter. q.

Meetings/Conferences:
1999 – San Diego, CA(Hilton Beach & Tennis)/March 4-6

American Ass'n of Anatomists *(1888)*
9650 Rockville Pike, Suite 2408
Bethesda, MD   20814
Tel: (301)571-8314   *Fax:* (301)571-0619
Web Site: http://www.faseb.org/anatomy
Members: 2,600 individuals
Staff: 4
Annual Budget: $500-1,000,000
Exec. Director: Andrea Pendleton

Historical Note
Established September 17, 1888 at Georgetown University, Washington, DC as the Ass'n of American Anatomists. Name changed in 1908 to American Ass'n of Anatomists. Incorporated in New York in 1947. Regular membership: $95/year; includes one journal.

Publications:
Anatomical Record. m.
Developmental Dynamics. m.

Meetings/Conferences:
Annual Meetings: in conjunction with FASEB experimental biology meeting/Spring
1999 – Washington, DC/April 17-21

American Ass'n of Attorney-Certified Public Accountants *(1964)*
24196 Alicia Parkway, Suite K
Mission Viejo, CA   92691-3926
Tel: (949)768-0336   *Fax:* (949)768-7062
E-Mail: aaacpa@attorney-cpa.com
Members: 1,300 individuals
Staff: 2
Annual Budget: $250-500,000
Exec. Director: Ronald M. DeVore, CAE

Historical Note
Members are individuals "dually licensed" as both lawyer and CPA. Membership: $90/year, first two years; $150/year thereafter.

Publications:
Membership Directory. a. adv.
The Attorney-CPA. 5/yr. adv.

Meetings/Conferences:
Semi-annual meetings: Spring and Fall

American Ass'n of Automatic Door Manufacturers *(1994)*
1300 Sumner Ave.
Cleveland, OH   44115-2851
Tel: (216)241-7333   *Fax:* (216)241-0105
E-Mail: aaadm@taol.com
Web Site: http://www.taol.com/aaadm
Members: 9 companies
Staff: 3
Annual Budget: $50-100,000
Exec. Director: John H. Addington

Historical Note
AAADM is a trade association of power operated automatic door manufacturers as defined and governed by ANSI/BHMA A156.10. The association promotes product safety by establishing uniform programs for training and certification of installers and service providers as well as inspection of installations. Membership: $9,000/year (company).

Meetings/Conferences:
Semi-annual Meetings: Spring and Fall

American Ass'n of Avian Pathologists *(1957)*
Univ. of Penn., New Bolton Center
382 West St. Road
Kennett Square, PA   19348-1692
Tel: (610)444-4282   *Fax:* (610)444-5387
Web Site: www.vm.iastate.edu/aaap
Members: 1000 individuals
Staff: 2
Annual Budget: $100-250,000
Secretary-Treasurer: Robert J. Eckroade, D.V.M.

Historical Note
Affiliated with the American Veterinary Medical Ass'n. Veterinarians specializing in poultry and their diseases. Membership: $70-90/year (individual).

Publications:
Avian Diseases. q. adv.
Directory. a.

Meetings/Conferences:
Annual Meetings: July, with the American Veterinary Medical Ass'n
1999 – New Orleans, LA/July 10-14

American Ass'n of Bank Directors *(1989)*
4719 Hampden Lane, Suite 300
Bethesda, MD   20814
Tel: (301)951-0583   *Fax:* (301)654-1733
Web Site: http://www.aabd.org
Exec. Director: David H. Baris
Membership Director: Laurin B. Morrison

Historical Note
AABD represents bank and thrift directors, providing educational programs and other services to its members. Membership: $695/year (directors); $795/year (associates).

Publications:
Bank Director News. q.
Course Guide-Institute for Bank Director Education. q.
Informational Booklet Series. q.
Newsletter. q.

American Ass'n of Behavioral Therapists *(1987)*
P.O. Box 1737
Ormond Beach, FL   32175
Tel: (904)248-0508
Members: 1000 individuals
Annual Budget: $25-50,000
President: Dan J. Allen, Ph.D

Historical Note
Therapists and counselors who use behavioral science techniques, such as biofeedback, hypnosis, conditioned learning, and behavior modification to effect positive changes for improved mental health, habit control and personal improvement. Membership: $45/year.

Publications:
Nat'l Directory of Behavioral Therapists. a.
Special Reports. irreg.
The Therapist Report. q.

American Ass'n of Bicycle Importers *(1975)*

Historical Note
Organization defunct in 1994.

American Ass'n of Bioanalysts *(1956)*
917 Locust St., Suite 1100
St. Louis, MO   63101-1413

Tel: (314)241-1445   *Fax:* (314)241-1449
E-Mail: aab1445@primary.net
Web Site: http://www.aab.org
Members: 900 individuals
Annual Budget: $500-1,000,000
Administrator: Mark S. Birenbaum, Ph.D.

Historical Note
Merger of Council of American Bioanalysts (founded in 1953) and the Nat'l Ass'n of Clinical Laboratories (founded in 1949). Absorbed Internat'l Soc. for Clinical Laboratory Technology in 1999. Members are directors, owners, managers, and supervisors of medical laboratories concerned with improving laboratory testing and procedures. Membership: $200/year (directors, owners), $60/year (managers, supervisors). AMS members include laboratory technologists and technicians.

Publications:
The AAB Bulletin. bi-m. adv.

Meetings/Conferences:

American Ass'n of Blacks in Energy *(1977)*
927 15th St., N.W., Suite 200
Washington, DC   20005-2304
Tel: (202)371-9530   *Fax:* (202)371-9218
Toll Free: (800)464 - 0204
E-Mail: aabe@erold.com
Web Site: http://www.aabe.org
Members: 950 individuals
Staff: 2
Annual Budget: $250-500,000
Exec. Director: Robert L. Hill
Director, National Projects: Dorita M. Dixon

Historical Note
AABE is a national association of energy professionals who are dedicated to include African American and other minorities into the discussion and development of energy policies, regulations, research and development technologies and environmental issues. Membership: $100/year (individual).

Publications:
AABE Energy News. q. adv.
Annual Report. bien.

Meetings/Conferences:
1999 – Los Angeles, CA(Marriott)/April 19-24/300
2000 – Atlanta, GA

American Ass'n of Blood Banks *(1947)*
8101 Glenbrook Road
Bethesda, MD   20814-2749
Tel: (301)907-6977   *Fax:* (301)907-6895
E-Mail: aabb@aabb.org
Web Site: http://www.aabb.org
Members: 8,500 individuals, 2,200 institutions
Staff: 75
Annual Budget: $5-10,000,000
Chief Executive Officer: Karen Shoos Lipton

Historical Note
Scientists, physicians, nurses, medical technologists and administrators concerned with blood banking and transfusion medicines. Has an annual budget of approximately $6.2 million. Membership $65-165/year (individual), $525-2,630/year (organization).

Publications:
Blood Bank Week. w.
News Brief. m. adv.
Transfusion Journal. 9/year. adv.

Meetings/Conferences:
Annual Meetings: Fall/7,500
1999 – San Francisco, CA/Nov. 6-10
2000 – Washington, DC/Nov. 4-8
2001 – San Antonio, TX/Oct. 13-17
2002 – Orlando, FL(Convention Center)/Oct. 26-30

American Ass'n of Botanical Gardens and Arboreta *(1940)*
351 Longwood Rd.
Kennett Square, PA   19348-1807
Tel: (610)925-2500   *Fax:* (610)925-2700
E-Mail: AABGA@voicenet.com
Web Site: http://www.aabga.mobot.org/aabga
Members: 2,400 individuals & institutions
Staff: 8
Annual Budget: $250-500,000
Exec. Director: Nancy Morin
Resource Center Coordinator: Carol Line

Historical Note
AABGA is a non-profit, membership organization serving North American botanical gardens and arboreta, their professional staffs and their work on behalf of the public and the profession. Membership: $60/year (individual), $150-1,000/year (organization).

Publications:
AABGA Newsletter. m.
The Public Garden: Journal of the AABGA. q. adv.

Meetings/Conferences:
Annual Meetings: Summer/350
1999 – Vancouver, British Columbia
2000 – Asheville, NC

American Ass'n of Bovine Practitioners *(1965)*
P.O. Box 1755
Rome, GA   30162-1755
Tel: (706)232-2220   *Fax:* (706)232-2232
Toll Free: (800)269 - 2227
E-Mail: aapbhq@aabp.org
Web Site: http://www.aabp.org
Members: 5,000 individuals
Staff: 2
Annual Budget: $500-1,000,000
Exec. V. President: Dr. James A. Jarrett

Historical Note
Membership is restricted to veterinarians. Membership: $95/year (individual).

Publications:
Bovine Practitioner. a. adv.
Proceedings of Annual Meeting. a. adv.

Meetings/Conferences:
Annual Meetings: Fall/1,400

American Ass'n of Business Valuation Specialists
P.O. Box 13089
Tallahassee, FL 32317
Tel: (850)878-3134   *Fax:* (850)878-1291
Annual Budget: $10-25,000
President and C.E.O.: Robert S. Rhinehart

Historical Note
Membership: $40-$80/year.

Publications:
AABVS Newsletter. q.

Meetings/Conferences:
Annual Meetings: Fall

American Ass'n of Candy Technologists
175 Rock Road
Glen Rock, NJ 07452
Tel: (201)652-2655   *Fax:* (201)652-3419
Members: 650 individuals
Annual Budget: under $10,000
Exec. Officer: Joan Rudolph

Historical Note
Has no paid officers or full-time staff. Membership: $30/year.

Meetings/Conferences:
Annual Meetings: September

American Ass'n of Cardiovascular and Pulmonary Rehabilitation *(1985)*
7611 Elmwood Ave., Suite 201
Middleton, WI 53562
Tel: (608)831-6989   *Fax:* (608)831-5122
E-Mail: aacvpr@tmahq.com
Web Site: http://www.aacvpr.org
Members: 2,400 individuals
Staff: 4
Annual Budget: $500-1,000,000
Exec. Director: Robin D. Brown

Historical Note
Established in New York and incorporated in Wisconsin, AACVPR is a multi-disciplinary professional society dedicated to the improvement of clinical practice, promotion of scientific inquiry and the advancement of education. Membership: $120/year.

Publications:
Directory of Cardiopulmonary Rehabilitaion Programs.
Journal of Cardiopulmonary Rehabilitation. m. adv.

Meetings/Conferences:
Annual Meetings: November

American Ass'n of Cereal Chemists *(1915)*
3340 Pilot Knob Rd.
St. Paul, MN 55121-2055
Tel: (651)454-7250   *Fax:* (651)454-0766
E-Mail: aacc@scisoc.org
Web Site: http://www.scisoc.org/aacc
Members: 4,000 individuals
Staff: 60
Annual Budget: $2-5,000,000
Exec. V. President: Steven C. Nelson, CMP
Coordinator, Meetings: Leslie Gibson
Meetings Coordinator: Faye LaBatt
Director, Finance: Larry Hartman
Director, Administration: Amy Hope
Manager, Membership Services: Michelle Bjerkness

Historical Note
Founded in 1915 at Kansas City, MO, it merged in 1923 with the American Soc. of Milling and Baking Technology; incorporated in Minnesota in 1956. AACC encourages research in cereal grains, related materials, processing and utilization. Membership: $82-$1102.50/year.

Publications:
Approved Methods of the AACC. a.
Cereal Chemistry. bi-m.
Cereal Foods World. m. adv.
Food Science Catalog. semi-a.

Meetings/Conferences:
Annual Meetings: Fall/1,900
1999 – Seattle, WA(Convention Center)/Oct. 30-Nov. 4

American Ass'n of Certified Allergists *(1968)*
85 W. Algonquin Road, Suite 550
Arlington Heights, IL 60005-4425
Tel: (847)427-8111   *Fax:* (847)427-1294
Members: 550 individuals
Staff: 2
Annual Budget: $10-25,000
Exec. Director: Rick Slawny

Historical Note
Membership: $75/year.

Publications:
President's Newsletter. semi-a.

Meetings/Conferences:

American Ass'n of Certified Appraisers *(1977)*
800 Compton Road, #10
Cincinnati, OH 45231
Tel: (513)729-1400   *Fax:* (513)729-1401
Members: 1,300 designates
Staff: 5
Annual Budget: $250-500,000
President: Craig Auberger

Historical Note
Members are real estate appraisers. Membership: $225/year (individual).

Publications:
Clipboard Newsletter. bi-m.
Educational Catalogue. semi-a.
Membership Directory. a. adv.

American Ass'n of Certified Orthoptists *(1940)*
501 Hill St.
Waycross, GA 31501
Tel: (912)285-2020   *Fax:* (912)285-8112
Members: 425 individuals
Staff: 1
Annual Budget: $25-50,000
President: Jill Clark

Historical Note
Founded October 8, 1940 in Cleveland as the American Ass'n of Orthoptic Technicians, it became American Ass'n of Certified Orthoptists in 1966. A charter member of the Internat'l Orthoptic Ass'n and member of the American Orthoptic Council. Membership: $85/year.

Publications:
AACO Directory. a.
American Orthoptic Journal. a. adv.
Prism. 3/year. adv.

Meetings/Conferences:
Annual Meetings: Fall, with American Academy of
          Ophthalmology

American Ass'n of Chairmen of Departments of Psychiatry *(1967)*
Historical Note
Address unknown in 1997.

American Ass'n of Children's Residential Centers *(1957)*
440 First St., N.W., 3rd Fl
Washington, DC 20001-2085
Tel: (202)628-1816   *Fax:* (202)638-4004
E-Mail: aacrc@dc.net
Members: 300 individuals, 100 institutions
Staff: 2
Acting Exec. Director: Allison Vickery

Historical Note
Concerned with maintaining and enhancing sound clinical practice in residential treatment for children with emotional problems. Membership includes psychologists, psychiatrists, social workers, educators and child care specialists, as well as residential treatment agencies. A member of the Nat'l Consortium for Child Mental Health Services. Membership: $95/year (individual); $750/year (agency).

Publications:
Contributions to Residential Treatment. a. adv.
Membership Directory. a.
Organizational Dirctory. a.
Residential News. q. adv.

Meetings/Conferences:
Annual Meetings: October/150
1999 – Portland, OR

American Ass'n of Christian Schools *(1972)*
P.O. Box 2189
Independence, MO 64055
Tel: (816)795-7709   *Fax:* (816)795-7462
Members: 1,250 schools
Staff: 7
Annual Budget: $250-500,000
President: Carl Herbster

Historical Note
Maintains school accreditation and teacher/administrator certification programs.

Publications:
AACS Directory. a.
AACS Newsletter. m.
The Builder. irreg. adv.

Meetings/Conferences:

American Ass'n of Classified School Employees *(1958)*
Historical Note
Address unknown in 1995.

American Ass'n of Clinical Endocrinologists *(1991)*
1000 Riverside Ave., Suite 205
Jacksonville, FL 32204-3339
Tel: (904)353-7878   *Fax:* (904)353-8185
Web Site: http://www.aace.com
Members: 2,700 individuals
Staff: 7
Annual Budget: $1-2,000,000
Exec. Director: Christopher R. Seymour
Director, Communications: Leora Legacy
Deputy to the Exec. Director: Jay Millson
Manager, Conventions: Sandra Martin
CME Director: Linda Kepner
Accountant: Ozi Snachez
General Counsel: Chris L. Nuland,, Esq.
Director, Membership: Jerry Rivero

Historical Note
AACE is a professional medical organization devoted to the field of clinical endocrinology. The mission of the Ass'n is to enhance the practice of clinical endocrinology. Members are physicians with special education, training and interest in the practice of clinical endocrinology. Membership: $150/year (individual).

Publications:
AACE on Line (internet).
Endocrine Practice Journal. bi-m. adv.
First Messenger Newsletter. bi-m. adv.

Meetings/Conferences:
1999 – San Diego, CA(Marriott & Marina)/April 28-May 2

American Ass'n of Clinical Urologists *(1969)*
1111 N. Plaza Dr., Suite 550
Schaumburg, IL 60173-6021
Tel: (847)517-1050   *Fax:* (847)517-7229
Members: 2,100 individuals
Staff: 6
Annual Budget: $250-500,000
Exec. Director: Wendy J. Weiser
Manager, Meetings and Projects: Kimberly Barnes
Manager, Membership and Programs: Deborah Tvaroh

Historical Note
AACU members are licensed physicians whose practices are devoted primarily to urology. The purpose of the Ass'n is to promote the science of urology in the best interests of the public and the medical medical profession by the study and evaluation of socioeconomic factors which affect the practice of urology. The Ass'n provides urologists with an opportunity to exert influence at a national level for the improvement of all aspects of the profession and to influence legislation and policies affecting the practice of medicine. Membership: $100/year (individual); $250/year (organization/company).

Publications:
AACU Fax. irreg.
AACU News. bi-m.

Meetings/Conferences:
Annual Meetings: Washington, DC/July with the American
          Urological Ass'n

American Ass'n of Code Enforcement *(1988)*
P.O. Box 15945-290
Lenexa, KS 66285-5945
Tel: (913)383-8811   *Fax:* (913)383-9299
E-Mail: saint@kcnet.com
Web Site: http://AACE1.Com
Members: 1,200 individuals
Annual Budget: $50-100,000
President: Kathy Dempsey

Historical Note
Membership: $45/year.

Publications:
Perspective. bi-m. adv.

Meetings/Conferences:
1999 – St. Louis, MO(Sheraton Westport Hotel)/250
1999 – Rapis City, SD(Holiday Inn)/May 6-7

American Ass'n of Colleges for Teacher Education *(1917)*
1307 New York Ave., N.W. Suite 300
Washington, DC 20005-4701
Tel: (202)293-2450   *Fax:* (202)457-8095
Web Site: http://www.aacte.org
Members: 706 institutions
Staff: 30
Annual Budget: $2-5,000,000
C.E.O.: David G. Imig
Senior Dir., Public Policy and Government Relations: Penelope M.
          Earley
Director, Meetings: Sonja D. Goree
Senior Dir., Professional Development: Susan E. Cimburek
Director, Finance: Jannie G. Taylor
Director, Membership-Human Resources: Patricia Goldman
Director, Publications: Elizabeth Foxwell

Historical Note
Formed by a merger of the American Ass'n of Teachers Colleges, the Nat'l Ass'n of Colleges and Departments of Education and the Nat'l Ass'n of Teacher Education Institutions of Metropolitan Districts. Affiliated with the ERIC Clearinghouse on Teacher Education.

Publications:
AACTE Briefs. 20/year. adv.
Journal of Teacher Education. bi-m. adv.

Meetings/Conferences:
Annual Meetings: February-March/2,000
1999 – Washington, DC(Marriott)/Feb. 24-27

American Ass'n of Colleges of Nursing *(1969)*
One Dupont Circle, N.W., Suite 530
Washington, DC 20036-1110
Tel: (202)463-6930   *Fax:* (202)785-8320
Web Site: http://www.aacn.nche.edu
Members: 525 schools of nursing
Staff: 17
Annual Budget: $1-2,000,000
Exec. Director: Geraldine Bednash
Director, Public Affairs: Dan Mezibov
Director, Governmental Affairs: G. Brockwel Heylin
Assoc. Exec. Director: Jennifer Ahearn
Director, Member Education: Anne M. Rhome
Coordinator, Membership: Fara Francis

Historical Note
Established to answer the need for a national organization devoted exclusively to furthering the goals of baccalaureate and graduate education in nursing. AACN members are schools of nursing at universities and four-year colleges. Member of the Federation of Ass'ns of Schools of the Health Professions.

Publications:
AACN Issue Bulletin. irreg.
Journal of Professional Nursing. bi-m.
Syllabus. bi-m. adv.
Syllabus Newsletter. bi-m.

Meetings/Conferences:
Semi-Annual Meetings: Washington, DC/Spring and Fall

American Ass'n of Colleges of Osteopathic Medicine *(1898)*
5550 Friendship Blvd., Suite 310

Chevy Chase, MD 20815-7231
Tel: (301)968-4100 *Fax:* (301)968-4191
Web Site: http://www.aacom.org
Members: 19 institutions
Staff: 18
Annual Budget: $2-5,000,000
President: Douglas L. Wood, D.O., Ph.D
Director, Research: Allen M. Singer, Ph.D.
Director, Govt. Relations: Michael J. Dyer
Director, Finance and Administration: Nancy C. Cioffari
Director, AACOMAS: William P. King
V. President: Carolyn Lee Decker

Historical Note
Established a national headquarters and permanent staff in 1972. Operates centralized application processing service. Represents the administration, faculty, and students of its member osteopathic medical schools in the U.S.

Publications:
College Information Booklet.
Debts and Career Plans of Osteopathic Medical Students.
Statistical Report. a.

Meetings/Conferences:
Semi-Annual Meetings: Summer and Winter

American Ass'n of Colleges of Pharmacy *(1900)*
1426 Prince St.
Alexandria, VA 22314-2841
Tel: (703)739-2330 *Fax:* (703)836-8982
Web Site: http://www.aacp.org
Members: 2,500 individuals, 81 institutions
Staff: 15
Annual Budget: $2-5,000,000
Exec. V. President: Richard P. Penna, Pharm.D.
V. President, Professional Affairs & Health Policy: C. Edwin Webb
Director, Government and Student Affairs: Mark D. Roesen
V. President, Graduate Education, Research & Scholar: Kenneth W. Miller
Director, Administration: Mary B. Bassler
Director, Finance and Systems: Ronald G. Linder
Senior V. Presidemt: Susan M. Meyer

Historical Note
Founded in May 1900 as the American Conference of Pharmaceutical Faculties. Became the American Ass'n of Colleges of Pharmacy in August 1925. Promotes pharmaceutical education and research. Includes a few foreign institutions. Member of the Coalition for Health Funding in Washington and the Federation of Associations of Schools of the Health Professions. Membership: $75/year (individual), $16,500 (institutions).

Publications:
AACP News. m. adv.
American Journal of Pharmaceutical Education. q. adv.

Meetings/Conferences:
1999 – Boston, MA(Westin Copley Place)/July 3-7
2000 – San Diego, CA(Sheraton Island)/July 6-12

American Ass'n of Colleges of Podiatric Medicine *(1932)*
1350 Piccard Drive, Suite 322
Rockville, MD 20850-4307
Tel: (301)990-7400 *Fax:* (301)990-2807
Toll Free: (800)922 - 9266
E-Mail: aacpm@aacpm.org
Web Site: http://www.aacpm.org
Members: 150 hospitals, 6 colleges
Staff: 12
Annual Budget: $500-1,000,000
President: Anthony J. McNevin, CAE

Historical Note
Established as the American Ass'n of Colleges of Chiropody, it then became the American Ass'n of Colleges of Podiatry and assumed its present name in 1968. Member of the Coalition for Health Funding in Washington and the Federation of Ass'ns of Schools of the Health Professions. Membership: $500/year (organization).

Meetings/Conferences:

American Ass'n of Collegiate Registrars and Admissions Officers *(1910)*
One Dupont Circle, N.W., Suite 520
Washington, DC 20036-1135
Tel: (202)293-9161 *Fax:* (202)872-8857
E-Mail: info@aacrao.com
Web Site: http://www.aacrao.com
Members: 9,200 individuals, 2,400 institutions
Staff: 16
Annual Budget: $2-5,000,000
Exec. Director: Jerry Sullivan
Asst. Exec. Director, Planning and Communications: Henrianne Wakefield
Consultant, Government Relations: Roger Swanson
Manager, Meetings/Conferences: Gloria Rutberg
Director, Marketing, Membership & Publications: Cassandra Tate
Manager, Membership: Satomi Matsumae

Historical Note
Founded in 1910 as the American Ass'n of Collegiate Registrars. AACRAO is a voluntary, nonprofit professional education association of degree-granting postsecondary institutions, government agencies and higher education coordinating boards, private educational organizations, and education- oriented businesses. Its goal is to promote higher education and further the professional development of members working in admissions, enrollment management, financial aid, institutional research, records, and registration. Membership: $125/year (individual); institutional dues vary according to size of enrollment.

Publications:
AACRAO Data Dispenser. 10/year. adv.
AACRAO Member Guide. a. adv.
College and University. q. adv.

Meetings/Conferences:
Annual Meetings: Spring/3,000
1999 – Charlotte, NC(Omni/Convention Center)/April 18-22
2000 – New Orleans, LA/April 2-6
2001 – Seattle, WA/April 22-26

American Ass'n of Community Colleges *(1920)*
One Dupont Circle, N.W., Suite 410
Washington, DC 20036-1176
Tel: (202)728-0200 *Fax:* (202)833-2467
E-Mail: dpierce@aacc.nche.edu
Web Site: http://www.aacc.nche.edu
Members: 1,120 two-year colleges
Staff: 40
Annual Budget: $5-10,000,000
President & CEO: David Pierce
Director, Communications: Norma Kent
Director, Government Relations: David Baime
Director, Meeting and Council Relations: Mary Ann Settlemire

Historical Note
Formerly (1972) American Ass'n of Junior Colleges and (1992) American Ass'n of Community and Junior Colleges. Membership $90-1,500 depending of type of member. Has an annual budget of approximately $6.1 million

Publications:
AACC Membership Directory. a.
Community College Journal. bi-m. adv.
Community College Times. bi-w. adv.
ITC News. q.

Meetings/Conferences:
Annual Meetings: April/2,500
1999 – Nashville, TN(Opryland)/April 7-10

American Ass'n of Community Psychiatrists *(1984)*
P.O. Box 28218
Dallas, TX 75228
Members: 500 individuals
Staff: 1
Admin. Director: Frances Roton

Historical Note
AACP members are psychiatrists practicing in community mental health centers, or in similar programs which provide community care to populations of the mentally ill unrestricted by financial or other exclusionary policies. AACP promotes excellence in the care of patients through the organization of psychiatrists in community health centers, helps clarify and solve problems related to the practice of psychiatry in community health settings, provide public education, establishes liaisons with related professional organizations, and encourages training and research in psychiatry. Membership: $75/year (individual).

Publications:
Community Psychiatry Newsletter.

Meetings/Conferences:
Semi-Annual Meetings: in conjunction with American Psychiatric Ass'n/Spring and Institute of Hospital and Community Psychiatry/Fall

American Ass'n of Community Theatre *(1986)*
4712 Enchanted Oaks Dr.
College Station, TX 77845-7649
Tel: (409)774-0611 *Fax:* (409)776-8718
E-Mail: info@aact.org
Web Site: http://www.aact.org
Members: 500 individuals, 700 organizations
Staff: 3
Annual Budget: $100-250,000
Exec. Director: Julie Angelo

Historical Note
Supersedes the American Community Theatre Ass'n. AACT members are community theater organizations and theater professionals and volunteers interested in community theater. Programs include community theatre festivals, insurance services, production and management resources, and other services. Membership: $25-65/year (individual); $40-250/year (organization).

Publications:
AACT Festival Handbook. bien.
AACT Membership Directory. a. adv.
Spotlight Magazine. bi-m. adv.

Meetings/Conferences:
Annual Meetings: June/350
1999 – Memphis, TN/July 8-12
2000 – New York, NY

American Ass'n of Concerned Engineers *(1973)*
Historical Note
Organization defunct in 1997.

American Ass'n of Cooperative/Mutual Insurance Socs. *(1979)*
One Nationwide Plaza, 3-14-05
Columbus, OH 43215-2220
Tel: (614)249-6347 *Fax:* (614)249-3090
Annual Budget: $250-500,000
Asst. Secretary: William Leffel

Historical Note
Formerly the North American Ass'n of the Internat'l Cooperative Insurance Federation. AAC/MIS membership is open to cooperative and mutual insurance companies in the Western Hemisphere who are also members of the international organization, Internat'l Cooperative and Mutual Insurance Federation. Membership fee varies; $500/year minimum.

Meetings/Conferences:
Annual Meetings: Fall

American Ass'n of Cosmetology Schools *(1924)*
901 N. Washington St., Suite 206
Alexandria, VA 22314-1535
Tel: (703)683-1700 *Fax:* (703)683-2376
Members: 550 schools
Staff: 3
Annual Budget: $250-500,000
President: Ronald E. Smith

Historical Note
Formerly (1991) Nat'l Ass'n of Cosmetology Schools and (1993) Ass'n of Accredited Cosmetology Schools. Membership: $750/year (single location); $475/year (additional locations).

Publications:
AACS News Report. 10/yr.
Membership Directory. a.

Meetings/Conferences:

American Ass'n of Critical-Care Nurses *(1969)*
101 Columbia
Aliso Viejo, CA 92656-1491
Tel: (714)362-2000 *Fax:* (714)362-2020
Toll Free: (800)899 - 2226
E-Mail: aacninfo@aacn.org
Web Site: http://www.aacn.org
Members: 76,900 individuals, 270 chapters
Staff: 104
Annual Budget: $10-25,000,000
C.E.O.: Sarah J. Sanford

Historical Note
Founded September 22, 1969 at the Second Cardiac Nursing Symposium, as the American Ass'n of Cardiovascular Nurses. Assumed its present name in 1972. Members are nurses in all areas of critical care, such as cardiac intensive care, medical/surgical critical care, and trauma. Membership: $78/year (individual).

Publications:
AACN Clinical Issues in Critical Care Nursing. q.
AACN Member Directory.
AACN News. m. adv.
AACN Nursing Scan in Critical Care. bi-m.
American Journal of Critical Care. bi-m. adv.
Critical Care Nurse. bi-m. adv.
Technology for Critical Care Nurses. bi-m.

Meetings/Conferences:
Annual Meetings: May-June/9,000-10,000

American Ass'n of Crop Insurers *(1983)*
One Massachusetts Ave., N.W., Suite 800
Washington, DC 20001-1431
Tel: (202)789-4100 *Fax:* (202)408-7763
E-Mail: aaci@erols.com
Web Site: http://www.AgInsurance.org
Members: 22 companies
Staff: 4
Annual Budget: $250-500,000
General Counsel & Exec. Director: Michael R. McLeod
Grassroots & Communications Manager: Kevin Collins
Government Relations: Laura L. Phelps
Manager: Stephen Frerichs

Historical Note
The American Ass'n of Crop Insurers is a nonprofit industry service organization representing the interests of reinsured companies, private agents, and adjusters involved in the Federal crop insurance program. AACI's reinsured company members write more than 81% of the multiple peril crop insurance sold by private companies nationwide.

Publications:
Crop Insurance Insider. m.

Meetings/Conferences:
Annual Meetings: Spring

American Ass'n of Dental Consultants *(1977)*
P.O. Box 3345
Lawrence, KS 66046-0345
Tel: (785)749-2727 *Fax:* (785)749-1140
Toll Free: (800)896 - 0707
E-Mail: JSALIS913@aol.com
Members: 420 individuals
Staff: 1
Annual Budget: $100-250,000
Exec. Director: Judith K. Salisbury

Historical Note
Members are dentists, insurance consultants, benefits programs administrators, and other dental professionals. Membership: $100/year.

Publications:
2nd Opinion. irreg. adv.
The Beacon. semi-a.

Meetings/Conferences:
Annual Meetings: Spring/350
1999 – Toronto, Ontario/May 20-22
2000 – Scottsdale, AZ(Marriott Mountain Shadows)/May 18-20
2001 – Scottsdale, AZ(Marriott Mountain Shadows)/May 17-19

American Ass'n of Dental Editors *(1931)*
1100 Lake St., Suite 240
Oak Park, IL 60301-1035
Tel: (708)445-0322 *Fax:* (708)445-0321
Members: 325 individuals
Staff: 1
Annual Budget: $10-25,000
Exec. Director: Detlef B. Moore

Historical Note
The AADE was chartered in 1931 and is composed of active, interested people who are dedicated to improving communication within the dental profession and to elevating the standards of dental journalism. The organization exists to establish and encourage responsible editorial policy. Member publications represent state dental associations, component societies, dental specialty groups, dental schools, alumni, dental auxiliaries, students, and commercial publications. Membership: $25/year (individual); $85/year (organization).

Publications:
Membership Directory. a.

Newsletter. 6/year.
Meetings/Conferences:
Annual Meetings: Fall, with the American Dental Ass'n

American Ass'n of Dental Examiners *(1883)*
211 E. Chicago Ave., Suite 760
Chicago, IL 60611
Tel: (312)440-7464　　　　　*Fax:* (312)440-3525
E-Mail: mnadler@aadexam.org
Members: 725 individuals
Staff: 3
Annual Budget: $100-250,000
Exec. Director: Molly Nadler
Historical Note
Formerly the National Association of Dental Examiners, members are present and former members of state dental examining boards.
Publications:
The Bulletin. q.
The Composite. a.
Meetings/Conferences:
Annual Meetings: With the American Dental Ass'n in the Fall.

American Ass'n of Dental Schools *(1923)*
1625 Massachusetts Ave., N.W., 6th Fl
Washington, DC 20036-2212
Tel: (202)667-9433　　　　　*Fax:* (202)667-0642
E-Mail: aads@aads.jhu.edu
Web Site: http://www.aads.jhu.edu
Members: 3,500 individuals, 180 institutions
Staff: 40
Annual Budget: $2-5,000,000
Exec. Director: Richard W. Valachovic, D.M.D.
Director, Office of Business and Financial Affairs: Joyce C. Keller
Asst. Exec. Director, Office of Women and Minority Affairs: Jeanne C. Sinkford, D.D.S., Ph
Historical Note
Founded in Omaha January 24, 1923 through the merger of the American Institute of Dental Teachers, Canadian Dental Faculties' Ass'n, Nat'l Ass'n of Dental Faculties and the Dental Faculties' Ass'n of American Universities. Incorporated in Illinois in 1960. Membership includes all U.S. dental schools and many other dental institutions in Canada and the U.S. Membership: $95/year (individual).
Publications:
Admission Requirements of U. S.
Bulletin of Dental Education. m. adv.
Directory of Institutional Members. a.
Journal of Dental Education. m. adv.
Opportunity for Minority Students in U. S.
Meetings/Conferences:
Annual Meetings: March/2,000
1999 – Vancouver, British Columbia/March 6-10

American Ass'n of Diabetes Educators *(1974)*
100 W. Monroe St., Suite 400
Chicago, IL 60603-1901
Tel: (312)424-2426　　　　　*Fax:* (312)424-2427
Members: 11,000 individuals
Staff: 6
Annual Budget: $2-5,000,000
Exec. Director: James J. Balija
Director, Communications: Mary Beach
Director, Education: Lois Book
Director, Finance: Janet Kosiba
Director, Member Services: Nadine Cunix
Historical Note
Nurses, dietitians, physicians, pharmacists and other allied health professionals involved in teaching self-management to people with diabetes. Membership: $275/year.
Publications:
AADE Newsletter. 10/year.
The Diabetes Educator. bi-m.
Meetings/Conferences:
Annual Meetings: August
1999 – Orlando, FL(Orange County Convention Center)/Aug. 18-22
2000 – San Diego, CA(San Diego Convention Center)/Aug. 9-13
2001 – Louisville, KY(Commonwealth Convention Center)

American Ass'n of Direct Human Service Personnel
1832 Litle Road
Parma, MI 49269-9506
Tel: (517)531-5820　　　　　*Fax:* (517)531-8055
E-Mail: aadhsp@aol.com
Vice President: Sharma J. Krauskopf
Publications:
Newsletter. q.
Meetings/Conferences:

American Ass'n of Directors of Psychiatric Residency Training *(1971)*
U of CT Health Center, Psychiatry Dept
10 Talcott Notch Road, East Wing
Farmington, CT 06030-6410
Tel: (860)679-6766　　　　　*Fax:* (860)679-6675
E-Mail: aadprt@psychiatry.uchc.edu
Members: 428 individuals
Staff: 2
Exec. Secretary: David A. Goldberg, M.D.
Coordinator: Lucille Meinsler
Historical Note
AADPRT was established to meet the needs of training directors, assistant/associate training directors, and residency training directors. Program directors generally hold institutional memberships. Programs with both general psychiatry and child/adolescent psychiatry training may hold combined memberships. Associate/Assistant directors hold individual memberships.

Publications:
Academic Psychiatry. q.
Newsletter. 3/yr.
Meetings/Conferences:
Annual Meetings: January-March/500
1999 – Santa Monica, CA(Loews)/March 11-14

American Ass'n of Early Childhood Educators *(1990)*
3612 Bent Branch Court
Falls Church, VA 22041
Tel: (703)941-4329
Members: 5,000 individuals
Staff: 3
Annual Budget: $10-25,000
Exec. Director: William J. Tobin, Ph.D.
Historical Note
AAECE members are directors, teachers and teacher aides working in licensed childcare centers. Membership: $10/year (individual); $500/year (organization/company).
Publications:
AAECE First Class Educator. q. adv.
Meetings/Conferences:
Annual Meetings: Spring

American Ass'n of Electrodiagnostic Medicine *(1953)*
421 First St. S.W., Suite 300-E
Rochester, MN 55902-3383
Tel: (507)288-0100　　　　　*Fax:* (507)288-1225
E-Mail: aaem@aaem.net
Web Site: http://www.aaem.net
Members: 4,200 individuals
Staff: 15
Annual Budget: $1-2,000,000
Exec. Director: Shirlyn A. Adkins
Manager, Communications: Elvina T. Jeffers
Manager, Education and Marketing: Cindy K. Cunzman
Assoc. Exec. Director: Lori H. Hattenhauer
Manager, Operations: Kathryn J. Smith
Manager, Member/Diplomate Services: Eric B. Erickson
Historical Note
Formerly American Ass'n of Electromyography and Electrodiagnosis; assumed its present name in 1989. The primary goal of AAEM is to increase the quality of patient care, specifically of those patients with disorders of skeletal muscle, neuromuscular function and the central and peripheral nervous systems, by contributing to the improvement in the methods of electrodiagnostic medicine through programs in education, research and quality assurance. Membership: $190/year (individual).
Publications:
Case Reports. irreg.
Minimonographs. irreg.
Muscle & Nerve Journal. m. adv.
Meetings/Conferences:
Annual Meetings: Fall
1999 – Vancouver, BC, Canada(Hyatt Regency)/Oct. 6-10
2000 – Philadelphia, PA(Marriott)/Sept. 13-17
2001 – Albuquerque, NM(Convention Center)/Oct. 3-7

American Ass'n of Endodontists *(1943)*
211 E. Chicago Ave., Suite 1100
Chicago, IL 60611-2691
Tel: (312)266-7255　　　　　*Fax:* (312)266-9867
Web Site: http://www.aae.org
Members: 5,000 individuals
Staff: 18
Annual Budget: $2-5,000,000
Exec. Director: Irma S. Kudo
Asst. Exec. Director: Jill B. Cochran
Manager, Meeting Services: Patt L. Moskal
Asst. Exec. Director: Laura L. Galusha
Historical Note
Established February 25, 1943 in Chicago. Incorporated in Illinois in 1955. Promotes research on pulp conservation and endodontic treatment. Sponsors the American Board of Endodontics and the AAE. Membership: $440/year; $50/year (student).
Publications:
Communique. q.
Endodontics: Colleagues for Excellence. semi.
Journal of Endodontics. m. adv.
Meetings/Conferences:
Annual Meetings: April/3,000
1999 – Atlanta, GA(Marriott Marquis)/April 21-25
2000 – Honolulu, HI(Hilton Hawaiian Village)/March 29-April 2
2001 – New Orleans, LA(Hilton)/March 28-April 1/3500
2002 – Chicago, IL(Hilton)/April 10-14/3500

American Ass'n of Engineering Societies *(1979)*
1111 19th St., N.W., Suite 403
Washington, DC 20036-3690
Tel: (202)296-2237　　　　　*Fax:* (202)296-1151
Toll Free: (800)658 - 8897
Web Site: http://www.aaes.org
Members: 28 societies
Staff: 9
Annual Budget: $1-2,000,000
Exec. Director: Thomas J. Price
Director, Government Relations and Media Affairs: Greg Schuckman
Manager, Government Relations: Pete Leon
Historical Note
Formerly the Engineers Joint Council, AAES is a multidisciplinary organization of engineering societies representing over 500,000 engineers in industry, government and education.
Publications:
Directory of Engineering Societies and Related Organizations. bien.
Engineering & Technology Enrollments. a.
Engineering and Technology Degrees. a.

Engineering Manpower Bulletin. 8/year.
Engineers' Salaries: Special Industry Report. a.
Learning for applications in Microelectronics. a.
Professional Income of Engineers. a.
Salaries of Engineers in Education. bien.
Update. 3/year.
Who's Who in Engineering. bien.
Meetings/Conferences:
Triannual Meetings: always Washington, DC/March, August, and December

American Ass'n of Enterprise Zones *(1985)*
1620 I St., N.W., Suite 300
Washington, DC 20006
Tel: (202)466-2687　　　　　*Fax:* (202)293-3109
Members: 60 organizations
Staff: 1
Exec. Director: Richard Cowden
Historical Note
AAEZ members are municipalities and other governmental organizations with an interest in promoting enterprise zones.
Meetings/Conferences:

American Ass'n of Entreprenurial Dentists *(1983)*
Historical Note
Address unknown in 1997.

American Ass'n of Equine Practitioners *(1955)*
4075 Iron Works Parkway
Lexington, KY 40511-8434
Tel: (606)233-0147　　　　　*Fax:* (606)233-1968
E-Mail: aaepoffice@aol.com
Web Site: http://www.aaep.org
Members: 6,200 individuals
Staff: 10
Annual Budget: $500-1,000,000
Exec. Director: Gary L. Carpenter, CAE
Dep. Exec. Dir/Conventions Manager: David L. Foley
Historical Note
Members are veterinarians who specialize in treating horses. Membership: $160/yr (individual), $25 (veterinary students).
Publications:
AAEP Report. m.
Member Directory. a.
Proceedings. a.
Scientific Abstracts. a.
Meetings/Conferences:
Annual Meetings: December/3,500

American Ass'n of Exporters and Importers *(1921)*
11 W. 42nd St., 30th Floor
New York, NY 10036
Tel: (212)944-2230　　　　　*Fax:* (212)382-2606
Members: 1,200 firms
Staff: 15
Annual Budget: $1-2,000,000
President: Eugene J. Milosh
Director, Administration: Cynthia L. Zigo
Senior Staff Attorney: Stuart Gerber
Editor: Liz Stern
Historical Note
Primary mission of the AAEI is the promotion of fair and open trade among nations. AAEI is the only nat'l ass'n specifically representing both U.S. exporters and importers before the Executive Branch, Congress, the U.S. Trade Representative, U.S. Customs Service and the regulatory agencies. Became the American Importers Ass'n in 1967 and assumed its present name in 1981. Membership fee: based on volume of business.
Publications:
Alertfax. d.
Customs Compliance Regulations Manual.
International Trade Alert. w.
International Trade Quarterly. q.
Membership Directory. a.
Textile Quota Report. w.
Meetings/Conferences:
Annual Meetings: Always New York, NY/May

American Ass'n of Eye and Ear Hospitals *(1983)*
1444 I St., N.W., Suite 410
Washington, DC 20005
Tel: (202)347-1993　　　　　*Fax:* (202)628-2310
E-Mail: rbetz@robertbetz.com
Members: 18 facilities
Annual Budget: $100-250,000
Exec. Director: Robert B. Betz
Historical Note
AAEEH represents specialty hospitals and related institutions emphasizing eye, ear, nose and throat patient care.
Meetings/Conferences:
Annual Meetings: Held in conjunction with the American Academy of Opthalmology.

American Ass'n of Family and Consumer Sciences *(1909)*
1555 King St., 4th Floor
Alexandria, VA 22314-2738
Tel: (703)706-4600　　　　　*Fax:* (703)706-4663
E-Mail: staff@aafcs.org
Web Site: http://www.aafes.org
Members: 14,000 individuals
Staff: 18
Annual Budget: $2-5,000,000
Exec. Director: Ann Collins Chadwick
Annual Meetings Coordinator: Monique Cooper
Director, Finance and Administration: Harold W. Johnson
Historical Note
Formerly (1994) American Home Economics Association, founded at Lake Placid, NY December 31, 1908 and incorporated in New

York in 1909. Reincorporated in the Distric of Columbia in 1951. The purpose of AAFCS is to improve the quality and standards of individual and family life through programs that educate, influence public policy, disseminate information and publish research findings. The association's members include; elementary, secondary and post-secondary educators and administrators; cooperative extension agents; other professionals in government, business and nonprofit sectors; and students preparing for the field. Membership: $82.50/year (active); $74.25/year (associate); $62/year (retired); $41.25/year (student).

Publications:
AAFCS Action. 5 year. adv.
Family and Consumer Sciences Research Journal. q. adv.
Family and Consumer Sciences Research Journal. q.

Meetings/Conferences:
Annual Meetings: late June/2,000
1999 – Seattle, WA/2000

American Ass'n of Family Businesses (1990)
P.O. Box 547217
Surfside, FL   33154
Tel: (305)864-1184   *Fax:* (305)864-1187
Staff: 2
President: Craig Gorson

Historical Note
AAFB represents the concerns and interests of family owned or operated businesses.

American Ass'n of Feed Microscopists (1953)
Historical Note
Became a division of American Oil Chemists' Soc. in 1997.

American Ass'n of Feline Practitioners (1970)
2701 San Pedro Dr., NE #7
Albuquerque, NM   87110-3300
Tel: (505)888-2424   *Fax:* (505)888-2688
E-Mail: KTAAFP@aol.com
Members: 1,600 individuals
Staff: 2
Annual Budget: $10-25,000
Exec. Director: Kristi Thomson

Historical Note
Veterinarians specializing in the treatment of cats. Membership: $100/yr.

Meetings/Conferences:
Annual Meetings: Semi-annual Meetings:
1999 – Big Sky, MT/Jan. 31-Feb. 2

American Ass'n of Food Stamp Directors (1975)
810 1st St., N.E., Suite 500
Washington, DC   20002-4267
Tel: (202)682-0100   *Fax:* (202)289-6555
Web Site: http://www.aphsa.org
Members: 300 individuals
Staff: 1
Annual Budget: under $10,000
Staff Contact: Larry Goolsby

Historical Note
An affiliate unit of the American Public Welfare Association which provides administrative support. Membership: $50/year

Meetings/Conferences:
Annual Meetings: Fall
1999 – Williamsburg, VA

American Ass'n of Franchisees and Dealers (1992)
P.O. Box 81887
San Diego, CA   92138-1887
Tel: (619)209-3775   *Fax:* (619)209-3777
Toll Free: (800)733 - 9858
E-Mail: benefits@aafd.org
Web Site: http://www.aafd.org
Members: 500 individuals, 5,000 individuals and companies
Staff: 9
Annual Budget: $500-1,000,000
Chairman and C.E.O.: Robert L. Purvin, Jr.
Co-op President: Mark Zuckerman
National Dir., Chapter Management: Jack Overton

Historical Note
AAFD represents owners of franchised businesses. Membership: $60-200/year (individual); $1,000-5,000/year (corporate).

Publications:
Annual Members Guide. a. adv.
Chapter Alert Newsletter. irreg. adv.
Franchisee Voice. q. adv.

Meetings/Conferences:
Annual Meetings: Spring
1999 – Las Vegas, NV(Golden Nugget Hotel)
2000 – San Diego, CA/April 30-May 1
2001 – Nashville, TN/April 30-May 1

American Ass'n of Fund-Raising Counsel (1935)
25 W. 43rd St., Suite 820
New York, NY   10036
Tel: (212)354-5799   *Fax:* (212)768-1795
Toll Free: (800)462 - 2372
E-Mail: aafrc@aol.com
Web Site: http://www.aafrc.org
Members: 32 companies
Staff: 4
Annual Budget: $500-1,000,000
Chair: Jimmie Alford
Project Manager: Molly Wasow
Director, Research: Ann Kaplan
Director, Member Services: Georgette Marshall

Historical Note
Members are consulting firms specializing in services to nonprofit organizations. Founded to promote ethical practice and professional standards in the fund-raising consultant field.

American Ass'n of Grain Inspection and Weighing Agencies (1944)
1629 K St., N.W., Suite 1100
Washington, DC   20006
Tel: (202)785-6740   *Fax:* (202)331-4212
Members: 60 agencies
Staff: 2
Annual Budget: $25-50,000
Exec. Director: Paul S. Weller, Jr.

Historical Note
Established to provide a liaison between the Federal Grain Inspection Service and designated agencies.

Publications:
Chaff Newsletter. bi-m.
Grain-Gram. bi-w.

Meetings/Conferences:
1999 – Williamsburg, VA

American Ass'n of Gynecological Laparoscopists (1972)
13021 E. Florence Ave.
Santa Fe Springs, CA   90670-4505
Tel: (562)946-8774   *Fax:* (562)946-0073
Members: 8,000 individuals
Staff: 13
Annual Budget: $500-1,000,000
Exec. Director: Jordan M. Phillips, M.D.
Meeting Coordinator: Jane Kalert

Historical Note
Obstetricians and gynecologists interested in gynecological endoscopy, the process by which the insides of organs are visualized. Membership: $195/year, (physician); $100/year, (resident).

Publications:
Journal of AAGL. q.

Meetings/Conferences:
Annual Meetings: Fall
1999 – Las Vegas, NV/Nov. 7-11

American Ass'n of Handwriting Analysts (1963)
P.O. Box 95
Southfield, MI   48037-0095
Tel: (248)746-0740   *Fax:* (248)746-0756
E-Mail: aahadoffice@aol.com
Web Site: http://www.handwriting.org/aaha/aahamain.htm
Members: 500 individuals
Annual Budget: $10-25,000

Historical Note
Members are proficient in the science of analyzing character through handwriting. Seeks public recognition of the usefulness of handwriting analysis in the authentication of documents and in describing the personality of a writer for counseling, therapy and personnel purposes. Membership: $50-55/year; $500/ Lifetime membership.

Publications:
AAHA Dialogue Newsletter. bi-m.
Annals. a.

Meetings/Conferences:
Annual Meetings: July/August
1999 – Denver, CO(Sheraton Denver West)/Aug. 5-7/100
2000 – Las Vegas, NV

American Ass'n of Health Plans (1959)
1129 20th St., N.W., Suite 600
Washington, DC   20036-3403
Tel: (202)778-3200   *Fax:* (202)331-7487
Web Site: Http://www.aahp.org
Members: 1,250 organizations
Staff: 100
Annual Budget: $10-25,000,000
President and C.E.O.: Karen M. Ignagni
V. President, Communications: Susan Pisano
V.President, Stratgic Communications: Mark Meritt
Exec. V.P., Govt. Affairs: Diana Dennett
V.President, Govt. Affairs: Julie Goon
V. President, Policy: Rick Smith
Senior V. President, Policy and Research: Dr. Donald Young
V. President, Finance and Oper.: Robert O. Borchardt
General Counsel: Lou Saccoccio
V.President, Member Services: Carlean Miller
V.President, Medical Affairs: Carmella Bocchino
Exec. V. President: Charles Stellar

Historical Note
AAHP was created by the merger of Group Health Federation of America(GHAA) and the American Managed Care and Review Ass'n (AMCRA). AAHP's mission is to advance health care quality and affordability through leadership in the health care community, advocacy and services to member plans. Members of the association are HMOs, PPOs and similar health plan providers.

Publications:
Healthplan Magazine.
Managed Care Overview.

Meetings/Conferences:
Annual Meetings: June/300
1999 – Washington, DC/Feb. 21-23

American Ass'n of Healthcare Consultants (1949)
11208 Waples Mill Road, Suite 109
Fairfax, VA   22030
Tel: (703)691-2242   *Fax:* (703)691-2247
Web Site: http://www.aahc.net
Members: 250 individuals, 70 firm members
Staff: 4
Annual Budget: $500-1,000,000
President: Vaughan A. Smith
V. President: Carolyn Shwidock

Historical Note
Formerly (1984) the American Ass'n of Hospital Consultants. Membership: $395 year (and/or a firm fee based on professional staff size).

Publications:
Directory. a.

American Ass'n of Hip and Knee Surgeons
6300 N. River Road, Suite 727
Rosemont, IL   60018-4226
Tel: (847)698-1693   *Fax:* (847)823-0536
Exec. Officer: Sandra Brahos

American Ass'n of Hispanic Certified Public Accountants (1972)
19726 E. Colima Rd., Suite 270
Roland Heights, CA   91748
Tel: (626)965-0643   *Fax:* (626)965-0653
E-Mail: aahcpa_national@compuserve.com
Web Site: http://www.aahcpa.org
Members: 700 individuals
Staff: 1
Annual Budget: $25-50,000
Exec. Director: John R. Hernandez

Historical Note
Members are certified public accountants of Hispanic descent and organizations. Membership: $50/year (individual).

Publications:
La Cuenta. bi-m. adv.
Membership Directory. a. adv.

Meetings/Conferences:

American Ass'n of Home-Based Businesses (1991)
P.O. Box 10023
Rockville, MD   20849-0023
Tel: (202)310-3130   *Fax:* (301)963-7042
Toll Free: (800)447 - 9710
E-Mail: aahbb@crosslink.net
Web Site: http://www.aahbb.org
Annual Budget: $10-25,000
President/Founder: Beverley Williams

Historical Note
AAHBB members are owners of home-based businesses and corporations with an interest in home-based businesses. Membership: $30/year, (home-based business); $135/year (corporate).

Publications:
Connector Newsletter. 4-6/yr. adv.

American Ass'n of Homes and Services for the Aging (1961)
901 E St., N.W., Suite 500
Washington, DC   20004-2011
Tel: (202)783-2242   *Fax:* (202)783-2255
E-Mail: info@aahsa.org
Web Site: http://www.aahsa.org
Members: 5,000 facilities
Staff: 95
Annual Budget: $5-10,000,000
V. President, Public Affairs: Scott L. Parkin
Sr. V.P., Govt./Public Affairs: Michael F. Rodgers
Director, Meetings and Conventions: Alison B. Owings
Sr. V. P., Professional/Organizational Development: Ann Gillespie
Sr. V.P., Admin./Operations: Patricia G. Kallsen, CAE
C.O.O.: Alan G. Rosenbloom
Chief Information Officer: Charles Robert Tremper
Director, Finance: Stanley M. Schwartz
V. President and Counsel, Public Policy: Suzanne M. Weiss
V.P., Services/Vendor Relations: Virginia D. Nuessle
Director, Internat'l Programs: Russell Roeding

Historical Note
Formerly (1994) American Ass'n of Homes for the Aging. Primary membership consists of community-based, non-profit nursing homes, independent housing, continuing care retirement communities, and homes and services for the aging; individuals with an interest in long term care and housing for the aged may join as associate members. Provides administrative support to the Internat'l Ass'n of Homes and Services for the Aging. Sponsors the Continuing Care Accreditation Commission. Membership: annual dues vary.

Publications:
Currents. m.
Legal Memo. bi-m.
Membership Directory. bien. adv.
Washington Report. bi-w.

Meetings/Conferences:
Semi-Annual Meetings: March-April in Washington, DC, and November
1999 – Washington, DC/April 20-23

American Ass'n of Hospital Dentists (1937)
211 E. Chicago Ave., Suite 948
Chicago, IL   60611
Tel: (312)440-2661   *Fax:* (312)440-2824
Members: 1000 individuals
Staff: 3
Annual Budget: $250-500,000
Exec. Director: John S. Rutkauskas, D.D.S., MS

Historical Note
Formerly (1968) American Ass'n of Hospital Dental Chiefs, Inc. Membership: $120/year (individual).

Publications:
Interface. q.
Special Care in Dentistry. bi-m. adv.

Meetings/Conferences:
1999 – Chicago, IL(Westin Hotel)/Mar. 26-28

American Ass'n of Hospital Podiatrists (1950)
420 74th St.

Brooklyn, NY 11209
Tel: (718)836-1017   *Fax:* (718)836-9555
Members: 800 individuals
Annual Budget: $25-50,000
Exec. Director: Louis J. Arancia, DPM

Historical Note
AAHP members are podiatrists affiliated with hospitals. Grants fellowship status to members who document 3 years of in-hospital privileges and pass an appropriate examination. Membership: $75/year (individual).

Publications:
Hospital Podiatrist. a. adv.
Newsletter. a. adv.

Meetings/Conferences:
Annual Meetings: in conjunction with the American Podiatric Medical Ass'n/August
1999 – Houston, TX
2000 – Philadelphia, PA

American Ass'n of Housing Educators (1965)
Historical Note
Address unknown in 1997.

American Ass'n of Immunologists (1913)
9650 Rockville Pike
Bethesda, MD 20814-3994
Tel: (301)530-7178   *Fax:* (301)571-1816
E-Mail: infoaai@aai.faseb.org
Web Site: http://www.sciencexchange.com/aai
Members: 5,390 individuals
Staff: 6
Annual Budget: $500-1,000,000
Exec. Director: M. Michelle Hogan, Ph.D.
Sr. Admin. Assistant: Linda Jean Comley
Public Affairs Officer: E. Patrick White
Business Manager: Tim Markwood
Coordinator, Membership: Lisa McFadden

Historical Note
Founded with 56 charter members, most of whom worked in the laboratories of Sir Almroth Wright, Mechnikov and Ehrlich. A member of the Federation of American Socs. for Experimental Biology since 1942. Membership: $210/year (domestic individual); $300/year (internat'l individual); $307/year (Canadian individual); $750-2000/year (organization/company).

Publications:
AAI Newsletter. bi-m.
Journal of Immunology. semi-m.

Meetings/Conferences:
Annual Meetings: With Federation of American Socs. for Experimental Biology/15,000
1999 – Washington, DC/Apr. 17-21

American Ass'n of Independent Newspaper Distributors (1971)
16 Santa Ana Place
Walnut Creek, CA 94598
Tel: (510)935-2026   *Fax:* (510)906-0922
Members: 700 individuals
Exec. Director: Deborah S. Dobbs, CAE

Historical Note
AAIND members are independent newspaper dealers and distributors.

Publications:
AAIND News Newsletter. bi-m.

Meetings/Conferences:

American Ass'n of Individual Investors (1979)
625 N. Michigan Ave., Suite 1900
Chicago, IL 60611-3110
Tel: (312)280-0170   *Fax:* (312)280-9883
Members: 180,000 individuals
Staff: 39
Annual Budget: $10-25,000,000
Chairman: James B. Cloonan
Meeting Coordinator: Arlene Zamudio

Historical Note
An independent non-profit corporation formed for the purpose of assisting individuals in becoming effective managers of their own assets through programs of education, information and research. Has an annual budget of approximately $12 million. Membership: $49/year.

Publications:
AAII Journal. m.
Computerized Investing. bi-w.
The Individual Investor.

Meetings/Conferences:
Annual Meetings: Summer
1999 – Chicago, IL(Palmer House)/July 24-25/500
2000 – San Diego, CA(Hyatt Regency)/Aug. 25-26/500
2001 – Chicago, IL(Chicago Marriott Downtown)/June 29-30/500

American Ass'n of Industrial Management (1899)
Stearns Bldg., 293 Bridge St.
Suite 324
Springfield, MA 01103
Tel: (413)737-8766   *Fax:* (413)737-9724
Members: 225 companies
Staff: 11
Annual Budget: $100-250,000
President: Christy Karr

Historical Note
Formerly (1964) Nat'l Metal Trades Ass'n. Concerned with labor and industrial relations, management training. Members are manufacturers, insurance companies and banks, town and city governments, universities and hospitals.

Publications:
Signs of the Times. q.

The Executive Manager. q.
Washington Newsletter.

American Ass'n of Industrial Social Workers (1982)
Historical Note
Organization defunct in 1996.

American Ass'n of Industrial Veterinarians (1954)
P.O. Box 488
Oskaloosa, KS 66066-0488
Tel: (785)863-2389   *Fax:* (785)863-3141
E-Mail: aaiv@ruralnet1.com
Members: 500 individuals
Staff: 1
Annual Budget: $25-50,000
Exec. Director: Peggy Miller

Historical Note
Formerly (1976) Industrial Veterinarian's Ass'n. Membership: $50/year.

Publications:
AAIV Newsline. 3/year.
Directory. a.

Meetings/Conferences:
Annual Meetings: July, with American Veterinary Medical Ass'n

American Ass'n of Insurance Management Consultants (1978)
221 Countrywood
Livingston, TX 77351
Tel: (409)327-2133   *Fax:* (409)327-5082
Members: 35 companies
Annual Budget: under $10,000
President: Roger E. Thomas, CIC

Historical Note
Founded to provide a platform for the exchange of information and the development of uniform standards and practices for firms and individuals providing professional consulting to the insurance industry. Has no paid officers or full-time staff.

Publications:
AAIMCO Connection. q.

Meetings/Conferences:

American Ass'n of Integrated Healthcare Delivery Systems (1993)
P.O. Box 4913
Glen Allen, VA 23058-4913
Tel: (804)747-5823   *Fax:* (804)747-5316
Web Site: http://www.aaihds.org
Members: 415 individuals
Staff: 18
Annual Budget: $500-1,000,000
President: W.C. Williams, III, M.D.

Historical Note
Founded as American Ass'n of Physician-Hospital Organizations; assumed its current name in 1997. AAIHDS members are physicians, hospital administrators, health plan executives and other individuals with an interest in physician-hospital organizations. Membership: $275/year (individual); $750/year (organization).

Publications:
Integrated Healthcare Delivery System Newsletter. q.

Meetings/Conferences:
Semi-Annual Meetings: Spring and Fall

American Ass'n of Language Specialists (1957)
1000 Connecticut Ave., N.W., Suite 9
Washington, DC 20036
Tel: (301)986-1542
Web Site: http://www.taals.net
Members: 150 individuals
Annual Budget: under $10,000
President: Doron Horowitz

Historical Note
Professional association representing interpreters, translators, and precis writers working at the international level, either for conferences on a free-lance basis or for international organizations as permanent staff. Has no paid officers or full-time staff. Membership: $80/year.

Publications:
Yearbook. a.

Meetings/Conferences:
Annual Meetings: December in New York, NY or Washington, DC

American Ass'n of Law Libraries (1906)
53 West Jackson Blvd., Suite 940
Chicago, IL 60604
Tel: (312)939-4764   *Fax:* (312)431-1097
E-Mail: aallhq@aall.org
Web Site: http://www.aallnet.org
Members: 5,000 individuals
Staff: 13
Annual Budget: $1-2,000,000
Exec. Director: Roger H. Parent
Director, Publications: Peter Beck
Director, Programs: Martha S. Brown
Director, Finance and Administration: Stephen Ligda

Historical Note
Members are librarians of law libraries in schools, law firms, associations, the government, court systems and other institutions. Membership: $133/year.

Publications:
AALL Spectrum. adv. adv.
Directory & Handbook. a.
Index to Foreign Legal Periodicals. q.
Law Library Journal. q. adv.

Meetings/Conferences:
Annual Meetings: Summer/2,600
1999 – Washington, DC(Convention Center)/July 17-22

American Ass'n of Legal Nurse Consultants (1989)
4700 W. Lake Ave.
Glenview, IL 60025-1485
Tel: (847)375-4713   *Fax:* (847)375-4777
E-Mail: assnmgmt@dial.cic.net
Members: 1,800 individuals, 15 companies
Annual Budget: $250-500,000
Exec. Director: Anne M. Cordes

Historical Note
Promotes the professional advancement of Registered Nurses practicing in a consulting capacity in the legal profession and provides educational opportunities for legal nurse consultants. Membership: $95/year (individual); $175/year (company).

Publications:
Journal of Legal Nurse Consulting. q. adv.
Network: News for the Legal Nurse Consultant. q. adv.

Meetings/Conferences:
Annual Meetings: April

American Ass'n of Limited Partners
4424 Montgomery Ave., Suite 102
Bethesda, MD 20814
Tel: (202)797-3763   *Fax:* (301)913-9146
Exec. Director: David S. O'Bryon, CAE

American Ass'n of Managed Care Nurses (1994)
4435 Waterfront Dr., Suite 101
P.O. Box 4975
Glen Allen, VA 23058-4975
Tel: (804)747-9698   *Fax:* (804)747-5316
Web Site: http://www.aamcn.org
Members: 1,500 individuals
Staff: 10
Annual Budget: $100-250,000
Exec. Director: Sloane Reed

Historical Note
AAMCN members are nurses and other professionals with an interest in managed healthcare. Membership: $65/year (individual).

Publications:
American Journal of Integrated Healthcare. q.
Nurses' Notes Newsletter. q. adv.

Meetings/Conferences:
1999 – Orlando, FL(Contemporary Resort Walt Disney)

American Ass'n of Managing General Agents (1926)
9140 Ward Parkway
Kansas City, MO 64114
Tel: (816)444-3500   *Fax:* (816)444-0330
Members: 260 managing firms, 165 assoc.
Staff: 10
Annual Budget: $500-1,000,000
Exec. V. President: Jerry Fogel, CAE
Executive Administrator: Mary Jo Bowman

Historical Note
Independent insurance managers with contractual authority to perform managerial functions on behalf of insurance companies and syndicates. Membership: $550-$750/year (company).

Publications:
AAMGA Newsletter. bi-m.
AAMGA Yearbook. a.
Annual Report. a.

Meetings/Conferences:
Annual Meetings: Spring/1,000
1999 – Colorado Springs, CO(The Broadmoor)

American Ass'n of Meat Processors (1939)
P.O. Box 269
One Meating Place
Elizabethtown, PA 17022
Tel: (717)367-1168   *Fax:* (717)367-9096
E-Mail: aamp@aamp.com
Web Site: http://www.aamp.com
Members: 1,800 firms
Staff: 9
Annual Budget: $250-500,000
Exec. Director: Stephen F. Krut
Director, Regulatory/Legislative Affairs: Bernard F. Shire
Convention Manager: Anne Tantum
American Cured Meat Championships, Membership: Jane Frey
Membership: Debbie Sinex

Historical Note
Founded as the Nat'l Frozen Food Locker Institute, it became successively the Nat'l Frozen Food Locker Ass'n, the Frozen Food Locker Institute, the Nat'l Institute of Locker and Freezer Provisioners, and in 1973 assumed its present name. North America's largest meat trade association, AAMP members are small to medium-sized meat, poultry, seafood and food businesses including packers, processors, wholesalers, home food service businesses, retailers, deli/catering operators, and industry suppliers. Membership: $150 (operator); $250/year (supplier); $75/year (Canadian); $100/year (international); $75/year (allied).

Publications:
AAMPlifier. semi-m.
Capitol Line Up. semi-m.
Membership Directory and Buyers' Guide. bi-a. adv.

Meetings/Conferences:
Annual Meetings: Summer
1999 – Springfield, IL(Crowne Plaza)/July 15-18
2000 – Lancaster, PA(Lancaster Host Resort)/Aug. 3-6
2001 – Nashville, TN(Opryland Hotel)/July 26-29

American Ass'n of Medical Assistants (1956)
20 North Wacker Drive, #1575

Chicago, IL 60606-2903
Tel: (312)899-1500   Fax: (312)899-1259
Web Site: http://www.aama-ntl.org
Members: 20,000 individuals
Staff: 21
Annual Budget: $1-2,000,000
Exec. Director/Counsel: Donald A. Balasa, JD,CAE
Director, Communications: Jean Lynch
Director, Operations: Deborah Murphy
Asst. Exec. Director: Anna Johnson
Historical Note
AAMA was established to promote the medical assisting profession
through continuing education and credentialing. Membership
includes medical assistants, medical secretaries, bookkeepers,
receptionists, technicians and office nurses. Administers CMA
(Certified Medical Assistant) certification program. Assistant.
Membership: $67/year (individual).
Publications:
The Professional Medical Assistant. bi-m.
Meetings/Conferences:
1999 – Nashville, TN/Oct. 1-6

American Ass'n of Medical Milk Commissions (1907)
1824 N. Hillhurst Ave.
Los Angeles, CA 90027
Tel: (213)664-1977   Fax: (213)664-0870
Members: 20 individuals
Annual Budget: under $10,000
President: Paul Fleiss, M.D.
Historical Note
Professional society of physicians on local Medical Milk
Commissions supervising production of Certified Milk from dairies
conforming to offical standards. Membership includes physicians,
pathologists, pediatricians and veterinarians. Affiliated with the
Certified Milk Producers Ass'n of America.
Publications:
Methods and Standards for the Production of Certified Milk.
    irreg.
Meetings/Conferences:
Semi-Annual Meetings: May, with Certified Milk Producers
    Ass'n of America, and September-October.

American Ass'n of Medical Soc. Executives (1947)
515 N. State St., 11th Floor
Chicago, IL 60610
Tel: (312)464-2555   Fax: (312)464-2467
E-Mail: aamse@aamse.org
Web Site: http://www.aamse.org
Members: 1,200 individuals
Staff: 4
Annual Budget: $500-1,000,000
Exec. Director: Robin Kriegel, CAE
Director, Education/Membership Services: Susan B. Turner
Historical Note
Professional organization of executives of medical societies.
Formerly Medical Soc. Executives Ass'n. Membership: $125/year
(individual).
Publications:
Hotline. m.
Who's Who in Medical Society Management - Directory. a.
    adv.
Meetings/Conferences:
Annual Meetings: Summer/325
1999 – New York, NY(Hilton)/Aug. 5-8
2000 – Seattle, WA

American Ass'n of Mental Health Professionals in Corrections (1940)
P.O. Box 160208
Sacramento, CA 95816-0208
Tel: (916)323-8305   Fax: (916)649-1080
Members: 2,000 individuals
Staff: 1
Annual Budget: $25-50,000
Nat'l President: J.S. Zil, M.D., J.D.
Historical Note
Formerly (1978) Medical Correctional Ass'n. Membership:
$55/year.
Publications:
Corrective and Social Psychiatry Monograph Series.
Meetings/Conferences:
Annual Meetings: With the American College of Forensic
    Psychiatry

American Ass'n of Minority Businesses (1992)
P.O. Box 35432
Charlotte, NC 28213
Tel: (704)376-2262   Fax: (704)921-2910
E-Mail: KAAMB@aol.com
Web Site: http://www.aamb.com
Members: 17,000 businesses/corporations
Staff: 3
Annual Budget: $250-500,000
President and C.E.O.: Charles L. Kelly
Historical Note
AAMB is a network of minority business owners. Membership:
$60/year (business owner); $100/year (associate); $1,000/year
(corporate member); $250/year (alliance and association
members).
Publications:
The Business Partner. q. adv.

American Ass'n of Motor Vehicle Administrators (1933)
4301 Wilson Blvd., Suite 400
Arlington, VA 22203
Tel: (703)522-4200   Fax: (703)522-1553
E-Mail: webmail@aamva.org

Web Site: http://www.aamva.org
Members: 150 agencies
Staff: 70
Annual Budget: $25-50,000,000
President and C.E.O.: Kenneth Beam, SPHR, CAE
Director, Legislative Affairs & Communications: Linda Lewis
President and C.O.O.: John Maxwell
Director, Human Resources and Administration: Iris Rogers
Director, Finance: John Mamone
Manager, Membership: Christine Auvenire
Historical Note
Membership composed of state and provincial agencies responsible
for the administration and enforcement of motor vehicle and traffic
laws in the U.S. and Canada. AAMVA is composed of 67
jurisdictions representing 150 agencies and thousands of
employees. Has an annual budget of approximately $22 million.
Publications:
AAMVA Bulletin. q.
Membership Directory of Member Jurisdictions. bi-a.
MOVE Magazine. q. adv.
netAFFECT. irreg.
Meetings/Conferences:
Annual Meetings: Fall

American Ass'n of Museums (1906)
1575 I St., N.W., Suite 400
Washington, DC 20005
Tel: (202)289-1818   Fax: (202)289-6578
Web Site: http://aam-us.org
Members: 14,000 individuals, 2,800 institutions, 1,000
    companies
Staff: 90
Annual Budget: $5-10,000,000
President and C.E.O.: Edward H. Able, Jr., CAE
Director, Marketing: Jeff Minett
Director, Government/Public Affairs: Jason Y. Hall
Director, Meetings/Continuing Ed.: Dean Phelus
Director, Education/Meetings: Margaret L. McCarthy, CMP
V. President, Finance/Administration: Edward T. Brenner
V. President, Programs/Policy: Patricia E. Williams
Director, Membership Services: Kathy Maxwell
Historical Note
AAM's institutional members include art museums, history
museums, natural history museums, science museums, children's
museums, historic buildings and sites, science/technology centers,
aquariums, zoos, botanical gardens, arboreta, and military and
maritime museums. Individual members include museum directors,
curators, registrars, educators, exhibit designers, public relations
officers, development officers, security managers, trustees, and
volunteers. Corporate members include individual consultants as
well as providers of commercial products and services. AAM's
services include: accreditation, museum assessment programs,
government affairs, technical information, continuing education,
publications, international programs, and vendor-provided services.
Affiliated with the Internat'l Council of Museums. Administers 12
standing professional committees, including the American Ass'n of
Museums Trustee Committee (1971). Has an annual budget of
approximately $7 million. Membership fee: Individual based on
salary; institution based on operating budget; corporate individual
based on salary, corporate company is flat fee.
Publications:
AAM Network News. semi-a.
Aviso. m. adv.
Museum News. bi-m. adv.
Official Museum Directory. a.
Meetings/Conferences:
Annual Meetings: Spring/5,000
1999 – Cleveland, OH/April 25-29

American Ass'n of Museums Trustee Committee (1971)
Historical Note
A Standing Committee of the American Ass'n of Museums, which
provides administrative support.

American Ass'n of Naturopathic Physicians (1986)
601 Valley St., Suite 105
Seattle, WA 98109-4229
Tel: (206)298-0126   Fax: (206)298-0129
Web Site: http://www.naturopathic.org
Members: 1,200 individuals, 47 companies
Staff: 7
Annual Budget: $500-1,000,000
Exec. Director: Sheila Quinn
Historical Note
AANP represents licensable naturopathic physicians in the United
States. It supports legislation to license and regulate naturopathic
physicians in all states, in order to distinguish properly trained
individuals. Provides referral service at: (206) 298-0125.
Membership: $395/year (individual), $1,800/year (organization).
Publications:
Journal of Naturopathic Medicine. a. adv.
Referral Directory. a.
The Naturopathic Physician. q. adv.
Meetings/Conferences:
Annual Meetings: Autumn/500
1999 – Coeur d'Alene, ID/Nov. 3-7

American Ass'n of Neurological Surgeons (1931)
22 S. Washington St.
Park Ridge, IL 60068-4287
Tel: (847)692-9500   Fax: (847)692-2589
E-Mail: info@aans.org
Web Site: http://www.neurosurgey.org
Members: 5,400 individuals
Staff: 65
Annual Budget: $10-25,000,000
Exec. Director: Robert E. Draba, Ph.D.
Director, Communications: Susan A. Nowicki, APR
Director, Government Affairs: Katie O. Orrico, JD
Assoc. Exec. Director, Programs: Laurie L. Behncke, CMP

Assoc. Exec. Director/Controller: Robert T. Cowan, CPA
Manager, Member Services: Chrystine Hanus
Historical Note
Founded October 10, 1931 as the Harvey Cushing Society.
Incorporated in Illinois in 1956 and name changed to American
Ass'n of Neurological Surgeons in 1967. Has an annual budget of
approximately $8.5 million. Membership: $620/year (individual).
Publications:
AANS Bulletin. q. adv.
Journal of Neurosurgery. m. adv.
Meetings/Conferences:
Annual Meetings: Spring
1999 – New Orleans, LA/April 24-29
2000 – San Francisco, CA/April 7-17
2001 – Toronto, ON, Canada/April 21-26

American Ass'n of Neuropathologists (1924)
Box 174 Mayo
University of Minnesota
Minneapolis, MN 55455
Tel: (612)625-0956   Fax: (612)625-0440
E-Mail: aanp@mail med.umn.edu
Web Site: www.aanp.gnen.com
Members: 810 individuals
Staff: 1
Annual Budget: $250-500,000
Secretary-Treasurer: H. Brent Clark, M.D., Ph.D
Historical Note
Founded as the Club of Neuropatholgists, this professional society
of physicians assumed its present name in 1932. Provides a forum
for the advancement of the study of diseases of the nervous system.
Membership: $125/year.
Publications:
Journal of Neuropathology & Experimental Neurology. m.
Membership Directory. a.
Neuropathology Newsletter. 3/year.
Meetings/Conferences:
Annual Meetings: Annual/June
1999 – Portland, OR(Hilton Hotel)/June 17-20/450
2000 – Atlanta, GA(Radisson Hotel)/June 8-11

American Ass'n of Neuroscience Nurses (1968)
224 N. Des Plaines St., Suite 601
Chicago, IL 60661-1134
Tel: (312)993-0043   Fax: (312)993-0362
E-Mail: AssnNeuro@aol.com
Web Site: http://www.aann.org
Members: 3,400 individuals
Staff: 4
Annual Budget: $500 1,000,000
Exec. Director: Shelly Johnson
Director, Communications: Tracy Bergfeld
Dept. Exec. Director: J.D. Mieacham
Historical Note
Membership is open to Registered Nurses who demonstrate an
active or primary interest in neurosurgical or neurological nursing.
Membership: $75/year (individual).
Publications:
Journal of Neuroscience Nursing. bi-m. adv.
Synapse. bi-m. adv.
Meetings/Conferences:
Annual Meetings: Spring/1,000

American Ass'n of Nurse Anesthetists (1931)
222 S. Prospect Ave.
Park Ridge, IL 60068
Tel: (847)692-7050   Fax: (847)692-6968
E-Mail: info@aana.com
Web Site: http://www.aana.com
Members: 28,000 individuals
Staff: 70
Annual Budget: $5-10,000,000
Exec. Director: John F. Garde, CRNA
Director, Public Relations: Christopher Bettin
Director, State Government Affairs: Mitchell H. Tobin, JD
Director, Programs and Meeting Services: Glen C. Ramsborg,
    CRNA,Ph.D.
Director, Continuing Education: Susan Smith Caulk, CRNA
Director, Education and Research: Lorraine M. Jordan, CRNA,
    PhD
Director, Finance: William E. Yeo, CPA, BBA
Director, Membership & Information Svcs.: Gregg R. Revak
Historical Note
Established in 1931 as the Nat'l Ass'n of Nurse Anesthetists.
Became the American Ass'n of Nurse Anesthetists in 1939.
Certifies nurse anesthetists and awards the CRNA (Certified
Registered Nurse Anesthetist) designation. Has an annual budget of
approximately $8 million. Sponsors and supports the CRNA
Political Action Committee. Membership: $380/year.
Publications:
AANA Journal. bi-m. adv.
AANA Newsbulletin. 11/year. adv.
Meetings/Conferences:
Annual Meetings: August
1999 – Boston, MA(Hynes Convention Center)/Aug. 7-12
2000 – Chicago, IL(Navy Pier & Hyatt)/Aug. 5-10
2001 – San Francisco, CA(Moscone Convention
    Center)/Aug. 11-16

American Ass'n of Nurse Attorneys (1982)
3525 Ellicott Dr., Suite N
Ellicott City, MD 21043--454
Tel: (410)418-4800   Fax: (410)418-4805
E-Mail: taana@assochq.com
Web Site: http://www.taana.org
Members: 575 individualsindividuals
Annual Budget: $50-100,000
Exec. Director: Belinda E. Puetz
: Janice Ward

Membership: Charles Dorsett

Historical Note
Members are individuals holding degrees in both nursing and law and members of either profession who are pursuing a second degree in the other field. Sponsors the TAANA Foundation to provide educational opportunities and recognize achievement in the field. Membership: $150/year (nurse/attorney),$150/year (affiliate/associate), $75/year (student).

Publications:
Inside TAANA. q.
Journal of Nursing Law.
Membership Directory. a.

Meetings/Conferences:

American Ass'n of Nurserymen *(1876)*

Historical Note
Became the American Nursery and Landscape Ass'n in 1997.

American Ass'n of Nutritional Consultants *(1980)*
810 Buffalo St.
Warsau, IN   46580
Toll Free: (888)828 - 2262
Members: 2,000 individuals
Staff: 1
Exec. Administrator: Wilma Johnson

Historical Note
Members are professional consultants in the field of nutrition. Also serves as administrative offices for the American Naturopathic Medical Ass'n. Membership: $50/year.

Publications:
Healthkeepers Journal. bi-m.
Journal of the ANMC and AANC. bi-m. adv.
Nutritionists Newsletter. bi-m.

Meetings/Conferences:

American Ass'n of Occupational Health Nurses *(1942)*
2920 Brandywine Rd., Suite 100
Atlanta, GA   30341-5539
Tel: (770)455-7757   *Fax:* (770)455-7271
E-Mail: aaohn@aaohn.org
Web Site: http://www.AAOHN.org
Members: 13,000 individuals, 183 chapters
Staff: 26
Annual Budget: $2-5,000,000
Exec. Director: Ann R. Cox, CAE
Director, Public Affairs: Geraldine C. Williamson, M.N., RNC,
Director, Professional Affairs: Frances Childre, MS, RNC, A
Director, Business Affairs: Thomas Dvorak

Historical Note
Founded in Philadelphia in 1942 and incorporated in New York in 1952. The professional association of occupational health nurses. Formerly (1977) the American Ass'n of Industrial Nurses, Inc. Incorporated in the state of Georgia in 1982. Membership: $95/year.

Publications:
AAOHN Journal. m. adv.
AAOHN News. m.

Meetings/Conferences:
Annual Meetings: April-May
1999 – New Orleans, LA/April 23-30
2000 – Philadelphia, PA/May 12-19
2001 – San Francisco, CA/April 20-27
2002 – Chicago, IL/April 12-19

American Ass'n of Office Nurses *(1988)*
109 Kinderkamack Road
Montvale, NJ   07645
Tel: (201)391-2600   *Fax:* (201)573-8543
E-Mail: aaonmail@aaon.org
Web Site: http://www.aaon.org
Members: 4,000 individuals
Staff: 3
Annual Budget: $250-500,000
Exec. Director: Joyce Logan

Historical Note
AAON members are registered nurses, nurse practitioners, nurse educators, licensed practical nurses, medical technicians, office managers and others working in the medical office setting. Membership: $35/year.

Publications:
NEON (Nurses Exchange Office News) Newsletter. q.
Office Nurse. 10/yr.

Meetings/Conferences:
1999 – San Diego, CA(Town & Country Hotel)/Sept. 22-26

American Ass'n of Oral and Maxillofacial Surgeons *(1918)*
9700 W. Bryn Mawr Ave.
Rosemont, IL   60018-5701
Tel: (847)678-6200   *Fax:* (847)678-6286
Web Site: http://www.aaoms.org
Members: 6,000 individuals
Staff: 49
Annual Budget: $5-10,000,000
Exec. Director: Dr. Bob Rinaldi
Manager, Marketing and Public Relations: Carol O'Brien
Assoc. Exec. Director, Education: Randi V. Andresen
Assoc. Exec. Director, Ops./Business: Scott Farrell

Historical Note
Formerly (1978) the American Soc. of Oral Surgeons. Members are surgeons specializing in treatment of the mouth and its related organs. Operates the Oral and Maxillofacial Surgery Political Action Committee (OMSPAC) and the Oral and Maxillofacial Surgery Foundation (OMSF). Has an annual budget of approximately $10 million. In addition to its annual meeting, AAOMS sponsors an annual 3-day Clinical Congress in late January-early February.

Publications:
AAOMS Today. bi-m.
Journal of Oral and Maxillofacial Surgery. m. adv.

Meetings/Conferences:
Annual Meetings: Fall/3,000-3,500
1999 – Boston, MA(Marriott)/Sept. 29-Oct. 3

American Ass'n of Oriental Medicine *(1983)*
443 Front St.
Catasauqua, PA   18032
Tel: (610)433-2448   *Fax:* (610)266-1433
E-Mail: aaom1@aol.com
Web Site: http://www.aaom.org
Members: 1,200 individuals, 100 companies
Staff: 3
Annual Budget: $250-500,000
Exec. Director: David Molony
Exec. Communications Manager: Alex Klo

Historical Note
Formerly (1996) American Ass'n of Acupuncture and Oriental Medicine. Advocates the recognition of acupuncture and Oriental medicine with acupuncture as a reliable, cost effective and viable form of treatment. Membership: $240/year (individual); $400/year (organization); $35/year (student).

Publications:
Membership Directory. a. adv.
The American Acupuncturist. semi-a. adv.
Update Bulletin. 5/yr. adv.

Meetings/Conferences:
Annual Meetings: Spring

American Ass'n of Orthodontists *(1900)*
401 North Lindbergh Blvd.
St. Louis, MO   63141-7816
Tel: (314)993-1700   *Fax:* (314)997-1745
Toll Free: (800)424 - 2841
Web Site: http://www.aaortho.org
Members: 13,000 individuals
Staff: 36
Annual Budget: $10-25,000,000
Exec. Director: Ronald S. Moen
Director, Communications and Marketing: Larry Mickey
Assoc. Exec. Director: James M. Drinan
Director, Meetings: Serena E. Leiser
Director, Finance and Administration: John J. Terranova
Coordinator, Membership and Due: Becky Yates

Historical Note
Formed in 1900 as The American Soc. of Orthodontists. Incorporated in Pennsylvania in 1917 as The American Ass'n of Orthodontists and later, in 1965 after the headquarters was established in St. Louis, incorporated in Missouri. Sponsors the American Ass'n of Orthodontists Foundation. Has an annual budget of approximately $10 million.

Publications:
American Ass'n of Orthodontists Bulletin. bi-m. adv.
American Journal of Orthodontics. m. adv.

Meetings/Conferences:
Annual Meetings: Spring/16,000
1999 – San Diego, CA(Convention Center)/May 14-18
2000 – Chicago, IL(McCormick Center)/Apr 29-May 3/20000
2001 – Toronto, Ontario(Metro Toronto Convention
Center)/May 5-9/15000

American Ass'n of Orthopaedic Medicine *(1982)*
90 South Cascade Ave., Suite 1190
Colorado Springs, CO   80903
Tel: (719)475-0032
Members: 600 individuals
Staff: 2
Annual Budget: $100-250,000
Exec. Director: Maylu Fleck

Historical Note
Professional association of physicians concerned with musculoskeletal system. Absorbed the Prolotherapy Association (founded in 1962). Membership: $195/year.

Publications:
Journal of Orthopaedic Medicine. 3/yr.
Newsletter. q.

Meetings/Conferences:
Annual Meetings: February or March
1999 – Las Vegas, NV(Alexis Park)/Feb. 18-20/300

American Ass'n of Owners and Breeders of Peruvian Paso Horses *(1962)*
P.O. Box 189
Ramona, CA   92065-0189
Tel: (760)789-5779
E-Mail: info@aaobpph.org
Web Site: http://www.aaobpph.org
Members: 500 individuals
Staff: 1
Annual Budget: $100-250,000
Exec. Secretary: Debbie Pye

Historical Note
Formed to establish a breed registry for the Peruvian Paso Horse (imported from Peru) and to encourage the breeding, training, and showing of the horse, as well as to inform the general public of the history and attributes of what has been called the "Cadillac of Pleasure Horses." Membership: $50/year.

Publications:
AAOBPPH Newsletter. 3/year. adv.
Owner/Breeder Membership Directory. a.

Meetings/Conferences:
Annual Meetings: With National Championship Show

American Ass'n of Pastoral Counselors *(1963)*
9504A Lee Highway
Fairfax, VA   22031-2303
Tel: (703)385-6967   *Fax:* (703)352-7725

E-Mail: info@aapc.org
Web Site: http://www.aapc.org
Members: 3,100 individuals
Staff: 6
Annual Budget: $500-1,000,000
Exec. Director: C. Roy Woodruff, Ph.D.
Director, Meetings and Publications: Barbara Gyomory

Historical Note
An international organization of clergy and other religious-oriented professionals whose ministry involves counseling and therapy.

Publications:
Directory. a. adv.
Newsletter. bi-m. adv.

Meetings/Conferences:
Annual Meetings: April-May/500-600
1999 – Albuquerque, NM

American Ass'n of Pathologists' Assistants *(1972)*
1711 County Rd. B., W. Suite 300N
Roseville, MN   55113-4036
Tel: (651)697-9264   *Fax:* (651)635-0307
Toll Free: (800)532 - 2272
Members: 500 individuals
Annual Budget: $25-50,000
Exec. Director: John Arlandson
AAPA Contact: Michelle Spindler

Historical Note
Established and incorporated in Ohio. Members have received training in anatomical pathology and related topics and provide a variety of technical services under the direction of a pathologist. Membership: $100/year (fellow); $150/year (affiliate); $10 one-time fee (student).

Publications:
AAPA Newsletter. q.

Meetings/Conferences:
Annual Meetings: October/150
1999 – Houston, TX(Doubletree)

American Ass'n of Petroleum Geologists *(1917)*
P.O. Box 979
Tulsa, OK   74101-0979
Tel: (918)584-2555   *Fax:* (918)584-0469
Toll Free: (800)364 - 2274
E-Mail: postmaster@aapg. org
Web Site: http://www.geobyte.com
Members: 30,030 individuals
Staff: 60
Annual Budget: $10-25,000,000
Exec. Director: Lyle F. Baie
Director, Communications: Larry M. Nation
Director, Meetings and Conventions: Michelle Mayfield
Director, Science: Jane Gallagher

Historical Note
Established in Tulsa in 1917 to provide for the dissemination of scientific and technical ideas and data in the field of geology as it relates to exploration for and production of oil, natural gas and engergy minerals and the environment. Originally the Southwestern Ass'n of Petroleum Geologists, it became the American Ass'n of Petroleum Geologists in 1918 and was incorporated in Colorado in 1924. A member society of the American Geological Institute. Has a budget of approximately $11 million. Membership: $62/year (full member); $10/year (student).

Publications:
AAPG Bulletin. m. adv.
AAPG Explorer. m. adv.
DEG Environment Geoscience. q. adv.
DEG Reporter. q. adv.

Meetings/Conferences:
Annual Meetings: Spring/7,600
1999 – Birmingham, England
1999 – San Antonio, TX/April 11-14
2000 – New Orleans, LA/April 16-19

American Ass'n of Pharmaceutical Scientists *(1986)*
1650 King St., Suite 200
Alexandria, VA   22314-2747
Tel: (703)548-3000   *Fax:* (703)684-7349
Web Site: http://www.aaps.org
Members: 7,500 individuals
Staff: 23
Annual Budget: $2-5,000,000
Exec. Director: John B. Cox, CAE
Director, Communications: Linda M. Williams
Director, Meetings and Expositions: Sharon R. Pichon
Director, Scientific Affairs: David Pang, Ph.D.
Director, Finance and Acting Director, Information Services:
    Maureen E. Downs

Historical Note
Incorporated in Washington, DC. AAPS members are pharmaceutical scientists in academia, industry, government and other research institutions. Membership: $100/year.

Publications:
AAPS Newsletter. adv. adv.
Journal of Pharmaceutical and Biomedical Analysis.
Journal of Pharmaceutical Marketing and Management. q.
Pharmaceutical Development and Technology.
Pharmaceutical Research. m. adv.

Meetings/Conferences:
Annual Meetings: October-November/5,000
1999 – New Orleans, LA(Convention Center)/Nov. 14-18

American Ass'n of Philosophy Teachers *(1978)*
9417 Doral Court, #2
Louisville, KY   40220
Tel: (606)233-8129   *Fax:* (606)233-8797
E-Mail: aapt@juno.com
Web Site: http://www.mnsfld.edu/depts/philosop/aapt.html
Members: 400 individuals
Annual Budget: $10-25,000

Exec. Director: Nancy S. Hancock

Historical Note
Incorporated in 1976, the AAPT is an internat'l organization with members in the US, Canada, Japan, South Africa and other countries. The organization is dedicated to the development and improvement of philosophy teaching at all levels of schooling. Sponsors a biennial International Workshop/Conference on Teaching Philosophy. Membership: $20/year (individual).

Publications:
AAPT News. 3 times/year. adv.

Meetings/Conferences:
Annual Meetings: With the American Philosophical Ass'n.

American Ass'n of Phonetic Sciences *(1973)*
Box 14095, Univ. Station
Gainesville, FL 32604
Tel: (352)392-2046   *Fax:* (352)392-6170
E-Mail: WSBROWN@CPD.UFL.EDU
Members: 150 individuals
Staff: 1
Annual Budget: under $10,000
Exec. Secretary: William S. Brown, Jr., Ph.D.

Historical Note
Affiliated with Internat'l Soc. of Phonetic Sciences. Membership: $15/year.

Publications:
Newsletter. semi-a. adv.

Meetings/Conferences:
Annual Meetings: Fall

American Ass'n of Physical Anthropologists *(1928)*
Dept. of Biological Anthropology
Duke University Medical Center
Durham, NC 27710
Tel: (919)684-2971   *Fax:* (919)684-8034
E-Mail: matt_cartmill@baa.mc.duke.edu
Members: 1,650 individuals
Staff: 3
Annual Budget: $25-50,000
President: Matt Cartwill

Historical Note
Founded in the District of Columbia in 1928. Affiliated with the Internat'l Ass'n of Human Biologists and the Soc. for the Study of Human Biology. Membership: $90/year (individual).

Publications:
American Journal of Physical Anthropology. m. adv.
Yearbook of Physical Anthropology. a.

Meetings/Conferences:
Annual Meetings: First week in April/800

American Ass'n of Physician Specialists *(1952)*
2296 Henderson Mill Rd., N.E.
Suite 206
Atlanta, GA 30345-2739
Tel: (770)939-8555   *Fax:* (770)939-8559
Toll Free: (800)447 - 9397
Members: 2,700 individuals
Staff: 10
Annual Budget: $1-2,000,000
Exec. Director: William J. Carbone
Manager, Certification: Trey Horton
Asst. Exec. Director: Martha White, CMP

Historical Note
Membership is open to D.O.'s and M.D.'s from all specialty categories. Formerly the American Academy of Osteopathic Surgeons, became American Ass'n of Osteopathic Specialists in 1984; assumed its current name in 1994. AAPS provides continuing medical education and board certification in 30 specialties. M.D.'s are accepted for associate membership. Membership: $450/year.

Publications:
Directory. a.
Newsletter. q.

Meetings/Conferences:
Annual Meetings: June
1999 - San Diego, CA(Sheraton)/June 10-13/150
2000 - San Juan, Puerto Rico(Ritz Carlton)/June 8-11/150

American Ass'n of Physician-Hospital Organizations
Historical Note
Becazme (1997) American Ass'n of Integrated Healthcare Delivery Systems.

American Ass'n of Physicists in Medicine *(1958)*
One Physics Ellipse
College Park, MD 20740-3846
Tel: (301)209-3350   *Fax:* (301)209-0862
E-Mail: aapm@aapm.org
Web Site: http://www.aapm.org
Members: 4,400 individuals
Staff: 11
Annual Budget: $250-500,000
Exec. Director: Salvatore Trofi, Jr.
Dep. Exec. Director: Angela R. Keyser
Director, Information Services: Michael Woodward

Historical Note
Founded in Chicago in 1958 and incorporated in Washington in 1965. Promotes the application of physics to medicine and biology. A member society of the American Institute of Physics and the American Institute for Medical and Biological Engineering. Membership: $165/year.

Publications:
Medical Physics. m. adv.

Meetings/Conferences:
1999 - Nashville, TN(Opryland)/July 25-29
2000 - Chicago, IL(Navy Pier)/July 23-28
2001 - Salt Lake City, UT(Salt Palace)/July 22-26
2002 - Montreal, Canada/July 14-18

American Ass'n of Physics Teachers *(1930)*
One Physics Ellipse
College Park, MD 20740-3845
Tel: (301)209-3300   *Fax:* (301)209-0845
Web Site: http://www.aapt.org
Members: 11,000 individuals
Staff: 25
Annual Budget: $2-5,000,000
Exec. Officer: Dr. Bernard V. Khoury
Director, Communications: Sina Kniseley
Director, Programs/Conferences/Exhibits: Maria Elena Khoury
Director, Meetings: Carol Heimpl
Director, Membership and Subscription Services: Ruth Spong

Historical Note
AAPT members are university, college, two-year college and high school physics teachers, students and friends. A member of the American Institute of Physics, AAPT is dedicated to advancing the teaching of physics and furthering the role of physics in our culture. Membership: $66-124/year (individual), $500/year (organization/company).

Publications:
AAPT Announcer. q. adv.
American Journal of Physics. m. adv.
Physics Today.
The Physics Teacher. 9/yr. adv.

Meetings/Conferences:
Semi-Annual Meetings: Winter & Summer, April with Am.
Physical Soc.
1999 - Anaheim, CA(Marriott)/Jan. 9-14

American Ass'n of Plastic Surgeons *(1921)*
2317 Seminole Road
Atlantic Beach, FL 32233
Tel: (904)359-3759
Members: 500 individuals
Staff: 1
Annual Budget: $100-250,000
Exec. Secretary: Fran Harris

Historical Note
Formerly (1942) American Ass'n of Oral and Plastic Surgeons.

Publications:
Plastic and Reconstructive Surgery. m. adv.

Meetings/Conferences:
Annual Meetings: Spring/650-700

American Ass'n of Podiatric Physicians and Surgeons *(1979)*
1328 Southern Ave., S.E., Suite 200
Washington, DC 20032
Tel: (202)562-2777   *Fax:* (202)562-5351
Web Site: http://www.infl1.com/aapps.html/index.html
Members: 1,500 individuals
Staff: 2
President: Dr. Richard Benjamin

Historical Note
Provides accreditation and certification for education and residency programs in podiatry. Membership: $185/year.

Publications:
AAPPS Newsletter. q. adv.

Meetings/Conferences:

American Ass'n of Poison Control Centers *(1958)*
3201 New Mexico Ave., N.W., Suite 310
Washington, DC 20016
Tel: (202)362-7217
Members: 50 individuals, 100 institutions
Administrator: Rose Ann G. Soloway

Historical Note
AAPCC represents poison control centers and personnel in the field of clinical toxicology. Certifies regional poison centers and individual practitioners; collects and publishes data on poison exposure in the U.S. Membership: $100/year (individual); $2,500/year (institution).

Publications:
Annual Report of the AAPCC's Toxic Exposure Surveillance
System. a.
The Poison Line.

Meetings/Conferences:
Annual Meetings: Fall/600

American Ass'n of Police Polygraphists *(1977)*
126 Silvery Ln.,
Vero Beach, FL 32960-5642
Tel: (561)978-7818
Members: 700 individuals
Staff: 1
Annual Budget: $25-50,000
Treasurer: Henry L. Canty

Historical Note
Polygraphists currently affiliated with a law enforcement, investigative agency or government service. Membership: $60/year.

Publications:
The Journal. q. adv.

Meetings/Conferences:
Annual Meetings: June

American Ass'n of Political Consultants *(1969)*
900 2nd St., N.E., Suite 217
Washington, DC 20002
Tel: (202)371-9585   *Fax:* (202)371-6751
Members: 650 individuals
Staff: 1
Annual Budget: $100-250,000
Exec. Director: Amy Marcenaro Heckman

Historical Note
Organized in Jan. 1969 in New York, AAPC is a bipartisan organization of political professionals members include strategy

consultants, media specialists, pollsters, campaign managers, corporate public affairs officers, elected and appointed public officials, academics, fundraisers, lobbyists, Congressional staff members, and vendors of products and services in the field of politics. Membership: $200/year (full member), $400/year (corporate).*

Publications:
Politea. q.

Meetings/Conferences:

American Ass'n of Port Authorities *(1912)*
1010 Duke St.
Alexandria, VA 22314-3589
Tel: (703)684-5700   *Fax:* (703)684-6321
E-Mail: info@aapa-ports.org
Web Site: www.aapa-ports.org
Members: 144 agencies, 232 firms & individual
Staff: 15
Annual Budget: $1-2,000,000
President and C.E.O.: Kurt J. Nagle
Director of Public Relations: Eileen E. Denne
Director of Government Relations: Stuart Binstock
Director, Membership Services: Edward L. O'Connell
Exec. V. President: Jean C. Godwin

Historical Note
Membership: $650/year (sustaining); dues for Ports, based on revenues.

Publications:
AAPA Advisory. w. adv.
AAPA Alert. w.
AAPA Handbook. a. adv.

Meetings/Conferences:
Annual Meetings: Fall
1999 - New York, NY/Sept. 27-Oct. 1
2000 - Veracruz, Mexico/Oct. 2-6
2001 - Quebec City/Oct. 1-5
2002 - Palm Beach, FL/Sept. 22-26

American Ass'n of Preferred Provider Organizations *(1983)*
Historical Note
Became the Ass'n of Managed Healthcare Organizations in 1996.

American Ass'n of Presidents of Independent Colleges and Universities *(1968)*
B346 ASB
Provo, UT 84602
Tel: (801)378-5625   *Fax:* (801)378-7521
Members: 175 individuals
Annual Budget: $50-100,000
Exec. Director: John B. Stohlton

Historical Note
Formerly (until 1969) known as the American Ass'n of Independent College and University Presidents. Membership: $225/year.

Publications:
Private Higher Education. irreg.

Meetings/Conferences:
Annual Meetings: Third weekend in February, usually in
Phoenix, AZ
1999 - Phoenix, AZ/Feb. 18-20

American Ass'n of Private Railroad Car Owners *(1977)*
421 New Jersey Ave., S.E.
Washington, DC 20003
Tel: (202)547-5696   *Fax:* (202)547-5697
Members: 512 individuals
Staff: 1
Annual Budget: $100-250,000
Exec. Director: M. Diane Elliott

Historical Note
Membership: $500/year (Amtrak-qualified owner), $350/year (non-Amtrak owner), $90/year (associate/non-owner).

Publications:
Private Varnish. bi-m. adv.
PV News Briefs. bi-m.

Meetings/Conferences:
Annual Meetings: Fall/250

American Ass'n of Professional Hypnotherapists *(1980)*
2443 Ash St., #D
Palo Alto, CA 94306-1858
Tel: (650)323-3224
Members: 1,500 individuals
Staff: 3
Annual Budget: $50-100,000
Exec. Director: William S. Brink

Historical Note
Members are hypnotherapists, clinical social workers, marriage and family therapists, psychologists, physicians, pastoral counselors, and others trained and experienced in the use of hypnosis in therapy. Membership: $55/year.

Publications:
Hypnotherapy Today. q. adv.
Nat'l Register of Professional Hypnotherapists. a.

American Ass'n of Professional Landmen *(1955)*
4100 Fossil Creek Blvd.
Fort Worth, TX 76137-2791
Tel: (817)847-7700   *Fax:* (817)847-7704
E-Mail: aapl@landman.org
Web Site: http://www.landman.org
Members: 8,000 individuals
Staff: 8
Annual Budget: $1-2,000,000
President: Don Clark
Director, Meeting Planning: Linda Wirt
Director, Education and Research: Robin Forte, CPL

Exec. V. President: Bruce Benes
Publications Editor: Le'ann Pembroke Callihan

Historical Note
A professional society of oil, gas and mining landmen, independent lease brokers, oil operators and company exploration managers. Formerly (1992) the American Ass'n of Petroleum Landmen. Membership: $75/year.

Publications:
AAPL United States Courthouse Directory. bien.
AAPL Update. bi-m.
Landmen's Directory & Guidebook. a. adv.
The Landman. bi-m. adv.

Meetings/Conferences:
Annual Meetings: Spring/2,500

American Ass'n of Professional Sales Engineers (1983)
55969 Jayne Drive
Elkhart, IN 46514-1325
Tel: (219)522-4837   *Fax:* (219)522-4837
Members: 600 individuals
Chairman/C.E.O.: Thomas S. Hill

Historical Note
Membership: $125/year (individual); $10/year (student).

Publications:
Newsletter.

American Ass'n of Professors of Yiddish (1974)
Historical Note
An "allied" organization of the Modern Language Ass'n. Has no paid staff. Membership: $15/year (individual).

American Ass'n of Psychiatric Administrators (1961)
1938 Peachtree Rd., N.W., Suite 505
Atlanta, GA 30309
Tel: (404)665-5664   *Fax:* (404)355-2917
Members: 413 individuals
Staff: 1
Annual Budget: $10-25,000
Exec. Director: Doreen Davis

Historical Note
Affiliated with the American Psychiatric Ass'n. Formerly (1975) Ass'n of Medical Superintendents of Mental Hospitals. Has no headquarters or permanent staff. Officers change annually. Membership: $40/year.

Publications:
Newsletter. q.

Meetings/Conferences:
Semi-Annual Meetings: Spring and Fall, always in conjunction
     with meetings of American Psychiatric Ass'n
1999 – Washington, DC
1999 – New Orleans, LA
2000 – Chicago, IL

American Ass'n of Psychiatric Services for Children (1948)
Historical Note
Address unknown in 1997.

American Ass'n of Psychiatric Technicians (1991)
336 Johnson Road, Suite 2
Michigan City, IN 46360
Tel: (219)861-0974   *Fax:* (219)879-1887
Toll Free: (800)391 - 7589
E-Mail: office@aapt.com
Web Site: http://www.aapt.com
Members: 7,500 individuals
Staff: 3
President and Exec. Director: George A. Blake

Historical Note
Dedicated to improving the quality of psychiatric facility care through training and certification of mental health workers. Awards the designation NCPT (Nationally Certified Psychiatric Technician. Membership: $24/year (individual); $200/year (corporate).

Publications:
AAPT News. q.
Journal of the AAPT. a. adv.

Meetings/Conferences:

American Ass'n of Public Health Dentistry (1937)
3760 S.W. Lyle Court
Portland, OR 97221
Tel: (503)242-0712   *Fax:* (503)242-0721
E-Mail: natoff@aol.com
Web Site: www.pitt.edu/aaphatilda/
Members: 750 individuals
Staff: 1
Annual Budget: $100-250,000
Exec. Administrator: James W. Toothaker, DDS, MPH

Historical Note
Formerly (1983) the American Ass'n of Public Health Dentists. Membership: $75/year.

Publications:
Communique. q. adv.
Journal of Public Health Dentistry. q. adv.

Meetings/Conferences:
Annual Meetings: usually in conjunction with American Dental
     Ass'n
1999 – Honolulu, HI/Oct. 6-8

American Ass'n of Public Health Physicians (1954)
515 N. State St.
Chicago, IL 60610
Tel: (312)464-4402   *Fax:* (312)464-5993
E-Mail: david_cloud@ama.assn.org
Members: 200 individuals
Staff: 1
Annual Budget: under $10,000

Exec. Director: David M. Cloud

Historical Note
Incorporated in the state of Texas. AAPHP advocates for physicians who plan, provide and administer preventive medicine and public health services in public, private or voluntary settings. Membership: $55/year; $13/year (AMA member).

Publications:
Bulletin. q.

Meetings/Conferences:
Annual Meetings: Spring

American Ass'n of Public Welfare Attorneys (1967)
810 1st St., N.E., Suite 500
Washington, DC 20002-4205
Tel: (202)682-0100
Members: 200 individuals
Annual Budget: under $10,000
Contact: Rosilyn King

Historical Note
An affiliate of the American Public Welfare Ass'n. Receives administrative support from APWA. Membership: $50/year.

Meetings/Conferences:

American Ass'n of Public Welfare Information Systems Management
810 1st St., N.E., Suite 500
Washington, DC 20002-4267
Tel: (202)682-0100   *Fax:* (202)289-6555
Members: 800 individuals
Annual Budget: $10-25,000
Contact: Rosslyn King

Historical Note
A constituent unit of the American Public Welfare Ass'n, which provides administrative support.

Meetings/Conferences:
Annual Meetings: Fall

American Ass'n of Radon Scientists and Technologists (1986)
1313 Dolley Madison Dr., Suite 402
McLean, VA 22101
Tel: (703)790-1745   *Fax:* (703)790-2672
E-Mail: aarst@burkinc.com
Web Site: http://www.aarst.com/aarst
Members: 1,100 individuals
Staff: 2
Annual Budget: $100-250,000
Exec. Director: Linda Hansen

Historical Note
AARST members are manufacturers, scientists and others concerned with radon gas testing and remediation. Membership: $75/year (individual); $250/year (company); $50/year (associate); $10/year/ (student).

Publications:
Radon Reporter. bim. adv.

Meetings/Conferences:
Annual Meetings: Fall/300

American Ass'n of Railroad Superintendents (1896)
18154 Harwood Ave.
Homewood, IL 60430
Tel: (708)799-4650
Members: 1000 individuals
Staff: 2
Annual Budget: $50-100,000
Secretary: Patricia Weissmann

Historical Note
Promotes continuing education among its members. Membership: $50/year.

Publications:
AARS News. q.
Proceedings. a. adv.

Meetings/Conferences:
Semi-annual Meetings: August and February
1999 – Duluth, MN(Radisson)/July 25-27

American Ass'n of School Administrators (1865)
1801 N. Moore St.
Arlington, VA 22209
Tel: (703)528-0700   *Fax:* (703)528-2146
Web Site: http://www.aasa.org
Members: 16,000 individuals
Staff: 50
Annual Budget: $5-10,000,000
Exec. Director: Paul D. Houston
Director, Marketing/Membership: C.J. Reid, II
Director, External Relations: Bruce Hunter
Director, Meetings and Conventions: Andrea Saris
Director, Administration: Donna Whisler
Director, Finance: Thuan Huynh
Dep. Exec. Director: E. Joseph Schneider
Director, Development: Darlene Pierce
Director, Information Technologies: K. David Weidner

Historical Note
Founded as the Nat'l Ass'n of School Superintendents, it became the Department of School Superintendence of the Nat'l Education Ass'n in 1870, the Department of Superintendents of NEA in 1907 and assumed its present name in 1937. Absorbed the County and Intermediate Unit Superintendents of NEA in 1968. Has an annual budget of approximately $9.5 million. Membership: $269/year (individual).

Publications:
Leadership News. bi. adv.
The School Administrator. m. adv.

Meetings/Conferences:
Annual Meetings: February-March/17,000
1999 – New Orleans, LA/Feb. 19-22

2000 – San Francisco, CA/March 3-6
2001 – Orlando, FL/Feb. 16-19

American Ass'n of School Librarians (1951)
50 E. Huron St.
Chicago, IL 60611-2795
Tel: (312)280-4386   *Fax:* (312)664-7459
Toll Free: (800)545 - 2433
E-Mail: aasl@ala.org
Web Site: http://www.ala.org/aasl
Members: 7,800 individuals
Staff: 11
Annual Budget: $250-500,000
Exec. Director: Julie A. Walker
Coordinator, Communications: Steven Hofman
Conference Planner: Cheryl Vargas
Coordinator, Member and Affiliate Services: Kathy Rogala

Historical Note
Membership composed of school library media specialists. A division of the American Library Association.

Publications:
Knowledge Quest. tri-m.
School Library Media. q. adv.

Meetings/Conferences:
1999 – Birmingham, AL(Convention Center)/Nov 10-14

American Ass'n of School Personnel Administrators (1940)
3080 Brickhouse Court
Virginia Beach, VA 23452-6859
Tel: (757)340-1217   *Fax:* (757)340-1889
Web Site: http://www.aspa.org
Members: 2,300 individuals
Staff: 3
Annual Budget: $250-500,000
Exec. Director: Esther Coleman

Historical Note
Founded as the American Ass'n of Examiners and Administrators of Educational Personnel, it assumed its present name in 1959. AASPA provides leadership in promoting effective human resource practices within education through professional development activities and a resource-based network. Membership: $100/year (individual).

Publications:
AASPA Members Handbook and Directory. a.
Handbook & Directory of Members in the U. S.
Prespectives. 11/year.
Promising Personnel Practices. a.
Research Publications.
Standards for School Personnel Administration.

Meetings/Conferences:
Annual Meetings: October/800
1999 – Pheonix AZ(Point Hilton Resort)/Oct. 21-24

American Ass'n of Sex Educators, Counselors and Therapists (1967)
P.O. Box 238
Mt. Vernon, IA 52314-0238
Tel: (319)895-8407   *Fax:* (319)895-6203
E-Mail: aasect@worldnet.att.net
Members: 1,750 individuals
Staff: 3
Annual Budget: $500-1,000,000
Exec. Director: Howard J. Ruppel, Jr., EdD,

Historical Note
Awards the designations Certified Sex Educator, Sex Counselor, Sex Therapist and Certified Supervisor to qualified members. Membership: $150/year (individual); $330/year (organizaton).

Publications:
Contemporary Sexuality. m. adv.
Journal of Sex Education and Therapy. q. adv.

Meetings/Conferences:
1999 – St. Louis, MO(Hyatt at Union Station)/Nov. 3-7/600

American Ass'n of Small Ruminant Practitioners (1968)
530 Church St., Suite 700
Nashville, TN 37219-2321
Tel: (615)254-3687   *Fax:* (615)254-7047
E-Mail: 74232.1077@compuserve.com
Members: 1,100 individuals
Annual Budget: $25-50,000
Administrator: Dee Ann Walker, CAE

Historical Note
Formerly (1988) American Ass'n of Sheep and Goat Practitioners. Primarily an association of veterinarians, AASRP also includes veterinary student members, foreign libraries, and owners of sheep, goats, llamas, deer, and more exotic small ruminants. It is an educational association which encourages research and dissemination of new knowledge to practicing veterinarians. Membership: $35/year (U.S.A.); $40/year (foreign); and $15/year (student U.S.A.); $20/year (student foreign).

Publications:
Proceedings. a.
The AASRP Newsletter, Wool & Wattles. q.

Meetings/Conferences:
Annual Meetings: With the AVMA
1999 – New Orleans, LA

American Ass'n of Spinal Cord Injury Nurses (1983)
75-20 Astoria Blvd.
Jackson Heights, NY 11370-1177
Tel: (718)803-3782   *Fax:* (718)803-0414
Web Site: http://www.aascin.org
Members: 1,300 individuals
Staff: 5
Annual Budget: $500-1,000,000
Exec. Administrator: Vivian Beyda, Ph.D.
Program Manager: Lisa Pollich

Historical Note
AASCIN members are nurses specializing in the care of spinal cord injuries. Limited to registered nurses (RN), licensed practical nurses (LPN), and licensed vocational nurses (LVN). Shares Administrative offices with American Paraplegia soc. Membership: $75/year (individual).

Publications:
SCI Nursing Journal. q. adv.

Meetings/Conferences:
Annual Meetings: September
1999 – Las Vegas, NV(Riviera)/Sept. 5-7
2000 – Las Vegas, NV(Riviera)/Sept. 5-7
2001 – Las Vegas, NV(Riviera)/Sept. 4-6

American Ass'n of Spinal Cord Injury Psychologists and Social Workers *(1986)*
75-20 Astoria Blvd.
Jackson Heights, NY   11370-1177
Tel: (718)803-3782   *Fax:* (718)803-0414
Web Site: http://www.aascipsw.org
Members: 530 individuals
Staff: 4
Annual Budget: $250-500,000
Exec. Administrator: Vivian Beyda, Ph.D.

Historical Note
Members are psychologists and social workers who treat individuals with spinal cord injuries. Shares administrative offices with American Paraplegia Soc. Membership: $75/year (individual).

Publications:
Compendium of Abstracts in Spinal Cord Medicine. 2/year.
Membership Directory. a.
SCI Psychosocial Process. q.

Meetings/Conferences:
1999 – Los Vegas, NV(Riviera)/Sept. 7-9
2000 – Los Vegas, NV(Riviera)/Sept. 5-7
2001 – Los Vegas, NV(Riviera)/Sept. 4-6

American Ass'n of State Climatologists *(1976)*
Oregon Climate Service
316 Strand Hall, Oregon State Univers.
Corvallis, OR   97331
Tel: (541)737-5705   *Fax:* (541)737-5710
E-Mail: taylor@oce.orst.edu
Web Site: http://www.ncdc.noaa.gov/ol/climate/aasc.html
Members: 130 individuals
Staff: 1
Annual Budget: under $10,000
President: George H. Taylor

Historical Note
Established in Asheville, NC, by 16 state climatologists as a method of interaction on climatological matters. AASC now includes 49 states. Has no paid officers or full-time staff. Membership: $15-25/year.

Publications:
State Climatology. q.

Meetings/Conferences:

American Ass'n of State Colleges and Universities *(1961)*
1307 New York Ave., NW
5th Floor
Washington, DC   20005
Tel: (202)293-7070   *Fax:* (202)296-5819
Web Site: http://www.aascu.org
Members: 425 institutions
Staff: 72
Annual Budget: $5-10,000,000
President: James B. Appleberry
Director, Communications: Gay Clyburn
V. President, Government Relations: Edward M. Elmendorf
Director,Meetings: Rosemary S. Lauth
V. President, Administration/Finance: Wendell Rayburn
Cheif Financial Officer: Wayne V. Sforza
Director, Membership, Services: Chris Bitting

Historical Note
Formerly the Ass'n of State Colleges and Universities. Absorbed the Ass'n of Upper Level Colleges and Universities and superseded the Ass'n of Teachers of Education Institutions founded in 1951. Has an annual budget of approximately $6.6 million. Membership fee based upon enrollment of institution.

Publications:
Memo: to the President. m.

Meetings/Conferences:
Annual Meetings: November/600
1999 – Puerto Rico

American Ass'n of State Highway and Transportation Officials *(1914)*
444 North Capitol St., N.W., Suite 249
Washington, DC   20001
Tel: (202)624-5800   *Fax:* (202)624-5806
Members: 52 state governmental agencies
Staff: 41
Annual Budget: $5-10,000,000
Exec. Director: Francis B. Francois
Director, Communications: Sunny Mays Schust
Director, Governmental Relations: Billy K. Higgins
Deputy Exec. Director: David J. Hensing

Historical Note
Founded as the American Ass'n of State Highway Officials, it was reorganized and renamed in 1973 to represent transportation agencies. AASHTO members are the state highway and transportation departments of the 50 states, Puerto Rico, and the District of Columbia. Annual budget is approximately $8.1 million.

Publications:
AASHTO Journal Weekly Transportation Report. w.
AASHTO Quarterly. q.

Meetings/Conferences:
1999 – Tulsa, OK(Doubletree Hotel)/Oct. 1-5
2002 – Nashville, TN(Opryland Hotel)/Sept. 28-Oct. 1

American Ass'n of State Social Work Boards *(1979)*
400 S. Ridge Pkwy., Suite B
Culpepper, VA   22701
Tel: (540)829-6880   *Fax:* (540)829-0142
E-Mail: info@aasswb.org
Web Site: http://www.aasswb.org
Members: 50 states, VI, DC, and Alberta, Can
Staff: 17
Annual Budget: $2-5,000,000
Exec. Director: Donna DeAngelis
Director, Communication: Troy Elliot
Meeting Planner: Dianne Wildgrube
Deputy Exec. Director: Kathleen Hoffman
Office Manager: Christine Breeden

Historical Note
Membership: based on number of licensed social works in each state.

Publications:
AASSWB Newsletter. bi-m.

Meetings/Conferences:
Semi-Annual Meetings: Spring and Fall
1999 – Minneapolis, MN(Radisson Plaza)/April 29-May 2/100
1999 – New Orleans, LA(Hotel Monteleone)/Dec. 10-12/100
2000 – Bismarck, ND(Holiday Inn)/April 27-30/100
2000 – Phoenix, AZ(Mesa Pavilion Hilton)/Nov. 10-12

American Ass'n of Stomatologists *(1993)*
c/o Lakewood Pathology Assocs.
1200 River Ave., Suite 10-E
Lakewood, NJ   08701
Tel: (732)901-7575
Members: 950 individuals
Annual Budget: under $10,000
President: Dr. David A. Lederman

Historical Note
Formerly (1987) the Federation of Dental Diagnostic Sciences and (1993) Academy of Oral Diagnosis/Radiology/Medicine, AAS is an umbrella organization for the American Academy of Dental Radiology, the American Academy of Oral Medicine and the Organization of Teachers of Oral Diagnosis. Purpose is to promote diagnostic science in dentistry in general and to obtain speciality recognition from the ADA specifically. Membership: $1,000/year (organization/company).

Publications:
AODRM Newsletter. 3/year. adv.

Meetings/Conferences:
Annual Meetings: March

American Ass'n of Stratigraphic Palynologists *(1967)*
c/o Amoco
P.O. Box 3092
Houston, TX   77253
Tel: (281)366-5399   *Fax:* (281)366-3195
E-Mail: dtpocknall@amoco.com
Web Site: http://www.geology.utoronto.ca/AASP
Members: 700 individuals, 110 institutions
Staff: 8
Annual Budget: $25-50,000
Secretary-Treasurer: David T. Pocknall, Ph.D.

Historical Note
Founded December 8, 1967 in Tulsa, Oklahoma with 32 charter members. Promotes the study of palynology-- the study of pollen and spores-- especially as it relates to stratigraphic applications and biostratigraphy. Has no paid staff. Membership: $30/year (individual); $40/year (institutional).

Publications:
Contribution Series. irreg.
Membership Directory. a.
Newsletter. q.
Palynology. a.

Meetings/Conferences:

American Ass'n of Suicidology *(1968)*
4201 Connecticut Ave., N.W., Suite 310
Washington, DC   20008
Tel: (202)237-2280   *Fax:* (202)237-2282
E-Mail: BERM101@ix.netcom.com
Web Site: http://www.cyberpsych.org
Members: 1000 individuals, 250 organizations
Staff: 3
Annual Budget: $250-500,000
Exec. Director: Dr. Alan L. Berman

Historical Note
Multi-disciplinary organization of professionals and concerned lay people. Makes available an up-to-date listing of suicide prevention centers and survivors' suicide support groups. Sponsors Nat'l Suicide Prevention Week. Membership: $100/year (individual), $200/year (organization).

Publications:
Newslink. q. adv.
Proceedings. a.
Suicide and Life Threatening Behavior. q. adv.
Surviving Suicide.

Meetings/Conferences:
Annual Meetings: Spring
1999 – Houston, TX(Doubletree)
2000 – Los Angeles, CA(Biltmore)

American Ass'n of Sunday and Feature Editors *(1948)*
803 Dogwood
Cedar Hill, TX   75104
Tel: (972)291-9998   *Fax:* (972)293-0830
E-Mail: judypat@classic.msn.com
Web Site: http://www.aasfe.org

Members: 250 individuals
Staff: 1
Annual Budget: $50-100,000
Administrative Secretary: Judy Stratton

Historical Note
Concerned with the improvement of Sunday newspapers and newspaper features. Membership: $100/year (organization).

Publications:
Feedback. q.
Style. semi-a.

Meetings/Conferences:
Annual Meetings: Fall
1999 – Vancouver, BC, Canada/Sept. 29-Oct. 2
2000 – New York, NY/Sept. 26-30
2001 – Chicago, IL/Sept. 25-29

American Ass'n of Surgeon Assistants *(1973)*
Historical Note
Name changed to American Ass'n of Surgical Physician Assistants (AASPA) in 1996.

American Ass'n of Surgical Physician Assistants *(1973)*
P.O. Box 867
Bernardsville, NJ   07924
Tel: (732)560-8378   *Fax:* (732)805-9582
Toll Free: (888)882 - 2772
E-Mail: surgicalpa@aol.com
Web Site: http://www.surgicalpa.com
Members: 540 individuals
Annual Budget: $50-100,000
Exec. Director: Susan E. Lusty

Historical Note
Formerly the American Ass'n of Surgeon Assistants. Membership: $115/year; $25/year (student).

Publications:
Membership Directory. a. adv.
Surgical Physician Assistant. m.
Sutureline. q. adv.

Meetings/Conferences:
Annual Meetings: Fall, with the American College of Surgeons Clinical Congress
1999 – San Francisco, CA/Oct. 9-10
2000 – Chicago, IL/Oct. 21-22

American Ass'n of Swine Practitioners *(1969)*
902 First St.
Perry, IA   50220
Tel: (515)465-5255   *Fax:* (515)465-3832
E-Mail: aasp@netins.net
Web Site: http://www.aasp.org
Members: 1,600 individuals
Staff: 2
Annual Budget: $250-500,000
Exec. Director: Thomas J. Burkgren, D.V.M.

Historical Note
Seeks to improve the quality of swine herd health programs and enhance the scientific knowledge to veterinarians through continued education. Members are graduate veterinarians. Membership: $95/year.

Publications:
"Swine Health and Production" Journal. bi-m. adv.
Proceedings of the AASP Annual Metting. a.

Meetings/Conferences:
Annual Meetings: March/800-900
1999 – St. Louis, MO(Adam's Mark)/Feb. 27-March 2
2000 – Indianapolis, IN(Westin)/March 11-14

American Ass'n of Teachers of Arabic *(1965)*
Brigham Young Univ.
280 HRCB
Provo, UT   84602
Tel: (801)378-3723   *Fax:* (801)378-5866
E-Mail: aata@byu.edu
Web Site:
    http://humanities.byu.edu/aata/aata_homepage.html
Members: 130 individuals
Staff: 5
Annual Budget: $10-25,000
Exec. Director: Kirk Belnap, Ph.D.

Historical Note
AATA's objective is to contribute to the enhancement of study, criticism and research in the field of Arabic language, literature and linguistics. Membership: $20/year (individual), $200/year (organization). Affiliated in 1964 with the American Council on Teaching of Foreign Languages and in 1970 with the Middle East Studies Association. Membership: $25/year (individual), $200/year (organization).

Publications:
AATA Newsletter. tri-a.
Al-Arabiyya. a. adv.

Meetings/Conferences:
Annual Meetings: with Middle East Studies Ass'n of North America

American Ass'n of Teachers of Esperanto *(1961)*
5140 San Lorenzo Drive
Santa Barbara, CA   93111-2521
Tel: (805)967-5241
Members: 60 individuals
Annual Budget: under $10,000
Editor, AATE Bulletin: Dorothy Holland

Historical Note
AATE members are persons who are teaching or have taught Esperanto, and educators interested in Esperanto. Affiliated with the Internat'l League of Esperantist Teachers. AATE has no paid staff. Membership: $25/year (individual).

Publications:
AATE Bulletin. q.

Meetings/Conferences:

American Ass'n of Teachers of French *(1927)*
MC-4510, So. Illinois Univ.
Carbondale, IL 62901-4510
Tel: (618)453-5731   *Fax:* (618)453-5733
Members: 10,000 individuals
Staff: 5
Annual Budget: $500-1,000,000
Exec. Director: Jayne Abrate

Historical Note
Member of the Joint Nat'l Committee on Languages. Sponsors programs for students such as the French honor society at the high school level, a national French contest, and summer scholarships placement service. Membership: $45/year (U.S.); $48/year (foreign); $22/year (student).

Publications:
AATF National Bulletin. q.
French Review. bi-m. adv.

Meetings/Conferences:
1999 - St. Louis, MO/July 11-14/350
2000 - Paris, France/700

American Ass'n of Teachers of German *(1926)*
112 Haddontowne Court, Suite 104
Cherry Hill, NJ 08034
Tel: (609)795-5553   *Fax:* (609)795-9398
E-Mail: aatg@bellatlantic.net
Web Site: http://www.aatg.org
Members: 7,000 individuals
Staff: 8
Annual Budget: $1-2,000,000
Exec. Director: Helene Zimmer-Loew

Historical Note
AATG sponsors a number of programs for students such as a national high school honor society, summer travel/study programs, and competitions. Also provides materials, awards, and placement for teachers. Membership: $30-50/yr. (based on salary)

Publications:
AATG Newsletter. q.
Die Unterrichtspraxis. semi-a. adv.
German Quarterly. q. adv.

Meetings/Conferences:

American Ass'n of Teachers of Italian *(1924)*
Dept. of Languages/Literatures
Arizona State University
Tempe, AZ 85287-0202
Tel: (602)965-6281   *Fax:* (602)965-0135
E-Mail: phaddini@asu.edu
Members: 1,200 individuals, 450 institutions
Staff: 1
Annual Budget: $25-50,000
Treasurer: Pier Raimondo Baldini

Historical Note
Allied with the Modern Language Ass'n and the American Council on the Teaching of Foreign Languages. Secretary-Treasurer serves for 4 years; others officers change triennially. Membership: $35/year (individual), $50/year (institution).

Publications:
AATI Newsletter. semi-a. adv.
Italica. q. adv.

Meetings/Conferences:
Annual Meetings: November, with the American Council on the Teaching of Foreign Languages/150

American Ass'n of Teachers of Slavic and East European Languages *(1941)*
1933 N. Fountain Park Drive
Tucson, AZ 85715
Tel: (520)885-2663   *Fax:* (520)885-2663
E-Mail: 76703.2063@compuserve.com
Web Site: http://clover.slavic.pitt.edu/ ~ aatseel
Members: 1,500 individuals
Staff: 2
Annual Budget: $50-100,000
Exec. Director: Gerard L. Ervin, Ph.D.

Historical Note
AATSEEL members are teachers of Slavic and East European languages. Membership: $40/year (administrators); $40/year (non-academic members); $30/year (asst. professors/instructors/lecturers); $25/year (secondary school teachers); $20/year (students).

Publications:
AATSEEL Newsletter. bi-m.
Slavic and East European Journal. q.

Meetings/Conferences:

American Ass'n of Teachers of Spanish and Portuguese *(1917)*
Univ. of Northern Colorado
210 Butler-Hancock Hall
Greeley, CO 80639
Tel: (970)351-1090   *Fax:* (970)351-1095
E-Mail: LSandste@bentley.unco.edu
Members: 13,000 individuals
Staff: 4
Annual Budget: $250-500,000
Exec. Director: Lynn A. Sandstedt, Ph.D.

Historical Note
Supports teachers of Spanish and Portugese at all levels through its publications, placement bureau, and other programs. Membership: $40/year.

Publications:
Enlace. 3/year.
Hispania. q. adv.

Meetings/Conferences:
Annual Meetings: August/500

1999 - Denver, CO(Marriott)July

American Ass'n of Teachers of Turkic Languages *(1985)*
Near Eastern Studies, 110 Jones Hall
Princeton University
Princeton, NJ 08544-1008
Tel: (609)258-1435   *Fax:* (609)258-1242
E-Mail: ehgilson@princeton.edu
Web Site: http://www.councilnet.org
Members: 160 individuals, 25 organizations
Annual Budget: under $10,000
Exec. Secretary-Treasurer: Erika H. Gilson, Ph.D.

Historical Note
AATT is a non-profit national association of professionals dedicated to the enhancement of study, criticism and research in the field of Turkic languages, literature and linguistics, and to improve and advance the teaching and learning of Turkic. Membership: $15/year (individual); $25-500/year (institution); $7/year (student).

Publications:
Bulletin. bi-a.

Meetings/Conferences:
Annual Meetings: Fall
1999 - Washington, DC(Sheraton)/Nov. 19-22

American Ass'n of Textile Chemists and Colorists *(1921)*
Box 12215
Research Triangle Pk, NC 27709-2215
Tel: (919)549-8141   *Fax:* (919)549-8933
E-Mail: daniels@aatcc.org
Web Site: http://www.aatcc.org
Members: 7,000 individuals, 300 organizations
Staff: 25
Annual Budget: $2-5,000,000
Exec. Director: John Y. Daniels
Director, Education: Peggy J. Pickett
Director, Membership Services: Birgit Patty
Editorial Director: Susan Keesee

Historical Note
Founded in Boston in 1921 with 270 charter members and incorporated in Massachusetts. Promotes the increase of knowledge of the application of dyes and chemicals in the textile industry and the use of textile wet processing machinery. Membership: $65/year(individual), $500/year (minimum for companies with sliding scale for size).

Publications:
AATCC Technical Manual. a.
Book of Papers from International Conference & Exhibition. a.
Membership Directory. a.
Textile Chemist & Colorist. m. adv.

Meetings/Conferences:
Annual Meetings: October/3,000
1999 - Charlotte, NC(Convention Center)/Oct. 12-15/3000
2000 - Winston-Salem, NC(Benton Convention Center)Oct. /3000
2001 - Greenville, SC(Palametto Expo Center)/Sept. 29-Oct. 2/3000

American Ass'n of Tissue Banks *(1976)*
1350 Beverly Road, Suite 220-A
McLean, VA 22101
Tel: (703)827-9582   *Fax:* (703)356-2198
Web Site: http://www.aatb.org
Members: 800 individuals & institutions
Staff: 4
Exec. Director: Jeanne Mowe

Historical Note
Incorporated in the State of Maryland. AATB members are individuals involved or interested in banking of tissues, cells or organs and institutions qualifying as accredited tissue banking facilities which participate in a tissue, cell or organ banking program including retrieval, processing, storage and distribution. AATB offers a program of Certification of Tissue Bank Personnel awarding the designation Tissue Bank Specialist (TBS). Membership: $150/year (individual); call for information on institutional membership.

Publications:
AATB Newsletter. q.
AATB Standards for Tissue Banking. irreg.
AATB Technical Manual for Tissue Banking. irreg.
AATB Tissue & Cell Report. semi-a. adv.

Meetings/Conferences:
Semi-annual Meetings: Spring and late August-early September
1999 - San Diego, CA(Sheraton)/August 21-25

American Ass'n of Trade and Industrial Instructors *(1969)*
Scioto County J.V.S.
P.O. Box 766
Lucasville, OH 45648
Tel: (614)259-5522   *Fax:* (614)259-2644
Members: 800 individuals
Annual Budget: under $10,000
Contact: Lynda Colley

Historical Note
Formerly (1995) Nat'l Ass'n of Trade and Industrial Instructors. AATII was formed to give the local teacher a voice as well as a responsiblity to provide input and direction in vocational education through the American Vocational Association. Membership: $5/year (individual).

Publications:
NATII News. 3/yr.

Meetings/Conferences:
Semi-annual Meetings: Summer with Vocational Industrial Clubs of America and Winter with American Vocational Association.

American Ass'n of University Administrators *(1970)*
P.O. Box 696
Heflin, AL 36264-0696
Tel: (205)463-2682   *Fax:* (205)463-1129
Members: 900 individuals
Staff: 2
Annual Budget: $50-100,000
General Secretary: Allan Watson, Ph.D.

Historical Note
A professional association of career educational administrators founded in Buffalo, New York. Membership: $90/year (individual), $400/year (institution).

Meetings/Conferences:
Annual Meetings: Summer

American Ass'n of University Affiliated Programs for Persons with Developmental Disabilities *(1968)*
8630 Fenton St., Suite 410
Silver Spring, MD 20910
Tel: (301)588-8252   *Fax:* (301)588-2842
E-Mail: AAUAPJ.org
Members: 80 universities
Staff: 15
Annual Budget: $1-2,000,000
Interim Exec. Director: Steve M. Eidelman
Director, Operations: Theresa Hosinski
Director, Legislative Affairs: Donna Ledder Meltzer

Historical Note
Members provide clinical settings in universities, teaching hospitals, and clinics operating exemplary services to teach graduate students and others studying developmental disorders such as mental retardation. Founded as the Ass'n of University Affiliated Facilities, it assumed its present name in 1975. Membership: $2,500-4,500/year (based on size of institution).

Publications:
AAUAP Network News. q. adv.

Meetings/Conferences:
Annual Meetings: Fall/350

American Ass'n of University Professors *(1915)*
1012 14th St., N.W., Suite 500
Washington, DC 20005-3465
Tel: (202)737-5900   *Fax:* (202)737-5526
Web Site: http://www.aaup.org
Members: 43,000 individuals
Staff: 45
Annual Budget: $2-5,000,000
General Secretary: Mary A. Burgan
Public Information and Member Development: Iris Molotsky
Director, Government Relations: Ruth Flower
Director, Meetings and Special Projects: Dori Binsted
Director, Organizing and Services: Patrick Shaw

Historical Note
Formed in New York City on the initiative of John Dewey. Promotes academic freedom and professional standards. Also represents the economic and legislative interests of full and part-time teachers, scholars, librarians and other academic professionals. Membership: $110/year (individual).

Publications:
Academe: Bulletin of AAUP. bi-m. adv.

Meetings/Conferences:
Annual Meetings: June/300-400
1999 - Washington, DC/June 9-14

American Ass'n of Utilization Management Nurses

Historical Note
Organization defunct in 1997.

American Ass'n of Variable Star Observers *(1911)*
25 Birch St.
Cambridge, MA 02138-1205
Tel: (617)354-0484   *Fax:* (617)354-0665
Toll Free: (800)642 - 3885
E-Mail: aavso@aavso.org
Web Site: http://www.aavso.org
Members: 11,000 individuals
Staff: 12
Annual Budget: $250-500,000
Director: Dr. Janet A. Mattei

Historical Note
Members are amateur and professional astronomers who gather and record data on stars which vary in brightness. Membership: $50/year.

Publications:
AAVSO Circular. m.
Alert Notices. irreg.
Bulletin. a.
Journal of AAVSO. semi-a.
Monographs. irreg.
Newsletter. semi-a.
Photoelectric Photometry Newsletter. q.
Reports of Variable Star Observations. irreg.
Solar Bulletin. m.

Meetings/Conferences:
1999 - Massachusetts

American Ass'n of Veterinary Anatomists *(1949)*
Dept. of Anatomy, Physiology & Pharma.
Auburn University
Auburn, AL 36849-5518
Tel: (334)844-4427   *Fax:* (334)844-4542
Members: 250 individuals
Annual Budget: under $10,000
Contact Officer: Paul F. Rumph, D.V.M.

Historical Note
Has no paid staff.

Publications:
AAVA Newsletter. semi-a.
Directory. bien.

Meetings/Conferences:

American Ass'n of Veterinary Clinicians (1958)
1024 Dublin Road
Columbus, OH 43215
Tel: (614)488-0617   Fax: (614)488-0352
Members: 476 individuals
Staff: 3
Annual Budget: $50-100,000
Exec. Director: Gene P. King

Historical Note
AAVC's purpose is three-fold: to provide for the ass'n of persons engaged in teaching clinical veterinary medicine, for the presentation and discussion of items of common interest and to further scientific progress by education and research in the field of clinical veterinary medicine. Membership: $8 (individual).

Publications:
1994-Arlington, VA(Hyatt Regency)/Oct. 1.
1995-Orlando, FL/May 17.

Meetings/Conferences:

American Ass'n of Veterinary Immunologists (1979)
USDA, ARS, 337 Bustad Hall
Washington State University
Pullman, WA 99164-7030
Tel: (509)335-6029   Fax: (509)335-8328
E-Mail: wgoff@vetmed.wsu.edu
Web Site: see text
Members: 260 individuals
Secretary-Treasurer: Dr. Will Goff

Historical Note
AAVI members are veterinarians and others with an interest in veterinary immunology. Membership: $15/year (individual); $5/year (student). AAVI's website id located at http://hsc.missouri.edu/vetmed/aavi/docs/aavihome.html

Publications:
AAVI Newsletter. irreg.

Meetings/Conferences:
1999 – Chicago, IL(Ramada Congress)/Nov. 8-10
2000 – Chicago, IL(Ramada Congress)/Nov. 7-9

American Ass'n of Veterinary Laboratory Diagnosticians (1958)
CVDLS, SVM, UC-Davis Turlock Branch Lab.
P.O. Box 1522
Turlock, CA 95381
Tel: (209)634-5837   Fax: (209)667-4261
E-Mail: abickfo@cvdls.ucdavis.edu
Members: 850 individuals
Annual Budget: $100-250,000
Secretary-Treasurer: Dr. Art Bickford

Historical Note
AAVLD, formerly the Conference of Veterinary Laboratory Diagnosticians, was organized in 1956 with the express purpose of: dissemination of information relating to the diagnosis of animal disease, coordination of diagnostic activities of regulatory research in service laboratories, establishment of uniform diagnostic techniques and the improvement of existing ones, and the development of a body that could act in a consultant capacity to the United States Animal Health Ass'n on uniform diagnostic criteria involved in regulatory animal disease programs. Has no paid staff. Membership: $50/year.

Publications:
Journal of Veterinary Diagnostic Investigation. q. adv.
Membership Directory. a. adv.
Newsletter. q. adv.
Proceedings. a. adv.

Meetings/Conferences:
Annual Meetings: October, with United States Animal Health Ass'n
1999 – San Diego, CA(Town and Country Hotel)/Oct. 8-15
2000 – Birmington, AL(Sheraton Hotel)/Oct. 20-27

American Ass'n of Veterinary Parasitologists (1956)
Box 708
Greenfield, IN 46140
Tel: (317)277-4439   Fax: (317)277-4532
E-Mail: snyder.daniel.E@Lilly.com
Web Site: http://www.vetmed.ufl.edu/users/aavp/aavp1.html
Members: 500 individuals
Staff: 1
Annual Budget: $25-50,000
Exec. Secretary-Treasurer: Dr. Daniel E. Snyder

Historical Note
Professional society for the promotion of veterinary parasitology and the dissemination of current scientific information. Affiliated with the American Veterinary Medical Ass'n. Membership: $20/year (individual).

Publications:
AAVP Newsletter. q.
Proceedings. a.

Meetings/Conferences:
Annual Meetings: With American Veterinary Medical Ass'n/200
1999 – New Orleans, LA
2000 – Salt Lake City, UT

American Ass'n of Veterinary State Boards (1957)
3100 Main St., Suite 208
Kansas City, MO 64111-1918
Tel: (816)931-1504   Fax: (816)931-1604
Web Site: http://www.aavsb.org
Members: 300 individuals, 53 jurisdictions
Staff: 1
Annual Budget: $50-100,000
Exec. Director: Charlotte P. Ronan

Historical Note
AAVSB members are members of state boards of veterinary examiners.

Publications:
AAVSB Newsletter. q.
Membership Directory. a.

Meetings/Conferences:
Annual Meetings: in conjunction with the American Veterinary Medical Ass'n

American Ass'n of Wildlife Veterinarians (1979)
Southeast. Coop. Wildlife Disease Study
Coll. of Vet. Med., Univ. of Georgia
Athens, GA 30602
Tel: (706)542-1741   Fax: (706)542-5865
Members: 483 individuals
Annual Budget: under $10,000
Secretary/Treasurer: Dr. Victor F. Nettles

Historical Note
Members are veterinarians specializing in the health of animals in their natural habitat.

Publications:
Membership Directory. irreg.
Newsletter. q.

Meetings/Conferences:
Annual Meetings: August, with the Wildlife Disease Ass'n.

American Ass'n of Women Dentists (1921)
645 N. Michigan Ave., Suite 800
Chicago, IL 60611
Tel: (312)280-9296   Fax: (312)280-9893
Toll Free: (800)920 - 2293
Members: 1000 individuals
Annual Budget: $100-250,000
Exec. Director: Sharon Gautschy

Historical Note
Founded as Ass'n of American Women Dentists; assumed its current name in 1979. Established to encourage women in the pursuit of a dental career.

Publications:
Chronicle. 5/year. adv.
Membership Directory. a. adv.

Meetings/Conferences:
Annual Meetings: Spring
1999 – Colorado
2000 – New England
2001 – Texas
2002 – Pacific Northwest

American Ass'n of Women Emergency Physicians (1983)
Historical Note
Address unknown in 1997.

American Ass'n of Zoo Keepers (1967)
Topeka Zoo, 635 S.W. Gage Blvd.
Topeka, KS 66606-2066
Tel: (785)273-1980
Toll Free: (800)242 - 4519
Members: 2,700 individuals
Staff: 3
Annual Budget: $50-100,000
Exec. Director: Ed Hansen
Administrative Secretary: Barbara Manspeaker
Managing Editor, AKF: Susan D. Chan

Historical Note
Membership: $35/year (professional keepers); $30/year (other individuals); $100/year (organization/company).

Publications:
Animal Keepers' Forum. m.
Conference Proceedings. a.

Meetings/Conferences:

American Ass'n of Zoo Veterinarians (1945)
6 North Pennell Road
Media, PA 19063
Tel: (610)892-4812   Fax: (610)892-4813
Web Site: http://www.worldzoo.org/aazv/
Members: 1,200 individuals
Staff: 4
Annual Budget: $100-250,000
Exec. Director: Dr. Wilbur Amand

Historical Note
Organized to advance programs of preventive medicine, husbandry and scientific research in the field of veterinary medicine dealing with captive and free-ranging wild animals. Membership: $60/year(student); $140/year (domestic); $155/year (overseas).

Publications:
Directory. a.
Newsletter. q.
Proceedings. a.
The Journal of Zoo and Wildlife Medicine. q. adv.

Meetings/Conferences:
Annual Meetings: Fall
1999 – Columbus, OH

American Ass'n of Zoological Parks and Aquariums
Historical Note
Became (1994) American Zoo and Aquarium Ass'n.

American Ass'n on Mental Retardation (1876)
444 North Capitol St. N.W., Suite 846
Washington, DC 20001-1512
Tel: (202)387-1968   Fax: (202)387-2193
Toll Free: (800)424 - 3688
E-Mail: aamr@access.digex.net
Web Site: http://www.aamr.org

Members: 9,200 individuals
Staff: 10
Annual Budget: $1-2,000,000
Exec. Director: M. Doreen Croser
Director, Meetings/Publications: Stephen H. Stidinger
Director, Programs: Paula A. Hirt
Director, Business and Finance: Paul D. Aitken
Membership Coordinator: Ana Montelieu

Historical Note
Organized June 6, 1876 in Elwyn, Pennsylvania as the Ass'n of Medical Officers of American Institutions for Idiotic and Feeble-Minded Persons. Name changed to American Ass'n for the Study of the Feeble-Minded in 1906 and became American Ass'n on Mental Deficiency in 1933. Became the American Ass'n on Mental Retardation in 1987. Incorporated in Pennsylvania in 1938. Affiliated with the Internat'l Ass'n for the Scientific Study of Mental Retardation. American Academy on Mental Retardation is the educational arm of AAMR. Membership: $80/year (individual).

Publications:
American Journal on Mental Retardation. bi-m. adv.
Innovations Series. irreg.
Mental Retardation. bi-m. adv.
Monograph Series. irreg.
News & Notes. bi-m. adv.

Meetings/Conferences:
Annual Meetings: May/2,000
1999 – New Orleans, LA(Hilton)/May 23-27
2000 – Washington, DC(Hilton)/May 30-June 3

American Assembly for Men in Nursing (1974)
CO-NYSNA
11 Cornell Rd.
Latham, NY 12110
Tel: (518)782-9400
E-Mail: AAMN@nysna.org
Members: 450 individuals
Annual Budget: $100-250,000

Historical Note
Founded as Nat'l Male Nurses Ass'n; assumed its current name in 1982. AAMN is a forum that enhances the nursing profession by supporting men in the profession. Membership: $60/year (R.N.s), $15/year (students).

Publications:
AAMN Interaction. q. adv.

Meetings/Conferences:

American Assembly of Collegiate Schools of Business
Historical Note
Became (1997) AACSB - the Internat'l Ass'n for Management Education,

American Association of Healthcare Administrative Management (1968)
1200 19th St., N.W., Suite 300
Washington, DC 20036-2401
Tel: (202)857-1100   Fax: (202)223-4579
E-Mail: scott_hall@dc.sba.com
Web Site: www.aaham.org
Members: 3,500 individuals
Staff: 4
Annual Budget: $500-1,000,000
Exec. Director: Dennis E. Smeage

Historical Note
APGAM's goal is to promote patient account management as an integral part of financial management in the health care industry. Provides educational and professional development for its members. Membership: $118/year (individual).

Publications:
Journal of Healthcare Administrative Management. 6/yea.
Legislative Currents. 6/year.

Meetings/Conferences:
Annual Meetings: October
1999 – Pheonix, AZ/Oct. 7-9

American Astronautical Soc. (1953)
6352 Rolling Mill Place, Suite 102
Springfield, VA 22152-2354
Tel: (703)866-0020   Fax: (703)866-3526
E-Mail: aas@astronautical.org
Web Site: http://www.astronautical.org
Members: 1,500 individuals
Staff: 4
Annual Budget: $250-500,000
Exec. Director: Carolyn F. Brown

Historical Note
Founded at the American Museum of Natural History in New York in November 1953 by a small group of engineers, scientists and others who wished to initiate an American activity similar to the British Interplanetary Society as spokesman for a substantive space program. Incorporated in the State of New York in 1954. Dedicated to the advancement of the astronautical sciences and spaceflight engineering and the encouragement of the astronautic arts. Regular memberships are for professionals involved in the field of astronautics with six years of related training and/or work experience. Membership: $75/year (individual).

Publications:
AAS History Series.
AAS Microfiche Series.
Advances in the Astronautical Sciences.
Journal of the Astronautical Sciences. q.
Science and Technology Series.
The Space Times/AAS Magazine. bi-m.

Meetings/Conferences:
Annual Meetings: November-December
1999 – Pasadena, CA(Pasadena Hilton)/Nov. 16-18/300

American Astronomical Soc. (1899)
2000 Florida Ave., N.W., Suite 400
Washington, DC 20009

Tel: (202)328-2010   *Fax:* (202)234-2560
E-Mail: aas@aas.org
Web Site: http://www.aas.org
Members: 6,400 individuals
Staff: 11
Annual Budget: $5-10,000,000
Exec. Officer: Dr. Robert W. Milkey
Associate Exec. Officer for Policy Programs: Dr. Kevin B. Marvel
Conference & Grants Manager: Diana Alexander
Financial Administrator: Barbara Cannon
Membership Coordinator: Sharon Savoy Thaxton

Historical Note
Organized September 6, 1899 at the Yerkes Observatory, Green Bay, Wisconsin as the Astronomical and Astrophysical Soc. of America. Name changed to American Astronomical Soc. in 1914. Incorporated in Illinois in 1928 and incorporated in DC in 1989. A member of the American Institute of Physics. Has an annual budget of $5.5 million. Membership: $105/year (individual); $30/first 2 years (junior); $750/year (corporate).

Publications:
AAS Job Register Newsletter. m.
AAS Membership Directory. a.
AAS Newsletter. 5/yr.
Astronomical Journal. m.
Astrophysical Journal. 3/m.
Bulletin of the American Astronomical Society. a.

Meetings/Conferences:
Semi-annual meetings: Winter and Summer
1999 – Austin, TX/Jan. 5-9
1999 – Chicago, IL/May 30-June 3
2000 – Atlanta, GA/Jan. 11-15

American Auditory Soc. (1973)
512 E. Canterbury Lane
Phoenix, AZ   85022
Tel: (602)789-0755   *Fax:* (602)942-1486
E-Mail: amandsoc@aol.com
Web Site: http://www.boystown.org/aas/
Members: 2,400 individuals
Annual Budget: $50-100,000
Secretary-Treasurer: Wayne J. Staab, Ph.D.

Historical Note
Formerly (1982) American Audiology Soc. Members are health professionals, audiologists, otolaryngologists, scientists, hearing aid manufacturers, educators of the hearing impaired and others with an interest in hearing. Membership: $55/year.

Publications:
Bulletin of the AAS. 3/year. adv.
Ear and Hearing. bi-m. adv.

Meetings/Conferences:
Annual Meetings: in conjunction with American Academy of Audiology
1999 – Scottsdale, AZ(Holiday Inn Sunspree Resort)/March 5-6/250

American Auto Racing Writers and Broadcasters Ass'n (1955)
922 North Pass Ave.
Burbank, CA   91505-2703
Tel: (818)842-7005   *Fax:* (818)842-7020
Web Site: http://www.RIS.Com
Members: 525 individuals
Staff: 1
Annual Budget: under $10,000
President: Norma "Dusty" Brandel

Historical Note
Established in Indianapolis in 1955 with 17 charter members. Members are professional journalists who regularly cover auto racing and related sports events. Membership: $45/year (individual); $65/year (affiliate); $300/year (association/corporation).

Publications:
Indiana All-America Team Program. a. adv.
Newsletter. m. adv.

Meetings/Conferences:
Annual Meetings: May, usually in Indianapolis, IN

American Automatic Control Council (1957)
Department of ECE, Northwestern Univ.
2145 Sheridan Road
Evanston, IL   60208-3118
Tel: (847)491-8175   *Fax:* (847)491-4455
E-Mail: aacc@ece.nwu.edu
Web Site: http://www.ece.nwu.edu/~ahaddad/aacc/
Members: 7 societies
Staff: 1
Annual Budget: $100-250,000
Secretary: Abraham H. Haddad, Ph.D.

Historical Note
Founded in Chicago, IL in March, 1957 as North American Control Council, it assumed its present name in October of that year. AACC is a federation of sponsoring societies, including: American Institute of Aeronautics and Astronautics, American Institute of Chemical Engineers, American soc. of Civil Engineers, American Soc. of Mechanical Engineers, Ass'n of Iron and Steel Engineers, Institute of Electrical and Electronic Engineers, Innternat'l Soc. for Measurement and Control, and the Soc. for Computer Simulation. Serves as the U.S. representative in Internat'l Federation of Automatic Control. Membership: $800/year (organization).

Publications:
AACC Newsletter. semi-a.
Proceedings of the American Control Conference. a.

Meetings/Conferences:
Annual Meetings: American Control Conference in June
1999 – San Diego, CA(Hyatt Regency)/June 2-4/1000
2000 – Chicago, IL(Hyatt Regency)/June 28-30/1000
2001 – Arlington, VA(Crystal Gateway Marriott)/June 18-20/1000

American Automobile Manufacturers Ass'n (1913)
1401 H St., N.W., Suite 900
Washington, DC   20005-2110
Tel: (202)326-5500   *Fax:* (202)326-5567
Web Site: http://www.aama.com
Members: 3 companies
Staff: 100
Annual Budget: $25-50,000,000
President and C.E.O.: Andrew H. Card, Jr.
V. President, Government Affairs: Robert E. Moss
Director, Administration: Linda M. Gambatesa
V. President & General Counsel: Phillip D. Brady

Historical Note
Formerly (1972) Automobile Manufacturers Ass'n and (1992) Motor Vehicle Manufacturers of the United States. The trade association of U.S. automakers, its member companies produce 80% of all domestic motor vehicles. Maintains and office in Detroit, Michigan and eight regional offices. Has an annual budget of approximately $30 million.

Publications:
Motor Vehicle Facts & Figures. a.
World Motor Vehicle Data Book. a.

Meetings/Conferences:
Annual Meetings: June

American Automotive Leasing Ass'n (1955)
700 13th St., N.W., Suite 350
Washington, DC   20005
Tel: (202)393-7292   *Fax:* (202)393-7293
E-Mail: aala@bolandmadigan.com
Members: 36 companies
Staff: 2
Annual Budget: $250-500,000
Exec. Director: Mary T. Tavenner

Historical Note
Formed in late 1955 by 19 charter auto leasing companies in response to an effort by the IRS to deny leasing companies capital gains treatment on the sale of their used vehicles. Members are large and small commercial leasing and fleet management companies.

Meetings/Conferences:
1999 – Colorado Springs, CO(The Broadmoor)/Sept. 26-28/40

American Bakers Ass'n (1897)
1350 Eye St., N.W., Suite 1290
Washington, DC   20005
Tel: (202)789-0300   *Fax:* (202)898-1164
Web Site: http://www.americanbakers.org
Members: 300 companies
Staff: 12
Annual Budget: $2-5,000,000
President: Paul C. Abenante
V. President, Government Relations: Robb S. MacKie, II
Manager, Conventions and Shows: Nikki Gayhart
V. President, Finance and Administration: Lisa B. Maloney

Historical Note
Formed at a meeting in Walter Baker & Co.'s room in the Mechanics' Building, Boston, October 20, 1897 at which eleven states and two Canadian provinces were represented. Known originally as the Nat'l Ass'n of Master Bakers and then the American Ass'n of the Baking Industry, it has operated under its present name since 1921. Incorporated in Illinois in 1917, it is affiliated with the American Institute of Baking. Supports the BREAD Political Action Committee.

Publications:
Bulletin. w.

Meetings/Conferences:
Annual Meetings: Spring
1999 – Scottsdale, AZ(Phoenician Resort)/April 18-22

American Bandmasters Ass'n (1929)
1521 S. Pickard Ave.
Norman, OK   73072-6316
Tel: (405)321-3373   *Fax:* (405)321-4117
E-Mail: thurston3@jumo.com
Web Site: http://www.uiowa.edu/~bands/aba/aba/html
Members: 325 individuals
Staff: 1
Annual Budget: under $10,000
Secretary-Treasurer: Richard E. Thurston, Ph.D.

Historical Note
Formed at a meeting on July 5, 1929 at the Hotel Pennsylvania in New York City. Incorporated March 13, 1930 in the State of New York.

Publications:
Directory. a.
Journal of Band Research. semi-a.

Meetings/Conferences:
Annual Meetings: March/300
1999 – Cocoa Beach, FL(Holiday Inn)/March 3-6/300
2000 – Austin, TX(Radisson)/March 1-4/300
2001 – Las Vegas, NV(Luxor)

American Bankers Ass'n (1875)
1120 Connecticut Ave., N.W.
Washington, DC   20036
Tel: (202)663-5382   *Fax:* (202)296-9258
Web Site: http://www.aba.com
Members: 9,000 individuals
Staff: 400
Annual Budget: $50-100,000,000
Exec. V. President: Donald G. Ogilvie
Exec. Director, Communications: Virginia Dean
Exec. Director, Government Relations: Edward L. Yingling
Director, Convention/Meeting Services: Paul R. Rossi
Director, Regulatory Compliance: Joseph V. Mock, Jr.

Historical Note
Organized in Saratoga, NY, July 20-22, 1875. Absorbed the Charge Account Bankers Ass'n and the Foundation for Full Service Banks in 1972. ABA represents over 90% of the nation's banks. The American Institute of Banking is a section of the ABA; BankPac is its political action committee, and the Bank Marketing Ass'n is an affiliate of ABA. Has an annual budget of approximately $66 million.

Publications:
ABA Bankers News. w.
ABA Banking Journal. m. adv.
Bank Insurance & Protection Bulletin. m.
Bank Personnel News. m.
Consumer Banking Digest. bi-m.
Consumer Credit Delinquency Bulletin q.
EB Quarterly.
Leaders Letter. m.
Management Update of Personal Trust & Private Banking. bi-m.
Trust Letter. m.

Meetings/Conferences:
Annual Meetings: Fall

American Bankruptcy Institute (1982)
44 Canal Center Plaza, Suite 404
Alexandria, VA   22314-1592
Tel: (703)739-0800   *Fax:* (703)739-1060
E-Mail: info@abiworld.org
Web Site: http://www.abiworld.org
Members: 6,300 individuals
Staff: 14
Annual Budget: $2-5,000,000
Exec. Director: Samuel J. Gerdano
Director, Communications: Michele E. Parisi
Meeting Planner: Beth Gilkenson
Membership Coordinator: Chris Thackston

Historical Note
Incorporated in Virginia. The ABI provides a multi-disciplinary forum for the exchange of ideas and information on bankruptcy issues. American Board of Certiofication is certifying organization sponsored by ABI. Membership: $170/year (private sector individual); $85/year (government/academic individual).

Publications:
ABI Directory. a. adv.
ABI Law Review.
ABI Newsletter. 10/year. adv.
Bulletins. irreg.

Meetings/Conferences:
Semi-Annual Meetings: May and December
1999 – Washington, DC(JW Marriott)/April 15-18/500

American Baptist Homes and Hospitals Ass'n (1935)
P.O. Box 851
Valley Forge, PA   19482-0851
Tel: (610)768-2411   *Fax:* (610)768-2470
Members: 112 institutions
Staff: 2
Exec. Director: Rosalie Norman-McNaney

Historical Note
ABHHA members are retirement/nursing homes, hospitals, children's homes.

Publications:
Directory. a.
Perspective Newsletter. q.

American Bar Ass'n (1878)
750 N. Lake Shore Drive
Chicago, IL   60611-4403
Tel: (312)988-5000   *Fax:* (312)988-6281
E-Mail: info@abanet.org
Web Site: http://www.abanet.org
Members: 375,000 individuals
Staff: 750
Annual Budget: $50-100,000,000
Exec. Director: Robert Stein
Assoc. Exec. Director: Marina Jacks
Assoc. Exec. Director, Communications: Sarina Butler
Assoc. Exec. Director, Administration: Elaine Weiss
Chief Financial Officer: John Hanle
Assoc. Exec. Director: Terry Kramer
General Counsel: Darryl L. DePriest
Director, Membership Benefits: Paula Cleave
Editor and Publisher: Gary Hengstler
Director, Editorial Services: E. Christine Tozer
Assoc. Exec. Director, Technology: Jay Ammerman

Historical Note
Represents more than 50% of practicing lawyers in the U.S. Federally approved accrediting agency for law schools. The American Law Student Ass'n is a division of the ABA. Maintains the nationally-honored Code of Professional Responsibility. Operates the Center for Professional Responsibility, and an information center for the bar admission and bar disciplinary agencies. Has an annual budget of $94 million. Membership: $15-$140/year (depending upon number of years admitted to the bar).

Publications:
American Bar Association Journal. m. adv.

Meetings/Conferences:
Semi-Annual Meetings: February and August
2000 – London, England/July 15-20

American Baseball Coaches Ass'n (1945)
108 S. University Ave., Suite 3
Mt. Pleasant, MI   48858-2327
Tel: (517)775-3300   *Fax:* (517)775-3600
E-Mail: abca@abca.org
Web Site: http://www.abca.org
Members: 5,000 individuals
Staff: 3
Annual Budget: $500-1,000,000
Exec. Director: Dave Keilitz

Historical Note
Formerly (1985) the American Ass'n of College Baseball Coaches. Founded in New York, NY. ABCA includes members from every division of amateur baseball. Membership: $30/year (U.S.); $35/year (North America); $40/year (overseas).
Publications:
Coaching Digest. semi-a. adv.
Covering All Bases. q.
Directory. a.
Meetings/Conferences:
Annual Meetings: January
1999 – Atlanta, GA(Marriott and Hyatt)/Jan. 2-5
2000 – Chicago, IL(Hyatt Regency)/Jan. 6-9

American Bashkir Curly Registry *(1971)*
P.O. Box 246
Ely, NY   89301
Tel: (702)289-4999   *Fax:* (702)289-8579
Members: 500 individuals
Staff: 4
Annual Budget: $10-25,000
V. President: Nancy Scott
Historical Note
Members are owners and breeders of rare horses with curly coats. Membership: $20/year (individual).
Publications:
Curly Cues. semi-a.
Meetings/Conferences:
Annual Meetings: June in Ely, NV(Bristlecone Convention
         Ctr.)/100
1999 – Ely, NV(Bristlecone Convention
         Center)/June 24-26/120
2000 – Alberta, Canada/June 19-21/150

American Basketball League
1900 Embarcadero Road
Palo Alto, CA   94303
Members: 9 teams
C.E.O.: Gary Cavalli

American Bearing Manufacturing Ass'n *(1933)*
1200 19th St., N.W., Suite 300
Washington, DC   20036
Tel: (202)429-5155   *Fax:* (202)828-6042
E-Mail: abma@de.sba.com
Web Site: http://www.abma-dc.org
Members: 35 companies
Staff: 4
Annual Budget: $250-500,000
President: Brian T. Borders
Coordinator, Membership: David S. Webber
Historical Note
Formerly (1993) the Anti-Friction Bearing Manufacturers Ass'n. Members are manufacturers of anti-friction bearings and of the major components used in their manufacture. Sponsors and supports the Bearing Technical Committee.
Publications:
U. S.
Meetings/Conferences:
Semi-Annual Meetings: Spring and Fall

American Beauty Ass'n *(1985)*
401 N. Michigan Ave.
Chicago, IL   60611-4206
Tel: (312)245-1595   *Fax:* (312)245-1080
Members: 250 corporations
Annual Budget: $500-1,000,000
Exec. Director: Paul D. Dykstra
Historical Note
Result of a merger of the Nat'l Beauty and Barber Manufacturers Ass'n and the UBA in 1985. The Nail Manufacturers Council, Manufacturers Representatives Task Force, and Esthetics Manufacturers and Distributors Alliance are divisions of ABA. Membership: $400/year.
Publications:
ABA Newsletter. bi-m.
Meetings/Conferences:

American Bed and Breakfast Ass'n *(1981)*
P.O. Box 1387
Midlothian, VA   23113-8387
Tel: (804)379-2222   *Fax:* (804)330-2729
E-Mail: info@abba.com
Web Site: http://www.abba.com
Members: 500 bed & breakfasts
Staff: 8
Annual Budget: $250-500,000
Director: Sarah Sonke
Historical Note
Acts as a clearinghouse of information on bed & breakfast accomodations, setting standards of operation and inspecting and rating B&B's. Membership: $300/year.
Publications:
Industry Sourcebook.
Inspected, Rated & Approved B&B's & Country Inns. a.
Shoptalk. bi-m.
Meetings/Conferences:
Annual Meetings: Not held.

American Bee Breeders Ass'n
Historical Note
Organization defunct in 1997.

American Beefalo World Registry *(1975)*
3770 121st Ave.
Allegan, MI   49010
Tel: (616)673-4966   *Fax:* (616)673-5008
Members: 250 individuals

Staff: 2
Annual Budget: $50-100,000
Exec. Director: Dan Coffindaffer
Historical Note
Formed in November, 1983 by a merger of the American Beefalo Ass'n (1975), the World Beefalo Ass'n and Internat'l Beefalo Breeders' Registry (1980). Absorbed the Bison Hybrid Internat'l Ass'n. Maintains a registry of full-blood and percentage Beefalo stock (full-blood is an exact 3/8 bison & 5/8 bovine cross); also maintains a registry for bison cross animals not qualifying as Beefalo, and a Beefalo Meat Registry. Membership: $65/year.
Publications:
American Beefalo World Registry Newsletter. bi-m.
Meetings/Conferences:
1999 – Missouri

American Beekeeping Federation *(1943)*
P.O. Box 1038
Jesup, GA   31598-1038
Tel: (912)427-4233   *Fax:* (912)427-8447
E-Mail: info@abfnet.org
Web Site: http://www.abfnet.org
Members: 1,850 individuals
Staff: 3
Annual Budget: $100-250,000
Exec. Director: Troy H. Fore, Jr.
Administrator/Bookkeeper: Christina Wright
Historical Note
Formerly Nat'l Federation of Beekeepers Ass'ns. Absorbed the Honey Industry Council of America in 1986. Members are honey producers, packers, shippers and suppliers. Membership: $200/year (commercial); $75/year (part-time); $25/year (hobbyist).
Publications:
ABF Newsletter. bi-m. adv.
Membership Directory. a. adv.
Meetings/Conferences:
Annual Meetings: January
1999 – Nashville, TN(Loews Vanderbilt)/500

American Belgian Blue Breeders Ass'n *(1988)*
P.O. Box 34663
Kansas City, MO   64116
Tel: (816)471-2583   *Fax:* (816)421-1991
E-Mail: JSpawn321@aol.com
Members: 240 individuals
Staff: 2
Annual Budget: $25-50,000
Exec. Director: James A. Spawn
Historical Note
ABBA members are breeders of Belgian Blue cattle. Maintains the national herd book registry for the Belgian Blue breed of beef cattle. Membership: $75/year.
Publications:
Belgian Blue Journal. q. adv.
Meetings/Conferences:

American Benefits Conference
Historical Note
Address unknown in 1995.

American Berkshire Ass'n *(1875)*
P.O. Box 2436
1769 US 52 West
West Lafayette, IN   47996-2436
Tel: (765)497-3618   *Fax:* (765)497-2959
Members: 500 individuals
Staff: 2
Annual Budget: $100-250,000
Historical Note
Breeders and promoters of Berkshire swine. Member of the Nat'l Pedigree Livestock Council. Membership: $20/year.
Publications:
The Berkshire News. 10/year. adv.
Meetings/Conferences:
Annual Meetings: July
1999 – Springfield, IL/July 9-10

American Beverage Institute *(1991)*
1775 Pennsylvania Ave., N.W., Suite 1200
Washington, DC   20006-4605
Tel: (202)463-7110   *Fax:* (202)463-7107
Toll Free: (800)843 - 8877
Web Site: http://www.abionline.org
Staff: 5
General Counsel: Richard B. Berman
Historical Note
Founded to represent the retail beverage industry, ABI shares accurate information with legislators, retailers, their employees, and the public regarding the responsible service and consumption of wine, beer, and distilled spirits.
Publications:
ABI News Letter. 9/year.

American Biological Safety Ass'n
1202 Allanson Road
Mundelein, IL   60060-3808
Tel: (847)949-1517   *Fax:* (847)566-4580
Exec. Director: Edward J. Stygar, Jr.
Publications:
ABSA Newsletter. q.
Journal of the American Biological Safety Ass'n.
Meetings/Conferences:
1999 – St. Louis, MO(Regal Riverfront)/Oct. 16-21/300

American Bison Ass'n *(1975)*

Historical Note
Became Nat'l Bison Ass'n in 1995.

American Black Book Writers Ass'n *(1980)*
Historical Note
Address unknown in 1997.

American Black Chiropractics Ass'n *(1980)*
Historical Note
Address unknown in 1995.

American Blind Lawyers Ass'n *(1971)*
c/o American Council of the Blind
1155 15th St., N.W., Suite 720
Washington, DC   20005
Tel: (202)467-5081   *Fax:* (202)467-5085
Toll Free: (800)424 - 8666
Web Site: http://www.acb.org
Members: 200 individuals
Annual Budget: under $10,000
President: Gary Austin
Historical Note
No paid staff. Officers change annually. Administrative services provided by the American Council of the Blind, located at the above address. Membership: $10-15/year.
Publications:
Newsletter. bi-m.
Meetings/Conferences:
Annual Meetings: July

American Blonde D'Aquitaine Ass'n *(1973)*
P.O. Box 12341
Kansas City, MO   64116-0341
Tel: (816)421-1991
E-Mail: JSpawn321@aol.com
Members: 150 individuals
Staff: 2
Annual Budget: $25-50,000
Exec. Director: James A. Spawn
Historical Note
Breeders and fanciers of Blonde D'Aquitaine cattle. Merged with the Nat'l Blonde D'Aquitaine Foundation in 1985. Membership: $50 for first year, $25/yr. thereafter.
Publications:
Blonde Bulletin. q. adv.
Membership Directory. a. adv.
Meetings/Conferences:

American Blood Resources Ass'n *(1971)*
P.O. Box 669
Annapolis, MD   21404-0669
Tel: (410)263-8296   *Fax:* (410)263-2298
E-Mail: 75463.3276@compuserve.com
Members: 95 companies
Staff: 10
Annual Budget: $1-2,000,000
President: James Reilly
Historical Note
Members are commercial plasma product processors, blood component collectors, distributors and manufacturers. Membership: $1,350/year (company, per each operating location).
Publications:
Annual Report. a.
FAX Letter. 10/year.
The Journal of the ABRA. q. adv.
Meetings/Conferences:
Annual Meetings: June, in Washington, DC/300
1999 – (Grand Hyatt)

American Board of Industrial Hygiene
6015 W. St. Joseph
Suite 102
Lansing, MI   48917-3980
Tel: (517)321-2638   *Fax:* (517)321-4624
E-Mail: ambrdih@ibm.net
Web Site: http://www.abih.org
Members: 18 boardmembers
Staff: 5
Annual Budget: $500-1,000,000
Exec. Director: Lynn O'Donnell, CIH
Historical Note
Certifies professionals who evaluate health and safety in the workplace employed by industry, labor unions, state, provincial and local governments, federal agencies, uniformed services and academia in the U.S., Canada, Australia and other countries. Membership: $70 (individual).
Publications:
Roster of Diplomats. a.

American Board of Medical Specialties *(1933)*
1007 Church St., Suite 404
Evanston, IL   60201-5913
Tel: (847)491-9091   *Fax:* (847)328-3596
Members: 24 organizations
Staff: 17
Annual Budget: $2-5,000,000
Exec. V. President: Stephen H. Miller, MPH
Director, Operations and Publications: Alexis L. Rodgers
Historical Note
Established as the Advisory Board for Medical Specialties, ABMS assumed its present name in 1970. As the parent organization for the 24 medical specialty Boards in the USA, it works closely with the American Hospital Ass'n, the Ass'n of American Medical Colleges, the American Medical Ass'n and the Council of Medical Specialty Societies in the accreditation of programs in graduate and continuing medical education. The mission of ABMS is to maintain and improve the quality of medical care by assisting the Member Boards in their efforts to develop and utilize professional and

educational standards for the evaluation and certification of physician specialists. The intent of the certification of physicians is to provide assurance to the public that a physician specialist certified by a Member Board of ABMS has successfully completed an approved educational program and an evaluation process which includes an examination designed to assess the knowledge, skills and experience required to provide quality patient care in that specialty. ABMS serves to coordinate the activities of its Member Boards and to provide information to the public, the government, the profession and its members concerning issues involving specialization and certification in medicine.

Publications:
Annual Report & Reference Handbook. a.
Directories for each medical specialty. bien.
The Official ABMS Directory of Board Certified Medical
 Specialists. a.

Meetings/Conferences:
Semi-Annual Meetings: Spring and Fall in Chicago at Hyatt
 O'Hare, O'Hare Westin or O'Hare Marriott/175

American Board of Nursing Specialties
4340 East-West Hwy., Suite 401
Bethesda, MD   20814-4411
Tel: (301)718-6514   *Fax:* (301)656-0989
E-Mail: abns@paimgmt.com
Members: 15 organizations
Staff: 3
Exec. Director: David Lewis, C.A.E.

Historical Note
ABNS promotes nursing certification and standards for nurse certification. Members are national nursing certification boards. Organizations which serve the nursing profession and are involved with credentialing issues are eligible for associate membership. Membership fee varies, $1,000-5,000/year.

Meetings/Conferences:
Semi-Annual Meetings: Spring and Fall/50

American Board of Periodontology (1939)
4157 Mountain Rd., Box 249
Pasadena, MD   21122
Tel: (410)437-3749   *Fax:* (410)437-4021
Members: 1,167 individuals
Staff: 2
Annual Budget: $250-500,000
Exec. Secretary-Treasurer: Gerald Bowers, D.D.S.

Historical Note
Membership: $95/year (individual).

Publications:
Directory. a.

Meetings/Conferences:
Annual Meetings: Fall/600-800

American Board of Podiatric Orthopedics and Primary Podiatric Medicine (1978)
22910 Crenshaw Blvd., Suite B
Torrance, CA   90505
Tel: (310)891-0100   *Fax:* (310)891-0500
E-Mail: ABPOPPMHQ@aol.com
Members: 2,850 individuals
Staff: 4
Annual Budget: $500-1,000,000
Exec. Director: Marc A. Benard, D.P.M.

Historical Note
An affiliate of American Podiatric Medical Ass'n, ABPOPPM is the certifying board responsible for non-surgical aspects of foot care. It offers comprehensive examinations in two specialty areas: podiatric orthopedics and primary podiatric medicine. APBOPPM emphasizes excellence in podiatric care and strives to further the cause of podiatry in general. Membership: $200/year (diplomate); $150/year (board-qualified member).

Publications:
Directory of Diplomates. a. adv.
Newsletter. semi-a. adv.

Meetings/Conferences:
Annual Meetings: with the American Podiatric Medical Ass'n

American Board of Preventive Medicine
9950 W. Lawrence Ave., Suite 106
Schiller Park, IL   60176-1310
Tel: (847)671-1750   *Fax:* (847)671-1751
Web Site: http://www.abprevenmed.org
Exec. Director: James Vanderpoge

American Board of Professional Psychology (1947)
2100 E. Broadway
Columbia, MO   65201-6082
Tel: (573)875-1267   *Fax:* (573)443-1199
E-Mail: ambra@abpp.org
Web Site: http://www.abpp.org
Members: 3,200 individuals
Staff: 4
Annual Budget: $250-500,000
Chief Administrative Officer: Nicholas Palo
Administrative Associate: Lorie Noe

Historical Note
Formerly the American Board of Examiners in Professional Psychology, ABPP awards its diploma in the areas of clinical psychology, counseling psychology, school psychology, industrial/organizational psychology, clinical neuropsychology, forensic psychology, family psychology, health psychology, behavioral psychology, psychoanalysis in psychology, and rehabilitation psychology. Applicants must have a minimum of three years postdoctoral and one year predoctoral full-time experience as a psychologist engaged in psychological services in the area of specialization. Membership: $110/year (individual).

Publications:
Diplomate. bi-a.

Meetings/Conferences:

American Board of Quality Assurance and Utilization Review Physicians (1977)
4890 W. Kennedy Blvd., Suite 260
Tampa, FL   33609
Tel: (813)286-4411   *Fax:* (813)286-4387
E-Mail: abqaurp@abqaurp.org
Web Site: http://www.abqaurp.org
Members: 8,236 individuals
Staff: 14
Annual Budget: $2-5,000,000
C.O.O.: H.E. Hartsell

Historical Note
ABQAURP provides education and certification programs in health care quality management and is accredited by the Accreditation Council for Continuing Medical Education (ACCME) for physicians. Membership: $245/year (physicians); $175/year (other healthcare professionals).

Publications:
ABQAURP Diplomate Directory. a. adv.
Diplomate Focus Newsletter. q. adv.

Meetings/Conferences:
Annual Meetings: November
1999 – San Diego, CA(Hyatt Regency La Jolla)/Nov. 6-7

American Board of Sexology (1986)
1929 18th St., N.W., Suite 1166
Washington, DC   20009
Tel: (202)462-2122   *Fax:* (202)642-2122
E-Mail: billeast@ct.net.net
Members: 2,000 individuals
Staff: 2
Annual Budget: $100-250,000
Exec. Director: W.B. Easterling

Historical Note
Earned doctorate required to be eligible for written and oral examinations leading to board certification. Membership: $200/trien.

Publications:
An Outline of Sexology.
Registry of Diplomates. a. adv.
The Diplomate. q. adv.

Meetings/Conferences:

American Board of Veterinary Practitioners (1978)
530 Church St., Suite 700
Nashville, TN   37219-2321
Tel: (615)254-3687   *Fax:* (615)254-7047
E-Mail: 74232.1077@compuserve.com
Members: 600 individuals
Staff: 2
Annual Budget: $100-250,000
Administrator: Dee Ann Walker, CAE

Historical Note
Certifying board for veterinarians who obtain advanced recognition through examination.

Publications:
ABVP News. q.

Meetings/Conferences:
1999 – Dallas, TX(DFW Hyatt)/June 25-27/300

American Boarding Kennels Ass'n (1977)
4575 Galley Road, Suite 400-A
Colorado Springs, CO   80915-2750
Tel: (719)591-1113   *Fax:* (719)597-0006
E-Mail: petsabka@aol.com
Web Site: http://abka.com
Members: 1,400 individuals
Staff: 6
Annual Budget: $500-1,000,000
Exec. Director: James J. Krack, CAE
Director Admin/Asst. Meeting Planner: Kathryn Eddy

Historical Note
Members are kennel suppliers, individuals or facilities that board pets, and others interested in the pet care industry. The association offers three levels of education and certification programs. The American Grooming Shop Association merged with ABKA in 1998. Membership: $165/year.

Publications:
Boarderline. bi-m. adv.
Pet Services Journal. bi-m.
Shoptalk. bi-m.

Meetings/Conferences:
Annual Meetings: Fall

American Boat and Yacht Council (1954)
3069 Solomon's Island Road
Edgewater, MD   21037-1416
Tel: (410)956-1050   *Fax:* (410)956-2737
Web Site: http://www.abycimc.org
Members: 700 individuals, 3,500 companies
Staff: 9
Annual Budget: $500-1,000,000
President: C.T. "Skip" Moyer, III
Manager, Education: Bonnie J. Michaels
V.P. and Technical Director: Thomas M. Hale
Manager, Finance: Elaine Mahaffey
Membership Coordinator: Sharon A. Busker

Historical Note
Members are companies and individuals concerned with the design, construction, and maintenance of recreational boats and related equipment. Develops standards and recommended practices. Membership: $75/year minimum (individual), $125/year minimum (company).

Publications:
American Boat and Yacht Council News. q.
Compliance Guidelines for Federal Boating Regulations. irreg.

Internat'l Navigation Rules (Inland). irreg.
Rules & Regulations for Recreational Boats. irreg.
Standards and Recommended Practices for Small Craft. irreg.

Meetings/Conferences:
Annual Meetings: February
1999 – Miami, FL

American Boat Builders and Repairers Ass'n (1943)
425 East 79th St., Suite 11B
New York, NY   10021-1006
Tel: (212)396-4246   *Fax:* (212)396-4243
E-Mail: ABBRA2@aol.com
Web Site: www.abbrayacht.com
Members: 350 individuals and companies
Staff: 1
Annual Budget: $50-100,000
Managing Director: Suzanne B. Sloan, CMM

Historical Note
Established as the Atlantic Coast Boat Builders and Repairers Ass'n, it assumed its present name in 1965. ABBRA was established to strengthen and encourage professionalism in the marine service industry. Membership: $100/year (individual); $375/year (company).

Publications:
Capstan. m.
Cruising and Repair Directory. a.

Meetings/Conferences:
1999 – Miami, FL(Radisson)/Jan. 16-19/70

American Boiler Manufacturers Ass'n (1888)
950 N. Glebe Road, Suite 160
Arlington, VA   22203-1824
Tel: (703)522-7350   *Fax:* (703)522-2665
E-Mail: abma@abma.com
Web Site: http://www.abma.com
Members: 114 companies
Staff: 10
Annual Budget: $1-2,000,000
President: Russell N. Mosher
Director, Public Affairs: Chris Rubsamen
Director, Meetings: Roselle Foley
V. President: W. Randall Rawson

Historical Note
Formerly (1960) American Boiler Manufacturers Ass'n. Incorporated in New Jersey. Members are manufacturers and suppliers of steam generating systems. Membership: $3,300/year (minimum).

Publications:
ABMA Buyers Guide.
ABMA News. m. adv.
Government Affairs Bulletin. m.

Meetings/Conferences:
Semi-Annual Meetings: January and June
1999 – Indian Wells, CA/Jan. 23-26
1999 – Orlando, FL/June 17-20

American Book Producers Ass'n (1980)
160 5th Ave., Suite 625
New York, NY   10010-7000
Tel: (212)645-2368   *Fax:* (212)989-7542
Toll Free: (800)209 - 4575
E-Mail: SKPASSOC@INTERNETMCI.COM
Members: 55 companies
Annual Budget: $25-50,000
President: David Rubel
Meetings Coordinator: John Campbell
Treasurer: Hiro Clark

Historical Note
Members are companies or individuals that develop concepts for books, and, based on a contractual agreement with a publisher, a business or other source, may produce finished books or production-ready film, camera-ready mechanicals, finished manuscripts, art and layouts. Membership: $500/year (company).

Publications:
American Book Producers Directory. a.
Newsletter. m.

Meetings/Conferences:
Monthly Meetings: 3rd Wednesday, except July and Aug.

American Booksellers Ass'n (1900)
828 South Broadway
Tarrytown, NY   10591
Tel: (914)591-2665   *Fax:* (914)591-2720
Web Site: http://www.bookweb.org
Members: 8,458 companies
Staff: 50
Annual Budget: $5-10,000,000
Exec. Director: Avin Domnitz
Director, Communications: Len Vlahos
Director, Government Affairs: Oren Teicher
Director, Professional Development/Education: Willard Dickerson
Assoc. Exec. Director, Operations: Eleanor Chang
Director, Research: Carol Miles
Director, Membership: Kathie Speer
Director, Book Publishing: Linda M. Miller

Historical Note
The trade association of U.S. retail bookstores. Started at the call of six booksellers in November, 1900, three from New York, and one from Grand Rapids, Cleveland and St. Paul. Formally organized the following year with an initial membership of 748. ABA represents the interests of booksellers through education, research, and the dissemination of information. Membership: $175/year.

Publications:
Book Buyer's Handbook. a.
Bookselling This Week. w. adv.

Meetings/Conferences:
Annual Meetings: June/38,000
1999 – Los Angeles, CA(Convention Center)/Apr. 30-May 1

American Border Leicester Ass'n
1039 SR 168
Darlington, PA 16115
Tel: (724)891-1440
E-Mail: ksavage@Timesnet.net
Members: 133 individuals
Annual Budget: under $10,000
Secretary/Treasurer: Kris Savage

Historical Note
Members are breeders of sheep. Maintains a breed registry, promotes sheep shows and education. Membership: $15/year.

Publications:
American Border Leicester Newsletter. q. adv.

Meetings/Conferences:
Annual Meetings: during the Maryland Sheep and Wool
   Festival/1st Saturday in May
1999 – Baltimore, MD(Howard County Fairgrounds)/50

American Brahman Breeders Ass'n *(1924)*
1313 La Concha Lane
Houston, TX 77054
Tel: (713)795-4444   *Fax:* (713)795-4450
E-Mail: abba@brahman.org
Web Site: http://www.brahman.org
Members: 1,800 individuals
Staff: 8
Annual Budget: $500-1,000,000
Exec. V. President: Jim Reeves
Director, Communications: Dala Dueitt

Historical Note
Breeders and fanciers of Brahman beef cattle. Member of the Nat'l Pedigree Livestock Council. Membership: $100/year (active membership).

Publications:
The Brahman Journal. m. adv.

Meetings/Conferences:
Annual Meetings: February, in Houston

American Brahmousin Council
P.O. Box 12363
North Kansas City, MO 64116
Tel: (816)421-1318   *Fax:* (816)421-1991
E-Mail: JSpawn321@aol.com
Members: 95 individuals
Exec. Director: James A. Spawn

Historical Note
Breeders of Brahmousin cattle.

Publications:
Brahmousin Connection. q. adv.

Meetings/Conferences:

American Bralers Ass'n *(1983)*
P.O.Box 75
Burton, TX 77835
Tel: (409)289-3021   *Fax:* (409)289-0170
Members: 200 individuals
Annual Budget: $25-50,000
President: Mark Brosche

Historical Note
Maintains a registry of Bralers (a crossbreed of Brahman and Salers cattle). Membership: $100/year.

Publications:
Bralers News. a. adv.

Meetings/Conferences:
Annual Meetings: February
1999 – Waller, TX

American Breed Ass'n *(1977)*
P.O. Box 853
Wagoner, OK 74477-0853
Tel: (405)257-3251
Members: 400 individuals
Annual Budget: under $10,000
Secretary-Treasurer: Sam Marker

Historical Note
Breeders and fanciers of cattle breed consisting of 1/2 Brahman, 1/4 Charolais, 1/8 Bison, 1/16 Hereford, and 1/16 Shorthorn. Member of the Nat'l Pedigree Livestock Council. Membership: $100/year (first year), $50/year (thereafter); $500 (lifetime).

Meetings/Conferences:
Annual Meetings: December-January

American Bridge Teachers' Ass'n *(1957)*
14840 Crystal Cove Ct. # 503
Fort Myers, FL 33919-7417
Tel: (941)437-4106
E-Mail: abta@juno.com
Members: 500 individuals
Staff: 1
Annual Budget: $25-50,000
Business Secretary-Treasurer: Pat Harrington

Historical Note
Membership: $35/year.

Publications:
ABTA Quarterly Magazine. q. adv.

Meetings/Conferences:
Annual Meetings: Precedes Summer Nationals of the American
   Contract Bridge League
1999 – San Antonio, TX(Marriott)/July 20-23
2000 – Anaheim, CA(Marriott)/Aug. 8-11
2001 – Toronto, ON, Canada/July 17-20

American Broncho-Esophagological Ass'n *(1917)*
S-2100 Med. Ctr. North
Vanderbilt Univ. Medical Center
Nashville, TN 37232-2559

Tel: (615)322-7267
E-Mail: james.duncavage@mcmail.vanderbilt.edu
Members: 350 individuals
Staff: 1
Annual Budget: under $10,000
Secretary: James Duncavage, M.D.

Historical Note
Established as the American Bronchoscopic Society, it assumed its present name in 1928. Affiliated with the American Academy of Otolaryngology - Head and Neck Surgery.

Publications:
Annals of Otolaryngology. adv. adv.

Meetings/Conferences:
Annual Meetings: Spring
1999 – Palm Desert, CA

American Brush Manufacturers Ass'n *(1918)*
1900 Arch St.
Philadelphia, PA 19103-1498
Tel: (215)564-3484   *Fax:* (215)564-2175
E-Mail: assnhqt@netoxs.com
Web Site: http://www.abma.org
Members: 165 companies
Staff: 3
Annual Budget: $250-500,000
Exec. Director: Kenneth R. Hutton

Historical Note
Absorbed the National Broom and Mop Council in 1982. Membership: $580-$7,200.

Publications:
"Brush Up" - ABMA Newsletter. q.

Meetings/Conferences:
Annual Meetings: March/300
1999 – Ponte Vedra Beach(Marriott Sawgrass)/March 17-20
2000 – San Diego, CA(La Costa Resort and
         Spa)/March 29-April 1
2001 – Florida
2002 – California(The Broadmore)
2003 – California

American Bryological and Lichenological Soc. *(1898)*
Dept. of Biology, MSN 321
George Mason University
Fairfax, VA 22030-4422
Tel: (703)993-1059   *Fax:* (703)993-1046
E-Mail: jlawrey@gmu.edu
Web Site: http://ucjeps.berkeley.edu/bryolab/ABLS.html
Members: 525 individuals
Annual Budget: $25-50,000
Secretary-Treasurer: James D. Lawrey

Historical Note
Originated in 1898 in Plymouth, New Hampshire, as the Sullivant Moss Chapter of the Agassiz Ass'n. Became independent in 1900 under the name of Sullivant Moss Soc. Name changed to American Bryological Soc. in 1949 and to the American Bryological and Lichenological Soc. in 1969. Incorporated in Missouri in 1965. Affiliated with American Institute of Biological Sciences. Devoted to the study of all aspects of bryophytes and lichens. Membership: $45/year, with publications (individual); $70/year, with publications (organization).

Publications:
Evansia. irreg.
The Bryologist. q.

Meetings/Conferences:
Annual Meetings: Summer
1999 – St. Louis, MO/Aug. 1-7

American Buckskin Registry Ass'n *(1962)*
Box 3850
Redding, CA 96049-3850
Tel: (530)223-1420
Members: 6,000 individuals
Staff: 3
Annual Budget: $25-50,000
Office Manager: Georgi Jones

Historical Note
Established as the Buckskin Registry Ass'n, it assumed its present name in 1965. Members are owners, breeders, and dealers of the Buckskin horse. Sponsors shows and other promotional events. Membership: $15/year (individual); $20/year (company).

Publications:
Newsletter. bi-m.

Meetings/Conferences:
Annual Meetings: early November

American Bureau of Metal Statistics *(1920)*
400 N. Main St., Suite 6
Manahawkin, NJ 08050
Tel: (609)597-3375   *Fax:* (609)597-6625
E-Mail: info@abms.com
Web Site: http://www.abms.com
Members: 6 companies
Staff: 5
Annual Budget: $500-1,000,000
Exec. Director: Brian Simpson

Historical Note
Formerly (1990) the American Bureau of Metal Statistics. Merged on January 1, 1975 with the Copper Institute (organized in 1927) and the United States Copper Association (established in 1934). Collects and disseminates statistical industry data on copper, lead, zinc and other non-ferrous metals. Collects and compiles statistical information for the Copper Development Ass'n and other non-ferrous metal trade associations. Membership: dues assessed pro-rata.

Publications:
Industry Reports. m.
Non-Ferrous Metal Data.
Yearbook of the ABMS. a.

Meetings/Conferences:
Semi-annual Meetings: April and September

American Bureau of Shipping and Affiliated Companies *(1862)*
Two World Trade Center, 106th Floor
New York, NY 10048
Tel: (212)839-5000   *Fax:* (212)839-5209
E-Mail: abs@eagle.org
Members: 750 individuals
Staff: 1470
Annual Budget: Over $100,000,000
Chairman/C.E.O.: Frank J. Iarossi
V.President, Info. Management Services: Gary A. Latin
Senior V. President, Technology: Donald Liu
V. President, Technology: John S. Spencer
President and C.O.O.: Robert D. Somerville
V. President, Treasurer & C.F.O.: Robert J. Bauerle
V. President and General Counsel/Secretary: Joseph E. Vorbach
V. President, Marketing and Communications: Stewart H. Wade
V. President, Human Resources: Donald M. Birney

Historical Note
Certifies the mechanical and structural fitness of ships, mobile and fixed offshore drilling units, and other marine structures. Publishes over 50 Rules and Guides related to the design, construction and operational maintenance of ships, mobile offshore drilling units, containers, machinery and other marine equipment. Has an annual budget of approximately $140 million.

Publications:
ABS Activity Report. m.
Annual Report. a.
Record of The American Bureau of Shipping. a.

Meetings/Conferences:
Annual Meetings: April, in New York, NY.
1999 – New York, NY

American Burn Ass'n *(1967)*
625 N. Michigan Ave., Suite 1530
Chicago, IL 60611
Tel: (312)642-9260   *Fax:* (312)642-9130
Toll Free: (800)548 - 2876
Web Site: http://www.ameriburn.org
Members: 4,000 individuals
Annual Budget: $25-50,000
Exec. Director: John Kirchbaum

Historical Note
Members are individuals concerned with the care, treatment and prevention of burns. Membership: $200/year (physicians); $125/year (non-physicians); plus initiation fee ($65).

Publications:
Annual Meeting Abstract. a.
Burn Care Resources in North America. bi-a.
Journal of Burn Care and Rehabilitation. bi-m. adv.
Roster of the ABA. a.

Meetings/Conferences:
Annual Meetings: Spring
1999 – Lake Buena Vista, FL(Coronada Springs
         Resort)/March 24-27
2000 – Las Vegas, NV(Mirage)/March 28-31

American Bus Ass'n *(1926)*
1100 New York Ave., N.W., Suite 1050
Washington, DC 20005-3934
Tel: (202)842-1645   *Fax:* (202)842-0850
Toll Free: (800)283 - 2877
E-Mail: abainfo@buses.org
Web Site: http://www.buses.org
Members: 3,000 companies
Staff: 23
Annual Budget: $2-5,000,000
President and C.E.O.: Peter J. Pantuso
V. President, Communications: Catharine King
Director, Marketing and Membership: Ginger D. Croce
Director, Government Relations: Jay Hansen
V. President: Sharon Stewart
Finance Officer: Ken Ryan
Director, Marketplace: Lynn M. Brewer
V. President, Publications: Mary Jo Shapiro

Historical Note
Formerly the Motor Bus Division and later the Nat'l Motor Bus Division of the American Automobile Ass'n. Name changed to the Nat'l Ass'n of Motor Bus Operators until 1960 when it became the Nat'l Ass'n of Motor Bus Owners. Assumed its present name on Sept. 19, 1977. Privately owned bus companies, bus manufacturers, accessory manufacturers, travel-tourism business and organizations and others concerned with bus service. Sponsors and supports the BusPac-Political Action Committee.

Publications:
ABA Regulatory Digest. m.
Destinations. m. adv.
Fast Facts. q.
Fast Fax. w.
The Motorcoach Marketer. a. adv.

Meetings/Conferences:
Annual Meetings: Fall

American Business Alliance for the Transition Economies of Eurasia
c/o Chamber of Commerce of the U.S.
1615 H St., N.W.
Washington, DC 20062-2000
Tel: (202)463-5473   *Fax:* (202)463-3114
E-Mail: europe@chamberusa.org
Members: 100 companies
Exec. Director: Gary Litman

Historical Note
Formed to consolidate the activities of several Chamber-supported divisions, including Polish-U.S. Economic Council, Romanian-U.S. Business Council, and Ukraine-U.S. Working Group. Members are

U.S. companies interested in developing business in the region.
Membership: $500/year.

American Business Conference (1980)
1730 K St., N.W., Suite 1200
Washington, DC   20006
Tel: (202)822-9300   Fax: (202)467-4070
Members: 100 individuals
Staff: 5
Annual Budget: $1-2,000,000
President: Barry K. Rogstad, Ph.D.

Historical Note
An association of 100 mid-size, high-growth companies, represented by their chief executive officers. Each member company generates from $25 million to $2 billion in revenue annually. Companies must maintain annual growth rates of approximately 15 percent a year to remain part of the ABC. Is concerned with tax and regulatory reform and preservation of the free enterprise system. Membership: $16,000/year.

Meetings/Conferences:

American Business Press (1906)
675 3rd Ave., Suite 415
New York, NY   10017-5704
Tel: (212)661-6360   Fax: (212)370-0736
Web Site: http://www.americanbusinesspress.com
Members: 180 companies & 1100 publications
Staff: 11
Annual Budget: $2-5,000,000
Manager, Membership: Carlese Weskock

Historical Note
Formed by a merger of Associated Business Publications (founded in 1906) and Nat'l Business Publications (founded in 1948). Members are specialized business magazines with audited circulation.

Publications:
ABP Fax.
ABP Newsletter. bi-m.

Meetings/Conferences:
Annual Meetings: Spring/350
1999 – Williamsburg, VA/May 10-13

American Business Women's Ass'n (1949)
9100 Ward Pkwy., Box 8728
Kansas City, MO   64114-0728
Tel: (816)361-6621   Fax: (816)361-4991
E-Mail: abwa@abwahq.org
Web Site: http://www.abwahq.org
Members: 70,000 individuals
Staff: 40
Annual Budget: $2-5,000,000
Exec. Director: Carolyn Bufton Elman
Director, Communications: Susan Fitch-Swanson
Manager, Convention: Stacey Smith
Director, Education: Mary Pebley
C.F.O.: Richard Baldwin
Director, Member Services: Susan Mizer

Historical Note
Dedicated to developing strong business skills in working women. Provides networking support. Membership: $35/year.

Publications:
Company Connection Business Owners Newsletter. q.
Leadership Edge Newsletter. q.
Prime Time Connection Retired Member Newsletter. q.
Women In Business Magazine. bi-m. adv.

Meetings/Conferences:
Annual Meetings: Fall
1999 – Kansas City, MO(Bartle Hall)/Oct. 6-10
2000 – Atlanta, GA(Hilton)/Nov. 1-5
2001 – Albuquerque, NM(Convention Center)/Oct. 31-Nov. 4
2002 – Nashville, TN(Opryland)/Nov. 6-10

American Butter Institute (1908)
2101 Wilson Blvd., Suite 400
Arlington, VA   22201
Tel: (703)243-6111   Fax: (703)841-9328
Members: 100 companies
Staff: 2
Annual Budget: $50-100,000
Exec. Director: Jerome J. Kozak
Program Administrator: Aniya Miner

Historical Note
Organized as the Nat'l Ass'n of Creamery Butter Manufacturers in 1908, ABI represents manufacturers and packagers of the majority of creamery butter and butter products. ABI is one of the nation's oldest dairy product associations.

Publications:
Butter Market Situation and Outlook. q.

Meetings/Conferences:
1999 – Chicago, IL(Marriott O'Hare)/April 25-27

American Buyers of Meeting and Incentive Travel (1989)
P.O. Box 1148
Wurstboro, NY   12790-1148
Tel: (914)888-4499   Fax: (914)888-0826
Members: 61 trade associations
Staff: 4
Annual Budget: $100-250,000
Exec. Director: Stanley Isaacs

Meetings/Conferences:
Annual Meetings: Early Spring

American Camping Ass'n (1910)
5000 State Rd. 67 North
Martinsville, IN   46151-7902
Tel: (765)342-8456   Fax: (765)342-2065
E-Mail: aca@aca.camps.org
Web Site: http://www.aca.camps.org

Members: 5,500 individuals
Staff: 39
Annual Budget: $2-5,000,000
Exec. Director: Peg L. Smith
Director, Public Relations: Bob Schultz
Deputy Director, Communications: Ruth Lister
Director, Conferences: Patricia Smilley
Deputy Director, Operations: Michael Dunbar
Director, Field Service: Karen Sivia
Dir., Standards, Development & Education: Connie Coutellier
Deputy Dir., Camp Services: Marge Scanlin

Historical Note
Established in 1910 as the Camp Directors Ass'n. Became the Camp Directors' Ass'n of America in 1924 and the American Camping Ass'n in 1935. Sponsors accreditation programs for camps and educational programs for camp director/owners. ACA offers over 250 products to camp and youth program directors through its direct-mail bookstore.

Publications:
Camping Magazine. bi-m. adv.
Guide to Accredited Camps. a. adv.

Meetings/Conferences:
Annual Meetings: Chicago, IL

American Cancer Soc. (1913)
1599 Clifton Rd. NE
Atlanta, GA   30329
Tel: (404)320-3333   Fax: (404)325-0230
Toll Free: (800)227 - 2345
Web Site: http://www.cancer.org
Members: 2,000,000 individuals
Staff: 4300
Annual Budget: Over $100,000,000
C.E.O.: John R. Seffrin, Ph.D.
Deputy Exec. V. President for Operations: Richard J. McGuinness, Jr.
Deputy Exec. V. President for Division Services and Field Operations: Donald E. Thomas
Deputy E.V.P., Research/Cancer Control: Harmon J. Eyre, M.D.

Historical Note
Formerly (1913) the American Soc. for the Control of Cancer. Incorporated in 1922. Name changed (1944) to American Cancer Soc. Inc. Has an annual budget of approximately $400 million.

Publications:
CA- a Cancer Journal for Clinicians. bi-m.
Cancer.
Cancer Facts and Figures. a.
Cancer Practice.

Meetings/Conferences:
Annual Meetings: Atlanta, GA in November

American Canine Sports Medicine Ass'n (1991)
P.O. Box 82433
Baton Rouge, LA   70884
E-Mail: acsma@acsma.com
Web Site: http://www.acsma.com
Members: 400 individuals
Staff: 1
President: Dr. Robert L. Gillette

Historical Note
Address unknown in 1996.

Publications:
Newsletter of the ACSMA. q.

Meetings/Conferences:
1999 – Kansas City, MO

American Car Rental Ass'n (1978)
1225 I St., N.W., Suite 500
Washington, DC   20005-3914
Tel: (202)682-4778   Fax: (202)789-4512
Members: 2,000 companies
Staff: 2
Annual Budget: $500-1,000,000
Exec. V. President: Jan M. Armstrong
Director, Operations: Melanie Penoyer

Historical Note
ACRA represents over 2,000 companies in the business of short-term renting and leasing of automobiles.

Publications:
ACRA Alert Legislative Bulletin. bi-m.
ACRA Report Newsletter. q.

Meetings/Conferences:
Annual Meetings: Spring
1999 – Las Vegas, NV(Ballys)

American Carbon Soc. (1957)
Historical Note
Address unknown in 1998.

American Cardiology Technologists Ass'n (1957)
Historical Note
A division of American Soc. of Extra-Corporeal Technology.

American Cargo War Risk Reinsurance Exchange (1939)
14 Wall St., Floor 8-A
New York, NY   10005
Tel: (212)233-3180   Fax: (212)240-0654
Members: 110 marine insurance companies
Staff: 2
Annual Budget: $100-250,000
Director: Edward K. Carpenter

Historical Note
During WW I, American insurance companies were dependent upon foreign insurers for reinsurance of war risks on cargo. In order to provide an independent domestic market for such risks, the Exchange was organized in June 1939, just prior to WW II. It has

provided a stable and economical reinsurance market for war risks on ocean cargoes since that time.

Meetings/Conferences:
Annual Meetings: April

American Cartographic Ass'n (1981)
Historical Note
A member organization of the American Congress on Surveying and Mapping.

American Cash Flow Ass'n (1990)
P.O. Box 2668
255 S. Orange Ave.,Suite 624 (ZIP 32801)
Orlando, FL   32802-2668
Tel: (407)843-2032   Fax: (407)648-9470
Toll Free: (800)253 - 1294
Web Site: http://www.acfa-cashflow.org
Members: 19,500 individuals, 1,500 companies
Staff: 7
Exec. Director: Deborah J. Bracknell
Coordinator, Communications: Judy Arndt
Coordinator, Member Enrichment: Sue Coles

Historical Note
Formerly (1997) the Nat'l Ass'n of Entrepreneurs, ACFA members are professionals working in fields related to cash flow and debt instruments. ACFA provides certification programs leading to the CMI (Certified Mortgage Investor), CFS (Certified Factoring Specialist), and DCFS (Diversified Cash Flow Specialist) designations. Membership: $199/year.

Publications:
American Cash Flow Journal Newspaper. m.
Cas Flow Connection Newsletter. m.
Industry Resource Guide. semi-a. adv.
Who's Who in the Diversified Cash Flow Industry. semi-a. adv.
Who's Who in the Factoring Industry. semi-a. adv.
Who's Who in the Private Mortgage Industry. semi-a. adv.

Meetings/Conferences:
Annual Meetings: Memorial Day weekend
1999 – Washington, DC/May 27-30

American Casual Furniture Fabric Ass'n
Historical Note
A division of the Industrial Fabrics Ass'n Internat'l.

American Catholic Correctional Chaplains Ass'n (1952)
409 Linden St.
Brooklyn, NY   11237
Tel: (718)821-1690   Fax: (718)386-4302
E-Mail: FWTP34A@prodigy.com
Members: 300 individuals
Annual Budget: under $10,000
Treasurer: Rev. John H. Wilkinson

Historical Note
Affiliated with The American Correctional Ass'n. Formerly the American Catholic Prison Chaplains Ass'n. Membership: $20/year $60/year (organization).

Publications:
Chap-lett. 3/year. adv.

Meetings/Conferences:
Annual Meetings: August, with the American Correctional Ass'n.
1999 – Denver, CO(Regis University)/Aug. 5-7/40
2000 – San Antonio, TX/Aug. 10-12
2001 – Philadelphia, PA/Aug. 9-11

American Catholic Historical Ass'n (1919)
Catholic Univ. of America
Mullen Library Rm. 318
Washington, DC   20064
Tel: (202)362-9620   Fax: (202)362-9624
Members: 1,096 individuals, 56 organizations
Staff: 2
Annual Budget: $25-50,000
Secretary-Treasurer: Rev. Robert Trisco

Historical Note
A professional society of those interested in the history of the Catholic church and the promotion of historical scholarship among Catholics. Founded in Cleveland, Ohio in December, 1919, by a small group of historians under the leadership of Peter Guilday and incorporated in the District of Columbia. Membership: $35/year.

Publications:
Catholic Historical Review. q. adv.

Meetings/Conferences:
Annual Meetings: January, with the American Historical Ass'n, which plans all meetings
1999 – Washington, DC(Marriot)/Jan. 8-10

American Catholic Philosophical Ass'n (1926)
Catholic University
Cardinal Station
Washington, DC   20064-0001
Tel: (202)319-5518
Members: 1000 individuals
Staff: 1
Annual Budget: $50-100,000
Nat'l Secretary: Therese-Anne Druart

Historical Note
Members are scholars and individuals interested in Catholic philosophy. Membership: $20-52/year (individual), $75/year (institution).

Publications:
Proceedings. a. adv.
The American Catholic Philosophical Quarterly. q.

Meetings/Conferences:
Annual Meetings: Spring

American Cemetery Ass'n (1887)

Historical Note
Became the Internat'l Cemetery and Funeral Ass'n in 1996.

American Center for Design *(1927)*
325 W. Huron St., Suite 711
Chicago, IL 60610
Tel: (312)787-2018   *Fax:* (312)649-9518
E-Mail: members@ac4d.org
Web Site: www.ac4d.org
Members: 2,500 individuals
Staff: 4
Annual Budget: $250-500,000
Exec. Director: Alan Freedman

Historical Note
Founded as the Society of Typographic Arts, the organization assumed its present name in 1989. ACD is composed of design and business professionals, educators and students. Acts as a primary resource for design-related information, supports quality design education, educates the business community on the value of design in meeting strategic objectives and builds public awareness of the role that design plays in shaping our culture. Membership: $125/year.

Publications:
American Center for Design Journal. a.
Design Year in Review. a.
Statements. semi-a. adv.

American Ceramic Soc. *(1898)*
735 Ceramic Place
P.O. Box 6136
Westerville, OH 43086-6136
Tel: (614)890-4700   *Fax:* (614)899-6109
E-Mail: customersrvc@acers.org
Web Site: http://www.acers.org
Members: 14,000 individuals, 385 companies
Staff: 55
Annual Budget: $5-10,000,000
Exec. Director: W. Paul Holbrook
Director, Communications: Mark Glasper
Director, Programs, Meetings, Expositions and Membership: Chris Schnitzer
Manager, Meeting Logistics: William R. Douglas
Manager, Promotions: Aimee F. Zerla
Director, Finance: Thomas Ciula
Assoc. Director: Lynn S. Moore
Director, MIS: Robert Mavros

Historical Note
Founded February 6, 1898 by Edward Orton, Jr. with 15 charter members. Incorporated in Ohio in 1905. The Nat'l Institute of Ceramic Engineers, the Ceramic Manufacturing Council and the Ceramic Education Council are affiliated classes of ACerS. Members include scientists, engineers and industrialists who produce products related to ceramics and related materials. Membership: $80/year (individual); $400/year (corporate).

Publications:
Ceramic Bulletin. m. adv.
Ceramic Engineering and Science Proceedings. bi-m.
Ceramic Source. a. adv.
Journal of the American Ceramic Society/Communications. m. adv.

Meetings/Conferences:
Annual Meetings: Spring/7,000
1999 – Indianapolis, IN(Convention Center)/April 25-29
2000 – St. Louis, MO/April 30-May 3
2001 – Indianapolis, IN/April 22-25
2002 – St. Louis, MO/April 28-May 1

American Chain Ass'n *(1971)*
6724 Lone Oak Blvd.
Naples, FL 34109-6834
Tel: (941)514-3441   *Fax:* (941)514-3470
E-Mail: rar@americanchainassn.org
Web Site: http://www.americanchainassn.org
Members: 7 companies
Staff: 3
Annual Budget: $50-100,000
Exec. Secretary: Robert A. Reinfried

Historical Note
Formerly (1971) American Sprocket Chain Manufacturers; successor to Ass'n of Roller and Silent Chain Manufacturers and Malleable Chain Manufacturers Institute. Membership: $2,500-15,000/year.

Publications:
Chains for Power Transmission and Material Handling. 1982. Identification,.
Indentification,.

Meetings/Conferences:
Annual Meetings: February/30
1999 – Litchfield Park, AZ(Wigwam)
2000 – Longboat Key, FL(Longboat Key Club)

American Chain of Warehouses *(1911)*
20500 South La Grange Road
Frankfort, IL 60423-1356
Tel: (815)469-4354   *Fax:* (815)469-2941
Web Site: http://acwiwarehouses.com
Members: 50 commercial warehouses
Staff: 2
Annual Budget: $100-250,000
Exec. V. President: Donald R. Greenland

Historical Note
Membership fees are set according to formula.

Publications:
Membership Directory. a.
Report for Members. m.

Meetings/Conferences:
Annual Meetings: May

American Chamber of Commerce Executives *(1914)*

4232 King St.
Alexandria, VA 22302-1507
Tel: (703)998-0072   *Fax:* (703)931-5624
Toll Free: (800)394 - 2223
E-Mail: info-request@acce.org
Web Site: http://www.acce.org
Members: 5,000 individuals, 1,200 state and local chambers
Staff: 36
Annual Budget: $2-5,000,000
President: Paul J. Greeley, Jr., CAE
V.President, Marketing and Communication Services: Marlies Mulckhuyse
V. President, Professional Development: Dina Lewis, CAE
Senior V. President, Operation and Ben. Services: Robert L. Eskridge
V. President, Executive Development Services: Eric L. Stowe
V. President, Internal Operations: Tamara Philibin

Historical Note
Merger of American Ass'n of Commercial Executives and Central Ass'n of Commercial Secretaries. Formerly (1949) Nat'l Ass'n of Commercial Organization Secretaries. Grants the professional CCE (Certified Chamber Executive) designation.

Publications:
Chamber Executive. m. adv.
Chamber JOBWATCH. bi-m. adv.
Quorum Call. q.

Meetings/Conferences:
1999 – Detroit, MI/Sept. 30-Oct. 4

American Cheese Soc. *(1982)*
P.O. Box 303
Delavan, WI 53115-0303
Tel: (414)728-4458   *Fax:* (414)728-1658
Web Site: http://www.cheesesociety.org
Members: 500 individuals
Staff: 1
Annual Budget: $10-25,000
Administrator: Laura Jacobs-Welch

Historical Note
ACS encourages the understanding, appreciation, and promotion of America's farmstead and specialty cheeses. Members include producers, distributors, retailers, and others with an interest in the cheese industry. Membership: $35-100/year (individual), $325-500/year (company).

Publications:
ACS Newsletter. bi-m.

Meetings/Conferences:
Annual Meetings: August
1999 – Shelburne, VT

American Chemical Soc. *(1876)*
1155 16th St., N.W.
Washington, DC 20036
Tel: (202)872-4600   *Fax:* (202)872-4615
Toll Free: (800)227 - 5558
Web Site: http://www.chemcenter.org
Members: 152,000 individuals
Staff: 1950
Annual Budget: Over $100,000,000
Exec. Director: John K. Crum, Ph.D.
Director, Communications: Denise Graveline
Director, Office of Legislative and Government Affairs: Flint H. Lewis
Head, Meetings and Divisional Activities: Christine P. Pruitt
Director, Education: Sylvia A. Ware
C.F.O.: Frank R. Young
Director, Membership: Nancy R. Gray
Counsel: Halley A. Merrell
Director, Information Systems: Terry Thornton

Historical Note
Founded in New York City on April 6, 1876. Incorporated in 1877. Granted a national charter by the Congress in 1937. Encourages the advancement of all branches of chemistry in the broadest and most liberal manner. Has an annual budget of approximately $250 million. Membership: $102/year.

Publications:
Accounts of Chemical Research. m.
Analytical Chemistry. semi-m. adv.
Analytical Chemistry News & Features. m.
Biochemistry. w. adv.
Bioconjugate Chemistry. bi-m. adv.
Biotechnology Process. bi-m. adv.
Chemical & Engineering News. w. adv.
Chemical Health & Safety. bi-m. adv.
Chemical Research in Toxicology. m. adv.
Chemical Reviews. m. adv.
Chemistry of Materials. m. adv.
CHEMTECH m. adv. adv.
Energy & Fuels. bi-m. adv.
Environmental Science & Technology. semi-m. adv.
Environmental Science & Technology News & Research Notes. m.
Industrial & Engineering Chemistry Research. m. adv.
Inorganic Chemistry. bi-w. adv.
Journal of Agricultural and Food Chemistry. m. adv.
Journal of Chemical and Engineering Data. bi-m. adv.
Journal of Chemical Information and Computer Sciences. bi-m. adv.
Journal of Combinatorial Chemistry. bi-m. adv.
Journal of Medicinal Chemistry. bi-w. adv.
Journal of Natural Products. m. adv.
Journal of Organic Chemistry. bi-w. adv.
Journal of Pharmaceutical Sciences. m. adv.
Journal of Physical & Chemical Reference Data. bi-m.
Journal of Physical Chemistry, A. w. adv.
Journal of Physical Chemistry, B. w. adv.
Journal of the American Chemical Society. w. adv.
Langmuir. bi-w. adv.
Macromolecules. bi-w. adv.
Modern Drug Discovery. bi-m. adv.
Organic Letters. bi-m. adv.
Organic Process Research & Development. bi-m. adv.
Organometallics. bi-w. adv.

Today's Chemists At Work. m. adv.

Meetings/Conferences:
Semi-Annual Meetings: Spring and Fall/10,000
1999 – Anaheim, CA/March 21-25
1999 – New Orleans, LA/Aug. 22-26
2000 – San Francisco, CA/March 26-31
2000 – Washington, DC/Aug. 20-25
2001 – San Diego, CA/April 1-6
2001 – Chicago, IL/Aug. 26-31
2002 – Orlando, FL/April 7-12
2002 – Boston, MA/Sept. 8-13

American Cheviot Sheep Soc. *(1924)*
R.R. 1, Box 100
Clarks Hill, IN 47930-9726
Tel: (317)523-2767
Members: 800 individuals
Staff: 1
Annual Budget: $10-25,000
Exec. Secretary: Ruth Bowles

Historical Note
Breeders and fanciers of Cheviot sheep. Member of the National Pedigree Livestock Council. Membership: $10 (lifetime).

Publications:
Breeders Directory. a.
Cheviot Journal. a.
The Banner. m. adv.

Meetings/Conferences:
Annual Meetings: November, in Louisville, KY

American Chianina Ass'n *(1972)*
Box 890
Platte City, MO 64079
Tel: (816)431-2808   *Fax:* (816)431-5381
E-Mail: aca@sound.net
Web Site: http://www.chicattle.org
Members: 1,044 individuals
Staff: 6
Annual Budget: $250-500,000
C.E.O.: Terry Atchison

Historical Note
Breeders and fanciers of Chianina beef cattle. Member of the Nat'l Pedigree Livestock Council. Membership: $50/year (individual and company).

Publications:
ACA Journal. 8/year. adv.

Meetings/Conferences:
Annual Meetings: Always, Louisville, KY in November

American Chiropractic Ass'n *(1930)*
1701 Clarendon Blvd.
Arlington, VA 22209
Tel: (703)276-8800   *Fax:* (703)243-2593
Toll Free: (800)986 - 4636
Web Site: http://www.amerchiro.org
Members: 22,000 individuals
Staff: 40
Annual Budget: $5-10,000,000
Exec. V. President: Garrett F. Cuneo
V.President, Communications: Cindy Yeast
Director, Communications: Felicity Feather
V. President, Government Relations: Pamela Phillips
Director, ACA-PAC: Steve LaPierre
Meetings Planner: Sue Ackley
V. President, Research: Dr. Christine Goertz
V. President, Member Services: Julie Warner de Martinez
Manager, Member Info. Center: Daniel Clancy
V. President, Managed Care and Insurance Relations: Andrew Aho

Historical Note
Founded in 1930 as the Nat'l Chiropractic Ass'n, it assumed its present name in 1963; chartered in Delaware. Sponsors the following specialty councils: Family Practice, Nutrition, Orthopedics, Neurology, Physiological Therapeutics, Sports Injuries and Physical Fitness, Diagnostic Imaging, Technique and Occupational Health. Promotes the philosophy, science and art of chiropractic, and the professional welfare of its members; promotes legislation defining chiropractic health care and public education of chiropractic. Conducts chiropractic survey and statistical study. Oversees the work of the ACA-PAC, its political action arm, and the American Chiropractic Foundation. Has an annual budget of approximately $7.7 million. Membership: $600/year.

Publications:
ACA Membership Directory. a.
ACA Today. m.
Journal of the ACA. m. adv.

Meetings/Conferences:
Annual Meetings: May-June

American Chiropractic Registry of Radiologic Technologists *(1982)*
2330 Gull Road
Kalamazoo, MI 49001
Tel: (616)343-6666
Members: 2,000 individuals
Staff: 2
Exec. V. President: Dr. Edward Maurer

Historical Note
Members are radiologic technologists working in chiropractic offices.

Publications:
Wavelengths Newsletter. bi-m.

American Choral Directors Ass'n *(1959)*
P.O. Box 6310
Lawton, OK 73506
Tel: (580)355-8161   *Fax:* (580)248-1465
Members: 19,000 individuals
Staff: 11
Annual Budget: $2-5,000,000

Nat'l Exec. Director: Gene Brooks, Ph.D.
Director, Development: Raymond W. Brock
Historical Note
A non-profit professional organization whose active membership is composed of choral musicians from schools, colleges and universities, community and industrial organizations, churches and professional groups. Active Membership: $55/year.
Publications:
The Choral Journal. 10/year. adv.
Meetings/Conferences:
Biennial Meetings: Odd years
1999 – Chicago, IL(Hyatt)/Feb. 24-27/8000

American Choral Foundation *(1954)*
Historical Note
A division of Chorus America, which provides administrative support.

American Cinema Editors *(1950)*
1041 N. Formosa Ave.
West Hollywood, CA   90046-6703
Tel: (213)850-2900   *Fax:* (213)850-2922
Members: 400 individuals
Staff: 1
Annual Budget: $100-250,000
Managing Director: Jenni McCormick
Historical Note
An honorary professional society. Presents the annual "Ace Eddie" award for film editing. Membership, though international, is concentrated in the Los Angeles area. Membership: $250/year.
Publications:
Cinemeditor. m. adv.
Meetings/Conferences:
Annual Meetings: Always Los Angeles, CA/4th Tuesday in June

American Classical League *(1919)*
Miami University
Oxford, OH   45056
Tel: (513)529-7741   *Fax:* (513)529-7742
Members: 4,000 individuals
Staff: 5
Annual Budget: $25-50,000
Manager: Geri Dutra
Historical Note
High school and college teachers of Latin and Greek. Supports the Junior Classical League – high school Latin and Greek students. Membership: $35/year (individual); $15/year (student); $25/year (retired).
Publications:
Classical Outlook. q. adv.
Meetings/Conferences:
Annual Meetings: Summer
1999 – Amherst, MA(Univ. of Mass)/June 24-26

American Cleft Palate-Craniofacial Ass'n *(1943)*
P.O. Box 2226
Chapel Hill, NC   27514-2226
Tel: (919)933-9044   *Fax:* (919)933-9604
E-Mail: cleftline@aol.com
Web Site: http://www.cleft.com
Members: 2,600 individuals
Staff: 4
Annual Budget: $250-500,000
Exec. Director: Nancy Smythe
Historical Note
Founded in Harrisburg, PA, April 4, 1943 as the American Academy of Cleft Prosthesis. Became the American Ass'n for Cleft Palate Rehabilitation in 1949 and later assumed its present name. Members consist of doctors, dentists and others concerned with facial birth defects. Membership: $125/year.
Publications:
ACPA/CPF Newsletter. q. adv.
Cleft Palate-Craniofacial Journal. bi-m. adv.
Directory. a.
Meetings/Conferences:
Annual Meetings: Spring/400-600
1999 – Scottsdale, AZ(Doubletree Paradise
       Valley)/April 13-18/600
2000 – Atlanta, GA(Crowne Plaza Ravinia)/April 10-15/550
2001 – Minneapolis, MN(Hilton and Towers)/April 23-28/550
2002 – Seattle, WA

American Clinical and Climatological Ass'n *(1884)*
Mayo Clinic, Room 1601 Guggenheim
Rochester, MN   55905
Tel: (507)284-3320   *Fax:* (507)284-2053
Members: 375 individuals
Annual Budget: $25-50,000
Exec. Officer: Sherry Linander
Historical Note
Members are engaged in the clinical study of disease. Has no paid staff. Membership: (invitation only) $100/yr.
Publications:
Transactions of the American Clinical and Climatological
   Ass'n. a.
Meetings/Conferences:
Annual Meetings: October/300-350
1999 – San Diego, CA(Rancho Bernardo)/Oct. 24-27

American Clinical Laboratory Ass'n *(1971)*
1250 H St., N.W., Suite 880
Washington, DC   20005
Tel: (202)637-9466   *Fax:* (202)637-2050
Members: 9 laboratories
Staff: 3
Annual Budget: $250-500,000
V.President, Government Relations: Jo Anne Glisson

Historical Note
Members are clinical laboratories licensed and regulated under Medicare and the Interstate Laboratory Program. Membership dues vary by organization size.

American Clinical Neurophysiological Soc. *(1946)*
One Regency Drive, P.O. Box 30
Bloomfield, CT   06002
Tel: (860)243-3977   *Fax:* (860)286-0787
Web Site: http://www.acns.org
Members: 1,450 individuals
Staff: 5
Annual Budget: $100-250,000
Exec. Director: Jacquelyn T. Coleman, CAE
Historical Note
Formerly (1996) American Electroencephalographic Soc. A professional society of electroencephalographers and neurophysiologists.
Publications:
Journal of Clinical Neurophysiology. 6/year.
Newsletter. semi-a.
Meetings/Conferences:
Annual Meetings: Fall
1999 – St. Louis, MO(Hyatt)/Oct. 28-Nov. 1/300

American Cloak and Suit Manufacturers Ass'n *(1919)*
450 Seventh Ave.
New York, NY   10123
Tel: (212)244-7300   *Fax:* (212)564-6166
Staff: 3
Annual Budget: $25-50,000
Exec. Director: Peter Conticelli
Historical Note
Membership concentrated in the New York metropolitan area. Major function is to represent its members in bargaining with labor.
Meetings/Conferences:
Executive Board meetings: Every six weeks.

American Coal Ash Ass'n *(1968)*
2760 Eisenhower Ave., Suite 304
Alexandria, VA   22314-4569
Tel: (703)317-2400   *Fax:* (703)317-2409
E-Mail: acaa-usa@msn.com
Web Site: http://www.aca.usa.org
Members: 100 companies
Staff: 6
Annual Budget: $500-1,000,000
Exec. Director: Samuel Tyson
Communications Coordinator: Gregg Deinhart
Historical Note
Incorporated in 1968 as the Nat'l Ash Ass'n in Washington, DC. ACAA moved to Alexandria, VA in 1994. ACAA has an international membership which includes both electric utility and non-utility producers of coal-combustion byproducts (CCBs), marketers, consultants, and other organizations. ACAA's mission is to advance the management and use of CCBs in ways that are technically sound, commercially competitive, and environmentally safe.
Publications:
Ash at Work. q.
Meetings/Conferences:

American Cocoa Research Institute *(1948)*
7900 Westpark Drive, Suite A320
McLean, VA   22102
Tel: (703)790-5011   *Fax:* (703)790-5752
Members: 13 companies
Staff: 5
Annual Budget: $1-2,000,000
President: Lawrence T. Graham
Senior V. President, Public & Legislative Affairs: Susan Snyder Smith
Director, Legislative Affairs: Stephen G. Lodge
Senior V. President, Scientific Affairs: Bruce R. Stillings, Ph.D.
Historical Note
Affiliate of Chocolate Manufacturers Ass'n of the U.S.A., which provides administrative support. ACRI provides industry leadership in all scientific areas related to cocoa and promotes the chocolate industry's interests through legislative and regulatory programs and public relations.
Meetings/Conferences:
Annual Meetings: with the Chocolate Manufacturers Ass'n

American Coke and Coal Chemicals Institute *(1944)*
1255 23rd St., N.W., Suite 850
Washington, DC   20037-1174
Tel: (202)452-1140   *Fax:* (202)833-3636
Members: 80 companies
Annual Budget: $500-1,000,000
President: David Saunders
Historical Note
Members are national and international firms representing companies which produce oven coke and metallurgical coal; producers and processors of chemicals derived from coal or tar; producers of integrated steel and builders of major components for the industry.
Publications:
ACCCI Update.
Foundry Facts.
Meetings/Conferences:
Semi-Annual Meetings: Spring and Fall/150

American Collectors Ass'n *(1939)*
4040 W. 70th St.
P.O. Box 39106
Minneapolis, MN   55439-0106
Tel: (612)926-6547   *Fax:* (612)926-1624
E-Mail: aca@collector.com
Web Site: http://www.collector.com
Members: 3,700 credit collection companies

Staff: 60
Annual Budget: $2-5,000,000
C.E.O.: Gary D. Rippentrop, CAE
Director, Communications: Wanda Lukaszewski
V.President, Government Relations: Carleton Fish
Director, Meetings and Conventions: Leslie Smith
Director, Education: Shari Baxter
Program Director: Ted M. Smith, CAE
V.President, Administration and Human Services: Margaret S.
   Kersteter, CAE
Controller: Kenneth Russell
V.President and General Counsel: Aimee Bissonette
Director, Membership: Judith Swanson
Managing Editor: Tim Dresser
Historical Note
ACA promotes the general welfare of the debt collection profession. Activities include education, publishing, research, public affairs, group buying, public relations, conventions and trade show. Sponsors and supports the American Collectors Political Action Committee (ACPAC). Membership: $200/year (minimum).
Publications:
Collector. m. adv.
Currents. bi-w.
HSP News. bi-w.
Pulse. m.
Roster. a.
Meetings/Conferences:
Annual Meetings: Summer
1999 – Chicago, IL(Marriott Downtown)/July 13-16
2000 – San Diego, CA(Hyatt Regency)/July 12-15

American College Counseling Ass'n *(1991)*
5999 Stevenson Ave.
Alexandria, VA   22304-3300
Tel: (703)823-9800   *Fax:* (703)823-0252
Members: 2,961 individuals
Staff: 2
Annual Budget: $10-25,000
Interim Exec. Director: Richard Yep
Historical Note
Members are those in higher education who have a professional identity in counseling and whose primary purpose is fostering student development. ACCA is a division of the American Counseling Ass'n which provides staff administrative support. Membership: $30/year, plus ACA dues (individual); $20/year (student/retired).
Publications:
Journal of College Counseling. q. adv.
Visions Newsletter. 3/year.
Meetings/Conferences:
Annual Meetings: with the American Counseling Ass'n
1999 – San Diego, CA/April 12-17
2000 – Washington, DC/March 22-25

American College for Advancement in Medicine *(1973)*
23121 Verdugo Drive, Suite 204
Laguna Hills, CA   92653-1339
Tel: (949)583-7666   *Fax:* (949)455-9679
Toll Free: (800)532 - 3688
Web Site: http://www.acam.org
Members: 965 individuals
Staff: 5
Annual Budget: $1-2,000,000
Exec. Director/C.E.O.: Edward A. Shaw, Ph.D.
Historical Note
Members are physicians interested in preventive and nutritional medicine. Membership: $260/year.
Publications:
Monthly Update. m. adv.
Quarterly Journal. q. adv.
Meetings/Conferences:
Semi-Annual Meetings: Spring and Winter
1999 – Orlando, FL

American College Health Ass'n *(1920)*
780 Elkridge Landing Rd.
Linthicum, MD   21090-2939
Tel: (410)859-1500   *Fax:* (410)859-1510
E-Mail: acha@access.digex.net
Members: 2,700 individuals, 900 institutions
Staff: 20
Annual Budget: $2-5,000,000
Exec. Director: Charles H. Hartman, CAE
Director, Education: Deborah Peoples
Director, Finance and Office Administration: Patricia Owens
Coordinator, Membership: Erica Wilson
Historical Note
Founded as the American Student Health Ass'n. ACHA and its regional affiliates represent and serve physicians, nurses, health educators, administrative and support staff who manage and staff college and university student health services. Membership: $105-135/year (professional); $30-60/year (student); $240-2,075/year (institution).
Publications:
Action. q.
Journal of American College Health. bi-m. adv.
Meetings/Conferences:
Annual Meetings: Spring/1,600
1999 – Philadelphia, PA(Marriott)/June 2-5

American College of Addictions Treatment Administrators *(1984)*
501 Randolph Drive
Lititz, PA   17543-9049
Tel: (717)581-1901   *Fax:* (717)581-1902
E-Mail: RHunsicker@naatp.org
Web Site: http://www.naatp.org
Members: 350 individuals
Staff: 1

Annual Budget: $50-100,000
Exec. Director: Ronald J. Hunsicker

Historical Note
ACATA members are executive officers and administrators of
addiction treatment facilities. The primary purpose of the College is
to provide standards of practice, conduct a professional certification
program and to provide opportunities for continuing professional
education. Membership: $100/year.

Publications:
Membership Directory. a. adv.
NAATP Visions. 10/yr. adv.

Meetings/Conferences:
Annual Meetings: June
1999 – Chicago, IL

American College of Allergy and Immunology (1942)

Historical Note
Became the American Academy of Allergy, Asthma and
Immunology in 1995.

American College of Allergy, Asthma and Immunology (1942)

85 W. Algonquin Road, Suite 550
Arlington Heights, IL 60005-4425
Tel: (847)427-1200   *Fax:* (847)427-1294
E-Mail: mail@acaai.org
Web Site: alllergy.mcg.edu
Members: 3,900 individuals
Staff: 14
Annual Budget: $5-10,000,000
Exec. Director: James R. Slawny
Director, Public Relations: JoAnn Faber
Director, Finance: Judith Nordtvedt
Director, Membership: Dianne Kubis

Historical Note
Formerly (1987) American College of Allergists and (1995)
American College of Allergy and Immunology. An organization of
qualified allergists, physicians and scientists who have a special
interest in allergy, asthma and/or immunology. Membership:
$265/year.

Publications:
ACAAI News. q.
Annals of Allergy, Asthma and Immunology. m. adv.
Fellow in Training News. q.
Practice Management. q.

Meetings/Conferences:
Annual Meetings: Winter/3,500
1999 – Chicago, IL/Nov. 12-17
2000 – Seattle, WA(Convention Center)/Nov. 3-8
2001 – Orlando, FL(Marriott World Center)/Nov. 16-21
2002 – San Antonio, TX(Convention Center)/Nov. 15-20

American College of Angiology (1954)

295 Northern Blvd., Suite 104
Great Neck, NY 11021-4701
Tel: (516)466-4055   *Fax:* (516)466-4099
Members: 1,700 individuals
Staff: 5
Annual Budget: $100-250,000
Exec. Director: Joan Shaffer

Historical Note
An interdisciplinary scientific organization composed of physicians
and scientists interested in the study of blood circulation, lymph
glands and the heart. Serves the growing need of medical, clinical
and research scientists by providing the opportunity for the
convenient interchange of technical research and clinical
experiences associated with circulatory diseases. Maintains and
sponsors the ACA Young Investigator Award Fund. Membership:
$285/year.

Publications:
Angiology, The Journal of Vascular Diseases. m. adv.
Vascular Surgery. 6/year. adv.

Meetings/Conferences:
Annual Meetings: Fall
1999 – Kamuela, HI(Mauna Kea Resort)/Oct. 3-8

American College of Apothecaries (1940)

P.O. Box 341266
Memphis, TN 38184-1266
Tel: (901)383-8119   *Fax:* (901)383-8882
Members: 1000 individuals
Staff: 5
Annual Budget: $500-1,000,000
Exec. V. President: Dr. D.C. Huffman, Jr.

Historical Note
Members are pharmacists owning ethical prescription pharmacies.
Membership: $295/year.

Publications:
A. C.
ACA Newsletter. special edition.
Patron's Newsletter. m.
Physician's Newletter. m.
Voice of The Pharmacist. q.

Meetings/Conferences:
Annual Meetings: Fall

American College of Bankruptcy (1989)

11350 Random Hills Road, Suite 800
Fairfax, VA 22030-6044
Tel: (703)934-6154   *Fax:* (703)802-0207
Members: 303 individuals
Staff: 1
Annual Budget: $100-250,000
Exec. Director: Suzanne A. Bingham

Historical Note
An honorary professional and educational ass'n of bankruptcy and
insolvency professionals. Its Fellows include commercial and
consumer banruptcy attorneys, insolvency accountants, corporate

turnaround and renewal specialists, law professors, judges,
government officals, and others involved in the bankruptcy and
insolvency community. Nominees are extended an invitation to join
based on a proven record of the highest standards of
professionalism.

Publications:
ACB Directory. a.
College Columns. q.

Meetings/Conferences:
Annual Meetings: May

American College of Cardiology (1949)

9111 Old Georgetown Road
Bethesda, MD 20814-1699
Tel: (301)897-5400   *Fax:* (301)897-9745
Toll Free: (800)253 - 4636
Web Site: http://www.acc.org
Members: 24,000 individuals
Staff: 156
Annual Budget: $25-50,000,000
Exec. V. President: Christine W. McEntee
Assoc. Exec. V. President, Advocacy: Karen J. Collishaw
Asst. Exec. V. President, Education Programs and Products: Barbara
  Kendrick
Senior Assoc. Exec. V. President, Education: Marcia J. Jackson,
  Ph.D.
Senior Assoc. Exec. V. President, Strategy, Finance and Operations:
  Penny S. Mills
*Senior Assoc. Exec. V. President, Clinical Practice adn Scientific
  Services:* Marie E. Michnich, Dr.P.H.
Asst. Exec. V. President, Operations: Cathleen C. Gates

Historical Note
Formed in 1949 and incorporated in the District of Columbia.
Sponsors cardiovascular specialists to discuss timely and relevant
topics through a variety of continuing medical education activities.
Has an annual budget of approximately $30 million. Membership:
$290/year.

Publications:
ACC Current Journal Review. bi-m. adv.
ACCEL (audiocassette). m.
Affiliates in Training. bi-m. adv.
Cardiology Newsletter. m. adv.
Journal of the American College of Cardiology. m. adv.
Learning Center Highlights. q.
Scientific Session News. a.

Meetings/Conferences:
Annual Meetings: Spring/23,000
1999 – New Orleans, LA/March 7-10
2000 – Anaheim, CA/March 12-15
2001 – Orlando, FL/March 18-21
2002 – Atlanta, GA/March 17-20

American College of Cardiovascular Administrators (1986)

30555 Southfield Road, Suite 150
Southfield, MI 48076
Tel: (248)540-4310   *Fax:* (248)645-0590
Members: 1,350 individuals
Staff: 8
Exec. Director: Thomas R. O'Donovan, Ph.D.

Historical Note
ACCA members are administrators in cardiovascular care. ACCA is
a chapter of the American Academy of Medical Administrators.
Membership: $145/year (individual).

Publications:
ACCA Journal of Cardiovascular Management. bi-m. adv.

Meetings/Conferences:
Management Conference: (also meets preceding the American
  College of Cardiology and American Heart Ass'n
  conventions)
1999 – New Orleans, LA/March 5-6
1999 – Atlanta, GA
2000 – Anaheim, CA/March 10-11
2000 – New Orleans, LA

American College of Chest Physicians (1935)

3300 Dundee Road
Northbrook, IL 60062
Tel: (847)498-1400   *Fax:* (847)498-5460
Toll Free: (800)343 - 2227
E-Mail: chestp@aol.com
Web Site: http://www.chestnet.org
Members: 16,000 individuals
Staff: 52
Annual Budget: $10-25,000,000
Exec. V. President/C.E.O.: Alvin Lever
V. President, Communications: Stephen J. Welch
V.President, Membership/Public Affairs: Lynne G. Marcus
Asst. V. President, Meetings/Exhibits: David Larsen
V.President, Education/Special Projects: David H. Eubanks, Ed.D.,
  RRT
V.President, Operations: Donald R. Jones
Assoc. V. President, Leadership Liaison: Darelene J. Buczak
V.President, Health/Science Policy: Sydney Parker, Ph.D.

Historical Note
Founded in 1935 and incorporated in Illinois in 1942. Promotes the
prevention of diseases of the chest.Membership: $324/year.

Publications:
CHEST. m. adv.
Chest Soundings. q.
Pulmonary Perspectives. q. adv.

Meetings/Conferences:
Annual Meetings: Fall/3,600
1999 – Chicago, IL(McCormick Palce)/Oct. 31-Nov. 4/3500
2000 – San Francisco, CA(Moscone Center)/Oct. 22-26/3500
2001 – Philadelphia, PA(Convention Center)/Nov. 4-8/3500
2002 – San Diego, CA(San Diego Convention
  Center)/Nov. 3-7/3500

American College of Chiropractic Orthopedists (1964)

1030 Broadway, Suite 101
El Centro, CA 92243
Tel: (619)370-9106   *Fax:* (619)352-3966
Web Site: http://www.accoweb.com
Members: 787 individuals
Annual Budget: $50-100,000
President and Exec. Director: Robin Futoran, D.C.

Historical Note
Members are chiropractic orthopedists and others with an interest
in the field. Membership: $70/year.

Publications:
Journal of the ACCO. q.
Membership Directory. bien.

Meetings/Conferences:
Annual Meetings: Spring.
1999 – Hilton Head, SC

American College of Clinical Pharmacology (1969)

3 Ellinwood Court
New Hartford, NY 13413-1105
Tel: (315)768-6117   *Fax:* (315)768-6119
E-Mail: ACCP1ssu@AOL.com
Web Site: http://www.ACCP1.org
Members: 1000 individuals
Staff: 1
Annual Budget: $250-500,000
Exec. Director: Susan Ulrich, R.Ph.

Historical Note
Members of the College are health care professionals and
biomedical/pharmaceutical scientists employed in academia, the
pharmaceutical industry, contract clinical research organizations,
private practice or government. There are four categories of
membership offered by the college.

Publications:
Directory. a.
Journal of Clinical Pharmacology. m. adv.
Newsletter. 3-4/yr.

Meetings/Conferences:
Annual Meetings: Fall
1999 – Rockville, MD(Doubletree)/Sept. 16-18/300
2000 – Chicago, IL(Drake Hotel)/Sept. 17-20/300

American College of Clinical Pharmacy (1979)

3101 Broadway, Suite 380
Kansas City, MO 64111
Tel: (816)531-2177   *Fax:* (816)531-4990
E-Mail: accp@accp.com
Web Site: http://www.accp.com
Members: 4,300 individuals
Staff: 14
Annual Budget: $2-5,000,000
Exec. Director: Robert M. Elenbaas, Pharm. D.
Director, Education/Member Services: Peggy Kuehl
Director, Publications: Warren S. Lacy

Historical Note
International society founded in October 1979 in Kansas City.
Promotes the rational use of medications in health care, the
advancement of knowledge regarding drug therapy and the
development of clinical pharmacy. Membership: $65-$150/year.

Publications:
ACCP Report. m.
Pharmacotherapy. bi-m.
PRN Report.
Residency & Fellowship Directory. a.

Meetings/Conferences:
1999 – Kansas City, MO(Marriott)/Oct. 24-27/1300
2000 – Los Angeles, CA/Nov. 5-8

American College of Construction Lawyers (1989)

1030 15th St., N.W. Suite 870
Washington, DC 20005
Tel: (202)638-3906   *Fax:* (202)393-0336
Members: 100 individuals
Staff: 4
Annual Budget: $50-100,000
Exec. Director: Marianne McDermott

Historical Note
ACCL is a national organization of lawyers who have demonstrated
skill and experience in the practice or teaching of construction law,
and are dedicated to the specialized practice of construction law.
The group provides advanced professional workshops and
educational programs. Membership: based upon nomination and
election.

Meetings/Conferences:
1999 – Tucson, AZ(Westin La Paloma)/Feb. 17-22

American College of Counselors (1984)

8038 Camellia Lane
Indianapolis, IN 46219
Tel: (317)898-3211
Members: 135 individuals
Staff: 3
Annual Budget: under $10,000
Exec. Director: Mary E. Oetjen

Historical Note
ACC members are professionals in counseling and related fields of
human services. Provides standards and guidelines common to all
specialties in the field. Membership: $100/year (individual).

Publications:
ACC Courier. 3/yr.
CON-TEXT - Journal of the ACC. a.

Meetings/Conferences:
Annual Meetings: Fall
1999 – Chicago, IL

American College of Critical Care Medicine (1988)

Historical Note
A division of the Soc. of Critical Care Medicine.

American College of Cryosurgery (1977)
Historical Note
Merged with American College of Mohs Micrographic Surgery and Cutaneous Oncology in 1997.

American College of Dentists (1920)
839 Quince Orchard Blvd., Suite J
Gaithersburg, MD   20878-1614
Tel: (301)977-3223   *Fax:* (301)977-3330
E-Mail: info@acdentists.org
Web Site: http://www.acdentists.org
Members: 7,000 individuals
Staff: 6
Exec. Director: Stephen A. Ralls, D.D.S.

Historical Note
Founded in Cedar Rapids in 1920 and incorporated in Maryland in 1970. Membership: $125/year.

Publications:
Journal of the American College of Dentists. q.
News and Views. q.

Meetings/Conferences:
Annual Meetings: Fall
1999 – Honolulu, HI
2000 – Chicago, IL

American College of Emergency Physicians (1968)
1125 Executive Cir
Dallas, TX   75038
Tel: (972)550-0911   *Fax:* (972)580-2816
Web Site: http://www.acep.org
Members: 19,675 individuals
Staff: 98
Annual Budget: $10-25,000,000
Exec. Director: Colin C. Rorrie, Jr., Ph.D.
PAC Director: Barbara Jackier
Director, Policy Division: W. Calvin Chaney
Director, Meetings: Michael M. Sheridan
Director, Academic Affairs: Rebecca Garcia, Ph.D.
Director, Professional and Educational Public: Tom Weilinich
Deputy Exec. Director: Michael E. Gallery, Ph.D., CAE
Director, Human Resource: Debbie Bridge
Director, Member Services Division: Elaine Jastram
Director, Member Services: Patty Stove

Historical Note
Provides courses in clinical practice and management to members in accordance with the continuing education requirements of the College. Sponsors and supports the Nat'l Emergency Medicine Political Action Committee and the Emergency Medicine Foundation. Has an annual budget of $14.5 million. Membership: $475/year.

Publications:
24/7 Quarterly.
ACEP News. m. adv.
Annals of Emergency Medicine. m. adv.
Em Today. bi-.
The Connection Quarterly.

Meetings/Conferences:
Annual Meetings: Fall
1999 – Las Vegas, NV(Hilton)/Oct. 11-14
2000 – Philadelphia, PA(Convention Center)/Oct. 23-26

American College of Epidemiology (1979)
401 E. Jefferson St., Suite 205
Rockville, MD   20850-2617
Tel: (301)251-0594   *Fax:* (301)279-6749
E-Mail: epiinfo@amcollepi.org
Web Site: http://www.amcollepi.org/ace/ace.htm
Members: 850 individuals
Staff: 7
Exec. Director: Judith C. Woodward, CAE
Manager, Meetings and Education: Dale Sandler, Ph.D.
Manager, Finance: Philip Nasca, Ph.D.

Historical Note
Members are physicians and other health professionals with an interest in the study of human disease. Membership: $120-150/year (individual).

Publications:
Annals of Epidemiology. bi-m.
Newsletter. q.

Meetings/Conferences:
Annual Meetings: Fall

American College of Eye Surgeons (1986)
700 N. Grant, Suite 702
Odessa, TX   79761
Tel: (915)335-0077   *Fax:* (915)335-0057
E-Mail: quality @acesabes.com
Web Site: acesabes.com
Members: 800 individuals, 40 organizations
Staff: 4
Exec. Director: Brenda S. Sheets

Historical Note
ACES promotes quality ophthalmic surgical care; also suports the American Board of Eye Surgery (ABES). ABES establishes sub-specialty certification programs for ophthalmic surgeons. Certification currently available in cataract/implant, refractive surgery (incisional keratotomy), and penetrating keratoplasty. Membership: $275/year (individual); $300/year (corporate).

Publications:
Clinical Guidelines. irreg.
Directory of Certified Physicians. a.
Newsletter. q.

Meetings/Conferences:
Annual Meetings: February/225 Whistler, B.C. Canada(Chateau Whistler)/Feb.18-21

American College of Foot and Ankle Orthopedics and Medicine (1949)
1988 Old Mission Dr. B1741
Solvang, CA   93463
Tel: (805)693-9137   *Fax:* (805)693-9758
Toll Free: (800)265 - 8263
E-Mail: ACFAOM@IBM.net or acfaom@acfaom.com
Web Site: http://www.acfaom.com
Members: 1,300 individuals
Staff: 3
Annual Budget: $250-500,000
Exec. Director: Judith A. Baerg

Historical Note
Formerly (1993) American College of Foot Orthopedists and American College of Foot and Ankle Orthopedic Medicine (1994). An education and research association of podiatrists specializing in diseases and deformities of the foot and ankle. Affiliated with the American Podiatric Medical Ass'n. Recognized educational arm of the American Board of Podiatric Orthopedic and Primary Podiatric Medicine. Membership: $295/year.

Publications:
ACFAOM Newsletter. q. adv.

Meetings/Conferences:
Annual Meetings: August with the American Podiatric Medical Ass'n
1999 – Los Angeles, CA(Westin Century Plaza Hotel)/Feb. 16-20

American College of Foot and Ankle Pediatrics (1977)
c/o Penn. College of Podiatric Medicine
8th at Race St.
Philadelphia, PA   19107
Tel: (215)625-5361   *Fax:* (215)629-0199
Members: 185 individuals
Staff: 1
Annual Budget: under $10,000
President: Philip J. Bresnahan, DPM

Historical Note
Established in Cleveland by a group of podiatrists and others interested in promoting children's foot health. Formerly American College of Podopediatrics; assumed its current name in 1994. Affiliated with the American Podiatric Medical Ass'n. Has no paid staff or permanent officers. Membership: $50/year.

Publications:
ACP Abstracts Newsletter. bi-m.

Meetings/Conferences:
Annual Meetings: August in conjunction with APMA National Meeting.

American College of Foot and Ankle Surgeons (1942)
515 Busse Hwy.
Park Ridge, IL   60068-3150
Tel: (847)292-2237   *Fax:* (847)292-2022
Toll Free: (800)421 - 2237
E-Mail: mall@acfas.org
Web Site: www.acfas.org
Members: 5,000 individuals
Staff: 10
Annual Budget: $2-5,000,000
Exec. Director: Thomas R. Schedler, CAE
Director, Mktg./Communications: Marsha Hinko
Director, Scientific Meetings: Mary Meyers
Director, Administration: Susan Couture
Director, Finance: Ronald Engelbreit

Historical Note
Formerly (1993) the American College of Foot Surgeons. ACFAS is a voluntary, educational and scientific organization devoted to the ethical and competent practice of podiatric surgery and to the provision of high quality care for the podiatric surgical patient. ACFAS presents extensive scientific and educational programs, promotes methods to ensure a high standard of surgical practice, disseminates surgical knowledge, and provides information to the general public. Membership: $300/year.

Publications:
Journal of Foot and Ankle Surgery. bi-m. adv.
The Bulletin. bi-m. adv.

Meetings/Conferences:
Annual Meetings: February-March/1,500
1999 – Beverly Hills, CA(Century Plaza)/Feb. 16-20/1200
2000 – Miami, FL(Hyatt Regency Miami)/Feb. 8-12/1400

American College of Forensic Examiners (1992)
611 E. Wells St.
Milwaukee, WI   53202
Tel: (414)226-2169   *Fax:* (414)276-8416
Toll Free: (800)423 - 9737
E-Mail: acfe@execinc.com
Web Site: http://www.acfe
Members: 10,000 Individuals
Staff: 8
Annual Budget: $500-1,000,000
Exec. Director: Robert L. O'Block, Ph.D.

Historical Note
ACFE members are forensic examiners mostly from the United States engaging in the scientific aspects of forensic examination. Membership: $100-125/year (individual).

Publications:
The Forensic Examiner. m.

Meetings/Conferences:
1999 – New York, NY(Waldorf Astoria)/1500

American College of Forensic Psychiatry (1981)
P.O. Box 5870
Balboa Island, CA   92662
Tel: (949)673-7773   *Fax:* (949)673-7710
Members: 350 individuals
Staff: 4
Directors: Ed and Debra Miller

Publications:
American Journal of Forensic Psychiatry. q. adv.

Meetings/Conferences:
1999 – Santa Fe, NM/April 22-25

American College of Gastroenterology (1932)
4900-B South 31st St.
Arlington, VA   22206-1656
Tel: (703)820-7400   *Fax:* (703)931-4520
Members: 5,900 individuals
Staff: 8
Annual Budget: $1-2,000,000
Exec. Director: Thomas F. Fise

Historical Note
With members in over 30 countries worldwide, ACG promotes scholarly practice, teaching, and research in the digestive disease specialties.

Publications:
American Journal of Gastroenterology. m. adv.

Meetings/Conferences:
1999 – Phoenix, AZ(Phoenix Convention Center)/Oct. 15-20

American College of Health Care Administrators (1962)
325 S. Patrick St.
Alexandria, VA   22314
Tel: (703)739-7900   *Fax:* (703)739-7901
Toll Free: (888)882 - 2422
Web Site: http://www.achca.org
Members: 6,500 individuals
Staff: 13
Annual Budget: $2-5,000,000
President/C.E.O.: Karen S. Tucker, CAE
Director, Professional Development & Development Affairs: Jan Lamoglia
Director, Finance/ Administration: Lyle N. Ankrapp, Jr.
Director, Membership/Marketing: Nancy Perrin

Historical Note
Formerly (1983) the American College of Nursing Home Administrators. ACHCA members manage and direct the daily operations of long-term care, subacute and assisted living facilities. Membership: $216/year, active (individual).

Publications:
Balance. 8/yr. adv.

Meetings/Conferences:
Annual Meetings: Spring/800
1999 – Providence, RI(Westin)/April 10-13

American College of Healthcare Executives (1933)
One N. Franklin St., Suite 1700
Chicago, IL   60606-3491
Tel: (312)424-2800   *Fax:* (312)424-0023
E-Mail: geninfo@ache.org
Web Site: http://www.ache.org
Members: 30,000 individuals
Staff: 100
Annual Budget: $10-25,000,000
President and C.E.O.: Thomas C. Dolan, PhD, FACHE
V.President, Communications: Ann Bartling, CHE
V. President, Division of Education: Arthur D. Neal, CHE, CAE
Exec. V. President and C.O.O.: Karen L. Hackett, CHE, CAE
V. President, Administration: Deborah J. Bowen, CHE, CAE
C.F.O.: Richard Harland, CPA, CAE
V.President, Membership: Cynthia Hahn, FACHE
V.President, Publications: Maureen Glass
V. President, Fund Development: Kathleen MacArthur
V.President, Mgmt. Information Systems/CIO: Kimberly Mosley
V. President, Regional Services: Charles Macfarlane, CHE, CAE
V. President, Research and Development: Peter Weil, Ph.D., FAC

Historical Note
ACHE is an international professional society of more than 30,000 healthcare executives. The College is known for its prestigious credentialing and educational programs. ACHE's annual Congress on Healthcare management draws more than 4,000 participants each year. Through its efforts, the College works toward its goal of improving the health status of society by advancing healthcare management excellence. Has an annual budget of over $16,000,000. Membership: $275/year (Fellow/Diplomate), $250/year (Associate).

Publications:
Directory. bien.
Frontiers of Health Services Management. q.
Health Services Research. 6/year.
Healthcare Executive. bi-m. adv.
Journal of Healthcare Management. bi.

Meetings/Conferences:
1999 – Chicago, IL/March 6-11/4000

American College of Healthcare Information Administrators
30555 Southfield Road, Suite 150
Southfield, MI   48076
Tel: (248)540-4310   *Fax:* (248)645-0590
E-Mail: info@aameda.org
Members: 166 individuals
Staff: 8
Exec. Director: Thomas R. O'Donovan, Ph.D.

Historical Note
ACHIA is a national chapter of the American Academy of Medical Administrators. ACHIA members are college graduates employed as managers of professionals who are providing healthcare information management or administration. Membership: $145/year (individual).

Publications:
AAMA Executive. bi-m.

Meetings/Conferences:
1999 – Atlanta, GA

American College of Home Health Administrators (1995)

Historical Note
Organization defunct in 1998.

American College of Internat'l Physicians (1975)

1101 Neal St., Suite 102
Cookesville, TN 38501
Tel: (931)526-8675 *Fax:* (931)526-8675
Members: 3,900 individuals
Staff: 3
Annual Budget: $100-250,000
Washington Counsel: Charles Brown, JD
Accountant: Thomas Abblett, CPA

Historical Note
Physicians educated in foreign countries and the U.S. who are licensed and practicing in the U.S. Main interests of the College are medical education, research, ethics and international activities. Absorbed the Nat'l Ass'n of Foreign Medical Graduates in 1976. Membership: $175/year (individual).

Publications:
Annual Program & Report.
International Physician Newsletter. q. adv.

Meetings/Conferences:
Annual Meetings: Summer
1999 – Virginia Beach, VA(Sheraton)/June 24-26

American College of Laboratory Animal Medicine (1957)

96 Chester St.
Chester, NH 03036
Tel: (603)887-2467 *Fax:* (603)887-0096
E-Mail: mwbaclam@gsi.net.net
Web Site: http://www.aclam.org
Members: 500 individuals
Staff: 2
Annual Budget: $100-250,000
Exec. Director: Dr. Melvin Balk

Historical Note
Founded in 1957 as the American Board of Laboratory Animal Medicine. Incorporated in Illinois in 1957. Affiliated with the American Veterinary Medical Ass'n and the American Ass'n for Laboratory Animal Science. Established to encourage education, training and research in laboratory animal medicine and to provide standards for veterinarians professionally concerned with the health of laboratory animals.

Publications:
ACLAM Newsletter. 5/yr.

Meetings/Conferences:
Annual Meetings: July, with American Veterinary Medical Ass'n
1999 – San Antonio, TX/May 2-5

American College of Legal Medicine (1960)

611 East Wells St.
Milwaukee, WI 53202-3816
Tel: (414)276-1881 *Fax:* (414)276-3349
Members: 1,500 individuals
Staff: 3
Annual Budget: $250-500,000
Director, Administration: Janet L. Haynes
Director, Accounting: Christina Aceredo

Historical Note
Founded and incorporated in Delaware September, 1960. Members are doctors, lawyers, and other health care professionals interested in the relationship between law and medicine. Fellows of the College must have both a medical and law degree or have performed significant service to the college over time. Membership: $270/year (fellow); $190/year (member/affiliate/corresponding); $35/year (student).

Publications:
ACLM Newsletter. q. adv.
Journal of Legal Medicine. q.
Legal Medicine Perspectives. bi-m. adv.
Medical Legal Lessons. bi-m.
Membership Directory. a.

Meetings/Conferences:
Semi-Annual Meetings: Spring/300 and Fall/150
1999 – New Orleans, LA(Westin Canal)/March 11-13

American College of Managed Care Administrators (1995)

30555 Southfield Road, Suite 150
Southfield, MI 48076
Tel: (248)540-4310 *Fax:* (248)645-0590
E-Mail: info@aameda.org
Web Site: http://www.aameda.org
Members: 175 individuals
Exec. Officer: Thomas R. O'Donovan, Ph.D.

Historical Note
Founded by the American Academy of Medical Administrators, ACMCA serves as a forum for exchanging information, credentialling and networking among managed care professionals. Membership: $140/year.

Meetings/Conferences:
1999 – Atlanta, GA/Nov. 4-6/50
2000 – New Orleans, LA/Nov. 9-11/50

American College of Managed Care Medicine

4435 Waterfront Dr., Suite 101
P.O. Box 4913
Glen Allen, VA 23058-4193
Tel: (804)527-1906 *Fax:* (804)747-5316
Toll Free: (800)722 - 0376
E-Mail: wmiller@namcp.org
Web Site: http://www.acmcm.org
Members: 1000 individuals
Staff: 17
Exec. Director: W.C. Williams, III, M.D.

Director, Communications: Whitney Miller
Director, Operations: Kelley Cuneo
Director, Member Services: Sloane Reed

Historical Note
ACMCM seeks to educate physicians about changes in health care environment and to prepare them to deliver cost-effective, appropriate managed care medicine to members of current and future health care delivery systems. Membership: $195/year (physicians); $250/year (other professionals); $1,500/year (organization).

Publications:
American Journal of Integrated Healthcare. bi-a. adv.
Journal of Managed Care Medicine. bi-a. adv.
Newsletter. m.

American College of Medical Physics (1982)

1891 Preston White Drive
Reston, VA 20191
Tel: (703)648-8966 *Fax:* (703)242-9313
Members: 400 individuals
Exec. Director: Suzanne Bohn

Meetings/Conferences:
1999 – Aspen, CO/May 24-30
2000 – Whistler, British Columbia/May 15-20

American College of Medical Practice Executives (1956)

104 Inverness Terrace East
Englewood, CO 80112-5306
Tel: (303)397-7869 *Fax:* (303)643-4427
Members: 3,000 individuals
Staff: 9
Annual Budget: $1-2,000,000
Sr. V. President: Andrea M. Rossiter
Director, Communications: Dennis L. Barnhardt
Director, Conference: Carol Wilke

Historical Note
Founded as the American College of Clinic Managers; became American College of Medical Group Administrators in 1976 and assumed its current name in 1993. A voluntary certification organization drawing its membership from the Medical Group Management Ass'n. Membership: $165/year (individual).

Publications:
The College Review.

Meetings/Conferences:
Annual Meetings: With Medical Group Management Ass'n
1999 – San Diego, CA

American College of Medical Quality (1973)

4334 Montgomery Ave., 2nd Floor
Bethesda, MD 20814
Tel: (301)913-9149 *Fax:* (301)913-9142
Toll Free: (800)924 - 2149
E-Mail: acmq@aol.com
Web Site: www.acmg.org
Members: 1000 individuals
Staff: 4
Annual Budget: $250-500,000
Exec. Vice President: Bridget Brodie

Historical Note
Formerly (1991) the American College of Utiliaztion Review Physicians. Organized and incorporated in the State of Pennsylvania, October 13, 1973 to set standards, provide continuing medical education and measure competence in the fields of quality assurance and utilization review. Members are doctors, related health personnel and hospitals. Membership: $300/year (first year membership), $395/year (full member/M.D.), $80/year (first year affiliate) $100/year (affiliate member).

Publications:
Focus. bi-m. adv.
Journal of the ACMQ. q. adv.

Meetings/Conferences:

American College of Medical Staff Development

6855 Jimmy Carter Blvd., Suite 2100
Norcross, GA 30071
Tel: (770)734-9904 *Fax:* (770)734-9709
Staff: 2
C.E.O.: Roger G. Bonds

American College of Medical Toxicology (1993)

777 East Park Drive
P.O. Box 8820
Harrisburg, PA 17105-8820
Tel: (717)558-7846 *Fax:* (717)558-7841
E-Mail: hmiller@pamedsoc.org
Web Site: www.acmt.net
Members: 235 individuals
Staff: 2
Exec. Director: Heather Miller

Historical Note
ACMT is a professional, non-profit organization of physicians, certified in medical toxicology, dedicated to advancing the science and practice of medical toxicology.

Publications:
Internet Journal of Medical Toxicology.

Meetings/Conferences:
Annual Meetings: in conjunction with North American Congress of Clinical Toxicology

American College of Medicine (1981)

4711 Golf Road, Suite 408
Skokie, IL 60076-1242
Tel: (847)568-1500 *Fax:* (847)568-1527
Annual Budget: $250-500,000
Co-Exec. Director: Randall T. Bellows, M.D.

Historical Note
Formerly (1984) the American College of General Practice. A professional society providing continuing education opportunities for physicians in general practice. Affiliated with the American Soc. of Contemporary Medicine and Surgery and the American Soc. of Contemporary Ophthalmology. Membership: $220/year (individual).

Publications:
Comprehensive Therapy. m. adv.

Meetings/Conferences:
Annual Meetings: with American Soc. of Contemporary Medicine and Surgery/April

American College of Mental Health Administration (1979)

7625 W. Hutchinson Ave.
Pittsburgh, PA 15218-1248
Tel: (412)244-0670 *Fax:* (412)244-9916
E-Mail: lawhel@aol.com
Web Site: http://www.acmha.org
Members: 200 individuals
Staff: 2
Annual Budget: $25-50,000
Exec. Director: Lawrence A. Heller, Ph.D.

Historical Note
ACMHA was established to further mental health administration as a practice and a profession, to foster research and provide opportunites for professional education and communication. ACMHA members are clinician–administrators with knowledge and experience in both the administration of mental health programs and clinical care. Membership: $175/year (individual).

Publications:
ACMHA Newsletter. q. adv.

Meetings/Conferences:
Annual Meetings: Spring
1999 – Sante Fe, NM(Inn at Loretto)/Mar. 17-20/125

American College of Mohs Micrographic Surgery and Cutaneous Oncology (1967)

930 N. Meacham Road
Schaumburg, IL 60173-6016
Tel: (847)330-0230 *Fax:* (847)330-0050
Members: 350 individuals
Staff: 2
Annual Budget: $100-250,000
Exec. Director: Sherryl Traficano

Historical Note
Formerly (1987) American College of Chemosurgery. Members are physicians utilizing chemosurgery for the microscopically controlled excision of skin cancers. Absorbed American College of Cryosurgery in 1997.

Publications:
Journal of Dermatologic Surgery.

Meetings/Conferences:
1999 – Miami Beach, FL(Fontainebleu Hotel)/May 17-19/400

American College of Musicians (1929)

808 Rio Grande St., Box 1807
Austin, TX 78767
Tel: (512)478-5775
Members: 115,000 individuals
Staff: 12
Annual Budget: $1-2,000,000
President: Richard Allison

Historical Note
A standardizing agency granting degrees and diplomas to worthy musicians, ACM consists of two divisions: the Nat'l Guild of Piano Teachers and the Nat'l Fraternity of Student Musicians. Members are individuals whose qualifications make them eligible to judge.

Publications:
Piano Guild Notes. bi-m.

Meetings/Conferences:
Annual Meetings: Not held

American College of Neuropsychiatrists (1939)

28595 Orchard Lake Road, Suite 200
Farmington Hills, MI 48334
Tel: (248)553-0010 *Fax:* (248)553-0818
Members: 600 individuals
Staff: 2
Annual Budget: $50-100,000
Exec. Director: Louis E. Rentz, DO, FACN

Historical Note
Affiliated with the American Osteopathic Association. Membership: $300/year (individual).

Publications:
ACN Journal. 2/year.
Journal Of The American College Of Neuropsychiatrists. q. adv.

Meetings/Conferences:
Semi-annual Meetings: Spring and Fall in coordination with the AOA
1999 – San Francisco, CA/Oct. 24-28
2000 – Orlando, FL/Oct. 29-Nov. 2
2001 – San Diego, CA/Oct. 21-25

American College of Neuropsychopharmacology (1961)

320 Centre Bldg., 2014 Broadway
Nashville, TN 37203
Tel: (615)322-2075 *Fax:* (615)343-0662
E-Mail: acnp@acnp.org
Web Site: http://www.acnp.org
Members: 713 individuals
Staff: 6
Annual Budget: $100-250,000
Secretary: Oakley Ray, M.D.

Meetings/Conferences:
Annual Meetings: December, by invitation only
1999 – Acapulco, Mexico/Dec. 13-17

American College of Nuclear Medicine (1972)
P.O. Box 175
Landisville, PA 17538-0175
Tel: (717)898-5008   Fax: (717)898-0713
E-Mail: tjj676@aol.com
Members: 500 individuals
Annual Budget: $50-100,000
Exec. Director: Thomas Johnson, Jr.

Historical Note
Members are scientists and physicians working in the field of nuclear medicine. Membership: $175/year.

Publications:
ACNM Report. q.

Meetings/Conferences:
Annual Meetings: March
1999 – Ft. Lauderdale, FL(Marina Marriott)/Feb. 5-7

American College of Nuclear Physicians (1974)
4400 Jenifer St., N.W., Suite 230
Washington, DC 20015-2113
Tel: (202)244-7904   Fax: (202)244-7355
Web Site: http://www.acnp.com
Members: 1,600 individuals
Staff: 6
Annual Budget: $500-1,000,000
Asst. Exec. Director: Haley Johnson

Historical Note
Members are physicians doing diagnostic work with radioactive pharmaceuticals. Members must pass a Specialty Board examination.

Publications:
ACNP Newsletter. bi-m.

Meetings/Conferences:
Semi-Annual Meetings: Fall and Winter

American College of Nurse Practitioners (1994)
503 Capitol Ct. NE, Suite 300
Washington, DC 20002
Tel: (202)546-4825   Fax: (202)546-4797
E-Mail: acnp@nurse.org
Web Site: http://www.nurse.org/acnp
President: Jean Johnson

Historical Note
ACNP members are nurse practitioners regardless of clinical specialty. Membership: $85/year (individual); $45/year (student).

Meetings/Conferences:
1999 – Washington, DC/Feb. 26-March 1

American College of Nurse-Midwives (1955)
818 Connecticut Ave, N.W., Suite 900
Washington, DC 20006
Tel: (202)728-9860   Fax: (202)728-9897
E-Mail: info@acnm.org
Web Site: http://www.midwife.org
Members: 6,800 individuals
Staff: 37
Annual Budget: $2-5,000,000
Exec. Director: Deanne Williams
Manager, Marketing and Public Relations: Janet Winer
Director, Financial: Joan Robertson
Exec. Director: Deanne Williams
Director, Member Services: John H. Boggess
Director, Special Projects: Debbie Armbruster

Historical Note
Formerly (1969) American College of Nurse-Midwifery. Membership: $250/year.

Publications:
Directory of Nurse-Midwifery Practices. adv. adv.
Journal of Nurse-Midwifery. bi-m. adv.
Quickening. bi-m.

Meetings/Conferences:
1999 – Anchorage, AK/May 28-June 3
2000 – Orlando, FL/May 5-11

American College of Nutrition (1959)
c/o Hospital for Joint Diseases
301 E. 17th St.
New York, NY 10003
Tel: (212)777-1037   Fax: (212)777-1103
Members: 1,200 individuals
Staff: 4
Annual Budget: $250-500,000
Exec. Director: Stanley Wallach, M.D.
Business/Office Manager: Santa Henriquez
Managing Editor: Sandy Allen

Historical Note
Merged with the American Nutritionists Ass'n in 1992. Members are physicians, bachelor and advanced degree nutritionists, and registered dieticians. Officers change annually. Membership: $115-140/year.

Publications:
ACN Newsletter. q.
Journal of ACN. bi-m. adv.

Meetings/Conferences:
Annual Meetings: Fall
1999 – Washington, DC(Washington Court Hotel)/Oct. 1-3/400
2000 – Las Vegas, NV(Alexis Park Resort)/Oct 13-15/400
2001 – Orlando, FL(Sheraton World Resort)/Oct. 5-7/400

American College of Obstetricians and Gynecologists (1951)
409 12th St., S.W.
PO Box 96920
Washington, DC 20024-2188
Tel: (202)638-5577   Fax: (202)863-4980
Web Site: http://www.acog.org
Members: 38,700 individuals

Staff: 185
Annual Budget: $25-50,000,000
Exec. V. President: Ralph W. Hale, M.D.
Director, Government Affairs: Kathy Bryant
V. President, Education: Gerald Holzman, M.D.
V. President, Administration: Elsa P. Brown
V. President and C.F.O: Richard Baily
General Counsel: Ann E. Allen

Historical Note
Doctors specializing in women's health care, including childbirth and female disorders. Formerly (1956) American Academy of Obstetrics and Gynecology. Promotes further education and standards of practice. Has an annual budget of approximately $37 million. Membership: $325/year.

Publications:
ACOG Clinical Review.
Obstetrics and Gynecology. m. adv.
Primary Care Update.

Meetings/Conferences:
Annual Meetings: Spring/7,000
1999 – Philadelphia, PA(Philadelphia Convention Center)/May 15-19
2000 – San Francisco, CA(Moscone)/May 20-24
2001 – Chicago, IL/April 28-May 2
2002 – Los Angeles, CA(LA Convention Center)

American College of Occupational and Environmental Medicine (1915)
55 W. Seegers Road
Arlington Heights, IL 60005-3916
Tel: (847)228-6850   Fax: (847)228-1856
Web Site: http://www.acoem.org
Members: 5,700 individuals
Staff: 22
Annual Budget: $500-1,000,000
Exec. V. President: Dr. Gene Handley
Meeting Planner: Nancy Kay Olson
Comptroller: Dick Schaszheck
Director, Membership Services: Lanny Hardy

Historical Note
Established in Illinois in 1915 as the American Ass'n of Industrial Physicians and Surgeons and chartered in Illinois in 1916. Became the Industrial Medical Ass'n in 1951, the American Occupational Medical Ass'n in 1974 and assumed its present name in 1988 on merging with the American Academy of Occupational Medicine. Membership: $260 year, plus $25 application fee (individual).

Publications:
ACOM Report. m.
Journal of Occupational Medicine. m. adv.

Meetings/Conferences:
Semi-Annual Meetings: Spring and Fall/4,000
1999 – New Orleans, LA/Apr. 23-30
2001 – Philadelphia, PA

American College of Oral and Maxillofacial Surgeons (1975)
1100 N.W. Loop 410, Suite 506
San Antonio, TX 78213-2266
Tel: (210)344-5674   Fax: (210)344-9754
Toll Free: (800)522 - 6676
Web Site: http://www.acoms.org
Members: 2,300 individuals
Staff: 3
Annual Budget: $500-1,000,000
Exec. Director: Emelie C. Schnettler

Historical Note
First called the Association of Diplomates of the American Board of Oral Surgery. Membership limited to Diplomates of the American Board of Oral and Maxillofacial Surgery, who actively practice in that specialty. Membership: $245/year (individual).

Publications:
ACOMS Review Newsletter. q.
British Journal of Oral and Maxillofacial Surgery. bi-m. adv.

Meetings/Conferences:
Annual Meetings: Spring
1999 – Orlando, FL
2000 – Washington, DC

American College of Osteopathic Emergency Physicians (1975)
142 East Ontario St., Suite 218
Chicago, IL 60611-2818
Tel: (312)587-3709   Fax: (312)587-3713
Members: 1,200 individuals
Staff: 1
Annual Budget: $100-250,000
Exec. Director: Janice Wachtler

Historical Note
Represents osteopathic emergency physicians in U.S. provide education, political representation, legal services, placement. Also represent students and residents. Membership: $375/year (individual).

Publications:
ACOEP Newsletter. q. adv.

Meetings/Conferences:
1999 – Scottsdale, AZ/Apr. 5-10

American College of Osteopathic Family Physicians (1950)
330 E. Algonquin Road, Suite 1
Arlington Heights, IL 60005
Tel: (847)952-5100   Fax: (847)228-9755
Members: 14,000 individuals
Staff: 8
Annual Budget: $2-5,000,000
Exec. Director: George V. Nyhart

Historical Note
Founded in California in 1950 and chartered in Illinois. Formerly the American College of General Practitioners in Osteopathic Medicine and Surgery (1993). An affiliate of the American Osteopathic Ass'n. Membership: $150/year (individual).

Publications:
Journal of Osteopathic Medicine.
Newsletter. m.

Meetings/Conferences:
Annual Meetings: Spring

American College of Osteopathic Internists (1943)
3 Bethesda Metro Center, Suite 508
Bethesda, MD 20814-5383
Tel: (301)656-8877   Fax: (301)656-7133
Toll Free: (800)327 - 5183
Members: 1,500 individuals
Staff: 2
Annual Budget: $250-500,000
Exec. Director: Brian J. Donadio

Historical Note
Educational association providing continuing medical education opportunities to a community of osteopathic internists. Membership: $300-350/year (individual).

Publications:
ACOI Annual Directory. a.
ACOInformation Newsletter. m. adv.

Meetings/Conferences:
Annual Meetings: Fall

American College of Osteopathic Obstetricians and Gynecologists (1934)
900 Auburn Rd.
Pontiac, MI 48342-3365
Tel: (248)332-6360   Fax: (248)332-4607
Toll Free: (800)875 - 6360
E-Mail: acog@mich.com
Web Site: http://www.acog.com
Members: 799 individuals
Staff: 4
Annual Budget: $250-500,000
Exec. Director: Jerry Polsinelli, D.O.

Historical Note
Formed in Wichita, Kansas during the annual meeting of the American Osteopathic Association by ten charter practicing obstetricians and gynecologists in the profession of osteopathic medicine. Originally the American College of Osteopathic Obstetricians, the present name was assumed in 1949. Chartered in the State of Missouri. Membership: $350/year.

Publications:
Membership Directory. a.
Newsletter. q.

Meetings/Conferences:
Semi-annual Meetings: March and September-October
1999 – Marco Island, FL/March 21-25

American College of Osteopathic Pain Management and Sclerotherapy (1938)
107 Maple Ave., Silverside Heights
Wilmington, DE 19809
Tel: (302)792-9280
Members: 190 individuals
Staff: 1
Annual Budget: under $10,000
Exec. Secretary: Judy Wilbank

Historical Note
Formerly (1995) American Osteopathic Academy of Sclerotherapy. Founded in 1938 as the American Osteopathic Soc. of Herniologists. Members are physicians who treat by injecting certain medications (sclerosants) to stimulate the production of fibrous connective tissue to strengthen weakened areas. Affiliated with American Osteopathic Ass'n.

Publications:
Get the Point. 2/year.

Meetings/Conferences:
Semi-Annual Meetings: Fall, in conjunction with American Osteopathic Ass'n, and annual seminar in the spring

American College of Osteopathic Pediatricians (1940)
5550 Friendship Blvd., Suite 300
Chevy Chase, MD 20815-7201
Tel: (301)968-4180
E-Mail: acop@osteohdq.org
Members: 500 individuals
Staff: 3
Annual Budget: $50-100,000
Exec. Director: David L. Kushner, CAE, CMP
Deputy Exec. Director: Debra Scheinberg

Historical Note
Organized in 1940 in California and incorporated in 1967 in Illinois. Administrative support provided by America Osteopathic Healthcare Ass'n. Membership: $250/year.

Publications:
Directory. a.
Newsletter. q.

Meetings/Conferences:
Annual Meetings: Spring
1999 – Chicago, IL(Drake Hotel)/April 15-18

American College of Osteopathic Surgeons (1927)
123 N. Henry St.
Alexandria, VA 22314-2903
Tel: (703)684-0416   Fax: (703)684-3280
Members: 1,500 individuals
Staff: 5
Annual Budget: $1-2,000,000
Exec. Director: Guy D. Beaumont, Jr.
Director, Education/Meetings: Caryl S. Grant

Director, Finance and Administration: Elizabeth F. Johnson
Director, Membership/Training: Lisa A. Glasgow

Historical Note
Organized June 1926 and incorporated in Missouri in 1927. Affiliated with the American Osteopathic Ass'n. Membership: $450/year (individual).

Publications:
ACOS News. m. adv.
Directory and By-Laws. a.

Meetings/Conferences:
Annual Meetings: Fall/1,000
1999 – Seattle, WA(Seattle Sheraton)/Oct. 2-5/1100
2000 – Boston, MA(Marriott Copley Place)/Sept. 21-24/1100
2001 – Palm Desert, CA(Marriott Desert Springs)/Oct. 4-7/1100
2002 – Orlando, FL(Hilton-Walt Disney World)/Sept. 19-22

American College of Physician Executives *(1975)*
4890 W. Kennedy Blvd., Suite 200
Tampa, FL 33609-2575
Tel: (813)287-2000   *Fax:* (813)287-8993
E-Mail: www.acpe.org
Web Site: http://www.acpe.org
Members: 11,000 individuals
Staff: 28
Annual Budget: $2-5,000,000
Exec. V. President: Kenneth C. Cummings
Director, Information Development: Susan McAllister Quinn
Director, Membership: Judy Rochell

Historical Note
Formerly (1988) the American Academy of Medical Directors, ACPE is the national professional and educational association for physicians in management positions within all sectors of the health care field. Recognized by the AMA House of Delegates as the national specialty society representing physicians in management. Membership: $185/year (individual).

Publications:
Membership Directory. a.
The College Digest. bi-m.
The Physician Executive. m.

Meetings/Conferences:

American College of Physician Inventors *(1992)*

Historical Note
Merged with Ass'n for the Advancement of Medical Instrumentation in 1997.

American College of Physicians-American Soc. of Internal Medicine *(1915)*
190 N. Independence Mall West
Philadelphia, PA 19106
Tel: (215)351-2400   *Fax:* (215)351-2829
Toll Free: (800)523 - 1546
Web Site: http://www.acponline.org
Members: 100,000 individuals
Staff: 300
Annual Budget: $25-50,000,000
Exec. V. President: Walter J. McDonald, M.D., F.A.
Senior V. President, Marketing and Communications: Janet Arneson
Director, Convention/ Meetings: Jean O'Donnell
Senior V. President, Education: Herbert S. Waxman, M.D., F.A.
Senior V. President, Operations: William Habingreither
Dep. Exec. V. President: John Tooker, M.D., FACP
Senior V. President, Finance: Charles Senior
Senior V. President, Membership & Special Advisor to the Exec. V. President: Joseph E. Johnson III, M.D., F.A.
Director, Membership Activities: Eve C. Swiacki
Senior V. President, Publications: Kathy Case

Historical Note
Merged with the Congress of Internal Medicine in 1925. Patterned after Great Britain's Royal College of Physicians, ACP was founded to foster communications among medical scientists, clinical researchers and practicing physicians. Members are practicing internists. "Fellows" are certified internists recognized by their colleagues for their scholarship and professional excellence. Has an annual budget of approximately $31 million.

Publications:
ACP Observer. 11/year. adv.
Annals of Internal Medicine. bi-m. adv.

Meetings/Conferences:
Annual Meetings: Spring/7,000
1999 – New Orleans LA/April 22-25

American College of Podiatric Radiologists *(1942)*
VA Medical Center
Route 9
Martinsburg, WV 25401
Tel: (304)263-0811   *Fax:* (702)733-1732
Members: 65 individuals
Annual Budget: under $10,000
President: Howard Nalin, M.D.

Historical Note
Established as the American College of Chiropodial Roentgenologists, it became the American College of Foot Roentgenologists in 1962 and assumed its present name in 1974. Affiliated with the American Podiatric Medical Ass'n. Membership: $110/year (individual).

Publications:
Journal. q.
Newsletter. m.

American College of Podopediatrics

Historical Note
Became American College of Foot and Ankle Pediatrics in 1994.

American College of Preventive Medicine *(1954)*
1660 L St., N.W., Suite 206
Washington, DC 20036-5603

Tel: (202)466-2044   *Fax:* (202)466-2662
Web Site: www.acpm.org
Members: 2,100 individuals
Staff: 8
Annual Budget: $500-1,000,000
Exec. Director: Jordon R. Richland
Director, Public Affairs: Suzanne Leous
Meetings Planner: Sherley Moore
Assoc. Exec. Director, Education: Carol O'Neill
Manager, Membership/Marketing: Jennifer Edwards

Historical Note
Physicians specializing in preventive medicine, occupational medicine, public health and aerospace medicine. Membership: $215/year.

Publications:
ACPM News. q.
American Journal of Preventive Medicine. bi-m.

Meetings/Conferences:
Annual Meetings: Spring

American College of Prosthodontists *(1970)*
211 E. Chicago, Suite 1000
Chicago, IL 60611-5217
Tel: (312)573-1260   *Fax:* (312)573-1257
Web Site: http://www.prosthodontics.org
Members: 2,700 individuals
Staff: 6
Annual Budget: $1-2,000,000
Exec. Director: Steve Hines
Director, Meetings/Conferences: Linda Wallenborn

Historical Note
Members are dentists who are diplomates of the American Board of Prosthodontics; board eligible prosthodontists; and students in prosthodontic training.

Publications:
Journal of Prosthodontics. q.
Newsletter. q.

Meetings/Conferences:
Annual Meetings: Fall
1999 – New York, NY
2000 – Hawaii

American College of Psychiatrists *(1963)*
732 Addison St., Suite B
Berkeley, CA 94710
Tel: (510)704-8020   *Fax:* (510)704-0113
E-Mail: aliceacp@aol.com
Members: 1000 individuals
Staff: 5
Annual Budget: $1-2,000,000
Exec. Director: Alice Conde

Historical Note
An honorary society limited to 1,000 members. Membership: $320/year (individual).

Publications:
Membership Directory. a.
Newsletter. q.
Proceedings. a.

Meetings/Conferences:
Annual Meetings: February/700
1999 – San Francisco, CA(Fairmont)/Feb. 17-21/800
2000 – Naples, FL(Registry)/Feb. 18-22
2001 – Tucson, AZ(El Conquistador)/Feb. 21-25/600
2002 – Mauna Lani, HI(Sheraton Orchid)/700

American College of Psychoanalysts *(1969)*
520 Breck Ct.
Benicia, CA 94510-1372
Tel: (707)745-2070   *Fax:* (707)746-7677
E-Mail: amercolpsa@aol.com
Members: 240 individuals
Staff: 1
Annual Budget: $10-25,000
Exec. Secretary: Angela Clark

Historical Note
ACP members are medical doctors practicing psychoanalysis.

Publications:
Bulletin. semi-a.

Meetings/Conferences:
Annual Meetings: May

American College of Radiation Oncology *(1989)*
2021 Spring Road, Suite 600
Oak Brook, IL 60521
Tel: (630)368-3733   *Fax:* (630)571-7837
E-Mail: info@acro.org
Web Site: http://www.acro.org
Staff: 4
Annual Budget: $100-250,000
Exec. Secretary: Torry Sansone

Historical Note
ACRO members are radiation oncologists, physicists and administrators. Membership: $300/year (individual); $180/year (associate).

Publications:
Newsletter. irreg.

Meetings/Conferences:
Annual Meetings: May
1999 – San Francisco, CA(Hyatt)/April 24-25

American College of Radiology *(1924)*
1891 Preston White Drive
Reston, VA 20191
Tel: (703)648-8900   *Fax:* (703)391-4397
E-Mail: info@acr.org
Web Site: http://www.acr.org
Members: 29,000 individuals
Staff: 150

Annual Budget: $10-25,000,000
Exec. Director: John J. Curry
Director, Public Relations: Michael Bernstein
Director, State Programs: James G. Potter
Director, Meeting Services: Barbara Ellen Rapp
Director, Education: Joann Bresch
Assoc. Exec. Director: Gary W. Price
C.F.O.: Peter Shavalay
Director, Administration and membership: Donna Kimball
General Counsel: William. Shields

Historical Note
Founded in June 1923 in San Francisco and incorporated in California in 1924. Purpose of the ACR is to improve the art and science of radiological practice through coordination of national radiological societies, promotion of research, standardization of procedures, safeguarding of patients and operators and continuing medical education. Has an annual budget of $18.2 million. Membership: $475/year.

Publications:
American College of Radiology Bulletin. m. adv.

Meetings/Conferences:
Annual Meetings: September/700
1999 – Washington, DC(Hilton)/September 23-27
2000 – New York, NY(Hilton)/Sept. 23-27
2001 – San Francisco, CA/September 6-12

American College of Real Estate Lawyers *(1978)*
1 Central Plaza
11300 Rockville Pike, Suite 903
Rockville, MD 20852-3034
Tel: (301)816-9811   *Fax:* (301)816-9786
Web Site: http://www.acrel.org
Members: 845 individuals
Staff: 2
Annual Budget: $500-1,000,000
Exec. Director: Jill H. Pace

Historical Note
ACREL members are attorneys with at least ten years of specialization in real estate law. Membership is by invitation.

Publications:
ACREL News. q.

Meetings/Conferences:
1999 – Vancouver, BC(Four Seasons)

American College of Rheumatology *(1934)*
60 Executive Park South, N.E., Suite 150
Atlanta, GA 30329-2229
Tel: (404)633-3777   *Fax:* (404)633-1870
Web Site: http://www.rheumatology.org
Members: 6,500 individuals
Staff: 25
Annual Budget: $2-5,000,000
Exec. V. President: Mark Andrejeski
V. President, Marketing: James E. Moody, Jr.
Director, Government Affairs: Steven Echard
Director, Conferences and Meetings: Ronald F. Olejko
Deputy Exec. V. President: Sherrie H. Cathcart, CAE
Director, Membership Services: Lynn Bonfiglio

Historical Note
The professional society for Rheumatologists and associated health professionals. Members are physicians, teachers, researchers, and individuals with an interest in diseases of the joints and connective tissues. Formerly (1989) American Rheumatism Ass'n. Membership: $313/year.

Publications:
ACR News. m. adv.
Arthritis and Rheumatism. m. adv.
Arthritis Care and Research. semi-m. adv.

Meetings/Conferences:
Annual Meetings: November

American College of Sports Medicine *(1954)*
ACSM National Center, Box 1440
Indianapolis, IN 46206-1440
Tel: (317)637-9200   *Fax:* (317)634-7817
E-Mail: pipacsm@acsm.org.
Web Site: http://www.acsm.org/sportsmed
Members: 17,000 individuals
Staff: 35
Annual Budget: $2-5,000,000
Exec. V. President: James R. Whitehead
Director, Public Information: David C. Ferrell
Director, Meetings: Amy Katzenberger
Director, Education: Sue Hilt
Director, Operations: Timothy Calvert
Director, Membership: Susan Yoder
Director, Publications: D. Mark Robertson

Historical Note
ACSM promotes sports medicine and exercise science and their capacity to maintain and enhance physical fitness and general health. Membership includes team physicians, orthopedic surgeons, athletic trainers and others. Affiliated with the Federation Internationale de Medicine Sportive. Membership: $145/year (professional); $60/year (student).

Publications:
ACSM Membership Directory. a.
ACSM Graduate Program Directory. a.
ACSM Undergraduate Program Directory.
Career Services Bulletin. m.
Exercise and Sports Sciences Review. a.
Medicine & Science in Sports & Exercise. m. adv.
Sports Medicine Bulletin. q.

Meetings/Conferences:
1999 – Seattle, WA(Convention Center)/June 2-5

American College of Surgeons *(1913)*
633 N. St. Claire St.
Chicago, IL 60611-3211
Tel: (312)202-5000   *Fax:* (312)202-5001

E-Mail: postmaster@facs.org
Web Site: http://www.facs.org
Members: 62,000 individuals
Staff: 210
Annual Budget: $25-50,000,000
Director: Paul A. Ebert, M.D.
Director, Communications: Linn Meyer
Director, Conventions/Meetings: Felix Niespodziewanski

Historical Note
Founded in 1913 and incorporated in Illinois. A professional association of surgeons devoted to advancing the science of surgery and its competent practice. Has an annual budget of approximately $38 million. Membership: $375/year (individual).

Publications:
Bulletin of the ACS. m.
Care of the Surgical Patient. irreg.
Journal of the American College of Surgeons. m. adv.

Meetings/Conferences:
Semi-Annual Meetings: Spring and Fall
1999 – Toronto, Ontario/April 25-28
1999 – San Francisco, CA/Oct. 10-15

American College of Tax Counsel (1980)
1030 15th St. N.W., Suite 870
Washington, DC 20005
Tel: (202)637-3243   Fax: (202)393-0336
Members: 625 individuals
Staff: 4
Annual Budget: $100-250,000
Administrative Manager: Marianne McDermott

Historical Note
The College was established to foster and recognize excellence and to elevate standards in the practice of tax law. ACTC provides additional mechanisms for input by tax professionals in the development of tax laws and facilitates scholarly discussion and examination of tax policy issues. Membership: $200/year.

Publications:
American Journal of Tax Policy. semi-a.

Meetings/Conferences:

American College of Theriogenologists (1970)
P.O. Box 2118
Hastings, NE 68902-2118
Tel: (402)463-0392   Fax: (402)463-5683
Members: 285 individuals
Annual Budget: under $10,000
Exec. Director: Don Ellerbee

Historical Note
ACT members are veterinarians specializing in animal reproduction.

Publications:
Directory. a.
Newsletter of ACT. bi-m.

Meetings/Conferences:
Annual Meetings: in conjunction with the Soc. for Theriogenology
1999 – Nashville, TN

American College of Toxicology (1977)
9650 Rockville Pike
Bethesda, MD 20814
Tel: (301)571-1840   Fax: (301)571-1852
E-Mail: ekagan@act.faseb.org
Web Site: http://landaus.com/toxicology/
Members: 850 individuals
Exec. Director: Carol Lemire
Asst. Exec. Director: Eveu Kagan

Historical Note
Incorporated in The State of Illinois. A multidisciplinary society composed of professionals having a common interest in toxicology. ACT educates and leads professionals in toxicology and related areas through exchange of information and other events.

Publications:
Acute Toxicity. bi-m. adv.
Internat'l Journal of Toxicology. bi-m. adv.
Newsletter. q.

Meetings/Conferences:
1999 – Vienna, VA(McLean Hilton)/Nov. 7-10

American College of Trial Lawyers (1950)
8001 Irvine Center Dr., Suite 960
Irvine, CA 92718-2919
Tel: (949)727-3194
Members: 4,620 individuals
Staff: 6
Annual Budget: $2-5,000,000
Exec. Director: Robert A. Young

Historical Note
An honorary society of lawyers, former lawyers and judges.

Meetings/Conferences:
Annual Meetings: April

American College of Trust and Estate Counsel (1949)
3415 S. Sepulveda Blvd., Suite 330
Los Angeles, CA 90034
Tel: (310)398-1888   Fax: (310)572-7280
Web Site: http://www.actec.org
Members: 3,000 individuals
Staff: 5
Annual Budget: $500-1,000,000
Exec. Director: Gerry Vogt

Historical Note
Membership, by invitation only, consists of lawyers specializing in probate, estate, and trust law, and related procedures. Formerly (1990) American College of Probate Counsel. Membership: $425/year.

Publications:
ACTEC Notes. q.
Membership Roster. a.

Studies. irreg.

Meetings/Conferences:
Annual Meetings: February-March/1,200
1999 – Maui, HI/March 2-7
1999 – Montreal, Canada/June 24-27
1999 – Boston, MA/Oct. 13-18

American College of Veterinary Dermatology (1982)
5610 Kearney Mesa Road, Suite B
San Diego, CA 92111
Tel: (619)560-9393
Members: 112 individuals
Annual Budget: $10-25,000
Exec. Secretary: Alexis Borich
Director, Meetings: Judy Schramm

Historical Note
ACVD's purpose is to certify veterinarians in the specialty of dermatology.

Meetings/Conferences:
1999 – Maui, HI/April 23-27

American College of Veterinary Internal Medicine (1972)
2750 S. Wadsworth Blvd., Suite C109
Denver, CO 80227-3400
Tel: (303)980-7136   Fax: (303)980-7137
Toll Free: (800)245 - 9081
E-Mail: ACVIM@aol.com
Web Site: http://www.vmth.ucdavis.edu/ACVIM
Members: 1,062 individuals
Staff: 5
Annual Budget: $250-500,000
Exec. Director: June Pooley
Exhibit Manager: Vicky L. Pelton
Exam Manager: Christine K. Hoeppner

Historical Note
Governing organization for veterinary specialists who deal with the diagnosis and non-surgical treatment of diseases of the internal organs. Encompasses internal medicine, cardiology, oncology, and neurology. Membership: $175/year.

Publications:
Directory. a.
Journal of Veterinary Internal Medicine. bi-m. adv.
Proceedings. a.
Specialists Newsletter. q. adv.

Meetings/Conferences:
Annual Meetings: Summer/4,000
1999 – Chicago, IL(Sheraton)/June 10-13
2000 – Seattle, WA(Convention Center)/May 25-28

American College of Veterinary Microbiologists (1962)
Historical Note
Address unknown in 1997.

American College of Veterinary Ophthalmologists (1969)
Dept. of Veterinary Clinical Sciences
Louisiana State University
Baton Rouge, LA 70803-8422
Tel: (504)346-3333   Fax: (504)346-5748
Web Site: http://www.acvo.com
Members: 184 individuals
Staff: 1
Annual Budget: $100-250,000
Secretary-Treasurer: Mary Belle Glaze, D.V.M.

Historical Note
The objectives of the ACVO are to advance ophthalmology in all phases of veterinary medicine, including training, continuing education, research and practice. Prerequisites for membership include graduation from an accredited college of veterinary medicine, two years of training in an approved residency program and successful completion of written, oral and practical examinations by the ACVO Examination Committee. Affiliated with The American Veterinary Medical Ass'n. Membership: $250/year.

Publications:
Veterinary and Comparative Ophthalmology. q. adv.

Meetings/Conferences:
Annual Meetings: Fall, with American Academy of Ophthalmology
1999 – Chicago, IL

American College of Veterinary Pathologists (1949)
19 Mantua Road
Mount Royal, NJ 08061
Tel: (609)423-0119   Fax: (609)423-3420
Web Site: http://www.afip.org/acup/index/html
Members: 1,288 individuals
Staff: 4
Annual Budget: $250-500,000
Exec. Director: Susan Whitehouse

Historical Note
Membership: $170/year.

Publications:
Membership Directory. a.
Proceedings. a.
Veterinary Pathology Journal. 6/year. adv.

Meetings/Conferences:
Annual Meetings: Fall

American College of Veterinary Radiology (1961)
P.O. Box 87
Glencoe, IL 60022
Tel: (847)251-5517
Members: 210 individuals
Staff: 1
Annual Budget: $50-100,000
Exec. Director: Dr. Myron Bernstein

Historical Note
Originally established as a specialty board in veterinary radiology under the jurisdiction of the American Veterinary Medical Ass'n, it had become the American Board of Veterinary Radiology with 11 charter members in 1966 and was incorporated in Illinois. Assumed its present name in 1969. Membership: $125/year.

Publications:
Ultrasound.
Veterinary Radiology. bi-m. adv.

Meetings/Conferences:
Annual Meetings: Every two out of three yrs. in Chicago, IL with the Radiological Soc. America; next year in conjunction with the American College of Veterinary Surgeons; final year scientific/resort meeting.
1999 – Chicago, IL(Marriott O'Hare)
2000 – Chicago, IL(Marriott O'Hare)

American College of Veterinary Surgeons (1965)
4401 East-West Hwy., Suite 205
Bethesda, MD 20814-4523
Tel: (301)913-9550   Fax: (301)913-2034
E-Mail: acvs@aol.com
Web Site: http://www.acvs.org
Members: 756 individuals
Staff: 2
Annual Budget: $500-1,000,000
Exec. Director: Ann T. Loew, Ed.M.

Historical Note
Maintains rigid membership requirements including certification by examination.

Publications:
Directory. bien. adv.
Newsletter. 3/year. adv.
Symposium Proceedings. a.

Meetings/Conferences:
1999 – San Francisco, CA(Hyatt Regency Embarcadero)/Sept. 30-Oct. 3
2000 – Arlington, VA(Hyatt Regency Crystal City)/Sept. 21-24
2001 – Chicago, IL(Hyatt Regency)/Oct. 11-14
2002 – San Diego, CA(Sheraton)/Oct. 17-20

American College Personnel Ass'n (1924)
One Dupont Circle, Suite 300
Washington, DC 20036-1110
Tel: (202)835-2272   Fax: (202)296-3286
E-Mail: info@acpa.nche.edu
Web Site: http://www.acpa.nche.edu
Members: 7,000 individuals
Staff: 5
Annual Budget: $1-2,000,000
Exec. Director: Carmen Guevara Neuberger, EdD, JD
Manager, Education/Publications: Donna M. Bourassa
Office Manager/Meeting Planner: Marguerite Clemons
Accounts Manager: Dorothy Seville
Manager, Membership Services: Lisa Mihalik
Asst. Systems Manager: Jeremy Baird

Historical Note
Established in 1924 to serve as a collective voice for the college student personnel profession, including teachers, counselors, administrators, deans, department heads and researchers. ACPA is an independent association with 16 commissions, 5 standing committees, and 32 state and international divisions. Membership: $90/year (general); $115-$800/year (organization/institute); $60/year (student); $34/year (graduate student).

Publications:
About Campus. bi-m. adv.
ACPA Developments Newsletter. q. adv.
The Journal of College Student Development. bi-m. adv.

Meetings/Conferences:
Annual Meetings: Spring
1999 – Atlanta, GA(Marriott Marquis)/March 20-24/3750
2000 – Washington, DC(Sheraton/Shoreham)/March 31-April 4/3750
2001 – Boston, MA(Sheraton/Marriott Copley)/March 2-7/4000
2002 – Long Beach, CA(Hyatt Regency)/March 13-17/3000

American Collegiate Retailing Ass'n (1948)
Dept. of Marketing, Georgia Southern U.
P.O. Box 8154
Statesboro, GA 30460
Tel: (912)681-5336   Fax: (912)871-1523
Members: 300 individuals
Annual Budget: under $10,000
President: William Bowlen

Historical Note
Established in 1948, ACRA is an organization of faculty from colleges with specialized curricula in retailing. Conducts annual Retail Management Conference with retail store executives, and attends the semi-annual meeting in New York each winter in conjunction with the Nat'l Retail Federation. Has no paid staff. Membership: $35/year.

Publications:
ACRA Newsletter. q.
Clearinghouse Directory. a.

Meetings/Conferences:
Semi-annual Meetings: January in New York, NY with Nat'l Retail Federation and April

American Colon Therapy Ass'n (1989)
Historical Note
Became the Internat'l Ass'n Colon Therapy in 1995.

American Commerce and Shipping Ass'n (1992)
1385 Iris Drive
Conyers, GA 30013
Tel: (770)929-3200   Fax: (770)929-3201
E-Mail: utsinfo@aol.com
Members: 1,025 individuals

C.E.O.: Anthony L. Keenan

Historical Note
Members are concerned with standards for interstate and international shipping. Membership: $100/year.

Publications:
Newsletter. q.

Meetings/Conferences:

American Commercial Collectors Ass'n *(1970)*

Historical Note
Became Internat'l Ass'n of Commercial Collectors in 1996.

American Commodity Distribution Ass'n *(1975)*

Historical Note
Address unknown in 1998.

American Community Cultural Center Ass'n *(1978)*
149 Cannongate III
Nashua, NH   03063-1953
Tel: (603)886-2748
Exec. Director: Milli Janz

Historical Note
ACCCA was founded to encourage the development of local cultural centers in the U.S. and abroad. Offers technical information and guidance on the development of cultural centers. Membership: $25/year.

American Comparative Literature Ass'n *(1960)*
Univ. of Alabama Box 870262
Tuscaloosa, AL   35487-0262
E-Mail: info@acla.org
Members: 800 individuals
Staff: 2
Annual Budget: under $10,000
Secretary-Treasurer: Dr. Elaine Martin

Historical Note
An allied organization of the Modern Language Ass'n. Membership: $30/year (individual); $100/year (institution); $7/year (student).

Publications:
ACLA Bulletin. semi-a.

Meetings/Conferences:
Annual Meetings: March

American Compensation Ass'n *(1955)*
14040 N. Northsight Blvd.
Scottsdale, AZ   05260 3627
Tel: (602)483-8352   *Fax:* (602)483-8352
E-Mail: aca@acaonline.org
Web Site: http://www.acaonline.org
Members: 25,000 individuals
Staff: 95
Annual Budget: $10-25,000,000
Exec. Director: Wallace J. Nichols, CCP
Director, Information and Publishing Services: Don Griffith
Manager, Meetings/Conferences: Lorraine Bergstorm, CMP
Senior Director, Education Services: Ted Sheneberger
Director, Finance and Administrative Support: DeAnn Rice
Director, Information Technology: Wilfredo Gumaru
Director, Global Operations Group: John Maxwell

Historical Note
Established as the Ohio Wage and Salary Association, it assumed its present name in 1957 and superseded the Midwest Compensation Association in 1963. Members are individuals responsible for the administration and management of all forms of employee compensation and benefits in their organization – wages, salaries, benefits, executive compensations and other forms of remuneration. Has a annual budget of approximately $15 million. Membership: $155/year (individual).

Publications:
ACA Journal.
ACA News. m.
Membership Directory. a.

Meetings/Conferences:
Annual Meetings: May/1100-1300
1999 – Boston, MA(Convention Center, Marriott & Westin)
2000 – Seattle, WA(Convention Center)

American Composers Alliance *(1937)*
170 W. 74th St.
New York, NY   10023
Tel: (212)362-8900   *Fax:* (212)362-8902
E-Mail: 75534.2232@compuserve.com
Members: 320 individuals
Staff: 5
Annual Budget: $100-250,000
Exec. Director: Bob Goldfarb
Manager, Operations: Donal Fergusson

Historical Note
Established in late 1937 by 48 musicians under the leadership of Aaron Copland, its first president, to protect the rights of its members and to promote the use and understanding of their music. Performing rights are assigned to Broadcast Music, Inc. Distributes members' music through its subsidiary, American Composers Edition. Membership: $75/yr.

Publications:
Catalogues of New Music.

Meetings/Conferences:
Annual Meetings: New York, NY/Dec.

American Concrete Institute *(1905)*
38800 Country Club Drive
Farmington Hills, MI   48331
Tel: (248)848-3700   *Fax:* (248)848-3701
Web Site: http://www.aci-int.org
Members: 17,500 individuals, 550 organizations
Staff: 70
Annual Budget: $5-10,000,000

Manager, Conventions/Meetings: Angie Legaspi
Director, Education: Peter J. Steiner
Director, Administrative Services: William R. Tolley
Associate Publisher/Editor: William J. Semioli, PE

Historical Note
Founded in 1905 as the Nat'l Ass'n of Cement Users; became the American Concrete Institute in 1913 and was incorporated in Michigan in 1964. ACI gathers and disseminates information for the improvement of the design, construction, manufacture and maintenance of concrete products and structures. Its members include designers, architects, civil engineers, educators, contractors, concrete craftsmen and technicians, materials suppliers, testing laboratories and manufacturers. Membership: $157/year (individual), $680/year (organization).

Publications:
ACI Materials Journal. bi-m.
ACI Structural Journal. bi-m.
Concrete Abstracts. bi-m.
Concrete International. m. adv.

Meetings/Conferences:
Semi-Annual Meetings: Spring and Fall

American Concrete Pavement Ass'n *(1964)*
5420 Old Orchard Road, Suite A-100
Skokie, IL   60077-1059
Tel: (847)966-2272   *Fax:* (847)966-9970
E-Mail: webmaster@pavement.com
Web Site: http://www.pavement.com
Members: 500
Staff: 14
Annual Budget: $250-500,000
President: Valentin Riva

Historical Note
Formerly (1988) the American Concrete Paving Association. ACPA is dedicated to promoting concrete pavement for use in interstate highways, state and county highways, local roads and airports. Membership: Dues depend on the type of member company.

Publications:
ACPA Action. m.
ACPA Today. q.
Concrete Pavement Progress. bi-m.

Meetings/Conferences:
Annual Meetings: late November or early December/300-400

American Concrete Pipe Ass'n *(1907)*
222 W. Las Colinas Blvd., Suite 641
Irving, TX   75039
Tel: (972)506-7216   *Fax:* (972)506-7682
Web Site: http://www.concrete-pipe.org
Members: 180 companies
Staff: 10
Annual Budget: $1-2,000,000
President: John J. Duffy
Director, Marketing: Mike Suabert
Government Relations Consultant: Cyril I. Malloy
Director, Services: Jeannie Williams
Director, Technical Services: Josh Beakley
Director, Services: Donna Hoye

Historical Note
The American Concrete Pipe Ass'n is an international trade association whose U.S. and Canadian members account for approximately 75% of the precast concrete pipe, box culvert and manhole production in North America. The association sponsors research and engineering investigations, educational programs and publishes technical and promotional literature. Provides administrative support to Concrete Pipe Ass'ns, a joint venture with American Concrete Pressure Pipe Ass'n (same address).

Publications:
Concrete Pipe News. q.
Membership Directory. a.
Newscast. irreg.
Resources. a.
The Locator. a.

Meetings/Conferences:
Annual Meetings: March/April
1999 – Florida/March 23-26

American Concrete Pressure Pipe Ass'n *(1950)*
11800 Sunrise Valley Dr., Suite 309
Reston, VA   20191-5302
Tel: (703)391-9135   *Fax:* (703)391-9136
Members: 7 companies
Staff: 2
Annual Budget: $500-1,000,000
President: David Prosser

Historical Note
Serves as the authoritative voice of the concrete pressure pipe industry, providing technical and educational information and activities.

Publications:
Concrete Pressure Pipe Digest. q.

Meetings/Conferences:

American Concrete Pumping Ass'n *(1974)*
7695 Kinneytuck Ct.
Lewis Center, OH   43035
Tel: (614)548-2351   *Fax:* (614)548-2352
Members: 360 companies
Staff: 4
Annual Budget: $250-500,000
Exec. Director: Donald Taylor

Historical Note
ACFA promotes concrete pumping and safety in concrete pumping. Membership: $100-300/year.

Publications:
Concrete Pumping & Placing. q.
Update (newsletter). bi-m.

Meetings/Conferences:
1999 – Las Vegas, NV
2000 – Las Vegas, NV
2001 – Las Vegas, NV

American Conference for Irish Studies *(1959)*
Liberal Arts, Nova Southwestern Univ.
3301 College Ave.
Fort Lauderdale, FL   33314
Tel: (954)262-8207   *Fax:* (954)262-3881
E-Mail: doan@polaris.acast.nova.edu
Members: 1,400 individuals
Annual Budget: $10-25,000
Secretary: James Doan

Historical Note
Formerly (1988) American Committe for Irish Studies. Members include scholars interested in Irish history, language and culture. Affiliated with the American Historical Ass'n and the Modern Language Ass'n of America. Membership varies.

Publications:
ACIS Newsletter.
Irish Literary Supplement. bien.

Meetings/Conferences:
Annual Meetings: Spring/200

American Conference of Academic Deans *(1944)*
1818 R St., N.W.
Washington, DC   20009
Tel: (202)387-3760   *Fax:* (202)265-9532
Web Site: http://www.acac.edu.org
Members: 685 individuals
Staff: 2
Annual Budget: $25-50,000
Exec. Director: Suzanne Hyers
Meeting Assistnt: Eliza Reilly

Historical Note
Academic deans and chief academic officers of four-year colleges, community colleges and two-year institutions. Membership: $50/year.

Publications:
Connections. a.
Peer Review. a.

Meetings/Conferences:
Annual Meetings: San Francisco, CA(Westin)/Jan./1000
1999 – San Francisco, CA/Jan. 28-30

American Conference of Cantors *(1953)*
140 Central Ave.
Lawrence, NY   11559-1417
Tel: (516)239-3650   *Fax:* (516)239-1318
E-Mail: accantors@aol.com
Members: 350 individuals
Staff: 4
Annual Budget: $50-100,000
Exec. V. President: Howard M Stahl

Historical Note
Members serve in Jewish congregations in the United States and Canada. Affiliated with the Union of American Hebrew Congregations. Membership: 1% of annual salary.

Publications:
Koleinu. bi-m.
Membership Directory. a.

Meetings/Conferences:
Annual Meetings: Summer
1999 – Cape Cod, MA/June 27-July 1

American Conference of Governmental Industrial Hygienists *(1938)*
1330 Kemper Meadow Dr., Suite 600
Cincinnati, OH   45240-1634
Tel: (513)742-2020   *Fax:* (513)742-3355
Web Site: http://www.acgih.org
Members: 5,500 individuals
Staff: 25
Annual Budget: $2-5,000,000
Exec. Director: Richard A. Strano, CAE
Director, Communications and Conferences: Sharon Ziegler
Director, Administration/Finance: Anthony Rizzuto

Historical Note
Formerly (1945) Nat'l Conference of Governmental Industrial Hygienists. A professional society of government and university employees engaged in full-time programs of industrial hygiene. Membership: $96/year (individual).

Publications:
Industrial Ventilation Manual. irreg.
Journal of Applied Occupational & Environmental Hygiene. m. adv.
Threshold Limit Values. a.

Meetings/Conferences:
Annual Meetings: May, with American Industrial Hygiene Ass'n/10,000
1999 – Toronto, Ontario, Canada(Convention Center)/June 5-11
2000 – Orlando, FL(Convention Center)
2001 – San Diego, CA(Convention Center)

American Congress of Rehabilitation Medicine *(1921)*
4700 W. Lake Ave.
Glenview, IL   60025-1485
Tel: (847)375-4725   *Fax:* (847)375-4777
E-Mail: info@acrm.org
Members: 1,700 individuals, 15 companies
Staff: 6
Annual Budget: $500-1,000,000
Exec. Director: Diane Burgher

Historical Note
Founded September 18, 1923 as the American College of Radiology and Physiotherapy. Name changed in 1926 to the American College of Physical Therapy and in 1930 to the American Congress

of Physical Therapy. In 1945 it again changed its name to the American Congress of Physical Medicine, and in 1953 it became the American Congress of Physical Medicine and Rehabilitation. In 1967 it adopted its present name. Incorporated in Illinois in 1930. Provides education and networking opportunities to professionals throughout the field of medical rehabilitation. Membership: $150-230/year (individual); $3,000/year (organization/company).

Publications:
Archives of Physical Medicine and Rehabilitation. m. adv.
Rehabilitation Outlook. q.

Meetings/Conferences:
Annual Meetings: Fall/200

American Congress on Surveying and Mapping (1941)
5410 Grosvenor Lane, Suite 100
Bethesda, MD   20814-2122
Tel: (301)493-0200   Fax: (301)493-8245
Web Site: http://www.survmap.org
Members: 8,000 individuals, 50 companies
Staff: 14
Annual Budget: $1-2,000,000
Exec. Director: John Lisack, Jr., CAE
Director, Communications and Government Affairs: Kevin Flynn
Convention Coordinator: Denise Calvert
Director, Finance: Richard T. Chinn
Director, Membership Services: Traci Little

Historical Note
Founded in the District of Columbia in 1941 and incorporated there in 1951. Composed of four member organizations: the Nat'l Soc. of Professional Surveyors, the Geographic Land Information Society and the American Cartographic Ass'n. Affiliated with state land surveyor societies, also the Accreditation Board for Engineering and Technology, and the National Council of Engineering Examiners. Member of the Internat'l Federation of Surveyors, the Internat'l Cartographic Ass'n and the Internat'l Soc. of Mine Surveyors. Promotes the profession of surveying and mapping science. Sponsors and supports the ACSM/NSPS Political Action Committee. Membership: $127-165/year (individual), $900/year (organization).

Publications:
ACSM Bulletin. bi-m. adv.
Cartography and Geographic Information Systems. q. adv.
Surveying and Land Information Systems. q. adv.

Meetings/Conferences:
Semi-annual Meetings: Spring and Fall
1999 – Portland, OR

American Connemara Pony Soc. (1956)
Historical Note
Address unknown in 1997.

American Construction Inspectors Ass'n (1959)
12995 6th St., Suite 69
Yucaipa, CA   92399
Tel: (909)795-3039   Fax: (909)795-4039
Toll Free: (888)876 - 2242
Web Site: http://www.acia.com
Members: 1,100 individuals, 30 companies
Staff: 2
Annual Budget: $100-250,000
Exec. Director: Woneta Carnes

Historical Note
Members are engineering, building, public works and other specialized construction inspectors. Supports and sustains the Board of Registered Construction Inspectors. Membership: $125/year (individual), $250/year (company).

Publications:
The Inspector Magazine. q. adv.

Meetings/Conferences:
Annual Meetings: November
1999 – Palm Desert, CA(Embassy Suites)/Oct. 28-31/100

American Consultants League (1984)
30466 Prince William St.
Princess Anne, MD   21853
Tel: (410)651-4869   Fax: (410)651-4885
Members: 1,025 individuals
Staff: 2
Annual Budget: $100-250,000
Exec. Director: Hubert Bermont

Historical Note
An association of part-time and full-time consultants in every field of expertise from all over the United States, Canada, and all foreign countries. Assists consultants in the setting up and managing of the business end of their consultancies by providing educational materials and continuing education through the Consultants Institute, a home study course which is the education arm of the League. Membership: $129/year.

Publications:
Consulting Intelligence (newsletter). bi-m.

Meetings/Conferences:
Annual Meetings: Not held.

American Consulting Engineers Council (1973)
1015 15th St., N.W., Suite 802
Washington, DC   20005-2605
Tel: (202)347-7474   Fax: (202)898-0068
Web Site: http://www.acec.org
Members: 5,000 firms
Staff: 45
Annual Budget: $5-10,000,000
Exec. V. President/C.E.O.: Howard M. Messner
Director, Communications: Sally Thompson
Dir., Government Affairs/General Counsel: John Kalavitrinos
Director, Meetings and Conventions: Susan L. Courtney
Director, Meetings/Conventions: Jeanmarie O'Sullivan
Director, Education Programs: Claire Brannen
Director, Administration: Kim Pham
Deputy EVP: Thomas E. Kern

Director, Member Services & Member Organization Affairs: Cynthia Pratt

Historical Note
Members are independent, private practice engineering companies. Provides information on federal legislation, insurance, business practices, international markets and public relations to member firms. Merger of the American Institute of Consulting Engineers (1910) and the Consulting Engineers Council of the U.S.A. (1956). Sponsors and supports the ACEC Political Action Committee and the Hazardous Waste Action Coalition.

Publications:
American Consulting Engineer. q. adv.
Guidelines to Practice.
Last Word. w.
Member Directory. a.
Resource Catalogue.
Special Reports. m.

Meetings/Conferences:
Semi-Annual Meetings: Spring and Fall
1999 – Traverse City, MI/Sept. 30-Oct. 2
1999 – Seattle, WA/May 9-12
2000 – Buffalo, NY/May 7-10/2000
2000 – San Diego, CA/Sept. 28-30
2001 – San Antonio, TX/May 13-16

American Copper Council (1974)
Two South End Ave., Suite 4C
New York, NY   10280
Tel: (212)945-4990   Fax: (212)945-4992
Members: 200 companies
Staff: 2
Annual Budget: $250-500,000
Exec. Director: Mary C. Boland

Historical Note
Organized in 1974 as the successor to the Committee for the Release of Stockpile Copper, the Council represents all segments of the industry. The Council sponsors four quarterly seminars of interest to members of the copper industry.

Publications:
Coppertalk Magazine. q.
Directory of Member Companies. a.

Meetings/Conferences:
1999 – Monterey, CA

American Corn Millers Federation (1918)
600 Maryland Ave., S.W., Suite 305-W
Washington, DC   20024
Tel: (202)484-2200   Fax: (202)488-7416
E-Mail: betsyfaga@aol.com
Members: 40 companies
Staff: 5
Annual Budget: $1-2,000,000
President: Betsy Faga

Historical Note
NAMA is comprised of companies engaged in grain milling.

Publications:
NAMA Newsletter. m.

Meetings/Conferences:
Semi-annual Meetings: Spring and Fall/40
1999 – Amelia Island, FL(Ritz Carlton)/Oct. 21-24/175

American Corporate Counsel Ass'n (1982)
1025 Connecticut Ave., N.W., Suite 200
Washington, DC   20036-5425
Tel: (202)293-4103   Fax: (202)293-4701
Web Site: http://www.acca.com
Members: 10,500 individuals
Staff: 28
Annual Budget: $2-5,000,000
President & C.O.O.: Frederick J. Krebs
Director, Communications: Deneen Stambone
Director, Education: Maria Volpe-Viles
Director, Finance & Administration: Kathie Cleary
Senior V. President & General Counsel: Susan Hackett
V. President, Chapter Relations and Membership: Bill Free
V. President: Anne Bracken
Director, Information Services: Karima Selehdar

Historical Note
Members are lawyers who practice law in a corporation or other private sector entity and who do not hold themselves out to the public for the practice of law. Organized in Dallas, Texas March 11, 1982 by 52 corporate attorneys from 45 companies. Membership: $150/year.

Publications:
ACCA News Newsletter. 2-4/year.
The ACCA Docket Magazine. bi-m. adv.

Meetings/Conferences:
1999 – San Francisco, CA(Fairmont)

American Correctional Ass'n (1870)
4380 Forbes Blvd.
Lanham, MD   20706-4322
Tel: (301)918-1800   Fax: (301)918-1900
Toll Free: (800)222 - 5646
Web Site: http://www.corrections.com/aca
Members: 20,000 individuals
Staff: 100
Annual Budget: $5-10,000,000
Exec. Director: James A. Gondles, Jr.
Director, Communications/Publications: Gabriella M. Daley
Legislative Liaison: Jim Turpin
Dir., Conventions/Advertising/Corp. Rel.: Marge Restivo
Director, Professional Development: Jack Greene
Director, Finance and Administration: Angela Rice
Dep. Exec. Director: Jeff Washington
Director, Membership: Faye Peterson
Director, Standards/Accreditation: Robert J. Verdeyen

Historical Note
Founded as the Nat'l Prison Ass'n. Became the American Prison Ass'n and assumed its present name in 1954. Member is open to all individuals and organizations actively working in the correctional profession including wardens, psychologists, sociologists, probation officers, etc. Has an annual budget of over $8 million. Membership: $35/year (individual); $300/year (non-profit organizations).

Publications:
Corrections Compendium. m.
Corrections Today. 7/year. adv.
Dir. Juvenile & Adult Co.
National Jail & Adult Detention Directory. bien.
On the Line Newsletter. 5/year.
Probation & Parole Directory. bien.
Proceedings. a.

Meetings/Conferences:
Semi-annual Meetings: January and August
1999 – Nashville, TN/Jan. 18-20/3000
1999 – Denver, CO/Aug. 8-12/5000

American Correctional Chaplains Ass'n (1885)
Historical Note
Address unknown in 1997.

American Correctional Food Service Ass'n (1969)
4248 Park Glen Road
Minneapolis, MN   55416
Tel: (612)928-4658   Fax: (612)929-1318
Members: 1,500 individuals
Staff: 4
Annual Budget: $250-500,000
Exec. Director: Karen Wesloh

Historical Note
An affiliate of the American Correctional Ass'n. Members are professional food service employees in government correctional institutions. Membership: $50/year (foodservice); $375/year (vendor).

Publications:
Directory. a. adv.
Insider Magazine. q. adv.

Meetings/Conferences:
Annual Meetings: August/1,000
1999 – Virginia Beach, VA/Aug. 14-18

American Correctional Health Services Ass'n (1975)
P.O. Box 10
Geln Dale, MD   20769
Tel: (301)918-1842   Fax: (301)918-0557
Toll Free: (877)918 - 1842
E-Mail: achsa@aca.org
Web Site: http://www.corrections.com/ACHSA
Members: 1000 individuals
Staff: 3
Annual Budget: $100-250,000
Administrator: Misty Mackey

Historical Note
Multidisciplinary society of health care professionals and representatives from diverse areas of the corrections field. An affiliate of the American Correctional Ass'n. Membership: $45/year (individual), $375/year (organization).

Publications:
CORHEALTH. bi-m.

Meetings/Conferences:
Annual conferences: Spring or Winter
1999 – Atlanta, GA(Radison Atlanta)/March 11-14/300

American Cotswold Record Ass'n (1878)
18 Elm Street, P.O. Box 59
Plympton, MA   02367
Tel: (781)585-2026
E-Mail: acrasheep@aol.com
Members: 110 individuals
Staff: 1
Annual Budget: under $10,000
Secretary: Vicki Rigel

Historical Note
Formerly (1904) American Cotswold Sheep Ass'n. Members are breeders of purebred Cotswold sheep. Maintains a breed registry.

Publications:
Cotswold News. a.
Directory. a.

Meetings/Conferences:
Annual Meetings: Louisville, KY/November

American Cotton Exporter's Ass'n (1975)
Historical Note
The Webb-Pomerene Act registration of American Cotton Shippers Ass'n.

American Cotton Shippers Ass'n (1924)
88 Union Center, Suite 1204
P.O. Box 3366
Memphis, TN   38173
Tel: (901)525-2272   Fax: (901)527-8303
E-Mail: acsa-mem-wmay@worldnet.att.net
Web Site: http://www.acsa-cotton.org
Members: 500 individuals
Staff: 10
Annual Budget: $10 25,000
V. President, Special Projects: Susan A. Braslow
V. President, Administration and Foreign Operations: William E. May

Historical Note
Members are cotton merchants, cotton shippers, and exporters of raw cotton and firms allied with the industry. Its membership is composed of four Federated Associations: Atlantic Cotton Ass'n; Southern Cotton Ass'n; Texas Cotton Ass'n; and the Western Cotton Shippers Ass'n. Maintains the Cotton States Arbitration

Board in conjunction with the American Textile Manufacturers Institute. Maintains a Washington office. Known as American Cotton Exporters Ass'n under Webb-Pomerene. Membership: $300/year.

Publications:
Directory. a.
Export News. irreg.
Washington Update Reports. irreg.

Meetings/Conferences:
Annual Meetings: Spring

American Council for Construction Education (1974)
1300 Hudson Lane, Suite 3
Monroe, LA   71201-6054
Tel: (318)323-2816   *Fax:* (318)323-2413
E-Mail: acce@iamerica.net
Members: 115 individuals, 50 ass'ns & organizations
Staff: 2
Annual Budget: $100-250,000
Exec. V. President: Daniel E. Dupree

Historical Note
ACCE is the accrediting agency for postsecondary construction education programs. Recognized by the Council for Higher Education Accreditation. Membership: $120/year (individual), $700/year (company), $4,000/year (association voting).

Publications:
Annual Report. a.
Newsletter. q.

Meetings/Conferences:
Semi-Annual Meetings: February and July
1999 – Monroe, LA/Feb. 17-20
1999 – Kansas City, MO/July 21-24

American Council for Southern Asian Art (1966)
926 Ridge Rd.
Hamden, CT   06517
Tel: (203)288-1995
Members: 280 individuals
Secretary: Richard Davis

Historical Note
Formerly the American Committee for South Asian Art, ACSAA members are academics and others with an interest in the art of India, Pakistan, Nepal, Bangladesh, Sri Lanka, and South East Asia. Membership: $25/year (individual); $30/year (institution); $10/year (student).

Publications:
Newsletter, semi-a.

American Council for the Arts (1960)
Historical Note
Name changed to Americans for the Arts in 1996.

American Council for Trade in Services (1994)
1030 15th St., N.W., Suite 1030
Washington, DC   20005
Tel: (202)842-1030   *Fax:* (202)842-1225
Members: 20 companies
Staff: 3
Annual Budget: $50-100,000
President and C.E.O.: Dr. Joy Cherian

Historical Note
ACTS represents the interests of service-industry companies involved in international trade. Membership: $6,000/year.

Publications:
ACTS Talks. m.

Meetings/Conferences:
1999 – Washington, DC(Capitol Hilton)/100

American Council of Applied Clinical Nutrition (1974)
P.O. Box 509
Florissant, MO   63032
Tel: (314)921-3997   *Fax:* (314)921-8485
Members: 500 individuals
Staff: 6
President: Clarence T. Smith, Ph.D.

American Council of Highway Advertisers (1936)
122 C St., N.W., Suite 310
Washington, DC   20001
Tel: (202)347-6787   *Fax:* (301)737-4727
E-Mail: rothgroup_@erols.com
Members: 70 companies
Staff: 2
Annual Budget: $100-250,000
President: Richard R. Roberts

Historical Note
Formerly (1949) American Highway Sign Ass'n and (1985) Roadside Business Ass'n. ACHA represents sign and billboard companies, hotels, motels, restaurants, tourist attractions, service stations and other businesses that depend on attracting highway travelers and customers. Supports the Highway Advertisers Political Action Committee (HAPAC).

Publications:
Bulletin. bi-m.
Legislative Alert Fax. irreg.
Morning Line Newsletter. m.

Meetings/Conferences:
Annual Meetings: Fall

American Council of Hypnotist Examiners (1980)
1147 E. Broadway, Suite 340
Glendale, CA   91205
Tel: (818)242-1159   *Fax:* (818)247-9379
Toll Free: (800)894 - 9766
E-Mail: hypnotherapy@gilboyne.com
Members: 9,200 individuals
Staff: 5
Annual Budget: $100-250,000

Exec. Director: Gil Boyne

Historical Note
Membership: $50-100/year (individual).

Publications:
American Hypnotherapy Report. a.
Directory of Certified Members.
Internat'l Hypnotherapy Report Magazine. q.
Newsletter. irreg.

Meetings/Conferences:
1999 – Glendale, CA(Red Lion)/April 15-18

American Council of Learned Societies (1919)
228 E. 45th St., 16th Floor
New York, NY   10017-3398
Tel: (212)697-1505   *Fax:* (212)949-8058
Web Site: http://www.acls.org
Members: 60 societies, 10 affiliated ass'ns
Staff: 20
Annual Budget: $2-5,000,000
President: John H. D'Arms

Historical Note
Organized in Washington DC September 19, 1919 by twelve scholarly organizations in the humanities and social sciences. Its immediate purpose was to provide U.S. representation in the International Academic Union. Its member organizations today are all national in scope and concerned with the advancement of fundamental research in humanistic studies.

Publications:
ACLS Newsletter. q.
Annual Report. a.
Occasional Papers. irreg.

Meetings/Conferences:
Annual Meetings: Spring

American Council of Life Insurance (1976)
1001 Pennsylvania Ave., N.W.
Suite 500
Washington, DC   20004-2599
Tel: (202)624-2000   *Fax:* (202)624-2319
Members: 538 insurance companies
Staff: 204
Annual Budget: $25-50,000,000
President and C.E.O.: Carroll A. Campbell, Jr.
Senior V. President, Policy: Nikki McNamee
General Counsel and Senior V. President, State and Federal Affairs:
   Mark R. Elam
Director, Meetings and Programs: Linda H. Cunningham
Treasurer: Gary A. Scheinkman

Historical Note
ACLI is a national trade association repesenting the interests of legal reserve life insurance companies in legislative, regulatory and judicial matters at the federal, state and municipal levels of government and at the NAIC. Its member companies hold more the 90 percent of the life insurance in force in the United States.

Publications:
ACLI Digest. bi-m.
Forum 500 Forecast. bi-m.

Meetings/Conferences:
Annual Meetings: Fall/1,200

American Council of Nanny Schools (1983)
Delta College
University Center, MI   48710
Tel: (517)686-9417
Members: 14 schools
Annual Budget: under $10,000
Director: Joy Shelton

Historical Note
ACNS is a coalition of accredited nanny schools which seeks to promote the professional status of nannies. The Council establishes educational standards, accredits new schools and provides professional support for nannies. Membership: $300/year (organization/company).

Publications:
ACNewS. semi-a.

Meetings/Conferences:
Semi-annual Meetings: Spring and Fall in conjunction with the Nat'l Ass'n for the Education of Young Children

American Council of Railroad Women (1944)
50 F Street, N.W., Suite 6101
Washington, DC   20001
E-Mail: AHAZELL@LMS.APR.ORG
Members: 150 individuals
Annual Budget: under $10,000
President: E.B. Anne Denman

Historical Note
Membership restricted to corporate officers and professional or high level supervisors/managers in the railroad industry. Established as Nat'l Ass'n of Railroad Women, it assumed its present name in 1952. Membership: $45/year; applicants are approved by the governing board.

Publications:
ACRW Bulletin. 3-4/year.

Meetings/Conferences:
Annual Meetings: Fall

American Council of State Savings Supervisors (1939)
P.O. Box 34175
Washington, DC   20043-4175
Tel: (703)922-5153   *Fax:* (703)922-6237
Members: 130 individuals
Staff: 1
Annual Budget: $100-250,000
Exec. Director: Diane Homiak

Historical Note
Formerly (1987) Nat'l Ass'n of State Savings and Loan Supervisors. Members are regulators of state-chartered thrift

institutions. Educational arm is the Institute for Supervisory Education. Associate membership includes approximately 100 state-chartered thrift institutions.

Publications:
The State Advisor. m. adv.

Meetings/Conferences:
Annual Meetings: May/June
1999 – Chicago, IL(Tremont Hotel)/June 13-15

American Council of Teachers of Russian (1974)
1776 Massachusetts Ave., N.W., Suite 700
Washington, DC   20036
Tel: (202)833-7522   *Fax:* (202)833-7523
E-Mail: general@actr.org
Web Site: http://www.actr.org
Members: 1,500 individuals, 275 sending institutions
Staff: 55
Annual Budget: $10-25,000
Exec. Director: Dan E. Davidson, Ph.D.
Govt. Relation Liaison: Carl A. Herrin
Director, Finance: Martin Nichols
Deputy Director: Lisa Choate
Senior Program Manager: Lauren Clarke
Manager, Human Resources: Kate Gottschall
Director, Development: Pamela Gerardi

Historical Note
ACTR is a private, non-profit educational ass'n and exchange organization devoted to improving education, professional training, and research within and about the Russian-speaking world, including both the Russian Federation and the many scores of non-Russian cultures and populations inhabiting the regions of central and eastern Europe and Eurasia. Over the past 20 years, ACTR has placed and supported U.S. students, teachers and scholars in many disciplines within the difficult political and logistical circumstances of the newly independent states (NIS). ACTR has administered intensive Russian-language immersion programs for U.S. undergraduates, graduate students, and teachers at institutes and universities in Moscow and St. Petersburg since 1976. In addition, ACTR administers programs for nationals of the NIS teaching, studying, and conducting research in the U.S. at the secondary, post-secondary, graduate, and post-graduate academic levels. Membership: $20/year (associate and full professors); $15/year (assistant professors, lecturers, and pre-college teachers); $10/year (students and retired persons); $200 (life membership); $100/year (institutions).

Publications:
ACTR Newsletter. 20/year. adv.
Russian Language Journal q. adv. adv.

Meetings/Conferences:
Annual Meetings: December 27-30, with the American Ass'n of Teachers of Slavic and Eastern European Languages and the Modern Languages Ass'n of America

American Council on Consumer Interests (1953)
240 Stanley Hall, University of Missouri
Columbia, MO   65211
Tel: (573)882-3817   *Fax:* (573)884-6571
E-Mail: acci@showme.missouri.edu
Members: 600 individuals, 650 institutions
Staff: 2
Annual Budget: $100-250,000
Exec. Director: Anita Metzen

Historical Note
Founded at the University of Minnesota as the Council on Consumer Information with 21 charter members for the purpose of stimulating the exchange of ideas among persons interested in the welfare of the consumer. The present name was adopted in 1969. ACCI is an affiliate member of the Internat'l Organization of Consumers Unions and the Consumer Federation of America. Membership: $70/year (individual); $150/year (organization); $35/year (student).

Publications:
Advancing the Consumer Interest. semi-a.
Consumer Interests Annual. a.
Consumer News and Reviews. bi-m.
Journal of Consumer Affairs. semi-a.

Meetings/Conferences:
Annual Meetings: March or April/250
1999 – Chicago, IL(Chicago City Centre)/March 24-27/200
2000 – San Antonio, TX
2001 – Washington, DC

American Council on Education (1918)
One Dupont Circle, N.W., Suite 800
Washington, DC   20036-1193
Tel: (202)939-9300   *Fax:* (202)833-4760
Web Site: http://www.acenet.edu
Members: 1,800 institutions and associations
Staff: 175
Annual Budget: $10-25,000,000
President: Stanley O. Ikenberry
V.P., Div. of Governmental Affairs: Terry W. Hartle
Annual Meetings Planner: Stephanie Marshall
V. President, Administration: Irene Gomberg
General Counsel: Sheldon Steinbach
V.President, External Affairs: James Murray

Historical Note
Organized by eleven national educational associations to coordinate the work of educational institutions during World War I. It has always placed particular emphasis on higher education and today plays a leading role in the resolution of questions regarding higher education and the Federal Government. Has an annual budget of approximately $17.6 million.

Publications:
Higher Education and National Affairs. semi-m.
Presidency. q.

Meetings/Conferences:
Annual Meetings: Winter/1,200
1999 – Washington, DC/Feb. 13-16

American Council on Exercise (1985)
5820 Oberlin Drive, Suite 102
San Diego, CA 92121-3787
Tel: (619)535-8227   *Fax:* (619)535-1778
Toll Free: (800)825 - 3636
Web Site: http://www.acefitness.org
Members: 46 individuals
Staff: 53
Annual Budget: $5-10,000,000
Exec. Director: Sheryl Marks Brown
V.President, Marketing/Public Relations: Jim Winters
V. President, Programs/Services: Mitch Sudy
C.O.O./Asst. Exec. Director: Norm Peck
Director, Administration/Human Resources: Anthony Spencer
V.President, Publications/Certification: Richard Cotton

Historical Note
The American Council on Exercise (ACE) is a not-for-profit, educational organization committed to enriching quality of life through safe and effective physical activity. It is the largest not-for-profit fitness certifying organization in the world, with over 65,000 instructors certified in 60 countries since 1986.

Publications:
ACE Ambassador Update.
ACE Certified News. bi-m.
ACE Fitness Matters. bi-m. adv.
ACE Leader Network.

American Council on Internat'l Personnel (1971)
515 Madison Ave., 15th Floor
New York, NY 10022-5403
Tel: (212)688-2437   *Fax:* (212)593-4697
E-Mail: info@acip.com
Web Site: http://www.acip.com
Members: 280 companies
Staff: 6
Annual Budget: $1-2,000,000
President: Arnold E. Eagle
Office Administrator: Joleen A. Hawkins

Historical Note
Membership is open to all companies and organizations that employ at least 1,000 persons worldwide, including overseas and U.S. affiliates and subsidiaries. ACIP's purpose is to serve the business community on immigration matters. Membership: $500/year.

Publications:
ACIP Newsletter. bi-m.
Employment of Foreign Nationals in the U. S.

Meetings/Conferences:
Annual Meetings: always Arlington, VA(Ritz-Carlton)/first week of June/175
1999 – Washington, DC

American Council on Pharmaceutical Education (1932)
311 West Superior St., Suite 512
Chicago, IL 60610
Tel: (312)664-3575   *Fax:* (312)664-4652
E-Mail: www.acpe-accredit.org
Members: 10 individuals
Staff: 7
Annual Budget: $100-250,000
Exec. Director: Daniel A. Nona

Historical Note
Established in 1932, chartered in Maryland in 1939. Sponsoring organizations are the American Ass'n of Colleges of Pharmacy, the American Pharmaceutical Ass'n, and the Nat'l Ass'n of Boards of Pharmacy. Accredits professional programs in pharmacy.

Publications:
Accredited Degree Programs. a.
Approved Providers of CE. a.

Meetings/Conferences:
Annual Meetings: Semi-annual Meetings

American Council on Schools and Colleges (1924)
13014 N. Dale Mabry, Suite 363
Tampa, FL 33618-2814
Tel: (813)926-5446
E-Mail: fredrick@tech-cezter.com
Members: 281 organizations
Staff: 2
Annual Budget: $50-100,000
Exec. Director: F. Richard O'Keefe, STD,D.Hum.

Historical Note
Formerly American Council on Education, Schools and Colleges. Represents private schools, institutes, trade schools, in-house training programs, consultants, publishers, other suppliers, vendors, and support organizations. Supports campus-oriented, open schools and other experimental programs. Not an accreditation organization. Membership: $65/year (individual), $150-$500/year (organization).

American Council on Science and Health (1978)
2nd Floor, 1995 Broadway
New York, NY 10023-5860
Tel: (212)362-7044   *Fax:* (212)362-4919
E-Mail: acsh@acsh.org
Web Site: http://www.acsh.org
Members: 2,500 individuals, 250 corporations
Staff: 10
Annual Budget: $1-2,000,000
President: Elizabeth M. Whelan, Sc.D., MPH

Historical Note
A consumer education organization providing the public with scientifically accurate evaluations of food, chemicals, the environment and health. Membership: $25/year (general), $50/year (sustaining), $1,000 and greater/year (organization).

Publications:
Priorities for Long Life & Good Health. q.
The ACSH Media Update. semi-a.

Meetings/Conferences:
1999 – New York, NY

American Council on the Teaching of Foreign Languages (1967)
6 Executive Plaza
Yonkers, NY 10701-6801
Tel: (914)963-8830   *Fax:* (914)963-1275
E-Mail: actflhq@aol.com
Web Site: http://www.actfl.org
Members: 7,500 individuals
Staff: 20
Annual Budget: $1-2,000,000
Exec. Director: C. Edward Scebold
Manager, Convention: Louise Patierno
Manager, Accounting: Sharon Denet
Manager, Membership: June Hicks

Historical Note
Founded in 1967 as part of the Modern Language Ass'n of America and incorporated in 1974. Became a separate organization in 1977. Membership: $65/year.

Publications:
ACTFL Foreign Language Education Series. a.
ACTFL Newsletter. q.
Foreign Language Annals. q. adv.

Meetings/Conferences:
Annual Meetings: November/5,000
1999 – Dallas, TX/Nov. 18-21

American Counseling Ass'n (1952)
5999 Stevenson Ave.
Alexandria, VA 22304-3300
Tel: (703)823-9800   *Fax:* (703)823-0252
E-Mail: aca@counseling.org
Web Site: http://www.counseling.org
Members: 52,000 individuals
Staff: 60
Annual Budget: $5-10,000,000
Interim Exec. Director: Richard Yep
Dir., Public Policy and Information: Scott Barstow
Director, Meeting Services: Andrew Miller
C.F.O./C.O.O.: Richard Mozier
Direcor, Operations: Amy Crank
Director, Publishing Systems: Michael Comlish

Historical Note
Formerly (1983) the American Personnel and Guidance Ass'n and (1992) American Ass'n for Counseling and Development, ACA is a private, non-profit organization dedicated to the growth and development of the counseling profession. ACA members, who must hold a master's degree or higher in counseling or a closely related field, work in education settings, mental health agencies, community organizations, correctional institutions, employment settings, rehabilitation programs, government, business, industry, research facilities, and private practice. Divisions include the following: American College Counseling Ass'n; American Mental Health Counselors Ass'n; American Rehabilitation Counseling Ass'n; American School Counselor Ass'n; Ass'n for Adult Development and Aging; Ass'n for Assessment in Counseling; Ass'n for Counselor Education and Supervision; Ass'n for Counselors and Educators in Government; Ass'n of Gay, Lesbian and Bisexual Issues in Counseling; Ass'n for Humanistic Education and Development; Ass'n for Multicultural Counseling and Development; Ass'n for Specialists in Group Work; Ass'n for Spiritual, Ethical and Religious Values in Counseling; Internat'l Ass'n of Addictions and Offender Counselors; Internat'l Ass'n of Marriage and Family Counselors; Nat'l Career Development Ass'n; and Nat'l Employment Counseling Ass'n. Has an annual budget of approximately $9.5 million. Membership: $106/year (professional); $80/year (retired/student).

Publications:
Counseling Today Newspaper. m. adv.
Journal of Counseling and Development. bi-m. adv.

Meetings/Conferences:
Annual Meetings: Spring/4,000
1999 – San Diego, CA/April 14-17
2000 – Washington, DC/March 22-25

American Countertrade Ass'n (1986)
818 Connecticut Ave., Suite 1200
Washington, DC 20006
Tel: (202)887-9011   *Fax:* (202)872-8324
E-Mail: aca@countertrade.org
Web Site: http://www.countertrade.org
Members: 500 individuals, 100 companies
Annual Budget: $50-100,000
Contact: Emily Creson

Historical Note
ACA members are NAFTA-based companies with an interest in countertrade. Membership: $350/year (corporate).

Publications:
ACA Newsletter. irreg.

Meetings/Conferences:
Semi-Annual Meetings: Spring and Fall
1999 – Miami Beach, FL/May 3-6

American Court and Commercial Newspapers (1930)
P.O. Box 430209
Pontiac, MI 48343-0209
Tel: (248)334-4329
Members: 71 newspapers
Staff: 1
Annual Budget: $50-100,000
Exec. Director/Meetings Manager: Sheila R. Ashcraft

Historical Note
Newspapers dealing primarily with court news, financial matters, real estate and business matters. Established as Associated Court and Commercial Newspapers, it assumed its present name in 1979. Membership: up to $2,100/year for 4 or more papers under common ownership.

Publications:
Bulletin. q.

Meetings/Conferences:
1999 – Sea Island, GA(The Cloister)/March 9-14
1999 – San Antonio, TX(The Crockett)/Oct. 12-17

American Craft Ass'n
Historical Note
A program of the American Craft Council.

American Craft Council (1943)
72 Spring St., 6th Fl.
New York, NY 10012-4019
Tel: (212)274-0630   *Fax:* (212)274-0650
Toll Free: (800)724 - 0859
Members: 30,000 individuals
Staff: 26
Annual Budget: $2-5,000,000
Exec. Director: Jeffrey Lavvis
Director, Finance: Michael W. McKay

Historical Note
Formerly the American Craftsmen's Council, ACC exists to encourage American artisans working in ceramics, wood, glass, metal, textiles, and other craft media, and to foster appreciation for their work. ACC programs include the American Craft Ass'n, American Craft Enterprises, American Craft Publishing, & the American Craft Information Center. Absorbed the American Craft Retailers Ass'n. The American Craft Museum is an affiliate of ACC. Membership: $40-1,000/year.

Publications:
American Craft. bi-m. adv.

Meetings/Conferences:
Annual Meetings: Summer

American Cranberry Growers Ass'n (1869)
Historical Note
Address unknown in 1997.

American Cream Draft Horse Ass'n (1944)
2065 Noble Ave.
Charles City, IA 50616-9108
Tel: (515)228-5308
Web Site: http://members.aol.com/creamdraft/file.html
Members: 45 individuals
Annual Budget: under $10,000
Secretary/Treasurer: Elizabeth A. Ziebell

Historical Note
Members are owners and breeders of American Cream Draft Horses. Has no paid staff. Membership: $10/year (individual).

Publications:
American Cream News. semi-a. adv.
Cream Newsletter. bi-a.

Meetings/Conferences:
1999 – Huxley, IA/July 9-10

American Criminal Justice Ass'n/Lambda Alpha Epsilon (1937)
Box 601047
Sacramento, CA 95860
Tel: (916)484-6553   *Fax:* (916)488-2227
E-Mail: acjalae@aol.com
Web Site: http://www.acjalae.org
Members: 3,750 individuals
Staff: 1
Annual Budget: $50-100,000
Exec. Secretary: Karen K. Campbell

Historical Note
Also known as Lambda Alpha Epsilon, its official title until 1970. Members include persons employed in an area concerned with the administration of criminal justice (e.g., law enforcement, corrections, courts, etc.) and persons enrolled in a program of study in the criminal justice field at a college or university. Membership: $30/year (renewal); $24/year.

Publications:
LAE Journal of the American Criminal Justice Ass'n. semi-a.
LAE Newsletter. semi-a.

Meetings/Conferences:
Annual Meetings: Spring
1999 – New Orleans, LA(Radisson Inn New Orleans Airport)/March 14-19/350

American Crop Protection Ass'n (1933)
1156 15th St., N.W., Suite 400
Washington, DC 20005
Tel: (202)296-1585   *Fax:* (202)463-0474
Web Site: http://www.acpa.org
Members: 86 companies
Staff: 28
Annual Budget: $5-10,000,000
President: Jay J. Vroom
V. President, Communications: Christopher Klose
V.P., Global Science & Regulat'y Affairs: Dr. John McCarthy
V. President, Legislative Affairs: Nancy E. Foster
Manager, State and Regulatory Affairs: Ab Basu
Secretary-Treasurer: Lawrence Norton
Director, Administration/Human Resources: Mary Kay Hindle
Senior V. President and General Counsel: Douglas T. Nelson

Historical Note
Formerly (1933) the Agricultural Insecticides and Fungicides Manufacturers' Association, (1949) the Agricultural Insecticide and Fungicide Association and (1994) the Nata'l Agricultural Chemicals Ass'n. ACPA is a trade association of the manufacturers, formulators, and distributors of agricultural crop protection and pest control products. Membership is composed of companies that produce, sell and distribute virtually all the active ingredients used in crop protection chemicals. Has an annual budget of approximately $7.3 million.

Publications:
Annual Report. a.
Growing Possibilities. q.

Meetings/Conferences:
Annual Meetings: White Sulphur Springs, WV(Greenbrier
    Hotel)/Fall/650 +

American Crossbred Pony Registery *(1957)*
22 Dove Island Road
Newton, NJ 07860
Tel: (973)383-3384
Members: 150 individuals
Staff: 1
Annual Budget: under $10,000
Registrar: Dr. George Yeaton

Historical Note
*Registry certifies and registers bloodlines of crossbred hunter and
driving ponies.*

Meetings/Conferences:
Annual Meetings: Not held.

American Crystallographic Ass'n *(1949)*
P.O. Box 96, Ellicott Station
Buffalo, NY 14205-0096
Tel: (716)856-9600   *Fax:* (716)852-4846
Web Site: http://www.awi.buffalo.edu/aca/
Members: 2,200 individuals
Staff: 2
Annual Budget: $250-500,000
Administrative Manager: Marcia Colquhoun

Historical Note
*Created in 1949 through a merger of the Crystallographic Soc. of
America and the American Soc. of X-ray and Electron Diffraction.
Incorporated in New York in 1971. Member of the American
Institute of Physics. Membership: $75/year (individual), $600/year
(company/organization), $15/year (student).*

Publications:
Newsletter. q.
Transactions of The A. C.

Meetings/Conferences:
Annual Meetings: Spring or Summer/800
1999 – Buffalo, NY(Convention Center)/May 22-27/800
2000 – St. Paul, MN
2001 – Los Angeles, CA(Westin Bonaventure)/800

American Culinary Federation *(1929)*
P.O. Box 3466
10 San Bartola Drive
St. Augustine, FL 32085-3466
Tel: (904)824-4468   *Fax:* (904)825-4758
Toll Free: (800)624 - 9458
E-Mail: acf@aug.com
Web Site: http://www.acfchefs.org/acf.html
Members: 24,000 individuals
Staff: 27
Annual Budget: $2-5,000,000
Director, Operations: John Waters
Director, Membership: Beverly Stuart

Historical Note
*Professional chefs and others serving the food service industry.
Awards the CEC (Certified Executive Chef) designation and the
Master Chef Program. Sponsors the American Academy of Chefs
(Honorary). Absorbed the American Institute of Chefs as well as the
Professional Chefs Association of America. Affiliated with the
Canadian Federation of Chefs and the World Ass'n of Cooks
Societies. Membership: $75/year (individual).*

Publications:
Nat'l Culinary Review. m. adv.

Meetings/Conferences:
Annual Meetings: July

American Cultural Resources Ass'n *(1995)*
6150 E. Ponce de Leon Ave.
Stone Mountain, GA 30083
Tel: (770)498-5159   *Fax:* (770)498-3809
E-Mail: tomwheaton@newsouthassoc.org
Web Site: http://www.acra-crm.org
Members: 120 firms, 30 associate members
Annual Budget: $50-100,000
Exec. Director: Thomas R. Wheaton

Historical Note
*ACRA provides professional support to firms in historic
preservation, architectural history, historical architecture,
landscape architecture, and related disciplines. Membership: $150-
1,000/year.*

Publications:
ACRA Newsletter. bi-m. adv.

Meetings/Conferences:
Annual Meetings: Fall
1999 – Princeton, NJ
2000 – Cincinnati, OH

American Custom Gunmakers Guild *(1983)*
P.O. Box 812
Burlington, IA 52601-0812
Tel: (319)752-6114   *Fax:* (319)752-6114
Members: 200 individuals, 100 custom gunmakers
Annual Budget: $25-50,000
Exec. Director: Jan Billeb

Historical Note
*ACGG was founded to be a viable association of craftsmen who are
actively engaged in custom gunmaking for the exchange of ideas,
views, techniques, and the promotion of public interest and
awareness of gun making as an art form. Membership: $100/year
(individual); $60/year (associate); $100/year (commercial
associate).*

Publications:
Directory of Custom Gunmaking Services. a.

Gunmaker. q. adv.
Membership Directory. a.

Meetings/Conferences:
Annual Meetings: Winter
1999 – Reno, NV(Silver Legacy)/Jan. 22-25

American Cutlery Manufacturers Ass'n *(1947)*
112-J Elden St.
Herndon, VA 20170-4809
Tel: (703)709-8253   *Fax:* (703)709-1036
E-Mail: acma@erols.com
Members: 50 companies
Staff: 4
Annual Budget: $50-100,000
Exec. Director: David W. Barrack

Historical Note
*Serves the cutlery manufacturing and marketing industry by
providing educational services, promoting communication and
cooperation between members and governmental agencies and by
sponsoring meetings and trade shows.*

Publications:
ACMA Newsletter. q.
Membership Directory. a.

Meetings/Conferences:
1999 – Longboat Key, FL(Longboat Key Club
    Resort)/April 28-May 1
2000 – Orlando, FL(The Villas of Grand Cypress)/May 3-6
2001 – LaQuinta, CA(LaQuinta Resort and Club)/May 2-5

American Dairy Ass'n *(1940)*
O'Hare International Ctr.
10255 W. Higgins Road, Ste. 900
Rosemont, IL 60018-5616
Tel: (847)803-2000   *Fax:* (847)803-2077
Web Site: http://www.dairyinfo.com
Members: 18 organizations
Staff: 7
Annual Budget: $500-1,000,000
C.E.O.: Thomas P. Gallagher

Historical Note
*A wholly-owned subsidiary of the United Dairy Industry Ass'n,
ADA represents 60% of the nation's dairy farmers and 65% of
domestic milk production. ADA conducts a $60 million annual
advertising and sales promotion program for domestic milk and
milk products on a non-brand basis.*

Meetings/Conferences:
Annual Meetings: September, with United Dairy Industry Ass'n

American Dairy Goat Ass'n *(1904)*
P.O. Box 865
Spindale, NC 28160
Tel: (704)286-3801   *Fax:* (704)287-0476
E-Mail: adgajdw2@aol.com
Members: 12,000 individuals
Staff: 12
Annual Budget: $1-2,000,000
Secretary-Treasurer: Ron Gelvin

Historical Note
*Breeders and fanciers of dairy goats. Formerly American Milch
Goat Record Association and American Milk Goat Record
Association. Member of the National Pedigree Livestock Council.
Membership: $35/year (full member), $10/year (junior member).*

Publications:
ADGA Directory. a.
ADGA Guidebook. a. adv.
ADGA News & Events Newsletter. q.

Meetings/Conferences:
Annual Meetings: Fall

American Dairy Goat Products Ass'n *(1991)*
Historical Note
Ceased operations in 1997.

American Dairy Products Institute *(1986)*
300 West Washington St., Suite 400
Chicago, IL 60606
Tel: (312)782-4888   *Fax:* (312)782-5299
E-Mail: AmerDairy@aol.com
Members: 220 companies
Staff: 8
Annual Budget: $500-1,000,000
C.E.O.: Warren S. Clark, Jr.

Historical Note
*Product of a merger between the American Dry Milk Institute and
the Whey Products Institute in 1986; the Evaporated Milk Ass'n
merged into Institute in 1987. Seeks to promote the acceptance and
utilization of processed dairy products,nationally and
internationally, to maintain liaison and represent the industry in
dealings with governmental agencies and regulatory bodies, to
support technical and marketing research and to assemble and
disseminate statistics and other information about processed dairy
products.*

Publications:
Dry Milk Products Utilization and Production Trends. a.
Whey Products-Utilization and Production Trends. a.

Meetings/Conferences:
Annual Meetings: Always in Chicago, IL metropolitan area in
    April
1999 – Chicago, IL(Marriott O'Hare)/April 25-28/550
2000 – Chicago, IL(Hilton & Towers)/April 30-May 3/550
2001 – Rosemont, IL(Hyatt Regency)/April 22-25/600
2002 – Chicago, IL(Fairmont)/April 20-24/600

American Dairy Science Ass'n *(1906)*
1111 N. Dunlap Ave.
Savoy, IL 61874
Tel: (217)356-3182   *Fax:* (217)398-4119
E-Mail: adsa@assochq.org
Web Site: http://www.adsa.uiuc.edu/

Members: 3,500 individuals, 2,000 institution & companies
Staff: 16
Annual Budget: $500-1,000,000
Exec. Director: M.E. Kelley
C.F.O.: Charles L. Sapp

Historical Note
*Incorporated in the District of Columbia in 1906. Members are
equipment manufacturers and suppliers, farmers, educators,
researchers and breeders interested in strengthening all aspects of
the dairy industry. Membership: $90/year (individual); $160/year
(organization/company).*

Publications:
Abstracts & Annual Meeting Program. a. adv.
Journal of Dairy Science. m. adv.
Newsletter. q.

Meetings/Conferences:
Annual Meetings: June-July
1999 – Memphis, TN/June 20-23/2000
2000 – Baltimore, MD/July 24-28/3000
2001 – Indianapolis, IN/July 24-28

American Dance Guild *(1956)*
Lenox Hill Station
New York, NY 10021
Tel: (212)932-2789   *Fax:* (212)675-9657
E-Mail: americandanceguild.org
Web Site: julia@americandanceguild.org
Members: 400 individuals
Staff: 1
Annual Budget: $25-50,000
President: Jana Feinman

Historical Note
*Members are performers, educators, critics, choreographers and
students of all forms of dance. Formerly (1956) known as Dance
Teachers Guild, (1966) Nat'l Dance Teachers Guild, and (1968)
Nat'l Dance Guild. Maintains a speakers bureau, job registry and
career counseling service. Has no paid officers or full-time staff.
Membership: $50/year (individual); $175/year (company).*

Publications:
Newsletter. q. adv.

Meetings/Conferences:
Annual Meetings: June

American Dance Therapy Ass'n *(1966)*
2000 Century Plaza, Suite 108
Columbia, MD 21044-3383
Tel: (410)997-4040   *Fax:* (410)997-4048
Members: 1,100 individuals
Staff: 2
Annual Budget: $100-250,000
Office Manager: Patricia Gardner

Historical Note
*Individuals and institutions concerned with the dance as a
therapeutic agent. Awards the DTR and the ADTR designations to
those meeting prescribed professional standards. Membership:
$54-102/year.*

Publications:
American Journal of Dance Therapy. semi-a. adv.
Newsletter. q. adv.

Meetings/Conferences:
Annual Meetings: Fall

American Defense Preparedness Ass'n *(1919)*
Historical Note
*Merged with Nat'l Security Industrial Ass'n in 1997 to form the
Nat'l Defense Industrial Ass'n.*

American Dehydrated Onion and Garlic Ass'n *(1956)*
221 Main St., 16th Floor
San Francisco, CA 94105-1906
Tel: (415)905-0200   *Fax:* (415)543-4940
Members: 3 companies
Staff: 3
Annual Budget: $250-500,000
Secretary-Treasurer: J. Dennis McQuaid

Historical Note
*Members are U.S. companies that dehydrate onions and garlic
serving industrial and food service customers. ADOGA members
account for 90% of dried onions and garlic produced in the United
States.*

Publications:
ADOGA News Bulletin. irreg.

American Dental Ass'n *(1859)*
211 East Chicago Ave.
Chicago, IL 60611-2678
Tel: (312)440-2500   *Fax:* (312)440-2800
E-Mail: online@ada.org
Web Site: http://www.ada.org
Members: 140,000 individuals
Staff: 400
Annual Budget: $50-100,000,000
Exec. Director: John S. Zapp, D.D.S.
Director, Inter. Relations: Helen Mck Cherrett, CMP
Membership Director: Paul W. Jarr

Historical Note
*Founded August 3, 1859 in Niagara Falls. United with the
Southern Dental Ass'n in 1897 and changed its name to the Nat'l
Dental Ass'n. In 1922 the name was changed to the American
Dental Ass'n. Incorporated in Illinois. Supports the American
Dental Political Action Committee. Maintains a Washington office.
Has an annual budget of approximately $50 million.*

Publications:
ADA News. Bi-w. adv.
Index to Dental Literature. q.
Journal of the ADA. m. adv.

Meetings/Conferences:
Annual Meetings: Fall/12,500

American Dental Assistants Ass'n *(1924)*
203 N. LaSalle St., Suite 1320
Chicago, IL 60601-1210
Tel: (312)541-1550   *Fax:* (312)541-1496
Members: 16,000 individuals
Staff: 11
Annual Budget: $1-2,000,000
Exec. Director: Lawrence H. Sepin
Director, Membership/Marketing: Doug McDonough
Meeting Planner: Tina Grikmanis

Historical Note
*Requires tripartite membership (local, state, and national).
Membership: $100/year.*

Publications:
The Dental Assistant. bi-m. adv.

Meetings/Conferences:
Annual Meetings: Summer/1,000
1999 – Salt Lake City, UT/July 21-25

American Dental Hygienists' Ass'n *(1923)*
444 North Michigan Ave., Suite 3400
Chicago, IL 60611
Tel: (312)440-8900   *Fax:* (312)440-8929
Web Site: http://www.adha.org
Members: 35,000 individuals
Staff: 40
Annual Budget: $2-5,000,000
Exec. Director: Stanley B. Peck
Director, Communications: Rosetta Gervasi
Director, Government Affairs: Jan Starr
Asst. Exec. Director: Isaac Carpenter
Director, Administration and Special Projects: Karen Dunn Caspers
Director, Membership: Kristin McGill
Director, Development: Rosalyn Averette Priester

Historical Note
*Membership: $145/year, plus constituent and component dues,
$500/year (organization/company).*

Publications:
Access. adv. adv.
Education Update. semi-a.
Journal of Dental Hygiene. adv. adv.

Meetings/Conferences:
Annual Meetings: June/1,000
1999 – San Diego, CA
2000 – Washington, DC
2001 – Nashville, TN

American Dental Interfraternity Council *(1923)*
13975 Connecticut Ave., Suite 306
Aspen Hill, MD 20906
Tel: (301)460-1777
Members: 4 dental fraternities
Staff: 1
Annual Budget: under $10,000

Historical Note
*A federation of professional Greek letter societies united to promote
better public relations for the dental profession.*

Meetings/Conferences:
Annual Meetings: Fall, in conjunction with the American Dental
Ass'n annual meeting.

American Dental Soc. of Anesthesiology *(1953)*
211 East Chicago Ave., Suite 780
Chicago, IL 60611
Tel: (312)664-8270   *Fax:* (312)642-9713
Web Site: http://www.adsa.org
Members: 3,500 individuals
Staff: 4
Annual Budget: $250-500,000
Contact: Knight Charlton

Historical Note
*Members are dentists with a special interest in pain control.
Membership: $175/year (active member); $25/year (student).*

Publications:
Anesthesia Progress. bi-m. adv.
Newsletter. bi-m.

Meetings/Conferences:
Annual Meetings: Spring/250
1999 – Washington, DC/Apr. 20-25

American Dental Trade Ass'n *(1882)*
4222 King St. West
Alexandria, VA 22302-1597
Tel: (703)379-7755   *Fax:* (703)931-9429
Members: 200 companies
Staff: 5
Annual Budget: $1-2,000,000
President and C.E.O.: Nikolaj M. Petrovic, CAE

Historical Note
Membership: $1,250-49,000/year.

Publications:
Update. bi-m.

Meetings/Conferences:
Annual Meetings: Fall/450

American Dermatologic Soc. for Allergy and Immunology *(1975)*
Historical Note
Organization defunct in 1998.

American Dermatological Ass'n *(1876)*
Historical Note
Address unknown in 1996.

American Desalting Ass'n *(1985)*
915 L St., Suite 1000
Sacramento, CA 95814
Tel: (916)442-9285   *Fax:* (916)442-0382
Web Site: http://www.desalting-ada.org
Members: 300 individuals
Staff: 5
Annual Budget: $25-50,000
Exec. Director: Karen L. Roberts
Editor, Newletter: Catherine Smith
Government Programs Coordinator: Chris Walker
Meeting Planner: Lorett Wire
Associate Administrative Director: Kathy Snelson

Historical Note
*ADA members are individuals, government agencies and
corporations with an interest in desalinization technology.*

Publications:
Conference Proceedings. bien.
Newsletter. m.

Meetings/Conferences:
Biennial Meetings: Fall and Late Summer.
1999 – San Diego, CA
2000 – Lake Tahoe, NV/Aug. 6-10

American Design Drafting Ass'n *(1959)*
P.O. Box 799
Rockville, MD 20848-0799
Tel: (301)460-6875   *Fax:* (301)460-8591
E-Mail: national@adda.org
Web Site: http://www.adda.org
Members: 2,000 individuals
Staff: 2
Annual Budget: $100-250,000
Exec. Director: Rachel H. Howard

Historical Note
*Formerly (1960) Ass'n of Professional Draftsmen and (1989)
American Institute for Design and Drafting. Membership includes
individuals, corporations and educational institutions and students.
Seeks to promote improved quality and efficiency in the
drafting/designing profession and industry. ADDA administers a
curriculum certification program for schools with design/drafting
programs and design/drafter certification programs. Membership:
$75/year (individual); $215/year(educational institutions);
$300/year (organization/company).*

Publications:
Design Drafting News. bi-m. adv.

Meetings/Conferences:
Annual Meetings: Spring
1999 – Denver, CO(Hyatt Regency)/May 6-7/150

American Dexter Cattle Ass'n *(1912)*
26804 Ebenezer Rd.
Concordia, MO 64020-9233
Tel: (660)463-7704
Members: 450 individuals
Staff: 1
Annual Budget: $25-50,000
Exec. Secretary-Treasurer: Rosemary Fleharty

Historical Note
*Established as the American Kerry and Dexter Club, it assumed its
present name in 1957. Indigenous to Ireland, the Dexter is a breed
used in both beef and dairy applications. Membership: $30/year
(new and associate); $20/year (renewal).*

Publications:
Bulletin. bi-m.
Herd Book. a.

Meetings/Conferences:
Annual Meetings: Summer
1999 – Wichita, KSJuly

American Diabetes Ass'n *(1940)*
National Office
1660 Duke St.
Alexandria, VA 22314-3447
Tel: (703)549-1500   *Fax:* (703)676-4065
Toll Free: (800)342 - 2383
Web Site: http://www.diabetes.org
Members: 1000,000 individuals
Staff: 800
Annual Budget: Over $100,000,000
C.E.O.: John H. Graham, IV
National V. President Communications and Public Relations: Jerry
     Franz
National V. President, Advocacy: Michael Mawby
Director of Meeting Services: Jacy Hanson
Director, Professional Education: Linda Cann
Chief Scientific & Medical Officer: Richard Kahn, Ph.D.
C.O.O.: Caroline Stevens
National V. President, Finance: Kevin Kavanaugh
Chief Field Operations Officer: Steve Hartley
Director, Membership/Subscription: William Outlaw

Historical Note
*Founded in 1940 in Cincinnati as a professional society of medical
doctors; converted in 1965 to a voluntary health agency. Operates
as a federation of affiliated associations, each of which is
responsible for fund raising and program activities within its
geographic region. ADA is the nation's leading voluntary health
organization concerned with the prevention and cure of diabetes. It
provides support to millions who have the disease and educates
health professinals and the general public.*

Publications:
Clinical Diabetes. bi-m. adv.
Diabetes. m. adv.
Diabetes Advisor. bi-m.
Diabetes Care. m. adv.
Diabetes Forecast. m. adv.
Diabetes Insider. m.
Diabetes Reviews. q. adv.
Diabetes Spectrum. bi-m.

Meetings/Conferences:
Annual Meetings: June/6,000
1999 – San Diego, CA(Hyatt and Marriott Hotels)/June 17-22

2000 – San Antonio, TX(Marriott Rivercenter)/June 8-13
2001 – Philadelphia, PA(Philadelphia Marriott)/June 20-26
2002 – San Francisco, CA(Marriott Marquis)/June 12-18

American Dialect Soc. *(1889)*
Dept. of English, MacMurray College
Jacksonville, IL 62650-2590
Tel: (217)479-7117   *Fax:* (217)245-0405
Web Site: http://www.americandialect.org
Members: 550 individuals, 280 institutions
Staff: 1
Annual Budget: $10-25,000
Exec. Secretary: Allan Metcalf

Historical Note
*Members are educators and others interested in the English
language in North America. Sponsors the Dictionary of American
Regional English. Membership: $35/year.*

Publications:
American Speech. q.
Newsletter of the American Dialect Society. 3/year. adv.
Publication of the American Dialect Society (PADS). a.

Meetings/Conferences:
Annual Meetings: With the Linguistic Soc. of America in
     January.
1999 – Los Angeles, CA(Bonaventure)/Jan. 7-9
2000 – Chicago, IL(Palmer House)/Jan. 6-8

American Diamond Industry Ass'n *(1982)*
589 Fifth Ave., Room 901
New York, NY 10017-1923
Tel: (212)935-1020   *Fax:* (212)753-2588
Members: 3 associations
Staff: 2
Annual Budget: $250-500,000
Chairman & President: Lloyd Jaffe

Historical Note
*AIDA, an umbrella organization for three diamond associations
(Diamond Dealers Club of New York, Diamond Manufacturers and
Importers Ass'n and Diamond Trade Ass'n), was established as an
information clearinghouse on diamonds and the diamond industry.*

Publications:
AIDA Newsletter. 3/year.

American Dietetic Ass'n *(1917)*
216 W. Jackson Blvd., Suite 800
Chicago, IL 60606-6995
Tel: (312)899-0040   *Fax:* (312)899-1758
Web Site: http://www.eatright.org
Members: 69,000 individuals
Staff: 165
Annual Budget: $10-25,000,000
C.O.O.: Connie Rivera
Director, Ext. Affrs/Fdn: Winthrop W. Hamilton
Public Relations: Maryanne Giustino
Legal and Government Affairs: Robert A. Schuckman
Services/Seminars: Gerri Salvatore
Education and Accreditation: Beverly Mitchell
Finance and Administration: Virgil Cole
Membership: Kay Manger-Hague
Publisher: Deborah L. McBride

Historical Note
*The nation's largest professional society of dietetics professionals.
Established in Cleveland, OH in 1917 and incorporated in Illinois in
1923. Members are employed in health care organizations, schools,
colleges, universities as well as in business institutions and industry.
The American Dietetic Ass'n Foundation, established 1967, is its
education and research arm. Sponsors and supports the American
Dietetic Ass'n Political Action Committee. Has an annual budget of
approximately $21.8 million. Membership: $150/year.*

Publications:
ADA Courier Newsletter. m. adv.
Journal of the American Dietetic Ass'n. m. adv.

Meetings/Conferences:
Annual Meetings: October/10,000
1999 – Atlanta, GA(Convention Center)/Oct. 18-21
2000 – Denver, CO(Convention Center)/Oct. 16-19
2001 – St. Louis, MO(Convention Center)/Oct. 22-25

American Dinner Theatre Institute *(1972)*
1275 E. Waterloo Rd.
Akron, OH 44306
Tel: (330)724-9855
Toll Free: (800)362 - 4100
Web Site: http://www.carouseldinnertheatre.com
Members: 12 theatres
Staff: 1
Annual Budget: $25-50,000
President: Prescott F. Griffith

Historical Note
*Founded at a conference of dinner theatre operators held in Dallas,
TX in October 1972. Acts as a clearinghouse for information on all
phases of dinner theatre operation.*

Publications:
Newsletter. m.

American Diopter and Decibel Soc. *(1960)*
Historical Note
Address unknown in 1996.

American Disc Jockey Ass'n *(1992)*
297 Route 72, W. Suite C-120
Manahawkin, NJ 08050-2890
Tel: (609)978-2180   *Fax:* (609)978-9363
E-Mail: djs2go@ameri-com.com
Web Site: http://www.adja.org
Members: 500 individuals
Staff: 8
President: Tony Valentine

Historical Note
ADJA represents the needs of professional mobile and night club DJ's and KJ's. The association promotes common standards, procedures and benefits for its members. *Membership:* $50/year (associate); $125/year (individual).

Publications:
ADJA News Newsletter. bi-m. adv.
Affiliate Directory. q.

American Dog Trainers Network *(1986)*
161 W. 4th St.
New York, NY 10014
Tel: (212)727-7257
E-Mail: dogs@inch.com
Web Site: http://www.inch.com/ ~ dogs
Members: 300 individuals
Staff: 4
Annual Budget: under $10,000
Director: Robin Kovary

Historical Note
Formerly (1995) Soc. of North American Dog Trainers.

Publications:
Newsletter. q.

American Donkey and Mule Soc. *(1967)*
2901 N. Elm St.
Denton, TX 76201-7631
Tel: (940)382-6845   *Fax:* (940)484-8417
E-Mail: adms@juno.com
Web Site: http://www.donkeys.com
Members: 6,000 individuals
Staff: 2
Annual Budget: $50-100,000
Secretary: Betsy Hutchins

Historical Note
Breeders, owners, and organizations interested in donkeys and mules. Maintains five registries for donkeys, mules and zebra hybrids, stud books, and prepares and disseminates educational books and literature. *Membership:* $20/year.

Publications:
The Brayer Magazine. bi-m. adv.

Meetings/Conferences:
1999 – Shelbyville, TN/(Celebration Showgrounds)

American Down Ass'n *(1983)*
3216 Eastwood Rd.
Sacramento, CA 95821-3101
Tel: (916)971-1135   *Fax:* (916)971-3151
Members: 22 companies
Staff: 2
Annual Budget: $25-50,000
Association Manager: Jeff Helms

Historical Note
Absorbed Feather and Down Ass'n in 1997. ADA members are suppliers, manufacturers, distributors and retailers of down-filled products.

Meetings/Conferences:

American Driver and Traffic Safety Education Ass'n *(1956)*
c/o Highway Safety Center
Indiana University of Pennsylvania
Indiana, PA 15705
Tel: (724)357-4051   *Fax:* (412)357-7595
Members: 1,600 individuals, 100 companies
Staff: 3
Annual Budget: $250-500,000
C.E.O.: Allen Robinson, Ph.D.

Historical Note
A professional society of driving and safety educators, it was established as the American Driver and Safety Education Ass'n, it became the American Driver Education Ass'n in 1957 and assumed its present name in 1963. Sponsors the Nat'l Student Safety Program. *Membership:* $25-100/year (individual), $400/year (organization/ company).

Publications:
ADTSEA New & Views. 4-7/yr.
Chronicle of the ADTSEA. q. adv.

Meetings/Conferences:
Annual Meetings: August/400-500

American Dry Pea and Lentil Ass'n *(1949)*
Historical Note
Merged with the USA Dry Pea and Lentil Council in 1994.

American Ecological Research Institute *(1985)*
Historical Note
Address unknown in 1996.

American Economic Ass'n *(1885)*
2014 Broadway, Suite 305
Nashville, TN 37203-2418
Tel: (615)322-2595   *Fax:* (615)343-7590
E-Mail: aeinfo@ctrvax.vanderbilt.edu
Web Site: http://www.vanderbilt.edu/AEA
Members: 21,600 individuals, 5,500 companies
Staff: 20
Annual Budget: $1-2,000,000
Secretary: John Seigfried
Administrative Director: Mary L. Winer
Counsel: Terry Calvani

Historical Note
Founded in Saratoga, NY in 1885. A member of the American Council of Learned Societies and affiliated with the Social Science Research Council, the American Ass'n for the Advancement of Science and the Internat'l Economic Ass'n. Encourages economic research, particularly historical and statistical studies of industrial life. The umbrella organization for U.S. economists. Regular

Membership: $56-78/year (individual); $132/year (organization/company).

Publications:
American Economic Review. q. adv.
Journal of Economic Literature. q. adv.
Journal of Economic Perspectives. q. adv.

Meetings/Conferences:
1999 – New York, NY/Jan. 3-5/7500
2000 – Boston, MA/Jan. 7-9/7500
2001 – New Orleans, LA/Jan. 5-7/7500

American Economic Development Council *(1926)*
9801 West Higgins Rd., Suite 540
Rosemont, IL 60018-4726
Tel: (847)692-9944   *Fax:* (847)696-2990
E-Mail: aedc@interaccess.com
Web Site: http://www.aedc.org
Members: 2,700 individuals
Staff: 14
Annual Budget: $2-5,000,000
President and C.E.O.: A. Bruce Wilson
Director, Public Affairs: Sally Duros
Director, Professional Development: Fred E. Straub
Director, Member Services: Christine Brenkus

Historical Note
AEDC is a tax-exempt incorporated organization of professionals active in the field of industrial and economic development. Founded in 1926 as the American Industrial Development Council, it assumed its present name in 1980. *Membership:* $305/year.

Publications:
AEDC Newsletter. m.
Economic Development Review Journal. 4/year.
Membership Directory. a.
Washington Report. m.

Meetings/Conferences:
Annual Meetings: June/750
1999 – Phoenix, AZ

American Education Finance Ass'n *(1975)*
5249 Cape Leyte Drive
Sarasota, FL 34242
Tel: (941)349-7580   *Fax:* (941)349-7580
E-Mail: GBABIGIAN@AOL.COM
Web Site: http://www.info.pitt.edu/ ~ aefa/aefa-wel.htm
Members: 650 individuals
Annual Budget: $250-500,000
Exec. Director: George R. Babigian

Historical Note
AEFA encourages communications among groups and individuals in the education finance field, including academicians, researchers, policy makers and practitioners. Serving as a forum for a broad range of issues and concerns, AEFA concerns include traditional school finance concepts, issues of public policy, and teaching school finance. *Membership:* $50/year (individual), $1,000/year (sustaining member).

Publications:
Conference Abstract. a. adv.
Journal of Education Finance. q.
Membership Directory. a. adv.
Newsletter. q. adv.
Yearbook of Education Finance. a.

Meetings/Conferences:
Annual Meetings: March-April
1999 – Seattle, WA/March 17 20
2000 – Austin, TX/March 8-11

American Educational Research Ass'n *(1915)*
1230 17th St., N.W.
Washington, DC 20036-3078
Tel: (202)223-9485   *Fax:* (202)775-1824
Web Site: http://www.aera.net
Members: 23,000 individuals
Staff: 20
Annual Budget: $2-5,000,000
Exec. Officer: William J. Russell, Ph.D.
Dir., Governmental/Professional Liaison: Gerald E. Stroufe
Director, Publications: Thomas J. Campbell

Historical Note
Founded in 1915 in Cincinnati as the Nat'l Ass'n of Directors of Educational Research, an affiliate of the Nat'l Education Ass'n. In 1930 the name was changed to the American Educational Research Ass'n. In 1968 the affiliation with NEA was dropped and the organization was incorporated in the District of Columbia. AERA is an international professional organization of educators, directors of research, testing, or evaluation in federal, state, and local agencies; counselors; evaluators; graduate students; and behavioral scientists concerned with educational research and its application to practice. Sponsors and supports the Nat'l Council on Measurement in Education. *Membership:* $45/year.

Publications:
American Educational Research Journal. q. adv.
Biographical Membership Directory. bien.
Educational Evaluation and Policy Analysis. q. adv.
Educational Researcher. 9/yr. adv.
Journal of Educational and Behavioral Statistics. q.
Review of Educational Research. q.
Review of Research in Education. a.

Meetings/Conferences:
Annual Meetings: Spring
1999 – Montreal, Quebec/April 19-23
2000 – New Orleans, LA/April 24-28

American Educational Studies Ass'n *(1968)*
Educational Policy Studies Dept.
University Plaza, Georgia State Univ.
Atlanta, GA 30303
Tel: (404)651-3294
Members: 600 individuals
Annual Budget: $10-25,000
President: Wayne Urban, Ph.D.

Historical Note
Concerned with the comprehensive view of education including the underlying philosophy, history, sociology and psychology of education and dedicated to research and the improvement of teaching in these areas. Has no paid staff. *Membership:* $35/year (regular), $20/year (emeritus, student), $100/year (institutional).

Publications:
AESA Newsletter. q.
Educational Foundations. 3/q.
Educational Studies. q. adv.

Meetings/Conferences:
Semi-annual Meetings: March with American Educational Research Ass'n, and November

American Egg Board *(1939)*
1460 Renaissance Dr., Suite 301
Park Ridge, IL 60068
Tel: (847)296-7044   *Fax:* (847)296-7007
E-Mail: LRaffel@aol.com
Web Site: http://www.aeb.org
Members: 18 individuals, 1000 producers
Staff: 20
Annual Budget: $10-25,000,000
President: Louis B. Raffel, CAE

Historical Note
Established as the Poultry and Egg Nat'l Board, a federation of egg producers. The name was changed in 1973 to the American Egg Board. An act of Congress in 1976 gave this official status, permitted dues check offs from egg producers, and the appointment by the Secretary of Agriculture of the members of the Board. Concerned with advertising, promotion and research activities for eggs and egg products. Has an annual budget of $14 million.

Publications:
Foodservice Newsletter. q.
News from AEB. m.

American Egyptian Chamber of Commerce *(1995)*
Historical Note
Address unknown in 1997.

American Electroencephalographic Soc.
Historical Note
Became (1996) American Clinical Neurophysiological Soc.

American Electrology Ass'n *(1958)*
106 Oak Ridge Rd.
Trumbull, CT 06611
Tel: (203)374-6667   *Fax:* (203)372-7134
Web Site: http://www.electrology.com
Members: 2,000 individuals
Staff: 2
Annual Budget: $50-100,000
Exec. Director: Teresa E. Petricca, CPE

Historical Note
Founded in New Jersey in Feb., 1958 as American Electrolysis Ass'n, it assumed its present name in 1986. Membership composed of electrologists (permanent hair removers). Sponsors national certification program, national accreditation program and continuing education. *Membership:* $100/year (individual).

Publications:
Electrology World. q. adv.
Journal of Electrology. semi-a.
Membership Directory. a.

Meetings/Conferences:
Annual Meetings: Fall
1999 – Savannah, GA(Marriott Reiverfront)

American Electronics Ass'n *(1943)*
5201 Great America Pkwy., Suite 520
Santa Clara, CA 95054
Tel: (408)987-4280   *Fax:* (408)986-1247
Toll Free: (800)284 - 4232
E-Mail: csc@aeanet.org
Web Site: http://www.aeanet.org
Members: 3,100 companies
Staff: 110
Annual Budget: $10-25,000,000
President and C.E.O.: William T. Archey
Senior V. President, Finance & Administration and C.F.O.: John Herrick
Senior V. President, Member Services: Michael E. McQuade
V. President, National Accounts: William R. Haerle
Senior V. President, International: Bill Krist
V. President, Asia & GII: Debra Waggoner

Historical Note
Founded in California in 1943 by 25 electronics manufacturers, it is now the largest trade association serving the electronics, software and information technology industries. Maintains a Washington office, one of its 19 offices in the U.S., and offices in Brussels, Tokyo and Beijing. Formerly (1971) the Western Electronic Manufacturers Ass'n (WEMA). Supports the American Electronics Ass'n ElectroPAC. Has an annual budget of over $15 million. *Membership:* dues vary with size of company.

Publications:
Council Newsletters.
Directory of Members. a. adv.
Impact (AEA activity update). bi-m.
Services Catalog. bi-m. adv.

Meetings/Conferences:
Annual Meetings: September

American Electroplaters and Surface Finishers Soc. *(1909)*
Central Florida Research Park
12644 Research Parkway
Orlando, FL 32826
Tel: (407)281-6441   *Fax:* (407)281-6446
Toll Free: (800)334 - 2052
E-Mail: aesf@worldnet.att.net

Members: 7,000 individuals
Staff: 25
Annual Budget: $2-5,000,000
Exec. Director: Ted Witt
Director, Communications: Sylvia Baxley
Manager, Meetings: Penny Harney
Coordinator, Education/Course: Anne Gaither
Asst. Exec. Director: W. Joan Harrison
Manager, Membership: Brenda Gross
Manager, Publication: Debbie J. Swank

Historical Note
Founded in New York City in 1909 as the Nat'l Electro-Platers Ass'n. Became American Electroplaters' Soc. in 1913 and assumed its present name in 1985. Incorporated in New Jersey in 1946. Promotes all aspects of electroplating and surface finishing. Membership: $70/year.

Publications:
AESF Shopguide. bien. adv.
Plating and Surface Finishing Journal. m. adv.
Proceedings of AESF/EPA Conference. a. adv.
Proceedings of Sur/Fin Conference. a. adv.

Meetings/Conferences:
Annual Meetings: Summer/4,500
1999 – Cincinnati, OH(Convention Center)/June 21-24
2000 – Chicago, IL(Navy Pier)/June 26-29
2001 – Nashville, TN(Opryland)/June 25-28

American Embryo Transfer Ass'n *(1981)*
P.O. Box 2118
Hastings, NE   68902-2118
Tel: (402)463-5691   *Fax:* (402)463-5683
Members: 363 companies and individuals
Annual Budget: $25-50,000
Exec. V. President: Don Ellerbee

Historical Note
Seeks to promote the use of embryo transfer as a means to improve livestock and encourages cooperative relationships among companies and individuals engaged in embryo transfer. Has developed a Certification Program for embryo transfer companies in order to identify those who meet certain criteria in their commercial activities.

Publications:
Closer Look. q.
Convention Proceedings. a.

Meetings/Conferences:
Annual Meetings: October

American Emu Ass'n
P.O. Box 740814
Dallas, TX   75374-0814
Tel: (214)559-2321   *Fax:* (218)238-6105
E-Mail: info@aea-emu.org
Web Site: www.aea-emu.org
Members: 1,600 individuals
Annual Budget: $50-100,000
Chairman of the Board: Margaret Painder

Historical Note
Members are emu, (a flightless bird), raisers. Membership: $100/year (individual).

Publications:
Emupdate. bi-m. adv.

Meetings/Conferences:
Annual Meetings: July
1999 – Biloxi, MS

American Endodontic Soc. *(1969)*
1440 N. Harbor Blvd. Suite 719
Fullerton, CA   92831-4120
Tel: (714)870-5590
Members: 7,000 individuals
Staff: 2
Annual Budget: $100-250,000
Exec. Director: Ramon Werts, D.D.S.

Historical Note
Members are dentists specializing in root canal work. Membership: $125/year.

Publications:
AES Newsletter. q.

Meetings/Conferences:
Annual Meetings: Fall

American Entomological Soc. *(1859)*
c/o Academy of Natural Sciences
1900 Ben Franklin Pkwy.
Philadelphia, PA   19103-1195
Tel: (215)561-3978   *Fax:* (215)299-1028
E-Mail: AES@say.acnatsci.org
Members: 400 individuals
Staff: 2
Annual Budget: $10-25,000
Office Manager: Suzanne McElroy

Historical Note
Founded as the Entomological Soc. of Phildelphia. In 1867 the name was changed to American Entomological Soc. The Society's library is housed and staffed by the Academy of Natural Sciences of Philadelphia. AES promotes the study of insects and publishes the results of pure research in the systematics and morphology of insects. Membership: $15/year (regular); $10/year (student).

Publications:
Entomological News. 5/yr. adv.
Memoirs of the AES. irreg.
Transactions of the AES. q.

Meetings/Conferences:
Annual Meetings: February, March, April, October and
    November in either Philadelphia, Pennsylvania or
    Newark, Delaware.

American Epilepsy Soc. *(1946)*

638 Prospect Ave.
Hartford, CT   06105-4203
Tel: (860)586-7505   *Fax:* (860)586-7550
E-Mail: info@aesnet.org
Web Site: http://aesnet.org
Members: 2,000 individuals
Staff: 3
Annual Budget: $1-2,000,000
Exec. Director: M. Suzanne C. Berry, CAE
Meeting Planner: Steve Rugens

Historical Note
Founded as the American League Against Epilepsy, it assumed its present name in 1959. Members are physicians, nurses, and scientists engaged in research and practice in epilepsy or closely related fields. Membership: $166/year (active member); $40 or $126/year (junior member); $125/year (outside North America).

Publications:
Epilepsia. m. adv.
Epilepsy Research. 9 times/year.
Journal of Epilepsy. 6 times/year.

Meetings/Conferences:
Annual Meetings: December
1999 – Orlando, FL(Disney Coronado Springs)/Dec. 3-9/2000
2000 – Los Angeles, CA/Dec. 3-9/2000

American Equilibration Soc. *(1955)*
8726 N. Ferris Avenue
Morton Grove, IL   60053
Tel: (847)965-2888   *Fax:* (847)965-4888
E-Mail: aesdental@sprynet.com
Members: 1000 individuals
Staff: 4
Annual Budget: $250-500,000
Office Director: Shel Marcus

Historical Note
Membership consists of dentists and physicians interested in the structure and functions of the temporomandibular region and related parts of the mouth. Membership: $285/year (individual).

Publications:
Directory. a.
Newsletter. 3/year.

Meetings/Conferences:
Annual Meetings: Chicago, IL(Marriott)/February/500
1999 – Chicago, IL(Marriott)/Feb. 17-18/500
2000 – Chicago, IL(Marriott)/Feb. 23-24/500

American Ethnological Soc. *(1842)*

Historical Note
Organized in 1842, "to make inquiries into the origin, progress and characteristics of the various races of man." Became inactive in the 1860s but was re-organized in 1871 as the Anthropological Institute, and shortly thereafter it assumed its present name. A section of the American Anthropological Ass'n.

American Evaluation Ass'n *(1986)*
P.O. Box 704
Point Reyes, CA   94956
Toll Free: (888)311 - 6321
E-Mail: amevalassn@aol.com
Web Site: http://www.eval.org
Members: 2,500 individuals
Annual Budget: $100-250,000
Exec. Director: Jeri Jacobson

Historical Note
Formed by the merger of the Evaluation Network and the Evaluation Research Soc. in 1985. AEA is an international organization of professionals involved in the practice or study of evaluation. Evaluation involves assessing the strengths and weaknesses of programs, policies, personnel, products and organizations to improve their effectiveness. AEA members represent many different disciplines including psychology, education, public administration and policy analysis, economics, public relations and marketing, auditing, health care, social work, sociology, and measurement and statistics. AEA's mission is to improve evaluation practice and methods, increase evaluation use and promote evaluation as a profession. Membership: $45/year (individual).

Publications:
Evaluation Practice. 3/year.
New Directions for Program Evaluation. q.

Meetings/Conferences:
1999 – Orlando, FL(Omni Rosen)/Nov. 2-6
2000 – Honolulu, HI(Sheraton Waikiki)/Nov. 1-4

American Factory Trawler Ass'n

Historical Note
Became (1997) At-sea Processors Ass'n.

American Family Therapy Academy *(1977)*
2020 Pennsylvania Ave, N.W., #273
Washington, DC   20006
Tel: (202)994-2776   *Fax:* (202)994-2775
E-Mail: afta@afta.org
Web Site: http://www.afta.org
Members: 950 individuals
Staff: 5
Annual Budget: $250-500,000
Executive Director: Barbro Miles

Historical Note
Formerly (1992) American Family Therapy Ass'n. Members are teachers, researchers, and clinical therapists specially trained to work with couples and families. Its purpose is to advance therapies and theories that regard the family as a unit within a broader context; to promote research in family therapy; and to make information available to the public and practitioners in other fields. Membership: $190/year.

Publications:
AFTA Newsletter. q. adv.
Membership Directory. a.

Meetings/Conferences:
Annual Meetings: June/400
1999 – Washington, DC(Hyatt Regency)/June 23-26

American Farm Bureau Federation *(1919)*
225 Touhy Ave.
Park Ridge, IL   60068-5874
Tel: (847)685-8600   *Fax:* (847)685-8896
Web Site: http://www.fb.com
Members: 48,000,000 individuals, 50 state & Puerto Rican
    bureaus
Staff: 160
Annual Budget: $10-25,000,000
President: Dean R. Kleckner
Director, Public Relations: Joseph Fields
Senior Director, Government Relations: J. Don Doggett
Director, Special Programs: Rolland Hayenga
Administrator: Dave Conover
Treasurer: Bill Broderick
General Counsel: John J. Rademacher
Director, Organization Division: David S. Christensen

Historical Note
Members are the state Farm Bureaus in 50 states and Puerto Rico. These, in turn, represent nearly 3,000 county Farm Bureaus and over 4.1 million families. The American Agricultural Marketing Ass'n, American Agricultural Insurance Company, and American Agricultural Communications System are affiliated companies. Has an annual budget of approximately $16 million.

Publications:
Farm Bureau News. w.

Meetings/Conferences:
Annual Meetings: January/6,000
1999 – Albuquerque, NM/Jan. 10-13/6000

American Farriers Ass'n *(1971)*
4059 Iron Works Parkway
Suite 2
Lexington, KY   40511
Tel: (606)233-7411   *Fax:* (606)231-7862
Members: 2,400 individuals, 100 manufacturers/suppliers
Staff: 2
Annual Budget: $250-500,000
Office Manager: Kelly L. Werner

Historical Note
An association of professional horseshoers. Membership: $100/year.

Publications:
AFA Newsletter. bi-m.
American Farriers Journal. bi-m. adv.

Meetings/Conferences:
Annual Meetings: Spring

American Fashion Ass'n *(1938)*

Historical Note
Organization defunct in 1997.

American Federation for Aging Research *(1979)*
1414 6th Ave., 18th Floor
New York, NY   10019-2514
Tel: (212)752-2327   *Fax:* (212)832-2298
E-Mail: age2327@aol.com
Web Site: http://www.afar.org
Staff: 5
Annual Budget: $1-2,000,000
Exec. Director: Stephanie Lederman

Historical Note
AFAR members are physicians, scientists and others with an interest in research on aging.

Publications:
AFAR Newsletter. irreg.

Meetings/Conferences:
Annual Meetings: with the American Geriatrics Soc.

American Federation for Clinical Research *(1940)*

Historical Note
Name changed to American Federation for Medical Research (AFMR) in 1996.

American Federation for Medical Research *(1940)*
1200 19th St., N.W., Suite 300
Washington, DC   20036-2422
Tel: (202)429-5161   *Fax:* (202)223-4579
E-Mail: afmr@dc.sba.com
Web Site: http://www.AFMR.org
Members: 5,000 individuals
Staff: 6
Annual Budget: $2-5,000,000
Exec. Director: Susan Eisenberg

Historical Note
Promotes research in clinical and laboratory medicine. Membership: $130/year.

Publications:
AFMR Newsletter. q.
Journal of Investigative Medicine. bi-m. adv.
Journal of Investigative Medicine Supplement. 3/yr. adv.

Meetings/Conferences:
Annual Meetings: Spring
1999 – Washington, DC(Convention
    Center)/April 17-21/9000

American Federation of Astrologers *(1938)*
P.O. Box 22040
6535 South Rural Road
Tempe, AZ   85285-2040
Tel: (602)838-1751   *Fax:* (602)838-8293
Toll Free: (888)301 - 7630
E-Mail: afa@msn.com
Web Site: http://www.astrologers.com

Members: 4,000 individuals
Staff: 12
Annual Budget: $500-1,000,000
Exec. Secretary: Robert W. Cooper

Historical Note
Organized to advance astrological education and research. Has members throughout the U.S. and in 54 foreign countries. Membership: $35/year.

Publications:
Today's Astrologer. m.
Today's Astrologer. m.

Meetings/Conferences:
Biennial Meetings: even years, July/August

American Federation of Government Employees *(1932)*
80 F St., N.W.
Washington, DC 20001-1528
Tel: (202)639-6435 *Fax:* (202)639-6441
Members: 200,000 individuals
Staff: 200
Annual Budget: $2-5,000,000
President: Bobby L. Harnage
Director, Communications: Magda Lynn Seymour
Exec. Ass't to National President: Brian DeWyngaert
National Secretary/Treasurer: Rita Mason
General Counsel: Mark Roth
Director, Membership & Organization: Sharon Pinnock

Historical Note
Established by dissidents from the Nat'l Federation of Federal Employees in 1932 who wished to extend the civil service classification system to skilled crafts in government. Chartered by the American Federation of Labor the same year. Sponsors and supports the American Federation of Government Employees Political Action Commitee. The largest union representing Federal and District of Columbia workers.

Publications:
AFGE Bulletin. m.
The Government Standard. bi-m.

Meetings/Conferences:
2000 – Orlando, FL

American Federation of Grain Millers Internat'l Union *(1936)*
4949 Olson Memorial Hwy.
Minneapolis, MN 55422
Tel: (612)545-0211 *Fax:* (612)545-5489
Members: 25,000 individuals
Staff: 25
Annual Budget: $2-5,000,000
President: Larry R. Jackson
General Secretary-Treasurer: Larry D. Barber

Historical Note
Merged(1999) with the Bakery, Confectionary and Tobacco Workers' International Union. Organized in Toledo, Ohio July, 1936 as the Grain Processors Council. Became the National Council of Grain Processors in 1939. Chartered by the American Federation of Labor July 26, 1948 under its present title.

Publications:
Grain Miller News. q.

Meetings/Conferences:
Quadriennial Meetings: (1999)

American Federation of Home Health Agencies *(1981)*
1320 Fenwick Lane, Suite 100
Silver Spring, MD 20910-3514
Tel: (301)588-1454 *Fax:* (301)588-4732
E-Mail: afhha@his.com
Web Site: www.his.com/afhha/usa.html
Members: 200 agencies
Staff: 2
Annual Budget: $100-250,000
Exec. Director: Ann B. Howard

Historical Note
Organized to represent the concerns of free-standing home health agencies (HHAs). Works to develop policies and implement the provisions of Medicare.

Publications:
Insider. semi-m.

Meetings/Conferences:
Semi-annual Meetings: Spring and Fall
1999 – Lake Tahoe, NV/Jan. 24-26

American Federation of Labor and Congress of Industrial Organizations *(1955)*
815 16th St., N.W.
Washington, DC 20006
Tel: (202)637-5000 *Fax:* (202)637-5058
Web Site: http://www.afl-cio.org
Members: 13,100,000 individuals
Staff: 200
Annual Budget: $50-100,000,000
President: John J. Sweeney
Secretary Treasurer: Richard L. Trumka
Exec. V. President: Linda Chavez

Historical Note
The American Federation of Labor was founded in 1886 by 13 national unions on the principle of autonomy for its members. Samuel Gompers was the first president and served 38 years. In 1935 nine of its unions broke away under the leadership of John L. Lewis to form the Congress of Industrial Organizations to push industrial (as opposed to craft) unionism. After 20 years of independence, the AFL and CIO were merged in 1955. The AFL-CIO consists of 78 international unions, 50 state organizations and about 45,000 local unions. Has an annual budget of approximately $72.3 million.

Publications:
America at Work. m.

Meetings/Conferences:
Biennial meetings: Odd years

American Federation of Musicians of the United States and Canada *(1896)*
1501 Broadway, Suite 600
New York, NY 10036
Tel: (212)869-1330 *Fax:* (212)764-6134
Members: 119,000 individuals
Staff: 85
Annual Budget: $5-10,000,000
President: Steve G. Young
Exec. Ass't to the President: Peter O'Shea
Director, Organizing and Education: Paul Frank
Secretary/Treasurer: Stephen R. Sprague
Ass't to the President: Barbara Nielsen

Historical Note
Organized October 19, 1896 in Indianapolis as the American Federation of Musicians and chartered by the American Federation of Labor the same year. Assumed its present name in 1965. Supports the A.F.M.-Tempo Political Contributions Committee.

Publications:
International Musician. m. adv.

Meetings/Conferences:
Biennial meetings: odd years
1999 – Las Vegas, NV(Riviera Hotel)

American Federation of Police and Concerned Citizens *(1966)*
3801 Biscayne Blvd.
Miami, FL 33137
Tel: (305)573-0202 *Fax:* (305)573-9819
Web Site: http://www.aphs.org
Members: 103,550 individuals
Staff: 22
Annual Budget: $2-5,000,000
Exec. Director: Donna M. Shepherd

Historical Note
Established as the United States Federation of Police, this is largely an educational organization, offering police survivor benefits, a placement service and various types of awards to its members. Merged with the American Law Enforcement Officers Association in 1977. Added "and Concerned Citizens" to its name in 1996. Maintains an office in Washington, DC. Membership: $36/year (active individual); $20/year (associate).

Publications:
Police Times Magazine. q.

Meetings/Conferences:
Biennial Meetings: even years

American Federation of Railroad Police
52-25 72nd Place
Maspeth, NY 11378
Tel: (718)898-0852
E-Mail: jpbrown@@pipeline.com
Web Site: http://www.pipeline.com/ ~ jpbrown/home.htm
Members: 325 individuals
Secretary-Treasurer: John Brown

Historical Note
Also known as the Amtrak Police Benevolent Ass'n, AFRP is the labor organization representing law enforcement professionals employed by the National Railroad Passenger Corporation. Has no paid officers or full-time staff.

American Federation of School Administrators *(1971)*
1729 21st St., N.W.
Washington, DC 20009-1101
Tel: (202)986-4209 *Fax:* (202)986-4211
Web Site: www.admin.org
Members: 13,000 individuals
Staff: 4
Annual Budget: $500-1,000,000
President: Joe L. Greene

Historical Note
Established in 1971 as the School Administrators and Supervisors Organizing Committee. Assumed its present name on July 7, 1976. Affiliated with the AFL-CIO in 1976. Memberhip: $56/year.

Publications:
AFSA News. 10/year.

Meetings/Conferences:
Triennial Meetings: Summer (2000)

American Federation of State, County and Municipal Employees *(1936)*
1625 L Street., N.W.
Washington, DC 20036
Tel: (202)452-4800 *Fax:* (202)429-1122
Web Site: http://www.afscme.org
Members: 1,300,000 individuals
Staff: 350
Annual Budget: $50-100,000,000
President: Gerald W. McEntee
Director, Public Affairs: Jean Nolan
Director, Finance: James L. O'Malley
Director, Info. Systems: Steven R. Cablk

Historical Note
Organized in Chicago December 9, 1935 and chartered by the American Federation of Labor the following year. Merged (April 1978) with the Civil Service Employees Ass'n of New York. Has an annual budget of approximately $88.2 million. Sponsors and supports the American Federation of State, County and Municipal Employees Political Action Committee.

Publications:
The Public Employee. bi-m.

Meetings/Conferences:
Biennial Meetings: Even years in late Spring

American Federation of Teachers *(1916)*
555 New Jersey Ave., N.W.
Washington, DC 20001
Tel: (202)879-4440 *Fax:* (202)879-4545
Toll Free: (800)238 - 1133
Web Site: http://www.aft.org
Members: 907,000 individuals
Staff: 200
Annual Budget: $50-100,000,000
President: Sandra Feldman
Director, Public Affairs: Donna Fowler
Political Director: Elizabeth M. Smith
Dir., Meetings & Travel: Sally Muravchik
Secretary-Treasurer: Edward McElroy
General Manager, Financial Operations: Ronald Krouse
Counsel: David J. Strom
Dir., Information Technology: Charles Stunson

Historical Note
Organized in Chicago, IL and affiliated with the AFL-CIO. Has an annual budget of approximately $71.2 million. The Federation of Public Employees is a division of AFT. Sponsors and supports the AFT Cope Political Action Committee.

Publications:
American Educator. q. adv.
American Teacher. 8/yr. adv.
Healthwire.
On Campus.
PSRP Reporter.
Public Service Reporter.

Meetings/Conferences:
Biennial Meetings: Quest Conference in odd years, Convention in even

American Federation of Television and Radio Artists *(1937)*
260 Madison Ave., 7th Floor
New York, NY 10016
Tel: (212)532-0800 *Fax:* (212)532-2242
Web Site: http://www.aftra.com
Members: 74,000 individuals
Staff: 50
Annual Budget: $2-5,000,000
Nat'l Exec. Director: Bruce A. York

Historical Note
Chartered August 16, 1937 by Associated Actors and Artistes of America as an autonomous branch union representing radio performers. It has since come to represent performers on live or videotaped TV programs as well. Merged with the Television Authority in 1950.

Publications:
AFTRA Magazine. q. adv.

Meetings/Conferences:
Biennial Meetings: Summer/350

American Federation of Violin and Bow Makers *(1980)*
250 West 54th St., Suite 709
New York, NY 10019
Toll Free: (800)633 - 2777
Web Site: http://www.afvbm.com
Members: 110 violin and bow makers
Staff: 9
Annual Budget: $50-100,000
President: James McKean

Historical Note
Professional society of individuals who make and restore violins and bows. Address changes bienially in conjunction with the President. Membership: $300/year (individual).

Publications:
Membership Directory. a.
Newsletter. q.

Meetings/Conferences:
Annual Meetings: April

American Feed Industry Ass'n *(1909)*
1501 Wilson Blvd., Suite 1100
Arlington, VA 22209-3199
Tel: (703)524-0810 *Fax:* (703)524-1921
E-Mail: mailafia@tomco.net
Web Site: http://www.afia.org
Members: 700 companies
Staff: 20
Annual Budget: $1-2,000,000
President: David A. Bossman
V. President, Public Relations: Rex A. Runyon
Senior V. President: Steven L. Kopperud
V. President: Barbara Estridge
Director, Administration: Dorann Towery

Historical Note
Formerly (1985) the American Feed Manufacturers Ass'n. Members are firms which manufacture formula feed to sell; firms which manufacture formula feed only for their own poultry or livestock; and firms which provide ingredients, services, equipment, and supplies to feed manufacturers. Absorbed the Midwest Feed Manufacturers Ass'n in 1975 and the Nat'l Feed Ingredients Ass'n in 1992.

Publications:
Membership Directory & Buyers Guide. a. adv.
Newsletters (Feedgram, Feed Control Comment, Feed Briefs, Feedline, Safety Gram).
Software Directory.

Meetings/Conferences:
Annual Meetings: Spring
1999 – Minneapolis, MN/May 17-19

American Fence Ass'n *(1962)*
5300 Memorial Drive, Suite 116
Stone Mountain, GA 30083
Tel: (404)299-5413 *Fax:* (404)299-8927
Toll Free: (800)822 - 4342
E-Mail: afa@mindspring.com

Web Site: http://www.americanfenceassoc.org
Members: 1,430 companies
Staff: 6
Annual Budget: $1-2,000,000
Exec. V. President: Frederick G. Dempsey, Jr., CAE

Historical Note
Formerly (1993) Internat'l Fence Industry Ass'n. Membership:
$365/year.

Publications:
Across the Fence. q.
ASTM Manual.
Buyer's Guide. a.
Fence Post. bi-m. adv.
Who's Who in Fencing. a. adv.

Meetings/Conferences:
Annual Meetings: January-February/5,940
1999 – Anaheim, CA(Anaheim Convention Center)/Jan. 27-30
2000 – Tampa, FL(Tampa Convention Center)/Jan. 26-29
2001 – San Antonio, TX(San Antonio Convention Center)
2002 – Las Vegas, NV(Convention Center)
2003 – Nashville, TN(Opryland)
2004 – Orlando, FL

American Fern Soc. *(1893)*
Milwaukee Public Museum
Milwaukee, WI   53233
Tel: (414)278-2760   *Fax:* (414)278-6100
E-Mail: ct@mpm.edu
Members: 819 individuals
Annual Budget: $10-25,000
Secretary: W. Carl Taylor

Historical Note
Founded in 1893 as the Linnaean Fern Chapter of the Aggasiz
Ass'n with 24 charter members. Became The American Fern Soc. in
1905 and was incorporated in the District of Columbia in 1936.
Affiliated with the American Institute of Biological Sciences. Has an
internat'l membership of pteridologists, botanists and others
interested in growing or studying ferns. Has no paid staff.
Membership: $8-15/year (individual), $20/year (organization).

Publications:
American Fern Journal. q.
Fiddlehead Forum Newsletter. bi-m.

Meetings/Conferences:
Annual Meetings: August, with the American Institute of
  Biological Sciences
1999 – St. Louis, MO(America's Center)/Aug. 1-7
2000 – Portland, OR

American Fiber Manufacturers Ass'n *(1933)*
1150 17th St., N.W., Suite 310
Washington, DC   20036
Tel: (202)296-6508   *Fax:* (202)296-3052
E-Mail: oday@afma.org
Web Site: http://www.afma.org
Members: 18 manufacturers
Staff: 11
Annual Budget: $1-2,000,000
President: Paul T. O'Day
V. President: Dr. Robert H. Barker
General Counsel: Donald Greeley, Esq.

Historical Note
Formerly (1988) the Man-Made Fiber Producers Ass'n. Members
are producers of chemically-based or cellulosic fibers such as
polyester, nylon, rayon, etc.

Publications:
Guide to Manufactured Fibers. a.
Manufactured Fiber Fact Book. a.
World Directory of Manufactured Fiber Products.

Meetings/Conferences:
Annual Meetings: October

American Fiberboard Ass'n *(1991)*
1210 W. Northwest Hwy.
Palatine, IL   60067-1897
Tel: (847)934-8394   *Fax:* (847)934-8803
Members: 6 manufacturers
Annual Budget: $50-100,000
Exec. Director: C. Curtis Peterson, CAE
Dir., Technical Service: Louis Wagner

Historical Note
Administrative assistance provided by the American Hardboard
Ass'n.

Meetings/Conferences:

American Film and Video Ass'n *(1943)*
Historical Note
Address unknown in 1995.

American Film Marketing Ass'n *(1980)*
10850 Wilshire Blvd., 9th Floor
Los Angeles, CA   90024-4321
Tel: (310)446-1000   *Fax:* (310)446-1600
Members: 125 companies
Staff: 29
Annual Budget: $2-5,000,000
President: Allen R. Frischkorn, Jr., CAE
V.President, Research/Publications: Melanie Moen
Exec. V. President: Jonathan Wolf
V. President, Member Services: Missy Huger
V.President, Research/Publications: William Anderson

Historical Note
Member companies are engaged in the international distribution,
marketing, and in some cases the production of independent
English language feature motion pictures. The association fosters
the interests of its members in areas of copyright protection and
trade barrier problems; operates the American Film Market in
February of each year in Los Angeles, CA. Membership:
$3,000/year.

Publications:
AFMA Market Newsletter. bi-m.
AFMA News Newsletter. 3/yr.
Anti-Piracy Guide. a.
Fact Book. a.

Meetings/Conferences:
Semi-annual meetings: Film Market in Los Angeles in March
  and meeting in September

American Filtration and Separations Soc. *(1987)*
P.O. Box 1530
Northport, AL   35476-6530
Tel: (205)333-6111   *Fax:* (205)333-6446
E-Mail: afs@afssociety.org
Web Site: http://www.afssociety.org
Members: 800 individuals, 80 companies
Staff: 4
Annual Budget: $250-500,000
Conference Coordinator: Charlotte Stripling

Historical Note
Formed as a U.S. section of the Filtration Soc. (U.K.); reorganized
as a separate organization in 1987. Members are engineers,
scientists and others with an interest in fluid particle separation
technology. Membership $75/year (individual-
U.S.)$85/year(individual-Canada and Mexico); $1,500/year
(company).

Publications:
AFS Newsletter. 3/year. adv.
Fluid Particle Separation Journal. 3/year.

Meetings/Conferences:
Annual Meetings: Spring/1,000
1999 – Boston, MA(Hynes Convention
  Center)/April 6-9/1200
2000 – Myrtle Beach, SC/1400

American Finance Ass'n *(1940)*
Blackwell Publishers
350 Main Street
Malden, MA   02148
Tel: (781)388-8200   *Fax:* (781)388-8232
Toll Free: (800)835 - 6770
E-Mail: PGree@Blackwellpub.com
Web Site: http://www.blackwellpub.com
Members: 4,500 individuals, 3,500 corporations & libraries
Staff: 2
Annual Budget: $250-500,000
Coordinator: Paulette Green

Historical Note
Established in 1940 and incorporated in Illinois in 1952.
Membership consists of both individuals and institutions interested
in finance. Affiliated with Allied Social Sciences Ass'n, which
manages the annual convention. Membership: $63/year
(individual), $80/year (organization).

Publications:
Journal of Finance. 6/year. adv.

Meetings/Conferences:
Annual Meetings: In conjunction with the Allied Social Sciences
  Ass'n
1999 – New York, NY/Jan. 3-5

American Financial Services Ass'n *(1916)*
919 18th St., N.W., 3rd Floor
Washington, DC   20006
Tel: (202)296-5544   *Fax:* (202)223-0321
Members: 530 companies
Staff: 23
Annual Budget: $2-5,000,000
President and C.E.O.: H. Randolph Lively, Jr.
Director, Communications: Lynne Strang
Sr. V. Pres., Government & Legal Affairs: Jeffrey A. Tassey
Director, Programs/ Conferences: Sheilah J. Harrison, CAE
President & C.E.O., AFSA Education Foundation: M. Susie Irvine
Exec. Sr. V. President: Thomas L. Thomas
V. President and General Counsel: Robert E. McKew
Corporate Secretary: Perla C. Mamel

Historical Note
The national trade association for providers of financial services to
consumers and small businesses. Its member companies are
consumer finance and sales finance companies, auto finance
companies, and diversified financial services firms. Merged (1971)
with the American Industrial Bankers Ass'n which had, in 1965,
absorbed the American Finance Conference. Established as the
National Consumer Finance Ass'n, it assumed its present name in
1983. Maintains the Consumer Credit Education Foundation and
the Consumer Finance Political Action Committee.

Publications:
Consumer Finance Law Bulletin. m.
Credit. m. adv.
Independent Operations. q.

Meetings/Conferences:
Annual Meetings: Fall/600

American Fine China Guild *(1955)*
c/o Lenox China, 100 Lenox Dr.
Lawrenceville, NJ   08648
Tel: (609)844-1332
Staff: 1
Annual Budget: under $10,000
V.P. and Secretary: Louis Fantin

Historical Note
Members are fine china manufacturers.

Meetings/Conferences:
Annual Meetings: usually November, New York, NY

American Fire Sprinkler Ass'n *(1981)*
12959 Jupiter Road, Suite 142
Dallas, TX   75238-3200
Tel: (214)349-5965   *Fax:* (214)343-8898
E-Mail: jennie@pbea.org

Web Site: http://www.pbea.org
Members: 600 companies
Staff: 13
Annual Budget: $1-2,000,000
President: Steve A. Muncy, C.A.E.
Director of Communications: Janet K. Knowles
Dir., Membership/Training: Lloyd M. Ivy
Director of Technical Services: Roland Huggins, P.E.

Historical Note
Members are contractors, manufacturers, and suppliers of fire
sprinkler systems, as well as fire protection consultant firms. Merit
shop orientation. Membership fee based on sales volume.

Publications:
Contractor Network. bi-m.
Membergram. m.
Sprinkler Age. m. adv.

Meetings/Conferences:
Annual Meetings: Fall

American Fisheries Soc. *(1870)*
5410 Grosvenor Lane, Suite 110
Bethesda, MD   20814-2199
Tel: (301)897-8616   *Fax:* (301)897-8096
E-Mail: main@fisheries.org
Web Site: http://www.fisheries.org
Members: 8,500 individuals
Staff: 23
Annual Budget: $2-5,000,000
Exec. Director: Paul Brouha
Director, Marketing: Terry Ames
Director, Administration & Finance: Betsy Fritz

Historical Note
Founded Dec. 20, 1870 in New York, NY as the American
Culturists' Ass'n, it became the American Fish Cultural Ass'n in
1878 and the American Fisheries Soc. in 1884; incorporated in the
District of Columbia in 1911. Promotes the conservation,
development and wise use of commercial and recreational fisheries.

Publications:
Fisheries - A Bulletin of the AFS. irreg.
Journal of Aquatic Animal Health. q.
North American Journal of Fisheries Management q.
Progressive Fish-Culturist. q.
Transactions of the American Fisheries Society. bi-m.

Meetings/Conferences:
Annual Meetings: August or September
1999 – Charlotte, NC/Aug. 30-Sept. 2
2000 – St. Louis, MO/Aug. 20-24
2001 – Phoenix, AZ/Aug. 19-23

American Fishing Tackle Manufacturers Ass'n *(1933)*
Historical Note
Merged into the American Sport Fishing Ass'n in 1995.

American Fitness Ass'n *(1987)*
1945 Palo Verde Ave., Suite 202
Long Beach, CA   90815-3445
Tel: (562)799-8333   *Fax:* (562)799-3355
Members: 4,000 individuals
Staff: 5
Annual Budget: $50-100,000
President: Dr. John Russell

Historical Note
A national association of health, sports and fitness professionals.
Membership: $75/year (individual); $250/year (organization).

Publications:
Newsletter. q.

American Flint Glass Workers Union *(1878)*
1440 South Byrne Rd.
Toledo, OH   43614
Tel: (419)385-6687   *Fax:* (419)385-8839
Members: 18,700 individuals
Staff: 25
Annual Budget: $2-5,000,000
National President: Richard Morgan

Historical Note
Organized in Pittsburgh July 1, 1878 as the United Flint Glass
Workers. Became the American Flint Glass Workers' Union of
North America in 1912 when it affiliated with the American
Federation of Labor. Adopted its present name in 1975.

Publications:
American Flint Magazine. m.
Trade Circular. m. adv.

Meetings/Conferences:
Triennial meetings: Odd years in June

American Flock Ass'n *(1985)*
230 Congress St., 3rd Floor
Boston, MA   02110
Tel: (617)542-8220   *Fax:* (617)542-2199
E-Mail: AmerFlock@aol.com
Web Site: http://www.flocking.org
Members: 66 companies
Staff: 3
Annual Budget: $50-100,000
Exec. Director: David Trumbull

Historical Note
AFA represents all aspects of the flock industry, including flock
suppliers, manufacturers and end users. Flock is very short fiber
primarily used in coating paper, fabric, plastic, objects, etc.
Membership: $600-1,800/year.

Publications:
American Flock Ass'n Directory. a.
Design with Flock in Mind.

Meetings/Conferences:
Annual Meetings: Fall, in conjunction with the Northern Textile
  Ass'n

American Floral Marketing Council (1969)

Historical Note
A council of the Soc. of American Florists.

American Florists Ass'n (1985)

Historical Note
Organization defunct in 1996.

American Folklore Soc. (1888)

c/o American Anthropological
4350 N. Fairfax Drive, Suite 640
Arlington, VA 22203-1620
Tel: (703)528-1902
Fax: (703)528-3546
Members: 1,500 individuals
Staff: 1
Annual Budget: $100-250,000
Exec. Secretary Treasurer: Shalom Staub

Historical Note
Organized in Cambridge, MA, January 4, 1888 to collect, publish and preserve original folklore material. An affiliate of the American Anthropological Association, which provides business and administrative support. Membership: $20/year (student or partner), $60/year (individual), and $800/year (life).

Publications:
American Folklore Society Newsletter. bi-m.
Journal of American Folklore. q. adv.

Meetings/Conferences:
Annual Meetings: October
1999 – Memphis, TN(Peabody)/Oct. 20-23
2000 – Columbus, OH(Hyatt Regency)/Oct. 25-29

American Football Coaches Ass'n (1921)

5900 Old McGregor Road
Waco, TX 76712-6166
Tel: (254)776-5900
Fax: (254)776-3744
Web Site: http://www.afca.com
Members: 8,000 individuals
Staff: 7
Exec. Director: Grant Teaff
Director, Communications and Marketing: Mel Pulliam
Director, Administration and Events: Sandi Atkinson

Historical Note
Originally organized to promote college football and to discuss mutual problems. Later interests include a voice in the rule making process, the promotion of safe techniques and the formulation and enforcement of a code of ethics. Membership: $40/year(coaches); $50/year (foreign members).

Publications:
Directory. a.
Proceedings Manual. a.
Summer Mannual. a.
The Extra Point. bi-m.

Meetings/Conferences:
Annual Meetings: January/3,500

American Forage and Grassland Council (1944)

P.O. Box 94
Georgetown, TX 78627
Tel: (512)238-0747
Fax: (512)869-0393
Members: 7,000 individuals
Staff: 3
Annual Budget: $50-100,000
Exec. Secretary: Dana Tucker

Historical Note
Established July 17, 1944 at Rutgers University as the Joint Committee on Grassland Farming. Reorganized on December 19, 1957 as the American Grassland Council. The name was changed July 15, 1968 to the American Forage and Grassland Council. Membership: $30/year (individual), $50-600/year (organization/company) based on type and size.

Publications:
AFGC News. q.
Membership Directory. a.
Proceedings. a.

Meetings/Conferences:
Annual Meetings: Spring
1999 – Omaha, NE/Feb. 21-26

American Foreign Law Ass'n (1925)

Fordham Law School
140 W. 62nd St.
New York, NY 10023
Tel: (212)636-6896
Fax: (212)636-6899
Members: 300 individuals
Staff: 2
Annual Budget: $10-25,000
President: Roger Gobel

Historical Note
AFLA promotes the advancement of learning through the study, understanding and practice of foreign, comparative and international law; cooperation with other professional societies interested in similar objectives; fostering legal research; and the publication and dissemination of legal materials. Membership: $90/year (individual); $40/year (foreign/non-resident); $35/year (student).

Publications:
AFLA Newsletter. 3/year.

Meetings/Conferences:
Monthly Luncheon Meeting: September to May in New York City
1999 – New York, NY

American Foreign Service Ass'n (1924)

2101 E St., N.W., 3rd Fl
Washington, DC 20037
Tel: (202)338-4045
Fax: (202)338-6820
Members: 11,000 individuals
Staff: 30

Annual Budget: $2-5,000,000
Exec. Director: Susan Reardon
Legal Counsel: Sharon Papp
Director, Membership: Janet Hedrick
Editor: Robert Guldin

Historical Note
Professional association of Foreign Service employees. Acts as the elected representative of all Foreign Service personnel in the AID, FAS, FCS and USIA and State Department bargaining units. Membership fee varies, based on service grade.

Publications:
Foreign Service Journal. m. adv.

Meetings/Conferences:
Annual Meetings: Washington, DC/late Fall

American Forensic Ass'n (1949)

Box 256
River Falls, WI 54022-0256
Tel: (715)425-3198
Fax: (715)425-9533
Toll Free: (800)228 - 5424
E-Mail: james.w.pratt@uwrf.edu
Members: 1,200 individuals
Staff: 2
Annual Budget: $50-100,000
Exec. Secretary: James Pratt

Historical Note
Established in 1949 to promote effective and responsible oral communication. Membership composed primarily of college and high school directors of debate and speech programs. Affiliated with the Speech Communication Ass'n. Membership: $45/year (individual), $55/year (organization/company).

Publications:
Journal. q. adv.
Newsletter. 3/year. adv.

Meetings/Conferences:
Annual Meetings: November, with Speech Communication Ass'n
1999 – Chicago, IL(Chicago Hilton)/Nov. 4-8

American Forest and Paper Ass'n (1993)

1111 19th St., N.W., Suite 800
Washington, DC 20036
Tel: (202)463-2700
Fax: (202)463-2785
Web Site: http://www.afandpa.org
Members: 1,500 companies and organizations
Staff: 156
Annual Budget: $25-50,000,000
C.E.O.: W. Henson Moore
V. President, Communications: Mary Joy Jameson
V. President, Governmental and External Affairs: John H. Dressendorfer
Director, Federal Relations: Jane L. Turner
C.F.O.: Ann W. Western
Senior Director, Human Resources and Development: Michael P. Hoagland
Manager, Membership Services: Kathleen M. Smith
Membership: Eric Horeff

Historical Note
Formed by the merger of the American Forest Council (1932), American Paper Institute (1964) and the Nat'l Forest Products Ass'n (1902) in 1993. AF&PA represents companies which grow, harvest and process wood and woodfiber; manufacture pulp, paper and paperboard products from both virgin and recovered fiber; and produce solid wood products. AF&PA divisions include: American Wood Council, Containerboard and Kraft Paper; Forest Resources, Paperboard, Paper and Pulp. Annual Budget: $36.4 million (1995). Membership: Dues are set and collected by each product group based on all member company primary paper sales, solid wood product sales and the cords of forest resources consumed in pulp production.

American Forests (1875)

P.O. Box 2000
Washington, DC 20013-2000
Tel: (202)955-4500
Fax: (202)955-4588
Members: 148,000 individuals
Staff: 35
Annual Budget: $2-5,000,000
Exec. Director: Deborah Gangloff
V.P., Communications: Daniel Smith
V. President, Policy: Gerald Gray
V.P., Administration: Lu N. Rose
V. President, Development: Rick Crouse

Historical Note
Formerly (1992) American Forestry Ass'n. Founded September 10, 1875 in Chicago, IL, for "the protection of the existing forests of the country from unnecessary waste, and the promotion of the propagation and planting of useful trees." Merged in 1882 with the American Forestry Congress. Membership: $30/year.

Publications:
American Forests. q.

Meetings/Conferences:
Annual Meetings: Fall
1999 – Seattle, WA

American Foundrymen's Soc. (1896)

505 State St.
Des Plaines, IL 60016-8399
Tel: (847)824-0181
Fax: (847)824-7848
Toll Free: (800)537 - 4237
Web Site: http://www.afsync.org
Members: 14,000 individuals, 600 corporate
Staff: 62
Annual Budget: $2-5,000,000
Exec. V. President: Charles H. Jones
Director, Public Relations/Meetings Coordinator: Kristy Glass
V. President, Education: Ian Kay
V. President, Finance: Maria P. Komon
Member Services Director: Marnelle Bragg
Publisher, Moder Casting: David Kanicki

V. President, Technology: John Lewinsky

Historical Note
Founded as the American Foundrymen's Ass'n, it assumed its present name in 1948. AFS is a technical and trade ass'n of individuals and companies concerned with the castings industry. The Cast Metals Institute is the educational arm of the AFS.

Publications:
Human Resource Report. bi-m.
Labor Agreement Settlement Data. 9-12/year.
Labor Case Comments. semi-m.
Modern Casting. m. adv.
Nat'l Survey of Wages and Benefits in the Foundry Industry. a.
Transactions. a.
Washington Focus. m.

Meetings/Conferences:
Annual Meetings: April-May
1999 – St. Louis, MO(Convention Center)/March 13-16/15000

American Fracture Ass'n (1938)

Route 6, Box 8
Bloomington, IL 61704
Tel: (309)828-2815
Fax: (309)828-1499
Members: 500 individuals
Staff: 2
Annual Budget: $50-100,000
Exec. Secretary: Sarah Olson

Historical Note
Founded in 1938 in Macomb, Illinois and was known as the Ambulatory Fracture Ass'n until 1952 when the name was changed to the American Fracture Ass'n. Membership limited to 500. Membership: $200/year (individual).

Publications:
JBJS. q.
Newsletter. bi-a.
Orthopedic Abstracts. a.

Meetings/Conferences:
Annual Meetings: Spring/200
1999 – Tucson, AZ(El Conquistador)/May 13-16
2000 – Trinidad, West Indies(Hilton)/May 13-16
2001 – Savannah, GA(Savannah Hyatt)/May 3-6/100
2002 – Williamsburg, VA(Colonial Williamsburg)/April 11-14/100

American Frozen Food Institute (1942)

2000 Corporate Ridge, Suite 1000
McLean, VA 22102-7805
Tel: (703)821-0770
Fax: (703)821-1350
E-Mail: AFFI@PORDN.NET
Web Site: http://www.affi.com
Members: 550 companies
Staff: 17
Annual Budget: $2-5,000,000
President & CEO: Steven C. Anderson
V. President, Communications: Christopher P. Krese
Director, Communications: Michelle Jacobs
Director, Industry/Government Affairs: Christin Bradshaw
V. President, Legislative Affairs: Dina Moses Land
Director, Covention Services/Statistical Services: M. Jean Bohannon
Senior V. President, Financial Operations: Joanne B. Cox
Exec. V. President and Staff Counsel: Leslie G. Sarasin
Director, Membership/Affilated Ass'n: Heather B. Schroeder
V.President, Scientific/Regulatory Aff's: Robert Garfield

Historical Note
Formerly (1970) Nat'l Ass'n of Frozen Food Packers. Absorbed the California Freezers Ass'n in 1967. Supports the AFFI Political Action Committee. Affiliated with the Internat'l Frozen Food Ass'n; Frozen Potato Products Institute; Nat'l Frozen Pizza Institute; and Nat'l Yogurt Ass'n.

Publications:
AFFI Letter. bi-w.
Membership Directory & Buyers Guide. a. adv.

Meetings/Conferences:
Annual Meetings: Fall/1,800
1999 – Boston, MA/Oct. 2-6

American Fur Merchant's Ass'n (1898)

Historical Note
A division of Fur Information Council of America, which provides administrative support.

American Furniture Manufacturers Ass'n (1905)

P.O. Box HP-7
High Point, NC 27261
Tel: (910)884-5000
Fax: (910)884-5303
Members: 375 companies
Staff: 15
Annual Budget: $1-2,000,000
Exec. V. President: Douglas L. Brackett
Director, Marketing/Communications: Nancy High

Historical Note
Manufacturers of household and institutional furniture. Founded as the Southern Furniture Manufacturers Ass'n. Assumed its current name in 1984 when it merged with the Nat'l Ass'n of Furniture Manufacturers. Maintains a government affairs office in Washington, DC. Divisions include Summer and Casual Furniture Manufacturers Ass'n, suppliers, transportation and logistics, marketing, finance, manufacturing, and human relations. Sponsors and supports the FurnPac political action committee.

Publications:
AFMA Membership Directory. a.
The Furniture Executive. m.

Meetings/Conferences:
Annual Meetings: Fall

American Galloway Breeders Ass'n (1888)

310 W. Spruce St.
Missoula, MT 59802

Tel: (406)728-5719   Fax: (406)721-6300
Members: 75 individuals
Annual Budget: under $10,000
Secretary: Bob Mullendore

Historical Note
Formed in Chicago, November 23, 1882 by U.S. and Canadian breeders of Galloway cattle. Incorporated in the State of Montana. Absorbed the Galloway Performance International in 1973. Membership: $75/year.

Publications:
Galloway Globe.
Midwest Galloway News.

Meetings/Conferences:
Annual Meetings: October

American Galvanizers Ass'n (1935)
12200 E. Iliff Ave., Suite 204
Aurora, CO 80014
Tel: (303)750-2900   Fax: (303)750-2909
Toll Free: (800)468 - 7732
E-Mail: aga@netway.net
Web Site: http://www.galvanizeit.org
Members: 150 companies
Staff: 8
Annual Budget: $500-1,000,000
Exec. Director: Philip G. Rahrig

Historical Note
Organized in 1933 and incorporated in 1935 in the Commonwealth of Pennsylvania. Represents the after-fabrication hot dip galvanizing industry whose members provide anti-corrosion coatings to steel products. Formerly (1989) American Hot Dip Galvanizers Ass'n.

Publications:
Directory. a.
Newsletter. bi-m.

Meetings/Conferences:
Annual Meetings: Spring/200
1999 - South Carolina(Kiawahh Island Resort)

American Gaming Ass'n (1995)
555 13th St., N.W., Suite 1010 East
Washington, DC 20004
Tel: (202)637-6500   Fax: (202)637-6507
Members: 17 companies
Staff: 8
President: Frank J. Fahrenkopf, Jr.
Senior V. President and Exec. Director: Judy Layne Patterson
V. President: John Shelk
V. President: Walton Chambers

Historical Note
Trade association representing the gambling industry.

Publications:
Inside the AGA. m.

Meetings/Conferences:

American Gas Ass'n (1918)
400 North Capitol St., N.W.
Washington, DC 20001
Tel: (703)841-8400   Fax: (703)841-8689
E-Mail: WEBMASTER@AGA.COM
Web Site: http://www.aga.com
Members: 3,000 individuals, 275 companies
Staff: 180
Annual Budget: $50-100,000,000
President and C.E.O.: David N. Parker, CAE
Managing Director, Communications: Julie Stewart
Senior V. President, Government Relations: Roger Cooper
Director, Congressional Relations: Deborah M. Estes
Director, Meeting Services: Mary E. Weekley
Manager, Meeting Services: Victoria R. Myers
C.F.O.: Kevin Hardardt
General Counsel/Corp. Secretary: David J. Muchow
Senior V. President, Membership Programs: Jay Copan
Director, Member Comm.: Lois Douthitt
Director, Membership Programs/Tech: Mark E. Stultz
Staff V. President: Karen Hill
Director, Information Systems: Gary Gardner

Historical Note
Formed by a merger of the Gas Institute and the Commercial Gas Ass'n in 1918. Connected with the Gas Employees Political Action Committee (GASPAC). Has an annual budget of approximately $56.3 million. Supports the Natural Gas Vehicle Coalition.

Publications:
American Gas Magazine. m. adv.
Financial Quarterly Review. q.
Gas Energy Review. m.
Operating Section Proceedings. a.
Pipeline Research Summary. a.
Research & Development Report. a.
The Natural Resource. q.

Meetings/Conferences:
Annual Meetings: Fall

American Gastroenterological Ass'n (1897)
7910 Woodmont Ave., 7th Floor
Bethesda, MD 20814-3015
Tel: (301)654-2055   Fax: (301)654-5920
Web Site: http://www.gastro.org
Members: 8,900 individuals
Staff: 50
Annual Budget: $10-25,000,000
Exec. Director: Robert Greenberg
V. President, Communications and Marketing: Dianne Bach, APR
V. President, Legal and Corporate Affairs: Lynne Robinson
V. President, Public Policy and Government Relations: Mary Berry Gerwin
V. President, Meetings: Pamela Magnani
V. President Finance and Administration: Thomas J. Serena

Historical Note
Membership: $250/year, plus $40 application fee (individual); $50/year (trainee).

Publications:
AGA News. m. adv.
Gastroenterology. m. adv.
GI Diseases Today.

Meetings/Conferences:
Annual Meetings: Spring

American Gear Manufacturers Ass'n (1916)
1500 King St., Suite 201
Alexandria, VA 22314-2730
Tel: (703)684-0211   Fax: (703)684-0242
E-Mail: webmaster@agma.org
Members: 400 companies
Staff: 13
Annual Budget: $1-2,000,000
President: Joe T. Franklin, Jr., CAE
V. President, Public Affairs: Wendy Allen
V. President, Technical Division: William Bradley
V. President, Administrative Division: Kurt Medert
V. President,Finance and Administration: Cathy Johnson

Historical Note
Members are gear manufacturers, makers of gear cutting and checking equipment, gearing teachers, suppliers to the industry and purchasers of gear products. Membership: $550/year (individual); $1,250-14,000/year, based on annual sales (company).

Publications:
News Digest. bi-m.

Meetings/Conferences:
Annual Meeting: March; Technical Meeting: October

American Gelbvieh Ass'n (1971)
10900 Dover St.
Westminster, CO 80021
Tel: (303)465-2333   Fax: (303)465-2339
E-Mail: aga@www.gelbvieh.org
Web Site: http://www.gelbvieh.org/2AbA
Members: 2,100 individuals
Staff: 12
Annual Budget: $1-2,000,000
Exec. Director: John T. Brink

Historical Note
Breeders and promoters of Gelbvieh cattle. Membership: $75/year (initial membership), $50/year (renewal).

Publications:
Gelbvieh World. m. adv.

Meetings/Conferences:
Annual Meetings: Denver, CO/Jan./300

American Gem and Mineral Suppliers Ass'n (1950)
P.O. Box 4065
Santa Monica, CA 90411-4065
Tel: (860)632-2020
Web Site: http://www.paleoart.com/agmsa/agmsahom.htm
Members: 90 companies
Staff: 1
Annual Budget: under $10,000
Exec. Director: Scott Petrillo

Historical Note
Provides an opportunity for members to become professional in their business activities through an exchange of ideas with each other. The purpose is to promote a high standard of ethics and business methods in the industry. Membership: $75/year.

Publications:
Newsletter. q.

Meetings/Conferences:
Semi-Annual Meetings: February/usually Tucson, AZ and August

American Gem Soc. (1934)
8881 W. Sahara Ave.
Las Vegas, NV 89117-5865
Tel: (702)255-6500   Fax: (702)255-7420
Web Site: http://www.AGS.org
Members: 3,600 individuals, 1,400 retail jewelry firms
Staff: 17
Annual Budget: $1-2,000,000
Exec. Director: Robert W. Bridel
Controller: Ruth Bennett
Manager, Membership Development: Yancy Weinrich

Historical Note
A professional association of U.S. and Canadian jewelers. Certifies members as Registered Jewelers, Certified Gemologists or Certified Gemologist Appraisers.

Publications:
Gems and Jewelry Fact Sheets. q.
Spectra. bi-m.

Meetings/Conferences:
Annual Meetings: Spring/800-1,000

American Gem Trade Ass'n (1981)
181 World Trade Center
P.O. Box 420643
Dallas, TX 75342
Tel: (214)742-4367   Fax: (214)742-7334
Members: 520 firms
Staff: 8
Annual Budget: $1-2,000,000
Exec. Director: Douglas K. Tucker
Director of Marketing: Shannon Woodmansee
Trade Show Manager: Mary Lou Keen

Historical Note
Established in Tucson, AZ and incorporated in New York, AGTA is a trade association for the colored gemstone industry in the United States and Canada. Membership: $125/year (affiliate), $500/year (firm).

Publications:
Directory. a.
Prism Newsletter. q.

Meetings/Conferences:
Annual Meetings: February, in Tucson, Arizona

American Genetic Ass'n (1903)
P.O. Box 257
Buckeystown, MD 21717
Tel: (301)695-9292   Fax: (301)695-9292
Members: 850 individuals, 1,500 institutions
Staff: 1
Exec. V. President: James Womack

Historical Note
Established as the American Breeders Ass'n in December 1903 in St. Louis by a committee from the Ass'n of Land Grant Colleges. Name changed in 1913 to the American Genetic Ass'n when it was incorporated in the District of Columbia. Affiliated with the American Ass'n for the Advancement of Science. A member society of the Internat'l Genetics Federation. Promotes the study of genetics and its application to plant and animal improvement and human welfare. Membership: $48/year (individual), $170/year (institutions), $24/year (student), $45/year (joint), foreign membership rates are available.

Publications:
Journal of Heredity. bi-m. adv.

Meetings/Conferences:
1999 - University Park, PA(Penn State University)

American Geographical Soc. (1851)
120 Wall St., Suite 100
New York, NY 10005-3904
Tel: (212)422-5456   Fax: (212)422-5480
E-Mail: amge.soc@earthlink.net
Members: 2,000 individuals
Staff: 6
Annual Budget: $500-1,000,000
Exec. Director: Mary Lynne Bird

Historical Note
Initiated in 1851 and incorporated on May 22, 1854 in New York as The American Geographical and Statistical Soc. Name changed to its present form in 1871. Over the years, sponsored research projects, symposia and lectures and published books, periodicals and maps, awards and travel programs. Membership: $38/year (individual);$45/year (institutional); $1,000/year (organization).

Publications:
Around the World Book Series. m.
Focus. q. adv.
Geographical Review. q. adv.
Ubique. 3/year.

Meetings/Conferences:
Annual Meetings: Not held.

American Geological Institute (1948)
4220 King St.
Alexandria, VA 22302-1502
Tel: (703)379-2480   Fax: (703)379-7563
E-Mail: agi@agiweb.org
Web Site: http://www.agiweb.org/
Members: 100,000 individuals, 32 societies
Staff: 45
Annual Budget: $2-5,000,000
Exec. Director: Marcus E. Milling
Director, Communications and Publications: Victor Van Beuren
Director, Government Affairs Program: David Applegate
Director, Human Resources/Career Dlvp: Marilyn J. Suiter
Director, Education: Michael J. Smith
Director, Information Systems: Sharon N. Tahirkheli

Historical Note
Founded in Washington in 1948 and operated as part of the Nat'l Academy of Sciences, 1948-1963. Incorporated as separate entity in 1963 in the District of Columbia. A federation of societies, the Institute is a member of the American Ass'n for the Advancement of Science, Commission on Professionals in Science and Technology, Board on Earth Sciences (NRC). Membership: $2/year/member (individual member societies); $2,500/year (organization/company).

Publications:
Bibliography and Index of Geology. m.
Directory of Geoscience Departments. a. adv.
Geotimes. m. adv.
Guide to Geoscience Departments. a. adv.

Meetings/Conferences:
Semi-Annual Meetings: Spring and Fall

American Geophysical Union (1919)
2000 Florida Ave., N.W.
Washington, DC 20009
Tel: (202)462-6900   Fax: (202)328-0566
Toll Free: (800)966 - 2481
E-Mail: service@.agu.org
Web Site: http://www.agu.org
Members: 36,000 individuals
Staff: 120
Annual Budget: $10-25,000,000
Exec. Director: Athelstan F. Spilhaus, Jr., Ph.D.
Director, Meetings: Brenda L. Weaver, CMP
Exhibits Coordinator: Karol B. Snyder

Historical Note
Incorporated in 1972 in Washington, DC. Members are individual research scientists and others, including some organizations, interested in supporting the objectives of AGU. AGU is dedicated to the study of Earth and its environment in space. Member society of the Renewable Natural Resources Foundation and the American Institute of Physics. Has an annual budget of over $20 million. Membership: $20/year (individual), $7/year (student).

Publications:
Earth in Space. 9/year.
Earth Interactions.

EOS, Transactions. w. adv.
Geomagnetism and Aeronomy Internat'l bi-m.
Geophysical Research Letters. semi-m.
Global Biogeochemical Cycles. q.
Journal of Geophysical Research. w.
Nonlinear Processes in Geophysics. q.
Paleoceanography. bi-m.
Radio Science. bi-m.
Reviews of Geophysics. q.
Tectonics. bi-m.
Water Resources Research. m.

Meetings/Conferences:
Semi-Annual Meetings: Spring and Fall
2000 – San Antonio, TX/Jan. 24-29
2000 – Tokyo, Japan/June 27-30

American Geriatrics Soc. *(1942)*
770 Lexington Ave., Suite 300
New York, NY   10021
Tel: (212)308-1414   *Fax:* (212)832-8646
Web Site: www.americangeriatrics.org
Members: 6,500 individuals
Staff: 18
Annual Budget: $2-5,000,000
Exec. V. President: Linda Hiddemen Barondess
Director, Communications: Bryan Conway
Director, Special Projects: Patricia Connelly
Director, Administration: Jill Chene
Director, Professional Services: Elaine Wong

Historical Note
Founded in Atlantic City in 1942. Incorporated in Rhode Island in 1952 and later in New York in 1963. Members are licensed physicians and allied health care professionals whose practice emphasis is in geriatric medicine and whose interests lie in geriatric medicine and gerontology. Membership: $195/year.

Publications:
AGS Membership Directory. a.
Geriatrics Review Syllabus. trien.
Journal of the American Geriatrics Society. m. adv.
Newsletter. bi-m. adv.
Proceedings of the Congress of Clinical Societies. a.

Meetings/Conferences:
Annual Meetings: Spring/2,000
1999 – Philadelphia, PA(Marriott)

American Glovebox Soc. *(1986)*
Historical Note
Address unknown in 1995.

American Goat Soc. *(1935)*
RD 1, Box 56
Esperance, NY   12066-9704
Tel: (518)875-6708
E-Mail: AMGOATSOC@aol.com
Members: 700 individuals
Staff: 1
Annual Budget: $10-25,000
Secretary: John Howland

Historical Note
Breeders and fanciers of pure bred dairy goats. Maintains herdbooks on eight breeds: French Alpine, Nubians, Saanens, Toggenburgs, LaMancha, Oberhasli, Pygmy and Nigerian Dwarf. Has an annual budget of approximately $20,000. Membership: $15/year.

Publications:
Buyers Guide. a. adv.
Roster of AGS Membership. a.
The Voice of AGS. q. adv.
Yearbook. a. adv.

Meetings/Conferences:
Annual Meetings: July
1999 – Texas
2000 – Springfield, MO

American Golf Sponsors Ass'n *(1970)*
Historical Note
Became the PGA Tour Tournaments Ass'n in 1997.

American Greenhouse Vegetable Growers Ass'n *(1982)*
Historical Note
Dissolved in 1997.

American Greyhound Track Operators Ass'n *(1946)*
Historical Note
Address unknown in 1996.

American Grooming Shop Ass'n *(1991)*
4575 Galley Road, Suite 400-A
Colorado Springs, CO   80915
Tel: (719)570-7788   *Fax:* (719)597-0006
E-Mail: agsa@abka.com
Members: 150 individuals
Staff: 3
Annual Budget: $50-100,000
Exec. Director: Kathryn Eddy

Historical Note
Services provided to members include a voluntary grooming shop accreditation program. Membership: $165/year.

Publications:
Pet Services Journal. bi-m. adv.
ShopTalk Newsletter. bi-m. adv.

Meetings/Conferences:

American Group Practice Ass'n *(1949)*
Historical Note
Merged with the Unified Medical Group Ass'n to form the American Medical Group Ass'n in 1996.

American Group Psychotherapy Ass'n *(1942)*
25 East 21st St., 6th Floor
New York, NY   10010
Tel: (212)477-2677   *Fax:* (212)979-6627
E-Mail: groupsinc@aol.com
Web Site: http://www.groupinc.org
Members: 4,500 individuals
Staff: 10
Annual Budget: $500-1,000,000
C.E.O.: Marsha S. Block, CAE
Director, Communications: Angela Moore James
Director, Membership: Jan I. Vadell

Historical Note
Includes psychiatrists, psychologists, social workers, psychiatric nurses and others in the mental health field interested in the theory, practice and research of group psychotherapy. Established June 16, 1942 in New York City at the Jewish Board of Guidance as the American Group Therapy Association. Membership: $85/year, minimum based on annual professional income (individual); $35/year (student).

Publications:
AGPA Membership Directory. a.
AGPA Newsletter q. adv. adv.
International Journal of Group Psychotherapy. q. adv.

Meetings/Conferences:
Annual Meetings: February/1,200
1999 – Houston, TX/Feb. 22-27

American Guernsey Ass'n *(1877)*
7614 Slate Ridge Blvd.
Reynoldsburg, OH   43068-0666
Tel: (614)864-2409   *Fax:* (614)864-5614
E-Mail: sethj@usguernsey.com
Web Site: http://www.usguernsey.com
Members: 1,427 individuals
Staff: 9
Annual Budget: $500-1,000,000
Exec. Secretary-Treasurer: Neil A. Jensen
Accountant: Cheri Foster
Membership Records: Ida Albert
Records Coordinator: Seth Johnson
Managing Editor: Becky Goodwin

Historical Note
Formerly (1987) American Guernsey Cattle Club. Members are breeders of Guernsey dairy cattle. Maintains herd registry. Member of the Nat'l Pedigree Livestock Council and the Purebred Dairy Cattle Ass'n. Membership: $150/lifetime or $15/year.

Publications:
Guernsey Breeder's Journal. 10/year. adv.
Guernsey Directory. every 18 mo.
Guernsey Sire Summary. semi-a.

Meetings/Conferences:
1999 – Columbus, OH/June 17-20
2000 – State College, PA
2001 – St. Paul, MN

American Guild of Hypnotherapists *(1975)*
2200 Veteran Blvd., #108
Kenner, LA   70062-4005
Tel: (504)468-2900   *Fax:* (504)468-3213
Members: 875 individuals
Staff: 3
Annual Budget: under $10,000
President: Reg Sheldrick, Ph.D.
Exec. V. President, Communications: Dr. Grayce Lee
Director, Education: Neil Feser

Historical Note
Membership: $50/year (initial registration); $35/year (renewal).

Publications:
Journal of Hypnotherapy. q.
Newsletter. irreg.

American Guild of Music *(1901)*
Historical Note
Address unknown in 1996.

American Guild of Musical Artists *(1936)*
1727 Broadway
New York, NY   10019-5284
Tel: (212)265-3687   *Fax:* (212)262-9088
Members: 5,700 individuals
Staff: 18
Annual Budget: $2-5,000,000
Nat'l Exec. Secretary: Louise J. Gilmore

Historical Note
Founded March 11, 1936 in New York City by Lawrence Tibbett and Jascha Heifetz. Became an autonomous branch union of Associated Actors and Artistes of America August 30, 1937 and merged at the same time with the Grand Opera Artists Ass'n. Absorbed the Grand Opera Choral Alliance in 1938. Now is the exclusive bargaining agent for concert musical artists, opera singers, ballet dancers, modern dancers, and stage personnel in those fields. Membership: $78/year (individual).

Publications:
AGMAzine. q.

American Guild of Organists *(1896)*
475 Riverside Drive Suite 1260
New York, NY   10115
Tel: (212)870-2310   *Fax:* (212)870-2163
E-Mail: info@agohq.org
Web Site: http://www.agohq.org
Members: 21,000 individuals
Staff: 10
Annual Budget: $1-2,000,000
Exec. Director: James Thomashower

Historical Note
Chartered by the Board of Regents of the University of the State of New York to conduct examinations of organists and choir-masters. Its purpose is to advance the cause of organ and choral music. Membership: $68/year.

Publications:
AGO News Newsletter. q.
The American Organist. m. adv.

Meetings/Conferences:
Biennial meetings: Even years/3,500
2000 – Seattle, WA

American Guild of Variety Artists *(1939)*
184 Fifth Ave., 6th Floor
New York, NY   10010
Tel: (212)675-1003   *Fax:* (212)633-0097
Members: 5,000 individuals
Staff: 15
Annual Budget: $250-500,000
President: Rod McKuen

Historical Note
An autonomous component of Associated Actors and Artistes of America (AFL-CIO).

American Gynecological and Obstetrical Soc. *(1981)*
Historical Note
AGOS declined to provide updated information for this edition.

American Hackney Horse Soc. *(1891)*
4059 Iron Works Pkwy., Suite 3
Lexington, KY   40511
Tel: (606)255-8694   *Fax:* (606)255-0177
Members: 850 individuals
Staff: 1
Annual Budget: $50-100,000
Exec. Secretary: Cheryl Shropshire

Historical Note
The registry for Hackney horses and ponies. Promotes the breeding, registering and showing of registered Hackney horses and Hackney ponies. Membership: $35/year (individual), $50/year (family), $15.00/year (junior).

Publications:
AHHS Newsletter. q.
AHHS Stud Book. bien.

Meetings/Conferences:

American Hair Loss Council
401 N. Michigan Ave.
Chicago, IL   60611-4267
Tel: (312)321-5128   *Fax:* (312)245-1080
Toll Free: (900)226 - 2452
E-Mail: info@ahlc.org
Web Site: http://www.ahlc.org
Exec. Director: Russell Bodnar

Historical Note
Membership: $220/year (individual); $550/year (organization/company).

Publications:
AHLC News. q.

Meetings/Conferences:

American Hampshire Sheep Ass'n *(1889)*
1557 173rd Ave.
Milo, IA   50166
Tel: (515)942-6402   *Fax:* (515)942-6402
Members: 900 individuals
Staff: 3
Annual Budget: $100-250,000
Exec. Secretary: Karey Claghorn

Historical Note
Breeders and fanciers of Hampshire sheep. Members of the Nat'l Pedigree Livestock Council.

Publications:
The Hampshire Heartbeat. q. adv.

Meetings/Conferences:
Annual Meetings: Fall

American Handwriting Analysis Foundation *(1967)*
P.O. Box 6201
San Jose, CA   95150-6201
Tel: (408)377-6775
Toll Free: (800)826 - 7774
Members: 300 individuals
Staff: 5
Annual Budget: $10-25,000
Contact: Dorothy W. Hodos

Historical Note
AHAF was established to educate the public and promote the growth of graphology. AHAF has established professional requirements for cetification. Membership: $50/year (individual), $60/year (foreign).

Publications:
AHAF Journal. bi-m. adv.

Meetings/Conferences:
Annual Meetings: summer
1999 – Denver, CO
2000 – Northern California
2001 – Northern New Jersey

American Hanoverian Soc. *(1971)*
4067 Iron Works Pkwy, Suite 1
Lexington, KY   40511-8462
Tel: (606)255-4141   *Fax:* (606)255-8467
Members: 1,500 individuals
Staff: 5
Annual Budget: $250-500,000
Exec. Director: Hugh Bellis-Jones

Historical Note
Members own and breed Hanoverian horses. Membership: $40-$60/year (individual).

Publications:
Stallion Directory and Yearbook. a. adv.
The Hanoverian. q. adv.
Yearbook. a. adv.

Meetings/Conferences:
1999 – Lexington, KY

American Hardboard Ass'n (1974)
1210 W. Northwest Hwy.
Palatine, IL 60067-1897
Tel: (847)934-8800   *Fax:* (847)934-8803
Members: 6 companies
Staff: 2
Annual Budget: $500-1,000,000
Exec. V. President: C. Curtis Peterson, CAE

Historical Note
A merger of the Acoustical and Insulating Materials Ass'n, founded in 1968, and the American Hardboard Ass'n founded in 1952. Became the American Board Products Ass'n in 1976. Changed to its present name in 1978. Represents most of the major U.S. producers of hardboard.

Publications:
Membership Directory.

Meetings/Conferences:
1999 – Palm Springs, CA(Hyatt Regency)/May 16-18/60

American Hardware Manufacturers Ass'n (1901)
801 N. Plaza Drive
Schaumburg, IL 60173-4977
Tel: (847)605-1025   *Fax:* (847)605-1093
Web Site: http://www.ahma.org
Members: 1,100 companies
Staff: 21
Annual Budget: $5-10,000,000
President and C.E.O.: William P. Farrell
Director,Events and Exposition: Chris Wehking
Manager, Industry Activities: Steven D. Johnson
General Counsel: John W. Stack

Historical Note
AHMA represents the manufacturing segment of America's hardlines industries, including producers and manufacturers' agents. Has an annual budget of approxiamtely $5.8 million.

Publications:
Eagle Newsletter. bi-m.
Employee Relations Report. m.
Executive Report. m.
Management Alert. m.

Meetings/Conferences:
Annual Meetings: National Hardware Show/Chicago, IL in August/70,000

American Hardwood Export Council (1989)
1111 19th St., N.W., Suite 800
Washington, DC 20036
Tel: (202)463-2720   *Fax:* (202)463-2787
Web Site: http://www.ahec.org
Members: 135 companies
Staff: 3
Annual Budget: $100-250,000
Exec. Director: Tracy Himmel Isham

Historical Note
Founded from the merger of Hardwood Export Trade Council and Nat'l Lumber Exporters Ass'n (1989). Exists to aid in the export of hardwoods and hardwood products overseas. A division of American Forest and Paper ass'n, which provides administrative support. Membership: $1,250-5,000/year (based on export value).

Meetings/Conferences:
Annual Meetings: In conjunction with the Nat'l Hardwood Lumber Ass'n

American Harp Soc. (1962)
6331 Quebec Dr.
Hollywood, CA 90068-2831
Tel: (323)463-0716   *Fax:* (323)464-2950
E-Mail: DRemsenAHS@aol.com
Web Site: http://www.harpsociety.org
Members: 3,300 individuals
Staff: 3
Annual Budget: $50-100,000
Exec. Secretary: Dorothy Remsen

Historical Note
Individuals interested in the lore and literature of the harp. Affiliated with the World Ass'n of Harpists (Paris France). Membership: $35/year.

Publications:
American Harp Journal. bien. adv.

Meetings/Conferences:
Annual Meetings: June-July
1999 – Los Angeles, CA(University of Southern California)
2000 – Cincinnati, OH

American Head and Neck Surgery Soc. (1959)
203 Lothrop St., Suite 519
Pittsburgh, PA 15213
Tel: (412)647-2227   *Fax:* (412)647-8944
E-Mail: rlwa@med.pitt.edu
Web Site: http://www.headandneckcancer.org
Members: 1,650 individuals
Staff: 1
Annual Budget: $50-100,000
Secretary: Jonas T. Johnson, M.D.

Historical Note
Members are fellows of the American College of Surgeons whose primary interest is head and neck surgery. Absorbed Soc. of Head and Neck Surgeons in 1998. Membership: $150/year.

Publications:
Proceedings. a. adv.

Meetings/Conferences:
Annual Meetings: Spring
1999 – Palm Desert, CA(Marriott)/April 26-28
2000 – San Francisco, CA(Marriott)/July 30-Aug. 3/2000

American Health and Beauty Aids Institute (1981)
401 N. Michigan Ave., 24th Floor
Chicago, IL 60611-4267
Tel: (312)644-6610   *Fax:* (312)527-6658
E-Mail: ahbai@sba.com
Web Site: http://www.proudlady.org
Members: 18 companies
Staff: 3
Annual Budget: $250-500,000
Exec. Director: Geri Duncan Jones

Historical Note
Members are makers of beauty products for ethnic minorities.

Publications:
Proud Lady Beauty Show Souvenir Journal. a. adv.
Salon Advantage News. q. adv.

Meetings/Conferences:
Semi-Annual Meetings: Spring and Fall

American Health Care Ass'n (1949)
1201 L St., N.W.
Washington, DC 20005
Tel: (202)842-4444   *Fax:* (202)842-3860
Web Site: http://www.ahca.org
Members: 11,000 state licensed facilities
Staff: 75
Annual Budget: $10-25,000,000
President: Paul R. Willging, Ph.D.
Director, Political Affairs: Rob Hartwell
V. President, Regulatory Affairs: David R. Seckman
V. President, Admin. and HR: Penny L. Prue
Director, Marketing: Deborah D. Ellsworth
Director, Finance: Paul Hensley
Senior Director, Affl. Relations/Member Services: Jennifer Souza

Historical Note
A federation of state associations of health care facilities formed by a merger of the American Ass'n of Nursing Homes and the Nat'l Ass'n of Registered Nursing Homes (founded in 1949). Formerly (1974) the American Nursing Home Ass'n. Absorbed (1984) Nat'l Council of Health Centers. Sponsors and supports the AHCA Political Action Committee. Membership: $7.55/bed/year.

Publications:
AHCA Notes. m.
Provider Magazine m. adv. adv.

Meetings/Conferences:
1999 – Honolulu, HI/Sept. 27-29

American Health Information Management Ass'n (1928)
919 N. Michigan Ave., Suite 1400
Chicago, IL 60611-1683
Tel: (312)787-2672   *Fax:* (312)787-9793
E-Mail: info@ahima.org
Web Site: http://www.ahima.org
Members: 38,000 individuals
Staff: 85
Annual Budget: $10-25,000,000
Exec. V. President: Linda L. Kloss, RRA
V.President, Mtkg/Creative Services: Steve McKenzie
V.President, Legislative/Public Policy: Kathleen A. Frawley
V. President, Education/Certification: Meride John
V.President, Professional Development: Patricia Thierry
V.President, Member/Volunteer Servs.: Susan Haack

Historical Note
Founded in Boston in 1928 as the Ass'n of Record Librarians of North America. Became the American Ass'n of Medical Record Librarians in 1935. Incorporated in Illinois in 1953, it became the American Medical Record Ass'n in 1969 and assumed its present name in 1992. Has an annual budget of approximately $8 million. Membership: $110/year (full member); $100/year (associate); $350/year (company); $15/year (student).

Publications:
AHIMA Advantage. bi-m. adv.
In Confidence. bi-m.
Journal of AHIMA. 10/year. adv.

Meetings/Conferences:
Annual Meetings: October/5,000
1999 – Anaheim, CA(Orange Cty. Conv. Center)/Oct. 2-7
2000 – Chicago, IL(McCormick Place)/Sept. 23-28
2001 – Miami, FL(Convention Center)/Oct. 12-18

American Health Lawyers Ass'n (1971)
1120 Connecticut Ave., N.W., Suite 950
Washington, DC 20036
Tel: (202)833-1100   *Fax:* (202)833-1105
Web Site: http://www.healthlawyers.org
Members: 10,000 individuals
Staff: 28
Annual Budget: $5-10,000,000
Exec. V. President and C.E.O.: Marilou M. King
Director, Membership and Marketing: Kerry B. Hoggard, CAE

Historical Note
Members are private, corporate, government and institutional lawyers involved with or practicing law in the health care field. Associate Membership is available to non-lawyers. Conducts non-partisan educational programs and publishes books and periodicals of interest to health attorneys and providers of health care. Membership: $215/year (full member), $55/year (student).

Publications:
Health Law Digest. m.
Health Lawyers News. m.

Meetings/Conferences:

American Health Planning Ass'n (1972)
7245 Arlington Blvd., Suite 300
Falls Church, VA 22042
Tel: (703)573-3103   *Fax:* (703)573-1276
Web Site: http://www.aphanet.org
Members: 150 organizations and individuals
Annual Budget: $50-100,000
Director: Dean Montgomery

Historical Note
State, regional and national health planning and other organizations. Formerly the Association of Areawide Health Planning Agencies and (1978) the American Association for Comprehensive Health Planning. Provides national voice for health care consumers, purchasers, providers and business and labor representatives who are interested in health planning to improve health care system. Has no paid staff. Membership: $50/year (individual); $500-1,000/year (organization); $250/year (affiliate).

Publications:
Directory. a.
Health Planning Bibliography.
Today in Health Planning. q.

Meetings/Conferences:
Annual Meetings: Annual conference, and annual meeting in conjunction with APHA
1999 – November

American Health Quality Ass'n (1973)
1140 Connecticut Ave., N.W., Suite 1050
Washington, DC 20036
Tel: (202)331-5790   *Fax:* (202)331-9334
E-Mail: ahqa@ahqa.org
Web Site: http://www.ahqa.org
Members: 1,200 individuals, 48 institutions
Staff: 10
Annual Budget: $1-2,000,000
Exec. V. President and C.E.O.: Josef J. Reum
Dir., Communications/External Rels.: Laura Kaloi
Manager of Meetings: Brian York
Director, Quality Improvement Programs: Regine Buchanan
Director, Membership Support Services: Lisa Weiss
Quality Management Associate: Elizabeth Schulz

Historical Note
Established as American Ass'n of Professional Standards Review Organizations; became American Medical Peer Review Ass'n in 1983, and assumed its present name in 1996. AHQA promotes health care quality through community-based, independent quality evaluation and improvement programs.

Publications:
Quality Advocate Newsletter. bi-m.

Meetings/Conferences:
1999 – Savannah, GA(Hyatt Regency)/Feb. 4-5
1999 – Chicago, IL(Hyatt Regency)/Sept. 9-11
2000 – Kissimmee, FL(Hyatt)/Feb. 11-12

American Healthcare Radiology Administrators (1973)
P.O. Box 334
111 Boston Post Road, Suite 215
Sudbury, MA 01776
Tel: (978)443-6911   *Fax:* (978)443-8046
E-Mail: info@ahraonline.com
Web Site: http://www.ahraonline.org
Members: 3,900 individuals
Staff: 6
Annual Budget: $2-5,000,000
Exec. Director: Mary S. Reitter
Director, Education Member Services: Laurie Graves

Historical Note
Formerly (1986) American Hospital Radiology Administrators. Membership: $120/year.

Publications:
Directory. a.
Link. m. adv.
Radiology Management. q. adv.

Meetings/Conferences:
Annual Meetings: August/1,300
1999 – Orlando, FL(Coronado Springs Resort)/July 25-29/2000

American Heart Ass'n (1924)
7272 Greenville Ave.
Dallas, TX 75231
Tel: (214)373-6300   *Fax:* (214)706-2139
Toll Free: (800)242 - 8721
Web Site: http://www.amhrt.org
Members: 29,506 individuals
Annual Budget: Over $100,000,000
Exec. V. President: M. Cass Wheeler
Senior V. President, Office of Communications & Public Advocacy: Brigid McHugh Sanner
Director, Strategic Planning: Vickie Peters
Director, Meetings & Exhibitions: James Youngblood
V. President, Comm. Programs and Development: John Paul
V. President, Field Operations and Development: Gordon McCullough
Senior V. President, Corporate Operations: Walter Bristol
Chief Staff Executive Officer: M. Cass Wheeler
V. President, Corporate Secretary and Counsel: David William Livingston
V. President, Information Technology: Steve Denny
Senior V. President, Office of Science and Medicine: Rod Starke,, M.D.
V. President, Office of Cardiovascular & Stroke Information: Larry Joyce
V. President, Production and Distribution: Robert Makawski

Historical Note
Incorporated in New York in 1924. Reorganized in 1948 as a national voluntary health agency. Maintains 14 scientific councils

which, through representatives to the AHA Research Committee, help determine the allocation of funds in research support, the nature and scope of professional education activities, and at which point knowledge is sufficiently advanced to be translated and applied to community-based education programs. Has an annual budget of approximately $318 million.

Publications:
Arteriosclerosis, Thrombosis and Vascular Biology. m. adv.
Cardiovascular Nursing. bi-m.
Circulation. bi-m. adv.
Circulation Research. m. adv.
Currents in Emergency Cardiac Care. q.
Hypertension. m. adv.
Stroke. m. adv.

Meetings/Conferences:
Scientific Session: Fall/25,000
1999 – Atlanta, GA/Nov. 7-10
2000 – New Orleans, LA/Nov. 12-15
2001 – Anaheim, CA/Nov. 11-14

American Heartworm Soc. (1974)
P.O. Box 667
Batavia, IL 60510-0667
Tel: (630)844-9676
Members: 1,200 individuals
Administrator: Eve C. Larocca

Historical Note
Members are practitioners and research scientists dedicated to research and dissemination of knowledge about canine heartworm disease. Membership: $25/year (member), $30/year (subscriber).

Publications:
American Heartworm Society Bulletin. q.
Proceedings of Heartworm Symposium. trien.

Meetings/Conferences:

American Helicopter Soc. (1943)
217 N. Washington St.
Alexandria, VA 22314-2538
Tel: (703)684-6777   *Fax:* (703)739-9279
E-Mail: ahs703@aol.com
Web Site: http://www.vtol.org
Members: 6,000 individuals, 120 companies
Staff: 5
Annual Budget: $1-2,000,000
Exec. Director: Morris E. Flater
Director, Meeting Planning: Stacey Clark
Deputy Director: Kim Smith

Historical Note
Founded and incorporated in 1943 in Connecticut.

Publications:
AHS Internat'l Directory. a. adv.
Annual Forum Proceedings. a.
Journal of the American Helicopter Society. q.
Vertiflite. 5 times/year. adv.

Meetings/Conferences:
Annual Meetings: May
1999 – Montreal, Quebec, Canada(Palais des
          Congres)/May 24-26/4500
2000 – Virginia Beach, VA(Pavilion)/May 1-3/4500
2001 – Washington, DC(Marriott Wardman Park)/May 13-15

American Herbal Products Ass'n (1981)
8484 Georgia Ave., Suite 370
Silver Spring, MD 20910 5601
Tel: (301)588-1171   *Fax:* (301)951-3205
Members: 220 companies
Staff: 3
Annual Budget: $250-500,000
Exec. Director: Jeffrey Michael Morrison

Historical Note
A trade association representing manufacturers, distributors, raw material suppliers and service associates of herbal products. Street address is 4733 Bethesda Ave., Suite 345, Bethesda MD 20814. Membership: $250-4,000/year (organization).

Publications:
Directory. a. adv.
Newsletter. bi-m.

Meetings/Conferences:

American Herbalists Guild (1989)
P.O. Box 70
Roosevelt, UT 84006-0070
Tel: (435)722-8434   *Fax:* (435)722-8452
E-Mail: ahgoffice@earthlink.net
Web Site: http://www.healthy.net/herbalists
Members: 500 individuals
Annual Budget: $10-25,000
President and Exec. Director: Steven Horne

Historical Note
AHG is a professional, peer-review organization for herbalists specializing in the medicinal use of plants. Membership: $85/year (professional); $50/year (associate); $35/year (student).

Publications:
Directory of Herb Education. a.
Herbalist Newsletter. q.
Recommended Reading List. a.

Meetings/Conferences:
Annual Meetings: Fall
1999 – Pocono, PA(Pocono Manor Inn)/Aug. 5-8

American Hereford Ass'n (1881)
P.O. Box 014059
Kansas City, MO 64101
Tel: (816)842-3757   *Fax:* (816)842-6931
E-Mail: records@hereford.org
Web Site: http://www.hereford.org
Members: 11,000 individuals
Staff: 70

Annual Budget: $5-10,000,000
Exec. V. President: Craig Huffhines

Historical Note
Breeders of Hereford beef cattle. Absorbed the American Polled Hereford Ass'n in 1995. Member of the Nat'l Pedigree Livestock Council. Annual Budget is approximately $6 million. Membership: $200/life.

Publications:
Hereford World. m. adv.

Meetings/Conferences:
Annual Meetings: November in Kansas City, MO

American Heren Ass'n (1980)
P.O. Drawer 1250
Lewisburg, WV 24901
Tel: (304)645-3773   *Fax:* (304)645-3755
Members: 15 individuals, 10 companies
Staff: 2
Annual Budget: under $10,000
Secretary-Treasurer: George L. Lemon

Historical Note
Members are dedicated to the preservation of herens in North America. Membership: $100/year.

Meetings/Conferences:
Annual Meetings: Summer.
2000 – Bern, Switzerland(Buhlor Matlen)/Sept. 9-21

American Hernia Soc. (1997)
P.O. Box 536544
Orlando, FL 32853-6544
Tel: (407)898-1695   *Fax:* (407)894-2312
E-Mail: williamsargmt@aol.com
Members: 340 individuals
Staff: 2
Annual Budget: $100-250,000
Exec. Director: Shelburn Wilkes

Historical Note
Membership: $100/year.

Publications:
Hernia. q. adv.

Meetings/Conferences:
1999 – Las Vegas, NV(Ceasars Palace)/Feb. 22-24/350
2000 – Toronto, ON, Canada(Royal York)
2001 – New Orleans, LA(Hilton Riverside)

American Highland Cattle Ass'n (1948)
200 Livestock Exchange Bldg.
4701 Marion St.
Denver, CO 80216
Tel: (303)292-9102   *Fax:* (303)292-9171
E-Mail: ahca@envision.net
Web Site: http://home.eznet.net/~highland/ahca.htm
Members: 900 individuals
Staff: 2
Annual Budget: $100-250,000
Operations Manager: Ginnah Moses

Historical Note
Formerly (1994) American Scotch Highland Breeder's Ass'n. Maintains a breed registry and promotes the Highland breed through research, education, and national events, including the Annual Show and Sale.

Publications:
The Bagpipe. q.

Meetings/Conferences:
1999 – Warsaw, IN

American Highway Users Alliance (1932)
1776 Massachusetts Ave., N.W., Suite 500
Washington, DC 20036-1993
Tel: (202)857-1200   *Fax:* (202)857-1220
E-Mail: gohighway@aol.com
Web Site: http://www.gohighway.com
Members: 150 companies and organizations
Staff: 12
Annual Budget: $2-5,000,000
President and C.E.O.: William D. Fay
V. President, Public Liaison/Development: David N. Lakin
V. President, Policy and Government Affairs: Taylor R. Bowlden
Director, Finance and Administration: Gzye Bennett
Manager, Member Relations/Marketing: Cheryl J. Hollins

Historical Note
Founded as Highway Users Federation for Safety and Mobility; assumed its current name in 1995. A consolidation of the Automotive Safety Foundation (1937), Auto Industries Highway Safety Committee (1946) and Nat'l Highway Users Conference (1932). Absorbed the Auto Dealers Traffic Safety Council in 1970. Members are users of highways who benefit from the movement of goods and people. Also includes manufacturers of vehicles, tires, and related accessories. membership: $250-$500,000/year (company/organization).

Publications:
Action Update. bi-w.
America's Highways. q.

Meetings/Conferences:

American Hispanic Owned Radio Ass'n (1991)
Historical Note
Ass'n inactive in 1997.

American Historical Ass'n (1884)
400 A St., S.E.
Washington, DC 20003
Tel: (202)544-2422   *Fax:* (202)544-8307
E-Mail: aha@theaha.org
Web Site: http://chnm.gmu.edu/aha
Members: 16,231 individuals
Staff: 27
Annual Budget: $1-2,000,000

Exec. Director: Sandria B. Freitag
Manager, Info. Systems/Communications: Robert Townsend
Asst. Director, Admin./Convention Director: Sharon K. Tune
Coordinator, Membership: Pamela Scott-Pinkney

Historical Note
An off-shoot of the American Social Science Ass'n which came into being at the annual meeting of the Ass'n in Saratoga, NY in 1884. Its founders were a group of historians who felt that the ASSA had over-specialized in such matters as prison reform, charity, etc. Incorporated by Congress in 1889 to promote historical studies, collect and preserve historical manuscripts and disseminate the fruits of historical research. A member of the American Council of Learned Societies. Membership: $30-120/year (individual); varies with income.

Publications:
American Historical Review. 5/year. adv.
Annual Report. a.
Directory of Affiliated Societies.
Directory of History Departments and Organizations. a.
Grants and Fellowships of Interest to Historians. a.
Perspectives (Newsletter). 9/year. adv.

Meetings/Conferences:
1999 – Washington, DC(Sheraton and Shoreham)
2000 – Chicago, IL(Sheraton and Marriott)
2001 – Boston, MA
2002 – San Francisco, CA

American Hockey Coaches Ass'n (1947)
7 Concord St.
Gloucester, MA 01930
Tel: (978)283-2662   *Fax:* (978)281-8021
Members: 700 individuals
Staff: 1
Annual Budget: $100-250,000
Exec. Director: Joe Bertanga

Historical Note
Resolves local and intersectional differences on rules, officiating and recruiting. Membership: $10-225/year (individual).

Publications:
American Hockey Coaches Directory. a.
Newsletter. 5/year.

Meetings/Conferences:
Annual Meetings: last week of April

American Hockey League (1936)
425 Union St. #D3
West Springfield, MA 01089-4108
Tel: (413)781-2030   *Fax:* (413)733-4767
Web Site: http://www.canoe.ca/ahl
Members: 19 clubs
Staff: 7
Annual Budget: $500-1,000,000
President & Treasurer: David A. Andrews

Historical Note
A professional ice hockey league functioning as a development league for the National Hockey League. Each member club is affiliated, or has a working agreement, with an NHL team.

Publications:
AHL Master Schedule. a. adv.
AHL Official Rule Book. a. adv.
Annual Media Guide & Play Off Guide. a. adv.

Meetings/Conferences:
Annual Meetings: end of June or July
1999 – Hilton Head, SC(Palmetto Dunes)

American Holistic Medical Ass'n (1978)
6728 Old McLean Village Drive
McLean, VA 22101-3906
Tel: (703)556-9728   *Fax:* (703)556-8729
E-Mail: ahma@degnon.org
Web Site: http://www.holisticmedicine.org
Members: 600 individuals
Staff: 2
Annual Budget: $100-250,000
Exec. Director: Dan Denton

Historical Note
Holistic medicine is a system of health care which emphasizes the necessity of looking at the whole person, when diagnosing and treating an illness, with emphasis on patient responsibility for self-health. Members are licensed physicians and medical and osteopathic students. Membership: $30-$275/year.

Publications:
Directory of Members. a.
Elective Rotations and Preceptorships in Holistic Medicine.
Holistic Medicine. bi-m. adv.
Nat'l Referral Directory.

Meetings/Conferences:
1999 – Washington, DC(Renissance Hotel)/May 5-9

American Holistic Nurses' Ass'n (1981)
P.O. Box 2130
Flagstaff, AZ 86003-2130
Tel: (520)526-2196   *Fax:* (520)526-2752
Toll Free: (800)278 - 2462
E-Mail: ahna-flag@flaglink.com
Web Site: http://www.ahna.org
Members: 3,500 individuals
Staff: 4
Annual Budget: $250-500,000
President: Susan Collins
Communications Coordinator: Michael French
Membership Coordinator: Doris Roger

Historical Note
AHNA is a non-profit, educational association for nurses and allied health care professionals embracing the concept of holistic health, a harmony between mind, body and spirit. Provides a support system, communications network, recognition and educational opportunities. Membership: $100/year.

Publications:
Beginnings (newsletter). bi.
Journal of Holistic Nursing. q.
Meetings/Conferences:
Annual Meetings: Summer
1999 – Scottsdale, AZ(Marriott Spa and Resort)/June 16-20

American Holistic Veterinary Medical Ass'n *(1982)*
2214 Old Emmorton Road
Bel Air, MD   21015
Tel: (410)569-0795
Fax: (410)569-2346
E-Mail: AHVMA@Compuserve.com
Members: 900 individuals
Staff: 2
Annual Budget: $100-250,000
Exec. Director: Carvel G. Tiekert, D.V.M.
Historical Note
Formerly (1985) the American Veterinary Holistic Medical Ass'n. AHVMA members have an interest in unconventional systems of veterinary medicine as a complement to conventional approaches.
Publications:
Journal of the AHVMA. q. adv.
Meetings/Conferences:
1999 – New Orleans(Radisson)/Sept. 12-15/350
2000 – Lihui, HI(Marriott)/Oct. 9-13

American Home Brewers Ass'n
736 Pearl St.
Boulder, CO   80302-5006
Tel: (303)447-0816
Fax: (303)447-2825
E-Mail: aha@aob
Web Site: http://beertown.org
President: Karen Barela

American Home Sewing and Craft Ass'n
Historical Note
Became (1997) Home Sewing Ass'n.

American Honey Producers Ass'n *(1969)*
Historical Note
Address unknown in 1997.

American Horse Council *(1969)*
1700 K St., N.W., Suite 300
Washington, DC   20006-3805
Tel: (202)296-4031
Fax: (202)296-1970
E-Mail: ANC@horsecouncil.org
Web Site: http://www.horsecouncil.org
Members: 2,000 individuals, 200 organizations
Staff: 5
Annual Budget: $500-1,000,000
President: James J. Hickey, Jr.
Director of Government Affairs: Steve Ralls
Director of Adminstration: Katherine A. Luedeke
Historical Note
The trade association of the equine industry. Members are organizations and individuals who need to be kept informed of tax and regulatory developments affecting such matters as breeding, racing, showing, pleasure riding, funding of livestock research, import-export restrictions and similar matters affecting those who live by horses. Membership: $100/year (individual), $1,000/year (organization).
Publications:
AHC Newsletter. bi-m.
Horse Industry Directory. a.
Tax Bulletin. bi-m.
Meetings/Conferences:
Annual Meetings: September

American Horse Publications Ass'n *(1970)*
49 Spinnaker Circle
South Daytona, FL   32119
Tel: (904)760-7743
Fax: (904)760-7728
Members: 200 publications
Staff: 1
Annual Budget: $50-100,000
Exec. Director: Christine W. Brune
Historical Note
An association of horse-oriented publications in the U.S. and Canada. Membership: $100-$200/year.
Publications:
AHP For the Record. q.
Meetings/Conferences:
Annual Meetings: Summer
1999 – Nashville, TN/May 20-23/100

American Horse Shows Ass'n *(1917)*
220 E. 42nd St.
New York, NY   10017-5876
Tel: (212)972-2472
Fax: (212)983-7286
Web Site: http://www.ahsa.org
Members: 71,000 individuals, 143 organizations
Staff: 65
Annual Budget: $5-10,000,000
Exec. Director: Katharine Jackson
Historical Note
Dedicated to equestrianism at all levels of proficiency. Has an annual budget of approximately $6 million. Membership: $35/year (junior); $40-85/year (senior); $125-$800/year (organization/competition).
Publications:
Horse Show Magazine. 11/year. adv.
Rule Book. bien.
Meetings/Conferences:

American Horticultural Marketing Council *(1982)*
Historical Note
Organization defunct in 1996.

American Horticultural Soc. *(1922)*
7931 East Boulevard Drive
Alexandria, VA   22308
Tel: (703)768-5700
Fax: (703)768-8700
Toll Free: (800)777 - 7931
E-Mail: info@ahs.org
Web Site: http://www.ahs.org
Members: 23,000 individuals
Staff: 20
Annual Budget: $2-5,000,000
President and C.E.O.: Linda D. Hallman
Manager, Communications: Tonda Phalen
Director, Marketing and Public Programs: Mary Ann Patterson
Director, Membership/Bus. Development: Darlene Oliver
Historical Note
Merged in 1926 with the Nat'l Horticultural Soc. Incorporated in 1932 in the District of Columbia and consolidated in 1959 with the American Horticultural Council. AHS educates and inspires people of all ages to become successful and environmentally responsible gardeners by advancing the art and science of horticulture. Membership includes the widest range of horticultural concerns, with individuals, scientific organizations, institutions and commercial enterprises spanning interests from technical research to advanced amateur gardening. Membership: $25/year (individual), $100-5,000/year (organization).
Publications:
The American Gardener. bi-m. adv.
Meetings/Conferences:
1999 – Boston, MA(Fairmont Copley Plaza)/June 9-13/350
2000 – Charleston, SC

American Horticultural Therapy Ass'n *(1973)*
909 York St.
Denver, CO   80206-3751
Toll Free: (800)634 - 1603
E-Mail: ahta@ahta.org
Web Site: http://www.ahta.org
Members: 900 individuals
Staff: 1
Annual Budget: $50-100,000
Historical Note
Formerly (1987) the Nat'l Council for Therapy and Rehabilitation Through Horticulture. Members are professional therapists, rehabilitation specialists and others using horticulture as a medium in rehabilitation. Membership: $40/year
Publications:
AHTA Membership Directory. a. adv.
Journal of Therapeutic Horticulture. a.
People Plant Connection. 6/year. adv.
Meetings/Conferences:

American Hospital Ass'n *(1898)*
1 North Franklin
Chicago, IL   60606
Tel: (312)422-3000
Fax: (312)422-4601
Web Site: http://www.aaha.org
Members: 50,000 individuals, 6,000 institutions
Staff: 800
Annual Budget: $50-100,000,000
President: Richard J. Davidson
Director, Continuing Education/Meetings: Bob Donovan
Sr. V. President and General Counsel: Fredric Entin
V. President, Spec. Membership Services: Deborah L. Frett
Director, Membership Dev.: Janet Brookman
Historical Note
Formerly (1906) Ass'n of Hospital Superintendents of the United States and Canada. Has an annual budget of approximately $81 million. Sponsors the AHA Political Action Committee, established in 1978.
Publications:
AHA Guide to the Health Care Field. a.
AHA News. w. adv.
Health Facilities Management. m.
Hospital Literature Index. q.
Hospital Statistics. a.
Hospitals & Health Networks. semi-m. adv.
Medical Staff Leader. m.
The Hospital Medical Staff. m.
Trustee. m. adv.
Meetings/Conferences:
Annual Meetings: Late Summer
1999 – Washington, DC(Hilton)/Jan. 29-Feb. 2

American Hotel and Motel Ass'n *(1910)*
1201 New York Ave., N.W., Suite 600
Washington, DC   20005-3931
Tel: (202)289-3100
Fax: (202)289-3199
E-Mail: infoctr@ahma.com
Web Site: http://www.ahma.com
Members: 12,000 properties/1.4 million rooms
Staff: 60
Annual Budget: $10-25,000,000
President: William P. Fisher
V.P., Communications/Mktg.: Maura Nelson
Director of Communications: Kathryn Potter
V. President, Industry Relations: Thierry G. Roch
Senior V. President, Government Affairs: John P. Connors
Director, Government Affairs: John Gay
Director, Governmental Affairs: Kevin Maher
Director, Conventions and Meetings: Stacey Chattman, CMP
President, American Hotel Foundation: Doug Viehland
Senior V.P./C.F.O.: Michael Gehrisch
Director, Member Relations: Sally Brasse
Publisher, Lodging Magazine: Lawrence Wilhelm
Director of Information Services: Daille G. Pettit
Director, Information Technology: Richard J. Jackson
Historical Note
A federation of state hotel & motel associations. Formerly (1917) American Hotel Protective Ass'n and (1962) American Hotel Ass'n.

Supports the American Hotel-Motel Political Action Committee. Has an annual budget of $18.4 million. Member of the Trade Show Bureau.
Publications:
AH&MA's Register. 10/year.
Construction & Modernization Report. m.
Directory of Hotel & Motel Companies. a. adv.
Lodging Magazine. 11/year. adv.
Meetings/Conferences:
Annual Meetings: Spring
1999 – Nashville, TN(Opryland)/Apr. 14-15

American Humor Studies Ass'n *(1974)*
English Department, Univ. of New Haven
300 Orange Avenue
West Haven, CT   06516
Tel: (203)932-7371
Members: 400 individuals
Annual Budget: under $10,000
Executive Director: David Sloane
Historical Note
Investigates American humor and popular culture topics to expand scholarship and understanding of American humor. An "allied" organization of the Modern Language Ass'n of America and the American Literature Ass'n. AHSA has no paid staff or permanent headquarters. Membership: $20/year
Publications:
Studies in American Humor. a. adv.
To Wit (newsletter). semi-a. adv.
Meetings/Conferences:
Semi-Annual: May with the A.L.A. and December with the M.L.A.

American Hungarian Educators Ass'n *(1974)*
P.O. Box 30288
Bethesda, MD   20824-0288
Tel: (301)384-4657
Members: 300 individuals
Staff: 1
Annual Budget: under $10,000
Exec. Director: Eniko Molnar Basa
Historical Note
Chartered in the State of Maryland in 1976. Educators concerned with the teaching and dissemination of Hungarian history, language, literature, art and music. Attempts to further Hungarian studies in American and Canadian universities. Officers are elected biennially. Membership: $15/year.
Publications:
American Hungarian Educator. 3/year.
Meetings/Conferences:
Annual Meetings: Spring

American Hydrogen Ass'n *(1989)*
1739 W. 7th Ave.
Mesa, AZ   85202-1906
Tel: (602)827-7915
Fax: (602)967-6601
E-Mail: aha@getnet.com
Web Site: http://www.clean-air.org
Members: 4,500 individuals
Staff: 2
Annual Budget: $50-100,000
President: Roy E. McAlister
Editor: Sherwin Berger
Historical Note
AHA is a non-profit association of individuals and institutions, technical and non-technical, with an interest in the promotion of renewable energy systems. Membership: $25-100/year(student-sustaining); $2,500/year (corporate).
Publications:
Hydrogen Today. bi-m. adv.
Meetings/Conferences:

American Hypnosis Ass'n *(1972)*
18607 Ventura Blvd., Suite 310
Tarzana, CA   91356
Tel: (818)344-4464
Fax: (818)344-2262
Toll Free: (800)990 - 0426
Members: 1,500 individuals
Staff: 6
Annual Budget: $25-50,000
President: George Kappas
Historical Note
AHA members are hypnotherapy professionals and other professionals with an interest in hypnosis and related fields. Membership: $25 initiation fee and $24/year (individual).
Publications:
AHA Newsletter. q.

American Imaging Ass'n *(1988)*
Historical Note
Address unknown in 1996.

American Immigration Lawyers Ass'n *(1946)*
1400 I St., N.W., Suite 1200
Washington, DC   20005
Tel: (202)371-9377
Fax: (202)371-9449
Web Site: http://www.aila.org
Members: 5,200 individuals
Staff: 20
Annual Budget: $2-5,000,000
Exec. Director: Jeanne A. Butterfield
Director, Advocacy: Judith Golub
Conference/Meetings Manager: Stacey Green
Sr. Director, Education: Amy R. Novick
Sr. Dir., Operations: Susan D. Quarles
General Counsel: H. Ronald Klasko
Dir., Membership/Marketing: Carol Ann Faber

Historical Note
Formerly (1981) the Ass'n of Immigration and Nationality Lawyers. Attorneys practicing in the field of immigration and nationality law. Membership: $225/year(less than three years of practice); $300/year(more than three years of practice).

Publications:
AILA Business Immigration News. q.
AILA Monthly Mailing. m. adv.
Directory. a. adv.
Immigration Journal. q. adv.

Meetings/Conferences:
Annual Meetings: June/2,000
1999 – Seattle, WA(Sheraton)/June 10-13
2000 – Chicago, IL
2001 – Boston, MA

American Import Shippers Ass'n *(1987)*
662 Main St.
New Rochelle, NY 10801
Tel: (914)633-3770 *Fax:* (914)633-4041
Members: 250 companies
Staff: 4
Exec. Director: Hubert Wiesenmaier

Historical Note
Members are small to medium-sized U.S. firms importing textiles and apparel. Membership: $75/year.

Publications:
ATTN - Apparel Trade & Transportation News. m.

Meetings/Conferences:

American Importers and Exporters Meat Products Group *(1955)*
One Atlanta Plaza
Elizabeth, NJ 07206
Tel: (908)351-8000 *Fax:* (908)351-0761
Members: 30 companies
Staff: 3
President: George Gellert

Historical Note
Formerly (1983) Meat Products Group of the American Ass'n of Exporters and Importers and (1992) American Importers Meat Products Group. Members are companies importing pork and pork products into the United States.

American In-vitro Allergy/Immunology Soc. *(1988)*
P.O. Box 341461
Bethesda, MD 20827-1461
Tel: (301)263-0703 *Fax:* (301)263-0770
E-Mail: aias@erols.com
Web Site: http://www.invitroallergy.com
Members: 200 individuals
Staff: 1
Annual Budget: $100-250,000
Exec. Director: Barbara Buchman

Historical Note
AIAIS is a professional society for physicians, scientists and allied health professionals who either utilize in-vitro techology in diagnosis and treatment of allergic/immunologic disorders or study its role in such areas. Membership: $150/year (MD, DO, PhD); $50/year (allied health professional).

Publications:
Newsletter. 2-3/yr.

Meetings/Conferences:
Annual Meetings: Summer/100
1999 – La Jolla, CA(Sea Lodge)/May 18-20

American Incense Manufacturers Ass'n *(1973)*
P.O. Box 4429
Yuma, AZ 85366
Tel: (520)343-1470 *Fax:* (520)343-1225
Toll Free: (800)266 - 6315
E-Mail: congax@primenet.com
Members: 4 companies
Annual Budget: under $10,000
President: Fred B. Block

Historical Note
AIMA members are companies manufacturing incense in the United States. Industry suppliers may join as associated members. Membership: $100/year.

Meetings/Conferences:
Annual Meetings: July

American Independent Refiners Ass'n *(1983)*
3315 Cummings Lane
Chevy Chase, MD 20815
Tel: (301)913-9012 *Fax:* (301)913-9041
Members: 12 companies
Staff: 2
Annual Budget: $100-250,000
Director: Raymond F. Bragg

Historical Note
Members are independent refiners. The product of a merger April 1, 1983 of the American Petroleum Refiners Ass'n (formed in 1961), the Independent Refiners Ass'n of America (formed in 1949) and the Independent Refiners Ass'n of California (formed in 1936).

Meetings/Conferences:
Annual Meetings: August

American Indian Council of Architects and Engineers *(1976)*
3820 N. Third St.
Phoenix, AZ 85012-2022
Tel: (602)222-8815 *Fax:* (602)222-9276
Members: 30 firms
Annual Budget: under $10,000
President: Stuart Fricke

Historical Note
Established in New Mexico, AICAE members are American Indian-owned architecture, engineering, and design firms and related professional businesses. Has no paid officers or full-time staff.

Publications:
AICAE Connections. semi-a. adv.
Membership Directory. a.

Meetings/Conferences:
1999 – Paris, France

American Indian Health Care Ass'n *(1975)*

Historical Note
Address unknown in 1996.

American Indian Science and Engineering Soc.
5661 Airport Blvd.
Boulder, CO 80301-1014
Tel: (303)939-0023 *Fax:* (303)939-8150
E-Mail: aiseshq@spot.colorado.edu
Members: 3,000 individuals
Staff: 20
Annual Budget: $2-5,000,000
Exec. Director: Norbert S. Hill, Jr.

Historical Note
Membership: $10/year (student); $40/year (professional).

Publications:
American Indian College Guide. a. adv.
College Newsletter. q. adv.
Education Newsletter. q. adv.

Meetings/Conferences:
Annual Meetings: Annual/Nov. Detroit, MI/2,000

American Indonesian Chamber of Commerce *(1949)*
711 3rd Ave., 17th Floor
New York, NY 10017
Tel: (212)687-4505 *Fax:* (212)867-9882
E-Mail: aicc@bigplanet.com
Web Site: http://www.aicc.globalnetlink.com
Members: 50 individuals, 175 companies
Staff: 2
Annual Budget: $100-250,000
Exec. Director: Wayne Forrest

Historical Note
The Chamber works to increase business and understanding between the United States and Indonesia and serves organizations and individuals involved commercially with Indonesia. Membership: $1000/year (corporate); $125/year (individual).

Publications:
Outlook Indonesia. q.

American Industrial Health Council *(1977)*
2001 Pennsylvania Ave., N.W., Suite 760
Washington, DC 20006-1850
Tel: (202)833-2131 *Fax:* (202)833-2201
Members: 46 companies
Staff: 10
Annual Budget: $1-2,000,000
Exec. Director: Gaylen M. Camera, CAE
V. President: Nancy G. Doerrer
Director, Administration and Membership: Anne P. Santalla

Historical Note
Formed to address the scientific issues related to proposed standards of federal agencies for identifying and regulating products suspected of being chronic health or environmental hazards. Members include producers and users of chemicals, manufacturers of textiles, pharmaceuticals, petroleum, metal products, business system machines, consumer products, motor vehicles, and individuals in the aerospace industry.

Publications:
AIHC Annual Meeting. a.
AIHC Newsletter. m.

Meetings/Conferences:
Annual Meetings: November/December, in Washington, DC

American Industrial Hygiene Ass'n *(1939)*
2700 Prosperity Ave., Suite 250
Fairfax, VA 22031
Tel: (703)849-8888 *Fax:* (703)207-3561
E-Mail: infonet@aiha.org
Web Site: http://www.aiha.org
Members: 13,000 individuals, 400 companies and
  organizations
Staff: 58
Annual Budget: $10-25,000,000
Exec. Director: O. Gordon Banks, CAE
Director, Communications: Anne Dees
Director, Government Affairs: Aaron Trippler
Director, Education and Meetings: Carol B. Tobin
Director, Administration: Barbara L. Morrison, CAE
Director, Marketing and Membership: Dr. Manuel Gomez
Director, Member Services: Donald Ethier, CAE

Historical Note
Promotes the study and control of environmental stresses arising in or from the work place or its products, in relation to the health or well-being of workers and the public. Has an annual budget of approximately $11 million. Membership: $100/year (individual); $250-475/year (organization).

Publications:
American Industrial Hygiene Association Journal. m. adv.
The Synergist. m. adv.
Who's Who in Industrial Hygiene. a. adv.

Meetings/Conferences:
Annual Meetings: Summer
1999 – Toronto, Canada/June 5-11

American Industrial Real Estate Ass'n *(1960)*
700 S. Flower, Suite 600
Los Angeles, CA 90017

Tel: (213)687-8777 *Fax:* (213)687-8616
Web Site: http://www.AIREA.com
Members: 1000 individuals
Staff: 17
Annual Budget: $1-2,000,000
C.O.O.: Ronald Surace
Administrative Asst.: Anna Ortega

Historical Note
Members are real estate brokers specializing in industrial/commercial properties.

Publications:
Bulletin. m.
Industrial Multiple. w.
Newsletter. q.

American Innerspring Manufacturers *(1966)*
1918 North Parkway
Memphis, TN 38112
Tel: (901)274-9030 *Fax:* (901)725-0510
Toll Free: (800)882 - 5634
Members: 15 companies
Staff: 2
Annual Budget: $100-250,000
Exec. Director: Arthur Grehan
Assoc. Exec. Director: George B. Gwin, Jr.

Historical Note
Formerly the Association of Innerspring Manufacturers. Members make and sell innerspring units and box springs to mattress manufacturers.

Meetings/Conferences:
Annual Meetings: Spring

American Institute for Archaeological Research *(1982)*
24 Cross Road
Mt. Vernon, NH 03057
Tel: (603)673-3005
Members: 300 individuals
Annual Budget: under $10,000
Chairman: Dorothy L. Hayden

Historical Note
Founded in New Hampshire in 1982 to carry out research in the fields of archaeology and anthropology with particular emphasis on stonework and inscriptions of North America from Pre-Columbian times. Has no paid officers or full-time staff. Membership: $25/year.

Publications:
Institute Newsletter. m.
On Site Magazine. irreg.

American Institute for Conservation of Historic and Artistic Works *(1973)*
1717 K St., N.W., Suite 301
Washington, DC 20006
Tel: (202)459-9545 *Fax:* (202)452-9328
E-Mail: info.alc@aol.com
Web Site: http://www.palimpsest.stanford.edu/aic/
Members: 3,000 individuals, 250 institutions
Staff: 5
Annual Budget: $250-500,000
Exec. Director: Elizabeth F. (Penny) Jones
Asst. Director: Beth Kline

Historical Note
Formerly (until 1973) an affiliate of the Internat'l Institute for Conservation of Historic and Artistic Works. The AIC is a professional organization of conservators, curators, educators, librarians and scientists. Purpose is to disseminate information on conservation, establish and encourage high standards of practice, and provide continuing education opportunities for conservators. Membership: $105/year (fellow or professional), $155/year (institution); $105/year (associate).

Publications:
Abstracts of Annual Meeting. a.
Directory. a. adv.
Journal. 3/yr. adv.
Newsletter. bi-m. adv.
Program of Annual Meeting. a. adv.

Meetings/Conferences:
Annual Meetings: June
1999 – St. Louis, MO(Adams Mark)/June 5-14
2000 – Philadelphia, PA(Adams Mark)
2001 – Dallas, TX(Adams Mark)

American Institute for CPCU - Insurance Institute of America *(1942)*
P.O. Box 3016
720 Providence Road
Malvern, PA 19355-0716
Tel: (610)644-2100 *Fax:* (610)640-9576
Toll Free: (800)644 - 2101
E-Mail: cserv@cpcuiia.org
Web Site: http://www.aicpcu.org
Members: 700 companies
Staff: 150
Annual Budget: $5-10,000,000
Chairman and C.E.O.: Dr. Norman A. Baglini, CPCU, CLU
Marketing/Communications Manager: Anne H. Swigart
Senior V. President, Chief Academic Officer: Christine L. Lewis, Ph.D.,CPCU
Senior V. President, Marketing: George A. White, CPCU, AIM
President and C.O.O.: Lawrence G. Brandon, CPCU, AIM
Treasurer: Francis J. Pedicone, CPA
Senior V. President, Director of Curriculum General Counsel: James J. Markham, JD, CPCU
Director, Marketing: James Matsoukas
V. President, Publications: Nancy W. Spellman

Historical Note
Formerly (1992) the American Institute for Property and Liability Underwriters. The American Institute for CPCU (AICPCU) and the Insurance Institute of America (IIA) are independent organizations

offering educational programs and professional certification to people in the property and liability insurance business. Chartered in 1942, AICPCU administers an education program that leads to the CPCU (Chartered Property Casualty Underwriter) designation. IIA programs offer both general education in insurance principles and specialist education in particular fields. The operations of IIA, founded in 1909, were merged with those of AICPCU of 1953; in 1996, a third arm, the Insurance Institute for Applied Ethics, was inaugurated.

Publications:
AICPCU/IIA Catalog. a.
AICPCU/IIA Key Information. a.
Report on Progress. a.
Solutions. Semi-a.
The Malvern Examiner. a.

Meetings/Conferences:
1999 – Boston, MA/Oct. 17-20
2000 – San Antonio, TX/Oct. 22-25

American Institute for Internat'l Steel *(1990)*
1325 G St., N.W., Suite 980
Washington, DC   20005
Tel: (202)628-3878   *Fax:* (202)737-3134
Members: 200 companies
Staff: 3
Exec. Director: David Phelps

Historical Note
An information-gathering organization keeping its members informed concerning trade and tariff legislation and importing concerns. Founded during the Korean War at government urging to help alleviate the then-current steel shortage. Members are U.S. companies or U.S. affiliates of foreign producers engaged in the import and export of steel. Membership concentrated on the East, West, and Gulf coasts. Membership: $2,500/year plus tonnage assessment (regular); $900/year (associate); $5,000/year (non-mill sales rep).

Meetings/Conferences:
Annual Meetings: usually first Monday after Thanksgiving

American Institute for Maghrib Studies *(1984)*
c/o Center for Internat'l Studies
P.O. Box 413
Milwaukee, WI   53201
Tel: (414)229-3757   *Fax:* (414)229-3626
E-Mail: tessler@csd.uwm.edu
Staff: 4
Annual Budget: $100-250,000
President: Mark Tessler, Ph.D.

Historical Note
AIMS members are individuals and institutions with an interest in the study of the Maghrib region of North Africa. Membership: $25/year (individual); $10/year (student); $500/year (institution).

Meetings/Conferences:
Annual Meetings: November

American Institute for Medical and Biological Engineering *(1992)*
Historical Note
Address unknown in 1996.

American Institute for Patristic and Byzantine Studies *(1967)*
12 Minuet Lane
Kingston, NY   12401
Tel: (914)336-8797   *Fax:* (914)336-5736
Members: 175 individuals
Staff: 3
Annual Budget: under $10,000
President: Dr. Constantine N. Tsirpanlis

Historical Note
Promotes research in eastern Patristic literature, history, theology, and culture. Founded as the American Society for Neo-Hellenic Studies, it assumed its present name in 1981. Membership: $45/year (individual), $50/year (organization).

Publications:
Patristic and Byzantine Review. a.

Meetings/Conferences:
Annual Meetings: 2nd week in October

American Institute for Shippers Ass'ns *(1961)*
P.O. Box 33457
Washington, DC   20033
Tel: (202)628-0933   *Fax:* (202)296-7374
Web Site: http://www.shippers.org
Members: 50 companies
Staff: 1
Annual Budget: $50-100,000
Exec. Director: Glenn Cella

Historical Note
Shippers associations are cooperatives formed for the purpose of consolidating freight to obtain volume transportation rates. Membership: $250-2,500/year, based on gross revenues.

Publications:
AISA Guide to Shipping Cooperatives. semi-a. adv.
AISA News. m.

Meetings/Conferences:
Annual Meetings: Spring-Early Summer/250
1999 – Marco Island, FL

American Institute of Aeronautics and Astronautics *(1963)*
1801 Alexander Bell Dr., Suite 500
Reston, VA   20191-4344
Tel: (703)264-7500   *Fax:* (703)264-7551
Toll Free: (800)639 - 2422
E-Mail: custserv@aiaa.org
Web Site: http://www.aiaa.org
Members: 35,000 individuals

Staff: 110
Annual Budget: $10-25,000,000
Exec. Director: Cort Durocher
Director, Communications: Michael J. Lewis
Events Manager: Joanne Hauser
Director, Technical Meetings: Cathy Chenevey
Treasurer and Secretary: David J. Quackenbush

Historical Note
Formed in 1963 by a merger of the American Rocket Soc. (1930) and the Institute of the Aeronautical Sciences (1932). Members are engineers, scientists, and students in the aerospace field. Maintains offices in New York and Los Angeles. Has an annual budget of over $15 million. Membership: $75/year (professional); $15/year (student).

Publications:
Aerospace America. m. adv.
AIAA Journal. m.
AIAA Student Journal. q.
International Aerospace Abstracts. m.
Journal of Aircraft. bi-m.
Journal of Guidance, Control and Dynamics. bi-m.
Journal of Propulsion and Power. bi-m.
Journal of Spacecraft and Rockets. bi-m.
Journal of Thermophysics and Heat Transfer. q.

Meetings/Conferences:

American Institute of Architects *(1857)*
1735 New York Ave., N.W.
Washington, DC   20006-5292
Tel: (202)626-7300   *Fax:* (202)626-7420
Web Site: http://www.aiaonline.com
Members: 58,000 individuals
Staff: 130
Annual Budget: $25-50,000,000
Exec. V. President/C.E.O.: Mark W. Hurwitz, Ph.D., CAE
V. President, Component Affairs & Membership: Nancy Somerville
V. President, Govt./Industry Affairs: James Dinegar
Director, Meeting Planning: Susan Finkel-Sexton
Director, Convention/Meeting Planning: John Gaillard
V. President, Education: Janet White
Director, Convention Education Programs: Brenda Henderson
Chief Financial/Operating Officer: Fred R. DeLuca
General Counsel: Jerald Jacobs
Director, Membership Development: Therese Crahan

Historical Note
Incorporated in New York April 15, 1857; incorporated The Western Ass'n of Architects in 1889. As the umbrella organization of the U.S. architectural profession, AIA promotes the standards of architecture and interests of architects. Supports the American Architectural Foundation and the Architects Quality Government Fund Political Action Committee. Has an annual budget of approximately $35 million. Membership: $175/year (full member architect); associate and allied memberships available.

Publications:
AIA News Service. m.
ARCHITECTURE. m. adv.
Memo. m.

Meetings/Conferences:
Annual Meetings: Late Spring/10,000-13,000
1999 – Dallas, TX/May 7-10

American Institute of Architecture Students *(1956)*
1735 New York Ave., N.W.
Washington, DC   20006
Tel: (202)626-7472   *Fax:* (202)626-7414
E-Mail: AIASNATL@AOL.COM
Members: 5,000 individuals
Staff: 2
Annual Budget: $500-1,000,000
Exec. Director: Thomas C. Osina

Historical Note
Formerly (1985) Ass'n of Student Chapters, American Institute of Architects and (1958) Nat'l Ass'n of Students of Architecture. Membership: $36/year (individual), $50/year (organization/company).

Publications:
CRIT: The Architectural Student Journal. semi-a.

Meetings/Conferences:
Annual Meetings: November, Thanksgiving week

American Institute of Baking *(1919)*
Historical Note
Research and educational center for the baking industry. Affiliated with the American Bakers Association.

American Institute of Bangladesh Studies *(1989)*
Juniata College, Box 974
Huntingdon, PA   16652-0999
Tel: (814)641-3646   *Fax:* (814)641-3695
E-Mail: Baxter@juniata.edu
Members: 17 institutions
Annual Budget: $10-25,000
President: Craig Baxter

Historical Note
Members of the Institute are colleges and universities. Membership: $250/year (institution).

Meetings/Conferences:
Annual Meetings: Spring

American Institute of Banking *(1900)*
Historical Note
A section of the American Bankers Ass'n.

American Institute of Biological Sciences *(1947)*
1444 I St., N.W., Suite 200
Washington, DC   20005
Tel: (202)628-1500   *Fax:* (202)628-1509
Web Site: http://www.reston.com/aibs.html
Members: 4,500 individuals, 4,000 institutions

Staff: 42
Annual Budget: $2-5,000,000
Exec. Director: Richard T. O'Grady, Ph.D.
Meetings Manager: Marilynn Maury
Editor-BioScience: Rebecca Chasen

Historical Note
Established within the Nat'l Academy of Sciences at a meeting of the Organizing Board in April, 1946. Incorporated as an independent, non-profit entity in the District of Columbia on January 12, 1955. Charter membership closed December 31, 1957. A federation of professional societies and research laboratories with an interest in the life sciences, AIBS also has individual members and promotes all aspects of the biological sciences, including agriculture, environment, and medicine. Absorbed the American Soc. of Professional Biologists in 1969. Membership: $70/year (individual), $125/year (library).

Publications:
Annual Meeting Program. a. adv.
BioScience. 11/year. adv.
Membership Directory. irreg.

Meetings/Conferences:
Annual Meetings: Summer/3,000

American Institute of Biomedical Climatology *(1958)*
1050 Eagle Rd.
Newtown, PA   18940-2818
Tel: (215)968-4483
Members: 58 individuals
Staff: 2
Annual Budget: under $10,000
Secretary: George W.K. King

Historical Note
Formerly (1987) the American Institute of Medical Climatology. Promotes the sciences of bioclimatology and biometerology, which address the relationship between climate, weather and the entire spectrum of life. Emphasizes human health and well-being. Membership: $45/year (individual); $250/year (corporate).

Publications:
AIBC Bulletin. q.
Med-Clime Currents. q.

Meetings/Conferences:
Annual Meetings: usually Philadelphia PA(Drexel Univ.)/late October

American Institute of Building Design *(1950)*
991 Post Road East
Westport, CT   06880
Tel: (203)227-3640   *Fax:* (203)227-8624
Toll Free: (800)366 - 2423
E-Mail: aibdnat@aol.com
Web Site: http://www.aibd.org
Members: 1,200 individuals
Staff: 4
Annual Budget: $250-500,000
Acting Exec. Director: Bobbie Currie

Historical Note
Established in California as United Designers Ass'n; assumed its present name in 1958. Seeks to unify the building design field, develop better design education standards, encourage inter-professional relations among designers and promote research into the aesthetic and technical aspects of the field. AIBD acts as a legislative watchdog for the building design profession, and provides professional support to residential design specialists. Membership: $140/year (individual); $1,200/year (company).

Publications:
Design Line Magazine.
Monthly Update. m.

Meetings/Conferences:
Annual Meetings: Summer
1999 – Asheville, NC(Radisson)/Aug. 2-6
2000 – San Diego, CA

American Institute of Certified Planners *(1978)*
1776 Massachusetts Ave., N.W.
Washington, DC   20036-1904
Tel: (202)872-0611   *Fax:* (202)872-0643
Web Site: http://www.planning.org
Members: 10,000 individuals
Staff: 5
Annual Budget: $1-2,000,000
Exec. Director: Frank So

Historical Note
The professional institute of the American Planning Ass'n. Members are those members of APA who have met the required qualifications of education, experience and examination in the field of city and regional planning. Awards the designation "AICP". Membership: $70/year, plus membership in APA.

Publications:
Planners Casebook. q.
Roster of Members. bi-a.

Meetings/Conferences:
Annual Meetings: Spring, with American Planning Ass'n
1999 – Seattle, WA
2000 – New York, NY
2001 – New Orleans, LA

American Institute of Certified Public Accountants *(1887)*
1211 6th Ave.
New York, NY   07311-3881
Tel: (201)938-3000   *Fax:* (201)938-3329
Web Site: http://www.aicpa.org
Members: 330,000 individuals
Staff: 625
Annual Budget: Over $100,000,000
President and C.E.O.: Barry C. Melancon
V. President, Public Relations and Communications: Geoffrey L. Pickard

V. President, State Societies and Regulatory Affairs: John M. Sharbaugh
Secretary and General Counsel: Richard F. Miller
V. President, Member Services: Jay L. Rothberg
V. President, Information Tech. CIO: Frank B. Kemp
Sr. V. President, Operations & Technology: Edward W. Niemicc

Historical Note
Founded as the American Ass'n of Public Accountants. Became the Institute of Accountants in the U.S.A. in 1916 and the American Institute of Accountants in 1917. Merged in 1937 with the American Soc. of Certified Public Accountants. Became the American Institute of Certified Public Accountants in 1957. Administers the national uniform CPA exam. Supports the AICPA Effective Legislation Committee. Has an annual budget over $100 million. Maintains offices in Jersey City, NJ and in Washington, DC.

Publications:
CPA Letter. m.
Journal of Accountancy. m. adv.
Practicing CPA. m.
Tax Adviser. m. adv.

Meetings/Conferences:
Annual Meetings: Fall
1999 – Washington, DC/May 2-5
1999 – Seattle, WA/Oct. 17-19

American Institute of Chemical Engineers *(1908)*
3 Park Ave.
New York, NY 10016-5901
Tel: (212)705-7045   *Fax:* (212)759-5977
Toll Free: (800)242 - 4363
Web Site: http://www.aiche.org
Members: 58,700 individuals
Staff: 108
Annual Budget: $10-25,000,000
Exec. Director: Glenn E. Taylor
Director, Sponsored Research and Meetings: Jack Weaver
Director, Education and Programming: Dean Kevlin
Director, Member Activities: Diana McCauley

Historical Note
Organized June 22, 1908 in Philadelphia and incorporated in New York in 1910. A member of the Accreditation Board for Engineering and Technology, the American Ass'n of Engineering Societies, the Chemical Heritage Foundation and related organizations. Sponsors research through its Center for Chemical Process Safety, Center for Waste Reduction Technologies, Process Data Exchange Institute, Design Institute for Physical Property Data, Research Institute on Food Engineering, and Design Institute for Emergency Relief Systems' Users' Group. A member society of the American Institute for Medical and Biological Engineering. Has an annual budget of approximately $21 million. Membership: $133/year.

Publications:
AIChE Activities Directory. a.
AIChE Directory. a.
AIChE Journal. m. adv.
AIChExtra. m.
Ammonia Plant Safety. a.
Biotechnology Progess. bi-m.
CHAPTER One. 8/year. adv.
Chemical Engineering Faculties. a.
Chemical Engineering Progress. m. adv.
Environmental Progress. q. adv.
Process Safety Progress. q. adv.
Symposium Series. bi-m.

Meetings/Conferences:
Annual Meetings: November/4,000 and Spring Nat'l Meeting

American Institute of Chemists *(1923)*
515 King St., Suite 420
Alexandria, VA 22314-1917
Tel: (703)836-2090   *Fax:* (703)836-2091
E-Mail: TheAIC@AOL.com
Web Site: http://www.TheAIC.org
Members: 5,000 individuals
Staff: 3
Annual Budget: $100-250,000
Exec. Director: Sharon Dobson

Historical Note
Founded in New York City in 1923 and incorporated in New York in 1926 and in Maryland in 1974. It engages in a broad range of programs for professional enhancement of the chemist and chemical engineer through it Fellow membership category, awards program, meetings, publications adn public relations activities. The AIC's National Certification Commission in Chemistry and Chemical Engineering (NCC) provides a professional credentialing system for members. Membership: $120/year (individual).

Publications:
Professional Directory. a. adv.
The Chemist. 6/yr. adv.

Meetings/Conferences:
Annual Meetings: Spring

American Institute of Commemorative Art *(1951)*
P.O. Box 43602
Middletown, KY 40253-0602
Tel: (502)254-1375   *Fax:* (502)254-1375
Members: 50 firms
Staff: 2
Annual Budget: $50-100,000
Exec. Director: Leland B. Longstreth

Historical Note
Members are devoted to high standards of design and ethics in the monument field. Limited to 50 member firms by its constitution. Membership: $400/year.

Publications:
Milestone. m.

Meetings/Conferences:

American Institute of Constructors *(1971)*
1300 North 17th St., 8th Floor

Rosslyn, VA 22209
Tel: (703)812-2021   *Fax:* (703)812-8234
E-Mail: AICNatl@aol.com
Web Site: http://aicnet.org
Members: 1000 individuals
Staff: 3
Annual Budget: $100-250,000
Exec. Director: Dominick Terrone
Exec. Administrator, Certification Commission: Maggie Green

Historical Note
Serves as the qualifying body for individuals in the construction profession. Was the founding organization for the American Council for Construction Education, the recognized agency for accrediting colleges and universities that grant 4-year degrees in construction. Membership: $60-125/year.

Publications:
American Professional Constructor. bian.
Newsletter. bi-m.

Meetings/Conferences:
1999 – Ashville, NC(Grove Park Inn)/April 8-11/250

American Institute of Engineers *(1990)*
4666 San Pablo Dam Road, Suite 8
El Sobrante, CA 94803-3142
Tel: (510)223-8911   *Fax:* (510)223-8911
Toll Free: (888)868 - 9243
E-Mail: aie@members-aie.org
Web Site: htttp://www.members-aie.org
Members: 1,200 individuals
Staff: 2
Annual Budget: $50-100,000
President: Martin S. Gottlieb

Historical Note
AIE is a two level professional association for engineers, mathematicians and scientists. Members hold a bachelor degree or higher in engineering or science, are members of another professional association, and are U.S. citizens. Membership: $50/year.

Publications:
AIE Perspectives. m. adv.
ATE Alumni Directory.
ATE Geographic Distribution Directory.
ATE Members' Directory. a. adv.

Meetings/Conferences:
Daily: Daily Via the Internet http://www.members-air.org

American Institute of Fishery Research Biologists *(1956)*
University of Texas, Dept. of Zoology
Austin, TX 78712
Tel: (512)471-1176   *Fax:* (512)471-9651
Members: 1,100 individuals
Staff: 1
Annual Budget: $10-25,000
President: Dr. Clark Hubbs
Treasurer: Joe Rachlin

Historical Note
Membership: $30/year, plus $10 initiation fee.

Publications:
BRIEFS. bi-m.

Meetings/Conferences:
Annual Meetings: Held in conjunction with American Fisheries Soc.

American Institute of Floral Designers *(1962)*
720 Light St.
Baltimore, MD 21230
Tel: (410)752-3318   *Fax:* (410)752-8295
Members: 550 individuals, 100 companies
Annual Budget: $250-500,000
Exec. Director: Thomas C. Shaner, CAE

Historical Note
Membership: $85/year.

Publications:
Focal Points. q.
Journal of Floral Design.

Meetings/Conferences:
Annual Meetings: July

American Institute of Food Distribution *(1928)*
28-12 Broadway
Fair Lawn, NJ 07410-3913
Tel: (201)791-5570   *Fax:* (201)791-5222
E-Mail: rpfaff@foodinstitute.com
Web Site: http://www.foodinstitute.com
Members: 5,500 individuals, 2,500 companies
Staff: 20
Annual Budget: $2-5,000,000
President: Rick Pfaff
V. President, Administration: Marge Salzano
Senior V. President: Brian Todd
V. President, Publications: Jim Gawley
Marketing Coordinator: Ivy Ellenberg

Historical Note
The Food Institute is an international food trade information and research organization serving, and maintained by, companies concerned with distribution of food products. Membership: $580/year (organization/company).

Publications:
Food Business Mergers & Acquisitions. a.
Food Industry Review. a.
Food Institute Report w.
HACCP & U. S.
Market Analysis Series. a.
Market Review Series. a.
OSHA Manual. a.
Recall Manual. a.

Meetings/Conferences:
Annual Meetings: Not held.

American Institute of Graphic Arts *(1914)*
164 Fifth Ave.
New York, NY 10010-5900
Tel: (212)807-1990   *Fax:* (212)807-1799
Web Site: http://www.aiga.org
Members: 10,000 individuals
Staff: 12
Annual Budget: $1-2,000,000
Exec. Director: Richard Grefe
Director, Finance and Administration: Gary Sisto

Historical Note
AIGA advances excellence in graphic design as a discipline, profession and cultural force. Members are involved in design and production of books, magazines and periodicals as well as corporate, environmental, and promotional graphics. AIGA provides leadership in the exchange of ideas and information, the encouragement of critical analysis and research, and the advancement of education and ethical practice. Conducts interrelated programs of competitions, exhibitions, publications and educational activities to promote excellence in graphic design. Has 37 chapters nationwide which provide local programs. Membership: $235/year.

Publications:
AIGA Journal. 3/year.
Graphic Design USA. a.

Meetings/Conferences:
Annual Meetings: Fall
1999 – Las Vegas, NV

American Institute of Homeopathy *(1844)*
801 N. Fairfax St., Suite 306
Alexandria, VA 22314-1757
Tel: (703)246-9501   *Fax:* (703)548-7792
E-Mail: rmartens@igc.apc.org
Members: 150 individuals
Annual Budget: $25-50,000
Treasurer: R. Martens, M.D.

Historical Note
Members are doctors of medicine, dentistry and osteopathy in the U.S. and Canada. Has no paid officers or full-time staff. Membership: $250/year.

Publications:
AIH Handbook & Directory of Active Members. a.
Journal of the AIH. q. adv.
Newsletter. m.

Meetings/Conferences:
Semi-annual Meetings: Spring and Fall

American Institute of Hydrology *(1981)*
2499 Rice St., Suite 135
St. Paul, MN 55113-3724
Tel: (651)484-8169   *Fax:* (651)484-8357
E-Mail: aihydro@aol.com
Web Site: http://www.aihydro.org
Members: 1000 organizations and individuals
Staff: 2
Annual Budget: $100-250,000
Exec. Director: Helen Klose

Historical Note
Incorporated March 1981 in the State of Minnesota. Registers and certifies hydrologists and hydrogeologists, provides a forum to discuss national and international issues, and provides educational courses. Membership: $65/year (individual); $180-330/year (organization/company).

Publications:
AIH Bulletin. q. adv.
Hydrological Science and Technology. q.

Meetings/Conferences:
Semi-Annual Meetings: Spring and Fall/200-300
1999 – San Francisco, CA(Cathedral Hill)/Nov. 7-10
2000 – Raleigh/Durham
2001 – Minneapolis/St. Paul

American Institute of Indian Studies *(1961)*
1130 E. 59th St.
Chicago, IL 60637
Tel: (773)702-8638   *Fax:* (773)702-6636
E-Mail: aiis@uchicago.edu
Members: 49 institutions
Staff: 2
President: Frederick M. Asher

Historical Note
Members include colleges and universities that support research in the art, archaeology and languages of India.

Meetings/Conferences:
Annual Meetings: With Asian Studies Conference

American Institute of Inspectors *(1989)*
P.O. Box 716
Carmichael, CA 95609-0716
Tel: (916)348-0607   *Fax:* (916)348-0607
Toll Free: (800)877 - 4770
Web Site: http://www.inspection.org
Members: 280 individuals
Annual Budget: $25-50,000
Exec. Director: Sarah Harrison

Historical Note
All members are home inspectors.

Publications:
AII Newsletter. bi-m. adv.
Roster. a.

Meetings/Conferences:
Annual Meetings: October

American Institute of Marine Underwriters *(1898)*

14 Wall St., Suite 820
New York, NY   10005
Tel: (212)233-0550   Fax: (212)227-5102
Members: 100 companies
Staff: 5
Annual Budget: $500-1,000,000
President: Walter M. Kramer

Historical Note
Tracing its origins to 1820, its member companies write ocean marine insurance in the United States.

Meetings/Conferences:
Annual Meetings: New York, NY in November

American Institute of Merchant Shipping
Historical Note
Became (1996) United States Chamber of Shipping.

American Institute of Mining, Metallurgical, and Petroleum Engineers (1871)
3 Park Ave., Suite 17
New York, NY   10016-5902
Tel: (212)419-7676   Fax: (212)371-9622
E-Mail: aimeny@aimeny.org
Web Site: http://www.aimeny.org
Members: 4 societies
Staff: 3
Annual Budget: $500-1,000,000
Exec. Director: Nellie E. Guernsey

Historical Note
Founded in Wilkes-Barre, Pennsylvania in 1871 as the American Institute of Mining Engineers to ''further the arts and sciences employed to recover the earth's minerals and convert them to useful products.'' Incorporated in 1905, the name was changed in 1919 to American Institute of Mining and Metallurgical Engineers after absorbing the American Institute of Metals. In 1957 the name American Institute of Mining, Metallurgical and Petroleum Engineers, Inc. was adopted and the Institute was reorganized into constituent societies: Minerals, Metals, & Materials Soc.; Soc. for Mining, Metallurgy, & Exploration; Soc. of Petroleum Engineers; and Iron and Steel Soc. In 1985, these societies became separately incorporated, autonomous organizations. Publications of these societies should be obtained directly from the society in question. A member of American Association of Engineering Societies.

Meetings/Conferences:
Annual Meetings: February/March
1999 – St. Louis, MO(Renaissance)/March 13-14

American Institute of Nutrition (1928)
Historical Note
Became the American Soc. for Nutritional Sciences in 1996.

American Institute of Oral Biology (1931)
P.O. Box 7184
Loma Linda, CA   92354-7184
Tel: (909)824-4671
Members: 650 individuals
Staff: 2
Annual Budget: $25-50,000
Exec. Secretary: June Barrientos

Historical Note
Registration: $325/year.

Publications:
Proceedings Manual. a.

Meetings/Conferences:
Annual Meetings: Always in Palm Springs, CA/Late October/120-140
1999 – (Hilton)/Oct. 22-25

American Institute of Organbuilders (1974)
P.O. Box 130982
Houston, TX   77219-0982
Tel: (713)529-2212
Members: 340 individuals
Staff: 1
Annual Budget: $25-50,000
Exec. Secretary: Howard Maple

Historical Note
AIO was established to educate professional builders of pipe organs through lectures, discussion and publication of technical information. Members are individuals professionally engaged in some facet of the building, servicing and maintaining of pipe organs, including organ company executives, pipe and cabinet makers, service and maintenance technicians. Membership: $75/year (individual).

Publications:
Journal of American Organbuilding. q. adv.

Meetings/Conferences:
Annual Meetings: October
1999 – Akron-Canton, OH/Akron-Canton, 0-Canton, 0

American Institute of Parliamentarians (1958)
P.O. Box 2173
Wilmington, DE   19899-2173
Tel: (302)762-1811   Fax: (302)762-2170
Toll Free: (888)664 - 0428
E-Mail: aip@aipparlipro.org
Web Site: http://www.aipparlipro.org
Members: 1,400 individuals
Staff: 2
Annual Budget: $50-100,000
Exec. Director: Ann Iona Warner

Historical Note
Promotes the teaching of parliamentary procedure, training and certification of parliametarians and the wider use of parliamentarians . Awards the designations CP (Certified Parliamentarian) and CPP (Certified Professional Parliamentarian). Membership: $45/year (regular); $50/year (associate); $20/year (full time student).

Publications:
Parliamentary Journal. q.
The Communicator. q.

Meetings/Conferences:
1999 – Annapolis, MD(Holiday Inn)/July 21-24

American Institute of Physics (1931)
1 Physics Ellipse
College Park, MD   20740-3843
Tel: (301)209-3000   Fax: (301)209-3153
E-Mail: aipinfo@aip.org
Web Site: http://www.aip.org
Members: 10 societies & 18 affiliated socs.
Staff: 500
Annual Budget: $50-100,000,000
Exec. Director: Marc H. Brodsky
Manager, Public Information Division: Alicia Torres
Senior Liaison, Government and Institutional Relations: Richard M. Jones
Exhibits Manager: Robert Finnegan
Manager, Education Division: Bo Hammer
Treasurer: Richard Baccante
Comptroller: Mary Ellen O'Connor

Historical Note
Organized in New York under the leadership of Karl Compton and George Pegram as a means of preserving communication within the community of physicists whose energies were being dispersed into an increasing number of special fields. A federation of ten societies in physics: Acoustical Soc. of America, American Ass'n of Physicists in Medicine, American Ass'n of Physics Teachers, American Astronomical Soc., American Crystallographic Ass'n, American Geophysical Union, American Physical Soc., American Vacuum Soc., Optical Soc. of America, and Soc. of Rheology. Incorporated in New York in 1932. Has a budget of approximately $60 million.

Publications:
Applied Physics Letters. w.
CHAOS: An Interdisciplinary Journal of Nonlinear Science. q.
Computers in Physics. bi-m. adv.
Current Physics Index. q.
Dir of Organizations with Physics, Astronomy & Geophysics Staff. bien.
Graduate Program Book.
Industrial Physicist. q.
JETP Letters. semi-m.
Journal of Applied Physics. m.
Journal of Chemical Physics. semi-m.
Journal of Experimental and Theoretical Physics. m.
Journal of Mathematical Physics. m.
Journal of Physical and Chemical Reference Data. q.
Low Temperature Physics. m.
Physics Education News (electronic newsletter). irreg.
Physics of Fluids. m.
Physics of Particles and Nuclei. bi-m.
Physics of Plasmas. m.
Physics of the Solid State. m.
Physics Today. m. adv.
Review of Scientific Instruments. m. adv.
Semiconductors. m.
Technical Physics. m.
Technical Physics Letters. m.

Meetings/Conferences:
Annual Meetings: Not held.

American Institute of Plant Engineers (1954)
Historical Note
Became the Ass'n for Facilities Engineering in 1996.

American Institute of Professional Bookkeepers
6001 Montrose Road, Suite 207
Rockville, MD   20852
Tel: (301)770-7300   Fax: (301)770-5626
Toll Free: (800)622 - 0121
E-Mail: info@aipb.org
Web Site: http://www.aipb.org
Members: 42,000 individuals
Staff: 6
President: Stanley I. Hartman

Historical Note
Members are bookkeepers.

Publications:
Journal of Taxation and Business. q.
The General Ledger. m.

American Institute of Professional Geologists (1963)
7828 Vance Drive, Suite 103
Arvada, CO   80003
Tel: (303)431-0831   Fax: (303)431-1332
E-Mail: aipg@aipg.org
Web Site: http://www.aipg.org
Members: 5,103 individuals
Staff: 4
Annual Budget: $500-1,000,000
Exec. Director: William V. Knight
Membership Services Manager: Karen Spaulding

Historical Note
Founded November 15, 1963 and incorporated in Colorado in 1964. A member of the American Geological Institute. Awards the designation Certified Professional Geologist (CPG). Provides continuing education and advocacy programs in support of the profession. Membership: $85/year.

Publications:
Membership Directory. a. adv.
The Professional Geologist. m. adv.

Meetings/Conferences:
Annual Meetings: late September-early October
1999 – Anchorage, AK/Oct. 5-8
2000 – Milwaukee, WI/Oct. 11-15

American Institute of Service Body Manufacturers

Historical Note
An affiliate of the Nat'l Truck Equipment Ass'n.

American Institute of Steel Construction (1921)
One E. Wacker Drive, Suite 3100
Chicago, IL   60601-2001
Tel: (312)670-2400   Fax: (312)670-5403
Web Site: http://www.aiscweb.org
Members: 2,750 individuals, 700 companies
Staff: 35
Annual Budget: $2-5,000,000
President: H. Louis Gurthet
Director, Membership: LeAnn Schmidt

Historical Note
Fabricators of structural steel.

Publications:
AISC Engineering Journal. q.
Modern Steel Construction. m. adv.

Meetings/Conferences:
Annual Meetings: Fall/400

American Institute of Stress (1979)
124 Park Ave.
Yonkers, NY   10703
Tel: (914)963-1200   Fax: (914)965-6267
E-Mail: stress124@earthlink.net
Web Site: http://www.stress.org
Members: 5,000 individuals
Staff: 4
Annual Budget: $50-100,000
President and Chairman: Paul J. Rosch, M.D.
Director of Communications: Robin Sacks

Historical Note
AIS is a multidisciplinary professional society composed of health professionals, academics and others with an interest in the study of stress and its treatment. Membership: $90/year (professional). Membership: $90/year (fellow); $70/year (individual).

Publications:
Health and Stress: The Newsletter of the AIS. m.

Meetings/Conferences:

American Institute of the History of Pharmacy (1941)
425 N. Charter St.
University of Wisconsin
Madison, WI   53706-1508
Tel: (608)262-5378
E-Mail: pills@aihp.org
Web Site: http://www.aihp.org
Members: 1000 individuals
Staff: 3
Annual Budget: $100-250,000
Director: Dr. Gregory J. Higby
Assistant Director: Elaine Stroud
Program Manager: Beth Fisher

Historical Note
Founded in Madison, WI as a non-profit agency specializing in the history of pharmacy and drugs, with emphasis on the USA. Individual memberships are nation-wide, governed by a nationally representative Council. The historical and publishing office has been at the University of Wisconsin School of Pharmacy since the founding. Fosters investigations, publications, teaching, and interest in the history of pharmacy; collects historical records and makes them available; sponsors awards and educational grants. Membership: $50/year (individual); $100/year (organization/company).

Publications:
AIHP Notes. q. adv.
Pharmacy in History. q.

Meetings/Conferences:
Annual Meetings: Spring, with American Pharmaceutical Ass'n
1999 – San Antonio, TX/Mar. 6-10
2000 – Washington, DC/Mar. 11-15
2001 – San Francisco, CA/Mar. 24-28
2002 – Philadelphia, PA/Mar. 16-20

American Institute of Timber Construction (1952)
7012 S. Revere Pkwy., Suite 140
Englewood, CO   80112
Tel: (303)792-9559   Fax: (303)792-0669
E-Mail: info@aitc-glulam.org
Web Site: http://www.aitc-glulam.org
Members: 410 companies and individuals
Staff: 6
Annual Budget: $500-1,000,000

Historical Note
Members are manufacturers and erectors of laminated structural timber, engineers, architects, etc. Membership: $50/year (individual); $150/year (installers); $500/year (suppliers); $150/year (associate).

Publications:
Lamlines. q.

Meetings/Conferences:
Annual Meetings: Spring
1999 – Lihue, HI(Outrigger Kauai Beach)/March 13-16

American Institute of Ultrasound in Medicine (1951)
14750 Sweitzer Lane, Suite 100
Laurel, MD   20707-5906
Tel: (301)498-4100   Fax: (301)498-4450
E-Mail: admin@aium.org
Members: 10,000 individuals
Staff: 30
Annual Budget: $2-5,000,000
Exec. Director: Carmine M. Valente, Ph.D., CAE
Director, Conventions/Education: Jenny Clark
Comptroller: Diane Eberle
Director of Committees and MIS: Glynis Harvey
Director, Marketing/Member Services: Stacey Day
Director, Development: Kelley Speros

Historical Note
Founded in Denver, CO, by 24 physicians attending the annual meeting of the American Congress of Physical Medicine and Rehabilitation who wished to expand the scope of physical medicine as a new specialty. Members are physicians, scientists, engineers and sonographers concerned with the use of diagnostic medical ultrasound. Membership: $195/year (physician); $125/year (non-physician).

Publications:
AIUM Reporter. m.
Journal of Ultrasound in Medicine. m. adv.
Scientific Meeting Abstracts. a.

Meetings/Conferences:
Annual Meetings: Spring/3,500
1999 – San Antonio, TX/march 14-17

American Institution of Nutrition
Historical Note
Became (1996) American Soc. for Nutritional Sciences.

American Institutions Food Service Ass'n *(1981)*
Historical Note
Address unknown in 1996.

American Insurance Ass'n *(1964)*
1130 Connecticut Ave., N.W., Suite 1000
Washington, DC 20036
Tel: (202)828-7100   *Fax:* (202)293-1219
Web Site: http://www.aiadc.org
Members: 270 companies
Staff: 150
Annual Budget: $10-25,000,000
President: Robert E. Vagley
Senior V. President, Public Affairs: Leigh Ann Pusey
Senior V. President, Government Affairs: George M. Mulligan
Director, Federal Affairs: Christina M. Cullinan
V. President, Federal Affairs: Richard C. Lawson
V. President, Finance and Administration: Carlos A. Munoz, Sr.
General Counsel & Senior V. President: Craig A. Berrington

Historical Note
Formed by a merger of the National Board of Fire Underwriters (founded in 1866), the Association of Casualty and Surety Companies (founded in 1927) and the old American Insurance Association (founded in 1953). Supports the American Insurance Association Political Action Committee. Has an annual budget of approximately $21.6 million. Membership fee based on market share.

Publications:
Briefing. bi-w.
Workers' Compensation Digest. a

Meetings/Conferences:
Annual Meetings: January

American Insurance Attorneys
Historical Note
Address unknown in 1997.

American Insurers Highway Safety Alliance *(1920)*
3025 Highland Pkwy., Suite 800
Downers Grove, IL 60515-1260
Tel: (630)724-2100
Members: 24 companies
President: Rodger S. Lawson
Exec. V. President: Greg Heidrich

Historical Note
Formerly (1977) Nat'l Ass'n of Automotive Mutual Insurance Companies. Members are automobile insurance companies.

Meetings/Conferences:
Annual Meetings: With Alliance of American Insurers

American Intellectual Property Law Ass'n *(1897)*
2001 Jefferson Davis Hwy., Suite 203
Arlington, VA 22202
Tel: (703)415-0780   *Fax:* (703)415-0786
E-Mail: aipla@aipla.org
Web Site: http://www.aipla.org
Members: 10,000 individuals
Staff: 10
Annual Budget: $2-5,000,000
Exec. Director: Michael K. Kirk
Director of Operations: Nancy Haley

Historical Note
Formerly (1914) Patent Law Ass'n of Washington and (1984) the American Patent Law Ass'n. Membership in this voluntary bar ass'n consists of lawyers whose specialty is trademark, copyright and patent law. Fields of concern are patent, trademark, and copyright patent laws, and the federal rules and regulations that administer them. A member of Nat'l Council of Patent Law Ass'ns. Membership: $195/year (active).

Publications:
AIPLA Quarterly Journal. q.
Bulletin of AIPLA. 3/yr. adv.
Economic Survey. bie.
Membership Directory. bien.

Meetings/Conferences:
Annual Meetings: always Arlington, VA(Marriott Crystal Gateway)/October
1999 – /Oct. 21-23
2000 – /Oct. 19-21
2001 – /Oct. 18-20

American Internat'l Automobile Dealers Ass'n *(1970)*
99 Canal Center Plaza, Suite 500
Alexandria, VA 22314-1538
Tel: (703)519-7800   *Fax:* (703)519-7810
Web Site: http://www.aiada.org
Members: 10,000 dealers
Staff: 20
Annual Budget: $2-5,000,000

President: Walter E. Huizenga
Director, Public Relations: Lori Weaver Barnes
V. President, Government Relations: Scott Lane
Manager, Meetings: Anne Nuttall
Director of Administration: Paul Giddings
V. President, Membership: Daniel C. Barson

Historical Note
Formed in 1970 as the Volkswagen American Dealers Ass'n. Assumed its present name in 1980. AIADA represents America's 10,000 international nameplate automobile dealers and their 330,000 employees who sell and service world-class automobiles. Only trade ass'n exclusively dedicated to representing the nation's international nameplate automobile dealers before Congress, the administration, the industry, the media and the American public.

Publications:
AIADA Newsletter. m.
Showroom Magazine. 8/year.

Meetings/Conferences:
Annual Meetings: Spring
1999 – Washington, DC/May 16-18

American Internat'l Charolais Ass'n *(1957)*
P.O. Box 20247
Kansas City, MO 64195
Tel: (816)464-5977   *Fax:* (816)464-5759
E-Mail: charusa@sound.net
Web Site: CHAROLAISUSA
Members: 4,500 individuals
Staff: 25
Annual Budget: $1-2,000,000
Exec. V. President: Dr. Bill V. Able
Dir. of Communications: Julie Olson
Accountant: Barbara Butki
Recording Secretary: Marilou Wegner

Historical Note
Formed (1957) by merger of American Charolais Breeders Ass'n and Internat'l Charolais Ass'n. Absorbed (1967) American Charbray Breeders Ass'n. Members are breeders and fanciers of Charolais beef cattle. Member of the National Pedigree Livestock Council and the United States Beef Breeds Council. Membership: $50 initial fee, $35/year.

Publications:
Charolais Journal. m. adv.

Meetings/Conferences:
Semi-Annual Meetings: 300

American Internat'l Freight Ass'n
3601 Eisenhower Ave., Suite 110
Alexandria, VA 22304
Tel: (703)329-9263   *Fax:* (703)329-9806
Members: 90
Staff: 6
C.E.O.: Robert A. Voltman
Communication and Policy Manager: Patrick Knight

Historical Note
AIFA members are frieght intermediaries engaged in international transportation by ocean, air and land. AIFA represents the interests of multi-modal freight transport operators, non-vessel operating common carriers, freight consolidation companies, shipper's agents, and similar professionals. AIFA is the American representative to FIATA, the international freight forwarding association. Membership: $250-1,250/year.

Publications:
AIFA Alert. irreg.
inside AIFA. m. adv.
Membership Directory. a. adv.

Meetings/Conferences:
1999 – San Diego, CA(Marriott)/Feb. 11-13

American Internat'l Marchigiana Soc. *(1973)*
Marky Cattle Ass'n
P.O. Box 198
Walton, KS 67151-0198
Tel: (316)837-3303
Members: 50 individuals
Staff: 1
Annual Budget: under $10,000
Exec. Secretary: Martie Knudsen

Historical Note
An association founded in 1973 to foster raising of the marchigiana breed of cattle in the United States. Also known as the Marky Cattle Ass'n. Membership: $35/year, $100 (regular member).

Publications:
The Marky Newsletter. m. adv.

Meetings/Conferences:
Annual Meetings: Kansas or Nebraska/March
1999 – Hutchinson, KS/March 10-13

American Iron and Steel Institute *(1855)*
1101 17th St., N.W., Suite 1300
Washington, DC 20036-4700
Tel: (202)452-7100   *Fax:* (202)463-6573
Web Site: http://www.steel.org
Members: 200 companies and assoc. members
Staff: 50
Annual Budget: $5-10,000,000
President and C.E.O.: Andrew G. Sharkey, III
V. President, Communications: Nancy Gravatt
V. President, Energy and the Environment: Bruce A. Steiner
V. President, Tax and Trade: Barry Solarz
Director, Government Relations: Sherri Zedd
V. President, Manufacturing and Technology: Larry Kavanaugh
V. President, Statistics: Janet K. Nash
Directotr, Finance: David E. Bell
Senior V. President and General Councel: Thomas M. Sneeringer
V. President, Market Development: David C. Jones

Historical Note
The American Iron Ass'n was founded in 1855 and absorbed by the American Iron and Steel Ass'n in 1864. This, in turn, was absorbed

in 1912 by the American Iron and Steel Institute which had been incorporated March 31, 1908 in New York. Promotes the interests of the iron and steel industry.

Publications:
Annual Statistical Report. a.

Meetings/Conferences:
1999 – New York, NY(Waldorf Historia)/May 25-27

American Iron Ore Ass'n *(1882)*
915 Rockefeller Bldg.
614 Superior Ave., West
Cleveland, OH 44113-1383
Tel: (216)861-0590   *Fax:* (216)241-8262
E-Mail: jearlywine@aioa.org
Web Site: http://www.aioa.org
Members: 8 companies
Staff: 2
Annual Budget: $50-100,000
Exec. Director: George J. Ryan
Asst. Secretary: Carol Ann Lane

Historical Note
Established as the Western Iron Ore Ass'n, it became the Lake Superior Iron Ore Ass'n in 1895 and assumed its present name in 1957. Members are iron ore mining companies in the United States and Canada.

Publications:
Iron Ore - Statistical. a.
Statistical Reports - Ore Consumed & Inventory. m.

Meetings/Conferences:

American Italian Historical Ass'n *(1966)*
209 Flagg Place
Staten Island, NY 10304
Tel: (718)852-2929
Members: 800 individuals
Annual Budget: under $10,000
Secretary: Dawn Esposito

Historical Note
AIHA members are academics and others with an interest in the study of the Italiean experience in North America. Has no paid officers or full-time staff. Membership: $35/year (individual); $15/year (student); $50/year (institution).

Publications:
Newsletter of AHIA. 3/year. adv.
Proceedings. a.

Meetings/Conferences:
Annual Meetings: Fall
1999 – San Francisco, CA
2000 – New Orleans, LA

American Jail Ass'n *(1981)*
2053 Day Road, Suite 100
Hagerstown, MD 21740-9795
Tel: (301)790-3930   *Fax:* (301)790-2941
E-Mail: jails@worldnety.att.net
Web Site: http://www.corrections.com/aja
Members: 4,600 individuals
Staff: 13
Annual Budget: $1-2,000,000
Exec. Director: Stephen J. Ingley
Director, Marketing: Patricia A. Cain
Director, Training and Membership: Sandy Prisak

Historical Note
Members are jail personnel and persons whose work is closely associated with jails. The result of a merger between the Nat'l Jail Ass'n (formed in 1929) and the Nat'l Jail Managers Ass'n (formed in 1973). Membership: $15/year (student); $30/year (individual, US); $36/year (Canada); $42/year (foreign); $100/year (affiliate); $250/year (organization/company).

Publications:
American Jails Magazine. bi-m. adv.
Jail Directory. bien.
Jail Managers Bulletin. m.
Jail Operations Bulletin. m.
Product Service Directory. a.
Write It Right Bulletin. q.

Meetings/Conferences:
Annual Meetings: Spring
1999 – Ft. Worth, TX/May 23-27
2000 – Phoenix, AZ/April 30-May 4
2001 – Columbus, OH/April 22-26
2002 – Milwaukee, WI

American Jersey Cattle Ass'n *(1868)*
6486 East Main St.
Reynoldsburg, OH 43068-2362
Tel: (614)861-3636   *Fax:* (614)861-8040
E-Mail: usjersey@iwaynet.net
Web Site: http://www.cattleofferings.com/usjersey.htm
Members: 2,550 individuals
Staff: 38
Annual Budget: $1-2,000,000
Exec. Secretary: Calvin Covington

Historical Note
Breeders of Jersey dairy cattle. Member of the National Pedigree Livestock Council. Membership: $100/lifetime.

Publications:
Jersey Directory. bien.
Jersey Handbook. bien.
Jersey Journal. m. adv.

Meetings/Conferences:
Annual Meetings: June
1999 – Minneapolis, MN(Hilton Airport)/June 24-28

American Jewish Correctional Chaplains Ass'n *(1937)*
c/o Westchester Jewish Center
Rockland & Palmer Aves.
Mamaroneck, NY 10543

Tel: (914)698-2960   *Fax:* (914)698-3610
Members: 50 individuals
Annual Budget: under $10,000
President: Rabbi Irving Koslowe

Historical Note
Affiliated with the American Correctional Ass'n and the American Correctional Chaplains Ass'n. Formerly Nat'l Council of Jewish Correctional Chaplains and Nat'l Council of Jewish Prison Chaplains. Membership: $10/year.

Publications:
Chaplaincy.

Meetings/Conferences:
Semi-annual Meetings: January and June

American Jewish Historical Soc. *(1892)*
2 Thornton Road
Waltham, MA   02154-7711
Tel: (617)891-8110   *Fax:* (617)899-9208
E-Mail: ajhs@ajhs.org
Web Site: http://www.ajhs.org
Members: 3,000 individuals
Staff: 9
Annual Budget: $500-1,000,000
Director: Michael Feldberg
: Libby Fonkelstein

Historical Note
The Society is a museum, library and archives and educational institution interested in public service. It is the repository for the archives of such organizations as the Council of Jewish Federations and the American Jewish Congress, and the Synagogue Council of America. Its collections provide information on current as well as past Jewish communal and institutional life, social welfare services, immigration, synagogue records, prominent Jewish individuals, the Colonial Period and the early 19th century, and the ties between American Jewry and events overseas. Members are historians, scholars, and lay people. Membership: $50/year.

Publications:
American Jewish History. q. adv.
Heritage (newsletter). irreg.

Meetings/Conferences:
Annual Meetings: Spring/300

American Jewish Press Ass'n *(1943)*
5307 Marsh Creek Dr.
Austin, TX   78759-6218
Tel: (512)795-9112   *Fax:* (512)795-9520
E-Mail: ajpamr@aol.com
Members: 50 individuals, 150 newspapers
Staff: 1
Annual Budget: $50-100,000
Administrator: Beverly Rodman

Historical Note
Members are Jewish community newspapers. Formerly the American Association of English Jewish Newspapers. Membership: $100/year (individual); $360/year (full newspaper).

Publications:
Membership Bulletin. m.
Membership Directory. a.

Meetings/Conferences:
Semi-annual meetings: spring and fall

American Journalism Historians Ass'n *(1981)*
4185 Corriente Place
Boulder, CO   80301
Tel: (303)443-7542
Members: 360 individuals, 160 institutional subscribers
Annual Budget: $10-25,000
Treasurer: Richard Scheidenhelm

Historical Note
AJHA members are academics and other individuals with an interest in the history of the media. Has no paid officers or full-time staff. Membership: $15/year (student/retiree); $30/year (individual); $30/year (organization/company)

Publications:
AJHA Intelligencer Newsletter. q.
American Journalism Journal. q. adv.

Meetings/Conferences:
Annual Meetings: October
1999 - Portland, OR

American Judges Ass'n *(1959)*
Nat'l Center for State Courts
300 Newport Ave., P.O. Box 8798
Williamsburg, VA   23187-8798
Tel: (757)259-1841   *Fax:* (757)259-1520
Members: 3,400 individuals
Staff: 2
Annual Budget: $50-100,000
Association Management Specialist: Shelley Rockwell

Historical Note
Formerly (1965) the Nat'l Ass'n of Municipal Judges and (1972) the North American Judges Ass'n. An independent organization of judges of all jurisdictions in the United States and Canada. Affiliated with the American Judges Foundation. Membership: $75/year.

Publications:
AJA Benchmark. q.
Court Review. q. adv.

Meetings/Conferences:
Annual Meetings: Fall/200-250
1999 - Cleveland, OH(Marriott Downtown)/Oct. 10-15/250
2000 - Kansas Ctiy, MO(Westin Crown Center)/Sept. 10-15
2001 - Reno, NV(Silver Legacy Resort)/Sept. 30-Oct. 5

American Judicature Soc. *(1913)*
180 N. Michigan Ave., Suite 600
Chicago, IL   60601-7401
Tel: (312)558-6900   *Fax:* (312)558-9175

E-Mail: ajs@interaccess.com
Web Site: http://www.ajs.org
Members: 20,000 individuals
Staff: 20
Annual Budget: $1-2,000,000
Exec. V. President: Sandra Ratcliff-Daffron
Director, Information & Program Services: Kathleen M. Sampson
Director, Development: Karen Rittenberg

Historical Note
Lawyers, judges, educators and others interested in the effective administration of justice. AJS goals include: greater public understanding of the role of the courts, the selection of judges primarily on their professional qualifications, the defense of judicial independence while ensuring that improper conduct will not be tolerated, and the application of modern management prinicples to court systems. Membership: $55/year.

Publications:
Judicature. bi-m. adv.
Judicial Conduct Reporter. q.
Judicial Discipline & Disability Digest 1960-1976 Supplement. a.

Meetings/Conferences:
Annual Meetings: in conjunction with American Bar Ass'n/Summer

American Karakul Sheep Registry *(1965)*
3026 Thomas Road
Rice, WA   99167
Tel: (509)738-6310   *Fax:* (509)738-4209
E-Mail: aksr@plix.com
Members: 125 individuals
Staff: 1
Annual Budget: under $10,000
Secretary: Julie DeVlieg

Historical Note
Formerly Karakul Fur Sheep Registry, (1979) Empire Karakul Registry and (1985) American Karakul Fur Sheep Registry. AKSR promotes and perpetuates the Karakul purebred, originally imported from Russia. Membership: $10/year (individual).

Publications:
Newsletter. 3-4/yr.

American Kennel Club *(1884)*
260 Madison Ave., 4th Floor
New York, NY   10016
Tel: (212)696-8200   *Fax:* (212)696-8299
E-Mail: info@akc.org
Web Site: http://www.akc.org
Members: 503 dog clubs
Staff: 410
Annual Budget: $10-25,000,000
President and C.E.O.: Alfred L. Cheaure
Director, Public Relations: Valerie Geiss
V. President, Public Education/Legislation: Noreen Baxter

Historical Note
The principal registry of pure-bred dogs in the United States and the regulatory agency for dog shows, the AKC was established to "advance the study, breeding, exhibiting, running and maintenance of the purity of thoroughbred dogs." Founded by show-giving clubs to bring order to the sport of dogs, the AKC has no individual members. Has an annual budget of approximately $20 million.

Publications:
Pure-Bred Dogs/American Kennel Gazette. m.

Meetings/Conferences:
Quarterly Meetings: Second Tuesday of every March, June, Sept. & Dec. in New York City, NY

American Kiddie Ride Ass'n *(1990)*
Historical Note
Organization defunct in 1995.

American Kinesiotherapy Ass'n *(1946)*
c/o Amer. Acad. of Physical Med. & Rehab
One IBM Plaza, Suite 2500
Chicago, IL   60611-3604
Toll Free: (800)296 - 2582
E-Mail: lhedrick@aapmr.org
Web Site: http://www.akta.org
Members: 500 individuals
Staff: 1
Annual Budget: $50-100,000
Administrative Officer: Lisa V. Hedrick

Historical Note
Formerly (1987) American Corrective Therapy Ass'n and (1967) Ass'n for Physical and Mental Rehabilitation. Professional society of kinesiotherapists and exercise therapists. Kinesiotherapy is the treatment of the effects of disease, injury and congenital disorders through the use of therapeutic exercise and education. Membership: $120/year (individual).

Publications:
Journal of Clinical Kinesiology. q. adv.
Mobility Newsletter. q. adv.

Meetings/Conferences:
Annual Meetings: Second week in July/150-200
1999 - Las Vegas, NV
2000 - Chicago, IL

American Ladder Institute *(1935)*
401 N. Michigan Ave.
Chicago, IL   60611-4206
Tel: (312)644-6610   *Fax:* (312)245-1053
Web Site: http://ali.sba.com/ali/
Members: 34 companies
Staff: 2
Annual Budget: $100-250,000
Exec. Director: Ronald Pietrzak

Historical Note
Represents U.S. companies engaged in the research, development, manufacture, and safety of ladders. Works with government bodies,

particularly ANSI, OSHA and CPSC, in addressing design and safety questions. Members include manufacturers of wood, metal, and fiberglass ladders. Suppliers to the industry are also eligible for membership as associates.

Publications:
Ladderlines. 3/year.

Meetings/Conferences:
1999 - Palm Springs, CA(Westin Mission Hills)
1999 - Las Vegas, NV(The Bellagio)

American Lamb Council
Historical Note
A division of the American Sheep Industry Ass'n.

American Laminators Ass'n *(1984)*
Historical Note
This organization is defunct.

American Land Rights Ass'n *(1978)*
P.O. Box 400
Battle Ground, WA   98604-0400
Tel: (360)687-3087   *Fax:* (360)687-2973
E-Mail: alra@pacifier.com
Web Site: http://www.landrights.org
Members: 18,000 individuals
Staff: 8
Annual Budget: $250-500,000
Exec. Director: Charles S. Cushman
Asst. Director: Elizabeth West

Historical Note
Formerly (1980) Nat'l Park Inholders Ass'n, (1993) Nat'l Inholders Ass'n. Members are individuals holding property, equity interest, grazing permits, leases or related claims to use on real estate in or adjacent to federally managed areas such as national parks, forests, refueges and other reserves in the public domain. Promotes the interests of these property owners and resource dependent communities through lobbying and activism. Maintains a Washington representative. Membership: $35/year.

Publications:
Congressional Directory. bien.
Land Rights Action Guide. bien.
Land Rights Advocate. bi-m. adv.
Land Rights Alert. m.
Private Property Congressional Vote Index. bien.

Meetings/Conferences:
Annual Meetings: Irregular

American Land Title Ass'n *(1907)*
1828 L St., N.W., Suite 705
Washington, DC   20036-5104
Tel: (202)296-3671   *Fax:* (202)223-5843
Toll Free: (800)787 - 2582
Web Site: http://www.alta.org
Members: 2,600 corporations
Staff: 15
Annual Budget: $2-5,000,000
Exec. V. President: James R. Maher
V. President, Public Affairs: Gary L. Garrity
Government Relations Director: Ann vom Eigen
Director, Meetings/Conferences: Liza Trey
Education Director: Patricia L. Berman
V. President, Administration: David R. McLaughlin
General Counsel: Edmond R. Browne, Jr.
Membership & Marketing Manager: M. Kathleen Hendrix
Director, Information Systems and Technology: Kelly Throckmorton

Historical Note
Membership is composed of title insurers, agents, title abstracters, lawyers and other specialists in real estate law. Formerly (1963) American Title Ass'n. Supports the Title Industry Political Action Committee.

Publications:
ALTA Update. irreg.
Capital Comment. 10/year.
TITLE News. bi-m. adv.

Meetings/Conferences:

American Landrace Ass'n *(1950)*
Box 2340
West Lafayette, IN   47906
Tel: (317)892-3134
Members: 165 individuals
Staff: 2
Annual Budget: $100-250,000
CEO: Darrell D. Anderson

Historical Note
Members are breeders and fanciers of landrace swine. Member of the Nat'l Pedigree Livestock Council. Membership: $50/year.

Publlcations:
America's Sowherd. q.
Landrace Commercial Yearbook. a.

Meetings/Conferences:
Annual Meetings: March

American Landscape Horticulture Ass'n *(1987)*
Historical Note
Address unknown in 1997.

American Laryngological Ass'n *(1878)*
S. 2100 Med. Center North, VU Med. Ctr.
Dept. of Otolaryngology
Nashville, TN   37232-2559
Tel: (615)322-6326
E-Mail: virginia.brightland@mcmail.vanderbilt.edu
Members: 250 individuals
Staff: 2
Annual Budget: $10-25,000
Secretary: Dr. Robert H. Ossoff, M.D.

Historical Note
Members are individuals concentrating on the advancement of medicine and surgery of the upper aerodigestive tract. Membership: $150/year.
Publications:
Transactions. a.
Meetings/Conferences:
Annual Meetings: Spring
1999 – Palm Desert, CA/April 24-25

American Laryngological, Rhinological and Otological Soc. (1895)
Boys Town Nat'l Res. Hospital
555 N. 30th St.
Omaha, NE 68131
Tel: (402)498-6666
Members: 1,100 individuals
Staff: 10
Annual Budget: $1-2,000,000
Exec. Director: Patrick Brookhauser
Historical Note
Organized June 19, 1895 and incorporated December 5, 1917. Also known as the Triological Soc. Membership: $110/year (individual).
Publications:
Laryngoscope. m. adv.
Triologistics. 3/yr.
Meetings/Conferences:
Annual Meetings: Spring

American Law Institute (1923)
4025 Chestnut St.
Philadelphia, PA 19104-3099
Tel: (215)243-1600   *Fax:* (215)243-1664
Toll Free: (800)253 - 6397
Web Site: http://www.ali.org
Members: 3,685 individuals
Staff: 85
Annual Budget: $5-10,000,000
Director: Geoffrey C. Hazard, Jr.
Director, Professional Relations/Marketing: Kathleen H. Lawner
Meetings Coordinator: Kathleen C. Peters
Director, Office of Administrative Services: Joseph A. Mendicino, Jr.
Deputy Director: Michael Greenwald
Membership Secretary: Helene Cohen
Deputy Director: Elena Capella
Exec. Director, ALI-ABA: Richard Carter
Historical Note
Membership, by invitation only, consists of lawyers, judges, educators and government officials interested in simplifying, clarifying, and improving the law. Institute produces restatements of the law, model codes, and recommendations for reform. Its program of education is conducted in close cooperation with the American Bar Ass'n through a joint committee known as the American Law Institute/American Bar Association Committee on Continuing Professional Education (ALI-ABA). Membership: $200/year (practicing lawyers); $100/year (teachers and judges).
Publications:
ALI Reporter. q.
ALI-ABA CLE Review. 11/year.
ALI-ABA Course Materials Journal. bi-m.
ALI-ABA Estate Planning Course Materials Journal. bi-m.
Annual Meeting Proceedings. a.
CLE Journal. bi-m.
Practical Lawyer. 8/year.
Practical Litigator. bi-m.
Practical Real Estate Lawyer. bi-m.
Practical Tax Lawyer. q.
The Audio Estate Planner. q.
Meetings/Conferences:
1999 – San Francisco, CA(The Fairmont)/May 17-20
2000 – Washington, DC(Mayflower)/May 15-18
2001 – Washington, DC(Mayflower)/May 14-17
2002 – Washington, DC(Mayflower)/May 13-16
2003 – Chicago, IL(The Fairmont)/May 12-15

American Law Student Ass'n (1949)
Historical Note
A Division of the American Bar Ass'n.

American League of Financial Institutions (1948)
Historical Note
Address unknown in 1998.

American League of Lobbyists (1978)
P.O. Box 30005
Alexandria, VA 22310
Tel: (703)960-3011
Members: 550 individuals
Staff: 1
Annual Budget: $100-250,000
Exec. Director: Patti Jo Baber
Historical Note
ALL is dedicated to enhancing the profession of lobbying throughout the United States. ALL helps its members to develop their professional skills, heighten their knowledge of the issues that affect them, and increase their exposure to the elected officials involved in public policy decisions. ALL also serves to inform the public about the substantive role of the lobbyist in the American governmental process. Membership: $175/year (regular), $85/year (government).
Publications:
ALL Directory. a. adv.
ALL News. 10/year. adv.
Meetings/Conferences:

American League of Professional Baseball Clubs (1900)

350 Park Ave.
New York, NY 10022
Tel: (212)339-7600   *Fax:* (212)593-7138
Members: 14 clubs
Staff: 9
Annual Budget: $5-10,000,000
President: Gene Budig
Publications:
American League Redbook. a.
Meetings/Conferences:
Annual Meetings: December

American Leather Chemists Ass'n (1903)
Tanners Building, P.O. Box 210014
University of Cincinnati
Cincinnati, OH 45221-0014
Tel: (513)556-1197   *Fax:* (513)556-2377
E-Mail: alca@leatherchemists.org
Web Site: http://www.leatherchemists.org
Members: 710 individuals
Staff: 5
Annual Budget: $50-100,000
Exec. Secretary: Loretta Anderson
Secretary/Treasurer: Kadir Donmez
Historical Note
Founded in 1903 and incorporated in New Jersey in 1937. Member of the Internat'l Union of Leather Chemists Societies. The association advances the knowledge of science and engineering as it applies to leather and leather products industries. Membership: $98/year.
Publications:
Journal of the American Leather Chemists Association. m. adv.
Meetings/Conferences:
Annual Meetings: June/350-400
1999 – Acme, MI(Grand Traverse Resort)/June 13-17/375

American Legal Studies Ass'n (1975)
341 Cushing
Northeastern University
Boston, MA 02115
Tel: (617)373-5211   *Fax:* (617)373-4691
E-Mail: lbuckle@lynx.neu.edu
Members: 429 individuals
Annual Budget: $10-25,000
Exec. Director: Suzann Thomas-Buckle
Historical Note
Members are professionals and institutions interested in the critical and interdisciplinary study of law and legal institutions. Membership: $32/year (individual).
Publications:
Legal Studies Forum: An Interdisciplinary Journal. q.
Transformations Newsletter. irreg.

American Legend Cooperative (1985)
P.O. Box 58308
Seattle, WA 98138
Tel: (425)251-3200
Members: 800 individuals
Staff: 5
Annual Budget: $1-2,000,000
C.E.O.: Edward Brenen
Historical Note
Formed in 1985 by a merger of the Great Lakes Mink Ass'n and the Emba Mink Breeders Ass'n (1942). ALC is producer-owned and promotes ranch-raised mink and fox fur. Membership: 2% of gross sales/year.
Publications:
American Legend Newsletter. m.
Meetings/Conferences:
Semi-Annual Meetings: Winter and Spring

American Library Ass'n (1876)
50 E. Huron St.
Chicago, IL 60611-2795
Tel: (312)280-3215   *Fax:* (312)944-3897
Members: 55,000 individuals
Staff: 265
Annual Budget: $25-50,000,000
Exec. Director: William R. Gordon
Director, Conference Services: Diedre Irwin Ross
Deputy Exec. Director: Mark Knoblauch
Assoc. Exec. Director, Member Programs/Services: Mary Ghikas
Historical Note
An educational association of U.S. libraries, librarians and library supporters, the ALA represents all types of libraries – state, public, school, academic and special libraries serving persons in government, commerce, armed services, hospitals, prisons and other institutions. ALA has 11 membership units (divisions) focusing on specific types of libraries or library services: American Ass'n of School Librarians, American Library Trustee Ass'n, Ass'n for Library Collections and Technical Services, Ass'n for Library Service to Children, Ass'n of College and Research Libraries, Ass'n of Specialized and Cooperative Library Agencies, Library Administration and Management Ass'n, Library Information and Technology Ass'n, Public Library Ass'n, Reference and Adult Services Division, and Young Adult Library Services Ass'n (see separate listings). ALA also counts 57 independent library associations in states, regions and territories of the U.S. as chapters. Twenty-two independent national and international organizations with purposes similar to the ALA are affiliates. Maintains a Washington, DC office. The annual budget of approximately $30 million. Membership: $21-85/year.
Publications:
ALA Washington Newsletter. 12/year.
American Libraries. 11/year. adv.
Booklist. semi-m. adv.
Choice. 11/year. adv.
College and Research Libraries. bi-m. adv.

College and Research Libraries News. 11/year. adv.
Documents to the People. bi-m. adv.
Information Technology and Libraries. q. adv.
Journal of Youth Services in Libraries. q. adv.
Library Personnel News. q.
Library Resources and Technical Services. q. adv.
Library Technology Reports. bi-m.
Newsletter on Intellectual Freedom. bi-m.
R Q. q. adv.
School Library Media Quarterly. q. adv.
Meetings/Conferences:
Semi-Annual Meetings: Winter and Summer
1999 – Philadelphia, PA/Jan. 22-28
1999 – New Orleans, LA/June 24-July 1
2000 – Chicago, IL/July 6-13

American Library Trustee Ass'n (1961)
50 East Huron St.
Chicago, IL 60611
Tel: (312)280-2161   *Fax:* (312)280-3257
Members: 1,750 individuals
Staff: 3
Annual Budget: $100-250,000
Contact: Alissa Hawkins
Historical Note
Originally founded in 1890 as a section of the American Library Ass'n, became a division of the ALA in 1961. Membership is restricted to ALA members. Membership: $50/year (individual).
Publications:
The Trustee Voice. q.
Meetings/Conferences:
Annual Meetings: Summer/250

American Licensed Practical Nurses Ass'n (1984)
1090 Vermont Ave., N.W., Suite 800
Washington, DC 20005-4905
Tel: (202)682-9000   *Fax:* (202)682-0168
Members: 5,000 individuals
Staff: 5
Annual Budget: $250-500,000
Exec. Director and General Counsel: Paul M. Tendler
Historical Note
A professional association of licensed practical/vocational nurses. Membership: $50/year (individual).
Publications:
ALPNA Newsletter. q.
Meetings/Conferences:

American Lighting Ass'n (1945)
2050 Stemmons Freeway, Suite 10046
P.O. Box 420288
Dallas, TX 75342-0288
Tel: (214)698-9898   *Fax:* (214)698-9899
Toll Free: (800)605 - 4448
Web Site: http://americanlightingassoc.com
Members: 1,100 firms
Staff: 8
Annual Budget: $1-2,000,000
President: Richard D. Upton
V. President, PR/Communications: Larry Lauck
Director, Meetings/Conventions: Beth Grandel
Director, Finance: Stan Thomas
V. President, Membership: Eric Jacobson
Historical Note
Members are manufacturers of lighting products, components, and accessories, manufacturers representatives, showrooms and distributors. Formerly (1989) American Home Lighting Institute. Membership: $325-$12,500 (organization/company).
Publications:
Light Up Your Kitchen & Bath.
Light Up Your Landscape.
Lighting Your Life.
Lightrays. bi-m.
Membership Directory. a. adv.
Meetings/Conferences:
Annual Meetings: Fall/550-600
1999 – Palm Springs, CA(Stouffer Esmeralda)/Sept. 25-28
2000 – Washington, DC(Omni Shoreham)/Oct. 13-16/600

American Literary Translators Ass'n (1978)
Univ. of Texas-Dallas
Box 830688, MC-35
Richardson, TX 75083-0688
Tel: (972)883-2093   *Fax:* (972)883-6303
E-Mail: ert@utdallas.edu
Members: 850 individuals
Staff: 5
Annual Budget: $10-25,000
Exec. Director: Eileen Tollett, Ph.D.
Historical Note
Members are translators into English of books in literature and the humanities. Maintains the Translation Clearinghouse and Translation Library. Membership fee varies, based on type.
Publications:
ALTA Newsletter. 3-4/year.
Translation Review. 3/year. adv.
Meetings/Conferences:
Annual Meetings: December/150

American Lithotripsy Soc. (1987)
70 Walnut St.
Wellesley Hills, MA 02481-2175
Tel: (781)239-8203   *Fax:* (781)239-7553
E-Mail: info@lithotripsy.org
Web Site: http://www.lithotripsy.org
Members: 900 individuals, 20 companies
Staff: 5
Annual Budget: $250-500,000
Exec. Director: Wesley E. Harrington, CAE

Historical Note
ALS was established to develop criteria for quality assurance and review, to validate and credential ESWL sites for training, establish training criteria, to provide support through data and experience to members for influencing third party reimbursers, to review and disseminate information on emerging ESWL technologies, to develop cost comparison data, establish liaison with related professional organizations, and to create a forum for the exchange of views regarding renal and billiary lithotripsy. Membership: $165/year (physician); $50/year (allied health care professional).

Publications:
Newsletter of the American Lithotripsy Soc. q.

Meetings/Conferences:
Annual Meetings: Spring/300
1999 – Ft. Lauderdale, FL(Hyatt Regency Pier 66)/March 11-14
2000 – San Antonio, TX(Hyatt Regency Hill Country)/March 16-19
2001 – Charleston, SC(Charleston Place Hotel)/March 10-13/375

American Littoral Soc. (1961)
Sandy Hook, Bldg. 18
Highlands, NJ 07732
Tel: (732)291-0055   *Fax:* (732)872-8041
Members: 9,500 individuals
Staff: 11000
Annual Budget: $100-250,000
Exec. Director: D.W. Bennett

Historical Note
Founded in 1961 at the Sandy Hook Marine Laboratory and incorporated in 1962 in New Jersey. Promotes the study and conservation of the coastal zone habitat. Membership: $25/year (regular).

Publications:
Coastal Reporter. semi-a.
Underwater Naturalist. q. adv.

Meetings/Conferences:
Annual Meetings: Fall
1999 – Chicoteaque, VA

American Logistics Ass'n (1920)
1133 15th St., N.W., Suite 640
Washington, DC 20005-2710
Tel: (202)466-2520   *Fax:* (202)296-4419
Members: 2,700 individuals, 600 companies
Staff: 12
Annual Budget: $2-5,000,000
President: Robert F. Swarts
V. President, Legislative Affairs: Robert W. Gaskin
President, Government Rels. Exch Affairs: Alan J. Burton
President, Government Relations: Alan Nissalke
V. President, MWR Affairs: Richard Tessier
V. President, Administration/Controller: Maurice Branch

Historical Note
A trade association of companies and individuals involved in marketing to the military - commissaries, exchanges, clubs, snack bars, ship's stores, mess halls, and service stations. Formerly the Quartermaster Ass'n and (1972) Defense Supply Ass'n. Membership: $75/year (individual); $1,995/year (company).

Publications:
Executive Briefing Newsletter. m.
Worldwide Directory. a. adv.

Meetings/Conferences:
Annual Meetings: Fall
1999 – Oct. 13

American Loudspeaker Manufacturers Ass'n (1965)
39 Ames Road
Groton, MA 01450-1963
Tel: (978)448-5658   *Fax:* (978)448-6851
E-Mail: cbous@ma.ultranet.com
Web Site: http://www.alma.org
Members: 70 companies
Staff: 1
Annual Budget: $50-100,000
Exec. Director: Carol Bousquet

Historical Note
Membership: $500/year.

Publications:
Buyers Guide. a. adv.
Manuals and Reports.
Statistical Program. q.

Meetings/Conferences:
Semi-Annual Meetings: Winter and Spring
1999 – Las Vegas, NV
1999 – Nashville, TN(Opryland)

American Luggage Dealers Ass'n (1970)
610 Anacapa St., Suite G
Santa Barbara, CA 93101
Tel: (805)966-6909   *Fax:* (805)966-5710
E-Mail: mjalda@aol.com
Web Site: http://www.luggagedealers.com
Members: 60 companies
Staff: 2
Annual Budget: $1-2,000,000
Exec. Director: Marion L. Jones

Historical Note
Formed to develop a progressive merchandise program such as publication of catalogs and specific merchandise opportunities for independent luggage retailers. Membership: $400/year (store); $100/year (additional store location).

Publications:
Fall Flyer. a.
Giftables Catalog. a.
Membership Roster. a.
Newsletter. q.
Spring Flyer. a.

Meetings/Conferences:
1999 – Orlando, FL/Feb. 16-17

American Lung Ass'n (1904)
1740 Broadway, 14th Floor
New York, NY 10019-4374
Tel: (212)315-8700   *Fax:* (212)315-6455
Web Site: http://www.lungusa.org
Members: 10,000 individuals, 57 constituent & 53 addiliate orgs
Staff: 150
Annual Budget: $10-25,000,000
C.E.O.: John R. Garrison

Historical Note
Established as the Nat'l Ass'n for the Study and Prevention of Tuberculosis, it became the Nat'l Tuberculosis Ass'n in 1918, the Nat'l Tuberculosis and Respiratory Disease Ass'n in 1968 and assumed its present name in 1973. The American Thoracic Soc. is the ALA's medical section. A federation of state and local associations, ALA is dedicated to the control and prevention of all lung diseases and some of their related causes, including smoking, air pollution and occupational lung hazards. Has an annual budget of $20 million.

Publications:
American Journal of Respiratory Cell and Molecular Biology. m. adv.
American Review of Respiratory Disease. m. adv.

Meetings/Conferences:
Annual Meetings: May
1999 – San Diego, CA/April 22-29

American Machine Tool Distributors Ass'n (1925)
1445 Research Blvd., Suite 450
Rockville, MD 20850
Tel: (301)738-1200   *Fax:* (301)738-9499
Toll Free: (800)818 - 2683
E-Mail: jallen@AMTDA.org
Web Site: http://www.amtda.org
Members: 475 companies
Staff: 17
Annual Budget: $2-5,000,000
President: Ralph J. Nappi, CAE
Director, Trade Shows: Gary Schiffres
Director, Finance and Administration: Pamela A. Obral
Senior Director, Member Resources: Gregory M. Safko, CAE
Director, Marketing Data: Gregory DuRoss

Historical Note
Founded in 1925 in Cincinnati by 22 charter distributors of machine tools.

Publications:
AMTDA Membership Directory. a.
Tool Talk. m.

Meetings/Conferences:
Annual Meetings: Spring
1999 – Orlando, FL(Walt Disney World Swan)/April 11-14

American Maine-Anjou Ass'n (1969)
760 Livestock Exchange Bldg.
Kansas City, MO 64102
Tel: (816)474-9555   *Fax:* (816)474-9556
E-Mail: anjou@ami.com
Web Site: http://www.maine-anjou.org
Members: 950 individuals
Staff: 5
Annual Budget: $250-500,000
Exec. V. President: John A. Boddicker
Director, Special Events: Susan Bomar

Historical Note
Formerly (1971) the Maine-Anjou Soc. and (1975) the Internat'l Maine-Anjou Ass'n. Members are breeders and fanciers of Maine-Anjou Beef Cattle. Member of the Nat'l Cattlemen's Ass'n. Membership: $35/year.

Publications:
American Maine-Anjou Voice. bi-m. adv.

Meetings/Conferences:

American Malacological Union (1931)
Dept. of Natural Science/Mathematics
Coastal GA. Comm. Coll., 3700 Altama Ave
Brunswick, GA 31520
Tel: (912)262-3089
Toll Free: (912)264 - 7280
Members: 600 individuals
Staff: 1
Annual Budget: $10-25,000
Treasurer: Dr. Eugene Keferl

Historical Note
An international society of individuals and organizations who are interested in the study of mollusks. Membership: $35/year (regular); $45/year (organization); $15/year (student).

Publications:
Bulletin. semi-a.
Newsletter. 3/year.

Meetings/Conferences:
Annual Meetings: Summer

American Malting Barley Ass'n (1945)
740N. Plankinton Ave., Suite 830
Milwaukee, WI 53203-2403
Tel: (414)272-4640   *Fax:* (414)272-9527
Web Site: http://www.ambainc.org
Members: 10 companies
Staff: 3
Annual Budget: $1-2,000,000
President: Michael P. Davis

Historical Note
Founded as the Midwest Barley Improvement Ass'n, it became the Malting Barley Improvement Ass'n in 1954 and assumed its present

---

name in 1982. Absorbed Malt Research Institute. Members are maltsters and brewers.

Publications:
Proceedings of Barley Improvement Conference. bien.
Proceedings Red River Valley Barley Day. bien.

Meetings/Conferences:
Annual Meetings: Usually December in Milwaukee, WI

American Managed Behavioral Healthcare Ass'n (1994)
700 13th St., N.W., Suite 950
Washington, DC 20005
Tel: (202)434-4565   *Fax:* (202)434-4564
Web Site: http://www.ambha.org
Members: 17 organizations
Staff: 2
Annual Budget: $250-500,000
Exec. Director: Pamela Greenberg, M.P.P.

Historical Note
AMBHA members are national and regional organizations managing the cost and quality of mental health and substance abuse services for 90 million subscribers. Contracting with HMOs or other health care delivery systems, AMBHA member organizations offer individualized care management, specialty networks, a continuum of care, quality management programs, consumer orientations and innovations in behavioral health care delivery. Membership:$5,000-$40,000/year (company).

Publications:
AMBHA Executive Director's Report. irreg.

Meetings/Conferences:
Annual Meetings: Always in association with the Institute for Behavioral Healthcare. Always May and September.

American Managed Care and Review Ass'n (1970)
Historical Note
Merged with Group Health Ass'n of America in 1995.

American Managed Care Pharmacy Ass'n (1975)
Historical Note
Became the Pharmaceutical Care Management Ass'n in 1996.

American Management Ass'n Internat'l (1923)
1601 Broadway
New York, NY 10019-7420
Tel: (212)586-8100   *Fax:* (212)903-8168
Toll Free: (800)262 - 9699
Web Site: http://www.amanet.org
Members: 4,464 corporate
Staff: 880
Annual Budget: $5-10,000,000
President & C.E.O.: George B. Weathersby
Corp. V. President and C.F.O.: Vivianna Guzman

Historical Note
Merger (1973) of the American Management Ass'n (1923), the American Foundation for Management Research (1960), the Internat'l Management Ass'n (1956), the Presidents Ass'n (1961) and the Soc. for Advancement of Management (1912) devoted to all types of management education. Maintains offices in Atlanta, GA; Watertown, MA; Chicago, IL; Hamilton, NY; Leawood, KS; New York, NY; San Francisco, CA; Saranac Lake, NY; and Washington, DC. Also maintains Internat'l offices and affiliated centers. AMA provides educational forums worldwide where members and their colleagues learn business skills and explore best practices of world-class organizations through interaction with each other and expert faculty practitioners.

Publications:
Compensation & Benefits Review. bi-m.
H R Focus. m.
Management Review. m. adv.
Organizational Dynamics. q.
The Take-Charge Assistant. m.

Meetings/Conferences:
1999 – Anaheim, CA/April 17-21

American Maritime Ass'n (1961)
380 Madison Ave., Suite 17
New York, NY 10017-2513
Tel: (212)557-9575   *Fax:* (212)557-9580
Members: 28 companies
Staff: 1
Annual Budget: $100-250,000
Administrator: Constance M. Oliva

Historical Note
An employer association created for the sole purpose of collective bargaining with the off-shore maritime unions.

Meetings/Conferences:
Annual Meetings: June, in New York City

American Maritime Congress (1977)
1300 I St., N.W., Suite 250-W
Washington, DC 20005
Tel: (202)842-4900   *Fax:* (202)842-3492
Staff: 8
Exec. Director: Gloria Cataneo Tosi
Director, Public Affairs: Michael D. Mason
Director of Policy and Planning: Thomas W. Scoville

Historical Note
AMC members are U.S. ship operating companies having contracts with the Nat'l Marine Engineers' Beneficial Ass'n, a maritime union.

Publications:
AMC Washington Letter. w.

American Marketing Ass'n (1937)
250 South Wacker Dr., Suite 200
Chicago, IL 60606-5819
Tel: (312)648-0536   *Fax:* (312)993-7542
Toll Free: (800)262 - 1150

E-Mail: info@ama.orf
Web Site: http://www.ama.org
Members: 45,000 individuals
Staff: 75
Annual Budget: $5-10,000,000
C.O.O.: Celeste Girolami
Director, Public Relations: Jamie Born
Senior Director, Profesional Development and Member Services:
  Patricia Goodridge
C.O.O. and C.F.O.: Les Girolami
Director, Membership Marketing: Nancy Costopoulos

Historical Note
*Formerly (1915) Nat'l Ass'n of Teachers of Advertising; (1926)
Nat'l Ass'n of Teachers of Marketing & Advertising; (1932) Nat'l
Ass'n of Teachers of Marketing; (1937) merged with American
Marketing Soc. to form the American Marketing Ass'n. The
Academy of Health Service Marketing was absorbed by the AMA in
1994. Has an annual budget over $7 million. No annual
convention or convocation, however hold a multiplicity of national
conferences, seminars and forums throughout the year.
Membership: $145/year (introductory); $25/year (student).*

Publications:
Journal of Health Care Marketing. q. adv.
Journal of International Marketing. semi-a.
Journal of Marketing. q. adv.
Journal of Marketing Research. q. adv.
Journal of Public Policy and Marketing. semi-a.
Marketing Educator. q. adv.
Marketing Health Services. q. adv.
Marketing Management. q. adv.
Marketing News. q. adv.
Marketing News (Collegiate Edition). 9/year. adv.
Marketing News (Professional Edition). 26/year. adv.
Marketing Research. q. adv.
Services Marketing Today. bi-m.

American Massage Therapy Ass'n *(1943)*
820 Davis St., Suite 100
Evanston, IL   60201-4444
Tel: (847)864-0123   *Fax:* (847)864-1178
E-Mail: info@inet.amtamassage.org
Web Site: http://www.amtamassage.org
Members: 28,000 individuals
Staff: 40
Annual Budget: $5-10,000,000
Exec. Director: Marlys Sperger
Director of Marketing and Communications: Elizabeth Lucas
Director of Government and Chapter Relations: Mark Tyle
Director of Meetings and Education: Karla Kreblein
Manager, Education Programs: Mary Beth Calverley
Director, Finance & Administration: Daniel Hoort
Director of Membership: Tanya Codulun

Historical Note
*Formerly (1983) American Massage and Therapy Ass'n. Provides
professional support to massage therapists. Membership fee varies.*

Publications:
AMTA Membership Registry. a.
Hand's On. q.
Massage Therapy Journal. q. adv.

Meetings/Conferences:
1999 – San Antonio, TX(Hilton)/Oct. 13-17
2000 – Phoenix, AZ(Crowne Plaza)

American Match Council *(1992)*
207 Peterborough St.
P.O. Box 457
Jaffrey, NH   03452-0457
Toll Free: (800)366 - 2824
Members: 5 match manufacturers
Staff: 1
Chairman: Mark Bean

Publications:
Match Points Newsletter. q.

American Mathematical Ass'n of Two Year Colleges *(1974)*
5983 Macon Cove
Memphis, TN   38134
Tel: (901)383-4643   *Fax:* (901)383-4651
E-Mail: amatyc@stim.tec.tn.us
Members: 3,000 individuals, 150 institutions
Annual Budget: $250-500,000
Exec. Assistant: Cheryl Cleaves
Publications Director: Carol Stoy

Historical Note
*A member of the Conference Board of the Mathematical Sciences
and the Council of Scientific Society Presidents, AMATYC is the
only national association exclusively devoted to improving
mathematical education in the first two years of college. AMATYC
members are teachers of mathematics and computer science in two-
year colleges. Membership: $50/year (individual); $250/year
(institution).*

Publications:
AMATYC News. 5/year.
AMATYC Review. semi-a.

Meetings/Conferences:
Annual Meetings: October-November
1999 – Pittsburg, PA(Convention Center)/Nov. 17-21

American Mathematical Soc. *(1888)*
P.O. Box 6248
Providence, RI   02940-6248
Tel: (401)455-4150   *Fax:* (401)455-4004
Toll Free: (800)321 - 4267
E-Mail: ams@ams.org
Web Site: http://www.ams.org
Members: 28,500 individuals, 485 institutions
Staff: 250
Annual Budget: $10-25,000,000
Exec. Director: John H. Ewing

Director of Marketing: Paul G. Chambers
Director of Meetings: H. Hope Daly
Assoc. Exec. Director, Finance/Administration: Gary G. Brownell
Membership and Customer Services Manager: Carol-Ann
  Blackwood

Historical Note
*Organized in New York City on November 24, 1888 by six
members of the mathematics department of Columbia University as
the New York Mathematical Soc. Became the American
Mathematical Soc. in 1894. Incorporated in the District of
Columbia in 1923. Has an annual budget of approximately $15.2
million. Membership: $132/year.*

Publications:
Abstracts of the AMS. bi-m.
Assistantships and Fellowships in the Mathematical Sciences.
  a.
Bulletin of the AMS. q.
Current Mathematical Publications. tri-w.
Employment Information in the Mathematical Sciences. bi-m.
Journal of the AMS. q.
Mathematical Reviews. m. adv.
Mathematics of Computation. q. adv.
Memoirs of the American Mathematical Society. bi-m.
Notices of the AMS. 10/year. adv.
Proceedings of the AMS. m.
Proceedings of the Steklov Institute of Mathematics. q.
Quarterly of Applied Mathematics.
St. Petersburg Mathemat.
Sugaku Expositions. semi-a.
Theory of Probability and Mathematical Statistics. 2/year.
Transactions of the AMS. m.
Transactions of the Moscow Mathematical Society. a.

Meetings/Conferences:
Annual Meetings: With The Mathematical Ass'n of
  America/Winter/2,800
1999 – San Antonio, TX(Convention Center)/Jan. 13-16

American Meat Institute *(1906)*
1700 N. Moore Street
Suite 1600
Arlington, VA   22209
Tel: (703)841-2400   *Fax:* (703)527-0938
Web Site: http://www.meatami.org
Members: 900 companies
Staff: 40
Annual Budget: $5-10,000,000
President & CEO: J. Patrick Boyle
Senior V. President, Legislative & Public Affairs: Sara Lilygren
V.P., Regulatory/Legislative Affairs: Karen Mogan
V. President, Legislative Affairs: Mike Brown
V. Pres, Education & Convention Services: Patricia L. Pines
Sr. VP, Admin, Convention & Member Svcs: Ronald L. Nunnery
Senior V. President, Regulatory Affairs: James H. Hodges
V. Preisdent, Internat'l Trade: Leonard W. Condon
Director, MIS: Pat T. Schuck

Historical Note
*The national trade organization of the meat and poultry packing
and processing industry. Founded in 1906 as the American Meat
Packers Ass'n, it became the Institute of American Meat Packers in
1919 and the American Meat Institute in 1940. Founded in 1944
as its research and education arm, the American Meat Institute
Foundation was reestablished in 1992. AMI merged with the
National Independent Meat Packers Association in 1982 and began
managing the U.S. Hide Skin and Leather Association in 1990. The
Nat'l Meat Canners Ass'n and the Western Hemisphere Ass'n of
Meat Marketers became affiliated with AMI in 1992. Connected
with the American Meat Institute Political Action Committee. Has
an annual budget of approximately $8 million.*

Publications:
A Guide to Practical Ergonomics. a.
AMI Newsletter. bi-w.
Crisis Manual. a.
Markets & Marketing Newsletter. w.
Meat Facts. a.
Recall Manual. a.

Meetings/Conferences:
1999 – Chicago, IL(McCormick Place)/Oct. 28-31/15000

American Meat Science Ass'n *(1948)*
9140 Ward Pkwy.
Suite 200
Kansas City, MO   64114
Tel: (816)444-3500   *Fax:* (816)444-0330
E-Mail: info@meatscience.org
Web Site: www.meatscience.org
Members: 1,066 individuals
Staff: 6
Annual Budget: $10-25,000
Exec. Director: Thomas Powell

Historical Note
*Established as the Reciprocal Meat Conference in 1948 and became
the American Meat Science Ass'n in 1964. Promotes education and
research in meat and related subjects. Membership: $100/year
(professional); $45/year (student).*

Publications:
AMSA Newsletter. q.
Directory of Members. a.
Proceedings of the Reciprocal Meat Conference. a.

Meetings/Conferences:
Annual Meetings: June, in a university environment
1999 – Stillwater, OK/June 20-23/500
2000 – Columbus, OH(OH State Univ.)/June 18-21/600
2001 – Indianapolis, IN(Convention Center)
2002 – East Lansing, MI(MI State Univ.)

American Medallic Sculpture Ass'n *(1982)*
56 North Plank Road, Suite 1-685
Newburgh, NY   12550
Tel: (914)634-4751
E-Mail: amsa@queenbee.net

Web Site: http://amsa.queenbee.net
Members: 365 individuals
Staff: 1
Annual Budget: $10-25,000
President: Anne S. Pollack

Historical Note
*Organized in February, 1982 in New York City by a group of
medallic artists to promote improvement in the art of the medal.
U.S. member of the Federation Internationale de la Medaille.
Sponsors exhibitions, symposia, and other events. Membership:
$35/year.*

Publications:
Medallic Sculpture. semi-a.
Members Exchange. bi-m.

Meetings/Conferences:
Semi-annual exhibitions: Fall and Spring

American Medical Ass'n *(1847)*
515 N. State St.
Chicago, IL   60610-4320
Tel: (312)464-5000   *Fax:* (312)464-4184
Web Site: http://www.ama-assn.org
Members: 287,338 individuals
Staff: 1200
Annual Budget: Over $100,000,000
V. President, Chief Information Officer: Robert A. Musacchio
V. President, Communications: Lewis S.W. Crampton
Director of Communications: Craig May
V. President, Federal Relations: Michael A. Murray
V. President, Corporate Services: Robert E. Hobart
V. President, Finance: William T. Zimmerman
V. President, Membership Division: Peter Lauer
Director, Strategic Memb. Prod.: Joy Mizell Cohn
Manager, Federation Development: David M. Cloud
Director, Membership Marketing: Renee Schleicher

Historical Note
*Established in Philadelphia in 1847 and incorporated in Illinois in
1897. Principal spokesman for the U.S. medical profession with
about 2,000 local and regional medical societies. AMA and its
affiliates support numerous political action committees throughout
the country, including the American Medical PAC.In 1994, AMA
absorbed the American Ass'n of Senior Physicians. Has an annual
budget of approximately $200 million. Membership: $420/year.*

Publications:
American Medical News. w. adv.
Archives of Dermatology. m. adv.
Archives of Family Medicine.
Archives of General Psychiatry. m. adv.
Archives of Internal Medicine. m. adv.
Archives of Neurology. m. adv.
Archives of Ophthalmology. m. adv.
Archives of Otolaryngology. m. adv.
Archives of Pediatric and Adolescent Medicine. m. adv.
Archives of Surgery. m. adv.
Journal of the American Medical Ass'n. w. adv.

Meetings/Conferences:
Semi-Annual Meetings: June and December
1999 – Chicago, IL(Hilton)/June 20-24

American Medical Directors Ass'n *(1976)*
10480 Little Patuxent Pkwy., Suite 760
Columbia, MD   21044-3506
Tel: (410)740-9743   *Fax:* (410)740-4572
Web Site: http://www.amda.com
Members: 6,900 individuals
Staff: 13
Annual Budget: $1-2,000,000
Exec. Director: Lorraine Tarnove
Dir., Federal Affairs: Susan Petty
Director of Education: Mary Logan
Director, Administration and Finance: J.Ann Beck
Director of Clinical Affairs: Cindy Hock

Historical Note
*Members are physicians who provide care to patients in long term
care facilities either as medical director or attending physician.
Awards the Certified Medical Director (CMD) designation.
Membership: $150/year (individual).*

Publications:
AMDA Reports Newsletter. 6/year.
Nursing Home Medicine: The Annals of Long Term Care.
  10/yr. adv.

Meetings/Conferences:
1999 – Orlando, FL(Walt Disney Dolphin)/March 4-7
2000 – San Francisco, CA(Marriott)/March 16-19

American Medical Electroencephalographic Ass'n *(1964)*
850 Elm Grove Rd.
Elm Grove, WI   53122
Tel: (414)784-3435   *Fax:* (414)782-8788
Members: 700 individuals
Staff: 4
Annual Budget: $100-250,000
Exec. Secretary: Michael Herzog

Historical Note
Membership: $175/year.

Publications:
Clinical EEG Journal. q.

Meetings/Conferences:
Annual Meetings: Fall

American Medical Group Ass'n *(1949)*
1422 Duke St.
Alexandria, VA   22314-3430
Tel: (703)838-0033   *Fax:* (703)548-1890
Web Site: www.amga.org
Members: 260 clinics
Staff: 30
Annual Budget: $1-2,000,000

C.E.O.: Donald W. Fisher, Ph.D., CAE
Editor, Corporate Communications: Laura Johnson
V. President of Political Affairs & Public Policy: Brent V. Miller
Historical Note
Formerly (1974) American Ass'n of Medical Clinics and (1996) American Group Practice Ass'n. AGPA merged with the Unified Medical Group Ass'n to form the American Medical Group Ass'n in 1996. Members are group practice medical clinics. Sponsors and supports the Group Practice Ass'n Political Action Committee (GROUPPAC).
Publications:
Directory. a.
Group Practice Journal. bi-m. adv.
Meetings/Conferences:
Annual Meetings: September/600

American Medical Informatics Ass'n *(1981)*
4915 St. Elmo Ave., Suite 401
Bethesda, MD   20814
Tel: (301)657-1291   *Fax:* (301)657-1296
E-Mail: mail@mail.amia.org
Web Site: http://www.amia.org
Members: 3,700 individuals
Staff: 3
Annual Budget: $1-2,000,000
Exec. Director: Dennis Reynolds
Director of Membership: Karen E. Greenwood
Meetings Manager: Pasha Cohen
Director of Education: Jeffrey Williamson
Asst. Exec. Director: Janice Kennedy
Director, Publications: Andria Brummitt
Historical Note
Formerly (1991) American Ass'n for Medical Systems and Informatics. The result of a merger between the Soc. for Advanced Medical Systems (1969) and the Soc. for Computer Medicine (1970) in 1981. Members are individuals interested in the application of information science and computer technology to all aspects of medical and health care, teaching and research. A member society of the American Institute for Medical and Biological Engineering. Membership: $175/year (individual), $1500-$10000/year (organization/company), $30/year (student).
Publications:
Abstracts of Spring Congress. a.
AMIA News Newsletter. q. adv.
Annual Membership Directory & Yearbook. a. adv.
JAMIA Journal. bi-m.
Proceedings of Symposium on Computer Applications in Medical Care. a.
Meetings/Conferences:
Annual Meetings: Spring Congress and Fall Symposium.
1999 – Washington, DC(Sheraton Washington)/Nov. 4-7
2000 – Washington, DC(Sheraton Washington)/Nov. 4-8
2001 – Washington, DC(Sheraton Washington)/Nov. 3-7
2002 – San Antonio, TX/Nov. 9-13

American Medical Peer Review Ass'n *(1973)*
Historical Note
Name changed to American Health Quality Ass'n in 1996.

American Medical Publishers' Ass'n *(1961)*
14 Fort Hill Road
Huntington, NY   11743
Tel: (516)423-0075   *Fax:* (516)423-0075
E-Mail: jillrudansky-ampa@msn.com
Web Site: http://www.am-pa.com
Members: 60 companies
Staff: 1
Annual Budget: $50-100,000
Exec. Director: Jill Rudansky
Historical Note
Formerly (1974) Ass'n of American Medical Book Publishers. Membership: $250-1,000/year, based on member's business.
Publications:
AMPA Newsletter. q. adv.
Directory. bien.
Meetings/Conferences:
Semi-annual Meetings: Philadelphia/February & March
1999 – Philadelphia, PA(Four Seasons)/Feb. 28-March 2

American Medical Rehabilitation Providers Ass'n *(1969)*
1606 20th St., N.W., 3rd Floor
Washington, DC   20009
Tel: (202)265-4404   *Fax:* (202)833-9168
Toll Free: (888)346 - 4624
Members: 740 facilities
Staff: 21
Annual Budget: $1-2,000,000
President and C.E.O.: Danny O'Malley
Director of Communications: Janet Estover
Director, Government Relations and General Counsel: Carolyn Zollar
Comptroller: John B. Henderson, CPA
V. President Member Services & Products: Joanne Dunne
V. President Public Policy: Bob Jarboe
Historical Note
Canadian and U.S. rehabilitation centers. Formed in 1969 by a merger of the Ass'n of Rehabilitation Centers (founded in 1952 as the Conference of Rehabilitation Centers and Facilities) and the Nat'l Ass'n of Sheltered Workshops and Homebound Programs (founded in 1954). Formerly (1975) Internat'l Ass'n of Rehabilitation Facilities, (1979) Ass'n of Rehabilitation Facilities, and (1994) Nat'l Ass'n of Rehabilitation Facilities. Represents medical, residential and vocational rehabilitation facilities.
Publications:
Rehab Report. m.
The Advocate. m.
Meetings/Conferences:
1999 – New Orleans, LA

American Medical Soc. for Sports Medicine *(1992)*
11639 Earnshaw St.
Overland Park, KS   66210-2763
Tel: (913)327-1415
Web Site: http://www.sportsmed.upnc.edu/amssn/
Members: 650 individuals
Staff: 2
Exec. Director: Jody Gold
Historical Note
AMSSM provides support and continuing educations specific to primary care, non-surgical spots medicine physicians. Membership: $275/year (physicians); $225 (fellows).
Meetings/Conferences:
1999 – Hilton Head, SC/April 24-28

American Medical Student Ass'n *(1950)*
1902 Association Drive
Reston, VA   20191
Tel: (703)620-6600   *Fax:* (703)620-5873
Toll Free: (800)767 - 2266
E-Mail: amsa@www.amsa.org
Web Site: http://www.amsa.org
Members: 30,000 individuals
Staff: 35
Annual Budget: $1-2,000,000
Exec. Director: Paul R. Wright
Historical Note
Founded as the Student American Medical Ass'n, it assumed its present name in 1975. Represents physicians-in-training from premedical students to residents. Membership: $55/5 years.
Publications:
New Physician. 9/year. adv.
Meetings/Conferences:
Annual Meetings: March
1999 – Chicago, IL(Palmer House Hilton)/March 10-14
2000 – Washington, DC(Hyatt Regency Crystal City)/March 15-19

American Medical Technologists *(1939)*
710 Higgins Road
Park Ridge, IL   60068
Tel: (847)823-5169   *Fax:* (847)823-0458
Toll Free: (800)275 - 1268
Members: 26,000 individuals
Staff: 20
Annual Budget: $1-2,000,000
Exec. Director: Gerard P. Boe, Ph.D.
Director, Publications and Meetings: Diane Powell
Coordinator, Member Services: Lisa Fried
Historical Note
Founded in 1939 and incorporated in New Jersey. Grants the MT (Medical Technologist), MLT (Medical Laboratory Technician), RMA (Registered Medical Assistant), RDA (Registered Dental Assistants) and RPT (Registered Phlebotomy Technician) designations. Membership: $85-115/year.
Publications:
AMT Events. 3/year. adv.
AMT Events Continuing Education Supplement. 3/year. adv.
AMT Newsletter. 3/year.
Meetings/Conferences:
Annual Meetings: June or July
1999 – Las Vegas, NV(Tropicana)
2000 – New Orleans, LA(Sheraton)
2001 – Nassau, Bahamas(Marriott)
2002 – Burlington, VT

American Medical Women's Ass'n *(1915)*
801 N. Fairfax St., Suite 400
Alexandria, VA   22314
Tel: (703)838-0500   *Fax:* (703)549-3864
E-Mail: emcgrath@amwa-doc.org
Web Site: http://www.amwa-doc.org
Members: 11,000 individuals
Staff: 22
Annual Budget: $2-5,000,000
Exec. Director: Eileen McGrath, CAE, JD
Director, Public Affairs/Government Relations: Kelly Mills
Director of Finance: Erma Logan
Director, Membership/Member Services: Germaine Ashton
Membership Director: Tangie Newborn
Historical Note
Founded November 1915 in Chicago and incorporated in Illinois in 1916 as the Medical Women's Nat'l Ass'n. Reincorporated in New York in 1924 and name changed to American Medical Women's Ass'n, Inc. in 1937. Membership restricted to women physicians, interns, residents and medical and osteopathic students. Friends of AMWA Category is open to both females and males. U.S. affiliate of the Medical Women's International Association. Membership: $225/year (physician), $80/year (resident), $50/year (associate) and $52/4 years (student).
Publications:
Journal of the American Medical Women's Association. q. adv.
What's Happening in AMWA. bi-m.
Meetings/Conferences:
Annual Meetings: November
1999 – San Fransisco, CA/Nov. 10-14

American Medical Writers Ass'n *(1940)*
9650 Rockville Pike
Bethesda, MD   20814-3998
Tel: (301)493-0003   *Fax:* (301)493-6384
E-Mail: amwa@amwa.org
Web Site: http://www.amwa.org
Members: 4,000 individuals
Staff: 2
Annual Budget: $500-1,000,000
Exec. Director: Lillian Sablack

Historical Note
Originated September 25, 1940 at Rock Island, IL as the Mississippi Valley Medical Editors' Ass'n; assumed its current name in 1948. Incorporated in Illinois in 1951. Concerned with the advancement and improvement of medical communications. Membership: $95/year (individual).
Publications:
AMWA Freelance Directory. bien.
AMWA Journal. q. adv.
AMWA Membership Directory. a.
Meetings/Conferences:
Annual Meetings: Fall
1999 – Philadelphia, PA(Marriott)/Oct. 26-Nov. 1

American Men's Studies Ass'n *(1991)*
22 East St.
Northampton, MA   01060
Tel: (413)584-8903
Members: 150 individuals
President: Sam Femiano
Historical Note
AMSA members are academics and others with an interest in the study of the male's social and historical context. Membership: $40/year (individual); $30/year (student).
Publications:
AMSA Newsletter. semi-a.
Meetings/Conferences:
1999 – Nashville, TN(Vanderbilt Univ.)/March 12-14

American Mental Health Counselors Ass'n *(1976)*
801 N. Fairfax St., Suite 304
Alexandria, VA   22314
Tel: (703)548-6002   *Fax:* (703)548-4775
Toll Free: (800)326 - 2642
E-Mail: amcha@pir.org
Web Site: http://ww.amhca.org
Members: 9,500 individuals
Staff: 6
Annual Budget: $1-2,000,000
Exec. Director: W. Mark Hamilton
Communications/Meeting Services: Erin Burnette
Director, Govt. Relations: Beth Powell
Director, Membership Information: Linda Morano
Historical Note
A division of the American Counseling Ass'n. Members are professional counselors working in a variety of community and non-school settings. Membership: $125/year (individual); $40/year (student).
Publications:
AMHCA Advocate. 8-10/year. adv.
Journal of Mental Health Counseling. q. adv.
Meetings/Conferences:
Annual Meetings: With the American Counseling Ass'n
1999 – Crystal City, VA(Doubletree)/July 22-24
2000 – Washington, DC/March 22-25

American Metal Detector Manufacturers Ass'n *(1978)*
1881 West State St.
Garland, TX   75042-6761
Tel: (972)494-6151   *Fax:* (972)494-1881
Members: 4 companies
Staff: 1
Annual Budget: under $10,000
President: Charles Garrett
Historical Note
Has no paid staff. Officers change periodically but the above will remain the address of the association.

American Meteorological Soc. *(1919)*
45 Beacon St.
Boston, MA   02108
Tel: (617)227-2425   *Fax:* (617)742-8718
Web Site: http://www.ametsoc.org
Members: 11,000 individuals, 125 corporations
Staff: 45
Annual Budget: $5-10,000,000
Exec. Director: Dr. Richard E. Hallgren
Director of Education: Ira Geer
Controller: Barry Mohan
Asst. Exec. Director: Todd Glickman
Historical Note
Founded December 29, 1919 in St. Louis and incorporated in the District of Columbia in 1920. Permanent headquarters were established in Boston in 1946 and the Society was reincorporated in Massachusetts in 1958. Certifies consulting meteorologists, and grants Seal of Approval to television and radio meteorologists. Has an annual budget of approxiamately $7 million. Membership: $30/year (individual); $400-$1500/year (organization/company).
Publications:
Bulletin of The AMS. m. adv.
Journal of Applied Meteorology. m.
Journal of Atmospheric and Oceanic Technology. semi-m.
Journal of Climate. m.
Journal of Physical Oceanography. m.
Journal of the Atmospheric Sciences. bi-m.
Meteorological and Geoastrophysical Abstracts. a.
Monthly Weather Review. m.
Weather and Forecasting. q.
Meetings/Conferences:
1999 – Dallas, TX/Jan. 10-15

American Methanol Institute *(1989)*
800 Connecticut Ave., N.W., Suite 620
Washington, DC   20006
Tel: (202)467-5050   *Fax:* (202)331-9055
E-Mail: ammethinst@aol.com
Web Site: http://www.methanol.org
Staff: 5

Annual Budget: $1-2,000,000
President and C.E.O.: John E. Lynn
Director, Communications: Gregory A. Dolan

Historical Note
AMI promotes use of methanol as an alternative fuel. Membership:
$10,000-125,000/year (company).

Publications:
Insider Report. w.

Meetings/Conferences:
1999 – Washington, DC/Feb. 4-5/200

American Microchemical Soc. *(1935)*

Historical Note
Organization inactive in 1996.

American Microscopical Soc. *(1878)*
P.O. Box 1897
Lawrence, KS   66044-1897
Tel: (785)843-1221   *Fax:* (785)843-1274
Web Site: http://www.umesci.maine.edu/ams/ams.htm
Members: 640 individuals
Staff: 1
Annual Budget: $10-25,000
Administrator: Robert Kerley

Historical Note
A professional society of microscopical biologists and microscopists established in 1878 to promote the use of the microscope in research and teaching. Membership: $36 + postage/year (individual); $75-100/year (company).

Publications:
Invertebrate Biology.

Meetings/Conferences:
Annual Meetings: January
1999 – Denver, CO/Jan. 6-10

American Mideast Business Associates *(1951)*
1137 S. Green St.
Tuckerton, NJ   08087
Tel: (609)296-4783
Members: 175 corporations
Staff: 2
Annual Budget: $500-1,000,000
President: I.F. Yusif, CAE

Historical Note
Established in New York, NY as the Egyptian American Soc. Became (1960) American Arab Ass'n for Commerce and Industry. Assumed its current name in 1987 to reflect growing membership interest in all Middle Eastern and North African countries. Members are both U.S and Arab transnationals. Provides consultation and translation services to non-members on a contract basis. Membership: $5,000/year (organization).

Publications:
Bulletin. m.

Meetings/Conferences:
Annual Meetings: Spring

American Milking Devon Ass'n *(1978)*
135 Old Bay Road
New Durham, NH   03855
Tel: (603)859-6611
Members: 85 individuals
Annual Budget: under $10,000
Secretary/Registrar: Susan Randall

Historical Note
In 1623, two heifers and a bull from north Devonshire, England, were received by a member of the Plymouth Colony. Today the breed is a dual-purpose animal adapted to survive on a low-quality, high forage diet in severe climatic conditions and provide up to 12,000 pounds of milk. AMDA members are breeders and interested individuals. Membership: $5/year.

Meetings/Conferences:
Annual Meetings: May

American Milking Shorthorn Soc. *(1920)*
Box 449
Beloit, WI   53512-0449
Tel: (608)365-3332   *Fax:* (608)365-6644
Web Site: http://www.spyder.net/cow
Members: 450 individuals
Staff: 2
Annual Budget: $100-250,000
Executive Secretary: Stuart Rowe

Historical Note
Breeders and fanciers of Milking Shorthorn dairy cattle. Formed in 1920 as the Milking Shorthorn Club within the framework of the American Shorthorn Breeders Ass'n. Adopted its present name and became incorporated as a separate association in 1948. Member of the Nat'l Pedigreed Livestock Council and the Purebred Dairy Cattle Ass'n. Membership: $40/year.

Publications:
Milking Shorthorn Journal. bi-m. adv.

Meetings/Conferences:
1999 – Indianapolis, IN
2000 – Illinois
2001 – Cortland, NY
2002 – Washington State
2003 – Minnesota

American Miniature Horse Ass'n *(1978)*
5601 S. I-35 West
Alvarado, TX   76009
Tel: (817)783-5600   *Fax:* (817)783-6403
Members: 8,700 individuals
Staff: 8
Annual Budget: $1-2,000,000
Exec. Secretary: Marlynn Gilcrest

Historical Note
Absorbed the Internat'l Miniature Horse Registry in 1985. Members own and breed American Miniature horses. AMHA promotes the breed and maintains a permanent registry, the largest for miniature horses in the world with over 40,000 currently registered. AMHA is member-owned and governed. Membership: $45/year (individual); $25/year (renewal).

Publications:
AMHA Newsletter. bi-m.
Miniature Horse World. bi-m. adv.

Meetings/Conferences:
Annual Meetings: Fall

American Mining Congress *(1897)*

Historical Note
Merged with the Nat'l Coal Ass'n to form the Nat'l Mining Ass'n in 1995.

American Mobile Telecommunications Ass'n *(1985)*
1150 18th St., N.W., Suite 250
Washington, DC   20036
Tel: (202)331-7773   *Fax:* (202)331-9062
E-Mail: arshark@aol.com
Web Site: http://www.amtausa.org
Members: 400 companies
Staff: 5
Annual Budget: $500-1,000,000
President: Alan R. Shark, CAE
V.P., Communications/Membership: Lynne Mallonee
V.P., Regulatory Relations: Jill Lyon
Controller & Administrative Director: Minerva Scott

Historical Note
Formerly (1990) the American SMR Network Ass'n. Established in Washington, DC, AMTA members are specialized mobile wireless operators and manufacturers. AMTA represents the interests of its members in federal regulatory and legislative activities; maintains data concerning the assignment and use of frequency assignments; and provides research services at a separate Gettysburg, PA office. In 1994, AMTA created an independent international association, the Internat'l Mobile Telecommunications Ass'n, which is headquartered at the same address. Membership: $350/year base fee, plus a sliding fee based on number of units in service

Publications:
AMTA Open Channels Newsletter. m. adv.
FCC Rules and Regulations (Abridged), Parts 90 & 17. a.
Membership Directory. adv. adv.
Membership News Bulletins. irreg.
Special Reports.

Meetings/Conferences:
Annual Meetings: June, Washington, DC

American Mold Builders Ass'n *(1973)*
701 East Irving Park Road, Suite 207
Roselle, IL   60172
Tel: (630)980-7667   *Fax:* (630)980-9714
Members: 430 organizations
Staff: 3
Exec. Director: Jeanette Bradley

Historical Note
Members are manufacturers of molds. Membership: $150 (organization).

Publications:
AMBA Membership Directory. a. adv.
AMBA News and Views. q. adv.

Meetings/Conferences:
Annual Meetings: March
1999 – Clearwater Beach, FL/March 2-7

American Montessori Soc. *(1960)*
281 Park Ave. South, 6th Floor
New York, NY   10010-6102
Tel: (212)358-1250   *Fax:* (212)358-1256
E-Mail: michael@amshq.org
Web Site: http://www.amshq.org
Members: 10,000 individuals, 800 schools
Staff: 15
Annual Budget: $1-2,000,000
Nat'l Director: Michael N. Eanes

Historical Note
Members are teachers, schools and others interested in the approach to early learning through self-motivation developed by Dr. Maria Montessori in 1907. Membership rates available upon request.

Publications:
Heads of Schools Newsletter. 3/year. adv.
Montessori Life. q. adv.

Meetings/Conferences:
Annual Meetings: April

American Monument Ass'n *(1904)*
30 Eden Alley, Suite 301
Columbus, OH   43215-2000
Tel: (614)461-5852   *Fax:* (614)461-1497
Members: 60 companies
Staff: 2
Annual Budget: $100-250,000
Exec. Director: Pennie L. Sabel

Historical Note
Founded as the Nat'l Ass'n of American Granite Producers, it became the American Granite Ass'n in 1914 and assumed its present name in 1946. Members are quarries, fabricators and dealers of memorial and monument stone.

Publications:
Stone in America Magazine. m. adv.

Meetings/Conferences:

American Morgan Horse Ass'n *(1909)*

122 Bostwick Road, P.O. Box 960
Shelburne, VT   05482-0960
Tel: (802)985-4944   *Fax:* (802)985-8897
E-Mail: amha@together.net
Web Site: http://www.morganhorse.com
Members: 12,000 individuals
Staff: 25
Annual Budget: $2-5,000,000
Exec. Director: Jesse M. Smith, Jr.
Dir., Mktg./Public Rels.: Jack Girompini
Registrar: Tyler Atwood
Dir., Membership/Programs: Erica Richard

Historical Note
Established as the Morgan Horse Club, Inc., it assumed its present name in 1971. Members are breeders, owners and trainers of the Morgan horse, a type of light horse which originated in Vermont around 1789. Membership: $30/year (individual), $10/year (junior).

Publications:
American Morgan Horse Register. a.
AMHA Network and Morgan Sales Network. m. adv.
The Morgan Horse Magazine. m. adv.

Meetings/Conferences:
Annual Meetings: February/400-500
1999 – Detroit, MI
2000 – Atlanta, GA
2001 – Denver, CO

American Mosquito Control Ass'n *(1935)*
2200 E. Prien Lake Road
Lake Charles, LA   70601-7975
Tel: (318)474-2723   *Fax:* (318)478-9434
Members: 2,000 individuals
Staff: 2
Annual Budget: $250-500,000

Historical Note
Established in 1935 as the Eastern Ass'n of Mosquito Control Workers and assumed its present name in 1944. Incorporated in New Jersey (1948), California (1974) and Louisiana (1986). Members are involved in the control of mosquitoes and other vectors. Has members throughout the world. Membership: $65/year (individual); $85/year (company).

Publications:
AMCA Newsletter. q.
Journal of the AMCA. q. adv.
Mosquito Systematics. q.

Meetings/Conferences:
Annual Meetings: Spring/700
1999 – St. Louis, MO
2000 – Atlantic City, NJ
2001 – Dallas, TX
2002 – Denver, CO

American Motility Soc. *(1980)*
6900 Grove Road
Thorofare, NJ   08086
Tel: (609)848-1000   *Fax:* (609)848-5274
E-Mail: ams@slackinc.com
Members: 250 individuals

Historical Note
AMS members are physicians with an interest in gastrointestinal motility. Membership: $25/year.

Meetings/Conferences:

American Motion Picture Export Company

Historical Note
Became (1995) Motion Picture Export Ass'n.

American Motorcyclist Ass'n
33 Collegeview Rd
Westerville, OH   43081
Tel: (614)891-2425   *Fax:* (614)891-5012
V. President, Government Relations: Robert Rasor

Historical Note
Membership: $29(Individual)

American Movers Conference

Historical Note
Became (1998) American Moving and Storage Ass'n.

American Moving and Storage Ass'n *(1953)*
1611 Duke St.
Alexandria, VA   22314-3482
Tel: (703)683-7410   *Fax:* (703)683-7527
Web Site: http://www.amconf.org
Members: 3,200 companies
Staff: 36
Annual Budget: $2-5,000,000
President: Joseph M. Harrison
V.P., Communications/Mktg.: George E. Bennett
Director, Marketing Services: Karen Climo
V. President, Programs and Services: Patricia T. Jennings
V. President, Administration: John B. Brewer

Historical Note
Formed by a merger of the Movers Conference of America (founded in 1943 as the Household Goods Carriers' Conference) and the American Movers Institute (founded in 1960). Founded in 1953 as the Household Goods Movers Group of ATA. Merged with Nat'l Moving and Storage Ass'n and assumed its current name in 1998. Affiliated with American Trucking Ass'ns. Membership: annual dues vary by size.

Publications:
AMC Membership Directory. a. adv.
Direction Magazine. m. adv.
Government Traffic Newsletter. m.
The Moving World. bi-w.

Meetings/Conferences:
1999 – San Diego, CA

American Murray Grey Ass'n (1970)
P.O. Box 34590
North Kansas City, MO 64116-0990
Tel: (816)421-1994   Fax: (816)421-1991
E-Mail: JSpawn321@aol.com
Members: 200 individuals
Staff: 1
Annual Budget: $25-50,000
Exec. Director: James A. Spawn

Historical Note
Established as a national breed registry for Murray Grey Cattle.
Members are breeders and fanciers of Murray Grey Beef Cattle.
Member of the Nat'l Pedigree Livestock Council. Membership:
$75/year.

Publications:
AMGA Herd Book. a. adv.
Murray Grey News. q. adv.

Meetings/Conferences:
Annual Meetings: Fall

American Mushroom Institute (1955)
1 Massachusetts Ave., N.W., Suite 800
Washington, DC 20001
Tel: (202)842-4344   Fax: (202)408-7763
E-Mail: ami@mwmlaw.com
Web Site: http://www.americanmushroominst.org
Members: 325 individuals
Staff: 3
Annual Budget: $250-500,000
President: Laura Phelps

Historical Note
AMI represents growers and marketers of cultivated mushrooms in
the United States. Its major purposes are research and information
dissemination, the development of better methods of growth and
marketing of mushrooms, representation of the industry to
governmental bodies and increasing the consumption of
mushrooms. Membership: $350-$16,000/year, based on
production; $300/year (non-growers).

Publications:
Membership Directory. a. adv.
Mushroom News. m. adv.
Mushroom News Flash. m. adv.

Meetings/Conferences:

American Music Conference (1947)
5790 Armada Drive
Carlsbad, CA 92008-4372
Tel: (760)431-9124   Fax: (760)438-7327
E-Mail: info@amc-music.com
Web Site: http://www.amc-music.com
Members: 180 organizations
Staff: 4
Annual Budget: $250-500,000
Exec. Director: Robert B. Morrison
Director of Development: Pat Page

Historical Note
AMC promotes the importance of music, music making and music
education to the general public. Membership: $50/year
(individual); $100/year, (supporter), $250/year (sponsor),
$500/year (Sustainer), $1,000/year (visionary).

Publications:
AMC News. q.
AMC Year in Review. a.

Meetings/Conferences:
Annual Meetings: July

American Music Therapy Ass'n (1950)
8455 Colesville Rd., Suite 1000
Silver Spring, MD 20910-3319
Tel: (301)589-3300   Fax: (301)589-5175
E-Mail: info@musictherapy.org
Web Site: http://www.musictherapy.org
Members: 5,000 individuals
Staff: 10
Annual Budget: $500-1,000,000
Exec. Director: Andrea H. Farbman, Ed.D.
Dir., Communications/Conferences: Al Bumanis
Dir., Membership Services: Angie Elkins

Historical Note
Founded as Nat'l Ass'n for Music Therapy; merged with American
Ass'n for Music Therapy and assumed its current name in 1998.
Seeks to develop the therapeutic use of music in hospital and
educational settings.

Publications:
Journal of Music Therapy. q.
Member Sourcebook. a. adv.
Music Therapy Matters. q.
Music Therapy Perspectives. semi-a.

Meetings/Conferences:
Annual Meetings: Fall
1999 – Washington, DC/Nov. 15-22/3000

American Musicians Union (1948)
8 Tobin Court
Dumont, NJ 07628
Tel: (201)384-5378
Members: 1000 individuals
Annual Budget: under $10,000
President: Ben Intorre

Historical Note
Formed by a small group of musicians who chose to remain
independent of the AFL-CIO merger of labor unions; joined the
Nat'l Federation of Independent Unions in 1961. Membership is
open to all musicians and vocalists; contract books are provided at
a modest cost, but members are not required to use the official
contract form nor a binding wage scale. Has no paid officers or full-
time staff. Membership: $27/year, plus $10 initiation fee.

Publications:
Quarternote. q. adv.

American Musicological Soc. (1934)
201 S. 34th St.
Philadelphia, PA 19104-6313
Tel: (215)898-8698   Fax: (215)573-3673
Toll Free: (888)611 - 4267
E-Mail: ams@sas.upenn.edu
Web Site:
     http://musdra.ucdavis.edu/Documents/AMS/AMS.html
Members: 3,500 individuals, 1,250 institutions
Staff: 2
Annual Budget: $100-250,000
Exec. Director: Robert Judd

Historical Note
In 1929 the American Council of Learned Societies, feeling that
"the history and science of music forms an important branch of
learning," formed a standing committee on musicology. Out of this,
the independent American Musicological Society was formed in
1934. It is a learned society of professional musicologists and
educators. Membership: $45-75/year (individual); $65/year
(organization).

Publications:
Directory. a.
Journal of The AMS. 3/year. adv.
Newsletter. semi-a.

Meetings/Conferences:
Annual Meetings: Fall
1999 – Kansas City, Mo(Hyatt)/Nov. 4-7/1800
2000 – Toronto, ON, Canada(Sheraton
         Centre)/Nov. 1-5/2300
2001 – Atlanta, GA(Marriott Marquis)
2002 – Columbus, OH(Hyatt)

American Mustang Ass'n (1962)
P.O. Box 338
Yucaipa, CA 92399
Tel: (805)946-8308
Members: 150 individuals
Staff: 1
Annual Budget: under $10,000
President: Janis Fisher

Historical Note
Members are owners and breeders of the Mustang horse of the
Western plains. Membership: $20/year.

Publications:
American Mustang World. q. adv.

American Name Soc. (1951)
Baruch College, Language/Comp. Lit. Dept
17 Lexington Ave., Box G-1224
New York, NY 10010-5526
Tel: (212)387-1597   Fax: (212)387-1591
E-Mail: Wayne_finke@baruch.cuny.edu
Members: 750 individuals and institutions
Staff: 1
Annual Budget: $10-25,000
Exec. Secretary-Treasurer: Wayne H. Finke, Ph.D.

Historical Note
A professional society of onomatologists and others interested in the
study of the origin and meaning of names, geographic, personal,
scientific, etc. Membership: $35/year (individual); $40/year
(company/organization); $45/year (foreign).

Publications:
ANS Newsletter. 3/year.
Names. q.

Meetings/Conferences:
Annual Meetings: with the Modern Language Ass'n

American Naprapathic Ass'n (1909)
5913 W. Montrose Ave.
Chicago, IL 60634
Tel: (312)685-6020
Members: 140 individuals
Staff: 1
Annual Budget: $10-25,000
Corresponding Secretary: Roy P. Krueger

Historical Note
Members are practitioners of naprapathy, the science and system of
manipulation (administered by the hands) designed to cure physical
ailments. Membership: $180/year (individual); $150/year
(organization/company).

Publications:
The Voice of Naprapathy. a.

Meetings/Conferences:
Semi-annual Meetings: 2nd Sunday in January and last
weekend in June

American Nat'l CattleWomen (1952)
P.O. Box 3881
Englewood, CO 80155-2851
Tel: (303)694-0313   Fax: (303)694-2390
Web Site: http://www.beef.org/ancw
Members: 5,300 individuals
Staff: 4

Historical Note
Members are women in the beef cattle industry. Promotes education
and legislation on behalf of the beef industry. Membership:
$25/year (individual); $100/year, $500/year or $1,000/year
(company).

Publications:
The American CattleWoman. bi-m.

Meetings/Conferences:
1999 – Charlotte, NC

American Nat'l Metric Council (1973)
4340 East-West Hwy., Suite 401

Bethesda, MD 20814-4408
Tel: (301)718-6508   Fax: (301)656-0989
E-Mail: anmc@paimgmt.com
Members: 200 individuals
Staff: 2
Annual Budget: $50-100,000
Exec. Director: Thomas Peno

Historical Note
Coordinates metric activities of commerce and industry.
Membership: $50/year (individuals); $50-2,500/year
(organization).

Publications:
Metric Reporter. bi-m.

American Nat'l Standards Institute (1918)
11 West 42nd St., 13th Floor
New York, NY 10036-8002
Tel: (212)642-4900   Fax: (212)398-0023
Web Site: http://www.ansi.org
Members: 1,030 companies & 275 organizations
Staff: 110
Annual Budget: $10-25,000,000
President/C.E.O.: Sergio Mazza

Historical Note
Originated in 1918 as the American Engineering Standards
Committee. Became the American Standards Ass'n in 1928 and the
United States of America Standards Institute in 1966. Incorporated
in New York in 1948. Became the American Nat'l Standards
Institute, Inc. in 1969. A member of the Internat'l Organization for
Standardization, the Pacific Area Standards Congress, and the
Internat'l Electrotechnical Commission. Promotes the knowledge
and voluntary use of approved standards for industry, engineering,
and safety design. Approves voluntary, private sector consensus
standards as American National Standards. Has an annual budget
of approximately $13 million. Membership: dues vary, based on
sales (corporate).

Publications:
ANSI Reporter. m.
Catalog of Approved American Nat'l Standards. a.
Standards Action. bi-w.

Meetings/Conferences:

American Natural Hygiene Soc.
P.O. Box 30630
Tampa, FL 33630-3630
Tel: (813)855-6607   Fax: (813)855-8052
E-Mail: anhs@anhs.org
Members: 7,000 individuals
Exec. Director: James Michael Lennon

Publications:
Health Science Magazine. 6/year

American Natural Soda Ash Corporation (1984)
15 Riverside Ave.
Westport, CT 06880-4214
Tel: (203)226-9056   Fax: (203)227-1484
Members: 6 companies
Staff: 27
Annual Budget: $5-10,000,000
President and C.E.O.: John Andrews
V.P., Administration: Douglas D. Gardner

Historical Note
A Webb-Pomerene Act association. ANSAC is the sole authorized
export organization for members' soda ash production.

American Nature Study Soc. (1908)
R.R. 2 Box 1010
Dingmams Ferry, PA 18328
Tel: (570)828-2319   Fax: (570)828-9695
E-Mail: peec@ptd.net
Web Site: http://www.peec.org
Members: 650 individuals
Staff: 1
Annual Budget: under $10,000
Secretary: Florence Mouro

Historical Note
Founded in 1908, ANSS quickly became the leading organization
serving and strengthening the Nature Study movement. Its main
concern is nature and conservation education. The Society works to
forge a bond between each generation of students and their natural
environment. Members are science, nature study, and
environmental education professionals. Membership: $25/year
(individual); $18/year (organization)

Publications:
ANSS Newsletter. q.
Nature Study. semi-a. adv.

Meetings/Conferences:
Annual Meetings: February, with American Ass'n for the
Advancement of Science

American Naturopathic Ass'n (1896)

Historical Note
Members are naturopathic physicians and others with an interest in
naturopathy. Membership: $100/year (individual); $150/year
(company).

American Naturopathic Medical Ass'n

Historical Note
Shares administrative offices with American Ass'n of Nutritional
Consultants.

American Nephrology Nurses Ass'n (1969)
East Holly Ave., Box 56
Pitman, NJ 08071-0056
Tel: (609)256-2320   Fax: (609)589-7463
Web Site: http://www.anna.inurse.com
Members: 11,000 individuals
Staff: 6
Annual Budget: $2-5,000,000

Exec. Director: Rick Grimes
Director, Public Relations: Gus Ostrum
Meetings/Conventions: Kristine Jannetti
Director of Professional Development: Linda J. Smith,
    MSN,RN,CNN
Director of Membership Services: Lou Ann Leary

Historical Note
Nurses specializing in the structure, function and diseases of the kidneys, as well as dieticians, physicians, social workers and technicians. Formerly the American Ass'n of Nephrology Nurses and Technicians. Assumed its present name in 1984. Membership: $60/year (individual), $2,500/year (organization/company).

Publications:
ANNA Journal. bi-m.
Publications List Available.
Update. bi-m.

Meetings/Conferences:
Annual Meetings: Spring
1999 – Baltimore, MD

American Network of Community Options and Resources *(1970)*
4200 Evergreen Lane, Suite 315
Annandale, VA 22003-3255
Tel: (703)642-6614   *Fax:* (703)642-0497
E-Mail: ancor@radix.net
Web Site: http://www.ancor.org
Members: 650 agencies
Staff: 6
Annual Budget: $500-1,000,000
Exec. Director: Joni Fritz
Director for Public Policy: Suellen Galbraith

Historical Note
Founded as Nat'l Ass'n of Private Residential Facilities for the Mentally Retarded. In 1987 became Nat'l Ass'n of Private Residential Resources. Adopted current name in 1993. Represents and assists agencies that provide private services and supports for people with disabilities. Affiliated with the American Ass'n on Mental Retardation, participates in the Commission on Accreditation of Rehabilitation Facilities; Accreditation Council on Services for People with Developmental Disabilities, and Nat'l Fire Protection Ass'n. Membership fee based on agency budget.

Publications:
ANCOR News and Notes. m.
Directory of Members. a.
Executive's Notebook. m.
LINKS. m. adv.

Meetings/Conferences:
Three Meetings Annually: May/June with American Ass'n on
    Mental Retardation, and Feb./March warm climate,
    Sept./Washington, DC
1999 – San Diego, CA/March 21-23

American Neurological Ass'n *(1875)*
5841 Cedar Lake Road, Suite 204
Minneapolis, MN 55416-1491
Tel: (612)545-6284   *Fax:* (612)545-6073
Web Site: http://www.aneuroa.org
Members: 1,100 individuals
Staff: 2
Annual Budget: $100-250,000
Exec. Director: Linda Wilkerson

Historical Note
Founded in 1875 and incorporated in Minnesota.

Publications:
Annals of Neurology. m. adv.

Meetings/Conferences:
Annual Meetings: September-October/700-900
1999 – Seattle, WA/Oct. 10-13

American Neuropsychiatric Ass'n *(1987)*
Historical Note
Address unknown in 1997.

American Neurotology Soc. *(1965)*
6550 Fannin, Suite 2001
Houston, TX 77030
Tel: (713)796-2001   *Fax:* (713)796-9172
Members: 480 individuals
Annual Budget: under $10,000
Secretary-Treasurer: Dr. Newton Coker

Historical Note
ANS members are otologists/neurotologists and allied health professionals as affiliate members with an interest in hearing and balance disorders. Has no paid officers or full-time staff.

Meetings/Conferences:

American North Country Cheviot Sheep Ass'n *(1962)*
P.O. Box 265
Lula, GA 30554
Tel: (770)869-7726   *Fax:* (770)869-1664
Members: 300 individuals
Staff: 1
Annual Budget: under $10,000
Exec. Secretary: Theresa H. Barefoot

Historical Note
Members are breeders of purebred North Country Cheviot Sheep. Maintains registry. Membership: $10/year.

Publications:
Breeders Directory. bien.
North Country News. q. adv.
North Country News. semi-a.

Meetings/Conferences:
Biennial Meetings: odd years

American Nuclear Insurers *(1957)*
29 S. Main St., Suite 300-S
West Hartford, CT 06107-2445

Tel: (860)561-3433   *Fax:* (860)561-4655
Members: 100 companies
Staff: 79
President and C.E.O.: George D. Turner

Historical Note
A merger in 1974 of the Nuclear Energy Property Insurance Ass'n and the Nuclear Energy Liability Insurance Ass'n both established in 1957. Formerly (until 1978) the Nuclear Energy Liability Property Insurance Ass'n.

Meetings/Conferences:
Annual Meetings: March
1999 – Hartford, CT(Sheraton)

American Nuclear Soc. *(1954)*
555 North Kensington Ave.
La Grange Park, IL 60526
Tel: (708)352-6611   *Fax:* (708)352-0499
E-Mail: nucleus@ans.org
Web Site: http://www.ans.org
Members: 12,000 individuals
Staff: 49
Annual Budget: $5-10,000,000
Exec. Director: Brian K. Hajek
Director, Public Communications: Sharon Kerrick
Director, Meetings and Exhibits: Mary Keenan
Comptroller: Christian Krapp
Publisher/Commercial Publications: Jon Payne
Publisher/Scientifc Publications: Mary Beth Gardner
Editor-in-Chief, Nuclear News: Gregg Taylor

Historical Note
Established December 11, 1954 in the Nat'l Academy of Sciences in Washington, DC to advance science and engineering relating to the atomic nucleus and allied sciences and arts. Has an annual budget of approximately $6.5 million. Membership: $32-80/year, based on age (individual).

Publications:
ANS News. m.
Fusion Technology. bi-m.
Nuclear News. m. adv.
Nuclear Science and Engineering. m.
Nuclear Standards News. m.
Nuclear Technology. m.
Radwaste Magazine. q.
re-actions. 5/year.
RSTD Proceedings. a.
Transactions. semi-a.
Utility Quarterly. q.

Meetings/Conferences:
Semi-annual Meetings: Spring and Fall
1999 – Boston, MA(Marriott Copley Place)/June 6-10
1999 – Long Beach, CA/Nov. 14-18
2000 – Orlando, FL(Marriott World Center)/June 18-22
2000 – Washington, DC(Sheraton Washington)/Nov. 12-17

American Numismatic Soc. *(1858)*
Broadway at 155th St.
New York, NY 10032-7598
Tel: (212)234-3130   *Fax:* (212)234-3381
E-Mail: info@amnumsoc.org
Web Site: http://www.amnumsoc2.org
Members: 2,135 individuals
Staff: 20
Annual Budget: $1-2,000,000
Exec. Director: Leslie A. Elam

Historical Note
Organized April 16, 1858 in New York City under the present name. Incorporated in 1865 as the American Numismatic and Archeological Society but reverted to the present name in 1907. Its purpose is "the collection and preservation of coins and medals, with an investigation into the history, and other subjects connected therewith." Maintains a significant numismatic library and museum. Membership: $40/year.

Publications:
American Journal of Numismatics. a.
Newsletter.
Numismatic Literature. semi-a.
Numismatic Notes and Monographs. irreg.
Numismatic Studies. irreg.
Sylloge Nummorum Graecorum. irreg.

Meetings/Conferences:
Quarterly Meetings: at ANS Headquarters.

American Nursery and Landscape Ass'n *(1876)*
1250 I St., N.W., Suite 500
Washington, DC 20005-3922
Tel: (202)789-2900   *Fax:* (202)789-1893
Web Site: http://www.anla.org
Members: 3,000 companies
Staff: 15
Annual Budget: $2-5,000,000
Exec. V. President: Robert J. Dolibois, CAE
Public Relations Director: Joel Albizo, APR
Director of Government Affairs: Benjamin C. Bolusky
Legislative Director: Bryce Quick
Director of Operations: Warren A. Quinn
Dir., Marketing and Retail Services: Clint Albin
Dir., Horticultural Res. Inst.: Ashby P. Ruden

Historical Note
Formerly (1887) the American Ass'n of Nurserymen, Florists and Seedmen and (1997) the American Ass'n of Nurserymen. Garden Centers of America, Horticultural Research Institute, Nat'l Ass'n of Plant Patent Owners, Nat'l Landscape Ass'n, and Wholesale Nursery Growers of America are divisions of ANLA. Supports the Nursery Industry Political Action Committee. Membership Fee: based on volume of business.

Publications:
AAN Today. bi-m.
Update. tri-w.
Who's Who in the Nursery Industry. a. adv.

Meetings/Conferences:
Annual Meetings: August/1,500-2,000
1999 – Philadelphia, PA/July 24-28
2000 – Vancouver, British Columbia/July 13-17

American Nursery and Landscape Ass'n - Landscape Division *(1939)*
1250 I St., N.W., Suite 500
Washington, DC 20005
Tel: (202)789-2900   *Fax:* (202)789-1839
Members: 700 landscaping companies
Staff: 2
Annual Budget: $50-100,000
Dir., Operations: Warren Quinn

Historical Note
Formerly (1972) Nat'l Landscape Nurserymen's Ass'n and (1997) Nat'l Landscape Ass'n, ANLA-LD affiliated with American Ass'n of Nurserymen in 1967.

Publications:
NLA Landscape How To/New Ideas.
NLA Landscape News.

Meetings/Conferences:
Annual Meetings: In conjunction with the American Ass'n of
    Nurserymen

American Nurses Ass'n *(1896)*
600 Maryland Ave., S.W., 100 West
Washington, DC 20024-2517
Tel: (202)651-7116   *Fax:* (202)488-8461
Toll Free: (800)274 - 4262
Web Site: http://www.ana.org
Members: 200,000 individuals
Staff: 170
Annual Budget: $10-25,000,000
Exec. Director: David W. Hennage, Ph.D.
Dir., Media Rels./Public Affairs: Joan Meehan, APR
Director, Federal Government Relations: Marjorie Vanderbilt
Director, State Government Relations: Theresa A. Gaffney
Director, Online Services: Garry Turner
Director, Office of Policy: David Keepnews
Director, Ethics and Human Rights: Colleen Scanlon
Director, Admin. Services and C.F.O.: James B. Elder, CPA
Director, Labor Relations: Anna Gilmore
General Counsel: Barbara Sapin
Membership Billing: Joseph A. Brown
Manager, Periodicals: Constance S. Helmlinger

Historical Note
Founded in New York City in 1896. Incorporated 1901 as the Nurses Associated Alumnae of the United States and Canada. Became the American Nurses' Ass'n in 1911 and was incorporated in the District of Columbia in 1917. The national professional organization of registered nurses, ANA is a federation composed of 53 constituent state and territorial associations and over 900 district associations of nurses. Sponsors and supports the ANA Political Action Committee. Has an annual budget of $22 million.

Publications:
Capital Update. bi-w.
CHN Communique. semi-a. adv.
CNR. 3/yr.
Cultural Connections. semi-a. adv.
In Touch. semi-a. adv.
Input/Output. semi-a. adv.
Oasis. q. adv.
Pacesetter. 3/yr. adv.
Synergy. 3/yr. adv.
The American Nurse. 10/yr. adv.
The Facilitator. 3/yr. adv.
Transitions. semi-a. adv.
Update. semi-a.

Meetings/Conferences:
Biennial meetings: even years in June

American Nurses in Business Ass'n *(1992)*
P.O. Box 741384
Houston, TX 77274-1384
Tel: (713)771-5016
Members: 30 individuals
President and C.E.O.: Sharon Mathis

Publications:
Choices. q. adv.

American Nursing Assistant's Ass'n *(1982)*
Historical Note
Address unknown in 1996.

American Oat Ass'n *(1988)*
415 Shelard Pkwy., Suite 101
Minneapolis, MN 55426
Tel: (612)542-9817   *Fax:* (612)397-7451
Members: 200 individuals
Exec. Director: Pat Henderson

Historical Note
AOA members are growers, users, traders, and processors of oats.

American Obesity Ass'n *(1995)*
1250 24th St., N.W., Suite 300
Washington, DC 20037-1124
Tel: (202)466-0577   *Fax:* (202)466-0525
Toll Free: (800)986 - 2373
Exec. Director: Morgan Downey

Historical Note
AOA is dedicated to promoting education, research, and community action that can improve the quality of life for people with obesity. Members include health professionals and others who are concerned with solving the problems of obesity. Membership: $25/year (individual); $50/year (health professional).

Publications:
AOA Newsletter. q. adv.

American Occupational Therapy Ass'n (1917)
P.O. Box 31220
4720 Montgomery Lane
Bethesda, MD 20824-1220
Tel: (301)652-2682   Fax: (301)652-7711
Toll Free: (800)668 - 8255
E-Mail: praota@aota.org
Web Site: http://www.aota.org
Members: 60,000 individuals
Staff: 160
Annual Budget: $10-25,000,000
Exec. Director: Jeanette Bair, OTR, FAOTA
Dir. Public Relations: Fred Whiting
Assoc. Exec. Director, Professional Development: Brena Manoly, Ph.D.
Assoc. Exec. Director, Professional Affairs: Frederick P. Somers
Assoc. Exec. Dir., Finance & Operations: Christopher M. Bluhm
Assoc. Exec. Director, Professional Resources: George Rowley
General Counsel: Thomas J. Steich
Managing Editor: David Zuckerman
Assoc. Exec. Director, Professional Affairs: Stephanie Hoover, Ed.D.
Director, Information Systems: Donald W. Brizendine

Historical Note
AOTA is a national professional society established to represent the interests and concerns of occupational therapy practicioners and to improve the quality of occupational therapy services. Occupational therapy is a vital health care profession whose pracititioners help to restore and sustain the highest quality of productive life to persons recovering from illnesses or injuries, or coping with developmental disabilities, mental illness or changes resulting from the aging process. Current AOTA membership numbers more than 60,000 including registered occupational therapists, certified occupational therapy assistants and occupational therapy students. AOTA's major programs are directed toward assuring the quality of occupational therapy services, improving consumer access to health care and promoting the professional development of its members. Has an annual budget of $18.2 million. Membership: $150/year (individual).

Publications:
American Journal of Occupational Therapy. m. adv.
AOTA Buyer's Guide. a. adv.
OT Practice. m. adv.
OT Week. w. adv.
Special Interest Section Newsletters. q.

Meetings/Conferences:
Annual Meetings: Spring/Summer/6-7,000
1999 – Indianapolis, IN/April 16-20

American Oil Chemists' Soc. (1909)
P.O. Box 3489
1608 Broadmoor Dr.
Champaign, IL 61826-3489
Tel: (217)359-2344   Fax: (217)351-8091
E-Mail: general@aocs.org
Web Site: http://www.aocs.org
Members: 5,400 individuals
Staff: 48
Annual Budget: $5-10,000,000
Exec. Director: James C. Lyon
Technical Director: Richard Cantrill
Meetings Manager: Jeffrey Newman
Exhibits Sales Manager: Scott Narug
Assoc. Exec. Director: Jean Wills
Admin. Services Director: Gloria Cook
Marketing and Membership Manager: Arleen Ward
Member Svcs. Manager: Kathy Atchley
Publications Director: Mary Lane

Historical Note
Founded in 1909 in Memphis, TN as the Soc. of Cotton Products Analysts. Incorporated in Louisiana in 1922 as the American Oil Chemists' Soc.American Ass'n of Feed Microscopists became a division of AOCS in 1997. Designed to be a forum for the exchange of ideas, information and experience for those with a professional interest in the sciences of fats, oils and related substances in ways that promote personal excellence and provide for a high standard of quality. Membership: $95/year (domestic), $110/year (foreign).

Publications:
INFORM (Internat'l News on Fats, Oils, and Related Materials). m.
Journal of Surfactants and Detergents.
Journal of the American Oil Chemists' Society. m.
Lipids. m.

Meetings/Conferences:
Annual Meetings: Spring/2,500
1999 – Orlando, FL(Marriott World Center)/May 9-12
2000 – San Diego, CA(Convention Center)

American Olive Oil Ass'n (1917)
Historical Note
A section of Ass'n of Food Industries.

American Ophthalmological Soc. (1864)
P.O. Box 193940
San Francisco, CA 94119
Tel: (415)561-8578   Fax: (415)561-8575
E-Mail: aos@aao.org
Members: 250 individuals
Staff: 3
Annual Budget: $25-50,000
Secretary-Treasurer: W. Banks Anderson, Jr., M.D.

Historical Note
The oldest specialty society in American medicine and the second oldest ophthalmology society in the world. Membership restricted to 225 active members. Awards the Howe Medal for distinguished service to ophthalmology. Membership: $200/year.

Publications:
Transactions of the AOS. a.

Meetings/Conferences:
Annual Meetings: May/250

1999 – Santa Barbara, CA(Four Seasons Biltmore)/May 23-26
2000 – Pebble Beach, CA(Inn at Spanish Bay)/March 21-24
2001 – Sea Island, GA(The Cloisters)/March 19-22/225

American Optometric Ass'n (1898)
243 N. Lindbergh Blvd.
St. Louis, MO 63141-7851
Tel: (314)991-4100   Fax: (314)991-4101
Toll Free: (800)365 - 2219
Web Site: http://www.aoanet.org
Members: 31,000 individuals, 550 local societies; 52 state ass'ns
Staff: 90
Annual Budget: $10-25,000,000
Exec. Director: Michael Jones
Director, Communications Center: Howard Hoskins
Director, Administration Center: Ramona L. Clymer
Associate Director, Sections: Laura M. Baumstark, CAE
Director, Finance Center: Thomas W. Meadows, CPA
Counsel: Thomas E. Eichhorst, CAE

Historical Note
Founded as the American Optical Ass'n in 1898. Became the American Optometric Ass'n in 1919. A federation of state optometric associations. Seeks to improve the quality, availability, and accessibility of eye/vision care, to represent the optometric profession to government, third parties and the public , and to assist members in conducting practices successfully in accordance with the highest standards of patient care and efficiency. Affiliated with the International Optometric and Optical League. Connected with the American Optometric Ass'n Political Action Committee. Has an annual budget of approximately $16 million.

Publications:
AOA News. semi-m. adv.
Journal of The American Optometric Association. m. adv.

Meetings/Conferences:
Annual Meetings: Summer
1999 – San Antonio, TX/June 23-27

American Optometric Student Ass'n (1968)
243 N. Lindbergh Blvd.
St. Louis, MO 63141
Tel: (314)991-4100   Fax: (314)991-4101
Web Site: http://home.earthlink.net/aosa/index.html
Members: 5,600 individuals
Staff: 2
Annual Budget: $10-25,000
Exec. Director: Carol Freihaut

Historical Note
AOSA promotes the profession of optometry and enhances the education and welfare of optometry students. Administrative support provided by American Optomoteric Ass'n. Membership: $25/year (individual); $100/year (company).

Publications:
AOSA Foresight: Optometry Looking Forward. semi-a.
Communicator Newsletter. a.

Meetings/Conferences:
Annual Meetings: Winter
1999 – Ft. Lauderdale, FL(Registry)/Jan. 6-9/1200
2000 – New York(Hilton Hotel and Towers)/Jan. 5-9/1(Hilton Hotel and Towers)/Jan. 5-9/1200

American Organization of Nurse Executives (1967)
One N. Franklin St., 32nd Floor
Chicago, IL 60606
Tel: (312)422-2800   Fax: (312)422-4503
Web Site: http://www.aone.org
Members: 6,000 individuals
Staff: 15
Annual Budget: $2-5,000,000
Exec. Director: Marjorie Beyers

Historical Note
Representing nurses in executive practice across the health care continuum, AONE is a corporate subsidiary of the American Hospital Ass'n. Formerly (1978) American Soc. for Hospital Nursing Service Administrators and (1985) American Soc. for Nursing Service Administrators. In 1994 AONE absorbed the Council of Nurse Manager Affiliates. Membership: $200/year.

Publications:
AONE News. m. adv.
AONE Update. every 3 weeks. adv.

Meetings/Conferences:
Annual Meetings: Spring
1999 – North Carolina/March 18-22

American Oriental Bodywork Therapy Ass'n (1990)
1010 Haddonfield-Berlin Road, Suite 408
Voorhees, NJ 08043
Tel: (609)782-1616   Fax: (609)782-1653
E-Mail: AOBTA@aol.com
Web Site: http://www.healthy.net/aobta
Members: 1,400 individuals
Staff: 2
Annual Budget: $25-50,000
President: David Lowenstein

Historical Note
Formerly (1990) American Shiatsu Ass'n. Especially concerned with the establishment of appropriate standards for practice of all forms of oriental bodywork therapy. Membership: $30-150/year (individual, varies according to type); $500/year (school).

Publications:
AOBTA Bulletin. q. adv.
Directory of Members. a.

Meetings/Conferences:
1999 – Clearwater, FL/May 14-17

American Oriental Soc. (1842)
Harlan Hatcher Library-Room 110D
Univ. of Michigan
Ann Arbor, MI 48109-1205

Tel: (934)647-4760
Members: 1,350 individuals
Staff: 4
Annual Budget: $50-100,000
Secretary-Treasurer: Jonathan Rodgers

Historical Note
Established in 1842 to encourage research in the languages and literatures of Asia and North Africa. Member of the American Council of Learned Societies. Membership: $50/year (regular); $1000 (life); $25/year (student); $90/year (organization).

Publications:
American Oriental Series. irreg.
AOS Newsletter. bi-a.
Journal of The American Oriental Society. q.

Meetings/Conferences:
Annual Meetings: Spring
1999 – Baltimore, MD(Sheraton Inner Harbor)/March 21-24
2000 – Portland, OR

American Ornithologists' Union (1883)
Nat'l Museum of Natural Hist., MRC-116
Smithsonian Institution
Washington, DC 20560-0116
Tel: (202)357-2051   Fax: (202)633-8084
E-Mail: aou@nmnh.si.edu
Web Site: http://www.nmnh.si.edu/BIRDNET/AOU/index.html
Members: 4,500 individuals
Annual Budget: $100-250,000
Secretary: Mary McDonald

Historical Note
Founded September 29, 1883 at the American Museum of Natural History in New York City with 21 charter members. Incorporated 1888 in the District of Columbia, reincorporated in 1987. Affiliated with the American Ass'n for the Advancement of Science. Officers change annually, but mailing address remains as above. Membership: $42/year.

Publications:
Checklist of North American Birds. irreg.
Membership List. trien.
Ornithological Monographs. irreg.
Ornithological Newsletter. bi-m.
The Auk. q. adv.

Meetings/Conferences:
Annual Meetings: August
1999 – Ithica, NY(Cornell University)/August 10-14
2000 – St. Johns, Newfoundland(Memorial University)/Aug. 14-20/600

American Orthodontic Soc. (1975)
Historical Note
Absorbed by Internat'l Ass'n for Orthodontics in 1995.

American Orthopaedic Ass'n (1887)
6300 N. River Road, Suite 300
Rosemont, IL 60018-4263
Tel: (847)318-7330   Fax: (847)318-7339
Web Site: http://www.aoassn.org
Members: 700 individuals
Staff: 7
Annual Budget: $1-2,000,000
Exec. Director: Hildegard A. Weiler

Historical Note
Founded in 1887, AOA is the oldest orthopaedic association in the world. Membership: $500/year.

Publications:
AOA News. semi-a.
Journal of Bone and Joint Surgery. 8/year. adv.

Meetings/Conferences:
Annual Meetings: Summer
1999 – Sun Valley, ID(Sun Valley Resort)/June 5-8

American Orthopaedic Foot and Ankle Soc. (1969)
1216 Pine St., Suite 201
Seattle, WA 98101-1944
Tel: (206)223-1120   Fax: (206)223-1178
Toll Free: (800)235 - 4855
Web Site: http://www.aofas.org
Members: 1,300 individuals
Staff: 7
Annual Budget: $1-2,000,000
Exec. Director: Richard Cantrall

Historical Note
Formerly (1983) American Orthopedic Foot Soc. AOFAS members are members of the American Academy of Orthopedic Surgeons with an interest the foot and ankle. Membership: $225/year (individual).

Publications:
In-Stride Newsletter. q.
Journal of the Foot and Ankle. m.

Meetings/Conferences:
1999 – Puerto Rico
2000 – Vail, CO

American Orthopaedic Soc. for Sports Medicine (1972)
6300 N. River Road, Suite 200
Rosemont, IL 60018-4229
Tel: (847)292-4900   Fax: (847)292-4905
Toll Free: (877)321 - 3500
E-Mail: aossm@aossm.org
Web Site: http://www.sportsmed.org
Members: 1,300 individuals
Staff: 7
Annual Budget: $500-1,000,000
Exec. Director: Irvin Bomberger
Director of Communications: Lisa Doty
Director, Operations and Meetings: Camille Petrick
President: Douglas Brown, M.D.

Historical Note
AOSSM members are orthopaedic surgeons and allied health professionals. AOSSM promotes the prevention, recognition and orthopedic treatment of sports injuries. Membership: $375/year.

Publications:
American Journal of Sports Medicine. bi-m. adv.
Sports Medicine Update. 3/year.

Meetings/Conferences:
Annual Meetings: Summer
1999 – Traverse City, MI(Grand Traverse)/June 19-22/900
2000 – Sun Valley, ID(Sun Valley Resort)/June 18-21/900
2001 – Keystone, CO(Keystone Resort)/June 28-July 1/1000
2002 – Orlando, FL(Contemporary Resort)/June 30-July 2/1000

American Orthopsychiatric Ass'n (1924)
330 7th Ave., 18th Floor
New York, NY 10001-5010
Tel: (212)564-5930   *Fax:* (212)564-6180
E-Mail: amerortho@aol.com
Members: 7,000 individuals
Staff: 7
Annual Budget: $500-1,000,000
Exec. Director: Gale Siegel, MSW

Historical Note
Founded in New York City in 1924 and incorporated in New York in 1937. Interdisciplinary association of mental health professionals concerned with the study of human behavior and development, and the promotion of mental health. Membership: $90/year (individual).

Publications:
American Journal of Orthopsychiatry. q. adv.
ORTHO UPDATE Newsletter. q.
Readings: A Journal of Reviews & Commentary in Mental Health. q. adv.

Meetings/Conferences:
Annual Meetings: Spring/1,500
1999 – Arlington, VA(Crystal Gateway Marriott)/Apr. 9-11

American Orthotic and Prosthetic Ass'n (1917)
1650 King St., Suite 500
Alexandria, VA 22314
Tel: (703)836-7116   *Fax:* (703)836-0838
Members: 1,600 companies
Staff: 8
Annual Budget: $1-2,000,000
Exec. Director: Robert T. Van Hook
Director of Government Relations: Martha L. Rinker
Director, Meetings: Annette Suriani
Dep. Exec. Director: Kimber Nation
Director, MIS: Jose Torres

Historical Note
AOPA is dedicated to quality patient care. The association represents companies that custom fit or manufacture componentry for patients with prostheses, artifical limbs, and orthoses, orthopedic braces. Membership: varies.

Publications:
AOPA in Advance. bi.
Journal of Prosthetics and Orthotics. q. adv.
O&P Almanac. m. adv.
The AOPA Yearbook. a. adv.

Meetings/Conferences:
Annual Meetings: Fall/1,500
1999 – Reno, NV(Hilton)/Oct. 6-9
2000 – Washington, DC(Marriott)/Oct. 4-7
2002 – Chicago, IL(Hyatt Regency)/Sept. 18-21

American Osteopathic Academy for Sports Medicine (1977)
7611 Elmwood Ave., Suite 201
Middleton, WI 53562-3161
Tel: (608)831-4400   *Fax:* (608)831-5122
E-Mail: aoasme@thahq.com
Members: 550 individuals
Staff: 2
Annual Budget: $50-100,000
Exec. Director: Sheila Endicott

Historical Note
An affiliate of the American Osteopathic Ass'n. Provides support and continuing education specific to primary care, nonsurgical sports medicine physicians. Membership: $275/year (physicians), $65/year (residents and interns).

Publications:
Clinical Journal of Sport Medicine. q. adv.
Membership Directory. a.
Sports Medicine Letter. 6/yr.

Meetings/Conferences:
1999 – Hilton Head, SC/April 21-25

American Osteopathic Academy of Addiction Medicine (1986)
5550 Friendship Blvd., Suite 300
Chevy Chase, MD 20815
Tel: (301)968-4170   *Fax:* (301)968-4199
Members: 225 individuals
Staff: 1
Exec. Director: David L. Kushner, CAE, CMP

Historical Note
Administrative support provided by American Osteopathic Healthcare Ass'n.

Publications:
AOAAM News and Advocate. q.

Meetings/Conferences:
Annual Meetings: Held in conjunction with the AOA's annual meeting and seminar (fall)
1999 – San Francisco, CA/Oct. 24-28/60
2000 – Orlando, FL/Oct. 29-Nov. 2
2001 – San Diego, CA/Oct. 21-25/60

American Osteopathic Academy of Orthopedics (1941)
P.O. Box 291690
Davie, FL 33329-1690
Tel: (954)262-1700   *Fax:* (954)262-1748
Members: 500 individuals
Staff: 2
Exec. Director: Morton Morris, D.O., J.D.

Historical Note
Affiliated with the American Osteopathic Ass'n. Membership: $350/year.

Publications:
The Orthopod. semi-a.

Meetings/Conferences:
Annual Meetings: Spring
1999 – Scottsdale, AZ/May 1-2

American Osteopathic Academy of Sclerotherapy

Historical Note
Became American College of Osteopathic Pain Management and Sclerotherapy in 1995.

American Osteopathic Ass'n (1897)
142 E. Ontario St.
Chicago, IL 60611-2864
Tel: (312)280-5810   *Fax:* (312)280-3894
Toll Free: (800)621 - 1773
Members: 28,500 individuals
Staff: 105
Annual Budget: $5-10,000,000
Exec. Director: John Crosby
Dir., Education Dept.: Konrad Retz, Ph.D.
Director, Finance: Frank Bedford
Dir., Member Services: Norbert W. Budde

Historical Note
Organized in April 1897 as the American Ass'n for the Advancement of Osteopathic Medicine. Became the American Osteopathic Ass'n in 1901 and was incorporated in Illinois in 1923. A federation of divisional societies organized within state boundaries, the present association has numerous affiliation with other osteopathic organizations. It constitutes the official structure of the osteopathic profession. Has an annual budget of approximately $7.5 million. Membership: $490/year (individual).

Publications:
The D. O. adv.
The Journal of the A. O. adv.
The Yearbook & Directory of Osteopathic Physicians. a. adv.

Meetings/Conferences:
Annual Meetings: Fall

American Osteopathic College of Allergy and Immunology (1975)

Historical Note
Address unknown in 1995.

American Osteopathic College of Anesthesiologists (1952)
17201 E. Hwy. 40, Suite 204
Independence, MO 64055
Tel: (816)373-4700   *Fax:* (816)373-1529
Members: 575 individuals
Staff: 4
Annual Budget: $100-250,000
Secretary-Treasurer: Bert M. Bez, D.O.

Historical Note
Advances the standards of practice and service in anesthesiology; aids in providing the opportunity for study and training in the specialty of anesthesiology. Membership: $300/year.

Publications:
Newsletter. 3/year.

Meetings/Conferences:
Semi-annual Meetings: Spring and Fall
1999 – Baltimore, MD/Oct. 3-6

American Osteopathic College of Dermatology (1955)
P.O. Box 7525
Kirksville, MO 63501-7525
Tel: (660)665-2184   *Fax:* (660)626-2714
Members: 200 individuals
Staff: 2
Annual Budget: $10-25,000
Exec. Director: Rebecca A. Mansfield

Historical Note
Membership: $200/year (individual); $3,000/year (organization).

Publications:
Directory. a.
Newsletter. q.

Meetings/Conferences:
Annual Meetings: Semi-Annual With American Osteopathic Ass'n
1999 – San Fransico, CA/Oct. 24-30
2000 – Orlando, FL/Oct. 29-Nov. 2
2001 – San Diego, CA/Oct. 21-25

American Osteopathic College of Occupational Preventive Medicine (1982)
5405 Alton Pkwy., Suite 5A-246
Irvine, CA 92604-3717
Tel: (949)653-8694   *Fax:* (949)654-0482
E-Mail: aocopm@ioc.net
Members: 400 individuals
Staff: 3
Annual Budget: $25-50,000
Exec. Director: Cathy M. Garris

Historical Note
Formerly (1995) American Osteopathic College of Preventive Medicine. Membership: $175/year (individual).

Publications:
Directory. a.
Newsletter. q.

Meetings/Conferences:

American Osteopathic College of Pathologists (1954)
Historical Note
Address unknown in 1997.

American Osteopathic College of Preventive Medicine (1982)
Historical Note
Became the American Osteopathic College of Occupational Preventive Medicine in 1995.

American Osteopathic College of Proctology (1927)
2320 Birch Run Court
Sylvania, OH 43560
Tel: (419)251-6520   *Fax:* (419)829-7122
E-Mail: adelman@ohiou.edu
Members: 100 individuals
Staff: 1
Annual Budget: under $10,000
Exec. Director: Michael Adelman, D.O.

Historical Note
Members specialize in disorders of the lower gastro-intestinal tract. Membership: $300/year.

Publications:
Procto-Topics. a. adv.

Meetings/Conferences:
Annual Meetings: Fall

American Osteopathic College of Radiology (1941)
119 E. 2nd St.
Milan, MO 63556-1331
Tel: (816)265-4011   *Fax:* (816)265-3494
Members: 800 individuals
Staff: 5
Annual Budget: $250-500,000
Exec. Director: Pamela A. Smith

Historical Note
Membership: $450/year.

Publications:
Membership directory. a.
View Box. q.
Washington Update. q.

Meetings/Conferences:
Annual Meetings: Fall/180

American Osteopathic College of Rehabilitation Medicine (1954)
2214 Elmira Ave.
Des Plaines, IL 60018-2630
Tel: (847)699-0048   *Fax:* (847)296-1366
Members: 125 individuals
Annual Budget: $10-25,000
Secretary: Julie Pickett

Historical Note
Affiliated with the American Osteopathic Ass'n. Formerly (1995) the American Osteopathic Academy of Physical Medicine and Rehabilitation and (1970) the American Osteopathic College of Physical Medicine and Rehabilitation.

Publications:
Directory. a.
Newsletter. irreg.

Meetings/Conferences:
Annual Meetings: in conjunction with the American Osteopathic Ass'n

American Osteopathic Colleges of Ophthalmology and Otolaryngology, Head and Neck Surgery (1916)
3 Mackoil Ave.
Dayton, OH 45403
Tel: (937)252-4958   *Fax:* (937)252-0968
Toll Free: (800)455 - 9404
E-Mail: aocoohns@aol.com
Web Site: http://www.aocoohns.org
Members: 565 individuals
Staff: 2
Annual Budget: $100-250,000
Administrator: Deborah Bailey

Historical Note
Formerly (1991) Osteopathic College of Ophthalmology and Otorhinolaryngology and (1993) Osteopathic Colleges of Ophthalmology and Otolaryngology and Head and Neck Surgery. Membership: $475/year.

Publications:
AOCOO-HNS Journal. a. adv.
Newsletter. q.

Meetings/Conferences:
Annual Meetings: Spring/300
1999 – Orlando, FL(Disney Swan)/April 21-25

American Osteopathic Healthcare Ass'n (1934)
5550 Friendship Blvd., Suite 300
Chevy Chase, MD 20815
Tel: (301)968-2642   *Fax:* (301)968-4195
E-Mail: aoha@aoha.org
Web Site: http://www.aoha.org
Members: 99 healthcare institutions
Staff: 15
Annual Budget: $500-1,000,000
President and C.E.O.: David L. Kushner, CAE, CMP
Dir., Government Relations: Paul C. Rettig
Coordinator, Member Svcs.: Margaret W. Townsend
Dir., Operations: Bobbi Brown Talisman
Coordinator, Membership Development: M.A. O'Donnell

Historical Note
Formerly (1993) the American Osteopathic Hospital Ass'n. Sponsors the AOHA Political Action Committee and The Foundation for Osteopathic Health Services. Affiliated with the College of Osteopathic Healthcare Executives. AOHA is dedicated to the interests of osteopathic hospitals and healthcare systems. The Assn's mission is to serve its members by promoting the health and welfare of the American public through effective leadership, serving as the unified voice in areas of common interest for the advancement of osteopathic health care, and providing advocacy and education to ensure members' success. AOHA's vision is to serve the osteopathic profession and its principles through a unified, collaborative organization that increases the recognition of osteopathic medicine and promotes excellence in the delivery of health care and medical education.

Publications:
Osteopathic Membership Directory. a.
Osteopathic Progress. bi-m.

Meetings/Conferences:
1999 – Chicago, IL/Apr. 24-27

American Ostrich Ass'n *(1987)*
PO Box 162627
Fort Worth, TX 76161-2627
Tel: (817)232-1200   *Fax:* (817)232-1390
E-Mail: aoa@flash.net
Web Site: http://www.ostriches.org
Members: 1,500 individuals
Staff: 4
Annual Budget: $500-1,000,000
Exec. Director: Mac Young
Communications Director: Janis L. Gary
Financial Manager: Sherrie Caraway
Membership Coordinator: Marilyn Phillips

Historical Note
AOA supports the ostrich industry through government relations, promotions, referral services, and other programs. Membership: $150/year (domestic); $200/year (international).

Publications:
American Ostrich Magazine. m. adv.

Meetings/Conferences:
Annual Meetings: October-November

American Otological Soc. *(1868)*
2720 Tartan Way
Springfield, IL 62707
Tel: (217)483-6966   *Fax:* (217)483-6966
E-Mail: segossard@aol.com
Members: 225 individuals
Annual Budget: $25-50,000
Secretary-Treasurer: Dr. Horst Conrad

Historical Note
AOS members are otologists and other health professionals with an interest in diseases of the ear. Membership: $400/year (individual).

Publications:
American Journal of Otology. bi-m. adv.
Transactions of the AOS. a. adv.

Meetings/Conferences:

American Oxford Sheep Ass'n *(1882)*
1960 East-2100 North Road
Stonington, IL 62567
Tel: (217)325-3515
Members: 500 individuals
Staff: 2
Annual Budget: under $10,000
Exec. Secretary: Mary Blome

Historical Note
Founded in Xenia, Ohio as the American Oxford Down Record Ass'n and assumed its present name in 1981. Membership: $10/year (senior members); $5/year (junior members).

Publications:
Newsletter. semi-a.
Oxford Newsletter. semi-a.

Meetings/Conferences:
Annual Meetings: Springfield, IL/third week in June

American Pain Soc. *(1978)*
4700 W. Lake Ave.
Glenview, IL 60025-1485
Tel: (847)375-4715   *Fax:* (847)375-4777
E-Mail: aps@amctec.com
Web Site: http://www.amctec.com/aps
Members: 3,400 individuals
Staff: 10
Annual Budget: $1-2,000,000
Exec. Director: Dr. Richard G. Muir

Historical Note
Physicians, dentists, psychologists, nurses, physical and occupational therapists and scientists interested in pain research and treatment. A national chapter of the Internat'l Ass'n for the Study of Pain. Incorporated in the District of Columbia in August, 1978. Mission is to serve people in pain by advancing research, education, treatment and professional practice. Membership: $100-$235/year, depending on income (individual); $40/year (student).

Publications:
APS Bulletin. bi-m. adv.
APS Membership Directory. a. adv.
APS Pain Facilities Directory. adv. adv.
Pain Forum. q. adv.

Meetings/Conferences:

American Paint Horse Ass'n *(1962)*
Box 961023
Fort Worth, TX 76161-0023
Tel: (817)834-2742   *Fax:* (817)838-7868
E-Mail: eroberts@apha.com
Web Site: http://www.apha.com

Members: 58,000 individuals
Staff: 130
Annual Budget: $2-5,000,000
Exec. Secretary: Ed Roberts
Business Manager: Steve Wasson

Historical Note
Merger of American Paint Stock Horse and American Paint Quarter Horse Ass'ns. Collects, records, and preserves the pedigrees of Paint horses. Member of the Nat'l Pedigree Livestock Council and the American Horse Council. Membership: $25/year.

Publications:
Down the Back Stretch. bi-m.
Member News. q.
Paint Perspective. q.
Stud Book and Registry. m. adv.
The Paint Horse Journal. q.

Meetings/Conferences:
Annual Meetings: Fall

American Pancreatic Ass'n *(1970)*
UCLA Sch. of Medicine, CHS72-259
10833 LeConte Ave.
Los Angeles, CA 90024
Tel: (805)259-1593
Members: 375 individuals
Annual Budget: under $10,000
Secretary-Treasurer: Howard A. Reber, M.D.

Historical Note
Formerly (1975) American Pancreatic Study Group. APA members are medical professionals with an interest in diseases of the pancreas. Has no paid officers or full-time staff.

Meetings/Conferences:
Annual Meetings: always Chicago, IL/November

American Paper Machinery Ass'n *(1933)*
111 Park Place
Falls Church, VA 22046-4513
Tel: (703)538-1787   *Fax:* (703)241-5603
E-Mail: apmahQ@aol.com
Members: 27 companies
Staff: 5
Annual Budget: $50-100,000
Exec. Director: Elizabeth B. Armstrong, CAE
Government Information Manager: Clay D. Tyerar
Meetings Manager: Judith O. Buzzerd
Member Services Coordinator: Sharon Kelly

Historical Note
Formerly (1971) Pulp and Paper Machinery Ass'n, and (1989) Pulp and Paper Machinery Manufacturers Ass'n. Membership: $1,700-$2,700/year.

Publications:
Newsletter (for members only). m.

Meetings/Conferences:
Semi-Annual Meetings: Spring and Fall
1999 – Delray Beach, FL/Feb. 11-14

American Paraplegia Soc. *(1954)*
75-20 Astoria Blvd.
Jackson Heights, NY 11370-1177
Tel: (718)803-3782   *Fax:* (718)803-0414
Web Site: http://www.apssci.org
Members: 400 individuals
Staff: 4
Annual Budget: $250-500,000
Exec. Administrator: Vivian Beyda, Ph.D.

Historical Note
APS members are physicians and scientists with an interest in injuries and diseases of the spinal cord. Membership: $100/year (individual).

Publications:
Compendium of Abstracts in Spinal Cord Medicine. 2/year.
Journal of Spinal Cord Medicine. q.

Meetings/Conferences:
1999 – Las Vegas, NV(Riviera)/Sept. 7-9
2000 – Las Vegas, NV(Riviera)/Sept. 5-7
2001 – Las Vegas, NV(Riviera)/Sept. 4-6

American Park and Recreation Soc. *(1966)*
22377 Belmont Ridge Road
Ashburn, VA 20148
Tel: (703)858-0784   *Fax:* (703)729-4753
Toll Free: (800)649 - 3042
E-Mail: nrpanesc@aol.com
Members: 6,900 individuals
Staff: 2
Annual Budget: $50-100,000
Director of National Programs: Kathy J. Spangler

Historical Note
Formed by a merger of the American Institute of Park Executives (1898) and American Recreation Soc. (1938). APRS members are professional park and recreation directors. APRS is the largest branch of the National Recreation and Park Association.

Publications:
APRS National Resource Directory. a.
Keeping You Current Newsletter. q.
Programmer's Information Network. q.

Meetings/Conferences:
1999 – Nashville, TN/Oct. 20-24

American Paso Fino Horse Ass'n *(1964)*
P.O. Box 2363
Pittsburgh, PA 15230
Tel: (724)437-5170   *Fax:* (724)438-4471
Members: 500 individuals
President: Warren R. Hull

Historical Note
Members are breeders and owners of Paso Fino horses. Maintains stud book and breed registry.

Publications:
American Paso Fino World. q.

Meetings/Conferences:
Annual Meetings: Fall

American Pathology Foundation *(1959)*
1202 Allanson Road
Mundelein, IL 60060-3808
Tel: (847)949-6055   *Fax:* (847)566-4580
Members: 600 individuals
Staff: 3
Exec. Director: Edward J. Stygar, Jr.

Historical Note
Formerly the Private Practitioners of Pathology Foundation. Members are board certified pathologists concerned with private practice. Membership: $175/year (individual).

Publications:
Directory. a.
Newsletter. q.

Meetings/Conferences:
1999 – Coelor D'Alene, ID/July 14-18

American Patient Ass'n *(1996)*
19545 Willowfield Court
Mokena, IL 60448
Tel: (708)479-8078
E-Mail: muehlbauer@aaos.org
Staff: 1
Annual Budget: under $10,000
Exec. Director: Eric J. Muehlbauer

Historical Note
Promotes a patient-active model of the healing process. Membership: $25-50/year.

American Payroll Ass'n *(1982)*
711 Navarro, Suite 100
San Antonio, TX 78205
Tel: (210)226-4600   *Fax:* (210)226-4027
Web Site: http://www.americanpayroll.org
Members: 14,000 individuals
Staff: 51
Annual Budget: $10-25,000,000
Exec. Director: Daniel J. Maddux
Public Rels. Manager: Kelly Johnson
Mgr., Events Planning: Carolyn Kobos
Dir., Education/Operations: Michael O'Toole
Dir., Finance/Training Development: Jim Medlock, CPP
Dir., Association Services: Rhonda Santamour

Historical Note
APA was established to increase the payroll professional's skill level through education and mutual support and to obtain recognition for payroll work as a professional discipline. Awards the designation Certified Payroll Professional (CPP). Has an annual budget of $8.1 million. Membership: $125/year (individual).

Publications:
APA Directory. 1/18m's.
Payroll Currently. (tax compliance new.
Payroll Views & News. (newspaper) bi-m. adv.
Paytech. (magazine) bi-m. adv.

Meetings/Conferences:
1999 – Las Vegas, NV(Bally's)/May 18-21

American Peanut Council *(1940)*
1500 King St., Suite 301
Alexandria, VA 22314-2730
Tel: (703)838-9500   *Fax:* (703)838-9089
E-Mail: peanutsusa@aol.com
Members: 225 producers and businesses
Staff: 8
Annual Budget: $2-5,000,000
President: Jeannette H. Anderson
Administrative Asst.: Anieca Lord

Historical Note
Formerly Nat'l Peanut Council (1998). Founded in June, 1940 and incorporated in Georgia in 1941, the Council counts among its members peanut farmers, shellers, brokers, special processors, the manufacturers of peanut products and peanut butter, as well as the allied support trades. As the umbrella for the entire peanut industry, the Council promotes increased peanut consumption, research and the dissemination of knowledge of new technology, as well as improved processing, storage, handling and packaging techniques. The Council also acts as a clearinghouse for information pertaining to actions by the federal government and is the industry forum for the exchange of ideas and information by the industry's leaders.

Publications:
American Peanut News.
Membership Directory. a.

Meetings/Conferences:
Annual Meetings: Spring/500

American Peanut Product Manufacturers *(1983)*
555 13th St., N.W.
Washington, DC 20004-1109
Tel: (202)637-5600   *Fax:* (202)637-5910
Members: 12 companies
Staff: 2

Historical Note
Members are food processors of products using peanuts.

Meetings/Conferences:
Annual Meetings: Not held.

American Peanut Research and Education Soc. *(1968)*
376 Ag Hall
Oklahoma State University
Stillwater, OK 74078
Tel: (405)744-9634   *Fax:* (405)744-5269
Members: 450 individuals
Staff: 2
Annual Budget: $50-100,000

Exec. Officer: J. Ronald Sholar, Ph.D.

Historical Note
Organized in Norfolk, Virginia July 1968 as the American Peanut Research and Education Ass'n as an outgrowth of the Peanut Improvement Working Group dating back to 1957. The present name was adopted in 1979. Membership, which is drawn from government, academia and private industry, now includes individuals from over 20 countries. Membership: $25/year (individual), $35/year (company).

Publications:
APRES Proceedings. a.
Peanut Research. q.
Peanut Science. semi-a.

Meetings/Conferences:
Annual Meetings: July
1999 – Sanannah, GA(Hyatt Regency Savannah)/July 13-16

American Peanut Shellers Ass'n *(1919)*
P.O. Box 70157
Albany, GA   31708-0157
Tel: (912)888-2508   *Fax:* (912)888-5150
E-Mail: info@peanut-shellers.org
Web Site: htpp://www.peanut-shellers.org
Members: 200 companies
Staff: 4
Annual Budget: $2-5,000,000
Exec. Director: John T. Powell
Events/Publications Dir.: Miriam Crosby

Historical Note
Formerly (1994) Southeastern Peanut Ass'n. Active members are companies engaged in peanut shelling and crushing; 198 associate members are firms serving the peanut industry in such areas as transportation, storage, insurance, implement manufacture, etc. Retains representation in Washington to promote the interests of the national peanut shellers. Membership: based on tonnage (active members); $400/year (associate member).

Publications:
Membership Directory. a.
Newsletter. m.

Meetings/Conferences:

American Pediatric Soc. *(1888)*
3400 Research Forest Drive, Suite B-7
The Woodlands, TX   77381-4259
Tel: (847)427-0206   *Fax:* (847)427-1305
E-Mail: info@aps-spr.org
Web Site: http://www.aps-spr.org
Members: 1,375 individuals
Staff: 4
Annual Budget: $50-100,000
Exec. Director: Debbie Anagnostelis
Asst.Exec. Director: Kathy A. Cannon

Historical Note
Organized September 18, 1888 and incorporated in New York in 1962. Membership: $185/year.

Publications:
Pediatric Research. m.

Meetings/Conferences:
Annual Meetings: Spring/4,500
1999 – San Francisco, CA(Hilton)/May 1-4/4500

American Pediatric Surgical Ass'n
13 Elm St.
Manchester, MA   01944-1314
Tel: (978)526-8330   *Fax:* (978)526-4018
Members: 600 individuals
Exec. Director: Kevin M. Cuff

Publications:
APSA Membership Directory. a.
Journal of Pediatric Surgery. m. adv.
Newsletter. a.

Meetings/Conferences:
Annual Meetings: May
1999 – Rancho Mirage, CA(Westin Mission Hills)/May 16-19/1000
2000 – Orlando, FL(WDW Swan)/May 25-28

American Pet Boarding Ass'n *(1989)*
22096 N. Pet Lane
Prairie View, IL   60069
Tel: (847)634-9444   *Fax:* (847)634-9460
Members: 189 individuals
Staff: 1
Annual Budget: $10-25,000
Exec. Director: Robert X. Leeds

Historical Note
APBA's goal is to define valid criteria for the humane boarding care of companion animals and to recognize operating boarding facilities that meet this criteria by conferring Accredited Membership to them. Membership: $35/year.

Publications:
Journal of Professional Pet Boarding. q. adv.

Meetings/Conferences:
Annual Meetings: Meetings are held during the first week in October.

American Pet Products Manufacturers Ass'n *(1958)*
255 Glenville Road
Greenwich, CT   06831-4148
Tel: (203)532-0000   *Fax:* (203)532-0551
Toll Free: (800)452 - 1225
Web Site: http://www.appma.org
Members: 500 companies
Staff: 9
Annual Budget: $2-5,000,000
Exec. V. President: William D. Schoolman
Director, Communications: Funda Alp
Gen. Counsel/Dir., Legis. Affairs: Gina Valeri

Director, Trade Shows & Special Events: Andrew Darmohraj
Dir. Member Services: Anne Ferrante

Historical Note
APPMA is a trade association for manufacturers and importers of pet products. Represents the pet products industry in the U.S., providing market research, legislative and regulatory monitoring, industry promotion, and other services to members.

Publications:
APPMA FaxBrief. bi-m.
APPMA Newsbriefs Update. q.
Nat'l Pet Owners Survey. bien.

Meetings/Conferences:
Annual Meetings: June
1999 – Nashville, TN(Opryland)/June 2-4/6000
2000 – Orlando, FL(Orange Cty. Convention Ctr.)/June 1-3/7000
2001 – San Diego, CA(Convention Ctr.)/June 7-9/7500
2002 – Chicago, IL(McCormick Place)/June 12-14/8000

American Petroleum Institute *(1919)*
1220 L St., N.W.,
Washington, DC   20005
Tel: (202)682-8000   *Fax:* (202)682-8115
Web Site: http://www.api.org
Members: 400 companies
Staff: 455
Annual Budget: $50-100,000,000
President: Charles J. DiBona
V. President, Public Affairs: Arthur E.F. Wiese
V.P., Government Affairs: Charles E. Sandler
Events Manager: Karen Halligan
Exec. V. President: William F. O'Keefe
V. President and General Counsel: G. William Frick
Director, Industry Services: James K. Walters

Historical Note
Incorporated March 20, 1919 in New York, NY. The petroleum industry's major trade ass'n, API is an umbrella organization for the major oil companies, independent oil producers and fuel distributors, service-station owners and other related concerns. Provides public policy development and advocacy, research, and technical services to help the industry meet the nation's energy needs . Maintains offices in New York, Dallas, and 33 state capitals. Has an annual budget of approximately $82.0 million. Membership: scale based on volume/sales.

Publications:
Numerous pamphlets and manuals.

Meetings/Conferences:
Annual Meetings: Rotates between Chicago, IL(every third year); New York, NY; San Francisco, CA; and Houston, TX in November

American Pewter Guild *(1958)*
c/o Fischer Pewter
11940 Old Buckingham Road
Midlothian, VA   23113-3728
Tel: (804)379-3282
Members: 36 manufacturers of pewter
Staff: 1
Annual Budget: $25-50,000
Exec. Director: Nellie M. Fischer

Historical Note
APG perpetuates the traditions of European craft guilds in order to maintain high standards of quality for pewter, to network with other international pewter guilds and trade organizations, and develop consumer awareness of the attributes of pewter products. Members represent both foreign and domestic concerns, large manufacturers, individual hobbyist, and suppliers to the industry. Membership fee varies.

Meetings/Conferences:
Semi-annual Meetings: Spring and Fall

American Pharmaceutical Ass'n *(1852)*
2215 Constitution Ave., N.W.
Washington, DC   20037-2985
Tel: (202)628-4410   *Fax:* (202)783-2351
Web Site: http://www.aphanet.org
Members: 50,000 individuals
Staff: 90
Annual Budget: $10-25,000,000
Exec. V. President & C.E.O.: John A. Gans, Pharm.D.
Director, Communications & Strategic Planning: Ronald L. Williams
Director, Policy and Legislation: Susan C. Winckler
Director, Expositions: Windy K. Christner
Director of Education: Elizabeth Keyes
V. President, Finance & Administration: Roger K. Browning
Director, Executive Office Operations: Linda Faison
General Counsel: Michael McConihe
V. President, Marketing & Membership: Robert A. Fulcher
Director, Information Services: Gail Whitaker

Historical Note
Founded in Philadelphia in 1852 and incorporated in the District of Columbia in 1888, APhA is a national professional society of pharmacists. Its constituent sections include: Academy of Pharmacy Practice and Management, Academy of Pharmaceutical Research and Science, and Academy of Students of Pharmacy. Sponsors and supports the APhA Political Action Committee. Membership: $165/year.

Publications:
Journal of Pharmaceutical Sciences. m. adv.
Journal of the American Pharmaceutical Ass'n. m. adv.
Pharmacy Student. q.
Pharmacy Today. m. adv.

Meetings/Conferences:
Annual Meetings: Spring/5,000
1999 – San Antonio, TX/March 6-10
2000 – Washington, DC/March 11-15
2001 – San Francisco, CA/March 17-21
2002 – Philadelphia, PA/March 16-20

American Pharmaceutical Product Managers Associates *(1991)*
Historical Note
Address unknown in 1995.

American Philatelic Soc. Writers Unit *(1967)*
2501 Drexel St.
Vienna, VA   22180
Tel: (703)560-2413
Members: 400 individuals
Staff: 1
Annual Budget: under $10,000
Secretary-Treasurer: George Griffenhagen

Historical Note
APSWU members are journalists and editors specializing in philately. APSWU is unit #30 of the American Philatelic Society. Membership: $10/year (USA); $17/year (outside the U.S.).

Publications:
Philatelic Communicator Journal. q.

Meetings/Conferences:
Annual Meetings: in conjunction with the American Philatelic Soc.

American Philological Ass'n *(1869)*
19 University Place,Rm.328
New York University
New York, NY   10003-4556
Tel: (212)998-3575   *Fax:* (212)995-4814
E-Mail: american.pilological@nyu.edu
Web Site: http://www.apaclassic.org
Members: 3,200 individuals
Staff: 3
Annual Budget: $500-1,000,000
Executive Director: John Marincola

Historical Note
Organized in Poughkeepsie, New York in July, 1869 by classical scholars from the Classical Section of the American Oriental Soc. and the Greek Club of New York City. A member of the American Council of Learned Societies and National Humanities Alliance. APA membership primarily comprises university and college teachers of classical languages, literature and history. Membership: $18-85/year (individual, based on salary); $55/year (organization).

Publications:
American Classical Studies. irreg.
Meeting Program. a.
Newsletter. bi-m.
Philological Monographs. irreg.
Positions for Classicals and Archaeologists. m.
Transaction and Proceedings. a.

Meetings/Conferences:
Annual Meetings: Always December 27-30
1999 – Dallas, TX/Dec. 27-30

American Philosophical Ass'n *(1900)*
University of Delaware
31 Amstel Ave.,
Newark, DE   19716-8690
Tel: (302)831-1112   *Fax:* (302)831-8690
E-Mail: apaOnline@udel.edu
Web Site: http://www.udel.edu/apa
Members: 9,600 individuals
Staff: 7
Annual Budget: $500-1,000,000
Exec. Director: Eric Hoffman
Meetings Coordinator: Janet Sample

Historical Note
Formed in New York City in November, 1901 with 98 charter members. Merged in 1927 with the Western Philosophical Ass'n, founded in 1900, and later with the Soc. of Philosophy, a Pacific Coast organization. Members are professors of philosophy at the college level, graduate students and others with a special interest in the field. A member of the American Council of Learned Societies and the Federation Internationale des Societes de Philosophie. Membership: $30-115/yr. (individual, by income).

Publications:
Computer Use in Philosophy Newsletter. semi-a.
Feminism & Philosophy Newsletter. semi-a.
Jobs for Philosophers. 5/year.
Philosophy & Law Newsletter. semi-a.
Philosophy & Medicine Newsletter. semi-a.
Philosophy and the Black Experience Newsletter. semi-a.
Proceedings and Addresses. 5/year. adv.
Teaching Philosophy Newsletter. semi-a.

Meetings/Conferences:
Three Meetings Annually: March, April and December
1999 – Berkeley, CA/March 31-April 3
1999 – Boston, MA/Dec. 27-30
1999 – New Orleans, LA(Hyatt Regency)/May 5-8
2000 – Chicago, IL(Palmer House)/April 19-22
2000 – New York, NY/Dec. 27-30

American Philosophical Soc. *(1743)*
Independence Mall East
104 South Fifth St.
Philadelphia, PA   19106-3387
Tel: (215)440-3400   *Fax:* (215)440-3436
Web Site: http://www.amphilsoc.org
Members: 700 individuals
Staff: 32
Annual Budget: $2-5,000,000
Exec. Officer: Alexander G. Bearn, Ph.D.

Historical Note
Founded 1743 in Philadelphia by Benjamin Franklin, APS evolved in 1769 through a merger of the American Philosophical Soc. and the American Soc. for Promoting Useful Knowledge; chartered in 1780 in Pennsylvania. The full name is the American Philosophical Society Held at Philadelphia for Promoting Useful Knowledge. A member of the American Council of Learned

Societies. Promotes and advances all useful branches of knowledge through: scholarly and scientific meetings (semi-annual); financial assistance to scholars; scholarly books, monographs, articles and newsletter; a library specializing in the history of science in America and its European background; and community service. The society, which includes about 100 Nobel laureates, recognizes excellence with awards and medals including the Magellanic Premium, the oldest scientific prize in America.

Publications:
APS News Newsletter. semi-a.
Memoirs. 6-8/year.
Proceedings. q.
Transactions. 6-8/year.
Yearbook. a.

Meetings/Conferences:
Semi-Annual Meetings: Spring and Fall
1999 – /April 22-24
1999 – /November 12-13
2000 – /April 27-29
2000 – /Nov. 10-11

American Phosphate Export Ass'n

Historical Note
Ass'n defunct in 1997.

American Photographic Artisans Guild (1966)
Box 699
Port Clinton, OH   43452-0699
Tel: (419)732-3290
E-Mail: allynr@dcache.net
Web Site: http://www.apag.com
Members: 200 individuals
Staff: 1
Annual Budget: $10-25,000
Exec. Secretary: Allyn Riznikove

Historical Note
Formerly Nat'l Professional Colorists of America. Affiliated with Professional Photographers of America. Membership: $45/year (U.S.); $50/year (Canada & Mexico); $55/year (foreign).

Publications:
Palette Page. q. adv.

Meetings/Conferences:

American Physical Soc. (1899)
One Physics Ellipse
College Park, MD   20740-3844
Tel: (301)209-3200   *Fax:* (301)209-0865
E-Mail: webmaster@aps.org
Web Site: http://www.aps.org
Members: 41,000 individuals
Staff: 170
Annual Budget: $25-50,000,000
Exec. Officer: Judy R. Franz, Ph.D.
Coordinator, Meetings and Publications: Donna Baudrau
Director of Education and Outreach Programs: Ramon Lopez
Treasurer: Thomas McIrath
Assoc. Exec. Officer: Barrett Ripin
Membership Manager: Trish Lettieri

Historical Note
Founded in 1899, the Society's objective is the advancement and diffusion of the the knowledge of physics. A constituent member of the American Institute of Physics. Has an annual budget of approximately $30 million. Membership: $25-90/year (individual).

Publications:
APS News. m.
Bulletin of the APS. m.
Physical Review Abstracts. bi-w.
Physical Review Letters. w.
Reviews of Modern Physics. q.
The Physical Reviews A-E. m.

Meetings/Conferences:
1999 – Atlanta, GA(Convention Center)/March 22-26
2000 – Minneapolis, MN/March 20-24
2001 – Seattle, WA/March 12-16
2002 – Indianapolis, IN/March 17-22

American Physical Therapy Ass'n (1921)
1111 N. Fairfax St.
Alexandria, VA   22314-1488
Tel: (703)684-2782   *Fax:* (703)684-7343
Toll Free: (800)999 - 2782
Web Site: http://www.apta.org
Members: 75,000 individuals
Staff: 170
Annual Budget: $25-50,000,000
C.E.O.: Francis J. Mallon
Senior V.P., Communications: Nancy Perkin Beaumont, CAE
Director, Public Relations: Alexis B. Waters
Director, Governance: Kristyanne Maldonado
Sr. V.P., Governance, Components, & Meetings: Bonnie Polvinale
Director, Meeting Services: Dobby Wall
Senior V.P., Education: Joseph P.H. Black, Ph.D.
Sr. Exec. V.P., Administration/Finance: Charles L. Martin, Jr., CAE
Senior V. President, Research: Cynthia M. Shewan, Ph.D.
Director, Ins/Member Benefits: Christie J. Susko
Senior V.P., Health Policy: Jerome Connolly

Historical Note
Founded as the American Women's Physical Therapeutic Ass'n, it became the American Physiotherapy Ass'n in the 1930s and assumed its current name in 1948. APTA is a professional association of physical therapists, physical therapist assistants and physical therapy students. Sponsors and supports the Physical Therapy Political Action Committee (PTPAC). Membership: $250/year, plus chapter dues.

Publications:
Physical Therapy Journal. m. adv.
PT Bulletin. w. adv.
PT, Magazine of Physical Therapy. m. adv.

Meetings/Conferences:
1999 – Seattle, WA/Feb. 3-7
1999 – Washington, DC/June 4-9
2000 – Indianapolis, IN/June 16-21

American Physical Therapy Ass'n - Private Practice Section (1955)
1710 Rhode Island Ave., NW, #800
Washington, DC   20036-3126
Tel: (202)457-1115   *Fax:* (202)457-9191
Web Site: http://www.pps.apfa.org
Members: 3,000 individuals
Staff: 5
Annual Budget: $1-2,000,000
C.E.O.: Lisa Wade

Historical Note
Consists of members of the APTA who are in private practice.

Publications:
IMPACT (monthly newsletter). m. adv.
Private Practice Section Membership Directory. a. adv.

Meetings/Conferences:
Annual Meetings: Fall
1999 – Marco Island, FL/Nov. 4-7

American Physicians Ass'n of Computer Medicine (1984)

Historical Note
Address unknown in 1997.

American Physiological Soc. (1887)
9650 Rockville Pike
Bethesda, MD   20814-3991
Tel: (301)530-7118   *Fax:* (301)571-8305
E-Mail: info@aps.faseb.org
Web Site: http://www.faseb.org/aps/
Members: 8,700 individuals
Staff: 70
Annual Budget: $10-25,000,000
Exec. Director: Martin Frank, Ph.D.
Publications Manager: Brenda Rauner
Public Affairs Coordinator: Alice Hellerstein
Coordinator, Membership Services: Linda Allen
Education Officer: Marsha Lakes Matyas, PhD
Business Manager: James C. Liakos

Historical Note
Founded December 30, 1887 at a meeting held in the physiology laboratory of the College of Physicians and Surgeons, New York City. Incorporated in Missouri in 1923. A member of the Federation of American Socs. for Experimental Biology (FASEB). Membership: $85/year (regular, corresponding); $60/year (affiliate); $15/year (students). Has an annual budget of over $10 million.

Publications:
Advances in Physiology Education. semi-a.
American Journal of Physiology (Consolidated). m.
American Journal of Physiology: Cell Physiology. m.
American Journal of Physiology: Cell Physiology. m. adv.
American Journal of Physiology: Endocrinology and
    Metabolism. m.
American Journal of Physiology: Gastrointestinal/Liver
    Physiology. m.
American Journal of Physiology: Heart and Circulatory
    Physiology. m.
American Journal of Physiology: Lung Cellular/Molecular
    Phys. m. adv.
American Journal of Physiology:
    Regulatory/Integrative/Comparative. m.
American Journal of Physiology: Renal Physiology. m.
Journal of Applied Physiology. m. adv.
Journal of Neurophysiology. m. adv.
News in Physiological Sciences. bi-m. adv.
Physiological Genomics.
Physiological Reviews. q. adv.
The Physiologist. bi-m. adv.

Meetings/Conferences:
Semi-Annual Meetings: Spring (with FASEB) and Fall
1999 – Washington, DC/April 17-21

American Phytopathological Soc. (1908)
3340 Pilot Knob Road
St. Paul, MN   55121-2097
Tel: (651)454-7250   *Fax:* (651)454-0766
E-Mail: aps@scisoc.org
Web Site: http://www.scisoc.org
Members: 5,000 individuals, 60 companies and organizations
Staff: 60
Annual Budget: $2-5,000,000
Exec. V. President: Steven C. Nelson
Public Relations: Kathleen Kogler
Director, Meetings: Faye Labatt
Director, Finance: Larry Hartman
Manager, Membership Marketing and Public Relations: Michelle
    Bjerkness
Dir., Scientific Services: Cindy Ash

Historical Note
Founded December 30, 1908 in Baltimore with 130 charter members and Incorporated in the District of Columbia in 1915. Promotes all aspects of knowledge of plant diseases and control. Membership: $61/year individual); $360/year (company).

Publications:
Directory. a. adv.
Molecular Plant-Microbe Interactions. 9/year. adv.
Phytopathology. m.
Phytopathology News. m. adv.
Plant Disease. m. adv.

Meetings/Conferences:
Annual Meetings: Summer/1,800-2,000
1999 – Montreal, PQ, Canada/Aug. 6-12
2000 – New Orleans, LA/Aug. 12-16
2001 – Salt Lake City, UT/Aug. 25-29

American Pilots' Ass'n (1884)
499 S. Capitol St., S.W., Suite 409
Washington, DC   20003
Tel: (202)484-0700   *Fax:* (202)484-9320
E-Mail: apaxdir@aol.com
Members: 59 state associations
Staff: 4
Annual Budget: $2-5,000,000
Exec. Director-General Counsel: Paul G. Kirchner

Historical Note
APA members are groups or state licensed maritime pilots or federally licensed pilots in the Great Lakes region. Membership: $1,040/year (individual).

Publications:
On Station. q.

Meetings/Conferences:
Biennial Meetings: Even years
2000 – New Orleans, LA

American Pinzgauer Ass'n (1973)
21555 State Rt. 698
Jenera, OH   45841
Tel: (419)326-8711   *Fax:* (419)326-5501
Toll Free: (800)914 - 9883
E-Mail: APinzgauer@aol.com
Web Site: http://www.afn.org/ ~ greatcow/
Members: 500 individuals
Staff: 1
Annual Budget: $25-50,000
Secretary: Peg Meents

Historical Note
Owners and breeders of the Pinzgauer breed of cattle, which originated in the Pinzgau Valley region of Austria. Membership: $35/year (individual); lifetime membership: $200.

Publications:
Pinzgauer Journal. q. adv.
Pinzgauer Newsline (newsletter). bi-m.

Meetings/Conferences:
Annual Meetings: Fall/100
1999 – Milwaukee, WI(Best Western)
2000 – Puyallup, WA/Sept. 15-20

American Pipe Fittings Ass'n (1938)
111 Park Place
Falls Church, VA   22046-4513
Tel: (703)538-1786   *Fax:* (703)241-5603
E-Mail: APFAHQ@aol.com
Members: 50 companies
Staff: 2
Annual Budget: $100-250,000
Exec. Director: Clay D. Tyeryar

Historical Note
Formerly Pipe Fittings Manufacturers Ass'n. Members are domestic producers of piping components and accessories and pipe hangers and supports. Seeks to promote use of American pipe fittings, contribute to development of standards, collect statistics, and cooperate with government agencies on matters affecting the industry.

Publications:
The Pipeline. 4-5/year.

Meetings/Conferences:
Semi-Annual Meetings: April and October/90

American Planning Ass'n (1909)
122 S. Michigan Ave., Suite 1600
Chicago, IL   60603-6107
Tel: (312)431-9100   *Fax:* (312)431-9985
Web Site: http://www.planning.org
Members: 29,000 individuals
Staff: 70
Annual Budget: $10-25,000,000
Exec. Director: Frank So
Director, Policy: Jeff Soule
Programs Director: Vicki Groat
Coord., Chapter/Student Services: Marsha Holub
Publications Director: Sylvia Lewis

Historical Note
Founded as the Nat'l Conference on City Planning, APA assumed its present name in 1978. Membership is open not only to practicing planners (city, local, state, regional, rural, privately or publicly employed), but to administrators, appointed commissioners, students and others. Includes the American Institute of Certified Planners, a professional institute which provides national certification of planners. Has an annual budget of approximately $11 million. Membership fee varies, based on annual salary: $80-156/year, plus chapter dues.

Publications:
JobMart. semi-m.
Journal of the American Planning Association. q.
Land Use Law and Zoning Digest. m.
Planning. m. adv.
Planning Advisory Service Memo. m.
Planning Advisory Service Reports. 8/year.
Zoning News. m.

Meetings/Conferences:
Annual Meetings: Spring/3,000
1999 – Seattle, WA
2000 – New York, NY
2001 – New Orleans, LA

American Plastics Council (1991)
1801 K St., N.W., Suite 701-L
Washington, DC   20006-1301
Tel: (202)974-5000   *Fax:* (202)296-7119
Web Site: http://www.plasticsresource.com
Members: 26 companies
Staff: 60
Annual Budget: $25-50,000,000

V. President, Communications: Susan P. Moore
V.P., State Govt. Affairs: Roger D. Bernstein
V. President, Government Affairs: Rodney Lowman
V. President, Technology: Ronald N. Liesemer
Dir., Operations: Susan Sherwood
General Counsel: W. Scott Ferguson

Historical Note
APC members include United States resin and monomer producers,
representatives of the plastics industry, processers and suppliers.
Focuses on resource-conservation issues, to ensure that the
industry is environmentally sustainable and responsible. A joint
initiative of Soc. of Plastics Industry. Membership fee varies, based
on sales volume.

Meetings/Conferences:

American Podiatric Circulatory Soc. (1979)
5704 18th Ave.
Brooklyn, NY 11204
Tel: (718)236-7952   Fax: (718)236-7953
Members: 900 individuals
President: Dr. Stanley Goldstein

Historical Note
Membership: $25/year (individual).

Publications:
APCS Bulletin. q. adv.

Meetings/Conferences:
1999 – San Juan, Puerto Rico(El San Jua)/Dec. 10-15/100

American Podiatric Medical Ass'n (1912)
9312 Old Georgetown Road
Bethesda, MD   20814-1698
Tel: (301)571-9200   Fax: (301)530-2752
E-Mail: apmadrop@apma.org
Web Site: http://www.apma.org
Members: 10,500 individuals
Staff: 57
Annual Budget: $5-10,000,000
Exec. Director: Glenn B. Gatswirth, D.P.M.
Director of Public Relations: George Tzamaras
Director/Governmental Affairs: John R. Carson
Annual Meeting Manager: Anne R. Martinez
Dir., Educational Services: Charles Kilczewski
Dir., Coucil on Pediatric Medical Education: Alan Tinkleman
Financial Director: David M. Gessner
General Counsel: Werner Strupp
Member Services Director: Beth McSweeney
Dir., Publications: David Zych
Dir., Development: Cheryl Reinhardt

Historical Note
Organized July 1, 1912 as the Nat'l Ass'n of Chiropodists.
Incorporated in New York in 1912; became the American Podiatry
Ass'n in 1958 and the American Podiatric Medical Ass'n in 1984.
Over 50 component podiatry societies and numerous affiliates.
Supports the Podiatry Political Action Committee, Fund for Podiatric
Medical Education, and Foot Health Foundation of America. Has
an annual budget of approximately $8 million. Membership:
$725/year (individual).

Publications:
APMA Alert. q.
APMA News. m. adv.
Journal of the American Podiatric Medical Association. m.
    adv.

Meetings/Conferences:
Annual Meetings: August/2,000
1999 – Houston, TX(Westin)/Aug. 12-14
2000 – Philadelphia, PA(Marriott)/Aug. 10-12

American Podiatric Medical Students' Ass'n
9312 Old Georgetown Road
Bethesda, MD   20814-1698
Tel: (301)493-9667   Fax: (301)530-2752
E-Mail: betsyAMPS@aol.com
Web Site: http://www.apmas.org
Exec. Director: Betsy Herman

Historical Note
APMSA represents all students enrolled at the seven colleges of
podiatric medicine. The association provides a forum to discuss
issues about the profession of podiatry.

Meetings/Conferences:
1999 – Cleveland, OH/Feb. 3-7

American Podiatric Medical Writers Ass'n (1985)
P.O. Box 750129
Forest Hills, NY 11375
Tel: (718)897-9700   Fax: (718)896-5747
E-Mail: bblock@prodigy.com
Members: 100 individuals
Staff: 3
Annual Budget: $10-25,000
Exec. Director: Dr. Barry Block

Historical Note
Established in New York City. Membership: $50/year (podiatrist);
$25/year (non-podiatrist).

Publications:
APMWA Newsletter. q.

Meetings/Conferences:
Semi-Annual Meetings: 0999-Houston, TX(Westin)/August
2000 – Philadelphia, PA

American Polarity Therapy Ass'n (1984)
2888 Bluff St., Suite 149
Boulder, CO   80301
Tel: (303)545-2080   Fax: (303)545-2161
Toll Free: (800)359 - 5620
E-Mail: SATVAHQ@aol.com
Members: 1,200 individuals
Annual Budget: $250-500,000
Exec. Director: Gary Peterson

Historical Note
Membership: $60/year (individual).

Publications:
Energy Newsletter. q. adv.

Meetings/Conferences:
Annual Meetings: June, plus two regional conferences

American Police Academy
Historical Note
Educational arm of the National Association of Chiefs of Police.

American Political Science Ass'n (1903)
1527 New Hampshire Ave., N.W.
Washington, DC   20036-1206
Tel: (202)483-2512   Fax: (202)483-2657
E-Mail: apsa@apsanet.org
Web Site: http://www.apsanet.org
Members: 14,500 individuals
Staff: 23
Exec. Director: Catherine E. Rudder
Convention Manager: Jennifer Hacha Richards
Director, Educational Programs: Sheilah Mann, Ph.D.
Deputy Director: Robert J.P. Hauck

Historical Note
Member of the American Council of Learned Societies. Membership:
$68-131/year (full member), $32/year (student), $147/year
(company).

Publications:
American Political Science Review. q. adv.
Membership Directory. trien.
Personnel Service Newsletter. m. adv.
PS: Political Science & Politics. q. adv.

Meetings/Conferences:
Annual Meetings: Fall
1999 – Atlanta, GA/Sept 2-5
2000 – Washington, DC/August 31-Sept 3

American Polled Hereford Ass'n (1901)
Historical Note
Merged into the American Hereford Ass'n in 1995.

American Polygraph Ass'n (1966)
P.O. Box 8037
Chattanooga, TN   37414-0037
Tel: (423)892-3992   Fax: (423)894-5435
Toll Free: (800)272 - 8037
Members: 2,500 individuals
Staff: 2
Annual Budget: $100-250,000
Manager: Robbie S. Bennett

Historical Note
A merger of Academy of Scientific Interrogation, American Academy
of Polygraph Examiners, and Nat'l Board of Polygraph Examiners.
Membership: $125/year.

Publications:
APA Membership Directory. a. adv.
APA Newsletter. bi-m.
Polygraph. q.

Meetings/Conferences:
Annual Meetings: August/400
1999 – Dallas, TX(Le Meridien)/Aug. 1-6
2000 – Fort Lauderdale, FLJuly
2001 – Albuquerque, NM

American Polypay Sheep Ass'n (1980)
609 South Central Ave., Suite 9
Sidney, MT   59270
Tel: (406)482-7768   Fax: (406)482-7768
Members: 225 individuals
Staff: 1
Annual Budget: $25-50,000
Exec. Secretary: Debbe Anderson

Historical Note
Breeders of polypay sheep, a breed developed to provide more
pounds of lamb, more frequently. Membership: $50/year.

Publications:
American Polypay Sheep News. q.
Breeders Directory. a. adv.

Meetings/Conferences:
Annual Meetings: Summer
1999 – Springfield, IL/June 17-19

American Pomological Soc. (1848)
102 Tyson Bldg.
University Park, PA   16802
Tel: (814)863-6163   Fax: (814)863-6139
E-Mail: aps@psu.edu
Members: 950 individuals
Staff: 1
Annual Budget: $10-25,000
Treasurer: Dr. Robert M. Crassweller

Historical Note
Formed in Buffalo September 1, 1848 at a conference called by the
New York Agricultural Soc. First called the North American
Pomological Convention, the group became the American
Pomological Congress in 1849 and the American Pomological Soc.
in 1852. The first U.S. national association to promote fruit variety
improvement. Membership: $25/year or $70/3 years.

Publications:
Fruit Varieties Journal. a. adv.

Meetings/Conferences:
Annual Meetings: With the American Soc. for Horticultural
    Science

American Portland Cement Alliance (1989)
1225 I St., N.W., Suite 300
Washington, DC   20005
Tel: (202)408-9494   Fax: (202)408-0877

Members: 40 companies
Staff: 12
President: Richard C. Creighton
Dir., Communications: Steve Kistucentz
V. President, Legislative Affairs: Peggy Renken Hudson
V. President, Environmental Affairs: Andrew O'Hare

Historical Note
Formerly (1989) American Cement Trade Alliance and (1993)
American Cement Alliance. Established and incorporated in the
District of Columbia to address issues relating to the portland
cement industry. Supported by companies who represent more than
a third of the U.S. cement production. Membership: assessed per
ton of clinker capacity.

Meetings/Conferences:

American Postal Workers Union (1971)
1300 L St., N.W.
Washington, DC   20005
Tel: (202)842-4200   Fax: (202)842-8530
E-Mail: apwu.hq@worldnet.att.net
Web Site: http//www.apwu.org
Members: 350,000 individuals
Staff: 90
Annual Budget: $10-25,000,000
President: Moe Biller
Director, Research and Education: Joyce B. Robinson

Historical Note
Merger (1971) of Nat'l Ass'n of Post Office and General Services
Maintenance Employees (1937); Nat'l Ass'n of Special Delivery
Messengers (1932); Nat'l Federation of Post Office Motor Vehicle
Employees (1925); Nat'l Postal Union; United Federation of Postal
Clerks (1966). Affiliated with AFL–CIO. Has a budget of about $18
million. Sponsors and supports the Committee on Political Action of
the American Postal Workers Union.

Publications:
The American Postal Worker. m. adv.

Meetings/Conferences:
Biennial Meetings: Even years in Summer

American Poultry Ass'n (1873)
133 Millville Street
Mendon, MA   01756
Tel: (508)473-8769
Members: 3,000 individuals
Staff: 1
Annual Budget: $25-50,000
Secretary-Treasurer: Lorna Rhodes

Historical Note
The oldest livestock organization in North America, established in
Buffalo, New York by a group of poultrymen interested in fostering
purebred poultry. Membership: $10/year (individual), $20/year
(organization/company), $25/year(international).

Publications:
APA Fancy Feathers. q.
APA Yearbook. a. adv.
News and Views.

Meetings/Conferences:

American Poultry Historical Soc. (1952)
Historical Note
Address unknown in 1994.

American Poultry U.S.A. (1978)
P.O. Box 16805
Jackson, MS   39236
Tel: (601)956-1715   Fax: (601)956-1755
Members: 13 companies
Staff: 5
Annual Budget: $50-100,000,000
V. President, Administration: Bob M. Anthony

Historical Note
A Webb-Pomerene Act association. Has an annual budget of $90
million.

Meetings/Conferences:
Triennial Meetings: Summer (1997)

American Precision Optics Manufacturers Ass'n (1986)
Historical Note
Organization defunct in 1995.

American Prepaid Legal Services Institute (1976)
541 N. Fairbanks Court
Chicago, IL   60611
Tel: (312)988-5751   Fax: (312)988-5710
E-Mail: lunealbrown@staff.abanet.org
Web Site: http://www.abanet.org/api
Members: 650 individuals
Staff: 4
Annual Budget: $250-500,000
Exec. Director: Alec M. Schwartz
Legislative Counsel: Jeremy Perlin

Historical Note
Founded by the American Bar Ass'n to serve as a national umbrella
organization dedicated to the growth and development of prepaid
legal services. Membership: $120/year (affiliate); $325/year
(organization/company); $75/year (provider).

Publications:
API Newsbriefs. m.
Publications List Available.
Regulation Reporter on Pre-Paid Legal Services. 6/yea.

Meetings/Conferences:
Annual Meetings: Spring/150
1999 – Myrtle Beach, SC(Wyndham MB
    Resort)/May 12-15/175
2000 – Vancouver, BC(Renaissance
    Vancouver)/May 17-20/175

American Preventive Medical Ass'n (1992)

459 Walker Road
Great Falls, VA 22066
Tel: (703)759-0662   *Fax:* (703)759-6711
Toll Free: (800)230 - 2762
E-Mail: apma@healthy.net
Web Site: http://www.healthy.net/apma
Members: 700 individuals
Staff: 2
Annual Budget: $250-500,000
Exec. Director: Candace Campbell

Historical Note
APMA members are primarily health care practitioners who use complementary therapies, nutritional supplements or other so-called alternatives to allopathic medicine; supplement manufacturers; and other individuals or businesses involved in the preventive health care industry. Membership: $300/year (practicing physicians); $145/year (allied health care practitioner [non-licensed]); $95/year (laymen).

Publications:
APMA Quarterly. q.
Director's Report Newsletter. m.

Meetings/Conferences:

American Printed Fabrics Council (1966)

Historical Note
Formed by members of the Textile Distributors Association to promote printed fabrics; administrative support provided by TDA.

American Printing History Ass'n (1974)
P.O. Box 4922, Grand Central Station
New York, NY 10163
Tel: (212)930-9220   *Fax:* (212)302-4815
Members: 900 individuals
Annual Budget: $25-50,000
Exec. Secretary: Stephen Crook

Historical Note
APHA members are academics and others with an interest in the history of printing and its related skills and technologies. Membership: $40/year (individual); $55/year (institution).

Publications:
APHA Newsletter. q.
Printing History. semi-a.

Meetings/Conferences:
Annual Meetings: Winter

American Probation and Parole Ass'n (1975)
P.O. Box 11910
Iron Works Pike
Lexington, KY 40578-1910
Tel: (606)244-8000   *Fax:* (606)244-8001
Web Site: http://www.acsp.uic.edu/IACO/Kv170227b.htm
Members: 2,500 individuals
Staff: 15
Annual Budget: $1-2,000,000
Exec. Director: Carl Wicklund
Staff Professional: Yolanda Swinford

Historical Note
Members are probation/parole professionals and others. Membership: $35/year or $90/3 years (individual); $150-$5,000/year (organization/company).

Publications:
Perspectives. q. adv.

Meetings/Conferences:
1999 – New York, NY(Marriott)/Aug. 22-25/2000
2000 – Phoenix, AZ(Convention Center)/July 23-26/2000
2001 – St. Paul, MN(The Broadmore)/2000
2002 – Denver, CO/(The Broadmore)/2000

American Producers of Italian Type Cheese Ass'n (1941)

Historical Note
Reported defunct in 1996.

American Production and Inventory Control Soc. (1957)

Historical Note
Became APICS - The Educational Soc. for Resource Management in 1997.

American Professional Needlework Retailers (1960)

Historical Note
Formerly the Midwest Professional Needlework Ass'n. Organization defunct in 1996.

American Professional Pet Distributors (1968)

Historical Note
Defunct in 1996.

American Professional Soc. on the Abuse of Children (1987)
407 S. Dearborn Ave., Suite 1300
Chicago, IL 60605
Tel: (312)554-0166   *Fax:* (312)554-0919
E-Mail: apsacexec@aol.com
Web Site: http://www.apsac.org
Members: 5,200 individuals
Staff: 12
Annual Budget: $500-1,000,000
Acting Exec. Director: Beverly Bradley
Conference Manager: Tifanni Sterdivant
Staff Accountant: Elmer McCaskill
Dir., Member Services: Cynthia Steele
Publications Manager: Maureen Kelly

Historical Note
APSAC's aim is to ensure that everyone affected by child maltreatment receives the best possible professional care. Members include psychologists, social workers, physicians, attorneys, nurses,

law enforcement officers, child protective service workers, administrators, researchers, and allied professionals who have dedicated a substantial portion of their professional lives to alleviating the problems caused by child maltreatment.
Membership: $35-100/year.

Publications:
APSAC Advisor. q. adv.
Child Maltreatment. q. adv.
State Chapter News. q.

Meetings/Conferences:
1999 – San Antonio, TX(Hyatt)/June 2-6
2000 – Chicago, IL(Hilton & Towers)/July 10-15

American Professional Soccer League (1987)

Historical Note
Address unknown in 1997.

American Prospect Research Ass'n

Historical Note
Became (1995) Ass'n of Professional Researchers for Advancement.

American Prosthodontic Soc. (1928)
919 North Michigan Ave., Ste. 2406
Chicago, IL 60611
Tel: (312)944-7618   *Fax:* (312)944-5147
Members: 1,250 individuals
Staff: 6
Annual Budget: $100-250,000
Exec. Director: Dr. Alan C. Keyes, DDS

Historical Note
Membership: $325/year (individual).

Publications:
Journal of Prosthetic Dentistry. m. adv.

Meetings/Conferences:
Annual Meetings: Winter, in conjunction with the Chicago
     Dental Soc.
1999 – Chicago, IL/Feb. 18-20

American Psychiatric Ass'n (1844)
1400 K St., N.W.
Washington, DC 20005
Tel: (202)682-6138   *Fax:* (202)682-6114
E-Mail: apa@psych.org
Web Site: http://www.psych.org
Members: 40,000 individuals
Staff: 200
Annual Budget: $25-50,000,000
C.F.O.: Kathleen Dempsey
Director, Public Affairs: John M. Blamphin
Special Counsel/Director, Govt. Relation: Jay B. Cutler, J.D.
Exec. V. President, APA Foundation: Lynn May, CAE
C.E.O. and Medical Director: Melvin Sabshin, M.D.
Deputy Director, Business Administration: Jack W. White, DBA
Assistant Director: Rosalind Keitt
Director, Administrative Services: Kenneth Robinson
Director, Membership: Kristine L. Bieg
Gen. Manager, American Psychiatric Press: Ronald E. McMillen
Dep. Medical Director: Robert T.M. Phillips, MD, Ph.D.
Dep. Medical Director: Harold A. Pincus
Dep. Medical Director: Deborah Zarin, MD

Historical Note
A professional society consisting solely of psychiatrists. The oldest national medical specialty society in the U.S., founded in Philadelphia in 1844 as the Ass'n of Medical Superintendents of American Institutions for the Insane. In 1892 it became the American Medico-Psychological Ass'n and in 1921 the American Psychiatric Ass'n. Incorporated in the District of Columbia in 1927. Has an annual budget of approximately $26.7 million. Membership: $540/year.

Publications:
American Journal of Psychiatry. m. adv.
Psychiatric News. bi-m. adv.
Psychiatric Services Journal. m. adv.

Meetings/Conferences:
Annual Meetings: Spring
1999 – Washington, DC/May 16-19
2000 – Chicago, IL/May 14-17

American Psychiatric Nurses Ass'n (1987)
1200 19th St., N.W., Suite 300
Washington, DC 20036
Tel: (202)857-1133   *Fax:* (202)223-4579
Members: 3,800 individuals
Staff: 2
Annual Budget: $500-1,000,000
Exec. Director: Timothy W. Gordon

Historical Note
APNA serves as a forum for dialogue among clinicians, teachers and researchers in the field of psychiatric nursing. Membership: $110/year (individual); $66/year (student).

Publications:
APNA News. q.
Journal of the APNA. m. adv.

Meetings/Conferences:
Annual Meetings: Fall

American Psychoanalytic Ass'n (1911)
309 E. 49th St.
New York, NY 10017
Tel: (212)752-0450   *Fax:* (212)593-0571
Web Site: http://www.apsa.org
Members: 3,026 individuals
Staff: 10
Annual Budget: $1-2,000,000
Admin. Director: Ellen Fertig
Manager, Meetings: Debra Eder

Historical Note
Formed to study and advance psychoanalysis; to advocate and maintain standards for the training and practice of psychoanalysis; and to foster the integration of psychoanalysis with other branches of medicine.

Publications:
A. Psa.
Journal of the A. Psa.
Roster of the A. Psa.

Meetings/Conferences:
1999 – Washington, DC(Washington
     Hilton)/May 12-16/1000
2000 – Chicago, IL/April 26-30/1000
2001 – New Orleans, LA/May 2-6/1000
2002 – Philadelphia, PA/May 15-19/1000

American Psychological Ass'n (1892)
750 First St., N.E.
Washington, DC 20002-4242
Tel: (202)336-5500   *Fax:* (202)336-5500
Toll Free: (800)374 - 2721
E-Mail: executiveoffice@apa.org
Web Site: http://www.apa.org
Members: 151,000 individuals
Staff: 500
Annual Budget: $50-100,000,000
Exec. V. President and C.E.O.: Raymond D. Fowler, Ph.D.
Director, Public Communications: Rhea K. Farberman
Asst. Exec. Director, Government Relations: Marilyn S. Richmond
Director, Government Affairs: Suzanne S. Wandersman
Convention Manager: Candy Won
Exec. Director, Education Affairs: Jill Reich
Chief Financial Officer: Charles McKay
Director, Office Services: Holly Holstrom
Director, Admin. Opers.: Skipwith C. Calvert
Director, Legal Affairs: James McHugh
Director, Membership: Joan Perrin, CAE
Member Services Manager: Pat K. Miyamoto

Historical Note
Established on July 8, 1892 and incorporated in the District of Columbia in 1925. Has a number of semi-autonomous divisions which collectively advance psychology as a science, profession and means of promoting human welfare. Divisions include: Addictions; Adult Development and Aging; American Psychology-Law Soc. (see separate listing); Applied Experimental and Engineering Psychology; Behavioral Neuroscience and Comparative Psychology; Child, Youth and Family Services; Clinical Neuropsychology; Clinical Psychology (see separate listing); Consulting Psychology; Counseling Psychology; Developmental Psychology; Educational Psychology; Evaluation, Measurement and Statistics; Exercise and Sport Psychology; Experimental Analysis of Behavior; Experimental Psychology; Family Psychology (see separate listing); General Psychology; Group Psychology and Group Psychotherapy; Health Psychology; History of Psychology; Humanistic Psychology; Media Psychology; Mental Retardation and Developmental Disabilities; Military Psychology; Peace Psychology; Population and Environmental Psychology; Psychoanalysis (see separate listing); Psychological Hypnosis; Psychologists in Independent Practice (see separate listing); Psychologists in Public Service; Psychology and the Arts; Psychology of Religion; Psychology of Women; Psychopharmacology and Substance Abuse; Psychotherapy; School Psychology; Rehabilitation Psychology; Soc. for Community Research and Action: Division of Community Psychology; Soc. for Consumer Psychology; Soc. for Industrial and Organizational Psychology (see separate listing); Soc. for the Psychological Study of Lesbian and Gay Issues; Soc. for the Psychological Study of Ethnic Minority Issues; Soc. for the Study of Men and Masculinity; Soc. for the Psychological Study of Social Issues (see separate listing); Soc. for the Teaching of Psychology; Soc. of Personality and Social Psychology; State Psychological Ass'n Affairs; and Theoretical and Philosophical Psychology. Membership: $160/year. Has an annual budget of approximately $62 million.

Publications:
American Journal of Community Psychology. bi-m. adv.
American Psychologist. m. adv.
APA Monitor. m. adv.
Clinical Psychology: Science & Practice. q.
Clinician's Research Digest Newsletter. m.
Consulting Psychology Journal: Practice and Research. q. adv.
Contemporary Psychology. m. adv.
Counseling Psychologist Journal. q. adv.
Educational Psychologist Journal. q. adv.
Experimental and Clinical Psychopharmacology. q. adv.
General Psychologist Bulletin. 3/yr.
Group Dynamics: Theory, Practice & Research Journal.
Health Psychology Journal. bi-m. adv.
Humanistic Psychologist Journal. 3/yr. adv.
Journal of Abnormal Psychology. q. adv.
Journal of Applied Psychology. q. adv.
Journal of Clinical Child Psychology. q.
Journal of Comparative Psychology. q. adv.
Journal of Consulting and Clinical Psychology. bi-m. adv.
Journal of Consumer Psychology. q. adv.
Journal of Experimental Psychology: Animal Behavior
     Processes. q. adv.
Journal of Experimental Psychology: Applied. q. adv.
Journal of Experimental Psychology: General. q. adv.
Journal of Family Psychology. q. adv.
Journal of Pediatric Psychology. q.
Journal of Social Issues. q.
Journal of Theoretical & Philosophical Psychology. semi-a.
Jrnl of Experimental Psych: Human Perception & Performance.
     bi-m. adv.
Jrnl of Experimental Psychology: Learning, Memory, &
     Cognition. q.
Law and Human Behavior Journal. bi-m. adv.
Military Psychology Journal. q. adv.
Neuropsychology. q. adv.
Peace & Conflict: Journal of Peace Psychology. q.
Professional Psychology: Research and Practice. bi-m. adv.
Psychoanalytic Abstracts Journal. q.
Psychoanalytic Psychology Journal. q.

Psychological Abstracts. m.
Psychological Assessment Journal. q. adv.
Psychological Bulletin Journal. bi-m. adv.
Psychological Hypnosis Bulletin. 3/yr.
Psychological Methods Journal.
Psychological Review. q.
Psychology and Aging. q. adv.
Psychology of Addictive Behaviors Journal. q. adv.
Psychology of Women Quarterly Journal. q. adv.
Psychology, Public Policy and Law. q. adv.
Psychopharmacology Newsletter. q.
Psychotherapy Bulletin Newsletter. q.
Psychotherapy: Theory Research & Practice Journal.
PsycSCAN: Applied Engineering and Human Factors.
PsycSCAN: Applied Psychology. q.
PsycSCAN: Behavior Analysis and Therapy. q.
PsycSCAN: Clinical Psychology. q.
PsycSCAN: Developmental Psychology. q.
PsycSCAN: LD/MR. q.
PsycSCAN: Neuropsychology. q.
PsycSCAN: Psychoanalysis. q.
Public Service Psychology Newsletter. 3/yr.
Recorder Newsletter. 3/yr.
Rehabilitation Psychology Journal. q. adv.
Rehabilitation Psychology News Newsletter. 3/yr.
Review of General Psychology Journal.
School Psychologist Newsletter. q.
School Psychology Quarterly Journal. q. adv.
Score Newsletter. q.
Soc. for the Teaching of.
SPSSI Newsletter. 3/yr.
State Psychological Ass'n Affairs Newsletter. 3-4/yr.
Teaching of Psychology Journal. q.

Meetings/Conferences:
Annual Meetings: August/18,000

American Psychological Ass'n - Division of Clinical Psychology (1946)

P.O. Box 1082
Niwot, CO 80544
Tel: (303)652-3126 Fax: (303)652-2723
E-Mail: 71202.1701@compuserve.com
Members: 6,600 individuals, 1 students
Staff: 2
Annual Budget: $250-500,000
Administrative Officer: Lynn Peterson

Historical Note
Division members are American Psychological Ass'n members who are active in the practice, research, teaching, administratioin and/or study in the field of clinical psychology. Sections include: Clinical Child Psychology; Clincial Geropsychology; Clinical Psychology of Women; Ethnic Minority Psychology; Soc. for a Science of Clinical Psychology; and Soc. of Pediatric Psychology. Membership: $40/year (individual); $22/year (student).

Publications:
Clinical Child Psychology Newsletter. 3/yr.
Clinical Geropsychology Newsletter. 3/yr.
Clinical Psychologist Newsletter. q. adv.
Clinical Psychology of Ethnic Minorities Newsletter. semi-a.
Clinical Psychology of Women Newsletter. semi-a.
Clinical Psychology: Science and Practice Journal. q. adv.
Clinical Science Newsletter. 3/yr.
Journal of Clinical Child Psychology. q. adv.
Journal of Pediatric Psychology. q. adv.

American Psychological Ass'n - Division of Family Psychology

Historical Note
Address unknown in 1998.

American Psychological Ass'n - Division of Psychoanalysis

4035 E. Fanfol Dr.
Phoenix, AZ 85028-5103
Tel: (602)912-5383 Fax: (602)957-4828
E-Mail: theadmin@theadmin.com
Web Site: http://www.divpsa.org
Members: 4,000 individuals, 32 local chapters
Staff: 1
Annual Budget: $250-500,000
Administrator: Ruth Helein

Historical Note
A semi-autonomous division of the American Psychological Ass'n, division members are professionally involved in psychoanaytic theory, research and practice. Sections include: Childhood and Adolescence; Family Therapy; Psychoanalysis and Groups; Psychoanalytic Research Soc.; Psychologist-Psychoanalyst Clinicians; Psychologist-Psychoanalyst Practitioners; Women and Psychoanalysis; Local Chapters; Membership: $70/year (individual).

Publications:
Psychoanalytic Abstracts. q.
Psychoanalytic Psychology Journal. q.
Psychologist-Psychoanalyst Newsletter. q.

Meetings/Conferences:
Semi-annual Meetings: Spring and in conjunction with APA Meeting

American Psychological Ass'n - Division of Psychologists in Independent Practice

919 W. Marshall Ave.
Phoenix, AZ 85013
Tel: (602)246-8714 Fax: (602)246-6577
E-Mail: div42apa@primnet.com
Members: 8,200 individuals
Staff: 1
Annual Budget: $250-500,000
Administrator: Jeannie Beeaf

Historical Note
A semi-autonomous division of the American Psychological Ass'n, the division focuses on issues affecting psychological services in all independent practice settings and advocates on behalf of consumers of these services. Members mbership: $25/year (individual).

Publications:
Independent Practioner Newsletter. q. adv.

Meetings/Conferences:
Semi-annual Meetings: March and in conjunction with APA meeting

American Psychological Ass'n - Division of Psychotherapy (1968)

4035 E. Fanfol Dr.
Phoenix, AZ 85028-5103
Members: 8,500 individuals
Management Exec.: Pauline Wampler

Historical Note
A semi-autonomous division of the American Psychological Ass'n. Membership: $40/year.

Publications:
Psychotherapy Bulletin. q. adv.
Psychotherapy Journal. q. adv.

Meetings/Conferences:
Semi-Annual Meetings: mid-Winter and Summer

American Psychological Practitioners Ass'n (1987)

PO Box 1585
Cape Canaveral, FL 32920
Tel: (407)783-8071
Members: 300 individuals
Staff: 5
Annual Budget: $25-50,000
President: Tim Grady

Historical Note
Mental health and psychological practitioners.

Publications:
APPA Directory/Register. irreg.
Psychological Practitioner. q. adv.

Meetings/Conferences:
Annual Meetings: Fall

American Psychological Soc. (1988)

1010 Vermont Ave., N.W., Suite 1100
Washington, DC 20005-4907
Tel: (202)783-2077 Fax: (202)783-2083
E-Mail: APS@APS.Washington.dc.us
Web Site: http://www.psychologicalscience.org
Members: 15,078 individuals
Staff: 12
Annual Budget: $1-2,000,000
Exec. Officer: Alan G. Kraut
Director, Communications: Elizabeth Ruksznis
Director, Government Relations: Sarah Brookhart
Director of Meetings: Melanie Weiner
Director, Accounting: Emily Moore
Director of Membership: Jacqueline Kennedy

Historical Note
APS addresses the needs and interests of scientifc and academic psychologists as distinct from members of the professional community primarily engaged in clinical practice. APS members include psychologists engaged in scientific research or the application of scientifically grounded research findings without regard for specialties. The Society promotes, protects and advances the interests of scientifically oriented psychology in research, applications and the improvement of human welfare. Membership: $120/year (regular); $40/year (student); $65/year (retiree); $250/year (comapny/organization).

Publications:
APS Observer Newsletter. 10/year.
Current Directions in Psychological Science Journal. bi-m. adv.
Membership Directory. a.
Psychological Science Journal. bi-m. adv.

Meetings/Conferences:
Annual Meetings: Spring
1999 – Denver, CO(Adams Mark)
2000 – Miami, FL/June 8-11
2001 – Toronto, ON, Canada/June 14-17

American Psychology-Law Soc. (1968)

238 Burnett Hall
University of Nebraska
Lincoln, NE 68588-0308
Tel: (402)472-3121 Fax: (402)472-4637
E-Mail: coslzly@unlinfo.unl.edu
Members: 2,700 individuals
Staff: 1
Annual Budget: under $10,000
Administrator: Cathy Oslzly

Historical Note
AP-LS promotes the contributions of psychology to the understanding of law and legal institutions, the education of psychologists in legal matters and law personnel in psychological matters, and the application of psychology in the legal system. AP-LS became a division of the American Psychological Ass'n in 1985.

Publications:
AP-LS Newsletter. 3/yr. adv.
Law and Human Behavior. bi-m. adv.

Meetings/Conferences:
Biennial Conference: (even years)

American Psychopathological Ass'n (1910)

Dept. of Psychology
University of Maryland
College Park, MD 20742
Tel: (301)405-5890 Fax: (301)914-9566
Members: 560 individuals

Staff: 1
Annual Budget: under $10,000
Secretary: Dr. Deborah Beidel

Historical Note
Founded in New York City in 1910. Promotes research on problems of psychopathology. Membership: $75/year.

Publications:
Comprehensive Psychiatry. bi-m. adv.

Meetings/Conferences:
Annual Meetings: New York, NY/March

American Psychosomatic Soc. (1943)

6728 Old McLean Village Drive
McLean, VA 22101
Tel: (703)556-9222 Fax: (703)556-8729
E-Mail: info@psychomatic.org
Members: 900 individuals
Staff: 3
Exec. Director: George K. Degnon, CAE
Associate Director: Laura Degnon

Historical Note
Organized in 1943 as the American Soc. for Research in Psychosomatic Problems and incorporated in 1944. Became The American Psychosomatic Soc., Inc. in 1948. APS members are specialists from all medical and health-related disciplines, the behavioral sciences and the social sciences. Membership: $75/year (regular); $25/year (student).

Publications:
Newsletter. semi-an.
Psychosomatic Medicine Journal. bi-m. adv.

Meetings/Conferences:
Annual Meetings: March
1999 – Vancouver, Canada(Westin Bayshore)/March 17-20
2000 – Savannah, GA(Westin)/March 1-4

American Psychotherapy Ass'n (1998)

611 E. Wells St.
Milwaukee, WI 53202
Tel: (414)276-4322 Fax: (414)276-8481
Members: 2,500 individuals
Staff: 2
Annual Budget: $100-250,000
Administrator: Jeanne Rhodes

Historical Note
APA promotes continuing education and training for psychotherapists, and serves as a voice for the profession. Awards the designation Certified Diplomate in Psychotherapy. Membership: $100/year.

Publications:
Annals of the APA. bi-m.

Meetings/Conferences:
Annual Meetings: Fall
1999 – New York, NY(Waldorf-Astoria)/Oct. 29-31

American Public Communications Council (1988)

10306 Eaton Pl., Suite 520
Fairfax, VA 22030-0000
Tel: (703)385-5300 Fax: (703)385-5301
Toll Free: (800)868 - 2722
Web Site: http://www.apcc.net
Members: 1,900 member companies
Staff: 12
Annual Budget: $2-5,000,000
Exec. Director: Lisa M. Roddy-Burns
Manager, Government Relations: Gregory V. Haledjian
Convention Manager: M. Drennan Lindsay
President: Vincent R. Sandusky
Editor: Tracey Guhl

Historical Note
Members are manufacturers, suppliers, distributors and operators of public communications equipment.

Publications:
APCC Conference and Expo Showguide. bien. adv.
Perspectives on Public Communication. m.

Meetings/Conferences:
Semi-annual Meetings: April and October

American Public Gas Ass'n (1961)

11094-D Lee Hwy., Suite 102
Fairfax, VA 22030-5014
Tel: (703)352-3890 Fax: (703)352-1271
Toll Free: (800)927 - 4204
E-Mail: bcave@apga.org
Web Site: http://www.apga.org
Members: 500 systems
Staff: 4
Annual Budget: $500-1,000,000
Exec. Director: Robert S. Cave

Historical Note
Members are municipal natural gas systems and their suppliers.

Publications:
Directory of Municipal Natural Gas Systems. a. adv.
Newsletter. semi-m.

Meetings/Conferences:
Annual Meetings: July/August
1999 – Burlington, VT(Radisson)/July 25-28/500

American Public Health Ass'n (1872)

1015 15th St., N.W., Suite 300
Washington, DC 20005
Tel: (202)789-5600 Fax: (202)789-5661
Web Site: http://www.apha.org
Members: 32,000 individuals
Staff: 65
Annual Budget: $5-10,000,000
Exec. Director: Mohammad N. Akhter, MD, MPH
Director, Public Relations: Carole Zimmerman
Director, Marketing Svcs: Karen G. DeLong

Assoc. Exec. Director, Programs and Policy: Richard Levinson, MD
Director, Government Relations: Mary Wallace
Director, Convention Services: Barbara A. Freel, CMP
Coordinator, Education: Ponnuswamy Swamidoss
Assoc. Exec. Director, Management: Kitty Hsu Dana
Director, Membership Services/Records: Barbara Reck
Director, Publications: Ellen Meyer

Historical Note
Established September 12, 1872 at Long Branch, NJ and incorporated in Massachusetts in 1918, APHA represents health professionals in over 40 disciplines in the development of health standards and policies. Member of the Coalition for Health Funding in Washington. Membership: $125/year (individual); $750/year (non-profit organization)

Publications:
American Journal of Public Health. m. adv.
The Nation's Health. m. adv.

Meetings/Conferences:
Annual Meetings: Fall/10,000-12,000
1999 - Chicago, IL/Nov. 7-11
2000 - Boston, MA/Nov. 12-16
2001 - Atlanta, GA/Oct. 21-25

American Public Human Services Ass'n *(1930)*
810 1st St., N.E., Suite 500
Washington, DC 20002-4267
Tel: (202)682-0100 *Fax:* (202)289-6555
Members: 4,000 individuals, 945 agencies
Staff: 50
Annual Budget: $2-5,000,000
Deputy Exec. Director: Linda Wolf
Director, Communications: Amy Tucci
Manager, Member Services and Conferences: Rosalyn King

Historical Note
Formerly American Public Welfare Ass'n (1998). APSHA represents the 50 cabinet-level, state human service departments; local public welfare agencies; and individuals concerned with social welfare policy and practice. APWA includes two councils, the Nat'l Council of State Human Service Administrators and the Nat'l Council of Local Public Human Service Administrators. It also includes nine affiliates representing separate professional disciplines within public welfare: the American Ass'n of Food Stamp Directors, the American Ass'n of Public Welfare Attorneys, the American Public Human Services Ass'n Information Systems Management, the Ass'n of Administrators of the Interstate Compact on the Placement of Children, the Nat'l Ass'n of Hearing Officials, the Nat'l Ass'n for Program Information and Performance Measurement, the Nat'l Ass'n of Public Child Welfare Administrators, the Nat'l Staff Development and Training Ass'n, and the Nat'l Ass'n of State Medicaid Directors. Membership: $50/year. (individual); agency dues vary.

Publications:
Policy and Practice Journal. q. adv.
Public Human Services Directory. a. adv.
This Week in Washington. w.
W-Memo. 6/year.

Meetings/Conferences:
1999 - Washington, DC(Hyatt Regency Capitol Hill)/400
1999 - Washington, DC(Hyatt Regency Capitol Hill)/400

American Public Power Ass'n *(1940)*
2301 M St., N.W., Suite 300
Washington, DC 20037-1484
Tel: (202)467-2900 *Fax:* (202)467-2910
Web Site: http://www.APPAnet.org
Members: 2,000 utilities
Staff: 60
Annual Budget: $5-10,000,000
Exec. Director: Alan H. Richardson
Director, Communications: Madalyn Cafruny
Assoc. Exec. Director, Governmetn Relations: James J. Nipper
Meetings Manager: Nancy Mooney
Director, Education: Jill Kennedy
Asst. Exec. Director, Information Services: Deborah Penn
Dep. Exec. Director: Dave Penn
Dir., Finance/Accounting: Bianca Donnally, CPA
Director, Membership/Marketing: Susan Ryba
Assoc. Exec. Director, Membership Services: Jeffrey Tarbert
Asst. Exec. Director, Publishing: Jeanne LaBella

Historical Note
Members are publicly-owned electric utility systems. Has an annual budget of approximately $8.0 million. Sponsors and supports the PowerPAC political action committee. Membership: based on kWh sales and revenues.

Publications:
Public Power. bi-m. adv.
Public Power Weekly. w.

Meetings/Conferences:
Annual Meetings: June/2,000
1999 - Salt Lake City, UT(Convention Center)/June 21-23

American Public Transit Ass'n *(1882)*
1201 New York Ave., N.W., Suite 400
Washington, DC 20005
Tel: (202)898-4000 *Fax:* (202)898-4070
Web Site: www.apta.com
Members: 1,100 organizations and indviduals
Staff: 80
Annual Budget: $10-25,000,000
President: William W. Millar
V.P., Communications/Mktg.: Rosemary Sheridan
Chief Counsel & V.President, Government Affairs: Daniel Duff
V. President, Member Services: Anthony M. Kouneski
Chief of Staff: Karol J. Popkin
V. President, Human Resources and Administration: Vivienne Williams

Historical Note
Founded in 1882 as the American Street Railway Ass'n, it became the American Street and Inter-Urban Railway Ass'n in 1905 and later the American Electric Railway Ass'n. The name was changed in 1910 to American Transit Ass'n which merged in 1974 with the Institute of Rapid Transit (1961) to form the present organization. APTA members include transit systems, manufacturers, consultants, state departments of transportation and others with an interest in the industry. Has an annual budget of approximately $13 million.

Publications:
Membership Directory. a.
Passenger Transport. w. adv.
Passenger Transport Index. a.
Transit Fact Book. a.

Meetings/Conferences:
Annual Meetings: Fall
1999 - Orlando, FL(Rosen/Peabody)/Oct. 10-14/15000
2000 - San Francisco, CA(Hilton)/Sept. 24-28/15000
2001 - Philadelphia, PA(Marriott)/Sept. 30-Oct. 4/15000
2002 - Las Vegas, NV(Hilton)/Sept. 22-26/15000

American Public Works Ass'n *(1894)*
2345 Grand Blvd., Suite 500
Kansas City, MO 64108-2641
Tel: (816)472-6100 *Fax:* (816)472-1610
E-Mail: apwa@apwa.net
Web Site: www.apwa.net
Members: 25,300 individuals
Staff: 44
Annual Budget: $5-10,000,000
Exec. Director: Peter B. King
Communications Manager: Joyce Junclans
Dir., Government Relations: Sarah Layton
Meetings Director: Dana Priddy
Dir., Member Services: Angie Tatum

Historical Note
Government officials, engineers, administrators and others engaged in some aspect of public works. Merger (1937) of American Soc. of Municipal Engineers and Internat'l Ass'n of Public Works Officials. Provides administrative support for Contract Sweepers Institute. Maintains a Washington office. Has an annual budget of approximately $7.2 million.

Publications:
APWA Reporter. 10/year. adv.

Meetings/Conferences:
Annual Meetings: September
1999 - Denver, CO/Sept. 18-23
2000 - Louisville, KY/Sept. 9-14
2001 - Philadelphia, PA/Sept. 8-13
2002 - Kansas City, MO(Bartle Hall)/Sept. 22-25

American Pulpwood Ass'n *(1934)*
600 Jefferson Plaza, Suite 350
Rockville, MD 20852
Tel: (301)838-9385 *Fax:* (301)838-9481
Web Site: http://www.apulpa.org
Members: 1,776 companies
Staff: 20
Annual Budget: $1-2,000,000
President: Richard Lewis, CAE
Manager, Communications: Neil A. Ward
Director, Finance and Administration: Linda Rosenberg
Director, Forestry Programs: Steve Jarvis

Historical Note
Members are consumers, producers and distributors of pulpwood. Membership fee varies, based on volume of wood handled.

Publications:
PR Alerts. m.
Pulpwood Highlights. m.
Safety Alerts. m.
Security Alerts. m.
Technical Releases. m.

Meetings/Conferences:
Annual Meetings: Spring/500
1999 - Orlando, FL/Apr. 10-13

American Purchasing Soc. *(1969)*
430 W. Downer Pl.
Aurora, IL 60506-5035
Tel: (630)859-0250 *Fax:* (630)859-0270
E-Mail: propurch@aol.com
Web Site: http://www.American-Purchasing.com
Members: 3,000 individuals
Staff: 4
Annual Budget: $250-500,000
President & Exec. Director: Harry E. Hough

Historical Note
APS members include purchasing agents, buyers, procurement specialists, purchasing managers, purchasing executives and others who buy goods and services. First organization to certify buyers and purchasing managers. APS is concerned with improving purchasing performance in business through the education of its membership and the development of ethical standards of conduct in the marketplace. Conducts third-party supplier evaluations. Membership: $115/year (individual), $225/year (organization/company).

Publications:
American Purchasing and Materials Management. a.
Annual Purchasing Benchmarking Report. a.
Professional Purchasing. m.
Purchasing Salaries and Employment Trends. a.

Meetings/Conferences:
Annual Meetings: September

American Pyrotechnics Ass'n *(1948)*
Box 213
Chestertown, MD 21620
Tel: (410)778-6825 *Fax:* (410)778-0304
Members: 170 companies
Staff: 2
Annual Budget: $250-500,000
Exec. Director: John A. Conkling, Ph.D.

Historical Note
Fireworks importers, distributors, suppliers and manufacturers. Incorporated in Delaware. Absorbed the Nat'l Pyrotechnic Distributors Ass'n in 1979.

Publications:
Bulletin. m.

Meetings/Conferences:
1999 - Washington, DC(Marriott Crystal Gateway)
2000 - Orlando, FL(Walt Disney World)

American Quarter Horse Ass'n *(1940)*
1600 Quarter Horse Drive
Amarillo, TX 79104-3406
Tel: (806)376-4811 *Fax:* (806)349-6409
E-Mail: aqhamail@aqha.org
Web Site: http://www.aqha.com
Members: 314,000 individuals
Staff: 270
Annual Budget: $50-100,000,000
Exec. V. President: Bill Brewer
Dir., Member Svcs./Public Policy: Ward Stutz
Meetings Manager: Karen Latta
Treasurer: Lee Calloway
Sr. Dir., Mktg./Member Services: Don Treadway
Dir., Marketing Services: Tom Persechino

Historical Note
Organized in 1940 to collect, register, and preserve the pedigree of American Quarter Horses. Member of the Nat'l Pedigree Livestock Council and the American Horse Council. Has an annual budget of $30 million. Membership: $25/year (new members); $55/3 years (new members); $20/year (renewal); $55/3 years (renewal).

Publications:
The Quarter Horse Journal. m. adv.
The Quarter Racing Journal. m. adv.

Meetings/Conferences:
Annual Meetings: First or second week in March
1999 - Atlanta, GA(Renaissance Waverly Hotel)

American Quaternary Ass'n *(1969)*
Illinois State Museum
1011 E. Ash Street
Springfield, IL 62703
Tel: (217)782-7475 *Fax:* (217)785-2857
E-Mail: styles@museum.state.il.us
Web Site: http://cc.usu.edu/~amqua/
Members: 1000 individuals
Staff: 1
Annual Budget: $10-25,000
Secretary: Bonnie Styles

Historical Note
Established in 1969 and held its first meeting at Montana State University in Bozeman in 1970. Members are natural scientists studying the history of the environment during the last two million years. Affiliated with The Internat'l Quaternary Ass'n. Membership: $8/year (individual); $4/year (student).

Publications:
Program with Abstracts. bien.
Quaternary Times Newsletter. semi-a.

Meetings/Conferences:
Biennial meetings: even years

American Rabbit Breeders Ass'n *(1910)*
P.O. Box 426
Bloomington, IL 61702
Tel: (309)664-7500 *Fax:* (309)664-0941
E-Mail: ARBApost@aol.com
Web Site: http://members.aol.com/arbanet/arba/web/
Members: 35,000 individuals
Staff: 6
Annual Budget: $500-1,000,000
Secretary: Glen C. Carr

Historical Note
Members are Commercial or Fancy breeders of rabbits and guinea pigs. Commercial breeders breed for profit and Fancy breeders breed for pleasure (about 90% of the membership). Founded as the Nat'l Breeders and Fanciers Ass'n, it became the American Pet Stock Ass'n in 1923, the American Rabbit and Cavy Ass'n in 1928 and assumed its present name in 1954. ARBA has chartered about 1100 affiliated clubs, for fanciers of various types of rabbits. Membership: $15/year (adult); $8/year (youth).

Publications:
ARBA Yearbook. a. adv.
Domestic Rabbits. bi-m. adv.

Meetings/Conferences:
Annual Meetings: Fall/4,000-5,000

American Radio Relay League
225 Main St.
Newington, CT 06111-1494
Tel: (860)594-0200 *Fax:* (860)594-0259
E-Mail: hq@arrl.org
Web Site: http://www.arrl.org
Members: 175,000 individuals
Staff: 110
Annual Budget: $5-10,000,000
Exec. V. President: David Sumner
C.F.O.: Barry J. Shelley

Publications:
NCJ. bi-m. adv.
QEX. bi-m. adv.
QST. m. adv.

Meetings/Conferences:
2000 - Dayton, OH(HARA Arena)/May 19-21/28000

American Radiological Nurses Ass'n *(1981)*
820 Joire Blvd.
Oak Brook, IL 60523
Tel: (630)571-9072 *Fax:* (630)571-7837
E-Mail: arna@rsna.org

Members: 1,476 individuals
Staff: 2
Annual Budget: $100-250,000
Exec. Secretary: Betty Rohr

Historical Note
ARNA members are professional nurses actively engaged in radiological nursing or with a radiological nursing background. Associate membership is available to licensed practical nurses actively employed in radiological nursing. Membership: $75/year (individual).

Publications:
ARNA Images. q. adv.
RN News. q. adv.

Meetings/Conferences:

American Radium Soc. *(1916)*
1891 Preston White Drive
Reston, VA   19107
Tel: (703)648-0698   *Fax:* (703)262-9313
Members: 850 individuals
Staff: 2
Annual Budget: $100-250,000
Executive Director: Suzanne Bohn

Historical Note
Founded in 1916 by physicians interested in radiation therapy. Promotes the study of cancer in all its aspects.

Publications:
Membership Directory. a.

Meetings/Conferences:
Annual Meetings: Spring/300

American Railway Bridge and Building Ass'n *(1891)*

Historical Note
Merged with Roadmasters and Maintenance of Way Ass'n of America to form American Railway Engineering and Maintenance of Way Ass'n in 1997.

American Railway Car Institute *(1915)*
700 North Fairfax St.
Alexandria, VA   22314-2098
Tel: (703)549-5662   *Fax:* (703)548-0058
E-Mail: RPI@RPI.ORG
Members: 30 companies
Staff: 2
Annual Budget: $50-100,000
Exec. Director: Robert A. Matthews

Historical Note
Administrative support provided by Railway Progress Institute (same address).

Meetings/Conferences:
Annual Meetings: Not held.

American Railway Development Ass'n *(1906)*
P.O. Box 44369
Eden Prairie, MN   55344-4369
Tel: (612)828-9750   *Fax:* (612)828-9751
E-Mail: tyck0001@aol.com
Web Site: http://amraildev.org
Members: 150 individuals
Annual Budget: $25-50,000
Exec. Director: E. Gilbert Tyckoson, Jr.

Historical Note
Members are marketing, real estate and industrial development officers of railroads. ARDA's objective is to foster the industrial, real estate, natural resources and market development activities of North American railroads and through the advancement of ideas and education of its members further promote the effectiveness of railway development and related work. Membership: $75/year (individual).

Publications:
ARDA Newsletter. 4-6/year.

Meetings/Conferences:
Annual Meetings: May/100
1999 – Montreal, Quebec
2000 – San Antonio, TX(Hyatt Regency)/May 23-26/150

American Railway Engineering and Maintenance of Way Ass'n *(1883)*
8201 Corporate Dr., Suite 1125
Landover, MD   20785
Tel: (301)459-3200   *Fax:* (301)459-8077
Members: 5,000 individuals
Staff: 7
Annual Budget: $50-100,000
Executive. Director: Charles Emely, Ph.D.,CMP,
Manager, Administration: W. Tayman
Coordinator, Membership: A. Padden

Historical Note
Formerly Roadmasters and Maintenance of Way Ass'n of America; absorbed American Railway Engineering Ass'n and American Railway Bridge and Building Ass'n and assumed its current name in 1997. Founded to raise the standards and improve the methods of track and roadway maintenance of American railways. Membership: $60/year.

Publications:
Newsletter. q.
Proceedings. a. adv.

Meetings/Conferences:
Annual Meetings: Fall
1999 – Chicago, IL
1999 – Baltimore, MD
2000 – Dallas, TX

American Railway Engineering Ass'n *(1899)*

Historical Note
Merged with Roadmasters and Maintenance of Way Ass'n of America to form American Railway Engineering and Maintenance of Way Ass'n in 1997.

American Rambouillet Sheep Breeders Ass'n *(1889)*
2709 Sherwood Way
San Angelo, TX   76901
Tel: (915)949-4414
Members: 500 individuals
Staff: 2
Annual Budget: $50-100,000
Secretary-Treasurer: Kenneth Blair

Historical Note
Breeders and fanciers of Rambouillet sheep. Its primary function is for registry of purebred Rambouillet sheep and secondarily to advertise and promote the breed. Membership: $15/year; $20 (after April 1).

Publications:
Bouillet Magazine. 3/year. adv.
Rambouillet Newsletter. q.

Meetings/Conferences:
Annual Meetings: July

American Real Estate and Urban Economics Ass'n *(1965)*
Indiana Univ. Sch. of Business
1309 E. Tenth St., Suite 461
Bloomington, IN   47405-1701
Tel: (812)855-7794   *Fax:* (812)855-8679
E-Mail: areuea@indiana.edu
Web Site: http://www.areuea.org
Members: 1,254 individuals
Staff: 1
Annual Budget: $10-25,000
Secretary-Treasurer: John L. Glascock

Historical Note
Established and incorporated in 1965 as American Real Estate Ass'n. Name changed in 1966 to American Real Estate and Urban Economics Ass'n. Individuals both academically and commercially involved in real estate and urban economics. Membership: $65/year (individual); $350/year (inst. sponsor); $125/year (library), $1,000 (inst. member); $30/year (student).

Publications:
Real Estate Economics. q. adv.

Meetings/Conferences:
Annual Meetings: January
1999 – New York, NY(Hilton)/Jan. 3-5

American Real Estate Soc. *(1985)*
Cleveland State Univ., Dept. of Finance
JamesJ. Nance College of Business,BU327E
Cleveland, OH   44114
Tel: (216)687-4732   *Fax:* (216)687-9331
Web Site: http://www.ARESnet.org
Members: 1,400 individuals, 150 companies
Annual Budget: $100-250,000
Exec. Director: James R. Webb
Meeting Planner: Arthur Schwartz
Secretary/Treasurer: Theron Nelson

Historical Note
ARES is concerned with real estate finance, real estate investment analysis and decision making, real estate valuation, real estate market analysis and other closely-related areas. Has no paid staff. Membership: $100/year (individual); $425/year (organization/company); $1,500-6,000/year (major real estate companies and organizations).

Publications:
ARES Annual Meeting Program. a.
ARES Membership Directory. on-line.
ARES Newsletter. semi-a. adv.
Journal of Real Estate Literature. semi-a. adv.
Journal of Real Estate Portfolio Management. 3/year.
Journal of Real Estate Practice & Education. a.
Real Estate Research Issues monograph series. a.
The Journal of Real Estate Research. bi-m. adv.

Meetings/Conferences:
1999 – Tampa, FL(West Shore, Hyatt)/April 15-18
2000 – Santa Barbara, CA/March 29-April 1
2001 – Coeur d'Alene, ID/April 18-21
2002 – Florida
2003 – Monterey, CA

American Recovery Ass'n *(1965)*
P.O. Box 6788
New Orleans, LA   70174
Tel: (504)366-7377   *Fax:* (504)367-6416
E-Mail: ara@repo.org
Web Site: http://www.repo.org
Members: 500 repossession companies
Staff: 6
Annual Budget: $1-2,000,000
Exec. Director: Catherine Rodi

Historical Note
The world's largest organization of professional finance adjusters and repossession specialists. ARA members represent banks, credit unions, finance companies, leasing companies, savings and loan associations and other financial institutions in the recovery of collateral on defaulted installment contracts. Formerly (1972) American Repossessors Ass'n, Inc.

Publications:
ARA News and Views Newsletter. m.
National Membership Directory. a. adv.

Meetings/Conferences:
Annual Meetings: July/250

American Recreation Coalition *(1979)*
1225 New York Ave., N.W., Suite 450
Washington, DC   20005

Tel: (202)682-9530   *Fax:* (202)682-9529
E-Mail: arc@funoutdoors.com
Web Site: http://www.funoutdoors.com
Members: 100 associations & companies
Staff: 4
Annual Budget: $250-500,000
President: Derrick A. Crandall

Historical Note
Formed by the recreation industry and related organizations to present a united approach to such topics of legislative interest as land use and energy, and to educate the government and the public about the value of recreation.

Meetings/Conferences:
1999 – Washington, DC

American Red Brangus Ass'n *(1956)*
3995 E. Hwy. 290
Dripping Springs, TX   78620-4205
Tel: (512)858-7285   *Fax:* (512)858-7084
Members: 2,700 individuals
Staff: 3
Annual Budget: $250-500,000
Office Manager: Cheryl Henderson

Historical Note
Founded in Austin, Texas. Breeders and fanciers of Red Brangus cattle, a crossbreed of Brahman and Angus cattle. Membership: $25/first year, dues thereafter based on stock size.

Publications:
Bull Pen. m.
Membership Directory. a.

Meetings/Conferences:
Annual Meetings: November

American Red Poll Ass'n *(1883)*

Historical Note
Breeders and fanciers of Red Poll beef cattle. Formerly (1976) Red Poll Cattle Club of America. Member of the Nat'l Pedigree Livestock Council. Absorbed The Red Poll Beef Breeders Internt'l in 1979.

American Registry of Certified Professionals in Agronomy, Crops and Soils

Historical Note
A membership activity of the American Soc. of Agronomy.

American Registry of Diagnostic Medical Sonographers *(1975)*
600 Jefferson Plaza, Suite 360
Rockville, MD   20852-1150
Tel: (301)738-8401   *Fax:* (301)738-0312
Toll Free: (800)541 - 9754
Web Site: http://www.ardms.org
Members: 35,000 individuals
Staff: 19
Annual Budget: $2-5,000,000
Exec. Director: Donald K. Gardiner, CAE
Director of Communications: Tamara Sloper
Director of Testing: Tim Sares
Manager of Registrant Services: Gwen Henderson

Historical Note
The ARDMS offers voluntary certification through examination to qualified sonographers and vascular technologists. Has certified over 35,000 individuals in these specialty areas: obstetrics & gynecology, abdomen, ophthamology, neurosonology, adult echocardiography, pediatric echocardiography and vascular technology. Membership: $45/year.

Publications:
ARDMS Directory. a.
Examination and Information & Application Booklet. a.
Registry Reports. q.

Meetings/Conferences:
Annual Meetings: Not held.

American Registry of Medical Assistants *(1950)*
69 Southwick Road, Suite A
Westfield, MA   01085-4729
Tel: (413)562-7336
Toll Free: (800)527 - 2762
Members: 5,500 individuals
Staff: 4
Director: Annette H. Heyman

Historical Note
ARMA provides updated information to its members, to advance the professional interests of medical assistants. Members include graduates of licensed medical assistant programs and other allied health professionals.Membership: $55 application fee; $25/year renewal.

Publications:
Medical Assistant. a. adv.
Registry Connection. q.

Meetings/Conferences:
Annual Meetings: September

American Rehabilitation Ass'n

Historical Note
Became (1998) American Medical Rehabilitation Providers Ass'n.

American Rehabilitation Counseling Ass'n *(1957)*
1835 Rohlwing Rd., Suite E
Rolling Meadows, IL   60008
Tel: (847)788-0848
Members: 1,772 individuals
Staff: 2
Annual Budget: $50-100,000
Exec. Director: Eda Holt

Historical Note
Members are rehabilitation counselors working with people with physical, mental or emotional disabilities. ARCA is a division of the American Counseling Ass'n, which provides administrative support.

Membership: $70/year (professional); $40/year (retired); $20/year (student).

Publications:
ARCA Newsletter. q. adv.
Rehabilitation Counseling Bulletin. q. adv.

Meetings/Conferences:
Annual Meetings: with American Counseling Ass'n
1999 – San Diego, CA/April 12-17
2000 – Washington, DC/March 22-25
2001 – San Antonio, TX
2002 – New Orleans, LA

American Rehabilitative Technology Ass'n

Historical Note
Address unknown in 1996; presumed inactive.

American Rental Ass'n *(1955)*
1900 19th St.
Moline, IL   61265-4198
Tel: (309)764-2475   *Fax:* (309)764-2747
Toll Free: (800)334 - 2177
Web Site: http://www.ararental.org
Members: 4,163 firms, 1,907 associates
Staff: 33
Annual Budget: $5-10,000,000
Exec. V. President: James R. Irish
V.P., Communications: Frederick Anderson
Director of Public Relations/Marketing: Sandy Howell
V.P., Conventions and Meetings: Darlene Summers
Director, Education: Trysh Mueller-Farber
C.F.O.: Kathleen A. Schwartz
Dept. Exec. V. President, Program Services: Joseph Lynch
Director of Field Services: Michael Moore

Historical Note
Founded as the Nat'l Rental Owners Mutual Ass'n, and formerly (1961) American Associated Rental Operators. In 1986, the Nat'l Rental Service Ass'n merged with ARA. ARA represents owners of privately owned or franchise rental businesses, and manufacturers and suppliers of rental products. The association covers most kinds of tangible personal properties found in the market today except apartments, cars, billboards or office space. Supports ARAPAC, its political action committee.

Publications:
ARA Alliance. bi-m.
ARA Washington News. q.
Inside Track. m.
Marketing Messages. bi-m.
Rental Management. m. adv.

Meetings/Conferences:
Annual Meetings: Late Winter/9,000
1999 – Las Vegas, NV/Feb. 8-11

American Resort Development Ass'n *(1969)*
1220 L St., N.W., Suite 500
Washington, DC   20005
Tel: (202)371-6700   *Fax:* (202)289-8544
Web Site: http://www.arda.org
Members: 950 companies
Staff: 30
Annual Budget: $5-10,000,000
President: Cynthia A. Huheey
Director, Communications: Christopher D. Larsen
Sr. V. President, Federal Govt. Relations: Michael F. Hussey
Director, Meetings: Chrissy Castles
Director, Education: Randy Goodhope
Director, Operations: Adrienne Riley
Corporate Counsel: Maria Deligiorgis
V. President, Member Services: Sandra Woolard
Director, Publications: Sheila Morris

Historical Note
Formerly (1985) the American Land Development Ass'n. Represents the recreational, resort and residential real estate development industry, including timesharing and R.V. camp resorts. Sponsors and supports the American Resort Development Ass'n Political Action Committee. Membership: $1,200-12,500/year, based on annual gross income (company).

Publications:
Developments Magazine. 11/year. adv.
Membership Directory. a.

Meetings/Conferences:
1999 – Orlando, FL(Marriott World Center)/April 11-14

American Restaurant China Council *(1957)*
P.O. Box 7601
McLean, VA   22106
Tel: (703)893-4631
Members: 5 companies
Staff: 1
Annual Budget: $50-100,000
Exec. Director: Helen D. Grayson

Historical Note
ARCC formulates positions and acts on issues affecting United States manufacturers of restaurant china and performs related promotional and educational activities.

American Retreaders' Ass'n *(1957)*

Historical Note
Became Internat'l Tire and Rubber Ass'n (ITRA) in 1996.

American Reusable Textile Ass'n *(1982)*
P.O. Box 801
Mulberry, FL   33860
Tel: (941)644-7477
Members: 55 companies and organizations
Annual Budget: $25-50,000
President: William J. Carroll, Ph.D.

Historical Note
ARTA members are producers and distributors of apparel, diapers, and other reusable textiles, manufacturers of laundry equipment,

and suppliers to the industry. Has no paid officers or full-time staff. Membership $500/year.

Meetings/Conferences:

American Rhinologic Soc. *(1954)*
Dept of Otolaryngology/Head & Neck Surg
1501 Kings Hwy., P.O. Box 33932
Shreveport, LA   71130-3932
Tel: (318)675-6263   *Fax:* (318)675-6260
Web Site: http://www.sinus.org/about/html
Members: 800 individuals
Staff: 1
Annual Budget: $50-100,000
Secretary: Fred J. Stucker, M.D., FACS

Historical Note
Formed in Chicago in 1954 by Dr. M.H. Cottle. Members are physicians who are diplomates of the American Board of Otolaryngology; promotes research and education on disorders and surgery of the nose. Membership: $200/year.

Publications:
American Journal of Rhinology.
Newsletter. q.

Meetings/Conferences:
Annual Meetings: Fall, with the American Academy of
    Otolaryngology
1999 – San Francisco, CA

American Risk and Insurance Ass'n *(1932)*
c/o Chase Communications
P.O. Box 9001
Mt. Vernon, NY   10552
Tel: (914)699-2020   *Fax:* (914)699-2025
Toll Free: (800)951 - 2020
Web Site: http://www.aria.org
Members: 1,700 individuals
Staff: 1
Annual Budget: $100-250,000
Exec. Director: Carole H. Acunto

Historical Note
A learned society devoted exclusively to furthering the science of risk and insurance through education, research, literature and communications. Formerly (1961) American Ass'n of University Teachers of Insurance. Membership: $75/year (individual), $90/year (organization); $500-$10,000/year (sponsoring institution).

Publications:
Journal of Risk and Insurance. q. adv.
Risk Management and Insurance Review. semi-a.

Meetings/Conferences:
Annual Meetings: August/300
1999 – Vancouver, BC, Canada

American River Management Soc. *(1988)*

Historical Note
Merged with the River Federation to form The River Management Soc. in 1996.

American Road and Transportation Builders Ass'n *(1902)*
1010 Massachusetts Ave., N.W.
Washington, DC   20001
Tel: (202)289-4434   *Fax:* (202)289-4435
Web Site: http://www.artba-hq.org
Members: 4,500 companies
Staff: 25
Annual Budget: $5-10,000,000
President and C.E.O.: T. Peter Ruane, CAE
V. President, Communications and Policy: William D. Toohey, Jr.
Director, Marketing: C. Patrick Sankey
Managing Director, Planning/Education: Robert M. Hinton
Managing Editor: Gail Schell

Historical Note
Founded as American Road Makers, it became the American Road Builders Association in 1910, absorbed the Better Highway Information Foundation in 1969 and assumed its present name in 1977. Sponsors the ARTBA Political Action Committee. Membership fee varies by division.

Publications:
ARTBA Newsletter. m.
Transportation Builder. m. adv.
Washington Newsline. w.

Meetings/Conferences:
1999 – Las Vegas, NV/March 24-28

American Rock Mechanics Ass'n *(1994)*
600 Woodland Terrace
Alexandria, VA   22302-3319
Tel: (703)683-1808   *Fax:* (703)683-1815
E-Mail: arma@tmn.com
Web Site: http://www.tmn.com/~arma
Members: 300 individuals, 5 companies
Staff: 1
Annual Budget: $10-25,000
Exec. Director: Peter Smeallie

Historical Note
ARMA is the U.S. affiliate of the Internat'l Soc. of Rock Mechanics, and represents professionals, firms, and students in the geosciences and related industries. Membership: $65/year (individual); $500-5,000/year (corporation); $15/year (student).

Publications:
ARMA News. q. adv.

Meetings/Conferences:
Annual Meetings: June
1999 – Vail, CO/June 6-9

American Roentgen Ray Soc. *(1900)*
44211 Slate Stone Court
Leesburg, VA   20116

Tel: (703)729-3353   *Fax:* (703)729-4839
Toll Free: (800)438 - 2777
Web Site: http://www.arrs.org
Members: 12,500 individuals
Staff: 21
Annual Budget: $2-5,000,000
Exec. Director: Paul R. Fullagar
Program Coordinator: Shannon Hamilton
Senior Director, Education: Susan Roberts, &1
Manager, Subscriber and Member Services: Leigh Myzk

Historical Note
Organized in 1900 in St. Louis as the Roentgen Soc. of the United States. Became the American Roentgen Ray Soc. in 1906. Incorporated in the District of Columbia in 1922. The purpose of the Society, as stated in its constitution, is the advancement of medicine through the science of radiology and its allied sciences. Membership: $200/year (individual).

Publications:
American Journal of Roentgenology. m. adv.
ARRS Memo. q.

Meetings/Conferences:
Annual Meetings: Spring/3,000
1999 – New Orleans, LA(Hilton & Towers)/May 9-14
2000 – Washington, DC(Sheraton Washington &
    Towers)/May 7-12
2001 – Seattle, WA(Sheraton Seattle)/April 29-May 4/3000

American Rolling Door Institute
P.O. Box 117
28 Lowry Drive
West Milton, OH   45383-0117
Tel: (937)698-4188   *Fax:* (937)698-6153
Exec. Director: Rosita S. Long

Meetings/Conferences:

American Romagnola Ass'n *(1974)*

Historical Note
Members are breeders of purebred Romagnola cattle, a beef breed originated in Italy. Maintains a breed registry. Membership: $100/year (lifetime).

American Romney Breeders Ass'n *(1909)*
P.O. Box 247
Corvallis, OR   97339
Tel: (541)754-3051
E-Mail: ewebetmccoy@proaxis.com
Members: 550 individuals
Staff: 1
Annual Budget: $25-50,000
Secretary-Treasurer: Wendy M. McCoy

Historical Note
Breeders and fanciers of Romney sheep. Maintains a registry of pedigrees. Has an annual budget of approximately $25,000. Membership: $10/year.

Publications:
Romney Ramblings. q. adv.

Meetings/Conferences:
Annual Meetings: November-December

American Saddlebred Horse Ass'n *(1891)*
4093 Iron Works Pkwy.
Lexington, KY   40511
Tel: (606)259-2742   *Fax:* (606)259-1628
Members: 7,000 individuals
Staff: 15
Annual Budget: $1-2,000,000
Registrar/Exec. Secretary: Marcia Carothers

Historical Note
Members are owners, breeders and others interested in American Saddlebred horses united to preserve a 5-generation pedigree of each horse of this breed in the world. Known as the American Saddle Horse Breeders Ass'n before 1980. Member of the Nat'l Pedigree Livestock Council. Membership: $50/year.

Publications:
American Saddle Horse Register. a.
American Saddlebred Magazine. bi-m. adv.
Membership Directory. a. adv.

Meetings/Conferences:
1999 – Lexington, KY/Feb. 5-7

American Safe Deposit Ass'n *(1924)*
P.O. Box 519
Franklin, IN   46131-0519
Tel: (317)738-4432   *Fax:* (317)736-5267
E-Mail: jmclin@aol.com
Members: 3,500 banks
Staff: 2
Annual Budget: $100-250,000
Exec. Manager: Joyce A. McLin

Historical Note
TASDA is a federation of regional and local associations of banks, trust companies and others engaged in the safe deposit business. Formerly (1947) Nat'l Safe Deposit Advisory Council.

Publications:
ACCESS Magazine. q. adv.
Educational Bulletin. q.

Meetings/Conferences:
Annual Meetings: Late Spring-Early Summer
1999 – Indianapolis, IN

American Salers Ass'n *(1974)*
7383 S. Alton Way, Suite 103
Englewood, CO   80112-2302
Tel: (303)770-9292   *Fax:* (303)770-9302
E-Mail: amsalers@aol.com
Web Site: http://www.salers.usa.org
Members: 1,900 individuals
Staff: 5

Annual Budget: $500-1,000,000
Exec. V. President: Sherry Doubet
Historical Note
Members are breeders of Salers cattle. Maintains registry of pedigreed Salers cattle. Membership: $50/year.
Publications:
American Salers. 9/yr. adv.
Trends Newsletter. semi-a. adv.
Meetings/Conferences:
Annual Meetings: January with the Nat'l Western Stock Show in Denver, CO
1999 – Denver, CO(Hyatt Regency)

American Salvage Pool Ass'n *(1985)*
P.O. Box 6749
12633 N. 49th Ave.,
Glendale, AZ   85304
Tel: (602)580-0610   *Fax:* (602)547-0246
E-Mail: hqtrs@aspa.com
Web Site: http://www.aspa.com
Members: 162 companies
Staff: 1
Annual Budget: $250-500,000
Exec. Director: Al Dimperio
President: Doug Owens
Historical Note
Incorporated in Florida. Members are firms specializing in the brokering of totally wrecked, water and hail damaged, and other recovered vehicles in conjunction with insurance companies and recovery personnel. Membership: $900-1,200/year (companies); $300/year (associates).
Publications:
ASPA Flash. 8-10/year.
ASPA Report. q.
Convention Program. a. adv.
Directory. a. adv.
Meetings/Conferences:
Annual Meetings: Spring/200
1999 – San Antonio, TX(Adams Mark)/April 7-10
2000 – Atlanta, GA

American School Band Directors' Ass'n *(1953)*
P.O. Box 696
Guttenberg, IA   52052-0696
Tel: (319)252-2500   *Fax:* (319)252-2500
E-Mail: asbda@netins.net
Members: 1,300 individuals
Staff: 1
Annual Budget: $25-50,000
Office Manager: Dennis L. Hanna
Historical Note
Organized in Cedar Rapids, Iowa, November 21-22, 1953. Members are professionally trained instrumental music teachers with at least seven years of experience. Officers change annually on September 1. Membership: $55/year (individual), $40/year (institution).
Publications:
Bandworld Magazine. bi-m.
Meetings/Conferences:
Annual Meetings: June/500
1999 – Milwaukee, WI(Embassy Suites)/July 7-10/300
2000 – Snowmass, CO/300
2001 – Honolulu, HI/300

American School Counselor Ass'n *(1952)*
801 N. Fairfax St., Suite 310
Alexandria, VA   22314
Tel: (703)683-2722   *Fax:* (703)683-1619
Toll Free: (800)306 - 4722
E-Mail: asca@erols.com
Web Site: http://www.schoolcounselor.org
Members: 13,000 individuals
Staff: 7
Annual Budget: $1-2,000,000
Exec. Director: Nancy Perry
Director of Operations: Kathleen A. Smith
Historical Note
ASCA promotes professional school counseling activities that affect personal, educational and career development of students. ASCA is an affiliate of the American Counseling Ass'n. Membership: $75/year (professional); $35/year (student/retired).
Publications:
ASCA Counselor. 5/year. adv.
Professional School Counseling. 5/year. adv.
Meetings/Conferences:
Semi-Annual Meetings: with American Counseling Ass'n/Spring, and June
1999 – Phoenix, AZ(The Pointe)/June 25-28
2000 – Cherry Hills, NJ(Hilton)/June 23-26
2001 – Portland, OR(DoubleTree)

American School Food Service Ass'n *(1946)*
1600 Duke St., 7th Floor
Alexandria, VA   22314-3436
Tel: (703)739-3900   *Fax:* (703)739-3915
Toll Free: (800)877 - 8822
Web Site: http://www.asfsa.org
Members: 60,000 individuals
Staff: 38
Annual Budget: $5-10,000,000
Exec. Director: Barbara S. Borschow, CAE
Dir., Communications: Maria Robertson
Dir., Government Affairs: Barry Sackin
Washington Counsel: Marshall Matz
Director, Meetings: Ann E. Singer, CMP
Manager, Exhibitions and Meetings: Robin R. Preston
Dir., Education and Nutrition: Suzanne Rigby, R.D.
Dir., School Food Service Foundation: Barbara Skillman
Dir., Finance: O.J. Byrnside

Dir., Mktg./Member Services: Patti Montague
Historical Note
Organized in 1946 when the school meals program was officially recognized and implemented through the National School Lunch Act. Members are individuals working in food services in elementary and secondary non-profit schools, state programs, CNP, and other non- profit community child nutrition programs. Seeks to encourage and promote children's health and nutrition, to promote united efforts between school personnel and the public and encourage nutrition projects and research development. Membership: $75/year (individual); $550/year (corporate sustaining).
Publications:
Research Review. bi-a.
School Foodservice and Nutrition. 11/year. adv.
Meetings/Conferences:
Annual Meetings: July/6,500
1999 – Denver, CO/July 23-28
2000 – St. Louis, MO(Convention Center)/July 14-19
2001 – Atlanta, GA(Convention Center)/July 13-18

American School Health Ass'n *(1927)*
7263 State Route 43
Box 708
Kent, OH   44240
Tel: (330)678-1601   *Fax:* (330)678-4526
E-Mail: asha@ashaweb.org
Web Site: http://www.ashaweb.org
Members: 4,000 individuals
Staff: 15
Annual Budget: $1-2,000,000
Exec. Director: Susan Wooley, Ph.D., CHE
Communications: Maria Kizer
Director, Editorial Services: Thomas M. Reed
Meetings/Conventions: Bob Synovitz
Education: Marcia Rubin
Membership: Pamela Quinn
Historical Note
Established in Cincinnati, OH in 1927 as the American Ass'n of School Physicians. Became the American School Health Ass'n in 1936. Incorporated in Ohio in 1971. ASHA supports and provides professional services to comprehensive school health programs, to protect and improve the health and well-being of children and youth. Membership: $95/year (individual), $130/year (institution).
Publications:
Journal of School Health. 10/year. adv.
The Pulse. q. adv.
Meetings/Conferences:
Annual Meetings: Fall/800
1999 – Kansas City, MO(Hyatt Regency Crown Center)/Oct. 27-31

American Schools Ass'n *(1914)*
P.O. Box 14260
Chicago, IL   60614-0260
Tel: (773)832-1318   *Fax:* (773)832-1319
Staff: 2
Annual Budget: $100-250,000
President: Carl M. Dye
Historical Note
Main purpose is to coordinate educational counseling and consulting; provide SAT, PSAT, and ACT preparation, home studies courses providing continuing education for professional certification maintenance.
Publications:
Directory of College Transfer Information. bien.
Meetings/Conferences:
Annual Meetings: Chicago, IL/August

American Schools of Oriental Research *(1900)*
656 Beacon St., 5th Floor
Boston, MA   02215-2006
Tel: (617)353-6570   *Fax:* (617)353-6575
E-Mail: asor@bu.edu
Web Site: http://www.asor.com
Members: 1,300 individuals, 130 institutions
Staff: 6
Annual Budget: $500-1,000,000
Exec. Director: Rudolph Dornemann
Publications Director: Billie Jean Collins
Senior Programs Coordinator: Holly Andrews
Historical Note
Universities and individuals involved in Middle Eastern research, especially Biblical archaeology, pre-history, ancient and medieval history. Membership: $40/year (min. per individual), $600/year (organization).
Publications:
Bulletin. q. adv.
Journal of Cuneiform Studies. a. adv.
Near Eastern Archaeology. q. adv.
Newsletter. q.
Meetings/Conferences:
Annual Meetings: November

American Scientific Glassblowers Soc. *(1952)*
302 Redbud Lane
Thomasville, NC   27360-1642
Tel: (336)882-0174
Members: 950 individuals
Staff: 2
Annual Budget: $100-250,000
Exec. Secretary: Jerry Cloninger
Historical Note
Founded in Wilmington, DE in 1952 and incorporated in Delaware in 1954. Membership: $65/year.
Publications:
Fusion. q. adv.
Symposium Proceedings. a.

Meetings/Conferences:
Annual Meetings: Summer
1999 – Princeton, NJ

American Seafood Distributors Ass'n
Historical Note
Organization defunct in 1997.

American Seed Trade Ass'n *(1883)*
601 13th St., N.W., Suite 570 South
Washington, DC   20005-3807
Tel: (202)638-3128   *Fax:* (202)638-3171
Toll Free: (888)890 - 7333
Web Site: http://www.amseed.com
Members: 800 companies
Staff: 10
Annual Budget: $1-2,000,000
Exec. V. President: Dean Urmston
V. President, Government Affairs: Leslie Cahill
V.P., Programs & Services: Robert Falasca
Director, Administrative Services: Terry Sullivan
V.P., Financial Services: Ann Jores
V.P., Internat'l Marketing: Mark Condon
Historical Note
Active members are producers of seeds for planting purposes. Affiliates are state seed associations, and the like, while associates are suppliers to the industry and corresponding members are overseas seed companies. Sponsors the American Seed Research Foundation.
Publications:
ASTA Newsletter.
Corn and Sorghum Seed Conference Proceedings. a.
Soybean Seed Conference Proceedings. a.
Meetings/Conferences:
Annual Meetings: June/1,000
1999 – Palm Springs, CA(Renaissance Esmeralda Resort)/June 20-24

American Seminar Leaders Ass'n *(1988)*
2405 E. Washington Blvd.
Pasadena, CA   91104-2040
Tel: (626)791-1211   *Fax:* (626)798-0701
E-Mail: info@asla.com
Web Site: http://www.asla.com
Members: 2,500 individuals
Annual Budget: $500-1,000,000
President: June Davidson
Vice President: Geri Rouse
Secretary-Treasurer: Richard Shaw
Historical Note
ASLA members are professional seminar and workshop leaders. Awards the CSL (Certified Seminar Leader) designation. Membership: $195 first year, $125/year renewal.
Publications:
Directory of Seminar Leaders. a.
Newsletter. bi-m. adv.
Meetings/Conferences:
Semi-Annual Meetings: East Coast/Summer and West Coast/Fall

American Seniors Housing Ass'n *(1991)*
1850 M St., N.W., Suite 540
Washington, DC   20036
Tel: (202)974-2300   *Fax:* (202)775-0112
Members: 250 firms
Exec. Director: David S. Schless
Historical Note
Created by the Nat'l Multi Housing Council, ASHA members are companies participating in the multi-family seniors housing industry including construction, finance, and property management.

American Sexually Transmitted Diseases Ass'n *(1934)*
P.O. Box 133118
Atlanta, GA   30333
Tel: (404)639-3559   *Fax:* (404)639-4664
Members: 450 individuals
Staff: 1
Annual Budget: $25-50,000
Secretary-Treasurer: Stephen Morse, M.D.
Historical Note
Member of the Internat'l Union Against Sexually Transmitted Infections. Founded as the American Neisserian Medical Ass'n; became American Veneral Disease Ass'n in 1967, and assumed its current name in 1996. Has no paid officers or full-time staff. Membership: $67/year (individual).
Publications:
Sexually Transmitted Diseases. 10/year. adv.
Meetings/Conferences:
1999 – Denver, CO(Adam's Mark)/July 11-14/1500

American Sheep Industry Ass'n *(1955)*
6911 S. Yosemite St.
Englewood, CO   80112-1415
Tel: (303)771-3500   *Fax:* (303)771-8200
Members: 80,000 individuals
Staff: 11
Annual Budget: $5-10,000,000
Exec. Director: John M. Olson
Director of Communications: Janice Grauberger
Director, Prod. Education: Paul Rodgers
Historical Note
ASI is a federation of state ass'ns dedicated to the welfare and profitability of the sheep industry. Formerly (1989) the American Sheep Producers Council, ASI merged with the Nat'l Wool Growers Ass'n in 1989. American Lamb Council and American Wool Council are divisions of ASI. Sponsors and supports RAMS-PAC. Has an annual budget of approximately $7 million.
Publications:
Lamb & Wool Market News. w.

Nat'l Wool Grower Magazine. m. adv.
Meetings/Conferences:

American Shetland Pony Club/American Miniature Horse Registry *(1888)*
81-B Queenwood Professional Court
Morton, IL   61550-2923
Tel: (309)263-4044   *Fax:* (309)263-5133
Members: 6,000 individuals
Staff: 9
Director of Operations: David Diemer
Financial Manager: Joe Schroeter
Historical Note
Member of ASPC are owners and breeders of Shetland ponies. A member of the Nat'l Pedigree Livestock Council. Founded by the American Shetland Pony Club, AMHR members are breeders and owners of American miniature horses. Membership: $45/year (individual).
Publications:
Journal. bi-m. adv.
Meetings/Conferences:
Annual Meetings: November
1999 – Baltimore, MD

American Shipbuilding Ass'n
600 Pennsylvania Ave., S.E., Suite 305
Washington, DC   20003-4345
Tel: (202)544-8170   *Fax:* (202)544-8252
Web Site: http://www.americanshipbuilding.com
Members: 6 shipyards
Annual Budget: $500-1,000,000
President: Cynthia Brown
Historical Note
ASA is a trade association comprising American private sector shipyards. Membership: $100,000/year.
Publications:
American Shipbuilder Newsletter. m.

American Shire Horse Ass'n *(1885)*
P.O. Box 739
Newcastle, CO   81647
Tel: (970)876-5980   *Fax:* (970)876-1977
E-Mail: secretary@shirehorse.org
Web Site: http://www.shirehorse.org
Members: 575 individuals
Staff: 1
Annual Budget: $25-50,000
Secretary: Sharon McLin
Historical Note
Members are owners and breeders of Shire horses. Records pedigrees of Shire draft horses and promotes their breeding. Membership: $25/years (domestic); $30/year (foreign); $200/5 years (company).
Publications:
A. S.
Directory of Shire Owners and Breeders. a.
Shire Newsletter. q.
Meetings/Conferences:
Annual Meetings: February

American Short Line and Regional Railroad Ass'n *(1913)*
1120 G St., N.W., Suite 520
Washington, DC   20005-3889
Tel: (202)628-4500   *Fax:* (202)628-6430
Members: 410 railroads, 260 assoc. companies
Staff: 10
Annual Budget: $1-2,000,000
President: William E. Loftus
Exec. Director, Federal and Industry Programs: Matthew B. Reilly
Exec. Director, Traffic and Tariffs: Grant Ozburn
Manager, Finance & Administration: Ann M. Coleman
Exec. Director, Membership Services: Kathleen M. Cassidy
Historical Note
Absorbed (1998) Regional Railroads of America. ASLRRA represents short line and regional railroads in legislative/regulatory matters and industry relations.
Publications:
Views & News. w.
Meetings/Conferences:
Annual Meetings: Fall/1,100
1999 – New York, NY(Marriott Marquis)

American Short Line Railroad Ass'n
Historical Note
Became American Short Line and Regional Railroad Ass'n in 1998.

American Shorthorn Ass'n *(1846)*
8288 Hascall St.
Omaha, NE   68124
Tel: (402)393-7200   *Fax:* (402)393-7203
E-Mail: hunsley@beefshorthornusa.com
Web Site: http://www.beefshorthornusa.com
Members: 2,500 individuals
Staff: 12
Annual Budget: $500-1,000,000
Exec. Secretary: Dr. Roger E. Hunsley
Historical Note
In 1991 ASA absorbed the American Polled Shorthorn Society. Breeders and promoters of Shorthorn Beef Cattle. It is a member of the Nat'l Pedigree Livestock Council, the U.S. Beef Breeds Council and the Nat'l Cattlemen's Ass'n. Membership: $35/year.
Publications:
Shorthorn Country. m. adv.
Meetings/Conferences:
1999 – Forth Worth, TX/Jun. 28-31/500
2000 – Louisville, KY(Executive Inn)/Nov. 15-18/500

American Shoulder and Elbow Surgeons *(1984)*
6300 N. River Rd., Suite 727
Rosemont, IL   60018-4226
Tel: (847)698-1629   *Fax:* (847)823-0536
Members: 168 individuals
Staff: 2
Society Director: Karen Jared
Historical Note
Members are orthopedic surgeons.
Publications:
Journal of Shoulder and Elbow Surgery.
Meetings/Conferences:
1999 – Philadelphia, PA(Four Seasons Hotel)

American Shrimp Processors Ass'n *(1962)*
P.O. Box 50774
New Orleans, LA   70150
Tel: (504)368-1571   *Fax:* (504)368-1573
Members: 51 companies
Staff: 3
Annual Budget: $25-50,000
Managing Director: William Chauvin
Historical Note
Formerly (1977) the American Shrimp Canners Ass'n and the American Shrimp Canners and Processors Ass'n. Assumed its present name in 1984. Membership: $500/year.
Publications:
Newsletter. m.
Meetings/Conferences:
Annual Meetings: Spring
1999 – Biloxi, MS/Apr. 15-17

American Shropshire Registry Ass'n *(1884)*
P.O. Box 635
Harvard, IL   60033-0635
Tel: (815)648-4750
Members: 1000 individuals
Staff: 1
Annual Budget: $10-25,000
Secretary-Treasurer: Dale E. Blackburn, D.V.M.
Historical Note
Breeders and fanciers of Shropshire sheep, which were introduced into the U.S. in 1855 from England and are bred both for their meat and wool production. The Association registers and records the pedigrees of all purebred Shropshire sheep bred in America.
Publications:
Shropshire Voice. 3/year. adv.
Meetings/Conferences:
Annual Meetings: Fall/100
1999 – Louisville, KY(KY Fair and Exposition Center)
2000 – Louisville, KY(KY Fair and Exposition Center)

American Sightseeing Internat'l *(1947)*
490 Post St., Suite 1701
San Francisco, CA   94102
Tel: (415)986-2082   *Fax:* (415)986-2703
Toll Free: (800)225 - 4432
E-Mail: info@sightseeing.com
Web Site: http://www.sightseeing.com
Members: 100 companies
Staff: 5
Annual Budget: $500-1,000,000
General Manager: Maria Polk
Historical Note
Established as the American Sightseeing Ass'n, it assumed its present name in 1971. Members are independent sightseeing companies worldwide, usually one per city.
Publications:
American Sightseeing-International Tariff. a.
ASI Worldwide Tour Planning Manual. a. adv.
Meetings/Conferences:
Annual Meetings: Fall
1999 – Strasbourg, France/Nov. 12-14

American Simmental Ass'n *(1969)*
One Simmental Way
Bozeman, MT   59715-8699
Tel: (406)587-4531   *Fax:* (406)587-9301
E-Mail: simmental@simmgene.com
Web Site: http://www.simmgene.com
Members: 8,702 individuals
Staff: 35
Annual Budget: $2-5,000,000
Exec. V. President: Jerry Lipsey
General Manager, Publications: Jeff Thomas
Historical Note
Members are breeders of Simmental and Simbrah cattle. ASA provides research and data in breed and cross-breed genetics, production methods, and other issues.
Publications:
American Simbrah. bi-a.
SimTalk. q. adv.
The Register. m.
Meetings/Conferences:
Annual Meetings: Winter
1999 – Denver, CO/Jan. 15-17

American Ski Federation *(1979)*
Historical Note
Reported inactive in 1996.

American Skin Ass'n *(1987)*
150 E. 58th St., 33rd Floor
New York, NY   10155-0002
Tel: (212)753-8260   *Fax:* (212)688-6547
Toll Free: (800)499 - 7546
E-Mail: AMERICANSKIN@COMPUSERV.COM

Members: 70 individuals
Staff: 2
Managing Director: Joyce Weidler
Historical Note
ASA supports research and educates the public on the prevention of skin disorders.
Publications:
Skin Facts Newsletter. q.
Meetings/Conferences:
Annual Meetings: always New York, NY/March
1999 – New York, NY

American Sleep Apnea Ass'n *(1990)*
1424 K St., N.W., Suite 302
Washington, DC   20005-2410
Tel: (202)293-3650   *Fax:* (202)293-3656
E-Mail: asaa@sleepapnea.org
Web Site: http://www.sleepapnea.org
Annual Budget: $100-250,000
Executive Director: Christin Engelhardt
Historical Note
ASAA exists to promote understanding and awareness of sleep apnea and to support care-givers and patients. The Ass'n is dedicated to reducing injury, disability, and death from sleep apnea and to enhancing the well-being of those affected by the disorder. Supports A.W.A.K.E., a network of mutual support groups. Membership: $25/year.
Publications:
WAKE-UP CALL: Wellness Letter for Snoring and Apnea. bi-m.
Meetings/Conferences:
Annual Meetings: none held.

American Sleep Disorders Ass'n *(1975)*
6301 Burdel Rd. Suite 101
Rochester, MN   55901-2200
Tel: (507)287-6006   *Fax:* (507)287-6008
E-Mail: asda@asda.org
Web Site: http://www.asda.org
Members: 3,000 individuals, 250 centers
Staff: 22
Annual Budget: $500-1,000,000
Exec. Director: Jerome A. Barrett
Communications Director: Judith B. Morton
Meeting Manager: Dede Landis
Director of Education: Sarah Myren
Research Coordinator: Dawn Welch
Accreditation Director: Kari Kubicek
Director of Finance: Beverly Stensvold
Membership Director: Gregory Mader
Historical Note
Formerly (1976) American Ass'n of Sleep Disorder Centers and (1987) Ass'n of Sleep Disorders Centers. ASDA members are institutions and individuals concerned with the clinical care of patients with sleep disorders. Membership: $170/year (individual), $1,000/year (center).
Publications:
Membership Directory. a.
Newsletter. q. adv.
Sleep. 8/yr. adv.
Meetings/Conferences:
Annual Meetings: In conjunction with the Sleep Research Soc.
1999 – Orlando, FL(Marriott)/June 19-24/3100
2000 – Las Vegas, NV(Bally's)/June 17-22/3100

American Soc. for Adolescent Psychiatry *(1967)*
P.O. Box 28218
Dallas, TX   75228-0218
Tel: (214)388-1310   *Fax:* (214)381-3509
Members: 850 individuals
Staff: 2
Annual Budget: $250-500,000
Exec. Director: Ann T. Loew, Ed.M.
Historical Note
In 1958 a group of New York psychiatrists formed the Soc. for Adolescent Psychiatry. Shortly thereafter similar groups were set up in Philadelphia, Los Angeles and Chicago. In 1967 these groups confederated into the present ASAP, which is now a confederation of psychiatric societies and members-at-large throughout the United States and Canada. Provides continuing education, clinical guidance, knowledge exchange, advocacy, and research support to professionals in adolescent psychiatry. Membership: $225/year.
Publications:
Annals of Adolescent Psychiatry. a.
Journal of Youth & Adolescence. bi-m.
Membership Directory. bi-a.
Newsletter. q. adv.
Meetings/Conferences:

American Soc. for Aesthetic Plastic Surgery *(1967)*
11081 Winner's Circle, Suite 200
Los Alamitos, CA   90720
Tel: (562)799-2356   *Fax:* (562)799-1098
E-Mail: asaps@surgery.org
Web Site: http://www.surgery.org
Members: 1,345 individuals
Staff: 22
Annual Budget: $2-5,000,000
Exec. Director: Robert G. Stanton
Director of Communications: Elizabeth Saolati
Education Coordinator: Eliana Silva-Reyes
Education Coordinator: Debra McCarty
Historical Note
Members are specialists in the area of aesthetic plastic surgery certified by the American Board of Plastic Surgery. Membership: $750/year.
Publications:
Aesthetic Surgery Journal.

Meetings/Conferences:
Annual Meetings: Spring/2,600
1999 – Dallas, TX(Anatole)/May 14-19
2000 – San Francisco, CA(Marriott)/April 13-18
2001 – New York, NY(Hilton & Towers)/April 27-May 2
2002 – Las Vegas, NV
2003 – Orlando, FL(Coronado Springs Resort)

American Soc. for Aesthetics (1942)
404 Cudahy Hall, Marquette University
P.O. Box 1881
Milwaukee, WI   53201-1881
Tel: (414)288-7831   Fax: (414)288-5415
Web Site: http://asastcar.vms.csd.mu.edu
Members: 1000 individuals, 1,750 institutions
Staff: 2
Annual Budget: $100-250,000
Exec. Director: Curtis L. Carter

Historical Note
Founded to advance the philosophical and scientific understanding of the arts and related fields, ASA promotes study, research, publication, and discussion of aesthetics. Member of the Council of Learned Societies. Membership: $50/year (individual); $75/year (organization).

Publications:
ASA Newsletter. 3/year.
Journal of Aesthetics and Arts Criticism. q. adv.

Meetings/Conferences:
Annual Meetings: Fall
1999 – Washington, DC(Phoenix Park Hotel)/Oct. 26-30

American Soc. for Amusement Park Security and Safety (1972)
Historical Note
Address unknown in 1997.

American Soc. for Apheresis (1981)
3900 E. Timrod St.
Tucson, AZ   85711
Tel: (520)327-8584   Fax: (520)322-6778
E-Mail: ASFA@AZstarnet.com
Members: 1000 individuals
Annual Budget: $50-100,000
Exec. Director: Phillip A. Gutt, CAE

Historical Note
Members are health professionals with an interest in the removal and separation of blood components. Membership: $30-95/year (individual).

Publications:
ASFA Newsletter. irreg.
Journal of Clinical Apheresis. q.

Meetings/Conferences:
Annual Meetings: Spring

American Soc. for Artificial Internal Organs (1955)
P.O. Box C
Boca Raton, FL   33429-0468
Tel: (561)391-8589   Fax: (561)368-9153
E-Mail: info@asaio.com
Web Site: http://www.asaio.com/
Members: 1,756 individuals
Staff: 3
Annual Budget: $250-500,000

Historical Note
Established June 1954, ASAIO members are physicians, scientists and engineers from academia, industry, research institutions and government agencies who have made a significant contribution to the development and/or understanding of of artificial organs. A member society of the American Institute for Medical and Biological Engineering. Membership: $225/year; $245/year (foreign); $50/year (students); $75 (foreign students).

Publications:
ASAIO Abstracts. a.
ASAIO Journal. bi-m. adv.

Meetings/Conferences:
Annual Meetings: Spring
1999 – San Diego, CA(Marriott)/June 2-5/1100

American Soc. for Ass'n Publishing
Historical Note
Became (1997) Ass'n Publishing and Fulfillment Services.

American Soc. for Automation in Pharmacy (1989)
P.O. Box 36972
Birmingham, AL   35236
Tel: (205)985-9488   Fax: (205)733-1006
Web Site: http://www.asapnet.org
Members: 150 companies
Staff: 3
Annual Budget: $50-100,000
Director: Bob Mosca

Historical Note
Members are software solutions providers serving the pharmacy industry. Supports implementation of standards for electronic data interchange between pharmacies and suppliers.

Publications:
Bite Line Newsletter. q. adv.

Meetings/Conferences:

American Soc. for Biochemistry and Molecular Biology (1906)
9650 Rockville Pike
Bethesda, MD   20814-3996
Tel: (301)530-7145   Fax: (301)571-1824
E-Mail: asbmb.faseb.org
Web Site: http://www.faseb.org/asbmb/
Members: 9,000 individuals
Staff: 17

Annual Budget: $10-25,000,000
Exec. Officer: Charles C. Hancock

Historical Note
Formerly (1987) American Soc. of Biological Chemists. Founded December 26, 1906 in New York City under the leadership of Drs. John J. Abel and C.A. Herter; incorporated in New York in 1919. Purpose is the extension and dissemination of knowledge about biochemistry and molecular biology. A founder and constituent society of the Federation of American Socs. for Experimental Biology as well as the Pan American Ass'n for Biochemistry and Molecular Biology. A member of the American Ass'n for the Advancement of Science and the Council of Academic Socs. of the American Ass'n of Medical Colleges. Has an annual budget of approximately $10 million. Membership: $100/year (regular); $60/year(student and associate).

Publications:
Journal of Biological Chemistry. w. adv.

Meetings/Conferences:
Annual Meetings: Spring
1999 – San Francisco, CA
2000 – Boston, MA
2001 – Orlando, FL
2001 – New Orleans, LA

American Soc. for Bioethics and Humanities
4700 W. Lake Ave.
Glenview, IL   60025-1485
Tel: (847)375-4700   Fax: (847)375-4777
E-Mail: info@asbh.org
Web Site: http://www.asbh.org
Members: 1,200 individuals and organizations
Account Executive: Richard Muir

Historical Note
ASBH promotes the exchange of ideas and fosters multidisciplinary, interdisciplinary, and interprofessional scholarship, research, teaching, policy development and collegiality among individuals engaged in all areas related to clinical and academic bioethics and the health-related humanities.

American Soc. for Bone and Mineral Research (1977)
1200 19th St., Suite 300
Washington, DC   20036-2422
Tel: (202)857-1161   Fax: (202)223-4579
E-Mail: ASBMR@DC.SBA.COM
Members: 3,000 individuals
Staff: 3
Annual Budget: $1-2,000,000
Exec. Director: Julia A. Janko
Public Relations Manager: Marlene Michael
Conventions Manager: Cele Fogarty
Membership Coordinator: Janet Stiles

Historical Note
ASBMR members are physicians and scientists who perform basic and clinical research in the fields of metabolic bone diseases and mineral metabolism. Membership: $155-172/year (individual); $75/year (trainee).

Publications:
Journal of Bone and Mineral Research. m. adv.
Membership Roster. bien. adv.
Primer on Metabolic Bone Diseases & Disorders of Mineral Metabolism.

Meetings/Conferences:
1999 – St. Louis, MO(Cervantes Convention Center)/Sept. 30-Oct. 4
2000 – Toronto, Ontario(Convention Center)/Sept. 22-26

American Soc. for Cell Biology (1960)
9650 Rockville Pike
Bethesda, MD   20814-3992
Tel: (301)530-7153   Fax: (301)530-7139
E-Mail: ascbinfo@ascb.org
Web Site: http://www.ascb.org/ascb
Members: 9,000 individuals
Staff: 14
Annual Budget: $2-5,000,000
Exec. Director: Elizabeth Marincola
Director, Public Policy: Tim Leshan
Director of Exhibits: Edward Newman
Director of Sales: Richard Sommer

Historical Note
Formed in 1960 and incorporated in New York in 1961. A member of The Federation of American Societies for Experimental Biology. Membership: $115/year.

Publications:
ASCB Directory. a.
ASCB Newsletter. m.
Molecular Biology of the Cell. m.

Meetings/Conferences:
Annual Meetings: Fall/6,000
1999 – Washington, DC(DC Convention Center)/Dec. 11-15/6000
2000 – San Francisco, CA(Moscone Convention Center)/Dec. 9-13
2001 – Washington, DC(DC Convention Center)/Dec. 8-12
2002 – San Francisco, CA(Moscone Convention Center)/Dec. 14-18

American Soc. for Clinical Evoked Potentials (1981)
14 Soundview Ave., #51
White Plains, NY   10606
Tel: (914)761-4713
Members: 410 individuals
Annual Budget: under $10,000
President: Laurian Jacoby

Historical Note
Promotes the study of the nervous system's electric transmissions, and the applications of such study to medical diagnosis and treatment. Membership: $95/year (individual); $1,000/year (organization/company).

Publications:
Electromyography & Clinical Neurophysiology. 8/yr. adv.
Membership Directory. irreg.

Meetings/Conferences:
Annual Meetings: Fall
1999 – New York City, NY(Cornell MedCenter)/April 22-24/100

American Soc. for Clinical Investigation (1909)
6900 Grove Road
Thorofare, NJ   08086-9447
Tel: (609)251-6976   Fax: (609)848-5274
E-Mail: asci@slackinc.comom
Web Site: http://www.asci-jci.org/ASCI
Members: 2,500 individuals
Staff: 5
Annual Budget: $1-2,000,000
Exec. Director: Susan J. Nelson
Manager, Meetings: Rhonda Simmons
Membership Manager: Peggy Gray

Historical Note
Founded in 1909 as the American Soc. for the Advancement of Clinical Investigation. Name changed to American Soc. for Clinical Investigation in 1916. ASCI's ojectives are to advance medical science, cultivate clinical research through the methods of natural science, correlate science with the art of medical practice and encourage scientific spirit amomng its members. Membership: $185/year.

Publications:
Journal of Clinical Investigation. m. adv.

Meetings/Conferences:
Annual Meetings: Spring
1999 – Chicago, IL(Fairmont Hotel)/April 23-25

American Soc. for Clinical Laboratory Science (1932)
7910 Woodmont Ave., Suite 530
Bethesda, MD   20814-3015
Tel: (301)657-2768   Fax: (301)657-2909
E-Mail: ascls@ascls.org
Web Site: http://www.ascls.org
Members: 17,500 individuals
Staff: 5
Annual Budget: $1-2,000,000
Exec. Director: Elissa Passiment, EdM
Director, Education: Jeannine Meloon

Historical Note
Formerly (1936) the American Soc. of Clinical Laboratory Technicians the American Soc. of Medical Technologists (1972) and the American Society for Medical Technology (1993). Members have an associate, a B.S. degree, and/or clinical training or experience in a branch of medical technology, or the medical laboratory sciences. Supports the American Soc. for Clinical Laboratory Science Political Action Committee. Membership: $80/year, plus state dues.

Publications:
ASCLS Today. m. adv.
Clinical Laboratory Science. bi-m. adv.

Meetings/Conferences:
1999 – San Juan, Puerto Rico/March 4-6

American Soc. for Clinical Nutrition (1959)
9650 Rockville Pike
Bethesda, MD   20814-3998
Tel: (301)530-7110   Fax: (301)571-1863
Web Site: http://www.faseb.org/ascn
Members: 1,550 individuals
Staff: 7
Annual Budget: $500-1,000,000
Exec. Director: Ann Marie W. Gebhart

Historical Note
The clinical division of the American Institute of Nutrition. Promotes training in clinical nutrition in the medical and health professions. Membership: $155/year (full); $2,500/year (organization).

Publications:
American Journal of Clinical Nutrition. m. adv.
Directory of Members.

Meetings/Conferences:

American Soc. for Clinical Pharmacology and Therapeutics (1900)
117 W. Ridge Pike, Suite 2
Conshohocken, PA   19428-1216
Tel: (610)825-3838   Fax: (610)834-8652
E-Mail: ascpt@aol.com
Web Site: http://www.ascpt.org
Members: 2,110 individuals
Staff: 3
Annual Budget: $250-500,000
Assistant Exec. Director: Denise Gavetti

Historical Note
Organized May 1, 1900 as the American Therapeutic Soc. Merged in 1969 with the American College of Clinical Pharmacology and Chemotherapy (founded in 1963) and incorporated in the District of Columbia under its present name. Approximately 60% of ASCPT members are from academia and private practice, 30% from industry and 10% from government. Two-thirds of members are clinicians with hospital staff appointments and a subspecialty interest in clinical pharmacology and therapeutics. Membership: $185/year.

Publications:
Clinical Pharmacology and Therapeutics. m.

Meetings/Conferences:
Annual Meetings: Spring/1,400
1999 – San Antonio, TX(Marriott Rivercenter)/March 18-20

American Soc. for Colposcopy and Cervical Pathology (1964)

20 W. Washington St., Suite 1
Hagerstown, MD   21740
Tel: (301)733-3640   *Fax:* (301)733-5775
Toll Free: (800)787 - 7227
Members: 3,500 individuals
Staff: 3
Annual Budget: $1-2,000,000
Administrative Director: Kathleen Graham Poole

Historical Note
Founded as American Soc. for Colposcopy and Colpomicroscopy to provide a forum for education in the diagnosis, etiology and treatment of pathologies of the cervix and lower genital tract. Members are gynecologists, pathologists, family phsysicians and others interested in promoting the study of female lower genital tract disease. Sponsors several continuing education programs throughout the year. Membership: $125/year (individual).

Publications:
Journal of Lower Genital Tract Disease. q. adv.
The Colposcopist. q. adv.
The Home Study Program. q.

Meetings/Conferences:
Biennial Meeting: (even years)
2000 – Lake Buena Vista, FL(Disney's Yacht and Beach
            Club)/March 13-16

American Soc. for Concrete Construction
Historical Note
Became (1998) American Soc. of Concrete Contractors.

American Soc. for Conservation Archaeology *(1974)*
Historical Note
Address unknown in 1996.

American Soc. for Cytotechnology *(1979)*
4101 Lake Boone Trail
Suite 201
Raleigh, NC   27607
Tel: (919)787-5181   *Fax:* (919)787-4916
Members: 1,800 individuals
Staff: 1
Annual Budget: $50-100,000
Exec. Director: Pamela D. Sproul

Historical Note
Members are individuals concerned with the evaluation of cells for early signs of malignancy. Full members must have passed a qualifying cytotechnology exam and have either graduated from a school of cytology or worked in the field for three years. Membership: $40/year.

Publications:
ACST Journal of Cytotechnology. q. adv.
ASCT News. m. adv.

Meetings/Conferences:
Annual Meetings: Spring; Held in conjunction with a regional
            Cytology Society.
1999 – Newport, RI(Hotel Viking)/March 19-21

American Soc. for Dental Aesthetics *(1976)*
635 Madison Ave., 12th Floor
New York, NY   10022
Tel: (212)371-4575   *Fax:* (212)308-5182
Web Site: http://www.asdatoday.com
Members: 160 individuals
Staff: 1
Annual Budget: $10-25,000
President: Irwin Smigel, D.D.S.

Historical Note
Members are dentists who have demonstrated excellence in an area of aesthetic dentistry. Applicants must be dentists for five years, then submit before- and-after photos of five cases for review. Fellowships to the Society are granted to members who have been active for five years and have advanced the Society's standards.

Publications:
Newsletter. q.

Meetings/Conferences:
Semi-annual Meetings: Spring and Fall
1999 – Bal Harbor, FL/Oct. 21-23

American Soc. for Dermatologic Surgery *(1970)*
930 N. Meacham Road
Schaumburg, IL   60173-4965
Tel: (847)330-9830   *Fax:* (847)330-0050
E-Mail: asds@neton-line.com
Web Site: http://www.asds-net.org
Members: 2,500 individuals
Annual Budget: $500-1,000,000
Exec. Director: Cheryl K. Nordstedt

Historical Note
ASDS was established to preserve and enhance the use of surgical modalities in the practice of dermatology. Membership: $225/year.

Publications:
Annual Meeting Program Book. a. adv.
Currents Newsletter. q.
Dermatologic Surgery m. adv. adv.

Meetings/Conferences:
1999 – Miami Beach, FL(Fountainbleau)/May 19-23

American Soc. for Eighteenth-Century Studies *(1969)*
Wake Forest U.
P.O. Box 7867
Winston-Salem, NC   27109
Tel: (336)727-4694   *Fax:* (336)727-4697
Web Site: http://direct.press.jhu.edu/associations/asecs
Members: 3,000 individuals
Staff: 1
Annual Budget: $250-500,000
Exec. Secretary: Byron Wells
Office Manager: Vickie B. Cutting

Historical Note
ASECS members are academics and others interested in the cultural history of the eighteenth century. Membership: $20-$65 (individual); $100-$130 (organization/company).

Publications:
ASECS Directory. quadren. adv.
ASECS News Circular.
ASECS Program of Annual Meeting. a. adv.
Eighteenth-Century Studies. q. adv.
Studies in Eighteenth Century Culture. a.

Meetings/Conferences:
1999 – Milwaukee, WI(Milwaukee Hilton)/March 31-April 4
2000 – Philadelphia, PA(Sheraton Society
            Hill)/April 12-16/600

American Soc. for Engineering Education *(1893)*
1818 N St., N.W., Suite 600
Washington, DC   20036
Tel: (202)331-3500   *Fax:* (202)265-8504
E-Mail: aseexec@asee.org
Web Site: http://www.asee.org
Members: 11,000 individuals, 550 institutions
Staff: 40
Annual Budget: $10-25,000,000
Exec. Director: Dr. Frank L. Huband
Manager, Public Affairs: Kathy Tollerton
Manager, Meetings & Conferences: Dyanne Hughes
Controller: Charlotte Watson
Membership Manager: Paige Polhill
Editor: Robert Black

Historical Note
Originated in 1893 as the Soc. for the Promotion of Engineering Education. Merged in 1946 with the Engineering College Research Ass'n to form the American Soc. for Engineering Education. Incorporated in Pennsylvania in 1943. A member of the American Ass'n of Engineering Societies, Accreditation Board for Engineering and Technology, the American Ass'n for the Advancement of Science and the American Council on Education. A participating society of the World Federation of Engineering Organizations. Membership: $60/year (individual); $750-900/year (organization).

Publications:
ASEE Conference Proceedings. a.
ASEE PRISM. 9/yr. adv.
Chemical Engineering Education. q. adv.
Civil Engineering Education. bi-a.
COED (Computers in Education Division) Journal. q.
College Industry Conference Proceedings.
Directory of Engineering Technology Statistics.
Directory of Graduate Engineering Statistics.
Directory of Key Engineering Administrators.
Directory of Undergraduate Engineering Statistics.
Engineering College Research and Graduate Directory. a. adv.
Engineering Design Graphics. 3/year. adv.
Engineering Economist. q.
Journal of Engineering Education. q.
Journal of Engineering Technology. semi-a.
Mechanical Engineering News. q. adv.

Meetings/Conferences:
Annual Meetings: June/3,000
1999 – Charlotte, NC/June 20-23
2000 – St. Louis, MO/June 18-21
2001 – Albuquerque, NM/June 24-27

American Soc. for Engineering Management *(1979)*
P.O. Box 820
Rolla, MO   65402
Tel: (573)341-2101
Members: 800 individuals
Staff: 1
Annual Budget: $100-250,000
MSCD Manager: Kellie Frohmader

Historical Note
Founded in 1979 by a group of engineering management professionals from academic, industrial, and governmental organizations to promote the development of engineering management as a professional discipline and academic specialty and to maintain a high professional standard among its members. Membership: $75/year (individual); $1,000-10,000/year (company).

Publications:
Engineering Management Journal. q.
Newsletter. q.
Proceedings of Annual Meeting. a.

Meetings/Conferences:
Annual Meetings: Fall

American Soc. for Enology and Viticulture *(1950)*
Box 1855
Davis, CA   95617-1855
Tel: (530)753-3142   *Fax:* (530)753-3318
Members: 2,200 individuals
Staff: 7
Annual Budget: $500-1,000,000
Exec. Director: Lyndie McHenry Boulton

Historical Note
Formerly (1984) the American Soc. of Enologists. ASEV is an international, professional society dedicated to the interests of enologists, viticulturists and others in the fields of wine and grape production. Membership: $130/year (domestic individual); $130/year (overseas individual); $250/year (company).

Publications:
American Journal of Enology and Viticulture. q. adv.

Meetings/Conferences:
Annual Meetings: June
1999 – Reno, NV(Hilton)/June 16-18
2000 – Seattle, WA(Convention Center)/June 21-23

American Soc. for Environmental History *(1976)*

c/o Forest History Soc.
701 Vickers Ave.
Durham, NC   27701
Tel: (919)682-9319   *Fax:* (919)682-2349
E-Mail: dwilliam@nov.snu.edu
Web Site: http://www.h-net.msu.edu/aseh
Members: 10,000 individuals
Annual Budget: under $10,000
Contact: Donald Pisani

Historical Note
ASEH members are teachers and researchers with an interest in human ecology and environmental history. Currently shares headquarters with Forest History Soc. Membership: $35/year (individual); $17.50/year (student); $30/year (organization/company).

Publications:
ASEH News. 3/yr.
Environmental History. q.

Meetings/Conferences:
1999 – Tuscon, AZ/April 14-18

American Soc. for Ethnohistory *(1953)*
Milwaukee Public Museum
800 W. Wells St.,
Milwaukee, WI   53233-1478
Members: 700 individuals
Annual Budget: $50-100,000
Secretary-Treasurer: Ann McMullen

Historical Note
Formerly (1966) known as the American Indian Ethnohistoric Conference. Members are anthropologists, historians, art historians, geographers and other professionals interested in the research of the cultural history of non-industrial peoples. Has no paid officers or full-time staff. Membership: $30/year (individual); $50/year (institution); $20/year (student/retired).

Publications:
Ethnohistory Journal. q. adv.
Meeting Program and Abstracts: a. adv. adv.

Meetings/Conferences:
Annual Meetings: November

American Soc. for Gastrointestinal Endoscopy *(1941)*
13 Elm St.
Manchester, MA   01944-1314
Tel: (978)526-8330   *Fax:* (978)526-4018
E-Mail: asge@shore.net
Web Site: http://www.asge.org
Members: 6,870 individuals
Staff: 10
Annual Budget: $1-2,000,000
Exec. Director: William T. Maloney, C.A.E.

Historical Note
Formerly American Gastropic Club. Seeks to advance the use of endoscopy as a diagnostic technique.

Publications:
Gastrointestinal Endoscopy. q. adv.

Meetings/Conferences:
1999 – Orlando, FL/May 18-19
2000 – San Diego, CA/May 23-24
2001 – Washington, DC/May 22-23
2002 – San Francisco, CA/May 21-22
2003 – Orlando, FL/May 20-21
2004 – New Orleans, LA/May 18-19

American Soc. for Geriatric Dentistry *(1964)*
211 E. Chicago Ave., Suite 948
Chicago, IL   60611
Tel: (312)440-2660   *Fax:* (312)440-2824
Members: 550 individuals
Staff: 2
Annual Budget: $250-500,000
Exec. Director: John S. Rutkauskas, D.D.S., MS

Historical Note
Established and incorporated in Chicago, IL. Membership: $120/year.

Publications:
ASGO Interface. q.
Special Care in Dentistry. bi-m. adv.

Meetings/Conferences:
Semi-annual Meetings: Spring in Chicago. Fall with the
            American Dental Ass'n.
1999 – Chicago, IL(Westin Hotel)/March 26-28

American Soc. for Health Care Marketing and Public Relations
Historical Note
Merged with the Soc. for Healthcare Planning and Marketing to form the Soc. for Healthcare Strategy and Marketing in 1996.

American Soc. for Healthcare Central Service Personnel *(1967)*
One N. Franklin
Chicago, IL   60606
Tel: (312)422-3750   *Fax:* (312)422-3846
Members: 1,300 individuals
Staff: 2
Annual Budget: $250-500,000
Director: J.D. Meacham

Historical Note
Formerly (1987) the American Soc. for Hospital Central Service Personnel. An affiliate of the American Hospital Ass'n. Membership: $75/year (individual).

Publications:
Healthcare Central Service. bi-m.

Meetings/Conferences:
Annual Meetings: Fall/300 +

American Soc. for Healthcare Education and Training (1970)

Historical Note
Defunct in 1997.

American Soc. for Healthcare Engineering (1962)

One N. Franklin, Suite 2700
Chicago, IL 60606-3420
Tel: (312)422-3000   *Fax:* (312)422-4571
Members: 6,000 individuals
Staff: 12
Annual Budget: $2-5,000,000
Exec. Director: Joseph J. Martori

Historical Note
Formerly (1995) American Soc. for Hospital Engineering. An affiliate of the American Hospital Ass'n. Supports the American Hospital Ass'n Political Action Committee (AHA-PAC). Membership: $95/year (individual from AHA member hospital); $105/year (individual from non-member hospital); $250/year (vendor/manufacturer), $25/year (retiree or student).

Publications:
Clinical Engineering Newsletter. bi-m.
Directory of Planning Professionals for Health Facilities. a.
Health Facilities Management Magazine. m.
Technical Document Series. m.
Yearbook. a.

Meetings/Conferences:
Annual Meetings: June-July

American Soc. for Healthcare Environmental Services (1986)

1 North Franklin
Chicago, IL 60606
Tel: (312)422-3860   *Fax:* (312)422-4572
Web Site: http://www.ashes.org
Members: 1,500 individuals
Staff: 7
Annual Budget: $500-1,000,000
Exec. Director: Katherine J. Svedman

Historical Note
An affiliate of the American Hospital Ass'n, ASHES members are managers of hospital environmental services, housekeeping, and laundry departments. Membership: $75/year (individual); $105-125/year (organization).

Publications:
Annual Conference Proceedings Manual. a.
ASHES Members Directory. a.
ASHES Newsletter. bi-m.
Healthcare Environmental Services. bi-m.
Hospitals and Health Network.

Meetings/Conferences:
Annual Meetings: September
1999 – Lake Bueno Vista, FL(Coronado Springs)/Sept. 19-23

American Soc. for Healthcare Food Service Administrators (1967)

1 North Franklin
31 Floor
Chicago, IL 60606
Tel: (312)422-3870   *Fax:* (312)422-4581
Web Site: www.ashffa.org
Members: 1,300 individuals
Staff: 3
Annual Budget: $250-500,000
Director: Patricia Burton, R.D.

Historical Note
An affiliate of the American Hospital Ass'n, ASHFSA advances the effectiveness of food and nutrition services administration in the healthcare setting.

Publications:
Newsletter. bi-m.

Meetings/Conferences:
Annual Meetings: Summer/500-600
1999 – Pheonix, AZ(Point Hilton Resort)/June 13-16

American Soc. for Healthcare Human Resources Administration (1964)

1 North Franklin
Chicago, IL 60606
Tel: (312)422-3720   *Fax:* (312)422-4579
Members: 2,800 individuals
Staff: 4
Annual Budget: $500-1,000,000
Exec. Director: Linda Brooks
Associate Director: Catherine Futrell

Historical Note
An affiliate of the American Hospital Ass'n. Formerly (1975) American Soc. for Hospital Personnel Directors. Dedicated exclusively to the education and professional development of hospital personnel administrators. Membership: $100/year.

Publications:
ADA Job Description Manual.
Consultants Directory. a. adv.
Human Resources Administration. bi-m.
Membership Roster. a.

Meetings/Conferences:
Annual Meetings: Summer/500

American Soc. for Healthcare Materials Management

Historical Note
Became Ass'n for Healthcare Resource Materials and Management in 1998.

American Soc. for Healthcare Risk Management (1980)

1 N. Franklin St., Suite 3100

Chicago, IL 60606-3491
Tel: (312)422-3980   *Fax:* (312)422-4580
E-Mail: chessle1@aha.org
Web Site: http://ashrm.org
Members: 3,500 individuals
Staff: 8
Annual Budget: $1-2,000,000
Exec. Director: Christy L. Kessler
Manager, Communications: Lynne Mangan
Manager, Meetings & Exhibits: Linda Moustis
Staff Associate, Membership: Cherrell Jackson

Historical Note
Formerly (1987) American Soc. for Hospital Risk Management. An affiliate of the American Hospital Ass'n. Members are hospital employees involved in risk management as well as insurance personnel, hospital administrators, attorneys, physicians and healthcare management consultants. Membership: $110/year.

Publications:
ASHRM Forum. bi-m.
Conference Proceedings. a.
Directory. a. adv.
Journal of Healthcare Risk Management. q.

Meetings/Conferences:
Annual Meetings: Fall/2,000
1999 – Chicago, IL(Hyatt Regency)/Oct. 3-6
2000 – New Orleans, LA(Hyatt regency)/Nov. 2-5
2001 – Boston, MA(Hynes Convention
          Center)/Oct. 28-31/2500
2002 – Seattle, WA(Seattle Convention Center)/2500

American Soc. for Histocompatability and Immunogenetics (1970)

P.O. Box 15804
Lenexa, KS 66285-5804
Tel: (913)541-0009   *Fax:* (913)541-0156
E-Mail: ashiamp@aol.com
Web Site:
          http://www.swmed.edu/home_pages/ASHI/ashi.html
Members: 1,150 individuals
Staff: 6
Annual Budget: $1-2,000,000
Exec. Director: Michael P. Flanagan
Meetings Coordinator: Joyce Miller

Historical Note
Physicians, blood banks and others involved in the testing of blood to determine its compatability with organs to be used in transplants. Formerly (1984) the American Ass'n for Clinical Histocompatibility Testing. Membership: $95/year (full member); $45/year (associate); $1,000/year (institution).

Publications:
ASHI Quarterly. q. adv.
Human Immunology. m.

Meetings/Conferences:
Annual Meetings: Fall
1999 – New Orleans, LA(Hilton Riverside)/Sept. 17-25
2000 – Orlando, FL(Walt Disney World
          Resort)/Sept. 17-24/1000

American Soc. for Horticultural Science (1903)

600 Cameron St.
Alexandria, VA 22314-2562
Tel: (703)836-4606   *Fax:* (703)836-2024
E-Mail: webmaster@ashs.org
Web Site: http://www.ashs.org
Members: 5,000 individuals
Staff: 11
Annual Budget: $2-5,000,000
Director, Meetings and Educational Programs: Teresa Alfaro
Director, Finance and Administration: Joan T. Herto
Director, Membership and Marketing: Lisa M. Preston
Publications Director: Michael W. Neff

Historical Note
Founded in 1903 in Boston and incorporated in 1961 in the District of Columbia. Promotes and encourages national and international interest in scientific research and education in all branches of horticulture (the production, marketing, processing, and utilization of fruits, nuts, vegetables, flowers, ornamental and landscape plants). Membership: $60/year (individual), $250-3,000/year (corporate).

Publications:
ASHS Newsletter. m. adv.
HortScience. m. adv.
HortTechnology. q. adv.
Journal of the ASHS. bi-m.

Meetings/Conferences:
1999 – Minneapolis, MN/July 28-31
2000 – Orlando, FL/July 23-26
2001 – Sacramento, CA/July 22-25

American Soc. for Hospital Engineering (1962)

Historical Note
Became the American Soc. for Healthcare Engineering in 1995.

American Soc. for Industrial Security (1955)

1625 Prince St.
Alexandria, VA 22314-2818
Tel: (703)522-5800   *Fax:* (703)519-6299
Web Site: http://www.asisonline.org
Members: 30,000 individuals
Staff: 52
Annual Budget: $5-10,000,000
Exec. Director: Michael J. Stack
Director, Marketing: Joseph Ricci
Director, Education Administration: Susan A. Melnicove
Manager, Education Programs: Valerie DiBenedetto
Director, Finance and Administration: Elizabeth Mewshaw
Director, Research & Development: Sandy Davidson
Director, Membership Services: Karen Reamy

Historical Note
Members include security professionals and company representatives for security products, and services. Awards the designation CPP (Certified Protection Professional). Operates The ASIS Foundation. Has an annual budget of approximately $8.5 million.

Publications:
Directory. a.
Dynamics. bi-m.
Security Management. m. adv.

Meetings/Conferences:
Annual Meetings: Fall
1999 – Las Vegas, NV/Sept. 27-30

American Soc. for Information Science (1937)

8720 Georgia Ave., Suite 501
Silver Spring, MD 20910-3602
Tel: (301)495-0900   *Fax:* (301)495-0810
E-Mail: asis@asis.org
Web Site: http://www.asis.org
Members: 3,800 individuals
Staff: 7
Annual Budget: $500-1,000,000
Exec. Director: Richard B. Hill
Dir., Marketing: Michele Devine
Manager, Membership Services: Vanessa O. Foss

Historical Note
Founded in Washington, DC in 1937 as the American Documentation Institute and incorporated in Delaware the same year. Became the American Soc. for Information Science in 1968. Promotes the creation and application of knowledge concerning information and its transfer. Membership: $95/year (individual), $350-550/year (company).

Publications:
Annual Review of Information Science and Technology. a.
ASIS Handbook and Directory. a. adv.
Bulletin of ASIS. bi-m. adv.
Journal of ASIS. 14/year. adv.
Proceedings. a.

Meetings/Conferences:
Semi-Annual Meetings: Fall and Spring

American Soc. for Investigative Pathology (1976)

9650 Rockville Pike
Bethesda, MD 20814-3993
Tel: (301)530-7130   *Fax:* (301)571-1879
E-Mail: asip@pathol.faseb.org
Web Site: http://asip.uthscsa.edu/
Members: 2,300 individuals
Staff: 2
Annual Budget: $250-500,000
Exec. Officer: Frances A. Pitlick, Ph.D.

Historical Note
Formed on July 1, 1976 by a merger of the American Soc. for Experimental Pathology (founded in 1913) and the American Ass'n of Pathologists and Bacteriologists (founded in 1900). Formerly (1992) American Ass'n of Pathologists. Membership: $160/year.

Publications:
American Journal of Pathology. m. adv.

Meetings/Conferences:
Annual Meetings: Spring, with ASBMB and American Ass'n of
          Immunologists
1999 – Washington, DC(Convention
          Center)/April 17-21/10000
2000 – San Diego, CA(Convention Center)/April 14-18
2001 – Anaheim, CA(Convention Center)/March 31-April 4

American Soc. for Laser Medicine and Surgery (1980)

2404 Stewart Square
Wausau, WI 54401
Tel: (715)845-9283   *Fax:* (715)848-2493
E-Mail: aslms@dwave.net
Web Site: http://www.aslms.org
Members: 3,200 individuals
Staff: 5
Annual Budget: $250-500,000
Secretary: Dr. Richard O. Gregory

Historical Note
Founded through an initial grant from the A. Ward Ford Memorial Institute in Wausau, and incorporated in the State of Wisconsin by 150 charter members.

Publications:
Lasers in Surgery and Medicine. bi-m.
Official ASLMS Newsletter. 2/year.

Meetings/Conferences:
1999 – Lake Buena Vista, FL(Buena Vista Palace)/April 15-18

American Soc. for Legal History (1956)

Department of History
Bowling Green State University
Bowling Green, OH 43403-0220
Tel: (419)372-2030   *Fax:* (419)372-7208
E-Mail: dnieman@bgnet.bgsu.edu
Members: 930 individuals, 300 institutions
Staff: 1
Annual Budget: $25-50,000
Secretary-Treasurer: Donald G. Nieman

Historical Note
A member of the American Council of Learned Societies. Originated as a special interest section of the American Ass'n of Law Schools. Membership: $35/year (individual), $50/year (institution), $12/year (student).

Publications:
Law & History Review. semi-a.
Newsletter. semi-a.

Meetings/Conferences:
Annual Meetings: Third week in October/250

American Soc. for Macro Engineering
Historical Note
Organization defunct in 1997.

American Soc. for Mass Spectrometry *(1969)*
1201 Don Diego Ave.
Santa Fe, NM   87505
Tel: (505)989-4517   *Fax:* (505)989-1073
E-Mail: asms@asms.org
Web Site: http://www.asms.org
Members: 5,500 individuals
Staff: 2
Annual Budget: $250-500,000
Exec. Director: Judith Sjoberg

Historical Note
Academic and industrial chemists and scientists who use the mass spectrograph as an analytical and physical tool. Membership: $65/year.

Publications:
Proceedings. a.

Meetings/Conferences:
Annual Meetings: Spring
1999 – Dallas, TX/June 13-18

American Soc. for Microbiology *(1899)*
1325 Massachusetts Ave., N.W.
Washington, DC   20005-4171
Tel: (202)737-3600   *Fax:* (202)942-9341
Web Site: http://www.asmusa.org
Members: 48,000 individuals
Staff: 110
Annual Budget: $25-50,000,000
Exec. Director: Michael I. Goldberg, Ph.D.
Director, Public Affairs: Janet Shoemaker
Dir., Communications: Barbara Hyde
Director, Meetings/Expo.: Nancy L. Elder
Director, Education & Training: Amy L. Chang
Director, American Academy of Microbiology: Carol Colgan
Director, Human Resources and Administration: Kim Shankle
Director, Member Services: Lorna D. Kent
Director of Journals: Linda Illig
Director, Mgmt. Info. Systems: Ron Butler

Historical Note
Founded in New Haven, CT in 1899 as the Soc. of American Bacteriologists. Became the American Soc. for Microbiology in 1960, and merged with the American Academy of Microbiology in 1969. Incorporated in the District of Columbia in 1947. A member of the Internat'l Union of Microbiological Societies. Promotes scientific knowledge of microbiology and related subjects through discussions, reports and publications. The American Academy of Microbiology is the professional services arm of the ASM.

Publications:
Antimicrobial Agents and Chemotherapy. m. adv.
Applied and Environmental Microbiology. m. adv.
ASM News. m. adv.
Clinical and Diagnostic Laboratory Immunology.
Clinical Microbiology Reviews.
Infection and Immunity. m. adv.
International Journal of Systematic Bacteriology. q. adv.
Journal of Bacteriology. bi-m. adv.
Journal of Clinical Microbiology. m. adv.
Journal of Virology. m. adv.
Microbiology and molecular biology. q. adv.
Molecular and Cellular Biology. m. adv.

Meetings/Conferences:
Annual Meetings: May
1999 – Chicago, Il/May 30-June 3

American Soc. for Neurochemistry *(1969)*
301 University Blvd., MRB 2.143
Galveston, TX   77555-1069
Tel: (409)772-2108   *Fax:* (409)772-2920
E-Mail: behaber@utmb.edu
Web Site: http://www/med.usf.edu/ASN/asn.html
Members: 1,200 individuals
Staff: 1
Annual Budget: $50-100,000
Secretary: Bernard Haber, Ph.D.

Historical Note
Organized in 1968-1969 by U.S., Canadian and Mexican members of the Internat'l Soc. for Neurochemistry and incorporated in the District of Columbia, August 6, 1969. Membership: $75/year.

Publications:
Membership Directory. a.
Transactions of the ASN. a. adv.

Meetings/Conferences:
Annual Meetings: Spring-Summer/800
1999 – New Orleans, LA/March 13-18
2000 – Portland, OR

American Soc. for Nondestructive Testing *(1941)*
1711 Arlingate Lane, P.O. Box 28518
Columbus, OH   43228-0518
Tel: (614)274-6003   *Fax:* (614)274-6899
Toll Free: (800)222 - 2768
Web Site: http://www.asnt.org
Members: 10,000 individuals, 400 corporate
Staff: 50
Annual Budget: $5-10,000,000
Exec. Director: Robert Windsor
Sr. Mgr., Conferences: Tina O'Donnell
Sr. Mgr., Finance & Accounting: Mary Potter
Mgr., Human Resources & Facilities: Cheryl-Lynn Matheny
Sr. Manager, Marketing: William Munk
Mgr., Membership Services: Ruth Dheez
Sr. Mgr., Communications: Paul McIntire
Sr. Mgr. Technical Services: Steven Hoyt
Sr. Mgr. Management Information Services: John Mottl

Historical Note
Founded in August 1941 with nine charter members as the American Industrial Radium and X-Ray Soc. In 1946 became officially known as The Soc. for Nondestructive Testing, Inc. and in 1967 the name was changed to the American Soc. for Nondestructive Testing, Inc. Incorporated in Ohio in 1988. Members are engineers, metallurgists and managers in the field of nondestructive testing for a variety of industries: chemicals, aerospace, construction, electronics, nuclear, metals, petroleum, food processing, transportation and automotive. Membership: $65/year (initial fee); $55/year (renewal).

Publications:
Materials Evaluation. m. adv.
Research in Nondestructive Evaluation.

Meetings/Conferences:
Semi-Annual Meetings: Spring and Fall
1999 – Orlando, FL(Marriott)/March 22-26/1500
1999 – Phoenix, AZ(Hyatt)/Oct. 7-14/2500

American Soc. for Nutritional Sciences *(1928)*
9650 Rockville Pike
Bethesda, MD   20814-3990
Tel: (301)530-7050   *Fax:* (301)571-1892
E-Mail: meyersp@asms.faseb.org
Web Site: http://www.faseb.org/asns
Members: 3,500 individuals
Staff: 5
Annual Budget: $1-2,000,000
Exec. Officer: Richard G. Allison

Historical Note
Founded as American Institute of Nutrition by members of the American Society of Biological Chemists to provide for the publication of the Journal of Nutrition. In 1934 AIN was reorganized as a membership society, with 178 charter members; assumed its current name in 1996. ASNS is a professional society of nutrition research scientists and a member of the Federation of American Socs. for Experimental Biology. Membership: $105/year.

Publications:
ASNS Nutrition Notes. q. adv.
Journal of Nutrition. m. adv.

Meetings/Conferences:
Annual Meetings: Spring, with Fed. of American Socs. for Experimental Biology/15,000
1999 – Washington, DC/April 17-21

American Soc. for Parenteral and Enteral Nutrition *(1975)*
8630 Fenton St., Suite 412
Silver Spring, MD   20910-3803
Tel: (301)587-6315   *Fax:* (301)587-2365
E-Mail: aspen@nutr.org
Web Site: http://www.clinnutr.org
Members: 6,700 individuals
Staff: 22
Annual Budget: $2-5,000,000
Exec. Director: Barney Sellers, CAE
Director of Policy and Research: Edward Bernstein
Meetings Manager: Katherine Hillegas
Director of Education/Professional Development: Janet Gannon
Membership/Chapters Director: Deborah Timmons

Historical Note
Physicians, dietitians, nurses, pharmacists, nutritionists, researchers, hospital administrators and others who work on hospital nutrition care teams. Concerned with the care of patients who cannot digest food normally, and therefore have to be fed parenterally (intravenously) or enterally (by tube). Membership: $100-$165/year.

Publications:
Journal of Parenteral and Enteral Nutrition. bi-m. adv.
Nutrition in Clinical Practice. bi-m. adv.

Meetings/Conferences:
Annual Meetings: Winter/3,000
1999 – San Diego, CA(Convention Center)/Jan 31-Feb. 3
2000 – Nashville, TN(Opryland)/Jan. 23-26
2001 – Chicago, IL/Jan. 21-24

American Soc. for Pediatric Neurosurgery *(1978)*
Univ. of New Mexico
Dept. of Neurosurgery, ACC2
Albuquerque, NM   87131-5341
Tel: (505)272-3401   *Fax:* (505)272-6091
Members: 50 individuals
Staff: 1
Annual Budget: under $10,000
Secretary: Bruce Storrs, M.D.

Historical Note
Membership: $100/year, new member initiation fee $100 additional.

Publications:
Newsletter. 4/year.

Meetings/Conferences:

American Soc. for Pharmacology and Experimental Therapeutics *(1908)*
9650 Rockville Pike
Bethesda, MD   20814-3995
Tel: (301)530-7060   *Fax:* (301)530-7061
E-Mail: aspetinfo@faseb.org
Web Site: http://www.faseb.org/aspet/
Members: 4,300 individuals
Staff: 8
Annual Budget: $1-2,000,000
Exec. Officer: Christine K. Carrico, Ph.D.
Director, Public Affairs: James Bernstein
Director, Journals: Richard Dohenhoff

Historical Note
Organized at Johns Hopkins University on December 28, 1908 with 18 charter members. Incorporated in Maryland in 1933. A member of the Federation of American Societies for Experimental Biology, Internat'l Union of Pharmacology, and American Ass'n for the Advancement of Science, and the U.S. Pharmacopeial Convention. Membership: $65/year.

Publications:
Clinical Pharmacology and Therapeutics. m. adv.
Drug Metabolism and Disposition. bi-m. adv.
Journal of Pharmacology and Experimental Therapeutics. m. adv.
Molecular Pharmacology. m. adv.
Pharmacological Reviews. q. adv.
The Pharmacologist. q. adv.

Meetings/Conferences:
1999 – Washington, DC/April 17-21
2000 – Boston, MA/June 4-8

American Soc. for Pharmacy Law *(1974)*
Historical Note
Address unknown in 1998.

American Soc. for Photobiology *(1972)*
1021 15th St., Suite 9
Augusta, GA   30901
Tel: (706)722-7511   *Fax:* (706)722-7515
E-Mail: maps@csra.net
Web Site: http://www.kumc.edu:80/asp/pol_vo1.htm
Members: 1,600 individuals
Staff: 6
Annual Budget: $250-500,000
Exec. Secretary: Sherwood M. Reichard, Ph.D.

Historical Note
Founded in 1972 to further the scientific study of the effects of light on all living organisms. Membership: $65/year.

Publications:
ASP Newsletter. bi-m.
Photochemistry and Photobiology. m. adv.

Meetings/Conferences:
Annual Meetings: Spring
1999 – Washington, DC
2000 – San Francisco, CA(Hyatt Regency)/July 1-6

American Soc. for Photogrammetry and Remote Sensing *(1934)*
5410 Grosvenor Lane, Suite 210
Bethesda, MD   20814-2160
Tel: (301)493-0290   *Fax:* (301)493-0208
E-Mail: asprs@asprs.org.
Web Site: http://www.asprs.org/asprs
Members: 7,600 individuals
Staff: 8
Annual Budget: $2-5,000,000
Exec. Director: Jim Plasker
Membership Manager: Sokhan Hing
Director, Publications: Kimberly A. Tilley

Historical Note
Founded as the American Soc. of Photogrammetry in Washington, DC in 1934 with 12 charter members and incorporated the same year in DC. Promotes the use of aerial photography and remote sensing. Membership: $75/year.

Publications:
Photogrammetric Engineering and Remote Sensing. m. adv.

Meetings/Conferences:
Semi-Annual Meetings: Spring and Fall
1999 – Portland, OR/May 17-21

American Soc. for Plasticulture *(1959)*
526 Brittany Dr.
State College, PA   16803-1420
Tel: (814)238-7045   *Fax:* (814)238-7051
E-Mail: pheuser@psu.edu
Members: 96 individuals, 23 companies
Staff: 1
Annual Budget: $25-50,000
Exec. Secretary: Patricia E. Heuser

Historical Note
Established in Lexington, KY as Nat'l Agricultural Plastics Ass'n; assumed its current name in 1990. Provides a forum for the investigation and discussion of the applications of plastics used in agricultural production and marketing systems. Membership: $50/year (grower); $40/year (academic); $150/year (company); $500/year (sponsor).

Publications:
Ag-Plastics Report. q. adv.
Conference Proceedings. every 14-20 mos.

Meetings/Conferences:
Annual Meetings: Every 14-20 months
1999 – Tallahassee, FL/May 19-22
2000 – Hershey, PA/Sept. 23-27

American Soc. for Political and Legal Philosophy *(1955)*
c/o Dept. Philosophy, Clark Univ.
Worcester, MA   01610
Tel: (508)793-7326   *Fax:* (508)793-7211
Members: 500 individuals
Secretary-Treasurer: Prof. Judith DeCew

Historical Note
ASPLP members are academics and others with an active professional interest in the field of political/legal philosophy. Membership: $40/year.

Publications:
Nomos. a.

Meetings/Conferences:

American Soc. for Precision Engineering *(1986)*
301 Glenwood Ave., Suite 205
Raleigh, NC   27603-1406
Tel: (919)839-8444   *Fax:* (919)839-8039
E-Mail: erika_layne@aspe.net

Web Site: http://www.aspe.net
Members: 800 individuals, 22 companies
Staff: 2
Annual Budget: $250-500,000
Exec. Director: Thomas A. Dow
Meetings and Membership Manager: Erika Deutsch-Layne
Manager, Office and Publications: Ilka Lee

Historical Note
Represents all facets of precision engineering from research to application. Members are from academia, government, and industry. Membership: $65/year (individual); $1,000/year (corporate).

Publications:
Journal of the American Soc. for Precision Engin.

Meetings/Conferences:
1999 – Monterey, CA(DoubleTree/Fisherman's Wharf)/Oct. 31-Nov. 5
2000 – Scottsdale, AZ(DoubleTree Paradise Valley)/Oct. 22-27

American Soc. for Pschoprophylaxis in Obstetrics

American Soc. for Public Administration (1939)
1120 G St., N.W., Suite 700
Washington, DC   20005-3885
Tel: (202)393-7878   *Fax:* (202)638-4952
E-Mail: info@aspanet.org
Web Site: http://www.aspanet.org
Members: 12,000 individuals
Staff: 13
Annual Budget: $1-2,000,000
Exec. Director: Mary Hamilton
Dir. of Communications: John Larkin
Deputy Director: Sarah Spradlin
Finance and Administration Director: Mahendra Shah
Director, Membership and Database Management: Patricia Woodward

Historical Note
A professional society dedicated to advancing excellence in public service and public management. Membership: $35-80/year (individual); $500-1,500/year (organization).

Publications:
Public Administration Review. bi-m. adv.
Public Administration Times. m. adv.

Meetings/Conferences:
Annual Meetings: Spring
1999 – Orlando, FL/April 10-14

American Soc. for Quality (1946)
P.O. Box 3005
611 East Wisconsin Ave.
Milwaukee, WI   53201-3005
Tel: (414)272-8575   *Fax:* (414)272-1734
Toll Free: (800)248-1946
E-Mail: asq@asq.org
Web Site: http://www.asq.org
Members: 133,000 individuals, 1,100 sustaining
Staff: 220
Annual Budget: $25-50,000,000
Exec. Director: Paul Borawski, CAE
Director, Market Research and Public Relations: Richard Sandretti
Manager, Conference/Exhibitions: Shirley A. Krentz
Manager, Education Services: Greg Weiler
Director, Programs and Operations: Brian LeHouillier
Director, Finance and Society Services: Christopher Bauman
Director, Business Development: Robert Krawisz
Director, Membership Services: Sheila Zelenski
Group Manager, Publications: William Tony

Historical Note
Formerly (1997) American Soc. for Quality Control. Founded and incorporated in New York State in 1946. ASQ is concerned with the development, promotion and application of quality-related information and technology for the quality profession, private sector, government and academia. ASQ's mission is to facilitate continuous improvement and increase customer satisfaction by identifying, communicating and promoting the use of quality principles, concepts and technologies. Has an annual budget of approximately $41 million. Membership: $77/year (individual); $450/year (sustaining).

Publications:
Journal of Quality Technology. q.
On Q Newsletter. bi-m.
Quality Engineer. q.
Quality Management Journal. q.
Quality Progress Magazine. m. adv.
Technometrics. q.

Meetings/Conferences:
Annual Meetings: May
1999 – Anaheim, CA(Hilton and Marriott)/May 24-26/4000
2000 – Indianapolis, IN/May 8-10
2001 – Charlotte, NC/May 7-9
2002 – Denver, CO/May 20-22

American Soc. for Quality Control
P.O. Box 3066
Milwaukee, WI   53201-3066
Tel: (414)272-8575   *Fax:* (414)272-1734
Manager, Adv. Sales: Phillip Edmunds

Historical Note
Became American Soc. for Quality in 1997.

American Soc. for Reconstructive Microsurgery
444 E. Algonquin Road
Arlington Heights, IL   60005-4654
Tel: (847)228-9717   *Fax:* (847)228-6509
Annual Budget: $100-250,000
Account Executive: Cathy Hay

American Soc. for Reproductive Medicine (1944)
1209 Montgomery Hwy.
Birmingham, AL   35216-2809
Tel: (205)978-5000   *Fax:* (205)978-5005
E-Mail: asrm@asrm.org
Web Site: http://www.asrm.org
Members: 10,000 individuals
Staff: 22
Annual Budget: $2-5,000,000
Exec. Director: Benjamin Younger
Administrative Director: Nancy C. Hayley

Historical Note
Founded and incorporated in 1944 in California as the American Soc. for the Study of Sterility, became American Fertility Soc. in 1966, assumed its present name in 1994. Promotes knowledge of all aspects of reproductive medicine including fertility. Provides administrative support to specialty divisions including Soc. for Assisted Reproductive Technology, Soc. of Reproductive Endocrinologists, and Soc. of Reproductive Surgeons. Membership: $195/year.

Publications:
ASRM News. q.
Fertility & Sterility. m. adv.
Membership Directory. bien. adv.
Menopausal Medicine.

Meetings/Conferences:
Annual Meetings: Fall
1999 – Tornoto, Canada(Convention Center)/Sept. 25-29/3500
2000 – San Diego, CA(Convention Center)/Oct. 21-25/3000
2001 – Orlando, FL(Convention Center)/Oct. 20-24/3000
2002 – Seattle, WA(Convention Center)/Oct. 12-16/3000

American Soc. for Stereotactic and Functional Neurosurgery (1968)
6624 Fannin St., Suite 1620
Houston, TX   77030-2328
Tel: (713)664-3592
Members: 280 individuals
Annual Budget: under $10,000
V. President: Philip L. Gildenberg, M.D.

Historical Note
Formerly (1972) the American Branch of the World Soc. for Research in Stereoencephalotomy. Members are surgeons using techniques for inserting delicate instruments into precise areas of the nervous system.

Publications:
Stereotactic and Functional Neurosurgery. 8/year. adv.

Meetings/Conferences:
Biennial Meetings: Odd years

American Soc. for Surface Mining and Reclamation (1973)
3134 Montavesta Road
Lexington, KY   40502
Tel: (606)257-8627   *Fax:* (606)257-2185
Members: 650 individuals
Annual Budget: $100-250,000
Exec. Secretary: Richard T. Barnhisel

Historical Note
Formerly (1978) Council for Surface Mining and Reclamation Research in Appalachia and (1982) American Council for Reclamation Research. ASSMR members are mining companies, federal and state agencies, academics and others with interest in reclamation of mined land. Membership: $50/year (individual); $120/year (organization/company); $10/year (student).

Publications:
CLRA/ASSMR Newsletter. semi-a.
IALR Newsletter. a.
Meeting Proceedings. a.
Membership Directory. a.

Meetings/Conferences:

American Soc. for Surgery of the Hand (1946)
6300 N. River Rd., Suite 600
Rosemont, IL   60018-4237
Tel: (847)384-8300   *Fax:* (847)384-1435
E-Mail: info@hand-surg.org
Web Site: http://www.hand-surg.org
Members: 1,556 individuals
Staff: 8
Annual Budget: $2-5,000,000
Exec. Director: Mark Anderson
Manager, Meetings (Education): Trudy Cohen

Historical Note
Established in 1946. Incorporated in Ohio in 1947. Membership: $570/year.

Publications:
Journal of Hand Surgery. bi-m. adv.

Meetings/Conferences:
Annual Meetings: Fall/2,500

American Soc. for Testing and Materials (1898)
100 Barr Harbor Dr.
West Conshohocken, PA   19428
Tel: (610)832-9500   *Fax:* (610)832-9555
E-Mail: service@astm.org
Web Site: http://www.astm.org
Members: 33,000 individuals
Staff: 220
Annual Budget: $10-25,000,000
President: James A. Thomas
V.P. Tech. Committee Ops.: Ken Pearson
V.P. Publications/Mktg.: Robert L. Meltzer

Historical Note
Originated in 1898 as the American Section of the Internat'l Ass'n for Testing Materials. Became the American Soc. for Testing and Materials in 1902 and incorporated in 1904. The world's largest source of voluntary consensus standards for materials, products, systems and services, ASTM also promotes related technical knowledge. Maintains Washington, DC and European offices. Has an annual budget of $21 million. Membership: $50/year.

Publications:
ASTM Standardization News. m. adv.
Book of Standards. a.
Cement and Concrete Aggregates Journal. semi-a.
Composites Technology & Research. q.
Geotechnical Testing Journal. q.
Journal of Forensic Science. q. adv.
Journal of Testing and Evaluation. bi-m.

American Soc. for the Advancement of Anesthesia in Dentistry (1929)
6 E. Union Ave.
Bound Brook, NJ   08805
Tel: (732)469-9050   *Fax:* (732)271-1985
E-Mail: info@sedatiom4dentists.com
Members: 650 individuals
Annual Budget: under $10,000
Exec. Secretary: David Crystal, D.D.S.

Historical Note
Founded in 1929 by Dr. M. Hillel Feldman for the training of dentists in the use of nitrous oxide and oxygen. Incorporated in New Jersey in 1929. As new drugs and techniques developed, the Society studied them and expanded its role to include all aspects of pain control. Formerly (1965) the American Soc. for the Advancement of General Established the Internat'l Federation of Dental Anesthetic and Sedation at the 101st Internat'l Dental Congress on Modern Dental Anesthesia in December, 1976 in Monaco. Membership: $85/year (individual), $35 initiation fee. (organization).

Publications:
Pain Control in Dentistry. semi-a. adv.

Meetings/Conferences:
Annual Meetings: Winter, New York, NY(Jacob Javitz Center)

American Soc. for the Study of Orthodontics (1945)
50-12 204th St.
Oakland Gardens, NY   11364
Tel: (718)224-8898
Members: 100 individuals
Staff: 1
Annual Budget: $10-25,000
President: Dr. Milton Bloch

Historical Note
Formerly (1962) New York Soc. for the Study of Orthodontics. Affiliated with the Federation of Orthodontic Ass'ns.

Publications:
International Journal of Orthodontics. irreg. adv.

Meetings/Conferences:
Annual Meetings: November in conjunction with the greater New York Dental Meeting.
1999 – New York, NY

American Soc. for Theatre Research (1956)
Dept. of Theatre, Brown Univ.
Box 1897
Providence, RI   02912
Tel: (401)863-3289   *Fax:* (401)863-7529
E-Mail: don_wilmeth@brown.edu
Members: 750 individuals
Staff: 1
Annual Budget: $25-50,000
Secretary: Don B. Wilmeth

Historical Note
Members are scholars of the theatre. Affiliated with the Internat'l Federation for Theatre Research. Membership: $45/year (regular), $25/year (student).

Publications:
ASTR Newsletter. semi-a.
Internat'l Bibliography of Theatre. a.
Ph. D.
Theatre Survey. semi-a.

Meetings/Conferences:
Annual Meetings: November

American Soc. for Therapeutic Radiology and Oncology (1955)
1891 Preston White Drive
Reston, VA   20191-4326
Tel: (703)295-6765   *Fax:* (703)476-8167
Toll Free: (800)962-7876
Web Site: http://www.astro.org
Members: 4,200 individuals
Staff: 4
Annual Budget: $500-1,000,000
C.O.O.: Gregg Robinson
Director, Meeting Management: Georgette Smith

Historical Note
Formerly (1984) the American Soc. of Therapeutic Radiologists. Members are physicians who limit their practice to radiation therapy. Membership: $235/year (active), $1,500/year (company/institution).

Publications:
ASTRO Newsletter. 3/year.
Internat'l Journal of Radiation, Oncology, Biology & Physics. 13/yr.

Meetings/Conferences:
Annual Meetings: Fall
1999 – San Antonio, TX(San Antonio Convention Center)/Oct. 31-Nov. 3
2000 – Boston, MA(Hynes Convention Center)/Oct. 22-26

American Soc. for Training and Development (1944)
1640 King St.
P.O. Box 1443
Alexandria, VA 22313
Tel: (703)683-8100   *Fax:* (703)683-9203
Toll Free: (800)628 - 2783
Web Site: http:www.dc.astd.org
Members: 66,000 individuals
Staff: 125
Annual Budget: $5-10,000,000
President and C.E.O.: Curtis E. Plott, CAE
V. President, Research: Laurie J. Bassi
Director of Education: Anne Blouin, CAE
Exec. V. President: Larry Randolph
Director, Finance and Administration: Debby Blazquez, CPA
V. President, Membership/Program Development: Pamela J. Schmidt
Manager, Member Forums: William J. Carroll, Jr.
Membership Svcs Manager: Maria Capestany
V. President, Publications: Nancy Olson

Historical Note
Formerly (1964) American Soc. of Training Directors. ASTD is a professional society of trainers and human resource development professionals. Has an annual budget of approximately $20 million. Membership: $150/year.

Publications:
ASTD Nat'l Report. semi-m.
Human Resource Development. q.
INFO-LINE. m.
Issues Trends and Resources Newsletter. q.
Technical & Skills Training Magazine. 8/year. adv.
Training and Development Magazine. m. adv.

Meetings/Conferences:

American Soc. for Value Inquiry (1970)
c/o Bergen Community Coll., Humanities
400 Paramus Rd
Paramus, NJ 07652-1595
Tel: (201)447-9282   *Fax:* (201)612-8225
E-Mail: jghaber@rockland.net
Members: 100 individuals
Annual Budget: under $10,000
Secrtary-Treasurer: Joram Graf Haber

Historical Note
ASVI members are academics with an interest in the study of values. Membership: $57/year.

Publications:
ASVI News. semi-a.
Journal of Value Inquiry. q.

Meetings/Conferences:

American Soc. for Virology (1981)
Dept. of Microbiology
8701 Watertown Plank Rd.
Milwaukee, WI 53226
Tel: (414)456-8104   *Fax:* (414)456-6566
E-Mail: lguarino@bioch.tamu.edu
Web Site: http://www.mcw.edu/asv
Secretary-Treasurer: Sydney Grossberg, Ph.D.

Historical Note
ASV members are individuals with advanced degrees who are actively engage in virological research. Membership: $75/year (full); $25/year (associate); $10/year (associate student).

Publications:
President's Newsletter. irreg.
Secretary-Treasurer's Newsletter. irreg.

Meetings/Conferences:

American Soc. of Abdominal Surgeons (1959)
675 Main St.
Melrose, MA 02176-3195
Tel: (781)665-6102   *Fax:* (781)665-4127
E-Mail: absurg@gis.net
Members: 4,000 individuals
Staff: 11
Annual Budget: $250-500,000
Exec. Secretary: Louis F. Alfano, M.D.

Historical Note
Founded and incorporated in Delaware in 1959. Membership: $150/year (individual).

Publications:
Journal of Abdominal Surgery. semi-a. adv.

Meetings/Conferences:
1999 – San Diego, CA(Clinical Congress)/May 6-9

American Soc. of Access Professionals (1980)
1444 I St., N.W., Seventh Floor
Washington, DC 20005
Tel: (202)712-9054   *Fax:* (202)216-9646
E-Mail: ASAP@bostromdc.com
Web Site: http://www.podi.com/asap
Members: 300 individuals
Staff: 1
Annual Budget: $100-250,000
Exec. Director: Claire Shanley

Historical Note
Members are government employees, lawyers, journalists and others concerned with access to government data under current personal privacy and public information statutes. Membership: $20/yr.

Publications:
ASAP Newsletter. irreg.

Meetings/Conferences:
Annual Meetings: Always Washington, DC/Fall

American Soc. of Addiction Medicine (1954)
4601 N. Park Ave.,Suite 101 Upper Arcade
Chevy Chase, MD 20815

Tel: (301)656-3920   *Fax:* (301)656-3815
E-Mail: email@asam.org
Web Site: http://www.asam.org
Members: 3,300 individuals
Staff: 11
Annual Budget: $1-2,000,000
Exec. V. President and C.E.O.: James F. Callahan, DPA
Director, Meetings and Conferences: Sandy Metcalfe
Credentialing Project Manager: Christopher Weirs
Director, Finance: Dennis Matus
Director of Membership: Catherine Davidge

Historical Note
ASAM serves as a medium for physicians and medical students who are interested in the diseases of alcoholism and drug dependency; to extend and disseminate knowledge and research in these fields; to encourage high quality care for individuals suffering from these problems; and to enlighten and inform medical opinion with regard to these issues. Maintains a certification program in addiction medicine. Membership: $200/year (individual).

Publications:
ASAM News. bi-m. adv.
Journal of Addictive Diseases. q. adv.
Principles of Addiction Medicine.

Meetings/Conferences:
Annual Meetings: Spring/1,500
1999 – New York, NY(Marriott Marquis)/April 29-May 2
2000 – Chicago, IL(Marriott)/April 12-16

American Soc. of Agricultural Appraisers (1980)
834 Falls Ave., Suite 1130
P.O. Box 186
Twin Falls, ID 83303
Tel: (208)733-2323   *Fax:* (208)733-2326
Toll Free: (800)488 - 7570
Members: 1000 individuals
Staff: 4
Annual Budget: $250-500,000
President: Jay Proost

Historical Note
The Society consists of three divisions: Internat'l Soc. of Livestock Appraisers, American Soc. of Farm Equipment Appraisers, and American Soc. of Equine Appraisers. Provides professional certification upon sucessful completion of of a divisional examination and subscription to a code of ethics. Membership: $295 initial plus $55 semi-annual renewal (association).

Publications:
Appraiser Newsletter. q.

Meetings/Conferences:
Meeting Sites: Chicago, Denver, Phoenix, Dallas, Boise,
    Atlanta

American Soc. of Agricultural Consultants (1963)
950 S. Cherry St., Suite 508
Denver, CO 80246-2664
Tel: (303)759-5091   *Fax:* (303)758-0190
E-Mail: asac@sgri-associations.org
Web Site: http:\\www.agri-associations.org\asac\
Members: 220 individuals
Staff: 3
Annual Budget: $100-250,000
Exec. V. President: Thomas E. Lipetzky

Historical Note
ASAC members are professional agricultural consultants with a minimum of two years consulting experience or have completed the required number of ASAC continuing courses. Associate and allied memberships are available for individuals and with a business tie to the industry. Operates a referral service for consultants. Membership: $285/year (consultant or associate); 500/year (allied).

Publications:
Membership Directory. a.
Newsletter. q.

Meetings/Conferences:
Annual Meetings: Fall
1999 – Reno, NV(Nugget)/Nov. 5-7

American Soc. of Agricultural Engineers (1907)
2950 Niles Road
St. Joseph, MI 49085-9659
Tel: (616)429-0300   *Fax:* (616)429-3852
E-Mail: moore@asae.org
Web Site: http://asae.org/
Members: 9,000 individuals
Staff: 26
Annual Budget: $2-5,000,000
Exec. V. President: M. Melissa Moore
Meetings Manager: Brenda West
Manager, Administrative Services: Mark D. Zielke
Manager, Member Services: Joseph A. Schulz
Director of Standards: Russell H. Hahn
Director of Publications: Donna M. Hull

Historical Note
Founded in Madison, WI in 1907 and incorporated in Michigan in 1935. ASAE is a professional and technical society for engineering in agriculture, food, and biological systems. Membership: $55-85/year (individual).

Publications:
Applied Engineering in Agriculture. q.
ASAE Standards. a.
Journal of Agricultural Safety & Health. q.
Resource. m. adv.
Transactions of the ASAE. bi-m.

Meetings/Conferences:
Annual Meetings: Summer/1,700
1999 – Toronto, ON, Canada(Sheraton Toronto
    Centre)/July 18-22
2000 – Milwaukee, WI/July 8-13

American Soc. of Agronomy (1907)

677 South Segoe Rd.
Madison, WI 53711-1086
Tel: (608)273-8080   *Fax:* (608)273-2021
E-Mail: rbarnes@agronomy.org
Web Site: http://www.agronomy.org
Members: 12,500 individuals
Staff: 30
Annual Budget: $1-2,000,000
Exec. V. President: Robert F. Barnes

Historical Note
ASA is a scientific and educational organization, dedicated to fostering research, communications education, high standards, and professionalism among people working in, or otherwise interested in agronomy and related activities. Offers individual certification for professional agronomists, crop science specialists, soil science specialists, soil classifiers, weed scientists, horticulturists, and plant pathologists through the American Registry of Certified Professionals in Agronomy, Crops and Soils. Membership: $64/year; $300/year (sustaining members).

Publications:
Agronomy Journal. bi-m. adv.
Agronomy News. m. adv.
Journal of Environmental Quality. q.
Journal of Natural Resources & Life Sciences Education. semi-
    a.
Journal of Production Agriculture. q.

Meetings/Conferences:
Annual Meetings: Fall/4,000
1999 – Salt Lake City, UT/Oct. 31-Nov. 4
2000 – Minneapolis, MN/Nov. 5-9
2001 – Charlotte, NC/Oct. 21-25

American Soc. of Andrology
74 New Montgomery Road, Suite 230
San Francisco, CA 94105
Tel: (415)764-4823   *Fax:* (415)764-4915
E-Mail: 105037.1120@compuserve.com
Web Site: http://godot.urol.uic.edu/ ~ androlog/
Members: 750 individuals
Staff: 4
Exec. Director: Carol Holland Parlette, CAE

Historical Note
ASA members are physicians specializing in the study of the male reproductive system. Membership: $85/year (individual).

Publications:
ASA Newsletter. q.
Journal of Andrology. bi-m. adv.

Meetings/Conferences:
1999 – Chicago, IL

American Soc. of Anesthesiologists (1905)
520 N. Northwest Hwy.
Park Ridge, IL 60068-2573
Tel: (847)825-5586   *Fax:* (847)825-1692
E-Mail: mail@asahq.org
Web Site: http://www.asahq.org
Members: 34,000 individuals
Staff: 45
Annual Budget: $10-25,000,000
Exec. Director: Glenn W. Johnson
Dir., Communications: Denise M. Jones
Director of Scientific Affairs: Frank W. Connell
Director of Administrative Affairs: Ronald A. Bruns
Asst. Exec. Director: William s. Marinko

Historical Note
Organized in 1905 in Brooklyn, NY as the Long Island Soc. of Anesthetists. Became the New York Soc. of Anesthetists in 1912 and incorporated in 1936 as the American Soc. of Anesthetists; assumed its current name in 1945. Membership: $350/year.

Publications:
Anesthesiology. m. adv.
Newsletter. m.

Meetings/Conferences:
Annual Meetings: Fall/15,000
1999 – Dallas, TX(Convention Center)/Oct. 9-13
2000 – San Francisco, CA(Convention Center)/Oct. 14-18

American Soc. of Animal Science (1908)
1111 N. Dunlap Ave.
Savoy, IL 61874
Tel: (217)356-3182   *Fax:* (217)398-4119
E-Mail: asas@assochq.org
Web Site: http://www.asas.org
Members: 4,000 individuals
Staff: 1
Annual Budget: $500-1,000,000
Exec. Director: Dr. Ellen Bergfeld

Historical Note
Founded in 1908 in Chicago as the American Soc. of Animal Nutrition. Became the American Soc. of Animal Production in 1912 and the American Soc. of Animal Science in 1941. Affiliated with the Nat'l Block and Bridle Club. Membership: $90/year (individual); $190/year (organization/company).

Publications:
Journal of Animal Science. m.

Meetings/Conferences:
Annual Meetings: Summer
1999 – Indianapolis, IN/July 21-24/2500
2000 – Baltimore, MD/July 24-28/2500

American Soc. of Appraisers (1936)
555 Herndon Pkwy., Suite 125
Herndon, VA 20170
Tel: (703)478-2228   *Fax:* (703)742-8471
Toll Free: (800)272 - 8258
E-Mail: asinfor@apo.com
Web Site: www.appraisers.org
Members: 6,500 individuals
Staff: 22

Annual Budget: $2-5,000,000
Exec. Director: Edwin W. Baker
Dir., Membership/Public Rels.: Donna Chowning Reid
Director, Conference/Meetings: Janet Coe, CMP
Director, Education: Patrick Christoff, Ed.D.
Director of Finance: Harriet Davis
Director, Information Systems: Howard S. Ducat
Director, Publications: Rebecca Ewing Maxey

Historical Note
Formed by a merger of the Soc. of Technical Appraisers (founded in 1939) and the American Soc. of Technical Appraisers. In 1985 the Ass'n of Governmental Appraisers merged with ASA. Awards the AM designation to appraisers with at least two years of full-time appraisal experience who pass written and oral examinations. Awards the ASA designation to individuals fulfilling the AM requirements with five years full-time appraisal experience. The FASA designation is awarded by the Board of Governors to ASA's in recognition of outstanding services to the appraisal profession or to the Society.

Publications:
Business Valuation Review. q.
Directory of Professional Appraisal Services. a.
Newsline. m.
Personal Property Journal. q.
Real Property Journal. 3/yea.
Valuation. a.

Meetings/Conferences:
Annual Meetings: August
1999 – Boston, MA
2000 – Pittsburgh, PA
2001 – San Diego, CA

American Soc. of Artists (1972)
P.O. Box 1326
Palatine, IL   60078
Tel: (312)751-2500
Members: 10,000 individuals
Staff: 14
Annual Budget: $50-100,000
President: Nancy J. Fregin

Historical Note
An organization of professional artists, which sponsors art and crafts festivals and a lecture/demonstration service and other services for members.

Publications:
A. S. adv.
Art Lovers' Art and Craft Fair Bulletin. q. adv.

Meetings/Conferences.
Annual Exhibits: 25-30

American Soc. of Ass'n Executives (1920)
1575 I St., N.W.
Washington, DC   20005-1168
Tel: (202)626-2723   *Fax:* (202)371-8825
E-Mail: pr@asaenet.org
Web Site: http://www.asaenet.org
Members: 24,000 individuals
Staff: 130
Annual Budget: $10-25,000,000
President: Michael S. Olson, CAE
V. President, Executive Management: Paul D. Meyer, LUTCF, CAE
Director, Public Relations: Ken Sommer
V.P., Public Policy: James L. Clarke
V. President, Professional Development: Gary A. LaBranche, CAE
Director, Education: Toni Crouch
Exec. V. President: Linda Chandler
General Counsel: Jerald A. Jacobs
V. President, Member Services: Debra Sher
V.P., Publishing: George Moffat
V. President, technology: George L. Tutt

Historical Note
Founded in Lenox, Massachusetts in 1920 as American Trade Ass'n Executives, a successor organization to the Nat'l Trade Organization Secretaries. Name changed in 1956 to American Soc. of Ass'n Executives. A professional society of paid employees of associations and societies, and suppliers of products and services to the association community. ASAE offers resources on association management, including education and training, publications, technology, research, career information, networking, and professional development. Certifies association executives and awards the CAE (Certified Association Executive) designation. Sponsors the ASAE Foundation and A-PAC. Membership: $215/year (associaton C.E.O.); $185/year (association staff); $315/year (associates/suppliers).

Publications:
AMC Forum. q.
Associate Member Update. q.
Association Educator. bi-m.
Association Law & Policy. bi-w.
Association Management. m. adv.
Chapter Relations. bi-m.
Communication News. m.
Copy-to-Go. q.
Dollars & Cents. m.
Executive IdeaLink. m.
Government Relations. bi-m.
International News. bi-m.
Marketing Forum. bi-m.
Meetings and Expositions. m.
Membership Developments. m.
Technoscope. bi-m.
Who's Who in Association Management. a. adv.

Meetings/Conferences:
SemiAnnual Meetings: August/4,000 and December/2,000

American Soc. of Asset Managers
P.O. Box 12528
San Antonio, TX   78212-0528
Tel: (210)225-2897   *Fax:* (210)225-8450
Toll Free: (800)486 - 3676

Members: 200 individuals
Staff: 4
Annual Budget: $50-100,000
President: Deborah J. Deane

Historical Note
Awards the designations AAM (Accredited in Asset Management) and SAM (Senior Asset Manager). Membership: $50/year (individual).

Publications:
Asset Manager. q.

Meetings/Conferences:
Annual Meetings: not held

American Soc. of Bakery Engineers

Historical Note
Became (1998) American Society of Baking.

American Soc. of Baking (1924)
2 N. Riverside Plaza, Suite 1733
Chicago, IL   60606-2607
Tel: (312)332-2246   *Fax:* (312)332-6560
Web Site: www.asbe.org
Members: 2,700 individuals
Staff: 2
Annual Budget: $250-500,000
President: Thomas J. Kuk

Historical Note
Formerly (1998) American Society of Bakery Engineers. Membership: $100/year.

Publications:
Newsletter. q.
Proceedings. a.
Technical Bulletins. q.

Meetings/Conferences:
Annual Meetings: Always in Chicago(Chicago
        Marriott)/March/1,300
1999 – Chicago, IL(Marriott)/Feb. 28-March 3
2000 – /March 5-8
2001 – /March 4-7

American Soc. of Bank Directors (1972)

Historical Note
Address unknown in 1998.

American Soc. of Bariatric Physicians (1950)
5600 South Quebec
Suite 109 A
Englewood, CO   80111-2210
Tel: (303)770-2526   *Fax:* (303)779-4834
E-Mail: bariatrc@asbp.org
Web Site: http://asbp.org/bariatrics
Members: 1,500 individuals
Staff: 7
Annual Budget: $500-1,000,000
Exec. Director: James F. Merker, CAE
Public Relations Director: J.P. Smith
Director of Meetings and Membership Services: Connie Maslow, CMP
Director, Continuing Medical Education: Hal Seim, M.D., M.P.

Historical Note
Formerly (1972) American Soc. of Bariatrics. Members are physicians specializing in the treatment of obesity. Membership: $395/year, ($295 first year).

Publications:
American Journal of Bariatric Medicine, The Bariatrician. q.
Membership Directory. a. adv.
News from ASBP. bi. adv.

Meetings/Conferences:
Annual Meetings: Fall/500
1999 – Las Vegas, NV(Riviera)/Oct. 14-16/450
2000 – Arlington, VA(Marriott Crystal City)/Oct. 5-7/550

American Soc. of Breast Disease (1976)
P.O. Box 140186
Dallas, TX   75214
Tel: (214)368-6836   *Fax:* (214)368-5719
Members: 600 individuals
Annual Budget: $25-50,000
President: Michael D. Lagios, M.D.

Historical Note
Formerly (1994) the Soc. for the Study of Breast Disease. Members are medical doctors, nurses, social workers, psychologists and others concerned with breast diseases. Has no paid officers or full-time staff. Membership: $150/year (doctors/psychologists), $100/yr (auxiliary).

Publications:
The Breast Journal. bi-m.

Meetings/Conferences:

American Soc. of Brewing Chemists (1934)
3340 Pilot Knob Rd.
St. Paul, MN   55121-2097
Tel: (651)454-7250   *Fax:* (651)454-0766
Members: 742 individuals
Staff: 2
Annual Budget: $100-250,000
Exec. Officer: Steven C. Nelson
Meeting Planner: Leslie Gibson

Historical Note
A professional society of brewing chemists. Formerly the Malt Analysis Standards Committee. Membership: $85/year (individual), $185/year (corporate); $25/year (student).

Publications:
Journal. a.
Newsletter. q. adv.

Meetings/Conferences:
Annual Meetings: Summer

1999 – Phoenix, AZ(Wigwam Resort)/June 19-23
2000 – Orlando, FL(Disney Coronado Springs)/June 23-27

American Soc. of Business Press Editors (1949)
107 W. Ogden Ave.
La Grange, IL   60525-2022
Tel: (708)352-6950   *Fax:* (708)352-3780
E-Mail: 71114.34@compuserve.com
Web Site: http://www.asbpe.org
Members: 500 individuals
Staff: 1
Annual Budget: $100-250,000
Exec. Director: Robert Mueller

Historical Note
Formerly (1964) Soc. of Business Magazine Editors. Membership: $65/year.

Publications:
ASBPE Annual Directory. a. adv.
ASBPE Byline. bi-m. adv.

Meetings/Conferences:
Annual Meetings: Summer
1999 – Chicago, IL(Marriott Hotel)/150

American Soc. of Cardiovascular Professionals/Soc. for Cardiovascular Management

Historical Note
Became Alliance of Cardiovascular Professionals in 1998.

American Soc. of Cataract and Refractive Surgery (1974)
4000 Legato Road, Suite 850
Fairfax, VA   22033-4003
Tel: (703)591-2220   *Fax:* (703)591-0614
E-Mail: ascrs@ascrs.org
Web Site: http://www.ascrs.org
Members: 7,000 individuals
Staff: 20
Annual Budget: $1-2,000,000
Exec. Director: David A. Karcher
Director, Communications: Shelly Hedrick
Director, Government Relations: Nancey Kaplan McCann
Meetings and Conventions Director: Jane Krause, CMP
Finance/Administration: Bernie Dellario

Historical Note
Incorporated in California as the American Intraocular Implant Soc. and assumed its present name in 1986. ASCRS serves to disseminate and facilitate the flow of information concerning anterior segment, cataract and refractive surgery. Membership is offered to physicians interested in anterior segment surgery and committed to the advancement of ophthalmology. Membership. $315/year.

Publications:
Journal of Cataract and Refractive Surgery. bi-m. adv.
Membership Roster. bien. adv.

Meetings/Conferences:
Annual Meetings: Spring/5,200
1999 – Seattle, WA(Washington State Conv.
        Center)/April 10-14
2000 – Boston, MA(Hynes Convention Center)/May 20-24

American Soc. of Certified Engineering Technicians (1964)
P.O. Box 1348
Flowery Branch, GA   30542-1348
Tel: (770)967-9173   *Fax:* (770)967-8049
Members: 3,000 individuals
Staff: 2
Annual Budget: $50-100,000
General Manager: Kurt Schuler

Historical Note
Society membership consists of certified and non-certified engineering technicians and technologists and registered professional engineers and land surveyors. Membership is also available to students enrolled in engineering technology degree programs belonging to an ASCET Student Chapter. Certified members have received certification verification of their skills through testing programs conducted by a number of independent certification societies. Membership: $40/year (individual), $250-500/year (organization/company).

Publications:
Certified Engineering Technician. bi-m. adv.

Meetings/Conferences:
Annual Meetings: last week in June
1999 – Kansas City, MO(Embassy Suites)/June 24-26
2000 – Austin, TX
2001 – Cleveland, OH
2002 – Philadelphia, PA

American Soc. of Church History (1888)
P.O. Box 8517
Red Bank, NJ   07701-8517
Tel: (732)345-1787   *Fax:* (732)345-1788
E-Mail: ASCHNOFF@aol.com
Members: 1,450 individuals
Staff: 2
Annual Budget: $50-100,000
Secretary-Treasurer: Henry W. Bowden

Historical Note
Affiliated with the American Historical Ass'n. Membership: $40-50/year (individual); $50-60/year (organization/company).

Publications:
Church History. q. adv.

Meetings/Conferences:
Semi-Annual Meetings: Spring, and early January, with
        American Historical Ass'n

American Soc. of Cinematographers (1919)
P.O. Box 2230

Hollywood, CA 90078
Tel: (213)876-5080   Fax: (323)882-6391
Toll Free: (800)448 - 0145
Members: 285 individuals
Staff: 12
Annual Budget: $1-2,000,000
Exec. Officer: Patty Armacost

Historical Note
Membership is by invitation.

Publications:
American Cinematographer Film Manual. every 7 years. adv.
American Cinematographer Magazine. m. adv.
American Cinematographer Video Manual. every 4 years. adv.

Meetings/Conferences:
Monthly Meetings: October through June

American Soc. of Civil Engineers (1852)
1801 Alexander Bell Drive
Reston, VA 20191-4400
Tel: (703)295-6000   Fax: (703)295-6351
Toll Free: (800)548 - 2723
Web Site: http://www.asce.org
Members: 120,000 individuals
Staff: 202
Annual Budget: $25-50,000,000
Exec. Director: James E. Davis
Director, Conference and Expos: Meggan Farrell
Managing Director; Professional, Educational anmd Technical
    Activities: Michael Kupferman, Ph.D.
President, Civil Engineering Research Foundation: Harvey M.
    Bernstein, CAE
Managing Director, Publications: David R. Dresia
Managing Director, Planning and Organization: Charles Day
Managing Director, Corporate Affairs: Grace Waldvogel

Historical Note
Founded November 5, 1852 in New York City as the American Soc.
of Civil Engineers and Architects. Dormant 1855-1867. Revived in
1868 as the American Soc. of Civil Engineers and incorporated in
New York in 1877. Membership: $135/year.

Publications:
ASCE News. m. adv.
ASCE Publications Abstracts. bi-m.
Civil Engineering. m. adv.
Journals of 25 Technical Divisions. m.
Transactions. a.

Meetings/Conferences:
Annual Meetings: Fall/1,750
1999 – Charlotte, NC/Oct. 17-20

American Soc. of Clinical Hypnosis (1957)
2200 E. Devon Ave., Suite 291
Des Plaines, IL 60018-4534
Tel: (847)297-3317   Fax: (847)297-7309
E-Mail: 70632.1663@compuserve.com
Members: 3,200 individuals
Staff: 7
Annual Budget: $1-2,000,000
Exec. V. President: Therese Sheehy

Historical Note
Established the American Soc. of Clinical Hypnosis-Education and
Research Foundation in 1962. Affiliated with the American Ass'n
for the Advancement of Science. Membership: $160/year.

Publications:
American Journal of Clinical Hypnosis. q.

Meetings/Conferences:
Annual Meetings: Spring/500-600

American Soc. of Clinical Oncology (1964)
225 Reinekers Lane, Suite 650
Alexandria, VA 22314-2875
Tel: (703)299-0150   Fax: (703)299-1044
E-Mail: asco@asco.org
Web Site: http://www.asco.org
Members: 11,500 individuals
Staff: 40
Annual Budget: $5-10,000,000
Exec. V. President: John R. Durant, M.D.
Director, Public Policy: Deborah Y. Kamin, Ph.D.
Director, Membership and Meeting Services: Jean Colvard
Director, Science and Education Programs: Michele K. Dinkel
V. President, Finance and Administration: Ron Beller, Ph.D.
Manager, Member Services: Linda Mock

Historical Note
Founded November 5, 1964 and incorporated in 1965 to promote
the study of neoplastic diseases, clinical research and patient care.
Members are academicians in universities, medical centers, teaching
and research facilities affiliated with cancer centers, major
hospitals, as well as physicians in community practice. Has an
annual budget of $8 million dollars. Membership: $200/year
(active U.S.); $215/year (active international); $50/year
(associate); $20/year (affiliate).

Publications:
ASCO News. q.
Educational Book. a.
Journal of Clinical Onclogy. m.
Policy Watch. m.
Proceedings. a.

Meetings/Conferences:
Annual Meetings: May/12,000
1999 – Atlanta, GA(GA World Congress Center)/May 15-18

American Soc. of Clinical Pathologists (1922)
2100 West Harrison St.
Chicago, IL 60612-3798
Tel: (312)738-1336   Fax: (312)738-1619
Toll Free: (800)621 - 4142
Web Site: http://www.ascp.org
Members: 77,000 individuals
Staff: 180

Annual Budget: $10-25,000,000
Executive V. President: Robert C. Rock, M.D.

Historical Note
ASCP's purpose is to promote public health and safety by
appropriate application of pathology and laboratory medicine in the
prevention diagnosis and treatment of disease, to conduct
educational programs and publish educational materials in the field
of clinical and anatomic pathology and laboratory medicine, and to
conduct a program for the examination and certification of medical
laboratory personnel. Has an annual budget of approximately $20
million. Membership: $260/year (pathologist), $50/year
(technologist).

Publications:
American Journal of Clinical Pathology. m. adv.
ASCP Newsletter. m. adv.
Laboratory Medicine m. adv. adv.
Pathology Patterns. semi-a.

Meetings/Conferences:
Semi-Annual Meetings: with the College of American
    Pathologists
1999 – Orlando, FL(Orlando Dolphin)/April 10-14
1999 – New Orleans, LA(NO Marriott)/Sept. 25-Oct. 1

American Soc. of Clinical Psychopharmacology (1992)
P.O. Box 2257
New York, NY 10116-2257
Tel: (212)268-4260   Fax: (212)268-4434
Web Site: http://www.ascpp.org
Members: 1,200 individuals
Staff: 2
Annual Budget: $250-500,000
Administrator: Melissa D'Agostino

Historical Note
Membership: $100/year.

Publications:
ASCP Update Newsletter. q.
Progress Notes Journal. q.

Meetings/Conferences:
Annual Meetings: May
1999 – St. Thomas, U.S. Virgin Islands

American Soc. of Colon and Rectal Surgeons (1899)
85 W. Algonquin Road, Suite 550
Arlington Heights, IL 60005-4425
Tel: (847)290-9184   Fax: (847)290-9203
Members: 1,800 individuals
Staff: 8
Annual Budget: $1-2,000,000
Exec. Director: James R. Slawny
Director, Administration/Convention Svcs: Dianne K. Kubis
Assoc. Exec. Director: Stella Zedalis
Bookkeeper: Ramsey Swenson

Historical Note
Founded in Columbus, Ohio in 1899 as the American Proctologic
Soc. with 12 charter members. Incorporated in Delaware in 1947.
Name changed in 1973 to the American Soc. of Colon and Rectal
Surgeons. Sponsored the formation of the American Board of Colon
and Rectal Surgery and in 1957 founded the American Soc. of
Colon and Rectal Surgeons Research Foundation. Membership:
$225/year (individual).

Publications:
Diseases of the Colon and Rectum. m. adv.

Meetings/Conferences:
Annual Meetings: Spring
1999 – Washington, DC(Hilton)/May 2-7
2000 – Boston, MA(Marriott Copley Place)/June 25-30

American Soc. of Comparative Law (1951)
Columbia Law School, Columbia University
435 W. 116th St.
New York, NY 10027
Tel: (212)854-4258   Fax: (212)854-7946
E-Mail: gbermann@law.columbia.edu
Members: 90 law schools
Annual Budget: $25-50,000
President: George A. Bermann

Historical Note
Formerly (1992) known as the American Ass'n for the Comparative
Study of Law. Membership: $700/year (organization/company).

Publications:
American Journal of Comparative Law. q. adv.

Meetings/Conferences:
1999 – Washington, DC(Georgetown Law Center)

American Soc. of Composers, Authors and Publishers (1914)
One Lincoln Plaza
New York, NY 10023
Tel: (212)621-6000   Fax: (212)721-0955
E-Mail: info@ascap.com
Web Site: http://www.ascap.com
Members: 75,000 individuals
Staff: 550
Annual Budget: Over $100,000,000
President: Marilyn Bergman
V. President, Communications: Karen Sherry
Chief Financial Officer: Jim Collins
Sr. V. President, Membership: Todd Brabec
V. President, Marketing: Philip Crosland
Chief Operating Officer: Al Wallace, & 1

Historical Note
America's first performing rights society, ASCAP was organized in
1914 by composer Victor Herbert and eight of his colleagues. The
goal of ASCAP was to license all commercial users of copyrighted
music so that the musical creative talent of this country and their
publishers might receive just financial returns. Has an annual
budget of approximately $500 million. Membership: $10/year
(writers), $50/year (publishers).

Publications:
Playback. 4-6/year. adv.

Meetings/Conferences:
1999 – Los Angeles, CA
1999 – New York, NY
1999 – Nashville, TN
1999 – New York, NY

American Soc. of Concrete Contractors (1964)
38800 Country Club Drive
Farmington Hills, MI 48331-3411
Tel: (248)848-3710   Fax: (248)848-3711
Toll Free: (800)877 - 2753
E-Mail: ascc@ascconc.org
Web Site: http://www.ascconc.org
Members: 325 companies and individuals
Staff: 3
Annual Budget: $250-500,000
Exec. V. President: Peter J. Steiner

Historical Note
Formerly (1998) American Soc. for Concrete Construction. ASCC is
a non-profit corporation founded in 1964 to enhance the
capabilities of those who build in concrete. Members of ASCC are
concrete contractors, material suppliers, equipment manufacturers,
and others involved in concrete construction. ASCC provides an
extensive Safety Program, concrete and safety hotlines, safety
videos, safety bulletins, troubleshooting newsletters, and The
Contractor's Guide to Quality Concrete Construction. Membership:
$100/year (individual); $520/year (company).

Publications:
Contractor's Guide to Quality Concrete Construction.
Employee Safety Handbook for Concrete Contractors.
Membership Bulletin. 3-4/year.
Membership Directory. a. adv.
Safety Bulletin. 3-4/year.
Safety Manual for Concrete Construction.
Troubleshooting Newsletter. 3-4/year.

Meetings/Conferences:
Semi-Annual Meetings: winter/50 and summer/50
1999 – Banff, AB(Banff Springs Hotel)/July 19-22
1999 – Las Vegas, NV(Hilton)/Jan. 17-21
2000 – Orlando, FL/Feb. 19-23
2000 – San Diego, CA/July 18-21

American Soc. of Consultant Pharmacists (1969)
1321 Duke St.
Alexandria, VA 22314-3563
Tel: (703)739-1300   Fax: (703)739-1321
E-Mail: twebster@ascp.com
Web Site: http://www.ascp.com
Members: 7,000 individuals, 120 companies
Staff: 45
Annual Budget: $5-10,000,000
Exec. Director: R. Tim Webster
Director, Communications: Bob Appel
Director, Government Affairs: Leigh Davitian
Director of Meetings & Conventions: Norinne Hessman
Director, Educational Affairs: Cindy Porter Huske, RPh
Director, Professional Affairs: Thomas Clark
Exec. Director, Education & Research Foundation: Janice Feinberg
Director of Finance: Doug McAdoo
Senior Director, Administration & Membership: Cheryl Rothbart
Managing Editor: Robin Bodishbaugh
Assoc. Exec. Director: Phyllis Moret

Historical Note
Pharmacists specializing in service to long-term care facilities and
geriatric institutions. Sponsors and supports the ASCP Political
Action Committee. Has an annual budget of approximately $7
million. Membership: $185/year (individual); $2,000/year
(company).

Publications:
Clinical Consult. m.
Consultant Pharmacist Journal. m. adv.
Update Newsletter. m.

Meetings/Conferences:
Annual Meetings: November

American Soc. of Consulting Arborists (1967)
15245 Shady Grove Road, Suite 130
Rockville, MD 20850-3222
Tel: (301)947-0483   Fax: (301)990-9771
Members: 306 individuals
Staff: 2
Annual Budget: $100-250,000
Exec. Director: Beth W. Palys, CAE

Historical Note
A professional society of individuals skilled in diagnosing problems
and appraising the value of shade and ornamental trees.
Membership: $225/year.

Publications:
Arboricultural Consultant. q.

Meetings/Conferences:
Annual Meetings: October/200
1999 – San Antonio, TX(Adams Mark)/Sept. 28-Oct 2
2000 – Newport, Rhode Island(Hotel Vikeag)/Dec. 3-6

American Soc. of Consulting Planners (1966)
122 South Michigan Ave.
Suite 1600
Chicago, IL 60603
Tel: (312)786-6371   Fax: (312)431-9985
Members: 50 firms
Staff: 1
Annual Budget: $10-25,000
Administrator: Barbara Baldwin

Historical Note
ASCP represents the interests of private planning firms as firms, not
as individuals. Incorporated in the District of Columbia. Members
are planning firms engaged in the private practice of planning.
Membership $100-$200/year depending on size of firm.

Publications:
Bulletin. m.
Membership Directory. a.

Meetings/Conferences:
Semi-annual Meetings: Fall, in conjunction with Nat'l
Planning Organization and Spring, with the American
Planning Ass'n

American Soc. of Contemporary Medicine Surgery and Ophthalmology (1977)

Historical Note
Absorbed by American College of Medicine in 1997.

American Soc. of Contemporary Ophthalmology (1977)

4711 Golf Rd., Suite 408
Skokie, IL 60076
Tel: (847)568-1500   *Fax:* (847)568-1527
Toll Free: (800)621 - 4002
Members: 6,500 individuals
Staff: 8
Annual Budget: $100-250,000
Director: Randall T. Bellows, M.D.

Historical Note
*Formerly (1989) the Internat'l Glaucoma Congress. Administrative
support provided by the American Soc. of Contemporary Medicine
and Surgery. Affiliated with the American College of Medicine. The
Internat'l Glaucoma Congress is a division of ASCO. Membership:
$175/year.*

Publications:
Annals of Opthalmology and Glaucoma. m. adv.

Meetings/Conferences:
Annual Meetings: March, with the ASCMS and the ACM.

American Soc. of Corporate Secretaries (1946)

521 5th Ave., 32nd Floor
New York, NY 10175
Tel: (212)681-2000   *Fax:* (212)681-2005
Web Site: http://www.ascs.org
Members: 3,700 individuals
Staff: 11
Annual Budget: $2-5,000,000
President: David W. Smith
V. President, Communications: Michael E. Goodman
Senior V. President, Finance & Administration: Sara Berman

Historical Note
*Members are principally corporate secretaries, assistant secretaries,
business executives and other persons involved in duties normally
associated with the corporate secretarial function. Membership:
$425/year (individual), $225/year for additional members from
same company.*

Publications:
Proxy Contacts. a.
Report on Shareholder Proposals. a.
The Corporate Secretary. q.

Meetings/Conferences:
Annual Meetings: Summer/1,000
1999 – White Sulphur Springs, WV(Greenbrier)/June 23-27

American Soc. of Crime Laboratory Directors (1974)

Historical Note
Address unknown in 1998.

American Soc. of Criminology (1941)

1314 Kinnear Road
Columbus, OH 43212
Tel: (614)292-9207   *Fax:* (614)292-6767
E-Mail: 76551.201@compuserve.com
Web Site: http://www.asc41.com
Members: 3,200 individuals
Staff: 1
Annual Budget: $250-500,000
Administrator: Sarah M. Hall

Historical Note
*Established in Berkeley, California as the Soc. for the Advancement
of Criminology, it absorbed the Ass'n of College Police Training
Officials in 1947 and assumed its present name in 1956. Affiliated
with the American Ass'n for the Advancement of Science, members
are criminologists, psychologists, sociologists and students in
institutions of higher learning. Membership: $30/year (student),
$60/year (active), $125/year (institution).*

Publications:
Criminology: An Interdisciplinary Journal. q. adv.
The Criminologist. bi-m. adv.

Meetings/Conferences:
Annual Meetings: November/1,000-1,100
1999 – Toronto, ON, Canada(Royal York)/Nov. 17-20
2000 – San Francisco, CA(Westin St. Fancis)/Nov. 7-10

American Soc. of Cytopathology (1951)

400 W. 9th St., Suite 201
Wilmington, DE 19801
Tel: (302)429-8802   *Fax:* (302)429-8807
E-Mail: asc@cytopathology.org
Web Site: http://www.cytopathology.org
Members: 3,600 individuals
Staff: 4
Annual Budget: $500-1,000,000
Exec. Secretary: Petrina M. Smith, R.N., M.B.

Historical Note
*Founded in 1951 as the Inter-Society Cytology Council.
Incorporated in Massachusetts in 1959. Became American Soc. of
Cytology in 1961, assumed current name in 1994. ASC members
are physicians, cytotechnologists, and scientists employing the
cytologic method of diagnostic pathology. Membership: $125/year
(individual).*

Publications:
Acta Cytologica. bi-m.

The ASC Bulletin. 8/year. adv.

Meetings/Conferences:
Annual Meetings: November
1999 – Sacramento, CA(Hyatt Regency)/Nov. 1-6
2000 – Philadelphia, PA(Wyndham Franklin Plaza)/Nov. 7-11
2001 – Kansas City, MO(Hyatt Crown Plaza)/Nov. 6-10

American Soc. of Dentistry for Children (1927)

875 N. Michigan Ave., Suite 4040
Chicago, IL 60611-1901
Tel: (312)943-1244   *Fax:* (312)943-5341
Toll Free: (800)637 - 2732
Members: 3,000 individuals
Staff: 5
Annual Budget: $500-1,000,000
Asst. Exec. Director: Carol A. Teuscher
Director, Membership Services/Meeting Planner: Slavka Sucevic

Historical Note
Membership: $200/year.

Publications:
ASDC Newsletter. bi-m.
Journal of Dentistry for Children. bi-m. adv.

Meetings/Conferences:
Annual Meetings: Fall

American Soc. of Dermatological Retailers (1989)

361 Hospital Road, Suite 428
Newport Beach, CA 92663-3501
Tel: (949)646-9098   *Fax:* (949)645-9848
Toll Free: (800)469 - 3739
Members: 10 individuals
Staff: 2
Annual Budget: $25-50,000
Medical Director: Jeffrey Lauber, M.D.

Historical Note
*ASDR members are board certified dermatologists concerned with
marketing standards for skin care products.*

Publications:
Contemporary Products. bi-m. adv.
Skin Saver Newsletter. bi-m. adv.

Meetings/Conferences:
Annual Meetings: December

American Soc. of Dermatology (1946)

411 Hamilton Blvd., Suite 1006
Peoria, IL 61602
Tel: (309)676-4074   *Fax:* (309)676-3522
Web Site: http://www.asd.org
Staff: 2
Exec. Director: M. John Hanni, Jr., CAE

Historical Note
*ASD is dedicated to perserving the practice of dermatology, freedom
in medicine and economic freedom.*

Meetings/Conferences:

American Soc. of Dermatopathology (1962)

930 N. Meacham Rd.
Schaumburg, IL 60173-6016
Tel: (847)330-9830   *Fax:* (847)330-1135
E-Mail: vprzybyszeski@aad.org
Web Site: http://path.mgh.harvard.edu/ASDP/
Members: 1,100 individuals
Staff: 1
Annual Budget: $250 500,000
Account Executive: Victoria Przybyszeski

Historical Note
*Members are pathologists or dermatologists who have extra
training or expertise in the study of skin biopsies. Membership:
$175/year.*

Publications:
Journal of Cutaneous Pathology. (published in Denma.

Meetings/Conferences:
1999 – La Jolla, CA(Sheraton Grande Torrey
Pines)/Oct. 28-31/600

American Soc. of Directors of Volunteer Services of the AHA (1968)

1 North Franklin St.
Chicago, IL 60606
Tel: (312)422-3939   *Fax:* (312)422-4575
E-Mail: nbrown1@aha.org
Web Site: http://www.asdvs.org
Members: 1,500 individuals
Staff: 4
Annual Budget: $250-500,000
Exec. Director: Nancy A. Brown
Meetings & Conventions: Ilse B. Almanza

Historical Note
*Sponsored by the American Hospital Ass'n. Members are directors
of volunteer resources in hospitals and other health care
institutions. Membership: $95/year.*

Publications:
Newsletter for Society Members. q.
Volunteer Services Administration. bi-m.

Meetings/Conferences:
Annual Meetings: Fall
1999 – Denver, CO(Adam's Mark)/Sept. 14-17
2000 – Orlando, FL

American Soc. of Echocardiography (1975)

4101 Lake Boone Trail, Suite 201
Raleigh, NC 27607-6518
Tel: (919)787-5181   *Fax:* (919)787-4916
E-Mail: ase@asecho.org
Members: 5,600 individuals
Staff: 5
Annual Budget: $1-2,000,000
Exec. Director: Sharon Perry, CAE

Historical Note
*Members are physicians, cardiac sonographers, and engineering
scientists concerned with ultrasound diagnosis of heart disease.
Incorporated in the state of Indiana. Membership: $75-120/year
(individual).*

Publications:
ASE Directory. a. adv.
Journal of the American Society of Echocardiography. 12
times/year.

Meetings/Conferences:
1999 – Washington, DC
2000 – Chicago, IL(Sheraton)

American Soc. of Electroneurodiagnostic Technologists (1959)

204 West 7th
Carroll, IA 51401-2317
Tel: (712)792-2978   *Fax:* (712)792-6962
E-Mail: aset@netins.net
Web Site: http://www.aset.org
Members: 2,650 individuals
Staff: 5
Annual Budget: $500-1,000,000
Exec. Director: M. Fran Pedelty

Historical Note
*Formerly (1987) the American Soc. of Electroencephalographic
Technologists. ASET members include technologists, students, lab
managers, physicians and institutions involved in EEG, evoked
potentials, polysomnography, nerve conduction studies, and related
electroneurodiagnostics. Membership: $65/year (individual),
$260/year (organization/company).*

Publications:
American Journal of Electroneurodiagnostic Technology. q.
adv.
ASET Newsletter. bi-m.
Who's Who in Electroneurodiagnostics. a. adv.

Meetings/Conferences:
Annual Meetings: August-September
1999 – Norfolk, VA(Marriott)/Aug. 9-13/650
2000 – Anaheim, CA(Marriott)/July 12-15/400

American Soc. of Electroplated Plastics (1966)

112-J Elden St.
Herndon, VA 20170-4809
Tel: (703)709-1034   *Fax:* (703)709-1036
E-Mail: namf@erols.org
Web Site: http://www.namf.org
Members: 60 companies
Staff: 2
Annual Budget: $50-100,000
Exec. Director: David W. Barrack

Historical Note
*Organized in 1966 and incorporated in 1967 in Pennsylvania. Part
of larger association, the National Association of Metal
Finishers(NAMF).*

Publications:
ASEP News & Views. q.
ASEP Standards and Guidelines for Electroplated Plastics.
Bulletin. q.
Directory. a.
Membership Directory. a.

Meetings/Conferences:

American Soc. of Equine Appraisers

Historical Note
A division of the American Soc. of Agricultural Appraisers.

American Soc. of Extra-Corporeal Technology (1964)

503 Carlaisle Dr., Suite 125
Herndon, VA 20170
Tel: (703)435-8556   *Fax:* (703)435-0056
Web Site: http://www.amsect.org
Members: 3,000 individuals
Staff: 5
Annual Budget: $500-1,000,000
Exec. Director: George M. Cate
Director, Government Relations: Lee Bechtel
Dep. Exec. Director: Judy luther
Treasurer: Ron Richards
Corporate Counsel: Michael L. Houliston
Managing Editor: Tara Hoke

Historical Note
*Perfusionists concerned with the function of heart-lung machines.
Formerly (until 1968) the American Soc. of Extracorporeal
Circulation Technicians. The American Cardiology Technologists
Ass'n is a division of the society. Membership: $225/year.*

Publications:
AmSect Today. 11/year. adv.
Journal of Extra-Corporeal Technology. q.

Meetings/Conferences:
Annual Meetings: Spring
1999 – New Orleans, LA(Hyatt)/April 8-11

American Soc. of Farm Equipment Appraisers

Historical Note
A division of the American Soc. of Agricultural Appraisers.

American Soc. of Farm Managers and Rural Appraisers (1929)

950 S. Cherry St., Suite 508
Denver, CO 80246-2664
Tel: (303)758-3513   *Fax:* (303)758-0190
E-Mail: asfmra@agri-associations.org
Web Site: agri-associations.org/asfrma/
Members: 3,000 individuals
Staff: 14
Annual Budget: $1-2,000,000
Exec. V. President and C.O.O.: Thomas Lipetzky

Manager, Publications: Maya Peterson
Meetings and Conventions Director: Debra West
Director, Education: Nancy Reeves Hardiman
General Counsel: Marlin Opperman

Historical Note
ASFMRA members are agricultural professionals with an interest in understanding the interaction between the land and the forces that influence its markets and products. Awards the AAC (Accredited Agricultural Consultant), AFM (Accredited Farm Manager) and ARA (Accredited Rural Appraiser) designations to members meeting field experience, educational, ethical requirements. Membership: $200-325/year.

Publications:
Journal of the ASFMRA. a.
Newsletter. bi-m.

Meetings/Conferences:
Annual Meetings: Fall/500-675
1999 – Reno, NV(Nugget)/Nov. 5-7

American Soc. of Forensic Odontology *(1975)*
239 Pearl St.
Burlington, VT 05401
Tel: (802)864-5315   *Fax:* (802)862-0274
Members: 425 individuals
Staff: 1
Annual Budget: $10-25,000
President: David Averill

Historical Note
Founded to further the study of forensic dentistry. Members are dentists and others interested in the study of teeth for identification purposes, particularly in relation to malpractice, child abuse, and bite mark identification. President elected annually, address changes accordingly. Membership: $40/year.

Publications:
Mannual of Forensic Odontology. irreg.
Newsletter. 3/year.
Worldwide Forensic Dental Contacts. irreg.

Meetings/Conferences:
Annual Meetings: February/1,500/In conjunction with the
    American Academy of Forensic Sciences.

American Soc. of Furniture Designers *(1981)*
P.O. Box 2688
High Point, NC 27261
Tel: (910)576-1273   *Fax:* (910)576-1573
E-Mail: asfd@ac.net
Web Site: http://www.asfd.com
Members: 200 individualscorporations
Staff: 1
Annual Budget: $25-50,000
Exec. Director: Christine Evans

Historical Note
Founded in High Point NC. It is the only nationwide, non-profit membership organization for furniture designers. Membership 225/year (individual), $600/year (organization/company).

Publications:
Bulletin. m.
Membership Directory. a.

Meetings/Conferences:
Annual Meetings: Held annually-High Point, NC/April &
    October

American Soc. of Gas Engineers *(1954)*
P.O. Box 66001, Suite 144
Anaheim, CA 92816
Tel: (714)666-0411   *Fax:* (714)666-0411
E-Mail: Dlhosler@aol.com
Web Site: http://www.asge-nat.org
Members: 500 individuals
Staff: 1
Annual Budget: $10-25,000
Exec. Director: Daryl Hosler

Historical Note
Formerly (1973) Gas Appliance Engineers Soc. Membership: $30-40/year (individual).

Publications:
ASGE News. q.

Meetings/Conferences:
Annual Meetings: Spring

American Soc. of General Surgeons *(1993)*
2122 Grove
Glenview, IL 60025
Tel: (847)998-4570   *Fax:* (847)998-4577
E-Mail: asgs-info@theasgs.org
Web Site: http://www.theasgs.org
Annual Budget: $50-100,000
Exec. Director: L. Jack Carow, III

Historical Note
ASGS members are board certified general surgeons and subspecialists who perform general surgery. Membership: $125/year (active); $50/year (candidate/corresponding); $50/year (resident); $100/year (senior).

Publications:
Issues & Insights Newsletter.
Legislative Hotline.

Meetings/Conferences:
1999 – San Francisco, CA(San Francisco
    Hilton)/March 14-18/400

American Soc. of Geolinguistics *(1965)*
Dept of Modern Languages, Box G-1224
Baruch College, CUNY, 17 Lexington Ave.
New York, NY 10010-5526
Tel: (212)387-1597   *Fax:* (212)387-1591
E-Mail: wayne_finke@baruch.cuny.edu
Members: 110 individuals, 16 organizations
Annual Budget: under $10,000

Corresponding Secretary: Wayne H. Finke, Ph.D.

Historical Note
The Society was founded by Mario A. Pei of Columbia University in 1965. The Society aims to gather and disseminate up-to-date knowledge concerning the world's present-day languages; their distribution and population use; their relative practical importance, usefulness and availability from the economic, political and cultural standpoints; their genetic, historical and geographic affiliations and relationships; and their identification and use in spoken and written form. Has no paid staff. Particularly interested in linguistic geography, languages in contact and conflict, language education and politics, language planning and macro-sociolinguistics. Membership fee: $30/year (regular); $25year (retired/student); $25/year (organization/company).

Publications:
Geolinguistics. a. adv.

Meetings/Conferences:
Quarterly Meetings: March, April, May, Sept., and Oct., Nov.
    in NY

American Soc. of Golf Course Architects *(1946)*
221 N. LaSalle St., 35th Floor
Chicago, IL 60601
Tel: (312)372-7090   *Fax:* (312)372-6160
Web Site: http://www.golfdesign.org
Members: 128 individuals
Staff: 1
Annual Budget: $25-50,000
Exec. Secretary: Paul Fullmer

Publications:
Suppliers Directory. a. adv.

Meetings/Conferences:
Annual Meetings: Spring
1999 – Charleston, SC
1999 – Charleston, SC

American Soc. of Group Psychotherapy and Psychodrama *(1942)*
301 N. Harrison St., Suite 508
Princeton, NJ 08540
Tel: (609)452-1339   *Fax:* (609)936-1659
E-Mail: asgpp@asgpp.org
Web Site: http://www.asgpp.org
Members: 600 individuals
Staff: 1
Annual Budget: $100-250,000
Exec. Director: Eduardo Garcia

Historical Note
Membership includes psychiatrists, psychologists, social workers, doctors, psychodramatists, sociologists and nurses. Membership: $35-80/year.

Publications:
Journal of Action Methods, Psychodrama, Skill Training & Role
    Playing.
Membership Directory. a. adv.
Psychodrama Network News. q. adv.

Meetings/Conferences:
Annual Meetings: Spring
1999 – Philadelphia, PA(Doubletree)/April 8-12
2000 – New York, NY

American Soc. of Hair Restoration Surgery
401 N. Michigan Ave.
Chicago, IL 60611-4267
Tel: (312)644-6610   *Fax:* (312)321-6869
Members: 1,600 individuals
Staff: 4

American Soc. of Hand Therapists *(1977)*
401 N. Michigan Ave.
Chicago, IL 60611-4267
Tel: (312)321-6866   *Fax:* (312)321-5194
Members: 1,585 individuals
Staff: 7
Annual Budget: $500-1,000,000
Exec. Director: Ruth Easterling
Director, Membership & Communications: Christine Kendal
National Meeting Planner: Joyce Gambino

Historical Note
Members are registered or licensed occupational or physical therapists specializing in working with patients with hand problems. Membership: $175/year (individual).

Publications:
ASHT News Newsletter. bi-m. adv.
ASHT Times. q.
Journal of Hand Therapy. q. adv.
Membership Directory. a.

Meetings/Conferences:
Annual Meetings: Fall

American Soc. of Head and Neck Radiology
820 Jorie Blvd.
Oak Brook, IL 60523
Tel: (630)368-7896   *Fax:* (630)571-7837
Web Site: http://www.asnr.org/ashnr
Members: 460 individuals
Exec. Secretary: Torry Mark Sansone

Historical Note
ASHNR members are physicians who are board certified in general radiology with an interest in the field of head and neck radiology. Membership: $250/year (individual).

Publications:
American Journal of Neuroradiology.

American Soc. of Health-System Pharmacists *(1942)*
7272 Wisconsin Ave.
Bethesda, MD 20814-1439
Tel: (301)657-3000   *Fax:* (301)657-8817
Web Site: http://www.ashp.com

Members: 30,000 individuals
Staff: 200
Annual Budget: $25-50,000,000
Exec. V. President/C.E.O.: Dr. Henri R. Manasse
Sr. V. President, Professional and Public Affairs: William Zellmer,
    M.P.H.
Director, Marketing/Communications: Michael Dodd
Director, Government Affairs: Brian Meyer
Director, Meeting Planning: Marilyn J. Sullivan
V. President, Meetings Administration Division: Stan Lowe
Director, Education Services Division: Barbara Hammonds
V. President, Finance: Norman Hochman
Controller: Dave Edwards
Corporate Counsel: Fern Zappala
Asst. V. President, Publications and Drug Information Systems: C.
    Richard Talley

Historical Note
Formerly (1994) American Soc. of Hospital Pharmacists. Founded in 1942 as an outgrowth of the Sub-Section of Hospital Pharmacy of the American Pharmaceutical Ass'n. Incorporated in the District of Columbia in 1955. Reincorporated in Maryland in 1984. Sponsors and supports the American Soc. of Health-System Pharmacists Research and Education Foundation and the ASHP Political Action Committee. Has an annual budget of approximately $30 million.

Publications:
AHFS Drug Information. a.
American Journal of Health-System Pharmacy. bi-w. adv.
ASHP Newsletter. m.
Home Care Highlights.
International Pharmaceutical Abstracts. bi-m.
Specialists Spectrum.
Student Line: Foundation News.

Meetings/Conferences:
Semi-Annual Meetings: June and December
1999 – Reno, NV/June 6-10
1999 – Orlando, FL/Dec. 5-9

American Soc. of Heating, Refrigerating and Air-Conditioning Engineers *(1894)*
1791 Tullie Circle, N.E.
Atlanta, GA 30329-2305
Tel: (404)636-8400   *Fax:* (404)321-5478
Toll Free: (800)527 - 4723
E-Mail: ashrae@ashrae.org
Web Site: http://www.ashrae.org
Members: 50,000 individuals
Staff: 98
Annual Budget: $10-25,000,000
Exec. Vice President: Frank M. Coda
Director of Communications/Publications: W. Stephen Comstock
Manager, Meetings: Judy Marshall
Director of Education: Anne Spengler
Dir., Administrative Svcs./Comptroller: Walter A. Glasser
Director, Member Services: Carolyn K. Kettering
Manager, Membership Development: Debra Canady-Foster
Director, Technology: Bruce D. Hunn

Historical Note
Organized in 1894 and incorporated in 1895 as the American Soc. of Heating and Ventilating Engineers. Became the American Soc. of Heating and Air-Conditioning Engineers in 1954. Merged in 1959 with the American Soc. of Refrigerating Engineers (established 1904) to form the American Soc. of Heating, Refrigerating and Air-Conditioning Engineers. Maintains a Washington office. Has an annual budget of approximately $10 million. Membership: $120/year (individual).

Publications:
ASHRAE Handbook. a.
ASHRAE Insights. m.
ASHRAE Journal. m. adv.
ASHRAE Transactions. semi-a.
HVAC&R Research Journal. q.

Meetings/Conferences:
Semi-Annual Meetings: Winter and Summer
1999 – Seattle, WA/June 19-23
1999 – Chicago, IL/Jan. 23-27
2000 – Dallas, TX/Feb. 5-9

American Soc. of Hematology *(1958)*
1200 19th St., N.W., Suite 300
Washington, DC 20036-2422
Tel: (202)857-1118   *Fax:* (202)857-1164
E-Mail: ash@dc.sba.com
Web Site: http://www.hematology.org
Members: 8,400 individuals
Staff: 6
Annual Budget: $2-5,000,000
Exec. Director: Martha L. Liggett
Regulatory and Legislative Affairs Coordinator: Maurice Mayrides
Exhibits Coordinator: Melissa Huston
Dir., Programs: Jenifer Hamilton
Membership Coordinator: Michelle Moody

Historical Note
Membership: $170/year renewal (active membership); $200/year renewal (foreign).

Publications:
Blood. semi-m. adv.
Meeting Program. a.
Membership Directory. a.
Newsletter. q.

Meetings/Conferences:
Annual Meetings: December
1999 – New Orleans, LA/Dec. 3-7/15000
2000 – San Francisco, CA/Dec. 1-5

American Soc. of Highway Engineers
113 Heritage Hills Road
Uniontown, PA 15401
Tel: (412)929-2760   *Fax:* (412)929-2234
Secretary: Terence D. Conner, P.E.

Meetings/Conferences:
Annual Meetings: Spring

American Soc. of Home Inspectors *(1976)*
932 Lee St., Suite 101
Des Plaines, IL 60016-6546
Tel: (847)759-2820   *Fax:* (847)759-1620
Toll Free: (800)743 - 2744
E-Mail: hg@ashi.com
Web Site: http://www.ashi.com
Members: 5,000 individuals
Staff: 10
Annual Budget: $2-5,000,000
Exec. Director: Robert J. Paterkiewicz, CAE
Publications Editor: Sandy Bourseau
Programs Administrator: Brad Nehls
Marketing Director: Carlos Tabora
Assistant Exec. Director: Noel Zak, CAE
Office Manager: Cindy Wittrock

Historical Note
*Sets standards for inspection professionals based on technical merit
and experience. Members are professional home inspectors; 2,000
full members and 3,000 candidates. Membership: $235/year
(candidate); $260/year (member).*

Publications:
Annual Conference Proceedings. a.
ASHI Reporter. m.
Technical Journal. a.

Meetings/Conferences:
Annual Meetings: Mid-January
1999 – Orlando, FL(Coronado Springs Resort)/Jan. 13-16
2000 – San Diego, CA(Town & Country)/Jan. 16-18/1000

American Soc. of Hospital Pharmicists *(1942)*
Historical Note
Became American Soc. of Health-System Pharmacists in 1995.

American Soc. of Human Genetics *(1948)*
9650 Rockville Pike
Bethesda, MD 20814-3998
Tel: (301)571-1825   *Fax:* (301)530-7079
Web Site:
          http://www.faseb.org/genetics/ashg/asahgmenu.html
Members: 6,000 individuals
Staff: 10
Annual Budget: $1-2,000,000
Exec. Director: Elaine Strass
Meetings Manager: Marsha Ryan
General Manager, Membership: Barbara Abbott

Historical Note
*Incorporated in North Carolina in 1952 and reincorporated in
Maryland in 1985. ASHG provides leadership in research,
education and service in human genetics. Membership: $120/year
(regular); $60/year (student).*

Publications:
American Journal of Human Genetics. m. adv.
Membership Directory. biennial.

Meetings/Conferences:
Annual Meetings: Fall

American Soc. of Hypertension *(1985)*
515 Madison Ave., Suite 1212
New York, NY 10022
Tel: (212)644-0650   *Fax:* (212)644-0658
Web Site: http://www.ash-us.org
Members: 3,200 individuals
Staff: 6
Annual Budget: $250-500,000
Exec. Director: Sandra Kuhach
Managing Editor: Joan Banes

Historical Note
*ASH members are individuals who have undertaken and
accomplished meritorious original scientific investigation in the field
of hypertension and/or related cardiovascular disease, and/or those
involved in the diagnosis and treatment of hypertension and related
cardiovascular disease.' Professionals, paraprofessionals and
students with a demonstrated interest in the field are elligible for
associate membership. Membership: $150/year (full), $75/year
(associate), $175/year (foreign), $15,000/year (corporate).*

Publications:
American Journal of Hypertension. m. adv.
Membership Directory. bien.

Meetings/Conferences:
Annual Meetings: Spring/2,600
1999 – New York, NY(Marriott Marquis)/May 19-22

American Soc. of Ichthyologists and Herpetologists *(1913)*
Grice Marine Bilogical Lab
205 Fort Johnson Rd.
Charleston, SC 29412
Tel: (843)406-4017   *Fax:* (843)406-4001
E-Mail: asih@uts.cc.utexas.edu
Web Site: http://www.utexas.edu/depts/asih/
Members: 2,600 individuals, 1000 institutions
Annual Budget: $100-250,000
Secretary: Robert K. Johnson

Historical Note
*Incorporated in the District of Columbia. Purpose is to advance the
study of fishes, amphibians and reptiles. Has no permanent
address; the Secretary stays in office 3-5 years. Membership:
$50/year (individual), $90/year (institutions), $25/year (student).*

Publications:
Copeia. q.

Meetings/Conferences:
Annual Meetings: Summer
1999 – University Park, PA(Penn State University)

American Soc. of Indexers *(1968)*
P.O. Box 39366
Phoenix, AZ 85069-9366
Tel: (602)979-5514   *Fax:* (602)530-4088
E-Mail: info@asindexing.org
Web Site: http://www.ASIndexing.org
Members: 1,100 individuals
Staff: 1
Annual Budget: $50-100,000
Dir., Communications: Lori Lathrop
Dir., Education: Kate Mertes
Dir., Membership: Bonnie Parks-Davies
Dir., Finance: Carolyn Weaver

Historical Note
*Founded in 1968, ASI is a nonprofit organization that promotes
excellence in indexing and provides information, guidance and aid
to indexers. Members include freelance and salaried indexers,
abstracters, librarians, editors, publishers and organizations
employing indexers. Membership: $120/year (individual),
$85/year (student), $250/year (organization).*

Publications:
Key Words Newsletter. bi-m. adv.

Meetings/Conferences:
Annual Meetings: Summer
1999 – Indianapolis, IN
2000 – Alburquerque, NM
2001 – Boston, MA

American Soc. of Industrial Medicine *(1946)*
15 East 26th St.
New York, NY 10010
Tel: (212)684-4670   *Fax:* (212)684-4741
Members: 100 individuals
Staff: 2
Annual Budget: under $10,000
President: Jay Rosenblum

Historical Note
*Formerly (1985) American Academy of Compensation Medicine
and (1991) American Academy of Legal and Industrial Medicine.
Promotes solutions and programs to aid the injured worker with
respect to fair compensation, rehabilitation, retraining, and other
issues. Membership: $50/year (Fellow); $25/year (non-doctor).*

Meetings/Conferences:

American Soc. of Interior Designers *(1975)*
608 Massachusetts Ave., N.E.
Washington, DC 20002
Tel: (202)546-3480   *Fax:* (202)546-3240
E-Mail: asid@asid.org
Web Site: http://www.asid.org
Members: 30,500 individuals
Staff: 33
Annual Budget: $5-10,000,000
Acting Exec. Director: Michael Alin
Dir. of Marketing and Communications: Jerry R. Harke
Dir. of Government and Public Affairs: Chris Ingram
Dir., Special Projects: Bettianne Welen
Dir., Education: Barbara Henn
Dir., Finance & Administration: Merk Douglas
Dir., Member Services: Chris Forst

Historical Note
*A consolidation of the American Institute of Interior Designers
(1931) and the Nat'l Soc. of Interior Designers (1957). ASID
promotes a professional code of ethics, presses for legislation
establishing minimum competency requirements, and instituting
educational standards for all designers. Membership: $225/year
(allied member); $365/year (professional), other rates may apply
based on number of years in service.*

Publications:
ASID Professional Designer. bi-m. adv.
Leadership Directory. a.

Meetings/Conferences:

American Soc. of Internal Medicine
Historical Note
Merged with American College of Physicians in 1998.

American Soc. of Internat'l Executives *(1964)*
Temple Univ., 13th St. & Cecil Moore Ave
373 Ritter Hall
Philadelphia, PA 19122
Tel: (215)204-6190   *Fax:* (215)204-5154
Members: 300 individuals
Staff: 2
Annual Budget: under $10,000
Acting President: Dr. Marvin Hirshfeld

Historical Note
*Founded in April 1964 under the sponsorship of the Foreign
Traders Ass'n of Philadelphia and incorporated in 1975, ASIE is a
professional society which sets standards, gives examinations and
bestows appropriate recognition through certification on career
personnel engaged in international trade. Awards the titles "CDS"
(Certified Documentary Specialist), "CIE" (Certified International
Executive), both through examination, and "EIE" (Experienced
International Executive). Membership: $25-$35/year (individual);
$75/year (corporate).*

Publications:
ASIE Bulletin. q.
Newsletter. semi-a.
Roster. a.

Meetings/Conferences:
Annual Meetings: Spring

American Soc. of Internat'l Law *(1906)*
2223 Massachusetts Ave., N.W.
Washington, DC 20008-2864
Tel: (202)939-6000   *Fax:* (202)797-7133
E-Mail: services@asil.org

Web Site: http://www.ASIL.org
Members: 4,300 individuals
Staff: 17
Annual Budget: $1-2,000,000
Exec. Director: Charlotte Ku

Historical Note
*Organized in 1906 and incorporated in 1950 by a special act of
Congress. Promotes international relations on the basis of law and
justice. Membership: $125/year (individual), $1,500/year
(organization).*

Publications:
American Journal of International Law. q. adv.
International Legal Materials. bi-m.
Newsletter. bi-m.
Proceedings of the ASIL. a.
Studies in Transnational Legal Policy. irreg.

Meetings/Conferences:
Annual Meetings: Spring/700
1999 – Washington, DC/March 27-29

American Soc. of Interpreters *(1965)*
Historical Note
Address unknown in 1996.

American Soc. of Irrigation Consultants *(1970)*
P.O. Box 426
Byron, CA 94514-0426
Tel: (510)516-1124   *Fax:* (510)516-1301
Web Site: http://www.asic.org/ask
Members: 200 individuals
Staff: 1
Annual Budget: $25-50,000
Exec. Secretary: Wanda M. Sarsfield

Historical Note
*ASIC was established to advance education and skills and to
exchange data, knowledge and experience related to landscape
irrigation. Members are irrigation consultants, suppliers, and
manufacturers involved in landscape irrigation. Membership:
$175/year.*

Publications:
Newsletter. q.

Meetings/Conferences:
Annual Meetings: Fall
1999 – Boston, MA

American Soc. of Journalists and Authors *(1948)*
1501 Broadway, Suite 302
New York, NY 10036
Tel: (212)997-0947   *Fax:* (212)768-7414
Web Site: http://www.asja.org
Members: 1000 individuals
Staff: 2
Annual Budget: $250-500,000
Exec. Director: Alexandra Owens

Historical Note
*Established in 1948 as the Soc. of Magazine Writers, Inc. Became
the American Soc. of Journalists and Authors, Inc. in 1975.
Members are freelance nonfiction writers whose bylines appear on
books and in leading periodicals. ASJA acts as an information
center on freelance rights, and provides other services to members.
Membership: $165/year.*

Publications:
ASJA Directory of Members. a.
Newsletter. m.

Meetings/Conferences:
Annual Meetings: New York, NY/Summer
1999 – New York, NY(Hilton)/May 1-2

American Soc. of Knitting Technologists *(1960)*
386 Park Ave. South
New York, NY 10016-8897
Tel: (212)683-7520   *Fax:* (212)532-0766
Members: 125 individuals
Staff: 1
Annual Budget: under $10,000
Secretary: David Gross

Historical Note
*Members are technologists employed in the knitting industry in
various capacities. Sponsored by the Nat'l Knitwear and Sportswear
Ass'n, the U.S. section of the Internat'l Federation of Knitting
Technologists, which is headquartered in Switzerland. Membership:
$50/yr.*

Meetings/Conferences:
Semi-annual Conferences: Spring and Fall

American Soc. of Laboratory Animal Practitioners *(1967)*
c/o University of Texas Medical School
6431 Fannin St., Room 1.132
Houston, TX 77030-1503
Tel: (713)500-7542   *Fax:* (713)500-0534
E-Mail: bgoodwin@admin4.hsc.uth.tmc.edu
Members: 950 individuals
Annual Budget: $10-25,000
Secretary-Treasurer: Bradford S. Goodwin, Jr., D.V.M

Historical Note
*ASLAP members are veterinarians engaged in laboratory animal
practice. Affiliated with the American Veterinary Medical Ass'n and
the American Ass'n for Laboratory Animal Science. Membership:
$30/year; $15/year (student).*

Publications:
Laboratory Animal Practitioner q. adv. adv.
Membership Roster. a.

Meetings/Conferences:
Semi-annual Meetings: Summer and Fall, in conjunction with
          AVMA and AALAS

American Soc. of Landscape Architects *(1899)*

636 I St., N.W.
Washington, DC 20001-3736
Tel: (202)898-2444   Fax: (202)898-1185
Web Site: http://www.asla.org
Members: 13,000 individuals
Staff: 45
Annual Budget: $5-10,000,000
Exec. V. President: Peter Kirsch
Manager, Government Relations: Stan Bowman
Manager, Meetings: JoAnn Brown
Manager, Continuing Education: Cheryl Wagner
Manager, Membership: Marc Selvitelli

Historical Note
Founded in New York City by eleven charter members and incorporated in Massachusetts in 1916. Absorbed the American Institute of Landscape Architects in 1982. Works closely with the Landscape Architecture Foundation. Has an annual budget of approximately $5.2 million. Membership: $195/year (individual) plus chapter dues.

Publications:
Landscape Architectural News Digest (LAND). 10/year. adv.
Landscape Architecture Magazine. m. adv.

Meetings/Conferences:
Annual Meetings: October
1999 – Boston, MA(Hynes Convention Center)/Sept. 12-14

American Soc. of Law Enforcement Trainers (1987)
102 Dock Road
P.O. Box 361
Lewes, DE 19958-0361
Tel: (302)645-4080   Fax: (302)645-4084
Members: 5,600 individuals
Staff: 5
Annual Budget: $500-1,000,000
Exec. Director: Stephen M. Bunting

Historical Note
ASLET represents law enforcement trainers, educators and administrators. Membership: $50/year, initial; $45/year, renewal.

Publications:
The ASLET Journal. bi-m.

Meetings/Conferences:
Annual Meetings: January
1999 – Alberquerque, NM(Alberquerque Convention Center)/Jan. 19-23/750

American Soc. of Law, Medicine and Ethics (1972)
765 Commonwealth Ave., 16th Floor
Boston, MA 02215
Tel: (617)262-4990   Fax: (617)437-7596
E-Mail: aslm@bu.edu
Web Site: http://www.aslme.org
Members: 4,500 individuals
Staff: 8
Annual Budget: $500-1,000,000
Exec. Director: Benjamin Moulton
Conference Planner: Lisa Bears
Administrator: Thomas Psidsikas
Office Manager: Victor Casey
President: John Lantos

Historical Note
An outgrowth of two founding organizations: the Massachusetts Soc. of Examining Physicians (1911) and the Massachusetts Soc. of Law and Medicine (1971). Formerly (1992) American Soc. of Law and Medicine. Multi-disciplinary membership of professionals concerned with the interrelation of law, medicine, and health care. Membership: $155/year (individual); $250/year (institution).

Publications:
American Journal of Law and Medicine. q.
Journal of Law, Medicine & Ethics. q.

Meetings/Conferences:
1999 – Cambridge, MA(Marriott)/Oct. 9-10

American Soc. of Limnology and Oceanography (1936)
5400 Bosque Blvd., Suite 680
Waco, TX 76710-4446
Tel: (254)399-9635   Fax: (254)776-3767
Toll Free: (800)929 - 2756
E-Mail: business@aslo.org
Web Site: http://aslo.org/
Members: 3,900 individuals
Staff: 3
Annual Budget: $500-1,000,000
Exec. Director: C. Susan Weiler, Ph.D.

Historical Note
Founded January 1, 1936 in St. Louis as the Limnological Soc. of America. Assumed its present name in 1949 and was incorporated in Wisconsin in 1956. Membership: $75/year (individual).

Publications:
ASLO Bulletin. 3/year. adv.
Limnology and Oceanography. 8/year.

Meetings/Conferences:
Semi-Annual Meetings: Winter and Summer at a University site
1999 – Santa Fe, NM(Sweeney Conv. Center)/Feb. 1-5

American Soc. of Lipo-Suction Surgery (1982)
401 N. Michigan Ave.
Chicago, IL 60611-4267
Tel: (312)527-6713   Fax: (312)644-1815
Members: 1,600 individuals
Staff: 4
Annual Budget: $500-1,000,000
Exec. Director: Jeffrey P. Knezovich

Historical Note
ASLSS members arre surgeons with an interest in the removal of fatty tissue by suction.

Publications:
American Journal of Cosmetic Surgery. q.

Membership Roster. a.
Newsletter. q.

American Soc. of Magazine Editors (1963)
919 Third Ave.
New York, NY 10022
Tel: (212)872-3700   Fax: (212)906-0128
E-Mail: asme@magazine.org
Web Site: http://www.magazine.org/asmeinfo.html
Members: 900 individuals
Staff: 3
Annual Budget: $250-500,000
Exec. Director: Marlene Kahan

Historical Note
A professional society of senior magazine editors designed to allow magazine editors to discuss matters of mutual concern. ASME's varied program includes The Nat'l Magazine Awards, The Magazine Internship Program, Conferences, Members Lunches, Seminars, The Junior Editorial Seminar Series, The American Magazine Conference, and Special Advertising Sections guidelines. Affiliated with the Magazine Publishers of America. Membership: $225/year.

Meetings/Conferences:
Annual Meetings: Fall, with the Magazine Publishers of America.
1999 – Boca Raton, FL

American Soc. of Mammalogists (1919)
Bean Museum of Life Sciences
Brigham Young University
Provo, UT 84602
Tel: (801)378-2492
Members: 3,600 individuals
Staff: 3
Annual Budget: $100-250,000
Secretary-Treasurer: H. Duane Smith, Ph.D.

Historical Note
Founded and incorporated in the District of Columbia in April 1919. Affiliated with the Internat'l Union for the Conservation of Nature. Membership: $30/year (individual), $45/year (organization/company).

Publications:
Journal of Mammalogy. q. adv.
Mammalian Species. a.

Meetings/Conferences:
Annual Meetings: June/800
1999 – Seattle, WA

American Soc. of Marine Artists (1977)
1461 Cathys Lane
North Wales, PA 19454
Tel: (215)283-0888
Members: 625 individuals
Staff: 1
Annual Budget: under $10,000
Exec. Director: Nancy Stiles

Historical Note
Members are artists, collectors and historians. Membership: $35/year (regular), $60/year (artist).

Publications:
ASMA News. q.

Meetings/Conferences:
Annual Meetings: Fall/various coastal locations on the East Coast

American Soc. of Master Dental Technologists (1976)
P.O. Box 248
Oakland Gardens, NY 11364-2614
Tel: (718)428-0075   Fax: (718)631-4509
Members: 125 individuals
Staff: 1
Annual Budget: under $10,000
Exec. Secretary: Susan Heppenheimer

Historical Note
A professional society formed to raise the educational standards of dental technicians. Awards the designation "MDT" (Master Dental Technologist). Membership: $100/year.

Meetings/Conferences:
Annual Meetings: Fall

American Soc. of Maxillofacial Surgeons (1947)
444 E. Algonquin Road
Arlington Heights, IL 60005
Tel: (847)228-8375   Fax: (847)228-6509
Members: 415 individuals
Staff: 1
Annual Budget: $100-250,000
Account Administrator: Rebecca Loden

Historical Note
ASMS is devoted to stimulating interest, advancing knowledge, and providing leadership and direction within the areas of maxillofacial and craniofacial surgery. Its members are dedicated to improving and promoting the highest levels of patient care. Membership: $300/year (individual).

Publications:
Journal of Plastic & Reconstructive Surgery. 14/yr. adv.
Maxillofacial News. 3/yr. adv.

Meetings/Conferences:
Annual Meetings: Fall, with the American Soc. of Plastic & Reconstructive Surgeons and the Plastic Surgery Educational Foundation
1999 – New Orleans, LA/Sept. 25-29
2000 – Los Angeles, CA/Nov. 4-8
2001 – Orlando, FL/Nov. 3-7

American Soc. of Mechanical Engineers (1880)
Three Park Avenue
New York, NY 10016-5990
Tel: (212)591-7000   Fax: (212)591-7674

E-Mail: infocentral@asme.org
Web Site: http://www.asme.org
Members: 125,000 individuals
Staff: 405
Annual Budget: $50-100,000,000
Exec. Director: David L. Belden, Ph.D.
Director, Member Services: Thomas G. Loughlin

Historical Note
Founded in 1880 and incorporated in New York in 1881, ASME is a technical society with 37 technical divisions and the Internat'l Gas Turbine Institute and extensive programs in the development of safety codes and equipment standards, educational guidance for student members, professional development, research and technology development and government relations. Conducts one of the largest technical publishing operations in the world. Has an annual budget of $60 million. Membership: $94/year.

Publications:
Applied Mechanics Reviews. m. adv.
ASME News. m. adv.
Heat Transfer - Recent Contents. bi-m.
Journal of Applied Mechanics. q. adv.
Journal of Biomechanical Engineering. q. adv.
Journal of Dynamic Systems, Measurement and Control. q. adv.
Journal of Electronic Packaging. q. adv.
Journal of Energy Resources Technology. q. adv.
Journal of Engineering for Gas Turbines and Power. q. adv.
Journal of Engineering for Industry. q. adv.
Journal of Engineering Materials and Technology. q. adv.
Journal of Fluids Engineering. q. adv.
Journal of Heat Transfer. q. adv.
Journal of Mechanical Design. q. adv.
Journal of Microelectromechanical Systems. q. adv.
Journal of Offshore Mechanics and Arctic Engineering. q. adv.
Journal of Pressure Vessel Technology. q. adv.
Journal of Solar Energy Engineering. q. adv.
Journal of Tribology. q. adv.
Journal of Turbomachinery. q. adv.
Journal of Vibration and Acoustics. q. adv.
Mechanical Engineering. m. adv.

Meetings/Conferences:
Semi-Annual Meetings: Summer and Winter
1999 – Nashville, TN(Opryland)/Nov. 14-19
2000 – Orlando, FL(Walt Disney World Dolphin)/Nov. 5-10
2001 – New York, NY(Hilton & Sheraton)/Nov. 11-16
2002 – New Orleans, LA(Hilton)/Nov. 17-22
2003 – Washington, DC(Sheraton and Omn.)/Nov. 16-21

American Soc. of Media Photographers (1944)
14 Washington Road, Suite 502
Princeton Junction, NJ 08550
Tel: (609)799-8300   Fax: (609)799-2233
Web Site: http://www.asmp.org
Members: 5,000 individuals
Staff: 7
Annual Budget: $1-2,000,000
Exec. Director: Richard Weisgrau
Communications Director: Peter Skinner
General Counsel and Managing Director: Victor Perlman
Director, Membership operations/Education: Bruce Blank

Historical Note
Known as Soc. of Photographers in Communications from 1971 to 1979, became American Soc. of Magazine Photographers, and assumed its current name in 1992. Actively lobbies on behalf of photographers at the state and federal levels. Has 35 chapters nationwide. Membership: $75-275/year (individual).

Publications:
ASMP Bulletin. m. adv.
ASMP White Papers. irreg.
Membership Directory. a. adv.

Meetings/Conferences:
Annual Meetings: Biennial meetings.
2000 – San Antonio, TX

American Soc. of Military Comptrollers (1949)
225 Reinekers Lane, Suite 250
Alexandria, VA 22314-2875
Tel: (703)549-0360   Fax: (703)549-3181
Members: 18,000 individuals
Staff: 3
Annual Budget: $250-500,000
Exec. Director: James F. McCall

Historical Note
Successor (1955) to Soc. of Military Accountants and Statisticians. Membership: $15/year (individual), $125/year (company).

Publications:
Armed Forces Comptroller. q.

Meetings/Conferences:
Annual Meetings: May-June
1999 – San Diego, CA/June 1-4

American Soc. of Missiology (1972)
Cloumbia Theological Seminary
P.O. Box 520
Decatur, GA 30031-0520
Tel: (404)687-4584   Fax: (404)377-9696
E-Mail: GunderD@CTSnet.edu
Members: 625 individuals
Annual Budget: $50-100,000
Secretary-Treasurer: Darrell Guder

Historical Note
Members are individuals interested in the scholarly study of theological, historical and social questions regarding the missionary dimension of the Christian church. Member of the Council of Socs. for the Study of Religion. Has no paid staff. Membership: $28/year.

Publications:
Missiology: an International Review. q. adv.

Meetings/Conferences:
Annual Meetings: Chicago, IL(Techny Towers)/third weekend in
June

American Soc. of Music Arrangers and Composers (1938)
P.O. Box 17840
Encino, CA 91316
Tel: (818)994-4661   Fax: (818)994-6181
Members: 325 individuals
Staff: 1
Annual Budget: $10-25,000
Exec. Secretary: Bonnie Janofsky

Historical Note
Professional society for musicians and composers specializing in
arrangement and orchestration, working in film, television and
other theater arts industries.

Publications:
Take One. m.

Meetings/Conferences:
Annual Meetings: Golden Score Awards Banquet.

American Soc. of Music Copyists (1960)
P.O. Box 2557, Times Square Station
New York, NY 10108
Tel: (212)262-3311   Fax: (212)961-9026
Members: 80 individuals
Secretary: Jennifer Brown

Historical Note
ASMC is a professional society of music copyists.

Publications:
ASMC Society Notes Newsletter. q.

Meetings/Conferences:
Annual Meetings: Triennial Meetings.

American Soc. of Naturalists (1883)
Historical Note
Address unknown in 1997.

American Soc. of Naval Engineers (1888)
1452 Duke St.
Alexandria, VA 22314-3458
Tel: (703)836-6727   Fax: (703)836-7491
E-Mail: asnehq.asne@mcimail.com
Web Site: http://www.jhuapl.edu/ASNE
Members: 6,500 individuals
Staff: 12
Annual Budget: $1-2,000,000
Exec. Director: Capt. Dennis K. Kruse, USN(Ret.)
Operations Manager: Dennis Pignotti
Manager, Meetings: Sara Ann Cook, CMP
Technical Director: Robert Steele
Manager, Membership: Judy Owen
Manager, Publications: Michael Cronin

Historical Note
Founded in the District of Columbia in 1888 and incorporated there
in 1946. Naval Engineering includes all arts and sciences as
applied in research, development, design, construction, operation,
maintenance, and logistic support of: surface/sub-surface ships and
marine craft; naval maritime auxiliaries; aviation and space
systems; combat systems including command and control
electronics, and ordnance systems; ocean structures; and associated
shore facilities which are used by the naval and other military
forces and civilian maritime organizations for the defense and well-
being of the nation. Membership: $70/year (individual).

Publications:
ASNE Newsletter. bi-m. adv.
Membership Directory. bien. adv.
Naval Engineers Journal. bi-m. adv.

Meetings/Conferences:
Annual Meetings: Spring
1999 – Arlington, VA(Hyatt Regency Crystal City)/May 21-22

American Soc. of Nephrology (1967)
1200 19th St., N.W., Suite 300
Washington, DC 20036-2422
Tel: (202)857-1190   Fax: (202)429-5140
E-Mail: judy_thomas@sba.com
Web Site: http://www.asn-online.com
Members: 6,200 individuals
Staff: 10
Annual Budget: $2-5,000,000
Exec. V. President: Judith A. Thomas
Public Rels. Manager: James Fennel
Dir., Government Relations: Jill Rathbun
Exec. Director: Sherri A. Mara
Conference Manager: Cele Fogarty

Historical Note
Members are nephrologists. Membership: $125/year (domestic),
$140/year (foreign); $25/year (associate).

Publications:
Highlights Newsletter. q.
Journal of American Soc. of Nephrology. adv.

Meetings/Conferences:
Annual Meetings: Fall
1999 – Miami, FL/Nov. 5-9
2000 – Toronto, ON, Canada

American Soc. of Neuroimaging (1977)
5841 Cedar Lake Rd., Suite 204
Minneapolis, MN 55416-1491
Tel: (612)545-6291   Fax: (612)545-6073
Members: 900 individuals
Staff: 2
Annual Budget: $250-500,000
Exec. Director: Linda Wilkerson

Historical Note
Established as the Soc. for Computerized Tomography and
Neuroimaging, it assumed its present name in 1980. Members are
specialists in CT scanning, MRI, neurosonology and other
neurodiagnostic techniques. Membership: $270/year (active
member); $85/year (junior member).

Publications:
Journal of Neuroimaging. q. adv.

Meetings/Conferences:
Annual Meetings: February
1999 – Scottsdale, AZ/Feb. 24-27

American Soc. of Neuroradiology (1962)
2210 Midwest Road, Suite 207
Oak Brook, IL 60521-8205
Tel: (630)574-0220   Fax: (630)574-0661
E-Mail: jgantenberg@asnr.org
Web Site: http://www.asnr.org
Members: 2,700 individuals
Staff: 15
Annual Budget: $2-5,000,000
Exec. Director and C.E.O.: James B. Gantenberg
Director, Communications and Media Management: Angelo
Artemaks
Manager of Scientific Meetings: Tim Moses
Ass'n Services Mgr.: Darcee Brown

Historical Note
ASNR was founded in 1962 to develop and support standards for
training in the practice of neuroradiology, to foster independent
research in neuroradiology, and to promote a closer fellowship and
exchange of ideas among neuroradiologists. Membership: $275-
$325/year.

Publications:
American Journal of Neuroradiology. 10/yr.

Meetings/Conferences:
Annual Meetings: Spring/1,200-1,800
1999 – San Diego, CA(San Diego Convention)/May 22-28
2000 – Atlanta, GA(Hyatt Regency)/April 2-8
2001 – Boston, MA(Hynes Convention Center)/April 21-27
2002 – Vancouver, BC(Vancouver Trade and Convention
Center)/May 11-17
2003 – Washington, DC(Washington Marriott
Park)/April 27-May 2

American Soc. of Newspaper Editors (1922)
11690-B Sunrise Valley Dr.
Reston, VA 20191
Tel: (703)453-1122   Fax: (703)453-1133
E-Mail: asne@asne.org
Web Site: http://www.infi.net/asne/
Members: 850 individuals
Staff: 6
Annual Budget: $500-1,000,000
Exec. Director: Lee Stinnett
Publications Director: Craig Branson
Meetings Planner: Mary Minnich
Finance/Membership Manager: Chris Schmidt

Historical Note
ASNE members are primarily directing editors with immediate
responsibility for editorial or news policies at daily newspapers, wire
services and other organizations in the U.S. and Canada.
Membership: $170-$525/year, varies by circulation.

Publications:
Editor's Exchange. 11/year.
The American Editor. 9/year.

Meetings/Conferences:
Annual Meetings: Spring
1999 – San Francisco, CA(Fairmont)/April 13-16
2000 – Washington, DC(JW Marriott)/April 11-14
2001 – Washington, DC(JW Marriott)/April 3-6
2002 – Washington, DC(JW Marriott)/April 9-12
2003 – New Orleans, LA(Fairmont)/April 8-11
2004 – Washington, DC(JW Marriott)/April 20-23
2005 – Washington, DC(JW Marriott)/April 12-15
2006 – Washington, DC(JW Marriott)/April 4-7
2007 – Seattle, WA/March 27-30
2008 – Washington, DC(JW Marriott)/April 8-11
2009 – Washington, DC(JW Marriott)/March 31-April 3
2010 – Washington, DC(JW MArriott)/April 13-16

American Soc. of Notaries (1965)
P.O. Box 5707
Tallahassee, FL 32314-5707
Tel: (850)671-5164   Fax: (850)671-5165
Toll Free: (800)522 - 3392
Members: 20,000 individuals
Staff: 2
Annual Budget: $250-500,000
Exec. Director: Lisa K. Fisher

Historical Note
ASN was organized to improve notarial practices and to uphold
high standards for notaries public. Membership: $21/year.

Publications:
American Notary. q.

Meetings/Conferences:
Annual Meetings: August-September
1999 – Annapolis, MD/July 28-30

American Soc. of Nuclear Cardiology (1993)
9111 Old Georgetown Road
Bethesda, MD 20814-1699
Tel: (301)493-2360   Fax: (301)493-2376
E-Mail: admin@asnc.org
Web Site: http://www.asnc.org
Members: 3,500 individuals
Staff: 5
Annual Budget: $1-2,000,000
Exec. Director: William D. Nelligan
Assoc. Exec. Director: Dawn Edgerton

Historical Note
Members are professionals in cardiology, nuclear medicine, and
radiology pursuing applications of nuclear science to cardiology.

Publications:
Journal of Nuclear Cardiology. bi-m. adv.
Membership Directory. bien.
Newsletter. bi-m.

Meetings/Conferences:
Annual Meetings: Fall
1999 – Washington, DC(Marriott Wardman Park)

American Soc. of Ocularists (1957)
493 8th Ave.
San Francisco, CA 94118
Tel: (415)399-0747   Fax: (415)399-9709
Exec. Director: Toni Zappone

Historical Note
ASO members are technicians specializing in the fitting and
fabrication of custom artifical eyes. Benefits of membership include
research, education and standards.

American Soc. of Ophthalmic Administrators (1986)
4000 Legato Road, Suite 850
Fairfax, VA 22033
Tel: (703)591-2222   Fax: (703)591-0614
Toll Free: (800)451 - 1339
Members: 1,800 individuals
Staff: 2
Annual Budget: $500-1,000,000
Exec. Director: Luz M. Santiago
Director, Membership & Special Projects: Don Bell
Director, Government Relations: Nancy McCann
Director, Meetings & Conventions: Jane Krause
Director of Finance: Bernie Dellario
MIS Manager: Mark Ehrick

Historical Note
A division of the American Soc. of Cataract and Refractive Surgery,
ASOA members are active administrators functioning in an
ophthalmologists's practice. Membership: $225/year (individual);
$550/year (organization/company).

Publications:
Administrative Eyecare. q. adv.

Meetings/Conferences:
Annual Meetings: Spring, with the American Soc. of Cataract
and Refractive Surgery
1999 – Seattle, WA(WA State Convention & Trade
Ctr.)/April 10-14/5000
2000 – Boston, MA(Hynes Convention
Center)/May 20-24/5000
2001 – San Diego, CA(San Diego Conference
Ctr.)/April 28-May 2/5000
2002 – Philadelphia, PA(Philadelphia Convention
Ctr.)/June 1-5/5500

American Soc. of Ophthalmic Plastic and Reconstructive Surgery (1969)
1133 W. Morse Blvd., Suite 201
Winter Park, FL 32789
Tel: (407)647-8839   Fax: (407)629-2502
Web Site: http://www.asoprs.org
Staff: 1
Exec. Director: Barbara Fitzgerald Beatty

Historical Note
ASOPRS members are surgeons specializing in plastic and
reconstructive surgery of the eyelids, orbits and lacrimal system.

Publications:
Ophthalmic Plastic and Reconstructive Surgery Journal. q.

Meetings/Conferences:
1999 – Scottsdale, AZ/May 16-19

American Soc. of Ophthalmic Registered Nurses (1976)
P.O. Box 193030
San Francisco, CA 94119
Tel: (415)561-8513   Fax: (415)561-8575
E-Mail: asorn@aao.org
Web Site: http://www.eye.ophth.uiowa.edu/asorn
Members: 1,500 individuals, 25 local chapters
Staff: 6
Annual Budget: $100-250,000
Exec. Administrator: Sue Brown
Meeting Manager: Lisa Brown
Client Services Coordinator: Jodi-Ann Nakayama

Historical Note
ASORN was established to assist the registered nurse involved in
ophthalmic care to achieve a necessary and distinctive role in the
health care system. Membership: $85/year.

Publications:
Insight. q.

Meetings/Conferences:
Annual Meetings: Fall, with the American Academy of
Ophthalmology/750
1999 – Orlando, FL/Oct. 23-26

American Soc. of Orthopaedic Physician's Assistants
6300 N. River Road, Suite 727
Rosemont, IL 60018-4226
Tel: (847)823-7186   Fax: (847)823-0536
Toll Free: (800)998 - 6022
Exec. Officer: Kathryn Grady

American Soc. of Outpatient Surgeons
Historical Note
Became (1996) American Ass'n of Ambulatory Surgery Centers.

American Soc. of Pain Management Nurses (1990)
7794 Grow Dr.
Pensacola, FL 32514

Tel: (850)473-0233   *Fax:* (850)484-8762
Toll Free: (888)342 - 7766
Members: 1,100 individuals
Annual Budget: $100-250,000
Exec. Director: Belinda E. Puetz
Government Relations Specialist: Robert Rupp
Dir., Convention Services: Henrietta Elston
Director, Education: Janice Ward
Publications Manager: Shay Stephens

Historical Note
The American Society of Pain Management Nurses is an organization of professional nurses dedicated to promoting and providing optimal care of patients with pain, including the management of its sequelae. This is accomplished through education, standards, advocacy, and research. Membership: $60/year (individual); $1000/year (organization/company).

Publications:
ASPMN Pathways. q.

Meetings/Conferences:
1999 – Washington, DC/April 15-18

American Soc. of Papyrologists *(1961)*
P.O. Box 15399
Atlanta, GA   30333-0399
Web Site: see text
Members: 175 individuals
Annual Budget: $25-50,000

Historical Note
The ASP is an association of scholars and students concerned with classical and Egyptian antiquity, in particular with the editing and study of texts preserved on papyrus. Affiliated with the Association Internationale de Papyrologues, Brussels, Belgium. Internet web site is http://scholar.cc.emory.edu/scripts/ASP/ASPMembForm. Has no paid staff. Membership: $40/year(regular); $30/year(associate).

Publications:
American Studies in Papyrology. irreg.
Bulletin of the ASP. q. adv.

Meetings/Conferences:
Annual Meetings: In conjunction with the American Philological Ass'n and the Archaeological Institute of America.

American Soc. of Parasitologists *(1924)*
c/o Univ. of Iowa Biology Dept.
Iowa City, IA   52422
Tel: (319)335-1061   *Fax:* (319)335-1069
E-Mail: george-cain@uiowa.edu
Web Site:
         http://www.museum.unl.edu/asp_image/aspjava.html
Members: 1,350 individuals
Staff: 1
Annual Budget: $50-100,000
Secretary-Treasurer: Dr. George D. Cain

Historical Note
Society started by Henry Baldwin Ward. Formed in Washington under the leadership of a group of parasitologists from the Baltimore-Washington area, December 30, 1924 at a meeting of the American Ass'n for the Advancement of Science. Incorporated in the District of Columbia in 1932. Membership: $35/year (student); $60 (individual); $160/year (organization/company).

Publications:
ASP Directory. a.
ASP Newsletter. q. adv.
Journal of Parasitology. 6/year.
Proceedings of the Annual Meeting of the ASP. a.

Meetings/Conferences:
Annual Meetings: Summer
1999 – Monterrey, CA(Monterrey Marriott)/July 5-8
2000 – Puerto Rico

American Soc. of Payroll Management *(1988)*
30 East 33rd St., # 5
New York, NY   10016
Tel: (212)686-2030   *Fax:* (212)686-4080
Members: 15,000 individuals
Staff: 1
President: Susan Berring

Historical Note
Membership: $350/year.

Publications:
ASPM Journal. q.

Meetings/Conferences:
1999 – Las Vegas, NV/May 18-22

American Soc. of Pediatric Hematology/Oncology *(1981)*
4700 W. Lake Ave.
Glenview, IL   60025-1485
Tel: (847)375-4716   *Fax:* (847)375-4777
E-Mail: info@aspho.org
Web Site: http://www.aspho.org
Members: 780 individuals
Staff: 5
Annual Budget: $250-500,000
Exec. Director: Cynthia S. Porter

Historical Note
Members are physicians and others with doctorates doing research in a relevant field. Affiliate members are other health professionals. ASPHO provides a forum for the interchange of information and promotes the advancement of knowledge concerning the treatment of diseases of the blood and cancer in children. Membership: $175/year (individual including quarterly journal).

Publications:
ASPHO News. q.
Journal of Pediatric Hematology/Oncology. bi-m.
Membership Directory. a.

Meetings/Conferences:
Annual Meetings: Chicago, IL

1999 – Montreal, Quebec(Montreal Marriott)/Sept. 13-18

American Soc. of Pediatric Nephrology
5938 N. Drake Ave.
Chicago, IL   60659-3203
Tel: (773)463-5520   *Fax:* (773)463-3552
Meeting Planner: Linda Campbell, CMP, CAE

Meetings/Conferences:

American Soc. of Pension Actuaries *(1966)*
4350 N. Fairfax Drive, Suite 820
Arlington, VA   22203
Tel: (703)516-9300   *Fax:* (703)516-9308
Web Site: www.aspa.org
Members: 3,000 individuals
Staff: 20
Annual Budget: $1-2,000,000
Exec. Director: Brian Graff
Desktop Publisher Administrator: Chip Chapot
Director, Meetings: Adele C. McCormack
Director, Education & Administration: Jane Grimm
Dir., Membership: Amy Emery

Historical Note
Awards the designations MSPA and FSPA (Member and Fellow of the Society of Pension Actuaries), QPA (Qualified Pension Administrator), and CPC(Certified Pension Consultant).

Publications:
The Pension Actuary. bi-m.

Meetings/Conferences:
Annual Meetings: Washington, DC(Grand Hyatt)/October

American Soc. of Perfumers *(1947)*

Historical Note
Address unknown in 1996.

American Soc. of Peri-Anesthesia Nurses *(1980)*
6900 Grove Road
Thorofare, NJ   08086-9447
Tel: (609)845-5557   *Fax:* (609)848-1881
E-Mail: aspan@slackinc.com
Members: 11,000 individuals
Staff: 10
Annual Budget: $1-2,000,000
Exec. Director: Kevin Dill

Historical Note
Formerly (1996) American Soc. of Post Anasthesia Nurses. ASPAN members are post-anesthesia, pre-anesthesia and ambulatory surgery nurses. Membership: $65/year (individual); $1,500/year (corporate).

Publications:
Breathline. bi-m.
Journal of Post-Anesthesia Nursing. bi-m. adv.

Meetings/Conferences:
Annual Meetings: April/2,000
1999 – Honolulu, HI/April 11-15

American Soc. of Petroleum Operations Engineers *(1976)*
673 S. Winding Rd.
Dover, PA   17315-2816
Tel: (717)308-0194   *Fax:* (717)432-0199
E-Mail: aspoe@aspoe.org
Members: 100 individuals
Staff: 1
Annual Budget: under $10,000
Exec. V. President: Walter Rimmer

Historical Note
ASPOE members are individuals concerned with the design, specification and maintenance supervision of petroleum marketing equipment. Membership: (by exam only) $250/year.

Publications:
Operations Briefs. bi-m.

Meetings/Conferences:
Semi-Annual Meetings: Spring, usually in Baltimore, MD, and Fall
1999 – Toronto, Ontario

American Soc. of Pharmacognosy *(1959)*
220 S. Ferris Dr.
Big Rapids, MI   49307
Tel: (616)592-2236   *Fax:* (616)592-3829
Web Site: http://www.phcog.org/
Members: 1000 individuals
Staff: 4
Annual Budget: $100-250,000
President: Dr. Gordon Craigg

Historical Note
Founded in 1959 and incorporated in the District of Columbia in 1965. Promotes the study of the composition, production, use and history of drugs of natural origin. Absorbed the Plant Science Seminar. Membership: $75/year.

Publications:
Journal of Natural Products Lloydia. m.
Newsletter. q.

Meetings/Conferences:
Annual Meetings: Summer/500

American Soc. of Photographers *(1937)*
P.O. Box 316
Williamantic, CT   06226-0316
Tel: (860)423-1402   *Fax:* (860)423-9402
E-Mail: ppanerl@aol.com
Members: 800 individuals
Staff: 1
Annual Budget: $50-100,000
Exec. Director: Roland Laramie

Historical Note
Membership in Professional Photographers of America is a pre-requisite for membership in ASP: members must be either a Master of Photography, a Photographic Craftsmen, or a Photographic Specialist. Membership: $70/year (individual).

Publications:
ASP Newsletter. q. adv.

Meetings/Conferences:
Annual Meetings: July-August
1999 – Atlanta, GA(Ga. World Congress Ctr.)/July 23-28

American Soc. of Picture Professionals *(1966)*
409 S. Washington St.
Alexandria, VA   22314-3629
Tel: (703)299-0219   *Fax:* (703)299-0219
E-Mail: aspp1@idsonline.com
Web Site: http://www.aspp.com
Members: 750 individuals
Annual Budget: $500-1,000,000
Exec. Director: Cathy D.P. Sachs

Historical Note
Members are image producers (e.g. photographers), stock photo agencies, and image users (publishers and independent photo editors and researchers). Provides networking and educational opportunities in the image transaction industry. Membership: $75/year.

Publications:
Membership Directory. bien. adv.
News Digest Newsletter. q.
The Picture Professional. q. adv.

Meetings/Conferences:
Regional Meetings: various locations within five regional chapters

American Soc. of Plant Physiologists *(1924)*
15501 Monona Drive
Rockville, MD   20855-2765
Tel: (301)251-0560   *Fax:* (301)279-2996
E-Mail: aspp@aspp.org
Web Site: http://www.aspp.org
Members: 5,200 individuals
Staff: 22
Annual Budget: $2-5,000,000
Exec. Director: John Lisack, Jr., CAE
Public Affairs Director: Brian M. Hyps
Dir., Finance/Administration: Susan K. Chambers
Director, Publications: Nancy Winchester

Historical Note
Founded at the University of Chicago in 1924 and incorporated in the District of Columbia the same year. Membership: $90/year (individual), $30/year (student).

Publications:
ASPP Newsletter. bi-m.
Plant Physiology m.
The Plant Cell. m.

Meetings/Conferences:
Annual Meetings: July-August
1999 – Baltimore, MD(Baltimore Convention Center)/July 24-28

American Soc. of Plant Taxonomists *(1936)*
Dep't of Botany
Iowa State University
Ames, IA   50011-1020
Tel: (515)294-8218   *Fax:* (515)294-1337
E-Mail: lgclark@iastate.edu
Web Site:
         http://www.csdl.tamu.edu/FLORA/aspt/aspthome.html
Members: 1,300 individuals
Annual Budget: $100-250,000
Secretary: Lynn G. Clark, Ph.D.

Historical Note
Founded in 1936 and incorporated in 1964. ASPT members are professional plant systematists and others interested in plant taxonomy and evolution. An affiliate of American Ass'n for the Advancement of Science, American Institute of Biological Sciences, Nat'l Research Council, Botanical Society of America, and Ass'n of Systematics Collections. Membership: $35/year (individual), $95/year (organization).

Publications:
ASPT Membership Directory. a.
ASPT Newsletter. 4/year.
Systematic Botany. q. adv.
Systematic Botany Monographs. irreg.

Meetings/Conferences:
Annual Meetings: August, with American Institute of Biological Sciences
1999 – St.Louis, MO(Convention Center)/August 1-7
2000 – Portland, OR

American Soc. of Plastic and Reconstructive Surgeons *(1931)*
444 E. Algonquin Road
Arlington Heights, IL   60005-4654
Tel: (847)228-9900   *Fax:* (847)228-9131
Web Site: http://plasticsurgery.org
Members: 4,000 individuals
Staff: 62
Annual Budget: $5-10,000,000
Exec. Director: Dave Fellers, CAE
Communications Director: John O'Brien
Manager, Government Relations: Adrian Hochstadt
Meetings Director: Carol L. Lazier, CMP
Education Director: Judith A. Northrup
Finance Director: Peter Kuhn
Director, Socioeconomic Affairs: Lousanne Lofgren

Historical Note
Founded in New York City in 1931 and incorporated in New York in 1945. Reincorporated in Illinois in 1975. Has an annual budget of

*approximately $8.6 million. Sponsors and supports the Plastic
Surgery Educational Foundation and the ASPRS Political Action
Committee.*

Publications:
Plastic and Reconstructive Surgery. m. adv.
Plastic Surgery News. m. adv.

Meetings/Conferences:
Annual Meetings: Fall/4,500

American Soc. of Plastic and Reconstructive Surgical Nurses *(1975)*

East Holly Ave., P.O. Box 56
Pitman, NJ　08071-0056
Tel: (609)256-2340　　　　　*Fax:* (609)589-7463
E-Mail: asprsn@mail.ajji.com
Web Site: http://www.asprsn.inurse.com
Members: 1,800 individuals
Staff: 2
Annual Budget: $250-500,000
Exec. Director: Gus Ostrum
Director, Membership: Maryanne Gawry

Historical Note
Membership: $75/year (individual), $1,500/year (company).

Publications:
ASPRSNews. bi-m.
Journal of Plastic and Reconstructive Surgical Nursing. q. adv.

Meetings/Conferences:
Annual Meetings: Fall
1999 – New Orleans, LA/October 25-29
2000 – Los Angeles, CA
2001 – Orlando, FL

American Soc. of Plumbing Engineers *(1964)*

3617 Thousand Oaks Blvd., Suite 210
Westlake, CA　91362-3649
Tel: (805)495-7120　　　　　*Fax:* (805)495-4861
E-Mail: aspehq@aol.com
Members: 6,800 individuals
Staff: 11
Annual Budget: $1-2,000,000
Exec. Director: Stanley Wolfson
Communications Manager: Paul McGuire

Publications:
Advanced Plumbing Technology.
ASPE Report Newsletter. bi-m.
Domestic Water Heating Design Manual.
Engineered Plumbing Design.
Model Plumbing Codes: A Comparison Study.
Plumbing Engineer. bi-m. adv.

Meetings/Conferences:
Biennial Meetings: Even years/4,500
2000 – Nashville, TN(Opryland)/Oct. 29-Nov. 2

American Soc. of Podiatric Dermatology *(1967)*

37443 Highland Court
Palmdale, CA　93552
Tel: (805)285-9378
Members: 300 individuals
Staff: 1
Annual Budget: $10-25,000
Exec. Director: Daniel J. McCarthy, DPM, Ph.D.

Historical Note
*Formerly (1973) the American Board of Chiropodical Dermatology.
An affiliate of the American Podiatric Medical Ass'n. Membership:
$50/year.*

Publications:
Newsletter. q.

Meetings/Conferences:
Annual Meetings: With the American Podiatric Medical Ass'n

American Soc. of Podiatric Executives

515 Busse Hwy.
Park Ridge, IL　60068-3263
Tel: (847)292-2237　　　　　*Fax:* (847)292-2022
Secretary/Treasurer: Thomas R. Schedler, CAE

Historical Note
*ASPE members are staff directors of podiatric regional and specialty
organizations.*

American Soc. of Podiatric Medical Assistants *(1964)*

2124 S. Austin Blvd.
Cicero, IL　60804
Tel: (708)863-6303　　　　　*Fax:* (708)863-5375
Toll Free: (888)882 - 7762
E-Mail: exaspma@aol.com
Members: 1,350 individuals
Annual Budget: $25-50,000
Exec. Director: Sandra Lohrentz, PMAC

Historical Note
*Members must be employed by podiatrists who are members of
APMA. Formerly (1985) American Soc. of Podiatric Assistants. An
affiliate of the American Podiatric Medical Ass'n. Membership:
$55/year.*

Publications:
The Journal of ASPMA.

Meetings/Conferences:
Annual Meetings: With the American Podiatric Medical
　　Ass'n/Aug.
1999 – Houston, TX(Westin Galleria)/Aug. 12-14/150
2000 – Philidelphia, PA(Marriott)/Aug. 10-12/150
2001 – San Francisco, CA

American Soc. of Podiatric Medicine *(1944)*

7331 Collins Ave.
Miami Beach, FL　33141
Tel: (305)866-9608　　　　　*Fax:* (305)866-1750
Members: 110 individuals
Annual Budget: under $10,000

Secrtary: Dr. Warren L. Simmonds

Historical Note
*An affiliate of the American Podiatric Medical Ass'n. Formerly
(1972) American College of Podiatric Medicine.*

Publications:
Newsletter. 3/year.

Meetings/Conferences:

American Soc. of Podiatry Executives

c/o Illinois Podiatric Medical Ass'n
53 W. Jackson Blvd., Suite 1103
Chicago, IL　60604-3608
Tel: (312)427-5810　　　　　*Fax:* (312)427-5813
Members: 35 individuals
Annual Budget: under $10,000
President: Mary S. Feeley

Historical Note
*Founded as Conference of Podiatric Executives; assumed its current
name in 1996. Members are directors of state podiatry
associations. Has no paid officers or full-time staff. Membership:
$125/year (individual).*

Meetings/Conferences:
Semi-annual Meetings: February and August
1999 – /February 26-27
1999 – Houston, TX

American Soc. of Post Anesthesia Nurses

Historical Note
Became American Soc. of Peri-Anesthesia Nurses in 1996.

American Soc. of Preventive Oncology *(1976)*

1300 University Ave., #7-C
Madison, WI　53706
Tel: (608)263-6809　　　　　*Fax:* (608)263-4497
E-Mail: JABowser@facstaff.wisc.edu
Members: 380 individuals
Staff: 1
Annual Budget: $100-250,000
Exec. Director: Judy Bowser

Historical Note
*ASPO is a multi-disciplinary society committed to cancer prevention
and control through scientific conferences and advocacy for cancer
prevention and control research funding. Membership: $150/year
(individual), $25/year (student).*

Publications:
Cancer Epidemiology, Biomarkers, and Prevention. m.

Meetings/Conferences:
Annual Meetings: Spring
1999 – Houston, TX(JW Marriott)/Mar. 13-17
2000 – Bethesda, MD(Hyatt Regency)
2001 – New York, NY
2002 – Bethesda, MD(Hyatt Regency)

American Soc. of Primatologists *(1976)*

California State Univ., Psychology Dept.
San Marcos, CA　92096
Tel: (760)750-4102
E-Mail: ncaine@mailhost1.csusm.edu
Web Site: http://www.asp.org
Members: 600 individuals
Staff: 1
Annual Budget: $10-25,000
President: Nancy Caine, Ph.D.

Historical Note
*Members are individuals specializing in the study of monkeys, apes,
and other primates. Membership: $30/year.*

Publications:
American Journal of Primatology. q.
The Bulletin of The ASP. bi-m.

Meetings/Conferences:
Annual Meetings: Usually at an academic center in the
　　summer/350

American Soc. of Professional Appraisers *(1984)*

430 Technology Pkwy.
Norcross, GA　30092-3406
Tel: (770)729-8400　　　　　*Fax:* (770)729-9296
Members: 2,463 individuals
Annual Budget: $50-100,000
Exec. Director: Lee I. McCutchan

Historical Note
*ASPA members are professionals concerned with residential and
commercial real estate appraisal. Membership: $85/year
(individual).*

Meetings/Conferences:
Annual Meetings: January

American Soc. of Professional Estimators *(1956)*

11141 Georgia Ave., Suite 412
Wheaton, MD　20902
Tel: (301)929-8848　　　　　*Fax:* (301)929-0231
Web Site: http://www.ASPEnational.com
Members: 3,000 individuals
Staff: 3
Annual Budget: $100-250,000
Director of Administration: Beverly S. Perrell
Meeting Planner: Darnell Ambrose

Historical Note
*Construction trade estimators. Membership: $110/year, plus
chapter dues.*

Publications:
Estimator Society Newsletter. bi-m. adv.
Estimator Technical Journal. q. adv.
Standard Estimating Practice. a.
The Estimator. m. adv.

Meetings/Conferences:
Annual Meetings: June-July

1999 – Cleveland, OH

American Soc. of Psychoanalytic Physicians *(1985)*

4804 Jasmine Dr.
Rockville, MD　20853
Tel: (301)929-1470　　　　　*Fax:* (301)929-1491
Web Site: http://pubweb.acns.nwu.edu/ ~ chessick/aspp.htm
Members: 280 individuals
Staff: 1
Annual Budget: under $10,000
Exec. Director: Janice Wright

Historical Note
*Formed by the merger of the American Soc. of Physician Analysts
and the American Ass'n of Psychoanalytic Physicians. Members are
involved in private practice of psychoanalysis and analytically-
oriented psychotherapy. Membership is by invitation.*

Publications:
Bulletin. semi-a. adv.

Meetings/Conferences:
Annual Meetings: May, in conjunction with the American
　　Psychiatric Ass'n

American Soc. of Psychopathology of Expression *(1964)*

74 Lawton St.
Brookline, MA　02446
Tel: (617)738-9821
Members: 100 individuals
Staff: 1
Annual Budget: under $10,000
President: Irene Jakab, M.D.

Historical Note
*Members are psychiatrists, psychologists, art therapists, artists, and
others interested in the problems of verbal and non-verbal
expression. Membership: $25/year.*

Publications:
Newsletter. semi-a.
Proceedings. bien.

Meetings/Conferences:

American Soc. of Questioned Document Examiners *(1942)*

P.O. Box 382684
Germantown, TN　38183-2684
Tel: (901)747-7751
E-Mail: ASQDE.org
Web Site: http://www.asqde.org
Members: 110 individuals
Staff: 1
Annual Budget: $10-25,000
President: Robert J. Muehlberg

Historical Note
*Purpose is to foster education; sponsor scientific research; establish
standards; and provide training in the field of questioned document
examination and promote justice in matters that involve questions
about documents. Membership: $100/year (individual).*

Publications:
ASQDE News. 3/year.
Journal of the ASQDE. semi a. adv.
Membership Directory. a.

Meetings/Conferences:
Annual Meetings: Summer/100-130
1999 – Los Angeles, CA

American Soc. of Radiologic Technologists *(1920)*

15000 Central Ave., S.E.
Albuquerque, NM　87123-3917
Tel: (505)298-4500　　　　　*Fax:* (505)298-5063
Toll Free: (800)444 - 2778
Web Site: http://www.asrt.org
Members: 73,000 individuals
Staff: 64
Annual Budget: $5-10,000,000
C.E.O.: Lynn May
Dir., Marketing: Carl Feak
Director, Communications: Nora Tuggle
Director, Government Relations: Duvonne Campbell
Meeting Administrator: Peggy Green
Dir., Continuing Education: Becky Kruse
Chief Financial Officer: Rick Linkous
Exec. V. President, Professional Development: Greg Morrison
Dir., Information Services: Dave Justice

Historical Note
*Founded in Chicago as American Ass'n of Radiologic Technicians,
it became American Soc. of Radiographers in 1930. Incorporated in
Minnesota in 1932. Became American Soc. of X-Ray Technicians
in 1934 and American Soc. of Radiologic Technologists, Inc. in
1936. Affiliated with the American Registry of Radiologic
Technologists. Promotes the science of radiation and imaging
specialties. Membership: $80 (initial year); $70/year (renewal).*

Publications:
ASRT Scanner. m.
Radiologic Technology. bi-m. adv.

Meetings/Conferences:
Annual Meetings: Summer/600
1999 – Portland, OR(Doubletree Jantzen Beach)/June 5-10
2000 – Albuquerque, NM(Hyatt)/June 3-6

American Soc. of Real Estate Counselors *(1953)*

Historical Note
Became Counselors of Real Estate in 1996.

American Soc. of Regional Anesthesia *(1976)*

1910 Byrd Ave., Suite 100
P.O. Box 11086
Richmond, VA　23230-1086
Tel: (804)282-0010　　　　　*Fax:* (804)282-0090
E-Mail: asra@societyhq.com

Members: 8,000 individuals
Annual Budget: $500-1,000,000
Exec. Secretary: John A. Hinckley
Communications: Hallie Townsend
Manager, Meetings and Conventions: Kevin Johns, CAE, CMP
Finance: David Vereen
Director, Operations: Stewart Hincilley, CMP
Membership: Daniel Gainyard

Historical Note
Physicians and anesthetists interested in the induction of
insensibility over a certain area by nerve blocking or field blocking,
regional anesthesia for pain, surgery and obstetrics. Membership:
$150/year (individual).

Publications:
Newsletter. q.
Regional Anesthesia and Pain Medicine. 6/year. adv.

Meetings/Conferences:
Annual Meetings: March/1,000
1999 – Philadelphia, PA(Marriott)/May 6-9/950
2000 – Orlando, FL(Walt Disney World
     Dolphin)/March 30-April 2/900
2000 – Quebec City, Canada(Convention
     Center)/May 30-June 2/1100

American Soc. of Roommate Services (1979)
250 W. 57th St., Suite 1629
New York, NY 10019
Tel: (212)489-6860   Fax: (212)582-6890
Exec. Officer: Michael Santomauro

Historical Note
ASRS members are roommate finding agencies.

Publications:
Ins & Outs of the Roommate Biz. 3/yr.

American Soc. of Safety Engineers (1911)
1800 East Oakton St.
Des Plaines, IL 60018-2187
Tel: (847)699-2929   Fax: (847)296-3769
E-Mail: 73244.562@compuserve.com
Web Site: http://www.asse.org
Members: 32,000 individuals
Staff: 52
Annual Budget: $5-10,000,000
Exec. Director: Fred Fortman

Historical Note
Founded in 1911 as the United Ass'n of Casualty Inspectors and
merged with the Nat'l Safety Council in 1924, becoming its
Engineering Section. It again became independent in 1947 as the
American Soc. of Safety Engineers and incorporated in Illinois in
1962. Membership is open to individuals whose employment,
education, and experience are safety-related. Has an annual budget
of approximately $8 million. Membership: $105/year.

Publications:
Professional Safety Journal. m. adv.
Society Update. m.

Meetings/Conferences:
Annual Meetings: June/1,900
1999 – Baltimore, MD(Convention Center)/June 13-16

American Soc. of Sanitary Engineering (1906)
28901 Clemens Road
Suite 100
Westlake, OH 44145
Tel: (440)835-3040   Fax: (440)835-3488
E-Mail: ASSE@ix.netcom.com
Web Site: www.asse-clemens.org
Members: 2,750 individuals
Staff: 5
Annual Budget: $50-100,000
Exec. Secretary: Diana Corcoran

Historical Note
Originated in January 1906 in the District of Columbia as the
American Soc. of Inspectors of Plumbing and Sanitary Engineers.
Became the American Soc. of Sanitary Engineering in 1914 and
incorporated in the District of Columbia in 1937. Membership:
$60-85/year (individual), $200/year (company).

Publications:
ASSE Yearbook. a. adv.
Newsletter. m.
Plumbing Standards Magazine. q. adv.
Technical Session Proceedings. a.

Meetings/Conferences:
Annual Meetings: Fall/250-300
1999 – Tampa Bay, FL

American Soc. of Scientific Glass Blowers
1123 N. Water St.
Milwaukee, WI 53202
Tel: (414)276-8788   Fax: (414)276-7704
Exec. Director: Jane A. Svinicki, CAE

American Soc. of Sephardic Studies (1963)
500 W. 185th St., Suite F H 419
New York, NY 10033
Tel: (212)960-5236   Fax: (212)960-5482
Members: 120 individuals
Annual Budget: under $10,000
Director: M. Mitchell Serels, Ph.D.

Historical Note
ASOSS members are academics with an interest in Sephardic Jewish
history, culture or language.

Publications:
Sephardic Scholar Journal. irreg.

Meetings/Conferences:
Annual Meetings: always New York City/March

American Soc. of Sugar Beet Technologists (1935)
800 Grant St., Suite 500

Denver, CO 80203
Tel: (303)832-4460   Fax: (303)832-4468
Members: 650 individuals
Staff: 2
Annual Budget: $10-25,000
Exec. V. President: Thomas K. Schwartz

Historical Note
Membership: $75/2 years.

Publications:
Journal of Sugar Beet Research. bi-a.

Meetings/Conferences:
Biennial Meetings: odd years in February-March
1999 – Orlando, FL(Hyatt Regency)/Feb. 10-13/500

American Soc. of Tax Professionals (1987)
P.O. Box 245
Centerville, IA 52544
Tel: (515)856-2294   Fax: (515)856-2294
Members: 150 individuals
Staff: 1
Annual Budget: $10-25,000
Exec. Director: Nancy Andrews

Historical Note
ASTP is a member-driven organization of tax preparers, devoted
primarily to education. ASTP supports the Certified Tax Preparer
(CTP) program. The Institute of Tax Consultants is the certifying
board for the ASTP. Formerly known as the Nat'l Ass'n of Income
Tax Preparers (1985). Assumed its present name in 1987.

Publications:
Tax Professionals Update. bi-m.

Meetings/Conferences:
Annual Meetings: September
1999 – Orlando, FL/Sept. 23-26
2000 – Las Vegas, NV

American Soc. of Theatre Consultants (1983)
12226 Mentz Hill Road
St. Louis, MO 63128
Tel: (314)843-9218   Fax: (314)843-4955
Members: 30 individuals
Annual Budget: $10-25,000
Secretary-C.F.O.: Edgar Lustig

Historical Note
ASTC members are consultants specializing in the planning and
design of theatres and other performing facilities.

Publications:
ASTC Newsletter. 2/year.

Meetings/Conferences:
1999 – Fort Worth, TX/February 20-21

American Soc. of Transplant Physicians
6900 Grove Road
Thorofare, NJ 08086-9447
Tel: (609)848-6205   Fax: (609)848-4016
E-Mail: astp@slackinc.com
Web Site: http://www.astp.org/
Members: 1,300 individuals
Staff: 9
Annual Budget: $1-2,000,000
Exec. Director: Susan J. Nelson
Meeting Manager: M. Pamela Ballinger
Exhibits: Betty Kehler
Manager, Registration: Christine Finken
Education: Kim Davis

Historical Note
Promotes and encourages education and research in transplantation
medicine and immunology, and provides a forum for the exchange
of scientific information related to the field. Membership:
$150/year.

Publications:
ASTP Decade of Transplantation.
ASTP Newsletter. q.
ASTP Primer on Transplantation.

Meetings/Conferences:

American Soc. of Transplant Surgeons (1974)
2000 L St., N.W., Suite 200
Washington, DC 20036
Tel: (202)416-1858   Fax: (202)833-3843
Web Site: http://www.asts.org
Members: 669 individuals
Staff: 6
Annual Budget: $250-500,000
Exec. Director: Katrina Crist

Historical Note
ASTS members are surgeons specializing in liver, heart, lung,
pancreas, and kidney transplants. Membership: $350/year
(individual).

Publications:
Chimera. q.
Transplantation. m.

Meetings/Conferences:
Annual Meetings: May-June
1999 – Chicago, IL/May 19-21

American Soc. of Transportation and Logistics (1946)
320 E. Water St.
Lock Haven, PA 17745-1419
Tel: (717)748-8515   Fax: (717)748-9118
E-Mail: info@astl.org
Web Site: http://www.astl.org
Members: 1,700 individuals
Staff: 4
Annual Budget: $100-250,000
Exec. V. President: Tricia Humphrey
Office Manager: Rene Russell

Historical Note
Organized in Chicago, IL, March 1, 1946 and incorporated later
the same year in the State of Indiana as the American Soc. of Traffic
and Transportation, ASTL assumed its present name in 1984. A
professional society of individuals involved in or concerned with the
various management functions of transportation, physical
distribution and logistics. Awards the CTL (Certified in
Transportation and Logistics) designation. Membership fee varies.

Publications:
ASTRALOG Newsletter. bi-m. adv.
Transportation Journal. q.

Meetings/Conferences:
Annual Meetings: Fall

American Soc. of Travel Agents (1931)
1101 King St., Suite 200
Alexandria, VA 22314
Tel: (703)739-2782   Fax: (703)549-7987
Web Site: www.astanet.com
Members: 25,000 individuals
Staff: 92
Annual Budget: $10-25,000,000
V. President, Government Affairs: John Bennison
Sr. V.P., Meetings/Conventions/Trade Shows: Chris P. Vranas
V. President, Industry Affairs and Travel Technology: Stephanie
    Kenyon
Sr. V.P., Finance/Administration: Nancy L. Dobberman
Sr. V.P., Sales & Marketing: Stephen McGillivray
Sr. V. President, Legal and Industry Affairs: Paul Ruden
General Counsel: Burton J. Rubin
V. President, Chapter/Member Services: Ray M. Greenly
Director, Membership Sales: Taryn Moore

Historical Note
Established in 1931 in New York as the American Steamship and
Tourist Agents' Ass'n. The name was changed in 1944 to American
Soc. of Travel Agents, Inc. Sponsors the American Soc. of Travel
Agents Political Action Committee. Has an international
membership of about 15%. Has an annual budget of approximately
$12 million.

Publications:
ASTA Agency Management. m.
Dateline ASTA. bi-w.

Meetings/Conferences:
Annual Meetings: Fall
1999 – Strasbourg, France

American Soc. of Trial Consultants (1982)
Mass Commmunication and Comm. Studies
Towson University
Towson, MD 21252
Tel: (410)472-0736   Fax: (410)830-3656
Members: 400 individuals
Staff: 2
Annual Budget: $50-100,000
Exec. Secretary: Ronald J. Matlon, Ph.D.

Historical Note
Organized in Phoenix, October, 1982. Formerly (1986) the Ass'n
of Trial Behavior Consultants, ASTC assumed its present name in
January, 1987. Members are trial consultants from a variety of
academic backgrounds who work within court systems on jury
selection, community surveys, continuing legal education,
courtroom visuals, witness preparation, language and law, legal
interviewing and negotiation, post trial juror interviews,
presentation strategy in the courtroom, trial simulations, voir dire
strategy, etc. Membership: $75/year (individual); $100/year (new
members), $180 + 60/year/person (company). Student
memberships $40/year.

Publications:
Annual Directory of Members. a.
Court Call Newsletter. q.

Meetings/Conferences:
Annual Meetings: October/100
1999 – San Diego, CA
2000 – St. Louis, MO

American Soc. of Tropical Medicine and Hygiene (1951)
60 Revere Dr., Suite 500
Northbrook, IL 60062-1577
Tel: (847)480-9592   Fax: (847)480-9282
E-Mail: astmh@astmh.org
Web Site: http://www.astmh.org
Members: 3,000 individuals
Staff: 4
Annual Budget: $1-2,000,000
Exec. Director: Joyce Paschall
Director, Conference: Lyn Maddox
Director, Administrative: Judy DeAcetis

Historical Note
Organized November 17, 1951 in Chicago as an amalgamation of
the American Soc. of Tropical Medicine, formed in 1903, and the
Nat'l Malaria Soc., founded in 1916. Incorporated in Delaware in
1952. Membership: $115/year (individual); $57.50/year (postdoctoral student); $38.33/year (pre-doctoral student).

Publications:
American Journal of Tropical Medicine and Hygiene. m.
Clinical Consultants Directory. a.
Directory of Internat'l Opportunities. a.
Program and Abstracts of the Annual Meeting. a.
Tropical Medicine and Hygiene News. bi-m.

Meetings/Conferences:
Annual Meetings: Winter/1,500
1999 – Washington, DC(Hilton & Towers)/Nov. 28-Dec. 2
2000 – Houston, TX(Westin Galleria)/Oct. 29-Nov. 2

American Soc. of TV Cameramen (1974)
2520 Lotus Hill Drive
Las Vegas, NV 89134-7855
Tel: (702)228-6704   Fax: (702)228-6701

Members: 500 individuals
Staff: 3
President: Robert Zweck
Director, Media Relations: Ruth Edna Feeney
Assoc. Director, CAMMY Awards: Nicole R.J. Spanos
Director, Professional Development: Janet Doka
Exec. Secretary: Morton Morje

Historical Note
A professional and fraternal society formed to bring together individuals of similar interests and experiences, and to promote standards of professionalism within the industry. Affiliated with the Internat'l Soc. of Videographers. Membership: $25/year (regular); $15/year (associate); $10/year (student).

Publications:
Directory. irreg.
Zoom Out! Newsletter. irreg.

Meetings/Conferences:
Annual Meetings: alternates between New York, NY and Las Vegas, NV/May
1999 – Las Vegas, NV

American Soc. of Veterinary Ophthalmology *(1957)*

1416 W. Liberty
Stillwater, OK   74075
Tel: (405)377-4388
Members: 200 individuals
Staff: 1
Annual Budget: under $10,000
Secretary-Treasurer: V.A. Schultz, D.V.M.

Historical Note
Founded in 1957 in Miami Beach during a meeting of the American Animal Hospital Association. Affiliated with American Veterinary Medical Ass'n. Membership: $25/year.

Publications:
Directory. a.
Newsletter. a.

Meetings/Conferences:
Annual Meetings: Spring, with American Animal Hospital Ass'n
1999 – Denver, CO

American Soc. of Wedding Professionals *(1992)*

268 Griggs Ave.
Teaneck, NJ   07666
Toll Free: (800)526 - 0497
Members: 100 individuals
Staff: 2
Exec. Officer: Brian D. Lawrence

Historical Note
ASWP members are professional wedding consultants. Membership: $129/year (individual).

Publications:
The Wedding Expert's Guide to Sales and Marketing.

American Soc. of Women Accountants *(1938)*

60 Revere Drive, Suite 600
Northbrook, IL   38119-7235
Tel: (847)205-1029   *Fax:* (847)480-9282
Toll Free: (800)326 - 2163
Members: 6,500 individuals
Staff: 15
Annual Budget: $250-500,000
Exec. Director: Debra Lynn Ross, CAE
Director, Communications: Angie Leondedis
Director, Membership: Rachel Airth

Historical Note
Composed of 108 chapters nationwide the association seeks to enable women in all fields of accounting to achieve their personal, professional, and economic potential as well as contributing to the future development of the profession. Membership: $79/year (regular),$22/year(associate), $15(retired).

Publications:
Membership Directory. a.
The Edge. 8/year adv. adv.

Meetings/Conferences:
Semi-annual Meetings: Late Spring and Fall
1999 – Seattle, WA
2000 – Baltimore, MD

American Soc. of Writers on Legal Subjects

Historical Note
See Scribes.

American Soc. of Zoologists *(1890)*

Historical Note
Became the Soc. for Integrative and Comparative Biology in 1996.

American Soc. on Aging *(1954)*

833 Market St., Suite 511
San Francisco, CA   94103-1824
Tel: (415)974-9600   *Fax:* (415)974-0300
Members: 10,000 individuals
Staff: 30
Annual Budget: $2-5,000,000
Exec. Director: Gloria Cavanaugh
Communications: Nancy Kaplan

Historical Note
Founded as the Western Gerontological Soc. ASA's goal is the well-being of older Americans and their families. Membership includes educators, service providers, researchers, health and social service professionals, administrators, policy makers, business executives, advocates, students, and elders. Membership: $110/year (individual), $250/year (organization).

Publications:
Aging and Spirituality. q.
Aging Today. bi-m. adv.
Dimensions. q.
Generations. q. adv.
Managed Care for the Elderly. q.

Maximizing Human Potential. q.
Networker. q.
Older Learner. q.
Outword. q.

Meetings/Conferences:
Annual Meetings: March/3,500

American Sociological Ass'n *(1905)*

1307 New York Ave., N.W.
Washington, DC   20005-4701
Tel: (202)833-3410   *Fax:* (202)785-0146
E-Mail: executive.office@asanet.org
Web Site: http://www.asanet.org
Members: 130,000 individuals
Staff: 25
Annual Budget: $2-5,000,000
Exec. Officer: Felice J. Levine
Dir., Academic & Professional Affairs and Deputy Exec. Officer: Carla Howery
Convention & Meetings Manager: Janet L. Astner
Dir., Customer Service/Membership: C. Connie Castillo
Director, Publication: Karen Edwards
Deputy Exec. Officer and Director of Administration: Phoebe Stevenson

Historical Note
The American Sociological Ass'n (ASA), founded in 1905, is a non-profit membership ass'n dedicated to serving sociologists in their work, advancing sociology as a scientific discipline and profession, and promoting the contributions and use of sociology to society. As the nat'l organization for over 13,000 sociologists, the Ass'n is well positioned to provide a unique set of benefits to its members and to promote the vitality, visibility, and diversity of the discipline. Working at the nat'l and internat'l levels, the Ass'n aims to articulate policy and implement programs likely to have the broadest possible impact for sociology now and in the future. Membership: $32-171/year (individual), $150-175/year (department).

Publications:
American Sociological Review. bi-m. adv.
ASA Employment Bulletin. m. adv.
ASA Footnotes. 9/year. adv.
Contemporary Sociology. bi-m. adv.
Employment Bulletin. m.
Journal of Health and Social Behavior. q. adv.
Social Psychology Quarterly. adv. adv.
Sociological Methodology. a.
Sociological Theory. semi-a. adv.
Sociology of Education. q. adv.
Teaching Sociology. q. adv.

Meetings/Conferences:
1999 – Chicago, IL/August 6-10
2000 – Washington, DC/August 12-16

American Software Ass'n *(1991)*

Historical Note
A division of the Information Technology Ass'n of America.

American Solar Energy Soc. *(1954)*

2400 Central Ave., #G-1
Boulder, CO   80301-2843
Tel: (303)443-3130   *Fax:* (303)443-3212
E-Mail: ases@ases.org
Web Site: http://www.ases.org/solar
Members: 4,500 individuals
Staff: 4
Annual Budget: $500-1,000,000
Exec. Director: Larry Sherwood

Historical Note
Established in 1970 and incorporated in Florida. Formerly (1982) the Internat'l Solar Energy Soc., American Section. Affiliated with the Internat'l Solar Energy Soc. Membership: $60/year (individual).

Publications:
Annual Proceedings. a.
Passive Proceedings. a.
Solar Today Magazine. bi-m. adv.

Meetings/Conferences:
Annual Meetings: Spring
1999 – Portland, ME

American Southdown Breeders Ass'n *(1882)*

HCR 13, Box 220
Fredonia, TX   76842
Tel: (915)429-6226   *Fax:* (915)429-6225
Members: 1000 individuals
Staff: 1
Annual Budget: $10-25,000
Secretary/Treasurer: Gary Jennings

Historical Note
Breeders and fanciers of Southdown sheep. Membership: $10 (initial fee), $5/year thereafter.

Publications:
Southdown Handbook. trien. adv.
The American Southdown Newsletter. 3/year. adv.

Meetings/Conferences:
Annual Meetings: Fall

American Soybean Ass'n *(1920)*

12125 Woodcrest Executive Dr., Suite 100
St. Louis, MO   63141-5009
Tel: (314)576-1770   *Fax:* (314)576-2786
Toll Free: (800)688 - 7692
Web Site: http://www.oilseeds.org/asa
Members: 31,500 individuals
Staff: 40
Annual Budget: $25-50,000,000
Chief Executive Officer: Steve Censky
Communications Director: Bob Callanan
Exec. Director: Jack Negens

Director, Membership and Mktg.: James L. Nagel
Exec. Director, Internat'l Marketing: Jim Guinn

Historical Note
Develops and implements policies to increase the profitability of its members and the entire soybean industry, including export/market expansion, education, research and legislative action.

Publications:
ASA Today. 10/year.
Leader Letter. w.
Washington Insider.

Meetings/Conferences:
1999 – Albuquerque, NM(Convention Center)/Feb. 18-20/4000
2000 – Orlando, FL/4000
2001 – San Antonio, TX/4000

American Spa and Health Resort Ass'n *(1982)*

Box 585
Lake Forest, IL   60045
Tel: (847)234-8851   *Fax:* (847)295-7790
Members: 70 companies
Annual Budget: under $10,000
Exec. Director: Melanie Ruehle

Historical Note
Incorporated in Illinois, ASHRA promotes the public awareness of spas/health resorts and sets standards for membership.

American Specialty Toy Retailing Ass'n *(1992)*

206 6th Avenue, Suite 900
Des Moines, IA   50309
Tel: (515)282-8192   *Fax:* (515)282-9117
E-Mail: astra@astratoy.org
Web Site: http://www.astratoy.org
Members: 770 individuals and companies
Annual Budget: $250-500,000
Exec. Director: Janet Koerner

Historical Note
ASTRA represents the needs and interests of the specialty toy industry and promotes the sale and use of specialty toys through marketing, research and education. Membership: $200-$5,000/year, based on gross sales (retailers); $200/year (others).

Publications:
Convention Program. a. adv.
Directory. a. adv.
Newsletter. q. adv.

Meetings/Conferences:
1999 – San Diego, CA(Catamara Resort Hotel)/April 29-May 2
2000 – St. Augustine, FL(World Golf Resort)/May 4-7

American Speech-Language-Hearing Ass'n *(1925)*

10801 Rockville Pike
Rockville, MD   20852-3226
Tel: (301)897-5700   *Fax:* (301)897-7358
Toll Free: (800)498 - 2071
Web Site: http://www.asha.org
Members: 96,000 individuals
Staff: 200
Annual Budget: $10-25,000,000
Exec. Director: Frederick T. Spahr, CAE
Director, Editorial Services: Barbara Goldberg
Dir., Conventions & Meetings: Cheryl Russell
Director, Education Programs: Babara Karpinski
Assoc. Dir. Operations: Charles Cochran
Assoc. Director, Audiology: Vic S. Gladstone
Dir., Membership/Career Development: Patricia Cole, PH.D.
Director, Information/Member Marketing: Thomas M. Smith
Dir., Publications Division: Joanne K. Jessen

Historical Note
ASHA is the professional, scientific and certifying association of speech-language pathologists and audiologists. Founded in 1925 as the American Academy of Speech Correction. Became the American Soc. for the Study of Disorders of Speech in 1927 and the American Speech Correction Ass'n in 1934. In 1947 the name was again changed to the American Speech and Hearing Ass'n and the organization was incorporated in Kansas. Changed to its present name in 1979. Member of the Council of Communication Societies and the Internat'l Ass'n of Logopedics and Phoniatrics. Has an annual budget of $14 million. Sponsors and supports the ASHA Political Action Committee. Membership: $150/year (individual).

Publications:
American Journal of Audiology.
American Journal of Speech-Language Pathology.
ASHA. q. adv.
Journal of Speech and Hearing Research. q.
Language, Speech and Hearing Services in Schools. q.

Meetings/Conferences:
Annual Meetings: Fall/13,000
1999 – San Francisco, CA/Nov. 18-21

American Spice Trade Ass'n *(1907)*

P.O. Box 1267
Englewood Cliffs, NJ   07632-1267
Tel: (201)568-2163   *Fax:* (201)568-7318
Members: 300 spice companies
Staff: 4
Annual Budget: $500-1,000,000
Exec. Director: Elizabeth Erman

Historical Note
ASTA is a trade association with worldwide membership comprised of leading firms in the spice industry. It protects the interests and promotes the welfare of the industry and encourages activities and programs leading to the continued growth in spice consumption.

Publications:
Membership Directory. a.
Spice Letter. m.

Meetings/Conferences:
Annual Meetings: Spring
1999 – Newport Beach, CA(Hyatt Newporter)/April 25-28

American Spinal Injury Ass'n (1975)
345 E. Superior Street, Suite 1436
Chicago, IL 60611
Tel: (312)908-1242   *Fax:* (312)503-0869
E-Mail: mars@merle.acns.nwu.edu
Web Site: http://www.asia-spinalinjury.org
Members: 500 individuals
Staff: 3
Annual Budget: $250-500,000
Exec. Secretary: Marianne G. Kaplan

Historical Note
ASIA members are Doctors of Medicine or Osteopathy and other allied health professionals. Membership: $200/year (doctor); $50/year (allied health professional).

Publications:
ASIA Bulletin. semi-a.

Meetings/Conferences:
Annual Meetings: Spring
1999 – Atlanta, GA(Hilton)/April 19-21/350
2000 – Chicago, IL(Westin)/April 14-16/350
2001 – Long Beach, CA(Hyatt)/May 18-20/350
2002 – Vancouver, BC(Hyatt)/May 4-7/400

American Sport Fishing Ass'n (1962)
1033 N. Fairfax St., Suite 200
Alexandria, VA 22314
Tel: (703)519-9691   *Fax:* (703)519-1872
E-Mail: amsportfish@delphi.com
Web Site: http://www.asafishing.org
Members: 700 companies
Staff: 25
Annual Budget: $2-5,000,000
President/C.E.O.: Mike Hayden
V. President, Gov't Affairs: Norville Prosser
V. President, Gov't Affairs: Mike Nussman
C.F.O.: Steve Knell

Historical Note
Formed by the merger in 1995 of the Sport Fishing Institute and the American Fishing Tackle Manufacturers Ass'n. ASA members are businesses that sell or manufacture any product used in serving and meeting the needs of recreational fishing and associated services including manufacturers, tackle and marine dealers, wholesalers, rep agencies, resource agencies, advocacy groups and publishers.

Meetings/Conferences:
1999 – Chicago, IL/July 9-11

American Sports Medicine Ass'n/Board of Certification (1978)
660 W. Duarte Road
Arcadia, CA 91007
Tel: (626)445-1978
Members: 3,550 individuals
Staff: 2
Annual Budget: $10-25,000
Board Chairman: Joe S. Borland, DO, RPT

Historical Note
Members are sports medicine trainers, skilled in the prevention and care of injuries as well as physical therapy under a physician's direction. Members must maintain their professional license annually. Provides continuing education and awards the designation CSMT (Certified Sports Medicine Trainer). Membership: $40/year.

Publications:
ASMA Newsletter. q. adv.

Meetings/Conferences:

American Sportscasters Ass'n (1979)
5 Beekman St.
New York, NY 10038
Tel: (212)227-8080   *Fax:* (212)571-0556
Members: 550 individuals
Staff: 3
Annual Budget: $100-250,000
President and Exec. Director: Louis O. Schwartz

Historical Note
Members are radio and TV sportscasters; the ASA is the forerunner of the American Sportscasters Charitable Trust. Founded the American Sportscasters' Hall of Fame in 1984. Membership: $50/year (individual), $250/year (company).

Publications:
Insiders Sportsletter. m.

Meetings/Conferences:
Annual Meetings: Annual Hall of Fame Awards Dinner

American Stamp Dealers' Ass'n (1914)
3 School St., Suite 205
Glen Cove, NY 11542
Tel: (516)759-7000   *Fax:* (516)759-7014
E-Mail: asda@erols.co,
Members: 1000 individuals
Staff: 4
Annual Budget: $250-500,000
Exec. V. President: Joseph B. Savarese

Historical Note
Members are retailer and wholesalers of stamps, albums and other philatelic materials. Membership: $300/year.

Publications:
A. S.
A. S.

Meetings/Conferences:

American Standardbred Breeders Ass'n (1953)
Historical Note
Organization defunct in 1997.

American Statistical Ass'n (1839)
1429 Duke St.

Alexandria, VA 22314-3402
Tel: (703)684-1221   *Fax:* (703)684-2036
E-Mail: ASAINFO@AMSTAT.ORG
Web Site: http://www.amstat.org
Members: 17,500 individuals
Staff: 42
Annual Budget: $2-5,000,000
Exec. Director/Secretary: Ray A. Waller, Ph.D.
Program Director for Support: Steve Porzio
Program Director for Services: Mary Fleming

Historical Note
Founded in Boston November 27, 1839 and incorporated in Massachusetts in 1841. ASA, a non-profit professional organization, fosters statistics and their application in the broadest manner, promotes unity and effective effort among all concerned with statistical problems and works to increase the contribution of statistics to human welfare. Membership: $74/year (regular); $25/year (student/senior member).

Publications:
American Statistician. q. adv.
AMSTAT News. m. adv.
Chance Magazine. q.
Current Index to Statistics. a.
Journal of Agricultural, Biological and Environmental
   Statistics. q.
Journal of Business and Economic Statistics. q. adv.
Journal of Computational & Graphical Statistics.
Journal of Educational & Behavioral Statistics. q.
Journal of the American Statistical Ass'n. q. adv.
LINK Newsletter.
Proceedings. a.
Stats-The Magazine for Students of Statistics. 3/yr. adv.
Technometrics. q.

Meetings/Conferences:
Annual Meetings: Summer
1999 – Baltimore, MD/Aug. 8-12
2000 – Indianapolis, IN/Aug. 13-17
2001 – Atlanta, GA/Aug. 5-9
2002 – New York, NY/Aug. 11-15

American Stock Exchange (1911)
86 Trinity Place
New York, NY 10006-1881
Tel: (212)306-1000   *Fax:* (212)306-1152
Toll Free: (800)843 - 2639
Members: 864 individuals521 associate
Staff: 781
Annual Budget: $5-10,000,000
Chairman: Richard S. Syron

Historical Note
Founded as an outdoor market in New York before 1800, it became successively the New York Market Agency in 1908, the New York Curb Market Ass'n in 1911, the New York Curb Market in 1921 with its move indoors, the New York Curb Exchange in 1929 and the American Stock Exchange in 1953. In 1998, AmEx merged with Nat'l Ass'n of Securities, forming the NASDAQ-AmEx Market Group, under which the two stock exchanges operate. Individual members are distinguished as regular members and options principal members.

Publications:
Annual Report.
Fact Book.

Meetings/Conferences:
Annual Meetings: New York City, 2nd Monday in April.

American Stock Yards Ass'n (1932)
Historical Note
Ass'n inactive in 1996.

American String Teachers Ass'n (1946)
1806 Robert Fulton Dr., Suite 300
Reston, VA 20191
Tel: (703)476-1316   *Fax:* (703)476-1317
E-Mail: gwixson@netcom.com
Members: 10,000 individuals
Staff: 2
Annual Budget: $250-500,000
Exec. Administrator: Galen Wikson

Historical Note
Founded in 1946 and incorporated in Iowa in 1955. An associate organization of the Music Educators Nat'l Conference and member of the Nat'l Music Council and Associated Councils of the Arts. Membership is open to teachers and performers of stringed instruments including guitar and harp, students, schools or libraries, and commercial institutions interested in supporting its programs. Sponsors a biannual National Solo Competition and summer workshops.

Publications:
American String Teacher. q. adv.

Meetings/Conferences:
Annual Meetings: With Music Educators Nat'l Conference

American Student Dental Ass'n (1971)
211 E. Chicago Ave., Suite 1160
Chicago, IL 60611
Tel: (312)440-2795   *Fax:* (312)440-2820
E-Mail: asda@asdaoffice.org
Web Site: http://www.asdanet.org
Members: 13,000 individuals
Staff: 6
Annual Budget: $500-1,000,000
Exec. Director: Karen S. Cervenka, CAE, CMP

Historical Note
Founded in Chicago, Illinois in 1971 at a national conference for dental students. Seeks to involve its members in the interprofessional activities of the dental profession. Membership: $40/year.

Publications:
ASDA Guides to Post-Doctoral Dental Programs, Vols I,II,III.
   bi-a.
ASDA Handbook. a. adv.
ASDA News. m. adv.
Dentistry. q. adv.
National Boards Examination Reprints.

Meetings/Conferences:
1999 – Denver, CO

American Studies Ass'n (1951)
1120 19th St., N.W., Suite 301
Washington, DC 20036
Tel: (202)467-4783   *Fax:* (202)467-4786
E-Mail: asastaff@erols.com.com
Web Site: http://georgetown.edu/crossroads
Members: 5,000 individuals, 150 institutions, 2000 libraries
Staff: 5
Annual Budget: $500-1,000,000
Exec. Director: John F. Stephens, Ph.D.
Coordinator, Publications: Reynolds Scott Childress

Historical Note
Founded in 1951 and incorporated in 1951 to foster the study of American culture and civilization as an entity rather than from the viewpoint of a single discipline. Admitted to membership in the American Council of Learned Societies in 1958.

Publications:
American Quarterly. q. adv.
ASA Newsletter. q. adv.
Connections: American History and Culture in Internat'l
   Perspective.
Guide to American Studies Resource. a. adv.
Meeting Program. a. adv.

Meetings/Conferences:
Annual Meetings: Fall/1,500
1999 – Montreal, Canada(Sheraton)/Oct. 28-31

American Subacute Care Ass'n (1993)
1720 Kennedy Causeway, Suite 109
North Bay Village, FL 33141
Tel: (305)864-0396   *Fax:* (305)864-0905
E-Mail: ascamail@aol.com
Members: 700 individuals
Staff: 5
Annual Budget: $100-250,000
Presisdent: Mike Freedman

Historical Note
Subacute patients are sufficiently stabilized to no longer require acute care services but are too complex for treatment in a conventional nursing center. Subacute care programs typically treat patients who are medically complex and require extensive physiological monitoring, intravenous therapy, or pre- or post-operative care. ASCA members are administrators, physicians, nurses, case managers, therapists, payors and other health professionals who work with subacute center throughout the U.S. Serves as a national vehicle for information, legislation and education that will enable its members to better serve persons with subacute needs. Membership: $99/year (individual), $500/year (organization/ company).

Publications:
ASCA. q. adv.
ASCA Directory. a. adv.

Meetings/Conferences:
Annual Meetings: Fall

American Subcontractors Ass'n (1966)
1004 Duke St.
Alexandria, VA 22314-3588
Tel: (703)684-3450   *Fax:* (703)836-3482
E-Mail: asaoffice@aol.com
Web Site: http://www.asaonline.com
Members: 6,900 companies
Staff: 15
Annual Budget: $2-5,000,000
Exec. V. President: E. Colette Nelson
Manager, Communications: David Mendes
Director, Government Relations: Brian T. Pallasch, CAE
Exec. Director: Steven W. Swafford
Manager, Membership: Julie Welch
Director, Chapter Services: Elizabeth Chisman Moon

Historical Note
ASA is a trade association representing subcontractors, specialty trade contractors, and material suppliers in the construction industry. Sponsors and supports the American Subcontractors Ass'n Political Action Committee. Membership: $190/year.

Publications:
The Subcontractor Magazine. m. adv.
Top Priority. bi-w.

Meetings/Conferences:
1999 – Miami, FL/March 13-16

American Suffolk Horse Ass'n
4240 Goehring Road
Ledbetter, TX 78946-5004
Members: 200 individuals
Staff: 1
Annual Budget: under $10,000
Secretary: Mary Margaret Read

Historical Note
Members are owners and breeders of Suffolk horses. Membership: $20-25/year.

Publications:
Directory of Suffolk Owners and Breeders. irreg.

Meetings/Conferences:

American Suffolk Sheep Soc. (1929)
Historical Note
Merged with Nat'l Suffolk Sheep Ass'n in 1998.

American Sugar Alliance (1983)
1225 I St., N.W., Suite 500
Washington, DC 20005
Tel: (202)457-1437   *Fax:* (202)408-0763
Members: 500 individuals
Staff: 2
Exec. Director: Vickie Rideout Myers
Director of Public Affairs: Joseph Terrell
Director of Economics: Jack Roney

Historical Note
A national coalition supporting America's cane, beet and corn farmers and dedicated to preserving a strong domestic sweetener industry.

Publications:
Washington Report. m.

Meetings/Conferences:

American Sugar Cane League of the U.S.A. (1922)
P.O. Drawer 938
Thibodaux, LA 70302
Tel: (504)448-3707   *Fax:* (504)448-3722
Members: 750 producers & 19 manufacturers
Staff: 6
Annual Budget: $1-2,000,000
President: Charles Melancon
General Counsel: Paul G. Borron, III

Historical Note
Formed by a merger of the Louisiana Sugar Planters Ass'n (founded in 1887), the American Cane Growers Ass'n (founded in 1919) and the Producers and Manufacturers Ass'n (founded in 1921). Sponsors the American Sugar Cane League Political Action Committee.

Publications:
Sugar Bulletin. m. adv.

Meetings/Conferences:
Annual Meetings: Thibodaux, LA/last Wednesday in February

American Sugarbeet Growers Ass'n (1975)
1156 15th St., N.W., Suite 1101
Washington, DC 20005
Tel: (202)833-2398   *Fax:* (202)833-2962
E-Mail: ASGA@aol.com
Web Site: http://hometown.aol.com/asga/sugar.htm
Members: 23 regional associations
Staff: 3
Annual Budget: $250-500,000
Exec. V. President: Luther A. Markwart

Historical Note
A federation of state and regional associations of sugarbeet growers. Formerly (1975) Nat'l Sugarbeet Growers Ass'n.

Meetings/Conferences:
Annual Meetings: Winter
1999 – Orlando, FL(Hotel Royal Plaza)/Feb. 9-11
2000 – Chandler, AZ/Jan. 30-Feb. 1
2001 – San Antonio, TX/Feb. 4-6

American Sulphur Export Corporation (1982)
Historical Note
Organization ceased operations in 1995.

American Supply and Machinery Manufacturers' Ass'n (1905)
1300 Sumner Ave.
Cleveland, OH 44115-2851
Tel: (216)241-7333   *Fax:* (216)241-0105
E-Mail: asmma@taol.com
Web Site: http://www.taol.com/asmma
Members: 525 companies
Staff: 2
Exec. Director: Charles M. Stockinger

Historical Note
Manufacturers of industrial, repair, production and operating supplies and machinery sold through industrial distributors.

American Supply Ass'n (1894)
222 Merchandise Mart Plaza, Suite 1360
Chicago, IL 60654-1202
Tel: (312)464-0090   *Fax:* (312)464-0091
E-Mail: asaemail@interserv.com
Web Site: http://asa.net
Members: 1000 companies
Staff: 20
Annual Budget: $5-10,000,000
Exec. Director: Maurice A. Desmarais, CAE
Director of Meetings and Conventions: Robert Jarvie
Director, Education Foundation: Eileen Robiso
Director, Finance: Catherine Fournier
Director, Center for Advancing Technology: Kevin Price

Historical Note
Merger (1970) of Central Supply Ass'n of Chicago and the American Institute of Supply Ass'ns. Members are plumbing, heating and cooling piping distributors and manufacturers. Sponsors and supports the ASA Political Action Committee.

Publications:
AMD News. bi-m. adv.
IPD News. q.
Membership Directory. a.
Operations Performance Report. a.

Meetings/Conferences:
Annual Meetings: Fall/6,000

American Surety Ass'n (1980)
910 Charles St.
Fredericksburg, VA 22401
Tel: (540)370-0106   *Fax:* (540)370-0015
E-Mail: SeanMce@aol.com
Members: 120 companies
Staff: 2

Annual Budget: $100-250,000
Exec. V. President: Peggy McElgunn

Historical Note
Members are surety companies, agents, attorneys and consultants interested in surety. Formerly (1984) the American Specialty Surety Council. Sponsors an annual specialty surety course. Membership: $400/yr. (agents); $1750/yr. (sureties).

Publications:
Bonding the Nation Newsletter. q.
Membership Directory. a.

Meetings/Conferences:
Semi-Annual Meetings: Spring and Fall
1999 – Tucson, AZ
1999 – Jekyll Island, GA

American Surgical Ass'n (1880)
13 Elm St.
Manchester, MA 01944
Tel: (978)526-8330   *Fax:* (978)526-4018
E-Mail: asa@prri.com
Members: 950 individuals
Staff: 1
Exec. Director: William T. Maloney, CAE

Historical Note
Founded in 1880 in Philadelphia as the American Surgical Soc., the name was subsequently changed to the American Surgical Ass'n.

Publications:
Annals of Surgery. semi-a. adv.
Transactions. a.

Meetings/Conferences:
Annual Meetings: Spring
1999 – San Diego, CA(Hyatt Regency)/April 15-17
2000 – Philadelphia, PA(Marriott)/April 13-15
2001 – Colorado Springs, CO(Broadmoor)/April 24-28/600

American Swimming Coaches Ass'n (1958)
2101 N. Andrews Ave., Suite 107
Fort Lauderdale, FL 33311
Tel: (954)563-4930   *Fax:* (954)563-9813
Toll Free: (800)356 - 2722
E-Mail: ASCA@LORNET.COM
Members: 5,200 individuals
Staff: 8
Annual Budget: $1-2,000,000
Exec. Director: John Leonard

Historical Note
Membership: $55/year (U.S.); $70/year (foreign).

Publications:
ASCA Magazine. m.
ASCA Newsletter. m.
Clinic Book. a.
High School Recruiters Directory. a.
Job Service. bi-w.
Journal of Swimming Research. a.

Meetings/Conferences:
Annual Meetings: September
1999 – San Diego, CA/Sept. 6-12

American Symphony Orchestra League (1942)
1156 15th St., N.W., Suite 800
Washington, DC 20005-1704
Tel: (202)776-0212   *Fax:* (202)776-0224
E-Mail: league@symphony.org
Members: 3,490 individuals, 901 orchestras & 706 organizations
Staff: 35
Annual Budget: $2-5,000,000
President: Charles Olton
V. President, Communications/Marketing: Jack McAuliffe
V. President, Government Affairs and Public Policy: John Sparks
Director, Meetings and Conferences: Jeri Royce
V. President, Professional and Artistic Services: Don Thulean
Director, Human Resources: Lisa Morton

Historical Note
Founded in 1942 and chartered by Congress in 1962, the purpose of the League is to ensure the artistic, organizational and financial strength of American orchestras. Services include: training programs, publications, research and analysis, technical assistance, and government relations for professional, avocational and youth orchestras, and for trustees, management staff, conductors, artistic staff and volunteers.

Publications:
SYMPHONY Magazine. bi-m. adv.

Meetings/Conferences:
Annual Meetings: June
1999 – Chicago, IL/June 9-12

American Tarentaise Ass'n (1973)
P.O. Box 34705
Kansas City, MO 64116-1105
Tel: (816)421-1993   *Fax:* (816)421-1991
E-Mail: JSpawn@aol.com
Members: 244 individuals
Staff: 2
Annual Budget: $50-100,000
Exec. Director: James A. Spawn

Historical Note
Tarentaise cattle originated in Southeastern France, and were recognized as a breed in 1866. The association is the official breed registry for Tarentaise cattle. Membership: $30/year.

Publications:
Tarentaise Journal. m. adv.

Meetings/Conferences:
Annual Meetings: January

American Taxation Ass'n (1975)

Historical Note
A section of the American Accounting Association, which provides administrative support. Members are university professors teaching courses dealing with federal tax matters.

American Technical Education Ass'n (1928)
North Dakota State College of Science
800 N. Sixth St.
Wahpeton, ND 58076-0002
Tel: (701)671-2240   *Fax:* (701)671-2260
Members: 2,250 organizations & individuals
Staff: 3
Annual Budget: $50-100,000
Exec. Director: Betty Krump

Historical Note
Established in 1928 as the American Ass'n of Technical High Schools and Institutes, it assumed its present name in 1950 and was incorporated in New York in 1960. From 1944 to 1969, the association was affiliated with the American Vocational Ass'n. Composed of post-secondary institutions, businesses and industrial concerns, ATEA is involved in expanding and improving the quality of technical education at the secondary level. Membership: $40/year (individual), $200/year (industry/business), $150/year (institution/agency)

Publications:
ATEA Journal. bi-m.

Meetings/Conferences:
Annual Meetings: Spring
1999 – Reno, NV(Nugget)/March 11-14
2000 – Louisville, KY(Galt House)/March 16-19

American Telemedicine Ass'n (1993)
901 15th St., N.W., Suite 230
Washington, DC 20005-3201
Tel: (202)408-0677   *Fax:* (202)408-1134
E-Mail: jlinkous@idi.net
Web Site: www.atmeda.org
Members: 1000 individuals
Annual Budget: $100-250,000
Exec. Director: Jonathan Linkous

Historical Note
Memerbship: $165/year.

Publications:
ATA Mews. q.
Telemed Journal. q. adv.

Meetings/Conferences:

American Telephone Fundraising Ass'n (1994)
Historical Note
Organization defunct in 1997.

American Teleservices Ass'n (1983)
4605 N. Lankershim Blvd., Suite 824
North Hollywood, CA 91602-1891
Tel: (818)766-5324   *Fax:* (818)766-8168
Members: 2,000 companies and individuals
Staff: 2
Annual Budget: $1-2,000,000
C.E.O.: J. Scott Thronton
Director, Convention Services: Lisa Levy

Historical Note
Founded as American Telemarketing Ass'n; assumed its current name in 1998. ATA members are business executives who have significant management responsibilities for telephone-assisted marketing/sales/service activities, own or operate telemarketing service agencies, or are suppliers of goods/services to the telemarketing industry. Membership: $400/year (individual), $1,000-2,000/year (corporate).

Publications:
ATA Membership Services Referral Directory. a.
Compendium of State Regulations. a.
Newsletter. m. adv.
On-Site Conference Program. semi-a. adv.

Meetings/Conferences:
Semi-Annual Meetings: Spring and Fall

American Textile Machinery Ass'n (1907)
111 Park Place
Falls Church, VA 22046-4513
Tel: (703)538-1789   *Fax:* (703)241-5603
E-Mail: atmahq@aol.com
Web Site: http://www.webmasters.net/atma/
Members: 100 companies
Staff: 5
Annual Budget: $250-500,000
Exec. V. President: Harry W. Buzzerd, Jr. CAE
Manager, Government Affairs: Clay D. Tyeryar
Manager, Meetings and Travel: Judith O. Buzzerd
Director, Member Services: Susan Denston

Historical Note
Formerly (1933) Nat'l Ass'n of Textile Machinery Manufacturers. Member, Machinery and Allied Products Institute. Sponsors and supports the Textile Machinery Good Government Committee.

Publications:
ATMA Executive Report. 6-8/year.
Product Directory Guide. every 4 years.

Meetings/Conferences:
1999 – Delray Beach, FL(Marriott)/Feb. 25-28/100

American Textile Manufacturers Institute (1949)
1130 Connecticut Ave., N.W., Suite 1200
Washington, DC 20036
Tel: (202)862-0500   *Fax:* (202)862-0570
Web Site: http://www.atmi.org
Staff: 36
Annual Budget: $2-5,000,000
Exec. V. President: Carlos F.J. Moore
Director, Communications: Gail A. Raiman
Director, Government Relations: Douglas W. Bulcao

Dir, Membership & Administrative Service: Ronald L. Floor

Historical Note

Merger in 1949 of the American Cotton Manufacturers Ass'n and the Cotton Textile Institute to form the American Cotton Manufacturers Institute. Absorbed the Nat'l Federation of Textiles in 1958. Current name adopted in 1962. Merged in 1964 with the Ass'n of Cotton Textile Merchants of NY. Absorbed the Nat'l Ass'n of Finishers of Textile Fabrics in 1965, and the Nat'l Ass'n of Wool Manufacturers in 1971. ATMI is the trade association for manufacturers of textile mill products made in the United States. Member companies operate in more the 30 states and account for 75% of all textile fibers consumed by mills in the U.S. Supports the American Textile Industry Committee for Good Government. Membership: Based upon percent of value added.

Publications:

ATMI Committee Directory.
ATMI Member Product Directory.
Global View.
Textile Fact File.
Textile Hi-Lights. q.
Textile Trends. w.

Meetings/Conferences:

Annual Meetings: Spring/300-400
1999 – Dana Pt., CA(Ritz Carlton Laguna
        Niguel)/March 11-13/500
2000 – Hamilton, Bermuda(Southampton
        Princess)/March 16-18/500

American Theatre and Drama Soc.

Historical Note

A focus group of the Ass'n for Theatre in Higher Education.

American Theatre Critics Ass'n *(1974)*

1011 Spring St.
Savannah, TN   38372-1227
Tel: (615)665-0595   *Fax:* (615)259-8057
Members: 345 individuals
Staff: 1
Annual Budget: under $10,000
Exec. Secretary: Clara Hieronymus

Historical Note

Organized at the O'Neill Theater Center in Waterford, CT in 1974 to make possible greater communication among theatre critics, to encourage freedom of expression in theater and theater criticism, to advance standards of criticism and to increase public awareness of the theater as a national resource. ACTA members are professional writers who have been employed for at least two years reviewing theatre on a regular and continuing basis for newspapers, magazines, radio or TV stations. Membership: $45/year.

Publications:

Critics Quarterly. q.

Meetings/Conferences:

Semi-annual Meetings: February in New York, NY and late
        May-June

American Theological Library Ass'n *(1947)*

820 Church St., Suite 400
Evanston, IL   60201-5603
Tel: (847)869-7788   *Fax:* (847)869-8513
Toll Free: (888)665 - 2852
E-Mail: atla@atla.com
Web Site: http://www.atla.com
Members: 550 individuals, 200 libraries
Staff: 33
Annual Budget: $1-2,000,000
Exec. Director: Dennis Norlin
Administrator, Financial Services: Pradeep Ganadia
Director of Member Services: Karen L. Whittlesey

Historical Note

An outgrowth of a Round Table on Libraries of the American Association of Theological Schools in 1947. International membership includes persons from Christian, Jewish and non-Judeo-Christian traditions interested in the practice, support or promotion of theological librarianship, information systems or bibliography. Membership: $30-100/year (individual), $75-500/year (company).

Publications:

Index to Book Reviews in Religion. a.
Newsletter. q.
Proceedings. a.
Religion Index One: Periodicals. semi-a.
Religion Index Two: Multi-Author Works. a.

Meetings/Conferences:

Annual Meetings: June
1999 – Chicago, IL(Loyola University, Lake Shore
        Campus)/June 10-12

American Therapeutic Ass'n *(1981)*

P.O. Box 612965
Dallas, TX   75261
Members: 500 individuals
Exec. Director: Tomas R. Aguila

Historical Note

ATA members are professional therapeutic practitioners in health care. Membership: $350 initial fee and $25/year renewal.

Publications:

Modalities.

American Therapeutic Recreation Ass'n *(1984)*

P.O. Box 15215
Hattiesburg, MS   39404-5215
Tel: (601)264-3442   *Fax:* (601)264-3337
Web Site: http://www.arta-tr.org
Members: 4,500 individuals, 50 companies
Staff: 3
Annual Budget: $500-1,000,000

Historical Note

Purpose is to advance the field of Therapeutic Recreation as an effective and efficient component of health care. Membership: $95/year (individual), $275/year (company).

Publications:

Annual in Therapeutic Recreation. a.
Employment Update. m. adv.
Newsletter. bi-m. adv.

Meetings/Conferences:

Semi-Annual Meetings: Spring and Fall
1999 – Portland, OR

American Thoracic Soc. *(1905)*

1740 Broadway, 14th Floor
New York, NY   10019-4374
Tel: (212)315-8778   *Fax:* (212)315-6498
Web Site: http://www.thoracic.org
Members: 13,500 individuals
Staff: 35
Annual Budget: $5-10,000,000
Exec. Director: Carl Booberg
Manager, Educational Programs: Francine Comi

Historical Note

Founded in 1905 as the American Sanatorium Ass'n. Became the American Trudeau Soc. in 1939. In 1960 the name was changed to the American Thoracic Soc. Acts as the medical section of the American Lung Ass'n. Has an annual budget of approximately $9.6 million.

Publications:

American Journal of Respiratory and Critical Care Medicine.
        m. adv.
American Journal of Respiratory Cell and Molecular Biology.
        m. adv.
ATS News. m.

Meetings/Conferences:

Annual Meetings: Spring, with the American Lung Ass'n
1999 – San Diego, CA/April 23-28
2000 – Toronto, ON, Canada/May 5-10

American Thoroughbred Breeders Alliance *(1989)*

Historical Note

Organization disbanded in 1995.

American Thyroid Ass'n *(1923)*

Montefiore Medical Center
111 East 210th St.
Bronx, NY   10467
Tel: (718)882-6047   *Fax:* (718)882-6085
E-Mail: admin@thyroid.org
Web Site: http://www.thyroid.org
Members: 741 individuals
Staff: 3
Annual Budget: $250-500,000
Secretary: Martin I. Surks, M.D.
Director, Meetings and Operations: Diane Miller

Historical Note

Founded as the American Ass'n for the Study of Goiter, it became the American Goiter Ass'n in 1948 and assumed its present name in 1959. ATA is a professional organization of physicians and scientists dedicated to treatment and education regarding thyroid function and disease. Membership: $80/year (basic dues), $175/year (dues plus journal).

Publications:

Annual Meeting Program Book. a.
Newsletter. q.
Thyroid, A Journal. q. adv.

Meetings/Conferences:

1999 – Palm Beach, FL
2000 – Japan
2001 – Washington, DC

American Tin Trade Ass'n *(1928)*

P.O. Box 53
Richboro, PA   18954
Tel: (215)504-9725   *Fax:* (215)504-9726
Members: 60 companies
Annual Budget: $10-25,000
Secretary: K. Salberg

Historical Note

Membership: $300/year.

Meetings/Conferences:

Semi-Annual Meetings: New York, NY/second Thursday in
        May and second Thursday in November/60

American Tinnitus Ass'n *(1971)*

P.O. Box 5
Portland, OR   97207-0005
Toll Free: (800)634 - 8978
E-Mail: tinnitus@ata.org
Web Site: http://www.ata.org
Members: 21,000 individuals
Staff: 7
Annual Budget: $500-1,000,000
Exec. Director: Gloria E. Reich, Ph.D.

Historical Note

Physicians, audiologists, hearing aid dispensers and individuals who suffer from tinnitus, noises in the head or ears. ATA supports tinnitus research, provides information and referral to professionals and support groups, conducts seminars for hearing professionals. Promotes public education regarding tinnitus. Membership: $25/year; $35/year (outside U.S.).

Publications:

Tinnitus Today. q.

Meetings/Conferences:

Annual Meetings: July

American Tort Reform Ass'n *(1986)*

1850 M St., N.W., Suite 1095

Washington, DC   20036
Tel: (202)682-1163   *Fax:* (202)682-1022
Toll Free: (800)306 - 2872
Web Site: http://www.atra.org
Members: 357 individuals
Staff: 7
Annual Budget: $2-5,000,000
President: Sherman Joyce
V. President and Dir., Legislative Affairs: Lissa M. Astilla
Exec. V. President: Diane K. Swenson

Historical Note

Members are individuals and organizations with a professional interest in the civil justice system.

Publications:

Leaders Update. bi-w.

Meetings/Conferences:

American Traffic Safety Services Ass'n *(1969)*

15 Riverside Parkway, Suite 100
Fredericksburg, VA   22406
Tel: (540)368-1701   *Fax:* (540)368-1701
E-Mail: general@atssa.com
Web Site: http://www.atssa.com
Members: 1,500 companies
Staff: 25
Annual Budget: $2-5,000,000
Exec. Director: Roger Wentz
Director, Training & Education: Michael Ireland
Manager, Government Relations: Robert Dingess
Director, Meetings & Conventions: Melanie Myers
Training Course Manager: Donna M. Clark
Director, Finance and Administration: Sandy Dayton
Director, Member Services: Douglas Curtis
Director, Chapter Relations: David McKee

Historical Note

Founded as the American Traffic Safety Control Devices Ass'n. Became the American Traffic Services Ass'n in 1971 and assumed its present name in 1984. Members are companies providing traffic control and safety devices to government and industry. Membership: $60/year (individual); $750/year minimum (organization/company).

Publications:

ATSSA Bulletin. irreg.
ATSSA Flash. a.
ATSSA Membership Directory. a.
ATSSA Signal. q.

Meetings/Conferences:

Annual Meetings: Winter
1999 – San Antonio, TX(Convention Center)/Feb. 14-16

American Train Dispatchers Ass'n *(1917)*

1370 Ontario St., Suite 1040
Cleveland, OH   44113-1701
Tel: (216)241-2770   *Fax:* (216)241-6286
E-Mail: afdabnfe@aol.com
Members: 2,600 individuals
Staff: 5
Annual Budget: $1-2,000,000
President: W. A. Clifford

Historical Note

First organized as a local union in Spokane, Washington on November 1, 1917. Shortly developed into the Western Train Dispatchers' Association and, before the end of 1918, The American Train Dispatchers Association was formed. Chartered by AFL-CIO in 1957. Affiliated with the Brotherhood of Locomotive Engineers in 1993. Membership: $678/year (individual).

Publications:

The Train Dispatcher 6/yr.

Meetings/Conferences:

Quadrennial Meetings: Fall (1995)

American Trakehner Ass'n *(1974)*

1520 W. Church St.
Newark, OH   43055
Tel: (740)344-1111   *Fax:* (740)344-3225
E-Mail: atahorses@aol.com
Members: 1,400 individuals
Staff: 3
Annual Budget: $100-250,000
General Manager: Charee L. Adams

Historical Note

Members are owners and breeders of Trakehner horses, a breed originating in Trakehnen, East Prussia in 1732. Membership: $65/year(individual); $650/year(lifetime member).

Publications:

American Trakehner. q. adv.
Handbook. a.
Newsletter.

Meetings/Conferences:

Annual Meetings: Fall

American Translators Ass'n *(1959)*

1800 Diagonal Road, Suite 220
Alexandria, VA   22314-2840
Tel: (703)683-6100   *Fax:* (703)683-6122
E-Mail: ata@atanet.org
Web Site: http://www.atanet.org
Members: 7,000 individuals
Staff: 8
Annual Budget: $1-2,000,000
Exec. Director: Walter W. Bacak, Jr.

Historical Note

Members are translators and interpreters. Has a testing and accreditation program. Membership: $95/year (individual), $120/year (institution); $175/year (corporate); $50/year (student).

Publications:

ATA Chronicle. m. adv.
Membership Directory. a.

Proceedings. a.
Translation Services Directory. a. adv.
Translator & Interpreter Training in the U. S.

Meetings/Conferences:
Annual Meetings: Fall
1999 – St. Louis, MO(Regal Riverfront)/1200
2000 – Orlando, FL(Buena Vista)/1300
2001 – Los Angeles, CA

American Trauma Soc. *(1968)*
8903 Presidential Pkwy., Suite 512
Upper Marlboro, MD   20772-2656
Tel: (301)420-4189   *Fax:* (301)420-0617
Toll Free: (800)556 - 7890
Members: 3,000 individuals
Staff: 5
Annual Budget: $1-2,000,000
Exec. Director: Harry Teter
Coordinator, Public Relations: JJ Kunkle
Office Administrator: Diana Colomo

Historical Note
Dedicated to reducing needless death and disability through public awareness/education on trauma system development and trauma prevention. Membership includes both lay and professional individuals, institutions, and corporations. Membership: $35/year (general member); $145 year/physician, $250/year sustaining and $2500 for lifetime membership.

Publications:
Promotional Media Resource Catalog. q.
Traumagram. q.

Meetings/Conferences:
Annual Meetings: May, in Washington, DC
1999 – Arlington, VA(Key Bridge Marriott)/April 29-May 1

American Truck Dealers *(1970)*
8400 Westpark Drive
McLean, VA   22102
Tel: (703)821-7116
Members: 2,000 companies
Director: James H. Westlake
Asst. Director: Eileen Boeing

Historical Note
A division of Nat'l Automobile Dealers Ass'n, ATD represents medium and heavy truck dealers. ATD members share in NADA's programs, services and benefits and can take advantage of ATD 20 Groups, a performance-based business forum for truck dealers.

Publications:
American Truck Dealer. m.

Meetings/Conferences:
1999 – San Diego, CA(Marriott)/April 10-13

American Truck Stop Operators Ass'n *(1981)*
P.O. Box 4949
Winston-Salem, NC   27115-4949
Tel: (910)744-5555   *Fax:* (910)744-1184
Members: 800 companies
Staff: 6
Annual Budget: $500-1,000,000
President: Lloyd L. Golding

Historical Note
Trade association of full facility truck stop operators. Membership: $500/year.

Publications:
Bulletin. m.

American Trucking Ass'ns *(1933)*
2200 Mill Road
Alexandria, VA   22314-4677
Tel: (703)838-1700   *Fax:* (703)684-5751
Web Site: www.trucking.org
Members: 4,200 associations & companies
Staff: 290
Annual Budget: $25-50,000,000
President and C.E.O.: Walter B. McCormick, Jr.
Director, Legislation Programs: Elisabeth A. Barna
Sr. V.P., Government Affairs: James B. Whittingbill
Sr. V. President, Government Affairs: John J. Collins
V.President, Conventions & Meeting Services: Julie Prazmark
V. President, Internat. Affairs: Linda Darr
V. President, Marketing: Samuel H. Gill
V. President Membership: Gene Pentimonti
Director, Member Services: Bonnie E. Cosby, NAFC
Director, Membership Operations: Richard Ware
Senior V. President, Federation Relations: Paul T. Stalknecht

Historical Note
A federation of state trucking associations, national truck conferences and individual motor carrier companies and suppliers. Formed by a merger of the American Highway Freight Ass'n and the Federated Truck Ass'ns of America. Sponsors and supports the political action committee TRUCK-PAC. The American Movers Conference is an afiliate of ATA. Has a budget of approximately $35 million.

Publications:
Financial & Operating Statistics: Annual Report. a.
Financial & Operating Statistics: Quarterly Report. q.
Government Traffic Bulletin. w.
Interstate Information Report. m.
Monthly Truck Tonnage Report. m.
Motor Carrier Professional Services Directory. a. adv.
Transport Topics. w. adv.
Trucking Safely. m. adv.
Trucksource: Sources of Trucking Industry Information. a.
Weekly Truck Tonnage Report. w.

Meetings/Conferences:
Annual Meetings: Fall/4,000

American Tube Ass'n/FMA *(1979)*

Historical Note
Merged with TPF/FMA to become TPA, The Tube and Pipe Ass'n, Internat'l in 1996.

American Tunaboat Ass'n *(1921)*
1 Tuna Lane
San Diego, CA   92101
Tel: (619)233-6405
Members: 25 companies
Staff: 4
Annual Budget: $250-500,000
President: Julius Zolezzi

Historical Note
Established as the American Fisherman's Protective Ass'n, ATA has also been known as American Fisherman's Tunaboat Ass'n (1929) and American Tunaboat Ass'n (1947). Sponsors the American Tunaboat Association Political Action Committee.

Publications:
Newsletter. irreg.

Meetings/Conferences:
Annual Meetings: December

American Turpentine Farmers Ass'n Co-op *(1936)*

Historical Note
Address unknown in 1996.

American Underground-Construction Ass'n *(1976)*
511 11th Ave. South, Suite 248
Minneapolis, MN   55415
Tel: (612)339-5403   *Fax:* (612)339-3207
Web Site: http://www.auca.org
Members: 700 individuals and firms
Staff: 2
Annual Budget: $100-250,000
Exec. Director: Susan R. Nelson

Historical Note
Formerly (1994) American Underground-Space Ass'n. Membership consists of owners, engineers, architects, planners, developers, contractors, equipment/materials manufacturers and others interested in the development of underground infrastructure and commercial, industrial, residential, and transport structures. Membership: $70/year (individual), $500/year (company/institution).

Publications:
AUA News. q. adv.

Meetings/Conferences:
2000 – Boston, MA(Boston Marriott)/June 6-11/500

American Urogynecologic Soc. *(1979)*
401 N. Michigan Ave.
Chicago, IL   60611
Tel: (312)644-6610   *Fax:* (312)527-6640
E-Mail: AUGS@sba.com
Members: 730 individuals
Staff: 4
Annual Budget: $500-1,000,000
Exec. Director: Deene Alongi
Convention Manager: Paul Pendola
Administrative Assistant: Chris Gephart

Historical Note
Membership: $230/year (individual).

Publications:
Quarterly Report. q.

Meetings/Conferences:
Annual Meetings: Fall/450-500
1999 – San Diego, CA(Hyatt Regency)/Oct. 13-17
2000 – Hilton Head, SC(Hyatt Regency)/Oct. 26-29

American Urological Ass'n *(1902)*
1120 N. Charles St.
Baltimore, MD   21201
Tel: (410)727-1100   *Fax:* (410)223-4370
E-Mail: aua@auanet.org
Web Site: http://www.auanet.org
Members: 10,200 individuals
Staff: 69
Annual Budget: $10-25,000,000
Exec. Director: G. James Gallagher
Director, Health Policy Department: Megan Cohen
Director, Conventions and Committee Affairs: Melanie Younger
Director, Finance: Mike Sheppard
Member Services Manager: Barbara Friedman
Director, Information Technology: Steve Burgess

Historical Note
Founded in 1902 and incorporated in Maryland. Has an annual budget of $12 million. Membership: $350/year.

Publications:
AUA News. m. adv.
Health Policy Brief. m.
Journal of Urology. m. adv.

Meetings/Conferences:
Annual Meetings: Spring/14,000
1999 – Dallas, TX(Convention Center/Loews
          Anatole)/May 1-6
2000 – Atlanta, GA(World congress center)/April 29-May 4
2001 – Anaheim, CA(Convention Center)/April 13-18

American Urological Ass'n Allied

Historical Note
Became (1995) Soc. of Urologic Nurses and Associates.

American Vacuum Soc. *(1953)*
120 Wall St., 32nd Floor
New York, NY   10005
Tel: (212)248-0200   *Fax:* (212)248-0245
Toll Free: (800)888 - 1021
E-Mail: avsnyc@vacuum.org

Web Site: http://www.vacuum.org
Members: 6,000 individuals
Staff: 7
Annual Budget: $2-5,000,000
Administrative Director: Yvonne Towse

Historical Note
Established in 1953 as the Committee on Vacuum Techniques. Incorporated in Massachusetts in the same year. Became the American Vacuum Soc. in 1958. A member of the American Institute of Physics, and affiliated with the Internat'l Union for Vacuum Science, Techniques and Applications. Membership: $75/year.

Publications:
Journal of Vacuum Science & Technology A. bi-m. adv.
Journal of Vacuum Science & Technology B. bi-m. adv.
Surface Science Spectra. bi-q.

Meetings/Conferences:
Annual Meetings: Fall
1999 – Seattle, WA/Oct. 25-29

American Venereal Disease Ass'n

Historical Note
Became (1996) American Sexually Transmitted Diseases Ass'n.

American Venous Forum
13 Elm St.
Manchester, MA   01944
Tel: (978)526-8330   *Fax:* (978)526-8330
E-Mail: avf@prri.com
Web Site: http://www.venous-info.com
Staff: 1
Exec. Director: Kevin M. Cuff

Meetings/Conferences:
1999 – Dana Point, CA(Marriott Laguna)

American Veterinary Dental Soc. *(1976)*
530 Church St., Suite 700
Nashville, TN   37219
Tel: (208)344-0194   *Fax:* (208)344-7333
Toll Free: (800)332 - 2837
Members: 1,200 individuals, 25 companies
Annual Budget: $25-50,000
Secretary: Carol Barnett

Historical Note
AVDS provides a common meeting ground and learning forum for those interested in veterinary dentistry with the objectives of furthering the knowledge and recognition of the importance of veterinary dentistry among practicing veterinarians, students of veterinary medicine and the general public. Membership: $60/year (individual).

Publications:
Journal of Veterinary Dentistry. q. adv.

Meetings/Conferences:
Annual Meetings: April

American Veterinary Distributors Ass'n *(1976)*
106 West 11th St., Suite 1200
Kansas City, MO   64105-1806
Tel: (816)221-5909   *Fax:* (816)842-2603
E-Mail: fries@qni.com
Web Site: avda.org
Members: 75 companies
Annual Budget: $100-250,000
Exec. Director: James L. Fries

Historical Note
AVDA members are distributors of animal healthcare products. Associate members are manufacturers.

Publications:
AVDA Distrubutor Newsletter. q.

Meetings/Conferences:
Annual Meetings: January-February

American Veterinary Exhibitors Ass'n *(1936)*
3831 N.E. Kincaid
Topeka, KS   66617-3628
Tel: (785)286-2996   *Fax:* (785)286-2996
Members: 100 companies
Annual Budget: $25-50,000
Exec. Director: James L. Fries

Historical Note
Members are firms which exhibit at veterinary meetings. Membership: $250/year.

Publications:
Newsletter. q.
Schedule of Veterinary Conventions. a.

Meetings/Conferences:
Annual Meetings: July, with the American Veterinary Medical Ass'n
1999 – N. American Veterinary Conference

American Veterinary Medical Ass'n *(1863)*
1931 N. Meacham Road, Suite 100
Schaumburg, IL   60173-4360
Tel: (847)925-8070   *Fax:* (847)925-1329
Web Site: http://www.avma.org
Members: 61,259 individuals
Staff: 114
Annual Budget: $10-25,000,000
Exec. V. President: Dr. Bruce Little
Director of Public Information: Michael E. Walters
Convention Manager: Dr. Cynthia L. Coursen
Director, Education & Research: Donald G. Simmons, DVM
Direcctor, Business: D.H. Murawski
Director, Membership: Karen M. Wernette, DVM
Editor-in-Chief & Director, Publications: Janis H. Audin, DVM
Director, Scientific Activities Division: Lyle Vogel, DVM
Assistant Exec. V. President: Arthur V. Tennyson, VMD

Historical Note
Founded in 1863 as the United States Veterinary Medical Ass'n, the name became American Veterinary Medical Ass'n in 1898. Incorporated in Illinois in 1917. Sponsors the American Veterinary Medical Foundation and the American Veterinary Medical Association Political Action Committee. Membership: $200/year (individual).

Publications:
American Journal of Veterinary Research. m. adv.
Journal of AVMA. semi-m. adv.

Meetings/Conferences:
Annual Meetings: July-August
1999 – New Orleans, LA/July 10-14
2000 – Salt Lake City, UT/July 22-26
2001 – Boston, MA/July 14-18

American Veterinary Soc. of Animal Behavior (1975)
201 Cedar Brook
Naperville, IL 60565
E-Mail: martinala@juno.com
Members: 600 individuals
Annual Budget: $10-25,000
Secretary-Treasurer: Dr. Laurie Martin

Historical Note
Formerly the American Soc. of Veterinary Ethology. Membership restricted to veterinarians, veterinary students, and animal behavior consultants. Has no paid staff. Membership: $40/year (full member); $7.50/year (student).

Publications:
Newsletter. q.

Meetings/Conferences:
Annual Meetings: in conjunction with American Veterinary Medical Ass'n
1999 – New Orleans, LA

American Vintners Ass'n (1978)
1200 G St., N.W., Suite 360
Washington, DC 20005
Tel: (202)783-2756   Fax: (202)347-6341
Toll Free: (800)879 - 4537
E-Mail: AVAAVA@aol.com
Members: 525 individuals
Staff: 4
Annual Budget: $250-500,000
President: Simon Siegl
V. President: Bill Nelson

Historical Note
Formerly (1992) the Ass'n of American Vintners. Members are wine producers.

Meetings/Conferences:
1999 – Washington, DC/March 15-16

American Vocational Ass'n (1926)
1410 King St.
Alexandria, VA 22314
Tel: (703)683-3111   Fax: (703)683-7424
Toll Free: (800)826 - 9972
E-Mail: avahq@avaonline.org
Web Site: http://www.avaonline.org
Members: 38,000 individuals
Staff: 40
Annual Budget: $2-5,000,000
Exec. Director: Bret D. Lovejoy
Asst. Exec. Director, Communications: Paul Plawin
Asst. Exec. Director, Govt. Relations: Nancy O'Brien
Director, Meetings: Julia Richardson
Manager of Trade Shows: Kristen Anderson
Meeting Planner: Elaine Adams
Asst. Exec. Director, Professional Development: Patricia Schwallie-Giddis, Ph.D.
Asst. Director, Membership: Don Reindhart
Assistant Exec. Director: Michael Shifflett

Historical Note
Founded in 1906 as the Nat'l Soc. for the Promotion of Industrial Education. Name changed in 1918 to the Nat'l Soc. for Vocational Education. Merged in 1925 with the Vocational Ass'n of the Middle West to form the American Vocational Ass'n and incorporated in Indiana in 1929. A federation of state vocational ass'ns. The Nat'l Ass'n of State Supervisors of Home Economics Education is a division of AVA. Membership: $40/year (individual).

Publications:
School-to-Work Reporter. m.
Techniques. 8/year. adv.
Vocational Education Weekly.

Meetings/Conferences:
Annual Meetings: December/8,000-10,000
1999 – Orlando, FL/Dec. 12-15

American Vocational Education Personnel Development Ass'n (1972)
P.O. Box 232
39 Bank St.
Chatham, VA 24531
Tel: (804)432-2761
Members: 250 individuals
Annual Budget: under $10,000
President: Lillian H. Daughtry, Ph.D.

Publications:
AVEPDA Review Newsletter. q.
Directory. a.

Meetings/Conferences:
Annual Meetings: in conjunction with the American Vocational Ass'n/December

American Vocational Education Research Ass'n (1966)
Univ. Of Georgia, 225 Rivers Crossing
850 College Station Rd
Athens, GA 30602-4809
Tel: (706)542-4078   Fax: (706)542-4054

Web Site: http://www.coe.uga.edu/occstudies/AVERA
Members: 500 individuals
Annual Budget: under $10,000
President: Dr. Wanda Stitt-Gohdes

Historical Note
Affiliated with the American Vocational Ass'n. Membership: $20/year (regular); $5/year (student).

Publications:
The Beacon. q.
The Journal of Vocational Education Research. q.

Meetings/Conferences:
Annual Meetings: Winter, with the American Vocational Ass'n

American Volleyball Coaches Ass'n (1981)
1227 Lake Plaza Dr., Suite B
Colorado Springs, CO 80906-7402
Tel: (719)576-7777   Fax: (719)576-7778
E-Mail: svivas@avca.org
Web Site: http://www.avca.org
Members: 3,100 individuals
Staff: 9
Annual Budget: $250-500,000
Exec. Director: Sandra L. Vivas
Dir., Informational Services: Kinda Asher
Director, Membership Services: Vivian Langley

Historical Note
AVCA is comprised of coaches from all levels who are committed to the development and advancement of volleyball throughout America. Membership: $50-$125/year (individual).

Publications:
American Volleyball. 12/year. adv.
AVCA Membership Directory. a. adv.
Coaching Volleyball. 6/year. adv.
Power Tips. m.
Volleyball Records Book. a.

Meetings/Conferences:
Annual Meetings: December
1999 – Honolulu, HI/Dec. 14-18
2000 – San Diego, CA/Dec. 19-23
2001 – Richmond, VA/Dec. 18-22

American Walnut Manufacturers Ass'n (1912)
P.O. Box 5046
Zionsville, IN 46077-5046
Tel: (317)873-8780   Fax: (317)873-8788
E-Mail: FhvaAwmaWc@CompuServe.com
Members: 10 companies
Staff: 1
Annual Budget: $10-25,000
Exec. Director: Larry R. Frye

Historical Note
First organized in 1912. AWMA is an international trade association representing manufacturers of walnut and other fine hardwood, lumber, dimension lumber, veneer, squares and gunstock blanks.

Meetings/Conferences:
Annual Meetings: Annual luncheon held in conjunction w/ the Nat'l Hardwood Lumber Ass'n

American Warehouse Ass'n (1891)

Historical Note
Became the Internat'l Warehouse Logistics Ass'n in 1997.

American Warmblood Registry (1981)
P.O. Box 127
Davis, CA 95617
Tel: (530)757-1377   Fax: (530)756-0892
E-Mail: sonjakl@aol.com
Web Site: http://www.americanwarmblood.com
Staff: 4
Annual Budget: $250-500,000
Exec. Director: Sonja K. Lowenfish

Historical Note
Members are owners and breeders of Warmblood horses. Membership: $70/year.

Publications:
Directory of Stallions at Stud. a.
Internet-with monthly upgrades of news. adv. adv.
Warmblood News Magazine. bi-m. adv.

Meetings/Conferences:

American Watch Ass'n (1933)
Box 464
Washington, DC 20044-0464
Tel: (703)759-3377
Members: 45 companies
Staff: 2
Annual Budget: $100-250,000
Exec. Director: Emilio G. Collado, III

Historical Note
Founded as the American Watch Assemblers Ass'n, it assumed its present name in 1951. Members are importers of watch and clock movements and cases; domestic manufacturers and assemblers.

Meetings/Conferences:
Annual Meetings: New York, NY/March

American Watchmakers-Clockmakers Institute (1960)
701 Enterprise Dr.
Harrison, OH 45030
Tel: (513)367-9800   Fax: (513)367-1414
Members: 6,300 individuals and institutions
Staff: 6
Annual Budget: $500-1,000,000
Exec. Director: William J. Ewbank
General Manager: Nancy Wellamn
Education & Technical Director: James E. Lubic

Historical Note
Formed by the merger of Horological Institute of America and United Horological Ass'n of America as the American Watchmakers Institute, it adopted its present name in 1992. Offers correspondence courses and bench courses in clockmaking, watchmaking, and micro-electronics for watches, and an examination and certification program for master watchmakers and clockmakers. Membership: $45/year.

Publications:
Horological Times. m.

Meetings/Conferences:

American Water Resources Ass'n (1964)
950 Herndon Pkwy., Suite 300
Herndon, VA 20170-5531
Tel: (703)904-1225   Fax: (703)904-1228
E-Mail: awrahq@aol.com
Members: 4,400 individuals
Staff: 5
Annual Budget: $500-1,000,000
Exec. V. President: Kenneth D. Reid, CAE
Director of Finance: Michael J. Kowalski
Director, Membership Services: Kerry L. Curtis
Dir. of Publications Production: Charlene E. Young

Historical Note
Incorporated in Illinois in March 1964, AWRA is a multidisciplinary non-profit scientific, educational association dedicated to the advancement of research, planning, management, development and education in water resources. Member society of the Renewable Natural Resources Foundation. Membership includes engineers, hydrologists, biologists, attorneys, chemists and social scientists. Membership: $120/year (individual), $325/year (company).

Publications:
Journal of the AWRA. bi-m.
Membership Directory. a.
Proceedings. a.
Water Resources Impact. bi-m.

Meetings/Conferences:
1999 – Seattle, WA/Dec. 4-9

American Water Works Ass'n (1881)
6666 W. Quincy Ave.
Denver, CO 80235-3098
Tel: (303)794-7711   Fax: (303)795-1989
Web Site: http://awwa.org
Members: 49,500 individuals, 4,800 organizations
Staff: 130
Annual Budget: $10-25,000,000
Exec. Director: Jack Hoffbuhr
Director, Communications and Marketing: Stephen Lewis
Chief Information Officer: Roberta Herman
Director, Legislative Affairs: Albert E. Warburton
Director of Meetings: Darline Daley, CMP
Director, Technical & Education: David Rossiter
Director, Sectiona and Educational Support: Paula Macilwaine
Director, Finance: Sylvia Luyten
C.F.O.: Linda Laskey
Director, Publishing: Monia Joda Baruth
Director, Customer Service: Suzanne Andrew
Director, Volunteer and Technical Support: Ed Baruth

Historical Note
Organized at Washington University, St. Louis, on March 29, 1881 and incorporated in Illinois in 1912. Has an annual budget of approximately $20 million. Membership: $90/year (individual); organizational fee varies by size.

Publications:
Journal. m. adv.
MainStream. m. adv.
Opflow. m.
WaterWeek. faxed newsletter.

Meetings/Conferences:
Annual Meetings: June
1999 – Chicago, IL/June 20-24
2000 – Denver, CO/June 11-15

American Waterways Operators (1944)
1600 Wilson Blvd., Suite 1000
Arlington, VA 22209-2597
Tel: (703)841-9300   Fax: (703)841-0389
Members: 375 companies
Staff: 22
Annual Budget: $2-5,000,000
President: Thomas A. Allegretti
Director, Public Affairs: Karen Coltrane
V. President, Legislative Affairs: John A. Moran
V. President, Government Affairs: Jennifer A. Kelly
C.F.O. and Senior V. President: Lee H. Hill
Manager. Member Services/Administration: Holly Fleming

Historical Note
Members include domestic carriers transporting commodities by water, shipyards, terminals, and affiliated businesses. Works to preserve the coastal and inland commercial navigable waterways system and promote waterborne transportation. Supports the American Waterways Operators PAC.

Publications:
Annual Report. a.
AWO Letter. bi-w.

Meetings/Conferences:

American Waterways Shipyard Conference (1976)
Historical Note
Became the Nat'l Shipyard Ass'n in 1997.

American Welara Pony Soc. (1981)
P.O. Box 401
Yucca Valley, CA 92286-0401
Tel: (760)364-2048   Fax: (760)364-2048
Members: 361 individuals, 3 organizations

Staff: 4
Annual Budget: under $10,000
Registrar: John H. Collins

Historical Note
AWPS was established to collect, record and preserve the pedigrees of Welara ponies (a cross of Arabian horse with Welsh pony), to publish a stud book, and to stimulate all other matters such as may pertain to the history, breeding, exhibiting, publicity, sale and improvement of the breed throughout the world. *Membership:* $16/year (individual); $28/year (organization).

Publications:
Registry Stud Book. bien. adv.
Welara Journal. semi-a. adv.

Meetings/Conferences:
Annual Meetings: late Spring/150
1999 – Portland, OR

American Welding Institute (1983)
Historical Note
Organization defunct in 1997.

American Welding Soc. (1919)
550 N.W. LeJeune Road
Miami, FL   33126
Tel: (305)443-9353   *Fax:* (305)443-7559
Toll Free: (800)443 - 9353
E-Mail: info@amweld.org
Web Site: http://www.amweld.org
Members: 49,000 individuals
Staff: 105
Annual Budget: $10-25,000,000
Exec. Director: Dr. Frank G. De Laurier, CAE
Director, Corporate Communications: Nannette Zapata
Managing Director, Technical Services: Charles R. Fassinger
Managing Director, Professional Services: Wendy Sue Reeve
Managing Director, Member/Customer Svcs.: Cassie Burrell
Managing Director, Sales and Marketing: Richard L. Alley
Managing Director, Publication Services: Jeff D. Weber

Historical Note
Organized in March 1919 as an outgrowth of the Welding Committee of the Emergency Fleet Corporation, U.S. Shipping Board. Incorporated in New York in 1932. Annual budget is over $17 million. *Membership:* $65/year.

Publications:
Welding Journal. m. adv.

Meetings/Conferences:
Annual Meetings: Spring/20,000
1999 – St. Louis, MO/Apr. 18-22
2000 – Chicago, IL/Apr. 2-6

American White/American Creme Horse Registry (1936)
RR 1, Box 20
Naper, NE   68755-9707
Tel: (402)832-5560
Members: 200 individuals
Staff: 1
Annual Budget: under $10,000
Secretary-Treasurer: Carley Daugherty

Historical Note
Founded as the American Albino Horse Club in 1936, became American Albino Ass'n in 1964, and Internat'l American Albino Ass'n in 1985. The Ass'n does business as the American White/American Creme Horse Registry. Serves as a promotional agency for the registered breeds American White and American Creme. *Membership:* $15/year (domestic individual), $25/year (domestic family), $20/year (overseas individual), $30/year (overseas family).

Publications:
American White/American Creme Newsletter. q.
American White/American Creme Yearbook and Directory. a. adv.

Meetings/Conferences:
Annual Meetings: Naper, NE(White Horse Ranch)/Father's Day Weekend

American Wholesale Booksellers Ass'n (1984)
702 S. Michigan St.
South Bend, IN   46601
Tel: (219)232-8500   *Fax:* (303)265-9292
Members: 26 publishers, 27 associates
Staff: 3
Annual Budget: $10-25,000
Exec. Secretary: Patricia Walsh

Historical Note
Members are wholesale distributors for whom book sales constitute at least 75% of total sales. *Membership:* $250-600/year (depending on size).

Publications:
Directory of Members. a.
Handbook for Small Presses.
Newsletter. q.

Meetings/Conferences:

American Wholesale Marketers Ass'n (1945)
1128 16th St., N.W.
Washington, DC   20036-4808
Tel: (202)463-2124   *Fax:* (202)463-6467
Members: 2,400 organizations
Staff: 22
Annual Budget: $2-5,000,000
President and C.E.O.: David E. Strachan, CAE
V. President, Government & Public Affairs: Jacqueline A. Cohen
V. President, Conventions and Meetings: Dorothea L. Russell, CAE
Exec. Director, Distributors Education Foundation: Robin Lempert
V. President, Operations: James M. Turner, III
Manager, Information Systems: Ann Marie Bitler

Historical Note
Formed by the merger of the Nat'l Candy Wholesalers Ass'n and the Nat'l Ass'n of Tobacco Distributors in 1992. AWMA promotes the interests of the wholesale distributors of convenience products and unites the members of the wholesale industry for its common good. In 1994 AWMA absorbed the Nat'l Ass'n of Service Merchandising. *Membership:* $240-$2,500/year (company).

Publications:
Buying Guide and AWMA Membership Directory.
Distribution Channels. m. adv.
Legistatus. 8/year.
Quick Topics Newsletter. m.

Meetings/Conferences:
Semi-Annual Meetings: Winter and Summer/10,000
1999 – Boston, MA/July 15-17
1999 – Orlando, FL(Orange County Center)/Feb. 25-27

American Wind Energy Ass'n (1974)
122 C St., N.W., 4th Floor
Washington, DC   20001
Tel: (202)383-2500   *Fax:* (202)383-2505
E-Mail: windmail@awea.org
Web Site: http://www.IGC.APC.ORG/AWEA/
Members: 650 individuals, 200 companies
Staff: 14
Annual Budget: $2-5,000,000
Exec. Director: Randall S. Swisher
Communications Director: Thomas Gray
Director, Governmental Affairs: Jaime Steve
Director, Finance: Patricia Mills
Director, Internat'l Programs: Kevin Rackstraw
Director of Membership: Laura Keelan

Historical Note
The trade association for the wind energy industry, AWEA is composed of manufacturers of wind systems and components, siting equipment, wind farm developers, investors, utilities and others with an interest in wind energy. *Membership:* $50/year (individual), $200 (academic), $750 (associate), $1000-3,000 (utility), $1,000-35,000 (corporate).

Publications:
Annual Conference Proceedings. a.
AWEA Wind Energy Weekly. w.
Membership Directory. a.
Windletter. m.

Meetings/Conferences:
1999 – Burlington, VT
2000 – Palm Springs, CA

American Wine Soc. (1967)
3006 Latta Road
Rochester, NY   14612-3298
Tel: (716)225-7613   *Fax:* (716)225-7613
Members: 5,000 individuals
Staff: 3
Annual Budget: $250-500,000
Exec. Director: Angel E. Nardone

Historical Note
AWS members include professional and amateur wine growers, winemakers, distributors, retailers and others with an interest in American wines to the public. *Membership:* $58/year (professional); $36/year (individual).

Publications:
AWS Journal. q. adv.
AWS News Newsletter. q. adv.
Home Wine Information. a.

Meetings/Conferences:
1999 – E. Burnswick, NY(Hilton Hotel)/Nov. 10-13/600
2000 – Cleveland, OH/November 8-11/600

American Wire Cloth Institute (1933)
P.O. Box 1018
Ossining, NY   10562
Tel: (914)962-9052
Members: 25 companies
Staff: 2
Secretary: Peter M. Miranda

Historical Note
Formerly (1978) the Industrial Wire Cloth Institute.

American Wire Producers Ass'n (1981)
515 King St., Suite 420
Alexandria, VA   22314-3137
Tel: (703)549-6003   *Fax:* (703)684-6048
E-Mail: ejohnson@clarionmr.com
Web Site: www.awpa.org
Members: 104 companies
Staff: 5
Annual Budget: $250-500,000
Exec. Director: Kimberly A. Korbel
Government Relations Coordinator: David Woodbury
Dir., Member Services: Emily M. Johnson

Historical Note
Founded as the Independent Wire Drawers Ass'n, it became the Independent Wire Producers Ass'n in 1975 and assumed its present name in 1981 when it merged with the Specialty Wire Ass'n. Members are companies producing wire by drawing metal through a die.

Publications:
Import Report. q.
Wireline. bi-m.

Meetings/Conferences:
Annual Meetings: Winter
1999 – Marco Island, FL(Marriott)/Jan. 30-Feb. 3

American Woman's Soc. of Certified Public Accountants (1933)
401 N. Michigan Ave.
Chicago, IL   60611
Tel: (312)644-6610   *Fax:* (312)245-1081
Toll Free: (800)297 - 2721
Members: 4,000 individuals
Staff: 6
Annual Budget: $250-500,000
Exec. Director: Susan Oster

Historical Note
AWSCPA provides programs and opportunites for professional networking at meetings and seminars, through publications and other services. The Society works to advance the professional interests and careers of women certified public accountants and to build a national presence for women CPA's throughout the country. *Membership:* $75/year.

Publications:
AWSCPA Newsletter. q.
Issues Paper. a.
Membership Directory. a.
Network. semi-a.

Meetings/Conferences:

American Women Composers (1970)
Historical Note
Became Internat'l Alliance of Women in Music in 1995.

American Women in Radio and Television (1951)
1650 Tysons Blvd., Suite 200
McLean, VA   22102
Tel: (703)506-3290   *Fax:* (703)506-3266
Members: 2,800 individuals
Staff: 4
Annual Budget: $250-500,000
Exec. Director: Terri Dickerson-Jones

Historical Note
Prior to 1951 a group known as the Ass'n of Women Broadcasters was an adjunct to the Nat'l Ass'n of Radio and Television Broadcasters, the predecessor to the Nat'l Ass'n of Broadcasters. AWB was discontinued in October, 1950. The present organization was established at the Hotel Astor in New York, April 6-8, 1951 and consists of individuals in numerous job categories in the radio-TV industry and its affiliated or supporting organizations. The Foundation of American Women in Radio and Television is an educational subsidiary. *Membership:* $115/year.

Publications:
Convention Program. a. adv.
Gracie Allen Awards Program. a adv. adv.
Membership Directory. a. adv.
News & Views. bi-m.
Women On The Job: Careers In The Electronic Media.

Meetings/Conferences:
Annual Meetings: late Spring
1999 – Chicago, IL(Drake)
2000 – Atlanta, GA

American Wood Chip Export Ass'n (1974)
c/o Stoel, Rives LLP
900 S.W. Fifth Ave., Suite 2600
Portland, OR   97204
Tel: (503)294-9507   *Fax:* (503)220-2480
Members: 5 companies
Staff: 1
Annual Budget: under $10,000
Secretary and Counsel: David P. Miller

Historical Note
A Webb-Pomerene Act association.

American Wood Council (1968)
Historical Note
A product group of the American Forests and Paper Ass'n.

American Wood Preservers Institute (1921)
2750 Prosperity Ave., Suite 550
Fairfax, VA   22031-4312
Tel: (703)204-0500   *Fax:* (703)204-4610
Toll Free: (800)356 - 2974
Web Site: http://www.awpi.org
Members: 111 companies
Staff: 6
Annual Budget: $1-2,000,000
President & CEO: Scott Ramminger
Manager, Communications: Sarah Ely
Manager, Legislative and Public Affairs: Anne Holloway
Director, Environmental and Regulatory Affairs: George Parris, Ph.D.
Membership/Meeting Coordinator: Tonja Tate-Taylor
Coordinator, Office and Publications: Nancy Melby

Historical Note
The government relations and environmental affairs arm of the wood preserving industry. Members are wood treating companies, manufacturers and formulators of wood preserving chemicals, and related industry suppliers and manufacturers.

Publications:
American Wood Preserver. bi.
AWPI letter. bi-m.

Meetings/Conferences:
Annual Meetings: October-November

American Wood-Preservers' Ass'n (1904)
P.O. Box 5690
Granbury, TX   76049
Tel: (817)326-6300   *Fax:* (817)326-6306
E-Mail: awpa@itexas.net
Web Site: http://www.awpa.com
Members: 1,200 individuals
Staff: 2
Annual Budget: $100-250,000
Exec. V. President: John Hall

Historical Note
The American Wood-Preserves' Association is an international, nonprofit, technical society founded in 1904 to provide a common forum for exchange of information for all segments of the industry.

The Association provides a link for technical interchange between industry, research and users of treated wood. Membership: $95/year.

Publications:
AWPA Book of Standards. a.
AWPA Proceedings. a. adv.

Meetings/Conferences:
Annual Meetings: Spring
1999 – Ft. Lauderdale, FL(Marriott Harbor Beach)/May 16-19
2000 – San Francisco, CA(Sheraton Palace)/May 7-10
2001 – Minneapolis, MN

American Wool Council (1954)

Historical Note
A division of the American Sheep Industry Ass'n.

American Yarn Spinners Ass'n (1967)

P.O. Box 99
Gastonia, NC 28053
Tel: (704)824-3522　　　　　Fax: (704)824-0630
Members: 100 companies
Staff: 4
Annual Budget: $100-250,000
Exec. V. President: Jim H. Conner

Historical Note
Merger of Carded Yarn Ass'n (1936) and Combed Yarn Spinners (1908). Affiliated with the Ass'n of Synthetic Yarn Manufacturers and the Craft Yarn Council of America. Absorbed the Long Staple Yarn Ass'n in 1974, the Yarn Dyers Ass'n in 1976, the Carpet Yarn Ass'n in 1981, and the Ass'n of Synthetic Yarn Manufacturers, Inc. in 1988.

Meetings/Conferences:
Annual Meetings: Sea Island, GA(Cloisters)/September
1999 – Sea Island, GA(The Cloister)/Sept. 8-11/300
2000 – Sea Island, GA(The Cloister)/Sept. 6-9/300

American Yorkshire Club (1935)

Historical Note
Club merged with the Hampshire Swine Registry and the United Duroc Swine Registry in 1996 and is now under the title of Nat'l Swine Registry.

American Zinc Ass'n (1990)

1112 16th St., N.W., Suite 240
Washington, DC 20036
Tel: (202)835-0164　　　　　Fax: (202)835-0155
E-Mail: gvary@zinc.org
Web Site: http://www.zinc.org
Members: 18 companies
Staff: 1
Annual Budget: $250-500,000
Exec. Director: George F. Vary

Historical Note
AZA's mission is to promote the general welfare of the zinc industry; serve as a spokesgroup and information center for zinc; monitor environmental and other issues pertinent to the zinc industry. Members are producers of zinc metal, oxide and dust selling in the United States.

Publications:
Zinc Essentials. semi-a.

Meetings/Conferences:
1999 – Palm Springs, CA(Marriot Rancho Las Palmas)/Feb. 28-March 3/475
2000 – Scottsdale, AZ(Camelback)

American Zoo and Aquarium Ass'n (1924)

8403 Colesville Rd., Suite 710
Silver Spring, MD 20910
Tel: (301)567-0777　　　　　Fax: (301)562-0888
Web Site: http://www.aza.org
Members: 6,500 individuals, 180 institutions
Staff: 19
Annual Budget: $1-2,000,000
Exec. Director: Sydney J. Butler
Public Affairs Director: Jane Ballentine
Legislative Affairs Specialist: Rob Howarth
Deputy Director and Dir. Government Affairs: Kristin L. Vehrs
Director,Finance and Administration: Gerald O. Kennedy
General Manager: Linda Boyd
Development & Marketing Director: Robert Ramin
Director of Conservation & Science: Michael Hutchins, PhD
Associate Director of Development & Marketing: Colleen R. Kelly

Historical Note
Formerly a branch of the American Institute of Park Executives and the National Recreation and Park Ass'n, it became an independent organization in 1971 as American Ass'n of Zoological Parks and Aquariums; assumed its current name in 1994.

Publications:
Annual Conference Proceedings. a.
Communique. m. adv.
Zoological Parks & Aquariums in the Americas. (directory) bien. adv.

Meetings/Conferences:
Annual Meetings: September/1,500

American-European Soda Ash Shipping Ass'n (1991)

c/o Coudert Brothers
1114 6th Ave. of the Americas
New York, NY 10036
Tel: (212)626-4496　　　　　Fax: (212)626-4120
Members: 7 companies
Secretary: Charles H. Critchlow

Historical Note
AESSA members are producers of soda ash in the United States. A Webb-Pomerene Act association, AESSA promotes the export of U.S. natural soda ash to countries in the European community through the provision of joint storage, transportation and other related logistical and technical support.

American-Israel Chamber of Commerce and Industry (1953)

310 Madison Ave., Suite 1103
New York, NY 10017
Tel: (212)661-4106　　　　　Fax: (212)661-7930
Web Site: http://www.amisbusiness.com
Members: 300 individuals
Staff: 2
Annual Budget: $100-250,000
Exec. V. President: Ronny Bassan

Historical Note
A U.S. non-profit trade association whose purpose is to foster the growth and expansion of economic relations between the U.S. and Israel and to promote U.S. investment in Israel, Israeli exports to the U.S. and U.S. exports to Israel. Membership: $250/year (individual); $500/year (organization).

Meetings/Conferences:

American-Southern Africa Chamber of Trade and Industry (1966)

1080 Park Ave., Suite 4W
New York, NY 10128-1167
Tel: (212)410-6560
Director: Dr. Robert John

American-Uzbekistan Chamber of Commerce (1993)

1800 Massachusetts Ave., N.W., Suite 600
Washington, DC 20036
Tel: (202)828-4317　　　　　Fax: (202)659-7010
E-Mail: aucc@erols.com
Web Site: http://www.erols.com/aucc
Members: 65 Companies
Staff: 2
Annual Budget: $100-250,000
Exec. Director: Robert S. Pace

Historical Note
AUCC promotes trade and investment between the U.S. and Uzbekistan. Membership: $2,500/year.

Publications:
AUCC Business Digest. m.

Meetings/Conferences:
1999 – Tashkent(Intercontinental)

Americans for the Arts (1960)

1000 Vermont Ave., N.W., 12th Floor
Washington, DC 20005
Tel: (202)371-2830　　　　　Fax: (202)371-0424
Web Site: http://www.artsusa.org
Members: 1,200 organizations
Staff: 20
Annual Budget: $1-2,000,000
President and C.E.O.: Robert L. Lynch
Dir., Communications: Jennifer Neiman
V.P., Govt. Affairs/Development: Nina Ozlu
Director, Finance: R. Brent Stanley

Historical Note
Formerly the American Council for the Arts; merged with Nat'l Assembly of Local Arts Agencies and assumed its current name in 1996. One of the nation's primary sources of legislative news affecting all the arts and serves as a leading advisor to arts administrators, educators, elected officials and the general public. Maintains one of the most complete arts libraries outside the university system. Promotes thoughtful public debate in various national, state and local fora. Communicates as a publisher of books, journals, newsletters, and commissioned papers to foundations, corporations, educators, artists, and mangers of arts organizations. Active in support of arts in schools. Addresses needs of individual artist in areas such as copyright, funding, etc. Established as Community Arts Councils Inc., it became Arts Councils of America in 1965, Associated Councils of the Arts in 1966, and American Council for the Arts in 1977. Membership: $50/year.

Publications:
ArtsLink.

Meetings/Conferences:
Annual Meetings: Spring
1999 – Atlanta, GA(Hilton)/June 5-8

Amerifax Cattle Ass'n (1977)

P.O. Box 149
Hastings, NE 68902-0149
Tel: (402)463-5289　　　　　Fax: (402)463-6652
Members: 150 individuals
Staff: 1
Annual Budget: $25-50,000
Secretary: John Quirk

Historical Note
Promotes the Amerifax breed of cattle. Maintains a herd book. Membership: $20/year, $50 initiation fee.

Publications:
Amerifax News. q. adv.

Meetings/Conferences:
January in Denver, CO

AMT - The Ass'n for Manufacturing Technology (1902)

7901 Westpark Drive
McLean, VA 22102-4269
Tel: (703)893-2900　　　　　Fax: (703)893-1151
Web Site: http://www.mfgtech.org
Members: 60 companies
Staff: 65
Annual Budget: $10-25,000,000
President: Albert W. Moore
V. President, Administration: Janie Galloway

Historical Note
Formerly (1989) the Nat'l Machine Tool Builders Ass'n, assumed present name in 1992. Supports the Machine-Tool Political Action Committee. Has an annual budget of approximately $12 million.

Publications:
Directory of Member Products: Machine Tools/Manufacturing Machinery/Re.
Economic Handbook of Machine Tool Industry. a.

Meetings/Conferences:
Semi-Annual Meetings: Spring and Fall
1999 – Orlando, FL(Walt Disney World Resort)/Apr. 11-14

Amusement and Music Operators Ass'n (1948)

401 N. Michigan Ave., 24th Floor
Chicago, IL 60611-4267
Tel: (312)245-1021　　　　　Fax: (312)245-1085
Members: 1,700 companies
Staff: 6
Annual Budget: $1-2,000,000
Exec. Director: Marian Long Griffin

Historical Note
Established as the Music Operators of America, it assumed its present name in 1977. Members are companies making, servicing or selling coin operated amusement, music, and vending equipment.

Publications:
Location Newsletter. bi-m.

Meetings/Conferences:
Annual Meetings: Fall/8,000

Amusement Manufacturers and Suppliers Internat'l (1926)

6916 22nd St. West
Bradenton, FL 34207
Tel: (941)751-5474　　　　　Fax: (941)752-1033
Web Site: http://aimsintl.org
Members: 61 companies
Staff: 2
Annual Budget: $50-100,000

Historical Note
Formerly (1934) Manufacturers Division, Nat'l Ass'n of Amusement Parks and (1997) American Recreational Equipment Ass'n. Members are makers of rides, walk-throughs and other equipment and devices purchased by carnivals, circuses and amusement parks. Membership: $300/year (individual): $100/year (associate).

Publications:
News Line. q.

Meetings/Conferences:
Annual Meetings: November, with Internat'l Ass'n of Amusement Parks

Analytical and Life Science Sytems Ass'n (1988)

225 Reinekers Lane, Suite 625
Alexandria, VA 22314-2875
Tel: (703)836-1360　　　　　Fax: (703)836-6644
Web Site: http://www.alssa.org
Members: 85 companies
Staff: 3
Annual Budget: $500-1,000,000
Exec. Director: Michael J. Duff

Historical Note
Formerly (1997) Analytical Instrument Ass'n, ALSSA is the trade association for suppliers of instruments and system, including consumables, reagents, software and informational databases as they relate to life sciences used for chemical and life science analysis and measurement. ALSSA is an affiliate of the SAMA Group of Ass'ns. Membership: Annual dues are based on sales volume (company).

Publications:
Membership Directory & Annual Report. a.
On the Agenda. q.

Meetings/Conferences:
Semi-Annual Meetings: Spring and October/55-70

Analytical Instrument Ass'n (1988)

Historical Note
Became the Analytical and Life Science Systems Ass'n in 1997.

Analytical Laboratory Managers Ass'n (1980)

1201 Don Diego Ave.
Santa Fe, NM 87505
Tel: (505)989-4683　　　　　Fax: (505)989-1073
E-Mail: professional_assn_management@compuserve.com
Web Site:
　　　http://www.STU.edu/departments/shops/almahome.html
Members: 450 individuals
Staff: 1
Annual Budget: under $10,000
Exec. Secretary: Judith Sjoberg

Historical Note
Created to promote the exchange of information about management and operation of analytical laboratories. Members include university, industrial and government laboratories. Founded as the University Laboratory Managers Ass'n, ALMA assumed its present name in 1981.

Publications:
ALMA Bulletin. 3/year.

Meetings/Conferences:
Annual Meetings: Fall

Aniline Ass'n (1982)

1815 H St., N.W., Suite 500
Washington, DC 20006
Tel: (202)296-6300　　　　　Fax: (202)775-5929
Members: 6 companies
Staff: 3
Annual Budget: $25-50,000
General Counsel: Joseph E. Hadley, Jr.

Historical Note
Members are chemical companies producing and/or using aniline.

Animal Behavior Soc. (1964)

2611 East 10th St, Suite 170
Indiana University
Bloomington, IN   47408-2603
Tel: (812)856-5541   *Fax:* (812)856-5542
E-Mail: aboffice@indiana.edu
Web Site: http://animalbehavior.org
Members: 3,000 individuals
Staff: 2
Annual Budget: $50-100,000
Secretary: Susan A. Foster

Historical Note
Professionals and students involved in animal behavior research. Affiliated with the American Soc. of Zoologists. Membership: $46/year (individual); $23/year (student).

Publications:
Animal Behaviour. m.
Newsletter. q.

Meetings/Conferences:
1999 – Bloomington, IN(Buckwell University)/June 26-30

Animal Health Institute *(1941)*
1325 G St., N.W., Suite 700
Washington, DC   20005
Tel: (202)637-2440   *Fax:* (202)393-1667
Web Site: http://www.ahi.org
Members: 26 companies
Staff: 16
Annual Budget: $2-5,000,000
President: Alexander S. Mathews
V. President, Regulatory, Scientific and International Affairs: Richard A. Carnevale, VMD

Historical Note
AHI is the U.S. industry trade association representing the manufacturers of the veterinary pharmaceuticals, biologicals, feed additives and animal pesticides used in agriculture and veterinary medicine. Sponsors and supports the AHI Political Action Committee.

Publications:
AHI Quarterly. q.
Annual Report. a.
Congressional Directory. bien.
Membership Directory. a.
Resource Book. bien.

Meetings/Conferences:

Animal Transportation Ass'n *(1976)*
10700 Richmond Ave., Suite 201
Houston, TX   77042
Tel: (713)532-2177   *Fax:* (713)532-2166
E-Mail: aata@npscmgmt.com
Web Site: http://www.npscmgmt.com/aata
Members: 180 individuals, 375 companies
Staff: 1
Annual Budget: $50-100,000
Administrator: Dean Newton
Director, Member Services: Rebecca Turner

Historical Note
Members include: transport manufacturers, carriers, and shippers; animal welfare groups and breeders; zoos; and animal forwarders. Organized to improve conditions for safe transportation of animals by air, sea and ground travel. Formerly (1989) Animal Air Transportation Ass'n. Membership: $180/year (individual), $375/year (company).

Publications:
AATA Newsletter. q. adv.
Conference Program. a. adv.

Meetings/Conferences:
Annual Meetings: Spring
1999 – London, England/April 18-23

Ankole Watusi Internat'l Registry *(1983)*
22484 W. 239th St.
Spring Hill, KS   66083-9306
Tel: (913)592-4050
E-Mail: watusi@aol.com
Web Site: http://members.aol.com/Watusi/index.html
Members: 144 individuals
Staff: 1
Annual Budget: $10-25,000
Exec. Secretary: Dr. Elizabeth Lundgren

Historical Note
Incorporated in Colorado. Breeders and fanciers of African Ankole Watusi cattle. Maintains pedigree registry and sponsors full blood and cross breeding programs. Membership: $25/year.

Publications:
Watusi. q. adv.

Meetings/Conferences:
Annual Meetings: Fall

Antenna Measurement Techniques Ass'n *(1979)*
6065 Roswell Road, Suite 2252
Atlanta, GA   30328
Tel: (707)864-3488   *Fax:* (707)864-3491
E-Mail: sally@aeroflex.com
Web Site: http://www.amta.org
Members: 400 individuals
Annual Budget: $50-100,000
Secretary: Jeff Way

Historical Note
Members are institutions and individuals concerned with the design and measurement of antennas. Membership: $30/year (individual).

Publications:
Membership List. a.
Newsletter. semi-a.
Proceedings of Annual Meeting. a.

Meetings/Conferences:
Annual Meetings: October/350
2000 – Philadelphia, PA

2001 – Denver, Co

Antennas and Propagation Soc.
Historical Note
A technical society of the Institute of Electrical and Electronics Engineers (IEEE). Membership in the Society, open only to IEEE members, includes subscription to a technical periodical in the field published by IEEE. All administrative support is provided by IEEE.

Antiquarian Booksellers Ass'n of America *(1949)*
20 W. 44th St., 4th Floor
New York, NY   10036-6604
Tel: (212)944-8291   *Fax:* (212)944-8293
E-Mail: abaa@panix.com
Members: 475 companies
Staff: 1
Annual Budget: $250-500,000
Exec. Director: Liane Wade

Historical Note
Members are rare book dealers. Affiliated with the Internat'l League of Antiquarian Booksellers. Membership: $350/year (individual).

Publications:
Membership Directory. a.

Meetings/Conferences:

Antique and Amusement Photographers Internat'l
5 Spring St.
P.O. Box 110
Eureka Springs, AR   72632-0110
Tel: (501)253-8425   *Fax:* (501)253-8225
Web Site: http://www.oldtimephotos.org
Members: 200 companies
Annual Budget: $10-25,000
Exec. Director: Gail Pierce Larimer

Historical Note
Members are photography studios and photographers, primarily in the U.S. and Canada, specializing in costume photography and suppliers to the industry. Membership: $75-150/year.

Publications:
AAPI Directory. a. adv.
Flash Bulletin. 9/year. adv.
Flash Newsletter. 3/year. adv.

Meetings/Conferences:
Annual Meetings: Winter
1999 – Las Vegas, NV
2000 – Las Vegas, NV

Antique Appraisal Ass'n of America *(1972)*
11361 Garden Grove Blvd.
Garden Grove, CA   92843
Tel: (714)530-7090
Members: 250 individuals
Staff: 1
Annual Budget: under $10,000
Contact: Helen Nolan

Historical Note
Certifies members to professionally appraise antiques.

Publications:
Newsletter. bi-m.

Meetings/Conferences:
Annual Meetings: Not held

Anxiety Disorders Ass'n of America *(1980)*
11900 Parklawn Drive, Suite 100
Rockville, MD   20852-2624
Tel: (301)231-9350   *Fax:* (301)231-7392
E-Mail: anxdis@aol.com
Web Site: http://www.addaa.org
Members: 4,000 individuals
Staff: 10
Annual Budget: $1-2,000,000
Administrative Director: Ivey Farber
Director, External Affairs: Jan Ross
Businesses & Finance Manager: Fred Palmai
Membership Services Manager: Carrie Plowden
Editor & Communications Manager: David Rapoport

Historical Note
Formerly (1990) Phobia Soc. of America. ADAA members includes people who suffer from anxiety disorders and professionals who study and treat them. Its purpose is to provide information, education and support. Membership: $30/year (consumer subscriber) , $125/year (professional).

Publications:
ADAA Reporter. q. adv.
Conference Program Book. a. adv.
National Directory. a. adv.

Meetings/Conferences:
Annual Meetings: Nat'l Conference and Training Institute on Anxiety Disorders in April
1999 – San Diego, CA(Hilton Beach & Tennis Resort)/March 25-28/600
2000 – Washington, DC(Loew's L'Enfant Plaza)/March 23-26

AOAC Internat'l *(1884)*
481 N. Frederick Ave., Suite 500
Gaithersburg, MD   20877-2417
Tel: (301)924-7077   *Fax:* (301)924-7089
E-Mail: aoac@aoac.org
Web Site: http://www.aoac.org
Members: 4,200 individuals
Staff: 31
Annual Budget: $2-5,000,000
Exec. Director and General Counsel: Ronald R. Christensen
Director of Marketing and Membership: Muri Dueppen
Director of Education/Meetings: Angelique Adams
Director, Technical Services: Scott Coates
Dir., Finance & Admin.: Vincent Conte
Dir., Publications: Krystyna McIver

Historical Note
Founded in 1884 as the Ass'n of Official Agricultural Chemists, became the Ass'n of Official Analytical Chemists in 1965 and assumed its present name in 1991. AOAC INTERNAT'L is an independent international association whose primary focus is coordination of the development and validation of chemical and microbiological analytical methods by expert scientists working in industry, academic, and government laboratories worldwide. These scientists work within three validation programs operated by AOAC Internat'l: the AOAC Official Methods Program, the AOAC Peer-Verified Methods Program, and the AOAC Performance-Tested Methods Program. Membership: $85/year (individual), $750/year (organization/company).

Publications:
AOAC INTERNAT'L Membership Directory. a. adv.
Inside Laboratory Management. m. adv.
Journal of AOAC INTERNAT'L. bi-m. adv.
Laboratory Products and Services Buyer's Guide. a. adv.
Official Methods of Analysis of AOAC INTERNAT'L.

Meetings/Conferences:
Annual Meetings: September/1,000
1999 – Houston, TX(Adam's Mark)/Sept. 26-30
2000 – Philadelphia, PA(Adam's Mark)/Sept. 10-14

APA - The Engineered Wood Ass'n *(1933)*
P.O. Box 11700
Tacoma, WA   98411-0700
Tel: (253)565-6600   *Fax:* (253)565-7265
Web Site: http://www.apawood.org
Members: 145 mills
Staff: 180
Annual Budget: $10-25,000,000
President: David L. Rogoway

Historical Note
Formerly (1964) Douglas Fir Plywood Ass'n and (1994) American Plywood Ass'n. Members are producers of plywood, oriented strandboard, and other engineered wood products. Members must meet the association's quality standards in order to use the APA Trademark on their products. Street address is 7011 S. 19th St., Tacoma, WA.

Publications:
Management Report. m.

Meetings/Conferences:
Annual Meetings: Fall

Apartment Owners and Managers Ass'n of America *(1966)*
Historical Note
Organization defunct in 1998.

Apiary Inspectors of America *(1932)*
Maryland Dept. of Agriculture
50 Harry S. Truman Pkwy.
Annapolis, MD   21401
Tel: (410)841-5920
Members: 60 individuals
Staff: 1
Annual Budget: under $10,000
Secretary: I. Barton Smith, Jr.

Historical Note
Members are state apiarists of the U.S. and Canada. Formerly Nat'l Apiary Inspectors. Membership: $35/year (individual), $100/year (state).

Publications:
Proceedings of the Annual Conference. a.

Meetings/Conferences:
Annual Meetings: January
1999 – Nashville, TN

APICS - The Educational Society for Resource Management *(1957)*
500 West Annandale Road
Falls Church, VA   22046-4274
Tel: (703)237-8344   *Fax:* (703)237-1087
Toll Free: (800)444 - 2742
Web Site: http://www.apics.org
Members: 70,000 individuals, 1,896 companies
Staff: 100
Annual Budget: $5-10,000,000
Exec. Director and C.O.O.: Jeffry W. Raynes, CAE
Director, Communications: Wendy Mann, CAE
Director, Conference and Meetings: Christopher Thiel
Director, Finance/CFO: Lynn Grossman Quinn, CPA
Dep. Exec. Director: John Vowell, CAE
Senior Editor: Lisa S. Jenkins
Senior Dir., Customer Service: Michael Clark, CPIM
Dir., Information Services: Kenneth Moser, CNA
Dir., Human Resources: Elizabeth Davis

Historical Note
Formerly (1997) American Production and Inventory Control Soc. APICS is an organization of professionals in the field of resource management. Sponsors Special Interest Groups (SIGs) for members interested in collecting, validating and disseminating information in areas not included in the existing body of knowledge. Conducts two voluntary certification programs leading to the "CPIM" (Certified in Production and Inventory Management) and "CIRM" (Certified in Integrated Resource Management) designations. Supports an Educational and Research Foundation. Has an annual budget of approximately $20 million. Membership: approximately $85/year.

Publications:
APICS Conference Proceedings. a.
APICS, The Performance Advantage. m.
Journal of Operations Management. q.
Production and Inventory Management Journal.

Meetings/Conferences:
Annual Meetings: Fall/5,000-8,000
1999 – New Orleans, LA/Oct. 24-27

APMI Internat'l *(1958)*

105 College Rd., East
Princeton, NJ   08540-6692
Tel: (609)452-7700   *Fax:* (609)987-8523
E-Mail: apmi@mpif.org
Web Site: http://www.mpif.org
Members: 3,000 individuals
Staff: 3
Annual Budget: $500-1,000,000
Exec. Director: Donald G. White
Manager; Membership, Programs and Services: Sandra E.
    Leatherman

Historical Note
*Formerly (1994) American Powder Metallurgy Institute. APMI is a
technical/professional societ representing engineers, chemists,
metallurgists, physicists, and other professionals involved in powder
metal and advanced particulate materials technology. Membership:
$75/year.*

Publications:
Internat'l Journal of Powder Metallurgy. 8/yr. adv.
Who's Who in P/M. a. adv.

Meetings/Conferences:
Annual Meetings: Spring, in conjunction with the Metal Powder
    Industries Federation.
1999 – Vancouver, BC(Vancouver Convention
    Center)/June 20-24
2000 – New York, NY(New York Hilton)/May 30-June 3
2001 – New Orleans, LA(Hilton)/May 13-17
2002 – Orlando, FL(Walt Disney Dolphin)/June 16-21

APPA: The Ass'n of Higher Education Facilities Officers
(1914)
1643 Duke St.
Alexandria, VA   22314-2818
Tel: (703)684-1446   *Fax:* (703)549-2772
E-Mail: lander@appa.org
Web Site: http://www.appa.org
Members: 4,500 individuals
Staff: 14
Annual Budget: $2-5,000,000
Exec. V. President: E. Lander Medlin, CAE
Director of Communications: Steve Glazner
Director of Education: Katherine Smith
Director of Finance: Chong-Hie Choi
Director of Membership: Tina Myers

Historical Note
*Formerly (1991) Ass'n of Physical Plant Administrators of
Universities and Colleges. Members are accredited non-profit
institutions of higher education with an independent facilities
department, and university or college system offices which supervise
the physical plants of two or more campuses. Membership: $240-
1,060/year (based on enrollment and gross institutional
expenditures).*

Publications:
Facilities Manager Magazine. q. adv.
Inside APPA. m. adv.
Job Express. adv. adv.
Membership Directory. m. adv.
Proceedings. a.

Meetings/Conferences:
Annual Meetings: Summer/1,600
1999 – Cincinnati, OH(Convention Center)/June 20-22
2000 – Ft. Worth, TX(Convention Center)/July 16-18
2001 – Montreal, Canada(Queen Ann)

Appalachian Hardwood Manufacturers *(1928)*
Box 427
High Point, NC   27261
Tel: (336)885-8315   *Fax:* (336)886-8865
Web Site: http://www.appalachiawood.org
Members: 200 companies
Staff: 3
Annual Budget: $100-250,000
Exec. V. President: Mark A. Barford

Publications:
Appalachian Hardwood Membership Directory. a.

Meetings/Conferences:
Annual Meetings: Spring
1999 – Sea Island, GA(The Cloister)/Feb. 18-21

Appaloosa Horse Club *(1938)*
5070 Hwy. 8W
Moscow, ID   83843
Tel: (208)882-5578   *Fax:* (208)882-8150
E-Mail: aphc@appaloosa.com
Web Site: http://www.appaloosa.com
Members: 28,800 individuals
Annual Budget: $2-5,000,000
C.E.O.: Roger L. Klamfoth
Director, Marketing: Pamela Samanego

Historical Note
*Owners and breeders of the Appaloosa horse. Member of the Nat'l
Pedigree Livestock Council. Appaloosas are descendents of horses
brought to America by Spanish explorers. Membership: $40/year
(individual).*

Publications:
Appaloosa Journal. m. adv.

Meetings/Conferences:
Annual Meetings: Summer

Apparel Decorators Ass'n Internat'l
Historical Note
Became (1995) Apparel Graphics Institute.

Apparel Graphics Institute *(1989)*
4972 Ocean Pines
Berlin, MD   21811
Tel: (410)641-7300   *Fax:* (410)641-6934
Members: 600 individuals
President: Mark L. Venit

Historical Note
*Formerly (1995) Apparel Decorators Ass'n Internat'l. AGI serves
constituents in the apparel graphics industry, including textile
screen printers, embroiderers, apparel retailers, as well as
manufacturers and distributors of garments, apparel decorating
equipment and supplies.*

Apparel Retailers of America *(1914)*
Historical Note
Absorbed by the Nat'l Retail Federation in 1995.

Apple Processors Ass'n *(1987)*
1629 K St., N.W., Suite 1100
Washington, DC   20006
Tel: (202)785-6715   *Fax:* (202)331-4212
Members: 80 individuals, 20 companies
Staff: 3
Annual Budget: $100-250,000
President: Paul S. Weller, Jr.

Historical Note
*APA is a national association dedicated to serving processors,
marketers and suppliers to the apple industry.*

Publications:
APAGram. bi-m.

Meetings/Conferences:
1999 – Cerromar, PR(Westin Rio Mar)/May 21-27
2000 – White Sulphur Springs, WV(Greenbrier)

Appliance Parts Distributors Ass'n *(1937)*
c/o NARDA, 10 E. 22nd St., Suite 310
Lombard, IL   60148
Tel: (630)953-8950   *Fax:* (630)953-8957
Toll Free: (800)621 - 0298
Members: 79 companies
Staff: 1
Annual Budget: $100-250,000
Exec. Director: Elly S. Valas

Historical Note
*Formerly Appliance Parts Jobbers Ass'n. Administrative support
provided by North American Retail Dealers Ass'n (same address).
Membership: based on the number of company branches.*

Meetings/Conferences:
Semi-Annual Meetings: Spring and Fall Kohala
    Coast,HI/March 31-April 5

Applied Research Ethics Nat'l Ass'n *(1986)*
132 Boylston St., 4th Floor
Boston, MA   02116
Tel: (617)423-4112   *Fax:* (617)423-1185
E-Mail: PRMR@Delphi.com
Web Site: www.aamc.org/research/primr/arena
Members: 875 individuals
Staff: 4
Annual Budget: $10-25,000
Exec. Director: Joan Rachlin

Historical Note
*ARENA is a nat'l service organization for professionals concerned
with issues relating to the protection of human subjects, the
humane care and treatment of animals, scientific misconduct,
ethical decision-making in healthcare, and other ethical issues
pertaining to biomedical and behavioral research. Members are
administrators, health research professionals and others with an
interest in the ethical aspects of biological research. Membership:
$55/year (individual); $150/year (company).*

Publications:
ARENA Newsletter. q.

Meetings/Conferences:
Semi-Annual Meetings: Spring and Fall
1999 – San Diego, CA(Paradise Point Resort)/March 21-23

Appraisal Institute *(1991)*
875 North Michigan Ave., Suite 2400
Chicago, IL   60611-1980
Tel: (312)335-4100   *Fax:* (312)335-4400
Web Site: http://www.appraisalinstitute.org
Members: 25,000 individuals
Staff: 100
Annual Budget: $10-25,000,000
Exec. V. President: John Ross
V. President, Education: Sean Hutchinson
V. President, Finance: Lisa Wassekman
V. President, Legal: Jeff Liskar
V. President, Membership: Larisa K. Phillips
V.P. Human Resources: Sheila Barnes
V. President, Information Systems: Ron Hamburger

Historical Note
*The result of the unification in 1991 of American Institute of Real
Estate Appraisers and Soc. of Real Estate Appraisers, the Appraisal
Institute is a professional association providing opportunities for
professional education and enforcing a code of ethics and uniform
standards of real estate appraisal practice. Sponsors and supports
the political action committee APPAC and an education trust. Offers
the designations MAI (Member, Appraisal Institute) and SRA
(Senior Residential Appraiser). Has an annual budget of
approximately $20 million.*

Publications:
Annual Directory of Designated Members. a.
Appraisal Journal. q.
Appraiser News in Brief.
Education Course Catalogue. a.
MarketSource. q.
Publications Catalogue. a.
Valuation Insights and Perspectives. q.

Meetings/Conferences:
1999 – Orlando, FL/June 20-29

Appraisers Ass'n of America *(1949)*
386 Park Ave. South, Suite 2000
New York, NY   10016-8804

Tel: (212)889-5404   *Fax:* (212)889-5503
Members: 1,200 individuals
Staff: 2
Annual Budget: $100-250,000
Exec. Director: Victor Wiener

Historical Note
A professional society primarily of personal property appraisers.

Publications:
The Appraiser. q.

Meetings/Conferences:
Annual Meetings: Fall, in New York, NY

Aquacultural Engineering Soc. *(1993)*
c/o Freshwater Institute
P.O. Box 1746
Shepherdstown, WV   25443
Tel: (304)876-1606   *Fax:* (304)876-6339
Web Site: http://www.cals.cornell.edu/dept/aben/aes
Members: 200 individuals
Annual Budget: under $10,000
Secretary-Treasurer: Steven T. Summerfelt, Ph.D.

Historical Note
*AES members are aquacultural engineers and others with an
interest in the field. Has no paid officers or full-time staff.
Membership: $75/year (individual).*

Publications:
AES Newsletter. bi-m. adv.
Aquacultural Engineering. bi-m.

Meetings/Conferences:

Aquatic Exercise Ass'n *(1987)*
P.O. Box 1609
Nokomis, FL   34274-1609
Tel: (941)486-8600   *Fax:* (941)486-8820
Toll Free: (888)232 - 9283
E-Mail: AEA@ix.netcom.com
Web Site: http://youth.net/aea
Members: 4,000 individuals
Staff: 50
Annual Budget: $500-1,000,000
Exec. Director: Angie Nelson

Historical Note
*AEA members are aquatic therapists or fitness professionals, facility
operators, manufacturers of pool/fitness products and others with
an interest in aquatic fitness and therapy programs. Membership:
$52/year (individual); $120/year (small business); $180/year
(company).*

Publications:
AKWA Letter Newsletter. bi-m. adv.

Meetings/Conferences:
1999 – Orlando, FL(Marriott)/May 11-16

Aquatic Plant Management Soc. *(1961)*
Historical Note
Address unknown in 1997.

Arabian Horse Registry of America, Inc. *(1908)*
12000 Zuni St.
Westminster, CO   80234
Tel: (303)450-4748   *Fax:* (303)450-2841
Web Site: http://www.theregistry.org
Members: 21,000 individuals
Staff: 28
Resident Officer: Ralph F. Clark

Historical Note
*Registers and transfers pure-bred Arabian Horses. Member of the
Nat'l Pedigree Livestock Council.*

Publications:
Registry News. q.

Meetings/Conferences:
Three Meetings/Year: March, July and November in
    Westminster, CO.

Archaeological Institute of America *(1879)*
656 Beacon St.
Boston, MA   02215-2006
Tel: (617)353-9361   *Fax:* (617)353-6550
E-Mail: aia@bu.edu
Members: 11,000 individuals
Staff: 30
Annual Budget: $5-10,000,000
Exec. Director: Mark J. Meister
Conference Manager: Shelley Griffin

Historical Note
*Founded in 1879 in Boston under the aegis of Charles Eliot Norton
and chartered by the US Congress in 1906. Member of the
American Council of Learned Societies and affiliate of the American
Ass'n for the Advancement of Science and numerous other societies
and institutes. Membership: $10-$250/year.*

Publications:
AIA Newsletter. q.
American Journal of Archaeology. q.
Archaeological Fieldwork Opportunities Bulletin. a.
Archaeology. bi-m. adv.

Meetings/Conferences:
Annual Meetings: Winter/2,200
1999 – Dallas, TX(Adams Mark)/Dec. 27-30/2200
2001 – San Diego, CA(San Diego Marriott)/Jan. 3-6/2300

Archery Manufacturers and Merchants Organization
(1946)
4131 NW 28th Lane, Suite 7
Gainesville, FL   32606-6681
Tel: (352)377-8262   *Fax:* (352)375-3961
Members: 523 companies
Staff: 3
Annual Budget: $100-250,000
President: Dick Lattimer

Historical Note
Founded as the Archery Manufacturers and Dealers Ass'n, it became the Archery Manufacturers Ass'n in 1952 and Archery Manufacturers Organization in 1965. Assumed present name in 1994. Members are producers and sellers to the archery consumer including manufacturers, distributors, sales representatives, dealers and the archery media. Supports the American Archery Council as its promotional arm. Membership: $150-15,000/year, based on archery sales (regular); $100/year (retail); $50-250/year (rep firm); $750/year (supporting).

Publications:
AMO News. q.

Meetings/Conferences:

Archery Manufacturers Organization (1946)

Historical Note
Became Archery Manufacturers and Merchants Organization in 1994.

Archery Range and Retailers Organization (1981)
156 N. Main
Oregon, WI 53575
Tel: (608)835-9060   *Fax:* (608)835-9360
Members: 115 companies
Staff: 2
Annual Budget: $50-100,000
Exec. Secretary: Lynn Stiklestad

Historical Note
Formerly (until 1980) known as the Archery Lane Operators Ass'n, ARRO is primarily a cooperative buying association. Membership: $400/year (company).

Meetings/Conferences:
Annual Meetings: January

Architectural Precast Ass'n (1966)
P.O. Box 08669
Fort Myers, FL 33908-0669
Tel: (941)454-6989   *Fax:* (941)454-6787
E-Mail: precrete@gate.net
Members: 100 companies
Staff: 6
Annual Budget: $50-100,000
Exec. Director: Fred L. McGee

Historical Note
Makers of precast concrete elements.

Publications:
The Architectural Precaster. bi-m.

Meetings/Conferences:
Annual Meetings: Spring
1999 – Acapulco, Mexico(Acapulco Princess)/March 12-15
1999 – Meredith, NH(Inn at Mill Falls)/Sept. 10-14

Architectural Spray Coaters Ass'n (1986)
895 Doncaster Dr.
West Deptford, NJ 08066
Tel: (609)848-6120   *Fax:* (609)251-1243
E-Mail: aseaassoc@erols.com
Web Site: http://ascassoc.com
Members: 25 companies
Staff: 1
Annual Budget: $50-100,000
Exec. Director: J. Jack Mohnacs

Historical Note
Formerly the Custom Kynar Coaters Group. ASCA is a national organization with members also in Canada and the Pacific Rim. Full members are contracting firms; membership is also available to suppliers and consultants in the field. Membership: $1,000-2,000/year.

Publications:
ASCA Specifications. a.
ASCA Spray Lites. q.

Meetings/Conferences:
Annual Meetings: Spring or Fall

Architectural Woodwork Institute (1953)
1952 Isaac Newton Square-W
Reston, VA 20190
Tel: (703)733-0600   *Fax:* (703)733-0584
E-Mail: jdusham@awinet.org
Web Site: http://www.awinet.org
Members: 800 companies
Staff: 6
Annual Budget: $1-2,000,000
Exec. V. President: Judith B. Durham
Director of Communcations: David Ritchey
Director of Conventions and Meetings: Kimberly Kennedy
Member Services Director: Greg Huer

Historical Note
Absorbed the Millwork Cost Bureau. Members are manufacturers and suppliers of paneling, fixtures, cases, laminates and doors. Membership: $600-3600/year (organization/company).

Publications:
Design Solutions Journal. q. adv.
National Membership Directory. a. adv.
Quality Standards. a.

Meetings/Conferences:
Annual Meetings: Fall/over 700
1999 – Portland, OR

Archivists and Librarians in the History of the Health Sciences (1975)
c/o Bakken Library of Electricity
3537 Zenith Ave. South
Minneapolis, MN 55416
Tel: (612)927-6508   *Fax:* (612)927-7265
E-Mail: lhrig@bakkenmuseum.org
Members: 220 individuals
Annual Budget: under $10,000

Secretary-Treasurer: Elizabeth Ihrig

Historical Note
Formerly (1992) the Ass'n of Librarians in the History of the Health Sciences. Members are librarians & archivists with responsibility for history of health science collections. Meets to discuss mutual concerns, view history of medicine collections, and to participate in continuing professional education. Membership $15/year (domestic); $21/year (overseas).

Publications:
The Watermark. q. adv.

Meetings/Conferences:
Annual Meetings: With the American Ass'n for the History of Medicine
1999 – New Brunswick, NJ/May 5-9

Argentina-American Chamber of Commerce (1919)
10 Rockefeller Plaza, Suite 1001
New York, NY 10020-1903
Tel: (212)698-2238   *Fax:* (212)698-2239
Members: 450 companies
Staff: 3
Annual Budget: $100-250,000
President: Carlos E. Alfaros

Historical Note
Membership: $280/year (individual), $550 (organization/company).

Publications:
Argentine News-Letter. m.
Argentine-American Business Review Directory. a. adv.
Business Watch. m. adv.
Directory. a.

Meetings/Conferences:
Annual Meetings: Spring in New York, NY/4-500

Armed Forces Broadcasters Ass'n (1982)
P.O. Box 447
Sun City, CA 92586-0447
Tel: (909)672-7299   *Fax:* (909)679-5484
Members: 600 individuals
Staff: 1
Annual Budget: under $10,000
President: Mary Carnes

Historical Note
Enhances camaraderie among former, present, and future members of the military broadcasting community; provides employment search assistance. Membership: $20/yr.

Publications:
Transmitter. q.

Meetings/Conferences:
Annual Meetings: April, in LA, following the Nat'l Ass'n of Broadcasters Convention.

Armed Forces Communications and Electronics Ass'n (1946)
AFCEA Internat'l Headquarters
4400 Fair Lakes Court
Fairfax, VA 22033-3899
Tel: (703)631-6100   *Fax:* (703)631-4693
Toll Free: (800)336 - 4583
E-Mail: service@afcea.org
Web Site: http://www.afcea.org
Members: 41,000 individuals, 1,040 corporations
Staff: 59
President and C.E.O.: Lt.Gen. C. Norman Wood, USAF(Ret.)
Exec. V. President-Treasurer: Maj.Gen. Tim Padden, USAF(Ret.)
V. President, Operations: Lawrence D. Pierce
Editor-in-Chief: Rob Robinson

Historical Note
Originated May 1946 as the Army Signal Ass'n. Name changed to Armed Forces Communications Ass'n in 1948 and to the Armed Forces Communications and Electronics Ass'n in 1954. Provides an ethical forum in which government and industry leaders and decision-makers can meet to exchange ideas and concepts, discuss current problems and solution and identify future requirements in the technical disciplines of communications, electronics, intelligence and information systems. Fosters cooperation between free world industries, governments and C3I professionals. Members include designers, planners, manufacturers, and systems testers. Has an annual budget of approximately $10 million. Membership: $20/year (individual); $5/year (student); $200-1,400/year (corporate).

Publications:
AFCEA Internation Press. irreg.
Signal Magazine. m. adv.

Meetings/Conferences:
Annual Meetings: June/25,000
1999 – San Diego, CA/Jan. 19-21

Armed Forces Marketing Council (1969)
3611-C Chain Bridge Road
Fairfax, VA 22030-3246
Tel: (703)273-6590
Members: 9 companies
Staff: 2
Annual Budget: $100-250,000
President: George "Rip" Rowan

Historical Note
Members are companies representing manufacturers who supply military and Coast Guard exchanges, commissaries, clubs and veterans canteens.

Meetings/Conferences:
Annual Meetings: March, in Washington, DC

Armed Forces Optometric Soc. (1970)

Historical Note
AFOS declined to provide updated information for this edition.

Army Aviation Ass'n of America (1957)

49 Richmondville Ave.
Westport, CT 06880-2000
Tel: (203)226-8184   *Fax:* (203)222-9863
Web Site: http://www.quad-a.org
Members: 13,500 individuals
Staff: 12
Annual Budget: $500-1,000,000
Exec. Director: William R. Harris, Jr.

Historical Note
Quad-A represents active and retired U.S. Army aviators and defense contractors. Membership: $21/year.

Publications:
Army Aviation. 10/year.

Meetings/Conferences:
Annual Meetings: Spring
1999 – Nashville, TN/May 9-12

Art and Antique Dealers League of America (1926)
353 East 78th St., Suite 19A
New York, NY 10021
Tel: (212)879-7558
Members: 94 dealers
Staff: 1
Annual Budget: $10-25,000
Secretary: Joseph H. Kilian

Historical Note
Oldest and principal antiques and fine arts organization in America. An outgrowth of the Antique Dealers Luncheon Club which on January 7, 1926 met at the Madison Hotel, New York City and formed the Antique and Decorative Arts League, which became the Art and Antique Dealers League of America, Inc., in 1942. Member of the Internat'l Art Dealers Confederation (CINOA - Confederation Internationale des Negociantes en Oeuvres d'Art), a worldwide organization encompassing 14 countries.

Meetings/Conferences:
Annual Meetings: Annual Dinner & General Meeting - New York, NY/late Jan./75

Art and Creative Materials Institute (1936)
100 Boylston St., Suite 1050
Boston, MA 02116-4610
Tel: (617)426-6400   *Fax:* (617)753-6185
E-Mail: acmi@guildassoc.com
Web Site: http://creative-industries.com/acmi
Members: 185 companies
Annual Budget: $500-1,000,000
Exec. V. President: Deborah Fanning, CAE
Assoc. Director: Deborah S. Gustafson
Director Membership/Certification: Brenda Welch

Historical Note
Formerly (1983) the Crayon, Water Color and Craft Institute and Art and Craft Materials Institute (1994). Members are makers of art and craft products. The Institute conducts a certification program to assure that these products are non-toxic or properly labelled if necessary. Membership fee varies, based on annual sales.

Publications:
Institute Items. m.
List of Certified Products. q.

Meetings/Conferences:
Annual Meetings: Spring

Art Dealers Ass'n of America (1962)
575 Madison Ave.
New York, NY 10022
Tel: (212)940-8590   *Fax:* (212)940-7013
E-Mail: artdeal@rosenman.com
Web Site: http://www.artdealers.org
Members: 152 dealers
Staff: 4
Admin. V. President: Gilbert S. Edelson
Director, Administrative: Donna Carlson

Historical Note
Non-profit membership organization of nation's leading dealers in the fine arts.

Publications:
Directory.

Meetings/Conferences:
Annual Meetings: Always held at a gallery in New York City.

Art Glass Suppliers Ass'n Internat'l (1986)
1100-H Brandywine Blvd., P.O. Box 3388
Zanesville, OH 43702-3388
Tel: (740)452-4541   *Fax:* (740)452-2552
E-Mail: agsa.info@offinger.com
Web Site: http://www.agsa.org
Members: 702 manufacturers
Staff: 6
Annual Budget: $100-250,000
Manager, Shows: Tricia Kidd

Historical Note
AGSA is the trade association of the art, decorative glass and ceramics industry. Members are retailers, wholesalers, studios of art glass and supplies. Membership: $250/year (manufacturer-wholesaler/distributor/publisher); $100/year (retailer-studio/consultant/designer/teacher).

Publications:
AGSA Trade Show Directory. a. adv.
Art Glass News Newsletter. q. adv.

Meetings/Conferences:
1999 – Long Beach, CA/June 9-13

Art Libraries Soc./North America (1972)
4101 Lake Boone Trail, Suite 201
Raleigh, NC 27607-7506
Tel: (919)787-5181   *Fax:* (919)787-4916
Toll Free: (800)637 - 7547
E-Mail: arusna@olsonmgmt.com
Web Site: www.libduke.edu/lilly/arlis/

Members: 1,200 individuals
Staff: 4
Annual Budget: $100-250,000
Exec. Director: Ashley Prather

Historical Note
A professional organization of art information specialists, the society includes individual (librarians, historians, curators, and students) and institutional (colleges and universities, museums and galleries, historical societies and libraries) members. Membership: (individual) $65-135/year based on income; $100/year (institutional).

Publications:
ARLIS/NA Update. bi-m. adv.
Art Documentation. bi-a. adv.
Conference Proceedings. a.
Handbook and List of Members. a. adv.
Occasional Papers. irreg.

Meetings/Conferences:
Annual Meetings: February-March/600
1999 – Vancouver, British Columbia(Hotel
       Vancouver)/March 25-31
2000 – Pittsburgh, PA(Hilton)/March 16-23

Arthroscopy Ass'n of North America (1982)
6300 N. River Road, Suite 104
Rosemont, IL   60018-4228
Tel: (847)292-2262   *Fax:* (847)292-2268
E-Mail: moreinfo@aana.org
Web Site: www.aana.org
Members: 1,300 individuals
Staff: 8
Annual Budget: $2-5,000,000
Exec. V. President: John B. McGinty, M.D.
Director, Meetings: Holly Albert
Director, Surgical Skills Education: Pamela Martens
Director, Finance: Edward Goss
Director, Committees: Donna K. Nikkel

Historical Note
Incorporated in the State of Illinois in 1982. Membership: by invitation only, $450/year.

Publications:
Arthroscopy, The Journal of Arthroscopic Related Surgery. bi-
     m. adv.
Journal of Arthroscopic Surgery. q. adv.
Membership Directory. a.
Newsletter-Inside AANA. bi-m.

Meetings/Conferences:
1999 – Vancouver, BC(Vancouver Trade
       Center)/April 15-18/1500
2000 – Miami, FL/April 13-16

Articulating Crane Council of North America
Historical Note
An affiliate of the Nat'l Truck Equipment Ass'n.

Artificial Flower Manufacturers Board of Trade (1938)
Historical Note
Merged with Pleaters, Stitchers and Embroiderers Ass'n in 1996.

Artist-Blacksmiths' Ass'n of North America (1973)
300 Cedar
P.O. Box 206
Washington, MO   63090-0206
Tel: (314)390-2133
E-Mail: abana@mail.us.mo.com
Web Site: http://www.abana.org
Members: 4,500 individuals
Exec. Director: Janelle Gilbert

Historical Note
Members are professional blacksmiths, artists and others with an interest in blacksmithing techniques. Membership: $45/year (individual).

Publications:
Anvil's Ring Journal. q.

Meetings/Conferences:
2000 – Flagstaff, AZ(Northern Arizona Univ.)/July 12-16

Asbestos Cement Product Producers Ass'n (1972)
1745 Jefferson Davis Hwy.
Crystal Square 4, Suite 406
Arlington, VA   22202
Tel: (703)412-1153   *Fax:* (703)412-1152
Members: 30 companies
Staff: 2
Annual Budget: $50-100,000
President: Bob J. Pigg

Historical Note
Formerly (1989) the Ass'n of Asbestos Cement Pipe Producers, and (1996) the Asbestos Cement Pipe Producers Ass'n. An international association incorporated in Pennsylvania in 1972. Represents international manufacturers of asbestos-cement products.

Publications:
A/C Advisory. irreg.
Special Reports. irreg.

Meetings/Conferences:
Annual Meetings: April

Asbestos Information Ass'n/North America (1970)
1745 Jefferson Davis Hwy.
Crystal Square 4, Suite 406
Arlington, VA   22202
Tel: (703)412-1150   *Fax:* (703)412-1152
Members: 10 companies
Staff: 2
Annual Budget: $250-500,000
President: Bob J. Pigg

Historical Note
Incorporated in 1971. The public relations arm of U.S. and Canadian asbestos producers and asbestos products manufacturers. Provides information on asbestos and health.

Publications:
Newsletter. m.

Meetings/Conferences:
Annual Meetings: Washington, DC area, second or third week
     in September

Aseptic Packaging Council (1989)
2111 Wilson Blvd., Suite 700
Arlington, VA   22201
Tel: (703)351-9750   *Fax:* (703)351-5062
Toll Free: (800)277 - 8088
President: Marshall Cohen
V. President, Communications: Erich Parker

Historical Note
Members are producers drink-boxes and other aseptic (plastic-coated paper) products.

ASFE: Professional Firms Practicing in the Geosciences (1969)
8811 Colesville Road, Suite G106
Silver Spring, MD   20910
Tel: (301)565-2733   *Fax:* (301)589-2017
E-Mail: info@asfe.org
Members: 350 companies, 1,300 branch offices
Staff: 9
Annual Budget: $500-1,000,000
Exec. V. President: John P. Bachner
Operations Director: Ann Reed
Membership Director: Joanna Ohring

Historical Note
Formerly (1975) Associated Soil and Foundation Engineers and (1987) Ass'n of Soil and Foundation Engineers and (1993) ASFE/ The Ass'n of Engineering Firms Practicing in the Geosciences. Seeks the enhancement of professionalism and the reduction of liability loss exposure. Membership: $750-7,500/year (company).

Publications:
Membership Directory. a.
Newslog. bi-m. adv.
PSA/UST Directory. a.

Meetings/Conferences:
Semi-annual Meetings: April and October
1999 – Atlanta
1999 – Tucson
2000 – New Orleans, LA
2000 – San Diego, CA

Asian American Certified Public Accountants (1979)
One Embarcadero Center, Suite 711
San Francisco, CA   94111
Tel: (415)981-1111   *Fax:* (415)982-1111
E-Mail: mlcpa@malhbuie.com
Members: 200 individuals
President: Jenny Siu

Historical Note
AACPA members are accountants of Asian ancestry.

Publications:
AACPA Newsletter. bi-m.
Directory of Accounting Firms. irreg.
Membership Directory. a.

Asian American Journalists Ass'n (1981)
1765 Sutter St.
San Francisco, CA   94115
Tel: (415)346-2051   *Fax:* (415)346-6343
E-Mail: national@aaja.org
Web Site: http://www.aaja.org
Members: 1,900 individuals
Staff: 5
Annual Budget: $250-500,000
Exec. Director: Sandra Michioku

Historical Note
Mission is to encourage Asian Pacific Americans to enter the journalism profession and work towards fair coverage of Asian Americans. AAJA members are journalists who receive the bulk of their economic support from employment as executives, reporters, editors, writers, photographers, producers, technicians and directors in news or news-oriented public affairs departments of print or broadcast companies. Members also include non-journalists who were at one time professional journalists and non-newsroom employers and students. Programs include scholarships, job referral, professional development, speakers bureau, fellowships and internship support. Membership: $55/year, full (professional journalist); $55/year (associate non-journalist); $20/year (retired); $15/year (student).

Publications:
AAJA Dateline. q. adv.
Directory. bien.

Meetings/Conferences:
1999 – Seattle WA/July 7-11

Asian American Manufacturers Ass'n (1980)
770 Menlo Ave., Suite 227
Menlo Park, CA   94025
Tel: (650)321-2262   *Fax:* (650)325-5499
E-Mail: aama@3wc.com
Web Site: http://www.3wc.com/aama/
Members: 650 individuals
Staff: 1
Annual Budget: $25-50,000
Exec. Director: Regina Lau

Historical Note
Members are Asian American manufacturers of high technology computer-related products. Membership: $50/year (individual manufacturer); $100/year (associate non-manufacturer); $450 (business) and $1,200/year (business associate).

Publications:
AAMA Newsletter. m.
Membership Directory. a.

Meetings/Conferences:
Annual Meetings: Fall

Asian American Psychological Ass'n (1971)
Historical Note
Address unknown in 1996; presumed inactive.

Asian/Pacific American Librarians Ass'n (1980)
Newport Beach Library
1000 Avocado Avenue
Newport Beach, CA   92660
Tel: (714)717-3824   *Fax:* (714)640-5681
E-Mail: sjung@city.newport-beach.ca.us
Web Site: http://www.uic.edu/ ~ rama/apala
Members: 219 individuals
Annual Budget: under $10,000
President: Dr. Abdulfazal M.F. Kabir

Historical Note
APALA members are librarians and other information specialists of Asian/Pacific heritage. Has no paid officers or full-time staff. Membership: $10/year (individual); $25/year (institution); $5/year (student).

Publications:
APALA Newsletter. q.
Membership Directory. a.

Meetings/Conferences:
Annual Meetings: in conjunction with the American Library
     Ass'n

ASM Internat'l (1913)
9639 Kinsman Road
Materials Park, OH   44073-0002
Tel: (440)338-5151   *Fax:* (440)338-4634
E-Mail: Mem-Serv@po.asm-intl.org
Web Site: http://www.asm-intl.org
Members: 43,000 individuals
Staff: 120
Annual Budget: $10-25,000,000
Managing Director: Michael J. DeHaemer
Dir., Marketing/New Services: Robert C. Uhl
Dir., Soc. Activities: Thomas S. Passek
Director, Education: Margaret M. Weir
Dir., Finance/Admin.: William S. Kornblau
Dir., Info. Systems/Technology: Dr. W. Douglas Knowles
Dir., Technical Services: Dr. William W. Scott, Jr.

Historical Note
Originated in Detroit as the Steel Treaters Club in 1913, it became the American Soc. for Steel Treating in 1920, the American Soc. for Metals in 1933 and assumed its present name in 1986. Incorporated in Ohio in 1920. ASM's mission is to gather, process and disseminate technical information on engineered materials through forums and meetings, education programs, publications and electronic media. Membership: $58/year (individual). Has a budget of about $12 million.

Publications:
Advanced Materials and Processes. m. adv.
ASM News. m. adv.
Internat'l Materials Review. bi-m.
Journal of Material Engineering & Performance. q.
Journal of Phase Equilibria. q.
Journal of Thermal Spray Technology. q.
Metallurgical Transactions A. m.
Metallurgical Transactions B. q.

Meetings/Conferences:
Annual Meetings: Fall
1999 – Cincinnati, OH/Nov. 1-4

Asociacion de Periodistas y Locutores Interamericanos (1980)
Historical Note
Address unknown in 1998.

Asphalt Emulsion Manufacturers Ass'n (1973)
3 Church Circle, Suite 250
Annapolis, MD   21401
Tel: (410)267-0023   *Fax:* (410)267-7546
E-Mail: Krissoff@compuserve.com
Web Site: http://www.aema.com
Members: 120 companies
Staff: 2
Annual Budget: $250-500,000
Exec. Director: Michael R. Krissoff

Historical Note
Members are manufacturers of asphalt emulsion (active) and suppliers to the industry (associate). Membership: $1,200 plus $100/additional plant/year, $4,500 maximum, (company); $1,750/year (associate).

Publications:
AEMA Directory. a. adv.
AEMA Newsletter. q. adv.

Meetings/Conferences:
Semi-Annual Meetings: March and November/250
1999 – Santa Fe, NM(Eldorado Hotel)/March 17-20
1999 – Washington, DC(Omni Shoreham Hotel)/Nov. 11-14
2000 – Amelia Island, FL(Amelia Island
     Plantation)/March 11-15
2001 – San Diego, CA(Loew's Coronado Bay
     Resort)/Feb. 21-24

Asphalt Institute (1919)
P.O. Box 14052
Research Park Dr.
Lexington, KY   40512-4052
Tel: (606)288-4971   *Fax:* (606)288-4999
E-Mail: emiller@asphaltinstitute.org
Web Site: http://www.asphaltinstitute.org

Members: 60 companies
Staff: 40
Annual Budget: $2-5,000,000
President: Edward L. Miller
Director of Research: Mike Anderson
Secy./Dir., Finance and Administration: Linda Botkin
Director of Marketing and Membership: Kelly Pinson

Historical Note
Founded as the Asphalt Ass'n, it assumed its present name in 1929. Members are companies that refine asphalt products, process finished asphalts, or are marketers with significant asphalt assets. Al affiliates include companies working with liquid asphalt through transporting, additive manufacturers, or equipment manufacturers. Al serves both users and producers of asphalt materials.

Publications:
ASPHALT Magazine. q.
Catalog of Publications and Audio-Visual Programs. a.

Meetings/Conferences:
Annual Meetings: December (by invitation only)

Asphalt Recycling and Reclaiming Ass'n *(1976)*
3 Church Circle, Suite 250
Annapolis, MD   21401-1902
Tel: (410)267-0023   *Fax:* (410)267-7546
E-Mail: Krissoff@Compuserve.com
Web Site: http://www.arra.org
Members: 200 companies
Annual Budget: $100-250,000
Exec. Director: Michael R. Krissoff

Historical Note
Promotes the collective interests of those individuals, firms or corporations engaged in the asphalt recycling industry as contractors, owners or manufacturers of equipment, engineers, suppliers and public highway officials. Membership: $1,350/year (organization/company).

Publications:
ARRA Newsletter. q. adv.
Membership Directory. a. adv.

Meetings/Conferences:
Semi-annual Meetings: Winter/200 and Fall
1999 – Southern California
1999 – Tempe, AZ(The Buttes Resort)/Feb. 17-20
1999 – Philadelphia, PA(Adam's Mark Hotel)/Oct. 26-28
2000 – Cancun
2000 – Vancouver, BC
2001 – San Diego, CA(Loew's Coronado Bay Resort)/Feb. 21-24
2002 – Tampa, FL(Saddlebrook Resort)
2003 – San Antonio, TX(Hyatt Regency Hill Country)

Asphalt Roofing Manufacturers Ass'n *(1919)*
4041 Powder Mill Road, Suite 404
Calverton, MD   20705
Tel: (301)348-2002   *Fax:* (301)348-2020
Members: 52 companies
Staff: 5
Annual Budget: $500-1,000,000
Exec. V. President: Richard D. Snyder, CAE
V. President, Communications/Public Affairs: Joseph Hobson
Director, Member Services & Meeting Planning: Sally A. Choquette

Historical Note
Formerly (1969) Asphalt Roofing Industry Bureau. ARMA members are manufacturers of roll roofing, built-up roofing, residential roofing, asphalt shingles, and modifed bitumen roofing.

Publications:
ARMA Newsletter. q.
Government Issues Newsletter. q.
Technical Bulletins. irreg.

Meetings/Conferences:
1999 – Amelia Island, FL(Ritz Carlton)/Nov. 10-12

Aspirin Foundation of America *(1981)*
1555 Connecticut Ave., N.W., Suite 200
Washington, DC   20036
Tel: (202)234-3154   *Fax:* (202)462-9043
Members: 8 companies
Staff: 1
Annual Budget: $1-2,000,000
President: Thomas E. Bryant, Sr., M.D.,

Meetings/Conferences:

Ass'n Chief Executive Council *(1988)*
8421 Frost Way
Annandale, VA   22003
Tel: (703)280-4622   *Fax:* (703)280-0942
E-Mail: kentonpl@aol.com
Members: 50 individuals
Annual Budget: $10-25,000
Exec. Director: Kenton Pattie

Historical Note
Council members are chief executive officers of trade & professional associations. Provides an exclusive and confidential trade & professional forum for C.E.O.'s to help solve leadership problems, work with boards & elected leaders, and give career development support. Membership: $200-$1,250/year.

Meetings/Conferences:
Monthly Meetings: usually in Washington, DC area

Ass'n for Academic Surgery *(1966)*
13 Elm St.
Manchester, MA   01944
Tel: (978)526-8330   *Fax:* (978)526-4018
E-Mail: aas@prri.com
Members: 3,000 individuals
Annual Budget: $100-250,000
Exec. Director: Kevin M. Cuff

Historical Note
Founded in 1966 as an organization serving the needs of academic surgeons, particularly those under 40 years of age. Dedicated to

interchange of scientific, educational, social and political information relative to the surgical profession. Membership: $95/year (regular); $15/year (senior, candidate).

Publications:
Journal of Surgical Research. m.

Meetings/Conferences:
Annual Meetings: November
1999 – Philadelphia, PA/November 18-20
2000 – Tampa, FL/November 1-3

Ass'n for Accounting Administration *(1983)*
136 South Keowee St.
Dayton, OH   45402
Tel: (937)222-0030   *Fax:* (937)222-5794
E-Mail: AAADayton@aol.com
Web Site: http://www.cpaadmin.org
Members: 500 individuals
Staff: 7
Annual Budget: $100-250,000
Exec. Director: Kimberly Fantaci

Historical Note
Formerly (1994) Ass'n of Accounting Administrators. Members are accounting administrators, high-level office managers and administrative partners in accounting firms and corporate accounting departments. Membership: $225/year (individual), $300/year (organization).

Publications:
AAA Report. bi-m. adv.
Membership Directory. a.

Meetings/Conferences:
Annual Meetings: June
1999 – Seattle, WA
2000 – Nashville, TN
2001 – San Antonio, TX

Ass'n for Accounting Marketing *(1989)*
9140 Ward Parkway, Suite 200
Kansas City, MO   64114
Tel: (816)444-3500   *Fax:* (816)444-0330
E-Mail: staff@accountingmarketing.org
Web Site: http://www.accountingmarketing.org
Members: 380 individuals
Staff: 3
Annual Budget: $100-250,000
Exec. Director: Lisa Daniels, CAE

Historical Note
Formerly (1993) Ass'n of Accounting Marketing Executives. AAM is a professional association serving individuals actively engaged in developing and implementing marketing programs for accounting firms. Executive membership is limited to full-time, in-house marketing executives; associate membership is available to in-house accounting firm personnel whose reponsibilities include marketing and consultants to the accounting profession; affiliate membership is also available. Membership: $250/year (first year), $200/year (renewal).

Publications:
MarkeTrends. bi-m.

Meetings/Conferences:
1999 – Kansas City, MO

Ass'n for Adult Development and Aging *(1986)*
5999 Stevenson Ave.
Alexandria, VA   22304
Tel: (703)823-9800   *Fax:* (703)823-0252
Toll Free: (800)347 - 6647
Members: 2,034 individuals
Staff: 2
Annual Budget: $25-50,000
Interim Exec. Director: Richard Yep

Historical Note
AADA is a division of the American Counseling Ass'n. Members are individuals who hold a masters degree in adult and/or gerontological counseling or an equivalent. Membership: $20/year (regular or associate), $20/year (student); $12/year (retired).

Publications:
ADULTSPAN Newsletter. q. adv.

Meetings/Conferences:
Annual Meetings: in conjunction with the American Counseling Ass'n
1999 – San Diego, CA/April 14-17
2000 – Washington, DC/March 22-25
2001 – San Antonio, TX
2002 – New Orleans, LA

Ass'n for Advanced Life Underwriting *(1957)*
1922 F St., N.W., 4th Floor
Washington, DC   20006
Tel: (202)331-6081   *Fax:* (202)331-2164
Members: 1,900 individuals
Staff: 8
Annual Budget: $1-2,000,000
Exec. V. President: David Stertzer
Director, Communications/Meetings: Karen Tyson
Director, Government Affairs: Thomas Korb
Assoc. Dir., Govt. Affairs: Sue Pechilio
Membership Director: Marilyn A. Maticic

Historical Note
A Conference of the Nat'l Ass'n of Life Underwriters. Members are individuals specializing in estate analysis, pension planning, employee benefit plans and similar fields involving the placement of a large volume of life insurance. Membership: $750/year.

Publications:
AALU Roster. a.
Quarterly Update.
Washington Report. 125/year.

Meetings/Conferences:
Annual Meetings: Spring in Washington, DC/700

Ass'n for Advancement of Behavior Therapy *(1966)*
305 Seventh Avenue, Suite 16A
New York, NY   10001-6008
Tel: (212)647-1890   *Fax:* (212)647-1865
E-Mail: aabt@aabt.org
Web Site: http://www.aabt.org/aabt
Members: 4,500 individuals
Staff: 10
Annual Budget: $500-1,000,000
Exec. Director: Mary Jane Eimer, CAE
Manager, Conventions: Mary Ellen Brown
Director, Publications: David Teisler, CAE

Historical Note
Founded and incorporated in New York in 1966 as the Ass'n for Advancement of the Behavioral Therapies. Assumed is present name in 1968. Membership: $142/year (full member); $25/year (student).

Publications:
Behavior Therapy. q. adv.
Cognitive and Behavioral Practice. semi-a. adv.
Directory of Psychology Internships. bien.
Graduate Study Directory. bien.
The Behavior Therapist. 10/year. adv.

Meetings/Conferences:
Annual Meetings: November
1999 – Toronto, Ontario, Canada/Nov. 11-14
2000 – New Orleans, LA(Hilton)/Nov. 16-19
2001 – Philadelphia, PA(Marriott)/Nov. 15-18
2002 – Reno, NV(Hilton)/Nov. 14-17

Ass'n for Africanist Anthropology

Historical Note
A section of the American Anthropological Ass'n.

Ass'n for Ambulatory Behavorial Healthcare *(1965)*
301 N. Fairfax St., Suite 109
Alexandria, VA   22314-2633
Tel: (703)836-2274   *Fax:* (703)836-0083
E-Mail: aabhgen@aol.com
Web Site: http://www.aabh.org
Members: 500 individuals, 1000 companies
Staff: 8
Annual Budget: $500-1,000,000
Exec. Director: Mark A. Knight, MSW
Government Relations Associate: Lawrence Best
Membership Associate: Brian Creamer

Historical Note
Formerly the American Ass'n for Partial Hospitalization. Began in the 1960's as the Partial Hospitalization Study Group; it adopted its present name in 1979 to reflect the fact that the organization had grown into an extensive national network. AAPH is a multidisciplinary organization whose members share a common interest in the development, growth and improvement of partial hospitalization within the continuum of psychiatric treatment. Membership: $105/year (individual); $450/year (organization).

Publications:
AABH Insurance Manual.
AAPH Bibliography. trien.
Continuum: Developments in Ambulatory Mental Health Care. q.
Inside AABH. bi-m.
Standards and Guidelines for Adult Partial Hospitalization.
Standards and Guidelines for Child/Adolescent Partial Hospitalization.
Standards and Guidelines for Geriatric Partial Hospitalization.

Meetings/Conferences:
Annual Meetings: August
1999 – Denver, CO/Aug. 4-7

Ass'n for Applied Psychoanalysis *(1952)*
116 Village Walk Drive
Royal Palm Beach, FL   33411
Tel: (561)793-0686
Members: 350 individuals
Staff: 2
Annual Budget: $10-25,000
Exec. Director: Dr. William D. Katz

Historical Note
Members are practicing psychoanalysts who must have had at least 300 hours of personal psychoanalysis. Membership: $35/year.

Publications:
American Imago. q. adv.
Directory. a.
Newsletter. q. adv.

Meetings/Conferences:
Annual Meetings: Spring

Ass'n for Applied Psychophysiology and Biofeedback *(1969)*
10200 West 44th Ave., Suite 304
Wheat Ridge, CO   80033
Tel: (303)422-8436   *Fax:* (303)422-8894
E-Mail: aapb@resourcenter.com
Web Site: http://www.aapb.org
Members: 1,900 individuals
Staff: 4
Annual Budget: $250-500,000
Exec. Director: Francine Butler, Ph.D., CAE
Dir., Communications: Michael P. Thompson
Dir., Meetings: Kate Holland, CMP
Dir., Finances: Chris Ruppert
Membership Director: Tom Noland

Historical Note
Formerly (1988) the Biofeedback Soc. of America. Members are psychologists and other health care professionals who treat stress-related disorders with biofeedback or other applied psychophysiology techniques. Membership: $115/year.

Publications:
Applied Psychophysiology and Biofeedback. q. adv.
Biofeedback: a Newsmagazine. q. adv.
Meetings/Conferences:
Annual Meetings: Spring
1999 – Vancouver, British Columbia/April 7-11

Ass'n for Arid Lands Studies (1977)
c/o Int'l Ctr Arid & Semi-Arid Lnd Stds
Texas Tech University, P.O. Box 41036
Lubbock, TX   79409-1036
Tel: (806)742-2218   *Fax:* (806)742-1954
Web Site: http://www.iaff.ttu.edu/AALS
Members: 250 individuals
Staff: 2
Exec. Director: Dr. Idris R. Traylor, Jr.
Historical Note
Members are scientists, social scientists and other academics with an interest in the study of arid and semi-arid lands. Membership: $20/year.
Publications:
Forum of the AALS. a.
Meetings/Conferences:
Annual Meetings: In conjunctiion with the Western Social Sciences Ass'n

Ass'n for Asian American Studies (1970)
420 Rockefeller Hall, Cornell University
Ithaca, NY   14853-2602
Tel: (607)255-3320   *Fax:* (607)254-4996
Members: 506 individuals
Staff: 1
President: Yen Le Espiritu
Historical Note
AAAS members are academics, students and others with an interest in the field. Membership: $30-80/year, varies by rank (faculty); $30/year (student).
Publications:
Anthology. a.
Occasional Papers Newsletter. q.
Meetings/Conferences:

Ass'n for Asian Performance
Historical Note
A focus group of the Ass'n for Theatre in Higher Education.

Ass'n for Asian Studies (1941)
1021 E. Huron St.
Ann Arbor, MI   48104
Tel: (734)665-2490   *Fax:* (734)665-3801
E-Mail: aasiamsc@org
Web Site: http://www.aasinst.org
Members: 8,000 individuals, 2,200 institutions
Staff: 10
Annual Budget: $250-500,000
Secretary-Treasurer: John C. Campbell
Conference Coordinator: Karen Fricke
Historical Note
Organized as the Far Eastern Association on June 9, 1941, the Ass'n for Asian Studies assumed its present name in 1957 to reflect a growing interest in Asia east of the Middle East. A member of the American Council of Learned Socs. Afghanistan Studies Ass'n is an affiliate of AAS. Membership: $25-90/year (individual).
Publications:
Asian Studies Newsletter. 5/year.
Bibliography of Asian Studies. a.
Journal of Asian Studies. q. adv.
Meeting Program. a. adv.
Membership Directory. a.
Meetings/Conferences:
Annual Meetings: Spring
1999 – Boston, MA(Marriott)/March 11-14

Ass'n for Assessment and Accreditation of Laboratory Animal Care Internat'l (1965)
11300 Rockville Pike, Suite 1211
Rockville, MD   20852-3035
Tel: (301)231-5353   *Fax:* (301)231-8282
Toll Free: (800)926 - 0066
Web Site: http://www.aaalac.org
Members: 610 units, 43 sponsoring societies
Staff: 8
Annual Budget: $1-2,000,000
Exec. Director: John G. Miller, Ph.D., DVM
Mktg./Communications Manager: Lori Wieder
Historical Note
Formerly (1996) American Ass'n for Accreditation of Laboratory Animal Care. Established and incorporated in Illinois, AAALAC promotes high quality animal care and use in programs of research, breeding, teaching and testing through a voluntary accreditation program.
Publications:
AAALAC Connection Newsletter.

Ass'n for Assessment in Counseling (1965)
5999 Stevenson Ave.
Alexandria, VA   22304-3300
Tel: (703)823-9800   *Fax:* (703)823-0252
Members: 2,233 individuals
Staff: 2
Annual Budget: $25-50,000
Interim Exec. Director: Richard Yep
Historical Note
A division of the American Counseling Ass'n. Formerly (1984) the Ass'n for Measurement and Evaluation in Guidance, and (1992) Ass'n for Measurement and Evaluation in Counseling and Development. Membership: $28/year, plus ACA dues; $9/year (student); $9/year (retired).

Publications:
AAC Newsnotes.
Measurement & Evaluation in Counseling & Development Journal. q. adv.
Meetings/Conferences:
Annual Meetings: With the American Counseling Ass'n
1999 – San Diego, CA/April 14-18
2000 – Washington, DC/March 22-25
2001 – San Antonio, TX
2002 – New Orleans, LA

Ass'n for Automated Reasoning (1984)
c/o Argonne Nat'l Lab./Math & Comp. Sci.
9700 S. Cass Ave.
Argonne, IL   60439-4844
Tel: (630)252-7224   *Fax:* (630)252-5986
Members: 400 individuals
President: Lawrence Wos, Ph.D.
Historical Note
Members are scientists with an interest in the field of automated reasoning.
Publications:
AAR Newsletter. q.

Ass'n for Behavior Analysis (1974)
213 West Hall, Western Michigan Univ.
1201 Oliver Street
Kalamazoo, MI   49008-5052
Tel: (616)387-8341   *Fax:* (616)387-8354
E-Mail: 76236.1312@compuserve.com
Members: 2,700 individuals
Staff: 3
Annual Budget: $100-250,000
Exec. Director: Maria E. Malott
Historical Note
Until 1979, known as the Midwestern Ass'n for Behavior Analysis. Members are individuals interested in the applied experimental and theoretical analysis of behavior and the enhancement of behavior analysis as a profession. Full members of ABA have at least a Master's degree in psychology or a related discipline and have demonstrated competence in either applied or experimental behavior analysis.
Publications:
ABA Newsletter. 3/yr. adv.
Behavior Analyst. bi-a. adv.
Journal of the Analysis of Verbal Behavior. a. adv.
Meetings/Conferences:
Annual Meetings: Annual/Memorial Weekend
1999 – Chicago, IL(Chicago Hilton & Towers)/May 26-30/2000
2000 – Washington, DC(Sheraton Washington)/May 25-30/2000
2001 – New Orleans, LA(Hyatt Regency New Orleans)/May 25-30/2000

Ass'n for Biology Laboratory Education (1979)
1153 Biochemistry Bldg., Purdue Univ.
West Lafayette, IN   47907-1153
Members: 400 individuals
Annual Budget: $10-25,000
President: Anna Wilson
Historical Note
ABLE's purpose is primarily to facilitate communication between college instructors actively involved with laboratory instruction in the various areas of biology and to encourage the development and dissemination of reliable laboratory exercises., Membership: $35/year.
Publications:
Labstracts Newsletter. 3/year.
Proceedings. a.
Meetings/Conferences:
Annual Meetings: June

Ass'n for Birth Psychology (1978)
Historical Note
Inactive in 1997.

Ass'n for Borderlands Studies (1976)
Ctr for Inter-American & Border Studies
5500 Campanile Dr.,
San Diego, CA   92182
Tel: (619)594-5423   *Fax:* (619)594-5474
Members: 3,000 individuals
Annual Budget: under $10,000
Exec. Secretary: Bertha Hernandez
Historical Note
Originally a scholarly organization studying the U.S.-Mexico border, ABS members now include academics and professionals concerned with other border regions as well. The executive officers change annually. Membership: $20/year (student); $45/year(professor).
Publications:
Journal of Borderlands Studies. semi-a.
La Frontera Newsletter. semi-a.
Meetings/Conferences:
Annual Meetings: last full weekend in April

Ass'n for Bridge Construction and Design (1976)
P.O. Box 23264
Pittsburgh, PA   15222
Tel: (412)281-9900
Members: 250 individuals, 30 companies
Annual Budget: $10-25,000
Historical Note
Has no paid staff. Membership: $15/yr. (individual); $125/yr. (company).
Publications:
Newsletter. bi-m.

Meetings/Conferences:
Annual Meetings: June, in Pittsburgh in conjunction with Internat'l Bridge Conference.

Ass'n for Business Communication (1935)
Historical Note
Address unknown in 1996.

Ass'n for Business Simulation and Experiential Learning (1974)
School of Business
Wayne State University
Detroit, MI   48202-3930
Tel: (313)577-4551   *Fax:* (313)577-5486
E-Mail: hughcannon@aol.com
Web Site: http://www.towson.edu/ ~ ABSEL/
Members: 225 individuals
Staff: 1
Annual Budget: $25-50,000
Exec. Director: Hugh M. Cannon, Ph.D.
Historical Note
ABSEL was created to encourage the association of business simulators and those interested in developing and using experiential learning techniques in the fields of business and administration. Membership: $65/year (individual).
Publications:
ABSEL News & Views. semi-a. adv.
Conference Program. a. adv.
Proceedings. a. adv.
Meetings/Conferences:
Annual Meetings: March
1999 – Philadelphia, PA/March 17-19
2000 – Savanah, GA
2001 – San Diego, CA

Ass'n for Canadian Studies in the United States (1971)
1317 F St., N.W., Suite 920
Washington, DC   20004-1105
Tel: (202)393-2580   *Fax:* (202)393-2582
E-Mail: acsus@nicom.com
Web Site: http://canada ~ acsus.plattsburg
Members: 1000 individuals
Staff: 3
Annual Budget: $100-250,000
Exec. Director: David N. Biette
Historical Note
Promotes the study of Canada at all educational levels. The core of its membership is comprised of university professors involved in teaching about Canada. Membership: $60/year (individual); $105/year (institution).
Publications:
American Review of Canadian Studies. q. adv.
Canadian Studies Update. q.
Directory. bien.
Meetings/Conferences:
Biennial Meetings: Odd years
1999 – Pittsburgh, PA(Westin William Penn)/Nov. 17-21

Ass'n for Central Asian Studies (1985)
Univ. of Wisconsin, 3211 Humanties Bldg.
4555 N. Park St.
Madison, WI   53706
Tel: (608)263-1825
Members: 85 individuals
Staff: 1
Annual Budget: under $10,000
President: Kemal H. Karpat
Historical Note
Professional society promoting the study of central Asia. Established in 1985 following a conference convened to awaken interest and promote the study of Central Asia. Membership: $15/year (individual); $25/year (organization).
Publications:
ACASIA. a. adv.
Meetings/Conferences:
Annual Meetings: in conjunction with MESA

Ass'n for Chemoreception Sciences (1979)
744 Duparc Circle
Tallahassee, FL   32312-1409
Tel: (850)531-0854   *Fax:* (850)531-0854
Members: 725 individuals
Program Chair: Gail Burd
Historical Note
Members are scientists interested in the physiological reception of chemical stimuli. Has no paid officers or full-time staff.
Publications:
AchemS Membership Directory. a.
Chemical Senses. bi-m.
Newsletter. semi-a.
Meetings/Conferences:
Annual Meetings: April
1999 – Sarasota, FL(Hyatt)

Ass'n for Child Psychoanalysis (1965)
P.O. Box 253
Ramsey, NJ   07446
Tel: (201)825-3138   *Fax:* (201)825-3138
E-Mail: 76422.3352@compuserve.com
Members: 600 individuals
Staff: 2
Annual Budget: $250-500,000
Administrator: Nancy Hall
Historical Note
Formerly (1971) American Ass'n for Child Psychoanalysis. Membership: $50/year (individual); $75/year (candidates).
Publications:
Abstracts. bien.

ACP Newsletter. q.
Meetings/Conferences:
Annual Meetings: Spring

Ass'n for Childhood Education Internat'l (1892)
17904 Georgia Ave., Suite 215
Olney, MD   20832-2277
Tel: (301)570-2111   *Fax:* (301)570-2212
Toll Free: (800)423 - 3563
E-Mail: aceihq@aol.com
Web Site: http://www.udel.edu/bateman/acei
Members: 16,000 individuals
Staff: 15
Annual Budget: $1-2,000,000
Exec. Director: Gerald C. Odland
Dir., Conferences/Marketing: Marilyn B. Gardner
Director, Membership: Julie Wisor
Editor/Director of Publications: Anne Watson Bauer

Historical Note
Established in 1892 as the Internat'l Kindergarten Union. In 1931 merged with the Nat'l Council of Primary Education and became Ass'n for Childhood Education Internat'l. ACEI is a professional organization for educators concerned with whole curriculum and whole child development from birth to age 13. It is the national accrediting body for university-level elementary education programs through the Nat'l Council for Accreditation of Teacher Education (NCATE). Membership: $45/year (individual), $55/year (institutional).

Publications:
ACEI Exchange Newsletter. 5/year.
Childhood Education. bi-m. adv.
Journal of Research in Childhood Education. semi-a. adv.

Meetings/Conferences:
Annual Meetings: Spring
1999 – San Antonio, TX

Ass'n for Clinical Pastoral Education (1967)
1549 Clairmont Road, Suite 103
Decatur, GA   30033-4635
Tel: (404)320-1472   *Fax:* (404)320-0849
E-Mail: 71210.2243@compuserve.com
Members: 3,500 individuals
Staff: 6
Annual Budget: $500-1,000,000
Exec. Director: Stuart Plummer, Ph.D.

Historical Note
A combination of four CPE organizations: the Lutheran Council of the U. S. A., the Association of Clinical Pastoral Educators, the Council for Clinical Training and the Institute of Pastoral Care became the ACPE in 1967 and assumed its present name in 1968. Membership: $67/year (individual), annual dues vary (institution).

Publications:
ACPE News. bi-m.
Journal of Pastoral Care. q. adv.

Meetings/Conferences:
Annual Meetings: Spring/600

Ass'n for College and University Religious Affairs (1959)
Northwestern University
1870 Sheridan Road
Evanston, IL   60208-1350
Tel: (847)491-7256
Members: 95 individuals
Annual Budget: under $10,000
Secretary-Treasurer: Timothy S. Stevens, Ph.D.

Historical Note
Formerly (1991) Ass'n for the Coordination of University Religious Affairs. An association of personnel involved in religious affairs at instutions of higher education. Membership: $30/year (individual); $60/year (institution).

Publications:
Dialogue on Campus. q.

Meetings/Conferences:
Annual Meetings: Fall

Ass'n for Commercial Real Estate
Historical Note
See NAIOP: The Ass'n for Commercial Real Estate.

Ass'n for Communication Administration (1971)
5105 Backlick Road, Bldg. E
Annandale, VA   22003
Tel: (703)750-0533   *Fax:* (703)914-9471
Members: 350 individuals
Staff: 2
Annual Budget: $25-50,000
Controller: N.J. Geiger

Historical Note
Founded in San Francisco as the Ass'n for Departments and Administrators in Speech Communication; it assumed its present name in 1975; incorporated in Virginia in 1982, and in Kentucky in 1990. Membership generally comprises administrators teaching Communication, Humanities, Theatre, Radio-TV, Journalism, or English at the college level. Membership: $30/year (individual), $75/year (academic unit).

Publications:
Communication Disciplines in Higher Education. a.
Directory of Theatre Programs. bien. adv.
Handbook for Theatre Department Chairs. irreg.
Journal of ACA (JACA). q.

Meetings/Conferences:
Annual Seminars: Fall/125

Ass'n for Community Based Education (1976)
1805 Florida Ave., N.W.
Washington, DC   20009
Tel: (202)462-6333

Members: 110 organizations
Staff: 7
Exec. Director: Christofer Zachariadis

Historical Note
Members are independent, community-based organizations providing educational opportunities to adults.

Publications:
CBE Report. m.
Directory of Community-Based Adult Literacy Providers. irreg.
Directory of Funding Sources. a.
Directory of Members. a.

Meetings/Conferences:
Annual Meetings: November

Ass'n for Commuter Transportation (1976)
1518 K St., N.W., Suite 503
Washington, DC   20005
Tel: (202)393-3497   *Fax:* (202)347-8847
E-Mail: acthg@aol.com
Web Site: http://www.tmi.cob.fsu.edu/act/
Members: 1,200 individuals
Staff: 5
Annual Budget: $250-500,000
Exec. Director: Kenneth M. Sufka

Historical Note
Formed in Savannah, Georgia in August 1976 by 31 charter van pool pioneers as the Nat'l Ass'n of Van Pool Operators; assumed its present name in 1984. Absorbed the Ass'n of Ridesharing Professionals in 1986. Members are corporations, employers, public agencies, transit authorities, vanpool management companies, real estate developers and individuals involved in promoting alternatives to drive-alone commuting. Membership: $200/year (individual); $400/year (organization/company).

Publications:
Directory of Transportation Management Associations.
Membership Directory. a. adv.
TDM Review. q. adv.

Meetings/Conferences:
Annual Meetings: September
1999 – Washington, DC
2000 – Orlando, FL

Ass'n for Comparative Economic Studies (1972)
Department of Economics
Arizona State Univ., Box 873806
Tempe, AZ   85287-3806
Tel: (602)965-6524   *Fax:* (602)965-0748
E-Mail: atjcb@asuvm.inre.asu.edu
Web Site: http://PUBLIC.ASU.EDU/ ~ ATJCB
Members: 700 individuals
Staff: 1
Annual Budget: $10-25,000
Exec. Secretary: Josef C. Brada

Historical Note
A member of the Allied Social Science Ass'ns. Merger of the Ass'n for the Study of Soviet-Type Economics (1959) and Ass'n for Comparative Economics (1963). Membership: $40/year (individual), $65/year (organization/company).

Publications:
Comparative Economic Studies. q. adv.
Journal of Comparative Economics. q. adv.

Meetings/Conferences:
Annual Meetings: With the Allied Social Science Ass'n
1999 – New York, NY(Hilton)/500
2000 – Boston, MA/Jan. 3-5

Ass'n for Computational Linguistics (1962)
75 Patterson St., Suite 9
New Brunswick, NJ   08901
Tel: (732)342-9100   *Fax:* (732)342-9339
E-Mail: acl@aclweb.org
Web Site: http://www.cs.columbia.edu/adl
Members: 1,750 individuals
Staff: 1
Annual Budget: $100-250,000
Business Manager: Priscilla Rasmussen

Historical Note
Formerly (1968) Ass'n for Machine Translation and Computational Linguistics. Affiliated with the Internat'l Committee on Computational Linguistics. Computational linguistics deals with algorithms, models, and computer systems or components of systems for research on language and scholarly investigation.

Publications:
Computational Linguistics. q.
Proceedings, Annual Meetings. a.
Proceedings, Conference on Applied Natural Language
     Processing. bien.
Proceedings, European Chapter Meetings. bien.

Meetings/Conferences:
1999 – College Park, MD(University of MD)/June 22-26

Ass'n for Computer Operations Management (1981)
Historical Note
Became Ass'n for Data Center, Network and Enterprise Systems Management in 1997.

Ass'n for Computers and the Humanities (1978)
P.O. Box 1885-CIS
Brown University
Providence, RI   02912
Tel: (401)863-7321
Web Site: http://www.ach.org
Members: 380 individuals
Annual Budget: under $10,000
Exec. Secretary: Elli Mylonas

Historical Note
Formed to foster computer-aided scholarship and teaching in the humanities and arts fields. Membership: $60/year.

Publications:
Computers and the Humanities. 6/year. adv.

Meetings/Conferences:
1999 – Charlottesville, VA/June 9-13

Ass'n for Computing Machinery (1947)
1515 Broadway
New York, NY   10036
Tel: (212)626-0500   *Fax:* (212)944-1318
Toll Free: (800)342 - 6626
E-Mail: acmhelp@acm.org
Web Site: http://www.acm.org
Members: 85,000 individuals
Staff: 94
Annual Budget: $25-50,000,000
Exec. Director: John White
Director, Financial Services: Michael Lichtenstein
Director, Membership: Lillian Israel
Director, Publications: Mark Mandelbaum

Historical Note
ACM was founded at Columbia University as the Eastern Ass'n for Computing Machinery. Its constitution and by-laws were adopted in 1949 and it was incorporated in Delaware in 1954. It is the oldest and largest international professional association of computer professionals. ACM's purpose is to advance the skills of information technology professionals and students. Membership $25/year (student), $84/year (full member).

Publications:
ACM Computing Surveys. q.
ACM Transactions on Database Systems. q.
ACM Transactions on Mathematical Software. q.
Collected Algorithms from ACM. q.
Communications of the ACM. m. adv.
Computing Reviews. m. adv.
Interactions. bi-m.
Journal of the ACM. bi-m.
Multimedia Systems. bi-m.
Networker. q.
StandardView. q.
Transactions on Computer Systems. q.
Transactions on Computer-Human Interaction. q.
Transactions on Graphics. q.
Transactions on Information Systems. q.
Transactions on Modeling and Computer Simulation. q.
Transactions on Networking. bi-m.
Transactions on Programming Languages and Systems. bi-m.
Transactions on Software Engineering & Methodology. q.
Wireless Networks. bi-m.

Meetings/Conferences:
Annual Meetings: February-March

Ass'n for Conservation Information (1938)
Div. of Fish Game And Wildlife
P.O. Box 400
Trenton, NJ   08625-0400
Tel: (609)984-6295   *Fax:* (609)984-1414
Members: 65 individuals, 45 gov't agencies & private orgs
Annual Budget: $10-25,000
Membership Director: David Chanda

Historical Note
Organized originally as the American Association for Conservation Information, ACI works to upgrade the quality of all forms of communication in and among agencies devoted to the protection and management of natural resources and wildlife. Members are officials of state fish and game departments, parks, recreation, soil and forestry organizations, as well as affiliates of federal and regional natural resource agencies. Has no paid staff or permanent address. Officers change annually. Membership: $25/year (individual), $100/year (organization).

Publications:
Membership Directory. a.
The Balance Wheel. q.

Meetings/Conferences:
Annual Meetings: Summer Conference
1999 – Arkansas

Ass'n for Consumer Research (1969)
Graduate School of Management, 632 TNRB
Brigham Young Univ.
Provo, UT   84602
Tel: (801)378-2080   *Fax:* (801)226-7650
E-Mail: nkhunt@byu.edu
Members: 1,600 individuals
Staff: 1
Annual Budget: under $10,000
Exec. Secretary: Keith Hunt

Historical Note
Business people, educators and government officials interested in consumer research. Membership: $30/year.

Publications:
Advances in Consumer Research. a.
Asia Pacific Advances in Consumer Research. bien.
European Advances in Consumer Research. bien.

Meetings/Conferences:
Annual Meetings: Even numbered years–Asia/Pacific; odd
                  numbered years–Europe

Ass'n for Continuing Higher Education (1939)
Trident Technical College
P.O. Box 118067, CE-M
Charleston, SC   29423-8067
Tel: (803)574-6658   *Fax:* (803)574-6470
E-Mail: zpbarrineau@trident.tec.sc.us
Web Site: http://Charleston.net/org/ACHE/
Members: 1,800 individuals
Staff: 1
Annual Budget: $50-100,000
Exec. V. President: Wayne L. Whelan

Historical Note
Established as Ass'n of University Evening Colleges by a group of evening college administrators attending the 1939 annual meeting of Ass'n of Urban Universities; assumed its present name in 1973. Membership consists of individuals whose prime commitment is continuing education and regionally accredited institutions of higher learning which have programming or administrative units responsible for continuing education. Absorbed Committee for Continuing Education for School Personnel in 1990. Membership: $60/year (individual), $240/year (institution).

Publications:
Five Minutes with ACHE. 10/year.
Journal of Continuing Higher Education. 3/year.
Membership Directory. a.
Proceedings. a.

Meetings/Conferences:
Annual Meetings: Fall/400
1999 – Cincinnati, OH
2000 – Myrtle Beach, SC

Ass'n for Continuing Legal Education (1964)
P.O. Box 4646
Austin, TX 78765
Tel: (512)453-4340   *Fax:* (512)451-2911
Members: 465 individuals
Staff: 2
Annual Budget: $250-500,000
Exec. Director: Donna Passons

Historical Note
Formerly (1964) the Nat'l Ass'n of Continuing Legal Education Administrators and (1995) Ass'n for Continuing Legal Education. Members are organizations and individuals involved in providing continuing legal education. Two meetings held each year. Membership: $150/year (individual); $135/year (adiitional members).

Publications:
Directory. a.
Newsletter. q.

Meetings/Conferences:
1999 – Santa Fe, NM/Feb. 6-9
1999 – Boston, MA

Ass'n for Convention Marketing Executives (1990)
1819 Peachtree St., NE, Suite 620
Atlanta, GA 30309-1848
Tel: (404)355-2400   *Fax:* (404)351-3348
Members: 175 individuals
Staff: 4
Annual Budget: $50-100,000
Exec. V. President: William H. Just, CAE, CMP

Historical Note
Active members are convention marketing executives affiliated with convention bureaus and centers whose chief objective is to establish and foster an effective marketing partnership. Membership: $195/year.

Publications:
Membership Directory. a. adv.
Newsletter. q. adv.

Meetings/Conferences:

Ass'n for Convention Operations Management (1988)
1819 Peachtree St., NE, Suite 620
Atlanta, GA 30309-1848
Tel: (404)351-3220   *Fax:* (404)351-3348
Members: 500 individuals
Staff: 4
Annual Budget: $250-500,000
Exec. V. President: William H. Just, CAE, CMP

Historical Note
Members are convention service directors and managers, associated with convention facilities and bureaus, and industry suppliers. Membership: $150/year (active member), $225/year (affiliate).

Publications:
ACOMmodate. q. adv.

Meetings/Conferences:

Ass'n for Corporate Growth (1954)
1926 Waukegan Road, Suite #1
Glenview, IL 60025-1770
Tel: (847)657-6730   *Fax:* (847)657-6819
Toll Free: (800)699 - 1331
E-Mail: acghq@tcag.com
Web Site: http://www.acg.org
Members: 4,200 individuals
Staff: 7
Annual Budget: $1-2,000,000
Exec. Director: Carl A. Wangman, CAE
Manager, Member Services: Janice H. Wangman

Historical Note
Founded as the Ass'n for Corporate Growth and Diversification by Peter Hilton and a group of businessmen as a professional society and forum for ideas related to both external and internal growth - joint ventures, acquisitions and divestitures, and new or expanded products and services. Members are mergers and acquisitions specialists. Membership: $250/year (individual, plus variable chapter dues).

Publications:
ACG Network Newsletter. m. adv.
Directory. a.

Meetings/Conferences:
Annual Meetings: Spring
1999 – Palm Springs, CA(Marriott Rancho Las
         Palmas)/April 21-24/650
2000 – Tampa, FL(Saddlebrook Resort)/April 12-15/700
2001 – Colorado Springs, CO(The Broadmaor)/May 2-5/700
2002 – Orlando, FL(Hyatt Regency)/April 10-13/700
2003 – San Diego, CA(Hotel del Coronado)/April 30-May 3

Ass'n for Correctional Research and Information Management (1971)
1129 Rivara Cir.
Sacramento, CA 95864-3720
Tel: (916)487-9334   *Fax:* (916)487-9929
E-Mail: Flylarry@aol.com
Web Site: http://www.happenings.com/lbennett
Members: 320 individuals
Annual Budget: under $10,000
Membership Chair: Lawrence Bennett, Ph.D.

Historical Note
Research branch of the American Correctional Ass'n. Formerly (1981) the Ass'n for Correctional Research. Purpose is to provide evaluation of problems that speak to correctional policy implications. Membership: $10/year.

Publications:
Newsletter. q.

Meetings/Conferences:
1999 – Nashville, TN
1999 – Denver, CO

Ass'n for Counselor Education and Supervision (1940)
5999 Stevenson Ave.
Alexandria, VA 22304-3300
Tel: (703)823-9800   *Fax:* (703)823-0252
Members: 2,711 individuals
Staff: 2
Annual Budget: $100-250,000
Interim Exec. Director: Richard Yep

Historical Note
ACES emphasizes the need for quality education and supervision of counselors for all work settings. A division of the American Counseling Ass'n. Membership: $40/year (professional); $20/year (student/retired).

Publications:
Counselor Education and Supervision. q. adv.
Spectrum. q.

Meetings/Conferences:
Annual Meetings: Spring, with the American Counseling Ass'n
1999 – San Diego, CA/April 12-17
2000 – Washington, DC/March 22-25
2001 – San Antonio, TX
2002 – New Orleans, LA

Ass'n for Counselors and Educators in Government (1984)
5999 Stevenson Ave.
Alexandria, VA 22304
Tel: (703)823-9800   *Fax:* (703)823-0252
Members: 722 individuals
Staff: 2
Annual Budget: $10-25,000
Interim Exec. Director: Richard Yep

Historical Note
An organizational affiliate of the American Counseling Ass'n, which provides administrative support. Formerly (1994) Military Educators and Counselors Ass'n. Members are counselors and educators working in local, state, or federal government agencies. Membership: $20/year (professional); $15/year (student).

Publications:
ACEG Newsletter.

Meetings/Conferences:
Annual Meetings: With the American Counseling Ass'n
1999 – San Diego, CA/April 14-17
2000 – Washington, DC/March 22-25
2001 – San Antonio, TX
2002 – New Orleans, LA

Ass'n for Creative Change (1968)
Historical Note
Address unknown in 1996.

Ass'n for Data Center, Network and Enterprise Systems Management (1981)
742 E. Chapman Ave.
Orange, CA 92866
Tel: (714)997-7966   *Fax:* (714)997-9743
Members: 2,800 individuals
Staff: 17
Annual Budget: $2-5,000,000
President: Leonard Eckhaus

Historical Note
Formerly (1997) Ass'n for Computer Operations Management, AFCOM members are managers of corporate and institutional computer facilities. Membership: $183/year.

Publications:
Annual Survey of Enterprise Systems Salaries. a.
Comminique Newsletter. bi-m.
Enterprise Systems Manager. bi-m. adv.

Meetings/Conferences:
Annual Meetings: Spring
1999 – Philadelphia, PA

Ass'n for Death Education and Counseling (1976)
638 Prospect Ave.
Hartford, CT 06105-4298
Tel: (860)586-7503   *Fax:* (860)586-7550
E-Mail: info@adec.org
Web Site: http://www.adec.org
Members: 2,150 individuals and institutions
Staff: 3
Annual Budget: $100-250,000
Managing Director: M. Suzanne C. Berry, CAE

Historical Note
ADEC members are individuals and institutions involved in counseling the dying and bereaved. Maintains a code of ethics and certification programs. Membership: $115/year (individual),

$230/year (institution), $60/year (student), $60/year (older citizen - 62 or older).

Publications:
Conference Proceedings. a.
Forum Newsletter. bi-m. adv.
Membership Directory. a.

Meetings/Conferences:
1999 – San Antonio, TX/March 11-14

Ass'n for Direct Instruction (1981)
P.O. Box 10252
Eugene, OR 97440
Tel: (541)485-1293   *Fax:* (541)683-7543
E-Mail: erica@adjhmoe.org
Web Site: http://www.adihmoe.org
Members: 2,500 individuals
President: Kathy Madigan

Historical Note
ADI members are public school teachers and university instructors with an interest in improving teaching methodology. Has no paid officers or full-time staff.

Publications:
Effective School Practices. q.

Meetings/Conferences:
Annual Meetings: always in Eugene, OR

Ass'n for Documentary Editing (1978)
c/o Papers of John Marshall
P.O. Box 8781
Williamsburg, VA 23188
Tel: (757)221-2413   *Fax:* (757)221-1287
E-Mail: snperd@facstaff.wm.edu
Members: 510 individuals, 40 institutions
Annual Budget: $10-25,000
Secretary: Susan Perdue

Historical Note
Members of the ADE are working on editions in history, literature, philosophy, the arts, and the sciences. Many members are teachers or archivists as well as editors; others are full-time editors. All share the goal of promoting documentary editing through cooperation and exchange of ideas. Membership: $25/year.

Publications:
Documentary Editing. q.
Membership Directory. a.

Meetings/Conferences:
Annual Meetings: Fall

Ass'n for Dressings and Sauces. (1926)
5775 Peachtree-Dunwoody Road, Suite 500-G
Atlanta, GA 30342-1558
Tel: (404)252-3663   *Fax:* (404)252-0774
E-Mail: ads@assnhq.com
Web Site: http://www.dressings-sauces.org
Members: 175 companies
Staff: 5
President: Richard E. Cristol

Historical Note
Formerly (1973) Mayonnaise and Salad Dressings Institute. Members are manufacturers of mayonnaise, dressings, and prepared sauces; associate membership is available to suppliers.

Publications:
ADS Information Heads Up. 3/year.

Meetings/Conferences:
Annual Meetings: Spring and Fall

Ass'n for Education and Rehabilitation of the Blind and Visually Impaired (1984)
P.O. Box 22397
Alexandria, VA 22304-9239
Tel: (703)823-9690   *Fax:* (703)823-9695
E-Mail: aernet@laser.net
Web Site: http://www.aerbzi.org
Members: 5,000 individuals
Staff: 5
Annual Budget: $250-500,000
Exec. Director: Denise Rozell
Manager, Education Services: Lorna A. Frazier-Lindsey

Historical Note
The result of a consolidation of the American Ass'n of Workers for the Blind (1895) and the Ass'n for Education of the Visually Handicapped (1905) in 1984. Membership: $110/year (individual).

Publications:
AER Report. bi-m.
Job Exchange. m.
Re: view. q.

Meetings/Conferences:
Annual Meetings: Summer
2000 – Denver, CO(Adam's Mark)

Ass'n for Education in Journalism and Mass Communication (1912)
Univ. of South Carolina
LeConte College, Room 121
Columbia, SC 29208-0251
Tel: (803)777-2005   *Fax:* (803)777-4728
E-Mail: aejmc@sc.edu
Web Site: http://www.aejmc.sc.edu
Members: 3,300 individuals
Staff: 7
Annual Budget: $250-500,000
Exec. Director: Jennifer McGill

Historical Note
Formerly (1951) American Ass'n for Teachers of Journalism. Membership: $85/year (individual); $125/year (organization); $600/year (council of affiliate member).

Publications:
AEJMC News. bi-m.

Journalism and Mass Communication Abstracts. a.
Journalism and Mass Communication Directory. a. adv.
Journalism and Mass Communication Educator. q. adv.
Journalism and Mass Communication Monographs. q.
Journalism and Mass Communication Quarterly. q. adv.

Meetings/Conferences:
Annual Meetings: Summer/over 700
1999 – New Orleans, LA/Aug. 4-7
2000 – Phoenix, AZ/Aug. 9-12
2001 – Washington, DC/Aug. 5-8

Ass'n for Educational Communications and Technology (1923)
1025 Vermont Ave., N.W., Suite 820
Washington, DC   20005
Tel: (202)347-7834   *Fax:* (202)347-7839
E-Mail: aect@aect.org
Web Site: http://www.aect.org
Members: 4,500 individuals
Staff: 8
Annual Budget: $1-2,000,000
Exec. Director: Stanley D. Zenor
Director, Marketing: Todd T. Shears
Director, Meetings: Lois J. Freeland
Director, Finance: Shannon Gordon
Director, Publications: Mary M. Twillman

Historical Note
Founded in 1923 as the Department of Visual Instruction of the Nat'l Education Ass'n. Incorporated in the District of Columbia in 1969. Reorganized in 1969 as a national affiliate of the Nat'l Education Ass'n and became independent as the Ass'n for Educational Communications and Technology in July 1974. Members are professionals such as microcomputer and audiovisual specialists, media services directors and television producers who require expertise in instructional technology. Membership: $75/year (individual).

Publications:
Educational Technology Research & Development. q.
TechTrends. 6/year. adv.

Meetings/Conferences:
Annual Meetings: Winter
1999 – Houston, TX/Feb. 10-14

Ass'n for Electronics Manufacturing of SME (1985)
P.O. Box 930
One SME Drive
Dearborn, MI   48121-0930
Tel: (313)271-1500   *Fax:* (313)271-2061
Web Site: http://www.sme.org/em.html
Members: 3,300 individuals
Association Manager: Sandra Marshall

Historical Note
Sponsored by the Soc. of Manufacturing Engineers, EM/SME has more than 3,300 individual members in 36 countries.

Publications:
Bibliography of Electronics Manufacturing Technical Resources.
Electronics Manufacturing Engineering Technical Quarterly. a.

Ass'n for Engineering Graphics and Imaging Systems (1954)
800 Enterprise Dr., Suite 202
Oak Brook, IL   60523
Tel: (630)574-8200
E-Mail: aegis1997@aol.com
Web Site: http://www.diazo.org/www.wfdic.org
Members: 52 companies
Staff: 5
Annual Budget: $250-500,000
Exec. Director: Brian McCarthy

Historical Note
Formerly (1969) Nat'l Ass'n of Blueprint & Diazotype Coaters and (1995) Ass'n of Reproduction Materials Manufacturers. AEGIS members are producers of wide format copiers and plotters; the paper, vellum, or film media used with this equipment; and software and systems used for the creation of images of all types.

Meetings/Conferences:
Annual Meetings: Fall
1999 – first week of Nov.

Ass'n for Enterprise Opportunity (1991)
70 E. Lake St., Suite 620
Chicago, IL   60601
Tel: (312)357-0177   *Fax:* (312)357-0180
E-Mail: aeochicago@aol.com
Members: 500 individuals
Staff: 7
Exec. Director: Christine M. Benuzzi
Dir., Strategic Services: Zulma Mustafa
Program Manager for Access to Market: Sarah Bobrow-Williams
Training Manager: Paula Mannillo

Historical Note
AEO is the national association of organizations committed to microenterprise development. AEO provides its members with a forum, information and a voice to promote enterprise opportunity for people and communities with limited access to economic resources. Membership: $150/year.

Publications:
AEO Exchange. m.
Membership Directory. irreg.

Meetings/Conferences:
Annual Meetings: May
1999 – Chicago, IL(Hyatt Regency Chicago)/May 5-8

Ass'n for Equine Sports Medicine (1982)
P.O. Box 4506
Santa Barbara, CA   93140-4506
Tel: (805)965-1028

Members: 350 individuals
Annual Budget: $50-100,000
Exec. Director: Nancy Bull

Historical Note
AESM members are veterinarians, health professionals, horse owners, horse trainers and others interested in the medical treatment of horses involved in athletic competition. Membership: $60/year (U.S.).

Publications:
AESM News. q. adv.
Conference Proceedings. a. adv.
Membership List. irreg.
Newsletter. q. adv.

Meetings/Conferences:
Annual Meetings: March
1999 – Sydney, Australia/Sept. 26-30/300
2000 – Sacramento, CA

Ass'n for Evolutionary Economics (1965)
300 Pultney St., Scandling Center
Hobart and William Smith Colleges
Geneva, NY   14456-3397
Tel: (315)781-3433   *Fax:* (315)781-3422
Members: 550 individuals, 1,300 libraries and organizations
Staff: 1
Annual Budget: $50-100,000
Secretary-Treasurer: William Waller

Historical Note
Includes institutional economists from the United States, Canada, Latin America, Western Europe, and Asia. Seeks to foster the development of economic study and of economics as a social science based on the complex interrelationships of man and society. A member of the Allied Social Science Ass'ns. Membership: $35/year (individual), $40/year (library/institution), $15/year (student).

Publications:
Journal of Economic Issues. q. adv.

Meetings/Conferences:
Annual Meetings: With the Allied Social Science Ass'ns
1999 – New York, NY/Jan. 3-5

Ass'n for Experiential Education (1972)
2305 Canyon Blvd., Suite 100
Boulder, CO   80302-5651
Tel: (303)440-8844   *Fax:* (303)440-9581
E-Mail: Sharon@AEE.ORG
Web Site: http://www.aee.org
Members: 2,000 individuals, 800 organizations
Staff: 8
Annual Budget: $500-1,000,000
Exec. Director: Sharon Heinlen
Director, Conferences and Finance: Teresa Brackett
Director, Accreditation: Sky Gray
Office Manager: Kate Robey
Coordinator for Accreditation: Bill Zimmerman
Director, Publications: Karyn Moore

Historical Note
A not-for-profit international professional organization with roots in adventure education committed to the development, practice, and evaluation of experiential learning in all settings. Membership: $50-75/year (individual), $175-250/year (organization).

Publications:
Jobs Clearinghouse. m.
Journal of Experiential Education. 3/yr.
The AEE Horizon Newsletter. q.

Meetings/Conferences:
Annual Meetings: Fall

Ass'n for Facilities Engineering (1954)
8180 Corporate Park Drive, Suite 305
Cincinnati, OH   45242-3309
Tel: (513)489-2473   *Fax:* (513)247-7422
Toll Free: (888)222 - 0155
E-Mail: mail@afe.org
Web Site: http://www.afe.org
Members: 9,000 individuals, 75 companies
Staff: 20
Annual Budget: $1-2,000,000
Exec. Director: Bruce Medaris
Communications Specialist/Editor: Gabriella Jacobs
Mgr., Education/Training: Cindy Taylor
Director, Finance and Operations: Merlyn Teague
Manager, Membership: Alma Fath

Historical Note
Formerly (1996) American Institute of Plant Engineers. Individuals involved in the full spectrum of facilities management required to create a product or provide a service. Membership: $120/year.

Publications:
AFE Journal Facilities. bi-m. adv.
AFE Newsline. bi-m.
Facilities Forum. bi-m.

Meetings/Conferences:
Annual Meetings: Fall
1999 – Chicago, IL/Oct. 16-20

Ass'n for Faculty in the Medical Humanities
Historical Note
A division of the Soc. for Health and Human Values.

Ass'n for Federal Information Resources Management (1979)
Historical Note
Address unknown in 1996.

Ass'n for Feminist Anthropology (1988)
Historical Note
A section of the American Anthropological Ass'n.

Ass'n for Financial Counseling and Planning Education
Historical Note
Adress unknown in 1998.

Ass'n for Financial Technology (1972)
Blendonview Office Park
5008-02 Pine Creek Drive
Westerville, OH   43081-4899
Tel: (614)895-1208   *Fax:* (614)895-3466
E-Mail: aft@fitech.org
Web Site: http://www.fitech.org
Members: 75 companies
Staff: 3
Annual Budget: $100-250,000
Exec. Director: James R. Bannister

Historical Note
Established as the Multi-Bank Data Processing Organization, it became Nat'l Ass'n of Bank Servicers in 1975 and assumed its present name in 1994. AFT member companies provide systems applications and outsourcing services to banks, thrifts, credit unions and other financial institutions. Membership also includes suppliers of computer hardware and software, and other related products and services. Membership: $750/year.

Publications:
Newsletter. semi-a. adv.

Meetings/Conferences:
Semi-annual Meetings: Spring and Fall/75
1999 – San Diego, CA/March 9-12
1999 – Amelia Island, FL(Inn & Conference Ctr.)/Sept. 21-24
2000 – Kiawah Island, SC(Inn & Conference Ctr.)
2000 – San Antonio, TX

Ass'n for Finishing Processes of SME (1975)
P.O. Box 930
One SME Drive
Dearborn, MI   48121-0930
Tel: (313)271-1500   *Fax:* (313)271-2861
Toll Free: (800)733 - 4763
E-Mail: SKOMCHE@.ORG
Web Site: http://www.sme.org/afp.html
Association Manager: Cheri Skomra
Administrator: Jackie Cook

Historical Note
Sponsored by the Soc. of Manufacturing Engineers, AFP/SME has more 2,000 members in 40 countries. AFP/SME members are technicians, engineers and scientists who use industrial finishes such as powder coating, waterborne high solids and other custom coatings. AFP/SME offers certification as either a Certified Manufacturing Engineer (CMfgE) or Certified Manufacturing Technologist (CMfgT) specializing in industrial finishing through the Manufacturing Engineering Certification Institute of SME. Membership: $72/year.

Publications:
Finishing Line. q. adv.

Meetings/Conferences:
Biennial Meetings: odd years in Fall
1999 – Cleveland, OH(I-X Center)/May 18-20

Ass'n for Forming and Fabricating Technologies of SME
P.O. Box 930
One SME Drive
Dearborn, MI   48121-0930
Tel: (313)271-1500   *Fax:* (313)271-2861
Toll Free: (800)733 - 4763
E-Mail: SKOMCHE@SME.ORG
Web Site: http://www.sme.org/fta.html
Ass'n Manager: Cheri Skomra
Administrator: Jackie Cook

Historical Note
Founded as Material Forming Group of SME; later became Forming Technologies Ass'n of SME, and assumed its current name in 1998. A professional group sponsored by the Soc. of Manufacturing Engineers, members have a special interest in metal fabrication and forming processes and the management of fabricating operations. Membership: $72/year.

Publications:
1998-Cleveland, OH(I-X Center)/Nov. 3-.
Forming and Fabricating. m. adv.

Meetings/Conferences:
Annual Meetings: Fall, plus Spring technical meeting

Ass'n for Gay, Lesbian and Bisexual Issues in Counseling (1974)
5999 Stevenson Ave.
Alexandria, VA   22304-3300
Tel: (703)823-9800   *Fax:* (703)823-9800
Toll Free: (800)347 - 6647
Members: 1,103 individuals
Staff: 2
Annual Budget: $25-50,000
Interim Exec. Director: Richard Yep

Historical Note
Formerly the Caucus of Gay Counselors and the Nat'l Caucus of Gay and Lesbian Counselors, AGLBIC is an association of members of the American Counseling Ass'n, which provides administrative support. AGLBIC educates counselors to the unique needs of client identity development. Membership: $35/year (professional); $15/year (student/retired).

Publications:
AGLBIC News. q. adv.

Meetings/Conferences:
Annual Meetings: Spring
1999 – San Diego, CA/April 12-17
2000 – Washington, DC/March 22-25
2001 – San Antonio, TX
2002 – New Orleans, LA

Ass'n for General and Liberal Studies (1961)

Ball State Univ., North Quad 327
Muncie, IN   47306-0125
Tel: (765)285-1511
E-Mail: 00btlowe@bsuvc.bsu.edu
Web Site: http://bsuvc.bsu.edu/home/00rfamato/agls.htm
Members: 550 individuals
Annual Budget: under $10,000
Exec. Director: B. Thomas Lowe

Historical Note
AGLS members are individuals with an interest in higher education liberal arts and general education programs. Has no paid officers or full-time staff; the Director's position changes every three years. Membership: $30/year.

Publications:
AGLS Newsletter. 3/year.

Meetings/Conferences:
Annual Meetings: October
1999 – Richmond, VA

Ass'n for Gerontology in Higher Education *(1974)*
1030 15th St., NW, Suite 240
Washington, DC   20005-1503
Tel: (202)289-9806   *Fax:* (202)289-9824
Web Site: http://www.aghe.org
Members: 320 institutions
Staff: 4
Annual Budget: $100-250,000
Exec. Director: Cathy Tompkins
Director, Membership/Information: Derek Stepp

Historical Note
The association grew out of a committee of educators interested in the development and improvement of gerontological programs and resources in institutions of higher education. Its membership comprises colleges and universities in the U.S. and Canada concerned with gerontological education, training and research. Membership: $250-440/year (institution).

Publications:
AGHE Exchange. q. adv.
Brief Bibliographies.
Nat'l Dir. of Educational Prog.

Meetings/Conferences:
Annual Meetings: February-March/500
1999 – St. Louis, MO(Regal Riverfront Hotel)/Feb. 25-28

Ass'n for Gnotobiotics *(1961)*
NCSU Sch. of Veterinary Medicine
4700 Hillsborough Ave.
Raleigh, NC   27606
Tel: (919)829-4278
Members: 400 individuals
Annual Budget: under $10,000
Contact: Dr. Edward Harrell

Historical Note
Members are scientists interested in germ-free research and applications. Formerly (1968) Ass'n for Applied Gnotobiotics. Has no paid officers or full-time staff. Membership: $20/year (individual), $250/year (organization).

Publications:
Annual Meeting Abstract. a.
Membership Directory. a.
Newsletter. a.

Meetings/Conferences:
Annual Meeting: held in either June or October-November

Ass'n for Governmental Leasing and Finance *(1981)*
1200 19th St., N.W., Suite 300
Washington, DC   20036-2412
Tel: (202)429-5135   *Fax:* (202)429-5113
Web Site: http://www.financenet.gov/aglf
Members: 295 individuals, 175 companies
Staff: 2
Annual Budget: $250-500,000
Exec. Director: B. Preston Rich

Historical Note
Provides an exchange of information among tax-exempt issuers, investment banking firms, commercial banks and third party lease brokers primarily concerned with the tax-exempt lease purchase marketplace. Informs members of recent changes in federal, state and local laws and regulations as they affect tax-exempt project finance. Membership: $120/year (governmental member); $600/year (organization).

Publications:
Fifty State Survey. a.
Tax Exempt Leasing Letter. bi-m.

Meetings/Conferences:
Semi-annual Meetings: Spring and Fall

Ass'n for Graphic Arts Training *(1987)*
P.O. Box 294
St. Petersburg, FL   33731
Toll Free: (800)214 - 1120
Web Site: http://www.napl.org.agat
Contact: Wanda Breeden

Historical Note
AGAT members are graphic arts trainers employed by printing companies, teachers and other individuals and companies with an interest in graphic arts instruction. Membership: $100/year (organization); $50/year (teacher).

Publications:
AGATe Lines Newsletter.

Meetings/Conferences:

Ass'n for Health Services Research *(1981)*
1130 Connecticut Ave., N.W., Suite 700
Washington, DC   20036
Tel: (202)223-2477   *Fax:* (202)835-8972
E-Mail: info@ahsr.org
Web Site: http://www.ahsr.org

Members: 2,500 individuals and organizations
Staff: 18
Annual Budget: $1-2,000,000
Acting C.E.O.: Marian Mankin
Assist. Director, Annual Meeting: Marian Mankin
Program Assoc. for Government Relations: Jennifer Rotchford
Financial Officer: Kathleen Kennelly
Assoc. Director: Lois Chester
Membership Manager: Suzan Meredith

Historical Note
AHSR members are individuals and organizations concerned with health services research. Membership: $90/year (individual), $1,500-$5,000 (institution).

Publications:
Health Service Research. bi-m.
HSR Reports. q. adv.

Meetings/Conferences:
1999 – Chicago, IL(Sheraton Chicago)/June 20-22

Ass'n for Healthcare Philanthropy *(1967)*
313 Park Ave., Suite 400
Falls Church, VA   22046
Tel: (703)532-6243   *Fax:* (703)532-7170
E-Mail: ahp@go-ahp.org
Web Site: http://www.go-ahp.org
Members: 2,500 individuals
Staff: 12
Annual Budget: $1-2,000,000
President: William C. McGinly, Ph.D.,CAE
Dir., Fondation & Gov't Relations: Barbara Smith
Dir., Education & Meetings: Monika Schulz
Finance & Office Manager: Jody McNamara
Dir., Membership & Board Relations: Amy Lightfield
V. President: Laura Fleming Jones

Historical Note
Established as Developartners, became Nat'l Ass'n for Hospital Development in 1968, and assumed its present name in 1991. A professional association of hospital and health care executives involved in hospital development and fund-raising programs. Membership: $350/year (individual), $600/year (organization).

Publications:
AHP Connect. 8/year. adv.
AHP Journal. semi-a. adv.
AHP Membership Directory & Buyers Guide. a. adv.

Meetings/Conferences:
Annual Meetings: Fall
1999 – San Diego, CA
2000 – Boston, MA(Sheraton)/Oct. 11-15
2001 – Chicago, IL(Sheraton)/Sept. 12-16
2002 – San Antonio, TX(Sheraton)/Sept. 25-29

Ass'n for Healthcare Resource Materials and Management *(1962)*
One N. Franklin, 30th Floor
Chicago, IL   60606-3420
Tel: (312)422-3840   *Fax:* (312)422-4573
Web Site: http://www.ahrmm.org
Members: 2,800 individuals
Staff: 5
Annual Budget: $1-2,000,000
Exec. Director: Albert Sunseri
Administrative Coordinator: Agatha Wharff

Historical Note
Affiliated with the American Hospital Ass'n. Formerly (1975) the American Soc. for Hospital Purchasing Agents, (1983) the American Soc. for Hospital Purchasing and Materials Management, (1994) American Soc. for Hospital Materials Management, (1998) American Soc. for Healthcare Materials Management. Membership: $75/year (regular), $130/year (associate).

Publications:
ASHMM Membership Roster.
Career Connection. m. adv.
Conference Proceedings. a.
Healthcare Materials Management Newsletter. m.
Hospital Materials Management News. bi-m.
Technical Articles. q.

Meetings/Conferences:
Annual Meetings: Summer
1999 – San Francisco, CA/Aug. 22-25

Ass'n for High Technology Distribution *(1985)*
1900 Arch St.
Philadelphia, PA   19103-1498
Tel: (215)564-3484   *Fax:* (215)564-2175
Members: 250 companies
Staff: 3
Annual Budget: $250-500,000
Exec. Director: Patricia A. Lilly

Historical Note
Formerly (1995) Ass'n of High Technology Distributors. AHTD members are distributors of industrial automation products; affiliate membership is available for manufacturers. Membership: $595/year (company).

Publications:
AHTD Network Newsletter. 3/yr.
Membership Directory. a.

Meetings/Conferences:
Semi-Annual Meetings: Spring and Fall

Ass'n for Hospital Medical Education *(1956)*
1200 19th St., N.W., Suite 300
Washington, DC   20036
Tel: (202)857-1196   *Fax:* (202)223-4579
Web Site: http://ahmc.med.edu
Members: 700 individuals, 300 hospitals
Staff: 2
Annual Budget: $100-250,000
Exec. Director: Dennis E. Smeage
Meetings/Membership: Jackie Spague

Historical Note
Formerly (1968) Ass'n of Hospital Directors of Medical Education. Members are hospital staff and administrators concerned with medical education, primarily at community hospitals. Membership: $250/year (individual), $800/year (institutional).

Publications:
AHME Congressional Record. bi-m.
AHME Directory. a.
AHME News. bi-m. adv.
Guide to Graduate Medical Education.
Transitional Year Program Directory. a.

Meetings/Conferences:
Semi-Annual Meetings: Spring and Fall
1999 – Hilton Head Island, SC

Ass'n for Humanist Sociology *(1976)*
Sociology Department, John Jay College
CUNY, 899 Tenth Ave.
New York, NY   10019
Tel: (212)237-8461   *Fax:* (212)237-8955
Members: 300 individuals
Annual Budget: $10-25,000
Treasurer: Don Goodman

Historical Note
AHS is an organization of sociologists disenchanted with conventional academic sociology and committed to making sociology relevant to human needs. AHS seeks to provide an active support network for sociologists committed to humanist values. Has no paid officers or full-time staff. Membership: $20-60/year, varies by annual income (individual); $50/year (organization).

Publications:
Humanist Sociologist Newsletter. q. adv.
Humanity and Society Jounal. q. adv.

Meetings/Conferences:
Annual Meetings: Fall

Ass'n for Humanistic Education and Development *(1952)*
5999 Stevenson Ave.
Alexandria, VA   22304-C300
Tel: (703)823-9800   *Fax:* (703)823-0252
Members: 1,767 individuals
Staff: 2
Annual Budget: $25-50,000
Interim Exec. Director: Richard Yep

Historical Note
AHEAD provides a forum to exchange information and promote changes that reflect the growing body of knowledge about humanistic principles applied to human development and potential. A division of the American Counseling Ass'n. Formerly (1975) Student Personnel Ass'n for Teacher Education. Membership: $30/year (professional); $15/year (student).

Publications:
Infochange. q.
Journal of Humanistic Education and Development. q. adv.

Meetings/Conferences:
Annual Meetings: Spring, with the American Counseling Ass'n
1999 – San Diego, CA/April 12-17
2000 – Washington, DC/March 22-25
2001 – San Antonio, TX
2002 – New Orleans, LA

Ass'n for Humanistic Psychology *(1962)*
45 Franklin St., Suite 315
San Francisco, CA   94102
Tel: (415)864-8850   *Fax:* (415)864-8853
E-Mail: ahpoffice@aol.com
Web Site: http://ahpweb.org
Members: 2,500 individuals
Staff: 3
Annual Budget: $250-500,000
Exec. Director: Georgia Berland

Historical Note
Founded in Palo Alto in December 1962 as the American Ass'n for Humanistic Psychology. Incorporated in California in 1965. Name changed to Ass'n for Humanistic Psychology in 1969. Purpose is to promote and protect the humanistic perspectives and practices worldwide. Membership: $39-59/year (individual), $149/year (organization).

Publications:
AHP Perspective. bi-m. adv.
Journal of Humanistic Psychology. q.

Meetings/Conferences:
Annual Meetings: July/August
1999 – Indianapolis, IN/March 19-21

Ass'n for Independent Music *(1971)*
147 E. Main St.
P.O. Box 988
Whitesburg, KY   41858-0988
Tel: (606)633-0946   *Fax:* (606)633-1160
Toll Free: (800)607 - 6526
E-Mail: pat@afim.org
Web Site: http://www.afim.org
Members: 1,300 companies
Staff: 5
Annual Budget: $250-500,000
Exec. Director: Pat Martin Bradley

Historical Note
Formerly (1997) Nat'l Ass'n of Independent Record Distributors and Manufacturers. Members are makers and distributors of records, tapes, music videos and compact discs, and suppliers and distributors in related fields. Membership fee varies according to type of membership, $300-1,500/year.

Publications:
Music Mix. m. adv.
State of Independents. m. adv.

Meetings/Conferences:
Annual Meetings: Spring
1999 – Atlanta, GA(Marriott Marrquis)/May 19-23

Ass'n for Individually Guided Education *(1972)*
Historical Note
Organization reported defunct in 1996.

Ass'n for Informal Logic and Critical Thinking *(1983)*
Philosophy and Religion Department
Baker University
Baldwin City, KS   66006
Tel: (913)594-6451   *Fax:* (913)594-2522
E-Mail: hatcher@harvey.bakeru.edu
Members: 250 individuals
Annual Budget: under $10,000
Treasurer: Dr. Donald L. Hatcher

Historical Note
*AILACT was established to promote whe quality of research,
teaching, and testing of informal logic and critical thinking at all
levels and to facilitate discussion between its members. AILACT
members are academics and teachers of courses in informal logic
and critical thinking. Membership: $6/year (individual).*

Ass'n for Information and Image Management International *(1943)*
1100 Wayne Ave., Suite 1100
Silver Spring, MD   20910-5603
Tel: (301)587-8202   *Fax:* (301)587-2711
E-Mail: aiim@aiim.org
Web Site: http://www.aiim.org
Members: 8,500 individuals
Staff: 50
Annual Budget: $10-25,000,000
President: John F. Mancini
Senior V. President, Information Content and Services: Priscilla
   Emery
V. President, Information Content and Services: Gary Robinson
V. President, Standards and Technical Services: Marilyn Wright
Senior V. President, Finance and Administration: J. Kenneth
   Althouse
V. President, Membership and Chapter Relations: Karen Clayton
   Carey
Senior V. President, Marketing and Events: Jeffrey V. Arcuri
Manager, Information Systems: Terrance Wilson

Historical Note
*Established and incorporated in Michigan as the Nat'l Microfilm
Ass'n, it became the Nat'l Micrographics Ass'n in 1975 and
assumed its present name in 1983. Members are users and
manufacturers of equipment, supplies and services for the document
management industry. Has an annual budget of approximately $12
million. Membership: $90/year (individual); $250-8,000/year
(company, based on gross revenue.)*

Publications:
Inform. m. adv.

Meetings/Conferences:
Annual Meetings: Spring/40,000
1999 – Atlanta, GA(Georgia World Congress
   Center)/April 12-15
2000 – New York, NY(Javits Convention Center)/April 10-13

Ass'n for Information Media and Equipment *(1986)*
134 Sunflower Ave.
Clarksdale, MS   38614-1173
Tel: (601)624-9355   *Fax:* (601)624-9366
E-Mail: info@gmi.net
Web Site: http://www.aime@gmi.net
Members: 19 companies, 125 institutions
Staff: 1
Annual Budget: $25-50,000
Exec. Director: Betty Gorsegner

Historical Note
*AIME is an association of producers and distributors of educational
films and video, companies who provide related equipment and
services, and others who use information media materials and
equipment. AIME is active in the areas of copyright, legislation to
benefit school media centers and funds for materials, market
research, new technology, and promotion of film and video as
effective instructional tools. Membership fee varies by category of
membership.*

Publications:
AIME News Newsletter. 4/year.

Meetings/Conferences:

Ass'n for Information Systems *(1995)*
P.O. Box 2712
Atlanta, GA   30301-2712
Tel: (404)651-0258   *Fax:* (404)651-4938
E-Mail: emclean@gsu.edu
Web Site: http://www.aisnet.org
Members: 1,400 individuals
Staff: 2
Exec. Director: Ephraim R. McLean

Historical Note
*AIS members are academics with an interest in information systems
and related fields.*

Publications:
Information Systems Journal. irreg.
Journal of Organizational Computing. irreg.
Management Information Systems Quarterly Journal. q.

Ass'n for Innovative Marketing *(1989)*
Historical Note
Address unknown in 1996.

Ass'n for Institutional Research *(1965)*
114 Stone Building
Florida State University
Tallahassee, FL   32306-3038

Tel: (904)644-4470   *Fax:* (904)644-8824
E-Mail: air@mailer.fsu.edu
Web Site: http://www.fsu.edu/air
Members: 2,700 individuals
Staff: 6
Annual Budget: $500-1,000,000
Exec. Director: Terrence R. Russell, Ph.D.
Coordinator, Continuing Education and Grants: Susan D. Gertel
Editor and Publications Coordinator: Christine Call
Coordinator, Information Systems and Office Manager: Norm
   Gravelle

Historical Note
*Members are involved in research to improve institutions of
postsecondary education. Membership: $90/year (individual);
$282/year (organization/company).*

Publications:
A. I.
Directory. a.
New Directions for Institutional Research. q.
Professional File. q.
Research in Higher Education. bi-m.
Resources in Institutional Research.

Meetings/Conferences:
Annual Meetings: Spring/1,250
1999 – Seattle, WA
2000 – Cincinnati, OH
2001 – Long Beach, CA
2002 – Toronto, Canada

Ass'n for Integrative Studies *(1979)*
School of Interdisciplinary Studies
Miami University
Oxford, OH   45056
Tel: (513)529-2213   *Fax:* (513)529-5849
E-Mail: newellwh@muohio.edu
Web Site: http://www.muohio.edu/ais/
Members: 1000 individuals
Staff: 1
Annual Budget: $10-25,000
Exec. Director: William H. Newell

Historical Note
*Established and incorporated in Ohio, AIS members are primarily
faculty and administrators engaged in interdisciplinary teaching
and research or who are interested in exploring interdisplinary
topics and methodology. Membership: $40/year (individual);
$100/year (institution), $15/year (student).*

Publications:
AIS Newsletter. q.
Issues in Integrative Studies. semi-a.

Meetings/Conferences:
Annual Meetings: Fall/125
1999 – Naperville, IL(North Central College)/Sept. 29-Oct. 3

Ass'n for Intelligent Systems Technology *(1986)*
Historical Note
Organization defunct in 1996.

Ass'n for Interactive Marketing *(1993)*
Historical Note
Merged with Direct Marketing Ass'n in 1998.

Ass'n for Internat'l Agricultural and Extension Education *(1984)*
204 Agriculture Administration Bldg.
2120 Fyffe Road, Ohio State Univ.
Columbus, OH   43210-1067
Tel: (614)292-0450   *Fax:* (614)292-7007
Members: 300 individuals
Annual Budget: under $10,000
President-Elect: Janet L. Henderson, Ph.D.

Historical Note
*AIAEE is a professional society composed of individuals working in
international education or extension programs. Has no paid officers
or full-time staff. Membership: $20/year (regular member);
$10/year (member from a developing country).*

Publications:
The Informer. 3/year.

Meetings/Conferences:
Annual Meetings: Spring

Ass'n for Investment Management and Research *(1990)*
P.O. Box 3668
5 Boar's Head Lane
Charlottesville, VA   22903-0668
Tel: (804)980-3668   *Fax:* (804)980-3616
Toll Free: (800)247 - 8132
E-Mail: info@aimr.org
Web Site: http://www.aimr.org
Members: 30,700 individuals
Staff: 116
Annual Budget: $25-50,000,000
President and C.E.O.: Thomas A. Bowman, CFA
*Senior V. President, Member/Society Communications & Global
   Affairs:* Raymond J. DeAngelo
Senior V. President, General Counsel: Michael S. Caccese
Senior V. President, Educational Products: Katrina F. Sherrerd, CFA
Director, Finance: George Payne, Jr., CFA
V. President, Operations: Moira Coleman Bourgeois
Manager, Member Services: Cindy S. Kent

Historical Note
*Formed by the merger in 1990 of the Financial Analysts Federation
with the Institute of Chartered Financial Analysts, AIMR is a
professional organizations for financial analysts and portfolio
managers. Awards the CFA (Certified Financial Analyst)
designation to members upon completion of three levels of testing
and the satisfaction of professional work experience and ethical
practice requirements. Membership: $125/year (non-CFA
charterholders); $200/year (CFA charterholders).*

Publications:
AIMR Newsletter. bi-m.
CFA Digest. q.
Financial Analysts Journal. bi-m. adv.
ISFA Digest. 2/year.

Meetings/Conferences:

Ass'n for Jewish Studies *(1969)*
MB0001, Brandeis University
P.O. Box 9110
Waltham, MA   02254-9110
Tel: (781)736-2981   *Fax:* (781)736-2982
Toll Free: (800)558 - 6958
E-Mail: ajs@brandeis.edu
Web Site: http://www.brandeis.edu/ajs
Members: 1,500 individuals
Staff: 1
Exec. Secretary: Dr. Aaron L. Katchen

Historical Note
*Founded in 1969, AJS is a learned society and professional
organization that seeks to promote, maintain and improve teaching,
research and related endeavors in Jewish Studies in colleges,
universities and other institutions of higher learning. AJS is a
constituent society of the American Council of Learned Societies.
Membership: $40/year (individual).*

Publications:
AJS Newsletter. irreg.
AJS Review. semi-a. adv.
Conference Program. a. adv.

Meetings/Conferences:

Ass'n for Library and Information Science Education *(1915)*
P.O. Box 7640
Arlington, VA   22207
Tel: (703)243-8040   *Fax:* (703)243-4551
E-Mail: sroger7@ibm.net
Web Site: http://www.si.umich.edu/ALISE/
Members: 700 individuals, 73 schools
Staff: 3
Annual Budget: $100-250,000
Exec. Director: Sharon Rogers

Historical Note
*Affiliate of American Library Ass'n and Internat'l Federation of
Library Ass'ns, Medical Library Ass'n, Special Libraries Ass'n, and
American Ass'n of Law Libraries. Formerly (until 1983) known as
the Ass'n of American Library Schools. Membership: $90/year
(full-time faculty member, librarian, researcher, administrator),
$50/year (part-time), $10/year (doctoral students).*

Publications:
Journal of Education for Library & Information Science. q.
Library and Information Science Education Statistical Report.
   a.
Membership Directory. a.

Meetings/Conferences:
Annual Meetings: January, prior to the Winter American Library
   Ass'n meeting
1999 – Philadelphia, Pa

Ass'n for Library Collections and Technical Services *(1957)*
50 E. Huron St.
Chicago, IL   60611
Tel: (312)280-5038   *Fax:* (312)280-5033
Toll Free: (800)545 - 2433
Web Site: http://www.ala.org.ALCTS
Members: 5,445 individuals
Staff: 5
Annual Budget: $250-500,000
Exec. Director: Karen Muller

Historical Note
*A division of the American Library Ass'n formerly known as the
Resources and Technical Services Division, ALCTS adopted its
name in 1989. Membership: $45/year, plus membership in ALA
(individual).*

Publications:
ALCTS Network News. irreg.
ALCTS Newsletter. bi-m.
Library Resources & technical Services. q. adv.

Meetings/Conferences:
Annual Meetings: in conjunction with the American Library
   Ass'n
1999 – New Orleans, LA/June 24-July 1
2000 – Chicago, IL/July 6-13
2001 – San Francisco, CA/June 14-20
2002 – Atlanta, GA/June 13-19

Ass'n for Library Service to Children *(1901)*
Historical Note
*A division of American Library Ass'n, which provides
administrative support.*

Ass'n for Living History Farms and Agricultural Museums *(1970)*
8774 Rte. 45 N.W.
North Bloomfield, OH   44450
Tel: (440)685-4410   *Fax:* (440)685-4410
Members: 950 individuals, 725 institutions
Annual Budget: $50-100,000
Secretary/Treasurer: Judy Sheridan

Historical Note
*Members include those involved in living history farms, house
museums, agricultural museums and outdoor museums of history
and folklife. Membership: $15/year; $40/year (organization).*

Publications:
Living Historical Farms Bulletin. q. adv.
Proceedings. a.

Meetings/Conferences:
Annual Meetings: June/250 Cooperstown, IN(Farmers Museum)/250
1999 – Kansas City, MO(Jewell College)/300
2000 – Mystic, CT(CT College)/300
2001 – Williamsburg, VA(William and Mary College)/350

Ass'n for Management Information in Financial Services (1980)
7950 E. La Junta Road
Scottsdale, AZ 85255-2798
Tel: (602)515-2160   Fax: (602)515-2101
E-Mail: ami@amifs.org
Web Site: http://www.amifs.org
Members: 600 individuals
Staff: 1
Annual Budget: $250-500,000
Executive Director: Nancy Basinger

Historical Note
Formerly (1990) the Nat'l Ass'n for Bank Cost Analysis and (1997) Nat'l Ass'n for Bank Cost and Management Accounting. Membership open to individuals employed by any commercial bank, trust company, Federal Reserve bank, bank holding company, credit union or thrift institution. Membership: $195/year.

Publications:
AMI Bulletin. q.
Journal for Bank Cost & Management Accounting. 3/year.

Meetings/Conferences:
Annual Meetings: May-June/300-350
1999 – Dallas, TX(Inter-Continental)/June 23-25/300

Ass'n for Manufacturing Excellence (1985)
380 West Palatine Road
Wheeling, IL 60090-5863
Tel: (847)520-3282   Fax: (847)520-0163
E-Mail: ame@ame.org
Web Site: http://www.ame.org
Members: 4,700 individuals
Staff: 5
Annual Budget: $2-5,000,000
Exec. Director: Tom Conley
Publications: JoAnn Weitzerfield

Historical Note
A not-for-profit organization founded to cultivate the understanding, analysis and exchange of world class productivity methods and their successful application in the pursuit of excellence. Membership: $125/year (individual).

Publications:
AME Newsletter. bi-m. adv.
Target. 5 times/yr.

Meetings/Conferences:
Annual Meetings: Fall
1999 – Portland, OR/Oct. 12-15
2000 – Boston, MA/Nov. 7-10

Ass'n for Maximum Service Television (1956)
1776 Massachusetts Ave., N.W., Suite 310
Washington, DC 20036
Tel: (202)861-0344   Fax: (202)861-0342
Web Site: http://www.mstv.org
Members: 300 television stations
Staff: 6
Annual Budget: $1-2,000,000
President: Margita E. White
Manager, Administration: April C.T. Lee

Historical Note
Formerly (1990) Ass'n of Maximum Service Telecasters. Individuals, partnerships, firms and corporations who own and operate TV stations, UHF or VHF seeking to assure the highest technical quality for local and nationwide free over-the-air television service.

Publications:
MSTV Membership Update. m.

Meetings/Conferences:
Annual Meetings: Spring/350

Ass'n for Molecular Pathology
9650 Rockville Pike
Bethesda, MD 20814-3993
Tel: (301)571-1880   Fax: (301)571-1879
E-Mail: amp@pathol.faseb.org
Web Site: http://zapruder.path.med.umich.edu/users/amp
Annual Budget: $100-250,000
Exec. Officer: Frances A. Pitlick, Ph.D.
Meetings Coordinator: Maricel M. Herrera

Historical Note
AMP are academics, scientists, researchers and others with an interest in molecular pathology. Membership: $120/year (M.D./Ph.D.); $75/year (BS or MS); $40/year (student/fellow/resident).

Publications:
AMP Membership Directory. a.
Newsletter. 3/yr.

Meetings/Conferences:
1999 – St. Louis, MO(Adams Mark)/Nov. 4-7

Ass'n for Multi-Image Internat'l (1974)
Historical Note
Became Ass'n for Multi-media Internat'l in 1994.

Ass'n for Multi-Media International (1974)
Historical Note
Address unknown in 1997.

Ass'n for Multicultural Counseling and Development (1971)
5999 Stevenson Ave.

Alexandria, VA 22304-3300
Tel: (703)823-9800   Fax: (703)823-0252
Members: 3,091 individuals
Staff: 2
Annual Budget: $25-50,000
Exec. Director: John L. Jaco

Historical Note
Formerly (1985) Ass'n for Non-White Concerns in Personnel and Guidance. AMCD strives to improve cultural, ethnic and racial empathy and understanding by designing programs to advance and sustain personal growth. AMCD is a division of the American Counseling Ass'n, which provides administrative support. Membership: $33/year (professional); $20/year (student/retired).

Publications:
AMCD Newsletter.
Journal of Multicultural Counseling and Development. q. adv.

Meetings/Conferences:
Annual Meetings: Spring, with the American Counseling Ass'n
1999 – San Diego, CA
2000 – Washington, DC/March 22-25
2001 – San Antonio, TX
2002 – New Orleans, LA

Ass'n for Persons with Severe Handicaps, The (1975)
29 W. Susquehannah Ave., Suite 210
Baltimore, MD 21204-5201
Tel: (410)828-8274   Fax: (410)828-6706
Members: 6,000 individuals
Staff: 6
Annual Budget: $500-1,000,000
Exec. Director: Nancy Weiss

Historical Note
Founded as the American Ass'n for the Education of the Severely-Profoundly Handicapped. It became the Ass'n for the Severely Handicapped in 1979 and assumed its present name in 1984. Members are teachers, social workers, psychologists, physical therapists, legal administrators, special education administrators, parents, self-advocates, and students. Membership: $85/year (individual); $190/year (organization/company).

Publications:
TASH Journal. q. adv.
TASH Newsletter. m. adv.

Meetings/Conferences:
Annual Meetings: Fall
1999 – Chicago, IL
2000 – Miami, FL

Ass'n for Philosophy of the Unconscious (1971)
Dept. of Philosophy, Georgetown Univ.
Washington, DC 20057
Tel: (202)687-7613
E-Mail: vereeckw@gunet.georgetown.edu
Members: 150 individuals
Annual Budget: under $10,000
President: W. Ver Eecke

Historical Note
APU members are academics and others with an interest in psychoanalysis and philosophy. Membership: $5/year (individual); $2/year (student).

Publications:
APU Newsletter. a.

Meetings/Conferences:
Annual Meetings: with American Philosophical Ass'n, Eastern Division in December

Ass'n for Physical and Systems Mathematics (1979)
Historical Note
Organization inactive in 1997.

Ass'n for Play Therapy (1982)
2100 N. Whitney Ave.
Suite 104
Fresno, CA 93727-2014
Tel: (559)252-2278   Fax: (559)252-2297
E-Mail: a4PT@sirius.com
Web Site: http://www.sirius.com/~a4pt/
Members: 7,600 individuals
Staff: 4
Annual Budget: $250-500,000
Exec. Director: Kevin O'Connor
General Manager: Kathryn Lebby

Historical Note
Membership: $55/year (individual); $100/year (organization); $45/year (affiliate).

Publications:
APT Newsletter. q. adv.
Internat'l Journal of Play Therapy. bi-a.

Meetings/Conferences:
Annual Meetings: October
1999 – Baltimore, MD(Renaissance Harbor Hotel)/Oct. 6-9/800

Ass'n for Political and Legal Anthropology (1976)
Historical Note
A section of the American Anthropological Ass'n. Established to foster communication and cooperation among scholars interested in the anthropological study of politics and the law.

Ass'n for Politics and the Life Sciences (1980)
Lake Superior State University
650 West Easterday Ave.,
Sault Ste. Marie, MI 49783-1699
Tel: (906)635-2757   Fax: (906)635-2111
E-Mail: apls@lakers.lssu.edu
Members: 450 individuals
Exec. Director: Dr. Gary R. Johnson

Historical Note
APLS members are individuals and institutions with an interest in the examination of relationship between the life sciences and politics.

Publications:
Politics and the Life Sciences Journal. semi-a.

Meetings/Conferences:

Ass'n for Population/Family Planning Libraries and Information Centers, Internat'l (1968)
c/o Family Health International
P. O. Box 13950
Research Triangle Pk, NC 27709
Tel: (215)898-5375   Fax: (215)898-2124
E-Mail: lnewman@pop.upenn.edu
Web Site: http://www.pop.upenn.edu/library/APLIC.html
Members: 120 individuals
Annual Budget: under $10,000
President: Lisa Newman

Historical Note
Members are librarians, information researchers, resource coordinators and the population and family-planning related agencies that they serve. Incorporated in the District of Columbia in May 1972. Membership: $25/year(individual).

Publications:
APLICommunicator. q. adv.

Meetings/Conferences:
1999 – New York, NY(Marriott Marquis)/March 23-25
2000 – Los Angeles, CA(Westin-Bonaventure)/April 11-13

Ass'n for Practical and Professional Ethics (1990)
618 E. Third St.
Bloomington, IN 47405-3602
Tel: (812)855-6450   Fax: (812)855-3315
E-Mail: appe@indiana.edu
Web Site: http://php.ucs.indiana.edu/~appe/home.html
Members: 500 individuals, 100 institutions
Staff: 2
Annual Budget: $100-250,000
Exec. Secretary: Brian Schrag

Historical Note
APPE members are academic and other professionals with an interest in the field of practical and professional ethics. Membership: $25-75/year (individual), $150/year (organization), $500 (sustaining).

Publications:
Ethically Speaking Newsletter. 3/yr.

Meetings/Conferences:
Annual Meetings: March
1999 – Washington, DC(National Airport Hilton)/Feb. 25-27

Ass'n for Practitioners in Infection Control (1972)
Historical Note
Became the Ass'n for Professionals in Infection Control and Epidemiology in 1996.

Ass'n for Preservation Technology Internat'l (1968)
P.O. Box 3511
Williamsburg, VA 23187
Tel: (540)373-1621
Members: 1,500 individuals
Annual Budget: $100-250,000
President: Harry Hunderman

Historical Note
APT Internat'l was organized in Canada in 1968 and relocated to the United States in 1988. Association members are preservationists, architects, conservators, consultants, contractors, craftspersons, curators, developers, educators, engineers, historians, landscape architects, technicians and others involved in the systematic application of methods and materials to the maintenance, conservation and protection of historic buildings, sites and artifact resources for future use and appreciation. Membership: Graduated scale, please call for information.

Publications:
APT Bulletin. q.
Communique. q. adv.

Meetings/Conferences:
Annual Meetings: September-October
1999 – Bampf, Canada/Oct. 20-23

Ass'n for Professionals in Infection Control and Epidemiology (1972)
1275 K Street, N.W., Suite 1000
Washington, DC 20005-4006
Tel: (202)789-1890   Fax: (202)789-1899
Toll Free: (888)278-2742
E-Mail: apicinfo@apic.org
Web Site: http://www.apic.org
Members: 11,500 individuals
Staff: 17
Annual Budget: $2-5,000,000
Exec. Director: Christopher E. Laxton
Technology and Information Services Manager: Joseph Harr
Information Resource Manager: Catherine Fleischman
Director, Government and Public Affairs: Jennifer Thomas
Mgr., Meetings/Member Services: Paula Ballard
Director of Education: Karen Harvey
Director, Finance & Administration: David Zinner
Director of Membership: Deborah Timmons
Managing Editor: Sharada Gilkey

Historical Note
Formerly (1996) Ass'n for Practitioners in Infection Control. APIC members are physicians, nurses, medical technologists, sanitarians and others professionally concerned with the practice and management of infection control and epidemiology in all health settings. Membership: $90/year (domestic), $1,500/year (patron member).

Publications:
American Journal of Infection Control. bi-m. adv.
APIC Directory. a. adv.
APIC News. bi-m. adv.
Infection Control in Long-Term Care Facilities. q. adv.
Membership Section Directories. a. adv.

Meetings/Conferences:
Annual Meetings: Spring/3,300
1999 – Baltimore, MD/June 20-24
2000 – Minneapolis, MN/June 18-22

Ass'n for Psychoanalytic Medicine *(1945)*
4560 Delafield Ave.
New York, NY   10471
Tel: (718)548-6088   *Fax:* (718)548-8302
Members: 240 individuals
Staff: 1
Annual Budget: under $10,000
Admin. Secretary: Terry Montgomery

Historical Note
Formerly Ass'n for Psychoanalytic and Psychosomatic Medicine. Affiliated with American Psychoanalytic Ass'n. Membership: $265/year.

Publications:
Bulletin. a.

Meetings/Conferences:
Annual Meetings: June, always in New York City

Ass'n for Psychological Type *(1979)*
9140 Ward Parkway, Suite 200
Kansas City, MO   64114
Tel: (816)444-3500   *Fax:* (816)444-0330
E-Mail: staff@aptcentral.org
Web Site: http://www.aptcentral.org/
Members: 6 individuals
Staff: 6
Annual Budget: $1–2,000,000
Exec. Director: Lisa Daniels, CAE

Historical Note
APT promotes the knowledge and ethical use of psychological type (such as the Myers-Briggs Type Indicator), and thereby growth for individuals and groups within society at large and, in particular, for professionals who use psychological type theory in their professional lives. Membership: $65/year (individual); $75/year (international); $45/year (student).

Publications:
Bulletin of Psychological Type. 8/yr.
Journal of Psychological Type. q.

Meetings/Conferences:
Biennial Meetings: (odd years)
1999 – Scottsdale, AZ(The Phoenician)/July 13-18/800

Ass'n for Public Health Statistics and Information Systems
Historical Note
Became (1997) Nat'l Ass'n for Public Health Statistics and Information Systems.

Ass'n for Public Policy Analysis and Management *(1979)*
Box 18766
Washington, DC   20036-8766
Tel: (202)261-5788   *Fax:* (202)223-1149
E-Mail: appam@ui.urban.org
Web Site: http://qsilver.queensu.ca/appamwww/
Members: 1,700 individuals
Staff: 2
Annual Budget: $250-500,000
Exec. Director: Dale Robinson

Historical Note
APPAM members are individuals with an interest in the teaching, research or practice of public policy analysis. Membership: $55-80/year (individual),$30/year (student) and $1,500/year (institution).

Publications:
Journal of Policy Analysis and Mangement. q.

Meetings/Conferences:
1999 – Washington, DC(ANA Hotel)/Nov. 4-6/1000
2000 – Seattle, WA(Westin)/Nov. 2-4/1000
2001 – Washington, DC(ANA Hotel)/Nov. 3-5
2002 – Atlanta, GA

Ass'n for Quality and Participation *(1977)*
801-B W. 8th Street, Suite 501
Cincinnati, OH   45203-1607
Tel: (513)381-1959   *Fax:* (513)381-0070
Toll Free: (800)733 - 3310
E-Mail: aqp@aqp.org
Web Site: http://www.aqp.org
Members: 6,400 individuals and organizations
Staff: 23
Annual Budget: $2-5,000,000
Exec. V. President: Cathy E. Kramer, Ph.D.
Mgr., Marketing/Communications/Membership: William E. Brewer
Manager, Conference & Education: Lisa Ohmer
Controller: Arleen Inger
Manager, Chapter Services: Jo Ann Jones
Editor: Christine Rogers
Manager, MIS: Michelle Poe

Historical Note
Formerly (1987) Internat'l Ass'n of Quality Circles. AQP promotes quality and participation in the workplace by providing education courses, an information center, conferences in-house training, publications and other resources. Membership: $120/year (individual); $550/year (group discount); $90/year (retired/student); $800-$2,000/year (site).

Publications:
Journal for Quality and Participation. bi-m. adv.

News for a Change. m. adv.
Transactions of the AQP Conference and Resource Mart. a.

Meetings/Conferences:
Semi-Annual meetings: Winter/Spring and Fall

Ass'n for Recorded Sound Collections *(1966)*
P.O. Box 543
Annapolis, MD   21404-0543
Tel: (410)757-0488   *Fax:* (410)349-0175
E-Mail: peters@umd5.umd.edu
Web Site: http://199.75.220.16/aacommg/arsc/arsc.htm
Members: 1,100 individuals
Staff: 1
Annual Budget: $25-50,000
Exec. Director: Peter Shambarger

Historical Note
ARSC serves the scholarly interests and concerns of the private collector, discographer, librarian, sound archivist, historian, recording preservation engineer, and specialty dealer and appraiser. ARSC fosters the development of discographic information in all fields and periods of recording and encourages the preservation of historical recordings. Membership: $40/year (institutional), $72/year (sustaining member),and $36(individual)

Publications:
Journal. semi-a. adv.
Membership Directory. bien. adv.
Newsletter. q. adv.

Meetings/Conferences:
Annual Meetings: Spring/150
1999 – Madison, WI/May 20-23

Ass'n for Regulatory Reform *(1985)*
Historical Note
Became the Manufactured Housing Ass'n for Regulatory Reform in 1997.

Ass'n for Research in Nervous and Mental Disease *(1920)*
630 W. 168th St., Box 23
New York, NY   10032
Tel: (212)740-7608   *Fax:* (212)305-4548
E-Mail: cpmcnet.columbia.edu/www/arnmd
Members: 750 individuals
Staff: 2
Annual Budget: $25-50,000
Exec. Director: Ann Louis Coodermuth

Historical Note
Established as the Neuropsychiatric Research Soc., it assumed its present name in 1922. Membership: $75/year.

Publications:
Proceedings. a.

Meetings/Conferences:
Annual Meetings: First Friday & Saturday in December in New York City

Ass'n for Research in Otolaryngology *(1973)*
19 Mantua Road
Mount Royal, NJ   08061
Tel: (609)423-0041   *Fax:* (609)423-3420
E-Mail: headquarters@aro.org
Web Site: http://www.aro.org
Members: 2,000 individuals
Annual Budget: $100-250,000
Exec. Secretary: Susan Whitehouse

Historical Note
ARO is a scientific society of researchers who investigate basic science and clincal problems associated with hearing, speech, the sense of balance, smell, taste and diseases of the head and neck. Membership: $30-50/year (individual).

Publications:
ARO Directory. a.
ARO News. 2/year.

Meetings/Conferences:
Annual Meetings: February, St. Petersburg, FL(Tradewinds)/1000
1999 – /Feb. 14-18

Ass'n for Research in Vision and Ophthalmology *(1928)*
9650 Rockville Pike, Suite 1502
Bethesda, MD   20814-3998
Tel: (301)571-1844   *Fax:* (301)571-8311
E-Mail: mem@arvo.org
Web Site: http://www.faseb.org/arvo
Members: 10,200 individuals
Staff: 9
Annual Budget: $2-5,000,000
Exec. Director: Joanne G. Angle

Historical Note
Founded as the Ass'n for Research in Ophthalmology and incorporated in New York in 1936; assumed its present name in 1970. Works to promote research opportunities in the vision sciences. Membership: $125/year (regular member); $45/year (student without journal); $75/year (student with IOVS).

Publications:
ARVO Newsletter. bi-a.
Investigative Ophthalmology and Visual Science. m. adv.
Membership Directory. bien.

Meetings/Conferences:
Annual Meetings: May
1999 – Ft. Lauderdale, FL(Broward County Convention Ctr)/May 9-14/8000
2000 – Ft. Lauderdale, FL(Broward County Convention Ctr)/April 30-May 5

Ass'n for Retail Technology Standards *(1992)*
P.O. Box 15066
Reading, PA   19612-5066

Tel: (610)929-7336
Web Site: http://www.retail-info.com/ARTS
Chairman: Richard E. Mader

Historical Note
ARTS members are retailers and vendors of retail and business systems and software. ARTS promotes the adoption of standards for techonology solutions in the retail sector. Membership: $750/year (retailer), $1,000-$1,500/year, varies by revenue (vendor).

Ass'n for School, College and University Staffing *(1934)*
Historical Note
Became American Ass'n for Employment in Education in 1996.

Ass'n for Social Anthropology in Oceania *(1967)*
2499 Kapiolani Blvd #2403
Honolulu, HI   96826
E-Mail: rensel@hawaii.edu
Web Site:
      http://www.soc.hawaii.edu/asao/pacific/hawaii.html
Members: 330 individuals, 30 institutions
Annual Budget: under $10,000
Secretary: Jan Rensel

Historical Note
Formerly known as the Ass'n for Social Anthropology in Eastern Oceania. Membership: $35/year (individual); $20/year (student).

Publications:
ASAO Newsletter. q.

Meetings/Conferences:
Annual Meetings: Alternates West & East Coasts & Hawaii/February
1999 – Hilo, HI(Hawaii Naniloa)/Feb. 2-6/200
2000 – US west coast
2001 – US east coast

Ass'n for Social Economics *(1941)*
College of Administration & Business
Louisiana Tech. Univ., Box 10318
Ruston, LA   71272
Tel: (318)257-3701   *Fax:* (318)257-4253
E-Mail: oboyle@lab.latech.edu
Web Site: http://www.lab.latech.edu/~oboyle/ase.home.htm
Members: 400 individuals
Annual Budget: $25-50,000
Secretary: Edward J. O'Boyle

Historical Note
Formerly (1965) Catholic Economic Ass'n. Has no paid officers or full-time staff. Membership: $35-45/year.

Publications:
Forum. semi-a.
Review of Social Economy. q.

Meetings/Conferences:
Annual Meetings: In January, with the Allied Social Science Ass'n
1999 – New York, NY
2000 – Boston, MA
2001 – New Orleans, LA

Ass'n for Specialists in Group Work *(1973)*
5999 Stevenson Ave.
Alexandria, VA   22304
Tel: (703)823-9800   *Fax:* (703)823-0252
Members: 3,980 individuals
Staff: 2
Annual Budget: $50-100,000
Interim Exec. Director: Richard Yep

Historical Note
ASGW provides professional leadership in the field of group work; establishes standards for professional and ethical practice; and supports research and dissemination of knowledge. A division of the American Counseling Ass'n which provides administrative support. Membership: $25/year (professional); $12.50/year (student/retired).

Publications:
ASGW Newsletter, Together. adv. adv.
Journal for Specialists in Group Work. q. adv.

Meetings/Conferences:
Annual Meetings: with the American Counseling Ass'n
1999 – San Diego, CA/April 12-17
2000 – Washington, DC/March 22-24
2001 – San Antonio, TX
2002 – New Orleans, LA

Ass'n for Spiritual, Ethical and Religious Values in Counseling *(1955)*
5999 Stevenson Ave.
Alexandria, VA   22304-3300
Tel: (703)823-9800   *Fax:* (703)823-0252
Members: 5,100 individuals
Staff: 2
Annual Budget: $10-25,000
Interim Exec. Director: Richard Yep

Historical Note
A division of the American Counseling Ass'n, which provides administrative support. Formerly (1958) Catholic Counselors in APGA; (1960) Nat'l Conference of Diocesan Guidance Councils; (1962) Nat'l Conference of Catholic Guidance Councils; (1978) Nat'l Catholic Guidance Conference; and (1993) Ass'n for Religious and Value Issues in Counseling. ASERVIC is devoted to professionals who believe that spiritual, ethical, religious and other human values are essential to the full development of the person, and to the discipline of counseling. Membership: $23/year (professional); $11/year (student).

Publications:
Counseling and Values Journal. 3/yr.
Interaction (ASERVIC newsletter).

Meetings/Conferences:
Annual Meetings: with the American Counseling Ass'n

1999 – San Diego, CA/April 14-17
2000 – Washington, DC/March 22-25
2001 – San Antonio, TX
2002 – New Orleans, LA

Ass'n for Supervision and Curriculum Development (1943)
1703 N. Beauregard St.
Alexandria, VA 22311-1714
Tel: (703)578-9600   Fax: (703)575-5400
Toll Free: (800)933 - 2723
E-Mail: info@ascd.org
Web Site: http://www.ascd.org
Members: 180,000 individuals
Staff: 155
Annual Budget: $10-25,000,000
Exec. Director: Gene R. Carter
Director, Public Information: Barbara Gleason
Government Relations Director: Don Ernst
Deputy Exec. Director: Dr. Diane G. Berreth

Historical Note
Merger in 1943 of the Soc. for Curriculum Study (1929) and the Department of Supervisors and Directors of Instruction of the Nat'l Education Ass'n to form the Department of Supervision and Curriculum Development of NEA. Changed to its present title in 1946. Became independent of NEA in 1975. Provides professional development in curriculum and supervision, initiates and supports activites to improve educational equity for all students, and serves as a leader in education information services. ASCD's members reside in more than 100 countries and include superintendents, supervisors, principals, teachers, professors of education, school board members, students, and parents who share a commitment to quality education and a belief that all students can learn in a well-planned educational program. Has an annual budget of approximately $20 million. Membership: $49-179/year.

Publications:
Curriculum Update Newsletter. q.
Education Update Newsletter. 8 times/year.
Educational Leadership. 8 times/year.
Journal of Curriculum and Supervision.

Meetings/Conferences:
Annual Meetings: March
1999 – San Francisco, CA/March 6-8

Ass'n for Surgical Education (1980)
SIU, School of Medicine
Dept. of Surgery, P.O. Box 19655
Springfield, IL 62794-1611
Tel: (217)785-3835
E-Mail: asc@fgi.net
Web Site: http://www.siumed.edu/surgery/ase.html
Members: 700 individuals and organizations
Staff: 2
Annual Budget: $100-250,000
Exec. Director: Susan Kepner

Historical Note
ASE works specifically to improve surgical education among medical students. Membership: $50/year (individual), $300/year (organization).

Publications:
Focus on Surgical Education. q. adv.

Meetings/Conferences:
Annual Meetings: April
1999 – Boston, MA/April 7-10

Ass'n for Symbolic Logic (1936)
Dept. of Mathematics, Univ. of Illinois
1409 West Green St., 331 Altgeld
Urbana, IL 61801-2975
Tel: (217)244-7902   Fax: (217)333-9576
E-Mail: asi@math.uiuc.edu
Web Site: http://www.aslonline.org
Members: 1,450 individuals
Staff: 2
Annual Budget: $250-500,000
Contact: Joanne Fetzner

Historical Note
Founded and incorporated in Rhode Island in 1936. Affiliated with the American Mathematical Soc., the Conference Board of the Mathematical Sciences and the Internat'l Union for the History and Philosophy of Science. Promotes research and studies in mathematical logic and related fields. Membership: $56/year (individual), $475/year (institution); $1050/year (corporate associate), $3,000/year (corporate), and $28/year (student).

Publications:
ASL Newsletter. q.
Bulletin of Symbolic Logic. q.
Journal of Symbolic Logic. q.

Meetings/Conferences:
1999 – San Diego, CA/March 20-23
2000 – Urbana, IL(University of Illinois, Urbana)/June 3-7

Ass'n for Systems Management (1947)

Historical Note
Formerly (1969) Systems and Procedures Ass'n. Members are managers and executives in the information systems and technology industry. Primary focus is promotion of education and professional growth in the systems profession, accomplished through more than 90 local chapters in the US and Canada; centrally-directed seminar program with over 150 2-5 day sessions annually; and an annual information systems management conference. Membership: $100/year.

Ass'n for Technology in Music Instruction (1975)
School of Music, Northwestern Univ.
711 Elgin Road
Evanston, IL 60208
Tel: (847)491-5740   Fax: (847)491-5260
Web Site: http://www.music.org/atmi
Members: 300 individuals

Staff: 1
Annual Budget: under $10,000
President: Peter Webster

Historical Note
Formerly (1986) Nat'l Consortium for Computer-Based Music Instruction. ATMI members are music teachers and others interested in the application of computers in music instruction. Membership: $40/year (individual); $40/year (foreign).

Publications:
ATMI Newsletter. q.
Technology Directory. a.

Meetings/Conferences:
Annual Meetings: in conjunction with the College Music Soc.
1999 – Denver, CO/Oct. 14-17

Ass'n for the Advancement of Applied Sport Psychology (1986)
Campus Box 6400
University of Memphis
Memphis, TN 38152-6400
Tel: (901)678-2147   Fax: (901)678-2579
E-Mail: jwhelan@memphis.edu
Members: 1000 individuals
Annual Budget: $100-250,000
Secretary-Treasurer: Jim Whelan, Ph.D.

Historical Note
AAASP promotes the development of psychological theory, research and intervention strategies in sport psychology; provides a forum for individuals who are interested in research and theory development and in the application of psychological principles in sport and exercise; and is also concerned with ethical and professional issues relating to the development of sport psychology and to the provision of psychological services in sport and exercise settings. Membership: $70/year (professional/affiliate); $40/year (student).

Publications:
AAASP Newsletter. 3/yr. adv.
Journal of Applied Sport Psychology. semi-a.

Meetings/Conferences:
Annual Meetings: September-October
1999 – Banff, AB, Canada/Sept. 22-26/650
2000 – Nashville, TN(Sheraton)October

Ass'n for the Advancement of Automotive Medicine (1957)
2340 Des Plaines Ave., Suite 106
Des Plaines, IL 60018-4602
Tel: (847)390-8927   Fax: (847)390-9962
E-Mail: aaami@aol.com
Web Site: http://www.carcrash.org
Members: 680 individuals
Staff: 5
Annual Budget: $250-500,000
Exec. Director: Elaine Petrucelli
Conference Manager, Meetings & Membership: Irene Herzau

Historical Note
Formerly (1988) the American Ass'n for Automotive Medicine. Organized in 1957 and incorporated in Florida. Encourages and promotes the growth and dissemination of new knowledge in the field of traffic and highway safety. Membership is composed of physicians, researchers, educators, engineers, administrators, and other highway and traffic medicine professionals. Membership: $200/year (individual), $2,000/year (company).

Publications:
Inroads. q.
Proceedings. a.

Meetings/Conferences:
Annual Meetings: Fall
1999 – Barcelona, Spain(Hotel Melia Gran)/Sept. 20-21
2000 – Chicago, IL(Drake Hotel)/Oct. 2-4/300

Ass'n for the Advancement of Baltic Studies (1968)
3465 E. Burnside St.
Portland, OR 97214-2050
Tel: (732)323-8265   Fax: (503)234-9082
E-Mail: aabs@teleport.com
Members: 900 individuals
Staff: 3
Annual Budget: $100-250,000
Senior Advisor: Janis Gaigulis

Historical Note
Formed to promote research and education in Baltic studies (history, literature, linguistics, social sciences), its membership is open to anyone wishing to support these aims. Membership: $50/year (individual), $100/year (institution), $2,000 (life member).

Publications:
Baltic Studies Newsletter. q. adv.
Journal of Baltic Studies. q. adv.

Meetings/Conferences:
2000 – Washington, DC

Ass'n for the Advancement of Health Education (1937)

Historical Note
Became the American Ass'n for Health Education in 1996.

Ass'n for the Advancement of Internat'l Education (1966)
Thompson House
Westminster College
New Wilmington, PA 16172
Tel: (724)946-7192   Fax: (724)946-7194
E-Mail: grellla@westminster.edu
Web Site: http://www.aaie.org
Members: 550 individuals, 350 schools, 50 companies
Staff: 2
Annual Budget: $250-500,000
Exec. Director: Lewis A. Grell, Ed.D.

Historical Note
AAIE is a support organization for American International schools abroad. Members include head administrators of American International schools located in major cities worldwide. U.S. membership includes superintendents of U.S. schools and college/university deans, presidents and others who have an interest in American international schools. Membership: $440/year (individual); $600/year (organization/company); $875/year (exhibitor).

Publications:
Inter-Ed. 4/year.

Meetings/Conferences:
Annual Meetings: Spring/550
1999 – Houston, TX(Hyatt Regency)/Feb. 22-26
2000 – San Francisco, CA(Hyatt Regency)/Feb. 28-March 2
2001 – Miami, FL/March 5-8/600
2002 – San Francisco, CA(Hyatt Regency)/March 4-7/600

Ass'n for the Advancement of Medical Instrumentation (1967)
3330 Washington Blvd., Suite 400
Arlington, VA 22201-4598
Tel: (703)525-4890   Fax: (703)276-0793
Toll Free: (800)332 - 2264
Web Site: http://www.aami.org
Members: 7,000 individuals
Staff: 35
Annual Budget: $2-5,000,000
President: Michael J. Miller, CAE
V. President, Publications and Communications: Mary Beth Hatem
V. President, New Business and Government Relations: Kathy Warye
V. President, Education and Conferences: Suzanne Stone
V. President, Standards: Theresa Zuraski
V. President, Finance and Administration: Sylvia E. Chandler
V. President, Membership and Marketing: Eileen Smith
Director, Membership and Marketing Services: Anne S. Wald
Exec. V. President: Elizabeth Bridgman

Historical Note
A non-profit multi-disciplinary association of engineering, medicine and government professionals and organizations involved in the development, use and management of medical instruments. Founded and incorporated in Massachusetts in 1967.Absorbed American College of Physician Inventors in 1997. A member society of the American Institute for Medical and Biological Engineering. Membership: $145/year (individual); $995/year (institutional/corporate).

Publications:
AAMI Membership Directory. a. adv.
AAMI News Newsletter. m. adv.
Biomedical Instrumentation & Technology Journal. bi-m. adv.
Medical Device Research Report Newsletter. m. adv.

Meetings/Conferences:
Annual Meetings: Spring and Fall
1999 – Boston, MA(Convention Center)/June 5-9

Ass'n for the Advancement of Psychoanalysis (1941)
329 East 62nd St.
New York, NY 10021
Tel: (212)838-8044
Members: 85 individuals
Staff: 1
Annual Budget: $10-25,000
President: Zoltan Norvay, PsyD

Historical Note
Membership: $200/year (individual).

Publications:
American Journal of Psychoanalysis. q.
Newsletter. q.

Meetings/Conferences:
Annual Meetings: Semi-Annual Meetings
1999 – New York, NY/60
1999 – New York, NY/60

Ass'n for the Advancement of Psychology (1974)
P.O. Box 38129
Colorado Springs, CO 80937-8129
Toll Free: (800)869 - 6595
Members: 6,000 individuals
Staff: 2
Annual Budget: $250-500,000
Exec. Director: Stephen M. Pfeiffer, Ph.D.
Administrator: Karen Rivard

Historical Note
Merged in 1975 with the Council for the Advancement of the Psychological Professions and Sciences (1971). Members are psychologists and educators. Works in close alliance with the American Psychological Ass'n. Primarily a government liaison operation. Supports Psychologists for Legislative Action Now (PLAN). Membership: $95/year (individual), $150/year (organization/company).

Publications:
AAP Advance Plan. q.

Meetings/Conferences:
Annual Meetings: August, with the American Psychological Ass'n.

Ass'n for the Advancement of Psychotherapy (1939)
Belfer Educational Center
1300 Morris Park Ave., Room 402
Bronx, NY 10461
Tel: (718)430-3503   Fax: (718)430-8907
Toll Free: (888)257 - 7924
Web Site: http://www.ajp.org
Members: 350 individuals
Staff: 2
Annual Budget: $100-250,000
President and Editor-in-Chief: T. Byram Karasu, M.D.
Business Manager: Robert Kennedy
Asst. Business Manager: Dianne Gabriele

Historical Note
AAP serves a forum for clinical and theoretical findings in the field of psychotherapy. Membership: $64/year (individual); $91/year (organization).

Publications:
American Journal of Psychotherapy. q.
Nat'l Academy of Psychotherapy Newsletter.

Meetings/Conferences:
Quarterly Meetings: always New York, NY

Ass'n for the Advancement of Wound Care (1995)
320 E. Towsontown Blvd., Suite 207
Baltimore, MD 21286-5331
Tel: (410)321-5557   *Fax:* (410)321-0695
Toll Free: (800)237 - 7285
E-Mail: AAWCLINE@aol.com
Web Site: http://members.aol.com/AAWCLINE/index.html
Staff: 1
Annual Budget: $50-100,000
Exec. Director: Diane Krasner, MS, RN, CE

Historical Note
AAWC is an interdisciplinary association serving medical professionals, patients and lay caregivers interested in wound care. Membership: $100/year (clinician); $50/year (student); $250/year (company) $25/year (patient/lay caregiver).

Publications:
AAWC Networking Directory. a.
AAWC Newsletter. q.
Ostomy/Wound Management. 9/year. adv.
Wounds. bi-m. adv.

Meetings/Conferences:
Annual Meetings: Spring

Ass'n for the Behavioral Sciences and Medical Education (1970)
Historical Note
Address unknown in 1998.

Ass'n for the Bibliography of History (1978)
Lockwood Library, Room 321
SUNY at Buffalo
Buffalo, NY 14260
Tel: (716)645-2817   *Fax:* (716)645-3859
E-Mail: lclcharl@ubvm.cc.buffalo.edu
Members: 150 individuals
Annual Budget: under $10,000
Exec. Secretary: Charles A. D'Aniello

Historical Note
Established in San Francisco at the 1978 annual meeting of the American Historical Ass'n. Members are historians and librarians interested in developing better bibliographic tools and skills for historical research. Membership: $10/year.

Publications:
ABH Bulletin. 3/year. adv.

Meetings/Conferences:
Annual Meetings: December, with American Historical Ass'n

Ass'n for the Care of Children's Health (1965)
19 Mantua Rd.
Mount Royal, NJ 08061-1006
Tel: (609)224-1742   *Fax:* (609)343-3420
Web Site: http://www.acch.org
Members: 4,000 individuals
Staff: 3
Annual Budget: $1-2,000,000
Exec. Director: Robert Talley

Historical Note
Promotes improved systems of health care for children and families. Supports the Community and Family Networks Project, the Nat'l Center for Family-Centered Care, and other programs that support the health and social services professions in service to children, families, and communities. Membership: $55/year (individual); $125-600/year (organization).

Publications:
ACCH News. q.
Children's Health Care. q. adv.

Meetings/Conferences:
Annual Meetings: Spring/1,600
1999 – Long Beach, CA/May 30-June 2

Ass'n for the Development of Computer-Based Instructional Systems (1968)
Historical Note
Address unknown in 1995.

Ass'n for the Development of Electronic Publishing Technique
Historical Note
Defunct in 1995.

Ass'n for the Development of Religious Information Systems (1971)
P.O. Box 210735
Nashville, TN 37221-0735
Tel: (615)662-5189   *Fax:* (615)662-5251
E-Mail: adrisnews@aol.com
Annual Budget: under $10,000
Editor: Edward W. Dodds

Historical Note
ADRIS provides a forum for the exchange of information on religious-topic databases and information systems, bringing together academic, religious and commercial users. Membership: $10-50/year.

Publications:
ADRIS Newsletter. q.
Internat'l Directory of Religious Information Systems.

Ass'n for the Education of Teachers in Science (1953)
East Carolina University
Greenville, NC 27858-4353
Tel: (252)328-4260   *Fax:* (252)328-4219
E-Mail: Pedersonj@mail.ecu.edu
Web Site: http://www.aets.unr.edu
Members: 850 individuals
Staff: 1
Annual Budget: $25-50,000
Exec. Secretary: Jon E. Pederson, Ph.D.

Historical Note
Affiliated with the Nat'l Science Teachers Ass'n. Has no paid staff. Membership: $70/year.

Publications:
AETS Newsletter. q.
Journal of Elementary Science Education. 2/year.
Journal of Science Teacher Education. 4/year.
Science Education. q. adv.

Meetings/Conferences:
Annual Meetings: Spring, with the Nat'l Science Teachers Ass'n
1999 – Austin, TX

Ass'n for the Environmental Health of Soils (1989)
150 Fearing St.
Amherst, MA 01002
Tel: (413)549-5170   *Fax:* (413)549-0579
Toll Free: (888)540 - 2347
E-Mail: aehs@aehs.com
Web Site: http://www.aehs.com
Members: 600 individuals
Staff: 6
Annual Budget: $250-500,000
Exec. Director: Paul T. Kostecki, Ph.D.

Historical Note
AEHS is a multi-disciplinary association providing a forum for individual professionals concerned with soil protection and cleanup. Fields represented include chemistry, geology, hydrogeology, law, engineering, modeling, toxicology, regulatory science, public health and public policy. Membership: $110/year (individual) and $55/year (student)

Publications:
International Journal of Phytoremediation. q.
Journal of Soil Contamination. bi-m. adv.
Matrix Newsletter. q. adv.
Soil & Groundwater Cleanup Magazine. 9/year.

Meetings/Conferences:
Annual Meetings: March
1999 – Oxnard, CA(Embassy Suites)/March 8-10/400

Ass'n for the Gifted, The
Historical Note
TAG is a division of the Council for Exceptional Children.

Ass'n for the Management of Organization Design (1989)
910 Charles Street
Fredericksburg, VA 22401-8048
Tel: (540)370-1722   *Fax:* (540)370-0015
E-Mail: SeanMcE@aol.com
Members: 210 individuals
Exec. Director: Peggy McElgunn

Historical Note
Membership: $85/year (individual).

Publications:
Gazette Newsletter. q.
Membership Directory.

Meetings/Conferences:

Ass'n for the Sociology of Religion (1938)
3520 Wiltshire Dr.
Holiday, FL 34691-1239
Tel: (813)844-5990   *Fax:* (813)844-7332
E-Mail: swatos@microd.com
Web Site: http://www.sociologyofreligion.com
Members: 757 individuals
Annual Budget: $50-100,000
Exec. Officer: William H. Swatos

Historical Note
Formerly (1971) American Catholic Sociological Soc. ASR is an international scholarly association that seeks to advance theory and research in the sociology of religion. Has no paid staff. Membership: $28/year (individual), $51.50/year (company).

Publications:
News & Announcements. q.
Religion and the Social Order. a.
Sociology of Religion: A Quarterly Review. q. adv.

Meetings/Conferences:
Annual Meetings: August, prior to the American Sociological
           Ass'n meeting/250
1999 – Chicago, IL(Essex House)/August 5-7
2000 – Washington, DC(Radison Barcello)/August 17-19
2001 – Anaheim, CA(Sheraton Anaheim)/Aug. 17-19
2002 – Chicago, IL

Ass'n for the Study of Afro-American Life and History (1915)
1407 14th St., N.W.
Washington, DC 20005-3704
Tel: (202)667-2822   *Fax:* (202)387-9802
E-Mail: asalh@earthlink.net
Web Site: http://www.asalh.org
Members: 2,500 individuals
Staff: 3
Annual Budget: $100-250,000
Nat'l President: Edward Beasley

Historical Note
Organized by Dr. Carter G. Woodson in Chicago September 9, 1915 as the Ass'n for the Study of Negro Life and History and incorporated in the District of Columbia the same year. Assumed its present name in 1973. Promotes an appreciation of the life and history of the Afro-American, creates an understanding of his present status and works to improve his promise for the future. Membership $40/year (general); $500/year (institutional); $1000/year (corporate).

Publications:
Journal of Negro History. 3/year. adv.
The Negro History Bulletin q. adv. adv.

Meetings/Conferences:
Annual Meetings: October
1999 – Detroit, MI

Ass'n for the Study of Dreams (1983)
P.O. Box 1600
Vienna, VA 22183
Tel: (703)242-0062   *Fax:* (703)242-8888
E-Mail: ASDreams@aol.com
Web Site: http://www.ASDreams.org
Members: 800 individuals
Staff: 1
Annual Budget: $25-50,000
Exec. Officer: Rita Dwyer

Historical Note
Incorporated in California, ASD was established as a multidisciplinary organization to promote the study of dreams. Members are individuals with serious interests in dreams, among the disciplines represented are: anthropology, comparative literature, education, medicine, psychology, religion, and social work. Membership: $85/year (individual); $55/year (student); $120/year (couple) and $150 (patron).

Publications:
Dream Time. q.
Dreaming Professional Journal. q.

Meetings/Conferences:
Annual Meetings: July
1999 – Santa Cruz, CA
2000 – Washington, DC

Ass'n for the Study of Food and Society (1986)
Family Nutrtion/Exercise Sciences Dept.
City Univ. of New York
Flushing, NY 11367
Tel: (718)997-4150   *Fax:* (718)997-4163
E-Mail: newman@qcvaxa.acc.qc.edu
Members: 90 individuals
Annual Budget: $10-25,000
President: Jacqueline M. Newman

Historical Note
ASFS is an interdisciplinary internat'l organization dedicated to the complex relationship between food and society. ASFS members are sociologists, anthropologists, nutritionists, dieticians and others with an interest in sociological aspects of food. Has no paid officers or full-time staff. Membership: $55/year;$30/year (student).

Publications:
Abstracts of Annual Meeting. a.
ASFS Newsletter. semi-a.
Directory. a.
Journal of the Ass'n for the Study of Food and Society. semi-a.

Meetings/Conferences:
Annual Meetings: Annual meetings in conjunction with the
           Food, Agriculture, and Human Values Society.
1999 – Toronto, Canada/June 3-6
2000 – New York City, NY

Ass'n for the Study of Higher Education
Univ. of Missouri/Educ. Leadership Dept.
211 Hill Hall
Columbia, MO 65211
Tel: (573)882-9645   *Fax:* (573)884-5714
E-Mail: ashe@tiger.coe.missouri.edu
Web Site: http://www.coe.missouri.edu/~ashe
Members: 1,100 individuals, 225 organizations
Staff: 1
Annual Budget: $50-100,000
Exec. Director: Julie Caplow

Historical Note
ASHE is a professional society of scholars, researchers, practitioners and graduate students dedicated to the advancement of higher education as a field of study. Membership: $70/year (individual); $50/year (student).

Publications:
ASHE Newsletter. q.
Directory of ASHE Members/Higher Education
           Programs/Faculty. trien.
Review of Higher Education. q.

Meetings/Conferences:
1999 – San Antonio, TX(Omni)/Nov. 18-21

Ass'n for the Study of Man-Environment Relations (1969)
Historical Note
Ass'n reported inactive in 1996.

Ass'n for the Study of Play (1974)
Willard Hall, Univ. of Delaware
Newark, DE 19716
Tel: (302)831-4598   *Fax:* (302)831-4445
E-Mail: hughesla@udel.edu
Web Site: http://www.uwm.edu/~aycock
Members: 180 individuals, 20 organizations
Annual Budget: under $10,000
Treasurer: Linda Hughes

Historical Note
Formerly (1987) Ass'n for the Anthropological Study of Play. TASP's broad focus includes many disciplines and scholarly

interests involved with the study of play. Has no paid officers or full-time staff. Membership: $20/year (professional membership), $15/year (student/retiree), $20/year (institution).

Publications:
TASP Newsletter. tri-a.

Meetings/Conferences:
Annual Meetings: Spring/200

Ass'n for the Treatment of Sexual Abusers (1985)
10700 S.W. Beaverton Hillsdale Hwy.
Suite 26
Beaverton, OR 97005-3035
Tel: (503)643-1023   *Fax:* (503)643-5084
E-Mail: atsa@atsa.com
Web Site: http://www.atsa.com
Members: 1,600 individuals
Staff: 2
Annual Budget: $250-500,000
Exec. Director: Connie D. Isaac

Historical Note
ATSA members are professionals treating sexual offenders and/or their victims. Among its activities are the development and dissemination of professional standards and practices in the field of sex offender research, evaluation and treatment. Membership: $95/year.

Publications:
Sexual Abuse: A Journal of Research and Treatment. q. adv.
The Forum: A Professional Newsletter. q.

Meetings/Conferences:
Annual Meetings: Fall
1999 – Orlando, FL(Hilton)/Sept. 22-25
2000 – San Diego, CA(Hyatt)
2001 – San Antonio, TX(Hyatt)/Nov. 7-10

Ass'n for Theatre in Higher Education (1986)
Historical Note
Address unknown in 1998.

Ass'n for Transpersonal Psychology (1971)
P.O. Box 3049
Stanford, CA 94305
Tel: (650)327-2066   *Fax:* (650)327-0535
Members: 2,600 individuals
Editor: Miles A. Vich

Historical Note
ATP members are professionals and others with an interest in transpersonal psychology.

Publications:
Journal of Transpersonal Psychology. semi-a.
Listing of Professional Members. a.
Listing of Schools and Programs. a.
Newsletter. q.

Ass'n for Transportation Law, Logistics and Policy (1929)
19564 Club House Rd
Montgomery Village, MD 20879-3002
Tel: (301)670-6733   *Fax:* (301)670-6735
E-Mail: atllp@aol.com
Web Site: http://www.transportlink.com/atllp
Members: 1,600 individuals
Staff: 3
Annual Budget: $100-250,000
Exec. Director: E. Dale Jones

Historical Note
Formerly (1929) Ass'n of Practitioners before the Interstate Commerce Commission; (1984) Ass'n of Interstate Commerce Commission Practitioners; and (1994) Ass'n of Transportation Practitioners. Membership includes attorneys, transportation and logistics professionals as well as faculty and students of transportation. Membership: $95/year (individual); $65/year (gov't/academic).

Publications:
Ass'n Highlights. bi-m. adv.
Journal of Transportation Law, Logistics and Policy. q. adv.
Transportation Law Institute Papers & Proceedings. a.

Meetings/Conferences:
Annual Meetings: Summer
1999 – Moran, WY(Jackson Lake Lodge)/June 20-23
2000 – Montreal, Quebec(Ritz Carlton)/June 23-28

Ass'n for Tropical Biology (1961)
Marie Selby Botanical Gardens
811 S. Palm Ave.
Sarasota, FL 34236
Tel: (941)955-7553   *Fax:* (941)951-1474
Members: 1,500 individuals, 400 libraries
Staff: 3
Annual Budget: $50-100,000
Corresponding Secretary/Treasurer: Dr. Margaret Lowman

Historical Note
Membership: $25-40/year (individual); $75 (library subscription).

Publications:
Biotropica. q.
Tropinet. q.

Meetings/Conferences:
Annual Meetings: August, with American Institute of Biological Sciences.

Ass'n for University and College Counseling Center Directors (1951)
University Counseling Center
Colorado State Univ.
Fort Collins, CO 80523-8010
Tel: (970)491-1613   *Fax:* (970)491-2382
Web Site: auccd.org
Members: 500 individuals
Treasurer: Charles Davidshofer

Historical Note
Members are directors of counseling centers on college and university campuses. Has no paid officers or full-time staff. Membership: $70/year.

Meetings/Conferences:
1999 – Miami, FL/Oct. 30-Nov. 3

Ass'n for University Business and Economic Research (1947)
Historical Note
Address unknown in 1997.

Ass'n for Unmanned Vehicle Systems Internat'l (1972)
1200 19th St., N.W., Suite 300
Washington, DC 20036-2401
Tel: (202)857-1889   *Fax:* (202)223-4579
E-Mail: auvsi@dc.sba.com
Members: 2,000 individuals
Staff: 4
Annual Budget: $500-1,000,000
Exec. Director: Daryl Davidson

Historical Note
Established in Dayton, Ohio as the National Ass'n for Remotely Piloted Vehicles, it assumed its present name in 1977. Members are companies and individuals concerned with the development and manufacture of unmanned vehicles. Membership: $40/year (domestic individual); $50/year (foreign); $300-750/year (company).

Publications:
Convention Proceedings. a.
Membership Directory. a. adv.
Unmanned Systems. q. adv.

Meetings/Conferences:
Annual Meetings: early summer/1,000
1999 – Washington, DC
2000 – Orlando, FL

Ass'n for Vital Records and Health Statistics (1933)
Historical Note
Became the Ass'n for Public Health Statistics and Information Systems in 1995.

Ass'n for Volunteer Administration (1960)
740 Florida Central Pkwy., Suite 1020
Longwood, FL 32750
Tel: (407)834-6688   *Fax:* (407)834-4747
Members: 1,850 individuals
Staff: 3
Annual Budget: $25-50,000
Exec. Director: Jone R. Sienkiewicz, CAE, CMP

Historical Note
Formerly (1981) American Ass'n of Volunteer Services Coordinators. Regular Membership: $100/year.

Publications:
Newsletter. bi-m.
The Journal of Volunteer Administration. q.

Meetings/Conferences:
Annual Meetings: October

Ass'n for Women Geoscientists (1977)
4779 126th St. North
St. Paul, MN 55110-5910
Tel: (651)426-3316   *Fax:* (651)426-5449
E-Mail: leete@macalester.edu
Web Site: http://www.awg.org
Members: 1,200 individuals
Staff: 1
Annual Budget: $50-100,000
Exec. Director: Dr. Jeanette H. Leete

Historical Note
Established in 1977 in San Francisco as the Ass'n of Women Geoscientists, AWG assumed its present name in 1982 and was incorporated in California in 1983. A member society of the American Geological Institute. Membership includes men and women from petroleum and mineral industries, geotechnical and hydrogeologic consulting, academic faculty, regulatory agencies and research institutions. Membership: $50/year (individual), $100/year (institution), $500/year (corporate), $25/year (students or reduced income members).

Publications:
Gaea Newsletter. bi-m. adv.

Meetings/Conferences:
Semi-Annual Meetings: May and October
1999 – Denver, CO

Ass'n for Women in Communications (1909)
1244 Ritchie Hwy., Suite 6
Arnold, MD 21012
Tel: (410)544-7442   *Fax:* (410)544-4640
E-Mail: Pat@womcom.org
Web Site: http://www.womcom.org
Members: 7,500 individuals
Staff: 8
Annual Budget: $500-1,000,000
Exec. Director: Patricia H. Troy
Support Services Coordinator: Debbie Caudill
Accounting Manager: Marilyn Taylor
Director, Membership: Nancy Badertscher

Historical Note
Founded as Theta Sigma Phi; absorbed Women in Communications, Inc., and assumed its current name in 1996. AWC seeks to improve opportunities for women in the communications industry. Membership: $90/year, plus local dues. Application fee: $50.

Publications:
Communicator's Connection. a. adv.
InterCom.
The Matrix. q. adv.

Meetings/Conferences:
Annual Meetings: Summer
1999 – Ft. Lauderdale, FL(Bahia Mar)/July 17-21/500
2000 – San Francisco, CA

Ass'n for Women in Computing (1978)
41 Sutter St., Suite 1006
San Francisco, CA 94104
Tel: (415)905-4663
E-Mail: awc@awe-hq.org
Web Site: http://www.awc-hq.org
Members: 1000 individuals, 12 chapters
Annual Budget: $10-25,000
National President: Sojn Hudson

Historical Note
AWC members are dedicated to the advancement of women in the computer industry fields, such as science and education. Membership: $12/year (individual).

Publications:
Nat'l Newsbytes. m. adv.
National Directory. a. adv.
The Source. q. adv.

Meetings/Conferences:
Annual Meetings: Spring
1999 – Oxford, OH
1999 – Houston, TX

Ass'n for Women in Development (1982)
666 11th St., N.W., Suite 450
Washington, DC 10005
Tel: (202)628-0440   *Fax:* (202)628-0442
E-Mail: AWID@igc.apc.org
Web Site: http://www.awid.org
Members: 1,200 individuals
Staff: 3
Annual Budget: $100-250,000
Exec. Director: Carol Garcia

Historical Note
AWID was founded in 1982 by a group of 26 North American scholars, practitioners and policy-makers at a Wingspread Conference in Racine, Wisconsin. Those who gathered at Wingspread created an organization dedicated to the full participation of women in the development process. Today AWID is an organization of over 1000 members providing a series of services and programs with the assistance of hundreds of dedicated volunteers. Membership: $15/year (income less than $10,000); $25/year (income between $10,000-$25,000); $60/year (income greater than $25,000); $150/year (organization).

Publications:
AWID Newsletter. q.
Mailing List. a.
Membership Directory. semi-a.
Trialogue. semi-a.

Meetings/Conferences:
1999 – Washington, DC

Ass'n for Women in Mathematics (1971)
4114 Computer & Space Sciences Bldg.
Univ. of Maryland
College Park, MD 20742-2461
Tel: (301)405-7892
Members: 4,500 individuals & institutions
Staff: 3
Annual Budget: $50-100,000
Director of Meetings and Marketing: Dawn Wheeler

Historical Note
Formerly (1973) Ass'n of Women Mathematicians. Members represent education, industry, business and government. Membership: $40/year (individual), $80-120/year (organization).

Publications:
AWM Newsletter. bi-m. adv.

Meetings/Conferences:
Annual Meetings: with American Mathematical Soc./Mathematical Ass'n of America/January
1999 – San Antonio, TX/Jan 13-Jan. 16
2000 – Washington, DC

Ass'n for Women in Psychology (1969)
423 N. Albany St.
Ithica, NY 14850
Tel: (607)735-1905
Members: 2,200 individuals
Annual Budget: $50-100,000
Recorder/Correspondent: Diane Maluso

Historical Note
Formerly (1970) Ass'n for Women Psychologists. Major objectives are to promote unbiased scientific research on gender in order to establish fact and eliminate myths and assumptions about the "natures" of women and men, to ensure equality of opportunity for women and men in the profession, and encourage research on issues of concern to women of color. Has no paid officers or full-time staff. Membership: $10-$75/year (individual).

Publications:
AWP Newsletter. q. adv.

Meetings/Conferences:
Annual Meetings: March
2000 – Salt Lake City, UT
2001 – Providence, RI
2002 – Fresno, CA
2003 – Orlando, FL

Ass'n for Women in Science (1971)
1200 New York Ave., N.W., Suite 650
Washington, DC 20005-3920
Tel: (202)326-8940   *Fax:* (202)326-8960
Toll Free: (800)886 - 2947
E-Mail: awis@awis.org
Web Site: http://www.awis.org
Members: 6,000 individuals

Staff: 5
Annual Budget: $250-500,000
Exec. Director: Catherine J. Didion
Manager, Administration: Lana Bilyeu
Manager, Membership and Publications: Deborah Morman

Historical Note
Founded in April, 1971 in Chicago, AWIS has 74 chapters in the U.S. Affiliated with the Federation of Organizations for Professional Women, the American Ass'n for the Advancement of Science, and the Nat'l Coalition for Women and Girls in Education. Sponsors the AWIS Predoctoral Awards. Membership: $15-60/year (varies with income).

Publications:
AWIS Magazine. bi-m. adv.

Meetings/Conferences:

Ass'n for Women in Sports Media (1987)

P.O. Box 17536
Fort Worth, TX 76102-0536
Tel: (817)390-7409
Members: 500 individuals
Annual Budget: $10-25,000
Secretary-Treasurer: Kathy Kudravi

Historical Note
AWSM members are professional women in sports media and the women and men who support them in their work. Membership: $35/year (individual); $20/year (student).

Publications:
AWSM Newsletter. q.
Membership Directory. a.

Meetings/Conferences:
Annual Meetings: Summer/120

Ass'n for Women Journalists

1206 S. State St.
Chicago, IL 60605
Tel: (312)321-2146   *Fax:* (312)321-3679
E-Mail: sysys@aol.com
Web Site: http://www.awjchicago.org
Members: 150 individuals
President: Susan Evans

Meetings/Conferences:
1999 – Nashville, TN/June 23-27
2000 – Alaska Cruise/June 3-9

Ass'n for Women Veterinarians (1947)

6200 Jefferson St., N.E., #117
Albuquerque, NM 87109-3431
Tel: (505)856-9016
Members: 600 individuals
Annual Budget: under $10,000
Secretary: Sherrilyn Wainwright

Historical Note
Founded as the Women's Veterinary Ass'n, it became the Women's Veterinary Medical Ass'n in 1950 and assumed its present name in 1980. Has no paid staff. Membership: $40/year.

Publications:
AWV Bulletin. q. adv.

Meetings/Conferences:
Annual Meetings: with the American Veterinary Medical Ass'n
1999 – New Orleans, LA

Ass'n for Work Process Improvement (1970)

185 Devonshire St., Suite 770
Boston, MA 02110-1407
Tel: (617)426-1167   *Fax:* (617)521-8675
Toll Free: (800)998 - 2974
E-Mail: info@tawpi.org
Web Site: http://www.tawpi.org
Members: 1,300 individuals, 1,100 companies
Staff: 10
Annual Budget: $1-2,000,000
President: Linda N. O'Hara
Director, Marketing: Gus Lodato
Director, Education and Convention Services: Melissa Comeau
Education Programs Coordinator: Kimberly Schwartz
Director, Finance and Operations: Kim Votta-Ali
Marketing and Membership Manager: Maria Paduano

Historical Note
Formed by the merger of the Recognition Technologies Users Ass'n, DEMA - The Ass'n for Input Technology and Management and the OCR/Scanner Fax Ass'n in 1993. Users and marketers of electronic processing equipment focusing on document (data capture and desktop), remittance, data entry, character, mark read, optical bar code, magnetic ink character, image processing and voice recognition technologies. Membership: $195/year.

Publications:
TODAY-Special Industry Focus Editions. semi-a. adv.
TODAY-The Journal of Work Process Improvement. 5/year. adv.

Meetings/Conferences:
Annual Meetings: Summer/1,500-2,000
1999 – Denver, CO/August 1-4

Ass'n for Worksite Health Promotion (1974)

60 Revere Drive, Suite 500
Northbrook, IL 60062
Tel: (847)480-9574   *Fax:* (847)480-9282
E-Mail: awhp@awhp.org
Web Site: http://www.awhp.org
Members: 2,800 individuals
Staff: 4
Annual Budget: $500-1,000,000
Exec. Director: Kevin R. Hacke
Conference Director: Liz Freyn
Member Services: Hyla Holmes
Administrative Director: Zoie Geleerd
Membership Director: Barbara Apgar
Publications Editor: Kristen Lambert

Historical Note
Founded as the American Ass'n of Fitness Directors in Business and Industry in 1974. Became the Ass'n for Fitness in Business in 1983; and assumed the name Ass'n for Worksite Health Promotion in 1992. Members include exercise facility managers, human resource directors, health educators, corporate wellness directors, non-profit organization wellness directors, health club owners, dietitians, organizational health consultants, benefits managers, fitness instructors/personal trainers, health and fitness management consultants, government and civic wellness directors, physical and occupational therapists, occupational health nurses, and physicians. Membership: $130/year (individual), $70/year (student), $250/year (company), $350/year (vendor company).

Publications:
AWHP Action Newsletter. bi-m. adv.
AWHP's Worksite Health Magazine. q. adv.

Meetings/Conferences:
Annual Meetings: Fall
1999 – Nashville, TN(Opryland Hotel)/Sept. 15-18/1600
2000 – Orlando, FL(Coronado Springs
        Hotel)/Sept. 13-16/1600

Ass'n of Academic Chairmen of Plastic Surgery

444 E. Algonquin Road
Arlington Heights, IL 60005-4654
Tel: (847)228-8375   *Fax:* (847)228-6509
Exec. Director: Catherine Hay

Meetings/Conferences:

Ass'n of Academic Health Centers (1969)

1400 16th St. NW, Suite 720
Washington, DC 20036
Tel: (202)265-9600   *Fax:* (202)265-7514
Web Site: http://www.ahcnet.org
Members: 104 institutions
Staff: 11
Annual Budget: $1-2,000,000
President and C.E.O.: Roger J. Bulger, M.D.
Assistant V. President, Programs: Elaine R. Rubin, Ph.D.
Exec. Vice President: Marian Ostenweis, Ph.D.
Manager, Administrative Services: Nancy L. Siegal
Manager, Information Technology: Serena R. Curry

Historical Note
Founded in 1969 and incorporated in Indiana as the Organization of University Health Center Administrators, name changed in 1971 to Ass'n for Academic Health Centers in 1971, and assumed its current name in 1980. Represents academic health centers in the U.S. and Canada. Sponsors study groups to address issues relevant to health care in the university setting.

Publications:
Directory. a.

Meetings/Conferences:

Ass'n of Academic Health Sciences Library Directors (1978)

2150 N. 107th St., Suite 205
Seattle, WA 98133-9009
Tel: (206)367-8704   *Fax:* (206)441-8262
Members: 125 institutions
Staff: 1
Annual Budget: $50-100,000
Exec. Director: Shirley Bishop

Historical Note
Formed to provide a medium for communication among academic health sciences library directors for addressing common concerns on planning, program and policy developments; to extend contacts nationally to provide a forum for joint action. Compiles statistics on medical school libraries in the U.S. and Canada annually. Membership: $300/year.

Publications:
AAHSLD News. q.
Annual Report. a.
Annual Statistics of Medical School Libraries. a.
Directory. a.

Meetings/Conferences:
Annual Meetings: Fall

Ass'n of Academic Physiatrists (1967)

5987 E. 71st Street, Ste. 112
Indianapolis, IN 46220
Tel: (317)845-4200   *Fax:* (317)845-4299
Web Site: http://www.physiatry.org
Members: 1,200 individuals
Staff: 5
Annual Budget: $250-500,000
Exec. Director: Carolyn L. Braddom, Ed.D.
Director, Meetings/Conventions: Lynn Lawson
Membership Services: Dennis Lawson, Sr.

Historical Note
Members are academic physicians specializing in physical medicine and rehabilitation. Affiliated with the Ass'n of American Medical Colleges. Membership: $150-450/year.

Publications:
American Journal of Physical Medicine & Rehabilitation. bi-m. adv.
Directory. a.
Newsletter. q.

Meetings/Conferences:
Annual Meetings: February
1999 – Orlando, FL(Caribe Royale)/Feb. 17-21/450
2000 – San Diego, CA(Sheraton Grand Torrey
        Pines)/Feb. 29-March 4
2001 – Hilton Head, SC

Ass'n of Administrative Law Judges (1970)

522 S.W. Fifth Ave., Suite 200
Portland, OR 97204-3275
Tel: (503)326-3275
Members: 700 individuals

Staff: 1
Annual Budget: $50-100,000

Historical Note
Formed to protect the decisional independence of Federal Administrative Law Judges, to provide ongoing judicial education, and defend the integrity of the hearing system. Incorporated in the State of Illinois in 1980, members are administrative law judges of the Social Security Agency of the U.S. Government. Officers are elected annually. Membership: $75/year.

Publications:
AALJ Newsletter. bi-m.

Meetings/Conferences:

Ass'n of Administrators of the Interstate Compact on the Placement of Children (1969)

810 First St., N.E., Suite 500
Washington, DC 20002-4267
Tel: (202)682-0100   *Fax:* (202)289-6555
Members: 50 states, DC and US Virgin Islands
Contact: Frank Barthel

Historical Note
An affiliate of the American Public Welfare Ass'n, AAICPC members are state administrators of the uniform law for the placement of children across state lines.

Publications:
Compact Administrators' Manual.
Guide to the ICPC.

Meetings/Conferences:

Ass'n of Advanced Rabbinical and Talmudic Schools (1971)

175 Fifth Ave., Suite 711
New York, NY 10010
Tel: (212)477-0950   212
Members: 56 institutions
Staff: 3
Annual Budget: $100-250,000
Exec. V. President: Bernard Fryshman, Ph.D.

Historical Note
Formerly (1971) the Council of Roshei Yeshivas.

Publications:
Handbook of the Accreditation Commission. a.

Meetings/Conferences:
Annual Meetings: Winter

Ass'n of African American Museums (1978)

P.O. Box 427
1350 Brush Row Rd.
Wilberforce, OH 45384-0548
Tel: (937)376-4611   *Fax:* (937)376-2007
E-Mail: NAAMCC@ERINET.com
Members: 200 individuals, 100 institutions
Staff: 5
Annual Budget: $10-25,000
Director of Operations: William Billingsley

Historical Note
Founded and incorporated in 1978 as African-American Museums Ass'n; assumed its current name in 1998. AAAM is the national voice of black museums in the U.S. AAAM helps its members in collecting, preserving, and interpreting the cultural objects and artifacts of black heritage worldwide. Membership is open to cultural organizations, historical societies and museums that collect, conserve, exhibit and interpret objects valuable to art, history, and science, as well as educational institutions and research centers. Membership: $15/year (student); $35/year (individual), $100-250/year (organization), $225-500/year (affiliates).

Publications:
AAAM News Update. q.
AAAM Professional Directory. a.
Survey Results - Profile of Black Museums. irreg.

Meetings/Conferences:
Annual Meetings: late Summer
1999 – Detroit, MI/Aug. 18-22

Ass'n of African Studies Programs (1972)

Historical Note
Address unknown in 1998.

Ass'n of African-American Women Business Owners (1982)

P.O. Box 13858
Silver Spring, MD 20911-0858
Tel: (301)585-8051
Members: 600 individuals
Staff: 4
Annual Budget: $100-250,000
Nat'l President: Brenda Alford

Historical Note
Formerly (1982) American Ass'n of Black Women Entrepreneurs. Purpose is to bring black women into the mainstream of the American economic system. Membership: $200/year (individual), $500/year (organization/company). $25 application fee. Send SASE business-sized envelope with written request for information.

Publications:
Chronicle of Minority Business. q. adv.

Meetings/Conferences:
Annual Meetings: Bien. Summer
2000 – Midwest

Ass'n of Agricultural Computer Companies (1984)

Historical Note
Organization defunct in 1998.

Ass'n of Air Medical Services (1980)

110 N. Royal St., Suite 307
Alexandria, VA 22314

Tel: (703)836-8732 *Fax:* (703)836-8920
E-Mail: Natloffice@aol.com
Web Site: http://www.aams.org
Members: 500 air medical service providers
Staff: 4
Annual Budget: $500-1,000,000
Exec. Director: Dawn Mancuso
Communications and Marketing Manager: Gerald Moczynski

Historical Note
Formerly (1988) ASHBEAMS (American Soc. of Hospital-Based Emergency Air Medical Services). Established in Houston, Texas and incorporated in Iowa, AAMS is an association of health care entities operating helicopter/fixed wing transport services. The composition of medical and aviation people who belong to AAMS includes administrators, pilots, mechanics, paramedics, respiratory therapists, physicians, communication specialists, nurses, Part 135 operators and aircraft manufacturers. Membership: $65/year (individual); $300-600/year (organization/company).

Publications:
AAMS News & Views Newsletter.
Air Medical Journal. m. adv.
AirMed. bi-m. adv.
Annual Membership Directory. a.

Meetings/Conferences:
Annual Meetings: Fall

Ass'n of Alternate Postal Systems *(1975)*
P.O. Box 1331
Gaylord, MI 43734
Tel: (517)732-9272 *Fax:* (517)732-8300
Members: 140 companies
Staff: 1
Annual Budget: $100-250,000
Exec. Director: Ken Bradstreet

Historical Note
Formerly (1990) the Ass'n of Private Postal Systems. Members are companies delivering advertising mail to consumers. Membership: $240/year, minimum.

Publications:
Update. m.

Meetings/Conferences:
Annual Meetings: February

Ass'n of Alternative Newsweeklies *(1978)*
1660 L St., N.W., Suite 316
Washington, DC 20036
Tel: (202)822-1955 *Fax:* (202)822-0929
Web Site: http://aan.org
Members: 113 newspapers
Staff: 5
Annual Budget: $500-1,000,000
Exec. Director: Richard Karpel

Historical Note
AAN represents alternative newspapers like the Village Voice, Boston Phoenix, LA Weekly and Chicago Reader. Membership: $500-$2500/year (company).

Publications:
AAN News. m. adv.

Meetings/Conferences:
Annual Meetings: June
1999 – Memphis, TN(The Peabody)/May 27-29/750
2000 – Phoenix, AZ/750
2001 – New Orleans, LA

Ass'n of America's Public Television Stations *(1980)*
1350 Connecticut Ave., N.W., Suite 200
Washington, DC 20036-1701
Tel: (202)887-1700 *Fax:* (202)293-2422
E-Mail: info@apts.org
Web Site: http://www.apts.org
Members: 165 Public television stations
Staff: 13
Annual Budget: $2-5,000,000
President: David J. Brugger
Director, Communications: Nancy F. Neubauer
V. President, Government Relations: Mary Dewhirst
Manager, Finance and Administration: Alan Steiner
Director, Legal Affairs: Lonna Thompson,. Esq.
General Counsel, V. President for Policy and Legal Affairs: Marilyn Mohrman-Gillis

Historical Note
Established in January, 1980 as the Ass'n for Public Broadcasting, became Nat'l Ass'n of Public Television Stations in July, 1980, later readopted its original name and then assumed its present name in 1991. APTS represents public television before the federal government and provides research, planning, and communicaions support to the industry. Members are public television licensees.

Publications:
Communique.
Transition.
Washington Update.

Meetings/Conferences:
Annual Meetings: Spring.
1999 – Washington, DC(Wyndham)/Feb. 28-March 3/250

Ass'n of American Cancer Institutes *(1959)*
Elm & Carlton Sts.
Buffalo, NY 14263
Tel: (716)845-3028 *Fax:* (716)845-8178
Members: 84 cancer centers
Annual Budget: $100-250,000
Secretary-Treasurer: Dr. Edwin A. Mirand

Historical Note
Formerly (1968) Ass'n of Cancer Institute Directors. AACI members are comprehensive, clinical and basic cancer centers. Membership: $1,500-$2,500/year (center).

Publications:
AACI Newsletter. a.

Meetings/Conferences:

Ass'n of American Chamber of Commerce in Latin America
1615 H St. N.W.
Washington, DC 20062
Tel: (202)463-5485 *Fax:* (202)463-3126
Exec. V. President: David T. Hirschmann

Meetings/Conferences:
1999 – Washington, DC(US Chamber of Commerce Building)/May 3-7

Ass'n of American Colleges and Universities *(1915)*
1818 R St., N.W.
Washington, DC 20009
Tel: (202)387-3760 *Fax:* (202)265-9532
Web Site: http://www.aacu-edu.org
Members: 675 institutions
Staff: 30
Annual Budget: $2-5,000,000
President: Carol Schneider
V. President, Communications: Joann Stevens
Meeting Coordinator: Suzanne Hyers
Membership Director: Tobin P. Comley

Historical Note
Formerly (1994) Ass'n of American Colleges. Strives to strengthen undergraduate curricula in liberal arts education and to revitalize classroom teaching and learning through research and development projects, publications, national and regional meetings and workshops and multi-campus partnerships and networks. Institutional membership fee based on sliding scale.

Publications:
Liberal Education. q.
On Campus with Women Newsletter. q.
Peer Review. q.

Meetings/Conferences:
Annual Meetings: Winter/900
1999 – San Francisco, CA/Jan. 28-30

Ass'n of American Editorial Cartoonists *(1957)*
4101 Lake Boone Trail, Suite 201
Raleigh, NC 27607-6518
Tel: (919)787-5181 *Fax:* (919)787-4916
Web Site: http://www.detnews.com/aaec
Members: 300 individuals
Staff: 2
Annual Budget: $25-50,000
General Manager: Shannon Parham

Historical Note
Membership: $100/year (individual).

Publications:
AAEC Notebook. q.
Membership Directory. trien.

Meetings/Conferences:
1999 – Chattanooga, TN

Ass'n of American Feed Control Officials *(1909)*
Office of IN State Chemist, Purdue Univ.
1154 Biochemistry Bldg.
West Lafayette, IN 47907-1154
Tel: (765)494-5900 *Fax:* (765)494-4331
E-Mail: noelr@isco.purdue.edu
Web Site: http://www.AAFCO.org
Members: 325 individuals
Secretary-Treasurer: Dr. Rodney Noel

Historical Note
Officials of government agencies at the State, Provincial, Dominion and Federal levels engaged in the regulation of production, analysis, labeling, distribution and sale of animal feeds and livestock remedies. Internet Home Page: http://www.uky.edu/Agriculture/RegulatoryServices/aafco.htm.

Publications:
Official Publication. a.

Meetings/Conferences:

Ass'n of American Geographers *(1904)*
1710 16th St., N.W.
Washington, DC 20009-3198
Tel: (202)234-1450 *Fax:* (202)234-2744
E-Mail: gaia@aag.org
Web Site: http://www.aag.org
Members: 7,000 individuals
Staff: 12
Annual Budget: $1-2,000,000
Exec. Director: Dr. Ronald F. Abler
Educational Affairs Director: Osa Brand
Comptroller: V. Veerappan
Membership Director: Kevin Klug
Annual Meeting Coordinator: Angie Jackson

Historical Note
Founded in Philadelphia in 1904 at a meeting of the American Ass'n for the Advancement of Science and incorporated in the District of Columbia in 1937. Merged in 1948 with the American Soc. for Professional Geographers. A member of the American Council of Learned Societies. Membership: varies according to income.

Publications:
AAG Newsletter.
Annals. q. adv.
The Professional Geographer. q. adv.

Meetings/Conferences:
Annual Meetings: Spring/3,500
1999 – Honolulu, HI(Hilton)/March 23-27
2000 – Pittsburg, PA/April 4-8

Ass'n of American Law Schools *(1900)*
1201 Connecticut Ave., N.W., Suite 800
Washington, DC 20036-2605

Tel: (202)296-8851 *Fax:* (202)296-8869
E-Mail: aals@aals.org
Web Site: http://www.aals.org
Members: 162 institutions
Staff: 20
Annual Budget: $2-5,000,000
Exec. V. President: Carl C. Monk

Historical Note
Organized in Saratoga Springs with 32 schools as charter members, AALS is an association of law schools and serves as the law teachers' learned society. AALS is legal education's principal representative to the federal government and to other national higher education organizations and learned societies. Incorporated in the District of Columbia in 1971. Membership: $4,190-16,760/year, varies by size of enrollment (school).

Publications:
AALS Newsletter. q.
Directory of Law Teachers. a.
Journal of Legal Education. q.
Placement Bulletin. bi-m.
Proceedings. a.

Meetings/Conferences:
Annual Meetings: January/3,000
1999 – New Orleans, LA(Hilton and Sheraton)/Jan. 6-10

Ass'n of American Medical Colleges *(1876)*
2450 N St., N.W.
Washington, DC 20037-1127
Tel: (202)828-0400 *Fax:* (202)828-1125
Web Site: http://www.aamc.org
Members: 125 schools, 92 socs., 400 hospitals
Staff: 200
Annual Budget: $25-50,000,000
President: Jordan J. Cohen
V. President for Communications: Susan Neely
Exec. V. President: Richard M. Knapp, Ph.D.
V. President, Administrative Services: Edwin L. Crocker
Director, Human Resources: Michele Fantt, SPHR
Director, Publications.: Dana Murphy
V. President, Information Resources: David Witter

Historical Note
Seeks the advancement of medical education, biomedical research and the nation's health. Has an annual budget of approximately $40 million.

Publications:
Academic Medicine. m. adv.
Reporter.
Washington Highlights.

Meetings/Conferences:
Annual Meetings: Fall, odd years in Washington, DC and even years in various cities
1999 – /Oct. 23-28
2000 – Chicago, IL/Oct. 27-Nov. 2
2001 – /Nov. 2-8
2002 – San Francisco, CA/Nov. 8-14

Ass'n of American Pesticide Control Officials *(1947)*
P.O. Box 1249
Hardwick, VT 05843
Tel: (802)472-6956 *Fax:* (802)472-6957
Web Site: http://aapaco.ceris.purdue.edu/doc/index.html
Members: 55 individuals
Staff: 1
Annual Budget: $10-25,000
Secretary: Philip H. Gray

Historical Note
An association comprised of state, pesticide regulatory officials dedicated to a uniform approach throughout the U.S. to the implementation of the Federal Insecticide, Fungicide, and Rodenticide Act, as amended. Formerly Ass'n of Economic Poisons Control Officials. Membership: $100/year.

Publications:
Official Publication. a.

Meetings/Conferences:
Annual Meetings: August/150
1999 – Omaha, NE(Doubletree Hotel)/Aug. 2-6
2000 – Charleston, WV

Ass'n of American Physicians *(1886)*
c/o UCSD Dept. of Medicine (O673)
9500 Gilman Drive
La Jolla, CA 92093-0673
Tel: (619)534-6651 *Fax:* (619)53 -6653
Members: 1,200 individuals
Staff: 1
Annual Budget: $10-25,000
Secretary: Jerrold Olefsky, M.D.

Historical Note
Members are medical school professors. Has no paid officers or full-time staff. Membership: $100/year.

Publications:
Transactions of the Association of American Physicians. a.

Meetings/Conferences:
Annual Meetings: Spring/4,500
1999 – Chicago, IL(Fairemont)/April 23-25/420

Ass'n of American Physicians and Surgeons *(1943)*
1601 North Tucson Blvd., Suite 9
Tucson, AZ 85716
Tel: (520)327-4885 *Fax:* (520)325-4230
E-Mail: 71161,1263@compuserve.com
Web Site: http://www.aapsonline.org
Members: 6,000 individuals
Staff: 3
Annual Budget: $100-250,000
Exec. Director: Jane M. Orient, M.D.

Historical Note
Represents physicians in the socio-economic aspects of medical practice. Supports the Ass'n of American Physicians and Surgeons Political Action Committee. Membership: $275/year (individual).

Publications:
AAPS News Newsletter. m.
Medical Sentinel. bi-m.

Meetings/Conferences:
Annual Meetings: Fall
1999 – Coeur d'Alene, ID/Oct. 12-16

Ass'n of American Plant Food Control Officials *(1946)*
Div. of Reg. Services, Univ. of Kentucky
Lexington, KY   40546-0275
Tel: (606)257-2668   *Fax:* (606)257-7351
E-Mail: dterry@ca.uky.edu
Members: 185 individuals
Staff: 1
Annual Budget: $10–25,000
Secretary: D.L. Terry

Historical Note
Formerly (1967) Ass'n of American Fertilizer Control Officials. Membership: $100/year.

Publications:
Official Publication of AAPFCO. a.

Meetings/Conferences:
Annual Meetings: 1st week in August
1999 – Omaha, NE(Doubletree Hotel)/Aug. 2-3
2000 – West Virginia
2001 – Kansas, MO

Ass'n of American Publishers *(1970)*
1718 Connecticut Ave., N.W.
7th Floor
Washington, DC   20009
Tel: (202)232-3335   *Fax:* (202)745-0694
Web Site: http://www.publishers.com
Members: 200 companies
Staff: 25
Annual Budget: $5–10,000,000
President: Patricia Schroeder
Director, Communications: Judith Platt
Exec. V. President: Thomas D. McKee

Historical Note
Formed by a merger of the American Educational Publishers Institute (founded in 1942 and formerly known as the American Textbook Publishers Institute) and the American Book Publishers Council (founded in 1946 and which included the former Technical, Scientific and Medical Book Publishers). The voice of the American publishing industry. Connected with the American Book Publishers Political Action Committee. Maintains a Washington office. Has an annual budget of approximately $6.3 million.

Publications:
AAP Monthly Report. m.
Industry Statistics Report.

Meetings/Conferences:
Annual Meetings: Spring
1999 – Washington, DC/March 17-18

Ass'n of American Railroads *(1934)*
50 F St., N.W.
Washington, DC   20001-1564
Tel: (202)639-2100   *Fax:* (202)639-2558
Web Site: http://www.aar.org
Members: 67 railroads
Staff: 450
Annual Budget: $25–50,000,000
President: Ed Hamburger
V. President, Media Relations: John J. Fitzpatrick
Senior V. President; Policy, Legislation and Economics: Karen Phillips
Manager, Meeting Services: Stephanie Kilfeather
Exec. V. President and C.F.O.: David B. Barefoot
General Attorney: Janet L. Bartelmay
Sr. VP & General Counsel: Louis P. Warchot
Manager, Publications/Bus. Services: Gregory Hill

Historical Note
Founded in 1934 through the merger of the American Railway Ass'n, the Ass'n of Railway Executives and several other rail organizations. The oldest predecessor organization was Master Car Builders Ass'n founded in 1867. AAR presently serves as the joint agency of its individual railroad members to assure an efficient nationwide rail system. Activity areas include standards, operations, maintenance, safety, theoretical and applied research, economics, finance, accounting, communications, electronic data exchanges and public affairs. Maintains the Transportation Technology Center near Pueblo, Colorado. As a wholly-owned subsidiary corporation, Transportation Technology Center, Inc. AAR has an annual budget of nearly $44 million. Membership dues: determined by members' annual revenues.

Publications:
Analysis of Class I Railroads. a.
Price List of Publications. a.
Railroad Facts. a.
Railroad Ten-year Trends. a.
Train It. bi-w.

Meetings/Conferences:
Annual Meetings: Not held; AAR divisions and departments meet separately.

Ass'n of American Seed Control Officials *(1946)*
North Carolina Dept. of Agriculture
P.O. Box 27647
Raleigh, NC   27611-7647
Tel: (919)733-3930   *Fax:* (919)733-1041
E-Mail: jim_warren@mail.agr.state.nc.us
Web Site:
http://www.isco.purdue.edu/aasco/index_aasco.htm
Members: 52 individuals
Annual Budget: under $10,000
President: James Warren

Historical Note
U.S. and Canadian officials who administer state/provincial seed regulations. One member from each state, one from Canada and one from the U.S. Dept. of Agriculture. Has no paid officers or full-time staff. Membership: $150/year (state organization).

Publications:
Administrative Practices Handbook.
Directory.
Seed Inspectors Handbook.

Meetings/Conferences:
Annual Meetings: Summer
1999 – Fayetteville, AR(Fayetteville Hilton Inn)/July 10-15

Ass'n of American State Geologists *(1906)*
Colorado Geological Survey
1313 Sherman St., Room 715
Denver, CO   80203
Tel: (303)866-2611   *Fax:* (303)866-2461
Web Site: http://www.kgs.ukans.edu/AASG.html
Members: 51 individuals
Annual Budget: under $10,000
Treasurer: Vicki J. Cowart

Historical Note
Founded in 1906 as the Ass'n of State Geologists of the Mississippi Valley; assumed its present name May 12, 1908 in the District of Columbia. Members of the association are chief executives of State Geological Surveys in the 50 states and Puerto Rico.

Publications:
AASG Fact Book. a.
The State Geologists Journal. a.

Meetings/Conferences:
Annual Meetings: late Spring
1999 – Alaska
2000 – Missouri
2001 – Montana
2002 – Iowa
2003 – Washington

Ass'n of American Universities *(1900)*
1200 New York Ave., N.W., Suite 550
Washington, DC   20005-3928
Tel: (202)408-7500   *Fax:* (202)408-8184
Members: 62 universities
Staff: 16
Annual Budget: $2–5,000,000
President: Nils Hasselmo, Ph.D.
Exec. V. President: John C. Vaughn

Historical Note
Members are chief executives of major research universities. Affiliated with the Association of Graduate Schools.

Meetings/Conferences:
Semi-Annual Meetings: Spring and Fall

Ass'n of American University Presses *(1937)*
71 W. 23rd St., Suite 901
New York, NY   10010-4102
Tel: (212)989-1010   *Fax:* (212)989-0275
Web Site: http://aaup.uchicago.edu/aaup_home.html
Members: 119 presses
Staff: 10
Annual Budget: $1–2,000,000
Exec. Director: Peter J. Givler
Assoc. Exec. Director: Hollis Holmes

Historical Note
AAUP members are university presses and a limited number of presses of non-degree-granting, non-profit scholarly institutions. The work of the Association is reflected in its committees, which currently cover such diverse fields as statistical surveys, computers, copyright, professional development, equal opportunity, government relations, national and international marketing, library relations, relations with private institutions, and scholarly journals. Applicant presses must have published at least ten scholarly books or journals in the twenty-four months prior to application and employ a minimum of three individuals on staff. Membership: $2–13,000/year.

Publications:
Directory. a.
The Exchange Newsletter. q.
University Press Books for Public & Secondary School Libraries. a.

Meetings/Conferences:
Annual Meetings: May-June/400-800
1999 – Austin, TX

Ass'n of American Veterinary Medical Colleges *(1965)*
1101 Vermont Ave., N.W., Suite 710
Washington, DC   20005-3521
Tel: (202)371-9195   *Fax:* (202)842-0773
E-Mail: aavmc@aavmc.org
Web Site: http://aavmc.org/
Members: 51 institutions
Staff: 4
Annual Budget: $250–500,000
Exec. Director: Dr. Curt J. Man, D.V.M.
Academic Affairs and Student Services Specialist: Paige Pence

Historical Note
AAVMC coordinates the affairs of veterinary medical colleges and addresses issues related to animal owners. In 1984, the association bylaws were amended to provide for only institutional membership. Membership: $13,000/year.

Publications:
Journal of Veterinary Medical Education. 4/year.
Professional Publishers, Bi.

Meetings/Conferences:
Annual Meetings: July/500

Ass'n of American Woodpulp Importers *(1911)*

Historical Note
Organization defunct in 1998.

Ass'n of Analytical Chemists *(1941)*
2017 Hyde Park Road
Detroit, MI   48207
Tel: (313)393-3685
E-Mail: 73230.1340@compuserve.com
Web Site:
ourworld.compuserve.com/homepages/Detroit_Chemists
Members: 250 individuals
Annual Budget: under $10,000
Contact: Ed Havlina

Historical Note
ANACHEM members are analytical chemists. Membership: $15/year. Website located at http://ourworld.compuserve.com/homepages/AnachNews

Meetings/Conferences:
Annual Meetings: always in Detroit, MI
1999 – Detroit, MI

Ass'n of Ancient Historians *(1974)*
History Department
San Diego State University
San Diego, CA   92182-8147
Tel: (619)594-4511   *Fax:* (619)594-7046
E-Mail: patricia.dintrone@sdsu.edu
Web Site:
http://www.weber01.u.washington.edu/tildaclio/aah
Members: 800 individuals
Annual Budget: under $10,000
Secretary-Treasurer: Patricia Dintrone

Historical Note
AAH was organized to provide ancient historians, as a group, an identity apart from classical philologists and to hold an annual meeting. Membership: $7.50/year (individual).

Publications:
Newsletter. 3/year.
Publications of the AAH (monograph series). irreg.

Meetings/Conferences:
Annual Meetings: Spring
1999 – New York, NY(Columbia University)/May 7-9

Ass'n of Applied Community Researchers *(1962)*
c/o ACCE, 4232 King St.
Alexandria, VA   22302
Tel: (703)998-0072   *Fax:* (703)931-5624
E-Mail: accra@acce.org
Web Site: http://www.accra.org
Members: 480 individuals
Staff: 4
Annual Budget: $250–500,000
ACCRA Manager: Christian D. Faulkner
Meetings Manager: Alison Donottue
Administrative Assistant: Andrea Meksher
COLI Fulfillment Administrator: Misrak Amde

Historical Note
Formerly (1992) American Chamber of Commerce Researchers Ass'n. Administrative support provided by American Chamber of Commerce Executives (same address). Promotes research in community development. Membership: $95/year.

Publications:
ACCRA Newsletter. q.
Applied Community Research Monographs Series.
Cost of Living Index. q.
Membership Directory. a.

Meetings/Conferences:
Annual Meetings: Spring
1999 – Pittsburgh, PA(Westin William Penn)/June 9-12
2000 – Minneapolis(Minneapolis Marriott City Center)/June 8-11/100

Ass'n of Applied Insect Ecologists *(1967)*
1008 10th St., Suite 549
Sacramento, CA   95814
Tel: (916)441-5224   *Fax:* (916)441-5224
E-Mail: plainaaieq/aol.com
Web Site: http://www.aaie.com
Members: 300 individuals
Staff: 1
Annual Budget: $25–50,000
Exec. Secretary: John F. Plain

Historical Note
Members are specialists in agricultural pest control. AAIE serves as a forum for the exchange of ideas on sound pest management practices. Membership: $100/year (professional); $50/year (general); $35/year (associate); $15/year (student).

Publications:
AAIE Bulletin. q. adv.
AAIE Conference Program. a. adv.

Meetings/Conferences:
Annual Meetings: Winter/300-400
1999 – Santa Barbara, CA(Red Lion)
2000 – Sacremento, CA(Raddisson)

Ass'n of Architectural Librarians *(1974)*
c/o Wentworth Library
550 Huntington Ave.
Boston, MA   02115-0898
Tel: (617)989-4042   *Fax:* (617)989-4091
E-Mail: biondip@wit.edu
Members: 80 individuals
Annual Budget: under $10,000
Secretary: Priscilla Biondi

Historical Note
Established in 1974, AAL promotes interaction between architects and architectural librarians as well as educational and professional development for its members. Membership: $25/year (individual).

Publications:
Newsletter. 3/year. adv.

Meetings/Conferences:
Annual Meetings: June
1999 – Chicago, IL(Prairie Avenue Bookshop)

Ass'n of Area Business Publications *(1979)*
5820 Wilshire Blvd., Suite 500
Los Angeles, CA 90036
Tel: (213)937-5514 *Fax:* (213)937-0959
Web Site: http://www.bizpubs.org
Members: 100 publications
Staff: 2
Annual Budget: $100-250,000
Exec. Director: C. James Dowden

Historical Note
Members are local and regional business newspapers and magazines. AABP provides a forum for local business publications to cooperate, exchange information, and promote their publications in the national business community. Membership: $500-2,100/year.

Publications:
AABP Directory. a.
AABP Newsletter. q.
Readership Survey. bien.

Meetings/Conferences:
Semi-Annual Meetings: Winter(publishers), Summer(editors & publishers)
1999 – Puerto Vallarta, Mexico(Camino Real)/Puerto 0-14

Ass'n of Art Museum Directors *(1916)*
41 E. 65th St.
New York, NY 10021
Tel: (212)249-4423 *Fax:* (212)535-5039
E-Mail: aamd@amn.org
Web Site: http://www.aamt.net
Members: 170 individuals
Staff: 4
Annual Budget: $100-250,000
Exec. Director: Millicent Hall Gaudieri

Historical Note
Works to establish and maintain high standards for members and the museums they represent. Membership: $1,400-5,400/year.

Publications:
AAMD Salary Survey. a.
Professional Practices in Art Museums.

Meetings/Conferences:

Ass'n of Artist-Run Galleries *(1974)*
Historical Note
Organization inactive in 1996.

Ass'n of Arts Administration Educators *(1975)*
Dept. of Performing Arts, American Univ.
4400 Mass. Ave., N.W.
Washington, DC 20016
Tel: (202)885-1000 *Fax:* (202)885-1092
E-Mail: vmorris@american.edu
Members: 60 university departments
Annual Budget: $10-25,000

Historical Note
Members are directors of graduate level programs in arts administration. Affiliate membership is available to directors of undergraduate programs and other interested individuals. Has no paid officers or full-time staff. Membership: $25/year (individual), $60/year (associate), $120/year (organization).

Publications:
Survey of Arts Administration Training. bien.

Meetings/Conferences:
Annual Meetings: Spring

Ass'n of Asphalt Paving Technologists *(1926)*
400 Selby Ave., Suite 1
St. Paul, MN 55102
Tel: (651)293-9188 *Fax:* (651)293-9193
E-Mail: aaptbev@aol.com
Members: 800 individuals
Staff: 1
Annual Budget: $100-250,000
Administrative Secretary: Beverly Winnie

Historical Note
Formed in Chicago in 1926 with 19 charter members and incorporated in Minnesota in 1969. Membership: $90/year.

Publications:
Asphalt Paving Technology. a.

Meetings/Conferences:
Annual Meetings: February-March
1999 – Chicago, IL(Palmer House)/March 8-10

Ass'n of Astronomy Educators *(1977)*
5103 Burt St.
Omaha, NE 68132
Members: 400 individuals
Exec. Director: Katherine Becker

Historical Note
AAE members are educators with an interest in astronomy education at all levels. Membership: $12/year.

Publications:
Astronomy Education Newsletter. q.

Meetings/Conferences:

Ass'n of Attorney-Mediators
One Galleria Tower
13355 Noel Road, Suite 500
Dallas, TX 75240
Tel: (972)869-1183 *Fax:* (214)739-2056
Toll Free: (800)280 - 1368

E-Mail: aam@counsel.com
Web Site: http://www.attorney-mediators.org
Staff: 1
Administrator: Lynn Rugoff

Historical Note
Members are attorneys who are qualified to provide mediation services.

Ass'n of Audio-Visual Technicians *(1975)*
Historical Note
Organization reported defunct in 1995.

Ass'n of Authors' Representatives *(1928)*
10 Astor Place
3rd Floor
New York, NY 10003
Tel: (212)353-3709
Web Site: http://www.aar-online.org
Members: 260 individuals
Annual Budget: $10-25,000
Administrative Secretary: Ginger Knowlton

Historical Note
Formerly (1991) the Society of Authors' Representatives, SAR merged with the Independent Literary Agents Ass'n (est. 1977) to form the Ass'n of Authors' Representatives. AAR membership is restricted to professional literary and dramatic agents.

Publications:
The Literary Agent. a.

Meetings/Conferences:
Annual Meetings: June

Ass'n of Automotive Aftermarket Distributors *(1977)*
5050 Poplar Ave., Suite 2020
Memphis, TN 38157-2001
Tel: (901)682-9090 *Fax:* (901)682-9098
E-Mail: partsplus@bellsouth.net
Web Site: http://www.partplus.com
Members: 35 distributors
Staff: 22
Annual Budget: $5-10,000,000
President: Mike Lambert
Marketing Manager: Gil Gunn
Advertising and Communications Manager: Laura Guy
Travel Coordinator: Mary Guice
Director of Training: Ed Pearson
Controller: Kerianne Schuster

Historical Note
Provides purchasing and marketing services for members.

Publications:
Car Care Center Newsletter. 6/year.
Parts Plus Magazine. 6/year.

Meetings/Conferences:
2000 – February

Ass'n of Average Adjusters of the U.S. *(1879)*
79 Palmer Drive
Livingston, NJ 07039-1314
Tel: (973)597-0824 *Fax:* (973)597-0824
Members: 800 individuals
Annual Budget: $25-50,000
Secretary: Raymond M. Hicks, Jr.

Historical Note
Marine insurance and general average adjusters, ship and cargo surveyors and admiralty lawyers. Has no paid staff. Membership principally in New York area.

Publications:
Bulletin. a.
Report of the Annual Meeting.

Meetings/Conferences:
Annual Meetings: October, in New York, NY

Ass'n of Avian Veterinarians *(1980)*
P.O. Box 811720
Boca Raton, FL 33481-1720
Tel: (561)393-8901 *Fax:* (561)393-8902
Web Site: http://www.aavcctrlofc.com
Members: 3,300 individuals
Staff: 8
Annual Budget: $250-500,000
Exec. Director: Adina Rae Freedman, CAE

Historical Note
Members are veterinarians, technicians, and members of allied professions. Membership: $85/year.

Publications:
AAV News and Clinical Forum. q.
Journal of Avian Medicine and Surgery. q. adv.

Meetings/Conferences:
Annual Meetings: August-September
1999 – New Orleans, LA

Ass'n of Aviation Psychologists *(1964)*
Dept. of Psych., San. Fran. State Univ.
1600 Holloway Avenue
San Francisco, CA 94132
Tel: (415)338-1059
Members: 225 individuals
Annual Budget: under $10,000
President: Dr. Kathy Mosier

Historical Note
AAP is an informal group whose members are psychologists, behavioral scientists, and pilots concerned with aviation psychology including such topics as pilot/controller performance and flight safety and related fields. Membership: $10/year.

Publications:
Membership Directory. a.
Newsletter. q.

Meetings/Conferences:
Annual Meetings: With the Human Factors Society

Ass'n of Battery Recyclers *(1976)*
P.O. Box 290286
Tampa, FL 33619
Tel: (813)626-6151 *Fax:* (813)622-8388
Members: 25 companies
Staff: 2
Annual Budget: $100-250,000
Exec. Secretary: Joyce Morales

Historical Note
Formerly (1990) the Secondary Lead Smelters Ass'n. Investigates means/methods to achieve compliance with OSHA and EPA regulations impacting the secondary lead smelting industry. Membership: $1,500/year (consultant); $4,500/year (associate); $2,500/month (secondary smelter).

Publications:
Minutes of Technical Sessions. semi.

Meetings/Conferences:

Ass'n of Bedding and Furniture Law Officials *(1936)*
c/oDept of Labor & Industry/Bedding Div.
7th & Foster Sts., Room 1539
Harrisburg, PA 17120
Tel: (717)787-6848 *Fax:* (717)787-6925
Members: 30 individuals
Annual Budget: under $10,000
President: A. Richard Geisler

Historical Note
Organized to secure the adoption of uniform bedding and upholstery laws; members supervise the inspection of bedding materials and upholstered furniture at the state and local levels. Has no permanent staff or address. Membership: $45/year.

Meetings/Conferences:
Annual Meetings: Spring
1999 – San Diego, CA(Bahia Hotel)/March 3-7/35

Ass'n of Biological Collections Appraisers *(1980)*
3493 Greenfield Place
Carmel, CA 93923
Tel: (408)624-5677
Members: 34 individuals
Annual Budget: under $10,000
President: Frank P. Sala

Historical Note
ABCA members specialize in the appraisal of biological specimen collections. ABCA establishes standards for appraisal and documentation, provides placement services and serves as an accrediting agency. Membership: $40/year (individual); $100/year (organization).

Ass'n of Biomedical Communications Directors *(1973)*
M.E.R.P., Indiana U School of Medicine
1226 W. Michigan St., BR156
Indianapolis, IN 46202
Tel: (317)274-4083 *Fax:* (317)274-4638
Members: 95 individuals
Staff: 1
Annual Budget: $10-25,000
Secretary: Beverly Hill

Historical Note
Members are directors of bio-medical communications units in a school or in an academic health science center, either of which must grant degrees in the field of health or life sciences. Membership: $75/year.

Publications:
ABCD Exchange. q. adv.
Annual Survey of ABCD.
Joint Membership Directory. a. adv.
The Journal of Biocommunication. q. adv.

Meetings/Conferences:
Annual Meetings: Summer

Ass'n of Biomolecular Resource Facilities *(1988)*
9650 Rockville Pike
Bethesda, MD 20814-3998
Tel: (301)571-8300
E-Mail: abrf@faseb.org
Web Site: http://www.abrf.com
Members: 800 individuals
Staff: 3
Contact: Delores Francis

Historical Note
ABRF members are laboratories and other facilities with an interest in biomolecular research. Administrative support is provided by the Federation of American Socs. for Experimental Biology.

Publications:
Directory. irreg.

Meetings/Conferences:
1999 – Durham, NC(Marriott at Civic Center)/March 19-22

Ass'n of Bituminous Contractors *(1968)*
1747 Pennsylvania Ave., N.W., Suite 1050
Washington, DC 20006
Tel: (202)785-4440
Members: 150 individuals
Staff: 1
Annual Budget: $100-250,000
Secretary and General Counsel: William H. Howe

Historical Note
General and independent contractors constructing coal mines and coal mine facilities. Bargains with the United Mine Workers. The above address is the law firm of Howe, Anderson and Steyer.

Meetings/Conferences:
Annual Meetings: March

Ass'n of Black Anthropologists *(1970)*

Historical Note
A section of the American Anthropological Ass'n.

Ass'n of Black Cardiologists (1974)
225 Peachtree St., N.E., Suite 1420
Atlanta, GA   30303-1729
Tel: (404)582-8777   *Fax:* (404)582-8778
E-Mail: dr.bwainekong@mindspring.com
Web Site: http://www.abcardio.org
Members: 667 individuals
Staff: 10
Annual Budget: $1-2,000,000
C.E.O.: B. Waine Kong, Ph.D., J.D
Director, Community Health Risk Reduction: Jacquilyn German

Historical Note
ABC members are primarily black cardiologists and other medical professionals with an interest in cardiovascular disease. Membership: $200/year (individual); $500/year (organization/company).

Publications:
ABC Directory. a.
ABC Newsletter. q.
Digest of Urban Cardiology. bi-m. adv.

Meetings/Conferences:
Annual Meetings: Semi Annual Meetings/Spring and Fall

Ass'n of Black Foundation Executives (1971)
Indiana Univ. Center on Philanthropy
550 W. North St., Suite 301
Indianapolis, IN   46202-3162
Tel: (317)274-4200   *Fax:* (317)684-2128
Members: 200 individuals

Historical Note
Membership is limited to the staff of grant-making foundations. Membership: $125/year (individual).

Meetings/Conferences:
1999 – New Orleans, LA/Apr. 19-21

Ass'n of Black Nursing Faculty in Higher Education (1987)
c/o ABNF Journal
5823 Queens Cove
Lisle, IL   60532
Tel: (630)969-3809   *Fax:* (630)969-3895
Members: 175 individuals
Annual Budget: $10-25,000
President: Bess B. Stewart, Ph.D.

Historical Note
Members are nursing faculty teaching at the college-level. Membership: $75/year (individual). Information concerning the ABNF Journal can be obtained by calling (630) 969-3809.

Publications:
ABNF Journal. bi-m. adv.
ABNF Newsletter. q. adv.

Meetings/Conferences:
Annual Meetings: Summer
1999 – Honolulu, HI

Ass'n of Black Psychologists (1968)
P.O. Box 55999
Washington, DC   20040-5999
Tel: (202)722-0808   *Fax:* (202)722-5941
Members: 1,500 individuals
Staff: 2
Annual Budget: $250-500,000
President: Dr. Samella Abdullah

Historical Note
Organized at the 1968 San Francisco meeting of the American Psychological Ass'n, ABPsi is an independent autonomous organization addressing the needs of black professionals and the mental health of the national black community by means of planning, programs, services, training and advocacy. Membership: $30/year (student), $90/year (individual), $200/year (company).

Publications:
Journal of Black Psychology. quarterly. adv.
Psych Discourse. m. adv.

Meetings/Conferences:
Annual Meetings: August
1999 – Charleston, SC(Sheridon)/Aug. 2-8

Ass'n of Black Sociologists (1970)
656 West Kirby Ave.   Room 3049 FAB
Wayne St. University
Detroit, MI   48202
Tel: (313)577-1811   *Fax:* (313)577-2976
Members: 400 individuals
Annual Budget: $100-250,000
Exec. Officer: Dr. Diana R. Brown

Historical Note
Formerly (1977) Caucus of Black Sociologists. Membership: $55/year (individual).

Publications:
ABS Newsletter. q.
Black Sociologist. semi-a.

Meetings/Conferences:
Annual Meetings: Last week in August

Ass'n of Black Women Entrepreneurs (1984)
1301 N. Kenter Ave.
P.O. Box 49368
Los Angeles, CA   90049
Tel: (213)624-8639
Members: 600 individuals, 10 companies
President: Dolores Ratcliffe

Historical Note
Acts as an information resource supporting Black women in business. Membership: $60/year (individual); $400/year (company).

Publications:
ABWE Means Business Newsletter. q. adv.
Mini-Updates. irreg.

Meetings/Conferences:
Biennial Meetings: late Summer-early Fall
1999 – S. California/Sept. 16-18

Ass'n of Boarding Schools, The (1976)
1620 L St., N.W., Suite 1100
Washington, DC   20036-5605
Tel: (202)973-9700   *Fax:* (202)973-9790
E-Mail: TABS@nais-schools.org
Web Site: http://www.schools.com
Members: 300 schools
Staff: 2
Annual Budget: $250-500,000
Director: Steven D. Ruzicka
Assoc. Director: Peter Pelham

Historical Note
Founded as Committee on Boarding Schools; assumed its current name in 1993. Sponsored by the Nat'l Ass'n of Independent Schools and the Secondary School Admission Test Board, TABS is colocated with NAIS but has its own dues structure and staff. Its members, essentially, are the members of NAIS who have boarding departments. Serves its member schools by improving public awareness of boarding schools, expanding the markets of students, and providing training for residential school staff. Membership: $800-2,000/year.

Publications:
Boarding Schools Directory. a.
The Tablet. 3/year.

Meetings/Conferences:
Annual Meetings: In conjunction with NAIS

Ass'n of Boards of Certification (1972)
208 5th St.,
Ames, IA   50010-6259
Tel: (515)232-3623   *Fax:* (515)232-3778
E-Mail: abc@abccert.org
Web Site: http://www.abccert.org
Members: 70 agencies
Staff: 7
Annual Budget: $250-500,000
Exec. Director: Stephen W. Ballou, Ph.D.

Historical Note
Formerly (1982) Ass'n of Boards of Certification for Operating Personnel in Water and Wastewater Utilities and (1986) Ass'n of Boards of Certification for Operating Personnel. Members are government agencies certifying operating personnel and laboratories concerned with water, pollution control and hazardous waste. Membership: $35/year (individual); $300-$1,800/year (organization/ company).

Publications:
Certifier. m. adv.
Directory. a.

Meetings/Conferences:
Annual Meetings: January
1999 – San Antonio, TX(Menger Hotel)/Jan. 26-29

Ass'n of Bone and Joint Surgeons (1947)
6300 N. River Rd., Suite 727
Rosemont, IL   60018-4226
Tel: (847)698-1636   *Fax:* (847)823-0536
Members: 270 individuals
Staff: 1
Annual Budget: $50-100,000
Society Manager: Colette Hohimer

Historical Note
Founded in Oklahoma City in April 1949 and incorporated the same year in Oklahoma.

Publications:
Clinical Orthopaedics and Related Research. m.
Orthopaedics Device Reference.

Meetings/Conferences:
Annual Meetings: Summer
1999 – Amelia Island, FL(Ameilia Island Resort)/May 5-9

Ass'n of Book Travelers (1884)
Historical Note
Address unknown in 1996.

Ass'n of Booksellers for Children (1985)
4412 Chowen Ave. South, Suite 303
Minneapolis, MN   55410
Tel: (612)296-6650
Toll Free: (800)421 - 1665
Members: 600 individuals
Staff: 1
Annual Budget: $250-500,000
Exec. Director: Caron Chapman

Historical Note
ABC offers a support network for professional children's booksellers. Membership: $60/year (bookstores); $50/year (others).

Publications:
Building Blocks Newsletter. q.

Meetings/Conferences:
Annual Meetings: May-June
1999 – Los Angeles, CA/500
2000 – Chicago, IL(Hilton)

Ass'n of Borderlands Scholars (1976)
Historical Note
Became the Ass'n for Borderlands Studies in 1997.

Ass'n of Boys and Girls Clubs Professionals (1953)
Historical Note
Address unknown in 1995; presumed inactive or defunct.

Ass'n of Bridal Consultants (1981)
200 Chestnutland Road
New Milford, CT   06776-2521
Tel: (860)355-0464   *Fax:* (860)354-1404
E-Mail: bridalassn@aol.com
Web Site: http://www.weddingchannel.com
Members: 2,100 companies and individuals
Staff: 6
Annual Budget: $500-1,000,000
President: Gerard J. Monaghan
V. President, Meeting Planner: Eileen P. Monaghan

Historical Note
Composed of independent consultants as well as owners and employees of wedding related businesses. Supersedes American Ass'n of Professional Bridal Consultants (1955-1980). Awards the designations Professional Bridal Consultant, Accredited Bridal Consultant, and Master Bridal Consultant. Membership: $125-500/year.

Publications:
Newsletter. bi-m. adv.
Retail Resource Directory. a.

Meetings/Conferences:
1999 – Indianapolis, IN(Hyatt Regency)/Oct. 30-Nov 2/300
2000 – Eastern site/Nov. 6-9
2001 – Pacific site/Nov. 5-8
2002 – Mountain site/Nov. 4-7

Ass'n of Business Officers of Preparatory Schools (1924)
Historical Note
Address unknown in 1997.

Ass'n of Business Products Manufacturers (1951)
P.O. Box 644
Millersville, MD   21108
Tel: (410)987-4847   *Fax:* (410)987-5442
E-Mail: vick@bayserve.net
Web Site: http://www.officeproducts.com
Members: 17 companies
Staff: 2
Annual Budget: $250-500,000
Exec. Director: John C. Vickerman

Historical Note
Formerly (1972) the Loose Leaf and Blank Book Manufacturers Ass'n. Became the Business Records Manufacturers Ass'n and assumed its present name in 1990.

Meetings/Conferences:
Semi-Annual Meetings: May and December

Ass'n of Business Support Services Internat'l (1981)
22875 Savi Ranch Parkway, Suite H
Yorba Linda, CA   92887-4619
Tel: (714)282-9398   *Fax:* (714)282-8630
Toll Free: (800)237 - 1462
E-Mail: ABSSI4YOU@aol.com
Web Site: http://www.abssi.org
Members: 1000 companies
Staff: 4
Annual Budget: $100-250,000
Exec. Director: Lynette M. Smith, CPS
Project Director: Denise C. Ross

Historical Note
Founded as Nat'l Ass'n of Secretarial Services; assumed its current name in 1997. Members are independent secretarial services, word processing services, telephone answering services, and related business support services. Membership: $132/year.

Publications:
Industry Focus Magazine. m.
National Membership Directory. a.

Meetings/Conferences:
Annual Meetings: Spring
1999 – Minneapolis, MN(Airport Marriott)/May 19-22/120
2000 – Atlanta, GA

Ass'n of Camp Nurses (1990)
8504 Thorsonveien, N.E.
Bemidji, MN   56601
Tel: (218)586-2633   *Fax:* (218)586-3630
E-Mail: acn@campnurse.org
Members: 300 individuals
Annual Budget: under $10,000
Exec. Director: Linda Ebner Erceg

Historical Note
Membership: $30/year (individual).

Publications:
Compasspoint. q.

Meetings/Conferences:
1999 – Benidji, MN
2000 – Albuquerque, NM

Ass'n of Career Management Consulting Firms Internat'l (1982)
1200 19th St., N.W., Suite 300
Washington, DC   20036
Tel: (202)857-1185   *Fax:* (202)857-1115
Web Site: www.aocfi.org
Members: 110 companies
Staff: 9
Annual Budget: $250-500,000
Exec. Director: Faye A. Malarkey

Historical Note
Formerly (1994) Ass'n of Outplacement Consulting Firms and (1997) Ass'n of Outplacement Consulting Firms Internat'l. Established at a dinner meeting at the Yale Club, New York City, on March 16, 1982 to promote standards of professional practice in the outplacement business. Supports and sustains an outplacement professional certification institute in conjunction with the Internat'l Ass'n of Career Management Porfessionals.

Publications:
Internal Newsletter.
Membership Directory.

Meetings/Conferences:

Ass'n of Caribbean Studies *(1978)*
P.O. Box 22202
Lexington, KY 40520
Tel: (606)257-6966   *Fax:* (606)323-1072
Members: 1,200 individuals
Annual Budget: under $10,000
Exec. Director: O.R. Dathorne, Ph.D.
Literature Committee: Lucy Wilson, Ph.D.

Historical Note
*Interdisciplinary scholarly society concerned with the Caribbean.
Membership: $50/year (individual); $200/year (organization).*

Publications:
ACS Abstracts. a.
Journal of Caribbean Studies. 2-3/year.
Newsletter. irreg.

Meetings/Conferences:
Annual Meetings: July/100
1999 – Guadeloupe

Ass'n of Catholic Colleges and Universities *(1899)*
One Dupont Circle, N.W., Suite 650
Washington, DC 20036
Tel: (202)457-0650   *Fax:* (202)728-0977
Web Site: http://www.accu.net.org
Members: 215 institutions
Staff: 4
Annual Budget: $250-500,000
Exec. Director: Dr. Monika Hellwig
Assoc. Exec. Director: Paul J. Gallagher

Historical Note
*Founded in 1899, ACCU in 1904 became the College and
University Department of the Nat'l Catholic Education Ass'n.
Although still a department of that latter organization, it reassumed
its former name in 1978.*

Publications:
Current Issues in Catholic Higher Education. semi-a.
Update. bi-m.

Meetings/Conferences:
Annual Meetings: February in Washington, DC at the Hyatt
     Regency/250
1999 – Washington, DC(Hyatt Regency)/Feb. 1-3/300

Ass'n of Catholic Diocesan Archivists *(1979)*
711 W. Monroe
Chicago, IL 60661
Tel: (312)831-0711   *Fax:* (312)831-0610
Members: 240 individuals
Annual Budget: $10-25,000
Treasurer: Mr. John Joseph Treanor

Historical Note
*Members are individuals responsible for the preservation of
diocesan records and historical materials. They are committed to
the active promotion of professionalism in the management of
diocesan archives. Membership: $15/year (individual).*

Publications:
ACDA Bulletin. q.

Meetings/Conferences:
Annual Meetings: Odd years with S.A.A., even years a summer
     meeting.
1999 – Pittsburgh, PA

Ass'n of Catholic TV and Radio Syndicators *(1975)*
518 S. Alandele
Los Angeles, CA 90036
Tel: (213)938-4861
Members: 35 companies
Annual Budget: under $10,000
V. President/Treasurer: Mary Jane Hopkins

Historical Note
*Affiliated with UNDA-USA, the U.S. arm of the international
association of Catholic broadcasters. Members are producers and
syndicators of Catholic radio and television programs. Has no paid
staff. Membership: $50/year (individual), $100/year
(organization).*

Publications:
Directory. bi-a.
Proceedings. bi-a.

Meetings/Conferences:
Annual Meetings: Held in July in San Francisco, CA

Ass'n of Celebrity Personal Assistants *(1992)*
340 Penn St., Suite 1
El Segundo, CA 90245
Tel: (310)322-4495   *Fax:* (310)414-0804
E-Mail: acpa1@aol.com
Members: 500 individuals
Staff: 3
Annual Budget: $25-50,000
President: Dinah Lary
Director of Job Bank: Lori Popovich

Historical Note
*A non-profit, membership-based organization representing
personal assistants to celebrities and other notables. Membership:
$100/year.*

Publications:
ACPA Membership Directory. a.
ACPA Service Directory. a. adv.
The Best Of The Best.
The Right Hand. bi-m. adv.

Ass'n of Certified Fraud Examiners *(1988)*
716 West Ave.
Austin, TX 78701

Tel: (512)478-9070   *Fax:* (512)478-9297
Toll Free: (800)245 - 3321
E-Mail: acfe@cfenet.com
Web Site: http://www.cfenet.com
Members: 15,000 individuals
Staff: 35
Program Director: James D. Ratley
General Counsel: John Gill

Historical Note
*Formerly (1993) the Nat'l Ass'n of Certified Fraud Examiners.
Members are individuals involved in the detection and prevention of
white collar crime. Awards the designation Certified Fraud
Examiner (CFE) to members successfully completing a
credentialing process. Membership: $200 initial examination fee,
$100/year thereafter (individual); $95/year (associate).*

Publications:
ACFE Journal. bi-m.

Meetings/Conferences:
Annual Meetings: August/400

Ass'n of Certified Professional Secretaries *(1985)*
P.O. Box 14281
Phoenix, AZ 85063-4281
Tel: (602)650-2659
Members: 300 individuals
Annual Budget: $10-25,000
President: Gail Corbiere

Historical Note
*Organized as a support network for individuals who have
successfully completed the Certified Professional Secretaries
examination administered by Professional Secretaries Internat'l.
Membership: $50/year.*

Publications:
ACPS Connection. Newsletter.

Meetings/Conferences:

Ass'n of Certified Trucking Schools

Historical Note
Address unknown in 1997.

Ass'n of Chairmen of Departments of Mechanics *(1970)*
Dept. of Theoretical & Applied Mechanics
Cornell University
Ithaca, NY 14853-1503
Tel: (607)255-7185
Members: 110 institutions
Staff: 1
Annual Budget: under $10,000
President: James T. Jenkins

Historical Note
Has no paid staff or permanent headquarters.

Meetings/Conferences:

Ass'n of Chartered Accountants in the United States *(1980)*
347 Fifth Ave., Suite 1406
New York, NY 10016
Tel: (212)481-7950   *Fax:* (212)481-7969
Web Site:
     http://ourworld.compuserve.com/homepages/ACAUS
Members: 650 individuals
Staff: 1
Annual Budget: $50-100,000
President: Connor Murphy

Historical Note
*ACAUS represents the interests of U.S.-based accountants
chartered by institutes in England and Wales, Scotland, Ireland,
Australia, Canada, New Zealand, and South Africa. Supports
research on international accounting and provides programs and
services linking its members to accounting practitioners worldwide.
Membership: $70/year (individual).*

Publications:
ACAUS Newsletter. a. adv.
Directory of Members. a. adv.

Meetings/Conferences:
Three Annual Dinners: New York, NY; Chicago, IL; and Los
     Angeles, CA

Ass'n of Child and Adolescent Psychiatric Nurses *(1971)*
1211 Locust St.
Philadelphia, PA 19107
Tel: (215)545-2843   *Fax:* (215)545-8107
Toll Free: (800)826 - 2950
E-Mail: acapn@nursecominc.com
Web Site: http://www.acapm.org
Members: 400 individuals
Annual Budget: $100-250,000
Exec. Director: Joseph Braden
Management Services Coordinator: Lanie Meriwether

Historical Note
Has no paid staff. Membership $90/year.

Publications:
ACAPN Newsletter. semi-a. adv.
Journal of Child and Adolescent Psychiatric Nursing. q. adv.

Meetings/Conferences:
1999 – Baltimore, MD/April 22-25

Ass'n of Children's Prosthetic-Orthotic Clinics
6300 N. River Road, Suite 727
Rosemont, IL 60018-4226
Tel: (847)698-1636   *Fax:* (847)823-0536
Members: 432 clinics
Staff: 3
Annual Budget: $25-50,000
Manager: Sheril King

*ACPOC supports clinic teams through education, clinical research
and annual meetings. Membership: $100/year (clinic chief);
$50/year (associate).*

Publications:
ACPOC Newsletter.

Meetings/Conferences:
Annual Meetings: at a host clinic
1999 – St. Petersburg Beach, FL/May 19-22
2000 – Banff, AB, Canada(Banff Springs
     Hotel)/April 27-29/250

Ass'n of Chiropractic Colleges *(1977)*
4424 Montgomery, Suite 102
Bethesda, MD 20814
Tel: (301)652-5066   *Fax:* (301)913-9146
Toll Free: (800)284 - 1062
E-Mail: obyronco@aol.com
Web Site: http://www.chirocolleges.org
Members: 18 individuals
Annual Budget: $250-500,000
Exec. Director: David S. O'Bryon, CAE

Historical Note
*Formerly (1985) Ass'n of Chiropractic College Presidents. ACC
members are presidents of chiropractic colleges.*

Publications:
Journal of Chiropractic Education. q.

Meetings/Conferences:
Semi-annual Meetings: January and June
1999 – Orlando, FL(Buena Vista Palace)
2000 – San Antonio, TX(Adams Mark)
2001 – San Diego, CA(Sheraton)

Ass'n of Christian Librarians *(1957)*
P.O. Box 4
Cedarville, OH 45314
Tel: (513)766-7842   *Fax:* (513)766-2337
E-Mail: ACL-info@cedarville.edu
Web Site: http://www.acl.org
Members: 400 individuals
Annual Budget: $25-50,000
Exec. Director: Nancy J. Olson

Historical Note
*Formerly (1981) Christian Librarians Fellowship. ACL members are
primarily evangelical Christian academic librarians, as well as other
interested librarians and individuals who subscribe to the purposes
and position of the association. ACL is an organization that
promotes the professional and spiritual growth of its members and
provides service to the academic library community worldwide.
Membership fee varies, based on salary: $50-$100/year.*

Publications:
Christian Librarian. 3/yr.
Christian Periodical Index. 3/year (last being.

Meetings/Conferences:
Annual Meetings: June
1999 – Cleveland, TN(Lee University)/June 8-11

Ass'n of Christian Schools Internat'l *(1978)*
P.O. Box 35097
Colorado Springs, CO 80935-3509
Tel: (719)528-6906   *Fax:* (719)531-0631
Web Site: http://www.acsi.org
Members: 4,200 schools
Staff: 125
Annual Budget: $10-25,000,000
Exec. V. President: James F. Burdick
Director, State Legislative Affairs: Burt Carney
V.President, Academic Affairs: Derek Keenan, Ed.D.
V. President, Finance: Glenn Meeter
President: Dr. Ken Smitherman

Historical Note
*Privately funded schools with a religious orientation that effectively
prepare students for life. The result of a merger on July 1, 1978 of
the Western Ass'n of Christian Schools, the Ohio Ass'n of Christian
Schools and the Nat'l Christian School Education Ass'n.*

Publications:
ACSI Directory. a.
Christian School Comment. m.
Christian School Education.
Legal/Legislative Update. bi-m.

Meetings/Conferences:

Ass'n of Christian Therapists
6728 Old McLean Village Dr.
McLean, VA 22101
Tel: (703)556-9222   *Fax:* (703)556-8729
Exec. Director: George K. Degnon, CAE

Ass'n of Cinema and Video Laboratories *(1953)*
1000 Hopor Blvd.
Pittsburgh, PA 15205
Tel: (412)937-7700   *Fax:* (412)922-2418
E-Mail: ghutchinson@CFI-hollywood.com
Web Site: http://www.acvl.org
Members: 61 laboratories
Staff: 3
Annual Budget: $50-100,000
President: Greg Thomas

Historical Note
*The ACVL provides an opportunity for the discussion and exchange
of ideas in connection with the technical, administrative and
managerial problems of the motion-picture and video laboratory
industry. The Association is concerned with government relations,
public and industry relations, product specifications, improvements
of technical practices and procedures and other interest areas for
film and video laboratories. Formerly Ass'n of Cinema Laboratories.*

Publications:
ACVL Handbook.

Meetings/Conferences:
Annual Meetings: June

Ass'n of Civilian Technicians *(1960)*
12510-B Lake Ridge Drive
Woodbridge, VA 22192
Tel: (703)494-4845 *Fax:* (703)494-0961
Members: 23,500 individuals
Staff: 8
Annual Budget: $1-2,000,000
President: John T. Hunter

Historical Note
ACT is the largest union representing civilian National Guard Technicians. Membership: 0.7% of base pay/bi-weekly.

Publications:
Technician Newsletter. m.

Meetings/Conferences:
Semi Annual Meetings: February and September/always in Washington D.C.

Ass'n of Clinical Research Professionals *(1977)*
1012 14th St., N.W., Suite 807
Washington, DC 20005-3406
Tel: (202)737-8100 *Fax:* (202)737-8101
Web Site: http://www.acrpnet.org
Members: 8,700 individuals
Staff: 12
Annual Budget: $2-5,000,000
Exec. V. President: Frederic Harwood, Ph.D.
Manager Communications: Tara A. Peterman
Meetings/Conventions: James Goodwin, II
Education/Certification: Sandra Sanford
Manager, Finance: Larry Medley
Exec. Director-Europe: Gina van Dijk
Membership: Marla Dockery

Historical Note
Founded as Associates of Clinical Pharmacology; assumed its current name in 1997. ACRP members are clinical researchers and related health professionals. Membership: $85/year(individual).

Publications:
ACRP Membership Directory. a. adv.
Monitor. q. adv.

Meetings/Conferences:
Annual Meeting: Spring
1999 – Washington, DC(Hilton)/May 25-28/3000
2000 – New Orleans, LA(Riverside Hilton)/May 13-17/3000
2001 – San Francisco, CA(Hilton)/April 28-May 3/3000
2002 – Toronto, Canada(Royal York)/April 14-17/3500

Ass'n of Clinical Scientists *(1949)*
P.O. Drawer 1287
Middlebury, VT 05753
Tel: (802)462-2507 *Fax:* (802)462-2673
E-Mail: 103040.3027@COMPUSERVE.COM
Members: 500 individuals
Staff: 1
Annual Budget: $100-250,000
Secretary-Treasurer: F. William Sunderman, Jr., M.D.

Historical Note
Organized as the Clinical Science Club in 1949. Became Ass'n of Clinical Scientists in 1956. Chartered by the State of Pennsylvania as a nonprofit scientific organization in 1957. Affiliated with the American Ass'n for the Advancement of Science and the Intersociety Pathology Council. Membership: $155/year (individual).

Publications:
Annals of Clinical and Laboratory Science. bi-m. adv.
Proceedings. a.

Meetings/Conferences:
Semi-Annual Meetings: Spring and Fall

Ass'n of Co-operative Educators *(1965)*
P.O. Box 64047
St. Paul, MN 55164
Tel: (651)451-5481 *Fax:* (651)451-5073
E-Mail: wnels@chslol.com
Members: 200 individuals
Annual Budget: $10-25,000
Exec. Administrator: William Nelson

Historical Note
Founded in Banff as the Ass'n for Cooperative Education, the name was changed in 1970 and reorganized in 1997 as a non-profit organization. Membership consists of individuals and organizations professionally engaged in educational, training or personnel programs of cooperative organizations. Membership: $25-40/year (individual); $100/year (organization/company).

Publications:
ACE News. q.
Membership List. a.
Newsletter. semi-a.

Meetings/Conferences:
Annual Meetings: Annual institutes in April or May.
1999 – Sakaton, Saskatchewan

Ass'n of College Administration Professionals *(1995)*
P.O. Box 1389
Staunton, VA 24402-1389
Tel: (540)885-1873 *Fax:* (540)885-6133
E-Mail: acap@cfw.com
Web Site: http://www.acap.org
Members: 1,500 individuals, 300 institutions
Staff: 3
Annual Budget: $250-500,000
President: Stan Clark

Historical Note
ACAP members are administrators in the business, student and academic services areas of colleges and universities. Membership: $65/year (individual); $195 (institution).

Publications:
Bulletin. m.

Meetings/Conferences:
Annual Meetings: February
1999 – San Diego, CA(Clarion Bayview)/Jan. 30-Feb. 3/250
2000 – Tampa, FL(Hyatt Regency)/Feb. 12-16/300

Ass'n of College and Research Libraries *(1938)*
50 E. Huron St.
Chicago, IL 60611-2795
Tel: (312)944-6780 *Fax:* (312)280-2520
Toll Free: (800)545-2433
Web Site: http://www.ala.org/acrl.html
Members: 10,000 individuals, 1000 libraries
Staff: 35
Annual Budget: $2-5,000,000
Exec. Director: Althea H. Jenkins
Publications: Hugh Thompson

Historical Note
Represents academic and research librarians and libraries. This includes all types of academic libraries - community and junior college, college, and university - as well as comprehensive and specialized research libraries and their professional staffs. Formerly Ass'n of College and Reference Libraries. A division of the American Library Ass'n. Individuals must belong to ALA in order to join ACRL. Membership: $50/year.

Publications:
C&RL News. 11/year. adv.
Choice. 11/year. adv.
College and Research Libraries. m. adv.
Rare Books & Manuscripts Librarianship. semi-a. adv.

Meetings/Conferences:
Semi-Annual Meetings: Mid-Winter, and Summer Annual Conference with American Library Ass'n
1999 – Detroit, MI(COBO/Westin)/April 9-12/3000

Ass'n of College and University Auditors *(1958)*
P.O. Box 968
Homewood, IL 60430
Tel: (708)922-1034 *Fax:* (708)922-0958
Web Site: http://www.acua.org
Members: 500 institutions
Annual Budget: $250-500,000
Executive Director: Lois B. May

Historical Note
Members are educational institutions with their own auditing staffs. Membership: $150/year (institution).

Publications:
Directory. a.
Homepage.
Ledger. 5x/year.
Newsletter. bi-m.

Meetings/Conferences:
Annual Meetings: September
1999 – St. Louis, MO(Hyatt Regency)
2000 – Montreal, Quebec(Queen Elizabeth)

Ass'n of College and University Housing Officers-Internat'l *(1951)*
364 W. Lane Ave., Suite C
Columbus, OH 43201-1062
Tel: (614)292-0099 *Fax:* (614)292-3205
Web Site: http://www.acuho.ohio-state.edu
Members: 5,200 individuals, 825 colleges & universities
Staff: 9
Annual Budget: $1-2,000,000
Exec. Director: Gary Schwarzmueller
Communications Coordinator: Mary Ellerbrock
Professional Development Coordinator: Kathy Froilan
Marketing Representative: Darcy Lehner
Manager of Operations: Robert Kearns

Historical Note
Organized in 1952 at the Univ. of California, Berkeley, as a direct outgrowth of the first Nat'l Campus Housing Conference held in 1949 at the Univ. of Illinois. Added International to its name in 1981. Members are college and university staff members with responsibility for student residence, food service, developmental programming, administration and related operations and independent residence hall operators. Membership: $102/year (individual), $154-952/year (institution), $29/year (student), $29/year (emeritus), $311/year (corporation).

Publications:
International Directory. a. adv.
Journal of College and University Student Housing. semi-a. adv.
Talking Stick. m. adv.

Meetings/Conferences:
Annual Meetings: Summer
1999 – Vancouver, BC(Univ. of British Columbia)/July 11-14
2000 – Pittsburg, PA/July 9-12

Ass'n of College and University Museums and Galleries *(1980)*
Oklahoma Museum of Natural History
1335 Asp Ave.
Norman, OK 73019-0606
Tel: (405)325-4712 *Fax:* (405)325-7699
E-Mail: pbtirrell@ou.edu
Web Site: http://www.omnh.ou.edu/acumg/
Members: 80 individuals, 196 institutions
Annual Budget: under $10,000
President: Peter B. Tirrell

Historical Note
ACUMG promotes the welfare of college and university museums and galleries of all disciplines as well as the welfare of the professional staffs of those museums and galleries. Membership: $20/year (individual); $35/year (institution); $50/year (corporate); $10/year (student).

Publications:
News and Issues. q.

Meetings/Conferences:
Annual Meetings: Spring, in conjunction with American Ass'n of Museums Cleveland, OH

Ass'n of College and University Printers *(1964)*
Arizona State University
Box 870401
Tempe, AZ 85287
Tel: (602)965-9833 *Fax:* (602)965-2234
E-Mail: iburxl@asu.edu
Members: 140 individuals
Annual Budget: $10-25,000
President: Bob Lane

Historical Note
An informal group of managers of printing services in colleges and universities, membership in which is achieved principally by attending the annual conference. Officers change annually in May.

Meetings/Conferences:
Annual Meetings: usually at a university location
1999 – Scottsdale, AZ/Apr. 11-15

Ass'n of College and University Telecommunications Administrators *(1971)*
152 W. Zandale Drive, Suite 200
Lexington, KY 40503-2486
Tel: (606)278-3338 *Fax:* (606)278-3268
Web Site: http://www.acuta.org
Members: 1,900 individuals
Staff: 10
Annual Budget: $1-2,000,000
Exec. Director: Jeri A. Semer, CAE
Communications Manager: Pat Scott
Meetings Planner: Lisa Cheshire
Business Manager: Eleanor Smith
Membership Development Manager: Kellie Bowman

Historical Note
Membership: $150-375/yr (college/university); $475-2,350/year (corporate affiliates); $150/year (associate).

Publications:
ACUTA News. m. adv.
Monographs Membership Directory.

Meetings/Conferences:
1999 – Nashville, TN/July 18-22

Ass'n of College Educators: Deaf and Hard of Hearing *(1975)*
National Technical Institute of the Deaf
Rochester Institute of Technology
Rochester, NY 14623
Tel: (716)475-6932 *Fax:* (716)475-6500
Members: 80 individuals
Annual Budget: under $10,000
President: Judy Egelston-Dodd

Historical Note
Has no paid staff. Membership: $40/year (individual).

Publications:
ACE-DHH News. q.

Meetings/Conferences:
Annual Meetings: February
1999 – San Diego, CA

Ass'n of College Honor Societies *(1925)*
4990 Northwind Dr., Suite 140
East Lansing, MI 48823-5031
Tel: (517)351-8335 *Fax:* (517)351-8336
E-Mail: dmitstifer@achsnatl.org
Web Site: http://achsnatl.org
Members: 60 societies
Staff: 1
Annual Budget: $10-25,000
Secretary-Treasurer: Dorothy I. Mitstifer

Historical Note
Organized in 1925 to consider problems of mutual interest, recommend action leading toward appropriate classification and stands. Acts as the coordinating agency for college and university honor societies. Membership fee varies, based on budget.

Publications:
Booklet of Information. trien.

Meetings/Conferences:
Annual Meetings: February
1999 – San Diego, CA(Radisson)/Feb. 18-21
2000 – Orlando, FL(Clarion Plaza)/Feb. 17-20

Ass'n of College Unions-Internat'l *(1914)*
120 W. 7th St., Suite 200
Bloomington, IN 47404-3925
Tel: (812)855-8550 *Fax:* (812)855-0162
Web Site: http://www.acuiweb.org
Members: 950 colleges and universities
Staff: 9
Annual Budget: $500-1,000,000
Exec. Director: Marsha Herman-Betzen
Director, Administrative Services: David Teske
Director, Membership & Development: Mary Ann Cannon

Historical Note
Founded as the Ass'n of College Unions, it assumed its present name in 1961. ACUI is a professional association dedicated to enhancing campus life through programs, services, and facilities with the goal of unifying the union and activities field. Membership: $42/year (individual); $110-$572/year (organization/ company) according to FTE.

Publications:
Bulletin. bi-m. adv.
The Union Wire. bi-m.

Meetings/Conferences:
Annual Meetings: Early Spring/1,000

1999 – Dallas, TX(Anatole)/March 21-24
2000 – New York, NY(Marriott)/March 12-15
2001 – Toronto, Canada(Sheraton)/March 18-21

Ass'n of Collegiate Business Schools and Programs *(1988)*
7007 College Blvd., Suite 420
Overland Park, KS   66211-1524
Tel: (913)339-9356   *Fax:* (913)339-6226
Web Site: http://okra.deltas.edu/acbsp
Members: 500 institutions
Staff: 5
Annual Budget: $500-1,000,000
Exec. Director: Dr. Harold W. Lundy

Historical Note
Accrediting organization for business schools and programs in colleges and universities. Membership: $900/year (institution).

Publications:
Update. q. adv.

Meetings/Conferences:
Annual Meetings: June

Ass'n of Collegiate Conference and Events Directors Internat'l *(1980)*
Colorado State University
Fort Collins, CO   80523-8037
Tel: (970)491-5151   *Fax:* (970)491-0667
E-Mail: acced@lamar.colostate.edu
Web Site: http://www.ColoState.edu/Depts/ACCED-I
Members: 900 individuals
Staff: 3
Annual Budget: $250-500,000
Exec. Director: Jill Lancaster

Historical Note
Formerly Ass'n of Conference and Events Directors International (1998). ACCED-I members are collegiate conference and events directors, professionals who design, coordinate and market conferences and special events at their institutions. Membership: $210/year (individual); $425/year (organization/company/institution).

Publications:
Communique. bi-m.

Meetings/Conferences:
Annual Meetings: March
1999 – St. Louis, MO(Adam's Mark)/March 21-24
2000 – San Diego, CA/March 25-29

Ass'n of Collegiate Licensing Administrators
638 Prospect Ave.
Hartford, CT   06105-4250
Tel: (860)586-7524   *Fax:* (860)586-7550
Members: 225 individuals
Staff: 2
Exec. Director: Pamela Hayes

Historical Note
Membership: $225/year (organization/company).

Publications:
Directory. a.

Meetings/Conferences:
1999 – Las Vegas, NV/May 3-6

Ass'n of Collegiate Schools of Architecture *(1912)*
1735 New York Ave., N.W., 3rd Floor
Washington, DC   20006
Tel: (202)785-2324   *Fax:* (202)628-0448
E-Mail: acsanatl@aol.com
Web Site: http://www.acsa-arch.org
Members: 3,500 individuals, 200 schools
Staff: 7
Annual Budget: $1-2,000,000
Exec. Director: G. Martin Moeller, Jr.

Historical Note
U.S. and Canadian faculties of professional architectural degree programs. Membership includes over 100 international schools.

Publications:
ACSA News. 9/year. adv.
Guide to Architecture Schools. quadren.
Journal of Architectural Education. q.

Meetings/Conferences:
Annual Meetings: Spring
1999 – Minneapolis, MN/March 20-23

Ass'n of Collegiate Schools of Planning *(1959)*
Drachman Institute
University of Arizona
Tuscon, AZ   85721
Tel: (520)621-1223
Members: 120 schools
Staff: 1
Annual Budget: $100-250,000
President: Sandra Rosenbloom

Historical Note
ACSP is a consortium of university-based programs offering degrees in urban and regional planning in the U.S. Supports research in planning curricula and instruction to promote the discipline. Membership: $225/year.

Publications:
ACSP Update. q. adv.
Journal of Planning Education and Research. q. adv.

Meetings/Conferences:
Annual Meetings: Fall/400
1999 – Chicago, IL
2000 – Boston, MA

Ass'n of Commercial Diving Educators *(1977)*
c/o Divers Institute
4315 11th Ave., N.W.
Seattle, WA   98107

Toll Free: (800)64 - 8377
Members: 5 institutions
Staff: 1
Exec. Director: John Ritter

Historical Note
Members are institutions and trade schools with programs training commercial divers. Membership: $500/year.

Publications:
Professional Divers' Logbook.

Meetings/Conferences:

Ass'n of Commercial Finance Attorneys
c/o Blank, Rome, Comisky & McCauley
210 Lake Dr. East, Suite 200
Cherry Hill, NJ   08002
Tel: (609)779-3644   *Fax:* (609)779-7647
Members: 353 individuals
Secretary: Peter Leibundgut

Historical Note
ACF members are attorneys specializing in commercial finance and bankruptcy law. Membership: $175/year.

Publications:
Annual Update Proceedings.

Meetings/Conferences:
Annual Meetings: 6-7 topical meetings/year; Legal Education Weekend/May

Ass'n of Commercial Records Centers *(1980)*

Historical Note
Became Professional Records and Information Services Management Internat'l in 1996.

Ass'n of Community Cancer Centers *(1974)*
11600 Nebel St., Suite 201
Rockville, MD   20852
Tel: (301)984-9496   *Fax:* (301)770-1949
Web Site: http://www.assoc-cancer-ctrs.org
Members: 500 institutions
Staff: 12
Annual Budget: $500-1,000,000
Exec. Director: Lee E. Mortenson
Director, Conferences and Member Services: David Walls, CMP
Conference Coordinator: Margaret May
Assoc. Director: Carol Kirkland

Historical Note
Voting members are primarily community hospitals with cancer-care programs. Membership: $100/year (individual); $650/year (hospitals).

Publications:
Community Cancer Programs in the U. S.
Oncology Issues. bi-m.

Meetings/Conferences:
1999 – Arlington, VA(Marriott)/March 24-27

Ass'n of Community College Trustees *(1972)*
1740 N St., N.W.
Washington, DC   20036-2907
Tel: (202)775-4667   *Fax:* (202)223-1297
Web Site: http://www.erols.com/acct
Members: 6,000 governing boards
Staff: 17
Annual Budget: $1-2,000,000
President: Ray Taylor
Director of Communications and Marketing: Alvin Major III
Director, Public Policy: J. Noah Brown
V. President: Marilyn Blocker
Director of Finance: Angela Summers

Historical Note
Formerly (1972) the Council of Community College Boards, National School Boards Ass'n. Membership: $545-2,185/year, based on enrollment (institution).

Publications:
Advisor. bi-m.
Trustee Quarterly. q. adv.

Meetings/Conferences:
Annual Meetings: Fall/1,500-2,000
1999 – Atlanta, GA/Oct. 13-16

Ass'n of Community Health Nursing Educators *(1978)*
7794 Grow Dr.
Pensacola, FL   32514
Tel: (850)484-9987   *Fax:* (850)484-8762
Members: 400 individuals
Staff: 2
Annual Budget: $50-100,000
Exec. Director: Belinda E. Puetz

Historical Note
Promotes the public's health by ensuring leadership and excellence in community and public health nursing education through excellence in practice and research. Membership: $90/year (individual), $450/year (organization/company).

Publications:
ACHNE Newsletter. q. adv.
Proceedings of Spring Institute. a.

Meetings/Conferences:
Annual Meetings: In conjunction with American Public Health Ass'n in the Spring.

Ass'n of Community Tribal Schools *(1982)*

Historical Note
Address unknown in 1998.

Ass'n of Computer Training Professionals

Historical Note
Address unknown in 1997.

Ass'n of Concert Bands *(1977)*

6613 Cheryl Ann Dr.
Independence, OH   44131-3718
Toll Free: (800)726 - 8720
E-Mail: acbsec@aol.com
Web Site: http://www.afn.org/encore
Members: 800 bands, companies and individuals
Staff: 1
Annual Budget: $25-50,000
Secretary: Nada Vencl

Historical Note
Formerly (1983) Ass'n of Concert Bands of America. Dedicated to the worldwide advancement of adult concert and community bands. Membership: $25/year (individual), $75/year (corporate), $50/year (organization), $400/lifetime membership.

Publications:
ACB National Directory of Bands.
Advance! ACB Magazine. q. adv.
Encore!ACC Newsletter.

Meetings/Conferences:
Annual Meetings: Spring
1999 – Salinas, CA/April 7-11
2000 – Milwaukee, WI(Hyatt Regency)/April 26-30
2001 – Pensacola, FL

Ass'n of Conservation Engineers *(1961)*
Arkansas Game & Fish Commission
#2 Natural Resources Dr.
Little Rock, AR   72205
Tel: (501)251-4306   *Fax:* (501)219-4315
Members: 310 individuals
Annual Budget: under $10,000
Secretary-Treasurer: Jim Price

Historical Note
Members are engineers and allied personnel employed by state, federal and provincial conservation and recreation departments, who have a specialized interest in the areas of fish, wildlife, parks, forests and related conservation-recreation fields. Membership: $15/year (individual).

Publications:
ACE Newsletter. semi-a. adv.
Membership Directory. a.

Meetings/Conferences:
Annual Meetings: Fall

Ass'n of Construction Inspectors
1224 No. Nokomis N.E.
Alexandria, MN   56308
Tel: (320)763-7525   *Fax:* (320)763-9290
Annual Budget: $1-2,000,000
Exec. Director: Robert G. Johnson

Historical Note
Membership: $165/year.

Meetings/Conferences:
Annual Meetings: Fall

Ass'n of Consulting Chemists and Chemical Engineers *(1928)*
P.O. Box 297
Sparta, NY   07871
Tel: (973)729-6671   *Fax:* (973)729-7088
E-Mail: info@chemconsult.org
Web Site: http://www.chemconsult.org
Members: 150 individuals
Annual Budget: $25-50,000
Exec. Secretary: Linda Townsend

Historical Note
Members are independent consulting chemists and chemical engineers. Chartered in 1928 in the state of New York. Membership: $250/year.

Publications:
Consulting Services Directory. bien.
Your Consultant. q.

Meetings/Conferences:
Annual Meetings: Fourth Tuesday in October/New York, NY

Ass'n of Consulting Foresters of America *(1948)*
723 North Washington St., Suite 4-A
Alexandria, VA   22314-2714
Tel: (703)548-0990   *Fax:* (703)548-6395
Toll Free: (888)540 - 8733
E-Mail: acf@igc.apc.org
Web Site: http://www.acf-foresters.com
Members: 550 individuals
Staff: 2
Annual Budget: under $10,000
Exec. Director: Loren R. Larson, II
Director, Administration: Lynn Wilson

Historical Note
Technically trained foresters who own their own businesses, demonstrate their professional competency and whose services are available to the general public on a fee or contract basis. Membership: $300/year.

Publications:
ACF Membership Specialization Directory. a.
ACF Newsletter. q.
The Consultant. q. adv.

Meetings/Conferences:
Annual Meetings: last week in June
1999 – Clymer, NY(Peak-N-Peak)/June 27-30/300

Ass'n of Container Reconditioners *(1940)*
8401 Corporate Dr., Suite 140
Landover, MD   20785-2224
Tel: (301)577-3786   *Fax:* (301)577-6476
Web Site: http://www.reconditioners.com
Members: 150 individuals
Staff: 2
Annual Budget: $500-1,000,000

President: Paul W. Rankin
Office Administrator: Joan Hunnam
Technical Director: Dana Worcester

Historical Note
Formerly (1987) Nat'l Barrel and Drum Ass'n. ACR members are reconditioners and dealers of steel and plastic drums, as well as intermediate bulk containers. Founding member of the Internation Confederation of Drum Reconditioners.

Publications:
Membership and Industrial Supply Directory. a. adv.
Reconditioner. m. adv.
Responsible Container Management.

Meetings/Conferences:
Annual Convention: Fall

Ass'n of Continuing Legal Education Administrators *(1964)*

Historical Note
Became the Ass'n of Continuing Legal Education in 1995.

Ass'n of Corporate Travel Executives *(1988)*
515 King St., Suite 330
Alexandria, VA 22314
Tel: (703)683-5322   *Fax:* (703)683-2720
E-Mail: info@acte.org
Web Site: http://www.acte.org
Members: 2,200 individuals
Staff: 4
Annual Budget: $500-1,000,000
Exec. Director: Nancy Holtzman

Historical Note
ACTE members are corporate travel managers, agency executives and supply representatives. Membership: $225/year (individual).

Publications:
ACTE Quarterly. q. adv.
Annual Report. a. adv.
Membership Directory. a. adv.

Meetings/Conferences:
1999 – Washington, DC/May 23-26
1999 – Istanbul, Turkey/Nov. 14-17

Ass'n of Cosmetologists and Hairdressers *(1985)*
2547 Monroe St.
Dearborn, MI 48124-3013
Tel: (313)563-0360   *Fax:* (248)669-0636
Members: 3,704 individuals, 47 companies
Staff: 4
Annual Budget: $2-5,000,000
President: Mary Ann Neuman

Historical Note
Membership includes hairdressers and cosmetologists, as well as wholesalers, manufacturers, buyers, distributors, and retailers. Membership: $150/year (individual).

Publications:
Newsletter. q.

Meetings/Conferences:
2000 – Monte Carlo, Monaco

Ass'n of Coupon Processors

Historical Note
Became (1996) Ass'n of Coupon Professionals.

Ass'n of Coupon Professionals *(1988)*
35 E. Wacker Dr., Suite 500
Chicago, IL 60601-2105
Tel: (312)782-5252   *Fax:* (312)236-1140
Web Site: http://www.couponpros.org
Members: 60 companies
Staff: 2
Annual Budget: $100-250,000
Admin. Manager: Melissa Wood

Historical Note
Founded as Ass'n of Coupon Processors; assumed its current name in 1996. ACP was established to improve industry business conditions, to assure continued use of coupons as a viable sales and marketing tool and to provide for the resolution of common industry concerns in the development, distribution and redemption of coupons. Membership fee varies, based on type: $500-3,000/year.

Publications:
Coupon Exchange. semi-a.

Meetings/Conferences:
Semi-annual Meetings: Spring and Fall
1999 – Denver, CO(Hyatt Regency)/March 15-17

Ass'n of Crafts and Creative Industries *(1976)*
1100-H Brandywine Blvd., P.O. Box 3388
Zanesville, OH 43702-3388
Tel: (740)452-4541   *Fax:* (740)452-2552
E-Mail: acci.info@creative-industries.com
Web Site: http://www.creative-industries.com/acci
Members: 6,400 individuals
Annual Budget: $250-500,000
Exec. Director: Walter Offinger
Show Director: Marrijane Jones

Historical Note
Formerly (1984) the Mid-America Craft Hobby Ass'n. Membership is composed of professionals in the craft supply and creative industries. Object of ACCI is to offer a means of exchange to all those engaged in the buying, selling or manufacturing of craft, art, framing, miniature, notions, needlework and floral hobby merchandise. Membership: $50-125/year.

Publications:
ACCI Topline Newsletter. bi-m.

Meetings/Conferences:
Annual: Trade Market/Trade Show & Convention
1999 – Rosemont, IL(Rosemont Convention Center)/June 4-7

Ass'n of Credit Union League Executives
Historical Note
Address unknown in 1998.

Ass'n of Cytogenetic Technologists
Historical Note
Became (1996) Ass'n of Genetic Technologists.

Ass'n of Dark Leaf Tobacco Dealers and Exporters *(1947)*
P.O. Box 638
Springfield, TN 37172
Tel: (615)384-4543   *Fax:* (615)384-6461
Members: 20 companies
Staff: 1
Annual Budget: under $10,000
President: Ed Alexander

Historical Note
An affiliate of Burley and Dark Leaf Tobacco Export Ass'n, ADLTDE was organized to promote the use of dark-fired and dark air-cured tobaccos both domestically and abroad.

Meetings/Conferences:
Semi-Annual Meetings: Spring and Fall Always Hopkinsville, KY(Hopkinsville Golf and Country Club)

Ass'n of Database Developers
5720 Kayron Dr.
Atlanta, GA 30328
Tel: (404)705-9440
E-Mail: add@inlingo.com
Web Site: http://www.addnet.org
Exec. V. President: Steve Davis

Historical Note
ADD provides mentoring and networking opportunities to promote the field of database design.

Ass'n of Defense Trial Attorneys *(1941)*
124 S.W. Adams St., Suite 600
Peoria, IL 61602
Tel: (309)676-0400   *Fax:* (309)676-3374
Members: 700 individuals
Staff: 1
Annual Budget: $25-50,000
Secretary: Gary M. Peplow

Historical Note
Formerly (1988) the Ass'n of Insurance Attorneys. ADTA members are attorneys who regularly represent insurance companies and self-insurers and are expert in the fields of law pertaining to dispute resolution for the insurance industry. A minimum of five years trial experience with insurance cases and insurance matters is required for admission. Membership is limited to one member selected from each city, town and municipality (with certain exceptions). A member's partners or associates may become associate members. Membership: $195/year (individual); $125/year (associate individual).

Publications:
Membership Roster. a.

Meetings/Conferences:
Annual Meetings: Spring/200

Ass'n of Defensive Spray Manufacturers *(1992)*
917 Locust St., Suite 1100
St. Louis, MO 63101-1413
Tel: (314)241-1445   *Fax:* (314)241-1449
Members: 15 corporate members
Annual Budget: $10-25,000
Exec. Director: Mark S. Birenbaum, Ph.D.

Historical Note
Purpose is to permit manufacturers of non-lethal chemical weapons to join together to promote the industry as well as to address safety, quality control, marketing and other views relevant to the industry. Membership: $1,000/year (corporate).

Ass'n of Departments of English *(1962)*
10 Astor Place
New York, NY 10003-6981
Tel: (212)614-6317   *Fax:* (212)533-0680
E-Mail: ade@mla.org
Web Site: http://www.ade.org
Members: 840 departments
Staff: 3
Director: David Laurence

Historical Note
Formerly Ass'n of Departments of English in American Colleges and Universities. ADE members are administrators of college and university-level departments of English. Sponsored by the Modern Language Ass'n of America. Membership: $100/year (company).

Publications:
ADE Bulletin. 3/year.
Job Information List. q.

Meetings/Conferences:
Annual Meetings: Summer

Ass'n of Departments of Foreign Languages *(1969)*
10 Astor Place
New York, NY 10003
Tel: (212)614-6319   *Fax:* (212)533-0680
E-Mail: adfl@mla.org
Web Site: http://www.adfl.org
Members: 1,050 academic departments
Staff: 4
Annual Budget: $50-100,000
Director: Elizabeth Welles

Historical Note
Members are administrators of foreign language departments at the college/university-level.

Publications:
ADFL Bulletin. 3/yr.

Meetings/Conferences:
1999 – Nashville, TN
1999 – Palo Alto, CA

Ass'n of Destination Management Executives *(1995)*
3333 Quebec, Suite 4050
Denver, CO 80207
Tel: (303)394-3905   *Fax:* (303)394-3450
Web Site: http://www.adme.org
Members: 70 companies
Staff: 2
Annual Budget: $500-1,000,000
Exec. V. President: Sylvia A. Rottman

Historical Note
ADME members are CEOs of destination management companies. Membership: $400/year.

Publications:
ADMExpressions. q. adv.

Meetings/Conferences:
1999 – Orlando, FL(Royal Plaza Hotel)/125

Ass'n of Diesel Specialists *(1956)*
9140 Ward Parkway
Kansas City, MO 64114
Tel: (816)444-3500   *Fax:* (816)444-0330
E-Mail: info@diesel.org
Web Site: http://www.diesel.org
Members: 750 companies
Staff: 6
Annual Budget: $500-1,000,000
Exec. V. President: Robert G. Stewart
Director, Meetings: Rosemary Hall
Director, Technical Education and Services: David A. Fehling
Member Services Coordinator: Barbi Oxley

Historical Note
Members are companies and individuals whose primary interest is the technology and service of diesel fuel injection, governor and turbocharger systems.

Publications:
Nozzle Chatter. bi-m.

Meetings/Conferences:
Annual Meetings: August/September
1999 – Las Vegas, NV(Mirage)/July 30-Aug. 3
2000 – Lake Buena Vista, FL(Disney Contemporary)/Aug. 4-8
2001 – Las Vegas, NV(Mirage)/Aug. 3-7

Ass'n of Direct Marketing Agencies *(1971)*
P.O. Box 3139, Grand Central Stn.
New York, NY 10163-3139
Tel: (212)644-8085   *Fax:* (212)644-0296
E-Mail: JWPgroup@aol.com
Members: 125 individuals, 60 agencies
Annual Budget: $25-50,000
Exec. Director: James W. Prendergast

Historical Note
Established as the Association of Direct Marketing Agencies and Consultants, it assumed its present name in 1971. Members are direct response advertising agencies. Membership: $350/year.

Meetings/Conferences:
Semi-Annual Meetings: January and June
1999 – Key West, FL
1999 – Charleston, SC

Ass'n of Directory Marketing *(1990)*
1187 Thorn Run Road, Suite 630
Moon Township, PA 15108-3198
Tel: (412)269-0663   *Fax:* (412)269-0655
E-Mail: admpghpa@aol.com
Web Site: http://www.admworks.org
Members: 115 companies
Staff: 8
Annual Budget: $500-1,000,000
President & C.E.O.: Herbert D. Gordon

Historical Note
ADM members are certified marketing representatives/agencies and directory publishers. Its mission is build advertisers' businesses and,in turn,industry revenues by maximizing the value of directory advertising. Membership: $2,500/year minimum, $500/$1 million billings (certified marketing representatives/agencies); $10,000/year (major publishers); $2,500/year (other publishers).

Publications:
ADM Flash.

Meetings/Conferences:
Annual Meetings: Spring
1999 – Orlando, FL(Hyatt Regency-Grand Cypress)/April 25-28

Ass'n of Directory Publishers *(1898)*
P.O. Box 157
Wrentham, MA 02093-0157
Tel: (508)384-0850   *Fax:* (508)384-0837
E-Mail: adp@ultranet.com
Web Site: http://www.adp.org
Members: 302 companies
Staff: 6
Annual Budget: $500-1,000,000
President: R. Lawrence Angove
V. President: Carol C. Hill
Convention Services Manager: Sue Chisholm
Executive Assistant: Sue LaChappelle

Historical Note
Formerly (1992) the Ass'n of North American Directory Publishers. Members are publishers of telephone, city and directories and special interest directories. Purpose is to foster and maintain high standards. Membership: $1,200-$15,000/year, based on gross advertising revenue.

Publications:
The Directory Journal. q.

Meetings/Conferences:
Semi-annual Meetings: Spring and Fall
1999 – Orlando, FL(Hyatt Cypress Gardens)/April 22-26/400
1999 – Las Vegas, NV(The Venetion)/Sept. 15-18/400
2000 – Kapalua, HI(The Ritz Carlton)/May 3-7/400
2000 – Traverse City, MI(Grand Traverse
Resort)/Sept. 9-12/400

Ass'n of Diving Contractors (1968)
3910 F.M. 1960 West, Suite 230
Houston, TX   77068
Tel: (281)893-8388   Fax: (281)893-5118
Toll Free: (888)232 - 4838
Members: 330 companies
Staff: 2
Annual Budget: $250-500,000
Exec. Director: Ross Saxon

Historical Note
Commercial diving and underwater contractors, manufacturers and
suppliers of diving equipment, diving schools and ROV owners and
operators. Membership: $25/year (individual); $250/year and up
(organization/ company) fee varies by volume.

Publications:
Underwater Magazine. q. adv.

Meetings/Conferences:
Annual Meetings: Winter
1999 – New Orleans, LA(Marriott)/Jan. 18-20/2000
2000 – Houston, TX(Adams Mark Hotel)/Jan. 24-26/2000

Ass'n of DSM Professionals

Historical Note
Became (1995) Ass'n of Energy Services Professionals.

Ass'n of Earth Science Editors (1967)
781 Northwest Drive
Morgantown, WV   26505
Tel: (304)285-4679   Fax: (304)285-4459
E-Mail: lessingk@aol.com
Web Site: http://www.odp.tamu.edu/publications/AESE
Members: 350 individuals
Annual Budget: $10-25,000
Secretary-Treasurer: Katherine B. Lessing

Historical Note
Founded to strengthen the profession of earth science editing, AESE
promotes the exchange of ideas on problems of selection, editing
and publication of research manuscripts, journals, serials,
periodicals and maps pertaining to earth sciences. Affiliated with
the American Geological Institute and the American Ass'n for the
Advancement of Science. Membership: $30/year (individual).

Publications:
Blueline. q.
Membership Directory. a.

Meetings/Conferences:
Annual Meetings: September or October/100

Ass'n of Ecosystem Research Centers (1985)
6182 Steele Hall
Darthmouth University
Hanover, NH   03755-3577
Tel: (603)646-1456
Members: 40 centers
Annual Budget: under $10,000
President: John O'Brien, Ph.D.

Historical Note
AERC was established to improve coordination and
communications among ecosystem research centers and to promote
and expand their research programs. President is elected annually.
Membership: $40/year (individual), $400/year (center).

Publications:
AERC Newsletter. semi-a.
Directory of Member Centers. bien.

Meetings/Conferences:

Ass'n of Edison Illuminating Companies (1885)
P.O. Box 2641
Birmingham, AL   35291-0992
Tel: (205)257-2530   Fax: (205)257-2540
E-Mail: aeic@apc.com
Web Site: http://www.aeic.org/index.htm
Members: 105 investor-owned utilities
Staff: 4
Annual Budget: $250-500,000
Exec. Director: Robert Huffman

Historical Note
Organized in 1885 by licensees of Thomas A. Edison for the
advancement of electric service to the public for light, heat and
power. Represents U.S. investor-owned utilities and international
electric utilities providing technical expertise and information.
Membership fee varies based on revenues; maximum $12,
275/year.

Publications:
AEIC Update. q.

Meetings/Conferences:
Annual Meetings: Fall

Ass'n of Editorial Businesses (1980)

Historical Note
Organization defunct in 1996.

Ass'n of Educators in Private Practice
N. 7425 Switzke Road
Watertown, WI   53094-9481
Tel: (920)699-8280
Toll Free: (800)252 - 3280
E-Mail: yelichris@aol.com
Web Site: http://www.execpc.com/ ~ aepp
Executive Director: Chris Yelich

Historical Note
Membership: $45/year (regular); $90/year (governing);
$200/year (corporate).

Publications:
AEPP Directory. a.
Enterprising Educators Newsletter. semi-a.

Meetings/Conferences:

Ass'n of Educators in Radiological Science (1967)
820 Jorie Blvd.,
Oak Brook, IL   60523-2251
Tel: (630)571-9183   Fax: (630)571-7837
E-Mail: aers@rsna.org
Web Site: http://www.aers.org
Members: 905 individuals
Exec. Secretary: Betty Rohr
Assoc. Exec. Secretary: Mary Beth Nardi

Historical Note
AERS members are professionals who have current registration with
ARRT, NMTCB, ARDMS, or equivalent credentials and are
employed in an educational position associated wioth an accredited
readiological sciences program. Membership: $50/year
(individual).

Publications:
AERS Quarterly Newsletter. q.
Radiologic Science and Education Journal.

Meetings/Conferences:
Annual Meetings: in conjunction with RSNA

Ass'n of Energy Engineers (1977)
4025 Pleasantdale Rd., Suite 420
Atlanta, GA   30340-4264
Tel: (770)447-5083   Fax: (770)446-3969
E-Mail: info@eecenter.org
Web Site: http://www.aeecenter.org
Members: 8,500 individuals
Staff: 12
Annual Budget: $1-2,000,000
Exec. Director: Albert Thumann
Information Director: Ruth Bennett Fowler

Historical Note
Licensed professional engineers, architects, utility managers and
consultants with experience in energy management and
cogeneration. Absorbed Energy Management and Controls Soc. in
1986. Membership: $125/year.

Publications:
Cogeneration & Competitive Power Journal. 3/yr.
Energy Engineering. bi-m. adv.
Energy Insight. semi-a.
Environmental News. q.
Strategic Planning for Energy and the Environment. q.

Meetings/Conferences:

Ass'n of Energy Service Companies (1956)
6060 North Central Expwy., Suite 428
Dallas, TX   75206-5205
Tel: (214)692-0771   Fax: (214)692-0162
Toll Free: (800)692 - 0771
Members: 800 companies
Staff: 4
Annual Budget: $250-500,000
Exec. Director: Robert Key
Communications Director: Kristin VanVeen

Historical Note
Formerly Ass'n of Oilwell Servicing Contractors (1996).

Publications:
Directory. a.
Field Reports Newsletter. m.
Workover/Well Servicing Magazine. bi-m. adv.

Meetings/Conferences:
Semi-Annual Meetings: February and July

Ass'n of Energy Services Professionals (1989)
7491 N. Federai Hwy., #C5
Boca Raton, FL   33487
Tel: (561)982-9903   Fax: (561)982-9905
E-Mail: eboardman@aesp.org
Web Site: http://www.aesp.org
Annual Budget: $500-1,000,000
Exec. Director: Elliot Boardman

Historical Note
Formerly (1994) Ass'n of DSM Professionals. Members are
professionals in the energy industry. Membership: $138/year.

Publications:
Journal of the AESP. q. adv.
Membership Directory. a. adv.
Strategies. q. adv.

Meetings/Conferences:
Annual Meetings: December/400

Ass'n of Engineering Geologists (1957)
Texas A-M University,#MS-3115
College Station, TX   77843-3115
Tel: (978)443-4639   Fax: (978)443-2948
Members: 3,100 individuals
Staff: 1
Annual Budget: $500-1,000,000
Exec. Director: Edwin A. Blackley, Jr.

Historical Note
Founded by 12 charter members in Sacramento, CA as the
California Ass'n of Engineering Geologists; assumed its present
name and became an international organization in 1957. A
member society of the American Geological Institute. Membership is
open to anyone possessing a college degree in geology or
engineering geology, or having a serious interest in the subject.
Membership: $80/year (full member); $70/year
(associate/affiliate); $25/year (student); $250/year (company).

Publications:
AEG Directory. a. adv.
AEG News. q. adv.
Environmental and Engineering Geoscience. q. adv.

Meetings/Conferences:
Annual Meetings: Fall
1999 – Salt Lake City, UT
2000 – San Francisco, CA

Ass'n of Environmental and Resource Economists (1979)
1616 P St., N.W., Suite 507
Washington, DC   20036
Tel: (202)328-5077   Fax: (202)939-3460
Web Site: http://www.ecu.edu/econ/aere/
Members: 800 individuals
Annual Budget: $25-50,000
Exec. Secretary: Marilyn Voigt

Historical Note
AERE serves as an information resource for economists involved in
natural resources policy planning and research. Membership:
$80/year (individual); $56.50/year (student).

Publications:
AERE Newsletter. semi-a. adv.
Journal of Environmental Economics and Management. bi-m.

Meetings/Conferences:
Annual Meetings: January, in conjunction with Allied Social
Science Ass'ns.

Ass'n of Environmental Engineering Professors (1963)
2208 Harrington Court
Champaign, IL   61821-6472
Tel: (217)398-6969   Fax: (217)355-9232
Web Site: http://www.aeep.org
Members: 650 individuals
Staff: 1
Annual Budget: $25-50,000
AEEP Business Office: Joanne Fetzner

Historical Note
Formerly (1972) American Ass'n of Professors in Sanitary
Engineering. Individuals working or teaching in the field of
environmental engineering, including water quality and treatment,
air quality, air pollution control and solid and hazardous waste
management. Officers change annually. Membership: $30-60/year
(individual); $250/year (company).

Publications:
AEEP Newsletter. q. adv.

Meetings/Conferences:
Annual Meetings: Fall with the Water Environment Federation

Ass'n of Episcopal Colleges (1962)
815 Second Avenue
Suite 315
New York, NY   10017-4594
Tel: (212)986-0989   Fax: (212)986-5039
Members: 11 colleges
Staff: 3
Annual Budget: $100-250,000
President: Linda Armstrong Chisholm, Ph.D.

Historical Note
Formerly (1965) Foundation for Episcopal Colleges, and (1966)
Fund for Episcopal Colleges. The Ass'n is a consortium of 12
colleges with historic and present ties to the Episcopal Church. Its
mission is the development of programs on and off campus which
enhance the spiritual, intellectual and ethical growth of college
students. Membership: $7,000/year (institution).

Publications:
Views & News. a.

Meetings/Conferences:
1999 – New York, NY/Apr. 22-23

Ass'n of Executive Search Consultants (1959)
500 Fifth Ave., Suite 930
New York, NY   10110-0900
Tel: (212)398-9556   Fax: (212)398-9560
Members: 160 firms
Staff: 5
Annual Budget: $500-1,000,000
President: Peter Felix

Historical Note
Established as the Ass'n of Executive Recruiting Consultants, it
assumed its present name in 1982.

Publications:
Code of Ethics.
Guidelines for Selecting an Executive Search Firm.
Journal of Executive Search Consulting. a. adv.
Membership Directory.
Professional Practice Guidelines.
Why Retain an AESC Firm.

Meetings/Conferences:
1999 – Palm Beach, FL(The Breakers)/April 8-11

Ass'n of Faculty Clubs Internat'l
3900 E. Timrod St.
Tucson, AZ   85711
Tel: (520)323-1533   Fax: (520)322-6778
Exec. Director: Phillip A. Gutt, CAE

Meetings/Conferences:

Ass'n of Family and Conciliation Courts (1963)
329 W. Wilson St.
Madison, WI   53703-3612
Tel: (608)251-4001   Fax: (608)251-2231
E-Mail: afcc@afccnet.org
Members: 1,600 individuals
Staff: 3
Annual Budget: $250-500,000
Exec. Director: Ann L. Milne

Historical Note
AFCC was established to: develop and improve the practice and procedures of family counseling as a complement to the judicial process; to promote ethical standards in court related marriage and divorce counseling; and to provide a forum for the exchange of ideas and assistance in establishing programs in this field. Members include lawyers, judges and marriage counselors. Membership: $125/year (individual); $300/year (institution); $40/year (student).

Publications:
Family and Conciliation Courts Review. q. adv.
Newsletter. q. adv.

Meetings/Conferences:
Annual Meetings: May
1999 – Vancouver, British Columbia

Ass'n of Family Practice Residency Directors (1990)
8880 Ward Pkwy.
Kansas City, MO   64114-2756
Tel: (816)333-9700   Fax: (816)333-9855
Toll Free: (800)274 - 2237
E-Mail: mesmith@aafp.org
Web Site: http://www.afprd.org
Members: 420 individuals
Staff: 2
Annual Budget: $50-100,000
Staff Exec.: Cathy Englund

Historical Note
Membership: $200/year.

Publications:
Highlights. 3/year. adv.

Meetings/Conferences:
Annual Meetings: always Kansas City, MO.
1999 – /June 13-15
2000 – /June 4-6

Ass'n of Farmworker Opportunity Programs (1971)
1611 N. Kent St., Suite 910
Arlington, VA   22209
Tel: (703)528-4141   Fax: (703)528-4145
E-Mail: AFOPMULL@AFOP.ORG
Members: 53 organizations
Staff: 15
Annual Budget: $2-5,000,000
Exec. Director: L. Diane Mull
Administrator/Special Programs Assistant: Laura Lull
DOL/PE Manager: Reid Maki
Finance Manager: Lowell Fogus

Historical Note
AFOP is a federation of non-profit organizations and state agencies using federal grants to provide training leading to full-time employment for eligible migrant and seasonal farmworkers. Membership: $50/year (individual); $850/year (organization/company).

Publications:
Ass'n of Farmworker Opportunity Programs Directory. a.
FAN Newsletter. q. adv.
Radio Social Marketing Publications. a. adv.

Ass'n of Federal Communications Consulting Engineers (1948)
P.O. Box 19333, 20th St. Station
Washington, DC   20036-0333
Tel: (703)569-7704   Fax: (703)569-6417
Web Site: http://www.afcce.org
Members: 250 individuals
Annual Budget: $25-50,000
President: Cynthia Jacobson

Historical Note
An organization of professional engineering consultants serving the telecommunications industry. Associate membership composed of engineering executives of communications companies and radio equipment manufacturers. AFCCE maintains close relationship with the Federal Communications Commission. Has no paid staff; officers change annually. Membership: $80-120/year.

Publications:
Membership Directory. a.
Newsletter. q.

Meetings/Conferences:
Annual Meetings: May-June

Ass'n of Field Ornithologists (1922)
P.O. Box 1897
Lawrence, KS   66044-1897
Tel: (785)843-1221   Fax: (785)843-1274
Members: 1,200 individuals
Administrator: Richard Walker

Historical Note
AFO members are individuals with an interest in the study of birds and their habitats, particularly through the use of bird banding.

Publications:
Journal of Field Ornithology. q.

Ass'n of Film Commissioners Internat'l (1979)
7060 Hollywood Blvd., Suite 614
Los Angeles, CA   90028-6931
Tel: (323)462-6092   Fax: (323)462-6091
Web Site: http://www.afciweb.org
Members: 250 individuals
Staff: 2
Annual Budget: $500-1,000,000
Managing Director: Barbara Shore

Historical Note
Formerly (1990) Ass'n of Film Commissioners. Members are officials serving as film commissioners. The purpose of the AFCI is to act as liaison between the visual communications industry and local governments or organizations in order to facilitate on-location production. Membership: $500/year.

Publications:
AFCI Newsletter. q.
Locations Magazine. a.

Meetings/Conferences:

Ass'n of Finance and Insurance Professionals (1989)
P.O. Box 212003
Bedford, TX   76095-8003
Tel: (817)428-2434   Fax: (817)428-2534
E-Mail: afip@aol.com
Web Site: http://www.afip.com
Annual Budget: $250-500,000
Exec. Director: David N. Robertson

Historical Note
AFIP supports finance/insurance personnel and the finance/insurance industry for franchised automobile dealers in the U.S. and 13 foreign countries. Membership: $95/year (individual); $1,500/year (company).

Publications:
Management and Technology. bi.

Ass'n of Financial Guaranty Insurors
122 S. Swan St.
Albany, NY   12210-1715
Tel: (518)449-4698   Fax: (518)432-5651
E-Mail: mackinco@albany.net
Web Site: http://www.agfi.org
Members: 9 corporations
Staff: 6
Exec. Director: Robert E. Mackin

Historical Note
AGFI members are firms who write financial guaranty insurance.

Ass'n of Financial Services Holding Companies (1985)
888 17th St., N.W., Suite 312
Washington, DC   20006
Tel: (202)223-6575   Fax: (202)331-3836
Members: 40 companies
Staff: 7
President: Patrick A. Forte
Government Relations Director: Geoffrey P. Gray
Counsel: Harding de C. Williams

Historical Note
Members are financial services holding companies; each member company owns at least one federally insured depository institution. AFSHC primarily serves as industry liaison with the United States Congress and regulatory agencies of the U.S. Government. Formerly (1990) Ass'n of Thrift Holding Companies.

Publications:
AFSHC Executive Report. irreg.

Ass'n of Firearm and Toolmark Examiners (1969)
Historical Note
Address unknown in 1996.

Ass'n of Flight Attendants (1945)
1275 K St., N.W., Suite 500
Washington, DC   20005-4090
Tel: (202)712-9799   Fax: (202)712-9798
Toll Free: (800)424 - 2401
Members: 42,000 individuals
Staff: 75
Annual Budget: $10-25,000,000
Internat'l President: Patricia A. Friend
Director, Communications: Jane Goodman
Director, Government Affairs: JoEllen Deutsch
Manager, Conventions/Meetings: Gail Stokes
Internat'l Secretary-Treasurer: Sharon E. Madigan
General Counsel: David Borer
Manager, Membership: Mary Beth Ziegler

Historical Note
Formerly (1973) the Steward and Stewardesses Division of the Air Line Pilots Ass'n, International. An independent affiliate of AFL-CIO (Washington, DC), organized to negotiate pay, working conditions, benefits, and work rules on behalf of flight attendants on the nation's commercial air carriers. Sponsors and supports the Flight PAC Political Action Committee. Has an annual budget of approximately $13 million. Membership: $39/month.

Publications:
Flight Log. q. adv.

Meetings/Conferences:
Annual Meetings: October

Ass'n of Food and Drug Officials (1896)
Box 3425
York, PA   17402-3425
Tel: (717)757-2888   Fax: (717)755-8089
E-Mail: afdo@blazenet.net
Web Site: http://www.foodsafety.org/afdu
Members: 600 individuals
Staff: 3
Annual Budget: $100-250,000
Exec. Administrator: Denise C. Rooney

Historical Note
Founded in 1896 to promote the passage of federal regulations to prevent the misbranding and adulteration of foods, drugs, cosmetics and devices, and to promote uniformity among the states in regulating the above. Members are individuals concerned with the development and enforcement of uniform food, drug and other consumer protection laws. Membership: varies; $35-300/year.

Publications:
Journal of the Ass'n of Food and Drug Officials. 5/year. adv.
News and Views Newsletter. q.

Meetings/Conferences:
Annual Meetings: June, hosted in rotation by the six regional chapters of the ass'n
1999 – San Antonio, TX/300

Ass'n of Food Industries (1906)

P.O. Box 545
5 Ravine Drive
Matawan, NJ   07747-0545
Tel: (732)583-8188   Fax: (732)583-0798
Members: 370 companies
Staff: 5
Annual Budget: $250-500,000
President: Richard J. Sullivan, CAE

Historical Note
Formed by a merger of the Bean Ass'n, the Dried Fruit Ass'n of New York and the Food Brokers Ass'n. Membership now composed of the American Olive Oil Ass'n, the Maraschino Cherry and Glace Fruit Processors, the Metropolitan Food Brokers Ass'n, Processed Foods and Nut and Agricultural Products. Formerly (1982) Ass'n of Food Distributors. Membership: $820-2,120/year.

Publications:
AFI Annual. a. adv.
AFI Newsletter. bi-m.
Bulletins. 2-3/wk.
Meeting Minutes. m.

Meetings/Conferences:
Annual Meetings: April/May
1999 – Phoenix, AZ(Pointe Hilton)/April 15-17/200

Ass'n of Food Journalists (1974)
38309 Genesee Lake Road
Oconomowoc, WI   53066
Tel: (414)965-3251
Members: 275 individuals
Staff: 1
Annual Budget: $50-100,000
Exec. Director: Carol DeMasters

Historical Note
Formerly (1994) the Newspaper Food Editors and Writers Ass'n. AFI members are food journalists for newspapers, magazines, broadcast and cable media, and cookbook authors. Membership: $75(individual).

Publications:
Newsletter. m.

Meetings/Conferences:
1999 – Orlando, FL(Disney Institute)/Orlando, 0-18
2000 – Kansas City, MO(Ritz Carlton)

Ass'n of Foreign Investors in Real Estate (1987)
1300 Pennsylvania Ave. N.W., Suite 880
Washington, DC   20004
Tel: (202)312-1400   Fax: (202)312-1401
E-Mail: afireinfo@afire.org
Web Site: http://www.afire.org
Members: 147 corporations
Staff: 3
Annual Budget: $250-500,000
Chief Executive: James A. Fetgatter, CPA
Programs Director: Carrie Hane

Historical Note
Formerly (1998) Ass'n of Foreign Investors in United States Real Estate. Members are foreign investors in U.S. real estate, and domestic firms providing services in the field. Membership: $4,000/year.

Publications:
AFIRE News. bi-m.

Meetings/Conferences:
Annual Meetings: Fall
1999 – Washington, DC/Oct. 3-5

Ass'n of Foreign Investors in United States Real Estate
Historical Note
Became (1998) Ass'n of Foreign Investors in Real Estate.

Ass'n of Foreign Trade Representatives (1984)
P.O. Box 300
New York, NY   10024-0300
Tel: (212)877-8900
E-Mail: mccabe@whoswho.com
Members: 200 individuals, 75 organizations
Staff: 2
Annual Budget: under $10,000
Exec. Director: John J. McCabe

Historical Note
Established in April, 1984 to provide a forum for the exchange of ideas and experiences relating to the advancement of trade. Members are consuls general, executive directors, trade commissioners, ministers and consuls, attaches, secretaries and officers from the commercial and information sections of sovereign states and provincial governments.

Ass'n of Forensic Document Examiners (1986)
100 E. Wisconsin Ave., Suite 1650
Milwaukee, WI   53202
Tel: (414)272-0048   Fax: (414)272-0240
E-Mail: bschwid@anagraphics.com
Web Site: http://www.anagraphics.com
Members: 40 individuals
Annual Budget: under $10,000
Membership Director: Bonnie L. Schwid

Historical Note
Established and incorporated in Illinois, AFDE provides continuing education in the field of forensic document examination and a forum for the exchange of information among colleagues. Admittance testing is required. AFDE provides a certification program involving the participation of non-members and members of the legal profession in the evaluation of candidates. Membership: $125/year (individual).

Publications:
AFDE Report. q.
Journal of Forensic Document Examination. a.

Meetings/Conferences:
Annual Meetings: October/75

1999 – Phoenix, AZ/Nov 4-7

Ass'n of Former Agents of the U.S. Secret Service (1970)
P.O. Box 848
Annandale, VA   22003
Tel: (703)256-0188   Fax: (703)256-1372
Toll Free: (800)392 - 4368
Members: 1,400 individuals
Staff: 4
Annual Budget: $25-50,000
Exec. Secretary: P. Hamilton Brown

Historical Note
Dedicated to welfare of former special agents of the U.S. Secret Service and of their families when in need; to the continuing improvement and effectiveness of law enforcement; and to awarding scholarships and honoring those law enforcement officers whose performance merits special recognition. Membership: $20/year.

Publications:
Directory. a.
Pipeline. q.

Meetings/Conferences:
Annual Meetings: Fall

Ass'n of Former Intelligence Officers (1975)
6723 Whittier Ave., Suite 303A
McLean, VA   22101
Tel: (703)790-0320   Fax: (703)790-0264
Toll Free: (800)234 - 6717
E-Mail: afio@his.com
Web Site: http://www.his.com/afio
Members: 2,800 individuals
Staff: 2
Annual Budget: $100-250,000
Exec. Director: Roy K. Jonkers

Historical Note
Founded in May 1975 by a group of intelligence professionals, who served with or retired from one of the U.S. intelligence organizations, civilian or military, concerned about the future of the U.S. intelligence system in consequence of the prevelant media reporting. Chartered originally as the Ass'n of Retired Intelligence Officers, the present name was adopted in December 1976. Incorporated as a non-profit organization in the State of Virginia. Membership: $40/year (individual); $1250/year (corporate).

Publications:
AFIO Weekly Intelligence Notes (e-mail).
Intelligencer. 3/yr.
Periscope Newsletter. 3/yr.

Meetings/Conferences:
Annual Meetings: Fall

Ass'n of Former OSI Special Agents
1444 I St., N.W., Suite 700
Washington, DC   20005
Tel: (202)216-9623   Fax: (202)216-9646
Manager: Ann Stockschlaeder

Historical Note
Membership fee: $25/year (individual), $15/year (associates).

Publications:
Global Alliance. a.

Ass'n of Fraternity Advisors (1976)
3901 W. 86th St., Suite 390
Indianapolis, IN   46268
Tel: (317)876-4691   Fax: (317)872-1134
E-Mail: afa29@mail.idt.net
Web Site: http://fraternityadvisors.org
Members: 1000 individuals
Staff: 1
Annual Budget: $500-1,000,000
Exec. Director: Gayle Webb

Historical Note
AFA was established to serve professionals in higher education who advise fraternities and sororities. Membership: $70/year (individual).

Publications:
Perspectives. 5/year. adv.

Meetings/Conferences:
Annual Meetings: December/500
1999 – Denver, CO(Adam's Mark)/Dec. 1-5
2000 – Phoenix, AZ(Pointe Hilton Squaw Peak)/Nov. 29-Dec. 3
2001 – Arlington, VA(Hyatt Regency Crystal City)/Nov. 28-Dec. 2

Ass'n of Free Community Papers (1950)
401 N. Michigan Ave.
Chicago, IL   60611-4657
Tel: (312)644-6610   Fax: (312)245-1083
Web Site: http://www.afcp.org
Members: 180 publishers
Staff: 2
Annual Budget: $250-500,000
Associate Director: Deirdre Flynn

Historical Note
Formerly (1987) Nat'l Ass'n of Advertising Publishers. Members are publishers of free-circulation community newspapers Membership: based on circulation.

Publications:
Ink Newsletter. adv. adv.

Meetings/Conferences:
Annual Meetings: June
1999 – Arlington, VA(Ritz Carlton at Pentagon City)/May 26-29/150

Ass'n of Freestanding Radiation Oncology Centers (1986)
1550 South Coast Hwy., Suite 201

Laguna Beach, CA   92651
Tel: (714)545-2087   Fax: (714)545-3643
Members: 300 individuals
Staff: 2
Exec. Director: Fred Droz

Historical Note
AFROC's focus is upon regulatory, legislative and socio-economic issues. AFROC has been highly successful in promoting independent, nonhospital-based cancer therapy centers, which are typically cost-effective for consumers and have high practice standards.

Publications:
Directory. a.
Source. q.

Meetings/Conferences:
Annual Meetings: June

Ass'n of Fund Raisers and Direct Sellers (1992)
5775 Peachtree-Dunwoody Rd., Suite 500-G
Atlanta, GA   30342-1558
Tel: (404)252-3663   Fax: (404)252-0774
Web Site: http://www.afrds.org
Members: 700 companies
Staff: 3
Annual Budget: $250-500,000
Exec. Director: Russell A. Lemieux

Historical Note
Formed in 1992 from the merger of Nat'l Ass'n of Product Fund Raisers and Nat'l Ass'n of Direct Sellers. AFRDS members are distributors, manufacturers, suppliers, and brokers to the product fund raising industry. Membership: $250-1,000/year, based on company's sales and function (i.e., distributor, supplier/manufacturer, or affiliate).

Publications:
AFRDS Advisor. q.
The Fundraising Edge. semi.

Meetings/Conferences:
Annual Meetings: January/1,600
1999 – Lake Buena Vista, FL(Disney Coronado Springs)/Jan. 4-8
2000 – Orlando, FL
2000 – Phoenix, AZ

Ass'n of Gay and Lesbian Psychiatrists (1985)
4514 Chester Ave.
Philadelphia, PA   19143-3707
Tel: (215)222-2800   Fax: (215)222-3881
E-Mail: aglpnat@aol.com
Web Site: http://members.aol.com/aglpnat/homepage.html
Members: 650 individuals
Staff: 1
Nat'l Office Director: Roy Harker

Historical Note
Successor to the Caucus of Gay, Lesbian and Bisexual Members of the American Psychiatric Ass'n, AGLP is an independent, professional organization of psychiatrists, psychiatric residents and medical students which serves as a voice for the concerns of lesbians and gay men within the psychiatric community. The organizations provides opportunities for affiliation and collaboration among psychiatrists who share these concerns.

Publications:
AGLP Newsletter. q.
Journal of Gay and Lesbian Psychotherapy. a.

Ass'n of Genetic Technologists (1975)
8310 Nieman Road
Lenexa, KS   66214
Tel: (913)541-0497   Fax: (913)541-0156
Members: 1,500 individuals
Exec. Director: Steven K. Bryant

Historical Note
Founded as Ass'n of Cytogenetic Technologists; assumed its current name in 1996.

Publications:
AGI International Laboratory Directory.
Journal of the Association of Genetic Technologists.

Meetings/Conferences:
Annual Meetings: June
1999 – Orlando, FL/June 17-20

Ass'n of Golf Merchandisers (1990)
8102 E. Culver St.
Mesa, AZ   85207
Tel: (602)373-8564   Fax: (602)373-8518
Members: 700 individuals and companies
Staff: 2
Annual Budget: $100-250,000
Exec. Director: Maggie Arendt

Historical Note
Membership: $225/year(individual); $450/year(organization/company).

Publications:
The Merchandiser. bi-m.

Meetings/Conferences:
1999 – Las Vegas, NV

Ass'n of Governing Boards of Universities and Colleges (1921)
One Dupont Circle, N.W., Suite 400
Washington, DC   20036
Tel: (202)296-8400   Fax: (202)223-7053
Web Site: http://www.agb.org
Members: 30,000 individuals, 1,700 tax exempt institutions
Staff: 30
Annual Budget: $2-5,000,000
President: Richard T. Ingram
V. President, Programs and Research: Thomas Longin
Senior V. Presdient: Richard D. Legon

V. President, Publications: Daniel J. Levin

Historical Note
Founded originally as an informal organization of public university trustees, AGB established an office in Washington with its first full-time staff in 1964. It now serves 30,000 trustees and regents on some 1,100 governing and coordinating boards of 1,700 public and private colleges and universities. Its purpose is to strengthen the performance of boards of higher education.

Publications:
Trustship magazine. bi-m.

Meetings/Conferences:
Annual Meetings: Spring
1999 – Seattle, WA(Sherton)/March 27-30
2000 – New Orleans, LA/March 18-19

Ass'n of Government Accountants (1950)
2208 Mount Vernon Ave.
Alexandria, VA   22301
Tel: (703)684-6931   Fax: (703)548-9367
Toll Free: (800)242 - 7211
Web Site: http://www.agacgfm.org
Members: 15,000 individuals
Staff: 13
Annual Budget: $2-5,000,000
Exec. Director: Charles W. Culkin, Jr., CGFM
Director, Communications: Marie S. Force
Director, Meetings and Expositions: Maria K. Donovan
Director, Professional Certification: Carol A. Codori
Controller: Thomas Raevis
Director, Membership and Marketing: Susan Fritzlen

Historical Note
Established in 1950 as the Federal Government Accountants Ass'n. The name was changed to Ass'n of Government Accountants in 1975. AGA implemented a "certified Government Financial Manager (CGFM)" program. Members are engaged in financial management at the federal, state and local levels of government. Membership: $60/year (individual).

Publications:
Financial Management Topics. m.
The Government Accountants Journal. q. adv.

Meetings/Conferences:
Annual Meetings: June
1999 – New Orleans, LA(Marriott)
2000 – San Franscisco, CA

Ass'n of Government Marketing Assistance Specialists (1986)
P.O. Box 1704
Orange, TX   77630
Tel: (409)886-0125   Fax: (409)886-2849
Members: 400 individuals
Staff: 4
President: J. Rick Evans

Publications:
The Connection. q. adv.

Meetings/Conferences:

Ass'n of Graduate Liberal Studies Programs (1975)
North Carolina State University
P.O. Box 7107
Raleigh, NC   27695-7107
Tel: (919)515-7965   Fax: (919)515-1828
E-Mail: korte@ncsu.edu
Members: 115 institutions
Annual Budget: $10-25,000
President: Charles Korte

Historical Note
AGLSP was founded in 1975 to promote the quality and growth of interdisciplinary graduate liberal studies programs at North American colleges and universities. Members are interested in maintaining the quality of interdisciplinary, graduate-level degree programs in liberal studies. Officers change annually in October. Membership: $15/year (affiliate); $150/year (associate/full member)

Publications:
Journal of Graduate Liberal Studies. bi.
The Presidents Report. q.

Meetings/Conferences:
Annual Meetings: Fall

Ass'n of Graduate Schools in Ass'n of American Universities (1948)
1200 New York Ave., N.W., Suite 550
Washington, DC   20005-3928
Tel: (202)408-7500   Fax: (202)408-8184
Members: 62 individuals
Staff: 2
Annual Budget: under $10,000
President: Nils Hasselmo, Ph.D.
Exec. v. President: John C. Vaughn

Historical Note
Members are deans of graduate studies of the sixty-two research universities belonging to the Ass'n of American Universities. Purpose is to consider matters of common interest relating to graduate study and research.

Meetings/Conferences:
Annual Meetings: Fall

Ass'n of Ground Water Scientists and Engineers (1985)
Historical Note
A division of the Nat'l Ground Water Ass'n.

Ass'n of Group Travel Executives (1965)
Historical Note
Organization defunct in 1997.

Ass'n of Halfway House Alcoholism Programs of North America (1966)

R.R. 2, Box 415
Kerhonkson, NY   12446-9603
Tel: (914)626-2684   *Fax:* (914)626-2685
E-Mail: ahhap@aol.com
Members: 300 individuals
President: Susan Blacksher

Historical Note
AHHAP members are halfway house programs and individuals with an interest in the halfway house movement.

Publications:
AHHAP Membership Directory. a.
Communications and Services Newsletter. q.
Conference Proceedings. a.

Meetings/Conferences:
1999 – Indianapolis, IN/April 27-May 2/400
2000 – Chicago, IL

Ass'n of Health Facility Survey Agencies (1968)

Historical Note
Formerly (1992) Ass'n of Health Facility Licensure and Certification Directors. AHFLCD members are directors of state and territorial agencies which license and/or certify health facilities. Has no paid officers or full-time staff.

Ass'n of Health Insurance Agents (1990)

1922 F St., N.W.
Washington, DC   20006-4387
Tel: (202)331-2160   *Fax:* (202)835-9604
Web Site: http://www.agentsonline.com/AHIA/ahia.htm
Members: 6,200 individuals
Staff: 4
Annual Budget: $1-2,000,000
Exec. V. President: Gary Sanders
Managing Director, Legislation: Diane Boyle
Director, Membership Marketing: Beverlee Jones

Historical Note
A conference of the Nat'l Ass'n of Life Underwriters, the mission of AHIA is to sustain and improve the business environment for insurance agents engaged in health underwriting. Also seeks to enhance the professional skills of those providing health products, and foster greater financial independence for the public. Membership: $75/year (individual).

Publications:
Health Insurance Matters. 10/year.
Health Legislative Report. m.

Meetings/Conferences:
Annual Meetings: September

Ass'n of Health Occupations Teacher Educators (1978)

Univ. of Louisville
Dept. of Occupational Training/Devel.
Louisville, KY   40292
Tel: (502)852-0608
Members: 28 individuals
Contact: Pat Leitsch

Historical Note
Membership: $10/yr (individual).

Publications:
Health Occupations Personnel: Teacher Educators. a.
Journal of Health Occupations Education. 2/year.

Meetings/Conferences:

Ass'n of Healthcare Internal Auditors (1981)

926 Great Pond Drive, Suite 1003
Altamonte Springs, FL   32714-7244
Tel: (407)786-8200   *Fax:* (407)774-6751
Toll Free: (888)275 - 2442
E-Mail: camco@iag.net
Web Site: http://www.ahia. org
Members: 1000 individuals
Staff: 2
Annual Budget: $250-500,000
Exec. Director: Thomas A. Monahan, CAE

Historical Note
Formerly (1989) Healthcare Internal Audit Group. HIAG was established to promote cost containment and increased productivity in healthcare institutions through internal auditing. Membership: $125/year (individual).

Publications:
New Perspectives. q. adv.

Meetings/Conferences:
Annual Meetings: Fall

Ass'n of High Medicare Hospitals (1988)

Historical Note
Address unknown in 1996.

Ass'n of High Technology Distributors (1985)

Historical Note
Became the Ass'n for High Technology Distribution in 1995.

Ass'n of Higher Education Facilities Officers

1643 Prince St.
Alexandria, VA   22314
Tel: (703)684-1446   *Fax:* (703)549-2772
E-Mail: webmaster@appa.org
Web Site: http://www.appa.org
Director, Communications: Steve Glazner
Dir., Education: Katherine J. Smith
Director, Finance & Administration: Chong-Hie Choi

Publications:
Facilities Manager. bi-m. adv.
Membership Directory. a. adv.
Proceedings of the Annual Meeting. a.

Meetings/Conferences:
1999 – Cincinnati, OH(Convention Center)/June 20-22
2000 – Ft. Worth, TX
2001 – Montreal, QB, Canada

Ass'n of Hispanic Arts (1975)

250 West 26th St., 4th Floor
New York, NY   10001
Tel: (212)727-7227
Members: 5,000 individuals, 250 companies
Staff: 5
Annual Budget: $500-1,000,000
Exec. Director: Sandra M. Perez
Development Associate: Adelita M. Medina
Director of Technical Assistance: Sandra Garcia
Financial Manager: Delia Montalvo

Historical Note
Founded in 1975 by a network of Hispanic Art Organization representatives for the purpose of addressing issues relevant to the growth and stability of the Hispanic Arts community; services are open to all Hispanic arts organizations and individual artists. Membership: $25/year (individuals), $40/year (organizations).

Publications:
AHA Hispanic Arts News. 9/year. adv.
Directory of Hispanic Arts Organizations. tri-a.

Meetings/Conferences:

Ass'n of Holistic Healing Centers

Historical Note
Address unknown in 1996; presumed inactive.

Ass'n of Home Appliance Manufacturers (1967)

20 N. Wacker Dr., Suite 1231
Chicago, IL   60606
Tel: (312)984-5800   *Fax:* (312)984-5823
E-Mail: ahamdc@aol.com
Web Site: http://www.aham.org
Members: 173 companies
Staff: 14
Annual Budget: $2-5,000,000
President: Joseph McGuire
V.President, Major Appliances: Marian D. Stamos
Director, Government Relations: Tracey A. Moorehead

Historical Note
Formed in 1967 by a merger of the Consumer Products Division of the Nat'l Electrical Manufacturers Ass'n and the American Home Laundry Manufacturers' Ass'n. Composed of manufacturers and suppliers to the major appliance and portable appliance industry. Sponsors and supports the AHAM Political Action Committee, and periodically sponsors action groups to address issues facing the industry. Technical information can be accessed through AHMA's fax-on-demand service: (312) 984-9950.

Publications:
Global Appliance Report. m.
Major Home Appliance Industry Factbook. a.

Meetings/Conferences:
Annual Meetings: Spring
1999 – Washington, DC/June 24-25

Ass'n of Hospital Employee Health Professionals

Historical Note
Became the Ass'n of Occupational Health Professionals in Healthcare in 1995.

Ass'n of Human Resource Systems Professionals (1980)

Historical Note
Merged with its Canadian counterpart and became the Internat'l Ass'n for Human Resource Information Management in 1996.

Ass'n of Image Consultants Internat'l (1990)

1000 Connecticut Ave., N.W., Suite 9
Washington, DC   20036-5032
Tel: (301)371-9021   *Fax:* (301)371-8847
Toll Free: (800)383 - 8831
E-Mail: aiciint@aici.org
Web Site: http://www.aici.org
Members: 600 individuals
Staff: 1
Annual Budget: $100-250,000
Administrative Assistant: Connie Coffey

Historical Note
Formed by the merger of the Ass'n of Image Consultants (1982) and the Ass'n of Fashion and Image Consultants (1983). AICI members include color and wardrobe analysts, personal shoppers, cosmetic and hair stylists, designers, manufacturers, retailers, product developers, etiquette and communications specialists, trainers, educators and students. Membership: $150/yr. (individual); $400/year (organization).

Publications:
AICI Image Update. q. adv.

Meetings/Conferences:
Annual Meetings: July

Ass'n of Immigration Attorneys (1983)

324 W. 14th Street
New York, NY   10014-5096
Tel: (212)989-0404   *Fax:* (212)633-0190
Members: 50 individuals
Legal Counsel: Antonio C. Martinez

Historical Note
AIA members are attorneys specializing in United States immigration law.

Ass'n of Importers-Manufacturers for Muzzleloading (1973)

Historical Note
Organization defunct in 1997.

Ass'n of Incentive Marketing (1956)

1620 Rt. 22
Union, NJ   07083
Tel: (908)687-3090   *Fax:* (908)687-0977
Members: 400 companies
Annual Budget: $250-500,000
Exec. Director: Gerri Hopkins
Public Relations Associate: Karen Kircher

Historical Note
Formerly (1990) the Nat'l Premium Sales Executives. Members are professional premium/incentive marketing executives. Membership: $595/year.

Publications:
AIM Newsletter. m.
Directory of Members. a. adv.

Meetings/Conferences:
Annual Meetings: Always in Chicago, IL(McCormick Place Complex)/Fall

Ass'n of Independent Airmen

Historical Note
Organization dissolved in 1995.

Ass'n of Independent Colleges of Art and Design (1991)

3957 22nd St.
San Francisco, CA   94114-3205
Tel: (415)642-8595   *Fax:* (415)642-8590
E-Mail: bbaicad@best.com
Web Site: www.aicad.org
Members: 34 institutions
Staff: 1
Annual Budget: $500-1,000,000
Exec. Director: William O. Barrett

Historical Note
Founded in 1991 as a result of the merger of three smaller art college consortia, AICAD seeks to enhance the professional education of visual artists and designers by fostering awareness and support of independent colleges of art and design and by strengthening their programs. Membership: $4,990-7,260/year.

Meetings/Conferences:
Annual Meetings: October

Ass'n of Independent Commercial Producers (1972)

11 E. 22nd St., 4th Floor
New York, NY   10010
Tel: (212)475-2600   *Fax:* (212)475-3910
E-Mail: AICP1@aol.com
Web Site: http://www.aicp.com
Members: 575 companies
Staff: 10
President: Matt Miller

Historical Note
Independent producers of television commercials and their suppliers.

Publications:
AICP National News Newsletter. bi-m.
Membership Directory. a. adv.

Meetings/Conferences:

Ass'n of Independent Corrugated Converters (1974)

P.O. Box 25708
Alexandria, VA   22313
Tel: (703)836-2422   *Fax:* (703)836-2795
E-Mail: aicc@aiccbox.org
Web Site: http://www.aiccbox.org
Members: 927 companies
Staff: 8
Annual Budget: $1-2,000,000
Exec. V. President: Steven Young
Director, Communications, Exhibits and Special Events: Bruce Hermit
Manager, Publications and Special Events: Melissa Lyman
Director, Education: Julie Briggs
Director, Membership Services: Tammy Reilly

Historical Note
AICC is an internat'l trade ass'n representing a majority of the independent corrugated packaging manufacturers and their suppliers in North America. AICC has 627 boxmaking members and 300 supplier member companies. Membership: $800/year (corporate).

Publications:
AICC Membership Directory. a. adv.
Annual Report. a.
Box Score. bi-m.
Packaging Design Awards Book. bien.
Profile of the Independent Corrugated Converter. a.
Salary Survey. bien.
Sales Compensation Survey. bien.

Meetings/Conferences:
Semi-Annual Meetings: Spring and Fall
1999 – Boca Raton, FL
1999 – Chicago, IL
2000 – Atlanta, GA

Ass'n of Independent Information Professionals (1987)

10290 Monroe, Suite 208
Dallas, TX   75229-5718
Tel: (609)730-8759   *Fax:* (609)730-8469
E-Mail: aiipinfo@aiip.org
Web Site: http://www.aiip.org
Members: 760 individuals
Annual Budget: $50-100,000
President: Renee Daulong

Historical Note
AIIP members are owners of firms providing information-related services including online and manual research, document delivery, database design, library support, consulting, writing and

---

publishing. Some members also provide other services such as document delivery, training and consulting, library support, indexing, writing, and publishing. Membership: $175/year (regular); $95/year(associate); $50/year(student).

Publications:
AIIP Connections. q. adv.
Membership Directory. a. adv.

Meetings/Conferences:
Annual Meetings: Spring
1999 – Berkeley, CA(Berkeley Radisson Marina)/April 22-25/150
2000 – Washington, DC(Georgetown Conference Center)/April 6-9/150

Ass'n of Independent Mailing Equipment Dealers (1975)

Historical Note
Merged with the Business Technology Ass'n in 1995.

Ass'n of Independent Research Institutes
Historical Note
Address unknown in 1997.

Ass'n of Independent Television Stations
Historical Note
Became (1996) Ass'n of Local Television Stations.

Ass'n of Independent Trust Companies (1989)
401 N. Michigan Ave.
Chicago, IL 60611
Tel: (312)527-6735   Fax: (312)527-6774
Members: 150 companies
Staff: 4
Annual Budget: $25-50,000
Exec. Director: Barbara Chalik

Historical Note
Founded to create a source for education, information and networking opportunities in order to have better resources to operate, manage and compete. Membership: $350-600/year.

Publications:
AITCo Advisor Newsletter. q. adv.

Meetings/Conferences:
Annual Meetings: Fall

Ass'n of Independent Video and Filmmakers (1974)
304 Hudson St., 6th Floor
New York, NY 10013
Tel: (212)807-1400   Fax: (212)463-8519
E-Mail: aivffivf@aol.com
Members: 5,000 individuals
Staff: 8
Annual Budget: $500-1,000,000
Exec. Director: Ruby Lerner

Historical Note
Membership is open to anyone involved in the independent video and film community. Foundation for Independent Video and Film is the educational arm of AIVF. Sponsors cultural programs with grants from the Nat'l Endowment for the Arts, the New York State Council on the Arts and other foundations and corporate support. Membership: $45/year (individual); $25/year (student); $100/year (non-profit organization); $150/year (business).

Publications:
Independent Films & Video Monthly. 10/year. adv.

Meetings/Conferences:
Annual Meetings: Always New York, NY/March-April/70-80

Ass'n of Industrial Metallizers, Coaters and Laminators (1970)
2166 Gold Hill Rd.,
Ft. Mill, SC 29715
Tel: (803)802-7820   Fax: (803)802-7821
E-Mail: aimcal@aimcal.org
Web Site: http://www.aimcal.org
Members: 120 companies
Staff: 1
Annual Budget: $250-500,000
Exec. Director: Craig Sheppard

Historical Note
AIMCAL represents companies who metalize, coat and laminate flexible substrates and their suppliers. Formerly (1973) Vacuum Metallizers Ass'n. Membership: $1,700/year (company).

Publications:
Fall Conference Proceedings. a.
Glossary of Terms.
Metallizing Technical Reference.
Newsletter. q.
Product/Service Directory.

Meetings/Conferences:
Semi-annual: Fall and Winter
1999 – Cerromar, PR(Westin Rio Mar)/March 18-21

Ass'n of Industrial Real Estate Brokers (1956)
710 E. Ogden Ave., Suite 600
Naperville, IL 60563
Tel: (630)369-2406   Fax: (630)369-2488
Web Site: http://www.aireb.org
Members: 400 individuals
Staff: 5
Annual Budget: $50-100,000
Exec. Director: Terry Stevenson
Administrative Director: Amy Elliott

Historical Note
Membership: $125/year (broker), $175/year (associate company).

Ass'n of Industry Manufacturers' Representatives (1972)
222 Merchandise Mart, Suite 1360

Chicago, IL 60654
Tel: (312)464-0092   Fax: (312)464-0091
Members: 270 firms
Staff: 2
Annual Budget: $100-250,000
Exec. Director: Eileen Robiso

Historical Note
AIM/R began as an auxiliary of the now defunct Ass'n of Independent Manufacturers, first becoming independent in June, 1976 in Minneapolis. Incorporated September 14, 1977. Formerly (1987) the Ass'n of Independent Manufacturers Representatives. Members are independent manufacturers' representatives throughout the the United States; membership draws heavily in the plumbing, heating, and air conditioning fields. Membership: $295/year (organization).

Publications:
AIM/R News. bi-m.
Membership Directory. a.

Meetings/Conferences:
1999 – Hilton Head, SC/Mar. 17-20

Ass'n of Information and Dissemination Centers (1968)
P.O. Box 8105
Athens, GA 30603
Tel: (706)542-6820   Fax: (706)542-0349
E-Mail: SECRETARIAT@ASIDIC.ORG
Web Site: http://www.asidic.org
Members: 64 organizations
Staff: 1
Annual Budget: $10-25,000
President: Thomas Hogan

Historical Note
Formerly (1976) the Ass'n of Scientific Information Dissemination Centers. Members are industrial, educational and government information centers which build, maintain, search and/or distribute online databases; online or computer database vendors, producers and high volume searchers. Membership: $135/year (full member), $85/year (associate). The above address is permanent although the president does change.

Publications:
ASIDIC Newsletters. semi-a.

Meetings/Conferences:
Semi-Annual Meetings: Spring and Fall/65
1999 – San Diego, CA(Wyndham Emerald Plaza)/March 14-16/65

Ass'n of Information Technology Professionals (1951)
315 S. Northwest Hwy
Park Ridge, IL 60068
Tel: (847)825-8124   Fax: (847)825-1693
Toll Free: (800)224 - 9371
Web Site: http://www.aitp.org
Members: 8,000 individuals, 4,000 students
Staff: 8
Annual Budget: $1-2,000,000
Office Manager: James M. Fitzgerald, Jr., CPA
Editor: Susan M. Smith
Exec. Secretary: Jane Shaffer
Director, Accounting & Finance: Jay Fitzgerald
Director, Membership: Annet Cannata

Historical Note
Formerly (1951) Nat'l Machine Accountants Ass'n, (1962) Data Processing Management Ass'n, and (1996) DPMA: the Ass'n of Information Systems Professionals. AITP represents systems professionals across the United States and Canada. Members serve in technical positions in business, industry and governmental organizations throughout the world. AITP's mission is to promote the effective, responsible management of information technology to the benefit of its members, their employers and society. AITP offers education programs, peer networking opportunities, local chapter affiliations, and member entitlement programs.

Publications:
Information Executive.

Meetings/Conferences:
Annual Meetings: Fall/250
1999 – Chicago, IL(Westin O'hare)/Oct. 14-17
2000 – Appleton, WI

Ass'n of Insolvency Accountants (1981)
132 W. Main St., Suite 200
Medford, OR 97501-2746
Tel: (541)858-9187   Fax: (541)858-1665
Members: 800 individuals
Staff: 2
Annual Budget: $100-250,000
Administrative Director: Shirley Stanfield

Historical Note
Members are certified and licensed public accountants, lawyers, examiners, trustees and receivers concerned with the application of accounting procedures to insolvency proceedings. Offers courses and examinations leading to the designation Certified Insolvency and Reorganization Accountant (CIRA). Membership: $150/year (individual), $225/year (CIRA designee), $105/year (associate), $75/year (government/education member).

Publications:
AIA Directory. a.
AIA Newsletter. q.
CIRA Courses: Parts 1-3.
CIRA Directory. a.
Distressed Business and Real Estate Newsletter. bi-m.

Meetings/Conferences:
Annual Meetings: Spring
1999 – San Diego, CA/June 9-12

Ass'n of Insurance Compliance Professionals (1985)
740 Florida Central Pkwy., Suite 1020
Longwood, FL 32750
Tel: (407)834-6688   Fax: (407)834-4747

Members: 800 individuals
Staff: 4
Annual Budget: $100-250,000
Exec. Director: Jone R. Sienkiewicz, CAE, CMP

Historical Note
Formerly Soc. of State Filers (1998). AICP represents individuals involved or interested in statutes, state filing methods, and/or regulatory requirements. Associate members are consultants, attorneys, association managers, education/service organizations and other interested individuals. Membership: $75/year.

Publications:
Newsletter. q.

Meetings/Conferences:

Ass'n of Interim Housing Providers
1 East Wacker Dr., Suite 3600
Chicago, IL 60601
Tel: (312)923-8500   Fax: (312)923-8509
Exec. Officer: Sharon R. Gorup, CAE

Ass'n of Internal Management Consultants (1971)
521 Fifth Ave., 35th Floor
New York, NY 10175-3598
Tel: (212)687-9463   Fax: (212)949-6571
Members: 250 individuals
Staff: 4
Annual Budget: $50-100,000
Exec. Secretary: Sonya Mendez

Historical Note
Established in Baltimore February 19, 1971 by forty-two charter members under the leadership of Walter J. Sistek of the Maryland National Bank. Incorporated in the State of New York in 1975. Individuals engaged in the practice of internal management consulting, with five or more years experience and operating at a senior or project leader level. Membership: $195/year (individual); $575/year (corporate), $125/year (additional corporate members).

Publications:
AIMC Forum. semi-a.
Membership Directory. a.

Meetings/Conferences:
Annual Meetings: Spring

Ass'n of Internat'l Agriculture and Rural Development (1964)
University of Illinois
109 Mumford Hall
Urbana, IL 61801
Tel: (217)333-1920   Fax: (217)244-6537
Members: 220 individuals
Staff: 1
Annual Budget: under $10,000
Secretary-Treasurer: Dr. Thomas A. McCowen

Historical Note
Formerly (1989) Ass'n of United States Directors of Internat'l Agriculture Programs. Members are international development professionals representing educational, research and extension interests in international agriculture. Affiliated with the Nat'l Ass'n of State Universities and Land Grant Colleges. Membership: $25/year.

Meetings/Conferences:
Annual Meetings: June/100

Ass'n of Internat'l Automobile Manufacturers (1964)
1001 19th St. North, Suite 1200
Arlington, VA 22209
Tel: (703)525-7788   Fax: (703)525-8817
Members: 18 manufacturers, 17 associates
Staff: 28
Annual Budget: $5-10,000,000
President: Philip A. Hutchinson, Jr.
Washington Representative: Morry B. Markowitz

Historical Note
Founded as the Imported Car Group, it became Automobile Importers of America in 1965 and assumed its present name in 1990. AIAM is the trade ass'n for U.S. subsidiaries of the international automobile companies. AIAM acts as the industry's voice and serves as a clearinghouse for industry-related information. Its purpose is to communicate the true makeup of today's automobile industry.

Ass'n of Internat'l Education Administrators (1981)
Washington State Univ.
P.O. Box 645120
Pullman, WA 99164-5120
Tel: (509)335-0921   Fax: (509)335-1471
Members: 329 individuals
Staff: 1
Annual Budget: $100-250,000
Director/Secretariat: V.N. Bhatia, Ph.D.

Historical Note
AIEA represents C.E.O.s at institutions of higher learning dedicated to the advancement of international education. Membership: $300/year (institutional); $30/year (associate).

Publications:
AIEA Directory. a.
Internat'l Education Forum. semi-a. adv.

Meetings/Conferences:
1999 – Merida, Yukatan, Mexico(Hyatt Regency)/Feb. 11-14

Ass'n of Internat'l Health Researchers (1982)
Historical Note
Address unknown in 1997.

Ass'n of Internat'l Healthcare Recruiters and Employers (1993)
Historical Note
Organization defunct in 1998.

Ass'n of Internat'l Photography Art Dealers (1979)
1609 Connecticut Ave., N.W., Suite 200
Washington, DC 20009
Tel: (202)986-0105   *Fax:* (202)986-0448
Members: 120 individuals
Annual Budget: $500-1,000,000
Exec. Director: Kathleen Ewing

Historical Note
Galleries and private dealers in fine art photography who have been in business for at least three years. Membership: $700/year, plus initiation fee (organization).

Publications:
Membership Directory. bien.
On Collecting Photographs. quinquen.
Show Art Catalogue. a. adv.

Meetings/Conferences:
Annual Meetings: Spring Trade Show in February or March

Ass'n of Investment Management Sales Executives (1978)
1211 Connecticut Ave., N.W., Suite 812
Washington, DC 20036-2701
Tel: (202)296-3560   *Fax:* (202)452-9370
Toll Free: (800)343 - 5659
E-Mail: psvenden@aimse.com
Web Site: http://www.aimse.com
Members: 1,400 individuals
Staff: 3
Annual Budget: $500-1,000,000
Exec. Director: Norbert Kraich

Historical Note
Incorporated in 1981, AIMSE provides marketing and sales educational programs for its members. Membership: $150/year (individual).

Publications:
Advisor Newsletter. q.
Membership Directory. a.

Meetings/Conferences:
Annual Meetings: April
1999 – Laquinta, CA(LaQuinta Resort)/May 2-5

Ass'n of Iron and Steel Engineers (1907)
Three Gateway Center, Suite 1900
Pittsburgh, PA 15222
Tel: (112)201 6222   *Fax:* (412)281-4657
Web Site: http://www.aise.org
Members: 11,500 individuals
Staff: 36
Annual Budget: $2-5,000,000
Managing Director: Lawrence G. Maloney
Advertising Sales and Convention Manager: Sam H. Seem
Manager of Finance and Administration: John L. Pierce

Historical Note
Originated in 1907 as the Ass'n of Iron and Steel Electrical Engineers; became the Ass'n of Iron and Steel Engineers in 1936. Promotes the technical and engineering phases of the production and processing of iron and steel. Membership: $60/year (domestic); $90/year (foreign)

Publications:
Convention Proceedings. a.
Directory of Iron and Steel Plants. a. adv.
Iron and Steel Engineer. m. adv.

Meetings/Conferences:
Annual Meetings: Fall/20,000
1999 – Cleveland, OH(Convention Center)/Sept. 27-30/20000
2000 – Chicago, IL(Navy Pier)/Sept. 11-13/5000
2001 – Cleveland, OH(Convention Center)/Sept. 24-27/20000

Ass'n of Jesuit Colleges and Universities (1970)
One Dupont Circle, N.W., Suite 405
Washington, DC 20036-1110
Tel: (202)862-9893   *Fax:* (202)862-8523
E-Mail: BLKROBE@AOL.COM
Web Site: http://www.ajcunet.edu
Members: 28 institutions
Staff: 4
Annual Budget: $100-250,000
President: Charles L. Currie, S.J.
Director, Federal Relations: Cyndy Littlefield
Director, Publications: George Chen

Historical Note
Formed in 1970 when the Jesuit Educational Ass'n split to form the Ass'n of Jesuit Colleges and Universities and the Jesuit Secondary Education Ass'n. Absorbed the Jesuit Research Council of America. A national voluntary service organization whose institutional members are the 28 Jesuit colleges and universities in the United States. The association respresents its members in shaping public policy for higher education, monitoring regulatory activities of government executive agencies and following the judicial decisions of the court.

Publications:
ACJU Higher Education Report. m.
AJCU/JSEA Directory. a.
International Resource Book.
Jesuit Degree Programs.

Meetings/Conferences:
Semi-annual Meetings: Small and closed to public

Ass'n of Jewish Aging Services (1960)
316 Pennsylvania Ave., S.E., Suite 402
Washington, DC 20003-1175
Tel: (202)543-7500   *Fax:* (202)543-4090
Members: 175 facilities
Staff: 2
Annual Budget: $500-1,000,000
President: Lawrence M. Zippin

Historical Note
Formerly (1997) the North American Ass'n of Jewish Homes and Housing for the Aging. AJAS members are non-profit organizations providing long term care and housing services for the aged.

Publications:
Directory. bien.
The Scribe. q.

Meetings/Conferences:
1999 – Colorado Springs, CO/March 13-16
2000 – Los Angeles, CA(Beverly Hilton)/Feb. 17-21/500

Ass'n of Jewish Book Publishers (1962)
c/o Jewish Lights Publishing
P.O. Box 237
Woodstock, VT 05091
Tel: (802)457-4000   *Fax:* (802)457-4004
Members: 40 publishing houses
Staff: 1
Annual Budget: under $10,000
President: Stuart M. Matlins

Historical Note
Membership: $85/year.

Meetings/Conferences:
Annual Meetings: Not held

Ass'n of Jewish Center Professionals (1918)
15 East 26th St., 10th Floor
New York, NY 10010-1505
Tel: (212)532-4949   *Fax:* (212)481-4174
Members: 1,100 individuals
Staff: 2
Annual Budget: $50-100,000
Exec. Director: Marilyn Altman

Historical Note
Formerly (1988) Ass'n of Jewish Center Workers.

Publications:
Conference Papers. a.
Kesher. q.
Max Tasgal Lecture.

Meetings/Conferences:
Annual Meetings: Summer

Ass'n of Jewish Family and Children's Agencies (1972)
3086 State Hwy. 27, Suite 1
Box 248
Kendall Park, NJ 08824-0248
Tel: (732)971-0909   *Fax:* (732)821-0493
Toll Free: (800)634 - 7346
E-Mail: AJFCA@aol.com
Web Site: http://www.ajfca.org
Members: 165 agencies
Staff: 8
Annual Budget: $500-1,000,000
Exec. V President: Bert J. Goldberg

Historical Note
Members are local Jewish family and children service agencies in the U.S. and Canada.

Publications:
Directory. a.
Executive Digest.

Meetings/Conferences:
Annual Meetings: April
1999 – Orlando, FL(Omni Rosen)
2000 – Seattle, WA(Madison)
2001 – Montreal, Canada(Boneventure)
2002 – San Antonio, TX

Ass'n of Jewish Family and Children's Agency Professionals (1965)
Historical Note
Became the Jewish Social Service Professionals Ass'n in 1996.

Ass'n of Jewish Libraries (1965)
15 E. 26th St. Room 1034
New York, NY 10010-1579
Tel: (212)678-8092   *Fax:* (212)678-8998
Members: 1,095 individuals
Staff: 1
Annual Budget: $25-50,000
President: Esther Nussbaum

Historical Note
Merger of the Jewish Library Ass'n (founded in 1946) and the Jewish Librarians Ass'n (founded in 1962). Membership: $30/year.

Publications:
AJL Newsletter. q. adv.
Judaica Librarianship. irreg. adv.

Meetings/Conferences:
Annual Meetings: June

Ass'n of Junior Leagues Internat'l (1921)
660 First Ave., 2nd Fl
New York, NY 10016-3295
Tel: (212)683-1515   *Fax:* (212)481-7196
E-Mail: info@ajli.org
Members: 192,000 individuals, 293 leagues
Staff: 50
Annual Budget: $5-10,000,000
Exec. Director: Holly Sloan, CAE
Director, Communications: Liz W. Quinlan
Director, Finance: Abraham A. Speiser

Historical Note
The first Junior League was established in New York City in 1901 to promote volunteer service in the settlement houses of the city. They founded the Junior League for the Promotion of Settlement Movements, later shortened to the Junior League. Subsequently, women in Boston, Brooklyn, Portland, Baltimore, Chicago and Cleveland began to organize Junior Leagues. From work in the settlement houses, early Junior Leagues rapidly expanded their programs to found well baby clinics, conduct classes in home nursing, establish orphanages and organize garment factories to employ needy women. The New York Junior League started the first residence for young working women. As Leagues multiplied, the need for an overall organization was recognized and, in 1921 the Association of the Junior Leagues of America was incorporated with 24 Leagues as charter members. Became the Ass'n of Junior Leagues in 1971 and added Internat'l in 1989. AJLI helps each member League to fulfill its mission, of promoting voluntarism, developing the potential of women, and improving communities through programs and activities.

Publications:
Association Update. 9/year.
What Works. 2/year.

Meetings/Conferences:
Annual Meetings: Spring/850
1999 – St. Louis, MO/April 21-24

Ass'n of Knitted Fabrics Manufacturers (1935)
c/o Steinbrecher & Ross
100 E. 42nd St.
New York, NY 10017
Tel: (212)867-5720   *Fax:* (212)986-8857
Members: 8 companies
Staff: 1
Annual Budget: under $10,000
Exec. Director: Jeffrey Russ

Ass'n of Labor Relations Agencies (1952)
110 Second St., S.E.
Room LA 200
Washington, DC 20540
Tel: (202)724-9250   *Fax:* (202)426-1913
Web Site: http://www.alra.org
Members: 65 agencies
Annual Budget: $50-100,000
President: Pamela Talkin

Historical Note
Formerly (1963) the Ass'n of State Mediation Agencies, and (1978) the Ass'n of Labor Mediation Agencies. Member agencies include those at the federal, state and local levels in the U.S. and federal and provincial levels in Canada. Has no paid officers or full-time staff. Membership: $250/year (organization/company).

Publications:
ALRA Advisor. q. adv.

Meetings/Conferences:
Annual Meetings: July/300
1999 – Phoenix, AZ

Ass'n of Latina and Latino Anthropologists
Historical Note
A section of the American Anthropological Ass'n.

Ass'n of Leadership Educators (1990)
ND State Univ., 311 Morril Hall
P.O. Box 5437
Fargo, ND 58105-5437
Tel: (701)231-9688   *Fax:* (701)231-8378
E-Mail: hdfndi@ndsuext.nodak.edu
Web Site: http://www.aces.uiuc.edu/ ~ ALE
Members: 200 individuals
Annual Budget: under $10,000
President: Karen Zotz

Historical Note
ALE members are educators with an interest in leadership development curricula. Membership: $50/year (individual).

Publications:
Annual Conference Proceedings. a.
Newsletter. q.

Meetings/Conferences:
1999 – San Diego, CA/July 8-11

Ass'n of Legal Administrators (1971)
175 E. Hawthorn Pkwy., Suite 325
Vernon Hills, IL 60061-1428
Tel: (847)816-1212   *Fax:* (847)816-1213
Members: 8,800 individuals
Staff: 32
Annual Budget: $2-5,000,000
Exec. Director: John J. Michalik
Director, Conferences and Meetings: Nancy M. Guthrie
Director, Professional Development: Pamela A. Strong
Director, Member Services: Jan M. Waugh

Historical Note
Members are individuals responsible for the management and administration of private law firms, corporate legal departments and government agencies. Membership: $240/year (individual).

Publications:
ALA News. 6/year. adv.
Compensation Survey. a.
Directory. a. adv.
Legal Management: Journal of the Ass'n of Administrators. 6/year. adv.

Meetings/Conferences:
Annual Meetings: Spring/1,700
1999 – Chicago, IL(Sheraton and Navy Pier)/April 19-22
2000 – Denver, CO(Adams Mark)/May 8-11
2001 – Baltimore, MD(Hyatt)/May 22-25
2002 – San Antonio, TX(Marriott)/May 21-24

Ass'n of Life Insurance Counsel (1913)
200 E. Berry St.
Fort Wayne, IN 46802
Tel: (219)455-5582   *Fax:* (219)455-5403
Members: 900 individuals
Annual Budget: $50-100,000
Secretary-Treasurer: J. Michael Keefer

Historical Note
Legal counsels of life insurance companies. Membership: $100/yr.
(individual).

Publications:
Proceedings of the ALIC. trien.

Meetings/Conferences:
Annual Meetings: May, in White Sulphur Springs,
WV(Greenbrier)
1999 – /May 23-25
2000 – /May 21-23
2001 – /May 20-22
2002 – /May 19-21

Ass'n of Literary Scholars and Critics (1994)
2039 Shattuck Ave., Suite 202
Berkeley, CA   94704-1116
Tel: (517)772-7228   Fax: (510)849-2492
E-Mail: alitsc@aol.com
Members: 2,000 individuals
Staff: 1
Annual Budget: $100-250,000
Exec. Director: Jeffrey Staiger

Historical Note
A professional society for the study of literature, ALSC serves as a
forum for anyone with serious critical or scholarly interests in
literature. Membership: $25/year (individual).

Publications:
ALSC Journal. q.
ALSC Newsletter. q.

Meetings/Conferences:
Annual Meetings: Fall

Ass'n of Local Air Pollution Control Officials (1971)
444 North Capitol St., N.W., Suite 307
Washington, DC   20001
Tel: (202)624-7864   Fax: (202)624-7863
E-Mail: 4clnair@sso.org
Web Site: http://www.4cleanair.org
Members: 220 local air pollution agencies
Staff: 4
Annual Budget: $100-250,000
Exec. Director: S. William Becker

Historical Note
ALAPCO represents air pollution control officials from over 150
major metropolitan areas across the United States. Shares
headquarters and staff with the State and Territorial Air Pollution
Program Administrators. In addition to its semi-annual meetings for
members, the association sponsors an annual Conference, Air
Toxics Control Conference.

Publications:
Washington Update. m.

Meetings/Conferences:
Semi-annual Meetings: Spring and Fall & Annual Air Toxics
Conf.
1999 – Tempe, AZ(Buttes)/May 15-19/150

Ass'n of Local Housing Finance Agencies (1982)
1200 19th St., N.W., Suite 300
Washington, DC   20036-2422
Tel: (202)857-1197   Fax: (202)857-1111
E-Mail: www.cais.com/alhfa
Web Site: http://www.cais.net/alhfa
Members: 350 organizations
Staff: 4
Annual Budget: $250-500,000
Exec. Director: John C. Murphy

Historical Note
Regular members of ALHFA are primarily county and city agencies
which finance, directly or indirectly, affordable housing through a
variety of means: tax-exempt and taxable bonds, federal grant
programs, and state and local subsidies. Affiliate members are
organizations providing technical assistance to local agencies.
Serves as an advocate before Congress and the Executive branch on
affordable housing issues. Provides a forum for information
exchange and capacity building.

Publications:
ALHFA Conference Program. bi-a. adv.
ALHFA Membership Directory. a.
Newsletter. bi-m.

Meetings/Conferences:
Semi-annual Meetings: Spring and Fall
1999 – San Antonio, TX/April 8-10
1999 – San Francisco, CA/Nov. 18-20

Ass'n of Local Telecommunications Services (1987)
888 17th St., N.W., Suite 900
Washington, DC   20006-3307
Tel: (202)969-2587   Fax: (202)969-2581
E-Mail: savage@alts.org
Web Site: http://www.alts.org
President: Heather Gold

Historical Note
ALTS promotes the opening of local telecommunications market to
full and fair facilities-based competition.

Meetings/Conferences:
1999 – Nashville, TN(Renaissance)/May 3-5

Ass'n of Local Television Stations (1972)
1320 19th St., N.W., Suite 300
Washington, DC   20036
Tel: (202)887-1970   Fax: (202)887-0950
Web Site: http://www.altv.org
Members: 300 companies
Staff: 7
Annual Budget: $2-5,000,000
President: James B. Hedlund
Dir., Congressional Relations: Angela Giroux
V. President, Legal/Legislative Affairs: David L. Donovan
V. President, Finance: Alan Petronio

V. President and General Counsel: James J. Popham

Historical Note
Founded as Ass'n of Independent Television Stations; assumed its
current name in 1996. Members include commercial local television
broadcasting stations not primarily affiliated with a national
broadcasting network; national sales representatives; program
distributors, and other related broadcasting companies and
organizations. Primary purpose is to act and speak for its members'
concerns before agencies of the government and in industry
councils.

Publications:
Capital Report. bi-w.

Meetings/Conferences:
Annual Meetings: Always in January/February
1999 – New Orleans, LA

Ass'n of Lutheran College Faculties (1935)
Luther College, Dept. of Nursing
700 College Dr.,
Decorah, IA   52101
Tel: (319)387-1453
E-Mail: kubeshdt@luther.edu
Members: 50 college faculties
Annual Budget: under $10,000
President: Donna Kubesh, Ph.D., RN

Historical Note
Interested faculty who teach in Lutheran church-related colleges
and universities.

Meetings/Conferences:
Annual Meetings: 1st weekend in October

Ass'n of Lutheran Secondary Schools (1944)
12555 Ryewater
Houston, TX   77089
Tel: (281)464-8299
Members: 70 schools
President: David Sommermeyer

Historical Note
Membership fees based on student enrollment.

Publications:
STYLE Newsletter. q.

Meetings/Conferences:
Annual Meetings: Second weekend in March
1999 – Portland, OR/March 4-8
2000 – San Antonio, TX/Feb. 4-8

Ass'n of Machinery and Equipment Appraisers (1983)
315 S. Patrick St.
Alexandria, VA   22314
Tel: (703)836-7900   Fax: (703)836-9303
E-Mail: amea@amea.org
Web Site: http://www.amea.org
Members: 285 individuals
Staff: 2
Annual Budget: $50-100,000
Exec. Director: Christine V. Druhan

Historical Note
Members are appraisers of metalworking machinery and capital
equipment. Conducts accreditation and certification programs for
members offering Level I Accredited Membership and Level II
Certified Membership. Membership: $300/year.

Publications:
AMEA Appraiser. q.
Auction Summaries. bi-a.
Membership Directory. a.

Meetings/Conferences:
Annual Meetings: May
1999 – Tucson, AZ

Ass'n of Major City Building Officials (1974)
505 Huntmar Park Drive, Suite 210
Herndon, VA   22070
Tel: (703)437-0100   Fax: (703)481-3596
Members: 36 cities and counties
Staff: 1
Annual Budget: under $10,000
Secretariat: Jill Moreschi

Historical Note
Provides a forum for the building officials of major cities and
counties in the U.S. to discuss mutual interests and seek solutions
to common problems in building code and public safety issues.
Membership: $300/year.

Meetings/Conferences:

Ass'n of Managed Care Dentists
1223 Wilshire Blvd., Suite 483
Santa Monica, CA   90403
Toll Free: (800)864 - 6848
Web Site: http://www.dentalgroup.com/amcd/
President: Gegory Kaplan, DDS

Historical Note
AMCD is a nonprofit organization that provides education,
representation and a forum for dentists. The association strives to
develop improved patient care, enhanced business strategies and
patient satisfaction.

Ass'n of Managed Healthcare Organizations (1983)
One Bridge Plaza, Suite 325
Ft. Lee, NJ   07024
Tel: (201)947-5545   Fax: (201)947-3808
Web Site: http://www.amho.org
Members: 1,100 individuals
Staff: 5
Annual Budget: $1-2,000,000
Exec. Director: Brad Kalish
Editor: Christina Li
V. President: Julie de Peyster

Historical Note
Formerly (1996) American Ass'n of Preferred Provider
Organizations. Members are actively involved in preferred provider
organizations. Membership: $495/year (individual), $995/year
(organization).

Publications:
Directory of Operational PPOs. a.
Healthcare Innovations, the Journal of the AAPPO. bi-m.
Summary of State Legislation. a.

Meetings/Conferences:
1999 – Miami, FL(Wyndham)/Oct. 10-12

Ass'n of Management (1975)
Historical Note
Name changed to Ass'n of Management and Internat'l Ass'n of
Management (AoM/IAoM) in 1996.

Ass'n of Management Analysts in State and Local Government (1963)
c/o Fels Center of Government
University of Pennsylvania
Philadelphia, PA   19104
Tel: (215)898-8216
Members: 650 individuals
Annual Budget: $25-50,000
Secretary-Treasurer: Tom Mills

Historical Note
Founded at the Univ. of Connecticut to promote the administrative
specialization of management analysis, primarily among state and
local governments. Has no paid staff; officers are elected annually.
Membership: $30/year (individual); $65/year (organization).

Publications:
MASLIG Messenger. q.

Meetings/Conferences:
Semi-Annual Meeting: Philadelphia, PA/Spring and
Rensselaer, NY/Fall

Ass'n of Management Consulting Firms (1929)
521 Fifth Ave., 35th Floor
New York, NY   10175-3598
Tel: (212)697-9693   Fax: (212)949-6571
E-Mail: info@amcf.org
Web Site: http://www.amcf.org
Members: 50 firms
Staff: 6
Annual Budget: $1-2,000,000
President and Exec. Director: Dudley C. Smith, CMC

Historical Note
Previously know as ACME-World Ass'n of Management Consulting
Firms; merged with Institute of Management Consultants to form
Council of Consulting Organizations in 1989. Oldest and largest
organization representing management consulting firms in the
world. Members are professional management consulting firms that
must meet demanding membership requirements and pledge to
uphold a strict and enforced code of professional conduct and
standards of practice. ACME member firms, 20% of which are
foreign-based, employ over 55,000 management consultants in
over 100 countries worldwide and have annual billings in excess of
$5 billion.

Publications:
ACME Carrer Kit.
ACME Directory of Members.
ACME Newsletter.
ACME U. S.
How to Select & Use Management Consultants.

Meetings/Conferences:
Annual Meetings: Fall

Ass'n of Management/Internat'l Ass'n of Management (1975)
P.O. Box 64841
Virginia Beach, VA   23467-4841
Tel: (757)482-2273   Fax: (757)482-0325
E-Mail: aomgt@infi.net
Web Site: http://www.aom-iaom.com
&http://cob.isu.edu/aom/
Members: 3,500 individuals
Staff: 12
Annual Budget: $250-500,000
President & C.E.O.: Dr. Willem A. Hamel, Ph.D.
Comptroller: T.J. Mills

Historical Note
Formerly the Ass'n of Management (AoM). Assumed its present
name in 1996. AoM/IAoM is a professional organization of
academic professionals and practitioners of management who are
taking scholarly pursuits toward bridging the management gap
worldwide. Membership: $85/year.

Publications:
AoM/IAoM Proceedings. a. adv.
Global Information Systems. q. adv.
Internat'l Association of Management Journal. q. adv.
Journal of Computer Science & Information Management. q.
adv.
Journal of Information Technology Management. q. adv.
Journal of Management Systems. q. adv.
Leadership and Leaders. q. adv.

Meetings/Conferences:
1999 – San Diego, CA/Aug. 5-8/900
2000 – San Antonio, TX/Aug. 2-5

Ass'n of Marine Engine Manufacturers (1945)
1819 L St., N.W., Suite 700
Washington, DC   20036-3830
Tel: (202)861-1180   Fax: (202)861-1181
Members: 34 companies
Staff: 2
Annual Budget: $500-1,000,000
V. President, Government Relations: Mick Blackistone
Director, Environmental & Safety Compliance: John McKnight

Historical Note
Established as the Outboard Motor Manufacturers Association, AMEM became the Marine Engine Manufacturers Ass'n in 1978 and assumed its present name in 1985. It is a ''partner-affiliate'' of the Nat'l Marine Manufacturers Ass'n, which provides AMEM with administrative support and with which it shares offices.

Meetings/Conferences:
Annual Meetings: Usually Chicago, IL/September

Ass'n of Master of Business Administration Executives *(1970)*
5 Summit Place
Branford, CT   06405
Tel: (203)315-5221   *Fax:* (203)483-6186
Members: 15,000 individuals
Staff: 11
President: Albert P. Hegyi

Historical Note
A membership organization providing career information and professional services.

Publications:
AMBA Network News. q.
MBA Employment Guide. adv. adv.

Ass'n of Maternal and Child Health Programs *(1944)*
1220 19th St., N.W., Suite 801
Washington, DC   20036-2435
Tel: (202)775-0436   *Fax:* (202)775-0061
Web Site: www.amchp1.org
Members: 400 individuals
Staff: 16
Annual Budget: $1-2,000,000
Exec. Director: Catherine A. Hess
Dir., Communications & Membership: Katrina Norfleet Brown
Asst. Director, Legislative Affairs: Betsy Langer
Director, Finance and Administration: Tess Esposito
Asst. Exec. Director for Policy and Programs: Karen VanLangdeghem

Historical Note
Established as the Ass'n of State and Territorial Maternal and Child Health and Crippled Children Directors, it assumed its present name in 1987. Membership: $50/year (individual); $250/year (associate).

Publications:
AMCHP Updates. 6/year.
Newsletter. q.

Meetings/Conferences.
Annual Meetings: Winter
1999 – Washington, DC/March 13-17

Ass'n of Medical Diagnostic Manufacturers *(1973)*
555 13th St., N.W.
Washington, DC   20004-1109
Tel: (202)637-6837   *Fax:* (202)637-5910
Web Site: http://www.amdm.org
Members: 75 companies
Staff: 1
Annual Budget: $25-50,000
Administrator: Debra Aleknavage

Historical Note
Formerly (1995) Ass'n of Microbiological Diagnostic Manufacturers. Membership open to any manufacturer, processor, repackager or distributor of medical diagnostic devices or device components. Membership: $500-1,250/year, based upon number of employees.

Publications:
AMDM News. q.

Meetings/Conferences:
Annual Meetings: October

Ass'n of Medical Education and Research in Substance Abuse *(1976)*
Historical Note
Address unknown in 1997.

Ass'n of Medical Illustrators *(1945)*
1819 Peachtree St., N.E., Suite 620
Atlanta, GA   30309-1848
Tel: (404)350-7900   *Fax:* (404)351-3348
Members: 900 individuals
Staff: 6
Annual Budget: $250-500,000
Exec. Director: William H. Just, CAE, CMP

Historical Note
Incorporated in the State of Illinois. AMI is dedicated to enhancing the professionalism and abilities of its members, and to advancing education and communication in medicine and health related fields. AMI has an international membership and operates an official placement service. Membership: $160/year.

Publications:
Medical Illustration Sourcebook. a.
Membership Directory. a.
Newsletter. bi-m. adv.
The Journal of Biocommunication. q.

Meetings/Conferences:
Annual Meetings: Late Summer

Ass'n of Medical School Pediatric Department Chairmen *(1961)*
c/o American Board of Pediatrics
111 Silver Cedar Court
Chapel Hill, NC   27514
Tel: (919)942-1993   *Fax:* (919)929-9255
Members: 145 individuals
Staff: 1
Annual Budget: $50-100,000
Coordinator: Jean M. Bartholomew

Historical Note
Chairmen of pediatrics of U.S. and Canadian accredited medical schools. Membership: $425/year (institution).

Publications:
Directory. a.

Meetings/Conferences:
Annual Meetings: Spring
1999 – Wesley Chapel, FL(Saddlebrook)/March 3-9
2000 – San Diego, CA(Rancho Bernardo Inn)/200
2001 – San Diego, CA(Sheraton San Diego)

Ass'n of Meeting Professionals *(1982)*
1255 23rd St., N.W.
Washington, DC   20037
Tel: (202)331-4267   *Fax:* (202)833-3636
Members: 400 individuals
Staff: 3
Annual Budget: $100-250,000
Exec. Director: Christopher M. Murphy

Historical Note
Membership: $110/year (individual); $185-295/year (organization/company).

Publications:
AMPS Directory. a. adv.
AMPS Update. q.

Ass'n of Membership and Marketing Executives *(1960)*
Historical Note
Address unknown in 1997.

Ass'n of Mental Health Administrators *(1959)*
Historical Note
Merged with Nat'l Council for Community Behavioral Healthcare in 1998.

Ass'n of Mental Health Clergy
Historical Note
Became Ass'n of Professional Chaplans in 1998.

Ass'n of Mental Health Librarians *(1964)*
c/o American Psychiatric Ass'n
1400 K St., N.W.
Washington, DC   20005
Tel: (202)682-6057
Members: 100 individuals
Annual Budget: under $10,000
President: Steve Parsons

Historical Note
Formed (1964) as the Soc. of Mental Health Librarians, it assumed its present name in 1980. The Ass'n provides an opportunity for the exchange of information and the continuing education of its members. Membership: $15/year.

Meetings/Conferences:
Annual Meetings: Fall

Ass'n of Mercy Colleges *(1982)*
St.Joseph College
1678 Asylum Avenue
West Hartford, CT   06117
Tel: (860)232-4571   *Fax:* (860)233-5695
Members: 19 colleges
President: Winifred Coleman

Historical Note
AMC members are colleges and universities established by the Religious Sister of Mercy.

Meetings/Conferences:
Annual Meetings: in conjunction with ACCU/summer

Ass'n of Metropolitan Sewerage Agencies *(1970)*
1000 Connecticut Ave., N.W., Suite 410
Washington, DC   20036-5302
Tel: (202)833-2672   *Fax:* (202)833-4657
Web Site: http://www.amsa-cleanwater.org
Members: 200 agencies
Staff: 13
Annual Budget: $2-5,000,000
Exec. Director: Ken Kirk, CAE
Manager, Communications and Public Affairs: Clavoine Bodin
Director, Government Affairs: Sam Hadeed
Manager, Conferences and Meetings: Linda Lohneis

Historical Note
Incorporated in the District of Columbia in 1970. Membership consists of sewerage agencies. Formed to exchange technical data of mutual benefit and deal with the Federal Government on environmental and regulatory matters. Membership:$1,500-$25,000 for individual municipal utilities.

Publications:
AMSA Clean Water News. m.
Legal Alert.
Legislative Alert. m.
Membership Directory. a.
Regulatory Alert. m.

Meetings/Conferences:
Annual Meetings: Spring in Washington, DC/300
1999 – Washington, DC(Marriott at Metro Center)/May 22-26
2000 – Washington, DC(Marriott at Metro Center)/May 20-24

Ass'n of Metropolitan Water Agencies *(1981)*
1717 K St., N.W., Suite 801
Washington, DC   20036
Tel: (202)331-2820   *Fax:* (202)785-1845
Members: 117 agencies
Staff: 4
Annual Budget: $250-500,000
Exec. Director: Diane VanDe Hei
Conference Coordinator: Eugenia Cadena

Historical Note
Established and incorporated in the District of Columbia, AMWA members are metropolitan, county and city water supply agencies serving populations of more than 150,000. Membership: based on population served.

Publications:
AMWA Monthly Report. m.

Meetings/Conferences:
Annual Meetings: Fall

Ass'n of Mezzanine Manufacturers *(1989)*
8720 Red Oak Blvd.
Charlotte, NC   28217-3992
Tel: (704)676-1190   *Fax:* (704)676-1199
Web Site: http://www.mhi.org
Members: 13 companies
Staff: 2
Managing Director: John B. Nofsinger

Historical Note
A product section of Material Handling Industry of America.

Publications:
Mezzanine Users Guide. irreg.

Meetings/Conferences:

Ass'n of Microbiological Diagnostic Manufacturers
Historical Note
Became Ass'n of Medical Diagnostic Manufacturers in 1996.

Ass'n of Military Banks of America *(1959)*
10205 Eisenhower Lane
Great Falls, VA   22066
Tel: (703)759-4037
Members: 110 banks
Annual Budget: $50-100,000
Exec. V. President: Wendell McHenry, Jr.

Historical Note
AMBA members are banks specializing in providing services to military personnel and banks operating on military bases.

Publications:
AMBA Newsletter. bi-m.
Banking Institutions Serving Military and Government Personnel. a.

Meetings/Conferences:
Annual Meetings: Fall

Ass'n of Military Colleges and Schools of the U.S. *(1914)*
9429 Garden Ct.
Potomac, MD   20854-3964
Tel: (301)765-0695   *Fax:* (301)983-0583
Members: 42 institutions
Staff: 1
Annual Budget: $25-50,000
Exec. Director: Dr. Lewis Sorley

Historical Note
Members are educational institutions with regionally accredited academic programs and Defense Department-approved military, naval, marine, or air programs. Absorbed the Nat'l Ass'n of Military Schools in 1972. Membership: varies from $500-1000/year, depending upon the size of the student body.

Publications:
Annual Meeting Program. a. adv.
Newsletter. m.

Meetings/Conferences:
Annual Meetings: March
1999 – Alexandria, VA(Holiday Inn Select)/Mar. 14-16/110

Ass'n of Military Surgeons of the U.S. *(1891)*
9320 Old Georgetown Road
Bethesda, MD   20814-1653
Tel: (301)897-8800   *Fax:* (301)530-5446
E-Mail: amsus@amsus.org
Web Site: http://www.amsus.org
Members: 11,000 individuals
Staff: 9
Annual Budget: $1-2,000,000
Exec. Director: RADM Frederic G. Sanford, MC, USN (R
Convention Manager: Linda L. Hines
Asst. Exec. Director: Col. Steven C. Mirick, USAF,MSC(R

Historical Note
Established in 1891 and incorporated by an act of Congress in 1903. Membership consists of health care professionals or civilians employed by the armed services, the Public Health Service or Dept. of Veterans Affairs, or medical consultants. Membership: $35-525 (individual), $500/year (institution).

Publications:
Military Medicine. m. adv.

Meetings/Conferences:
Annual Meetings: Fall/7,000
1999 – Anaheim, CA(Convention Center)/Nov. 7-12
2000 – Las Vegas, NV(Convention Center)/Nov. 5-10

Ass'n of Minority Health Professions Schools *(1981)*
507 Capitol Ct., N.E., Suite 200
Washington, DC   20002
Tel: (202)544-7499   *Fax:* (202)546-7105
Members: 8 schools
Staff: 1
Washington Representative: Dale P. Dirks

Historical Note
AMHPS assists its member institutions in expanding and enhancing educational opportunities for minorities in the health professions. AMHPS also seeks to encourage majority institutions to expand minority enrollment and to enhance health programs which will improve the health status of minority groups.

Ass'n of Modeling, Planning and Simulation

Historical Note
Defunct in 1996.

Ass'n of Moving Image Archivists *(1990)*
8949 Willshire Blvd.
Beverly Hills, CA 90211
Tel: (310)550-1363
E-Mail: amia@ix.netcom.com
Web Site: http://www.amianet.org
Members: 500 individuals
Annual Budget: $50-100,000
Secretary: Gregory Lukow

Historical Note
AMIA members are archivists, scholars, and institutions concerned with the preservation of film and video resources. Founded as Film and Television Archives Advisory Committee; assumed its current name in 1990. Has no paid officers or full-time staff. Membership: $50/year (individual); $150/year (non-profit); $300/year (company).

Publications:
AMIA Newsletter. q. adv.

Meetings/Conferences:
1999 – Montreal, PQ, Canada/Nov. 1-6

Ass'n of Muslim Scientists and Engineers *(1969)*
Box 38
Plainfield, IN 46168
Tel: (317)839-8157   *Fax:* (317)839-1840
Members: 590 individuals
Staff: 1
Annual Budget: $25-50,000
Director: Iqbal Unus

Historical Note
Established and incorporated in Indiana. Membership: $25/year (regular); $15/year (student).

Publications:
AMSE Newsletter. bi-m. adv.
Directory of Members. irreg. adv.
Internat'l Journal of Science and Technology. semi-a. adv.
Proceedings of AMSE Annual Conference. a. adv.

Meetings/Conferences:
Annual Meetings: October

Ass'n of Muslim Social Scientists *(1972)*
P.O. Box 669
Herndon, VA 22070
Tel: (703)471-1133   *Fax:* (703)471-3922
E-Mail: amss@iiit.org
Members: 300 individuals
Annual Budget: under $10,000
Secretarial Assistant: Muggedar Khan

Historical Note
AMSS members are professors and graduate students in the social sciences, united to disseminate Islamic positions relevant to their various academic disciplines. Seeks to present an accurate portrayal and understanding of Islamic thought. Membership: $45/year (professional); $30/year (student).

Publications:
American Journal of Islamic Social Sciences. q. adv.

Meetings/Conferences:
Annual Meetings: October

Ass'n of Nat'l Advertisers *(1910)*
708 Third Ave.,
New York, NY 10017
Tel: (212)697-5950   *Fax:* (212)661-8057
Web Site: http://www.ana.net
Members: 250 companies
Staff: 35
Annual Budget: $2-5,000,000
President and C.E.O.: John J. Sarsen, Jr.
Senior V. President, Communications/Systems: Robin Webster
Senior V. President, Government Relations: Philip C. Shyposh
Senior V. President, Communications: Robert D. Liodice

Historical Note
Founded in 1910 as Ass'n of Nat'l Advertising Managers, it assumed its present name four years later. A.N.A. is dedicated exclusively to serving the interest of companies which advertise either regionally or nationally. Maintains a Washington office to lobby against restrictions of advertisers' rights. Membership fee based on advertiser's expenditures.

Publications:
Catalog of A. N.
Compendium of Legislative/Regulatory Issues. a.
The Advertiser. q.

Meetings/Conferences:
Annual Meetings: Fall
1999 – Amelia Island, FL(Ritz Carlton)/Oct. 2-6

Ass'n of Natural Resource Enforcement Trainers
c/o Nova Scotia Natural Resources
1701 Hollis St., Box 698
Halifax, NS B0N 2-S0
Tel: (902)424-8925
Members: 50 individuals
Exec. Director: Chuck Moore

Ass'n of Naval Aviation *(1975)*
2550 Huntington Ave., #201
Alexandria, VA 22303-1400
Tel: (703)960-2490   *Fax:* (703)960-4490
President: V.Adm. Richard C. Allen, USN(Ret.)

Historical Note
Seeks to support a strong U.S. maritime air posture. Membership: $35/year (individual), $2,000/year (organization/ company).

Publications:
Wings of Gold. q. adv.

Meetings/Conferences:
1999 – Washingto, DC
2000 – Pensacola, Fl

Ass'n of Naval R.O.T.C. Colleges and Universities *(1946)*
Box 270041 Administration Bldg.
University of Rochester
Rochester, NY 14627-0041
Tel: (716)275-4111   *Fax:* (716)275-8531
Members: 62 institutions
Staff: 1
Annual Budget: $10-25,000
Administrator: Sarah Williams

Historical Note
Membership: $200/year (institution).

Meetings/Conferences:
Annual Meetings: Fall/75-100
1999 – Pensacola, FL

Ass'n of Neurosurgical Physician Assistants *(1991)*
P.O. Box 559
Bernardsville, NJ 07924
Toll Free: (888)942 - 6772
E-Mail: surgicalpa@aol.com
Web Site: http://www.anspa.org
Annual Budget: under $10,000
Exec. Director: Susan Lusty

Historical Note
A specialty organization affiliated with the American Academy of Physician Assistants, ANSPA educates professionals and the lay public with respect to neurological surgery and the role of the physician assistant. Membership: $50/year (individual); $500/year (company).

Publications:
Member Directory. a.
Newsletter. q. adv.

Meetings/Conferences:
Annual Meetings: May

Ass'n of North American Missions *(1942)*
Historical Note
Address unknown in 1997.

Ass'n of Nurses in AIDS Care *(1987)*
11250 Roger Bacon Dr., Suite 8
Reston, VA 20190-5202
Tel: (703)925-0081   *Fax:* (703)435-4390
E-Mail: aidsnurses@aol.com
Web Site: http://www.anacnet.org/aids/
Members: 3,100 individuals
Staff: 7
Annual Budget: $500-1,000,000
Exec. Director: Randall C. Price, CAE
Director, Meetings: Amy Doyle
Administrator: Lisa J. Fox
Director, Finance: H. Allen Beam

Historical Note
ANAC members are nurses and other health professionals with an interest in the care of individuals with HIV. Membership: $60/year (individual); corporate dues vary.

Publications:
Journal of ANAC. q.
Newsletter. 4-8/yr.

Meetings/Conferences:
Annual Meetings: Fall
1999 – San Diego, CA(Sheraton)/800
2000 – Puerto Rico
2001 – Minneapolis, MN
2002 – San Francisco, CA

Ass'n of Occupational and Environmental Clinics *(1987)*
1010 Vermont Ave., N.W., Suite 513
Washington, DC 20005-1503
Tel: (202)347-4976   *Fax:* (202)347-4950
E-Mail: aoec@aoec.org
Web Site: http://occ-env-med.mc.duke.edu/oem/aoec.htm
Members: 300 individuals, 64 companies
Staff: 4
Annual Budget: $500-1,000,000
Exec. Director: Katherine H. Kirkland
Program Coordinator: Sheila Brown Arbury

Historical Note
Established to enhance practice of occupational/environmental medicine through information sharing and research. Membership criteria include commitment to teaching, research and public health response to occupational and environmental conditions. Individual membership is open to those who share the goals of AOEC. Membership: $40/year (individual), $250/year (clinic).

Publications:
Newsletter. q.

Meetings/Conferences:
Annual Meetings: Fall, in conjunction with American Public Health Ass'n
1999 – Chicago, IL

Ass'n of Occupational Health Professionals (in Healthcare)
11250 Roger Bacon Drive, Suite 8
Reston, VA 20190-5202
Tel: (703)437-4377   *Fax:* (703)435-4390
Toll Free: (800)362 - 4347
E-Mail: aohpi@aol.com
Web Site: http://www.aohpi.org/aohp/
Members: 1,561 individuals
Staff: 7
Annual Budget: $250-500,000

Exec. Director: Randall Price, CAE
Director, Communications: Peggy Gartner
Administrator: Maureen Thompson
Comptroller: Allen Beam

Historical Note
Formerly (1994) Ass'n of Hospital Employee Health Professionals. AOHP members are employee and occupational health professionals, safety officers, human resource administrators, risk managers, infection control practitioners and hospital administrators. Membership: $90/year (individual).

Publications:
Journal of the AOHP. bi-m. adv.

Meetings/Conferences:
1999 – Chicago, IL(Palmer House Hilton)/Oct. 6-9/400
2000 – Albuquerque, NM(Hyatt Regency)

Ass'n of Official Racing Chemists *(1947)*
P.O. Box 296, Pte. Claire
Quebec, H9R -4N9
Tel: (514)697-7578   *Fax:* (514)694-7421
E-Mail: aorc.mclellan@sumpatico.ca
Members: 150 individuals
Staff: 1
Annual Budget: $25-50,000
Exec. Director: Sharon K. McLellan

Historical Note
Formed in Chicago by a group of chemists from the United States and several other countries. The international membership consists of individuals concerned with detection of drugs in racing samples. Affiliated with the Ass'n of Racing Commissioners Internat'l. There are currently 150 active members and 15 emeritus and honorary members.

Publications:
Proceedings. a.

Meetings/Conferences:
1999 – New Orleans, LA/March 10-15
2000 – Cambridge, U.K./Aug. 1-8

Ass'n of Official Seed Analysts *(1908)*
P.O. Box 81152
Lincoln, NE 68501-1152
Tel: (402)476-3852   *Fax:* (402)476-6547
E-Mail: assoc@navix.net
Members: 55 individuals
Staff: 2
Annual Budget: $100-250,000
Account Administrator: Tami Greer

Historical Note
Established in 1908 by 16 states, the U.S. Department of Agriculture and Canada. Cooperates with the Internat'l Seed Testing Ass'n, the Soc. of Commercial Seed Technologists and the Commercial Seed Analysts Ass'n of Canada. Membership: $100/year (individual), $250/year (organization).

Publications:
Seed Technologist News.
Seed Technology. semi-a.

Meetings/Conferences:
Annual Meetings: Summer/250-300
1999 – Omaha, NE(Downtown Doubletree Hotel)

Ass'n of Official Seed Certifying Agencies *(1919)*
BARC
10300 Baltimore Ave., Bld. 003, Rm. 124
Beltsville, MD 20705
Tel: (301)504-5903   *Fax:* (301)504-6016
Members: 450 individuals, 45 agencies
Staff: 2
Annual Budget: $100-250,000
Exec. V. President: Dr. James Elgin

Historical Note
Formerly (1968) The Internat'l Crop Improvement Ass'n. Members are state seed certifying agencies and their employees.

Publications:
Annual Proceedings. a.
Newsletter. 3/yr.
Production Publications. irreg.
Variety Publications. irreg.

Meetings/Conferences:

Ass'n of Oil Pipe Lines *(1947)*
1101 Vermont Ave., N.W., Suite 604
Washington, DC 20005
Tel: (202)408-7970   *Fax:* (202)408-7983
E-Mail: aopl@aopl.org
Web Site: http://www.aopl.org
Members: 59 companies
Staff: 3
Annual Budget: $500-1,000,000
Exec. Director: Benjamin S. Cooper

Historical Note
Founded as the Committee for Pipe Line Companies, a voluntary, unincorporated association of common carrier pipeline companies, the name was later changed to the Committee for Oil Pipe Lines, and in 1960 to Ass'n of Oil Pipe Lines.

Publications:
Oil Pipelines of the U. S.
Shifts in Petroleum Transportation. a.

Meetings/Conferences:
Semi-Annual Meetings: Winter in Washington, DC and June
1999 – Traverse Village, MI(Grand Traverse)/June 27-29
2000 – Carlsbad, CA(La Costa)/June 18-20
2001 – Hot Springs, VA(The Homestead)/June 17-19

Ass'n of Oilwell Servicing Contractors *(1956)*
Historical Note
Became Ass'n of Energy Service Companies (AESC) in 1996.

Ass'n of Old Crows *(1964)*

1000 North Payne St.
Alexandria, VA 22314-1696
Tel: (703)549-1600   *Fax:* (703)549-2589
Web Site: http://www.aochq.org
Members: 17,000 individuals, 100 companies
Staff: 5
Annual Budget: $1-2,000,000
Exec. Director: Vern Luke
Director, Conventions: Carolyn Wood-Holmes
Director, Administration: Carole Vann
Director, Membership: Andy Vittoria

Historical Note
AOC is a professional association comprised of individuals engaged in the science of electronic warfare, information warfare and related disciplines. Members include scientists, engineers, managers, operators, educators, and military personnel in all grades. Grew from a similar World War II organization whose symbol was the raven. Membership: $25/year.

Publications:
Journal of Electronic Defense. m. adv.

Meetings/Conferences:
Annual Meetings: Fall/4,000
1999 – Anaheim, CA(Marriott)/Nov. 14-18

Ass'n of On-Line Professionals (1994)
6096 Franconia Road, Suite D
Alexandria, VA 22310
Tel: (703)924-5800   *Fax:* (703)924-5801
E-Mail: info@aop.org
Web Site: http://www.aop.org
Members: 700 individuals
Staff: 3
Annual Budget: $250-500,000
Exec. Director: David P. McClure
Director, Member Services: Susan Merkel

Historical Note
Membership: $150/year (individual);$1000-$25,000/year (company/organization).

Publications:
AOP Newsletter. m.

Meetings/Conferences:
Annual Meetings: Fall

Ass'n of Oncology Social Work (1984)
1910 E. Jefferson St.
Baltimore, MD 21205
Tel: (410)614-3990   *Fax:* (410)614-3991
Web Site: http://www.aosw.org
Members: 900 individuals
Annual Budget: $50-100,000
Admin. Coordinator: Kimberly Bell

Historical Note
Formerly the Nat'l Ass'n of Oncology Social Workers. AOSW was established to enable professional social workers in oncology to better address the needs of clients, practitioners, managers, educators and researchers in the cancer field. Membership: $85/year (full member); $65/year (student/retired).

Publications:
AOSW News Newsletter. q.
Journal of Psychosocial Oncology. q. adv.

Meetings/Conferences:
Annual Meetings: Spring/400
1999 – New Orleans, LA(Hyatt Regency)/May 26-29
2000 – Vancouver, British Columbia(Hyatt Regency)/April 5-8
2001 – Cleveland, OH

Ass'n of Operating Room Nurses (1954)
2170 S. Parker Road, Suite 300
Denver, CO 80231-5711
Tel: (303)755-6300   *Fax:* (303)750-2927
Toll Free: (800)755 - 2676
Web Site: http://www.aorn.org
Members: 43,000 individuals
Staff: 160
Exec. Director: Lola M. Fehr, CAE
Meetings & Event Manager: Jody Zeman
C.F.O.: Peter Derchang
Dep. Exec. Director: Pat Palmer, RN MS MNM
Director, Member Services: Jody Foss, CAE
Publisher: Warren Kolber
Manager, Exhibits: Christine Lindmark
Health Policy Analyst: Candace Romig
Corporate Director of Marketing: Fred Perner

Historical Note
Professional organization that unites its members by providing education, representation, and standards for quality patient care. Membership: $65/year (individual).

Publications:
AORN Journal. m. adv.
AORN Standards and Recommended Practices. a.
O. R.
Surgical Services Management. m. adv.

Meetings/Conferences:
Annual Meetings: Late Winter-Early Spring
1999 – San Francisco, CA/March 28-April 2
2000 – New Orleans, LA/April 2-7
2001 – Dallas, TX/March 11-16

Ass'n of Operative Millers (1895)
5001 College Blvd., Suite 104
Leawood, KS 66211
Tel: (913)338-3377   *Fax:* (913)338-3553
E-Mail: aom@sky.net
Members: 1,500 individuals
Staff: 3
Annual Budget: $250-500,000
Exec. V. President: Harvey L. McCray
Director, Ass'n Services: Roger D. Gelsinger

Historical Note
Millers, superintendents, engineers, plant managers, and others in the flour milling, cereal milling, and grain and seed industry. Membership: $100/year (domestic); $130/year (internat'l).

Publications:
Membership Directory. a. adv.
Technical Bulletin. m.

Meetings/Conferences:
Annual Meetings: Spring/1,000 May 6-10/1300

Ass'n of Optometric Educators (1970)
Historical Note
Address unknown in 1997.

Ass'n of Organ Procurement Organizations (1984)
8110 Gatehouse Road, Suite 101 West
Falls Church, VA 22042
Tel: (703)573-2676   *Fax:* (703)573-0578
Web Site: http://www.aopo.com
Members: 51 organizations
Staff: 2
Annual Budget: $250-500,000
Exec. Director: Daniel Whiteside, D.D.S.

Historical Note
AOPO members are organizations which obtain and transport vascular organs for transplantation. Membership: $4,500/year (organization).

Publications:
Newsletter Update. m.

Meetings/Conferences:
1999 – Providence, RI/June 16-18
2000 – Asheville, NC/June 7-9

Ass'n of Osteopathic Directors and Medical Educators (1962)
5550 Friendship Blvd., Suite 300
Chevy Chase, MD 20815
Tel: (301)968-4170   *Fax:* (301)968-4199
E-Mail: aodme@osreondg.org
Members: 150 individuals
Staff: 1
Annual Budget: $25-50,000
Exec. Director: David L. Kushner, CAE, CMP
Director, Government Relations: Paul Rettig

Historical Note
Formerly (1992) Academy of Osteopathic Directors of Medical Education. Members are medical directors and/or directors of medical education or other qualified individuals charged with this responsibility by the governing body of an osteopathic hospital. Grants fellowships and offers certificates of accomplishment in medical education. Administrative support provided by American Osteopathic Healthcare Ass'n. Membership: $200/year (active), $150/year (associate).

Publications:
Osteopathic Progress. bi-m. adv.

Meetings/Conferences:
1999 – Chicago, IL(The Drake Hotel)/April 24-27/100

Ass'n of Osteopathic State Executive Directors (1918)
3520 Guion Rd. Suite 202
Indianapolis, IN 46222-1672
Tel: (317)926-3009   *Fax:* (317)926-3984
Members: 58 individuals
Annual Budget: $10-25,000
President: Mike Claphan, CAE

Historical Note
Regular members are Osteopathic State executive directors; affiliate members include related medical associations. Has no paid officers or full-time staff.

Publications:
AOSED News. q. adv.

Meetings/Conferences:
Annual Meetings: Fall, with the American Osteopathic Ass'n
1999 – San Francisco, CANovember
2000 – Orlando, Fl/Oct. 29-Nov. 2/50

Ass'n of Otolaryngology Administrators (1982)
PO Box 315033
Iowa City, IA 52244-3150
Members: 760 individuals
Staff: 1
Annual Budget: $100-250,000
Exec. Secretary: Beth M. Williams

Historical Note
Active members are individuals responsible for the business aspects of an otolaryngology practice. Membership: $90/year.

Publications:
Oto's Scope. q. adv.

Meetings/Conferences:
Annual Meetings: Fall
1999 – New Orleans, LA/Sept. 23-26/210
2000 – Washington, DC/Sept. 21-24/210
2001 – Denver, CO/Sept. 6-9/210
2002 – San Diego, CA/Sept. 19-22/210

Ass'n of Outplacement Consulting Firms Internat'l
Historical Note
Became (1997) Ass'n of Career Management Consulting Firms Internat'l.

Ass'n of Paid Circulation Publications (1964)
P.O. Box 10669
Rockville, MD 20849-0669
Tel: (301)260-1646   *Fax:* (301)424-1253
Staff: 1
Annual Budget: $10-25,000
Exec. Director: Kimberly Scott

Historical Note
Established in 1964 as the Paid Circulation Committee, it changed its name in 1965 to the Paid Circulation Council. In 1974 it became the Ass'n of Second Class Mail Publications, in 1979 the Ass'n of Second Class Mail Publishers and in 1982 assumed its present name. Members are national periodical publishers and associated businesses.

Publications:
Washington Report. m.

Ass'n of Paroling Authorities, Internat'l (1961)
Northwest Corner, Courthouse Square
P.O. Box 211
California, MO 65018
Tel: (314)796-2113   *Fax:* (314)796-2114
E-Mail: ghdh@aol.comm
Members: 350 individuals
Staff: 1
Annual Budget: $50-100,000
Exec. Secretary: Gail D. Hughes

Historical Note
Affiliate of the American Correctional Ass'n. Membership is made up of paroling authorities, which includes both individuals and agencies. Membership: $50/year (individual) and $300/year (agency).

Publications:
APAI News. q.

Meetings/Conferences:
1999 – Biloxi, MS(Isle of Capri)/April 18-21/150
2000 – Canada/400

Ass'n of Part-Time Professionals (1978)
7700 Leesburg Pike, Suite 216
Falls Church, VA 22043-2615
Tel: (703)734-7975   *Fax:* (703)734-7405
Members: 750 individuals
Staff: 4
Annual Budget: $25-50,000
C.F.O.: Laura B. King

Historical Note
Members are individuals and organizations concerned with flexible work options. Encourages employers to hire professionals on a permanent part-time basis and to pay pro-rated benefits. Incorporated in the Commonwealth of Virginia. Membership: $20-45/year (individual); $45-75/year (company).

Publications:
Working Options Newsletter. m.

Meetings/Conferences:
Annual Meetings: Winter

Ass'n of Partners for Public Lands (1977)
8375 Jumpers Hole Road, Suite 104
Millersville, MD 21108-1255
Tel: (410)647-9001   *Fax:* (410)647-9003
E-Mail: appl@nps.gov
Members: 72 organizations
Staff: 4
Annual Budget: $250-500,000
Exec. Director: Paula A. Degen

Historical Note
APPL supports its members in their missions of service and stewardship of America's public lands through education, information, and representation. APPL provides training courses, publications, a biennial convention and trade show, and other programs to foster professional management practices and facilitate partnership among members and the federal agencies they serve.

Publications:
Annual Report. a.
Membership Directory. 2/.
Newswire. m.
The Exchange. 3/year.

Meetings/Conferences:
Biennial Meetings: even years/February-March
2000 – Anchorage, AK/1000

Ass'n of Pathology Chairs (1967)
9650 Rockville Pike
Bethesda, MD 20814-3993
Tel: (301)571-1880   *Fax:* (301)571-1879
Members: 140 departments of pathology
Staff: 1
Annual Budget: $50-100,000
Administrator: Frances A. Pitlick, Ph.D.

Historical Note
Formerly (1976) American Ass'n of Chairmen of Medical School Departments of Pathology, Inc. Membership: $400/yr. (institution).

Publications:
Newsletter. q.

Meetings/Conferences:

Ass'n of Pediatric Oncology Nurses (1976)
4700 W. Lake Ave.
Glenview, IL 60025-1485
Tel: (847)375-4724   *Fax:* (847)375-4777
E-Mail: info@apon.org
Web Site: http://www.apon.org
Members: 1,700 individuals, 2 companies
Annual Budget: $250-500,000
Exec. Director: M. Kathleen Klaeser, CAE

Historical Note
Members are nurses specializing in care for children and adolescents with cancer and their families. Membership: $65/year (individual); $85/year (foreign individual); $3,000/year (company).

Publications:
APON Newsletter. q. adv.
Journal of Pediatric Oncology Nursing. q. adv.

Meetings/Conferences:
Annual Meetings: Fall/700
1999 – Phoenix, AZ/Oct. 21-23
2000 – Orlando, FL/September 7-9
2001 – Memphis, TN/October 4-6

Ass'n of Pediatric Oncology Social Workers (1977)
Children's Hospital
1056 E. 19th Ave., B-220
Denver, CO 80218
Tel: (303)861-6959
Members: 180 individuals
Annual Budget: $25-50,000
President: Karen Tilley

Historical Note
APOSW members are professional social workers employed in the field of pediatric oncology. Membership: $45/year (individual).

Publications:
Newsletter. q.

Meetings/Conferences:
Annual Meetings: April
1999 – Chicago, IL/March 17-20

Ass'n of Pediatric Program Directors
6728 Old McLean Village Dr.
McLean, VA 22101
Tel: (703)556-9222   *Fax:* (703)556-8729
Exec. Director: George K. Degnon, CAE

Meetings/Conferences:
Annual Meetings: May

Ass'n of Performing Arts Presenters (1957)
1112 16th St., N.W., Suite 400
Washington, DC 20036-4823
Tel: (202)833-2787   *Fax:* (202)833-1543
Web Site: http://www.artspresenters.org/artspresenters
Members: 1,400 organizations
Staff: 20
Annual Budget: $1-2,000,000
Exec. Director: Susan Farr
Communications Director: Micheal J. Conaty
Government Affairs Coordinator: Shana Meehan
Meeting Planner: Elizabeth Pickard
Director, Professional Development: Sara Picillo
Membership Manager: Jane Roxbury
Senior Director, Cultural Participation Programs: Tony Tapia

Historical Note
Formerly (1974) Ass'n of College and University Concert Managers, and (1989) Ass'n of College, University and Community Arts Administrators. Members are arts organizations who present the professional, touring performing arts and managers of artists involved in the performing arts. Membership: $325-$1,200/year (organization).

Publications:
Bulletin. 6/year.
Inside Arts. bi-m. adv.
Presenters Reports. 9/yr.

Meetings/Conferences:
Annual Meetings: always New York, NY/2,000

Ass'n of Personal Computer User Groups
4798 S. Florida Ave.
Suite 24
Lakeland, FL 33813-2181
Tel: (941)646-1390   *Fax:* (941)648-9584
Web Site: www.apcug.org
Staff: 1
Exec. Director: Sam Gardner

Ass'n of Petroleum Re-refiners (1950)
P.O. Box 584
Buffalo, NY 14231-0584
Tel: (716)631-8246   *Fax:* (716)631-8246
E-Mail: gbooth@adelphia.net
Web Site: http://www.veol.com/recycling/congress
Annual Budget: under $10,000

Historical Note
Membership consists of companies recycling used oils by re-refining back to lubricant quality, as well as suppliers to the industry. APR is primarily involved with sponsoring educational conferences.

Meetings/Conferences:

Ass'n of Pharmaceutical Publishers
1358 Busch Pkwy.
Buffalo Grove, IL 60089
Tel: (847)459-8480
Toll Free: (847)459 - 6644
Exec. Director: Michael Anisfeld

Ass'n of Philosophy Journal Editors (1971)
Journal of Philosophy, Columbia Univ.
1150 Amsterdam Ave., MC 4972
New York, NY 10027
Tel: (212)666-4419   *Fax:* (212)932-3721
Members: 95 journal members
Staff: 1
Annual Budget: under $10,000
Secretary-Treasurer: Michael Kelly

Historical Note
Membership: $10/year.

Meetings/Conferences:
Annual Meetings: With the American Philosophical Ass'n, Eastern Division

Ass'n of Photo CD Imagers

Historical Note
Organization defunct in 1998; superseded by Digital Imaging Marketing Ass'n.

Ass'n of Physician Assistant Programs (1972)
950 North Washington St.
Alexandria, VA 22314-1552
Tel: (703)548-5538   *Fax:* (703)684-1924
E-Mail: apap@aapa.org
Members: 104 programs
Staff: 4
Annual Budget: $50-100,000
Coordinator: Timi Agar-Barwick
Director, Government & Professional Affairs: Nicole Gara

Historical Note
APAP represents Physician Assistant educational programs in the U.S. It provides for communications with and coordination of educational programs that train physician assistants.

Publications:
Physician Assistant Programs Directory. a.

Meetings/Conferences:
Semi-annual Meetings: May-June and October
1999 – Atlanta, GA/May 29-June 3

Ass'n of Physician Assistants in Cardiovascular Surgery (1981)
P.O. Box 4834
Denver, CO 80155
Tel: (303)770-6048   *Fax:* (303)771-2550
Toll Free: (877)221 - 5651
Web Site: http://www.apacvs.org
Members: 500 individuals
Staff: 2
Annual Budget: $50-100,000
Exec. Director: Carol A. Goddard

Historical Note
APACVS members are surgical physician assistants specializing in cardiovascular surgery. Membership: $125/year (individual); $25/year (student).

Publications:
CardioVision. q. adv.
Membership Directory. a. adv.
Salary & Benefits Survey. a.

Meetings/Conferences:
Annual Meetings: usually prior to Soc. of Thoracic Surgeons meeting/January
1999 – San Antonio, TX(Adam's Mark)/Jan. 22-24/150

Ass'n of Plastic Surgery Assistants
444 E. Algonquin Road
Arlington Heights, IL 60005
Tel: (847)228-8376   *Fax:* (847)228-6509
Members: 650 individuals
Account Executive: Mary Jo Harrold

Meetings/Conferences:

Ass'n of Polysomnographic Technologists (1978)
P.O. Box 14861
Lenexa, KS 66285-4861
Tel: (913)541-1991   *Fax:* (913)541-0156
E-Mail: jsutter@applmeapro.com
Web Site: http://www.aptweb.org
Members: 1,800 individuals
Annual Budget: $100-250,000
Exec. Director: Julie Sutter

Historical Note
A constituent society of the Ass'n of Professional Sleep Societies. Membership: $60/year (individual).

Publications:
A2Z Newsletter. q. adv.
Membership Directory. a.

Meetings/Conferences:
Annual Meetings: June
1999 – Orlando, FL/June 19-23
2000 – Las Vegas, NV

Ass'n of Practical Theology (1950)
Loyola Institute of Pastoral Studies
Loyola Univ. Chicago; 6525 N. Sheridan
Chicago, IL 60626
Tel: (773)508-2320   *Fax:* (773)508-2319
Toll Free: (800)424 - 1238
E-Mail: kdolphi@orion.it.luc.edu
Members: 100 individuals
Annual Budget: under $10,000
Secretary-Treasurer: Kathleen Dolphin

Historical Note
Formerly (1970) Ass'n of Seminary Professors in the Practical Fields and (1984) Ass'n of Professional Education for Ministry. APT promotes the professional development of those involved in the education of ministers and priests. Membership: $25/year (individual); $12.50/year (student).

Publications:
Newsletter. irreg.
Report of Annual Meeting. a.

Meetings/Conferences:
2000 – St. Louis, MO(Mercy Center)/April 7-9

Ass'n of Presbyterian Colleges and Universities (1983)
100 Witherspoon St., Room M040
Louisville, KY 40202-1396
Tel: (502)569-5605   *Fax:* (502)569-8766
Members: 66 institutions
Staff: 2
Annual Budget: $50-100,000
President: Duncan S. Ferguson
Program Coordinator: William Peterson

Historical Note
The product of a merger of the Ass'n of Presbyterian Colleges and Presbyterian College Union.

Publications:
Directory. a.
Point of View. q.

Meetings/Conferences:
1999 – Wooster, OH/March 6-9

Ass'n of Private Pension and Welfare Plans (1967)
1212 New York Ave., N.W., Suite 1250
Washington, DC 20005-3987
Tel: (202)289-6700   *Fax:* (202)289-4582
E-Mail: appwp@aol.com
Web Site: http://www.appwp.org
Members: 400 individuals
Staff: 10
Annual Budget: $1-2,000,000
President: James A. Klein

Historical Note
Focus is on government regulations and legislation concerning private, voluntary retirement savings and welfare benefit arrangements. Members are investment firms, attorneys, benefits administrators, banks, actuaries, associations, accounting firms and employer/plan sponsors. Sponsors and supports the Ass'n of Private Pension and Welfare Plans Political Action Committee.

Publications:
Benefits Brief.
Health Notes.
Legislative Alert.
Pension Notes.
Special Alerts.

Meetings/Conferences:
Annual Meetings: Annual spring legislatie meeting-Washington, DC

Ass'n of Productivity Specialists (1977)
521 Fifth Ave., Suite 1700
New York, NY 10175
Tel: (212)286-0943
Members: 1,200 individuals, 30 companies
Staff: 2
Annual Budget: $10-25,000
Chairman: Robert Jacobson

Historical Note
Membership: $50/year (individual); $1,500-4,000/year (organization/company).

Ass'n of Professional Ball Players of America (1924)
12062 Valley View St., Suite 211
Garden Grove, CA 92845
Tel: (714)892-9900   *Fax:* (714)897-0233
E-Mail: apbpa@gte.net
Web Site: home1.gte.net/apbpa
Members: 6,000 individuals
Staff: 2
Annual Budget: $250-500,000
Secretary-Treasurer: Richard Beverage

Historical Note
ACBPA members are professional baseball players, managers, coaches, scouts, and umpires.

Meetings/Conferences:
Annual Meetings: December

Ass'n of Professional Baseball Physicians (1970)

Historical Note
Address unknown in 1996.

Ass'n of Professional Bridge Players (1982)
606 Western
Petaluma, CA 94952
Tel: (707)766-5021   *Fax:* (707)763-2612
Members: 150 individuals
Annual Budget: $50-100,000
President: Ron Feldman

Historical Note
Established and incorporated in California, APBP is the oldest accredited professional organization of the American Contract Bridge League. Membership: $50/year (individual); $1,500/year (organization/company).

Meetings/Conferences:
Annual Meetings: Fall

Ass'n of Professional Chaplains
1701 E. Woodfield Rd., Suite 311
Schaumburg, IL 60173
Tel: (847)240-1014   *Fax:* (847)240-1015
Web Site: http://www.professionalchaplains.org
Members: 3,300 individuals
Staff: 4
Annual Budget: $500-1,000,000
Exec. Administrator: Josephine N. Schrader

Historical Note
Formerly (1975) Ass'n of Mental Hospital Chaplains. An interfaith organization for ministers, priests and rabbis professionally concerned with mental health. The first meeting was held in Washington, DC with the American Psychiatric Ass'n, and the AMHC retains close affiliative ties with that organization. Certifies competence in mental health ministry among clinically trained clergy serving in psychiatric facilities, community mental health centers, facilities for the developmentally handicapped, and religious congregations. Membership: $90/year (full member); $45/year (associate); $25/year (student).

Publications:
Cura Animarum. a.
Journal of Pastoral Care. q. adv.

Meetings/Conferences:
Annual Meetings: Spring, with the American Psychiatric Ass'n
1999 – Kansas City, MO/Feb. 27-March 3

Ass'n of Professional Chaplains (1946)
1701 E. Woodfield Road, Suite 311

Schaumburg, IL   60173
Tel: (847)240-1014   *Fax:* (847)240-1015
E-Mail: cochpln@aol.com
Web Site: http://www.members.aol.com/cochpln/home.htm
Members: 3,000 individuals
Staff: 3
Annual Budget: $250-500,000
Exec. Administrator: Josephine N. Schrader

Historical Note
Formerly (1968) Chaplains Ass'n of the American Protestant Hospital Ass'n and College of Chaplains (1998). An interfaith, multicultural, professional pastoral care ass'n promoting excellence in pastoral care. Members are ministers serving as chaplains in specialized settings, such as hospitals or other institutions. Membership: $30-175/year.

Publications:
APC News. bi-m. adv.
Caregiver Journal. q. adv.
Chaplaincy Today. bi. adv.
Journal of Pastoral Care. q. adv.

Meetings/Conferences:
Annual Meetings: Spring/600

Ass'n of Professional Color Imagers *(1968)*
3000 Picture Place
Jackson, MI   49201
Tel: (517)788-8146   *Fax:* (517)788-8371
Members: 725 companies
Staff: 2
Annual Budget: $100-250,000
Exec. Director: Roy S. Pung

Historical Note
Formerly (1997) Ass'n of Professional Color Laboratories. Members are laboratories doing processing for professional photographers. A section of Photo Marketing Ass'n-Internat'l, which provides administrative support.

Publications:
Colorgram. m.
Glossary of Terms. a.
Membership Roster. a.

Meetings/Conferences:
Annual Meetings: late Winter

Ass'n of Professional Color Laboratories
Historical Note
Became (1997) Ass'n of Color Imagers.

Ass'n of Professional Communication Consultants *(1983)*
C/O The Oak Group
1317 Jamestown Rd., Suite 101
Williamsburg, VA   23185
Tel: (757)564-8750   *Fax:* (757)564-8747
E-Mail: 71233.1664@compuserve.com
Web Site: http://www.apcc-online.org
Members: 200 individuals
Annual Budget: under $10,000
President: Sherry Scott

Historical Note
Formerly (1995) Ass'n of Professional Writing Consultants. Members are full-time independent writing and communications consultants, part-time consultants who primarily teach in colleges and universities, in-company consultants, training professionals, and freelance writers and editors. Its purpose is to provide a network and group services for writing and communications consultants, to ensure the quality of seminars and other consulting practices, and to inform business and industry about the value of writing and communicating effectively. Membership: $50/year.

Publications:
Bibliography. a.
Consulting Success.
Getting Started in Consulting. irreg.
Membership Directory. a.
Resources for Writing Consultants. irreg.

Meetings/Conferences:
Annual Meetings: November
1999 – Los Angeles, CA

Ass'n of Professional Design Firms *(1985)*
P.O. Box 29166
San Francisco, CA   94129-0166
Tel: (415)561-2733   *Fax:* (415)561-2734
E-Mail: apdf@lexitech.com
Web Site: http://www.apdf.org
Members: 75 companies
Staff: 1
Annual Budget: $50-100,000
Director: Stephanie Allen

Historical Note
Membership is open to firms engaged in graphic, industrial, and commercial interior design. APDF officers are elected annually. Membership: $1000/yr. minimum, based on number of employees.

Publications:
Financial Survey. a.

Meetings/Conferences:
Annual Meetings: April
1999 – Chatham, MA/May 20-23

Ass'n of Professional Directors of YMCAs in the United States *(1871)*
8200 Humboldt Ave., Suite 111
Bloomington, MN   55431
Tel: (612)885-0273   *Fax:* (612)885-0227
Members: 4,500 individuals
Staff: 2
Annual Budget: $250-500,000
Exec. Director: James G. Stooke

Historical Note
Formerly (1969) Ass'n of Secretaries, Young Men's Christian Ass'ns of North America.

Publications:
Perspective. 8/year. adv.

Meetings/Conferences:
Biennial Meetings: Fall (1999)
2000 – San Diego, CA

Ass'n of Professional Energy Managers *(1982)*
143 S. Citrus St.
Orange, CA   92868
Tel: (714)771-6311   *Fax:* (714)532-2435
Toll Free: (800)543 - 3563
E-Mail: apem@aol.com
Web Site: http://www.apem.org
Members: 500 individuals
Admin. Assistant: Teri Berry

Historical Note
APEM members are individuals responsible for energy production, consumption or management decisions, including professional consultants, in all types of organizations. Promotes sustainable resource use through the exchange of information. Membership: $125/year (individual); $1,250/year (corporate).

Publications:
Membership Directory. a.
Professional Energy Manager. bi-m. adv.

Meetings/Conferences:

Ass'n of Professional Genealogists *(1979)*
Historical Note
APG declined to provide updated information for this edition.

Ass'n of Professional Insurance Women *(1976)*
Historical Note
Address unknown in 1997.

Ass'n of Professional Investigative Photographers
Historical Note
APIP is a not-for-profit organization designed to disseminate information and to provide training to law enforcement/military imaging specialists. Membership: $35 (initial membership fee); $25/year (individual); $15/year (associate).

Ass'n of Professional Landscape Designers *(1987)*
104 S. Michigan Ave., Suite 1500
Chicago, IL   60603
Tel: (312)201-0101   *Fax:* (312)201-0214
E-Mail: info@apld.com
Web Site: http://apld.com
Members: 550 individuals
Annual Budget: $10-25,000
Administrator: Jack L. Lagershausen

Historical Note
APLD members are professional landscape designers, allied vendors and students of landscape design. Awards Professional Landscape Designer Certification. Membership: $125/year.

Publications:
APLD News Newsletter. q. adv.

Meetings/Conferences:
Semi-annual Meetings: February and August
1999 – San Francisco, CA
1999 – Long Island, NY

Ass'n of Professional Material Handling Consultants *(1959)*
8720 Red Oak Blvd., Suite 201
Charlotte, NC   28217
Tel: (704)676-1184   *Fax:* (704)676-1199
E-Mail: 102512.1772@compuserve.com
Web Site: http://www.mhia.org/apmhc
Members: 40 individuals
Staff: 1
Annual Budget: under $10,000
Exec. Director: Eugene C. Curtis

Historical Note
Independent material handling consultants, and those who coordinate material handling within multi-plant operations. Membership: $250/year (individual).

Publications:
Newsletter. q.

Meetings/Conferences:
Semi-annual Meetings: Spring and Fall Forum

Ass'n of Professional Model Makers *(1992)*
6502 Shiner St.
Austin, TX   78729-7520
Tel: (512)257-0730   *Fax:* (415)957-1107
Web Site: http://www.modelmakers.org
Members: 1000 individuals
Staff: 3
Annual Budget: $50-100,000
Exec. Director: Wendy Sommers

Historical Note
APMM promotes the practice of model-making as an important component of design and manufacturing processes. Membership: $100/year (individual); $900/year (organization).

Publications:
APMM Directory. a. adv.
Prototype. 6x/year. adv.
Vendor Directory. a. adv.

Meetings/Conferences:
Annual Meetings: Austin, TX(Driskill)/April 6/300

Ass'n of Professional Researchers for Advancement *(1988)*
414 Plaza Drive, Suite 209

Westmont, IL   60559-1265
Tel: (630)655-0177   *Fax:* (630)655-0391
E-Mail: apra@adminsys.com
Members: 1,600 individuals
Staff: 5
Annual Budget: $500-1,000,000
Exec. Director: Judith K. Keel

Historical Note
An outgrowth of the Minneapolis Prospect Research Ass'n,formerly (1995) American Prospect Research Ass'n. APRA members are professionals (including prospect researchers, directors of development, executive directors and consultants) who work in donor research at non-profit institutions throughout the nation. Membership: $100/year.

Publications:
Bulletin. m.
Connections. q.

Meetings/Conferences:
Annual Meetings: August
1999 – Atlanta, GA

Ass'n of Professional Schools of Internat'l Affairs *(1989)*
1779 Massachusetts Ave., N.W.
Washington, DC   20036
Tel: (202)939-2390   *Fax:* (202)483-1542
E-Mail: APSIA@erols.com
Web Site: http://www.apsia.org/
Members: 30 institutions
Staff: 3
Annual Budget: $100-250,000
Exec. Director: Kay King

Historical Note
Members are graduate institutions providing professional education in international affairs. Membership: $1,000-7,500/year (institution).

Publications:
APSIA News. semi-a.
Journal of Public & International Affairs. a.

Meetings/Conferences:

Ass'n of Professional Writing Consultants
Historical Note
Became (1995) Ass'n of Professional Communication Consultants.

Ass'n of Professors and Researchers in Religious Education *(1970)*
Historical Note
Address unknown in 1997.

Ass'n of Professors of Cardiology *(1990)*
9111 Old Georgetown Road
Bethesda, MD   20814-1699
Tel: (301)493-2330   *Fax:* (301)897-9745
E-Mail: sthayer@acc.org
Members: 116 institutions
Staff: 2
Annual Budget: $25-50,000
Administrative Coordinator: Susan C. Thayer

Historical Note
APC states its purpose as to promote and engage in educational and scientific activities with respect to the science of cardiology. Members are Directors of Divisions of Cardiology of each accredited school in the United States and Puerto Rico. Membership: $350/year (institution).

Meetings/Conferences:
Semi-Annual Meetings: March and November
1999 – New Orleans, LA
1999 – Atlanta, GA
2000 – Anaheim, CA
2000 – New Orleans, LA

Ass'n of Professors of Gynecology and Obstetrics *(1962)*
409 12th St., S.W.
Washington, DC   20024
Tel: (202)863-2507   *Fax:* (202)863-2514
E-Mail: webmaster@APgo.org
Web Site: http://www.apgo.org
Members: 1,500 individuals
Staff: 5
Annual Budget: $250-500,000
Exec. Director: Donna Wachter
Director, Communications: Pamela Johanssen
Publications and Meetings: Anne Large
Membership Services: Danice Beal

Historical Note
Members are drawn from faculties of medical school departments of obstetrics and gynecology. Membership: $110/year (individual); $1,000/year (member departments); $750/year (institutional departments).

Publications:
Academic Positions Report. q.
APGO Newsletter. q.
Care of Aging Woman. 5/years.
Instructional Objectives. trien.
Manual & Workbook on Infectious Diseases. 5/years.
Medical Legal Issues. 5/years.

Meetings/Conferences:
Annual Meetings: February-March/600 Alubquerque, NM(Convention Center)/March 6-9
1999 – San Diego, CA(Marriott Hotel and Marina)/Feb. 20-23/700
2000 – New Orleans, LA/March 1-4
2001 – Lake Buena Vista, FL(Disney Contemporary Resort)/March 7-10
2002 – Dallas, TX(Adam's Mark)/March 6-9

Ass'n of Professors of Medicine (1954)
2501 M St., N.W., Suite 550
Washington, DC   20037-1308
Tel: (202)861-7700   *Fax:* (202)861-9731
E-Mail: APM@im.org
Web Site: http://www.im.org/apm
Members: 150 individuals
Staff: 4
Annual Budget: $100-250,000
Exec. Director: Tod Ibrahim
Legislative Coordinator: Jeff Coughlin

Historical Note
Chairpersons of medical school departments of medicine.

Publications:
American Journal of Medicine. m. adv.
APM Update. q.

Meetings/Conferences:
1999 – Pasadena, CA(Ritz Carlton)/Feb. 24-27

Ass'n of Professors of Mission (1952)
Wheaton Graduate School
Wheaton, IL   60187
Tel: (708)752-5948   *Fax:* (708)752-5935
Members: 190 individuals
Staff: 1
Annual Budget: under $10,000
Secretary-Treasurer: Dr. Doug McConnell

Historical Note
Professors teaching in the field of mission in colleges and seminaries. Member of the Council on the Study of Religion. Membership: $15/year.

Meetings/Conferences:
Annual Meetings: June/usually in Chicago, IL/80-100

Ass'n of Program Directors in Internal Medicine (1978)
2501 M St., N.W., Suite 550
Washington, DC   20037
Tel: (202)887-9450   *Fax:* (202)887-9447
Toll Free: (800)622 - 4558
Members: 1,100 individuals, 430 institutions
Staff: 4
Annual Budget: $250-500,000
Exec. Director: Dema C. Daley
Coordinator, Meetings: Wendy Harris

Historical Note
Seeks to advance medical education through assisting accredited hospital internal medicine education programs. Membership: $600/year (institution); $60/year (individual).

Publications:
APDIM. q. adv.
Chief Resident Handbook. a. adv.
Educational Clearinghouse Catalogue. bien. adv.
Program Directors Handbook. a. adv.

Meetings/Conferences:
Semi-annual Meetings: Spring with American College of
    Physicians and Fall with Ass'n of American Medical
    Colleges
1999 – New Orleans, LA(Fairmont)/Apr. 19-22/900
2000 – Philadelphia, PA(Wyndham Plaza)/Apr. 9-12/900
2001 – Atlanta, GA(Hilton)/March 24-29/1000
2002 – Philadelphia, PA(Wyndham)

Ass'n of Program Directors in Radiology (1993)
820 Joire Blvd.
Oak Brook, IL   60523
Tel: (630)368-3737   *Fax:* (630)571-7837
E-Mail: thomas@rsna.org
Web Site: http://www.rsna.org/about/societies.html
Members: 285 individuals
Chief Administrator: Jennifer K. Boylan

Historical Note
APDR members are directors of resident training in radiology.

Publications:
Academic Radiology.

Meetings/Conferences:
Annual Meetings: Spring
1999 – San Diego, CA(Sheraton)/March 10-14

Ass'n of Program Directors in Surgery
4900-B South 31st St.
Arlington, VA   22206-1656
Tel: (703)820-7400   *Fax:* (703)931-4520
Members: 500 individuals
Exec. Director: Thomas F. Fise

Publications:
Current Surgery. irreg.

Meetings/Conferences:

Ass'n of Progressive Rental Organizations (1980)
9015 Mountain Ridge Dr., Suite 220
Austin, TX   78759-7252
Tel: (512)794-0095   *Fax:* (512)794-0097
Web Site: http://www.apro/rto.com
Members: 3,800 companies
Staff: 11
Annual Budget: $1-2,000,000
Exec. Director: Bill Keese
Communications Director: Julie Stephens Sherrier
Director, Marketing: Cindy Ganther
Director, Government Affairs: Ron Waters
Membership Director: Carolyn Fitzsimmons

Historical Note
Members are television, appliance and furniture dealers who rent merchandise with an option to purchase. Membership: $450-100,000/year (dealers), $500/year (suppliers).

Publications:
APRO Show Guide. a. adv.
Network News. bi-m. adv.
Progressive Rentals. bi-m. adv.
Who's Who in Rent to Own Directory. a. adv.

Meetings/Conferences:
Annual Meetings: Summer

Ass'n of Promotion Marketing Agencies Worldwide (1969)
750 Summer St.
Stamford, CT   06901-1020
Tel: (203)325-3911   *Fax:* (203)969-1499
E-Mail: mccapma@aol.com
Web Site: http://www.apmaw.org
Members: 75 agencies
Staff: 3
Annual Budget: $250-500,000
Exec. V. President: Vincent Sottosanti

Historical Note
Formerly (1995) Council of Sales Promotion Agencies. A trade association of sales promotion agencies with at least two years experience. 50% of APMA membership is foreign. Membership: $3,300/year (full member); $825/year (associate).

Publications:
APMA Newsletter. q.
Membership Roster. bi-a.

Meetings/Conferences:
Semi-annual Meetings: Spring and Fall
1999 – London, England(Marriott)/April 25-29/90
1999 – Chicago, IL(Four Seasons)/Oct. 3-6/115
2000 – Rome, Italy/90
2001 – Sydney, Australia/90
2001 – October

Ass'n of Proposal Management Professionals
P.O. Box 1172
Idyllwild, CA   92549-1172
Tel: (909)659-0789   *Fax:* (909)659-8589
Web Site: http://www.apmp.org
Members: 1,500 individuals
Staff: 1
Annual Budget: $250-500,000
Exec. Director: David L. Winton

Historical Note
Thirteen chapters located throughout the United States. Membership: $75/year.

Publications:
Conference Proceedings. a.
Perspective Newsletter. 6/yr.

Meetings/Conferences:
Annual Meetings: Semi-Annual.
1999 – San Diego, CA/May 25-29
2000 – Orlando, FL

Ass'n of Psychology Postdoctoral and Internship Centers (1968)
733 15th St., N.W., Suite 719
Washington, DC   20005-2112
Tel: (202)347-0022   *Fax:* (202)347-8480
Members: 580 internship sites
Staff: 1
Annual Budget: $100-250,000
Administrative Director: Connie Hercey

Historical Note
Formerly (1990) the Ass'n of Psychology Internship Centers. Members are programs in psychology. APPIC was formed to foster the sharing of information about mutual concerns and interests with respect to internship training interests within the American Psychological Ass'n. Membership: $300/year.

Publications:
APPIC Newsletter. semi-a.
Internship & Postdoctoral Programs in Professional
    Psychology. a.

Meetings/Conferences:
Annual Meetings: August, with APA

Ass'n of Public Data Users (1975)
c/o DBER, Univ. of New Orleans
New Orleans, LA   70148
Tel: (504)280-3154   *Fax:* (504)280-6094
E-Mail: APDUDB@uno.edu
Web Site: http://www.apdu.org
Members: 350 individuals, 200 organizations
Staff: 1
Annual Budget: $50-100,000
Exec. Director/Administrator: Patricia J. Connor

Historical Note
Facilitates the utilization of public data through the sharing of knowledge about files and applicable software, and exchange of documentation. APDU is committed to increasing the knowledge base of its members about new sources of information and increasing the awareness of Federal agencies about the requirements of data users. Membership: $375/year (organization).

Publications:
APDU Membership Directory. a.
APDU Newsletter. m.

Meetings/Conferences:
Annual Meetings: Fall, in the Washington, DC area

Ass'n of Public Health Laboratories (1951)
1211 Connecticut Ave., N.W., Suite 608
Washington, DC   20036-2701
Tel: (202)822-5227   *Fax:* (202)887-5098
Web Site: http://www.aphl.org
Members: 75 states, city and county lab dir.

Staff: 16
Annual Budget: $2-5,000,000
Exec. Director: Scott Becker
Associate Exec. Director, Finance/Operations: Carol Clark, CPA

Historical Note
Formerly Ass'n of State and Territorial Public Health Laboratory Directors (1998). APHL works cooperatively with private and governmental groups to improve the quality of laboratory testing through training and national conferences, and extends such programs to the international community.

Publications:
Consolidated Annual Report of State Laboratory Testing. a.
Human Retrovirus Testing Conference Proceedings. a.
Neonatal Screening Symposium Proceedings. a.
Pay & Classification Report of State Public Health Lab
    Personnel. bi-m.

Meetings/Conferences:
Annual Meetings: Summer
1999 – Washington, DC

Ass'n of Public-Safety Communications Officials-Internat'l (1935)
2040 S. Ridgewood Ave.
South Daytona, FL   32119-8437
Tel: (904)322-2500   *Fax:* (904)322-2501
E-Mail: apco@apcoint.org
Web Site: http://www.apcointl.org
Members: 12,000 individuals
Staff: 49
Annual Budget: $2-5,000,000
Exec. Director: Chris Bevevino
Government Affairs Coordinator: Allison Kasold
Conference and Exposition Administration: Ann M. Armitage
Director, APCO Institute: Kevin R. Duffy
C.F.O.: Tim Ryan
Director, Operations: John Ramsey
Publisher & Editor: Alan W. Chase

Historical Note
The oldest and largest public safety communications group, APCO is recognized by the Federal Communications Commission as the frequency coordination body for police, local government and 800 MHZ public safety radio services. Member of the Land Mobile Communications Council. Offers various training courses.

Publications:
The APCO Bulletin. m. adv.

Meetings/Conferences:
Annual Meetings: Summer
1999 – Minneapolis, MN
2000 – Boston, MA
2001 – Salt Lake City, UT
2002 – Nashville, TN

Ass'n of Publication Production Managers (1939)
P.O. Box 5106, Grand Central Station
New York, NY   10163-5106
Tel: (212)522-2121   *Fax:* (212)522-0800
E-Mail: Michael_Arpino@Timeinc.com
Members: 350 individuals
Annual Budget: under $10,000
President: Michael Arpino
Secretary: Mark Abraham
Treasurer: David Orlin
Membership Chairperson: Wanda Ziembinski

Historical Note
Members are production managers of periodicals. Membership: $60/year (individual).

Publications:
Membership Roster. a.

Meetings/Conferences:
Monthly Luncheon: New York City, October-May

Ass'n of Publicly Traded Companies (1973)
1200 19th St., N.W., Suite 300
Washington, DC   20036
Tel: (202)857-1114   *Fax:* (202)828-6024
Members: 900 companies
Staff: 3
Annual Budget: $250-500,000
President: Brian T. Borders

Historical Note
Formerly (1990) the Nat'l Ass'n of OTC Companies. APTC members are companies that issue stock into the public capital markets. Individuals, private firms and closely held corporations may join as associate members. Membership: $1,350-2,300/year.

Publications:
Alerts. irreg.
Newsletter. m.

Meetings/Conferences:
Annual Meetings: Summer

Ass'n of Racing Commissioners Internat'l (1934)
2343 Alexandria Dr., Suite 200
Lexington, KY   40504
Tel: (606)224-7070   *Fax:* (606)224-7071
E-Mail: Tony@ARCI.com
Web Site: http://www.ARCI.com
Members: 500 individuals
Staff: 5
Annual Budget: $1-2,000,000
President: R. Anthony Chamblin
Business Manager: Eva M. Waters

Historical Note
Formerly (1988) Nat'l Ass'n of State Racing Commissioners. Represents all forms of flat racing, as well as jai alai, and harness and greyhound racing. Member of the American Horse Council.

Publications:
Statistical Reports on Greyhound Racing. a.
Statistical Reports on Horse Racing. a.

Statistical Summary of Pari-Mutuel Wagering. a.
Weekly News Bulletins. w.

Meetings/Conferences:
Annual Meetings: Spring/400
1999 – New Orelans, LA

Ass'n of Railroad Advertising and Marketing *(1924)*

Historical Note
Organization defunct in 1998.

Ass'n of Railway Communicators *(1922)*

327 E. Mason Avenue
Alexandria, VA   22301
Tel: (703)548-3451   *Fax:* (703)548-1768
Members: 55 individuals
Staff: 1
Annual Budget: under $10,000
Secretary-Treasurer: Ron Shumate

Historical Note
*Established as Railway Employees' Magazine Ass'n, it became the
Conference of Railway Editors in 1924, the American Railway
Magazine Editors Ass'n in 1925, the Ass'n of Railroad Editors in
1964 and assumed its present name in 1985. Membership:
$100/year.*

Publications:
Proof. irreg.

Meetings/Conferences:
Annual Meetings: Fall/45

Ass'n of Railway Museums *(1961)*

P.O. Box 370
Tujunga, CA   91043-0370
Tel: (818)951-9151
Members: 100 museums
Annual Budget: under $10,000
Secretary: Ellen Fishburn

Historical Note
*Members are museums displaying electric and steam railway
equipment. Has no full-time staff. Professional Affiliate Member of
American Ass'n of Museums. Membership: $100/year (museum);
$60/year (non-profit affiliate); $175/year (commercial affiliate).*

Publications:
Railway Museum Quarterly. q.

Meetings/Conferences:
Annual Meetings: Fall/200
1999 – Vancouver, British Columbia(Renaissance
    Vancouver)Sept.

Ass'n of Rain Apparel Contractors *(1948)*

500 Seventh Ave., 2nd Floor
New York, NY   10018
Tel: (212)819-1011
Members: 1 individuals
Staff: 3
Exec. Director: Arnold R. Harris

Historical Note
Members are manufacturers of women's coats and rainwear.

Ass'n of Real Estate License Law Officials *(1930)*

4170 Carmichael Ct.
Montgomery, AL   36106-2871
Tel: (334)260-2902   *Fax:* (334)272-7128
E-Mail: mailbox@arello.org
Web Site: www.arello.org
Members: 61 jurisdictions
Staff: 6
Annual Budget: $250-500,000
Exec. V. President: Stephen J. Francis

Historical Note
*Formerly Nat'l Ass'n of License Law Officials, as well as formerly
the Nat'l Ass'n of Real Estate License Law Officials. An association
of all the Real Estate Commissions in the United States and
territories. Purpose is to upgrade the states' regulation of the real
estate industry.*

Publications:
ARELLOgram. q.
Digest of Real Estate License Laws. a.
Directory. a.

Meetings/Conferences:
Annual Meetings: Fall
1999 – Savannah, GA/400
2000 – Salt Lake City, UT/400

Ass'n of Real Estate Women *(1978)*

250 W. 57th St., Suite 2301
New York, NY   10107
Tel: (212)265-4652   *Fax:* (212)265-4974
Members: 300 individuals
Staff: 5
Annual Budget: $100-250,000
Exec. Director: Ann L. Woodfield

Meetings/Conferences:
Annual Meetings: None held.

Ass'n of Records Managers and Administrators *(1975)*

4200 Somerset Dr., Suite 215
Prairie Village, KS   66208-0540
Tel: (913)341-3808   *Fax:* (913)341-3742
Toll Free: (800)422 - 2762
E-Mail: hq@arma.org
Web Site: http://www.arma.org
Members: 10,000 individuals
Staff: 25
Annual Budget: $2-5,000,000
Exec. Director/C.E.O.: Peter R. Hermann, CAE
Director, Communications and Editor: Cynthia Launchbaugh
Director, Public Rels./Advocacy: Mary Hodges
Director, Meetings: Michael Toohey, CAE
Director, Education: Gwen A. Wright

Director, Finance & Administration: Richard Todd
Member Services Director: Elizabeth Usovicz

Historical Note
*Formerly (1975) American Records Management Ass'n. Absorbed
(1975) Ass'n of Records Executives and Administrators. Affiliated
with the Institute of Certified Records Managers. Membership:
$115/year.*

Publications:
InfoPro. q. adv.
Information Management Journal. q. adv.
Membership Directory. a. adv.

Meetings/Conferences:
Annual Meetings: Fall/3,000
1999 – Cincinnati, OH/Oct. 17-20
2000 – Las Vegas, NV/Oct. 22-25
2001 – Montreal, Quebec/Sept. 30-Oct. 3
2002 – New Orleans, LA/Sept. 29-Oct. 2

Ass'n of Refrigerant Desuperheater Manufacturers *(1985)*

7050 Overland Road
Orlando, FL   32810
Tel: (407)292-4400   *Fax:* (407)290-1329
Members: 20 companies
Staff: 1
Annual Budget: $10-25,000
Exec. Director: Rodney Weaver

Historical Note
*ARDM was established to promote the use of desuperheaters as an
energy saving device. Membership: $500/year company),
$250/year (institution), $200/year (associate).*

Publications:
Directory. a.
hotExchanger. irreg.

Meetings/Conferences:

Ass'n of Rehabilitation Nurses *(1974)*

4700 W. Lake Ave.
Glenview, IL   60025-1485
Tel: (847)375-4710   *Fax:* (847)375-4777
E-Mail: info@rehabnurse.org
Web Site: http://rehabnurse.org
Members: 8,000 individuals
Staff: 8
Annual Budget: $1-2,000,000
Exec. Director: Anne M. Cordes
Director, Communications: Dot Vartan
Director, Meetings: Kay V. Granath, CMP
Director, Education: Marta MacDonald
Director, Finance: Ron Kruskol
Manager, Membership Records: Kay Warskow

Historical Note
*ARN members are registered nurses concerned with or involved in
the practice of rehabilitation nursing; non-voting membership is
available for others interested in the field. Formed and supports the
Rehabilitation Nursing Foundation as its research arm.
Membership: $95/year (individual); $2,000/year (corporate).*

Publications:
ARN Network Newsletter. bi-m.
Rehabilitation Nursing. bi-m. adv.

Meetings/Conferences:
Annual Meetings: Fall
1999 – Minneapolis, MN(Hilton Convention
    Center)/Nov. 3-7/2000
2000 – Reno, NV(Reno Hilton)/Oct. 11-15/2000

Ass'n of Rehabilitation Programs in Computer Technology *(1978)*

Michigan Career and Technical Institute
P.O. Box 232
Plainwell, MI   49080
Tel: (616)664-9230   *Fax:* (616)664-5850
E-Mail: cmsi@aol.com
Web Site: http://www.arpct.org
Members: 53 organizations
Annual Budget: under $10,000
President: Dr. Robert Leneway

Historical Note
*Formerly (1994) Ass'n of Rehabilitation Programs in Data
Processing. Membership includes rehabilitation programs as well as
individuals interested in promoting computer technology as a career
for persons with disabilities. Has no permanent office or staff;
officers elected annually. Membership: $75/year (individual);
$275/year (organziation).*

Publications:
Viewpoint. 2/yr.

Meetings/Conferences:

Ass'n of Reporters of Judicial Decisions *(1982)*

7909 Roswell Drive
Falls Church, VA   22043
Tel: (202)479-3390   *Fax:* (202)479-3240
Members: 75 individuals
President: C. Clifford Allen

Historical Note
*ARJD is composed of attorneys and their staffs employed by the
appellate courts who edit and publish judicial opinions.
Membership: $50/year (reporter); $30/year (staff).*

Publications:
Catchline Newsletter. 3/yr.
Directory. a.

Meetings/Conferences:
1999 – Philadelphia, PA(Park Hyatt at the Bellvue)/Aug. 5-9
2000 – Lake Tahoe, NV/Aug. 5-7
2001 – Point Clear, AL/Aug. 2-6

Ass'n of Reproduction Materials Manufacturers

Historical Note
*Became the Ass'n for Engineering Graphics and Imaging Systems in
1995.*

Ass'n of Reproductive Health Professionals *(1963)*

2401 Pennsylvania Ave., N.W., Suite 350
Washington, DC   20037
Tel: (202)466-3825   *Fax:* (202)466-3826
E-Mail: ARHP@aol.com
Web Site: http://policy.net/arhp
Members: 1,875 individuals
Staff: 8
Annual Budget: $2-5,000,000
President/C.E.O.: Wayne C. Sheilds
Conference Coordinator: Amy McCormick

Historical Note
*Members are physicians, advanced practice clinicians, and other
professionals in reproductive health. Formerly (1973) American
Ass'n of Planned Parenthood Physicians and (1987) Ass'n of
Planned Parenthood Professionals. Membership: $60/year
(advanced practice clinicians), $100/year (physicians).*

Publications:
Clinical Proceedings.
Health & Sexuality. q.
NARHP Newsletter. q. adv.

Meetings/Conferences:
Annual Meetings: Fall

Ass'n of Research Directors *(1945)*

Historical Note
Organization defunct in 1998.

Ass'n of Research Libraries *(1932)*

21 Dupont Circle, N.W., Suite 800
Washington, DC   20036
Tel: (202)296-2296   *Fax:* (202)872-0884
E-Mail: arihq@arl.org
Web Site: http://arl.cni.org
Members: 122 libraries
Staff: 22
Annual Budget: $2-5,000,000
Exec. Director: Duane Webster

Historical Note
*The Association's primary function is to identify and solve problems
fundamental to large research libraries. Membership:
$13,500/year.*

Publications:
ARL Preservation Statistics. a.
ARL Salary Survey. a.
ARL Statistics. a.
ARL: A Bimonthly Newsletter of Research Library
    Issues/Actions. bi-m.
Directory of Electronic Journals, Newsletters, and Discussion
    Lists.
Proceedings of the Meeting. semi-a.

Meetings/Conferences:
Semi-Annual Meetings: May and October
1999 – Kansas City, MO(Ritz Carlton)/May 11-14
1999 – Washington, DC(Marriott)/Oct. 13-15
2000 – Newark, DE
2000 – Washington, DC
2001 – Toronto, Canada
2001 – Washington, DC

Ass'n of Residents in Radiation Oncology *(1983)*

1101 Market st., 14th Floor
Philadelphia, PA   19107
Tel: (215)574-3155
E-Mail: arro@acr.org
Web Site: http://www.arro.org
Members: 515 individuals
Exec. Secretary: Ann Marie Webster

Historical Note
*ARRO members are residents and clinical fellows in accredited
radiation oncology programs.*

Meetings/Conferences:
Annual Meetings: With American Soc. for Therapeutic
    Radiology and Oncology

Ass'n of Retail Marketing Services *(1957)*

3 Caro Court
Red Bank, NJ   07701-2315
Tel: (732)842-5070   *Fax:* (732)219-1938
Members: 140 individuals, 125 companies
Staff: 6
Annual Budget: $250-500,000
Exec. Director: Gerri Hopkins
Public Relations Director: George Meredith
Legal Counsel: Raymond M. Patt

Historical Note
*Formerly (1982) Trading Stamp Institute of America and TSIA,
Inc., The Ass'n of Retail Marketing Services. Assumed its present
name in 1983. ARMS is a market-information network for suppliers
of premium and continuity plans, customer incentive programs, and
motivation techniques for sales personnel. Membership: $350/year.*

Publications:
ARMS Retail Promotion Show Directory. a.
Creative Marketing. q.
Directory of Members. a.

Meetings/Conferences:
1999 – Chicago, IL(Ramada Congress)/Jan. 8-11/1500
2000 – Chicago, IL(Congress Plaza Hotel)/Jan. 14-17/1500

Ass'n of Retail Travel Agents *(1963)*

501 Darby Creek Road, Suite 47
Lexington, KY   40509-1604
Tel: (606)263-1194   *Fax:* (606)264-0368
Toll Free: (800)969 - 6069
E-Mail: artahdq@aol.com

Web Site: http://www.artaonline.com/ARTA
Members: 4,500 individuals
Staff: 3
Annual Budget: $250-500,000
President: John K. Hawks, APR
V. President, Administration: Pat Funk

Historical Note
ARTA represents small and independent professional travel agents. Its two primary activities are providing educational and training opportunities to agents and representing their point of view before industry, governmental and consumer organizations. Membership: $75/year (individual); $250/year (company).

Publications:
ARTAFAX. w.
The ARTA Agent. bi-m.

Meetings/Conferences:
1999 – Myrtle Beach, SC(Kingston
Plantation)/March 4-7/500

Ass'n of Rheumatology Health Professionals *(1965)*
1800 Century Pl., N.E., Suite 250
Atlanta, GA 30345-4300
Tel: (404)633-3777   *Fax:* (404)633-1870
E-Mail: JEPPS@RHEUMATOLOGY.ORG
Members: 750 individuals
Staff: 4
Annual Budget: $250-500,000
Exec. Director: Julie Epps
Education Manager: Joan Tyree
Exec. Assistant: Jan McCart

Historical Note
Formerly (1994) Arthritis Health Professions Ass'n. A professional membership society, the organization works to establish and disseminate scientific knowledge relevant to issues of access, quality and provision of appropriate arthritis care. Membership: $115/year (individual), $115/year (internat'l), $75/year (associate).

Publications:
Arthritis Care & Research. q. adv.

Meetings/Conferences:
Annual Meetings: Fall, in conjunction with the American
College of Rheumatology

Ass'n of Rotational Molders *(1976)*
2000 Spring Road, Suite 511
Oak Brook, IL 60523-1850
Tel: (630)571-0611   *Fax:* (630)571-0616
Members: 440 companies
Staff: 5
Annual Budget: $1-2,000,000
Exec. Director: Charles D. Frederick
Director, Administration and Member Services: Janet Popp

Historical Note
Plastic fabricators employing Rotational Molding.

Publications:
Rotation Magazine. q. adv.

Meetings/Conferences:
Semi-Annual Meetings: April and October
1999 – Cleveland, OH(Renaissance)/Oct. 24-27

Ass'n of Sales Administration Managers *(1981)*
PO Box 1356
Laurence Harbor, NJ 08879
Tel: (732)264-7722   *Fax:* (732)264-0232
E-Mail: ASAMNET@AOL.COM
Web Site: http://www.members.aol.com/ASAMnet/index.html
Members: 88 individuals
Annual Budget: under $10,000
Secretary-Treasurer: Bill Martin

Historical Note
Independent consultants and corporate employees providing sales and marketing services including: establishing broker/representative sales networks, field sales management, marketing and administrative services, retail management, meeting management, etc. Members provide a full range of services from product introduction to promotional programs to support the sales effort. Operating primarily in the Consumer Packaged Goods field, both Private Label and Branded, in all classes of trade. Members are open for selective consulting assignments.

Ass'n of Sales and Marketing Companies *(1904)*
2100 Reston Pkwy., Suite 400
Reston, VA 20191-1218
Tel: (703)758-7790   *Fax:* (703)758-7787
E-Mail: info@asmc.org
Web Site: http://www.asmc.org
Members: 1000 companies
Staff: 21
Annual Budget: $2-5,000,000
President: Robert C. Schwarze
Assoc. Director, Communications: Julie Legg
Director, Meeting Services: Sandra Savino
Director, Education/Prgm Dev: SueEllan L. Cantwell
V. President, Finance/Administration: Rachna Metha
V. President, Exec. Dir., Foodservice: Rick Abraham

Historical Note
Formerly (1997) Nat'l Food Brokers Ass'n. Members are sales representatives for producers of food, packaged goods, and other consumer products. The mission of the ASMC is to: maintain a highly respected position in those industries served by its members; advocate ethical and professional practices among principals, customers, and members; and lead its members in their continuing development of effective sales and marketing organizations so that they are the preferred method to market products and services. Sponsors the ASMC Education and Training Foundation. Membership: $750-$100,000/year, based on broker revenues (corporate).

Publications:
ASMC Directory. a.
Newsline. m.

SMQ (Sales and Marketing Quarterly). q.

Meetings/Conferences:
1999 – Chicago, IL/Oct. 6-9
2000 – Chicago, IL/Oct 29-Nov. 1

Ass'n of School Business Officials Internat'l *(1910)*
11401 North Shore Drive
Reston, VA 20190-4200
Tel: (703)478-0405   *Fax:* (703)478-6968
E-Mail: ditharpe@sprynet.com
Web Site: http://www.asbointl.org
Members: 7,000 individuals
Staff: 18
Annual Budget: $2-5,000,000
Exec. Director: Don I. Tharpe, Ed.D.
Communications Director: Scott Bisco
Director, Membership & Professional Programs: Alex Graham
Director, Finance and Administration: Noel E. Montesa

Historical Note
ASBO members are school district level business executives, professors of business and education, students, and businessmen of school-related firms. Members are dedicated to the professional stewardship of the investment in education, both public and private. Membership: $125/year.

Publications:
ASBO Accents Newspaper. m. adv.
Directory. a. adv.
School Business Affairs. m. adv.

Meetings/Conferences:
Annual Meetings: Fall
1999 – Orlando, FL
2000 – Minneapolis, MN/Sept. 30-Oct. 4
2001 – Baltimore, MD/Oct. 12-16
2002 – Phoenix, AZ

Ass'n of Schools and Colleges of Optometry *(1941)*
6110 Executive Blvd., Suite 510
Rockville, MD 20852
Tel: (301)231-5944   *Fax:* (301)770-1828
E-Mail: admini@opted.org
Web Site: http://www.opted.org
Members: 22 institutions, 20 corporations
Staff: 6
Annual Budget: $500-1,000,000
Exec. Director: Martin A. Wall, CAE
Director, Member & Public Affairs: Patricia O'Rourke
Student & Academic Affairs: Joan J. Anson, M.S. Ed.
Program Manager: Carol A. Brubaker

Historical Note
ASCO represents professional programs of optometric education in the U.S. and abroad. Membership: $21,400/year (institution); $3,000/year (corporate); $1,000/year (affiliate).

Publications:
Eye on Education Newsletter. bi-m.
Journal of Optometric Education. q. adv.
Ophthalmic Educational Software Guide. irreg.
Optometric Faculty Directory. a.
Residency and Graduate Program Directory. a.
Survey of Optometric Education. a.
Trends in Optometric Education. irreg.

Meetings/Conferences:
Annual Meetings: June, with the American Optometric Ass'n

Ass'n of Schools of Allied Health Professions *(1967)*
1730 M St., N.W., Suite 500
Washington, DC 20036
Tel: (202)293-4848   *Fax:* (202)293-4852
Web Site: http://hsc.missouri.edu/~shrp/asahp
Members: 750 schools, programs & individuals
Staff: 6
Annual Budget: $500-1,000,000
Exec. Director: Thomas W. Elwood

Historical Note
Formerly (1974) Ass'n of Schools of Allied Health Professions and (1992) American Soc. of Allied Health Professions. Membership includes allied health schools and programs, associations, and individual educators. Membership: $95-125/year (individual); $3,500/year (institution).

Publications:
Journal of Allied Health. q. adv.
Trends. m.

Meetings/Conferences:
1999 – San Juan, Puerto

Ass'n of Schools of Journalism and Mass Communication *(1917)*
Univ. of SC
LeConte College, Room 121
Columbia, SC 29208-0251
Tel: (803)777-2005   *Fax:* (803)777-4728
E-Mail: AEJMC@SC.EDU
Web Site: http://www.aejmc.edu
Members: 203 institutions
Staff: 7
Exec. Director: Jennifer McGill
Convention/Communications Manager: Fred Williams
Business Manager: Richard Burke
Membership/Sub. Mgr: Pamella Price

Historical Note
Founded as the Ass'n of Accredited Schools and Departments of Journalism, it became the American Ass'n of Schools and Departments of Journalism in 1954 and assumed its present name in 1983. Absorbed the American Soc. of Journalism School Administrators in 1984. Affiliated with the Ass'n for Education in Journalism and Mass Communication. Membership: $50/year (individual); $350/year (institution).

Publications:
ASJMC/Administrator Demographic Survey. a.

Annual Meetings: Summer/2,000
1999 – New Orleans, LA(Sheraton)/Aug. 4-7
2000 – Phoenix, AZ(Hyatt Regency)/Aug. 8-12
2001 – Washington, DC(Grand Hyatt)/Aug. 5-8

Ass'n of Schools of Public Health *(1953)*
1660 L St., N.W., Suite 204
Washington, DC 20036-5603
Tel: (202)296-1099   *Fax:* (202)296-1252
E-Mail: info@asph.org
Web Site: http://www.asph.org
Members: 28 schools
Staff: 18
Annual Budget: $500-1,000,000
Exec. Director: Michael K. Gemmell, CAE
Director, Finance and Administration: Allison Foster
Project Coordinator: Andrew McCachran

Historical Note
The only national organization representing administration, faculty, and students of the country's accredited schools of public health. Established in 1941 to facilitate communication among leadership of the schools. Membership: $14,000/year (organization).

Publications:
Graduate Education for Public Health. bien.

Meetings/Conferences:
Annual Meetings: Spring

Ass'n of Science Museum Directors *(1960)*
c/o Illinois State Museum
Spring and Edwards Sts.
Springfield, IL 62706-5000
Tel: (217)782-7011   *Fax:* (217)782-1254
E-Mail: rbm@museum.state.il.us
Web Site: http://www.musuem.state.il.us
Members: 72 individuals
Annual Budget: under $10,000
Secretary-Treasurer: Dr. R. Bruce McMillan

Historical Note
Has no paid officer or full-time staff. Membership: $100 or $200/year, depending on museum operating budget.

Publications:
Science Museum News. bi-a.

Meetings/Conferences:
Annual Meetings: With American Ass'n of Museums

Ass'n of Science-Technology Centers *(1973)*
1025 Vermont Ave., N.W., Suite 500
Washington, DC 20005-3516
Tel: (202)783-7200   *Fax:* (202)783-7207
E-Mail: info@astc.org
Web Site: www.astc.org
Members: 520 institutions
Staff: 24
Annual Budget: $2-5,000,000
Exec. Director: Bonnie VanDorn
Deputy Director: Wendy Pollock
Director, Government Relations: Ellen Griffee
Manager, Meetings/Conferences: Valerie Royal
Director, Education: Sally Middlebrooks
Chief Financial Officer: John Mericsko
Membership Coordinator: Diane Frendak
Manager, Membership and Human Resources: Franklin Boyd

Historical Note
Members are science museums and related institutions united to increase public understanding of science and technology. Works to improve the operation and delivery of services of member institutions, with a special interest in informal education and programs targeted to traditionally underserved communities and constituencies. Membership: $300 to $3,000/year (based on budget and type of membership).

Publications:
ASTC Directory. a.
ASTC Newsletter. bi-m. adv.

Meetings/Conferences:
Annual Meetings: Mid-October/1,400
1999 – Tampa, FL(Museum of Science & Industry)/Oct. 2-5
2000 – Cleveland, OH(Great Lakes Science
Center)/Oct. 14-17
2001 – Phoenix, AZ(Arizona Science Center)

Ass'n of Senior Anthropologists
Historical Note
A section of the American Anthropological Ass'n.

Ass'n of Service and Computer Dealers Internat'l *(1981)*
1045 E. Atlantic Ave. #206
Delray Beach, FL 33483
Tel: (561)266-9016   *Fax:* (561)266-9017
E-Mail: jmarion@ix.netcom.com
Web Site: http://www.ascdi.com
Members: 160 members
Staff: 4
Annual Budget: $100-250,000
President: Joseph Marion
Director, Conventions: Ruth Stramberg

Historical Note
Formerly (1994) American Soc. of Computer Dealers. Members are dealers, leasing companies, brokerage firms and refurbishment maintenance companies. Membership: $900/year (company).

Publications:
Membership Directory. a.

Meetings/Conferences:

Ass'n of Seventh-day Adventist Educators *(1970)*
Historical Note
Address unknown in 1996.

Ass'n of Seventh-Day Adventist Librarians *(1978)*
Weis Library, Columbia Union College
7600 Flower Ave.
Takoma Park, MD   20912-7796
Tel: (301)891-4222   *Fax:* (301)891-4204
E-Mail: LWISEL@cuc.edu
Web Site: http://andrews.edu/asdal
Members: 150 individuals
Annual Budget: $10-25,000
Treasurer: Lee Marie Wisel

Historical Note
Promotes librarianship and library services to Seventh-Day Adventist institutions. Sponsors the D. Glenn Hilts Scholarship Program. Has no paid officers or full-time staff. Membership: $10/year.

Publications:
ASDAL Action Newsletter. semi-a.
Seventh-Day Adventist Periodical Index. a.

Meetings/Conferences:
1999 – Montemorelos, Mexico(Montemorelos Univ.)
2000 – Berrien Spring, MI(Andrews Univ.)/50
2001 – Angwin, CA(Pacific Union College)/50

Ass'n of Ship Brokers and Agents (U.S.A.) *(1934)*
75 Main St., Suite 104
Millburn, NJ   07041
Tel: (973)376-4144   *Fax:* (973)376-4145
Members: 105 individuals
Staff: 2
Annual Budget: $100-250,000
Exec. Director: Virginia D. Redstone

Historical Note
Founded as the Ass'n of Ship Brokers and Agents on January 9, 1934. Incorporated in 1954 and assumed its present name in 1970. Members are ship brokers and ship agents. Offers correspondence courses in chartering available to the general public. Membership: $700/year (individual); $350/year (affiliate); $250/year (associate).

Publications:
American Tanker Rate Schedule. a.
ASBA Newsletter. q.
Yearbook. bi-a.

Meetings/Conferences:
Annual Meetings: always New York, NY/2nd Tuesday in
            January

Ass'n of SIDS and Infant Mortality Programs *(1987)*
c/o Center for Infant and Child Loss
630 W. Fayette St., Room 5-0684
Baltimore, MD   21201
Tel: (410)706-5062   *Fax:* (410)706-0146
Members: 75 individuals
President: Jodi Shaefer, Ph.D.

Historical Note
Founded as Ass'n of SIDS Program Professionals; assumed its current name in 1996. Members are health care and human service professionals providing services to those affected by Sudden Infant Death Syndrome and related conditions. Has no paid officers or full-time staff. Membership: $65/year (full); $40/year (associate).

Publications:
Newletter. a.

Meetings/Conferences:

Ass'n of SIDS Program Professionals
Historical Note
Became (1996) Ass'n of SIDS and Infant Mortality Programs.

Ass'n of Small Business Development Centers *(1980)*
3108 Columbia Pike, #300
Arlington, VA   22204-4304
Tel: (703)271-8700   *Fax:* (703)271-8701
Members: 950 centers
Staff: 3
Annual Budget: $500-1,000,000
Exec. Director: Kathleen Dawson

Historical Note
SBDCs are small business development centers which provide management and technical assistance to small business concerns and are jointly funded by federal and state governments. Previously the Small Business Development Center Directors Ass'n.

Publications:
ASBDC News. m.

Meetings/Conferences:
Semi-annual Meetings: Spring and Fall (one always in
            Washington, DC)
1999 – San Diego, CA

Ass'n of Small Research, Engineering and Technical Service Companies *(1983)*
36 S. Charles St., 20th Floor
Baltimore, MD   21201-3020
Tel: (410)363-4949   *Fax:* (410)647-5424
Members: 200 companies
Staff: 2
Exec. Director: Daniel T. Arnold

Historical Note
ASRET members are companies engaged in research, engineering and technical services. ASRET promotes teaming, strategic partnering, contracting and subcontracting among member companies and to voice the concerns of small high tech companies. Membership: $200-600/year, varies by number of employees (corporate); $750/year (large business); $750/year (professional services); $50/year (associate).

Publications:
ASRET News. m. adv.

Meetings/Conferences:
Monthly Meetings: Washington, DC metro area

Ass'n of Smoked Fish Processors *(1963)*
5 Hayward St.
Quincy, MA   02171
Tel: (617)328-7600   *Fax:* (617)770-0957
Members: 5 companies
Staff: 2
Technical Director: Dr. George W. Bierman

Historical Note
Members are food processors with an interest in smoked fish.

Ass'n of Social and Behavioral Scientists *(1935)*
Historical Note
Address unknown in 1996.

Ass'n of Southern Baptist Colleges and Schools *(1915)*
7348 Charlotte Pike, Suite C
Nashville, TN   37209
Tel: (615)354-1398   *Fax:* (615)354-1331
Members: 71 institutions
Staff: 1
Annual Budget: $25-50,000
Interim Director: Tim Fields

Historical Note
Consists of the presidents and chief academic officials of Southern Baptist colleges, universities, seminaries, Bible schools and academies. Formerly known as the Southern Ass'n of Baptist Colleges and Schools.

Publications:
Southern Baptist Educator. m.

Meetings/Conferences:
Annual Meetings: June/150 St. Luis, MO/June 14-16/100

Ass'n of Specialists in Cleaning and Restoration Internat'l *(1946)*
10830 Annapolis Junction Rd., Suite 312
Annapolis Junction, MD   20701-1120
Tel: (301)604-4411   *Fax:* (301)604-4713
Toll Free: (800)272 - 7012
E-Mail: info@ascr.org
Web Site: http://www.ascr.org
Members: 1,050 companies
Staff: 6
Annual Budget: $1-2,000,000
Exec. Director: Kimberly Howard
Technical Director: Eric Bae

Historical Note
Formerly (1984) the Ass'n of Interior Decor Specialists. Divisions: Carpet & Upholstery Cleaning Institute (1971); Drapery Specialists Institute (1971); Mechanical Systems Hygiene Institute (1993); Nat'l Institute of Disaster Restoration (1968); Nat'l Institute of Rug and Drapery Cleaning (1946); and Water Loss Institute (1994). ASCRI is made up of owners, executives, and companies whose primary business purpose is to offer cleaning and restoration services and products. Membership: $300-800/year.

Publications:
Cleaning & Restoration. m. adv.
Directory of Cleaning & Restoration Firms. a.

Meetings/Conferences:
Annual Meetings: Spring/400
1999 – Palm Springs, CA(Wyndham Palm
            Springs)/March 9-13
2000 – Nashville, TN(Opryland)/March 14-19
2001 – Colorado Springs, CO(Broadmoor)/March 6-13/600

Ass'n of Specialized and Cooperative Library Agencies *(1944)*
50 East Huron St.
Chicago, IL   60611
Tel: (312)280-4395   *Fax:* (312)944-8089
Members: 1,220 libraries
Staff: 3
Annual Budget: $50-100,000
Exec. Director: Cathleen Bourdon

Historical Note
Division of the American Library Ass'n. Formerly known as the Ass'n of State Library Agencies, the Ass'n of Hospital and Institution Libraries (until 1974), and Health and Rehabilitative Library Services (until 1978). Membership:$40 (individual); $50 (organization).

Publications:
Interface. q.

Meetings/Conferences:
Annual Meetings: With the American Library Ass'n

Ass'n of Specialized and Professional Accreditors *(1993)*
1020 W. Byron St., Suite 8-G
Chicago, IL   60613-2987
Tel: (773)525-2160   *Fax:* (773)525-2162
E-Mail: aspacd@aol.com
Web Site: http://nait.org/aspa
Members: 42 individuals
Staff: 1
Annual Budget: $100-250,000
Exec. Director: Cynthia A. Davenport

Historical Note
ASPA represents the interests of specialty and professional accreditation organizations to higher education and to government. Membership fee varies based on size of organization; $6,000/year maximum.

Publications:
Membership Directory. a.
Newsletter. semi-a.

Meetings/Conferences:
Semi-Annual Meetings: Spring and Fall
1999 – Washington, DC

1999 – Washington, DC(Ritz-Carlton, Pentagon
            City)/March 4-6/30
2000 – Chicago, IL/April 2-4
2000 – /Sept. 10-12
2001 – Washington, DC/March 25-27
2001 – /Sept. 9-11
2002 – Chicago, IL/April 7-9
2002 – /Sept. 8-10

Ass'n of Specialty Cut Flower Growers *(1988)*
MPO Box 268
Oberlin, OH   44074-0268
Tel: (440)774-2887   *Fax:* (440)774-2435
Web Site: http://www.ascfg.org
Members: 600 individuals
Staff: 1
Exec. Director: Judy M. Laushman

Historical Note
Mission of ASCFG is to unite and inform growers in the production and marketing of field and specialty floral crops. Membership: $125/year (individual); $150/year (international member); $25/year (student).

Publications:
Cut Flower Quarterly. q. adv.

Meetings/Conferences:
1999 – Worcester, MA/Oct. 20-24

Ass'n of State and Interstate Water Pollution Control Administrators *(1962)*
750 First St., N.E., Suite 1010
Washington, DC   20002
Tel: (202)898-0905   *Fax:* (202)898-0929
E-Mail: admin1@asiwpca.org
Web Site: http://www.asiwpca.org
Members: 56 state government organizations
Staff: 6
Annual Budget: $250-500,000
Exec. Director: Roberta (Robbi) Savage

Historical Note
The chief water pollution control administrators from 50 states, Guam, Virgin Islands, Puerto Rico, the District of Columbia, and 4 interstate agencies. Establishes objectives, policies, and standards for state water pollution control and groundwater protection.

Meetings/Conferences:
1999 – Kenne Bunk Port, MN

Ass'n of State and Provincial Psychology Boards *(1961)*
P.O. Box 4389
400 S. Union St., Suite 295
Montgomery, AL   36103-4389
Tel: (334)832-4580   *Fax:* (334)269-6379
Toll Free: (800)448 - 4069
E-Mail: asppb@asppb.org
Web Site: http://www.aspbb.org
Members: 40 individuals, 61 agencies
Staff: 12
Annual Budget: $1-2,000,000
Exec. Officer/General Counsel: Randolph P. Reaves, JD
Associate Exec. Officer: Amy E. Campbell

Historical Note
ASPPB represents psychology regularotry baords in the U.S. and Canada. It creates the Examination for Professional Practice in Psychology; provides a means fo psychology boards to work together on common concerns; and serves as a clearinghouse for information on licensing requirements, professional discipline, and other topics. Formerly (1992) the American Ass'n of State Psychology Boards. Membership: $350 (base) + $3 per licensee, maximum $2,750 (agency); $35/year (individual).

Publications:
AASPB Newsletter. q.
Handbook of Licensing & Certification Requirements. a.
Psychologists in North America. a.

Meetings/Conferences:
Annual Meetings: October/100

Ass'n of State and Territorial Dental Directors *(1947)*
Arizona Department of Health Services
1740 W. Adams, Room 10
Phoenix, AZ   85007-2670
Tel: (602)542-1866   *Fax:* (602)542-2936
E-Mail: daltman@hs.state.AZ.US
Members: 59 individuals
Annual Budget: $50-100,000
Secretary-Treasurer: Don Altman

Historical Note
An affiliate of Ass'n of State and Territorial Health Officials. Has no paid officers or full-time staff. Membership: $100/year (full member); $50/year (associate).

Publications:
ASTDD News Briefs. q. adv.

Meetings/Conferences:
Annual Meetings: Spring/200

Ass'n of State and Territorial Directors of Health Promotion and Public Health *(1946)*
1015 15th St., N.W., Suite 410
Washington, DC   20005
Tel: (202)289-6639   *Fax:* (202)408-9815
E-Mail: director@astshppe.org
Web Site: http://www.astdhpphe.org
Members: 75 individuals
Staff: 2
Annual Budget: $100-250,000
Exec. Director: Rose Marie Matulionis, MSPH

Historical Note
Founded as Conference of State and Territorial Directors of Public Health Education; became Ass'n of State and Territorial Directors of

Public Health Education in 1996; assumed its current name in 1998. Membership: $25/year (individual); $200/year (organization).

Meetings/Conferences:

Ass'n of State and Territorial Directors of Nursing (1935)

900 S.W. Jackson, Suite 665
Topeka, KS 66612-1290
Tel: (785)296-7100
Fax: (785)296-1231
Members: 54 individuals
Annual Budget: under $10,000
President: Abby Horak

Historical Note

Established in 1935 as a council of the American Public Health Ass'n, it later became Ass'n of State and Territorial Directors of Public Health Nursing. In 1966 the name was changed to Ass'n of State and Territorial Directors of Nursing. Affiliated with Ass'n of State and Territorial Health Officials. Has no paid staff or permanent address. The president is elected for a 1-year term. Membership: $35/year (individual).

Meetings/Conferences:
Annual Meetings: May

Ass'n of State and Territorial Directors of Public Health Education (1946)

Historical Note

Became (1997) Ass'n of State and Territorial Directors of Health Promotion and Public Health.

Ass'n of State and Territorial Health Officials (1942)

1275 K St., N.W., Suite 800
Washington, DC 20005-4006
Tel: (202)371-9090
Fax: (202)371-9797
E-Mail: sturner@astho.org
Web Site: http://www.astho.org
Members: 57 individuals
Staff: 23
Annual Budget: $2-5,000,000
Exec. V. President: Cheryl A. Beversdorf, RN, MHS, C
Senior Dep. Director: Shannon Turner
Assoc. Director, Public Relations/Membership/Marketing: Sandra Cutts
Dep. Director, Policy and Programs: Jacalyn L. Bryan
Senior Director, Government Relations: Joseph S. Green

Historical Note

Formerly (1975) Ass'n of State and Territorial Health Officers. Members are executive officers at public health agencies of the U.S. states and territories. Its purpose is to formulate and influence sound public health policy, and to promote policies that improve health and prevent disease, injury, and disability.

Publications:
ASTHO Report. Bi-m.
SHO-time. bi-m.
State Health Agency Directory. bi-a.
Washington Report. bi-w(in session).

Meetings/Conferences:
Annual Meetings: Fall

Ass'n of State and Territorial Public Health Nutrition Directors (1952)

1015 15th St., N.W. Suite 403
Washington, DC 22605
Tel: (202)408-1257
Fax: (202)789-1259
Members: 121 individuals
Staff: 1
Annual Budget: $100-250,000
President: Margaret Tate

Historical Note

Members are directors of nutrition programs in the state and territorial public health agencies. Affiliated with the Ass'n of State and Territorial Health Officials. Membership: $300/year.

Publications:
ASTPHND Newsletter. q.
Resource Directory. a.

Meetings/Conferences:
Annual Meetings: Spring
1999 - Indianapolis, IN

Ass'n of State and Territorial Solid Waste Management Officials (1974)

444 North Capitol St., N.W., Suite 315
Washington, DC 20001
Tel: (202)624-5828
Fax: (202)624-7875
Members: 56 states and territories
Staff: 9
Annual Budget: $1-2,000,000
Exec. Director: Thomas J. Kennedy
Director, Government Affairs: Thomas Kennedy

Historical Note

Members are state employees who manage the regulatory solid waste and remedial action programs of state government.

Publications:
Directory of State Waste Management Program Officials. a.

Meetings/Conferences:
Two Annual Meetings: Spring and Fall

Ass'n of State Correctional Administrators (1960)

213 Court St., Sixth Fl.
Middletown, CT 06457-2906
Tel: (860)704-6410
Members: 58 individuals
Staff: 4
Annual Budget: $100-250,000
Exec. Director: Camille G. Camp

Historical Note

Formerly (1967) Correctional Administrators Ass'n of America. ASCA's membership consists of the directors of all fifty state correctional agencies, the Federal Bureau of Prisons, and several large urban prison systems. Its purpose is to provide leadership and direction on national correctional policy and practice. Membership: $750/year.

Meetings/Conferences:
1999 - Nashville, TN

Ass'n of State Dam Safety Officials (1984)

450 Old Vine St., 2nd Floor
Lexington, KY 40507
Tel: (606)257-5140
Fax: (606)323-1958
E-Mail: damsafety@aol.com
Web Site: http://members.aol.com/damsafety/homepage.htm
Members: 1000 individuals, 600 companies
Staff: 3
Annual Budget: $500-1,000,000
Exec. Director: Lori Spragens
Director, Membership and Conference Coordinator: Susan Sorrell

Historical Note

ASDSO was established to provide a forum for the exchange of ideas and experiences on dam safety issues; to foster interstate cooperation; provide information and assistance to state dam safety programs; provide representation of state interests before Congress and federal agencies; and improve the efficiency and effectiveness of state dam safety programs. Full voting membership is restricted to one state official from each of the 50 states and U.S. territories who is responsible for administering and managing dam safety programs. Associate membership is available for other state, local and federal and federal officials concerned with dam safety. Affiliate membership is available for individuals representing the private sector. Membership: $200/year (full voting); $20/year (associate); $200/year (company affiliate); $50/year (individual affiliate); $25/year (retired); $5/year (student).

Publications:
Annual Report.
ASDSO Newsletter. bi-m. adv.
Conference Proceedings. a.
Publication on State Requirements. a.
State Dam Safety Programs Update. a.
Summary of Laws on Dam Safety.

Meetings/Conferences:
Annual Meetings: Fall
1999 - St. Louis, MO(Hyatt)/650

Ass'n of State Drinking Water Administrators (1984)

1120 Connecticut Ave., N.W., Suite 1060
Washington, DC 20036-3902
Tel: (202)293-7655
Fax: (202)293-7656
E-Mail: asdwa@erols.com
Web Site: http://www.asdwa.org
Members: 50 states and 6 territories
Staff: 5
Annual Budget: $500-1,000,000
Exec. Director: Vanessa M. Leiby

Historical Note

Members include 50 states and six territories; individuals who work for state water regulatory agencies or local health departments are also eligible for associate membership.

Publications:
Newsletter. bi-m.

Meetings/Conferences:
1999 - Orlando, FL(Hotel Royal Plaza)/Oct. 4-7

Ass'n of State Floodplain Managers (1977)

4233 W. Beltline Hwy.
Madison, WI 53711-3814
Tel: (608)274-0123
Fax: (608)274-0696
E-Mail: asfpm@floods.org
Web Site: http://www.floods.org
Members: 1000 individuals, 2,500 chapter affiliates
Staff: 3
Annual Budget: $100-250,000
Exec. Director: Larry A. Larson
Executive Office Manager: Diane Alicia Watson
Administrative Assistant: Debra Pond

Historical Note

ASFPM is an organization of professionals involved in floodplain management, flood hazard mitigation, multi-objective watershed management, the National Flood Insurance Program and flood preparedness, warning and recovery. Membership: $50/year (individual); $100/year (agency); $100-400/year, based on number of employees (corporate sponsorship).

Publications:
Insider. bi-m.
Nat'l Directory of Floodplain Managers. a.
News & Views Newsletter. 6/year. adv.
Proceedings of Annual Conference. a.

Meetings/Conferences:
1999 - Portland, OR(Marriott)/May 23-28
2000 - Austin, TX(Hyatt Regency)/June 16-25

Ass'n of State Supervisors of Mathematics (1961)

Dept. of Education
165 Capital Ave.
Hartford, CT 06106
Tel: (860)566-4588
Fax: (860)566-5625
Members: 100 individuals
Annual Budget: under $10,000
President: Charles Watson

Historical Note

ASSM promotes interest in the study and teaching of mathematics. Has no paid officers or full-time staff. Membership: $30/year.

Publications:
ASSM Newsletter. q.

Ass'n of State Wetland Managers (1984)

P.O. Box 269
Berne, NY 12023-9746
Tel: (518)872-1804
Fax: (518)872-2171
Web Site: http://www.aswm.org
Members: 950 individuals
Staff: 4
Annual Budget: $100-250,000
Exec. Director: Jon A. Kusler

Historical Note

Members are professionals involved in wetlands protection and management programs including members of the federal, state, local, private, not-for-profit and academic communities addressing wetland protection issues. Membership: $30/year (individual); $100/year (organization/company).

Publications:
Wetland News Newsletter. q. adv.

Meetings/Conferences:

Ass'n of Statisticians of American Religious Bodies (1934)

1121 Seneca Rd.
Benton Harbor, MI 49022
Tel: (616)925-0695
Members: 30 individuals
Annual Budget: under $10,000
Secretary-Treasurer: Greta Lauria

Historical Note

Members are persons at the denominational or national level with responsibility for gathering, compiling and publishing statistics of and for their religious bodies. The association provides a forum for the exchange of information and seeks to bring about such measure of standardization as may be necessary and possible for the correlation of religious statistical data. Has no paid staff. Membership: $35/year (individual).

Meetings/Conferences:
Annual Meetings: Fall
1999 - St. Louis, MO

Ass'n of Steel Distributors (1943)

401 N. Michigan Ave.
Chicago, IL 60611-4267
Tel: (312)644-6610
Fax: (312)245-1083
E-Mail: asd@sba.com
Web Site: http://www.steeldistributors.org/osd
Members: 157 companies
Staff: 4
Annual Budget: $250-500,000
Exec. Director: Ron Pietrzak
Public Relations Manager: Lori Seaberg
Manager, Convention: Neela Thakrar

Historical Note

Members are service centers, warehouses, processors, traders and mills. Membership: $1,350/year.

Publications:
ASD News & Views. q. adv.

Meetings/Conferences:
Semi-annual: Spring and Fall
1999 - Scottsdale, AZ(Scottsdale Princess)/April 25-28/150
1999 - Orlando, FL(Disney's Board Walk)/Oct. 17-20/100
2000 - Maui, HI(Grand Wailela)/April 1-4/150

Ass'n of Supervisory and Administrative School Personnel (1989)

1300 Mercantile Lane, Suite 144
Largo, MD 20774
Tel: (301)925-7047
Fax: (301)925-2774
Members: 585 individuals
Staff: 2
Annual Budget: $250-500,000
Exec. Director: Doris A. Reed

Historical Note

Formerly Ass'n of School Based Administrators and Supervisors (1994). Membership: $390/year.

Publications:
AWARE newsletter. 6/year.

Ass'n of Surfing Professionals (1983)

P.O. Box 309
Huntington Beach, CA 92648
Tel: (949)851-2774
Fax: (949)851-2773
E-Mail: aspintl@earthlink.net
Web Site: http://www.aspworldtour.com
Members: 1,200 individuals
Staff: 10
Annual Budget: $1-2,000,000
Exec. Director: Graham Stapelberg
Manager, Events and Projects: Meg Bernaido

Historical Note

ASP is dedicated to the promotion and excellence of surfing events throughout the world. Seeks to promote the sport of professional surfing for the benefit of its members, the sanctioned World Tour events, the professional surfers and the public. Membership is open to professional and amateur surfers.

Publications:
ASP Media Guide. a.
ASP Newsletter. m.

Meetings/Conferences:
1999 - Sydney, Australia

Ass'n of Surgical Technologists (1969)

7108-C S. Alton Way,
Englewood, CO 80112-2106
Tel: (303)694-9130
Fax: (303)694-9169
E-Mail: ast@ast.org
Web Site: http://www.ast@ast.org

Members: 17,000 individuals
Staff: 25
Annual Budget: $1-2,000,000
Exec. Director: William J. Teutsch
Marketing Manager: Ron Carter
Assistant Exec. Director: Bob Caruthers
Accounting Manager: Ron Miller
Membership Manager: Laura Parker

Historical Note
AST's primary concerns center on ensuring that surgical technologists are educationally qualified to administer surgical patient care through the support of accreditation, certification and continuing education. Membership $70/year.

Publications:
Surgical Technologist. m. adv.

Meetings/Conferences:
1999 – Las Vegas, NV/May 31-June 3

Ass'n of Systematics Collections (1972)
1725 K St., N.W., Suite 601
Washington, DC   20006-1401
Tel: (202)835-9050   *Fax:* (202)835-7334
E-Mail: asc@ascoll.org
Web Site: http://www.ascoll.org
Members: 83 institutions, 25 societies
Staff: 2
Annual Budget: $100-250,000

Historical Note
Members are museums, zoos, botanic gardens and other systematic collections housed at universities, non-profit research institutions, state-funded institutions and governmental agencies. Professional societies of individuals interested in the systematics of organisms are also included in the membership. Membership: $600, 1,900 or 5,000/year (based on size of organization). Affiliate Membership: $100/year.

Publications:
ASC Newsletter. bi-m. adv.
Washington Initiative. m.

Meetings/Conferences:
1999 – Beltsville, MD/July 26-30
1999 – St. Louis, MO/August 1-7

Ass'n of Talent Agents (1937)
9255 Sunset Blvd., Suite 930
Los Angeles, CA   90069-3381
Tel: (310)274-0628   *Fax:* (310)274-5063
E-Mail: agentassoc@aol.com
Members: 120 companies
Staff: 2
Annual Budget: $250-500,000
Exec. Director: Karen Stuart

Historical Note
Founded in 1937 as the Artists Managers Guild with the purpose of professionalizing the agency business. Assumed is present name in 1979. ATA member companies currently represent approximately 85% of the creative talent in the SAG, AFTRA, Equity, DGA and WGA fields. Membership: $320/year (minimum).

Publications:
Newsletter. m.

Ass'n of Teacher Educators (1920)
1900 Association Dr., Suite ATE
Reston, VA   20191-1502
Tel: (703)620-3110   *Fax:* (703)620-9530
Members: 4,000 individuals
Staff: 4
Annual Budget: $250-500,000
Exec. Director: Dr. Gloria Chernay

Historical Note
The ATE serves as a national voice for issues related to preservice, graduate and inservice teacher education and provides opportunities for professional development through its publications and national conferences, workshops and academies. Membership: $75/year (individual); $60/year (library).

Publications:
Action in Teacher Education. q. adv.
ATE Newsletter. bi-m.

Meetings/Conferences:
Annual Meetings: February/1,500
1999 – Chicago, IL(Hilton)/Feb. 13-17
2000 – orlando, FL(Corondo Springs)/Feb. 12-16
2001 – New Orleans, LA(Hilton)/Feb. 17-21

Ass'n of Teachers of Japanese (1963)
Box 279 Dept. of East Asian Lang. & Lit.
University of Colorado
Boulder, CO   80309-0279
Tel: (303)492-5487   *Fax:* (303)492-5856
E-Mail: ATJ@colorado.edu
Web Site: http://www.colorado.edu/ealld/atj
Members: 1,300 individuals
Staff: 3
Annual Budget: $25-50,000
President: Laurel Rasplica Rodd

Historical Note
Members have professional interests in the teaching of Japanese as a foreign language and in the allied fields of Japanese linguistics and literature. Membership: $35/year (individual); $45/year (organization).

Publications:
ATJ Newsletter. q. adv.
Journal of The Association of Teachers of Japanese. semi-a. adv.

Meetings/Conferences:
1999 – Boston, MA(Hilton)/March 11-14

Ass'n of Teachers of Latin American Studies (1970)
P.O. Box 620754

Flushing, NY   11362-0754
Tel: (718)428-1237   *Fax:* (718)428-1237
E-Mail: DJMUGAN@AOL.com
Members: 727 individuals
Staff: 2
Annual Budget: $50-100,000
Exec. Director: Daniel J. Mugan
Treasurer: Dr. Norman Binder
Secretary: Ms. Rosa Salinas

Historical Note
An organization of educators and other persons interested in the promotion of study about Latin America in our education institutions. Incorporated in 1973. Membership: $12/year.

Publications:
Curriculum Guides on Ecuador, Brazil, Argentina, Venezuela, and Chile.
Perspective (newsletter). q. adv.

Meetings/Conferences:

Ass'n of Teachers of Maternal and Child Health (1968)
2000 15th St. North, Suite 701
Arlington, VA   22201-2617
Tel: (703)524-7802
Members: 200 individuals
Annual Budget: under $10,000
Secretariat: Katrina Holt

Historical Note
ATMCH members are academics in the field of maternal and child health. Administrative support provided by the Nat'l Center for Education in Maternal and Child Health (same address). Membership: $35/year.

Publications:
ATMCH News Newsletter. semi-a.

Meetings/Conferences:
Semi-annual Meetings: Fall with APHA and Spring with AMCHP

Ass'n of Teachers of Preventive Medicine (1942)
1660 L St., N.W., Suite 208
Washington, DC   20036-5603
Tel: (202)463-0550   *Fax:* (202)463-0555
Members: 500 individuals, 110 institutions
Staff: 11
Annual Budget: $250-500,000
Exec. Director: Barbara J. Calkins
Manager, Membership/Marketing: Linda Grande Brady

Historical Note
Teachers of preventive medicine and community health in medical schools. Sponsors the ATPM Foundation. Affiliated with the Ass'n of American Medical Colleges and the Council on Education for Public Health. Membership: $125/year (individual); $500/year (institution).

Publications:
American Journal of Preventive Medicine. q.
ATPM E-mail Newsletter. w.
ATPM Newsletter. q.
ATPM Roster. a.

Meetings/Conferences:
Annual Meetings: Spring, with American College of Preventive Medicine
1999 – Washington, DC/March 18-21

Ass'n of Teachers of Technical Writing (1973)
Dept. Of English, Eastern Michigan U.
P.O. Box 25000
Ypsilanti, MI   48197
Tel: (734)487-4221
Members: 1,200 individuals
Contact: Ann Blakeslee

Historical Note
ATTW provides communication among teachers of technical writing and develops technical communications as an academic discipline. Begun in 1973 with a dozen or so members, ATTW is now an international organization. Membership includes teachers and students from all levels and all types of educational institutions, and technical writers from government and industry. Has no paid staff. Membership: $30/year (USA), $35/year (foreign), $50/year (library), $15/year (student).

Publications:
ATTW Bulletin Newsletter. semi-a.
Technical Communication Quarterly Journal. q. adv.

Meetings/Conferences:
Annual Meetings: in conjunction with Conference on College Composition & Communication

Ass'n of Technical and Supervisory Professionals (1972)
1912 Katie Court
Joliet, IL   60435
Tel: (815)439-0072   *Fax:* (815)439-0766
Members: 420 individuals
Annual Budget: under $10,000
Nat'l Secretary: Paul V. Wolseley

Historical Note
ATSP members are individuals involved in the Department of Agriculture's meat and poultry inspection programs. ATSP was formed to give members consultation rights with the Department of Agriculture, Meat and Poultry Inspection Managment Program and to promote the importance of a safe and sanitary supply of meat and poultry. Has no office or full time staff. Membership: $62.50/year (individual).

Publications:
ATSP Newsletter. q.

Ass'n of Technical Personnel in Ophthalmology (1969)

Historical Note
ATPO members are certified and other technical personnel in ophthamology.

Ass'n of Telemedicine Service Providers
7276 SW Beaverton-Hillsdale Hwy.
Box 400
Portland, OR   97225
Tel: (503)222-2406   *Fax:* (503)223-7581
E-Mail: info@atsp.org
Web Site: http://www.atsp.org

Ass'n of TeleServices Internat'l (1942)
1200 19th St., N.W., Suite 300
Washington, DC   20036-2401
Tel: (202)857-1100   *Fax:* (202)223-4579
Web Site: http://www.atsi.org
Members: 900 companies
Staff: 3
Annual Budget: $500-1,000,000
Exec. V. President: Herta Tucker

Historical Note
Formerly the Association of Telemessaging Services International (1998). Formed to represent the telephone answering service industry, ATSI has expanded with the industry and now represents the full range of messaging and communications service bureaus, including TAS, voice mail, voice store, forward, fax mailboxes, and interactive and broadcast fax. Formerly (1986) Associated Telephone Answering Exchanges. Membership: $600-1,800/yr. (company).

Publications:
TeleCommunicator. bi-w. adv.
The Answer. q. adv.

Meetings/Conferences:
Annual Meetings: May/June
1999 – San Francisco, CA(Fairmont)/June 9-12/500
2000 – Washington, DC(Radisson)/June 28-July 1/500

Ass'n of Test Publishers (1992)
1201 Pennsylvania Ave., N.W., Suite 300
Washington, DC   20004
Tel: (202)857-8444
Toll Free: (800)922 - 7343
Members: 41 companies
Annual Budget: $100-250,000
Exec. Director: Dr. William G. Harris

Historical Note
Formerly (1993) Ass'n of Personal Test Publishers. Members are publishers of standardized tests for use in educational, industrial, and clinical situations, as well as providers of assessment services and products. Membership: $250-15,000/year.

Publications:
Test Publisher. q.

Meetings/Conferences:

Ass'n of the Nonwoven Fabrics Industry

Historical Note
See INDA, Ass'n of the Nonwoven Fabrics Industry.

Ass'n of the United States Army (1950)
2425 Wilson Blvd.
Arlington, VA   22201-3385
Tel: (703)841-4300   *Fax:* (703)525-9039
Toll Free: (800)336 - 4570
Web Site: http://www.ausa.org
Members: 112,000 individuals
Staff: 75
Annual Budget: $10-25,000,000
President & C.O.O.: Gen. Jack N. Merritt, USA(Ret.)
Director, Government Affairs: John M. Molino
V. President, Meetings & Membership: Lt.Gen. Thomas Rhame, USA(Ret.)
V. President, Education: Lt.Gen. Theodore G. Stroup, Jr., USA(R
V. President, Finance and Administration: Arthur S. Welch, CAM
Director, Marketing: Millie Hurlbut

Historical Note
Formed by a merger of the U.S. Infantry Ass'n and the U.S. Field Artillery Ass'n in 1950. Absorbed (1955) the U.S. Antiaircraft Ass'n. Active, retired and reserve military personnel. Has an annual budget of $12 million.

Publications:
Army Magazine. m. adv.
AUSA News. m. adv.
Washington Update. m.

Meetings/Conferences:
Annual Meetings: always Washington, DC(Wardman Park Marriott/Omni Shoreham)/October/26
1999 – /Oct. 10-14

Ass'n of the Wall and Ceiling Industries-Internat'l (1918)
803 W. Broad St., Suite 600
Falls Church, VA   22046-3108
Tel: (703)534-8300   *Fax:* (703)534-8307
E-Mail: info@awci.org
Web Site: http://www.awci.org
Members: 1000 companies, 17 chapters
Staff: 12
Annual Budget: $2-5,000,000
Exec. V. President: Steven A. Etkin, CAE
Director, Communications: Laura Porinchak
Director, Meetings & Exhibits: Margaret Jenkins Roberts

Historical Note
AWCI represents acoustics systems, ceiling systems, drywall systems, exterior insulation/finishing systems, fireproofing, flooring systems, insulation and stucco contractors, suppliers and manufacturers; and those in allied trades. Membership accounts for nearly 25% of related wall and ceiling construction volume in the United States. Membership: annual dues vary through chapters; $585/year (At-Large), $295/year (foreign contractors).

Publications:
Construction Dimensions. m. adv.

Members Only. m.
Tech Notes. m.
Who's Who in the Wall and Ceiling Industry. a.

Meetings/Conferences:
Annual Meetings: Spring
1999 – Washington, DC

Ass'n of Theatrical Press Agents and Managers (1928)
165 West 46th St., Suite 700
New York, NY 10036
Tel: (212)719-3666 *Fax:* (212)302-1585
Toll Free: (800)858 - 3667
E-Mail: atpam@erols.com
Members: 750 individuals
Staff: 5
Annual Budget: $500-1,000,000
Secretary-Treasurer: Gordon Forbes

Historical Note
Labor Union affiliated with the AFL-CIO. Membership: $105/year (individual).

Publications:
Hi-Lites.

Meetings/Conferences:
Triannual Meetings: always in New York, NY in Jan., April and
October

Ass'n of Theological Schools in the United States and Canada (1918)
10 Summit Park Drive
Pittsburgh, PA 15275-1103
Tel: (412)788-6505 *Fax:* (412)788-6510
E-Mail: ats@ats.edu
Web Site: http://www.ats.edu
Members: 237 institutions
Staff: 18
Annual Budget: $2-5,000,000
Exec. Director: Rev. David O. Aleshire, Ph.D.
Director, Communications: Nancy Merrill
Director, Accreditation/Ed. Technology: Katherine Amos
Director, Business Affairs: Stephanie Sweeney
Information Systems Manager: Deena Malone
Grant Programs Coordinator: Matthew Zyniewicz

Historical Note
ATS is a membership organization of graduate schools of theology in the U.S. and Canada. The primary purpose of ATS is the improvement of theological schools, which it seeks to attain by accrediting schools and by providing programs and services to its membership. Member institutions are Protestant, Roman Catholic, and Orthodox schools of theology, both university-related divinity schools and freestanding seminaries. ATS is recognized by the U.S. Department of Education and by the nongovernmental Council for Higher Education Accreditation. The Ass'n began in 1918 as a small annual conference of predominantly Protestant theological schools. In 1936 it became an ass'n and adopted standards for judging quality in theological education, and in 1938 it established its first list of accredited schools.

Publications:
Bulletin. bi-a.
Colloquy Newsletter. 5/yr.
Fact Book on Theological Education. a.
Membership List. a.
Theological Education Journal. bi-en.

Meetings/Conferences:
2000 – Toronto, Ontario, Canada(Hilton)/June 17-19/350

Ass'n of Third World Studies (1983)
P.O. Box 1232
Americus, GA 31709-1232
Tel: (912)931-2078 *Fax:* (912)931-2270
Members: 600 individuals
Staff: 1
Annual Budget: $25-50,000
Founder: Harold Isaacs, Ph.D.

Historical Note
ATWS members are academics, development specialists and others with an interest in 'third world' countries. Membership: $35/year.

Publications:
ATWS Conference Proceedings. a.
ATWS Newsletter. 3/year.
Journal of Third World Studies. bi-a. adv.

Meetings/Conferences:

Ass'n of Tongue Depressors (1978)
100 East Maple St.
Teaneck, NJ 07666
Tel: (201)692-3250 *Fax:* (201)387-1288
Members: 28 companies
Staff: 1
Annual Budget: $25-50,000
Contact: Matthew Schorr

Historical Note
Health care firms, researchers and manufacturers of tongue depressors.

Publications:
Wooden Stick. q.

Ass'n of Tour Professionals
Historical Note
Address unknown in 1995.

Ass'n of Training and Employment Professionals (1967)
Historical Note
Organization defunct in 1998.

Ass'n of Traumatic Stress Specialists (1989)
7338 Broad River Road
Irmo, SC 29063

Tel: (803)781-0017 *Fax:* (803)781-3899
E-Mail: www.atss-nq.comm
Members: 900 individuals
Staff: 5
Annual Budget: $50-100,000
Exec. Director: Ritchie Tidwell

Historical Note
Founded as Internat'l Ass'n of Trauma Counseling; assumed its current name in 1997. ATSS members are actively engaged in the field of trauma counseling treatment. Offers certfication in three specializations: Certified Trauma Specialist, Associate in Trauma Support, and Certified Trauma Responder. Membership: $70/year (individual).

Publications:
Frontline Counselor Newsletter. q. adv.
Trauma Line. q.

Meetings/Conferences:
1999 – Charleston, SC/Feb. 4-7

Ass'n of Travel Marketing Executives (1980)
Historical Note
Address unknown in 1997.

Ass'n of Trial Lawyers of America (1946)
1050 31st St., N.W.
Washington, DC 20007
Tel: (202)965-3500 *Fax:* (202)625-7312
Web Site: www.atlanet.org
Members: 60,000 individuals
Staff: 155
Annual Budget: $10-25,000,000
Exec. Director: Thomas H. Henderson, Jr., CAE
Director, Media Relations: Carlton Carl
Senior Director of Public Affairs: Linda Lipsen
Senior Director, Natioanl Advocacy: Margie Lehrman
Director, Human Resources/Administration: Valerie Thomas
Senior Director, Finance/Administration: Donald L. Walker
Director, Marketing: Melissa Duprat
Director Legal Affairs: Robert S. Peck
Senior Director, Member Services: Ann P. Casso

Historical Note
Founded as the NACCA Bar Ass'n (Nat'l Ass'n of Claimant's Compensation Attorneys); became the American Trial Lawyers Ass'n in 1964 and the Ass'n of Trial Lawyers of America in 1972. Sponsors ATLA PAC, a political action committee; the Nat'l College of Advocacy; and publishes legal books and tapes through ATLA Press. Sponsors the Roscoe Pound Foundation (public policy research, seminars and publications) and the Civil Justice Foundation (grants in areas of injury prevention). Has an annual budget of approximately $19 million.

Publications:
ATLA Advocate. 10/year.
ATLA Law Reporter. 10/year. adv.
Products Liability Law Reporter. 10/year.
Professional Negligence Law Reporter. 10/year.
Trial. m. adv.

Meetings/Conferences:
Semi-annual Meetings: Summer/13,900 and Winter/1,500

Ass'n of Universities for Research in Astronomy (1957)
1200 New York Ave, N.W., Suite 350
Washington, DC 20005
Tel: (202)483-2101 *Fax:* (202)483-2106
Web Site: www.aura.astronomy.org
Members: 31 institutions
Staff: 11
Annual Budget: $2-5,000,000
President: Goetz Oertel, Ph.D.
Director, Corporate Relations: J. Lorraine Reams

Historical Note
A consortium of universities managing government-sponsored observatories in the U.S. and abroad. One-time membership fee: $10,000 per university.

Meetings/Conferences:
Annual Meetings: Spring

Ass'n of University Anesthesiologists (1953)
2150 N. 197th St., Suite 205
Seattle, WA 98133-9009
Tel: (206)367-8704 *Fax:* (206)367-8777
Members: 700 individuals
Staff: 5
Annual Budget: under $10,000
Exec. Secretary: Shirley Bishop

Historical Note
Formerly (1990) Ass'n of University Anesthetists.

Ass'n of University Architects (1955)
c/o Facilities Plng., Fla Gulf Coast U.
10501 FGCU Blvd. South
Fort Myers, FL 33965-6565
Tel: (941)590-1000 *Fax:* (941)590-1010
Members: 150 individuals
Annual Budget: $10-25,000
Past President: Jack Fenwick, Jr.

Historical Note
Licensed architects whose full-time job is the development of the university or system employing them. Has no paid officers or full-time staff. Membership: $50/year (individual).

Publications:
Annual Report. a.
Newsletter/Roster. a.

Meetings/Conferences:
Annual Meetings: June, at various university locations

Ass'n of University Environmental Health/Sciences Centers (1980)
Columbia Univ. School of Public Health

60 Haven Ave., Suite B-1
New York, NY 10032
Tel: (212)305-1678 *Fax:* (212)305-4012
Members: 14 centers
Director: Joseph Graziano, Ph.D.

Historical Note
Members are environmental health science centers supported by the Nat'l Institute of Environmental Health Sciences.

Ass'n of University Interior Designers (1979)
Univ. of Missouri, Facility Operations
8 Defoe Hall
Columbia, MO 65201
Tel: (573)882-7211 *Fax:* (573)882-9189
Members: 101 individuals
Annual Budget: $10-25,000
Publicist: Harriet Green-Sappington

Historical Note
Members are designers, architects, facility managers, etc., employed by universities to do in-house design work. Has no paid officers or full-time staff. Membership: $25/year (individual).

Publications:
Clerestory. a.

Meetings/Conferences:
Semi-Annual Meetings: June and October
1999 – Lawrence, KS/50
2000 – Ames, IA/50

Ass'n of University Professors of Ophthalmology (1966)
P.O. Box 420369
San Francisco, CA 94142-0369
Tel: (415)561-8548 *Fax:* (415)561-8575
Members: 250 individuals
Staff: 3
Exec. V. President: Steven Podos, M.D.
Client Services Coordinator: Denise DeLosada

Publications:
Membership Directory. a.
News & Views. q.

Meetings/Conferences:
1999 – Captiva Island, FL(South Seas
Plantation)/Jan. 28-30/250

Ass'n of University Programs in Health Administration (1948)
1110 Vermont Ave., N.W., Suite 220
Washington, DC 20005
Tel: (202)822-8550 *Fax:* (703)525-4791
E-Mail: AUPHA@AUPHA.COM
Web Site: http://www.AUPHA-LC.com
Members: 1,200 individuals, 145 university programs
Staff: 16
Annual Budget: $2-5,000,000
President and C.E.O.: Henry A. Fernandez, JD
Director, International Programs: Bernardo Ramirez, MD
Director, Education and Special Projects: John Kress
Director, Finance and Administration: Jim Evans
Director, Development: Lydia Middleton Reed

Historical Note
AUPHA is an internat'l consortium of educational centers for health care services management, policy and research. It also administers nat'l scholarships and fellowships. AUPHA was incorpated in the U.S., Canada, and Costa Rica and has affiliates in 37 countries. AUPHA has additional offices in Washington, Ottawa, and Bogota. Membership: $50/year (individual), $1,100/year (organization).

Publications:
AUPHA Exchange. bi-m. adv.
Health Services Administration Education. bien.
Journal of Health Administration Education. q.

Meetings/Conferences:
Annual Meetings: Spring
1999 – Chicago, IL(Drake)/June 18-20

Ass'n of University Programs in Occupational Health and Safety (1981)
Univ of Illinois Sch. of Public Health
2121 W. Taylor St., Rm. 215, M/C 922
Chicago, IL 60612-7260
Tel: (312)996-7887 *Fax:* (312)413-7369
Members: 14 universities
Annual Budget: $25-50,000
President: Daniel Hryhorczuk, M.D.

Historical Note
Members are fourteen universities who have graduate, NIOSH-funded programs in such areas as occupational medicine, nursing, industrial hygiene and safety engineering.

Meetings/Conferences:
Semi-annual Meetings: Spring and Fall

Ass'n of University Radiologists (1953)
2021 Spring Road, Suite 600
Oak Brook, IL 60521
Tel: (630)368-3730 *Fax:* (630)571-7837
Members: 1,500 individuals
Staff: 2
Annual Budget: $25-50,000
Exec. Director: Jennifer Bolan

Historical Note
Members are full-time academic radiologists, involved in teaching and laboratory and clinical investigation. An associate member of Coalition for Health Funding (Washington, DC). Membership: $130 (individual).

Publications:
Academic Radiology. m.

Meetings/Conferences:
Annual Meetings: Spring/450
1999 – San Diego, CA/March 10-14

Ass'n of University Related Research Parks (1986)

1730 K St., N.W., Suite 700
Washington, DC 20006
Tel: (202)828-4167   Fax: (202)828-4192
E-Mail: AURRP@urbandevelopment.com
Web Site: http://www.aurrp.org
Members: 300 companies and non-profits
Staff: 5
Annual Budget: $250-500,000
Exec. Director: Jason Jordan
Editor: Katie Burns

Historical Note
Serves as a central clearing house for the exchange of information on the planning, construction, marketing, and management of university related research parks and technology incubators. Promotes university-industry relations and helps to facilitate the transfer of technology to the private sector. Works to promote technology-led economic development for communities. Membership: $650/year (organization/company).

Publications:
The Reasearch Park Forum. m.

Meetings/Conferences:
Annual Meetings: Summer
1999 – Madison, WI/June 9-12
2000 – Boulder, CO

Ass'n of University Summer Sessions (1917)

Summer Sessions & Special Programs,
Maxwell Hall 254, Indiana University
Bloomington, IN 47405
Tel: (812)855-5048   Fax: (812)855-3815
Members: 50 institutions
Staff: 1
Annual Budget: under $10,000
Recorder: Leslie J. Coyne, Ph.D.

Historical Note
Formerly (1964) Ass'n of Summer Sessions Deans and Directors. Membership is by invitation only. Has no paid officers or full-time staff.

Meetings/Conferences:
Annual Meetings: October

Ass'n of University Technology Managers (1974)

49 East Ave.
Norwalk, CT 06851-0493
Tel: (203)845-9015   Fax. (203)847 1304
E-Mail: autm@i.netcom.com
Members: 1,800 individuals
Staff: 2
Annual Budget: $100-250,000
Administrator: Penny Dalziel

Historical Note
Incorporated as a non-profit group in the state of Connecticut. Formerly (1989) Soc. of University Patent Administrators. AUTM helps protect faculty inventions, fosters positive social and legislative climate for university technology transfer, and assists in licensing academic technologies. Members are individuals overseeing the marketing and sale of the results of government-financed research at educational institutions. Membership: $100/year (regular); $125/year (affiliate).

Publications:
AUTM Journal. a.
AUTM Membership Directory. a.
AUTM Newsletter. q.

Meetings/Conferences:
Annual Meetings: February-March
1999 – San Diego, CA

Ass'n of Vacuum Equipment Manufacturers Internat'l (1969)

71 Pinon Hill Place
Albuquerque, NM 87122-1914
Tel: (505)856-6924   Fax: (505)856-6716
E-Mail: aveminfo@avem.org
Web Site: http://www.avem.org
Members: 63 companies
Annual Budget: $50-100,000
Exec. Secretary: Vivienne Harwood Mattox

Historical Note
Membership: $425-1,650/year.

Publications:
Directory/Index of Products and Services. a.
Spectrum. q.

Meetings/Conferences:
Annual Meetings: Fall, with the American Vacuum Soc.

Ass'n of Vascular and Interventional Radiographers (1988)

820 Joire Blvd.
Oak Brook, IL 60523
Tel: (630)571-2266   Fax: (630)571-7837
E-Mail: avir@rsna.org
Members: 1,469 individuals
Staff: 2
Exec. Secretary: Betty Rohr

Historical Note
AVIR members are cardiovascular and interventional radiographers and allied health care professionals. Membership: $50/year (active); $40/year (associate); $20/year (student); $75/year (international).

Publications:
AVIR Newsletter. q.

Meetings/Conferences:
1999 – Orlando, FL/March 21-25
2000 – San Diego, CA

Ass'n of Vegetarian Dietitians and Nutrition Educators (1983)

3835 State Route 414
Burdett, NY 14818
Tel: (607)546-7171   Fax: (607)546-4091
E-Mail: g.eisman@juno.com
Web Site:
         http://www.clarityconnect.com/webpages5/g.eisman
Members: 300 individuals
Annual Budget: under $10,000
Exec. Director: George Eisman

Historical Note
VEGEDINE provides a network for vegetarian health professionals to exchange information and provide the general public with an education in vegetarian nutrition.

Ass'n of Vision Science Librarians (1968)

Wills Eye Hospital
900 Walnut St.
Philadelphia, PA 19107
Tel: (215)928-3288   Fax: (215)928-7247
Members: 80 individuals
Annual Budget: under $10,000
Chairman: Judith Schaeffer Young

Historical Note
Established in Beverly Hills, California at the 1968 meeting of the American Academy of Optometry. Members are librarians whose collections or services collections provide information services in the field of vision science. Has no paid officers or staff. Officers serve for two years.

Meetings/Conferences:
Annual Meetings: With the Medical Library Ass'n in May and the American Academy of Optometry in December

Ass'n of Visual Communicators

Historical Note
Became (1997) Internat'l Ass'n of Audio Visual Communicators.

Ass'n of Visual Merchandise Representatives (1983)

307 Cove Creek
Houston, TX 77042-1023
Tel: (713)782-5533   Fax: (713)785-1114
Members: 30 individuals
Annual Budget: under $10,000
President: Tom Raguse

Historical Note
Members are sales representatives for manufacturers of mannequins and other products used in retail sales displays. Membership. $50/year (individual).

Publications:
Newsletter. irreg.

Ass'n of Visual Science Librarians (1968)

Historical Note
Name changed to Ass'n of Vision Science Librarians in 1996.

Ass'n of Volleyball Professionals (1983)

330 Washington Blvd., Suite 600
Marina del Rey, CA 90292
Tel: (310)577-0775   Fax: (310)577-0777
Members: 150 individuals
Staff: 15
Annual Budget: $5-10,000,000
Interim C.E.O.: William Berger

Historical Note
Founded to organize sanctioned events for pro beach volleyball players, AVP now co-sponsors the AVP Tour, negotiates broadcast coverage of Tour events, and represents the Tour's players and sponsors. Membership: %5 of prize winnings.

Publications:
AVP Tour Guide.
AVP Tour Yearbook. a.
Newsletter. bi-m during season.

Meetings/Conferences:
Annual Meetings: Fall

Ass'n of Water Technologies (1985)

8201 Greensboro Drive, Suite 300
McLean, VA 22102
Tel: (703)610-9012   Fax: (703)610-9005
E-Mail: awt@awt.org
Web Site: http://www.awt.org
Members: 1,500 individuals, 435 companies
Staff: 3
Annual Budget: $500-1,000,000
Exec. Director: John M. Schulte
Director of Communications: Laura Sako

Historical Note
The purpose of AWT is to provide small to medium-sized independent water treatment companies with technical education, industry communication, access to information, group purchasing discounts, legislative affairs, and sound management techniques. It also provides certification of professional water technologists as well as regulatory monitoring. Membership: $625/year (associate member company); $375/year (full member company); $425/year (consultants/manufacturers representatives).

Publications:
Analyst. q. adv.
Annual Membership Directory and Buyer's Guide. a.

Meetings/Conferences:
1999 – Palm Springs, CA/Oct. 26-30
2000 – Hawaii

Ass'n of Water Transportation Accounting Officers (1912)

Historical Note
Address unknown in 1997.

Ass'n of Winery Suppliers (1983)

21 Tamal Vista Blvd., Suite 196
Corte Madera, CA 94925
Tel: (415)924-2640   Fax: (415)927-0608
Members: 50 companies
Staff: 1
Exec. Director: John G. Warner

Historical Note
Members are suppliers of materials and services to wineries with a minimum of 20 active accounts.

Publications:
Credit Report. m.

Meetings/Conferences:
Annual Meetings: Fall, always in Marin County, CA.

Ass'n of Women in Natural Foods (1985)

Historical Note
Organization defunct in 1997.

Ass'n of Women in the Metal Industries (1981)

515 King St., Suite 420
Alexandria, VA 22314-3137
Tel: (703)739-8335   Fax: (703)684-6048
E-Mail: ejohnson@clarionmr.com
Web Site: http://www.awmi.com
Members: 2,000 individuals
Staff: 4
Annual Budget: $100-250,000
Exec. Director: Stephanie Trapp

Historical Note
Founded in Oakland CA, AWMI fosters the professional growth of women in the metal industries. Membership: $100/year.

Publications:
AWMI Coast to Coast. q. adv.
Nat'l Membership Directory. a. adv.

Meetings/Conferences:
Annual Meetings: Fall

Ass'n of Women Soil Scientists (1981)

1525 N. Elms Rd.
Flint, MI 48532-2034
Tel: (810)230-8766
E-Mail: kbloser@mi.nrcs.usda.gov
Members: 200 individuals
Annual Budget: under $10,000
Secretary-Treasurer: Kristin Bloser

Historical Note
AWSS goals are to identify women employed as soil scientists and in the sciences in general, to share technical and career information, to enhance communication among members, and to assist and encourage women seeking employment in the field. Membership: $10/year (individual or company).

Publications:
Membership Directory.
Newsletter. q.

Meetings/Conferences:
Annual Meetings: Held w/Soil and Water Conservation Soc.and American Soc. of Agronomy

Ass'n of Women Surgeons (1981)

414 Plaza Drive, Suite 209
Westmont, IL 60559
Tel: (630)655-0392   Fax: (630)655-0391
E-Mail: aws@adminsys.com
Members: 1,200 individuals
Annual Budget: $250-500,000
Exec. Director: Judith K. Keel

Historical Note
Membership: $150/year.

Publications:
AWS Newsletter. q.
Membership Directory. a.

Meetings/Conferences:
1999 – Hershey, PA(Hurshey Hotel)/July 15-17
2000 – Avon, CO(Hyatt Regency Bever Creek)/July 13-15
2001 – Coeurd'Alene, ID(Coeurd'Alene Hotel)/July 26-28

Ass'n of Women's Health, Obstetric and Neonatal Nurses (1969)

2000 L St., N.W., Suite 740
Washington, DC 20036
Toll Free: (800)673 - 8499
Web Site: http://www.awhonn.org
Members: 22,000 individuals
Staff: 37
Annual Budget: $5-10,000,000
Exec. Director: Gail G. Kincaide, CAE
Mgr., Marketing and Communications: Lisa DeMatteo
Dir., Education and Meetings: Fran Weed

Historical Note
Founded as Nurses Ass'n of the American College of Obstetricians and Gynecologists; became an independent organization and assumed its current name in 1993. Members specialize in women's health, obstetric, or neonatal nursing. Membership: $90-130/year.

Publications:
AWHONN Lifelines. bi-m. adv.
Journal of Obstetric, Gynecologic and Neonatal Nursing. bi-m. adv.

Meetings/Conferences:
1999 – Chicago, IL/June 13-16
2000 – Seattle, WA/June 4-7
2001 – Charlotte, NC/June 10-13

Ass'n of Women's Music and Culture

Historical Note
Organization defunct in 1998.

Ass'n of Woodworking and Furnishings Suppliers (1976)
5800 S. Eastern Ave., Suite 330
Los Angeles, CA 90040-4020
Tel: (323)838-9440   Fax: (323)838-9443
Toll Free: (800)946-2937
Members: 450 companies
Staff: 5
Annual Budget: $1-2,000,000
Exec. Director: Dale K. Silverman, CAE, SPHR

Historical Note
Originally a chapter of the California Furniture Manufacturers Ass'n, it became independent as the Ass'n of Western Furniture Suppliers in 1978. Adopted its present name in 1990 to reflect the geographic broadening of its membership and the importance of woodworking machinery suppliers to the industry. Membership: $300/year (company).

Publications:
Buyers Guide/Membership Directory. bien. adv.
Suppliers Edge. bi-m.

Meetings/Conferences:
Annual Meetings: November-December and Biennial Trade Show/August (odd years)
1999 - Anaheim, CA(Convention Center)/25000

Ass'n of Yarn Distributors (1915)
Historical Note
Disbanded in 1997.

Ass'n of Youth Museums (1962)
1775 K St., N.W., Suite 595
Washington, DC 20006
Tel: (202)466-4144   Fax: (202)466-4233
E-Mail: aymdc@aol.com
Web Site: http://www.aym.org
Members: 385 museums and individuals
Staff: 5
Annual Budget: $250-500,000
Exec. Director: Janet Rice Elman
Director, Education and Programs: Sharon Witting
Coordinator, Member Services: Susanne D'Andrea

Historical Note
Formerly (1967) the Ass'n of Youth Museum Directors and (1988) the the American Ass'n of Youth Museums. Membership composed of museums with hands-on exhibits and programs of which most of the participants are children. Membership: $250-1,000/year (museum, based on annual budget), $250/year (individual).

Publications:
AYM News Newsletter. bi-m.
Hand to Hand Journal. q.
Membership Directory. a.

Meetings/Conferences:
Annual Meetings: Spring, prior to American Ass'n of Museums annual meeting
1999 - New York City, NY(New York University)/May 21-23/650
2000 - Baltimore, MD(Omni)/May 11-13/500

Ass'n on Higher Education and Disability (1977)
Box 21192
Columbus, OH 43221-0192
Tel: (614)488-4972   Fax: (614)488-1174
Members: 2,200 individuals
Staff: 8
Annual Budget: $500-1,000,000
Exec. V. President: Ed Suddath
Coordinator of Marketing: Kim Kaller

Historical Note
Members are committed to improving postsecondary educational opportunities for handicap students. Members are committed to improving postsecondary educational opportunities for handicapped students. Membership: $75/year (individual); $187.50/year (institution); $35/year (student). Formerly (1992) Ass'n on Handicapped Student Service Programs in Postsecondary Education.

Publications:
ALERT Newsletter. bi-m.
Journal of Postsecondary Education & Disability. q.
Membership Directory. a.
Proceedings of AHSSPPE Annual Conference. a.

Meetings/Conferences:
Annual Meetings: Summer
1999 - Atlanta, GA

Ass'n on Programs for Female Offenders (1960)
500 E. Fourth St.
Chester, PA 19013
Tel: (610)490-1340
Members: 150 individuals
Annual Budget: under $10,000
President: Mary V. Leftridge Byrd

Historical Note
APFO members are corrections professionals and others with an interest in programs for female offenders. Membership: $15/year (individual).

Publications:
APFO Newsletter. irreg. adv.

Meetings/Conferences:
Annual Meetings: in conjunction with the American Correctional Ass'n

Ass'n Publishing and Fulfillment Services (1986)
Historical Note
Address unknown in 1997.

Ass'n Retail Travel Agents
501 Darby Creek Road, Suite 47

Lexington, KY 40509
Tel: (606)263-1194   Fax: (606)264-0368
President: John Hawks
V. President, Operations: Pat Funk

Meetings/Conferences:
1999 - Myrtle Beach, SC/March 4-7

Ass'n to Advance Ethical Hypnosis (1956)
2675 Oakwood Drive
Cuyahoga Falls, OH 44221
Tel: (330)923-8880
Members: 1,200 individuals
Staff: 1
Annual Budget: under $10,000
Exec. Director: Nell R. Orndoff, MA

Historical Note
A non-profit professional society incorporated in New Jersey, AAEH is concerned with upholding ethics and standards in the practice of hypnosis. AAEH maintains a certification program; an approved school program, to assure adequate training and instruction; and actively opposes state legislation which would restrict the professional practice of hypnosis to the medical community. Membership: $45/year (individual).

Publications:
Suggestion. q. adv.

Meetings/Conferences:
Annual Meetings: October

Ass'ns Council of the Nat'l Ass'n of Manufacturers (1907)
1331 Pennsylvania Ave., N.W., Suite 600
North Lobby
Washington, DC 20004-1790
Tel: (202)637-3104   Fax: (202)637-3182
E-Mail: associations@nam.org
Members: 225 associations
Staff: 3
Annual Budget: $250-500,000
Exec. Director: David W. Rohn

Historical Note
A Division of the Nat'l Ass'n of Manufacturers, the Council is composed of associations representing manufacturers in specific industries.

Publications:
Ass'ns Council Membership Directory. a.
Associations Council Connections. m.
Manufacturing Trade Ass'ns. bien.
Operating Ratio Report for Manufacturing Trade Ass'ns. bien.

Meetings/Conferences:
Semi-annual Meetings: June even years, July-Aug. odd years and Dec.

Ass'ns for Community Design (1977)
c/o American Institute of Architects
1735 New York Ave., N.W.
Washington, DC 20006
Tel: (202)626-7532   Fax: (202)626-7365
Web Site: www.aiaonline.com
Members: 50 organizations
Staff: 1
Annual Budget: under $10,000
AIA Liaison: Stephanie Bothwell

Historical Note
Formed to strengthen goals and address common problems of Community Design Centers which are non-profit, community-based organizations that provide architectural design, planning and related technical assistance to community groups and individuals who could not afford such services. Affiliated with the American Institute of Architects. Formerly the Community Design Center Directors Ass'n, ACD assumed its present name in 1989.

Publications:
Directory.
Newsletter.

Meetings/Conferences:
Annual Meetings: Washington, DC/AIA Headquarters/May

Assembly of Episcopal Hospitals and Chaplains (1951)
Historical Note
Address unknown in 1996.

Assisted Living Facilities Ass'n of America (1991)
Historical Note
Became Assisted Living Federation of America in 1996.

Assisted Living Federation of America (1991)
10300 Eaton Place, Suite 400
Fairfax, VA 22030-2239
Tel: (703)691-8100   Fax: (703)691-8106
E-Mail: info@alfa.org
Web Site: http://www.alfa.org
Members: 4,500 organizations and companies
Staff: 26
Annual Budget: $2-5,000,000
Exec. Director: Karen A. Wayne
Director, Media and Public Relations: Whitney Redding
Director, Government Affairs: Leslie Kilgannon
Senior V. President: Larry Johnson
Director, Education and Training: Jane Mayfield
V. President, Finance/Administration: Becky Heath
Director, Membership: Ron Plamondon

Historical Note
Absorbed NARCF in 1997. Formerly (1996) Assisted Living Facilities Ass'n of America, ALFA members are providers of assisted living, organizations whose members are providers of assisted living, and other businesses with an interest in the industry.

Publications:
ALFA Advisor Newsletter. m.

Assisted Living Today. bi-m.
Overview of the Assisted Living Industry. a.

Meetings/Conferences:
Semi-Annual Meetings: Spring and Fall
1999 - Dallas, TX(Wyndham)/Apr. 18-20
2000 - Orlando, FL(Walt Disney World Resort)/Apr. 2-4
2001 - Las Vegas, NV(Venetian)

Associated Accounting Firms Internat'l (1966)
Historical Note
Ceased non-profit operations in 1997.

Associated Actors and Artistes of America (1919)
165 West 46th St.
New York, NY 10036
Tel: (212)869-0358   Fax: (212)869-1746
Members: 120,000 individuals, 7 national unions
Staff: 2
Annual Budget: $50-100,000
President: Theodore Bikel

Historical Note
Affiliated with AFL-CIO. Chartered by the American Federation of Labor on August 28, 1919, 4As is the successor organization to the White Rats Actors Union of America (established in 1910). An umbrella coordinating organization comprising autonomous branches: Actors' Equity Ass'n, American Federation of Television and Radio Artists, American Guild of Musical Artists, American Guild of Variety Artists, Hebrew Actors Union, Italian Actors Union and screen Actors Guild.

Meetings/Conferences:
Biennial Meetings: Uneven years, at 4As headquarters in New York, NY, second Thursday in June.

Associated Air Balance Council (1965)
1518 K St., N.W., Suite 503
Washington, DC 20005
Tel: (202)737-0202   Fax: (202)638-4833
E-Mail: AABCHQ@aol.com
Web Site: http://www.aabchq.com
Members: 130 companies
Staff: 5
Annual Budget: $500-1,000,000
Exec. Director: Kenneth M. Sufka

Historical Note
Members are independent testers of air handling systems.

Publications:
Annual Membership Directory. a.
TAB Journal. q.

Meetings/Conferences:
Annual Meetings: Fall

Associated Antique Dealers of America
Historical Note
Became World Antique Dealers Ass'n in 1996.

Associated Bodywork and Massage Professionals (1987)
28677 Buffalo Park Road
Evergreen, CO 80439-7347
Tel: (303)674-8478   Fax: (303)674-0859
Toll Free: (800)458-2267
E-Mail: expectmore@abmp.com
Web Site: http://www.abmp.com
Members: 24,000 individuals
Staff: 19
Annual Budget: $2-5,000,000
Exec. Director: Les Sweeney

Historical Note
ABMP members are massage therapists, bodyworkers, somatic therapists and estheticians practicing a wide variety of massage and bodywork styles. Membership: $229/year (certified/esthetician); $199/year (professional/practitioner), $75/year (supporting), $39/year (student).

Publications:
ABMP Successful Business Handbook. a. adv.
ABMP Touch Training Directory. a. adv.
ABMP Yellow Pages. a. adv.
Different Strokes. bi.
Massage & Bodywork Magazine. bi-m.

Meetings/Conferences:

Associated Builders and Contractors (1950)
1300 North 17th St., Suite 800
Rosslyn, VA 22209
Tel: (703)812-2000   Fax: (703)812-8200
Web Site: http://www.abc.org
Members: 21,000 companies
Staff: 80
Annual Budget: $5-10,000,000
Interim Exec. V. President: Robert P. Hepner
Director, Communications: Scott Brown
V. President, Public Affairs: Richard Haas
V. President, Government Affairs: Charlotte W. Herbert
Director, Legistative Affairs: Jennifer Boucher
Director, Government Relations: William B. Spencer
Director, Meetings/Conventions: Kristin Harrison
National Education Director: Dan Mosser
V. President, Member Services: Robert P. Hepner
Director, Information Systems: Mary S. Schroer

Historical Note
Incorporated in Baltimore, MD in 1950. Members are merit shop construction companies. Sponsors and supports the Associated Builders and Contractors Political Action Committee. Has an annual budget of approximately $7.2 million. Membership fee varies by volume and is collected at chapter level.

Publications:
ABC Today. bi-w. adv.
National Membership Directory. a. adv.

Meetings/Conferences:
Annual Meetings: January
1999 – Maui, HI/Jan. 27-Feb. 3
2000 – Baltimore, MD/May 4-6

Associated Business Writers of America (1945)
3140 S. Peoria St., Suite 295
Aurora, CO   80014
Tel: (303)841-0246   Fax: (303)751-8593
Members: 230 individuals
Staff: 2
Annual Budget: $10-25,000
Exec. Director: Sandy Whelchel

Historical Note
An affiliate of the National Writers Ass'n. The Associated Business
Writers of America was established in 1946. The ABWA is
composed of freelance writers whose aim is to better the image of
the profession, to improve relations and communication with editors
and other clients, and to strive for higher pay scales and more
considerate handling of manuscripts. Membership: $80/year
(individual); $250/year (group.)

Publications:
Authorship. bi-m.
Flash Market News. m.
Membership Directory. a. adv.

Meetings/Conferences:
Annual Meetings: with the Nat'l Writers Ass'n/June

Associated Church Press (1916)
P.O. Box 21749
Washington, DC   20009-1749
Tel: (202)332-5544   Fax: (202)332-4559
E-Mail: jroos@erds.com
Web Site: http://www.thelutheran/aco/index.html
Members: 40 individuals, 200 periodicals
Staff: 1
Annual Budget: $50-100,000
Exec. Director: Joe Roos

Historical Note
Formerly (1937) Editorial Council of the Religious Press.
Protestant, Anglican, Catholic and Orthodox church-affiliated and
independent periodicals in North America. Membership: $35/year
(individual), $123-706, depending on circulation (company).

Publications:
Associated Church Press Directory. a. adv.
Newslog.

Meetings/Conferences:
Annual Meetings: Spring
1999 – Portland, OR(Portland Marriott)/April 18-21/100
2000 – Chicago, IL/March 29-April 1/100

Associated Collegiate Press, Nat'l Scholastic Press Ass'n (1921)
2221 University Ave., S.E., Suite 121
Minneapolis, MN   55414
Tel: (612)625-8335   Fax: (612)626-0720
E-Mail: info@studentpress.org
Web Site: http://www.studentpress.org
Members: 2,000 publications
Staff: 5
Annual Budget: $250-500,000
Exec. Director: Tom E. Rolnicki

Historical Note
Also known as the Nat'l Scholastic Press Ass'n. Founded to
promote the growth and quality of high school and college student
publications.

Publications:
Trends in College Media. 3/year. adv.
Trends in High School Media. q. adv.

Meetings/Conferences:
Annual Meetings: Fall
1999 – Albuquerque, NM/Apr. 8-11
1999 – Atlanta, GA/Nov. 18-21
1999 – Atlanta, GA/Oct. 30-31

Associated Construction Distributors Internat'l (1974)
4595 Towne Lake Pkwy., Bldg. 300-230
Woodstock, GA   30189-5518
Tel: (770)516-1636   Fax: (770)516-1303
Members: 36 construction distributors
Staff: 4
Annual Budget: $50-100,000
Exec. V. President: Tom Goetz

Historical Note
Members are distributors of construction supplies and equipment.

Publications:
ACDI Bulletin. m.
ACDI Directory. a.

Meetings/Conferences:
Semi-annual Meetings: Spring and Fall

Associated Construction Publications (1938)
30 Technology Pkwy. South
Suite 100
Narcoss, GA   30092
Tel: (404)782-0960   Fax: (404)417-4138
Toll Free: (800)486 - 0014
Members: 14 regional publications
Staff: 4
Annual Budget: $2-5,000,000
Exec. V. President: John Weatherhead

Meetings/Conferences:
Semi-annual Meetings: January and June

Associated Cooperage Industries of America (1915)
2100 Gardiner Lane, Suite 100-E
Louisville, KY   40205-2947
Tel: (502)459-6113   Fax: (502)459-6113

Members: 72 companies
Staff: 1
Annual Budget: $10-25,000
Secretary-Treasurer: Ida Austin

Historical Note
Promotes the interests of cooperage manufacturers and of those
who use wooden barrels.

Publications:
Newsletter. m.

Meetings/Conferences:
Annual Meetings: Fall
1999 – Key West, FL/Oct. 23-26
2000 – San Diego, CA

Associated Corset and Brassiere Manufacturers Ass'n (1933)
1430 Broadway, Suite 1603
New York, NY   10018-3308
Tel: (212)354-0707   Fax: (212)221-3540
Members: 27 companies
Staff: 2
Annual Budget: $50-100,000
Exec. Director and Counsel: Alex J. Glauberman

Historical Note
Membership is concentrated in the Eastern United States - New
York, New Jersey and Pennsylvania.

Associated Credit Bureaus (1906)
1090 Vermont Ave., N.W., Suite 200
Washington, DC   20005-4905
Tel: (202)371-0910   Fax: (202)371-0134
Web Site: http://www.acb_credit.com
Members: 1,100 bureaus, 4900 collection agencie
Staff: 22
Annual Budget: $5-10,000,000
President: D. Barry Connelly
V. President, Public Relations: Norman Magnuson
V. President, Government Relations: Stuart Pratt
Program Administration: Carrie Bright

Historical Note
Founded as Nat'l Ass'n of Retail Credit Agencies, it became the
Nat'l Ass'n of Mercantile Agencies in 1908 and the Associated
Credit Bureaus of America in 1937; assumed its present name in
1968. Membership is divided into three classes: Credit Reporting
Offices, Collection Service Offices, and Specialized Reporting
Services. Supports the ACB Political Action Committee.

Publications:
Communicator. m.

Meetings/Conferences:
Annual Meetings: June

Associated Equipment Distributors (1919)
615 West 22nd St.
Oak Brook, IL   60523
Tel: (630)574-0650   Fax: (630)574-0132
E-Mail: jtm@macknet.com
Web Site: http://www.aednet.org
Members: 1,200 companies
Staff: 20
Annual Budget: $2-5,000,000
Exec. V. President: Toby Mack
Exec. Director, AED Foundation: Robert C. Holt

Historical Note
Distributors and manufacturers of construction, mining, logging,
and road maintenance equipment. Formerly Nat'l Distributors
Ass'n of Construction Equipment. Affiliated with the Canadian
Ass'n of Equipment Distributors. Connected with the AED
Foundation, Inc.

Publications:
Construction Equipment Distribution. m. adv.
Contact. m.

Meetings/Conferences:
Annual Meetings: Winter/3,000

Associated Funeral Directors, Internat'l (1939)
PO Box 1382
Largo, FL   34779
Tel: (813)593-0709   Fax: (813)593-9937
Toll Free: (800)346 - 7151
Members: 2,500 funeral homes
Staff: 5
Annual Budget: $50-100,000
Exec. Director: Richard A. Santore

Historical Note
Formerly (1992) the Associated Funeral Directors Service.
Membership fee based on population of member's service area.

Publications:
AFDI Membership Directory. a. adv.
Styx. bi-m. adv.
Today in Funeral Service. bi-m. adv.
Update Newsletter.

Meetings/Conferences:
Annual Meetings: October

Associated Fur Manufacturers (1911)
Historical Note
A division of Fur Information Council of America, which provides
administrative support.

Associated Gas Distributors (1963)
1001 Pennsylvania Ave., N.W.
Washington, DC   20004
Tel: (202)466-5329   Fax: (202)628-5116
Members: 50 companies
Staff: 2
Counsel and Secretary: Frederick Moring

Historical Note
Natural gas distributors, no pipelines or producers or affiliates of
major interstate pipelines. Mailing address is the law firm of Crowell
and Moring.

Publications:
Directory. a.

Meetings/Conferences:

Associated General Contractors of America (1918)
1957 E St., N.W.
Washington, DC   20006-5107
Tel: (202)393-2040   Fax: (202)347-4004
E-Mail: info@agc.org
Web Site: http://agc.org
Staff: 90
Annual Budget: $10-25,000,000
Exec. V. President: Stephen E. Sandherr
Exec. Director, Convention & Meeting Services: Rick Brown
Exec. Director, Training & Educational Services: John Heffner
C.O.O.: David R. Lukens
C.F.O.: Ralph Willett
General Counsel: Michael E. Kennedy
Exec. Director, Publications: Donald A. Scott

Historical Note
Members are contracting firms responsible for the construction of
commercial buildings, highways, industrial complexes and
municipal-utilities and heavy-engineering facilities. Has an annual
budget of approximately $10.3 million. Sponsors and supports the
AGC Political Action Committee.

Publications:
CONSTRUCTOR. m. adv.
Directory and Buyers Guide. a. adv.
National Newsletter. bi-w.

Meetings/Conferences:
Semi-Annual Meetings: March and Fall
1999 – Las Vegas, LV/March 22-26

Associated Glass and Pottery Manufacturers (1874)
373 Maple Drive
Greensburg, PA   15601
Tel: (724)834-8822
Members: 18 companies
Staff: 1
Annual Budget: under $10,000
Secretary: Mildred A. Wible

Historical Note
Manufacturers of semi-vitrified and vitrified ceramic and glass
dinnerware and tableware. Membership: $75/year
(organization/company).

Associated Landscape Contractors of America (1961)
150 Elden St., Suite 270
Herndon, VA   20170-4831
Tel: (703)736-9666   Fax: (703)736-9668
Toll Free: (800)395 - 2522
Members: 1,600 firms
Staff: 15
Annual Budget: $2-5,000,000
Exec. Director: Debra A. Holder
Director, Marketing and Communications: Laurie Saunders
Director, Education: Elise J. Lindsey, CMP

Historical Note
ALCA represents the interior and exterior landscape maintenance,
installation and design-build contractor. Membership: $375-
$5000/year based on volume of lanscape contracting business;
$500/year (supplier); $25/year (student).

Publications:
ALCA Advantage.
Landscape Contractor News. m. adv.
Who's Who in Landscape Contracting. a. adv.

Meetings/Conferences:
1999 – Ft. Lauderdale, FL/Jan. 20-23/400

Associated Locksmiths of America (1956)
3003 Live Oak St.
Dallas, TX   75204
Tel: (214)827-1701   Fax: (214)827-1810
E-Mail: aloa@anet-dfw.com
Members: 10,000 individuals
Staff: 20
Annual Budget: $1-2,000,000
Exec. Director: Charles W. Gibson, Jr., CAE
Government Affairs Manager: Tim McMullen
Meetings Manager: Jessica Vasquez
PRP/Education Manager: David Lowell, CML, CMS
Comptroller: Kathy Romo
Membership Manager: Brandon Durrett
Communications: Anne McDonald Davis

Historical Note
Membership: $125/year (individual); $500/year (company).

Publications:
Keynotes. m. adv.

Meetings/Conferences:
Annual Meetings: Summer/6,000
1999 – Cincinnati, OH(Regal Hyatt Hotels)/July 25-31
2000 – Las Vegas, NV(Hilton)/July 24-30
2001 – Baltimore, MD(Hyatt)/July 16-21
2002 – Rosemont, IL(Hyatt)/July 22-28

Associated Luxury Hotels (1986)
1000 16th St., N.W., Suite 503
Washington, DC   20036
Tel: (202)887-7020   Fax: (202)887-0085
E-Mail: meetings@alhi.com
Members: 52 hotels and resorts
Staff: 23
President: Liz Jackson

Associated Owners and Developers (1991)

P.O. Box 4163
McLean, VA 22103
Tel: (703)734-2397   *Fax:* (703)734-2908
Web Site: http://www.constructionsite.net
Members: 1,500 individuals, 200 companies
Staff: 2
Annual Budget: $10-25,000
President and Exec. Director: Steve Beattie

Historical Note
AOD represents owner/developers from both the private and public sectors, enhancing their business opportunities through interaction with other owner/developers and assisting them in producing and maintaining projects which make economic sense. Membership: $250/year (individual), $500/year (company).

Publications:
AOD News Newsletter. q.

Meetings/Conferences:

Associated Pipe Organ Builders of America (1941)
c/o C.B. Fisk, Inc.
18 Kondelin Road
Gloucester, MA 01930
Tel: (978)283-1909   *Fax:* (978)283-2938
Web Site: http://www.tneorg.com/apoba/
Members: 33 companies
Annual Budget: $10-25,000
President: Steven Dieck

Historical Note
Formerly Associated Organ Builders of America. Formed originally to get metal priorities during World War II. Has no permanent address or staff; officers rotate trienally.

Meetings/Conferences:
Annual Meetings: Spring
1999 – Lincoln, NE/May 14-15

Associated Press Managing Editors (1933)
50 Rockefeller Plaza
New York, NY 10020
Tel: (212)621-1552   *Fax:* (212)621-1567
Web Site: http://www.apme.com
Members: 2,000 individuals
Staff: 1
Annual Budget: $100-250,000
Exec. Liaison: Bruce Nathan

Historical Note
Members are editors of Associated Press newspapers.

Publications:
APME News. q.

Meetings/Conferences:
Annual Meetings: Fall
1999 – Memphis, TN(Peabody)/Oct. 13-16
2000 – San Antonio, TX(Marriott Rivercenter)/Oct. 18-21

Associated Professional Sleep Socs. (1986)
6301 2 Bondel Rd., Suite 101
Rochester, MN 55901-0246
Tel: (507)287-6006   *Fax:* (507)287-6008
Web Site: http://www.asda.org
Members: 2 societies
Staff: 12
Annual Budget: $250-500,000
Exec. Director: Jerome Barrett
Meeting Coordinator: Jennifer Gemelke

Historical Note
A partnership comprising two sleep societies: Sleep Research Soc., and the American Sleep Disorders Ass'n. APSS provides a joint annual meeting and publications. Formerly (1993) Ass'n of Professional Sleep Societies.

Publications:
Sleep. bi-m. adv.

Meetings/Conferences:
Annual Meetings: May/June
1999 – Orlando, FL/June 21-24

Associated Regional Accounting Firms
Historical Note
Merged with (1998) TGI Internat'l and made Polaris Internat'l.

Associated Risk Managers Internat'l (1970)
816 Congress Ave., Suite 990
Austin, TX 78701-2443
Tel: (512)479-6886   *Fax:* (512)479-0577
Web Site: http://www.arminet.com
Members: 375 companies
Staff: 6
Annual Budget: $500-1,000,000
Exec. Director: James Sanders

Historical Note
ARMI members are state/province affiliates representing independent agencies united to market insurance/risk management services to targeted industries, associations, professional societies and other organizations.

Publications:
ARMI Messenger. q.

Meetings/Conferences:
Annual Meetings: May
1999 – Las Vegas, NV(Luxor)/April 28-May 2/125

Associated Schools of Construction (1965)
119 Dudley Hall
Auburn University
Auburn, AL 36849-5315
Tel: (334)844-5383   *Fax:* (334)844-5386
E-Mail: molhend@mail.auburn.edu
Web Site: http://www.ascweb.org
Members: 92 schools
Annual Budget: $50-100,000
Exec. Director: Hendrick D. Mol

Historical Note
ASC is a professional association for the development and advancement of construction education. Members are colleges and universities which have programs in the field of construction. Membership: $400/year.

Publications:
ASC Annual Conference Proceedings. a.
Journal of Construction Education. q.

Meetings/Conferences:
Annual Meetings: April
1999 – San Luis Obispo, CA(California Poly State Univ)/April 15-17

Associated Specialty Contractors (1950)
3 Bethesda Metro Center, Suite 1100
Bethesda, MD 20814-5372
Tel: (301)657-3110   *Fax:* (301)215-4500
Members: 8 associations
Staff: 1
Annual Budget: $25-50,000
President: Daniel Walter

Historical Note
A federation of construction specialty associations: Mechanical Contractors Ass'n of America; Nat'l Ass'n of Plumbing-Heating-Cooling Contractors; Nat'l Electrical Contractors Ass'n; Sheet Metal and Air Conditioning Contractors' Nat'l Ass'n; Mason Contractors Ass'n of America; Nat'l Insulation Contractors Ass'n; Nat'l Roofing Contractors Ass'n; and Painting and Decorating Contractors of America. Formerly (1973) Council of Mechanical Specialty Contracting Industries, Inc. Membership: $1,500/year.

Meetings/Conferences:
Semi-Annual Meetings: May and November

Associated Surplus Dealers (1950)
2950 31st St., Suite 100
Santa Monica, CA 90405
Tel: (310)396-6006   *Fax:* (310)399-2662
Toll Free: (800)421 - 4511
Members: 475 individuals
Staff: 35
Annual Budget: $10-25,000,000
V. President and Administrator: Sam Bundy

Historical Note
Has an annual budget of approximately $10 million.

Publications:
ASD/AMD Trade News. m. adv.

Meetings/Conferences:

Associated Wire Rope Fabricators (1976)
Historical Note
AWRF declined to provide updated information for this edition.

Associated Writing Programs (1967)
George Mason University
Tallwood House, Mail Stop 1E3
Fairfax, VA 22030
Tel: (703)993-4301   *Fax:* (703)993-4302
Members: 17,000 individuals, 300 universities
Staff: 6
Annual Budget: $500-1,000,000
Exec. Director: D.W. Fenza
Publications Manager: David Sherwin

Historical Note
An organization of writers, teachers, students and educational institutions concerned with creative and professional writing. Founded at Brown University. Membership: $45/year (individual), $200-500/year (institution).

Publications:
AWP Catalogue of Writing Programs. bien.
AWP Chronicle. 6/year.
Job List. 7/year.

Meetings/Conferences:
Annual Meetings: Spring

At-sea Processors Ass'n (1985)
4039 21st Ave. West, Suite 400
Seattle, WA 98199
Tel: (206)285-5139   *Fax:* (206)285-1841
Web Site: http://www.atsea.org
Members: 15 companies
Staff: 5
Annual Budget: $1-2,000,000
Exec. Director: Paul MacGregor
Director, Communications: Barbara Nombalais
Director, Public Affairs: James L. Gilmore
Exec. Secretary: Ann Revelle

Historical Note
Formerly (1997) American Factory Trawler Ass'n. Represents firms operating at-sea processing fleets, providing regulatory and legislative advocacy.bodies.

Publications:
AFTA Words. q.

Meetings/Conferences:
Annual Meetings: December

Athletic Equipment Managers Ass'n (1974)
P.O. Box 2093
Ann Arbor, MI 48106-2093
Tel: (734)523-2362
Members: 675 individuals
Staff: 1
Annual Budget: $10-25,000
President: Terry Schlatter

Historical Note
Membership: $60/year (individual).

Publications:
Newsletter. q.

Meetings/Conferences:
Annual Meetings: June/300
1999 – Charlotte, NC(Adams Mark Hotel)/June 9-12
2000 – Pasadena, CA(Hilton, Doubletree & Holiday Inn)
2001 – Las Vegas, NV(Riviera Hotel)

Athletic Footwear Ass'n (1982)
200 Castlewood Drive
North Palm Beach, FL 33408
Tel: (561)842-4100   *Fax:* (561)863-8984
E-Mail: JHSGMA@aol.com
Web Site: www.sportlink.com
Members: 105 companies
Staff: 6
Annual Budget: $250-500,000
Exec. Director: Gregg Hartley

Historical Note
AFA represents the interests of manufacturers and/or distributors of athletic footwear in the North American market place.

Meetings/Conferences:
1999 – Breakers, FL

Athletic Goods Team Distributors (1970)
Historical Note
A division of the National Sporting Goods Association.

Atlantic Independent Union (1938)
2700 W. Passyunk Ave., 2nd Floor
Philadelphia, PA 19145
Tel: (215)339-0076   *Fax:* (215)339-0146
Toll Free: (800)346 - 4731
Members: 500 individuals
Staff: 2
President: John W. Kerr

Historical Note
Independent union representing workers in the petroleum and chemical industries.

Publications:
IU News Newspaper. a. adv.

ATP Tour (1972)
200 ATP Tour Blvd.
Ponte Vedra Beach, FL 32082
Tel: (904)285-8000   *Fax:* (904)285-5966
Toll Free: (800)527 - 4811
Members: 800 individuals
Staff: 125
Annual Budget: $50-100,000,000
C.E.O.: Mark Miles
V. President, Communications: Peter Alfano
CFO: Philip Galloway
General Counsel: Mark Young
Director, Tour Services: Weller Evans

Historical Note
Founded in 1972 at Forest Hills, New York, as Ass'n of Tennis Professionals; assumed its current name in 1990. Membership restricted to male touring professional tennis players and tournament members. Operates the official computerized player ranking system. Administers entry system for international tennis circuit and staffs tournaments. Also features approximately 77 tournaments in 34 countries. In 1990, ATP Tour began the ATP World Championship. Has an annual budget of approximately $51 million. Membership: $300/year (Division II Player), $1000/year (Division I Player).

Publications:
International Tennis. m. adv.
International Tennis Weekly. w. adv.
Player Guide. a.

Meetings/Conferences:
Annual Meetings: November

Auction Marketing Institute (1976)
8880 Ballentine St.
Overland Park, KS 66214
Tel: (913)541-8115   *Fax:* (913)894-5281
E-Mail: aucmktinst@aol.com
Web Site: http://www.auctionweb.com/ami
Members: 1000 individuals
Staff: 3
Annual Budget: $250-500,000
Exec. V. President and Secretary: Ann C. Wood
Dir., Membership: Sara Schoehle

Historical Note
Formerly (1994) Certified Auctioneers Institute. An educational association offering the CAI, AARE, and GPPA professional designations for practicing auctioneers and appraisers. Membership: $150/year.

Publications:
Auction Insider.
Auction Insights.
CAI Directory. a.

Meetings/Conferences:
Annual Meetings: Summer/1,200
1999 – Grand Rapids, MI
2000 – Norfolk, VA
2001 – Boise, ID
2002 – Orlando, FL

Audio Engineering Soc. (1948)
60 East 42nd St., Rm. 2520
New York, NY 10165
Tel: (212)661-8528   *Fax:* (212)682-0477
Toll Free: (800)541 - 7299
Web Site: http://www.aes.org
Members: 11,780 individuals, 175 companies
Staff: 19
Annual Budget: $2-5,000,000
Exec. Director: Roger K. Furness

Historical Note
Members are professionals throughout the world active in audio engineering or acoustics. Membership: $75/year (individual); $750/year (organization/company).
Publications:
Journal of the Audio Engineering Society. 10/yr. adv.
Meetings/Conferences:
1999 – New York, NY/Sept. 24-27

Audio Publishers Ass'n *(1986)*
627 Aviation Way
Manhattan Beach, CA 90266
Tel: (310)372-0546   *Fax:* (310)374-3342
E-Mail: apaonline@aol.com
Web Site: http://www.audiopub.org
Members: 200 companies
Exec. Director: Jan Nathan
Historical Note
APA represents the concerns of audiobook publishers, collects data on the industry, and provides promotional opportunities to members.
Publications:
APA Newsletter. q.
Customer Attitude and Usage Study. a.

Audit Bureau of Circulations *(1914)*
900 N. Meacham Road
Schaumburg, IL 60173-4968
Tel: (847)605-0909   *Fax:* (847)605-0483
Web Site: http://www.accessabc.com
Members: 4,700 members
Staff: 250
Annual Budget: $10-25,000,000
President and Managing Director: Michael J. Lavery
Director, Meetings: Susan Thomas
Senior V. President, Audit Services: Richard Bennett, & 1
Senior V. President, Communications: John R. Payne
Senior V. President, Marketing: Mark Wachowicz
Historical Note
Members are newspapers and periodicals, advertisers and advertising agencies. Purpose is to audit claimed circulation figures and publish the results. Has an annual budget of approximately $22 million. Through a wholly-owned subsidiary, Audit Bureau of Verification Services, Inc., audits Web site activity, trade show attendance and demographics, and other alternative, advertiser-supported, census-based media.
Publications:
Audit Reports. a.
Canadian Circulation of U. S.
Canadian Newspaper Factbook. a.
County Penetration Report. semi-a.
FAS-FAX. semi-a.
Magazine Coverage Reports. a.
Magazine Trends Report. a.
News Bulletin. 3/year.
Publisher's Statements. semi-a.
Rate Book. a.
Meetings/Conferences:
Annual Meetings: November/600

Augustinian Secondary Educational Ass'n *(1987)*
Providence Catholic Highschool
1800 W. Lincoln Hwy.
New Lenox, IL 60451
Tel: (815)415-2136   *Fax:* (815)485-2709
E-Mail: jpejza@ix.netcom.com
Web Site:
        http://www.geocities.com/Athens/1534/osaschoo.ht
        m/
Members: 9 schools
Staff: 1
Annual Budget: under $10,000
Exec. Secretary: Richard McGrath
Historical Note
Members are secondary schools administered by the Augustinian order.
Meetings/Conferences:
Annual Meetings: Easter

Authors Guild *(1921)*
330 West 42nd St., 29th Floor
New York, NY 10036-6902
Tel: (212)563-5904   *Fax:* (212)564-8363
E-Mail: staff@authorsguild.org
Web Site: http://www.authorsguild.org
Members: 7,400 individuals
Staff: 12
Annual Budget: $500-1,000,000
Exec. Director: Paul Aiken
Historical Note
A component organization of the Authors League of America. Membership is available to any individual who has had a book published by an established American publisher within seven years prior to application, or who has had three works of fiction or non-fiction published by magazines of general circulation within 18 months prior to application. Members receive free assistance with contract negotiations and publishing disputes, current information on the publishing industry, and access to group health insurance and other benefits. Membership: $90/year (first year).
Publications:
Bulletin. q.
Meetings/Conferences:
Annual Meetings: February in New York, NY

Authors League of America *(1912)*
330 West 42nd St., 29th Floor
New York, NY 10036-6902
Tel: (212)564-8350   *Fax:* (212)564-8363
Members: 14,500 individuals

Staff: 9
Exec. Director: Paul Aiken
Historical Note
Promotes the professional interests of authors and dramatists in such areas as taxation, copyright and freedom of expression. Affiliated with the Authors Guild and the Dramatists Guild. Membership: $90/year.
Publications:
Authors Guild Bulletin. q.
Dramatists Guild Quarterly. q.
Meetings/Conferences:
Annual Meetings: Late-February

Auto Internat'l Ass'n *(1981)*
P.O. Box 13966
Research Triangle Pk, NC 27709-3966
Tel: (919)549-4800   *Fax:* (919)549-4824
Members: 300 companies
Staff: 10
Annual Budget: $100-250,000
Exec. Director: Steve Moore
Historical Note
Members are manufacturers, importers, distributors and retailers of parts and accessories for imported vehicles. Shares administrative staff with Motor and Equipment Manufacturers Ass'n. Membership: $100-1,000/year.
Publications:
AIA Update. m.
Meetings/Conferences:
Annual Meetings: Las Vegas, NV(Convention Center)/Oct. or Nov./50,000
1999 – Las Vegas, NV

Autobody Representatives Council *(1988)*
9600 Delmar
Overland Park, KS 66207
Tel: (913)383-1713   *Fax:* (913)383-9299
E-Mail: sainte@kanet.com
Web Site: http://www.pbea.org
Members: 40 companies
Staff: 2
Annual Budget: $10-25,000
Exec. Director: Jennie Ison
Historical Note
Independent manufacturers' representatives specializing in paint, body, equipment and other automotive repair/refinishing products. Membership: $400/year.
Publications:
PBEA Extra. 6/year.
Meetings/Conferences:
1999 – Dallas, TX(Westin Galleria)/Sept. 23-28

Automated Builders Consortium *(1993)*
P.O. Box 5586
Buffalo Grove, IL 60089-5586
Tel: (847)398-7756   *Fax:* (847)590-5241
Members: 100 companies
Staff: 2
Annual Budget: $10-25,000
Exec. Director: Sheila Wertz
Historical Note
Incorporated in Illinois. ABC is a national group of firms involved in factory-built housing. Promotes the establishment of such factories in economically distressed areas, and similar economic initiatives. Membership: $150-500/year.
Publications:
The Module. q.
Meetings/Conferences:
Annual Meetings: Summer

Automated Electrified Monorail Product Section - Material Handling Institute *(1990)*
8720 Red Oak Blvd., Suite 201
Charlotte, NC 28217
Tel: (704)676-1190   *Fax:* (704)676-1199
Web Site: http://www.mhia.org
Members: 5 companies
Staff: 2
Annual Budget: under $10,000
Managing Director: Thomas A. Carbott
Historical Note
A section of the Material Handling Institute.

Automated Imaging Ass'n *(1984)*
900 Victors Way, Box 3724
Ann Arbor, MI 48106
Tel: (734)994-6088   *Fax:* (734)994-3338
Web Site: http//:www.automated-imaging.org
Members: 200 companies
Staff: 10
Annual Budget: $500-1,000,000
Executive Director: Jeffrey A. Burnstein
Historical Note
Established and managed by the Automation Technologies Council. Formerly (1989) the Automated Vision Ass'n. Members are imaging manufacturers, users or suppliers of related equipment and services for the machine vision industry. Membership: $300-2,000/yr.
Publications:
AIA Today. q.
Machine Vision Market Study. a.
Machine Vision Systems Integrator Directory. a.
Meetings/Conferences:
1999 – San Jose, CA(Convention Center)/Oct. 5-7/3000

Automated Mapping/Facilities Management Internat'l

Historical Note
See AM/FM Internat'l.

Automated Procedures for Engineering Consultants *(1966)*
40 W. 40th St., Suite 2100
Dayton, OH 45402
Tel: (937)228-2602   *Fax:* (937)228-5652
Members: 200 companies
Staff: 3
Annual Budget: $250-500,000
Exec. Director: Doris J. Wallace
Historical Note
Formerly Automated Procedures for Engineering Consultants. APEC is an international non-profit ass'n of professional design firms who have been developing computer software for use in building systems design through volunteer cooperative efforts. Membership: $600-1,800/year (based on firm size).
Meetings/Conferences:

Automated Storage/Retrieval Systems *(1967)*
8720 Red Oak Blvd., Suite 201
Charlotte, NC 28217-3957
Tel: (704)676-1190   *Fax:* (704)676-1199
Web Site: www.mhia.org
Members: 16 companies
Staff: 2
Annual Budget: $25-50,000
Managing Director: Richard E. Ward, Ph.D.
Historical Note
A product section of the Material Handling Industry of America. Formerly (1975) Controlled Mechanical Storage Systems.
Meetings/Conferences:
Semi-Annual Meetings: Spring & Fall, with MHIA

Automatic Fire Alarm Ass'n *(1953)*
P.O. Box 951807
Lake Mary, FL 32795-1807
Tel: (407)322-6288   *Fax:* (407)322-7488
Web Site: http://www.afaa.org
Members: 1,100 companies & individuals
Staff: 3
Annual Budget: $500-1,000,000
Exec. Director & President: Larry Neibauer
Training Director: Tom Hammerberg
Historical Note
Manufacturers, installers, and others interested in fire alarm and detection equipment.
Publications:
AAFA Newsletter. m.
Meetings/Conferences:
Annual Meetings: March San Diego, CA/March 12-13

Automatic Guided Vehicle Systems *(1979)*
8720 Red Oak Blvd., Suite 201
Charlotte, NC 28217-3957
Tel: (704)676-1190   *Fax:* (704)676-1199
Web Site: http://www.mhia.org
Members: 14 companies
Staff: 2
Annual Budget: $25-50,000
Managing Director: Richard E. Ward, Ph.D.
Historical Note
A product section of the Material Handling Industry of America.
Meetings/Conferences:
Semi-Annual Meetings: Spring and Fall with MHIA

Automatic Indentification Manufacturers USA *(1972)*
Historical Note
See AIM USA.

Automatic Meter Reading Ass'n *(1987)*
60 Revere Drive, Suite 500
Northbrook, IL 60062
Tel: (847)480-9628   *Fax:* (847)480-9282
E-Mail: amra@amra-intl.org
Web Site: http://www.amra-intl.org
Members: 980 individuals
Staff: 4
Annual Budget: $500-1,000,000
Exec. Director: Joyce Paschall
Communications Director: Marcie Valerio
Administrative Director: Carol Scott
Historical Note
AMRA serves to advance the state of telemetry technology for meter reading, distribution, and control, and to provide a forum for research and development of standards, guidelines and practices. Membership: $200/year (full member), $115/year (associate).
Publications:
AMR Products and Services Directory. a. adv.
AMRA News. m.
Meetings/Conferences:
1999 – Reno, NV(Hilton)/Sept. 26-29/1500
2000 – Tampa, FL(Marriott and Convention Center)/Spet. 25-28/1500

Automatic Transmission Rebuilders Ass'n *(1954)*
2472 Eastman Ave., Suite 23
Ventura, CA 93003-5776
Tel: (805)654-1700   *Fax:* (805)654-0970
Web Site: http://www.atra-gears.com
Members: 3,200 individuals
Staff: 21
Annual Budget: $1-2,000,000
Exec. Director: G. Stephen Gray
Historical Note
Members are rebuilders and suppliers. Membership: $129/quarter.

Publications:
Directory. a.
Gears Magazine. 9/yr.
Good Guys Newsletter. 9/yr.
Tech Mailings. bi-m.
Meetings/Conferences:
Semi-annual Meetings: Spring and Fall
1999 – Orlando, FL/Sept. 24-26

Automation Forum (1984)
1300 North 17th St., Suite 1847
Rosslyn, VA 22209
Tel: (703)841-3294 *Fax:* (703)841-3394
Members: 10 individuals, 90 companies
Staff: 2
Annual Budget: $250-500,000
Exec. Director: Bill Snyder
Historical Note
The Forum provides an opportunity for senior managers to advance the manufacturing competitiveness of their organizations through networking, plant tours and exposure to leading-edge applications of best practices. Membership: $100/year (individual); $500/year (corporate).
Publications:
AFNET MBR Directories. a.
Newsletter. q.
Selected Reading Series. As required.
Meetings/Conferences:
Annual Meetings: Spring
1999 – New Orleans, LA/March 9-10

Automation Technologies Council (1974)
900 Victors Way, Box 3724
Ann Arbor, MI 48106
Tel: (734)994-6088 *Fax:* (734)994-3338
E-Mail: ria@robotics.org
Web Site: http://www.robotics.org
Members: 160 companies
Staff: 10
Annual Budget: $1-2,000,000
Exec. V. President: Donald A. Vincent, CAE
Director, Marketing and Public Relations: Jeffrey A. Burnstein
Historical Note
Established in 1974 as Robot Institute of America, incorporated in Washington, DC; became Robotic Industries Ass'n in 1980. In 1997, became Automation Technologies Council. ATC represents the automation industry in North America. Concerned with developing industry guidelines and collecting and dispensing accurate information on research and applications. Robotic Industries Ass'n is now a specialty division of ATC; other divisions include Automated Imaging Ass'n, Internat'l Service Robot Ass'n and Ass'n for Robots in Hazardous Environments. Membership: $350-10,000/yr. (depending on class).
Publications:
Machine Vision Systems Integrator Directory. a.
RIA Robotics Statistics Report. q.
Robot Times. q.
Robotics Supplier Directory. a.
Meetings/Conferences:
Semi-Annual Meetings: Spring and Fall
1999 – Detroit, MI(Cobo Hall)/May 14-16

Automobile Dealers Ass'n (1917)
8400 Westpark Drive
McLean, VA 22102
Tel: (703)821-7000 *Fax:* (703)821-7075
Members: 19,500 individuals
Staff: 400
Annual Budget: $10-25,000,000
President: Frank E. McCarthy
Exec. Director, Communications/Public Rels.: Denise Patton-Pace
Exec. Director, Conventions/Member Svcs.: Stephen R. Pitt
Chief Counsel: William A. Newman
Director, Membership: G. William MacLeod, CAE
Exec. Director, Industry Relations: Jake Kelderman
Director, Dealers Election Action Committee: Gregory Knopp
Historical Note
Organized in Chicago, June 10-11, 1917 as the result of the U.S. entry into World War I and a proposed luxury tax of 5% on automobiles. Incorporated in Illinois the same year, it represents dealers franchised by manufacturers and importers to sell and service new cars and trucks. Affiliated with Nat'l Automobile Dealers Ass'n Used Car Guide Company. Connected with the Dealers Election Action Committee and the Nat'l Automobile Dealers Charitable Foundation. The American Truck Dealers Ass'n is a division of the NADA. Has an annual budget of approximately $19.8 million.
Publications:
Automotive Executive. m. adv.
Convention Daily Newspaper. during convention. adv.
NADA Official Used Car Guide. m.
NADA Wholesale Used Car Trade-In Guide. bi-w.
Meetings/Conferences:
Annual Meetings: Winter
1999 – San Francisco, CA/Feb. 6-9

Automotive Body Parts Ass'n (1980)
P.O. Box 820689
Houston, TX 77282-0689
Tel: (281)531-0809 *Fax:* (281)531-9411
Toll Free: (800)323 - 5832
E-Mail: autobpa@infohwi.com
Members: 375 companies
Staff: 3
Annual Budget: $250-500,000
Exec. Director: Stanley A. Rodman
Historical Note
Founded and incorporated in California in 1980; re-incorporated in Texas in 1987. Formerly (1984) the Aftermarket Body Parts Distributors Ass'n and (1990) the Aftermarket Body Parts Ass'n.

Absorbed (1997) Bumper Recycling Ass'n of North America. Members are companies that distribute, supply and/or manufacture automotive bumpers and other auto body crash parts for auto dealers, body shops and garages. Membership: $400-750/year (company); $200/year (associate).
Publications:
Body Language Newsletter. m. adv.
Collision Parts Journal. q. adv.
Meetings/Conferences:
Semi-annual Meetings: Spring and Fall

Automotive Booster Clubs Internat'l (1921)
1806 Johns Drive
Glenview, IL 60025-1657
Tel: (847)729-2227 *Fax:* (847)729-3670
Members: 500 individuals
Staff: 2
Annual Budget: $50-100,000
Exec. V. President: Donn R. Proven
Historical Note
Founded in Boston, MA. Members are salespersons of auto replacement parts, supplies, tools/equipment and accessories for the automotive aftermarket. Membership: $31/year.
Publications:
Booster Bulletin. q.
Meetings/Conferences:

Automotive Chemical Manufacturers Council (1985)
1225 New York Ave., N.W., Suite 300
Washington, DC 20005
Tel: (202)393-6362 *Fax:* (202)737-3742
E-Mail: JCarney@MEMA.ORG
Members: 50 companies
Staff: 2
Annual Budget: $25-50,000
Group Executive: John W. Carney
Historical Note
ACMC represents domestic manufacturers of automotive chemical products. Membership: $450/year.
Publications:
ACMC News. m.
Meetings/Conferences:
1999 – Palm Beach Gardens, FL

Automotive Communications Council (1941)
25 Northwest Point Blvd., 4th Floor
Elk Grove Village, IL 60007-1035
Tel: (847)228-1310 *Fax:* (847)228-1510
E-Mail: richn@aftmktusa.org
Members: 65 companies
Staff: 1
Annual Budget: $10-25,000
Director, Finance: Richard Niebrzydowski
Historical Note
Formerly (1993) the Automotive Advertisers Council. Administrative services provided by the Automotive Service Industry Ass'n. Promotes research to increase advertising effectiveness. Chief executive is the President, who is elected annually. Membership: $225/year (individual).
Publications:
ACC Newsletter. semi-a.
Meetings/Conferences:
Semi-annual Meetings: May and October

Automotive Cooling System Institute (1976)
P.O. Box 13966
Research Triangle Park
Durham, NC 27709-3966
Tel: (919)549-4800 *Fax:* (919)549-4824
Members: 20 companies
Staff: 1
Annual Budget: $25-50,000
Exec. Secretary: Brent Hazelett
Historical Note
A service activity of the Motor and Equipment Manufacturers Ass'n. Informs the motoring public of the need for and benefits of proper care and maintenance of vehicle cooling systems.
Meetings/Conferences:

Automotive Engine Rebuilders Ass'n
Historical Note
Became (1995) AERA - Engine Rebuilders Ass'n.

Automotive Exhaust Systems Manufacturers Council (1970)
Historical Note
Organization defunct in 1997.

Automotive Fleet and Leasing Ass'n (1969)
21061 S. Western Ave.
Torrance, CA 90501
Tel: (310)533-2400 *Fax:* (310)533-2503
Members: 275 individuals
Staff: 2
Annual Budget: $50-100,000
Exec. Director: Rose Finch
Historical Note
AFLA is designed to improve communications among buyers, sellers, fleet administrators, lending institutions, lessors, used vehicle marketers and allied automotive service companies. Membership: $140/year.
Publications:
AFLA Conference Journal. a. adv.
The Forum Newsletter. m.
Meetings/Conferences:
1999 – New Orleans, LA(Le Meridien)/April 29-May 1/350
1999 – San Antonio, TX(St. Anthony)/Sept. 30-Oct. 2/200

2000 – Nashville, TN(Sheraton Music City)/April 13-15/350

Automotive Industry Action Group (1982)
26200 Lahser Road, Suite 200
Southfield, MI 48034
Tel: (810)358-3570 *Fax:* (810)358-3253
Web Site: http://www.aiag.org
Members: 1,500 companies
Staff: 60
Annual Budget: $10-25,000,000
Managing Director: Darlene Miller
Historical Note
Composed of major North American vehicle manufacturers and their suppliers, the AIAG's goal is to reduce costs and to improve productivity within the industry. Generally, activities focus on the automotive chain. The AIAG provides a forum for suppliers and manufacturers to indentify and solve common business problems. Membership: fees are based on annual corporate sales.
Publications:
Actionline. m. adv.
Buyer's Guide. a.
Meetings/Conferences:
1999 – Detroit, MI(Cobo Hall)/Aug. 31-Sept. 1/3300

Automotive Lift Institute (1945)
P.O. Box 33116
Indialantic, FL 32903-3116
Tel: (407)722-9993 *Fax:* (407)722-9931
E-Mail: autolift@iu.net
Web Site: http://autolift.org
Members: 25 companies
Staff: 3
President: E.K. (Chic) Fox
Historical Note
ALI is a trade association of U.S./Canadian manufacturers and exclusive distributors of automotive lifts that are used to completely raise motor vehicles for undercarriage service. Members sell more than 90% of the lifts marketed in the U.S. ALI promotes public awareness of safety in the use of lifts.
Publications:
ALI/ETL Listing of Certified Lifts. q.
Lifting It Right-Industry Generic Safety Manual. irreg.
Membership List. irreg.
National Safety Standard for Auto Lifts.
Standard for Operation, Inspection & Maintenance of Automotive Lifts.
Vehicle Lifting Points/Quick Reference Guide. a.
Meetings/Conferences:
Semi-annual Meetings: Open only to members and invited guests.

Automotive Maintenance and Repair Ass'n (1994)
1444 I St., N.W., Suite 700
Washington, DC 20005
Tel: (202)712-9038 *Fax:* (202)216-9646
Staff: 4
Annual Budget: $250-500,000
President: Lawrence S. Hecker, CAE
Communication Director: Mark Wright
Program Coordinator: Tom Placek
Accreditation Manager: Kim Harrison
Historical Note
AMRA represents automotive repair stores, manufacturers, trade groups, retailers and distributors. Activities includes developing standards of service, uniform inspection procedures, shop accreditation programs, and dispute resolution mechanisms. Membership: $100/year, minimum (organization/company).
Publications:
Directions Newsletter. q.
Meetings/Conferences:
1999 – Las Vegas, NV/200

Automotive Market Research Council (1966)
P.O. Box 13966
Research Triangle Pk, NC 27709-3966
Tel: (919)549-4800 *Fax:* (919)549-4824
Members: 375 individuals, 110 companies
Annual Budget: $50-100,000
Contact: Frank Hampshire
Historical Note
AMRC is a professional association for companies that manufacture autos and automotive parts, components, subassemblies, or accessories for sale as original or replacement equipment. Marketing research is a primary responsibility of the personnel who represent their companies in the council. Has no paid staff; administrative support is provided by the Motor and Equipment Manufacturers Ass'n. All officers change annually. Membership: $450/year (individual); $75/year (additional members from the same organization/ company).
Publications:
Newsletter. 2/year.
Press release. semi-a.
Meetings/Conferences:
Semi-annual meetings: Spring and Fall

Automotive Occupant Protection Ass'n (1978)
21251 E. Cuba Rd.
Kildeer, IL 60047
Tel: (847)215-9050
Members: 4 companies
Staff: 1
Annual Budget: $10-25,000
President: Jack Martens
Historical Note
Members are manufacturers interested in promoting auto safety equipment in general, and auto air bags in particular.

Automotive Occupant Restraints Council (1961)
3367 Tates Creek Road

Lexington, KY 40502
Tel: (606)269-4240   *Fax:* (606)269-4241
Members: 55 companies
Staff: 4
Annual Budget: $100-250,000
Administrator: Jill P. Mulholland

Historical Note
Formerly (1977) the American Safety Belt Council and (1989) American Seat Belt Council. Supersedes the Automobile Safety Belt Council. Membership: $3,000-15,000/year

Meetings/Conferences:
Annual Meetings: March
1999 – San Diego, CA(LaCosta)/March 17-20

Automotive Oil Change Ass'n (1987)
12860 Hillcrest, Suite 229
Dallas, TX 75230
Tel: (972)458-9468   *Fax:* (972)458-9539
Toll Free: (800)331 - 0329
E-Mail: aoca@onramp.net
Web Site: http://www.aoca.org
Members: 1000 companies
Staff: 5
Annual Budget: $1-2,000,000
Exec. Director: Stephen M. Christie, CAE
Director, Meetings/Conventions: Joyce A. Laurie
Director, Education: Jeff Pohlman

Historical Note
Formerly (1993) Nat'l Ass'n of Independent Lubes. AOCA members are owners of independent and franchise automobile oil and lubrication businesses. Membership: $250/year, minimum (corporate).

Publications:
Oil Changing Times. bi-m.

Meetings/Conferences:
1999 – Albuquerque, NM
2000 – Atlanta, GA((Westin)
2001 – Fort Worth, TX

Automotive Parts and Accessories Ass'n (1967)
4600 East-West Hwy., Suite 300
Bethesda, MD 20814-3415
Tel: (301)654-6664   *Fax:* (301)654-3299
E-Mail: apaa@apaa.com
Web Site: www.apaa.org
Members: 1,700 companies
Staff: 23
Annual Budget: $2-5,000,000
President/CEO: Alfred L. Gaspar
Managing Dir., Public Rels./Communications: John Reilly
V. President, Regulatory & Government Affairs: Aaron Lowe
V. President, Government Affairs & Trade: Lee Kadrich
Manager, Meetings and Events: Michael E. Barratt
Chief Finance/Operations Officer: Susan Medick, CPA
Senior Director, Membership/Marketing: Yvonne D.H. Dock, CAE
Director, EIS: James A. Hilbert

Historical Note
Members are manufacturers, distributors, retailers and manufacturers' representatives who market automotive replacement parts and accessories and services. Membership: $200-3,500/year (organization).

Publications:
APAA Aftermarket Factbook. a. adv.
APAA In-Brief. q. adv.
APAA Mini-Monitor. a.
AutoFax. w.
Reptalk. m.

Meetings/Conferences:
Trade Show: Las Vegas, NV
1999 – (MGM Grand)/Nov. 1-5
2000 – (MGM Grand)/Oct. 30-Nov. 3

Automotive Parts Rebuilders Ass'n (1941)
4401 Fair Lakes Court, Suite 210
Fairfax, VA 22033-3848
Tel: (703)968-2772   *Fax:* (703)968-2878
E-Mail: mail@apra.org
Web Site: http://www.apra.org
Members: 2,100 companies
Staff: 12
Annual Budget: $2-5,000,000
President: William C. Gager
V. President: Jeanie Magathan
Director, Membership: Judy Chandler

Historical Note
Membership: $195-$3,500/year (based on number of employees).

Publications:
APRA Membership Directory. a.
Data Link Newsletter. m.
Global Sourcing Directory. a.
The Electrical Connection. m.
The Mechanical Messenger. m.

Meetings/Conferences:
Annual Meetings: Fall

Automotive Presidents Council
1225 New York Ave., N.W., Suite 300
Washington, DC 20005
Tel: (202)393-6362   *Fax:* (202)737-3742
Members: 55 individuals
Staff: 1
Vice President and Exec. Director: Christopher M. Bates

Historical Note
A division of Motor and Equipment Manufacturers Ass'n, which provides administrative support. Members are chief executive officers of MEMA-member companies.

Meetings/Conferences:
Semi-annual Meetings: Spring and Fall.

Automotive Products Emissions Committee
Historical Note
Inactive in 1996.

Automotive Public Relations Council (1974)
P.O. Box 13966
Research Triangle Park
Durham, NC 27709-3966
Tel: (919)549-4800   *Fax:* (919)549-4824
E-Mail: rkitchin@mema.com
Members: 63 individuals
Staff: 1
Annual Budget: under $10,000
Exec. Secretary: Rosemarie Kitchin

Historical Note
An activity of the Motor and Equipment Manufacturers Ass'n, APRC members are corporate and agency communicators. Membership: $225/year.

Meetings/Conferences:
Semi-annual Meetings: Spring and Fall
1999 – Washington, DC
1999 – Detroit, MI

Automotive Recyclers Ass'n (1943)
3975 Fair Ridge Drive, Suite 20
Terrace Level North
Fairfax, VA 22033-2924
Tel: (703)385-1001   *Fax:* (703)385-1494
Web Site: www.autorecyc.org
Members: 2,000 companies
Staff: 7
Annual Budget: $2-5,000,000
Exec. V. President: William P. Steinkuller
Manager, Communications: Gail Schell
Manager, Public Relations and Marketing: Veronica M. Dove
Manager, Governmental Affairs: Michael Wilson
Director, Member Services: Isabel F. Sullivan
Manager, Membership and Certification: Kelly C. Badillo

Historical Note
Incorporated in the State of New York. Formerly (1973) Nat'l Auto and Truck Wreckers Ass'n, (1975) Ass'n of Auto and Truck Recyclers, and (1989) Automotive Dismantlers and Recyclers; assumed its current name in 1993. Members are recyclers of domestic and foreign automobile, truck, and motorcycle parts. Supports its international membership through education programs, legislative representation, and professional certification. Membership: $320-600/year (company); $395/year (individual).

Publications:
Annual Convention Program Guide. a. adv.
Automotive Recycling. bi-m. adv.
Membership Directory/Buyers Guide. a. adv.

Meetings/Conferences:
Semi-Annual Meetings: Spring and Fall

Automotive Refrigeration Products Institute (1983)
P.O. Box 470462
Fort Worth, TX 76147-9462
Tel: (817)338-1100   *Fax:* (817)338-1451
Members: 10 companies
Staff: 4
Annual Budget: $250-500,000
Exec. Director: Frank Allison

Historical Note
Trade association of companies engaged in the manufacture, distribution and/or packaging of automotive refrigeration products. Administrative support provided by Internat'l Mobile Air Conditioning Ass'n (same address).

Meetings/Conferences:
1999 – Fort Worth, TX(Fort Worth Convention
         Center)/Nov. 16-19

Automotive Service Ass'n (1986)
P.O. Box 929
1901 Airport Freeway
Bedford, TX 76095-0929
Tel: (817)283-6205   *Fax:* (817)685-0225
Toll Free: (800)272 - 7467
E-Mail: wahert@asa.dataorg.com
Web Site: http://www.asashop.org
Members: 14,000 businesses
Staff: 39
Annual Budget: $5-10,000,000
President and Chief Executive Officer: George W. Merwin, III
V.President, Communications: Ken Roberts
Curriculum Specialist: John L. Berry
V. President, Finance/Controller: Mark Hale
Director, Membership: John Scully

Historical Note
Consolidation of Automotive Service Councils, Inc. (formed in 1955) and Independent Automotive Service Ass'n (formed in 1949). Members are businesses providing automotive service in mechanical, auto body and transmission, along with other fields. Membership: $150/year.

Publications:
AutoInc. m. adv.
Division Bulletins. bi-w.

Meetings/Conferences:
Annual Meetings: Spring and Trade Show/late Fall
1999 – Bermuda/March 16-20/425
2000 – Point Clear, AL(Marriott)
2001 – Hawaii

Automotive Service Industry Ass'n (1959)
25 Northwest Point Blvd., 4th Floor
Elk Grove Village, IL 60007-1035
Tel: (847)228-1310   *Fax:* (847)228-1510
E-Mail: asia@aftmktusa.org
Web Site: http://www.aftmkt.org/asia
Members: 1,800 companies

Staff: 22
Annual Budget: $2-5,000,000
President: Gene A. Gardner
Director, Communications: Gary D. McCoy
Director, Conventions & Meetings: Alice M. Moore
Director, Finance and Administration: Richard Niebrzydowski
Director, Member Services: William A. Potter
Director, Communications: Robert F. Sigel

Historical Note
Merger (1959) of Nat'l Standard Parts Ass'n and Motor Equipment Wholesalers Ass'n. Absorbed (1974) Automotive Electric Ass'n. Members are manufacturers, remanufacturers, manufacturers' reps, distributors and jobbers in seven divisions: automotive, heavy duty, trim, paint/body equipment, automotive electric, tool and equipment, and manufacturers reps. Sponsors and supports the Automotive Aftermarket Political Action Committee (AAPAC). Membership fee based on sales volume.

Publications:
Aftermarket Today.
Eight Divisional newsletters. m.
Membership Directory. bi-a.
Washington Insights, legislative newsletter. m.

Meetings/Conferences:
Annual Meetings: Fall/3,000

Automotive Technicians Ass'n Internat'l (1984)
Historical Note
Organization defunct in 1997.

Automotive Trade Ass'n Executives (1917)
8400 Westpark Drive
McLean, VA 22102
Tel: (703)821-7072   *Fax:* (703)556-8581
Members: 107 associations
Staff: 2
Annual Budget: $100-250,000
Exec. Director: C. Alan Marlette

Historical Note
Members are executives of state and local automobile dealer associations.

Meetings/Conferences:
Semi-Annual Meetings: February and July
1999 – Lake Tahoe, NV

Automotive Training Managers Council (1984)
13505 Dulles Technology Drive, Suite 2
Herndon, VA 20171-3421
Tel: (703)713-1113   *Fax:* (703)713-3848
Members: 155 individuals
Staff: 3
Annual Budget: $50-100,000
V. President, Programs: Lloyd W. "Bill" Brown

Historical Note
ATMC members are automotive aftermarket manufacturing and distributing concerns, each represented by a training department executive. ATMC provides a forum for the exchange of views and opinions regarding the training needs of the automotive trade; encourages study and research of training effectiveness; and promotes quality training. Membership: $250/year (corporate).

Meetings/Conferences:
Semi-Annual Meetings: Spring and Fall

Automotive Warehouse Distributors Ass'n (1947)
9140 Ward Pkwy., Suite 200
Kansas City, MO 64114
Tel: (816)444-3500   *Fax:* (816)444-0330
Web Site: http://www.awda.org
Members: 400 companies
Staff: 15
Annual Budget: $1-2,000,000
President: Jack Creamer
Director, Meetings/Operations: Rosemary Hall
Coordinator, Membership: David Madole
Editor: Lisa Sorenson

Historical Note
Distributors and manufacturers of automotive parts and supplies. Sponsors and supports the Automotive Warehouse Distributors Association Political Action Committee.

Publications:
AWDA Leadership Directory. a.
AWDA News. bi-m.
AWDA University Catalog. a.

Meetings/Conferences:
Annual Meetings: Las Vegas, NV/Fall

Automotive Wholesalers Ass'n Executives (1954)
958 S. Perry St.
Montgomery, AL 36104
Tel: (334)834-1848   *Fax:* (334)834-1860
Web Site: http://www.awag.org
Members: 725 organizations
Staff: 5
Annual Budget: $10-25,000
President: Randall H. Ward

Historical Note
Members are automotive parts dealers referred to as the automotive aftermarket. Membership: $210-420/year (based on sales volume).

Meetings/Conferences:
1999 – Orlando, FL(Peabody)/July 7-9

Aviation Distributors and Manufacturers Ass'n Internat'l (1943)
1900 Arch St.
Philadelphia, PA 19103-1498
Tel: (215)564-3484   *Fax:* (215)564-2175
Members: 90 companies
Annual Budget: $100-250,000
Exec. Director: Patricia A. Lilly

Historical Note
Promotes friendly business relations and mutual confidence among its members and others in the industry; represents the distributors and manufacturers of aviation parts, supplies and equipment in all matters of national importance; and cooperates with various government agencies, including the Federal Aviation Administration. Membership fee varies, based on sales volume.

Publications:
Aviation Education News Bulletin. a.

Meetings/Conferences:
Semi-Annual Meetings: Spring and Fall

Aviation Insurance Ass'n *(1976)*
899 S. College Mall Rd., Suite 375
Bloomington, IN   47401
Tel: (812)323-7955   *Fax:* (812)323-7956
Toll Free: (800)354 - 7918
Members: 435 firms
Staff: 2
Annual Budget: $250-500,000
Exec. Director: John P. Donica

Historical Note
Membership: $225/year per firm.

Publications:
Membership Directory. a.
Newsletter-The Binder. q.

Meetings/Conferences:
1999 – San Antonio, TX(Hyatt Hill Country)/May 22-25/550
2000 – Washington, DC(Omni Shoreham)/May 6-9
2001 – Phoenix, AZ(Hilton South Mountain)
2001 – London, England(Tower Thistle)

Aviation Maintenance Foundation Internat'l *(1971)*
P.O. Box 2826
Redmond, WA   98073-2826
Members: 6,000 individuals, 100 companies
Staff: 8
Annual Budget: $500-1,000,000
President and Exec. Director: Richard S. Kost

Historical Note
Formerly (1988) the Aviation Maintenance Foundation. Incorporated in March, 1972. Members are aviation maintenance personnel, schools, companies and related organizations. Membership: $40/yr. (individual); $420 (Life membership).

Publications:
AMFI Technical Bulletin. irreg.
China Aerospace News Digest. m.
Industry News. m.
Industry Statistical Surveys. a.
SAMOLYOT (Russian Aviation/Aerospace). semi-a.
World of Aviation Maintenance. a.

Meetings/Conferences:
Annual Meetings: Fall/1,200

Aviation Safety Institute *(1973)*
PO Box 690
Worthington, OH   43085-0690
Tel: (614)885-4242   *Fax:* (614)793-1708
E-Mail: 110364.3550@compuserve.com
Web Site: http://www.asionline.org
Members: 510 individuals, 35 companies
Staff: 5
Annual Budget: $100-250,000
President: Edward Wachs
Editor: Mike Overly

Historical Note
A not-for-profit research organization that depends primarily upon tax-deductible contributions and consequently serves as a wholly independent "third party" in the promotion of aviation safety. Membership: $25/year (individual), $250/year (company).

Publications:
Monitor. m.

Meetings/Conferences:

Aviation Technician Education Council *(1961)*
2090 Wexford Court
Harrisburg, PA   17112-1579
Tel: (717)540-7121   *Fax:* (717)540-7121
Members: 155 schools
Staff: 1
Annual Budget: $50-100,000
Exec. Director: R. Dumaresq, Ph.D.

Historical Note
ATEC members are FAA approved schools training aviation maintenance technicians.

Publications:
ATEC Newsletter. 3/yr.

Meetings/Conferences:
1999 – Las Vegas, NV
2000 – Seattle, WA
2001 – Orlando, FL

Aviation/Space Writers Ass'n *(1938)*
Historical Note
Organization defunct in 1997.

Awards and Recognition Ass'n *(1980)*
35 E. Wacker Dr., Suite 500
Chicago, IL   60601-2105
Tel: (312)782-5252   *Fax:* (312)236-1140
Members: 4,500 companies
Annual Budget: $2-5,000,000
Exec. Director: Ralph J. Bloch

Historical Note
Began in San Francisco, CA in 1966 as Bay Area Trophy Dealers; incorporated in California in 1967 as Trophy Dealers of Northern California; eventually expanded its membership to become the

Trophy Dealers of America, Inc. Merged with American Awards Manufacturers Ass'n in 1980 and became Trophy Dealers and Manufacturers Ass'n; assumed its current name in 1993. Membership: $150/yr. (retail dealer); $380/yr. (manufacturing supplier)

Publications:
Recognition Review. m. adv.

Meetings/Conferences:
1999 – Las Vegas, NV(MGM Grand)/February 8-11
2000 – Las Vegas, NV(Las Vegas Convention
          Center)/Feb. 22-25

Ayrshire Breeders' Ass'n *(1875)*
P.O. Box 1608
Brattleboro, VT   05302-1608
Tel: (802)254-7460   *Fax:* (802)257-4332
E-Mail: ayrshire@gbla.com
Web Site: http://www.gbla.com/ayrshire
Members: 1,100 individuals
Staff: 3
Annual Budget: $100-250,000
Executive Secretary: Robert E. Schrull
Manager: Jennifer Carpenter

Historical Note
Breeders and fanciers of Ayrshire dairy cattle. Member of the Nat'l Soc. of Livestock Record Ass'ns. Membership: $25/year.

Publications:
Ayrshire Digest. bi-m. adv.

Meetings/Conferences:
Annual Meetings: Spring

Bakery, Confectionery and Tobacco Workers' Internat'l Union *(1886)*
10401 Connecticut Ave.
Kensington, MD   20895-3961
Tel: (301)933-8600   *Fax:* (301)946-8452
Members: 120,000 individuals
Staff: 40
President: Frank Hurt
Director of Public Relations: Carolyn Jacobson

Historical Note
Organized on January 13, 1886 in Pittsburgh and chartered by the American Federation of Labor on February 23, 1887. Merged (1969) with American Bakery and Confectionery Workers' Internat'l Union. Affiliated with AFL-CIO, CLC. Formerly (until 1978) known as the Bakery and Confectionery Workers Internat'l Union of America. Merged with the Tobacco Workers Internat'l Union in August, 1978, and assumed its present name at that time. Sponsors and supports the Bakery, Confectionery and Tobacco Workers International Union Political Action Committee.

Publications:
BC&T News. 9/year.
BC&T Report. m.

Meetings/Conferences:
Quadrennial Convention: 1998

Baking Industry Sanitation Standards Committee *(1949)*
1400 W.Devon Ave., Suite 422
Chicago, IL   60660
Tel: (773)761-4100   *Fax:* (773)274-3032
E-Mail: bakesan@aol.com
Web Site: http://www.baking-sanitation.com
Members: 130 registered companies, 6 ass'ns
Staff: 2
Annual Budget: $50-100,000
Secretary/Treasurer: Bonnie Sweetman

Historical Note
Founded and supported by the American Bakers Ass'n (ABA), the American Institute of Baking (AIB), the American Soc. of Baking (ASB), the Bakery Equipment Manufacturers Ass'n (BEMA), the Biscuit and Cracker Manufacturers Ass'n (B&CMA),and Retail Bakers of America (RBA). Primary purpose is to develop, publish and promote the use of voluntary sanitation standards covering the design and construction of machinery and equipment used in the baking industry. Registration fee: $300/year (company).

Publications:
BISSC Bulletin. semi-a.
BISSC Design Handbook for Easily Cleanable Equipment.
BISSC Standards Book. quadren.
Directory of Registered Companies. a.

Meetings/Conferences:
Annual Meetings: Winter/30
1999 – Chicago, IL(Marriott)/30
2000 – Chicago, IL(Marriott)/30

Balloon Manufacturers Ass'n
Historical Note
A division of the Industrial Fabrics Association International.

Bank Administration Institute *(1924)*
1 N. Franklin St.
Chicago, IL   60606
Tel: (312)553-4600   *Fax:* (312)683-2434
E-Mail: http://www.bai.org
Web Site: www.bai.org
Members: 1,500 banks
Staff: 90
Annual Budget: $5-10,000,000
President and C.E.O.: Thomas P. Johnson
C.F.O.: John Nitschke
Director, Marketing: Deborah L. Bianvcci

Historical Note
Provides information for member bankers in areas such as human resources, finance, strategic planning and marketing, accounting, corporate services, audit, taxes, retail, operations and technology, through its series of emerging issues studies, professional conferences and education programs.

Publications:
Bank Fraud Newsletter. m.
Bank Strategies Magazine.
Compliance Alert Newsletter. m.

Meetings/Conferences:
Annual Meetings: not held

Bank Marketing Ass'n *(1915)*
1120 Connecticut Ave., N.W.
Washington, DC   20036
Tel: (202)663-5268   *Fax:* (202)828-4540
Toll Free: (800)433 - 9013
Members: 3,000 individuals
Staff: 15
Annual Budget: $5-10,000,000
Exec. Director: J. Douglas Adamson
Assoc. Director, Programs & Products: Catherine Nelson
Managing Director: Michael Riley
Division Manager, Membership: Cindy Sheridan
Publisher, Periodicals: Larry Price

Historical Note
Formerly (1947) the Financial Advertisers Ass'n, (1965) the Financial Public Relations Ass'n and (1970) the Bank Public Relations and Marketing Ass'n. Membership: $950/year.

Publications:
Bank Marketing Magazine. m. adv.

Meetings/Conferences:
Annual Meetings: Fall
1999 – Orlando, FL/October 23-26

Bankcard Services Ass'n
Historical Note
Became (1997) Electronic Transactions Ass'n.

Bankers Institute
Historical Note
Address unknown in 1997.

Bankers Roundtable, The *(1958)*
805 15th St., N.W., Suite 600
Washington, DC   20005
Tel: (202)289-4322   *Fax:* (202)289-1903
Members: 115 companies
Annual Budget: $1-2,000,000
Exec. Director: Anthony T. Cluff, Ph.D.
Senior Legislative Director: Alfred Pollard
Administrative Director: Marguerite A. Cox
General Counsel: Richard M. Whiting

Historical Note
Product of a merger in 1993 of the Ass'n of Bank Holding Companies and the Ass'n of Reserve City Bankers.

Publications:
Government Affairs Newsletter. m.
Newsletter. m.

Meetings/Conferences:
Semi-Annual Meetings: Spring and Fall

Bankers' Ass'n for Foreign Trade *(1921)*
2121 K St., N.W., Suite 701
Washington, DC   20037-1801
Tel: (202)452-0952   *Fax:* (202)452-0959
Members: 155 banks
Staff: 5
Annual Budget: $500-1,000,000
Exec. Director: Mary Condeelis
Director, Communications/Issues Management: John D. Bierman
General Counsel: Thomas L. Farmer
Director, Conferences: Deborah Smith

Historical Note
BAFT is an association of banking institutions dedicated to fostering and promoting international trade, finance, and investment between the United States and its trading partners. BAFT has played a unique role in bringing together financial institutions worldwide which have an interest in business, commerce and finance in the United States. Membership fee varies, based on assets.

Publications:
BAFT Update. m. adv.
For Your Information. q.

Meetings/Conferences:
Annual Meetings: April/May
1999 – Phoenix, AZ(The Biltmore)/May 16-19

Baptist Communicators Ass'n *(1954)*
P.O. Box 270187
Nashville, TN   37227-0187
Tel: (615)904-0152   *Fax:* (615)904-0183
Members: 450 individuals
Annual Budget: $10-25,000
Admin. Coordinator: Keith Beene

Historical Note
Founded as Baptist Public Relations Ass'n; assumed its current name in 1997. Main purpose is educational. Membership: $60/year.

Publications:
BPRA Directory. a.
BPRA Newsletter. bi-m.

Meetings/Conferences:
Annual Meetings: Spring
1999 – Jacksonville, FL/April 20-22

Baptist Hospital Ass'n
Historical Note
Became (1998) Palmetto Baptist Medical Center.

Baptist Public Relations Ass'n

Historical Note
Became (1997) Baptist Communicators Ass'n.

Barbecue Industry Ass'n *(1958)*
710 E. Ogden Ave., Suite 600
Naperville, IL   60563-8603
Tel: (630)369-2404   *Fax:* (630)369-2488
Members: 60 companies
Staff: 2
Annual Budget: $250-500,000
Exec. Director: Ann E. Spehar, CAE

Historical Note
Formerly (1966) Wood Charcoal Briquet Producers Ass'n, (1969) Barbecue Briquet Institute, (1977) Charcoal Briquet Institute, and (1978) Charcoal Barbecue Industry Ass'n. Member companies manufacture and sell barbecue products. BIA's primary purpose is promoting consumer barbecuing. Membership: $1,925/year (corporate).

Publications:
Barbecue Bulletin. q.

Meetings/Conferences:
Semi-annual Meetings: Spring and Fall

Baromedical Nurses Ass'n *(1985)*
Historical Note
BNA members are nurses assisting in the practice hyperbaric medicine. Membership: $50/year (individual); $250/year (corporate).

Barre Granite Ass'n *(1889)*
P.O. Box 481, 51 Church St.
Barre, VT   05641
Tel: (802)476-4131   *Fax:* (802)476-4765
Members: 81 companies
Staff: 4
Annual Budget: $500-1,000,000
President and Manager, Administration and Finance: John Castaldo

Historical Note
Members are granite quarriers and manufacturers, dedicated to the production of granite monuments and other products. BGA provides a cemetery planning assistance program designed to expand cemetery areas or establish new cemetery sections.

Publications:
Barre Life. q.

Meetings/Conferences:
Annual Meetings: usually Barre, VT/May

Barzona Breeders Ass'n of America *(1968)*
P.O. Box 631
Prescott, AZ   86302-0631
Tel: (520)445-5150   *Fax:* (520)445-5150
Members: 80 individuals
Staff: 1
Annual Budget: $25-50,000
Exec. Secretary: Karen Halford

Historical Note
Breeders and fanciers of Barzona cattle. Officers elected annually. Membership: $75/year.

Meetings/Conferences:

Baseball Writers Ass'n of America *(1908)*
78 Olive Street
Lake Grove, NY   11755
Tel: (516)981-7938   *Fax:* (516)585-4669
E-Mail: bbwaa@aol.com
Members: 800 individuals
Staff: 1
Annual Budget: under $10,000
Secretary-Treasurer: Jack O'Connell

Historical Note
Members are sports writers on direct assignment to major league teams. Membership: $35/year (individual).

Meetings/Conferences:
Annual Meetings: In October at the site of the World Series and in July at the All-Star Game.

Basic Acrylic Monomer Manufacturers Ass'n *(1986)*
1250 Connecticut Ave.
Suite 800
Washington, DC   20005
Tel: (202)637-9040   *Fax:* (202)637-9178
Members: 5 manufacturers
Staff: 2
Annual Budget: $500-1,000,000
Exec. Director: Elizabeth K. Hunt

Historical Note
Members are producers of the basic acrylic monomers. BAMM addresses health, environmental and regulatory issues concerning acrylic monomers.

Bath Enclosure Manufacturers Ass'n
2945 S.W. Wanamaker Dr., Suite A
Topeka, KS   66614-5321
Tel: (785)271-0208   *Fax:* (785)271-0208
E-Mail: bema@glasswebsite.com
Web Site: http://www.glasswebsite.com/bema
Annual Budget: $50-100,000
Exec. Director: William J. Birch

Historical Note
Membership: $200-400/year.

Meetings/Conferences:

Battery Council Internat'l *(1924)*
401 N. Michigan Ave.
Chicago, IL   60611-4267
Tel: (312)644-6610   *Fax:* (312)321-6869
Members: 200 companies
Annual Budget: $500-1,000,000

Exec. Secretary: Edward M. Craft
Convention Manager: Irene Condon

Historical Note
Established as the Nat'l Battery Manufacturers Ass'n. Became the Ass'n of American Battery Manufacturers in 1940, and the Battery Council Internat'l in 1969. Distributors, manufacturers and suppliers to the electrical storage battery industry. Maintains a Washington office. Membership dues based on sales volume.

Publications:
Battery Replacement Data Book.
Membership Directory. a.
Newletter. q.
Service Manual. irreg.
Technical Manual. irreg.

Meetings/Conferences:
Annual Meetings: Spring/600
1999 – Nashville, TN(Opryland Hotel)/May 2-5/500
2000 – San Francisco, CA(Hyatt Regency)/April 16-19/550

Bearing Specialist Ass'n *(1966)*
800 Roosevelt Road, Bldg. C, Suite 20
Glen Ellyn, IL   60137-5833
Tel: (630)858-3838   *Fax:* (630)790-3095
Members: 80 companies
Staff: 3
Annual Budget: $250-500,000
Exec. Director: Richard W. Church
Exec. Secretary: Jerilyn J. Church,, CAE

Historical Note
Merger of Anti-Friction Bearing Distributors Ass'n and Ass'n of Bearing Specialists. BSA serves as a forum for professionals in the bearing industry to exchange information, network and focus on problems relevant to the industry.

Publications:
News and Views. bi-m.

Meetings/Conferences:
Annual Meetings: Spring
1999 – Tucson, AZ(Loewe's Ventana Canyon)/April 25-28

Bearing Technical Committee
Historical Note
A committee of the American Bearing Manufacturing Ass'n.

Beauty and Barber Supply Institute *(1904)*
11811 N. Tatum Blvd.
Suite 1085
Phoenix, AZ   85028-1625
Tel: (602)401-1000   *Fax:* (602)404-8900
Toll Free: (800)468 - 2274
E-Mail: spano@bbsi.org
Web Site: http://www.bbsi.org
Members: 1,400 firms
Staff: 21
Annual Budget: $2-5,000,000
Exec. Director: Michael A. Spano
Director, Communications: Denise M. Rucci
Director, Trade Shows/Education: Eric Z. Horn
Director, Finance: Steve Sleeper
Director, Marketing: Jill Kohler

Historical Note
Formerly the Barber Supply Dealers of America. Maximizes the potential of the professional salon industry. Membership: $400/year.

Publications:
Beauty Inc. bi-m. adv.

Meetings/Conferences:
Semi-annual Meetings: Winter and Summer
1999 – Las Vegas, NV(Las Vegas Conv. Ctr.)/Aug. 4-7/12000
2000 – Las Vegas, NV(Las Vegas Conv. Ctr.)/Aug. 2-5/12000
2001 – Las Vegas, NV(Las Vegas Conv. Ctr.)/July 18-21/12000

Bedding Plants International *(1969)*
206 6th Ave., Suite 900
Des Moines, IA   50309-4018
Tel: (515)282-8192
Toll Free: (800)647 - 7742
Members: 2,500 individuals
Staff: 10
Annual Budget: $500-1,000,000
C.E.O.: John F. Greenslit

Historical Note
Formerly known as Bedding Plants, Inc. Members are growers, wholesalers, retailers, educators, and allied tradesmen of the bedding plant and flowering potted plant industry.

Publications:
PPGA News. m.

Meetings/Conferences:
Annual Meetings: Fall

Beef Friesian Soc.
25377 Weld County Rd. 17
Johnstown, CO   80534
Tel: (970)587-2252
Members: 50 individuals
Annual Budget: under $10,000
Director-President: Maurice W. Boney

Historical Note
Members are breeders of Beef Friesian (Irish Black) cattle. Has no paid officers or full-time staff.

Publications:
BFS Newsletter. irreg.

Beef Improvement Federation *(1968)*
Department of Animal and Range Science
South Dakota State University
Brookings, SD   57007
Tel: (605)688-5166
Members: 80 organizations

Staff: 1
Annual Budget: $25-50,000
Exec. Director: Donn Boggs

Historical Note
Membership, by organization, consists of groups of beef cattle breeders and state improvement associations. Membership: $50-600/year.

Publications:
Genetic Prediction Proceedings. quinquen.
Guidelines for Uniform Beef Improvement Programs. quinquen.
Ideas into Action - BIF 25 Year History.
Proceedings - BIF Symposium and Annual Meeting. a.

Meetings/Conferences:
Annual Meetings: Spring/300

Beef Industry Council
Historical Note
Merged with the Nat'l Cattlemen's Ass'n in 1996 to form the Nat'l Cattlemen's Beef Ass'n.

Beefmaster Breeders United *(1961)*
6800 Park Ten Blvd., Suite 290 West
San Antonio, TX   78213
Tel: (210)732-3132   *Fax:* (210)732-7711
Members: 6,400 individuals
Staff: 14
Annual Budget: $1-2,000,000
Exec. V. President: Wendell E. Schronk

Historical Note
Formerly Beefmaster Breeders Universal; absorbed Foundation Beefmaster Ass'n and assumed its current name in 1996. Owners and breeders of Beefmaster cattle. Member of the Nat'l Pedigree Livestock Council. Membership: $60/year.

Publications:
Directory of BBU Members. a. adv.
The Beefmaster Cowman. m. adv.

Meetings/Conferences:
Annual Meetings: Fall
1999 – Knoxville, TN/Oct. 14-17

Beefmaster Breeders Universal
Historical Note
Became Beefmaster Breeders United in 1996.

Beer Institute *(1986)*
122 C St., N.W., Suite 750
Washington, DC   20001
Tel: (202)737-2337   *Fax:* (202)737-7004
Toll Free: (800)379 - 2739
Web Site: http://www.beerinst.org
Members: 165 brewers and suppliers
Staff: 8
Annual Budget: $1-2,000,000
President: Raymond J. McGrath
V. President, Alcohol Issues: Jeffrey G. Becker
Exec. V. President and General Counsel: Arthur DeCelle
Director, Information and Statistical Services: Matthew Hein

Historical Note
Successor organization to the United States Brewers Ass'n, formerly (1944) United Brewers Industrial Foundation and (1961) United States Brewers Foundation. Members are the major national breweries and suppliers to the brewing industry.

Publications:
Brewers Almanac. a.
Export Bulletin. m.
Import Statistics. m.
State Consumption Almanac. m.

Meetings/Conferences:
Annual Meetings: Not held.

Beet Sugar Development Foundation *(1945)*
800 Grant St., Suite 500
Denver, CO   80203
Tel: (303)832-4460   *Fax:* (303)832-4468
Members: 15 companies
Staff: 30
Annual Budget: $250-500,000
Exec. V. President: Thomas K. Schwartz

Historical Note
Members are U.S. and Canadian sugar beet companies and primary suppliers of sugar beet seed.

Meetings/Conferences:
Annual Meetings: Semi-Annual Meetings.

Behavior Genetics Ass'n *(1972)*
Inst. for Psych. & Behavioral Genetics
Virginia Commonwealth Univ., Box 98003
Richmond, VA   23290-0003
Tel: (804)828-8145   *Fax:* (804)828-8801
E-Mail: hmaes@hydro.psi.vcu.edu
Web Site: http://www.bga.org
Members: 500 individuals
Annual Budget: $10-25,000
Secretary: Hermine Maes

Historical Note
Organized May 9, 1972 in Illinois to promote scientific study of the interrelationships of genetic mechanisms and behavior of both animal and human; to aid and encourage education and training in the field; and interpret and disseminate knowledge to the public. Affiliated with the International Genetics Association, American Association for the Advancement of Science (AAAS). Has no paid staff. Membership: $55/year (full member); $30/year (student).

Publications:
Behavior Genetics. bi-m. adv.

Meetings/Conferences:
Annual Meetings: Summer/175

1999 – Vancouver, British Columbia(Coast Plaza
  Suites)/July 4-7
2000 – Burlington, VT

Behavioral Pharmacology Soc. *(1957)*
Yerkes Reg. Primate Research Center
Behavioral Biology Div., Emory Univ.
Atlanta, GA 30322
Tel: (404)727-7730   *Fax:* (404)727-1266
E-Mail: byrd@rmy.emory.edu
Members: 200 individuals
Annual Budget: under $10,000
President: Larry D. Byrd, Ph.D.

Historical Note
*BPS members are research scientists involved in studies to
determine the effects of drugs on the central nervous system and
behavior. Membership: $100/year (individual).*

Meetings/Conferences:
Annual Meetings: May

Belarus-U.S. Working Group
Historical Note
*Became (1997) American Business Alliance for the Transition
Economies of Eurasia.*

Belgian American Chamber of Commerce in the United States *(1925)*
1330 Ave. of the Americas, 26th Floor
New York, NY 10019-5400
Tel: (212)969-9940   *Fax:* (212)969-9942
E-Mail: bacc@ix.netcom.com
Web Site: http://www.belchan.org
Members: 282 companies and organizations
Staff: 2
Annual Budget: $100-250,000
Exec. Director: George Ugeux

Historical Note
*Membership: $350/year (individual), $750/year (coporate),
$1500/year (sustaining).*

Publications:
BACC News. a. adv.
Listing of Belgian Companies in the United States. irreg.
Listing of Belgian Exporters/Importers. irreg.

Meetings/Conferences:
Annual Meetings: Held annually during June in New York, NY

Belgian Draft Horse Corp. of America *(1887)*
Box 335
125 Southwood Drive
Wabash, IN 46992-0335
Tel: (219)563-3205
Web Site: belgincorp.com
Members: 5,500 individuals
Staff: 2
Annual Budget: $250-500,000
Secretary-Treasurer: Vicki Knott

Historical Note
*Originated as the American Ass'n of Importers and Breeders of
Belgian Draft Horses and assumed its present name in 1937. The
pedigree ass'n for owners and breeders of Belgian Draft Horses.
Membership: $100/lifetime membership.*

Publications:
Belgian Newsletter. 3/year.
Belgian Review. a. adv.

Meetings/Conferences:
Annual Meetings: December in Wabash, Indiana

Belt Ass'n *(1934)*
145 W. 45th St., Suite 800
New York, NY 10036
Tel: (212)398-5700   *Fax:* (212)398-7818
Members: 90 companies
Staff: 2
Annual Budget: $50-100,000
Exec. Director: Sheldon M. Edelman

Historical Note
*Membership originally consisted of manufacturers of ladies' belts.
Absorbed the Ass'n of Men's Belt Manufacturers in 1986.*

Publications:
Trade Directory. a.

Belted Galloway Soc. *(1951)*
P.O. Box 56
Hollis Springs, MS 38635
Tel: (601)252-5744
Members: 650 individuals
Staff: 1
Annual Budget: $50-100,000
Secretary: Joanne Huff-Ritts

Historical Note
*A non-profit association of United States breeders of Belted
Galloway cattle, known for the economical production of beef under
range conditions. Maintains a pedigree registry and promotes the
breed. Membership: $40/year, plus $50 initiation fee.*

Meetings/Conferences:
Annual Meetings: Fall/50-100

BEMA - An Internat'l Ass'n Serving the Baking and Food Industries *(1918)*
401 N. Michigan Ave.
Chicago, IL 60611
Tel: (312)644-6610   *Fax:* (312)527-6640
E-Mail: bema@sba.com
Web Site: http://www.bema.org
Members: 165 companies
Staff: 2
Annual Budget: $250-500,000
Exec. Director: Mark Hanson, CAE

Public Relations Coordinator: Kristin Schroeder
Account Coordinator: Carmalita Collier

Historical Note
*Formerly (1993) Bakery Equipment Manufacturers Ass'n. BEMA is
an internat'l, nonprofit trade association representing bakery and
food equipment manufacturers and suppliers. The ass'n is
committed to furthering the professionalism of its members with
programs that enhance communications and promote technological
advancement, education, safety, sanitation, marketing and good
manufacturing practices. Membership: $1,000/year (corporate).*

Publications:
Bakery Equipment Guide.
BEMA Newsletter. q.
Industry Regulations Bulletin.
Internat'l Bulletin.

Meetings/Conferences:
Annual Meetings: Summer
1999 – Monterery, CA(Monterery Plaza)
2000 – Puerto Rico(El Conquistador Resort)

Benchmarking Network Ass'n *(1992)*
4606 FM 1960 West, Suite 300
Houston, TX 77069
Tel: (281)440-5044   *Fax:* (281)440-6677
E-Mail: benchmar@well.com
Web Site: http://www.benchmarkingnetwork.com
Members: 520 individuals
Staff: 14
Annual Budget: $1-2,000,000
President: Mark T. Czarnecki

Historical Note
*TBNA assists in benchmarking activities and promotes
communication between professionals in corporations involved in
benchmarking. Members span industries and functional expertise.
TBNA sponsors a number of specialty groups, including Health
Care Benchmarking, Human Resources Benchmarking, Electric
Utility Benchmarking, Accounting and Finance Benchmarking,
Telecommunications Benchmarking, Automotive Supplier
Benchmarking, Procurement and Supply Chain Benchmarking, and
Internat'l Governmental Benchmarking. Membership: $149/year
(individual).*

Meetings/Conferences:
Annual Meetings: August
1999 – Miami, FL

Beta Alpha Psi *(1919)*
1211 Avenue of the Americas, 6th Floor
New York, NY 10036-8775
Tel: (212)596-6090   *Fax:* (212)596-6284
Web Site: http://www.bap.org
Members: 170,000 individuals
Staff: 3
Annual Budget: $250-500,000
Executive Director: Elizabeth Walsh
National Coordinator: Jodi Mutnansky

Historical Note
*An honorary, professional accounting fraternity. Organized
February 12, 1919 at the University of Illinois. Membership:
$45/year.*

Publications:
Newsletter. semi-a.

Meetings/Conferences:
Annual Meetings: August, before the convention of the
  American Accounting Ass'n
1999 – San Diego, CA(Sheraton Harbor Island)/August 13-14
2000 – Washington, DC(Crystal Gateway
  Marriott)/August 11-12

Beta Beta Beta *(1922)*
P.O. Box 428
Ocean Grove, NJ 07756
E-Mail: tribeta@bellatlantic.net
Members: 11,000 individuals
Staff: 1
Annual Budget: $50-100,000
Secretary-Treasurer: Dawn B. Rohrs

Historical Note
*TriBeta is an honorary, professional society of biology professionals
and students of the biological sciences. TriBeta alumni number over
140,000 since 1922.*

Publications:
Bios Journal. q. adv.

Meetings/Conferences:
Biennial Meetings: even years

Beta Phi Mu *(1948)*
School of Information Studies
Florida State University
Tallahassee, FL 32306-2100
Tel: (850)644-3907   *Fax:* (850)644-6253
E-Mail: Beta_Phi_Mu@lis.fsu.edu
Members: 24,000 individuals
Exec. Secretary: F. William Summers, Ph.D.

Historical Note
Professional society for library studies.

Publications:
Newsletter. semi-a.

Meetings/Conferences:
Annual Meetings: Winter, usually with American Library Ass'n

Better Lawn and Turf Institute *(1957)*
3020 Roswell Road, Suite 200
Marietta, GA 30062-4987
Web Site: http://www.lawninstitute.com
Members: 200 companies
Staff: 2
Annual Budget: $50-100,000
Director: James R. Brooks

Historical Note
*Organized originally by midwestern bluegrass harvesters but soon
sprea to include growers of improved turfgrasses in the Northwest
and included distributor groups, associations and suppliers such as
fertilizer, chemical and equipment companies. Known also as The
Lawn Institute. Membership: $150/year.*

Publications:
Lawn-O-Gram. q.
Press Kits. q.

Meetings/Conferences:
Annual Meetings: Fall

Beverage Network *(1986)*
4437 Concord Lane
Skokie, IL 60076
Tel: (847)673-4614   *Fax:* (847)673-4644
Members: 100 companies
President: Russell G. Hopkins

Historical Note
*Members are distributors of specialty non-alcoholic beverages and
also some specialty foods.*

Bibliographical Soc. of America *(1904)*
P.O. Box 1537
Lenox Hill Station
New York, NY 10163-0397
Tel: (212)452-2710
E-Mail: bsa@bibsocamer.org
Members: 1,200 individuals
Annual Budget: $100-250,000
Exec. Secretary: Michele G. Randall

Historical Note
*Organized in Washington, D.C. as an outgrowth of the
Bibliographical Soc. of Chicago. Incorporated in 1927. A member
of the American Council of Learned Societies. Membership is open
to all interested in bibliographical problems and projects.
Membership: $50/year.*

Publications:
Papers. q. adv.

Meetings/Conferences:
1999 – New York, NY

Bicycle Manufacturers Ass'n of America *(1965)*
Historical Note
Address unknown in 1997.

Bicycle Product Suppliers Ass'n *(1940)*
1900 Arch St.
Philadelphia, PA 19103-1498
Tel: (215)564-3484   *Fax:* (215)963-9785
E-Mail: assnhqt@netaxs.com
Members: 100 companies
Staff: 2
Annual Budget: $50-100,000
Exec. Director: Elizabeth Barnett Franks

Historical Note
*Formerly (1960) Cycle Jobbers Ass'n and (1997) Bicycle Wholesale
Distributors Ass'n.*

Publications:
Newsletter. q.

Meetings/Conferences:
1999 – San Diego, CA(Catamaran Resort)/Jan. 22-24/200

Bicycle Wholesale Distributors Ass'n
Historical Note
Became (1997) Bicycle Product Suppliers Ass'n.

Billiard and Bowling Institute of America *(1940)*
200 Castlewood Drive
North Palm Beach, FL 33408
Tel: (561)840-1120   *Fax:* (561)863-8984
Members: 100 manufacturers and distributors
Staff: 2
Annual Budget: $50-100,000
Exec. Director: Sebastian DiCasoli

Historical Note
*A component of the Sporting Goods Manufacturers Ass'n.
Membership: $325-$550/year (organization/company).*

Publications:
BBIA Newsline. m.
Directory of Membership and Products Made. a.

Meetings/Conferences:
Annual Meetings: Spring
1999 – Hilton Head, SC(Hyatt Regency)/April 10-14/150
2000 – Incline Village, NV(Hyatt Regency)/May 6-10/150
2001 – San Antonio, TX(Hyatt Regency)/May 19-23/150

Billiard Congress of America *(1948)*
910 23rd Ave.
Coralville, IA 52241-1221
Tel: (319)351-2112   *Fax:* (319)351-7767
E-Mail: bca@netins.net
Web Site: http://bca-pool.com
Members: 40,000 individuals, 1,250 companies
Staff: 15
Annual Budget: $2-5,000,000
Exec. Director: Bruce Cottew
Marketing & Public Relations: Jason Akst
Deputy Exec. Director: Steve Kahl

Historical Note
*As the billiard industry's governing body, it is the stated mission of
BCA to promote and sanction events and help increase awareness of
and participation in the sport to all people, while working with all
members to increase the overall growth of billiards. Membership:
$25/year (individual); $100-1,000/year (company).*

Publications:
BCA Break. q.
Official Rule and Record Book. a.

Meetings/Conferences:
1999 – Las Vegas, NV(Sands Convention
    Ctr)/July 18-20/5000
2000 – Kansas City, MO(KC Convention
    Cener)/July 15-17/6000
2001 – Las Vegas, NV

Billings Ovulation Method Ass'n of the United States (1990)

316 N. 7th Ave.
St. Cloud, MN   56303
Tel: (320)252-2100   *Fax:* (320)252-2877
Toll Free: (888)637 - 6371
Members: 50 individuals
Staff: 3
President/Program Coordinator: Kay Ek

Historical Note
BOMA members are teachers of the Billings Ovulation Method and others with an interest in natural family planning. Membership: $50/year (organization); $35/year (associate); $25-50/year (teacher).

Publications:
BOMA News. q.
BOMA Teachers Directory. a.
Science Notes Newletter. bi-m.
Victoria Bulletin. q.

Meetings/Conferences:
1999 – Orlando, FL/Apr. 28-May 2

Binding Industries of America (1955)

70 E. Lake St.
Chicago, IL   60601
Tel: (312)372-7606   *Fax:* (312)704-5025
E-Mail: bia1@ix.net.com
Web Site: http://www.bindingindustries.org
Members: 350 companies
Staff: 2
Annual Budget: $250-500,000
Exec. Director: Don Dunham

Historical Note
A special industry group of Printing Industries of America. Formerly (1971) Trade Binders and Loose Leaf Division of P.I.A. Members are trade binders and loose leaf manufacturers or suppliers. Membership: $395-850/year.

Publications:
Binders Bulletin. m.
The Binding Edge. q. adv.

Meetings/Conferences:
Annual Meetings: March
1999 – Palm Desert, CA(Marriott)/March 12-17/325
2000 – San Francisco, CA(Hyatt)/March 24-29

BioCommunications Ass'n (1931)

1819 Peachtree St., Suite 620
Atlanta, GA   30309
Tel: (404)351-6300   *Fax:* (404)351-3348
Web Site: http://www.bpa.org
Members: 650 individuals
Staff: 2
Annual Budget: $250-500,000
Vice President: William H. Just, CAE, CMP

Historical Note
Formerly (1997) Biological Photographic Ass'n. Membership: $100/year (individual), $250-1,000/organization (based on gross sales).

Publications:
BPA News. q.
Journal of Biological Photography. q.

Meetings/Conferences:
Annual Meetings: Summer/300

Bioelectrical Repair and Growth Soc.

Historical Note
Became Soc. for Physical Regulation in Biology and Medicine in 1994.

Bioelectromagnetics Soc. (1978)

7519 Ridge Road
Frederick, MD   21702
Tel: (301)663-4252   *Fax:* (301)371-8955
E-Mail: 75230.1222@compuserve.com
Web Site: bioelctromagnetics.org
Members: 800 individuals
Staff: 2
Annual Budget: $250-500,000
Exec. Director: William G. Wisecup

Historical Note
A scientific society promoting research concerned with the interaction of electromagnetic energy with biological systems. Membership: $50/year (individual); $500/year (organization).

Publications:
Annual Meeting Abstract Book. a.
Bioelectromagnetics Journal. bi-m.
Bioelectromagnetics Newsletter. bi-m. adv.

Meetings/Conferences:
Annual Meetings: June
1999 – Long Beach, CA(Hyatt Regency)/June 20-24/500
1999 – California
2000 – Munich, Germany(Tech University)/June 10-16/500

Biological Photographic Ass'n

Historical Note
Became (1997) BioCommunications Ass'n.

Biological Stain Commission (1922)

Univ. of Rochester Medical Center
Dept. of Pathology, Box 626
Rochester, NY   14642-0001
Tel: (716)275-6335   *Fax:* (716)422-8993
E-Mail: dpenney@cc.urmc.rochester.edu
Web Site:
    www.urmc.rochester.edu/smd/path/bsc/contents.htm
    l
Members: 80 individuals, 20 societies
Staff: 5
Annual Budget: $100-250,000
Treasurer: David P. Penney, Ph.D.
Secretary: Dr. James Powers

Historical Note
To standardize biological stains and promote their perfection and use. Originated as a special committee of the Nat'l Research Council and later became the Commission on Biological Stains. Incorporated in New York in 1943 as the Biological Stain Commission, Inc. Tests samples submitted by manufacturers and those approved are awarded the Certified Biological Stain distinction. Membership: $35/year (individual).

Publications:
Biotechnic & Histochemistry. bi-m. adv.

Meetings/Conferences:
Annual Meetings: June
1999 – Rochester, NY

Biomedical Engineering Soc. (1968)

Box 2399
Culver City, CA   90231
Tel: (310)618-9322
Members: 2,000 individuals
Staff: 3
Annual Budget: $100-250,000
Exec. Director: Rita Schaffer

Historical Note
Incorporated February 1, 1968 in order to give equal representation to those interested in biomedical and engineering issues. A member society of the American Institute for Medical and Biological Engineering. Membership: $95/year.

Publications:
Annals of Biomedical Engineering. bi-m. adv.
BMES Bulletin. q.
BMES Membership Directory. a.

Meetings/Conferences:
Annual Meetings: Fall/800

Biomedical Marketing Ass'n

10293 N. Meridian St., Suite 175
Indianapolis, IN   46290-1073
Tel: (317)816-1640   *Fax:* (317)816-1833
Web Site: http://bmdonline.org
Members: 700 individuals
Staff: 5
Annual Budget: $250-500,000
Exec. Officer: Michael F. Ward, CAE

Historical Note
Members are dignostic marketers in the biomedical field. Membership: $225/year (domestic); $275/year (international).

Publications:
1999-Chicago, IL/March 22-23.
Diagnostic Insight. q. adv.
Membership Directory. a. adv.

Meetings/Conferences:

Biophysical Soc. (1957)

9650 Rockville Pike, Suite 0512
Bethesda, MD   20814-3998
Tel: (301)530-7114   *Fax:* (301)530-7133
Web Site: http://www.biophysics.org/biophys
Members: 5,400 individuals
Staff: 8
Annual Budget: $2-5,000,000
Exec. Director: Kampman Rosalba

Historical Note
Founded in Columbus, Ohio in 1957. Members are individuals interested in applying physical laws and techniques to the investigation of biological phenomena. Membership: $130/year (individual).

Publications:
Biophysical Journal. m. adv.
Call for Papers. a. adv.
Directory. a. adv.
Newsletter. q. adv.

Meetings/Conferences:
Annual Meetings: Winter/4,000
1999 – Baltimore, MD(Baltimore Convention
    Center)/Feb. 13-17/3500
2000 – New Orleans, LA(Morial Convention
    Center)/Feb. 12-16/3500
2001 – Boston, MA(Boston Convention
    Center)/Feb. 17-21/3700
2002 – San Francisco, CA(San Francisco Convent.
    Center)/Feb. 23-27/4000

Biotech Medical Management Ass'n (1993)

12300 Perry Hwy., Suite 309
Wexford, PA   15090
Tel: (724)934-8440   *Fax:* (724)934-8449
Toll Free: (888)990 - 2662
E-Mail: mljones@fyi.net
Web Site: http://www.bmma.org
Members: 600 individuals
Staff: 2
Exec. Director: Suzanne Butera
Manager, Membership and Operations: Michelle L. Jones

Historical Note
Formerly U.S. Biotech Medical Management Association (1998). BMMA creates a forum for the open exchange of ideas and information between the biotechnology-oncology manufactures and the insurance payor community. Members include managed care professionals and others concern about biotechnology and oncology.

Publications:
BMMA Journal. q. adv.
BMMA Newsletter.

Meetings/Conferences:
1999 – Phoenix, AZ(Wigwam Resort)/Sept. 22-25

Biotechnology Industry Organization (1993)

1625 K St., N.W., Suite 1100
Washington, DC   20006-1604
Tel: (202)857-0244   *Fax:* (202)857-0237
Web Site: www.bio.org
Members: 720 companies
Staff: 34
Annual Budget: $5-10,000,000
President: Carl B. Feldbaum
V. President, Communications: Daniel G. Eramian
V. President, Government Relations: Chuck Ludlam
Director, Meetings: Jean Dougherty Mills
Dir., Finance/Administration: Terri Stewart
Director, Marketing: Susan G. Rathbone
Dir., Technical Affairs: Alan Goldhammer, Ph.D.

Historical Note
Product of the merger of the Industrial Biotechnology Ass'n and the Ass'n of Biotechnology Companies in 1993. BIO represents biotechnology companies, academic institutions and state biotechnology centers in 47 states and more than 20 nations. BIO members are involved in the research and development of health care, agricultural and environmental biotechnology products.

Publications:
BIO Bulletin. m.
Bio News. bi-m.
Directory. a.
Editors' and Reporters' Guide to BioTechnology. a.

Meetings/Conferences:
Annual Meetings: April-May
1999 – Seattle, WA/May 16-20

Biscuit and Cracker Distributors Ass'n (1944)

401 N. Michigan Ave.
Chicago, IL   60611-4267
Tel: (312)644-6610   *Fax:* (312)527-6783
E-Mail: bcda@sba.com
Members: 53 companies
Staff: 2
Annual Budget: $100-250,000
Exec. Director: Margaret Laport

Historical Note
Membership: $100-975/year.

Publications:
BCDA Newsletter.

Meetings/Conferences:
1999 – Orlando, Fl(Orange City Conv.)/Jan. 8-10

Biscuit and Cracker Manufacturers' Ass'n (1901)

8484 Georgia Ave., Suite 700
Silver Spring, MD   20910-5604
Tel: (301)608-1552   *Fax:* (301)608-1557
Web Site: http://www.thebcma.org
Members: 350 companies
Staff: 5
Annual Budget: $500-1,000,000
President: Francis P. Rooney
Director, Government Relations: Christina Blue
Director, Education: Stacey Sharpless
Dir., Finance/Membership: Shelley Sullivan

Historical Note
Established in Cincinnati in 1901, B&CMA promotes the cookie and cracker baking indutry. Absorbed the Biscuit Bakers Institute in 1965. Membership: annual dues vary, based on gross sales (bakers); $750/year (suppliers to bakers).

Publications:
BCMA Bulletin. semi-m.
BCMA Membership Directory. a.

Meetings/Conferences:
Semi-Annual: April Convention and October Technical
    Conference
1999 – Williamsburg, VA(Willamsburg Inn &
    Lodge)/April 25-28
1999 – Cincinnati, OH(Omni Netherland)/Oct. 3-6

Bituminous and Aggregate Equipment Bureau (1960)

111 East Wisconsin Ave., Suite 1000
Milwaukee, WI   53202
Tel: (414)272-0943   *Fax:* (414)272-1170
E-Mail: technical@cimanet.com
Members: 30 companies
Staff: 2
Annual Budget: under $10,000
Secretary/Director, Technical Services: Edward L. Roszkowski, P.E.

Historical Note
A Bureau of the Construction Industry Manufacturers Ass'n. Formerly (1976) the Bituminous Equipment Manufacturers Bureau. Members are manufacturers of equipment used in asphalt paving and aggregate processing industries.

Bituminous and Aggregate Equipment Council

Historical Note
A council of the Equipment Manufacturers Institute.

Bituminous Coal Operators Ass'n (1950)

918 16th St., N.W., Suite 303
Washington, DC   20006-2971
Tel: (202)783-3195   *Fax:* (202)783-4862
Members: 6 company groups
Staff: 8
Annual Budget: $2-5,000,000
President: Joseph P. Brennan

Historical Note
BCOA was formed in 1950 to represent mine operators in negotiation of the National Bituminous Coal Wage Agreement, in order to avoid the chaotic situation resulting from separate company negotiations with the United Mine Workers of America. Dues are established by the Board of Directors, using tonnage produced as the basis.

BKR Internat'l (1972)
40 Exchange Place, Suite 1100
New York, NY   10005-2701
Tel: (212)809-5796   Fax: (212)809-5965
Web Site: http://www.bkr.com
Members: 107 companies
Staff: 5
Annual Budget: $500-1,000,000
Exec. Director: Maureen M. Schwartz

Historical Note
Formerly known as the Nat'l Group of CPA Firms and (1989) The Nat'l CPA Group. BKR is an international affiliation of accounting firms in 140 cities formed to provide services to its member firms: professional development programs, exchange of management information, development of technical and promotional materials, interfirm peer reviews, availability of specialized knowledge, marketing brochures, comprehensive marketing programs for specialized services, newsletters on personal finance planning, year-end tax planners, office technology and benefits surveys. Membership: 0.8% of collections, minimum $1.2 million-maximum $2.2 million (company).

Publications:
Directory of Members. a.
Directory of Specialists. bien.
Marketing Materials. q.
Newsletter. bi-m.

Meetings/Conferences:
Semi-annual Meetings: Spring and Fall/150
1999 – Paris, France

Black Broadcasters Alliance
711 W. 40th St., Suite 301
Baltimore, MD   21211
Tel: (410)662-4536   Fax: (410)662-0816
E-Mail: e-mail@thebba.org
Web Site: http://www.thebba.org
Executive Director: Eddie Edwards Sr.

Historical Note
The BBA promotes equality and opportunities for African Americans and others employed in the broadcasting industry. Membership: $50/year (individual), $1,000/year (company), $25/year (student).

Publications:
The Communique. bi-a.

Black Caucus of the American Library Ass'n (1970)
East Cleveland Public Library
14101 Euclid Ave.
Cleveland, OH   44112
Tel: (216)541-4128   Fax: (216)541-1790
E-Mail: glr@ben.net
Members: 1,100 individuals
Staff: 1
Annual Budget: $50-100,000
President: Gregory L. Reese

Historical Note
Organized in 1970 at the midwinter meeting of the American Library Ass'n in Chicago, IL. Has no paid officers or full-time staff. Membership: $20/year.

Publications:
BCACA Newsletter. bi-m. adv.
Membership Directory. bien.

Meetings/Conferences:
1999 – Las Vegas, NV(Luxor Hotel)/July 19-22

Black Coaches Ass'n (1986)
5223 Citrus Blvd., #T-341
River Ridge, LA   70123-7229
Members: 3,000 individuals
Annual Budget: $250-500,000
Exec. Director: Alex Woods

Historical Note
BCA members are African-American and other minority athletic coaches at the college, junior college and secondary school levels. Membership: $60/year (individual).

Publications:
BCA Journal. q.
Newsletter. q.

Meetings/Conferences:
Annual Meetings: May
1999 – Orlando, FL(Hilton)

Black Communicators of America (1989)
Historical Note
Address unknown in 1995; presumed inactive or defunct.

Black Data Processing Associates (1976)
1111 14th St., N.W., Suite 700
Washington, DC   20005
Tel: (202)789-1540   Fax: (202)789-1592
Toll Free: (800)727 - 2372
Web Site: http://www.bdpa.org
Members: 2,000 individuals
Staff: 2
Annual Budget: $100-250,000
Office Manager: Patricia F. Drumming

Historical Note
Dedicated to being the premier provider of Information Technology resources to the African American Community. BDPA is a professional organization open to all persons without regard to race

or sex in accordance with existing national and local chapter bylaws. Membership: $75/year (individual); $15/year (student).

Publications:
Nat'l Journal. q. adv.
Quarterly Chapter Publications. adv. adv.

Meetings/Conferences:
Annual Meetings: Summer
1999 – Atlanta, GA(Hyatt Regency)/Aug. 19-22

Black Entertainment and Sports Lawyers Ass'n (1979)
1502 Fairlakes Place
Mitchelleville, MD   20721
Tel: (301)333-0003
Web Site: http://www.besla.com
Members: 350 individuals
Staff: 1
Annual Budget: $50-100,000
President: Darell D. Miller

Historical Note
Founded by a group of prestigious black lawyers to encourage attorneys to develop an expertise in the fields of entertainment and sports law and related areas of specialization and to nurture and enhance individuals' aptitudes in these fields. BESLA members represent leading celebrities and professionals in entertainment and sports industries. Membership: $100/year (attorney); $75/year (associate); $25/year (law students).

Publications:
BESLA Bulletin.

Meetings/Conferences:
Annual Meetings: November
1999 – Mexico/Oct. 27-Nov. 2

Black Filmmaker Foundation (1978)
670 Broadway, Suite 304
New York, NY   10012
Tel: (212)253-1690   Fax: (212)253-1689
Members: 3,200 individuals
Staff: 2
Annual Budget: $250-500,000
Director: Sarah Khan

Historical Note
BFF supports emerging African-American filmmakers and builds audiences for their work. BFF programs and services include screenings, speakers series, showcases, mixers, film courses, and a talent directory. Maintains offices in New York

Meetings/Conferences:
Annual Meetings: Spring
1999 – Acapulco, Mexico/June 7-13/1000

Black Psychiatrists of America (1969)
866 Carlston Ave.
Oakland, CA   94610
Tel: (510)834-7103   Fax: (415)695-9830
E-Mail: wlawsonpsy@aol.com
Members: 650 individuals
Annual Budget: $25-50,000
President: Ramona Davis, M.D.

Historical Note
Organized in Miami, Florida and incorporated in New York, BPA membership includes black psychiatrists in the United States, Canada, and the Caribbean. BPA is a non-profit, professional organization promoting excellence within the field with particular emphasis on the concerns of ethnic minority groups and the economically depressed. Has no paid staff. Membership: $150/year(individual).

Publications:
BPA Annals. a. adv.
BPA Newsletter. q. adv.

Meetings/Conferences:
Semi-annual Meetings: Odd years with APA/May, even years with NMA/Aug.

Black Retail Action Group (1970)
P.O. Box 1192
Rockefeller Center Station
New York, NY   10085
Tel: (212)308-6017   Fax: (718)325-8737
Members: 300 individuals
Annual Budget: $50-100,000
V.P. Operations: Earl Rodney Holman

Historical Note
Founded by members of the former Nat'l Negro Retail Advisory Group, BRAG promotes the participation of Blacks and other minorities in retailing, especially in managerial and executive positions, and provides professional development, networking, and educational opportunities. Membership: $50/year (individual), $25/year (student).

Publications:
BRAG About Progress. semi-a.
BRAG Journal. a. adv.

Meetings/Conferences:
Annual Meetings: Fall, always New York City.
1999 – New York, NY

Black Theatre Ass'n
Historical Note
A focus group of the Ass'n for Theatre in Higher Education.

Black Theatre Network (1986)
2603 N.W. 13th St., #312
Gainesville, FL   32609
Tel: (352)495-2116   Fax: (352)495-2051
E-Mail: manicho@aol.com
Members: 500 theater companies/subscribers
Annual Budget: $10-25,000
President: Lorna Littleway
Newsletter Editor: Dr. Hely M. PÈrez

Historical Note
BTN is dedicated to increasing awarenes, appreciation, and production of Black Theatre in the African Diaspora. Network members are theatre professionals and academics. Membership: $75/year (individual); $35/year (retired/student); $110/year (institution).

Publications:
Black Theatre Connections. q. adv.
Black Theatre Directory. bien.
Black Theatre Network News/BTNews. q. adv.
Dissertation Concerning Black Theatre. a.

Meetings/Conferences:
1999 – Winston-Salem, NC(Radisson Marque)

Black Tie Bureau
401 N. Michigan Ave.
Chicago, IL   60611-4267
Tel: (312)644-6610   Fax: (312)321-5144
Administrative Manager: Karin S. Aeschliman

Publications:
Formalwords. bi-m. adv.

Meetings/Conferences:

Black Top and Nat'l Delaine-Merino Sheep Breeders Ass'n (1885)
3 Kelso Road
McDonald, PA   15057
Tel: (724)745-1075
Members: 8 individuals
Staff: 1
Annual Budget: under $10,000
Secretary-Treasurer: Irwin Y. Hamilton

Historical Note
The product of a merger between the National Delaine Merino Sheep Ass'n and the Black Top Sheep Breeders Ass'n.

Meetings/Conferences:
Annual Meetings: Washington, PA in March

Black Women in Publishing (1979)
P.O. Box 6275, FDR Station
New York, NY   10150
Tel: (212)772-5951
E-Mail: bwip@hotmail.org
Web Site: http://www.bwip.org
Members: 100 individuals
Annual Budget: under $10,000
President: Valerie C. Dixon

Historical Note
BWIP is a professional ass'n of women and men of color who work in the print media including editors, writers, designers, photographers, publicists, financial analysts, production managers, personnel directors and freelancers. Membership: $75/year.

Publications:
Interface. q.

Meetings/Conferences:
Annual Meetings: January

Blue Cross and Blue Shield Ass'n (1946)
225 N. Michigan Ave.
Chicago, IL   60611
Tel: (312)297-6000   Fax: (312)297-6609
Web Site: http://www.bluecares.com
Members: 55 companies
Staff: 700
Annual Budget: Over $100,000,000
President: Bernard Tresnowski

Historical Note
Formerly Blue Cross Ass'n and Nat'l Ass'n of Blue Shield Plans; merged in 1978 to become the Blue Cross and Blue Shield Ass'n. Members must be medical and/or hospital plans and operate according to established standards. Offers information, consulting, representation and operation services to members. Member plans represent over 68.1 million health care consumers. Has an annual budget of approximately $131 million.

Publications:
Inquiry. q.

Meetings/Conferences:
Annual Meetings: November

Board of Certified Safety Professionals (1969)
208 Burwash Ave.
Savoy, IL   61874-9510
Tel: (217)359-9263   Fax: (217)359-0055
Annual Budget: $1-2,000,000
Exec. Director: Roger L. Brauer, Ph.D.

Historical Note
Members are safety professionals. BCSP provides standards for the industry and conducts certification examinations.

Publications:
BCSP Newsletter. semi-a.

Board of Trade of the City of New York (1882)
4 World Trade Center
New York, NY   10048
Tel: (212)742-6000   Fax: (212)748-4321
Toll Free: (800)433 - 4348
E-Mail: csce@ix.netcom.com
Web Site: http://www.csce.com
Members: 527 full membership seats, 250 assoc
Staff: 200
President: James J. Bowe
V. President, Marketing and Communications: Janet E. Troy
V. President, Finance, Asst. Treasurer: Brett Harootunian
Senior V. President, Finance & Administration: Walter J. Hines
V. President, Corporate Secretary: Regina Rocker
Senior V. President, General Counsel: Audrey Hirschfeld
Exec. V. President, Floor Operations & Systems: Patrick L. Gambaro

Historical Note
Formerly Coffee, Sugar and Coca Exchange (1998). New York Cotton Exchange merged with the Coffee, Sugar and Coca Exchange(CSCE) to form the Board of Trade of the City of New York. Founded as the Coffee Exchange of the City of New York. Originally created to trade coffee futures, the Exchange added the trading of sugar futures in 1914 to replace European raw sugar markets closed by World War I. In 1916, the Exchange changed its name to the New York Coffee and Sugar Exchange, Inc. On September 28, 1979, the Exchange merged with the New York Cocoa Exchange, Inc. and officially became the Coffee, Sugar & Cocoa Exchange, Inc. The New York Cocoa Exchange opened for business on October 1, 1925, establishing the world's first exchange for trading in cocoa beans. The Exchange is the world's leading marketplace for futures and options trading in these commodities. In 1993, the CSCE expanded its product base with the introduction of cheddar cheese and nonfat dry milk futures and options trading and added the trading of milk futures and options in 1995. The Exchange's 527 membership seats are held by representatives from every segment of the coffee, sugar and cocoa industries as well as by floor brokers and futures commission merchants. The Exchange is regulated by the federal Commodity Futures Trading Commission (CFTC), created in 1974. With the creation of the CFTC, internationally traded commodities were brought under federal regulation for the first time.

Publications:
Annual Report. a.
Statistical Annual. a.

Board of Trade of the Wholesale Seafood Merchants (1933)
7 Dey St., Suite 805
New York, NY 10007
Tel: (212)732-4340   *Fax:* (212)732-6644
Members: 400 individuals
Staff: 2
Annual Budget: $25-50,000
Exec. Secretary: Albert Altesman

Historical Note
The credit exchange for U.S. and Canadian wholesale seafood merchants.

Meetings/Conferences:
Annual Meetings: New York, NY

Boating Writers Internat'l (1970)
P.O. Box 10
Greentown, PA 18426
Tel: (717)857-1557   *Fax:* (717)857-1012
Members: 350 individuals
Staff: 1
Annual Budget: $10-25,000
Exec. Director: Alex Zidock, Jr.

Historical Note
Individuals who write about boating and allied outdoor sports for magazines, newspapers, television and radio. Reports on legislation affecting boating and seeks to encourage boating as a recreational and competitive sport. Membership: $30/yr. (active), $40/yr. (associate), $150/yr. (supporting).

Publications:
Boating Writers Journal. m.

Meetings/Conferences:
Tri-annual Meetings: Jan., in conjunction with the New York Boat Show Sept., with the Internat'l Marine Trades and Exhibit Conference in Chicago; and in Feb., annual meeting in conjunction with the Miami Internat'l Boat Show.

Body and Hoist Manufacturers Committee
Historical Note
An affiliate of the Nat'l Truck Equipment Council.

Bond Market Ass'n (1977)
40 Broad St., 12th Floor
New York, NY 10004-2373
Tel: (212)809-7000   *Fax:* (212)440-5260
Web Site: http://www.psa.com
Members: 400 individuals
Staff: 60
Annual Budget: $10-25,000,000
President: Heather L. Ruth
V. President/Dir., Conferences: Rusty Loiseaux
V. President, C.F.O. and C.A.O.: Hugh Moore

Historical Note
Formerly (1997) Public Securities Ass'n. Members are dealers and dealer banks who underwrite and trade federal, state and local government securities and mortgage-backed securities. Absorbed the GNMA Dealers Ass'n in 1980 and the Ass'n of Primary Dealers in U.S. Government Securities in 1983. Sponsors and supports the PSA Political Action Committee. Has an annual budget of approxiamtely $10.8 million.

Publications:
Agency Action Line Faxletter. as necessary.
Government Manual. a.
Government Securities Newsletter. m.
Management Update Newsletter. q.
Money Market Newsletter. q.
Mortgage-Backed Securities Newsletter. m.
Municipal Market Developments. q.
Municipal Securities Newsletter. m.
PSA Quarterly Review.
Stan'd Formulas Anal. of Mortgage-Backed.
Unif. Prac.
Washington Legislative Update. w.

Meetings/Conferences:
Annual Meetings: April/700

Book Components Manufacturers Ass'n
P.O. Box 644
Millersville, MD 21108
Tel: (410)987-4847   *Fax:* (410)987-5442

E-Mail: vick@bayserve.net
Members: 13 companies
Staff: 2
Annual Budget: $50-100,000
Exec. V. President: John C. Vickerman

Book Industry Study Group (1976)
160 Fifth Ave., Suite 625
New York, NY 10010
Tel: (212)929-1393   *Fax:* (212)989-7542
E-Mail: http://www.bisg.org
Members: 200 individuals and organizations
Staff: 2
Annual Budget: $100-250,000
Managing Agent: Sandra K. Paul

Historical Note
Members are publishers, manufacturers, suppliers, wholesalers, retailers, librarians and others engaged professionally in the development, production and dissemination of books and journals. Purpose is to sponsor and encourage research within and about the publishing industry, to increase readership, improve distribution of books of all kinds, and expand the market for books.

Publications:
Book and Serials Industry Communications (Basic Minutes).
Book Industry Trends. a.
Research Reports. irreg.

Meetings/Conferences:
Annual Meetings: September, in New York, NY

Book Manufacturers Institute (1920)
65 William St., Suite 300
Wellesley, MA 02481-3800
Tel: (781)239-0103   *Fax:* (781)239-0106
Members: 100 companies
Staff: 3
Annual Budget: $250-500,000
Exec. V. President: Stephen P. Snyder

Historical Note
Established as the Employing Bookbinders of America, it assumed its present name in 1933. Membership fee varies, based on sales volume.

Publications:
Directory. a.
Newsletter. q.

Meetings/Conferences:
Annual Meetings: Fall/250
1999 Scottsdale, AZ

Botanical Soc. of America (1906)
Botanical Soc. of America Business Off.
1735 Neil Avenue
Columbus, OH 43210-1293
Tel: (614)292-3519   *Fax:* (614)292-3519
Web Site: www.botany.org
Members: 2,800 individuals
Staff: 2
Annual Budget: $250-500,000
Business Manager: Kimberly Hiser

Historical Note
The American Botanical Club was organized in 1883 as a segment of the American Ass'n for the Advancement of Science. In 1894, 25 members of this group constituted themselves the Botanical Soc. of America. This merged in 1906 with the Soc. for Plant Morphology and Physiology (formed in 1896) and the American Mycological Soc. (formed in 1903) and at a meeting in New York City the present Society was formed and later incorporated in Connecticut in 1939. An affiliate of the American Ass'n for the Advancement of Science and an adherent society of the American Institute of Biological Sciences. Goals are to promote research and teaching, cooperation among scientists and to disseminate knowledge of plants for application to practical problems. Membership: $65/year.

Publications:
Abstracts. a.
American Journal of Botany. m. adv.
Botany For The Next Millennium.
Directory and Handbook. a.
Guide to Graduate Study in the U. S.
Plant Science Bulletin. q.

Meetings/Conferences:
Annual Meetings: August

Bow Tie Manufacturers Ass'n (1952)
Historical Note
Address unknown in 1998.

Bowling (1943)
5301 South 76th St.
Greendale, WI 53129-1127
Tel: (414)421-6400   *Fax:* (414)421-1194
Members: 32 organizations
Annual Budget: $1-2,000,000
Exec. Director: Darold Dobs

Historical Note
Formerly (1995) Nat'l Bowling Council. BI serves as an umbrella organization for all facets of the sport of bowling: equipment manufacturers, bowling centers, and players' associations. Its purpose is to promote the sport of bowling. Membership: $5,000/year (organization/company).

Bowling Proprietors Ass'n of America (1932)
Box 5802
Arlington, TX 76005-5802
Tel: (817)649-5105   *Fax:* (817)633-2940
Members: 3,300 individuals
Staff: 20
Annual Budget: $2-5,000,000
C.E.O.: Don A. Harris, CAE
Dir., Meetings: Carmen Murphey

Dir., Operations: Michele Byers
Dir., Tournaments/Education: Carey Tosello
Dir., General Services/MIS: Richard Cairns

Historical Note
Supports the Bowling Proprietors' Ass'n of America Political Action Committee.

Meetings/Conferences:
Annual Meetings: Summer
1999 – Orlando, FL(Omni Rosen)/June 13-19/4000
2000 – Las Vegas, NV
2001 – Las Vegas, NV

Bowling Writers Ass'n of America (1934)
10350 W. Park Ridge Ave.
Wauwatosa, WI 53222
Tel: (414)616-4990
Members: 280 individuals
Staff: 1
Annual Budget: under $10,000
Exec. Director: Rory Gillespie

Historical Note
Formerly (1931) Nat'l Bowling Writers' Ass'n. Membership: $20/year (full member); $30/year (associate).

Publications:
BWAA Newsletter. semi-a.

Meetings/Conferences:
Annual Meetings: With American Bowling Congress tournament
1999 – Syracuse, NY/March 15-20
2000 – Albuquerque, NM/March 13-18
2001 – Reno, NV
2002 – Billings, MT

Box Office Management Internat'l
Historical Note
Became Internat'l Ticketing Ass'n in 1996.

BPA Internat'l (1931)
270 Madison Ave.
New York, NY 10016-0699
Tel: (212)779-3200   *Fax:* (212)779-3615
Web Site: http://www.bpai.com
Members: 200 companies
Staff: 85
Annual Budget: $5-10,000,000
President and C.E.O.: Michael Marchesano
Communications Manager: Jeffrey Yacker
Continuing Ed. Manager: Jane O'Connor
Sr V.P. Finance/Administration: Edward L. Macrini

Historical Note
Formerly Controlled Circulations Audit and (1991) Business Publications Audit of Circulation. Provider of circulation marketing intelligence for business publications and special interest consumer magazines. Through annual audits, BPA Internat'l verifies circulation claims for 1,600 publications and provides the information to advertiser companies and advertising agencies. Serves members in 13 countries outside of the U.S. Has an annual budget of approximately $9 million.

Publications:
Business TRAC.
Consumer TRAC.

Meetings/Conferences:
1999 – Orlando, FL
1999 – Santa Monica, CA

Brake Manufacturers Council (1973)
P.O. Box 13966
Research Triangle Pk, NC 27709-3966
Tel: (919)549-4800   *Fax:* (919)458-4824
Members: 31 companies
Staff: 2
Annual Budget: $50-100,000
Exec. Director: Jim Lawrence

Historical Note
A product line group of Motor and Equipment Manufacturers Ass'n. Formed by a group of companies making brake systems parts to expand the market for their productsand to conduct friction material testing. Formerly (1994) Brake System Parts Manufacturers Council.

Meetings/Conferences:
Annual Meetings: Spring, Fall and Winter

Brass and Bronze Ingot Manufacturers (1989)
200 S. Michigan Ave., Suite 1100
Chicago, IL 60604-2480
Tel: (312)372-4000   *Fax:* (312)939-5617
Members: 9 companies
Staff: 1
Annual Budget: $10-25,000
Exec. Director: P. Bowman
Admnistrative Assistant: Celine Stachura

Historical Note
Formed by members of Brass and Bronze Ingot Institute and Ass'n of Brass & Bronze Manufacturers in 1989. Has no paid officers or full-time staff; the above address is the law firm of Defrees and Fiske.

Braunvieh Ass'n of America
P.O. Box 6396
Lincoln, NE 68506
Tel: (402)421-2960   *Fax:* (402)421-2994
Members: 350 individuals
Exec. Secretary: Iola Doeschot

Publications:
Braunvieh World.

Braunvieh Breeders Internat'l
1912 Clay St.
North Kansas City, MO 64116
Tel: (816)421-1991

E-Mail: jspawn321@aol.com

Brazilian American Chamber of Commerce (1968)
509 Madison Ave., Suite 304
New York, NY 10022-5501
Tel: (212)751-4691   Fax: (212)921-1078
E-Mail: info@brazilcham.com
Web Site: http://www.brazilcham.com
Members: 700 organizations and individuals
Staff: 5
Annual Budget: $500-1,000,000
Exec. Director: Sueli Bonaparte

Historical Note
Founded as the Brazilian-American Association, it incorporated and assumed its present name in 1968. Members are Brazilian and U.S. business persons concerned with promoting trade and investment between the business communities of both nations. Membership: $850/year (corporate); $1,650/year (contributing); $5,000/year (sponsor); $10,000/year (patron).

Publications:
Brazilian American Business Review/Directory. a. adv.
Brazilian-American Who's Who's. bi-a. adv.
News Bulletin. m.

Meetings/Conferences:

Brazilian Studies Ass'n (1994)
University of New Mexico
Latin American & Iberian Institute
Albuquerque, NM 87131-1016
Tel: (505)277-2961   Fax: (505)277-5989
E-Mail: brasa@unm.edu
Members: 1,200 individuals
Staff: 3
Annual Budget: $10-25,000
Exec. Director: Jon M. Tolman, Ph.D.
Secretary-Treasurer: Robyn Cote-Schmader

Historical Note
BRASA members are academics and others with an interest in the study of Brazil. Membership: $70/year (institution); $40/year (faculty); $20/year (academic); $15/year (student).

Publications:
Fagulha Newsletter. semi-a. adv.

Meetings/Conferences:
2000 – Recife, Brazil/June 22-24

Brewers' Ass'n of America (1941)
601 Madison St., Suite 200
Alexandria, VA 22314-1756
Tel: (703)467-6350   Fax: (703)684-4638
Members: 150 individuals, 150 companies
Staff: 1
Annual Budget: $100-250,000
President: Gary Galanis

Historical Note
Founded as the Small Brewers Ass'n, it assumed its present name on September 11, 1952. Members are breweries and suppliers to the industry. Focus is on sales marketing and issues affecting the industry.

Publications:
Bulletin. m.
Legal Newsletter. m.
Special Studies.

Meetings/Conferences:
Annual Meetings: November
1999 – San Diego, CA

Brick Industry Ass'n (1934)
11490 Commerce Park Drive
Reston, VA 22091-1525
Tel: (703)620-0010   Fax: (703)620-3928
E-Mail: brickinfo@bia.org
Web Site: http://www/bia.org
Members: 200 companies
Staff: 16
Annual Budget: $2-5,000,000
President: Nelson J. Cooney
Director, Engineering and Research: Gregg Borchelt
Director, Marketing: Norman Farley
Director, Marketing: Charles N. Farley

Historical Note
Founded as Structural Clay Products Institute and became Brick Institute of America in 1972; merged with Nat'l Ass'n of Brick Distributors and assumed its current name in 1997.

Publications:
BIA News. m.
Brick in Architecture. q.
Brick Quarterly. q.
Technical Notes on Brick Construction.

Meetings/Conferences:
Annual Meetings: Spring
1999 – Phoenix, AZ/March 28-April 1

Brick Institute of America

Historical Note
Merged with Nat'l Ass'n of Brick Distributors in 1997 to form Brick Industry Ass'n.

Bridge Grid Flooring Manufacturers Ass'n (1985)
231 S. Church St.
Mount Pleasant, PA 15666
Tel: (412)547-2660   Fax: (412)547-2660
E-Mail: BGFMA@aol.com
Members: 5 companies
Staff: 1
Annual Budget: $100-250,000
Exec. Director: Daniel H. Copeland

Historical Note
BGFMA serves to educate and inform bridge owners and engineers regarding the use of bridge grid flooring systems, including open steel grid, grid reinforced concrete, and exodermic bridge decks.

Publications:
Bridge Grid Flooring Systems.
Gridline. q.

Meetings/Conferences:

Bright Belt Warehouse Ass'n (1945)
P.O. Box 12004
Raleigh, NC 27605
Tel: (919)828-8988   Fax: (919)821-2092
Members: 180 warehouses
Staff: 2
Annual Budget: $50-100,000
Managing Director: Mac Dunkley

Historical Note
Represents the flue-cured tobacco warehouse industry.

Meetings/Conferences:
Annual Meetings: June
1999 – Hilton Head, SC/June 21-23

British-American Chamber of Commerce (1920)
52 Vanderbilt Ave., Suite 20
New York, NY 10017-3808
Tel: (212)661-4060   Fax: (212)661-4074
Web Site: http://www.bacc.org
Members: 2,000 individuals
Staff: 9
Annual Budget: $500-1,000,000
Chief Executive Officer: Richard Fursland
Dir., Marketing and Membership: Molly Hays
Director of Special Events: Kiki Walker

Historical Note
BACC is a business organization that encourages trade and investments, and cultivates reciprocal interest in, and comity between the United States and the United Kingdom. Managed by its New York and London offices, the Chamber provides promotional opportunities, business contacts and information services to its member companies. Membership: $2,200/year (sponsor), $850/year (corporate), $375/year (associate).

Publications:
Membership Directory. a.
New York - London Briefing. q. adv.
The Trade Monitor. 6-8 times/year. adv.
The U. K.
UK and USA Magazine q. adv. adv.

Meetings/Conferences:
Annual Meetings: June

Broadcast Cable Credit Ass'n (1972)
701 Lee St., Suite 640
Des Plaines, IL 60016
Tel: (847)827-9330   Fax: (847)827-1653
E-Mail: info@bcfm.com
Web Site: http://www.bcfm.org
Members: 400 stations
Staff: 8
Annual Budget: $1-2,000,000
President: Buz Buzogany
Coordinator, Membership: Terry Jerman

Historical Note
A subsidiary of the Broadcast Cable Financial Management Ass'n, Inc. Formerly known as BCA-Credit Information from 1976 to 1985. Became the Broadcast Credit Ass'n in 1985 and assumed its present name in 1990.

Publications:
Credit and Collection Survey. bien.
Creditopics. bi-m. adv.
Membership Directory. a. adv.
The Financial Manager. bi-m. adv.

Meetings/Conferences:
Annual Meetings: Febraury
1999 – Amelia Island, FL(Ritz-Carlton)/Feb. 15-17

Broadcast Cable Financial Management Ass'n (1961)
701 Lee St., Suite 640
Des Plaines, IL 60016-4571
Tel: (847)296-0200   Fax: (847)296-7510
E-Mail: info@bcfm.com
Web Site: http://www.bcfm.com
Members: 1,280 individuals
Staff: 5
Annual Budget: $1-2,000,000
President: Buz Buzogany
Meetings Manager: Mary Teister
Manager, Membership Services: Kim Falk

Historical Note
Formerly the Institute of Broadcasting Financial Management. Became the Broadcast Financial Management Ass'n in 1977 and assumed its present name in 1990. Membership fee varies, base $310/year (individual).

Publications:
Membership Directory. a. adv.
Monthly Update. m.
The Financial Manager. bi-m. adv.

Meetings/Conferences:
Annual Meetings: May/800-1,200
1999 – Las Vegas, NV(MGM Grand)/May 17-20
2000 – San Diego, CA(Sheraton)/May 21-24
2001 – Toronto, Ontario(Sheraton)/May 20-23

Broadcast Designers' Ass'n (1978)
2029 Century Park East, Suite 555
Los Angeles, CA 90067
Tel: (310)712-0040   Fax: (310)712-0039
Web Site: http://www.bdonline.org
Members: 2 individuals

Staff: 4
Annual Budget: $1-2,000,000
President: David Snapp

Historical Note
BDA members are designers, artists, illustrators and others involved design for electronic media and screen design. BDA fosters an exchange of ideas, information and experience, while serving as a resource for young talent interested in the televison communications arts/design field. Membership: $225/year (professional), $375/year (company), $500/year (corporate), $2,500/year (corporate patron).

Publications:
BDA Awards Annual. a. adv.
BDA Directory. a. adv.
BDAfax. bi-w. adv.
DIEM Magazine. q. adv.

Meetings/Conferences:
Annual Meetings: June
1999 – San Francisco, CA(Convention
    Center)/June 9-12/9000
2000 – New Orleans, LA(Convention
    Center)/June 14-17/10000

Broadcast Education Ass'n (1955)
1771 N St., N.W.
Washington, DC 20036
Tel: (202)429-5354   Fax: (202)775-2981
Web Site: http://www.beaweb.org
Members: 1,200 individuals, 350 institutions, 25 associates
Staff: 2
Annual Budget: $250-500,000
Exec. Director: Louisa A. Nielsen
Manager, Marketing: Judy Hawkins

Historical Note
Formerly (1973) Ass'n for Professional Broadcasting Education. Institutional members are colleges and universities with degree-granting programs in radio and television, film, multi-media telecommunications, and communications. Individual members are full and part-time faculty and industry professionals.

Publications:
Feedback. q.
Journal of Broadcasting & Electronic Media. q.

Meetings/Conferences:
Annual Meetings: Spring, with Nat'l Ass'n of Broadcasters
1999 – Las Vegas, NV/April 16-19

Broadcast Technology Soc.

Historical Note
A technical society of the Institute of Electrical and Electronics Engineers (IEEE). Membership in the Society, open only to IEEE members, includes a subscription to a technical periodical published by IEEE. All administrative support provided by IEEE.

Broker Management Council (1980)
P.O. Box 150229
Arlington, TX 76015
Tel: (817)561-7272   Fax: (817)561-7275
E-Mail: assnhgtrs@aol.com
Web Site: www.bmcsales.com
Members: 25 food marketing companies
Staff: 2
Annual Budget: $50-100,000
Exec. Director: William R. Bess

Historical Note
Independent institutional food service brokers who specialize in institutional deli, bakery, school, hotel and restaurant food service products.

Publications:
Management Letter. m.

Meetings/Conferences:
1999 – Naples, FL
1999 – Minneapolis, MN
2000 – Palm Springs, CA

Brotherhood of Locomotive Engineers (1863)
1370 Ontario St., Mezzanine Level
Cleveland, OH 44113-1702
Tel: (216)241-2630   Fax: (216)241-6516
Members: 52,500 individuals
Staff: 40
Annual Budget: $2-5,000,000
President: Clarence V. Monin

Historical Note
Established in Detroit May 8, 1863 as Division Number One, Brotherhood of the Footboard, the nation's senior labor union. After 1864 became the Grand Internat'l Division of the Brotherhood of Locomotive Engineers. Later the BLE was affiliated with the AFL-CIO and Canadian Labor Congress. Sponsors and supports the Brotherhood of Locomotive Engineers Political Action Committee.

Publications:
Locomotive Engineer Newsletter. m.
Locomotive Engineers Journal. q.

Meetings/Conferences:
Quinquennial Meetings: (2001)

Brotherhood of Maintenance of Way Employees (1887)
26555 Evergreen Rd., Suite 200
Southfield, MI 48076-4225
Tel: (248)948-1010   Fax: (248)948-7150
Members: 55,000 individuals
Staff: 50
Annual Budget: $2-5,000,000
President: Mac A. Fleming

Historical Note
Established in July 1887 in Alabama as the Order of Railroad Trackmen. On October 13, 1891 the Brotherhood of Railway

Section Foremen of North America, founded in La Porte City, Iowa, merged with the Order of Railroad Trackmen to become the International Brotherhood of Railway Track Foremen of America. Became the Brotherhood of Railway Trackmen in 1896 and absorbed the United Brotherhood of Railroad Trackmen (Canadian) in 1900, affiliating with the American Federation of Labor the same year. Became the United Brotherhood of Maintenance of Way Employees and Railway Shop Laborers in 1918 and assumed its present name in 1925. Has a budget of about $8 million.

Publications:
BMWE Journal. m.

Meetings/Conferences:
Quadriennial Meetings: July, 1994

Brotherhood of Railroad Signalmen *(1901)*
601 West Golf Road, Box U
Mount Prospect, IL   60056
Tel: (847)439-3732   *Fax:* (847)439-3743
E-Mail: signalman@brs.org
Web Site: http://www.brs.org
Members: 11,000 individuals
Staff: 20
Annual Budget: $1-2,000,000
President: W.D. Pickett

Historical Note
Organized in the signal tower of the Altoona, Pennsylvania railroad yard in 1901 and chartered by the American Federation of Labor in 1914. Sponsors and supports the Brotherhood of Railroad Signalmen Political Action Committee.

Publications:
The Signalmen's Journal. bi-m. adv.

Meetings/Conferences:
Triennial Meetings: Summer 1994

Brotherhood of Shoe and Allied Craftsmen *(1933)*
Box 390
East Bridgewater, MA   02333
Tel: (508)587-2606   *Fax:* (508)588-9735
Members: 700 individuals
Annual Budget: $50-100,000
President: Albert R. Hamlen

Historical Note
Independent labor union.

Brotherhood of Traveling Jewelers *(1891)*
c/o Loye, Christie Co,
342 Madison Ave.
New York, NY   10173
Tel: (212)869-9162
Members: 300 individuals
Staff: 1
Exec. Secretary: Barbara Perrin

Meetings/Conferences:
Annual Luncheon: February.

Brotherhood Railway Carmen/TCU *(1888)*
3 Research Place
Rockville, MD   20850-3279
Tel: (301)948-4910   *Fax:* (301)948-1369
Members: 50,000 individuals
Staff: 11
President: R.A. Johnson

Historical Note
The result of a merger on September 9, 1890 of the Brotherhood of Car Repairers of North America (founded in Cedar Rapids October 27, 1888) and the Carmen's Mutual Aid Ass'n (founded in Minneapolis on November 23, 1888). Merged with the Car Inspectors, Repairers and Oilers Mutual Benefit Association in 1891 and with the Brotherhood of Railway Carmen of Canada the next year. Affiliated with the American Federation of Labor in 1910. Merged with Transportation Communications Int'l Union in 1988. Sponsors and supports the Railway Carmen Political League Political Action Committee. Membership: $318/year (individual).

Publications:
TCU Interchange. m.

Meetings/Conferences:
Quadrennial Meetings: Summer (1999)

Brown Swiss Cattle Breeders Ass'n of the U.S.A. *(1880)*
800 Pleasant St.
P.O. Box 1038
Beloit, WI   53512-1038
Tel: (608)365-4474   *Fax:* (608)365-5577
Members: 907 individuals
Staff: 15
Annual Budget: $500-1,000,000
Exec. Secretary: John M. Meyer
Administrative Assistant: Robin Lindenberg

Historical Note
Breeders and fanciers of Brown Swiss dairy cattle. Member of the Nat'l Soc. of Livestock Record Ass'ns. Membership: $50/lifetime (individual); $50/10 years (company).

Publications:
Brown Swiss Bulletin. m. adv.
Sire Summary. 2 times/year.

Meetings/Conferences:
Annual Meetings: July
1999 – Maryland
2000 – Pennsylvania

Budget Furniture Forum
Historical Note
A forum of the Nat'l Office Products Ass'n.

Builders Hardware Manufacturers Ass'n *(1925)*
355 Lexington Ave., 17th Floor
New York, NY   10017-6603

Tel: (212)661-4261   *Fax:* (212)370-9047
E-Mail: assocmgmt@aol.com
Web Site: www.buildershardware.com
Members: 80 companies
Staff: 3
Annual Budget: $250-500,000
Exec. Director: Peter S. Rush
Program Director: Maria Ungaro

Historical Note
Formerly (1961) Hardware Manufacturers Statistical Ass'n.

Publications:
ANSI/BHMA Standards.
Directory of Certified Door Closers. a.
Directory of Certified Electromagnetic & Delayed Egress Locks. a.
Directory of Certified Exit Devices. a.
Directory of Certified Locks & Latches. a.
Membership Directory. a.

Meetings/Conferences:
Semi-Annual Meetings: Spring and Fall

Building Environment and Thermal Envelope Council
Historical Note
An affiliated council of Nat'l Institute of Building Sciences, which provides administrative support.

Building Material Dealers Ass'n *(1915)*
12246 S.W. Garden Pl.
Tigard, OR   97223-8246
Tel: (503)624-0561   *Fax:* (503)620-1016
Toll Free: (800)666 - 2632
Web Site: bmda@bmda.com
Members: 1,200 individuals, 850 companies
Staff: 20
Exec. Director: Marie Escamilla

Historical Note
Members are companies that retail building materials. Membership fee varies.

Publications:
Oregon & Washington Law Manuals. bi-en.

Building Officials and Code Administrators Internat'l *(1915)*
4051 W. Flossmoor Road
Country Club Hills, IL   60478-5795
Tel: (708)799-2300   *Fax:* (708)799-4981
Web Site: http://www.bocai.org
Members: 15,000 individuals
Staff: 110
Annual Budget: $10-25,000,000
C.E.O.: Paul K. Heilstedt, P.E.
V. President, Professional Development Services: Kathleen Mihelich
V. President, Member Services: Terrence A. Leppellere

Historical Note
Formerly (1970) Building Officials Conference of America, Inc., BOCAI is the oldest organization of building officials and code administrators in the country. Promulgates and maintains model building codes, promotes the use of safe, suitable and modern construction techiques and materials and related educational services, provides members assistance in the use and interpretation of codes. Membership: $150/year (individual),$120/year(organization).

Publications:
BOCA. bi-m. adv.
BOCA Bulletin. bi-m. adv.
The Building Official. m. adv.

Meetings/Conferences:
Annual Meetings: Summer-Fall/600-700
1999 – St. Louis, MO

Building Owners and Managers Ass'n Internat'l *(1907)*
1201 New York Ave., N.W., Suite 300
Washington, DC   20005
Tel: (202)326-6351   *Fax:* (202)371-0181
Web Site: http://www.boma.org
Members: 16,500 individuals and companies
Staff: 34
Annual Budget: $5-10,000,000
Executive V. President: Robert Angle
V.P, Communications/Membership: Lisa M. Prats, CAE
V.P, Government/Industry Affairs: Gerard Lavery Lederer, CAE
V.P, Education/Convention/Meetings: Patricia M. Areno, CAE
Director, Education and Meetings: Janine Pesci
V.P, Finance: Thomas Harrison
Sr. V.P: Henry Chamberlain, CAE
Director, MIS: Edward C. Turner

Historical Note
Formerly (1968) Nat'l Ass'n of Building Owners and Managers. International membership consists of building owners, developers, managers, service companies, investors, brokers, and third-party management firms. Members include 94 federated associations in North America and around the world. The Building Owners and Managers Institute Internat'l, an associated trade institute, provides educational programming (see separate listing). Has an annual budget of approximately $7 million. Membership fee varies.

Publications:
Convention Directory. a. adv.
Experience Exchange Report. a.
Potomac Currents. bi-w.
Skylines. m. adv.

Meetings/Conferences:
Annual Meetings: June
1999 – Atlanta, GA/June 18-20

Building Owners and Managers Institute Internat'l *(1970)*
1521 Ritchie Hwy.
Arnold, MD   21012

Tel: (410)974-1410   *Fax:* (410)974-1935
Toll Free: (800)235 - 2664
Web Site: www.bomi/edu.org
Members: 30,000 individuals
Staff: 55
Annual Budget: $2-5,000,000
Chairman: Lorraine Kucinski
C.F.O.: Amy C. McMonagle
Publisher: Mark T. Laurenson

Historical Note
BOMI provides course materials and professional certification for building managers (RPA - Real Property Administrator), building engineers (SMA - Systems Maintenance Administrator), and corporate facilities managers (FMA - Facilities Management Administrator). BOMI serves developers, fee managers, multinational corporations and governments in 8 countries.

Publications:
BOMI Institute Update. semi-a.
Institute Educator. bi-m.
SPP Journal. semi-a.

Meetings/Conferences:
Annual Meetings: June, with Building Owners and Managers Ass'n Internat'l
1999 – Atlanta, GA(Georgia World Conference Center)/June 20-22

Building Seismic Safety Council
Historical Note
An affiliated council of Nat'l Institute of Building Sciences, which provides administrative support.

Building Service Contractors Ass'n Internat'l *(1965)*
10201 Lee Highway, Suite 225
Fairfax, VA   22030
Tel: (703)359-7090   *Fax:* (703)352-0493
Toll Free: (800)368 - 3414
Web Site: http://www.bscai.org
Members: 2,500 companies
Staff: 20
Annual Budget: $2-5,000,000
Exec. V. President: Carol A. Dean
Director of Advertising and Special Exhibitions: Jon S. Shonerd
Director, Government Affairs: Philip J. Ufholz
Director of Meetings: Karen Bilak, CMP
Manager, Meetings/Exhibitions: Ann M. Diven
V.P, Admin./Finance: Gail R. McCawley
V. President, Administration/Finance: Peggy Hummel
Director, Membership Services: Gail McCauley
Director of Publications: Donald Tepper, APR

Historical Note
Formerly (1974) Nat'l Ass'n of Building Service Contractors. Members are companies offering cleaning, maintenance, security and janitorial services, and their suppliers. Awards the designations CBSE (Certified Building Service Executive), RBSM (Registered Building Service Manager), and CSSP (Certified Sanitary Supply Professional). Membership: $55-1,400/year (based on annual gross service sales of prior business year.)

Publications:
Annual Report. a.
Insider. m.
SERVICES magazine. m. adv.
Who's Who in Building Service Contracting. a. adv.

Meetings/Conferences:
Annual Meetings: Spring

Building Service Managers Institute *(1957)*
Historical Note
A component of the Environmental Management Association.

Building Stone Institute *(1919)*
P.O. Box 507
Purdys, NY   10578
Tel: (914)232-5725   *Fax:* (914)232-5259
Members: 400 companies
Staff: 5
Annual Budget: $500-1,000,000
Exec. V. President: Dorothy Kender

Historical Note
Formerly (1955) Internat'l Cut Stone Quarrymen's Ass'n. Stone dealers, contractors, quarry owners and importers/exporters. Membership: based on sales volume.

Publications:
Building Stone Magazine. q. adv.
Stone Industry News Update. m. adv.
Who's Who in the Stone Business. a. adv.

Meetings/Conferences:
Annual Meetings: February
1999 – Las Vegas(The Mirage)/Feb. 2-6/200

Building Systems Councils of the Nat'l Ass'n of Home Builders *(1943)*
1201 15th St., N.W.
Washington, DC   20005-2800
Tel: (202)822-0576   *Fax:* (202)861-2141
Staff: 4
Exec. Director: Barbara K. Martin
Communications Manager: Holly Blumenthal

Historical Note
Formerly Prefabricated Home Manufacturers Institute, (1971) Home Manufacturers Ass'n, (1976) Nat'l Ass'n of Building Manufacturers, (1982) Nat'l Ass'n of Home Manufacturers and (1987) Home Manufacturers Councils of Nat'l Ass'n of Home Builders. BSC/NAHB consists of four divisions: Modular Building Systems Council, Log Homes Council, Panelized Building Systems Council, and Associate Members Council.

Publications:
Building Systems Review. m.

Meetings/Conferences:

Building Systems Industry Forum (1984)
Historical Note
Organization defunct in 1998.

Building Systems Institute
Historical Note
Became (1995) Building Systems Industry Forum.

Bulgaria-United States Working Group
Historical Note
Became (1997) American Business Alliance for the Transition Economies of Eurasia.

Bulk Carrier Conference (1956)
6405 Waveland Way
Columbia, MD   21045
Tel: (410)381-7844   *Fax:* (410)381-3213
Members: 20 individuals
Staff: 1
Annual Budget: $100-250,000
General Manager: Reginald Mutter

Bumper Recycling Ass'n of North America (1969)
Historical Note
Merged with Automotive Body Parts Ass'n in 1997.

Bureau of Wholesale Sales Representatives (1946)
1101 Spring St., N.W., Suite 700
Atlanta, GA   30309
Tel: (404)870-7600   *Fax:* (404)870-7601
Web Site: www.bwsr.com
Members: 10,000 individuals
Staff: 12
Annual Budget: $500-1,000,000
Exec. Director: Michael A. Wolyn
Director, Government Relations and Political Action: Michael
    Blackman
Membership Services Coordinator: Lisa Clark

Historical Note
Mission is to act as the advocate and resource for wholesale sales representatives, providing insurance plans specifically tailored to the industry at group rates and to lobby Congress on issues that affect small businesses. Members are wholesale sales representatives in product lines including apparel, ski/outdoor gear, gifts, furniture, and footwear. Formerly Nat'l Ass'n of Men's and Boys' Apparel Club (NAMBAC) and the Nat'l Ass'n of Women's and Children's Apparel Salesmen (The NAWCAS Guild). Absorbed the Bureau of Salesmen's Nat'l Ass'ns in 1994. Membership: $125/year.

Publications:
Bureau News. m. adv.
Compass. q. adv.

Meetings/Conferences:
1999 – Washington, DC/April 30-May 8
2000 – Washington, DC/April 30-May 8

Burlap and Jute Ass'n (1923)
Drawer 8
322 Davis Ave.
Dayton, OH   45401
Tel: (937)476-8272   *Fax:* (937)258-0029
Members: 7 companies, 6 associates
Annual Budget: under $10,000
Secretary-Treasurer: Susan Spiegel

Historical Note
Members are importers of burlap and jute. Membership: $250/year (corporate). Above address is that of Chadbourne & Parke, legal counsel to BJA.

Meetings/Conferences:
Annual Meetings: New York City, in November-December/20
1999 – Amelia Island, FL

Burley and Dark Leaf Tobacco Ass'n (1947)
1100 17th St., N.W., Suite 900
Washington, DC   20036
Tel: (202)296-6820   *Fax:* (202)467-6349
E-Mail: bdlta@tomco.net
Members: 5 associations
Staff: 1
Annual Budget: $250-500,000
Manager, Federal Affairs: Claire Edwards

Historical Note
Formerly (1990) Burley and Dark Leaf Tobacco Export Ass'n. A federation of associations. Directors of these constitute the membership.

Meetings/Conferences:
Annual Meetings: Fall

Burley Auction Warehouse Ass'n (1946)
620 South Broadway, Suite 201
Lexington, KY   40508-3150
Tel: (606)255-4504   *Fax:* (606)255-4534
Members: 225 companies
Staff: 2
Annual Budget: $50-100,000
Exec. Director: Denny Wilson

Historical Note
Members are warehouse companies selling burley tobacco at auction in the eight burley-producing states. Membership: $200/per million pounds burley tobacco sold.

Meetings/Conferences:
Annual Meetings: June
1999 – Asheville, NC(Grove Park Inn)/June 12-15

Burley Tobacco Growers Cooperative Ass'n (1922)
620 South Broadway

Lexington, KY   40508
Tel: (606)252-3561   *Fax:* (606)231-9804
Members: 500,000 individuals
Staff: 9
Annual Budget: $250-500,000
C.E.O.: Danny McKinney

Meetings/Conferences:
1999 – Lexington, NY(Marriott's Griffin Gate)/400
2000 – Lexington, KY(Marriott's Griffin Gate)/400
2001 – Lexington, KY(Marriott's Griffin Gate)/400
2002 – Lexington, KY(Marriott's Griffin Gate)/400

Buses Internat'l Ass'n (1981)
P.O. Box 9337
Spokane, WA   99209-9337
Tel: (509)328-2494   *Fax:* (509)325-5396
Members: 100 individuals
Staff: 1
Annual Budget: under $10,000
Exec. Director: William A. Luke

Historical Note
Members are management-level personnel in the bus industry or its suppliers. Membership: $30/year.

Publications:
Buses International. q.

Meetings/Conferences:
Annual Meetings: Not held.

Business and Institutional Furniture Manufacturers Ass'n Internat'l (1973)
2680 Horizon Dr., S.E., Suite A-1
Grand Rapids, MI   49546-7500
Tel: (616)285-3963   *Fax:* (616)285-3765
E-Mail: treardon@bifma.com
Web Site: http://www.bifma.com
Members: 306 companies
Staff: 5
Annual Budget: $500-1,000,000
Exec. Director: Thomas Reardon
Manager, Communications and Government Affairs: Bradley Miller
Manager, Administration and Statistical Information: Michael
    Reagan
Manager of Technical Services: Dick Driscoll

Historical Note
The voice of the office furnishings industry, BIFMA members are manufacturers, rep firms, and suppliers of goods and services to the industry.

Publications:
Membership Directory. a. adv.
Newsletter. q. adv.

Meetings/Conferences:

Business and Professional Women/USA (1919)
2012 Massachusetts Ave., N.W.
Washington, DC   20036
Tel: (202)293-1100   *Fax:* (202)861-0298
Web Site: http://www.bpwusa.org
Members: 80,000 individuals
Staff: 28
Annual Budget: $1-2,000,000
Exec. Director: Gail Schaffer
Communications Manager: Julie Smith
Director, Public Policy Programs: Suzanne Stokes
Dir., Education/Training: Irma Burks
Dep. Exec. Director and C.F.O.: Deborah Story
Director, Membership: Vivian Dandridge Charles

Historical Note
Formerly (1998) National Federation of Business and Professional Women/USA. The membership is divided among about 2,800 local chapters and 53 state and territorial organizations. Sponsors the Business and Professional Women's Foundation and the Business and Professional Women's Political Action Committee. Membership: varies by type of membership.

Publications:
BPW/USA Foundation Directory. a.
National Business Woman. q. adv.

Meetings/Conferences:
Annual Meetings: Summer
1999 – Rochester, NY(Rochester Riverside Convention
    Center)/July 15-20

Business Council (1933)
888 17th St., N.W., Suite 506
Washington, DC   20006
Tel: (202)298-7650   *Fax:* (202)785-0296
Web Site: http://www.businesscouncil.com
Members: 300 individuals
Staff: 2
Annual Budget: $500-1,000,000
Exec. Director: Philip E. Cassidy

Historical Note
Established originally as the Business Advisory Council to the Department of Commerce, it assumed its present name in 1961 and broke away from the Department of Commerce. The Business Council is a forum for the exchange of ideas between top corporate executives and government officials.

Meetings/Conferences:
Tri-annual Meetings: one in Washington and two in
    Williamsburg, VA

Business Education Research of America
Historical Note
Address unknown in 1995, probably defunct.

Business Espionage Controls and Countermeasures Ass'n (1990)
P.O. Box 44260
Fort Washington, MD   20749

Tel: (301)292-6430   *Fax:* (301)292-4635
E-Mail: tsainc@erols.com
President: Glenn Whidden

Historical Note
BECCA members fall into two categories. One consists of counterespionage security practitioners. The other consists of persons and organizations who have a need for protection against espionage. Its mission is to make life as difficult and dangerous as possible for the espionage practitioner. It does that by publishing information on the nature and extent of the espionage threat. It operates the Certified Confidentiality Officer (CCO) program. Membership: $125/year.

Publications:
The Business Espionage Report. m.

Business Forms Management Ass'n (1958)
319 SW Washington
Suite 710
Portland, OR   97204
Tel: (503)227-3393   *Fax:* (503)274-7667
E-Mail: bfma@bfma.org
Web Site: http://www.bfma.org
Members: 1,300 individuals
Staff: 3
Annual Budget: $250-500,000
Exec. Director: Andrew Palatka, CAE
Manager, Communications: Porter Huddleston

Historical Note
An international, non-profit association of individuals interested in the effective management of forms and related information resources management. Members are form designers, analysts, systems managers and IS managers. Membership: $105/year (member-at-large), $135/year (chapter member).

Publications:
BFMA Directory. a.
Infocus. 10 times/year. adv.
News and Views. 10 times/year.

Meetings/Conferences:
Annual Meetings: May/500
1999 – Orlando, FL(Disney's Coronado
    Springs)/May 23-27/500
2000 – Minneapolis, MN(Hyatt Regency)/May 21-25/500

Business Higher Education Forum (1979)
One Dupont Circle, N.W., Suite 800
Washington, DC   20036-1193
Tel: (202)939-9345   *Fax:* (202)833-4723
E-Mail: BHEF@ACE.NCHE.EDU
Web Site: http://www.acenet.edu/programs/bhef/bhef.html
Members: 55 individuals
Staff: 3
Annual Budget: $1-2,000,000
Acting Director: Judy Irwin

Historical Note
An alliance of corporate CEO's and university presidents dedicated to cooperative links between higher education and corporate America. Studies education's relation to workplace competitiveness and other issues of mutual interest to business and education.

Publications:
Meeting Highlights. semi-a.

Meetings/Conferences:
Semi-Annual Meetings: February and September
1999 – Tucson, AZ/June 17-19

Business History Conference (1954)
Dept. of Economics
College of William and Mary
Williamsburg, VA   23187-8795
Tel: (757)221-2381   *Fax:* (757)221-2390
Members: 525 individuals
Staff: 1
Annual Budget: under $10,000
Exec. Secretary: William J. Hausman

Historical Note
Membership: $15/year.

Publications:
Business and Economic History. semi-a.

Meetings/Conferences:
Annual Meetings: March, in a university environment
1999 – Chapel Hill, NC/150

Business Identity Council of America
12729 Layhill Road, Suite 102
Silver Spring, MD   20906
Tel: (301)946-2022   *Fax:* (301)946-2077
Members: 54 corporations
Annual Budget: $25-50,000
President: Bill Delaney

Historical Note
BICA members are companies that use signs to identify, advertise and promote their businesses.

Meetings/Conferences:
Annual Meetings: Spring

Business Marketing Ass'n (1922)
150 N. Wacker Dr., Suite 1760
Chicago, IL   60606-1607
Tel: (312)409-4262   *Fax:* (312)409-4266
Toll Free: (800)664 - 4262
E-Mail: bma@marketing.org
Web Site: http://www.marketing.org
Members: 4,500 individuals
Staff: 4
Annual Budget: $10-25,000,000
Exec. Director: Richard I. Kean

Historical Note
Formerly the Business/Professional Advertising Ass'n. Membership: $150/year.

Publications:
BMA Membership Directory & Marketing Services Guide. a.
The Business-to-Business Marketer Newsletter. 10/yea.

Meetings/Conferences:
1999 – San Jose, CA(DoubleTree Hotel)/June 9-12

Business Products Credit Ass'n *(1875)*
119 Hill Ave.
Manchester, MO   63011-4349
Tel: (314)394-7777   *Fax:* (314)394-7099
E-Mail: bpca@bpca.org
Web Site: http://www.bpca.org
Members: 341 companies
Staff: 5
Annual Budget: $500-1,000,000
President and C.E.O.: C. David Schmucker

Historical Note
Founded in 1875 as Stationers and Publishers Board of Trade (Incorporated in 1879); became Stationery & Office Equipment Board of Trade, Inc., and amended its certificate of incorporation in 1994 to become Business Products Credit Association, Inc. A credit and financial reporting bureau servicing its membership of manufacturers, factors, and wholesaler in the office products, filing supplies, office furniture, graphic arts, writing supplies, advertising specialty, janitorial and sanitary supply and forms industries. Also involved in consulting with members' debtors, including out of court reorganizations and liquidations.

Meetings/Conferences:

Business Products Industry Ass'n *(1904)*
301 North Fairfax St.
Alexandria, VA   22314-2696
Tel: (703)549-9040   *Fax:* (703)683-7552
Toll Free: (800)542 - 6672
Members: 2,000 companies
Staff: 24
Annual Budget: $2-5,000,000
President: James A. McGarry
Director, Communications: Simon De Groot
Alliance Executive: Sandra Williams
Manager, Conventions: Randall P. Horshok
Director of Finance & Administration: Graziella Jacobs
Director, Member Benefits: Camille Kelly

Historical Note
Established in 1904. Ass'n composed of the following alliances: Business Products Wholesalers Alliance, Furniture Manufacturers Alliance, Office Furniture Dealers Alliance, Office Products Dealers Alliance, Office Products Manufacturers Alliance, Office Products Representatives Alliance. Members are manufacturers, wholesalers and retailers of office equipment, supplies and furniture. Membership dues vary, based on annual sales volume (company).

Publications:
Business Products Industry Report. bi-m. adv.

Meetings/Conferences:
Annual Meetings: Fall

Business Professionals of America *(1966)*
5454 Cleveland Ave.
Columbus, OH   43231-4021
Tel: (614)895-7277   *Fax:* (614)895-1165
E-Mail: bpa@ix.netcom.com
Web Site: http://www.bpa.org/bpa.html
Members: 55,000 individuals
Staff: 8
Annual Budget: $500-1,000,000
President and C.E.O.: Gary L. Hannah
Director of Communications: Stephen Dziura
V. President: Becky Stokesbury
Director of Educational Programs: Deborah Paul

Historical Note
Formerly (1988) Office Education Ass'n. A non-profit vocational student organization for students enrolled in high school and post secondary business and/or office education programs. Membership: $9/year (individual).

Publications:
Advisors Bulletins. bi-m. adv.
Communique. 4/yr. adv.

Meetings/Conferences:
Annual Meetings: Spring/4,000 (Two divisions meet back to
    back).
1999 – Philadelphia, PA
2000 – Minneapolis, MN
2001 – Anaheim, CA
2002 – Chicago, IL

Business Software Alliance *(1988)*
1150 18th Street, Suite 700
Washington, DC   20036-4910
Tel: (202)872-5500   *Fax:* (202)872-5501
E-Mail: BSA@software.org
Web Site: http://www.bsa.org
Members: 14 companies
Staff: 50
President: Robert W. Holleyman, II
V.P., Public Affairs: Diane Smiroldo
V.P., Public Policy: Rebecca M. Gould
V.P of Enforcement: Robert M. Kruger

Historical Note
BSA members are producers of business software for personal computers. BSA promotes the continued growth of the software industry through its international programs. Its public policy, education, and enforcement programs are designed to eradicate software piracy, advance strong intellectual property protection, and remove other barriers to international markets.

Business Systems Ass'n *(1974)*
1411 Peterson Ave., Suite 101
Park Ridge, IL   60068-5000
Tel: (847)696-1784   *Fax:* (847)825-8445
Toll Free: (800)809 - 0272

Members: 35 servicers and sellers
Staff: 1
Annual Budget: under $10,000
Exec. Director: Ann Walk

Historical Note
Formerly (1992) Business Systems and Security Management Ass'n. Also known as Business Systems Ass'n. Members are sellers and servicers of record management systems, filing supplies and equipment.

Publications:
BSA Newsletter. m.
Official Roster. a.

Meetings/Conferences:
1999 – St. Augustine, FL/June 28-31

Business Systems Sales Marketing Ass'n *(1974)*
Historical Note
Name changed to Business Systems Ass'n in 1996.

Business Technology Ass'n *(1926)*
12411 Wornall Road
Kansas City, MO   64145
Tel: (816)941-3100   *Fax:* (816)941-2829
E-Mail: execdir@btanet.org
Web Site: http://www.btanet.org
Members: 2,750 companies
Staff: 35
Annual Budget: $5-10,000,000
Exec. Director: Michael R. Wukitsch
Director of Education: Ellen Eruin
Director of Administration: Harold Durheim
General Counsel: Robert C. Goldberg
Dir., Marketing & Member Services: Robin Keller
Dir., Integration Channels: Angela Williams

Historical Note
Founded in 1926 as the Nat'l Ass'n of Typewriter Dealers. Became the Nat'l Typewriter and Office Machine Dealers Ass'n and later Nat'l Office Machine Dealers Ass'n. Assumed its present name in 1994 after a merger with LANDA (Local Area Network Dealers Ass'n). Absorbed the Ass'n of Independent Mailing Equipment Dealers in 1995. Sponsors and supports the Business Technology Political Action Committee (BTA-PAC). Has an annual budget of approximately $5 million. Membership: $275/year (organization).

Publications:
Business Technology Solutions. adv. adv.
Hotline. bi-w. adv.
The Who's Who Directory. a.

Meetings/Conferences:
Annual Meetings: Spring/22,000
1999 – Las Vegas, NV(Convention Ctr.)
2000 – Orlando, FL
2001 – Las Vegas, NV

Cab Manufacturers Council
Historical Note
A council of the Equipment Manufacturers Institute.

Cable and Telecommunications Ass'n for Marketing *(1976)*
201 N. Union St., Suite 440
Alexandria, VA   22314-2642
Tel: (703)549-4200   *Fax:* (703)684-1167
E-Mail: ctam@ctam.com
Web Site: http://www.ctam.org
Members: 5,600 individuals
Staff: 25
Annual Budget: $2-5,000,000
President and C.O.O.: Char Beales
V. President, Communications: M.C. Antil
V. President, Research: Barbara Gural
V.P., Finance/Administration: Dana Lee Beales
V. President, Marketing: Seth Morrison
Mgr., Member Services: Marsha Cran

Historical Note
Founded as Cable and Television Administration and Marketing Soc.; became (1995) Cable and Telecommunications: A Marketing Soc. in 1995, and assumed its current name in 1996. Supports marketing executives and management in the cable and telecommunications industry through numerous programs, publications, conferences, and other activities. Membership: $240/year.

Publications:
CTAM Probe. q.
CTAM Pulse. q.
CTAM Quarterly Journal. q. adv.

Meetings/Conferences:
Annual Meetings: July-August/2,500
1999 – San Francisco, CA(Marriott)/July 18-21/2500

Cable and Telecommunications: A Marketing Soc.
Historical Note
See Cable and Telecommunications Ass'n for Marketing.

Cable Telecommunications Ass'n *(1973)*
P.O. Box 1005
3950 Chain Bridge Road
Fairfax, VA   22030-1005
Tel: (703)691-8875   *Fax:* (703)691-8911
Web Site: http://www.CATAnet.org
Members: 250 cable companies
Staff: 7
Annual Budget: $1-2,000,000
President: Stephen R. Effros
V. President, Communications: Anne Cowan
Exec. V. President: James H. Ewalt, CAE

Historical Note
Formerly (1994) the Community Antenna Television Ass'n, CATA is an association of over 3,000 cable television systems serving over

40 million subscribers. Street address is 3950 Chain Bridge Rd., Fairfax, VA. Membership: dues vary by size of company.

Publications:
CATAbrief. bi-m.
CATAcable. m.

Meetings/Conferences:
Annual Meetings: Not held.

Cable Television Administration and Marketing Soc. *(1976)*
Historical Note
Became Cable and Telecommunications: A Marketing Soc. in 1995.

Cable Tray Institute *(1991)*
4101 Lake Boone Trail, Suite 201
Raleigh, NC   27607-6518
Tel: (919)787-5181   *Fax:* (919)787-4916
Toll Free: (800)883 - 8883
Members: 9 companies
Staff: 2
Annual Budget: $100-250,000
Exec. Director: Michael R. Borden

Historical Note
CTI members are cable tray manufacturers, cable manufacturers and companies in associated fields. Cable tray technology is an alternative to traditional wiring and support systems. Membership: $6,500/year.

Publications:
Cablegram. 6/year.
Installation Guidelines.
Technical Bulletins.

Meetings/Conferences:
Annual Meetings: January

Cabletelevision Advertising Bureau *(1980)*
830 Third Ave., 2nd Floor
New York, NY   10022-7522
Tel: (212)508-1200   *Fax:* (212)832-3268
Web Site: www.cabletvadbureau.com
Members: 200 companies
Staff: 27
Annual Budget: $2-5,000,000
President/C.E.O.: Joseph W. Ostrow
Manager, Communications: Susan Eck
V. President, Planning & Communications: Steve Raddock
V. President, Finance & Administration: Kenneth Damsky
V. President, Member Services: Lynne Nordone

Historical Note
CAB's purpose is to assist members in maximizing advertising revenues and to promote the use of cable as an advertising medium. Members include systems operators representing more than 85% of the nation's cable subscribers and virtually all ad-supported cable programming services.

Publications:
Cable Network Profiles.
Cable TV Facts. a.
Guide to Associate Members' Products & Services. a.

Meetings/Conferences:
1999 – New York, NY(Marriott Marquis)
1999 – Chicago, IL(Hyatt Regency)/June 5-7

CADD Council
Historical Note
An affiliated council of Nat'l Institute of Building Sciences, which provides administrative support.

Cajal Club *(1947)*
Historical Note
A program of American Ass'n of Anatomists, which provides administrative support.

Calendar Marketing Ass'n *(1989)*
710 E. Ogden Ave., Suite 600
Naperville, IL   60563-8603
Tel: (630)369-2406
E-Mail: cma@b-online.com
Web Site: http://www.CalendarMarketplace.com
Members: 150 companies
Staff: 5
Exec. V. President: Ann E. Spehar, CAE
Exec. Director: Maria Tuthill
Director of Marketing: Richard Mikes

Historical Note
Members are calendar designers, printers, publishers, marketers and distributors. Membership: $149/year (individual); $350/year (organization/company).

Publications:
Calendar News. q. adv.
State of the Calendar. a.

California Dried Fruit Export Ass'n *(1925)*
710 Striker Ave.
Sacramento, CA   95834-1112
Tel: (530)561-5900   *Fax:* (530)561-5906
Members: 33 companies
Staff: 3
Annual Budget: $25-50,000
C.E.O.: Richard W. Novy

Historical Note
A Webb-Pomerene Act Ass'n of dried fruit and tree nut exporters.

Meetings/Conferences:

California Redwood Ass'n *(1916)*
405 Enfrente Drive, Suite 200
Novato, CA   94949-7206
Tel: (415)382-0662   *Fax:* (415)382-8531
Toll Free: (888)225 - 7389
E-Mail: cfgrover@worldnet.att.net

Web Site: http://www.calredwood.org
Members: 6 companies
Staff: 8
Annual Budget: $1-2,000,000
Exec. V. President: Christopher Grover

Historical Note
CSA promotes the use of redwood, providing technical services to manufactures, specifiers and builders and maintaining high product quality through its Redwood Inspection Service division in Eureka, California.

Publications:
Redwood Reporter. q.

Meetings/Conferences:
Annual Meetings: September

Callerlab-Internat'l Ass'n of Square Dance Callers *(1971)*
829 Third Ave., S.E., Suite 285
Rochester, MN 55904-7313
Tel: (507)288-5121   *Fax:* (507)288-5827
Members: 3,000 individuals
Staff: 6
Annual Budget: $250-500,000
Exec. Director: George White

Historical Note
An organization of currently active square dance callers. Incorporated in the State of California. Has an international membership. Membership: $75/year.

Publications:
Direction. bi-m.

Meetings/Conferences:
Annual Meetings: Mon.-Wed. before Easter
1999 – Dallas, TX(Dallas Grand)

Calorie Control Council *(1966)*
5775 Peachtree-Dunwoody Rd., Suite 500-G
Atlanta, GA 30342-1558
Tel: (404)252-3663   *Fax:* (404)252-0774
E-Mail: ccc@assnhq.com
Web Site: http://www.caloriecontrol.org
Members: 60 companies
Staff: 5
Annual Budget: $500-1,000,000
Exec. V. President: Lyn O'Brien Nabors
Dir., Communications: Keith C. Keeney

Historical Note
An international association of manufacturers of low-calorie and reduced fat foods and beverages. Objectives include maintaining and enhancing communication between the low-calorie food and beverage industry, government and regulatory bodies, scientific and medical professionals and consumers.

Publications:
Calorie Control Commentary. semi-a.
Calorie Control Focus. m.

Meetings/Conferences:
Annual Meetings: November
1999 – Palm Beach, FL(Breakers)

Calorimetry Conference *(1947)*
Coll. of Pharmacy, Florida A&M Univ.
Tallahassee, FL 32307
Tel: (850)561-2672   *Fax:* (850)599-3731
Members: 250 individuals
Annual Budget: $10-25,000
Secretary-Treasurer: Renee Reams

Historical Note
Scientists interested in the measurement of heat. Formerly (1950) the Low Temperature Calorimetry Conference. Membership: $20/year.

Meetings/Conferences:
Annual Meetings: Late Summer or Early Fall

CAMEO *(1978)*

Historical Note
Organization dissolved in 1995 and reorganized as a for-profit production company, Celestial Visions. Not a trade association.

Campus Computer Resellers Alliance

Historical Note
A division of Nat'l Ass'n of College Stores, which provides administrative support.

Campus Safety Ass'n

Historical Note
Became (1996) Campus Safety, Health, and Environmental Division.

Campus Safety Division of the Nat'l Safety Council *(1954)*
1121 Spring Lake Drive
Itasca, IL 60143-3201
Tel: (630)775-2026   *Fax:* (630)775-2185
Web Site: http://www.nsc.org
Members: 800 individuals, 550 schools
Staff: 1
Annual Budget: $100-250,000
Exec. Officer: Eve Brouwer

Historical Note
A division of Nat'l Safety Council. Founded as Campus Safety Ass'n; became Campus Safety, Health, and Environmental Division in 1996, and assumed its current name in 1997. CSHEMA represents college and university safety professionals. Promotes the image and importance of the field, defines responsibilities, provides opportunities to learn and to mentor, develops skills and sets up ideal situations for networking. Membership: $100/year (individual); $200/year (organization).

Publications:
Campus Safety Newsletter. bi-m.
Conference Proceedings. a.

Meetings/Conferences:
Annual Meetings: June-July
1999 – Madison, WI(Univ. of Wisconsin)

Can Manufacturers Institute *(1938)*
1625 Massachusetts Ave., N.W., Suite 500
Washington, DC 20036-2212
Tel: (202)232-4677   *Fax:* (202)232-5756
Web Site: http://www.cancentral.com
Members: 120 companies
Staff: 9
Annual Budget: $2-5,000,000
President: Robert B. Budway

Historical Note
Absorbed the Carbonated Beverage Container Manufacturers Ass'n in 1974. Has an annual budget of approximately $11 million.

Publications:
Executive Focus. m.
Legislative Review. w.
Metal Can Shipments Report. m.
Specs. 9/year.
Specs Technology. 9/year.

Meetings/Conferences:
Annual Meetings: Washington, DC/Spring

Canada-United States Business Ass'n

Historical Note
Address unknown in 1996.

Canadian-American Business Council *(1987)*
1629 K St., N.W., Suite 1100
Washington, DC 20006
Tel: (202)785-6717   *Fax:* (202)331-4212
E-Mail: canambusco@aol.com
Members: 130 individuals
Staff: 3
Exec. Director: Paul S. Weller, Jr.

Historical Note
Founded to represent businesses and individuals with business interests in Canada.

Publications:
Membership Directory. a.
Newsletter. bi-m.

Meetings/Conferences:

Cancer Biotherapy Research Group *(1987)*
P.O. Box 680757
Franklin, TN 37068-0757
Tel: (615)791-6393   *Fax:* (615)791-4719
Toll Free: (888)791 - 6393
Members: 100 individuals
Staff: 5
Annual Budget: $250-500,000
Exec. Director: Rosalie A. Crispin
Manager, Clinical Affairs: Carol DePriest,, R.N.
Business Manager: Angela Gettys

Historical Note
Formerly (1997) Nat'l Biotherapy Study Group. CBRG members are oncologists and other cancer specialists with an interest in the use of biologicals in cancer therapy.

Meetings/Conferences:

Canned and Cooked Meat Importers Ass'n

Historical Note
Became (1995) Western Hemisphere Ass'n of Meat Marketers.

Canon Law Soc. of America *(1939)*
Catholic University
Caldwell Hall, Room 431
Washington, DC 20064
Tel: (202)269-3491   *Fax:* (202)319-5719
E-Mail: CLSA@tidalwave.net
Web Site: www.CLSA.ORG
Members: 1,600 individuals
Staff: 2
Annual Budget: $250-500,000
Exec. Coordinator: Patrick J. Cogan

Historical Note
Individuals interested in the study of church law and ecclesiastical jurisprudence. Membership: $100/year.

Publications:
CLSA Newsletter. q.
Proceedings. a.
Roman Replies and CLSA Advisory Opinions. a.

Meetings/Conferences:
Annual Meetings: Fall/450
1999 – Minneapolis, MN(Marriott City Center)/Oct. 4-7/500
2000 – Arlington, VA(Hyatt Regency Capitol
       City)/Oct. 2-5/500

Cantors Assembly *(1947)*
c/o Jewish Theological Seminary
3080 Broadway, Suite 613
New York, NY 10027
Tel: (212)678-8834   *Fax:* (212)662-8989
E-Mail: caoffice@jtsa.edu
Members: 460 individuals
Staff: 3
Annual Budget: $250-500,000
Exec. Administrator: Abraham B. Shapiro

Historical Note
Promotes and advances the traditions of Conservative Judaism. Membership: $500/year.

Publications:
Journal of Synagogue Music. semi-a.

Proceedings. a.

Meetings/Conferences:
1999 – Monticello, NY(Kutchev's)/April 18-25/500
2000 – Detroit, MI(Hyatt Regency)

Captive Insurance Companies Ass'n *(1973)*
4248 Park Glen Road
Minneapolis, MN 55416-4758
Tel: (612)927-9220   *Fax:* (612)929-1318
Toll Free: (800)999 - 4505
Members: 125 companies
Staff: 2
Annual Budget: $50-100,000
Exec. Director: Ed A. Harrington, CAE

Historical Note
Single insurance companies completely owned by a parent organization or industry. Membership: $500/year (company).

Publications:
Captive Insurance Legal Update.
CICA Membership Directory. a.
Newsletter.

Meetings/Conferences:

Car Care Council *(1968)*
42 Park Drive
Port Clinton, OH 43452
Tel: (419)734-5343   *Fax:* (419)732-3780
E-Mail: carcare@infinet.com
Web Site: http://www.carecarecouncil.org
Members: 150 companies
Staff: 5
Annual Budget: $250-500,000
President: Donald B. Midgley
Director of Operations: Donna Wagner

Historical Note
CCC members are automotive aftermarket manufacturers, distributors, jobbers, service providers, associations and communications organizations. CCC provides public service messages on auto maintenance to radio, television, newspapers and magazines. Coordinates National Care Care Month each October.

Publications:
Car Care Corner. q.
Car Care Quarterly. q.
Car Care Supplement. bi-a.
On the Air with Car Care. bi-a.

Meetings/Conferences:
Annual Meetings: November, with the Automotive Aftermarket
       Industry Week

Car Department Officers Ass'n *(1901)*
5 Berkshire Dr.
St. Charles, MO 63301
Tel: (314)723-9947   *Fax:* (314)947-3750
Members: 500 companies and individuals
Staff: 1
Annual Budget: $10-25,000
Secretary-Treasurer: Charles Funesti

Historical Note
Companies and individuals involved in the construction, maintenance and repair of freight and passenger railway cars. Founded as Interchange Car Inspectors, it became the Railway Car Department Officers Ass'n the same year, the Master Car Builders Ass'n in 1926 and assumed its present name in 1928. Membership: $20/year (individual); $100/year (company)

Publications:
Proceedings. a.

Meetings/Conferences:
Annual Meetings: September

Career Apparel Institute *(1970)*
1156 Ave. of the Americas, Suite 700
New York, NY 10036
Tel: (212)869-0670   *Fax:* (212)575-2847
Web Site: http://www.naumd.com
Members: 450 companies
Staff: 5
Annual Budget: $250-500,000
Exec. Director: Bernard J. Lepper

Historical Note
Members are manufacturers of uniforms, mills, fibre producers, and dealers. CAI is a division of the Nat'l Ass'n of Uniform Manufacturers and Distributors.

Publications:
Membership Listing. a.

Meetings/Conferences:
Annual Meetings: February, with Nat'l Ass'n of Uniform
       Manufacturers and Distributors
1999 – San Diego, CA(Sheraton)/Feb. 26-March 3

Career College Ass'n *(1912)*
10 G St. N.E., Suite 750
Washington, DC 20002-4213
Tel: (202)336-6700   *Fax:* (202)336-6828
E-Mail: cca@career.org
Web Site: http://www.career.org/career.html
Members: 750 institutions
Staff: 20
Annual Budget: $2-5,000,000
President: Omer E. Waddles
V. President of Government Affairs: Bruce Leftwich
Director of Operations: Marty Byrne
General Counsel: Nancy Broff
Membership Specialist: Katie Calabrese

Historical Note
In 1950 the Nat'l Ass'n and Council of Accredited Commercial Schools and the Nat'l Council of Business Schools merged to form the Nat'l Ass'n and Council of Business Schools. This, in turn, merged with the American Ass'n of Business Schools (formerly the

American Ass'n of Commercial Colleges) to form the United Business Schools Ass'n in 1962. Became the Ass'n of Independent Colleges and Schools in 1973. Assumed its present name after the Ass'n of Independent Colleges and Schools consolidated with the Nat'l Ass'n of Trade and Technical Schools in 1991. Sponsors and supports the CCA Political Action Committee.

Publications:
CCA Link. m.
Connector. m.

Meetings/Conferences:
1999 – Los Angeles, CA

Career Pilots Ass'n

Historical Note
Address unknown in 1998.

Career Planning and Adult Development Network (1979)
4965 Sierra Road
San Jose, CA 95132
Tel: (408)441-9100   Fax: (408)441-9101
E-Mail: info@careertrainer.com
Members: 1000 individuals
Staff: 1
Annual Budget: $50-100,000
Exec. Director and Editor: Richard L. Knowdell

Historical Note
CPADN members are career counselors, educators and human resource specialists. Membership: $49/year (individual); $64/year (foreign).

Publications:
Career Planning & Adult Development Journal. q.
Carrer Planning & Adult Development Newsletter. m.

Meetings/Conferences:
Annual Meetings: late October-early November
1999 – San Diego, CA(Town & Country)/Nov. 1-5
2000 – San Francisco, CA(Hyatt Regency)

Cargo Airline Ass'n (1947)
1220 19th St., N.W., Suite 400
Washington, DC 20036-2405
Tel: (202)293-1030   Fax: (202)293-4377
E-Mail: cargoair@aol.com
Members: 25 companies
Annual Budget: $100-250,000
President: Stephen A. Alterman

Historical Note
Founded as Air Freight Forwarders Ass'n; became Air Freight Ass'n of America in 1977, and assumed its current name in 1997.

Meetings/Conferences:
Annual Meetings: June or August in Washington, DC

Cargo Reinsurance Ass'n (1965)
14 Wall St., Floor 8-A
New York, NY 10005
Tel: (212)233-3180
Annual Budget: $100-250,000
Director: Edward K. Carpenter

Historical Note
Organized to facilitate the exchange of marine reinsurance among members.

Meetings/Conferences:
Annual Meetings: April

Caribbean Studies Ass'n (1974)

Historical Note
Address unknown in 1996.

Caribbean-American Chamber of Commerce and Industry (1985)

Historical Note
Address unknown in 1996.

Carpet and Rug Institute (1969)
310 S. Holiday Ave.
P.O. Box 2048
Dalton, GA 30722-2048
Tel: (706)278-3176   Fax: (706)278-8835
Toll Free: (800)882 - 8846
Web Site: www.carpet-rug.com
Members: 151 companies
Staff: 24
Annual Budget: $1-2,000,000
President: Ronald E. VanGelderen
Controller: Jerry L. Hullander
Membership Director: Doug Thompson
Director of Technical Services: Ken McIntosh
Director of Seal of Approval Program: Gary Kenworthy
Director of Marketing: Dick Corelitz

Historical Note
Formed by a merger of the American Carpet Institute (1928) and the Tufted Textile Manufacturers Ass'n (1945).

Meetings/Conferences:
Annual Meetings: Fall

Carpet and Upholstery Cleaning Ass'n (1971)

Historical Note
A division of the Ass'n of Specialists in Cleaning and Restoration.

Carpet Cushion Council (1976)
P.O. Box 546
Riverside, CT 06878-0546
Tel: (203)637-1312   Fax: (203)698-1022
Web Site: www.carpetcushion.org
Members: 35 individuals, 32 companies
Staff: 1
Annual Budget: $100-250,000

Exec. Director: William Oler

Historical Note
Involved in public relations to encourage distribution and use of separate carpet cushions. Works with regulatory agencies at the national, state, and local levels. Formerly a division of the Carpet and Rug Institute, the Council is now independent and incorporated in the District of Columbia. Membership: based on sales volume.

Publications:
Fact Sheets. bi-m.

Meetings/Conferences:
Annual Meetings: November-December/50

Carwash Owner's and Supplier's Ass'n (1983)
1822 South St.
Racine, WI 53404
Tel: (414)639-2289   Fax: (414)639-4393
Members: 234 individuals, 56 companies
Staff: 3
Annual Budget: $10-25,000
Director: Ed Holbus

Historical Note
COSA's primary objective is to raise the public image of the industry. Membership: $300/year.

Publications:
COSA's Questions & Answers. m. adv.

Meetings/Conferences:

Case Management Soc. of America (1990)
8201 Cantrell Road, Suite 230
Little Rock, AR 72227-2448
Tel: (501)225-2229   Fax: (501)221-9068
Web Site: www.cmsa.org
Members: 8,500 individuals
Staff: 16
Annual Budget: $1-2,000,000
Exec. Director: Jeanne H. Boling
Membership/Chapter Services: Danielle Marshall
Sr. Director of Operations: Randall Van Den Berghe
General Counsel: Terrence Hutton

Historical Note
CSMA is an international professional society of health care professionals engaged in case management on all levels. Absorbed (1996) Individual Case Management Ass'n. Membership: $125/year (individual); $1,250-7,500/year (organization).

Publications:
CMSA Membership Directory. a.
Journal of Care Management. bi-m.
The Case Manager. bi-m.

Meetings/Conferences:
Annual Meetings: late Winter
1999 – Minneapolis, MN/June 16-19

Cashmere and Camel Hair Manufacturers Institute (1984)
230 Congress St.
Boston, MA 02110
Tel: (617)542-7481   Fax: (617)542-2199
E-Mail: cashccmi@aol.com
Web Site: www.cashmere.org
Members: 11 companies
Staff: 2
President: Karl H. Spilhaus

Historical Note
Trade association of manufacturers of cashmere and camel hair products.

Casino and Theme Party Operators Ass'n (1990)
2120-G S. Highland Drive
Las Vegas, NV 89102
Tel: (702)385-2963   Fax: (702)385-6963
E-Mail: GAMECO@VEGAS.QUIK.COM
Members: 36 individuals
Annual Budget: under $10,000
Resident Director: Marty Wolf

Historical Note
CTPOA members are casino and theme party operators, planners, suppliers and others with an interest in the industry. Membership: $100/year (organization/company).

Publications:
Membership Directory. a.
Newsletter. q.
Suppliers & Manufacturers Directory. irreg.

Meetings/Conferences:

Casket and Funeral Supply Ass'n of America (1913)
8707 Skokie Blvd., Suite 306
Skokie, IL 60077-2281
Tel: (847)763-1541   Fax: (847)763-1547
Members: 200 companies
Staff: 3
Annual Budget: $250-500,000
Exec. Director: George W. Lemke

Historical Note
Formerly (1993) Casket Manufacturers Ass'n of America. Membership fee based on sales volume.

Publications:
CFSA Newsletter. m.

Meetings/Conferences:
Annual Meetings: Fall/190-200
1999 – Lake Tahoe, NV(Harrah's)/Sept. 22-26
2000 – Amelia Island, FL(Amelia Island Plantation)/Oct. 4-7

Cast Iron Soil Pipe Institute (1949)
5959 Shallow Ford Road, Suite 419
Chattanooga, TN 37421
Tel: (423)892-0137   Fax: (423)892-0817
Members: 4 foundries
Staff: 9

Annual Budget: $500-1,000,000
Exec. V. President: William H. LeVan

Historical Note
Manufacturers of cast iron soil pipe and fittings.

Meetings/Conferences:
Annual Meetings: November/December

Cast Metals Institute

Historical Note
Not a trade assocation. The educational branch of the American Foundrymen's Society.

Cast Stone Institute (1927)
10 W. Kimball St.
Winder, GA 30680-2535
Tel: (770)868-5909   Fax: (770)868-5910
E-Mail: staff@caststone.org
Web Site: www.caststone.org
Members: 19 producers, 13 associates
Staff: 3
President: James Edwards

Historical Note
CSI represents manufacturers of cast stone and the architects, engineers, concrete technologists, and contractors who specify, design, and use cast stone.

Casting Industry Suppliers Ass'n (1919)
455 State St., Suite 104
Des Plaines, IL 60016
Tel: (847)824-7878   Fax: (847)824-7908
E-Mail: cisa@ix.netcom.com
Members: 70 companies
Staff: 3
Annual Budget: $250-500,000
Exec. Director: Darla Boudjenah

Historical Note
Formerly (1984) Foundry Equipment Manufacturers Ass'n and (1986) Casting Industry Suppliers Ass'n. Founded as the result of common industry problems during and after World War I. Members are makers of foundry equipment and supplies. Merged in 1963 with the Foundry Supply Manufacturers Group. Affiliate export group is CISA Export Trade Group, Inc. (CETGI) which was founded in 1988, has an annual budget of $200,000 and has 30 member companies. Membership: $2,500/year (CISA); $3,750/year (CISA Export Trade Group).

Publications:
Bulletin. m.
Directory. a.

Meetings/Conferences:

Casual Furniture Retailers (1980)
710 E. Ogden Ave., Suite 600
Naperville, IL 60563-8614
Tel: (630)369-2406   Fax: (630)369-2488
Toll Free: (800)956 - 2237
E-Mail: tim@b-online
Web Site: http://www.casualfurniture.org
Members: 400 retailers
Annual Budget: $100-250,000
Exec. Director: Tim Seeden
Exec. Admistrative Director: Amy Elliott

Historical Note
Formerly (1998) {Nat'l Ass'n of Casual Furniture Retailers}. Incorporated in Illinois, members are retailers; manufacturers and sales representatives qualify as associate members.

Publications:
Ad Book. a.
Casual Affairs. q. adv.
Membership Directory. a.
Newsletter. q.

Meetings/Conferences:
Annual Meetings: Fall
1999 – Orlando, FL(Caribe Royale)/Feb. 5-8/250
2000 – Cancun, Mexico(Moon Palace)/250

Casualty Actuarial Soc. (1914)
1100 N. Glebe Road, Suite 600
Arlington, VA 22201
Tel: (703)276-3100   Fax: (703)276-3108
E-Mail: office@casact.org
Web Site: http://www.casact.org
Members: 2,700 individuals
Staff: 15
Annual Budget: $2-5,000,000
Exec. Director: James H. Tinsley
Meeting Planner: Kathleen Liller
Manager, Finance and Adminstration: Todd P. Rogers
Manager, Administration: J. Thomas Downey

Historical Note
Formerly (1921) Casualty Actuarial and Statistical Soc. of America. Membership contigent upon examination. Actuaries dealing in casualty and fire insurance, to the exclusion of life insurance. Affiliated with the American Academy of Actuaries. Membership: $260/year.

Publications:
Actuarial Review. q.
Discussion Paper Program. a.
Forum. semi-a.
Proceedings. a.
Syllabus Examination. a.
Yearbook. a.

Meetings/Conferences:
Semi-annual Meetings: May and Nov./700
1999 – Toronto, Ontario, Canada(Sheraton Centre)/Nov. 8-11/500

Catecholamine Club (1969)
Sch. of Pharmacy, Dept. of Pharm. & Tox.
University of Kansas

Lawrence, KS 66045-2505
Tel: (785)864-3951 Fax: (785)864-5219
E-Mail: prvulliet@ucdavis.edu
Members: 350 individuals
Annual Budget: $10-25,000
Secretary-Treasurer: Walter R. Dixon, Ph.D.
Historical Note
Members are researchers in neuroscience interested in the properties of the ammonia-based chemical compounds known as catecholamines.
Meetings/Conferences:
Annual Meetings: in conjunction with Society for Neuroscience 1999 – Washington, DC(Cosmos Club)

Catfish Farmers of America (1968)
1100 Highway 82 East, Suite 202
Indianola, MS 38751
Tel: (601)887-2699 Fax: (601)887-6857
Members: 450 farms
Staff: 3
Annual Budget: $250-500,000
Exec. V. President: Hugh Warren, III
Historical Note
CFA represents the national farm-raised catfish industry.
Publications:
The Catfish Journal. m. adv.
Meetings/Conferences:
Annual Meetings: Winter in the Southeastern United States 1999 – New Orleans, LA(Monteleon)/Feb. 18-20

Catfish Institute (1986)
P.O. Box 247
118 Hayden St.
Belzoni, MS 39038
Tel: (601)247-4913 Fax: (601)247-2644
Web Site: http://www.catfishinstitute.com
Historical Note
CI members are catfish farmers and processors.

Cathodic Protection Industry Ass'n (1980)
Box 227
Hawthorne, NJ 07507
Tel: (973)427-8540
Members: 20 companies
Staff: 1
Annual Budget: $10-25,000
President: Edgar W. Dreyman
Historical Note
Members manufacture, sell, install and maintain electronic anti-corrosion systems, which are affixed to such areas as docks and pipelines.
Publications:
CPIA News. irreg.
Meetings/Conferences:
Annual Meetings: Spring, with the Nat'l Ass'n of Corrosion Engineers.

Catholic Actors Guild of America (1914)
729 7th Ave. 10th Floor
New York, NY 10019-6831
Tel: (212)398-1868
Members: 750 individuals
Annual Budget: $50-100,000
Treasurer: Martin Kiffel
Historical Note
Strives to promote the best interests of theatre by bringing members of the profession together on spiritual and professional lines. Has no paid staff. Membership: $20/year, $150/life
Publications:
Call Board. 12/year. adv.
Meetings/Conferences:
Semi-annual Meetings: always New York, NY/50-100

Catholic Audio-Visual Educators (1955)
Historical Note
Address unknown in 1997.

Catholic Biblical Ass'n of America (1936)
Catholic University, 297 Leahy Hall
620 Michigan Ave., N.E.
Washington, DC 20064
Tel: (202)319-5519 Fax: (202)319-4799
E-Mail: cua-cathbib@cua.edu
Web Site: http://www.cua.edu/www/org/cbib
Members: 1,300 individuals
Staff: 2
Annual Budget: $250-500,000
Exec. Secretary: Joseph Jensen, O.S.B.
Historical Note
Members are Catholic and non-Catholic Biblical scholars. Member of the Council of Societies for the Study of Religion. Membership: $27/year (individual).
Publications:
Catholic Biblical Quarterly. q. adv.
Old Testament Abstracts. 3/yr. adv.
Meetings/Conferences:
Annual Meetings: August in a university setting
1999 – Scranton, PA(University of Notre Dame)/Aug. 7-10

Catholic Book Publishers Ass'n (1987)
2 Park Ave., Suite 206
Manhasset, NY 11030-2442
Tel: (516)869-0122 Fax: (516)627-1381
E-Mail: cbpa1@aol.com
Web Site: http://www.cbpa.org
Members: 80 book publishers
Annual Budget: $25-50,000
Exec. Director: Charles Roth

Historical Note
Members are publishers specializing in books of interest to the Catholic community. CBPA faciliates the exchange of professional information and cooperation concerning Catholic book publishing in the United States and abroad. Membership: $250-750/year (publisher); $200/year (service company); $150/year (individual).
Publications:
CPBA Directory. bien.
The Spirit of Books Catalog. semi-a. adv.
Meetings/Conferences:
Annual Meetings: May
1999 – Anaheim, CA

Catholic Campus Ministry Ass'n (1969)
300 College Park Ave.
Dayton, OH 45469-2515
Tel: (937)229-4648 Fax: (937)229-4024
E-Mail: William@checkov.hm.udayton.edu
Members: 1,200 individuals
Staff: 6
Annual Budget: $100-250,000
Historical Note
Formerly (1968) Nat'l Newman Chaplains Ass'n. CCMA is a national organization of individuals and groups of campus ministers who associate to foster their theological and professional growth and to promote the ministry of the Catholic Church in higher education. Membership: $110/year (individual); $125/year (organization).
Publications:
CCMA Directory. a.
Crossroad. m.
Meetings/Conferences:

Catholic Charities USA (1910)
1731 King St., Suite 200
Alexandria, VA 22314
Tel: (703)549-1390 Fax: (703)549-1656
Members: 3,000 individuals, 1,400 agencies/institutions
Staff: 35
Annual Budget: $1-2,000,000
President: Fred Kammer, S.J.
Director of Communications: Alexandra Peeler
Dep. to the President for Social Policy: Sharon Daly
Director of Convening & Special Programs: Bro. Joseph Berg
Director, Social Services: Ruth Delassandri
Chief Administrative Officer: David T. Feeley
Director, Disaster Response: Jane Gallagher
Historical Note
Formerly (1986) Nat'l Conference of Catholic Charities. Catholic Charities USA is a network of agencies, institutions and individuals who seek to support families, reduce poverty and empower communities. Membership: $25/year (individual); Agency/institutional dues vary.
Publications:
Charities USA. q.
Meetings/Conferences:
Annual Meetings: Fall

Catholic Fine Arts Soc. (1955)
Molloy College, Maria Regina Hall
1000 Hempstead Ave.
Rockville Center, NY 11570-1199
Tel: (516)678-5000 Fax: (516)678-7295
Members: 400 individuals
Staff: 5
Annual Budget: under $10,000
President: Sr. Jean Dominici de Maria, O.P.
Historical Note
Founded at Catholic University, Washington DC in 1955 to facilitate the exchange of ideas among artists, art educators, and other professionals interested in the spiritual dimension of fine arts. Has no paid staff or permanent address; its affairs are directed by a biennially-elected President. Membership: $15/year.
Publications:
CFAS Newsletter. q.
Meetings/Conferences:
Annual Meetings: Columbus Day Weekend

Catholic Health Ass'n of the United States (1915)
4455 Woodson Road
St. Louis, MO 63134-3797
Tel: (314)427-2500 Fax: (314)427-0029
Web Site: http://www.chausa.org
Members: 600 hospitals, 300 nursing homes
Staff: 80
Annual Budget: $10-25,000,000
President & CEO: Rev. Michael D. Place, STD
Dir., Communications: Susan Hume
Dir., Public Affairs: Fred Caesar
Dir., Meetings & Travel: Roger Cook
C.F.O.: Brian Camey
Historical Note
Formerly (1979) Catholic Hospital Ass'n. Has an annual budget of approximately $13 million.
Publications:
Catholic Health World. bi-w.
Health Progress. bi-m.
Meetings/Conferences:
Annual Meetings: June
1999 – Orlando, FL
2000 – San Francisco, CA/June 11-14/1500

Catholic Library Ass'n (1921)
100 North St., Suite 224
Pittsfield, MA 01201-5109
Tel: (413)443-2252 Fax: (413)442-2252
E-Mail: cla@vgernet.net
Members: 1000 individuals and institutions

Staff: 9
Annual Budget: $100-250,000
Exec. Director: Jean R. Bostley, SSJ
Historical Note
CLA extends its membership to all librarians for the purpose of initiating, fostering and encouraging any activity or library program which will promote literature and libraries, not only of a Catholic nature but also an ecumenical spirit. Membership: $45-500/year (individual); $75-125/year (institution/company).
Publications:
Catholic Library World. q. adv.
Catholic Periodical and Literature Index.
Convention Program. a. adv.
Membership Directory/Handbook. a. adv.
Meetings/Conferences:
Annual Meetings: With Nat'l Catholic Educational Ass'n
1999 – New Orleans, LA(Doubletree)/April 6-9
2000 – Baltimore, MD/April 25-28
2001 – Milwaukee, WI/April 17-20
2002 – /April 2-5
2003 – St. Louis, MO/April 22-25

Catholic Press Ass'n (1911)
3555 Veterans Memorial Hwy., Suite O
Ronkonkoma, NY 11779-7636
Tel: (516)471-4730 Fax: (516)471-4804
Web Site: http://www.catholicpress.org/index.html
Members: 258 individuals, 300 publications
Staff: 6
Annual Budget: $250-500,000
Exec. Director: Owen P. McGovern
Historical Note
Founded in Columbus, Ohio, August 24-25, 1911 by forty-seven charter member publications. Incorporated the following year in New York. Membership: based on size and frequency of publications.
Publications:
Catholic Journalist. m. adv.
Catholic Press Directory. a. adv.
Meetings/Conferences:
Annual Meetings: Spring
1999 – Chicago, IL/May 26-28

Catholic Theological Soc. of America (1946)
Creighton University
2500 California Plaza
Omaha, NE 68178
Tel: (402)280-2505
Members: 1,400 individuals
Staff: 1
Annual Budget: $10-25,000
Exec. Secretary: Maryanne Stevens
Historical Note
Members are individuals engaged in scholarly research, writing, and teaching of theology in seminaries and universities. Membership: $50/year (individual); $56/year (outside North America).
Publications:
CTSA Proceedings. a.
Meetings/Conferences:
Annual Meetings: June/500

Caucus for Producers, Writers and Directors (1974)
Historical Note
Address unknown in 1997.

Caucus for Women in Statistics (1970)
Historical Note
Address unknown in 1996.

CAUSE
Historical Note
Became (1998) EDUCAUSE.

CBA (1950)
P.O. Box 200
Colorado Springs, CO 80901-0200
Tel: (719)576-7880 Fax: (719)576-0795
Members: 3,300 stores and companies
Staff: 40
Annual Budget: $5-10,000,000
President: William R. Anderson
Meetings Director: Judy Kohles
Member Services Director: Mark Kuyper
Historical Note
Founded as Christian Booksellers Ass'n; assumed its current name in 1997. CBA is worldwide network of 2500 Christian stores. CBA supplies its member store owners with training, publications, trade shows and market research.
Publications:
CBA Frontline. m. adv.
CBA Marketplace. m. adv.
Meetings/Conferences:
Annual Meetings: July/13,000

CDLA: the Computer Leasing and Remarketing Ass'n (1981)
Historical Note
See Computer Leasing and Remarketing Ass'n.

CDPD Forum
Historical Note
Became (1998) Wireless Data Forum.

Cedar Shake and Shingle Bureau (1915)
P.O. Box 1178
Sumas, WA 98295-1178

Tel: (604)462-8961   Fax: (604)462-9386
Web Site: www.cedarbureau.org
Members: 525 companies
Staff: 10
Annual Budget: $1-2,000,000
President and C.E.O.: Jack W. Davidson
Marketing Manager: Lynne Christensen
Executive Assistant: Darlene Jacuk

Historical Note
Founded in 1915 as Shingle Branch of West Coast Lumber
Manufacturers Ass'n. Incorporated as the Red Cedar Shingle
Bureau in 1926. Absorbed (1963) the Hand Split Red Cedar Shake
Ass'n. Adopted its present name in 1988.

Publications:
Certi-Talk and Manager's Report. newsletters.
Membership Directory and Buyers Guide. a. adv.

Meetings/Conferences:
1999 – Whistler, British Columbia(Delta)/130
2000 – Victoria, British Columbia(Laurel)/150

Ceilings and Interior Systems Construction Ass'n (1950)
1500 Lincoln Highway, Suite 202
St. Charles, IL   60174
Tel: (630)584-1919   Fax: (630)584-2003
Web Site: http://www.cisca.org
Members: 600 firms
Exec. Director: Jan Foxen, CAE, CDT
Communications Manager: Karen Newman

Historical Note
Formerly (1970) Nat'l Acoustical Contractors Ass'n. Membership:
$520/year and up.

Publications:
Interior Construction. bi-m. adv.

Meetings/Conferences:
Annual Meetings: Spring/6-700

Cell Kinetics Soc. (1977)
c/o Dept. of Surgery
Medical Coll of Ohio, P.O. Box 10008 CS
Toledo, OH   43699-0008
Tel: (419)383-3970   Fax: (419)381-3057
Members: 330 individuals
Annual Budget: $10-25,000
President: David C. Allison

Historical Note
A multidisciplinary professional society of individuals with an
interest in cell kinetics and the application of kinetics information to
other disciplines. Membership: $45/year (individual), $500/year
(sustaining company).

Publications:
Cell Proliferation.
Membership Directory. a.

Meetings/Conferences:

Cellular Telecommunications Industry Ass'n (1984)
1250 Connecticut Ave., N.W., Suite 700
and 800
Washington, DC   20036
Tel: (202)785-0081   Fax: (202)467-6990
Web Site: http://www.wow-com.com
Members: 396 companies
Staff: 100
Annual Budget: $10-25,000,000
President and C.E.O: Thomas E. Wheeler
Sr. V.P., Public Afrs/Communications: Margaret Tutwiler
Sr. V.P., Congressional Affairs: Steven K. Berry
Director of Federal Relations: Jo-Anne R. Basile
V.P., Industry Affairs: Elizabeth Maxfield
Sr. V.P., Policy/Administration: Brian Fontes
V. President and General Counsel: Michael F. Altschul

Historical Note
Formerly (1984) the Cellular Communications Industry Ass'n.
Members are companies holding licenses, permits or having a
reasonable expectation of receiving a cellular authorization from the
FCC. Absorbed the Cellular Radio Communications Ass'n in 1985.
The CTIA represents more than 90% of licensed cellular operators,
as well as manufacturers of cellular equipment and other interests
providing services and products to the cellular industry.
Membership: $1,000-135,000/year (based on size of market).
Annual Budget approx. $10,000,000.

Meetings/Conferences:
1999 – New Orleans, LA/Feb. 8-10
2000 – New Orleans, LA/Feb. 28-March 1

Cellulose Insulation Manufacturers Ass'n (1982)
136 S. Keowee St.
Dayton, OH   45402
Tel: (937)222-2462   Fax: (937)222-5794
Toll Free: (888)881 - 2462
E-Mail: cima@dayton.net
Web Site: http://www.cellulose.org
Members: 32 companies
Staff: 3
Annual Budget: $250-500,000
Exec. Director: Daniel Lea
Finance and Administration: E.H. Carl

Historical Note
Formerly (1992) Cellulose Industry Standards Enforcement
Program. Founded in 1982 as the Cellulose Industry Standards
Enforcement Program to enforce and document compliance with
government and industry standards for cellulose insulation by
member companies. Originally devoted exclusively to standards
development through ASTM and ISO.

Cement Employers Ass'n (1936)
122 E. Broad St., 2nd Floor
Bethlehem, PA   18018
Tel: (610)868-8060

Members: 40 companies
Staff: 2
Annual Budget: $100-250,000
Exec. V. President: Eugene O. Chomicky

Historical Note
A grouping of cement companies united to promote personnel and
industrial relations.

Publications:
Newsletter. w.

Meetings/Conferences:
Annual Meetings: Fall/50-60
1999 – Kiawah Escand, SC(Kiawah Escand
            Resort)/Sept. 14-17/65
2000 – Lake Tahoe, CA

Cement Kiln Recycling Coalition
1225 I St., N.W., Suite 300
Washington, DC   20005
Tel: (202)789-1945   Fax: (202)408-9392
Web Site: http://www.ckrc.org
Members: 19 organizations
Staff: 5
Annual Budget: $1-2,000,000
Exec. Director: Michel R. Benoit

Historical Note
CKRC has adopted a comprehensive Environmental Policy
Statement which mandates that its members be responsible
stewards of the environment and conduct their businesses in a
manner protective of human health and the environment. Members
include most of the major cement companies engaged in the use of
hazardous waste-derived fuel as well as companies involved in the
collection, processing, management and marketing of such fuel for
use in cement kilns.

Cemented Carbide Producers Ass'n (1955)
30200 Detroit Road
Cleveland, OH   44145-1967
Tel: (440)899-0010   Fax: (440)892-1404
Members: 24 companies
Staff: 2
Annual Budget: $50-100,000
Commissioner: J. Jeffery Wherry

Historical Note
Members are makers of sintered carbide containing tungsten.

Center for Computer/Law (1978)
Historical Note
Address unknown in 1996.

Center for Exhibition Industry Research (1978)
4350 East West Highway, Suite 401
Bethesda, MD   20814
Tel: (301)907-7626   Fax: (301)907-0277
E-Mail: ceir@aol.com
Web Site: http://www.ceir.org
Members: 1000 companies
Staff: 5
Annual Budget: $500-1,000,000
President and C.E.O.: Douglas Ducate
Dir., Marketing Communications: Courtney Chamberlain

Historical Note
Formerly (1995) the Trade Show Bureau. CEIR promotes the
growth of the exhibitions industry through research, information,
and communications. Membership: $550/year.

Publications:
Catalog. a.
Membership Directory. a. adv.
Newsletters. bi-m.
Research Reports. bi-m.

Meetings/Conferences:

Center for Management Advisors (1997)
111 E. Wacker Dr., Suite 990
Chicago, IL   60601
Tel: (312)729-9900   Fax: (312)729-9800
E-Mail: info@pencormazur.com
Web Site: http://www.cpaselect.com/center
Members: 137 individuals
Staff: 10
Exec. Director: George A. Buckley, Jr.
Director, Communications: Michelle Durham

Historical Note
The Center is an association of CPAs that provides its members with
the educational, networking and marketing resources they need to
expand their role as CPAs and become value-added management
advisors to clients. The Center offers Certified Professional
Management Advisor (CPMA) certification.

Publications:
Journal for Management Advisors. bi-m.
The Source. q.

Center for Waste Reduction Technologies (1991)
3 Park Avenue
New York, NY   10016-5901
Tel: (212)591-7462   Fax: (212)591-8895
E-Mail: cwrt@aiche.org
Web Site: http://www.aiche.org/cwrt
Members: 27 individuals
Staff: 3
Director: Joseph E.L. Rogers

Historical Note
CWRT is an international non-profit professional organization,
affiliated with the American Institute of Chemical Engineers. The
Center promotes the chemical, petroleum and pharmaceutical
manufacturing industries.

Publications:
Wastenotes. q.

Meetings/Conferences:
Tri-Annual Meetings: with AIChE meetings

Central Conference of American Rabbis (1889)
355 Lexington Ave., 18th Floor
New York, NY   10017-6603
Tel: (212)972-3636   Fax: (212)689-0819
Web Site: http://www.ccarnet.org
Members: 1,650 individuals
Staff: 10
Annual Budget: $1-2,000,000
Exec. V. President: Rabbi Paul J. Menitoff

Historical Note
Professional rabbinic organization of Reform Judaism.

Publications:
CCAR Yearbook. a.
Journal of Reform Judaism. q. adv.

Meetings/Conferences:
Annual Meetings: Spring
1999 – Pittsburgh, PA(William Penn Hotel)/May 23-27

Central Office Executives Ass'n of the Nat'l Panhellenic Conference (1943)
Historical Note
A division of Nat'l Panhellic Council, which provides administrative
support. Members are the executive directors of the fraternities
which constitute the NPC.

Central Station Alarm Ass'n (1950)
440 Maple Ave., Suite 201
Vienna, VA   22180
Tel: (703)242-4670   Fax: (703)242-4675
Web Site: http://www.csaaul.org
Members: 150 companies
Staff: 10
Annual Budget: $1-2,000,000
Exec. V. President: Stephen P. Doyle
Director of Communications: Frank McNeirney
Director of Meetings and Conventions: Christina Jones
Comptroller: Madeline Fullerton

Historical Note
Underwriters Laboratories listed central stations and suppliers to
the burglar/fire alarm industry. Formerly (1989) Central Station
Electrical Protection Ass'n.

Publications:
CS News Newsetter. bi-m.
Directory. a.

Meetings/Conferences:
Annual Meetings: Fall

Ceramic Educational Council (1926)
Historical Note
Formerly (1938) the Ass'n of Ceramic Educators. Education arm of
the American Ceramic Soc. Membership open only to ACerS
members.

Ceramic Manufacturers Ass'n (1925)
1100-H Brandywine Blvd.
P.O. Box 3388
Zanesville, OH   43702-3388
Tel: (740)452-4541   Fax: (740)452-2552
E-Mail: cerma.info@offinger.com
Members: 150 companies
Annual Budget: $10-25,000
Exec. Director: Larry Bell
Association Manager: Jody Spencer

Historical Note
Formerly (1991) American Ass'n of Ceramic Industries. CerMA is a
trade association representing manufacturers of ceramic products.
Members are corporations and individuals in the ceramic industry.
Membership: $95/year (individual); $350/year (corporate).

Publications:
CerMA Member Directory. a. adv.
CerMA Member News Newsletter. q.

Meetings/Conferences:
Semi-annual Meetings: Spring and Fall

Ceramic Tile Distributors Ass'n (1978)
800 Roosevelt Road, Bldg. C, Suite 20
Glen Ellyn, IL   60137
Tel: (630)545-9415   Fax: (630)790-3095
Toll Free: (800)938 - 2832
Web Site: http://www.CTDAhome.org
Members: 600 companies
Staff: 3
Annual Budget: $500-1,000,000
Exec. Director: Richard W. Church

Historical Note
A national trade association of wholesale distributors of ceramic
tile. Incorporated in Illinois. Its goals are to increase members'
professionalism through information, education and product
knowledge and to promote use of ceramic tile in the U.S.
Membership: $550/year.

Publications:
News & Views. q.
Quick Notes. m.

Meetings/Conferences:
1999 – San Antonio, TX/Nov. 4-7
2000 – Amelia Island, FL/Nov. 9-12

Ceramic Tile Institute of America (1957)
12061 Jefferson Blvd.
Culver City, CA   90230
Tel: (310)574-7800   Fax: (310)821-4655
Members: 150 companies
Annual Budget: $250-500,000
Exec. Director: Gray LaFortune

Historical Note
Formerly Ceramic Tile Institute. Members are installers and makers of ceramic tiles. Membership: Dues vary.
Publications:
Tile Industry News. bi-m. adv.
Meetings/Conferences:
Annual Meetings: October

Certification Board for Urologic Nurses and Associates (1972)
East Holly Ave., P.O. Box 56
Pitman, NJ 08071-0056
Tel: (609)256-2351   *Fax:* (609)589-7463
E-Mail: cbuna@mail.ajj.com
Members: 500 individuals
Staff: 1
Exec. Secretary: Marlene Diedrich
Historical Note
Founded as American Board of Urologic Allied Health Professionals; assumed its current name in 1996.
Meetings/Conferences:
1999 – Dallas, TX/Apr.30-May 0-May 4/2500

Certified Alfalfa Seed Council
Historical Note
Became Alfalfa Council in 1998.

Certified Ballast Manufacturers Ass'n (1939)
355 Lexington Ave., 17th Floor
New York, NY 10017
Tel: (212)661-4261   *Fax:* (212)370-9047
E-Mail: assocmgmt@aolcom
Web Site: http://www.certbal.org
Members: 7 manufacturers
Staff: 2
Annual Budget: $100-250,000
Secretary: Maria Ungaro
Historical Note
CBM certifies performance of fluorescent lamp ballasts to ANSI standards through independent laboratory testing. Promotes the CBM certification as an assurance of quality performance.
Publications:
CBM News. q.
Flourescent Lamp Ballast Primer.
Meetings/Conferences:

Certified Claims Professional Accreditation Council (1980)
P.O. Box 441110
Fort Washington, MD 20749-1110
Tel: (301)292-1988   *Fax:* (301)292-1787
Members: 300 individuals
Annual Budget: $10-25,000
Administrator: Dale L. Anderson
Historical Note
CCPAC was established to certify individuals in all levels of the domestic and international transportation industry. Membership: $50/year (individuals); $200/year (company).
Publications:
Passport to Claims Professionalism. bien.
Pocket CCPAC Directory. bien.
Proclaim. q. adv.
Meetings/Conferences:
Annual Meetings: in conjunction with the Transportation Claims and Prevention Council

Certified Contractors NetWork (1995)
715 Brooke Road
Wayne, PA 19087-4708
Tel: (610)293-1475   *Fax:* (610)293-1475
E-Mail: info@contractors.net
Web Site: http://www.contractors.net
Members: 100 companies
Staff: 5
Annual Budget: $500-1,000,000
Exec. V. President: Richard Kaller
Historical Note
CCN provides training and consulting services to independent contractors.

Certified Milk Producers Ass'n of America (1908)
8300 Pines Ave.
Chino, CA 91710
Tel: (909)393-0960   *Fax:* (909)393-0284
Members: 6 farms
Staff: 2
Annual Budget: under $10,000
President: Boyd Clarke
Historical Note
Members are farms producing raw "certified" (pure, but unpasteurized) milk. CMPAA is affiliated with the American Ass'n of Medical Milk Commissions. Membership fee based on production.
Publications:
Newsletter. q.
Meetings/Conferences:
Annual Meetings: May, with American Ass'n of Medical Milk Commissions.

Certified Professional Insurance Agents Soc. (1968)
P.O. Box 35718
Richmond, VA 23235
Tel: (804)674-6466   *Fax:* (804)276-1300
Web Site: http://www.cpia.com
Members: 500 individuals
Staff: 1
Annual Budget: $100-250,000
Exec. Director: Kitty Ambers, CIC, CPSR,

Historical Note
CPIA educates agents in the property casualty insurance profession about sales skills and provides a forum for agents to exchange sales and marketing ideas. Awards the CPIA (Certified Professional Insurance Agent) designation to members successfuly completing an educational program. Membership: $195/year (individual).
Publications:
Bright Ideas from CPIA Fax. m.
Membership Directory & Networking Guide. a.
Quik Sales Tip Fax. bi-w.
The Selling Edge. q. adv.
Meetings/Conferences:
Annual Meetings: Spring
1999 – Tucson, AZ/March 25-27

Cervical Spine Research Soc.
6300 N. River Road, Suite 727
Rosemont, IL 60018-4226
Tel: (847)698-1628   *Fax:* (847)823-0536
Exec. Officer: Jackie O'Brien

CHA - Certified Horsemanship Ass'n (1967)
5318 Old Bullard Road
Tyler, TX 75703-3612
Tel: (903)509-2473   *Fax:* (903)509-2474
Toll Free: (800)399 - 0138
Web Site: http://www.cha-ahse.org
Members: 2,500 individuals, 300 organizations
Staff: 4
Annual Budget: $250-500,000
Exec. Director: LaJuan Skiver
Historical Note
Formerly (1990) the Camp Horsemanship Ass'n and The Ass'n for Horsemanship Safety and Education (1998). Founded in Texas in 1967 and incorporated in Michigan in 1980. Members are camp owners, camp directors, colleges, stables, riding instructors and others interested in riding instruction and safety. CHA provides manuals and safety equipment for riding programs and also conducts certification clinics for riding instructors. Membership: $100/year (organization); $30/year (individual).
Publications:
CHA News & Views Newsletter. q. adv.
Membership Directory. a. adv.
Meetings/Conferences:
Annual Meetings: Fall
1999 – Standford, WA

Chain Drug Marketing Ass'n (1926)
P.O. Box 995
Novi, MI 48376-0995
Tel: (248)449-9300   *Fax:* (248)449-9396
E-Mail: cdma1@aol.com
Web Site: http://www.chaindrug.com
Members: 101 organizations
Staff: 13
Annual Budget: $2-5,000,000
President: James R. Devine
Coordinator, Meetings: Kelly Doran
Historical Note
CDMA members are regional drug chains from across North America. Association markets over 800 products under the name Quality Choice to its members. Membership: $200/month (individual); corporate dues vary by size.
Publications:
Making the Connection. q.
President's Update. m. adv.
Meetings/Conferences:
1999 – Ft. Lauderdale, FL(Convention Center)/March 17-20/500

Chain Link Fence Manufacturers Institute (1960)
9891 Broken Land Pkwy., Suite 300
Columbia, MD 21046
Tel: (301)596-2584   *Fax:* (301)596-2594
Members: 54 companies
Staff: 2
Annual Budget: $100-250,000
Exec. V. President: Mark Levin
Publications:
Linkletter. m.
Meetings/Conferences:
Annual Meetings: Summer
1999 – Bozeman, MT(Big Sky Resort)/July 21-23/150

Chamber Music America (1977)
305 7th Ave., 5th Floor
New York, NY 10001-6008
Tel: (212)242-2022   *Fax:* (212)242-7955
E-Mail: info@chamber-music.org
Web Site: http://www.chamber-music.org
Members: 12,000 individuals\
Staff: 14
Annual Budget: $2-5,000,000
Exec. Director: Dean K. Stein
Historical Note
Incorporated in New York in September, 1977. Members are conductorless ensembles, one musician to a part (instrumental or vocal), performing concerts for professional fees, presenters of chamber music concerts, training institutions and individuals and businesses interested in the development and growth of the chamber music field. Membership: $30-80/year (individual), $110-360/year (organization).
Publications:
Chamber Music Magazine. bi-m.
CMA Matters. q.
Directory of Summer Festivals, Workshops and Schools. bien.
Flying Together. 3/year.
Management Monographs.
Membership Directory. a.

New Music Repertoire Directory. a.
Meetings/Conferences:
Annual Meetings: January
1999 – New York, NY(Crowne Plaza Manhattan)/Jan. 15-17

Chamber of Commerce of the Apparel Industry (1936)
570 Seventh Ave., 10th Floor
New York, NY 10018-0000
Tel: (212)354-0907   *Fax:* (212)768-4732
Members: 1,300 individuals
President: Howard Birne
Historical Note
Membership concentrated in the New York City area. Primary purpose is the administration of workers' compensation for the industry, as authorized by the New York State Insurance Fund.

Chamber of Commerce of the United States of America (1912)
1615 H St., N.W.
Washington, DC 20062-2000
Tel: (202)659-6000   *Fax:* (202)463-5836
Members: 18,392 businesses and organizations
Staff: 1100
Annual Budget: $50-100,000,000
President and C.E.O.: Thomas J. Donohue
Senior V. President, Communications Group: Carl N. Grant
V. President, Media Relations: Frank Coleman
Senior V.P., Administration: Lawrence B. Kraus
V. President and General Counsel: Stephen A. Bokat
Editor, Nation's Business: Mary McElveen
V. President, Public Liaison & Special Assistant to President: Milton E. Mitler
Exec. Director, Office of Chamber Relations: Richard Loomis
V. President Congressional Relations: Lonnie Taylor
Historical Note
Organized at a conference called by President Taft on April 22, 1912 in Washington, DC. The Chamber was formed on the recommendation of President Taft, who saw the need for a "central organization" to give Congress the benefit of the thinking of the business community on national problems and issues affecting the economy. Now, it is generally regarded as the spokesgroup for U.S. business. It is the world's largest business federation, composed of more than 215,000 companies, plus 3,000 local and state chambers of commmerce and 1,200 trade and professional associations. Sponsors and supports the Nat'l Chamber Alliance for Politics. Has an annual budget of approximately $65.8 million.
Publications:
Nation's Business. m. adv.
The Business Advocate. bi-m. adv.
Meetings/Conferences:

Chamber of Shipping of America (1968)
1730 M St., N.W., Suite 407
Washington, DC 20036-4517
Tel: (202)775-4399   *Fax:* (202)659-3795
Members: 15 companies
Staff: 4
Annual Budget: $500-1,000,000
President/C.E.O.: Joseph J. Cox
Dir., Maritime Affairs: Kathy J. Metcalf
Coordinator of Public Relations: Renee Reynolds
Historical Note
Founded as American Institute of Merchant Shipping as the result of the merger of Committee of American Steamship Lines (1952), Pacific American Steamship Ass'n (1919) and American Merchant Marine Institute (1938). Became U.S. Chamber of Shipping in 1996, and assumed its current name in 1998. CSA members are U.S.-based companies which own, operate, or charter oceangoing tankers, container ships, and other merchant vessels engaged in domestic or international trade. Represents members' interests in dealings with international and domestic agencies concerned with merchant shipping.
Meetings/Conferences:
Annual Meetings: usually Washington, DC

Chartered Property and Casualty Underwriters Soc. (1944)
720 Providence Rd.
P.O. Box 3009
Malvern, PA 19355-0709
Tel: (610)251-2728   *Fax:* (610)251-2775
Toll Free: (800)932 - 2728
Web Site: http://www.cpcusociety.org
Members: 28,088 individuals
Staff: 45
Annual Budget: $5-10,000,000
Exec. V. President: James R. Marks, CPCU, AIM
V. President, Communications: Robert Trometter
V. President, Finance & Administration: Joseph Wisniewski
Director, Meeting Services: Liliana Rizzo
Sr. V.P., Continuing Education: Cynthia R. Ziegler, CPCU
V. President, Member/Chapter Services: Mark Gaydos
Historical Note
Formerly (1995) Soc. of Chartered Property and Casualty Underwriters. Insurance professionals who have passed the 10 exams of the American Institute for Chartered Property Casualty Underwriters and have become a Chartered Property Casualty Underwriter (CPCU). Has an annual budget of approximately $6 million. Membership: $115/year.
Publications:
CPCU Journal. q.
CPCU News. 10/year.
CPCU Yearbook. a.
Directory. bien.
Meetings/Conferences:
Annual Meetings: Fall/3,500
1999 – Boston, MA/Oct. 17-19

Cheese Importers Ass'n of America (1943)

460 Park Ave.
New York, NY 10022
Members: 160 companies
Staff: 2
Secretary: Virginia Sheahan
Publications:
Bulletin. semi-m.
Year Book. a. adv.

Chefs de Cuisine Ass'n of America (1916)

Historical Note
Formerly (1964) Executive Chefs de Cuisine Ass'n of America. Membership concentrated in the New York area. Membership: $60/year.
Publications:
Newsletter. m.

Cheiron: The Internat'l Soc. for the History of Behavioral and Social Sciences (1968)

P.O. Box 2000
Kenosha, WI 53141
Tel: (414)595-2112   *Fax:* (414)595-2602
E-Mail: harrisb@uwp.edu
Web Site: www.yorku.ca/dept/psych/cheiron/
Members: 350 individuals
Staff: 2
Annual Budget: under $10,000
Exec. Officer: Benjamin Harris
Historical Note
Scholars in the United States and other countries interested in the history of the behavioral and social sciences. Membership: $20/year.
Publications:
Cheiron Newsletter. semi-a. adv.
Meetings/Conferences:
Annual Meetings: Third Week in June/80-120
1999 – Ottawa, Ontario(Carleton, University)
2000 – Gorham, ME(University of Southern Maine)

Chemical Coaters Ass'n Internat'l (1970)

P.O. Box 54316
Cincinnati, OH 45254
Tel: (513)624-6767   *Fax:* (513)624-0601
Members: 1000 individuals and companies
Staff: 4
Annual Budget: $100-250,000
Exec. Director: Anne Goyer
Historical Note
Users and suppliers of industrial cleaners, paints, coatings and equipment. Membership: $65/year (domestic individual), $1,000/year (domestic corporation); $135/year (individual, overseas), $1,500/year (corporation, overseas); $15 one-time membership processing fee.
Publications:
Finishing Touch.
Newsletter. q.
Meetings/Conferences:
Annual Meetings: Spring
1999 – Las Vegas, NV/May 20-22

Chemical Communications Ass'n (1964)

Robert J. Gurney Industries,Inc.
219 E. 69th St., PH F
New York, NY 10021-5457
Members: 130 individuals
Annual Budget: under $10,000
President: Phillip P. Fried
Historical Note
An organization of editors, writers, corporate public relations and agency people who work in and around the chemical industry, mostly in the New York area. Has no paid officers or full-time staff. Membership: $60/year.
Publications:
Membership Directory. a.
Meetings/Conferences:
Annual Meetings: Not held.

Chemical Fabrics and Film Ass'n (1927)

1300 Sumner Ave.
Cleveland, OH 44115-2851
Tel: (216)241-7333   *Fax:* (216)241-0105
E-Mail: cffa@taol.com
Web Site: http://www.taol.com/cffa
Members: 18 manufacturers, 19 associates
Staff: 2
Exec. Secretary: Charles M. Stockinger
Historical Note
Established as the Pyroxylin Coated Fabric Manufacturers, CFFA became the Vinyl Fabrics Institute and assumed its present name in 1971. Members are manufacturers of vinyl and urethane products.

Chemical Industry Institute of Toxicology (1974)

P.O. Box 12137
6 Davis Drive
Research Triangle Pk, NC 27709-2137
Tel: (919)558-1202   *Fax:* (919)558-1400
E-Mail: McClellanciit.org
Web Site: http://www.ciit.org
Members: 36 companies
Staff: 160
Annual Budget: $10-25,000,000
C.E.O. and President: Roger O. McClellan, DVM
Communications Specialist: Robert Nellis
Controller: David Althaus
Manager, Information Services: Rusty Bramlage, MPH, MBA

Historical Note
Studies toxicological and human health risk issues associated with the manufacture, distribution and disposal of industrial chemicals. Has an annual budget of approximately $17 million.
Publications:
CIIT Activities Newsletter. m.
CIIT Impact. bi-m.
Meetings/Conferences:
Annual Meetings: May

Chemical Management and Resources Ass'n (1940)

1255 23rd St., N.W.
Washington, DC 20037-1125
Tel: (202)452-1620   *Fax:* (202)833-3636
E-Mail: mjccmra@earthcom.net
Web Site: http://www.cmra.org/cmra
Members: 900 individuals
Exec. Director: Christopher Murphy
Historical Note
Formerly (1945) Chemical Market Research Ass'n and (1965) Chemical Marketing Research Ass'n; assumed its current name in 1990. Members are professionals within the chemical and allied process industries concerned with marketing, management, business development, business intelligence, market research and planning. Presents the CMRA Award for Executive Excellence annually to recognize accomplishments in the industry. Membership: $160/year (individual).
Publications:
CMRA Directory. a.
Meeting Papers. 2-3/year.
Newsletter. 2-3/year.
Meetings/Conferences:

Chemical Manufacturers Ass'n (1872)

1300 Wilson Blvd.
Arlington, VA 22209-2307
Tel: (703)741-5000   *Fax:* (703)741-6000
Web Site: http://www.cmahq.com
Members: 190 companies
Staff: 285
Annual Budget: $25-50,000,000
President and C.E.O.: Frederick L. Webber
Director, Meetings/Conventions: Edie Fleming
Exec. V. President and C.O.O.: Charles W. Van Vlack
Director, Business Services: Michael McGraw
V. President/General Counsel: David F. Zoll
V. President, Internat'l Affairs: Kathleen Ambrose
Historical Note
Assumed its present name in 1979. Formerly known as Manufacturing Chemists' Ass'n (1950). Absorbed the Plastic Materials Manufacturers Ass'n in 1950. Began admitting Canadian companies to membership in 1953. Includes programs such as Ethylene Oxide Industry Council. Administers research on specific chemicals germane to industry activity. Has a core budget of approximately $28 million.
Publications:
Chemecology. m.
CMA News. 10/yr.
Meetings/Conferences:
Annual Meetings: Always White Sulphur Springs, WV/June
1999 – /June 2-4

Chemical Producers and Distributors Ass'n (1975)

1430 Duke St.
Alexandria, VA 22314
Tel: (703)548-7700   *Fax:* (703)548-3149
Members: 100 companies
Staff: 5
Annual Budget: $500-1,000,000
President: Warren E. Stickle, Ph.D.
Director, Legislative Affairs: Diane Schute
Regulatory Affairs Manager: Ted Wang
Meetings and Membership: Kelly Potter
Historical Note
Until 1979, Pesticide Formulators Ass'n, and formerly the Pesticide Producers Ass'n, CPDA assumed its present name in 1987. Incorporated in the District of Columbia in 1975. Member are small to medium sized pesticide formulators, manufacturers and distributors.
Publications:
Executive News. m.
FAX-Flashed. bi-w.
Legislative and Regulatory Journal. m.
Meetings/Conferences:
Semi-Annual Meetings: February in Washington, DC and
          August in varying locations
1999 – San Diego, CA
2000 – Banff, Alberta, Canada

Chemical Sources Ass'n (1972)

500 Plaza Drive
P.O.Box 3189
Secaucus, NJ 07096-3189
Tel: (201)392-8900   *Fax:* (201)348-3877
E-Mail: patrick@njlegalink.com
Members: 170 individuals, 74 companies
Staff: 3
Annual Budget: $25-50,000
Counsel: Daniel R. Thompson
Historical Note
Created to seek sources of supply and encourage production of aroma chemicals used as flavoring ingredients. Membership: $200/year.
Publications:
Newsletter. q.
Patent Compendiums. a.
Meetings/Conferences:
Annual Meetings: Spring

Chemical Specialties Manufacturers Ass'n (1914)

1913 I St., N.W.
Washington, DC 20006-2111
Tel: (202)872-8110   *Fax:* (202)872-8114
E-Mail: info@csma.org
Web Site: http://www.csma.org
Members: 400 companies
Staff: 36
Annual Budget: $2-5,000,000
President: Ralph Engel
Director, Member Services: Paul Pierpoint
Controller: James A. Councilor
V.P., Dept. of Legal Affairs: Stephen S. Kellner
Historical Note
Established as the Nat'l Ass'n of Insecticide and Disinfectant Manufacturers, it assumed its present name in 1948. Sponsors the Chemical Specialties Manufacturers Association Political Action Committee (Chem-PAC).
Publications:
Chemical Times and Trends. q. adv.
Executive Newswatch, Legislative Report. w.
Meetings/Conferences:
Semi-Annual Meetings: April-May and December

Chemical Waste Transporation Institute (1982)

Historical Note
A division of the Hazardous Waste Management Ass'n.

Cherry Marketing Institute (1988)

P.O. Box 30285
Lansing, MI 48909-7785
Tel: (517)669-4264   *Fax:* (517)669-3354
Web Site: http://www.cherrymkt.org
Members: 3 state associations
Staff: 11
Annual Budget: $500-1,000,000
President: Philip J. Korson, II
Historical Note
Serves as the national promotional organization for cherry growers in Michigan, Utah, and Wisconsin. Provides marketing information, research, product development, and product promotion for its members.
Publications:
Newsletter. m.
Meetings/Conferences:
Annual Meetings: January
1999 – Travers City, MI(Grand Travers Resort)

Chester White Swine Record Ass'n (1930)

P.O. Box 9758
Peoria, IL 61612-9758
Tel: (309)691-6301   *Fax:* (309)691-0168
Members: 1,050 individuals
Staff: 3
Annual Budget: $250-500,000
Dir., Promotions: Jack Wall
Historical Note
Breeders of Chester White swine. The Chester White Breed originated in Chester County, PA, in the early 19th century. Member of the Nat'l Pedigree Livestock Council.
Publications:
Chester White Journal. m. adv.
Meetings/Conferences:

Chi Eta Phi Sorority (1932)

3029 13th St., N.W.
Washington, DC 20009
Tel: (202)232-3858   *Fax:* (202)232-3460
Members: 7,000 individuals
Staff: 1
Annual Budget: $100-250,000
Nat'l Secretary: Anita Love
Historical Note
A professional sorority of registered and student nurses, Chi Eta Phi was established to develop a corps of nursing leaders, encourage continuing education, recruit for the nursing and health professions, develop working relationships with other professional groups, and stimulate a close and friendly relationship among members. Membership: $75/year.
Publications:
Chi Line Newsletter. semi-a.
Directory. a.
Glowing Lamp. a.
Meetings/Conferences:
Annual Meetings: July/500
1999 – Pittsburg, PA

Chief Administrators of Catholic Education

Historical Note
An affiliate of the Nat'l Catholic Educational Ass'n which provides administrative support.

Chief Executives Organization (1958)

7920 Norfolk Ave., Suite 400
Bethesda, MD 20814
Tel: (301)656-9220   *Fax:* (301)651-0060
Members: 1,400 individuals
Staff: 15
Annual Budget: $2-5,000,000
Exec. Director: Wendy S. Pangburn
Historical Note
Members are individuals formerly in the Young Presidents' Organization who have become 49, the mandatory retirement age. Formerly (1983) Chief Executives Forum. Membership: $900/year.
Publications:
Compasss.

Meetings/Conferences:
Semi-Annual Meetings: Spring and Fall
1999 – Britain
1999 – Italy

Chief Officers of State Library Agencies (1973)
167 W. Main St., Suite 600
Lexington, KY 40507
Tel: (606)514-9169   Fax: (606)231-1928
E-Mail: pmclaughlon@amrinc.net
Web Site: www.csl.ctstateu.edu/cosla
Members: 52 individuals
Staff: 1
Annual Budget: $50-100,000
Ass'n Manager: Piper McLaughlin

Historical Note
*An independent organization of the chief officers of state and
territorial agencies designated as the state library administrative
agency and responsible for statewide library development. It
provides a continuing mechanism for dealing with the problems and
challenges faced by the heads of the state agencies which are
responsible for statewide library development.*

Publications:
COSLA Directory. a.

Meetings/Conferences:
1999 – Washington, DC
1999 – Indianapolis, IN

Chief Petty Officers Ass'n (1969)
5520-G Hempstead Way
Springfield, VA 22151-4009
Tel: (703)941-0395   Fax: (703)941-0397
Members: 12,000 individuals
Staff: 2
Annual Budget: $100-250,000
Chief Administrator: Thomas R. Scaramastro

Historical Note
*Chief Petty Officers of the U.S. Coast Guard, active, retired and
reserve. Constituent member of the Combined Organization of
Military Ass'ns. Membership: $18/year.*

Publications:
The Chief. q.

Meetings/Conferences:
Annual Meetings: August
1999 – Las Vegas, NV(Hotel California)/150

Chief Warrant and Warrant Officers Ass'n, United States Coast Guard (1929)
James Creek Marina
200 V St., S.W.
Washington, DC 20024
Tel: (202)554-7753   Fax: (202)484-0641
Members: 3,300 individuals
Staff: 1
Annual Budget: $50-100,000
Executive Director: Robert Lewis

Historical Note
*CWOA members are active, reserve and retired warrant officers and
chief warrant officers.*

Publications:
Newsletter. m.

Meetings/Conferences:
Annual Meetings: April

Child Neurology Soc. (1971)
3900 Northwoods Dr., Suite 175
St. Paul, MN 55112-6966
Tel: (651)486-9447   Fax: (651)486-9436
E-Mail: cns@tc.umn.edu
Web Site: http://www.umn.edu/cns
Members: 1,300 individuals
Staff: 2
Annual Budget: $100-250,000
Exec. Director: Mary E. Currey

Historical Note
*Established in Minneapolis, MN, the Society advances child
neurology by providing a scientific forum for professionals in the
field. Membership: $225/year (active).*

Publications:
Annals of Neurology. m. adv.
CNS Newsletter. q. adv.

Meetings/Conferences:
1999 – Nashville, TN/Oct. 13-16

Child Welfare League of America (1920)
440 1st St., N.W., Suite 310
Washington, DC 20001
Tel: (202)638-2952   Fax: (202)638-4004
Web Site: www.cwla.org
Staff: 120
Annual Budget: $5-10,000,000
Exec. Director: David S. Liederman
Communications Director: Mary J. Layton
Public Policy Director: Karabelle Pizzigati
Conference Management Director: Lydell Broom
Training Director: Maureen Leighton
Finance Director: Dick Geldof
General Counsel: Cynthia Seymour
Deputy Director: Shirley Marcus Allen
Publications Director: Susan Brite
Dep. Director: Michael Petit
Research Director: Patrick Curtis
Co-Director, Consultation: Earl Stuck
Co-Director, Consultation: Robert McKeagney

Historical Note
Has an annual budget of approximately $15 million.

Publications:
Child Welfare: Journal of Policy, Practice & Program. bi-m.
        adv.
Children's Voice Magazine. q. adv.
CWLA Children's Monitor Newsletter. m.
CWLA Directory of Member Agencies. a.
Washington Social Legislation Bulletin. semi-m.

Meetings/Conferences:
Annual Meetings: always Washington, DC/March

Children's Book Council (1945)
568 Broadway
New York, NY 10012
Tel: (212)966-1990   Fax: (212)966-2073
E-Mail: staff@cbcbooks.org
Web Site: http://www.CBCbooks.org
Members: 80 publishers
Staff: 8
Annual Budget: $1-2,000,000
President: Paula Quint
Member Programs Manager: Ellen Yurish
Information Services Manager: Stephen Christensen
Director of Liaison and Member Programs: Allan Marshall
Director of Business and Operations: Barry Klein

Historical Note
*CBC is a trade association of producers of children's books and
related materials promoting reading and literature for children.
Sponsors Nat'l Children's Book Week each November.*

Publications:
CBC Features. semi-a.

Meetings/Conferences:
Annual Meetings: September

Children's Literature Ass'n (1972)
P.O. Box 138
Battle Creek, MI 49016-0138
Tel: (616)965-8180   Fax: (616)965-3568
E-Mail: chla@mlc.lib.mi.us
Web Site: http://ebbs.english.vt.edu/chla
Members: 550 individuals, 200 institutions
Staff: 1
Annual Budget: $50-100,000
President: Sylvia Iskander

Historical Note
*The ChLA promotes serious scholarship and criticism in children's
literature. Members are teachers, academics, critics, scholars,
students, librarians, and institutions. Presents annual awards for
excellence in children's literature. Membership: $70/year
(individual), $110/year (institution).*

Publications:
Children's Literature: An International Journal. a.
ChLA Quarterly. q.

Meetings/Conferences:
Annual Meetings: Annual meetings in June/July
1999 – Calgary, AB, Canada(University of Calgary)/July 5-9

Childrenswear Marketing Ass'n (1976)
236 Rte. 38 West
Moorestown, NJ 08057
Tel: (609)231-8500   Fax: (609)231-4664
E-Mail: cma@ahint.com
Web Site: http://www.childrenswear-assoc.org
Members: 150 companies
Annual Budget: $100-250,000
Exec. V. President: Robert Waller, Jr.
Exec. Director: Linda Lauer

Historical Note
*CMA promotes the childrenswear industry through communication,
education and expansion of the industry. Membership: $100-
500(individuals, retailers); $375-$1200(corporations).*

Publications:
Newsletter. irreg.

Chilled Foods Ass'n (1988)
5775 Peachtree-Dunwoody Rd., Suite 500-G
Atlanta, GA 30342-1558
Tel: (404)252-3663   Fax: (404)252-0774
E-Mail: CFA@AssnHQ.com
Staff: 6
Annual Budget: $100-250,000
Exec. Director: Andrew G. Ebert, Ph.D.

Historical Note
*CFA members are manufacturers, retailers, food service operators,
distributors and suppliers involved in the chilled foods industry.
Membership: $1,000-15,000/year (organization).*

Meetings/Conferences:
Annual Meetings: Fall

China Clay Producers Ass'n (1978)
7183 Jonesboro Road, Suite 101
Morrow, GA 30260-2940
Tel: (770)961-7680   Fax: (770)961-7767
Web Site: www.kaoloin.com
Members: 5 companies
Staff: 1
Annual Budget: $250-500,000
Exec. Director: Kenneth W. Jackman

Historical Note
*A trade group of kaolin producers. Supports the China Clay
Producers Group Political Action Committee.*

Meetings/Conferences:
Annual meetings: September
1999 – Hilton Head, SC(Westin)

China, Glass and Giftware Ass'n (1948)

Historical Note
Organization defunct in 1997.

Chinese American Food Soc. (1975)
P.O. Box 161
Palatine, IL 60078-0161
Tel: (314)982-2631
Web Site: http://www.griffin.peachnet.edu/cafs
Members: 300 individuals
Annual Budget: under $10,000

Historical Note
*CAFS is an academic and professional organization which brings
together professionals residing in North America with interests in
food science and technology, as well as in Chinese culture to
provide technical consultation to industry and organizations. Has
no paid officers or full-time staff. Membership: $20/year
(individual).*

Publications:
CAFS Newsletter. q. adv.
Science & Technology Monograph Series.

Meetings/Conferences:

Chinese American Medical Soc. (1962)
281 Edgewood Ave.
Teaneck, NJ 07666
Tel: (201)833-1506   Fax: (201)833-8252
Web Site: http://www.camsociety.org
Members: 860 individuals
Annual Budget: $25-50,000
Exec. Director: H.H. Wang, M.D.

Historical Note
*Formerly (1985) American Chinese Medical Soc. CAMS members
are physicians of Chinese ancestry residing in the United States or
Canada. Has no paid officers or full-time staff. Membership:
$100/year (individual); $25/year (residency).*

Publications:
CAMS Newsletter. 3-4/year.
Membership Directory. a.

Meetings/Conferences:
Semi-Annual Meetings: Spring and Fall, usually in New York,
        NY/150
1999 – New York, NY

Chinese Language Teachers Ass'n (1962)
c/o Kalamazoo College
1200 Academy St.
Kalamazoo, MI 49006
Tel: (616)337-7001   Fax: (616)337-7251
Members: 800 individuals and organizations
Staff: 1
Annual Budget: $25-50,000
Exec. Director: Madeline Chu
Assistant to the Exec. Director: Qingshun Sun

Historical Note
*Affiliated with the Ass'n for Asian Studies, the Modern Language
Ass'n, and the American Council for the Teaching of Foreign
Languages. Membership: $50/year (individual); $80/year
(organization).*

Publications:
Journal of The Chinese Language Teachers Association.
        3/year. adv.
Monograph. irreg.
Newsletter. 3/year. adv.

Meetings/Conferences:
Annual Meetings: November, with the American Council for the
        Teaching of Foreign Languages.
1999 – Dallas, TX/Nov. 19-21
2000 – Boston, MA/Nov. 17-19

Chinese-American Librarians Ass'n (1973)
3111 Cedarbrook Rd.
Ann Arbor, MI 48105-3407
Tel: (734)332-0390   Fax: (734)332-4480
E-Mail: sheilalai@csus.edu
Members: 700 individuals
Annual Budget: $10-25,000
Exec. Director: Amy Seetoo

Historical Note
*Formerly the Mid-West Chinese American Librarians Association.
Affiliated with the American Library Association. Membership:
$20/year (individual), $45/year (organization).*

Publications:
CALA Newsletter. 3/year.
Journal of Library and Information Science. semi-a.
Membership Directory. a. adv.

Meetings/Conferences:
Semi-Annual Meetings: with American Library Ass'n
1999 – New Orleans, LA/June 24-July 1

Chlorinated Paraffins Industry Ass'n (1984)
1250 Connecticut Ave., N.W.
Suite 700
Washington, DC 20036
Tel: (202)637-9040   Fax: (202)637-9178
E-Mail: regnet@ricochet.net
Members: 4 companies
Staff: 2
Annual Budget: $100-250,000
Exec. Director: Robert J. Fensterheim

Historical Note
*Manufacturers, distributors, and users of chlorinated parafins, used
in lubricants, plastics, and flame retardants. Membership:
$7,000/year (company).*

Publications:
Status Report. irreg.

Chlorine Chemistry Council (1992)
1300 Wilson Blvd.
Arlington, VA 22209
Tel: (703)741-5000   Fax: (703)741-6084
Annual Budget: $5-10,000,000

V. President and Exec. Director: Clifford T. Howlett, Jr., CMA
Director, Public Affairs: Janet Flynn
Director, Operations and Finance: Frank Hurd
Director, International Affairs: Warner Braun
Assistant General Counsel: David Fischer
Director of State Affairs: Greg Merrill
Director of Science: Ann Mason

Historical Note
A council of the Chemical Manufacturers Ass'n. Membership: based on production/use of chlorine.

Publications:
Newsline. w.

Chlorine Institute *(1924)*
2001 L St., N.W., Suite 506
Washington, DC 20036-4919
Tel: (202)775-2790 *Fax:* (202)223-7225
Web Site: http://www.CL2.COM
Members: 226 companies
Staff: 12
Annual Budget: $2-5,000,000
President: Robert G. Smerko
Director, Public Relations/Membership Communication: Gardner B. Bates
Director, Administration: Christine B. Kelly

Historical Note
Members are producers of gaseous and liquid chlorine and others associated in some way with manufacture, processing, packaging, transporting, and use. The Halogenated Solvents Industry Alliance became affiliated with the Institute in 1992. Membership: $2,700/year.

Publications:
Annual Report. a.
Insider. m.

Meetings/Conferences:
Annual Meetings: February/March/April
1999 – Washington, DC(JWMarriott)/April 11-15/300
2000 – Houston, TX/March 19-22/300

Chlorobenzene Producers Ass'n *(1978)*
1850 M St. N.W. Suite 700
Suite 1090
Washington, DC 20036
Tel: (202)721-4160 *Fax:* (202)296-8120
Members: 5 companies
Staff: 2
Annual Budget: $100-250,000
Exec. Director: Richard E. Opatick, CAE

Historical Note
An affiliate of the Synthetic Organic Chemical Manufacturers Ass'n.

Publications:
None.

Meetings/Conferences:
Annual Meetings: None held.

Chocolate Manufacturers Ass'n of the U.S.A. *(1923)*
7900 Westpark Drive, Suite A320
McLean, VA 22102-4297
Tel: (703)790-5011 *Fax:* (703)790-5752
Web Site: http://www.candyusa.org/who_cma.html
Members: 11 companies
Staff: 10
Annual Budget: $100-250,000
President and C.E.O.: Lawrence T. Graham
Senior V. President, Public & Legislative Affairs: Susan Smith
Manager, Legislative Affairs: Mark Finch
Senior V. President, Scientific Affairs: Bruce R. Stillings, Ph.D.
Director, Membership and Meetings: Libby Taylor
Corp. Secretary: Joy Kennedy Hughes

Historical Note
Founded as the Ass'n of Cocoa and Chocolate Manufacturers of the United States, it assumed its present name in 1958.

Meetings/Conferences:

Choristers Guild *(1949)*
2834 W. Kingsley Road
Garland, TX 75041-2498
Tel: (972)271-1521 *Fax:* (972)840-3113
E-Mail: choristers@choristerguild.org
Web Site: http://www.choristersguild.org
Members: 8,500 individuals
Staff: 6
Annual Budget: $500-1,000,000
Exec. Director: George Eison

Historical Note
Members are directors of children's and youth choirs in churches and schools seeking to enhance the religious and musical training of their students. Incorporated in the states of Tennessee and Texas. Membership: $48/year.

Publications:
The Chorister. 10/year.

Meetings/Conferences:
1999 – Liberty, MO(William Jewell College)

Chorus America *(1977)*
1156 15th St., N.W., Suite 310
Washington, DC 20005-1704
Tel: (202)331-7577 *Fax:* (202)331-7599
E-Mail: chorusam@libertynet.org
Web Site: http://www.libertynet.org/~chorusam
Members: 900 organizations and individuals
Staff: 5
Annual Budget: $500-1,000,000
Projects Director: Jennifer Sherwood
Member Services Director: Amy Young

Historical Note
Formerly (1987) the Ass'n of Professional Vocal Ensembles. Professional members are choral organizations which employ a minimum of 25% of the total ensemble membership or twelve professional singers. Chorus America promotes the professional growth and quality of the choral art, and occupational respectability and opportunity for its performers. Administers the American Choral Foundation (see separate listing). Membership: $50/year (individual), .01% of operating budget or $100 minimum (organization), with $500 maximaum.

Publications:
The Voice of CHORUS AMERICA. q. adv.

Meetings/Conferences:
1999 – Minneapolis, MN(Radisson)

Christian Booksellers Ass'n *(1950)*
Historical Note
Became CBA in 1997.

Christian College Consortium *(1971)*
50 Stark Hwy. South
Dunbarton, NH 03045-4406
Tel: (603)774-6623 *Fax:* (603)774-6628
E-Mail: tenglund@aol.com
Members: 13 colleges
Staff: 1
Annual Budget: $50-100,000
President: Thomas H. Englund

Historical Note
Organized in 1971, the Consortium consists of thirteen colleges united by regional accreditation, concentration upon liberal arts studies, educational strengths that can be shared, nationwide distribution and a common affirmation of faith.

Meetings/Conferences:
Annual Meetings: March

Christian Educators Ass'n Internat'l *(1953)*
P.O. Box 41300
Pasadena, CA 91114-8300
Tel: (626)798-1124 *Fax:* (626)798-2346
E-Mail: feedback@ceai.org
Web Site: http://www.ceai.org
Exec. Director: Forrest L. Turpen

Historical Note
CEAI members are professionals serving in public and private education.

Meetings/Conferences:
1999 – Colorado Springs, CO/July 29-Aug. 1

Christian Labor Ass'n of the United States of America *(1931)*
Box 65, 405 Centerstone Ct.
Zeeland, MI 49464
Tel: (616)772-9164 *Fax:* (616)772-9830
E-Mail: chrlabor@eagledesign.com
Members: 3,000 individuals
Staff: 12
Annual Budget: $250-500,000
President: Doug Reese
Nat'l Representative: Mike Koppenol

Historical Note
Independent labor union. Works to support Christian principles in the workplace and promote cooperation between management and labor.

Meetings/Conferences:
Annual Meetings: Holland, MI in March

Christian Legal Soc. *(1961)*
4208 Evergreen Lane, Suite 222
Annandale, VA 22003-3235
Tel: (703)642-1070 *Fax:* (703)642-1075
E-Mail: cls@interramp.com
Web Site: http://www.clsnet.com
Members: 5,000 individuals
Staff: 5
Annual Budget: $1-2,000,000
Exec. Director: Samuel B. Casey
Dir., Center for Law & Religious Freedom: Steven T. McFarland
Manager, Membership Services: Kristin Murphy

Historical Note
A Christian organization of lawyers, judges, law professors and students, and interested laypeople, advocating justice and religious freedom. Membership: $25-175/year (individual).

Publications:
Christian Lawyer. q.
The Defender. 5/year.

Meetings/Conferences:
1999 – San Antonio, TX

Christian Management Ass'n *(1976)*
P.O. Box 4638
Diamond Bar, CA 91765
Tel: (909)861-8861 *Fax:* (909)860-8247
Toll Free: (800)959 - 6774
Members: 3,000 individuals
Staff: 5
Annual Budget: $1-2,000,000
C.E.O.: John Pearson
Dir., Member Dev./Training: Jackie Tsujimoto
Director, Publications and Education: Sandy Scruggs

Historical Note
Formerly Christian Ministries Management Ass'n; assumed its present name in 1990. Non-profit organization assisting C.E.O.'s and managers of churches and Christian organizations. Membership: $149/year.

Publications:
Christian Management Report. bi-m. adv.
Christian Ministries Salary Survey.

Membership Directory. a. adv.
Publications List Available.

Meetings/Conferences:
Annual Meetings: February
1999 – Colorado Springs, CO/Feb. 15-18

Christian Medical and Dental Soc. *(1931)*
P.O. Box 5
Bristol, TN 37621-0005
Tel: (423)844-1000 *Fax:* (423)844-1005
E-Mail: main@christian-doctors.com
Web Site: http://www.cmds.org
Members: 12,000 individuals
Staff: 40
Annual Budget: $2-5,000,000
Exec. Director: David Stevens, M.D.
Assoc. Director: Gene Rudd, M.D.

Historical Note
Members are Christian medical and dental personnel, some of whom serve as medical missionaries. Membership: $250/year (individual practicing member), $75/year (missionary), $25/year (student), $150/year (new member).

Publications:
CMDS Incision. q.
CMDS Today's Christian Doctor. q.

Meetings/Conferences:
Annual Meetings: May
1999 – Toronto, Ontario(Sheraton Centre)/April 28-May 2/650
2000 – Orlando, FL(Clarion Plaza Hotel)/May 3-7/650

Christian Schools Internat'l *(1920)*
3350 E. Paris Ave.
Grand Rapids, MI 49512
Tel: (616)957-1070 *Fax:* (616)957-5022
E-Mail: CSI@gospelcom.net
Web Site: http://www.christianschoolsint.org
Members: 460 protestant private schools
Staff: 35
Annual Budget: $1-2,000,000
Exec. Director: Daniel R. Vander Ark
Director of Support Services: Robert Van Wieren
Director of Business Administration: Thomas D. Glover

Historical Note
Established as the National Union of Christian Schools, it assumed its present name in 1978. Serves Christian schools of the Reformed tradition, providing employee benefit programs, curriculum and periodical publications, and services to school boards and administrators.

Publications:
Administrator. q.
Christian Home and School. bi-m. adv.
Christian School Directory. a.
Intercom. q.
The Agenda.

Meetings/Conferences:
Annual Meetings: July/August

Church and Synagogue Library Ass'n *(1967)*
Box 19357
Portland, OR 97280-0357
Tel: (503)244-6919 *Fax:* (503)977-3734
Toll Free: (800)542 - 2752
E-Mail: CSLA@worldaccess.com
Web Site: http://www.worldaccessnet.com/ncsla
Members: 1,900 libraries
Staff: 1
Annual Budget: $10-25,000
Administrator: Judith M. Janzen

Historical Note
An outgrowth of library workshops held for several years by the library school of Drexel University in Philadelphia, CSLA provides educational guidance for library services in religious institutions. A member of the Council of National Library Ass'ns. Membership: $25-$45/year (individual); $45-$55/year (church); $175/year (institution).

Publications:
Church & Synagogue Libraries. bi-m. adv.

Meetings/Conferences:
Annual Meetings: June/July
1999 – Orlando, FL(Airport Hyatt Regency)/July 25-27
2000 – Kansas City, MO/July 23-25

Church Music Publishers Ass'n *(1926)*
P.O. Box 158992
Nashville, TN 37215
Tel: (615)791-0273
Members: 30 companies
Annual Budget: $10-25,000
Exec. Secretary: Diane Cobb

Historical Note
Formerly Church and Sunday School Music Publishers Ass'n. Members publish music for Christian churches and schools. Membership: $450/year (organization).

Meetings/Conferences:
Annual Meetings: Spring

Cider Ass'n of North America *(1973)*
Historical Note
Address unknown in 1997.

CIES, The Food Business Forum *(1953)*
5549 Lee Highway
Arlington, VA 22207-1613
Tel: (703)534-8880 *Fax:* (703)534-9080
Web Site: http://www.cismet.com
Members: 500 companies
Staff: 30
Annual Budget: $1-2,000,000

General Manager: Jonathan Berger
Exec. V. President: Denise Larking-Coste
V. President, Conventions/Meetings: Werner Dahne
Senior V. President: Jacques LeRoux

Historical Note
Formerly the Internat'l Ass'n of Chain Stores - North American Headquarters, Internat'l Center for Companies of the Food Trade and Industry-North America Headquarters (1989) and Food Business Forum (1996). Provides management research on problems related to food distribution and serves as an international forum where food chain store executives can meet to exchange ideas and information. Membership: $900-$16,000/year based on sales volume (organization).

Publications:
EURO Food Focus. 10/yr.
Food Business News. 10/yr.
Wasteline. q.

Meetings/Conferences:
1999 – Stockholm, Sweden/June 6-8

Cigar Ass'n of America *(1937)*
1100 17th St., N.W., Suite 504
Washington, DC 20036
Tel: (202)223-8204 *Fax:* (202)833-0379
Members: 80 companies
Staff: 5
Annual Budget: $2-5,000,000
President: Norman F. Sharp

Historical Note
Established in 1937 as the Cigar Manufacturers Ass'n of America, Inc. Became the Cigar Ass'n of America, Inc. in 1974 through a merger of the Cigar Research Council, the Cigar Manufacturers Ass'n of America, the Cigar Institute of America and the State and Local Tax Council. Represents the producers of about 95% of the cigars sold in the U.S. Sponsors the Cigar Political Action Committee.

Publications:
Imports of Cigars and Leaf Tobacco. m.
Statistical Bulletin. m.
Trademark Bulletin. m.

Meetings/Conferences:
Annual Meetings: November
1999 – Aventura, FL(Turnberry Isle)/200

CIM --The Business Owners Forum *(1959)*
Commerce Industrial Chemical, Inc.
5611 W. Woolworth Ave.
Milwaukee, WI 53218
Tel: (414)353-3630
Members: 200 individuals
Annual Budget: $10-25,000
Exec. Secretary: Donna Kitlass

Historical Note
Formerly (1998) Council of Independent Managers. CIM members are owners of small to medium-sized companies. Membership: $490/year (individual).

Publications:
CIM Diretory. a.

Circuits and Systems Soc.
Historical Note
See IEEE Circuits and Systems Soc.

Circulation Managers of America *(1991)*
Historical Note
Organization defunct in 1994.

CISA Export Trade Group, Inc. *(1988)*
Historical Note
A division of Casting Industry Suppliers Ass'n (CISA).

City and Regional Magazine Ass'n *(1978)*
5820 Wilshire Blvd., Suite 500
Los Angeles, CA 90036
Tel: (213)937-5514 *Fax:* (213)937-0959
Members: 50 companies
Annual Budget: $100-250,000
Exec. Director: C. James Dowden

Historical Note
Membership composed of ABC or BPA-audited, general news, paid subscription city and regional magazines. CRMA represents member magazines on major national and regional policy issues, encourages high editorial and journalistic standards, provides professional development and training opportunities, compiles industry research and data, and promotes city and regional magazines as a major media market. Associate memberships are available to any person, firm, or corporation engaged in a business allied to the publishing of city or regional consumer magazines. Membership: $400-3,500/year (magazine).

Publications:
Communicator. q.
Media Watch. m.

Meetings/Conferences:
Annual Meetings: Spring/150-200
1999 – Indianapolis, IN(Hyatt Regency)/May 15-18

Civil Aviation Medical Ass'n *(1948)*
P.O. Box 23864
Oklahoma City, OK 73123-2864
Tel: (405)840-0199 *Fax:* (405)848-1053
Web Site: http://www.awgnet.com/safety/cama.htm
Members: 800 individuals
Staff: 1
Annual Budget: $25-50,000
Exec. V. President: James L. Harris, M.Ed.
Secretary/Treasurer: Floyd F. McSpadden

Historical Note
Established in 1948 as the Airline Medical Examiners Ass'n, it assumed its present name in 1955. CAMA is composed of physicians concerned with the welfare and growth of civil aviation, including aviation medical examiners and physicians who are pilots, aviation medical educators, flight instructors, and fixed-base operators. Membership: $80/year (individual), $250/year (organization/company).

Publications:
CAMA Bulletin. q.
Flicht Physician. bi-m.

Meetings/Conferences:
Annual Meetings: Fall
1999 – Toronto, ON, Canada/Sept. 15-18/200

Classical Music Broadcasters Ass'n *(1969)*
c/o WCLV, 26501 Renaissance Pkwy.
Cleveland, OH 44128
Tel: (216)464-0900 *Fax:* (216)464-2206
Members: 125 stations
Annual Budget: $50-100,000
Contact: Richard Marschner

Historical Note
Formerly (1993) Concert Music Broadcasters Ass'n. Organization of radio stations playing classical music on a commercial basis more than twenty hours per week. Has no permanent headquarters or paid staff. Mail to the above address will be forwarded. Purpose is assist classical radio stations in selling the classical format. Addresses problems concerning classical stations, provides assistance in conducting market research, and acts as a clearinghouse for information on engineering, new radio equipment, etc. Membership: $225/year.

Publications:
CMBA Directory. a.

Meetings/Conferences:
Annual Meetings: First Week in May

Classification and Compensation Soc. *(1969)*
1730 K St., N.W., Suite 713
Washington, DC 20006
Tel: (202)296-1900 *Fax:* (202)296-1910
Web Site: http://www.classandcomp.org
Members: 500 individuals
Staff: 3
Annual Budget: $100-250,000
National President: Richard Bell
Director of Administration: Caldwell Coleman

Historical Note
CCS members are persons in the public and private sector involved in personnel/human resources management activities who have an interest in compensation management, job analysis/evaluation, staffing, or organization design. Membership: $50/year (individual); $300/year (organization/company).

Publications:
Classifiers Column. bi-m.
Directory of Members. a.

Meetings/Conferences:

Classification Soc. of North America *(1969)*
IDS Dept., Univ. of Illinois M/C 294
601 S. Morgan St.
Chicago, IL 60607-7124
Tel: (312)996-2676 *Fax:* (312)413-0385
E-Mail: slsclove@uic.edu
Web Site: http://www.pitt.edu/csna/csna.html
Members: 300 individuals
Annual Budget: $10-25,000
Business Manager: Stanley L. Sclove, Ph.D.

Historical Note
A non-profit, interdisciplinary organization whose purposes are to promote the scientific study of classification and clustering, including systematic methods of creating classifications from data, and to disseminate scientific and educational information related its fields of interest. Members are researchers in the fields of psychology, statistics, computer science, biology, business applications, education, engineering, mathematics and sociology. Membership: $60/year (individual).

Publications:
Classification Literature Automated Search Service. a.
Journal of Classification. 2/year. adv.

Meetings/Conferences:
1999 – Pittsburg, PA(Univ. of Pittsburg)/June 10-13/120

Classroom Publishers Ass'n *(1948)*
107 Park Washington Court
Falls Church, VA 22046-4519
Tel: (703)532-9255 *Fax:* (703)532-0300
Members: 6 companies
Staff: 1
Annual Budget: $50-100,000
General Counsel: Stephen F. Owen, Jr.

Historical Note
Founded as the Classroom Periodical Publishers Ass'n, it assumed its present name in 1978. Has no permanent office; the above address is the law firm of Stephen F. Owen, Jr.

Clay Minerals Soc. *(1962)*
P.O. Box 4416
Boulder, CO 80306-4416
Tel: (303)444-6405 *Fax:* (303)444-2260
E-Mail: peberl@clays.org
Members: 1000 individuals
Staff: 1
Annual Budget: $250-500,000
Manager: Patricia Eberl

Historical Note
Incorporated in the District of Columbia July 18, 1962. Supersedes the Committee on Clay Minerals of the National Academy of Sciences/National Research Council. Members are individuals concerned with the scientific study and applications of clays and related silicate minerals. Membership: $60/year (subscribing member); $30/year (non-subscribing member); $165/year (company/organization); $180/year (company/ organization-outside of NA).

Publications:
Clays and Clay Minerals. bi-m.
CMS News. q. adv.
Meeting Abstracts. a.
Workshop Lecture Series.

Meetings/Conferences:
Annual Meetings: September-October/250

Cleaning Equipment Trade Ass'n *(1980)*
2440 Charles St., N., #220
St. Paul, MN 55109-3013
Tel: (651)777-4177 *Fax:* (651)777-4114
Toll Free: (800)441 - 0111
Members: 350 companies
Staff: 3
Annual Budget: $500-1,000,000
Exec. Director: Michael Lund
Convention Manager: Carol Wasieleski

Historical Note
Formerly the Cleaning Equipment Manufacturers Ass'n, CETA assumed its present name in 1990. Members are manufacturers, distributors and component suppliers of powered cleaning systems. Membership: $325-1,000/year (company).

Publications:
Newsletter.

Meetings/Conferences:
Annual Meetings: Winter
1999 – Reno, NV(Nugget Hotel)/November 3-16

Cleaning Management Institute *(1985)*
c/o Nat'l Trade Publications
13 Century Hill Dr.
Latham, NY 12110-2197
Tel: (518)783-1281 *Fax:* (518)783-1386
E-Mail: robin@cmexpo.com
Web Site: http://www.cmexpo.com
Members: 2,000 individuals
Staff: 4
Annual Budget: $250-500,000
Director: Robin Granger
Publisher: Alice J. Savino
Membership Coordinator: Marion Thompson

Historical Note
Successor organization to the American Institute of Maintenance (1958) in 1985. Members are individuals and companies involved in building cleaning and maintenance management. Membership: $95/year.

Publications:
Cleaning & Maintenance Management Magazine. m. adv.
Networking Directory. a.
NETWORKING Newsletter. m.
Training Publications and Testing.

Meetings/Conferences:
Annual Meetings: Spring
1999 – San Francisco, CA(Hyatt Fisherman's Wharf)/June 2-4
1999 – Arlington, VA(Hyatt Regency)/June 6-9

Clear Channel Broadcasting Service *(1934)*
1776 K St., N.W., Suite 1100
Washington, DC 20006
Tel: (202)429-7070 *Fax:* (202)429-7207
Members: 40 stations
Legal Counsel: John Bartlett

Historical Note
Membership composed of Class I-A and I-B Clear Channel standard broadcast (AM) stations. Has no permanent headquarters or staff. The above address is the law firm of Wiley, Rein & Fielding.

Meetings/Conferences:
Annual Meetings: In conjunction with the Nat'l Ass'n of Broadcasters

Cleveland Bay Horse Soc. of America *(1885)*
Historical Note
Became Cleveland Bay Horse Soc. of North America in 1994.

Clinical Immunology Soc. *(1986)*
611 E. Wells St.
Milwaukee, WI 53202-3816
Tel: (414)224-8095 *Fax:* (414)276-3349
E-Mail: cis@globaldialog.com
Web Site: http://www.globaldialog.com/ ~ cis
Members: 900 individuals
Staff: 4
Annual Budget: $250-500,000
Exec. Director: John J. Reichertz

Historical Note
CIS is devoted to fostering multidisciplinary approaches to clinical immunology. Members are M.D.s and Ph.D. working or researching in the field. Membership: $120-205/year (individual).

Publications:
Journal of Immunology.
Membership Directory. bien.
The Immunologist. bi-m.

Meetings/Conferences:

Clinical Laboratory Management Ass'n *(1971)*
989 Old Eagle School Rd., Suite 815
Wayne, PA 19087
Tel: (610)995-9580 *Fax:* (610)995-9568
E-Mail: glinial@clma.org
Web Site: http://clma.org
Members: 9,000 individuals

Staff: 25
Annual Budget: $1-2,000,000
Exec. V. President: George T. Linial, C.A.E.
Director, Information and Knowledge Development: Colette Steward, Ph.D.

Historical Note
Established as the American Ass'n of Clinical Laboratory Supervisors and Administrators, it assumed its present name in 1976. Members are laboratory executives and their suppliers. Membership: $90/year.

Publications:
Clinical Laboratory Management Review. bi-m. adv.
Management Briefs. m.

Meetings/Conferences:
Annual Meetings: Fall
1999 – Dallas, TX/June 17-20
2000 – Anaheim, CA/June 25-28

Clinical Ligand Assay Soc. *(1974)*
3139 S. Wayne Rd.
Wayne, MI   48184-1220
Tel: (734)722-6290   *Fax:* (734)722-7006
E-Mail: clas@clas.org
Web Site: http://www.clas.org
Members: 750 individuals
Staff: 3
Annual Budget: $250-500,000
Exec. Director: Daisy S. McCann
Office Manager: Diane Shaw

Historical Note
Founded as the Clinical Radioassay Soc., CLAS assumed its present name in 1981. Ligand assay is a specialty of clinical laboratory medicine by which substances (drugs, hormones, etc.) are measured in minute quantities. Membership: $95/year (regular), $40/year (associate).

Publications:
Journal of Clinical Ligand Assay. q. adv.
Newsletter. bi-m. adv.
Proceedings (Sullabus). a.

Meetings/Conferences:
Annual Meetings: Spring
1999 – Philadelphia, PA(Adam's Mark)/May 5-8
2000 – Boston, MA(Boston Park Plaza)/May 31-June 3

Clinical Orthopaedic Soc. *(1912)*
401 N. Michigan Ave., Suite 2400
Chicago, IL   60611
Toll Free: (800)843 - 9735
E-Mail: cos@sba.com
Web Site: http://www.cosociety.org
Members: 750 individuals
Staff: 3
Annual Budget: $100-250,000
Exec. Secretary: Catherine Carey

Historical Note
Members are orthopaedic surgeons. Membership: $165/year (individual).

Publications:
Directory. a.
Journal of the Southern Orthopaedic Ass'n. q.

Meetings/Conferences:
Annual Meetings: Fall/250
1999 – Orlando, FL/Sept. 29-Oct. 2
2000 – Birmingham, AL
2001 – Seattle, WA

Clinical Soc. of Genito-Urinary Surgeons *(1921)*
Dept. of Urology, University of Iowa
200 Hawkins Drive, 3123 RCP
Iowa City, IA   52242-1089
Tel: (319)353-0760   *Fax:* (319)353-8564
Members: 50 individuals
Annual Budget: under $10,000
Secretary-Treasurer: Richard D. Williams, M.D.

Publications:
Newsletter. 2/year.
Program. a.

Meetings/Conferences:

Clinical Social Work Federation *(1971)*
P.O. Box 3740
Arlington, VA   22203
Tel: (703)522-3866   *Fax:* (703)522-9441
Members: 11,000 individuals
Staff: 1
Annual Budget: $100-250,000
Administrative Coordinator: Linda O'Leary

Historical Note
Formerly (1997) the Nat'l Federation of Socs. for Clinical Social Work, CSWF is an advocacy organization for state societies of social workers.

Publications:
Managed Care News. bi-m.
Progress Report. 2-3/year. adv.

Meetings/Conferences:
Annual Meetings: Spring and Fall
1999 – Arlington, VA/April 30-May 2

Clock Manufacturers and Marketing Ass'n *(1985)*
710 E. Ogden Ave., Suite 600
Naperville, IL   60563
Tel: (630)369-2406   *Fax:* (630)369-2488
Members: 82 individuals, 50 companies
Staff: 2
Annual Budget: $25-50,000
Exec. Director: Janet Helfrich

Historical Note
Incorporated in Illinois, CMMA members are manufacturers, marketers and industry suppliers. Membership: $750/year (manufacturer), $400/year (supplier), $100/year (marketing representative).

Meetings/Conferences:
Annual Meetings: With the Internat'l Housewares Exposition in Chicago, IL/April

Closed Circuit Television Manufacturers Ass'n *(1986)*
2500 Wilson Blvd.
Arlington, VA   22201-3834
Tel: (703)907-7500   *Fax:* (703)907-7501
Members: 40 manufacturers
Staff: 7
Annual Budget: $50-100,000
Contact: Pete Walsh

Historical Note
Affiliated with the Electronic Industries Ass'n which provides administrative support. Membership dues vary, based on income.

Closure Manufacturers Ass'n *(1981)*
1627 K St., N.W., Suite 800
Washington, DC   20006
Tel: (202)223-9050   *Fax:* (202)785-5377
E-Mail: cmadc@erols.com
Members: 33 companies
Staff: 1
Annual Budget: $250-500,000
V. President, Closure Activities: Darla J. Williamson

Historical Note
Founded as the Closure Committee of the Glass Packaging Institute, CMA in 1981 became an independent affiliate of the Institute. Members are companies which make metal and plastic closures for all types of containers. Associate members are allied suppliers.

Publications:
The Closure Report (newsletter). 3/year.

Meetings/Conferences:
Semi-annual Meetings: Spring and Fall (Members Only)
1999 – Longboat Key, FL(Longboat Key Club)/Feb. 27-March 1

Clothing Manufacturers Ass'n of the U.S.A. *(1933)*
730 Broadway, 9th Floor
New York, NY   10003
Tel: (212)529-0823
Members: 100 companies
Staff: 2
Annual Budget: $100-250,000
Exec. Director: Robert A. Kaplan

Historical Note
Recognized by the Federal Government as the official liaison and spokesperson for the U.S. men's and boy's tailored clothing manufacturing industry. Represents employer members in national collective bargaining negotiations with the Union. Conducts annual problem-solving seminar. Membership: annual dues based on sales volume; $297/year (U.S. supplier); $397/year (supplier outside U.S.).

Publications:
Annual Statistical Report. a.
Publications List Available.
Statistical Report on Sales, Production, and Profit in Men's and Boy's.
Tailored Clothing Industry. a.

Clowns of America, Internat'l *(1960)*
P.O. Box 6468
Lee's Summit, MO   64064-6468
Tel: (816)373-5696   *Fax:* (816)522-5696
Toll Free: (888)522 - 5696
E-Mail: coai@coai.org
Web Site: http://www.clown.org
Members: 7,000 individuals
Annual Budget: $50-100,000
President: Judith Quest

Historical Note
Formerly (1968) Clown Club of America and Circus Clown Club. Members are amateur, semi-professional and professional clowns. Membership: $25/year (new members), $20/year (individual), $10/year (family).

Publications:
New Calliope. bi-m. adv.

Meetings/Conferences:
Annual Meetings: April
1999 – Bloomington, MN/April 27-May 2

Club Managers Ass'n of America *(1927)*
1733 King St.
Alexandria, VA   22314-2720
Tel: (703)739-9500   *Fax:* (703)739-0124
Web Site: http://www.cmaa.org
Members: 5,500 individuals
Staff: 30
Annual Budget: $2-5,000,000
Exec. V. President: James B. Singerling, CCM,CEC
Manager, Public Affairs: Bridget Gorman
Director, Conference and Exhibitions: Nancy L. Clare
V. President, Education/Professional Development: Gordon Welch
V. President: Kathi Driggs

Historical Note
Established and incorporated in Michigan in 1927. CMAA is the professional association for managers of the leading private membership clubs in the US and abroad. Membership: $520/year.

Publications:
At Your Service.
Club Management. m. adv.
Outlook. m.

Club Pool Ass'n *(1998)*
776 21st Ave. North
St. Petersburg, FL   73704
Tel: (727)896-7946   *Fax:* (727)896-3933
E-Mail: cpa@shamrockgroup.com
Web Site: shamrockgroup.com
Members: 80 businesses
Annual Budget: under $10,000
Exec. Director: Steve Graves

Historical Note
Formerly (1998) Nat'l Swim and Recreational Ass'n. Became (1980) Swim Facility Operators of America. NSRA members are operators of swim clubs and related facilities.

Publications:
Newsletter. bi-m.

Meetings/Conferences:
1999 – Monterey, CA/Nov. 4-6

Clydesdale Breeders of the United States *(1879)*
17346 Kelly Road
Pecatonica, IL   61063
Tel: (815)247-8780   *Fax:* (815)247-8337
E-Mail: clydesusa@aol.com
Web Site: http://members.aol.com/clydesusa/
Members: 800 individuals
Staff: 2
Annual Budget: $100-250,000
Secretary: Betty J. Groves

Historical Note
Members own and breed Clydesdale horses. Formerly the American Clydesdale Ass'n and Clydesdale Breeders Ass'n of the U.S. CBUS is responsible for all registration of eligible horses and the transfer of ownership.

Publications:
Clydesdale. a. adv.
The Clydesdale News. adv. adv.
The Lead Horse.
The Stud Book.

Meetings/Conferences:
Annual Meetings: always in Springfield, IL

Coal and Slurry Technology Ass'n *(1975)*
1156 15th St., N.W., Suite 525
Washington, DC   20005
Tel: (202)296-1133   *Fax:* (202)223-3504
Members: 30 companies
Staff: 2
Annual Budget: $100-250,000
Exec. Director: Stuart D. Serkin
V. President: Barbara A. Sakkestad

Historical Note
Organized in Houston, August, 1975. Pipeline and energy companies and manufacturers interested in pipeline delivery of solids, coal liquid mixtures and direct firing of coal. Formerly the Slurry Transport Ass'n and Slurry Technology Ass'n. Assumed present name in 1988. Membership: $2,000-15,000/year.

Publications:
Coal & Slurry Technology Bibliography. irreg.
Inside Pipeline. m.
Proceedings, International Technical Conference. a.

Meetings/Conferences:
Annual Meetings: Clearwater, FL(Sheraton Sand Key)/March or April
1999 – Clearwater, FL(Sheraton Sand Key)/March 8-11/300

Coal Exporters Ass'n of the United States *(1945)*
1130 17th St., N.W., 5th Floor
Washington, DC   20036
Tel: (202)463-2639   *Fax:* (202)833-9636
Web Site: www.nma.org
Members: 40 companies
Staff: 1
Annual Budget: $25-50,000
Exec. Director: Moya Phelleps

Historical Note
Affiliated with Nat'l Mining Ass'n.

Publications:
Bulletin. m.

Meetings/Conferences:
Annual Meetings: June, with the Nat'l Coal Ass'n
1999 – Lisbon, Portugal

Coalition for Christian Colleges and Universities *(1976)*
329 8th St., N.E.
Washington, DC   20002-6158
Tel: (202)546-8713   *Fax:* (202)546-8913
E-Mail: coalition@cccu.org
Web Site: http://www.cccu.org
Members: 91 institutions
Staff: 34
Annual Budget: $5-10,000,000
President: Robert C. Andringa
Director of Communications: Julie Peterson
V. President, Professional Development Programs: Dr. Karen Longman
V.P., Finance/Administration: Kyle Royer
Asst. to the President/Memebership Secretary: Jennifer M. Jukarovich
V. President, Student Development Programs: Richard Gathro

Historical Note
Incorporated in the District of Columbia as Christian College Coalition in 1982; assumed its current name in 1995. CCCU members are accredited four-year colleges and universities that apply a Christ-centered philosophy to higher education. Membership fee varies, $1,800-8,600/year, based on full-time enrollment.

Publications:
Resource Guide to Christian Higher Education. a.
The News. m.

Meetings/Conferences:
Annual Meetings: Winter
1999 – Washington, DC(Washington Court)

Coalition for Government Procurement (1979)
1990 M St., N.W., Suite 400
Washington, DC 20036
Tel: (202)331-0975   *Fax:* (202)822-9788
E-Mail: coalgovpro@aol.com
Web Site: http://www.washmg.com/cgp
Members: 220 companies, 10 associations
Staff: 3
Annual Budget: $100-250,000
Exec. Director: Larry Allen

Historical Note
Members are firms who provide commercial goods to the federal government, and related associations. Formerly (1988) the Coalition for Common Sense in Government Procurement.

Publications:
Off the Shelf. m.

Meetings/Conferences:
2000 – Washington, DC(Omni Shoreham)

Coalition for Intelligent Manufacturing Systems (1991)
1400 I St., N.W., Suite 540
Washington, DC 20005-2241
Tel: (202)638-4434   *Fax:* (202)296-1074
E-Mail: wmorin@sayer.com
Web Site: http://www.sayer.com/cims
Members: 20 individuals
Staff: 2
Annual Budget: under $10,000
Exec. Director: William G. Morin

Historical Note
CIMS provides a coordinated U.S. industry response to the proposed Intelligent Manufacturing Systems (IMS) program. CIMS currently administers U.S. participation in IMS projects.

Coalition for Juvenile Justice (1974)
1211 Connecticut Ave., N.W., Suite 414
Washington, DC 20036
Tel: (202)467-0864   *Fax:* (202)887-0738
E-Mail: juvjustice@aol.com
Staff: 7
Annual Budget: $500-1,000,000
Exec. Director: David Doi
Director, Public Policy: H. Pamela Allen
Director, Conference Planning: Rene Madigan
Operations Manager: Michael Hurlocker

Historical Note
Formerly (1994) Nat'l Coalition of State Juvenile Justice Advisory Groups.

Publications:
Annual Report. a.
Juvenile Justice Monitor. bi-m.

Meetings/Conferences:
Annual Meetings: Spring
1999 – Portland, OR(Doubletree)/Feb. 18-21
1999 – Bethesda, MD(Hyatt Regency)/April 8-13

Coalition of Automotive Ass'ns

Historical Note
Non-profit organization formed to provide administrative support for the Specialty Equipment Market Ass'n and Auto Internat'l Ass'n.

Coalition of Black Trade Unionists (1972)
P.O. Box 66268
Washington, DC 20035-6268
Tel: (202)429-1203   *Fax:* (202)429-1102
Members: 26 chapters
Exec. Director: Will Duncan
President: William Lucy

Historical Note
Organized to bring more blacks into the labor movement.

Publications:
CBTU Bulletin. q.

Meetings/Conferences:
1999 – New Orleans, LA

Coalition of Higher Education Assistance Organizations (1980)
1101 Vermont Ave., N.W., Suite 400
Washington, DC 20005
Tel: (202)289-3910   *Fax:* (202)371-0197
Web Site: http://coheao.com
Members: 340 organizations
Annual Budget: $50-100,000
Exec. Director: Ellin Nolan

Historical Note
COHEAO members are colleges/universities, billers and collectors of student loans. Specialty conferences are held as necessary.

Publications:
Torch Newsletter. m.

Meetings/Conferences:
Semi-Annual Meetings: Annual/January and Mid-
      Year/August

Coalition of Labor Union Women (1974)
1126 16th St., N.W.
Washington, DC 20036
Tel: (202)466-4610   *Fax:* (202)776-0537
Web Site: http://www.cluw.org
Members: 210,000 individuals
Staff: 2
Annual Budget: $100-250,000
Exec. Director: Chrystl L. Bridgeforth

Historical Note
Founded in 1974 to work towards full equality of opportunities and rights for employed women. Members are women in the labor movement, and others interested in advancing the participation of women within unions. Concerned with such issues as labor law reform, passage of ERA, child care, safety in the workplace and pay equity. Membership: $25/year.

Publications:
CLUW News. bi-m.

Meetings/Conferences:
1999 – Chicago, IL/Sept. 2-5

Coalition of Publicly Traded Partnerships (1983)
805 15th St., N.W., Suite 500
Washington, DC 20005
Tel: (202)371-9770   *Fax:* (202)371-6601
Members: 20 companies
Staff: 2
Annual Budget: $100-250,000
President: Letitia Chambers
Tax Counsel: Mary Lyman

Historical Note
CPTP is a trade association representing publicly traded partnerships, corporations which are general partners of PTP's and attorneys, accountants and investment bankers who work with them. Sponsors and supports the Coalition of Publicly Traded Partnerships Political Action Committee. Membership: $15,000/year (large PTP's); $11,000 (small PTP's); $6,000/year (all others).

Meetings/Conferences:

Coalition of Service Industries (1982)
805 15th St., N.W., Suite 1110
Washington, DC 20005
Tel: (202)289-7460   *Fax:* (202)775-1726
E-Mail: csi@uscsi.org.net
Web Site: http://www.uscsi.org
Members: 65 companies
Staff: 7
Annual Budget: $250-500,000
President: J. Robert Vastine, Jr.
Director, Conferences: Bonnie Jessup
Program Director: Brian Cook

Historical Note
Promotes public awareness of the service industry in the U.S. Service industries include: health fields, accounting, banking, financial services, insurance, engineering, construction, communications, advertising, professional services and transportation. Membership: $3,000-$20,000/year.

Publications:
CSI Reports Newsletter. q.
Occasional Papers.
Professional Services World Update. q.
Service Economy. q.
World Services Gazette. a.

Meetings/Conferences:

Coated Abrasives Manufacturers' Institute (1933)
30200 Detroit Road
Cleveland, OH 44145-1967
Tel: (440)899-0010   *Fax:* (440)892-1404
Members: 5 companies
Staff: 2
Managing Director: J.J. Wherry

Historical Note
Members are individuals, partnerships or corporations that manufacture coated abrasives and coated abrasive products.

Meetings/Conferences:
1999 – Ft. Lauderdale, FL(Marriott Harbor Beach)/April 17-20
1999 – Cleveland, OH(Ritz Carlton)/Nov. 8-9

Coblentz Soc. (1954)

Historical Note
Address unknown in 1995.

Cocoa Merchants' Ass'n of America (1924)
26 Broadway, Suite 707
New York, NY 10004-1703
Tel: (212)363-7334   *Fax:* (212)363-7678
Members: 114 corporations
Annual Budget: $250-500,000
Exec. Director: Laurie Trimarchi

Historical Note
CMAA regular members are importing dealers of cocoa beans and cocoa products. Associate membership is available for chocolate manufacturers, merchants domiciled in foreign countries, domestic commission houses, service companies and government agencies. Has no paid staff. Membership: $750-$4,000/year (organization/company).

Publications:
Annual Report.

Meetings/Conferences:

Cognitive Science Soc. (1979)
Univ. of Michigan, 525 E. University
Ann Arbor, MI 48109-1109
Tel: (734)763-0210   *Fax:* (734)763-7480
E-Mail: cogsci@umich.edu
Web Site: http://www.umich.edu/~cogsci/

Members: 1,400 individuals
Annual Budget: $50-100,000
Exec. Officer: Colleen Seifert

Historical Note
Members are university and industrial researchers with doctorates. Has no paid officers or full-time staff. Membership: $55/year.

Publications:
Cognitive Science (Journal). q.
Conference Proceedings. a.

Meetings/Conferences:
1999 – Vancouver, BC, Canada
2000 – Philadelphia, PA

Coin Laundry Ass'n (1960)
1315 Butterfield Road, Suite 212
Downers Grove, IL 60515
Tel: (630)963-5547   *Fax:* (630)963-5864
E-Mail: info@coinlaundery.org
Web Site: http://www.coinlaundry.org
Members: 3,000 individuals
Staff: 8
Annual Budget: $1-2,000,000
Exec. Director: John Vassiliades
Dir., Communications: Brian Wallace
Director, Administration: Kathy Yolles
Deputy Exec. Director: George Pistona
Director, Membership and Meeting: Sue Lally
Editor: Maureen Knight

Historical Note
Established as the National Automatic Laundry and Cleaning Council, it assumed its present name in 1983. Members are self-service laundry and dry cleaning establishments together with manufacturers and distributors of the equipment, services and supplies they use. Membership: $175/year (individual); $550-6,500/year (company).

Publications:
CLA Journal. m. adv.
CLA Management Guidelines. m.
Manufacturer & Supply Directory. a. adv.

Meetings/Conferences:
Annual Meetings: Spring Trade Show/22,000
1999 – San Diego, CA(Doubletree Mission Valley)/Feb. 5-7

COLA
9881 Broken Land Pkwy., Suite 200
Columbia, MD 21046-1172
Tel: (410)381-6581   *Fax:* (410)381-8611
Toll Free: (800)981 - 9883
E-Mail: info@cola.org
Web Site: http://www.cola.org
Members: 7,500 individuals
Staff: 65
C.E.O.: Dr. J. Stephen Kroger
Corporate Communications Specialist: Julie A. Owings
Information Resource Center Supervisor\: Kenya Cousin

Historical Note
Formerly (1997) Commission on Office Laboratory Accreditation. Sponsors programs and services to support excellence in medicine and patient care.

Cold Finished Steel Bar Institute (1971)
700 14th St., N.W., Suite 900
Washington, DC 20005-2010
Tel: (202)508-1030   *Fax:* (202)508-1010
Members: 21 companies
Staff: 1
Annual Budget: $100-250,000
Admin. Secretary: Barbara N. Shoemaker

Meetings/Conferences:
Semi-annual Meetings: Washington, DC(Watergate)/June and
      November/50

Coleopterists Soc.
3294 Meadowview Road
Sacramento, CA 95832-1448
Tel: (916)262-1160   *Fax:* (916)262-1190
Web Site: http://www.nhm.ukan.edu/ksem/beetles/
Members: 570 individuals
Annual Budget: $25-50,000
Treasurer: Terry Seeno

Historical Note
A professional society organized exclusively for scientific and educational purposes, members are concerned with the study of living and fossil beetles. Membership: $30/year (individual); $50/year institutional subscription to Coleopterists Bulletin.

Publications:
Coleopterists Bulletin. q.

Meetings/Conferences:
Annual Meetings: December/with the Entomological Soc. of
      America

Collectibles and Platemakers Guild (1977)
77 E. Washington St., Suite 1507
Chicago, IL 60602-2902
Tel: (708)272-0028   *Fax:* (708)272-4388
Members: 80 companies
Staff: 1
Annual Budget: $25-50,000
Managing Director: Hunter Haines

Historical Note
Formerly (1988) the Collector Platemakers Guild. CPG is a trade associaiton of makers or importers of commemorative or limited edition plates who wish to encourage plate collecting as a hobby.

Publications:
Newsletter. m.

Meetings/Conferences:
Annual Meetings: July
1999 – Rosemont, IL(Convention Center)
2000 – Rosemont, IL(Convention Center)

Collector Car Appraisers Internat'l (1980)

24 Myrtle Avenue
Buffalo, NY 14204
Tel: (716)855-1931
Members: 25 individuals
Staff: 3
Annual Budget: $25-50,000
President: James T. Sandoro

Historical Note
Members are licensed and bonded individuals with at least ten years experience handling antique, classic, special interest collector cars, trucks, motorcycles, etc. Certifies members to act as expert witnesses in law suits and arbitration. Maintains a 3,740 volume library. Membership: $1,000/yr.

Publications:
Actual Cash Value, Car Guide. a.

Meetings/Conferences:

College and Universities Systems Exchange (1971)

Historical Note
See CAUSE.

College and University Computer Users Conference (1956)

Historical Note
See CUMREC.

College and University Personnel Ass'n (1946)

1233 20th St., N.W., Suite 301
Washington, DC 20036-1250
Tel: (202)429-0311   *Fax:* (202)429-0149
Web Site: http://www.cupa.org
Members: 1,750 individuals, 1,700 colleges and universities
Staff: 25
Annual Budget: $2-5,000,000
Exec. Director: Susan Jurow
Director, Communications: Audrey R. Rothstein
Director, Government Relations: Michael P. Aitken
Mgr., Member Development: Susan E. Cipollini
Director, Professional Development: Susan Reichbart
Director, Research: John Quinley

Historical Note
Members are colleges and universities united to improve the effectiveness of their human resource management. Membership: $140/year (individual); $205-1,013/year (organization, depending on budget).

Publications:
Administrative Compensation Survey. a.
CEO Survey.
CUPA Directory. a. adv.
CUPA News. semi-m. adv.
Faculty Salary Surveys. a.
The Journal of the College and University Personnel Ass'n. q. adv.

Meetings/Conferences:
Annual Meetings: Late Summer or early Fall/1,000
1999 – Seattle, WA(Westin)/Oct. 3-6
2000 – Nashville, TN(Opryland Hotel)/Oct. 22-25

College Art Ass'n (1911)

275 Seventh Ave., 18th Floor
New York, NY 10001-6708
Tel: (212)691-1051   *Fax:* (212)627-2381
E-Mail: nyoffice@collegeart.org
Members: 13,000 individuals
Staff: 17
Annual Budget: $2-5,000,000
Exec. Director: Susan Ball
Manager of Finance & Operations: Denise Mitchell
Membership Services Coordinator: Theresa Smyth
Director, Publications: Elaine Koss

Historical Note
Founded at the Cincinnati Art Museum in May, 1911 at a meeting of the Western Drawing and Manual Training Ass'n. A professional organization of art historians, studio artists and museum personnel united to improve the standards of art scholarship, art teaching and art history. Member of the American Council of Learned Socs., Nat'l Humanities Alliance, American Arts Alliance and the American Council on the Arts. Membership: $25-125/year (individual); $150/year (institution).

Publications:
Art Journal. q. adv.
CAA Newsletter. bi-m.
Position Listings. bi-m.
The Art Bulletin. q.

Meetings/Conferences:
Annual Meetings: Winter
1999 – Los Angeles, CA
2000 – New York, NY
2001 – Chicago, IL

College Athletic Business Management Ass'n (1951)

19009-398 Laurel Park Road
Rancho Dominguez, CA 90220-6066
Tel: (310)637-0560   *Fax:* (310)637-0560
Web Site: http://www.cabma.com
Members: 474 individuals, 530 individuals and institutions
Staff: 5
Annual Budget: $10-25,000
Secretary-Treasurer: Janet La Casse

Historical Note
Affiliated with Nat'l Collegiate Athletic Ass'n. Members are business and ticket managers, directors of athletics and their assistants, fundraisers, facilities managers, systems managers, and individuals performing similar duties under different titles. Has no paid staff. Membership: $90/year (individual), $270/year (institution).

Publications:
Convention Notes. a.

Meetings/Conferences:
Annual Meetings: January, with Nat'l Collegiate Athletic Ass'n
1999 – Tucson, AZ(Tucson Marriott)/Jan. 9-12/200

College Band Directors Nat'l Ass'n (1941)

823 Congress Ave., Suite 1300
Austin, TX 78701
Tel: (512)479-0425   *Fax:* (512)495-9031
Members: 1000 individuals
Annual Budget: $25-50,000
Exec. Director: Michael T. Marks

Historical Note
Membership: $40/year.

Publications:
Journal. semi-a.
Newsletter. q.

Meetings/Conferences:
1997: Odd years

College English Ass'n (1939)

English Department
Winthrop University
Rock Hill, SC 29733
Tel: (803)323-4633   *Fax:* (803)323-4837
E-Mail: wilcoxe@winthrop.edu
Web Site: http://www.winthrop.edu
Members: 1,200 individuals, 325 libraries
Staff: 6
Annual Budget: $25-50,000
Exec. Director: Earl Wilcox, Ph.D.

Historical Note
Concerned with practical applications of scholarship to teaching English literature and language at the college level. Membership: $30/year (individual); $30/year (institution).

Publications:
The CEA Critic. 3/year.
The CEA Forum. bi-a. adv.

Meetings/Conferences:
Annual Meetings: April
1999 – Philadelphia, PA/April 2-5

College Football Ass'n (1977)

Historical Note
Ceased operation in 1997.

College Fraternity Editors Ass'n (1923)

P.O. Box 6277
Oxford, OH 45056
Tel: (513)523-7591   *Fax:* (513)523-2381
Web Site: http://www.cfea.org
Members: 100 fraternities and sororities
Annual Budget: $10-25,000
President: Judy Hare Thorne

Historical Note
Organized December 1, 1923 in New York City. Membership consists of full-time editors of fraternity magazines. Officers change annually in July.

Publications:
CFEA Directory. a.
The Editor's Edition. 3/yr.
The Fraternity Editor. q.

Meetings/Conferences:
Annual Meetings: Summer
1999 – Tampa, FL/July 8-10

College Gynmastics Ass'n (1950)

Historical Note
Address unknown in 1996.

College Language Ass'n (1937)

Clark Atlanta University
Fair St. & J.P. Brawley Dr., S.W.
Atlanta, GA 30314
Tel: (404)880-8524
Members: 700 individuals
Annual Budget: $10-25,000
Secretary: Lucy Grigsby

Historical Note
Established as the Ass'n of Language Teachers in Negro Colleges, it assumed its present name in 1949. An "allied" organization of the Modern Language Ass'n, the Nat'l Council of Teachers of English and the Conference on College Composition and Communications. Has no paid staff. Membership: $35/year (individual), $100/year (insitution).

Publications:
CLA Journal. q. adv.

Meetings/Conferences:
Annual Meetings: April

College Media Advisers (1954)

University of Memphis, MJ-300
Dept. of Journalism
Memphis, TN 38152
Tel: (901)678-2403   *Fax:* (901)678-4798
Members: 750 individuals
Staff: 2
Annual Budget: $50-100,000
Exec. Director: Ronald E. Spielberger

Historical Note
Established as the Nat'l Council of College Publication Advisors, it assumed its present name in 1983 to reflect the growing importance of electronic media. Members are advisers to college student newspapers, yearbooks, magazines, radio and TV stations. Membership: $60/year.

Publications:
CMA Newsletter. m.
College Media Review. q. adv.

Meetings/Conferences:
Semi-annual Meetings: Mid-March in New York City and Fall
1999 – New York, NY/March 17-20
1999 – Atlanta, GA/Nov. 3-7
2000 – New York, NY/March 15-18
2000 – Washington, DC/Nov. 8-12

College Music Soc. (1958)

202 W. Spruce St.
Missoula, MT 59802-4202
Tel: (406)721-9616   *Fax:* (406)721-9419
Members: 6,500 individuals
Staff: 8
Annual Budget: $500-1,000,000
Exec. Director: Robby D. Gunstream
Director, Meetings: Tod Trimble

Historical Note
CMS members are college teachers of music. CMS is a professional consortium of college, conservatory and university faculty dedicated to gathering, considering and disseminating ideas on the philosophy and practice of music as an integral part of higher education, and to developing and increasing communication among the various disciplines of music. Membership: $65/year (individual).

Publications:
CMS Newsletter. bi-m. adv.
CMS Reports. irreg.
College Music Symposium. a. adv.
Directory of Music Faculties. a.
Monographs and Bibliographies in American Music. irreg.
Music Vacancy List. w.

Meetings/Conferences:
Annual Meetings: Fall
1999 – Denver, Co(Hyatt Regency)/Oct. 14-17/350
2000 – Toronto, Canada(Sheridan)/Nov. 2-5/2500

College of American Pathologists (1947)

325 Waukegan Road
Northfield, IL 60093-2719
Tel: (847)832-7000   *Fax:* (847)446-5011
E-Mail: lvanbre@cap.org
Web Site: http://www.cap.org
Members: 15,600 individuals
Staff: 356
Annual Budget: $50-100,000,000
Exec. V President: Lee VanBremen, Ph.D.,CAE
V. President, Communications/Marketing: Sandra Orcar
Director, Education and Meetings: Margaret Maczulski
V.P., Finance & Administrative Svcs.: Terry Sidlow
V. President, Member Services: Pamela M. Cramer, CAE
Manager, Publications: Joe Schramm
V. President, Div. of Laboratory Improvement: Dana Procsal, Ph.D.
Director, Governance Services: Elizabeth Cramer
V. President, Division of Information Services: C. Roger Brooks

Historical Note
Founded and incorporated May 14, 1947. Fellowship is restricted to pathologists certified by the American Board of Pathology. Has an annual budget of approximately $75 million. Membership: $250/year.

Publications:
CAP Today. m. adv.

Meetings/Conferences:
Semi-Annual Meetings: Spring and Fall with American Soc. of Clinical Pathologists
1999 – Lake Buena Vista, FL(Dolphin)
1999 – New Orleans, LA(Marriott)

College of Diplomates of the American Board of Orthodontics (1979)

427 Kenwood Ave.
Delmar, NY 12054-1805
Tel: (518)439-0981   *Fax:* (518)439-0980
Members: 1,800 individuals
Staff: 1
Annual Budget: $50-100,000
Management Exec.: Elizabeth V. Matterson

Historical Note
Limited to diplomates of the American Board of Orthodontics. Promotes continuing education and certification among orthodontists. Membership: $50/yr.

Publications:
Newsletter. semi-a.

Meetings/Conferences:
Annual Meetings: July

College of Optometrists in Vision Development (1970)

243 N. Lindbergh Blvd.
St. Louis, MO 63141-7851
Tel: (314)991-4007   *Fax:* (314)991-1167
Toll Free: (888)268 - 3770
Web Site: http://www.covd.org
Members: 1,593 individuals
Staff: 3
Annual Budget: $250-500,000
Exec. Director: Stephen C. Miller, O.D.

Historical Note
Optometrists concerned with vision therapy, particularly in the area of learning-related vision problems and visual information processing problems. Affiliated with the American Optometric Ass'n. Formed by a merger of the Nat'l Optometric Soc. for Developmental Vision Care, the Nat'l Soc. for Vision and Perception Training and the Southwest Developmental Vision Soc.

Publications:
Journal of Optometric Vision Development. q. adv.

Meetings/Conferences:
Annual Meetings: Fall

College of Osteopathic Healthcare Executives (1954)
5550 Friendship Blvd., Suite 300
Chevy Chase, MD 20815
Tel: (301)968-2642
Members: 150 individuals
Staff: 15
Annual Budget: $100-250,000
Coordinator of Meetings and Memberships: Debra Scheinberg

Historical Note
COHE provides continuing education for executives of osteopathic health care facilities to ensure their professional excellence. It also certifies their levels of educational achievement. Administrative support provided by American Osteopathic Healthcare Ass'n.

Publications:
Annual Report and Directory. a.
COHE Notes.

Meetings/Conferences:
Annual Meetings: Spring/250-350

College Placement Council (1956)

Historical Note
Became the Nat'l Ass'n of Colleges and Employers in 1995.

College Reading and Learning Ass'n (1967)
The Learning Center
University of Nebraska
Kearney, NE 68849
Tel: (308)865-8214
Members: 1000 individuals
Annual Budget: $25-50,000
President: Kathy Carpenter

Historical Note
Formerly Western College Reading Ass'n and Western College Reading and Learning Ass'n. CRLA members are educators involved in college and adult literacy and learning programs.

Publications:
CRLA Newsletter. q.
Journal of College Reading & Learning. semi-a.

Meetings/Conferences:

College Savings Plans Network
c/o Nat'l Ass'n of State Treasurers
2760 Research Park Drive
Lexington, KY 40578-1910
Tel: (606)244-8175   *Fax:* (606)244-8053
E-Mail: nast@csg.org
Web Site: http://www.collegesavings.org
Annual Budget: $10-25,000
Director: Pamela Taylor
Manager, Research and Publications: Kathy Tyson

Historical Note
CSPN members are state government officials who manage higher education tuition savings programs. Membership: $500-$1,000/year.

Publications:
Special Report on State College Savings Plans. a.

Meetings/Conferences:
1999 – Portland, OR(Hilton)

College Sports Information Directors of America (1957)
Campus Box 114-A, Texas A&M Univ.
Kingsville, TX 78363
Tel: (512)593-3908   *Fax:* (512)592-0389
Members: 1,800 individuals
Annual Budget: $25-50,000
Secretary: Fred Nuesch

Historical Note
Originally a section of the American College Public Relations Ass'n. Became independent in 1957. Selects Academic All-American teams in football, basketball, baseball, volleyball, and softball and a post-graduate scholarship.

Publications:
CoSIDA Digest. m. adv.
CoSIDA Directory. a. adv.

Meetings/Conferences:
Annual Meetings: Summer
1999 – Orlando, FL(Marriott)

College Swimming Coaches Ass'n of America (1922)
3077 Nichols Hwy.
Galizants Ferry, SC 29544
Tel: (843)358-0145   *Fax:* (843)358-0154
E-Mail: fin@sccoast.net
Web Site: http://www.users.sccoast.net.fin/cscaa.html
Members: 850 individuals
Staff: 3
Annual Budget: $100-250,000
Exec. Director: G. Robert Boettner

Historical Note
Chartered in the State of Florida, September 14, 1967. Officers rotate trienially. Membership: $50-100/year.

Publications:
CSCAA Newsletter. bi-m. adv.
Top Teams Poll. bi-m. adv.
Top Times Listing. bi-m. adv.

Meetings/Conferences:
Annual Meetings: September

College Theology Soc. (1954)
Box 5150
Saint Mary's College of California
Moraga, CA 94575
Tel: (510)631-4403   *Fax:* (510)631-9510
E-Mail: adoval@stmarys-ca.edu
Members: 850 individuals
Staff: 1

Annual Budget: $25-50,000
Secretary: Alexis Doval

Historical Note
Formerly (1967) Soc. of Catholic College Teachers of Sacred Doctrine. Member of the Council on the Study of Religion. Members are devoted to the study and the teaching of religion. Membership: $30 (Joint professional); $25 (Full professional).

Publications:
Horizons: The Journal of the College Theology Society. semi-a. adv.
Trade Book. a.

Meetings/Conferences:
Annual Meetings: Summer
1999 – De Pere, WI(St. Norbert Cull)/June 3-6/200

Collegiate Commissioners Ass'n (1939)
28th Floor
2201 Stemmons Fwy.
Dallas, TX 75207
Tel: (510)932-4411   *Fax:* (510)932-4601
Members: 32 individuals
Annual Budget: $50-100,000
Secretary-Treasurer: Britton Banowsky

Historical Note
Members are commissioners and staffs of the major collegiate athletic conferences of the U.S. Founded as the National Association of Football Commissioners, it became the National Association of Collegiate Commissioners in 1948 and assumed its present name in 1965. Publishes a number of annual handbooks for officials. Has no paid staff or permanent headquarters. Membership fee: $500/year.

Publications:
Basketball Officials' Manual. a.
Basketball Officials' Manual for 2 and 3-Man Crews. a.
Basketball Officials' Manual for 3-Man Crew. a.
Collegiate Commissioners Ass'n Directory. a.
Football Officials' Manual for 4-Man Crew. a.
Football Officials' Manual for 5-Man Crew. a.
Football Officials' Manual for 6-Man Crew. a.
Football Officials' Manual for 7-Man Crew. a.
Football Rules Illustrated for Coaches, Players and Fans. a.
Manual of Football Officiating. a.

Colombian American Ass'n (1927)
150 Nassau St.
Room 2015
New York, NY 10038
Tel: (212)233-7776   *Fax:* (212)233-7779
Members: 100 individuals, 55 companies
Staff: 3
Annual Budget: $25-50,000
Treasurer: Paul E. Calvet

Historical Note
Seeks to facilitate commerce and trade between the Republic of Colombia and the United States, to foster and advance cultural relations and good will between the two nations, and to encourage safe and sound investments. Membership: $250/year (individual), $500/year (corporate), $850/year (supporting).

Publications:
Colombian Newsletter. m.

Color Ass'n of the United States (1915)
409 W. 44th St.
New York, NY 10036-4402
Tel: (212)582-6884   *Fax:* (212)757-4557
Web Site: http://www.colorassociation.com
Members: 1000 companies
Staff: 8
Annual Budget: $100-250,000
Exec. Director: Marielle Bancou
Assoc. Director: Margaret Walch
Director, Membership: Karyn Valino

Historical Note
Formerly (1954) The Textile Color Card Ass'n of the U.S., Inc. The Color Ass'n or the US (CAUS), is an internat'l organization that represents leaders in every branch of fashion, textiles, design industries and general trade in which color is a factor. The ass'n serves as the authority and arbiter of commercial colors in the US. Membership: $325/year (individual); $675/year (company).

Publications:
CAUS Color Design/Newsletter. m.
Seasonal Color Forecasts. bi-a.
Standard Color Reference of America. Every 10 yrs.
Trend Reports.

Meetings/Conferences:
Annual Meetings: New York,NY

Color Marketing Group (1962)
5904 Richmond Hwy., Suite 408
Alexandria, VA 22303-1864
Tel: (703)329-8500   *Fax:* (703)329-0155
Web Site: http://www.colormarketing.org
Members: 1,500 individuals
Staff: 8
Annual Budget: $1-2,000,000
Exec. Director: Nancy A. Burns, CAE
Dir., Mktg./Communications: Lexy Bodreau

Historical Note
Membership: $650/year.

Meetings/Conferences:
Semi-Annual Meetings: Spring and Fall
1999 – Chicago, IL(Palmer House)/Apr. 18-20
1999 – Palm Springs, CA(Esmeralda Hotel)/Oct. 24-26

Color Pigments Manufacturers Ass'n (1922)
300 N. Washington St., Suite 102
Alexandria, VA 22314
Tel: (703)684-4044   *Fax:* (703)684-1795
Members: 60 companies

Staff: 5
Annual Budget: $500-1,000,000
President: J. Lawrence Robinson, CAE

Historical Note
Formerly (1993) the Dry Color Manufacturers Ass'n. Manufacturers of organic and inorganic color pigments.

Publications:
Newsletter. m.

Meetings/Conferences:
Annual Meetings: White Sulphur Springs, WV/June

Colorado Ranger Horse Ass'n (1938)
R.D. #1, Box 1290
Wampum, PA 16157-9610
Tel: (724)535-4841
E-Mail: crha@telisphere.com
Members: 2,700 individuals
Staff: 1
Annual Budget: under $10,000
Exec. Secretary: Laurel Kosior

Historical Note
Members are owners, breeders and enthusiasts of Colorado Ranger horses. Records and registers horses that can trace unbroken and direct descent from one of two foundation sires, Patches 1 and Max 2. Membership: $20/year (new member), $15/year (renewal).

Publications:
CRHA Bloodhorse.
CRHA Brochure. irreg.
Rangerbred News. 6-10/year. adv.

Meetings/Conferences:
Annual Meetings: September

Columbia Sheep Breeders Ass'n of America (1942)
Box 272
Upper Sandusky, OH 43351
Tel: (614)482-2608
Members: 1000 individuals
Staff: 1
Annual Budget: $50-100,000
Office Manager: Phyllis Gerber

Historical Note
Breeders and fanciers of Columbia sheep. Member of the Nat'l Soc. of Livestock Record Ass'ns.

Publications:
Speaking of Columbias. m. adv.

Meetings/Conferences:

Combustion Institute (1954)
5001 Baum Blvd., Suite 635
Pittsburgh, PA 15213-1851
Tel: (412)687-1366   *Fax:* (412)687-0340
Members: 4,000 individuals
Staff: 2
Exec. Secretary: Sue Terpack

Historical Note
An international organization with sections in several foreign countries, including Canada. Absorbed the Standing Committee on Combustion Symposia in 1954. The Institute is a non-profit, educational organization with the purpose of promoting and disseminating, knowledge in the field of combustion science.

Publications:
Combustion and Flame. m.
Proceedings. bien.

Meetings/Conferences:
Biennial Meetings: even years
2000 – Edinburgh, Scotland/July 30-Aug. 4

Comedy Writers and Performers Ass'n (1977)
P.O. Box 23304
Brooklyn, NY 11202-3304
Tel: (718)855-5057
Annual Budget: under $10,000
Director: Robert Makinson

Historical Note
Formerly Comedy Writers Ass'n (1996). Membership open to anyone who can create comedy and market it. Membership: $24/year.

Publications:
Being a Comedian. (booklet.
Comedy Buyer's Bulletin. a.
Comedy Writer's Bulletin. a.
Comedy Writers Ass'n Newsletter. q.
Humor & Public Speaking. (booklet.
Latest Jokes. m.

Meetings/Conferences:
Annual Meetings: New York, NY(Rehearsal Studio)

Comics Magazine Ass'n of America (1954)
355 Lexington Ave., 17th Floor
New York, NY 10017-6603
Tel: (212)661-4261   *Fax:* (212)370-9047
E-Mail: AssocMgmt@aol.com
Members: 10 companies
Annual Budget: $50-100,000
Exec. Director: Holly J. Munter-Koenig

Historical Note
Sponsors the Comics Code Authority, an agency for pre-publication evaluation of all editorial and advertising matter appearing in comic books.

Meetings/Conferences:
Annual Meetings: Winter in New York, NY

Commercial Development Ass'n (1943)
1850 M St., N.W., Suite 700
Washington, DC 20036
Tel: (202)721-4110   *Fax:* (202)296-8120
E-Mail: info@commercialdevelopment.com

Web Site: http://www.commercialdevelopment.com
Members: 750 individuals
Staff: 2
Annual Budget: $100-250,000
Exec. Director: Jack Murray
Operations Manager: Caroline McLean

Historical Note
Formerly (1970) Commercial Chemical Development Ass'n. CDA represents the chemical and allied industries and is dedicated to improving the commerical development process. The association advances commercial development skills at the managerial level through education, professional meetings, sharing of best practices and networking. It also strives to maximize success associated with bringing new products and technologies to market. Membership: $185/year.

Publications:
CDAdvisor. q.

Meetings/Conferences:
Semi-annual Meetings: March/200 and October/200
1999 – Hilton Head, SC(Hyatt)/Oct. 10-13/150
1999 – Boston, MA(Westin)/March 21-24/150
2000 – Philadelphia, PA(Sheraton Society
        Hill)/March 12-15/150
2000 – Panama City, FL(Marriott)/Oct. 15-18/150
2001 – Philadelphia, PA(Sheraton Society
        Hill)/March 18-21/150

Commercial Finance Ass'n (1943)
225 West 34th St., Suite 1815
New York, NY 10122
Tel: (212)594-3490   Fax: (212)564-6053
Web Site: http://www.cfa.comm
Members: 312 banks & commercial institutions
Staff: 12
Annual Budget: $2-5,000,000
Exec. Director & Secretary: Leonard Machlis
Deputy Exec. Director: Bruce H. Jones
Government Relations Director: Bryan Cove
Education Director: Michael Keller
Chapter/Membership Coordinator: Betty Ann Pillsworth

Historical Note
Founded as the Nat'l Conference of Commercial Receivable Companies, it became the Nat'l Commercial Finance Conference in 1953, the Nat'l Commercial Finance Ass'n in 1983, and assumed its present name in 1991. Members are banks and commercial finance and factoring companies. Membership: $1,500-6,000/year (organization).

Publications:
Compendium of Commercial Finance Law. a.
Secured Lender. bi-m. adv.

Meetings/Conferences:
Annual Meetings: Fall/1,400
1999 – Toronto, Ontario, Canada(Sheraton)/Nov. 3-5/1500
2000 – New Orleans, LA(Hilton)/Oct. 18-20/1500

Commercial Food Equipment Service Ass'n (1963)
9247 North Meridian St., Suite 216
Indianapolis, IN 46260
Tel: (317)844-4700   Fax: (317)844-4745
Members: 200 companies
Staff: 3
Annual Budget: $100-250,000
Exec. Director: Carla M. Helm

Historical Note
Members are companies with a minimum of three years experience servicing or repairing food preparation equipment for hotels, restaurants or institutions.

Publications:
Directory. a.
Newsletter. bi-m.

Meetings/Conferences:
Semi-annual Meetings: May and September

Commercial Internet Exchange Ass'n (1991)
1041 Sterling Road, Suite 104-A
Herndon, VA 20170
Tel: (703)709-8200   Fax: (703)709-5249
E-Mail: helpdesk@cix.org
Web Site: http://www.cix.org
Members: 160 companies
Annual Budget: $1-2,000,000
President: Barbara A. Dooley

Historical Note
The Commercial Internet Exchange Ass'n is a non-profit, 501(c)6 trade ass'n of Public Data Internetwork service providers promoting and encouraging development of the public data communications internetworking services industry in both nat'l and internat'l markets. CIX members are organizations which offer TCP/IP or OSI data internetworking to the general public.

Publications:
Cixtra. m.

Meetings/Conferences:

Commercial Law League of America (1895)
150 N. Michigan Ave., Suite 600
Chicago, IL 60601
Tel: (312)781-2000   Fax: (312)782-2010
Toll Free: (800)978 - 2552
E-Mail: clla@clla.org
Web Site: http://www.clla.org
Members: 5,000 individuals
Staff: 10
Annual Budget: $1-2,000,000
Exec. V. President: Max G. Moses
Meetings Planner: Katie Munley
Director of Membership & Marketing: Mark V. Matz

Historical Note
CLLA members are commercial and bankruptcy law professionals. Participates with the American Board of Certification (Alexandria,

VA), which certifies attorneys specializing in bankruptcy and creditors' rights law. Membership: $195/year.

Publications:
Bankruptcy & Insolvency Section Newsletter. m.
Commercial Law Bulletin. bi-m. adv.
Commercial Law Journal. q. adv.

Meetings/Conferences:
Annual Meetings: July/600-800
1999 – Mont Tremblant, Quebec(Chateau Mont
        Tremblant)/500
2000 – Monterey, CA(Hyatt Monterey)/500

Commercial Real Estate Women

Historical Note
See Nat'l Network of Commercial Real Estate Women.

Commercial Refrigerator Manufacturers Ass'n (1933)
1200 19th St., N.W., Suite 300
Washington, DC 20036-2422
Tel: (202)857-1145   Fax: (202)223-4579
E-Mail: sharon_butalla@dc.sba.com
Members: 44 companies
Staff: 3
Exec. Director: Sharon Butalla

Historical Note
Members include individuals and corporations who manufacture commercial refrigerators for sale in the U.S. and industry suppliers. Membership fee is determined by company's sales volume.

Publications:
CRMA Voluntary Standards.

Meetings/Conferences:
Semi-Annual Meetings: January and June

Commercial Travelers Ass'n (1993)
P.O. Box 9
Glasgow, KY 42142-0009
Tel: (502)651-9362   Fax: (502)651-9142
Toll Free: (800)378 - 4400
E-Mail: cta@ctrav.org
Web Site: http://www.ctrav.org
Members: 21,000 individuals
President: James P. Haynes

Historical Note
Founded in 1993 to form political base for business travelers.

Publications:
Fax Broadcasts. m.
Newsletter. q.

Commercial Vehicle Safety Alliance (1982)
5430 Grosvenor Lane, Suite 130
Bethesda, MD 20814-2142
Tel: (301)564-1623   Fax: (301)564-0588
E-Mail: cvsahq@aol.com
Web Site: http://www.cvsahq.org
Members: 67 agencies
Staff: 7
Annual Budget: $500-1,000,000
Exec. Director: William R. Fiste
Director of Administration: Larry D. Stern

Historical Note
Members are state, territorial and provincial agencies responsible for motor vehicle safety enforcement in the U.S., Canada and Mexico. Membership: $500/year (trucking and bus companies and safety supplier), $700/year (organization), $3,750/year (state/province).

Publications:
The Guardian. bi-m.

Meetings/Conferences:

Commercial Weather Services Ass'n (1987)
1600 Duke St., Suite 220
Alexandria, VA 22314
Tel: (703)519-0390   Fax: (703)519-1807
E-Mail: CWSA@wpa.org
Web Site: http://www.weather-industry.org
Members: 43 companies
Staff: 2
Annual Budget: $25-50,000
Exec. Director: Jeffrey C. Smith
Director, Government Relations: Amy Taylor
Program Director: Laura Norfolk

Historical Note
Formerly the Ass'n of Private Weather Related Companies, CWSA adopted its present name in 1989. Established in Washington, DC, CWSA is the national trade association for the private weather services industry. Membership: based on number of employees.

Publications:
CWSA Washington Report. m.

Meetings/Conferences:
1999 – Washington, DC(Capital Hill Club)/50

Commercial-Investment Real Estate Institute (1950)
430 N. Michigan Ave., Suite 800
Chicago, IL 60611-4092
Tel: (312)321-4460   Fax: (312)321-4530
Toll Free: (800)621 - 7027
Web Site: http://www.ccim.com
Members: 10,000 individuals
Staff: 40
Annual Budget: $5-10,000,000
Exec. V. President: Susan J. Groeneveld, CAE
Public Relations Director: R.J. Sirois
Director, Education Marketing: Ann M. Pellegrini

Historical Note
An affiliate of the Nat'l Ass'n of Realtors; incorporated in Chicago in 1967. CIREI functions as a professional association of real estate practitioners who have successfully completed its certification program or are striving toward it. Awards Certified Commercial-

Investment Member (CCIM) designation upon completion of its curriculum. Membership: $300/year (designees), $200/year (candidates). Has an annual budget of approximately $6 million.

Publications:
CCIM Red Book. a. adv.
CCIM/Landauer Investment Trends Quarterly. q.
Commercial Investment Real Estate Journal. bi-m. adv.

Meetings/Conferences:

Commerical Real Estate Secondary Market and Securitization Ass'n (1993)
11050 Roe Ave., Suite 200
Overland Park, KS 66211-1216
Tel: (913)339-6330   Fax: (913)339-6338
E-Mail: administrator@cssacmbs.org
Web Site: http://www.cssacmbs.org
President: Stacey N. Berger

Historical Note
The organization represents and promotes an orderly and ethical global institutional secondary market for the sale of commerical mortage loans and equity investments.

Commission of Accredited Truck Driving Schools (1987)
1725 Duke St., Suite 600
Alexandria, VA 22314-3457
Tel: (703)549-0124   Fax: (703)299-9115
E-Mail: cataldo2ix@netcom.com
Members: 20 schools
Staff: 2
Exec. Director: Carol Cataldo

Publications:
CATDS Scan Newsletter. m.
Report to Members. m.

Commission on Accreditation for Law Enforcement Agencies (1979)
10306 Eaton Place, Suite 320
Fairfax, VA 22030-2201
Tel: (703)352-4225   Fax: (703)591-2206
Toll Free: (800)368 - 3757
E-Mail: calea@calea.org
Web Site: http://www.calea.org
Members: 800 law enforcement agencies
Staff: 12
Annual Budget: $2-5,000,000
Exec. Director: Richard F. Kitterman, Jr.
Manager, Administrative Services: Antonio T. Beatty

Historical Note
Membership fee varies, based on size of agency.

Publications:
Commission Update. irreg.
Standards for Law Enforcement Agencies. irreg.

Meetings/Conferences:
Tri-annual Meetings: March, July and November
1999 – Denver, CO/March 17-20
1999 – Montreal, CN
1999 – Atlanta, GA

Commission on Accreditation of Allied Health Education Programs (1994)
35 E. Wacker Drive, Suite 1970
Chicago, IL 60601-2208
Tel: (312)553-9355   Fax: (312)553-9616
E-Mail: caahep@caahep.org
Web Site: http://caahep.org
Members: 70 health programs
Staff: 4
Annual Budget: $500-1,000,000
Exec. Director: Kathleen Megivern
Communications Editor: Wendi A. Williams

Historical Note
CAAHEP is the national accrediting agency for health programs in 18 occupations. Formerly (1994) the Committee on Allied Health Education and Accreditation. Membership: $300/year (individual); $3,000/year (institution).

Publications:
Communique. m.

Meetings/Conferences:
1999 – /April 23-24
2000 – /April 21-22

Commission on Certification of Work Adjustment and Vocational Evaluation Specialists (1981)
1444 I St., N.W., Suite 700
Washington, DC 20005-2210
Tel: (202)466-7444
Web Site: http://cewaves.org
Members: 2,000 individuals
Staff: 1
Annual Budget: $50-100,000
Exec. Director: Ramon A. Estrada

Historical Note
CCWAVES offers qualified candidates the opportunity to obtain certification in vocational evaluation. The primary purpose of this certification is to provide assurances that those professionals engaged in vocational evaluation can meet acceptable standards of quality to service the best interests of clients, other practitioners, individuals in allied professions and the public.

Publications:
Wavelengths. q.

Meetings/Conferences:

Commission on Office Laboratory Accreditation (1988)

Historical Note
Became COLA in 1997.

Commission on Professionals in Science and Technology (1953)
1200 New York Ave., N.W., Suite 390
Washington, DC 20005
Tel: (202)326-7080   *Fax:* (202)842-1603
Web Site: http://www.cpst.org
Members: 700 individuals, 40 corporate, 20 societies
Staff: 2
Annual Budget: $250-500,000
Exec. Director: Catherine D. Gaddy

Historical Note
Formerly (1986) Scientific Manpower Commission. A private non-profit corporation formed by 14 scientific societies to provide data on the education and employment of scientists and engineers. Concerned with the recruitment, training and utilization of scientific personnel. Membership: $85/year (individual associate); $600/year (society); $700/year (corporate).

Publications:
CPST Comments. 8/year.
Preparing for 21st Century: Human Resources in Science & Technology.
Professional Women & Minorities: A Manpower Data Resource Service. a.
Salaries of Scientists, Engineers & Technicians. a.

Meetings/Conferences:
Commissioners' Meetings: May and November/Washington, DC

Commission on Recognition of Postsecondary Accreditation

Historical Note
Dissolved in 1996. Succeeded by the Council for Higher Education Accreditation in 1997.

Commissioned Officers Ass'n of the United States Public Health Service (1947)
8201 Corporate Dr., Suite 560
Landover, MD 20785
Tel: (301)731-9080   *Fax:* (301)731-9084
E-Mail: mikecoa@aol.com
Web Site: http://www.coausphs.org
Members: 7,000 individuals
Staff: 5
Annual Budget: $250-500,000
Exec. Director: Cmdr. Michael W. Lord, USN (Ret)
Director of Administration: Lucille Clay

Historical Note
Membership: $60/year.

Publications:
C. O.
Proceedings Program. a. adv.

Meetings/Conferences:
1999 – Alexandria, VA(Radisson Plaza)/June 5-9

Committee for Private Offshore Rescue and Towing (C-PORT) (1987)
1600 Duke St., Suite 220
Alexandria, VA 22314
Tel: (703)519-1713   *Fax:* (703)519-1716
E-Mail: c-port@c-port.org
Web Site: http://www.c-port.org
Members: 160 companies
Staff: 2
Annual Budget: $50-100,000
Exec. Director: Jeffrey C. Smith
Director, Government Relations: Amy Taylor
Programs Director: Laura Norfolk

Historical Note
Established in Washington, DC, C-PORT is the trade association for the small boat towing and salvage industry. C-PORT administers the ACAPT Industry Certification Program. Membership: $300/year minimum.

Publications:
C-PORT News. m.

Meetings/Conferences:
1999 – Miami, FL(DoubleTree Biscayne Bay)/Feb. 8-10

Committee of 200 (1982)
625 N. Michigan Ave., Suite 500
Chicago, IL 60611-3108
Tel: (312)751-3477   *Fax:* (312)943-9401
Web Site: http://www.c200.org
Members: 370 individuals
Staff: 3
Annual Budget: $500-1,000,000
President: Anna K. Lloyd
Director of Programs and Communications: Amy White
Director, Membership and Educational Programs: Lauren Herho
Business Manager: Melissa Knepp

Historical Note
C200 is an international organization of leading business women. Three-quarters of members are entrepreneurs, most others are senior executives of major corporations. Members are a diverse group drawn from across the spectrum of business and industry. Encourages entrepreneurship and seeks to promote women in executive positions. Membership: $1,200/year (individual).

Publications:
Network. m.
Update. semi-a.

Meetings/Conferences:
Semi-Annual Meetings: Spring and Fall/125

Committee of American Axle Producers
c/o Harris, Ellsworth & Levin
2600 Virginia Ave., NW, Watergate, #1113
Washington, DC 20037-1905
Tel: (202)337-8338   *Fax:* (202)337-6885

Counsel: Herbert E. Harris, II

Committee of Annuity Insurers
c/o Davis & Harmon
1455 Pennsylvania Ave., N.W., Suite 1200
Washington, DC 20004
Tel: (202)347-2230   *Fax:* (202)393-3310
E-Mail: cai@davis-harman.com
Web Site: http://www.annuity-insurers.org
Counsel: Joseph F. McKeever III

Committee of Domestic Steel Wire Rope and Specialty Cable Manufacturers
c/o Harris, Ellsworth & Levin
2600 Virginia Ave., NW, Watergate, #1113
Washington, DC 20037-1905   *Fax:* (202)337-6885
Counsel: Herbert E. Harris, II

Committee on Lesbian and Gay History (1979)
Human Studies, Alfred Univ.
Saxon Drive
Alfred, NY 14802
Tel: (607)871-2217
E-Mail: veaklor@bigvax.alfred.edu
Members: 350 individuals and organizations
Annual Budget: under $10,000
Co-Chair: Vicki Ealor

Historical Note
CLGH members are academics from a variety of disciplines and others with an interest in the study of homosexuality in the past and present. CLGH also seeks to prevent discrimination against gay and lesbian historians. Membership: $10/year (individual); $25/year (organization).

Publications:
CLGH Newsletter. 3x/year. adv.

Meetings/Conferences:
Annual Meetings: in conjunction with AHA annual meeting

Committee on State Taxation (1967)
122 C St., N.W., Suite 330
Washington, DC 20001
Tel: (202)484-5222   *Fax:* (202)484-5229
Web Site: http://www.statetax.org
Members: 400 multi state corporate taxpayers
Staff: 8
Annual Budget: $1-2,000,000
Exec. Director: J. William McArthur, Jr.
Tax Counsel: Kendall Houghton

Historical Note
Organized as an advisory committee to the Council of State Chambers of Commerce in 1967, COST became separately incorporated in in 1991. COST members are state and local tax officials of multistate and multinational corporate taxpayers. COST provides educational programs and government affairs representation for its members. Membership: $2,000/year.

Publications:
Judicial Report. m.
State Tax Report. m.

Meetings/Conferences:
Annual Meetings: Fall

Commodity Exchange (1933)

Historical Note
See New York Mercantile Exchange.

Communications Fraud Control Ass'n (1985)
3030 N. Central Ave., Suite 804
Phoenix, AZ 85012-2715
Tel: (602)265-2322   *Fax:* (602)265-1015
E-Mail: fraud@cfca.org
Members: 150 individuals, 150 companies
Staff: 4
Annual Budget: $250-500,000
Exec. Director: Frances Feld, CAE

Historical Note
CFCA represents companies and individuals in the telecommunications industry, and agencies and professionals involved in the investigation of telecommunications fraud. Membership: $50-150/year (individual); $600-1,800/year (company).

Publications:
CFCA Communicator. q.
Fraud Alert. w.

Meetings/Conferences:

Communications Managers Ass'n (1948)
1201 Mt. Kemble
Morristown, NJ 07960
Tel: (973)425-1400   *Fax:* (973)425-0777
Web Site: http://www.cma.org
Members: 800 individuals, 200 companies
Managing Director: Catherine Takacs

Publications:
Newsletter. q.

Meetings/Conferences:
1999 – New York, NY(Hilton)/Nov. 15-18

Communications Marketing Ass'n (1974)
2417 Aztec. Rd. N. E.
Albuquerque, NM 87107
Tel: (505)345-8674   *Fax:* (505)345-2812
Web Site: http://www.commktga.comforward/cma.htm
Members: 400 individuals
Staff: 1
Annual Budget: $25-50,000
President: Joe O'Connal

Historical Note
CMA members are independent manufacturers, independent sales representative firms and distributors of two-way mobile radio equipment.

Publications:
CMA Update Newsletter. q.

Meetings/Conferences:
Annual Meetings: November, 2 weeks before Thanksgiving
1999 – Dallas, TX(DFW Harvey Hotel)/Nov. 11-14

Communications Media Management Ass'n (1946)
Box 227
607 Arbor Ave.
Wheaton, IL 60189
Tel: (630)653-2772   *Fax:* (630)653-2882
E-Mail: cmma@cmma.net
Web Site: http://www.cmma.net
Members: 160 individuals
Staff: 1
Annual Budget: $50-100,000
Exec. Director: David W. Roe

Historical Note
Formerly (1980) known as the Industrial Audio-Visual Ass'n and (1994) Audio Visual Management Ass'n. It is a professional society of individuals managing comunications media departments in business and education. Membership: $275/year.

Publications:
CMMA Visions. q.

Meetings/Conferences:
Semi-Annual Meetings: Spring and Fall
1999 – Key Biscayne, FL/Oct. 30-Nov. 3/175
1999 – Cincinnati, OH(Royal Cincinnati)/May 8-11/100
2000 – Texas/100
2000 – Minneapolis, MN/175

Communications Research Council

Historical Note
Address unknown in 1995.

Communications Soc. (1952)

Historical Note
See IEEE Communications Soc.

Communications Supply Service Ass'n (1976)
5700 Murray St.
Little Rock, AR 72209
Tel: (501)562-7666   *Fax:* (501)562-7616
Web Site: www.cssa.net
Members: 258 companies
Staff: 27
Annual Budget: $5-10,000,000
President: Larry Hoagland

Historical Note
CSSA members are small independent telephone companies.

Publications:
Link. m.

Meetings/Conferences:
Annual Meetings: in conjunction with the Nat'l Telephone Cooperative Ass'n.

Communications Workers of America (1938)
501 Third St., N.W.
Washington, DC 20001-2797
Tel: (202)434-1100   *Fax:* (202)434-1139
Web Site: http://cwa-union.org
Members: 630,000 individuals
Staff: 600
Annual Budget: $50-100,000,000
President: Morton Bahr
Director, Public Affairs: Jeffrey M. Miller

Historical Note
Established in Chicago June 5, 1938 as the Nat'l Federation of Telephone Workers, it was named the Communications Workers of America in 1947; joined the Congress of Industrial Organizations in 1949 and merged with Telephone Workers Organizing Committee. Has a budget of approximately $65 million. Sponsors and supports the CWA-COPE Political Action Committee. Absorbed (1987) the Internat'l Typographical Union, (1990) United Telegraph Workers.

Publications:
CWA News. m.
CWA Newsletter. bi-w.
The Sector News. m. adv.

Meetings/Conferences:
Annual Meetings: Spring/4,000
1999 – Miami Beach, FL/July 12-14

Community Ass'ns Institute (1973)
1630 Duke St.
Alexandria, VA 22314
Tel: (703)548-8600   *Fax:* (703)684-1581
Web Site: http://www.caionline.org
Members: 16,000 firms and associations
Staff: 39
Annual Budget: $2-5,000,000
Exec. V. President: Barbara A. Keenan, CAE
Staff V.P., Communications/Mktg.: Deborah Bass
V.P., Govt./Public Affairs: Rodney D. Clark
V.P., Education: Cathy McCarty
Senior V. President: Doris Fee, CAE
V.P., Chapter Development/Services: Mark Robbins

Historical Note
Sponsored by the Nat'l Ass'n of Home Builders and the Urban Land Institute. Composed of community and condominium owners, builders and managers. Absorbed (1975) Nat'l Federation of Condominium Ass'ns and the Condominium Research and Education Soc. Membership: $50-265/year (home owner/associations), $315-550/year (professionals/firms).

Publications:
Common Ground Magazine. bi-m. adv.
Community Association Law Reporter. m.
Community Living of California. m.
Community Living of Florida. m. adv.
Community Management. bi-m.
Ledger Quarterly. q.

Meetings/Conferences:
Semi-annual Meetings: Spring and Fall
1999 – Denver, CO/May 16-21
1999 – Atlanta, GA/Oct. 24-29

Community Banking Advisory Network (1995)
111 E. Wacker Dr., Suite 990
Chicago, IL 60601
Tel: (312)729-9900   *Fax:* (312)729-9800
Toll Free: (800)869 - 0491
E-Mail: info@pencormazur.com
Web Site: http://www.cpaselect.com/cban
Members: 22 firms
Staff: 10
Exec. Director: George A. Buckley, Jr., CAE
Director of Communications: Michelle Durham

Historical Note
CBAN is an association of CPA firms that concentrate a substantial portion of their business on providing financial and consulting services to community banks.

Publications:
Community Banking Advisor. q.
Members' Bulletin. q.

Meetings/Conferences:
1999 – Las Vegas, NV/June 23-25

Community College Ass'n for Instruction and Technology (1971)
New Mexico Military Institute
101 W. College Blvd.
Roswell, NM 88201-5173
Tel: (505)624-8381   *Fax:* (505)624-8390
E-Mail: klopfer@yogi.nmmi.cc.nm.us
Members: 250 individuals
Annual Budget: under $10,000
President: Bruce McLaren
V. President: Jerry Klopfer

Historical Note
Members are instructional technology professionals working in community colleges. Membership: $10/year (individual); $20/year (institution).

Publications:
CCAIT Newsletter. q. adv.

Meetings/Conferences:
1999 – Houston, TX

Community College Business Officers
200 Norman Hall, Univ. of Florida
P.O. Box 117049L
Gainesville, FL 32611-7049
Tel: (352)392-0745   *Fax:* (352)392-3664
E-Mail: ccbo@coe.ufl.edu
Annual Budget: $50-100,000
Exec. Director: Dale F. Campbell
Membership Coordinator: Mike Petko

Historical Note
Membership: $200/year.

Publications:
Bottom Line.

Meetings/Conferences:
Annual Meetings: October-November

Community College Journalism Ass'n (1968)
3376 Hill Canyon Ave.
Thousand Oaks, CA 91360-1119
Tel: (805)492-4440   *Fax:* (805)492-9800
E-Mail: ames@robles.calluthern.edu
Members: 300 individuals
Annual Budget: under $10,000
Exec. Secretary-Treasurer: Steven Ames

Historical Note
Formerly the Junior College Journalism Ass'n, members are journalism instructors in community and junior colleges. Affiliated with the Ass'n for Education in Journalism. Membership: $35/year.

Publications:
Community College Journalist. q. adv.
Newsletter. q.

Meetings/Conferences:
Semi-annual Meetings: Aug. with AEJMC and Fall with CMA
1999 – New Orleans, LA/August 4-7

Community Colleges Humanities Ass'n (1979)
Essex County College
303 University Ave.
Newark, NJ 07102
Tel: (973)877-3577   *Fax:* (973)877-3578
E-Mail: bozecale@essex.edu
Web Site: http://www.ccha_asoc.org
Members: 850 individuals
Staff: 3
Annual Budget: $25-50,000
Exec. Director: David A. Berry

Historical Note
Members are administrators and humanities faculty from two-year colleges. Membership: $35/year (individual); $250-$850/year (institution).

Publications:
Community College Humanist. 3/year.
Community College Humanities Review Journal. a.

Meetings/Conferences:
Biennial Meetings: (1999)

Community Development Soc. (1969)
1123 North Water St.
Milwaukee, WI 53202
Tel: (414)276-7106   *Fax:* (414)276-7704
Members: 1000 individuals
Staff: 2
Annual Budget: $50-100,000
Acct. Executive: Lisa Betancourt

Historical Note
CDS members are academics and pratitioners in community development. Membership: $25/year (student); $55/year (individual); $200/year (organization/company).

Publications:
CDS Membership Directory. a.
Journal of the CDS. semi-a.
Practice Series. q.
Vanguard Newsletter. q.

Meetings/Conferences:

Community Development Venture Capital Ass'n (1995)
302 W. Superior St., Suite 700
Duluth, MN 55802
Tel: (218)725-6834   *Fax:* (218)725-6800
E-Mail: jburton@cdvca.org
Members: 47 corporations and organizations
Staff: 1
Administrator: Judy Burton

Historical Note
CDVCA is an alliance of venture capital funds, community development corporations, and other organizations dedicated to entreprenurial solutions to community development and long-term investment in economically disadvantaged areas. Acts as a source of information and technical assistance to members. Membership: $500/year.

Publications:
CDVCA Ventures. semi-a.

Meetings/Conferences:
Annual Meetings: Winter

Community Transportation Ass'n of America (1989)
1341 G St., N.W., Suite 600
Washington, DC 20005
Tel: (202)628-1480   *Fax:* (202)737-9197
Toll Free: (800)527 - 8279
Web Site: http://www.ctaa.org
Members: 100 individuals, 1,200 companies and systems
Staff: 20
Annual Budget: $2-5,000,000
Exec. Director: Dale Marsico
Communications Director: Scott Bogren
Financial Director: Donald Browner
Membership Director: Caryn Souza

Historical Note
CTAA is a professional association focusing on serving transit agencies in rural areas, small cities and wherever elderly, disabled or poor persons do not have access to conventional public transit. CTAA members include transit operators, human service agencies, consultants, industry suppliers and state officials. Membership: $100/year (individual); $200/year (organization); $125, plus $10/vehicle/year (transit system); $500/year (associate).

Publications:
Community Transportation Magazine. 9/year. adv.

Meetings/Conferences:
Annual Meetings: Spring
1999 – New Orleans, LA/May 23-28

Compact Loader Council
Historical Note
A council of the Equipment Manufacturers Institute.

Comparative and Internat'l Education Soc. (1956)
Institute of International Education
1400 K St., N.W.
Washington, DC 20005-2403
Tel: (202)326-7759   *Fax:* (202)326-7763
Members: 1,500 individuals, 1,500 institutions
Staff: 1
Annual Budget: $25-50,000
Secretary: Paige Baldwin

Historical Note
Formerly (1974) Comparative Education Soc. CIES members are comparative educators and others who work in the more applied areas of international education. Membership: $35/year (individual); $67/year (organization),; $20/year (students).

Publications:
CIES Newsletter. tri-a.
Comparative Education Review. q. adv.

Meetings/Conferences:
Annual Meetings: March

Competitive Telecommunications Ass'n (1981)
1900 M St., N.W., Suite 800
Washington, DC 20036-4001
Tel: (202)296-6650   *Fax:* (202)296-7585
Web Site: http://www.comptel.org
Members: 175 companies
Staff: 3
Annual Budget: $2-5,000,000
Exec. V.P. and General Counsel: Genevieve Morelli
Director, Communications: Jennifer H. Christie
V. President, Legislative and Regulatory Affairs: Carol Ann Bischoss
Director, State Affairs: Andrew Regitsky
Director, Member Affairs: Jennifer H. Christie

Historical Note
Members are providers of long distance telephone services. Formed by a merger of Ass'n of Long Distance Telephone Companies and the American Council for Competitive Telecommunications in 1984. Absorbed Operator Service Providers of America in 1990.

Membership: $1700/year (flat-rate associate); $2,800-52,800/year (carriers, based on revenues); $2,800- 16,500/year (suppliers, based on revenues).

Publications:
COMPTEL Bulletin Series. w.
COMPTEL Definitive List of Long-Distance Telephone Companies. m.

Meetings/Conferences:
Annual Meetings: February/1,000
1999 – Atlanta, GA(Westin Peachtree)/Feb. 7-10

Components, Packaging, and Manufacturing Technology Soc. (1950)
P.O. Box 1331
445 Hoes Lane
Piscataway, NJ 08855-1331
Tel: (732)562-5529   *Fax:* (732)981-1769
E-Mail: m.tickman@ieee.org
Web Site: http://www.cpmt.org
Members: 3,900 individuals
Exec. Director: Marsha S. Tickman

Historical Note
Formerly (1996) the Components, Hybrids and Manufacturing Technology Soc. A technical society of the Institute of Electrical and Electronics Engineers.

Publications:
Circuits and Devices Magazine. bi-m.
Transactions on Advanced Packaging. q.
Transactions on Components and Packaging Technologies. q.
Transactions on Semiconductor Manufacturing. q.
Transasctions on Manufacturing. q.

Composite Can and Tube Institute (1933)
1630 Duke St.
Alexandria, VA 22314
Tel: (703)549-2233   *Fax:* (703)549-4912
E-Mail: cctiwdc@erols.com
Web Site: http://www.cctiwdc.org
Members: 80 companies
Staff: 3
Annual Budget: $250-500,000
Exec. V. President: Kristine J. Garland
Director, Administration: Cynthia Wigfall
Manager, Publications and Programs: Andrea Ball

Historical Note
Formed in New York, NY as the Nat'l Fibre Can and Tube Institute, it assumed its present name in 1970. Members are manufacturers of composite (paperboard) cans, tubes, spools, cores, fibre drums, ribbon blocks, mailing packages, cones and bobbins, and suppliers to those manufacturers. Membership: $1,700/year (supplier); manufacturers' dues based on sales volume.

Publications:
Cantube Bulletin. m. adv.
Industry Directory. a.
Membership Directory. a.
Performance Report.
Technical Notebook.
Tube and Core Statistical Report.
Wages and Benefits Survey.

Meetings/Conferences:
Annual Meetings: Spring/100
1999 – Ponta Verda, FL/May 12-16

Composite Panel Ass'n (1960)
18928 Premiere Court
Gaithersburg, MD 20879-1569
Tel: (301)670-0604   *Fax:* (301)840-1252
E-Mail: info@pbmdf.com
Web Site: http://www.pbmdf.com
Members: 31 companies
Staff: 13
Annual Budget: $2-5,000,000
President: Rich Margosian
V. President, Communications: Thomas A. Julia
V. President, Technical Affairs, Research & Standards: Daniel Hare
V. President, Quality Assurance: John Bradfield

Historical Note
Formed by the consolidation of the Nat'l Particleboard Ass'n and Canadian Particleboard Ass'n in 1997, CPA represents North American particleboard and medium density fiberboard manufacturers.

Publications:
Buyers & Specifiers Guide to Particleboard & MDF. bien.
Membership Directory. a.
North American Particleboard/MDF Plant Capacity. a.
U. S.

Meetings/Conferences:

Composites Fabricators Ass'n (1979)
1655 Ft. Myer Dr., Suite 510
Arlington, VA 22209-3108
Tel: (703)525-0511   *Fax:* (703)525-0743
Web Site: http://www.cfa-hq.org
Members: 750 companies
Staff: 11
Annual Budget: $1-2,000,000
Exec. Director: Missy Henriksen
Dir., Govt. Affairs: Steve McNally
Dir., Advertising/Exhibits: Tiana Hickman
Dir., Education: Sabeena Sharma
Dir., Member Services: Jennifer Jones
Editor: Andy Rusnak

Historical Note
Formerly (1992) Fiberglass Fabrication Ass'n. Membership is open to any person, firm or corporation performing the hand layup or sprayup method of fiberglass fabrication in open or closed molds or engaged in filament winding or resin transfer molding. Incorporated in 1979 in Washington, DC. Membership Fee: based on sales volume.

Publications:
Composites Fabrication. m. adv.
Membership Directory/Buyers Guide. a. adv.

Meetings/Conferences:
Annual Meetings: Fall/2,000
1999 - Chicago, IL(Hyatt Regency)

Composites Institute (1946)
600 Mamaroneck Ave.
Harrison, NY 10528
Tel: (914)381-3572   Fax: (914)381-1253
E-Mail: crandazz@socplas.org
Web Site: http://www.composites.org
Members: 415 companies
Staff: 7
Annual Budget: $250-500,000
Exec. Director: Catherine A. Randazzo

Historical Note
Formerly (1986) Reinforced Plastics/Composites Institute. Division of the Soc. of the Plastics Industry. Members are molders and fabricators of glass and other fibre-reinforced plastics as well as materials suppliers.

Publications:
CI Insider. m.
Proceedings. a.

Meetings/Conferences:
1999 - Cincinnati, OH(Convention Center)/May 10-13

Composites Manufacturing Ass'n of SME
P.O. Box 930
One SME Drive
Dearborn, MI 48121-0930
Tel: (313)271-1500   Fax: (313)271-2861
Toll Free: (800)733 - 4763
E-Mail: SKOMCHE@SME.ORG
Web Site: http://www.sme.org/cma.html
Association Manager: Cheri Skomra

Historical Note
Sponsored by the Soc. of Manufacturing Engineers, CMA/SME has nearly 2,000 members in 35 countries. CMA/SME is concerned with the intergration of fiber reinforced plastics/composites into the manufacturing sector including issues of design, tooling, assembly, producibility, supportability, and in materials and hardware. Membership: $72/year (individual).

Publications:
Composites in Manufacturing. q. adv.

Meetings/Conferences:
Annual Meetings: February, usually in Anaheim, California

Composting Council (1990)
4424 Montgomery Ave., Suite 102
Bethesda, MD 20814
Tel: (301)913-2885   Fax: (301)913-9146
Web Site: http://compostingcouncil.org
Members: 155 businesses
Staff: 3
Annual Budget: $250-500,000
Exec. V. President: David O'Bryon
Director of Operations: Randall Monk

Historical Note
Formerly (1993) the Solid Waste Composting Council. Members are generators, composters, users, marketers and others who aim to develop standards for compost products, define compost products as recycled materials, and serve as an information clearinghouse. Membership: $7,500/year (regular); $250/year (small business); $2,500/year (affiliate); $250/year (non-profit organizations).

Publications:
Newsletter. q.

Meetings/Conferences:
Annual Meetings: November
1999 - New Orleans, LA/Jan 6-8

Compressed Air and Gas Institute (1915)
1300 Sumner Ave.
Cleveland, OH 44115-2851
Tel: (216)241-7333   Fax: (216)241-0105
E-Mail: cagi@taol.com
Web Site: http://www.taol.com/cagi
Members: 36 companies
Staff: 3
Annual Budget: $250-500,000
Secretary-Treasurer: John H. Addington

Historical Note
The Compressed Air and Gas Institute is a non-profit organization of companies which manufacture air and gas compressors, air or gas dryers, or pneumatic tools and machinery; products which have many applications in construction, manufacturing, mining, and the process and natural gas industries. The forerunner of the present Institute, the Compressed Air Society, was formed in 1915 to provide an instrument for solving the problems common to all member companies and to promote the industry. In 1933 the group became the Compressed Air Institute. The name Compressed Air and Gas Institute was adopted in 1945.

Meetings/Conferences:
1999 - Amelia Island, FL(The Plantation)/April 30-May 3
2000 - Kiawah Island, SC(Kiawah Island
    Resort)/April 28-May 3

Compressed Gas Ass'n (1913)
1725 Jefferson Davis Hwy., Suite 1004
Arlington, VA 22202-4102
Tel: (703)412-0900   Fax: (703)412-0128
E-Mail: cga@cganet.com
Web Site: http://www.cganet.com
Members: 230 companies
Staff: 18
Annual Budget: $2-5,000,000
President: Carl T. Johnson
Manager, Meetings and Membership: Nancy Flower

Technical Director: Roger Smith
Chief Administrative Officer: Michael Tiller

Historical Note
Established as the Compressed Gas Manufacturers Ass'n, it assumed its present name in 1949; absorbed the Internat'l Acetylene Ass'n. CGA member companies include manufacturers, distributors and transporters of compressed, liquefied and cryogenic gases, as well as manufacturers of valves, cylinders, transportation equipment and other products related to the compressed gas industry. CGA's main concern is the promotion of safety in the compressed gas industry. Membership: based on annual sales/revenues.

Publications:
Compressions. m.
Membership Directory. a.
Publications Catalog. a.

Meetings/Conferences:
Annual Meetings: February-March
1999 - Rancho Mirage, CA(Westin Mission Hills)/Feb. 21-24

Computer Aided Manufacturing-Internat'l
Historical Note
Became (1997) Consortium for Advanced Manufacturing Internat'l.

Computer and Automated Systems Ass'n of SME (1975)
P.O. Box 930
One SME Drive
Dearborn, MI 48121-0930
Tel: (313)271-1500   Fax: (313)271-2861
Web Site: http://www.sme.org/casa.html
Members: 12,000 individuals, 124 companies
Staff: 2
Association Manager: Sandra Marshall

Historical Note
Sponsored by the Soc. of Manufacturing Engineers, CASA/SME has 14,000 members in 35 countries. CASA/SME was founded in 1975 to provide comprehensive coverage of computers and automation in the overall advancement of manufacturing. Since that time, CASA/SME has become an organizational home for engineers, managers, and other professionals involved with computers and automated systems. CASA/SME is application-oriented and addresses all phases of research, design, installation, operation, and maintenance of the total manufacturing enterprise. With a goal of continuing education for manufacturing engineers and managers, CASA/SME activities include major conference and expositions, short courses, local chapter participation, and publications. Membership: $60/year (individual), $185/year (company).

Publications:
Bibliography of CASA/SME Related Technical Papers.
CIM Series Booklets. irreg.

Meetings/Conferences:
Annual Meetings: AUTOFACT Conference &
    Exposition/Fall/25,000

Computer and Communications Industry Ass'n (1972)
666 11th St., N.W., Suite 600
Washington, DC 20001-4542
Tel: (202)783-0070   Fax: (202)783-0534
E-Mail: ccia@aol.com
Web Site: http://www.ccianet.org
Members: 30 companies
Staff: 10
Annual Budget: $1-2,000,000
President: Edward J. Black
Manger, Communications: Mark Lewis
Financial Officer: Carolyn Queen
Exec. V. President: Glenn K. Davidson

Historical Note
Formerly (1976) Computer Industry Ass'n. Members are manufacturers and providers of computer information processing and telecommunications-related products and services. Companies are represented by senior executives. It represents the interests of its members in domestic and foreign trade, federal procurement policy, telecommunication and technology policy, and intellectual property issues. Membership: $3,500-55,000/year (company).

Publications:
CEO Report. bi-w.
Executive Briefing Book. q.
Federal Procurement Policy Update. irreg.
Intellectual Property Report. irreg.
International Trade Report. irreg.
Technology Report. irreg.
Telecommunications Report. irreg.

Meetings/Conferences:
1999 - Tempe, AZ

Computer Assisted Language Instruction Consortium (1983)
214 Centennial Hall, 601 University Dr.
San Marcos, TX 78666
Tel: (512)245-1417   Fax: (512)245-9089
E-Mail: info@calico.org
Web Site: http://www.calico.org.
Members: 780 individuals, 220 companies
Staff: 1
Annual Budget: $50-100,000
Exec. Director: Robert Fischer

Historical Note
Formerly (1991) Computer Assisted Language Learning and Instruction and (1995) Computer Assisted Learning and Instruction Consortium. Established at Brigham Young University, CALICO is a consortium of academic, business, research, manufacturing and government members involved in the field of computer-assisted language instruction. Membership: $50/year (individual); $90/year (institution); $140/year (corporation).

Publications:
CALICO Monograph Series. a.

CALICO Proceedings. a. adv.
Resource Guide. a. adv.
The CALICO Journal. q. adv.

Meetings/Conferences:
Annual Meetings: Spring/450
1999 - Oxford, OH(Miami Univ.)/June 1-5/400

Computer Dealer Forum (1987)
Historical Note
Formerly (1987) Ass'n of Computer Retailers, CDF is a department of the Business Products Industry Ass'n.

Computer Ethics Institute
P.O. Box 42672
Washington, DC 20015
Staff: 1
Exec. Director: Patrick Sullivan

Historical Note
CEI serves as a forum that focuses on the ethical issues raised by computer and information technology. Members are firms and individuals active in the computer industry.

Meetings/Conferences:

Computer Event Marketing Ass'n (1990)
490 Boston Post Road
Sudbury, MA 01776-3301
Tel: (978)443-3330   Fax: (978)443-4715
E-Mail: cema@ndegree.com
Members: 420 individuals
Staff: 1
Annual Budget: $100-250,000
Exec. Director: Leigh Walker

Historical Note
Membership: $260/year (individual); $545/year (company).

Publications:
CEMA Communicator. m.

Meetings/Conferences:
Annual Meetings: July
1999 - PQ, Canada(Chateau Mont Tremblant)

Computer Law Ass'n (1971)
3028 Javier Road, Suite 402
Fairfax, VA 22031
Tel: (703)560-7747   Fax: (703)207-7028
E-Mail: clanet@aol.com
Web Site: http://www.cla.org
Members: 2,000 individuals
Staff: 2
Annual Budget: $50-100,000
Exec. Director: Barbara Fieser

Historical Note
Members are concerned with legal problems arising from the invention, evolution, production, marketing, acquisition and use of computer communications technology. Membership: $100/year.

Publications:
Computer Law Ass'n Newsletter. q.
Membership Directory. a.

Meetings/Conferences:
1999 - Reston, VA(Hyatt)/March 14-17
1999 - Chicago, IL(Drake)/Nov. 4-5

Computer Leasing and Remarketing Ass'n
Historical Note
Became (1997) Information Technology Resellers Ass'n.

Computer Measurement Group (1975)
151 Fries Mill Rd., Suite 104
Turnersville, NJ 08012-2016
Tel: (609)401-1700   Fax: (609)401-1708
Members: 3,000 individuals
Staff: 10
Annual Budget: $2-5,000,000
Exec. Director: Maryann Milner

Historical Note
Membership: $125/year (U.S); $175/year (Canada); $200/year (International).

Publications:
CMG Bulletin. q.
CMG Proceedings. a.
CMG Transactions. q.

Meetings/Conferences:
Annual Meetings: December/2,000
1999 - Reno, NV/Dec. 6-10

Computer Oriented Geological Soc. (1982)
P.O. Box 269
Golden, CO 80402-0269
Tel: (303)697-6864   Fax: (303)279-0909
E-Mail: tbrez@csn.org
Web Site: http://www.csn.net/~tbrez/cogs
Members: 1000 individuals
Exec. Officer: Tom Bresnahan

Historical Note
COGS is a professional society composed of geologists who are using computers in their research. Membership: $30/year (individual); $15/year (student).

Publications:
COGSletter. irreg.

Computer Press Ass'n (1983)
2 Apollo Way
Flanders, NJ 07836
Tel: (973)252-4037
E-Mail: information@computerpress.org
Web Site: http://www.computerpress.org
Members: 280 individuals
Staff: 1
Annual Budget: $10-25,000

Administrator: Michele Zatorski
Historical Note
*CPA members are writers and editors regularly covering the
computer industry. Membership: $75/year (individual); $300/year
(company).*
Publications:
CPA Network News. q.
Meetings/Conferences:
Annual Meetings: New York City in April

Computer Security Institute *(1974)*
600 Harrison St.
San Francisco, CA   94107
Tel: (415)905-2626   *Fax:* (415)905-2218
E-Mail: csi@mfi.com
Web Site: http://www.gocsi.com
Members: 3,000 individuals
Staff: 13
Annual Budget: $1-2,000,000
Exec. Director: Patrice Rapalus
Historical Note
*Membership services designed for data processing managers,
security officers, auditors and others with an interest in computer
security. Membership: $197/year (domestic and Canada);
$237/year (international).*
Publications:
Computer Security Alert Newsletter. m.
Computer Security Buyers Guide. a.
Computer Security Journal. q.
Meetings/Conferences:
Semi-Annual Meetings: June and November
1999 – St. Louis, MO/June 12-18
1999 – Washington, DC/Nov. 13-19

Computer Soc. *(1946)*
Historical Note
See IEEE Computer Soc.

Computer Soc. of the Institute of Electrical and Electronics Engineers *(1951)*
Historical Note
See IEEE Computer Soc.

Computer Use in Social Services Network *(1981)*
Box 19129
Arlington, TX   76019-0129
Tel: (817)273-3964   *Fax:* (817)794-5795
Web Site: http://www.uta.edu/cussn/cussn.html
Staff: 1
Annual Budget: under $10,000
Coordinator: Dick Schoech
Historical Note
*Members share expertise and resources in the application of
computers in human service settings. Provides software distribution
service and an electronic network.*
Publications:
Computers in Human Services. q.
Meetings/Conferences:
1999 – Budapest, Hungary

Computer Users in Speech and Hearing *(1981)*
Historical Note
Organization defunct in 1995.

Computer-based Patient Record Institute *(1992)*
4915 Elm Ave., Suite 401
Bethesda, MD   20814
Tel: (301)657-5918   *Fax:* (301)657-1296
E-Mail: margaret@cpri.org
Web Site: http://www.cpri.org
Annual Budget: $250-500,000
Exec. Director: Margret Amatayakul
Historical Note
*CPRI promotes routine use of information technology to improve
healthcare quality, cost, and access. In particular, CPRI supports
companies and institutions using computer-based patient record
systems (CPRs), and promotes advances in technology that allow
for improved record-keeping and patient profiles.*
Publications:
CPR Recognition Symposium Proceedings. a.
CPRI-Mail. bi-m.
Meetings/Conferences:

Computerized Medical Imaging Soc. *(1977)*
Georgetown Univ. Medical Center
3900 Reservoir Road, N.W., Rm. LR-3
Washington, DC   20007
Tel: (202)687-2121   *Fax:* (202)687-1662
Web Site: www./nvrf.georgetown.edu/pir
Members: 25 individuals
Staff: 1
Annual Budget: under $10,000
Editor in Chief: Dr. Robert S. Ledley
Historical Note
*Formerly (1988) the Computerized Radiology Soc. Members are
radiologists interested in using the computer to scan X-rays of
selected planes of the body. Membership: $60/year.*
Publications:
Computerized Medical Imaging & Graphics. bi-m. adv.
Meetings/Conferences:
Annual Meetings: With American Ass'n for the Advancement of
Science

Computerized Meeting Management Ass'n *(1992)*
Historical Note
Address unknown in 1993.

Computing Research Ass'n *(1972)*
1100 17th St., N.W., Suite 507
Washington, DC   20036-4632
Tel: (202)234-2111   *Fax:* (202)667-1066
E-Mail: info@cra.org
Web Site: http://www.cra.org
Members: 180 academic depts, ind labs & socs
Staff: 5
Annual Budget: $500-1,000,000
Exec. Director: William Aspray
Communications Manager: Stacy Cholewinski
Director, Government Affairs: Lisa Thompson
Director of Administration: Kimberly Peaks
Historical Note
*Formerly (1986) Computing Science Board and (1990) Computing
Research Board. CRA members are U.S. and Canadian academic
departments of computer science and computer engineering and
industrial and government laboratories engaging in basic computer
research. Membership: $650-10,000/year (organization).*
Publications:
Computing Research News. 5/yr. adv.
Meetings/Conferences:

Computing Technology Industry Ass'n *(1982)*
450 E. 22nd St., Suite 230
Lombard, IL   60148-6158
Tel: (630)268-1818   *Fax:* (630)268-1384
Web Site: http://www.comptia.org
Members: 7,500 companies
Staff: 22
Annual Budget: $2-5,000,000
Exec. V.P. and C.E.O.: John A. Venator
Director, Public Policy: Bruce Hahn
Manager, Publications: Bill Carey
Historical Note
*Formerly (1986) Ass'n of Better Computer Dealers and ABCD: The
Microcomputer Industry Ass'n (1993). Members are
microcomputer resellers who provide technical assistance, training
and full maintenance to customers and leading microcomputer
software and hardware manufacturers and distributors.
Membership: $150-10,000/year (corporation).*
Publications:
Computing Channels. m.
Directory. a.
Meetings/Conferences:
Annual Meetings: Fall

Comsource Independent Foodservice Companies
Historical Note
*Ceased non-profit operations in 1997, and reorganized as a for-
profit company, Uni-Pro Food Service.*

Concord Grape Ass'n *(1969)*
5775 Peachtree-Dunwoody Rd., Suite 500-G
Atlanta, GA   30342-1558
Tel: (404)252-3663   *Fax:* (404)252-0774
E-Mail: cga@assnhq.com
Members: 10 companies
Staff: 4
Annual Budget: $25-50,000
Exec. Director: Pamela A. Chumley
Manager, Client Services: Nancy Marlin
Historical Note
*Founded as the Concord Grape Council, it became the American
Concord Grape Ass'n in 1974 and assumed its present name in
1980. Members are firms engaged in the processing of a
substantial quantity of Concord grapes in North America.*
Publications:
Membership Directory. a.
Meetings/Conferences:

Concrete Anchor Manufacturers Ass'n *(1995)*
1603 Boonslick Road
St. Charles, MO   63301
Tel: (314)925-2212   *Fax:* (314)946-3336
Members: 22 companies
Staff: 1
Annual Budget: $25-50,000
Exec. Director: James A. Borchers
Meetings/Conferences:

Concrete Foundations Ass'n *(1975)*
107 First St. West
Mount Vernon, IA   52314-1602
Tel: (319)895-6940   *Fax:* (319)895-8830
Members: 200 companies
Staff: 3
Annual Budget: $100-250,000
Exec. Director: J. Edward Sauter
Historical Note
*Formerly (1990) the Poured Concrete Wall Contractors Ass'n of
America. Membership: $150-600/year.*
Publications:
Newsletter. q.
Meetings/Conferences:
Annual Meetings: January-February
1999 – Durango, CO(Tamarron)/July 7-10/250

Concrete Modifications Contractors Ass'n
P.O. Box 1142
Livermore, CA   94551
Members: 13 companies
Annual Budget: $25-50,000
Exec. Director: Susan Dyer
Publications:
Newsletter. bi-a.

Concrete Pipe Ass'ns
Historical Note
*Formed to handle matters of common concern to American Concrete
Pipe Ass'n and American Concrete Pressure Pipe Ass'n.
Administrative support provided by ACPA.*

Concrete Plant Manufacturers Bureau *(1958)*
900 Spring St.
Silver Spring, MD   20910
Tel: (301)587-1400   *Fax:* (301)585-4219
Members: 12 companies
Staff: 2
Annual Budget: $50-100,000
Exec. Secretary: Robert A. Garbini
Administrator: Nicole R. Maher
Historical Note
*An affiliate of the Nat'l Ready Mixed Concrete Ass'n. Primary
purpose is developing engineering standards.*
Publications:
Concrete Plant Mixer Standards of the CPMB.
Concrete Plant Standards of the CPMB.
Meetings/Conferences:
Annual Meetings: always April in Phoenix, AZ

Concrete Reinforcing Steel Institute *(1924)*
933 N. Plum Grove Road
Schaumburg, IL   60173-4758
Tel: (847)517-1200   *Fax:* (847)517-1206
Web Site: http://www.crsi.org
Members: 270 firms
Staff: 17
Annual Budget: $2-5,000,000
President: Charels E. Slater
Manager, Administration: Linda Ross
Historical Note
*Firms engaged in the production and fabrication of reinforcing bars
and accessories. Absorbed the Associated Reinforcing Bar
Producers in 1982 and the Fusion Bonded Coaters Ass'n in 1985.*
Publications:
Shop Talk. q.
Meetings/Conferences:
1999 – La Jolla, CA(Sheraton Grande Torrey Pines)/May 1-6
2000 – Hilton Head Island, SC(Hilton at Palmetto
     Dunes)/April 29-May 4
2001 – Indian Wells, CA(Renaissance Esmeralda
     Resort)/April 21-26

Concrete Sawing and Drilling Ass'n *(1972)*
6089 Frantz Road, Suite 101
Dublin, OH   43017
Tel: (614)798-2252   *Fax:* (614)798-2255
E-Mail: paddyobie@aol.com
Web Site: http://www.csda.org
Members: 370 companies
Staff: 3
Annual Budget: $500-1,000,000
Exec. Director: Patrick A. O'Brien
Historical Note
*Contractors of concrete sawing and drilling and producers of
diamond sawblades, drills, and equipment. Sponsors operator
certification and other continuing education programs.
Membership: $375-$1,450/year, based on construction volume
(contractor); $750-$1,500/year, based on manufacturing volume
(manufacturer); $475/year (associate).*
Publications:
Concrete Openings Magazine. q. adv.
Meetings/Conferences:
Annual Meetings: always 1st quarter.
1999 – Las Vegas, NV(Las Vegas Convention
     Center)/Jan. 19-22
2000 – Nassau, Bahamas(Atlantis)/Jan. 23-26/350
2001 – Tucson, AZ(Sheraton)/Jan. 21-24/350

Conductors Guild *(1975)*
103 S. High St., Suite 6
West Chester, PA   19382-3262
Tel: (610)430-6010   *Fax:* (610)430-6034
E-Mail: conguild@aol.com
Web Site: http://www.conductorsguild.org
Members: 1,700 individuals, 120 institutions
Staff: 4
Annual Budget: $100-250,000
Administrative Director: Judy A. Voois
Historical Note
*Formerly a sub-group of the American Symphony Orchestra
League, the Guild became an independent entity in 1985. Guild
members are conductors, students and institutions with an interest
in the field. Membership: $70/year (regular/associate); $40/year
(student); $80/year (institution).*
Publications:
Conductor Opportunities Bulletin. m.
Conductors Guild Directory. a.
Journal of the Conductors' Guild. semi-a.
Podium Notes Newsletter. q.
Meetings/Conferences:
1999 – Los Angeles, CA(Intercontinental Hotel)/Jan. 7-10

Conference Board of the Mathematical Sciences *(1960)*
1529 18th St., N.W.
Washington, DC   20036
Tel: (202)293-2270   *Fax:* (202)265-2384
E-Mail: lkolbe@maa.org
Members: 14 organizations
Staff: 2
Annual Budget: $25-50,000
Administrative Officer: Ronald C. Rosier

Historical Note

A group of professional societies formed to present their point of view to the Government, CBMS consists of: American Mathematical Soc., Ass'n for Symbolic Logic, Institute of Mathematical Statistics, Mathematical Ass'n of America, Nat'l Council of Teachers of Mathematics, Soc. for Industrial and Applied Mathematics, American Mathematical Ass'n of Two-Year Colleges, American Statistical Ass'n, Ass'n for Women in Mathematics, Nat'l Council of Supervisors of Mathematics, Soc. of Actuaries, Institute for Operations Research and the Management Sciences, Ass'n of State Supervisors of Mathematics, Nat'l Ass'n of Mathematicians and Benjamin Banneker Ass'n.

Meetings/Conferences:
Semi-annual Meetings: May and December/35

Conference for the Study of Political Thought (1969)
Department of Politics
Pitzer College
Claremont, CA   91711
Tel: (909)607-3178   *Fax:* (909)621-8481
E-Mail: ssnowiss@pitzer.edu
Members: 500 individuals
Annual Budget: under $10,000
Secretary-Treasurer: Sharon Nickel-Snowiss

Historical Note
CSPT members are academics and others with an interest in the study of political theory. Membership: $18-30/year (individual); $12/year (student).

Publications:
CSPT Newsletter. semi-a.
Proceedings. a.

Meetings/Conferences:
1999 – New Haven, CT(Yale University)

Conference of Ass'n Soc. Executives (1987)
Historical Note
Address unknown in 1998.

Conference of Business Economists
28790 Chagrin Blvd., Suite 350
Cleveland, OH   44122
Tel: (216)464-2137   *Fax:* (216)464-0397
E-Mail: dwilliams@Admgt.com
Exec. Director: David L. Williams

Publications:
Directory. a.

Meetings/Conferences:
Annual Meetings: Quarterly Meetings

Conference of Casualty Insurance Companies
Historical Note
Became(1998) Property Casualty Conferences.

Conference of Chief Justices (1949)
Nat'l Center for State Courts
300 Newport Ave.
Williamsburg, VA   23187-8798
Tel: (757)259-1841   *Fax:* (757)259-1520
Members: 58 individuals
Staff: 1
Secretariat: Brenda A. Williams

Historical Note
Administration provided by the Nat'l Center for State Courts.

Meetings/Conferences:

Conference of Consulting Actuaries (1950)
1110 W. Lake Cook Road, Suite 235
Buffalo Grove, IL   60089-1968
Tel: (847)419-9090   *Fax:* (847)419-9091
E-Mail: cca@ccactuaries.org
Web Site: http://www.ccactuaries.org
Members: 1000 individuals
Staff: 5
Annual Budget: $250-500,000
Exec. Director: Rita K. DeGraaf

Historical Note
Formerly (1991) Conference of Actuaries in Public Practice. CCA is a professional membership organization for actuaries working as consultants in life, health, property and casualty insurance and in the pension planning and employee benefits fields. Affiliated with the American Academy of Actuaries and Soc. of Actuaries. Awards the designations "FCA", "MCA", and "ACA" (Fellow, Member, and Associate of the Conference of Consulting Actuaries). Membership: $240/year.

Publications:
The Consulting Actuary. q.
The Proceedings. a.

Meetings/Conferences:
Annual Meetings: Fall
1999 – Boca Raton, FL(Boca Raton Resort)/Oct. 10-13

Conference of Educational Administrators of Schools and Programs for the Deaf (1868)
P.O. Box 1778
St. Augustine, FL   32085-1778
Tel: (904)810-5200   *Fax:* (904)810-5525
E-Mail: innceasd@aug.com
Members: 800 individuals
Annual Budget: $50-100,000
Exec. Director: Joseph P. Finnegan, Jr.
President: Dr. Gertrude S. Galloway

Historical Note
CEASD's purpose is to promote effective management of educational programs for the deaf. Orginially known as the Ass'n of Superintendents and Principals, a splinter group from the Convention of American Instructors of the Deaf (established 1850). Formerly (until 1980) known as the Conference of Executives of

American Schools for the Deaf, Inc. CEASD is a member of the Council on Education of the Deaf.

Publications:
American Annals of the Deaf. 5/year. adv.

Meetings/Conferences:
Biennial Meetings: with Convention of American Instructors of the Deaf
1999 – Pittsburgh, PA

Conference of Educational Administrators Serving the Deaf (1868)
Historical Note
Name changed to Conference of Educational Administrators of Schools and Programs for the Deaf (CEASD) in 1996.

Conference of Funeral Service Examining Boards of the United States
Historical Note
Became (1998) International Conference of Funeral Service Examining Boards.

Conference of Major Superiors of Men, U.S.A. (1956)
8808 Cameron St.
Silver Spring, MD   20910
Tel: (301)588-4030   *Fax:* (301)587-4575
E-Mail: postmaster@cmsm.org
Web Site: http://www.cmsm.org
Members: 275 individuals
Staff: 6
Annual Budget: $250-500,000
Exec. Director: Rev. Steven Henrich
Director of Communications: Jeanean D. Merkel
Assoc. Director, Justice & Peace: Rev. Ted Keating
Assoc. Director, Planning: Ann Carville, OSF

Historical Note
Formerly the Conference of Major Superiors of Men's Institutes. Members are major superiors of the various Roman Catholic religious orders of men in the U.S.

Publications:
CMSM Bulletin. m.
CMSM Forum. q.
Directory. a.
Justice and Peace Alert. m.

Meetings/Conferences:
Annual Meetings: August
1999 – Danvers, MA(Taras Ferncroft Resort)/Aug. 4-7/200
2000 – New Orleans, LA/Aug. 9-12/200
2001 – Pittsburg, PA(Convention Center)

Conference of Minority Public Administrators (1971)
1120 G St., N.W., Suite 700
Washington, DC   20005
Tel: (202)393-7878   *Fax:* (202)638-4952
Web Site: http://www.compa.org
Members: 500 individuals
Annual Budget: $25-50,000
Section Chair: Michael Massiah
Editor, Newsletter: Audrey Matthews
Treasurer: Edwin Cook

Historical Note
A section of the American Soc. for Public Administration, COMPA members are minority ASPA members and others concerned with the advancement of minorities in public administration. Membership: $19/year (individual).

Publications:
COMPA Spectrum. q. adv.
Journal of Public Management and Social Policy. q. adv.

Meetings/Conferences:
Annual Meetings: February, in conjunction with ASAP
1999 – Pittsburg, PA/March 10-14

Conference of Minority Transportation Officials (1971)
1725 DeSales St., N.W., Suite 808
Washington, DC   20036
Tel: (202)289-0567   *Fax:* (202)289-1214
E-Mail: mharper@comto.com
Web Site: http://www.comto.com
Members: 2,000 individuals
Staff: 4
Annual Budget: $250-500,000
Exec. Director: Margareth C. Harper

Historical Note
The Conference of Minority Transportation Officials(COMTO) is a nationwide association of professionals from a wide spectrum of transportation related industries and backgrounds. Membership, as the name suggests, is predominantly made up of minority professionals and organizations who have joined the association to continue the development of professional growth and influence through interaction with COMTO's programs and its people. Membership: $60/year (individual); $1,000-5,000 (organization/company).

Publications:
Cable Express. m. adv.

Meetings/Conferences:
1999 – Boston, MA/July 6-11

Conference of Philosophical Societies (1976)
Keene State College
Keene, NH   03435-1402
Tel: (603)352-1909   *Fax:* (603)358-2777
Web Site:
    http://www.people.memphis.edu/~philos/sjp/philcal
Members: 95 societies
President: Sander Lee

Historical Note
COPS members are philosophical societies. Has no paid officers or full-time staff.

Publications:
COPS Newsletter. semi-a.
Directory of Philosophical Socs. irreg.
Philosophical Calendar. bi-m.

Meetings/Conferences:
1999 – Washington, DC

Conference of Podiatry Executives (1960)
Historical Note
Became the American Soc. of Podiatry Executives in 1996.

Conference of Public Health Veterinarians (1946)
Historical Note
Address unknown in 1995.

Conference of Radiation Control Program Directors (1968)
205 Capitol Ave.
Frankfort, KY   40601-2832
Tel: (502)227-4543   *Fax:* (502)227-7862
Members: 980 individuals
Staff: 10
Annual Budget: $500-1,000,000
Exec. Director: Charles M. Hardin

Historical Note
Members are or have been employed by state, local or foreign radiation control programs. The CRCPD provides a forum for the exchange of information between radiation control programs of states, and between the states and federal government. Membership: $25-75/year.

Publications:
Annual Proceedings. a.
Directory of Radiological Health Program Directors. a.
Newsbrief. m. adv.
Profile of State & Local Radiation Control Programs in the U. S.
Radon Bulletin. q.

Meetings/Conferences:
Annual Meetings: Spring
1999 – Louisville, KY/May 9-12
2000 – Tampa Bay, FL/May 14-17

Conference of Research Workers in Animal Diseases (1920)
Colorado State University
Dept. of Microbiology
Fort Collins, CO   80523
Tel: (970)491-5740   *Fax:* (970)491-1815
E-Mail: rellis@cvmbs.colostate.edu
Web Site:
    www.cvmbs.colostate.edu/microbiology/crwad/crwad.htm
Members: 700 individuals
Staff: 1
Annual Budget: $25-50,000
Exec. Director: Dr. Robert P. Ellis

Historical Note
Approximately 400 presentations of unpublished research results of studies in animal heath and disease are presented annually. Membership: $40/year.

Publications:
Newsletter @website. a.
Proceedings of the CRWAD Annual Meeting. a.

Meetings/Conferences:
Annual Meetings: Chicago, IL(Congress Hotel)/November/700
1999 – Chicago, IL(Congress Hotel)/Nov. 8-10
2000 – Chicago, IL(Congress Hotel)/Nov. 12-14

Conference of State Bank Supervisors (1902)
1015 18th St., N.W., Suite 1100
Washington, DC   20036-5725
Tel: (202)296-2840   *Fax:* (202)296-1928
Toll Free: (800)886 - 2727
E-Mail: nmilner@csbsdc.org
Members: 54 state regulatory organizations
Staff: 25
Annual Budget: $2-5,000,000
President & C.E.O.: Neil Milner, CAE
V.P., Communications: Ellen C. Lamb
Sr. V.P., Policy: Lisa McGreery
Sr. V.P., Regulatory: Montrice Godard
Sr. V.P., Education: Roger Stromberg
Asst. V.P., Administration: Merry C. Lo

Historical Note
Founded in 1902 as the Nat'l Ass'n of Supervisors of State Banks. Current name assumed in 1970. The professional organization of the state bank regulators of the 50 States, Guam, Puerto Rico, the Virgin Islands, and Washington, DC. Associate membership offered, to state-chartered commercial and mutual savings banks.

Publications:
A Profile of State Chartered Banking. bien.
CSBS Examiner. w.
State of the State Banking System Report. a.

Meetings/Conferences:
Annual Meetings: Spring
1999 – Wlliamsburg, VA(Inn & Lodge at Colonial Williamsburg)/June 2-5
2000 – San Francisco, CA(Fairmont Hotel)
2001 – Traverse City, MI(Grand Traverse Resort)
2002 – Salt Lake City, UT(Little America)

Conference of State Court Adminstrators (1955)
Nat'l Center for State Courts
300 Newport Ave., P.O. Box 8798
Williamsburg, VA   23187-8798
Tel: (757)259-1841   *Fax:* (757)259-1520
E-Mail: cosca@ncsc.com
Members: 56 individuals
Staff: 1
Association Manager: Shelley Rockwell

Historical Note
Established as Nat'l Conference of Court Administrative Officers, it became Nat'l Conference of State Court Administrators in 1972 and assumed its present name in 1975. Administration provided by Nat'l Center for State Courts.
Meetings/Conferences:
Annual Meetings: Late Summer/100
1999 – Williamburg, VA(Williamsburg Lodge)/Aug 1-5
2000 – Rapid City, SD(Holiday Inn Rushmore
    Plaza)/July 30-Aug. 3
2001 – Seattle, WA

Conference on Asian History *(1953)*
East Asian Studies Center
Indiana University
Bloomington, IN 47405
Tel: (812)855-3765   *Fax:* (812)855-7762
E-Mail: easc@indiana.edu
Members: 100 individuals
Chairman: Prof. George M. Wilson
Historical Note
An affiliate of the American Historical Ass'n, Conference members are historians specializing in the history of Asia. Membership: $5/year.
Meetings/Conferences:
Annual Meetings: in conjunction with American Historical Ass'n

Conference on College Composition and Communication *(1949)*
1111 W. Kenyon Road
Urbana, IL 61801
Tel: (217)328-3870   *Fax:* (217)328-0977
Toll Free: (800)369 - 6283
Web Site: http://www.ncte.org
Members: 8,000 individuals, 1,500 institutions
Staff: 1
Annual Budget: $250-500,000
Exec. Secretary-Treasurer: Faith Z. Schullstrom
Historical Note
A subsidiary of the Nat'l Council of Teachers of English, to which members of the Conference must first belong and which provides administrative support. Members are teachers of freshman English at the college level. Membership: $48/year (individual).
Publications:
College Composition and Communication. q. adv.
Meetings/Conferences:
Semi-annual Meetings: Spring/3,000 and Winter Workshop
1999 – Atlanta, GA(Hilton)/March 24-27
2000 – Minneapolis, MN(Hilton)/April 5-8
2001 – Denver, CO(Adam's Mark)/March 14-17
2002 – Chicago, IL(Palmer House)/March 20-23
2003 – New York, NY(Hilton)/March 14-22
2006 – Chicago, IL(Palmer House)/March 22-25
2007 – New York, NY(Hilton)/March 21-24

Conference on Consumer Finance Law *(1927)*
Oklahoma City University School of Law
Box 117-A, 2501 N. Blackwelder
Oklahoma City, OK 73106
Tel: (405)521-5363   *Fax:* (405)521-5089
F-Mail: ccflqr@lec.okcu.edu
Web Site: http://www.theccfl.com
Members: 1,200 lawyers & financial institutions
Staff: 1
Annual Budget: $25-50,000
Editor: Alvin C. Harrell
Historical Note
Formerly (1984) Conference on Personal Finance Law. The objects of the Conference are to encourage research in the commercial law, banking, and consumer finance fields, to promote by discussion and publication the improvement of legal procedures affecting credit law and installment finance, and to afford a forum at which lawyers may meet and exchange opinions. Membership: $75/year.
Publications:
Consumer Finance Law Quarterly Report. q. adv.
Meetings/Conferences:
Semi-Annual Meetings: Spring, and August with American
    Bar Ass'n

Conference on English Education *(1963)*
1111 W. Kenyon Road
Urbana, IL 61801-1096
Tel: (217)328-3870   *Fax:* (217)328-0977
Web Site: www.ncte.org
Members: 3,000 individuals, 900 institutions
Staff: 1
Annual Budget: under $10,000
Secretary-Treasurer: Faith Z. Schullstrom
Public Information: Lori Bianchini
Historical Note
A subsidiary of the Nat'l Council of Teachers of English, to which all members of the Conference must first belong and which provides administrative support. Members are state and local supervisors of English instruction and college English education teachers. Membership: $45/year.
Publications:
English Education. q. adv.
Meetings/Conferences:
Semi-annual Meetings: Fall with NCTE and Spring
1999 – Cincinnati, OH(Convention Center)/March 3-6
1999 – Denver, CO(Adams Mark)/Nov. 18-23/8000
2000 – New York, NY(Hilton)/Mar. 15-18/3000
2000 – Milwaukee, WI(Hilton)/Nov. 16-21/8000
2001 – Birmingham, AL(Convention Center)/Mar. 22-24/3000
2001 – Baltimore, MD(Omni Inner Harbor)/Nov. 15-20/8000

Conference on English Leadership *(1970)*
1111 W. Kenyon Road
Urbana, IL 61801-1096

Tel: (217)328-3870   *Fax:* (217)328-0979
Toll Free: (800)369 - 6283
Web Site: http://www.ncte.org
Members: 1,400 individuals, 50 institutions
Staff: 1
Annual Budget: $50-100,000
Secretary-Treasurer: Faith Z. Schullstrom
Historical Note
Formerly (1992) the Conference for Secondary School English Department Chairpersons. A subsidiary of the National Council of Teachers of English, to which all members of the Conference must first belong, and which provides administrative support. Membership: $45/year (individual).
Publications:
English Leadership Quarterly. q.
Meetings/Conferences:
Annual Meetings: November, with the Nat'l Council of Teachers
    of English
1999 – Denver, CO(Adam's Mark)/Nov. 18-23
2000 – Milwaukee, WI(Hilton)/Nov. 16-21

Conference on Faith and History *(1967)*
Department of History
Indiana State University
Terre Haute, IN 47809
Tel: (812)237-2707   *Fax:* (812)877-6693
E-Mail: hipier@ruby.indstate.edu
Members: 600 individuals
Secretary-Treasurer: R.V. Pierard
Historical Note
Incorporated in 1969. CFH represents professional historians and others with an interest in the relationship of faith and history. Membership: $20/year (individual); $15/year (student/retired).
Publications:
Fides et Historia. 3/year.
Newsletter. semi-a.
Meetings/Conferences:
Annual Meetings: in conjunction with American Historical Ass'n
    meeting

Conference on Jewish Social Studies *(1933)*
Stanford University, Bldg. 240, Room 103
Stanford, CA 94305-2190
Tel: (650)725-0829   *Fax:* (650)725-2920
E-Mail: jss@leland.stanford.edu
Members: 1,400 individuals
Staff: 2
President: Steven J. Zipperstein
Historical Note
Academics and others with an interest in Jewish social studies.
Publications:
Jewish Social Studies. 3/yr.

Conference on Latin American History *(1926)*
Historical Note
Address unknown in 1997.

Conference on the Safe Transportation of Hazardous Articles *(1972)*
7811 Carrleigh Parkway
Springfield, VA 22152
Tel: (703)451-4031   *Fax:* (703)451-4207
E-Mail: mail@costha.com
Web Site: http://www.costha.com
Exec. Director: Beth W. Palys, CAE
Historical Note
COSTHA represents shippers, carriers, manufactures annd others in the transportation industry. The association is dedicated to promoting regulatory compliance and safety in the hazaradous materials transportation industry.
Publications:
Newsletter. q.
Meetings/Conferences:
1999 – Orlando, FL(Walt Disney Resort)

Conflict Resolution Education Network *(1984)*
1527 New Hampshire Ave. N.W.
Washington, DC 20005
Tel: (202)667-9700
E-Mail: nid@igc.apc.org
Members: 1,250 individuals
Staff: 2
Annual Budget: $100-250,000
Interim Staff Director: Terry Wheeler
Historical Note
Formerly (1995) the Nat'l Ass'n for Mediation in Education, CREnet is a program of the Nat'l Institute for Dispute Resolution. Members are educators with an interest in teaching conflict resolution skills. Membership: $65/year (individual); $150/year (organization); $20/year (student).
Publications:
CREnet Directory of Members.
Fourth R Newsletter. 5/yr.
Resource Guide for Selecting a Trainer.
Meetings/Conferences:

Congress of Chiropractic State Ass'ns
P.O. Box 2054
Lexington, SC 29071
Tel: (803)356-6809   *Fax:* (803)356-6826
E-Mail: jjordan@chirolink.com
Web Site: http://www.cocsa.org
Members: 45 organizations
Staff: 1
Annual Budget: $50-100,000
Exec. Director: Janet Jordan

Historical Note
CCSA represents the state organizations which support the profession and science of chiropractic in the U.S. Membership: $300/year.
Publications:
Congress Connection. q.
Meetings/Conferences:
Annual Meetings: November
1999 – San Diego, CA/Nov. 4-7

Congress of Independent Unions *(1958)*
303 Ridge St.
Alton, IL 62002
Tel: (618)462-2447   *Fax:* (618)462-5579
Members: 10 independent labor unions
Staff: 6
Annual Budget: $250-500,000
President: R. Richard Davis
Publications:
CIU News. a.
Meetings/Conferences:
Annual Meetings: October/November

Congress of Lung Ass'n Staff *(1912)*
1726 M St., N.W., Suite 902
Washington, DC 20036-4502
Tel: (202)785-3355   *Fax:* (202)452-1805
Members: 800 individuals
Staff: 2
Annual Budget: $100-250,000
Exec. Director: Janet M. Widmer
Historical Note
Formerly Nat'l Conference of Tuberculosis Workers, and (1973) Nat'l Respiratory Disease Conference. Members are professional staff of American Lung Ass'n offices throughout the country. Membership: $25/year (individual).
Publications:
CLAS Action Report. q.
Meetings/Conferences:
Annual Meetings: May
1999 – San Diego CA/April 23-25

Congress of Nat'l Black Churches *(1978)*
1225 I St., N.W., Suite 750
Washington, DC 20005-3914
Tel: (202)371-1091   *Fax:* (202)371-0908
Members: 8 denominations
Staff: 45
Annual Budget: $2-5,000,000
Exec. Director: Sullivan Robinson
Project Director: Lean M. West
Historical Note
CNBC is a coalition of eight major historically black denominations. CNBC promotes unity, charity and fellowship among the member denominations and provides the opportunity for collective action. CNBC also has an Atlanta, GA office.
Publications:
Visions. semi-a.
Meetings/Conferences:
Annual Meetings: December

Congress of Neurological Surgeons *(1951)*
UAB Division of Neurosurgery
1813 Sixth Ave. South, MEB 516
Birmingham, AL 35294-3295
Tel: (205)934-3546   *Fax:* (205)934-3559
Members: 3,500 individuals
Staff: 1
Annual Budget: $500-1,000,000
Secretary: Mark Hadley, M.D.
Historical Note
A professional society with members both from the United States and a number of foreign countries. Membership: $230/year.
Publications:
Clinical Neurosurgery. a.
Concepts. adv. adv.
Neurosurgery. m. adv.
Newsletter. q.
Video Perspectives in Neurological Surgery. 4/y.
Meetings/Conferences:
Annual Meetings: Fall
1999 – Boston, MA
2000 – San Antonio, TX
2001 – San Diego, CA

Congress of Religious Credit Unions *(1993)*
Historical Note
Address unknown in 1996.

Congress on Ministry in Specialized Settings *(1987)*
c/o American Ass'n of Pastoral Counselor
9504-A Lee Highway
Fairfax, VA 22031
Tel: (703)385-6967
Members: 27 companies
Annual Budget: $10-25,000
President: Larry Seidl
Historical Note
Membership: 100/year (organization/company).
Publications:
Journal of Pastoral Care. q. adv.
Meetings/Conferences:
Annual Meetings: Always Washington, DC/first weekend in
    December/100

Congress on Research in Dance *(1965)*
c/o Dance Department

SUNY College at Brockport
Brockport, NY 14420-2939
Tel: (716)395-2590   Fax: (716)395-5413
Members: 822 individuals, 500 institutions
Staff: 1
Annual Budget: $25-50,000
Administrative Director: Ginger Macchi Carlson

Historical Note
Formerly (until 1979) known as the Committee on Research in Dance. Members are dance scholars who conduct research in dance and dance-related fields such as anthropology, body sciences, education, film, history, music, philosophy, psychology, sociology, theatre and the visual arts. CORD also has an international membership. Membership: $60/year (regular), $72/year (institution), $30/year (student/retired), $42-84(international).

Publications:
Dance Research Journal. bi-a. adv.
Newsletter. bi-a. adv.

Meetings/Conferences:

Connected Int'l Meeting Professionals Ass'n (1980)
9200 Bayard Place
Fairfax, VA 22032
Tel: (703)978-6287   Fax: (703)978-5524
E-Mail: 74117.351@compuserv.com
Web Site: http://www.cimpa.org
Members: 1,200 individuals
Staff: 6
Annual Budget: $2-5,000,000
President: Andrea Sigler, Ph.D.
Counsel: Alan Schlaifer

Historical Note
CIMPA members are conference and convention planners who completed the certification course on convention management. Awards the CIMP (Certified Internet Meeting Professional) designation. Membership: $95/year.

Publications:
Course Catalogue. q.
Internat'l Meetings Newsletter. bi-m. adv.

Meetings/Conferences:
2000 – Marrakecg, Morocco

Conservative Orthopedics Internat'l Ass'n (1982)
2547 Monroe St.
Dearborn, MI 48124-3013
Tel: (313)563-0360   Fax: (248)669-0636
Members: 3,620 individuals
Staff: 4
Annual Budget: $2-5,000,000
President: Dr. Stephen R. Castor

Historical Note
Doctors of medicine, chiropractic, osteopathy, and other individuals interested in non-surgical treatment for the prevention and rehabilitation of musculoskeletal related disorders. Membership: $175/year.

Publications:
Bulletin. bi-m.
Newsletter. m.

Meetings/Conferences:
Annual Meetings: Winter
1999 – Hong Kong

Consolidated Tape Ass'n (1974)
c/o New York Stock Exchange
11 Wall St., 21st Floor
New York, NY 10005
Tel: (212)656-2052   Fax: (212)656-5848
Members: 9 organizations
Annual Budget: under $10,000
Administrator: John F. Cipriano

Historical Note
CTA members are 7 stock exchanges and the Nat'l Ass'n of Securities Dealers. CTA melds the reporting of transactions from the various stock exchanges.

Publications:
Activity Report. m.
Statistical Releases. w.

Consortium for Advanced Manufacturing Internat'l (1972)
3301 Airport Fwy., Suite 324
Bedford, TX 76021-6032
Tel: (817)860-1654   Fax: (817)275-6450
Web Site: http://www.cam-i.org
Members: 100 companies and organizations
Staff: 10
Annual Budget: $1-2,000,000
President: Woody Noxon

Historical Note
Founded as Computer Aided Manufacturing-Internat'l; assumed its current name in 1997. Members are companies throughout the world interested in computer-assisted manufacturing and the general field of robotics. About two-thirds of the membership is from the United States. Membership: $25,000/year.

Publications:
CIE Journal. q.
CMS Review Journal. q.
Library Catalogue. a.

Consortium for Graduate Study and Management (1966)
200 S. Hanley Road, Suite 1102
St. Louis, MO 63105-3415
Tel: (314)935-5011   Fax: (314)935-5014
Toll Free: (888)658 - 6814
Web Site: http://www.wuolin.wustl.edu:8010/
C.E.O.: Phyllis Scott Buford

Historical Note
CGSM is an eleven university alliance working to faciliate the entry of minorities into mangerial positions in business.

Consortium for School Networking
1555 Connecticut Ave., N.W., Suite 200
Washington, DC 20036-1103
Tel: (202)466-6296   Fax: (202)462-9043
Annual Budget: $250-500,000
Exec. Director: Keith Krueger
Meetings: Sawanee Nivasabut
Membership: Toni Miller

Historical Note
CoSN promotes the development and use of telecommunications in K-12 education. Members are educational, institutional and commercial organizations, all whom share to goal of promoting the state of the art in computer networking technologies in schools.

Publications:
CoSN News (print newsletter). 3 times/year.
CoSNotes (electronic newsletter). 10 times/year.

Consortium of College and University Media Centers (1971)
121 Pearson Hall-ITC
Iowa State University
Ames, IA 50011-2203
Tel: (515)294-1811   Fax: (515)294-8089
E-Mail: ccumc@ccumc.org
Web Site: http://www.indiana.edu/~ccumc/
Members: 450 individuals, 400 libraries and media centers
Staff: 1
Annual Budget: $100-250,000
Exec. Director: Don A. Rieck

Historical Note
Members are college and university media center managers, film/video rental librarians, film/video producers, distributors and individuals. Membership: $160/year (company/institution).

Publications:
CCUMC Leader Newsletter. q.
College and University Media Review. semi-a.
Directory. a.

Meetings/Conferences:
Semi-annual Meetings: Spring and Fall
1999 – Burlington, VT(Radison Hotel)/Oct 21-26
2000 – Fairborn, OH(Holiday Inn)/Oct 19-24
2001 – Denton, TX(Radison Hotel)

Consortium of Social Science Ass'ns (1981)
1522 K St., N.W., Suite 836
Washington, DC 20005
Tel: (202)842-3525   Fax: (202)842-2788
E-Mail: socscience@aol.com
Web Site:
     http://members.aol.com/socscience/COSSAindex.htm
Members: 95 orgnizations
Staff: 4
Annual Budget: $250-500,000
Exec. Director: Howard J. Silver

Historical Note
Established and incorporated in the District of Columbia, COSSA represents the full range of the social and behavioral science disciplines with 12 member and 26 affiliate scholarly associations and 54 contributing universities/independent research institutions. Originally created to lobby for the restoration of funds for social and behavioral science research cut from the Nat'l Science Foundation budget, COSSA now monitors research and research funding in most federal agencies which award significant external grants. COSSA provides information and guidance for social science groups unfamiliar with government processes and represents the social sciences in legislative relations.

Publications:
COSSA Washington Update. bi-w.

Meetings/Conferences:

Construction and Agricultural Film Manufacturers Film Ass'n
104 S. Michigan, 15th Fl.
Chicago, IL 60603-1210
Tel: (312)201-0101   Fax: (312)201-0214
Annual Budget: $50-100,000
Exec. Director: James C. Stanley

Historical Note
Membership: $5,000-7,000/year.

Publications:
CAFMA Special Bulletin. semi-a.

Construction Equipment Council
Historical Note
A council of the Equipment Manufacturers Institute.

Construction Equipment Electronics Bureau
Historical Note
A bureau of the Construction Industry Manufacturers Ass'n.

Construction Financial Management Ass'n (1981)
707 State Road 223
Princeton, NJ 08540-1413
Tel: (609)683-5000   Fax: (609)683-4821
E-Mail: execdirector@cfma.org
Web Site: http://www.cfma.org
Members: 6,000 individuals, 80 chapters
Staff: 13
Annual Budget: $2-5,000,000
Exec. Director: William M. Schwab
Communications Manager and Editor: Paula A. Wristen
Conference and Education Manager: Cynthia L. Rupprecht
Accounting & Technology Manager: Erica Pugliese
Membership Manager: Susan Dunham
Chapter Relations Manager: Michael Molaro

Historical Note
Members are accountants, controllers, financial managers and CPAs in the construction industry concerned with financial management tax, technology and risk management issues. Officers are elected annually. Membership: $195/year

Publications:
Annual Financial Survey Report. a.
CFMA Building Profits. bi-m. adv.
Computerization Survey for the Construction Industry.
Financial Management Accounting for the Construction Industry. a.
THE SOURCE Directory. a. adv.

Meetings/Conferences:
1999 – Atlanta, GA(Hyatt Regency)/May 16-19/1000
2000 – Nashville, TN(Renaissance Nashville)/April 30-May 3/1000

Construction Industry CPA/Consultants Ass'n (1991)
111 E. Wacker Dr., Suite 990
Chicago, IL 60601
Tel: (312)729-9900   Fax: (312)729-9800
Toll Free: (800)869 - 0491
E-Mail: info@pencormazur.com
Web Site: http://www.cicpac.com
Members: 61 firms
Staff: 10
Director, Communications: Michelle Durham

Historical Note
CICPAC is an association of CPA firms that provide services to construction contractors beyond traditional compliance work. Members are accepted on a territorially excluse basis with a limit of one member in each Metropolitan Statistical Area.

Publications:
Construction Industry Advisor (Client Newsletter). q.
Members Bulletin. q.

Meetings/Conferences:
1999 – Las Vegas, NV(Caesar's Palace)/June 23-25

Construction Industry Management Board (1974)
Historical Note
Ceased operations in 1996.

Construction Industry Manufacturers Ass'n (1911)
111 E. Wisconsin Ave., Suite 1000
Milwaukee, WI 53202-4879
Tel: (414)272-0943   Fax: (414)272-1170
E-Mail: cima@cimanet.com
Web Site: http://www.cimanet.com
Members: 500 companies
Staff: 25
Annual Budget: $2-5,000,000
Exec. V.P. and C.O.O.: Dennis J. Slater
Director, Public Relations: Patricia E. Monroe
Director, Technical Services: Edward L. Roszkowski, P.E.
C.F.O.: John L. Nowak
Director, Strategic Info. Services: Charles H. Frey
V. President, Marketing and Member Services: Albert A. Cervero
Director, Statistical Services: Antoinette Vnuk

Historical Note
Members are manufacturers of off-road earthmoving and materials handling equipment and related off-road components used in the general construction, housing, roadbuilding, mining, energy and forestry fields (i.e. bulldozers, cranes, motor-graders, etc.) as well as providers of construction related services. Subsidiaries include: Bituminous and Aggregate Equipment Bureau; Construction Equipment Electronics Bureau; Contractors Pump Bureau; Light Equipment Group; Mounted Breakers Manufacturers Bureau; Portable and Stationary Crushing Bureau; Power Crane and Shovel Ass'n; Rock Drill Bureau; Marketing Communication Council; Parts/Service/Training Councils; International Council; Product Safety Council; Compaction & Paving Machinery Technical Committee; Earth Moving Machinery Technical Committee; Engine Emissions Committee; Product Security Committee; and Technical Liaison/Regulations Committee. Maintains a Washington office.

Publications:
Activities Report.
Catalog Safety, Technical & Info Materials on Off-Road Constr Machines.
Directory.
Newsletter.

Meetings/Conferences:
1999 – Las Vegas, NV(Convention Center)/March 23-27

Construction Industry Sales (1979)
202 East Huron St., Suite 206
Ann Arbor, MI 48104-1915
Tel: (313)769-8169   Fax: (313)769-0755
E-Mail: 74367.3504@compuserve.com
Members: 12 companies
Staff: 1
Annual Budget: under $10,000
Secretary-Manager: John Hancock

Historical Note
Established in Atlanta in 1979 to support independent sales representatives specializing in construction products and supplies. Provides ongoing contact with other sectors of the construction industry. Membership: $100/year.

Meetings/Conferences:
Annual Meetings: Winter

Construction Management Ass'n of America (1981)
7918 Jones Branch Drive, Suite 540
McLean, VA 22102
Tel: (703)356-2622   Fax: (703)356-6388
Web Site: http://www.access.digix.net/~cmaa
Members: 1000 firms and individuals
Staff: 4
Annual Budget: $250-500,000
Exec. Director: Ted Simpson

Assoc. Director: Karen Hermann
Historical Note
The Association is comprised of firms and individuals that provide total Management of a construction project from conception through completion as a professional service.
Publications:
CM Adviser. bi-m.
Meetings/Conferences:
Annual Meetings: Fall
1999 – Boston, MA/Sept. 19-22

Construction Marketing Research Council *(1992)*
3225 S. MacDill Ave., #129-137
Tampa, FL 33629-8171
Tel: (813)873-4345   *Fax:* (813)839-2035
Web Site: http://cmrc.net
Members: 25 companies
Staff: 1
Annual Budget: $10-25,000
Treasurer: Sita Monti
Historical Note
CMRC members are professionals in the construction products industry with responsibilites for their firms' corporate strategic planning and the conduct of marketing research activities. Membership is restricted to the highest level marketing research or planning professional within a company. Associate non-voting membership is available for other individuals in difeerent groups within the same company. Membership: $425/year (corporate).
Meetings/Conferences:
Semi-annual Meetings: April and October

Construction Metrication Council
Historical Note
An affiliated council of Nat'l Institute of Building Sciences, which provides administrative support.

Construction Owners Ass'n of America *(1994)*
229 Peachtree N.W., Suite 1212
International Tower
Atlanta, GA 30303
Toll Free: (800)994 - 2622
Members: 200 individuals
Staff: 1
Administrator: Sally Coulter
Historical Note
Membership: $250/year (regular); $1000/year (associate).
Publications:
COAA Briefing. q. adv.
Newsletter.
Meetings/Conferences:
Annual Meetings: Semi-Annual Meetings
1999 – Amelia Island, FL/May 6-7
1999 – Phoenix, AZ

Construction Specifications Institute *(1948)*
601 Madison St.
Alexandria, VA 22314-1791
Tel: (703)684-0300   *Fax:* (703)684-8436
Toll Free: (800)689 - 2900
Web Site: http://www.csinet.org
Members: 17,421 individuals
Staff: 57
Annual Budget: $5-10,000,000
Exec. Director: Gregory Balestrero
Manager, Education Programs: Roger Doucette
Director, New Business Dev.: Gregory Cunningham
Manager, Member Customer Service: Mary H. Bailey
Manager, Human Resources: Sarah Phaneuf
Historical Note
A not-for-profit technical organization dedicated to the advancement of construction technology through communication, research, education, and service. CSI serves the interests of architects, specifiers, engineers, contractors, product manufacturers, and others in the construction industry. Has an annual budget of approximately $7 million. Membership: $155/year.
Publications:
Construction Specifier. m. adv.
CSI Newsdigest. m.
Meetings/Conferences:
Annual Meetings: Spring
1999 – Los Angeles, CA/June 24-27

Construction Writers Ass'n *(1957)*
P.O. Box 5586
Buffalo Grove, IL 60089-5586
Tel: (847)398-7756   *Fax:* (847)590-5241
Members: 200 individuals
Staff: 2
Annual Budget: $10-25,000
Secretary-Treasurer: Sheila Wertz
Historical Note
Membership: $50/year (individual); $100/year (company).
Publications:
CWA News Newsletter. q. adv.
Meetings/Conferences:
Semi-Annual Meetings: Washington, DC/May and
     Chicago,IL/October
1999 – Washington, DC(National Press Club)/50
1999 – Chicago, IL(Tower Club)/50

Consular Law Soc. *(1940)*
Historical Note
Address unknown in 1995.

Consultant Dietitians in Health Care Facilities *(1975)*
90 S. Cascade Ave., Suite 1190
Colorado Springs, CO   80903

Tel: (719)475-1320   *Fax:* (719)475-8748
E-Mail: Heck@Heckcorporation.com
Members: 5,800 individuals
Annual Budget: $100-250,000
: Maelo Heck
Historical Note
A dietetic practice group of the American Dietetic Ass'n. Membership: $20/year (individual), plus ADA membership.
Publications:
The Consultant Dietitian Newsletter. q.
Meetings/Conferences:
Annual Meetings: in conjunction with the American Dietetic Ass'n

Consultants Consortium *(1992)*
Historical Note
Address unknown in 1997.

Consumer Bankers Ass'n *(1919)*
1000 Wilson Blvd., Suite 3012
Arlington, VA 22209-3908
Tel: (703)276-1750   *Fax:* (703)528-1290
Web Site: http://www.cbanet.org
Members: 750 banks
Staff: 21
Annual Budget: $2-5,000,000
President: Joe Belew
V.P., Communications/Public Rels.: Friedrich M. Elmendorf
V.P./Dir., Govt. Relations: Marcia Zucker Sullivan
V.P./Admin. & Dir., Conferences: Jayne E. Hunt
V. President, Senior Counsel: Steven I. Zeisel
V.P., Membership/Mktg.: Jerry R. Baugh
Historical Note
Formerly (1947) Morris Plan Bankers Ass'n. Sponsors and supports the Consumer Bankers Ass'n Political Action Committee (CONPAC). Members are federally-insured financial institutions with a primary interest in retail banking.
Publications:
CBA Reports. bi-w.
Meetings/Conferences:
Annual Meetings: Fall
1999 – Palm Springs, CA(Marriott Desert Springs)/Oct. 22-25

Consumer Credit Insurance Ass'n *(1951)*
542 South Dearborn, Suite 400
Chicago, IL 60605
Tel: (312)939-2242   *Fax:* (312)939-8287
Members: 180 companies
Staff: 6
Annual Budget: $1-2,000,000
Exec. V. President: William F. Burfeind, III
Historical Note
Members are insurance companies that provide insurance in connection with credit transactions.
Meetings/Conferences:
Annual Meetings: Spring
1999 – Las Vegas/Feb. 3-5

Consumer Electronics Manufacturers Ass'n *(1996)*
2500 Wilson Blvd.
Arlington, VA 22201
Tel: (703)907-7600   *Fax:* (703)907-7692
Web Site: http://www.cemacity.org
President: Gary J. Shapiro
V. President, Communications: Jeff Joseph
Director, Government and Legal Affairs: Joe Peck
V. President, Government and Legal Affairs: Gary S. Klein
V. President, Member Relations: Glyn Finley
Historical Note
Formerly the Consumer Electronics Group of the Electronic Industries Ass'n, CEMA became a section of EIA in 1996.

Consumer Electronics Soc.
Historical Note
See IEEE Consumer Electronics Soc.

Consumer Federation of America *(1967)*
1424 16th St., N.W., Suite 604
Washington, DC 20036
Tel: (202)387-6121
Members: 240 organizations
Staff: 12
Annual Budget: $1-2,000,000
Exec. Director: Stephen Brobeck
Historical Note
A broad coalition of consumer groups united to advance consumer interests. Membership consists of consumer organizations, labor unions, rural-electric cooperatives and state and local consumer protection officials. Supports the C.F.A. Political Action Fund.
Publications:
CFA News. m.
Consumer Health and Safety Update.
Indoor Air News. q.
Voting Record of U. S.
Meetings/Conferences:
Annual Meetings: Consumer Assembly, Washington, DC

Consumer Product Brokers Ass'n
Historical Note
Became (1998) NAGMR Consumer Product Brokers.

Contact Lens Ass'n of Ophthalmologists *(1963)*
721 Papworth Ave., Suite 205-206
Metairie, LA 70005-4906
Tel: (504)835-3937   *Fax:* (504)833-5884
Web Site: http://www.clao.org
Members: 2,200 individuals
Staff: 4

Annual Budget: $500-1,000,000
Exec. Director: John S. Massare
Historical Note
Founded in New York, NY, by a group a members of the American Academy of Ophthalmology. CLAO provides comprehensive ophthalmologists and other eyecare professionals with education and training in contact lenses, refractive surgery, and related eyecare science. Membership: $240/year.
Publications:
CLAO Journal. q. adv.
CLAOGram. m.
ContactPoint-Newsletter for Ophthalmogogy Residents & Fellows.
Meetings/Conferences:
Annual Meetings: usually Las Vegas, NV/January
1999 – Las Vegas, NV(Ceasear's Palace)/Jan. 25-27

Contact Lens Institute *(1982)*
8201 Corporate Drive, Suite 850
Landover, MD   20785
Tel: (301)459-1800   *Fax:* (301)459-1802
Toll Free: (800)884 - 4252
E-Mail: clc@us.net
Web Site: http://www.iglobal.com/clc
Members: 8 organizations
Staff: 3
Annual Budget: $500-1,000,000
Exec. Director: Edward L. Schilling, III
Director, Communications: Karen Schut
Historical Note
CLI members are contact lens manufacturers, producers and professional associations with an interest in the safe use of contact lenses and public education on vision correction. Membership: $20,000-$80,000(organization).

Contact Lens Manufacturers Ass'n *(1962)*
4400 East-West Hwy., Suite 33
Bethesda, MD   20814-4501
Tel: (301)654-2229   *Fax:* (301)654-1611
E-Mail: clma@mindspring. com
Web Site: http://www.contact.inter.net
Members: 130 companies
Staff: 1
Annual Budget: $100-250,000
Managing Director: Janis C. Marshall
Historical Note
CLMA members are contact lens laboratories, as well as material, solution and equipment manufacturers. Membership fee based upon annual sales.
Publications:
Contact Report Newsletter. bi-m. adv.
Meetings/Conferences:
Annual Meetings: Fall

Contact Lens Soc. of America *(1955)*
441 Carlisle Dr.
Reston, VA   22070
Tel: (703)437-5100   *Fax:* (703)437-0727
Members: 1,200 individuals and companies
Staff: 2
Annual Budget: $100-250,000
Exec. Director: Tina M. Schott
Historical Note
Members are fitters, as well as manufacturers, of contact lenses. Membership: $130/year (individual); $500/year (company).
Publications:
CLSA Eyewitness Newsletter. q.
Meetings/Conferences:
Annual Meetings: Spring
1999 – New Port Beach, CA/march 24-28

Containerization and Intermodal Institute *(1960)*
185 Fairfield Ave., Suite 2-D
West Caldwell, NJ 07006
Tel: (201)226-0160   *Fax:* (201)364-1212
Members: 300 companies
Annual Budget: under $10,000
Exec. Director: Barbara Spector Yeninas
Historical Note
Formerly (1960) Bulk Packaging and Containerization Institute, and (1967) The Containerization Institute. Membership includes: transportation carriers; domestic and import-export lessors of containers and unit-load devices; terminal and port managers; and importers and exporters.
Meetings/Conferences:
Annual Meetings: September

Continental Ass'n of CPA Firms
Historical Note
Became AGN Internat'l - North America in 1997.

Continental Ass'n of Funeral and Memorial Socs.
Historical Note
Became (1995) Funeral and Memorial Socs. of America.

Continental Basketball Ass'n *(1946)*
400 N. Fifth St., Suite 1425
Phoenix, AZ 85004
Tel: (602)254-6677
E-Mail: cbahoops.com
Web Site: http://www.cbahoops.com
Members: 9 clubs
Staff: 13
Annual Budget: $1-2,000,000
Commissioner: Gary Hunter
Historical Note
Established April 23, 1946 as the Eastern Basketball League, it later became the Eastern Basketball Ass'n and assumed its present

name on Jan. 1, 1978. Supported as a feeder league by the Nat'l Basketball Ass'n.

Publications:
CBA Media Guide. a.

Meetings/Conferences:
Semi-annual Meetings: June and October

Continental Dorset Club (1898)
P.O. Box 506
North Scituate, RI   02857
Tel: (401)647-4676   *Fax:* (407)647-4679
Members: 1,700 individuals
Staff: 1
Annual Budget: $50-100,000
Exec. Secretary/Treasurer: Debra Hopkins

Historical Note
Breeders and fanciers of Dorset sheep. Member of the Nat'l Pedigree Livestock Council.

Publications:
C. D.

Contract Furnishings Forum
Historical Note
A forum of the Business Products Industry Ass'n.

Contract Manufacturers Ass'n (1985)
Historical Note
Address unknown in 1998.

Contract Packagers Ass'n (1992)
481 Carlisle Drive
Herndon, VA   20170-4830
Tel: (703)318-8969   *Fax:* (703)318-0310
Members: 75 companies
Annual Budget: $50-100,000
Exec. Director: William C. Pflaum

Historical Note
An organization for contract packaging firms that aims to help its members lower their operating costs and improve their performance. Membership: $500/year (active membership); $250/year (associate).

Publications:
Newsletter. q.

Meetings/Conferences:
Semi-annual Meetings: April and October

Contract Services Ass'n of America (1965)
1200 G St., N.W., Suite 750
Washington, DC   20005-3802
Tel: (202)347-0600   *Fax:* (202)347-0608
E-Mail: gary@csa-dc.org
Web Site: http://www.csa-dc.org
Members: 280 companies
Staff: 8
Annual Budget: $1-2,000,000
President: Gary D. Engebretson
V. President, Public Policy: Cathy Garman
Legislative Associate: Adnew Fortin
Administrative Assistant: John M. Barton
Accountant: Sally H. Birge
Director, Business Management: Kurt C. McMillan
Director, Membership Services: Paul Baebler

Historical Note
CSA members are companies performing technical and support services for federal, state, and local governments. CSA supports committment of Contracting-Out, and greater reliance on the private sector to perform services for the government. Sponsors and supports the CSA Political Action Committee. Membership: $300-16,000/year (company, based on gross revenue).

Publications:
Build America. m.
CSA Insider. q.
Maintenance Contracting Initiative. q.
News Update. m.
Quarterly Report. q.
Service Scope. m.

Meetings/Conferences:
Semi-annual Meetings: Winter and Summer

Contract Stationers Forum
Historical Note
A forum of the Business Products Industry Ass'n.

Contractors Pump Bureau (1938)
111 E. Wisconsin Ave.
Milwaukee, WI   53202-4806
Tel: (414)272-0943   *Fax:* (414)272-1170
E-Mail: cima@cimanet.com
Web Site: www.cimanet.com
Members: 14 companies
Annual Budget: $25-50,000
Contact: Steve Biersdorf

Historical Note
Members are manufacturers of contractor type pumps and manufacturers of pump engines involved in the construction industry. A bureau of the Construction Industry Manufacturers Ass'n.

Publications:
CPB Pump Selection Guidebook.
Pump Safety Manual.

Meetings/Conferences:
1999 – Charleston, SC(Charleston Place)/15

Control Systems Soc. (1954)
Historical Note
See IEEE Control Systems Soc.

Controlled Environment Testing Ass'n
1518 K St., N.W., Suite 503
Washington, DC   20005-0000
Tel: (202)737-0202   *Fax:* (202)638-4833
Exec. Director: Kenneth M. Sufka

Publications:
Performance Review. q.

Meetings/Conferences:

Controlled Release Soc. (1973)
1020 N. Milwaukee Ave., Suite 335
Deerfield, IL   60015
Tel: (847)808-7071   *Fax:* (847)808-7073
E-Mail: crs@crsadmhdq.org
Web Site: http://www.crsaadmhdq.org/
Members: 2,500 individuals
Staff: 4
Exec. Director: M. Judith Roseman

Historical Note
Members are firms and individuals concerned with basic and applied research on controlled release delivery systems. Maintains an office in Geneva, Switzerland and Tokyo, Japan. Membership: $80/year (individual); $300/year (company).

Publications:
Journal of Controlled Release. q.
Newsletter. 3/yr.
Proceedings. a.

Meetings/Conferences:
1999 – Boston, MA(Marriott)
2000 – Paris, France
2001 – San Diego, CA

Controllers Council (1985)
10 Paragon Drive
Montvale, NJ   07645-1760
Tel: (201)573-9000   *Fax:* (201)573-8185
Toll Free: (800)638 - 4427
E-Mail: migs@imanet.org
Web Site: http://www.imanet.org
Members: 2,000 individuals
Staff: 2
Annual Budget: $250-500,000
Contact: Michelle Nicolato

Historical Note
Established in New Jersey in January, 1985, the Council is a special interest section of the Institute of Management Accountants. Membership: $75/year (individual).

Publications:
Controllers Update Newsletter. m.

Meetings/Conferences:

Convenient Automotive Services Institute (1983)
P.O. Box 7010
Silver Spring, MD   20907-7010
Tel: (301)588-9077   *Fax:* (301)588-9076
E-Mail: casinet@aol.com
Web Site: http://www.fastoil.com
Members: 2,600 service centers
Staff: 2
Annual Budget: $250-500,000
Exec. Director: G. Lawrence Northup

Historical Note
Founded by owners and operators of quick oil change and lubrication service stores to promote the growth of the industry through government relations, consumer education, technician certification, education and management support services. Membership: $300/year (minimum).

Publications:
CASI Report. q.

Meetings/Conferences:
Annual Meetings: September
1999 – Key West, FL(Marriott Casa Marina)/Sept. 26-28

Convention Liaison Council (1949)
10200 West 44th Ave., Suite 310
Wheat Ridge, CO   80033
Tel: (303)422-8522   *Fax:* (303)422-8894
Members: 26 associations
Staff: 3
Annual Budget: $500-1,000,000
Exec. Director: Francine Butler, Ph.D., CAE

Historical Note
Members are associations which are directly involved in the convention, exposition, trade show, and meeting industry, and travel and tourism generally. Provides a focal point for the industry to exchange information, recommend solutions to industry problems, develop programs to serve the industry and to create a public awareness of the size of the industry. Sponsors Certified Meeting Professional (CMP) Program and Hall of Leaders Recognition. Membership: $1,600/year.

Publications:
Convention Liason Manual.
Legal Review Newsletter. q.

Meetings/Conferences:
Semi-Annual Meetings: May and November

Convention of American Instructors of the Deaf (1850)
P.O. Box 377
Bedford, TX   76095
Tel: (817)354-8414
E-Mail: caid@swbell.net
Web Site: http://www.caid.org
Members: 1,250 individuals
Staff: 1
Annual Budget: $50-100,000
President: Harvey J. Corson

Historical Note
Incorporated in 1897 by act of Congress. Members are teachers, administrators, educational interpreters, residential personnel and other concerned professionals involved in the education of the deaf. CAID is a member of the Council on Education of the Deaf, the Council of Organizational Representatives, and the Coalition of Citizens with Disabilities. Membership: $75/year (individual).

Publications:
American Annals of the Deaf. q. adv.
American Annals of the Deaf (Reference issue). a. adv.
Conference Proceedings. bien. adv.
News'n Notes Newsletter. q. adv.

Meetings/Conferences:
Biennial Meetings: Uneven years/June
1999 – Los Angeles, CA(Los Angeles Hilton &
        Towers)/July 14-18
1999 – Los Angeles, CA

Converting Equipment Manufacturers Ass'n (1984)
66 Morris Ave., Suite 2A
Springfield, NJ   07081
Tel: (973)379-1100   *Fax:* (973)379-6507
Members: 75 companies
Staff: 3
Annual Budget: $50-100,000
Exec. Director: Richard Alampi

Historical Note
Membership open to any company or corporation engaged on a commercial scale in the manufacture of coaters, laminators, slitters/rewinders, printing press, metalizers, sheeters, extruders, calenders, forming, bag or envelope machinery used to perform a complete web converting function. Membership: $1,000/yr. (full); $700/yr. (associate).

Publications:
CEMA Scope. q.

Meetings/Conferences:
Annual Meetings: May or June

Conveyor Equipment Manufacturers Ass'n (1933)
6724 Lone Oak Blvd.
Naples, FL   34109-6834
Tel: (941)514-3441   *Fax:* (941)514-3470
E-Mail: staff@cemanet.org
Web Site: http://cemanet.org
Members: 91 companies
Staff: 4
Annual Budget: $250-500,000
Exec. V. President: Robert A. Reinfried

Historical Note
Founded as the Ass'n of Conveyor and Material Preparation Equipment Manufacturers, it became the Conveyor Ass'n in 1935 and assumed its present name in 1945. A member of the Machinery and Allied Products Institute.

Publications:
Bulletin.
Directory. a.

Meetings/Conferences:
Semi-Annual Meetings: March and September/150
1999 – Litchfield Park, AZ(Wigwam)
2000 – Naples, FL(Registry)
2001 – Rancho Mirage, CA(Nestin Mission Hills Resort)

Cookie and Snack Bakers Ass'n (1962)
P.O. Box 3720
Cleveland, TN   37320
Tel: (423)472-1561
Members: 25 processors
Staff: 1
Exec. Director: Craig Parrish

Historical Note
Members are bakery and snack food processors.

Meetings/Conferences:
Annual Meetings: Fall

Cookware Manufacturers Ass'n (1922)
P.O. Box 531335
Mountain Brook, AL   35253
Tel: (205)802-7600   *Fax:* (205)802-7610
E-Mail: hrushing@cookware.org
Web Site: http://www.cookware.org
Members: 25 companies
Staff: 1
Annual Budget: $100-250,000
Exec. V. President: Hugh J. Rushing

Historical Note
Formerly (until 1963) the Aluminum Wares Ass'n and (until 1981) the Metal Cookware Manufacturers Ass'n.

Publications:
Consumer Guide to Cookware.
Enginnering Standards Manual for Cookware/Bakeware.

Meetings/Conferences:
Annual Meetings: Spring/60
1999 – Ojai, CA(Ojai Valley Inn)
2000 – Williamburg, VA(Williamsburg Inn)
2001 – La Quinta, CA(La Quinta Resort)

Cooling Tower Institute (1950)
Box 73383
Houston, TX   77273
Tel: (281)583-4087   *Fax:* (281)537-1721
E-Mail: vmanser@cti.org
Web Site: http://www.cti.org
Members: 400 corporations
Staff: 2
Annual Budget: $500-1,000,000
Administrator: Virginia A. Manser

Historical Note
Promotes improvement in technology, design, performance and maintenance of cooling towers. Also concerned with water and air pollution and conservation of water as a natural resource. Membership: $420/year.
Publications:
CTI Journal. semi-a. adv.
CTI News. q.
Meetings/Conferences:

Cooperative Education Ass'n *(1963)*
8640 Guilford Road, Suite 215
Columbia, MD 21046-2615
Tel: (410)290-3666   *Fax:* (410)290-7084
E-Mail: jleim@aol.com
Members: 1,200 individuals
Staff: 3
Annual Budget: $250-500,000
Exec. Director: Dawn Pettit
Historical Note
Represents all aspects of cooperative education, the integration of classroom work and practical experience in an organized college program. CEA's primary goal is to promote opportunities for students to integrate periods of academic study with curriculum-related, paid, productive work experiences that maximize benefits to all students, employers and educators involved. Membership: $110/year (individual); $290/year (organization).
Publications:
CEA Membership Directory. a.
Experience Magazine. 2-3/year.
Journal of Cooperative Education. 3/yr.
President's Newsbrief. q.
Meetings/Conferences:
Annual Meetings: Spring
1999 – Washington, DC(Hyatt Regency)/July 4-7/1000

Cooperative Whole Grain Education Ass'n *(1978)*
Historical Note
Address unknown in 1996.

Coordinating Council for Women in History *(1969)*
Glendale College
1500 North Verdugo Road
Glendale, CA 91208
Tel: (818)240-1000   *Fax:* (818)549-9436
Members: 800 individuals
Staff: 1
Annual Budget: $10-25,000
Exec. Director: Marguerite Renner
Historical Note
Formerly (1995) Coordinating Committee on Women in the Historical Profession/Conference Group on Women's History. CCWH is concerned with the advancement of women at all levels in the profession and with the study of women's history. Membership: $15-$50/year, based on salary (individual); $10/year (graduate student).
Publications:
CCWH Newsletter. 5/yr. adv.
Meetings/Conferences:
Annual Meetings: in conjunction with AHA annual
             meeting/January
1999 – Washington, DC/Jan. 7-10

Coordinating Research Council *(1942)*
219 Perimeter Center Pkwy., Suite 400
Atlanta, GA 30346
Tel: (770)396-3400   *Fax:* (770)396-3404
E-Mail: tbellian@crcao.com
Members: 800 individuals, 2 companies
Staff: 8
Annual Budget: $1-2,000,000
Exec. Director: Alan E. Zengel, CAE
Historical Note
Coordinates research between the petroleum, automotive equipment and transportation industries.
Publications:
Annual Report.
Meetings/Conferences:
Annual Meetings: None held.

Copier Dealers Ass'n *(1977)*
Historical Note
Address unknown in 1997; presumed inactive.

Copper and Brass Fabricators Council *(1964)*
1050 17th St., N.W., Suite 440
Washington, DC 20036-5561
Tel: (202)833-8575   *Fax:* (202)331-8267
Members: 23 companies
Staff: 3
Annual Budget: $250-500,000
President: Joseph L. Mayer
Government Affairs Counsel: John E. Arnett
Historical Note
Formerly (1966) Copper & Brass Fabricators Foreign Trade Ass'n, Inc. The CBFC was organized to stem the flood of unlawful imports of brass mill products, minimize the compliance costs of federal regulations, and deal with brass mill industry problems. Membership: dues vary according to company size.
Meetings/Conferences:
Annual Meetings: February
1999 – New York, NY(Waldorf Astoria)

Copper and Brass Servicenter Ass'n *(1951)*
994 Old Eagle School Road, Suite 1019
Wayne, PA 19087-1802
Tel: (610)971-4850   *Fax:* (610)971-4859
E-Mail: fbrown@cbsa.copper-brass.org

Web Site: http://www.cbsa.copper-brass.org
Members: 85 individuals, 82 companies
Staff: 2
Annual Budget: $250-500,000
Exec. V. President: R. Franklin Brown, Jr.
Historical Note
Formerly (1976) Copper and Brass Warehouse Ass'n. CBSA is composed of wholesale distributors (Servicenters) of fabricated copper and brass mill products; the associate members are mills (fabricators) who manufacture such products.
Publications:
CBSA Capsules Newsletter. m.
Guide for Marketing Copper, Brass, and Bronze. 5/year.
Guide to American Brass Mills. 3/year.
Membership Directory. a.
Report - Statistical Survey. m.
Sources Handbook. bien.
Meetings/Conferences:
Annual Meetings: Spring
1999 – Marco Island, FL(Marriott Marco)/March 17-20/275
2000 – Kamuela, HI(Hapuna Prince)/March 29-April 1

Copper Development Ass'n *(1963)*
260 Madison Ave.
New York, NY 10016-2401
Tel: (212)251-7200   *Fax:* (212)251-7234
Toll Free: (800)232 - 3282
E-Mail: r.payne@cdacopper.org
Web Site: http://www.copper.org
Members: 71 companies
Staff: 31
Annual Budget: $10-25,000,000
President: Robert M. Payne
Historical Note
Supersedes the Copper and Brass Research Ass'n as the market and technical development arm of the copper and brass industry. Membership is open to copper producers worldwide and to brass mill, wire mill and foundry fabricators of copper and copper alloys with production facilities in the USA. Has an annual budget of approximately $11 million.
Publications:
Annual Data. a.
Copper Topics. q.
Meetings/Conferences:
Annual Meetings: June and December

Copyright Soc. of the U.S.A. *(1953)*
1133 Ave. of the Americas
New York, NY 10036-6910
Tel: (212)354-6401   *Fax:* (212)354-2847
E-Mail: barpan@interport.net
Web Site: http://www.csusa.org
Members: 850 individuals
Staff: 2
Annual Budget: $100-250,000
Administrator: Barbara Pannone
Historical Note
Established to foster interest in and advance the study of copyright law and of rights in literature, music, art, the theatre, motion pictures and other forms of intellectual property. Established the Walter J. Derenberg Copyright Library in 1976. Membership: $175/year (individual); $700-1,200/year (company).
Publications:
Journal of the CSUSA. q.
Meetings/Conferences:
Semi-Annual Meetings: January-March and June
1999 – Bolton Landing, NY(Sagamore Hotel)/June 13-15/400
2000 – Bolton Landing, NY(Sagamore Hotel)/June 11-14/400

Copywriter's Council of America *(1964)*
7 Putter Ln., Communications Bldg.
P.O. Box 102
Middle Island, NY 11953-0102
Tel: (516)924-8555   *Fax:* (516)924-3890
Members: 5,550 individuals
Staff: 6
Exec. Director: Roger Dextor
Historical Note
CCA members are professional copywriters, photojournalists, writers, marketing and public relations consultants, copy editors, proofreaders and others with an interest in print, broadcast, and public relations communications. Membership: $125/year (professional); $95/year (associate); $200/year (company).
Publications:
Digest. q.
Meetings/Conferences:

Cordage Exporters Ass'n
Historical Note
A Webb-Pomerene association, organized to promote commodity export, CEA is operated by the Cordage Institute.

Cordage Institute *(1920)*
350 Lincoln St.
Hingham, MA 02043
Tel: (781)749-1016   *Fax:* (781)749-9783
E-Mail: ropecord@aol.com
Web Site: http://www.ropecord.com/
Members: 50 companies
Staff: 2
Annual Budget: $250-500,000
Exec. Director: G.P. Foster
Historical Note
Membership consists of manufacturers of natural and synthetic cordage (rope, twine and netting) and fiber and machinery suppliers. Merged with the American Cordage and Netting Manufacturers in 1990. Membership: annual dues vary based on class.

Publications:
Newsletter. bi-m.
Rope Cord Directory. m.
Ropecord News. bi-m. adv.
Standards, Technical Information Manual.
Meetings/Conferences:
1999 – Chandler, AZ(Sheraton)/April 21-24/100

Corel WTA Tour *(1973)*
1266 E. Main St.
Fourth Floor
Stamford, CT 06902-3546
Tel: (203)978-1740   *Fax:* (203)978-1702
Members: 500 individuals
Staff: 32
Annual Budget: $2-5,000,000
C.E.O.: Bara McGuire
Historical Note
Originally Women's Tennis Ass'n, became (1986) Women's Internat'l Tennis Ass'n, reverted to its original name in 1990. Absorbed WTA Tour Players Ass'n and assumed its current name in 1995. Members are professional women tennis players. Sponsors tournaments in 22 countries worldwide. Full membership: $750/year.
Publications:
Media Guide. a.

Corn Refiners Ass'n *(1913)*
1701 Pennsylvania Ave., N.W., Suite 950
Washington, DC 20006-5805
Tel: (202)331-1634   *Fax:* (202)331-2054
E-Mail: details@corn.org
Web Site: http://www.corn.org
Members: 9 companies
Staff: 8
Annual Budget: $1-2,000,000
President: Charles F. Conner
Director, Communications: Shannon Shoesmith
Director, Congressional Affairs: Sherri K. Lehman
V. President: Kyd D. Brenner
Director, Technical Affairs: Jennifer White
Historical Note
Formerly (1923) American Manufacturers' Ass'n of Products from Corn; (1932) Associated Corn Products Manufacturers; (1966) Corn Industries Research Foundation. Represents the corn wet milling industry in the U.S. Members operate plants which produce corn syrup, corn starch, dextrose, corn oil and various animal feed ingredients.
Publications:
Corn Annual. a.

Corporate Facility Advisors
P.O. Box 30583
Santa Barbara, CA 93130-0583
Tel: (510)886-1662   *Fax:* (510)582-6513
Members: 805 individuals, 67 firms
Annual Budget: $100-250,000
Exec. Director: Kate Canon
Historical Note
CORFAC Internat'l member firms, located in 46 major North American cities, 35 European cities and Hong Kong, provide a full spectrum of coordinated commercial real estate services, including brokerage, counseling valuation, finance, project management and asset management. Membership: $3500/year (organization).
Meetings/Conferences:
Semi-annual Meetings: February and September/150-170

Corporate Transfer Agents Ass'n *(1946)*
c/o AFLAC
1932 Wynton Road
Columbus, GA 31999
Tel: (706)596-3385   *Fax:* (706)596-3488
Members: 240 individuals
Annual Budget: $50-100,000
President: Joan M. DiBlasi
Historical Note
Members are corporate employees responsible for the transfer of stock, shareholder services and related functions. Membership: $225/year (organization/company).
Publications:
CTAA Roster & Bylaws. irreg.
Output Newsletter. q.
Meetings/Conferences:
Annual Meetings: May Palm Beach, FL(PGA National)/June 1-4

Correctional Education Ass'n *(1945)*
4380 Forbes Blvd.
Lanham, MD 20706
Tel: (301)918-1915   *Fax:* (301)918-1846
Members: 3,000 individuals
Staff: 2
Annual Budget: $250-500,000
Exec. Director: Stephen J. Steurer
Historical Note
One of the largest affiliates of the American Correctional Ass'n and one of two with a national headquarters and paid staff, CEA is a nonprofit professional association serving educators and administrators who provide services to students in correctional settings. Its members include adult and juvenile educational administrators, academic and vocational educators, correctional officers, counselors, clinicians, researchers and librarians. (institution). Membership: $50/year (individual), $85/year (library), and $85/year (institution), $275/year (corporate/life).
Publications:
CEA Newsletter. q. adv.
CEA Yearbook. a.
Directory. a.
Journal of Correctional Education. q. adv.

Meetings/Conferences:
Annual Meetings: July
1999 - Philidelphia, PA(Adams Mark Hotel)/Aug. 1-4

Correctional Industries Ass'n *(1942)*
1420 W. Charles St.
Suite CH415
Baltimore, MD 21201
Tel: (410)837-5036   *Fax:* (410)837-5039
Web Site: http://www.corrections.com/industries
Members: 2,100 individuals
Staff: 1
Annual Budget: $25-50,000
Exec. Director: Gwyn Smith Ingley

Historical Note
Members are personnel in prison industries. Affiliated with the American Correctional Association and Jail Industries Ass'n Representatives. Membership: $25/year (individual); $200/year (organization).

Publications:
CIA Directory. a. adv.
CIA Newsletter. q. adv.

Meetings/Conferences:
Annual Meetings: August, with American Correctional Ass'n

Correctional Service - U.S. Federation *(1962)*

Historical Note
Formerly (1993) Correctional Service Federation U.S.A. Affiliate of the American Correctional Ass'n and International Prisoners Aid Ass'n. CSF represents the private sector in corrections, usually providing contracted direct service to correctional clients or impacting state or national level legislative processes. Membership: $5/year (individual), $50/year (organization).

COSMEP, Internat'l Ass'n of Independent Publishers *(1968)*

Historical Note
Address unknown in 1996.

Cosmetic Executive Women *(1954)*
20 East 69th Street, Suite 5-C
New York, NY 10021
Tel: (212)717-2415   *Fax:* (212)717-2419
Members: 850 individuals
Staff: 1
President: Jean Hoehn-Zimmerman

Historical Note
Organized in 1954 and incorporated in New York in 1959. Membership is limited to women who have served at least 3 years in an executive capacity in business, and presently in the cosmetic industry. Formerly (1981) Cosmetic Career Women.

Publications:
CEW Wavelength. q.

Meetings/Conferences:
Annual Meetings: always New York, NY

Cosmetic, Toiletry and Fragrance Ass'n *(1894)*
1101 17th St., N.W., Suite 300
Washington, DC 20036-4702
Tel: (202)331-1770   *Fax:* (202)331-1969
Web Site: http://www.ctfa.org
Members: 525 companies
Staff: 50
Annual Budget: $10-25,000,000
President: E. Edward Kavanaugh
V. President, Public Affairs: Irene L. Malbin
V. President, Legislative Relations: Michael J. Patrina, Jr.
Director, meetings: Jean Knarr, CMP
Dir., Administration: Cheryl Schiappa
V. President/General Counsel: Thomas J. Donegan, Jr.

Historical Note
Founded as the Manufacturing Perfumers Ass'n of the United States, it became the American Manufacturers of Toilet Articles in 1921, the Associated Manufacturers of Toilet Articles in 1932, the Toilet Goods Ass'n in 1935 and assumed its present name in 1971. Sponsors the Cosmetic, Toiletry and Fragrance Ass'n Political Action Committee. Founded the CTFA Foundation in 1986. Has an annual budget of approximately $10.5 million.

Publications:
Annual Report. a.
CIR Development. q.
CTFA Newsletter. bi-w.
Tech/Reg. Notes.
Who's Who Membership Directory. a. adv.

Meetings/Conferences:
Annual Meetings: usually Boca Raton, FL(Boca Raton
          Resort)/February-March
1999 - /Feb. 25-28

Cost Management Group
10 Paragon Dr.
Montvale, NJ 07645-1760
Tel: (201)573-9000   *Fax:* (201)573-8185
Toll Free: (800)638 - 4427
E-Mail: migs@imanet.org
Web Site: http://www.imanet.org
Members: 1,300 individuals
Staff: 2
Contact: Michelle Nicolato

Historical Note
CMG is a member interest group of the Institute of Management Accountants. Membership: $75/year.

Publications:
Cost Management Update. m.

Costume Jewelry Salesmen's Ass'n *(1951)*
3 Davol Sq., Suite B101
Mail Unit #117

Providence, RI 02903
Tel: (401)272-3090   *Fax:* (401)274-5114
Members: 102 individuals
Staff: 1
Annual Budget: $1-2,000,000
President and Managing Director: Louis Cohn

Historical Note
Membership: $100/year.

Meetings/Conferences:

Costume Soc. of America *(1973)*
55 Edgewater Drive
P.O. Box 73
Earleville, MD 21919-0073
Tel: (410)275-2329   *Fax:* (410)275-8936
Toll Free: (800)272 - 9447
Web Site: http://www.costumesocietyamerica.com
Members: 1,700 individuals
Staff: 2
Annual Budget: $100-250,000
President: Phyllis Specht
Manager: Kaye Kittle Boyer, CAE

Historical Note
CSA members are costume professionals and enthusiasts interested in the study, collection, preservation, presentation and interpretation of dress and appearance in societies of the past, present and future. Membership: $60/year (individual); $40/year (student); $95/year (institution); $35/year (library); $90/year (sustaining); $350/year (corporate).

Publications:
CSA Bibliography. irreg.
CSA Membership Directory. a.
CSA News. q.
Dress Journal. a.
Symposium Abstract. a.

Meetings/Conferences:
Annual Meetings: May-June

Cottage Industry Miniaturists Trade Ass'n *(1980)*
P.O. Box 42849
Evergreen Park, IL 60805
Tel: (773)233-5522   *Fax:* (773)223-5506
Toll Free: (800)492 - 4682
E-Mail: CIMTA@tradeshownet.com
Web Site: http://www.cimta.com
Members: 300 individuals
Annual Budget: $10-25,000
President: Frank Morze

Historical Note
Members are handcrafters of dollhouse miniatures. Sponsors trade shows and seminars for members. Membership: $100/year.

Publications:
CIMTA Newsletter. q.

Meetings/Conferences:
1999 - Las Vegas, NV
1999 - Arlington, VA

Cotton Council Internat'l *(1956)*
1521 New Hampshire Ave., N.W.
Washington, DC 20036-1205
Tel: (202)745-7805   *Fax:* (202)483-4040
E-Mail: cottonusa@cotton.org
Web Site: http://www.cottonusa.org
Members: 21 companies
Staff: 20
Annual Budget: $10-25,000,000
Exec. Director: Allen Terhaar
Communications Coordinator: Tommy Horton
Fiscal Director: Debrise A. Winter

Historical Note
The overseas operations arm of the Nat'l Cotton Council of America. CCI's primary goal is to increase exports of American-grown cotton.

Publications:
Buyers Guide to U. S.
CCI FAX. w.
Cotton USA Global Fax.
U. S.

Meetings/Conferences:
1999 - Memphis, TN(Peabody)/Feb. 4-8

Cotton Warehouse Ass'n of America *(1969)*
1156 15th St., N.W., Suite 1103
Washington, DC 20005
Tel: (202)331-4337   *Fax:* (202)331-4330
Members: 125 companies
Annual Budget: $100-250,000
Exec. V. President: Donald L. Wallace, Jr.

Historical Note
Merger (1969) of the American and the National Cotton Compress and Cotton Warehouse Ass'ns. Supports the Cotton Warehouse Government Relations Committee.

Publications:
Cotton Comments. m.

Meetings/Conferences:
Annual Meetings: June
1999 - Sun Valley, ID(Sun Valley Resort)
2000 - Charleston, SC
2001 - Acapulco, Mexico(The Princess)

Council for Adult and Experiential Learning *(1974)*
243 S. Wabash Ave., Suite 800
Chicago, IL 60604-2302
Tel: (312)922-5909   *Fax:* (312)922-1769
E-Mail: skrone@cael.org
Web Site: http://www.cael.org
Members: 700 institutions and individuals
Staff: 80

Annual Budget: $2-5,000,000
President: Pamela Tate
V. President for Public Policy: Samuel Leiken

Historical Note
Established in 1974 as Council for the Advancement of Experiential Learning (CAEL), it assumed its present name in 1985 to reflect changing program priorities. A non-profit, higher education association whose basic mission is the advancement of experiential learning and the improvement of services to adult learners. Membership: $75/year (individual); $275-475/year (institution); $275/year (organization).

Publications:
CAEL Forum & News. q. adv.

Meetings/Conferences:
Annual Meetings: November

Council for Advancement and Support of Education *(1974)*
1307 New York Ave., NW, Suite 1000
Washington, DC 20005-4701
Tel: (202)328-5900   *Fax:* (202)387-4973
Web Site: http://www.case.org
Members: 14,500 individuals, 2,950 institutions
Staff: 90
Annual Budget: $10-25,000,000
President: Eustace D. Theodore
V.P., Communications: Sarah Hardesty Bray
Director, Public and State Relations Affairs: Micahel McDowell
Director, Gov't. Relations: Eric Wentworth
Director, Conference Services: Sheryl Brannon
V. President, Education: Patricia Jackson
V.P., Finance and Admin.: Charles Lee
Manager, Member Services: Minnie de la Paz
Dir., Membership Development: A. Cedric Calhoun
Publisher and Editor in Chief: Mary Dalheim
Online and Media Rels. Director: Steve Weiss
V. President, Strategic Initiatives: Thomas Grabau
V. President, Marketing: Julie Landes
Dir., Int'l Programs: Janet Sailian

Historical Note
Merger (1974) of American College Public Relations Ass'n and American Alumni Council. Formerly (1975) AAC/ACPRA. Has an annual budget of approximately $10 million.

Publications:
CASE CURRENTS. 10/year. adv.

Meetings/Conferences:
Annual Meetings: Summer
1999 - Boston, MA

Council for Affordable and Rural Housing *(1980)*
1300 19th St., N.W., Suite 410
Washington, DC 20036
Tel: (202)296-5159   *Fax:* (202)785-2008
E-Mail: CARH@worldweb.net
Web Site: http://www.worldweb.net/ ~ carh
Members: 231 individuals, 10 state organizations
Exec. Director: Colleen M. Fisher
Membership Coordinator: Dorothy Fernandes

Historical Note
CARH is a trade association representing managers and developers of affordable housing.

Meetings/Conferences:
1999 - Ft. Lauderdale, FL(Largo Mar Resort)/Jan. 24-26

Council for Agricultural Science and Technology *(1972)*
4420 W. Lincoln Way
Ames, IA 50014-3447
Tel: (515)292-2125   *Fax:* (515)292-4512
E-Mail: cast@cast-science.org
Web Site: http://www.cast-science.org
Members: 3,000 individuals, 36 scientific societies
Staff: 5
Annual Budget: $500-1,000,000
Exec. V. President: Richard E. Stuckey
Communications Director: Robert J. Ver Straeten
Director, Development: Candi Kelly

Historical Note
Chartered in the State of Iowa as a non-profit corporation to provide accurate information, based on agricultural science and technology, to the government, the news media and the public about national or regional agricultural subjects of broad concern. Membership: $40-100/year (individual); dues vary (organization/company).

Publications:
Issue Papers, irreg.
NewsCAST. q.
Special Publications, irreg.
Task Force Reports. irreg.

Council for American Private Education *(1971)*
18016 Mateny Road, Suite 140
Germantown, MD 20874-2112
Tel: (301)916-8460   *Fax:* (301)916-8485
E-Mail: cape@impresso.com
Members: 13 organizations
Staff: 2
Annual Budget: $100-250,000
Exec. Director: Joseph W. McTighe

Historical Note
Represents national organizations for private elementary and secondary schools. Actively voices private school positions on public policy issues affecting private education.

Publications:
Outlook. m.

Meetings/Conferences:
Semi-annual Meetings: Washington, DC in March and
          October

Council for Art Education

100 Boylston St., Suite 1050
Boston, MA 02116-4610
Tel: (617)426-6400   *Fax:* (617)426-6639
Annual Budget: $25-50,000
Exec. Secretary/Clerk: Deborah Fanning, CAE
Youth Art Month Coordinator: Deborah S. Gustafson

Historical Note
*CAE promotes art education and school art programs, primarily
through the Nat'l Youth Art Month program.*

Publications:
YAM News. q.

Meetings/Conferences:
Annual Meetings: Summer

Council for Basic Education *(1956)*

1319 F St., N.W., Suite 900
Washington, DC 20004-1152
Tel: (202)347-4171   *Fax:* (202)347-5047
E-Mail: info@c-b-e.org
Web Site: http://www.c-b-e.org
Members: 3,500 individuals
Staff: 25
Annual Budget: $2-5,000,000
President: Christopher T. Cross
Vice President: Elsa M. Little
Director of Communications: Selina Newell Winchester
Director, Publications: Madelyn Holmes
Director, Development: Julie Slavik

Historical Note
*National advocate of the liberal arts for all elementary and
secondary school students. Primarily concerned with strengthening
the position of the basic curriculum - English, Math, Science,
Foreign Languages, History and the Arts. Membership: $50/year.*

Publications:
Basic Education. 10/year.
CBE Advocate. 3/year.
Independent Study in the Humanities: Directory of Fellows. a.
Perspective. irreg.

Meetings/Conferences:
Annual Meetings: Semi-Annual
1999 – Washington, DC(CBE office)
2000 – Washington, DC(CBE office)

Council for Chemical Research *(1980)*

1620 L St., N.W., Suite 825
Washington, DC 20036
Tel: (202)429-3971   *Fax:* (202)429-3976
Members: 204 organizations
Staff: 3
Annual Budget: $500-1,000,000
Exec. Director: Janis L. Tabor, CAE

Historical Note
*CCR members are university, government, and private industry
laboratories engaged in research.*

Publications:
CCR News. q.

Council for Children with Behavioral Disorders

Historical Note
CCBD is a division of the Council for Exceptional Children.

Council for Early Childhood Professional Recognition *(1985)*

2460 16th St., N.W.
Washington, DC 20009-3575
Tel: (202)265-9090   *Fax:* (202)265-7309
Toll Free: (800)424 - 4310
E-Mail: cda@cdacouncil.org
Web Site: http://www.cdacouncil.org
Members: 100,000 individuals
Staff: 35
Annual Budget: $2-5,000,000
Exec. Director: Carol B. Phillips, Ph.D.

Historical Note
*Formerly (1987) Child Development Associate Nat'l Credentialing
Program. Concerned with improving the standards of child care
through establishing standards and credentialing staff of child care
facilities.*

Publications:
CDA Information Mannual.
Council News & Views. 3/yr.
Essentials.
Improving Childcare.
Nat'l Directory of Early Childhood Teacher Preparation
    Institutions.

Meetings/Conferences:
Annual Meetings: None held.

Council for Educational Development and Research

Historical Note
Became (1997) Nat'l Education Knowledge Industry Ass'n.

Council for Educational Diagnostic Services

Historical Note
CEDS is a division of the Council for Exceptional Children.

Council for Electronic Revenue Communication Advancement

1800 Diagonal Road, Suite 600
Alexandria, VA 22314
Tel: (703)684-3147
Members: 75 companies
Staff: 4
Annual Budget: $250-500,000
Exec. Director: Michael Cavanagh

Historical Note
*CERCA members are companies with an interest in advancing
electronic commerce with government revenue agencies.
Membership: $25-$75/year (individual); $500-$2,000/year,
based on sales (corporate); $2,000/year (government agency).*

Publications:
CERCA News. q.

Council for Elementary Science Internat'l *(1920)*

Dept. of EDCI-TAMU
Texas A & M University
College Station, TX 77843-4232
Tel: (409)845-7088   *Fax:* (409)845-9663
E-Mail: djanke@tamu.edu
Members: 1,200 individuals
Annual Budget: $10-25,000
President: Delmar Janke

Historical Note
*CESI members are teachers, administrators and others with an
interest in the teaching of science at the preschool, elementary and
middle school levels. Membership: $16/year.*

Publications:
CESI Directory. a.
CESI News. q. adv.
CESI Updates. irreg.
Mongraph. a.

Meetings/Conferences:
Annual Meetings: in conjunction with the Nat'l Science
    Teachers Ass'n

Council for Ethics in Economics *(1982)*

125 E. Broad St.
Columbus, OH 43215-3605
Tel: (614)221-8661   *Fax:* (614)221-8707
Web Site: http://www.businessethics.org
Annual Budget: $250-500,000
President: David C. Smith, Ph.D.

Historical Note
*The Council is an association of leaders in business, education and
other professions, working together to strengthen the ethical fabric
of business and economic life. Membership:$100 (individual);
moving scale prices for organizations.*

Publications:
Ethics in Economics. q. adv.

Meetings/Conferences:
1999 – Columbus, OH

Council for European Studies *(1970)*

807-807A International Affairs Bldg.
Columbia University
New York, NY 10027
Tel: (212)854-4172   *Fax:* (212)854-8808
E-Mail: ces@columbia.edu
Web Site: http://www.columbia.edu/cu/ces
Members: 900 individuals, 75 institutions
Staff: 2
Annual Budget: $250-500,000
Exec. Director: Ioannis Sinanoglou

Historical Note
*Members are social scientists interested in modern Europe and
colleges and universities that have programs dealing with the
history, culture and economics of Western Europe. Membership:
$20/year (student); $25/year (individual); $300/year (institution).*

Publications:
European Studies Newsletter. bi-m. adv.

Meetings/Conferences:
Biennial Meetings: (even years)

Council for Exceptional Children *(1922)*

1920 Association Drive
Reston, VA 20191-1589
Tel: (703)620-3660   *Fax:* (703)264-9494
Toll Free: (888)232 - 7733
E-Mail: cec@cec.sped.org
Web Site: http://www.cec.sped.org
Members: 51,000 individuals
Staff: 80
Annual Budget: $5-10,000,000
Exec. Director: Nancy Safer
Assistant Exec. Director, Public Policy: B. Joseph Ballard
Asst. Exec. Director, Professional Standards & Practice: Richard
    Mainzer
Dep. Exec. Director: Bruce A. Ramirez
Asst. Exec. Director, Financial Affairs and Operations: Eugene
    Sullivan
*Asst. Exec. Director. Membership and Unit Development/Constituent
    Services:* Grace Z. Duran, Ed.D.

Historical Note
*Formerly (1958) International Council for Exceptional Children.
CEC is a professional organization whose members include
teachers, administrators, teacher educators, students, support
services, professionals and parents. Its goals include the promotion
of professional standards of practice for persons involved in the
education of exceptional persons; the extension of special education
services to exceptional children not presently being served; and the
support of the development and advancement of new knowledge,
technology, methodology, curriculum and materials. Special
divisions within CEC (which publish their own periodicals, see
below) include: Council for Children with Behavioral Disorders;
Career Development; Council for Educational Diagnostic Services;
Mental Retardation; Children with Communication Disorders; Early
Childhood; Administrators of Special Education; Ass'n for the
Gifted; Technology and Media; Research; and Council of
Administrators of Special Education. Hosts symposia, and the ERIC
Clearinghouse on Disabilities and Gifted Education. Sponsors and
supports the CEC Children's Action Network (CEC-CAN).*

Publications:
Behavioral Disorders. q.
Career Development for Exceptional Individuals. semi-a.
Diagnostique. q.
Education and Training of the Mentally Retarded. q.
Exceptional Child Education Resources. q.
Exceptional Children. q. adv.
Journal for the Education of the Gifted. q.
Journal of Childhood Communication Disorders. semi-a.
Journal of Special Education Technology.
Journal of the Division for Early Childhood. semi-a.
Learning Disabilities Research. semi-a.
Learning Disability Focus. semi-a.
Teacher Education and Special Education. q.
Teaching Exceptional Children. bi-m. adv.

Meetings/Conferences:
Annual Meetings: Spring

Council for Higher Education Accreditation *(1974)*

One Dupont Circle, N.W., Suite 510
Washington, DC 20036-1135
Tel: (202)955-6126   *Fax:* (202)955-6129
E-Mail: chea@chea.org
Web Site: http://www.chea.org
Members: 56 accrediting bodies
Staff: 2
Annual Budget: $100-250,000
President: Judith Eaton
V. President: Dr. Phillis Safman
Government Relations: Gregory Fusco
Office Manager: Micheal Shipiro

Historical Note
*Successor organization to the Council on Postsecondary
Accreditation which dissolved in 1993 and the Commission on
Recognition of Postsecondary Accreditation which dissolved in
1996. CHEA is an organization of colleges and universities serving
as the national advocate for voluntary self-regulation through
accreditation. It is supported by member institutions and regional,
national and specialized/professional accrediting bodies.*

Publications:
Accredited Institutions of Postsecondary Education. a.
Annual Directory. a.

Meetings/Conferences:
1999 – San Diego, CA/Jan. 31-Feb. 2

Council for Internat'l Business Risk Management *(1980)*

Historical Note
Organization defunct in 1995.

Council for Jewish Education *(1926)*

111 8th Ave.
New York, NY 10011-5201
Tel: (212)284-6950
Members: 350 individuals
Annual Budget: $25-50,000
Secretary: Solomon Goldman, Ph.D.

Historical Note
*Formerly (until 1981) the Nat'l Council for Jewish Education.
Members are college and university teachers of Hebrew and faculty
of Jewish teacher training schools.*

Publications:
Journal of Jewish Education (English). 3/year.

Meetings/Conferences:
Annual Meetings: Joint meetings with CJCS.

Council for Learning Disabilities *(1968)*

P.O. Box 40303
Overland Park, KS 66204
Tel: (913)492-8755   *Fax:* (913)492-2546
Web Site: http://coe.winthrop.edu/cld/
Members: 2,000 individuals
Annual Budget: $100-250,000
Exec. Secretary: Kirsten McBride

Historical Note
*CLD members are educators, diagnosticians, psychologists,
physicians, optometrists, and speech, occupational and physical
therapists working with individuals having specific disorders
involving reading, writing, speaking, listening, thinking and
mathematics. A member of the Nat'l Joint Committee on Learning
Disabilities, CLD promotes and encourages high standards for
serving the learning disabled and for conducting research including
taking positions on legislation and professional practices.
Membership: $45/year (individual)*

Publications:
Learning Disability Quarterly. q. adv.

Meetings/Conferences:
1999 – Minneapolis, MN(Radisson)/Oct. 13-15/800
2000 – Austin, TX(Hyatt)/Oct. 18-21/800

Council for Marketing and Opinion Research *(1992)*

170 North Country Road
Port Jefferson, NY 11777-2180
Tel: (516)928-6206   *Fax:* (516)928-6041
Annual Budget: $500-1,000,000
President: Diane K. Bowers

Historical Note
*CMDR was established by four major industry associations to
address the critical issues of government affairs and respondent
cooperation.*

Council for Museum Anthropology *(1975)*

c/o American Anthropological Ass'n
4350 North Fairfax Drive, Suite 640
Arlington, VA 22203
Tel: (703)528-1902   *Fax:* (703)528-3546
Members: 450 individuals
Annual Budget: $10-25,000
President: Sally Yerkovich

Historical Note
*Members are anthropologists, institutions and others with an
interest in the field. CMA is a section of American Anthropological*

Ass'n and an Affiliated Professional Organization of American Ass'n of Museums. Membership: varies based on the type of membership

Publications:
Museum Anthropolgy Journal. 3/year. adv.

Meetings/Conferences:
Semi-Annual Meetings: in conjunction with AAM/Spring and AAA/Fall

Council for Near-Infrared Spectroscopy (1986)
Bldg. 200, Rm. 218
NCML, USDA, BARC East
Beltsville, MD 20705
Tel: (301)504-8294   *Fax:* (301)504-8162
Web Site: http://kerouac.pharm.uky.edu/asrg/cnirs/cnirs.html
President: Jim Reeves

Historical Note
Affiliated with the Soc. for Applied Spectroscopy.

Publications:
North American Overtones Newsletter. irreg.

Meetings/Conferences:
1999 – Somerset, NJ(Garden State Convention Center)/Nov. 14-19

Council for Periodical Distributors Ass'ns (1955)
Historical Note
Defunct in 1996.

Council for Responsible Nutrition (1973)
1300 19th St., N.W., Suite 310
Washington, DC 20036-1609
Tel: (202)872-1488   *Fax:* (202)872-9594
E-Mail: info@crnusa.org
Web Site: http://www.crnusa.org
Members: 90 companies
Staff: 11
Annual Budget: $2-5,000,000
President/C.E.O.: John B. Cordaro
Director, Administration: Kenneth Schoppmann
Programs Manager: Christi Jenulsen
Conference Manager: Kathleen Carr-Smith

Historical Note
Manufacturers and distributors of dietary supplements, ingredients, and other nutritional products. Membership: cost based on annual supplement sales.

Publications:
CRN News Newsletter. bi-m.

Meetings/Conferences:
Annual Meetings: Fall
1999 – Palm Springs, CA/Oct. 3-6

Council for Spiritual and Ethical Education (1898)
1465 Northside Dr., N.W., Suite 220
Atlanta, GA 30318-4225
Tel: (404)355-4460   *Fax:* (404)355-4435
E-Mail: info@csee.org
Web Site: www.csee.org
Members: 340 schools
Staff: 3
Annual Budget: $250-500,000
Director: Peter W. Cobb

Historical Note
CRIS provides independent school leaders, chaplains, community service coordinators, and teachers with publications, programs and information to initiate, evaluate and improve the teaching of religion and ethics. Incorporated in the District of Columbia. Membership: $226-646/year.

Publications:
Chaplain's Craft. 3 times/year.
Network News. q.
Newsletter. 10/yr.

Meetings/Conferences:
Annual Meetings: Spring

Council for the Advancement of Standards in Higher Education (1979)
c/o SD School of Mines & Technology
501 E. St. Joseph St.
Rapid City, SD 57701-3995
Tel: (605)394-2416   *Fax:* (605)394-2914
E-Mail: dlange@silver.sdsmt.edu
Members: 100,000 individuals, 32 organizations
Secretary: Douglas Lange

Historical Note
CAS members are professional organizations whose members are involved in providing higher education services.

Publications:
CAS Roster of Members and Directors. a.

Meetings/Conferences:
Semi-Annual Meetings: April and November

Council for Tobacco Research-U.S.A. (1954)
900 3rd Ave., Suite 400
New York, NY 10022
Tel: (212)421-8885
Members: 15 companies
Staff: 20
Annual Budget: $10-25,000,000
President/Chairman: Dr. James Glenn

Historical Note
Organized by tobacco companies as the sponsoring agency for a program of research into questions of the effects of tobacco on human health. Originally the Tobacco Industry Research Committee, it assumed its present name in 1965. Has an annual budget of approximately $19 million.

Publications:
Annual Report.

Council for Urban Economic Development (1967)
1730 K St., N.W., Suite 700
Washington, DC 20006
Tel: (202)223-4735   *Fax:* (202)223-4745
Web Site: http://OUED.org
Members: 1,700 individuals
Staff: 20
Annual Budget: $1-2,000,000
Exec. Director: Jeff Finkle
Deputy Executive Director: Chris Mead

Historical Note
Established as the HUB Council, became the Council for Urban Economic Development in 1971 and assumed its present name in 1974. Members are concerned with urban revitalization and economic development, including state and local development professionals and elected officials, community organization and chamber of commerce leaders, utility executives, and others.

Publications:
Commentary. q.
Economic Development Abroad. bi-m.
Economic Development Commentary. q. adv.
Economic Developments. bi-w.
Information Service Report. irreg.
Legislative Report. irreg.

Meetings/Conferences:

Council of 1890 College Presidents and Chancellors (1913)
c/o office of President
University of Kentucky, E. Main St.
Frankfort, KY 40601
Tel: (502)227-6260   *Fax:* (502)227-6490
E-Mail: gwreid@gwmail.kysu.edu
Members: 20 individuals
Staff: 1
Annual Budget: under $10,000
Secretary-Treasurer: George W. Reid, Ph.D.

Historical Note
Presidents of land grant colleges with predominantly black enrollment. Formerly (1955) known as the Conference of Presidents of Negro Land Grant Colleges, (1979) the Council on Cooperative College Projects, and (1991) Council of 1890 College Presidents. Membership: $500/year.

Meetings/Conferences:
Annual Meetings: November
1999 – San Antonio, TX

Council of Administrators of Special Education
615 16th St., N.W.
Albuquerque, NM 87104-1303
Tel: (505)243-7622   *Fax:* (505)247-4822
E-Mail: case@aol.com
Web Site: http://www.members.aol.com/case/index.htm
Members: 5,300 individuals
Staff: 2
Exec. Officer: Jo Thomason

Historical Note
A division of the Council for Exceptional Children.

Meetings/Conferences:

Council of Advisers to Foreign Students and Scholars
Historical Note
A section of NAFSA: Ass'n of Internat'l Educators.

Council of American Building Officials (1972)
5203 Leesburg Pike, Suite 708
Falls Church, VA 22041
Tel: (703)931-4533   *Fax:* (703)379-1546
E-Mail: staff@intlcode.org
Web Site: http://www.cabo.org
Members: 3 associations
Staff: 4
Annual Budget: $500-1,000,000
C.E.O.: Richard P. Kuchnicki

Historical Note
Merged with International Code Council. Members are the Southern Building Code Congress International, Building Officials and Code Administrators International, and the International Conference of Building Officials. The Council represents the interests of these organizations in Washington.

Meetings/Conferences:
1999 – St. Louis, MO/Sept. 12-16

Council of American Jewish Museums (1978)
330 7th Ave., 21st Floor
New York, NY 10001
Tel: (212)629-0500   *Fax:* (212)629-0508
E-Mail: cajm@jewishculture.org
Members: 60 museums
Staff: 1
Annual Budget: under $10,000
Program Associate: Deborah Schneider

Historical Note
Founded and administered by the Nat'l Foundation for Jewish Culture, CAJM represents a broad spectrum of Jewish community museums and galleries which recognize professional standards of operation and programming. CAJM fosters collaborative efforts to improve scholarship, conservation and exhibition of Jewish art and artifacts. Membership: $75-150/year.

Publications:
CAJM Newsletter. semi-a.

Meetings/Conferences:
Semi-annual Meetings: January and June
1999 – Jackson, MS

Council of American Kidney Socs.
Historical Note
CAKS declined to provide updated information for this edition.

Council of American Maritime Museums (1974)
c/o Chesapeake Bay Maritime Museum
Mill St. - P.O. Box 636
St. Michaels, MD 21663-0636
Tel: (410)745-2916   *Fax:* (410)745-6088
Web Site: http://www.mystic.org/camm
Members: 67 museums
Annual Budget: under $10,000
President: John R. Valliant

Historical Note
Affiliated with the Internat'l Congress of Maritime Museums and the American Ass'n of Museums. Membership: $75/year.

Publications:
Gamming Newsletter. semi-a.

Meetings/Conferences:
1999 – Philadelphia, PA(Independence Seaport Museum)/Sept. 12-18

Council of American Master Mariners (1936)
#5 Dwars Kill Lane
Norwood, NJ 07648
Tel: (201)768-1757   *Fax:* (201)768-6455
E-Mail: alsonmar@aol.com
Members: 1,600 individuals
Staff: 2
Annual Budget: $25-50,000
Nat'l Secretary-Treasurer: Capt. John T. Lemily

Historical Note
CAMM is a professional non-profit organization of shipmasters who now command or have commanded American Flag ocean-going vessels. The stated objective of the Council is to render a public service by voicing, as the need arises, the opinion of Master Mariners concerning professional subjects of common interest to them and of concern to the Maritime Industry. Membership: $50/year.

Publications:
Sidelights. q.

Meetings/Conferences:
Annual Meetings: Spring
2000 – San Francisco, CA

Council of American Overseas Research Centers (1980)
1100 Jefferson Drive, S.W., Suite 3123
Washington, DC 20560
Tel: (202)842-8636   *Fax:* (202)786-2430
Web Site: www.caorc.org
Members: 15 centers
Staff: 3
Annual Budget: $50-100,000
Exec. Director: Mary Ellen Lane

Historical Note
Established to "advance higher learning and scholarly research by providing a forum for communication and cooperation among American overseas advanced research centers."

Meetings/Conferences:
1999 – Washington, DC

Council of American Survey Research Organizations (1975)
3 Upper Devon Belle Terre
Port Jefferson, NY 11777
Tel: (516)928-6954   *Fax:* (516)928-6041
Members: 180 companies
Staff: 5
Annual Budget: $500-1,000,000
Exec. Director: Diane K. Bowers

Historical Note
CASRD is the national trade association of full-service, for profit survey research companies in the United States. Membership: $750-3,500/year.

Meetings/Conferences:
Annual Meetings: Fall

Council of Archives and Research Libraries in Jewish Studies (1974)
330 7th Ave., 21st Floor
New York, NY 10001
Tel: (212)629-0500   *Fax:* (212)629-0508
E-Mail: nfjc@jewishculture.org
Members: 34 institutions
Annual Budget: under $10,000
Program Associate: Deborah Schneider

Historical Note
Founded by the Nat'l Foundation for Jewish Culture in conjunction with the Nat'l Endowment for the Humanities, CARLJS members include the Jewish divisions of major North American municipal, university and Jewish community libraries and archives. CARLJS fosters cooperative efforts to enhance preservation of and access to collections. Membership: $100/year (full).

Meetings/Conferences:
Annual Meetings: June

Council of Better Business Bureaus (1970)
4200 Wilson Blvd., Suite 800
Arlington, VA 22203-1838
Tel: (703)247-9318   *Fax:* (703)525-8277
E-Mail: cbbb@bbb.org
Web Site: http://www.bbb.org
Members: 500 companies & BB Bureaus
Staff: 145
Annual Budget: $10-25,000,000
President and C.E.O.: James L. Bast
Director, Public Relations and Communications: Holly Thompson Cherico
V. President and Chief Information Officer: Stephen L. Rose
V. President and C.F.O.: Joseph E. Dillon
V. President, Administration and Operations: Mary Reilly

Senior V. President, General Counsel and Corp. Secretary: Steven J. Cole
V. President, Marketing: Russell Bodoff
V. President, National Advertising Division: Andrea Levine
V. President, Children's Advertising Review Unit: Elizabeth Lascoutx
Senior V. President, Bureau Affairs Division: Ron Berry
V. President, Philanthropic Advisory Service: Bennett Weiner

Historical Note
Merger (1970) of the Ass'n of Better Business Bureaus (1921) and the Nat'l Better Business Bureau (1912). Membership consists of national companies and local Better Business Bureaus. Promotes sound business-consumer relations and a self-regulating environment for ethical business practice.

Publications:
Council of Better Business Bureaus Annual Report. a.
Do's and Don'ts in Advertising Copy. m.
Give But Give Wisely. bi-m.

Meetings/Conferences:
Annual Meetings: Fall

Council of Biology Editors (1957)
11250 Roger Bacon Dr., Suite 8
Reston, VA 20190-5202
Tel: (703)437-4377   Fax: (703)435-4390
Members: 1,200 individuals
Staff: 5
Annual Budget: $250-500,000
Exec. Director: Cathy Hoskins

Historical Note
Founded in 1957 and incorporated in 1965 in the District of Columbia. Membership consists of individuals concerned with writing, editing and publishing in the life sciences and related fields. Membership: $95/year (individual).

Publications:
CBE Views. bi-m. adv.
Membership Directory. a.

Meetings/Conferences:
Annual Meetings: Spring/250
1999 – Montreal, Quebec(Queen Elizabeth)/May 21-25

Council of Chief State School Officers (1927)
One Massachusetts Ave., N.W., Suite 700
Washington, DC 20001-1431
Tel: (202)408-5505   Fax: (202)408-8076
Web Site: www.ccsso.org
Members: 56 individuals
Staff: 70
Annual Budget: $10-25,000,000
Exec. Director: Gordon M. Ambach
Dir., Strategic Planning & Communications: Billie Rollins
Director, Federal/State Relations: Carnie Hayes
Chief of Staff: Pamela Reynolds
Director, Administration and Finance: Bruce Buterbaugh, CPA

Historical Note
Established in 1927 as the National Council of Chief State School Officers, it assumed its present name in 1954. Members head departments of elementary and secondary education in every state, U.S. extra-state jurisdictions and the District of Columbia, and the U.S. Department of Defense Dependents Schools. CCSSO members develop consensus on major education issues which the Council advocates before the President, Federal agencies, Congress and the public. CCSSO creates and coordinates seminars for the professional growth and development of its members and their management teams. Has an annual budget of approximately $13.5 million.

Publications:
Chief Line. w.
Hill Notes. w.
State Education Agency Directory. a.
The Council 1998.

Meetings/Conferences:
Annual Meetings: November

Council of Colleges of Acupuncture and Oriental Medicine (1982)
1010 Wayne Ave., Suite 1270
Silver Spring, MD 20910-5600
Tel: (301)608-9175   Fax: (301)608-9576
Members: 33 schools
Staff: 1
Annual Budget: $50-100,000
Administrator: Amy Kaufman

Historical Note
Formerly (1992) Nat'l Council of Acupuncture Schools and Colleges. Founded in Chicago and incorporated in the District of Columbia. Membership is open to all established 3-year residential acupuncture training programs providing classroom and clinical instruction. Membership: $5,000/year.

Publications:
CCAOM News.

Meetings/Conferences:
Semi-Annual Meetings: May and October

Council of Colleges of Arts and Sciences (1965)
Arizona State University
P.O. Box 873901
Tempe, AZ 85287-3901
Tel: (602)727-6064   Fax: (602)727-6078
E-Mail: epeck@asu.edu
Members: 1,400 individuals
Staff: 2
Annual Budget: $250-500,000
Exec. Director: Ernie Peck

Historical Note
Organized in 1965 by the arts and sciences deans from the Nat'l Ass'n of State Universities and Land-Grant Colleges (NASULGC). Until 1988, CCAS members were deans of arts and sciences at state-supported colleges and universities. Membership eligibility was changed in 1988 to include arts and science deans at all

accredited, bachelor degree granting-institutions. Membership: $115-345/year (based on the number of BA/BS degrees awarded).

Publications:
CCAS Annual Meeting Program. a.
CCAS Member Directory. a.
CCAS Newsletter. bi-m. adv.

Meetings/Conferences:
Annual Meetings: November/500-600
1999 – Seattle, WA(Westin)/Nov. 10-13/500
2000 – Toronto, ON(Sheraton Eaton Center)/Nov. 8-11/500
2001 – Washington, DC(Hilton)/Nov. 7-10/500
2002 – San Francisco, CA(Hyatt)/Nov. 13-16/500

Council of Communication Management (1955)
333-B Rte. 46 West, Suite B-201
Fairfield, NJ 07004
Tel: (973)575-1444   Fax: (973)575-1445
Members: 240 individuals
Annual Budget: $50-100,000
Acct. Manager: Susan Dunkelman

Historical Note
Formerly (1985) the Industrial Communication Council. CCM provides a network through which managers, consultants and educators, who work at the policy level in organizational communication can help one another advance the practice of communication in business. Membership: $250/year.

Publications:
CCM Communicator. m.

Meetings/Conferences:

Council of Community Blood Centers (1962)
Historical Note
Name changed to America's Blood Centers (ABC) in 1996.

Council of Consulting Organizations (1989)
Historical Note
Formed as an umbrella organization with two divisions: ACME, the Ass'n of Management Consulting Firms and the Institute of Management Consultants (listed separately). An affiliate organization is the Foundation for Excellence in Consulting and Management. ACME-The Ass'n of Management Consulting Firms became a division of CCO in 1989.

Council of Dance Administrators (1967)
250 Art & Arch. Center, Univ.of Utah
Salt Lake City, UT 84112
Tel: (801)581-6764   Fax: (801)585-3066
Members: 25 individuals
President: Phyllis Haskell

Historical Note
Members are administrators of dance departments in educational institutions.

Meetings/Conferences:
Annual Meetings: November

Council of Defense and Space Industry Ass'ns (1964)
1250 I St., N.W., Suite 1200
Washington, DC 20005
Tel: (202)371-8414   Fax: (202)371-8470
Members: 10 associations
Staff: 3
Annual Budget: $50-100,000
Admin. Officer: Ruth W. Franklin

Historical Note
Established June 30, 1964 by industry ass'ns having common interests in the defense and space fields, CODSIA functions as a voluntary, coordinating, non-profit, consultative body. It addresses policies, regulations, directives and procedures relating to the supplier-purchaser relationship between government and industry. Members are Aerospace Industries Ass'n of America, American Defense Preparedness Ass'n, American Electronics Ass'n, American Shipbuilding Ass'n, Contract Services Ass'n, Electronic Industries Ass'n, Manufacturers' Alliance for Productivity and Innovation, Nat'l Security Industrial Ass'n, Professional Services Council, and Shipbuilders Council of America.

Council of Development Finance Agencies (1984)
1200 19th St., N.W., Suite 300
Washington, DC 20036-2401
Tel: (202)857-1162   Fax: (202)429-5113
E-Mail: aaron_mindel@dc.sba.com
Members: 165 agencies
Staff: 2
Annual Budget: $250-500,000
Exec. Director: Aaron Mindel

Historical Note
Formerly (1992) Council of Industrial Development Bond Issuers. Established and incorporated in the District of Columbia, CIDBI members are state, city, county public agencies and special authorities whose primary purpose is the provision of economic development financing. Membership fee varies based on type and volume of business: $250/year.

Publications:
Newsletter. bi-m.

Meetings/Conferences:
Annual Meetings: Fall

Council of Educational Facility Planners, Internat'l (1921)
8687 E. Via de Ventura, Suite 311
Scottsdale, AZ 85258-3347
Tel: (602)948-2337   Fax: (602)948-4420
E-Mail: cefpi@cefpi.com
Web Site: http://www.cefpi.com
Members: 2,500 companies and individuals
Staff: 7
Annual Budget: $500-1,000,000
Exec. Director and C.E.O.: Thomas A. Kube

Marketing and Communications Manager: Barbara C. Worth
Director of Operations: Deborah Moore

Historical Note
Formerly (1967) Nat'l Council on Schoolhouse Construction. Members are companies and persons who plan, design, build, equip and maintain educational facilities. Membership: $230 new, $180/year renewal (individual);$600 new, $500/year renewal (company).

Publications:
Consultants Directory.
Educational Facility Planner. q. adv.
The Communicator. q. adv.

Meetings/Conferences:
Annual Meetings: Fall
1999 – Baltimore, MD(Hyatt Regency)/Nov. 1-4
2000 – Orlando, FL(Coronado Springs)Sept.

Council of Engineering and Scientific Soc. Executives (1949)
c/o Society of Petroleum Engineers
222 Palisades Creek Drive
Richardson, TX 75080
Tel: (972)952-9393   Fax: (972)952-9435
Toll Free: (800)456 - 6863
Members: 850 individuals
Annual Budget: $100-250,000
President: Dan Adamson

Historical Note
Formerly (1972) Council of Engineering and Scientific Soc. Secretaries. Has no paid staff or permanent office.

Publications:
CESSE Quill. 3/year.

Meetings/Conferences:
Annual Meetings: Summer/800
1999 – Cleveland, OH/July 19-23
2000 – New York, NY/July 11-14
2001 – Houston, TX/July 17-20
2002 – San Jose, CA/July 23-26

Council of Fashion Designers of America (1963)
1412 Broadway, Suite 2006
20th Floor
New York, NY 10018
Tel: (212)302-1821   Fax: (212)768-0515
Members: 208 individuals
Staff: 5
Annual Budget: under $10,000
Exec. Director: Fern Mallis

Historical Note
CFDA represents the fasion industry, sponsoring campaigns and initiatives that advance the artistic and professional standards of the industry. CFDA Foundation is a subsidiary of CFDA which sponsors charitable activities on behalf of its members. Members are professionals in apparel and accessory design.

Meetings/Conferences:
Annual Awards Ceremony: Always in New York, NY

Council of Federal Interior Designers
Historical Note
Merged with the Internat'l Interior Design Ass'n in 1995.

Council of Fleet Specialists (1967)
315 Delaware St.
Kansas City, MO 64105-1247
Tel: (816)421-2600   Fax: (816)421-7532
E-Mail: cfshq@gmi.com
Web Site: http://www.cgshq.com
Members: 210 individuals
Staff: 6
Annual Budget: $250-500,000
Exec. V. President: Bud Reese

Historical Note
Members are distributors of parts and servicers for heavy-duty trucks. Membership: $800/year.

Publications:
Parts/Equipment Buyers' Guide & Services Directory. a. adv.

Meetings/Conferences:
Annual Meetings: Spring/1,100
1999 – Las Vegas, NV/April 18-21
2000 – Kansas City, MO/March 25-29
2001 – Atlanta, GA(Hyatt)/Apr. 22-25

Council of Food Processors Ass'n Executives (1937)
1350 I St. N.W., Suite 300
Washington, DC 20005
Tel: (202)639-5900   Fax: (202)639-5932
Members: 30 individuals
Staff: 1
Annual Budget: under $10,000
Contact: John R. Cady

Historical Note
Formerly (1962) Ass'n of Canners' State and Regional Secretaries, and (1979) Council of Canning Ass'n Executives. Members are paid staff members of associations serving the food processing industry. Administrative support provided by Nat'l Food Processors Ass'n. Membership: $25/year (organization/company).

Council of Governors' Policy Advisors (1964)
Historical Note
Organization defunct in 1998.

Council of Graduate Schools (1961)
One Dupont Circle, N.W., Suite 430
Washington, DC 20036-1173
Tel: (202)223-3791   Fax: (202)331-7157
E-Mail: jlapidus@cgs.nche.edu
Web Site: http://www.cgsnet.org
Members: 430 institutional members

Staff: 13
Annual Budget: $2-5,000,000
President: Jules B. LaPious, Ph.D.
V. President and Director for Government and Association Relations: Thomas J. Linney, Jr.
V. President, Finance/Administration: Nancy A. Gaffney
V. President, Research and Information Services: Peter D. Syverson

Publications:
Directory. a.
Membership Directory. a.
Newsletter. m.

Meetings/Conferences:
Annual Meetings: Winter
1999 - Washington, DC(J.W.Marriott)/600

Council of Graphological Socs. *(1974)*

Historical Note
Address unknown in 1997.

Council of Growing Companies *(1988)*

8260 Greensboro Drive, Suite 260
McLean, VA 22102-3806
Tel: (703)893-5343 *Fax:* (703)893-5222
Toll Free: (800)929 - 3165
E-Mail: bobcgc@ibm.net
Web Site: http://www.ceolink.org
Members: 1,300 individuals
Staff: 3
Annual Budget: $1-2,000,000
President: Robert S. Morgan, CAE
V. President: C.J. Kupec
Exec. V. President and President, Foundation for Entrepreneurship: Doreen Ruyak
Director of Member Services: Theresa Ronk

Historical Note
Members are CEOs of companies with over $5 million in annual revenues. Members form chapters throughout the U.S. and abroad. Provides lobbying, education, and networking opportunities. Maintains the on-line service CEOLink for members and Foundation for Entrepreneurship. Membership: $1000/year.

Publications:
Agenda. 3/yr.
Progress Newsletter. m.

Meetings/Conferences:
Annual Meetings: Fall

Council of Hotel and Restaurant Trainers *(1971)*

P.O. Box 211
Avon-by-the-Sea, NJ 07717
Toll Free: (800)463 - 5918
E-Mail: e_jordan@msn.com
Web Site: http://www.chart.org
Members: 250 organizations
Staff: 1
Annual Budget: $25-50,000
Chief Staff Officer: Tara Davey

Historical Note
CHART members are training or human resource professionals employed by multi-unit food service and lodging organizations with the authority and responsibility for the design and implementation of training and development programs. Membership: $195/year, plus initiation fee.

Publications:
FlipCHART Newsletter. m.

Meetings/Conferences:
Semi-Annual Meetings: March and August
1999 - Savannah, GA(Hyatt)/March 6-9

Council of Independent Colleges *(1956)*

One Dupont Circle, N.W., Suite 320
Washington, DC 20036-1110
Tel: (202)466-7230 *Fax:* (202)466-7238
Web Site: www.cic.edu
Members: 441 colleges
Staff: 18
Annual Budget: $1-2,000,000
President: Allen P. Splete, Ph.D.
V.P., Communications: Stephen G. Pelletier
Government Relations Counsel: Howard E. Holcomb
Conference Coordinator: Elizabeth Bishop
Exec. V. President: Russell Y. Garth
Business Manager: Suzanne Naples-Nye
Manager, Membership: Kelly A. Sennewald

Historical Note
Formerly (1981) the Council for the Advancement of Small Colleges. Members are independent four-year colleges of liberal arts and sciences and state, regional, and national organizations with an interest in these colleges. Sponsoring memberships are available for corporations and foundations. CIC provides leadership and faculty development programs and sponsors projects on curricular reform and other educational topics. Acquired the Consortium for the Advancement of Private Higher Education in 1993. Membership: $1,560-4,740/year, based on enrollment (institution); $225/year (affiliate).

Publications:
CIC Independent Newsletter. q.

Meetings/Conferences:
Annual Meetings: January

Council of Independent Managers

Historical Note
Became CIM--The Business Owners Forum in 1998.

Council of Industrial Boiler Owners *(1978)*

6035 Burke Center Pkwy., Suite 360
Burke, VA 22015-3717
Tel: (703)250-9042 *Fax:* (703)239-9042
E-Mail: bessette@cibo.rog
Web Site: http://www.cibo.org
Members: 103 companies
Staff: 5
Annual Budget: $500-1,000,000
President: Robert D. Bessette
Manager of Communications & Marketing: Robert E. Simonski
Manager, Meetings/Administration: B.J. Ogden

Historical Note
CIBO was founded to address technical and public policy issues affecting industrial boilers. Members are owners and operators of non-utility boilers as well as manufacturers, consultants and suppliers. In addition to its annual meeting, CIBO sponsors several technical conferences each year. Membership: $9,000/year (active); $4,500/year (associate); $1,000/year (university/educational affiliate).

Publications:
CIBO Newsletter. 2-4/year.
Seminar/Conference Proceedings.

Meetings/Conferences:
Annual Meetings: October/85-100
1999 - Scottsdale, AZ(SunBurst Resort)/Oct. 20-22/100

Council of Infrastructure Financing Authorities *(1988)*

805 15th St., N.W., Suite 500
Washington, DC 20005
Tel: (202)371-9694 *Fax:* (202)371-6601
Exec. Director: James N. Smith

Historical Note
CIFA is an organization of state and local agencies that have authority to assist and facilitate the issuance of debt financing for public infrastructure purposes. It is the only nat'l organization dedicated exclusively to the service and representation of public environmental financing authorities, many of which issue debt, manage state loan funds, and provide various mechanisms to enhance credit arrangement and generally facilitate public financing. Membership: $1,000-5,000/year (Full member); $1,000/year (associate member); $250-5,000/year (affiliate member).

Meetings/Conferences:
Semi-Annual Meetings: Legislative Conference/Spring & Workshop/Fall

Council of Institutional Investors *(1985)*

1730 Rhode Island., N.W., Suite 512
Washington, DC 20036-3117
Tel: (202)822-0800 *Fax:* (202)822-0801
E-Mail: info@cii.org
Web Site: http://www.cii.org
Members: 115 individuals, 115 companies
Staff: 7
Annual Budget: $1-2,000,000
Exec. Director: Sarah A.B. Teslik

Historical Note
Members include employee benefit plans, non-profit foundations and non-profit endowment funds. The Council studies and discusses issues, policies and practices affecting its membership.

Publications:
Alerts. w.
CII Central. m.

Meetings/Conferences:
Semi-Annual Meetings: Spring and Fall
1999 - San Francisco, CA/Sept. 27-28
1999 - Washington, DC/Mar. 29-30

Council of Insurance Agents and Brokers *(1913)*

701 Pennsylvania Ave., N.W., Suite 750
Washington, DC 20004-2608
Tel: (202)783-4400 *Fax:* (202)783-4410
E-Mail: ciab@ciab.com
Web Site: http://www.ciab.com
Members: 300 corporate members
Staff: 14
Annual Budget: $2-5,000,000
President: Ken A. Crerar
Director, Industry Affairs: Coletta I. Kemper
Director, Communications and Marketing: Karen R. Seidman
Senior V. President, Government Affairs: Joel Wood
Director, Meetings: Ann Steadman
Dir., Financial Svcs/Administration: Traci Krial
Dir., Membership: Alison Bowman

Historical Note
Formerly (1993) the Nat'l Ass'n of Casualty and Surety Agents. The Council represents 300 of the nation's largest commercial property and casualty insurance agencies and brokerage firms. Council members annually place some 75% of the commercial property/casualty insurance premiums in the United States. Council members, who operate both nationally and internationally, specialize in a wide range of insurance products and risk management services for business, industry, government and the public.

Publications:
Council Advocate. m.

Meetings/Conferences:
Annual Meetings: Always at White Sulphur Springs, WV(Greenbrier)/Oct./1,500

Council of Insurance Company Executives *(1911)*

701 Pennsylvania Ave., N.W., Suite 750
Washington, DC 20004-2608
Tel: (202)783-4400 *Fax:* (202)783-4410
E-Mail: ciab@ciab.com
Web Site: http://www.ciab.com
Members: 67 firms
President: Ken Crerar

Historical Note
Foremerly (1996) Nat'l Ass'n of Casualty and Surety Executives. The object and purpose of CICE is to afford insurance companies an opportunity to discuss industry problems with insurance agents and brokers so the insurance business may better serve the insuring public. A standing committee of the Council of Insurance Agents and Brokers, CICE co-hosts the annual Insurance Leadership Forum.

Meetings/Conferences:
Annual Meetings: always White Sulphur Springs, WV(Greenbrier)/Fall
1999 - /Oct. 2-6
2000 - /Sept. 30-Oct. 4
2001 - /Oct. 6-10

Council of Internat'l Investigators *(1955)*

300 Welsh Road, Bldg. 4, Suite 200
Horsham, PA 19044-2248
Tel: (215)657-6258 *Fax:* (215)657-6247
Toll Free: (888)759 - 8884
E-Mail: email@c112.org
Web Site: http://cii2.org
Members: 350 individuals
Staff: 2
Annual Budget: $25-50,000
Exec. Secretary-Treasurer: Norman A. Willox, Jr.

Historical Note
Membership is open to any individual within a firm, partnership, or corporation engaged in private investigation, private patrol operation or related security positions. Membership: $150/year.

Publications:
Councillor. bi-m.
Internat'l Focus. q. adv.
Roster. a.

Meetings/Conferences:
1999 - Grand Cayman, Cayman Islands(Hotel Los Fariones)/March 9-13
1999 - Chicago, IL(Drake Hotel)/Aug. 22-28
2000 - Sydney, Australia
2001 - Las Vegas, NV

Council of Jewish Federations *(1932)*

111 Eighth Ave., Suite 11E
New York, NY 10011-9596
Tel: (212)284-6500 *Fax:* (212)284-6835
E-Mail: frank_strauss@cjfny.org
Web Site: http://jewishfedna.org
Members: 200 organizations
Staff: 80
Exec. V. President: Jay Yoskowitz
Dir., Communications: Frank Strauss

Meetings/Conferences:
1999 - Atlanta, GA/Nov. 16-28

Council of Jewish Theatres *(1980)*

Historical Note
Organization defunct in 1997.

Council of Landscape Architectural Registration Boards *(1961)*

12700 Fair Lakes Circle, Suite 110
Fairfax, VA 22033-4905
Tel: (703)818-1300 *Fax:* (703)818-1309
E-Mail: MRankin@clarb.org
Web Site: http://www.clarb.org
Members: 45 state boards
Staff: 7
Annual Budget: $500-1,000,000
Exec. Director: Clarence L. Chaffee
Director, Communications: Elizabeth A. Isbell
Director, Public Relations and Marketing: Matt Rankin

Historical Note
An independent service organization whose only members are the legally constituted state regulatory agencies, the Council's main objectives are to: promote high standards for landscape architecture registration; foster the enactment of uniform laws for landscape architecture; compile, maintain and transmit certified records of qualified practitioners for registration; and equalize and improve examination of applicants through a uniform national licensing examination. Membership: $1,800/year (state board).

Meetings/Conferences:
Annual Meetings: September/75

Council of Large Public Housing Authorities *(1981)*

601 Pennsylvania Ave.,N.W., Suite 825 S.
Washington, DC 20004-2612
Tel: (202)638-1300 *Fax:* (202)638-2364
Members: 56 individuals, 56 public housing authorities
Staff: 5
Annual Budget: $500-1,000,000
Exec. Director: Sunia Zaterman
Research Director: Debbie Gross
Office Manager: Patricia Redmon
General Counsel: Gordon Cavanaugh
Research Coordinator: Marlene Kwitowski

Historical Note
Established in response to the perceived threat to funding of the nation's low-income housing programs, CLPHA members are large public housing authorities. CLPHA works to improve public, low-income housing stock through legislation in Congress and administrative actions by federal agencies. Membership: dues vary by number of units managed.

Publications:
CLPHA Mailer.
Newsletter. m.

Meetings/Conferences:
Annual Meetings: Fall

Council of Literary Magazines and Presses *(1967)*

154 Christopher St., Suite 3C
New York, NY 10014-2839
Tel: (212)741-9110 *Fax:* (212)741-9112
Members: 500 literary publishers
Staff: 4
Annual Budget: $500-1,000,000

Exec. Director: Celia O'Donnell

Historical Note
Formerly (1990) Coordinating Council of Literary Magazines. Membership open to any noncommercial literary magazine or press that publishes at least one issue or one book per year. Sponsors granting programs, regional meetings, publications, technical assistance and an advertising program. Membership fee varies, $45-600/year, based on annual budget.

Publications:
CLMPages Newsletter. q.
Directory of Literary Magazines. a.

Council of Logistics Management *(1963)*
2805 Butterfield Road, Suite 200
Oak Brook, IL 60523
Tel: (630)574-0985   *Fax:* (630)574-0989
E-Mail: clmadmin@clm1.org
Web Site: www.clm1.org
Members: 15,000 individuals
Staff: 25
Annual Budget: $5-10,000,000
Exec. V. President: George A. Gecowets
Director, Communications/Research: Elaine M. Winter
Director of Conferences: Louise A. Pochelski
V. President, Operations: Maria A. McIntyre
General Counsel: Eugene Ruark
Director of Roundtable: Kathleen L. Hedland

Historical Note
Formerly (1985) Nat'l Council of Physical Distribution Management. A professional organization of individuals concerned with transportation, warehousing, inventory, materials, logistics and/or physical distribution management. Has an annual budget of approximately $8 million. Membership: $200/year (individual).

Publications:
Conference Proceedings. a.
Journal of Business Logistics. semi-a.
Logistics Bibliography. a.
Logistics Comment. bi-m.
Survey of Logistics Software. a.

Meetings/Conferences:
Annual Meetings: Fall/5,500
1999 – Toronto, Ontario, Canada(Convention Center)/Oct. 17-20
2000 – New Orleans, LA(Morial Convention Center)/Sept. 24-27
2001 – Kansas City, MO(Convention Center)/Sept. 30-Oct. 3
2002 – Kansas City, MO(KC Convention Center)/Sept. 30-Oct. 3
2003 – Chicago, IL(McCormick Place on the Lake)/Sept. 21-24

Council of Medical Specialty Socs. *(1965)*
51 Sherwood Terrace, Suite M
Lake Bluff, IL 60044-2232
Tel: (847)295-3456   *Fax:* (847)295-3759
E-Mail: mailbox@cmss.org
Web Site: http://www.cmss.org
Members: 17 medical societies
Staff: 2
Annual Budget: $250-500,000
Exec. V. President: Rebecca R. Gschwend, MA, MBA

Historical Note
Founded as the Tri-College Council by the American College of Obstetricians and Gynecologists, the American College of Physicians and the American College of Surgeons. As other specialty societies joined, the present name was adopted in 1967. Incorporated in the state of Illinois in 1976. Each member society represents one of the 25 specialties with a certifying board sanctioned by the American Board of Medical Specialties. Provides a forum for discussion, action and policy formulation on national issues affecting medical practice. Membership: $1/year.

Publications:
CMSS Report. q.

Meetings/Conferences:
Semi-Annual Meetings: Spring in Chicago, IL and Fall
1999 – Chicago, IL(Doubletree)/March 12-14
1999 – Rosemont, IL(Westin Hotel O'hare)/Nov. 19-20

Council of Musculoskeletal Specialty Socs.
6300 N. River Road, Suite 727
Rosemont, IL 60018-4226
Tel: (847)698-1629   *Fax:* (847)823-0536
Exec. Officer: Penelope Johnson

Council of Nephrology Nurses and Technicians
Historical Note
A professional council of the Nat'l Kidney Foundation.

Council of Nephrology Social Workers
Historical Note
A professional council of the Nat'l Kidney Foundation.

Council of Nurse Manager Affiliates of the American Organization of Nurse Executives *(1988)*
Historical Note
Absorbed by the American Organization of Nurse Executives in 1994.

Council of Petroleum Accountants Socs. *(1961)*
P.O. Box 1190
Denison, TX 75021-1190
Tel: (903)463-5463   *Fax:* (903)463-5473
E-Mail: jgear@copas.org
Web Site: http://www.copas.org
Members: 3,200 individuals, 24 societies
Staff: 3
Exec. Director: Jon H. Gear

Historical Note
Members are accountants involved in, or closely related to, the oil and gas industry. Sponsors the Nat'l Oil and Gas Accounting

School with the Professional Development Institute at University of North Texas.

Publications:
Bulletins. irreg.
COPAS Accounts. q. adv.
Interpretations. irreg.
Research Papers. irreg.

Meetings/Conferences:
Semi-annual Meetings: April and October
1999 – Wichita Falls, TX(Holiday Inn)/April 26-May 1
1999 – Fort Worth, TX(Worthington Hotel)/Oct. 11-15
2000 – Wichita, KN
2000 – Artesia, NM

Council of Planning Librarians *(1957)*
101 N Wacker Drive., Suite CM-190
Chicago, IL 60606
Tel: (312)409-3349   *Fax:* (312)263-7417
Members: 86 individuals, 55 institutions
Staff: 2
Annual Budget: $25-50,000
Administrator: Ena Dahm

Historical Note
Originally an ad-hoc committee of librarians interested in planning materials convened in 1957; became an official organization in 1960. Members are librarians, academics, professional planners, and public and private planning agencies. Cooperates with several other professional associations, including the Council of Nat'l Library Ass'ns, the Internat'l City Management Ass'n. CPL is affiliated with the American Planning Ass'n. Membership: $35/year (individual), $55/year (institution).

Publications:
Membership Directory.

Meetings/Conferences:
Annual Meetings: Spring/50
1999 – Minneapolis, MN/June 5-10

Council of Professional Ass'ns on Federal Statistics *(1980)*
1429 Duke Street, Suite 402
Alexandria, VA 22314-3402
Tel: (703)836-0404   *Fax:* (703)684-3410
Web Site: http://www.members.aol.com/copafs
Members: 17 organizations, 50 affiliates
Staff: 2
Annual Budget: $100-250,000
Exec. Director: Edward J. Spar

Historical Note
Established to monitor the priorities, scope and compatibility of the Federal statistical effort. Has a multidisciplinary membership of associations and also has 60 affiliate organizations. Membership: $2,000-15,000/year (associations), $1,000-3,000/year (other organizations).

Publications:
News From COPAFS. q.

Meetings/Conferences:
Quarterly Meetings: Washington, DC

Council of Protocol Executives *(1988)*
101 West 12th St., Suite PHH
New York, NY 10011
Tel: (212)633-6934
Members: 200 individuals
President: Page Kjellstrom

Historical Note
COPE members coordinate executive meetings in the public and private sectors. Has no paid officers or full-time staff. Membership: $150/year.

Publications:
Newsletter. q.
Protocol Directory. a.

Meetings/Conferences:
Annual Meetings: Winter

Council of Rehabilitation Specialists *(1979)*
Historical Note
Organization defunct in 1995.

Council of Sales Promotion Agencies
Historical Note
Became the Ass'n of Promotion Marketing Agencies Worldwide in 1996.

Council of Scientific Soc. Presidents *(1973)*
1155 16th St., N.W., Suite 1040
Washington, DC 20036-4800
Tel: (202)872-4452   *Fax:* (202)872-4079
E-Mail: cssp@acs.org
Web Site: http://www.science-presidents.org
Members: 100 societies and 3 federations
Staff: 3
Annual Budget: $250-500,000
President: Martin A. Apple, Ph.D.

Historical Note
Formerly (1977) Committee of Scientific Soc. Presidents. Members are past and current presidents and presidents-elect of scientific societies. CSSP is a leadership-development organization that exists to promote science, improve national science policy, and focus on related issues.

Publications:
CSSP Congressional Sourcebook. a.
CSSP News. q.
CSSP News OnLine. 3.
Email Directory of Members and Alumni. bi.

Meetings/Conferences:
Semi-Annual Meetings: Washington, DC/May and December

Council of Socs. for the Study of Religion *(1969)*
Valparaiso University
Valparaiso, IN 46383-6493
Tel: (219)464-5515   *Fax:* (219)464-6714
Toll Free: (888)422 - 2777
E-Mail: david.truemper@valpo.edu
Web Site: http://www.cssr.org
Staff: 4
Annual Budget: $100-250,000
Exec. Director: David G. Truemper

Historical Note
Formerly (1985) Council on the Study of Religion. An umbrella group for learned societies concerned with the study of religion. Membership fee varies, based number of constituents.

Publications:
Bulletin of CSSR. q. adv.
Directory of Departments of Religion. a.
Religious Studies Review. q. adv.

Meetings/Conferences:
Annual Meetings: Fall

Council of State Administrators of Vocational Rehabilitation *(1940)*
P.O. Box 3776
Washington, DC 20007
Tel: (202)638-4634
Members: 100 individuals
Staff: 2
Annual Budget: $250-500,000
Exec. Director: Joseph H. Owens, Jr.
General Counsel: Jack G. Duncan

Historical Note
Composed of the chief administrators of the public vocational rehabilitation agencies for physically and mentally handicapped persons in the states, District of Columbia, and the territories.

Meetings/Conferences:
Semi-Annual Meetings: Spring, various locations/Fall, Washington, DC

Council of State and Territorial Epidemiologists *(1951)*
2872 Woodcock Blvd., Suite 303
Atlanta, GA 30341
Tel: (770)458-3811   *Fax:* (770)458-8516
E-Mail: forr102w@cdc.gov
Web Site: http://www.cste.org
Members: 400 individuals, 62 states and territories
Staff: 20
Annual Budget: $2,000,000-5,000,000
Exec. Director: Donna Knutson
Business Manager: Clara Jenkins

Historical Note
Formerly (1986) Conference of State and Territorial Epidemiologists. Affiliated with Ass'n of State and Territorial Health Officials. Members are public health epidemiologists employed by the various states and territories. Membership: $450-650/year (state/territory); $15/year (individual).

Publications:
Newsletter. q.

Meetings/Conferences:
Annual Meetings: Spring
1999 – Madison, WI/June 28-July 1

Council of State Ass'n Presidents *(1975)*
P.O. Box 140046
Austin, TX 78714
Tel: (512)452-4571   *Fax:* (512)452-5255
E-Mail: bnksmiller@aol.com
Members: 48 States
Staff: 2
Annual Budget: $25-50,000
Manager: Chilton Roberts

Historical Note
Membership: $225/year (organiztion).

Meetings/Conferences:
1999 – Asheville, NC
1999 – San francisco, CA

Council of State Chambers of Commerce *(1967)*
20 Wacker Drive, Suite 1950
Chicago, IL 60606
Tel: (312)236-1361   *Fax:* (312)853-6165
Members: 43 chambers
Staff: 5
Annual Budget: $500-1,000,000
President: Richard Aplend

Historical Note
A federation of state and regional chambers of commerce founded as the Nat'l Ass'n of State Chambers of Commerce. It assumed its present name in 1948.

Meetings/Conferences:
Annual Meetings: Fall
1999 – Ashville, NC

Council of State Community Development Agencies *(1974)*
444 North Capitol St., N.W., Suite 224
Washington, DC 20001
Tel: (202)624-3630   *Fax:* (202)624-3639
Web Site: www.sso.org/coscda
Members: 48 state agencies
Staff: 4
Annual Budget: $250-500,000
Exec. Director: John Sidor

Historical Note
Members are employees of state community affairs agencies representing all 50 states. Formerly (1992) Council of State Community Affairs Agencies.

Publications:
National Line.
State Line.
Meetings/Conferences:
Annual Meetings: September

Council of State Governments *(1933)*
P.O. Box 11910
Lexington, KY 40578-1910
Tel: (606)244-8000 *Fax:* (606)244-8001
Web Site: http://www.csg.org
Members: 50 states, 5 territories
Staff: 190
Annual Budget: $10-25,000,000
Exec. Director: Daniel M. Sprague
Deputy Exec. Director & Chief Operating Officer: Shari
Hendrickson
Dir., Program, Policy & Membership Services: Bob Silvanik
Deputy Director, Marketing & Sales: Phyllis Santos
Historical Note
*Founded as the American Legislators Ass'n, it assumed its present
name in 1933. The Council seeks to preserve and strengthen the
role of the state in the federal system; it serves as a research and
service agency for 50 state governments and associations of state
officials. Has an annual budget of approximately $11-$12 million.*
Publications:
Journal of State Government. q.
State Government News. m.
State Leadership Directories.
The Book of the States. bien.
Meetings/Conferences:
Annual Meetings: December

Council of State Science Supervisors *(1963)*
Historical Note
Address unknown in 1996; presumed inactive or defunct.

Council of Teaching Hospitals
Historical Note
A council of the Ass'n of American Medical Colleges.

Council of the Americas *(1958)*
680 Park Ave.
New York, NY 10021
Tel: (212)628-3200 *Fax:* (212)517-6247
E-Mail: as-coa.org
Web Site: counciloftheamericas.org
Members: 235 corporations
Staff: 11
Annual Budget: $1-2,000,000
President: Amb. Thomas E. McNamara
Dir., Communications: David Wernick
Dir., Government Relations: Josh Collet
Senior V. President: James W. Trowbridge
Senior Director, Administration and Finance: Michael H. Rothkin
V. President: Susan Kaufman-Purcell, Ph.D.
Historical Note
*Founded in New York City in 1958 as the United States Inter-
American Council, Inc. The name was changed in 1965 to Council
for Latin America, Inc. and in 1970 to Council of the Americas, Inc.
Members are corporations doing business in Latin America.
Maintains a Washington office. Affiliate of The Americas Soc.
Membership: $7,500-45,000/year.*
Publications:
Americas Society Update.
Washington Report. q.
Meetings/Conferences:
Annual Meetings: May in Washington, DC

Council of the Great City Schools *(1961)*
1301 Pennsylvania Ave., N.W., Suite 702
Washington, DC 20004-1701
Tel: (202)393-2427 *Fax:* (202)393-2400
E-Mail: mcasserly@cgcr.org
Web Site: www.cgcs.org
Members: 51 school districts
Staff: 15
Annual Budget: $1-2,000,000
Exec. Director: Michael D. Casserly
Director of Communications: Henry Duvall
Director, Legislative: Jeff Simmering
Director, Research: Sharon Lewis
Director of Finance, Administration, & Conferences: Teresita T.
Valecruz
Director, Management Affairs: Robert Carlson
Historical Note
*Members are large city school districts. Formerly known as the
Research Council of the Great Cities Program for School
Improvement. Membership. $25-37,000/year.*
Publications:
Council Directory. a.
The Urban Educator. bi-w.
Urban Indicators and Administrators Report. m.
Meetings/Conferences:
1999 – Dayton, OH(Crowne Plaza Hotel)/Oct. 13-17/400
2000 – New York, NY

Council of Theatre Chairs and Deans
Historical Note
A focus group of the Ass'n for Theatre in Higher Education.

Council of Vehicle Ass'ns *(1992)*
Historical Note
Address unknown in 1998.

Council of Writers Organizations *(1979)*
12724 Sagamore Road
Leawood, KS 66209

Tel: (913)451-9023 *Fax:* (913)451-4866
E-Mail: cwo@sound.net
Web Site: http://www.councilofwriters.com
Members: 20 organizations
Staff: 1
Annual Budget: under $10,000
Exec. Director: Beverly Hurley
Historical Note
*CWO is an umbrella group for writing groups with 20,000
members. Acts as a communications network for members groups,
circulating information of interest to writers and organizations
representing writers' interests. Membership: $100-300/year.*
Publications:
World Wrap. bi-.
Meetings/Conferences:
Annual Meetings: Fall, usually New York, NY/10-20
1999 – New York, NY(Williams Club)

Council of Writing Program Administrators *(1978)*
Historical Note
See Nat'l Council of Writing Program Administrators.

Council on Anthropology and Education
Historical Note
A section of the American Anthropology Ass'n.

Council on Botanical and Horticultural Libraries *(1970)*
c/o Nat'l Agricultural Library, USDA
Beltsville, MD 20705-2351
Tel: (301)504-5724 *Fax:* (301)504-6409
E-Mail: jgates@nalusda.gov
Members: 275 libraries
Annual Budget: under $10,000
Secretary: Jane P. Gates
Historical Note
*Members are libraries and individuals with an interest in botanical
and horticultural subjects. Membership: $30/year (individual);
$75/year (organization).*
Publications:
Bibliographies. irreg.
Directory of Member Libraries. a.
Newsletter. 3-4/year.
Meetings/Conferences:
Annual Meetings: Spring
1999 – Albuquerque, NM(Rio Grande Bot. Garden)
2000 – Beltsville, MD(Nat'l Agriculture Library)
2001 – Denver, CO(Denver Botanic Gardens)

Council on Chiropractic Education *(1971)*
7975 N. Hayden Road, Suite A-210
Scottsdale, AZ 85258-3246
Tel: (602)443-8877 *Fax:* (602)483-7333
E-Mail: CCEoffice@aol.com
Members: 16 programs and institutions
Staff: 5
Annual Budget: $500-1,000,000
Exec. V. President: Paul D. Walker, Ph.D.
Historical Note
*Members are indtutions offering the doctor of chiropractic degree.
Provides accreditation. Membership fee varies, based on enrollment;
$45 per FTE/year.*
Publications:
CCE Biennial Report. bien.
Meetings/Conferences:
Annual Meetings: January/60
1999 – Scottsdale, AZ(Doubletree)/Jan. 22-24
2000 – Scottsdale, AZ(Doubletree)

Council on Chiropractic Orthopedics *(1967)*
190 East 100 South
Provo, UT 84606
Tel: (801)373-2240 *Fax:* (801)373-5239
Members: 650 individuals
Annual Budget: $50-100,000
Treasurer: Phil L. Aiken, D.C.
Historical Note
*A division of the American Chiropractic Ass'n. Members are
chiropractors with an interest in orthopedics. Membership:
$75/year (individual).*
Publications:
Directory. a.
Orthopedic Briefs. bi-m.
Meetings/Conferences:
Annual Meetings: November

Council on Chiropractic Physiological Therapeutics and Rehabilitation *(1920)*
Palmer College, 1000 Brady St.
Davenport, IA 52803
Tel: (319)884-5000 *Fax:* (319)884-5470
Members: 200 individuals
Staff: 2
Annual Budget: under $10,000
President: Clay MacDonald
Historical Note
*Members are chirprators with an interest in the application of
physiotherapy and rehabilitation to the practice of chiropractic. Has
no paid officers or full-time staff.*
Publications:
Physiotherapy Briefs. irreg.
Meetings/Conferences:
Annual Meetings: June

Council on Diagnostic Imaging to the A.C.A. *(1936)*
P.O. Box 25
Palatine, IL 60067

Tel: (847)705-1177 *Fax:* (847)705-1178
Members: 1,500 individuals
Staff: 1
Annual Budget: $100-250,000
Secretary/Treasurer: Dr. Lawrence Pyzik
Historical Note
*A part of the American Chiropractic Ass'n. Founded as the Nat'l
Council of Chiropractic Roentgenologists, it later became the
Council on Roentgenography, (1964) the American Council on
Chiropractic Roentgenology, (1968) the Council on Roentgenology
to the A.C.A. and assumed its present name in 1986. Membership:
$50/year.*
Publications:
TDI. q. adv.
Topics in Diagnostic Radiology and Advanced Imaging.
Meetings/Conferences:

Council on Education of the Deaf *(1960)*
52 Loews Memorial Drive
Bldg. LBJ, Room 2630
Rochester, NY 14623
Tel: (716)475-6371 *Fax:* (716)475-7410
Members: 12 representatives
Annual Budget: $25-50,000
Chair, Comm on Prof Prep & Certification: Gail Rothman-Marshall,
Ph.D.
Historical Note
*An umbrella organization of associations concerned with education
of the deaf, including the Alexander Graham Bell Ass'n for the
Deaf, the Convention of American Instructors of the Deaf, the
Conference of Educational Administrators Serving the Deaf, the
Ass'n of College Educators: Deaf and Hard of Hearing, the Nat'l
Ass'n of the Deaf, and the American Soc. for Deaf Children.
Maintains certification programs for teacher education programs
and individual professionals.*
Meetings/Conferences:
Annual Meetings: First week in December at Galludet University
in Washington, DC.

Council on Electrolysis Education *(1972)*
Historical Note
Organization defunct in 1997.

Council on Employee Benefits *(1946)*
1212 New York Ave., N.W., Suite 1225
Washington, DC 20005
Tel: (202)408-3192 *Fax:* (202)408-3289
E-Mail: vschieber@ceb.org
Web Site: http://www.ceb.org
Members: 160 companies
Staff: 2
Annual Budget: $250-500,000
Exec. Director: Vicki A. Schieber
Historical Note
*An employer organization for the exchange of information on all
aspects of employee benefit plans. Founded as the Federation of
Employee Benefit Associations, it became the Council on Employee
Benefit Plans in 1950 and assumed its present name in 1961.
Membership: $1,000/year (company).*
Publications:
Reporter. q.
Meetings/Conferences:
Semi-Annual Meetings: Spring and October
1999 – Ft. Myers, FL(Sanibel Harbor Resort)/April 18-21

Council on Fine Art Photography *(1982)*
5613 Johnson Ave.
West Bethesda, MD 20817-3503
Tel: (301)897-0083
Members: 50 individuals
Staff: 14
Exec. Director: Lowell Anson Kenyon
Historical Note
*Members are fine art photographers employing silver processes.
The Internat'l Museum Photographers Ass'n is a divisioin of CFAP.*
Publications:
Contemporary Photographer. m.
Daguerre Report. m.
Perspective on Photography.
Meetings/Conferences:
Annual Meetings: always Washington, DC/June

Council on Forest Engineering *(1978)*
620 S.W. 4th St.
Corvallis, OR 97333
Tel: (541)754-7558 *Fax:* (541)754-7559
Members: 400 individuals
Admin. Secretary: Sylvia Aulerich
Historical Note
*COFE members are individuals with an interest in forest
engineering. Membership: $10/year (individual).*
Publications:
Newsletter. semi-a.
Proceedings. a.
Meetings/Conferences:

Council on Foundations *(1949)*
1828 L St., N.W., Suite 300
Washington, DC 20036-5168
Tel: (202)466-6512 *Fax:* (202)785-3926
Web Site: http://www.cof.org
Members: 1,700 foundations & giving programs
Staff: 90
Annual Budget: $5-10,000,000
President and C.E.O.: Dorothy S. Ridings
V.P., Membership/Marketing/Communication: Sunshine Janda
Overkamp
V. President & General Counsel: John A. Edie

V. Pres., Educat'l Programs & International: Christopher Harris
V.P., Finance/Administrative Services: Phillipa P. Taylor
Exec. V. President: Judith O'Connor
Editor: Jody Curtis
Director, Management Info. Services: Michael Q. Cannon

Historical Note
Founded in 1949 as a non-profit membership association for grantmaking foundations and corporations. Membership includes independent foundations, community foundations, corporate grantmakers, public foundations, operating foundations and foreign foundations. COF promotes responsible and effective philanthropy, secures public policy supportive of philanthropy and provides advisory services to its members. Has an annual budget of $9.6 million.

Publications:
Annual Report. a.
Communications Update. q.
Community Foundation Quarterly. q.
Corporate Update.
Council Columns Newsletter. bi-w.
Foundation Management Report. bien.
Foundation News Magazine. bi-m. adv.
Foundation Salary Update. a.
International Dateline. q.
Regional Review. irreg.
Washington Update. irreg.

Meetings/Conferences:
Annual Meetings: Spring
1999 - New Orleans, LA/April 19-21

Council on Geriatric Cardiology (1986)
c/o Le Jacq Communications
777 West Putnam Ave.
Greenwich, CT 06830
Tel: (203)531-0916   *Fax:* (203)531-0533
Web Site: http://www.sgcard.org
Members: 500 individuals
Staff: 8
Annual Budget: $25-50,000
Exec. Director: Sarah Howell

Historical Note
CGC was incorporated to meet the problems resulting from cardiovascular diseases in increasing numbers of aging men and women in the United State and around the world. Membership is open to all health care professionals who have demonstrated a commitment to geriatric cardiology and who have been certified in their area of professional expertise by an appropriate agency. Membership: $50/year (physician); $40/year (non-physicians); $75/year (fellowship).

Publications:
American Journal of Geriatric Cardiology. bi-m. adv.
CGC News Brief. q.

Meetings/Conferences:
Annual Meetings: March
1999 - New Orleans, LA

Council on Governmental Ethics Law (1978)
10951 W. Pico Blvd., Suite 120
Los Angeles, CA 90064-2126
Tel: (310)470-6590   *Fax:* (310)475-3752
E-Mail: sternecgs.org
Web Site: http://www.cogel.org
Members: 40 individuals, 160 companies
Staff: 2
Administrator: Robert M. Stern

Historical Note
Established in Minneapolis, COGEL is the international professional association for agencies and individuals with responsibilities in governmental ethics, elections, campaign finance, freedom of information, and lobby law regulation. Membership: $100/year (individual); $350/year (agency).

Publications:
Campaign Finance. a.
COGEL Guardian. q.
Ethics & Lobbying. a.

Council on Hotel, Restaurant and Institutional Education (1946)
1200 17th St., N.W., 1st Fl
Washington, DC 20036-3097
Tel: (202)331-5990   *Fax:* (202)785-2511
Web Site: http://www.chrie.org
Members: 2,500 individuals, 18 chapters
Staff: 15
Annual Budget: $500-1,000,000
Exec. V. President: Dale Gaddy, CAE

Historical Note
Founded as a non-profit organization for schools, colleges, and universities offering programs of study in hotel and restaurant management, foodservice management and culinary arts. Also includes the enhancement of professionalism at all levels of the hospitality and tourism industry, or businesses that provide food, lodging and travel services. Founded as the Nat'l Council on Hotel and Restaurant Education, it assumed its present name in 1959. Membership: $135/year (individual), $500/year (organization).

Publications:
CHRIE Communique. m.
Conference Proceedings. a. adv.
Guide to College Programs in Hospitality & Tourism. a. adv.
HOSTEUR Magazine. semi-a.
Journal of Hospitality and Tourism Education. q. adv.
Journal of Hospitality Research Journal. q. adv.

Meetings/Conferences:
Annual Meetings: Summer/1,000
1999 - Albuquerque, NM/August 4-7

Council on Library-Media Technicians (1967)
Cuyahoga Community College
SSC-400, 2900 Community College Avenue

Cleveland, OH 44115
Tel: (216)987-4655   *Fax:* (216)987-4404
Members: 800 individuals and institutions
Annual Budget: under $10,000
Exec. Secretary: Margaret R. Barron

Historical Note
Formerly (1973) Council on Library Technology, (1977) Council on Library Technical-Assistants, and (1989) Council on Library-Media Technical-Assistants. Affiliated with the American Library Ass'n. Members are library employees responsible for audio-visual, interactive, and other non-book holdings. Membership: $25/year (individual); $50/year (organization).

Publications:
Conference Proceedings. a.
Library Mosaics. bi-m. adv.
Membership Directory and Data Book. a.

Meetings/Conferences:
1999 - Detroit, MI/April 7-10

Council on Licensure, Enforcement and Regulation (1980)
403 Marquis Ave., Suite 100
Lexington, KY 40502-2140
Tel: (606)269-1289   *Fax:* (606)231-1943
E-Mail: clear@uky.campus.mci.net
Web Site: http://www.clearhq.org
Members: 480 individuals and agencies
Staff: 7
Annual Budget: $500-1,000,000
Exec. Director: Pamela Brinegar

Historical Note
Formerly (1991) Nat'l Clearinghouse on Licensure, Enforcement and Regulation. Members include licensing boards and agencies in the 50 states, territories and Canada. Its mission is to improve the quality and understanding of professional and occupational regulation. Membership: $150/year (individual), $150-2,000/year (board/agency).

Publications:
Clear Exam Review. semi-a.
CLEAR News. q.
Resource Briefs. a.

Meetings/Conferences:
1999 - Portland, OR/Aug. 30-Sept. 4

Council on Nutritional Anthropology (1974)
Historical Note
A section of the American Anthropological Ass'n. CNA promotes interest and research in the anthropological study of food and nutrition.

Council on Occupational Education
41 Perimeter Center East, NE, Suite 640
Atlanta, GA 30346
Tel: (770)396-3898   *Fax:* (770)396-3790
Toll Free: (800)917 - 2081
E-Mail: bowman@council.org
Web Site: http://www.council.org
Members: 352 institutions
Staff: 9
Exec. Director: Dr. Harry L. Bowman

Historical Note
Formerly Commission on Occupational Education Institutions (1971). Members are postsecondary schools and institutions who are committed to career and workforce development.

Publications:
The Councilor. q.

Meetings/Conferences:

Council on Oceanic Engineering Soc.
Historical Note
A subsidiary of the Institute of Electrical and Electronics Engineers. Membership in the Society, open only to IEEE members, includes subscription to a technical periodical in the field published by IEEE. All administrative support is provided by IEEE.

Council on Packaging in the Environment
Historical Note
Reported defunct in 1997.

Council on Renal Nutrition
Historical Note
A professional council of the Nat'l Kidney Foundation.

Council on Resident Education in Obstetrics and Gynecology (1967)
P.O. Box 96920
Washington, DC 20090-6920
Tel: (202)863-2554   *Fax:* (202)863-4994
Toll Free: (800)673 - 8444
E-Mail: dnehra@acog.org
Web Site: www.acog.org
Members: 7 societies
Annual Budget: $500-1,000,000
Assoc. Director: DeAnne Nehra

Historical Note
Founded by the American College of Obstetricians and Gynecologists, CREOG members are specialty professional societies with an interest in residency training in obstetrics and gynecology.

Publications:
Basic Science Monographs in Obstetrics & Gynecology. irreg.
CREOG Council News Newsletter. 3/year.
Directory of Obstetric/Gynecologic Residency Programs & Directors. a.

Meetings/Conferences:
1999 - San Diego, CA(Marriott Marina)/Feb. 19-23
2000 - New Orleans, LA(Hyatt Regency)/Feb. 29-March 4

Council on Social Work Education (1952)
1600 Duke St., Suite 300
Alexandria, VA 22314-3421
Tel: (703)683-8080   *Fax:* (703)683-8099
E-Mail: info@cswe.org
Web Site: http://www.cswe.org
Members: 3,500 individuals
Staff: 25
Annual Budget: $2-5,000,000
Exec. Director: Donald W. Beless
Director, Conferences/Member Services: Rochelle P. Gershenow
Director, Finance: Wanda L. Moore

Historical Note
Accredits Baccalaureate and Masters degree programs of social work at colleges and universities. Formed by a merger of the Nat'l Ass'n of Schools of Social Administration and the American Ass'n of Schools of Social Work.

Publications:
Journal of Education for Social Work. 3/yr. adv.
Statistics on Social Work Education. a.
Summary Information on Master of Social Work Programs. a.
The Reporter. 3/yr.

Meetings/Conferences:
Annual Meetings: February/March
1999 - San Francisco, CA
2000 - New York, NY
2001 - Dallas, TX

Council on Superconductivity (1987)
700 13th St., N.W., Suite 400
Washington, DC 20005
Tel: (202)849-0374   *Fax:* (202)347-0785
Members: 40 companies
Staff: 3
Annual Budget: $250-500,000
Exec. Director: Lawrence Grossman

Historical Note
Formerly (1994) Council on Superconductivity for American Competitiveness. Established to serve as the focal point and public policy voice of the emerging American superconductor industry, CSAC is the principal national trade association for the industry. Members include organizations from industry and academia who are engaged in the development and commercialization of superconductivity in the United States. Membership: $2,500-9,500/year.

Publications:
CSAC Superconductors. bi-m.

Meetings/Conferences:
Annual Meetings: Irreg.

Council on Technology Teacher Education (1950)
Old Dominion U. Occup./Technical Studies
108 Technology Bldg., 4608 Hampton Blvd.
Norfolk, VA 23529-0498
Tel: (757)683-4305   *Fax:* (757)683-5227
E-Mail: jritz@odu.edu
Web Site: http://teched.edtl.vt.edu/ctte/
Members: 900 individuals
Annual Budget: $10-25,000
President: John M. Ritz, Ph.D.

Historical Note
Formerly (1986) American Council on Industrial Arts Teacher Education. Has no paid staff. An affiliate of the Internat'l Technology Education Ass'n (ITEA). Membership: $25/year, plus ITEA membership.

Publications:
CTTE Newsletter. semi-a.
CTTE Yearbook. a.
Journal of Technology Education. semi-a.

Meetings/Conferences:
Annual Meetings: March, with Internat'l Technology Education Ass'n
1999 - Indianapolis, IN/March 28-30

Counselors of Real Estate (1953)
430 N. Michigan Ave.
Chicago, IL 60611-4089
Tel: (312)329-8427   *Fax:* (312)329-8881
E-Mail: cre@interaccess.com
Web Site: http://www.cre.org/
Members: 1000 individuals
Staff: 8
Annual Budget: $1-2,000,000
Exec. V. President: Mary Walker Fleischmann
Dir., Communications: Camilla Ashley
Conventions/Meetings: Gloria Bowman
Dir., Publications: Faye Porter

Historical Note
Formerly (1996) the American Soc. of Real Estate Counselors. CRE is the professional consulting affiliate of the Nat'l Ass'n of Realtors. Members are awarded the CRE (Counselor of Real Estate) designation. CRE's are a respected source for professional advice on all types of property and land-related matters.

Publications:
CRE Member Directory. a.
Real Estate Issues. semi-a.
Technical Monographs and Bulletins. irreg.
The Counselor. bi-m.

Meetings/Conferences:
Annual Meetings: With Nat'l Ass'n of Realtors
1999 - Orlando, FL(Disneyland Contemp. Resort)/Nov. 7-10

Country Day School Headmasters Ass'n of the U.S. (1912)
Historical Note
Address unknown in 1996.

Country Music Ass'n (1958)

One Music Circle South
Nashville, TN 37203
Tel: (615)244-2840 *Fax:* (615)726-0314
Web Site: www.countrymusic.org
Members: 7,000 individuals, 700 organizations
Staff: 18
Annual Budget: $1-2,000,000
Exec. Director: Edwin W. Benson, Jr.
Senior Director, Communications: Teresa George
Senior Dir., Operations: Tammy Genovese
Manager, Membership Development: Becky Sowers
Senior Director, International Business Development: Jeff Green

Historical Note
Membership is open to any individual or organization deriving income from country music. Membership: $50-$100/year (individual), $125-$5,000/year (organization).

Publications:
Close-Up. m.

Meetings/Conferences:
Annual Meetings: always Nashville, TN/Fall

Country Radio Broadcasters (1970)
819 18th Ave. South
Nashville, TN 37203-3218
Tel: (615)327-4487 *Fax:* (615)329-4492
Web Site: www.crb.org
Members: 2,000 individuals
Staff: 4
Annual Budget: $500-1,000,000
Exec. Director: Paul Allen

Historical Note
Members are country radio broadcasters, music industry personnel, record label officials and related industry executives. Sponsors panels, workshops, speakers, and presentations to expose members to all facets of the broadcasting and music industries.

Publications:
CRS Program Book and Directory. a. adv.

Meetings/Conferences:
Annual Meetings: always March in Nashville,
TN(Opryland)/1,500
1999 – /March 10-13

County Executives of America (1970)
1010 Massachusetts Ave., N.W., Suite 100
Washington, DC 20001
Tel: (202)289-4805 *Fax:* (202)289-4809
Members: 611 individuals
Staff: 5
Annual Budget: $100-250,000
Exec. Director: Michael G. Griffin

Historical Note
Founded as Nat'l Council of Elected County Executives; assumed its current name in 1997. Represents the chief elected officers of over 600 counties throughout the U.S.

Publications:
County Executive Summary.

Meetings/Conferences:

CPA Associates Internat'l (1957)
301 Route 17 North, Seventh Floor
Rutherford, NJ 07070-2574
Tel: (201)804-8686 *Fax:* (201)804-9222
E-Mail: homeoffice@spaai.com
Web Site: http://cpaai.com/
Members: 96 companies
Staff: 2
Annual Budget: $500-1,000,000
President: James F. Flynn
Manager of Member Services: Patricia Reeves

Historical Note
Members are accounting firms.

Publications:
Business Advisory Client Newsletter. q.
Construction Newsletter. q.
CPA Associates Directory. a.
Law Firm Client Newsletter.
Medical Client Newsletter. q.
Not For Profit Client Newsletter.
Outlook. q.
Tax Outlook. q.
Year-End Tax Planning Guide. a.

Meetings/Conferences:

CPA Auto Dealer Consultants Ass'n (1996)
111 E. Wacker Dr., Suite 990
Chicago, IL 60601
Tel: (312)729-9900 *Fax:* (312)729-9800
Toll Free: (800)869 - 0491
E-Mail: info@pencormazur.com
Web Site: http://www.cpaselect.com/cadca
Members: 22 firms
Staff: 10
Director, Communications: Michelle Durham

Historical Note
CADCA is an assocoition of CPA firms that concentrate a substantial portion of their business on providing financial and consulting services to auto dealers.

Publications:
Auto Focus. q.
Members' Bulletin. q.

Meetings/Conferences:
1999 – Las Vegas, NV/June 23-25

CPA Manufacturing Services Ass'n (1995)
111 E. Wacker Dr., Suite 990
Chicago, IL 60601
Tel: (312)729-9900 *Fax:* (312)729-9800
Toll Free: (800)869 - 0491

E-Mail: info@pencormazur.com
Web Site: http://www.cpaselect.com/msa
Members: 22 firms
Staff: 10
Director, Communications: Michelle Durham

Historical Note
NSA is a national association of CPA firms that provide industry specific services to manufactures. Membership is on a territorially protected basis.

Publications:
Manufacturing Monitor Newsletter. q.
Members' Bulletin q.

Meetings/Conferences:
1999 – Las Vegas, NV/June 23-25

Cranberry Institute (1952)
266 Main St.
Wareham, MA 02571-2172
Tel: (508)295-4132 *Fax:* (508)291-1511
Web Site: jdd@capecod.net
Members: 1,200 growers and handlers
Staff: 2
Annual Budget: $100-250,000
Exec. Director: Jere Downing

Historical Note
Members are cranberry growers and handlers in the United States and Canada. Membership: $50-100/year (individual); by assessment (organization/company).

Publications:
Cranberry Institute Newsletter. bimonthly.

Crane Certification Ass'n of America (1984)
8810 Pierce Dr.
Buena Park, CA 90620
Tel: (714)828-0363 *Fax:* (714)828-8929
Toll Free: (800)447 - 3402
Staff: 1
Exec. Director: Janet C. Huber, CAE

Historical Note
Promotes crane safety through improvements to the certification process and participation in government forums. Membership: $250/year.

Publications:
CCAA Newsletter. q. adv.

Meetings/Conferences:

Crane Manufacturers Ass'n of America (1927)
8720 Red Oak Blvd., Suite 201
Charlotte, NC 28217-3992
Tel: (704)676-1190 *Fax:* (704)676-1199
E-Mail: Hal_Vandiver@MHIA.ORG
Web Site: http://www.mhia.org
Members: 24 companies
Staff: 24
Annual Budget: $25-50,000
Managing Director: F. Hal Vandiver

Historical Note
Formerly (1968) Electric Overhead Crane Institute. A member of the Manufacturers Alliance, CMAA is product section of the Material Handling Institute (same address).

Meetings/Conferences:
Annual Meetings: With the Material Handling Institute

Cranial Academy (1947)
8202 Clearvista Pkwy., Suite 9D
Indianapolis, IN 46256-1457
Tel: (317)594-0411 *Fax:* (317)594-9299
Members: 1,200 individuals
Staff: 2
Annual Budget: $250-500,000
Exec. Director: Patricia Crampton

Historical Note
Affiliated with the American Academy of Osteopathy. Formerly (1960) Osteopathic Cranial Ass'n. Members are osteopaths, physicians, dentists, and students who have studied osteopathy in the cranial field.

Publications:
Cranial Letter. q.
Directory. a.

Meetings/Conferences:
Annual Meetings: June/150
1999 – San Antonio, TX(Holiday Inn Riverwalk)
2000 – Philadelphia, PA(Adam's Mark)

Creative Education Foundation (1954)
1050 Union Road, Suite 4
Buffalo, NY 14224-3402
Tel: (716)675-3181 *Fax:* (716)675-3209
E-Mail: cefhq@cef-cpsi.org
Web Site: http://www.cef-cpsi.org

Historical Note
Members are corporations and individuals using and developing innovative problem-solving strategies for business, education, medicine, and the arts. Membership: $60/year (domestic); $70/year (foreign); $250/year (organization/company).

Publications:
Creativity in Action. newsletter.
The Journal of Creative Behavior. q.

Meetings/Conferences:
Annual Meetings: Buffalo, NY/Summer
1999 – /June 20-25
1999 – La Jolla, CA/Jan. 6-10

Credit Professionals Internat'l (1930)
525B N. Laclede Station Road
St. Louis, MO 63119
Tel: (314)961-0031 *Fax:* (314)961-0040
Members: 3,000 individuals

Staff: 4
Annual Budget: $100-250,000
Exec. V. President: Esther Worthington
Communications Coordinator: Sharon Baebler
Membership/Meetings Coordinator: Pam Richter

Historical Note
Formerly (1987) Credit Women - Internat'l and (1990) CWI: Credit Professionals. Members are persons employed in credit or collections departments of business firms, professional offices or companies. Membership: $55/year.

Publications:
CPI Connection Newsletter. q.
CPI Education Manual. a. adv.
Credit Line Legislative Update. q.
Credit Professional Magazine. semi-a. adv.

Meetings/Conferences:
Annual Meetings: Summer/600

Credit Research Foundation (1949)
8815 Centre Park Drive, Suite 200
Columbia, MD 21045-2117
Tel: (410)740-5499 *Fax:* (410)740-5574
E-Mail: paulm@nacm.org
Members: 600 corporations
Staff: 4
Annual Budget: $500-1,000,000
C.O.O.: Paul J. Mignini, Jr., CAE
V. President: William Terence Callahan, CCE

Historical Note
CRF is a membership organization dedicated to developing and enhancing the skills, talents and knowledge of credit professionals. Members are cash managers, credit executives, treasurers, and others responsible for any portion of the credit function in an organization. Sponsors research and education programs to advance the industry. Affiliated with the Nat'l Ass'n of Credit Management. Membership: $595/year (corporate).

Publications:
Benchmarking Report for Credit and A/R.
Compensation of Credit Executives. bien.
Credit and Financial Management Review.
Nat'l summary of Domest Trade Receivables. q.
Technical Reference Manual.

Meetings/Conferences:
Annual Meetings: May

Credit Union Executives Soc. (1962)
P.O. Box 14167
Madison, WI 53714-0167
Tel: (608)271-2664 *Fax:* (608)271-2303
Toll Free: (800)252 - 2664
E-Mail: cues@cues.org
Web Site: http://www.cues.org
Members: 3,500 individuals
Staff: 42
Annual Budget: $5-10,000,000
President/C.E.O.: Fred Johnson
Sr. V.P., Conferences/Meetings: Linda Stemper, CMP
V.P., Professional Development: Franck Schurrmans, Ph.D.
Director, Administration: Trish Kienitz, PHR
Sr. V.P./C.F.O.: Edward Peirick
Senior V. President, Membership Services: Barbara Kachelski
V.P., Publications: Mary Arnold

Historical Note
Formerly (1970) CUES Managers Soc. Members are credit union executives. CUES divisions include Directors Educational Forum and Financial Suppliers Forum. Membership: $456/year.

Publications:
Credit Union Director Magazine. q. adv.
Credit Union Directory. a.
Credit Union Management Magazine. m. adv.
FYI Management Memo. semi-m.

Meetings/Conferences:
Annual Meetings: June
1999 – Honolulu, HI(Sheraton Waikiki)/May 1-4

Credit Union Nat'l Ass'n (1934)
P.O. Box 431
Madison, WI 53701-0431
Tel: (608)231-4000 *Fax:* (608)231-4263
E-Mail: JKarban@cuna.com
Web Site: http://www.cuna.org
Members: 51 state credit union leagues
Staff: 600
Annual Budget: $25-50,000,000
President and C.E.O.: Daniel A. Mica
V. President, Meetings & Special Events: Dean Archer
Exec. V. President, Corporate Services and Chief Staff Officer: Pete Crear
Senior V. President and Chief Economist: William Hampel
Sr. V.P., Finance and Administration: Greg Moser
Senior V.President, Administration: Harley Skjervem
Exec. V.P., Ass'n Services: John Gregoire
Senior V. President, Consumer Relations & Corporate Responsibility: Lucy Harr
Senior V. President: Brenda Furlow

Historical Note
Formerly (1970) CUNA Internat'l Inc. CUNA is the principal national trade association serving the nation's 12,300 credit unions through leagues in 50 states and the District of Columbia. Its affiliate organizations, including CUNA Service Group, provide financial products and services for credit unions. Certifies qualified credit union employees and awards the CCUE (Certified Credit Union Executive) designation. Sponsors and supports the Credit Union Legislative Action Council (CULAC). Street address is 5710 Mineral Point Rd., Madison 53701. Has an annual budget over $30 million.

Publications:
Credit Union Executive. bi-m. adv.
Credit Union Manager. bi-w.
Credit Union Newswatch. w.

Credit Union Report. a.
Directors Newsletter. m.
Everybody's Money. q.
News About Credit Unions. m.
The Credit Union Magazine. m. adv.
Meetings/Conferences:
Annual Meetings: October-November

Cremation Ass'n of North America *(1913)*
401 N. Michigan Ave.
Chicago, IL 60611-4267
Tel: (312)644-6610   *Fax:* (312)245-1081
E-Mail: Jack_Springer@sba.com
Members: 1,250 individuals
Staff: 3
Annual Budget: $500-1,000,000
Exec. Director: Jack M. Springer
Historical Note
*Formerly (1976) Cremation Ass'n of America. Members are
crematories, cemeteries, funeral directors and suppliers.
Membership: $275/year (regular, consultant, association,
supplier); $250/year (associate); $140/year (affiliate).*
Publications:
CANA Update Newsletter. bi-m.
Cremationist Magazine. q. adv.
Meetings/Conferences:
Annual Meetings: August
1999 – Baltimore, MD(Marriott Harbour)/Aug. 25-28/500
2000 – Keystone, CO(Keystone Resort)/Aug. 23-26/500

Crop Insurance Research Bureau *(1964)*
9200 Indian Creek Pkwy., Suite 220
Overland Park, KS 66210-2008
Tel: (913)338-0470   *Fax:* (913)661-1640
Web Site: http://www.cropinsurance.org
Members: 32 companies
Staff: 5
Annual Budget: $250-500,000
President: Paul L. Horel
Historical Note
*Members are crop insurance and other related companies. Sponsors
CIRB-PAC and crop insurance industry research. Provides industry
liaison to the U.S. Department of Agriculture.*
Publications:
CIRB Notes. m. adv.
Meetings/Conferences:
Annual Meetings: February

Crop Science Soc. of America *(1955)*
677 South Segoe Rd.
Madison, WI 53711
Tel: (608)273-8080   *Fax:* (608)273-2021
E-Mail: rbarnes@agronomy.org
Web Site: http://www.crops.org
Members: 5,800 individuals
Staff: 30
Annual Budget: $250-500,000
Exec. V. President: Robert F. Barnes
Historical Note
*Founded in 1955 and incorporated in Wisconsin in 1963. Shares
headquarters with the American Soc. of Agronomy and the Soil
Science Soc. of America. Membership: $64/year.*
Publications:
Agronomy News. m.
Crop Science. bi-m.
Journal of Environmental Quality. q.
Journal of Natural Resources & Life Sciences Education. semi-
a.
Journal of Production Agriculture. q.
Meetings/Conferences:
Annual Meetings: Fall, with American Soc. of Agronomy and
        Soil Science Soc. of America
1999 – Salt Lake City, UT/Oct. 30-Nov. 4
2000 – Minneapolis, MN/Nov. 5-10
2001 – Charlotte, NC/Oct. 21-25

Cross Country Ski Areas Ass'n *(1976)*
259 Bolton Road
Winchester, NH 03470
Tel: (603)239-4341   *Fax:* (603)239-6387
E-Mail: ccsaa@xcski.org
Web Site: www.xcski.org
Members: 250 ski areas
Staff: 2
Annual Budget: $10-25,000
President: Chris Frado
Historical Note
*Formerly (1983) Nat'l Ski Touring Operators Ass'n and (1988)
Cross Country Ski Areas of America. CCSAA is the industry
representative of cross country ski area operators. It was formed to
promote cross country skiing in North America, protect the interests
of operators and establish guidelines for ski area operations.
Membership: $350/year.*
Publications:
Best of Cross Country Skiing. a.
Nordic Network. q. adv.
Meetings/Conferences:
Annual Meetings: always at member ski areas/April
1999 – W. Yellowstone, MT(Holiday Inn)/April 16-17

Cruise Lines Internat'l Ass'n *(1975)*
500 Fifth Ave., Suite 1407
New York, NY 10110
Tel: (212)921-0066   *Fax:* (212)921-0549
Web Site: http://www.cruising.org
Members: 24 cruise lines, 23,000 agencies
Staff: 21
Annual Budget: $5-10,000,000
President: James G. Godsman

Historical Note
*Founded as Internat'l Passenger Ship Ass'n; assumed its current
name in 1984. CLIA promotes cruise and passenger vessel
vacationing to selling agents and the buying public.*
Meetings/Conferences:

Cryogenic Engineering Conference *(1954)*
Fermilab
P.O. Box 500, MS347
Batavia, IL 60510-0500
Tel: (708)840-3238   *Fax:* (708)840-4989
E-Mail: theilacker@fnal.gov
Web Site: cec-icmc.org
Members: 1000 individuals
Annual Budget: $100-250,000
Secretary: Jay Theilacker
Historical Note
*CEC members are scientists and engineers involved in research on
extreme cold.*
Publications:
Advances in Cryogenic Engineering. bien.
Meetings/Conferences:
Biennial Meetings: odd years.
1999 – Montreal, Quebec, Canada/July 12-16
2001 – Madison, WI/July 16-20

Cryogenic Soc. of America *(1964)*
c/o Huget Advertising
1033 South Blvd.
Oak Park, IL 60302
Tel: (708)383-6220   *Fax:* (708)383-9337
E-Mail: csa@huget.com
Web Site: www-csa.Fnal.gov
Members: 500 individuals, 100 corporate
Staff: 2
Annual Budget: $50-100,000
Exec. Director: Laurie Huget
Historical Note
*Founded in Los Angeles in September, 1964 and incorporated in
California the same year. Reincorporated in Illinois in 1984.
Absorbed the Helium Soc. in 1971. Promotes the engineering and
science of low temperatures. Membership: $50/year (individual),
$200/year minimum (corporate).*
Publications:
Cold Facts. q.

Cultured Pearl Ass'n of America *(1954)*
321 E. 53rd St.
New York, NY 10022
Tel: (212)688-5580
Members: 50 importers
Staff: 2
Annual Budget: $50-100,000
Exec. Secretary: Devon Macnow
Historical Note
*A group of cultured pearl importers in the New York area united for
promotion and public relations.*
Meetings/Conferences:
Quarterly Meetings: Always in New York, NY

CUMREC Internat'l *(1956)*
1244 Blossom St.
Columbia, SC 29208
Tel: (803)777-6890   *Fax:* (803)777-4760
Members: 3,000 individuals
Staff: 3
Annual Budget: $100-250,000
Coordinator: Fred Goebeler
Historical Note
*Founded in 1956 and known as CUMREC, (College University
Machine Records Conference) the organization later became the
College and University Computer Users Ass'n (CUCUA). However,
the organization maintains the acronymn CUMREC as its trade
name. Members are adminstrators of records management and data
processing in colleges and universities. Membership: $280/year.*
Publications:
Directory of Attendance. bien.
Newsletter. q.
Proceedings. a.
Meetings/Conferences:
Annual Meetings: May/Always hosted by a local
        university/600-1,000

CUNA Internat'l *(1934)*
Historical Note
See the Credit Union National Association.

Custom Electronic Design and Installation Ass'n
        (1989)
9202 N. Meridian St., Suite 200
Indianapolis, IN 46260-1810
Tel: (317)571-5602   *Fax:* (317)571-5603
Toll Free: (800)669 - 5329
Web Site: http://www.cedia.org/cedia
Members: 1,400 companies
Staff: 8
Annual Budget: $1-2,000,000
Exec. Director: Billilynne Keller
Conference Coordinator: Kristin Ross
Director, Education & Membership: Jennifer Carnahan
Historical Note
*Members are residential installers of custom designed electronic
systems. Membership: $500/year (designers and installers);
$1,000/year (manufacturers); $250/year (sales representatives);
$500/year (affiliates); $250/year (regional distributors);
$1,000/year (nat'l distributors).*
Publications:
Newsletter. q.

Annual Meetings: September
1999 – Indianapolis, IN/Sept. 22-26

Custom Tailors and Designers Ass'n of America *(1881)*
P.O. Box 53052
Washington, DC 20009
Tel: (202)387-7220   *Fax:* (202)387-7713
Members: 350 individuals
Staff: 1
Annual Budget: $100-250,000
Exec. Director: Suzanne Kilgore
Historical Note
*Trade association for men's custom tailoring industry. Formerly the
Merchant Tailors and Designers Association of America.
Membership: $295/year.*
Publications:
The Custom Tailor. 3/year. adv.
Meetings/Conferences:
Annual Meetings: late Winter/200
1999 – Atlanta, GA/Feb. 10-14

Customer Relations Institute *(1986)*
P.O. Box 880774
San Diego, CA 92168-0774
Tel: (619)656-6400   *Fax:* (619)656-2389
E-Mail: cri@swmall.com
Staff: 12
Annual Budget: $500-1,000,000
President: Thomas D. Hinton, Jr.
Director, Education: Alicia Pettersen
V.P., Finance: Jean Greer
Historical Note
*An international training and consulting consortium specializing in
customer service, team building, leadership and performance
excellence in the workplace. CRI also conducts customer satisfaction
surveys.*
Publications:
Customer Focus. q.
Leadership Lessons. q.
Meetings/Conferences:
1999 – Los Angeles, CA(Inter-Continental)
2000 – San Diego, CA(Hotel del Coronado)

Customs and Internat'l Trade Bar Ass'n *(1917)*
475 Park Ave. South
New York, NY 10016
Tel: (212)725-0200   *Fax:* (212)889-4135
Members: 600 individuals
Annual Budget: $25-50,000
President: Rufus E. Jarman, Jr.
Historical Note
*Attorneys admitted to practice before the United States Court of
Internat'l Trade (previously the United States Customs Court) and
specializing in Customs and Internat'l Trade law in the United
States. Formerly (until 1982) The Ass'n of the Customs Bar.
Membership: $50/year (individual).*
Publications:
Newsletter. a.
U. S.

Cutting Die Institute *(1946)*
Historical Note
Address unknown in 1995.

Cycle Parts and Accessories Ass'n *(1906)*
Historical Note
Organization defunct in 1998.

Cystic Fibrosis Foundation *(1955)*
6931 Arlington Road
Bethesda, MD 20814
Tel: (301)951-4422   *Fax:* (301)951-6378
Toll Free: (800)344 - 4823
E-Mail: info@cff.org
Web Site: http://www.cff.org
Members: 56 chapters
Staff: 80
President and C.E.O.: Robert Beall, Ph.D.
Historical Note
*The Cystic Fibrosis Foundation was established in 1955 to assure
the development of the means to cure and control cystic fibrosis and
to improve the quality of life for those with the disease.*
Publications:
Annual Report. a.
Commitment. bien.
Meetings/Conferences:
Annual Meetings: North American C.F. Conference

Czech and Slovak-United States Economic Council
        (1975)
Historical Note
*Became (1997) American Business Alliance for the Transition
Economies of Eurasia.*

Dairy and Food Industries Supply Ass'n *(1919)*
Historical Note
Became Internat'l Ass'n of Food Industry Suppliers in 1997.

Dairy Management *(1994)*
10255 W. Higgins Road, Suite 900
Rosemont, IL 60018-5616
Tel: (847)803-2000   *Fax:* (847)803-2077
Members: 20 member organization units
Staff: 86
Annual Budget: $1-2,000,000
Chief Executive Officer: Thomas P. Gallagher
Group Executive, Nutrition and Product Research: Linda Racicot

Group Executive, Planning and Research: Gordon McDonald
Group Executive, Finance and Administration: Daniel J. Chavka
Group Executive, Member Relations: William Piggott

Historical Note
Formed by the merger of the United Dairy Industry Ass'n and the Nat'l Dairy Promotuion and Research Board, Dairy Management Inc. increases the demand for dairy products through the development and execution of an industry-wide, market-driven business plan that invests resources in a strategic manner and provides the best possible economic advantage to dairy farmers.

Publications:
Catalogue of Nutrition Education Materials. a.
Dairy Council Digest. bi-m.
Nutrition News. q.

Meetings/Conferences:
Annual Meetings: September

Dairy Soc. Internat'l *(1946)*
7185 Ruritan Drive
Chambersburg, PA   17201-9242
Tel: (717)375-4392
Members: 200 companies and associations
Staff: 2
Annual Budget: under \$10,000
Manging Director: George W. Weigold

Historical Note
Founded as the Dairy Industry Societies, Internat'l, it assumed its present name in 1956. Members are associations and companies interested in expanding world consumption of milk and milk products. Has an international membership. Is the official dairy cooperator with USDA Foreign Agriculture Service to expand sales of U.S. dairy products. Membership: \$20/year (individual), \$200/year (company).

Meetings/Conferences:
Annual Meetings: Fall, usually with another dairy organization.

Dalton Floor Covering Market Ass'n *(1979)*
210 W. Cuyler St.
Dalton, GA   30720-8209
Tel: (706)278-4101   *Fax:* (706)278-5323
Toll Free: (800)288 - 4101
E-Mail: dfcma@alltel.net
Web Site: http://www.carpets.org
Members: 180 companies
Staff: 2
Annual Budget: \$50-100,000
Exec. Director: Wanda Ellis

Historical Note
Formerly (1991) Carpet Manufacturers Marketing Ass'n, DFCMA provides marketing services, employee benefits programs, and other services to members of the floor covering industry nationwide. Membership: \$300-500/year.

Publications:
Directory. a.
Newsletter. q.

Meetings/Conferences:
1999 – Dalton, GA(N.W.GA Trade Center)/Sept. 14-16/3000

Dance Critics Ass'n *(1974)*
C/O Dance Alloy
5530 Penn Ave.
Pittsburgh, PA   15206
Tel: (510)548-7474
Members: 266 individuals
Annual Budget: \$10-25,000
President: Stacy Prickett

Historical Note
Professionals who review dance either on a regular basis or freelance; teachers, historians, publicists and others interested in dance writing. Conducts workshops on subjects of practical interest to dance critics, also holds symposiums and mini-conferences.Alternative address is P.O. Box 1882, Old Chelsea Station, New York, NY 10011. Membership: \$40/year (individual); \$20/year (student); \$65/year (organization).

Publications:
DCA News. q.
Membership Directory. bien.

Meetings/Conferences:
Annual Meetings: usually New York, NY/June-July

Dance Educators of America *(1932)*
P.O. Box 607
Pelham, NY   10803-0607
Tel: (914)636-3200   *Fax:* (914)636-5895
Toll Free: (800)229 - 3868
E-Mail: dancedea@aol.com
Members: 2,000 individuals
Staff: 4
Annual Budget: \$50-100,000
Exec. Director: Vickie Sheer

Historical Note
Promotes the education of teachers in the performing arts, including dance and stage arts. Conducts seminars and workshops to advance the theory and practice of dance education. Membership: \$125/year (individual); \$200/year (couple).

Publications:
DEA News. semi-a. adv.
DEA Tap Dancing Dictionary. a.
DEA Workshops and Competitions. a.

Meetings/Conferences:
Three Meetings Annually: Summer, various locations
1999 – Las Vegas, NV

Dance Masters of America *(1884)*
P.O. Box 610533
Bayside, NY   11631
Tel: (718)225-4013   *Fax:* (718)225-4293
E-Mail: dmamann@aol.com

Web Site: http://www.dma-national.org
Members: 2,500 individuals
Staff: 2
Annual Budget: \$250-500,000
Exec. Secretary: Robert Mann

Historical Note
An organization of dance teachers. Formerly (until 1926) known as the American Nat'l Ass'n, Masters of Dancing. Membership: \$62/year, plus local chapter dues (individual).

Publications:
DMA Bulletin. q.
DMA Bulletin. bi-m. adv.
DMA Magazine. q. adv.

Meetings/Conferences:
Annual Meetings: July/500
1999 – Anaheim, CA(Marriott)
2000 – New Orleans
2001 – NYC, NY(Marriott Marquis)
2002 – Orlando, FL(Coronado Springs Hotel Disney)

Dance/USA *(1982)*
1156 15th St., N.W., Suite 820
Washington, DC   20005-1704
Tel: (202)833-1717   *Fax:* (202)833-2686
E-Mail: danceusa@artswire.org
Web Site: http://www.danceusa.org/danceusa
Members: 300 organizations and individuals
Staff: 6
Annual Budget: \$500-1,000,000
Exec. Director: Martin D. Cohen
General Manager: Carolynn Jennings

Historical Note
Dance/USA, the national service organization for not-for-profit, professional dance, seeks to advance the artform of dance by addressing the needs, concerns and interests of professional dance. Dance/USA members include ballet, modern, ethnic, jazz, culturally specific, traditional and tap companies as well as dance service organizations and other organizations concerned with non-profit professional dance. Membership: \$75-\$250/year (individual), \$150-\$7,350/year (organization/company).

Publications:
Dance/USA Journal. q. adv.
Dance/USA Membership Directory. m.
Member Bulletin. 11/yr. adv.

Meetings/Conferences:

Danish-American Chamber of Commerce (USA) *(1931)*
885 2nd Ave., 18th Floor
New York, NY   10017
Tel: (212)980-6240   *Fax:* (212)754-1904
E-Mail: daccny@interport.net
Members: 160 companies
Staff: 1
Annual Budget: \$50-100,000
Exec. Director: Hanne Hochheim

Historical Note
Formed through a merger of the Danish-American Trade Council (1964) and the Danish Luncheon Club (1931). Members are concentrated in the New York City area. Membership: \$80/year (individual); \$350/year (corporate), sustaining members \$1,000/year.

Publications:
Newsletter. 5/year. adv.

Meetings/Conferences:
Monthly Meetings: in New York City

Data Administration Management Ass'n Internat'l *(1988)*
P.O. Box 5786
Bellevue, WA   98006-5786
Tel: (425)562-2636   *Fax:* (425)562-0376
E-Mail: members4u@compuserve.com
Web Site: http://www.dama.org
Members: 3,000 individuals
Annual Budget: \$25-50,000
President: Wayne Olsen

Historical Note
Promotes understanding, development, and practice of managing information and data as a key enterprise asset.

Publications:
DAMA Internat'l. bi-m. adv.

Meetings/Conferences:

Data Interchange Standards Ass'n *(1987)*
1800 Diagonal Road, Suite 200
Alexandria, VA   22314-2852
Tel: (703)548-7005   *Fax:* (703)548-5738
Web Site: http://www.disa.org
Members: 800 companies
Staff: 37
Annual Budget: \$5-10,000,000
President: Judy A. Kilpatrick
Dir., Communications/Marketing: Carmella Baccari
Dir., Meetings/Expositions: Connie Shaw
Director of Business Development: William Myers
Director, Education: Lisa D. Clowers
Dir., Finance and Administration: Brenda Pritz

Historical Note
DISA is a not-for-profit corporation that serves the electronic commerce community by providing education about EDI and related technologies, and managing the development of industry standards for electronic data interchange.

Publications:
DISAGram. bi-m. adv.

Meetings/Conferences:
1999 – Las Vegas, NV(Caesar's Palace)/April 12-14/2000

Deciduous Tree Fruit Disease Workers

Historical Note
Largely inactive, DTFDW declined to provide updated information for this listing.

Decision Sciences Institute *(1969)*
Georgia State U., College of Business
35 Broad St.
Atlanta, GA   30303
Tel: (404)651-4000   *Fax:* (404)651-4008
Members: 3,500 individuals, 1000 libraries and companies
Staff: 2
Annual Budget: \$250-500,000
Exec. Director: Carol J. Latta

Historical Note
Formerly (1985) American Institute for Decision Sciences. Membership consists mainly of business school faculties and management specialists who use quantitative and behavioral techniques to apply theories of administrative decision-making. Membership: \$59/year (U.S.); \$59/year (U.S. and international).

Publications:
Decision Line. bi-m. adv.
Decision Sciences Journal. bi-m. adv.

Meetings/Conferences:
Annual Meetings: Fall/1,500
1999 – New Orleans, LA

Decorative Laminate Products Ass'n *(1956)*

Historical Note
Dissolved in 1995. DLPA members voted to join the Kitchen Cabinet Manufactures Ass'n.

Decorative Window Coverings Ass'n *(1988)*
10521 St. Charles Rock Road, Suite 1
St. Ann, MO   63074-1838
Tel: (314)429-4267   *Fax:* (314)429-0334
Members: 30 companies
Staff: 2
Annual Budget: \$25-50,000
Exec. V. President: Rosemary Jost

Historical Note
DWCA is a trade association of wholesale fabricators and distributors of all window treatment. Stresses industry cooperation through adherence to a Code of Ethics and retailer certification; provides benefits including credit card merchant discounts and cooperative purchasing of long distance service. Membership: \$400-1,600/year (company).

Publications:
On Track. bi-m.

Meetings/Conferences:
Semi-Annual Meetings: Winter and Early Spring

Deep Foundations Institute *(1976)*
120 Charlotte Place, 3rd Floor
Englewood Cliffs, NJ   07632-2607
Tel: (201)567-4232   *Fax:* (201)567-4436
E-Mail: dfihq@idt.net
Web Site: http://www.dfi.org
Members: 912 individuals and organizations
Staff: 2
Annual Budget: \$250-500,000
Exec. Director: Manuel A. Fine
Operations Manager: Geordie Compton

Historical Note
Incorporated in New Jersey in January, 1976. Concerned with the design, installation and stability of deep foundations of all types. Members are project owners, consulting engineers, contractors, educators and suppliers. Membership: \$95/year (individual); corporate membership scaled by sales volume and/or number of employees.

Publications:
Deep Foundation News. bi-m.
Foundations Industry Desk Directory. a.
Membership Roster. a.

Meetings/Conferences:
Annual Meetings: Fall/150-250
1999 – Dearborn, MI(Hyatt Regency)/Oct. 14-16

Defense Credit Union Council *(1963)*
805 15th St., N.W., Suite 300
Washington, DC   20005-2207
Tel: (202)682-5993   *Fax:* (202)682-9054
Members: 330 credit unions
Staff: 2
Annual Budget: \$250-500,000
President and C.E.O.: Capt. David C. Lundahl, USN(Ret.)

Historical Note
Members are credit unions serving military and civilian employees of the Department of Defense.

Publications:
Alert. m. adv.
Director of Defense Credit Unions. bien.
Statistical Report of Defense Credit Unions. a.

Meetings/Conferences:
Annual Meetings: September
1999 – Orlando, FL(Marriott)/Aug. 1-4/300
2000 – San Francisco, CA(Hyatt Embarcadeso)/Aug. 18-22/300
2001 – Portland, OR

Defense Fire Protection Ass'n
P.O. Box 1310
Falls Church, VA   22041-0310
Tel: (703)521-3926   *Fax:* (703)521-0849
E-Mail: dfpa@aol.com
Exec. Director: Ron Fisher
Director, Government Affairs: David A. Johnston

Meetings/Conferences:

Defense Research Institute *(1960)*
750 N. Lake Shore Drive, Suite 500
Chicago, IL 60611-4403
Tel: (312)944-0575   *Fax:* (312)944-2003
Web Site: http://www.dri.org
Members: 22,000 individuals
Staff: 28
Annual Budget: $2-5,000,000
Exec. Director: John Kouris
Historical Note
Members are defense lawyers, insurance and manufacturing executives, and defendants. The Institute's primary purpose is to increase the professional skill and enlarge the knowledge of defense lawyers. Products and professional liability, insurance, environmental and equal opportunity law are some of the subjects with which members are concerned. Operates an arbitration service and provides a Brief Bank Index and Expert Witness Index. Membership: $125/year.
Publications:
For the Defense. m.
Meetings/Conferences:
Annual Meetings: With Internat'l Ass'n of Defense Counsel
1999 – New York, NY/Oct. 6-10

Delta Dental Plans Ass'n *(1965)*
1515 W. 22nd St., Suite 1200
Oak Brook, IL 60521
Tel: (630)574-6001   *Fax:* (630)574-6999
Members: 50 dental plans
Staff: 19
Annual Budget: $5-10,000,000
President & CEO: Kim E. Volk
V. President & Chief Financial Officer: Steven White
V. President & Gen. Manager: Bruce Skaggs
Historical Note
Formerly the Nat'l Ass'n of Dental Service Plans. A group of dental service corporations providing group dental benefit programs to the public. Membership: dues vary by premium revenue.
Publications:
Membership Directory. a.
Newsletters. q.
Meetings/Conferences:
Annual Meetings: June

Delta Nu Alpha Transportation Fraternity *(1940)*
530 Church St., Suite 700
Nashville, TN 37219-2321
Tel: (615)251-0933   *Fax:* (615)244-3170
Members: 5,000 individuals
Staff: 6
Annual Budget: $100-250,000
Management Exec.: Dee Ann Walker, CAE
Historical Note
Professional fraternity. Membership: $50-$100/year (individual).
Publications:
Journal of Transportation. semi-a.
Proceedings. a.
The Alphian. q.
Meetings/Conferences:
Annual Meetings: Fall

Delta Omicron Foundation, Inc. *(1909)*
57 Orchard Drive
Worthington, OH 43085
Tel: (614)436-5258   *Fax:* (614)436-4776
E-Mail: doexof@aol.com
Web Site: http://deltaomicron.people.virginia.edu
Members: 25,000 individuals
Staff: 1
Annual Budget: $25-50,000
Exec. Secretary: M. Diane Blaine
Historical Note
An international music fraternity founded September 6, 1909 at the Cincinnati Conservatory of Music and incorporated in the State of Ohio the same year.
Publications:
The Wheel of Delta Omicron. q.
The Whistle. a.
Meetings/Conferences:
1990: Spartanburg, SC(Converse College)/August

Delta Phi Epsilon *(1920)*
P.O. Box 25401
Washington, DC 20007
Tel: (202)337-7116
Members: 7,000 individuals
General Secretary: Terrence Boyle
Historical Note
Professional foreign service fraternity.
Publications:
Membership Directory. bien.
The Galley. a.
The Sun. q.
The Tramp. a.

Delta Pi Epsilon *(1936)*
P.O. Box 4340
Little Rock, AR 72214
Tel: (501)562-1233   *Fax:* (501)562-1293
E-Mail: dpe@ipa.net
Web Site: http://www.dpe.org
Members: 11,000 individuals
Staff: 2
Annual Budget: $100-250,000
Exec. Director: Dr. Robert B. Mitchell

Historical Note
Professional society in graduate business education. Founded at New York University in 1936 and incorporated in the State of New York, December 3, 1937. Reincorporated in Minnesota in 1983 and in Arkansas in 1988. Members are teachers of business subjects. National Membership: $30/year.
Publications:
Business Education Index. a.
DPE Journal. q.
Meetings/Conferences:
Annual Meetings: November

Delta Psi Kappa *(1916)*
P.O. Box 90264
Indianapolis, IN 46290
Tel: (317)255-4379   *Fax:* (317)253-5067
Members: 16,000 individuals
Staff: 1
Annual Budget: $10-25,000
Exec. Director: Harriet Rodenberg
Historical Note
Professional fraternity in health, physical education, recreation, dance and allied fields.
Meetings/Conferences:
Biennial Meetings: Spring (even years)

Delta Sigma Delta *(1882)*
W323 S3380 Highway E
Dousman, WI 53118
Tel: (414)968-2030   *Fax:* (414)968-5850
Toll Free: (800)335 - 8744
Members: 26,000 individuals
Staff: 2
Annual Budget: $100-250,000
Secretary: John H. Prey, D.D.S.
Historical Note
A professional dental fraternity founded at the University of Michigan November 15, 1882. Membership: By invitation.
Publications:
Desmos of Delta Sigma Delta. q.
Meetings/Conferences:
Annual Meetings: Fall/150-200
1999 – Turtle Bay, HI(Hilton)/Oct. 6-9/175
2001 – Chicago, IL/Oct. 12-15/175

Delta Sigma Pi *(1907)*
330 South Campus Ave., Box 230
Oxford, OH 45056-0230
Tel: (513)523-1907   *Fax:* (513)523-7292
Members: 161,000 individuals
Staff: 16
Annual Budget: $1-2,000,000
Exec. V. President: William Loftus
Exec. Director: William C. Schilling
Historical Note
Professional fraternity, commerce and business administration, founded at New York University November 7, 1907.
Publications:
The Deltasig. q.
Meetings/Conferences:
Biennial Meetings: Odd years/750
1999 – Houston, TX/Aug. 18-22

Delta Soc. *(1977)*
289 Perimeter Road East
Renton, WA 98055-1329
Tel: (206)226-7357   *Fax:* (206)235-1076
Toll Free: (800)869 - 6898
E-Mail: deltasociety@cis.compuserve.com
Web Site: www.deltasociety.org
Members: 5,000 individuals, 300 companies and organizations
Staff: 8
Annual Budget: $1-2,000,000
Acting President: Maureen Frederickson
Director, Finance: Jon Eastlake
Historical Note
The Society is an international, educational, research and service resource on the relationships between people, animals and nature. Members include veterinarians, psychiatrists, health workers, volunteers, administrators, teachers, and pet owners. Membership: $35/year, with subscription.
Publications:
Alert. bi-m.
Anthrozoos: Journal of the Delta Society. q.
InterActions. q.
Pet Partners Newsletter. bi-m.
Meetings/Conferences:
Annual Meetings: October
1999 – Ohio

Delta Theta Phi *(1900)*
21330 Center Ridge Rd., Suite 32
Rocky River, OH 44116
Tel: (440)895-9990   *Fax:* (440)895-9994
Toll Free: (800)783 - 2600
Members: 100,000 individuals
Staff: 2
Annual Budget: $100-250,000
Exec. Director: Cate K. Smith
Historical Note
Professional legal fraternity formed at the Cleveland Law School of Baldwin University in 1900 as Delta Phi Delta. On September 27, 1913 created Delta Theta Phi. A merger of Alpha Kappa Phi, Delta Phi Delta and Theta Lambda Phi. Merged with Sigma Nu Phi legal fraternity in 1989. Membership: $50 (one time student initation fee); $60(alumni-one time fee)
Publications:
Adelphia Law Journal. a.

The Paper Book. q.
Meetings/Conferences:
Biennial Meetings: Odd years in Summer
1999 – Washington, DC/Aug. 10-15

Delta Waterfowl Foundation *(1911)*
R.R. 1, Box 1
Portage La Prairie
Manitoba,Canada, R1N 3-A1
Tel: (204)239-1900   *Fax:* (204)239-5950
E-Mail: delta@deltawaterfowl.com
Web Site: http://www.deltawaterfowl.com
Members: 4,500 companies and individuals
Staff: 12
Annual Budget: $1-2,000,000
Exec. V. President: Jonathan Scarth
Historical Note
Formerly (1935) American Game Protective Ass'n, (1946) American Wildlife Institute, (1951) American Wildlife Foundation, and North American Wildlife Foundation (1993). Aims to help maintain, restore and advance sound natural resource and wildlife management programs. Supported by both individual and corporate members interested in its aims.
Meetings/Conferences:

Dental Dealers of America *(1944)*
123 S. Broad St., Suite 2030
Philadelphia, PA 19109-1020
Tel: (215)731-9975   *Fax:* (215)731-9984
Members: 55 wholesale distributors
Staff: 2
Annual Budget: $25-50,000
Exec. Director: Edward B. Shils, Ph.D.
Associate Director: Kathleen A. LaMar
Historical Note
Founded to help educate the dental industry suppliers about industry problems and marketing and distribution trends. Membership: $225-$5000/year (organization).
Publications:
DDA Membership Directory. bi-a.
Meetings/Conferences:
Annual Meetings: February in Chicago at the Fairmont, held in conjunction with the Dental Manufacturers of America. Meeting in the Fall held with the American Dental Association.
1999 – Chicago, IL(Fairmont)/100
2000 – Chicago, IL(Fairmont)/100

Dental Gold Institute *(1981)*
Historical Note
Organization defunct in 1997.

Dental Group Management Ass'n *(1951)*
DGMA 220, P.O.Box 42036
Phoenix, AZ 85080
Tel: (602)465-5691   *Fax:* (602)465-5691
Members: 200 individuals
Staff: 1
Annual Budget: $10-25,000
Contact: Vince Cedola
Historical Note
Dental group business managers and others concerned with group practice management. Membership: $150/year.
Publications:
DGMA Communicator Newsletter. q. adv.
Directory. a.
Meetings/Conferences:
Annual Meetings: with American Academy of Dental Group Practice Palm Springs, CA(Doubletree Resort)/Feb. 3-6/300

Dental Manufacturers of America *(1932)*
123 S. Broad St., Suite 2030
Philadelphia, PA 19109-1020
Tel: (215)731-9975   *Fax:* (215)731-9984
E-Mail: staff@dmanews.org
Web Site: http://www.dmanews.org
Members: 215 companies
Staff: 4
Annual Budget: $250-500,000
Exec. Director: Edward B. Shils, Ph.D.
Associate Director: Kathleen A. LaMar
Historical Note
DMA serves the dental manufacturing industry through dissemination of market research, sales and exporting information, standards and GMP's as they relate to the Safe Medical Devices Act and the ISO 9000 series. Membership: $1,400-6,000/year (organization).
Publications:
Membership Directory. bien.
Meetings/Conferences:
Annual Meetings: Summer. Also meets with the Dental Dealers of America in February and with the American Dental Association in the fall.

Dermatology Nurses Ass'n *(1982)*
East Holly Ave., Box 56
Pitman, NJ 08071-0056
Tel: (609)256-2330   *Fax:* (609)589-7463
Toll Free: (800)454 - 4362
E-Mail: dna@mail.ajj.com
Web Site: http://www.dna.inurse.com
Members: 1,300 individuals
Staff: 2
Annual Budget: $500-1,000,000
Exec. Director: Cynthia R. Nowicki
Manager, Conferences: Michael Brennan
Director, Education: Donna Gloe

Historical Note
Founded in New Orleans in December, 1982 and incorporated in the State of New Jersey. Membership: $60/year.

Publications:
Dermatology Nursing. bi-m.
DNA Focus. bi-m. adv.
Membership Directory. a.
Product Guide. a.

Meetings/Conferences:
Annual Meetings: February or March
1999 – New Orleans, LA(Hyatt Regency)/March 17-22
2000 – San Francisco, CA(Hyatt Regency)/March 8-12
2001 – Crystal City, VA/Feb. 28-March 4/700
2002 – New Orleans, LA(Hyatt Regency)/Feb. 20-25

Design Management Institute *(1976)*
29 Temple Place
Boston, MA   02111-1350
Tel: (617)338-6380   *Fax:* (617)338-6570
E-Mail: epowell@dmi.org
Web Site: http://www.dmi.org
Members: 700 designing teams and firms
Staff: 7
Annual Budget: $500-1,000,000
President: Earl N. Powell
Programs Coordinator: Chris Handcock
V. President of Operations: John Tobin

Historical Note
Members are in-house design teams and consulting design firms. Sponsors the Centers for Research, Education & Information, and other operations focusing on current issues in design management. Membership: $350/year (individual); $400/year (academic); $1,500-6,000/year (company).

Publications:
Conference Notebooks. 2-3/year.
Design Management Journal. q. adv.
Directory of Members. a.
DMI Newsletter. q. adv.
Salary Survey and Profession Profile. a.

Meetings/Conferences:
1999 – Amsterdam, March 14-16/Amsterdam, 0-16
1999 – Pasadena, CA/April 25-27
1999 – Montreal, Canada/June 20-22
1999 – Chatham, MA

Design Professionals Ass'n *(1986)*
247 Bryant Ave.
Glen Ellyn, IL   60137
Tel: (630)858-9500   *Fax:* (630)858-0700
E-Mail: mail@leatzow.com
President: Jim Leatzow

Historical Note
Members are professionals involved in landscape design, including landscape architects, planners, and irrigation consultants.

Design-Build Institute of America *(1993)*
1010 Massachusetts Ave., N.W., Suite 350
Washington, DC   20001
Tel: (202)682-0110   *Fax:* (202)682-5877
E-Mail: dbia@dbia.org
Web Site: http://dbia.org
Members: 500 companies
Staff: 17
Annual Budget: $2-5,000,000
Exec. Director: Jeffrey L. Beard
Director of Technical Programs: David A. Johnston
Dir., Meetings & Conferences: Donald R. Jessup
Executive Assistant: Stacey E. Anderson
Dir., Member Services: Christina M. Elsner

Historical Note
DBIA is a professional association founded to promote Design-Build project delivery and to develop practices for users and practitioners. Design-Build includes professional design and construction (and frequently additional services such as finance, real estate and operation) under a single source responsiblity contract. Members include companies and individuals concerned with integrated architecture, engineering and construction services. Membership: $500-$7,500/year, dues vary based on annual volume.

Publications:
Design Build Magazine.
Design-Build Dateline. m.
Design-Build Documents.
FYI. q.
Membership Directory. a.

Meetings/Conferences:
Annual Meetings: Fall
1999 – Dallas, TX(Adam's Mark)/Oct. 13-15/1100
2000 – San Diego, CA(Sheraton)/Oct. 4-6/1200
2001   Boston, MA
2002 – Denver, CO

Design-Build Manufacturers Ass'n *(1986)*
2938 Columbia Ave., Suite 1102
Lancaster, PA   17603
Tel: (717)295-0033   *Fax:* (717)299-2154
E-Mail: dbminfo@dbm-assoc.com
Web Site: http://www.dcenter.com
Members: 13,500 individuals
Staff: 7
Annual Budget: $1-2,000,000
Exec. Director: Amy Z. Thorn
V. President, Operations: Jerry Fulkerson
Manager, Administration: Chris Sensenick
V. President, Business Development: Thomas Cozzoli

Historical Note
DBM members are companies and professional involved in warehousing and distribution, including warehouses, manufacturers of equipment, construction companies and material handling professionals and consultants. DBM conducts a certificate program

sponsored by several universities. Membership: $400/year (corporate); $45/year (individual).

Publications:
Warehouse of the Future News Newsletter. 3/year. adv.

Meetings/Conferences:
1999 – Orlando, FL/June 7-9

Developmental Disabilities Nurses Ass'n *(1992)*
1720 Willow Creek Circle, Suite 515
Eugene, OR   97402
Tel: (541)485-0477   *Fax:* (541)485-7372
Toll Free: (800)888 - 6733
Members: 1000 individuals
Annual Budget: $250-500,000
Exec. Director: Randy Bryson, R.N.

Historical Note
DDNA members are registered, licensed practical and licensed vocational nurses with an interest in developmental disabilities nursing. Administers a professional certification program for achievement of the Certified Developmental Disabilities Nurse (CDDN) credential. Membership: $55/year (individual).

Publications:
DDNA News Network. q. adv.

Meetings/Conferences:
1999 – Nashville, TN

Devon Cattle Ass'n *(1918)*
Route 1, Box 93
Bunkie, LA   71322-9709
Tel: (318)876-3630
Members: 125 individuals
Staff: 1
Annual Budget: under $10,000
Exec. Director: Stewart H. Fowler, Ph.D.

Historical Note
Breeders of Devon beef cattle. Formerly (1971) American Devon Cattle Club.

Publications:
DCA Newsletter. q.

Meetings/Conferences:
Annual Meetings: Fall

Diamond Council of America *(1944)*
9140 Ward Parkway
Kansas City, MO   64114
Tel: (816)444-3500   *Fax:* (816)444-0330
Members: 71 exec members, 1,700 locations
Annual Budget: $250-500,000
Exec. Director: Jerry Fogel, CAE

Historical Note
Conducts correspondence course in Gemology and Diamontology. Certifies employees as Guild Gemologist and Certified Diamontologist. Established the Diamond Council University in 1988. Supplies members with merchandising tools, advertising copy, displays, etc. to feature diamonds and other gems as a professional specialty.

Publications:
The Diamontologist. bi-m.

Meetings/Conferences:
1999 – Las Vegas, NV(The Mirage)/125

Diamond Manufacturers and Importers Ass'n of America *(1932)*
111 Great Neck Road
Great Neck, NY   11021
Tel: (212)944-2066
Members: 150 companies
Staff: 2
Annual Budget: $10-25,000
Counsel: Ben Kinzler

Historical Note
Formerly the Diamond Manufacturers Ass'n. Members are importers, cutters and polishers of rough diamonds.

Diamond Trade and Precious Stone Ass'n of America *(1940)*
11 W. 47th St.
New York, NY   10036
Tel: (212)790-3806   *Fax:* (212)768-8656
Members: 500 individuals
Staff: 6
Annual Budget: $100-250,000
Secretary: Hank Frydman

Historical Note
Formerly (1991) Diamond Trade Ass'n of America.

Meetings/Conferences:
Annual Meetings: 2nd week in January/New York, NY

Diamond Wheel Manufacturers Institute *(1963)*
30200 Detroit Road
Cleveland, OH   44145-1967
Tel: (440)899-0010   *Fax:* (440)892-1404
Web Site: http://www.dwmi.org
Members: 11 companies
Staff: 2
Manager: J. Jeffery Wherry
Meetings/Conventions: Donna Haders

Historical Note
Members are makers of grinding wheels, rotary dressers, core drills and hones, for use in applications outside the construction industry, in which the abrasive used is diamond or cubic boron nitride, in all bond types. Acts as the representative for the superabrasives industry in the U.S. and worldwide.

Publications:
Publish a series of booklets on techniques, procedures & safety tips.

Meetings/Conferences:
1999 – Ft. Lauderdale, FL(Marriott Harbor
   Beach)/April 17-20/80
1999 – Cleveland, OH(Ritz-Carlton)/Nov. 9-10/80

Dibasic Esters Group *(1995)*
1850 M St., N.W., Suite 700
Washington, DC   20036
Tel: (202)721-4160   *Fax:* (202)296-8120
E-Mail: DBE@socma.com
Staff: 2
Annual Budget: $100-250,000
Exec. Director: Richard E. Opatick, CAE

Historical Note
An affiliate of the Synthetic Organic Chemical Manufacturers.

Die Set Manufacturers Service Bureau *(1951)*
Historical Note
Organization defunct in 1998.

Diecasting Development Council *(1987)*
9701 W. Higgins Rd., #855
Rosemont, IL   60018-4703
Tel: (847)292-3625   *Fax:* (847)292-3613
Web Site: www.diecasting.org/ddc
Members: 133 companies
Staff: 2
Exec. Director: Leo J. Baran

Historical Note
DDC members are companies supplying custom die casting production and related services to original equipment manufacturers and supplier companies to the die casting industry.

Publications:
Capabilities Directriy of Custom Die Casters & Suppliers. q.
NADCA Product Specification Standards for Die Casting.
Product Design for Die Castings Manual.

Dielectrics and Electrical Insulation Soc.
Historical Note
A technical society of the Institute of Electrical and Electronics Engineers (IEEE). Membership in the Society, open only to IEEE members, includes a subscription to a technical periodical in the field published by IEEE. All administrative support is provided by IEEE.

Dietary Managers Ass'n *(1960)*
406 Surrey Woods Dr.
St. Charles, IL   60174-2386
Tel: (630)587-6336   *Fax:* (630)587-6308
Web Site: http://www.dmaonline.org
Members: 16,000 individuals
Staff: 23
Annual Budget: $1-2,000,000
Exec. Director: William S. St. John, CAE
Director, Education: Elaine L. Fisher
Controller: Jennifer Denil

Historical Note
Formerly (1984) the Hospital, Institution and Educational Food Service Soc. DMA is an organization of professionals dedicated to excellence in the food service industry. Sponsors and supports the DMA Political Action Committee. Membership: $70/year (active); $75/year (associate); $90/year (certified).

Publications:
Dietary Manager Magazine. bi-m. adv.

Meetings/Conferences:
Annual Meetings: August
1999 – San Francisco, CA(Hyatt Regency)/July 4-8

Diethyl Ether Producers Ass'n *(1993)*
1250 Connecticut Ave., N.W., Suite 700
Washington, DC   20036
Tel: (202)637-9040   *Fax:* (202)637-9178
Members: 4 manufacturers
Annual Budget: $25-50,000
Exec. Director: Elizabeth K. Hunt

Digital Distribution of Advertising for Publications *(1990)*
2090 Casa de Vereda
Vista, CA   92084-4223
Tel: (760)758-9460   *Fax:* (760)758-5401
Members: 1000 companies
Staff: 2
Annual Budget: $50-100,000
Secretary-Treasurer: Patrice M. Dunn

Historical Note
The DDAP committee is a consortium of industry professionals working together to develop a standard for the digital distribution of advertising for publications (DDAP). Membership comprised of representatives from major corporations, advertising agencies, design firms, trade shops, services bureaus, printers and publishers. Membership: $250/year (individual), $2,500/year (organization/company)

Publications:
Newsletter. irreg.

Meetings/Conferences:

Digital Imaging Marketing Ass'n
Historical Note
A section of the Photo Marketing Ass'n-Internat'l.

Digital Printing and Imaging Ass'n *(1992)*
10015 Main St.
Fairfax, VA   22031-3489
Tel: (703)385-1339   *Fax:* (703)359-1336
E-Mail: dpi@dpia.org
Web Site: http://www.dpia.org
Members: 800 companies
Staff: 2

Annual Budget: $500-1,000,000
Coordinating Director: John S. Shaw
Director of Communications: Bruce H. Joffe
V. President, Government Affairs: Marci Kinter
V. President, Conventions and Conference: Sylvia Hall
V. President, Finance: Carole E. Cook
Historical Note
Formerly an independent association, DPI affiliated with the Screenprinting and Graphic Imaging Ass'n Internat'l in 1995. DPI's membership represents large format digital outpur firms, reprographic companies, photo labs, screen printers, service bureaus, quick printers, lithographic printers and other commercial printers/suppliers. Its mission is to serve as a forum to advance the electronic imaging field by: helping all graphic industry segments that provide or use digital printing devices to become more productive; responding to industry needs and concerns; promoting progress and excellence in digital pre-press, printing, and imaging, as well as related processes and techniques; and improving the industry's ability to serve its markets and customers. SGIA provides administrative support. Membership: $250-$1,000/year (organization/company).
Publications:
KwikScan. 8/yr.
RIP Newsletter. q.
Meetings/Conferences:
Annual Meetings: March
1999 – Reno, NV(Nugget)/March 10-13
2000 – Dallas, TX(Anatole)/March 8-11/3000

Digital Publishing Ass'n *(1992)*
Historical Note
Address unknown in 1996; presumed inactive.

Digital Video Disc Special Interest Group
Historical Note
A special interest group of the Interactive Multimedia Ass'n.

Diplomatic and Consular Officers, Retired *(1952)*
1801 F St., N.W.
Washington, DC 20006-4497
Tel: (202)682-0500   *Fax:* (202)842-3295
Toll Free: (800)344 - 9127
E-Mail: dacor@ix.netcom.com
Members: 2,300 individuals
Staff: 2
Annual Budget: $250-500,000
Exec. Director: William W. Lehfeldt
Historical Note
Established as the Retired Foreign Service Officers Association, it assumed its present name in 1954. Members are principally active and retired Foreign Service officers. Now accepts members with overseas experience from other government agencies and operates Dacor Bacon House in Washington.
Publications:
Dacor Bulletin. m.
Meetings/Conferences:
Annual Meetings: Washington, DC in Spring.

Direct Mail Fundraisers Ass'n *(1972)*
Historical Note
Members are primarily direct mail managers for charity organizations. Has no paid staff; officers change annually. Membership: $75/year.

Direct Marketing Ass'n *(1917)*
1120 Ave. of the Americas
New York, NY 10036-6700
Tel: (212)768-7277   *Fax:* (212)302-6714
Web Site: http://www.the-dma.org
Members: 6,517 individuals, 3,626 companies
Staff: 150
Annual Budget: $10-25,000,000
President and C.E.O.: H. Robert Wientzen
Sr. V.P., PR/Communications: Connie F. LaMotta
Historical Note
Formerly (1983) Direct Mail/Marketing Ass'n and Direct Mail Advetising Ass'n. Absorbed the Business Mail Foundation and the Mailing List Users and Suppliers Ass'n. Sponsors and supports the DMA Political Action Committee. Has an annual budget of approximately $17.4 million.
Publications:
Dateline: DMA (Members Only). q.
Direct Line (Members Only). 10/year. adv.
DMA Insider.
Fact Book. a.
Journal of Direct Marketing. q.
The DMA Publications Catalog. bien.
Washington Report (Members Only). m.
Washington Update. m.
Meetings/Conferences:

Direct Marketing Credit Ass'n *(1965)*
Historical Note
Address unknown in 1996.

Direct Marketing Insurance and Financial Services Council
Historical Note
DMIFSC is a council of Direct Marketing Ass'n, which provides administrative support. DMIFSC members are DMA members who market insurance and financial services.

Direct Marketing Insurance Council
Historical Note
Became the Direct Marketing Insurance and Financial Services Council in 1995.

Direct Selling Ass'n *(1910)*
1666 K St., N.W., Suite 1010
Washington, DC 20006-2808
Tel: (202)293-5760   *Fax:* (202)463-4569
E-Mail: noffen@dsa.org
Web Site: http://www.dsa.org
Members: 400 companies
Staff: 30
Annual Budget: $5-10,000,000
President: Neil H. Offen, CAE
Director of Communications: Elizabeth M. Doherty
Director, Government Relations/Sr. Attorney: Teresa Jennings
V. President, Government Relations: Joseph N. Mariano
Director, Education and Meeting Services: Melissa K. Brunton
Controller: Kathy Lindner
Manager, Operations: Jennifer Dunleavy
Vp., Membership/Development: Eileen O'Neill
Historical Note
Formerly (1969) Nat'l Ass'n of Direct Selling Companies. Manufacturers and distributors retailing products via door-to-door, party plan and other direct-to-consumer methods. Supports the Direct Selling Ass'n Political Action Committee and the Direct Selling Education Foundation. Serves as the Secretariat for the World Federation of Direct Selling Ass'ns. Membership: $1,500-120,000/year (corporate).
Publications:
Action Needed Bulletin. irreg.
Advisory Memorandum. irreg.
Annual Report. a.
At Home wih Consumers. q.
Internat'l Bulletin. 3/yr.
Legigram. q.
News from Neil. m.
State Status Sheet. w.
Meetings/Conferences:
Annual Meetings: Spring/550

Directional Crossing Contractors Ass'n *(1991)*
13355 Noel Road, L.B. #39
Dallas, TX 75240
Tel: (972)386-9545   *Fax:* (972)386-9547
E-Mail: dcca@rickgump.com
Web Site: http://www.dcca.org
Members: 67 organizations
Staff: 2
Exec. Secretary: Richard A. Gump, Jr.
Historical Note
DCCA is a trade association promoting the interests of the directional crossing contracting industry. Associate membership is available for providers of equipment, materials or services incident to the industry. Membership: $1,500/year (regular); $1,000/year (associate).
Publications:
Pipeline Digest.
Meetings/Conferences:
Semi-annual Meetings: Symposium/April&Planning
         Meeting/Dallas, TX/Fall

Directors Educational Forum
Historical Note
A division of the Credit Union Executives Soc.

Directors Guild of America *(1936)*
7920 Sunset Blvd.
Los Angeles, CA 90046
Tel: (310)289-2000   *Fax:* (310)289-2029
Members: 9,313 individuals
Staff: 85
Annual Budget: $5-10,000,000
Exec. Director: Jay Roth
Historical Note
Independent labor union.
Publications:
DGA Directory of Members.
DGA Magazine.
Meetings/Conferences:
Biennial meetings: Odd years

Directory Publishers' Forum - North America *(1991)*
Historical Note
The organization is defunct.

Disaster Preparedness and Emergency Response Ass'n *(1962)*
P.O. Box 280795
Denver, CO 80228-0795
Tel: (970)532-3362   *Fax:* (970)532-2979
E-Mail: dera@disasters.org
Web Site: http://www.disasters.org
Members: 1,100 individuals
Staff: 3
Annual Budget: $25-50,000
Exec. Director: Bascombe J. Wilson
Dir., Govt. Liaison: Steve Keene
Dir., Education and Training: Robert Dockery
Membership Coordinator: James K. Lucas
Historical Note
DERA is an international network of individuals and organizations active in disaster preparedness and response. Sponsors research projects, technical publications, and other programs to inform members. Membership: $35/year (individual); $150/year (company).
Publications:
Disaster Resource Center Update. irreg.
DisasterCom Newsletter. q.

Disaster Recovery Institute Internat'l *(1988)*
1810 Craig Road, Suite 125

St. Louis, MO 63146-4758
Tel: (314)434-2272   *Fax:* (314)434-1260
E-Mail: jayb@dr.org
Web Site: www.dr.org
Members: 1,725 individuals
Staff: 4
Annual Budget: $500-1,000,000
Exec. Director: Jay G. Bender
Dir., Education: William Langendorfer
Dir., Membership Services: John Mangiameli
Historical Note
DRI represents professionals and organizations working in disaster recovery, contingency planning, and business continuity planning. Awards the designations CBCP (Certified Business Continuity Professional), ABCP (AssociateBusiness Continuity Planner), and MBCP (Master Business Continuity Professional Planner). Membership: $50-75/year.
Publications:
DRI Quarterly Newsletter. q.
Meetings/Conferences:
Annual Meetings: Semi-Annual Meetings in March and
         Septmember
1999 – San Diego, CA(Sheraton)/March 21-26/175
1999 – Orlando, FL(Hyatt)/175

Display Distributors Ass'n *(1968)*
Daniels Display
1267 Mission Street
San Francisco, CA 94103-2766
Tel: (415)861-4400   *Fax:* (415)861-4496
Toll Free: (800)862 - 4400
Members: 16 companies
Staff: 2
Annual Budget: $50-100,000
President: Daniel Benjamin
Historical Note
Members are companies manufacturing or distributing display products and store fixtures. Incorporated in the State of Illinois. Membership: $1,200/year (organization).
Meetings/Conferences:
Semi-annual Meetings: New York, NY/June & Chicago,
         IL/December
1999 – Chicago, IL

Distance Education and Training Council *(1926)*
1601 18th St., N.W.
Washington, DC 20009-2529
Tel: (202)234-5100   *Fax:* (202)332-1386
E-Mail: detc@detc.org
Web Site: http://www.detc.org
Members: 70 home study schools
Staff: 5
Annual Budget: $500-1,000,000
Exec. Director: Michael P. Lambert
Historical Note
Founded as Nat'l Home Study Council; assumed its current name in 1994. A federally-recognized accrediting agency and trade association whose members serve 80-90% of all correspondence students.
Publications:
DETC News. 2/year.
DETC Report. 2/year.
Directory of Accredited Institutions. a.
Meetings/Conferences:
Annual Meetings: Spring/200
1999 – Boston, MA(Copley Plaza)/April 10-13

Distilled Spirits Council of the U.S. *(1933)*
1250 I St., N.W., Suite 400
Washington, DC 20005
Tel: (202)628-3544   *Fax:* (202)682-8876
Web Site: http://www.discus.health.org
Members: 22 companies
Staff: 55
Annual Budget: $10-25,000,000
President/C.E.O.: Frederick A. Meister
Sr. V.P., Ofc. of Public Communs.: Mary K. Young
General Counsel: Lynne J. Omlie
Historical Note
DISCUS represents producers and marketers of distilled spirits. Merger of the Distilled Spirits Institute (1933), the Bourbon Institute (1958), and Licensed Beverage Industries (1946). Absorbed the Tax Council-Alcoholic Beverage Industries. Connected with the Distilled Spirits Council Political Action Committee (DISPAC). Has an annual budget of approximately $10 million.
Publications:
Summary of State Laws and Regulations.
Meetings/Conferences:

Distillers Feed Research Council
Historical Note
Became (1997) Distillers Grain Technology Council.

Distillers Grains Technology Council *(1945)*
c/o Academic Bldg., Room 435
Univ. of Louisville
Louisville, KY 40292
Tel: (502)852-1575   *Fax:* (502)852-1577
Toll Free: (800)759 - 3448
E-Mail: chstaf01@ulkyum.louisville.edu
Members: 7 companies
Staff: 2
Annual Budget: $50-100,000
Exec. V. President: Charlie Staff
Historical Note
Formerly (1997) Distillers Feed Research Council. Members are beverage and ethanol distillers who process by-products of the distilling process for other uses (e.g., livestock feed, fuel additives, pharmaceutical products).

Meetings/Conferences:
Annual Meetings: Spring/70

Distillery, Wine and Allied Workers' Internat'l Union (1940)

Historical Note
Became a division of United Food and Commercial Workers Internat'l Union in 1996.

Distribution and LTL Carriers Ass'n (1939)
211 N. Union St., Suite 102
Alexandria, VA 22314-2643
Tel: (703)739-3101   *Fax:* (703)739-3105
Members: 200 companies
Staff: 6
C.E.O.: Kevin M. Williams
President: A.D. Gearner, Jr.

Historical Note
Founded as Regular Common Carriers Conference; merged with Regional and Distribution Carriers Conference and assumed its current name in 1997. Members are highway common carriers and less-than-truckload haulers of general commodity freight. An autonomous affiliate of American Trucking Ass'ns.

Publications:
Highway Motor Carrier Newsletter. bi-w.

Meetings/Conferences:
Semi-Annual Meetings: Fall and Winter/100

Distribution Contractors Ass'n (1961)
Woodcreek Plaza
101 West Renner Road, Suite 250
Richardson, TX 75082-1318
Tel: (972)680-0261   *Fax:* (972)680-0461
E-Mail: dca@airmail.net
Web Site: www.dca-online.org
Members: 180 companies
Staff: 5
Annual Budget: $500-1,000,000
Exec. V. President: Dennis J. Kennedy
Administrative Assistant/Accounting: Teri Korson
Manager, Member Services: Cindy Savage
Publications Manager: John Churchill

Historical Note
Membership consists of firms engaged in underground pipeline construction and manufacturers and suppliers of construction equipment to the gas distribution industry. Membership: $1,700/year (full member); $500/year (associate).

Publications:
DCA Benchmark. a.
DCA Directory. a. adv.
DCA News Newsletter. m.
DCA Update. m.

Meetings/Conferences:
Annual Meetings: January-February
1999 – Coronado, CA(Loew's)/Feb. 17-21/400
2000 – St. Thomas, Virgin Islands(Frenchmen's Reef Marriott)/Feb. 16-20

Distributive Education Clubs of America (1947)
1908 Association Drive
Reston, VA 20191
Tel: (703)860-5000   *Fax:* (703)860-4013
Members: 186,000 individuals
Staff: 20
Annual Budget: $2-5,000,000
Exec. Director: Edward L. Davis, Ph.D.
Meeting Planner: Jackie Karovic

Historical Note
Members are students and educators concerned with distribution, marketing, merchandising and management.

Publications:
DECA Advisor. m. adv.
DECA Dimensions. q. adv.

Meetings/Conferences:
Annual Meetings: Spring, Meets in two divisions, High School and College
1999 – Orlando, FL(Conv. Cntr.)/April 24-27/12000
2000 – Louisville, KY(Conv. Cntr.)/Apr. 20-23/12000
2001 – Anaheim, CA(Conv. Cntr.)/April 25-28/13000
2002 – Salt Lake City(Conv. Cntr.)/Apr. 20-23/12(Conv. Cntr.)/April 20-23/12000

Diving Equipment and Marketing Ass'n (1972)
2050 S. Santa Cruz St., Suite 1000
Anaheim, CA 92805-6816
Tel: (714)939-6399   *Fax:* (714)939-6398
Web Site: www.dema.org
Members: 1,575 companies
Staff: 9
Annual Budget: $1-2,000,000
Exec. Director: Robert C. Watts, Jr.
Dir., Education/Market Research: Shelley Anne Chase

Historical Note
Formerly (1994) Diving Equipment Manufacturers Ass'n. Membership: $300-12,000/year.

Publications:
Trade Show Directory. a.

Meetings/Conferences:
Annual Meetings: January/10,000
1999 – New Orleans, LA/Jan. 13-16
2000 – Las Vegas, NV
2001 – Miami, FL

Document Management Industries Ass'n (1946)
433 E. Monroe Ave.
Alexandria, VA 22301-1693
Tel: (703)836-6225   *Fax:* (703)836-2241
Web Site: ww.dmia.org

Members: 2,400 companies
Staff: 48
Annual Budget: $5-10,000,000
Exec. V. President: Peter L. Colaianni, CAE
V. President, Information Services & Technical Programming: Dennis McGarry
V. President, Meetings/Expositions: Michael E. Pramstaller, CFC,CAE
Director of Education: Harriet Carter
V. President; Membership, Regionalization & Education: Debbie Ayres
V. President, Operations: Marj Green, CFC, CPSS
V. President, New Media: Brad Holt

Historical Note
Formerly (1996) Nat'l Business Forms Ass'n. Has an annual budget of approximately $5.2 million.

Publications:
Business Printing Technologies Report. bi-m.
FORM. m. adv.
Independent Management Report. m.
Who's Who in Business Printing and Information Management Services. a.

Meetings/Conferences:
Annual Meetings: October/700
1999 – Las Vegas, NV(Hilton)/Oct. 3-5

Dog Writers' Ass'n of America (1935)
173 Union Road
Coatesville, PA 19320
Tel: (610)384-2436   *Fax:* (610)384-2471
E-Mail: rhydowen@aol.com
Web Site: dwaa.org
Members: 525 individuals
Annual Budget: under $10,000
Secretary: Pat Santi

Historical Note
DWAA members write professionally on the subject of dogs. Membership: $40/year (individual).

Publications:
Members Bulletin. m.
Membership Roster. a.
Newsletter. m.

Meetings/Conferences:
Annual Meetings: always in New York, NY/2nd weekend in February/200

Door and Access Systems Manufacturers' Ass'n, Internat'l (1968)
1300 Sumner Ave.
Cleveland, OH 44115-2851
Tel: (216)241-7333   *Fax:* (216)241-0105
E-Mail: dasma@taol.com
Web Site: http://www.taol.com/dasma
Members: 80 companies
Staff: 5
Annual Budget: $100-250,000
Exec. Director: John H. Addington

Historical Note
Formerly (1972) Midwest Garage Door Manufacturers Ass'n and Nat'l Ass'n of Garage Door Manufacturers, merged with Door and Operator Remote Controls Manufacturers Ass'n and assumed its current name in 1996. DASMA is organized into three product specific divisions: Commercial and Residential Garage Door Division, Operator and Electronics Division, and Rolling Door Division. Membership: $2,550/year (minimum).

Publications:
Door & Access Systems. q. adv.

Meetings/Conferences:
Annual Meetings: Winter/200
1999 – Carlsbad, CA(La Costa)/Feb. 3-6
2000 – Orlando, FL(Disney Swan)/Feb. 2-5
2001 – Tucson, AZ(Loews Ventana Canyon)/Jan. 17-20

Door and Hardware Institute (1934)
14170 Newbrook Drive
Chantilly, VA 20151-2232
Tel: (703)222-2010   *Fax:* (703)222-2410
Web Site: www.dhi.org
Members: 5,200 individuals, 500 companies
Staff: 20
Annual Budget: $2-5,000,000
Exec. Director: Jerry Heppes, CAE
Director of Communications: Donna Munari, CAE
Dir., Meetings/Conventions: Mindy McAllister, CMP
Dir., Finance/Administration: Suzanne Shomers
Marketing Manager: Lynn Meloche

Historical Note
Founded as the Nat'l Contract Hardware Ass'n, it became the Nat'l Builders Hardware Ass'n in 1954. The Door and Hardware Institute is the result of a merger with the American Soc. of Architectural Hardware Consultants in 1975. Distributors and manufacturers of doors and builders' hardware, and architectural hardware and certified door consultants. Membership: $170/year.

Publications:
DHI Membership Directory/Buyer's Guide. a.
Doors and Hardware. m. adv.
The Plan Room.

Meetings/Conferences:
Annual Meetings: Fall/3,500-4,000
1999 – Dallas, TX(Wyndham Anatole)/Oct. 16-18

Door and Operator Dealers Ass'n (1973)

Historical Note
Became (1997) Internat'l Door ass'n.

Door Operator and Remote Controls Manufacturers Ass'n (1959)

Historical Note
Merged (1996) with Nat'l Ass'n of Garage Door Manufacturers to form Door and Access Systems Manufacturers Ass'n Internat'l.

DPMA: the Ass'n of Information Systems Professionals
Historical Note
Became (1996) Ass'n of Information Technology Professionals.

Draft Horse and Mule Ass'n of America (1980)
Historical Note
Address unknown in 1996.

Dramatists Guild (1921)
1501 Broadway, Suite 701
New York, NY 10036
Tel: (212)398-9366   *Fax:* (212)944-0420
Members: 6,500 individuals
Staff: 11
Annual Budget: $500-1,000,000
Acting Exec. Director: Chris Wilson

Historical Note
An affiliate of the Authors League of America. The Guild is the professional association of playwrights, composers and lyricists. Members are entitled to use the Guild's "Approved Production Contract". Membership: $75-125/year.

Publications:
Dramatists Guild Quarterly. semi-a.
Newsletter. semi-a.
The Dramatists Guild Newsletter. semi-a. adv.

Meetings/Conferences:
1999 – New York, NY(Headquarters)

Drapery Specialists Institute (1971)
Historical Note
A division of the Ass'n of Specialists in Cleaning and Restoration Internat'l.

Dredging Contractors of America (1935)
643 S. Washington St.,
Alexandria, VA 22314
Tel: (703)518-8408   *Fax:* (703)518-8490
E-Mail: mdsdca@kreative.net
Members: 50 companies
Staff: 2
Annual Budget: $250-500,000
Exec. Director: Mark D. Sickles
Assistant Director: Rosemary Lynch

Historical Note
Formerly the Nat'l Ass'n of Dredging Contractors.

Meetings/Conferences:
Annual Meetings: March

Drilling Engineering Ass'n
c/o Chevron Petroleum Technology Company
P.O. Box 4450
Houston, TX 77210
Tel: (281)230-2706   *Fax:* (281)230-2669
E-Mail: meak@chevron.com
Web Site: http:www.dea.main.com
Members: 50 Companies
Secretary and Treasurer: Michael E. Akins

Historical Note
DEA was established to advance the technology related to drilling wells. Membership: One time fee, $500(full);$200 (associate).

Meetings/Conferences:
Annual Meetings: Quarterly Meetings

Drilling Equipment Manufacturers Ass'n (1929)
Historical Note
Merged (1995) with Internat'l Drilling Federation and Nat'l Drilling Contractors Ass'n to form Nat'l Drilling Ass'n.

Driver Employer Council of America (1967)
1225 I St., N.W., Suite 1000
Washington, DC 20005
Tel: (202)371-0100   *Fax:* (202)842-0011
Members: 43 companies
Staff: 1
Annual Budget: $50-100,000
General Counsel: Peter A. Susser

Historical Note
Formerly (1992) the Driver Leasing Council of America. Members are companies leasing truck drivers to motor carriers.

Publications:
Labor Relations Report. bi-m.
Newsletter. 3/year.

Meetings/Conferences:

Driving School Ass'n of America (1973)
111 W. Pomona Blvd.
Monterey Park, CA 91754
Tel: (213)728-2100   *Fax:* (213)722-0485
E-Mail: ERHENSEL@earthlink.com
Web Site: www.californiadrivingsch.com
Members: 275 firms
Annual Budget: $100-250,000
Co-Founder & Editor: George R. Hensel

Historical Note
Trade association of professional, state-licensed driving schools in the U.S. and Canada, as well as spokesmen of state associations. Affiliated with the IVV, an international organization of driving schools headquartered in Europe. Membership: $250/year.

Publications:
Dual News. q. adv.
Dual News Bulletin. bi-m.

Meetings/Conferences:
Annual Meetings: November

Drug and Alcohol Nursing Ass'n (1979)
Historical Note
Merged with Nat'l Nurses Soc. on Addiction in 1998.

Drug and Alcohol Testing Industry Ass'n (1995)
1600 Duke St., Suite 220
Alexandria, VA 22314
Tel: (703)548-0901 *Fax:* (703)519-1716
Toll Free: (800)355 - 1257
E-Mail: datia@wpa.org
Web Site: www.datia.org
Members: 1000 individuals
Staff: 4
Exec. Officer: Jeffrey C. Smith
Dir., Gov't Relations: Amy Taylor
Programs Director: Laura Norfolk
Historical Note
Founded as the Nat'l Ass'n of Correction Sites. Represents its members on Capital Hill as well as to market its members to the public.
Publications:
Drug-Alcohol Testing Industry News. bi-m.
Meetings/Conferences:
1999 – St. Louis, MO(Regal Riverfront)/April 22-24/300
2000 – Washington, DC/300

Drug and Alcohol Testing Industry Ass'n (1995)
1600 Duke St., Suite 220
Alexandria, VA 22314
Tel: (703)548-0901 *Fax:* (703)519-1716
Toll Free: (800)355 - 1257
E-Mail: datia@wpa.org
Web Site: http://www.datia.org
Members: 1000 companies
Staff: 3
Annual Budget: $100-250,000
President: Jeffrey Smith
Director of Congressional & Regulatory Affairs: Amy Taylor
Program Director: Laura Norfolk
Historical Note
Founded as National Association of Collection Sites(1995), DATIA represents drug and alcohol service providers, including collection sites, laboratories and testing manufactures. Membership:$5-$1500.
Publications:
Collection Site Industry News. bi-m.
Drug-Alcohol Testing Industry Directory and Buyers' Guide
a.
Meetings/Conferences:
Annual Meetings: Spring

Drug Information Ass'n (1965)
501 Office Center Dr.,
Fort Washington, PA 19034-3211
Tel: (215)628-2288 *Fax:* (215)641-1229
E-Mail: info@diahome.org
Web Site: http://www.diahome.org
Members: 20,000 individuals
Staff: 8
Annual Budget: $1-2,000,000
Exec. Director: Joseph R. Assenzo, Ph.D.
Historical Note
Members are individuals from the pharmaceutical industry, government, and academia responsible for processing and disseminating information on medicine and drugs in medicine, biology, pharmacy, and allied human/animal fields. Maintains a computer-access information line: (215) 628-9999. Membership: $65/year (individual).
Publications:
Drug Information Journal. q. adv.
Newsletter. q. adv.
Meetings/Conferences:
Annual Meetings: June/1,800-2,000
1999 – Baltimore, MD(Convention Center)/June 27-July 1

Drug, Chemical and Allied Trades Ass'n (1890)
510 Rte. 120, Suite B1
East Windsor, NJ 08520
Tel: (609)448-1000 *Fax:* (609)609-4481
Toll Free: (800)640 - 3228
Members: 600 companies
Staff: 2
Annual Budget: $1-2,000,000
Director, Membership Services: William Cleary
Historical Note
Until 1962, the Drug, Chemical and Allied Trades Section of the New York Board of Trade. Represents all segments of the drug, chemical and cosmetics industries, such as manufacturers, packaging agents and brokers. Membership dues based on number of employees in the company.
Publications:
Annual Report.
Digest. m.
FYI. m.
Washington Update. q.
Meetings/Conferences:
Annual Meetings: October/350-400

Ductile Iron Pipe Research Ass'n (1915)
245 Riverchase Pwky. East, Suite 0
Birmingham, AL 35244
Tel: (205)402-8700 *Fax:* (205)402-8730
E-Mail: info@dipra.org
Web Site: http://www.dipra.org
Members: 7 companies
Staff: 22
President: Troy F. Stroud
Administrator: Joan Goodwine

Historical Note
Established as the Cast Iron Pipe Publicity Bureau, it later became the Cast Iron Pipe Institute, and the Cast Iron Pipe Research Association in 1928. Assumed its present name in 1979.
Publications:
Ductile Iron Pipe Installation Guide.
Ductile Iron Pipe News. semi-a.
Meetings/Conferences:
Semi-Annual Meetings: April and October.

Ductile Iron Soc. (1958)
28938 Lorain Road, Suite 202
North Olmstead, OH 44070-4014
Tel: (440)734-8040 *Fax:* (440)734-8182
Web Site: www.ductile.org
Members: 90 companies
Staff: 2
Annual Budget: $100-250,000
Exec. Director: John V. Hall
Historical Note
Ductile Iron is a casting material having properties similar to cast steel and processing characteristics similar to cast iron. Membership: $1,800 - $6,000/year (foundaries); $1760/year associate.
Publications:
Ductile Iron News. 3/year.
Meetings/Conferences:
Semi-annual Meetings: Spring and Fall
1999 – South Bend, IN/May 19-21

Dude Ranchers' Ass'n (1926)
P.O. Box 471
LaPorte, CO 80535
Tel: (970)223-8440 *Fax:* (970)223-0201
E-Mail: duderanches@compuserve.com
Web Site: http://www.duderanch.org
Members: 100 guest ranches
Staff: 2
Annual Budget: $100-250,000
Exec. Directors: Bobbi & Jim Futterer
Historical Note
Organized in Bozeman, Montana in November 1926 to protect the image of the dude ranch industry, promote ranch properties as a tourist vacation, work with public lands, game and fish departments and preserve the Western way of life. Membership: $750-2,200/year.
Publications:
The Dude Rancher Directory. a.
Meetings/Conferences:
Annual Meetings: January, by vote of the previous convention

Dutch Warmblood Ass'n (1983)
P.O. Box O
Sutherlin, OR 97479
Tel: (541)459-3232 *Fax:* (541)459-2967
E-Mail: nawpn@rosenet.net
Web Site: http://www.nawpn.org
Members: 1,200 individuals
Exec. Director: J.Ashton Moore
Historical Note
Also known as The Dutch Warmblood Studbook in North America. Subscribers are owners and breeders of purebred Dutch Warmblood horses.
Publications:
Breeder's Directory. a.
FAST ADS. m.
NA/WPN Newsletter. bi-m.
Stallion Directory. a.
Meetings/Conferences:
Annual Meetings: late March

Early Sites Research Soc. (1973)
Long Hill
Rowley, MA 01969
Tel: (508)948-2410
Members: 250 individuals
Staff: 1
Annual Budget: under $10,000
Director: James Whittall
Historical Note
Membership, concentrated in the Northeast, is composed of archaeologists involved in exploring unidentified antiquities.
Publications:
Early Sites Bulletin. semi-a.
Newsletter. bi-m.
Work Report. irreg.
Meetings/Conferences:
Semi-annual Meetings: Spring and Fall

Earthmoving Equipment Manufacturers Council
Historical Note
A council of the Equipment Manufacturers Institute.

Earthquake Engineering Research Institute (1948)
499 14th St., Suite 320
Oakland, CA 94612-1934
Tel: (510)451-0905 *Fax:* (510)451-5411
E-Mail: eeri@eeri.org
Web Site: http://www.eeri.org
Members: 2,300 individuals
Staff: 8
Annual Budget: $1-2,000,000
Exec. Director: Susan Tubbesing
Financial Manager: Sonya Hollenbeck
Membership Coordinator: Martha Martinez
Special Projects Manager: Marjorie Green

Historical Note
EERI advances the science and practice of earthquake engineering to protect people and property from the effects of damaging earthquakes. EERI's programs draw on its unique interdisciplinary membership, fostering communication among those disciplines to bridge the gap between new knowledge, design, practice, and policy. Membership: $150/year (individual); $275/year (organization).
Publications:
Earthquake Spectra Journal. q.
EERI Newsletter. m.
Proceedings – Nat'l Conference. 1/4yrs.
Roster(Directory). a.
Meetings/Conferences:
1999 – San Diego, CA
2000 – St. Louis, MO

Ecological and Toxilogical Ass'n of the Dyestuffs Manufacturing Industry (1982)
Historical Note
An international trade association; the United States Operating Committee of ETAD is the U.S. affiliate (1993).

Ecological Soc. of America (1915)
2010 Massachusetts Ave., N.W., Suite 400
Washington, DC 20036-1023
Tel: (202)833-8773 *Fax:* (202)833-8775
E-Mail: esahq@esa.org
Web Site: http://esa.sdsc.edu
Members: 7,500 individuals
Staff: 26
Annual Budget: $2-5,000,000
Exec. Director: Katherine McCarter
Assoc. Director, Public Affairs: Nadine Cavender
Director, Programs: Mary Barber
Historical Note
Organized December 1915 in Columbus, Ohio at the annual meeting of the American Association for the Advancement of Science. A professional society of individuals interested in the study of living things in relation to their environment. Member society of the American Institute of Biological Sciences. Represented on the Council of the American Ass'n for the Advancement of Science and the Nat'l Research Council. Membership: $20-80/year, varies by income (individual); special rates for students and for individuals in developing countries.
Publications:
Bulletin of the Ecological Soc. of America.
Ecological Applications. q.
Ecological Monographs. q.
Ecology. 8/year.
Meetings/Conferences:
1999 – Spokane, WA(Convention Center)/Aug. 8-12
2000 – Snowbird, UT
2001 – Madison, WI

Econometric Soc. (1930)
Dept. of Economics, Northwestern Univ.
2003 Sheridan Road
Evanston, IL 60208-2600
Tel: (847)491-3615 *Fax:* (847)491-5427
Members: 4,000 individuals, 3,000 institutions
Staff: 2
Annual Budget: $100-250,000
Exec. Director: Julie Gordon, Ph.D.
Historical Note
An international society for the advancement of economic theory in its relation to mathematics and statistics. Organized in Cleveland, Ohio, December 29, 1930 with Professor Irving Fisher of Yale University as the first president.
Publications:
Econometrica. bi-m. adv.
Meetings/Conferences:

Economic History Ass'n (1940)
Univ. of Kansas Dept. of Economics
Lawrence, KS 66045
Tel: (785)864-2847 *Fax:* (785)864-5270
E-Mail: eha@falcon.cc.ukans.edu
Members: 1,029 individuals, 2,230 Institutes
Annual Budget: $100-250,000
Exec. Director: Thomas Weiss
Meetings Coordinator: Martha Olney
Historical Note
A member of American Council of Learned Societies. Has no paid officers or full-time staff. Membership: $15-40/year (individual), $98/year (organization/company).
Publications:
Journal of Economic History. q. adv.
Meetings/Conferences:
Annual Meetings: September

Ecotourism Soc. (1990)
P.O. Box 755
North Bennington, VT 05257-0755
Tel: (802)447-2121 *Fax:* (802)447-2122
E-Mail: ecomail@ecotourism.org
Web Site: http://www.ecotourism.org
Members: 1,200 individuals
Staff: 4
President: Megan Epler Wood
Workshop and Marine Program Coordinator: Elizabeth Halpenny
Membership & Book Program Director: Nicole R. Otte
Historical Note
Society members include park managers, tour operators, conservation professionals and others with an interest in the development of ecology-centered tourism. Membership: $50/year (professional); $100/year (organization).
Publications:
International Membership Directory. a.

TES Quarterly Newsletter. q.

ECRI (1955)
5200 Butler Pike
Plymouth Meeting, PA   19462
Tel: (610)825-6000   *Fax:* (610)834-1275
Web Site: www.healthcare.ecri.org
Members: 3,800 hospitals
Staff: 210
Annual Budget: $10-25,000,000
President: Dr. Joel J. Nobel
V. President, Planning: Jeffrey Lerner, Ph.D.
V. President, Technology Planning: Anthony Montagnolo
V. President, Technology Assessment: Vivian Coates
V. President, Finance: Dan Downing
V. President, Legal Affairs: Ronni Solomon, J.D.

Historical Note
Offers evaluation, testing, and technical assistance services related to health care technology, clinical engineering and healthcare environmental management. Founded as the Graduate Pain Research Institute in 1968 and assumed its present name in 1980. Has an annual budget of approximately $13 million. Membership: $595-2,595/year.

Publications:
Health Care Environmental Management. m.
Health Devices. m.
Health Devices Alerts. w.
Health Devices Sourcebook. q.
Health Standards Directory. a.
Healthcare Hazardous Materials Management. m.
Hospital Risk Control. bi-m.
Laboratory Products, Imaging and Radiology Products, and.
Operating Room Products. m.
Product Comparison System in: Hospital Products, Clinical.
Technology in Health Care Newsletter Series. q.

Ecuadorean American Ass'n (1932)
150 Nassau St.
Room 2015
New York, NY   10038
Tel: (212)233-7776   *Fax:* (212)233-7779
Members: 27 individuals, 30 companies
Staff: 3
Annual Budget: $25-50,000
Secretary: Linda Calvet

Historical Note
Promotes greater knowledge and understanding of modern Ecuador; seeks to disseminate information on current events and on economic and financial matters of concern to investors in Ecuador; and promotes commercial and cultural relations and good will among the people of the two countries. Membership: $150/year (individual), $350/year (corporate), $1,000/year (sustaining).

Publications:
News Digest. m.

Edison Electric Institute (1933)
701 Pennsylvania Ave., N.W.
Washington, DC   20004-2696
Tel: (202)508-5000   *Fax:* (202)508-5360
Web Site: http://www.eei.org
Members: 206 companies
Staff: 280
Annual Budget: $50-100,000,000
President: Thomas R. Kuhn, CAE
Dir., Public Policy/Communications: Susan E. Clark
V. President, Communications and Marketing: M. William Brier
Exec. V.P., Membership and External Relations: Walker F. Nolan
Senior V. President, Technical: David L. Swanson
V. President, External Affairs: Randal H. Ihara
V. President, Government Affairs: E. John Neumann
Executive V. President, Business Operations: David K. Owens
Executive V. President, Policy Issues Management and Internal Operations: Lynn H. LeMaster
V. President, Finance and Information Technology: Patric O'Kelley
V. President, General Council: Edward H. Comer
V. President, Member Relations & Corporate Security: Edwin R. Anthony
Director, Member Services: Carol Ann Linder
V. President, Human Resources and Corporate Services: Carl D. Behnke
V. President, International Programs: John J. Easton, Jr.

Historical Note
EEI's members are the nation's shareholder-owned electric utility companies, who generate and distribute more than three-fourths of the country's electricity. Membership also includes international affiliates, made up of power companies in every part of the world, and associates, who are electric power industry suppliers. EEI provides national leadership in legislative and regulatory arenas on public policy issues affecting its members and in promoting the development and use of efficient electrotechnologies. The association's other activities include administering the Power Political Action Committee (POWERPAC), providing forums for its members to exchange information and ideas, and serving as the authoritative information source on the shareholder-owned electric utility industry. Has an annual budget of $63.8 million.

Publications:
EEI Washington Letter. w.

Meetings/Conferences:
Annual Meetings: Spring/2,000
1999 – San Francisco, CA/June 6-9
2000 – Boston, MA/June 4-7
2001 – New Orleans, LA/June 3-6

Edison Welding Institute (1984)
1250 Arthur E. Adams Dr.
Columbus, OH   43221
Tel: (614)688-5000   *Fax:* (614)688-5001
Web Site: http://www.ewi.org/
Members: 400 companies
Staff: 165
Annual Budget: $10-25,000,000

Exec. Director: Karl Graff, Ph.D.
Communications: Karen Malone
Govt. Relations: David Edmonds
Meetings/Conventions: Renee Dickinson
Education: Rich Green
Finance/Admin.: Frank Chasar
Member Services: Jay Eastman

Historical Note
EWI provides continuing technical support and professional services to firms and manufacturers using welding and materials joining technologies. Operates the U.S. Navy Joining Center, and the Alliance for Nat'l Excellence in Materials Joining. Has an annual budget of approximately $22 million.

Publications:
Insights Newsletter. irreg.
Research Reports. m.

Meetings/Conferences:
Annual Meetings: Fall
1999 – Portugal
2000 – Itlay

Editorial Freelancers Ass'n (1974)
71 West 23rd St., Suite 1504
New York, NY   10010
Tel: (212)929-5400   *Fax:* (212)929-5439
Web Site: http://www.the-efa.org
Members: 1000 individuals
Staff: 1
Annual Budget: $100-250,000
Office Administrator: David Bell

Historical Note
EFA is a professional organization comprising editors, writers, indexers, proofreaders, researchers, translators and other self-employed workers in the publishing and communications industries. Membership concentrated in New York City. Membership: $75-105/year.

Publications:
EFA Membership Directory. a.
EFA Newsletter. bi-m. adv.
EFA Rates Survey. a.

Meetings/Conferences:
Annual Meetings: always New York, NY(EFA Offices)/June/60-100

EdPress--The Ass'n of Educational Publishers (1895)
Rowan University
201 Mullica Hill Road
Glassboro, NJ   08028-1701
Tel: (609)256-4610   *Fax:* (609)256-4926
E-Mail: edpress@aol.com
Web Site: http://www.edpress.org
Members: 750 individuals
Staff: 24
Annual Budget: $250-500,000
Exec. Director: Charlene F. Gaynor

Historical Note
Formerly (1998) Education Press Ass'n of America. Members are CEOs, editorial, marketing and public relations professionals in education publishing. Membership: $195/year (individual); corporate fee varies.

Publications:
Edpress News. m.

Meetings/Conferences:
Annual Meetings: early Summer
1999 – Washington, DC(Mayflower)/June 9-11

Education Credit Union Council (1972)
P.O. Box 7558
Spanish Fort, AL   36577
Tel: (334)626-3399
Members: 350 credit unions
Staff: 1
Annual Budget: $250-500,000
Exec. Director: Lorraine B. Webster

Historical Note
Members are credit unions serving educational institutions. Membership: $100/yr. (organization).

Publications:
Chalktalk. m.
Directory of Educational Credit Unions. bien.

Meetings/Conferences:
Annual Meetings: February
1999 – Orlando, FL/Feb. 13-16
2000 – New Orleans, LA/Feb. 19-22
2001 – San Francisco, CA(Hyatt Regency Embarcadero)/Feb. 17-20
2002 – San Antonio, TX/Feb. 16-19
2003 – Anaheim, CA/Feb. 15 18

Education Law Ass'n (1954)
300 College Park
Dayton, OH   45469-2280
Tel: (937)229-3589   *Fax:* (937)229-3845
E-Mail: ela@udayton.edu
Web Site: http://www.educationlaw.org
Members: 1,750 individuals
Staff: 5
Annual Budget: $250-500,000
Exec. Director: Robert Wagner

Historical Note
Formerly (1996) Nat'l Organization on Legal Problems of Education. Membership consists of law professors, school administrators, school attorneys, etc. Purpose is to promote research and publication in the field of school law. Membership: $95/year; $35/year (student).

Publications:
NOLPE Case Citation Series. a.
School Law Reporter.
Yearbook of Education Law. a.

Meetings/Conferences:
Annual Meetings: November
1999 – Chicago, IL(Swissotel)/Nov. 4-6
2000 – Atlanta, GA(Swissotel)/Nov. 9-11
2001 – Alberquerque, NM(Hyatt)/Nov. 15-17

Education Soc.
Historical Note
See IEEE Education Soc.

Education Writers Ass'n (1947)
1331 H St., N.W., Suite 307
Washington, DC   20005
Tel: (202)637-9700   *Fax:* (202)637-9707
E-Mail: ewa@crosslink.net
Web Site: http://www.ewa.org
Members: 900 individuals
Staff: 4
Annual Budget: $250-500,000
Exec. Director: Lisa J. Walker
Administrative Coordinator: Tracee Eason
Assistant Director of Education: Lori Crouch
Membership Coordinator: Tracy Williams

Historical Note
Members work for newspapers, magazines and broadcasting stations and freelance. Absorbed the Nat'l Council for the Advancement of Education Writing in 1975. Membership: $50/year.

Publications:
Buskin Education Lecture. a.
Covering the Education Beat. irreg.
EWA Membership Directory. a.
Nat'l Award for Education Reporting. a. adv.
The Education Reporter. bi-m.
The Literacy Beat. irreg.

Meetings/Conferences:
Annual Meetings: Spring/200
1999 – Chicago, IL/Apr. 15-17

Educational Dealers and Suppliers Ass'n Internat'l (1984)
711 West 17th St., Suite J-5
Costa Mesa, CA   92627
Tel: (714)642-3986   *Fax:* (714)642-7960
E-Mail: edsaintl@aol.com
Members: 1,300 companies
Staff: 7
Annual Budget: $2-5,000,000
Director: Allen Warren

Historical Note
EDSA Internat'l was formed and incorporated in California with the goal of providing member services in a cost-effective manner to all sectors of the educational product market. Membership: $100/year (dealers/reps); $225/year (suppliers).

Publications:
EDSA International Magazine. bi-m. adv.
Membership Directory. a. adv.

Meetings/Conferences:
Annual Meetings: Spring/1,600
1999 – Portland, OR/April 9-11
2000 – Milwaulke, MN/April 5-9/1400

Educational Paperback Ass'n (1975)
P.O. Box 1399
East Hampton, NY   11937
Tel: (212)879-6850
Toll Free: (888)833 - 2665
Members: 70 companies
Staff: 1
Exec. Secretary: Marilyn Abel

Historical Note
Membership: $350/year (wholesaler); $500/year (publisher).

Publications:
EPA Newsnetwork. q.

Meetings/Conferences:
Annual Meetings: January
1999 – Key West, FL(Marriott)/Jan. 20-23/130

Educational Press Ass'n of America
Historical Note
Became EdPress - The Ass'n of Educational Publishers in 1998.

Educational Theatre Ass'n (1988)
Historical Note
The Educational Theatre Ass'n is made of two components. The Internat'l Thespian Society (for students) and the Theatre Education Ass'n for adults.

EDUCAUSE (1998)
1112 16th St., N.W., Suite 600
Washington, DC   20036-4823
Tel: (202)872-4200   *Fax:* (202)872-4318
Web Site: http://www.educause.edu
Members: 130 corporations, 600 institutions
Staff: 11
Annual Budget: $5-10,000,000
President: Brian L. Hawkins

Historical Note
A non-profit consortium of colleges, universities and other nonprofit institutions to facilitate the introduction, use and management of information technology. Formerly (1984) the Interuniversity Communications Council. Has an annual budget of approximately $6 million. Membership: for institutions, varies with full time enrollment.

Publications:
Cause/Effect. q.
EDUCOM Review. bi-m.

Meetings/Conferences:
Annual Meetings: October

EDUCAUSE (1962)
4840 Pearl East Circle, Suite 302-E
Boulder, CO 80301
Tel: (303)449-4430 *Fax:* (303)440-0461
E-Mail: info@educause.edu
Web Site: http://www.educause.edu/
Members: 3,600 individuals, 1,400 institutions
Staff: 35
Annual Budget: $2-5,000,000
President: Jane N. Ryland
Director of Publicity: James Roche
Dir., Conferences and Meetings: Deborah K. Smith, CMP
Dir., Finance and Administration: Denton K. Farnsworth
Dir., Information Services: Randy Richter

Historical Note
EDUCAUSE works to enhance the administration and delivery of higher education through the effective management and use of information resources. Member representatives typically are responsible for managing, computing, networking, and telecommunications on college and university campuses in North America and internationally. Membership: $250-7,000/year.

Publications:
CAUSE/EFFECT Magazine. q.
EDUCAUSE Monographs. irreg.
Educom Review magazine. 6/year.
Proceedings. a.

Meetings/Conferences:
Annual Meetings: December

Egg Ass'n of America
Historical Note
Address unknown in 1996.

EIFS Industry Members Ass'n (1981)
3000 Corporate Center Dr., Suite 270
Morrow, GA 30260-4116
Tel: (770)968-7945 *Fax:* (770)968-5818
Toll Free: (800)294 - 3462
Web Site: www.eifsfacts.com
Members: 400 companies
Staff: 4
Annual Budget: $1-2,000,000
Exec. Director: Stephan E. Klamke

Historical Note
Formerly (1993) the Exterior Insulation Manufacturers Ass'n. Established for EIFS (exterior insulation finish systems) manufacturers only, EIFS Industry Members Ass'n includes manufacturers, suppliers, distributors, applicator/contractors, and affiliated building professionals. EIMA is a trade association representing member firms involved in the exterior insulation and finish systems (EIFS) industry. Membership: dues vary by type of member on a sliding scale.

Publications:
Generic Technical Publications.
Outside/In. q.

Meetings/Conferences:

Eight Sheet Outdoor Advertising Ass'n (1953)
P.O. Box 2680
Bremerton, WA 98310-0344
Toll Free: (800)874 - 3387
Members: 130 companies
Staff: 2
Annual Budget: $100-250,000
Exec. Director: David Jacobs

Historical Note
Members are owners of eight-sheet outdoor poster panels (Jr 8 Poster Panels) which are small 6' x 12' panels used in outdoor advertising. Formerly (until 1979) known as the Junior Panel Outdoor Advertising Ass'n.

Publications:
Eight-Sheet Report. m.
Rate and Allotments Book. a.
Sources. a.

Meetings/Conferences:
1999 – Puerto Rico

Elastic Fabric Maunfacturers Council (1915)
Historical Note
A council of the Northern Textile Ass'n.

Electric Generation Ass'n
Historical Note
Became the Electric Power Supply Ass'n in 1997.

Electric Power Research Institute (1972)
3412 Hillview Ave.,
Palo Alto, CA 94304-1395
Tel: (650)855-2000 *Fax:* (650)855-2800
E-Mail: kyeager@epri.com
Web Site: http://www.epri.com
Members: 660 utilities
Staff: 750
Annual Budget: Over $100,000,000
President and C.E.O.: Kurt Yeager

Historical Note
Research relating to the production, transmission, distribution and utilization of electric power. Members both publicly and privately held electric utility organizations. Maintains a Washington office. Has an annual budget of approximately $400 million.

Publications:
EPRI Journal. 8/year.

Electric Power Supply Ass'n (1997)
1401 H St., N.W., Suite 760
Washington, DC 20005-2110
Tel: (202)789-7200 *Fax:* (202)789-7201
E-Mail: epsa@mindspring.com
Web Site: http://www.epsa.org
Members: 85 companies
Staff: 12
Annual Budget: $2-5,000,000
Exec. Director: Lynne H. Church
Director, Public Affairs and Marketing: Mark Stultz
Director, Legislative Affairs: Eugene Peters
Mgr., Meetings: Laurie Martin
Manager, Finance and Administration: Julie Greene Smith

Historical Note
Formerly (1987) Congeneration Coalition of America; became (1991) Cogeneration and Independent Power Coalition of America; merged with Independent Power Producers Working Group and became Electric Generation Ass'n in 1992; merged with Nat'l Independent Energy Producers and assumed its current name in 1997. EPSA is primarily concerned with encouraging federal and state legislation and regulation favorable to the development of full wholesale and retail competition. Members are competitive electric generators, power markets and suppliers to the industry. Membership: $10,500-$65,000 (organization/company).

Publications:
EPSA Report q.
Restructing Matters. m.

Meetings/Conferences:
1999 – Tucson, AZ(Lowe's Ventana)

Electric Utility Cost Group
Historical Note
Name changed to EUCG in 1996.

Electric Vehicle Ass'n of the Americas (1990)
601 California St., Suite 502
San Francisco, CA 94108-2810
Tel: (415)249-2690 *Fax:* (415)249-2699
E-Mail: ev@evaa.org
Web Site: www.evaa.org
Members: 45 companies & agencies
Staff: 7
Exec. Director: Robert Hayden
Communications Manager: Leah R. Reich

Historical Note
Advances commercialization of electric vehicles in the United States, Canada and Latin America through comprehensive public information and market development programs.

Publications:
EV Update. bi-m.

Meetings/Conferences:
Biennial Meetings: even years
1999 – December

Electrical Apparatus Service Ass'n (1933)
1331 Baur Blvd.
St. Louis, MO 63132
Tel: (314)993-2220 *Fax:* (314)993-1269
E-Mail: tjraynes@aol.com
Web Site: EASA.COM
Members: 2,900 firms
Staff: 14
Annual Budget: $2-5,000,000
Exec. V. President: Linda J. Raynes
Director, Promotion & Public Relations: Carl M. Fields
Manager of Meetings and Exhibitions: Michael Toohey
Controller: Richard Tutka

Historical Note
Established as the Nat'l Industrial Service Ass'n, it assumed its present name in 1961. Members are firms selling, servicing and rebuilding electric motors, generators, transformers and related equipment. Membership: $280-$745/year (active), $690/year (associate).

Publications:
Currents - Newsletter. m.
Equipment Bulletin. m. adv.
Yearbook - Directory. a.

Meetings/Conferences:
1999 – Toronto, ON(Royal York)/June 27-30/4900
2000 – Anaheim, CA(Marriott)/April 2-5/5200
2001 – Chicago, IL(Chicago and Palmer House Hiltons)/June 24-27

Electrical Equipment Representatives Ass'n (1948)
P.O. Box 419264
Kansas City, MO 64141-6264
Tel: (816)753-0210 *Fax:* (816)753-1954
Members: 100 companies
Staff: 1
Annual Budget: $100-250,000
Exec. Director: John S. McDermott, CAE

Historical Note
Founded to advance the quality and increase the effectiveness of Manufacturers Representatives in the Electrical Equipment Industry. Membership: $800/year.

Publications:
EERA Directory. a.

Meetings/Conferences:
Annual Meetings: May/235
1999 – Palm Beach Gardens, FL(PGA National)/May 9-13/215
2000 – Rancho Mirage, CA(Marriott's Rancho Las palmas)/May 4-11/215

Electrical Generating Systems Ass'n (1965)
1650 S. Dixie Highway, Fifth Floor
Boca Raton, FL 33432
Tel: (561)750-5575 *Fax:* (561)750-5316
Members: 330 companies

Staff: 2
Exec. Director: David L. Kellough

Historical Note
Founded as the Engine Generator Set Manufacturers Ass'n, it became the Electrical Generating Systems Marketing Ass'n in 1973 and assumed its present name in 1985. Formed in 1965 by 14 companies manufacturing engine generator sets, who were interested in standardizing specifications for products to be purchased by the U.S. government, primarily the military. In 1972, dealers and distributors of electrical generating equipment were invited to become full members, and the focus of the ass'n was changed to developing programs which would be of benefit to them. Membership is international. Membership: $180-725/year (company)

Publications:
Membership/Product Directory. a.
Powerline. bi-m.

Meetings/Conferences:
Annual Meetings: Spring and Fall

Electrical Insulation Conference (1957)
P.O. Box 792
Lewiston, NY 14092
Tel: (905)682-6288 *Fax:* (905)682-0087
Members: 200 individuals
Staff: 1
Exec. Director: John Bullivant

Historical Note
EEIC is a non-profit organization directed by industrial volunteers under the auspices of the Dielectrics and Electrical Insulation Soc. of IEEE and the Nat'l Electrical Manufacturers Ass'n. Formerly Electrical Insulation Conference.

Meetings/Conferences:
Biennial Meeting: Fall, with the Electrical Manufacturing and Coil Winding Ass'n

Electrical Manufacturing and Coil Winding Ass'n (1977)
P.O. Box 278
Imperial Beach, CA 91933
Tel: (619)575-4191 *Fax:* (619)575-5009
Members: 300 individuals, 215 companies
Staff: 2
Annual Budget: $1-2,000,000
Exec. Director: Charles E. Thurman

Historical Note
Formerly the North American Council of the Internat'l Coil Winding Ass'n and (1993) Internat'l Coil Winding Ass'n. Membership: $35/year (individual), $200/year (organization/company)

Publications:
Conference Proceedings. a.
EMCWA News Letter. bi-m.
Membership Directory. a. adv.

Meetings/Conferences:
Annual Meetings: September-October
1999 – Cincinnati, OH(Convention Center)/Oct. 26-28/9000
2000 – Cincinnati, OH(Convention Center)/Oct. 31-Nov. 2

Electrical Overstress/Electrostatic Discharge Ass'n (1982)
7900 Turin Road, Suite 2, Bldg. 3
Rome, NY 13440-2069
Tel: (315)339-6937 *Fax:* (315)339-6793
Toll Free: (800)562 - 6434
E-Mail: eosesd@aol.com
Web Site: http://www.eosesd.org
Members: 2,300 individuals
Staff: 4
Annual Budget: $100-250,000
Secretary: Sue Ohrman
Administrator: Lisa Pimpinella

Historical Note
EOS/ESD is concerned with the advancement of the theory and practice of electrical overstress avoidance, with emphasis on electrostatic discharge phenomena. Members are government, industry and academic organizations involved in research and development; electronic equipment manufacturers and users; and manufacturers and users of EOS/ESD effects reduction products and methods. Also known as the ESD Ass'n and Electrostatic Discharge Ass'n. Membership: $35/year (U.S.); $45/year (foreign).

Publications:
EOS/ESD Standards. irreg.
EOS/ESD Symposium Proceedings. a.
Membership Roster. a.
Threshold. bi-m.
Tutorial Note. a.

Meetings/Conferences:

Electrical Women's Round Table
Historical Note
Became (1998) Women's Internat'l Network of Utility Professionals.

Electrical-Electronics Materials Distributors Ass'n (1970)
5024-R Campbell Blvd.
Baltimore, MD 21236-5974
Tel: (410)931-8100 *Fax:* (410)931-8111
Members: 22 distributors, 17 manufacturers
Staff: 3
Annual Budget: $50-100,000
Exec. V. President: Celeste Powers, CAE

Historical Note
Distributors of electrical-electronic materials and industry suppliers. Affiliated with the Nat'l Ass'n of Wholesaler-Distributors.

Publications:
EEMDA Circuits. 3/year.

Meetings/Conferences:
Annual Meetings: April/150

Electricity Consumers Resource Council *(1976)*
1333 H St., N.W., 8th Floor
Washington, DC 20005-4707
Tel: (202)682-1390   *Fax:* (202)289-6370
E-Mail: elcon@elcon.org
Web Site: www.elcon.org
Members: 38 member companies & 7 affiliates
Staff: 6
Annual Budget: $500-1,000,000
Exec. Director: John A. Anderson
Director of Government and Public Affairs: Marc Yacker
Director of Technical Affairs: John P. Hughes

Historical Note
Members are industrial consumers of electricity who support regulatory practices that assure adequate supplies of electricity at prices based on cost of service.

Publications:
ELCON Report. q.
Profiles on Electricity Issues.

Meetings/Conferences:
Annual Meetings: Washington, DC/October

Electrochemical Soc. *(1902)*
10 South Main St.
Pennington, NJ 08534-2896
Tel: (609)737-1902   *Fax:* (609)737-2743
E-Mail: ecs@electrochem.org
Web Site: http://www.electrochem.org
Members: 7,000 individuals
Staff: 18
Annual Budget: $2-5,000,000
Exec. Director and C.E.O.: Roque J. Calvo, CAE
Meetings and Programs Manager: Brian E. Rounsavill

Historical Note
Formed in Philadelphia April 3, 1902 as the American Electrochemical Soc., it became the Electrochemical Soc., Inc. in 1930 and incorporated in New York. Membership: $90/year (individual); $600-2,000-5,000/year (organization/company).

Publications:
Electrochemical and Solid State Letters. m.
Electrochemical Soc. Interface. adv.
Journal of The Electrochemical Society. m.

Meetings/Conferences:

Electrocoat Ass'n
6915 Valley Avenue
Cincinnati, OH 45244
Tel: (513)527-8977   *Fax:* (513)527-8950
Toll Free: (800)950 - 8977
Web Site: http://www.electrocoat.org
Members: 50 companies
Staff: 1
Exec. Director: Cindy Goodridge

Historical Note
Members represent associations, corporations and individuals who have an economic or educational interest in electrocoating.

Meetings/Conferences:
2000 - Orlando, Fl/April 26-28

Electromagnetic Compatibility Soc. *(1957)*
Historical Note
See IEEE Electromagnetic Compatibility Soc.

Electromagnetic Energy Ass'n *(1984)*
1255 23rd St., N.W., Suite 850
Washington, DC 20037-1174
Tel: (202)452-1070   *Fax:* (202)833-3636
Members: 30 companies
Staff: 5
Exec. Director: Dinah D. McElfresh

Historical Note
Formerly (1994) Electromagnetic Energy Policy Alliance, EEA represents manufacturers and users of electronic and electrical systems that utilize non-ionizing electromagnetic energy in telecommunications, broadcasting, manufacturing and consumer services. Its primary objective is to work for a responsible and rational public policy regarding electromagnetic energy. Membership: $800/year (individual); $2,000-6,500/year (corporate).

Publications:
EMF Bulletin.

Meetings/Conferences:
Annual Meetings: Spring

Electron Devices Soc. *(1951)*
Historical Note
A technical society of the Institute of Electrical and Electronics Engineers (IEEE). Membership in the Society, open only to IEEE members, includes subscriptions to technical periodicals in the field published by IEEE. All administrative support is provided by IEEE.

Electronic Banking Economics Soc. *(1980)*
Historical Note
Organization inactive in 1997.

Electronic Data Interchange Ass'n *(1968)*
Historical Note
Ceased operations in 1995.

Electronic Data Processing Auditors Ass'n *(1969)*
Historical Note
See Information Systems Audit and Control Ass'n.

Electronic Design Automation Consortium
111 W. St. John St., Suite 200
San Jose, CA 95113
Tel: (408)287-3322   *Fax:* (408)283-5283
E-Mail: information@edac.org
Web Site: http://www.edac.org
Members: 50 companies
Exec. Director: Pamela Parrish

Historical Note
EDAC members are companies engaged in the development, manufacture and sale of design tools to the electronic engineering community. The Consortium's mission is to foster communication and cooperation between EDA companies, customers and stakeholders, driving industry-wide solutions to industry-wide problems.

Meetings/Conferences:
Annual Meetings: January

Electronic Distribution Show Corporation *(1935)*
222 South Riverside Plaza, Suite 2160
Chicago, IL 60606
Tel: (312)648-1140   *Fax:* (312)648-4282
E-Mail: eds@edsc.org
Web Site: edsc.org
Members: 500 companies
Staff: 5
Annual Budget: $500-1,000,000
Show Manager: Gretchen A. Oie

Historical Note
Formerly (1996) Electronic Industry Show Corporation. Members are manufacturers who sell their products through electronics distributors. EDSC's main purpose is to conduct an annual trade show for these manufacturers. Affiliated with Electronic Industries Ass'n, Electronic Representatives Ass'n, and Nat'l Electronic Distributors Ass'n.

Publications:
Bulletin. m.

Meetings/Conferences:
Annual Meetings: April/7,500-8,000
1999 - Las Vegas, NV(Hilton)/May 18-20
2000 - Las Vegas, NV(Hilton)/May 16-18
2001 - Las Vegas, NV(Hilton)/May 15-17
2002 - Las Vegas, NV(Hilton)/May 14-16

Electronic Forum on Sound Technology *(1994)*
c/o Ass'n for Computing Machinery
1515 Broadway
New York, NY 10036
Tel: (212)626-0500   *Fax:* (212)944-1318
Toll Free: (800)342 - 6626
E-Mail: soundrequest@acm.org
Members: 4,000 individuals
Staff: 120
Assoc. Director: Patrick McCarren

Historical Note
A division of Ass'n for Computing Machinery, which provides program support. SIGSOUND provides an electronic forum for the exchange of data on digitally-generated or -manipulated audio.

Electronic Funds Transfer Ass'n *(1977)*
950 Herndon Pkwy., Suite 390
Herndon, VA 22070-5531
Tel: (703)435-9800   *Fax:* (703)435-7157
Web Site: http://www.efta.org
Members: 180 companies
Staff: 7
Annual Budget: $500-1,000,000
Exec. Director: H. Kurt Helwig

Historical Note
EFTA is an inter-industry trade association involved in analyzing and addressing the broad range of issues affecting the evolving service of electronic transfers. Its specific mission is to provide leadership for the domestic and international advancement of electronic value transfer systems, technologies and services. Members include financial institutions; EFT networks; bank card associations; retailers; information processors; equipment, card and software manufacturers and vendors; Internet providers; telecommunications companies; state governments; and federal agencies. Membership varies with the type of participation: $150/year (special interest group); $2,500/year (council); $6,000 (corporate); $15,000 (sustaining).

Publications:
EFTA News Fax. m.

Meetings/Conferences:
Annual Meetings: Spring/1,200 +

Electronic Industries Ass'n *(1924)*
2500 Wilson Blvd.
Arlington, VA 22201
Tel: (703)907-7500   *Fax:* (703)907-7501
Web Site: http://www.eia.org
Members: 1,500 companies
Staff: 200
Annual Budget: $25-50,000,000
President: David McCurdy, CAE
V. President, Public Affairs: Mark V. Rosenker
V. President, Government Division: Dan C. Heinemeier
V. Preisdent, Government and Legal Affairs: Gary Klein
V. President, Finance: Elizabeth A. Hartnett
V. President, Member Relations: T.Glyn Finley
V. President, General Counsel & Secretary: John J. Kelly
Manager, Member Relations: Gretchen Lenz

Historical Note
Formerly Radio Manufacturers Ass'n (1924-50); Radio-Television Manufacturers Ass'n (1950-53); Radio-Electronics-Television Manufacturers Ass'n (1953-57). Became Electronic Industries Ass'n on August 5, 1957. Includes former Magnetic Recording Industry Ass'n. Absorbed Ass'n of Electronic Manufacturers in 1975, Institute of High Fidelity in 1980, amd Mobile Electronics

Ass'n in 1992. Consumer Electronics Manufacturers Ass'n and Electronic Components, Assemblies, Equipment and Supplies Ass'n are sections of EIA. Sponsors the Joint Electron Device Engineering Council, the Electronics Political Action Committee, the Electronic Industries Foundation, and Consumer Electronics Shows. Members are companies involved in the manufacture of electronic components, parts, systems and equipment for communications, industrial, government and consumer uses. Has an annual budget of approximately $42 million.

Publications:
Annual Report. a.
EIA Trade Directory. a.
Executive Report. q.
Market Data Book. a.
Market Trends. m.
Publication Index. bien.

Meetings/Conferences:
Semi-annual meetings: Spring in Washington, DC and Fall on the West Coast
1999 - Washington, DC/March 21-24

Electronic Industry Show Corporation
Historical Note
Became (1996) Electronic Distribution Show Corporation.

Electronic Media Rating Council *(1964)*
Historical Note
Became the Media Rating Council in 1997.

Electronic Messaging Ass'n *(1983)*
1655 N. Ft. Myer Drive, Suite 500
Arlington, VA 22209
Tel: (703)524-5550   *Fax:* (703)524-5558
Web Site: http://www.ema.org
Members: 550 companies
Staff: 15
Annual Budget: $2-5,000,000
President and C.E.O.: Kerry C. Stackpole, CAE

Historical Note
Formerly (1993) the Electronic Mail Ass'n. Members are corporate users plus telecommunications carriers, computer equipment and software manufacturers, and consultants. Membership: $1000-10,000/year.

Publications:
EMA ALERT (via E-Mail). bi-w.
EMA Membership Directory. a.
Messaging Magazine. bi-m.

Meetings/Conferences:
Annual Meetings: Spring/4,000
1999 - Dallas, TX/March 20-April 2

Electronic Publishing Special Interest Group *(1986)*
Historical Note
Organization defunct in 1997.

Electronic Retailing Ass'n *(1990)*
1225 New York Ave., N.W., Suite 1200
Washington, DC 20005
Tel: (202)289-6462   *Fax:* (202)682-0603
Toll Free: (800)987 - 6462
E-Mail: lmyers@retailing.org
Web Site: http://www.retailing.org
Members: 400 companies
Staff: 12
Annual Budget: $2-5,000,000
President and C.E.O.: Elissa Matulis Myers, CAE
V. President, Communications: Joseph Cavarretta
V. President, Meeting Services: Amy Ledoux

Historical Note
Formerly (1994) Nat'l Infomercial Marketing Ass'n and (1998) NIMA Internat'l. ERA promotes the growth, development and acceptance of the electronic retailing insudtry. Members (direct response companies and their suppliers) are involved in infomercial and short-form commercials, television shopping channels, internet nd multimedia marketing. Membership: $1,000-$23,000/year (corporate).

Publications:
Membership Directory. a. adv.
NIMA News Newsletter. m.

Meetings/Conferences:
Annual Meetings: Fall
1999 - Las Vegas, NV(Venetian)
2000 - Las Vegas, NV

Electronic Transactions Ass'n *(1990)*
2841 Main
Kansas City, MO 64108
Tel: (816)221-8488   *Fax:* (816)472-7765
Toll Free: (800)695 - 5509
Web Site: www.electran.org
Members: 175 companies
Staff: 4
Annual Budget: $250-500,000
Exec. Director: Kenneth R. Bowman
Dir., Communications: Melanie Brown
Assoc. Director: Sheila R. Navis, CAE

Historical Note
Founded as Bankcard Services Ass'n; assumed its current name in 1996. ETA members are bankcard service providers who are actively engaged in providing a full range of services to qualified merchants, who act as intermediaries between merchants and settlement banks. Other classes of membership include: credit card issuers and suppliers to the industry (associate); and financial institutions.

Publications:
Transaction Trends. q. adv.

Meetings/Conferences:
1999 - Waikoloa, HI(Waikoloa Hilton)/March 12-17/600

Electronics Representatives Ass'n *(1935)*

444 N. Michigan Ave., Suite 1960
Chicago, IL   60611
Tel: (312)527-3050   *Fax:* (312)527-3783
E-Mail: info@era.org
Web Site: http://www.era.org
Members: 10,000 individuals, 1,500 companies
Staff: 13
Annual Budget: $1-2,000,000
Exec. V. President & CEO: Raymond J. Hall
Staff Vice President: Janet Hipp

Historical Note
Founded as the Representatives of Radio Parts Manufacturers, it became the Representatives of Electronic Parts Manufacturers in 1942 and assumed its present name in 1959.

Publications:
Locator of Manufacturer's Representatives. a. adv.
The Representor. q. adv.

Meetings/Conferences:
1999 – Maui, HI(Aston Wailea Resort)/April 6-11

Electronics Technicians Ass'n Internat'l *(1978)*

602 N. Jackson St.
Greencastle, IN   46135
Tel: (765)653-8262   *Fax:* (765)653-8262
Toll Free: (800)288 - 3824
E-Mail: eta@indy.tdsnet.com
Web Site: http://www.eta-sda.com
Members: 1,850 individuals
Staff: 5
Annual Budget: $250-500,000
President: Dick Glass
Communications: Carolyn Lentz
Government Relations: Thomas Glass
Meetings: Teresa Maher
Education: Lynda Shute

Historical Note
Incorporated November 14, 1978 in the State of Indiana. Members are involved in such fields as medical, industrial, computer, and military electronics, as well as satellite communications, sound equipment and other electronic service. Operates a Certified Electronics Technician Program. One of seven organizations appointed by the FCC to administer FCC commercial license exams. Absorbed the Satellite Dealers Ass'n (SDA), and the Indiana Electronic Service Ass'n (IESA) in 1996. Membership: $25-42/year (individual), $175/year (company).

Publications:
EEA Training Program. m.
High Tech News. m.
Management Update. m.

Meetings/Conferences:
Annual Meetings: Summer
1999 – Orlando, FL

Electrophoresis Soc. *(1980)*

Univ. of Iowa-Dept. of BioChemistry
4403 BSB 51 Newtown Road
Iowa City, IA   52242
Tel: (319)335-7896
Members: 5,000 individuals
Staff: 1
Annual Budget: $10-25,000
Administrator: Nancy Stellwagen

Historical Note
Members are scientists striving to promote scientific advances in electrophoretic theory and applications. Membership: $90/year.

Publications:
Applied and Theoretical Electrophoresis. q. adv.
Electrophoresis Soc. Newsletter.

Meetings/Conferences:

Elevator Industries Ass'n *(1947)*

425 Hampton Road, #12
Southampton, NY   11968-3017
Tel: (516)287-7360   *Fax:* (516)287-7358
Exec. Consultant: Richard M. Wheeler

Embalming Chemical Manufacturers Ass'n *(1951)*

Historical Note
Organization disbanded in 1997.

Embroidery Council of America *(1973)*

596 Anderson Ave.
Clifford Park, NJ   07010-1831
Tel: (201)943-7757   *Fax:* (201)943-7793
Members: 200 companies
Staff: 2
Exec. V. President: I. Leonard Seiler

Historical Note
Formerly Schiffli Lace and Embroidery Institute. Members are manufacturers of machine-made embroidery and laces under union contract.

Meetings/Conferences:
Annual Meetings: None held.

Embroidery Trade Ass'n *(1990)*

13760 Noel Rd., Suite 500
Dallas, TX   75240
Tel: (972)419-7966   *Fax:* (972)455-8865
Toll Free: (800)727 - 3014
E-Mail: ETA@emfi.com
Web Site: http://www.etab.mfi.com
Members: 2,000 companies
Staff: 6
Annual Budget: $100-250,000
Exec. Director: Peggy A. Brock

Historical Note
ETA members are companies and individuals involved in the embroidery industry. Sponsorship: $115/year (individual); $1,200/year (company).

Publications:
Embroidery and Monogramming. adv. adv.

Meetings/Conferences:
1999 – Ft. Worth, TX
1999 – Long Beach, CA

Emerald Green Miniature Golf Ass'n *(1997)*

3726 Vermilion Ct., S.
Eagan, MN   55122-3153
Annual Budget: under $10,000
President: Terry Damron

Historical Note
Founded to organize a schedule of tournament play for miniature golf professionals, EGMGA offers memberships to both courses and professional golfers. Membership: $35/year (individual); $100/year (company); $200-500/year (course/sponsor).

Emergency Medicine Residents' Ass'n *(1974)*

1125 Executive Circle
Irving, TX   75038
Tel: (214)550-0911   *Fax:* (214)580-2829
Toll Free: (800)798 - 1822
Web Site: http://www.emra.org
Members: 4,400 individuals
Staff: 2
Annual Budget: $250-500,000
Exec. Director: Elizabeth A. Sibley

Historical Note
Members are physicians training in the specialty of emergency medicine and medical students interested in emergency medicine. Membership: $45/year.

Publications:
Antibiotic Handbook.
EM Resident. bi-m.
EMRA Job Catalog. a.

Meetings/Conferences:
Semi-Annual Meetings: Spring and Fall

Emergency Nurses Ass'n *(1970)*

216 Higgins Road
Park Ridge, IL   60068-5736
Tel: (847)698-9400   *Fax:* (847)698-9406
Web Site: http://www.ena.org
Members: 25,000 individuals
Staff: 65
Annual Budget: $5-10,000,000
Exec. Director: Pat Blake
Director, Communication Services: Ronald Lehmann
Director, Marketing/Public Relations: Jim McCormack
Director, Meeting Services: Kathleen Rossell
Director, Financial Services: Sandra I. Thomas
Director, Membership Services: Rebecca White

Historical Note
Formerly (1974) Nat'l Emergency Department Nurses Ass'n and the Emergency Department Nurses Ass'n. Assumed its present name in 1984. Members are registered nurses committed to emergency nursing. Membership: $80/year.

Publications:
Etcetera. bi-m. adv.
Journal of Emergency Nursing. bi-m. adv.
Management Update. q.

Meetings/Conferences:
Annual Meetings: Fall/4,000
1999 – Washington, D.C.(D.C. Convention
       Center)/Sept. 29-Oct. 3
2000 – Chicago, IL/Sept. 20-24

Emerging Markets Traders Ass'n *(1990)*

63 Wall St., 20th Floor
New York, NY   10005
Tel: (212)908-5000   *Fax:* (212)908-5039
E-Mail: emtammc@aol.com
Web Site: http://www.emta.org
Members: 170 institutions
Staff: 20
Annual Budget: $5-10,000,000
Exec. Director: Michael M. Chamberlin
Public Relations/Marketing: Rachael Mark
Finance Director: Donald Goecks
Director, Research: Jonathan Murmo
Senior Legal Counsel: Aviva Werner

Historical Note
EMTA promotes the orderly development of fair, efficient and transparent trading markets for Emerging Markets instruments and the integration of emerging capital marketsinto the global financial marketplace. Full members are institutions that, directly or through affiliates, act as traders, brokers or dealers in Emerging Markets instruments; memberships are also available to firms who participate in local markets or otherwise have a strong interest in the Emerging Markets trading industry. Membership: $20,000/year (full member); $10,000/year (associate); $5,000 (local markets); $3,000 (affiliate).

Publications:
Bulletin Newsletter. q. adv.
Trading Volume Survey. q.

Meetings/Conferences:
Annual Meetings: December
1999 – London, England

Employee Assistance Professionals Ass'n *(1971)*

2101 Wilson Blvd., Suite 500
Arlington, VA   22201-3062
Tel: (703)522-6272   *Fax:* (703)522-4585
E-Mail: capmain@aol.com
Members: 7,000 individuals, 900 companies

Staff: 18
Annual Budget: $2-5,000,000
C.O.O.: Sylvia A. Straub, Ph.D., CAE
Editor, The Exchange and Director of Communications: Kay
       Springer
Director, Legislation and Public Policy: Sheila Macdonald
Director, Accreditation & Certification: Joni Reed Cooley, CEAP
Manager, Resource Center: Janice Laughlin
Director, Membership/Chapter Services: Mary Craigie

Historical Note
Members are individuals involved in employee assistance programs. Formerly (1989) Ass'n of Labor-Management Administrators and Consultants on Alcoholism. Sponsors continuing education and awards the designation CEAP (Certified Employee Assistance Professional). Membership: $115/year (individual); $205/year (organization/company).

Publications:
EAPA Exchange. bi-m. adv.
Member Resource Directory. a.

Meetings/Conferences:
Annual Meetings: November

Employee Assistance Soc. of North America *(1984)*

435 N. Michigan Ave., Suite 1717
Chicago, IL   60611-4067
Tel: (312)644-0828   *Fax:* (312)644-8557
E-Mail: EASNA@bostrom.com
Members: 300 individuals
Annual Budget: $100-250,000
Administrative Officer: Roxanne Dwyer

Historical Note
EASNA members are professionals involved in employee assistance. Membership: $90/year (U.S.), $120/year (Canada), $50/year (student), $55/year (student/Canada).

Publications:
EASNA Membership Directory. bien. adv.
Employee Assistance Quarterly.
The Source. q. adv.

Meetings/Conferences:

Employee Benefit Research Institute *(1978)*

2121 K St., N.W., Suite 600
Washington, DC   20037-1896
Tel: (202)659-0670   *Fax:* (202)775-6312
Web Site: http://www.ebri.org
Members: 300 companies
Staff: 30
Annual Budget: $2-5,000,000
President: Dallas L. Salisbury
Director, Administration: Patsy D'Amelio
Director, Public Relations: Danny Devine

Historical Note
Plan sponsors, consultants and others interested in employee benefit plans. The Institute's main purpose is to conduct public policy research, particularly in the area of retirement, health, and welfare plans. Established September 1978 in Washington DC. Membership: $4,000-28,500/year.

Publications:
EBRI's Benefit Outlook.
EBRI's Washington Bulletin.
Employee Benefit Notes. m.
Issue Briefs. m.
Quarterly Pension Investment Report. q.

Meetings/Conferences:

Employee Involvement Ass'n *(1942)*

740 Florida Central Pkwy., Suite 1020
Longwood, FL   32750
Tel: (407)834-6688   *Fax:* (407)834-4747
Members: 700 companies
Annual Budget: $250-500,000
Exec. Director: Jone R. Sienkiewicz, CAE, CMP

Historical Note
Formerly (1992) Nat'l Ass'n of Suggestion Systems. EIA represents manager and administrators of programs and/or systems which are designed to encourage employee involvement through the recognition of employee ideas and suggestions for company improvement. Membership: $225/year (initial membership); $220/year (renewal).

Publications:
Membership Directory. a. adv.
New Horizons. q.
Roster and Statistical Report. a. adv.

Meetings/Conferences:
Annual Meetings: Fall

Employee Relocation Council *(1964)*

1720 N St., N.W.
Washington, DC   20036
Tel: (202)857-0857   *Fax:* (202)466-2384
Web Site: http://www.erc.org
Members: 13,000 individuals
Staff: 40
Annual Budget: $5-10,000,000
Exec. V. President: H. Cris Collie, III
Director, Conference Management: Cynthia Thompson
Director, Professional Development/Research: Karen A. Reid
Director, Finance and Administration: Laura Macary Fitch
Director, Research: Jan Hatfield Goldman
Manager, Membership Development: Polly Smith

Historical Note
Organized by a handful of large companies who wished to lessen the impact of relocation on their employees' productivity, efficiency and morale. Formerly (1973) Employee Relocation Real Estate Advisory Council.

Publications:
ERC Directory. a.
Mobility. m.

Meetings/Conferences:
1999 – Las Vegas, NV/May 4-7

Employee Stock Ownership Ass'n *(1979)*
Historical Note
See ESOP Ass'n.

Employers Council on Flexible Compensation *(1981)*
927 15th St., N.W., Suite 1000
Washington, DC 20005
Tel: (202)659-4300
E-Mail: infoecfc@ecfc.org
Web Site: www.ecfc.org
Members: 650 companies and organizations
Staff: 9
Annual Budget: $1-2,000,000
Exec. Director: Kenneth E. Feltman, CAE
Chief Operating Officer: Bonnie Whyte, CAE
Historical Note
A national, non-profit association committed to the promotion and improvement of flexible compensation plans. Professional membership is open to public and private employers, including non-profit organizations, companies, accounting firms, consulting actuaries, and others that design or administer flexible benefit plans. Membership fee based upon size and type of organization.
Publications:
CapitoLetter. m.
ECFC Bulletins. bi-w.
Flex Reporter.
Legislative Alerts.
Meetings/Conferences:
Annual Meetings: March, in Washington, DC area
1999 – Washington, DC(Crystal Gateway
    Marriott)/March 25-26

Employment Management Ass'n *(1969)*
1800 Duke St.
Alexandria, VA 22314-3499
Tel: (703)548-3440   *Fax:* (703)836-0367
Toll Free: (800)283 - 7476
Web Site: http://www.shrm.org/ema
Members: 4,100 individuals
Annual Budget: $500-1,000,000
Manager, EMA Operations: Rebecca R. Hastings, SPHR
Historical Note
EMA members are employment and human resource executives. "Third party" professionals (providers of support services to the employment process) are eligible as affiliate, non-voting members. EMA became a unit of the Soc. for Human Resource Management in 1996. Membership: $75/year, with SHRM membership of $160/year.
Publications:
EMA Journal. q. adv.
EMA Reporter. bi-m.
Membership Directory. a. adv.
National Cost/Hire Survey Report. a. adv.
Meetings/Conferences:
Annual Meetings: Spring
1999 – San Diego, CA(Sheraton San Diego Hotel and
    Marino)/April 28-30

Employment Management Ass'n *(1969)*
Historical Note
Became the Soc. for Human Resource Management/Employment Management Ass'n upon merging into SHRM in 1996.

Emulsion Polymers Council *(1995)*
1250 Connecticut Ave., NW, Suite 800
Washington, DC 20005-3305
Tel: (202)637-9040   *Fax:* (202)637-9178
E-Mail: regnet@ricochet.net
Members: 11 companies
Staff: 2
Annual Budget: $100-250,000
Exec. Director: Robert J. Fensterheim
Historical Note
EPC represents regulatory professionals at companies which produce emulsion polymers, chemical compounds used in a variety of coating and other industrial applications. Membership: Base on production.

Endocrine Fellows Foundation *(1990)*
401 N. Michigan Ave., Suite 2400
Chicago, IL 60611
Toll Free: (888)340 - 8711
E-Mail: eff@sba.com
Web Site: http://www.endocrinefellows.org
Members: 600 individuals
Staff: 3
Annual Budget: $500-1,000,000
Exec. Director: Marilyn Fishman
Historical Note
EEF provides support to endocrine fellows in education, research grant funding and career guidance. The foundation also provides fellows and endocrinology professionals with research results on developments in endocrinology, metabolism and diabetology.
Publications:
EndoTrends. q.
Meetings/Conferences:
Annual Meetings: Summer

Endocrine Soc. *(1916)*
4350 East West Highway, Suite 500
Bethesda, MD 20814-4426
Tel: (301)941-0200   *Fax:* (301)941-0259
Toll Free: (888)363 - 6274
E-Mail: endostaff@endo-society.org
Web Site: http://www.endo-society.org
Members: 9,000 individuals

Staff: 43
Annual Budget: $10-25,000,000
Exec. Director: Scott Hunt
Director, Public Affairs: David Thomas
Director, Meetings: Cathy L. Scheck
Director, Professional Affairs: Barbara Hollis
Manager, Professional Affairs and Membership: Suzanne Rogers
Asst. Exec. Director and Director, Finance & Administration: Cindy
    A. Bodin
Director, Journal Publications: Lenne Miller
Director, Information Systems: Nancy Gold
Historical Note
Founded as the Ass'n for Study of Internal Secretions, the Endocrine Soc. is a professional society of scientists, educators, clinicians, practicing physicians, nurses and students with an interest in research, study and clinical practice of endocrinology. Has an annual budget of approximately $8 million. Membership: $105/year.
Publications:
Endocrine Reviews. bi-m. adv.
Endocrine Society News. bi-m. adv.
Endocrinology. m. adv.
Journal of Clinical Endocrinology and Metabolism. m. adv.
Molecular Endocrinology. m. adv.
Meetings/Conferences:
Annual Meetings: June/5,000
1999 – San Diego, CA(Convention Center)/June 16-19/5000
2000 – Toronto, Canada(Metropolitan Convention
    Center)/June 21-24/5000
2001 – Denver, CO(Colorado Convention Cneter)/June 20-23
2002 – San Francisco, CA(Moscone Convention
    Center)/June 19-22

Energy Efficient Building Ass'n *(1982)*
1300 Spring Street Suite 500
Silver Spring, MD 20910
Tel: (301)589-2500   *Fax:* (301)588-0854
E-Mail: info@eeba.org
Web Site: http://www.eeba.org
Members: 700 individuals
Staff: 6
Annual Budget: $500-1,000,000
Exec. Director: James Golden
Historical Note
EEBA members are architects, builders, building material suppliers, and others with an interest in energy efficient construction. Membership: $150/year (individual); $275/year (small business); $475/year (corporate).
Publications:
EEBA Excellence Newsletter. q.
Meetings/Conferences:
Annual Meetings: Fall

Energy Efficient Lighting Ass'n *(1997)*
P.O. Box 727
Princeton Junction, NJ 08550
Tel: (609)799-4900   *Fax:* (609)799-7032
E-Mail: eela@eela.com
Web Site: http://www.eela.com
Members: 40 companies
Staff: 6
Exec. Director: Jeffrey E. Barnhart
Historical Note
Members are manufacturers, installers, designers, specifiers and professional users of energy-efficient lighting equipment. EELA distributes publications and technical information on the industry to promote the use of energy-efficient lighting.
Publications:
On a Lighter Note. m.
Meetings/Conferences:

Energy Frontiers Internat'l *(1980)*
1110 N. Glebe Road, Suite 610
Arlington, VA 22201-4714
Tel: (703)276-6655   *Fax:* (703)276-7662
Members: 30 companies
Staff: 3
Annual Budget: $250-500,000
President: Michael Koleda
Historical Note
Formerly (1996) the Council on Alternate Fuels. Energy Frontiers Internat'l is a joint effort by companies in the energy industry to augment their internal efforts to keep abreast of advances in a broad range of emerging energy technologies worldwide.
Publications:
Alternate Fuel News. m. adv.
Proceedings for Annual Spring Meeting. a.
Meetings/Conferences:

Energy Telecommunications and Electrical Ass'n
   (1928)
P.O. Box 639
Tomball, TX 77375-0639
Tel: (281)357-8700   *Fax:* (281)357-8777
Toll Free: (888)503 - 8701
E-Mail: entelec@pdq.net
Web Site: http://www.entelec.org
Members: 170 companies
Staff: 5
Annual Budget: $500-1,000,000
Meeting Services/Print Production: John D. Fike
Senior Advisor: Loyce Hurley, CAE
Historical Note
Formerly (until 1978) the Petroleum Industry Electrical Ass'n. Members are companies and corporations in the energy industries employing personnel having managerial, engineering or technical responsibility in the electrical, electronics, communications and allied fields. Membership: $300/year.

Publications:
ENTELEC Bound Technical Papers. a.
ENTELEC News. q. adv.
Meetings/Conferences:
Annual Meetings: March
1999 – Houston, TX(Hyatt Regency)/March 28-31
2000 – Dallas, TX(Hyatt Regency)/March 19-22

Energy Traffic Ass'n *(1941)*
907 Kiowa Drive East
Gainesville, TX 76240
Tel: (940)668-7735   *Fax:* (817)668-7212
E-Mail: vmusick@nortexinfo.netm
Members: 100 companies
Annual Budget: $25-50,000
Exec. Director: Virgil O. Musick
Historical Note
Formerly (1997) Shippers Oil Field Traffic Ass'n.
Publications:
Membership Directory. a.
SOFTA Newsletter. m.
Meetings/Conferences:

Engine Manufacturers Ass'n *(1968)*
401 N. Michigan Ave.
Chicago, IL 60611-4206
Tel: (312)644-6610   *Fax:* (312)321-5111
Members: 35 companies
Staff: 5
Annual Budget: $5-10,000,000
Exec. Director: Glenn F. Keller
Historical Note
Formerly (1968) Internal Combustion Engine Institute. Members are manufacturers of internal combustion engines used for any purpose except aircraft or passenger car use. Membership: $20-100,000/year (corporate).
Publications:
Lubricating Oils Data Book. bi-a.

Engine Service Ass'n *(1970)*
210 Allen Dr.
Exton, PA 19341
Tel: (610)363-3844   *Fax:* (610)363-3817
E-Mail: esajohn@bee.net
Web Site: engineservice.com
Members: 35 companies
Staff: 2
Annual Budget: $50-100,000
Exec. Director: John W. Kane
Historical Note
Members are central warehouse distributors of air-cooled internal combustion engines.
Publications:
Newsletter. bi-m.
Meetings/Conferences:
Annual Meetings: Fall
1999 – Bermuda(Marriott Castle Harbor Resort)/Oct. 24-28

Engineered Wood Ass'n
Historical Note
See APA - The Engineered Wood Ass'n.

Engineering College Magazines Associated *(1920)*
133 Ward Hall, Kansas State Univ.
Manhattan, KS 66506-2508
Tel: (785)532-4996   *Fax:* (785)532-6952
E-Mail: mdorcey@ksu.edu
Members: 40 colleges
Staff: 1
Annual Budget: under $10,000
Exec. Secretary: Mike Dorsey
Historical Note
Members are engineering colleges that publish engineering journals for students. ECMA promotes communication skills, good journalism and publishing practices, and comradery among students. Membership: $150/year.
Meetings/Conferences:
Annual Meetings: Spring
1999 – Washington, DC

Engineering Contractors' Ass'n *(1963)*
8310 Florence Ave.
Downey, CA 90240
Tel: (562)861-0929   *Fax:* (562)923-6179
E-Mail: eca@phlash.net
Members: 250 individuals
Staff: 3
Annual Budget: $1-2,000,000
Exec. Director: Gary Futral
Historical Note
Promotes the interest of member contractors in matters involving labor, government, and legislation. Sponsors and supports the ECA Political Action Committee.
Publications:
ECA. m. adv.
Meetings/Conferences:
Annual Meetings: May
1999 – Las Vegas, NV

Engineering in Medicine and Biology Soc. *(1950)*
Historical Note
A technical society of the Institute of Electrical and Electronics Engineers (IEEE). Membership in the Society, open only to IEEE members, includes subscription to a technical periodical in the field published by IEEE. All administrative support provided by IEEE.

Engineering Management Soc. *(1950)*

Historical Note
A technical society of the Institute of Electrical and Electronics Engineers (IEEE). Membership in the Society, open only to IEEE members, includes subscription to a technical periodical in the field published by IEEE. All administrative support provided by IEEE.

Engraved Stationery Manufacturers Ass'n *(1911)*
P.O. Box 290249
Nashville, TN 37229-0249
Tel: (615)366-1094 *Fax:* (615)366-4192
Members: 150 companies
Staff: 1
Annual Budget: $50-100,000
Manager: Harris B. Griggs

Historical Note
Founded in 1911 as the Nat'l Ass'n of Steel and Copper Plate Engravers; assumed its present name in 1938. Administrative support provided by Printing Industry Ass'n of the South (same address).

Publications:
ESMA Newsletter. m.

Meetings/Conferences:
Semi-annual Meetings: Winter and Summer

Enlisted Ass'n of Nat'l Guard of the United States
1219 Prince St.
Alexandria, VA 22314
Tel: (703)519-3846 *Fax:* (703)519-3849
Toll Free: (800)234 - 3264
E-Mail: EANGUS@EANGUS.ORG
Web Site: WWW.EANGUS.ORG
Members: 75,000 individuals
Staff: 5
Annual Budget: $500-1,000,000
Exec. Director: Michael P. Cline

Historical Note
EANGUS represents enlisted men and women of the Army and Air Force National Guard. Membership: $6/year (individual); $100-1000/year (organization/company).

Publications:
Air Force Times. w. adv.
Army Times. w. adv.
Congressional Report. d.
Legislative Updates. q. adv.
New Patriot Magazine. q. adv.
New Patriot Newsletter. bi-m. adv.

Meetings/Conferences:
1999 - Des Moines, IA(Convention Center)/August 21-26/1500
2000 - Bismarck, ND(Radisson Inn)/August 19-23/1500

Enteral Nutrition Council *(1983)*
Historical Note
Members are manufacturers and marketers of enteral formulas, foods for special dietary use, and medical foods.

Enterprise Computer Telephony Forum *(1995)*
39355 California St., Suite 307
Fremont, CA 94538
Tel: (510)608-5915 *Fax:* (510)608-5917
E-Mail: ectf@ectf.org
Web Site: http://www.ectf.org
Members: 70 companies
Exec. Director: Lisa Winkler

Historical Note
ECTF members are suppliers, developers, systems integrators and users of computer telephony integration technology. Promotes international standards for computer telephony technology and implementation of such standards throughout the industry. Membership: $12,000/year (principal); $6,000/year (small company principal); $2,500/year (auditing/user).

Meetings/Conferences:
1999 - Los Angeles, CA/Jan. 25-27

Entertainment Services and Technology Ass'n *(1987)*
875 Sixth Ave., Suite 2302
New York, NY 10001
Tel: (212)244-1505 *Fax:* (212)244-1502
E-Mail: info@esta.org
Web Site: http://www.esta.org
Members: 400 companies
Staff: 4
Annual Budget: $500-1,000,000
Exec. Director: Lori Rubinstein

Historical Note
Formerly (1994) Theatrical Dealers Ass'n. ESTA's members are manufacturers, dealers, distributors, production companies, service companies, consultants, designers and others providing goods and services to the live entertainment industry in North America and around the world. These companies work in the areas of lighting, sound, rigging, soft goods, scenery, props, electrical distribution, costumes, special effects, computer software and show control.

Publications:
Membership Directory. a. adv.
Protocol. q. adv.

Entomological Soc. of America *(1889)*
9301 Annapolis Road
Lanham, MD 20706-3115
Tel: (301)731-4535 *Fax:* (301)731-4538
E-Mail: info@entsoc.org
Web Site: http://www.entsoc.org
Members: 8,500 individuals
Staff: 21
Annual Budget: $2-5,000,000
Exec. Director: Douglas M. Kleine
Meeting Manager: Judy Miller
Director, Services: Kaye Meckley
Director, Publications: Beth Staehle

Historical Note
Formed in 1953 by the consolidation of the American Ass'n of Economic Entomologists (1889) and the Entomological Soc. of America (1906). Incorporated in the District of Columbia in 1954. The Entomological Foundation is the development arm of ESA. In 1992 the American Registry of Professional Entomologists became the certification program for the ESA. Provides Board Certification for interested individuals. Membership: $94.50/year.

Publications:
American Entomologist. q. adv.
Annals of ESA. bi-m. adv.
Arthropod Management Tests. a.
Environmental Entomology. bi-m. adv.
ESA Newsletter. m.
Journal of Economic Entomology. bi-m. adv.
Journal of Medical Entomology. bi-m. adv.

Meetings/Conferences:
Annual Meetings: December
1999 - Atlanta, GA(Hyatt Regency Atlanta)/Dec. 12-16/3000
2000 - Montreal, QB, Canada/3000

Envelope Institute of America *(1943)*
Historical Note
Address unknown in 1997.

Envelope Manufacturers Ass'n *(1933)*
300 N. Washington St., Suite 500
Alexandria, VA 22314-2530
Tel: (703)739-2200 *Fax:* (703)739-2209
Members: 250 companies
Staff: 7
Annual Budget: $1-2,000,000
President: Maynard H. Benjamin, C.A.E.
Coordinator, Meeting and Membership: Kim Moses
Director, Industry Services: Douglas Roorbach
Director, Membership Services: Tonya Muse

Historical Note
A merger of the American Envelope Manufacturers Association (founded in 1909) and the Bureau of Envelope Manufacturers Association of America (founded in 1916). Formerly (1995) Envelope Manufacturers Ass'n of America.

Publications:
Newsletter. m.

Meetings/Conferences:
Semi-annual Meetings: Spring and Fall/250

Envelope Manufacturers Ass'n of America
Historical Note
Became Envelope Manufacturers Ass'n in 1995.

Environmental and Engineering Geophysical Soc. *(1992)*
10200 W. 44th Ave., Suite 304
Wheat Ridge, CO 80033-2840
Tel: (303)422-7905 *Fax:* (303)843-6232
E-Mail: eegs@resourcenter.com
Web Site: www.esd.ornl.gov/EEGS
Members: 700 individuals
Staff: 3
Exec. Officer: Jerry Bowman

Historical Note
Members are individuals and corporation with an interest in geophysics and applied environmental engineering. Membership: $70/year (individual); $15/year (student); $700/year (corporate).

Publications:
Directory. a.
EEGS Newsletter. q.
Journal of Engineering and Environmental Geophysics. q.

Meetings/Conferences:

Environmental Assessment Ass'n
1224 No. Nokomis Ave.
Alexandria, VA 56308
Tel: (320)763-4320 *Fax:* (320)763-9290
Annual Budget: $1-2,000,000
Exec. Director: Robert G. Johnson
Assoc. Director: Joan Powell
Assoc. Director: Troy Johnson
Editor: David Held

Historical Note
Membership: $195-225/year.

Publications:
Environmental Times. m. adv.

Meetings/Conferences:
Annual Meetings: Las Vegas, NV(Aladdin Hotel)/Sept. 28-Oct. 2

Environmental Bankers Ass'n *(1994)*
110 N. Royal St., Suite 301
Alexandria, VA 22314
Tel: (703)549-0977 *Fax:* (703)548-5945
E-Mail: envirobank@aol.com
Web Site: http://envirobank.org
Members: 60 institutions
Staff: 3
Exec. Co-Directors: D.J. and T.C. Telego

Historical Note
EBA members are banks, trust companies, credit unions, savings and loan ass'ns, and other financial services organizations with an interest in environmental risk management and related issues. Active participants are bankers from Trust or Credit offices with responsibility for environmental liability, and financial services officers with environmental interests. Membership: $500-$900/year.

Publications:
Bank Notes. m.
Directory. bien. adv.
Your Bank, Your Business & the Environment.

Meetings/Conferences:
Semi-annual Meeting: January and June
1999 - Tucson, AZ
1999 - Detroit, MI

Environmental Business Ass'n, The *(1989)*
1150 Connecticut Ave., N.W., 9th Floor
Washington, DC 20036
Tel: (202)862-4363 *Fax:* (202)828-4130
Members: 55 companies
Annual Budget: $50-100,000
President: William H. Bode

Historical Note
TEBA members represent all segments of the environmental industry -- consultants, laboratories, remediation companies, disposal firms, recyclers and technology innovators. TEBA facilitates arrangements and information exchange among members to develop business opportunities. Services include sponsoring seminars, monthly meetings, industry trends, changes in technology and legislation. Membership: $500/year (individual); corporate dues vary based on revenue.

Meetings/Conferences:
Annual Meetings: June

Environmental Design Research Ass'n *(1968)*
P.O. Box 7146
Edmond, OK 73083-7146
Tel: (405)330-4863 *Fax:* (405)330-4150
E-Mail: edra@telepath.com
Web Site: www.telepath.com/edra/home.html
Members: 700 individuals
Staff: 3
Annual Budget: $100-250,000
Exec. Director: Janet Singer

Historical Note
Mission is to advance the art and science of environmental design research, to improve understanding of the interrelationships between people and their built and natural surroundings, and to help create environments responsive to human needs. EDRA members are designers and other professionals with an interest in environmental design research. Membership: $100/year (individual); $65/year (student); $300/year (organization/company).

Publications:
Design Research News. q.
Proceedings of Annual Meeting. a.

Meetings/Conferences:
Annual Meetings: Spring-Summer
1999 - Orlando, FL /June 2-6

Environmental Industry Ass'ns *(1968)*
4301 Connecticut Ave., N.W., Suite 300
Washington, DC 20008
Tel: (202)244-4700 *Fax:* (202)966-4818
Members: 2,000 companies
Staff: 85
Annual Budget: $10-25,000,000
President and C.E.O.: Bruce J. Parker
Director, Public Affairs: Allen Blakey
Manager, Legislative Affairs: William H. Sells
Chief Operating Officer: Lawson L. Hockman
Comptroller: Gene Olexa
Assistant Counsel: David Biderman

Historical Note
Formerly (1994) Nat'l Solid Wastes Management Ass'n. Restructured in 1994. EIA now includes the National Solid Waste Management Ass'n, the Hazardous Waste Management Ass'n, and the Waste Equipment Technology Ass'n. Sponsors and supports the Environemental Industry Ass'ns Political Action Committee (WASTE PAC).

Publications:
Infectious Waste News. bi-w.
Recycling Times. bi-w. adv.
Waste Age. m. adv.

Meetings/Conferences:
Annual Meetings: Spring/14,000
1999 - Dallas, TX(Convention Center)/June 8-11

Environmental Industry Council *(1976)*
Historical Note
Organization defunct in 1995.

Environmental Information Ass'n *(1983)*
4915 Auburn Ave., Suite 303
Bethesda, MD 20814
Tel: (301)961-4999 *Fax:* (301)961-3094
Members: 850 individuals, 280 companies
Staff: 5
Annual Budget: $250-500,000
Exec. Director: Martha J. Lockwood, CAE, APR
Manager, Development and Communication: Kelly Rutt

Historical Note
Formerly (1991) Nat'l Asbestos Council and (1993) NAC/The Environmental Information Ass'n. Serves as an information clearinghouse for building owners, environmental professionals, and the public concerning asbestos and other environmental health hazards to building occupants, industrial sites and other facilities. Membership: $150/year (individual); $400/year (corporate).

Publications:
EIA Technical Journal. q. adv.
Environmental Choices. bi-m. adv.
Environmental Quarterly. q. adv.
Lead/Asbestos Fact Sheet. q. adv.
Membership Directory. a.
Technical Supplement. semi-a. adv.

Meetings/Conferences:
Annual Meetings: Spring 1998-Las Vegas, NV(Aladdin Hotel)/Mar. 22-26
1999 - San Antonio, TX(Omni Hotel)/March 27-31

Environmental Management Ass'n (1977)

530 W. Ionia St., Suite C
Lansing, MI 48933-1062
Tel: (517)485-5715   *Fax:* (517)371-1170
Members: 35 manufacturers
Staff: 3
Annual Budget: $50-100,000
Exec. Director: Cindy Schnetzler

Historical Note
Founded as Liquid and Solid Industrial Control Ass'n; assumed its current name in 1995. Members are industrial waste generators, consultants, transporters, site operators, hygienists and environmental attorneys. Membership: $600/year (organization/company); $125/year (individual).

Publications:
EMA Commentary. m.

Meetings/Conferences:
Annual Meetings: Usually in Detroit, MI/Fall/250-500

Environmental Management Ass'n (1957)

1721 Pheasant Lane
Jeffersonville, PA 19403-3333
Tel: (610)539-8588   *Fax:* (610)539-9999
E-Mail: emapres@aol.com
Members: 700 individuals
Annual Budget: $50-100,000
President: Barry M. Dressler, CPMBG,HCFC

Historical Note
Formed by a merger of Ass'n of Food Industry Sanitarians, Industrial Sanitation Management Ass'n, and Nat'l Ass'n of Bakery Sanitarians. Formerly Institute of Sanitation Management. EMA serves as a clearinghouse for information that would be useful to facilities management, maintenance and sanitation professionals. Membership is composed of administrators and managers responsible for facilities planning and design, purchasing, maintenance and operations, building systems, waste management/recycling, and industrial sanitation in educational facilities, municipalities, food and other processing plants, health care facilities, convention centers, office buildings, religious facilities, hotels and other commercial establishments. Food Sanitation Institute and Building Service Managers Institute are components of EMA. Membership: $150/year (professional), $125/year (associate), $375/year (company).

Publications:
Environmental Management. q. adv.

Meetings/Conferences:
Annual Meetings: Fall
1999 – St. Petersburg Beach, FL(Tradewinds Resort)/135
2000 – St. Petersburg Beach, FL(Tradewinds Resort)/Oct. 28-Nov. 1/135
2001 – St. Petersburg Beach, FL

Environmental Mutagen Soc. (1969)

11250 Roger Bacon Dr., Suite 8
Reston, VA 20190-5202
Tel: (703)437-4377   *Fax:* (703)435-4390
E-Mail: emsdmg@aol.com
Web Site:
        http://www.ornl.gov.techresources/ems/hmepg.html
Members: 1,500 individuals
Staff: 7
Annual Budget: $250-500,000
Exec. Director: Randall C. Price, CAE
Administrator: Maureen Thompson

Historical Note
Members are scientists of diverse backgrounds and varied interests who are working in the field of molecular genetics and mutagenesis, whether in academia, industry or government. Focus is to encourage the study of mutagens in the human environment, particularly as they affect public health. Membership: $75/year (individual - U.S., Canada and Mexico).

Publications:
EMS Newsletter. bi-a.
Environmental and Molecular Mutagenesis. 8/yr.
Membership Roster. irreg.

Meetings/Conferences:
Annual Meetings: Spring
1999 – Washington, DC(Capitol Hilton)

Environmental Sciences Ass'n

Historical Note
Ceased nonprofit operations in 1997.

Environmental Technology Council (1982)

734 15th St., N.W., Suite 720
Washington, DC 20005
Tel: (202)783-0870   *Fax:* (202)737-2038
Web Site: http://www.etc.org
Members: 15 companies
Staff: 3
Annual Budget: $1-2,000,000
Exec. Director: David R. Case

Historical Note
Established in Washington, DC and incorporated in Delaware. Formerly (1994) Hazardous Waste Treatment Council. Trade association of environmental management firms engaged in waste treatment, recycling and disposal as well as engineering and consulting firms engaged in the cleanup of contaminated sites. Membership: $8,000-96,000/year, based on revenues (company); $2,500/year for firms outside the industry.

Publications:
Conference Proceedings. a.
Environmental Technology Council Reports. bi-w.

Meetings/Conferences:
Quarterly Meetings: Washington, DC/January, April, July, and October

Environmental Transportation Ass'n (1991)

Historical Note
Organization defunct in 1995.

EPS Molders Ass'n (1994)

2128 Espey Ct., Suite 4
Crofton, MD 21114
Tel: (410)451-8341   *Fax:* (410)451-8343
Toll Free: (800)607 - 3772
E-Mail: bdecamp@aol.com
Web Site: http://epsmolders.org
Staff: 4
Annual Budget: $250-500,000
Exec. V. President: Carl A. Wangman, CAE

Historical Note
EPS Molders ass'n represents the views of the manufactures of expanded polystyrene and insulation product and associated industry groups. Membership fee varies.

Meetings/Conferences:

Epsilon Sigma Phi (1927)

P.O. Box 626
Battle Lake, MN 56515
Tel: (218)864-8678   *Fax:* (218)864-8064
E-Mail: jscarlson@aol.com
Members: 10,000 individuals
Staff: 2
Annual Budget: $100-250,000

Historical Note
A fraternity of professional staff in U.S. land grant universities and U.S. Department of Agriculture Extension programs. Established in Montana January 10, 1927. Membership: $20/year (active); $100/lifetime membership.

Publications:
Journal of Extension.
Newsletter.
The People and the Profession. q.

Meetings/Conferences:
1999 – Indianapolis, IN

Equipment and Tool Institute (1947)

1806 Johns Drive
Glenview, IL 60025-1657
Tel: (847)729-8550   *Fax:* (847)729-3670
Members: 90 companies
Staff: 2
Annual Budget: $500-1,000,000
Exec. Manager: Donn R. Proven

Historical Note
Members are manufacturers of automotive service equipment and tools.

Meetings/Conferences:
Annual Meetings: Fall

Equipment Leasing Ass'n of America (1961)

4301-N Fairfax Dr., Suite 550
Arlington, VA 22203-1608
Tel: (703)527-8655   *Fax:* (703)522-7099
Web Site: http://www.elaonline.com
Members: 720 companies
Staff: 21
Annual Budget: $2-5,000,000
President: Michael J. Fleming, CAE
Director, Communications: Suzanne Jackson
Director, Federal Government Relations: Steven I. Fier
Director, State Government Relations: Dennis Brown, CAE
Meetings and Conventions Director: Sally A. Maloney
Assoc. Director/Professional Development: Lesley Sterling
Asst. Dir. Information/Professional Development: Cecillia Beverina
Director, Finance & Administration: Chris Busky, CPA
Director, Membership: Katie Plona
Coordinator, Membership: Charles Britt
Director, Information/Professional Development: Ralph A. Petta

Historical Note
Founded as Ass'n of Equipment Lessors, it became American Ass'n of Equipment Lessors in 1974 and assumed its present name in 1992. Members are companies whose principal business is leasing equipment to business users. Sponsors the Equipment Leasing Ass'n Capital Investment-Lease Political Action Committee.

Publications:
Equipment Leasing Today. m. adv.
Journal of Equipment Lease Finance. semi-a.

Meetings/Conferences:
Annual Meetings: Fall

Equipment Maintenance Council (1980)

P.O. Box 528
Stroud, OK 74079-9013
Tel: (918)968-1077   *Fax:* (918)968-9621
E-Mail: motherrd@fullnet.net
Web Site: http://www.coneq.com
Members: 1,200 individuals
Staff: 2
Annual Budget: $100-250,000
Exec. Director: Stan Orr, CAE

Historical Note
EMC members are equipment managers from all equipment-intensive industries: construction, wood products, municipalities, utilities, gas and oil exploration, mining, solid waste, commercial farming, aviation ground equipment maintenance, and vocational technical schools. EMC works to establish a positive relationship between users, manufacturers, government agencies and educators involved in the design and operation of equipment. Membership: $95/year (individual); $300-400/year (company).

Publications:
Management Digest. bi-a.
Membership Directory. a.
Newsletter. bi-m. adv.
Tech Tips. bi-m.
Up & Running. 6/year. adv.

Meetings/Conferences:
Annual Meetings: Spring
1999 – Colorado Springs, CO/260
2000 – Atlanta, GA

Equipment Manufacturers Institute (1894)

10 S. Riverside Plaza, Suite 1220
Chicago, IL 60606-3710
Tel: (312)321-1470   *Fax:* (312)321-1480
E-Mail: emi@emi.org
Web Site: http://www.emi.org
Members: 375 companies
Staff: 11
Annual Budget: $2-5,000,000
President: Emmett Barker
V. President: Tim Metzger

Historical Note
Established in 1893. Formerly Nat'l Ass'n of Agricultural Implement and Vehicle Manufacturers, (1933) Nat'l Ass'n of Farm Equipment Manufacturers and (1965) Farm Equipment Institute. Merged (1969) with Industrial Equipment Manufacturers Council to form the Farm and Industrial Equipment Institute. Adopted its present name in 1989 to reflect expanded product coverage. Maintains the following councils: Bituminous and Aggregate Equipment, Cab Manufacturers, Compact Loader, Construction Equipment, Earthmoving Equipment, Farm Equipment, Farmstead Equipment Ass'n, Forestry Equipment, Grain Equipment Manufacturers, Horizontal Earth Boring Equipment Manufacturers, Industrial/Ag Mower Manufacturers, Manufacturers Elevating and Work Platform, Manufacturers of Aerial Devices and Digger-Derricks, Manufacturers of Telescoping and Articulating Cranes, Milking Machine Manufacturers, Mini-Compact Excavators Manufacturers, Power Crane Shovel Ass'n, Rough Terrain Forklifts Council, Rubber Tired Backhoe Loader and Attachments, Tillage Equipment, and Underground Equipment.

Publications:
First of the Week. bi-m.
Membership Roster. a.
Newsletter. m.
Retail Sales Reports. m.
State of the Industry. semi-a.

Meetings/Conferences:
Annual Meetings: September-October
1999 – Braselton, GA/Oct. 9-11

Equipment Service Ass'n (1960)

206 6th Ave., Suite 900
Des Moines, IA 50309-4018
Tel: (515)282-8192   *Fax:* (515)282-9117
E-Mail: dms@ascoc-mgmt.com
Web Site: http://www.assoc-mgmt.com/users/esa/esa.html
Members: 225 companies
Annual Budget: $50-100,000
Exec. Director: Carole Thompson, CAE

Historical Note
Organized as the Internat'l Hydraulic Equipment Rebuilders Ass'n at a meeting of hydraulic jack rebuilders convoked by the Hydraulic Jack Manufacturers Ass'n. Members are companies who rebuild pneumatic, electric and hydraulic equipment. Membership: $225/year.

Publications:
Bulletin. m.
Membership Directory. a.

Meetings/Conferences:
Annual Meetings: Spring/200
1999 – Las Vegas, NV(Monte Carlo)/June 10-12/125

Equity Asset Managers Ass'n, The

564 Mission St., Box 406
San Francisco, CA 94105-2918
Tel: (415)928-4555
Web Site: http://www.teama.org
Secretary: Dede Satten

Historical Note
TEAM A members are institutional asset managers who work with commercial real estate portfolios owned or managed by banks, federal savings banks, pension fund advisors, real estate investment trusts, life insurance companies and commercial real estate investment companies. Membership: $65/year (individual); $250/year (service providers).

Publications:
Membership Directory. a.
TEAM A News Newsletter. q.

Meetings/Conferences:

ERISA Industry Committee (1977)

1400 L St., N.W., Suite 350
Washington, DC 20005
Tel: (202)789-1400   *Fax:* (202)789-1120
E-Mail: eric@eric.org
Web Site: http://www.eric.org
Members: 125 individuals
Staff: 7
President: Mark J. Ugoretz
V. President: Janice M. Gregory

Historical Note
ERIC represents the employment benefit and retirement security interests of America's major enterprises. Members administer private sector retirement, health plans and other benefits for some 25 million active and retired workers and their beneficiaries.

Publications:
ERIC Executive Report Newsletter. bi-m.

ESOP Ass'n (1979)

1726 M St., N.W., Suite 501
Washington, DC 20036
Tel: (202)293-2971   *Fax:* (202)293-7568
E-Mail: esop@the-esop-emplowner.org
Web Site: http://www.the-esop-emplowner.org

Members: 2,000 companies and professionals
Staff: 9
Annual Budget: $2-5,000,000
President: J. Michael Keeling, CAE
Director, Communications: Jim Leut Kemeyer
Director of Meetings and Conferences: Rosemary A. Clements
V. President, Administration: Gwenn E. Rosenthal
C.F.O.: Barbara S. Neider
Director, Membership and Marketing: Lisa Reckstraw
Publications Coordinator: Heather Oestlike

Historical Note
Formed in May 1979 as the ESOP Ass'n of America through a merger of the Nat'l Ass'n of ESOP Companies and the Employee Stock Ownership Council of America, both formed in 1977; assumed its present name in July, 1982. Incorporated in California. Members are companies with employee stock ownership plans as well as professionals who specialize in these plans. Sponsors and supports ESOP PAC. Membership: $330-8,000/year.

Publications:
ESOP Report. m.
Profiles. m.

Meetings/Conferences:
Annual Meetings: May-June/1,000
1999 – Washington, DC(Marriott)/May 12-14

Estuarine Research Federation *(1969)*
490 Chippingwood Drive, Suite 2
Port Republic, MD   20676
Tel: (410)586-0997   *Fax:* (410)586-9226
Web Site: www.erf.org
Members: 2,000 individuals
Staff: 1
Annual Budget: $100-250,000
Exec. Director: Joy A. Bartholomew

Historical Note
ERF is a multidisciplinary organization of individuals who study the structure and function of estuaries, and the effect of human activities on these environments. Promotes research in estuarine and coastal waters, and is available as a source of advice in matters concerning estuaries and the coastal zone. Membership: $80/year (individual); $245-600/year (institutional, domestic).

Publications:
Estuaries. q.
Newsletter. q.

Meetings/Conferences:
Biennial Meetings: Odd years
1999 – New Orleans, LA/Sept. 26-Oct. 1

Ethics Officer Ass'n *(1992)*
30 Church St., Suite 331
Belmont, MA   02478-1301
Tel: (617)484-9400   *Fax:* (617)484-8330
Web Site: http://WWW.EOA.ORG
Exec. Director: Edward Petry, Ph.D.
Director of Communications: Amanda Mujica

Historical Note
Membership: $500/year (individual); $2,000/year (organization/company).

Meetings/Conferences:
Annual Meetings: Semi-Annual/April and November
1999 – Washington, DC(Mayflower)/Oct. 6-8

Ethylene Oxide Industry Council
Historical Note
A program of the Chemical Manufacturers Ass'n.

Ethylene Oxide Sterilization Ass'n *(1995)*
1815 H St., N.W., Suite 500
Washington, DC   20006-3604
Tel: (202)296-6300   *Fax:* (202)775-5929
Members: 46 companies
Staff: 3
Annual Budget: $100-250,000
General Counsel: Joseph E. Hadley, Jr.

Historical Note
Members are companies in the medical and scientific instruments industries. Membership fee varies, based on sales: $195-1,475/year.

Meetings/Conferences:
Three Meetings Annually: usually in conjunction with AAMI

EUCG
710 E. Ogden Ave., Suite 600
Naperville, IL   60563
Tel: (630)369-0609   *Fax:* (630)369-2488
Members: 80 companies
Staff: 3
Annual Budget: $100-250,000
Exec. Director: Ann E. Spehar

Historical Note
Founded as Electric Utility Cost Group. Assumed its current name in 1996. Membership: $950-5,300/year.

Meetings/Conferences:

European-American Business Council *(1989)*
1333 H St., N.W., Suite 630
Washington, DC   20005
Tel: (202)347-9292   *Fax:* (202)628-5498
E-Mail: eabc@eabc.org
Web Site: http://www.eabc.org
Members: 80 companies
Staff: 6
Annual Budget: $500-1,000,000
President: Willard M. Berry
Manager, Government Relations: Chris Mustain
Govt. Affairs Representative: Jeffrey Werner
Manager, Business and Finance: Agnes Mannarelli

Historical Note
Formerly (1992) the European Community Chamber of Commerce in the United States and (1997) the European-American Chamber of Commerce. EABC members are European and American companies concerned with U.S. and European political activity affecting transatlantic trade. Membership: $10,000/year.

Publications:
Abstracts. w.
Jobs, Trade & Investment. a.
Official Journal. semi-a.

Meetings/Conferences:

European-American Chamber of Commerce *(1989)*
Historical Note
Became the European-American Business Council in 1997.

Evangelical Christian Publishers Ass'n *(1974)*
1969 E. Broadway Road, Suite 2
Tempe, AZ   85282
Tel: (602)966-3998   *Fax:* (602)966-1944
E-Mail: dross@ecpa.org
Web Site: http://www.ecpa.org
Members: 207 companies
Staff: 6
Annual Budget: $500-1,000,000
President and C.E.O.: Douglas Ross
Dir., Operations and Events: Sandy Ross
Manager, Membership Services: Jo Meegan

Historical Note
ECPA is an international, non-profit trade organization serving its industry by promoting excellence and professionalism, sharing relevant data, stimulating Christian fellowship, raising the effectiveness of member houses, and equipping them to meet the need of the changing marketplace. Membership: $1,200-$6,000/year.

Publications:
Footprints.

Meetings/Conferences:
Semi-Annual Meetings: April-May and October-November
1999 – Palm Springs, CA/Nov. 6-10
1999 – West Coast U.S./April 24-28
2000 – Scottsdale, AZ/April 22-26
2000 – New York Area/Nov. 4-8
2001 – Hilton Head Island, SC/April 28-May 2

Evangelical Church Library Ass'n *(1970)*
P.O. Box 353
Glen Ellyn, IL   60138-0353
Toll Free: (800)223 - 0001
E-Mail: eclalib@aol.com
Web Site: http://members.aol.com./ECLASSOC/index.html
Members: 350 individuals
Staff: 1
Annual Budget: $10-25,000
President: Mary Bechtel

Historical Note
Established to assist churches in setting up and maintaining library resource centers. Membership: $25-28/year (individual); $75/year (publishers).

Publications:
Church Libraries. q. adv.

Meetings/Conferences:
Annual Meetings: Yearly-Wheaton, IL(Wheaton Bible Church)/October/150-200

Evangelical Press Ass'n *(1948)*
314 Dover Rd.
Charlottesville, VA   22901-1014
Tel: (804)973-5941   *Fax:* (804)973-2710
E-Mail: 74463.272@compuserve.com
Web Site: http://www.epassoc.org
Members: 375 individuals
Staff: 2
Annual Budget: $100-250,000
Exec. Director: Ronald Wilson

Historical Note
EPA is a fellowship of more than 300 Christian magazines, newspapers, and newsletters, including editors and publishers. Membership: $60/year (individual); $120-$325/year (organization).

Publications:
Liaison. bi-m.
Membership Directory. a. adv.

Meetings/Conferences:
Annual Meetings: May
1999 – Orlando, FL(Sheraton World Resort)/May 2-5/300
2000 – Nashville, TN
2001 – San Diego, CA

Evangelical Training Ass'n *(1930)*
110 Bridge St., Box 327
Wheaton, IL   60189-0327
Tel: (630)668-6400   *Fax:* (630)668-8437
Toll Free: (800)369 - 8291
E-Mail: EVTRAIN@aol.com
Web Site: http://www.ETAWorld.org
Members: 200 colleges and seminaries
Staff: 13
Annual Budget: $250-500,000
President: Jonathan Thigpen
Financial Services Manager: Brenda Dumper
Director of Educational Ministries: Yvonne E. Thigpen

Historical Note
Active member seminaries and colleges present courses using ETA materials to prepare students for professional church leadership and to train church volunteers. These courses lead to the Associate Teacher Diploma, the Standard Teacher Diploma or the Graduate Teacher Diploma. Formerly (1990) Evangelical Teacher Training Ass'n. Membership: $100/year (organization).

Publications:
Journal of Adult Training. 2/year.
Profile. q.

Meetings/Conferences:
Biennial Meetings: Odd years in February

Evaporative Cooling Institute *(1989)*
P.O. Box 3ECI
Las Cruces, NM   88003-8001
Tel: (505)646-4104   *Fax:* (505)646-2960
E-Mail: eci@solar.nmn.edu
Web Site: http://www.solar.nmsu.edu/eci/
Members: 60 companies
Annual Budget: under $10,000
Exec. Officer: Robert Foster

Historical Note
Promotes research in and applications of evaporative air conditioning. Membership: $60/year (individual); $300/year (organization).

Publications:
Cool Air News. a. adv.
Membership Services Directory. a. adv.

Meetings/Conferences:
1999 – Chicago, IL
1999 – Seattle, WA
2000 – Dallas, TX
2000 – Minneapolis, MN
2001 – Atlanta, GA
2001 – Cincinnati, OH

Evidence Photographers Internat'l Council *(1968)*
600 Main St.
Honesdale, PA   18431
Tel: (717)253-5450   *Fax:* (717)253-5011
Toll Free: (800)356 - 3742
Web Site: http://www.epic-photo.org
Members: 2,000 individuals
Staff: 5
Annual Budget: $500-1,000,000
President: Robert Jennings

Historical Note
EPIC is a non-profit educational and scientific organization dedicated to the advancement of forensic photography in civil evidence and law enforcement. Membership: $75/year.

Publications:
Journal of Evidence Photography. semi-a. adv.
Newsletter. q.

Meetings/Conferences:
1999 – California(School of Evidence Photography)

Executive Suite Ass'n *(1986)*
438 E. Wilson Bridge Road, Suite 200
Columbus, OH   43085-2382
Tel: (614)431-8295   *Fax:* (614)431-8258
Toll Free: (800)237 - 4741
E-Mail: ESACentral@aol.com
Web Site: http://www.execsuites.org
Members: 640 companies
Staff: 4
Annual Budget: $250-500,000
Exec. Director: Jeanine Windbigler
Director, Member Services: Lisa Pearce

Historical Note
Formerly (1993) Executive Suite Network, ESA is a member-owned trade association for owners and operators of executive suite businesses. ESA provides professional development, continuing education and coordinated office reservation services to its members. Membership: $395/year.

Publications:
ESA World. m.

Meetings/Conferences:
1999 – Phoenix, AZ(Hilton)/Sept. 22-25
2000 – Orlando, FL(Hilton)/Sept. 20-23

Executive Women Internat'l *(1938)*
515 South 700 East, Suite 2-E
Salt Lake City, UT   84102-2801
Tel: (801)355-2800   *Fax:* (801)355-2852
E-Mail: ewi@executivewomen.org
Web Site: www.executivewomen.org
Members: 6,000 individuals
Staff: 5
Annual Budget: $500-1,000,000
Business Manager: Rose Defa
Marketing/Meeting Planning Specialist: Vanessa Elias

Historical Note
Formerly (until 1978) Executives' Secretaries, Inc. Members are firms, each of which is represented by individuals engaged in executive and administrative positions. EWI provides an environment for the promotion of member firms, the enhancement of personal and professional development, and the encouragement of community involvement. Membership is by invitation only and through company representation.

Publications:
Pulse. q. adv.

Meetings/Conferences:
Annual Meetings: September
1999 – Cleveland, OH
2000 – Calgary, Alberta

Exercise-Safety Ass'n *(1978)*
10151 University Blvd., Suite 138
Orlando, FL   32817-1981
Tel: (330)995-5161   *Fax:* (330)995-5160
Members: 20,000 individuals
Staff: 5
Director: Carol Wagner

Historical Note
ESA is a professional training organization, providing safety training and certification for fitness instructors and health facilities. Membership: $25/year.

Publications:
ESA Catalogue Directory. a. adv.
ESA News Newsletter. q. adv.

Exhibit Designers and Producers Ass'n *(1954)*
5775 Peachtree-Dunwoody Road, N.E.
Suite 500-G
Atlanta, GA   30342-1507
Tel: (404)303-7310   *Fax:* (404)252-0774
Members: 265 companies
Staff: 2
Annual Budget: $250-500,000
Exec. Director: Mike Levin

Historical Note
Designers and builders of displays for exhibits and trade shows. Sets standards for creators of exhibits and promotes education in the use of three-dimensional media. Member of the Center for Exposition Industry Research.

Publications:
EDPA ActionNews. bi-m.
Membership Directory. a. adv.

Meetings/Conferences:
Annual Meetings: December/150

Exhibition Validation Council *(1981)*

Historical Note
Established by the Center for Exhibition Industry Research to develop a standardized form for reporting attendance and other data from trade shows, and to act as a clearinghouse where information on trade shows can be registered. A subsidiary of the Center for Exhibition Industry Research.

Exotic Wildlife Ass'n *(1967)*
P.O. Box 705
Ingram, TX   78025-0705
Tel: (830)895-4997   *Fax:* (830)895-4998
E-Mail: ewa@hilconet.com
Web Site: http://www.hilconet.com/~ewa
Members: 500 individuals
Staff: 2
Annual Budget: $100-250,000
Exec. Director: Ike Sugg

Historical Note
Membership: $100/year (individual).

Publications:
The Fence Line. bi-m. adv.

Meetings/Conferences:
1999 – Kerrville, TX(Holiday Inn)/March 18-21

Expanded Shale, Clay and Slate Institute *(1952)*
2225 E. Murray Holladay Road, Suite 102
Salt Lake City, UT   84117
Tel: (801)272-7070   *Fax:* (801)272-3377
E-Mail: escsi@consuper.net
Web Site: http://www.concreteworld.com/ecsci
Members: 50 companies
Staff: 2
Annual Budget: $250-500,000 .
Exec. Director: John P. Ries, P.E.
Administrator: Cerise Llewelyn

Historical Note
Founded as the Expanded Shale Institute, it assumed its present name in 1955. Members are manufacturers of rotary kiln produced expanded shale, clay and slate lightweight aggregate. ESCSI promotes the extensive use of rotary kiln produced lightweight aggregate in the concrete masonry, ready-mix and precast markets. Based on research and development, educational material is disseminated to all phases of the building industry. The ass'n works closely with other technical organizations to maintain product quality, life-safety and professional integrity throughout the construction industry and related building code bodies.

Publications:
Information Sheets. irreg.

Meetings/Conferences:
Annual Meetings: October
1999 – Boston, MA/60

Expansion Joint Manufacturers Ass'n *(1954)*
25 N. Broadway
Tarrytown, NY   10591-3201
Tel: (914)332-0040   *Fax:* (914)332-1541
Members: 9 companies
Staff: 2
Annual Budget: $10-25,000
Secretary: Richard C. Byrne

Historical Note
EIMA's Technical Committee prepares industry standards. Cooperates with ASME in the development of engineering standards for metallic expansion joints for use in piping systems.

Expediting Management Ass'n *(1975)*
18 S. Bertrand Road
Mount Arlington, NJ   07856
Tel: (973)398-6616   *Fax:* (973)770-2423
E-Mail: Expediterhjkeworldnet.atl.net
Web Site: http://www.expedite.org/
Members: 200 companies
Annual Budget: $10-25,000
Exec. Administrator: Harry J. Kelly, CEM

Historical Note
Established in Greenwich, Connecticut and incorporated in Texas, EMA members are individuals actively engaged in managerial or supervisory positions in the profession of expediting. Membership: $90/year (individual).

Publications:
EMAnator. q. adv.
Expediter Training Manual.
Expeditors Checklist Handbook.
Managers Handbook.

Meetings/Conferences:
Annual Meetings: September
1999 – Washington, DC

Explosive Distributors Ass'n *(1971)*

Historical Note
Organization reported defunct in 1996

Export Processing Industry Coalition

Historical Note
Defunct in 1997.

Exposition Service Contractors Ass'n *(1970)*
400 S. Houston St., Suite 210
Dallas, TX   75202
Tel: (214)742-9217   *Fax:* (214)741-2519
Members: 150 firms
Annual Budget: $100-250,000
Exec. Director: E. Dan Dobson

Historical Note
Members are full-service general exposition contractors, as well as specialty firms to the exposition service industry such as security, audio-visual, electrical and floral companies. Member of the Trade Show Bureau. Has no paid officers or full-time staff. Membership: $500-700/year.

Publications:
Annual Guide to Exposition Service. a. adv.
ESCA Voice Newsletter. q. adv.

Meetings/Conferences:
Semi-Annual Meeting: December, with Internat'l Ass'n for
    Exposition Management, and Summer Educational
    Conference
1999 – San Diego, CA

Express Carriers Ass'n *(1991)*
P.O. Box 4307
Bethlehem, PA   18018
Tel: (610)740-5857   *Fax:* (610)740-3174
Members: 70 companies
Staff: 2
Annual Budget: $50-100,000
Exec. Director: Cheryle Williamson

Historical Note
A national association of shippers, carriers and vendors of products and services of the transportation industry. Membership: $520/year (organization).

Publications:
Quarterly Newsletter Expressions. q.
Service Directory. a. adv.

Meetings/Conferences:

Eye Bank Ass'n of America *(1961)*
1001 Connecticut Ave., Suite 601
Washington, DC   20036-5504
Tel: (202)775-4999   *Fax:* (202)429-6036
Members: 112 eye banks
Staff: 8
Annual Budget: $1-2,000,000
President: Patricia Aiken-O'Neill
Development Officer, Meetings and Marketing: Gail Reggio
Manager, Finance: Dorothy Robinson

Historical Note
Established in 1961 by the Committee on Eye Banks of the American Academy of Ophthalmology to obtain, medically screen and deliver donor eyes to surgeons for corneal transplantation, and to research centers to aid in the discovery of the causes and cures of many types of blindness. EBAA represents eye banks nationwide and internationally.

Publications:
Insight. 8/year.
Membership Directory. a.

Meetings/Conferences:
1999 – Newport Beach, CA/June 23-26

Fabric Salesmen's Ass'n *(1982)*
McAlpin House
50 West 34th St., Suite 17A8
New York, NY   10001
Tel: (212)594-4283   *Fax:* (212)594-4284
Members: 375 individuals
Staff: 2
Annual Budget: $50-100,000
President: Chester Blyn

Historical Note
Membership concentrated in New York City area. Formerly (1982) the Piece Goods Salesmen's Ass'n and the Fabric Salesmen's Guild, the FSA is a fraternal organization dedicated to the betterment of the textile and wearing appearel industries and the New York City Garment District. Membership: $50/year.

Publications:
Newsletter. m.
The Fabric Salesman. a. adv.

Meetings/Conferences:

Fabricators and Manufacturers Ass'n, Internat'l *(1970)*
833 Featherstone Road
Rockford, IL   61107
Tel: (815)877-7633   *Fax:* (815)399-7279
Members: 3,000 individuals
Staff: 66
Annual Budget: $5-10,000,000
President and C.E.O.: John P. Nandzik, CAE
Director, Education: Gary Schott

Director, Membership Conference and Customer Service: Lynn
    Olexy
V. President: Mike Hedges

Historical Note
The primary educational organization serving the metal-forming and fabricating industry. Services focus on providing technical information through publications, conferences and seminars, expositions, newsletters and the Technical Information Center to companies and individuals involved in sheet metal fabricating, presswork, roll forming, coil processing, plate and structural fabricating. Formerly known as the Fabricating Machinery Ass'n, it became the Fabricating Manufacturers Ass'n in 1975 and assumed its present name in 1985. Has an annual budget of $5.3 million. Membership: $95-795/year (based on company size).

Publications:
Discover FMA. bi-m.
FMA Member Directory. a.
Radius Newsletter. 6/year.
Stamping Journal. 6/year.
The Fabricator. 12/year. adv.
TPJ, The Tube & Pipe Journal. 6/year.

Meetings/Conferences:

Family and Consumer Science Education Ass'n *(1927)*
Central Washington Univ.
Family/Consumer Sci., 400 E. 8th Ave.
Ellensburg, WA   98926-7565
Tel: (509)963-2766   *Fax:* (509)963-2787
E-Mail: bowersj@cwu.edu
Web Site: http://ww.cwu.edu/~fandcs/fcsea/
Members: 1000 individuals
Staff: 2
Annual Budget: $50-100,000
Exec. Director: Jan Bowers, Ph.D.

Historical Note
Established as Dept. of Supervisors and Teachers of Home Economics of the Nat'l Education Ass'n, it became the Dept. of Home Economics in 1938, Home Economics Education Ass'n in 1969, and assumed its current name in 1995. It is a nongovernance affiliate of the NEA. Membership: $20/year.

Publications:
Bulletin. semi-a.
Newsletter. semi-a.

Meetings/Conferences:
Semi-annual Meetings: June with American Home Economics
    Ass'n December with American Vocational Ass'n

Family Firm Institute *(1986)*
221 N. Beacon St.
Boston, MA   02135-1943
Tel: (617)789-4200   *Fax:* (617)789-4220
E-Mail: ffi221@msn.com
Web Site: http://www.ffi.org
Members: 1,100 individuals
Staff: 2
Annual Budget: $500-1,000,000
Exec. Director: Judy L. Green

Historical Note
FFI members include practitioners, academics, and other individuals who advise, study, research and consult with family-owned businesses. Provides educational and networking opportunities for individuals and organizations interested in issues pertinent to family-owned business. Membership: $340/year (consultant/advisor); $175/year (educator), $1,200/year (organizational), $60/year (student).

Publications:
Conference Proceedings. a.
Directory of Consultants & Speakers. a.
Family Business Bibliography. a.
Family Business Matters. q.
Family Business Review. q.
FFI Newsletter. q. adv.
Membership Directory. a.

Meetings/Conferences:
Annual Meetings: Fall
1999 – Chicago, IL
2000 – Washington, DC/Oct. 25-28

Family Therapy Network *(1982)*
7705 13th St., N.W.
Washington, DC   20012
Tel: (202)829-2452   *Fax:* (202)726-7983
Members: 65 individuals
Staff: 7
Director: Richard Simon

Publications:
Family Therapy Networker Magazine. bi-m. adv.

Meetings/Conferences:
Annual Meetings: always Washington, DC/Spring

Farm Credit Council *(1983)*
50 F St., N.W., Suite 900
Washington, DC   20001
Tel: (202)626-8710   *Fax:* (202)626-8718
Members: 8 district councils
Staff: 12
Annual Budget: $5-10,000,000
President: William Weber

Historical Note
Represents the Farm Credit System and its 230 local credit association members, who make loans available to agricultural producers, rural homebuyers, farmer cooperatives, and rural utilities.

Publications:
Farm Credit File. q.

Meetings/Conferences:
Annual Meetings: January
1999 – San Antonio, TX/Jan. 18-21

Farm Equipment Council

Historical Note
A council of the Equipment Manufacturers Institute.

Farm Equipment Manufacturers Ass'n *(1950)*
1000 Executive Parkway, Suite 100
St. Louis, MO 63141
Tel: (314)878-2304   *Fax:* (314)878-1742
E-Mail: FEMA@aol.com
Web Site: http://www.farmEquip.org
Members: 750 companies
Staff: 6
Annual Budget: $500-1,000,000
Exec. V. President: Robert K. Schnell
Director, Membership Services: Vernon F. Schmidt
Convention Manager: Chris M. Schulte
Director, Special Projects: Craig Sims

Historical Note
Founded as the Allied Farm Equipment Manufacturers Ass'n, it assumed its present name in 1956. Membership: $235-920/year (company).

Publications:
Shortliner. semi-m.

Meetings/Conferences:
Semi-Annual Meetings: Spring and Fall
1999 – Palm Springs, CA(Doubletree)/March 12-15

Farm Equipment Wholesalers Ass'n *(1945)*
P.O. Box 1347
Iowa City, IA 52244
Tel: (319)354-5156   *Fax:* (319)354-5157
E-Mail: info@fewa.org
Web Site: http://www.fewa.org
Members: 71 companies
Staff: 2
Annual Budget: $100-250,000
Exec. V. President: Patricia Collins
Office Manager: Jane L. Holtz

Historical Note
FEWA is the internat'l trade ass'n of independent wholesale distributors engaged in marketing farm and related power equipment products including light industrial, commercial, irrigation, lawn and garden products. Membership: dues based on a sliding scale.

Publications:
FEWA Cross Index. a
FEWA Membership Directory. a.
TIPS Newsletter. m.

Meetings/Conferences:
Annual Meetings: November
1999 – Houston, TX(Hyatt)/Nov. 7-10
2000 – Reno, NV(Hilton)/Nov. 5-8
2001 – Denver, CO(Adams Mark)/Nov. 4-7

Farmers Educational and Co-operative Union of America *(1902)*
11900 E. Cornell Ave.
Aurora, CO 80014-3194
Tel: (303)337-5500   *Fax:* (303)368-1390
Toll Free: (800)347 - 1961
E-Mail: nfu.denver@nfu.org
Web Site: http://www.nfu.org
Staff: 35
Annual Budget: $1-2,000,000
President: Leland H. Swenson
Communcations Director: Marilyn Wentz
Education Director: Leesa Christensen

Historical Note
Also known as Nat'l Farmers Union, Farmers Union. Maintains a Washington Office. Members are farm families throughout the nation united for legislative, cooperative and educational purposes.

Publications:
National Farmers Union News. m.

Meetings/Conferences:
Annual Meetings: 1,200-1,500
1999 – Springfield, IL/March 5-8
2000 – Salt Lake City, UT/Feb. 25-28

Farmstead Equipment Ass'n Council *(1945)*

Historical Note
Merger (1967) of Barn Cleaner, Cattle Feeder, Silo Unloader Ass'n and Barn Equipment Ass'n. A council of the Equipment Manufacturers Institute.

Fashion Accessories Shippers Ass'n
330 5th Ave., Suite 205
New York, NY 10001
Tel: (212)947-3424   *Fax:* (212)629-0361
Web Site: http://www.accessoryweb.com
Members: 100 companies
Staff: 5
Exec. Director: Harold Sachs

Meetings/Conferences:
1999 – New York, NY

Fashion Ass'n, The *(1955)*
475 Park Ave. South, 9th floor
New York, NY 10016
Tel: (212)683-5665   *Fax:* (212)545-1709
Members: 400 companies
Staff: 8
Annual Budget: $1-2,000,000
Exec. Director: Eric Hertz
Fashion Marketing Director: Elena Hart
Convention Services Director: Mina K. Henry
Comptroller: Nina Gerbakher
Account Executive: Tiffany Ellzy

Associate Creative Director: Zena J. Zahran

Historical Note
Founded as the American Institute of Men's and Boy's Wear, it became the Men's Fashion Ass'n of America in 1970, and assumed its present name in 1993. TFA serves as a public relations and marketing arm of the men's, women's, and childrens fashion industry. In addition to fashion TFA offers information about style and lifestyle. Membership varies.

Publications:
Fahion Press Releases. bi-w.
Membership Information.

Meetings/Conferences:
Annual Meetings: TFA hosts the Aldo Awards for Fashion Journalism, The American Image Awards, and Men's and Women's Fashion Trend seminars/shows 2x/year.

Fashion Group Internat'l *(1931)*
597 Fifth Ave.
New York, NY 10017
Tel: (212)593-1715   *Fax:* (212)593-1925
E-Mail: info@fgi.org
Web Site: http://www.fgi.org
Members: 6,000 individuals
Staff: 8
Annual Budget: $1-2,000,000
President: Margaret Hayes
Director of Regional Services: Gloria Ingrassia
Legal Counsel: Kay S. Hadley
Director of Membership: Trish Maffei

Historical Note
Members are women executives with a minimum of three years experience representing all facets of the fashion industry including manufacturing, marketing, designing, retailing communications and education. Includes 30 U.S. chapters and 11 chapters overseas. Membership: $100-$150/year.

Publications:
Fashion Trend Report. 4-6/year.
Membership Directory. a. adv.
The 'FGI' Newsletter. bi-m.

Meetings/Conferences:
Annual Meetings: New York, NY/December
1999 – New York, NY

Fashion Jewelry Ass'n of America *(1985)*
3 Davol Sq., Unit 177
Providence, RI 02903
Tel: (401)331-7630   *Fax:* (401)521-7488
Web Site: http://unitedjewelryshow.com
Members: 200 individuals
Staff: 1
Annual Budget: $10-25,000
Office Secretary: Barbara McCaffrey

Historical Note
Founded as the Manufacturing Jewelers Sales Ass'n in 1952; assumed its present name in 1985. Membership: $125/year.

Meetings/Conferences:
Quarterly Trade Shows: usually Providence, RI

Fastener Industry Coalition
1717 E. 9th St., Suite 1185
Cleveland, OH 44114
Tel: (216)579-1571   *Fax:* (216)579-1531
Members: 9 associations
Annual Budget: under $10,000
Secretariat: Dave Merrifield

Historical Note
A coalition of regional and national fastener associations. Has no paid officers or full-time staff.

Meetings/Conferences:

FCIB-NACM Corp. *(1919)*
Koll Corp. Plaza
485-A Rte. One South, Suite 100
Iselin, NJ 08830-3009
Tel: (732)283-8606   *Fax:* (732)283-8613
E-Mail: fcib_info@nacm.org
Web Site: http://www.fcibnacm.com
Members: 748 companies & institutions
Staff: 6
Annual Budget: $1-2,000,000
President and C.O.O.: Leonard J. Satkowski, CCE

Historical Note
A subsidiary of the Nat'l Ass'n of Credit Management. Formerly (1967) the Foreign Credit Interchange Bureau. Membership: $840/year (corporate).

Publications:
Country Credit Reports. on demand.
Credit and Collection Survey. q.
FCIB Bulletin. m.
FCIB Minutes of Round Table Conference. m.

Meetings/Conferences:
Annual Meetings: European Meetings - 3/year in various cities;
   North American Meetings - 5/year in various cities
   and 5/year in New York, NY
1999 – New York, NY(Hilton Towers)/200

Feather and Down Ass'n *(1964)*

Historical Note
Merged with American Down Ass'n in 1997.

Federal Administrative Law Judges Conference *(1947)*
2000 Pennsylvania Ave., N.W., Suite 263
Washington, DC 20006
Tel: (202)675-3065   *Fax:* (703)569-2515
Members: 360 individuals
Annual Budget: $10-25,000
Exec. Manager: Joel M. Paul

Historical Note
Formerly (1973) Federal Trial Examiners Conference. Members are judges who preside at administrative hearings within federal agencies. Has no permanent staff. Officers are elected annually. Membership: $65/year.

Publications:
Directory. a.
Newsletter. q.

Meetings/Conferences:
Annual Meetings: September

Federal Bar Ass'n *(1920)*
2215 M. St., N.W.
Washington, DC 20037
Tel: (202)785-1614   *Fax:* (202)785-1568
E-Mail: FBA@FEDBAR.ORG
Web Site: http://www.fedbar.org
Members: 15,000 individuals
Staff: 20
Annual Budget: $1-2,000,000
Exec. Director: Michael E. Campiglia
Dep. Exec. Director: Lee Ann Chrostowski

Historical Note
Members are attorneys currently or formerly employed by the Federal Government or who have a substantial interest in federal law as evidenced by admission to practice before a federal court or agency. Membership: $86/year (attorneys admitted to first bar five or more years); $44/year (retired attorneys or those admitted to first bar less than five years); $11/year (law student), plus section/committee dues where applicable.

Publications:
Job Placement Bulletin Board. m.
The Federal Lawyer. 10/year. adv.

Meetings/Conferences:
Annual Meetings: Summer
1999 – Sacramento, CA
2000 – Cleveland, OH/Sept. 19-24/250

Federal Bureau of Investigation Agents Ass'n *(1981)*
P.O. Box 250
New Rochelle, NY 10801
Tel: (914)235-7580   *Fax:* (914)235-8235
Members: 8,500 individuals
Staff: 2
President: John J. Sennett

Historical Note
Membership: $78/year; $26/year (retired or associate).

Publications:
Newsletter. 3/year.

Meetings/Conferences:
Biennial Meetings: (1997)

Federal Communications Bar Ass'n *(1936)*
1722 I St., N.W., Suite 300
Washington, DC 20006-3705
Tel: (202)736-8640   *Fax:* (202)736-8740
E-Mail: fcba@fcba.org
Web Site: www.fcba.org
Members: 3,300 individuals
Staff: 3
Annual Budget: $500-1,000,000
Exec. Director: Paula G. Friedman

Historical Note
FCBA members are involved in the development, interpretation, implementation and practice of communications law and policy. Voting members are members in good standing of the Bar of any state and who are (a) eligible to practice before an agency of government or (b) employees of an agency of the government. Non-voting membership is available to professionals in allied fields, including engineers, consultants, economists, government relations officials, foreign lawyers and law students at accredited law schools. Membership: $100/year (individual).

Publications:
FCBA Directory. a.
FCBA News. m.
Federal Communications Law Journal. q.
Internat'l Telecommunications Practice Handbook.

Meetings/Conferences:
Annual Meetings: May, usually in mid-Atlantic region
1999 – Hershey, PA(Hershey Resort)/May 7-9

Federal Education Ass'n *(1956)*
1101 15th St., N.W., Suite 1002
Washington, DC 20005
Tel: (202)822-7850   *Fax:* (202)822-7867
Web Site: http://www.feaonline.org
Members: 5,500 individuals
Staff: 10
Annual Budget: $500-1,000,000
Exec. Director: H.T. Nguyen

Historical Note
Formerly Overseas Education Ass'n (1996). A Federal labor union affiliated with the Nat'l Education Ass'n, FEA represents teachers on overseas and stateside military bases. Membership: $300/year.

Publications:
Journal. q.

Meetings/Conferences:
Annual Meetings: July

Federal Energy Bar Ass'n *(1946)*
1350 Connecticut Ave., N.W., Suite 300
Washington, DC 20036
Tel: (202)223-5625   *Fax:* (202)833-5596
Members: 1,800 individuals
Staff: 1
Annual Budget: $250-500,000
Administrator: Lorna Johnston Wilson

Historical Note
Lawyers engaged in promoting proper administration of federal laws relating to the production, development, conservation, transmission, and economic regulation of energy. Formerly (1977) the Federal Power Bar Ass'n. Membership: $80/year (private practitioner); $20/year (gov't/academic/student).

Publications:
Court-Related Opinions.
Directory. a.
Energy Law Journal. semi-a. adv.

Meetings/Conferences:
Annual Meetings: Semi-Annual, held in May and November
1999 – Washington, DC(Capitol Hilton)

Federal Facilities Council *(1952)*
c/o Nat'l Research Council
2101 Constitution Ave., N.W. (HA 274)
Washington, DC 20418
Tel: (202)334-3378 *Fax:* (202)334-3370
Members: 130 individuals, 18 agencies
Staff: 2
Annual Budget: $500-1,000,000
Director: Lynda Stanley

Historical Note
Formerly (1994) Federal Construction Council. Members are professional employees of federal agencies and members of the Board on Infrastructure and the Constructed Environment of the Nat'l Research Council. Encourages cooperation among the sponsoring federal agencies. Sponsors six standing committees composed of federal agency employees and private-sector liaisons.

Federal Investigators Ass'n *(1953)*

Historical Note
Information could not be confirmed.

Federal Judges Ass'n *(1982)*
111 W. Washington St., Suite 1100
Chicago, IL 60602
Tel: (312)641-1441 *Fax:* (312)641-1128
Contact: Kevin M. Forde

Historical Note
Formed "to seek the highest quality of justice for the people of the United States," the Association seeks to preserve the ability of the federal judiciary to attract and retain the best qualified people for judicial service and to preserve the independence of the judiciary from intrusion, intimidation, coercion or domination from any source. At the outset, the overriding focus was for increased compensation for members of the federal judiciary, but other issues such as survivors' benefits, travel reimbursement and health coverage have also been crucial. Membership: $200/year (individual).

Publications:
In Camera. q.

Federal Law Enforcement Officers Ass'n *(1978)*
P.O. Box 508
East Northport, NY 11731-0472
Tel: (516)368-6117 *Fax:* (516)368-6429
E-Mail: fleoa@juno.com
Web Site: http://www.fleoa.com
Members: 14,500 individuals
Staff: 2
Annual Budget: $500-1,000,000
Corporate Services Director: Josephine Klein

Historical Note
FLEOA represents roughly 35% of all the men and women in Federal law enforcement as law enforcement officers and criminal investigators. Retired Federal officers, resigned officers, and other interested people are also members. Membership: $75/year (regular), $30/year (retiree, resignee), $40/year(associate).

Publications:
FLEOA Newlettter. m.

Meetings/Conferences:

Federal Librarians Roundtable *(1972)*
c/o American Library Ass'n, Wash. Ofc.
1301 Pennsylvania Ave., N.W., Suite 403
Washington, DC 20004
Tel: (202)628-8410 *Fax:* (202)628-8419
Members: 550 individuals
Staff: 1
Annual Budget: under $10,000
Staff Liaison: Patricia Muir

Historical Note
An affiliate of the American Library Ass'n. A Round Table is a membership unit established to promote a field of librarianship not within the scope of any single division of the ALA. Individuals may join the FLRT after first joining the ALA. Membership: $12/year (individual); $20/year (institution).

Publications:
The Federal Librarian. q. adv.

Meetings/Conferences:
Annual Meetings: in conjunction with the American Library Ass'n
1999 – New Orleans, LA/June 24-July 1
2000 – Chicago, IL/July 6-13

Federal Managers Ass'n *(1913)*
1641 Prince St.
Alexandria, VA 22314-2818
Tel: (703)683-8700 *Fax:* (703)683-8707
E-Mail: fma@ix.netcom
Members: 15,000 individuals
Staff: 6
Annual Budget: $1-2,000,000
Chief Operations Officer: Frances Webb
Legislative Director: Mark Gable
Dir., Administration: Kate DiBitetto

Historical Note
Organized in 1913 in Washington, DC as the Nat'l Ass'n of Supervisors, with members solely from the U.S. Navy. Disbanded in 1922, but was reactivated in 1933. In 1950, the ass'n became the Nat'l Ass'n of Supervisors, Department of Defense; in 1968 became the Nat'l Ass'n of Supervisors, Federal Government; and in 1979 assumed its present name. Membership includes managers and supervisors in all federal agencies. Membership: $52/year.

Publications:
The Federal Manager. q. adv.
The Washington Report. bi-w.

Meetings/Conferences:
1999 – Vienna, VA(Sheraton Premiere)/March 17-24/225

Federal Physicians Ass'n *(1979)*
P.O. Box 45150
Washington, DC 20026-5150
Tel: (703)455-5947 *Fax:* (703)455-8282
Toll Free: (800)403 - 3374
E-Mail: fedphy@aol.com
Web Site: www.fedphy.org
Members: 500 individuals
Staff: 1
Annual Budget: $25-50,000
Exec. Director: Dennis W. Boyd, & 1

Historical Note
Founded by a group of physicians concerned with the worsening situation of the physician in federal government employment, FPA has focused it efforts on ensuring that highly qualifed doctors will continue to consider federal employement both rewarding and desirable. A key component of FPA's program has been promotion of the Physician's Comparability Allowance, an annual bonus granted to physicians in various capacities among the various U.S. government agencies. FPA is a member of the Public Employees Roundtable. Membership: $75/year (individual).

Publications:
Federal Physician. bi-m.

Meetings/Conferences:
Annual Meetings: Fall

Federal Probation and Pre-trial Officers Ass'n *(1955)*

Historical Note
Address unknown in 1996.

Federal Water Quality Ass'n *(1941)*
P.O. Box 44163
Washington, DC 20026
Tel: (202)260-5827 *Fax:* (202)260-0116
Members: 300 individuals
Annual Budget: under $10,000
President: Karen Waldvogel

Historical Note
Formerly the Federal Sewage Research Ass'n; now affiliated with the Water Environment Federation. Membership consists of federal employees, consultants, industry and association representatives concerned with sewage/industrial waste treatment and disposal, non-point source pollution, water quality, and other environmental concerns. 80% of members are in the Washington area. Membership: $12/year (WEF members); $15/year (non-WEF members). Has no paid staff.

Publications:
FWQA Newsletter. 6-8/year.

Federally Employed Women *(1968)*
1400 I St., N.W., Suite 425
Washington, DC 20005
Tel: (202)898-0994 *Fax:* (202)898-0998
E-Mail: fewinc@the-hermes.net
Web Site: http://www.few.org
Members: 360 chapters
Staff: 5
Annual Budget: $500-1,000,000
Exec. Director: Alma Esparza

Historical Note
Most members are employees of the Federal government. The association's goal to end sex discrimination and increase job opportunities for women in government service. Membership: $20/year (national dues, plus regional and chapter dues); $30/year (member-at-large).

Publications:
FEW News and Views. bi-m. adv.

Meetings/Conferences:
Annual Meetings: July
1999 – Phoenix, AZ

Federated Ambulatory Surgery Ass'n *(1974)*
700 N. Fairfax St., Suite 306
Alexandria, VA 22314-2040
Tel: (703)836-8808
Web Site: http://www.fasa.org
Members: 3,594 individuals, 803 facilities, 54 companies
Staff: 3
Annual Budget: $500-1,000,000
Exec. Director: Kathy Bryant

Historical Note
First incorporated in Arizona in 1974 as the Society for the Advancement of Freestanding Ambulatory Surgical Care, became the Freestanding Ambulatory Surgery Ass'n in 1984 and assumed its present name in 1986. Membership: $250/year (individual), $500-2,000/year (facility), $ $500/year (auxiliary).

Publications:
FASA Update. bi-m.

Meetings/Conferences:
Annual Meetings: Spring/600
1999 – Orlando, FL/May 13-15

Federated Pecan Growers' Ass'ns of the U.S.

Historical Note
Became Nat'l Pecan Growers Council in 1995.

Federation of American Controlled Shipping *(1958)*

Historical Note
Organization defunct in 1997.

Federation of American Health Systems *(1966)*
1111 19th St., N.W., Suite 402
Washington, DC 20036
Tel: (202)833-3090 *Fax:* (202)861-0063
Web Site: www.fahs.com
Members: 1,400 hospital & health care systems
Staff: 26
Annual Budget: $5-10,000,000
President: Thomas A. Scully
Senior V. President, Communications and Administration: W. Campbell Thomson
V. President, Communications: Lauren Maddox
Exec. V. President and C.O.O.: Laura Ison Thevenot

Historical Note
Formerly (1986) the Federation of American Hospitals. Originally an association of investor-owned hospitals, FAHS members now include a broad range of health-care delivery systems. Sponsors the Federation of American Hospitals Political Action Committee (FedPAC).

Publications:
Annual Report. a.
Directory. a.
Hospital Outlook. m.
State-to-State. m.

Meetings/Conferences:
Annual Meetings: Spring/1800
1999 – Orlando, FL/April 19-21

Federation of American Scientists *(1945)*
307 Massachusetts Ave., N.E.
Washington, DC 20002
Tel: (202)546-3300 *Fax:* (202)675-1010
E-Mail: fas@fas.org
Web Site: http://www.fas.org
Members: 3,000 individuals
Staff: 10
Annual Budget: $500-1,000,000
President: Jeremy J. Stone

Historical Note
Engages in research and advocacy on science-and-society issues, especially global security. Works to help insure humanitarian use of atomic energy, a rational national defense and the human rights of scientists around the world. Membership: $15/year (student); $25/year (individual); $75/year(supporting member).

Publications:
Arms Sales Monitor. bi-m.
FAS Public Interest Report. bi-m.
Secrecy & Government Bulletin. m.

Meetings/Conferences:
Annual Meetings: December

Federation of American Socs. for Experimental Biology *(1912)*
9650 Rockville Pike
Bethesda, MD 20814-3998
Tel: (301)530-7090 *Fax:* (301)530-7049
E-Mail: mjackson@execofc.faseb.org
Web Site: http://www.faseb.org
Members: 11 member societies
Staff: 110
Annual Budget: $10-25,000,000
Exec. Director: Dr. Michael J. Jackson
Dir., Communications: Edward P. Rekas
Dir., Public Affairs: Dr. Howard H. Garrison
Dir., Meetings/Conferences: Geri Swindle
Comptroller: John Rice

Historical Note
In 1912 the American Physiological Soc., the American Soc. of Biological Chemists and the American Soc. of Pharmacology and Expermental Therapeutics formed the Federation of American Societies for Experimental Biology (FASEB). The Federation was joined by the American Soc. of Experimental Pathology (now known as American Ass'n for Investigative Pathology) in 1913, the American Institute of Nutrition in 1940, the American Ass'n of Immunologists in 1942, the American Soc. for Cell Biology and the Biophysical Soc. in 1991, the American Ass'n of Anatomists in 1993, and The Protein Soc. in 1995. Incorporated in the District of Columbia in 1954. Has an annual budget of approximately $16 million.

Publications:
FASEB Directory. a. adv.
FASEB Journal. m. adv.
FASEB Newsletter. m. adv.

Federation of Analytical Chemistry and Spectroscopy Societies *(1972)*
1201 Don Diego Ave.
Santa Fe, NM 87505-4115
Tel: (505)820-1648 *Fax:* (505)989-1073
E-Mail: professional_assn_management@compuserve.com
Web Site: http://www.facss.org.info.html
Members: 7 organizations
Staff: 2
Annual Budget: $100-250,000
Administrator: Judith Sjoberg

Historical Note
Members are the analytical division of the American Chemical Soc., the Chromatography Forum of the Delaware Valley, the Coblentz Soc., the Instrument Soc. of America, the Soc. for Applied Spectroscopy, the Ass'n of Analytical Chemists, and the analytical division of the Royal Soc. of Chemistry. Purpose is to provide a

national forum for analytical chemistry through an exhibition and technical papers.

Meetings/Conferences:
Annual Meetings: Fall
1999 – Vancouver, British Columbia/Oct. 24-28

Federation of Ass'ns of Regulatory Boards *(1973)*
P.O. Box 4389
Montgomery, AL 36103
Tel: (334)834-2415   *Fax:* (334)269-6379
Members: 100 individuals, 12 associations
Annual Budget: $50-100,000
Exec. Director: Randolph P. Reaves

Historical Note
Formerly (1985) Federation of Ass'ns of Health Regulatory Boards, the association is now open to any regulated profession. Membership: $75/year (individual); $750/year (association).

Publications:
FARB Facts Newsletter. 3/yr.

Meetings/Conferences:
Annual Meetings: January-February
1999 – Long Beach, CA/Feb. 4-8

Federation of Behavioral, Psychological and Cognitive Sciences *(1980)*
750 First St., N.E., Suite 5007
Washington, DC 20002-4242
Tel: (202)336-5920   *Fax:* (202)336-5953
Members: 18 societies & 118 academic depts.
Staff: 3
Annual Budget: $100-250,000
Exec. Director: Dr. David H. Johnson
Asst. Director: Patrice O'Toole

Historical Note
A coalition of scientific societies and academic departments. Members are research scientists who study behavioral, psychological and cognitive processes and the physiological bases of these processes with an aim to apply their research to health, education and human development. Membership: $11/year per member (societies); $200-$500/year (academic departments).

Publications:
Annual Report. a.
Federation News Newsletter. m.
Science Seminar Public Policy Transcripts. 6/yr.

Meetings/Conferences:
Annual Meetings: always Washington, DC/December

Federation of Diocesan Liturgical Commissions
P.O. Box 29039
Washington, DC 20017-0039
Tel: (202)635-6990
E-Mail: fdlcnatoff@aol.com
Web Site: http://www.fdlc.org
Members: 24 individuals
Staff: 1
Exec. Director: Michael J. Spillane

Historical Note
FDLC is an association of diocesan liturgical commissions in the United States.

Publications:
Pertinent Liturgical Issues. 6/yea.

Meetings/Conferences:
1999 – Cleveland, OH/Oct. 10-14
2000 – /Oct. 3-7

Federation of Environmental Technologists *(1981)*
Historical Note
FET declined to provide updated information for this edition.

Federation of Government Information Processing Councils *(1979)*
3601 Chain Bridge Road, Suite E
Fairfax, VA 22030-3243
Tel: (703)218-1955   *Fax:* (703)218-1960
E-Mail: fgipc@fgipc.org
Web Site: http://www.fgipc.org
Members: 49,000 individuals, 15 organizations
Staff: 4
Annual Budget: $500-1,000,000
Exec. Director: Mary Ann Emely, CAE

Historical Note
FGIPC is the U.S. representative in the Internat'l Council for Information Technology in Government Administration (ICA). Members are information resources management councils as well as professionals at various government positions and levels. FGIPC is parent to the Industry Advisory Council which has 195 corporate members; dues $500-$5,000/year (company).

Publications:
Federation Facts Newsletter. q. adv.
IAC Connector. q.

Meetings/Conferences:
Annual Meetings: Spring-Summer
1999 – Dallas, TX(Sheraton Park Central)/June 21-23

Federation of Insurance and Corporate Counsel *(1936)*
301 Centre Lane, P.O. Box 111
Walpole, MA 02081-0111
Tel: (508)668-6859   *Fax:* (508)668-6892
E-Mail: jolhshan@otw.com
Web Site: http://thefederation.org
Members: 1,283 individuals
Staff: 2
Annual Budget: $500-1,000,000
Exec. Director: Joseph R. Olshan

Historical Note
Founded in 1936 as the Federation of Insurance Counsel; incorporated in Illinois in 1973 and assumed its present name in 1985. Members are lawyers who are actively engaged in the legal aspects of the insurance business, officials and executives of insurance companies, and corporate counsel engaged in defense of claims. Membership: $250/yr.

Publications:
FICC Quarterly. q.

Meetings/Conferences:
Semi-Annual Meetings: Winter and Summer
1999 – San Antonio, TX(Hyatt Regency Hill Country)/Feb. 28-March 7
1999 – Whistler, BC, Canada(Chateau Whistler)/July 25-Aug

Federation of Internat'l Trade Ass'ns *(1985)*
1851 Alexander Bell Drive
Reston, VA 20191
Tel: (703)620-1588   *Fax:* (703)391-0159
Toll Free: (800)969 - 3482
E-Mail: info@fita.org
Web Site: http://www.fita.org
Members: 250 clubs and associations
Staff: 5
Annual Budget: $250-500,000
Chairman: Nelson T. Joyner

Historical Note
FITA's members are world trade clubs and international trade associations located throughout North America.

Publications:
Membership Directory. a.
Newsletter. irreg.

Meetings/Conferences:
Annual Meetings: Not held.

Federation of Materials Socs. *(1972)*
1899 L St., N.W., Suite 500
Washington, DC 20036
Tel: (202)296-9282   *Fax:* (202)833-3014
E-Mail: betsyhou@ix.netcom.com
Web Site: http://www.foms.org
Members: 14 societies
Annual Budget: $50-100,000
Exec. Director: Betsy Houston

Historical Note
Promotes cooperation among societies concerned with the understanding, development and application of materials and processes.

Publications:
FMS Update. w..

Meetings/Conferences:
2000 – Washington, DC(Georgetown University)/May 21-23

Federation of Modern Painters and Sculptors *(1940)*
234 West 21st St.
New York, NY 10011
Tel: (212)255-4858
Members: 51 individuals
Annual Budget: under $10,000
Co-President: Haim Mendelson

Historical Note
Professional painters and sculptors. Purpose is to improve the economic and working conditions of professional artists and facilitate the exhibition of their work. Has no permanent headquarters or paid staff. Membership concentrated in the New York area. Membership: $25/year.

Federation of Nurses and Health Professionals *(1978)*
555 New Jersey Ave., N.W.
Washington, DC 20001
Tel: (202)879-4491   *Fax:* (202)879-4597
Toll Free: (800)238 - 1133
E-Mail: fnhpaft@aft.org
Web Site: http://www.aft.org
Staff: 7
Annual Budget: $2-5,000,000
Director: Mary Lehman MacDonald
Legislative Director: Jerry Morris
Assoc. Director: Janet Bass
In-House Counsel: David J. Strom
Assistant to Pres. for Organizing: Phil Kugler

Historical Note
FNHP, the health care division of the American Federation of Teachers,is a union which organizes and represents a wide spectrum of health care professionals, including registered nurses, LPNs, medical technologists and technicians and school nurses.

Publications:
Healthwire. bi-m.
Stat. q.

Meetings/Conferences:
1999 – New York, NY(New York Hilton)/May 20-23
2000 – Washington, DC

Federation of Organizations for Professional Women *(1972)*
1825 I St., N.W., Suite 400
Washington, DC 20006
Tel: (202)328-1415   *Fax:* (301)949-3459
E-Mail: fopw@dgs.dgsys.com
Members: 30 organizations, 200 associate
Annual Budget: $10-25,000
Exec. Director: Viola Young-Horvath

Historical Note
A federation of affiliated women's organizations to promote equal status for women in all education levels and career fields. Membership: $30/year (individual); $50-200/year (organization).

Publications:
ALERT. bi-m.
On the Line: Professional Woman's Information Network. bien.
Woman's Yellow Directory. bien.

Meetings/Conferences:
Annual Meetings: Always Washington, DC/November-December

Federation of Podiatric Medical Boards *(1936)*
1729 Glastonberry Road
Potomac, MD 20854
Tel: (301)424-1001
Members: 50 states
Staff: 1
Exec. Director: Larry I. Shane

Historical Note
FPMB represents the collective interests of the state licensing boards for podiatric medicine. It is responsible for the administrative aspects of the Podiatric Medical Licensing Examination for STATES (PMLExis), and maintains a file of state board, public record disciplinary findings. Membership fee varies, based on number of state licensees.

Publications:
Directory of State Licensing Examination Information and Directory. a.
Federation News. q. adv.

Meetings/Conferences:

Federation of Socs. for Coatings Technology *(1922)*
492 Norristown Rd.
Blue Bell, PA 19422-2307
Tel: (215)940-0777   *Fax:* (215)940-0292
Web Site: www.coatingstech.org
Members: 7,000 individuals
Staff: 16
Annual Budget: $2-5,000,000
Exec. V. President: Robert F. Ziegler
Director, Meetings/Conventions: Victoria Graves

Historical Note
Established June 15, 1922 as the Federation of Paint and Varnish Production Clubs. Became the Federation of Societies for Paint Technology in 1959. The name was later changed to Federation of Societies for Coatings Technology. Membership: $25/year.

Publications:
Convention Program Book. a. adv.
FSCT Focus. q.
Journal of Coatings Technology. m. adv.
Membership Directory. a. adv.

Meetings/Conferences:
Annual Meetings: Fall/8,000
1999 – Dallas, TX(Convention Center)/Oct. 20-22

Federation of Special Care Organizations
211 E. Chicago Ave., Suite 948
Chicago, IL 60611-3810
Tel: (312)440-2660   *Fax:* (312)440-2824
Members: 1,500 individuals
Staff: 3
Annual Budget: $250-500,000
Exec. Director: John S. Rutkauskas, D.D.S., MS

Historical Note
Membership: $120/year (individual).

Publications:
Interface Newsletter. m. adv.
Special Care in Dentistry Journal. bi-m. adv.

Meetings/Conferences:
Annual Meetings: April
1999 – Chicago, IL(westin Hotel)/March 26-28

Federation of Spine Ass'ns
6300 N. River Road, Suite 727
Rosemont, IL 60018-4226
Tel: (846)698-1628   *Fax:* (847)823-0536
Exec. Officer: Jackie O'Brien

Federation of State Boards of Physical Therapy
509 Wythe St.
Alexandria, VA 22314-1917
Tel: (703)299-3100   *Fax:* (703)299-3110
Web Site: http://www.ssept.org
Members: 200 individuals
Staff: 8
C.E.O.: William Hatherill
Coordinator, Meetings: Anna K. Hayes

Meetings/Conferences:
1999 – San Antonio, TX/March 5-8

Federation of State Humanities Councils *(1977)*
1600 Wilson Blvd., Suite 902
Arlington, VA 22209-2505
Tel: (703)908-9700   *Fax:* (703)908-9706
Members: 56 councils
Staff: 3
Annual Budget: $500-1,000,000
President: Gail Leftwich
Administrator, Conferences and Finance: Elizabeth Paine, CMP

Historical Note
FSHC assists state councils in achieving their common mission: the integration of the humanities into American life. FSHC monitors Congressional legislation and plans legislative forums. The Federation also forms partnerships with other national organizations on behalf of the state councils and coordinates an annual national conference of state humanities councils.

Meetings/Conferences:
Annual Meetings: Fall/350-400
1999 – Denver, CO/Sept. 30-Oct 3

Federation of State Medical Boards of the U. S. *(1912)*

---

400 Fuller Wiser Road, Suite 300
Euless, TX   76039-3855
Tel: (817)868-4000   *Fax:* (817)868-4099
Members: 69 boards
Staff: 100
Annual Budget: $10-25,000,000
Exec. V. President: James R. Winn, M.D.
Asst. V. President, Public Relations, Education and Publications: Carol
   Clothier
Asst. V. President, Member Support Services: Deborah Modesette
Deputy Exec. V. President: Dale L. Austin
Comptroller: Randy McCullough
Asst. V. President, Exam and Board Action Services: William Finical
Historical Note
*Voluntary national organization of state medical boards, the
Federation was organized at the Congress Hotel, Chicago on
February 29, 1912 with a charter membership of ten boards and
eighteen fellows. It was incorporated in 1966. Maintains
disciplinary information submitted by state boards on physicians. In
collaboration with the Nat'l Board of Medical Examiners offers
United States Medical Licensing Examination--the only medical
licensing examination in the U.S. for allopathic physicians. Keeps
statistics regarding requirements for licensure for ready reference to
inquiries. Has an annual budget of $10 million. Membership:
$2,000/year (state board).*
Publications:
Directory. a.
FSMB Newsline. m.
Guide to the Essentials of a Modern Medical Practice.
Guidebook on Medical Discipline. a.
The EXCHANGE. trien.
The Federation Bulletin. q.
Meetings/Conferences:
Annual Meetings: Spring
1999 – St. Louis, MO(Hyatt Regency)/April 22-24/500
2000 – Dallas, TX(Wyndham)/April 13-15/500

Federation of Straight Chiropractors and Organizations *(1978)*
642 Broad St.
Clifton, NJ   07013
Tel: (973)777-1197   *Fax:* (973)777-0739
Toll Free: (800)521 - 9856
E-Mail: FSCO@juno.com
Members: 1,200 individuals
Staff: 1
Annual Budget: $100-250,000
Chairman: Dr. Joseph Donofrio
Historical Note
*FSCO members are chiropractors and others with an interest in the
practice of traditional chiropractic. Traditional chiropractic is
defined as the correction of vertebral sudluxations to improve
function and potential for health. Membership: $400/year.*
Publications:
FSCO Insider. bi-m.
President's Update. bi-m.
Meetings/Conferences:
1999 – Greenville, SC

Federation of Tax Administrators *(1937)*
444 North Capitol St., N.W., Suite 348
Washington, DC   20001
Tel: (202)624-5890   *Fax:* (202)624-7888
Members: 52 agencies
Staff: 6
Annual Budget: $500-1,000,000
Exec. Director: Harley Duncan
Historical Note
*Established by the Nat'l Ass'n of Tax Administrators, the North
American Gasoline Tax Conference and the Nat'l Tobacco Tax
Ass'n. FTA subsequently absorbed all three founding organizations.
Members are the tax agencies of the 50 state governments, the
District of Columbia and New York City.*
Publications:
Directory of State Tax Administrators. a.
Tax Administrators News. m.
Meetings/Conferences:
Annual Meetings: June

Fellowship of United Methodists in Music and Worship Arts *(1956)*
P.O. Box 840
Nashville, TN   37202
Tel: (615)749-6875   *Fax:* (615)749-6874
E-Mail: FUMMWA@aol.com
Members: 2,500 individuals
Staff: 1
Annual Budget: $100-250,000
Administrator: David L. Bone
Historical Note
*Formerly (1974) Nat'l Fellowship of United Methodist Musicians,
(1979) Fellowship of United Methodist Musicians, and (1995)
Fellowship of United Methodists in Worship, Music and Other Arts.
Membership: $50/year.*
Publications:
Worship Arts. bi-m. adv.
Meetings/Conferences:
Biennial meetings: Uneven years
1999 – Nashville, TN(Holiday Inn-Vanderbilt)
2001 – Washington, DC

Fellowship of United Methodists in Worship, Music and Other Arts
Historical Note
*Became (1995) Fellowship of United Methodists in Music and
Worship Arts.*

Felt Manufacturers Council *(1961)*

Historical Note
A council of the Northern Textile Ass'n.

Ferroalloys Ass'n *(1971)*
900 2nd St., N.E., Suite 201
Washington, DC   20002-3557
Tel: (202)842-0292   *Fax:* (202)842-4840
Web Site: http://amc.aticorp.org/tfa
Members: 20 companies
Staff: 4
Annual Budget: $100-250,000
President: Edward J. Kinghorn, Jr.
Historical Note
*Organized to promote the general welfare of the ferroalloy industry
in the areas of technology, international trade, environment and
health, saftey and government relations.*
Meetings/Conferences:
1999 – La Quinta, CA(La Quinta Resort)/Feb. 24-27/20

Fertilizer Institute *(1970)*
501 2nd St., N.E.
Washington, DC   20002
Tel: (202)675-8250   *Fax:* (202)544-8123
Members: 200 individuals, 325 companies
Staff: 30
Annual Budget: $2-5,000,000
President: Gary D. Myers
V. President, Public Affairs: Ron Phillips
Director, Public Affairs: Kathleen O'Hara Mathers
V. President, Government Relations: Ford B. West
Director of Conventions: Linda McAbee
Secretary/Treasurer and V. President of Administration: P. Whitney
   Yelverton
Historical Note
*Merger of the Nat'l Plant Food Institute (1955) and Agricultural
Nitrogen Institute (1951). Formerly (1970) Nat'l Plant Food
Institute. Members are brokers, producers, importers, dealers and
manufacturers of fertilizer and fertilizer-related equipment. Supports
the FERT Political Action Committee.*
Publications:
Action. m.
Meetings/Conferences:
Annual Meetings: February
1999 – Dallas, TX(Windham Hotel)/Feb. 7-9

Fiber Soc. *(1941)*
Sch. of Textiles Fibers & Polymer Sci.
161 Sirrene Hall, Clemson Univ.
Clemson, SC   29634-1307
Tel: (864)656-5957   *Fax:* (864)656-5973
Members: 400 individuals
Staff: 1
Annual Budget: $10-25,000
Secretary-Treasurer: Bhuvenesh C. Goswami, Ph.D.
Historical Note
*A professional group of researchers on fibers, fiber products and
fibrous compounds. Membership: $15/year.*
Meetings/Conferences:
1999 – Philadelphia, PA/100
1999 – Clemson, SC(Madison Center)/120
2000 – Guamaraes, Portugal/2000

Fiberglass Petroleum Tank and Pipe Institute
Historical Note
Became (1995) Fiberglass Tank and Pipe Institute.

Fiberglass Tank and Pipe Institute *(1987)*
11150 S. Wilcrost Dr.
Suite 101
Houston, TX   77099-4343
Tel: (281)568-4100   *Fax:* (281)568-4500
Members: 6 companies
Staff: 2
Annual Budget: $250-500,000
Exec. Director: Sullivan D. Curran
Historical Note
*Formerly (1995) Fiberglass Petroleum Tank and Pipe Institute, FTPI
promotes and protects the interests and image of the fiberglass-
reinforced thermosetting plastic tank and pipe manufacturing
industry. In addition, the Institute develops, exchanges and
disseminates information of benefit to its members. Members are
domestic manufacturers. Membership: $4,400 minimum.*
Meetings/Conferences:
Semi-Annual Meetings: Spring and Fall
1999 – Houston, TX(Hyatt)/12

Fibre Box Ass'n *(1940)*
2850 Golf Road
Rolling Meadows, IL   60008
Tel: (847)364-9600   *Fax:* (847)364-9639
Members: 170 companies
Staff: 8
Annual Budget: $1-2,000,000
President: Bruce Benson
Historical Note
*Members are makers of corrugated boxes. FBA represents 90% of
the U.S. corrugated paper board packing industry.*
Publications:
Labor Bulletin. m.
Statistical Report. m.
Statistical Summary. m.
Meetings/Conferences:
Annual Meetings: Spring
1999 – Houston, TX(Four Seasons Hotel)/May 2-4

Fibre Channel Ass'n *(1993)*
2570 W. El Camino Real, Suite 304
Mountain View, CA   94040
Tel: (650)949-6730   *Fax:* (650)949-6735

Toll Free: (800)272 - 4618
E-Mail: fca@fibrechannel.com
Web Site: http://www.fibrechannel.com
Exec. Director: P.J. Stegen
Historical Note
*FCA was formed to encourage the utilization of Fibre Channel and
to complement the activities of the American Nat'l Standards
Institute T11 committee by providing a support structure for system
integrators, peripheral manufacturers, software developers,
component manyufacturers, communications companies and
computer service providers.*
Publications:
FCA Newsletter. q.
Meetings/Conferences:
1999 – Beverly Hills, CA/Jan. 19-21

Fibre Drum Technical Council *(1974)*
Historical Note
Became the Internat'l Fibre Drum Institute in 1994.

Field Services Marketing Ass'n *(1982)*
8566 Laureldale Dr.
Laurel, MD   20724-2008
Tel: (410)792-2744   *Fax:* (410)792-2949
Toll Free: (800)338 - 6232
E-Mail: fmsa@smart.net
Web Site: www.fmsanet.com
Members: 165 individuals
Staff: 1
Annual Budget: $50-100,000
President: Virginia M. Hook
Historical Note
*Formerly (1996) Nat'l Ass'n of Demonstration Companies. FMSA
was established to strengthen the direct marketing industry by
improving and stimulating the acceptance, performance, reputation
and use of in-store demonstrations, as well as a range of other
marketing assistance services. Membership: $300-850/year
(demonstration company); $3,000/year (marketing company), plus
initiation fee.*
Publications:
The Communicator. q. adv.
Meetings/Conferences:
Annual Meetings: Spring
1999 – Palm Springs, CA(Wyndam Hotel)/April 18-21/200

Film and Bag Federation *(1986)*
1801 K. St., N.W., Suite 600K
Washington, DC   20006
Tel: (202)974-5218
Web Site: http://www.plasticbag.com
Members: 50 companies
Staff: 2
Annual Budget: $100-250,000
Exec. Director: Donna Dempsey
Historical Note
*Formerly Plastic Bag Ass'n (1998). Members are U.S. and
Canadian manufacturers and suppliers of plastic retail bags.
Membership: $2,000/year.*
Publications:
Newsletter. q.
Meetings/Conferences:

Filter Manufacturers Council *(1971)*
P.O. Box 13966
Research Triangle Park
Durham, NC   27709-3966
Tel: (919)549-4800   *Fax:* (919)549-4824
Members: 24 companies
Staff: 1
Annual Budget: $100-250,000
Exec. Director: Gregory K. Griggs
Historical Note
Formerly (1989) Automotive Filter Manufacturers Council.
Publications:
Technical Service Bulletins. q.
Meetings/Conferences:
Semi-annual Meetings: Spring and Fall/70-75

Financial Executives Institute *(1931)*
10 Madison Avenue, P.O. Box 1938
Morristown, NJ   07962-1938
Tel: (973)898-4600   *Fax:* (201)538-6144
E-Mail: pnroy@fei.org
Web Site: http://www.fei.org
Members: 14,000 individuals
Staff: 40
Annual Budget: $5-10,000,000
President: P. Norman Roy
Director, Conferences: Maureen E. Campbell
V. President, Professional Development: Susan Koski-Grafer
Asst. Secretary: Barbara Chanes
Dir., Member/Chapter Relations: David Lewis
Historical Note
*Formed by eight corporate controllers in New York City as the
Controllers Institute of America, December 29, 1931 and
incorporated December 31 in the District of Columbia. Assumed its
present name in 1962. A professional organization of individuals
performing the duties of C.F.O., Controller, Treasurer or Vice
President of Finance. Has an annual budget of $5.5 million.
Membership: $425year.*
Publications:
FEI Members Directory. bien.
Financial Executive. bi-m. adv.
Meetings/Conferences:
Annual Meetings: October/1,000
1999 – Vancouver, BC/May 26-29

Financial Housing Division-Manufactured Housing Institute
Historical Note
Became Manufactured Housing Institute in 1994.

Financial Institutions Insurance Ass'n
21 Tamal Vista Blvd., Suite 125
Corte Madera, CA 94925-1130
Tel: (415)924-8122 *Fax:* (415)924-1447
E-Mail: fiia@ix.netcom.com
Web Site: http://www.fiia.org
Annual Budget: $1-2,000,000
Exec. Director: Alice G. Berreyesa

Historical Note
FIIA members are financial institutions marketing insurance products as an integral part of their retail banking strategy including: commercial banks, thrifts, credit unions, mortgage companies, finance companies, and their affiliates and subsidiaries. Associate membership is available to all organizations providing products and services to financial institutions marketing insurance, academia, government agencies, and other industry trade associations. Membership: $500-$875/year, varies by company assets; $1,000/year (associate).

Publications:
Bank Insurance Executives Directory. a.
Bank Insurance Marketing Magazine. q.
Bank Insurance Services & Suppliers Directory. a.
FIIA Membership Directory. a.

Meetings/Conferences:
1999 – Scottsdale, AZ/April 18-20

Financial Institutions Marketing Ass'n *(1965)*
Historical Note
Organization defunct in 1997.

Financial Management Ass'n *(1970)*
College of Business Administration
University of South Florida
Tampa, FL 33620
Tel: (813)974-2084 *Fax:* (813)974-3318
E-Mail: fma@coba.usf.edu
Web Site: http://www.fma.org
Members: 12,000 individuals and institutions
Staff: 6
Annual Budget: $500-1,000,000
Exec. Director: Jack S. Rader
Special Events Coordinator: Karen Wright

Historical Note
Members are college professors of financial management and corporate and organizational financial officers. Membership: $80/year (individual); $100/year (organization).

Publications:
Contemporary Finance Digest. q.
Financial Management. q. adv.
Financial Practice and Education. 3/year. adv.

Meetings/Conferences:
Annual Meetings: October/1,200

Financial Management for Data Porcessing *(1988)*
Historical Note
Became IS Financial Management Ass'n in 1997.

Financial Managers Soc. *(1949)*
230 W. Monroe St., Suite 2205
Chicago, IL 60606-4901
Tel: (312)578-1300 *Fax:* (312)578-1308
Toll Free: (800)275 - 4367
E-Mail: dyingst@fmsinc.org
Web Site: http://www.fmsinc.org
Members: 1,700 individuals
Staff: 10
Annual Budget: $1-2,000,000
President: Richard A. Yingst
Director of Marketing: Dirk L. Behrends
V. President, Administration: Diane Urbanski
V. President, Director of Member Services: Diane Walter

Historical Note
Formerly (1967) The Soc. of Savings and Loan Controllers, (1974) The Nat'l Soc. of Controllers and Financial Officers of Savings Institutions and (1982) The Financial Managers Soc. for Savings Institutions. FMS is dedicated to providing the technical information needed by financial executives in savings and loans, banks, credit unions, and other financial institutions. FMS has 25 chapters throughout the United States. Membership: $375/year (individual), $420/year (affiliate).

Publications:
FMS Update. bi-weekly. adv.

Meetings/Conferences:
Annual Meetings: May
1999 – Philadelphia, PA(Wyndham)/May 9-12
2000 – Orlando, FL(Hilton Disney Village)/May 14-16
2001 – Chicago, IL(Westin Chicago)/May 13-16

Financial Marketing Ass'n
Historical Note
A division of the Credit Union Executives Soc.

Financial Markets Ass'n *(1990)*
7799 Leesburg Pike, Suite 800-N
Falls Church, VA 22043-2413
Tel: (703)749-1579 *Fax:* (703)749-1688
E-Mail: dpearce@securagroup.com or dp-fma@erols.com
Members: 350 individuals
Staff: 1
Annual Budget: $100-250,000
Managing Director: Jo Dorcas Pearce

Historical Note
FMA focuses on the educational and training needs of professionals working with financial institution treasury and capital markets, securities investing and fiduciary activities. Unlike other organizations, FMA works for individual bankers, not member banks. Membership: $150 (new); $99 (renewal).

Publications:
Market Solutions. q.

Financial Operation Ass'n
Historical Note
A division of the Credit Union Executives Soc.

Financial Services Council *(1987)*
1776 I St., N.W., Suite 735
Washington, DC 20006-3700
Tel: (202)785-1500 *Fax:* (202)785-1562
Staff: 4
Annual Budget: $500-1,000,000
President: Samuel J. Baptista

Historical Note
A broad-based coalition of U.S. financial institutions; supports comprehensive, structural reform of the financial services industry that would remove artificial barriers to competition.

Financial Services Technology Network
8 S. Michigan Ave., Suite 1000
Chicago, IL 60603
Tel: (312)782-4951 *Fax:* (312)580-0165
Web Site: www.gss.net/fstn
Members: 62 corporate
Staff: 10
Annual Budget: $250-500,000
Exec. Director: Kathleen Lukasik

Historical Note
Previously known as Nat'l Trust Aids Systems Ass'n. Members are companies involved in technology services.

Meetings/Conferences:
1999 – Philadelphia, PN/June 27-29

Financial Stationers Ass'n *(1952)*
1200 19th St., N.W., Suite 300
Washington, DC 20036-2422
Tel: (202)857-1144 *Fax:* (202)223-4579
E-Mail: fsa@dc.sba.com
Members: 60 companies
Staff: 2
Annual Budget: $100-250,000
Exec. Director: Gary T. Satterfield

Historical Note
Formerly Bank Stationers Section of Lithographers and Printers Nat'l Ass'n and the Bank Stationers Ass'n, FSA assumed its present name in 1984. Absorbed the Payment Systems Education Ass'n in 1990.

Publications:
Chek Up Newsletter. q.
FSA FACTS (broadcast fax).
Guideline to Enhanced Check Security.

Meetings/Conferences:
1999 – Amelia Island, SC/April 18-21
2000 – Tucson, AZ(Omni Tucson)

Financial Suppliers Forum
Historical Note
A division of the the Credit Union Executives Soc.

Financial Women Internat'l *(1921)*
200 N. Glebe Road, Suite 820
Arlington, VA 22203
Tel: (703)807-2007 *Fax:* (703)807-0111
Web Site: http://www.fwi.org
Members: 10,000 individuals
Staff: 10
Annual Budget: $1-2,000,000
Exec. Director: Penny Dudley
Director of Communications: Judith C. Marden
Membership Director: Marcia Cram
Publication Manager: Kathleen Robeson

Historical Note
Formerly (1989) the Nat'l Ass'n of Bank Women. Members are managers, directors and officers from all sectors of the financial services industry. FWI's mission is to serve women in the financial services industry who seek to expand their personal and professional capabilities through self-directed growth in a supportive environment. Membership: $96/year (individual).

Publications:
Financial Woman Today. m. adv.
FWInfo.

Meetings/Conferences:
Annual Meetings: Fall/500
1999 – Pittsburg, PA(Weston William Penn)/Sept. 25-28

Fine Hardwood Veneer Ass'n *(1933)*
Historical Note
Merged with Hardwood, Plywood, & Veneer Ass'n in 1998.

Fine Hardwoods-American Walnut Ass'n *(1971)*
Historical Note
Became two independent ass'ns in 1994: American Walnut Manufacturers Ass'n and Fine Hardwood Veneer Ass'n.

Fine Particle Soc. *(1968)*
Historical Note
Address unknown in 1997.

Finishing Contractors Ass'n *(1997)*
2000 L St. N.W., Suite 200
Washington, DC 20036

Tel: (202)530-5200 *Fax:* (202)530-5201
Members: 500 companies
Staff: 3
Annual Budget: $250-500,000
Exec. V. President: James R. Baxter

Historical Note
FCA members are union contractors. FCA represents companies which are signatory to agreements with the Internat'l Brotherhood of Painters and Allied Trades. Areas covered include painting, drywall, glass, flooring, and signs. Membership: $275/year.

Publications:
Finishing News Newsletter. m.

Meetings/Conferences:
Annual Meetings: Winter
1999 – Las Vegas, NV/April 16-17

Finnish American Chamber of Commerce *(1948)*
866 United Nations Plaza
New York, NY 10017-1822
Tel: (212)821-0225 *Fax:* (212)750-4417
E-Mail: info@finlandtrade.com
Web Site: http://www.finlandtrade.com
Members: 200 companies
Staff: 1
Annual Budget: $25-50,000
Secretary: Anne Aunio

Historical Note
Membership: $50/year (individual); $350/year (company); $1,000/year (sustaining).

Publications:
Finnish-American Headlines. q. adv.

Meetings/Conferences:
Annual Meetings: always New York, NY/May-June/50

Fire Apparatus Manufacturers Ass'n *(1946)*
P.O. Box 397
Lynnfield, MA 01940-0397
Tel: (781)334-2911 *Fax:* (781)334-2911
Web Site: http://www.fama.org
Staff: 1
Annual Budget: $50-100,000
Admin. Assistant: Karen H. Burnham

Historical Note
Formerly a division of the Nat'l Truck Equipment Ass'n, FAMA became an independent organization in 1997. Members are manufacturers of fire suppression material and equipment and other firefighting components. Membership: $1,000/year (company).

Publications:
FAMA Flyer. q.

Meetings/Conferences:
1999 – Orlando, FL/April 24-27
1999 – San Antonio, TX/Sept. 23-25

Fire Equipment Manufacturers Suppliers Ass'n *(1966)*
11250 Roger Bacon Dr., Suite 8
Reston, VA 20190
Tel: (703)437-4377 *Fax:* (703)435-4390
Web Site: http://www.femsa.org
Members: 150 companies
Staff: 2
Annual Budget: $50-100,000
Deputy Exec. Director: Richard A. Guggolz

Historical Note
Formerly (1990) the Fire Equipment Manufacturers and Services Ass'n. Established and incorporated in Delaware, FEMSA members are companies that manufacture vehicles, protective clothing, hoses and nozzles, breathing apparatus, rescue tools and other products and services used by fire fighters. FEMSA's primary public policy concern is federal product liability.

Publications:
FEMSA news. q.

Meetings/Conferences:
1999 – San Antonio, TX(Marriott)/Sept. 22-25
2000 – Newport Beach, RI(Marriott)/Oct. 4-7
2001 – Palm Springs, CA/Oct. 3-6
2002 – New Orleans, LA/Oct. 9-12

Fire Equipment Manufacturers' Ass'n *(1925)*
1300 Sumner Ave.
Cleveland, OH 44115-2851
Tel: (216)241-7333 *Fax:* (216)241-0105
E-Mail: fema@taol.com
Web Site: http://www.taol.com/fema
Members: 27 companies
Staff: 2
Annual Budget: $100-250,000
Exec. Director: John H. Addington

Historical Note
Established as the Fire Extinguisher Manufacturers' Ass'n, Inc., it assumed its present name in 1936. Members are companies making devices that control or extinguish fires in residential or commercial buildings. Membership: sliding scale.

Meetings/Conferences:
Annual Meetings: Fall/50
1999 – Tarpon Springs, FL(Innisbrook)/Oct. 21-23

Fire Marshals Ass'n of North America *(1906)*
Batterymarch Park
Quincy, MA 02269-9101
Tel: (617)984-7424 *Fax:* (617)984-7056
Members: 1,600 individuals
Staff: 2
Exec. Secretary: Steven Sawyer

Historical Note
Founded in 1906, it reorganized as a section of the Nat'l Fire Protection Ass'n in 1927. Members are fire marshals, fire prevention officers or similar government officials charged with investigating or preventing fires.

Publications:
Fire Marshals Directory.. quinquen..
Fire Marshals.. q.
Meetings/Conferences:
Semi-annual Meetings: with the Nat'l Fire Protection Ass'n
    Cincinatti, OH/May 17-20

Fire Retardant Chemicals Ass'n *(1973)*
851 New Holland Ave., Box 3535
Lancaster, PA   17604
Tel: (717)291-5616   *Fax:* (717)295-9637
Members: 40 companies
Staff: 2
Annual Budget: $50-100,000
Exec. V. President: Russell Kidder
Historical Note
Promotes fire safety while creating and maintaining the best possible industry climate for member companies to individually market their products and services. Membership fee varies, based on sales volume.
Publications:
Newsletter. q.
Proceedings. bi-a.
Meetings/Conferences:
Annual Meetings: Spring and Fall
1999 – New Orleans, LA/March 14-17
1999 – Tucson, AZ(OMNI Tucson)/Oct. 24-27

Fire Suppression Systems Ass'n *(1982)*
5024-R Campbell Blvd.
Baltimore, MD   21236-5974
Tel: (410)931-8100   *Fax:* (410)931-8111
E-Mail: fssahq@aol.com
Web Site: http://www.podi.com/fssa
Members: 94 installers, 21 manufacturers
Staff: 3
Annual Budget: $100-250,000
Exec. Director: Celeste Powers
Historical Note
Founded in Chicago and incorporated in the State of Illinois, members are designers, suppliers and installers of special hazard fire suppression equipment, gases and dectectors.
Publications:
FYI.. bi-m.
Membership Directory..
Meetings/Conferences:
Annual Meetings: Winter
1999 – Puerto Vallarta, Mexico(Westin)/Feb. 10-14

Firearm and Security Trainer Management Ass'n *(1985)*
Historical Note
Organization defunct in 1998.

Firearms Research and Indentification Ass'n *(1978)*
21465 E. Fort Bowie Drive
Walnut, CA   91789
Tel: (909)598-8919   *Fax:* (909)598-5666
President: John Armand Caudron
Historical Note
FRIA members are individuals concerned with provenance, history and functional analysis of firearms.

First Amendment Lawyers Ass'n *(1970)*
125 S. Wacker Dr., Suite 2700
Chicago, IL   60606
Tel: (312)332-6000   *Fax:* (312)332-6008
E-Mail: wayneb@mcs.net
Web Site: http://www.fala.org
Members: 130 individuals
Staff: 1
Annual Budget: $10-25,000
Contact: Wayne Giampietro
Historical Note
Lawyers concentrating on defending clients under the 1st Amendment to the Constitution - free speech, assemblage, petition, etc. Membership: based on number of attorneys nominated for FALA membership from same firm: $140/year (1st member); $90/year (2nd member); $40/year (3rd & 4th members).
Publications:
Bulletin. irreg.
Directory. a.
Meetings/Conferences:
Semi-annual Meetings: Winter and Summer

Fitness Trade Ass'n *(1979)*
P.O. Box 2378
Corona, CA   91718-2378
Tel: (909)371-0606   *Fax:* (909)371-0608
Members: 2,000 fitness facilities
Staff: 8
President: Wally Boyko
Historical Note
Formerly (1987) Nat'l Fitness. Ass'n Members are fitness facilities.
Publications:
Nat'l Fitness Trade Journal. q. adv.
Meetings/Conferences:
Annual Meetings: Always in Las Vegas, NV(Tropicana)/Fall
1999 – Las Vegas, NV(The Venetian)/Aug. 5-7/2500

Fixed Income Analysts Soc. *(1975)*
151 Herricks Road, Suite 1
Garden City Park, NY   11040-5200
Tel: (516)739-2510   *Fax:* (516)739-3803
Toll Free: (800)284 - 6228
Web Site: http://www.fiasi.org
Members: 300 individuals
Staff: 5

Annual Budget: $50-100,000
Exec. Director: Harry A. Hansen
Historical Note
FIASI members are individuals regularly engaged as fixed income professionals, including persons who specialize in credit research as well as those specializing in quantitative research. Membership: $160/year, plus $50 initiation (individual).
Publications:
Bonds-Eye. q.
Meetings/Conferences:
Annual Meetings: June
1999 – New York, NY

Flavor and Extract Manufacturers Ass'n of the United States *(1909)*
1620 I St., N.W., Suite 925
Washington, DC   20006
Tel: (202)293-5800   *Fax:* (202)463-8998
Members: 850 individuals, 150 companies
Staff: 18
Annual Budget: $2-5,000,000
Attorney and Exec. Secretary: Daniel R. Thompson
Director, Government Relations: Glenn Roberts
Meeting Planner: Kim Prentice
Association Manager: Margaret J. Mount
Historical Note
Formerly the Flavoring Extract Manufacturers Ass'n of the U.S. Merged with the Nat'l Manufacturers of Beverage Flavors in 1965.
Publications:
Regulatory and Legislative Update. q.
Meetings/Conferences:

Flexible Intermediate Bulk Container Ass'n *(1984)*
P.O. Box 2206
Macon, GA   31203-2206
Tel: (912)757-1006   *Fax:* (912)757-9444
Members: 54 companies
Annual Budget: $50-100,000
Exec. V. President: Bruce Cuthbertson
Historical Note
Members are companies manufacturing flexible intermediate bulk containers, and their suppliers. Membership: $1,500/year.
Meetings/Conferences:
1999 – Chicago, IL(Rosemont Suites)

Flexible Packaging Ass'n *(1950)*
1090 Vermont Ave., N.W., Suite 500
Washington, DC   20005-4960
Tel: (202)842-3880   *Fax:* (202)842-3841
E-Mail: fpa@flexpack.org
Web Site: http://www.flexpack.org
Members: 200 companies
Staff: 20
Annual Budget: $2-5,000,000
President: Glenn E. Braswell
Director, Public Relations and Marketing: Marjorie Valin
Director, Government Relations: Rick Thornburg
Meeting Planner: Judi Rosenburg
Director, Finance and Administration: Liz Dixon
Historical Note
Includes former Industrial Bag and Cover Ass'n and Waxed Paper Institute. Formerly (until 1979) known as Nat'l Flexible Packaging Ass'n. FPA is a trade association of manufacturers, converters and suppliers of paper, metal foil, and plastic or cellulose film. Membership: dues vary by sales (company).
Publications:
FPA Update. m.
Membership Directory.. a.
Right-to-Know Compliance Manual..
State of the Industry Report.. a.
Technical Specifications Directory..
Web and Roll Defects Glossary.. a.
Meetings/Conferences:
Annual Meetings: March/200
1999 – Carlsbad, CA(Four Seasons)/March 3-5

Flexicore Manufacturers Ass'n *(1952)*
Historical Note
Organization inactive in 1996.

Flexographic Technical Ass'n *(1958)*
900 Marconi Ave.
Ronkonkoma, NY   11779-7212
Tel: (516)737-6020   *Fax:* (516)737-6813
Web Site: http://www.fta-fta.org
Members: 1,400 printers and other businesses
Staff: 22
Annual Budget: $2-5,000,000
President: William C. Dowdell
V. President: Mark Cisternino
Dir., Meetings & Exhibits: Diane R. Euler
Historical Note
Members are printers and suppliers to the flexographic process, a method of rotary printing using flexible plates and fast-drying inks. Membership: $325-650/year.
Publications:
FLEXO. m. adv.
FLEXO Espanol. q. adv.
Meetings/Conferences:
Annual Meetings: Spring/2,000
1999 – San Antonio, TX(Marriott)/May 2-5

Flight Engineers' Internat'l Ass'n *(1948)*
1926 Pacific Coast Hwy., Suite 202
Redondo Beach, CA   90277-6145
Members: 20 individuals
Staff: 1
Annual Budget: under $10,000

President: Jerry L. Austin
Historical Note
Affiliated with AFL-CIO; Internat'l Transport Workers' Federation; Flight Safety Foundation; and the Soc. of Accident Investigators.
Meetings/Conferences:
Annual Meetings: Fall

Flight Safety Foundation *(1945)*
601 Madison St., Suite 300
Alexandria, VA   22314
Tel: (703)739-6700   *Fax:* (703)739-6708
Web Site: http://www.flightsafety.org
Members: 630 airlines, orgs. & individuals
Staff: 20
Annual Budget: $2-5,000,000
Chairman, President and C.E.O.: Stuart Matthews
Comptroller: Liby Kirby
Director, Membership: Jane Berrin
Director, Publications: Roger Rozelle
Director, Technical Projects: Robert Vandel
Historical Note
An international, independent non profit association supported by airlines, aerospace manufacturers, aviation professionals, corporate flight departments and others interested in flight safety. Membership: $100/year (indiv.); $1,000-25,000/year (company)
Publications:
Accident Prevention Bulletin. bi-m.
Airport Operations Safety Bulletin. bi-m.
Aviation Mechanics Bulletin. bi-m.
Cabin Crew Safety Bulletin. bi-m.
Corporate Seminar Proceedings. a. adv.
FSF Flight Safety Digest. m.
Helicopter Safety Bulletin. bi-m.
Human Factors Bulletin. bi-m.
Internat'l Seminar Proceedings. a. adv.
Newsletter. bi-m.
Meetings/Conferences:
Three Annual Meetings: two in Spring and one in Fall
1999 – Amsterdam/March 8-10
1999 – Cincinnati, OH/Apr. 27-28
1999 – Rio de Janero, Brazil/Nov. 8-11

Floatation Tank Ass'n *(1984)*
P.O. Box 1396
Grass Valley, CA   95945-1396
Tel: (916)432-4502   *Fax:* (916)477-1953
Members: 100 individuals, 125 companies
Staff: 1
Annual Budget: under $10,000
President: Lee Perry
Historical Note
Members are manufacturers of floatation tanks and operators of floatation tank facilities, owners of floatation tanks and users of floatation tanks. FTA establishes and maintains principles and standards for fair, safe and equitable operation of floatation tanks and promotes and encourages interest in floating. Membership: $75/year (company); $25/year (individual).

Floor Covering Installation Contractors Ass'n *(1982)*
Box 948
Dalton, GA   30722-0948
Tel: (706)226-5488   *Fax:* (706)226-1775
E-Mail: fcica@catt.com
Members: 234 companies
Staff: 1
Annual Budget: $100-250,000
Administrative Coordinator: Deborah Ratcliff
Historical Note
Established in 1982 and incorporated in Georgia. FCICA represents the floor covering installation industry. Membership: $250-500/year (full member), $50-500/year (associate).
Publications:
FCICA Newsletter. m.
Membership Directory. q. adv.
Meetings/Conferences:
Annual Meetings: Spring
1999 – Orlando, FL(Disney's Coronado
    Springs)/April 14-17/125
2000 – San Diego, CA

Floral Marketing Ass'n
P.O. Box 6036
Newark, DE   19714-6036
Tel: (302)738-7100   *Fax:* (302)731-2409
E-Mail: CDonofrio@mail.pma.com
Web Site: www.pma.com
Members: 650 companies
Staff: 2
Annual Budget: $250-500,000
Director: Carolyn Donofrio
Historical Note
FMA is a division of Produce Marketing Ass'n serving the mass-market floral industry. Membership: dues vary, $725/year (minimum).
Publications:
Floraline. m.
Membership Directory/Buyer's Guide. a. adv.
Meetings/Conferences:
1999 – Atlanta, GA(Georgia World Congress
    Center)/Jan. 7-10/5000

Flue-Cured Tobacco Cooperative Stabilization Corporation *(1946)*
P.O. Box 12300
Raleigh, NC   27605
Tel: (919)821-4560   *Fax:* (919)821-4564
Web Site: http://www.ustobaccofarmer.org
Members: 50,000 individuals
Staff: 55

Annual Budget: $1-2,000,000
General Manager: Lionel Edwards

Historical Note
Flue-cured tobacco producers' marketing cooperative for six southern states and adminstrator of federal price support program for flue-cured tobacco. Membership: $5/year (individual).

Publications:
Newsletter. m.

Meetings/Conferences:
Annual Meetings: Always in Raleigh, NC(Scott Pavilion, NC State Fairgrounds)/last Friday in May/800-1,000

Fluid Controls Institute *(1921)*
1300 Sumner Ave.
Cleveland, OH   44115-2851
Tel: (216)241-7333   Fax: (216)241-0105
E-Mail: fci@taol.com
Web Site: http://www.taol.com/fci
Members: 68 companies
Staff: 3
Annual Budget: $25-50,000
Exec. Secretary: John H. Addington

Historical Note
Manufacturers of devices for fluid control, such as temperature and pressure regulators, strainers, gauges, control valves, solenoid valves, steam traps, etc. Established as the Nat'l Ass'n of Steam and Fluid Specialty Manufacturers, it became the Nat'l Steam Specialty Club in 1941 and assumed its present name in 1955.

Publications:
News and Views. q.

Meetings/Conferences:
Semi-annual Meetings: Spring and Fall
1999 – Palm Desert, CA(Marriott's Palm Desert)/May 22-26

Fluid Fertilizer Foundation *(1982)*

Historical Note
The research and educational arm of the Agricultural Retailers Ass'n.

Fluid Power Distributors Ass'n *(1974)*
P.O. Box 1420
Cherry Hill, NJ   08034-0054
Tel: (609)424-8998   Fax: (609)424-9248
Web Site: http://www.fpda.org
Members: 475 companies
Staff: 7
Annual Budget: $300-1,000,000
Exec. Director: Mary Connor
Director of Meetings: Kathleen A. DeMarco
Member Services Coordinator: Cheryl Smithers

Historical Note
Membership is composed of distributors and manufacturers of hydraulic and pneumatic equipment. Services provided to members include management training, technical information updates, and statistical and financial information. Membership: $350-850/year (corporate).

Publications:
Buyers Guide. a.
Directory. a.
FPDA News. m.

Meetings/Conferences:
Semi-Annual Meetings: Spring and Fall
1999 – Tuscon, AZ(Loews Ventana)/Feb. 20-24/600
2000 – Acapulco, Mexico(Acapulco Princess)/Feb. 19-23/600

Fluid Power Soc. *(1957)*
2433 N. Mayfair Rd., Suite 111
Milwaukee, WI   53226-1406
Tel: (414)257-0910   Fax: (414)257-4092
E-Mail: fpsociety@ad.com
Web Site: http://www.ifps.org
Members: 2,600 individuals
Staff: 6
Annual Budget: $500-1,000,000
Exec. V. President: Paul F. Prass

Historical Note
FPS is the international organization for fluid power (hydraulics, pneumatics, vacuum and electronics technologies) and motion control professionals. The Society provides education, certification and professional services. Membership: $55/year (initial fee), $50/year (renewal).

Publications:
Certification Directory..
Fluid Power Journal.. m. adv.
Membership Directory..

Meetings/Conferences:
Annual Meetings: January-February

Fluid Sealing Ass'n *(1933)*
994 Old Eagle School Road, Suite 1019
Wayne, PA   19087-1802
Tel: (610)971-4850   Fax: (610)971-4859
E-Mail: INFO@fluidsealing.com
Web Site: http://www.fluidsealing.com
Members: 100 companies
Staff: 5
Annual Budget: $250-500,000
Exec. Director: Robert H. Ecker

Historical Note
Formerly (1970) Mechanical Packing Ass'n, FSA is an international association of manufacturers of mechanical packings, sealing devices, gaskets, rubber expansion joints, and allied products.

Publications:
Newsletter.. semi-a.
Technical Manuals & Standards..

Meetings/Conferences:
1999 – Hawaii(Hapuna Beach Hotel)/April 28-May 1

1999 – Asheville, NC(Grove Park Inn)/Oct. 13-15

Foil Stamping and Embossing Ass'n *(1992)*
P.O. Box 12090
Portland, OR   97212
Tel: (503)331-6221   Fax: (503)331-6928
E-Mail: FSEAmail@aol.com
Web Site: http://www.FSEA.com
Members: 350 companies
Staff: 4
Annual Budget: $500-1,000,000
Exec. Director: Mary P. Fuller

Historical Note
FSEA is a non-profit international trade association of foil stampers, embossers, diecutters and industr suppliers working together for the advancement of the industry. Membership: $175-500/year (active); $250-750/year (associate). Rates are dependant upon the number of employees.

Publications:
FSEA Annual Directory.. a. adv.
Inside Fishing Magazine.. q. adv.

Meetings/Conferences:
Annual Meetings: October-November
1999 – Miami Beach, FL(Wyndham Miami Beach Resort)/Jan. 20-22

Food and Drug Law Institute *(1949)*
1000 Vermont Ave., N.W., Suite 200
Washington, DC   20005-4903
Tel: (202)371-1420   Fax: (202)371-0649
E-Mail: comments@fdli.org
Web Site: http://www.fdli.org
Members: 498 companies
Staff: 28
Annual Budget: $2-5,000,000
President: John C. Villforth
V. President, Conference Program: Anna Belousovitch
V. President, Publications & Academic Programs: Julia K. Ogden
Director, Finance and Administration: Carol D. Gavin
Exec. V. President: Joseph Arcarese
Director, Marketing & Membership: Constance Sayers

Historical Note
Formerly (1965) Food Law Institute. FDLI is a non-profit, educational organization working to promote an understanding of the laws, regulations, and policies affecting the public health aspects of foods, drugs, cosmetics, medical devices, biological products, and veterinary medical products. Members are manufacturers, suppliers, law firms, consultants, associations, research groups, public relations firms and others associated with the food, drugs, medical devices, cosmetics and biologics industries. Membership: $500-12,000/year.

Publications:
Directory of Lawyers and Consultants. a.
Directory of the Food and Drug Administration. a.
Food and Drug Law Institute Update. semi-a.
Food and Drug Law Journal. q.

Meetings/Conferences:
Annual Meetings: always Washington, DC/December

Food Business Forum *(1953)*

Historical Note
Became CIES, The Food Business Forum in 1996.

Food Distribution Research Soc. *(1960)*
LSU Department of Ag. Economics
101 Agricultural Admin. Bldg.
Baton Rouge, LA   70808
Tel: (504)388-2753   Fax: (504)388-2716
E-Mail: rhinson@agctr.lsu.edu
Members: 200 individuals, 50 companies
Annual Budget: $25-50,000
Secretary-Treasurer: Dr. Virgil P. Culver

Historical Note
Informally established in 1960 as the Food Distribution Research Conference, the organization became formally recognized and assumed its present name in 1967. The Society encourages and implements food distribution research and serves as an information clearinghouse for past, current, and future food industry issues. Has no paid staff. Membership fee: $40/year (student); $35/year (professional/academic/government); $50/year (library); $135/year (company).

Publications:
Journal of Food Distribution Research. 3/year. adv.
Newsletter. 3/year. adv.

Meetings/Conferences:
1999 – San Antonio, TX/Oct. 17-20

Food Distributors Internat'l *(1906)*
201 Park Washington Court
Falls Church, VA   22046-4521
Tel: (703)532-9400   Fax: (703)538-4173
Members: 325 companies
Staff: 40
Annual Budget: $5-10,000,000
President: John R. Block
V. President, Communications and Marketing: Robert Gatty
V. President, Government Relations: Kevin Burke
Senior V. President, Industry Relations: Paul Schulz
V. President, Education and Operational Services: Dennis Madsen
V. President, Finance and Administration and C.F.O.: Mary E. Jorgenson
Exec. V. President/IFDA President/General Counsel: John Gray

Historical Note
Formerly (1996) Nat'l-American Wholesale Grocers' Ass'n. Absorbed the Institutional Food Distributors of America (founded in 1956) and United States Wholesale Grocers' Ass'n (founded in 1892) in 1969. The Internat'l Foodservice Distributors Ass'n is a partner ass'n with FDI. FDI provides educational, research and governmental services to wholesale grocers servicing independent

retail grocers and foodservice distributors. Sponsors and supports the Food Distributors Voice in Politics Political Action Committee. Has an annual budget of approximately $8 million.

Publications:
Capitol Report. q.
Dateline Washington. bi-w.
Food Distributor. bi-m. adv.

Meetings/Conferences:
1999 – Dallas, TX/March 6-10
1999 – Coronado, CA/Sept. 26-29
1999 – St. Louis, MO/Oct. 31-Nov. 3

Food Equipment Manufacturers Ass'n
401 N. Michigan Ave.
Chicago, IL   60611
Tel: (312)644-6610   Fax: (312)527-6658
E-Mail: maxine_couture@SBA.com
Members: 27 companies
Staff: 2
Annual Budget: $25-50,000
Exec. Secretary: Maxine Lee Couture

Historical Note
Members are fabricators of commercial kitchen equipment. Membership: $650/year.

Meetings/Conferences:

Food Industries Suppliers' Ass'n

Historical Note
Became (1996) Food Industry Suppliers' Ass'n.

Food Industry Ass'n Executives *(1927)*
P.O. Box 2510
Flemington, NJ   08822
Tel: (908)782-7833   Fax: (908)782-6907
Members: 170 individuals
Staff: 2
Annual Budget: $100-250,000
President/C.E.O.: Barbara McConnell

Historical Note
Formerly (1959) the Nat'l Grocery Secretaries Ass'n. Members are executives of retail grocer associations on the national, state and local levels. Membership: $150-650/year (active); $500/year (affiliate).

Publications:
Execunews. bi-m.
FIAE. m.
Membership Directory. a.

Meetings/Conferences:
1999 – Scottsdale, AZ(Gaudensis Resort)/Nov. 9-14

Food Industry Suppliers Ass'n *(1968)*
1207 Sunset Dr.
Greensboro, NC   27408
Tel: (336)274-6311   Fax: (336)691-1839
Members: 120 companies
Staff: 2
Annual Budget: $50-100,000
Exec. Director: Stella Jones

Historical Note
Formerly (1996) Food Industries Supplers' Ass'n. Affiliated with Nat'l Ass'n of Wholesaler-Distributors. Members are distributors who sell equipment and supplies to the food processing industry. Membership: $650/year (distributor/manufacturer); $325/year (associate).

Publications:
FISA Distributor News. q.

Meetings/Conferences:
Annual Meetings: Fall/150

Food Ingredient Network Development *(1995)*

Historical Note
Defunct in 1997.

Food Machinery Service Institute *(1932)*

Historical Note
Established as the United Saw Service Association, it assumed its present name in 1983. An autonomous division of the Meat Industry Supplier Ass'n.

Food Marketing Institute *(1977)*
800 Connecticut Ave., N.W., Suite 500
Washington, DC   20006-2701
Tel: (202)452-8444   Fax: (202)429-4519
E-Mail: fmi@fmi.org
Web Site: http://www.fmi.org
Members: 1,500 companies
Staff: 140
Annual Budget: $25-50,000,000
President and C.E.O.: Timothy Hammonds
Sr. V. President, Communications: Karen H. Brown
Media Relations Director: Carole Throssell
Sr. V. President, Conventions: Brian Tully
Manager, Intl Conv. Marketing: Suzanne B. Duvall
Director, Education Conferences: Patricia Shinko
Sr. V. President, Industry Rels./Education: Michael Sansolo
Director, Administration & Convention Conferencing: Jack Woolley
Director, Membership: Patrick A. Davis
Director, Editorial Services: William Greer

Historical Note
Formed Jan. 3, 1977 by a merger of the Super Market Institute, Inc. and the Nat'l Ass'n of Food Chains. Members are food retailers and wholesalers. Supports the Food Marketing Institute Political Action Committee. Has an annual budget of approximately $32 million.

Publications:
FMI Issues Bulletin. m.
Reference Point: Food Industry Abstracts. m.

Meetings/Conferences:
1999 – Chicago, IL(McCormick Place)/May 2-4

Food Processing Machinery and Supplies Ass'n *(1885)*
200 Daingerfield Road
Alexandria, VA 22314-2884
Tel: (703)684-1080   Fax: (703)548-6563
Toll Free: (800)331 - 8816
E-Mail: fpmsa@clark.net
Web Site: http://www.fpmsa.org
Members: 500 companies
Staff: 10
Annual Budget: $250-500,000
President and C.E.O.: George O. Melnykovich, Ph.D.
Director, International Programs: Sacha Helfand
Exec. Director, IEFP: Nancy Janssen

Historical Note
Formerly (1968) Canning Machinery and Supplies Ass'n. Absorbed the Beverage Machinery Manufacturers Ass'n in 1987. Membership: $1,250 (biennially).

Publications:
Blue Book Buyer's Guide. a. adv.

Meetings/Conferences:
1999 – Las Vegas, NV/Oct. 18-20

Food Processors Institute *(1973)*

Historical Note
A division of the Nat'l Food Processors Ass'n, the FPI meets the educational and training needs of the food processing industry. Also known as the Nat'l Food Processors Institute.

Food Sanitation Institute *(1957)*

Historical Note
A component of the Environmental Management Association.

Food Service Marketing Institute *(1987)*

Historical Note
FSMI seeks to increase professionalism in the food service wholesale distribution industry. Members include management, sales, purchaseing and marketing professionals in the industry. Membership: $90/year (individual); $250/year (company).

Foodservice and Packaging Institute *(1933)*
1550 Wilson Blvd., Suite 701
Arlington, VA 22209-2435
Tel: (703)527-7505   Fax: (703)527-7512
Web Site: http://www.fpi.org/fpi
Members: 50 companies
Staff: 7
Annual Budget: $1-2,000,000
President: John R. Burke
Mgr. Communication Technologies: Celia Besore
Director, Public Affairs: Ann Mattheis
Office Manager: Lucille Davis

Historical Note
Formerly (1987) the Single Service Institute. Manufacturers of one-time use cups, plates, bowls, wraps, straws and other similar products used for food service; nestable containers, placemats, prepackaging trays, egg cartons, etc made from paper, plastic aluminum and other materials. Formed by the merger in 1966 of the Paper Cup and Container Institute (1933), the Paper Plate Ass'n (1948) and the Linen and Lace Paper Institute (1954). Absorbed the Food Tray and Board Ass'n in 1971 (formerly Pulp and Paper Prepackaging Ass'n.) Absorbed the Egg Packaging Ass'n in 1975. Membership: varies by sales volume.

Publications:
Member Product Directory. semi-a.
Single Service News. bi-m.

Meetings/Conferences:
1999 – San Antonio, TX(Hyatt Hill
    Country)/March 17-21/125
1999 – Arlington, VA(Ritz-Carlton/Pentagon
    City)/Oct. 20-21/80

Foodservice Consultants Soc. Internat'l *(1979)*
304 W. Liberty St., Suite 201
Louisville, KY 40202-3011
Tel: (502)583-3783   Fax: (502)589-3602
E-Mail: fcsi@fcsi.org
Web Site: http://www.fcsi.org
Members: 1,200 individuals
Staff: 5
Annual Budget: $500-1,000,000
Exec. Director: David L. Drain
Director of Communications: Matt Hickey
Dir., Admninistration: Wade Koehler
Exec. V. President: Phillip S. Cooke
Director of Member Services: Monica Fehribach

Historical Note
The result of a merger in 1979 between the Food Facilities Consultants Soc. (founded in 1955) and the Internat'l Soc. of Food Service Consultants (founded in 1958). A professional society for consultants in design, equipment, engineering and management in the foodservice industry and furthers reseach, development and education in the foodservice field. Membership: $385/year (individual), $450-1,900/year (company).

Publications:
The Consultant. q. adv.

Meetings/Conferences:
1999 – Dallas, TX(Fairmont)/Sept. 29-Oct. 1/350

Foodservice Equipment Distributors Ass'n *(1933)*
223 W. Jackson Blvd., Suite 620
Chicago, IL 60606
Tel: (312)427-9605   Fax: (312)427-9607
Web Site: www.cfeda.com
Members: 300 companies
Staff: 6
Annual Budget: $100-250,000
Exec. Director: Raymond W. Herrick, II, CAE

Historical Note
Formerly (1972) Food Service Equipment Industry, Inc. Dealers in and distributors of foodservice equipment and supplies.

Publications:
FEDA News & Views. bi-m. adv.

Meetings/Conferences:
Annual Meetings: March
1999 – Tuscon, AZ/March 24-28

Foodservice Group *(1978)*
P.O. Box 76533
Atlanta, GA 30358
Tel: (770)977-1476   Fax: (770)973-6662
E-Mail: kwr@fsgroup.com
Web Site: www.fsgroup.com
Members: 47 companies
Staff: 1
Annual Budget: $50-100,000
Exec. Director: Kenneth W. Reynolds

Historical Note
Formerly (1978) Nat'l Foodservice Marketing Associates. Members are independent food service brokers.

Football Writers Ass'n of America *(1941)*
18652 Vista Del Sol
Dallas, TX 75287
Tel: (972)713-6198
Members: 825 individuals
Staff: 1
Exec. Director: Steve Richardson

Historical Note
Established to improve working conditions in college press boxes. Now picks All-America Football team, national championship football team, college coach of the year, winner of the Outland Award, and college football defensive player of the year. Membership: $25/year.

Publications:
The 5th Down. 5/year.

Meetings/Conferences:

Footwear Distributors and Retailers of America *(1944)*
1319 F St., N.W., Suite 700
Washington, DC 20004
Tel: (202)737-5660   Fax: (202)638-2615
E-Mail: fdra@fdra.org
Web Site: http://www.fdra.org
Members: 80 companies
Staff: 4
Annual Budget: $500-1,000,000
President: Peter T. Mangione
Director of Communications: Margaret A. Lew
Meeting Planner: Mary Ellen Smoczynski
Bookkeeper: Faith Lewis
Director, Member Services: Carrie D. Bright

Historical Note
Founded as the Popular Price Shoe Retailers Ass'n, it became the Nat'l Ass'n of Shoe Chain Stores in 1965, the Volume Footwear Retailers Ass'n in 1969, the Volume Footwear Retailers of America in 1972, Footwear Retailers of America in 1985 and assumed its present name in 1985. Absorbed Internat'l Footwear Ass'n in 1990. Sponsors and supports the FDRA Political Action Committee.

Publications:
Bulletin. w.
Customs. m.
Employee Relations. bi-m.
Labor Digest. bi-w.

Meetings/Conferences:
Annual Meetings: Spring
1999 – Sarasota, FL(Longboat Key Club)/April 14-17

Footwear Industries of America *(1869)*
1420 K St., N.W.
Suite 600
Washington, DC 20005
Tel: (202)789-1420   Fax: (202)789-4058
E-Mail: fawn@fia.org
Web Site: http://www.fia.org
Members: 150 companies
Staff: 9
Annual Budget: $1-2,000,000
President: Fawn K. Evenson
V. President, Education and Communications: Barbara Singer
V. President, Finance and Administration: Milt Girdner

Historical Note
Formerly (1905) the Nat'l Boot and Shoe Manufacturers Ass'n; (1965) the Nat'l Shoe Manufacturers Ass'n; (1969) Nat'l Footwear Manufacturers Ass'n. Merged in 1972 with the New England Footwear Ass'n (1869) to form the American Footwear Industries Ass'n Inc. and assumed its present name in 1982 after merging with the American Shoe Center. Incorporated in Massachusetts. Represents nonrubber shoe manufacturers and distributors and their suppliers. Membership: $1,000/year minimum, based on sales.

Publications:
Executive Digest.. m.
Shoe Stats.. a.
Sole Source..

Meetings/Conferences:
Annual Meetings: Spring

Footwear Traffic and Distribution Council *(1964)*

Historical Note
Sponsored by the Footwear Industries of America and the Volume Footwear Retailers of America. Formerly (1969) the Footwear Industry Traffic Council, and (1979) the Footwear Industry Traffic and Distribution Council. Concentrates on tariffs, taxes and physical distribution problems of the shoe industry. Has no dues structure, staff or permanent headquarters.

Foragers of America *(1897)*
135 E. 55th St., 8th Floor
New York, NY 10022
Tel: (212)582-1658
Members: 150 individuals
Annual Budget: $10-25,000
President: Jacqueline Smith

Historical Note
Organization of cosmetic buyers and sales executives with membership concentrated in New York City. Membership: $25/year.

Meetings/Conferences:
Annual Meetings: always New York, NY

Foreign Press Ass'n *(1918)*
110 E. 59th St.
New York, NY 10022
Tel: (212)751-3068   Fax: (212)751-3081
E-Mail: FPANEWYORK@AOL.COM
Members: 450 individuals
Staff: 1
Annual Budget: under $10,000
Director: Suzanne Adams

Historical Note
FPA members are foreign newspaper and broadcast correspondents stationed in the United States. Membership: $50/year (individual).

Publications:
FPA Directory of Members. a. adv.
FPA News Newsletter. bi-m.

Forest Farm and Community Tree Network *(1981)*
c/o Winrock International
38 Winrock Dr.
Morrilton, AR 72110-9537
Tel: (501)727-5435   Fax: (501)727-5417
E-Mail: forestry@winrock.org
Web Site: www.winrock.org/forestry/factnet.htm
Members: 1000 individuals
Staff: 3
Annual Budget: $250-500,000
Contact: Mark Powell

Historical Note
Founded as Nitrogen Fixing Tree Ass'n; assumed its current name in 1996. Encourages research and development efforts concerning the use of nitrogen fixing trees to provide firewood, forage, green manure, and other products that benefit people and relieve pressure on dwindling natural forests. Membership: $35/year (individual), $70/year (institution).

Publications:
FFCT Highlights. 4-8/year.
FFCT Tree Research Reports. a.
FFTC Newsletter. semi-a.

Meetings/Conferences:
Annual Meetings: February

Forest History Soc. *(1946)*
701 Vickers Ave.
Durham, NC 27701
Tel: (919)682-9319
E-Mail: steven@acpub.duke.edu
Web Site: http://www.lib.duke.edu/forest
Members: 2,000 individuals
Staff: 6
Annual Budget: $250-500,000
President and Secretary: Steve Anderson

Historical Note
Preceded by two unincorporated organizations, the Forest Products History Foundation (1946-52) and the American Forest History Foundation (1951-55), the Forest History Soc. was incorporated in Minnesota in 1955. In 1984 it affiliated with Duke University and moved to Durham, NC. A non-profit educational institution advancing the historical understanding of mankind's interaction with the physical environment. Membership: $35/year (individual); $250/year (corporate); $50/year (institution).

Publications:
Environmental History. q.
Forest History Today. a.

Forest Industries Telecommunications *(1947)*
871 Country Club Rd., Suite A
Eugene, OR 97401
Tel: (541)485-8441   Fax: (541)485-7556
E-Mail: license@landmobil.com
Web Site: www.landmobile.com
Members: 1,800 companies
Staff: 6
Annual Budget: $500-1,000,000
Exec. V. President: Kenton E. Sturdevant
Asst. Coordinator: Jackie Jacobson
Manager, Special Services: Teresa Ziemer
Exec. Secretary: Kathy Colley
Membership Services Manager: Angela Baker

Historical Note
Organized in 1947 to assist the forest industry in radio matters before the FCC. Recognized by the FCC as the official representative of the Forest Products Radio Service.

Publications:
Two Way Transmissions. m.

Meetings/Conferences:
Annual Meetings: Fall
1999 – Eugene, OR

Forest Products Safety Conference *(1934)*
c/o IHS Consulting
1525 N.W. Almira
Roseburg, OR 97470
Tel: (541)673-3822
Members: 120 companies

Annual Budget: $25-50,000
Chairman: Jose Phillips

Historical Note
A group of U.S. and Canadian lumber companies united to promote safer working conditions. Established as the Western States Safety Conference, it became the Western Safety Conference in 1938, the Western Forest Products Safety Conference in 1945 and assumed its present name in 1951. Has no paid officers or full-time staff.

Publications:
Conference Proceedings. a.

Meetings/Conferences:

Forest Products Soc. (1947)
2801 Marshall Court
Madison, WI   53705
Tel: (608)231-1361   Fax: (608)231-2152
E-Mail: info@forestprod.org
Web Site: www.forestprod.org
Members: 2,500 individuals
Staff: 11
Annual Budget: $1-2,000,000
Exec. V. President: Arthur B. Brauner

Historical Note
Formerly (1995) Forest Products Research Society. Focus is on wood industry development, research, production, distribution and use, including all phases from logging to finished product and use of by-products.

Publications:
Forest Products Journal. m. adv.
Wood Design Focus. q. adv.

Meetings/Conferences:
Annual Meetings: Summer/400-500
1999 – Boise, ID(Grove Hotel)/June 27-30
2000 – Lake Tahoe, NV(Harvey's Casino & Resort Hotel)/June 18-21

Forest Products Traffic Ass'n (1911)
Historical Note
Ass'n inactive in 1996.

Forest Products Trucking Council (1984)
Historical Note
Organization defunct in 1996.

Forestry Conservation Communications Ass'n (1944)
444 N. Capitol St., N.W.
Washington, DC   20001
Tel: (202)624-5416   Fax: (202)624-5407
E-Mail: fcca@SSO.org
Members: 200 organizations
Staff: 2
Annual Budget: $50-100,000
Secretary: John M. Kenty

Historical Note
Certified by the FCC as the radio frequency coordinator for the Forestry Conservation Radio Service. Has no paid officers or full-time staff.

Publications:
FCAA Newsletter. q.

Meetings/Conferences:
Annual Meetings: July
1999 – Layfatte, LA(Arcadian)/July 11-14/200

Forestry Equipment Council
Historical Note
A council of the Equipment Manufacturers Institute.

Forex U.S.A.: the Financial Markets Ass'n (1958)
Bank Polska, Kasa Opiek S.A.
470 Park Ave. South
New York, NY   10016
Tel: (212)725-8834   Fax: (212)679-5910
Members: 600 individuals
Secretary: Derek J. Ridout

Historical Note
Formerly (1988) Forex Ass'n of North America, and (1997) Forex U.S.A. Members are foreign exchange and money market traders and brokers. Membership: $200/year.

Meetings/Conferences:
Annual Meetings: June

Forging Industry Ass'n (1913)
Landmark Office Towers, Suite 300
25 Prospect Ave., West
Cleveland, OH   44115-1040
Tel: (216)781-6260   Fax: (216)781-0102
E-Mail: info@forging.org
Web Site: http://www.forging.org
Members: 200 companies
Staff: 12
Annual Budget: $1-2,000,000
Exec. V. President: Charles H. Hageman
Communications: Donald Farley
Director, Industry Meetings: Cynthia Korzun
Education/Training: George Mochnal
Finance/Administration: Diane Rothaermel
Director, Membership Development: Karen Lewis Taylor

Historical Note
Formerly Drop Forging Ass'n. Producers of forgings and raw materials, major equipment and supplies used in the forging industry. In addition to its annual meeting, FIA sponsors Forge Fair, an international symposium, triennially.

Publications:
Environmental Update. q.
FIA Directions. bi-m.
Labor and Employment Update. q.
Safety and Health Newsletter. bi-m.

Meetings/Conferences:
Annual Meetings: May
1999 – Tucson, AZ(Loews Ventana Canyon Resort)/May 8-11

Forming Technologies Ass'n of SME

Forum for Health Care Planning (1950)
314 Vista de Valle
Mill Valley, CA   94941-4017
Tel: (415)381-1846   Fax: (415)381-1104
E-Mail: 73503.2616@compuserve.com
Members: 600 individuals
Staff: 2
Annual Budget: $100-250,000
Exec. Director: Jane Drever

Historical Note
Formerly (1986) American Ass'n for Hospital Planning. The Forum is a national membership organization committed to strengthening the planning for hospitals and health care delivery systems to meet community needs. Its members include health care practitioners, executives, consultants, architects, managers, voluntary community leaders, planners, teachers and researchers in the health care field. Membership: $145/year.

Publications:
Membership Directory. a.
Newsletter. q.

Meetings/Conferences:

Forum for Investor Advice
7200 Wisconsin Ave., Suite 709
Bethesda, MD   20814-4811
Tel: (301)656-7998   Fax: (301)656-5019
Members: 70 organizations
Staff: 6
Annual Budget: $500-1,000,000
Exec. Director: Barbara Levin
Director of Communications: Arthur Siddon
Manager, Administrative and Member Services: Adrienne Varieur

Historical Note
Formerly Mutual Fund Forum, FIA is an association of financial services organizations that distribute mutual funds or other investment products. The organization's primary role is to provide information and research to its constituencies, which include its member firms, the investing public, financial advisors, and the financial press.

Publications:
Media Guide. a..
Mutual Fund Forum..

Meetings/Conferences:
1999 – New York/150

Foster Family-Based Treatment Ass'n
1415 Queen Anne Road
Teaneck, NJ   07666
Toll Free: (800)414 - 3382
Web Site: http://www.ffta.org
Staff: 3
Administrator: David Schild

Historical Note
FFTA supports administrators, researchers, educators, treatment foster parents, and others interested in strengthening family-based child care and treatment.

Meetings/Conferences:
1999 – Minneapolis, MN/July 11-14

Foundation Beefmaster Ass'n (1971)
Historical Note
Merged with Beefmaster Breeders United in 1996.

Foundation for Advances in Medicine and Science (1983)
P.O. Box 832
Mahwah, NJ   07430-0832
Tel: (201)818-1010   Fax: (201)818-0086
Toll Free: (800)443 - 0263
E-Mail: scanning@fams.com
Web Site: http://www.scanning-fams.org
Members: 400 individuals
Staff: 3
Annual Budget: $250-500,000
Director: Tony Bourgholtzer

Historical Note
FAMS supports and distributes information on cardiology research and education, and sponsors research on the readability of patient education materials used in the profession. Members are physicians, scientists and others with an interest in clinical medicine and science. Membership: $195/year (individual); $500/year (company).

Publications:
Clinical Cardiology. m. adv.
Scanning. 8/year. adv.

Meetings/Conferences:
Annual Meetings: Spring
1999 – Chicago, IL(Hyatt Regency O'Hare)

Foundation for Independent Higher Education (1958)
11 S. LaSalle St., Suite 1730
Chicago, IL   60603-1301
Tel: (312)849-9400   Fax: (312)849-9151
Members: 600 colleges/universities, 38 ass'ns
Staff: 10
Annual Budget: $1-2,000,000
Director of Program Development: Ruth Frey
Director of Development: John T. Carr
Director of Finance and Operations: Michael W. Elews

Historical Note
Formerly (1987) Independent College Funds of America. The Foundation is the national headquarters for a federation of 38 state and regional associations representing 600 independent colleges and universities. One of the nation's largest fund-raising organizations for independent higher education, it is dedicated to broadening financial support and understanding of independent higher education and its contributions to the nation.

Publications:
Annual Report. a.
Directory of State Associations and Colleges Represented. a.

Meetings/Conferences:
1999 – Baltimore, MD/April 11-13

Foundation for Internat'l Meetings (1983)
1110 N. Glebe Road, Suite 580
Arlington, VA   22201
Tel: (703)908-0707   Fax: (703)908-0709
Members: 140 individuals
Staff: 2
Annual Budget: $50-100,000
President: Jack C. Sammis
Director of Operations: Joan Buser

Historical Note
Founded in Washington, DC in early 1983. Members are C.E.O.'s of associations and corporations which have ongoing international meeting or trade programs. Membership: $475/year, (by invitation).

Publications:
Internat'l Meetings. q.

Meetings/Conferences:
Annual Meetings: Washington, DC

Foundation for Pavement Rehabilitation and Maintenance Research
1200 19th St., N.W., Suite 300
Washington, DC   20036-2422
Tel: (202)429-5146   Fax: (202)429-5113
Acct. Executive: John Fiegel

Foundation of the American Soc. of Ass'n Executives (1963)
Historical Note
Established in 1963 by the American Society of Association Executives and incorporated in the District of Columbia in 1967. Receives its support from business organizations and associations whose executives are members of ASAE. Supports research on the future of association operations and provides information to increase the effectiveness of voluntary associations.

Fourdrinier Wire Council (1924)
Historical Note
Name changed to Paper Machine Clothing Council (PMCC) in 1996.

Fragrance Foundation (1949)
145 East 32nd St.
New York, NY   10016-6002
Tel: (212)725-2755   Fax: (212)779-9058
E-Mail: info@fragrance.org
Web Site: http://www.fragrance.org
Members: 200 companies
Staff: 11
Annual Budget: $1-2,000,000
President: Annette Green
Public Relations: Karen Peterson
Director: Mary Ellen Lapsansky
Exec. Administrator, Olfactory Res. Fund: Terry Molnar

Historical Note
The educational arm of the perfume industry. Membership fee based on annual sales volume.

Publications:
Directory. a.
Fragrance Forum. q.
Recognition Awards Journal. a. adv.

Meetings/Conferences:
Annual Meetings: usually New York, NY

Fragrance Materials Ass'n of the United States (1979)
1620 I St., N.W., Suite 925
Washington, DC   20006
Tel: (202)293-5800   Fax: (202)463-8998
Members: 65 companies
Staff: 12
Annual Budget: $500-1,000,000
Attorney and Exec. Secretary: Daniel R. Thompson

Historical Note
FMA promotes the U.S. fragrance industry through legislative and regulatory work. Its activities are closely coordinated with those of the Research Institute for Fragrance Materials, which undertakes scientific research to support product safety for the industry.

Publications:
FMA Bulletin. m.
Regulatory and Legislative Update. q.

Meetings/Conferences:

Franchise Consultants Internat'l Ass'n (1987)
5147 South Angela Road
Memphis, TN   38117
Tel: (901)368-3333   Fax: (901)368-1144
E-Mail: FRANMARK@MSN.COM
Members: 3,126 individuals
Staff: 5
Annual Budget: $100-250,000
President: William C. Richey

Historical Note
FCIA members are sales, marketing, advertising, legal, placement, finance, and administrative consultants to the franchising industry. Membership: $315/year (individual).

Publications:
Franchise Logistics. a.
Franchise Manuals. a.

Franchise News. m. adv.
Legal Issues-Legal Rewards. a.
Meetings/Conferences:
1999 – Orlando. Fl

Fraternal Field Managers Ass'n (1935)
4321 North Ballard Rd.
Appleton, WI   54919-0001
Tel: (920)734-5721   *Fax:* (920)730-3763
Members: 75 individuals
Staff: 1
Annual Budget: $10-25,000
Secretary-Treasurer: Fred Ebbesen
Historical Note
Members are sales managers of fraternal life insurance societies. Awards the designation FIC (Fraternal Insurance Counselor). A section of the Nat'l Fraternal Congress of America, it sponsors the Nat'l Ass'n of Fraternal Insurance Counselors. Has no paid staff. Membership: $50/yr.
Meetings/Conferences:

Fraternity Executives Ass'n (1930)
5939 Castle Creek Pkwy Dr. North
Indianapolis, IN   46250-4343
Tel: (317)579-5050
Web Site: http://www.fea-inc.org
Members: 72 fraternities
Annual Budget: $100-250,000
President: Nancy H. Leonard
Historical Note
Formerly (1970) College Fraternity Secretaries Ass'n. Serves chief executive officers of fraternal organizations. Has no paid officers or full-time staff.
Publications:
News and Notes. m.
Meetings/Conferences:
Annual Meetings: Normally with College Fraternity Editors
Ass'n, usually in Summer
1999 – Wesley Chapel, FL(Saddlebrook Resort)/July 10-13

Freelance Editorial Ass'n (1983)
P.O. Box 380835
Cambridge, MA   02238-0835
Tel: (617)576-8797
Members: 300 individuals
Annual Budget: $25-50,000
Contact: Eileen Kramer
Historical Note
Members are self-employed contractors, or consultants, with expertise in editorial functions such as copyediting, indexing, translation, researching, proofreading, desktop publishing, project management and writing. Membership: $90/year (individual).
Publications:
Code of Fair Practice.
FEA Yellow Pages. a.
Freelance Editorial Ass'n News Newsletter. q.

Freestanding Insert Council of North America
4700 W. Lake Ave.
Glenview, IL   60025-1485
Tel: (847)375-4700   *Fax:* (847)375-4777
Exec. Officer: Mark T. Engle

French-American Chamber of Commerce (1896)
1350 Avenue of the Americas
New York, NY   10019
Tel: (212)765-4460   *Fax:* (212)765-4650
Members: 3,000 domestic companies, 600 abroad
Staff: 10
Annual Budget: $1-2,000,000
Managing Director: Kathy Baiardi
Historical Note
Formerly (1977) French Chamber of Commerce in the United States. Furthers trade and fosters economic, commercial and financial relations between the U.S. and France. Also provides a forum for French and American business and professional people with international interests. Operates eighteen chapters in the U.S. and an office in Paris. Membership: $200-$650/year.
Publications:
Directory. a. adv.
News. bi-m. adv.

Fresh Produce and Floral Council (1966)
6301 Beach Blvd., Suite 150
Buena Park, CA   90621-2800
Tel: (714)739-0177   *Fax:* (714)739-0226
E-Mail: fpfc@aol.com
Members: 500 individuals, 300 companies
Staff: 3
Annual Budget: $500-1,000,000
President: Linda Stine
Event Coordinator: Carissa Mace
Historical Note
Formerly (1994) Fresh Produce Council. Incorporated in California, FPFC's primary purpose is promoting, through communication and education, fresh fruit, vegetable and floral products. It also acts as a trade organization providing an environment for better communication within the industry. Membership: $450/year.
Publications:
FPFC Digest. 6/yr. adv.
Issues in Food Safety. 2-3/year.
Meetings/Conferences:
1999 – Anaheim, CA(Disneyland Hotel)/700

Fresh Produce Ass'n of the Americas (1944)
P.O. Box 848
Nogales, AZ   85628
Tel: (520)287-2707   *Fax:* (520)287-2948
E-Mail: leef@fpaota.org

Web Site: http://www.fpaota.org
Members: 125 individuals
Staff: 5
Annual Budget: $500-1,000,000
President: Lee Frankel
Director, Communications: Kathleen Vandervoet
Event Coordinator: Jessica Ruiz
Historical Note
Formerly known as West Mexico Vegetable Distributors Association, FPAA represents U.S. firms engaged in the marketing of Mexican-grown fruits and vegetables to international markets. Membership: $500/year.
Publications:
Newsletter. w.
Meetings/Conferences:
Annual Meetings: May

Friction Materials Standards Institute (1948)
588 Monroe Turnpike
Monroe, CT   06468
Tel: (203)452-1877   *Fax:* (203)452-7951
Members: 90 companies
Staff: 2
Annual Budget: $100-250,000
Exec. Director: Gilbert N. Laycock
Historical Note
Formerly Brake Lining Manufacturers Ass'n. Manufacturers of brake linings and clutch facings.
Publications:
Automotive Data Book. a.
Brake Block Identification Catalog. a.
Meetings/Conferences:
Annual Meetings: June
1999 – Longboat Key, FL(Longboat Key Club)/June 4-7

Frozen Potato Products Institute (1958)
2000 Corporate Ridge
Suite 1000
McLean, VA   22102
Tel: (703)821-0770   *Fax:* (703)821-1350
Members: 7 companies
Staff: 2
Annual Budget: $50-100,000
Exec. Director: Heather B. Schroeder
Meetings/Conferences:

Frozen Vegetable Council (1983)
Historical Note
Defunct in 1997.

FSC/DISC Tax Ass'n (1982)
One Barker Ave.
White Plains, NY   10601
Tel: (914)328-5656   *Fax:* (914)328-5757
Members: 400 individuals
Staff: 4
Annual Budget: $500-1,000,000
Exec. Director: Robert H. Ross, CAE
Historical Note
Members are companies and individuals with an interest in the operation of Foreign Sales Corporations and Domestic Internat'l Sales Corporations. Membership: $345/year (individual); $500/year (company).
Publications:
FSC Leasing News Newsletter.. q.
FSC/DISC News Newsletter.. q.
International Tax Newsletter..
Multistate Tax Newsletter.. q.

FTD Ass'n (1994)
33031 Schoolcraft Road
Livonia, MI   48150-1618
Toll Free: (888)419 - 1515
Web Site: http://www.ftdassociation.org
Members: 20,292 individuals
Staff: 49
Annual Budget: $5-10,000,000
Managing Exec. and C.E.O.: Jim Jordan
Director, Value Added Services: William Golden
Assoc. Managing Exec.: David Vaillancourt
Group Director, Finance: John Gauss
Director, Networking: Ron Smith
Historical Note
Formerly Florists Telegraph Delivery Ass'n (1998). A partner of InterFlora, Inc., the international florists' delivery organization. Has an annual budget of approximately $140 million. Membership: $800/year.
Publications:
Florist. m. adv.
FTD Family. m.
Meetings/Conferences:
Annual Meetings: August
1999 – Las Vegas, NV(Bellagio)/Aug. 1-4

Fuel Cell Institute (1993)
P.O. Box 65481
Washington, DC   20035-5481
Tel: (301)681-3532   *Fax:* (301)681-4896
Members: 50 individuals and corporations
Annual Budget: $10-25,000
Secretary/Treasurer: Martin Gutstein
Historical Note
FCI supersedes the Fuel Cell Ass'n. Members are developers, designers, manufacturers, researchers and others with an interest in fuel cell applications. The Institute disseminates timely and reliable information about the benefits of fuel cells to the general public. Membership: $150/year (individual); $1,000/year (organization/company).

Publications:
Fuel Cell News Newsletter. q. adv.
Meetings/Conferences:
Annual Meetings: June

Fulfillment Management Ass'n (1948)
60 East 42nd St., Suite 1146
New York, NY   10165
Tel: (212)277-1597   *Fax:* (212)277-1530
Web Site: http://www.fmanational.org
Members: 425 individuals
Annual Budget: $50-100,000
Contact: Bruce Barone
Historical Note
Established as the Subscription Fulfillment Managers Ass'n, it assumed its present name in 1972. Members are direct mail fulfillment, marketing and circulation executives. Membership is concentrated in New York, Chicago, and Washington, DC. Has no paid staff. Membership: $125/year; $95/year (early bird rate).
Publications:
Job Listings Bulletin. m.
Membership Directory. a.
Meetings/Conferences:
Monthly Meetings: New York, NY(Grand Hyatt)/3rd
Wednesday

Funeral and Memorial Socs. of America (1963)
P.O. Box 10
Hinesburg, VT   05461
Tel: (802)482-3437   *Fax:* (802)482-5246
Toll Free: (800)765 - 0107
E-Mail: famsa@funerals.org
Web Site: http://www.funerals.org/famsa
Members: 150 societies
Staff: 3
Annual Budget: $50-100,000
Exec. Director: Lisa Carlson
Historical Note
Formerly (1995) Continental Ass'n of Funeral and Memorial Socs. Members are non-profit consumer groups dedicated to protecting a consumers right to choose a meaningful, affordable funeral. Membership fee varies, based on group membership dues collected.
Publications:
FAMSA Directory of Member Societies. irreg.
Newsletter. q.
Meetings/Conferences:
Biennial Meetings: Even years/100

Fur Commission USA (1944)
426 Orange Ave., Suite 506
Coronado, CA   92118-2619
Members: 45 organizations
Staff: 4
Annual Budget: $100-250,000
Legislative Director: Robert Buckler
Communications Director: Marsha Kelly
Historical Note
Formerly (1995) Nat'l Board of Fur Farm Organizations, Fur Farm Animal Welfare Coalition, Mink Farmers Research Foundation. Members are U.S. mink and fox farmers.
Publications:
Fur Farm Letter. m.
Meetings/Conferences:
Annual Meetings: Fall

Fur Conservation Institute of America (1970)
Historical Note
A subsidiary of the Fur Information Council of America.

Fur Industry Marketing Institute (1962)
Historical Note
A subsidiary of the Fur Information Council of America.

Fur Information Council of America (1985)
447-A Carlisle Dr.
Herndon, VA   20170
Tel: (703)471-5238   *Fax:* (703)471-6485
Web Site: http://www.fur.org
Members: 300 individuals
Staff: 5
Annual Budget: $500-1,000,000
Exec. Director: Carol Wynne
Director, Public Relations: Stephanie Kenyon
Membership Services Director: Susan P. Giardina
Historical Note
Absorbed (1962) Fur Industry Marketing Institute, (1971) Fur Conservation Institute of America, and (1972) American Fur Industry. Formerly known as Fur Information and Fashion Council; assumed its current name in 1985. FICA is the largest organization representing the fur trade. Member retailers and manufacturers account for over 80% of U.S. fur sales.
Publications:
Fur Fashion Trends Media Kit. a.
Newsletter. bi-w.
Meetings/Conferences:
Annual Meetings: usually New York, NY/February

Furniture Manufacturers Alliance
Historical Note
An alliance of the Business Products Industry Ass'n.

Fusion Power Associates (1979)
2 Professional Drive, Suite 249
Gaithersburg, MD   20879
Tel: (301)258-0545   *Fax:* (301)975-9869
E-Mail: fpa@compuserve.com
Web Site: http://fusionpower.org
Members: 400 individuals, 45 companies

Staff: 3
Annual Budget: $250-500,000
President: Stephen O. Dean, Ph.D.
V. President, Administration & Finance: Ruth Watkins

Historical Note
Incorporated in California in 1979, the association is concerned with the development of practical applications of fusion science and technology. Membership: $50/year (individual), $400/year (small business), $900/year (non-voting institution), $1,600/year (voting institution).

Publications:
Executive Newsletter. m.
Fusion Facilities Directory. a.

Meetings/Conferences:

Futon Ass'n Internat'l *(1984)*
P.O. Box 6548
Chico, CA 95927-6548
Tel: (530)534-7833 *Fax:* (530)534-7875
Toll Free: (800)327 - 3262
Web Site: http://www.fainet.com
Members: 520 manufacturers and distributors
Staff: 3
Annual Budget: $250-500,000
Admin. Director: Timothy A. Jacobs

Historical Note
Formerly (1990) the Futon Ass'n of North America. futon furniture and bedding. Members are manufacturers, distributors and retailers of futon furniture and bedding. Membership: sliding scale based on sales.

Publications:
Membership Directory. a.
Newsletter. q.

Meetings/Conferences:
1999 – Las Vegas, NV

Future Business Leaders of America-Phi Beta Lambda *(1942)*
1912 Association Drive
Reston, VA 20191-1591
Tel: (703)860-3334 *Fax:* (703)758-0749
Toll Free: (800)325 - 2946
E-Mail: general@fbla.org
Members: 270,000 individuals
Staff: 11
Annual Budget: $2-5,000,000
President and C.E.O.: Jean M. Buckley
Conference Director: Lori Schirpke
Membership Director: Jennifer Seavey

Historical Note
Future Business Leaders of America-Phi Beta Lambda is a nonprofit 501(c)(3) educational ass'n of student members preparing for careers in business and business-related fields. The ass'n has four divisions: FBLA for high school students; FBLA-Middle Level for junior high and intermediate students; PBL for postsecondary students;and a Professional Division for Business people, educators, and parents who suport the goals of the ass'n. Membership: $4/year (middle level); $6/year (high school); $10/year (college); $23/year (professional).

Publications:
Middle Connection. q. adv.
PBL Business Leader. 3 times/year.
The Adviser's Hotline. q. adv.
The Professional Edge. q. adv.
Tomorrow's Business Leader. q. adv.

Meetings/Conferences:
Annual Meetings: July

Future Homemakers of America *(1945)*
1910 Association Drive
Reston, VA 20191-1584
Tel: (703)476-4900 *Fax:* (703)860-2713
E-Mail: NATLHDQTRS@FHAHERO.ORG
Web Site: http://www.fhahero.org
Members: 230,000 individuals
Staff: 23
Annual Budget: $2-5,000,000
Exec. Director: Alan T. Rains, Jr.
Director, Programs & Communications: Carolyn W. Brown
Director, Finance & Administration: Mary Lou Seigfried

Historical Note
Sponsored by the Department of Education and the American Ass'n of Family and Consumer Sciences. Members are family and consumer sciences students through grade 12. Absorbed the New Homemakers of America in 1965. Membership: $6/year.

Publications:
Teen Times. q.
The Adviser. 3/year.

Meetings/Conferences:
Annual Meetings: July
1999 – Boston, MA
2000 – Orlando, FL
2001 – Anaheim, CA
2002 – Minneapolis, MN
2003 – Philadelphia, PA

Futures Industry Ass'n *(1955)*
2001 Pennsylvania Ave., N.W., Suite 600
Washington, DC 20006-1850
Tel: (202)466-5460 *Fax:* (202)296-3184
E-Mail: info@fiafii.org
Web Site: http://www.fiafii.org
Members: 100 brokerage houses, 130 associates
Staff: 12
Annual Budget: $2-5,000,000
President: John M. Damgard
V. President, Communications: Mary Ann Burns
Director, Futures Industry Institute: Paula A. Tosini
V. President, Administration: Julia Greenway, CMP

Exec. V. President & General Counsel: Barbara Wierzynski

Historical Note
Formerly (1975) Ass'n of Commodity Exchange Firms. Founded to represent the brokerage community, FIA now acts as a principal spokesman for the futures and options industry in general.

Publications:
Bulletin. w.
Futures Industry Magazine. bi-m. adv.
Futures Trading Volume Report. m.
Marketbeat Newsletter. m.

Meetings/Conferences:
1999 – Boca Raton, FL(Boca Raton Resort)/March 17-20

Galiceno Horse Breeders Ass'n *(1959)*
Box 219
Godley, TX 76044
Tel: (817)389-3547
Members: 600 individuals
Annual Budget: under $10,000
Secretary: Chris Giles

Historical Note
Members are owners and breeders of Galiceno horses. Membership: $20/year.

Publications:
Newsletter. m.

GAMA Internat'l *(1951)*
1922 F St., N.W.
Washington, DC 20006
Tel: (202)331-6088 *Fax:* (202)785-5712
Toll Free: (800)345 - 2687
Members: 9,200 individuals
Staff: 15
Annual Budget: $2-5,000,000
Acting Exec. V. President: Renee Pietrangelo, Ph.D.
Director, Education: Carol Walsh

Historical Note
Founded as General Agents and Managers Conference of NALU; became General Agents and Managers Ass'n in 1991, and assumed its current name in 1997. Provides educational and training opportunities for those engaged in field management within the life insurance industry. Membership: $90/year.

Publications:
GAMA News Journal. bi-m. adv.
Leaders Letter. bi-m.
Showcase (audio series). 8/year.

Meetings/Conferences:
Annual Meetings: March/2,500

Game Manufacturers Ass'n *(1975)*
P.O. Box 1210
Scottsdale, AZ 85252
Tel: (602)945-6917 *Fax:* (602)994-1170
E-Mail: ed@gama.org
Web Site: http://www.gama.org
Members: 231 companies
Annual Budget: $100-250,000
Exec. Director: Murray Nuckols

Historical Note
Formerly (1986) GAMA. Members are companies that manufacture historical, fantasy, science fiction, and adult games which are played on tables, computers, boards, or plain paper for the adventure game, hobby, and game markets. Membership: $300/year (full member); $100/year (associate); $50/year (retail or distributor); $25/year (communicating).

Publications:
GAMA Source Directory. a.
Newsletter. q.

Meetings/Conferences:
Semi-Annual Meetings: Spring and Summer
1999 – Las Vegas, NV/March 23-25
2000 – Columbus, OH(Convention Center)/July 13-16
2001 – Columbus, OH(Convention Center)/July 5-8

Gamma Iota Sigma *(1965)*
2586 Oakstone Drive
Columbus, OH 43231-7628
Tel: (614)891-4242
Members: 500 individuals
Staff: 1
Annual Budget: $25-50,000
Treasurer: George Gummer

Historical Note
Student professional insurance fraternity. Member of Professional Fraternity Association.

Publications:
The Sextant. semi-a.

Meetings/Conferences:
Annual Meetings: Spring
1999 – Dallas, TX/April 8-11

Garage Door Council *(1982)*

Historical Note
A federation available to trade groups of companies making and distributing garage doors and components; main task is conducting public information campaigns.

Garage Door Hardware Ass'n

Garden Centers of America *(1972)*
1250 I St., N.W., Suite 500
Washington, DC 20005
Tel: (202)789-2900 *Fax:* (202)789-1893
Members: 1000 companies
Staff: 2
Annual Budget: $100-250,000
Exec. V. President: Robert J. Dolibois, CAE

Historical Note
GCA is the retail division of the American Nursery and Landscape Ass'n.

Publications:
Garden Centers of America Newsletter. bi-m.

Meetings/Conferences:
Semi-Annual Meetings: February and with ANLA/July

Garden Writers Ass'n of America *(1948)*
10210 Leatherleaf Court
Manassas, VA 20111-4245
Tel: (703)257-1032 *Fax:* (703)257-0213
E-Mail: assnctr@earthlink.net
Web Site: http://www.gwaa.org
Members: 1,600 individuals
Staff: 4
Annual Budget: $250-500,000
Exec. Director: Robert C. LaGasse, CAE

Historical Note
Membership: $75/year, (individual); $250/year, (organization).

Publications:
Quill & Trowel Newsletter. bi-m.

Meetings/Conferences:
Annual Meetings: Fall
1999 – Toronto, ON(Royal York Hotel)/Aug. 19-25
2000 – Philadelphia, PA

Gas Appliance Manufacturers Ass'n *(1935)*
1901 N. Moore St., Suite 1100
Arlington, VA 22209-1706
Tel: (703)525-9565 *Fax:* (703)525-0718
E-Mail: information@gamanet.org
Web Site: http://www.gamanet.org
Members: 256 companies
Staff: 18
Annual Budget: $1-2,000,000
President: C. Reuben Autery
Manager, Member/Communications Services: Sydney Ashley
Director of Gov't Affairs: Joseph M. Mattingly
Manager, Government Affairs: Gina J. Rigby
Director, Technical Services: Frank A. Stanonik
Director, Administrative Services: John R. Heberlein

Historical Note
Founded as the Association of Gas Appliance and Equipment Manufacturers, it assumed its present name in 1946 and absorbed the Institute of Appliance Manufacturers (founded in 1872) in 1967. Manufacturers of residential, commercial and industrial gas and oil appliances and equipment; gas, electric and oil-fired water heaters; oil-fired central furnaces and equipment used in the production, transmission and distribution of natural gas.

Publications:
Gama Reports. bi-m.
Patent Digest. m.
Statistical Highlights. m.

Meetings/Conferences:
Annual Meetings: Spring/500
1999 – Ponte Verde Beach, FL(Marriott at Sawgrass)/April 25-28
2000 – La Qunita, CA(La Quinta Resort & Club)/May 14-17
2001 – Palm Beach, FL(The Breakers)/April 22-25

Gas Processors Ass'n *(1921)*
6526 E. 60th St.
Tulsa, OK 74145-9202
Tel: (918)493-3872 *Fax:* (918)493-3875
E-Mail: gpa@gasprocessors.com
Members: 150 companies
Staff: 8
Annual Budget: $500-1,000,000
Exec. Director: Mark Sutton
Director, Industry Affairs: Johnny Dreyer
Secretary: Ronald G. Bruner

Historical Note
Established in 1921 as Ass'n of Natural Gasoline Manufacturers and became Natural Gasoline Ass'n of America in 1922. The name was changed to Natural Gas Processors Ass'n in 1961 and Gas Processors Ass'n in 1974. Membership consists of firms handling natural gasoline and other hydrocarbon products at gas-processing plants.

Publications:
Proceedings. a.

Meetings/Conferences:
Annual Meetings: March/2,000
1999 – Nashville, TN/March 15-17
2000 – Atlanta, GA/March 13-15
2001 – San Antonio, TX/March 12-14
2002 – Dallas, TX/March 11-13
2003 – San Antonio, TX/March 10-12
2004 – New Orleans, LA/March 8-10
2005 – San Antonio, TX/March 14-16

Gas Processors Suppliers Ass'n *(1927)*
6526 E. 60th St.
Tulsa, OK 74145-9202
Tel: (918)493-3872 *Fax:* (918)493-3875
E-Mail: gpsa@gasprocessors.com
Members: 350 companies
Staff: 6
Annual Budget: $100-250,000
Treasurer: Mark Sutton

Historical Note
Formerly (1974) Natural Gas Processors Suppliers Ass'n. GPSA is comprised of companies that provide supplies, equipment, or services to the gas processing industry. Membership: $200/yr.

Publications:
Engineering Data Book.

Meetings/Conferences:
Annual Meetings: with Gas Processors Ass'n/3,000

Gas Research Institute (1976)
8600 W. Bryn Mawr Ave.
Chicago, IL   60631-3562
Tel: (773)399-8100   Fax: (773)399-8170
Web Site: http://www.gri.org
Members: 335 companies
Staff: 180
Annual Budget: Over $100,000,000
President and C.E.O.: Stephen D. Ban
V. President, Customer Relations/Communications: Susan Newman
Principal Manager, Customer Relations and Communications: Sandy Hagen
V. President and C.F.O.: Robert G. Eady
V. President and General Counsel: William H. Kockenmeister
V. President and General Manager, Distrbution End Use/LDC Business Unit: William M. Burnett

Historical Note
Members are companies involved in the production, transmission and distribution of natural gas. Manages research, development, demonstration and deployment of new gas technologies. Has an annual budget of approximately $160 million.

Publications:
Baseline Projection of U. S.
GRI Annual Report. a.
GRI Catalogue of Technical Reports. irreg.
GRI Digest. q.
IGRC Proceedings. irreg.
R&D Plan and R&D Program. a.
Technology Profiles. irreg.

Meetings/Conferences:
Annual Meetings: April

Gas Turbine Ass'n (1995)
1050 Thomas Jefferson St., N.W.
Washington, DC   20007
Tel: (202)298-1806   Fax: (202)338-2416
E-Mail: advocates@erols.com
Members: 12 companies
Staff: 3
Annual Budget: $100-250,000
Exec. Director: Jeffrey S. Abboud

Historical Note
GTA's mission is to represent the industry before public, governmental amd quasi-governmental bodies; to collect and publish industry, economic and other statistical data; to encourage the use of gas turbines in specific markets through promotional and/or market development programs; to help member companies solve common environmental, health and safety problems; to develop recommended industry standards; to increase public knowledge and understanding of gas turbines and the industry through educational and information programs. Membership: $20,000/year (organization/company).

Gasification Technologies Council (1995)
1110 N. Glebe Road, Suite 610
Arlington, VA   22201
Tel: (703)276-0110   Fax: (703)276-7662
E-Mail: JMCHIL@AOL.COM
Web Site: http://www.gasification.org.
Members: 25 individualscompanies
Exec. Director: James M. Childress

Historical Note
GTC members are companies involved in the gasification of coal, coke and heavy oils. Membership: $15,000/year (regular); $10,000/year (associate); $5,000/year (affiliate).

Gasket Fabricators Ass'n (1979)
994 Old Eagle School Road, Suite 1019
Wayne, PA   19087-1802
Tel: (610)971-4850   Fax: (610)971-4859
E-Mail: info@gasketfab.com
Web Site: http://www.gasketfab.com
Members: 110 companies
Staff: 5
Annual Budget: $100-250,000
Exec. Director: Robert H. Ecker

Historical Note
National trade association of gasket fabricators whose products include metallic and non-metallic sealing devices and allied products. Membership: $900/year.

Publications:
Newsletter.
Technical Handbook.

Meetings/Conferences:
Semi-Annual Meetings: Spring and Fall
1999 – Ponte Vedro, FL(Sawgrass)/April 14-16
1999 – Scottsdale, AZ(Camelback)/Sept. 22-24

Gasoline and Automotive Service Dealers Ass'n (1931)
9520 Seaview Ave.
Brooklyn, NY   11236-5432
Tel: (718)241-1111   Fax: (718)763-6589
Members: 860 companies, 120 associates
Staff: 7
Annual Budget: $250-500,000
Exec. Director: Stanley M. Schuer

Historical Note
Formerly (1977) Gasoline Merchants. Members are owners and/or operators of service stations or auto repair facilities. GASDA seeks to strengthen professionalism in the industry. Membership: $175/year (individual), $420/year (company).

Publications:
Bulletin. m.
Directory and Buyers Guide. a.
Newsletter. irreg.

Gasoline Pump Manufacturers Ass'n (1934)
P.O. Box 33882
Washington, DC   20033-0882

Tel: (202)467-7000
Members: 5 companies
Staff: 1
Annual Budget: $25-50,000
General Counsel: Mark R. Joelson

Gastroenterology Research Group (1955)
6900 Grove Road
Thorofare, NJ   08086-9447
Tel: (609)848-1000   Fax: (609)848-5274
E-Mail: grg@slackinc.com
Members: 1,200 individuals
Staff: 1
Annual Budget: $10-25,000
Exec. Director: Debra Maines

Historical Note
Affiliated with American Gastroenterological Ass'n and American Ass'n for the Study of Liver Disease. Membership: $10/yr.

Publications:
GRG Newsletter. semi-a.

Meetings/Conferences:
Semi-Annual Meetings: Spring and Fall

Gastrointestinal Pathology Soc. (1979)
Historical Note
Organization defunct in 1998.

Gay and Lesbian Press Ass'n (1981)
Historical Note
Organization defunct in 1997.

Gelbray Internat'l (1981)
Rt.1, Box 273C
Madille, OK   73446
Tel: (580)223-5771   Fax: (580)226-5773
Members: 150 ranches
Annual Budget: $10-25,000
Secretary: Don M. Yeager

Historical Note
Gelbray Internat'l was established for registering and promoting Gelbray cattle. Membership: $25/year (individual).

Publications:
American Beef Cattleman. a. adv.
Gelbray Newsletter. irreg. adv.

Meetings/Conferences:

Gemological Institute of America (1931)
5345 Armada Dr.
Carlsbad, CA   92008
Tel: (760)603-4000   Fax: (760)603-4080
Toll Free: (800)421 - 7250
Web Site: http://www.gia.org
Members: 350 gem manufacturers
Annual Budget: $10-25,000,000
Exec. Director: Susan B. Johnson
Manager, Public Information: Victoria Morrison

Historical Note
Has an annual budget of approximately $12.0 million.

Publications:
Gems & Gemology. q.

Meetings/Conferences:

General Agents and Managers Ass'n
Historical Note
Became GAMA Internat'l in 1997.

General Aviation Manufacturers Ass'n (1970)
1400 K St., N.W., Suite 801
Washington, DC   20005
Tel: (202)393-1500   Fax: (202)842-4063
Members: 53 companies
Staff: 13
Annual Budget: $1-2,000,000
President: Edward M. Bolen
Director, Communications: Shelly R. Snyder
Government Affairs Director: Darby Becker

Historical Note
An outgrowth of the former Utility Aircraft Council of the Aerospace Industries Association, members of GAMA are manufacturers of general aviation aircraft equipment and components. Works on airport/airway technical matters, product liability, and safety issues to develop a better climate for growth of general aviation. Supports the General Aviation Political Action Committee (GAMAPAC).

General Federation of Women's Clubs (1890)
1734 N St., N.W.
Washington, DC   20036-2990
Tel: (202)347-3168   Fax: (202)835-0246
E-Mail: gfwc@gfwc.org
Web Site: http://www.gfwc.org
Members: 300,000 individuals, 8,000 clubs
Staff: 25
Annual Budget: $1-2,000,000
President: Maxine Scarbro
Public Relations Director: Sally Kranz
Director, Public Policy: Sarah Albert
Director, Meetings and Conventions: Natasha Kalteis
Program Director: Pat Nolan
Finance Director: Beverly Bradshaw
Membership Director: Debbe Gladstone

Historical Note
GFWC is a non-denominational, non-partisan, international service organization of volunteer women's clubs dedicated to community service. Membership: $4/year.

Publications:
GFWC Clubwoman Magazine. q. adv.

Meetings/Conferences:
Annual Meetings: June/1,000

1999 – San Francisco, CA(Fairmont Hotel)
2000 – Boston, MA

General Merchandise Distributors Council (1970)
1275 Lake Plaza Drive
Colorado Springs, CO   80906
Tel: (719)576-4260   Fax: (719)576-2661
E-Mail: info@gmdc.org
Web Site: http://www.gmdc.org
Members: 870 companies
Staff: 14
Annual Budget: $2-5,000,000
President and CEO: Richard W. Tilton
Director, Information Services: Kathie D. Zorman
Sr. V. President: David T. McConnell
V. President, Education: Roy White
Manager, Finance and Administration: Ann McConnell
V. President, Membership: Jerry G. Barnes

Historical Note
Founded as a national trade association for the general merchandise and health and beauty care operations of wholesale grocers and supermarket retailers and suppliers of these products to the retail trade. Membership: $1,500/year.

Publications:
Membership Directory. a.
The Focus. bi-m.

Meetings/Conferences:
1999 – Palm Desert, CA/May 21-26
1999 – Marco Island, FL/Sept. 24-29

Generic Pharmaceutical Industry Ass'n (1981)
1620 I St., N.W., Suite 800
Washington, DC   20006-4005
Tel: (202)833-9070   Fax: (202)833-9612
E-Mail: info@gpia.org
Members: 45 companies
Staff: 6
Annual Budget: $1-2,000,000
President: Alice E. Till
V. President of Federal Government Affairs: Henry W. Menn, III

Historical Note
GPIA members are manufacturers and distributors of generic medicines, as well as the providers of technical services and goods to these firms. Membership: dues based on sales volume.

Meetings/Conferences:
1999 – New York, NY(Palace)/March 26-28

Genetic Toxicology Ass'n (1977)
Historical Note
Address unknown in 1996.

Genetics Soc. of America (1931)
9650 Rockville Pike
Bethesda, MD   20814
Tel: (301)571-1825   Fax: (301)530-7079
Web Site: http://www.faseb.org/genetic/gsa/gsamenu.html
Members: 4,000 individuals
Staff: 12
Annual Budget: $1-2,000,000
Exec. Director: Elaine Strass

Historical Note
Organized in 1931 in New Orleans as an outgrowth of the Genetics Section of the American Soc. of Zoologists and the Botanical Soc. of America. Incorporated in Maryland in 1984. Membership: $105/year (full member), $50/year (student).

Publications:
Genetics. m.
Membership Directory. bien.

Meetings/Conferences:

Geochemical Soc. (1955)
Oak Ridge Nat'l Laboratory
P.O. Box 2008
Oak Ridge, TN   37831-6110
Tel: (423)574-6903
E-Mail: www@geochemsoc.org
Web Site: http://www.geochemsoc.org
Members: 1,600 individuals
Staff: 3
Annual Budget: $25-50,000
Secretary: David J. Wesolowski

Historical Note
Founded November 7, 1955 and incorporated in the District of Columbia in 1956. Encourages the application of chemistry to the solution of geological and cosmological problems.

Publications:
Geochemical News. q.
Geochimica et Cosmochimica Acta. semi-m. adv.

Meetings/Conferences:

Geological Soc. of America (1888)
3300 Penrose Place, Box 9140
Boulder, CO   80301
Tel: (303)447-2020   Fax: (303)447-1133
E-Mail: admin@geosociety.org
Web Site: http://www.geosociety.org
Members: 15,258 individuals
Staff: 68
Annual Budget: $5-10,000,000
Exec. Director: Donald M. Davidson, Jr.
Communications Coordinator: Karlon G. Blythe
Meetings Manager: Kathy Lynch
Coordinator for Educational Programs: Edward E. Geary
Manager, Membership Services: T. Michael Moreland

Historical Note
Founded in 1888 and incorporated in New York in 1929. Soc. includes topical divisions: Archaeological Geology, Coal Geology, Engineering Geology, Geophysics, Geoscience Education, History of Geology, Hydrogeology, International Division, Planetary Geology,

Quaternary Geology and Geomorphology, Sedimentary Geology, and Structural Geology and Tectonics. Also has six regional sections, each of which holds its own annual meeting in the spring. A member society of the American Geological Institute. Membership: $42/year (members/fellows).

Publications:
Environmental & Engineering Geoscience. q.
Geological Society of America Bulletin.
Geology. m. adv.
GSA Today. m. adv.
Membership Directory. a.

Meetings/Conferences:
Annual Meetings: Fall
1999 – Denver, CO/Oct. 25-28
2000 – Reno, NV/Nov. 13-16
2001 – Boston, MA/Nov. 5-8
2002 – Denver, CO/Oct. 28-31
2003 – Seattle, WA/Nov. 2-5

Geoscience and Remote Sensing Soc. (1962)
Historical Note
A technical society of the Institute of Electrical and Electronics Engineers (IEEE). Membership in the Society, open only to IEEE members, includes a subscription to a technical periodical in the field published by IEEE. All administrative support provided by IEEE.

Geoscience Information Soc. (1965)
c/o American Geological Institute
4220 King Street
Alexandria, VA   22302
Tel: (703)379-2480
Web Site: http://www.lib.berkeley.edu/GIS
Members: 200 individuals, 40 corporate members
Annual Budget: $10-25,000
Secretary: Shaun Hardy

Historical Note
Founded in Kansas City, GIS was incorporated in the District of Columbia in 1966. Affiliated with the Geological Soc. of America and the American Geological Institute. GIS membership includes national and international representation from colleges and universities, business and industry, publishing, geological surveys, geological societies and other aspects of the field. Membership: $40/year (individual), $75/year (institution), $15/year (student or retired), $100/year sustaining).

Publications:
GIS Newsletter. bi-m.
Membership Directory. a.
Proceedings. a.

Meetings/Conferences:
Annual Meetings: Fall, with the Geological Soc. of America, and quadrennial Internat'l Conference on Geological Information (1998).
1999 – Denver, CO/Oct. 25-28

Geospatial Information and Technology Ass'n (1982)
14456 E. Evans Ave.
Aurora, CO   80014
Tel: (303)337-0513   *Fax:* (303)337-1001
E-Mail: staff@gita.org
Web Site: http://www.gita.org
Members: 2,000 individuals, 244 organizations
Staff: 12
Annual Budget: $1-2,000,000
Exec. Director: Robert Samborski
Director, Communications: John Kayser
Director, Education: Henry Rosales
Director, Administration: Marilyn Seal
Director, Member Services: Rose Seemann

Historical Note
GITA is a non-profit, educational association which fosters information exchange, educational opportunities and scientific research and development in the field of geospatial information technology with emphasis on infrastructure-based applications. Membership: $85/year (individual).

Publications:
Conference Proceedings. a.
GITA Networks. bi-m. adv.
IT Magazine. q.
Membership Directory. a.

Meetings/Conferences:
Annual Meetings: Spring/3,200
1999 – Charlotte, NC(Convention Cneter)/April 25-28
2000 – Denver, CO(Convention Center)/March 26-29
2001 – San Diego, CA/March 4-7
2002 – Tampa, FL/March 18-21

Geothermal Energy Ass'n (1987)
1025 Thomas Jefferson St.
Suite 109
Washington, DC   20007
Tel: (202)944-8564
E-Mail: GEA@Geotherm.org
Web Site: http://www.geotherm.org
Members: 50 corporations
Staff: 7
Annual Budget: $250-500,000
Exec. Director: Karl Gawell
Director, Outreach Programs: Perle M. Dorr

Historical Note
Founded as Nat'l Geothermal Ass'n; assumed its current name in 1994. Shares administrative offices with Geothermal Resources Council. GEA is composed of U.S. companies who support the expanded use of geothermal energy and are developing geothermal resources worldwide for electrical power generation and direct heat uses. Membership: $500/year (individual); $1000/year corporate); $5000/year (board); $75/year (associate).

Publications:
First Alert Newsletter. m.
GEA Newsletter. bi-m.

Meetings/Conferences:
Annual Meetings: October

Geothermal Resources Council (1972)
P.O. Box 1350
Davis, CA   95617-1350
Tel: (530)758-2360   *Fax:* (530)758-2839
E-Mail: grc@geothermal.org
Web Site: http://www.geothermal.org
Members: 900 individuals
Annual Budget: $500-1,000,000
Exec. Director: Ted J. Clutter
Meeting Coordinator: Grace Mata
Accountant and Exec. Secretary: David MacMillan
Online Librarian: Estela Smith

Historical Note
Members are individuals interested in the development and production of geothermal energy. Street address is 4365 Executive Dr., Suite 900, San Diego, CA. Membership: $100/year (individual); $480/year (institution/company).

Publications:
Annual Meeting Transactions. a.
Membership Directory. a. adv.
Special Reports. irreg.
The GRC Bulletin. 9/year. adv.

Meetings/Conferences:
Annual Meetings: Fall
1999 – Reno, NV/Oct. 17-20
2000 – Reno, NV

German American Business Ass'n (1990)
103 Ross Alley
Alexandria, VA   22314-3129
Tel: (703)836-6120   *Fax:* (703)836-6160
Members: 250 individuals, 200 companies
Staff: 4
Annual Budget: $100-250,000
President: Charles W. Zschock

Historical Note
GABA is a business league promoting business between Germany and the United States. Membership: $195/year (individual); $345-650/year (corporate).

Publications:
Focus on Germany Newsletter. m. adv.
Membership Directory. a.

Meetings/Conferences:
Annual Meetings: May

German American Chamber of Commerce (1947)
40 West 57th St., 31st Floor
New York, NY   10019-4001
Tel: (212)974-8857   *Fax:* (212)974-8863
Members: 2,000 corporations
Staff: 32
Annual Budget: $2-5,000,000
President & C.E.O.: Werner Walbrol

Historical Note
Established as a guide and liaison for U.S. and German businesses who want to practice in both the United States and Germany. Now acts as a service organization for members and non-members. Membership: $500/yr.

Publications:
American Subsidiaries of German Firms. a. adv.
German American Trade. a. adv.
Membership Directory. a. adv.
U. S. adv.
United States-German Economic Yearbook. adv. adv.

Meetings/Conferences:
Annual Meetings: March, New York, NY/June, Bonn, Germany

Gerontological Soc. of America (1945)
1030 15th St., N.W., Suite 250
Washington, DC   20005-1503
Tel: (202)842-1275   *Fax:* (202)842-1150
E-Mail: geron@geron.org
Web Site: http://www.geron.org
Members: 6,500 individuals
Staff: 17
Annual Budget: $2-5,000,000
Exec. Director: Carol A. Schutz

Historical Note
An outgrowth of the Club for Research in Aging, organized in 1939. Incorporated in New York in 1945 to promote scientific study of aging; Reincorporated in Washington, DC in 1980. A member of the American Ass'n for the Advancement of Science, and the Internat'l Ass'n of Gerontology. Members are researchers, educators and professionals in the field of aging. Membership: $120/year.

Publications:
Gerontology News. m.
Journal of Gerontology: Series A: Biological & Medical Sciences. bi-m. adv.
Journal of Gerontology: Series B: Psychological & Social Sciences. bi.
The Gerontologist. bi-m. adv.

Meetings/Conferences:
Annual Meetings: Fall/3,500
1999 – San Francisco, CA(Hilton Square)/Nov. 19-23
2000 – Washington, DC(Sheraton)/Nov. 17-21

Gift Ass'n of America (1952)
608 W. Broad St.
Bethlehem, PA   18018-5221
Tel: (610)861-9445
Members: 800 individuals
Staff: 1
Annual Budget: $50-100,000
Exec. Director: Lenore Staffieri Pitsilos

Historical Note
Offers programs and continuing education to professionals in the gift industry. Fomerly (1982) Gift and Decorative Accessories Ass'n of America. Membership: $50/year (retail), $100/year (wholesale).

Publications:
GAA Newsletter. q.
Membership Directory. bien. adv.

Meetings/Conferences:
Semi-annual Meetings: always New York, NY/January & August/25 & 100

Gift Retailers, Manufacturers and Representatives Ass'n
Historical Note
Organization defunct in 1995.

Giftware Associates Interchange (1974)
1100 Main St.
Buffalo, NY   14209
Tel: (716)878-2873   *Fax:* (716)878-2866
Members: 185 companies
Staff: 6
Manager, Marketing and Membership Services: J. Warren Wright

Historical Note
Formerly (1995) Giftware Associates Interchange. Members are manufacturers and importers of giftware and china. Membership: $495/year.

Publications:
Directory. irreg.

Meetings/Conferences:
Semi-Annual Meetings: March in Dallas, TX and October in Toronto, Ontario, Canada

Giftware Manufacturers Credit Interchange (1970)
Historical Note
Became Giftware Associates Interchange in 1995.

Girls Incorporated (1945)
120 Wall St., 3rd Floor
New York, NY   10005-3904
Tel: (212)689-3700   *Fax:* (212)683-1253
Web Site: http://www.girlsinc.org
Members: 350,000 individuals, 133 centers
Staff: 25
Annual Budget: $2-5,000,000
Nat'l Exec. Director: Isabel C. Stewart

Historical Note
Formerly (1989) Girls Clubs of America. Established in 1945 by nineteen charter clubs serving young women. Serves over 300 centers serving 250,000 girls aged 6-18 Maintains a National Resource Center in Indianapolis, IN.

Publications:
Girls Ink. q.

Meetings/Conferences:
Annual Meetings: Spring/250-275

Glass Art Soc. (1971)
1305 4th Ave., Suite 711
Seattle, WA   98101-2401
Tel: (206)382-1305   *Fax:* (206)382-2630
E-Mail: glassartsoc@earthlink.net
Web Site: http://www.glassart.org
Members: 1 individuals
Staff: 3
Annual Budget: $100-250,000
Exec. Director: Penny Berk

Historical Note
A professional society of artists working in glass, as well as critics, collectors, and educators interested in the medium. Membership: $40/year minimum (individual); $15/year (student); $250/year (organization/company).

Publications:
Conference Program. a. adv.
Glass Art Society Journal. a. adv.
Membership Roster. a.
Newsletter. q.

Meetings/Conferences:
1999 – Tampa, FL(Tampa Convention Center)
2000 – Brooklyn, NY
2001 – Corning, NY

Glass Ass'n of North America (1994)
2945 S.W. Wanamaker Dr., Suite A
Topeka, KS   66614-5321
Tel: (785)271-0208   *Fax:* (785)271-0166
Members: 135 companies
Staff: 8
Annual Budget: $500-1,000,000
Exec. V. President: William J. Birch

Historical Note
Formed by the merger of the Flat Glass Marketing Ass'n (1949), the Glass Tempering Ass'n (1958), and the Laminators Safety Glass Ass'n (1971) in 1994. Membership: $600-$4,300/year (corporate).

Publications:
Glass Reflections. m.
Safety Bulletins. m.

Meetings/Conferences:
Semi-Annual Meetings: March and Fall

Glass Packaging Institute (1945)
1627 K St., N.W., Suite 800
Washington, DC   20006
Tel: (202)887-4850   *Fax:* (202)785-5377
E-Mail: gpidc@pop.erols.com
Web Site: http://www.gpi.org
Members: 9 companies, 26 associate members

Staff: 8
Annual Budget: $2-5,000,000
President: Lewis D. Andrews, Jr.
Exec. V. President and Corp. Secretary: Joseph J. Cattaneo
Historical Note
Formerly (1976) Glass Container Manufacturers Institute, Inc. Has an annual budget of approximately $5 million.
Meetings/Conferences:

Glass, Molders, Pottery, Plastics and Allied Workers International Union *(1988)*
608 East Baltimore Pike, Box 607
Media, PA 19063
Tel: (610)565-5051   *Fax:* (610)565-0983
Members: 80,000 individuals
Staff: 75
Annual Budget: $5-10,000,000
Internat'l President: James H. Rankin
Historical Note
Product of a merger between the Glass, Pottery, Plastics and Allied Workers and the Internat'l Molders and Allied Workers Union in 1988. Supports the Glass, Molders, Pottery, Plastics and Allied Workers Political Education League. Membership: $14/month (individual).
Publications:
GMP Horizons. m.
Meetings/Conferences:
Quadrennial Convention: (2000)

Glazing Industry Code Committee *(1983)*
2945 S.W. Wanamaker Dr., Suite A
Topeka, KS 66614-5321
Tel: (785)271-0208   *Fax:* (785)271-0166
E-Mail: gicc@glasswebsite.com
Web Site: http://www.glasswebsite.com/gicc
Members: 13 companies
Staff: 8
Annual Budget: $50-100,000
Administrator: William J. Birch
Historical Note
GICC represents the glass and glazing industry before the model building codes. Members are industry companies and associations.
Meetings/Conferences:

Global Health Council *(1971)*
1701 K St., N.W., Suite 600
Washington, DC 20006-1503
Tel: (202)833-5900   *Fax:* (202)833-0075
E-Mail: ghc@globalhealthcouncil.org
Web Site: http://www.ncih.org
Members: 2,200 individuals, 130 organizations
Staff: 14
Annual Budget: $1-2,000,000
President and C.E.O: Dr. Nils Daulaire
Senior Communications Officer: Karen Farrell
Director, Advocacy and Political Affairs: Carol Miller
Director, Global AIDS Program: Ron MacInnis
Director, Membership: Kathy Downes
Historical Note
Formerly Nat'l Council for International Health (1998). GHC seeks to promote and improve people's health worldwide through advocacy and leadership in identifying and sharing best practices to serve the needs of those who have yet adequately benefited from the globalized world economy.Membership: $120/year (individual, regular); $60/year (student/retiree); $500-5,000/year (organization).
Publications:
AIDSlink Newsletter. bi-m.
Career Network. m. adv.
Directory of Organizations in Internat'l Health. bi-a.
Global Healthlink bi. m. adv.
Membership Directory.
Meetings/Conferences:
Annual Meetings: June
1999 – Alexandria, VA(Crystal Gateway Marriott)/June 20-22

Glycerine and Oleochemicals Ass'n *(1983)*
Historical Note
A division of the Soap and Detergent Ass'n.

Gold Institute *(1976)*
1112 16th St., N.W., Suite 240
Washington, DC 20036
Tel: (202)835-0185   *Fax:* (202)835-0155
E-Mail: info@goldinstitute.org
Web Site: http://www.goldinstitute.org
Members: 83 companies
Staff: 12
Annual Budget: $500-1,000,000
President: John H. Lutley
Exec. V. President: Paul W. Bateman
Historical Note
The Gold Institute, incorporated in the U.S. with an international membership, is the developmental, technical and information arm of leading producers of gold and products using gold. Maintains a financial office in Toronto.
Publications:
The Gold News/Nouvelles de l'Or. bi-m.
Meetings/Conferences:
Annual Meetings: Spring

Golf Coaches Ass'n of America *(1942)*
P.O. Box 215
Raymore, MO 64083
Tel: (816)322-4666   *Fax:* (816)942-5989
Toll Free: (800)925 - 1687
Members: 500 individuals
Staff: 2

Annual Budget: $250-500,000
Exec. Director: Jim Hames
Historical Note
Formerly (1969) NCAA Golf Coaches Ass'n. Members are coaches at 4-year colleges and universities which are members of the Nat'l Collegiate Athletic Ass'n. Membership: $100/year.
Publications:
Coach Approach. q. adv.
Meetings/Conferences:
Annual Meetings: Held in Orlando, FL late January of each year in conjunction with the PGA Merchandise Show/225

Golf Course Builders Ass'n of America *(1970)*
920 Airport Road, Suite 210
Chapel Hill, NC 27514-2619
Tel: (919)942-8922   *Fax:* (919)942-6955
E-Mail: gcbaa@aol.com
Web Site: http://www.gcbaa.com
Members: 200 companies
Staff: 3
Annual Budget: $100-250,000
Exec. V. President: Philip A. Arnold
Historical Note
Formerly (1991) Golf Course Builders of America. A trade association representing all segments of the golf course construction industry. Membership: $1,000/year (company); $500/year (associate); $100/year affiliate.
Publications:
Directory. a. adv.
Earth Shaping News Newsletter.
Meetings/Conferences:
1999 – Orlando, FL
2000 – New Orleans, LA
2001 – San Diego, CA

Golf Course Superintendents Ass'n of America *(1926)*
1421 Research Park Dr.
Lawrence, KS 66049-3859
Tel: (785)841-2240   *Fax:* (785)832-4449
Toll Free: (800)472 - 7878
E-Mail: infobox@gcsaa.org
Web Site: http://www.gcsaa.org
Members: 19,000 individuals
Staff: 114
Annual Budget: $10-25,000,000
C.E.O.: Stephen F. Mona, CAE
Director of Communications: Teri Harris
Government Relations Counsel: Cynthia Kelly Smith, CAE
Senior Director, Corporate Marketing & Sales/Conference and Show: Robert Shively
Director, Learning Systems, Innovation and Design: Deena Amont
Sr. Director, Career Development: Kim Heck
Senior Manager, Education: Hannes Combest
Director, Research: Jeff Nus, Ph.D.
C.F.O.: Julian M. Arredondo
C.O.O.: Joseph A. O' Brien
Director of Member/Chapter Services: Don Bretthauer
Director,Information Service: David M. Bishop
Historical Note
GCSAA strives to provide education programs either in formal educational settings or at home or office through the use of videotapes, educational cassettes, and computers as well as conventional printed matter. Has a U.S. and international membership. Membership: $250/year (individual or organization); $55/year (student).
Publications:
Briefax. m.
GCSAA Membership Directory-Source Book. a.
Golf Course Management. m. adv.
Leader Board. semi-m.
Newsline. m.
Professional Development Catalogue.
Meetings/Conferences:
Annual Meetings: Winter/22,000
1999 – Orlando, FL(Convention Center)
2000 – New Orleans, LA(Convention Center)
2001 – Dallas, TX(Convention Center)

Golf Range and Recreation Ass'n of America *(1991)*
P.O. Box 1265
New Canaan, CT 06840-1265
Tel: (212)865-0050   *Fax:* (212)865-4513
E-Mail: rangeassoc@aol.com
Web Site: http://www.golfrange.org
Members: 600 individuals
Annual Budget: $250-500,000
President: Steven J. DiCostanzo
Historical Note
Membership: $125/year.
Publications:
Golf Range Magazine. bi-m. adv.
Meetings/Conferences:
1999 – Orlando, FL(Clarion Plaza Hotel)
2000 – Orlando, FL(Clarion Plaza)

Golf Writers Ass'n of America *(1946)*
10210 Greentree Rd.
Houston, TX 77042-1232
Tel: (713)782-6664   *Fax:* (713)781-2575
E-Mail: MHauser80beaol.com
Members: 800 individuals
Staff: 1
Annual Budget: $10-25,000
Secretary-Treasurer: Melanie Hauser
Historical Note
Membership: $50/year.
Publications:
Newsletter. 10/year.

Meetings/Conferences:
Semi-annual Meetings: Augusta, GA/April (Masters Tournament) and June in conjunction with the U.S. Open Golf Tournament

Gospel Music Ass'n *(1964)*
1205 Division Street
Nashville, TN 37203
Tel: (615)242-0303   *Fax:* (615)254-9755
Members: 5,800 individuals
Staff: 9
Annual Budget: $2-5,000,000
President: Frank Breeden
Dir., Convention Svcs./Meetings: Kristy Nelson
Director, Operations and Finance: Justin Lawson
Director, Development & special Projects: Karen Berry
Historical Note
GMA was established to provide a common ground for the various facets of the gospel music industry. As an umbrella organization, GMA members include recording and publishing executives, artists, church musicians, broadcasters, retailers and others. The Nat'l Christian Radio Seminar, a forum of Christian broadcasters, and the Nat'l Christian Promoters Roundtable, an organization of professional concert promoters/producers, are affiliate organizations. Membership: $75/year (professional individual); $50/year (associate).
Publications:
GMA Today. bi-m.
The Christian Music Networking Guide. a. adv.
Meetings/Conferences:

Government Finance Officers Ass'n of the United States and Canada *(1906)*
180 N. Michigan Ave., Suite 800
Chicago, IL 60601-7476
Tel: (312)977-9700   *Fax:* (312)977-4806
E-Mail: JEsser@gfoa.org
Web Site: http://www.gfoa.org
Members: 13,500 individuals
Staff: 65
Annual Budget: $5-10,000,000
Exec. Director: Jeffrey L. Esser
Meeting Planner: Eric Nygren
Dir., Professional Development: Kevin Smith
Director, Finance and Operations: Barbara G. Mollo
Historical Note
Formerly (1984) Municipal Finance Officers Ass'n of the United States and Canada. Members are finance officers from city, county, and state governments, school, and other special districts; retirement systems and others in the U.S. and Canada interested in government finance.
Publications:
GAAFR Review. m.
Government Finance Review. bi-m. adv.
Newsletter. semi-m.
Pension & Benefits Update. bi-m.
Public Investor. m.
Meetings/Conferences:
Annual Meetings: Spring
1999 – Nashville, TN/May 23-26
2000 – Chicago, IL/June 11-14
2001 – Philadelphia, PA/June 3-6
2002 – Denver, CO/June 16-19

Government Management Information Sciences *(1971)*
P.O. Box 421
Kennesaw, GA 30144-0421
Tel: (770)975-0729   *Fax:* (770)975-0719
Toll Free: (800)460 - 7454
E-Mail: GMISHdqrs@mindspring.com
Web Site: http://www.gmis.org
Members: 400 government agencies
Staff: 1
Annual Budget: $50-100,000
Exec. Secretary: Herschel Strickland
Historical Note
GMIS is an organization of local governments involved in data processing and educational institutions dealing in the affairs of state, county, or municipal governments which are involved in data processing. GMIS has 18 state chapters established and several others in process. Membership: $75-400/year, (based on agency's EDP budget).Alternative email: gmis@mail.co.catawda.nc.us
Publications:
General Education Material Newsletter. bi-m. adv.
Meetings/Conferences:
Annual Meetings: Summer/300
1999 – Charlotte, NC

Governmental Research Ass'n *(1914)*
Samford University
402 Samford Hall
Birmingham, AL 35229-7017
Tel: (205)870-2482   *Fax:* (205)870-2900
Members: 165 individuals
Annual Budget: under $10,000
Secretary: James W. Williams, Jr.
Historical Note
Members work in privately sponsored government research organizations, universities, chambers of commerce and governmental agencies. Membership: $75/year.
Publications:
GRA Directory. a.
GRA Reporter. q.
Meetings/Conferences:
1999 – Birmingham, AL

Graduate Management Admission Council *(1970)*
8300 Greensboro Dr., Suite 750

McLean, VA   22102-3604
Tel: (703)749-0131   *Fax:* (703)749-0169
E-Mail: gmailmail@gmac.com
Web Site: http://www.gmat.org
Members: 131 institutions
Staff: 12
President: David Wilson

Historical Note
Members are graduate schools of management or business administration.

Publications:
GMAC Bulletin of Information. a.
GMAC Selections. 3/year.

Meetings/Conferences:
Annual Meetings: June
1999 – Washington, DC(Hyatt)

Grain Elevator and Processing Soc. *(1930)*
Box 15026
Minneapolis, MN   55415-0026
Tel: (612)339-4625   *Fax:* (612)339-4644
E-Mail: info@geaps.com
Web Site: http://www.geaps.com
Members: 3,000 individuals
Staff: 6
Annual Budget: $1-2,000,000
Exec. V. President: David Krejci
Director, Marketing/Communications: Kathryn L. Hendricks
Manager, Administrative Services: Joanne Rabatin

Historical Note
Formerly Soc. of Grain Elevator Superintendents. GEAPS provides information, networking, and other services to grain handling and processing operations. Regular members are individuals who are associated directly with the grain, feed, milling and processing industries in an operations management or supervisory capacity. Affiliate membership is available for academics and government officials. Associate membership is available to suppliers of products, equipment or services to the industry. Membership: $115/year.

Publications:
Directa Souce: Member, Equipment, Product & Services
     Directory. a.
In-Grain (newsletter). m.

Meetings/Conferences:
Annual Meetings: late Winter/1,800
1999 – Tampa, FL(Convention Center)/March 6-9
2000 – Kansas City, MO(Convention Center)/Feb. 26-29
2001 – Phoenix, AZ(Convention Center)/March 3-6
2002 – Vancouver, British Columbia(Convention
     Center)/March 3-5

Grain Equipment Manufacturers Council
Historical Note
A council of the Equipment Manufacturers Institute.

Graphic Artists Guild Nat'l *(1967)*
90 John St., Suite 403
New York, NY   10038-3202
Tel: (212)791-3400   *Fax:* (212)791-0333
E-Mail: execdir@gag.org
Web Site: http://www.gag.org/
Members: 3,000 Individuals
Staff: 6
Annual Budget: $500-1,000,000
Exec. Director: Paul Basista, CAE
Communications Director: Brett Harvey

Historical Note
The Guild is a labor organization working to improve industry conditions and standards, and to protect the economic interests of member artists. The long-range goals of the Guild are: financial & professional respect, education & research, valued benefits, and organizational development. Full membership is open to any creators of original work intended for graphic presentation, either in original form or in reproduction. Members are illustrators, graphic designers, surface designers, production artists, cartoonists, computer artists and designers of accesories and wearable art. Associate members are professional in allied fields. Has absorbed the Illustrators Guild, Cartoonist Guild, and Textile Designers Guild. Membership: $55-$270/year.

Publications:
Directory of Illustration. a. adv.
Graphic Artists Guild Handbook: Pricing and Ethical
     Guidelines. bien.
National Guild NEWS. bi-m. adv.

Meetings/Conferences:

Graphic Arts Employers of America *(1887)*
Historical Note
A division of Printing Industries of America, of which it was the originating organization. Represents graphic arts firms whose production departments are partially or wholly organized. Formerly (1981) the Graphic Arts Union Employers of America (UEA).

Graphic Arts Marketing Information Service *(1966)*
100 Daingerfield Road
Alexandria, VA   22314-2888
Tel: (703)519-8179   *Fax:* (703)548-3227
E-Mail: jbland@printing.org
Web Site: http://printing.org
Members: 75 companies
Staff: 2
Annual Budget: $500-1,000,000
Exec. Director: Jacqueline M. Bland

Historical Note
GAMIS is a section of market researchers of Printing Industries of America dedicated to providing its members with current, relevant market data and information on graphic arts through member-directed research studies. Membership: $2,750-6,600/year (organization/company).

Publications:
Source Book for Graphic Arts Industry Information.
Statistical Handbook for the Graphic Arts.

Meetings/Conferences:
1999 – Lake Tahoe, NV(Hyatt)/June 27-30/70

Graphic Arts Professionals *(1913)*
P.O. Box 3139, Grand Central Stn.
New York, NY   10163-3139
Tel: (212)644-8085   *Fax:* (212)644-0296
E-Mail: JWPgroup@aol.com
Members: 100 individuals, 25 corporate members
Annual Budget: $10-25,000
Exec. Director: James W. Prendergast

Historical Note
Founded as Sales Ass'n of the Graphic Arts; assumed its current name in 1996. Membership, concentrated in the New York area, is composed of sales professionals specializing in graphic arts equipment and supplies. Membership: $100/year (individual); $300/year (corporate).

Publications:
Press Proof. q.

Meetings/Conferences:

Graphic Arts Sales Foundation *(1983)*
113 E. Evans St.
West Chester, PA   19380-3336
Tel: (610)431-9780   *Fax:* (610)436-5238
Members: 1,800 individuals
Staff: 5
Annual Budget: $250-500,000
C.E.O.: Richard Gorelick
Administrator: Judy M. Warren

Historical Note
This is the largest training organization in the graphic arts industry offering industry-specific education programs for C.E.O.'s, marketing executives, sales managers, salespeople, print buyers, customer service representatives, estimators, and production supervisors. GASF also was the first organization to offer a professional certification program for sales professionals in the graphic arts industry.

Publications:
Monographs. bi-m.

Graphic Arts Technical Foundation *(1924)*
200 Deer Run Road
Sewickley, PA   15143-2600
Tel: (412)741-6860   *Fax:* (412)741-2311
Toll Free: (800)910 - 4283
E-Mail: info@gatf.org
Web Site: http://www.gatf.org
Members: 7,000 individuals
Staff: 72
Annual Budget: $5-10,000,000
President: George H. Ryan
Public Relations Manager: Alissa Gould
Conference Coordinator: Amy Ciminel
Dir., Training Program: James Workman
V.P. and Dir., Research: Richard D. Warner
Member Services Coordinator: Amy Magnis

Historical Note
Formerly (1963) Lithographic Technical Foundation. GATF is a non-profit, member supported and directed educational, research, and technical organization. It serves the graphic communications industries worldwide. Absorbed the Nat'l Scholarship Trust Fund for the Printing and Publishing Industry in 1966, and reconstituted it as Nat'l Scholarship Trust Fund of the Graphic Arts, a division of GATF, in 1992. Membership: corporate fee based on sales volume.

Publications:
GATFWORLD Magazine. bi-m.
Products Catalogue. semi-a.
Training Programs Catalogue. semi-a.

Meetings/Conferences:
Annual Meetings: Fall
1999 – Pittsburgh, PA/Jan. 31-Feb. 2

Graphic Communications Ass'n *(1966)*
100 Daingerfield Road
Alexandria, VA   22314-2888
Tel: (703)519-8160   *Fax:* (703)548-2867
E-Mail: info@gca.org
Web Site: http://www.gca.org
Members: 325 companies and organizations
Staff: 15
Annual Budget: $2-5,000,000
President: Norman W. Scharpf

Historical Note
Organized as Graphic Communications Computer Ass'n, GCA assumed its present name in 1981. Has a broad-based membership of printing, publishing, fulfillment and list management, supplier/manufacturer and government organizations and advertising agencies. Seeks productivity, technical and market improvements in the creation, production and distribution of publications and printed materials. Affiliated with Printing Industries of America.

Publications:
GCA Bar Code Reporter. q.
GCA Conference Audiocassettes.
GCA Membership Directory. a.
GCA Review. m.
TAG: The SGML Newsletter. 6/year.
TECHinfo. q.

Meetings/Conferences:

Graphic Communications Internat'l Union *(1983)*
1900 L St., N.W., 9th Floor
Washington, DC   20036
Tel: (202)462-1400   *Fax:* (202)721-0600
Members: 200,000 individuals

Staff: 60
Annual Budget: $2-5,000,000
President: James J. Norton
Managing Editor: Herald Grandstaff
Meeting Planner: Kathy Durgam
Director, Safety and Health Department: Brian J. Bobal
Director, Contract and Research Department: Victor Ciuccio

Historical Note
The Amalgamated Lithographers of America and the Internat'l Photoengravers Union of North America merged on September 7, 1964 to form the Lithographers and Photoengravers Internat'l Union. This, in turn, merged September 4, 1972 with the Internat'l Brotherhood of Bookbinders (founded 1892) to form the Graphic Arts Internat'l Union which merged July 1, 1983 with the Internat'l Printing and Graphic Communications Union to form the present organization. Affiliated with AFL-CIO, Canadian Labour Congress and Internat'l Graphical Federation. Sponsors and supports the Graphic Communications Internat'l Union Political Contributions Committee.

Publications:
GraphiCommunicator. 8/year.

Meetings/Conferences:
Quadrennial Meetings: (2000)

Gravure Ass'n of America *(1947)*
1200-A Scottsville Rd.
Rochester, NY   14624
Tel: (716)436-2150   *Fax:* (716)436-7689
E-Mail: GAA@GAA.org
Web Site: http://www.gaa.org
Members: 212 companies
Staff: 11
Annual Budget: $1-2,000,000
Exec. V. President: Richard H. Dunnington
Meeting Planner: Denise Klos, CMP
Director, Member Services: Bill Sunter
Editor: Laura Hatch Smith

Historical Note
Formed (1988) through the merger of the Gravure Technical Ass'n and the Gravure Research Insitute. Members are gravure printers, converters, suppliers, and users. Supports the Gravure Education Foundation, established in 1979.

Publications:
GAA Member Alert. 8/year.
Gravure Environmental Reporter. m.
Gravure Magazine. q. adv.

Meetings/Conferences:
Annual Meetings: Spring
1999 – Cincinnati, OH(Regal Hotel and Convention
     Center)/April 20-23
2000 – Alexandria, VA(Radisson Mark Center)/April 4-7

Greater Blouse, Skirt and Undergarment Ass'n *(1933)*
225 West 34th St.
New York, NY   10122
Tel: (212)563-5052   *Fax:* (212)563-5373
Members: 500 companies
Staff: 6
Annual Budget: $500-1,000,000
Exec. Director: Charles Wang

Historical Note
Formerly (1967) Greater Blouse and Skirt Contractors Ass'n. Membership: $1020/year (company)

Publications:
Anniversary Journal. a. adv.
Greater Voice Newsletter. q. adv.

Meetings/Conferences:
Annual Meetings: Early Fall

Greater Clothing Contractors Ass'n *(1932)*
31 West 15th St.
New York, NY   10011
Tel: (212)924-5670   212
Members: 50 manufacturers
Staff: 10
Annual Budget: $100-250,000
President: Dino Bonacasa

Historical Note
Major purpose is to represent its members in union negotiations.

Greek Food and Wine Institute *(1992)*
825 Eighth Ave.
New York, NY   10019-7498
Tel: (212)474-5588   *Fax:* (212)474-5196
Members: 18 companies
Annual Budget: $100-250,000
Communications Director: Lisa Cutick

Historical Note
The Greek Food and Wine Institute was created in 1992 to expand and enrich our connections with Greek cuisine. Through its educational activities, the Institute seeks to broaden our understanding of Greece's food, wine and agricultural traditions-- and the connections of these traditions to Greek history, culture, the arts and human health. Members are producers, importers and distributors of Greek food, wine, and spirits in both the United States and Greece. Membership: $5,000/year (member); $25,000/year (board member); $1,000 (restaurant member).

Publications:
Gastronomia Newsletter. semi-a.

Meetings/Conferences:
Annual Meetings: Athens, Greece

Green Olive Trade Ass'n
325 14th St.
Carlstadt, NJ   07072
Tel: (201)935-0233   *Fax:* (201)935-8792
Members: 3 companies
Staff: 1
Annual Budget: under $10,000

President: Edward Culleton

Historical Note
Formerly Ass'n of American Importers of Green Olives and (1969) Ass'n of American and Canadian Importers of Green Olives.

Greeting Card Ass'n *(1941)*
1200 G St., N.W., Suite 760
Washington, DC 20005
Tel: (202)393-1778 *Fax:* (202)393-0336
Members: 170 companies
Staff: 5
Annual Budget: $500-1,000,000
Exec. V. President: Marianne McDermott

Historical Note
Originally founded as the Greeting Card Industry to confront the paper shortage during World War II, it became the Nat'l Ass'n of Greeting Card Publishers in 1967 and assumed its original name in 1983. Membership fee based on annual sales volume.

Publications:
Card News. m.
Directory of Greeting Card Sales Representatives. a.
Industry Directory of Publishers and Suppliers. a.

Meetings/Conferences:
Annual Meetings: Fall

Grinding Wheel Institute *(1914)*
30200 Detroit Road
Cleveland, OH 44145-1967
Tel: (440)899-0010 *Fax:* (440)892-1404
Web Site: http://www.gwi.org
Members: 22 companies
Staff: 2
Annual Budget: $100-250,000
Manager: J. Jeffery Wherry

Historical Note
Formerly (1948) Grinding Wheel Manufacturers Ass'n.

Meetings/Conferences:
1999 – Ft. Lauderdale(Marriott Harbor beach)/April 17-20/80
1999 – Cleveland, OH(Ritz Carlton)/80

Grocery Manufacturers of America *(1908)*
1010 Wisconsin Ave., N.W., Suite 900
Washington, DC 20007-3694
Tel: (202)337-9400 *Fax:* (202)337-4508
E-Mail: webmaster@gmabrands.com
Web Site: http://www.gmabrands.com
Members: 145 companies
Staff: 43
Annual Budget: $5-10,000,000
President/C.E.O.: C. Manly Molpus
V. President, Communications: Gene Grabowski
Industry Communications Manager: Lisa McCue
Senior V. President, Government Affairs: Mary Sophos
Senior V. President, Industry Relations and Productivity: Patrick Kiernan
V. President, Organizational Development: Steve Sibert
V. President, Member Relations and Administration: Hilarie Hoting
V. President and General Counsel: James H. Skiles

Historical Note
Members are manufacturers of branded products sold in grocery stores and retail outlets. Sponsors and supports the GMA Political Action Committee (GMA-PAC). Has an annual budget of approximately $8.0 million.

Publications:
State Legislative Reporting and Analysis Service. w.

Meetings/Conferences:
Annual Meetings: White Sulphur Springs, WV in June

Ground Water Protection Council *(1983)*
827 N.W. 63rd St., Suite 103
Oklahoma City, OK 73116-7639
Tel: (405)516-4972 *Fax:* (405)516-4973
E-Mail: Mike@gwpc.site.net
Web Site: gwpc.site.net
Members: 1,500 individuals
Staff: 7
Annual Budget: $1-2,000,000
Exec. Director: Michel J. Paque, CAE
Assoc. Director: Benjamin D. Grunewald
Member Services Director: Jeff Bryant

Historical Note
GWPC provides a forum for discussion of ground water protection, source water and wellhead protection, and underground injection practices. Forums and projects bring together state and federal regulatory agencies and the industries subject to regulation to work on issue resolution. Membership: $75/year (individual); corporate fee varies.

Publications:
Directory. a.
Journal. q.
Newsletter. q.
Proceedings. a.

Meetings/Conferences:
1999 – New Orleans, LA/Jan. 12-13

Groundwater Management Districts Ass'n *(1975)*
P.O. Box 905
Colby, KS 67701
Tel: (785)462-3915 *Fax:* (785)462-2693
Members: 140 individuals
Staff: 1
Annual Budget: under $10,000
Exec. Secretary: Wayne Bossert

Historical Note
Membership includes districts, consulting organizations and individuals concerned with the management and conservation of water resources. Seeks effective information transfer between member districts, associations, and organizations responsible for water resource management. Affiliated with the Nat'l Water

Resources Ass'n. Membership: $20/year (individual); $90/year (affiliate); $150/year (organization); $200/year (district).

Publications:
Proceeding of Annual Conference. a.

Meetings/Conferences:
Annual Meetings: In conjunction with the Nat'l Water Resources Ass'n

Group Health Ass'n of America

Historical Note
Became American Ass'n of Health Plans in 1996.

Guild of American Luthiers *(1972)*
8222 South Park
Tacoma, WA 98408
Tel: (253)472-7853 *Fax:* (253)472-7853
E-Mail: tim@luth.org
Web Site: http://www.luth.org
Members: 3,000 individuals
Staff: 6
Annual Budget: $100-250,000
President/Editor: Timothy L. Olsen

Historical Note
Non-profit educational organization. Members are professional and amateur builders and repairers of string musical instruments and other interested individuals. Membership: $39/year (domestic); $49/year (overseas).

Publications:
American Lutherie. q. adv.

Meetings/Conferences:

Guild of Book Workers *(1906)*
521 Fifth Ave., Suite 1740
New York, NY 10175
Tel: (212)292-4444
Members: 900 individuals
Staff: 1
Annual Budget: $10-25,000
President: Karen Crisali

Historical Note
Established to continue and foster the growth of the hand book crafts, including binding, calligraphy, illumination, papermaking and printing. An affiliate of the American Institute of Graphic Arts from 1948 to 1978. Has no paid staff; all contact handled through mail. Membership: $40/year.

Publications:
Guild of Book Workers Journal. semi-a.
Newsletter. bi-m.

Meetings/Conferences:
Annual Meetings: Fall

Guild of Natural Science Illustrators *(1968)*
Box 652, Ben Franklin Station
Washington, DC 20044
Tel: (301)309-1514 *Fax:* (301)309-1514
Members: 1,200 individuals
Staff: 1
Annual Budget: $25-50,000
Admin. Asst.: Leslie Becker

Historical Note
Originially formed by illustrators at the Smithsonian Institution, the GNSI now includes foreign members. The Guild's purpose is to promote the techniques and understanding of scientific illustration and to encourage professionalism among its members. Membership: $45/year.

Publications:
Journal of Natural Science Illustration. a.
Membership Directory. a.
Newsletter. 10/year. adv.

Meetings/Conferences:
Annual Meetings: Summer

Guild of Temple Musicians *(1974)*
Historical Note
Address unknown in 1995; presumed inactive.

Guitar and Accessories Marketing Ass'n *(1924)*
38 West 21st St., Room 1106
New York, NY 10010-6906
Tel: (212)924-9175 *Fax:* (212)675-3577
E-Mail: assnhdqs@aol.com
Members: 46 companies
Staff: 2
Annual Budget: $25-50,000
Exec. V. President: Jerome Hershman

Historical Note
Established as the Nat'l Ass'n of Musical Merchandise Manufacturers, it became the Guitar and Accessory Manufacturers of America in 1963, became the Guitar and Accessories Music Marketing Ass'n in 1982 and assumed its present name in 1992. Members are distributors of domestic fretted instruments and allied accessories.

Publications:
Newsletter. q.

Meetings/Conferences:
Annual Meetings: With Nat'l Ass'n of Music Merchants in Anaheim, CA(Marriott)/Jan./50
1999 – Los Angeles, CA(Bonaventure)

Gummed Industries Ass'n *(1920)*
Historical Note
Organization inactive in 1996.

Gunite/Shotcrete Contractors Ass'n *(1951)*
940 Doolittle Dr.
San Leandro, CA 94577
Tel: (510)568-8112 *Fax:* (510)568-1601

Members: 55 individuals
Staff: 1
Annual Budget: under $10,000
Exec. Director: Larry Totten

Historical Note
Trade association of contractors specializing in the application of concrete under pressure. Affiliated with the American Concrete Institute. Membership: $250/year (individual), $750/month (organization).

Publications:
Membership List. q.

Meetings/Conferences:

Gynecologic Laser and Advanced Technology Soc. *(1979)*
Historical Note
Became the Gynecologic Surgery Soc. in 1995.

Gynecologic Oncology Group *(1970)*
1234 Market St., Suite 1945
Philadelphia, PA 19107
Tel: (215)854-0770 *Fax:* (215)854-0716
Members: 45 institutions
Staff: 10
Annual Budget: $500-1,000,000
Administrative Director: John R. Kellner

Historical Note
Members are teaching hospitals and research institutions.

Meetings/Conferences:
Semi-Annual Meetings: January/700 and July/700
1999 – San Antonio, TX
1999 – Phoenix, AZ

Gynecologic Surgery Soc. *(1979)*
6900 Grove Road
Thorofare, NJ 08086-9431
Tel: (609)848-1000 *Fax:* (609)848-5274
E-Mail: gss@slackinc.com
Members: 1000 individuals
Staff: 1
Annual Budget: $100-250,000
Administrator: Audra Rival

Historical Note
Formerly (1993) Gynecologic Laser Soc. and (1995) Gynecologic Laser and Advanced Technology Soc. Membership: $95/year (individual).

Publications:
GLS Newlsetter. q. adv.
Journal of Gynecologic Surgery. q. adv.

Meetings/Conferences:
Biennial Meetings: even years/Spring

Gypsum Ass'n *(1930)*
810 First St. N.E., Suite 510
Washington, DC 20002
Tel: (202)289-5440 *Fax:* (202)289-3707
E-Mail: jwalker@gypsum.org
Web Site: gypsum.org
Members: 13 companies
Staff: 10
Annual Budget: $1-2,000,000
Exec. Director: Jerry A. Walker
Government Relations: Susan Chana
Director of Promotion: Steve Meima
Asst. Exec. Director: Robert A. Wessel

Historical Note
Members are U.S. and Canadian manufacturers of gypsum board products. Membership fee based on tonnage of gypsum calcined.

Meetings/Conferences:
Annual Meetings: Fall

Hack and Band Saw Manufacturers Ass'n of America *(1959)*
1300 Sumner Ave.
Cleveland, OH 44115-2851
Tel: (216)241-7333 *Fax:* (216)241-0105
E-Mail: hbs@taol.com
Web Site: http://www.taol.com/hbs
Members: 4 companies
Staff: 2
Secretary-Treasurer: Charles M. Stockinger

Historical Note
Formed by a merger of the Hack Saw Ass'n (1928) and the Metal Cutting Band Saw Ass'n.

Hair Internat'l *(1924)*
P.O. Box 273
Palmyra, PA 17078-0273
Tel: (717)838-0795 *Fax:* (717)838-0796
E-Mail: hairint@nbn.net
Web Site: http://www.hairinternational.com
Members: 1000 individuals
Staff: 2
Annual Budget: $500-1,000,000
President: Franz Singer

Historical Note
Formerly (1987) Associated Master Barbers and Beauticians of America/Hair Internat'l. A professional organization of barbers and cosmetologists. Membership: $158/year (individual), $150/year (organization).

Publications:
Hair International News. bi-m. adv.

Meetings/Conferences:
Triannual Meetings: 2000

Halogenated Solvents Industry Alliance *(1980)*
2001 L St., N.W., Suite 506A
Washington, DC 20036-4919

Tel: (202)775-0232   Fax: (202)833-0381
Web Site: www.hsia.org
Members: 250 companies
Exec. Director: Steven P. Risotto
Manager, Administration: Debra B. Jackson
Historical Note
A division of The Chlorine Institute since 1992, HSIA members are producers, users, distributors and equipment manufacturers for the industry. Membership: $50-500/year.
Publications:
HSIA Newsletter. bi-m.
HSIA Solvents Update. m.
Meetings/Conferences:

Halon Alternatives Research Corp.
2111 Wilson Blvd., Suite 850
Arlington, VA   22201-3001
Tel: (703)524-6636   Fax: (703)243-2874
Members: 50 companies
Staff: 1
Annual Budget: $100-250,000
Exec. Director: Tom Cortina
Historical Note
A trade association representing producers, distributors, users of halons and others with an interest in finding replacement agents. Membership: $5,000/year (organization); $900/year (company).
Publications:
HARC News. 2-4/yr.

Hampshire Swine Registry (1893)
Historical Note
Registry merged with the United Duroc Swine Registry and the American Yorkshire Club in 1996 and is now under the title of Nat'l Swine Registry.

Hand Knitting Ass'n
Historical Note
A committee of the Nat'l Needlework Ass'n.

Hand Tools Institute (1935)
25 N. Broadway
Tarrytown, NY   10591-3201
Tel: (914)332-0040   Fax: (914)332-1541
E-Mail: HTI@HTI.org
Web Site: http://www.HTI.org
Members: 60 companies
Staff: 3
Annual Budget: $250-500,000
Exec. Director: Richard C. Byrne
Historical Note
Absorbed the Vise Manufacturers Ass'n in 1969. Formerly (1973) Service Tools Institute.
Publications:
Directory. a.
Meetings/Conferences:
Semi-annual Meetings: February and September

Handweavers Guild of America (1969)
3327 Duluth Hwy., Suite 201
Duluth, GA   30096
Tel: (770)495-7702   Fax: (770)495-7703
E-Mail: 73744,202@compuserve.com
Web Site: http://www.weavespindye.org
Members: 9,000 individuals
Staff: 5
Annual Budget: $250-500,000
Exec. Director: Sandra Bowles
Public Relations: Pat King
Business Manager: Marian K. Allen
Historical Note
Individuals, companies and organizations promoting interest in and creation of handcrafted textiles. Membership: $35/year (domestic), $40/year (foreign).
Publications:
Shuttle Spindle & Dyepot. q. adv.
Meetings/Conferences:
Biennial Meetings: Even years
1999 – Gatlinburg, TN(Arrowmont School of Arts & Crafts)/Oct. 6-10/500
2000 – Cincinatti, OH/June 20-26
2002 – Vancouver, British Columbia

Hard Fibers Ass'n
Metcalf Agency
P.O. Box 250
Skaneateles, NY   13152-0250
Tel: (315)685-5088   Fax: (315)685-5077
E-Mail: PFMetcalf@aol.com
Members: 5 companies
Annual Budget: under $10,000
President: Peter F. Metcalf
Historical Note
Importers and distributors of sisal, abaca and other hard fibers.

Hardwood Distributors Ass'n (1933)
P.O. Box 988
North Tonawanda, NY   14120-0988
Tel: (716)694-0562   Fax: (716)694-0966
Members: 75 companies
Staff: 1
Annual Budget: $10-25,000
Secretary-Treasurer: Christopher A. Miller
Historical Note
Formerly (1985) Nat'l Wholesale Lumber Distribution Yard Ass'n, HDA members are wholesale hardwood distributing yards. Membership: $200/year (company).
Meetings/Conferences:
Annual Meetings: October, with Nat'l Hardwood Lumber Ass'n

Hardwood Manufacturers Ass'n (1935)
400 Penn Center Blvd., Suite 530
Pittsburgh, PA   15235-5605
Tel: (412)829-0770   Fax: (412)829-0844
Web Site: http://www.hardwood.org
Staff: 7
Annual Budget: $500-1,000,000
Exec. V. President: Susan Regan
Historical Note
Formerly Southern Hardwood Producers Inc. and the Southern Hardwood Lumber Manufacturers Ass'n. Assumed present name in 1984. Southern Cypress Manufacturers Ass'n is a division HMA.
Publications:
Hardwood Expressions. q.
Link Newsletter. m.
Meetings/Conferences:
Annual Meetings: March

Hardwood Plywood and Veneer Ass'n (1921)
P.O. Box 2789
Reston, VA   20195
Tel: (703)435-2900   Fax: (703)435-2537
E-Mail: hpva@hpva.org
Web Site: http://www.hpva.org
Members: 196 companies
Staff: 11
Annual Budget: $500-1,000,000
President: E.T. "Bill" Altman
Manager, Natural Resources Issues: Brent McClendon
Manager, Convention Planner and Membership Services: Ketti Tyree
Technical Director: Gary Gramp
Financial Manager: Myrna Downey
Director, Environmental Policy & Veneer Member Services: Brent McClendon
Marketing Manager: Curt Alt
Historical Note
Absorbed (1998) Fine Hardwood Veneer Association. Established in Chicago in 1921 as the Plywood Manufacturers Ass'n. Formerly Plywood Manufacturing Institute, (1964) Hardwood Plywood Institute, and (1992) Hardwood Plywood & Veneer Ass'n. Absorbed the Southern Plywood Manufacturers Ass'n in 1953. HPVA members include plywood manufacturers, veneer facilities, industry suppliers and wholesale stocking distributors. Affiliated with American Forest and Paper Ass'n, Internat'l Conference of Building Officials, Southern Building Code Congress, Building Officials and Code Administrators Internat'l, and the U.S. Dept. of Commerce Nat'l Voluntary Laboratory Accreditation Program. Street address is: 1825 Michael Faraday Dr., Reston, VA. Membership: dues based on sales volume.
Publications:
Catalyst Newsletter.
Executive Brief. q.
Hardwood Plywood & Veneer News. m.
Where to Buy Hardwood Plywood and Veneer. a.
Meetings/Conferences:
Semi-Annual Meetings: Spring and Fall

Hardwood Research Council (1953)
Historical Note
A program of the Nat'l Hardwood Lumber Ass'n.

Harness Horsemen Internat'l (1964)
14 Main St.
Robbinsville, NJ   08691-1410
Tel: (609)259-3717
Members: 40,000 individuals, 23 associations
Staff: 2
Annual Budget: $250-500,000
Exec. Director: Michael Izzo
Historical Note
HHI represents owners, trainers, and drivers of standardbred racehorses working in the U.S. and Canada.
Publications:
Careers in Harness Racing. irreg.
Directory of Associations. irreg.
News from Harness Horsemen Internat'l. irreg.
Meetings/Conferences:
Semi-Annual Meetings: Winter and Summer
1999 – Orlando, FL

Harness Tracks of America (1954)
4640 E. Sunrise Dr., Suite 200
Tucson, AZ   85718-4576
Tel: (520)529-2525   Fax: (520)529-3235
E-Mail: harness@azstarnet.com
Members: 35 pari-mutuel harness tracks
Staff: 4
Annual Budget: $500-1,000,000
Exec. V. President: Stanley F. Bergstein
Historical Note
A trade association for North American harness race tracks. Issues monthly economic studies, reports, position papers, daily newsletters, and special surveys on legal and legislative matters affecting the sport and industry.
Publications:
Directory. a. adv.
Surveys. m.
Track Topics. bi-m.
Meetings/Conferences:
Annual Meetings: Winter

Harvey Soc. (1905)
Mt. Sinai School of Medicine
One Gustave L. Levy Place, Box 1496
New York, NY   10029
Tel: (212)824-7728   Fax: (212)803-6740
Members: 1,700 individuals
Staff: 1

Annual Budget: $25-50,000
Secretary: Savio Woo, Ph.D.
Historical Note
Named after William Harvey, British physician who discovered the circulation of the blood in the 17th century, the Society consists of individuals interested in or capable of making a contribution to the literature of medicine. Membership: $40/year.
Publications:
The Harvey Lectures. a.
Meetings/Conferences:
Annual Meetings: Always in New York, NY

Hazardous Materials Advisory Council (1978)
1101 Vermont Ave., N.W., Suite 301
Washington, DC   20005
Tel: (202)289-4550   Fax: (202)289-4074
Toll Free: (800)634 - 1598
E-Mail: hmalinfo@hmac.org
Web Site: http://www.hmac.org
Members: 280 companies
Staff: 10
Annual Budget: $1-2,000,000
President: Jonathan Collom
Director of Communications and Public Relations: Kimberly Seitz
Director of Education and Training: E. Vaughn Arthur
Director, Technical Support: Michael Morrissette
Historical Note
Formerly (1978) a committee of the Transportation Ass'n of America. HMAC represents shippers, carriers of all modes, container manufacturers and reconditioners, emergency response and waste clean-up companies, and other firms and associations involved in hazardous materials transportation. Membership: $1000-2600/year (organization).
Publications:
Courier. m.
Directory. a.
Federal Register Extract. bi-m.
Meetings/Conferences:
Semi-Annual Meetings: May and November
1999 – St. Louis, MO(Hyatt Regency)/Nov. 17-19
2000 – Savannah, GA(DeSoto Hilton)/Nov. 8-10
2001 – New Orleans, LA(Intercontinental)/Nov. 7-9

Hazardous Materials Control Resources Institute (1976)
Historical Note
Organization dissolved in 1995.

Headmasters Ass'n (1893)
Historical Note
HMA declined to provide updated information for this edition.

Headwear Information Bureau (1955)
302 W. 12th St., PH-C
New York, NY   10014
Tel: (212)627-8333
E-Mail: MILICASE@aol.com
Web Site: http://www.hatsny.com
Members: 85 individuals, 80 individuals and companies
Staff: 2
Annual Budget: $10-25,000
Exec. Director: Casey Bush
Historical Note
Formerly (1989) Millinery Institute of America and (1997) Millinery Information Bureau, HIB members are designers and manufacturers/importers of women's hats and suppliers to the industry. HIB promotes women's fashion headwear. Membership: $20-$125/month.
Publications:
Milli Gram Newsletter. bi-m.
Meetings/Conferences:
Annual Meetings: Not held.

Health and Personal Care Distribution Conference
1090 12th St.
Vero Beach, FL   32960
Tel: (561)778-7782   Fax: (561)778-4111
Web Site: http://www.moran.hpcdc@aol.com
Members: 70 companies
Exec. Director: William Moran
Historical Note
H&PCDC members are shippers of drugs, medicines, toilet preparations, and health and personal care products.
Meetings/Conferences:
Semi-Annual: Spring and Fall
1999 – Philadelphia, PA(Ritz Carlton)/Apr. 19-21
1999 – Longboat Key, FL(Longboat Key Club)/Oct. 4-7

Health Care Institute
Historical Note
A component of the Environmental Management Association.

Health Care Material Management Soc.
Historical Note
Became (1996) Health Care Resource Management Soc.

Health Care Resource Management Soc. (1982)
P.O. Box 29253
Cincinnati, OH   45229-0253
Tel: (513)520-1058   Fax: (513)872-6158
E-Mail: hcrms@choice.net
Web Site: http://hcrms.com
Members: 1,500 individuals
Staff: 1
Annual Budget: $50-100,000
Exec. Director: Steven Goetz

Historical Note
Formerly (1996) Health Care Material Management Soc. Originally a part of the Internat'l Material Management Soc., HCRMS became an independent society in 1982. Members are resource management professionals employed in the health care/hospital field. Membership: $75/year (individual).

Publications:
Change & Exchange Newsletter. q.
Directions. a.
Membership Directory. a.

Meetings/Conferences:
1999 – Jacksonville, FL(Hilton)/Sept. 12-15

Health Industry Business Communications Council (1984)
2525 East Arizona Biltmore Cir.
Suite 127
Phoenix, AZ 85016
Tel: (602)381-1091   *Fax:* (602)381-1093
E-Mail: info@hibcc.org
Web Site: http://www.hibcc.org
Members: 900 individuals, 300 companies
Staff: 20
Annual Budget: $500-1,000,000
President: Robert A. Hankin, Ph.D.
Communications Director: Beverly Kieffer

Historical Note
Membership: $150/year (individual); $2,500/year (organization).

Publications:
Health Industry Lines. q. adv.

Meetings/Conferences:

Health Industry Distributors Ass'n (1902)
66 Canal Center Plaza, Suite 520
Alexandria, VA 22314-1591
Tel: (703)549-4432   *Fax:* (703)549-6495
Members: 1000 companies
Staff: 27
Annual Budget: $5-10,000,000
President and C.E.O.: S. Wayne Kay
Sr. V. President, Membership Services, Marketing, and Communications: Matthew J. Rowan
V. President, Meetings and Trade Show: Catherine K. Roper
V. President, HIDA Educational Fdtn.: Elizabeth B. Hilla
Chief Financial Officer: John G. Wooldridge
V. President, Membership Services: Christopher N. Pancratz
Dir., Home Care/Long Term Care: Cara C. Bachenheimer

Historical Note
Founded as the American Surgical Trade Ass'n, it assumed its present name in 1983. Trade association for all sectors of the medical products distribution and home care industries. Sponsors the HIDA Educational Foundation, the Health Industry Distributors Ass'n Political Action Committee (HIDA-PAC), and the HIDA Service Corporation. Membership fee varies, based on annual sales.

Publications:
Capitol Connection. m.
Government Report. m.
HIDA Headlines. m.
Medical Products Sales Magazine. m. adv.
Repertoire Magazine.

Meetings/Conferences:
Annual Meetings: Fall/7,500

Health Industry Group Purchasing Ass'n (1990)
1444 I St., N.W., Suite 410
Washington, DC 20005
Tel: (202)393-7306   *Fax:* (202)628-2310
Contact: Jack Rowley

Historical Note
Members are organizations providing economies of scale to health care providers through group purchasing.

Meetings/Conferences:

Health Industry Manufacturers Ass'n (1903)
1200 G St., N.W., Suite 400
Washington, DC 20005-3814
Tel: (202)783-8700   *Fax:* (202)783-8750
Web Site: http://www.himanet.com
Members: 800 companies
Staff: 60
Annual Budget: $10-25,000,000
President: Alan H. Magazine
Senior V. President, Technology and Regulatory Affairs: James S. Benson
V. President, Finance & Operations: Kristen M. Bogenrief
V. President, Membership Development and Communications: James F. Jorkasky
Exec. V. President, Technology/Regulatory Affairs: James S. Benson
Sr. V. President of Payment and Health Care Delivery: Ted R. Mannen
Sr. V. President, Global Strategy/Analysis: Edward M. Rozynski

Historical Note
Established as the Wholesale Surgical Trade Ass'n. Became Manufacturers Surgical Trade Ass'n in 1944 and the Medical-Surgical Manufacturers Ass'n in 1967. Merged in 1974 with the Health Industries Ass'n to form the Health Industry Manufacturers Ass'n. Represents manufacturers of health care technology, including medical devices, diagnostic products, and health care information systems. Has an annual budget of approximately $10 million. Membership fee based on domestic sales volume.

Publications:
Directory. a.
In Brief. bi-w.
President's Letter.

Meetings/Conferences:
Annual Meetings: March (open only to member companies)
1999 – Bal Harbor, FL/March 13-16

Health Industry Representatives Ass'n (1978)

6740 E. Hampden Ave., Suite 306
Denver, CO 80224
Tel: (303)756-8115   *Fax:* (303)756-5699
Members: 185 companies, 65 associates
Staff: 2
Annual Budget: $100-250,000
Exec. Director: Karen A. Hone

Historical Note
Independent manufacturers representatives who sell medical equipment and other products in the health care field. Formerly (1985) Health Associated Representatives.

Publications:
Communicator. m.

Meetings/Conferences:
Annual Meetings: Summer

Health Insurance Ass'n of America (1956)
555 13th St., N.W., Suite 600-E
Washington, DC 20004-1109
Tel: (202)824-1600   *Fax:* (202)824-1722
Web Site: http://www.hiaa.org
Members: 245 companies
Staff: 100
Annual Budget: $25-50,000,000
President: Bill Gradison, Jr.
V. President, Public Affairs: J. Peter Segall
Director, Communications: Richard Coorsh
Exec. V. President, Governmental Affairs: Ron Souters
Senior V. President, Federal Affairs: Sharon Cohen
Director, Meeting Planning\: Norene M. Yoch

Historical Note
Formed by a merger of the Bureau of Accident and Health Underwriters and the Health and Accident Underwriters Conference. Members are accident and health insurance companies. Sponsors the Health Insurance Political Action Committee (HIPAC). Has annual budget of approximately $26.9 million.

Publications:
Executive Report.

Meetings/Conferences:

Health Physics Soc. (1956)
1313 Dolley Madison Blvd., Suite 402
McLean, VA 22101-3926
Tel: (703)790-1745   *Fax:* (703)790-2672
E-Mail: hps@BurkInc.com
Web Site: http://www.hps.org
Members: 7,000 individuals
Staff: 12
Annual Budget: $1-2,000,000
Exec. Director: Richard J. Burk, Jr.

Historical Note
Founded and incorporated in the District of Columbia in 1956. Reincorporated in Tennessee in 1969. Fosters the protection of man and the environment from radiation. Affiliated with the Internat'l Radiation Protection Ass'n. Membership: $75/year.

Publications:
Health Physics Journal. m. adv.
Membership Handbook. a.
Newsletter. m.

Meetings/Conferences:
Annual Meetings: Summer
1999 – Philidelphia, PA

Health Sciences Communications Ass'n (1959)
1 Wedgewood Drive, Suite 28
Jewett City, CT 06351-2428
Tel: (860)376-5915   *Fax:* (860)376-6621
E-Mail: HeSCAOne@aol.com
Web Site: http://www.hesca.washington.edu
Members: 250 individuals, 80 institutions
Staff: 2
Annual Budget: $100-250,000
Exec. Director: Ron Sokolowski

Historical Note
Organized in 1959 as the Council on Medical Television as part of the Institute for Advancement of Medical Communication. Incorporated in North Carolina in 1964 under its own charter. Became the Health Sciences Communications Ass'n in 1972. A professional association of individuals interested in application of educational technology to the health sciences field. Membership: $150/year (individual); $195/year (organization).

Publications:
HeSCA Feedback. 5/year.
Journal of Biocommunication. q. adv.
Membership Catalog. a.

Meetings/Conferences:
Annual Meetings: Spring
1999 – Phoenix, AZ(Camelback Marriott)/June 9-12/125

Healthcare Billing and Management Ass'n
7315 Wisconsin Ave., Suite 424-East
Bethesda, MD 20814
Tel: (301)961-8680   *Fax:* (301)961-8681
Exec. V. President: Sanford J. Hill

Historical Note
Founded as Internat'l Billing Ass'n; assumed its current name in 1998. Members are companies providing third-party medical billing services.

Healthcare Compliance Packaging Council (1990)
7799 Leesburg Pike, Suite 900 N.
Falls Church, VA 20043
Tel: (703)847-9396   *Fax:* (703)538-6305
Web Site: http://www.unitdose.org
Members: 70 corporations and individuals
Staff: 3
Annual Budget: $100-250,000
Staff Director: Peter G. Mayberry
Staff Consultant: Kathleen Hemming

Historical Note
Members are companies and individuals in the pharmaceutical packaging industry with an interest in promoting unit-dose blister packaging. Membership: $5,000/year (corporate); $2,500/year (associate); $500/year (educational institution); $1,000/year (trade association); $195/year (individual).

Publications:
Compliance News & Views. q. adv.
Unit-Dose Alert. bi-m.

Meetings/Conferences:
Semi-Annual Meetings: Washington, DC/Fall and Philadelphia, PA/Spring

Healthcare Convention and Exhibitors Ass'n (1930)
5775 Peachtree-Dunwoody Rd., Suite 500-G
Atlanta, GA 30342-1558
Tel: (404)252-3663   *Fax:* (404)252-0774
E-Mail: hcea@assnhq.com
Web Site: http://www.hcea.org
Members: 600 companies
Staff: 7
Exec. Director: Robert C. Gelardi
Director, Meetings: Carol Wilson

Historical Note
Formerly (1973) Medical Exhibitors Ass'n and (1990) Health Care Exhibitors Ass'n. Members are manufacturers and distributors of products exhibited at surgical, medical, dental and hospital meetings. Member of the Center for Exhibition Industry Research, Convention Liaison Council, and other industry organizations. Membership: $495/year (domestic); $595/year (overseas).

Publications:
Action Memo Newsletter.
Conventional Wisdom.
Guidelines for Healthcare Conventions.
Handbook: Directory of Healthcare Meetings/Conventions. semi-a. adv.
Insight.

Meetings/Conferences:
Annual Meetings: June

Healthcare Finance Study Group (1973)
c/o O'Connor & Hannan
1919 Pennsylvania Ave., N.W., Suite 800
Washington, DC 20006
Tel: (202)887-1400   *Fax:* (202)466-2198
Annual Budget: $100-250,000
Counsel: Michael Colopy

Historical Note
Formerly (1981) the Hospital Financing Study Group. Group members are firms involved in providing financing for healthcare institutions, especially access to tax-exempt financing for hospitals. Primarily concerned with federal legislative and regulatory initiatives which impact on the healthcare financing industry.

Publications:
Newsletter. m.

Meetings/Conferences:
Annual Meetings: January

Healthcare Financial Management Ass'n (1946)
Two Westbrook Corporate Center
Suite 700
Westchester, IL 60154-5700
Tel: (708)531-9600   *Fax:* (708)531-0032
Toll Free: (800)252 - 4362
E-Mail: dclarke@hfma.org
Web Site: http://www.hfma.org
Members: 35,000 individuals
Staff: 80
Annual Budget: $10-25,000,000
President and C.E.O.: Richard L. Clarke, FHFMA
Director, Marketing and Public Relations: Elaine B. Krieger
Director, Professional Development: Harold Prink
C.O.O.: Thom D. Freyer

Historical Note
Formerly (1946) the American Ass'n of Hospital Accountants and (1982) the Hospital Financial Management Ass'n. Offers designation of Fellow and Certified Healthcare Financial Professional. Members are directly or indirectly associated with financial management in healthcare organizations in the U.S., Canada, and several other countries, and belong to one of 70 local chapters. Membership: $185/year.

Publications:
Healthcare Financial Management. m. adv.
Patient Accounts. m.

Meetings/Conferences:
Annual Meetings: June/1,500
1999 – Anaheim, CA(Hilton)/June 20-24
2000 – Orlando, FL(Dolphin)/June 25-29

Healthcare Forum, The (1927)
425 Market St., 16th Floor
San Francisco, CA 94105
Tel: (415)356-4300   *Fax:* (415)356-9300
E-Mail: thf@healthonline.com
Web Site: http://www.thf.net.org
Members: 1,300 organizations and individuals
Staff: 60
Annual Budget: $5-10,000,000
President and C.E.O.: Kathryn E. Johnson, CAE
Dir., Mktg./Communications: Jan Emerson
Meetings and Conventions: Linda Milks
Senior V. President: Robert G. Stein, CAE

Historical Note
Founded as the Ass'n of Western Hospitals, THF is a provider of executive education and applied research for healthcare leaders. Forum members, individuals and organizations, are drawn from all 50 states and countries around the world. Has an annual budget of over $9 million. Membership: $500/year (individual); $1,600/year (organization).

Publications:
Healthcare Forum Journal. bi-m. adv.
Meetings/Conferences:
Annual Meetings: Spring/2,900
1999 – San Francisco, CA(Marriott & Moscone
      Center)/April 17-20
2000 – Orlando, FL(Dolphin)/April 29-May 4

Healthcare Information and Management Systems Soc. *(1961)*
230 E. Ohio St., Suite 500
Chicago, IL   60611
Tel: (312)664-4467   *Fax:* (312)664-6143
E-Mail: himss@himss.org
Web Site: http://www.himss.org
Members: 12,500 individuals
Staff: 24
Annual Budget: $10-25,000,000
Exec. Director: John A. Page
Education Manager: Sandra Burbridge
Assoc. Director for Education: Pamela Barrett
Asst. Director, Business: Marcia Zitowski
Asst. Director for Membership and Editorial: Sandra Spears
Manager, Editorial Svcs.: Julie R. Foreman

Historical Note
*Formerly (1987) Hospital Management Systems Soc. HIMSS
provides leadership in health care for the management of systems,
information and change. Members include CIO's, Information
Systems, Management Engineering, Clinical Systems, and
Telecommunications. Membership: $110/year; (individual
members); $195/year (foreign membership).*

Publications:
Directory.
Healthcare Information Management. q.
HIMSS News. m.
Leadership Survey: Trends in Health Care Information
      Systems.
Proceedings of Annual Conference. a.
Proceedings of other Conferences.
Salary Survey.
Meetings/Conferences:
Annual Meetings: February-March
1999 – Atlanta, GA(World Congress Center)

Healthcare Leadership Council *(1990)*
900 17 st. N.W. Suite 600
Washington, DC   20006
Tel: (202)452-8700   *Fax:* (202)296-9561
Web Site: http://www.hlc.org
Staff: 5
President: Pamela G. Bailey
V. President, Communications: Michael V. Freeman
V. President, Public Affairs: Ginny Grenham
V. President, Policy: Kathy Means
Exec. V. President: Tim Burns
Director, Administration: Sylvia Bramante

Historical Note
*A coalition of health care providers including physicians, health
insurers, hospitals, pharmceutical companies and medical
technology firms. Affiliated with the Nat'l Committee for Quality
Healthcare.*

Healthcare Marketing and Communications Council *(1934)*
333-B Rte. 46 West, Suite B-206
Fairfield, NJ   07004-2427
Tel: (973)575-9555   *Fax:* (973)575-1239
E-Mail: rsawyer@hnc-council.org
Members: 1,200 individuals
Staff: 1
Annual Budget: $500-1,000,000
Exec. Director: Richard D. Sawyer

Historical Note
*Founded as Pharmaceutical Advertising Club; later became
Pharmaceutical Advertising Council, and assumed its current name
in 1995. Membership, concentrated in the mid-Atlantic region,
consists of marketing and communications professionals serving the
health care industry. Membership: $150/year.*

Publications:
HMC News. 9/year.
Membership Directory. a. adv.
Meetings/Conferences:
Monthly Meetings: various mid-Atlantic locations (8/year)

Hearing Industries Ass'n *(1955)*
515 King St., Suite 420
Alexandria, VA   22314-3103
Tel: (703)684-5744   *Fax:* (703)684-6048
E-Mail: crogin@clarionmr.com
Members: 34 companies
Staff: 4
Annual Budget: $500-1,000,000
President: Carole M. Rogin
Director of Government Relations: David E. Woodbury
Director of Member Services: Melinda A. Watters

Historical Note
Formerly (1977) the Hearing Aid Industry Conference.
Publications:
HIA Update. m.
The Marketing Edge. q.
Meetings/Conferences:
Annual Meetings: February/100
1999 – Phoenix, AZ(The Wigman)/Feb. 17-21/100

Hearth Products Ass'n *(1980)*
1601 N. Kent St., Suite 1001
Arlington, VA   22209-2105
Tel: (703)522-0086   *Fax:* (703)522-0548
E-Mail: HPAMAIL@HEARTHASSOC.ORG

Web Site: http://www.hearthassoc.org
Members: 2,500 companies
Staff: 17
Annual Budget: $2-5,000,000
President and C.E.O.: Carter E. Keithley
Director, Meetings and Exhibits: Joan Letchworth
Director of Education & Communications: Susan Kalish
Technical Director: Michael Van Buren
Dir., Publications & Promotions: Betteanne Leahy
Dir., Membership Services: Micahel Winn
Comptroller/Exec. Assistant: Cathy Centra

Historical Note
*HPA is the North American trade association representing the
hearth industry. Member firms come from all segments of the
industry: manufacturer, distributor, retailer, service and associated
companies. Formerly (1992) the Wood Heating Alliance, the
product of a merger of the Wood Energy Institute, founded in 1974,
and the Fireplace Institute, founded in 1973.*

Publications:
HPA Journal. q.
HPA Membership Directory. a.
Meetings/Conferences:
Annual Meetings: Spring/9,000
1999 – Phoenix, AZ
2000 – Baltimore, MD

Heat Exchange Institute *(1933)*
1300 Sumner Ave.
Cleveland, OH   44115-2851
Tel: (216)241-7333   *Fax:* (216)241-0105
E-Mail: hei@taol.com
Web Site: http://www.taol.com/hei
Members: 16 companies
Staff: 3
Annual Budget: $50-100,000
Secretary-Treasurer: John H. Addington

Historical Note
*Members are manufacturers of heat exchange and/or vacuum
apparatus such as steam jet ejectors, steam surface condensers,
closed feedwater heaters, power plant heat exchangers and
deaerators.*
Meetings/Conferences:
1999 – Ojai, CA(Ojai Valley Inn)/Feb. 28-March 2
2000 – Tucson, AZ(Westin La Paloma)/Feb. 26-29

Heavy Duty Brake Manufacturers Council
P.O. Box 13966
Research Triangle Pk, NC   27709-3966
Tel: (919)549-4800   *Fax:* (919)549-4824
Members: 12 companies
Staff: 2
Exec. Director: Jim Lawrence

Historical Note
*A product line group of Motor and Equipment Manufacturers Ass'n.
Coordinates research in heavy duty brake standards and testing
procedures.*

Heavy Duty Business Forum *(1977)*
P.O. Box 13966
Research Triangle Park
Durham, NC   27709-3966
Tel: (919)549-4800   *Fax:* (919)549-4824
Members: 50 individuals
Staff: 2
Annual Budget: $50-100,000
Exec. Secretary: James J. Conner, III

Historical Note
*A discussion group affiliated with the Motor and Equipment
Manufacturers Ass'n and the Heavy Duty Manufacturers Ass'n
concerned with issues affecting makers of products for heavy duty
vehicles. Membership, by invitation only, is composed of top-level
management and marketing executives and is limited to fifty
members.*
Meetings/Conferences:
1999 – Carmel, CA(Quail Lodge)/May 5-7/95
1999 – Sheraton O'Hare Gateway Suites/Nov. 11-12/95
2000 – Amelia Island, FL(Amelia Island
      Resort)/April 25-28/95
2000 – /Nov. 25-28

Heavy Duty Manfacturers Ass'n *(1983)*
P.O. Box 13966
Research Triangle Pk, NC   27709-3966
Tel: (919)549-4800   *Fax:* (919)549-4824
Members: 115 companies
Staff: 3
Annual Budget: $2-5,000,000
Exec. V. President: James J. Conner, III

Historical Note
*HDMA is the heavy duty division of the Motor and Equipment
Manufacturers Ass'n and was formed to provide a focus on issues
involving manufacturers of components and equipment for class 6,7
and 8 trucks, buses and off-road equipment. Membership: $900-
$12,000/year, based on annual sales volume.*
Publications:
Heavy Duty Newsletter. 6/year.
Meetings/Conferences:
Annual Meetings: March, and Biennial Heavy Duty Dialogue
      Conference in February
1999 – Louisville, KY(Fair & Expo Center)
2000 – Atlanta, GA(Airport Hilton & Towers)/Feb. 7-8

Heavy Duty Representatives Ass'n *(1974)*
4015 Marks Road, Suite 2B
Medina, OH   44256
Tel: (330)725-7160   *Fax:* (330)722-5638
Members: 65 companies
Staff: 1
Annual Budget: $25-50,000

Exec. Director: Cara R. Giebner
Historical Note
*Independent sales agents, representing manufacturers of parts,
equipment and accessories for the heavy-duty vehicle and
equipment market. Associate membership opened to manufacturers
in the heavy- duty trucking industry.*
Publications:
Between the Lines. m.
Meetings/Conferences:

Hebrew Actors Union *(1887)*
31 East 7th St.
New York, NY   10003
Tel: (212)674-1923
Members: 225 individuals
Staff: 3
Annual Budget: $10-25,000
President: Seymour Rexite

Historical Note
*An autonomous branch union of Associated Actors and Artists of
America. An affiliate of the AFL-CIO. Membership: $20/year.*
Meetings/Conferences:
Semi-annual Meetings: New York, NY in March and
      September/60-100

Helicopter Ass'n Internat'l *(1948)*
1635 Prince St.
Alexandria, VA   22314-2818
Tel: (703)683-4646   *Fax:* (703)683-4745
Toll Free: (800)435 - 4976
Web Site: www.rotor.com
Members: 1,300 individuals, 1,400 organizations
Staff: 26
Annual Budget: $2-5,000,000
President: Roy Resavage
Director, Communications and Editor, Rotor Magazine: Marilyn
      McKinnis
Legislative Assistant: Bill Wannamaker
V. President, Expositions and Marketing: Meg Ellacott
V. President, Information Systems: Edward DiCampli
Exec. V. President, Administration: Elizabeth W. Meade
Comptroller/C.F.O.: Henry J. D'Souza
V. President, Operations: Glenn Rizner
Director, Membership: Kate Miller Haselby

Historical Note
*Began as the California Helicopter Ass'n with seven charter
members. Became the Helicopter Ass'n of America in 1951 and
assumed its present name in 1981. Now has an international
membership from over 60 countries. Membership consists of
companies that own and operate helicopters for hire, use helicopters
for private and corporate transport and helicopters in public service.
Associate members are manufacturers and servicers to the industry.
Membership: annual dues vary, based on helicopter fleet size
(regular); annual dues vary, based on company's gross revenue
(associate); $60/year (individual sustaining); $40/year
(pilot/mechanic/technician); $35/year (student).*
Publications:
Helicopter Annual a. adv. adv.
Operations Update. m.
Rotor Magazine. q. adv.
Meetings/Conferences:
Annual Meetings: Winter/13,000-14,000
1999 – Dallas, TX/Feb 21-23
1999 – Las Vegas, NV/Jan. 24-26

Helicopter Loggers Ass'n *(1980)*
P.O. Box 206
Wilsonville, OR   97070
Tel: (503)678-1222
Members: 4 companies
Annual Budget: $50-100,000
Secretary-Treasurer: Steve Martin

Historical Note
*Members are logging companies using helicopters. Has no paid
officers or full-time staff. Membership fee varies, based on
operating expenses.*

Hellenic-American Chamber of Commerce *(1947)*
960 Avenue of the Americas, Suite 1204
New York, NY   10001-2112
Tel: (212)629-6380   *Fax:* (212)564-9281
Members: 250 companies
Administrator: Joanne Pateas

Help Desk Institute *(1989)*
650 Townsend St., Floor 3
San Francisco, CA   94103-4908
Tel: (415)528-4200   *Fax:* (415)528-4250
Toll Free: (800)248 - 5667
E-Mail: ekobylec@sbforums.com
Web Site: http://www.helpdeskinst.com
Members: 5,300 individuals
Exec. Director: Bill Rose

Historical Note
*Institute members are software support sites and professionals
involved in the provision of telephonic software support services.
Membership: $275/year (individual); $495/year
(organization/company).*

Publications:
Help Desk Buyers Guide. a.
Liferaft. bi-m.
Meetings/Conferences:

Herb Growing and Marketing Network *(1990)*
P.O. Box 245
Silver Spring, PA   17575-0245
Tel: (717)393-3295   *Fax:* (717)393-9261
E-Mail: herbworld@aol.com

Web Site: http://www.herbnet.com/or
//www.hgmn.com/internet/
Members: 2,000 companies/individuals
Staff: 3
Annual Budget: $100-250,000
Director: Maureen Rogers

Historical Note
*HGMN was designed to provide practical information on all
segments of the industry with an emphasis on marketing and
locating wholesale sources. Members are growers, distributors,
retailers and suppliers of materials to the industry. Membership:
$75/year (full member); $48/year (newsletter only).*

Publications:
Herbal Connection Newsletter. m.
Herbal Green Pages. a. adv.

Meetings/Conferences:
1999 – Florida
2000 – Sedona, AZ

Herpetologists' League *(1936)*
Florida Int. University
College of Art & Science
North Miami, FL   33181
Tel: (305)919-5651   *Fax:* (305)919-5964
Members: 1,800 individuals and institutions
Annual Budget: $50-100,000
Secretary: Maureen A. Donnelly

Historical Note
*International membership organization. Fosters the study of the
biology of amphibians and reptiles. Regular membership: $50/year
(individual), $90/year (organization).*

Publications:
Herpetologica. q.
Herpetological Monographs. a.

Meetings/Conferences:

Hickory Handle Ass'n *(1900)*
Historical Note
Defunct in 1996.

High Speed Ground Transportation Ass'n
1010 Massachusetts Ave., N.W.
Washington, DC   20001
Tel: (202)784-8107   *Fax:* (202)789-8109
E-Mail: hsgt@mindspring.com
Web Site: http://www.hsgt.org
Members: 1,500 individuals
Staff: 4
President: Mark Dysart

Historical Note
Supersedes High Speed Rail/Maglev Ass'n.

Publications:
Speedlines.

Meetings/Conferences:
1999 – Seattle, WA

High Speed Rail/Maglev Ass'n *(1983)*
Historical Note
*Defunct in 1997; superseded by High Speed Ground Transportation
Ass'n.*

Highway Sign Support Ass'n *(1975)*
Historical Note
Organization defunct in 1998.

Highway Users Federation for Safety and Mobility
Historical Note
Became (1995) American Highway Users Alliance.

Hispanic Ass'n of Colleges and Universities *(1986)*
4204 Gardendale, Suite 216
San Antonio, TX   78229
Tel: (210)692-3805   *Fax:* (210)692-0823
Members: 200 colleges and universities
Staff: 31
Annual Budget: $2-5,000,000
President: Antonio R. Flores, Ph.D.
Dir., Public Affairs: Diana Marin
Conference Coordinator: Gloria Cummnins
Acting Director, Education Collaboratives: Rene Gonzalez
C.F.O.: Vijay Jain
General Counsel: Vincent Lazaro
Director of Resource Development and Membership: Lisa Beltran

Historical Note
*HACU members are U.S. and Puerto Rican colleges and universities
with a minimum Hispanic enrollment of 25%. Membership fee
varies based on enrollment: $825-2,200/year.*

Publications:
Annual Report. a.
HACU Newsletter. m.
The Voice of Hispanic Higher Education. m. adv.

Meetings/Conferences:
Annual Meetings: October/800
1999 – Puerto Rico
2000 – Albuquerque, NM

Hispanic Dental Ass'n
188 W. Randolph St., Suite 1811
Chicago, IL   60601-3001
Tel: (312)634-9018   *Fax:* (312)634-0228
Toll Free: (800)852 - 7921
Web Site: www.hadssoc.org
Annual Budget: $100-250,000
Exec. Director: Sandy Reed

Historical Note
Membership: $85/year (individual); $15/year (student).

Publications:
HDA News. q. adv.
Meetings/Conferences:

Hispanic Elected Local Officials *(1976)*
c/o Nat'l League of Cities
1301 Pennsylvania Ave., N.W., Suite 550
Washington, DC   20004
Tel: (202)626-3169   *Fax:* (202)626-3043
Web Site: http://www.nlc.org
Members: 100 individuals
Annual Budget: under $10,000
Manager: Mary France Gordon

Historical Note
*HELO serves as a forum for communication and exchange among
Hispanic local government officials within the framework of the
Nat'l League of Cities. HELO objectives include encouraging
participation of Hispanic officials in NLC, identifying qualified
Hispanic officials for service in NLC as well as for other national
positions, promoting issues of interest to Hispanics, and
establishing liaisons with other state and national organizations
concerned with municipal government or issues of particular
concern to the Hispanic community. Membership: $35-55/year
(individual).*

Publications:
Constituency and Member Group Report. q.
HELO Membership Directory. a.

Meetings/Conferences:
Annual Meetings: March and December, during Nat'l League of
Cities meetings
1999 – Los Angeles, CA(Convention Center)

Hispanic Nat'l Bar Ass'n *(1972)*
P.O. Box 66105
Washington, DC   20035-6105
Tel: (202)293-1507   *Fax:* (202)293-1508
Web Site: http://www.hnba.com
Members: 22,000 individuals
Staff: 1
Annual Budget: $100-250,000
Interim Exec. Director: Elizabeth Giordano

Historical Note
*Founded in California as LaRaza Nat'l Bar Ass'n; assumed present
name in 1980; and was re-incorporated in Washington, DC in
1983. Members are Hispanic attorneys, judges, law professors and
law students. Membership: $45-100/year (individual), $200/year
(affiliate).*

Publications:
Noticias. q. adv.

Meetings/Conferences:
Annual Meetings: Fall
1999 – Dallas, TX/Oct. 14-16
2000 – Chicago, IL

Hispanic Organization of Latin Actors *(1977)*
250 West 65th St.
New York, NY   10023-6403
Tel: (212)595-8286   *Fax:* (212)799-6718
E-Mail: holagram@aol.com
Members: 400 individuals
Staff: 2
Annual Budget: $50-100,000
Exec. Director: Manuel Alfaro

Historical Note
*HOLA is an arts service organization committed to exploring and
expanding available opportunities for projecting Hispanic artists
and their culture into the mainstream of Anglo-American industry
and culture. Membership: $50/year (individual).*

Publications:
Directory of Hispanic Talent. bi-a. adv.
For Our Members Only. 18/yea.
La Nueva Ola Newsletter. m.

Meetings/Conferences:
Biennial Meetings: January (odd years)

Histamine Research Soc. of North America *(1946)*
Historical Note
Address unknown in 1997.

Histochemical Soc. *(1950)*
Dept. Neurology, UW Box 356465
University of Washington, School of Med.
Seattle, WA   98195
Tel: (206)764-2088
E-Mail: wlstahl@u.washington.edu
Members: 550 individuals
Annual Budget: $50-100,000
Exec. Director: William Stahl, Ph.D.

Historical Note
*Founded in 1950 and incorporated in 1963 in New York. Affiliated
with the Internat'l Federation of Socs. for Histochemistry and
Cytochemistry. Society members are qualified scientists who employ
histochemical and cytochemical techniques in their research.
Organization encourages scientific research to advance and
promulgate knowledge concerning the interrelationship of chemical
constitution and detailed morphologic structure of organisms in
normal and pathologic states. Membership: $98/year (individual);
$88/year (student).*

Publications:
Newsletter. semi-a.
Proceedings. a.
The Journal of Histochemistry and Cytochemistry. m. adv.

Meetings/Conferences:

Historians Film Committee *(1970)*
Popular Culture Center
Route 3, Box 80
Cleveland, OK   74020

Tel: (918)243-7637   *Fax:* (918)243-5995
E-Mail: RollinsPC@aol.com
Members: 1000 individuals and libraries
Chair: Peter C. Rollins

Historical Note
*Members are academics and others with an interest in the use of
film and television in historical teaching and research. Membership:
$25/year (individual); $35/year (institution).*

Publications:
Film & History: Interdisciplinary Journal of Film & Television
Studies.

Meetings/Conferences:
Annual Meetings: in conjunction with AHA, PCA/ACA, and OAH
annual meetings

Historians of American Communism *(1982)*
P.O. Box 1216
Washington, CT   06793
Tel: (212)737-2715   *Fax:* (212)741-6790
Members: 165 individuals
Annual Budget: under $10,000
General Secretary: Daniel Leab

Historical Note
*HAC members are academics and others with an interest in the
study of American communism. Membership: $20/year
(individual); $25/year (organization/company).*

Publications:
Newsletter of the HAC. q. adv.

Meetings/Conferences:
Annual Meetings: in conjunction with AHA and OAH annual
meetings

History of Earth Sciences Soc. *(1982)*
History Dept., Texas Tech Univ.
Lubbock, TX   79409
Tel: (806)742-3744   *Fax:* (806)742-1060
E-Mail: J3Ron@ttac.ttu.edu
Members: 500 individuals, 100 institutions
Staff: 1
Annual Budget: $10-25,000
Secretary: Ronald Rainger

Historical Note
*Seeks to foster the study of all phases of history of the earth
sciences. Membership: $30/year (individual); $50/year
(institution), $35/year (foreign individual); $55/year (foreign
institution).*

Publications:
Earth Sciences History. semi-a.

Meetings/Conferences:
Annual Meetings: Summer

History of Economics Soc. *(1972)*
Univ. Of Tenn., Business Admin. Bldg.
Martin, TN   38238
Tel: (901)587-7228
Web Site: http://cs.muohio.edu/~HisEcSoc/
Members: 400 individuals
Annual Budget: under $10,000
Secretary-Treasurer: Prof. John Bethune

Historical Note
Membership: $30/year (individual).

Publications:
Journal of the History of Economic Thought. semi-a. adv.

Meetings/Conferences:
Annual Meetings: Summer
1999 – Greensboro, NC/June 26-28

History of Education Soc. *(1960)*
Univ. of Oregon, Coll. of Education
Eugene, OR   97403
Tel: (541)346-1367
Members: 600 individuals
Staff: 2
Annual Budget: $50-100,000
Managing Editor: C.H. Edson

Historical Note
*For the advancement of interest, study and research in the history
of education Membership: $30/year (individual), $57/year
(institution).*

Publications:
History of Education Quarterly. q. adv.
The Network. m.

Meetings/Conferences:
Annual Meetings: Fall

History of Science Soc. *(1924)*
Univ. of Washington, Box 351330
Seattle, WA   98195-1330
Tel: (206)543-9366   *Fax:* (206)685-9544
E-Mail: hssexec@u.washington.edu
Web Site: http://www.weber.u.washington.edu/uhssexec
Members: 3,000 individuals
Staff: 3
Annual Budget: $250-500,000
Exec. Secretary: Keith R. Benson

Historical Note
*Founded in 1924 to foster interest in the history of science and its
social and cultural relations. Member American Council of Learned
Societies. Membership: $57/year (individual), $24/year (student
and retired), $153/year (institution).*

Publications:
Current Bibliography. a.
HSS Newsletter. q. adv.
Isis. q.
Osiris. a. adv.

Meetings/Conferences:
Annual Meetings: Fall

1999 – Pittsburgh, PA(Westin William Penn)/Nov. 3-7/900
2000 – Vancouver, BC, Canada(Hyatt Regency)/Nov. 1-5
2001 – Denver, CO(Adam's Mark)/Nov. 7-11
2002 – Milwaukee, WI

Hobby Industry Ass'n of America *(1940)*
319 E. 54th St.
P.O. Box 348
Elmwood Park, NJ   07407
Tel: (201)794-1133						*Fax:* (201)797-0657
E-Mail: hia@ix.netcom.com
Web Site: http://www.webcreations.com/hia
Members: 3,800 corporations
Staff: 20
Annual Budget: $5-10,000,000
Exec. Director: Patricia S. Koziol
Asst. Exec. Director, Communications: Susan Brandt
Director of Meetings & Expositions: Susan L. Danker
Certification and Education Manager: Anita Bolen Collins
Marketing Manager: Adrienne Coppola
Historical Note
Founded in Chicago as the Model Industry Association with 87 charter members, it assumed its present name in 1956. The Hobby Industry Association is a grouping of manufacturers, wholesalers, retailers, publishers and others affiliated with the craft and hobby industry. Annual Budget: $5.5 million.
Publications:
Horizons. m.
Nationwide Consumer Survey. a.
Size of Industry Survey.
The Directory. a.
Meetings/Conferences:
Annual Meetings: Held during trade show in Winter
1999 – Dallas, TX(Convention Center)/Feb. 4-7
2000 – Anaheim, CA(Convention Center)/Jan. 30-Feb. 2

Hoist Manufacturers Institute *(1968)*
8720 Red Oak Blvd., Suite 201
Charlotte, NC   28217-3992
Tel: (704)676-1190						*Fax:* (704)676-1199
E-Mail: Hal_Vandiver@mhia.org
Web Site: http://www.mhia.org
Members: 15 companies
Staff: 3
Annual Budget: $25-50,000
Managing Director: F. Hal Vandiver
Historical Note
Formerly Hoist Manufacturers Ass'n. A product section of the Material Handling Institute.
Meetings/Conferences:
Annual Meetings: With the Material Handling Institute

Holistic Dental Ass'n *(1980)*
P.O. Box 5007
Durango, CO   81301
Tel: (970)259-1091						*Fax:* (970)259-1091
E-Mail: HDA@Frontier.net
Web Site: HollisticDental.org
Members: 200 individuals
Staff: 1
Annual Budget: $25-50,000
Exec. Director: Dr. R.S. Shepard
Historical Note
Members are dentists and other health professionals with an interest in a holistic approach to the practice of dentistry. Membership: $250/year.
Publications:
Communicator Newsletter. q. adv.
Meetings/Conferences:
Annual Meetings: Spring
1999 – Denver, CO/May 15-17

Hollow Metal Door and Buck Ass'n *(1938)*
Historical Note
Organization defunct in 1997.

Holstein Ass'n USA *(1885)*
One Holstein Place
Brattleboro, VT   05302-0808
Tel: (802)254-4551						*Fax:* (802)254-8251
Toll Free: (800)952 - 5200
E-Mail: skerr@holstein.com
Web Site: www.holsteinusa.com
Members: 50,000 individuals
Staff: 215
Annual Budget: $10-25,000,000
Exec. Secretary and C.E.O.: Stephen R. Kerr
Marketing Director: David Hollis
Exec. Director, Human Resources: Carol Adams
Exec. Assistant: Thomas J. Moses
Exec. Director, Information Services: Richard Cronce
Historical Note
Formerly (1988) Holstein-Friesian Ass'n of America, (1994) Holstein Ass'n U.S.A. Members are breeders of Holstein dairy cattle. Member of the National Pedigreed Livestock Council. Has an annual budget of approximately $15 million. Membership: $25/year.
Publications:
Holstein Association News. m.
Holstein World. bi-m. adv.
Meetings/Conferences:
Annual Meetings: June/1,500-2,000
1999 – Boise, ID(Grove Hotel)/June 19-22/1500
2000 – Columbus, OH(Hyatt Hotel)/June 30-July 1/1500
2001 – Cedar Rapids, IA(Four Seasons)/June 27-30/1500
2002 – Atlantic City, NJ(Taj Mahal)/June 23-26/1500

Home Automation Ass'n *(1988)*
1444 I St., N.W., Suite 700

Washington, DC   20005-2210
Tel: (202)712-9050						*Fax:* (202)216-9646
E-Mail: haa@bostromdc.com
Web Site: http://www.homeautomation.org
Members: 320 companies
Staff: 2
Annual Budget: $100-250,000
Exec. Director: Charles A. McGrath, CAE
Historical Note
The trade association of the home control industry, HAA members are dealers, installers, architects, manufacturers, utilities, home builders, designers and developers of home automation products. Membership: $195-5,000/year (organization/company).
Publications:
Home Automation News. bi-m.
Membership Directory. a. adv.
Meetings/Conferences:
1999 – Orlando, FL/3000

Home Baking Ass'n *(1943)*
10841 S. Parker Rd., Suite 105
Englewood, CO   80111
Tel: (303)840-8787						*Fax:* (303)840-6871
E-Mail: HBAPatton@aol.com
Members: 38 companies
Staff: 4
Annual Budget: $100-250,000
Administrator: Charlene Patton
Historical Note
An association of the millers of wheat flour and corn meal, manufacturers of branded food ingredients used in home baking, and their allied trades formed for the purpose of conducting an educational program on behalf of those products. Formerly Self Rising Flour Institute and (1989) Self-Rising Flour and Corn Meal Program.
Meetings/Conferences:
Annual Meetings: Fall

Home Builders Institute
Historical Note
A subsidiary of the Nat'l Ass'n of Home Builders of the U.S.

Home Care Aide Ass'n of America
228 7th St., S.E.
Washington, DC   20003-4306
Tel: (202)547-7424						*Fax:* (202)547-9559
Web Site: http://www.nahc.org/HCA/home.html
Exec. Director: Deborah McNeal Arrindell
Historical Note
An affiliate of the Nat'l Ass'n for Home Care.
Meetings/Conferences:
1999 – San Diego, CA/Oct. 9-13

Home Economists in Business *(1923)*
Historical Note
Address unknown in 1995.

Home Energy Rating Systems Council *(1993)*
1511 K St., N.W., Suite 600
Washington, DC   20005
Tel: (202)638-3700						*Fax:* (202)393-5043
E-Mail: herscdc@aol.com
Web Site: www.hers-council.org
Members: 100 individuals
Staff: 3
Annual Budget: $250-500,000
Exec. Director: Cynthia J. Gardstein
Historical Note
The mission of HERS Council is to increase energy efficiency in housing by serving as an education and research resource and by establishing guidelines for uniformity of HERS and establishing a voluntary program for accrediting systems and certifying tools that assign home energy efficiency ratings to facilitate access to energy efficient mortgages and other programs. Membership: $200-1,000/year, varies by type of industry (organization)
Publications:
HERSC News. q.
Meetings/Conferences:
Semi-Annual Meetings: Winter and Spring

Home Executives Nat'l Networking Ass'n *(1992)*
Historical Note
Organization defunct in 1996.

Home Fashion Products Ass'n *(1968)*
355 Lexington Ave., 17th Floor
New York, NY   10017-6603
Tel: (212)661-4261						*Fax:* (212)370-9047
Members: 125 companies
Annual Budget: $50-100,000
Exec. Director: Holly J. Munter
Historical Note
Formerly (until 1981) the National Curtain, Drapery and Allied Products Ass'n. Members are producers of all window and bed decor products and related accessories as included in a curtain or drapery retail assortment. Membership: $475/year.
Meetings/Conferences:
Semi-annual Meetings: New York, NY(members' showrooms)/Spring and Fall

Home Furnishings Internat'l Ass'n *(1923)*
P.O. Box 420807
Dallas, TX   75342-0807
Tel: (214)741-7632						*Fax:* (214)742-9103
Toll Free: (800)942 - 4663
Members: 1,500 individuals
Staff: 15
Annual Budget: $2-5,000,000

President: Mary Frye
Director, Membership: Christy Hodges
Historical Note
HFIA members are officers, managers and employees of stores which stock home furnishings for retail sales. Associate members are consulting, design, manufacturing and supplier firms; affiliate members are individuals with an interest in the industry. Membership: $180/year, minimum; $320/year (associate); $180/year (affiliate).
Publications:
Homefurnishings Review. m. adv.
Meetings/Conferences:
Annual Meetings: January and July Markets

Home Health Services and Staffing Ass'n *(1978)*
115-D S. St. Asaph St.
Alexandria, VA   22314-3119
Tel: (703)836-9863						*Fax:* (703)836-9866
E-Mail: mbenner@hhssa.org
Web Site: http://www.hhssa.org
Members: 2,000 firms
Staff: 2
Annual Budget: $500-1,000,000
Exec. Director: Mara Benner
Director of Marketing: Lauren Young
Manager, Government Relations: Seth Johnson
Director of Membership: Suzy Brown, CMP
Membership Marketing Representative: Kelly Verberg
Historical Note
Provides leadership on federal and state issues affecting the proprietary home health/supplemental care & nursing industry in the U.S. Membership: $400-84,000/year, based on gross annual sales.
Publications:
Federal Activities Report. m.
State Activities Update. w.
Status Report. m. adv.
Meetings/Conferences:
Annual Meetings: Fall

Home Healthcare Nurses Ass'n *(1993)*
7794 Grow Drive
Pensacola, FL   32514
Tel: (850)474-1066						*Fax:* (850)484-8762
Toll Free: (800)558 - 4462
E-Mail: hhna@aol.com
Members: 2,500 individuals
Annual Budget: $250-500,000
Exec. Director: Belinda F. Puetz Ph.D,
Director, Convention Services: Henrietta Elston
Director, Education: Janice Ward
Member Services Representative: Christie Herrington
Manager, Publications: Shay Stephens
Historical Note
HHNA promotes the specialty of home healthcare nursing. Membership: $75/year.
Publications:
HHNA Forum. bi-m. adv.
Home Healthcare Nurse. m. adv.
Meetings/Conferences:
Annual Meetings: Spring
1999 – Arlington, VA/April 22-25

Home Improvement Lenders Ass'n *(1988)*
1625 Massachusettes Ave., N.W.
Suite 601
Washington, DC   20036-2244
Tel: (202)328-9171						*Fax:* (202)265-4435
E-Mail: Gpeth@aol.com
Web Site: http://www.hila.com
Members: 200 individuals
Staff: 5
Annual Budget: $250-500,000
Exec. Director: Peter H. Bell
Historical Note
Formerly (1998) the Title I Home Improvement Lenders Ass'n. Members are financial institutions which make federally insured loans under the Federal Housing Administration Title I program.
Meetings/Conferences:
1999 – Palm Springs, CA(Marriott Desert Springs)

Home Improvement Research Institute *(1981)*
3922 Coconut Palm Dr.
Tampa, FL   33619
Tel: (813)627-6750						*Fax:* (813)627-7063
Web Site: http://www.hiri.org
Members: 53 companies
Staff: 2
Annual Budget: $250-500,000
Exec. Director: Fred Miller
Member Services Coordinator: Amy Rosanova
Historical Note
Formerly (1990) the Do-It-Yourself Research Institute. Members are manufacturers, wholesalers and retailers, trade associations and trade publications involved in the home improvement market (e.g. home repair and renovation, landscaping/gardening, etc.). Membership: $8,000/year.
Publications:
Home Imporvement Market: A Reference Guide. a.
Newsletter. q.
Product Purchase Tracking Study. bien.
Professional Remodeler Segmentation Study. bien.
Size of Industry Study. q.
Meetings/Conferences:
Annual Meetings: Fall
1999 – September

Home Office Ass'n of America *(1994)*

Gracie Station, P.O. Box 806
New York, NY   10028-0082
Tel: (212)980-4622   *Fax:* (800)315-4622
Toll Free: (800)809 - 4622
E-Mail: hoaa@aol.com
Exec. Director: Eileen Jaffe
Marketing Vice President: Angela Costa

Historical Note
Represents the interests of home office operators. Membership:
$49/year.

Publications:
Home Office Connections. m.

Home Office Life Underwriters Ass'n *(1930)*
2300 Windy Ridge Pkwy., Suite 600
Atlanta, GA   30339-8443
Tel: (770)984-3715   *Fax:* (770)984-6417
Members: 1,200 individuals
Staff: 1
Annual Budget: $250-500,000
President: Sam White

Historical Note
Membership: $75/year (domestic); $100/year (overseas).

Publications:
On the Risk Magazine.
Proceedings. a.

Meetings/Conferences:
Annual Meetings: Spring
1999 – Chicago, IL(Hyatt Regency
        Riverwalk)/April 25-28/800
2000 – Toronto, Canada(Toronto Sheraton)/April 30-May
        3/700
2001 – Orlando, FL(Renaissance Orlando
        Resort)/May 6-9/800
2002 – Seattle, WA(Sheraton Seattle)/May 6-9/700

Home Sewing Ass'n *(1928)*
1350 Broadway, Suite 1601
New York, NY   10018
Tel: (212)714-1633   *Fax:* (212)714-1655
E-Mail: administration@sewing.org
Web Site: http://www.sewing.org
Members: 900 companies
Staff: 5
Annual Budget: $1-2,000,000
Exec. V. President: Joan Carter Campbell, CAE
Dir., Marketing & Communications: Cathleen Campbell
Special Projects Manager: Anneke van Zanten
Manager, Special Projects: Donna Pierson

Historical Note
Formerly (1976) the Nat'l Notion Ass'n; a new Nat'l Notion Ass'n
was incorporated at this time with different objectives and a
separate organization called the Nat'l Home Sewing Ass'n (NHSA)
was formed. In 1978 NHSA merged with the American Home
Sewing Council to create American Home Sewing Ass'n; became
American Home Sewing and Craft Ass'n in 1990. Absorbed the
Internat'l Sewing Machine Ass'n in 1996; assumed its current
name in 1997. Members are manufacturers of all types of home
sewing items, as well as fabric stores, wholesalers and chains.
Affiliate members include manufacturers' representatives,
educators, and buying offices. Asssociate members include
manufacturers of display equipment and supplies. Membership:
varies according to sales volume or number of stores.

Publications:
Inside HSA. bi-m.
Trade and Show Journal semi-a. adv. adv.

Meetings/Conferences:
Semi-Annual Meetings: Spring and Fall(Trade Show)/4,000

Home Wine and Beer Trade Ass'n *(1979)*
P.O. Box 1373
Valrico, FL   33595
Tel: (813)685-4261   *Fax:* (813)681-5625
E-Mail: hwbta@aol.com
Web Site: http://www.hwbta.org
Members: 521 individuals
Staff: 1
Annual Budget: $50-100,000
Exec. Director: Dee Roberson

Historical Note
HWBTA members are manufacturers, distributors, retailers and
others with an interest in the home brewing/home winemaking
trade. Membership: $50/year (retailer); $250/year
(wholesaler/manufacturer).

Publications:
HWBTA Advocate Newsletter. q. adv.

Meetings/Conferences:

Home Workers Ass'n *(1990)*
7235 Saddle Creek Circle
Sarasota, FL   34241-9543
Tel: (813)925-1909
Members: 2,300 individuals
Annual Budget: $10-25,000
Exec. Director: Francine DiFilippo

Historical Note
Begun as a national network of self-employed researchers who act
as independent contractors. Provides job referrals and discounts as
member benefits began to be shared.

Publications:
Fox Net News. adv. adv.

Hoo-Hoo Internat'l
Historical Note
See Internat'l Concatenated Order of Hoo-Hoo.

Hop Growers of America *(1956)*
Box 9218

Yakima, WA   98909
Tel: (509)248-7043   *Fax:* (509)248-7044
Members: 240 growers, state associations
Staff: 3
Annual Budget: $100-250,000
Exec. Director: Sean McGree

Historical Note
HGA provides marketing statistics, promotion, and research to U.S.
hop growers, and serves as liaison between its membership and the
world brewing industry. Membership is concentrated in
Washington, Oregon, and Idaho. Membership: $100/year (full
member); associate memberships available.

Publications:
Newsletter. m.

Meetings/Conferences:
Annual Meetings: January

Horizontal Earth Boring Equipment Manufacturers Council
Historical Note
A council of the Equipment Manufacturers Institute.

Horsemen's Benevolent and Protective Ass'n *(1940)*
20801 Biscayne Blvd., Suite 442
Aventura, FL   33180
Tel: (305)935-4700   *Fax:* (305)933-2233
E-Mail: racing@hbpa.org
Web Site: http://www.hbpa.org
Members: 70,000 individuals
Staff: 3
Annual Budget: $100-250,000
Exec. Director: Scott Savin

Historical Note
Members are owners and trainers of thoroughbred horses.

Meetings/Conferences:
Semi-annual meetings: Summer and Winter

Horticultural Research Institute *(1962)*
1250 I St., N.W., Suite 500
Washington, DC   20005
Tel: (202)789-2900   *Fax:* (202)789-1893
Members: 255 companies 25 associations
Staff: 2
Annual Budget: $250-500,000
Administrator: Ashby P. Ruden

Historical Note
The research arm of the American Nursery and Landscape Ass'n,
HRI supports and stimulates environmental horticultural research to
benefit the nursery and landscape industry. Membership:
$200/year (individual); $300/year (association).

Publications:
Journal of Environmental Horticulture. q.
New Horisons Newsletter. q.

Meetings/Conferences:
Annual Meetings: July, with American Nursery and Landscape
Ass'n

Hospice and Palliative Nurses Ass'n *(1986)*
Medical Center East, Suite 375
211 N. Whitfield St.
Pittsburgh, PA   15206-3031
Tel: (412)361-2470   *Fax:* (412)361-2425
E-Mail: hnafan@pipeline.com
Web Site: http://www.roxane.com/HNA
Members: 2,500 individuals
Staff: 4
Annual Budget: $250-500,000
Exec. Director: Marty Ayers
Asst. Director for Administrative Affairs: Donna J. Carothers
Membership Coordinator: Patricia Rowan

Historical Note
Formerly (1997) the Hospice Nurses Ass'n, HPNA members are
registered nurses specializing in hospice and palliative care.
Associate members are professionals, para-professionals, and/or
volunteers engaged in or interested in palliative and hospice care.
Membership: $60/year (voting); $25/year (student).

Publications:
Hospice & Palliative Care Clinical Practice Protocols. bien.
Hospice Nurses Certification Examination Review Manual a.
Journal of Hospice & Palliative Nursing.
Standards of Hospice Nursing Practice and Professional
    Performance. a.

Meetings/Conferences:
Annual Meetings: Spring
1999 – Clearwater Beach, FL/Feb. 10-13

Hospice Ass'n of America *(1985)*
228 7th St, S.E.
Washington, DC   20003
Tel: (202)546-4759   *Fax:* (202)547-9559
Web Site: http://www.nahc.org
Members: 2,500 hospices
Exec. Director: Karen Woods
Director, Public Relations: Suzanne Kieffer

Historical Note
HAA members are hospices, related healthcare organizations, and
medical professionals.

Publications:
Hospice Forum Newsletter. bi-w. adv.

Meetings/Conferences:
Annual Meetings: in conjunction with NAHC/Fall and
    Educational Conference/Feb.
1999 – San Diego, CA/Oct. 9-13

Hospice Nursing Ass'n *(1986)*

Historical Note
Formerly (1986) Hospice Nurses Association; became the Hospice
and Palliative Nurses Ass'n in 1997. Members of the association
promote excellence in hospice and palliative nursing, and fosters the
professional development of nurses. Membership:$60 (individual).

Hospital Presidents Ass'n *(1983)*
801 Main St.
Suite 9
Concord, MA   01742
Tel: (978)369-1290   *Fax:* (978)369-5101
Members: 65 individuals
Staff: 1
Annual Budget: $25-50,000
President: Joel P. Davidson

Historical Note
HPA is an educational association dedicated to the design and
presentation of programs for the most advanced practitioners of
health care management among the Chief Executive Officers of
hospitals in the U.S. and abroad. Has no paid officers or full-time
staff. Membership: $500/year.

Meetings/Conferences:

Hospitality Financial and Technology Professionals *(1953)*
11709 Boulder Lane, Suite 110
Austin, TX   78726
Tel: (512)249-5333   *Fax:* (512)249-1533
Web Site: http://www.hftp.org
Members: 3,700 individuals
Staff: 15
Annual Budget: $1-2,000,000
Exec. V. President and C.E.O.: Frank I. Wolfe, CAE
Dir., Communications: Jennifer Carr, CAE
Assoc. V. President, Meetings and Expositions: Doris Roach

Historical Note
A professional society of hotel, motel, casino, restaurant and club
controllers and financial officers. Founded as the Nat'l Ass'n of
Hotel Accountants, it later became the Nat'l Ass'n of Hotel-Motel
Accountants; became Internat'l Ass'n of Hospitality Accountants in
1975, and assumed its current name in 1997. Sponsors HITEC
(Hospitality Industry Technology Exposition and Conference), an
annual event showcasing the use of technology in hospitality.
Membership: $150/year (individual).

Publications:
Bottom Line. bi-m. adv.

Meetings/Conferences:
Annual Meetings: Fall
1999 – Atlanta, GA/June 22-24
1999 – San Antonio, TX/Oct. 20-23

Hospitality Sales and Marketing Ass'n Internat'l *(1927)*
1300 L St., N.W., Suite 1020
Washington, DC   20005
Tel: (202)789-0089   *Fax:* (202)789-1725
Members: 6,500 individuals
Staff: 9
Annual Budget: $2-5,000,000
Exec. V. President and C.E.O.: Robert A. Gilbert
Director, Marketing: Kenneth P. Esthus

Historical Note
Formerly (1983) Hotel Sales Management Ass'n Internat'l and
(1992) Hotel Sales and Marketing Ass'n Internat'l. Awards the
CHME (Certified Hospitality Marketing Executive) designation.
Membership: $195/year (individual).

Publications:
HSMAI Marketing Review. q.
HSMAI Update. m.

Meetings/Conferences:

Hotel Electronic Distribution Network Ass'n *(1991)*
303 Freeport Road
Pittsburgh, PA   15215-3131
Tel: (412)781-3255   *Fax:* (412)781-2871
E-Mail: Bill@hakanson.com
Web Site: http://www.hedna.org
Members: 175 corporations
Exec. Director: William P. Hakanson, CAE

Hotel Employees and Restaurant Employees Internat'l Union *(1891)*
1219 28th St., N.W.
Washington, DC   20007
Tel: (202)393-4373   *Fax:* (202)333-0468
E-Mail: hereiu@pop.erols.com
Web Site: www.hereiu.org
Members: 250,000 individuals
Staff: 125
Annual Budget: $25-50,000,000
Gen'l President: Edward T. Hanley

Historical Note
Founded in April 1891 as the Waiters and Bartenders Nat'l Union.
Became the Hotel and Restaurant Employees Nat'l Alliance in 1892
and the Hotel and Restaurant Employees' Internat'l Alliance and
Bartenders' Internat'l League of America in 1898. Merged in 1935
with the Food Workers Industrial Union to become the Hotel and
Restaurant Employees and Bartenders Internat'l Union and
assumed its present name in 1982. Has an annual budget of
approximately $26.2 million. Sponsors and supports the HEREIU
"TIP" (To Insure Progress) a Political Action Committee.

Publications:
Catering Industry Employee. bi-m.

Meetings/Conferences:
Quinquennial Meetings: 1996

Hotel Motel Brokers of America *(1959)*
10220 N. Executive Hills Blvd. Suite 610
Kansas City, MO   64153-2312
Tel: (816)891-7070   *Fax:* (816)891-7071

Toll Free: (800)825 - 5191
E-Mail: bob@hmba.com
Web Site: http://www.hmba.com
Members: 145 individuals, 45 firms
Staff: 5
Annual Budget: $500-1,000,000
Exec. V. President: Robert H. Kralicek, CAE
Director of Marketing: Sharon Lemon
Director of Administration: Elaine Lindsey

Historical Note
Founded as the Motel Brokers of America in 1959; became the American Hotel and Motel Brokers in 1984 and assumed its present name in 1985. Members are real estate agents specializing in the sale of motel and hotel properties. Membership: $550/year (individual); $5,160/year (company).

Publications:
Inside Issues. q.
TransActions by HMBA. a.

Meetings/Conferences:
Semi-Annual Meetings: Winter and Summer
1999 – Ft. Lauderdale, FL(Largo Mar Resort)/Jan. 7-10/125

Household Goods Forwarders Ass'n of America (1962)
2320 Mill Road, Suite 102
Alexandria, VA   22314
Tel: (703)684-3780   Fax: (703)684-3784
E-Mail: HHGFA@aol.com
Members: 1,400 individuals
Staff: 5
Annual Budget: $1-2,000,000
President: Terry Head
Director, Government Affairs: David Germroth

Historical Note
Active members (97) are companies transporting household goods by the door-to-door container method for the Department of Defense, national accounts and individuals. Associate members (1300) are suppliers and related organization, here and abroad. Membership: $250/month (active), $300/year (associate).

Publications:
Military Forwarder. m.
The Portal. bi-m.

Meetings/Conferences:
Annual Meetings: Fall/1,000
1999 – Washington, DC

Human Behavior and Evolution Soc. (1988)
Social Science Dept. Cal Poly Univ.
San Luis Obispo, CA   93407
Tel: (805)756-1173   Fax: (805)756-5748
E-Mail: pmckim@calpoly.edu
Web Site: http://157.242.64.83/hbes.htm
Treasurer: Patrick McKim

Historical Note
HBES is an interdisciplinary organization founded to promote the exchange of ideas and research findings using evolutionary theory to better understand human nature. Has no paid officers or full-time staff. Membership: $60/year (individual); $30/year (student).

Publications:
Ethology and Sociobiology Journal. bi-m. adv.
Membership Directory. a.
News of the Society Newsletter. q.

Human Biology Ass'n (1974)
University of Mass. at Amherst/Dept. of Anthropology
Machmer Hall, Box 34805
Amherst, MA   01003-4805
Tel: (413)545-1186   Fax: (413)545-9494
E-Mail: leidy@anthro.umass.edu
Web Site: http://www.cwru.edu/cwru/dept/artsci/anth/hba/
Members: 600 individuals
Annual Budget: $25-50,000
Secretary-Treasurer: Dr. Lynette E. Leidy

Historical Note
Formerly (1995) Human Biology Council. HBA promotes research and teaching in human biology and related fields, encourages human biological disciplines. Council members are physical anthropologists, medical doctors, dentists, public health officers, geneticists, nutritionists and related professions. Membership: $70/year (fellow); $35/year (student).

Publications:
American Journal of Human Biology. bi-m. adv.

Meetings/Conferences:
Annual Meetings: Spring
1999 – Columbus, OH/Apr. 27-28

Human Factors and Ergonomics Soc. (1957)
P.O. Box 1369
Santa Monica, CA   90406-1369
Tel: (310)394-1811   Fax: (310)394-2410
E-Mail: hfes@compuserve.com
Web Site: http://hfes.org
Members: 5,400 individuals
Staff: 7
Annual Budget: $1-2,000,000
Exec. Director: Lynn Strother

Historical Note
A multidisciplinary society of those engaged in research on problems of the safety, comfort and convenience of people in the environment. Established in 1957 in Tulsa. Formerly known as the Human Factors Soc. of America and the Human Factors Soc. (1992). Membership: $115/year (individual); $30/year (student).

Publications:
Bulletin. m. adv.
Cumulative Index. quinquen.
Directory. a. adv.
Ergonomics in Design. q. adv.

Human Factors. bi-m.
Proceedings of Annual Meeting.

Meetings/Conferences:
Annual Meetings: October
2000 – San Diego, CA(Marriott)/July 30-Aug. 1

Human Resource Planning Soc. (1977)
317 Madison Ave., Suite 1509
New York, NY   10017
Tel: (212)490-6387   Fax: (212)682-6851
Web Site: http://www.hrps.org
Members: 3,500 individuals
Staff: 7
Annual Budget: $1-2,000,000
Exec. Director: Walter J. Cleaver
Director, Communications: Beverly Pinzon
Director of Meeting Services: Dillan Waldron

Historical Note
Manpower planning and development specialists, staffing analysts, business planners and others concerned with planning for employee recruitment, development and utilization. Membership: $200/year (individual); $1,500/year (organization); $1,000/year (research sponsor).

Publications:
Case Studies of HR Planning Practice. irreg.
Human Resource Planning. q.
Membership Directory. a.
Research Symposium Proceedings. bi-a.

Meetings/Conferences:
Annual Meetings: March/April
1999 – San Diego, CA/March 28-31

Human Resources Research Organization
66 Canal Center Plaza, Suite 400
Alexandria, VA   22314-1591
Tel: (703)549-3611   Fax: (703)549-9025
Program Manager: Deirdre Knapp, Ph.D.

Hungarian-United States Business Council (1974)
Historical Note
Became (1997) American Business Alliance for the Transition Economies of Eurasia.

Hybrids and Manufacturing Technology Components Soc.
Historical Note
A subsidiary of the Institute of Electrical and Electronics Engineers. Membership in the Society, open only to IEEE members, includes subscription to a technical periodical in the field published by IEEE. All administrative support is provided by IEEE.

Hydraulic Institute (1917)
9 Sylvan Way
Parsippany, NJ   07054-3802
Tel: (973)267-9700   Fax: (973)267-9055
E-Mail: rasdal@pump.org
Members: 96 manufacturers of pumps
Staff: 8
Annual Budget: $500-1,000,000
Exec. Director: Robert K. Asdal
Meeting Planner: Christine Schneider
Comptroller: Laura DiPrimo
Membership Director: Gary Miller

Historical Note
Members of the Hydraulic Institute are major United States pump manufacturers. HI develops and disseminates standards for the industry, encourages continued technical development, and pursues appropriate activities in support of the industry. Membership: dues based on company revenue.

Publications:
Engineering Data Book.
Membership Directory. a.
Pump Forum. bi-m.
Pump Standards.

Meetings/Conferences:
Tri-annual Meetings: Annual Meeting/February
1999 – Tucson, AZ(Sheraton El
             Conquistador)/Feb. 20-23/200
1999 – Pinehurst, NC(Pinehurst Resort)/Sept. 16-19/135

Hydraulic Tool Manufacturers Ass'n (1974)
1509 Rapids Dr.
Racine, WI   53404-2383
Tel: (414)633-3454   Fax: (414)637-8582
Members: 12 companies
Staff: 1
Annual Budget: under $10,000
Exec. Secretary: John W. Petersen

Historical Note
Members are firms who market portable hydraulic-powered tools under their own brand name. HTMA establishes and publishes voluntary standards for several aspects of the hydraulic tool industry. Has no paid staff. Membership: $300/year (corporate).

Meetings/Conferences:
Semi-Annual Meetings: Spring and Fall/20

Hydrogen Industry Council
1800 McGill College Ave., Suite 2610
Montreal, PQ   H3A 3-J6
Tel: (514)288-5139
Members: 30 companies and organizations
President: Richard D. Champagne

Hydronics Institute Division of GAMA (1915)
35 Russo Place
P.O. Box 218
Berkeley Heights, NJ   07922
Tel: (908)464-8200   Fax: (908)464-7818
E-Mail: gamaorg@aol.com

Web Site: http://www.gamanet.org
Members: 63 companies
Staff: 4
Annual Budget: $500-1,000,000
Office Manager: Janine Bosnak

Historical Note
Merger (1970) of Better Heating-Cooling Council (1950) and Institute of Boiler and Radiator Manufacturers (1915). Became a division of the Gas Appliance Manufacturers Ass'n in 1995. The Institute is a trade association of manufacturers of hydronic heating and cooling equipment including boilers, various types of heating units, their accessories and controls.

Meetings/Conferences:
Semi-Annual Meeting: Absecon, NJ(Seaview Country
             Club)/October
1999 – /Oct. 19-22

Hydroponic Merchants Ass'n (1997)
10210 Leatherleaf Court
Manassas, VA   20111-4245
Tel: (703)392-5890   Fax: (703)257-0213
Annual Budget: $50-100,000
Exec. Officer: Robert C. LaGasse
Director, Membership: J.C. McGowan

Historical Note
HMA addresses the needs of retail, manufacturing, wholesale and other interests in the hydroponic industry. Membership: $250/year (company).

Publications:
HMA Newsletter. q.
Industry and Market Surveys. irreg.
Membership Directory. a.

Meetings/Conferences:
Annual Meetings: June
1999 – Orlando, FL(Airport Marriott)/June 17-23/200

Hydroponic Soc. of America (1978)
PO Box 1183
El Cerrito, CA   94530-1183
Tel: (510)232-2323   Fax: (510)232-2384
Web Site: www.hsa.hydroponics.org
Members: 700 companies and individuals
Staff: 1
Annual Budget: $50-100,000
Operations Manager: Patty Bates

Historical Note
Organized to promote the development of hydroponics - the growing of plants in nutrient solutions, without soil. Membership: $40/year (in North America), $60/year (outside North America)

Publications:
Conference Proceedings. a.
Directory.
Newsletter. bi-m. adv.

Meetings/Conferences:
Annual Meetings: Spring
1999 – Oakland, CA/July 30-Aug. 2

I2O Special Interest Group (1996)
404 Balboa St.
San Francisco, CA   94118
Tel: (415)750-8352   Fax: (415)751-4829
E-Mail: info@i2osig.org
Web Site: http://www.i2osig.org
Members: 110 companies

Historical Note
I2O SIG members are computer system/network/peripheral interface card, operating system, and independent software/tools vendors committed to the design, promotion, maintenance, extension and certification of the intelligent I/O driver specification. Membership: $5,000/year (contributing); $2,000/year (associate).

IBFI, The Internat'l Ass'n for Document and Information Management Solutions (1953)
100 Daingerfield Road
Alexandria, VA   22314-2888
Tel: (703)684-9606   Fax: (703)684-9675
Toll Free: (888)999 - 4234
E-Mail: ecover@ibfi.org
Web Site: http://www.ibfi.org
Members: 600 companies
Annual Budget: $1-2,000,000
President: Thomas C. Playford
Dir., Communications and Vice President: Eva Cover, CAE

Historical Note
Formerly Internat'l Business Forms Industries; it became IBFI, The Internat'l Ass'n Serving the Forms, Information Management, Systems Automation and Printed Communications Requirements of Business in 1994, and assumed its present name in 1997. Members are manufacturers of business forms, information management service providers, and suppliers to the industry. Founded in 1953 as a section of Printing Industries of America, IBFI is now a self-sustaining, wholly incorporated organization. Maintains a European Operations Office in Berne, Switzerland. Membership: dues based on sales volume.

Publications:
Business Conditions Survey. q.
IBFI Perspective. m.
IBFI Ratio Study. a.
Papertronix Magazine, merging paper & electronics.
Sales Index. m.

Meetings/Conferences:
1999 – Marco Island Marriott

ICAAAA Coaches Ass'n (1919)
3927 Benton St., N.W.
Washington, DC   20007
Tel: (202)965-1907   Fax: (202)466-8987
Members: 115 schools
Annual Budget: under $10,000

Secretary-Treasurer: Walter Krolman

Historical Note
Track and field coaches from eastern colleges and universities affiliated with the Intercollegiate Ass'n of Amateur Athletes of America (ICAAAA). Has no paid staff. Membership: $15/year (individual).

Publications:
None.

Meetings/Conferences:
Three Meetings Annually: March, May and September

Ice Skating Institute *(1959)*
17120 Dallas Pkwy.,Suite 140
Dallas, TX   75248-1187
Tel: (972)735-8800   *Fax:* (972)735-8815
E-Mail: skateISI@aol.com
Web Site: http://www.skateisi.com
Members: 60,000 individuals
Staff: 11
Annual Budget: $1-2,000,000
Exec. Director: Peter Martell
Managing Dir., Member Svcs/Prgms.: Patti Feeney
Publications Manager: Dianne Powell

Historical Note
Membership comprised of ice rink owners, operators, instructors, builders/suppliers, skaters and retail shops. Sponsors educational seminars and judge certification, as well as the annual World Recreational Team Championships in August and an annual Winter Classic in January, the trade show/conference (listed below) and consumer shows in conjunction with the national skating events. Membership: $5/year (individual), $225/year (ice rink), $375/year (builder/supplier).

Publications:
Directory. a.
ISI EDGE. bi-m. adv.
Resreational Ice Skating. q. adv.

Meetings/Conferences:
Annual Meetings: May
1999 – Las Vegas, NV(Ceasar's Palace)/May 31-June 3

Icelandic American Chamber of Commerce *(1986)*
c/o Cons. General of Iceland
800 Third Ave., 36th Floor
New York, NY   10022-7604
Tel: (212)593-2700   *Fax:* (212)593-6269
E-Mail: icecon.ny@utn.stjr.is
Web Site: http://www.icelandtrade.com
Members: 110 companies
Staff: 1
Annual Budget: $25-50,000
Exec. Director: Magnus Bjarnason

Historical Note
Facilitates businesses relationships between Iceland and U.S. firms. Membership: $60/year (individual), $200/year (company).

Publications:
Newsletter. q.

Meetings/Conferences:
1999 – New York, NY

IDEA, The Health and Fitness Source *(1982)*
6190 Cornerstone Court E., Suite 204
San Diego, CA   92121-3773
Tel: (619)535-8979   *Fax:* (619)535-8234
Members: 23,000 individuals
Staff: 53
C.E.O.: Peter Davis
Communications Director: David Gilroy
Meetings and Conventions: Dawn Norman
Education: Gary McCoy
Exec. Director: Kathie Davis
Membership: Cheryl Nelson

Historical Note
Formerly (1990) Internat'l Dance-Exercise Ass'n, (1993) IDEA: The Ass'n for Fitness Professionals, and (1997) IDEA, the internat'l ass'n of fitness professionals. Provides continuing education and services for fitness professionals. IDEA members include aerobics instructors, personal trainers, program directors, and club/studio owners and managers. Membership fees vary, based on type.

Publications:
IDEA Fitness Edge. 5/year.
IDEA Fitness Manager Newsletter. 5/year.
IDEA Health and Fitness Source. 10/year. adv.
IDEA Personal Trainer Magazine. 10/yr. adv.

Meetings/Conferences:
1999 – Las Vegas, NV/July 27-30

IDEA, the internat'l ass'n of fitness professionals
Historical Note
Became (1997) IDEA, The Health and Fitness Source.

IEEE Circuits and Systems Soc.
Historical Note
A technical society of the Institute of Electrical and Electronics Engineers (IEEE). Membership in the Society, open only to IEEE members, includes a subscription to a technical periodical in the field published by IEEE. All administrative support is provided by IEEE.

IEEE Communications Soc. *(1952)*
305 East 47th St.
New York, NY   10017
Tel: (212)705-8900   *Fax:* (212)705-8909
E-Mail: comsoc-techsupport@ieee/org
Web Site: http://www.comsoc.org
Members: 50,000 individuals
Staff: 20
Exec. Director: Jack Howell

Historical Note
A subsidiary of the Institute of Electrical and Electronics Engineers, ComSoc members are industry professionals with a commoninterest in communications technologies. Membership in the Society is open only to IEEE members. Administrative support is provided by IEEE.

Publications:
IEEE Communications Magazine. m. adv.
IEEE Network, The Magazine of Computer Communications. q.
IEEE Personal Communications: Nomadic Communications & Computing. bi-.
IEEE/ACM Transactions on Networking Journal. bi-m.
Journal on Selected Areas in Communications. 9/yr.
Transactions on Communications Journal. m.

IEEE Computer Soc. *(1946)*
1730 Massachusetts Ave., N.W.
Washington, DC   20036-1992
Tel: (202)371-0101   *Fax:* (202)728-9614
Web Site: http://computer.org
Members: 94,000 individuals
Staff: 109
Annual Budget: $25-50,000,000
Exec. Director: T. Michael Elliott, Ph.D.
Director, Finance and Administration: Violet S. Doan
Director, Information Technology and Services: Robert Care
Mgr., Research and Planning: John C. Keaton

Historical Note
IEEE membership represents more than 94,000 of the world's computer professionals. Two out of five members live and work outside the United States in 147 countries. The Computer Society generates a diverse array of 20 application and research oriented periodicals, publishes a variety of books, and holds as many as 150 conference proceedings per year. Programs in education, accreditation, standards, and technical activities are also services provided to members and the profession. Offices include: Washington, DC; Los Alamitos, CA; Brussels, Belgium; Tokyo, Japan. Other service centers include: Beijing, China; Budapest, Hungary; Moscow, Russia. Membership: $67/year (Society only); $123-145/year (IEEE and Society membership).

Publications:
Computer Magazine. m. adv.
IEEE Annals of the History of Computing. q.
IEEE Computer Graphics & Applications. bi-m. adv.
IEEE Computing in Science & Engineering. q. adv.
IEEE Concurrency. q. adv.
IEEE Design & Test. q. adv.
IEEE Intelligent Systems. bi-m. adv.
IEEE Internet Computing. bi-m. adv.
IEEE MICRO. bi-m. adv.
IEEE Multimedia. q. adv.
IEEE SOFTWARE. bi-m. adv.
IEEE Transactions on Computers. m.
IEEE Transactions on Knowledge and Data Engineering. bi-m.
IEEE Transactions on Multimedia. q.
IEEE Transactions on Networking KS. bi-m.
IEEE Transactions on Parallel and Distributed Systems. m.
IEEE Transactions on Pattern Analysis and Machine Intelligence. m.
IEEE Transactions on Software Engineering. q.
IEEE Transactions on Visualization and Computer Graphics. q.
IEEE Transactions on VLSI. q.
IT Professional. bi-m.

Meetings/Conferences:
Annual Meetings: The Computer Society organizes more than 125 conferences, symposia, and technical workshops each year throughout the world.

IEEE Consumer Electronics Soc. *(1965)*
Historical Note
A technical society of the Institute of Electrical and Electronics Engineers (IEEE). Membership in the Society, open only to IEEE members, includes a subscription to a technical periodical in the field published by IEEE. All administrative support is provided by IEEE.

IEEE Control Systems Soc. *(1954)*
Historical Note
A technical society of the Institute of Electrical and Electronics Engineers (IEEE). Membership in the Society, open only to IEEE members, includes a subscription to a technical periodical in the field published by IEEE. All administrative support is provided by IEEE.

IEEE Education Soc. *(1963)*
Historical Note
A technical society of the Institute of Electrical and Electronics Engineers (IEEE). Membership in the Society, open only to IEEE members, includes a subscription to a technical periodical in the field published by IEEE. Administrative support provided by IEEE.

IEEE Electromagnetic Compatibility Soc. *(1957)*
Historical Note
A technical society of the Institute of Electrical and Electronics Engineers (IEEE). Membership in the Society, open only to IEEE members, includes a subscription to a technical periodical in the field published by IEEE. All administrative support is provided by IEEE.

IEEE Industry Applications Soc.
3685 Motor Ave., Suite 240
Los Angeles, CA   90034-5750
Tel: (310)287-1826   *Fax:* (310)287-1851
Web Site: http://www.engine.ieee.org/society/ia.html
Members: 11,500 individuals
Administrator: Robert Myers

Historical Note
IAS members are individuals interested in the global development, design, manufacture and application of electrical systems, apparatus, devices and controls to the processes and equipment of industry and commerce; the promotion of safe, reliable and economic installations; industry leadership in energy conservation and environmental, health and safey issues; the creation of voluntary engineering standards and recommended practices; and professional development. IAS is a technical society of the Institute of Electrical and Electronics Engineers (IEEE). Membership in IAS is open only to IEEE members.

Publications:
Transactions on Industry Applications Journal. m.

Meetings/Conferences:
Annual Meetings: Fall

IEEE Instrumentation and Measurement Soc.
3685 Motor Ave., Suite 240
Los Angeles, CA   90034-5750
Tel: (310)287-1826   *Fax:* (310)287-1851
E-Mail: bob.myers@ieee.org
Web Site: http://engine.ieee.org/im
Members: 5,500 individuals
Annual Budget: $250-500,000
Exec. Director: Robert Myers

Historical Note
The I&M Soc. is a technical society of the Institute of Electrical and Electronics Engineers (IEEE). Provides support to scientists and technicians working in the design and development of electrical and electronic instruments and equipment to measure, monitor, and/or record physical phenomena of all types. Membership: $18/year (IEEE members).

Publications:
I&M Newsletter. q. adv.
IEEE Instrumentation & Measurement Magazine.
Transactions on Instrumentation and Measurement. bi-m.

Meetings/Conferences:
1999 – Venice, Italy

IEEE Magnetics Soc. *(1964)*
445 Hoes Lane
Piscataway, NJ   08855
Tel: (908)981-0060   *Fax:* (908)981-9667
Web Site: http://yara.ecn.purdue/~smag/
Members: 3,500 individuals
Annual Budget: $500-1,000,000
Editor in Chief: Ron Goldfarb

Historical Note
Members are interested in theory, design and applications of magnetic materials and devices. A technical society of the Institute of Electrical and Electronics Engineers (IEEE). Membership in the Society is open only to IEEE members. Administrative support is provided by IEEE. Membership: $30/year.

Publications:
IEEE Transactions on Magnetics. bi-m. adv.

Meetings/Conferences:
1999 – Seoul, Korea/May 18-21
2000 – Toronto, Ontario(Royal York)/April 9-12
2001 – San Antonio, TX(Marriott)/Jan. 8-11

IEEE Microwave Theory and Techniques Soc.
Historical Note
A technical society of the Institute of Electrical and Electronics Engineers (IEEE). Membership in the Society, open only to IEEE members, includes a subscription to a technical periodical in the field published by IEEE. All administrative support provided by IEEE.

IEEE Power Electronics Soc. *(1987)*
3685 Motor Ave., Suite 240
Los Angeles, CA   90034-5750
Tel: (310)287-1826   *Fax:* (310)287-1851
E-Mail: bob.myers@ieee.org
Web Site: http://www.ieee-pels.vt.edu/HTMLpages/PELS
Members: 5,000 individuals
Staff: 3
Annual Budget: $250-500,000
Administrator: Robert Myers

Historical Note
A technical society of the Institute of Electrical and Electronics Engineers. Supports professionals working in the field of power electronics technology, including electronic components, circuit theory and design techniques, and the development of analytical tools for electronic power conversion. Membership: $18/year.

Publications:
PELS Newsletter. q.
Transactions on Power Electronics. q.

Meetings/Conferences:
1999 – Charleston, SC(Omni)/400

IEEE Power Engineering Soc.
445 Hoes Lane
Piscataway, NJ   08855
Tel: (732)562-3883   *Fax:* (732)981-1769
E-Mail: m.olken@ieee.org
Web Site: http://engine.ieee.org/power
Members: 21,286 individuals
Exec. Director: Melvin I. Olken

Historical Note
IEEE/PES members are engineers with an interest in the planning, research, development, design, application, construction, installation and operation of apparatus, equipment, structures, materials and systems for the generation, transmission, distribution, conversion, measurement and control of electric energy. A technical society of the Institute of Electrical and Electronics Engineers. Membership in the Society, open only to IEEE members, includes subscription to a technical periodical in the field published by IEEE.

Publications:
Power Engineering Review. m.
Transaction on Power Delivery. q.
Transactions on Energy Conversion. q.
Transactions on Power Electronics. q.

Transactions on Power Systems. q.

Meetings/Conferences:
Semi-annual Meetings: winter and summer
1999 – New York, NY
1999 – Edmonton, Canada

IEEE Signal Processing Soc. (1948)
445 Hoes Lane
Piscataway, NJ 08855-1331
Tel: (908)562-3888   Fax: (908)235-1627
E-Mail: sp.info@ieee.org
Web Site: http://www.ieee.org/sp/index.html
Members: 19,000 individuals
Staff: 6
Annual Budget: $2-5,000,000
Exec. Director: Mercy Kowalczyk

Historical Note
Formerly the Acoustics, Speech and Signal Processing Soc., SPS members are interested in the theory and application of filtering, coding, transmitting, estimating, detecting, analyzing, recognizing, sythesizing, recording and reproducing signals by digital or analog devices or techniques. SPS is a technical society of the Institute of Electrical and Electronic Engineers (IEEE). Membership: $20/year (IEEE members).

Publications:
Signal Processing Letters. m.
Signal Processing Magazine. bi-m. adv.
Transactions on Image Processing. m.
Transactions on Multimedia. q.
Transactions on Signal Processing Journal. m.
Transactions on Speech and Audio Processing. bi-m.

Meetings/Conferences:
1999 – Phoenix, AZ/March 14-18
2000 – Istanbul, Turkey

IFPA- Film and Video Communicators (1957)
Historical Note
Acronym for Information Film Producers of America, Inc.

IHPA - The Internat'l Wood Products Ass'n (1956)
4214 King St., West
Alexandria, VA 22302
Tel: (703)820-6696   Fax: (703)820-8550
E-Mail: info@ihpa.org
Web Site: http://www.ihpa.org
Members: 190 companies
Staff: 5
Annual Budget: $250-500,000
Exec. V. President: Wendy J. Baer

Historical Note
Formerly (1982) Imported Hardwood Plywood Ass'n and Imported Hardwood Products Ass'n and (1993) Internat'l Hardwood Products Ass'n. IHPA is committed to the promotion and enhancement of trade in all imported wood and wood products. Membership consists of U.S. importers, overseas suppliers, manufacturers, ports, steamship companies, wholesalers, custom brokers, consultants, retailers, sales representatives, agents and other organizations and government agencies related to the forest products industry. Sponsors and supports the International Hardwood Products Ass'n Political Action Committee.

Publications:
Directory. a.
IHPA Newsletter. m.
Import Wood Statistics. q.

Meetings/Conferences:
1999 – Tampa, FL(Saddlebrook Resort)/March 17-19/350

Illuminating Engineering Soc. of North America (1906)
120 Wall St., 17th Floor
New York, NY 10005-4001
Tel: (212)248-5000   Fax: (212)248-5017
E-Mail: whanley@IESNA.org
Web Site: IESNA.org
Members: 10,000 individuals
Staff: 20
Annual Budget: $2-5,000,000
Exec. V. President: William H. Hanley, CAE
Marketing Director: Beth Bay, CAE
Member Services Manager: Valerie Landers
Director, Educational & Tech Development: Rita Harrold
Controller: Bruce Sohl
Editor: Mark Newman

Historical Note
Organized February 13, 1906 with 178 charter members and incorporated in New York in 1907. Membership: $150/year (individual); $500 1st year (company).

Publications:
Journal of the Illuminating Engineering Society. semi-a.
Lighting Design and Application. m. adv.

Meetings/Conferences:
Annual Meetings: Summer/700
1999 – New Orleans, LA(Sheraton)/Aug. 9-11/750
2000 – Washington, DC(Renaissance)
2001 – Ottawa, ON
2002 – Salt Lake City, UT(Little America)

Illustrators' Guild
Historical Note
A division of the Graphic Artists Guild Ass'n for free-lance illustrators.

Image Industry Council Internat'l (1988)
Historical Note
Address unknown in 1997.

IMAGE Soc. (1987)
P.O. Box 6221
Chandler, AZ 85246-6221
Tel: (602)839-8709

E-Mail: image@asu.edu
Web Site: http://www.public.asu.edu/ ~ image/Image.html
Members: 600 individuals, 40 corporate
Staff: 1
President: Eric G. Monroe

Historical Note
Members are individuals concerned with visual and related simulation technologies and applications.

Publications:
Images Newsletter. semi-a. adv.
Proceedings. a. adv.
Resource Guide. a. adv.

Meetings/Conferences:

Imaging Products Remanufacturing Ass'n
Historical Note
Address unknown in 1998.

Imaging Supplies Coalition for Internat'l Intellectual Property Protection (1994)
P.O. Box 8378
Lexington, KY 40533-8378
Tel: (606)278-3032   Fax: (606)278-1244
E-Mail: iscenright@aol.com
Web Site: http://www.isc-inc.org
Members: 9 companies
President: William R. Duffy

Historical Note
ISC represents manufacturers, distributors, licensees, and other companies in the imaging industry. Works to eliminate counterfeiting and telemarketing fraud in the imaging supplies industry.

Publications:
ISC Newsletter. q.

Meetings/Conferences:
1999 – September

Imaging Technologies Ass'n (1911)
Historical Note
Address unknown in 1997.

Immigration and Ethnic History Soc. (1965)
University of Cincinnati
3410 Bishop St.
Cincinnati, OH 45220
Tel: (513)861-7462   Fax: (513)556-7901
E-Mail: june.alexander@uc.edu
Members: 800 individuals
Staff: 1
Annual Budget: under $10,000
Secretary: June G. Alexander

Historical Note
Historians, sociologists, economists and others interested in immigration to the U.S. and Canada. Affiliated with the American Historical Ass'n and the Organization of American Historians. Membership: $30/year (individual), $15/year (student), $72/year (organization/company).

Publications:
Immigration History Newsletter. semi-a.
Journal of American Ethnic History. q.

Meetings/Conferences:
Annual Meetings: April, with the Organization of American Historians
1999 – Toronto, Canada(Sheraton Centre)/April 22-25
2000 – St. Louis, MO

In-Tix
Historical Note
See Internat'l Ticketing Ass'n.

Incentive Federation (1984)
3 Caro Court
Red Bank, NJ 07701-2315
Tel: (908)233-4009   Fax: (908)687-0977
Members: 150 companies
Staff: 2
Annual Budget: $50-100,000
Exec. Director: Howard C. Henry, CAE

Historical Note
Membership: $100-3,000/year (corporate).

Publications:
Newsletter. q.

Meetings/Conferences:
Annual Meetings: usually Spring/New York, NY(Javits Convention Center)

Incentive Manufacturers Representatives Ass'n (1963)
1805 N. Mill St., Suite A
Naperville, IL 60563-1275
Tel: (630)369-3466   Fax: (630)369-3773
Members: 325 companies
Staff: 4
Annual Budget: $250-500,000
Exec. Director: Ross Ament, CAE
Administrative Director: Carol Lopat

Historical Note
Formerly (1977) Nat'l Premium Manufacturers Representatives, Inc. Members are incentive marketing specialists. Membership: $495/year.

Publications:
Inside IMRA. m. adv.
News and Views. q. adv.

Meetings/Conferences:
Annual Meetings: Spring
1999 – La Hoya, CA/April 4-10

INDA, Ass'n of the Nonwoven Fabrics Industry (1968)

1001 Winstead Drive, Suite 460
Cary, NC 27513
Tel: (919)677-0060   Fax: (919)677-0211
Web Site: inda.org
Members: 187 companies
Staff: 13
Annual Budget: $1-2,000,000
President: Ted Wirtz
Marketing Director: Peggy Blake
Director, Government Affairs: Peter G. Mayberry
Administrative Assistant: Lori Reynolds
Education Coordinator: Deanna Lovell
Technical Director: Chuck Lovell
Sales Coordinator: Marilyn Bellinger

Historical Note
Formerly (1972) the Disposables Ass'n and (1977) the Internat'l Nonwovens and Disposables Ass'n. Suppliers of fibers, adhesives, chemicals, fluff pulp, plastic film and related materials; roll goods producers; machinery and equipment suppliers; finishers and converters; and marketers of finished products. Membership: Based upon revenues.

Publications:
Disposability Conference Papers. a.
Filtration Conference Papers. a.
Highloft Conference Papers. a.
IDEA Conference Papers. every 3 years.
INDA-Tec. a.
International Directory of the Nonwoven Fabrics Industry. bien. adv.
Needlepunch Conference Papers. a.
Nonwoven Handbooks.

Meetings/Conferences:
1999 – Palm Beach, FL/Feb. 28-March 4

Independent and Reinsurance Underwriters Ass'n
Historical Note
Became (1998) Intermediaries and Reinsurance Underwriters Ass'n.

Independent Armored Car Operators Ass'n (1973)
102 E. Ave. J.
Lancaster, CA 93535
Tel: (805)726-9864   Fax: (805)949-7877
E-Mail: iacoasec@afas.net
Web Site: http://www.iacoa.com
Members: 63 companies, 59 associates
Staff: 1
Annual Budget: $100-250,000
Secretary: John Margaritis

Historical Note
IACOA's purpose is to promote the high standards within the entire armored transportation/services industry. Membership: $450/year.

Publications:
IACOA Newsletter. q.

Meetings/Conferences:
Annual Meetings: Fall
1999 – Tucson, AZ/Sept. 17-22

Independent Ass'n of Questioned Document Examiners (1969)
403 W. Washington
Red Oak, IA 51566-2146
Tel: (712)623-9130
Members: 150 individuals
Contact: Robert Larson

Historical Note
Members are professional examiners of questionned documents.

Publications:
IAQDE Journal. q.
IAQDE Membership Directory & Bylaws. a.
IAQDE Newsletter. m.

Meetings/Conferences:
Annual Meetings: Always in September or October.

Independent Automotive Damage Appraisers Ass'n (1947)
P.O. Box 1166
Nixa, MO 65714-1166
Tel: (417)725-8080   Fax: (417)725-3479
Toll Free: (800)369 - 4232
E-Mail: Bud@iada.org
Web Site: http://www.iada.org
Members: 125 companies
Staff: 3
Annual Budget: $100-250,000
Exec. Director: Bud Nickl

Historical Note
Founded by a group of independent appraisers sponsored and screened in selected areas after World War II by the Ass'n of Casualty and Surety Companies and the Ass'n of Mutual Companies.

Publications:
IADA News. q.
IADA Service Directory. a.
Watchline. q.

Meetings/Conferences:
Annual Meetings: June/200
1999 – Washington, DC/June 24-25

Independent Bakers Ass'n (1967)
1223 Potomac St., N.W.
Washington, DC 20007-3212
Tel: (202)333-8190   Fax: (202)337-3809
E-Mail: independentbaker@mindspring.com
Web Site: www.mindspring.com/ ~ independentbaker
Members: 350 companies
Staff: 2
Annual Budget: $250-500,000

President: Robert N. Pyle

Historical Note
Members are baking companies not part of any national chain. Sponsors BakePAC, a political action committee.

Publications:
The Independent.

Meetings/Conferences:
Three Meetings Annually: February, usually in Florida, June in Washington, DC and November, usually in California.

Independent Bankers Ass'n of America *(1930)*
One Thomas Circle, Suite 950
Washington, DC 20005-5802
Tel: (202)659-8111   *Fax:* (202)659-9216
Toll Free: (800)422 - 8439
E-Mail: Info@IBAA.ORG
Web Site: http://www.ibaa.org
Members: 5,300 financial institutions
Staff: 60
Annual Budget: $10-25,000,000
Exec. V. President: Kenneth A. Guenther
Director for Communications: Jennifer Rulew
Director of Legislative Affairs: Ronald C. Ence
Sr. Legislative Representative: Rubin Jackson
Regulatory Counsel: Robert Rowe
IBPAC Administrator: Alexandra Maroulis-Cronmiller
Agriculture/Rural America Representative: Mark Scanlan
Director of Payment Systems: Viveca Ware

Historical Note
Membership consists of community financial institutions. Supports the Independent Bankers Political Action Committee. Has an annual budget of approximately $13 million. Membership fee based upon the size of the institutioy.

Publications:
Community Bank Director. q.
The Independent Banker. m. adv.
Washington Weekly Report. w.

Meetings/Conferences:
Annual Meetings: Spring
1999 – San Francisco, CA(Marriott)/March 14-18
2000 – San Antonio, TX(Marriott Riven Walk)/March 5-9

Independent Battery Manufacturers Ass'n *(1955)*
100 Larchwood Drive
Largo, FL 34640
Tel: (813)586-1408   *Fax:* (813)586-1400
Members: 306 manufacturers and suppliers
Staff: 5
Annual Budget: $500-1,000,000
Exec. Secretary: Celwyn E. Hopkins

Historical Note
Founded as the Independent Battery Manufacturers of America. Incorporated in Ohio. The present name was assumed in 1966 to reflect increased foreign membership. Membership: $300/year (organization/company).

Publications:
SLIG Buyers' Guide. bi-a. adv.
The Battery Man. m. adv.

Meetings/Conferences:

Independent Business Alliance *(1995)*
111 John St., 12th Floor
New York, NY 10038
Tel: (212)513-1446   *Fax:* (212)285-1639
Toll Free: (800)559 - 2580
Web Site: http://www.ibaonline.com
Members: 27,000 individuals
Staff: 18
Founding Chairman and C.E.O.: Robert J. Levine

Historical Note
IBAA members are home-based and other small businesses. Membership: $24/year.

Independent Cash Register Dealers Ass'n *(1948)*
1900 Crossbeam Drive
Charlotte, NC 28217-2820
Tel: (704)357-3124   *Fax:* (704)357-3127
E-Mail: icrda@ix.netcom.com
Web Site: http://www.icrda.org
Members: 480 companies
Staff: 18
Annual Budget: $5-10,000,000
Exec. Director: William K. Bussard

Historical Note
Established in 1948 in protest to an arbitrary ceiling on prices of used cash registers. Formally organized in 1948 in Dayton, Ohio. Membership: $300/year.

Publications:
Data Link Newsletter. m. adv.
Membership Directory. a. adv.

Meetings/Conferences:
Semi-Annual Meetings: Winter and Summer

Independent Coin Payphone Ass'n
Historical Note
Address unknown in 1995.

Independent Computer Consultants Ass'n *(1976)*
11131 S. Towne Square, Suite F
St. Louis, MO 63123-7817
Tel: (314)892-1675   *Fax:* (314)487-1345
Toll Free: (800)774 - 4222
E-Mail: 70007.1407@compuserve.com
Web Site: http://www.icca.org
Members: 1,500 individuals and firms
Staff: 3
Annual Budget: $250-500,000
Exec. Director: Joyce Burkard

Historical Note
ICCA is a national network of independent computer consultants representing a wide variety of resources serving computer-related needs. ICCA's goal is to support the success of independent computer consultants in providing professional services to their clients. Through chapters, educational conferences and programs, gov't and vendor relations activities, publications and electronic forums, ICCA encourages high standards of performance, increases understanding of computer resources, and enhances recognition of the computer consulting profession. Membership: $175/year (for 1 member firm), $225/year (for 2-9 member firm), $275/year (for 10 member firm).

Publications:
The Independent. bi-m. adv.

Meetings/Conferences:
Annual Meetings: Spring
1999 – San Jose, CA(San Jose Doubletree)/June 11-13

Independent Computer Services Ass'n of America
7235 Saddle Creek Circle
Sarasota, FL 34241
Tel: (941)925-1909
E-Mail: DiFiKent@aol.com
Members: 45 companies
Staff: 2
Annual Budget: $25-50,000
Exec. Director: Francine DiFilippo

Independent Cosmetic Manufacturers and Distributors *(1974)*
1220 W. Northwest Hwy.
Palatine, IL 60067-1803
Tel: (847)991-4499   *Fax:* (847)991-8161
Toll Free: (800)334 - 2623
E-Mail: info@icmad.org
Web Site: http://www.icmad.org
Members: 660 individuals and companies
Staff: 5
Annual Budget: $250-500,000
Exec. Director: Penni Jones

Historical Note
Membership fee based upon annual sales volume.

Publications:
Digest. m.
Labeling Guide.

Meetings/Conferences:
Annual Meetings: June
1999 – New York, NY

Independent Data Communications Manufacturers Ass'n *(1971)*
Historical Note
Organization defunct in 1997.

Independent Distributors Ass'n *(1958)*
13370 Branch View Lane, Suite 100
Dallas, TX 75234-5771
Tel: (972)241-1124   *Fax:* (972)484-3599
E-Mail: ida_@onramp.net
Members: 450 companies
Staff: 2
Annual Budget: $100-250,000
Exec. Director: Nancy Estes

Historical Note
Formerly (1987) Associated Independent Distributors. Manufacturers and distributors of replacement parts for construction equipment.

Publications:
Universal. bi-m.

Meetings/Conferences:
Annual Meetings: Fall/450
1999 – Atlanta, GA

Independent Educational Consultants Ass'n *(1976)*
4085 Chain Bridge Road, Suite 401
Fairfax, VA 22030-4106
Tel: (703)591-4850   *Fax:* (703)591-4860
Toll Free: (800)808 - 4322
E-Mail: IECAAssoc@aol.com
Web Site: http://www.educationalconsulting.com
Members: 300 individuals, 800 affiliates
Staff: 4
Annual Budget: $500-1,000,000
Exec. Director: Mark H. Sklarow
Conference Manager: Susan Milburn
Member Services Coordinator: Rebecca Peck

Historical Note
Formerly (1987) the Independent Educational Counselors Ass'n. Consultants who work directly with students and parents in school, therapeutic and college placements for a fee, and are not affiliated with any educational institution. Individuals must have a minumum of three years of substantial independent practice or three years of experience as a responsible admissions officer and one year of independent practice to be elligible for membership. Membership: $600/year; $300/year (provisional membership); $165/year (affiliated institutions).

Publications:
IECA Directory. a.
Newsletter. m.

Meetings/Conferences:
Semi-Annual Meetings: Spring and Fall.
1999 – Columbus, OH(Hyatt Regency)/May 11-14
1999 – Baltimore, MD(Hyatt Regency)/Nov. 13-16
2000 – Providence, RI(RI Convention Center)/May 9-13/750
2000 – San Antonio, TX(Westin La Cantera Resort)/Nov. 11-15/650

Independent Electrical Contractors *(1958)*
2010-A Eisenhower Ave.,
Alexandria, VA 22314
Tel: (703)549-7351   *Fax:* (703)549-7448
Toll Free: (800)456 - 4324
Web Site: http://www.ieci.org
Members: 3,200 companies and 74 chapters
Staff: 7
Annual Budget: $2-5,000,000
Exec. V. President: Dwight L. Casey
Director, Government Affairs and Public Relations: Anthony Bedell
Director, Education and Industry Relations: Lawrence W. Mullins
Director, Administration: Assefa Checol
Director, Apprenticeship/Training: Robert W. Baird
Director, Membership: Torrey E. Hairston

Historical Note
Formerly (1981) Associated Independent Electrical Contractors of America. A federation of state and local groups promoting the common business interests of the electrical construction industry, particularly the independent electrical contractor. Membership: $195/year (individual); $100/year (company).

Publications:
Directory. a. adv.
Executive Exchange. m.
IEC Magazine. bi-m. adv.
IEC Quarterly. q. adv.

Meetings/Conferences:
Annual Meetings: September
1999 – Denver, CO(Marriott City Center)/Sept. 15-18/1000
2000 – San Antonio, TX(Marriott Riverwalk)/Sept. 18-21/1200

Independent Feature Project *(1979)*
104 W. 29th St., 12th Floor
New York, NY 10001-5310
Tel: (212)465-8200   *Fax:* (212)465-8525
E-Mail: ifpny@ifp.org
Web Site: http://www.ifp.org
Members: 3,800 individuals
Staff: 5
Annual Budget: $1-2,000,000
Exec. Director: Michelle Byrd

Historical Note
IFP members are independent feature film directors and producers. Membership: $65/year (student), $100/year (individual).

Publications:
Filmmaker. q. adv.

Meetings/Conferences:
Annual Meetings: September-October
1999 – New York, NY

Independent Forest Products Ass'n *(1947)*
14780 SW Osprey Drive, Suite 270
Beaverton, OR 97007-8424
Tel: (503)590-5559   *Fax:* (503)590-1555
Members: 125 companies
Staff: 7
Annual Budget: $500-1,000,000
President: Frank M. Gladics
V. President, Policy and Communications: Laura Cleland
V. President, Operations: Becca Merritt

Historical Note
Founded as Western Forest Industries Ass'n by a merger of the Pacific Lumber Remanufacturing Ass'n and the Portland Western Ass'n of Lumbermen and Loggers; assumed its current name in 1995. IFPA represents small, independent forest products manufacturers before government and the public in order to maintain a sustainable and economic supply of lumber from public and private lands.

Publications:
Out-of-the Woods Newsletter. bi-m.

Meetings/Conferences:
Annual Meetings: March
1999 – Portland, OR

Independent Free Papers of America *(1980)*
P.O. Box 69
Covington, OH 45318
Tel: (937)473-2028   *Fax:* (937)473-3299
Toll Free: (800)441 - 4372
Web Site: http://www.ifpa.com
Members: 300 free newspapers
Staff: 1
Annual Budget: $250-500,000
Secretary-Treasurer: Gary L. Godfrey

Historical Note
Publishers of locally distributed and independently owned free circulation shopping guides and community newspapers. Membership: $75/year.

Publications:
The Independent Publisher. m. adv.

Meetings/Conferences:
Semi-Annual Meetings: St. Louis, MO(Airport Marriott)/March & Sept.
1999 – Orlando, FL/March 18-20

Independent Innkeepers Ass'n *(1971)*
P.O. Box 150
Marshall, MI 49068
Tel: (616)789-0393   *Fax:* (616)789-0970
Toll Free: (800)344 - 5244
Members: 334 individuals
Staff: 4
Annual Budget: $250-500,000
Exec. Director: Sue C. Moore

Historical Note
Members are independent, full-service inns in the U.S. and Canada.

Publications:
Innkeepers Register. a.
Tidings. bi-m.

Meetings/Conferences:
Annual Meetings: November

Independent Insurance Agents of America *(1896)*
127 S. Peyton St.
Alexandria, VA 22314-2803
Tel: (703)683-4422 *Fax:* (703)683-7556
Web Site: www.independentagent.com
Members: 28,000 agencies
Staff: 65
Annual Budget: $10-25,000,000
C.E.O. of Industry and State Relations: Jeffrey M. Yates
Director, Marketing: Ryan Harris
Education Programs Manager: Betsy Kurtz
Asst. V. President, Finance and Treasurer: Frances Shelburne
Ass. V. President of Meetings and Events: Jill A. Kriser
Sr. V. President of Assoc. Affairs & Chief Info. Officer: Len Brevik
Historical Note
Formerly (1976) Nat'l Ass'n of Insurance Agents, Inc. Supports the Nat'l Agents Political Action Committee (Insur-PAC). Has an annual budget of approximately $12.4 million.
Publications:
Independent Agent Magazine. m. adv.
Meetings/Conferences:
Annual Meetings: Fall/4,000

Independent Investors Protective League *(1970)*
P.O. Box 5031
Fort Lauderdale, FL 33310
Tel: (954)749-1551 *Fax:* (954)749-1553
Members: 3,000 individuals
Staff: 2
Annual Budget: $25-50,000
Exec. V. President: Merrill Sands
Historical Note
Membership: $5/year (individual).
Meetings/Conferences:
Annual Meetings: December

Independent Jewelers Organization *(1972)*
Historical Note
Ceased non-profit operations in 1997.

Independent Laboratory Distributors Ass'n
1521 S. Third St.
Terre Haute, IN 47802
Tel: (812)235-9953 *Fax:* (812)235-3050
Members: 76 companies
Staff: 3
Annual Budget: $100-250,000
Ass'n Manager: Anne Dean
Historical Note
ILDA is a trade association representing small businessmen (revenues between $500,000 and $40 million) whose primary endeavor is stocking and reselling products used by research, industrial, life science, education and/or government laboratories. Membership: $550-2,200/year, varies by annual sales volume (distributor member); $1,650-$2,200, varies by annual sales volume (associate member).
Publications:
ILDA Distributor Newsletter. q.
ILDA Update News. m.
Meetings/Conferences:

Independent Liquid Terminals Ass'n *(1974)*
1133 15th St., N.W., Suite 650
Washington, DC 20005
Tel: (202)659-2301 *Fax:* (202)466-4166
E-Mail: jprokop@ilta.org
Web Site: http://www.ilta.org
Members: 90 terminals, 375 suppliers
Staff: 7
Annual Budget: $500-1,000,000
President: John Prokop
Director of Administration: Mrs. E. Bruce Calvert
Historical Note
Owners and lessors of bulk storage tank space for oil, chemicals, edibles and other liquid commodities.
Publications:
Directory of Bulk Liquid Terminals and Storage Facilities. a.
Directory of Suppliers of Equipment and Services. a.
Newsletter. m.
Meetings/Conferences:
Annual Meetings: November/80-90
1999 – Savannah, GA(Hyatt Regency)/Nov. 18-19

Independent Lubricant Manufacturers Ass'n *(1948)*
651 S. Washington St.
Alexandria, VA 22314
Tel: (703)684-5574 *Fax:* (703)836-8503
E-Mail: ilma@ilma.org
Web Site: http://www.ilma.org
Members: 295 companies
Staff: 6
Annual Budget: $1-2,000,000
Exec. Director: Richard H. Ekfelt
Advertising Manager: Bruce Levine
Historical Note
Independent blenders and compounders of lubricants, metalworking fluids, and greases. Until 1980 known as the Independent Oil Compounders Ass'n. Membership: $1,050/year (regular member); $1150/year (associate); $1150 (international).
Publications:
ILMA Compoundings. m. adv.
ILMA Membership Directory. a. adv.
Meetings/Conferences:
Semi-annual Meetings: Spring and Fall
1999 – Scottsdale, AZ(The Phoenician)

Independent Manufacturers Representative Forum
Historical Note
A forum of the Business Products Industry Ass'n.

Independent Medical Distributors Ass'n *(1978)*
5800 Foxridge Dr., Suite 115
Mission, KS 66202-2333
Tel: (913)262-2114 *Fax:* (913)262-0174
Members: 100 companies
Staff: 3
Annual Budget: $100-250,000
Exec. Director: Frank A. Bistrom, CAE
Conference Manager: Betchie Bistrom, CAE
Historical Note
Members are firms dealing in high-technology, sophisticated, medical equipment.
Publications:
Update. m.
Meetings/Conferences:
Annual Meetings: January/150
1999 – Scottsdale, AZ
2000 – Charleston, SC(Charleston Place)/Jan. 26-30
2001 – Palm Springs, CA

Independent Music Ass'n *(1987)*
Historical Note
Address unknown in 1998.

Independent Music Producers Syndicate *(1991)*
Historical Note
Organization defunct in 1996.

Independent Music Retailers Ass'n
Historical Note
Address unknown in 1998.

Independent Pet and Animal Transportation Ass'n Internat'l *(1978)*
Rte. 1, Box 747
Big Sandy, TX 75755
Tel: (903)769-2267 *Fax:* (903)769-2867
E-Mail: intl 1pata@aol.com
Members: 75 companies
Annual Budget: $25-50,000
Administrative Coordinator: Cherie Derouin
Historical Note
Companies providing animal transportation services. Membership: $150/year (organization/company).
Publications:
Membership Directory. a.
Paw Prints Newsletter. bi-m.
Meetings/Conferences:
Annual Meetings: October

Independent Petroleum Ass'n of America *(1929)*
1101 16th St., N.W.
Washington, DC 20036-4803
Tel: (202)857-4722 *Fax:* (202)857-4799
Web Site: http://www.ipaa.org
Members: 8,500 companies
Staff: 30
Annual Budget: $2-5,000,000
President: Gil Thurm
V. President, Communications: Paula Barnett
Dir., Meetings: Tina Hamlin
V. President, Administration/Special Projects: Cindy Grisso
V. President and General Counsel: Barry Russell
V. President, Membership and Marketing: Ronald Whitmire
Director, Membership and Meetings Services: LuAnne O. Tyler
V. President, Information Services: Scott Espenshade
V. President, Public Resources: Bernie Dillon
Historical Note
Members are small producers of oil and natural gas and their suppliers. Sponsors and supports the Independent Petroleum Political Action Committee. Has an annual budget of approximately $3 million.
Publications:
Petroleum Independent. m. adv.
Meetings/Conferences:
1999 – Dallas, TX/Nov. 3-6

Independent Photo Imagers *(1982)*
44-489 Town Center Way, #D-102
Palm Desert, CA 92260
Tel: (760)340-6482 *Fax:* (760)779-9935
E-Mail: info@ipiphoto.com
Web Site: http://www.ipiphoto.com
Exec. Officer: Roger Steitman
Historical Note
IPI members are independent photofinishing laboratories and imaging business owners.

Independent Professional Painting Contractors Ass'n of America *(1982)*
P.O. Box 1759
Huntington, NY 11743-0630
Tel: (516)423-3654
Members: 45 companies
Annual Budget: under $10,000
Exec. Director: Heinz K. Hoffmann
Historical Note
Founded as an alternative to Painting and Decorating Contractors of America, IPPA represents open-shop painting contractors. Has no paid officers or full-time staff. Membership concentrated in the New York/Long Island metropolitan area. Membership: $125/year (full member); $85/year (associate); $45/year (outside New York metro area).

Publications:
Independent Brush Stroke. m.
Meetings/Conferences:
Annual Meetings: Meetings every second Thursday of the month

Independent Professional Representatives Organization *(1988)*
1073 Deenwood Lane
Weston, FL 33326
Tel: (954)217-8532
Toll Free: (800)420 - 4268
E-Mail: ipromail@aol.com
Members: 70 individuals, 70 companies
Staff: 1
Annual Budget: $25-50,000
Exec. Director/Treasurer: Tex Morton
Historical Note
Established and incorporated in Missouri, I-PRO members are independent manufacturers' representatives of audio-visual specialty products. Membership: $550/year, average (corporate).
Meetings/Conferences:
1999 – Atlanta, GA

Independent Reinsurance Underwriters Ass'n
Historical Note
Became (1998) Intermediaries & Reinsurance Underwriters Ass'n.

Independent Research Libraries Ass'n *(1972)*
c/o Library Company of Philadelphia
1314 Locust St.
Philadelphia, PA 19107
Tel: (215)546-3181 *Fax:* (215)546-5167
E-Mail: jcvh@librarycompany.org
Members: 16 institutions
Staff: 1
Annual Budget: under $10,000
President: John C. Van Horne, Ph.D.
Historical Note
Members are independently-supported research libraries that are not part of a larger institution (e.g., a university). Has no paid officers or full-time staff.
Meetings/Conferences:
Annual Meetings: always hosted by a member institution

Independent Scholars of Asia *(1981)*
2321 Russell St., #3-C
Berkeley, CA 94705-1959
Tel: (510)849-3791
E-Mail: rih@juno.com
Members: 132 organizations and individuals
Staff: 6
Annual Budget: under $10,000
National Director: Ruth-Inge Heinze, Ph.D.
Historical Note
A non-profit, non-partisan professional organization affiliated with the Association for Asian Studies. Represents specialists in Asian affairs who prefer to stay independent, are looking for a tenured position in academia, are considering an alternative career, or are planning a career in the field of Asian studies. ISA disseminates information on upcoming events, vacancies, available grants and fellowships, inquiries, reports on research in progress, and book reviews. ISA also maintains a referral file. Has no paid staff. Membership fees: $15/year (general); $10/year (supportive or student); $15/year (organization/company).
Publications:
Independent Scholars of Asia Newsletter. 3/yr. adv.
Proc'gs of the Internat'l Conf. on the Study of Sham.
Meetings/Conferences:
Annual Meetings: Spring
1999 – Boston, MA

Independent Sealing Distributors
105 Eastern Ave., Suite 104
Annapolis, MD 21403-3300
Tel: (410)263-1014 *Fax:* (410)263-1659
Members: 170 companies
Staff: 6
Annual Budget: $250-500,000
Exec. Director: Joseph M. Thompson, Jr.
Conference and Communications Director: Kristin B. Thompson
Business Services Manager: Diana J. Crumpton,, CPA
Membership & Resources Manager: Wendy Blumenthal
Program Services Director: Barbara Colburn
Historical Note
ISD is an internat'l trade association representing distributors and manufacturers of mechanical and hydraulic seals and gaskets. ISD is a member of the Nat'l Ass'n of Wholesaler Distribution (NAW). Membership: $250-1,750/year (corporate).
Publications:
ISD Annual Membership Directory. a. adv.
ISD Insider Newsletter. q. adv.
Meetings/Conferences:
Semi-Annual Meetings: Fall and Spring
1999 – Palm Springs, FL(Westin Hotel)/250

Independent Sector *(1980)*
1828 L St., N.W., Suite 1200
Washington, DC 20036
Tel: (202)223-8100 *Fax:* (202)416-0580
E-Mail: info@indepsec.org
Web Site: http://www.indepsec.org
Members: 850 institutions
Staff: 35
Annual Budget: $2-5,000,000
President: Dr. Sara E. Melendez
V. President, Communications: John H. Thomas
Senior V. President, Government Relations: Bob Smucker
V. President, Research: Patrice Flynn, Ph.D.

V. President, Research: Virginia Hodgkinson
V. President, Membership and Development: Char Mollison
Exec. V. President: Arnold W. de Beaufort
V. President, Leadership and Management: Sandra Trice Gray, CAE
Historical Note
Formed from a merger of the Coalition of Nat'l Voluntary Organizations and the Nat'l Council on Philanthropy. Purpose is to encourage giving, volunteering and not-for-profit initiative.
Meetings/Conferences:
Annual Meetings: Fall/600-800

Independent Service Network Internat'l
Historical Note
Became (1998) Service Industry Ass'n.

Independent Terminal Operators Ass'n *(1970)*
1150 Connecticut Ave., N.W., 9th Floor
Washington, DC   20036-4104
Tel: (202)828-4100   *Fax:* (202)828-4130
Members: 15 companies
Staff: 1
Annual Budget: $10-25,000
Secretary & General Counsel: William H. Bode
Historical Note
Has no office beyond the above, the law firm of William H. Bode & Associates.

Independent Turf and Ornamental Distributors Ass'n *(1990)*
Historical Note
Address unknown in 1997.

Independent X-ray Dealers Ass'n *(1971)*
Historical Note
Address unknown in 1996.

Independent Zinc Alloyers Ass'n *(1959)*
1000 16th St., N.W., Suite 400
Washington, DC   20036
Tel: (202)785-0558   *Fax:* (202)785-0210
Members: 11 companies
Staff: 2
Annual Budget: $50-100,000
Exec. Director: Richard M. Cooperman
Historical Note
Producers and suppliers of zinc alloy.
Meetings/Conferences:
Annual Meetings: None held.

India-American Chamber of Commerce (N.Y.) *(1990)*
P.O. Box 414
New York, NY   10150
Tel: (212)906-2446
President: Rajiv Khanna
Historical Note
Members include leading U.S. multinational corporations and Indian companies engaged in all facets of Indo-U.S. commercial activities. Membership: $495/year (individual); $495/year (company with revenues under $5 million); $795/year (company with revenues over $5 million).
Meetings/Conferences:
Monthly Meetings: New York, NY

Indian Arts and Crafts Ass'n *(1974)*
122 La Veta Dr., N.E., Suite B
Albuquerque, NM   87108-1613
Tel: (505)265-9149   *Fax:* (505)265-8251
E-Mail: iaca@ix.netcom.com
Web Site: http://www.iaca.com
Members: 750 companies and craftpersons
Staff: 4
Annual Budget: $250-500,000
Exec. Director: Roger Wilcox
Director, Education and Membership: Maria Kramer
Historical Note
IACA promotes, protects and preserves Native American Indian arts and crafts. Membership: $175/year (retailers); $50-60/year (artists and collectors).
Publications:
Directory. a. adv.
Newsletter. m. adv.
Meetings/Conferences:

Indian Dental Ass'n (USA) *(1983)*
146-02 89th Ave.
Jamaica, NY   11435
Tel: (718)523-8438
Members: 275 individuals
Annual Budget: under $10,000
President: Raj Singla, D.D.S.
Historical Note
IDA(USA) members are dentists of Asian-Indian heritage.
Publications:
IDA Newsletter. m. adv.
Meetings/Conferences:

Indian Educators Federation *(1967)*
P.O. Box 2020
Farmington, NM   87499
Tel: (505)327-7733   *Fax:* (505)327-9558
Toll Free: (800)443 - 3358
Members: 360 individuals
Staff: 1
Annual Budget: $100-250,000
Treasurer: John McDonald
Field Representative: Bernadette Rolfs

Historical Note
Formerly the Nat'l Council of BIA Educators. IEFW members are teachers in schools operated by the Bureau of Indian Affairs. Affiliated with the American Federation of Teachers.
Publications:
Union Educator. m. adv.
Meetings/Conferences:

Indiana Limestone Institute of America *(1928)*
Stone City Bank Bldg., Suite 400
Bedford, IN   47421
Tel: (812)275-4426   *Fax:* (812)279-8682
E-Mail: jim@iliai.com
Web Site: http://www.iliai.com
Members: 60 companies
Staff: 2
Annual Budget: $50-100,000
Exec. Director: Jim Owens
Historical Note
Incorporated in 1928, ILI is the successor to the Quarryman's Club, an outgrowth of the Bedford Stone Club, which had been formed for promotional and political reasons. Absorbed the National Association for Indiana Limestone. As now constituted, ILI is the promotional arm of the Indiana Limestone Industry for limestone used as a building product and sets standards of quality and workmanship.
Publications:
Indiana Limestone Handbook. bien.
Meetings/Conferences:
Semi-annual Meetings: Spring/Fall

Industrial Ass'n of Juvenile Apparel Manufacturers *(1933)*
1430 Broadway, Room 1603
New York, NY   10018-3308
Tel: (212)244-2953   *Fax:* (212)221-3540
Members: 4 companies
Staff: 1
Annual Budget: $100-250,000
General Counsel: Alex J. Glauberman
Historical Note
A subsidiary of United Infants' and Children's Wear Ass'n. Membership: Based on sales volume.
Meetings/Conferences:
Annual Meetings: Not held.

Industrial Chemical Research Ass'n *(1985)*
2547 Monroe St.
Dearborn, MI   48124
Tel: (313)563-0360   *Fax:* (248)669-0636
Members: 3,974 individuals, 74 companies
Staff: 5
Annual Budget: $2-5,000,000
President: Harold Castor
Historical Note
Members are manufacturers, marketers, researchers, formulators, salesmen, executive officers, and suppliers of industrial chemicals united to promote research, safe practices, and increased selling efficiency in the industrial chemical industry. Membership: $175/yr.
Publications:
Bulletin Update. irreg.
Newsletter. bi-m.
Meetings/Conferences:
2000 - London, England

Industrial Designers Soc. of America *(1965)*
1142- Walker Road, Suite E and F
Great Falls, VA   22066
Tel: (703)759-0100   *Fax:* (703)759-7679
E-Mail: IDSA@EROLS.com
Web Site: http://www.idsa.org
Members: 2,900 individuals
Staff: 8
Annual Budget: $1-2,000,000
Exec. Director: Robert T. Schwartz
Manager, Communications & Chapter Development: Gunilla Girardo
Director, Meetings: Celia Weinstein
Dep. Exec. Director: Kristina Goodrich
Director, Financial operations: Larry W. Allen
Program Manager: Cordelia Chu
Historical Note
Merger of American Soc. of Industrial Designers (1944), Industrial Designers Institute (1938) and Industrial Design Education Ass'n. Membership: $148-238/year plus chapter dues ($22-55/year).
Publications:
Design Perspectives. m. adv.
Innovation: the Journal of IDSA. q. adv.
Membership Directory. a. adv.
Meetings/Conferences:
Annual Meetings: Early Fall
1999 - Chicago, IL(Drake)
2000 - New Orleans, LA(Fairmont)

Industrial Diamond Ass'n of America *(1946)*
P.O. Box 1070
Skyland, NC   28776
Tel: (704)684-1986   *Fax:* (704)684-7372
E-Mail: Gray3@Juno.Com
Web Site: http://www.superabrasives.org
Members: 190 individuals
Staff: 2
Annual Budget: $100-250,000
Exec. Director: Fred A. Gray
Historical Note
Members are concerned with industrial diamonds, either as material suppliers, importers, dealers or manufacturers of diamond tools.

Publications:
Finer Points. q.
Meetings/Conferences:
Annual Meetings: Spring
1999 - Marco Island, FL
2000 - Vancover, British Columbia

Industrial Distribution Ass'n *(1988)*
1277 Lenox Park Blvd., Suite 275
Atlanta, GA   30319
Tel: (404)266-3991   *Fax:* (404)266-8311
E-Mail: idainc@pop.mindspring.com
Web Site: http://www.ida-assoc.org
Members: 2,130 companies
Staff: 7
Annual Budget: $2-5,000,000
Exec. V. President: Gary L. Buffington
Director, Meetings/Conventions: Mary R. Ritchie
Membership Manager: Donna Hufferd
Historical Note
Formerly Southern Industrial Distributors, Nat'l Supply and Machinery Distributors Ass'n, and (1988) Nat'l Industrial Distributors Ass'n. IDA represents wholesalers of industrial equipment in North America. Membership: $300-3,000/year (company).
Publications:
IDA Management Bulletin. m.
IDA Member Profitability Report. a.
Just-In-Time Management Journal. bi-m.
Report on Business. m.
Meetings/Conferences:
Annual Meetings: June

Industrial Electronics Soc. *(1974)*
Historical Note
A technical society of the Institute of Electrical and Electronics Engineers (IEEE). Membership in the Society, open only to IEEE members, includes a subscription to a technical periodical in the field published by IEEE. All administrative support is provied by IEEE.

Industrial EMS Soc.
Historical Note
A division of the Nat'l Ass'n of Emergency Medical Technicians.

Industrial Fabrics Ass'n Internat'l *(1912)*
1801 County Road B W
Roseville, MN   55113-4061
Tel: (651)222-2508   *Fax:* (651)631-9334
Toll Free: (800)225 - 4324
E-Mail: generalinfo@ifai.com
Web Site: http://www.ifai.com
Members: 2,100 companies
Staff: 70
Annual Budget: $5-10,000,000
President: Stephen M. Warner
Director, Conference Management: Susan Larson
V. President, Finance and Administration: John Langlais
Director, Communications/Publisher: Mary Hennessy
V. President, Membership Services: Frank M. McGinty
Historical Note
Founded as the Nat'l Canvas Goods Manufacturers Ass'n, it became the Canvas Products Ass'n Internat'l in 1956 and assumed its present name in 1980. IFAI is a trade association comprised of fiber producers, weavers, coaters, laminators, finishers, dyers, non-woven producers, and producers of goods made from industrial fabrics. Divisions include: American Casual Furniture Fabric Ass'n, Awning Division, Banner and Flag Ass'n, Geosynthetic Materials Ass'n, Marine Division, Marine Fabricators Ass'n, Narrow Fabrics Institute, Safety and Protective Fabrics Division, Tent Rental Division, Transportation Division, Truck Cover & Tarp Ass'n, Division, and United States Industrial Fabrics Institute. Annual budget is $6 million. Membership: $55/year (student); $110/year (individual or affiliate); $220-750/year (company).
Publications:
Buyers' Guide. a. adv.
Fabrics & Architecture. bi-m. adv.
Geosynthetics International. q.
Geotechnical Fabrics Report. m. adv.
IFAI Membership Directory.
In-Tents. q.
Industrial Fabric Products Review. m. adv.
Marine Fabricator. q.
Meetings/Conferences:
Annual Meetings: Fall/6,500
1999 - San Diego, CA/Oct.28-30(San Diego Convention Center)
2000 - Orlando, FL/Oct. 26-28

Industrial Fasteners Institute *(1931)*
1717 East 9th St., Suite 1105
Cleveland, OH   44114
Tel: (216)241-1482   *Fax:* (216)241-5901
E-Mail: indfast@aol.com
Web Site: http://www.industrial-fasteners.org
Members: 154 individuals, 140 companies
Staff: 9
Annual Budget: $1-2,000,000
Managing Director: Robert J. Harris
Sr. Staff Engineer: Frank W. Akstens
Director, Engineering: Charles J. Wilson
Office Manager & Treasurer: Jewetta Haselbuch
Historical Note
An association of leading North American manufacturers of bolts, nuts, screws, rivets and all types of special formed parts. Also, suppliers of equipment, materials and services used in fastener manufacturing.
Publications:
Fastener Application Advisory. 10 times/yea.

Meetings/Conferences:
Annual Meetings: Spring

Industrial Foundation of America

16420 Park Ten Place, Suite 520
Houston, TX 77084-5052
Tel: (713)398-0082   Fax: (281)398-0263
Toll Free: (800)592 - 1433
Members: 650 individuals
Staff: 6
Exec. Director: William C. Smith, Jr

Historical Note
IFA represents different construction, trucking, oil drilling and retail interests throughout the United States.

Industrial Heating Equipment Ass'n (1929)

1901 N. Ft. Myer Dr.
Arlington, VA 22209
Tel: (703)525-2513   Fax: (703)525-2515
E-Mail: ihea@ihea.org
Web Site: http://www.ihea.org
Members: 55 companies
Staff: 2
Annual Budget: $100-250,000
Exec. V. President: James J. Houston, CAE

Historical Note
Manufacturers of industrial furnaces, ovens, combustion equipment, induction and dielectric heaters. Formerly (1954) Industrial Furnace Manufacturers Ass'n. Membership: $1,700-6,200/year (organization).

Publications:
Combustion Technology Manual.
IHEA Newsletter. q.
Legislative and General News Reports. irreg.
Membership and Information Directory. a.
News Compendium. irreg.

Meetings/Conferences:
Annual Meetings: February-March/120
1999 – Scottsdale, AZ(Hyatt)/March 14-18/100
2000 – Desert Springs, CA(Marriott)/March 16-20/100

Industrial Mathematics Soc. (1949)

Box 159
Roseville, MI 48066
Tel: (810)591-1619
Members: 50 individuals
Annual Budget: under $10,000
Secretary-Treasurer: Leo S. Parry

Historical Note
Established in 1949 in Detroit. Members are individuals interested in extending the understanding and application of mathematics in industry. Has no paid staff. Membership: $22/year.

Publications:
Industrial Mathematics. semi-a.

Meetings/Conferences:
Meetings: held irregularly.

Industrial Metal Containers Ass'n

8720 Red Oak Blvd., Suite 201
Charlotte, NC 28217-3957
Tel: (704)676-1190   Fax: (704)676-1199
E-Mail: ahowie@mhia.org
Members: 10 companies
Staff: 2
Managing Director: Allan M. Howie

Historical Note
A product section of the Material Handling Industry of America.

Meetings/Conferences:
Semi-Annual Meetings: Spring and Fall with MHIA

Industrial Perforators Ass'n (1961)

P.O. Box 19
Newburg, WI 53060-0019
Members: 23 companies
Staff: 2
Annual Budget: $50-100,000
Secretary-Treasurer: Dolores Morris

Historical Note
Members are companies making perforated metal products.

Meetings/Conferences:

Industrial Relations Research Ass'n (1947)

4233 Social Sciences Bldg.
Univ. of Wisconsin, 1180 Observatory Dr.
Madison, WI 53706-1393
Tel: (608)262-2762   Fax: (608)265-4591
E-Mail: irra@macc.wisc.edu
Web Site: http://www.irra.ssc.wisc.edu
Members: 4,200 individuals
Staff: 5
Annual Budget: $250-500,000
Administrator: Kay B. Hutchison

Historical Note
Affiliated with Internat'l Industrial Relations Ass'n and a member of Allied Social Science Ass'ns. Membership $75 /year (United States); $87/year (foreign).

Publications:
IRRA Newsletter. q.
Membership Directory. quadrennial.
Perspectives on Work. bi.
Proceedings. semi-a.
Volume of Research. a.

Meetings/Conferences:
Semi-Annual Meetings: Spring and January, with Allied Social Science Ass'ns
1999 – New York, NY(Grand Hyatt)/Jan. 3-5
2000 – Boston, MA/Jan. 7-9
2001 – New Orleans, LA

Industrial Research Institute (1938)

1550 M St., N.W.
Suite 1100
Washington, DC 20005-1712
Tel: (202)296-8811   Fax: (202)776-0756
Web Site: http://www.iriinc.org
Members: 285 companies
Staff: 11
Annual Budget: $2-5,000,000
Exec. Director: Charles F. Larson
Director, Communications and Information Services: Ludita H. Vallarta
Director, Professional Development Service: Robert E. Burkart
Manager, Administrative Services: Patricia Tiede
Director, Research Services: Margaret R. Grucza

Historical Note
Founded in 1938 under the auspices of the Nat'l Research Council and incorporated in New York in 1945. A company-membership ass'n to improve the management of technological innovation in industry and to promote interaction among industry, government and academe in science and technology. Membership: $3,600/year (company).

Publications:
Research Technology Management. bi-m.

Meetings/Conferences:
Annual Meetings: Spring/500-600
1999 – Williamburg, VA/May 23-26
2000 – Palm Desert, CA/May 7-10
2001 – Boca Raton, FL/May 20-23
2002 – Palm Beach, FL/May 5-8

Industrial Telecommunications Ass'n (1953)

1110 N. Glebe Road, Suite 500
Arlington, VA 22201-5720
Tel: (703)528-5115   Fax: (703)524-1074
Toll Free: (800)482 - 8282
Web Site: http://www.ita-relay.com
Members: 7,500 partnerships & corporations
Staff: 30
Annual Budget: $1-2,000,000
President and C.E.O.: Mark E. Crosby
Director of Communications: J. Sharpe Smith
Director, Government Relations: Frederick J. Day, Jr.
Exec. V. President: Cynthia T. Chappell
V. President, Member Relations, Marketing & Education: Karin L. Norton

Historical Note
Formerly (1992) the Special Industrial Radio Service Ass'n, ITA was designated by the FCC in 1986 as the official Frequency Advisory Committee for the Special Industrial Radio Service and the 850/900 mHz industrial/land transportation pool. Incorporated in the District of Columbia, ITA members are licensees authorized to operate radio communication facilities in the Special Industrial Radio Service and other private land radio services. ITA represents the interests of its members concerning 2-way radio communications. Membership: $85-2,000/year, varies by number of radio units.

Publications:
Telecommunication Exchange & Telecom Express. m. adv.

Meetings/Conferences:
Annual Meetings: Fall

Industrial Truck Ass'n (1951)

1750 K St., N.W., Suite 460
Washington, DC 20006
Tel: (202)296-9880   Fax: (202)286-9884
E-Mail: indtrk@earthlink.net
Web Site: http://www.indtrk.org
Members: 30 manufacturers, 80 assoc. firms
Staff: 5
Annual Budget: $1-2,000,000
Exec. Director: William J. Montwieler

Historical Note
Founded as the Electric Industrial Truck Ass'n, it assumed its present name in 1951. Members are manufacturers of powered and non-powered lift trucks as well as their major component suppliers. Membership: $6000-$100,000 (organization/company).

Publications:
Membership Directory. a.

Meetings/Conferences:
Annual Meetings: Fall/300
1999 – Tucson, AZ(El Conquistador)Oct.
2000 – Lake Tahoe, NV(Squawcreek)/Sept. 12-15

Industrial Union of Marine and Shipbuilding Workers of America (1933)

719 E. Fort Ave., #23
Baltimore, MD 21230-4724
Tel: (410)837-0056
Members: 800,000 individuals
Staff: 7
Annual Budget: $1-2,000,000
Trustee: Robert Thayer
President: Dave Libby

Historical Note
Organized in Quincy, Massachusetts in September 1934. Affiliated with AFL-CIO. Merged with the Internat'l Ass'n of Machinists and Aerospace Workers in 1988.

Meetings/Conferences:
Biennial meetings: Even years

Industrial Water Conditioning Institute (1965)

Historical Note
Organization defunct in 1997.

Industrial/Ag Mower Manufacturers Council

Historical Note
A council of the Equipment Manufacturers Institute.

Industry Coalition on Technology Transfer (1984)

1400 L St., N.W., Suite 800
Washington, DC 20005-3502
Tel: (202)371-5994
Members: 5 organizations
Staff: 3
Annual Budget: $50-100,000
Exec. Secretary: Eric L. Hirschhorn

Historical Note
ICOTT is composed of trade associations whose members' products and technical data are subject to United States export controls. ICOTT advises U.S. Government officials of industry concerns about export controls.

Industry Council for Tangible Assets (1983)

P.O. Box 1365
Severna Park, MD 21146-8365
Tel: (410)626-7005   Fax: (410)626-7007
Members: 400 firms
Staff: 2
Annual Budget: $100-250,000
Exec. Director: Eloise Ullman

Historical Note
Promotes the interests of those individuals, partnerships, firms, associations and corporations who are engaged in the business of manufacturing, importing, distributing or selling at retail any tangible asset, including any precious metal, coin, antique or art object. Membership: $250/year minimum (based on sales volume).

Publications:
Washington Wire. q.

Meetings/Conferences:
Annual Meetings: No conventions held - Board of Directors meets three times a year.
1999 – Orlando, FL(Jan.6)

Infant and Juvenile Manufacturers Ass'n (1912)

575 Lexington Ave., 19th Floor
New York, NY 10022-6102
Tel: (212)754-3100   Fax: (212)986-8851
Members: 18 companies
Staff: 1
Annual Budget: $10-25,000
Exec. Director: Bernard Ferster

Meetings/Conferences:
Annual Meetings: New York, NY/1st Tuesday in December

Infants', Children's and Girls' Sportswear and Coat Ass'n (1934)

500 Seventh Ave., 2nd Floor
New York, NY 10018-4502
Tel: (212)819-1011
Members: 1 company
Staff: 2
Annual Budget: $100-250,000
Exec. Director: Frederick T. Johnson

Historical Note
Formerly (until 1978) the Infants' and Children's Coat Ass'n. A member of the Federation of Apparel Manufacturers.

Meetings/Conferences:
Annual Meetings: December

Infectious Diseases Soc. of America (1963)

99 Canal Center Plaza, Suite 210
Alexandria, VA 22314
Tel: (703)299-0200   Fax: (703)299-0204
E-Mail: info@idsociety.org
Web Site: http:\\www.idsociety.org
Members: 5,100 individuals
Staff: 9
Annual Budget: $2-5,000,000
Exec. Director: Mark Leasure
Dir., Communications: Loyce Craft
Dir., Conventions & Meeting Services: Sandra Harwood
Dir., Finance: Donna Wilds
Dir., Administration: Annette Murha

Historical Note
IDSA represents physicians, scientists, and other health care professionals primarily involved with infectious disease treatment and related disciplines. Membership: $195/year (domestic); $270/year (overseas); $95/year (fellow-in-training).

Publications:
Clinical Infectious Diseases. m. adv.
Journal of Infectious Disease. m. adv.

Meetings/Conferences:
Annual Meetings: Fall/3,500
1999 – Philadelphia, PA(Convention Center)/Nov. 18-21/3500
2000 – New Orleans, LA(Convention Center)/Sept. 7-10/3750

Inflatable Advertising Dealers Ass'n

136 S. Keowee St.
Dayton, OH 45402
Tel: (937)222-1024   Fax: (937)222-5794
Members: 145 individuals
Exec. Director: Kimberly Fantaci

Meetings/Conferences:
1999 – Las Vegas, NV

Inflatable Boat Ass'n

Historical Note
A division of Industrial Fabrics Ass'n Internat'l.

Inflight Food Service Ass'n

Historical Note
Became (1996) Internat'l Inflight Food Ass'n.

Information Industry Ass'n (1969)

1625 Massachusetts Ave., N.W., Suite 700
Washington, DC 20036-2212

Tel: (202)986-0280   Fax: (202)638-4403
E-Mail: info@infoindustry.org
Web Site: www.infoindustry.org
Members: 500 companies
Staff: 20
Annual Budget: $2-5,000,000
V. President, Government Relations: Daniel C. Duncan
V. President of Operations & Programming: Sheri Rene Robey

Historical Note
Trade association representing companies interested and involved in the business opportunities associated with the generation, distribution, processing and provision of information products, services and technologies. These firms participate in four IIA divisions which develop programs to meet their needs in Databases and Publishing, Electronic Services, Financial Information Services and Voice Information Services. Directory Publishers Alliance (DPA) is now a part of IIA. Membership: $500-45,000/year (depending on revenues).

Publications:
Friday Memo. m.
Information Sources. a.

Meetings/Conferences:
Annual Meetings: Fall

Information Processing Administratrators of Large School Systems

Historical Note
IPALSS is a functional affiliate of the Internat'l Soc. for Technology in Education.

Information Systems Audit and Control Ass'n (1969)
3701 Algonquin Rd., Suite 1010
Rolling Meadows, IL 60008
Tel: (708)253-1545   Fax: (708)253-1443
E-Mail: exec@isaca.org
Web Site: http://www.isaca.org
Members: 19,000 individuals
Staff: 38
Annual Budget: $5-10,000,000
Exec. Director: Susan M. Caldwell
Director, Communications: Jane Seago
Director, Professional Practices: Terence Trsar
Director, Finance: Scott Artman
Director, Membership Services: Deborah Pincon
Director, Information Systems: Ronald Riba
Director, Research & Academic Relations (Foundation): Thomas
     Lamm
Director, Education: Nancy Doubek

Historical Note
Formerly (1994) EDP Auditors Ass'n, ISACA was formed to provide continuing professional education and development in information systems audit techniques and standards to its membership of auditors, managers and systems specialists. Maintains a research and education subsidiary, Internat'l Systems Audit and Control Foundation. Membership: $100/year, plus $30 new member processing fee.

Publications:
CISA Review Manual. a.
Global Communique. bi-m. adv.
IS Audit and Control Journal. bi-m. adv.

Meetings/Conferences:
Annual Meetings: Summer
1999 – Denver, CO

Information Systems Consultants Ass'n (1986)
P.O. Box 467190
Atlanta, GA 30346
Tel: (770)491-1500   Fax: (404)634-3819
Toll Free: (800)832 - 7767
E-Mail: President@isco.org
Web Site: http://www.isca.org
Members: 170 individuals
Annual Budget: under $10,000
President: Earl Sabot

Historical Note
ISCA members are individuals providing consulting services related to business information systems. Companies which market information systems products or services are eligible for affiliate membership. Companies and individuals with an interest in the field are eligible for associate membership. Membership: $120/year (individual); $150/year (corporate).

Publications:
Consultants Connection Resource Directory. a.
ISCA Consultants Connection. q. adv.
ISCA News Newsletter. m. adv.

Meetings/Conferences:
Annual Meetings: December

Information Systems Security Ass'n (1981)
7044 S. 13th St.
Oak Creek, WI 53154
Tel: (414)768-8000   Fax: (414)768-8001
Toll Free: (800)370 - 4772
E-Mail: issah@ix.netcom.com
Members: 2,000 individuals
Staff: 7
Annual Budget: $250-500,000
Managing Director: Meg Marredeth

Historical Note
Members are professionals responsible for the protection of information databases. Membership: $70/year (individual).

Publications:
Guideline for Information Valuation.
Password. bi-m. adv.

Meetings/Conferences:
Annual Meetings: March
1999 – Orlando, FL/March 15-17

Information Technologies Credit Union Ass'n (1959)

P.O. Box 160
Del Mar, CA 92014-0160
Tel: (619)792-3883   Fax: (619)792-3884
Members: 300 credit unions
Annual Budget: $100-250,000
Exec. Director: Katherine E. Clark

Historical Note
Formerly (1993) the Internat'l Telephone Credit Union Ass'n. Members are credit unions serving telephone companies.

Publications:
Connection Newsletter. q.
Telephone Credit Union Directory. a.

Meetings/Conferences:
1999 – Boston, MA(Marriot Copley Place)/500

Information Technology and Telecommunications Ass'n (1961)
74 New Montgomery, St., Suite 230
San Francisco, CA 94105
Tel: (415)777-4647   Fax: (415)777-5292
E-Mail: info@tca.org
Web Site: http://www.tca.org
Members: 900 individuals, 1,050 companies
Staff: 3
Annual Budget: $2-5,000,000
Exec. Director: Sherilyn Clayes

Historical Note
Formerly (1996) TeleCommunications Ass'n. TCA is a national associaion of businesses that represent the interests of end users of information technology including voice, data, video and imaging. TCA is a strategic industry resource for regulatory issues, peer-to-peer networking and educational opportunities. Members are organizations utilizing voice and data communications products and services for internal purposes.

Publications:
Membership/Peer-to-Peer Networking Directory.
New Connections. m.
Users Manual.

Meetings/Conferences:

Information Technology Ass'n of America (1961)
1616 N. Ft. Myer Drive, Suite 1300
Arlington, VA 22209-3106
Tel: (703)522-5055   Fax: (703)525-2279
E-Mail: hmiller@itaa.org
Web Site: ITAA.org
Members: 5,000 individuals
Staff: 20
Annual Budget: $2-5,000,000
President and C.E.O.: Harris Miller
V. President, Communications: Bob Cohen
V. President, Government Affairs/General Counsel: Marc A. Pearl
Conference Planner: Kelly Cultar
V. President of Marketing: Paul Green
V. President, Information Technology Services: Amy Callahan
V. President, Information Services and Electronic Commerce: Mark
     Unscapher

Historical Note
Formerly (1985) the Ass'n of Data Processing Service Organizations and (1991) ADAPSO, the Computer Software and Services Industry Ass'n. Consists of four divisions: American Software Ass'n, Information Technology Services, Processing and Network Services, and Systems Integration. Absorbed the Ass'n of Independent Software Companies in 1972. Member of the Nat'l Commission on Software Issues in the Eighties. Membership fee based on size of company.

Publications:
Agenda. m.
Membership Directory. a. adv.
New Products Guide. q. adv.

Meetings/Conferences:
Semi-Annual Meetings: Spring and Fall

Information Technology Industry Council (1916)
1250 I St., N.W., Suite 200
Washington, DC 20005-3922
Tel: (202)737-8888   Fax: (202)638-4922
Web Site: http://www.itic.org
Members: 29 companies
Staff: 30
Annual Budget: $2-5,000,000
President: Rhett B. Dawson
V. President, Technology Policy: John S. Wilson
V. President and Chief Council: Fiona Branton
Exec. V. President: Oliver R. Smoot
Director, Administration: Jane C. Lewicki, CAE

Historical Note
Formerly (1962) Office Equipment Manufacturers Institute, (1973) Business Equipment Manufacturers Ass'n, and (1994) Computer and Business Equipment Manufacturers Ass'n. ITI represents providers of computers, business and telecommunications equipment, software and services. Acts on domestic and international issues that affect the high-technology industry. ITI serves as the Secretariat for the American Nat'l Standards Institute Committee, Information Technology (X3).

Publications:
Annual Report. a.
ITI Washington Letter. bi-w.

Meetings/Conferences:
Semi-annual Meetings: Spring and Fall

Information Technology Resellers Ass'n (1981)
11921 Freedom Dr., Suite 550
Reston, VA 20190
Tel: (703)904-4337   Fax: (703)904-4339
Web Site: http://www.itra.net/welcome.cfm
Members: 125 companies
Staff: 2
Annual Budget: $500-1,000,000

Exec. V. President: David E. Poisson
Director, Operations: Melanie Haske

Historical Note
Formed by a merger of the Computer Dealers Ass'n (est. 1972) and the Computer Lessors Ass'n (est. 1968) as Computer Dealers and Lessors Ass'n in 1992; became Computer Leasing and Remarketing Ass'n in 1996, assumed its current name in 1997. Members are buyers, lessors and sellers of computers. Sponsors and supports the CDLA Political Action Committee. Membership:$975(organization).

Meetings/Conferences:
Semi-Annual Meetings: Spring and Fall

Information Technology Training Ass'n
8400 N. Mopac, Suite 201
Austin, TX 78759-5321
Tel: (512)502-9300   Fax: (512)502-9308
Web Site: http://www.itta.org
Staff: 2
Annual Budget: $1-2,000,000
Exec. Director: Doug Upchurch

Meetings/Conferences:
1999 – San Antonio, TX(Hyatt Riverwalk)/Apr. 29-May 1

Information Theory Soc.

Historical Note
A technical society of the Institute of Electrical and Electronics Engineers (IEEE). Membership in the Society, open only to IEEE members, includes a subscription to a technical periodical in the field published by IEEE. All admninistrative support is provided by IEEE.

Infrared Data Ass'n (1993)
P.O. Box 3883
Walnut Creek, CA 94598
Tel: (925)943-6546   Fax: (925)943-5600
E-Mail: info@irda.org
Web Site: http://www.irda.org
Members: 150 companies
Staff: 3
Exec. Director: John A. LaRoche
Dir., Operations: Daphne Terrell

Historical Note
IrDA is a consortium of companies united to develop and promote interoperable, low-cost infrared data connection standards that support a broad range of appliances, computers, and communication devices.

Publications:
IRDA SIR Standard. a.

Meetings/Conferences:
1999 – San Francisco, CA(Airport Crowne Plaza)/Jan. 25-28

Inland Marine Underwriters Ass'n (1930)
111 Broadway, 15th Floor
New York, NY 10006
Tel: (212)233-7958   Fax: (212)732-3451
Members: 413 companies
Staff: 2
Annual Budget: $500-1,000,000
President and C.E.O.: James E. Mooney

Historical Note
Addresses problems of common concern to companies doing Inland Marine insurance business. Membership: $2,500/year (minimum).

Publications:
Impact. q.
Inland Marine Insurance Fact Book. bien.

Meetings/Conferences:
Annual Meetings: Spring/130
1999 – Ponte Vedra Beach, FL/May 2-5

Inland Rivers Ports and Terminals (1974)
P.O. Box 105353
Jefferson City, MO 65110-5353
Tel: (573)634-2028   Fax: (573)634-2038
E-Mail: admin@irpt.com
Web Site: http://www.irpt.com
Members: 150 ports and terminals
Staff: 1
Annual Budget: $50-100,000
Exec. Secretary: Kathy Pabst

Historical Note
Incorporated in the State of Missouri to represent the interests of inland waterway ports, terminals and associated activities, throughout the U.S. Membership: $100-300/year.

Publications:
Newsletter. bi-m.

Meetings/Conferences:
Annual Meetings: March/April
1999 – Washington, D.C.
2000 – Pittsburgh, PA

Insect Screening Weavers Ass'n (1940)
Historical Note
Defunct in 1997.

Institute for Alternative Agriculture
Historical Note
See Henry A. Wallace Institute for Alternative Agriculture.

Institute for Applied Iridology (1995)
1278 Gleneyre, Suite 153
Laguna Beach, CA 92651
Tel: (714)362-4959   Fax: (714)362-4959
Toll Free: (888)886 - 8985
E-Mail: WOLFANGEL@AOL.COM & BOBBAROBBA@AOL.COM
Annual Budget: $50-100,000
Administrator: Robert Grad

Publications:
IAI Newsletter. q.

Meetings/Conferences:
1999 – Santa Ana, CA/May 13-16

Institute for Brewing Studies *(1983)*
P.O. Box 1679
Boulder, CO   80306-1679
Tel: (303)447-0816   *Fax:* (303)447-2825
E-Mail: ibs@aob.org
Web Site: http://www.beertown.org
Members: 1,350 individuals
Staff: 4
Annual Budget: $250-500,000
Director: David S. Edgar

Historical Note
Formerly (1988) Institute for Fermentation and Brewing Studies. Subsidiary of Ass'n of Brewers (same address). Members are professional brewers at micro, regional, large and pub breweries, suppliers to the industry, and other interested individuals. Publishes information on brewing techniques and brewery operations. Membership: $135/year (minimum, based on affiliation to industry), $195/year (company/organization, minimum).

Publications:
Brewers Resource Directory. a. adv.
Brewery Planner.
New Brewer. bi-m. adv.

Meetings/Conferences:
Annual Meetings: Spring
1999 – Phoenix, AZ/Apr. 28-May 1

Institute for Briquetting and Agglomeration *(1949)*
179 Riverview Acres Rd.
Hudson, WI   54016
Tel: (715)549-6342   *Fax:* (715)549-5678
Members: 225 individuals, 150 companies
Staff: 1
Annual Budget: $50-100,000
Exec. Director: Ralph W. Weggel

Historical Note
Organized in 1949 as Internat'l Briquetting Ass'n, the present name was assumed in 1967. Members shape and form materials such as charcoal, lime, ores, chemicals, metal swarf and powders, coal fines, coke breeze, wood waste, etc. which require size enlargement for efficient use. Membership: $30/year (individual), $60/year (organization/company).

Publications:
Newsletter. semi-a.
Proceedings. bien. adv.

Meetings/Conferences:
Biennial Meetings: odd years

Institute for Business and Home Safety
175 Federal St., #500
Boston, MA   02110-2210
Tel: (617)292-2003   *Fax:* (617)292-2022
Web Site: http://www.bhf.org
Members: 78 insurance groups
Staff: 26
President and C.E.O.: Harvey G. Ryland

Historical Note
Members are firms in the property/casualty insurance industry. IBHS promotes building code enforcement and research on effective code formulation to reduce property losses from natural disasters.

Publications:
Update. q.

Meetings/Conferences:
1999 – Memphis, TN/Oct. 27-28

Institute for Business Innovation
7235 Saddle Creek Circle
Sarasota, FL   34241-9543
Tel: (813)925-1909
Members: 1,850 individuals
Annual Budget: $25-50,000
Exec. Director: Francine DiFilippo

Historical Note
Reviews technology options and how they can influence economic development in the medium and small-business community.

Publications:
Newsletter. bi-m.

Institute for Certification of Computing Professionals *(1973)*
2200 E. Devon Ave., Suite 247
Des Plaines, IL   60018
Tel: (847)299-4227   *Fax:* (847)299-4280
E-Mail: 74040.3722@compuserve.com
Web Site: http://www.iccp.org
Members: 27 associations
Staff: 3
Annual Budget: $500-1,000,000
President: Joann Ward
Coordinator, Marketing: Sharon Frank
Director, Finance and Administration: Cynthia A. Bleaise

Historical Note
ICCP is supported by 27 major international computer societies. It exams and certifies professionals within the computer information processing industry, operating certification programs which lead to the designations: Certified Computing Professional (CCP) and Associate Computing Professional (ACP). Membership: $50/year (individual).

Publications:
ICCP Certification News. 3/year. adv.

Meetings/Conferences:
Annual Meetings: Third Week in January

Institute for Certification of Tax Professionals
1832 Stratford Place
Pomona, CA   91768

Tel: (909)629-1460
E-Mail: bobv@aviastar.net
Web Site: http://www.inter-american.com
Staff: 1
Exec. Director: Robert C. Verkler

Historical Note
Members are accountants, auditors, enrolled agents, and other professionals in tax administration. Provides continuing education. Awards the designations Certified Tax Consultant (CTC) and Certified Tax Accountant).

Publications:
The Tax Professional. m.

Institute for Computer Capacity Management

Historical Note
Ceased membership operations in 1998.

Institute for Hospital Clinical Nursing Education *(1967)*

Historical Note
Address unknown in 1996.

Institute for Interconnecting and Packaging Electronic Circuits *(1957)*
2215 Sanders Road, Suite 250
Northbrook, IL   60062-6135
Tel: (847)509-9700   *Fax:* (847)509-9798
E-Mail: info@ipc.org
Web Site: http://www.ipc.org
Members: 2,300 companies
Staff: 82
Annual Budget: $10-25,000,000
President: Thomas J. Dammrich
Director, Marketing/Communications: Kim Sterling
Director, Public Policy: Christopher Rhodes
Director, Convention Services: Stephen D. Evans, CAE
Director, Education: John Riley
V. President, Technical Programs: David W. Bergman, CAE
V. President, Industry Programs: Anthony Hilvers
Director, Environmental/Health/Safety: Holly Evans
V. President, Administration: Clint Swift
V. President, Operatons: Melinda Robinson
Director, Publishing and Production: Lee Combes
Director, Information Services: Karla Dahan

Historical Note
Established as the Institute of Printed Circuits, it became the Institute for Interconnecting and Packaging Electronic Circuits in 1978, more commonly known as IPC. Members are designers, manufacturers, and users of printed circuits and electronics manufacturing service providers. Has an annual budget of approximately $11.5 million. Membership: $1,000/year (company).

Publications:
IPC Review. m.

Meetings/Conferences:
Semi-Annual Meetings: April and October

Institute for Internat'l Human Resources *(1991)*
1800 Duke Street
Alexandria, VA   22314
Tel: (703)548-3440   *Fax:* (703)836-0367
E-Mail: intldiv@shrm.org
Web Site: http://www.shrmglobal.org
Members: 4,800 individuals
Staff: 5
Annual Budget: $1-2,000,000
V. President, Internat'l Programs: Brian J. Glade

Historical Note
IIHR members are individuals responsible for international personnel administration. A division of the Soc. for Human Resource Management. Membership: $95/year (regular), $20/year (student).

Publications:
Internat'l HR Update Newsletter. bi-m.

Meetings/Conferences:
Annual Meetings: Spring
1999 – Orlando, FL(Renaissance Hotel)/April 11-14/600

Institute for Investment Management Consultants *(1986)*
10214 N. Tatum Blvd., Suite A-700
Phoenix, AZ   85028
Tel: (602)922-0090   *Fax:* (602)922-0391
Toll Free: (800)449 - 4462
E-Mail: info@theiimc.org
Web Site: http://www.theiimc.org
Members: 820 individuals
Staff: 3
Administrator: Judith A. Allen

Historical Note
Membership: $250/year (individual); $350/year (organization).

Publications:
Directory. a.
Network Newsletter. m. adv.

Meetings/Conferences:
1999 – New York, New York/June 15-18
1999 – San Diego, CA

Institute for Municipal Engineering *(1966)*

Historical Note
Organization defunct in 1998.

Institute for Operations Research and the Management Sciences *(1952)*
901 Elkridge Landing Road, Suite 400
Linthicum Heights, MD   21090-2920
Tel: (410)850-0380   *Fax:* (410)684-2963

Toll Free: (800)446 - 3676
E-Mail: informs@mail.informs.org
Web Site: http://www.informs.org
Members: 12,000 individuals
Staff: 21
Annual Budget: $2-5,000,000
Exec. Director: Mark Doherty, CAE
Director, Marketing: Lisa Klose
Director, Public Relations: Barry List
Director, Administrative Operations: Ellen Duncan
Director, Member and Subdivision Services: Mary Thomas Magrogan

Historical Note
Formerly Operations Research Soc. of America; merged with the Institute of Management Sciences and assumed its current name in 1995. Founded in 1952 and incorporated in the District of Columbia. A member society of the Internat'l Federation of Operational Research Societies. Members are investigators, students, teachers and managers that deal with the application of scientific methods to decision making, especially to the allocation of resources. Also maintains an office at: 2 Charles St., Suite 300, Providence, RI 02904, Tel: (401) 274-2525, Fax: (401) 274-3189. Membership: $90/year; $23/year (retired); $23/year (student).

Publications:
Information Systems Research Journal. q. adv.
INFORMS Meeting Program. semi-a. adv.
Interfaces Journal. bi-m. adv.
Journal on Computing. q. adv.
Management Science Journal. m. adv.
Marketing Science Journal. q. adv.
Mathematics of Operations Research Journal. q.
Operations Research Journal. bi-m. adv.
OR/MS Today Magazine. bi-m. adv.
Organization Science Journal. q. adv.
Transportation Science Journal. q. adv.

Meetings/Conferences:
Semi-Annual Meetings: Spring and Fall
1999 – Cincinatti, OH

Institute for Polyacrylate Absorbents *(1985)*
1850 M St., N.W., Suite 700
Washington, DC   20036
Tel: (202)721-4190   *Fax:* (202)296-8210
Members: 20 companies
Staff: 2
Annual Budget: $500-1,000,000
Exec. Director: Richard E. Opatick, CAE

Historical Note
IPA represents manufacturers and users of absorbent polymers made of cross-linked polyacrylates and manufacturers and users of acrylic acid or its salts. It addresses the scientific, regulatory and related issues which are likely to impact the manufacture, use and disposal of fluid-absorbing polyacrylates.

Institute for Professionals in Taxation *(1976)*
3350 Peachtree Road, N.E., Suite 280
Atlanta, GA   30326-1040
Tel: (404)240-2300   *Fax:* (404)240-2315
Web Site: www.IPT.org
Members: 3,800 individuals
Staff: 15
Annual Budget: $2-5,000,000
Exec. Director: Billy D. Cook
Asst. Director: Brenda Pittler

Historical Note
Formerly (1997) Institute of Property Taxation. Members are corporate sales/property tax representatives and attorneys, accountants and other professionals representing corporate clients in these fields. Membership: $175-350/year.

Publications:
IPT Membership Directory. a.
Property Tax Report. m.
Sales Tax Report. m.

Meetings/Conferences:
Annual Meetings: June
1999 – Toronto, ON, Canada

Institute for Responsible Housing Preservation *(1989)*
1255 23rd St., N.W., Suite 800
Washington, DC   20037
Tel: (202)973-7739   *Fax:* (202)973-7750
E-Mail: IRHP@aol.com
Members: 60 companies
Staff: 1
Annual Budget: $100-250,000
Exec. Director: Candace Kerman

Historical Note
IRHP members are owners and managers of Low Income Housing Preservation and Resident Housing Act (1990) housing and ELIHPA housing and concerned professionals. Membership: $5/unit/year.

Publications:
Responsible Owner. m.
Washington Alert. irreg.

Meetings/Conferences:

Institute for the Advancement of Engineering *(1967)*

Historical Note
Address unknown in 1995. Presumed inactive or defunct.

Institute of Ass'n Management Companies *(1963)*

Historical Note
Name changed to Internat'l Ass'n of Ass'n Management Companies (IAAMC) in 1996.

Institute of Behavioral and Applied Management
Wilkes University
Wilkes-Barre, PA   18766
Tel: (717)408-4706   *Fax:* (717)408-4917
E-Mail: stepanov@wilkes1.wilkes.edu

Members: 150 individuals
Annual Budget: $10-25,000
President: Pamela Hopkins Stepanovich, Ph.D.

Historical Note
IBAM members are educators and other professionals interested in organizational behavior and management theory. Has no paid officers or full-time staff. Membership: $50/year.

Publications:
Proceedings. a. adv.

Meetings/Conferences:
Annual Meetings: Fall
1999 - Annapolis, MD(Holiday Inn)/Nov. 4-6

Institute of Business Appraisers *(1978)*
P.O. Box 1447
Boynton Beach, FL 33425-1447
Tel: (561)732-3202 *Fax:* (561)732-4304
Toll Free: (800)299 - 4130
E-Mail: IBAHq@instbusapp.org
Web Site: http://www.instbusapp.org
Members: 3,000 individuals
Staff: 7
Annual Budget: $500-1,000,000
Exec. Director: Michele G. Miles, Esq.
Technical Director: Raymond C. Miles
Mgr., Member Services: Tana Ewing

Historical Note
Members are actively involved in the valuation and appraisal of midsize and smaller businesses. Membership: $250/year.

Publications:
IBA Directory. a.
IBA Newsletter. q.

Meetings/Conferences:
1999 - Disney World in Florida(Royal Plaza Hotel)/Feb. 3-8

Institute of Caster Manufacturers *(1933)*
104 South Michigan Ave., Suite 1500
Chicago, IL 60603
Tel: (312)201-0101 *Fax:* (312)201-0214
Members: 40 companies
Staff: 2
Annual Budget: $50-100,000
Exec. Secretary: Jack L. Lagershausen

Historical Note
Formerly (1990) Caster and Floor Truck Manufacturers Ass'n. Trade association represents industrial casters and wheels.

Publications:
Guide to Industrial Casters and Wheels. irreg.

Meetings/Conferences:
1999 - Palm Springs, CA
1999 - Oak Brook Hills, IL

Institute of Certified Business Counselors *(1975)*
P.O. Box 70326
Eugene, OR 97401
Tel: (541)345-8064 *Fax:* (541)349-0753
E-Mail: cbc@continet.com
Members: 160 individuals
Annual Budget: $25-50,000
President: George Abraham

Historical Note
ICBC members are primarily professional intermediaries specializing in assisting clients in the successful operation sale or purchase of businesses. Membership: $295/year.

Publications:
CBC Counselor - The Certified Business Counselor. bi-m. adv.

Meetings/Conferences:
Annual Meetings: Fall

Institute of Certified Financial Planners *(1973)*
3801 E. Florida Ave., Suite 708
Denver, CO 80210-2571
Tel: (303)759-4900 *Fax:* (303)759-0749
Members: 12,000 individuals
Staff: 35
Annual Budget: $2-5,000,000
Exec. Director: David Brand
Director of Public Relations: Brigid O'Connor
Director, Government Relations: Duane Thompson
Director of Corporate Development and Relations: Amy Tougaw
Director of Education: Mare Canfield
Comptroller: Curt Niepoth
Director of Board Relations: Judy Wallace
Asst. Exec. Director: Marvin W. Tuttle, CAE
Director of Society Relations: Heather Caldwell
Publications Manager: Maureen E.P. Irish
Director of Marketing: Lauren Schadle
Director, Society Relations: Marsha Temple

Historical Note
Established in Denver with 75 charter members. Accepts members who have qualified for the CFP (Certified Financial Planner) designation. Membership: $375/year (CFP member). $150/year (licensed less than a year), $175/year (licensed one to two years), $225/year (sustaining).

Publications:
Journal of Financial Planning. bi-m. adv.

Meetings/Conferences:

Institute of Certified Healthcare Business *(1975)*
330 S. Wells St., Suite 1422
Chicago, IL 60606-7105
Tel: (312)360-0384 *Fax:* (312)360-0388
Toll Free: (800)447 - 1684
E-Mail: ICPBC@aol.com
Members: 340 individuals
Staff: 2
Exec. Director: Barbara Boden

Historical Note
Formerly Institute of Certified Professional Business Consultants (1998). Members provide business management or consulting services to physicians, dentists and other medical professionals. Awards the CPBC (Certified Professional Business Consultant) designation.

Publications:
ICHBC Directory.

Meetings/Conferences:
Annual Meetings: With the Nat'l Ass'n of Health Care Consultants and the Soc. of Medical-Dental Consultants

Institute of Certified Management Accountants *(1972)*
10 Paragon Drive
Montvale, NJ 07645-1760
Tel: (201)573-9000 *Fax:* (201)573-8438
Web Site: http://www.imanet.org
Members: 25,000 individuals
Staff: 8
Managing Director: Priscilla Payne

Historical Note
Formerly (1985) Institute of Management Accounting. Affiliated with the Institute of Management Accountants (formerly) the National Ass'n of Accountants. Awards the designations Certified Management Accountant (CMA) and Certified in Financial Management (CFM) to accountants successfully completing a course of study an examination and meeting employment experience requirements. Continuing professional development is required to retain the CMA designation.

Meetings/Conferences:
1999 - Seattle, WA/June 20-23

Institute of Certified Professional Managers *(1974)*
James Madison University
Harrisonburg, VA 22807
Tel: (540)568-3247 *Fax:* (540)568-3587
Toll Free: (800)568 - 4120
E-Mail: cob.jmu.edu/icpm
Web Site: http://www.jmu.edu/icpm
Members: 91,000 individuals
Staff: 5
Annual Budget: $250-500,000
Exec. Director: Robert Keid
Director of Marketing: Colin Steele
Director of Administration: Dianne Little

Historical Note
Members are professional supervisors and managers. Offers professional education and certification upon successful completion of an examination.

Publications:
Newsletter. 2/yr.

Meetings/Conferences:
Annual Meetings: Spring

Institute of Certified Records Managers *(1975)*
P.O. Box 8188
Prairie Village, KS 66208
Toll Free: (800)825 - 4276
Members: 680 individuals
Staff: 1
Annual Budget: $50-100,000
President: Don Chewie

Historical Note
Developed by the American Records Management Ass'n in 1966, the ICRM was incorporated in 1975. It is a separate and independent organization from its sponsoring associations which include: Ass'n of Records Managers and Administrators, Nat'l Ass'n of Government Archivists and Records Administrators, the Soc. of American Archivists, and the Ass'n for Information and Image Management. ICRM is a certifying organization of professional records managers and administrative officers who specialize in the field of Records and Information Management Programs. All members have received the Certified Records Manager (CRM) designation. ARMA provides administrative support for the ICRM secretariat. Membership: $100/year (regular); $10/year (retired).

Publications:
CRM Examiniation Handbook. irreg.
ICRM Newsletters. semi-a.
Membership Directory. a.

Meetings/Conferences:
Annual Meetings: Fall
1999 - Cincinnati, OH(Convention Center)/Oct. 18-22

Institute of Certified Travel Agents *(1964)*
P.O. Box 812059
148 Linden St.
Wellesley, MA 02482-0012
Tel: (781)237-0280 *Fax:* (781)237-3860
Toll Free: (800)542 - 4282
Web Site: www.icta.com
Members: 7,000 individuals
Staff: 23
Annual Budget: $2-5,000,000
President: Robert W. Lepisto, CTC
Director, Finance & Administration: H. William Donnelly
Director, Member Services: Anita Alden, CTC

Historical Note
A non-profit, educational institution chartered in Washington in 1964 to promote professionalism in the travel industry. Now based in Wellesley, Massachusetts, it conducts a training program leading to certification and the CTC ("Certified Travel Counselor") designation, various geography courses and entry-level training. Membership: $95/year(individual).

Publications:
Travel Counselor Magazine. bi-m. adv.

Meetings/Conferences:

Institute of Chemical Waste Management
Historical Note
A division of the Hazardous Waste Management Ass'n.

Institute of Clean Air Companies *(1960)*
1660 L St., N.W., Suite 1100
Washington, DC 20036-5603
Tel: (202)457-0911 *Fax:* (202)333-1388
E-Mail: jsmith@icac.com
Web Site: http://www.icac.com
Members: 61 individuals
Staff: 4
Annual Budget: $250-500,000
Exec. Director: Jeffrey C. Smith
Deputy Director: E.J. Campobenedetto, Ph.D.

Historical Note
Formerly (1992) the Industrial Gas Cleaning Institute. Members are manufacturers of industrial air pollution control and monitoring equipment for stationary sources. Membership: $4500/year.

Publications:
Clean Air Technology News. bi-an.
Executive Update. w.
Market Forecast. a.
Organization Directory. a.
Statistical Reports. q.

Meetings/Conferences:
Annual Meetings: Spring
1999 - Amelia Island, FL

Institute of Diving *(1977)*
17314 Panama City Beach Pkwy.
Panama City Beach, FL 32413-2020
Tel: (850)235-4101 *Fax:* (850)235-4101
E-Mail: subraces@panamacity.com
Web Site: www.iod.ycg.org
Members: 600 individuals and companies
Staff: 2
Annual Budget: $100-250,000
Newsletter Editor: Dorothy Parkinson
Director: Douglas R. Hough

Historical Note
Members are sports, commercial and military divers, individuals, organizations and corporations interested in diving and diving-related activities. Supports the Museum of Man in the Sea which is dedicated to the preservation of artifacts, equipment, and archives of subjects ranging from diving history to aquaculture, marine biology, life support systems, remotely operated vehicles, oceanography, photography, and the ecology of the sea. Membership: $25/year.

Publications:
IOD Newsletter. q. adv.

Meetings/Conferences:
Annual Meetings: Always Panama City, FL/Spring

Institute of Electrical and Electronics Engineers *(1884)*
445 Hoes Ln.
Piscataway, NJ 08855-1331
Tel: (732)562-3998 *Fax:* (732)981-1721
Web Site: http://www.ieee.org
Members: 320,000 individuals
Staff: 700
Annual Budget: Over $100,000,000
Exec. Director: Daniel J. Senese
Staff Exec., Business Administration: Dick Schwartz
Managing Dir., Educational Act.: Pete Lewis
Managing Director, Technical Act.: Mary Ward-Callan
Staff Director, Information Technology: John Witsken
Managing Director, Standards Act.: Judith Gorman
Strategic Planning & Ins't Research: Henry Shein

Historical Note
Merger (1963) of the American Institute of Electrical Engineers (1884) and Institute of Radio Engineers (1912). Includes sections in Canada and throughout the rest of the world, with members in over 150 countries. Maintains and provides administrative support for the following subsidiary groups: Aerospace and Electronic Systems Soc.; Antennas and Propagation Soc.; Broadcast Technology Soc.; Circuits and Systems Soc.; Communications Soc.; Components, Packaging and Manufacturing Technology Soc.; Computer Soc.; Consumer Electronics Soc.; Control Systems Soc.; Dielectrics and Electrical Insulation Soc.; Education Soc.; Electromagnetic Compatibility Soc.; Electron Devices Soc.; Engineering Management Soc.; Engineering in Medicine and Biology Soc.; Geoscience and Remote Sensing Soc.; Industrial Electronics Soc.; Industry Applications Soc.; Information Theory Soc.; Instrumentation and Measurement Soc.; Lasers and Electro-Optics Soc.; Magnetics Soc.; Microwave Theory and Techniques Soc., Neural Networks Council; Nuclear and Plasma Sciences Soc.; Oceanic Engineering Soc.; Power Electronics Soc.; Power Engineering Soc.; Professional Communications Soc.; Reliability Soc.; Robotics and Automation Council; Signal Processing Soc.; Soc. on Social Implications of Technology; Solid-State Circuits Council; Systems, Man and Cybernetics Soc.; Ultrasonics, Ferroelectrics and Frequency Control Soc.; and Vehicular Technology Soc. Has an annual budget of over $110 million. In addition to its New York City headquarters, the IEEE maintains a library, the Center for the History of Electrical Engineering at Rutgers University in New Brunswick, New Jersey; a multi-department complex called the IEEE Operations Center in Pisacataway, NJ; and an office in Washington, DC.

Publications:
IEEE Potentials. q.
Institute. bi-m.
Proceedings. m.
Spectrum. m. adv.

Institute of Electrical and Electronics Engineers Computer Soc.

Historical Note
See IEEE Computer Soc.

Institute of Environmental Sciences and Technology (1954)
940 East Northwest Hwy.
Mount Prospect, IL   60056
Tel: (847)255-1561   *Fax:* (847)255-1699
E-Mail: iest@iest.org
Web Site: http://iest.org
Members: 3,000 individuals
Staff: 11
Annual Budget: $500-1,000,000
Exec. Director: Julie Kendrick
Assoc. Dir., PR./Marketing: Joan Harpham
Assoc. Director of Education Programs: Corrie Roesslein
Coordinator, Membership Services: Geri Heath

Historical Note
Formed by a merger of the Institute of Environmental Engineers (founded in 1955) and the Soc. of Environmental Engineers. Absorbed the American Ass'n for Contamination Control in 1973. IEST is an international professional society that serves members and the industries they represent through education and the development of recommended practices and standards. Membership: $80/year (individual).

Publications:
Journal of the Institute of Environmental Sciences. bi-m. adv.
Proceedings. a.

Meetings/Conferences:
Annual Meetings: Spring

Institute of Financial Education (1922)
55 W. Monroe, Suite 2800
Chicago, IL   60603
Tel: (312)364-0100   *Fax:* (312)364-0190
Toll Free: (800)946 - 0488
E-Mail: ifego@theinstitute.com
Web Site: www.theinstitute.com
Members: 40,000 individuals
Staff: 16
Annual Budget: $2-5,000,000
President: Dennis Graham

Historical Note
Established as the American Savings and Loan Institute, it assumed its present name in 1975. Membership: $8/year.

Meetings/Conferences:

Institute of Food Technologists (1939)
221 N. LaSalle St., Suite 300
Chicago, IL   60601-1291
Tel: (312)782-8424   *Fax:* (312)782-8348
E-Mail: info@ift.org
Web Site: http://www.ift.org
Members: 28,000 individuals
Staff: 50
Annual Budget: $5-10,000,000
Exec. Director: Daniel E. Weber
Director, Science Communications: Joyce Nettleton
Director, Meetings and Expo. Services: Stan Butler
Director, Professional Development: Dean Duxbury
Director, Finance and Administration: Michael R. Cernauskas
Director of Marketing and Membership Development: Steven Sertling
Associate Publisher: Frances Katz
Director, Information Services: Paul Grassman
Director, Field Services: Pamela Pierson

Historical Note
Founded in 1939 and incorporated in Illinois. Promotes the application of science and engineering to the production, processing, packaging, distribution, preparation, evaluation and utilization of food. About 60% of IFT members work for food processors or ingredient manufacturers, principally in R&D, quality control, technical sales, or corporate management. Has an annual budget of approximately $10 million. Membership: $90/year (individual).

Publications:
Food Technology. m. adv.
Journal of Food Science. bi-m.

Meetings/Conferences:
Annual Meetings: Summer/19,000
1999 – Chicago, IL(Convention Center)/July 24-28
2000 – Dallas, TX(Convention Center)/June 10-14

Institute of Gas Technology (1941)
1700 S. Mount Prospect Road
Des Plaines, IL   60018-1804
Tel: (847)768-0500   *Fax:* (847)768-0501
E-Mail: sen@igt.org
Web Site: http://www.igt.org
Members: 200 organizations
Staff: 200
Annual Budget: $25-50,000,000
President: Bernard S. Lee, D.Ch.E.
V. President, Education: Robert Remick
Senior V. President, Research: Stanley S. Borys
V. President, Operations: James Dunne

Historical Note
IGT is an independent center for energy and environmental research and education in the areas of energy supply, energy utilization, and environmental protection and remediation. Its main functions are to perform research and development work, provide educational programs and services, and disseminate scientific and technical information. Approximately 150 energy-related organizations are members of IGT; more than 40 others are international associates. Has an annual budget of $30 million.

Publications:
Gas Abstracts. m.
LNG Observer. q.

Meetings/Conferences:

Institute of Hazardous Materials Management (1984)
11900 Parklawn Drive, Suite 450
Rockville, MD   20852
Tel: (301)984-8969
Members: 9,000 individuals
Staff: 10
Annual Budget: $500-1,000,000
Exec. Director: Robert Teitler
Examination Coordinator: Shelley Wolf
Asst. Exec. Director: Betty Fishman

Historical Note
Professional Certification Board certifies for Certified Hazardous Materials Manager upon successful completion of qualifications and test. Annual maintenance fee: $45.

Publications:
Directory of Hazardous Materials Management. a.
Handbook on Hazardous Materials Management.
Newsletter. q. adv.

Meetings/Conferences:

Institute of Home Office Underwriters (1937)
Historical Note
Address unknown in 1996.

Institute of Industrial Engineers (1948)
25 Technology Park/Atlanta
Norcross, GA   30092-2901
Tel: (770)449-0460   *Fax:* (770)441-3295
Toll Free: (800)494 - 0460
E-Mail: cs@www.iienet.org
Web Site: http://www.iienet.org
Members: 2,400 individuals
Staff: 45
Annual Budget: $5-10,000,000
Exec. Director: David Levy
Director, Conferences and Seminars: Judy Stech
Director, Finance: Patrick Neagle
Director, Marketing: Paula Edmondson
Director, Membership: Lisa Zaken

Historical Note
Founded and chartered in Columbus, Ohio as the American Institute of Industrial Engineers; assumed its present name in 1981. Member of the Accreditation Board for Engineering and Technology and the Council of Engineering Examiners. Absorbed the Industrial Management Soc. in 1982. Has an annual budget of approximately $5 million. Membership: $75/year.

Publications:
IIE Transactions. q.
Industrial Engineering Solutions. m. adv.
Industrial Management. bi-m. adv.
Student I. E.
The Engineering Economist. q.

Meetings/Conferences:
Annual Meetings: May/2,000

Institute of Inspection Cleaning and Restoration (1972)
2715 East Mill Plain Blvd.
Vancouver, WA   98661
Tel: (360)693-5675   *Fax:* (360)693-4858
E-Mail: IICRC@E-Z.NET
Web Site: WWW.IICRC.ORG
Members: 16,000 individuals, 4,500 companies
Staff: 8
Annual Budget: $1-2,000,000
Exec. Administrator: Kenway Mead

Historical Note
Formerly (1993) the Internat'l Institute of Carpet and Upholstery Certification. Members are firms and individuals concerned with fabric restoration. IICR establishes standards, codifies ethics and certifies companies and individuals.

Publications:
International Directory of Certified Professionals. a.
Newsletter. 2/year.

Institute of Intermodal Repairers (1983)
450 Sansome St., Suite 600
San Francisco, CA   94111-3306
Tel: (415)398-2120   *Fax:* (415)398-3610
Members: 70 companies
Staff: 1
Annual Budget: $50-100,000
President: Mark C. North

Historical Note
Begun in 1983 by approximately 40 repair companies from the U.S. and Canada to develop the industry in such areas as new repair techniques and to unify industry response to other trade associations and industry groups. Membership: $700/year.

Publications:
IIR Newsletter. q. adv.

Meetings/Conferences:

Institute of Internal Auditors (1941)
249 Maitland Ave.
Altamonte Springs, FL   32701-4201
Tel: (407)830-7600   *Fax:* (407)831-5171
E-Mail: custserv@theiia.org
Web Site: http://www.theiia.org
Members: 60,000 individuals
Staff: 90
Annual Budget: $10-25,000,000
President: William G. Bishop, III
Manager, Marketing & Public Rels.: Trish W. Harris
Manager, Meeting Planning: Louise Whitsett
Manager, Academic Relations: Candy Murray
V. President, Learning Center: John J. Fernandes
Manager, Professional Issues: Steve Jameson
Manager, Educational Products: Stacy Hurt
Manager, Research: Roland L. Laing
Director, Finance/Administration: Walter E. Liss
Director, Membership Services: Judith K. Burke
Director, Technology: Charles H. LeGrand

Historical Note
IIA provides professional development and educational services, certification standards and research to the internal auditing profession. Membership composed of internal auditors, comptrollers and accountants in companies, government and organizations. Grants the CIA (Certified Internal Auditor) designation. Has an annual budget of approximately $14.5 million. Membership: $70-125/year.

Publications:
CSA Sentinel tri. a.
IIA Educator. semi-a.
IIA Today. bi-m.
Pistas de Auditoria. bi-m.
The Internal Auditor. bi-m. adv.

Meetings/Conferences:
Annual Meetings: Summer
1999 – Montreal, Quebec/June 20-23
2000 – New York, NY
2001 – Buenos Aires, Argentina

Institute of Internat'l Bankers (1966)
299 Park Ave., 17th Floor
New York, NY   10171
Tel: (212)421-1611   *Fax:* (212)421-1119
Web Site: http://www.iib.org
Members: 230 banks
Staff: 10
Annual Budget: $2-5,000,000
Exec. Director-General Counsel: Lawrence R. Uhlick
Director, Communications: William Goodwin

Historical Note
The Institute is a trade association engaged in lobbying on behalf of foreign banks doing business in the United States.

Publications:
Internat'l Banking Focus. 11/year.

Meetings/Conferences:
Annual Meetings: always Washington, DC/March

Institute of Internat'l Container Lessors (1971)
630 Old Post Road
Bedford Consultants Bldg., Box 605
Bedford, NY   10506
Tel: (914)234-3696   *Fax:* (914)234-3641
E-Mail: info@iicl.org
Web Site: http://www.iicl.org
Members: 12 companies
Staff: 7
Annual Budget: $500-1,000,000
Secretary & Counsel: Edward A. Woolley
Asst. Director, Examinations: Carolyn Baron
Director, Publications & Examinations: Linda S. Rae

Historical Note
Members lease marine cargo containers and container chassis to ship operators and others on a broad international basis. Sponsors an inspectors' certification and examination testing program; distributes technical manuals; and is active in regulatory, tax, communications and customs fields.

Publications:
IICL Inspection Directory. a. adv.
News from IICL Newsletter. semi-a.

Institute of Internat'l Finance (1983)
2000 Pennsylvania Ave., N.W., Suite 8500
Washington, DC   20006-1812
Tel: (202)857-3600   *Fax:* (202)775-1430
Web Site: http://www.iif.com
Members: 300 institutions
Staff: 65
Annual Budget: $2-5,000,000
Managing Director: Charles H. Dallara
Membership Administrator: Carla H. Cronin

Historical Note
Created as a center for the dissemination of information to member organizations and a forum in which lending institutions can communicate with borrowing countries, multilateral organizations and regulators, in order to improve the processs of international lending. Members include commercial banks from developed and developing countries. Associate members include development banks, trading companies, export credit agencies and multinational corporations.

Publications:
Capital Flows to Emerging Market Economies. 2/year.
Comparative Country Statistics. a.
Survey of Debt Restructuring. 2/year.

Meetings/Conferences:
Semi-Annual Meetings: Usually at Washington, DC headquarters

Institute of Judicial Administration (1952)
40 Washington Sq. South
New York University School of Law
New York, NY   10012-1005
Tel: (212)998-6196   *Fax:* (212)995-4036
Members: 1,600 individuals
Staff: 8
Annual Budget: $500-1,000,000
Exec. Director: Samuel Estreicher

Historical Note
Founded by Arthur T. Vanderbilt in 1952 at the New York University Law Center. Members are judges, lawyers and others concerned with improving the operation of the court system. Membership is by invitation. Membership: $30-500.

Institute of Makers of Explosives (1913)
1120 19th St., N.W., Suite 310
Washington, DC 20036-3605
Tel: (202)429-9280   *Fax:* (202)293-2420
Web Site: http://IME.org
Members: 32 companies
Staff: 8
Annual Budget: $1-2,000,000
President: J. Christopher Ronay
Historical Note
Members are U.S. and Canadian producers of commercial explosives. Sponsors the I.M.E. Political Action Committee. Membership: based on sales.
Publications:
Publications List Available.
Meetings/Conferences:
Annual Meetings: Fall

Institute of Management Accountants (1919)
10 Paragon Drive
Montvale, NJ 07645-1760
Tel: (201)573-9000   *Fax:* (201)573-8185
Toll Free: (800)638 - 4427
Web Site: http://www.imanet.org
Members: 76,000 individuals
Staff: 94
Annual Budget: $10-25,000,000
Exec. Director: Richard Swanson
Managing Director, Finance/Administration: Catherine Stanke
Managing Director, Regional Operations: Jack A. Vaccaro
Sr. Director, Information Technology: Anthony Plescia
Historical Note
A professional association of accountants established as the National Ass'n of Cost Accountants, became the Nat'l Ass'n of Accountants in 1957 and assumed its current name in 1991. Has an annual budget of approximately $16.1 million. Awards the designations CFM (Certified in Financial Management) or CMA (Certified Management Accountant) to managment accountants or financial managers who pass the examinations, have at least two years experience, and agree to comply with the IMA's standards of ethical conduct. Controllers Council and Cost Management Group are special interest groups supported by IMA. Membership: $130/year (individual).
Publications:
Controller's Quarterly. m.
Cost Management Update. m.
IMA Focus. bi-m.
Management Accounting. m. adv.
Meetings/Conferences:
Annual Meetings: June
1999 – Seattle, WA(The Westin Hotel)/June 20-23
2000 – Philadelphia, PA(Marriott)/June 14-17

Institute of Management Consultants (1968)
521 5th Ave., 35th Floor
New York, NY 10175-3598
Tel: (212)697-8262   *Fax:* (212)949-6571
Web Site: http://www.imcusa.org
Members: 2,800 individuals
Staff: 8
Annual Budget: $500-1,000,000
Exec. Director: Joanne E. Dunne
Manager, Marketing & Programs: Melissa Cole
Historical Note
IMC members are individual management consultants. IMC awards the CMC (Certified Management Consultant) designation. Offers free CMC Referral Service. Presents consulting skills workshop in major U.S. cities. A member of the Internat'l Council of Management Consulting Institutes. Membership: $300/year (certified member); $150/year (member); $75/year (student).
Publications:
Directory of Members.
Journal of Management Consultants. a.
Management Consulting Times. m.
Meetings/Conferences:
Annual Meetings: April-May/150

Institute of Mathematical Statistics (1935)
Business Office
3401 Investment Blvd., Suite 7
Hayward, CA 94545-3819
Tel: (510)783-8141   *Fax:* (510)783-4131
E-Mail: ims@stat.berkely.edu
Web Site: http://www.imstat.org
Members: 3,500 individuals
Staff: 4
Annual Budget: $500-1,000,000
Business Manager: Elyse R. Gustafson
Historical Note
Established September 12, 1935 during the joint meeting of the American Mathematical Soc. and the Mathematical Ass'n of America in Ann Arbor. Member of the Conference Board of the Mathematical Sciences. Membership: $60/year (individual); $450/year (institution); $750/year (corporate).
Publications:
Annals of Applied Probability. q.
Annals of Probability. q.
Annals of Statistics. bi-m.
Institute of Mathematical Statistics Bulletin. bi-m. adv.
Statistical Science. q.
Meetings/Conferences:
Annual Meetings: Summer
1999 – Baltimore, MD
2000 – Guanajuato, Mexico/May 15-20
2001 – Atlanta, GA

Institute of Medicine (1970)

2101 Constitution Ave., N.W.
Washington, DC 20418
Tel: (202)334-2169   *Fax:* (202)334-1412
Web Site: http://www2.nas.edu/iom
Members: 1,200 individuals
Staff: 100
Annual Budget: $10-25,000,000
President: Kenneth I. Shine, M.D.
Director, Office of Congressional and Government Affairs: Jim Jensen
Exec. Officer: Susanne Stoiber
Director, Office of Membership Services: Jana Surdi
Historical Note
Private membership organization established in 1970 under the charter of the Nat'l Academy of Sciences to address issues associated with public policies for the advancement of human health.
Publications:
IOM News. bi-m.
Meetings/Conferences:
Annual Meetings: October in Washington, D.C.

Institute of Merger and Acquisition Professionals
Historical Note
Address unknown in 1995.

Institute of Metal Repair (1985)
Historical Note
Address unknown in 1997.

Institute of Nautical Archaeology (1973)
Drawer HG
College Station, TX 77841-5137
Tel: (409)845-6694   *Fax:* (409)847-9260
E-Mail: nautical@tamu.edu
Web Site: http://nautarch.tamu.edu/NAPINA.HTM
Members: 1000 individuals
Staff: 26
Annual Budget: $500-1,000,000
President: George F. Bass, Ph.D.
Historical Note
Originally called the American Institute of Nautical Archaeology. Members are interested in underwater archaeological excavation. Membership: $30/year (individual); $100/year (organization).
Publications:
INA Quarterly Newsletter. q.
Meetings/Conferences:

Institute of Navigation (1945)
1800 Diagonal Road, Suite 480
Alexandria, VA 22314-2840
Tel: (703)683-7101   *Fax:* (703)683-7105
Web Site: http://www.ion.org
Members: 4,000 individuals
Staff: 6
Annual Budget: $1-2,000,000
Director, Operations: Lisa Beaty
Historical Note
Members are individuals interested in advancing the science of space, land, air, and marine navigation. Membership: $45/year (individual); $350-750/year (organization).
Publications:
Navigation. q. adv.
Newsbulletin. 4-6/year.
Proceedings. 3/yr.
Meetings/Conferences:
Annual Meetings: Technical/Jan., Membership/June, Global Positioning System/Sept.
1999 – Cambridge, MA/June 28-30

Institute of Noise Control Engineering (1971)
Box 3206
Arlington Branch
Poughkeepsie, NY 12603
Tel: (914)462-4006   *Fax:* (914)463-0201
E-Mail: hq@ince.org
Web Site: http://ince.org
Members: 1,100 individuals, 7 companies
Annual Budget: $100-250,000
Managing Director: G.C. Maling, Jr.
Historical Note
Incorporated in Washington, DC, INCE is a non-profit professional organization concerned with the advancement of noise control technology with particular emphasis on engineering solutions to environmental noise problems. Has no paid staff. Membership: $70/yr.
Publications:
Noise Control Engineering Journal. bi-m.
Noise/News International. q. adv.
Meetings/Conferences:
Triennial Convention: Winter (1997)

Institute of Nuclear Materials Management (1958)
60 Revere Drive, Suite 500
Northbrook, IL 60062
Tel: (847)480-9573   *Fax:* (847)480-9282
E-Mail: bscott5465@aol.com
Members: 800 individuals
Staff: 2
Annual Budget: $250-500,000
Exec. Director: Barbara A. Scott
Historical Note
Individuals and companies concerned with the managing and safeguarding of nuclear materials. Membership: $50/year.
Publications:
Journal of Nuclear Materials Management. q. adv.
Proceedings. a.

Meetings/Conferences:
Annual Meetings: Summer

Institute of Nuclear Power Operations (1979)
700 Galleria Parkway, N.W.
Atlanta, GA 30339-5957
Tel: (770)644-8000   *Fax:* (770)644-8549
Members: 44 members, 33 participants
Staff: 400
Annual Budget: $50-100,000,000
C.E.O.: James Rhodes
Director, Communications: Philip N. McCullough
Director, Government Relations: William J. Hastie
Meetings Coordinator: Karen L. Rowley
Exec. V. President: Alfred C. Tollison, Jr.
Historical Note
Established in late 1979, incorporated in Delaware, to promote the highest levels of safe and reliable nuclear power plant operation. Members are electric utilities owning a share in a nuclear power plant, operating one, or holding a license to construct one. Has an annual budget of over $50 million.
Publications:
Review. semi-m.
The Nuclear Professional. q.
Meetings/Conferences:
Annual Meetings: March

Institute of Outdoor Advertising
Historical Note
The marketing/promotion arm of the Outdoor Advertising Ass'n of America.

Institute of Packaging Professionals (1989)
481 Carlisle Dr.
Herndon, VA 20170
Tel: (703)318-8970   *Fax:* (703)814-4961
Toll Free: (800)432 - 4085
Members: 7,000 individuals
Staff: 22
Annual Budget: $2-5,000,000
Exec. Director: William C. Pflaum
Meeting & Exhibitions Manager: Jill J.K. Retz
Finance and Administration Manager: Erin Edwards
Manager, Awards and Honors: Kathy Deeney
Historical Note
Formed in 1989 by a merger of the Packaging Institute Internat'l (1939) and the Soc. of Packaging Professionals (1946), the Institute is a society of individuals whose objectives include educating the packaging professional, advancing packaging technology, and increasing the value of packaging in the marketplace. Membership: $125/year (individual).
Publications:
Directory of Consultants. a.
PACK-INFO. bi-m.
Packaging Technology and Engineering. m. adv.
Who's Who and What's What in Packaging. a. adv.
Meetings/Conferences:

Institute of Paper Science and Technology (1929)
500 10th St., N.W.
Atlanta, GA 30318-5794
Tel: (404)894-5700   *Fax:* (404)894-4778
Toll Free: (800)558 - 6611
Web Site: http://www.ipst.edu
Members: 50 manufacturers
Staff: 225
Annual Budget: $10-25,000,000
President: James Ferris
Continuing Education Coordinator: Dani Denton
Director, Academic Affairs: Dr. Barry Crouse
Director, Information Services Division: Ray Cunningham
V. President, Research: Dr. Jim Ferris
Historical Note
Formerly (1989) the Institute of Paper Chemistry (Appleton, WI). Name affiliated with Georgia Tech, IPST is an educational research center for manufacturers of pulp paper. Has an annual budget of approximately $20 million.
Publications:
Abstract Bulletin.
Meetings/Conferences:
Annual Meetings: Atlanta, GA/Spring

Institute of Political Campaign Consultants
P.O. Box 2502
San Rafael, CA 94912-4155
Tel: (415)485-1463   *Fax:* (415)460-1921
Annual Budget: under $10,000
Exec. Director: Don L. Organ, CAE
Historical Note
IPCC was established to provide public education about the services of political campaign consultants and techniques.
Publications:
Campaign Materials. irreg.

Institute of Property Taxation (1976)
Historical Note
Became the Institute for Professionals in Taxation in 1997.

Institute of Public Utilities (1965)
Michigan State University
410 Eppley Ctr.
East Lansing, MI 48824-1121
Tel: (517)355-1876   *Fax:* (517)355-1854
Web Site: http://www.bus.msu.edu/ipu
Members: 28 companies
Staff: 3
Annual Budget: $250-500,000
Director: Pamela Prairie

Associate Director, Communications and Education: Michelle F. Wilsey
Administrative Secretary and Conference Coordinator: Margie Gray

Historical Note
IPU members are regulated and competitive utility companies. An independent research organization, IPU promotes study, research, teaching, and training in the field of public utilities. $3,000-6,000/year (company).

Meetings/Conferences:

Institute of Real Estate Management (1933)
430 N. Michigan Ave.
Chicago, IL 60611-4090
Tel: (312)329-6000   *Fax:* (312)661-0217
Toll Free: (800)837 - 0706
E-Mail: custserv@irem.org
Web Site: http://www.irem.org
Members: 1,400 individuals, 670 firms
Staff: 75
Annual Budget: $10-25,000,000
Sr. Staff V. President: Nancye Kirk
Public Affairs Manager: Mariwyn Evans
Staff V. President., Legislation & Spec. Services: Charles Achilles
Meetings/Convention Manager: Phyllis Coneset
V. President, Education/Communications: Joyce Travis Copess
Staff V. President, Finance and Controller: Kenneth M. Paul
Manager, Member Services: Ann Arnott
Staff V. President, Management Information Systems: Carole J. Hansen

Historical Note
An affiliate of Nat'l Ass'n of REALTORS, IREM represents and supports individuals and companies that manage real estate. Awards three professional designations: Certified Property Manager (CPM); Accredited Residential Manager (ARM); and Accredited Management Organization (AMO). Membership: $395/year (individual); $425/year (organization).

Publications:
Income/Expense Analyses. a.
Inside IREM. bi-m.
Journal of Property Management. bi-m. adv.

Meetings/Conferences:
Annual Meetings: Fall with the Nat'l Ass'n of Realtors
1999 - Orlando, FL(Buena Vista Palace)/Nov. 8-12
2000 - San Francisco, CA(Hilton)/Nov. 6-10

Institute of Roofing and Waterproofing Consultants Internat'l (1972)
401 N. Michigan Ave
Chicago, IL 60611
Tel: (312)321-6864   *Fax:* (312)644-0310
Toll Free: (800)837 - 4792
E-Mail: KevinGammonley@sba.com
Web Site: http://www.irwc.org
Members: 75 individuals
Staff: 3
Annual Budget: $25-50,000
Exec. Director: Kevin Gammonley
Marketing Director: Kevin Grant

Historical Note
IRWCI members are professional roofing and waterproofing consultants. Affiliate membership is available for others with an interest in the industry. Awards the CPRC (Certified Professional Roofing Consultant) and CPWC (Certified Professional Waterproofing Consultant) designations. Membership: $450/year.

Publications:
IRWC Newsletter. q. adv.
Membership Directory. a. adv.
Technical Bulletins. bi-m.

Meetings/Conferences:
Annual Meetings: February

Institute of Scrap Recycling Industries (1987)
1325 G St., N.W., Suite 1000
Washington, DC 20005-3104
Tel: (202)737-1770   *Fax:* (202)626-0900
Members: 1,500 companies
Staff: 38
Annual Budget: $5-10,000,000
Exec. Director: Robin K. Wiener
Director, Communications: Evelyn L. Haught
Director, Federal and State Programs: Clare Hessler
Manager, Legislative & Int'l Affairs: Mark Reiter
Director, State and Local Programs: James Caffey
Education/Meetings Manager: Lisa Ness
Director, Programs and Services: Patricia Adair
Director, Administration and Finance: Kenneth M. Fox
Counsel & Managing Director, Government Relations: Scott Horne
Director, Membership: John Weaver
Publisher and Editorial Director: James Fowler

Historical Note
Merger (1987) of the Institute of Scrap Iron and Steel (founded 1928) and the Nat'l Ass'n of Recycling Industries (founded 1913). Membership includes processors, brokers, and consumers of scrap metal, paper, textiles, glass, rubber and plastics. Sponsors and supports the ISRI Political Action Committee.

Publications:
ISRI Digest.
Membership Directory. a.
Phoenix.
Scrap Magazine. bi-m. adv.

Meetings/Conferences:
Annual Meetings: April
1999 - Orlando, FL(Marriott's Orlando World Center)/April 13-17

Institute of Shortening and Edible Oils (1936)
1750 New York Ave., N.W., Suite 120
Washington, DC 20006
Tel: (202)783-7960   *Fax:* (202)393-1367

E-Mail: info@iseo.org
Members: 22 companies
Staff: 2
Annual Budget: $100-250,000
President: Robert M. Reeves

Historical Note
ISEO is a trade association representing the refiners of edible fats and oils in the United States. Its members represent approximately 90-95% of the edible fats and oils produced domestically which are used in numerous foods including margarine, shortening, cooking and salad oils, confections and toppings in addition to being used as ingredients in a wide variety of foods. Formerly the Institute of Shortening Manufacturers.

Publications:
Directory of Edible Oil Industry in the U. S.
Food Fats and Oils. quinquenn..
Treatment of Waste Water from Food Oil Plants. quinquenn..

Meetings/Conferences:
Annual Meetings: Late Winter/Early Spring
1999 - Rancho Mirage, CA(Ritz Carlton)/March 21-23/50
2000 - Tucson, AZ(Tucson National)/March 10-15/50
2001 - San Antonio, TX/March 16-20/50

Institute of Store Planners (1961)
25 N. Broadway
Tarrytown, NY 10591-3201
Tel: (914)332-1806   *Fax:* (914)332-1541
E-Mail: HTI@HTI.org
Web Site: http://www/ISPO.org
Members: 1,100 individuals
Staff: 2
Annual Budget: $100-250,000
Exec. Director: Richard C. Byrne

Historical Note
Members are store planners and designers, visual merchandisers, educators, as well as contractors and suppliers to the industry. Membership: $150/year (professional), $250/year (trade).

Publications:
ISP Newsletter. q.

Institute of Tax Consultants (1980)

Historical Note
The Institute is the certifying board for the American Soc. of Tax Professionals.

Institute of the Ironworking Industry (1977)
1750 New York Ave., N.W.
Washington, DC 20006
Tel: (202)783-3998   *Fax:* (202)393-1507
Members: 35 organizations
Staff: 4
Annual Budget: $250-500,000
Exec. Director: John J. McMahon

Historical Note
Began operations on April 4, 1977 as the joint creation of the Iron Workers Employers Ass'n of Washington, DC and the Internat'l Ass'n of Bridge, Structural and Ornamental Iron Workers (AFL-CIO). Co-participants are 37 regional associations of steel fabricators and erectors. The Institute was formed to enhance the development of the Ironworking industry; its mission is, in part, "to assist workers and employers in the Ironworking industry in solving problems of mutual concern not susceptible to resolution within the collective bargaining process; to study and explore ways of eliminating potential problems which reduce competitiveness and inhibit the economic development of the industry."

Publications:
Directory. irreg.

Meetings/Conferences:
Semi-annual Meetings: Washington, DC/June and November

Institute of Transportation Engineers (1930)
525 School St., S.W., Suite 410
Washington, DC 20024-2797
Tel: (202)554-8050   *Fax:* (202)863-5486
E-Mail: info@vax.ite.org
Web Site: http://www.ite.org
Members: 15,000 individuals
Staff: 23
Annual Budget: $5-10,000,000
Exec. Director: Thomas W. Brahms
Director, Communications and Marketing: Shannon Gore Peters
Deputy Exec. Director: Mark R. Norman
Assoc. Exec. Dir., Admin./Finance: Peter W. Frentz

Historical Note
Founded in Pittsburgh in 1930 and incorporated in 1954 in Connecticut as the Institute of Traffic Engineers; assumed its present name in 1976. Members are individual professionals responsible for planning, designing, and operating surface transportation facilities.

Publications:
ITE Journal. m. adv.

Meetings/Conferences:
Annual Meetings: August-September
1999 - Las Vegas, NV(Hilton)/Aug. 1-4
2000 - Nashville, TN(Opryland)/Aug. 6-9
2001 - Chicago, IL(Hyatt Regency)/Aug. 19-22

Institute on Religion in an Age of Science (1954)
56 Hawes St.
Brookline, MA 02446
Tel: (617)738-7723
E-Mail: Jgoodbrook@aol.com
Members: 330 individuals
Annual Budget: $25-50,000
Secretary: Joan Goodwin

Historical Note
IRAS aims to understand, interpret, and advance in the light of the sciences and critical scholarship the continuing functions of evolving religion that guide humanity's relation to the ultimate

conditions of its destiny. Has no paid officers or full-time staff. Member of the Council on the Study of Religion. Affiliate Society of the American Ass'n for the Advancement of Science. Membership: $60/year (individual); $65/year (joint); $100/year (organization); $40/year (student).

Publications:
IRAS Newsletter. 3/year.
Science and Spirit.
Zygon, Journal of Religion and Science. q. adv.

Meetings/Conferences:
Annual Meetings: Always Star Island, NH in July or August/50

Institutional and Municipal Parking Congress (1976)

Historical Note
Became the Internat'l Parking Institute in 1995.

Institutional and Service Textile Distributors Ass'n (1944)
1609 Connecticut Ave., N.W., Suite 200
Washington, DC 20009
Tel: (202)986-0105   *Fax:* (202)986-0448
Members: 18 companies
Annual Budget: $50-100,000
Exec. Secretary: Kathleen Ewing

Historical Note
Members are wholesale distributors of U.S. textiles to hospitality and health care industries such as hospitals, hotels, nursing homes and restaurants. Member sales total approximately $750 million annually. Membership: $1,000-3,000/year minimum, based on sales.

Meetings/Conferences:
Semi-Annual Meetings: Winter and Spring

Institutional Carpet Maintenance Council (1971)

Historical Note
A division of the Ass'n of Specialists in Cleaning and Restoration.

Instructional Systems Ass'n (1978)
4952 Warner Ave., Suite 243
Huntington Beach, CA 92649
Tel: (714)846-6012   *Fax:* (714)846-3987
E-Mail: isainfo@aol.com
Web Site: http://www.isaconnection.org
Members: 150 companies
Staff: 3
Annual Budget: $250-500,000
Exec. Director: Terry K. Broomfield

Historical Note
Members are training industry firms which produce generic and/or custom-designed training programs or consult for business and industry.

Publications:
Intercom. 3/year.

Meetings/Conferences:
Annual Meetings: March
1999 - Amelia Island, FL(Amelia Island Plantation)/March 21-24/175

Instructional Telecommunications Council (1977)
One Dupont Circle, Suite 410
Washington, DC 20036-1176
Tel: (202)293-3110   *Fax:* (202)833-2467
E-Mail: cdalziel@aacc.nche.edu
Members: 500 institutions
Staff: 2
Annual Budget: $100-250,000
Exec. Director: Christine Dalziel

Historical Note
Founded as Instructional Telecommunications Consortium; assumed its current name in 1993. Members are educators and organizations involved in higher education instructional telecommunications and distance learning. Membership: $525/year (insititution); $125/year (individual).

Publications:
ITC News. 10/yr. adv.

Meetings/Conferences:
Annual Meetings: April/50-100
1999 - Austin, TX/Oct. 10-13

Instrument Contracting and Engineering Ass'n (1986)
P.O. Box 42558, Northwest Station
Washington, DC 20015-0558
Tel: (301)933-7430
Members: 35 individuals, 51 companies
Annual Budget: $25-50,000
Exec. Director: Walter M. Kardy, C.A.E.

Historical Note
A group of contractors who install automated controls and controls for robotics in power stations and other heavy industrial installations. Incorporated in Washington, DC. Membership: $100/year.

Meetings/Conferences:
Annual Meetings: Spring

Instrument Soc. of America (1998)
67 Alexander Dr., Box 12277
Research Triangle Pk, NC 27709
Tel: (919)549-8411   *Fax:* (919)549-8288
E-Mail: info@isa.org
Web Site: www.isa.org
Members: 49,000 individuals
Staff: 120
Annual Budget: $10-25,000,000
Exec. Director: Glenn F. Harvey
Assoc. Exec. Director, Conferences and Exhibits: Jan Holman
Assoc. Exec. Director: T.S. Lee
Assoc. Exec. director, Marketing & International Development: Fred W. Gebarowski

Assoc. Exec. Director of Standards, Training, and Publications: James D. Converse
Assoc. Exec. Director, Corporate Development: E.V. Burlchulder

Historical Note
Formerly (1998) Internat'l Soc. for Measurement in America. Founded in Pittsburgh on April 28, 1945 by representatives of 18 local instrument societies from the U.S. and Canada as Instrument Soc. of America; became Internat'l Soc. for Measurement and Control in 1994, and assumed its current name in 1997. Incorporated in Pennsylvania. A charter member of the American Automatic Control Council, an affiliate of the American Institute of Physics, member of American Nat'l Standard Institute and U.S. representative to the Internat'l Measurement Confederation. Formed a subsidiary, ISA Services, Inc. in 1986. Has a budget of approximately $21 million. Membership: $60/year.

Publications:
Industrial Computing. m. adv.
InTech. m. adv.
ISA Directory of Instrumentation. a.
ISA Proceedings. a.
ISA Transactions. q.
Motion Control. m. adv.

Meetings/Conferences:
Annual Meetings: Fall/32,000
1999 – Philadelphia, PA/Oct. 5-7
2000 – Houston, TX/Oct. 16-19
2001 – New Orleans, LA/Oct 2-4

Insulated Cable Engineers Ass'n *(1925)*
P.O. Box 440
South Yarmouth, MA   02664
Tel: (508)394-4424   *Fax:* (508)394-1194
Web Site: www.icea.net
Members: 100 individuals
Staff: 4
Annual Budget: $50-100,000
Secretary-Treasurer: Edward E. McIlveen

Historical Note
Formerly (1979) known as the Insulated Power Cable Engineers Ass'n, Inc. ICEA is a professional society of engineers who develop standards to promote the reliability of insulated wire and cable. Membership: $1,500/year.

Publications:
ICEA Activities.
Publications List Available.

Meetings/Conferences:
Annual Meetings: usually September
1999 – Pocono, PA(Pocono Manor)/Sept. 13-16/50
2000 – Charleston, SC/Sept. 11-14/50

Insulated Steel Door Institute *(1975)*
30200 Detroit Road
Cleveland, OH   44145-1967
Tel: (440)899-0010   *Fax:* (440)892-1404
Web Site: http://www.isdi.org
Members: 6 companies
Staff: 2
Managing Director: J. Jeffery Wherry

Historical Note
Formerly (1991) Insulated Steel Door Systems Institute. Members are producers of insulated steel door systems.

Insulation Contractors Ass'n of America *(1977)*
1321 Duke St., Suite 303
Alexandria, VA   22314
Tel: (703)739-0356   *Fax:* (703)739-0412
Web Site: insulate.org
Members: 300 companies
Staff: 2
Annual Budget: $250-500,000
Exec. Director: Michael Kwart

Historical Note
Incorporated in the District of Columbia in December 1977, with 32 charter members. Residential and commercial insulation contractors and suppliers. Membership: $600-5,000/year (organization, based on gross sales).

Publications:
Insulation Contractors Report. bi-m.
Member Bulletin. bi-m.
Membership Directory. a.

Meetings/Conferences:
Annual Meetings: September-October
1999 – Phoenix, AZ

Insurance Accounting and Systems Ass'n *(1928)*
P.O. Box 51340
Durham, NC   27717
Tel: (919)489-0991   *Fax:* (919)489-1994
E-Mail: info@iasa.org
Web Site: www.iasa.org
Members: 1,700 companies
Staff: 2
Annual Budget: $500-1,000,000
Secretary-Treasurer: Elaine S. Powell

Historical Note
Formed as the Insurance Accounting and Statistical Ass'n at a meeting of representatives of 8 Illinois and Indiana life insurance companies at Peoria, IL on April 14, 1928. Adopted the name Insurance Accounting and Systems Ass'n in 1983 and incorporated in 1986. The IASA serves life, property and liability, reinsurance and health care companies through the study, research, and development of modern insurance theory, practice, and procedures. Membership: $250/year (company).

Publications:
Interpreter. bi-m.

Meetings/Conferences:
Annual Meetings: May or June
1999 – San Diego, CA/June 6-9
2000 – Washington, DC/June 4-7

2001 – San Antonio, TX/June 3-6

Insurance Conference Planners Ass'n *(1958)*
Suite 106, 260 W. Esplanade
North Vancouver, BC   V7M 3-G7
Tel: (604)988-2054   *Fax:* (604)988-4743
Members: 400 individuals
Staff: 1
Exec. Director: Karen Hopkinson
Administrative Assistant: Helen Peters

Historical Note
Established as the Insurance Convention Planners Ass'n, it assumed its present name in 1976. Membership: $150/year.

Publications:
Directory. a.

Meetings/Conferences:
Annual Meetings: November/500
1999 – Boca Raton, FL(Boca Raton Resort)/Nov. 15-19/500
2000 – Colorado Springs, CO(The Broadmoor)/Nov. 6-10

Insurance Consumer Affairs Exchange *(1976)*
P.O. Box 746
Lake Zurich, IL   60047
Tel: (847)320-2522
Members: 120 individuals, 62 companies
V. President: Nancy Brebner

Historical Note
Forum for dialogue with professionals interested in consumer-related matters in the insurance industry and issues of consumer affairs in general. Membership: $100/year (individual); $250/year (organization/company).

Publications:
ICAE Catalyst. q.

Meetings/Conferences:
1999 – Dallas, TX/April 18-21
1999 – Washington, DC

Insurance Information Institute *(1959)*
110 William St., 24th Floor
New York, NY   10038
Tel: (212)669-9200   *Fax:* (212)732-1916
E-Mail: iiilibrary@aol.com
Web Site: http://www.iii.org
Members: 275 individuals and companies
Staff: 38
Annual Budget: $5-10,000,000
President: Gordon C. Stewart
Sr. V. President, Communications Division: Steven Goldstein
V. President, Issues Analysis: Ruth Gastel, CPCU
Sr. V. President, Programs & Operations: Cary Schneider
Manager, Administrative Services: Diane Portantiere
V. President and Economist: Robert Hartwig, Ph.D.

Historical Note
An association of property and casualty insurance companies whose activities include public education, information dissemination, and media relations. Maintains library data base, as well as a toll-free consumer hotline. Has an annual budget of approximately $5 million.

Publications:
III Insurance Daily. d.
Insurance Facts. a.
Insurance Issues Update. m.

Meetings/Conferences:
Annual Meetings: January
1999 – New York, NY(Waldorf Astoria)/Jan. 12-13

Insurance Institute for Highway Safety *(1959)*
1005 N. Glebe Road, Suite 800
Arlington, VA   22201-4751
Tel: (703)247-1500   *Fax:* (703)247-1678
Web Site: http://www.hwysafety.org
Members: 3 automobile insurers
Staff: 70
Annual Budget: $10-25,000,000
President: Brian O'Neill
Director of Communications: Julie Rochman
Senior V. President, Research: Adrian K. Lund, Ph.D.
Senior V. President, Research: Allan F. Williams, Ph.D.
V. President, Vehicle Research Center: Charles Anthony Preuss
Sr. V. President: Stephen L. Oesch
General Counsel: Michele Fields
Director, Publications: Anne Fleming
V. President, Research: Susan A. Ferguson
V. President, Research: David S. Zuby

Historical Note
An independent non-profit research and communications organization working to reduce property losses, deaths and injuries on the nation's highways. Supported by automobile insurers Has an annual budget of approximately $10.3 million.

Publications:
Status Report. m.
The Year's Work. a.

Meetings/Conferences:
Annual Meetings: Not held.

Insurance Loss Control Ass'n *(1931)*
c/o NAMIC
P.O. Box 68700
Indianapolis, IN   46268-0700
Tel: (317)875-5250   *Fax:* (317)879-8408
Members: 350 individuals
Staff: 1
Annual Budget: under $10,000
Education Manager: Donna Moore

Historical Note
Established as the Ass'n of Mutual Fire Insurance Engineers, it became the Ass'n of Mutual Insurance Engineers in 1968 and assumed its present name in 1980. ILCA enables loss control

---

professionals to increase their knowledge about fire prevention and protection. Membership: $20/year (individual).

Publications:
ILCA Help Newsletter. q. adv.

Meetings/Conferences:
Annual Meetings: Fall
1999 – Harrisburg, PA/Oct. 18-20

Insurance Marketing Communications Ass'n *(1923)*
9710 N. 80th Place
Scottsdale, AZ   85258-1740
Tel: (602)443-8860   *Fax:* (602)443-1911
E-Mail: imca1@juno.com
Web Site: http://www.imcanet.com
Members: 180 companies
Staff: 1
Annual Budget: $100-250,000
Exec. Director: William T. Hadley

Historical Note
Members represent mutual, stock and direct writer, property and casualty insurance companies. Formerly the Insurance Advertising Conference. Assumed its present name in 1984. Membership: $500/year (company).

Publications:
Membership Roster. a.
Update. bi-m.

Meetings/Conferences:
Annual Meetings: June
1999 – Keystone, CO(Keystone Resort)/June 27-30/250
2000 – Hilton Head, NC/June 25-28/250

Integrated Waste Services Ass'n *(1991)*
1401 H St., N.W., Suite 220
Washington, DC   20005
Tel: (202)467-6240   *Fax:* (202)467-6225
E-Mail: iwsa@ix.netcom.com
Members: 50 companies
Staff: 3
Annual Budget: $1-2,000,000
President: Maria Zannes

Historical Note
IWSA, representing the waste-to-energy industry, promotes integrated solutions to municipal solid waste management problems.

Meetings/Conferences:

Intellectual Property Owners Ass'n *(1972)*
1255 23rd St., N.W., Suite 850
Washington, DC   20037
Tel: (202)466-2396   *Fax:* (202)466-2893
E-Mail: info@ipo.org
Web Site: http://www.ipo.org
Members: 400 institutions and individuals
Staff: 5
Annual Budget: $500-1,000,000
Exec. Director: Herbert C. Wamsley

Historical Note
founded as intellectual property Owners; assumed its current name in 1997. Members are holders of patents, trademarks and copyrights. Primary concern is to strengthen patent, trademark and copyright laws as an increased incentive for innovation and creativity. Membership: $110-240/year (individual); $410-12,000/year (institution).

Publications:
IPO Directory of Members. a.
IPO News and Analysis. irreg.
IPO Washington Brief. semi-m.

Meetings/Conferences:
Annual Meetings: Washington, DC/December

Intelligent Buildings Institute *(1986)*
Historical Note
Address unknown in 1996.

Intelligent Transportation Soc. of America *(1991)*
400 Virginia Ave., S.W., Suite 800
Washington, DC   20024-2730
Tel: (202)484-4847   *Fax:* (202)484-3483
Toll Free: (800)374 - 8472
E-Mail: webmaster@itsa.org
Web Site: http://www.itsa.org
Members: 1,150 organizations
Staff: 50
Annual Budget: $5-10,000,000
Exec. V. President: James Constantino, Ph.D.
Director, Communications: Gerald M. Bastarache
Director, Finance/Administration: Bonnie Jessup
Director, Finance/Administration: Alan Hutchins
Director of Policy & Partnerships: Craig Roberts
Director, Marketing/Member Services: Paul Gannon
Director, Membership Development: Melinda Mount
Director of Operations: Donna Nelson
Director of Administration: Bill Collier

Historical Note
Formerly (1994) Intelligent Vehicle Highway Soc. of America, ITS America fosters the acceleration of the development and deployment of intelligent transporation systems. ITS refers to the application of advanced computer, information and communication technologies to surface transportation. Members include transportation systems manufacturers, academic research centers and public transportation agencies. Composed of 24 state chapters in 17 states. Membership: $500-15,000/year (organization/company).

Publications:
Annual Report. a.
APTS Quarterly. q.
CVO Update. q.
Intermodal News. q.
ITS America News. m.
ITS Quarterly. q.

Proceedings of Annual Meeting. a.
The Standards Quarterly. q.

Meetings/Conferences:
Annual Meetings: Spring
1999 – Washington, DC(Sheraton)/April 19-22
2000 – Boston, MA/May 1-3

Inter American Press Ass'n (1942)
2911 N.W. 39th St.
Miami, FL 33142-5191
Tel: (305)634-2465   *Fax:* (305)635-2272
Web Site: http://www.pdiarios.com/pag4.html
Members: 1,300 publications
Staff: 7
Annual Budget: $1-2,000,000
Exec. Director: Julio E. Munoz

Meetings/Conferences:
1999 – Kingston, Jamaica/March 1-5
1999 – Houston, TX/Oct. 16-20

Inter-America Travel Agents Soc. (1954)
248 S. Allen St.
Philadelphia, PA 19139
Tel: (215)471-5321   *Fax:* (215)471-5473
E-Mail: jussery@compuserve.com
Members: 392 individuals
Annual Budget: $10-25,000
Exec. Director: Joanne Ussery

Historical Note
ITAS members are African-American owned and operated travel agencies and agents. Has no paid officers or full-time staff. Membership: $100-$150/year (individual); $300/year (organization/company).

Publications:
ITAS Newsletter. q. adv.

Meetings/Conferences:
1999 – Jacksonville, FL

Inter-American Bar Ass'n (1940)
1211 Connecticut Ave., N.W., Suite 202
Washington, DC 20036
Tel: (202)393-1217   *Fax:* (202)393-1241
Members: 3,000 individuals
Staff: 3
Annual Budget: $100-250,000
Secretary General: Louis G. Ferrand
Office Manager: Patricia De La Riva

Historical Note
Founded in 1940 by a group of jurists and laywers representing 44 professional organizations throughout 17 nations of the Western hemisphere to fill the need for an unbiased and professional forum for the discussion of comparative law. Membership: $90/year (junior); $120/year (senior); $45/year (student).

Publications:
Newsletter. q.
Proceedings. a.

Meetings/Conferences:
Annual Meetings: Spring

Inter-Industry Conference on Auto Collision Repair (1979)
3701 W. Algonquin Road, Suite 400
Rolling Meadows, IL 60008-3118
Tel: (847)590-1191   *Fax:* (847)590-1215
Toll Free: (800)422 - 7872
Members: 120 individuals
Staff: 68
Annual Budget: $5-10,000,000
Exec. V. President: Thomas M. Mack
Director of Marketing & Field Operations: David Heckeler
Manager, Meetings and Travel: Irene Erickson
Education Foundation Exec. Director: Ron Ray
Director, Operations: Mary Dickson
Manager, Corporate Administration: Margaret Knell
Human Resources Manager: Shirley Pincus
Technical Director: Thomas McGee

Historical Note
I-CAR's mission is to research, develop and deliver technical education programs on collision repair, in order to raise the level of available knowledge and improve communication within the collision repair, insurance and related industries. Members are major auto manufacturers, insurance companies, auto collision repair shops, tool, equipment, and supply manufacturers and related industry and trade associations. Membership: $200/year (individual); $600 (organization/company).

Publications:
I-CAR Advantage. 6/year.
I-CAR Connection. q.

Meetings/Conferences:
Annual Meetings: Summer
1999 – Chicago, IL/July 22-25

Inter-Society Color Council (1931)
11491 Sunset Hills Rd., Suite 301
Reston, VA 20190
Tel: (703)318-0263   *Fax:* (703)318-0514
Members: 860 individuals, 25 organizations
Staff: 2
Annual Budget: $50-100,000
Secretary: Danny C. Rich, Ph.D.

Historical Note
Members are concerned with descriptions and specifications of color and their application to color problems. Established December 29, 1931 at the Museum of Science and Industry in New York City. Membership: $45/year (individual); $100-500/year (organization).

Publications:
ISCC Newsletter. 6 times/year.

Meetings/Conferences:
Annual Meetings: Spring
1999 – St. Louis, MO

Interactive Audio Special Interest Group (1994)
c/o MIDI Manufacturers Ass'n
P.O. Box 3173
La Habra, CA 90632-3171
Tel: (714)736-9774   *Fax:* (714)736-9775
Web Site: http://www.iasig.com
Managing Director: Tom White

Historical Note
Formerly the Ass'n of Interactive Audio and Music Professionals, IA-SIG is an autonomous organization sponsored by the MIDI Manufacturers Ass'n. IA-SIG members are companies and individuals involved in interactive audio development. Membership: $150/year (non-MMA corporate members); $75/year (MMA corporate members); $25/year (individual).

Meetings/Conferences:
1999 – Los Angeles, CA(LACC)

Interactive Digital Software Ass'n (1994)
1775 I St. 420
Washington, DC 20006
Tel: (202)833-4372   *Fax:* (202)833-4431
E-Mail: info@idsa.com
Web Site: http://www.idsa.com
Members: 44 companies
Staff: 10
President: Douglas S. Lowenstein
Senior V. President: Carolyn Rauch
Senior V. President and General Counsel: Gail Markels

Historical Note
IDSA represents interactive entertainment software publishers. Created the autonomous Entertainment Software Rating Board, which reviews product content to promote informed purchasing decisions by entertainment software consumers. Services include: annual industry trade show, anti-piracy program, industry research, and government relations.

Meetings/Conferences:

Interactive Marketing Ass'n
Historical Note
Merged into the Ass'n for Interactive Media in 1997.

Interactive Multimedia Ass'n (1988)
Historical Note
Organization defunct in 1997

Interactive Services Ass'n
Historical Note
Became Internet Alliance in 1998.

Interactive Television Ass'n (1993)
Historical Note
Name changed to Ass'n for Interactive Media (AIM) in 1996.

Intercoiffure America (1933)
540 Robert E. Lee Blvd.
New Orleans, LA 70124
Tel: (504)282-4907   *Fax:* (504)282-5531
E-Mail: johnjay@gs.net
Members: 260 companies
Staff: 3
Annual Budget: $100-250,000
Secretary: Dee Ferina

Historical Note
Formerly (1966) Internat'l des Coiffures de Dames. The North American section of Intercoiffure Mondiale (founded 1912). Members are beauty salon owners. Membership: $650/year.

Meetings/Conferences:
Semi-Annual Meetings: Spring and Fall in New York, NY
1999 – New York, NY/May 24-25
1999 – New York, NY/Oct. 23-25

Intercollegiate Broadcasting System (1940)
367 Windsor Hwy
New Windsor, NY 12553-7900
Tel: (914)565-0003   *Fax:* (914)565-7446
E-Mail: ibshq@aol.com
Web Site: http://www.ibsradio.org
Members: 732 stations
Staff: 8
Annual Budget: $100-250,000
Director, Operations: Fritz Kass

Historical Note
IBS is a nationwide, non-profit association of college and university broadcasting stations. Membership: $95/year.

Publications:
IBS Station Manager's Newsletter. m.
Journal of College Radio. q.

Meetings/Conferences:
Annual Meetings: March
1999 – Washington, DC/March 5-7
2000 – New York, NY/March 10-12

Intercollegiate Men's Choruses, an Internat'l Ass'n of Male Choruses (1915)
229 McCain Auditorium
Kansas State Univ.
Manhattan, KS 66506-4706
Tel: (785)532-5740   *Fax:* (785)532-7004
Members: 70 choruses
Staff: 1
Annual Budget: under $10,000
Exec. Director: Gerald Polich

Historical Note
Formerly (1988) the Intercollegiate Musical Council, The Nat'l Ass'n of Male Choruses. Promotes research, publication and production of quality music for male choruses. Inactive during and after World War II, the Council was revived in 1952; annual seminars have been held since 1954. Membership: $30/year (minimum).

Publications:
Quodlibet (Newsletter). 3/year.

Meetings/Conferences:
Biennial Meetings: odd years with the American Choral Directors Ass'n

Intercollegiate Tennis Ass'n (1956)
P.O. Box 71
Princeton, NJ 08544-0071
Tel: (609)258-6332   *Fax:* (609)258-2935
E-Mail: tennisita@aol.com
Web Site: http://www.tennisonline.com/ita
Members: 2,300 individuals
Staff: 5
Annual Budget: $500-1,000,000
Exec. Director: David A Benjamin
Media Director: Casey Angle
Associate Director: Nina Miller

Historical Note
Formerly (1958) Nat'l Collegiate Tennis Coaches Ass'n and (1992) the Intercollegiate Tennis Coaches Ass'n. The governing body of collegiate tennis administers a number of national championships; administers a comprehensive ranking system for teams, singles and doubles; and awards honors to players and coaches. Membership: $95-170/year (coach); $500/year (corporation); $65/year (associate); $55/year (collegiate parent), $40/year (junior); $200/year (federation).

Publications:
Ass'n News included in Tennis Week.
ITA Coaches Directory. a.
ITA Newsmagazine. q.
ITA Yearbook. a.

Meetings/Conferences:
Annual Meetings: December/300

Interior Design Educators Council (1962)
9202 N. Meridian St., Suite 200
Indianapolis, IN 46260
Tel: (317)816-6261   *Fax:* (317)571-5603
Web Site: http://www.idec.org
Members: 500 individuals
Staff: 2
Annual Budget: $250-500,000
Exec. Director: Leigh Anne Gede

Historical Note
IDEC members are teachers of interior design in colleges and universities in the U.S. and Canada concerned with the advancement of education and research in interior design. IDEC concentrates on the establishment and strengthening of lines of communication among educators, practitioners, professional institutions and other organizations concerned with interior design education. Membership: $250/year (individual).

Publications:
IDEC Record. q.
The Journal of Interior Design Education and Research. semi-a.

Meetings/Conferences:
Annual Meetings: Spring/300
1999 – Clearwater, FL(Doubletree Surfside)
2000 – Calgary, Alberta

Interior Design Soc. (1973)
Historical Note
A division of Nat'l Home Furnishings Ass'n, which provides administrative support.

Interlocking Concrete Pavement Institute (1993)
1444 I St., NW, Suite 700
Washington, DC 20005-2210
Tel: (202)712-9036   *Fax:* (202)408-0285
Toll Free: (800)241 - 3652
E-Mail: ICPI@bostromdc.com
Web Site: http://icpi.org/ICPI
Members: 200 companies
Staff: 5
Annual Budget: $500-1,000,000
Director: Charles McGrath

Historical Note
ICPI members are manufacturers, distributors and users of interlocking concrete pavement. Membership: $500/year (small contractor); $1,500/year (distributor/contractor); $3,000/year (associate); $1,500 to $16,000/year (North American manufacturer); $1,000/year (international manufacturer).

Publications:
ICPI Tech Specs Bulletin. 1-2/year.
Interlocking Concrete Pavement Magazine. q. adv.
Membership Directory. a.
Newsletter. q.

Meetings/Conferences:
Semi-Annual Meetings: Winter and Summer
1999 – Orlando, FL/Feb. 22-25
1999 – Winnipeg, MN, Canada

Intermarket Ass'n of Advertising Agencies (1967)
1605 N. Main St.
Dayton, OH 45405
Tel: (513)278-0681   *Fax:* (513)277-1723
Members: 22 companies
Staff:
Annual Budget: $25-50,000
President: Walter Ohlmann

Historical Note
Founded in 1967 as a network for small to medium agencies, the organization is comprised primarily of shops ranging from $2-30 million in billings. Membership: $1,500/year.

Publications:
Newsletter. m.

Meetings/Conferences:
Semi-Annual Meetings: Winter and Summer/25
1999 – Charleston, SC(Charleston Place)/Feb. 17-21/25
1999 – Seattle, WA

Intermediaries and Reinsurance Underwriters Ass'n
223 Courtyard Dr.
Somerville, NJ   08876-4247
Tel: (908)203-0211   *Fax:* (908)203-0213
E-Mail: mkclancy@trua.com
Web Site: http://www.irua.com
Staff: 3
Exec. Director: Mary K. Clancy

Historical Note
Formerly Intermediary and Reinsurance Underwriters Ass'n (1998). Membership: $2,500/year (company).

Publications:
Journal of Reinsurance. q.

Intermodal Ass'n of North America (1991)
7501 Greenway Center Drive, Suite 720
Greenbelt, MD   20770
Tel: (301)982-3400   *Fax:* (301)982-4815
E-Mail: IANA@intermodal.org
Web Site: http://www.intermodal.org
Members: 700 companies
Staff: 15
Annual Budget: $2-5,000,000
President: Joanne Casey
Dir., Interchange Svcs./Convention Management: Constance Sheffield
Director, Research and Policy: Tina Casgar
Director, Info. Systems: George Mundell

Historical Note
Formed by the merger of the Intermodal Transportation Ass'n with the Intermodal Marketing Ass'n and the Nat'l Railroad Intermodal Ass'n in 1991. Members are motor, rail and water transportation companies and allied services. IANA promotes the benefits of intermodal freight transportation and encourages its growth through innovation and dialogue. Membership: dues vary according to intermodal revenues.

Publications:
IMC Market Activity Report. m.
Intermodal Insights Newsletter. m. adv.
Intermodal Product and Supplier Directory. a. adv.
Membership Handbook. a. adv.
Rail Intermodal Terminal Directory. a. adv.

Meetings/Conferences:
Semi-annual Meetings: Spring and Fall

Intermodal Conference
Historical Note
A conference of the Transportation Intermediaries Ass'n.

Internat'l Academy for Child Brain Development (1958)
8801 Stenton Ave.
Wyndmoor, PA   19038
Tel: (215)233-2050   *Fax:* (215)233-1530
Toll Free: (800)736 - 4663
E-Mail: NHarveyP@AOL.comm
Web Site: http://www.IAHP.ORG
Annual Budget: under $10,000
Secretary: Neil Harvey, Ph.D.

Historical Note
IACBD members are physicians, psychologists and other professionals with an interest in child brain development.

Meetings/Conferences:
Annual Meetings: always last week in November

Internat'l Academy of Behavioral Medicine, Counseling and Psychotherapy (1979)
3208 N. Academy Blvd. #160
Colorado Springs, CO   80917
Tel: (719)597-5959   *Fax:* (719)597-0166
Members: 1000 individuals
Annual Budget: $25-50,000
Exec. Director: Dr. Gary Forrest

Historical Note
Formerly (1988) the American Academy of Behavioral Medicine. Incorporated in the State of Texas as an outgrowth of a regional group of southwestern therapists, the Academy has a membership of psychologists, psychiatrists and others interested in the general field of behavioral medicine and health care. Membership: $60/year.

Publications:
Journal of the AABM. irreg.
Membership Roster. a.
Newsletter. q.

Meetings/Conferences:
1999 – Colorado Springs, CO

Internat'l Academy of Compounding Pharmacists
P.O. Box 1365
Sugar Land, TX   77487
Toll Free: (800)927 - 4227
Web Site: http://www.compassnet.com/ ~ iacp
Exec. Director: Gina Ford

Historical Note
IACP members are state-licensed pharmacists who provide and promote compounding services utilizing their knowledge and skill in the art of preparing, mixing, assembling, packaging, or labeling drugs/devices.

Publications:
Contemporary Compounder Journal. q.

Meetings/Conferences:
1999 – Houston, TX/Jan. 14-16

Internat'l Academy of Gnathology - American Section (1964)
1428 Medical and Dental Building
Seattle, WA   98101
Tel: (206)624-2535   *Fax:* (206)622-2722
Members: 3,000 individuals
President: Olin Loomis, D.D.S.

Historical Note
Members are dentists.

Publications:
Journal of Gnathology. a.

Meetings/Conferences:
Annual Meetings: Biennial Meetings

Internat'l Academy of Health Care Professionals (1984)
70 Glen Cove Road, Suite 209
Roslyn Heights, NY   11577
Tel: (516)621-0620
Members: 40 individuals
Staff: 1
Annual Budget: under $10,000
Chief Staff Officer: Henry H. Reiter, M.D.

Historical Note
IAHCP members are physicians, nurses and other health care professionals.

Publications:
Newsletter. irreg.

Internat'l Academy of Nutrition and Preventive Medicine (1987)
Historical Note
Absorbed by Internat'l and American Ass'ns of Clinical Nutritionists in 1997.

Internat'l Academy of Oral Medicine and Toxicology (1984)
P.O. Box 608531
Orlando, FL   32860-8531
Tel: (407)298-2450   *Fax:* (407)298-3075
Web Site: http://www.iaomt.org
Members: 310 individuals
Staff: 1
Annual Budget: $100-250,000
Exec. Director: Michael F. Ziff, D.D.S.
Meetings Chair: Janet Stopka, D.D.S.
Education Chair: David W. Regiani, D.D.S.
Treasurer: S.W. Eccles, D.D.S.
Legal Counsel: Aaron J. Rynd, Ph.D.
Membership Chair: Ronald M. Dressler, D.D.S.

Historical Note
IAOMT members are dentists and other medical professionals with an interest in the biocompatibility of materials. Membership: $300 (initial); $22y/year (renewal).

Publications:
Bio-Probe Newsletter. bi-m.
In Vivo Newsletter. q.
Membership Directory.

Meetings/Conferences:
1999 – Atlanta, GA/Oct. 8-9

Internat'l Academy of Pathology (1906)
Historical Note
Address unknown in 1998.

Internat'l Academy of Podiatric Medicine (1994)
1324 State St. Suite J-221
P.O. Box 39
Santa Barbara, CA   93101
Tel: (805)693-9137   *Fax:* (805)693-9758
Toll Free: (800)367 - 4276
Exec. Director: Judith A. Baerg

Historical Note
Membership: $250/year (fellow); $150/year (associate).

Internat'l Academy of Sports Vision (1984)
200 S. Progress Ave.
Harrisburg, PA   17109
Tel: (717)652-8080   *Fax:* (717)652-8878
E-Mail: nasv@mindspring.com
Web Site: http://www.iasv.net
Members: 1000 individuals
Staff: 5
Annual Budget: $100-250,000
Exec. Director: Dr. A.I. Garner
Meetings & Conventions: Dorrie Clark

Historical Note
Founded as Nat'l Academy of Sports Vision; assumed its current name in 1992. Members are health professionals, physical education professionals, eyewear manufacturers, and others involved in comprehensive vision care for amateur and professional athletes of all ages and abilities in every sports field. Membership: $125/year (individual), $200/year (company).

Publications:
Journal. semi-a.
Membership Directory. a.
SportsVision Magazine. q. adv.
Update. q.

Meetings/Conferences:
1999 – San Jose, CA/May 14-16

Internat'l Academy of Trial Lawyers (1954)
5041 Cedar Lake Rd., Suite 204
Minneapolis, MN   55416
Tel: (612)546-2364   *Fax:* (612)545-6073
E-Mail: wilkeson@compuserve.com
Members: 600 individuals
Staff: 2
Annual Budget: $500-1,000,000
Exec. Director: Linda Wilkerson

Historical Note
Members are defense and plaintiff attorneys who have had a minimum of 12 years of trial or appellate practice. The Academy works for the enhancement and protection of the jury system and the enhancement of integrity within the profession. Membership: $600/year (individual).

Publications:
Dean's Address. a.
IATL Bulletin. 3/year.
Student Advocacy Report. a.

Meetings/Conferences:
Annual Meetings: Spring/200
1999 – West Palm Beach, FL/March 24-28

Internat'l Academy of Twirling Teachers (1971)
Historical Note
Organization defunct in 1998.

Internat'l Advertising Ass'n (1938)
521 Fifth Ave., Suite 1807
New York, NY   10175
Tel: (212)557-1133   *Fax:* (212)983-0455
E-Mail: iaaglobal@worldnet.att.net
Web Site: http://www.iaaglobal.org
Members: 5,100 individuals, 97 companies, 63 orgs, 61 chapters
Staff: 8
Annual Budget: $1-2,000,000
Director General: Norman Vale
Mgr., Communications/Prof. Development: Pamela Yaeger
Exec. Director: Richard M. Corner
Director, Membership Services: Marie J. Scotti

Historical Note
Formerly (1954) Export Advertising Ass'n. IAA is the only global partnership of advertisers, agencies, the media, and related service providers. Its principal objectives are to protect freedom of commercial speech and consumer choice, to promote the value of advertising and to encourage self-regulation. Membership: $175/year, plus initiation fee of $50 and local chapter dues where applicable (individual), $7,000/year, plus initiation fee of $5,000 (corporate); $350/year (organization).

Publications:
IAA Annual Report and Membership Directory. a. adv.
IAA Perspectives. bi-m.
IAA World News: Newsletter for Int'l Marketing Executives. q.

Meetings/Conferences:
Annual Meetings: even years
2000 – London, England

Internat'l Affiliation of Independent Accounting Firms (1978)
9200 South Dadeland Blvd., Suite 510
Miami, FL   33156-2703
Tel: (305)670-0580   *Fax:* (305)670-3818
E-Mail: iaintl@accountants.org
Web Site: http://www.accountants.org
Members: 135 companies
Staff: 4
Annual Budget: $500-1,000,000
Exec. Director: Arthur D. Goessel, CAE

Historical Note
Provides services to a global network of independent accounting firms. Maintains an educational foundation that administers scholarship grants to students seeking careers in accounting. Membership: $3,000/yr (average); $7,000/yr (maximum).

Publications:
Internat'l Tax Summary. a.
Membership Directory. a.
Newsletter. m.
Talent Bank and Resource Guide. a.

Meetings/Conferences:
Annual Meetings: May
1999 – Brussels, Belgium
2000 – Buenos Aires, Argentina

Internat'l Agricultural Aviation Foundation (1978)
P.O. Box 1607
Mount Vernon, WA   98273
E-Mail: AGPILOT@CNW.com
Members: 4,781 individuals
Staff: 5
Annual Budget: $1-2,000,000
Exec. Director: Tom J. Wood

Historical Note
Pilots and aircraft owners licensed by the FAA as agricultural aviators (crop dusters). Membership: $119/year.

Publications:
AG-Pilot Internat'l Magazine. m. adv.
North American Applicator Journal.

Meetings/Conferences:
Annual Meetings: December 8-11

Internat'l Air Cargo Ass'n
3111 SW 27th Ave.
P.O. Box 330669
Coconut Grove, FL   33233-0669
Tel: (305)443-9696   *Fax:* (305)443-9698
E-Mail: secgen@tiaca.org
Web Site: http://www.tiaca.org

Secretary General: Garth H. Davies
Director, Public Relations: Connie Crowthor
Director, Meetings and Exhibition: Arthur L. Werdy
Director, Membership: Richard Jones

Historical Note
TIACA members are individuals and companies in the air logistics industry with an interest in global commerce through air distribution. Membership:$250/year (individual); $1,000/year (company).

Publications:
TIACA Times. q.

Meetings/Conferences:
1999 – Los Angeles, CA
2000 – Washington, DC(Marriott Wardman Park)

Internat'l Alliance for Women in Music *(1976)*
George Washington U., Dept. of Music
801 22nd St., N.W., Suite B-144
Washington, DC 20052-2515
Tel: (202)994-6338   *Fax:* (202)994-9038
E-Mail: sasha@gwis2.circ.gwu.edu
Web Site: http://music.acu.edu/www/iawm/home.hml
Members: 300 individuals
Staff: 1
Annual Budget: under $10,000
Administrator: Sasha D. Kennison

Historical Note
Formerly (1995) American Women Composers. Members are women composers, performers, musicologists, and their supporters. Maintains a music library and holds various symposia and concerts throughout the year. The organization was formed to establish a network of support and encouragement for female musicians; to gain status and recognition for female musicians; to offer financial assistance for female efforts in the compositional arena; and to provide a forum for the interchange of ideas through workshops, meetings, and performances. Membership: $20/year (senior/student); $40/year (individual); $50/year (organization/company); $75/year (board affiliate).

Publications:
IAWM Journal. q.
News/Updates. bi-a.
Women and Music: A Journal of Gender and Culture.

Internat'l Alliance of Theatrical Stage Employees and Moving Picture Technicians of the U.S. and Canada *(1893)*
1515 Broadway, Suite 601
New York, NY 10036
Tel: (212)730-1770   *Fax:* (212)921-7699
Web Site: http://www.iatse.lm.com
Members: 70,000 individuals
Staff: 30
Annual Budget: $2-5,000,000
President: Thomas Short

Historical Note
Established in New York City on July 20, 1893 as the Nat'l Alliance of Theatrical Stage Employees of the United States and chartered by the American Federation of Labor in 1894. In 1899, with the acceptance of two Canadian locals, the words "and Canada" were added, and in 1902 "International" was subsituted for "National." When the union was granted jurisdiction over motion picture projectionists in 1914, the present name was adopted.

Publications:
The Official Bulletin. q.

Meetings/Conferences:
Biennial Meetings: odd years.
1999 – Puerto Rico

Internat'l Alliance: An Ass'n of Executive and Professional Women, The *(1980)*
P.O. Box 20236
Baltimore, MD 21284
Tel: (410)472-4221   *Fax:* (410)472-2920
E-Mail: info@t-i-a.com
Web Site: http://www.t-i-a.com
Members: 7,000 individuals
Staff: 2
Annual Budget: $100-250,000
Exec. V. President: Marian E. Goetze

Historical Note
Alliance members are executive and professional women. Membership: $125/year, plus $25 initiation fee (individual); $400-2,000/year (group).

Publications:
Alliance Newsletter. bi-m. adv.
Membership Directory. a.

Meetings/Conferences:
1999 – October

Internat'l Allied Printing Trades Ass'n *(1909)*
1900 L St., N.W., 8th Floor
Washington, DC 20036
Tel: (202)462-1400
Members: 2 labor unions
Secretary-Treasurer: Gerald Deneau

Historical Note
Exercises jurisdiction throughout the United States and Canada in regard to the Allied Printing Trades Label. Member unions are the Graphic Communications Internat'l Union and the Printing, Publishing & Media Workers Sector of the C.W.A. Adopted and owned by the Association, the label designates the products of the labor of its members.

Internat'l Aloe Science Council *(1981)*
PO Box 141837
Irving, TX 75014-1837
Tel: (972)258-8772   *Fax:* (972)258-8777

E-Mail: iasc@airmail.net
Web Site: http://www.iasc.org
Members: 175 individuals
Staff: 2
Annual Budget: $100-250,000
Managing Director: Gene Hale

Historical Note
Formerly known as the Nat'l Aloe Science Council (1990). Membership: $300-500/year (organization/company).

Publications:
Inside Aloe. 8/year. adv.

Meetings/Conferences:
Annual Meetings: Annual Meetings in September

Internat'l American Albino Ass'n *(1936)*
Historical Note
The Internat'l American Albino Ass'n does business and is listed as the American White/American Creme Horse Registry (AWACHR).

Internat'l Analgesia Soc.
Historical Note
Address unknown in 1996.

Internat'l and American Ass'ns of Clinical Nutritionists *(1983)*
16775 Addison Road #102
Dallas, TX 75248
Tel: (972)407-9089   *Fax:* (972)250-0233
Web Site: http://www.iaacn.org
Staff: 5
Annual Budget: $250-500,000
Exec. Secretary: Winna Henry, CCN
Associate Exec.: James Robert Henry
Continuing Education Officer: Janice Mugo
Finance Officer: Linda McElvain
Records Officer: Jane Volkmer

Historical Note
IAACN represents clinical nutritionists in all of the licensed health care fields. Merged with Internat'l Academy of Nutrition and Preventive Medicine in 1997. Sponsors the Certified Clinical Nutritionist (CCN) designation through the Clinical Nutrition Certification Board and Columbia Assessment Services, Inc. Five levels of membership. Professional: $295/year (individual).

Publications:
IAACN Insight. q. adv.
Journal of Applied Nutrition. q. adv.
Your Health Newsletter. bi-m. adv.

Meetings/Conferences:
Annual Meetings: Fall/750
1999 – Orlando, FL(Marriott World Center)/Sept. 2-5/500
2000 – Las Vegas, NV
2001 – Orlando, FL(Marriott World Center)/Aug. 30-Sept. 2/600

Internat'l Anesthesia Research Soc. *(1922)*
2 Summit Park Dr., Suite 140
Cleveland, OH 44131-2553
Tel: (216)642-1124   *Fax:* (216)642-1127
E-Mail: iarshq@iars.org
Web Site: www.iars.org
Members: 16,000 individuals
Staff: 6
Exec. Director: Anne F. Maggiore

Publications:
Anesthesia & Analgesia. m. adv.

Meetings/Conferences:
Annual Meetings: Spring
1999 – Los Angeles, CA(Century Plaza)/March 12-16
2000 – Honolulu, HI(Hilton Hawaiian Village)/March 10-14
2001 – Ft. Lauderdale, FL/March 16-20
2002 – San Diego, CA(Marriott)/March 16-20

Internat'l Animated Film Soc. *(1972)*
725 S. Victory
Burbank, CA 91502
Tel: (818)842-8330   *Fax:* (818)842-5645
E-Mail: asifa@earthlink.net
Web Site: http://www.home.earthlink.com/asifa
Members: 1,200 individuals
Staff: 2
Annual Budget: $250-500,000
President: Antran Manoogian

Historical Note
U.S. chapter of the international organization. ASIFA members are professional animators and others with an interest in film animation. Sponsors programs for film preservation and exhibition. Membership: $45/year (individual); $20/year (student).

Publications:
Annie Awards Annual Program Book. a. adv.
Calendar of Animation. m. adv.
Inbetweener. q. adv.

Internat'l Apple Institute
Historical Note
Became (1996) U.S. Apple Ass'n.

Internat'l Arabian Horse Ass'n *(1950)*
10805 E. Bethany Dr.
Aurora, CO 80014
Tel: (303)696-4500   *Fax:* (303)696-4599
E-Mail: iaha.laha.com
Web Site: iaha.com
Members: 30,000 individuals
Staff: 70
Annual Budget: $5-10,000,000
Exec. V. President: Carol Alm
Communications Manager: Susan Bavaria
Manager, Membership & Youth: Lorie Liddicoat

Historical Note
Promotes the Arabian breed, and registers Half-Arabians and Anglo-Arabians. Maintains show records of Arabian horse placings, produces films and videotapes, compiles statistics, and sponsors national competitions for adult and youth competitors. Membership: $80/year (regular); $40/year (affiliate); $15/year (youth); $50/year (farm/ranch); $1,000 (lifetime membership).

Publications:
International Arabian Horse. 8/year.

Meetings/Conferences:
Annual Meetings: November-December/800

Internat'l Arthroscopy Ass'n *(1974)*
Historical Note
Merged with Internat'l Soc. of the Knee to form Internat'l Soc. of Arthroscopy, Knee Surgery, and Orthopaedic Sports Medicine in 1995.

Internat'l Ass'n Colon Hydro Therapy *(1989)*
P.O. BOX 461285
San Antonio, TX 78246-1285
Tel: (210)366-2888   *Fax:* (210)366-2999
E-Mail: iact@healthy.net
Web Site: http://www.2-act.org
Annual Budget: $100-250,000
President: William T. Tiller, N.D.

Historical Note
Formerly (1995) the American Colon Therapy Ass'n. IACT members are colon hygiene therapists and other health care professionals. Educational certification is provided by the group. Membership: $150.

Publications:
IACT Membership Directory. a.
IACT Newsletter. q. adv.

Meetings/Conferences:
Annual Meetings: Colorado Springs, CO/May
1999 – Virginia Beach, VA(Doubletree)/May 13-16/400

Internat'l Ass'n for Aquatic Animal Medicine *(1969)*
Historical Note
Address unknown in 1997.

Internat'l Ass'n for Computer Information Systems *(1960)*
College of Business
Oklahoma State Univ.
Stillwater, OK 74078
Tel: (405)744-8632
E-Mail: dnord@okway.okstate.edu
Members: 600 individuals, 200 organizations
Annual Budget: $25-50,000
Managing Director: Dr. G. Daryl Nord

Historical Note
Formerly (1987) Soc. for Data Educators and (1990) Ass'n for Computer Educators. IACIS members are individuals with a particular interest in all levels computers. Membership: $50/year (individuals); $75/year (institutions).

Publications:
Journal of Computer Information Systems. q. adv.

Meetings/Conferences:
Annual Meetings: September-October

Internat'l Ass'n for Computer Systems Security *(1981)*
6 Swarthmore Lane
Dix Hills, NY 11746
Tel: (516)499-1616   *Fax:* (516)462-9178
E-Mail: iacssja@aol.com
Web Site: http://www.iacss.com
Members: 800 individuals
Staff: 16
Annual Budget: $100-250,000
President: Robert J. Wilk

Historical Note
Members are organizations and individuals with an interest in the security of computer information systems. Certifies individuals as Computer Systems Security Professionals.

Publications:
Computer Security Guidebook.
Computer Security Workbook.
Computer Systems Security Newsletter. q.
Proceedings Region 1 IACSS Conference. a.
Proceedings Region 2 IACSS Conference. a.
Security and Control of your PC/Micro Network.

Meetings/Conferences:
Annual Meetings: International Seminars 10/yr., Workshops, Consulting Work

Internat'l Ass'n for Continuing Education and Training *(1968)*
1200 19th St., N.W., Suite 300
Washington, DC 20036-2422
Tel: (202)857-1122   *Fax:* (202)223-4579
Web Site: www.iacet.org
Members: 720 individuals
Staff: 3
Annual Budget: $100-250,000
Exec. Director: Drew W. Allbritten
Administrator: Rachel Hunter
Membership Coordinator: Elizabeth Longstreet

Historical Note
Formerly (1990) the Council on the Continuing Education Unit. Members are educational institutions, hospitals, professional societies and others providing continuing education. Seeks to standardize and improve the quality of continuing education and training.

Publications:
IACET Reporter Newsletter. q.
Membership Directory. a.

Research Papers. a.

Meetings/Conferences:
1999 – Fort Lauderdale, Florida/Oct. 4-6

Internat'l Ass'n for Dental Research (1920)

Historical Note
See American Ass'n for Dental Research.

Internat'l Ass'n for Exposition Management (1928)
P.O. Box 802425
Dallas, TX 75380-2425
Tel: (972)458-8002 *Fax:* (972)458-8119
E-Mail: 73363.1264@compuserve.com
Web Site: http://www.iaem.org
Members: 3,500 individuals
Staff: 17
Annual Budget: $1-2,000,000
President: Steven G. Hacker, CAE
Director of Communications/Marketing: Keith J. Vincent
Director, Communications: Renee Berres
Director, Conventions and Expositions: Vicki Simmons
Education Coordinator: Marcia Wisocki
Sr. V. President: John Swinburn, CAE
Director, Chapter Relations and Membership: Cathy Breden, CAE, CMP
Exec. Director: Dana Murphy, CAE
Editorial Director: Julie Nelson

Historical Note
Originated in Cleveland in June 1928 and incorporated in 1947 as the Nat'l Ass'n of Exhibit Managers; became the Nat'l Ass'n of Exposition Managers in 1969; and adopted its present name in 1992. Members are managers of shows, exhibits and expositions; associate members are industry suppliers. Awards the designation CEM (Certified in Exposition Management). Member of the Center for Exhibition Industry Research. IAEM Services, Inc. is a for-profit subsidiary, offering publications and other services. Operates a fax-on-demand service: (214) 353-6140. Membership: $215/year (exposition manager); $325/year (associate).

Publications:
IAEM World Wide Directory of Members.

Meetings/Conferences:
Semi-Annual Meetings: June and December
1999 – Chicago, IL/June 15-18
1999 – Eastern U.S./Nov. 30-Dec. 3
2000 – San Diego, CA/Dec. 5-8
2000 – Eastern U.S.
2001 – Eastern U.S.
2001 – Chicago, IL/Dec. 4-7
2002 – Central U.S.
2002 – Eastern U.S.
2003 – Eastern U.S.
2003 – Western U.S.
2004 – Western U.S. Summer
2004 – Central U.S.
2005 – Central U.S.
2005 – Eastern U.S.
2005 – Western U.S.
2006 – Eastern U.S.

Internat'l Ass'n for Financial Planning (1969)
5775 Glenridge Drive, N.E., Suite B-300
Atlanta, GA 30328-5364
Tel: (404)845-0011 *Fax:* (404)845-3660
Toll Free: (800)945 - 4237
E-Mail: info@iafp.org
Web Site: http://www.iafp.org
Members: 17,000 individuals
Staff: 30
Annual Budget: $5-10,000,000
Exec. Director: Janet G. McCallen, CAE
Director, Communications: Paul Ryan
Director, Corp/Government Affairs: Dale E. Brown, CAE
Govt. Affairs Manager: Michael Herndon
Education/Program Development: Bud Elsea
Director, Administration: Ricardo D. Sanchez
Director, Membership: Sean Walters

Historical Note
Established in Denver in 1969. Members work with individuals in the areas of personal and/or corporate financial advice or provide services to those who work directly with individuals. Membership includes accountants, financial planners, lawyers, bankers, stockbrokers, insurance professionals and others involved in the financial services industry. Membership: $225/year (individual), $5,000/year (company).

Publications:
Chapter Leaders Resource. 8/year.
Financial Planning.
IAFP Leadership Letter.
Planning Matters. m.
Referral Notes. 10/year.

Meetings/Conferences:
Annual Meetings: Fall/2,000
1999 – San Antonio, TX/Oct. 23-26

Internat'l Ass'n for Healthcare Security and Safety (1968)
P.O. Box 637
Lombard, IL 60148
Tel: (630)953-0990 *Fax:* (630)950-1786
Members: 1,700 individuals
Staff: 5
Annual Budget: $250-500,000
President: Edward Flores

Historical Note
Formerly (1991) Internat'l Ass'n for Hospital Security. An affiliate of the American Hospital Association. Membership: $75/year.

Publications:
IAHSS Newsletter. q.
Journal of Healthcare Protection Management. bi-a.

Meetings/Conferences:
1999 – Portland, ME(Marriott Sable Oaks)/June 27-20
2000 – Chicago, IL, British Columbia
2001 – Vancouver, British Columbia

Internat'l Ass'n for Human Resource Information Management (1978)
401 N. Michigan Ave.
Chicago, IL 60611-4255
Tel: (312)321-5141 *Fax:* (312)245-1080
E-Mail: moreinfo@ihrim.org
Web Site: http://www.ihrim.org
Members: 6,000 individuals
Staff: 13
Annual Budget: $2-5,000,000
Exec. Director: Bernadette Patton
Marketing/Communications Manager: Stephanie Crombie

Historical Note
Formerly the Ass'n of Human Resource System Professionals (HRSP), HRSP unified with its Canadian counterpart (CHRSP) in 1996 and assumed its current name. IHRIM members are human resource or information systems professionals concerned with the development, maintenance and operation of human resource information and management systems. Membership: $195/year (individual).

Publications:
IHRIM Journal. q.
IHRIM Link. bi-m. adv.

Meetings/Conferences:
Annual Meetings: Spring
1999 – Salt Lake City, UT(Salt Palace)/June 13-16
2000 – Boston, MA/June 18-21

Internat'l Ass'n for Hydrogen Energy (1975)
Box 248266
Coral Gables, FL 33124
Tel: (305)284-4666 *Fax:* (305)284-4792
Members: 2,600 individuals
Staff: 2
Annual Budget: $100-250,000
President: T. Nejat Veziroglu, Ph.D.

Historical Note
Established at the Hydrogen Economy Miami Energy Conference in Miami in March 1974 and incorporated in Florida in 1975. Members, hailing from 86 countries, are scientists and engineers professionally involved in the development of hydrogen energy. Membership: $80/year (individual); $65/year (associate); $550/year (institution).

Publications:
Conference Proceedings. a.
International Journal of Hydrogen Energy. m. adv.

Meetings/Conferences:
Annual Meetings: Buenos Aires, Argentina/June
2000 – Beijing, China
2002 – Montreal, Canada

Internat'l Ass'n for Identification (1915)
2535 Pilot Knob, Suite 117
Mendota Heights, MN 55120-1120
E-Mail: IAISECTY@aol.com
Members: 4,000 individuals
Staff: 4
Annual Budget: $250-500,000
Exec. Secretary: Joseph P. Polski
Education Program Planner: Curt Shane

Historical Note
Organized in 1915 in Oakland, CA as the Internat'l Ass'n for Criminal Identification, it assumed its present name in 1920. Absorbed the Internat'l Ass'n for Voice Identification in 1981. Membership consists of persons engaged in forensic identification, investigation and scientific examination of physical evidence. IAI promotes research in forensic sciences and is responsible for six international certification programs for Latent Print Examiners, Voice Print Examiners, Crime Scene Technicians, Bloodstain Pattern Analysis, Footwear and Tiretrack Examination and Forensic Art. Membership: $60/year.

Publications:
I. A. adv.
Journal of Forensic Identification. bi-m.

Meetings/Conferences:
Annual Meetings: Summer
1999 – Milwaukee, WI(Hilton)/July 11-17/1000
2000 – Charleston, WV(Embassy Suites)/July 23-29/1000
2001 – Miami, FL(Doral Resort)/July 22-28/1200

Internat'l Ass'n for Impact Assessment (1980)
c/o Inst. for Business-Industry Dev.
North Dakota State Univ.
Fargo, ND 58105-5256
Tel: (701)231-1006 *Fax:* (701)231-1007
E-Mail: rhamm@ndsuext.nodak.edu
Web Site: http://IAIA.ext.NoDak.edu/IAIA/
Members: 1,400 individuals
Staff: 3
Annual Budget: $50-100,000
Exec. Director: Rita Hamm

Historical Note
Founded and chartered in Atlanta, GA, IAIA is a professional society of those who assess environmental, social and technological impact for both the private and public sectors. Members are corporate planners and managers, public interest advocates, government planners and administrators, private consultants and policy analysts, and university teachers and their students. Membership: $70/year (individual), $175/year (subscriber), $1250/year (institution).

Publications:
IAIA Newsletter. q.
Impact Assessment & Project Appraisal. q. adv.

Meetings/Conferences:
1999 – Glasgow, Scotland(Univ. of Strathclyde)/June 15-19/500
2000 – Hong Kong

Internat'l Ass'n for Insurance Law - United States Chapter (1963)
c/o Chase Communications
P.O. Box 9001
Mt. Vernon, NY 10552
Tel: (914)699-2020 *Fax:* (914)699-2025
Members: 700 individuals
Annual Budget: $50-100,000
V. President: Stephen C. Acunto

Historical Note
The national affiliate of the Association Internationale de Droit des Assurances (AIDA), U.S. Chapter members are attorneys, professors, regulators and others who are interested in interantional or comparative aspects of insurance law and regulation. In addition to supporting the work of AIDA on an international basis, the U.S. Chapter sponsors seminars on regulation, publishes a regular bulletin of the international working group on pollution, publishes a newsletter, and serves as a vehicle through which its members can become involved with international projects or make contact with fellow professionals overseas. Membership: $100/year (individual).

Publications:
AIDA-US Newsletter. q.

Meetings/Conferences:

Internat'l Ass'n for Learning Laboratories (1965)
Humanities Resource Ctr., 1600 Grand Ave
Macalester College
St. Paul, MN 55105
Tel: (651)696-6336 *Fax:* (651)696-6336
Web Site: http://www.polyglot.lss.wisc.edu/IALL/
Members: 700 individuals
Staff: 1
Annual Budget: under $10,000
Business Manager: Thomas Browne

Historical Note
Members are involved in the administration or operation of machine aided learning facilities and foreign language programs. Founded as the Nat'l Ass'n of Language Laboratory Directors, it became the Nat'l Ass'n Learning Lab Directors before assuming its present name in 1982. Affiliated with the American Council on the Teaching of Foreign Languages and the Ass'n for Educational Communications and Technology. Membership: $40/year.

Publications:
IALL Journal of Language Learning Technologies. 3/year.
Membership Directory. a.

Meetings/Conferences:
1999 – College Park, MD(Univ. of MD)/June 22-26

Internat'l Ass'n for Mathematical Geology (1968)
c/o Exxon Production Research Co.
P.O. Box 2189
Houston, TX 77252-2189
Tel: (713)431-6546 *Fax:* (713)431-6336
Members: 500 individuals
Annual Budget: $50-100,000
Secretary-General: Thomas A. Jones

Historical Note
Founded at the XXIII Internat'l Geological Congress, Prague, Czechoslovakia in 1968. Professional geologists, mathematicians and others interested in the application and use of mathematics in geological research and technology. Affiliated with the Internat'l Statistical Institute and the Internat'l Union of Geological Sciences. Has no paid officers or full-time staff.

Publications:
Computers & Geosciences. 10/year.
Mathematical Geology. 8/year.
Nonrenewable Resources. q.
Studies in Mathematical Geology Series.

Meetings/Conferences:
1999 – Trondheim, Norway(University of Technology)/Aug. 15-19/250
2000 – Rio De Janeiro

Internat'l Ass'n for Modular Exhibitry (1987)
155 West St., Unit 3
Wilmington, MA 01887-3064
Tel: (978)988-1100
Members: 47 companies
Annual Budget: $100-250,000
Exec. Director: Irving Sacks

Historical Note
IAME members are companies with an interest in promoting the use of modular exhibits for trade shows and museums.

Publications:
Newsletter. q.

Internat'l Ass'n for Near Death Studies (1981)
P.O. Box 502
East Windsor Hill, CT 06028
Tel: (860)644-5216 *Fax:* (860)644-5759
Web Site: http://www.iands.org
Members: 1,200 individuals
Staff: 1
Exec. Director: Janet Scollo

Historical Note
IANDS promotes research into the experiences of persons claiming to have had an out-of-body experience related to traumatic injury or medical emergency. Membership: $45/year (general), $80/year (researcher), $35/year (senior/student).

Publications:
Journal of Near-Death Studies. q.
Vital Signs. q.

Meetings/Conferences:
Annual Meetings: Summer

Internat'l Ass'n for Orthodontics *(1961)*
1100 Lake St., Suite 240
Oak Park, IL 60301-1035
Tel: (708)445-0320   *Fax:* (708)445-0321
E-Mail: iaode.dent@syslink.mcs.com
Web Site: http://www.iaoortho.com
Members: 2,100 individuals
Staff: 3
Annual Budget: $500-1,000,000
Exec. Director: Detlef B. Moore

Historical Note
*Formerly Internat'l Academy of Orthodontics. IAO trains general
and pediatric dentists in the practice of orthodontics. Membership:
$125/year.*

Publications:
IAO Straight Talk. m.
Membership Directory. a.
Orthodontic Suppliers Directory. a.
The Journal of General Orthodontics. q. adv.

Meetings/Conferences:
Annual Meetings: Fall/500-600
1999 – Orlando, FL(Contemporary Resort)/April 14-18

Internat'l Ass'n for Oxygen Therapy *(1898)*
P.O. Box 1360
Priest River, ID 83856
Tel: (208)448-2504   *Fax:* (208)448-2657
Toll Free: (800)909 - 7855
E-Mail: oxytherapies@nidunk.com
Web Site: http://www.oxytherapies.com
Members: 3,500 individuals
Staff: 15
Annual Budget: $500-1,000,000
Secretary-Treasurer: Nicole Sacks

Historical Note
*Founded as Institute for Oxygen Therapy. IAOT members are
oxydation therapists and other interested parties. Membership:
$50/year (individual).*

Publications:
Oxydation News Newsletter. q. adv.

Meetings/Conferences:
1999 – Las Vegas, NV
2000 – Priest Lake, ID(Hills Resort)

Internat'l Ass'n for Philosophy and Literature *(1976)*
Historical Note
Address unknown in 1997.

Internat'l Ass'n for Philosophy of Law and Social Philosophy - American Section *(1963)*
2530 Dole St.
College of Philosophy, Univ. of Hawaii
Honolulu, HI 96822-2383
Tel: (808)956-9228   *Fax:* (808)956-8954
Members: 370 individuals
Annual Budget: under $10,000
Exec. Director: Ken Kipnis

Historical Note
*AMINTAPHIL members are professors of philosophy, law and the
social sciences in the United States and Canada. Membership:
$15/year (individual).*

Publications:
Conference Proceedings. bien.
Newsletter. q.

Internat'l Ass'n for the Study of Organized Crime *(1984)*
Univ. of IL at Chicago, OICJ (M/C 777)
Suite 500, 1033 W. Van Buren St.
Chicago, IL 60607-2919
Tel: (312)996-0159   *Fax:* (312)413-0458
E-Mail: U62206@UICVM
Members: 550 individuals
Annual Budget: under $10,000

Historical Note
*Researchers, investigators, and educators interested in the study of
organized crime. Has no paid staff. Membership: $25/year
(individual); $35/year (organization).*

Publications:
Criminal Organizations Newsletter. q. adv.

Meetings/Conferences:
Annual Meetings: in conjunction with American Criminal Justice
     Soc./October-November

Internat'l Ass'n for the Study of Pain *(1973)*
909 NE 43rd St., Suite 306
Seattle, WA 98105-6020
Tel: (206)547-6409   *Fax:* (206)547-1703
E-Mail: IASP@locke.hs.washington.edu
Web Site: www.halcyon.com/iasp
Members: 6,300 individuals, 25 companies
Staff: 10
Annual Budget: $1-2,000,000
Exec. Officer: Louisa E. Jones

Historical Note
*Founded in Seattle, Washington, IASP was incorporated in
Washington, DC in 1974. Members are scientists, physicians and
other health professionals actively engaged in pain research and
those who have a special interest in diagnosis and treatment of pain
syndromes. Membership: $110-175/year (individual).*

Publications:
Directory of Members. a.
IASP Newsletter. bi-m.
Pain. m. adv.
Pain: Clinical Updates. 3/year.

Meetings/Conferences:
1999 – Vienna, Austria(Austria CTR)/Aug. 22-27/3500
2002 – San Diego, CA(San Diego Conv. Cntr.)/Aug. 17-22

Internat'l Ass'n of Addictions and Offender Counselors *(1974)*
c/o American Counseling Ass'n
5999 Stevenson Ave.
Alexandria, VA 22304
Tel: (336)676-1139   *Fax:* (336)676-0442
Toll Free: (800)364 - 2262
Members: 3,000 individuals
Staff: 2
Annual Budget: $25-50,000
President: Sandra Ritter

Historical Note
*Formerly (1990) Public Offenders Counselors Ass'n. IAAOC
advocates the development of effective counseling and rehabilitation
programs for people with substance abuse problems, other
addictions and adult and/or juvenile public offenders. A division of
the American Counseling Ass'n. Membership: $35/year
(professional); $17.50/year (student/retired).*

Publications:
IAAOC Newsletter. bi-m. adv.
Journal of Addictions & Offender Counseling. semi-a. adv.

Meetings/Conferences:
Annual Meetings: Spring, with the American Counseling Ass'n
1999 – San Diego, CA
2000 – Washington, DC/March 22-25

Internat'l Ass'n of Administrative Professionals *(1942)*
10502 NW Ambassador Drive
P.O. Box 20404
Kansas City, MO 64195-0404
Tel: (816)891-6600   *Fax:* (816)891-9118
E-Mail: twatters@iaap-hq.org
Web Site: iaap-hq.org
Members: 40,000 individuals
Staff: 27
Annual Budget: $2-5,000,000
Exec. Director: Thomas A. Watters, CAE
Convention Manager: Dale Shuter
Manager, Education and Professional Dev.: Susan Fenner, Ph.D.
Accounting Manager: Suzanne Tuff
Manager, Membership Services: Robin Parrish
Manager, Information Systems: Fred Frederick
Admin. Asst. to Exec. Director: Krista Cunningham

Historical Note
*Formerly (1998) Professional Secretaries Internat'l. Formerly
(1901) Nat'l Secretaries Ass'n (Internat'l). Incorporated in the State
of Missouri, PSI is a non-profit professional association sponsoring
the Institute for Certifying Secretaries which awards the designation
"Certified Professional Secretary" (CPS). PSI services include the
PSI Research and Educational Foundation, a nonprofit trust which
coordinates and authorizes research, distributes findings and
provides public instruction related to the secretarial profession.
Membership: $15 initial fee; $45/year renewal.*

Publications:
Office Pro. 9/yr. adv.

Meetings/Conferences:
Annual Meetings: Summer/1,700
1999 – Portland, OR(Convention Center)/July 25-28
2000 – Chicago, IL(Hilton Towers)/July 23-26
2001 – Toronto, Ontario, Canada(Sheraton Centre
     Hotel)/July 15-18
2002 – Nashville, TN(Opryland Hotel)/July 21-24
2003 – Albuquerque, NM(Convention Center)/July 20-23

Internat'l Ass'n of Airport Duty Free Stores *(1970)*
1200 19th St., N.W., Suite 300
Washington, DC 20036-2422
Tel: (202)857-1184   *Fax:* (202)429-5154
E-Mail: IAADFS@DC.SBA.COM
Web Site: http://www.IAADFS.ORG
Members: 475 companies
Staff: 3
Annual Budget: $500-1,000,000
Exec. Director: Michael L. Payne
Director of Membership: Steven G. Antolick

Historical Note
*Provides market research and professional development to member
stores and suppliers. Membership: $350/year.*

Publications:
Membership Directory. a.
Passport. q.
Trademarket Handbook and Membership Directory. a. adv.

Meetings/Conferences:
Annual Meetings: Spring
1999 – Orlando, FL(Orlando World Center
     Marriott)/Mar. 21-25

Internat'l Ass'n of Allergology and Clinical Immunology *(1951)*
611 E. Wells St.
Milwaukee, WI 53202
Tel: (414)276-6445   *Fax:* (414)272-6070
E-Mail: iaaci@global.dialog.com
Members: 49 national societies
Staff: 3
Exec. Secretary: Rick Iber

Historical Note
*Founded at the First Internat'l Congress of Allergology, Zurich,
Switzerland, IAACI is an international umbrella organization
representing national societies of allergology and clinical
immunology around the world. IAACI promotes allergology and
clinical immunology for the improvement of public health practice,
medical practice within the discipline, and medical research and
practice in other specializations.*

Publications:
ACI Internat'l. bi-m. adv.
Directory.

Meetings/Conferences:
2000 – Sydney, Australia/Oct. 15-20

Internat'l Ass'n of Amusement Parks and Attractions *(1920)*
1448 Duke St.
Alexandria, VA 22314-3403
Tel: (703)836-4800   *Fax:* (703)836-4801
Web Site: http://www.iaapa.org
Members: 5,000 companies
Staff: 26
Annual Budget: $5-10,000,000
President/CEO/Counsel: John R. Graff
V. President, Government Relations: Randall P. Davis
V. President, Convention Services: Joseph Rubel
Director, Education and Information: Eamon Conner
V. President, Finance: James Fox
Director, Association Relations: Susan E. Mosedale

Historical Note
*Formed as Nat'l Ass'n of Amusement Parks, Pools and Beaches
through a merger of the Nat'l Ass'n of Amusement Parks and the
American Ass'n of Pools and Beaches, it became (1964) the
Internat'l Ass'n of Amusement Parks and assumed its present name
in 1972. Absorbed the Nat'l Water Slide Ass'n in 1982. Sponsors
and supports the Internat'l Ass'n of Amusement Parks and
Attractions Political Action Committee.*

Publications:
Directory and Guide. a. adv.
Family Entertainment Center.
Funworld. m. adv.

Meetings/Conferences:
Annual Meetings: Fall

Internat'l Ass'n of Approved Basketball Officials *(1921)*
12321 Middlebrook Rd.,
Germantown, MD 20815-1300
Tel: (301)601-8013   *Fax:* (301)601-8018
E-Mail: info@iaabo.org
Web Site: http://www.iaabo.org
Members: 14,600 individuals
Staff: 3
Annual Budget: $250-500,000
Exec. Director: Paul Loube

Historical Note
*A recruiting and training association for basketball officials.
Membership: $25/year (individual).*

Publications:
Basketball Handbook. a.
Sportorials. 7/year.

Meetings/Conferences:
Semi-Annual Meetings: Spring and Fall
1999 – Newport, RI

Internat'l Ass'n of Aquaculture Economics and Mangement
Dept. of Ag. & Resource Econ, University of Hawaii
3050 Maile Way, Gilmore 115
Honolulu, HI 96822
Tel: (808)956-8533   *Fax:* (808)956-2811
Members: 200 individuals
Annual Budget: $10-25,000
President: Yung C. Shang, Ph.D.

Historical Note
Membership fee varies, based on location.

Publications:
Aquaculture Economics and Management. q. adv.

Meetings/Conferences:
Biennial Meetings: (1998)

Internat'l Ass'n of Aquatic and Marine Science Libraries and Information Centers *(1975)*
Harbor Branch Oceanographic Institution
c/o Library, 5600 U.S. 1 North
Fort Pierce, FL 34946
Tel: (561)465-2400   *Fax:* (561)465-2446
Toll Free: (800)333 - 4264
E-Mail: iamslic@ucsd.edu
Web Site: http://siolib-155.ucsd.edu/iamslic/
Members: 295 libraries and information ctrs.
Annual Budget: under $10,000
Contact: Kristen Metzger

Historical Note
*Formerly (1975) the Marine Science Library Ass'n became the
Internat'l Ass'n of Marine Science Libraries and Information
Centers and assumed its present name in 1991. Membership:
$35/year.*

Publications:
Directory of Marine Science Libraries and Information
     Centers. irreg.
Newsletter. 4/yr.
Proceedings. a.

Meetings/Conferences:
Annual Meetings: Fall
1999 – Woods Hole, MA
2000 – Rimouski, Brittish Columbia

Internat'l Ass'n of Arson Investigators *(1949)*
300 S. Broadway, Suite 100
St. Louis, MO 63102-2808
Tel: (314)621-1966   *Fax:* (314)621-5125
Members: 7,500 individuals
Staff: 16
Annual Budget: $500-1,000,000
Exec. Director: Benny King
Director, Education: Bill Buxton

Historical Note
Formed at Purdue University by U.S. and Canadian representatives of the insurance industry, fire services, law enforcement agencies and law firms. Membership: $65/year (individual or company) and $15 initiation fee.

Publications:
I. A.
The Fire and Arson Investigator. q. adv.

Meetings/Conferences:
Annual Meetings: Spring
1999 – Las Vegas, NV/500
2000 – Grand Rapids, MI/500

Internat'l Ass'n of Ass'n Management Companies *(1963)*
414 Plaza Dr., Suite 209
Westmont, IL   60559-9000
Tel: (630)655-1669   *Fax:* (630)655-0391
Toll Free: (800)648 - 8861
Web Site: http://www.iaamc.org
Members: 115 companies
Annual Budget: $250-500,000
Exec. V. President: Judith K. Keel

Historical Note
Founded as the Multiple Ass'n Management Institute in 1963, it assumed the name IAMC in 1977, then assumed its present name, IAAMC, in August, 1996 to better fit the organization's mission. Membership consits of companies engaged in the management of two or more organizations on a professional client basis. Membership: $350-3,000/year (ranges according to total aggregate clients budgets).

Publications:
Associate Directory. a.
IAAMC News Update. q.
Management Information Survey - Operations Exec.
    Compensation.
Membership Directory. a.

Meetings/Conferences:
1999 – New Orleans, LA(Marriott)/Feb. 18-20

Internat'l Ass'n of Assembly Managers *(1923)*
4425 West Airport Freeway, Suite 590
Irving, TX   75062-5835
Tel: (972)255-8020   *Fax:* (972)255-9582
Toll Free: (800)935 - 4226
E-Mail: jack.zimmer@iaam.org
Web Site: http://www.iaam.org
Members: 2,502 individuals
Staff: 20
Annual Budget: $2-5,000,000
Exec. Director: John R. Zimmer, CAE
Director, Communications: Julie Herrick
Director, Meetings/Expos: Marsha Willox
Director, Education and Research: Don Hancock, Ph.D., CAE
Director, Membership: J.D. Wilson

Historical Note
Formerly (1996) Internat'l Ass'n of Auditorium Managers. IAAM members are managers of auditoriums, arenas, convention centers, stadiums and performing arts centers representing the most prominent sports, entertainment and convention facilities. Sponsors executive development courses in public assembly facility management. Member of the Center for Exhibition Industry Research and the Convention Liaison Council. Membership: $275/year (active); $400/year (allied).

Publications:
Facility Manager. bi-m. adv.
IAAM Guide to Members and Services. a. adv.
IAAM News. bi-w. adv.

Meetings/Conferences:
Annual Meetings: Summer/2,500
1999 – Toronto, Ontario(Convention Centre)/July 23-28
2000 – Nashville, TN(Opryland)/July 21-26
2001 – Los Angeles, CA(Convention Center)/Aug. 3-7
2002 – Atlanta, GA(Convention Center)/July 25-31

Internat'l Ass'n of Assessing Officers *(1934)*
130 East Randolph St., Suite 850
Chicago, IL   60601-6001
Tel: (312)819-6100   *Fax:* (312)819-6149
E-Mail: webmaster@iaao.org
Web Site: http://www.iaao.org
Members: 8,500 individuals
Staff: 32
Annual Budget: $2-5,000,000
Exec. Director: Eugene Jackson
Director, Communications: Annie Aubrey
Director, Conference and Meetings: Lori Edmunds
Director, Professional Development: James Culver

Historical Note
Formerly (1959) the Nat'l Ass'n of Assessing Officers. Members are professionals involved in the administration of property taxes. Awards the CAE (Certified Evaluater), RES (Residential Evaluation Specialist), Cadasreal Mapping Specialist (CMS), Personal Property Specialist (PPS) and Assessment Administration Specialist (AAS) designations. Sponsors numerous educational programs. Membership: $125/year.

Publications:
Assessment Journal. bi-m.
IAAO Opportunities Newsletter.
Property Tax Information Service. bi-m.

Meetings/Conferences:
Annual Meetings: Fall/1,500
1999 – Las Vegas, NV/Sept. 27-30

Internat'l Ass'n of Astacology *(1972)*
P.O. Box 44650
Univ. of Southwestern Louisiana
Lafayette, LA   70504-4650
Tel: (318)482-5239   *Fax:* (318)482-5395

Members: 300 businesses and individuals
Annual Budget: under $10,000
General Manager: Jay Huner

Historical Note
Members are concerned with the study and economic development of freshwater crayfish. Has no paid officers or full-time staff. Membership: $35/2 yrs.(individual); $70/2 yrs. (institution), $17/2 yrs. (student).

Publications:
Directory. bien.
Freshwater Crayfish: Journal of Astacology. 2/3 years.
IAA Newsletter. q.

Meetings/Conferences:
Biennial Meetings: even-numbered years

Internat'l Ass'n of Attorneys and Exec. in Corporate Real Estate *(1990)*
20106 South Sycamore Drive
Frankfort, IL   60423
Tel: (815)464-6019   *Fax:* (815)464-6019
E-Mail: lisacarreas@ameritech.net
Web Site: http://www.aecre.org
Members: 250 individuals
Staff: 3
Annual Budget: $50-100,000
Exec. Director: Lisa Carreras

Historical Note
AECRE promotes the improvment of knowledge for executives and attorneys involved in the legal issues of real estate. The organization sponsors different educational programs, including workshops. Membership: $250 (individual).

Publications:
Corporate Real Estate and The Law. q.

Meetings/Conferences:
1999 – San Diego, CA(La Costa)/April 22-24/150

Internat'l Ass'n of Audio Visual Communicators *(1957)*
9531 Jamacha Blvd., Suite 263
Spring Valley, CA   91977-5628
Tel: (619)461-1600   *Fax:* (619)461-1606
E-Mail: sheemonw@cindys.com
Web Site: http://www.iaavc.org
Members: 4,500 individuals
Staff: 2
Annual Budget: $500-1,000,000
Exec. Officer: Sheemon Wolfe

Historical Note
Founded as Industry Film Producer Ass'n; later became Information Film Producers of America. Became (1985) Ass'n of Visual Communicators, and assumed its current name in 1997. Members are audio-visual professionals using the media of film, video, slides, filmstrips, multi-image and interactive media to communicate information. Membership: $100/year (regular), $20/year (full-time student).

Meetings/Conferences:

Internat'l Ass'n of Auditorium Managers *(1924)*
Historical Note
Became Internat'l Ass'n of Assembly Managers in 1996.

Internat'l Ass'n of Auto Theft Investigators *(1953)*
P.O. Box 1176
Cross City, FL   32628-1176
Tel: (352)498-3446   *Fax:* (352)498-0021
E-Mail: IAATIEXDIR@aol.com
Web Site: http://www.IAATI.org
Members: 3,000 individuals
Staff: 1
Annual Budget: $50-100,000
Exec. Director: H. Lee Ballard

Historical Note
Established and incorporated at the University of Oklahoma in Norman, OK. Active members include local and state police officers and national government agents. Affiliate members are from the insurance industry, car rental firms, and various automobile associations. Membership: $25 (first year), $20/year (renewal).

Publications:
APB. q.
Training & Education Bulletin. q.

Meetings/Conferences:
Annual Meetings: Summer
1999 – Dearborn, MI(Hyatt Regency)/500
2000 – Vancouver, British Columbia/500

Internat'l Ass'n of Black Professional Fire Fighters *(1970)*
8700 Central Ave., Suite 306
Landover, MD   20785-4831
Tel: (301)808-0804   *Fax:* (301)808-0807
E-Mail: iabpff@msn.com
Web Site: http://www.iabpff.org
Members: 8,000 individuals
Staff: 3
Annual Budget: $100-250,000
Acting Exec. Director: Romeo O. Spaulding

Historical Note
Members are black firefighters and related professionals. Membership: $20/year (individual); $60/year (organization); $350/year (corporation).

Publications:
National Express.

Meetings/Conferences:
Biennial Meetings: even years
2000 – Barbados, West Indies/Aug. 13-18

Internat'l Ass'n of Boards of Examiners in Optometry *(1919)*

4401 East-West Hwy., Suite 205
Bethesda, MD   20814-4411
Tel: (301)913-0641   *Fax:* (301)913-2034
Web Site: http://www.iabopt.org
Members: 54 boards
Staff: 2
Annual Budget: $250-500,000
Exec. Director: James Vrac

Historical Note
Affiliated with the Federation of Ass'ns of Regulatory Boards, and Clearinghouse on Licensure, Enforcement and Regulation. The IAB is the association of state, provincial, and territorial boards that license optometrists. Its mission is to present and assist members in regulating the practice of optometry for the public welfare. Membership: $475-$675/year, depending on number of licensees (board).

Publications:
Directory of Boards of Optometry. a.
IAB "Greensheet" Newsletter. q.

Meetings/Conferences:
Annual Meetings: With the American Optometric Ass'n
1999 – San Antonio, TX/June 20-22/100
2000 – Las Vegas, NV/June 18-20/100

Internat'l Ass'n of Bomb Technicians and Investigators *(1973)*
P.O. Box 8629
Naples, FL   34101
Tel: (941)353-6843   *Fax:* (941)353-6841
E-Mail: iabtimain@aol.com
Members: 3,671 individuals
Staff: 2
Annual Budget: $250-500,000
Exec. Director: Glenn E. Wilt

Historical Note
Membership: $50/year

Publications:
Directory. bi-an.
Newsletter. bi-m.

Meetings/Conferences:
Annual Meetings: Spring
1999 – Biloxi, MS

Internat'l Ass'n of Bridge, Structural and Ornamental Iron Workers *(1896)*
Historical Note
Became the Internat'l Ass'n of Bridge, Structural, Ornamental and Reinforcing Iron Workers in 1997.

Internat'l Ass'n of Bridge, Structural, Ornamental and Reinforcing Iron Workers *(1896)*
1750 New York Ave., N.W., Suite 400
Washington, DC   20006
Tel: (202)383-4800   *Fax:* (202)638-4856
Members: 135,000 individuals
Staff: 70
Annual Budget: $10-25,000,000
President: Jake West

Historical Note
Organized in Pittsburgh, PA on February 4, 1896 as the Internat'l Ass'n of Bridge and Structural Iron Workers. Chartered by the American Federation of Labor in 1903. Formerly (1917) the Internat'l Ass'n of Bridge, Structural and Ornamental Iron Workers and Pile Drivers and (1997) Internat'l Ass'n of Bridge, Structural and Ornamental Iron Workers.

Publications:
The Iron Worker. m.

Meetings/Conferences:
Quinquennial Meetings: August (1996)

Internat'l Ass'n of Broadcast Monitors *(1981)*
P.O. Box 27
Union City, PA   16348-0027
Tel: (814)694-3718
Toll Free: (800)236 - 1741
E-Mail: iabm@juno.com
Web Site: http://www.iabm.com
Members: 110 companies
Staff: 1
Exec. Director: Joy Helmuth

Historical Note
Members are companies that monitor radio and/or television programming, print media and advertising. Membership: $300/year (domestic); $250/year (foreign).

Publications:
Membership Directory. a.

Meetings/Conferences:
1999 – Seattle, WA/Sept. 30-Oct. 3

Internat'l Ass'n of Business Communicators *(1970)*
1 Hallidie Plaza, Suite 600
San Francisco, CA   94102-2818
Tel: (415)433-3400   *Fax:* (415)362-8762
Toll Free: (800)776 - 4222
Web Site: http://www.iabc.com
Members: 13,000 individuals
Staff: 34
Annual Budget: $2-5,000,000
President and C.E.O.: Elizabeth J. Allan, CAE, ABC
Head of Communications: Gloria Gordon
Education and Development Group Leader: Chris Grossgart
Chief Financial Officer, Finance and Operations: Sherman Smith

Historical Note
Merger (1970) of the International Council of Industrial Editors (1941) and the American Association of Industrial Editors (1938). Absorbed the Corporate Communicators Canada (1942) in 1974. Members are communication and public relations professionals. Membership: $180/first year, $150/year thereafter.

Publications:
Communication World. m. adv.

Meetings/Conferences:
Annual Meetings: Spring/1,500
1999 – Washington, DC/June 20-23
2000 – Vancouver, British Columbia/June 25-28

Internat'l Ass'n of Business Forecasting *(1986)*
c/o Conrail, 2001 Market St., Suite 7-B
Philadelphia, PA 19101-1407
Tel: (215)209-7842
Members: 500 individuals
President: Howard Keen

Historical Note
Has no paid officers or full-time staff. Membership: $30/year.

Publications:
IABF Forum. q. adv.
Membership Directory. a.

Meetings/Conferences:
Annual Meetings: Fall

Internat'l Ass'n of Campus Law Enforcement Administrators *(1958)*
638 Prospect Ave.
Hartford, CT 06105-4298
Tel: (860)586-7517   *Fax:* (860)586-7550
E-Mail: info@iaclea.org
Web Site: www.iaclea.org
Members: 900 institutions
Staff: 4
Annual Budget: $100-250,000
Exec. Director: Peter J. Berry, CAE

Historical Note
Formerly Nat'l Ass'n of College and University Security Directors, and (until 1980) Internat'l Ass'n of College and University Security Directors.

Publications:
Campus Law Enforcement Journal. bi-m. adv.
Membership Directory. a. adv.

Meetings/Conferences:
Annual Meetings: Summer
1999 – San Diego, CA/June 23-26
2000 – Boston, MA/June 25-27

Internat'l Ass'n of Career Consulting Firms *(1987)*
1910 Cochran Road, Suite 844
Pittsburgh, PA 15220
Toll Free: (800)565 - 2182
Annual Budget: $25-50,000
President: Faye M. Cornell

Historical Note
Founded as nat'l Ass'n of Career Development Consultants; assumed its current name in 1992 An association of career consulting firms comitted to client service and satisfaction; professional and ethical standards; and advancement of the industry. Membership: $300(organization).

Publications:
IACCF Newsletter. q.

Internat'l Ass'n of Career Management Professionals *(1989)*
2400 E. Arizona Biltmore Circle
Suite 2250
Phoenix, AZ 85016
Tel: (602)381-0011   *Fax:* (602)381-8146
Members: 1,250 individuals
Annual Budget: $25-50,000
President: Allen O'Conner

Historical Note
Founded as Internat'l Ass'n of Outplacement Professionals; assumed its current name in 1994. Established to build the professionalism and to meet the professional needs of outplacement practitioners; and to achieve recognition for that profession. Membership: $40/year (individual).

Publications:
IACMP Highlighter. m.
IACMP Networks Newsletter. q.

Meetings/Conferences:

Internat'l Ass'n of Chiefs of Police *(1893)*
515 N. Washington St., Suite 400
Alexandria, VA 22314-2340
Tel: (703)836-6767   *Fax:* (703)836-4543
Toll Free: (800)843 - 4227
Web Site: http://www.theiacp.org
Members: 16,000 individuals
Staff: 85
Annual Budget: $5-10,000,000
Exec. Director: Daniel N. Rosenblatt
Director, Information and Services: Charles Higginbotham
Public Information Specialist: Sara Johnson
Marketing Specialist: Elisa B. Cohen
Legislative Counsel: Gene Voegtlin
Manager, Conference and Exhibits: Chrissy Hart
Director, Financial Management/Administration: Michele M. Henry
Dep. Exec. Director: Eugene R. Cromartie
Coordinator, Membership Services: Carol A. Bennette

Historical Note
Formerly (1895) Nat'l Chiefs of Police Union; (1898) Nat'l Ass'n of Chiefs of Police; (1902) Chiefs of Police of the United States and Canada. Has an annual budget of approximately $7 million. Membership: $100/year (individual).

Publications:
The Police Chief. m. adv.

Meetings/Conferences:
Annual Meetings: Fall/6,000
1999 – Charlotte, NC/Oct. 30-Nov 4
2000 – San Diego, CA/Nov. 11-16

2001 – Milwaukee, WI/Nov. 3-8

Internat'l Ass'n of Clerks, Recorders, Election Officials and Treasurers *(1971)*
P.O. Box 1525
Houston, TX 77251-1525
Toll Free: (800)890 - 7368
Members: 2,000 individuals and companies
Staff: 5
Annual Budget: $50-100,000
President: John F. Chafin

Historical Note
IACREOT was established to provide a forum for the exchange of information among county officials, to improve the standards of operation that will best serve the public, to encourage the passage of uniform laws governing the operation of county offices, and to provide a unified voice on matter of importance to county officials. Membership: $100/year (elected and appointed members), $50/year (deputy and associate members).

Publications:
IACREOT News. q. adv.

Meetings/Conferences:
Annual Meetings: Summer
1999 – Scottsdale, AZ

Internat'l Ass'n of Clothing Designers and Executives *(1911)*
475 Park Ave. South, 17th Floor
New York, NY 10016-2820
Tel: (212)685-6602   *Fax:* (212)545-1709
Members: 400 individuals
Staff: 3
Annual Budget: $250-500,000
Exec. Director: Norman Karr

Historical Note
Founded as the Nat'l Ass'n of Clothing Designers, changed its name in 1919 to Internat'l Ass'n of Clothing Designers, and assumed present name in 1994. Membership figure includes both designers and industrial members. Membership: $300/year (full member); $600/year (supplier).

Publications:
Bulletin. q.
IACDE Annual Directory. a. adv.
International Designer. a.
Style Forecast. semi-a.

Meetings/Conferences:
Semi-annual Meetings: May and September
1999 – Key Biscayne, FL(Sonesta Beach)/April 8-11/300
2000 – Montreal, Quebec(Marriott Champlain)/350

Internat'l Ass'n of Cold Storage Contractors *(1981)*
7315 Wisconsin Ave.
#1200 N
Bethesda, MD 20814
Tel: (301)652-5674   *Fax:* (301)652-7269
E-Mail: email@iarw.org
Members: 70 companies
Staff: 2
Annual Budget: $50-100,000
Exec. Director: J. William Hudson

Historical Note
Trade association for the low-temperature facility construction industry. Formerly (1989) Nat'l Ass'n of Cold Storage Contractors. Membership: $700/year.

Publications:
Directory. a.
Manual of Standards of Practice.
Newsletter. q.

Meetings/Conferences:
Annual Meetings: Fall
1999 – Tempe, AZ(The Buttes)/Nov. 10-14

Internat'l Ass'n of Color Manufacturers *(1972)*
1620 I St., N.W., Suite 925
Washington, DC 20006
Tel: (202)221-5765   *Fax:* (202)221-0755
Members: 15 companies
Staff: 5
Annual Budget: $250-500,000
Attorney: John B. Hallagan

Historical Note
Manufacturers of certified colors for food, drugs, and cosmetics. Formerly (1993) the Certified Color Manufacturers Ass'n.

Internat'l Ass'n of Commercial Collectors *(1970)*
Historical Note
Organization defunct in 1998.

Internat'l Ass'n of Conference Center Administrators *(1976)*
9482 Glengarriff Drive
Brewerton, NY 13029-9529
Tel: (315)676-4130   *Fax:* (315)676-2598
Web Site: http://www.iacc.org
Members: 270 individuals
Staff: 1
Annual Budget: $50-100,000
Exec. Secretary: Al Meyer

Historical Note
Membership: $145/year (executive); $100/year (associate); $45/year (student/retiree).

Publications:
Association News. q.
IACCA Journal. irreg.
Journal. q.
Take Ten. q.

Meetings/Conferences:
1999 – Hunt, TX(Mo Ranch Conf. Center)

Internat'l Ass'n of Conference Centers *(1981)*
243 N. Lindbergh Blvd., Suite 315
St. Louis, MO 63141
Tel: (314)993-8575   *Fax:* (314)993-8919
E-Mail: tbolman@iacc.iacconline.com
Web Site: http://www.iacconline.com
Members: 128 individuals, 265 facilities
Staff: 3
Annual Budget: $500-1,000,000
Exec. V. President: Thomas E. Bolman, CAE
Director of Communications: Steven M. Smith
Director of Member Services: Jerry L. White

Historical Note
Membership: $450/year (individual), $700-3,000/year (organization).

Publications:
Center Lines. q.
Membership Directory. a.

Meetings/Conferences:
Annual Meetings: Annual/Spring Olympic Valley, CA(The Resort at Squaw Creek)/April 10-14/350

Internat'l Ass'n of Convention and Visitor Bureaus *(1914)*
2000 L St., N.W., Suite 702
Washington, DC 20036-4490
Tel: (202)296-7888   *Fax:* (202)296-7889
E-Mail: info@iacvb.org
Web Site: http://www.iacvb.org
Members: 420 convention & visitor bureaus
Staff: 15
Annual Budget: $2-5,000,000
President and C.E.O.: Edward Nielsen
V. President, Communications: Robert Ensinger
Manager of Communications: Gina Barrett
Director, Meetings and Events: Elaine Fellin
Director, Education: Cynthia Fisher
Manager of Finance: Linda Black

Historical Note
Formerly (1975) Internat'l Ass'n of Convention Bureaus. Represents 420 member bureaus in 29 countries. Founded in 1914 to promote sound professional practices in the solicitation and servicing of meetings and conventions. IACVB runs the on-line Convention Industry Network (CINET(R)) with a broad spectrum of data on client meetings, sponsors three "Destinations Showcase(TM)" tradeshow events where IACVB members exhibit their destinations to meeting professionals, offers educational programs for members, provides public relations for the industry, and represents CVBs on legislative and regulatory issues. Member bureaus represent all significant travel/tourism-related businesses at the local and regional level, and also serve as the primary contact points in their destinations for a broad universe of convention and meeting professionals and tour operators. IACVB is also involved with a variety of travel and tourism organizations such as the Travel Industry Ass'n of America and many meetings-and-convention-oriented ass'ns such as Meeting Professionals Internat'l, American Soc. of Ass'n Executives, and the Professional Convention Management Ass'n.

Publications:
Crossroads. 6/year. adv.
Crossroads for Meeting Professionals. q. adv.
IACVB Directory of Destinations. a. adv.
Membership Directory. a. adv.

Meetings/Conferences:
Annual Meetings: Summer
1999 – Las Vegas, NV(Caesar's Palace)/July 11-14

Internat'l Ass'n of Coroners and Medical Examiners *(1927)*
Historical Note
Address unknown in 1997.

Internat'l Ass'n of Corporate and Professional Recruiters *(1978)*
Historical Note
Became Internat'l Ass'n of Corporate and Professional Resources in 1995.

Internat'l Ass'n of Corporate and Professional Recruitment *(1976)*
1001 Green Bay Road, Suite 308
Winnetka, IL 60093
Tel: (847)441-1644   *Fax:* (847)441-7551
E-Mail: iacpr@aol.com
Web Site: http://www.iacpr.org
Members: 300 individuals
Staff: 3
Annual Budget: $100-250,000
Exec. Director: Susan Roberts

Historical Note
Formerly (1991) the Nat'l Ass'n of Corporate and Professional Recruiters and (1995) Internat'l Ass'n of Corporate and Professional Recruiters. Founded in New York and incorporated in Kentucky, IACPR was established to address the common concerns of corporate staffing executives and executive search consultants. Members are professionals with at least ten years experience in the recruiting of executives. Membership: $400/year (individual).

Publications:
Impact. semi-a.
Quick Takes. q.

Meetings/Conferences:
Annual Meetings: Fall
1999 – Philadelphia, PA(Rittenhouse Hotel)/Sept. 28-30/100

Internat'l Ass'n of Corporate and Professional Resources *(1976)*

Historical Note
Name changed to Internat'l Ass'n of Corporate and Professional Recruitment in 1996.

Internat'l Ass'n of Correctional Officers *(1977)*
P.O. Box 81826
Lincoln, NE 68501-1826
Tel: (402)464-0602   *Fax:* (402)464-5931
Members: 13,000 individuals
Staff: 3
Annual Budget: $25-50,000
President: Mel Grieshaber
Administrator: Cece Hill

Historical Note
Officers in federal, state and local correctional facilities. Formerly (1978) the American Ass'n of Correctional Facility Officers and (until 1986), the American Ass'n of Correctional Officers. Membership: $35/year (individual), $20/year (supporting), $10/year (student).

Publications:
The Keeper's Voice. q. adv.

Meetings/Conferences:
Annual Meetings: None Held.

Internat'l Ass'n of Correctional Training Personnel *(1974)*
P.O. Box 47264
Lake Monroe, FL 32747-1264
Tel: (407)321-3215
E-Mail: Iactp@aol.com
Members: 450 individuals
Annual Budget: under $10,000
President: Cindy Boyles

Historical Note
Formerly (1992) the American Ass'n of Correctional Training Personnel. Formed in Carbondale, IL to improve the quality of correctional training. An affiliate of the American Correctional Ass'n and The American Jail Ass'n. Membership: $25/yr. in the U.S. (individual); $30/yr. (foreign); $20/yr. (full-time student); $50/yr. (agency/library).

Publications:
Correctional Training Journal. q. adv.

Meetings/Conferences:
Annual Meetings: with the Internat'l Trainer's Conference in October and in April at the site of upcoming conference.
1999 – Baltimore, MD
2000 – Atlanta, GA/300

Internat'l Ass'n of Counseling Services *(1972)*
101 S. Whiting St., Suite 211
Alexandria, VA 22304-3416
Tel: (703)823-9840   *Fax:* (703)823-9843
E-Mail: IACS@gmu.edu
Web Site: http://wwwmason.gmu.edu/ ~ iacs
Members: 170 centers and agencies
Staff: 2
Annual Budget: $50-100,000
Exec. Officer: Nancy E. Roncketti

Historical Note
Formerly the American Board on Professional Standards in Vocational Counseling; the American Board on Counseling Services. Established to evaluate counseling services. Accredits university/college counseling centers, and public and private couseling agencies. Accreditation fee: $550/year (company).

Publications:
Directory of Counseling Services. a.
IACS Newsletter. q.
Professional Series. irreg.

Meetings/Conferences:
Annual Meetings: With American College Personnel Ass'n

Internat'l Ass'n of Counselors and Therapists *(1990)*
10915 Bonita Beach Road, SE, Suite 2142
Bonita Springs, FL 34135
Tel: (941)498-9710   *Fax:* (941)498-1215
Web Site: http://www.georgebien.com/iact.htm
Members: 5,000 individuals
Staff: 2
Annual Budget: $50-100,000
President: Jillian R. LaVelle

Historical Note
IACT provides a forum in which helping and healing professionals may exchange informatiuon, techniques, and methodologies. Membership: $50/year (individual).

Publications:
Unlimited Human! Magazine. q. adv.

Meetings/Conferences:
2000 – Atlanta, GA(Holiday Inn Select)/April 30-May 2/250

Internat'l Ass'n of Credit Card Investigators
Historical Note
Became (1996) Internat'l Ass'n of Financial Crimes Investigators.

Internat'l Ass'n of Culinary Professionals *(1978)*
304 West Liberty St., Suite 201
Louisville, KY 40202
Tel: (502)581-9786   *Fax:* (502)589-3602
E-Mail: IACP@AOL.COM
Members: 2,700 individuals, 200 schools, 50 corporations
Staff: 11
Annual Budget: $500-1,000,000
Exec. V. President: Daniel D. Maye

Historical Note
Founded in 1978 as the Ass'n of Cooking Schools; became (1985) Internat'l Ass'n of Cooking Schools; (1988) Internat'l Ass'n of Cooking Professionals; assumed its current name in 1990. The IACP is a not-for-profit professional society of individuals employed

in, or providing services to, the culinary industry (cooking schools, cooking educators, cooking students, culinary specialists, caterers, and food writers). IACP's mission is to be a resource and support system for food professionals, and to help its members achieve and sustain success at all levels of their careers through education, information and peer contacts in an ethical, responsible and professional climate. Membership: $175/year (individual), $300-$875/year (corporate).

Publications:
Directory of Cooking Schools. a.
Food Forum. q. adv.
Research Reports. semi-a.

Meetings/Conferences:
Annual Meetings: Spring/600

Internat'l Ass'n of Defense Counsel *(1920)*
1 N. Franklin, Suite 2400
Chicago, IL 60606
Tel: (312)368-1494   *Fax:* (312)368-1854
E-Mail: office@iadclaw.org
Web Site: http://www.iadclaw.org
Members: 2,800 individuals
Staff: 12
Annual Budget: $1-2,000,000
Exec. Director: Jennifer Panagopoulos, Ph.D.
Director, Education: Carmela Balice
Director, Finance: James Cronwall
Director, Membership: Sally Fitzgerald
Director, MIS: Edward Christensen
Assistant to Executive Director: Dolores J. Rothenberger

Historical Note
Formerly (1986) Internat'l Ass'n of Insurance Counsel. Members are defense attorneys and insurance and corporate counsel; membership is by invitation only. Membership: $620/year.

Publications:
Defense Council Journal. q.
IADC News.

Meetings/Conferences:
Semi-Annual Meetings: Summer & Winter with Defense Research Institute
1999 – Chateau Whistler, Canada
2000 – Greenbrier, VA

Internat'l Ass'n of Diecutting and Diemaking *(1972)*
P.O. Box 1587
Crystal Lake, IL 60039-1587
Tel: (815)455-7519   *Fax:* (815)455-7510
Toll Free: (800)828 - 4233
E-Mail: staff@iadd.org
Web Site: http://www.iadd.org
Members: 700 individuals, 399 firms
Staff: 3
Annual Budget: $250-500,000
Exec. Director: Cynthia C. Crouse
Facilitator, Technical and Education: Nick Crabtree
Meetings Assistant: Heidi Poplin

Historical Note
Founded as the Diemakers and Diecutters Ass'n, it became the Nat'l Ass'n of Diemakers and Diecutters in 1980 and assumed its present name in 1991. Members are firms involved in diemaking, diecutting and related equipment and supply areas. Membership: $325/year (company); $60/year (associate); $600/year (patron).

Publications:
Cutting Edge Newsletter. m. adv.
Directory of Members. a.

Meetings/Conferences:
Semi-Annual Meetings: February & September
1999 – Chicago, IL(Hotel Intercontinental)/Sept. 23-25/200
1999 – Hilton Head, SC(The Westin Resort)/March 23-25
2000 – Scottsdale, AZ(The Sunburst Resort)/March 22-24/150

Internat'l Ass'n of Directory Publishers *(1984)*
Historical Note
Address unknown in 1998.

Internat'l Ass'n of Dive Rescue Specialists *(1978)*
P.O. Box 479
Windsor, CO 80550
Tel: (970)686-0815   *Fax:* (970)686-0815
Toll Free: (800)423 - 7791
E-Mail: iadrs@fia.net
Web Site: www.iadrs.org
Members: 3,000 individuals
Staff: 6
Annual Budget: $50-100,000
Exec. Director: Steven J. Linton

Historical Note
IADRS is an information network for dive rescue authorities including state and federal agencies, military, coast guard, police and fire departments, equipment manufacturers and volunteer teams. Membership: $25/year (individual).

Publications:
Searchlines. bi-m. adv.

Meetings/Conferences:
1999 – West Point, NY

Internat'l Ass'n of Drilling Contractors *(1940)*
Box 4287
Houston, TX 77210-4287
Tel: (281)578-7171   *Fax:* (281)578-0589
Web Site: http://www.iadc.org
Members: 1000 companies
Staff: 25
Annual Budget: $2-5,000,000
President: A. Lee Hunt, Jr.

Historical Note
Formerly (1972) American Ass'n of Oilwell Drilling Contractors. Sponsors and supports the IADC Political Action Committee.

Publications:
Drill Bits Newsletter. m.
Drilling Contractor. bi-m. adv.
Trainer's Digest.

Meetings/Conferences:
Annual Meetings: Fall
1999 – Houston, TX/Sept. 29-Oct. 1

Internat'l Ass'n of Eating Disorders Professionals *(1985)*
427 Whooping Loop, Suite 1819
Altamonte Springs, FL 32701-3448
Tel: (407)831-7099   *Fax:* (407)831-2661
Toll Free: (800)800 - 8126
E-Mail: iaedp@aol.com
Web Site: http://www.iaedp.com
Members: 800 individuals, 38 organizations
Staff: 3
Annual Budget: $250-500,000
Exec. Director: Marie C. Shafe, Ed. D.

Historical Note
IAEDP members are professionals working in the field of eating disorders. Awards the designation Certifed Eating Disorders Specialist or Certified Eating Disorders Associate upon completion requirements. Membership: $100/year (individual); $500/year (organization).

Publications:
Bulletin.
Certification Manual.
Connections Newsletter. q. adv.
Guidelines for Eating Disorders in Higher Education.

Meetings/Conferences:
1999 – Phoenix, AZ(WigWam Resort)/Aug. 13-17/400

Internat'l Ass'n of Electrical Inspectors *(1928)*
901 Waterfall Way, Suite 602
Richardson, TX 75080-0848
Tel: (972)235-1455   *Fax:* (972)235-3855
E-Mail: 76226.563@compuserve.com
Web Site: http://www.iaei.com
Members: 26,000 individuals
Staff: 14
Annual Budget: $1-2,000,000
Exec. Director: Philip H. Cox

Historical Note
Members consist of inspectors, utilities, insurance groups, dealers, contractors, electricians, manufacturers and testing laboratories. IAEI cooperates in the formulation of standards for the safe installation and use of electrical materials, devices, and appliances. Membership: $40/year (individual); $200-5,000/year (organization/company).

Publications:
1&2 Family Electrical Systems.
Analysis of National Electrical Code. trien.
Analysis of National Electrical Code (video). trien.
Ferm's Fast Finder Index.
IAEI News. bi-m. adv.
Membership Directory. a. adv.
Soares Grounding. trien.

Meetings/Conferences:
Annual Meetings: September and October

Internat'l Ass'n of Electronic Keyboard Manufacturers *(1963)*
c/o Korg USA
316 S. Service Road
Melville, NY 11747-3201
Tel: (516)333-9100   *Fax:* (516)333-9108
Members: 20 companies
Staff: 1
Annual Budget: under $10,000
President: Mike Kovins

Historical Note
Founded as the Nat'l Ass'n of Electronic Organ Manufacturers. Became the Nat'l Ass'n of Electronic Keyboard Manufacturers in 1983 and assumed its present name in 1990. Affiliated with the American Music Conference. Membership: $800/year.

Meetings/Conferences:
Annual Meetings: Trade Shows with the Internat'l Ass'n of Music Merchants/Jan. and June

Internat'l Ass'n of Emergency Managers *(1952)*
111 Park Place
Falls Church, VA 22046-4513
Tel: (703)538-1795   *Fax:* (703)241-5603
E-Mail: iaem@aol.com
Web Site: http://www.emassociation.org
Members: 1,700 individuals
Staff: 3
Annual Budget: $100-250,000
Exec. Director: Elizabeth B. Armstrong, CAE
Newsletter Editor: Shari Coffin
Government Information Manager: Clay D. Tyeryar
Meetings and Travel Manager: Judith O. Buzzerd
Membership Director: Sharon Kelly

Historical Note
Founded as United States Civil Defense Council; became Nat'l Coordinating Council on Emergency Management in 1983, and assumed its current name in 1998. Members are representatives of city and county government departments responsible for civil defense and emergency management. Membership: $100-$250/year.

Publications:
Bulletin. m.

Meetings/Conferences:
1999 – Louisville, KY/November 13-16

Internat'l Ass'n of Enviromental Testing Laboratories *(1988)*

Historical Note
Address unknown in 1998.

Internat'l Ass'n of Equine Dental Technicians *(1987)*
2207 Concord Pike, Suite 501
Wilmington, DE   19803-2098
Tel: (500)776-6095   *Fax:* (500)776-6096
Toll Free: (800)334 - 6095
Web Site: http://www.iaedt.com
Members: 50 individuals
Annual Budget: $10-25,000
Exec. Officer: Carl Mitz

Historical Note
Membership: $100/year.

Publications:
Newsletter. q. adv.

Meetings/Conferences:
Annual Meetings: Fall.
1999 – Portland, OR/September 23-25

Internat'l Ass'n of Ethicists *(1985)*

Historical Note
Address unknown in 1996

Internat'l Ass'n of Fairs and Expositions *(1920)*
Box 985
Springfield, MO   65801
Tel: (417)862-5771   *Fax:* (417)862-0156
Members: 2,300 fairs and organizations
Staff: 15
Annual Budget: $1–2,000,000
Exec. V. President: Lewis Miller

Historical Note
Membership consists of individual agricultural fairs and regional ass'ns of agricultural fairs. Member of the Trade Show Bureau.

Publications:
Directory. a.
Fairs and Expositions. 10/yr. adv.

Meetings/Conferences:
Annual Meetings: Always Las Vegas, NV/Fall/5,000

Internat'l Ass'n of Family Entertainment Centers *(1993)*
36 Symonds Road
Hillsboro, NH   03244
Tel: (603)464-6498   *Fax:* (603)464-6497
Toll Free: (888)464 - 6498
E-Mail: IAFECNH@aol.com
Web Site: http://www.iafec.org
Members: 550 companies
Staff: 4
Annual Budget: $250-500,000
Exec. Director: Carole Sjolander, CAE

Historical Note
IFECA members are owners and operators of family and location-based family entertainment centers, as well as developers and suppliers who serve the family entertainment center industry. Provides research, education, and publications to promote successful center operations. Membership: $225-350/year.

Publications:
Fun Extra. m. adv.
Membership Directory and Buyers' Guide. a. adv.

Meetings/Conferences:
Annual Meetings: Fall/8,500
1999 – Las Vegas, NV(Convention Center)/Sept. 27-30

Internat'l Ass'n of Family Sociology *(1972)*
Dept. of Sociology
Northern Illinois University
DeKalb, IL   60115-2854
Tel: (815)753-6423   *Fax:* (815)753-6302
Members: 250 individuals
Staff: 1
Annual Budget: under $10,000
General Secretary: Man Singh Das

Historical Note
Sociologists interested in the field of family and marriage.

Publications:
IAFS Newsletter. q.
International Journal of Modern Sociology. semi-a.
International Journal of Sociology of the Family. semi-a.

Meetings/Conferences:
Quinquennial Meetings: (2000)

Internat'l Ass'n of Financial Crimes Investigators *(1968)*
385 Bel Marin Keys Blvd., Suite H
Novato, CA   94949
Tel: (415)884-6600   *Fax:* (415)884-6605
E-Mail: admin@iafci.org
Web Site: http://iafci.org
Members: 3,700 individuals
Staff: 2
Annual Budget: $100-250,000
Exec. Director: Susan L. Sylstra
Membership Services Coordinator: Renee Woolard

Historical Note
Founded as Internat'l Ass'n of Credit Card Investigators; assumed its current name in 1996. IAFCI promotes the establishment of effective international card and cheque security programs, the suppression of fraudulent use of cards and travelers cheques, and the detection and apprehension of those responsible. Membership: $50/year (regular); $35/year (law enforcement members).

Publications:
IAFCI News. q. adv.

Meetings/Conferences:

Internat'l Ass'n of Fire Chiefs *(1873)*
4025 Fair Ridge Dr., Suite 300
Fairfax, VA   22033-2868
Tel: (703)273-0911   *Fax:* (703)273-9363
Web Site: http://www.iafc.org
Members: 11,700 individuals
Staff: 27
Annual Budget: $2-5,000,000
Exec. Director: Garry L. Briese, CAE
Director, Communications: Dale Smith
Director, Government Relations: Allen Caldwell
Director, Professional Development: Dave Gudinas
Director, Finance: Sharon Southerland Smith
Director, Membership Services: Tracy Barron

Historical Note
Formerly (1926) Nat'l Ass'n of Fire Engineers. Members are chief fire officers, equipment manufacturers and others concerned with fire prevention, protection and emergency services management. Membership: $105-123/year (individual), $90/year (renewal), $750/year (company).

Publications:
On-Scene Newsletter. bi-w. adv.

Meetings/Conferences:
Annual Meetings: Fall

Internat'l Ass'n of Fire Fighters *(1918)*
1750 New York Ave., N.W.
Washington, DC   20006-5395
Tel: (202)737-8484   *Fax:* (202)737-8418
Web Site: www.iaff.org
Members: 225,000 individuals
Staff: 65
Annual Budget: $10-25,000,000
General President: Alfred K. Whitehead
Director of PR & Communications: George Burke
Director of Governmental Affairs: Fred Nesbitt
Director of Special Events: Richard Hyatt
Education Director: Dwight Horkheimer

Historical Note
Organized in Washington February 26, 1918 and chartered by the American Federation of Labor the same year. Sponsors and supports the Fire Fighters Interested in Registration and Election Political Action Committee (FIREPAC), the John P. Redmond Educational Foundation, and the IAFF Burn Foundation. Has an annual budget of $10 million.

Publications:
The International Fire Fighter. bi-m.

Meetings/Conferences:
Biennial Meetings: Even years in August
2000 – Chicago, IL

Internat'l Ass'n of Fish and Wildlife Agencies *(1902)*
444 North Capitol St., N.W., Suite 544
Washington, DC   20001
Tel: (202)624-7890   *Fax:* (202)624-7891
E-Mail: iafwa@sso.org
Web Site: sso.org/iafwa
Members: 300 individuals
Staff: 12
Annual Budget: $500-1,000,000
Exec. V. President: R. Max Peterson
Legislative Director: Gary J. Taylor

Historical Note
Established as the Nat'l Ass'n of Game Commissioners and Wardens, it became the Internat'l Ass'n of Game, Fish and Conservation Commissioners in 1917 and assumed its present name in 1976. Membership: $25/year (individual), $250/year (organization).

Publications:
Newsletter. q.
Proceedings. a. adv.

Meetings/Conferences:
Annual Meetings: September/250

Internat'l Ass'n of Fitness Professionals *(1982)*

Historical Note
See IDEA, the Health and Fitness Source.

Internat'l Ass'n of Food Industry Suppliers *(1911)*
1451 Dolley Madison Blvd.
McLean, VA   22101-3850
Tel: (703)761-2600   *Fax:* (703)761-4334
E-Mail: info@iafis.org
Web Site: www.iafis.org
Members: 750 companies
Staff: 21
Annual Budget: $2-5,000,000
President: Charles W. Bray
V. President, Marketing: Heidi McNeal
Director, Communications: Mary G. O'Dea
Annual Conference Coordinator: Dorothy Brady
V. President, Expositions: Liz Overstreet
C.F.O.: Daniel J. Hilleary

Historical Note
Formerly the Dairy and Ice Cream Machinery and Supplies Ass'n, the Dairy Industries Supply Ass'n, and (1963) Dairy and Food Industries Supply Ass'n. Absorbed the Nat'l Ass'n of Food and Dairy Equipment Manufacturers in 1976. Members are manufacturers and distributors of dairy and food industry machinery, equipment, ingredients, and supplies. Membership: $300-$4,600/year (company).

Publications:
Dairy Processor Directory Series. a.
Global Food Megatrends. q.
IAFIS Reporter. m.
Technical Bulletin. q.

Meetings/Conferences:
Annual Meetings: Spring/400

Internat'l Ass'n of Forensic Nurses *(1992)*
6900 Grove Road
Thorofare, NJ   08086-9447
Tel: (609)848-8356   *Fax:* (609)848-5274
E-Mail: iafn@slackinc.com
Members: 1,100 individuals
Staff: 5
Annual Budget: $100-250,000
Exec. Director: Debi Maines

Historical Note
IAFN members are registered nurses participating in the application of nursing science to public or legal proceedings, including assault nurse examiners, clincal trauma nurses, correctional nurse specialists, crisis intervenors, death investigators, forensic clinical nurse specialists, forensic geriatric nurses, forensic gynecology specialists, forensic psychiatric nurses, grief counselors, legal nurse consultants, nurse attorneys, and other nursing roles defined as forensic practice. Membership: $75/year (individual).

Publications:
On the Edge. q.

Meetings/Conferences:
1999 – Phoenix, AZ(Hilton)/350
2000 – Calgary, AL

Internat'l Ass'n of Geophysical Contractors *(1971)*
Box 460209
Houston, TX   77056-0209
Tel: (713)850-7981   *Fax:* (713)850-7984
Members: 235 companies
Staff: 2
Annual Budget: $100-250,000
President: Charles F. Darden

Historical Note
Companies involved in oil exploration. Affiliated with the Canadian Ass'n of Geophysical Contractors; operates chapters in Far East, Australia and Europe, Africa and Middle East (EAME) regions. Membership: Fee based on gross geophysical expenditures or revenues.

Publications:
IAGC Newsletter. q.

Meetings/Conferences:
Annual Meetings: May
1999 – London, England

Internat'l Ass'n of Golf Administrators *(1968)*
c/o Southern California Golf Ass'n
3740 Cahuenga Blvd.
North Hollywood, CA   91604
Tel: (818)980-3630
Members: 170 individuals
Staff: 1
Annual Budget: $50-100,000
Managing Director: Robert Myers

Historical Note
Members are executives of state, regional, or national amateur golf associations. Membership: $125-150/year.

Publications:
IAGA Roster. a.

Meetings/Conferences:
Annual Meetings: November-December
1999 – Casa de Campo, Dominican Republic/Nov. 13-17/120
2000 – Amelia Island, FL(Amelia Island Plantation)/Nov. 12-15

Internat'l Ass'n of Graphics Arts Consultants *(1976)*
Historical Note
Defunct in 1996.

Internat'l Ass'n of Healthcare Central Service Material Management *(1958)*
213 W. Institute Place, Suite 307
Chicago, IL   60610
Tel: (312)440-0078   *Fax:* (312)440-9474
Toll Free: (800)962 - 8274
E-Mail: mailbox@iahcsmm.com
Web Site: www.iahcsmm.com
Members: 9,000 individuals
Staff: 4
Annual Budget: $500-1,000,000
Exec. Director: Betty Hanna

Historical Note
Established in 1958 as the Nat'l Ass'n of Hospital Central Service Personnel. Became the Internat'l Ass'n of Hospital Central Service Management in 1969 and adopted its present name in 1989. Membership consists of persons serving in a technical, supervisory or management capacity in hospital departments responsible for the management and distribution of supplies. Affiliate members are technicians who have achieved a passing grade in national exam. Membership: $35-$60/year.

Publications:
Communique. bi-m.

Meetings/Conferences:
Annual Meetings: May
1999 – Philadelphia, PA(Adams Mark)/May 2-5
2000 – Reno, NV(John Ascuaga's Nugget)/May 7-10
2001 – St. Louis, Mo(Hyatt)/April 29-May 2/300

Internat'l Ass'n of Heat and Frost Insulators and Asbestos Workers *(1904)*
1776 Massachusetts Ave., N.W., Suite 301
Washington, DC   20036-1989
Tel: (202)785-2388   *Fax:* (202)429-0568
Members: 21,000 individuals
Staff: 15
Annual Budget: $2-5,000,000

President: William G. Bernard

Historical Note
Chartered on September 22, 1904 by the American Federation of Labor as the Nat'l Ass'n of Heat, Frost, General Insulators and Asbestos Workers of America. The word "International" came into the title after the acceptance of Canadian locals in 1910. Sponsors and supports the Internat'l Ass'n of Heat and Frost Insulators and Asbestos Workers Political Action Committee.

Publications:
The Asbestos Worker. q.

Meetings/Conferences:

Internat'l Ass'n of Holistic Health Practitioners (1970)

Historical Note
Ass'n inactive in 1997.

Internat'l Ass'n of Home Safety and Security Professionals (1992)

P.O. Box 2044
Erie, PA   16512-2044
Tel: (814)454-6029
E-Mail: director@iahssp.org
Web Site: http://www.iahssp.org
Exec. Director: Bill Phillips

Historical Note

Publications:
Home Safety & Security Experts Directory. a.
The Home Protector. 10/year.

Meetings/Conferences:
Annual Meetings: Spring

Internat'l Ass'n of Homes and Services for the Aging

Historical Note
A division of the American Ass'n of Homes and Services for the Aging, which provides administrative support.

Internat'l Ass'n of Hospitality Accountants

Historical Note
Became (1997) Hospitality Financial and Technology Professionals.

Internat'l Ass'n of Hydrogeologists (1956)

2614 Checkerberry Court
Reston, VA   22091
Tel: (703)648-6600   *Fax:* (703)648-6683
Members: 300 individuals
President: P. Patrick Leahy
Secretary-Treasurer: John F. Harsh

Historical Note
Membership: $55/year (individual); $24/year (student); $210/year (corporate).

Publications:
Hydrogeology. q.

Meetings/Conferences:
Annual Meetings: Fall

Internat'l Ass'n of Hygienic Physicians (1978)

4620 Euclid Blvd.
Youngstown, OH   44512-1633
Tel: (330)788-0526   *Fax:* (330)788-0093
E-Mail: boar_mah@access-k12.org
Web Site: http://www.cisnet.com/iahp
Members: 50 individuals
Staff: 1
Annual Budget: $10-25,000
Secretary-Treasurer: Mark A. Huberman

Historical Note
Founded as Internat'l Ass'n of Professional Natural Hygienists; assumed its current name in 1995. IAHP promotes the clinical advancement of its profession, ethical responsibility, certification of other professionals and the accredation of schools or training programs, and the health freedom of its membership. Members are limited to Primary Care Doctors specializing in the supervision of fasting as an integral part of Natural Hygienic care. Members must be graduates of a university and have a medical practice. Membership: $200/year.

Publications:
IAPNH Newsletter. q.

Meetings/Conferences:
Annual Meetings: Summer

Internat'l Ass'n of Ice Cream Vendors (1969)

1900 Arch St.
Philadelphia, PA   19103-1498
Tel: (215)564-3484   *Fax:* (215)963-9785
Members: 115 companies
Annual Budget: $100-250,000
Exec. Director: Charlene Mayfield
Director, Administrative: Kim Soldavin

Historical Note
IAICV is dedicated to the education and communication of responsible and ethical practice in the ice cream vending industry. The ass'n promotes and enhances a quality image for safe ice cream vending and the success of the industry. Membership: $300/year (individual), $500/year (company).

Publications:
Chimes. 3/year. adv.
Directory. a. adv.

Meetings/Conferences:
Annual Meetings: November/300
1999 – Tucson, AZ(Sheraton El Conquistador)/Nov. 17-20

Internat'l Ass'n of Industrial Accident Boards and Commissions (1914)

1201 Wakarusa Dr., Suite C-3
Lawrence, KS   66049-3889

Tel: (785)840-9103   *Fax:* (785)840-9107
E-Mail: workcomp@iaiabc.org
Web Site: http://www.iaiabc.org
Members: 3,000 individuals, 450 companies and organizations
Staff: 10
Annual Budget: $1-2,000,000
Dept. Director: Jamie Beletz
Director, Education and Research: Melody Curtiss Cathey

Historical Note
Members are governmental units, companies and others interested in improving workers compensation laws and their administration. Membership: $1000-10,000/year (active), $1000/year (associate).

Publications:
IAIABC Journal. semi-a.
IAIABC Newsletter. bi-m.

Meetings/Conferences:
Annual Meetings: Fall
2000 – Seattle, WA
2001 – Portland, OR

Internat'l Ass'n of Insurance Receivers

5800 Foxridge Dr., Suite 115
Mission, KS   66202-2333
Tel: (913)262-4510   *Fax:* (913)262-0174
Annual Budget: $50-100,000
Exec. Director: Frank A. Bistrom, CAE

Historical Note
Membership: $150/year.

Publications:
The Insurance Receiver. q.

Meetings/Conferences:
Annual Meetings: December
1999 – San Fransisco, CA(S.F. Marriott)/Dec. 11-15/100
2000 – Boston, MA(Marriott & Westin)/Dec. 2-6/100

Internat'l Ass'n of Insurance Supervisors (1994)

444 N. Capitol St., N.W., Suite 701
Washington, DC   20001
Tel: (202)624-7790   *Fax:* (202)624-8579
Web Site: http://www.naic.org
Members: 53 individuals
Staff: 30
Exec. Officer: Kevin Cronin

Historical Note
IAIS members are international insurance regulators. The Nat'l Ass'n of Insurance Commissioners serves as the Secretariat.

Meetings/Conferences:
1999 – Washington, DC

Internat'l Ass'n of Jazz Educators (1968)

P.O. Box 724
Manhattan, KS   66505
Tel: (785)776-8744
Web Site: http://www.iaje.org
Members: 7,000 individuals
Staff: 6
Annual Budget: $500-1,000,000
Exec. Director: Dr. William F. Lee, III

Historical Note
Formerly the Nat'l Ass'n of Jazz Educators, it became international in 1989. Music teachers at all educational levels, librarians, musicians, and representatives from the music industry. A member of the Music Educators National Conference. Membership: $50/year (individual); $160-5000/year (company).

Publications:
Jazz Educators Journal. bi-m. adv.

Meetings/Conferences:
Annual Meetings: January/3,500
1999 – Anaheim, CA(Disneyland Hotel)/Jan. 6-9
2000 – New Orleans, LA
2001 – Philadelphia, Pa

Internat'l Ass'n of Jewish Vocational Services (1939)

1845 Walnut St., Suite 640
Philadelphia, PA   19103-4701
Tel: (215)854-0233   *Fax:* (215)854-0212
E-Mail: iajvs@jevs.org
Members: 26 affiliate agencies
Staff: 2
Annual Budget: $100-250,000
Exec. Director: Jenie Cohen

Historical Note
Formerly (1976) the Jewish Occupational Council and (1990) Nat'l Ass'n of Jewish Vocational Services. Voluntary Jewish vocational guidance, employment, training and rehabilitation organizations in the U.S., Canada and Israel.

Publications:
Administrators' Newsletter. irreg.
Conference Proceedings. a.
Newsletter. q.

Meetings/Conferences:

Internat'l Ass'n of Knowledge Engineers (1987)

973 Russell Ave., Suite D
Gaithersburg, MD   20879-3276
Tel: (301)948-5390   *Fax:* (301)926-4243

Historical Note
Established and incorporated in the District of Columbia, IAKE is a non-profit, international association of computer professionals concerned with the design of reasoning machines and computer systems to receive, organize and maintain human knowledge; and with the synthesis of new and graduated human knowledge from this knowledge base. IAKE promotes the definition and standardization of educational and experience qualifications for Knowledge Engineers; the development of technical and social standards in the field of reasoning machine science; the encouragement of documentation of the science through publishing

opportunities for members. Membership: $65/year (individual in the United States), and $90/year (individual overseas).

Meetings/Conferences:

Internat'l Ass'n of Law Enforcement Firearms Instructors (1981)

25 Country Club Road, Suite 707
Gilford, NH   03246-6909
Tel: (603)524-8787   *Fax:* (603)524-8856
Web Site: http://www.ialefi.com
Members: 4,500 individuals
Annual Budget: $500-1,000,000
Exec. Officer: Robert D. Bossey

Historical Note
IALEFI members are certified fierarms instructors from police departments, security agencies, etc. Membership: $50/year (individual); $500/year (sponsor).

Publications:
Firearms Instructor Magazine. q.
IALEFI Directory. a.

Meetings/Conferences:
Annual Meetings: Fall

Internat'l Ass'n of Law Enforcement Intelligence Analysts (1980)

P.O. Box 6385
Lawrenceville, NJ   08648-0385
Tel: (609)984-1035   *Fax:* (609)896-9577
E-Mail: peterson@ialeia.org
Web Site: http://www.ialeia.org
Members: 1,200 individuals
Staff: 1
Annual Budget: $25-50,000
President: Marilyn B. Peterson

Historical Note
IALEIA members are presently or formerly employed in a specialized law enforcement intelligence capacity, sworn or civilian, by a government entity. Membership: $35/year (individual); $150/year (corporate).

Publications:
IALEIA Journal.
Intelscope Magazine. q. adv.
Member Directory. a. adv.

Meetings/Conferences:
Annual Meetings: in conjunction with the Internat'l Ass'n of Chiefs of Police
1999 – Alexandria, VA(Holiday Inn)/June 21-25
1999 – Charlotte, NC/Oct. 31-Nov. 4/125

Internat'l Ass'n of Lighting Designers (1969)

Suite 487, Merchandise Mart
200 World Trade Center
Chicago, IL   60654
Tel: (312)527-3677   *Fax:* (312)527-3680
E-Mail: iald@iald.org
Web Site: http://www.iald.org
Members: 600 individuals
Staff: 2
Annual Budget: $500-1,000,000
President: Morag Fullilove
Member Services Manager: Renee Campbell

Historical Note
The Internat'l Ass'n of Lighting Designers (IALD) is an internationally recognized organization dedicated solely to the concerns of independent, professional lighting designers. Founded in 1969, the IALD now has 600 members worldwide. As the only global organization that focuses on independent lighting design, the IALD provides a worldwide forum for the accomplished lighting designer as well as those just entering the position.

Publications:
Membership Directory. a.
Newsletter. bi-m.

Meetings/Conferences:
1999 – San Francisco, CA/May 11-13
2000 – New York, NY(Javits)/15000
2001 – Las Vegas, NV(Convention Center)/15000

Internat'l Ass'n of Lighting Management Companies (1952)

431 E. Locust St., Suite 202
Des Moines, IA   50309-1999
Tel: (515)243-2360   *Fax:* (515)243-2049
Web Site: http://www.nalmco.org
Members: 150 individuals
Annual Budget: $250-500,000
Exec. V. President: Fred Nicholson
Assoc. Director: Nancy Taylor

Historical Note
Formerly (until 1978) the Nat'l Ass'n of Lighting Maintenance Contractors and (1987) Internat'l Ass'n of Lighting Maintenance Contractors. Companies that clean, repair, maintain and manage commercial and industrial lighting fixtures. Offers members a tradeshow and convention, various educational products, videos, certification programs and seminars. Membership: $500-2,050/year (based on sales which must be more that $10,000).

Publications:
Directory. a. adv.
LM&M. 6/year. adv.

Meetings/Conferences:
Annual Meetings: Annual meetings in April or May.
1999 – Vancouver, British Columbia(Hotel Vancouver)/May 2-5
2000 – New Orleans, LA(Hilton Riverside)/May 21-24

Internat'l Ass'n of Machinists and Aerospace Workers (1888)

9000 Machinists Place
Upper Marlboro, MD   20772-2687

Tel: (301)967-4500   Fax: (301)967-4588
Web Site: www.iamaw.org
Members: 650,000 individuals
Staff: 225
Annual Budget: Over $100,000,000
President: R. Thomas Buffenbarger
Director of Communications: Robert J. Kalaski
Dir. of Legislative & Pol. Action: Richard P. Michalski
General Secretary Treasurer: Donald E. Wharton
General Counsel: Allison Beck
Director of Strategic Resources: Stephen R. Sleigh

Historical Note
Founded May 5, 1888 in Atlanta, Georgia as the Order of United
Machinists and Mechanical Engineers. Became the Nat'l Ass'n of
Machinists in 1889 and the Internat'l Ass'n of Machinists in 1891.
Absorbed the Industrial Union of Marine and Shipbuilding Workers
of America in 1988. Assumed its present name in 1964. Sponsors
and supports the Internat'l Ass'n of Machinists and Aerospace
Workers Political Action Committee. On October 1, 1991 the
Pattern Makers' League of North America was merged with
IAMAW. In 1994 IAMAW merged with the Internat'l Woodworkers
of America - U.S. Has an annual budget of approximately $101.3
million. Membership: $326/year minimum (individual).

Publications:
IAM Journal. q.

Meetings/Conferences:

Internat'l Ass'n of Marriage and Family Counselors (1989)
5999 Stevenson Ave.
Alexandria, VA   22304-3300
Tel: (703)823-9800   Fax: (703)823-0252
Members: 7,540 individuals
Staff: 3
Annual Budget: $50-100,000
Exec. Director: John L. Jaco

Historical Note
A division of the American Counseling Ass'n, IAMFC was formed to
meet the need to focus on the problems connected with marital and
family issues. IAMFC members are ACA members whose primary
work-related responsibilities or interests are in the area of marriage
and family, specifically marriage counseling, marital therapy,
divorce counseling, mediation, and family counseling or therapy.
Membership: $24/year (student, retired); $39/year (professional).

Publications:
Family Digest Newsletter.
The Family Journal: Counseling and Therapy for Couples &
    Families. q.

Meetings/Conferences:
Annual Meetings: Spring, with the ACA
1999 - San Diego, CA/April 14-17
2000 - Washington, DC/March 22-25
2001 - San Antonio, TX
2002 - New Orleans, LA

Internat'l Ass'n of Medical Science Educators
6878 Fleetwood Road, Suite D
McLean, VA   22101-3618
Tel: (703)442-8780   Fax: (703)448-6914
Exec. Officer: Dr. Armand B. Weiss, CAE

Internat'l Ass'n of Merger and Acquisition Consultants (1973)
Historical Note
Became Internat'l Merger and Acquisition Professionals in 1995.

Internat'l Ass'n of Milk Control Agencies (1935)
Dept. of Agriculture
Div. of Dairy Industry Services
Albany, NY   12235
Tel: (518)457-5731   Fax: (518)485-5816
Members: 26 agencies
Annual Budget: $25-50,000
Secretary-Treasurer: Charles Huff

Historical Note
Membership: $150/year.

Publications:
Membership Directory. a.
Proceedings. a.

Meetings/Conferences:
Annual Meetings: Summer
1999 - Quebec City, Quebec(Lowes LeConcorde)/June 27-30
2000 - Albany, NY(Albany Omni Hotel)/July 23-26

Internat'l Ass'n of Milk, Food and Environmental Sanitarians (1911)
6200 Aurora Ave., Suite 200-W
Des Moines, IA   50322-2863
Tel: (515)276-3344   Fax: (515)276-8655
Toll Free: (800)369 - 6837
E-Mail: iamfes@iamfes.org
Web Site: http://www.iamfes.org
Members: 2,800 individuals
Staff: 12
Annual Budget: $1-2,000,000
Exec. Director: David W. Tharp
Director, Communications: Carol F. Mouchka
Director, Finance/Admin.: Lisa K. Backer

Historical Note
Founded as the Internat'l Ass'n of Dairy and Milk Inspectors, it
became the Internat'l Ass'n of Milk Sanitarians in 1938, the
Internat'l Ass'n of Milk and Food Sanitarians in 1949 and assumed
its present name in 1966. Members are professionals from the
industry, government, and academia with an interest in sanitary
dairy and food product handling practices. Membership: $85-
140/year (individual); $525/year (sustaining); $95-165/year
(Canada and Mexico); $110-$210(international).

Publications:
Dairy, Food and Environmental Sanitation. m. adv.

Journal of Food Protection. m. adv.
Meetings/Conferences:
Annual Meetings: August/1,100
1999 - Dearborn, MI(Hyatt Regency)/Aug. 1-4
2000 - Atlanta, GA(Hilton Tower Hotel)/Aug. 1-4

Internat'l Ass'n of Music Libraries, United States Branch (1955)
Music Library, Lincoln Hall
Cornell University
Ithaca, NY   14853-4101
Tel: (607)255-7126
E-Mail: LFC1@cornell.edu
Members: 415 individuals and libraries
Annual Budget: under $10,000
President: Lenore Coral

Historical Note
Membership: $38/year (individual); $60/year (organization).

Publications:
Fontes Artis Musicae. q. adv.

Meetings/Conferences:
Annual Meetings: in conjunction with the Music Library Ass'n
1999 - Los Angeles, CA/March 3-6/30
2000 - Louisville, KY/Feb. 23-26

Internat'l Ass'n of Natural Resource Pilots (1972)
200 Patrick St., S.W.
Vienna, VA   22180-6703
Tel: (703)560-1271
Members: 225 individuals
Public Affairs Off. & Newsletter Editor: Maj. Francis N. Satterlee,
    USAF(Ret.)

Historical Note
IANRP members are pilots and aircrew members employed by
federal, state and provincial natural resource/conservation agencies
in the United States and Canada. Membership: $15/year.

Publications:
Conservation Aeronautics. q. adv.

Meetings/Conferences:
Annual Meetings: August

Internat'l Ass'n of Non-Vessel Operating Common Carriers (1972)
33WO54 Stearns Road
Elgin, IL   60120
Tel: (847)697-3788   Fax: (847)697-3556
Members: 100 non-vessel carriers
Annual Budget: $100-250,000
Exec. Director: Laurie Zack-Olson

Historical Note
Established as a trade association representing non-vessel
operating common carriers (NVOCCs) before Congress and federal
agencies.

Publications:
Newsletter. q.

Meetings/Conferences:
Semi-Annual Meetings: Spring and Fall

Internat'l Ass'n of Ocular Surgeons (1981)
Historical Note
A division of American Soc. of Contemporary Ophthalmology,
which provides administrative support.

Internat'l Ass'n of Official Human Rights Agencies (1949)
444 North Capitol St., N.W., Suite 536
Washington, DC   20001
Tel: (202)624-5410   Fax: (202)624-8185
Members: 200 agencies
Staff: 1
Annual Budget: $100-250,000
President: William Hale

Historical Note
Members are state and local government human rights and human
relations agencies responsible for human rights law enforcement.
Provides support services and training for human rights
professionals.

Publications:
IAOHRA Newsletter. q.
Membership Directory. a.

Meetings/Conferences:
1999 - Des Moines, IA

Internat'l Ass'n of Optometric Executives
1000 Corporate Center Dr., Suite 240
Morrow, GA   30260
Tel: (770)961-9866   Fax: (770)961-9965
Members: 125 individuals
Annual Budget: under $10,000
President: Georgia Anne Bearden

Historical Note
Formerly called the Society of Association Optometric Executives.
Membership: $30-105/year.

Meetings/Conferences:
Semi-Annual Meetings: June, with American Optometric Ass'n
    and Fall

Internat'l Ass'n of Pallet Recyclers (1990)
Historical Note
Merged with the Nat'l Wooden Pallet and Container Ass'n in June
1996.

Internat'l Ass'n of Pediatric Laboratory Medicine
6728 Old McLean Village Dr.
McLean, VA   22101
Tel: (703)556-9222   Fax: (703)556-8729
E-Mail: iaplme@degnon.org

Members: 100 individuals
Staff: 2
Exec. Officer: George K. Degnon, CAE

Internat'l Ass'n of Personal Protection Agents (1990)
458 W. Kenwood
Brighton, TN   38011-6294
Tel: (901)837-1915   Fax: (901)837-4949
E-Mail: 103222.2541@compuserve.com
Web Site: http://www.tiac.net/users/jmking
Members: 600 individuals
Staff: 3
Annual Budget: $10-25,000
Exec. Director: James A. King, Ph.D.

Historical Note
Founded as Internat'l Bodyguard Ass'n; assumed its current name
in 1997. IAPPA represents members in 50 countries worldwide.
Members are professional bodyguards with at least one year of
experience working for a public or private organization.
Membership: $40/year (individual); $250/year (company).

Publications:
Bodyguard. q. adv.
Membership Directory. a.

Meetings/Conferences:
Annual Meetings: always Las Vegas, NV/December

Internat'l Ass'n of Personnel in Employment Security (1913)
1801 Louisville Road
Frankfort, KY   40601-3922
Tel: (502)223-4459   Fax: (502)223-4127
Toll Free: (800)662 - 2255
E-Mail: iapes@aol.com
Web Site: http://www.iapes.org
Members: 21,000 individuals
Staff: 4
Annual Budget: $500-1,000,000
Exec. Director: J. Roger Detweiler
Administrative Services Manager: Mary Riddell
Member Services Manager: Pam Quincey

Historical Note
Formerly (1952) Internat'l Ass'n of Public Employment Services.
Members are involved in unemployment compensation and job
placement in local, state and federal agencies. Membership:
$30/year (individual).

Publications:
Proceedings. a.
Workforce. 10/yr. adv.

Meetings/Conferences:
Annual Meetings: June-July/1,500
1999 - Providence, RI(Westin)/June 20-25

Internat'l Ass'n of Pet Cemeteries (1971)
13 Cemetery Lane
P.O. Box 163
Ellenburg Depot, NY   12935
Toll Free: (800)952 - 5541
Members: 165 cemeteries
Staff: 2
Annual Budget: $50-100,000
Exec. Director: Peter Drown

Historical Note
Founded in Chicago as the Nat'l Ass'n of Pet Cemeteries, it
assumed its present name in 1978. Membership: $110/year
(individual); $150/year (organization/company).

Publications:
News and Views. bi-m. adv.

Meetings/Conferences:

Internat'l Ass'n of Physicians and Health Care Professionals
P.O. Box 13089
Tallahassee, FL   32317
Tel: (904)878-3134   Fax: (904)878-1291
Annual Budget: $50-100,000
Exec. Director: Robert S. Rhinehart

Historical Note
Membership: $50/year.

Publications:
Newsletter.

Meetings/Conferences:
1999 - Tampa, FL

Internat'l Ass'n of Physicians in AIDS Care (1995)
225 W. Washington, Suite 2200
Chicago, IL   60606-4183
Tel: (428)419-7074   Fax: (312)419-7160
E-Mail: iapac@iapac.org
Web Site: http://www.iapac.org
Members: 5,500 individuals
Staff: 5
Annual Budget: $500-1,000,000
President: Gordon Nary

Historical Note
Membership: $60/year (individual); $3,000/year (corporate).

Publications:
Journal of IAPAC. adv. adv.

Meetings/Conferences:
1999 - Vienna, Austria/Oct. 10-14

Internat'l Ass'n of Plastics Distributors (1956)
4707 College Blvd., Suite 105
Leawood, KS   66211-1667
Tel: (913)345-1005   Fax: (913)345-1006
E-Mail: iadp@iapd.org
Web Site: http://www.iadp.org
Members: 412 companies
Staff: 6

Annual Budget: $1-2,000,000
Exec. Director: Deborah M. Hamlin, CAE
Historical Note
Formerly United Plastics Distributors Ass'n and (1970) Nat'l Ass'n of Plastics Distributors. Membership: $550/year (company).
Publications:
The IAPD Magazine. bi-m.
Meetings/Conferences:
Annual Meetings: Fall
1999 – Toronto, Ontario(Sheraton)/Aug. 11-15
2000 – Phoenix, AZ(Pointe at South Mountain)/750
2001 – Nashville, TN(Opryland Hotel)/Sept. 11-17/750
2002 – Anaheim, CA(Disneyland)/Oct.` 16-Oct. 20/750

Internat'l Ass'n of Plumbing and Mechanical Officials *(1926)*
20001 Walnut Drive South
Walnut, CA 91789-2825
Tel: (909)595-8449   *Fax:* (909)594-3690
E-Mail: iapmo@earthlink.net
Web Site: http://www.iapmo.org
Members: 3,000 individuals
Staff: 26
Annual Budget: $2-5,000,000
Exec. Director: G.P.Russ Chaney
Director, Codes/Education: John M. Halliwill
Director, Standards: Mike Kobel
Director, IAPMD Research and Testing: Bill Schreiber
Director, Administration: Donald D. Laughlin
Membership Registrar: Debbie Martinez
Historical Note
Formerly (1966) Western Plumbing Officials Ass'n. IAPMO members are government officials, agencies, industry and others interested in the promotion of the Uniform Plumbing Codes, which IAPMO sponsors and publishes. Membership: $30/year (individual); $350/year (organization/company).
Publications:
Directory of Listed Plumbing Products. m.
Directory of Listed Plumbing Products for Manufactured
    Housing & RVs. irreg.
Directory of Water Conserving Products. m.
Minutes of Annual Meeting. a.
Newsletter. irreg.
Official Magazine. bi-m. adv.
Uniform Plumbing Codes. trien.
Uniform Solar Energy Code. trien.
Uniform Swimming Pool, Spa & Hot Tub Code. trien.
Meetings/Conferences:
Annual Meetings: Spring and Fall
1999 – Salt Lake City, UT
1999 – Washington, DC

Internat'l Ass'n of Printing House Craftsmen *(1919)*
7042 Brooklyn Blvd.
Minneapolis, MN 55429-1370
Tel: (612)560-1620   *Fax:* (612)560-1350
Toll Free: (800)466 - 4274
E-Mail: kkeane1069@aol.com
Web Site: http://www.iaphc.org
Members: 6,000 individuals
Staff: 2
Annual Budget: $250-500,000
C.E.O.: Kevin P. Keane
Historical Note
IAPHC is open to persons employed in or retired from the graphic arts industry. Membership: $100/year.
Publications:
Craftsmen Communicator. irreg.
Know More Notes. irreg.
Meetings/Conferences:
Annual Meetings: August/1,000
1999 – St. Louis, MO(Hyatt Regency)/Aug. 6-11
2000 – Reno, NV

Internat'l Ass'n of Professional Natural Hygienists
Historical Note
Became (1995) Internat'l Ass'n of Hygienic Physicians.

Internat'l Ass'n of Professional Security Consultants *(1984)*
1444 I St., N.W., Suite 700
Washington, DC 20005
Tel: (202)216-9623   *Fax:* (202)223-9569
Members: 77 individuals
Staff: 2
Annual Budget: $25-50,000
Exec. Director: Claire Shanley
Historical Note
Members are independent, non-product affiliated, security management technical and forensic consultants. Membership: $240/year.
Publications:
Membership Directory.
Newsletter.
Meetings/Conferences:
Annual Meetings: March

Internat'l Ass'n of Psychosocial Rehabilitation Services
10025 Governor Warfield Pkwy., Suite 301
Columbia, MD 21044-3357
Tel: (410)730-7190   *Fax:* (410)730-5965
E-Mail: iapsrs33@aol.com
Web Site: http://www.accessv.com/~iapsrson
Members: 1,700 individuals, 447 agencies
Staff: 8
Annual Budget: $500-1,000,000
Exec. Director: Ruth A. Hughes, Ph.D.
Director, Operations/Conventions: David Issing

Membership: $26/year (associate), $80/year (individual), $130-2,200/year, according to budget (organization).
Publications:
PSR Connection. q. adv.
Psychosocial Rehabilitation Journal.
Meetings/Conferences:
1999 – Minneapolis, MN(Hyatt Regency)/May 10-14

Internat'l Ass'n of Pupil Personnel Workers *(1911)*
2940 N. Stratham Point
Hernando, FL 34442-5442
Tel: (352)637-0653   *Fax:* (352)637-0926
E-Mail: William@CHMELA.com
Members: 400 individuals, 100 libraries
Annual Budget: $10-25,000
Exec. Director: Bill Chmela
Historical Note
Pupil personnel workers, social workers and others concerned with school attendance. Formerly (1957) known as the Nat'l League to Promote School Attendance. Membership: $35/year.
Publications:
IAPPW Journal for Truancy and Dropout Prevention. semi-a.
Meetings/Conferences:
Annual Meetings: October
1999 – Knoxville, TN(Hyatt)

Internat'l Ass'n of Railway Operating Officers *(1892)*
Historical Note
Address unknown in 1996.

Internat'l Ass'n of Refrigerated Warehouses *(1891)*
7315 Wisconsin Ave., Suite 1200 North
Bethesda, MD 20814-3322
Tel: (301)652-5674   *Fax:* (301)652-7269
E-Mail: email@iarw.org
Web Site: http://www.iarw.org
Members: 700 companies
Staff: 10
Annual Budget: $1-2,000,000
President: J. William Hudson
Historical Note
Formerly (1972) Nat'l Ass'n of Refrigerated Warehouses. Members are operators of public refrigerated warehouses. Membership: varies by size of operation.
Publications:
Annual Directory of Public Refrigerated Warehouses. a. adv.
Cold Facts. bi-m.
Meetings/Conferences:
Annual Meetings: Spring/650
1999 – Puerto Rico(Westin Rio Mar)/April 10-15
2000 – Phoenix, AZ(Arizona Biltmore)/April 29-May 4
2001 – Boca Raton, FL(Boca Raton Resort & Club)/May 5-10
2002 – San Antonio, TX(Western La Cantera)/Apr. 13-18

Internat'l Ass'n of Residential and Community Alternatives
Historical Note
Became (1995) Internat'l Community Corrections Ass'n.

Internat'l Ass'n of Satellite Users and Suppliers *(1980)*
45681 Oakbrook Court, Suite 107
Sterling, VA 20166-9215
Tel: (703)759-2094   *Fax:* (703)759-5094
Members: 100 companies
Staff: 6
Annual Budget: $500-1,000,000
Exec. Director: A. Fred Dassler
Historical Note
IASUS members are users and suppliers of satellite telecommunications technology and services. Membership: $55/year (organization/company).
Publications:
Catalogue of Telecommunications Equipment. bi-m.

Internat'l Ass'n of School Librarianship *(1971)*
P.O. Box 34069, Dept. 300
Seattle, WA 98124-1069
Tel: (604)925-0266   *Fax:* (604)925-0566
E-Mail: iasl@rockland.com
Web Site: http://www.rhi.hi.is/~anne/iasl.html
Members: 700 individualscompanies
Staff: 1
Annual Budget: $50-100,000
Exec. Director: Dr. Ken Haycock
Historical Note
IASL members are librarians, administrators, and others concerned with school library media programs and services. Membership: $50/year.
Publications:
IASL Conference Proceedings. a.
IASL Newsletter. q. adv.
School Libraries Worldwide. semi-a. adv.
Meetings/Conferences:
Annual Meetings: July
1999 – Birmingham, AL/Nov. 10-14/500

Internat'l Ass'n of Security Services *(1973)*
Historical Note
Address unknown in 1997.

Internat'l Ass'n of Severe Weather Specialists *(1992)*
P.O. Box 31808
Tucson, AZ 85751
Tel: (520)751-9964
Web Site: www.stormchaser.com
Members: 50 individuals

Staff: 5
Annual Budget: $10-25,000
Director: Warren Faidley
Historical Note
IASWSI members are profesional meteorologists and others with an interest in extreme weather conitions. Membership: $25/year (individual).
Publications:
ISSI Journal. semi-a.
Meetings/Conferences:

Internat'l Ass'n of Special Investigation Units
5024-R Campbell Blvd.
Baltimore, MD 21236-5974
Tel: (410)931-8100   *Fax:* (410)931-8111
Exec. Director: Calvin K. Clemons, CAE, CMP

Internat'l Ass'n of Sports Museums and Halls of Fame *(1971)*
4400-A Ambassador Caffery Pkwy.,
Suite 200
Lafayette, LA 70508
Tel: (318)856-0643   *Fax:* (318)856-0643
E-Mail: iasmhf@net-connect.net
Web Site: http://www.sportshall.com
Members: 125 organizations
Staff: 1
Annual Budget: $25-50,000
Admin. Assistant: Teri Cober
Historical Note
Formerly the Ass'n of Sports Museums and Halls of Fame, the association adopted its present name in 1989. Membership: $100/year.
Publications:
Membership Directory. adv. adv.
Newsletter. bi-m. adv.
Organizing a Sports Museum/Hall of Fame.
Meetings/Conferences:
Annual Meetings: Fall, usually at a Hall of Fame
1999 – Lake Placid, NY
2000 – Toronto, Canada

Internat'l Ass'n of Structural Movers *(1983)*
P.O. Box 1213
Elbridge, NY 13060-1213
Tel: (315)689-9498   *Fax:* (315)689-9498
E-Mail: carlt@baldcom.net
Web Site: http://iasm.org
Members: 340 individuals, 300 companies
Staff: 1
Annual Budget: $100-250,000
Exec. Officer: Carl Tuxill
Historical Note
Founded at the Marriott Hotel, Atlanta, Georgia January 15, 1983. Members are movers of heavy structural products, trusses, barns, houses and machinery. Has a small international membership. Membership: $150/year (organization/company).
Publications:
The Structural Mover. 3/year. adv.
Meetings/Conferences:
Annual Meetings: February
1999 – San Diego, CA(Cataamaran Hotel)/Feb. 17-21
2000 – Ft. Myers, FL(Amtel Marina Hotel &
    Suites)/Feb. 9-13/350
2001 – Ft. Worth, TX

Internat'l Ass'n of Sublimation Printers *(1990)*
Historical Note
Defunct in 1996.

Internat'l Ass'n of Tool Craftsmen *(1953)*
3718 Wright Ave.
Racine, WI 53405
Tel: (414)637-4371
Members: 200 individuals
Staff: 1
Annual Budget: $10-25,000
President: Michael Loomis
Historical Note
Independent labor union.
Publications:
Tool and Die Journal. q.
Meetings/Conferences:
Biennial meetings: Uneven years in Fall

Internat'l Ass'n of Tour Managers - North American Region *(1961)*
65 Charnes Drive
East Haven, CT 06513-1225
Tel: (203)466-0425
Members: 1,700 individuals
Staff: 2
Annual Budget: $250-500,000
Exec. Director: G. Domenic Passarelli
Historical Note
Affiliated with American Soc. of Travel Agents and Universal Federation of Travel Agents Ass'n. Professional association of tour managers; tour operators are associate members. Membership: $75/yr.
Publications:
Professional Tour Manager. q.
Meetings/Conferences:
Annual Meetings: Fall/500-600

Internat'l Ass'n of Trauma Counseling
Historical Note
Became (1997) Ass'n of Traumatic Stress Specialists.

Internat'l Ass'n of Travel Exhibitors (1973)
P.O. Box 2309
Gulf Shores, AL   36547-2309
Tel: (334)948-6690   Fax: (334)948-6690
E-Mail: iateinfo@gulftel.com
Members: 125 individuals
Staff: 1
Annual Budget: under $10,000
Secretary-Treasurer: William R. Burton
Administrative Asst.: Sue Burton

Historical Note
Members are government agencies and private businesses engaged in promotion through travel shows. Membership: $100/year (state agency or show producer), $75/year (travel related).

Publications:
Listing of Shows. a.
Membership List. semi-a.
Newsletter. q.
Show Survey. a.

Meetings/Conferences:
Annual Meetings: Fall

Internat'l Ass'n of Trichologists (1973)
37320 22nd St.
Kalamazoo, MI   49009
Tel: (616)375-4430   Fax: (616)372-3224
Web Site: www.zip.com.au/~stingray/IAT
Members: 250 individuals
Staff: 2
Annual Budget: under $10,000
Director: David Salinger

Historical Note
IAT was formed to promote the study, research and legitimate practice in all aspects pertaining to the treatment and care of the human hair and scalp in health and disease, and to supply instruction, training, and aid in the professional application of these specialties. Awards the designations Certified Trichologist (IAT) and Master Certified Trichologist (MIAT). Membership: $150/year.

Publications:
Newsletter. bi-m.

Meetings/Conferences:

Internat'l Ass'n of Wildland Fire (1983)
E. 8109 Bratt
Fairfield, WA   99012-0328
Tel: (509)523-4003   Fax: (509)523-5001
E-Mail: greenlee@cet.com
Web Site: http://www.wildfiremagazine.com
Exec. Director: Jason M. Greenlee, Ph.D.

Historical Note
IWAF members are academics and professionals with an interest in wildland fires.

Publications:
Current Titles in Wildland Fire. m.
Internat'l Bibliography of Wildland Fire. q.
Internat'l Directory of Wildland Fire.
Internat'l Journal of Wildland Fire. q.
Wildfire Magazine. m.

Internat'l Ass'n of Women Chefs and Restaurateurs
Historical Note
Became (1997) Women Chefs and Restaurateurs.

Internat'l Ass'n of Women Ministers (1919)
579 Main St.
Stroudsburg, PA   18360
Tel: (717)421-7751   Fax: (717)421-7718
E-Mail: cjk@epix.net
Web Site: http://www.hesinc.com/seater/iawm1.html
Members: 300 individuals
Annual Budget: $10-25,000
Treasurer: Carol Brown

Historical Note
IAWM active members are ordained, licensed and recorded women clergy and women who meet the requirements for ordination, but whose denominations do not authorize women to serve as ministers. Other membership categories are retired, student, fraternal and sustaining. Membership: sliding scale (based on income).

Publications:
Woman's Pulpit. q.

Meetings/Conferences:
Annual Meetings: July
1999 – Pittsburgh, PA/July 26-29

Internat'l Ass'n of Women Police (1915)
5413 W. Sunnyside Ave.
Chicago, IL   60630
Tel: (773)736-3405
Members: 2 individuals
Annual Budget: $100-250,000
President: Constance J. Maki

Historical Note
Originally founded as the Internat'l Policewoman's Ass'n in 1915 and disbanded in 1932; reorganized under its present name in 1956. Members are full-time law enforcement officers with powers of arrest. Men have been eligible for full membership since 1976. Membership: $40/year (U.S. and Canada), $15/year (foreign).

Publications:
Women Police. a. adv.

Meetings/Conferences:
Annual Meetings: Fall

Internat'l Atherosclerosis Soc. (1979)
6565 Fannin, Suite A-601
Houston, TX   77030
Tel: (713)797-9620   Fax: (713)797-9507
E-Mail: ajackson@bcm.tmc.edu

Web Site: http://www.athero.med.bcm.tmc.edu/ias/
Members: 7,350 individuals
Staff: 1
Annual Budget: $100-250,000
Exec. Director: Ann Stephens Jackson

Historical Note
IAS promotes, at an internat'l level, the advancement of science, research and teaching in the field of atherosclerosis. Members are physicians, scientist and other health professionals. Membership: $10/year (individual); $3 x the number of members/year (organization/company).

Publications:
IAS Newsletter. semi-a.
Proceedings of Symposia. trien.

Meetings/Conferences:
2000 – Stockholm, Sweden

Internat'l Aviation Women Ass'n (1989)
P.O. Box 4491, Grand Central Station
New York, NY   10163-4491
Tel: (212)774-7415   Fax: (212)370-4453
E-Mail: info@iawa.org
Members: 150 individuals
Annual Budget: $10-25,000
President: Katherine B. Posner

Historical Note
IAWA members are women who are senior aviation defense attorneys, executives and managers in the aviation insurance industry, the aviation/aerospace manufacturing industry, airlines and related government agencies. Membership: $65/year (individual).

Publications:
IAWA Newsletter. q.
Membership Directory. a.

Meetings/Conferences:
Annual Meetings: September-October
1999 – Montreal, Canada/Oct. 7-8

Internat'l Balloon Ass'n
Historical Note
Address unknown in 1997.

Internat'l Banana Ass'n (1983)
1929 39th St., N.W.
Washington, DC   20007
Tel: (202)223-1183   Fax: (202)223-1194
Members: 8 companies
Staff: 3
Annual Budget: $1-2,000,000
President: Robert M. Moore

Historical Note
Trade association of the banana industry.

Internat'l BBSing and Electronic Communications Conference
P.O. Box 21766
Denver, CO   80221-0766
Tel: (303)426-1847   Fax: (303)429-0449
E-Mail: ibecc@ibecc.org
Web Site: http://www.ibecc.org
Exec. Officer: Marshall Barry

Historical Note
Members are organizations and individuals involved in electronic bulletin boards and similar developments in electronic messaging.

Publications:
IBECC Newsletter. irreg.

Internat'l Beverage Dispensing Equipment Ass'n (1971)
P.O. Box 1285
White Plains, MD   20695-1285
Tel: (301)932-9075   Fax: (301)932-9149
E-Mail: ibdea@aol.com
Web Site: http://www.olg.com/ibdea
Members: 200 individuals, 225 companies
Staff: 1
Annual Budget: $100-250,000
Exec. Director: Edna Sendish Peters

Historical Note
Established as the Nat'l Soda Dispensing Equipment Ass'n; beacme Nat'l Beverage Dispensing Equipment Ass'n in 1982, and assumed its current name in 1996. Members are companies which sell, rent or service beverage dispensing equipment. Membership: $295-835/year (regular); $570/year (associate).

Publications:
IBDEA Annual Membership Directory. a. adv.
IBDEA News, Periodical.
IBDEA Report. q. adv.

Meetings/Conferences:
Annual Meetings: March
1999 – Hilton Head Island, SC(Crowne Plaza)/March 6-10
2000 – Newport Beach, CA

Internat'l Billing Ass'n
Historical Note
Became Healthcare Billing and Management Ass'n in 1998.

Internat'l Biometric Soc. (1947)
1444 I St., N.W., Suite 700
Washington, DC   20005-2210
Tel: (202)712-9049   Fax: (202)216-9646
E-Mail: tibs@bostromdc.com
Web Site: http://www.tibs.org
Members: 6,600 individuals
Staff: 3
Annual Budget: $500-1,000,000
Exec. Director: Charles A. McGrath, CAE
Administrative Director: David Sanini

Historical Note
The Biometric Soc., was founded at Woods Hole, September 1947 as a result of a report at the First Internat'l Biometric Conference. Became the Internat'l Biometric Soc. in 1994. Promotes the application of mathematical and statistical methods and applications in pure and applied biological sciences. Membership: $50/year (individual); $300/year (organization/company).

Publications:
Biometric Bulletin. q. adv.
Biometrics. q. adv.
Journal of Agricultural, Biological and Environmental Statistics. q.
Membership Directory. bi-a. adv.

Meetings/Conferences:
Annual Meetings: March and June, and International Meetings biennially, even years
2000 – San Francisco, CA(University of California at Berkley)/600

Internat'l Biotechnology Scientific Ass'n (1989)
Historical Note
Address unknown in 1996; presumed inactive.

Internat'l Black Writers Conference (1970)
P.O. Box 1030
Chicago, IL   60690
Members: 2,000 individuals
Staff: 2
Annual Budget: $25-50,000
Exec. Director: Mable J. Terrell

Historical Note
IBWC is a writers organization formed to address the needs of black and other minority-group writers. Membership: $15/year (individual), $50/year (company).

Publications:
Black Writer Magazine. q. adv.
In-Touch Newsletter. m. adv.
Urban Voices Poetry Book. a.

Meetings/Conferences:
Annual Meetings: June

Internat'l Bluegrass Music Ass'n (1985)
207 E. 2nd St.
Owensboro, KY   42303
Tel: (502)684-9025   Fax: (502)686-7863
Toll Free: (888)438 - 4262
E-Mail: ibma1@occ.uky.campus.mci.net
Web Site: http://www.ibma.org
Members: 2,500 individuals
Staff: 3
Annual Budget: $250-500,000
Exec. Director: Dan Hays
Special Projects Director: Nancy Cardwell
Member Services: Susan Cooke

Historical Note
Bluegrass music trade association representing musicians, disc jockeys, record manufacturers and distributors, writers and promoters. Membership: $25-$50/year (individual); $125/year (organization/company).

Publications:
Blue Hot. m.
Internat'l Bluegrass. bi-m.

Meetings/Conferences:
Annual Meetings: September
1999 – Louisville, KY(Galt House)/Oct. 18-24/2000

Internat'l Bodyguard Ass'n
Historical Note
Became (1997) Internat'l Ass'n of Personal Protection Agents.

Internat'l Bottled Water Ass'n (1958)
1700 Diagonal Road, Suite 650
Alexandria, VA   22314
Tel: (703)683-5213   Fax: (703)683-4074
Toll Free: (800)928 - 3711
Members: 1,200 companies
Staff: 14
Annual Budget: $2-5,000,000
President: Sylvia Swanson
V. President of Communications: Adele Logan Galen
V. President of Membership, Conventions and International Affairs: Carol Kinkdale
V. President of Research, Science and Technical Affairs: Cindy Jengeleski

Historical Note
Membership consists of owners and operators of bottled water plants, dealers, distributors and industry suppliers. Established as The American Bottled Water Ass'n, it assumed its present name in 1982. Membership fee based on sales.

Publications:
Bottled Water Reporter. bi-m. adv.
Membership Roster. a. adv.
Newsletter. bi-m.
Technical Newsletter. q.

Meetings/Conferences:
Annual Meetings: November/3,000
1999 – New Orleans, LA/Nov. 11-13

Internat'l Bowling Pro Shop and Instructors Ass'n
P.O. Box 5634
Fresno, CA   93755-5634
Tel: (559)275-9245   Fax: (559)275-9250
Toll Free: (800)659 - 9444
Members: 630 retailers, 96 manufacturers
Exec. Director: Sue Haws

Historical Note
Formerly the Internat'l Bowling Pro Shop Ass'n (1994). IBPSA members are retailers, manufacturers and interested individuals.

Membership: $200/year (U.S, Mexican and Canadian retailers); $400/year (U.S., Mexican and Canadian wholesalers); $275/year (foreign); $475/year (foreign associates).

Publications:
Pro Shop Today. bi-m. adv.

Meetings/Conferences:
Annual Meetings: November
1999 – Las Vegas, NV/July 1-3

Internat'l Brangus Breeders Ass'n *(1949)*
P.O. Box 696020
San Antonio, TX 78269-6020
Tel: (210)696-8231 *Fax:* (210)696-8718
Members: 1,925 individuals
Staff: 12
Annual Budget: $500-1,000,000
Exec. V. President: J. Neil Orth
Director of Jr. Activities/Promotions: Terri Barber
Director of Administration: Nancy Bolzle

Historical Note
Breeders and merchandisers of Brangus beef cattle. Member of the National Society of Livestock Record Associations. Membership: $70/year.

Publications:
Brangus Journal. m. adv.

Meetings/Conferences:
Annual Meetings: Always, Houston, TX/February

Internat'l Bridge, Tunnel and Turnpike Ass'n *(1932)*
2120 L St. N.W., Suite 305
Washington, DC 20037
Tel: (202)659-4620 *Fax:* (202)659-0500
E-Mail: IBTTA @IBTTA.org
Web Site: http://www.ibtta.org
Members: 250 companies and organizations
Staff: 7
Annual Budget: $1-2,000,000
Exec. Director: Neil D. Schuster
Director, Public Affairs: Bruce Cannon
Director, Government Affairs: Neil Gray
Assistant Meeting Planner: Nicole Neuman
Research Manager: Rob Pitzer
Asst. Exec. Director: Robert Davis
Dir., Technology Programs: Tim McGuckin

Historical Note
Founded as the American Toll Bridge Ass'n, it became the American Bridge, Tunnel and Turnpike Ass'n in 1948 and assumed its present name in 1964. Membership consists of public agencies, private companies, and support organizations operating toll facilities. Membership: sliding scale.

Publications:
Eye on Washignton. q.
Proceedings. a.
Toll Industry Statistics. a.
Tollways. m.

Meetings/Conferences:
Annual Meetings: Fall/700
1999 – Halifax, Nova Scotia(Sheraton)
2000 – Spain

Internat'l Brotherhood of Boilermakers, Iron Ship Builders, Blacksmiths, Forgers and Helpers *(1880)*
753 State Ave., Suite 570
New Brotherhood Bldg.
Kansas City, KS 66101
Tel: (913)371-2640 *Fax:* (913)281-8101
Members: 80,000 individuals
Staff: 150
Annual Budget: $25-50,000,000
International President: Charles W. Jones
Director, Communications and Manageing Editor of Publications: Don Caswell
Admin. Asst. to Internat'l President: Joseph A. Stinger
Director, Research and Collective Bargaining: L.G. Beauchamp
Internat'l Secretary-Treasurer: Jerry Willburn
Director, Organizing: W.M. Creeden
Director, Construction Division: Joseph Meredith

Historical Note
Organized in Chicago August 6, 1881 as the Nat'l Boilermaker and Helpers Protective and Benevolent Union. Renamed the Internat'l Brotherhood of Boilermakers and Iron Ship Builders Protective and Benevolent Union of the United States and Canada in 1883. Merged with the Nat'l Brotherhood of Boilermakers in 1893 to form the Internat'l Brotherhood of Boilermakers and Iron Ship Builders of America. Chartered by the American Federation of Labor in 1897, it became the Internat'l Brotherhood of Boilermakers, Iron Ship Builders and Helpers of America in 1912 and merged in 1951 with the Internat'l Brotherhood of Blacksmiths, Forgers and Helpers and adopted its present name. Merged with United Cement, Lime, Gypsum and Allied Workers Internat'l Union in 1984; Stove, Furnace and Allied Appliance Workers and Western Energy Workers in 1994; and the Metal Polishers, Buffers, Platers and Allied Workers Internat'l Union in 1997. Has a budget of about $27 million. The union represents 85,000 members in 420 lodges across the United States and Canada. Members perform work in contruction, shipbuilding, railroad, manufacturing, and service industries.

Publications:
Boilermaker Reporter. bi-m.

Meetings/Conferences:
Annual Meetings: Every 5 years (2001)

Internat'l Brotherhood of Correctional Officers

Historical Note
A unit of the Nat'l Ass'n of Government Employees.

Internat'l Brotherhood of Electrical Workers *(1891)*
1125 15th St., N.W.
Washington, DC 20005
Tel: (202)833-7000 *Fax:* (202)467-6316
E-Mail: ibewnet@compuserve.com
Web Site: http://www.ibew.org
Members: 750,000 individuals
Staff: 250
Annual Budget: $5-10,000,000
International President: John J. Barry
Director, Media Relations: C. James Spellane
Director, Legislative Affairs: Michael Emig
Director, Political Affairs: Rick Diegel
Director, Education Dept.: Martha H. Letsinger
Internat'l Secretary: Edwin D. Hill

Historical Note
Established in St. Louis November 21, 1891 as the Nat'l Brotherhood of Electrical Workers and chartered by the American Federation of Labor the same year. Assumed its present name in 1899 after the acceptance of the first Canadian local. Sponsors and supports the Internat'l Brotherhood of Electrical Workers Committee on Political Education.

Publications:
IBEW Journal. m.

Meetings/Conferences:
2001 – San Francisco, CA

Internat'l Brotherhood of Firemen and Oilers

Historical Note
Became Nat'l Conference of Firemen and Oilers in 1996.

Internat'l Brotherhood of Magicians *(1922)*
11137-C Southtowne Sq.
St. Louis, MO 63123-7819
Tel: (314)845-9200 *Fax:* (314)845-9220
E-Mail: No1inMagic@aol.com
Web Site: http://www.magician.org
Members: 15,000 individuals, 300 local groups
Staff: 8
Annual Budget: $100-250,000
Exec. Secretary: Darleen Eads

Historical Note
Includes an international membership of professional and amateur magicians and their suppliers. Membership: $30/year (domestic).

Publications:
Linking Ring. m. adv.

Meetings/Conferences:
Annual Meetings: late June-July
1999 – Little Rock, AR/June 30-July 3

Internat'l Brotherhood of Painters and Allied Trades *(1887)*
1750 New York Ave., N.W.
8th Floor
Washington, DC 20006
Tel: (202)637-0700 *Fax:* (202)637-0771
Members: 130,000 individuals
Staff: 125
Annual Budget: $10-25,000,000
General President: Michael E. Monroe

Historical Note
Organized in Baltimore March 15, 1887 as the Brotherhood of Painters and Decorators. Became the Brotherhood of Painters, Decorators and Paperhangers of America in 1890. Absorbed the United Scenic Artists, the Nat'l Paperhangers Ass'n and the Nat'l Union of Sign Painters. Merged with the Amalgamated Glass Workers Internat'l Ass'n in 1915. Assumed its present name in 1969. Has an annual budget of approximately $12 million. Sponsors and supports the IBPAT Political Action Together-Political Action Committee.

Publications:
Directory. a.
The Painters and Allied Trades Journal. 6/year.

Meetings/Conferences:
Quinquennial Meetings: (1998)

Internat'l Brotherhood of Police Officers

Historical Note
A division of the Nat'l Ass'n of Government Employees.

Internat'l Brotherhood of Teamsters, AFL-CIO *(1903)*
25 Louisiana Ave., N.W.
Washington, DC 20001-2198
Tel: (202)624-6800 *Fax:* (202)624-6918
Web Site: www.teamster.org
Members: 1,400,000 individuals
Staff: 300
Annual Budget: $50-100,000,000
Director, Legislative Department: Bob Nicholas
General Counsel: David Neigus

Historical Note
Established in Niagara Falls, New York in 1903 as the International Brotherhood of Teamsters through the merger of the Teamsters National Union (founded in 1902) and the Team Drivers International Union (founded in 1899). Became the Internat'l Brotherhood of Teamsters, Chauffeurs, Warehousemen and Helpers of America in 1940 and assumed its present name in 1991. Formerly affiliated with the American Federation of Labor, it was expelled for corruption in 1957. After 30 years as an independent union, it reaffiliated with the AFl-CIO in 1987. Has an annual budget of approximately $87.8 million. As of press time, general election results for the presidency were unsettled.

Publications:
The NEW Teamster. 8/year.

Meetings/Conferences:
Quinquennial Meetings: Summer, next 1996.

Internat'l Buckskin Horse Ass'n *(1971)*
P.O. Box 268
Shelby, IN 46377
Tel: (219)552-1013
Members: 3,000 individuals
Staff: 4
Annual Budget: $100-250,000
Exec. Secretary: Richard E. Kurzeja

Historical Note
IBHA was incorporated in 1971 to register, preserve the pedigree, and promote activity of buckskin, dun, red dun and grulla horses. IBHA has proven to be the largest and most progressive registry for these types of horses, creating interest and demand through national, state, family and individual activities plus increased marketability of IBHA registered horses. Maintains a registry of Buckskin, Dun, Red Dun and Grulla horses. Membership: $25/year.

Publications:
Horse Circuit News. m. adv.

Meetings/Conferences:
1999 – Indianapolis, IN(Best Western Waterfront)/Feb. 18-20/200

Internat'l Builders Exchange Executives *(1948)*
P.O. Box 2274
Rapid City, SD 57709
Tel: (605)341-3380 *Fax:* (605)341-6099
E-Mail: sfernn@dtg.net.com
Members: 82 individuals
Staff: 1
Annual Budget: under $10,000
Exec. V. President: Fern Nagel

Historical Note
Members are executive heads of local building trade associations in the United States and Canada.

Publications:
Construction Executive Report. bi-m.

Meetings/Conferences:
Annual Meetings: June
1999 – New Orleans, LA/Feb. 25-28
1999 – Williamsburg, VA/June 23-27

Internat'l Business Brokers Ass'n *(1984)*
11250 Roger Bacon Drive, suite 8
Reston, VA 20190
Tel: (703)437-7464 *Fax:* (703)435-4390
Members: 150 individuals, 700 companies
Staff: 2
Annual Budget: $100-250,000
Exec. Director: Robert MacDicken

Historical Note
Members are individuals and companies specializing in the sales of businesses of all sizes.

Publications:
IBBA Journal. semi-a. adv.
Membership Directory. a. adv.
Newsletter. q.

Meetings/Conferences:
Semi-Annual Meetings: Spring and Fall
1999 – Bloomington, MN(Radisson)/June 7-12
1999 – Las Vegas, NV(Alexis Park)/Nov. 8-13

Internat'l Business Forms Industries *(1953)*

Historical Note
Became IBFI - The Internat'l Ass'n Serving the Forms, Information Management, Systems Automation and Printed Communications Requirement of Business in 1994.

Internat'l Business Music Ass'n *(1971)*
P.O Box 940
Franklin, NC 28744
Tel: (828)369-2322 *Fax:* (828)369-2322
Web Site: http://www.ibma.net
Members: 67 businesses
Annual Budget: $10-25,000
President: F. Joseph Elum

Historical Note
IBMA is an organization dedicated to serving business music and sound contracting companies by providing a vehicle for the exchange of ideas on matters of common interest and by promoting the interest and general welfare of the business music industry. Membership: $175/year (organization/company).

Publications:
IBMA Newsletter. q. adv.

Meetings/Conferences:
Annual Meetings: September or October
1999 – Scottsdale, AZ(Mountain Shadows Resort)Sept.

Internat'l Cadmium Ass'n *(1980)*
P.O. Box 924
Great Falls, VA 22066-0924
Tel: (703)759-7400 *Fax:* (703)759-7003
E-Mail: cadmium.na@worldnet.att.net
Members: 25 U.S. & 25 overseas companies
Staff: 2
Annual Budget: $250-500,000
President, North America: Hugh Morrow

Historical Note
Formerly a committee of the Zinc Institute, the ass'n is the marketing, research and promotional arm of the cadmium industry. The Internat'l Cadmium Ass'n (ICdA) was formed by the merger of the Cadmium Council (North America) and the Cadmium Ass'n (Europe). Separate annual meetings are held in the United States and Europe. Members are producers and consumers of cadmium. Membership fee based on annual cadmium production or consumption.

Meetings/Conferences:
Annual Meetings: June

Internat'l Cake, Candy, and Party Supply Ass'n *(1991)*

Historical Note
Organization defunct in 1995.

Internat'l Card Manufacturers Ass'n *(1990)*
P.O. Box 727
Princeton Junction, NJ   08550-1028
Tel: (609)799-4900   *Fax:* (609)799-7032
E-Mail: jbarnhart@icma.com
Web Site: http://www.icma.com
Members: 195 companies
Staff: 6
Annual Budget: $500-1,000,000
Exec. Director: Jeffrey E. Barnhart
Communications Manager: Mary Kay Metcalf
Public Relations Manager: Jennifer Szwalek
Ass'n Manager: Lynn McCullough

Historical Note
Principal members of ICMA are manufacturers of credit cards, automatic teller machine cards, and other plastic cards used in commercial transactions; associate members are material suppliers and card-issuing organizations. ICMA serves as an information resource to members, both for technical information on manufacturing standards and for the commercial applications of plastic cards. Membership: $500-2,500/year.

Publications:
Card Flash (Fax). m.
Card Manufacturing. 8/year. adv.
Directory. a. adv.

Meetings/Conferences:
Annual Meetings: Fall

Internat'l Cargo Gear Bureau *(1966)*
90 West St., Suite 1612
New York, NY   10006
Tel: (212)267-4242   *Fax:* (212)267-4250
Members: 35 companies
Staff: 20
Annual Budget: $1-2,000,000
President: Charles G. Visconti

Historical Note
Members are makers and users of material handling equipment ashore and afloat.

Publications:
Directory. bien.

Internat'l Cartridge Recycling Ass'n *(1991)*
P.O. Box 2411
Norcross, GA   30091-2411
Members: 450 companies
Staff: 2
Annual Budget: $250-500,000
President: Gary M. Bruce

Historical Note
Formerly (1990) Internat'l Computer Products Remanufacturing Ass'n. ICRA members are companies actively engaged in the remanufacturing of laser toner cartridges, ribbons, ink jets or other computer products. Membership: $150/year (company).

Publications:
ICRA Re-News. bi-m.

Meetings/Conferences:
Semi-Annual Meetings: Spring and Fall

Internat'l Carwash Ass'n *(1953)*
401 N. Michigan Ave.
Chicago, IL   60611
Tel: (312)321-5199   *Fax:* (312)321-6869
Toll Free: (888)422 - 8422
E-Mail: ica@sba.com
Web Site: http://www.carwas.com/ica
Members: 3,000 companies
Staff: 18
Annual Budget: $2-5,000,000
Exec. Director: Mark O. Thorsby

Historical Note
Formerly American Auto Laundry Ass'n (1958) and Automatic Car Wash Ass'n Internat'l (1975); absorbed the Nat'l Car Wash Council in 1982 and Professional Detail Ass'n in 1996. Membership: $35-195/year (individual); $395-800/year (company).

Publications:
ICA News. m.
Membership Directory/Buyers Guide. a. adv.

Meetings/Conferences:
Annual Meetings: Spring
1999 – Nashville, TN(Opryland)/April 21-24

Internat'l Cast Polymer Ass'n *(1974)*
8201 Greensboro Drive, Suite 300
McLean, VA   22102
Tel: (703)610-9034   *Fax:* (703)610-9005
Web Site: http://www.icpa-hq.com
Members: 330 companies
Annual Budget: $500-1,000,000
Exec. V. President: Tim Rugh
Director, Communications: Jeanne Molumby
Government Relations: Steve McNally
Meetings and Membership Manager: Mary A. Johnson
Director, Industry Affairs: Jill Johnson

Historical Note
Formerly (1993) Cultured Marble Institute. Manufacturers and suppliers of polyester resin-based synthetic marble, onyx and granite-densified products. ICPA promotes quality in the cast polymer products industry. Membership: $650-1,850/year (based on annual volume).

Publications:
Cast Polymer Connection. bi-m. adv.
Membership Directory-Supplier's Guide. a.

Meetings/Conferences:
Annual Meetings: February
1999 – Nashville, TN(Renaissance)/Feb. 17-20/1200

2000 – Phoenix, AZ(Hyatt Regency
      Phoenix)/March 9-12/1300

Internat'l Castor Oil Ass'n *(1957)*
656 Linwood Ave.
Ridgewood, NJ   07450
Tel: (201)652-0889   *Fax:* (201)652-7383
E-Mail: ICOA@ICOA.org
Web Site: http://www.ICOA.org
Members: 52 individuals, 38 companies
Annual Budget: $25-50,000
Secretary-Treasurer: David P. Dingley

Historical Note
Formed in New York City May 1, 1957 by members of the former Linseed-Castorseed Association of New York and incorporated in the State of New Jersey in 1963. Includes foreign members. Crushers of castor seed and exporters, importers, processors, consumers and distributors of castor oil. Membership: $50/year (associate); $700/year (service); $700/year (members).

Publications:
Annual.
The Chemistry of Castor Oil and Its Derivatives and Their
      Applications.
The Processing of Castor Meal for Detoxicification and
      Deallergeration.

Meetings/Conferences:
Annual Meetings: Spring

Internat'l Cemetery and Funeral Ass'n *(1887)*
1895 Preston White Dr., Suite 220
Reston, VA   20191-5434
Tel: (703)391-8400   *Fax:* (703)391-8416
Toll Free: (800)645 - 7700
Members: 4,800 individuals
Staff: 16
Annual Budget: $2-5,000,000
Exec. V. President and C.O.O.: Linda Christenson
Director, Communications/Membership Services: Joseph W.
      Budzinski
Manager, Conventions & Meetings: Pamela J. Davis
Director, Business and Finance Affairs: Scott E. Shaffer
General Counsel: Robert M. Fells
Manager, Membership Services: Nancy E. Paul
Managing Editor: Linda Acorn

Historical Note
Formerly (1944) the Ass'n of American Cemetery Superintendents, (1945) the Ass'n of American Cemeteries and (1996) the American Cemetery Ass'n. Merged with the Nat'l Ass'n of Cemeteries in 1980. Absorbed the Pre-Arrangement Ass'n of American in 1996. Members are cemetery and funeral owners and managers.

Publications:
Internat'l Cemetery Management Magazine. m. adv.
Legal Compass Newsletter. m.

Meetings/Conferences:
1999 – Houston, TX(Hyatt Regency)/March 24-28

**Internat'l Center for Companies of the Food Trade and
Industry-North America Headquarters**
Historical Note
Became Food Business Forum (1994).

Internat'l Ceramic Ass'n *(1958)*
5428 Birch Rd.
Minnetonka, MN   55345-4305
Tel: (410)923-3425
Members: 3,000 suppliers, distributors & manuf.
Annual Budget: $10-25,000
Chairperson: Olevia Higgs

Historical Note
Suppliers of raw materials, manufacturers, distributors and teachers of ceramics. Maintains the Internat'l Ceramics Ass'n Educational Foundation. Incorporated in the State of Illinois in August, 1958 as the Nat'l Ceramics Ass'n, it assumed its present name in 1982.

Publications:
Blue Book. a.
Trade Journal. bi-m. adv.

Meetings/Conferences:
Annual Meetings: Summer

Internat'l Chemical Workers Union
Historical Note
Merged with United food and Commercial Workers Internat'l Union in 1996 to become Internat'l Chemical Workers Union Council/UFCW.

Internat'l Chemical Workers Union Council/UFCW
(1944)
1655 West Market St.
Akron, OH   44313
Tel: (330)867-2444   *Fax:* (330)867-0544
Members: 35,000 individuals
Staff: 83
Annual Budget: $2-5,000,000
President: Frank D. Martino

Historical Note
The International Council of Chemical and Allied Industries Union was formed in Akron, Ohio September 7, 1940. Renamed the International Chemical Workers Union, this organization received a charter from the American Federation of Labor in September, 1944. Merged with United Food and Commercial Workers Internat'l Union and assumed its current name in 1996. Maintains a Washington office. Sponsors and supports the Labor Investment of Voter Education Political Action Committee. Membership fee varies.

Meetings/Conferences:
Biennial meetings: Even years
1999 – Las Vegas, NV(Riveria)/April 15-23/400

Internat'l Childbirth Education Ass'n *(1960)*

P.O. Box 20048
Minneapolis, MN   55420-0048
Tel: (612)854-8660   *Fax:* (612)854-8772
Web Site: http://www.icea.org
Members: 10,000 individuals
Staff: 9
Annual Budget: $250-500,000
Administrator: Doris Olson

Historical Note
Association concerned with family-centered maternity care with minimal medical intervention. An international group functioning in 32 countries, ICEA membership is predominantly concentrated in the U.S. Membership: $30/year (individual).

Publications:
ICEA Bookmarks. q.
Internat'l Journal of Childbirth Education. q. adv.
Membership Directory. bi-a. adv.

Meetings/Conferences:
Annual Meetings: Summer
1999 – Los Angeles, CA/Aug. 5-8

Internat'l Chiropractors Ass'n *(1926)*
1110 N. Glebe Road, Suite 1000
Arlington, VA   22201
Tel: (703)528-5000   *Fax:* (703)528-5023
Members: 8,000 individuals
Staff: 15
Annual Budget: $2-5,000,000
Exec. V. President: Ronald M. Hendrickson
Deputy Exec. V. President for Programs: Molly Rangnath
General Counsel: James D. Harrison
Director, Membership Services: Jody Hunter

Historical Note
Established in 1926 as the Chiropractic Health Bureau, it assumed its present name in 1941. A professional society of Doctors of Chiropractic which supports the International Chiropractors Political Action Committee (ICPAC). Membership: $460/year (doctor).

Publications:
FACTS Bulletin. irreg.
ICA Membership Directory. a. adv.
ICA Today. q. adv.
Internat'l Review of Chiropractic. bi-m. adv.

Meetings/Conferences:
Annual Meetings: Spring

Internat'l City/County Management Ass'n *(1914)*
777 North Capitol St., N.E., Suite 500
Washington, DC   20002-4201
Tel: (202)289-4262   *Fax:* (202)962-3500
Web Site: http://www/icma.org
Members: 8,300 individuals
Staff: 120
Annual Budget: $10-25,000,000
Exec. Director: William H. Hansell, Jr.
Deputy Director: Elizabeth Kellar
Director, Finance: Wayne Sommer
Director, Member Services: Betsy D. Sherman
Director, MIS: Aubrey Charles

Historical Note
Founded as the Internat'l City Managers Ass'n, it became the Internat'l City Management Ass'n in 1969 and assumed its present name in 1991. Also known as ICMA - The Professional Local Government Management Ass'n. A professional society of local government administrators. Has an annual budget of approximately $15 million.

Publications:
ICMA Newsletter. bi-w. adv.
Management Information Service. m.
Municipal Year Book. a.
Public Management. m. adv.
Urban Data Service. m.

Meetings/Conferences:
Annual Meetings: Fall
1999 – Portland, OR/Sept. 26-29
2000 – Cincinnati, OH/Sept. 17-20
2001 – Salt Lake City, UT/Sept. 23-26

Internat'l Claim Ass'n *(1909)*
1255 23rd St., N.W., Suite 850
Washington, DC   20037-1125
Tel: (202)452-8100   *Fax:* (202)833-3636
Members: 425 companies
Staff: 1
Annual Budget: $250-500,000
Director, Administration: Christopher M. Murphy

Historical Note
Members are life and health insurance companies represented by claims employees and officers. Membership: $300/year.

Publications:
ICA News. q.
Proceedings. a.

Meetings/Conferences:
Annual Meetings: Fall

Internat'l Clarinet Ass'n *(1990)*
P.O. Box 7683
Shawnee Mission, KS   66207-0683
Tel: (913)268-3064   *Fax:* (913)268-3064
Members: 3,600 individuals
Annual Budget: $25-50,000
Membership Coordinator: Elena Lence-Talley

Historical Note
ICA members include teachers, manufacturers, amateur musicians and others with an interest in the clarinet. Membership: $35/year (general); $25/year (student).

Publications:
Clarinet Journal. q. adv.

Meetings/Conferences:
Annual Meetings: early July
1999 – Belgium

Internat'l College of Applied Kinesiology (1975)
6405 Metcalf Ave., Suite 503
Shawnee Mission, KS   66202-3929
Tel: (913)384-5336   *Fax:* (913)384-5112
E-Mail: icakusa@usa.net
Web Site: http://www.icakusa.com
Members: 600 individuals
Staff: 4
Annual Budget: $250-500,000
Exec. Director: Terry Kay Underwood

Historical Note
Membership: $400/year.

Publications:
AK Review Journal. semi-a. adv.
Membership Directory. a. adv.

Meetings/Conferences:

Internat'l College of Cranio-Mandibular Orthopedics
619 N. 35th St., Suite 307
Seattle, WA   98103
Tel: (206)633-4355
Toll Free: (800)446 - 1763
Staff: 1
Exec. Secretary: Hallie Truswell

Internat'l College of Dentists, U.S.A. Section (1928)
51 Monroe St., Suite 1501
Rockville, MD   20850-2408
Tel: (301)251-8861   *Fax:* (301)738-9143
E-Mail: info@icd.org
Web Site: http://www.icd.org
Members: 7,000 individuals
Staff: 2
Secretary General and Registrar: Richard G. Shaffer, D.D.S.

Historical Note
Members are dentists who have made an outstanding contribution to the profession of dentistry.

Publications:
Globe. a.
Key. a.
Keynotes. semi-an.

Meetings/Conferences:
Annual Meetings: Fall
1999 – Honolulu, HI

Internat'l College of Real Estate Consulting Professionals (1972)
Historical Note
Defunct in 1996.

Internat'l College of Surgeons (1935)
1516 N. Lake Shore Drive
Chicago, IL   60610-1694
Tel: (312)642-3555   *Fax:* (312)787-1624
Toll Free: (800)766 - 3427
E-Mail: infor@icsglobal.org
Web Site: http://www.icsglobel.org
Members: 14,000 individuals
Staff: 7
Annual Budget: $100-250,000
Exec. Director: Max C. Downham
Director, International Membership: Patricia Binfa

Historical Note
Founded in Geneva, Switzerland 1935 and incorporated in the District of Columbia in 1940, ICS is a federation of general surgeons and surgical specialists. Has an annual budget of approximately $1.5 million.

Publications:
International Surgery. q. adv.

Meetings/Conferences:
Annual Meetings: Spring (U.S. Section) and Biennial
International Meetings

Internat'l Commercial Flooring Specifiers
Historical Note
See COMSPEC - Internat'l Commercial Flooring Specifiers.

Internat'l Commission on Natural Health Products (1994)
Historical Note
Organization defunct in 1998.

Internat'l Communication Ass'n (1950)
Box 9589
Austin, TX   78766-9589
Tel: (512)454-8299   *Fax:* (512)451-6270
E-Mail: icahq@uts.cc.utexas.edu
Web Site: http://www.icahdq.org
Members: 3,238 individuals
Staff: 2
Annual Budget: $250-500,000
Exec. Director: Robert L. Cox

Historical Note
Founded December 1950 in Chicago as the Nat'l Soc. for the Study of Communication. Adopted its present name in 1969 when it was incorporated in Ohio. A founding member of the Council of Communication Societies and affiliate of the American Ass'n for the Advancement of Science. Encourages the systematic study of communication theories, processes and skills. Not to be confused with the Internat'l Communications Ass'n.

Publications:
Communication Theory. q.
Human Communication Research. q.

ICA Newsletter. q. adv.
Journal of Communication. q.
Membership Directory. bien. adv.

Meetings/Conferences:
Annual Meetings: Spring
1999 – San Francisco, CA/May 27-31

Internat'l Communications Agency Network (1950)
1649 County Road 12
P.O. Box 490
Rollinsville, CO   80474
Tel: (303)258-9511   *Fax:* (303)258-3090
E-Mail: gary@icomagencies.com
Web Site: http://www.icomagencies.com
Members: 72 agencies
Staff: 2
Annual Budget: $250-500,000
Exec. Director: Gary Burandt

Historical Note
Chartered in California as the Nat'l Federation of Advertising Agenciesl. It changed its name to International Federation of Advertising Agencies in 1979 and assumed its present name in 1998. Members are non-competing local advertising agencies, about 32% of which are American. Membership: $1,500-5,000/year (.1% of annual revenue)

Publications:
Client Directory. a.
Membership Directory. a.
Newsletter. a.

Meetings/Conferences:
1999 – London, England(Intercontinal)/50

Internat'l Communications Ass'n (1948)
2735 Villa Creek Drive, Suite 200
Dallas, TX   75234-7419
Tel: (972)620-7020   *Fax:* (972)488-9985
Toll Free: (800)422 - 4636
E-Mail: information@ICAnet.com
Web Site: http://www.ICAnet.com
Members: 450 companies
Staff: 3
Annual Budget: $250-500,000
Exec. Manager: R.L. Harper
Manager, Conferences & Meetings: Jan Hall
Legal Counsel: Brian Moir
Manager, Members Services/Systems: Steve Brown

Historical Note
Founded as the Nat'l Committee of Communications Supervisors. Became the Industrial Communications Ass'n in 1953 and assumed its present name in 1966. Membership consists of representatives responsible for telecommunications services and/or facilities of companies, corporations, and other organizations who do not predominantly produce, sell, or rent communications services or equipment. Membership: $25/year (students), $100/year (affiliate/educator), $975/year (company).

Publications:
Communique. q.
Membership Roster. a.
Survey of North American Telecommunications Issues. a.

Meetings/Conferences:
Annual Meetings: Spring
1999 – Atlanta, GA(Georgia World Congress
Center)/June 6-10

Internat'l Communications Industries Ass'n (1939)
11242 Waples Mill Road, Suite 200
Fairfax, VA   22030
Tel: (703)273-7200   *Fax:* (703)278-8082
Toll Free: (800)659 - 7469
E-Mail: icia@icia.org
Web Site: http://www.usa.net/Icia
Members: 1,018 companies, 438 associates
Staff: 21
Annual Budget: $2-5,000,000
Exec. Director: Walter G. Blackwell
V. President, Conventions and Education: Klaus Winkler
V. President, Education/Prof. Development: Randal Lemke
V. President, Finance and Administration: Dana Hargbol
Director, Marketing: James M. Cudahy
Director, Operations: Kristen Young
V. President, Marketing/Membership Services: Rick Harris
Director, Membership: Susan U. Capozzi
Manager, Membership Svcs.: Sue Capozzi
Manager, System Operations: Pat Pluto

Historical Note
Commercial members are video, audio-visual and computer dealers; equipment manufacturers and video and computer software producers; educational and training publishers; video and A-V rental firms; designers and installers of video and sound systems. Associate membership open to end-users in business, education, health care, and government. Cooperates with other industry associations on projects such as legislation, copyright, international marketing, statistics, and technical standards. Awards the CTS (Certified Technology Specialist) designation. Sponsors and supports the Audio-Visual Communications Fund Political Action Committee. Operates the Educational Communications Foundation. Absorbed the Ass'n of Media Producers in 1982. The Independent Media Producers Ass'n became a council within ICIA in 1985. Formerly (1983) the Nat'l Audio-Visual Ass'n. Headquarters for INFOCOMM Internat'l, an annual trade expo for video, multimedia presentation, A-V, audio, & computer dealers. ICIA also sponsors INFOCOMM Asia a communications technology exposition held in Singapore.

Publications:
Communications Industries Report. m.

Meetings/Conferences:
1999 – Orlando, FL(Orange County Convention
Center)/June 10-12

Internat'l Community Corrections Ass'n (1964)

P.O. Box 1987
La Crosse, WI   54602-1987
Tel: (608)785-0200   *Fax:* (608)784-5335
E-Mail: icca@exepc.com
Web Site: http://www.iccaweb.org
Members: 1,100 individuals, 300 agencies
Staff: 3
Annual Budget: $250-500,000
Exec. Director: Peter Kinziger

Historical Note
An affiliate of the American Correctional Ass'n. Formerly (1989) Internat'l Halfway House Ass'n; and (1995) Internat'l Ass'n of Residential and Community Alternatives. Members are public and private agencies involved in providing community based correctional programming and services. Membership: $25/year (individual); $150-950/year (organization).

Publications:
Directory of Residential Programs. bien.
ICCA Journal. bi-m. adv.
Research Conference Proceedings. a.

Meetings/Conferences:
Annual Meetings: Fall
1999 – Cincinnati, OH/600

Internat'l Compact Disc Interactive Ass'n (1991)
5623 Spring Grove Drive
Solon, OH   44139
Tel: (440)349-9661   *Fax:* (440)349-3311
E-Mail: paul.holmes@icdia.org
Web Site: www.icdia.org
Members: 550 individuals
Staff: 2
Annual Budget: $100-250,000
Exec. Director: Paul G. Holmes

Historical Note
Formerly (1994) CD-I Ass'n of North America. ICDIA promotes interactive compact disc (CD-I) technology and its various applications in consumer, business, government, and educational settings. Membership: $250/year (individual); $1,000/year (corporate).

Publications:
Plug & Play.

Meetings/Conferences:
Annual Meetings: October, location alternates between U.S. and
Europe

Internat'l Compressor Remanufacturers Ass'n (1965)
7603 Jarboe
P.O. Box 33092
Kansas City, MO   64114
Tel: (816)333-7205   *Fax:* (816)822-8826
E-Mail: mapgc_os@msn.com
Members: 60 individuals, 53 companies
Annual Budget: $10-25,000
Exec. Secretary: Olive L. Snider
Technical Coordinator: John Clark

Historical Note
ICRA was established to foster the trade, commerce and interest of those engaged in the business of remanufacturing compressors and repairing similar equipment. Membership: $500/year (organization/company).

Publications:
Newsletter. q.

Meetings/Conferences:
Annual Meetings: Winter
1999 – New York, NY

Internat'l Computer Music Ass'n (1974)
2040 Polk St., Suite 330
San Francisco, CA   94109
Tel: (650)493-9448   *Fax:* (650)493-8045
E-Mail: icma@email.sjsu.edu
Web Site: http://www.//,music.dartmouth.edu/~icma/
Members: 700 individuals
Staff: 2
Contact: Allen Strange

Historical Note
ICMA are computer hardware/software companies, composers, musicians and others with an interest in computer music. Membership: $50/year (individual); $15/year (student); $150/year (corporation).

Publications:
Array Newsletter. 3/yr. adv.
ICMA Membership Directory.

Internat'l Concatenated Order of Hoo-Hoo (1892)
Box 118
Gurdon, AR   71743-0118
Tel: (870)353-4997   *Fax:* (870)353-4151
Members: 6,000 individuals
Staff: 2
Annual Budget: $100-250,000
Exec. Secretary: Beth A. Thomas

Historical Note
Does business under "Hoo-Hoo Internat'l" and "Internat'l Order of Hoo-Hoo". Members are represenatives of the forest products and lumber industry, lumber associations and lumber press. Originated in Gurdon, Arkansas when several lumber executives were stranded by a railroad washout. International in scope with chapters in Canada, Australia, and New Zealand. Membership: $21.99/year (membership is based on recommendation by a current member).

Publications:
Log & Talley. q. adv.

Meetings/Conferences:
Annual Meetings: September

Internat'l Concrete Repair Institute (1988)
1323 Shepard Dr., Suite D

Sterling, VA   20164-4428
Tel: (703)450-0116   *Fax:* (703)450-0119
E-Mail: mcollins@icri.org
Web Site: http://www.icri.org
Members: 1,200 companies and individuals
Staff: 6
Annual Budget: $500-1,000,000
Exec. Director: Milton J. Collins
Technical Director: Lawrence F. Hagan

Historical Note
ICRI members are contractors, manufacturers, engineers and others concerned with improving the quality of concrete repairs through communication and education. Formerly (1993) Internat'l Ass'n of Concrete Repair Specialists. Membership: $100-2,000/year.

Publications:
Concrete Repair Bulletin. bi-m. adv.
Who's Who in Concrete Repair Membership Directory. a. adv.

Meetings/Conferences:
1999 – Chicago, IL(Hotel Inter-Continental)/March 11-12/150
1999 – Baltimore, MD/Oct. 28-29

Internat'l Conference of Building Officials *(1922)*
5360 Workman Mill Rd.
Whittier, CA   90601-2298
Tel: (562)699-0541   *Fax:* (562)692-6031
Web Site: http://www.icbo.org
Members: 16,000 individuals
Staff: 110
Annual Budget: $10-25,000,000
President: Jon S. Traw
Operations Manager: Mark Johnson

Historical Note
Membership in the Conference is open to all governmental units as well as all other segments of the building construction industry. Publishes the Uniform Building Code, related code documents and educational texts; maintains a products/systems evaluation service; and sponsors an educational program leading to inspector certification. Has an annual budget of approximately $16 million. Membership: $90/year (individual); $150 year (organization/company).

Publications:
Building Standards Magazine. bi-m. adv.
Building Standards Newsletter. bi-m.
ICBO Evaluation Reports. irreg.
Membership Roster. a.

Meetings/Conferences:
Annual Meetings: Fall
1999 – St. Louis, MO/Sept. 12-17

Internat'l Conference of Funeral Service Examining Boards *(1900)*
P.O. Box E
Huntsville, AR   72740-0130
Tel: (501)738-1915   *Fax:* (501)738-1922
E-Mail: khat@CFSEB.org
Web Site: http://www.cfseb.org
Members: 130 individuals, 50 state/41 school members
Staff: 4
Annual Budget: $250-500,000
Exec. Director: Kevin Hatfield
Registrar: Tracy Easterling

Historical Note
Formerly (1998) Conference of Funeral Service Examining Boards of the United States. Members are executive secretaries and board members of state and provincial agencies, licensing embalmers and funeral directors in the U.S. and Canada. Associate members are mortuary science schools accredited by the American Board of Funeral Service. Membership: $250/year (organization/company).

Meetings/Conferences:
1999 – Kansas City, KS(Westin Hotel)/Oct. 25-30
2000 – Baltimore, MD/Oct. 9-14
2001 – Orlando, FL/Oct. 1-6
2002 – San Antonio, TX/Oct. 14-19

Internat'l Conference of Police Chaplains *(1973)*
P.O. Box 5590
Destin, FL   32540
Tel: (850)654-9736   *Fax:* (850)654-9742
E-Mail: icpc@compuserve.com
Web Site: http://www.eskimo.com/gwmon/icpchome.html
Members: 2,180 individuals
Staff: 3
Annual Budget: $100-250,000
Exec. Director: David W. DeRevere

Historical Note
ICPC members are volunteer and paid law enforcement chaplains. Assists law enforcement agencies seeking to start chaplaincy programs. Membership: $75/year.

Publications:
Chaplains Handbook. irreg.
Directory of Police Chaplains. m.
Newsletter. 9/year.

Meetings/Conferences:
Annual Meetings: July/600
1999 – Columbus, OH(Radisson)/July 19-23
2000 – Mobile, AL(Adams Mark)
2001 – South Bend, IN

Internat'l Conference of Symphony and Opera Musicians *(1962)*
4 W. 31st St., #921
New York, NY   10001
Tel: (212)594-1636
Web Site: http://www.icsom.org
Members: 4,500 individuals
Annual Budget: $250-500,000
Secretary: Lucinda Lewis

Historical Note
Professional symphony, opera and ballet musicians united to promote the welfare of and make more rewarding the livelihood of the orchestral performer and to disseminate inter-orchestra information through correspondence and a newsletter. Affiliated with the American Federation of Musicians. Membership: varies.

Publications:
Senza Sordino. bi-m.

Meetings/Conferences:
Annual Meetings: August
1999 – Vail, CO
2000 – Vail, CO
2001 – Vail, CO

Internat'l Congress of Oral Implantologists *(1975)*
248 Lorraine Ave., 3rd Floor
Upper Montclare, NJ   07043
Tel: (973)783-6300   *Fax:* (973)783-1175
E-Mail: icoi@dentalimplants.com
Web Site: http://www.icoi@dentalimplants.com
Members: 6,000 individuals
Staff: 7
Annual Budget: $1-2,000,000
Exec. Director: R. Craig Johnson

Historical Note
ICOI is a dental implant education and research organization. Members are dentists, oral surgeons, research personnel and others involved in oral implant procedures. Sponsors several seminars and meetings annually. Membership: $350/year (U.S.); $275/year (overseas); $150/year (Affiliate Society).

Publications:
Implant Dentistry Journal q.
Newsletter. q.

Meetings/Conferences:
1999 – Buenos Aires(Sheraton Hotel)/May 14-16/500
2000 – Berlin, Germany(Maritim Hotel)/Sept. 14-16/500
2001 – Las Vegas, NV(Belagic Hotel)/May 28-31/700

Internat'l Coordinating Committee on Solid State Sensors and Actuators Research *(1981)*
c/o Berkeley Sensor & Actuator Center
Univ. of California
Berkeley, CA   94720-1770
Tel: (510)642-0614
Members: 35 organizations
Staff: 1
Annual Budget: $250-500,000
Chairman: Richard Muller

Historical Note

Publications:
Digest of Internat'l Conference on Sensors & Actuators. bien.

Meetings/Conferences:
1999 – Sendai, Japan
2001 – Munich, Germany
2003 – Boston, MA

Internat'l Copper Ass'n *(1960)*
260 Madison Ave., 16th Floor
New York, NY   10016
Tel: (212)251-7240   *Fax:* (212)251-7245
E-Mail: ica@copper.org
Members: 33 companies, 9 associate members
Staff: 12
Annual Budget: $10-25,000,000
President: Jan Smolders
Director of Communications: Catherine Bolton
V. President, Administration/Finance: Gerald J. McGee

Historical Note
Internat'l Copper Ass'n, Ltd. (ICA) was organized in 1989 when the copper industry's worldwide research arm, the Internat'l Copper Research Ass'n, Inc. (INCRA), was restructured to include market development activities. ICA, formed by primary copper producing and fabricating companies throughout the world, assists the copper industry in maintaining the use of copper where traditionally utilized, in meeting competition from other materials, in expanding and extending markets inot established and new areas, and in developing new applications for the metal. Has an annual budget of approximately $15 million. Membership fee: $2.50/ton/year (producer); $50,000/year (associate).

Meetings/Conferences:
Annual Meetings: usually New York City in June
1999 – New York, NY

Internat'l Corrugated Case Ass'n *(1962)*
Historical Note
Address unknown in 1997.

Internat'l Corrugated Packaging Foundation *(1985)*
P.O. Box 25708
Alexandria, VA   22313
Tel: (703)549-8580   *Fax:* (703)549-8670
Web Site: http://www.aiccbox.org
Staff: 2
Annual Budget: $100-250,000
President: Robin Jackson

Historical Note
Established in Virginia and incorporated in Illinois, ICPF is a not-for-profit foundation formed for the purposes of research, education and scholarship for the corrugated packaging industry. The foundation is supported by donations.

Publications:
Newlstter 'Preview'. 6/yea.

Meetings/Conferences:
Annual Meetings: Semi-annual.
1999 – Boca Raton, FL/Apr. 21-24
1999 – Chicago, IL/Nov. 3-6

Internat'l Council for Computer Communication *(1972)*
Box 9745
Washington, DC   20016-9745
Tel: (703)836-7787   *Fax:* (703)836-7787
E-Mail: office@iccgovernors.org
Web Site: http://www.icccgovernors.org
Members: 125 individuals
Annual Budget: $50-100,000
Treasurer: John D. McKendree

Historical Note
ICCC is a professional society of computer communication professionals (senior managers, academic leaders, policy analysts and legal analysts) affiliated with the Internat'l Federation for Information Processing. Has no paid officers or full-time staff.

Publications:
Computer Networks and ISDN Systems. m. adv.

Meetings/Conferences:
1999 – Tokyo, Japan/Sept. 14-16/500

Internat'l Council for Small Business *(1956)*
3674 Lindell Blvd.
St. Louis University
St. Louis, MO   63108
Tel: (314)977-3628   *Fax:* (314)977-3627
E-Mail: icsb@slu.edu
Web Site: http://www.icsb.org
Members: 1,800 individuals
Staff: 2
Annual Budget: $50-100,000
Exec. Administrator: Sharon Bower

Historical Note
Formerly (1977) Nat'l Council for Small Business Management Development. Questions concerning the Journal should be directed to: Editor, Tom Witt at the Bureau of Business Research, West Virginia University, P.O. Box 6025, Morgantown, WV 26506-6025. Membership: $65/year (individual); $500/year (organization/company).

Publications:
ICSB Bulletin. q.
Journal of Small Business Management. q. adv.

Meetings/Conferences:
Annual Meetings: June
1999 – Naples, Italy

Internat'l Council of Air Shows *(1968)*
751 Miller Dr., Suite F-4
Leesburg, VA   20175
Tel: (703)779-8510   *Fax:* (703)779-8511
Members: 950 companies and organizations
Staff: 5
Annual Budget: $500-1,000,000
President: John Cudahy

Historical Note
Members consist of event orgainzers, producers and air show performers and event service organizations. Membership: $175/year.

Publications:
Airshows Magazine. q. adv.
Directory. a.
Newsletter. 8/year.

Meetings/Conferences:
Annual Meetings: Las Vegas, NV/December/1,500

Internat'l Council of Cruise Lines *(1965)*
1211 Connecticut Ave., N.W., Suite 800
Washington, DC   20036-2701
Tel: (202)296-8463   *Fax:* (202)296-1676
E-Mail: bserchake@iccl.org
Members: 17 cruise lines
Staff: 8
Annual Budget: $1-2,000,000
President: Cynthia A. Colenda
Director of Communications: Bridget Ann Serchak

Historical Note
Formerly the Internat'l Committee of Passenger Lines. ICCL is a trade association representing about 90% of oceangoing, overnight major cruise line companies. Membership: $35,000/year (company).

Publications:
Even Keel. q.

Internat'l Council of Employers of Bricklayers and Allied Craftworkers *(1987)*
821 15th St., N.W., Suite 1002
Washington, DC   20005
Tel: (202)783-3791   *Fax:* (202)383-3122
Members: 5,000 companies
Annual Budget: $100-250,000
Exec. Director: Walter M. Kardy, CAE

Historical Note
Formerly (1996) Internat'l Council of Employers of Bricklayers and Allied Craftsmen. Members are contractors who are signatory to collectively-bargained labor agreements with the Internat'l Union of Bricklayers and Allied Craftworkers.

Meetings/Conferences:
Annual Meetings: Fall

Internat'l Council of Fine Arts Deans *(1964)*
P.O. Box 1013
Kent, OH   44240-0020
Tel: (330)673-6734   *Fax:* (330)673-3466
Members: 250 individuals
Annual Budget: $50-100,000
Exec. Director: Linda L. Moore

Historical Note
Members are deans of university schools of the arts. Membership: $50/year (individual); $250/year (institutional).

Publications:
Forum. semi-a.
Membership Roster. a.
Update Newsletter. 3/yr.

Meetings/Conferences:
Annual Meetings: November
1999 – Pittsburgh, PA(Doubletree)
2000 – Miami, FL(Hyatt Regency)

Internat'l Council of Library Ass'n Executives (1975)
c/o California Library Ass'n
717 K St., Suite 300
Sacramento, CA 95814-3477
Tel: (916)447-8541   Fax: (916)447-8394
Members: 30 individuals
Staff: 1
Annual Budget: under $10,000
Convener: Mary Sue Ferrell

Historical Note
Formerly Council of Library Ass'n Executives, the Council assumed its present name in 1983. Members are executive directors, or equivalent, of state, provincial and regional library associations. Membership: $10/year.

Meetings/Conferences:
Semi-annual Meetings: In conjunction with the American
    Library Ass'n
1999 – Philadelphia, PA/Jan. 22-28
1999 – New Orleans, LA/June 24-July 1

Internat'l Council of Psychologists (1941)
c/o Department of Psychology
Southwest Texas State University
San Marcos, TX 78666-4601
Tel: (512)245-7605   Fax: (512)245-3153
Members: 1,200 individuals
Staff: 2
Annual Budget: $50-100,000
Secretary General: John M. Davis, Ph.D.

Historical Note
Established as Nat'l Council of Women Psychologists in the U.S.A. Became (1947) Internat'l Council of Women Psychologists, and (1959) Internat'l Council of Psychologists. Purpose is to advance psychology and the applicaton of its scientific findings throughout the world. ICP seeks to strengthen internat'l bonds between psychologists and to widen, deepen, and clarify channels of communication between individual psychologists. Membership: $44/year (individual).

Publications:
Convention Proceedings. a.
Directory of Members. trien-quadren.
International Psychologist. q. adv.
World Psychology. q.

Meetings/Conferences:
Annual Meetings: July-August/250

Internat'l Council of Regional School Accrediting Commissions (1995)
P.O. Box 246
Coopersburg, PA 18036
Tel: (610)282-8064
Members: 20 individuals
Annual Budget: $50-100,000
C.E.O.: John A. Stoops

Historical Note
Members are chairpersons and directors of evaluation from seven accrediting commissions. ICSAC is dedicated to the establishment of reliable standards of quality and the improvement of educational programs through voluntary school evaluation.

Internat'l Council of Shopping Centers (1957)
665 Fifth Ave.
New York, NY 10022-5302
Tel: (212)421-8181   Fax: (212)486-0849
Web Site: http://www.icsc.org
Staff: 132
Annual Budget: $25-50,000,000
President: John T. Riordan
Director of Communications and Media: Mark Schoifet
V. President, Marketing/Publg: Ellis E. Rowland
Staff V. President, Conventions and Conferences: Lorraine Mazza
Sr. V. President, Programs/Services: Marvin Morrison
V. President, Research and Statistics: John Konarski, III
Sr. Staff V. President, Operations: Robert A. Mallia
V. President & Controller: Steven Holub
Staff V. President and General Counsel: Edward Sack

Historical Note
Owners, developers, managers, retailers and suppliers of shopping centers. Sponsors professional accreditation programs for Certified Shopping Center Manager (CSM), Certified Marketing Director (CMD) and Certified Leasing Specialist (CLS). Sponsors and supports the ICSC Political Action Committee. Research analysts produce updates on the economic impact of U.S. and Canadian shopping centers, tenant sales in malls and center revenues and expenses. The ICSC Library contains information from surveys, periodicals, reference texts and computer data bases on most areas of shopping center retailing activities. ICSC holds 200 seminars and conferences annually. An ICSC ON-LINE service was introduced to members this year. Membership: $100/year (individual), $500/year (company).

Publications:
Directory of Products & Services. a. adv.
Government Affairs Report. q.
Journal of Shopping Center Research. semi-a.
Legal Update. tri-a.
Membership Directory. a.
Monthly Mall Merchandise Index. m.
National Issues Update. m.

Research Quarterly. q.
Retail Challenge. q.
Shopping Centers Today. m. adv.

Meetings/Conferences:
Semi-annual Meetings: Spring and Fall
1999 – Las Vegas, NV

Internat'l Council on Education for Teaching (1953)
1000 Capitol Dr.
Wheeling, IL 60090
Tel: (847)465-0191   Fax: (847)465-5617
Staff: 4
Annual Budget: $250-500,000
Exec. Director: Dr. Darrell Bloom

Historical Note
ICET is an internat'l, non-governmental ass'n of educational organizations, institutions, and individuals dedicated to the improvement of teacher education and all forms of education and training related to nat'l development. ICET works to foster internat'l cooperation in improving the quality of the preparation of teachers and education specialists, to promote cooperation between higher education, government, and the private sector to develop a world-wide network of resources, and to provide and internat'l forum for the exchange of information. Membership: $40/year (individual); $400/year (organization/company).

Publications:
Internat'l Yearbook on Teacher Education. a.
Newsletter. q.
Proceedings. a.

Meetings/Conferences:
2000 – Southern Africa, Nimbia(World Conference)

Internat'l Council on Systems Engineering (1990)
2150 N 107th St., Suite 205
Seattle, WA 98133
Tel: (206)367-8704   Fax: (206)441-8262
Toll Free: (800)366 - 1164
Members: 2,000 individuals, 20 companies
Managing Executive: Shirley Bishop

Publications:
Insight Newsletter. q. adv.
Journal.

Meetings/Conferences:

Internat'l Credit Ass'n (1912)
243 N. Lindbergh Blvd.
St. Louis, MO 63141-1757
Tel: (314)991-3031   Fax: (314)991-3029
Web Site: www.ica-credit.org
Members: 4,000 individuals
Staff: 12
Annual Budget: $500-1,000,000
President: Howard H. Hoemann
Director, Communications: Janet Protzel
Director, Education: Diane Lambert
Director, Membership: Linda Bynan

Historical Note
Originally (1912) Nat'l Retail Credit Ass'n; most recently (1985) Internat'l Credit Ass'n. Certifies through its Soc. of Certified Credit Executives. Membership: $100/year.

Publications:
Consumer Trends. m.
Credit World. bi-m. adv.

Meetings/Conferences:
Annual Meetings: June
1999 – Toronto, ON, Canada
2000 – Chicago, IL

Internat'l Crystal Federation
c/o Collier, Shannon Rill & Scott
3050 K St., N.W., Suite 400
Washington, DC 20007
Tel: (202)342-8580   Fax: (202)342-8451
Web Site: www.colshan.com
Counsel: Michael R. Kershow

Internat'l Customer Service Ass'n (1981)
401 N. Michigan Ave.
Chicago, IL 60611-4267
Tel: (312)321-6800   Fax: (312)321-6869
Toll Free: (800)360 - 4272
E-Mail: icsa@sba.com
Web Site: http://www.icsa.com
Members: 3,200 individuals
Staff: 10
Annual Budget: $2-5,000,000
Exec. Director: Brenda Anderson

Historical Note
Members are customer service management professionals. Incorporated in Illinois May 13, 1981. Membership: $195/year.

Publications:
Benchmarking Study. bien.
Compensation Study. bien.
ICSA Journal. semi-a. adv.
ICSA News. bi-m.
Membership Directory. a.

Meetings/Conferences:
Annual Meetings: Fall/1,000
1999 – Las Vegas, NV(The Mirage)/Sept. 26-29
2000 – San Antonio, TX(San Antonio Marriott)/Sept. 16-19

Internat'l Dairy Foods Ass'n (1990)
1250 H St., N.W., Suite 900
Washington, DC 20005-3952
Tel: (202)737-4332   Fax: (202)331-7820
Web Site: http://www.idfa.org
Members: 800 companies
Staff: 45
Annual Budget: $2-5,000,000

President and C.E.O.: E. Linwood Tipton
V. President, Communications and Meetings: Susan E. Ruland
Manager, Communications: Wendy McDavid
Manager, Communication: Jennifer Korolishi
Senior Director, Congressional Affairs: Michael Torrey
V. President, Regulatory Affairs: Cary Frie
Manager, Meetings and Trade Show: David B. Anderson
Sr. V. President: Constance E. Tipton
Finance and Administration: Sam J. DiCarlo
Membership and Development Officer: William H. Chambliss
V. President: Kurt S. Graetzer
V. President and Of Counsel: Janet A. Nuzum

Historical Note
IDFA is the umbrella organization for three separate associations: Milk Industry Foundation, Nat'l Cheese Institute, Internat'l Ice Cream Ass'n, and manages the American Butter Institute. IDFA is the dairy foods trade association working with industry, legislators, regulators and the public on issues affecting the dairy processing industry. Sponsors and supports the Ice Cream, Milk, and Cheese Political Action Committee.

Publications:
Alert! irreg.
Hotline. irreg.
IDFA Membership Directory. a.
News Update. m.
Washington Update/State News Update. m.

Meetings/Conferences:
Annual Meetings: Fall
1999 – Chicago, IL/Oct. 28-31

Internat'l Dairy-Deli-Bakery Ass'n (1964)
313 Price Pl, Suite 202
P.O. Box 5528
Madison, WI 53705-0528
Tel: (608)238-7908   Fax: (608)238-6330
Web Site: http://www.iddba.org
Members: 1,200 companies
Staff: 18
Annual Budget: $2-5,000,000
Exec. Director: Carol L. Christison
Director, Education: Mary Kay O'Connor
Membership Director: Lucie Arendt

Historical Note
Formerly (1985) the Internat'l Cheese and Deli Ass'n, (1991) Internat'l Dairy-Deli Ass'n. Members are companies involved in the production, processing or selling of deli, dairy and bakery products. Membership: $450/year (company).

Publications:
Dairy-Deli-Bakery Digest. m.
Dairy-Deli-Bakery Wrap Up. q.
Legisletter Newsletter.
Research Publication. a.
What's In Store. a.

Meetings/Conferences:
Annual Meetings: June
1999 – New Orleans, LA/June 6-8
2000 – Anaheim, CA/June 4-6
2001 – Charlotte, NC/JUne 3-5

Internat'l Desalination Ass'n (1973)
Box 387
Topsfield, MA 01983
Tel: (978)887-0410   Fax: (978)887-0411
Web Site: www.ida.bm
Members: 600 firms, individuals & agencies
Staff: 3
Annual Budget: $250-500,000
Secretary General: Patricia A. Burke

Historical Note
Established as the Nat'l Water Supply Improvement Ass'n, became the Water Supply Improvement Ass'n in 1982, and assumed its present name in 1985 upon merging with the Internat'l Desalination and Environmental Ass'n. Members are producers and users of water desalinization equipment. In addition to the biennial meetings, the associaton holds regional affiliate meetings in even years and several seminars/workshops. Membership: $85/year (individual), $675/year (corporation), $450/year (small firms), $25/year (student/library).

Publications:
Desalinization Directory. bi-a.
International Desalination and Reuse Quarterly. q.
Inventory Report. bi-a.
Membership Directory. a.
Newsletter. m.
Proceedings of Biennial Conference. bien.

Meetings/Conferences:
1999 – San Diego, CA/Aug. 29-Sept. 2

Internat'l Development Research Council (1961)
35 Technology Park, Suite 150
Norcross, GA 30092-2906
Tel: (770)446-8955   Fax: (770)263-8825
Web Site: http://www.idrc.org
Members: 2,300 individuals
Staff: 22
Annual Budget: $2-5,000,000
Exec. Director: Michael E. Palmer
Deputy Director/Meetings: Martha Finlay
Deputy Director, Education: Bruce Margine
Sr. Director, Member Services: Emma Lee B. Durham
Membership Development Manager: Cathy Pierce
Deputy Director, Research: Robert Materna

Historical Note
Formerly (1994) Industrial Development Research Council. IDRC members are executives of industrial corporations engaged in corporate real estate site selection and facility planning. Membership: $395/year (active), $495/year (associate).

Publications:
IDRC Communicator. m.
Site Selection. bi-m.

Meetings/Conferences:
Semi-annual Meetings: Spring and Fall

Internat'l Digital Imaging Ass'n (1990)
170 Township Line Rd.
Belle Mead, NJ 08502-4107
Tel: (908)359-3924   *Fax:* (908)359-7619
E-Mail: idia@blast.net
Members: 300 individuals, 525 companies
Staff: 3
Annual Budget: $250-500,000
Exec. Director: April L. Pennacchio
Exec. Administrator: Erica Hunter

Historical Note
Formerly (1994) Ass'n of Imaging Service Bureaus. Absorbed Typographers Internat'l Ass'n in 1996. IDIA is a trade association serving the digital imaging industry. Membership: $295/year (consultant/company); $150/year (educator/instructor); $1,000-$5,000/year, based on gross sales of desktop/prepress products (vendor).

Publications:
Annual Directory. a.
Bulletin. m.
Executive Update. q.
Glitch Report. m. adv.

Meetings/Conferences:
Annual Meetings: February, usually in conjunction with
    CONCEPPTS convention.

Internat'l Disk Drive Equipment and Materials Ass'n (1986)
3255 Scott Blvd., Suite 2-102
Santa Clara, CA 95054-3013
Tel: (408)720-9352   *Fax:* (408)720-9380
Members: 100 individuals, 600 companies
Staff: 6
Annual Budget: $2-5,000,000
Exec. Director: Joan Pinder
Director, Communications: Suzanne Wynn
Director, Meetings: Debbie Lee
Director, Finance: Gloria Rodrigues

Historical Note
IDEMA was founded to promote the disk drive industry by holding trade shows, conferences and meetings and by setting industry standards. Membership: $125/year (individual); $450-895/year (organization/company).

Publications:
Insight. bi-m. adv.

Meetings/Conferences:
Annual Meetings: Usually in San Jose, CA in September

Internat'l District Energy Ass'n (1909)
1200 19th St., N.W., Suite 300
Washington, DC 20036-2422
Tel: (202)429-5111   *Fax:* (202)429-5113
E-Mail: IDEA@dc.sba.com
Web Site: http://www.energy.rochester.edu/IDEA
Members: 850 individuals, 300 businesses
Staff: 3
Annual Budget: $1-2,000,000
President: John L. Fiegel

Historical Note
Formerly (1969) Nat'l District Heating Ass'n, (1985) Internat'l District Heating Ass'n, and (1994) Internat'l District Heating and Cooling Ass'n. Absorbed (1988) North American District Heating and Cooling Institute. Members are owners/operators of District (central) heating and cooling systems, suppliers of centralized piping systems and appurtenances that produce hot water, and architects/engineers associated with the design of such systems.

Publications:
District Energy. q. adv.
District Energy Now. m.
Proceedings. a.

Meetings/Conferences:
Annual Meetings: June
1999 – Boston, MA(Boston Park Plaza Hotel)/June 12-15/500
2000 – Montreal, Quebec(Bonaventure
    Hilton)/June 17-20/500

Internat'l Documentary Ass'n (1982)
1551 South Robertson Blvd.
Suite 201
Los Angeles, CA 90035
Tel: (310)284-8422   *Fax:* (310)785-9334
E-Mail: ida@artnet.net
Web Site: http://www.documentary.org
Members: 1,900 individuals
Staff: 7
Annual Budget: $250-500,000
Exec. Director: Betsy McLane, Ph. D.
Editor: Timothy J. Lyons
Public Relations: Stephanie Mandesich
Special Projects Coordinator: Grace Ouchida
Membership Coordinator: Dale Zackery

Historical Note
The International Documentary Association is a non-profit association founded in 1982 to promote non-fiction film and video, to support the efforts of documentary film and video makers around the world and to increase public appreciation and demand for documentary film and television programs. Our international membership includes producers, directors, writers, editors, camera operators, musicians, researchers, technicians, journalists, broadcast and cable programmers, academics, distributors and members of the general public. Membership: $70/year (individual); $200/year (organization/company).

Publications:
IDA Membership Directory & Survival Guide. bien.
Internat'l Documentary Magazine. 10/year.

Meetings/Conferences:
Annual Awards Dinner: Los Angeles, CA/October/350

Internat'l Doll Restoration Artists Ass'n (1987)
Historical Note
Became the Small Antique Restoration Ass'n in 1996.

Internat'l Door Ass'n (1973)
P.O. Box 246
28 Lowry Drive
West Milton, OH 45383
Tel: (513)698-8042   *Fax:* (513)698-6153
Toll Free: (800)355 - 4432
E-Mail: chrislong@wesnet.com
Members: 1,300 individuals
Staff: 10
Annual Budget: $1-2,000,000
Managing Director: Christopher S. Long

Historical Note
Formerly (1986) Door and Operator Dealers of America and (1997) Door and Operator Dealers Ass'n and Far Western Garage Door Ass'n. Members are producers and installers of garage door systems.

Publications:
International Door and Operator Industry. bi. m.

Meetings/Conferences:
Annual Meetings: Summer
1999 – Toronto, Ontario

Internat'l Double Reed Soc. (1972)
2423 Lawndale Rd.
Finksburg, MD 21048-1401
Tel: (410)871-0658   *Fax:* (410)871-0659
E-Mail: norma4IDRS@erols.com
Web Site: http://idrs.colorado.edu
Members: 4,600 individuals
Staff: 1
Annual Budget: $50-100,000
Exec. Secretary-Treasurer: Lowry Riggins

Historical Note
Members are performers, teachers, students and manufacturers of double reed instruments(e.g., bassoon, oboe). Membership: $30-250/year.

Publications:
Double Reed. 3/year. adv.
The Journal. a. adv.

Meetings/Conferences:
Annual Meetings: Annual/Summer
1999 – Madison, WI(University of
    Wisconsin)/Aug. 10-14/800
2000 – Buenos Aires, AR/Aug. 10-14
2001 – Morgantown, WV(University of West
    Virginia)/Aug. 11-15

Internat'l Downtown Ass'n (1954)
910 17th St., N.W., Suite 210
Washington, DC 20006-2603
Tel: (202)293-4505   *Fax:* (202)293-4509
E-Mail: question@ida-downtown.org
Web Site: www.ida-downtown.org
Members: 575 individuals
Staff: 4
Annual Budget: $500-1,000,000
President: Elizabeth Jackson
Office/Business Manager: Rita Lewis
Information Specialist: Kate Seiver

Historical Note
Formerly (1986) Internat'l Downtown Executives Ass'n. Members are downtown development organizations represented by chief executive officer; city, county or state agencies involved with downtown economic development; and individuals and corporations with an interest in downtown development. Operates a subsidiary for program development, the Downtown Development Foundation. Membership: $295/year (individual); $95-2,495/year, based on budget (company).

Publications:
Downtown News Briefs. m. adv.

Meetings/Conferences:
Annual Meetings: Fall/400
1999 – Meza, AZ
1999 – Charlotte, NC(Radisson Plaza Hotel)/May 15-17
1999 – Philadelphia, PA(Philadelphia Marriott)/Oct. 2-5
2000 – Los Angeles, CA(The Regal Biltmore)/Sept. 16-19
2001 – Pittsburgh, PA

Internat'l Drapery Ass'n (1965)
Historical Note
Defunct in 1996.

Internat'l Drilling Federation (1980)
Historical Note
Merged (1995) with Drilling Equipment Manufacturers Ass'n and Nat'l Drilling Contractors Ass'n to form Nat'l Drilling Ass'n.

Internat'l Drycleaners Congress (1959)
4 West Central Avenue
Oxford, OH 45056
Tel: (513)523-4121   *Fax:* (513)523-1370
Members: 1000 individuals
Staff: 5
Annual Budget: $50-100,000
Exec. Director: William Pulley

Historical Note
IDC is a world-wide organization of fabric care industry leaders in 45 countries who believe they can and should make a contribution to international understanding and goodwill. Membership: $75/year.

Publications:
IDC News. bi-m.

Meetings/Conferences:
1999 – Toronto, Ontario

Internat'l Dwarf Fruit Tree Ass'n (1958)
14 S. Main St.
Middleburg, PA 17842
Tel: (570)837-1551   *Fax:* (570)837-0090
Staff: 2
Annual Budget: $100-250,000
Business Director: Charles J. Ax, Jr.

Historical Note
Founded in Hartford, Michigan in 1958. Membership: $50/year (domestic), $60/year (foreign), $35/year (student).

Publications:
Compact Fruit Tree, Proceedings of the Annual Conference.
Compact News, Newsletter. irreg.

Meetings/Conferences:
Annual Meetings: February-March

Internat'l Dyslexia Ass'n (1949)
Chester Building, Suite 382
8600 La Salle Rd.
Baltimore, MD 21286-2044
Tel: (410)296-0232   *Fax:* (410)321-5069
Toll Free: (800)222 - 3123
E-Mail: info@interdys.org
Web Site: http://www.interdys.org
Members: 12,500 individuals
Staff: 16
Annual Budget: $1-2,000,000
Exec. Director: J. Thomas Viall
Director, Marketing and PR: Susan Brickley
Director, Conferences and Publications: Cindy Ciresi
Director, Membership and Branch Services: Lin Baumann

Historical Note
Formerly (1997) The Orton Dyslexia Soc., IDA is an international organization disseminating information on specific language disabilities-dyslexia. Membership: $55/yr. (individual); $90/yr. (family); $125 (institution).

Publications:
Annual Conference Program. a. adv.
Journal - Annals of Dyslexia. a.
Newsletter - Perspectives on Dyslexia. q. adv.

Meetings/Conferences:
Annual Meetings: Fall
1999 – Chicago, IL(Marriott Downtown)/Nov. 3-6
2000 – Washington, DC(Omni Shoreham)/Nov. 8-11
2001 – Albuquerque, NM(Convention Center)/Oct. 24-27

Internat'l Electrical Testing Ass'n (1972)
P.O. Box 687
106 Stone St.
Morrison, CO 80465
Tel: (303)697-8441   *Fax:* (303)697-8431
E-Mail: neta@compuserve.com
Web Site: http://www.electricnet.com/neta
Members: 600 individuals, 60 companies
Staff: 1
Annual Budget: $250-500,000
Exec. Director: Mary R. Jordan, Ed.D.

Historical Note
Formerly the Nat'l Electrical Testing Ass'n. Members are independent firms in testing, analysis and maintenance of electical power systems; associate members are firms supplying services for the power systems industry. Membership: Based on employees (company), $75/yr. (individual).

Publications:
NETA Conference Program. a. adv.
NETA World. q. adv.

Meetings/Conferences:
Annual Meetings: March
1999 – Pittsburg, PA(Sheraton Station
    Square)/March 9-12/250

Internat'l Electrology Educators (1979)
132 Great Road, Suite 200
Stow, MA 01775-1189
Tel: (978)461-0313   *Fax:* (978)897-5442
Members: 60 schools and educators
Staff: 3
Annual Budget: $100-250,000
Exec. Secretary: Lauren A. Hunte

Historical Note
A committee affiliate of Soc. of Clnical and Medical Electrologists (same address). IEE members are electrology schools and educators. Membership: $75/year (individual).

Publications:
IEE Directory of Schools. irreg.

Meetings/Conferences:
1999 – Nashville, TN

Internat'l Electronic Article Surveillance Manufacturers Ass'n
1420 16th St., N.W.
Washington, DC 20036-2218
Tel: (202)797-9854   *Fax:* (202)332-2301
Members: 12 companies
Staff: 7
Annual Budget: $250-500,000
Exec. V. President: Randy Dyer, CAE

Historical Note
IEASMA members are manufacturers of equipment which provides inventory security for retail and industrial stores or outlets. Membership: varies, based on gross sales.

Publications:
IEASMA Newsletter. bi-m.

Meetings/Conferences:

Internat'l Electronic Packaging Soc. *(1977)*
Historical Note
Merged with the Internat'l Soc. for Hybrid Microelectronics to form Internat'l Microelectronics and Packaging Soc. in 1996.

Internat'l Embryo Transfer Soc. *(1974)*
1111 N. Dunlap Ave.
Savoy, IL 61874
Tel: (217)356-3182   *Fax:* (217)398-4119
E-Mail: iets@assochg.org
Web Site: http://www.iets.uiuc.edu
Members: 1,100 individuals
Staff: 2
Annual Budget: $100-250,000
Business Manager: Charles L. Sapp

Historical Note
Active members are persons interested in the technology of embryo transfer with a veterinary, master's or doctorate degree in a field related to embryo transfer. Membership: $80/year(individual/organization); $40 (student).

Publications:
Embryo Transfer Newsletter. q. adv.

Meetings/Conferences:
Annual Meetings: January
1999 – Quebec City, Quebec(Convention Center)/Jan. 10-12
2000 – Maastricht, Netherlands(Convention
         Center)/Jan. 16-18/600
2001 – Omaha, NE(Holiday Inn)/Jan. 14-17/600

Internat'l Engineering Consortium *(1944)*
549 W. Randolph St., Suite 600
Chicago, IL 60661-2208
Tel: (312)559-4100   *Fax:* (312)559-3329
Web Site: www.iec.org
Members: 73 universities
Staff: 50
Exec. Director: Robert M. Janowiak

Historical Note
Formerly (1974) Nat'l Electronics Conference and (1993) Nat'l Engineering Consortium. A engineering education organization sponsored by major technological universities.

Publications:
Annual Review of Communications. a.

Internat'l Entertainment Buyers Ass'n *(1970)*
P.O. Box 128376
Nashville, TN 37212
Tel: (615)244-0628   *Fax:* (615)244-6228
Toll Free: (888)999 - 4322
E-Mail: info@ieba.org
Web Site: http://www.ieba.org
Annual Budget: $25-50,000
Exec. Director: Kymberle Pearson

Historical Note
IEBA is dedicated to entertainment buyers, artists, managers and publicity persons. Membership: $100/year.

Publications:
Membership Directory.
Newsletter. m.

Meetings/Conferences:
1999 – Nashville, TN(Doubletree)/June 11-14/200
2000 – Nashville, TN(Doubletree)/June 10-13

Internat'l Environmental Technology Ass'n
Historical Note
Address unknown in 1996; presumed inactive.

Internat'l Erosion Control Ass'n *(1972)*
P.O. Box 4904
Steamboat Springs, CO 80477-4904
Tel: (970)879-3010   *Fax:* (970)879-8563
Toll Free: (800)455 - 4322
E-Mail: ecinfo@ieca.org
Web Site: http://www.ieca.org
Members: 1,900 individuals, 1,100 companies
Staff: 5
Annual Budget: $500-1,000,000
Exec. Director: Ben Northcutt

Historical Note
Landscape contractors, architects, engineers, and suppliers, as well as government officials concerned about soil erosion. Membership: $95/year (individual), $295/year (corporate).

Publications:
Erosion Control Journal. bi-m. adv.
IECA Compilations.
Membership Directory. a.
Newsletter. q.
Proceedings. a.
Products/Services Directory. bi-a.

Meetings/Conferences:
1999 – Nashville, TN(Stouffer)/Feb. 22-26
2000 – Pasadena, CA

Internat'l Exchangors Ass'n *(1978)*
Drawer L
Rancho Santa Fe, CA 92067
Tel: (619)756-1441   *Fax:* (619)756-1111
Members: 5,500 individuals
Staff: 2
Annual Budget: $250-500,000
Chairman: Dr. A.D. Kessler

Historical Note
Professionals involved in exchanging real estate. Awards the C.E. (Certified Exchanger) designation.

Publications:
Creative Real Estate Magazine. m.

Internat'l Directory of Exchange Groups.
Listing Book. m.
Roster of Exchangors. q.
Meetings/Conferences:
Annual Meetings: Spring

Internat'l Executive Housekeepers Ass'n *(1930)*
1001 Eastwind Dr., Suite 301
Westerville, OH 43081-3361
Tel: (614)895-7166   *Fax:* (614)895-1248
Toll Free: (800)200 - 6342
E-Mail: excel@ieha.org
Web Site: http://www.ieha.org
Members: 6,300 individuals
Staff: 10
Annual Budget: $1-2,000,000
C.E.O.: Beth B. Risinger
Convention/Meetings Director: Carolyn Dollison
Membership Team Manager: Tisha Gildee

Historical Note
Formerly (1996) Nat'l Executive Housekeepers Ass'n. A professional organization for administrators of housekeeping programs in commercial, institutional and industrial facilities. Membership: $115/year (individual).

Publications:
Executive Housekeeping Today. m. adv.

Meetings/Conferences:
Biennial Meetings: Even years, in Summer

Internat'l Exhibitors Ass'n
Historical Note
Became (1996) Trade Show Exhibitors Ass'n.

Internat'l Fabricare Institute *(1972)*
12251 Tech Road
Silver Spring, MD 20904-1976
Tel: (301)622-1900   *Fax:* (301)622-1568
E-Mail: communication@iti.org
Web Site: http://www.ifi.org
Members: 9,000 companies
Staff: 39
Annual Budget: $2-5,000,000
Chief Exec. Officer: William E. Fisher
V. President, Communications: David J. Uchic
Contributing Editor: Jill Handman
Manager, Government Affairs: Mary Scalco
V. President, Finance: Nadine Harris
Sr. V. President, Membership/Marketing: Roger L. Schilling
V. President: Jon Meijer
Director, Garment Analysis: Jacqueline Stephens

Historical Note
Merger (1972) of the American Institute of Laundering (1883) and the Nat'l Institute of Drycleaning (1907). The national and international association for drycleaners and launderers. Members also include manufacturers and suppliers of cleaning equipment, retailers, garment manufacturers, and others concerned with professional garment cleaning and serviceability. Membership: $179-1,150/year.

Publications:
Clothes Care Gazette. m.
Fabricare Magazine. m. adv.
Fabricare Resources. bi-m.

Meetings/Conferences:
Biennial Meetings: April-July, odd years/25,000.

Internat'l Facility Management Ass'n *(1980)*
One E. Greenway Plaza, Suite 1100
Houston, TX 77046-0194
Tel: (713)623-4362   *Fax:* (713)623-6124
Web Site: http://www.ifma.org
Members: 15,000 individuals, 124 chapters
Annual Budget: $5-10,000,000
President: Dennis L. Longworth
Director, Communications: Donald A. Young
Director, Event Management: Cynthia James
Director, Education: William W. Back
Director, Technology: Pamela Ewton
V. President, Finance/Administration: David Brady
Associate Director of Membership Services: Linda Beverly
Director, Internat'l Development: John Henson

Historical Note
Founded as the Nat'l Facility Management Ass'n, it assumed its present name in 1982. Regular membership is open to any individual who is an in-house member or manager of a department responsible for facility planning, design, or management. Membership: $195/year (individual), $360/year (allied), $210/year (affiliate).

Publications:
Conference Proceedings. a.
Directory. a.
Facility Management Journal. bi-m. adv.
IFMA News. m.

Meetings/Conferences:
Annual Meetings: Fall
1999 – Los Angeles, CA/Oct. 3-5

Internat'l Facsimile Counsultative Council *(1986)*
4019 Lakeview Drive
Lake Havasu City, AZ 86406
Tel: (520)453-9234   *Fax:* (520)453-9234
Members: 1,500 individuals, 150 companies
Staff: 5
Exec. Director: David Day

Historical Note
IFAXA members are corporations directly involved in the facsimile industry.

Publications:
Facsimile Facts and Figures. a. adv.

Meetings/Conferences:
Annual Meetings: Not Held.

Internat'l Family Recreation Ass'n *(1982)*
P.O. Box 520
Gonzales, FL 32560-0520
Tel: (850)944-7992   *Fax:* (850)944-0081
E-Mail: nrvockws@spydee.net
Members: 9,610 individuals
Staff: 4
Annual Budget: $50-100,000
Exec. Officer: K.W. Stephens

Historical Note
Commercial and individual advocates of family recreation and the management of an organized customer base. Supports recommendations and legislation advantageous to recreation, leisure and travel. Promotes recreation, leisure, and travel safety policies and public participation in family recreational, leisure and travel activities. Membership: $49/year (family/individual); $100(commercial).

Publications:
The Recreation Advisor. 5/year. adv.
The Recreation Digest. q. adv.

Meetings/Conferences:
Annual Meetings: November
1999 – Atlanta, GA
2000 – Dallas, TX
2001 – New Orleans, LA

Internat'l Federation for Business Education *(1988)*
Historical Note
Organization defunct in 1997.

Internat'l Federation for Choral Music *(1982)*
Univ. of Illinois Performing Arts Dept.
1040 W. Harrison St., Room L-018
Chicago, IL 60607-7130
Tel: (312)996-8744   *Fax:* (312)996-0954
E-Mail: mja@uic.edu
Web Site: choralnet.org
Members: 2,000 individuals, 100 organizations
Staff: 3
Annual Budget: $1-2,000,000
Deputy Secretary-General: Dr. Michael J. Anderson

Historical Note
The Federation was formed to strengthen cooperation between national and international organizations interested in choral music, encourage formation of new choral organizations, promote international exchange programs and the inclusion of choral music in general education, and to inform the public of occurrences in the choral field. Membership: $40/year (individual); $125-2,500 (organization/company).

Publications:
International Choral Bulletin. q. adv.
World Census of Choral Music. a.

Meetings/Conferences:
1999 – Rottedam, Netherlands/3000
1999 – Rotterdam, Netherlands/3000

Internat'l Federation of Inspection Agencies - Americas Committee
3942 N. Upland St.
Arlington, VA 22207
Tel: (703)533-9539   *Fax:* (703)533-1612
E-Mail: ifianac@aol.com
Annual Budget: $25-50,000
Exec. Director: Milton M. Bush, JD, CAE

Historical Note
IFIA-NAC monitors standards, safety procedures, and rules and regulations to determine their impact on member companies and suggest potential improvements. Membership: $7,668/year (company).

Internat'l Federation of Leather Guilds *(1966)*
Historical Note
Address unknown in 1995.

Internat'l Federation of Nurse Anesthetists *(1985)*
222 South Prospect Avenue
Park Ridge, IL 60068
Tel: (847)692-7050   *Fax:* (847)692-6968
E-Mail: ifna@aana.com
Web Site: http://www.aana.com/ifna
Members: 45,000 individuals
Staff: 1
Exec. Director: Ronald F. Caulk, CRNA

Historical Note
IFNA represents and promotes nurse anesthetists internationally through the education activities and continuing education programs.

Internat'l Federation of Pharmaceutical Wholesalers *(1984)*
c/o Goetz, Loeher, Shields & Mittman
3915 Old Lee Highway, Suite #22-A
Fairfax, VA 22030-2432
Tel: (703)352-0808   *Fax:* (703)352-6905
E-Mail: ifpwusa@ifpw.com
Web Site: www.ifpw.com
Members: 110 companies
Annual Budget: $250-500,000
President: William Goetz
Director of Finance and Technology: Christopher Goetz
Director of Administration: Samantha Beaty

Historical Note
Membership: $250-$5,000/year (corporate).

Publications:
Focus. bi-w.
Update. bi-w.

Meetings/Conferences:
Annual Meetings: September
1999 – Naples, FL/Sept. 28-29

Internat'l Federation of Professional and Technical Engineers (1918)
8630 Fenton St., Suite 400
Silver Spring, MD 20910-3803
Tel: (301)565-9016   Fax: (301)565-0018
Web Site: http://www.ifpte.org
Members: 30,000 individuals
Staff: 12
Annual Budget: $1-2,000,000
President: Paul E. Almeida
Secretary-Treasurer: Gregory J. Junemann
General Counsel: Julia A. Clark

Historical Note
Founded in Washington, DC, July 1, 1918 as the Internat'l Federation of Draftsmen's Unions and affiliated with the American Federation of Labor. Became the Internat'l Federation of Technical Engineers' Architects' and Draftsmen's Unions in 1919, the American Federation of Technical Engineers in 1953 and assumed its present name in 1973.

Publications:
Outlook. bi-m.

Meetings/Conferences:
Triennial Meetings: July
2000 – Seattle, WA

Internat'l Federation of Women's Travel Organizations (1969)
13901 N. 73rd St., Suite 210-B
Scottsdale, AZ 85260-3125
Tel: (602)596-6640   Fax: (602)596-6638
E-Mail: ifwtohq@primenet.com
Web Site: http://www.ifwto.trav.org
Members: 5,000 individuals, 70 organizations
Staff: 2
Annual Budget: $50-100,000
Exec. Administrator: Mary Beth McClellan

Historical Note
Seeks to improve and make more effective the status of women within the travel industry through the exchange of ideas and personal participation. Membership is comprised of organizations which have been in existence at least one year and whose members are engaged in the sale and/or promotion of passenger travel. Membership: $25/year (individual); $100/year (organization/company).

Publications:
Directory. a.
Federation Footnotes. q.

Meetings/Conferences:
Annual Meetings: Spring
1999 – Alaska(Holland America Cruise)/May 8-15/450
2000 – Ottawa, Ontario(Westin)/April 12-16/350

Internat'l Festivals and Events Ass'n (1956)
115 E. Railroad Ave., Suite 302
Port Angeles, WA 98362-0336
Tel: (360)457-3141   Fax: (360)452-4695
E-Mail: Bruce@Ifea.com
Web Site: http://www.ifea.com
Members: 2,400 individuals
Staff: 15
Annual Budget: $1-2,000,000
President: Bruce Skinner
V. President, Communications: Mark A. Tucker
Marketing Director: Alexis Sorensen
V. President, Events: George Hill
Director, Administrative Services: Jennifer Charles
Finance Director: Julie Hester
Director, Membership Services: Shelly Sukert

Historical Note
Members are individuals employed by the administrations of community and civic festivals. Membership: $125-650/year.

Publications:
Chapter Newsletters. q.
Festivals. q.

Meetings/Conferences:
1999 – Phoenix, AZ(Biltmore Hotel)/Sept. 22-26/1100

Internat'l Festivals Ass'n (1956)
Historical Note
Became the Internat'l Festivals and Events Ass'n in 1997.

Internat'l Fibre Drum Institute (1974)
c/o HMT Associates, LLC
1850 K St., N.W., Suite 200
Washington, DC 20006
Tel: (202)463-3511   Fax: (202)463-3512
Members: 6 companies
Staff: 2
Annual Budget: $25-50,000
Technical Advisor: Gordon Rousseau

Historical Note
An Formerly (1994) the Fibre Drum Technical Council, IFDI is an international association of fibre drum manufacturers which addresses issues affecting the manufacture and use of fibre drums for the transportation of industrial liquid and solid commodities. IFDI devotes primary attention to regulatory codes governing the packaging of dangerous goods which are established by national authorities and international bodies. The law firm of Winston & Strawn (Washington, DC) provides Secretariate services to IFDI.

Internat'l Financial Services Ass'n (1924)
One World Trade Center, Suite 2269
New York, NY 10048
Tel: (212)466-3352   Fax: (212)432-0544
Web Site: http://www.intlbanking.org

Members: 300 businesses
Staff: 5
Annual Budget: $1-2,000,000
President: Dan Taylor
V. President, Education: Patricia Barry

Historical Note
Formerly (1998) United States Council om Internat'l Banking. USCIB members are banks involved in international operations.

Publications:
FYI. m.
IFSA Newsletter. 3-4/yr.

Meetings/Conferences:
1999 – San Antonio, TX/Oct. 10-14

Internat'l Fire Photographers Ass'n (1964)
143 40th St.
New Orleans, LA 70124
Members: 300 individuals
Annual Budget: under $10,000
President: Chris Mickel

Historical Note
Fire photographers affiliated with fire departments, law enforcement, insurance, and related services dedicated to promoting the use of photography in fire investigations and in fire prevention education. Also works to establish harmonious relationships with news media and related agencies. Has no paid staff. Certification program awards designations of Journeyman, Craftsman and Master Fire Photographer. Non-voting corporate membership is available to manufacturers, dealers and distributors of photographic equipment. Membership: $35/year; $37.50/year (Canadian); $40/year (overseas); $75/year (company).

Publications:
Fire Photography Journal. q. adv.
Membership Manual. a. adv.

Meetings/Conferences:
Annual Meetings: Summer

Internat'l Firestop Council
25 N. Broadway
Tarrytown, NY 10591-3201
Tel: (914)332-0040   Fax: (914)332-1541
Members: 26 comapnies
Staff: 3
Annual Budget: $50-100,000
Exec. Director: Richard C. Byrne

Internat'l Floor Covering Representatives Ass'n (1994)
Historical Note
Address unknown in 1997.

Internat'l Food Additives Council (1980)
5775 Peachtree-Dunwoody Rd., Suite 500-G
Atlanta, GA 30342-1558
Tel: (404)252-3663   Fax: (404)252-0774
E-Mail: IFAC@ASSNHQ.COM
Members: 11 companies
Staff: 1
Annual Budget: $100-250,000
President: Andrew G. Ebert, Ph.D.

Historical Note
Information clearing house concerning the use in food and safety of food additives. Members are companies engaged in the manufacture, sale, reformulation and commercial use of food additives. Serves as a regulatory and scientific liaison for industry concerning food additives.

Publications:
Food Additives.

Meetings/Conferences:

Internat'l Food Information Council (1985)
1100 Connecticut Ave. NW, Suite 430
Washington, DC 20036
Tel: (202)296-6540   Fax: (202)296-6547
E-Mail: foodinfo@ifichealth.org
Web Site: http://ificinfo.health.org
Members: 28 companies
Staff: 19
Annual Budget: $1-2,000,000
President: Sylvia B. Rowe
Assoc. Director, Communications: Ann G. Bouchoux
Director, Media Relations: Tmelia Steiner
Director, Administration: Geraldine M. Carbo

Historical Note
IFIC serves as an information and educational resource on food safety and nutrition.

Publications:
Food Insight. bi-m.

Meetings/Conferences:

Internat'l Food Service Executives' Ass'n (1901)
1100 S. State Rd. 7, Suite 103
Margate, FL 33068
Tel: (954)977-0767   Fax: (954)977-0874
E-Mail: HQ@IFSEA.ORG
Web Site: http://www.ifsea.org
Members: 5,000 individuals
Staff: 3
Annual Budget: $250-500,000
President: Edward H. Manley, CFE,DHFSA

Historical Note
The oldest food service trade association. Formerly (1957) Internat'l Stewards' and Caterers' Ass'n and (1977) Food Service Executives' Ass'n, Inc. Administers the Certified Food Executive (CFE) program. Membership: $125/year.

Publications:
Hotline. q. adv.

Meetings/Conferences:
Annual Meetings: Summer

1999 – San Diego, CA(Town & Country)/March 11-14/1000
2000 – Chicago, IL(Hyatt O'hare)/April 6-9/1000
2001 – Anaheim, CA(Marriott)/March 2-5/1000
2002 – Tampa Bay, FL(Marriott)/March 21-24/1000

Internat'l Food, Wine and Travel Writers Ass'n (1956)
P.O. Box 13110
Long Beach, CA 90803
Tel: (562)433-5969   Fax: (562)438-6384
Members: 465 individuals
Staff: 2
Annual Budget: $100-250,000
Exec. Director: Ron Hodges

Historical Note
Established in Paris. Headquarters moved to California in 1981. Members are freelance and/or staff writers, editors, and photographers specializing in food, wine and/or travel writing. Associate memberships are available for individuals or companies in the travel and hospitality industries. Membership: $95/year (regular member), $150/year (associate), plus $50 initiation fee.

Publications:
Press Pass. m.
Windows to the World. a.

Meetings/Conferences:

Internat'l Foodservice Brokers Ass'n
Historical Note
Became (1998) Internat'l Foodservice Brokers Ass'n/Ass'n of Sales & Marketing Companies.

Internat'l Foodservice Brokers Ass'n/Ass'n of Sales & Marketing Companies (1994)
2100 Reston Pkwy., Suite 400
Reston, VA 20191-1218
Tel: (703)758-7790   Fax: (703)758-7787
E-Mail: Abraham@asmc.org
Web Site: http://www.asmc.org
Members: 600 companies
Staff: 25
Annual Budget: $5-10,000,000
Exec. Director and C.E.O./IFBA: Rick Abraham
V. President of Marketing and Members Services: Karen Connell

Historical Note
An association for food service agencies and food service manufacturers using sales and marketing representation.

Publications:
Sales & Marketing Quarterly.

Meetings/Conferences:
1999 – Chicago, IL
1999 – San Juan, Puerto Rico

Internat'l Foodservice Distributors Ass'n (1956)
Historical Note
A division of Food Distributors Internat'l in 1996.

Internat'l Foodservice Editorial Council (1956)
P.O. Box 491
Hyde Park, NY 12538-0491
Tel: (918)452-4345   Fax: (918)452-0532
E-Mail: ifec@aol.com
Members: 250 individuals
Staff: 2
Annual Budget: $100-250,000
Exec. Director: Carol Lally Metz

Historical Note
IFEC is a non-profit international organization of communicators working in the foodservice industry. Its purpose is to facilitate the exchange of ideas between editors and other communicators and help advance the foodservice industry through media communications. Members include editors, publicists, marketers, educators, representatives of multi-unit operations, foodservice home economists, consultants and others active in foodservice communications. Membership: $225/year (individual).

Publications:
Directory. a.
IFEC Newsletter. m.

Meetings/Conferences:
Annual Meetings: Fall
1999 – Miami, FL(Hyatt Regency)

Internat'l Foodservice Manufacturers Ass'n (1952)
Two Prudential Plaza
180 N. Stetson Ave., Suite 4400
Chicago, IL 60601
Tel: (312)540-4400   Fax: (312)540-4401
Web Site: foodserviceworld.com/ifma
Members: 600 companies
Staff: 20
Annual Budget: $5-10,000,000
President: Michael J Licata
V. President, Communications: Janet E. Rustigan
V. President of Educational Programs: John P. Daschler
Sr. V. President & C.F.O.: Anthony J. Marchese

Historical Note
Founded as the Institutional Food Manufacturers of America, it became the Institutional Food-Service Manufacturers Association in 1964 and assumed its present name in 1970. Members are manufacturers of food, equipment and supplies for the away-from-home feeding market. Has an annual budget of $6 million.

Publications:
IFMA World. 9/year.
Membership Directory. a.

Meetings/Conferences:
Annual Meetings: late February
1999 – Palm Beach, FL(Breakers)/Nov. 7-10

Internat'l Formalwear Ass'n (1973)
401 N. Michigan Ave.

Chicago, IL 60611
Tel: (312)644-6610   *Fax:* (312)245-1081
E-Mail: IFA@SBA.COM
Web Site: http://www.formalwear.org
Members: 325 companies
Staff: 2
Annual Budget: $250-500,000
Exec. Director: Jack M. Springer
Administrative Director: Karin S. Aeschliman

Historical Note
Formerly a division of the Menswear Retailers of America, became autonomous in 1981 as the American Formalwear Ass'n. Assumed its present name in 1987. Membership: $195-695/year.

Publications:
Formalwords Newsletter. bi-m. adv.
Membership Roster. a. adv.

Meetings/Conferences:
1999 – Reno, NV(Nugget)/Sept. 15-18/1500
2000 – San Francisco, CA(Marriott)/Sept. 13-16/1500

Internat'l Formula Council *(1970)*
5775 Peachtree-Dunwoody Rd., Suite 500-G
Atlanta, GA 30342-1558
Tel: (404)252-3663   *Fax:* (404)252-0774
Members: 3 companies
President: Robert C. Gelardi
Exec. Director: Mardi K. Mountford

Historical Note
Formerly the Infant Formula Council and Enteral Nutrition Council. IFC is an international association of formulated nutrition products, infant formula and adult nutritionals.

Meetings/Conferences:
Annual Meetings: February-March

Internat'l Foundation for Telemetering *(1964)*
5959 Topanga Canyon Blvd., Suite 150
Woodland Hills, CA 91367
Tel: (818)884-9568
Treasurer: D.R. Andelin

Historical Note
IFT is a technical organization concerned with the theory and practice of telemetry. Has no paid officers or full-time staff.

Publications:
ITC Proceedings. a.

Meetings/Conferences:

Internat'l Foundation of Employee Benefit Plans *(1954)*
P.O. Box 69
Brookfield, WI 53008-0069
Tel: (414)786-6700   *Fax:* (414)786-8670
E-Mail: mbrshp@ifebp.org
Web Site: http://www.ifebp.org
Members: 35,000 individuals
Staff: 140
Annual Budget: $10-25,000,000
C.E.O.: John A. Altobelli
Director, Public Relations/Advertising: Terri L. Bannon
Sr. Director, Education: Mary Just
Sr. Director, CEBS: Daniel Graham
Director, Administration: John W. Steinbach
Marketing and Membership Senior Director: Dean D. Ossanna
Director, Publications: Dee Birschel

Historical Note
Formerly (1973) Nat'l Foundation of Health, Welfare and Pension Plans. Membership consists of individuals working in the field of employee benefits. Has an annual budget of approximately $20 million. Membership: $495/year.

Publications:
Benefits Quarterly.
Canadian Legal-Legislative Benefits Reporter. m.
Digest. m.
Employee Benefits Journal. q.
Legal-Legislative Reporter News Bulletin. m.

Meetings/Conferences:
Annual Meetings: Fall/6,000
1999 – October

Internat'l Franchise Ass'n *(1960)*
1350 New York Ave., N.W., Suite 900
Washington, DC 20005-4709
Tel: (202)628-8000   *Fax:* (202)628-0812
E-Mail: info@franchise.org
Web Site: http://www.franchise.org
Members: 32,000 companies
Staff: 28
Annual Budget: $5-10,000,000
President: Don J. DeBolt, CAE
V. President, Communications and Media Relations: Terry Hill
V. President, Public Affairs and Emerging Markets: Terrian Barnes
Director, Government Affairs & Assoc. Counsel: Maureen Riehl
Director, State Government Relations and Small Business Initiatives: Greg Smith
V. President, Operations: Debra A. Moss
Exec. V. President, Marketing: John R. Reynolds, CAE
Director, International Development and Global Marketing: Marcel Portmann
V. President and Chief Counsel: Matt Shay
Exec. V. Prsident, Membership: Scott Lehr

Historical Note
Membership consists of companies franchising the distribution of their goods or services, unit owners (franchisees) and companies supplying products and services to franchise businesses. Sponsors and supports the Franchising Political Action Committee and the IFA Educational Foundation.

Publications:
Franchise Opportunities Guide. semi-a.
Franchising World Magazine. bi-m.
IFA Insider Newsletter. bi-w.

Meetings/Conferences:
Annual Meetings: Fall/1,200-1,500
1999 – Miami Beach, FL(Fontainebleau Hilton)/March 4-6

Internat'l Fresh-cut Produce Ass'n *(1987)*
1600 Duke St., Suite 440
Alexandria, VA 22314
Tel: (703)299-6282   *Fax:* (703)299-6288
Web Site: http://www.fresh-cuts.org
Members: 525 companies
Staff: 6
Annual Budget: $500-1,000,000
President: Edith H. Garrett
Director, Meetings: Justina Brewer
Manager, Membership Services: Jennifer Golisch

Historical Note
Members are companies involved in the processing of fresh fruits and vegetables for commercial distribution. Membership: $550-975/year (organization/company); $125 (government/university/individual).

Publications:
Cutting Edge Newsletter. q.
Directory & Buyer's Guide. a. adv.

Meetings/Conferences:
1999 – Tampa, Fl(Tampa Convention
          Center)/April 15-17/1350
2000 – Dallas, TX(Wyndham Anatore)/March 9-11/1350
2001 – Pheonix, AZ(Pheonix Civic Center)/April 5-7/1350

Internat'l Frozen Food Ass'n *(1974)*
2000 Corporate Ridge, Suite 1000
McLean, VA 22102
Tel: (703)821-0770   *Fax:* (703)821-1350
Members: 60 companies and associations
Staff: 2
Annual Budget: $10-25,000
Director General: Steven C. Anderson
Deputy Director General: Leslie G. Sarasin
Deputy Director General: Kimberly H. Ramsey

Historical Note
Federation of ass'ns and companies involved in distribution, production or marketing of frozen food for internat'l markets. Affiliated with the American Frozen Food Institute.

Publications:
IFFA World Review.

Meetings/Conferences:
Biennial Meetings: (1999)

Internat'l Function Point Users Group *(1984)*
Blendonview Office Park
5008-28 Pine Creek Drive
Westerville, OH 43081-4899
Tel: (614)895-7130   *Fax:* (614)895-3466
Members: 650 companies
Staff: 5
Annual Budget: $500-1,000,000
Exec. Director: Rick Bannister

Historical Note
Members are companies and individuals employing the function point measurement process for business management. Membership: $250/year.

Publications:
IFPUG Newsletter. semi-a. adv.

Meetings/Conferences:
Semi-Annual Meetings: Spring and Fall

Internat'l Furnishings and Design Ass'n *(1947)*
1200 19th St., N.W., Suite 300
Washington, DC 20036-2422
Tel: (202)857-1897   *Fax:* (202)828-6042
Members: 2,000 individuals
Staff: 2
Annual Budget: $250-500,000
Exec. Director: Jennifer A. Lewis

Historical Note
Formerly (1987) Nat'l Home Fashions League. IFDA members are executives from diverse industries related to residential and commercial furnishings including interior and product design, communications, manufacturing, retailing, education, architecture and finance. Membership: $225/year (individual).

Publications:
IFDA Directory a. adv. adv.
IFDA Network. q. adv.

Meetings/Conferences:
Annual Meetings: 250

Internat'l Furniture Rental Ass'n *(1964)*
9202 N. Meridian St., Suite 200
Indianapolis, IN 46260
Tel: (317)571-5613   *Fax:* (317)571-5603
Members: 45 companies
Annual Budget: $100-250,000
Exec. Director: Jerry Gorup, CAE

Historical Note
Founded as Furniture Rental Ass'n of America; assumed its current name in 1994. Incorporated 1972 in Massachusetts, IFRA is the only trade association serving the furniture renting and leasing industry exclusively. Represents approximately two-thirds of the industry. Associate Membership: $500/yr. (supplier); Voting Membership fee based on number of showrooms.

Publications:
IFRA Newsletter. bi-m.

Meetings/Conferences:
Annual Meetings: Spring

Internat'l Gas Turbine Institute, ASME *(1946)*
5775 B Glenridge Dr. Suite 370
Atlanta, GA 30328-5380

Tel: (404)847-0072   *Fax:* (404)847-0151
Web Site: http://www.asme.org
Staff: 15
Annual Budget: $2-5,000,000
Managing Director: Ann McClure, CAE
Manager, Expositions: Scott J. Moore, CAE

Historical Note
An eductional and technical institute of the American Soc. of Mechanical Engineers.

Publications:
Annual Who's Who in Gas Turbine Technology. a.
Global Gast Turbine News Newsletter. bi-m.
Technology Report. a. adv.

Meetings/Conferences:
1999 – Indianapolis, IN(Convention Center)

Internat'l Gay and Lesbian Franchise Ass'n *(1995)*

Historical Note
Address unknown in 1997.

Internat'l Glaucoma Congress *(1977)*

Historical Note
A division of the American Soc. of Contemporary Ophthalmology.

Internat'l Glutamate Technical Committee *(1969)*
1101 15th St., N.W., Suite 202
Washington, DC 20005-5002
Tel: (202)785-3232   *Fax:* (202)223-9741
E-Mail: ebertan@assnhq.com
Members: 60 individuals, 20 companies
Staff: 3
Annual Budget: $100-250,000
Chairman: Dr. Andrew G. Ebert, Ph.D.

Historical Note
Composed of phyicians and/or scientists employed by producers or users of glutamic acid and its salts or doing research on it in university laboratories. Membership: $2,000/year.

Meetings/Conferences:
Annual Meetings: Fall
2000 – Taiwan

Internat'l Graphic Arts Education Ass'n *(1923)*
200 Deer Run Road
Sewickley, PA 15143-2328
Tel: (412)749-9165
Web Site: http://www.igaea.org
Members: 800 individuals
Annual Budget: $25-50,000
Contact: James Workman

Historical Note
Founded in 1936 as the Nat'l Graphic Arts Education Ass'n. Adopted the present name in 1950 and was incorporated in 1969. Members are teachers of printing, photography and the graphic arts. Membership: $15/year (individual); $150/year (organization/company).

Publications:
Research & Resource Report. 3/year.
The Communicator. bi-m.
Visual Communications Journal. a.

Meetings/Conferences:
Annual Meetings: Summer, always in a university setting

Internat'l Graphoanalysis Soc. *(1929)*
111 N. Canal St.
Chicago, IL 60606
Tel: (312)930-9446   *Fax:* (312)930-5903
E-Mail: headquarters@igas.com
Web Site: http://www.igas.com
Members: 15,000 individuals
Staff: 60
Annual Budget: $250-500,000
Administrator: Brett Hallongren

Historical Note
Graphoanalysis is the analysis of handwriting for personality assessment. Used in such areas as testing for employment and education counseling. Absorbed the American Institute of Grapho Analysis in 1949. Membership: $90/year.

Publications:
Journal of Graphoanalysis. m.

Meetings/Conferences:
Semi-annual meetings: Attendance 1,000

Internat'l Graphological Soc. *(1983)*
3530 Forest Lane, Suite 155
Dallas, TX 75234
Tel: (214)351-3668
Toll Free: (800)960 - 1034
Members: 1,100 individuals
Annual Budget: $100-250,000
Director: Patricia J. Johnson
Exec. Director: Allan Coursey

Historical Note
IGS members are graphologists, document examiners and others with an interest in handwriting analysis. Membership: $20/year.

Publications:
Document Examiner. q.
Quill. q. adv.

Meetings/Conferences:
Annual Meetings: November
1999 – Kansas City, MO

Internat'l Grooving and Grinding Ass'n *(1972)*

Historical Note
Address unknown in 1997.

Internat'l Ground Source Heat Pump Ass'n *(1987)*
490 Cordell South

Oklahoma State University
Stillwater, OK 74078
Tel: (405)744-5175   *Fax:* (405)744-5283
Toll Free: (800)626 - 4747
E-Mail: jbose@master.ceat.okstate.edu
Members: 2,800 individuals
Staff: 20
Annual Budget: $500-1,000,000
Exec. Director, Program Coordinator: James Bose
Marketing, Membership & Training: James D. Netherton
Historical Note
Members are manufacturers, distributors and installers of heat pumps making use of ground water in the exchange process. Membership: $70/year (individual); $330-1,100/year (company).
Publications:
1997 IGSHPA Membership Directory. a. adv.
The Source. q. adv.
Meetings/Conferences:

Internat'l Group of Agencies and Bureaus (1986)
6845 Parkdale Place, Suite A
Indianapolis, IN 46254-5605
Tel: (317)297-0872   *Fax:* (317)387-3387
Web Site: http://www.igab.org
Members: 115 speakers bureaus and agents
Staff: 5
Annual Budget: $50-100,000
Exec. V. President: James D. Montoya, CAE
Historical Note
Formerly (1991) Internat'l Group of Agents and Bureaus. Members are bureaus, agencies or management companies who actively book professional speakers. Membership: $225/year.
Publications:
Bureau Talk. m.
Meetings/Conferences: *Annual Meetings:* April/75
1999 – Vancouver, B.C.(The Sutton Marc Hotel)/April 29-May 2

Internat'l Guards Union of America (1947)
602 Fallon Ave.
Monticello, MN 55362
Tel: (612)295-8036   *Fax:* (612)295-8536
E-Mail: igua@soncom.com
Members: 2,600 individuals
Staff: 1
Annual Budget: $10-25,000
General Secretary: William A. Malone
Historical Note
Originally affiliated with the Building Services Employees Internat'l Union, IGUA became an independent union in 1948. Independent labor union. Guards, watchmen and others hired to protect personnel and property. Membership: $4/month (individual).
Publications:
IGUA Newsletter. q.
Meetings/Conferences:
1999 – Las Vegas, NV

Internat'l Guild of Candle Artisans (1961)
867 Browning Ave. South
Salem, OR 97302
Tel: (503)589-0650   *Fax:* (503)371-0494
Members: 700 companies and individuals
Staff: 1
Annual Budget: $25-50,000
Editor: Eleanor Wulff
Historical Note
IGCA members are individuals and companies with an interest in candle making. Membership: $50 first year, $30/year renewal.
Publications:
Candlelighter Newsletter. m. adv.
Candlelighter Yearbook and Buyers Guide. m.
Meetings/Conferences:
1999 – Pittsburgh, PA

Internat'l Guild of Professional Electrologists (1979)
803 N. Main St., Suite 8
High Point, NC 27262-3921
Toll Free: (800)830 - 3247
Web Site: http://www.bworks.com/igpe/
Members: 2,000 individuals
Staff: 4
Annual Budget: $100-250,000
President: Trudy Brown, LE,CPE
Historical Note
A public relations organization whose members are professional electrologists and manufacturers of hair-removing equipment as well as owners and teachers of schools of electrolysis. Membership: $85/year (individual); $290/year (schools and manufacturers).
Publications:
IGPE Newsletter. q. adv.
Meetings/Conferences:
Annual Meetings: Fall

Internat'l Guild of Symphony, Opera and Ballet Musicians
5802 16th Ave., N.E.
Seattle, WA 98105
Tel: (206)524-7050
Members: 400 individuals
President: R.L. Baunton
Historical Note
Independent labor union. Has no paid officers or full-time staff.

Internat'l Hand Protection Ass'n (1902)
7315 Wisconsin Ave., Suite 424-East
Bethesda, MD 20814

Tel: (301)961-8680   *Fax:* (301)961-8681
Members: 65 companies
Staff: 3
Annual Budget: $100-250,000
Exec. Director: Sanford J. Hill
Historical Note
Formerly (1967) the Work Glove Institute, and (1991) Work Glove Manufacturers Ass'n.
Publications:
InTouch Newsletter. bi-m.
Meetings/Conferences:
Annual Meetings: June
1999 – Marco Island, FL/(Marriott Marco Island)/June 18-23

Internat'l Hard Anondizing Ass'n (1989)
P.O. Box 579
Moorestown, NJ 08057-0579
Tel: (609)234-0330   *Fax:* (609)727-9504
Members: 30 companies
Staff: 4
Annual Budget: $10-25,000
Exec. Director: Dennis C. Neff
Historical Note
IHAA was formed by companies in the hard anodizing business to provide a forum for the exchange of technical information and to act as a clearing house for information about the industry. Membership: $400/year (corporate).
Meetings/Conferences:
Biennial Meetings: Fall
2000 – Barcelona, Spain

Internat'l Hardware Distributors Ass'n (1993)
401 N. Michigan Ave., Suite 2200
Chicago, IL 60611-4267
Tel: (312)644-6610   *Fax:* (312)527-6640
E-Mail: IHDA@SBA.COM
Members: 60 wholesale hardware distributors
Annual Budget: $250-500,000
Managing Director: Glen R. Anderson
Historical Note
Formed by the consolidation of the American Wholesale Hardware Ass'n and the Nat'l Wholesale Hardware Ass'n in 1993. Membership fee varies, based on annual sales volume.
Publications:
NewsFax. m.
Meetings/Conferences:
Annual Meetings: Spring

Internat'l Health Evaluation Ass'n (1972)
6412 Dahlonega Rd.
Bethesda, MD 20816
Tel: (301)765-1179   *Fax:* (301)765-0829
E-Mail: mfloor@cpcug.org
Members: 400 individuals, 50 organizations
Annual Budget: $50-100,000
Exec. V. President and Secretary: Marianne K. Floor, M.D., MPH
Historical Note
A non-profit international organization devoted to the development and practice of preventive medicine using computer-based techniques for data gathering and/or data analysis. Members include medical directors, industrial physicians, computer experts, administrators, HMOs, system and biomedical equipment suppliers, mobile test van operators, educators, and individual practicing physicians. NHEA strives to maintain an important balance of providers and suppliers. Has no paid staff. Membership fee: $350/year (group), $100/year (professional), $30/year (student).
Publications:
Meeting Proceedings. a. adv.
Newsletters. 3/year.
Meetings/Conferences:
Annual Meetings: September/October

Internat'l Health, Racquet and Sportsclub Ass'n (1981)
263 Summer St., 8th Fl.
Boston, MA 02210
Tel: (617)951-0055   *Fax:* (617)951-0056
Toll Free: (800)228 - 4772
E-Mail: ihrsa@aol.com
Web Site: http://www.ihrsa.org
Members: 350 companies, 4600 clubs
Staff: 50
Annual Budget: $5-10,000,000
Exec. Director: John McCarthy, CAE
Director, Public Relations: Catherine Masterson McNeil
Director, Government Relations: Helen A. Durkin
Director, Marketing and Meetings: William Dussor
Education Manager: Janice De Groot
Financial/Business Director: Anita Horne Lawlor
Director, Operations: Rick Devereux
Historical Note
Formed as Internat'l Racquet Sports Ass'n as the result of a merger between the Nat'l Court Clubs Ass'n and the Nat'l Tennis Ass'n; became IRSA-the Ass'n of Quality Clubs in 1991, and assumed its current name in 1995. Members are commercial, for-profit health and sport clubs, as well as manufacturers and suppliers. Has an annual budget of approximately $7.8 million. Membership fee varies, based on annual revenues.
Publications:
Club Business Internat'l. m.
Meetings/Conferences:
Annual Meetings: Spring
1999 – San Diego, CA(Marriott)/March 24-27
2001 – San Francisco, CA(Marriott)/March 21-24

Internat'l Hearing Soc. (1951)
20361 Middlebelt Road
Livonia, MI 48154
Tel: (734)522-7200   *Fax:* (734)522-0200

Toll Free: (800)521 - 5247
Web Site: http://www.hearingins.org
Members: 4,000 individuals
Staff: 10
Annual Budget: $1-2,000,000
Exec. Director: Robin Holm
Director, Marketing/Public Relations: Glenn L. Peacock
Assoc. Director: Phyllis Wilson
Historical Note
Formerly (1992) the Nat'l Hearing Aid Soc., prior to that was called the Soc. of Hearing Aid Audiologists until 1966. Professional association of hearing instrument specialists. Membership: $200/year.
Publications:
Audecibel. q. adv.
Directory. a.
Meetings/Conferences:
Annual Meetings: Fall
1999 – Philadelphia, PA(Marriott)/Oct. 13-17

Internat'l Herb Ass'n
P.O. Box 317
Mundelein, IL 60060-0317
Tel: (847)949-4372   *Fax:* (847)949-5896
E-Mail: IHAOFFICE@aol.com
Web Site: http://www.herb-pros.com
Members: 700 individuals
Exec. Director: Cathy Sebastian
Historical Note
Formerly (1994) Internat'l Herb Growers and Marketers Ass'n. Membership: $100/year.
Publications:
IHA Newsletter. 6 times/year. adv.
Meetings/Conferences:
1999 – East Lansing, MI(Kellogg Conference Ctr.)/July 8-11

Internat'l Hockey League (1945)
1577 N. Woodward Ave., Suite 212
Bloomfield Hills, MI 48304-2820
Tel: (248)258-0580   *Fax:* (248)258-0940
E-Mail: ihl@mindspring.com
Web Site: http://www.TheIhl.com
Members: 19 teams
Staff: 16
Annual Budget: $2-5,000,000
President: Doug Moss
Director, Communications: Jim Anderson
Chief Financial Officer: Joe Fada
Historical Note
Professional ice hockey league. In addition to participating in IHL league play, many IHL franchises serve as feeders to Nat'l Hockey League franchises.
Publications:
Hockey Schedule. a.
Media Guide.
Meetings/Conferences:
Semi-Annual Meetings: January and June
1999 – /Jan. 6-11

Internat'l Home Furnishings Marketing Ass'n
P.O. Box 5687
High Point, NC 27262-5687
Tel: (336)889-0203   *Fax:* (336)889-7460
Members: 2,300 exhibitors
Staff: 2
C.E.O.: Richard Barentine
Historical Note
Formerly (1989) the Furniture Factories' Marketing Ass'n of the South. IHFMA acts as the introductory wholesale market for a range of finished products, including home furnishings, gift and decorative accessories, lighting, and area floor covering.
Meetings/Conferences:
Annual Meetings: High Point, NC
1999 – /April 15-23
2000 – /April 6-14
2001 – /April 19-27
2002 – /April 18-26
2003 – /April 3-11
2004 – /April 22-30
2005 – /April 14-22
2006 – /April 27-May 5
2007 – /April 19-27
2008 – /April 10-18
2009 – /April 23-May 1
2010 – /April 15-23

Internat'l Home Furnishings Representatives Ass'n (1934)
P.O. Box 670
High Point, NC 27261-0670
Tel: (336)889-3920   *Fax:* (336)883-8245
Members: 3,200 individuals, 33 chapters
Staff: 5
Annual Budget: $250-500,000
Exec. Director: Kelly R. Crisco, CHR
Business Manager: Kimberly Huneycutt
Historical Note
Formerly (1967) Nat'l Wholesale Furniture Salesmens' Ass'n and (1972) Nat'l Home Furnishings Representatives Ass'n. A federation of local home furnishings representatives associations. Membership: $105-$205/year, national + chapter dues, (individual); $105/year (at-large).
Publications:
Contact Magazine. m. adv.
Opportunity Center. m. adv.
Meetings/Conferences:
Annual Meetings: Spring

Internat'l Horn Soc. (1970)
8180 Thunder St.
Juneau, AK 99801
Tel: (907)789-5477   Fax: (907)790-4066
E-Mail: hvogel@ptialaska.net
Web Site: www.wmich.edu/horn
Members: 3,200 individuals
Annual Budget: $50-100,000
Exec. Secretary: Heidi Vogel

Historical Note
IHS members are professional players, instructors and students of the French horn. Membership: $30/year (individual); $45/year (organization/company).

Publications:
Horn Call Journal. q. adv.
IHS Membership Directory. a. adv.
IHS Newsletter. q. adv.

Meetings/Conferences:
Annual Meetings: Annual Membership Meetings-
          Spring/Summer
1999 – Athens, GA(University)/May 18-23/550
2000 – Beijing, China

Internat'l Hot Rod Ass'n (1970)
P.O. Box 708
Norwalk, OH 44857
Tel: (419)663-6666   Fax: (419)663-4472
Members: 12,000 individuals
Staff: 14
Annual Budget: $1-2,000,000
General Manager: Bill Bader
Director, Communications: Ron Colson
Accountant: Anita Freeman

Historical Note
Sanctioning body for professional drag racing strips, providing rules, regulations, and guidelines. Members are drivers and their sponsors, tracks, and spectators.

Publications:
Drag Review Newspaper. bi-w.
Official Drag Racing Rule Book. a.

Internat'l Hydrofoil Soc. (1970)
P.O. Box 51
Cabin John, MD 20818-0051
E-Mail: foiler@erols.com
Web Site: http://www.erols.com/foiler
Annual Budget: under $10,000
Secretary: Kenneth B. Spaulding
Editor: Barney C. Black

Historical Note
Represents organizations and individuals interested in the design, construction, and operation of hydrofoil craft. In addition to the e-mail address listed above, IHS maintains a web site at: http://ourworld.compuserve.com/homepages/barneycblack. Membership: $20/year (regular); $2.50/year (student).

Publications:
Newsletter. q.

Meetings/Conferences:
Annual Meetings: Spring

Internat'l Hydrolized Protein Council (1976)
555 13th St., N.W.
Washington, DC 20004-1109
Tel: (202)637-5881   Fax: (202)637-5910
Members: 14 companies
General Counsel: Richard S. Silverman

Historical Note
Members are companies producing or using hydrolized proteins.

Internat'l Ice Cream Ass'n (1900)
1250 H St., N.W., Suite 900
Washington, DC 20005
Tel: (202)737-4332   Fax: (202)331-7820
Members: 175 companies
Staff: 38
Annual Budget: $1-2,000,000
President & CEO: E. Linwood Tipton
Director, Communications: Susan E. Ruland
Senior V. President & PAC Chairperson: Constance E. Tipton
Manager, Trade Show & Meetings: David B. Anderson
Asst. Director, Membership & Education: John M.E. Rice
Senior V. President, Executive Director: Jerome J. Kozack
V. President: Thomas M. Balmer
Director, Finance: Sam J. DiCarlo
V. President & Counsel: Janet A. Nuzum
Manager, Membership Administration: Cindy F. Cavallo

Historical Note
Established as the Nat'l Ass'n of Ice Cream Manufacturers, it became the Internat'l Ass'n of Ice Cream Manufacturers in 1933 and assumed its present name in 1986. IICA represents manufacturers, distributors, and marketers of ice cream, frozen yogurt and other frozen desserts. IICA's activities range from legislative and regulatory advocacy to market research, industry training and education. Administrative support provided by Internat'l Dairy Foods Ass'n. Membership fee based on volume.

Publications:
The Latest Scoop. a.

Meetings/Conferences:
Annual Meetings: in conjunction with the Internat'l Dairy Foods Ass'n/Fall

Internat'l Inflight Food Service Ass'n (1965)
304 W. Liberty St., Suite 201
Louisville, KY 40202
Tel: (502)583-3783   Fax: (502)589-3602
Members: 450 businesses
Staff: 5
Annual Budget: $250-500,000

Exec. Administrator: Phillip S. Cooke
Director, Communications: Matt Hickey
Director, Administration: Nick Vaccaro
Director, Member Services: Holly Hartford

Historical Note
Members are domestic and international airlines, caterers and their suppliers. Membership: $100-1,000/year.

Publications:
IECA/IFSA Review. q. adv.
Membership Directory. a.

Meetings/Conferences:
Annual Meetings: Spring
1999 – San Antonio, TX(Marriott)/May 5-8/900
2000 – Boca Raton, FL(Boca Resort & Club)/May 14-17/900
2001 – Phoenix, AZ(Hyatt & Civic Plaza)/April 29-May 2/900

Internat'l Information Management Congress (1962)
1650 38th St., Suite 205W
Boulder, CO 80301-2638
Tel: (303)440-7085   Fax: (303)440-7234
E-Mail: info@iimc.org
Web Site: http://www.iimc.org
Members: 470 companies and organizations
Staff: 9
Annual Budget: $1-2,000,000
President and C.E.O.: Paul Carman
Sr. V. President, Meetings/Exhibitions: Marlene Goldman
V. President of Marketing: Rick Mitchell

Historical Note
IMC's goal is to communicate document-based technologies and applications to an inernational audience through conferences, exhibitions, publications, and various membership interactions. Membership: $85/year (individual); $350-5,100/year (organization).

Publications:
Document World.

Meetings/Conferences:
1999 – Amsterdam/June 8-10

Internat'l Institute for Bio-Energetic Analysis (1956)
144 East 36th St.
New York, NY 10016
Tel: (212)532-7742   Fax: (212)532-5331
Web Site: http://www.bioenergetictherapy.com
Members: 1,600 individuals
Staff: 2
Annual Budget: $100-250,000
Administrator: Donna M. Dempsey

Historical Note
A professional society of individuals concerned with the energy processes of the human body and their effect on physical and mental health. Formerly (until 1979) known as the Institute for Bio-Energetic Analysis. Membership: $75/year (member), $50/year (associate).

Publications:
Bioenergetic Analysis Journal. a.
Directory. bien.
Newsletter. 3/year.

Meetings/Conferences:
Biennial Meetings: even years.
2000 – Canada

Internat'l Institute for Lath and Plaster (1976)
3127 Los Feliz Blvd.
Los Angeles, CA 90039
Tel: (213)660-4411   Fax: (213)660-6259
E-Mail: pruter@ix.netcom.com
Members: 52 individuals, 20 organizations
Staff: 2
Annual Budget: $25-50,000
President: Walter F. Pruter

Historical Note
Formed by merger of the Associated Institute for Lath and Plaster and the Internat'l Council for Lathing and Plastering (founded 1952 and formerly the Nat'l Bureau for Lathing and Plastering). A federation of organizations representing contractors, unions and makers of lathing and plastering supplies.

Meetings/Conferences:
1999 – Anaheim, CA
2000 – Washington, DC

Internat'l Institute for Safety in Transportation (1977)
Historical Note
Address unknown in 1995.

Internat'l Institute of Ammonia Refrigeration (1971)
1200 19th St., N.W., Suite 300
Washington, DC 20036-4303
Tel: (202)857-1110   Fax: (202)223-4579
E-Mail: iiar@dc.sba.org
Web Site: http://www.iiar.org
Members: 1,300 members
Staff: 6
Annual Budget: $1-2,000,000
President: M. Kent Anderson
Communications Manager: Bob Armstrong
Program Administrator: Kathleen Sidwell
Convention Manager: Cele Forgarty
Dir., Member Services: Mary Ann Grant

Historical Note
Established in 1971 to promote the safe use of ammonia as a refrigerant. IIAR's purposes include public education, promotional and standards development programs, and legislative/regulatory concerns. Membership includes manufacturers, contractors, consulting engineers, wholesalers, and end users of ammonia refrigeration products. Membership: $500-800/year (company).

Publications:
Annual Meeting Proceedings. a.

IIAR Newsletter. bi-m.
Membership Directory. a.
Standards & Safety Bulletins. irreg.

Meetings/Conferences:
Annual Meetings: March/900 +
1999 – Dallas, TX(Anatole)/March 21-24
2000 – Nashville, TN(Sheraton Renaissance)/March 19-22

Internat'l Institute of Connector and Interconnection Technology (1958)
P.O. Box 399
Waretown, NJ 08758
Tel: (908)233-7278   Fax: (609)693-1614
Toll Free: (800)854 - 4248
E-Mail: IICITDIR@msn.com
Web Site: iicit.org
Members: 2,500 individuals, 140 companies
Staff: 4
Annual Budget: $250-500,000
Managing Director: Suzanne Parker

Historical Note
Formerly (1988) the Electronic Connector Study Group, IICIT members are engineers, manufacturers, sales reptesentatives or anyone involved with any type of connector or interconnection application. IICIT has members from 90% of the major connector manufacturers and various interconnection related companies such as wire manufacturers, platers, testing and evaluation labs, etc. Membership: $35/year (individual); $225-$1,100 (corporate).

Publications:
IICIT News. q.
Proceedings. (also on CD-Rom) a.

Meetings/Conferences:
Annual Meetings: Fall/1,000
1999 – Anaheim, CA(Disneyland)/Sept. 27-29
2000 – Orlando, FL(Buena Vista Palace)/Oct. 23-25
2001 – Anaheim, CA(Disneyland)/Oct. 1-3
2002 – Orlando, FL(Buena Vista Palace)/Oct. 7-9

Internat'l Institute of Convention Management
Historical Note
Became (1998) Connected Internat'l Meeting Professionals Ass'n

Internat'l Institute of Fisheries Economics and Trade (1982)
Dept of Agricultural & Resource Economic
Oregon State University
Corvallis, OR 97331-3601
Tel: (541)737-1416   Fax: (541)737-2563
E-Mail: Ann.L.Shriver@orst.edu
Web Site: http://www.orst.edu/Dept/IIFET
Members: 400 individuals
Exec. Director: Ann L. Shriver

Historical Note
The IIFET is organized to promote the discussion of factors which affect international trade in seafoods, and fisheries policy questions. Designed to be attractive to individuals from governments, industries, and universities from all over the world, a major goal of the organization is to facilitate cooperative research and data exchange. Membership: $40/year (individual); $250/year (organization).

Publications:
IIFET Newsletter. semi-a.
Membership Directory. bien.

Meetings/Conferences:
2000 – Corvallis, OR(Oregon State University)/July 10-13

Internat'l Institute of Forecasters (1981)
Dept. of Resource Economics
Univ. of Massachusetts
Amherst, MA 01003
Tel: (413)545-5715   Fax: (413)545-5853
E-Mail: allen@resecon.umass.edu
Web Site: http://forecasting.cwru.edu/institute.htm
Members: 600 individuals
Annual Budget: $250-500,000
Contact: Geoff Allen

Historical Note
Members are decision makers, forecasters and researchers involved with forecasting in the management, social, engineering and behavioral sciences. IIF is interested in research on forecasting methods and processes. Membership: $75/year (individual); $175/year (organization/library).

Publications:
International Journal of Forecasting. q. adv.
Newsletter. q.

Meetings/Conferences:
Annual Meetings: Summer/650
1999 – Washington, DC/June 27-30

Internat'l Institute of Municipal Clerks (1947)
1212 N. San Dimas Canyon Road
San Dimas, CA 91773-1223
Tel: (909)592-4462   Fax: (909)592-1555
Members: 10,000 individuals
Staff: 11
Annual Budget: $500-1,000,000
Exec. Director: John R. Devine

Historical Note
Founded in 1947 at French Lick, Indiana as the Nat'l Institute of City and Town Clerks. Became the Nat'l Institute of Municipal Clerks in 1949 and the Internat'l Institute of Municipal Clerks in 1960. Membership consists of persons serving as Clerks, Secretaries or Recorders at the state, provincial, county or local level of government. Awards the CMC (Certified Municipal Clerk) designation. Membership: $30-450/yr. (varies by population).

Publications:
Case Studies. irreg.
Directory. a.

IIMC News Digest. m.
Ordnance Compilations. irreg.
Technical Bulletins. irreg.
Meetings/Conferences:
Annual Meetings: May
1999 – Ottawa, Ontario/May 23-27

Internat'l Institute of Synthetic Rubber Producers *(1960)*
2077 South Gessner, Suite 133
Houston, TX   77063-1123
Tel: (713)783-7511   *Fax:* (713)783-7253
E-Mail: rjkillian@iisrp.com
Web Site: http://www.iisrp.com
Members: 49 companies
Staff: 6
Annual Budget: $1-2,000,000
Managing Director: Richard J. Killian
Information Systems Director: Britt D. Theismann
Deputy Managing Director: James L. McGraw
Administrative Supervisor: Peggy Ballinger
Senior Advisor: Larry Turner
Historical Note
Has an international membership. Membership: $17,000/year (organization/company).
Publications:
Proceedings. a.
Synthetic Rubber Manual. trien.
Synthetic Rubber: End Use Survey. a.
Worldwide Rubber Statistics. a.
Meetings/Conferences:
Annual Meetings: April or May/250-300
1999 – Taipei, Taiwan/May 9-13
2000 – Germany

Internat'l Insurance Council *(1946)*
900 19th St., N.W., Suite 250
Washington, DC   20006-2105
Tel: (202)682-2345   *Fax:* (202)218-7730
Web Site: www.iicdc.org
Members: 85 companies and trade associations
Staff: 6
Annual Budget: $1-2,000,000
President: Gordon J. Cloney
Historical Note
Formerly (1988) Internat'l Insurance Advisory Council. Operated under the aegis of the U.S. Chamber of Commerce until 1987. IIC unites the domestic property & casualty, life insurance, reinsurance, and insurance services industries to build trade and investment relations with overseas markets. Membership: $4,750-20,000/year.
Publications:
Report. bi-a.
Meetings/Conferences:
Annual Meetings: May

Internat'l Insurance Soc. *(1965)*
101 Murray St., 4th Floor
New York, NY   10007-2165
Tel: (212)815-9290   *Fax:* (212)815-9297
Members: 1,200 individuals, 200 companies
Staff: 4
Annual Budget: $1-2,000,000
President & C.E.O.: John P. Meyerholz
Exec. Director: Linda C. Bock
Historical Note
IIS facilitates international understanding, the transfer of ideas and innovations, and the development of personal networks across insurance markets through a joint effort of leading executives and academics on a worldwide basis. Membership: $100/year (individual); $1,500/year (corporate).
Publications:
Governors' Journal Newsletter. q.
Seminar and Proceedings Manual. a.
Meetings/Conferences:
1999 – Berlin, Germany(Hotel Inter-Continental)/July 11-14

Internat'l Intellectual Property Alliance *(1984)*
1747 Pennsylvania Ave., N.W., #825
Washington, DC   20006-4604
Tel: (202)833-4198   *Fax:* (202)872-0546
E-Mail: smimet@iipa.com
Web Site: http://www.iipa.com
Members: 7 associations
Staff: 4
President: Eric H. Smith
Historical Note
IIPA is an umbrella organization of trade associations representing the publishing, recording, business/entertainment software, and motion picture industries. Concerned with copyright protection on both the national and international levels.
Publications:
Copyright Industries in the U. S.

Internat'l Intellectual Property Ass'n *(1930)*
1255 23rd St., N.W., Suite 850
Washington, DC   20037
Tel: (202)785-1814   *Fax:* (202)466-2893
Members: 650 individuals
Management Exec.: Sheldon Hauck
Historical Note
Formerly (1990) Internat'l Patent and Trademark Ass'n. IIPA is the American section of the Internat'l Ass'n for the Protection of Industrial Property. IIPA members are lawyers specializing in the international protection of patents, trademarks, copyrights, and other intellectual property. Has no paid officers or full-time staff. Membership: $150/year (individual), $275/year (organization).

Publications:
IIPA Notes. q.
Membership Directory. a.
Meetings/Conferences:
Annual Meetings: always Washington, DC

Internat'l Interactive Communication Soc. *(1983)*
39355 California St.,Suite 307
Fremont, CA   94538-1447
Tel: (510)608-5930   *Fax:* (510)608-5917
E-Mail: worldhq@iics.org
Web Site: http://www.iics.org
Members: 3,000 individuals
Staff: 3
Annual Budget: $250-500,000
Managing Director: Debra L. Palm
Historical Note
IICS is an association of communications industry professional dedicated to the advancement of interactive technologies. The Society provides a forum to share ideas, applications and techniques for effective use of interactive media. Has a total of 26 chapters in the U.S., Canada, Japan, and Denmark. Membership: $120/year (individual); $675/year (corporate); $75/year (student).
Publications:
IICS Newsline. m. adv.
Membership Directory. a. adv.
Meetings/Conferences:

Internat'l Interior Design Ass'n *(1969)*
341 Merchandise Mart
Chicago, IL   60654-1104
Tel: (312)467-1950   *Fax:* (312)467-0779
Toll Free: (800)799 - 4432
E-Mail: iidahq@aol.com
Web Site: http://www.iida.com
Members: 9,700 individuals, 34 chapters
Staff: 17
Annual Budget: $2-5,000,000
Exec. Director: Elisabeth G. Houston
Sr. Director, Communications: Deborah Barron
Sr. Director, Membership Development: Dennis Krause
Historical Note
Formed (1994) by the merger of Council of Federal Interior Designers, Institute of Business Designers, and Internat'l Soc. of Interior Designers. Members are professionals from various facets of the interior design industry/.
Publications:
Advantage. 8/year.
Perspective. q. adv.
Meetings/Conferences:
Annual Meetings: June/Chicago, IL

Internat'l Isotope Soc. *(1986)*
Historical Note
IIS declined to provide updated information for this edition.

Internat'l Jazz Festival Directors
Historical Note
Address unknown in 1995; presumed inactive or defunct.

Internat'l Jelly and Preserve Ass'n *(1918)*
5775 Peachtree-Dunwoody Rd., Suite 500-G
Atlanta, GA   30342-1558
Tel: (404)252-3663   *Fax:* (404)252-0774
E-Mail: ijpa@assnhq.com
Members: 78 companies
Staff: 4
Annual Budget: $100-250,000
President: Pamela A. Chumley
Manager, Client Services: Nancy Marlin
Historical Note
Formerly (1978) the National Preservers Ass'n. Members are producers of fruit jams, preserves, jellies, marmalades, pie fillings, fruit butters and manufacturers of bakers supplies or processed fruit products used as industrial ingredients; brokers; and suppliers of packaging materials or equipment to the preserving industry.
Publications:
Direct Line. q.
Meetings/Conferences:
Annual Meetings: March

Internat'l Jewish Media Ass'n *(1988)*
5307 Marsh Creek Dr.
Austin, TX   78759-6218
Tel: (512)795-9112   *Fax:* (512)795-9520
E-Mail: ajpamr@aol.com
Members: 250 individuals
Staff: 2
Annual Budget: $10-25,000
Exec. Director: Beverly Rodman
Historical Note
Coordinating association of professional Jewish journalists worldwide. Founded in Jerusalem. The American Jewish Press Ass'n and its members represent U.S. journalists in IJMA. Principal activities: bi-annual internship, conference of Jewish journalists, in Israel, assembling world's Jewish journalists for meetings with Israeli government and civil leaders. Membership: $35/year (U.S. individual).
Meetings/Conferences:

Internat'l Juvenile Officers Ass'n *(1957)*
P.O. Box 56
Easton, CT   06612
Tel: (203)377-4424   *Fax:* (203)377-2769
Members: 343 individuals
Staff: 1
Annual Budget: $10-25,000

Exec. Director: Mark Pastor
Historical Note
Members are law enforcement officers who handle offenses committed by or against juveniles. Membership: $20/year.
Publications:
IJOA Reporter. 3/yr.
Resource Directory. a.
Meetings/Conferences:
Annual Meetings: Last week in June. Also sponsors two seminars.

Internat'l Kitchen Exhaust Cleaning Ass'n *(1988)*
7101 Wisconsin Ave., Suite 901
Bethesda, MD   20814
Tel: (301)656-4950
Members: 100 companies
Staff: 4
Annual Budget: $50-100,000
Historical Note
Promotes fire safety in restaurants and professionalism in the kitchen exhaust cleaning industry. Membership: $375/year (company).
Publications:
Scratch Pad. q. adv.
Meetings/Conferences:

Internat'l Labor Communications Ass'n *(1955)*
815 16th St., N.W.
Washington, DC   20006
Tel: (202)637-5068
Members: 870 individuals
Staff: 1
Annual Budget: $100-250,000
Secretary-Treasurer: Susan Phillips
Historical Note
Formerly (1984) Internat'l Labor Press Ass'n. Formed by a merger of the Internat'l Labor Press of America (1911) and the CIO Editors and Public Relations Conference (1940). Members are editors of union papers. Membership: $300-1,000/year.
Publications:
Reporter. bi-m.
Meetings/Conferences:
Biennial Conventions: Odd years

Internat'l Lactation Consultant Ass'n *(1984)*
4101 Lake Boone Trail, Suite 201
Raleigh, NC   27607-7506
Tel: (919)787-5181   *Fax:* (919)787-4916
E-Mail: ILCA@erols.com
Web Site: http://www.ilca.org
Members: 4,600 individuals
Staff: 2
Annual Budget: $250-500,000
Exec. Director: Susan Van der Weert
Historical Note
Members are professionals working to prevent and solve breastfeeding problems and to encourage a social environment that effectively supports breastfeeding families; including lactation consultants, midwives, breastfeeding specialists, childbirth educators, physicians, nurses, and community-based service providers. Membership: $70/year (individual).y
Publications:
Journal of Human Lactation. q. adv.
The Globe. q.
Meetings/Conferences:
Annual Meetings: July-August/1,000
1999 – Scottsdale, AZ(Scottsdale Princes Hotel)July
2000 – Washington, DC
2001 – Acapulco, Mexico
2002 – Boca Raton, FL

Internat'l Ladies Garment Workers Union
Historical Note
Became the Union of Needletrades, Industrial and Textile Employees in 1995.

Internat'l Laser Display Ass'n *(1986)*
4301 32nd St., West, Suite B-23
Bradenton, FL   34205
Tel: (941)758-6881   *Fax:* (941)758-1605
E-Mail: ildadirect@aol.com
Web Site: http://www.ilda.wa.org
Members: 28 individuals, 125 companies
Staff: 1
Annual Budget: $25-50,000
Exec. Director: Linda Hare
Historical Note
ILDA members are individuals involved in the laser entertainment and display industry. Membership: $125/year (individual); $50/year (student); corporate and affiliate membership varies, maximum $1,000/year.
Publications:
Laserist. q. adv.
Meetings/Conferences:
Annual Meetings: November

Internat'l Lead Zinc Research Organization *(1958)*
P.O. Box 12036
2525 Meridian Parkway
Research Triangle Pk, NC   27709-2036
Tel: (919)361-4647   *Fax:* (919)361-1957
Web Site: http://www.ilzro.org
Members: 43 companies
Staff: 16
Annual Budget: $5-10,000,000
President: Dr. Jerome F. Cole
Director, Communication: Rob Putnam
Finance and Administration: G. Scott Mooneyham

V. President, Materials Sciences: Frank Goodwin

Historical Note
Established in New York and incorporated in North Carolina, ILZRO members are miners and refiners of lead and zinc. Trade ass'n of the lead and zinc industry worldwide. Focus on research and development to detect new uses for the metals and refine existing uses. Has an annual budget of approximately $5.3 million.

Publications:
Annual Review. a.
Environmental Health Newsletter. q.
R&D Focus. q.

Meetings/Conferences:
Annual Meetings: November
1999 – Scottsdale, AZ(Doubletree)/April 26-May 1/100
1999 – Shanghai, China/Nov. 1-6/100

Internat'l League of Dermatological Socs. *(1889)*
7045 S. Tamiami Trail, Suite 2-B
Sarasota, FL 34231
Tel: (941)927-6565   *Fax:* (941)927-1936
E-Mail: mtgmgr@gte.net
Members: 79 nat'l societies, 18 int'l soc.
Staff: 2
Annual Budget: $250-500,000
Exec. V. President: Barbara C. Nichols

Historical Note
ILDS encourages the worldwide advancement of dermatological education, care and sciences.

Publications:
Congress/Proceedings. quinquennial.
Dermatology International. q.
Directory. a.

Meetings/Conferences:
2002 – Paris, France/July 1-5

Internat'l League of Electrical Ass'ns *(1936)*
2901 Metro Dr., Suite 203
Bloomington, MN 55425-1556
Tel: (612)854-4405   *Fax:* (612)854-7076
Members: 35 organizations
Staff: 1
Annual Budget: $10-25,000
Exec. Director: Dale Yohnke

Historical Note
A federation of state, province and local organizations in the electrical industry. Until 1979 known as the Internat'l Ass'n of Electrical Leagues. Membership: $250/year.

Publications:
Bulletins. irreg.
Contacts Newsletter. bi-m.
Membership Directory. a.

Meetings/Conferences:

Internat'l League of Professional Baseball Clubs *(1884)*
55 S. High St., Suite 202
Dublin, OH 43017
Tel: (614)791-9300   *Fax:* (614)791-9009
Web Site: http://www.ilbaseball.com
Members: 14 clubs
Staff: 3
Annual Budget: $250-500,000
President: Randy Mobley

Historical Note
The oldest minor league in baseball.

Publications:
Record Book. a.

Meetings/Conferences:
1999 – Anaheim, CA

Internat'l Leather Goods, Plastics, Novelty, and Service Workers' Union *(1937)*
265 West 14th Street
Suite 711
New York, NY 10011
Tel: (212)675-9240   *Fax:* (212)675-6896
Members: 5,000 individuals
Staff: 5
Annual Budget: $500-1,000,000
President: Rosemary Behrman

Historical Note
Chartered March 5, 1937 by the American Federation of Labor as the International Ladies' Handbag, Pocketbook and Novelty Workers Union. Became Internat'l Leather Goods, Plastics and Novelty Workers Union in 1955, and adopted its present name in 1992.

Meetings/Conferences:

Internat'l Licensing Industry Merchandisers' Ass'n *(1985)*
350 Fifth Ave., Suite 2309
New York, NY 10118-0110
Tel: (212)244-1944   *Fax:* (212)563-6552
Web Site: http://www.licensing.org
Members: 700 companies
Staff: 4
Annual Budget: $1-2,000,000
Exec. Director: Charles Riotto
Director, Communications: Jodi S. Levin

Historical Note
Formerly Licensing Industry Merchandisers Ass'n. Formed by a merger of the Licensing Industry Ass'n (1980) and the Licensed Merchandisers' Ass'n (1983) in 1985. LIMA members are companies and individuals engaged in the marketing of licensed properties, both as agents and as property owners, including manufacturers, consultants, publications, lawyers, accountants, and retailers.

Publications:
Licensing Resource Directory. a. adv.
LIMA Bottomline Newsletter.

Meetings/Conferences:
Annual Meetings: June
1999 – New York, NY(Javits Center)/June 8-10/15000

Internat'l Listening Ass'n *(1979)*
P.O. Box 25324
Overland Park, KS 66225-5324
Tel: (913)685-9228   *Fax:* (913)685-9235
Toll Free: (800)452 - 4505
E-Mail: ilistening@aol.com
Web Site: http://www.listen.org
Members: 400 individuals
Staff: 1
Annual Budget: $50-100,000
Exec. Director: Diana Corley Schnapp

Historical Note
ILA members are academics and others with an interest in expanding our understanding of effective listening. Membership: $75/year (individual); $425/year (organization).

Publications:
Internat'l Journal of Listening. a.
Listening Post. q. adv.

Meetings/Conferences:
Annual Meetings: Spring
1999 – Albuquerque, NM(Sheraton Old Town)/March 14-16
2000 – Virginia Beach, VA/March 8-10/2000

Internat'l Liver Transplantation Soc. *(1992)*
6900 Grove Road
Thorofare, NJ 08086-9447
Tel: (609)848-8497   *Fax:* (609)848-5274
E-Mail: ilts@slackinc.com
Members: 700 individuals
Staff: 1
Annual Budget: $50-100,000
Administrative Manager: Audra Rival

Historical Note
Membership: $95/year (physician); $65/year (non-physician).

Publications:
ILTS Newsletter. q. adv.
Liver Transplantation and Surgery. bi-m. adv.

Meetings/Conferences:

Internat'l Livestock Identification Ass'n *(1946)*
4701 Marion St., Suite 201-LXB
Denver, CO 80216-2102
Tel: (303)294-0895   *Fax:* (303)294-0918
Members: 27 states and provinces
Annual Budget: under $10,000
Secretary-Treasurer: Cara Strain

Historical Note
An ass'n of government agencies and independent livestock organizations committed to provide the livestock owner protection against livestock theft through brand registration, ownership inspection and theft investigation. State employees and livestock associations' executives (in the U.S. and Canada) concerned with the use of livestock brands. Formerly (1969) the Nat'l Livestock Brand Conference, (1982) Internat'l Livestock Brand Conference, (1988) Internat'l Livestock Brand and Theft Conference, and (1992) the Internat'l Livestock Identification and Theft Investigators Ass'n. Also interested in the identification of ownership, theft and movement of livestock. Membership: $75/year (state/province).

Meetings/Conferences:
1999 – Albuquerque, NM

Internat'l Livestock Theft Investigators Ass'n *(1978)*
c/o Colorado Brand Board
4701 Marion St., 201 Livestock Exchange
Denver, CO 80216-2139
Tel: (303)294-0895   *Fax:* (303)294-0918
Members: 28 states
Contact: Cara Strain

Historical Note
ILTIA members are police specializing in livestock theft. The association's primary function is the issuing of bulletins concerning livestock theft to members in the United States and Canada.

Meetings/Conferences:

Internat'l Llama Ass'n

Internat'l Longshoremen's and Warehousemen's Union *(1937)*
1188 Franklin St.
Fourth Floor
San Francisco, CA 94109
Tel: (415)775-0533   *Fax:* (415)775-1302
Members: 55,000 individuals
Staff: 20
Annual Budget: $1-2,000,000
President: Brian McWilliams

Historical Note
ILWU was founded by Harry R. Bridges and NLRB certified as the Internat'l Longshoremen's and Warehousemen's Union. Members are longshoremen, warehousemen, bargemen, cannery workers, chemical/chemical processing workers, shipscalers, fishermen, and tourism employees. Inlandboatmen's Union of the Pacific is its Marine Division. Affiliated with the AFL-CIO in 1988.

Publications:
The Dispatcher. 11/year.

Meetings/Conferences:
Triennial Meetings: Spring

Internat'l Longshoremen's Ass'n *(1892)*
17 Battery Place, Room 1530

New York, NY 10004
Tel: (212)425-1200   *Fax:* (212)425-2928
Members: 116,000 individuals
Staff: 30
Annual Budget: $5-10,000,000
President: John Bowers

Historical Note
Established in Detroit in 1892 as the Nat'l Longshoremen's Ass'n of the United States. Became the Internat'l Longshoremen's Ass'n in 1895 and was chartered by the American Federation of Labor in 1896. Expelled for corruption and racketeering by the AFL in 1953, the ILA was an independent union until 1959, when it re-affiliated with AFL-CIO.

Publications:
Directory. bien.
ILA Newsletter. 4-5/year.

Meetings/Conferences:
1999 – Lake Buena Vista, FL

Internat'l Magnesium Ass'n *(1943)*
1303 Vincent Place, Suite 1
McLean, VA 22101-3615
Tel: (703)442-8888   *Fax:* (703)821-1824
E-Mail: ima@bellatlantic.net
Web Site: http://www.intlmag.org/
Members: 120 companies
Staff: 3
Annual Budget: $500-1,000,000
Exec. V. President: Byron B. Clow
Meeting Manager: Sandra Lynn Hughes

Historical Note
The purpose of the association is to develop and increase the international use and acceptance of magnesium metal and its alloys in all product forms. Regular membership is open to organizations or individuals directly engaged in the production, manufacture or marketing of metallic magnesium in some product form; or those supplying materials, equipment or services to the industry. Membership: $2,500 (regular), $1,500 (associate).

Publications:
Annual Conference Proceedings. a.
Magnesium Buyer's Guide. a.
Magnesium Newsletter. m.

Meetings/Conferences:
Annual Meetings: May-June
1999 – Rome, Italy

Internat'l Maintenance Institute *(1961)*
P.O. Box 751896
Houston, TX 77275-1896
Tel: (281)481-0869   *Fax:* (281)481-8337
Web Site: http://www.imionline.org
Members: 2,500 individuals
Staff: 1
Annual Budget: $100-250,000
Exec. Secretary: Joyce Rhoden

Historical Note
Membership: $50/year, plus chapter dues.

Publications:
The Maintenance Journal. bi-m. adv.

Meetings/Conferences:
1999 – Myrtle Beach, SC/March 26-27

Internat'l Management Council *(1935)*
430 S. 20th St., Suite 3
Omaha, NE 68102-2506
Tel: (402)345-1904   *Fax:* (402)345-4480
E-Mail: IMCOFFICE@msn.com
Web Site: http://www.imc-ymca.org
Members: 3,100 individuals
Staff: 1
Annual Budget: $100-250,000
Nat'l Administrator: Jodeen M. Sterba

Historical Note
IMC provides individuals with opportunities to develop their leadership and management skills throug a network of shared experiences and education. Sponsored by the Young Men's Christian Ass'n as the Nat'l Council of Foremen's Clubs, it became the Nat'l Council of Industrial Management Clubs in 1948 and assumed its present name in 1971. Membership: $20/year.

Publications:
IMC Management Forum. q.

Meetings/Conferences:
Annual Meetings: Spring
1999 – San Francisco, CA

Internat'l Manufacturers Representatives Ass'n *(1958)*
P.O. Box 702678
Tulsa, OK 74170
Tel: (918)743-5443   *Fax:* (918)743-5443
Members: 29 individuals
Annual Budget: under $10,000
Secretary-Treasurer: Mert Dale

Historical Note
IMRA members are manufacturers representatives of autobody repair and refinishing products and automotive detailing products that sell to wholesale distributors only.

Meetings/Conferences:
Annual Meetings: Annual meetings in Fall

Internat'l Map Trade Ass'n *(1981)*
P.O. Box 1789
Kankakee, IL 60901
Tel: (815)939-4627   *Fax:* (815)933-8320
E-Mail: imta@maptrade.org
Web Site: http://www.maptrade.org
Members: 800 companies
Staff: 2
Exec. Director: Norman Strasma

Conference Coordinator: Linda Mickle

Historical Note
Formerly (1993) the Internat'l Map Dealers Ass'n. Membership comprised of retail stores featuring maps; distributors; manufacturers; wholesalers; and publishers. The purposes of the association are to stimulate the sale and use of maps and related material, to promote high standards of professional competence, conduct, and ethics, and to foster communication and cooperation among publishers, wholesalers, retailers, and others in the map industry. Incorporated in Florida. Membership: $150/year.

Publications:
Membership Directory. a.
Newsletter. m.

Meetings/Conferences:
Annual Meetings: Fall
1999 – Sydney, Australia/June 3-6

Internat'l Maple Syrup Institute *(1975)*

Historical Note
Address unknown in 1998.

Internat'l Marina Institute *(1986)*
720 Albee Road West
Nokomis, FL 34275-2533
Tel: (941)480-1212   *Fax:* (941)480-0081
E-Mail: imimarina@aol.com
Web Site: www.imimarina.com
Annual Budget: $250-500,000
President and Managing Director: Paul E. Dodson

Historical Note
Membership: $115/year (individual); $360/year (organization/company)

Publications:
Dock Lines. bi-w.
IMI Catalog. a.

Meetings/Conferences:
Annual Meetings: December.
1999 – Nashville, TN

Internat'l Marine Transit Ass'n *(1976)*
34 Otis Hill Road
Hingham, MA 02043
Tel: (781)749-0078
Members: 300 companies
Annual Budget: $100-250,000
Secretary-Treasurer: Martha A. Reardon

Historical Note
Membership includes ferry operators, naval architects, manufacturers, suppliers, shipyards, government agencies, support services, marine engineering and planning consultants, and specialists in marine transit. Membership: $40/year (individual); $150/year (company).

Publications:
Conference Proceedings. a. adv.
IMTA LogLine. semi-a.

Meetings/Conferences:
Annual Meetings: Fall
1999 – Cebu City, Phillipines

Internat'l Masonry Institute *(1970)*
42 East St.
Annapolis, MD 21401
Tel: (410)263-5596
Toll Free: (800)464 - 0988
E-Mail: hrbradford@imiweb.org
Web Site: http://www.imiweb.org
Staff: 150
Annual Budget: $10-25,000,000
President: Joan B. Calambokidis
Administrative Manager: Lynn O'Brien
Chief of Staff: Cristina Morse

Historical Note
A Labor/Management Trust established between the Internat'l Union of Bricklayers and Allied Craftsmen and contractors who employ BAC members. IMI conducts market development, research and development, training and labor/management relations programs. Not a membership organization.

Publications:
IMI Today. q.

Meetings/Conferences:

Internat'l Mass Retail Ass'n *(1965)*
1700 N. Moore St., Suite 2250
Arlington, VA 22209
Tel: (703)841-2300   *Fax:* (703)841-1184
Web Site: http://www.imra.org
Members: 170 mass retailers, 600 suppliers
Staff: 20
Annual Budget: $1-2,000,000
President: Robert J. Verdisco
Manager, Communications: Jennifer Roberts
Sr. V. President, Govt. Affairs: Morrison Cain
Sr. V. President, Industry Affairs & Trade Development: Robin Lanier
Sr. V. President, Education, Exhibits and Conventions: Susan H. Dove
Exec. V. President: Joe Mosgkowicz

Historical Note
Formerly (1969) Mass Merchandising Research Foundation, (1976) Mass Retailing Institute and (1988) Nat'l Mass Retailing Institute. Absorbed the Ass'n of General Merchandise Chains in 1987. Membership fee based on sales volume.

Publications:
Mass Retail News. m.

Meetings/Conferences:
Annual Meetings: May/2,500
1999 – Orlando, FL(Orange Cty. Convention Center)/May 22-25

Internat'l Memorialization Supply Ass'n *(1955)*
P.O. Box 8250
Columbus, OH 43201-0250
Tel: (614)294-3761   *Fax:* (614)299-2324
Members: 102 companies
Staff: 1
Annual Budget: $10-25,000
Secretary: David Beck

Historical Note
Formerly (until 1980) known as the Cemetery Supply Ass'n and (until 1994) the Internat'l Cemetery Supply Ass'n. Suppliers of equipment, materials and services to the cemetery industry united to improve the quality of materials made available to and by cemetery suppliers; to improve communication with the public; and to meet needs of access to information. Membership: $100/year (company).

Meetings/Conferences:
Semi-annual: with American Cemetery Ass'n

Internat'l Merger and Acquisition Professionals *(1973)*
3232 Cobb Parkway, Suite 437
Atlanta, GA 30339
Tel: (770)319-7797   *Fax:* (770)319-9838
E-Mail: imap@imap.com
Web Site: http://www.imap.com
Members: 42 Companies
Staff: 1
Annual Budget: $25-50,000
Exec. Director: Deborah Martin

Historical Note
Formerly (1982) Nat'l Ass'n of Merger and Acquisition Consultants and (1995) Internat'l Ass'n of Merger and Acquisition Professionals. Members are specialists in selling, buying, and merging medium-sized public and private businesses.

Publications:
M&A Insider. q.

Meetings/Conferences:
Semi-annual Meetings: Spring and Fall/50
1999 – San Diego, CA/May 7-8

Internat'l Microelectronics and Packaging Soc. *(1967)*
1850 Centennial Park Dr., Suite 105
Reston, VA 20191-1517
Tel: (703)758-1060   *Fax:* (703)758-1066
E-Mail: IMAPS@aol.com
Web Site: http://www.imaps.org
Members: 5,400 individuals, 600 companies
Staff: 13
Annual Budget: $2-5,000,000
Exec. Director: Richard M. Breck
Exec. Director, Development: Janet Kingston
Director of Marketing: Nancy Stengel

Historical Note
Formed in 1996 by the merger of the Internat'l Soc. for Hybrid Microelectronics and the Internat'l Electronic Packaging Soc., IMAPS promotes close interaction between the complementary technologies of ceramics, thin and thick films, semiconductor packaging, surface mount technology, multichip modules, semiconductor devices, and monolithic circuits. Formed in the fall of 1967 by a small group of engineers in the San Francisco Bay area. Membership: $55/year (individual), $330/year (organization); $150/year (associate organization); $100/year (affiliate organization).

Publications:
Advancing Microelectronics. bi-m. adv.
Directory of IMAPS Members. a.
IMAPS Journal. q. adv.
Industry Guide. a. adv.
Technical Proceedings. a. adv.

Meetings/Conferences:
Annual Meetings: Fall
1999 – Chicago, IL(Chicago Hilton)/Oct. 26-28

Internat'l Microwave Power Institute *(1966)*
10210 Leatherleaf Court
Manassas, VA 20111-4245
Tel: (703)257-1415   *Fax:* (703)257-0213
E-Mail: assnetr@earthlink.net
Web Site: http://www.impi.org
Members: 700 individuals
Staff: 2
Annual Budget: $100-250,000
Exec. Director: Robert C. LaGasse, CAE
Director, Administration: Kim Thies

Historical Note
Members are engineers, educators, home economists and scientists interested in non-communication aspects of microwave power. Membership: $120/year (individual); $175 (individual-joint); $1,500/year (organization).

Publications:
Journal of Microwave Power. q.
Microwave World. tri.

Meetings/Conferences:
Annual Meetings: July
1999 – Washington, DC

Internat'l Military Community Executives Ass'n *(1971)*
1125 Duke St.
Alexandria, VA 22314-3513
Tel: (703)548-0093   *Fax:* (703)548-0095
Members: 800 individuals
Staff: 3
Annual Budget: $250-500,000
Exec. Director: Donald Pavlik
Director of Advertising: Karen E. Burke
Managing Editor, MWR Today: Deborah Cornutt

Historical Note
Formerly (1990) the Internat'l Military Club Executives Ass'n. Founded in 1971 for management personnel including all branches of the armed services. Some benefits of joining include training programs and certification. IMCEA is open to all personnel involved in morale, welfare and recreation, (MWR) activities, including clubs, bowling and golf managers. Membership: $295/year (regular), $345/year (associate).

Publications:
Annual Directory. a. adv.
MWR Today. m. adv.

Meetings/Conferences:
Regional Meetings: throughout U.S., Europe, and the Far East

Internat'l Minilab Ass'n *(1985)*

Historical Note
Organization defunct in 1998.

Internat'l Mobile Air Conditioning Ass'n *(1958)*
P.O. Box 9000
Fort Worth, TX 76147-2000
Tel: (817)338-1100   *Fax:* (817)338-1451
E-Mail: imaca@iamerica.net
Web Site: http://www.imaca.org
Members: 500 companies
Staff: 4
Annual Budget: $250-500,000
Exec. Director: Frank Allison
Manager, Marketing Services: Joan M. Jones

Historical Note
Formerly (1970) Automotive Air Conditioning Ass'n, Inc. Members include manufactures and suppliers of air conditioning units, component parts, supplies and related services and tools for motor vehicles, as well as automotive air conditioning service facilities. Membership: $600/year (manufacturer/supplier); $175 (distributor, installation and service facilities); $250/year (international) and $200/year (allied industries).

Publications:
Shop Talk. bi-m.

Meetings/Conferences:

Internat'l Mobile Telecommunications Ass'n *(1994)*
1150 18th St., N.W., Suite 250
Washington, DC 20036
Tel: (202)331-7773   *Fax:* (202)331-9062
E-Mail: imta@erols.com
Web Site: http://www.imta.org
Members: 600 companies
Staff: 8
Annual Budget: $250-500,000
President and C.E.O.: Alan R. Shark, CAE
V. President, Communications and Associations: Louise Tucker
V. President, Regulatory Relations: Jill M. Lyon
V.President, Research and Information Services: Robyn K. Shalhoub

Historical Note
Founded in 1994 as an international counterpart to Nat'l Mobile Telecommunications Ass'n (same address); incorporated as a separate organization in 1996. IMTA provides industry input on government regulations for the commercial trunked radio industry in the 60+ countries where specialized mobile radio systems operate. Sponsors several international meetings and seminars throughout the year. Membership: $500/year (individual); $1,000/year (organization).

Publications:
Global Channels. m.
Global Digest. q.

Internat'l Motion Picture and Lecturers Ass'n *(1970)*
1455 Royal Blvd.
Glendale, CA 91207
Tel: (818)243-7043   *Fax:* (818)241-1720
Members: 60 individuals
Staff: 7
Annual Budget: $10-25,000
President: Sandy Mortimor

Historical Note
Members produce personally narrated travel films.

Publications:
Membership Roster. a.
President's Newsletter. q.

Meetings/Conferences:
Annual Meetings: December

Internat'l Motor Press Ass'n *(1962)*
1756 Broadway, Room 26-J
New York, NY 10019
Tel: (212)315-4900   *Fax:* (212)315-4903
Members: 500 individuals
Staff: 1
Annual Budget: $50-100,000
President: Jerry Flint

Historical Note
A professional group of writers and editors producing auto articles for the press, radio or TV. Concentrated in the New York area. U.S. Chapter of the Internat'l Federation of Automotive Journalists. Membership: $50/year.

Publications:
IMPAct. m.

Meetings/Conferences:
Monthly Meetings: Third Thursdays

Internat'l Municipal Lawyers Ass'n *(1935)*
1110 Vermont Ave., N.W., Suite 200
Washington, DC 20005-3522
Tel: (202)466-5424   *Fax:* (202)785-0152
E-Mail: info@imla.org
Web Site: http://www.imla.org
Members: 1,500 cities and counties
Staff: 11
Annual Budget: $1-2,000,000
Exec. Director and General Counsel: Henry W. Underhill, Jr.

Deputy Exec. Director: Veronica Kleffner
Sr. Associate Counsel: Walter Wilson

Historical Note
*Formerly (1995) the Nat'l Institute of Municipal Law Officers.
Founded by municipal attorneys attending an annual conference of
the United States Conference of Mayors in 1935 as an organization
of municipalities acting through their chief legal officer. Participates
in federal and state cases of nation-wide importance and serves as a
source of local government legal information. Membership fee based
on population.*

Publications:
The Municipal Lawyer. bi-m.

Meetings/Conferences:
Annual Meetings: Fall/700
1999 – Toronto, ON(Westin Harbour)
2000 – San Francisco, CA(Hyatt Embaracadero)

Internat'l Municipal Signal Ass'n (1896)
P.O. Box 539
165 E. Union St.
Newark, NY   14513
Tel: (315)331-2182   *Fax:* (315)331-8205
Toll Free: (800)723 - 4672
E-Mail: INFO@IMSASAFETY.ORG
Web Site: http://www.imsasafety.org
Members: 5,000 individuals
Staff: 5
Annual Budget: $500-1,000,000
Exec. Director: Marilyn E. Lawrence
Technical Training Coordinator: Sharon Earl

Historical Note
*Members are government employees and municipal contractors
involved in public safety operations: traffic signal installation and
maintenance, fire alarm systems, street lights, radio
communications, etc. Sustaining membership is available to persons
in private corporations responsible for promoting public safety.
Membership: $50/year (individual); $40/year (3 or more
individuals from the same agency); $350/year (sustaining).*

Publications:
IMSA Journal. bi-m. adv.

Meetings/Conferences:
Annual Meetings: July-August
1999 – Hamilton, ON, Canada(Hamilton Convention
        Centre)/Aug. 13-20

Internat'l Museum Theater Alliance (1990)
Museum of Science
Science Park
Boston, MA   02114-1099
Tel: (617)589-0449   *Fax:* (617)589-0454
E-Mail: imtal@a1.mos.org
Web Site: www.mos.org/imtal/
Members: 150 individuals
Annual Budget: under $10,000
Exec. Director: Catherine Hughes

Historical Note
*The International Museum Theatre Alliance, formed in 1990, is a
professional resource and networking organization for museum and
theatre professionals using theatre as an interpretive technique.
Membership: $15/year (student); $25/year (artist); 35/year
(museum professional); $50-75/year (institution).*

Publications:
Insights. q. adv.

Meetings/Conferences:
1999 – Cleveland, OH

Internat'l Music Products Ass'n (1901)
5790 Armada Dr.
Carlsbad, CA   92008-4391
Tel: (760)438-8001   *Fax:* (760)438-7327
Web Site: http://www.namm.comm.namm
Members: 6,500 companies
Staff: 40
Annual Budget: $5-10,000,000
President and C.E.O.: Larry R. Linkin
Communications Director: John Maher
Director, Trade Shows: Kevin Johnstone
Director, Professional Development: Randy Beck
Director, Membership: Judy I. Bohlim

Historical Note
*Founded as Nat'l Ass'n of Music Merchants; became IMPA in
1997. Members are musical instrument retailers and manufacturers
and their suppliers. Membership: $150/year (retail); $100/year
(commercial).*

Publications:
Compesation and Benefits.
Cost of Doing Business Report. a.
Music USA. m.
Playback. m.

Meetings/Conferences:
Semi-Annual Trade Shows: Winter Market/Anaheim,
        CA/60,000, and Summer Session/Nashville,
        TN/20,000

Internat'l Nanny Ass'n (1985)
900 Haddon Ave., Suite 438
Collingswood, NJ   08108-2101
Tel: (609)858-0808   *Fax:* (609)858-2519
Toll Free: (800)297 - 1477
E-Mail: INA@nanny.org
Web Site: www.nanny.org
Members: 700 individuals
Annual Budget: $100-250,000
Exec. Director: Diane O'Mara

Historical Note
*INA members are nannies, nanny placement agencies and others
with an interest in the field. Membership: $49-255/year, based on
membership level.*

Publications:
Directory of Agencies, Programs, and Services. a. adv.
INA Vision Newsletter. bi-m. adv.

Meetings/Conferences:
Annual Meetings: June
1999 – Atlanta, GA(Hilton)/June 17-20/200

Internat'l Narcotic Enforcement Officers Ass'n (1958)
112 State St., Suite 1200
Albany, NY   12207
Tel: (518)463-6232   *Fax:* (518)432-3378
Web Site: http://www.ineoa.org
Members: 10,000 individuals
Staff: 6
Annual Budget: $250-500,000
Exec. Director: John J. Bellizzi
Editor/Public Relations Manager: Celeste Morga

Historical Note
*Established in Albany, NY in October, 1960, and incorporated in
the state of New York in the same year. In recognition of its growing
international membership, the present name was adopted in 1963.
Membership: $35/year.*

Publications:
International Drug Report. q. adv.
Narc Officer. bi-m. adv.

Meetings/Conferences:
Annual Meetings: Ocotber
1999 – Albany, NY

Internat'l Natural Sausage Casing Ass'n (1964)
10400 Conecticut Ave., Suite 507
Kensington, MD   20895
Tel: (301)962-8400   *Fax:* (301)962-7630
E-Mail: insca@aol.com
Web Site: http://www.insca.org
Members: 248 companies
Staff: 2
Annual Budget: $250-500,000
Exec. Secretary: Glenn Fellman

Historical Note
*Formerly (1965) Natural Casing Institute. Membership: $1,250
(organization/company).*

Publications:
Newsletter. q.
Yearbook. a. adv.

Meetings/Conferences:
Semi-Annual Meetings: Spring in Europe, Fall in North
        America

Internat'l Neural Network Soc. (1987)
19 Mantua Road
Mount Royal, NJ   08061
Tel: (609)423-0162   *Fax:* (609)423-3420
E-Mail: innshq@inns.smarthub.com
Web Site: http://www.inns.org
Members: 3,000 individuals
Staff: 4
Annual Budget: $100-250,000
Exec. Director: Dale B. Zeigler

Historical Note
*INNS promotes research into models of brain and behavioral
processes, and the development of computing applications which
utilize concepts obtained from neural modelling. Members are
neural network scientists and other professionals interested in
neurocomputing and theoretical neuroscience. Membership:
$80/year (individual); $55/year (student).*

Publications:
INNS Newsletter. m.
Journal of Neural Networks. m.

Meetings/Conferences:
1999 – Washington, DC/July 10-16

Internat'l Neuropsychological Soc. (1967)
700 Ackerman Road, Suite 550
Columbus, OH   43202-1559
Tel: (614)263-4200   *Fax:* (614)263-4366
E-Mail: osu_ins@postbox.acs.ohio-state.edu
Web Site: http://med.ohio-state.edu/ins/
Members: 3,425 individuals
Staff: 2
Exec. Secretary: Robert Bornstein, Ph.D.

Publications:
Journal of the Internat'l Neuropsychological Society. 6/year.
        adv.

Meetings/Conferences:
Annual Meetings: Semi-Annual meetings.
1999 – Boston, MA/Feb. 10-13
1999 – Durban, S. Africa/June 23-26

Internat'l Newspaper Financial Executives (1947)
21525 Ridgetop Circle, Suite 200
Sterling, VA   20166
Tel: (703)421-4060   *Fax:* (703)421-4068
E-Mail: INFE@AOL.COM
Web Site: http://www.infe.org
Members: 1000 individuals
Staff: 4
Annual Budget: $500-1,000,000
V. President/Exec. Director: Robert J. Kasabian

Historical Note
*Formerly (1984) Institute of Newspaper Controllers and Finance
Officers. The international newspaper association for financial
accounting and business management. Membership: $210-
550/year (individual).*

Publications:
Newspaper Financial Executive Newsletter. m.
Newspaper Financial Executives Quarterly. q.

Meetings/Conferences:
Annual Meetings: June
1999 – Las Vegas, NV(Ceasar's Palace)/June 13-16

Internat'l Newspaper Group (1974)
39 Mouacdie Drive
Pearl River, NY   10965
Members: 250 individuals
Staff: 1
Annual Budget: $50-100,000
Secretary-Treasurer: Martin Donner

Historical Note
*ING members are individuals involved in newspaper production and
operations.*

Publications:
Information Flyer. semi-a.

Meetings/Conferences:
Annual Meetings: October

Internat'l Newspaper Marketing Ass'n (1930)
12770 Merit Dr., Suite 330
Dallas, TX   75251-1215
Tel: (972)991-5900   *Fax:* (972)991-3151
E-Mail: inma@connect.net
Web Site: http://www.inma.org
Members: 1,200 individuals
Staff: 6
Annual Budget: $500-1,000,000
Exec. Director: Earl Wilkinson
Membership Manager: Andrea Loubier

Historical Note
*Founded in 1930 as the Nat'l Newspaper Promotion Ass'n. The
name was changed in 1967 to the Internat'l Newspaper Promotion
Ass'n to reflect the makeup of the membership from more than 40
countries including the United States and Canada. In 1987, INMA
assumed its present name. INMA's mission is to provide papers
with professional leadership and assistance in creating effective
marketing of the total newspaper. Membership fee based on
newspaper circulation size.*

Publications:
Best in Print. a.
IDEAS Magazine. m. adv.
Research Primer.
Strategic Newspaper Marketing.

Meetings/Conferences:
Annual Meetings: May/500-600
1999 – Miami, FL/May 23-26

Internat'l Nubian Breeders Ass'n (1956)
773 Cherokee Road
Inman, KS   67546-8931
Tel: (316)585-2215
Members: 400 individuals
Annual Budget: under $10,000
Secretary-Treasurer: Barbara Regehr

Historical Note
*Monitors and proposes revisions to the breed standard, awards
outstanding animals and breeders, and provides a forum for
breeders to learn about, advertise, and promote their breed. Has no
paid officrs or full-time staff. Membership: $10/year (domestic),
$14/year (foreign).*

Publications:
Nubian Newsletter. q.

Meetings/Conferences:
Annual Meetings: October/November

Internat'l Oculoplastic Soc. (1978)
630 Park Ave.
New York, NY   10021
Tel: (212)734-1010
Members: 3,000 individuals
Staff: 4
Annual Budget: $100-250,000
Secretary: Andre Smith

Historical Note
*IOS is an interspecialty surgical society with an international
constituency. Members are eye, plastic, otolaryngylogic and
dermatology surgeons. Membership: $1,000/year (individual).*

Publications:
IOS Journal. q.
Newsletter. m. adv.

Meetings/Conferences:
Annual Meetings: Spring

Internat'l Oil Mill Superintendents Ass'n (1894)
2099 Loganberry Drive
Fayetteville, NC   28302
Tel: (910)487-2568   *Fax:* (910)433-4929
Members: 600 individuals
Staff: 1
Annual Budget: $25-50,000
Secretary-Treasurer: Tom Richardson

Historical Note
*Founded in Waco, Texas May 2, 1894 as the Oil Mill
Superintendents Ass'n of Texas. Several years later the name was
changed to the Nat'l Oil Mill Superintendents Ass'n to reflect the
fact that the membership included individuals from other cotton-
growing states. In the 1950s the present name was assumed
because the membership had come to include individuals from other
countries growing edible oil seeds. Absorbed the Internat'l Oil Seed
Superintendents Ass'n and the Tri-States Oil Mill Superintendents
Ass'n in 1996. Membership: $60/year (domestic), $65/year
(foreign).*

Publications:
Oil Mill Gazetteer. m. adv.

Meetings/Conferences:
Annual Meetings: June
1999 – Orlando, FL/June 26-29

2000 – Santa Fe, NM

Internat'l Oil Scouts Ass'n (1924)
P.O. Box 272949
Houston, TX 77277
Tel: (512)472-7173
Web Site: http://www.iosa.org
Members: 100 individuals
Annual Budget: under $10,000
President: Terry Strang

Historical Note
Formerly (1960) Nat'l Oil Scouts and Landmen's Ass'n. Federation of regional ass'ns of oil scouts and landmen. Records production in oil and gas fields and compiles exploratory well listings, in the U.S., Canada, and abroad. Membership: $85/year. Requests for the IOSA Yearbook should be directed to: Mason Map Service, Yearbook Editor, P.O. Box 338, Austin, TX 78767.

Publications:
Directory. a. adv.
IOSA Newsletter. q.
Magazine. a. adv.
Yearbook. semi-a.

Meetings/Conferences:
Annual Meetings: June
1999 – Biloxi, MS
2000 – Banff Alta Canada

Internat'l Organization for the Education of the Hearing Impaired (1967)
Historical Note
A section of the Alexander Graham Bell Ass'n for the Deaf.

Internat'l Organization of Citrus Virologists (1959)
Dept. of Plant Pathology
Univ. of California
Riverside, CA 92521
Tel: (909)684-0934   Fax: (909)684-4324
E-Mail: chester.r@worldnet.att.net
Members: 270 individuals
Annual Budget: under $10,000
Secretary: C.N. Roistacher

Historical Note
Members are individuals engaged in research of citrus virus diseases and related disorders that reduce production of citrus. Membership: $30/3 year period.

Publications:
Proceedings of Conference. Tri-en.

Meetings/Conferences:
2001 – Nicosea, Cyprus

Internat'l Organization of Masters, Mates and Pilots (1887)
700 Maritime Blvd.
Linthicum Heights, MD 21090
Tel: (410)850-8700   Fax: (410)850-0973
E-Mail: iommp@bridgedeck.org
Web Site: http://www.bridgedeck.org
Members: 6,800 individuals
Staff: 50
Annual Budget: $2-5,000,000
President: Capt. Timothy A. Brown
Communications Director: Karl D. Schwartz
International Comptroller: John A. Gorman
Exec. Director, MITAGS: Glen Paine
International Counsel: Ernest Allen Cohen

Historical Note
Affiliated with the AFL-CIO. Supports the Maritime Institute for Research and Industrial Development.

Publications:
Master, Mate & Pilot. m.

Internat'l Orthokeratology Soc. (1985)
Historical Note
Address unknown in 1997.

Internat'l Oxygen Manufacturers Ass'n (1943)
14701 Detriot Ave., Suite 385
Cleveland, OH 44107-4109
Tel: (216)228-2166   Fax: (216)228-5810
E-Mail: RCroy@worldnet.att.net
Web Site: http://www.iomaweb.org
Members: 190 companies
Staff: 2
Annual Budget: $250-500,000
Exec. Director: Richard S. Croy

Historical Note
IOMA members are the manufacturers of all of the industrial and medical gases (oxygen, nitrogen, argon, acetylene, carbon dioxide, hydrogen, etc.) or of equipment and supplies (plants, cylinders, valves, tanks, etc.) used by the industrial gas companies.

Publications:
IOMA Broadcaster. bi-m.

Meetings/Conferences:
Annual Meetings: Fall/350
1999 – San Diego, CA(Loews Coronado)/Oct. 30-Nov. 3/320
2000 – Monte Carlo, Monaco(Loews)/Sept 23-Sept. 27
2001 – Boca Raton, FL(Boca Raton Club)/Nov. 3-7/350
2002 – Dorado, PR(Hyatt Cerromar)/Oct. 24-30/350

Internat'l Ozone Ass'n-Pan American Group Branch (1976)
31 Strawberry Hill Ave.
Stamford, CT 06902
Tel: (203)348-3542   Fax: (203)967-4845
Web Site: http://www.int-ozone-assoc.org
Members: 900 individuals, 70 companies
Staff: 2
Annual Budget: $50-100,000

Exec. Director: Margit H. Istok
Historical Note
Formerly (1978) the Internat'l Ozone Institute, Inc., IOA-PAGB represents the interests of environmental and other scientific communities, application engineers, users, manufacturers of ozone generation and contacting equipment, ozone analyzers, monitors and control equipment, as well as the interests of various supporting industries and professions. International Coordinating office located in Lille, France. Membership: $80/year (individual), $180-600/year (organization).

Publications:
Ozone Science and Engineering: The Journal of IOA. bi-m. adv.
OZONews. bi-m. adv.

Meetings/Conferences:
Biennial World Congress: Odd years

Internat'l Parking Institute (1962)
P.O. Box 7167
Fredericksburg, VA 22404-7167
Tel: (540)371-7535   Fax: (540)371-8022
Members: 1,250 organizations
Staff: 10
Annual Budget: $1-2,000,000
President: David L. Ivey
Director, Communications: Lucia Cobo
Director, Marketing: Jenny Price
Director, Professional Development: Kim E. Jackson

Historical Note
Formerly known as the Internat'l Municipal Parking Congress and (1995) Institutional and Municipal Parking Congress; until 1962 IPI was a branch of the National League of Cities. Members are cities, colleges, hospitals, airports, port authorities, civic centers, state/federal government agencies, commercial parking operators and others concerned with parking, as well as suppliers and consultants. Membership: $375-545/year.

Publications:
Guide to Parking Consultants. a.
Parking Buyers Guide. a. adv.
The Parking Professional. m. adv.
Who's Who in Parking Yearbook. a.

Meetings/Conferences:
Annual Meetings: Spring/1,600
1999 – New Orleans, LA(Ernest Morial Convention Center)/May 30-June 2
2000 – Fort Lauderdale, FL(Broward County Convention Center)/May 20-24
2001 – Las Vegas, NV(Las Vegas Convention Center)/June 3-6

Internat'l Pediatric Nephrology Ass'n (1971)
111 E. 210th St.
Bronx, NY 10467
Tel: (718)655-1120   Fax: (718)652-3136
Members: 1,600 individuals
Annual Budget: $250-500,000
Secretary General: Ira Greifer, M.D.

Historical Note
IPNA members are physicians specializing in pediatric kidney disease. Has no paid officers or full-time staff. Membership: $125/year.

Publications:
Pediatric Nephrology Journal. bi-m. adv.
Proceedings. trien.

Meetings/Conferences:
2001 – Seattle, WA(Hyatt Regency)

Internat'l Pension and Employee Benefits Lawyers Ass'n (1987)
4424 Montgomery Ave., Suite 201
Bethesda, MD 20814
Tel: (301)654-6499   Fax: (301)654-3739
Toll Free: (800)227 - 5210
E-Mail: imi@imimtg.com
Web Site: http://www.websmart.com/IPEBLA/
Annual Budget: $2-5,000,000
Administrator: Amy Amerson

Historical Note
IBEPLA members are lawyers and other legal professionals with a practical interest in the legal aspects of pension plans and other employee benefit arrangements. Membership: $200/two years.

Publications:
IPEBLA Pension Lawyer Newsletter. q. adv.

Meetings/Conferences:
1999 – Florence, Italy(Sheraton)/May 24-27

Internat'l Perimetric Soc. (1974)
University of Iowa
Dept. of Neurology
Iowa City, IA 52242
Tel: (319)356-8758   Fax: (319)356-4505
Web Site: http://www.webye.ophth.uiowa.edu/ips/index.html
Members: 300 individuals
Annual Budget: $25-50,000
Secretary: Michael Wall, M.D.

Historical Note
Members are ophthamologists and other professionals working in the area of visual field testing.

Publications:
Proceedings. bien.

Meetings/Conferences:
Biennial Meetings: even years

Internat'l Periodical Distributors Ass'n (1972)
P.O. Box 3540
Allentown, PA 18106-0540
Members: 12 companies
Staff: 2
Annual Budget: $250-500,000

Consulting Director: Robert B. Alleger
Historical Note
Members are consumer magazine and paperback book distributors. Membership fee varies by share of total dollar volume of market in the U.S., Canada, and internationally.

Internat'l Personnel Management Ass'n (1906)
1617 Duke St.
Alexandria, VA 22314
Tel: (703)549-7100   Fax: (703)684-0948
Toll Free: (800)220 - 4762
E-Mail: ipma-hr.org
Web Site: http://www.ipma-hr.org
Members: 4,500 individuals, 1,400 agencies
Staff: 20
Annual Budget: $2-5,000,000
Exec. Director: Neil E. Reichenberg, CAE
Sr. Director, Ass'n Services: Sarah Shiffert
Manager, Government Affairs: Tina Ott
Director, Publications: Karen Smith
Director, Personnel Research: Eleanor Trice

Historical Note
Formerly (1906) Civil Service Assembly of the United States and Canada; (1957) Public Personnel Ass'n; and (1973) consolidated with Soc. for Personnel Administration. Membership: $100/year (individual); corporate membership fee varies.

Publications:
Agency Issues. bi-w.
IPMA News. m.
Public Personnel management. q. adv.

Meetings/Conferences:
Annual Meetings: Fall/700
1999 – Washington, D.C.(J.W. Marriott)/Oct. 17-21/600

Internat'l Petroleum Credit Ass'n (1923)
P.O. Box 59149
Minneapolis, MN 55459-0149
Tel: (612)384-2552
Members: 600 individuals
Annual Budget: $250-500,000
Exec. Director: John Finnessy

Historical Note
Members are credit and financial executives with companies whose product is a petroleum derivative. Allied members are vendors to the industry. Formerly (1992) the American Petroleum Credit Ass'n. Membership: $175/year (individual).

Publications:
IPCA Journal. 3/year.

Meetings/Conferences:
Annual Meetings: October

Internat'l Pharmaceutical Excipients Council (1991)
1655 N. Ft. Myer Dr., Suite 700
Arlington, VA 22209
Tel: (703)875-2127   Fax: (703)525-5157
E-Mail: ipecamer@aol.com
Members: 27 companies
Annual Budget: $250-500,000
Exec. Officer: Alan Mercill

Historical Note
IPEC members are companies with an interest in the otherwise inert chemicals used as vehicles for medicines. Membership: $14,000/year (full corporate); $9,000/year (associate).

Publications:
Guidelines. irreg.
Newsletter. q.

Meetings/Conferences:
Annual Meetings: Fall

Internat'l Philatelic Press Club (1963)
Historical Note
Members are professionals who write or edit news about stamps and stamp collecting. Associate members are persons or organizations who edit or publish catalogs or other materials intended to publicize profit-making philatelic enterprises. Formerly (1978) Philatelic Press Club. Membership: $12.50/year (individual), $60/year (organization).

Internat'l Phototherapy Ass'n (1981)
Photo Therapy Centre
1300 Richards St., Suite 205
Vancouver, BC V6B 3-G6
Tel: (604)689-9709   Fax: (604)689-9709
E-Mail: jweiser@istar.ca
Members: 225 individuals
Chairperson/Director: Judy Weiser

Historical Note
IPA members are psychologists, psychiatric nurses, social workers, therapists and other professionals with an interest in the use of still and moving pictures as tools for treatment, personal growth and reconciliation of emotional conflict.

Publications:
Magazine. 2-3/yr.

Internat'l Physical Fitness Ass'n (1960)
415 W. Court St.
Flint, MI 48503
Tel: (810)239-2166   Fax: (810)239-9390
Members: 2,000 fitness centers
Staff: 1
Annual Budget: $10-25,000
Contact: Stacy Sparkf

Historical Note
Formerly (1975) Universal Gym Affiliates. Principal purpose at present is to facilitate the transfer of memberships from one center to another. Membership: $100/year (center).

Publications:
Membership Roster. a.
Meetings/Conferences:
Annual Meetings: None held

Internat'l Piano Guild (1929)
808 Rio Grande St., Box 1807
Austin, TX 78767-1807
Tel: (512)478-5775
Members: 115,000 individuals
Staff: 11
Annual Budget: $1-2,000,000
President: Richard Allison
Historical Note
A division of the American College of Musicians. Professional society of piano teachers and music faculty members. Sponsors national examinations. Formerly (1981) the National Guild of Piano Teachers.
Publications:
Piano Guild Notes. bi-m. adv.
Meetings/Conferences:
Annual Meetings: Not held.

Internat'l Planetarium Soc. (1970)
c/o Arthur Storer Planetarium
600 Dares Beach Rd.
Prince Frederick, MD 20678
Tel: (410)535-7339
Web Site: http://www.ips-planetarium.org
Members: 620 individuals
Annual Budget: $25-50,000
Treasurer: Shawn Laatsch
Historical Note
Members are planetarium personnel and suppliers. Until 1976 known as the Internat'l Soc. of Planetarium Educators. Has no paid staff. Membership: $34/year (individual), $125/year (institution).
Publications:
Planetarian. q.
Meetings/Conferences:
Biennial Meetings: Even years

Internat'l Plant Propagation Soc. (1950)
Washington Park Arboretum
2300 Arboretum Dr.
Seattle, WA 98112
Tel: (206)543-8602   Fax: (206)527-2796
Web Site: www.ipps.org
Members: 3,200 individuals
Secretary: John A. Wott
Historical Note
IPPS is an educational organization representing members in 40 countries worldwide. Members are professionals in the science of plant propagation. Membership fee varies.
Publications:
Combined Proceedings. a.
Meetings/Conferences:
Annual Meetings: Regional Meetings Held in 10 Regions. See Web Site.

Internat'l Plasma Products Industry Ass'n
P.O. Box 669
Annapolis, MD 21404-0669
Tel: (410)268-2011   Fax: (410)263-2298
Members: 6 corporations
Staff: 2
Exec. Director: Robert W. Reilly

Internat'l Plate Printers', Die Stampers' and Engravers' Union of North America (1893)
3957 Smoke Road
Doylestown, PA 18901-1556
Tel: (215)340-2843
Members: 450 individuals
Staff: 2
Annual Budget: $10-25,000
Secretary-Treasurer: James Kopernick
Historical Note
Organized in Boston in 1892 as the Nat'l Steel and Cooper Plate Printers of the United States of America and affiliated with the American Federation of Labor in 1898. Accepted Canadian members in 1901 and became the Internat'l Plate Printers and Die Stampers Union of North American in 1921. A merger with the Internat'l Steel and Copper Plate Engravers League in 1925 resulted in adoption of the present title. Members are employed in the printing of U.S. and Canadian currency as well as stocks, bonds and foreign currency.
Meetings/Conferences:
Biennial Meetings: Odd years
1999 – Lake George, NY(Holiday Inn Turf Motel)
2000 – Ottawa, Canada

Internat'l Platform Ass'n (1831)
P.O. Box 250
Winnetka, IL 60093-0250
Tel: (847)446-4321   Fax: (847)446-7186
Web Site: http://www.internationalplatform.com
Members: 5,000 corporations and organizations
Staff: 5
Annual Budget: $250-500,000
Exec. Director: Luvie M. Owens
Historical Note
An outgrowth of the American Lyceum Ass'n founded by Daniel Webster and Josiah Holbrook. Professional association of those interested in oratory and the power of the spoken word – including lecturers, musicians, actors, program chairman and booking agents, bringing together all facets of the American lecture circuit. Members are corporations and associations that hire speakers. Membership: $45/year.

Publications:
Podium (Newsletter). q.
Meetings/Conferences:
Annual Meetings: Summer
1999 – /August 4-8

Internat'l Pot and Kettle Club (1924)
4107 Harbor Ridge Road N.E.
Tacoma, WA 98422
Tel: (206)927-6003
Members: 150 individuals
Staff: 1
Annual Budget: $25-50,000
Exec. Secretary/Treasurer: Mildred Johnson
Historical Note
Established in Los Angeles in January, 1924 as the Associated Pot and Kettle Clubs of America and incorporated in the State of California in 1926. The present name was assumed in 1979. The club is an association of individuals engaged in buying and selling non-food hard goods and kindred lines. It was originally organized to abate the animosity then existing between buyers for retail and wholesale establishments. Most charters are in the West. Membership: $50/year (individual); $100/year (organization/company).
Publications:
Hints. semi-m. adv.
Membership Directory. a.
Meetings/Conferences:
Annual Meetings: last week in June

Internat'l Precious Metals Institute (1976)
Suite 18
4400 Bayou Blvd.
Pensacola, FL 32503-1908
Tel: (850)476-1156   Fax: (850)476-1548
Web Site: http://www.ipmi.org
Members: 1000 individuals, 185 companies
Staff: 3
Annual Budget: $250-500,000
Exec. Director: David E. Lundy
Historical Note
Members are miners, refiners, producers and users of precious metals, as well as research scientists and mercantilists. The Institute was formed Nov. 18, 1976, to encourage the exchange of information and information in the precious metals industry. Cooperates with the American Soc. for Metals, the American Electroplaters' Soc., the American Institute of Mining Engineers, the American Soc. for Testing and Materials and the Manufacturing Jewelers and Silversmith Ass'n. Membership: $90/year (individual), $750-2,000/year (corporate).
Publications:
Buyers Guide. a. adv.
IPMI Membership Directory. a.
IPMI News and Reviews. m.
Meetings/Conferences:
Annual Meetings: June/400-450
1999 – Acapulco, Mexico(Princess)/June 20-23
2000 – Williamsburg, VA(Marriott)/June 11-14

Internat'l Prepress Ass'n (1896)
7200 France Ave. South, Suite 327
Edina, MN 55435
Tel: (612)896-1908   Fax: (612)896-0181
E-Mail: info@ipa.org
Web Site: http://www.ipa.org
Members: 500 companies
Staff: 6
Annual Budget: $1-2,000,000
President: Henry L. Hatch
Director, Member Services: Steven Bonoff
Historical Note
Members produce pre-press material for the graphics industry. Formerly (1968) the American Photoengravers Ass'n and (1980) the American Photoplatemakers Ass'n and (until 1984) Internat'l Ass'n of Photoplatemakers. Merged with PERI, Inc. (1980) and Graphic Preparatory Ass'n (1988).
Publications:
Images. m.
The Prepress Bulletin. bi-m. adv.
Meetings/Conferences:
Annual Meetings: Fall
1999 – Maui, HI/Oct. 3-6

Internat'l Printers Supply Salesmen's Guild (1913)
Historical Note
Organization defunct in 1995.

Internat'l Produce Federation (1993)
Historical Note
Organization defunct in 1995.

Internat'l Professional Groomers (1988)
1108 W. Devon
Elk Grove Village, IL 60007
Tel: (847)895-6630
Toll Free: (800)258 - 4765
Members: 300 individuals
Staff: 5
Annual Budget: under $10,000
President: Judy Kurpiel
Historical Note
IPG represents the professional pet grooming industry, providing continuing education to members and information to the public on the proper care and humane treatment of pets. Awards the designation Certified Master Groomer (CMG) to individuals successful completing a certification program. Membership: $50/year (individual), $25/year (company).

Publications:
Newsletter. q. adv.
Meetings/Conferences:

Internat'l Professional Rodeo Ass'n (1957)
P.O. Box 83377
Oklahoma City, OK 73148
Tel: (405)235-6540   Fax: (405)235-6577
Toll Free: (800)458 - 4772
E-Mail: iprainfo@intprorodeo.com
Web Site: http://www.intprorodeo.com
Members: 3,500 individuals
Staff: 9
Annual Budget: $1-2,000,000
Exec. Director: Ronnie Williams
Membership: Pam Queen
Editor: Todd Newville
Historical Note
Formerly Interstate Rodeo Ass'n (1963) and the Internat'l Rodeo Ass'n (1983). Governing body for professional rodeo. Membership: $225/year.
Publications:
IFR Program. a. adv.
Newsletter. m.
Pro Rodeo World. m. adv.
Meetings/Conferences:
Annual Meetings: in conjunction with International Finals Rodeo January
1999 – Oklahoma City, OK(Radisson)/Jan. 14-16

Internat'l Psychogeriatric Ass'n (1981)
550 Frontage Rd., Suite 2820
Northfield, IL 60093
Tel: (847)784-1701   Fax: (847)784-1705
E-Mail: ipa@ipa-online.org
Web Site: http://www.ipa-online.org
Members: 1,200 individuals
Staff: 4
Annual Budget: $100-250,000
Exec. Director: Fern Finkel
Meetings Coordinator: Margaret Brown
Program Administrator: Dorthy E. Zoller
Historical Note
Members are health care professionals and academics with an interest in developments in mental health care related elderly. Membership: $95/year (individual), $190/year (organization/company).
Publications:
Internat'l Psychogeriatrics. q.
IPA Bulletin. q.
Meetings/Conferences:
Annual Meetings: 2002
1999 – Vancouver, British Columbia/Aug. 15-20
2000 – Newcastle upon Tyre, England/April 4-7
2001 – Nice, France/Sept. 9-14
2003 – Chicago, IL/Aug. 17-22

Internat'l Psychohistorical Ass'n (1976)
266 Monroe Ave.
Wyckoff, NJ 07481-1915
Tel: (201)891-4980
Members: 250 individuals
Staff: 1
Annual Budget: under $10,000
Secretary: Henry Lawton
Historical Note
Membership is open to scholars from all disciplines who are interested in advancing the study and practice of psychohistory. Membership: $25/year.
Publications:
Convention Directory. a.
Membership Directory. a.
Psychohistory News. q. adv.
Meetings/Conferences:
1999 – New York, NY

Internat'l Public Relations Ass'n - United States Chapter (1955)
c/o Fazio Internat'l Ltd.
430 Plaza Real, Suite 275
Boca Raton, FL 33432
Tel: (561)416-5870
Members: 1000 individuals
Annual Budget: $500-1,000,000
President Elect: Carolyn Fazio
Director, Administrators: Pam Lemaire
Historical Note
IPRA members are senior public relations professionals. International headquarters is in London, England. Membership: GBP 225/year (individual).
Publications:
Internat'l Public Relations Review. q.
IPRA Gold Papers. trien.
IPRA Members Register. a.
IPRA News.
Meetings/Conferences:
1999 – Tokyo, Japan/800
2000 – Chicago, IL/2500

Internat'l Public Works Federation
Historical Note
A division of American Public Works Ass'n, which provides administrative support.

Internat'l Publishing Management Ass'n (1964)
1205 West College St.
Liberty, MO 64068-3733
Tel: (816)781-1111   Fax: (816)781-2790

E-Mail: ipmainfo@ipma.org
Web Site: http://www.ipma.org
Members: 2,000 individuals
Staff: 5
Annual Budget: $500-1,000,000
Exec. Director: Larry E. Aaron, CAE
Financial Coordinator: Cindy Pyles

Historical Note
Founded as the In-Plant Printing Management Ass'n, it became
IPMA-A Graphic Communications Management Ass'n in 1982 and
In-Plant Management Ass'n in 1986; assumed its current name in
1994. IPMA Internat'l is the professional association for corporate
publishing (creation, production, distribution) professionals who
work for educational institutions, government, and private industry.
It exists to provide corporate publishing and distribution
professionals the resources to attain greater productivity and cost
effectiveness through education, certification and information
exchange and to promote the value of in-house publishing and
distribution while advocating high ethical standards, environmental
and safety awareness. Membership: $160/year (individuals);
$320/year (vendors/associates).

Publications:
Inside IPMA. m.
Perspectives. m. adv.

Meetings/Conferences:
Annual Meetings: Spring
1999 – Minneapolis, MN(Hyatt Regency)/May 23-26

Internat'l Quorum of Film and Video Producers (1966)
c/o Film House
810 Dominican Dr.
Nashville, TN 37228
Tel: (615)255-4000   Fax: (615)255-4111
E-Mail: results@filmhouse.com
Members: 80 companies
Staff: 1
Annual Budget: $25-50,000
Exec. Officer: Curt Hahn

Historical Note
Membership composed of non-theatrical motion picture producers
making films and video for industry and government. Founded as
the Internat'l Quorum of Motion Picture Producers, it assumed its
present name in 1983.

Publications:
Quorum Quotes. q.

Meetings/Conferences:
Annual Meetings: Fall

Internat'l Radio and Television Soc. Foundation (1939)
420 Lexington Ave. (Suite 1714)
New York, NY 10170
Tel: (212)867-6650   Fax: (212)867-6653
Web Site: http://www.irts.org
Members: 1,900 individuals
Staff: 6
Annual Budget: $500-1,000,000
President: Joyce M. Tudryn
Director of Marketing: Maggie Davis
Manager, Press Relations and Membership Services: Jim Cronin
Senior Director, Program Administration: Maria De Leon Fisher
Comptroller: Vilma McPherson

Historical Note
Formerly (1962) Radio and Television Executives Soc. Originally
formed by a merger in 1952 of the Radio Executives Club (1939)
and the American Television Soc. (1940). Members are
professionals in radio, television, cable, advertising, and related
areas, as well as interested members of the general public. The IRTS
Foundation stages educational programs about electronic media.
Membership: $100/year NY members ($45/year for those under
age 30).

Publications:
Gold Medal Annual. a. adv.
Yearbook and Directory. a. adv.

Meetings/Conferences:
1999 – New York, NY(Marriott East Side)/Feb. 24-28

Internat'l Reading Ass'n (1956)
800 Barksdale Road, P.O. Box 8139
Newark, DE 19714-8139
Tel: (302)731-1600   Fax: (302)731-1057
E-Mail: Pubinfo.reading.org
Web Site: http://www.reading.org
Members: 90,000 individuals
Staff: 90
Annual Budget: $5-10,000,000
Exec. Director: Alan E. Farstrup
Dir., Publications: Joan M. Irwin

Historical Note
Founded January 1, 1956 through a merger of the Internat'l
Council for the Improvement of Reading Instruction and the Nat'l
Ass'n for Remedial Teaching. Members are classroom teachers,
reading specialists, consultants, administrators, supervisors, college
teachers, researchers, psychologists, librarians - persons who
promote the study of reading techniques and teaching methods and
literacy worldwide. Has an annual budget of approximately $8.0
million. Membership: $30/year, minimum.

Publications:
Journal of Adolescent & Adult Literacy. 8/year. adv.
Lectura y Vida. q.
Reading Research Quarterly. q.
Reading Teacher. 8/year. adv.
Reading Today. bi-m. adv.

Meetings/Conferences:
Annual Meetings: April/May
1999 – San Diego, CA/May 2-7
2000 – Indianapolis, IN/April 30-May 5
2001 – New Orleans, LA

Internat'l Real Estate Federation - American Chapter (1951)
2000 N. 15th St., Suite 101
Arlington, VA 22201
Tel: (703)524-4279   Fax: (703)528-2392
E-Mail: snewman@fiabci-usa.com
Web Site: http://www.fiabci-usa.com
Members: 1000 individuals
Staff: 1
Annual Budget: $100-250,000
Secretary General: Susan Newman

Historical Note
Members are real estate professionals and those in related fields.
U.S. chapter of FIABCI, headquartered in Paris, with 6,000
members in 52 countries worldwide. Membership: $435-485/year
(individual); $2,000/year (national associations).

Publications:
FIABCI Directory. a.
Newsletter. q.

Meetings/Conferences:
Semi-Annual Meetings: usually December/Paris, France and
May/various

Internat'l Real Estate Institute (1975)
1224 No. Nokomis N.E.
Alexandria, MN 56308
Tel: (320)763-4648   Fax: (320)763-9290
E-Mail: irei@iami.org
Web Site: http://iami.org/irei/html
Members: 5,000 individuals
Staff: 16
Annual Budget: $1-2,000,000
Exec. Director: Robert G. Johnson

Historical Note
Formerly (1984) the Internat'l Institute of Valuers. The primary
objective of IREI is to provide professional recognition and a method
to easily network with real estate professionals both internationally
as well as within your own nation. The Institute is also committed
to providing the most current international real estate information
possible through various publications and conferences. Members
represent the area of real estate valuation, finance investment and
development and management on an international level.
Membership: $195/year (individual); $1,200/year (corporate);
$150/year (associate).

Publications:
International Real Estate Journal. semi-a. adv.
Registry of Members. a.
The Internat'l Property Report.
The Internat'l Real Estate Newsletter. q. adv.

Meetings/Conferences:
Annual Meetings: May

Internat'l Reciprocal Trade Ass'n (1979)
175 W. Jackson Blvd., Suite 625
Chicago, IL 60604
Tel: (312)461-0236   Fax: (312)461-0474
E-Mail: admin1@irta.net
Web Site: http://www.irta.net
Members: 180 organizations
Staff: 2
Annual Budget: $100-250,000
Chief Executive Officer: Paul E. Suplizio

Historical Note
Formerly (1994) Internat'l Ass'n of Trade Exchanges. Members are
organizations serving as clearinghouses for the barter exchange of
goods and services among business firms, or who act as principals
or intermediaries in the barter exchange of goods and services
nationally and internationally. Formed to foster the common
interests of the commercial barter industry worldwide. Supports the
Barter Political Action Committee (BARTERPAC). Membership:
$450-3,500/year.

Publications:
Barter Statistics for North America, 1974-present. a.
IRTA Update. m.
The Trader. irreg.
Trade Wire Fax Newsletter. irreg.

Meetings/Conferences:
Semi-Annual Meetings: Spring and Fall

Internat'l Recording Media Ass'n (1970)
182 Nassau St., Suite 204
Princeton, NJ 08542-7005
Tel: (609)279-1700   Fax: (609)279-1999
E-Mail: info@recordingmedia.org
Web Site: http://www.recordingmedia.org
Members: 450 companies
Staff: 6
Annual Budget: $1-2,000,000
Exec. V. President: Charles Van Horn
Director, Operations: Richard Bennett
Manager, Research and Member Services: Brian Lewin

Historical Note
Formerly (1995) ITA - Internat'l Ass'n of Magnetic and Optical
Recording Manufacturers and Associated Industries. Founded as the
Internat'l Tape Ass'n, it became the Internat'l Tape/Disc Ass'n in
1981. Members are manufacturers of audio and video tape and
equipment, blank computer software and optical/laser media.
Membership: Based on volume, $480-6,000/year (company).

Publications:
ITA International Source Directory. a. adv.
ITA Membership Newsletter.
ITA Seminar Proceedings. a.

Meetings/Conferences:
Annual Meetings: March
1999 – Amelia Island, FL(Ritz Carlton)/March 10-14
2000 – LaQuinta, CA(La Quinta Resort and
     Club)/March 15-19

2001 – Tucson, AZ(Loews Ventana Canyon
     Resort)/March 28-April 1

Internat'l Regional Magazine Ass'n (1960)
P.O. Box 125
Annapolis, MD 21404
Tel: (410)451-2892
Members: 42 publications
Staff: 1
Annual Budget: $50-100,000
Exec. Director: Patrick Hornberger

Historical Note
Formerly (1994) Regional Publishers Ass'n. Founded to foster the
interchange of publishing knowledge among regional magazines.
IRMA provides a means by which members can assist one another
in solving problems unique to regional publishing. In most cases,
members are not competing for the same markets, so they discuss
matters frankly and trade information freely. IRMA members are
publishers of state and regional, as opposed to municipal,
magazines. Membership: $375/year.

Publications:
The IRMA Report. q.

Meetings/Conferences:

Internat'l Reprographic Ass'n (1927)
800 Enterprise Dr., Suite 202
Oak Brook, IL 60521-1929
Tel: (630)571-4685   Fax: (630)571-4731
Web Site: http://www.irga.com
Members: 900 companies
Staff: 7
Annual Budget: $1-2,000,000
Exec. Officer: Brian A. McCarthy
Manager, Communications: Jennifer Karabetsos
Manager, Convention: Mary Jo Sager
Business Manager: Lily McKinney

Historical Note
Membership consists of blueprint service companies and
engineering reproduction equipment manufacturers and suppliers. Formerly (until
1973) known as the Internat'l Ass'n of Blue Print and Allied
Industries and (1973-1980) as the Internat'l Reprographic
Blueprint Ass'n. Membership: $150-900/year (based on employee
count).

Publications:
Repro Report. m. adv.

Meetings/Conferences:
Annual Meetings: Annual/May
1999 – Long Beach, CA/May 5-8/2600
2000 – Lake Buena Vista, FL(Coronado Springs
     Resort)/April 26-30
2001 – Minneapolis, MN(Minneapolis Convention
     Center)/May 2-5/2700

Internat'l Research Council of Neuromuscular Disorders (1982)
1600 Sheridan Dr.
Lancaster, OH 43130
Tel: (740)653-1098   Fax: (740)687-5003
Members: 60 individuals
Annual Budget: $100-250,000
Exec. Director: James R. Grilliot, D.C.

Historical Note
IRCND members are health professionals with an interest in
diseases of the neuromuscular system.

Publications:
Newsletter. a.

Meetings/Conferences:

Internat'l REST Investigators Soc. (1983)
Medical College of Ohio, Dept. of Psych.
Ruppert Hall Cntr., 3120 Glendale Ave.
Toledo, OH 43614
Tel: (419)383-5695   Fax: (419)383-3031
Members: 175 individuals, 4 companies
Annual Budget: $10-25,000
President: Thomas Fine

Historical Note
IRIS's purpose is to exchange information among researchers of
restricted environmental stimulation techniques (REST), form
research groups and present findings. Membership: $30/year.

Publications:
Conference Proceedings. bien.
IRIS Bulletin. 3/yea.

Meetings/Conferences:
Biennial Conference: Odd Years

Internat'l Right of Way Ass'n (1934)
13650 Gramercy Place
Gardena, CA 90249-2453
Tel: (310)538-0233   Fax: (310)538-1471
Members: 8,000 individuals
Staff: 16
Annual Budget: $1-2,000,000
Exec. V. President: Raymond H. Rosenberg, CAE
Director, Education: Armando Apodaca
Director, Membership: Bonnie Gray
Editor: David M. Roman

Historical Note
Members are individuals responsible for acquiring land over which
to run power and telephone lines, pipelines, and roads. Founded as
the Southern California Right of Way Ass'n. Formerly (1980)
known as the American Right of Way Ass'n. Membership:
$130/year (individual).

Publications:
Right of Way. bi-m. adv.

Meetings/Conferences:
Annual Meetings: June/1,000
1999 – Albuquerque, NM(Hyatt)/June 20-24

2000 – Orlando, FL(Disney Resort)/June 18-22
2001 – Vancover, BC(Hyatt)/June 17-21
2002 – Mobile, AL(Adams Mark)/June 16-20

Internat'l Road Federation *(1948)*
2600 Virginia Ave., N.W., Suite 208
Washington, DC   20037-1905
Tel: (202)338-4641   *Fax:* (202)338-8104
Members: 750 companies & government agencies
Staff: 8
Annual Budget: $2-5,000,000
Director General: Gerald P. Shea
Dep. Director General: Wayne McDaniel
Director, Programs: Amy Englehart

Historical Note
An internat'l organization representing road associations in over 70 countries. Provides consulting and administrative services in highways and transportation. Membership: $500/15,000/year (organization).

Publications:
Annual Report. a.
Fellowship Directory. a.
Proceedings of World and Regional Meetings.
Who's Who. a.
World Highways. bi-m. adv.

Meetings/Conferences:
1999 – Las Vegas, NV(Ceasars Palace)/March 25-26

Internat'l Safe Transit Ass'n *(1948)*
1400 Abbott Road, Suite 310
East Lansing, MI   48823-1900
Tel: (517)333-3437   *Fax:* (517)333-3813
E-Mail: ista@ista.org
Web Site: http://www.ista.org
Members: 620 companies
Staff: 6
Annual Budget: $100-250,000
Exec. Director: Edward Church
Member Services Manager: Meredith L. Young

Historical Note
Formerly (1974) Nat'l Safe Transit Committee, Inc. Members are shippers, carriers, manufacturers, packagers, package designers, and testing laboratories interested in reducing damage to goods in transit. Formerly (1992) the Nat'l Safe Transit Ass'n. Formerly (1994) Nat'l/Internat'l Safe Transit Ass'n. Membership: $475/yr. (company).

Publications:
Directory. a. adv.
Preshipment Testing Newsletter. q. adv.
Proceedings/Projects.

Meetings/Conferences:
Annual Meetings: April-May
1999 – Orlando, FL(Disney's Coronado Springs Resort)/April 6-9

Internat'l Sanitary Supply Ass'n *(1923)*
7373 North Lincoln Ave.
Lincolnwood, IL   60646-1799
Tel: (847)982-0800   *Fax:* (847)982-1012
Toll Free: (800)225 - 4772
E-Mail: issa@info.com
Web Site: http://www.ISSA.COM
Members: 4,400 companies
Staff: 23
Annual Budget: $5-10,000,000
Exec. Director: John P. Garfinkel
Director, Legislative Affairs: William C. Balek
Director, Conventions/Meetings: Lee Ann Nowling
Manager of Education & Training: Susan Tansey
Manager, Finance: Donna Tode
Director, Operations/Membership Services: Joan Cook
Director, Publications: Lisa Veeck
Manager of Technology: Lori Crane

Historical Note
Formerly Nat'l Sanitary Supply Ass'n. Members are manufacturers, distributors, wholesalers, manufacturer representatives, publisher and associate members engaged in the manufacture and/or distribution of cleaning and maintenance products. Sponsors and supports the Sanitary Supply Political Action Committee (Clean-PAC) and the ISSA Foundation, its educational arm. Membership: $390-2,800/year.

Publications:
Education Catalog. a.
ISSA Legislative and Regulatory Update. m.
ISSA Today. m. adv.
ISSAlert. irreg.
Membership Directory. a.

Meetings/Conferences:
Annual Meetings: Fall/15,000
1999 – Chicago, IL/Oct. 12-15
2000 – Atlanta, GA/Oct. 11-14
2001 – Orlando, FL/Oct. 16-19
2002 – Las Vegas, NV/Oct. 15-18

Internat'l Saw and Knife Ass'n *(1965)*
505 Van Ness
Fresno, CA   93721
Tel: (209)237-0809
Members: 150 companies
Annual Budget: $10-25,000
Secretary: Kirk Wetchey

Historical Note
Members are companies repairing, selling, manufacturing, or servicing large band and circular saws, paper knives, shear blades, circular slitters, and metal cutting bands. Formerly the Nat'l Ass'n of Saw Shops, assumed its present name in 1983. Has no paid officers or full-time staff. Membership: $125-250/year (individual).

Publications:
Membership List. a.

Newsletter.
Meetings/Conferences:
1999 – Seattle, WA

Internat'l Security Management Ass'n *(1982)*
66 Charles St., Suite 280
Boston, MA   02114
Tel: (319)381-4008   *Fax:* (319)381-4283
Toll Free: (800)368 - 1894
E-Mail: isma3@aol.com
Members: 280 individuals
Staff: 1
Annual Budget: $100-250,000
President: David Burrill
Business Manager: Susan Pohlmann

Historical Note
ISMA members are corporate security directors and executives of full service security service firms.

Publications:
Membership Directory. a.

Meetings/Conferences:
Semi-annual Meetings: January and June

Internat'l Security Officers, Police and Guards Union *(1937)*
321 86th St.
Brooklyn, NY   11209
Tel: (718)836-3508
Members: 7,000 individuals
Staff: 2
Annual Budget: $50-100,000
President: Frank W. Mancini, Jr.

Historical Note
An independent labor union founded as Independent Watchmen's Ass'n. The present name was assumed around 1981-82. Represents guards and security personnel in all phases of private industry and those employed on the city, state, or federal levels.

Meetings/Conferences:
Annual Meetings: Quinquennial Meetings

Internat'l Service Robot Ass'n *(1984)*
Historical Note
Organization defunct in 1998.

Internat'l Sewing Machine Ass'n *(1952)*
Historical Note
Absorbed by the American Home Sewing and Craft Ass'n in 1996.

Internat'l Shooting Coaches Ass'n *(1984)*
P.O. Box 91782
Lakeland, FL   33804
Tel: (941)682-0716
Members: 400 individuals
President: Lance R. Miller

Historical Note
Formerly (1985) American Shooting Coaches Ass'n. Members are archery, pistol, rifle and shotgun coaches. Membership: levels based on certification and national standing.

Publications:
On Target Newsletter. q.

Meetings/Conferences:

Internat'l Sign Ass'n *(1944)*
707 N. St. Asaph St.
Alexandria, VA   22314
Tel: (703)836-4012   *Fax:* (703)836-8353
Web Site: http://www.signs.org
Members: 1,250 manufacturers
Staff: 16
Annual Budget: $2-5,000,000
President and C.E.O.: Mark Lappen
V. President of Government Relations: Suzanne C. Beamer
V. President of Conventions: K. Brian McNamara
Exec. V. President of Conventions and Educations: E.G. (John) Johnson, CAE
V. President of Finance: Jill Tompkuis
V. President of Membership: Jennifer Branslans

Historical Note
Formerly (1995) Nat'l Electric Sign Ass'n, ISA members are manufacturers of all types of on-premise signs and the materials for them. They are also suppliers to the industry. Membership fee varies, based on company size.

Publications:
ISA Directory a. adv. adv.
Perspectives Newsletter. q.
Signals Newsletter. bi-m.
Signline.

Meetings/Conferences:
Annual Meetings: Spring/12-15,000
1999 – Las Vegas, NV(City Wide/Conv. Cntr.)/April 29-May 1/15000
2000 – Orlando, FL(City Wide/Conv. Cntr.)/April 26-29/15000
2001 – Las Vegas, NV(City Wide/Conv. Cntr.)/Mar. 22-24/15000
2002 – Orlando, FL(City Wide/Conv. Cntr.)/Apr. 3-6/15000

Internat'l Silk Ass'n *(1950)*
c/o Soritex
One Madison St.
East Rutherford, NJ   07073
Tel: (973)472-4200   *Fax:* (973)472-0222
Members: 25 silk converters and importers
Staff: 1
Annual Budget: $10-25,000
President: William Katterman

Meetings/Conferences:
Annual Meetings: Fall

Internat'l Skeletal Soc. *(1973)*
Department of Radiology, USCF
San Francisco, CA   94143-0628
Tel: (415)476-4864   *Fax:* (415)476-8550
Members: 428 individuals
Annual Budget: $500-1,000,000
Secretary: Dr. Harry Genant

Historical Note
ISS members are physicians and researchers with an interest in skeletal radiology. ISS's purpose is (a) to advance the science and art of skeletal radiology through an educational non-profit society of radiologists and individuals in related fields of medicine and science (b) to bring together radiologists and individuals in related fields to improve the understanding, research and teaching of skeletal radiology, and (c) to promote closer fellowship and exchange of ideas. Membership: $175/year.

Publications:
Membership Directory. a.
Newsletter. 2/year.
Skeletal Radiology. 8/year. adv.

Meetings/Conferences:
1999 – Barcelona, ESP

Internat'l Sleep Products Ass'n *(1915)*
333 Commerce St.
Alexandria, VA   22314
Tel: (703)683-8371   *Fax:* (703)683-4503
Web Site: http://www.sleepproducts.org
Members: 700 companies
Staff: 17
Annual Budget: $2-5,000,000
Exec. V. President: Russell L. Abolt
V. President of Communications: Andrea Herman
Director, Communications: Douglas B. McAllister
Director, Government Affairs/Issues Management: Shawn Conrad
V. President, Meetings/Expositions: Susan E. Perry
C.O.O.: Brian Dulmaine
V. President of Membership Services: Patricia Martin

Historical Note
Formerly (1986) Nat'l Ass'n of Bedding Manufacturers. Affiliate organizations include the Better Sleep Council and the Sleep Products Safety Council.

Publications:
Bed Times. m. adv.

Meetings/Conferences:

Internat'l Slurry Surfacing Ass'n *(1962)*
1200 19th St., N.W., Suite 300
Washington, DC   20036
Tel: (202)857-1160   *Fax:* (202)223-4579
E-Mail: issa@dc.sba.com
Web Site: www.history.rochester.edu/issa
Members: 235 companies
Staff: 2
Annual Budget: $100-250,000
Exec. Director: John L. Fiegel

Historical Note
Formerly known as the Internat'l Slurry Seal Ass'n (1990). Members are contractors and suppliers of asphalt slurry seal. Provides information, technical assistance, and networking opportunities. Membership: $350/year (associate), $1,700/year (active); $75/year (government); $1,100/year (international).

Publications:
Convention Proceedings. a.
ISSA Report. bi-m.
Membership Directory. a.

Meetings/Conferences:
1999 – Puerto Vallarta, Mexico(Marriott Casa Magna)/March 7-12
2000 – Amelia Island, FL(Amelia Island Plantation)/March 12-16

Internat'l Small Satellite Organization
Historical Note
Organization defunct in 1997.

Internat'l Snowmobile Industry Ass'n *(1965)*
Historical Note
Became the Internat'l Snowmobile Manufacturers Ass'n in 1995.

Internat'l Snowmobile Manufacturers Ass'n *(1995)*
1640 Haslett Rd., Suite 170
Haslett, MI   48840
Tel: (517)339-7788   *Fax:* (517)339-7798
E-Mail: EKlim@aol.com
Web Site: http://Snowmobile.org/
Members: 4 manufacturers
Staff: 2
Annual Budget: $500-1,000,000
President: Edward J. Klim

Historical Note
Formerly (1995) the Internat'l Snowmobile Industry Ass'n. Organized and incorporated in Michigan. ISMA serves the interests of the snowmobile manufacturing industry as well as recreational snowmobiling.

Meetings/Conferences:
Annual Meetings: Late Spring in Canada or the U.S.
1999 – Reno, NV/June 9-13
2000 – Nasua, NH/June 10-14

Internat'l Soc. for Adolescent Psychiatry *(1985)*
730 Soundview Ave.
Bronx, NY   10473
Tel: (718)542-0394
E-Mail: rlandy7257@aol.com
Members: 800 individuals
Staff: 1
Annual Budget: $50-100,000

Administrative Director: Rosalie Landy
Historical Note
ISAP members are psychiatrists and allied professionals specializing in adolescence. Membership: $100/year (individual).
Publications:
ISAP Newsletter. 2/y.
Meetings/Conferences:
1999 – Aix-en-Provence, France/July 0-en-Provence, 0

Internat'l Soc. for Analytical Cytology
c/o Sherwood Group
60 Revere Drive, Suite 500
Northbrook, IL 60062
Tel: (847)480-9080   *Fax:* (847)480-9282
Members: 1,800 individuals
Staff: 3
Annual Budget: $500-1,000,000
Exec. Director: Richard Koetke
Historical Note
Members are scientists interested the study of the cell. Membership: $110/year (individual).
Publications:
Cytometry. m. adv.
Journal of Cytometry. bi-m.
Meetings/Conferences:
2000 – France

Internat'l Soc. for Artificial Organs *(1977)*
10 W. Erie St., Suite 200
Painesville, OH 44077-3270
Tel: (440)358-1102   *Fax:* (440)358-1104
Members: 1000 individuals
Staff: 3
Annual Budget: $100-250,000
Editor-in-Chief: Yukihiko Nose, M.D., PhD
Historical Note
Members are involved in the research, development or application of artificial organs. Membership: $125/year.
Publications:
Artificial Organs. m. adv.
Meetings/Conferences:
Biennial Meetings: Odd years

Internat'l Soc. for Cardiovascular Surgery - North American Chapter
13 Elm St.
Manchester, MA 01944
Tel: (978)526-8330   *Fax:* (978)526-1010
E-Mail: naiscvs@prri.com
Web Site: http://www.vascsyrg.org
Members: 1,540 individuals
Staff: 20
Annual Budget: $25-50,000
Exec. Director: William T. Maloney, CAE
Historical Note
Membership: $150/year (active); $50/year (senior).
Publications:
Journal of Vascular Surgery. bi.
Meetings/Conferences:
Annual Meetings: June
1999 – Washington, DC(Sheraton)/June 6-9/1300
2000 – Toronto, Ontario(Sheraton/Westin)/June 11-14/1500

Internat'l Soc. for Chronobiology *(1937)*
University of Texas, Medical Branch
Dept. of Anatomy and Neurosciences
Galveston, TX 77555-1069
Tel: (409)772-1294   *Fax:* (409)772-1832
Members: 300 individuals
Annual Budget: $10-25,000
Secretary-Treasurer: Norma H. Rubin, Ph.D.
Historical Note
Founded at Ronneby, Sweden as Societas pro Studio Rhythmi Biologici, it assumed its present name in 1971. Seeks to further the development of studies on temporal parameters of biological variables (chronobiologic variation) and to pursue related scientific and educational purposes; to encourage the development of centers of chronobiological research; and to work toward the establishment of chronobiology as an academic discipline in its own right. Its principal activity is sponsorship of international conferences. Scientific Membership: $82/year.
Publications:
Chronobiology International. q. adv.
Meetings/Conferences:

Internat'l Soc. for Clinical Laboratory Technology *(1962)*
Historical Note
Merged with American Ass'n of Bioanalysts in 1999.

Internat'l Soc. for Developmental Psychobiology *(1967)*
Dept. of Psychology
Virginia Tech
Blacksburg, VA 24061-0436
Tel: (540)231-5346   *Fax:* (540)231-3652
Members: 307 individuals
Annual Budget: $10-25,000
Secretary: Robert Lickliter
Historical Note
Formed to promote research into the relationship between behavioral and biological aspects of the developing organism at all levels of organization; membership open to any person engaged in the scientific study of human or animal development and holding a doctorate degree. Membership: $65/year.
Publications:
Developmental Psychobiology. bi-m. adv.

Membership Directory. a. adv.
Newsletter. 3/yr. adv.
Meetings/Conferences:
Annual Meetings: October-November/200

Internat'l Soc. for Ecological Economics *(1989)*
P.O. Box 1589
Solomons, MD 20688
Tel: (410)326-7263   *Fax:* (410)326-7354
E-Mail: beckman@cbl.umces.edu
Web Site: http://kabir.cbl.cees.edu/ISEE/ISEEhome.html
Members: 2,000 individuals
Staff: 3
Annual Budget: $100-250,000
Dir., Publications and Development: Lisa Speckhardt
Dir., Membership/Conf. Services: Jennifer Beckman
Managing Editor, Ecological Economics: Janis King
Historical Note
Members are researchers, academics, and other professionals who study the impact of econmoic models and policies on the environment. Membership: $15-102/year.
Publications:
Ecological Economics Bulletin. q. adv.
Ecological Economics Journal. m.
Meetings/Conferences:
2000 – Canberra, Australia

Internat'l Soc. for Ecological Modelling-North American Chapter *(1983)*
Environmental Sci., Washington State U.
2710 University Dr.
Richland, WA 99352
Tel: (509)372-7388   *Fax:* (509)372-7471
E-Mail: erykiel@tricity.wsu.edu
Web Site: http://ecomod.tamu.edu/ecomod/isem.html
Members: 150 individuals
Annual Budget: under $10,000
President: Dr. T King, Ph.D.
Historical Note
The International Society for Ecological Modelling promotes the international exchange of general knowledge, ideas and scientific results in the area of the application of systems analysis and simulation to ecology, environmental science and natural resource management using mathematical and computer modelling of ecological systems.
Publications:
ECOMOD Newsletter. q.
Meetings/Conferences:
Annual Meetings: August

Internat'l Soc. for Educational Planning *(1970)*
Historical Note
Address unknown in 1997.

Internat'l Soc. for Environmental Toxicology and Cancer *(1983)*
P.O. Box 134
Park Forest, IL 60466
Tel: (708)758-3242   *Fax:* (708)758-3276
Members: 700 individuals
Secretary-Treasurer: George Scherr, Ph.D.
Historical Note
ISETC members are researchers concerned with environmental toxicology and cancer.
Publications:
Journal of Environmental Pathology, Toxicology and Oncology. bi-m.

Internat'l Soc. for Experimental Hematology *(1972)*
1200 19th St., N.W., Suite 300
Washington, DC 20036
Tel: (202)857-1890   *Fax:* (202)851-1102
E-Mail: iseh@dc.sba.com
Web Site: http://www.iseh.org
Members: 1,400 individuals, 14 corporate
Staff: 1
Annual Budget: $500-1,000,000
Account Manager: Seth Goldman
Historical Note
ISEH promotes the scientific knowledge and clinical application of basic hematology and immunology through research, publications, and other activities. Incorporated in Texas in 1972. Membership: $130/year (full member); $26/year (associate); $5,000/year (corporate).
Publications:
Experimental Hematolgy. 13/year. adv.
Meetings/Conferences:
Annual Meetings: Summer
1999 – Monte Carlo, Monaco/July 10-14/1500
2000 – Tampa, FL(Convention Center)/July 8-12/1500
2001 – Japan/1
2002 – Montreal, Canada

Internat'l Soc. for General Semantics *(1943)*
P.O. Box 728
Concord, CA 94522
Tel: (925)798-0311   *Fax:* (925)798-0312
E-Mail: isgs@a.crl.com
Web Site: http://www.crl.com/~isgs/isgshome.html
Members: 2,500 individuals
Staff: 2
Annual Budget: $100-250,000
Exec. Director: Paul Johnston
Historical Note
Members are educators, trainers, writers and scientists interested in how language shapes thought, behavior and communication with others. The Society stimulates and sponsors research in colleges

and universities and other institutions through the publication of papers, articles, and books. Membership: $30/year.
Publications:
ETC: A Review of General Semantics. q. adv.
Meetings/Conferences:
Annual Meetings: One every two-three years

Internat'l Soc. for Heart and Lung Transplantation *(1981)*
14673 Midway Road, Suite 108
Addison, TX 75001
Tel: (972)490-9495   *Fax:* (972)490-9499
E-Mail: ishlt@aol.com
Members: 2,200 individuals
Staff: 2
Annual Budget: $1-2,000,000
Exec. Director: Amanda W. Rowe
Historical Note
Formerly (1991) Internat'l Soc. for Heart Transplantation. Encourages and stimulates discussion of problems of interest and concern in the field of heart and lung transplantation, and promotes educational opportunities for professionals in the field. Membership: $230/year (individual).
Publications:
Journal of Heart and Lung Transplantation. m. adv.
Meetings/Conferences:
Annual Meetings: Spring
1999 – San Francisco, CA/April 21-24/1700

Internat'l Soc. for Hybrid Microelectronics *(1967)*
Historical Note
Merged with the Internat'l Electronic Packaging Soc. to form the Internat'l Microelectronics and Packaging Soc. in 1996.

Internat'l Soc. for Infectious Diseases
181 Longwood Ave.
Boston, MA 02115
Tel: (617)525-0777   *Fax:* (617)731-1541
E-Mail: isid@aol.org
Web Site: http://www.isid.com
Members: 30,000 individuals
Staff: 2
Exec. Director: Norman R. Stein
Meetings/Conferences:
Annual Meetings: Biannual.
2000 – Buenos Aires, Argentina

Internat'l Soc. for Intelligent Systems
1313 Dolley Madison Blvd., Suite 402
McLean, VA 22101-3926
Tel: (703)790-1745   *Fax:* (703)790-9063
Exec. Director: Richard J. Burk, Jr.

Internat'l Soc. for Intercultural Education, Training and Research *(1974)*
P.O. Box 467
Putney, VT 05346
Tel: (802)387-4785   *Fax:* (802)387-5783
E-Mail: ctar@sover.net
Members: 1,900 individuals, 60 institutions
Staff: 2
Annual Budget: $250-500,000
Exec. Director: David L. Santini
Membership Coordinator: Diane K. Frendak
Historical Note
Founded as the Soc. for Intercultural Education, Training and Research in 1974, it added "International" to its name in 1985. An international professional association of individuals concerned with understanding the interaction between peoples of different national, cultural, racial and ethnic backgrounds. Membership: $125/year (indvidual); $485/year (organization/company); $70/year (student).
Publications:
Communique. q. adv.
International Journal of Intercultural Relations. q.
Meetings/Conferences:
Annual Meetings: Spring
1999 – Toronto, Ontario
2000 – Mexico City, Mexico

Internat'l Soc. for Magnetic Resonance in Medicine *(1994)*
2118 Millvia, Suite 201
Berkeley, CA 94704
Tel: (510)841-1899   *Fax:* (510)841-2340
E-Mail: info@ismrm.org
Members: 5,000 individuals
Staff: 9
Annual Budget: $2-5,000,000
Exec. Director: Jane Tiemann
Publications Coordinator: Sheryl Liebscher
Meetings Coordinator: Cordie Miller
Education Coordinator: Robert Goldstein
Membership Coordinator: Lynn Williams
Assistant Director: Jennifer Olson
Historical Note
Formed as a merger of the Soc. for Magnetic Resonance Imaging and the Soc. of Magnetic Resonance in Medicine in 1994. Name changed from Soc. of Magnetic Resonance to Internat'l Soc. for Magnetic Resonance in Medicine in 1996. Membership consists of physicians and scientists promoting the applications of magnetic resonance techniques to medicine and biology. Membership: $165/year (individual).
Publications:
Journal of Magnetic Resonance Imaging. bi-m. adv.
Magnetic Resonance in Medicine. m. adv.
MR Pulse Newletter. 3/year. adv.
Proceedings of the Scientific Meeting. y. adv.

Meetings/Conferences:
Annual Meetings: Annual/April/May
1999 – Philadelphia, PA(Pennsylvania Convention Center)/May 22-28
2000 – Denver, CO(Colorado Convention Center)/April 1-7
2001 – Glasgow, Scotland(Scottish Exhibition & Conf Center)/April 21-27
2002 – Honolulu, HI(Convention Center)/May 18-24
2003 – Toronto, ON, Canada(Metro Toronto Convention Center)/May 10-16

Internat'l Soc. for Measurement and Control

Historical Note
Became (1997) ISA: Internat'l Soc. for Measurement and Control.

Internat'l Soc. for Molecular Plant Microbe Interactions *(1990)*

3340 Pilot Knob Road
St. Paul, MN 55121
Tel: (612)454-7250 *Fax:* (612)454-0766
Members: 400 individuals
Exec. V. President: Steven C. Nelson

Historical Note
Membership: $25/year (individual); $10/year (student).

Publications:
Molecular Plant-Microbe Interactions Journal. bi-m. adv.

Meetings/Conferences:

Internat'l Soc. for Performance Improvement *(1962)*

1300 L St., N.W., Suite 1250
Washington, DC 20005
Tel: (202)408-7969 *Fax:* (202)408-7972
E-Mail: info@ispi.org
Web Site: http://www.ispi.org
Members: 6,000 individuals
Staff: 10
Annual Budget: $2-5,000,000
Exec. Director: Richard D. Battaglia, CAE
Director, Publications: Matthew Davis
Deputy Exec. Director: Tom Omri
Director, Marketing: Megan Spillane

Historical Note
Formerly (1973) Nat'l Soc. for Programmed Instruction and (1995) Nat'l Soc. for Performance and Instruction. ISPI is dedicated to increasing performance in the workplace through the application of performance technologies. ISPI members include performance technologists, training directors, human resource managers, instructional technologists, human factors practitioners and organizational development consultants working in a variety of settings including business, industry, universities, government agencies, health services, banks and the armed forces. ISPI has 60 chapters located throughout the world. Membership: $125/year.

Publications:
Performance Improvement Journal. 10/yr. adv.
Performance Improvement Quarterly. q.

Meetings/Conferences:
Annual Meetings: Spring
1999 – Long Beach, CA(Long Beach Convention Center)/March 23-26/13000

Internat'l Soc. for Peritoneal Dialysis *(1984)*

3800 Reservoir Rd., N.W.
Suite F6003-PHC
Washington, DC 20007
Tel: (202)784-3662 *Fax:* (202)687-2808
E-Mail: jwinch@dcez.com
Web Site: http://www.ispd.org
Members: 1,300 individuals
Annual Budget: $250-500,000
Secretary-Treasurer: R. Krediet

Historical Note
Stimulated by the growth of continuous ambulatory peritoneal dialysis, which is now used for renal failure management of 30,000 patients worldwide. Members are MD's, RN's, scientists, dieticians and social workers or those who have experience in peritoneal dialysis for the treatment of renal failure. ISPD's purpose is to promote teaching, research, and patient care in dialysis. Membership: $120/year (M.D.); $60/year (RN, M.D. in training).

Publications:
PD Newsletter. 3/year. adv.
Peritoneal Dialysis International. bi-m. adv.

Meetings/Conferences:

Internat'l Soc. for Pharmaceutical Engineering *(1980)*

3816 W. Linebaugh Ave., Suite 412
Tampa, FL 33624-4702
Tel: (813)960-2105 *Fax:* (813)264-2816
Web Site: http://www.ispe.org
Members: 9,000 individuals
Staff: 22
Annual Budget: $2-5,000,000
Exec. Director: Paul N. D'Eramo
Director, Education: Laurie J. Mask, CMP
Director, Administration: Susan Humphreys Klein
Director, Chapter/Membership Services: Connie Muia

Historical Note
Formerly (1991) Internat'l Soc. of Pharmaceutical Engineers. Members are individuals concerned with the construction of pharmaceutical plants, particularly such matters as pure water, sterile environments, anti-pollution measures, etc. U.S. members comprise 80% of membership. Membership: $130/year (individual).

Publications:
Annual Report. a.
ISPE Membership Directory and By-Laws. a. adv.
ISPEAK. m. adv.
Pharmaceutical Engineering. bi-m. adv.

Meetings/Conferences:
Annual Meetings: November

Internat'l Soc. for Pharmacoeconomics and Outcomes Research *(1995)*

20 Nassau, Suite 307
Princeton, NJ 08543-5256
Tel: (609)252-1305 *Fax:* (609)252-1306
Web Site: http://www.ispor.org
Members: 2,000 individuals
Staff: 3
Annual Budget: $500-1,000,000
Exec. Director: Marilyn Dix Smith
Director, Meetings/Committees: Jennifer Olson

Historical Note
Founded as Ass'n for Pharmacoeconomics and Outcomes Research; absorbed Internat'l Soc. for Economic Evaluation of Medicines and assumed its current name in 1998. Members are researchers who study the relative effectiveness of treatments and procedures. Membership: $75/year (individual); $25/year (student).

Publications:
ISPOR News. bi-m. adv.

Meetings/Conferences:
Annual Meetings: Spring
1999 – Arlington, VA(Crystal City Hyatt)

Internat'l Soc. for Plastination *(1984)*

Anatomical Serv. Div., Schl of Med. UMAB
B.R.B. Rm. B-026, 655 West Balt. St.
Baltimore, MD 21201
Tel: (410)706-3313 *Fax:* (410)706-8107
Web Site: http://www.kfunigraz.ac.at/amawww/plast/index.html
Members: 200 individuals
Exec. Secretary: Ronn Wade

Historical Note
Members are professional with an interest in the use of curable polymers in the preparation of biological specimens. Membership: $75/2-years.

Publications:
Journal of the Internat'l Soc. of Plastination.

Meetings/Conferences:
2000 – Etienne, France/July 2-7

Internat'l Soc. for Preventive Oncology *(1980)*

217 East 85th St., Suite 303
New York, NY 10028
Tel: (212)534-4991
Members: 600 individuals
Staff: 6
Annual Budget: $100-250,000
Secretary General: Herbert E. Neiburgs, M.D.

Historical Note
ISPO members are medical doctors, scientists and other professionals who are actively involved in preventive oncology.

Publications:
Cancer Detection & Prevention. bi-m.
Proceed of Int'l Symposium on Prevention & Detection of Cancer. bien.

Meetings/Conferences:
2000 – Vienna, Austria/Nov. 2-5

Internat'l Soc. for Professional Hypnosis *(1970)*

RDI P.O. Box 72
Hillcrest Dr.
Towanda, PA 18848
Tel: (717)265-7378
Members: 1,200 individuals
Staff: 1
Annual Budget: $25-50,000

Publications:
Conference Tapes. a.
Internat'l Journal of Professional Hypnosis. q.

Internat'l Soc. for Prosthetics and Orthotics, United States Nat'l Member Soc. *(1970)*

1650 King St., Suite 500
Alexandria, VA 22314
Tel: (703)836-7114 *Fax:* (703)836-0838
Members: 310 individuals
Staff: 1
Annual Budget: $10-25,000
US-ISPO Coordinator: Heather Rogers

Historical Note
Established in Copenhagen, Denmark. Incorporated in Dover, Delaware. Has no paid staff. Membership: $110/year.

Publications:
Membership Directory. irreg.
Prosthetics and Orthotics International. 3/yr. adv.

Meetings/Conferences:
Annual Meetings: January, plus triennial international congress (1989)

Internat'l Soc. for Quality-of-Life Studies *(1995)*

Marketing Dept, Pamplin Col of Business
Virginia Tech
Blacksburg, VA 24061-0236
Tel: (540)231-5110 *Fax:* (540)231-3076
E-Mail: isqols@vt.edu
Web Site: http://www.cob.vt.edu/market/isqols
Members: 200 individuals
Annual Budget: under $10,000
Exec. Director and Secretary: M. Joseph Sirgy

Historical Note
ISQOLS was founded to stimulate interdisciplinary research in quality-of-life studies and closer cooperation among scholars. Members are academic and government social/behavioral science researchers drawn from such fields as marketing, management, applied psychology, applied sociology, political science, economics, public administration, educational administration, family/child development, leisure/recreation studies, and technology management. Membership: $20/year (individual); $60/year (corporate/institutional); $15/year (student/retired researchers).

Publications:
ISQOLS Newsletter. q. adv.
Journal of Macromarketing. semi-a. adv.
Social Indicators Network News. q.
Social Indicators Research. 10/yr. adv.

Meetings/Conferences:
Annual Meetings: Fall

Internat'l Soc. for Systems Sciences *(1954)*

Historical Note
Originated in 1954 as the Soc. for the Advancement of General Systems Theory and incorporated in Michigan in 1955. Became the Soc. for General Systems Research in 1957 and the Internat'l Soc. for General Systems Research in 1987 and assumed its present name in 1989. Affiliated with American Ass'n for the Advancement of Science, United Nations Educational, Scientific and Cultural Organization, Internat'l Federation for Systems Research, and World Internat'l Systems Institutional Network (WISINET). Promotes the development of theoretical systems applicable to more than one of the traditional fields of knowledge. Membership: $65/year (individual), $ 35/year (retired/student), $155/year (organization/company).

Internat'l Soc. for Technology in Education *(1979)*

1787 Agate St.
Eugene, OR 97403-1923
Tel: (541)346-4414 *Fax:* (541)346-5890
Toll Free: (800)336 - 5191
E-Mail: iste@oregon.uoregon.edu
Web Site: http://www.iste.org
Members: 12,000 individuals
Staff: 32
Annual Budget: $500-1,000,000
Exec. Officer: David Moursund
General Manager: Tom Magness

Historical Note
Product of a merger in 1989 of the Internat'l Council for Computers in Education and the Internat'l Ass'n for Computing in Education. Maintains six special interest groups: Special Interest Group for Logo Educators (SIGLogo), Special Interest Group for Teacher Educators (SIGTE), Hyper/Multi-Media Special Interest Group (HyperSIG), Special Interest Group for Computer Science (SIGCS), Special Interest Group for Telecommunications (SIG/Tel), and Special Interest Group for Technology Coordinators (SIGTC). The Information Processing Administrators of Large School Systems ia a functional affiliate of ISTE. Membership: $58/year (domestic); $78/year (overseas), plus SIG dues.

Publications:
Computer Assisted English Language Learning Journal. q.
HyperNEXUS (publication of HyperSIG). q.
Journal of Computer Science Education (publication of SIGCS). q.
Journal of Computing in Teacher Education (publication of SIGTE). q.
Journal of Research on Computing in Education. q.
Learning & Leading with Technology. 8/year. adv.
Logo Exchange (publication of SIGLogo). q.
SIGTC Connections (publication of SIGTC). q.
Telecommunications in Education News (publication of SIG/Tel). q.
Update: People, Events & News in Education Technology. 7/yr.

Meetings/Conferences:
Semi-annual Meetings: November-December and June
1999 – Atlantic City, NJ(Convention Center)/June 22-24

Internat'l Soc. for the Comparative Studies of Civilizations *(1961)*

History Dept.
Univ. of Missouri, Rolla
Rollaton, MO 65401
Tel: (314)341-4815
E-Mail: wbledsoe@umr.edu
Members: 491 individuals
Annual Budget: under $10,000
President: Wayne Bledsoe, Ph.D.

Historical Note
Founded in 1961 in Salzburg, Austria. Moved its headquarters to the U.S. in 1970 and was reconstituted over a two-year period. Members are scholars and other individuals interested in the study of the history and evolution of world cultures. Membership fee: $25/year (individual); $35/year (organization).

Publications:
Comparative Civilizations Review. semi-a. adv.
ISCSC Newsletter. 2-3/year.

Meetings/Conferences:
1999 – Rolla, MO(Univ. of Missouri, Molla)
2000 – New Jersey(Rutgers University)

Internat'l Soc. for the Performing Arts *(1949)*

P.O. Box 909
Rye, NY 10580-0909
Tel: (914)971-1550 *Fax:* (914)971-1593
E-Mail: info@ispa.org
Web Site: http://ispa.org
Members: 700 individuals and organizations
Staff: 2
Annual Budget: $250-500,000
Exec. Director: Michael Hardy

Historical Note
ISPA represents executives and directors of concert and performance halls, festivals, performing companies,and artist competitions; government cultural officials; artists' managers; and other interested parties with a professional involvement in the performing arts, internationally. Membership: $500/year (individual).

Publications:
Forum. bi-m.
Membership Directory. a.

Meetings/Conferences:
Semi-Annual Meetings: June, international; December, New York, NY
1999 – Vancouver, Canada/June 17-20/300
2000 – Berlin, Germany/June 22-26/325

Internat'l Soc. for the Study of Dissociation (1984)

60 Revere Dr., Suite 500
Northbrook, IL   60062
Tel: (847)480-0899   *Fax:* (847)480-9282
E-Mail: issd@issd.org
Members: 1,600 individuals
Annual Budget: $250-500,000
Exec. Director: Richard Koepke

Historical Note
Formerly (1994) Internat'l Soc. for the Study of Multiple Personality and Dissociation. Incorporated in Georgia, ISSD members are professionals in psychology, psychiatry, medicine, nursing, sociology, social work, anthropology, philosophy, theology and other disciplines seriously involved in the study and treatment of multiple psychological processes. Membership: $105/year (regular); $50/year (affiliate); $45/year (student/ retiree).

Publications:
Dissociation Journal. q.
Guidelines for Treatment.
Membership Directory. a.
Newsletter. bi-m.

Meetings/Conferences:
Annual Meetings: November
1999 – Miami, FL(Inter-Continental)/Nov. 10-13/300

Internat'l Soc. for the Study of Subtle Energies and Energy Medicine (1989)

356 Goldco Circle
Golden, CO   80403
Tel: (303)278-2228   *Fax:* (303)279-3539
Members: 1,400 individuals
Staff: 4
Annual Budget: $250-500,000
Exec. Director: C. Penny Hiernu

Historical Note
ISSSEEM members are interested in integrating traditional knowledge about subtle energies and the healing process with modern scientific method and theory. Membership: $50/year (individual); $150/year (organization).

Publications:
Bridges Magazine. q.
Subtle Energies & Energy Medicine Journal. 3/yr.

Meetings/Conferences:
Annual Meetings: June
1999 – Boulder, CO(Regal Harvest House)/June 17-23/400

Internat'l Soc. for Third-Sector Research (1992)

Johns Hopkins U., Wyman Park Bldg. 559
3400 N. Charles St.
Baltimore, MD   21218-2688
Tel: (410)516-4678   *Fax:* (410)516-4870
E-Mail: istrmbd@jhunix.hcf.jhu.edu
Web Site: http://www.jhu.edu/~istr
Members: 540 individuals & institutions
Staff: 2
Annual Budget: $250-500,000
Exec. Officer: Margery Berg Daniels

Historical Note
ISTR members are academics and others with an interest in studying non-profit organizations, philanthropy and volunteerism. Membership: $75-$85/year (individual); $50-$60/year (student); $175/year (institution).

Publications:
Inside ISTR Newsletter. q.
Membership Directory. a.
Voluntas Journal. q.

Meetings/Conferences:
2000 – Dublin, Ireland(Trinity College)/July 5-8

Internat'l Soc. for Traumatic Stress Studies (1985)

60 Revere Drive, Suite 500
Northbrook, IL   60062
Tel: (847)480-9028   *Fax:* (847)480-9282
E-Mail: istss@istss.org
Web Site: http://www.istss.com
Members: 2,200 individuals
Annual Budget: $250-500,000
Exec. Director: Greg Schultz

Historical Note
Formerly (1991) Soc. for Traumatic Stress Studies. Established in Washington and incorporated in Ohio. Society members include mental health, social service, clergy and legal professionals who work with combat veterans, victims of crime and other forms of violence, survivors of natural and technological disasters, persons suffering from duty-related stress, and individuals who have suffered physical trauma. Membership: $100/year.

Publications:
Journal of Traumatic Stress. q. adv.
Traumatic StressPoints Newsletter. q. adv.

Meetings/Conferences:
Annual Meetings: November
1999 – Miami. FL(InterContinental)/Nov. 13-17
2000 – San Antonio, TX(Hyatt)/Nov. 15-19

Internat'l Soc. of Air Safety Investigators (1964)

Technology Trading Park
Five Export Drive
Sterling, VA   20164
Tel: (703)430-9668   *Fax:* (703)450-1745
E-Mail: isasi@erols.com

Members: 1,400 individuals, 80 companies
Staff: 1
Annual Budget: $100-250,000
Office Manager: Ann Schull
Treasurer: Tom McCarthy
Secretary: Keith Hagy

Historical Note
Established August 31, 1964 in Washington, DC to promote development of improved aircraft accident investigation procedures. Has an international membership from 41 countries. Formerly (1977) the Soc. of Air Safety Investigators. Membership: $60/year (individual), $500/year (company).

Publications:
The Forum. q.

Meetings/Conferences:
Annual Meetings: Fall
1999 – Boston, MA(Hyatt Harborside)/400
2000 – Shannon, Ireland(Dunratty Castle)/Sept. 29-Oct. 4/400

Internat'l Soc. of Applied Intelligence (1993)

SW TX State U., Dept. of Computer Science
601 University Drive
San Marcos, TX   78666-4616
Tel: (512)245-3409   *Fax:* (512)245-8750
E-Mail: ma04@swt.edu
Web Site: http://pirates.cs.swt.edu/isai/
Members: 100 individuals
Annual Budget: $50-100,000
President: Moonis Ali, Ph.D.
Administrative Assistant: Cheryl Morris

Historical Note
ISAI members are academics, computer scientists and others with an interest in the applications of artificial intelligence. Membership: $100/year (individual); $50/year (student); $500/year (institution).

Publications:
IEA/AIE Conference Proceedings. a.
Internat'l Journal of Applied Intelligence. bi-m.
ISAI Newsletter. q. adv.

Meetings/Conferences:
1999 – Cairo, Egypt(Le Meridien Cairo Hotel)/May 31-June 3
2000 – New Orleans, LA
2001 – Oxford, England(Oxford University)

Internat'l Soc. of Appraisers (1979)

Riverview Plaza Office Park, Suite 102
16040 Christensen Road
Seattle, WA   98188-2965
Tel: (206)241-0359   *Fax:* (206)241-0436
Toll Free: (888)472 - 4732
E-Mail: ISA_HQ@compuserve.com
Web Site: ISA-APPRAISERS.org
Members: 1,375 individuals
Staff: 6
Annual Budget: $500-1,000,000
Exec. Director: Christian A. Coleman
Coordinator, Membership: Suzi Farley

Historical Note
Founded and chartered in Illinois, ISA members are appraisers, specializing in Fine Arts, gems, and jewelry, antiques and collectibles, household items, and machinery and equipment. ISA offers courses in appraisal principles, theory, practice, adn various speciality courses. ISA became a non profit in 1993 and tax exempt in 1995. Membership: $390 /year (initiation); $315/year (renewal).

Publications:
ISA Membership Directory. a.
Professional Appraisers Information Exchange bi.

Meetings/Conferences:
Annual Meetings: Spring
1999 – Troy, MI(Marriott)/May 2-5

Internat'l Soc. of Arboriculture (1924)

PO Box 3129
Champaign, IL   61826-3129
Tel: (217)355-9411   *Fax:* (217)355-9516
E-Mail: isa@isa-arbor.com
Web Site: http://www.ag.uiuc.edu/~isa/
Members: 12,000 individuals
Staff: 15
Annual Budget: $2-5,000,000
Exec. Director: William P. Kruidenier

Historical Note
Formerly (1976) Internat'l Shade Tree Conference. Membership: $85/year (individual), $500/year (company, U.S).

Publications:
Arborist Equipment.
Journal of Arboriculture/Arborist News. m. adv.
Member Directory. a.
Municipal Tree Ordinance Manual.
Tree and Shrub Transplanting Manual. a.

Meetings/Conferences:
Annual Meetings: August/800-900
1999 – Stamford, CT/Aug. 1-4

Internat'l Soc. of Arthroscopy, Knee Surgery and Orthopaedic Sports Medicine (1977)

6300 N. River Rd., Suite 727
Rosemont, IL   60018-4226
Tel: (847)698-1632   *Fax:* (847)823-0536
Members: 1,200 individuals
Staff: 2
Annual Budget: $100-250,000
Manager: Kathryn Grady

Historical Note
Formerly Internat'l Soc. of the Knee; merged with Internat'l Arthroscopy Ass'n and assumed its current name in 1995.

Membership: $125/year (domestic); $200/year (overseas); membership is by invitation only.

Meetings/Conferences:
Biennial Meetings: (1997)

Internat'l Soc. of Barristers (1965)

3586 East Huron River Drive
Ann Arbor, MI   48104
Tel: (734)763-0165   *Fax:* (734)764-8309
E-Mail: reedj@umich.edu
Members: 700 individuals
Staff: 1
Annual Budget: $100-250,000
Admin. Secretary: John W. Reed

Historical Note
Members are trial lawyers interested in encouraging advocacy under the adversary system and preserving the right to a jury trial. Membership: $500/year.

Publications:
ISOB Quarterly. q.
Newsletter.

Meetings/Conferences:
Annual Meetings: Late Winter
1999 – Kailua-Kona, HI(Four Seasons Resort)/Feb. 28-March 6/180
2000 – Carlsbad, CA(Four Season Resort)/Feb. 27-March 4/250
2001 – Nevis, West Indies(Four Seasons Resort)/March 11-17/180

Internat'l Soc. of Bassists (1974)

4020 McEwen, Suite 105
Dallas, TX   75244-5019
Tel: (972)233-9107   *Fax:* (972)490-4219
Members: 2,700 individuals
Annual Budget: $50-100,000
General Manager: Madeleine Crouch

Historical Note
Members are teachers, students, reseachers and manufacturers of the double bass. ISB also serves to stimulate public interest in the double bass and improve performance standards. Membership: $35/year (domestic), $40/year (overseas).

Publications:
International Society of Bassists. tri-a.

Meetings/Conferences:
Biennial Meetings: Spring/Summer (1999)
1999 – Iowa City, IA

Internat'l Soc. of Beverage Technologists (1953)

113 Heron Point Lane
Hartfield, VA   23071
Tel: (804)776-7315   *Fax:* (804)776-9230
E-Mail: isbt@corsslink.net
Web Site: http://www.bevtech.org
Members: 1000 individuals
Staff: 2
Annual Budget: $100-250,000
Exec. Director: Anthony J. Meushaw

Historical Note
Formerly (1995) Soc. of Soft Drink Technologists ISBT is a professional society of individuals engaged in the soft drink industry. Membership: $75/year.

Publications:
Annual Meeting Proceedings. a.
Newsletter. q.

Meetings/Conferences:
Annual Meetings: April-May
1999 – Ft. Lauderdale, FL(Marina Marriott)/May 3-5/400

Internat'l Soc. of Certified Electronics Technicians (1970)

2708 West Berry St.
Fort Worth, TX   76109-2356
Tel: (817)921-9101   *Fax:* (817)921-3741
E-Mail: iscetFW@aol.com
Members: 2,000 individuals
Staff: 5
Annual Budget: $100-250,000
Exec. Director: Clyde W. Nabors
Director, Member Services: Alice Brown

Historical Note
An affiliate of the Nat'l Electronic Service Dealers Ass'n. Tests for and awards the CET (Certified Electronics Technician) designation. Publishes technical information, conducts technical training and product serviceability inspections. Only CETs are eligible for membership. Membership: $35/year.

Publications:
ISCET Update. bi-m.
ProService. bi-m. adv.
ProService Directory. a. adv.
Technical Log. q.

Meetings/Conferences:
Annual Meetings: With the Nat'l Electronic Service Dealers Ass'n in August.
1999 – Dallas, TX(Intercontinental)/Aug. 2-7/800
2000 – Reno, NV(Nugget Hotel)/Aug. 7-12/800

Internat'l Soc. of Certified Employee Benefit Specialists (1981)

18700 W. Bluemound Rd.
Brookfield, WI   53008-0209
Tel: (414)786-8771   *Fax:* (414)786-8650
E-Mail: ISCEBS@ifebp.org
Web Site: http://www.ifebp.org/ceiscebs.html
Members: 4,000 individuals
Staff: 4
Annual Budget: $1-2,000,000
Exec. Director: Daniel W. Graham

Director, Chapter Services and Development: Pamela White Wu
Historical Note
An affiliate of the Internat'l Foundation of Employee Benefit Plans, ISCEBS members are graduates of a professional certification program co-sponsored by the Foundation and the Wharton School, Univ. of Pennsylvania. Membership: $145/year (individual).
Publications:
Benefits Quarterly.
ISCEBS Membership Directory. a.
ISCEBS Newsbriefs. bi-m.
Meetings/Conferences:
1999 – Orlando, FL(Buena Vista Palace)/Oct. 3-6
2000 – San Diego, CA(Hyatt Regency)/Sept. 17-20
2001 – Boston, MA(Sheraton Boston)/Sept. 9-12

Internat'l Soc. of Chemical Ecology *(1983)*
Department of Entomology
University of California
Riverside, CA 92521
Tel: (909)787-5821   *Fax:* (909)787-3086
Web Site: http://www.isce.ucr.edu/society
Members: 750 individuals
Annual Budget: $50-100,000
Secretary: Jocelyn G. Millar
Historical Note
Formed to promote the understanding of the origin, function, and significance of natural chemicals that mediate interactions with and among organisms. Has no paid staff. Membership: $35/year.
Publications:
Annual Conference Abstracts/Proceedings. a. adv.
ISCE Newsletter. 3/yr. adv.
Journal of Chemical Ecology. m. adv.
Meetings/Conferences:
Annual Meetings: Summer
1999 – Marseilles, France
2000 – Brazil
2001 – Lake Tahoe, NV

Internat'l Soc. of Cleaning Technicians *(1970)*
4965 W. 14th St.
Speedway, IN 46224
Tel: (317)244-9183   *Fax:* (317)241-5931
Toll Free: (800)949 - 4728
E-Mail: whyisct@aol.com
Web Site: http://www.isct.com
Members: 325 companies
Staff: 3
Annual Budget: $50-100,000
Exec. Director: Joel Reets
Historical Note
Added Internat'l to name in 1993. Members are professional on-site carpet and upholstery cleaners and suppliers to the industry. ISCT is affiliated with the Institute of Inspection, Cleaning and Restoration Certification. Membership: $275/year.
Publications:
ISCT Monitor. 10/year.
Membership Directory. bien.
Pro-Pac. 10/year.
Read Book Directory. a.
Meetings/Conferences:
Annual Meetings: August

Internat'l Soc. of Communication Specialists *(1984)*
201 Blue Sky Drive
Marietta, GA 30068-3511
Tel: (770)973-0662   *Fax:* (770)973-1410
E-Mail: ECSAI@aol.com
Members: 70 companies
Annual Budget: $100-250,000
Exec. Director: Ed Sanner
Historical Note
ISCS members are companies that represent on-location audio and video recording services for the association community. Membership: $275/year (company).
Publications:
On Location. q. adv.
Meetings/Conferences:
Annual Meetings: January
1999 – New Orleans, LA

Internat'l Soc. of Copier Artists *(1982)*
759 President St., #2H
Brooklyn, NY 11215
Tel: (718)638-3264
Members: 125 individuals, 26 museums and libraries
Annual Budget: under $10,000
Director: Louise Neaderland
Historical Note
Founded to promote the use of the copier as a creative tool. Membership: $30/year (contributing artist), $90-110/year (supporting member).
Publications:
ISCA Quarterly. q.
Newsletter. irreg.
Meetings/Conferences:
Annual Meetings: Not held.

Internat'l Soc. of Crime Prevention Practitioners *(1978)*
266 Sandy Point Road
Emlenton, PA 16373-2524
Tel: (724)867-1000   *Fax:* (724)867-1200
E-Mail: iscpp@compuserve.com
Members: 1,300 individuals
Staff: 2
Annual Budget: $100-250,000
Exec. Director: Jim Howell

Historical Note
Membership includes practitioners from civic organizations, law enforcement, private security, business, government, education, mass media, and other groups and agencies. ISCPP's mission is to establish and support a permanent network of crime prevention practitioners who can provide leadership, foster cooperation, encourage information exchange, and extend and improve crime prevention education and programs internationally. Absorbed Nat'l Crime Prevention Institute in 1997. Membership: $35/year (individual).
Publications:
Basic Crime Prevention Curriculum. upon request.
Practitioner Newsletter. bi-m. adv.
Meetings/Conferences:
Annual Meetings: October
1999 – Pittsburgh, PA(Holiday Inn)
2000 – Milwaukee, WI

Internat'l Soc. of Facilities Executives *(1989)*
200 Corporate Place, Suite 2B
Peabody, MA 01960
Tel: (978)536-0108   *Fax:* (978)536-0199
E-Mail: isfe@isfe.org
Web Site: http://www.isfe.org
Annual Budget: $100-250,000
Chairman: Kreon L. Cyros
Historical Note
ISFE, founded by the Massachusetts Institute of Technology, is a professional organization for senior facilities executives with ultimate responsibilities for their corporate and institutional assets. ISFE provides a forum to exchange knowledge and experience in asset management. Membership: $290/year (professional).
Publications:
Executive Briefs. q.
Executive Updates. m.
Membership Directory. a.
Meetings/Conferences:
Annual Meetings: always Cambridge, MA(Royal Sonesta)/200
1999 – /Apr. 25-27
2000 – /Apr. 23-25

Internat'l Soc. of Financiers, Inc. *(1979)*
P.O. Box 18508
Asheville, NC 28814
Tel: (828)252-5907   *Fax:* (828)251-5061
Members: 300 individuals
Staff: 1
Annual Budget: $50-100,000
President & Chairman of Board of Advisors: Ronald I. Gershen
Historical Note
A professional society of brokers, consultants, investors and corporate lenders active in financial projects and transactions. 40% of the membership resides in the United States. Membership: $1,000/year (individual).
Publications:
International Financier Newsletter. m. adv.
Meetings/Conferences:
Annual Meetings: Not held.

Internat'l Soc. of Fine Arts Appraisers *(1979)*
Historical Note
Address unknown in 1995; presumed inactive or defunct.

Internat'l Soc. of Fire Service Instructors *(1960)*
P.O. Box 2320
Stafford, VA 22555-2320
Tel: (540)657-9375   *Fax:* (540)657-0154
Toll Free: (800)435 - 0005
Members: 7,000 individuals, 300 companies
Staff: 30
Annual Budget: $2-5,000,000
C.E.O.: Robert Fleming
Historical Note
Founded as Internat'l Soc. of Fire Service Instructors; became Alliance for Fire and Emergency Management in 1995, and resumed its original name in 1997. Individuals responsible for the training of fire, police, ambulance and rescue personnel, and the public. Membership: $60/year (individual)
Publications:
The Voice. m. adv.
Meetings/Conferences:

Internat'l Soc. of Hepato-Biliary Pancreatic Radiology *(1989)*
1891 Preston White Drive
Reston, VA 20191-4397
Tel: (703)648-8948   *Fax:* (703)648-9176
F-Mail: robertb@acr.org
Members: 165 individuals
Exec. Director: Bridgette Bienacker
Historical Note
ISHBPR members are radiologists with an interest in bililary disorders, especially when their subspecialty orientation may be in other areas, such as ultrasonography, gastrointestinal or interventional radiology.

Internat'l Soc. of Hotel Ass'n Executives *(1974)*
115 West Washington Street #1165
Indianapolis, IN 46204-3418
Tel: (317)673-4207   *Fax:* (317)673-4210
Members: 100 individuals
Staff: 2
Annual Budget: $25-50,000
Manager: Jan Bledsoe
Historical Note
Formerly (1974) American Hotel Trade Ass'n Executives. Affiliated with the American Hotel and Motel Ass'n. Members include Executive Directors of hotel and motel ass'ns in the U.S. and

Canada. No permanent address. Officers change annually. Membership: $125 year.
Meetings/Conferences:

Internat'l Soc. of Industrial Fabric Manufacturers *(1974)*
1337 Garden Circle Drive
Newberry, SC 29108
Tel: (803)939-8513
Members: 350 individuals
Staff: 1
Annual Budget: under $10,000
Secretary-Treasurer: Sandy Saye
Historical Note
Engineers, executives, technicians and salespersons in the yarn industry. Formerly (1980) Internat'l Soc. of Industrial Yarn Manufacturers.
Meetings/Conferences:
Semi-annual meetings: Spring and Fall

Internat'l Soc. of Introduction Services *(1986)*
P.O. Box 4876
West Hills, CA 91308
Tel: (818)222-1367
Members: 50 dating services
Staff: 3
President: Patricia Moore
Historical Note
ISIS members are introduction and dating services. ISIS works to curb misrepresentations of the dating service industry, and to promote its code of member ethics. Membership: $100/year.

Internat'l Soc. of Livestock Appraisers
Historical Note
A division of the American Soc. of Agricultural Appraisers.

Internat'l Soc. of Orthopaedic Surgery - U.S. Chapter
6300 N. River Road, Suite 727
Rosemont, IL 60018-4226
Tel: (847)698-1628   *Fax:* (846)823-0536
Exec. Officer: Leslie Hanson

Internat'l Soc. of Parametric Analysts *(1979)*
P.O. Box 6402
Chesterfield, MO 63006-6402
Tel: (314)527-2955   *Fax:* (314)256-8358
E-Mail: clydeperry@aol.com
Web Site: www.ispa-cost.org
Members: 400 individuals
Staff: 1
Annual Budget: $100-250,000
Business Manager: Clyde Perry
Historical Note
Members are estimators, project managers, cost analysts, and other professionals working principally in the field of defense and weapons systems. Membership: $45/year.
Publications:
Annual Conference Proceedings. a. adv.
Annual Conference Tutorials. a. adv.
ISPA Directory. a. adv.
Journal of Parametrics. semi-a. adv.
Parametric World Newsletter. 4-6/yr. adv.
Meetings/Conferences:
1999 – San Antonio, TX(Hilton)/June 8-11
2000 – Noardwijk, The Netherlands(Hotel Huis Fer Duin)/June 16-20/200

Internat'l Soc. of Political Psychology *(1978)*
1050 N. Mills St.
Pitzer College
Claremont, CA 91711
Tel: (909)621-8442   *Fax:* (909)607-7880
E-Mail: dward@pitzer.edu
Web Site: http:\\www.pitzer.edu\~dward\ispp
Members: 1,300 individuals
Staff: 2
Annual Budget: $50-100,000
Historical Note
ISPP members include psychologists, political scientists, psychiatrists, historians, sociologists, economists, anthropologists, as weel as journalists, government officials and others. Membership: $65/year.
Publications:
ISPP News Newsletter. semi-a. adv.
Members Directory. bien.
Political Psychology Journal. q. adv.
Meetings/Conferences:
Scientific Conference: usually July/400
1999 – Amsterdam, Netherlands
2000 – Seattle, WA

Internat'l Soc. of Psychiatric Consultation Liaison Nurses *(1986)*
7794 Grow Drive
Pensacola, FL 32514
Tel: (904)474-4147   *Fax:* (904)484-8762
Members: 250 individuals
Annual Budget: $25-50,000
Exec. Director: Belinda E. Puetz, Ph.D.
Historical Note
ISPCLN provides a forum for the discussion of psychiatric issues within the nursing community. Membership: $75/year.
Publications:
Connections. q. adv.
Meetings/Conferences:

Internat'l Soc. of Refractive Surgery
1175 Springs Centre South Blvd.,

Suite 152
Altamonte Springs, FL   32714
Tel: (407)786-7446   *Fax:* (407)786-7447
Web Site: http://www.isrs.org
Members: 1,500 individuals
Staff: 5
Annual Budget: $5-10,000,000
Exec. Director: Elizabeth Best
Director, On-Line Communications: Wayne Bennett
Director, Meetings/Corporation Sponsorship: Marianna Shanne
Director, Membership & Marketing: Keri Molyneaux

Historical Note
Formerly (1995) the Internat'l Soc. of Refractive Keratoplasty. ISRS promotes research, education, and exchange to advance the ethical practice of refractive surgery. Membership: $385/year.

Publications:
Journal of Refractive Surgery. bi-m. adv.

Meetings/Conferences:
1999 – Miami, FL/July 16-18
1999 – Orlando, FL/Oct. 22-23

Internat'l Soc. of Restaurant Ass'n Executives
P.O. Box 30073
Long Beach, CA   90853
Tel: (562)438-0991   *Fax:* (562)438-0991
Members: 147 individuals
Annual Budget: $100-250,000
President: Peter Meersman

Historical Note
Membership limited to executive staff of state and national restaurant associations.

Publications:
ISRAE Newsletter. semi-a.

Meetings/Conferences:
1999 – Chicago, IL(Hyatt Regency)/May 21-24
1999 – Williamsburg, VA(Kingsmill)/July 18-21

Internat'l Soc. of Speakers, Authors and Consultants
P.O. Box 6432
Kingwood, TX   77325-6432
Tel: (713)354-4440   *Fax:* (713)361-7163
E-Mail: issac@icsi.net
Web Site: issac.com
Members: 763 individuals
Staff: 3
Exec. Director: Bernard Hale Zick

Publications:
Professional Advisor Newsletter. m.

Meetings/Conferences:

Internat'l Soc. of Statistical Science *(1982)*
536 Oasis Drive
Santa Rosa, CA   95407
Tel: (707)575-3529
E-Mail: shvyrkov@jps.net
Members: 100 individuals
Staff: 2
Annual Budget: under $10,000
Chairman: Vladislav V. Shvyrkov

Historical Note
Formerly (1992) Internat'l Soc. of Statistical Science in Economics. IS-SS goal is to build statistical science on four axioms not on unwarranted assumptions. Membership: $15/year (individual).

Publications:
ISSS Directory. a.
Newsletter. q. adv.
Proceedings. a. adv.
Quantity and Quality in Statistical Research. a. adv.

Meetings/Conferences:
Annual Meetings: August

Internat'l Soc. of Stress Analysts *(1973)*
Historical Note
Address unknown in 1997.

Internat'l Soc. of Technology Assessment in Health Care *(1985)*
Historical Note
Members include researchers and clinicians working in scientifically-based technologies in health care, including drugs and medical procedures. Additionally, the organization focuses on professional and social implications of new technologies.

Internat'l Soc. of the Knee
Historical Note
Merged with Internat'l Arthroscopy Ass'n to form Internat'l Soc. of Arthroscopy, Knee Surgery and Orthopaedic Sports Medicine in 1995.

Internat'l Soc. of Transport Aircraft Trading *(1983)*
5517 Talon Ct.
Fairfax, VA   22032-1737
Tel: (703)978-8156   *Fax:* (703)503-5964
E-Mail: istat@istat.org
Web Site: http://www.istat.org
Members: 600 individuals, 58 companies
Staff: 1
Annual Budget: $500-1,000,000
Exec. Director: Dawn O'Day Foster

Historical Note
ISTAT provides a communications medium for those engaged in the purchase, sale, financing, appraisal or insuring of transport category aircraft. Membership: $350/year (individual); $1,500/year (corporate).

Publications:
Conference Proceedings.
JeTrader. bi-m.
Membership Directory.

Meetings/Conferences:
Annual Meetings: March
1999 – San Diego, CA/400

Internat'l Soc. of Travel and Tourism Educators *(1980)*
19364 Woodcrest
Harper Woods, MI   48225
Tel: (313)526-0710   *Fax:* (313)526-0710
E-Mail: ISTTE@aol.com
Web Site:
     http://MEMBERS.AOL.com/ISTTE/TRAVEL/INDEX.HT
     ML
Members: 300 individuals
Staff: 3
Annual Budget: $100-250,000
Exec. Director: Joanne Bruss

Historical Note
Founded as Soc. of Travel and Tourism Educators; assumed its current name in 1997. ISTTE members are teachers and administrators of programs that offer degrees in the areas of travel and tourism. Membership: $75/year (individual); $125/year (organization/company).

Publications:
News and Views. q. adv.
Travel and Tourism Books in Print. a. adv.
World Directory. a.

Meetings/Conferences:

Internat'l Soc. of Weekly Newspaper Editors *(1954)*
Dept. of Journalism
South Dakota State University
Brookings, SD   57007-0596
Tel: (605)688-4171   *Fax:* (605)688-5034
E-Mail: leer@ur.sdstate.edu
Members: 300 individuals
Annual Budget: $10-25,000
Secretary-Treasurer: Richard W. Lee

Historical Note
Sponsors the Golden Quill Award for excellence in writing of editorials in weekly newspapers and the Eugene Cervi Award for that weekly newspaper person who has served as the conscience of the community. Membership: $50/year.

Publications:
Grassroots Editor. q.
Newsletter. m.

Meetings/Conferences:
Annual Meetings: July

Internat'l Soc. of Weighing and Measurement *(1916)*
10 W. Kimball St.
Winder, GA   30680-2535
Tel: (770)868-5300   *Fax:* (770)868-5301
E-Mail: staff@iswm.org
Web Site: www.iswm.org
Members: 1,500 individuals
Staff: 3
Annual Budget: $250-500,000
Exec. Director: Mimi Harlan

Historical Note
Formerly (1985) Nat'l Men's Scale Ass'n. Members are engaged in the weighing and measurement industry. Membership: $70/year (individual), $165/year (dealers), $385/year (manufacturers).

Publications:
ISWM News. q. adv.
Membership Directory and Product Guide. a.

Meetings/Conferences:
1999 – Atlanta, GA(Hyatt Regency)/June 9-12/1200
2000 – Las Vegas, NV

Internat'l Spa and Fitness Ass'n *(1991)*
546 E. Main St.
Lexington, KY   40508
Tel: (606)226-4260   *Fax:* (606)226-4424
Toll Free: (888)651 - 4772
E-Mail: walker@mgtserv.com
Web Site: http://www.globalspaguide.com
Members: 800 companies
Staff: 3
Annual Budget: $500-1,000,000
Exec. Director: Lynne Walker

Publications:
Pulse Profile. m. adv.

Meetings/Conferences:
1999 – Tampa, FL(Saddlebrook)/2000

Internat'l Special Events Soc. *(1986)*
9202 N. Meridian St.,   Suite 200
Indianapolis, IN   46260-1810
Tel: (317)571-5601   *Fax:* (317)571-5603
Toll Free: (800)688 - 4737
E-Mail: kelleher@in.net
Web Site: http://www.ises.com
Members: 2,400 individuals
Staff: 7
Annual Budget: $500-1,000,000
Exec. Director: Debra W. Kelleher
Director, Education: Abigail E. Helmer
Director, Membership/Publications: Beth A. Sewell
Director, Special Projects: Ali Bayes

Historical Note
ISES is an umbrella organization for the many different disciplines comprising the special event industry. ISES members include caterers, decorators, special event producers, meeting planners, destination management companies, rental agencies, hotel sales managers, convention center managers, and other professionals. 24 chapters provide professional and networking services to members worldwide. Membership: approximately $349/year (individual).

Publications:
Eventworld. m.

International Fax.
Membership Directory. a. adv.
Meetings/Conferences:

Internat'l Sport Show Producers Ass'n *(1970)*
P.O. Box 480084
Denver, CO   80248-0084
Tel: (303)892-6800   *Fax:* (303)892-6322
Web Site: http://www.exposonline.com/isspa
Members: 25 individuals
Staff: 7
Annual Budget: under $10,000
Exec. Secretary: Dianne Seymour

Historical Note
ISSPA members are producers of public events featuring outdoor recreation products.

Publications:
Sports & Vacation Show Directory & Calendar. a.

Meetings/Conferences:
Annual Meetings: Summer

Internat'l Sports Massage Federation *(1983)*
2156 Newport Blvd.
Costa Mesa, CA   92627-1710
Tel: (949)642-0735   *Fax:* (949)642-1729
Annual Budget: under $10,000
President: M.K. Hungerford, Ph.D.

Historical Note
Formerly (1993) the Sports Massage Therapists Ass'n. Also known as U.S. Sports Massage Federation. Represents China, Australia, Canada and Russia as well as the United States. Membership: $25 application fee; $100/year membership.

Publications:
Journal. q. adv.

Meetings/Conferences:
Annual Meetings: Summer

Internat'l Sprout Growers Ass'n
Historical Note
Address unknown in 1995.

Internat'l Staple, Nail and Tool Ass'n *(1966)*
512 W. Burlington Ave., Suite 203
La Grange, IL   60525-2245
Tel: (708)482-8138   *Fax:* (708)482-8186
Members: 19 companies
Staff: 5
Exec. V. President: John Kurtz

Historical Note
Founded as the Industrial Stapling Manufacturer's Institute, it became the Industrial Stapling and Nailing Technical Association in 1972 and assumed its present name in 1982. Financed and directed by manufacturers of machine-driven staples, nails and similar fasteners and their power tools.

Publications:
Evaluation Reports. bien.
Safety Standards. every 5 years.

Meetings/Conferences:

Internat'l Stress Management Ass'n *(1973)*
University of Hawaii at Manoa
Dept. of Psychology, 2430 Campus Rd.
Honolulu, HI   96822
Tel: (808)956-6006
Members: 750 individuals
Staff: 1
Annual Budget: under $10,000
Chairman: John G. Carlson

Historical Note
Formerly (1980) American Ass'n for the Advancement of Tension Control and (1992) Internat'l Stress and Tension Control Ass'n. ISMA members are individuals with an interest in the dissemination and acquisition of scientific knowledge for stress management, related disorders and tension control strategies.

Publications:
Convention Proceedings. a.
Internat'l Journal of Stress Management. q. adv.
Newsletter. q.

Meetings/Conferences:
Annual Meetings: Spring
1999 – Houston, TX/Sept. 28-Oct. 3

Internat'l Studies Ass'n *(1959)*
324 Social Sciences
University of Arizona
Tucson, AZ   85721
Tel: (520)621-7715   *Fax:* (520)621-5780
E-Mail: isa@arizona.edu
Web Site: http://www.isanet.org
Members: 3,500 individuals
Staff: 9
Annual Budget: $250-500,000
Exec. Director: Thomas J. Volgy
Administrative Director: Dana B. Larsen

Historical Note
A professional society with multinational and multidisciplinary membership concerned with the communication of national, international, and transnational issues, concerns, and ideas. Special areas of interest are directed within sectional subunits. Membership: based upon annual income.

Publications:
International Studies Notes. tri-annual.
International Studies Quarterly. q.
ISA Newsletter. 8/yr. adv.
Mershon International Studies Review. semi-annual.

Meetings/Conferences:
1999 – Washington, DC(Omni Shoreham)/Feb. 16-20/2000

2000 – Los Angeles, CA(Westin Bonaventure)/March 7-11

Internat'l Swaps and Derivatives Ass'n (1985)
600 Fifth Ave., 27th Floor
New York, NY 10020
Tel: (212)332-1200　　　　*Fax:* (212)332-1212
E-Mail: isda@isda.org
Web Site: http://www.isda.org
Members: 370 firms and institutions
Staff: 27
Exec. Director: Richard E. Grove, Jr.
Director, Communications/Press: Milton Bellis
Director, North American Policy: Susan Hinko
Director, European Program: Matthew Elderfield
Co-Director, Conferences: Alison Smythe
Director, Member Relations: Mary Cunningham
Director, Administration: David Lafleur
General Counsel: Robert G. Pickel

Historical Note
Founded as Internat'l Swap Dealers Ass'n; assumed its current name in 1993. Represents firms, primarily financial institutions, corporations and government entities who deal in privately-negotiated derivatives, as well as firms who provide services to such institutions. ISDA's mission is to encourage the productive development of interest rate, currency, commodity, and equity swaps as financial products. Has an annual budget of approximately $10 million. Membership fee varies, based on type of firm and degree of activity.

Publications:
Market Survey. semi-a.
Newsletter. 5/year.

Meetings/Conferences:
1999 – Vancouver, BC, Canada/March 24-26

Internat'l Tanning Manufacturers Ass'n (1979)
3820 Premier Ave.
Memphis, TN 38118
Tel: (901)368-3333
Members: 8 companies
Annual Budget: under $10,000
President: William C. Richey

Historical Note
Members are manufacturers of suntanning equipment. Purpose of ITMA is to promote quality and safety in the products manufactured by members. Membership: $300/year (company).

Meetings/Conferences:
Annual Meetings: Winter

Internat'l Tax Institute (1961)
1177 Ave. of the Americas
New York, NY 10036
Tel: (212)596-8217　　　　*Fax:* (212)596-8871
Members: 75 individuals
Staff: 1
Annual Budget: $50-100,000
President: Kenneth H. Kral

Historical Note
Formerly (1971) Institute on U.S. Taxation of Foreign Income. A professional organization of tax executives, lawyers and accountants concerned with taxation of international business income. Membership: $175/year (individual), $400/year (corporate).

Meetings/Conferences:
Annual Meetings: Meetings and seminars held throughout the year

Internat'l Taxicab and Livery Ass'n (1917)
3849 Farragut Ave.
Kensington, MD 20895
Tel: (301)946-5701　　　　*Fax:* (301)946-4641
E-Mail: itla@itla-info.org
Web Site: http://www.taxinetwork.com
Members: 985 individuals, 925 companies
Staff: 5
Annual Budget: $500-1,000,000
Exec. V. President: Alfred B. LaGasse
Director, Member Services: Harold E. Morgan
Director, Publications: Nancy Murphy

Historical Note
Formed in 1966 by a merger of the American Taxicabs Ass'n (1942), the Nat'l Ass'n of Taxicab Owners (1917), and the Cab Research Bureau (1938). Members are owners of taxi cab, limousine, van, livery and minibus fleets. Sponsors the Internat'l Taxicab Ass'n Political Action Committee. Membership: $18/vehicle/year; minimum $120/year, maximum $4,500.

Publications:
Taxi and Livery Management. q. adv.

Meetings/Conferences:
Annual Meetings: Fall/600
1999 – Chicago, IL(Hyatt Regency)/Oct. 13-17/900
2000 – Las Vegas, NV

Internat'l Technical Caramel Ass'n (1975)
Historical Note
Address unknown in 1998.

Internat'l Technology Education Ass'n (1939)
1914 Association Drive
Reston, VA 20191-1539
Tel: (703)860-2100　　　　*Fax:* (703)860-0353
E-Mail: itea@iris.org
Web Site: http://www.iteawww.org
Members: 7,000 individuals
Staff: 10
Annual Budget: $1-2,000,000
Exec. Director: Kendall N. Starkweather
Meeting Planner: Michelle Judd
Membership Coordinator: Lari Price
Editor-in-Chief: Kathleen Sheehan

ITEA has an international membership, primarily from North America. Membership consists of teachers, supervisors and university faculty interested in advancing technology and science education. Affiliates of the ITEA are: Technology Education for Children Council, Council on Technology Teacher Education and Council for Supervisors. Membership: $60/year (individual), $180/year (institution).

Publications:
Curriculum Brief.
Technology & Children.
The Technology Teacher. m. adv.

Meetings/Conferences:
Annual Meetings: Spring
1999 – Indianapolis, IN(Convention Center)/March 28-30

Internat'l Teleconferencing Ass'n (1982)
100 Four Falls Corporate Ctr., Suite 105
West Conshohocken, PA 19428
Tel: (610)941-2020　　　　*Fax:* (610)941-2015
Web Site: http://www.itca.org
Members: 1,900 individuals
Staff: 3
Annual Budget: $100-250,000
President and C.O.O.: Henry S. Grove
Manager, Member Services: Marcia Kaplan

Historical Note
Non-profit corporation founded to provide a clearinghouse for the exchange of information between users, researchers, and providers in the field of teleconferencing. Absorbed Nat'l Telecommuting and Telework Ass'n in 1994. Membership: $100/year (individual), $500/year (organizational); $250/year (small business), $30/year (student).

Publications:
Classroom of the Future. a.
ITCA Connections Newsletter. m.
ITCA Membership Directory.
ITCA Videoconferencing Room Directory. a.
Teleconferencing in State Government Guide. a.
Yearbook. a.

Meetings/Conferences:
1999 – San Hose, CA/March 8-11

Internat'l Teleproduction Soc. (1986)
527 Maple Ave. E., Suite 204
Vienna, VA 22192
Tel: (703)319-0800　　　　*Fax:* (703)319-1120
Members: 410 companies
Staff: 7
Annual Budget: $1-2,000,000
Exec. Director: Terence J. Rainey
Director, Conferences: Monica Mathis
Dir., Membership: Joyce Summers

Historical Note
ITS member firms provide creative and technical services in film, video and sound to the television and motion picture industry. Membership: $500-5,000/year (company).

Publications:
Industry Financial Profile. a.
ITS Directory of Members. a. adv.
ITS Handbook Recommended Standards Procedures. a. adv.
ITS Newsletter. m.
ITS Pocket Agenda. a.
Monitor Awards Journal. a.

Meetings/Conferences:
1999 – New York, NY(Waldorf-Astoria Hotel)/July 19-24

Internat'l Television Ass'n (1968)
6311 N. O'Connor Road, Suite 230
Irving, TX 75039
Tel: (972)869-1112　　　　*Fax:* (972)869-2980
E-Mail: itvahq@worldnet.att.net
Web Site: http://www.itva.org
Members: 8,000 individuals
Staff: 6
Annual Budget: $1-2,000,000
Exec. Director: Fredrick M. Wehrli, CAE, CEM
Director, Communications/Publications: Rene Chapin

Historical Note
National organization of professional video communicators: individuals in non-broadcast video who use videotape and equipment in organizational settings producing, writing and editing video programs. Founded in 1968 as the Nat'l Industrial Television Ass'n. Merged in 1973 with the Industrial Television Society to become the Internat'l Industrial Television Ass'n. Assumed current name in 1978. Membership: $150/year (individual), $425/year (organization).

Publications:
Handbook of Forms.
ITVA News. bi-m. adv.
Membership Directory. a.

Meetings/Conferences:
1999 – Washington, DC/June 2-5/2000

Internat'l Test and Evaluation Ass'n (1980)
4400 Fair Lakes Court
Fairfax, VA 22033-3899
Tel: (703)631-6220　　　　*Fax:* (703)631-6221
E-Mail: itea@itea.org
Web Site: http://www.itea.org
Members: 2,000 individuals
Staff: 5
Annual Budget: $100-250,000
Exec. Director: R. Alan Plishker

Historical Note
A professional society of engineers and testers concerned with the technology, process and management of test and evaluation. Members are concerned primarily with industrial and defense products (autos, tanks, aircraft, spacecraft, command and control,

simulation, weapon systems, etc). Membership: $40/year (individual); $625/year (corporate).

Publications:
Journal of Test and Evaluation. q. adv.
Symposium Proceedings. a. adv.

Meetings/Conferences:
Annual Meetings: Fall

Internat'l Textile and Apparel Ass'n (1944)
P.O. Box 1360
Monument, CO 80132-1360
Tel: (719)488-3716
Members: 1000 individuals
Staff: 1
Annual Budget: $100-250,000
Exec. Director: Sandra S. Hutton

Historical Note
An outgrowth of regional conferences of textile and clothing professors held under the auspices of the Home Economics Section of the Ass'n of Land-Grant Colleges, ITAA was established in 1970. As a part of this change, the Ass'n was incorporated in Oklahoma. Active members are persons engaged in college or university instruction, research, and/or administration in textiles, clothing or a related area. Formerly (1991) Ass'n of College Professors of Textiles and Clothing. Membership: $95/year (individual).

Publications:
ITAA Monographs. irreg.
ITAA Newsletter. q. adv.
ITAA Proceedings. a.
The Clothing & Textiles Research Journal. q.

Meetings/Conferences:
Annual Meetings: November/500
1999 – Santa Fe, NM
2000 – Cincinnati, OH

Internat'l Theatre Equipment Ass'n (1971)
244 West 49th St., Suite 200
New York, NY 10019
Tel: (212)246-6460　　　　*Fax:* (212)265-6428
Web Site: http://www.itea.com
Members: 150 companies
Staff: 2
Annual Budget: $250-500,000
Exec. Director: Robert Sunshine

Historical Note
Merger of Theatre Equipment Dealers Ass'n and the Supply Manufacturers Ass'n founded in 1933. Added Internat'l to its name in 1996. Membership: $300/year.

Publications:
ITEA Newsletter. q.

Meetings/Conferences:
1999 – Squaw Valley, ID/Aug. 29-Sept. 2

Internat'l Thermal Storage Advisory Council (1986)
Historical Note
Defunct in 1996.

Internat'l Thermographers Ass'n (1973)
100 Daingerfield Road
Alexandria, VA 22314-2804
Tel: (703)519-8122　　　　*Fax:* (703)548-3227
Members: 84 companies
Staff: 1
Annual Budget: $100-250,000
Exec. Director: Frank S. Wilton

Historical Note
A section of the Printing Industries of America, composed of members who specialize in thermography (heat-raised printing). Membership: $140-660/year.

Publications:
Thermogram. q.

Meetings/Conferences:
Annual Meetings: Fall/125

Internat'l Ticketing Ass'n (1980)
250 West 57th St., Suite 722
New York, NY 10107
Tel: (212)581-0600　　　　*Fax:* (212)581-0885
E-Mail: info@intix.org
Web Site: http://www.intix.org
Members: 1,400 individuals
Staff: 6
Annual Budget: $1-2,000,000
President: Patricia G. Spira, CAE
Director, Communications & Marketing: Kerry O'Donnell
Deputy Director: Kathleen O'Donnell
Special Projects Director: Ann Gennardo
Administrative Manager: Paul Gamner
Comptroller: Cindy Wong
Attorney: Daniel Wasser
Administrative Services: Diane Raboud

Historical Note
Incorporated as Box Office Management Internat'l, INTIX members are box office managers, treasurers, marketing and systems directors and other administrators from the performing arts and sports fields; performing arts centers; entertainment facilities; and industry vendors and suppliers. Membership: $180-500/year.

Publications:
Conference Proceedings Manuals. a. adv.
INTIX Directory. a.
INTIX Newsletter. 8/year. adv.

Meetings/Conferences:
1999 – Dublin, Ireland(Burlington Hotel)/March 25-27/400
1999 – Portland, OR(Hilton)/June 9-11/150
1999 – Nashville, TN(Renaissance)/Jan. 26-29
2000 – Albuquerque, NM(Hyatt Regency)/Jan. 25-28/800

Internat'l Tire and Rubber Ass'n (1957)
Box 37203
Louisville, KY 40233-7203
Tel: (502)968-8900   *Fax:* (502)964-7859
Toll Free: (800)426 - 8835
E-Mail: itra@aol.com
Web Site: www.itra.com
Members: 1,500 companies
Staff: 12
Annual Budget: $1-2,000,000
Exec. Director: Marvin F. Bozarth
Convention/Meeting Director: Gretchen Schrantz
Technical Director: Bill Gragg
Member Services: Jean Murphy

Historical Note
Founded as the Central States Retreaders' Ass'n; became American Retreaders Ass'n in 1964, and assumed its current name in 1996. Organized to provide its members with technical, marketing and management programs and continuing education. Membership: $250/year (domestic); $300/year (international).

Publications:
Commercial Tire Service Update. m. adv.
ITRA Industry Update. bi-m.
Tire Retreading/Repair Journal. m. adv.

Meetings/Conferences:
Annual Meetings: Annual World Tire Conference and
    Exhibition. Louisville, KY(Kentucky Fair and
    Exposition Center)/April/5,000
1999 – Nashville, TN/June 9-12
2000 – /April 13-15

Internat'l Titanium Ass'n (1984)
1871 Folsom St., Suite 200
Boulder, CO 80302-5714
Tel: (303)443-7515   *Fax:* (303)443-4406
E-Mail: AFitz@titanium.net
Web Site: http://www.titanium.org
Members: 400 individuals, 100 companies
Staff: 4
Annual Budget: $250-500,000
Exec. Assistant: Amy K. Fitzgerald

Historical Note
Founded as Titanium Development Ass'n; assumed its current name in 1995. Formed to promote titanium metal; seeks to expand existing markets and develop new markets for titanium.

Publications:
Buyers Guide. a.
Conference Proceedings.
Products and Services Guide. a.
Statistics. a.
Titanium Newsletter. q.

Meetings/Conferences:

Internat'l Trade Commission Trial Lawyers Ass'n (1984)
601 13th St., N.W.
Washington, DC 20005
Tel: (202)626-6361   *Fax:* (202)783-2331
E-Mail: admin@itcta.org
Web Site: http://www.itcta.org
Members: 350 individuals
Staff: 1
Annual Budget: under $10,000
Exec. Director: Judith B. Oken

Historical Note
Composed of attorneys who practice or are otherwise interested in Section 337 cases before the Internat'l Trade Commission. Membership: $80/year (government attorneys); $50/year (non-government attorneys and students).

Publications:
337 Reporter. m.

Meetings/Conferences:
Annual Meetings: Washington, DC/Nov.

Internat'l Trademark Ass'n (1878)
1133 Ave. of the Americas, 33rd Fl
New York, NY 10036
Tel: (212)768-9887   *Fax:* (212)768-7796
E-Mail: executivedirector@inta.org
Web Site: http://www.inta.org
Members: 4,500 firms and organizations
Staff: 35
Annual Budget: $5-10,000,000
Exec. Director: Allen Drewsen
Meetings Manager: Feikje van Rein
Office Manager: Melissa Star
Publications Manager: Mary McGrane
Managing Editor: Charlotte Jones

Historical Note
Established in New York City as The United States Trademark Association in 1878 by twelve manufacturers responding to the need to protect their trademarks. Incorporated in the state of New York January 8, 1887. INTA is the largest international membership organization that supports and advances trademarks as essential to commerce throughout the world. Changed to the Internat'l Trademark Ass'n in 1993. INTA is located in 120 countries. Membership: $850/year (regular), $700/year (associate).

Publications:
Bulletin. tri-m.
Trademark Checklist. a.
Trademark Reporter. bi-m.

Meetings/Conferences:
Annual Meetings: April-May/5,000
1999 – Seattle, WA(Washington State Con. & Trade
    Center)/May 22-26

Internat'l Transactional Analysis Ass'n (1958)
450 Pacific Ave., Suite 250
San Francisco, CA 94133
Tel: (415)989-5640   *Fax:* (415)989-9343
E-Mail: itaa@itaa-net.org
Web Site: http://www.itaa-net.org
Members: 4,000 individuals
Staff: 3
Annual Budget: $500-1,000,000
Exec. Director: Susan D. Sevilla
Meetings: Lillian Tan
Membership: Ken Fogleman

Historical Note
Founded in 1950-1951 by Dr. Eric Berne as the San Francisco Social Psychiatry Seminars, Inc. Became Internat'l Transactional Analysis Ass'n, Inc. in 1958. ITAA is a scientific organization established to investigate and promote the use of transactional analysis (TA) in psychotherapy, education, business and other fields of human interaction. Professional membership includes individuals from the fields of psychotherapy, business, education, religion, medicine and industry. Associate membership is available for those whose interest is not related to their profession. Membership: $86/year, regular (individual); $62/year, associate (individual).

Publications:
Membership Directory. a. adv.
Script Newsletter. 9/yr. adv.
Transactional Analysis Journal. q. adv.

Meetings/Conferences:
Semi-annual Meetings: Annual Conference and Spring
    Meeting.

Internat'l Transplant Nurses Soc. (1992)
651 Holiday Dr.
Foster Plaza Bldg. 5, Suite 300
Pittsburgh, PA 15220
Tel: (412)928-3667   *Fax:* (412)928-4951
E-Mail: JNLA74A@prodigy.com
Web Site: http://www.trans.org/ITNS
Members: 1,300 individuals
Staff: 2
Annual Budget: $100-250,000
Exec. Director: Beth A. Kassalen, MBA

Historical Note
ITNS active members are registered nurses, LVN's and LPN's licensed to practice in the United States with an interest in the specialty of transplantation nursing. Associate memberships available. Membership: $40/year (active); $20/year (associate).

Publications:
ITNS Newsletter. q. adv.

Meetings/Conferences:

Internat'l Trauma Anesthesia and Critical Care Soc. (1988)
P.O. Box 4826
Baltimore, MD 21211
Tel: (410)235-7697   *Fax:* (410)235-8084
Members: 1000 individuals
Exec. Director: Christopher M. Grande, M.D., MPH

Historical Note
ITACCS members are health care professionals with an interest in trauma/critical care anesthesiology. Membership: $100/year (individual); $1,000/year (corporate); $40/year (student).

Publications:
Trauma Care. semi-a.

Internat'l Travel Writers and Editors Ass'n (1972)
1224 No. Nokomis Ave.
Alexandria, MN 56308
Tel: (320)763-4919   *Fax:* (320)763-9290
Members: 3,000 individuals
Staff: 3
Annual Budget: $500-1,000,000
Exec. Director: Robert G. Johnson

Historical Note
Membership: $85/year (individual).

Meetings/Conferences:
Annual Meetings: Spring

Internat'l Trombone Ass'n (1971)
College of Music, Univ. of North Texas
P.O. Box 11367
Denton, TX 76203
Tel: (817)565-2791   *Fax:* (817)382-3435
Members: 3,500 individuals
Annual Budget: $50-100,000
Secretary-Treasurer: Dr. Vern Kagarice

Historical Note
Members are instrument makers, music publishers, professional performers, students, teachers and amateurs of the trombone.

Publications:
Journal. q.
Membership Directory. a.

Meetings/Conferences:

Internat'l Truck Parts Ass'n (1974)
7127 Braeburn Place
Bethesda, MD 20817
Tel: (202)544-3090   *Fax:* (301)229-7331
Members: 120 companies
Staff: 1
Annual Budget: $10-25,000
Exec. Director: Venlo J. Wolfsohn

Historical Note
Members are dealers in used and rebuilt parts for heavy duty trucks. Membership: $400/year.

Publications:
Membership Directory. a.
Newsletter. m.

Internat'l Trumpet Guild (1975)
Western Michigan University
School of Music
Kalamazoo, MI 49008
Tel: (616)387-4700   *Fax:* (616)387-5809
Members: 8,000 individuals
Annual Budget: $250-500,000
President: Kim Dunnick

Historical Note
ITG members are professional and amateur trumpet players. Membership:$ $40(individual and organization).

Publications:
ITG Journal Newsletter. q.

Meetings/Conferences:
Annual Meetings: Summer
1999 – Richmond, VA

Internat'l Turfgrass Soc. (1969)
c/o Royal Canadian Golf Ass'n
Golf House, RR2
Oakville, ON L6J 4-Z3
Tel: (905)849-9700   *Fax:* (905)845-7040
Members: 325 individuals
Secretary: Teri Yamada

Historical Note
ITS members are academics and others with an interest in turfgrass science. Has no paid officers or full-time staff. Membership: $30/quadrennially.

Publications:
Proceedings of Conference.

Meetings/Conferences:
2001 – Canada

Internat'l Union of Allied Novelty and Production Workers (1965)
1950 W. Erie St.
Chicago, IL 60622
Tel: (312)738-0822   *Fax:* (312)738-3553
Members: 34,000 individuals
Staff: 2
Annual Budget: $250-500,000
President: Hermes Ruiz

Historical Note
Labor union affiliated with AFL-CIO. Formerly (1978) Internat'l Union of Dolls, Toys, Playthings, Novelties and Allied Products of the United States and Canada.

Meetings/Conferences:
Quinquennial Conventions: (2001)

Internat'l Union of Bricklayers and Allied Craftsmen (1865)
815 15th St., N.W.
Washington, DC 20005
Tel: (202)783-3788   *Fax:* (202)393-0219
Web Site: www.bacweb.org
Members: 100,000 individuals
Staff: 65
Annual Budget: $5-10,000,000
President: John T. Joyce
Exec. Director of Finance: Michael E. Sparrough

Historical Note
Organized October 16, 1865 in Painters Hall, Philadelphia as the Bricklayers International Union of the United States of North America. Around 1870 it was renamed the National Union of Bricklayers of the United States of America. About 1880 it became the Bricklayers and Masons International Union of America and, after plasterers were included in 1910, the Bricklayers, Masons and Plasterers' International Union of America. It affiliated with the American Federation of Labor in 1916 and assumed its present name in 1975. Sponsors and supports the International Union of Bricklayers and Allied Craftsmen Political Action Committee.

Publications:
Chalkline. bi-m.
Journal. bi-m.

Meetings/Conferences:
Quinquennial Meetings: (2000)

Internat'l Union of Electronic, Electrical, Salaried Machine, and Furniture Workers (1949)
1126 16th St., N.W.
Washington, DC 20036
Tel: (202)785-7200   *Fax:* (202)785-7448
Web Site: iue.org
Members: 150,000 individuals
Staff: 200
Annual Budget: $10-25,000,000
President: Edward Fire
Director of Communications: Laure Asplen
Director of Research & Int'l Affairs: Douglas Meyer
Comptroller: Berry Allan
General Counsel: Peter Mitchell
Director of Social Action: Gloria Johnson

Historical Note
Chartered November 2, 1949 by the Congress of Industrial Organizations after the expulsion, on grounds of being a Communist front, of the United Electrical, Radio and Machine Workers of America. In 1987 United Furniture Workers of America merged with IUE to form the Furniture Division of IUEETSMW. Has a budget of about $17 million. Founded as the International Union of Electrical, Radio and Machine Workers (AFL-CIO), it became the Internat'l Union of Electronic, Electrical, Technical, Salaried and Machine Workers (AFL-CIO) in 1983, and assumed its present name in 1987.

Publications:
Convention Proceedings. bien.

IUE News. m.
News Wire. semi-m.
Meetings/Conferences:
Quadrennial meetings: Fall (2000)

Internat'l Union of Elevator Constructors *(1901)*
5565 Sterret Place, Clarke Bldg.
Suite 310
Columbia, MD 21044
Tel: (410)997-9000   *Fax:* (410)997-0243
Web Site: www.iuec.org
Members: 25,000 individuals
Staff: 11
Annual Budget: $2-5,000,000
President: John N. Russell

Historical Note
Established in Pittsburg July 18, 1901 as the National Union of Elevator Constructors. Became the International Union of Elevator Constructors in 1903 and received a charter from the American Federation of Labor.

Publications:
The Elevator Constructor. m.

Meetings/Conferences:
Quinquennial Conventions: (2001)

Internat'l Union of Gospel Missions *(1913)*
1045 Swift Ave.
North Kansas City, MO 64116-4127
Tel: (816)471-8020   *Fax:* (816)471-3718
Web Site: http://www.iugm.org
Members: 1,200 individuals, 265 rescue ministries
Staff: 10
Annual Budget: $1-2,000,000
Exec. Director: Rev. Stephen E. Burger
Director of Communications: Phil Rydman
Director of Education: Michael Liimatta
Business Administrator: Len Conner
Exec. Secretary: Masdeleine Wooley

Historical Note
Members are rescue mission directors, staff and others. Membership: $40/year (individual), $150-3,000/year (organization/ company).

Publications:
Executive Report. bi-m.
Happenings Newsletter. m. adv.
IUGM Directory. bien.
Rescue Magazine. bi-m. adv.

Meetings/Conferences:
Annual Meetings: Spring and Summer
1999 – Spokane, WA(Red Lion Convention Center)/May 22-26/1000
2000 – Orlando, FL(Hyatt Airport)/May 27-31
2001 – Phoenix, AZ(Doubletree Paradise Valley)

Internat'l Union of Industrial Service Transport Health Employees *(1970)*
18 East 31st St.
New York, NY 10016
Tel: (212)696-5545   *Fax:* (212)696-5556
Members: 10,600 individuals
Staff: 22
Annual Budget: $2-5,000,000
President: William Perry

Historical Note
Labor union formerly known as the Internat'l Federation of Health Professionals. Assumed its present name in 1990. Members are medical personnel, blue and white collar workers and transport workers united to oppose the influence of "third party" health insurance organizations destructive of the classical doctor- patient relationship.

Publications:
District 6 Voice. m.

Meetings/Conferences:
Quadrennial Meetings: Summer (2000)

Internat'l Union of Journeymen Horseshoers of the United States and Canada *(1874)*
120 Gladstone St.
East Boston, MA 02128-2635
Tel: (617)569-4876
Toll Free: (800)872 - 4854
Members: 480 individuals
Staff: 2
Annual Budget: $10-25,000
Secretary-Treasurer: Paul C. Brooker

Historical Note
Provides training and information on efficient, proper and humane horseshoes to the professional and amateur horseman as well as working to obtain equitable wages for horseshoers. Membership is $720/year (individual).

Publications:
Newsletter. irreg.

Meetings/Conferences:
Triennial Meetings: (1998)

Internat'l Union of Operating Engineers *(1896)*
1125 17th St., N.W.
Washington, DC 20036
Tel: (202)429-9100   *Fax:* (202)778-2616
Web Site: www.ioue.org
Members: 360,000 individuals
Staff: 160
Annual Budget: $10-25,000,000
General President: Frank Hanley

Historical Note
Established in Chicago, IL on December 7, 1896 as the Nat'l Union of Steam Engineers and received a charter from the American Federation of Labor the following year. Became the Internat'l Union

of Steam Engineers in 1898 following the acceptance of Canadian locals. Responding to changes in technology, it was renamed the Internat'l Union of Steam and Operating Engineers, which in 1927 merged with the Internat'l Brotherhood of Steam Shovel and Dredgemen, assuming its present name in 1928. Absorbed the United Welders Internat'l Union in 1969. Has an annual budget of approximately $15 million. Sponsors and supports the Engineers Political Education Committee.

Publications:
International Operating Engineer. bim.

Meetings/Conferences:
Quinquennial Meetings: April (1997)

Internat'l Union of Petroleum and Industrial Workers *(1945)*
8131 E. Rosecrans Ave.
Paramount, CA 90723
Tel: (562)630-6232
Members: 6,500 individuals
Staff: 8
Annual Budget: $1-2,000,000
Internat'l President: George R. Beltz

Historical Note
Founded and incorporated in 1945 as the Independent Petroleum Workers Union; affiliated with the Seafarer's Internat'l Union of North America (AFL-CIO) in 1962; adopted its present name in 1971.

Publications:
IUPIW Views. bi-m.

Meetings/Conferences:
Quinquennial Meetings: (2000)

Internat'l Union of Police Ass'ns, AFL-CIO *(1978)*
1421 Prince St.
Suite 330
Alexandria, VA 22314
Tel: (703)549-7473   *Fax:* (703)683-9048
Members: 45,000 individuals
Staff: 15
Annual Budget: $500-1,000,000
President: Sam A. Cabral
International Secretary-Treasurer: Rich A. Estes

Historical Note
Members are individual police local unions in the U.S. Established December, 1978 in Washington, DC, when those members who wanted to affiliate with the AFL-CIO split away from the Internat'l Conference of Police Ass'ns. Affiliated with the AFL-CIO in February, 1979.

Publications:
Police Union News. m.
The Law Officer.

Meetings/Conferences:
Biennial meetings: even years

Internat'l Union of Security Officers *(1945)*
2404 Merced St.
San Leandro, CA 94577
Tel: (510)895-9905   *Fax:* (510)895-6974
Members: 5,000 individuals
Staff: 10
Annual Budget: $250-500,000
President: Robert Ulrich

Historical Note
An independent labor union. Until 1980 known as the Internat'l Union of Guards and Watchmen.

Publications:
News Letter. bi-m.

Meetings/Conferences:
Annual Meetings: None held

Internat'l Union, United Automobile, Aerospace and Agricultural Implement Workers of America *(1935)*
8000 East Jefferson Ave.
Detroit, MI 48214
Tel: (313)926-5000   *Fax:* (313)331-1520
Web Site: http://www.uaw.org
Members: 750,000 individuals
Staff: 800
Annual Budget: Over $100,000,000
President: Stephen P. Yokage

Historical Note
Chartered by the American Federation of Labor August 26, 1935 in Detroit under the name, United Automobile Workers of America. Joined the Congress of Industrial Organizations in 1938, then became independent (after the formation of AFL-CIO) in 1968. Affiliated with the AFL-CIO in 1981. Has an annual budget of approximately $389.7 million.

Publications:
Skill. q.
Solidarity. m.

Meetings/Conferences:

Internat'l Union, United Plant Guard Workers of America *(1948)*
25510 Kelly Road
Roseville, MI 48066
Tel: (810)772-7250   *Fax:* (810)772-9644
Toll Free: (800)228 - 7492
Members: 20,000 individuals
Staff: 20
Annual Budget: $1-2,000,000
President: Eugene P. McConville

Historical Note
Independent labor union representing security professionals.

Publications:
The Security Link. semi-a.

Meetings/Conferences:
Quinquennial Meetings: (2000)

Internat'l VAR Ass'n *(1963)*
Historical Note
Organization defunct in 1997.

Internat'l Veterinary Acupuncture Soc. *(1974)*
Historical Note
Address unknown in 1988.

Internat'l Visual Literacy Ass'n *(1968)*
Navarro Coll. Dept. of Learning Resources/Spec. Collections
3200 W. 7th Ave.
Corsicana, TX 75110
Tel: (903)874-6501 Ext: 320   *Fax:* (903)874-4636
E-Mail: et@ivla.org
Web Site: http://www.ivla.org
Members: 200 individuals
Staff: 1
Annual Budget: under $10,000
Exec. Treasurer: Darrell Beauchamp

Historical Note
Professionals involved in visual communication and visual literacy in relation to education. Affiliated with the Ass'n for Educational Communications and Technology. Incorporated in New York in 1968, IVLA's purpose is to provide a multidisciplinary forum for exploration, presentation, and discussion of visual communication; to serve as an organizational base for professionals interested in visual literacy projects, programs, and research; to promote and evaluate projects intended to increase the use of visuals in education and communications. Membership: $40/year (individual in U.S. or Canada), $45/year (individual foreign), $20/year (student), $200 (life).

Publications:
Journal of Visual Literacy. semi-a.
Proceedings. a.
Visual Literacy Review. q.

Meetings/Conferences:
Semi-Annual Meetings: Late Winter and Fall

Internat'l Warehouse Logistics Ass'n *(1891)*
1300 West Higgins Road, Suite 111
Park Ridge, IL 60068-5764
Tel: (847)292-1891   *Fax:* (847)292-1896
E-Mail: logistx@aol.com
Web Site: http://www.warehouselogistics.org
Members: 625 companies
Staff: 18
Annual Budget: $2-5,000,000
President and C.E.O.: Michael L. Jenkins
Coordinator, Marketing/Public Relations: Ben Stephens
Director, Education/Asst. General Counsel: Ann Christopher
V. President/Director, Member Services: Kevin McNulty

Historical Note
A merger of the American Warehouse Ass'n and the Canadian Ass'n of Warehousing and Distribution Sevices, IWLA represents the warehouse logistics industry.

Publications:
IWLA Newsgram. m.
Resource Guide to Logistic Professionals. a.

Meetings/Conferences:
Annual Meetings: Spring/550
1999 – Palm Desert, CA/Jan. 24-27/600

Internat'l Water Lily Soc.
Historical Note
Became (1998) Internat'l Waterlily and Watergardening Soc.

Internat'l Water Resources Ass'n *(1972)*
4535 Faner Hall
Southern Illinois University
Carbondale, IL 62901-4516
Tel: (618)453-5138   *Fax:* (618)453-2671
E-Mail: iwra@siu.edu
Web Site: http://www.iwra.siu.edu
Annual Budget: $50-100,000
Exec. Director: Ben Dziegielewski

Historical Note
IWRA members are individuals and organizations with an interest in water resource development. Membership: $65/year (individual); $30/year (student/retiree); $250/year (institution); $400/year (corporation).

Publications:
IWRA Update Newsletter. q.
Water Internat'l. q.

Meetings/Conferences:
2000 – Melbourne, NM(Melbourne Conv. Ctr.)/March 11-17/2000

Internat'l Waterlily and Watergardening Soc. *(1984)*
President: Barbara Davies

Historical Note
Formerly (1988) the Water Lily Soc. and (1998) Internat'l Water Lily Soc. Established and incorporated at Lilypons, MD, the Society is concerned with all aspects of water gardening. Membership: $24/year (individual), $150/year (organization).

Publications:
Water Garden Journal. q.

Meetings/Conferences:
Annual Meetings: August
1999 – Germany

Internat'l Webmasters Ass'n *(1996)*
556 S. Fair Oaks Ave., Suite 101-200
Pasadena, CA 91105
Tel: (626)449-3709   *Fax:* (626)449-8308
Web Site: http://www.iwanet.org

Annual Budget: $100-250,000
Exec. Director: Richard S. Brinegar

Historical Note
IWA is a membership association organized to benefit its members. Membership include Webmasters, web site developers, graphic designers, multimedia specialists and others who participate in the development, monitoring and management of Web sites. Membership: $50/year (regular); $25/year (associate).

Internat'l Weed Science Soc. *(1972)*
107 Crop Science Bldg.
Oregon State Univ.
Corvallis, OR 97331-3002
Tel: (541)737-4715   Fax: (541)737-3407
Members: 550 individuals, 60 institutions
Secretary-Treasurer: Dr. Carol Mallory-Smith

Historical Note
Members are institutions and individuals concerned with the study of weeds and their control. IWSS is a sponsor of the International Weed Control Congress, held quadrennially.

Publications:
Newsletter. semi-a.
Symposia Proceedings. irreg.

Meetings/Conferences:
Annual Meetings: Held in conjunction with the Weed Science
    Society of America
2000 – Fox do Iguassu, Brazil/June 6-11

Internat'l Wholesale Furniture Ass'n *(1929)*
P.O. Box 2482
High Point, NC 27261-2482
Tel: (336)884-1566   Fax: (336)884-1350
E-Mail: iwfa@northstate.net
Members: 135 companies
Staff: 2
Annual Budget: $100-250,000
Exec. Director: Mike Herschel

Historical Note
Organized under the auspices of the Nat'l Ass'n of Furniture Manufacturers, members are wholesale furniture distributors. Formerly (1992) Nat'l Wholesale Furniture Ass'n. Street address: 164 S. Main St. Suite 404, High Point, NC.

Publications:
Distributor's Pre-Market Report. q. adv.
Newsletter. m.
Who's Who in Furniture Distribution. a.

Meetings/Conferences:
1999 – Scottsdale, AZ(Camelback)/Jan. 27-31/125

Internat'l Wild Rice Ass'n *(1969)*
2061 Freeway Dr., Suite G
Woodland, CA 95776-9580
Tel: (530)669-0150   Fax: (530)668-9317
Members: 100 individuals
Staff: 1
Annual Budget: $10-25,000
General Manager: Carlos Zambello

Historical Note
Membership: $100/year.

Publications:
Manomin News. q.

Meetings/Conferences:
Annual Meetings: January
1999 – Woodland, CA

Internat'l Window Cleaning Ass'n *(1989)*
7801 Suffolk Ct.
Alexandria, VA 22315-4029
Tel: (703)971-7771   Fax: (703)971-7772
Toll Free: (800)875 - 4922
E-Mail: IWCA@aol.com
Web Site: http://www.iwca.org
Members: 500 companies
Staff: 3
Annual Budget: $100-250,000
Exec. Director: Shannon M. Van Winter

Historical Note
Trade association of the window cleaning industry with members in the United States and foreign countries, IWCA provides opportunities for networking, seminars and a trade show at its annual convention. Lobbies on issues that affect the industry and works to upgrade the image of the industry. Offers liability insurance and group medical coverage to members. Membership: $125-750/year, based on gross sales (corporate).

Publications:
American Window Cleaner Magazine. bi-m. adv.
IWCA News Newsletter. bi-m.

Meetings/Conferences:
Annual Meetings: February
1999 – Nashville, TN/Feb. 3-6

Internat'l Window Film Ass'n *(1991)*
P.O. Box 3871
Martinsville, VA 24115
Tel: (540)666-4932   Fax: (540)666-4933
Members: 1,200 individuals
Annual Budget: $500-1,000,000
Exec. Director: Darrell Smith

Historical Note
IWFA members are manufacturers, distributors, and installers of solar film for windows. Membership: $150/year (installer); $5000/year, plus assessment (manufacturer).

Publications:
Legislative Bulletin. irreg.
Legislative Chart. 3/year.
Newsletter. q.

Meetings/Conferences:
Annual Meetings: always Las Vegas, NV/Fall

1999 – November

Internat'l Wire and Machinery Ass'n
Historical Note
Address unknown in 1995.

Internat'l Women's Writing Guild *(1976)*
Box 810, Gracie Stn.
New York, NY 10028-0082
Tel: (212)737-7536   Fax: (212)737-9469
E-Mail: iwwg@iwwg.com
Web Site: http://www.iwwg.com
Members: 3,200 individuals
Staff: 3
Annual Budget: $100-250,000
Exec. Director: Hannelore Hahn

Historical Note
A broad-based, grass roots alliance open to all women connected with the written word, regardless of previous professional accomplishments. A network for the personal and professional empowerment of women through writing. Membership: $35/year (domestic); $45/year (foreign).

Publications:
Network. 6/year. adv.

Meetings/Conferences:
Annual Summer Conference: Saratoga Springs, NY(Skidmore
    College), 2nd week in August/450

Internet Alliance *(1992)*
1825 I St., N.W., Suite 400
Washington, DC 20035-5782
Tel: (202)955-8091   Fax: (202)955-8081
E-Mail: ia@internetalliance.org
Web Site: http://www.internetalliance.org
Members: 350 companies
Staff: 7
Annual Budget: $500-1,000,000
Exec. Director: Jeff B. Richards
Manager, IT and Communication: Tim Jordan
Director, Public Policy and Media Relations: Brian O'Shaughnessy
Director of Meetings: Patti McKnight
Director, Administration and Finance: Susan C. Hoch
V. Chairman, Board of Directors: Bill Burrington
Dep. Policy Counsel: Tim Jordan
Member Services Assistant: Sheri Key

Historical Note
The Alliance is the successor to Videotex Industry Ass'n (founded 1981). Founded as Interactive Services Ass'n; merged with the Nat'l Ass'n for Interactive Services in 1994, and assumed its current name in 1998. Promotes the personal use of network-based interactive electronic services in homes, offices, and public locations. Membership consists of companies developing mass market electronic information and transaction services and all other components of the industry. Membership: $1,000-15,000/year (company).

Publications:
Annual Conference Proceeding. a.
ISA Update Newsletter. m.
Membership Directory & Handbook. a. adv.

Meetings/Conferences:
Annual Meetings: Summer

Internet Local Advertising and Commerce Ass'n
130 Webster St., Suite 100
Oakland, CA 94607-3723
Tel: (510)893-5565   Fax: (510)452-5033
E-Mail: info@ilac.net
Web Site: http://www.ilac.net
Members: 75 individuals
Exec. Director: Hal Logan

Historical Note
ILAC members are Internet service providers and other companies using the Internet as an advertising medium. Membership: $750-$6,000/year, varies by annual revenue/expenses (corporate).

Meetings/Conferences:

Internet Soc. *(1992)*
12020 Sunrise Valley Drive, Suite 210
Reston, VA 22091-3429
Tel: (703)648-9888   Fax: (703)648-9887
E-Mail: isoc@isoc.org
Web Site: http://www.isoc.org
Members: 6,000 individuals, 140 companies/organizations
Staff: 14
Annual Budget: $2-5,000,000
President and C.E.O.: Donald M. Heath
Director, Conferences and Education: Torryn P. Brazell, ACA
Exec. Director: Martin Burack

Historical Note
ISOC members are technologists, developers, educators, researchers, government representatives, business people and others with an interest in internet technologies and applications. Membership: $1,000-50,000/year (corporate); $35/year (individual); $25/year (student).

Publications:
ISOC Forum (electronic).
OnTheInternet Magazine. bi-m. adv.

Meetings/Conferences:
Annual Meetings: Summer
1999 – San Jose, CA(Convention Center)/June 22-25

Intersocietal Commission for the Accreditation of Vascular Laboratories *(1994)*
8840 Stanford Blvd., Suite 4900
Columbia, MD 21045-5852
Tel: (410)872-0100   Fax: (410)872-0030
Web Site: www.icabl.org
Members: 400 laboratories
Exec. Director: Sandy Katanick

Historical Note
Establishes standards for the accreditation of laboratories performing testing for vascular disease and publishes study material for laboratories interested in the accreditation process.

Intersociety Committee on Pathology Information *(1957)*
4733 Bethesda Ave., Suite 730
Bethesda, MD 20814
Tel: (301)656-2944   Fax: (301)656-3179
E-Mail: isicpi@erols.com
Web Site: pathologytraining.org
Members: 5 societies
Staff: 2
Annual Budget: $100-250,000
Information Counsel: Eileen M. Lavine

Historical Note
Incorporated in 1968, the Committee serves as a central source of information about pathology and careers in pathology.

Publications:
Directory of Pathology Training Programs. a.

Interstate Conference of Employment Security Agencies *(1937)*
444 North Capitol St., N.W., Suite 142
Washington, DC 20001-1512
Tel: (202)434-8020   Fax: (202)434-8033
E-Mail: ederocco@icesa.org
Web Site: http://www.icesa.org
Members: 53 state agencies
Staff: 11
Annual Budget: $1-2,000,000
Exec. Director: Emily S. DeRocco
Info. Technology Communications Director: Jaime Fall
Director, Employment, Training, & Congressional Relations: Kathleen
    A. Cashen
Unemployment Insurance Director: Richard A. Hobbie
Director, Labor Market Information/Research: Mary Susan Vickers
Fiscal/Admin. Director: Marcia R. Larson

Historical Note
Administrators of state agencies responsible for employment and training programs, unemployment insurance, and labor market information. Formerly (1939) the Interstate Conference of Unemployment Compensation agencies. Membership: $18,000/year.

Publications:
One-Stop-Wonders Newsletter (on-line).

Meetings/Conferences:
1999 – Ft. Lauderdale, FL
2000 – Salt Lake City, UT

Interstate Council on Water Policy *(1959)*
1299 Pennsylvania Ave., N.W., 8th fl, W.
Washington, DC 20004-2400
Tel: (202)218-4196   Fax: (202)842-0621
Members: 70 agencies, businesses and ass'ns
Staff: 4
Annual Budget: $50-100,000
Exec. Director: Susan Gilson
Meeting/Conference Coordinator: Sheila Reilly
Membership Services Director: Kerry Keene

Historical Note
Established in 1959 and incorporated in Washington, DC in 1977. Formerly (1990) the Interstate Conference on Water Policy. Members are state and regional agencies concerned with conservation, development and administration of water and land-related resources. Multi-state, interstate and intrastate agencies, as well as non-profit organizations and educational institutions, are eligible for associate membership; business and trade associations may apply for affiliate membership. Membership: $500/year (affiliate); $1,250/year (associate), $1,875-$3,750/year (state).

Publications:
ICWP Bulletin.
ICWP Policy Statement & Bylaws. a.
Membership Directory. a.
Proceedings. a.

Meetings/Conferences:
1999 – Pitsburg, PA

Interstate Natural Gas Ass'n of America *(1944)*
10 G St., N.E., Suite 700
Washington, DC 20002
Tel: (202)216-5900   Fax: (202)216-0877
Web Site: http://www.ingaa.org
Members: 39 companies
Staff: 26
Annual Budget: $5-10,000,000
President: Jerald V. Halvorsen
V. President, Legislative Affairs: Gay Friedmann
Director, Legislative Affairs: Martin E. Edwards, III
Sr. V. President, Regulatory Affairs: S. Lorraine Cross
Meetings Coordinator: Lynne M. Turschmann
Sr. V. President, Finance and Administration: John G. Ams
Exec. V. President, Rate & Policy Analysis: R. Skip Horvath

Historical Note
Established in Kansas City, Missouri on January 11, 1944 as the Independent Natural Gas Ass'n of America by representatives of fourteen natural gas companies. In 1974 it assumed its present name and limited its voting membership to gas transmission companies, producers and distributors becoming associate members. Sponsors the Interstate Natural Gas Ass'n of America Political Action Committee (INGAA-PAC). Has an annual budget of approximately $5.3 million.

Publications:
Regulatory Update. q.

Meetings/Conferences:
Annual Meetings: Fall/400
1999 – Florida/Oct. 3-5

Interstate Oil and Gas Compact Commission *(1935)*
Box 53127
Oklahoma City, OK   73152-3127
Tel: (405)525-3556   *Fax:* (405)525-3592
Toll Free: (800)822 - 4015
E-Mail: iogcc@oklaosf.state.ok.us
Members: 700 individuals
Staff: 10
Annual Budget: $1-2,000,000
Exec. Director: Christine Hansen
Meeting Planner: Rosemary Marmen
Director, Training/Education: Barbara Skelton

Historical Note
Formerly (1991) the Interstate Oil Compact Commission. IOGCC members are states that produce oil or gas; associate states support the conservation of America's energy resources. Establishes rules and guidelines for the proper maintenance of wells.

Publications:
Compact Comments,IOGCC Newsletter. m.
Directory of Interstate Oil Commission and State Gas
    Agencies. a.
Marginal Oil and Gas: Fuel for Economic Growth. a.

Meetings/Conferences:
Semi-annual Meetings: June and December
1999 – Jackson Hole, WY(Snow King Resort)/June 6-8/300
1999 – New Orleans, LA(Omni Royal Orleans)/400
2000 – San Antonio, TX(Omni San Antonio
    Hotel)/Dec. 3-5/400
2000 – Lexington, KY(Radisson Plaza Hotel)/June 11-13/300
2001 – Anchorage, AK(Captain Cook Hotel)/May 13-15

Interstate Producers Livestock Ass'n *(1962)*
1705 W. Luthy Drive
Peoria, IL   61615
Tel: (309)691-5360
Members: 19,100 individuals
Staff: 185
Annual Budget: $2-5,000,000
Exec. V. President: E.J. Strasma

Historical Note
Absorbed the Producers Livestock Marketing Association in 1968. A cooperative marketing organization.

Meetings/Conferences:
Annual Meetings: Chicago, IL/December

Interstate Towing Ass'n
Historical Note
Part of the Towing and Recovery Ass'n of America.

Interstate Truckload Carriers Conference
Historical Note
Became the Truckload Carriers Ass'n in 1997.

Intersure, Ltd. *(1966)*
3 Hotel St.
Warrenton, VA   20186
Tel: (540)349-0969   *Fax:* (540)349-0971
E-Mail: intersur@citizen.infi.net
Web Site: http://www.intersurepartners.com
Members: 45 insurance agencies
Staff: 2
Annual Budget: $50-100,000
Exec. Officer: Millie Curtis

Historical Note
Formerly (1980) the Ass'n of Internat'l Insurance Agents; became Intersure: The Internat'l Insurance Agents Ass'n; assumed its present title in 1985.

Meetings/Conferences:

Intimate Apparel Manufacturers Ass'n *(1931)*
1430 Broadway, Suite 1603
New York, NY   10018-3308
Tel: (212)354-0707   *Fax:* (212)221-3540
Members: 15 companies
Staff: 1
Annual Budget: $10-25,000
Exec. Director-Counsel: Alex J. Glauberman

Historical Note
Membership concentrated in the New York area. Major purpose is labor negotiations with the International Ladies Garment Workers Union. Formed by the merger of the Lingerie Manufacturers Ass'n and the Negligee Manufacturers Ass'n in 1984.

Intravenous Nurses Soc. *(1973)*
Fresh Pond Square, 10 Fawcett St.
Cambridge, MA   02138
Tel: (617)441-3008   *Fax:* (617)441-3009
Toll Free: (800)694 - 0298
E-Mail: ins@ins1.org
Web Site: http://ins1.org
Members: 7,000 individuals
Staff: 21
Annual Budget: $1-2,000,000
C.E.O.: Mary Alexander, CRNI
Director of Marketing: Chris Hunt
Controller: Jim Mathson

Historical Note
Formerly the Nat'l Intravenous Therapy Ass'n. The name was changed to the Intravenous Nurses Soc. in 1987. Membership consists primarily of Registered Nurses involved in the clinical practice of intravenous therapies. Membership: $90/year.

Publications:
Convention Program. a.
INS Newsline. bi-m.
Journal of Intravenous Nursing. bi-m.

Meetings/Conferences:
Annual Meetings: Spring
1999 – Charlotte, NC/May 1-6/1500

2000 – Minneapolis, MN/May 6-11/1500
2001 – Indianapolis, IN/April 28-May 3/1500

Investigative Reporters and Editors *(1975)*
138 Neff Hall Annex
University of Missouri
Columbia, MO   65211
Tel: (573)882-2042   *Fax:* (573)882-5431
Web Site: http://www.ire.org
Members: 3,500 individuals
Staff: 2
Annual Budget: $500-1,000,000
Exec. Director: Brant Houston
Conference Coordinator: Lisa Barnes

Historical Note
A non-profit educational organization of individuals involved or concerned with investigative journalism. Membership: $40/year (regular), $25/year (student), $25/year (journal subscription only).

Publications:
IRE Book. bien.
IRE Journal. bi-m.
Uplink. m.

Meetings/Conferences:
Annual Meetings: June/1,000

Investment Casting Institute *(1950)*
8350 North Central Expressway
Suite M-1110
Dallas, TX   75206-1625
Tel: (214)368-8896   *Fax:* (214)368-8852
Members: 180 companies
Staff: 5
Annual Budget: $500-1,000,000
Exec. Director: Henry T. Bidwell
Editor, INCAST Magazine: Leland Martin

Historical Note
Formed in 1950 and holding its first annual meeting in 1953, ICI members are companies employing the precision, investment casting process and suppliers to the industry.

Publications:
Incast Magazine. m. adv.

Meetings/Conferences:
Semi-annual Meetings: Spring and Fall

Investment Company Institute *(1940)*
1401 H St., N.W., Suite 1200
Washington, DC   20005-2148
Tel: (202)326-5800   *Fax:* (202)326-5806
E-Mail: fink@ici.org
Web Site: http://www.ici.org
Members: 7,114 companies
Staff: 180
Annual Budget: $25-50,000,000
President: Matthew P. Fink
Director, Information Systems: Robert Bryce
Exec. V. President: Julie Domenick
Conference Director: Reece Thompson
Manager, Meetings and Seminars: Lauren J. Graham
V. President, Administration: Thomas S. Simmons
Senior V. President, Management: Lawrence Maffia
General Counsel: Craig S. Tyle
Membership Director: Virginia S. Echeverria
Assit. V. President/Director, Publications: Susan J. Duncan

Historical Note
Members are open-end and closed-end investment companies registered under the Investment Company Act of 1940, and their advisers and principal underwriters, as well as unit investment trust sponsors. Formerly (1961) Nat'l Ass'n of Investment Companies. Absorbed the Ass'n of Mutual Fund Plan Sponsors in 1973, the Unit Investment Trust Ass'n in 1985, and the Ass'n of Publicly Traded Investment Funds in 1987. Has an annual budget of approximately $30 million. Sponsors the Investment Management Political Action Committee (IMPAC).

Publications:
Board Bulletin. bi-m.
Guide to Mutual Funds. a.
Mutual Fund Fact Book. a.
Mutual Fund News. 5/yr.
Mutual Fund Trends. m.
Portfolio. bi-m.
Service Directory. a.

Meetings/Conferences:
Annual Meetings: Spring in Washington, DC

Investment Counsel Ass'n of America *(1937)*
1050 17th St., N.W., Suite 725
Washington, DC   20036-5503
Tel: (202)293-4222   *Fax:* (202)293-4223
E-Mail: icaa@icaa.org
Web Site: http://www.icaa.org
Members: 230 firms
Staff: 4
Annual Budget: $500-1,000,000
Exec. Director: David Tittsworth
Assit. Director: Kimberly Fridrich
General Counsel: Karen Barr

Historical Note
ICAA is a non-for-profit association that exclusively represents the interests of federally registered investment adviser firms. Membership: $2,000-$6,500/year(based on assets under management).

Publications:
Blue Sky Survey. a.
Directory of Member Firms. a.
ICAA Investment Adviser. irreg.
ICAA Newsletter. m. adv.

Meetings/Conferences:
Annual Meetings: April

1999 – Scottsdale, AZ(Scottsdale Princess)
2000 – Atlanta, GA(Ritz Carlton Buckhead)/April 3-7

Investment Management Consultants Ass'n *(1985)*
9101 E. Kenyon Ave., Suite 3000
Denver, CO   80237-1855
Tel: (303)770-3377   *Fax:* (303)770-1812
Members: 1,700 individuals
Staff: 9
Annual Budget: $2-5,000,000
Exec. Director: Evelyn L. Brust, CAE
Government Relations: Bonny Brill
Director of Education: Kathryn Meyer
Membership Services: Betty Hepp

Historical Note
Incorporated in Colorado, IMCA was established to provide opportunities for the exchange of information and education; encourage the practice of high standards of professional conduct; broaden public understanding, and protect the interests of the profession. Membership: $375/year (individual).

Publications:
The Journal of Investment Consulting.
The Monitor. bi-m.

Meetings/Conferences:
Semi-Annual Meetings: Spring and Fall
1999 – San Francisco, CA(Sheraton)
1999 – Denver, CO(Marriott)

Investment Program Ass'n *(1985)*
1101 17th st. N.W., Suite 703
Washington, DC   20036
Tel: (202)775-9750   *Fax:* (202)331-8446
Members: 150 companies
Staff: 4
Annual Budget: $500-1,000,000

Historical Note
Formerly (1991) Investment Partnership Ass'n. A national trade association for direct investment program sponsors, broker/dealers and partnership services firms. Serves as the industry advocate before Congress, regulatory agencies, and the media. Sponsors and supports the Invest America Political Action Committee. Membership: $2,500/year (minimum).

Publications:
Roundtable Newsletter. irreg.
Technical Bulletin.

Meetings/Conferences:
1999 – CA(Swan Hill)/April 22-24

Investment Recovery Ass'n *(1981)*
5800 Foxridge Dr., # 115
Mission, KS   66202-2333
Tel: (913)262-4597   *Fax:* (913)262-0174
E-Mail: ira@invrecovery.org
Web Site: http://www.invrecovery.org
Members: 210 companies
Staff: 5
Annual Budget: $100-250,000
Exec. Director: Jane Male, CAE

Historical Note
Members are firms that have an established investment recovery program providing for the disposition of recyclable products, capital assets, or surplus materials. Membership: $300/year; $450/year(associate).

Publications:
Member Directory. a. adv.
Newsletter. q. adv.

Meetings/Conferences:
Semi-annual Meetings: April-May and October-November

Iota Tau Sigma *(1902)*
P.O. Box 792
Kirksville, MO   63501
Tel: (816)665-7741
Secretary-Treasurer: Wilson P. Bailey

Historical Note
Professional fraternity promoting osteopathic medicine. This organization is reorganizing.

Publications:
Gozzle Nipper. semi-a.

Iota Tau Tau *(1925)*
641 Benfield Road
Severna Park, MD   21146
Tel: (410)647-6781
Members: 500 individuals
Staff: 1
Annual Budget: $10-25,000
Exec. Officer: Catherine M. Osborne

Historical Note
Founded November 11, 1925 at Southwestern University, Los Angeles. Originally an honorary legal sorority, now also open to men. Has no permanent address or paid staff. The officers change every two years. Membership: $20/year.

Publications:
The Double Tau. bien.

Meetings/Conferences:
1999 – Atlanta, GA/July /75

Ireland Chamber of Commerce in the United States *(1988)*
1305 Post Road
Fairfield, CT   06430-6016
Tel: (203)255-4774   *Fax:* (203)255-6752
Web Site: ICCUSA.org
Members: 500 individuals
Annual Budget: $250-500,000
Exec. Director: Bernard F. Lynch

Historical Note
ICCUSA is a corporate and professional membership organization promoting the interests of Ireland and expanding trade opportunities between the U.S. and Ireland. Membership: $500/year (individual), $1,000/year (company).

Publications:
Ireland Info Fax Line.
Newsletter. q. adv.
Trade Directory. a. adv.
Trade Leads Bulletin. m.

Iron and Steel Soc. (1974)
410 Commonwealth Drive
Warrendale, PA 15086-7512
Tel: (412)776-1535   *Fax:* (412)776-0430
E-Mail: mailbag@issource.org
Web Site: www.issource.org
Members: 9,000 individuals
Staff: 33
Annual Budget: $2-5,000,000
Exec. Director: David Kanagy
Manager, Meeting Services: Cheryll Mayes
Controller: Nicholas G. Stratigos
Manager, Membership Services: Kathryn Kost

Historical Note
One of the four member societies of the American Institute of Mining, Metallurgical, and Petroleum Engineers. Concerned with steel, castings, and ferroalloy production from raw material handling to the finished products. Membership: $75/year.

Publications:
Iron and Steelmaker. m. adv.

Meetings/Conferences:
1999 – Chicago, IL(Chicago Hyatt Regency)/Mar. 21-24/1500
1999 – Pittsburgh, PA(Pittsburgh Conv. Cntr.)/Nov. 14-16/2000

Irrigation Ass'n (1949)
8260 Willow Oaks Corp. Dr., Suite 120
Fairfax, VA 22031-4513
Tel: (703)573-3551   *Fax:* (703)573-1913
Web Site: http://www.irrigation.org
Members: 1,200 companies
Staff: 11
Exec. V. President: Thomas Kimmell
Director, Communications: Laura Dorsey
Director, Meetings: Denise Stone
Director, Education: Tim Wilson
Director, Membership and Finance: Debra Chmara

Historical Note
Formerly the Sprinkler Irrigation Association, it adopted its present name in 1976 and absorbed the Drip Irrigation Association in 1979. Members are manufacturers, designers, suppliers, consultants, and contractors of all irrigation systems. Membership: $100/year (individual), $350-$14,000/year (company).

Publications:
Conference Proceedings. a.
Irrigation Business & Technology Magazine. bi-m. adv.
Membership Directory and Buyers Guide. a. adv.
The Fax of Irrigation. bi-m.

Meetings/Conferences:
Annual Meetings: Fall
1999 – Orlando, FL/Nov. 7-9

IRSA - the Ass'n of Quality Clubs (1981)
Historical Note
Became International Health, Raquet and Sportsclub Association in 1996.

IS Financial Management Ass'n (1988)
P.O. Box 27543
145 San Benito Way
San Francisco, CA 94127
Tel: (415)731-3706
Members: 950 individuals
Staff: 1
Annual Budget: $100-250,000
President & Director: Terence A. Quinlan

Historical Note
Formerly (1996) Finanacial Managment for Data Processing. ISFMA provides educational programs and services for the financial management of information services organization. Services include seminars, education certificates, conferences and job clearinghouse service. Membership: $50/year (individual); $300-500 (facility).

Publications:
Journal of IS Financial Management. q.
Membership Directory. a.

Meetings/Conferences:
Annual Meetings: Spring
1999 – Hershey, PA(Hershey Hotel)/April 19-22/150
1999 – Orlando, FL(Grand Floridian)/July 6-9/350

ISA: Internat'l Soc. for Measurement and Control
Historical Note
Became (1998) Instrument Society of America.

ISDA - The Office Systems Cooperative (1973)
37 W. Yokuts St., Suite A-4
Stockton, CA 95207
Tel: (209)474-0919   *Fax:* (209)474-0663
E-Mail: info@isadnet.net
Web Site: http://www.isadnet.net
Members: 125 companies
Staff: 4
Annual Budget: $500-1,000,000
Exec. V. President: William N. Highfill

Historical Note
Formerly (1981) Internat'l Systems Dealers Ass'n. Members are dealers of office filing systems and microfilm equipment. Membership: $300-960/year (organization/company).

Publications:
News & Views. q. adv.
Office Systems Management. q. adv.

Meetings/Conferences:

ISEA-The Safety Equipment Ass'n (1933)
1901 N. Moore St., Suite 808
Arlington, VA 22209
Tel: (703)525-1695   *Fax:* (703)528-2148
E-Mail: isea@safetycentral.org
Web Site: http://www.safetycentral.org/isea
Members: 80 companies
Staff: 6
Annual Budget: $500-1,000,000
President: Daniel K. Shipp
Public Affairs Director: Bruce R. Clash
Technical Director: Janice Comer Bradley, CSP

Historical Note
Members manufacture and market all types of apparel, supplies and equipment used for the protection of workers.

Publications:
ISEA Buyers Guide. a.
ISEA Washington Report. m.
Membership Directory. a.
Safety Exporter Newsletter. q.
Safety Signals Newsletter. 6/year.

Meetings/Conferences:
Annual Meetings: May and November
1999 – Palm Beach, FL(Ritz Carlton)/May 16-18/200

Islamic Medical Ass'n (1967)
950 75th Street
Downers Grove, IL 60516
Tel: (630)852-2122   *Fax:* (630)435-1429
Members: 2,000 individuals
Staff: 2
Annual Budget: $100-250,000
Exec. Director: Khursheed Mallick, M.D.
Business Manager: Syed Mansoor Uddin

Historical Note
IMA members are Muslim physicians and health professionals. Membership: $150/year (individual); $1,500 (life membership).

Publications:
Journal. q.
Newsletter. q.

Meetings/Conferences:

Issues Management Ass'n (1982)
2040 Nat'l Press Blvd., N.W.
Washington, DC 20045
Tel: (202)342-1050   *Fax:* (500)776-2020
Members: 450 individuals
Staff: 1
Annual Budget: $50-100,000
President: William Renfro

Historical Note
Members are corporate/government executives and academics concerned with the foresight, analysis and effect of public issues on corporate, government and organization, policy. Membership: $100/year (individual); $500/year (organization/company).

Publications:
The IMA Newsletter. q.
The Issue Commentary. irreg.

Meetings/Conferences:
Annual Meetings: Fall

ITA-Internat'l Ass'n of Magnetic and Optical Recording Manufacturers and Associated Industries (1970)
Historical Note
Became ITA-Internat'l Recording Media Ass'n in 1995.

Italian Actors Union (1938)
2105 64th St.
Brooklyn, NY 11204-3063
Tel: (212)517-1764   *Fax:* (212)352-1815
Members: 100 individuals
Staff: 1
Annual Budget: under $10,000
President: Olga Barbato

Historical Note
An autonomous component of Associated Actors and Artistes of America, which chartered it in 1938. Founded in 1936 as the Lega di Miglioramento fra gli Artisti della Scena in New York City. Membership: $56/year.

Meetings/Conferences:
Semi-Annual Meetings: July and December in New York City.

Italy-America Chamber of Commerce (1887)
730 Fifth Ave., Suite 600
New York, NY 10019
Tel: (212)459-0044   *Fax:* (212)459-0090
E-Mail: iacc@ix.netcom.com
Web Site: http://www.italian-chamber.com
Members: 1,200 individuals
Staff: 9
Annual Budget: $1-2,000,000
Exec. Secretary: Francesco DeAngelis
Marketing Manager: Piersandro Rao
Director, Trade Show: Carlo Santoro

Historical Note
Formerly American Chamber of Commerce for Trade with Italy, it is the oldest foreign trade chamber in the U.S. An independent, private, not-for-profit corporation devoted to fostering trade between Italy and the U.S. through information, education, and travel services. Affiliated with the U. S. Chamber of Commerce and is a founding member of the European-American Chamber of Commerce. Membership: $500/year.

Publications:
IACC Inform. m. adv.
Target Italy. q. adv.
Trade with Italy. bi-m. adv.
US-Italy Trade Directory. a. adv.

Meetings/Conferences:
Annual Meetings: June
1999 – Sardinia, Italy

IUA - The CA-IDMS Database and Applications User Ass'n

Japan Automobile Manufacturers Ass'n (1967)
1050 17th St., N.W., Suite 410
Washington, DC 20036-5503
Tel: (202)296-8537   *Fax:* (202)872-1212
Web Site: http://www.japanauto.com
Gen. Director: William Duncan

Historical Note
JAMA supports the production of Japanese made automobiles and vehicles.

Jean Piaget Soc./Soc. for the Study of Knowledge and Development (1970)
Larsen Hall, Dept. of Human Development
Harvard Univ.
Cambridge, MA 02138
Tel: (617)495-3446   *Fax:* (617)495-3626
E-Mail: Kurt_fischer@harvard.edu
Web Site: http://www.piaget.org
Members: 600 individuals
Staff: 1
Annual Budget: $10-25,000
General Office Manager: Kurt W. Fischer

Historical Note
Membership includes researchers and practitioners in the fields of psychology, education, philosophy and psychiatry who are interested in the nature of human knowledge. Has no paid officers or staff. General correspondence may be sent to the address above; membership correspondence should be sent to William Gray, Dept. of Educational Psychology, Univ. of Toledo, Toledo, OH 43606-3390. Membership: $30/year (student); $70/year (regular).

Publications:
Newsletter.
Symposium Proceedings.

Meetings/Conferences:
Annual Meetings: late May-June
1999 – Mexico City, Mexico/June 2-5

Jesuit Ass'n of Student Personnel Administrators (1954)
Rockhurst College
1100 Rockhurst Road
Kansas City, MO 64110
Tel: (816)501-4125   *Fax:* (816)501-4822
E-Mail: kramer@vax2.rockhurst.edu
Members: 28 institutions
Annual Budget: under $10,000
President: Dr. Elizabeth Kramer

Historical Note
Members are administrators of student personnel programs in Jesuit universities/colleges. Has no paid officers or full-time staff. Membership: based on a sliding scale.

Publications:
Directory. a.
JASPA Newsletter. 6/year.

Meetings/Conferences:
Annual Meetings: Spring

Jesuit Secondary Education Ass'n (1970)
1616 P St., N.W.
Suite 400
Washington, DC 20036-1405
Tel: (202)667-3888   *Fax:* (202)328-9212
Members: 45 schools
Staff: 6
Annual Budget: $100-250,000
President: Carl E. Meirose, S.J.

Historical Note
Formerly, with the Ass'n of Jesuit College and Universities, a part of the Jesuit Education Ass'n.

Publications:
AJCU/JSEA Directory. a.
JSEA News Bulletin. 8/year.

Meetings/Conferences:

Jewelers Board of Trade (1884)
95 Jefferson Blvd.
Warwick, RI 02888-1046
Tel: (401)467-0055   *Fax:* (401)467-1199
Members: 3,200 businesses
Staff: 90
Annual Budget: $2-5,000,000
President: Nathaniel C. Earle

Historical Note
A credit reporting agency, JBT also provides collection services and mailing lists specific to the jewelry industry. Membership: $740/year (company).

Publications:
J. B.
New Name Bulletin. w.
Service Bulletin. w.

Meetings/Conferences:
1999 – Providence, RI

Jewelers of America (1957)
1185 Ave. of the Americas, 30th Floor
New York, NY   10036
Tel: (212)768-8777   *Fax:* (212)768-8087
Toll Free: (800)223 - 0673
E-Mail: jewelersam@aol.com
Web Site: http://www.Jewelers.org
Members: 12,500 stores
Staff: 16
Annual Budget: $2-5,000,000
Exec. Director: Matthew A. Runci
Director of Communications: Misha Glezin
Director of Education: Beverly Hori-Ankrom
Deputy Director of Operations: David Rocha
Director of Membership & Affiliates: Rossana Aguilar
Director of Prof. Certification: Mark Mann
Historical Note
Formed as Retail Jewelers of America; the result of a merger between American Nat'l Retail Jewelers Ass'n (founded 1906) and Nat'l Jewelers Ass'n (founded 1942); assumed its current name in 1980. Membership: based on annual sales.
Publications:
J Report. 10/year.
Meetings/Conferences:
Semi-Annual Meetings: February and July in New York, NY

Jewelers Shipping Ass'n (1962)
125 Carlsbad St.
Cranston, RI   02920
Tel: (401)943-6020   *Fax:* (401)943-1490
Members: 1,500 companies
Staff: 50
Annual Budget: $1-2,000,000
Manager: James Sell
Historical Note
Membership: $10/year.
Publications:
Journal of Commerce. d.
Meetings/Conferences:
Annual Meetings: Providence, RI/Fall

Jewelers Vigilance Committee (1912)
25 West 45th St.
New York, NY   10036
Toll Free: (800)564 - 6582
E-Mail: amsjvc@aol.com
Web Site: http://www.jvc.legal.org
Members: 3,000 companies
Staff: 6
Annual Budget: $500-1,000,000
Exec. V. President & General Counsel: Cecilia L. Gardner
Historical Note
JVC is the "legal arm and guardian of the jewelry industry, advocating legal compliance and ethical practices." JVC monitors legislation, provides government agency liaison, trade liason, and consumer dispute resolution services.
Publications:
Annual Directory. a.
News and Views.
Meetings/Conferences:
Annual Meetings: July/New York, NY(Javits Center)

Jewelers' Security Alliance of the U.S. (1883)
6 E. 45th St.
New York, NY   10017
Tel: (212)687-0328   *Fax:* (212)808-9168
Toll Free: (800)537 - 0067
Members: 14 business locations
Staff: 6
Annual Budget: $500-1,000,000
President: John J. Kennedy
Manager, Marketing and Communications: Paul K. Silverman
Manager, Membership Services: Helen M. Buck
Historical Note
Founded by 17 manufacturing jewelers in New York, NY to offer crime prevention assistance to traveling salespersons. Membership: $85-3000/year.
Publications:
Crime Bulletin. 10-15/year.
JSA Manual of Jewelry Security. bien.
Meetings/Conferences:
Annual Meetings: January, New York City

Jewelry Industry Council
Historical Note
Superseded (1995) by Jewelry Industry Center.

Jewelry Industry Distributors Ass'n (1946)
11812-A N. 56th St.
Tampa, FL   33617
Tel: (813)988-0737   *Fax:* (813)988-5837
Members: 135 companies
Staff: 2
Annual Budget: $50-100,000
Exec. Director: Michael Streeper
Historical Note
Formerly (1984) the Watch Material and Jewelry Distributors Ass'n of America.
Publications:
News and Views. q.
Meetings/Conferences:
Annual Meetings: Spring, with American Jewelry Marketing Ass'n

Jewelry Information Center (1946)
1185 Ave. of the Americas, 30th Floor
New York, NY   10036-2601

Tel: (212)398-2319   *Fax:* (212)398-2324
Toll Free: (800)459 - 0130
E-Mail: jewelryjic@aol.com
Web Site: jewelryinfo.org
Members: 700 companies
Staff: 4
Annual Budget: $500-1,000,000
President and C.E.O.: Lynn Ramsey
Historical Note
The promotional and education arm of the fine jewelry industry, JIC provides news, trends, and statistics about the fine jewelry industry to the media and otherwise promotes fine jewelry. JIC members are manufacturers, importers, refiners, equipment and tool suppliers, stone dealers, precious metal fabricators and retailers with a 60/30 split between suppliers and retailers. Membership: $95-10,000/year (based on number of employees).
Publications:
LINK. q.

Jewelry Manufacturers Ass'n (1919)
c/o Austern & Paul
18 E. 48th St.
New York, NY   10017
Tel: (212)753-1717
Members: 20 companies
Staff: 1
Annual Budget: $25-50,000
General Counsel: Steven Orgell
Historical Note
Established as Jewelry Crafts Ass'n, it assumed its present name in 1961. Major activity is to conduct collective bargaining with the Jewelry Workers Union.
Meetings/Conferences:
Annual Meetings: January, in New York City

Jewelry Manufacturers Guild (1981)
P.O. Box 46099
Los Angeles, CA   90046
Tel: (909)769-1820   *Fax:* (909)769-1920
Toll Free: (800)359 - 0340
Members: 100 companies
Annual Budget: $10-25,000
Operations Manager: Paula Glick Hill
Historical Note
JMG was established to promote and improve conditions in the fine jewelry manfacturing industry; to provide a medium of communication for the interchange of ideas; and to promote a high standard of ethics. Membership: $250/year (company).
Publications:
Credit Reports. m.
Sales Representative Network.

Jewish Book Council
15 East 26th St., 10th Floor
New York, NY   10010-1579
Tel: (212)532-4949   *Fax:* (212)481-4174
Staff: 1
Director: Carolyn Hessel
Historical Note
Formerly an affiliate of Jewish Community Centers Ass'n of North America; became an independent organization in 1996.
Publications:
Jewish Book World. 3/year.

Jewish Community Centers Ass'n of North America (1917)
15 East 26th St., 10th Floor
New York, NY   10010-1579
Tel: (212)532-4949   *Fax:* (212)481-4174
Web Site: http://jcca.org
Members: 260 agencies
Staff: 40
Annual Budget: $2-5,000,000
Exec. V. President: Allan Finkelstein
Historical Note
An association of Jewish Community Centers, YM-YWHAs and Camps. Founded as the Nat'l Jewish Welfare Board, it absorbed the Council of Young Men's Hebrew and Kindred Ass'ns in 1921. Assumed the name JWB in 1977 and its present name in 1990.
Publications:
Briefing for JCC Presidents. 5/year.
Circle. q.
Meetings/Conferences:
Biennial Meetings: Even years/1,200
2000 – Boston, MA/May 7-10
2002 – Los Angeles, CA/April 21-24

Jewish Education Service of North America (1939)
111 Eighth Ave.
11th Floor
New York, NY   10011
Tel: (212)284-6950   *Fax:* (212)284-6951
Members: 2,000 individuals
Staff: 22
Annual Budget: $1-2,000,000
Exec. V. President: Jonathan Woocher, Ph.D.
Director, Marketing & Communications: Jessica Kurk
Director, Finance, Operations & Information Management: David Shriner-Cahn
Historical Note
Formerly (1981) the American Ass'n for Jewish Education. The Jewish education, advocacy, planning, coordinating and service agency for the federated Jewish community in North America. Helps local federations and central agencies for Jewish education undertake activities in research, program and human service development, information and resource dissemination, and consultations. Membership: $100/year (individual); for institutions, fee varies by size.

Publications:
Agenda: Jewish Education. q.
Directory of Central Agencies for Jewish Education. a.
JESNA Update.
Trends. q.

Jewish Educators Assembly (1951)
106-06 Queens Blvd.
Flushing, NY   11375-4248
Tel: (718)268-9452   *Fax:* (718)520-4369
Members: 450 individuals
Staff: 3
Annual Budget: $100-250,000
Historical Note
The Jewish Educators Assembly is an organization of Jewish education professionals, including educational directors of congregational schools, day school headmasters, youth directors, educational consultants, bureau directors, college professors, camp directors, family educators, academicians, and nursery directors functioning within the Conservative movement. Membership: $150/year (basic), $25/year (retired, student).
Publications:
V'Aleh Hachadashot. 3/year.
Meetings/Conferences:

Jewish Funeral Directors of America (1927)
Seaport Landing, 150 Lynnway, Suite 506
Lynn, MA   01902
Tel: (781)477-9300   *Fax:* (781)477-9393
Members: 125 firms
Staff: 1
Annual Budget: $250-500,000
Exec. Director: Florence Pressman, CAE
Historical Note
JFDA's purpose is to preserve the traditions and customs of the Jewish funeral service as recognized and practiced by those of the Jewish faith; to enrich and strengthen its association as an exemplar of Jewish values; to fomulate and advocate the highest principles, ideals and ethics of the funeral profession; to conduct a Jewish funeral association for the mutual benefit of its members and the performance of its religious functions though professional cooperation to foster other activities for the perpetuation and advancement of the funeral profession and its relationship to Judaism.
Publications:
JFDA Newsletter. 3/yr.
The Jewish Funeral Director. a. adv.
Meetings/Conferences:
Annual Meetings: November
1999 – Puerto Rico

Jewish Ministers Cantors Ass'n of America (1895)
Historical Note
Address unknown in 1998.

Jewish Music Council (1944)
Historical Note
Organization inactive in 1996.

Jewish Social Service Professionals Ass'n (1965)
3086 State Hwy. 27, Suite 11
P.O. 248
Kendall Park, NJ   08824-0148
Tel: (908)828-0909   *Fax:* (908)828-0493
Members: 300 individuals
Staff: 1
Annual Budget: $10-25,000
President: Alan Goodman
Historical Note
Established in 1964 as the Nat'l Ass'n of Jewish Family, Children's and Health Services. Known as Nat'l Ass'n of Jewish Family, Children's and Health Professionals until 1987. Membership: $25-100/year (individual).
Publications:
JSSPA Update. irreg.
Our JSSPA Connection Newsletter. tri-a.
Meetings/Conferences:
Annual Meetings: May

Jewish Teachers Ass'n-Morim (1924)
45 East 33rd. St., Suite 604
New York, NY   10016
Tel: (212)684-0556
Members: 15,000 individuals
Annual Budget: $25-50,000
Staff Assoc.: Dawny David
Historical Note
Jewish teachers in public and private schools. Has no paid staff.
Publications:
Morim Bulletin. q.
Meetings/Conferences:
Annual Meetings: Always New York, NY

Jockey Club (1894)
40 E. 52nd St., 15th Floor
New York, NY   10022
Tel: (212)371-5970   *Fax:* (212)371-6123
Toll Free: (800)444 - 8521
Web Site: http://www.jockeyclub.com
Members: 100 individuals
Staff: 14
Chairman: Hans Stahl
Historical Note
A service organization to the racing industry which encourages the development of thoroughbred horses, establishes regulations governing them and sets the foundation for rules adopted by all racing states. Members are individual owners/breeders and others connected with the racing industry.

Publications:
The American Stud Book. irreg.

Meetings/Conferences:
Annual Meetings: Quarterly Meetings Held.

Jockeys' Guild (1940)
PO Box 250
Lexington, KY 40588-0250
Tel: (606)259-3211   Fax: (606)252-0938
Members: 1,065 individuals
Staff: 13
Annual Budget: $1-2,000,000
Nat'l Manager/Secretary: John Giovanni

Historical Note
Established as the Jockey's Community Fund and Guild, it assumed
its present name in 1946. Members are licensed flat riding jockeys.
Major thrust is to offer financial aid to needy members.

Publications:
Jockey News. bi-m.

Meetings/Conferences:
Annual Meetings: First week in December

Joint Council of Allergy, Asthma and Immunology (1975)
50 N. Brockway St. #3-3
Palatine, IL 60067
Tel: (847)934-1918   Fax: (847)934-1820
Members: 2 organizations
Annual Budget: $250-500,000
Exec. Director: Joseph J. Lotharius

Historical Note
The political affairs arm for the two major national allergy
organizations: the American Academy of Allergy, Asthma &
Immunology and the American College of Allergy, Asthma &
Immunology. Membership: $120/year.

Publications:
JCAAI Reports. q.

Meetings/Conferences:
1999 – Chicago, IL

Joint Electron Device Engineering Council (1941)
2500 Wilson Blvd.
Arlington, VA 22201
Tel: (703)907-7558   Fax: (703)907-7583
Web Site: http://www.jedec.org
Members: 300 companies
Staff: 6
Annual Budget: $1-2,000,000
Contact: Ingrid Taylor

Historical Note
Affiliated with the Electronic Industries Ass'n. Manufacturers of
solid state products. Membership: $3,000-6,000/year.

Publications:
JEDEC Engineering Publications.

Meetings/Conferences:
Semi-annual Meetings: Spring and Fall

Journalism Education Ass'n (1924)
Kansas State University
103 Kedzie Hall
Manhattan, KS 66506-1501
Tel: (785)532-5532   Fax: (785)532-5484
Web Site: http://www.jea.org
Members: 1,900 individuals
Staff: 2
Annual Budget: $250-500,000
Exec. Director: Linda S. Puntney

Historical Note
Established as Nat'l Ass'n of Journalism Directors in 1924, it
became a division of Nat'l Education Ass'n in 1937; it has since
severed this tie, and in 1963 assumed its present name. Members
are principally secondary school journalism teachers and advisers.
Membership: $35/year (individual); $40/year (institution).

Publications:
Communication: Journalism Education Today. q. adv.
Newswire. 3/year. adv.

Meetings/Conferences:
Semi-annual Meetings: April and November/3,000-3,500
1999 – Albuquerque, NM/April 8-11
1999 – Atlanta, GA/Nov. 18-21
2000 – Anaheim, CA/April 6-9
2000 – Kansas City, MO/Nov. 1-4
2001 – San Francisco, CA/April 4-8
2001 – Boston, MA/Nov. 1-4

Judge Advocates Ass'n (1943)
6800 Chapins Road
Bloomsburg, PA 17185
Tel: (717)752-2027   Fax: (717)752-2097
E-Mail: Jaassn@sunlink.net
Members: 800 individuals
Staff: 1
Annual Budget: $25-50,000
Exec. Director: Col. Eileen M. Albertson, USMC(Ret.)

Historical Note
Members are lawyers who serve or have served in the Armed Forces
or who practice before the U.S. Court of Appeals for the Armed
Forces. Fosters the development of an efficient military legal and
judicial system. Membership: $40/year.

Publications:
The Military Advocate. q.

Meetings/Conferences:
Annual Meetings: With the American Bar Ass'n
1999 – Atlanta, GA
2000 – London, England

Justice Research and Statistics Ass'n (1974)
777 North Capitol St., N.E., Suite 801

Washington, DC 20001
Tel: (202)842-9330   Fax: (202)842-9329
E-Mail: cjinfo@jrsa.org
Web Site: www.jrsa.org
Members: 200 individuals
Staff: 4
Annual Budget: $1-2,000,000
Exec. Director: Joan C. Weiss
Assistant Director, Information Services: Karen F. Maline
Meeting Coordinator: Charleen Cook
Director of Training and Technical Assistance: James Zepp
Asst. Director for Special Projects: Kellie Dressler
Senior Research Associate: Stan Orchowsky, Ph.D.

Historical Note
Funded primarily from Justice Department grants, JRSA members
are directors of state criminal justice statistics analysis centers and
individuals engaged in applied statistical analysis in criminal justice
agencies and academia. Purpose is to foster standardization and
promote the exchange of criminal justice statistics in the states, to
promote multi-state research, and to provide training. Membership:
$60/year (individual), $300/year (organization), $35/year
(student).

Publications:
Directory of Criminal Justice Issues in the States. a.
JRSA Forum. q.

Meetings/Conferences:

Jute Carpet Backing Council (1959)
Drawer 8
322 Davis Ave.
Dayton, OH 45401
Tel: (937)476-8272   Fax: (937)258-0029
Members: 7 companies
Annual Budget: under $10,000
Secretary: Susan Spiegel

Historical Note
Has no paid officers. Members are importers of jute carpet
backings; purpose is to promote their product for use by domestic
carpet mills in the manufacturing of tufted carpeting. Membership:
$125/year, (importer members).

Meetings/Conferences:
Annual Meetings: November in New York, NY at 30 Rockefeller
   Plaza
1999 – Amelia Island, FL

Juvenile Products Manufacturers Ass'n (1962)
236 Rte. 38 West, Suite 100
Moorestown, NJ 08057
Tel: (609)231-8500   Fax: (609)231-4664
E-Mail: jpma@ahint.com
Web Site: www.jpma.org
Members: 250 companies
Staff: 7
Annual Budget: $1-2,000,000
Exec. V. President: Robert Waller, Jr.
Director, Public Relations: Kathy Baier
Director of Meetings: Karen Feder
Director of Trade Shows & Conventions: Ruthann Little
Director, Member Services: Kandi Mell

Historical Note
Members are makers of baby furniture, carriages and related
products.

Publications:
Connections. q.

Meetings/Conferences:
Annual Meetings: Early Spring

JWB Jewish Chaplains Council (1946)
15 East 26th St., 10th Floor
New York, NY 10010-1579
Tel: (212)532-4949   Fax: (212)481-4174
Members: 400 individuals
Annual Budget: under $10,000
Exec. Director: Rabbi David Lapp

Historical Note
Members are Jewish chaplains in the Army, Air Force, and Veterans
Administration. Formerly Ass'n of Jewish Chaplins of the Armed
Forces. Has no paid officers or full-time staff. Membership:
$10/year.

Publications:
CHAPLINES Newsletter. q.

Meetings/Conferences:
Annual Meetings: January-February
1999 – Ft. Belvoir, VA

Kamut Ass'n of North America (1990)
295 Distribution St.
San Marcos, CA 92069
Tel: (760)752-5234   Fax: (760)752-1322
Members: 45 individuals
Staff: 1
Annual Budget: $25-50,000
Exec. V. President: Bob Andersen

Historical Note
KANA members are growers, processors and distributors of kamut
grain.

Publications:
Golden Kernel. q.

Meetings/Conferences:

Kappa Delta Epsilon (1933)
2561 Rocky Ridge Rd.
Birmingham, AL 35243-4442
Tel: (205)822-4106
Members: 38,000 individuals
Staff: 1
Annual Budget: $50-100,000
Nat'l Exec. Director: Dr. Frances Tunnell Carter

Historical Note
An honorary professional educational fraternity founded in
Washington, DC, March 25, 1933. KDE recognizes through its
membership outstanding students preparing to enter the teaching
profession and those actively engaged in teaching or related
professions. Membership: $10/year, plus $25 initiation fee.

Publications:
The Current. 3/year.

Meetings/Conferences:
Biennial National Meeting: odd-numbered years
1999 – Baltimore, MD

Kappa Delta Pi (1911)
1601 W. State St.
P.O. Box A
West Lafayette, IN 47906-0576
Tel: (765)743-1705   Fax: (765)743-2202
Toll Free: (800)284 - 3167
Members: 60,000 individuals, 540 chapters
Staff: 14
Annual Budget: $2-5,000,000
Exec. Director: Michael P. Wolfe

Historical Note
Educational honor society. Membership: $28/year.

Publications:
Educational Forum. q. adv.
Kappa Delta Pi Record. q. adv.
New Teacher Advocate. q. adv.

Meetings/Conferences:
Biennial Meetings: Odd-numbered Years

Kappa Kappa Iota (1921)
1875 East 15th St.
Tulsa, OK 74104-4610
Tel: (918)744-0389   Fax: (918)744-0389
Members: 8,800 individuals
Staff: 2
Annual Budget: $100-250,000
Exec. Director: Pat Fluegel

Historical Note
Established in Stillwater, OK, Kappa Kappa Iota is an organization
formed to promote the advancement of education by providing an
effective network for the exchange of education and teaching
practices by educators. Membership: $14 plus state and local
dues/year (individual).

Publications:
Kappa Profile. q.

Meetings/Conferences:
Annual Meetings: June/100
2000 – Houston, TX(Marriott)/June 19-26

Kappa Psi Pharmaceutical Fraternity (1879)
P.O. Box 26901
Oklahoma City, OK 73190
Tel: (405)271-6942   Fax: (405)271-3830
E-Mail: robert-magarian@ouhsc.edu
Members: 56,000 individuals
Staff: 2
Annual Budget: $100-250,000
Exec. Director: Robert A. Magarian, Ph.D.

Historical Note
Founded at Russell Military Academy, New Haven, CT. Kappa Psi is
a professional fraternity in pharmacy. Street address: Central Office,
College of Pharmacy, University of Oklahoma Health Sciences
Center, 1110 N. Stonewall, Oklahoma City, OK 73117-1223.
Membership: $35/year (individual).

Publications:
The Mask. q. adv.

Meetings/Conferences:
Biennial Meetings: August (odd years)
1999 – Kalispell, MT

Karaoke Internat'l Sing-Along Ass'n
Historical Note
Address unknown in 1997.

Kart Marketing Ass'n of America
Historical Note
Organization defunct in 1994.

Keramos Fraternity (1902)
2226 Daley Dr.
Longmont, CO 80501-1300
Tel: (303)702-1672   Fax: (303)702-1682
E-Mail: pmanderson@nrcorp.com
Members: 8,000 individuals
Annual Budget: under $10,000
General Secretary: Paul M. Anderson

Historical Note
A professional fraternity of ceramic engineers. Has no paid officers
or full-time staff. Membership: $10/year (individual).

Publications:
Keragram. q.

Meetings/Conferences:
Annual Meetings: Spring
1999 – Indianapolis, IN/Apr. 24-28

Kerato-Refractive Soc. (1979)
P.O. Box 796728
Dallas, TX 75379-6728
Tel: (972)601-5750   Fax: (972)713-9722
Members: 2,000 individuals
Exec. Secretary: Ronald A. Schacher, M.D.

Historical Note
KRS members are ophthamologists and other professionals
interested in keratorefractive surgical techniques.

Publications:
Newsletter. semi-a.
Meetings/Conferences:

Keyboard Teachers Ass'n Internat'l *(1963)*
361 Pin Oak Lane
Westbury, NY 11590-1941
Tel: (516)333-3236   *Fax:* (516)997-9531
Web Site: http://www.516Web.com/Music/Ktai
Members: 250 individuals
Annual Budget: under $10,000
President: Albert DeVito, Ph.D.

Historical Note
Formerly (1979) Nat'l Ass'n of Organ Teachers, Inc. and (1986) Internat'l Ass'n of Organ Teachers USA. Sponsors the Nat'l Soc. of Student Keyboardists. Membership: $25/year (individual); variable fee for organizations.

Publications:
The Keyboard Teacher. q.
Meetings/Conferences:
Annual Meetings: Summer

Kitchen Cabinet Manufacturers Ass'n *(1955)*
1899 Preston White Drive
Reston, VA 20191-5435
Tel: (703)264-1690   *Fax:* (703)620-6530
E-Mail: dtitus@kcma.org
Web Site: http://www.kcma.org
Members: 360 manufacturers
Staff: 5
Annual Budget: $500-1,000,000
Exec. V. President: C. Richard Titus
Director of Member Services: Janet Titus

Historical Note
Formerly Nat'l Institute of Wood Kitchen Cabinets. Became the Nat'l Kitchen Cabinet Ass'n in 1962. Assumed its present name in 1990. Members are manufacturers of assembled prefinished kitchen cabinets. Absorbed the Decorative Laminate Products Ass'n in 1995. Membership: $535/year (minimum, based on member company's sales volume).

Publications:
Directory of Certified Cabinet Manufacturers. a.

Meetings/Conferences:
Annual Meetings: May
1999 – Williamsburg, VA(Williamsburg Hotel)/April 25-28

Kite Trade Ass'n Internat'l *(1983)*
P.O. Box 115
Rose Lodge, OR 97372-0115
Tel: (541)994-3453   *Fax:* (541)994-3459
E-Mail: info@kitetrade.org
Web Site: kitetrade.org
Members: 300 companies
Staff: 3
Annual Budget: $100-250,000
Exec. Director: Maggie Vohs, CAE

Historical Note
Membership: $75-450/year (organization/company).

Publications:
Directory. a.
Tradewinds. q. adv.

Meetings/Conferences:
Annual Meetings: January
1999 – Clearwater, FL(Harborview Center)

Knitted Textile Ass'n *(1965)*
386 Park Avenue South, 9th Floor
New York, NY 10016
Tel: (212)689-3807   *Fax:* (212)889-6160
E-Mail: kta386@aol.com
Web Site: http://www.kta-usa.org
Members: 165 companies
Staff: 3
Annual Budget: $250-500,000
Exec. Director: Peter Adelman

Historical Note
Established as the Knitted Fabric Group, it assumed its present name in 1971. Affiliated with the American Fiber, Textile & Apparel Coalition. Members are makers of knitted fabrics of all types, and their suppliers. Membership: $500/year minimum (company).

Publications:
Resources Guide. q.

Meetings/Conferences:
1999 – /March 18-21

Knitting Guild of America *(1984)*
Box 1606
Knoxville, TN 37901-1606
Tel: (423)524-2401   *Fax:* (423)524-8677
Toll Free: (800)274 - 6034
E-Mail: tkga@tkga.com
Web Site: www.tkga.com
Members: 10,000 individuals
Staff: 5
Annual Budget: $500-1,000,000
President: Carol Wigginton
Meeting Planner: Sandy Reeves
Membership Services: Mae Archer

Historical Note
Provides a source for communication and education to those persons wishing to advance the quality of workmanship and creativity in their knitting. Membership: $23/year.

Publications:
Cast On. 5/year. adv.

Meetings/Conferences:
Annual Meetings: Spring
1999 – San Diego, CA(Town & Country)/March 16-22/500

Knitwear Employers Ass'n *(1959)*
75 Livingston St.
Brooklyn, NY 11201
Tel: (718)875-2300
Members: 12 companies
Staff: 1
Annual Budget: under $10,000
General Counsel: Leonard Brodsky

Historical Note
Major purpose is labor negotiations. Membership: $600/year.

Meetings/Conferences:
Annual Meetings: None held.

Label Packaging Suppliers Council
4509 Willet Drive
Annandale, VA 22003
Tel: (703)323-1790   *Fax:* (703)425-7462
E-Mail: 103006.643@compuserve.com
Web Site: www.lpsc.com
Members: 80 individuals
Staff: 1

Meetings/Conferences:
1999 – Phoenix, AZ(The Wigwam)/65

Label Printing Industries of America *(1976)*
100 Daingerfield Road
Alexandria, VA 22314
Tel: (703)519-8122   *Fax:* (703)548-3227
E-Mail: lpia@printing.org
Members: 40 companies
Staff: 1
Annual Budget: $100-250,000
Exec. Director: Frank S. Wilton

Historical Note
A special industry section of Printing Industries of America. Members are companies printing labels to be attached to food and consumer products. Membership: $600-3,000/year.

Publications:
Label Industry Facts and Guidelines. irreg.
Labelgram. 6/year.

Meetings/Conferences:
Semi-Annual Meetings: Spring and Fall
1999 – Toronto, Canada(Royal York)

Laboratory Animal Management Ass'n *(1984)*
P.O. Box 1744
Silver Spring, MD 20902
Tel: (765)494-7592   *Fax:* (765)494-0781
Members: 550 individuals
Annual Budget: under $10,000
President: Fred Douglas

Historical Note
Formerly the Laboratory Animal Manager Ass'n. LAMA members are managers of laboratory animal facilities. Has no paid officers or full-time staff.

Publications:
LAMA Lines. bi-m. adv.
Membership Directory. a.
The LAMA Review. q.

Laboratory Products Ass'n *(1988)*
225 Reinekers Lane, Suite 625
Alexandria, VA 22314
Tel: (703)836-1360   *Fax:* (703)836-6644
E-Mail: membershipservice@lpanet.org
Web Site: http://www.lpanet.org
Members: 125 companies
Staff: 3
Annual Budget: $500-1,000,000
Exec. Director: William C. Strackbein
Manager, Meeting/Member Services: Katherine French Carter

Historical Note
Originally part of the Scientific Apparatus Makers Ass'n (SAMA) which was founded in 1914 and reorganized in 1988.

Meetings/Conferences:
Semi-annual Meetings: Spring/125 and Fall/125
1999 – Boston, MA(Royal Sonesta)/April 19-20
1999 – Naples, FL(Ritz Carlton)/Nov. 7-9

Laborers' Internat'l Union of North America *(1903)*
905 16th St., N.W.
Washington, DC 20006-1765
Tel: (202)737-8320   *Fax:* (202)737-2754
Web Site: www.liuna.org
Members: 750,000 individuals
Staff: 150
Annual Budget: $50-100,000,000
General President: Arthur A. Coia
Director, Public Affairs: Linda Fisher
Legislative and Political Director: Daniel J. Kaniewski
Director, Research & Labor: Greg Giebel
Director, Laborers-AGC Ed. & Training Trust Fund: James M. Warren
Exec. Director/Laborers-Employers Cooperation-Education Trust: Chris Engquist
Comptroller: Ralph Adams
Director, Jurisdiction: Steve Hammond
General Counsel: Michael S. Bearse
Exec. Dir./Laborers Health & Safety Fund: Brian McQuade
Director, Organizing: Mason Warren
Director, International Affairs: Michael D. Boggs
Director, Construction Maintenance & Service Trades: Jim Thomas
Chief of Staff: Terence M. O'Sullivan
Asst. to the General President and V. President: Carl E. Booker

Historical Note
Organized in Washington DC April 13, 1903 as the International Hod Carriers and Building Laborers' Union of America and chartered by the AFL-CIO. Reflecting the expanding scope of its organizing it changed its name twice in 1912, first to the

International Hod Carriers' and Common Laborers' Union of America and next to the International Hod Carriers', Building and Common Laborers' Union of America. Merged in 1918 with the Compressed Air and Foundation Workers' International Union (founded in 1904) and in 1929 with the Tunnel and Subway Constructors' International Union (founded in 1910). Adopted its present name September 20, 1965. Has an annual budget of approximately $57.4 million. Sponsors and supports the Laborers' Political League, Laborers' Health & Safety Fund on North America, Laborers-Employers Cooperation and Education Trust, Laborers-ACG-Education and Training Fund.

Publications:
The Laborer. q.

Meetings/Conferences:
Quinquennial Conventions: Fall

Lacrosse USA *(1935)*
113 W. University Pkwy.
Baltimore, MD 21210
Tel: (410)235-6882   *Fax:* (410)366-6735
E-Mail: info@lacrosse.org
Web Site: http://www.lacrosse.org
Members: 1,200 individuals
Annual Budget: $25-50,000
Secretary-Treasurer: Jody Martin

Historical Note
Formerly (1997) United States Lacrosse Coaches Ass'n. Promotes the sport of lacrosse on all levels through coaching clinics, clinic notes, award presentation and grants.

Publications:
Lacrosse Magazine. 9/year.

Meetings/Conferences:

Ladies Apparel Contractors Ass'n *(1933)*
450 Seventh Ave., Suite 1009
New York, NY 10123
Tel: (212)564-6161   *Fax:* (212)564-6166
Members: 150 companies
Staff: 2
Annual Budget: $100-250,000
Exec. Director: Sidney Reiff

Historical Note
Founded as the United Popular Dress Manufacturers Ass'n. Formerly (1977) the Popular Price Dress Contractors Ass'n, Inc. Membership is concentrated in the New York, New Jersey and Connecticut area.

Meetings/Conferences:
Annual Meetings: Spring in New York, NY with the Sportswear Apparel Ass'n.

Ladies Professional Golf Ass'n *(1950)*
100 International Golf Drive
Daytona Beach, FL 32124
Tel: (904)274-6200   *Fax:* (904)274-1099
Web Site: http://www.lpga.com
Members: 1,200 professional golfers
Staff: 60
Annual Budget: $25-50,000,000
Commissioner: Jim Ritts
Director of Communications: Leslie King
Director, Education: Betsy Clark, Ph.D.
Director, Finance/Administration: Terri McCracken
V. President of Business Affairs: Ty M. Votaw
Deputy Commissioner: Jim Webb

Historical Note
The LPGA is the governing body for women's professional golf in the United States. In its 47th season, the LPGA is expected to play an international schedule of approximately 43 golf tournaments for a combined purse exceeding $32.5 million. Separated into two divisions: teaching and tournament professionals.

Publications:
Annual Media Guide. a. adv.
LPGA Golf. a. adv.
Pro Shop Merchandise Catalogue.

Meetings/Conferences:
Annual Meetings: Winter

Lake Carriers' Ass'n *(1892)*
915 Rockefeller Bldg.
614 Superior Ave. West
Cleveland, OH 44113-1383
Tel: (216)621-1107   *Fax:* (216)241-8262
Members: 11 companies
Staff: 5
Annual Budget: $250-500,000
President: George J. Ryan
Communications Director: Glen Nekvasil
V. President, Operations: Richard W. Harkins
Secretary-Treasurer: Carol Ann Lane

Historical Note
Established in 1892 as the successor organization to Cleveland Vessel Owners Ass'n (1880) and Lake Carriers' Ass'n of Buffalo (1885). Members are Great Lakes vessel operators engaged in transportation of iron ore, coal, grain, limestone, cement and petroleum products.

Publications:
Annual Report. a.

Meetings/Conferences:
Annual Meetings: With Canadian Shipowners Ass'n
1999 – Tampa, FL(Saddlebrook Resort)/Feb. 7-9

Lamaze International *(1960)*
1200 19th St., N.W., Suite 300
Washington, DC 20036
Tel: (202)857-1128   *Fax:* (202)223-4579
Toll Free: (800)368 - 4404
Web Site: www.lamaze.childbirth.com
Members: 4,600 individuals
Staff: 4

Annual Budget: $500-1,000,000
Exec. Director: Linda L. Harmon, MPH
Manager, Convention Services: Leigh McMillan
Education Coordinator: Crystal Huegle
Director of Membership Services: Chrystal Farmer
Certification Coordinator: Dawn Schultz

Historical Note
Formerly (1998) the American Society for Psychoprophylaxis in Obstetrics. Founded and incorporated in New York in 1960. Begun as a medical society, the membership now includes childbirth educators, parents and physicians. Promotes prepared childbirth by the Lamaze method. Membership: $40/year (parent), $95/year (professional), $95/year (phycisian/nurse midwife).

Publications:
GENESIS. q.
The Journal of Perinatal Education. q. adv.

Meetings/Conferences:
Annual Meetings: Fall
1999 – Canada, Toronto/Oct. 8-10

Lambda Alpha Epsilon *(1937)*

Historical Note
See American Criminal Justice Association.

Lambda Kappa Sigma *(1913)*
2284 Diamond Point Dr.
Alpena, MI   49707-4617
Tel: (517)356-8797
Toll Free: (800)557 - 1913
E-Mail: lks@iks.org
Members: 18,000 individuals
Staff: 3
Annual Budget: $100-250,000
Exec. Director: Joan Rogala, CAE

Historical Note
Lambda Kappa Sigma promotes the profession of pharmacy among women, promoting the advancement of women in the profession and contributing to philanthropic endeavors of interest to its members. Membership: $40/year (students); $70/year (alumni).

Publications:
Blue & Gold Triangle. 3/yr. adv.

Meetings/Conferences:
Biennial Meetings: Summer

Lambda Omicron Gamma Medical Society *(1924)*
636 Argyle Road
Wynnewood, PA   19096
Tel: (610)649-8086
Members: 1,200 individuals
Staff: 1
Annual Budget: $10-25,000
Exec. Secretary: Lisa Michell

Historical Note
Formerly Lambda Omicron Gamma Nat'l Fraternity. Professional fraternity in osteopathy, committed to providing a lifetime experience that will foster the development, skills, and attitudes necessary to be a complete, caring osteopathic physician through the enhancement of personal and professional growth and responsibility. Membership: $75/year (individual).

Publications:
LOG Newsletter. 3/yr. adv.
LOG Yearbook. a. adv.

Meetings/Conferences:
Annual Meetings: Spring

Laminating Materials Ass'n *(1985)*
116 Lawrence St.
Hillsdale, NJ   07642-2730
Tel: (201)664-2700   *Fax:* (201)666-5665
E-Mail: info@LMA.org
Web Site: http://www.LMA.org
Members: 150 companies
Staff: 1
Annual Budget: $50-100,000
Exec. Director: George M. Carter

Historical Note
Represents manufacturers and importers who produce one or more of six decorative surfacing materials and edge banding to be use on wood substances. Collects production and import statistics for the six materials in the United States and Canada. Membership: $500/year.

Publications:
Annual Statistical Report.
Glossary of Terms.
Source of Supply Directory. q.

Meetings/Conferences:
Annual Meetings: Fall Santa Fe, NM(Hilton)Nov. 9-11/100 New Orleans, LA/Nov. 8-10/100
1999 – Louisville, KY(Kentucky Fair Center)
2000 – Atlanta, GA(Atlanta Airport Hilton & Towers)/Feb. 7-8

Laminators Safety Glass Ass'n *(1977)*
2945 S.W. Wanamaker Dr., Suite A
Topeka, KS   66614-5321
Tel: (913)266-7014   *Fax:* (913)266-0272
Members: 22 companies
Staff: 8
Annual Budget: $50-100,000
Exec. V. President: William J. Birch

Historical Note
Makers or distribution of flat laminated safety glass.

Publications:
Glass Reflections. q.
Membership Roster. bien.

Meetings/Conferences:
Semi-Annual Meetings: Spring and Fall

Land Mobile Communications Council *(1967)*

1110 N. Glebe Road, Suite 500
Arlington, VA   22201
Tel: (703)528-5115
Members: 22 organizations
Staff: 1
Annual Budget: $100-250,000
Secretary-Treasurer: Mark E. Crosby

Historical Note
Members are organizations representing users of mobile radio communication apparatus such as railroads, business, trucking companies and public safety services. Wishes to insure the reservation of a sufficient part of the radio spectrum to meet their requirements. Has no paid staff or permanent headquarters. The above address is the law firm of Keller & Heckman.

Meetings/Conferences:
Annual Meetings: Spring in Washington, DC

Land Trust Alliance *(1982)*
1319 F St., N.W., Suite 501
Washington, DC   20004-1106
Tel: (202)638-4725   *Fax:* (202)638-4730
Web Site: http://www.lta.org
Members: 2,057 organizations and individuals
Staff: 27
Annual Budget: $1-2,000,000
President: Jean Hocker
Director, Communications: Martha Nudel
Director, Public Policy: Russell Shay
Director, Training and Conferences: Andrea Freeman
V. President, Administration: Phil Jones
V. President, Development: John Chappell
Manager, Info. Technology: Xantippe Humphries

Historical Note
Formerly (1991) Land Trust Exchange. Members are local and regional non-profit land conservation groups and other concerned organizations and individuals. Membership: $35-1,000/year (individual); $150-1,250/year (organization).

Publications:
Exchange. q.
Landscape. q. adv.
Nat'l Directory of Conservation Land Trusts.

Landscape Nursery Council *(1952)*

Historical Note
Address unknown in 1996.

Laser and Electro-Optics Manufacturers' Ass'n *(1985)*
123 Kent Rd.
Pacifica, CA   94044-3923
Tel: (650)738-1492   *Fax:* (650)738-1592
Web Site: http://www.leoma.com
Staff: 1
Exec. Director: C. Breck Hitz

Historical Note
Formerly (1991) Laser Ass'n of America. Members are companies with an interest in laser technology.

Publications:
Newsletter. irreg.

Laser Disc Ass'n

Historical Note
Became (1997) Optical Video Disc Ass'n.

Laser Institute of America *(1968)*
12424 Research Pkwy., Suite 125
Orlando, FL   33826
Tel: (407)380-1553   *Fax:* (407)380-5588
Toll Free: (800)345 - 2737
Web Site: http://www.laserinstitute.org
Members: 1,657 individuals, 186 companies
Staff: 12
Annual Budget: $1-2,000,000
Exec. Director: Peter M. Baker
Manager, Marketing: Richard Greene
Meetings Coordinator: Ms. Daryl Flynn
Accounting Coordinator: Jeannette Gabay
Membership Coordinator: Karen Wente

Historical Note
Established in February 1968 in California as the Laser Industry Ass'n by a group of laser pioneers, inventors, and industry leaders. The name was changed to Laser Institute of America in 1972. The Institute is dedicated to fosering lasers, laser applications and laser safety worldwide as well as sponsoring educational and training courses, conferences and symposia on laser related information. Membership: $60/year (individual); $550/year (corporation); $350/year (institution).

Publications:
ANSI 2136 Series of Laser Safety Standards. irreg.
ICALEO Proceedings.
Journal of Laser Applications. 6 times/year. adv.
Members' Newsletter. bi-m. adv.
Membership Directory. a. adv.

Meetings/Conferences:
Annual Meetings: Fall
1999 – San Diego, CA(Catamaran Resort)/Nov. 15-18/400
2000 – Detroit, MI(Hyatt Dearborn)/Oct. 8-11/600

Lasers and Electro-Optics Soc. *(1964)*

Historical Note
A technical society of Institute of Electrcal and Electronics Engineers, which provides administrative support.

Latex Advisors Ass'n *(1989)*
27127 Valle Arroyo
Suite 1902
San Juan Capistrano, CA   92693
Tel: (949)487-1772   *Fax:* (949)487-7271
Toll Free: (877)877 - 8780

Members: 2,100 comapnies
Staff: 3
Annual Budget: $100-250,000
Managing Director: James A. Murphy
Assistant Director: Mike Hammond
Legal Counselor: Ron Nelson

Historical Note
The association merged with Glove Shippers Ass'n (1998).LAA members are manufacturers and distributors of gloves and related medical products. Membership: $500/year.

Publications:
Latex Advisor. q. adv.
Medical and Latex Newsletter.

Meetings/Conferences:
Annual Meetings: Spring
1999 – Long Beach, CA(Hyatt Hotel)/Feb. 2-4/1000

Latin American Management Ass'n *(1973)*
419 New Jersey Ave., S.E.
Washington, DC   20003-4007
Tel: (202)546-3803   *Fax:* (202)546-3807
Members: 500 companies
Annual Budget: $1-2,000,000
President and C.E.O.: Steve Dillenger

Historical Note
Formerly (1990) Latin American Manufacturers Ass'n. LAMA is dedicated to the goal of advancing opportunities for the Hispanic and minority community. Seeks to promote the interests of Hispanic and other minority-owned business firms through marketing and procurement information, education and training activities, publication, advocacy initiatives, outreach programs and electronic bulletin board services. Members cover the entire business spectrum, from manufacturing and high technology firms to service and construction. Membership: $100-10,000/year.

Publications:
Watch on Washington Newsletter. m. adv.

Meetings/Conferences:
Annual Meetings: usually Washington, DC/Fall
1999 – Washington, DC

Latin American Studies Ass'n *(1966)*
946 William Pitt Union
Univ. of Pittsburgh
Pittsburgh, PA   15260
Tel: (412)648-7929   *Fax:* (412)624-7145
E-Mail: LASA + @PITT.EDU
Web Site: http://www.pitt.edu/ ~ lasa/
Members: 4,800 individuals, 100 institutions
Staff: 4
Annual Budget: $100-250,000
Exec. Director: Reid Reading

Historical Note
Members are both teachers and scholars concerned with the promotion of Latin American Studies. Membership: $30-78/year, based on income (individual), $150/year (non-profit organizazation); $250/year (for-profit organization).

Publications:
LASA Forum. q. adv.
Latin American Research Review. 3/yr. adv.

Meetings/Conferences:
Annual Meetings: Every 18 months
2000 – Miami, FL(Hyatt Regency)

Latin Business Ass'n *(1976)*
5400 E. Olympic Blvd., Suite 130
Los Angeles, CA   90022
Tel: (323)721-4000   *Fax:* (323)722-5050
Toll Free: (800)371 - 4522
E-Mail: lba@worldnet.att.net
Web Site: www.lbausa.com
Members: 2,000 individuals
Exec. Director: Adela Soriano

Publications:
LBA Business Journal. m.

Latin Chamber of Commerce of U.S.A. *(1965)*
P.O. Box 350824
1417 W. Flagler
Miami, FL   33135
Tel: (305)642-3870   *Fax:* (305)642-0653
Members: 2,500 businesses
Staff: 35
Annual Budget: $500-1,000,000
President: Luis Sabines

Historical Note
Formerly (1990) Latin Chamber of Commerce.

Publications:
Members Directory. bien.
Revista Camacol. m.

Meetings/Conferences:
Annual Meetings: always last week in April

Laundry and Dry Cleaning Internat'l Union *(1959)*
307 Fourth Ave., Suite 405
Pittsburgh, PA   15222
Tel: (412)471-4829
E-Mail: ldciu@aol.com
Members: 17,500 individuals
Staff: 15
Annual Budget: $250-500,000
President: Mary O'Brien

Historical Note
Organized in Washington May 12, 1959 by locals formerly members of the Laundry, Dry Cleaning and Dye House Workers' International Union (which had been expelled from the AFL-CIO in December, 1957). Chartered by the AFL-CIO. Sponsors and supports the League of Voter Education Political Action Committee.

Meetings/Conferences:
Quinquennial Conventions: (1997)

Law and Society Ass'n *(1964)*
Hampshire House, Box 33615
University of Massachusetts
Amherst, MA   01003-3615
Tel: (413)545-4617   *Fax:* (413)545-1640
E-Mail: lsa@legal.umass.edu
Web Site: http://www.lawandsociety.org
Members: 1,500 individuals
Staff: 2
Annual Budget: $100-250,000
Exec. Officer: Ronald M. Pipkin
Exec. Officer: Ronald M. Pipkin
Administrative Coordinator: Lisa Ganter
Membership Coordinator: Judy Rose
Historical Note
Members are social science and legal professionals and others interested in exploring the relationships between law and society. Membership: $25-110/year (individual); $124/year (organization/company).
Publications:
Law and Society Newsletter. q.
Law and Society Review. q. adv.
Meetings/Conferences:
Annual Meetings: Spring
1999 – Chicago, IL(Renaissance)/May 27-30/900
2000 – Miami Beach, FL(Loews)/May 25-29/1200

Law Firm Services Ass'n *(1994)*
111 E. Wacker Dr., Suite 990
Chicago, IL   60601
Tel: (312)729-9900   *Fax:* (312)729-9800
Toll Free: (800)869 - 0491
E-Mail: info@pencormazur.com
Web Site: http://www.cpaselect.com/lfsa
Members: 26 firms
Staff: 10
Director, Communications: Michelle Durham
Historical Note
LFSA is an association of CPA firms that provide services to law firms beyond traditional compliance work. Members are accepted on a territorial exclusive bases with a limit of one member in most metropolitan statistical areas.
Publications:
Law Firm Management Survey Report (Client Newsletter).
Lawyer's Business Journal Client Newsletter. q.
Members Bulletin. q.
Meetings/Conferences:
1999 – New Orleans, LA/Jan. 7-8
1999 – Las Vegas, NV/June 23-25

Lawn and Garden Dealers' Ass'n *(1985)*
P.O. Box 700868
Tulsa, OK   74170-0868
Tel: (918)749-1600   *Fax:* (918)749-1718
Toll Free: (800)752 - 5296
E-Mail: LGDA@aol.com
Members: 2,000 companies
Staff: 5
Annual Budget: $500-1,000,000
Exec. Director: Ryan S. Carter
Marketing Director: Lola Conley
Director, Financial Services: Adell T. Nellis
Director, Customer Service: Mollie Steensland
Historical Note
Members are in the professional lawn and garden industry and include lawn equipment dealers, nurseries, small engine repair, and landscape and irrigation companies. Membership fee: $45/year. Street address is 2411 East Skelly, Suite 105, Tulsa, OK, 74105.
Publications:
Lawn & Garden Newsletter. q. adv.
Meetings/Conferences:
Annual Trade Show: always Lexington, KY/last weekend in July

Lawn and Garden Marketing and Distribution Ass'n *(1969)*
1900 Arch St.
Philadelphia, PA   19103-1498
Tel: (215)564-3484   *Fax:* (215)564-2175
E-Mail: assnhqt@netaxs.com
Web Site: http://www.lgmda.org
Members: 300 companies
Staff: 3
Annual Budget: $250-500,000
Exec. Director: John D. McGreevey, Jr.
Historical Note
Founded as Lawn and Garden Distributors Ass'n; became Nat'l Lawn and Garden Distributors Ass'n in 1979, and assumed its current name in 1997. Members are wholesale distributors and manufacturers of lawn and garden supplies. There is also an affiliate classification. Promotes the growth and profitability of the lawn and garden industry through effective and efficient marketing and distribution of products and services. Membership: $300-500/year (depending on classification).
Publications:
Grassroots. q.
Membership Directory. a.
Meetings/Conferences:
Annual Meetings: June/July
1999 – Hilton Head, SC/July 18-21
2000 – San Francisco, CA
2001 – Nashville, TN

Lawn Institute
Historical Note
See Better Lawn and Turf Institute.

Lead Industries Ass'n *(1928)*
13 Main St.,
Sparta, NJ   07871
Tel: (973)726-5323   *Fax:* (973)726-4484
E-Mail: miller@leadinfo.com
Web Site: http://www.leadinfo.com
Members: 61 companies
Staff: 2
Annual Budget: $1-2,000,000
Exec. Director: Jeffrey T. Miller
Historical Note
LIA serves as the marketing and promotional arm and technical information resource for the lead industry in North America.
Publications:
The Newsleader. bi-m.
Meetings/Conferences:
1999 – Washington, DC(The Williard)/March 17-19

Leading Jewelers Guild *(1957)*
2050 South Bundy Drive, Suite 210
Los Angeles, CA   90025
Tel: (310)820-3386   *Fax:* (310)820-3530
Members: 29 companies and 180 stores
Staff: 10
Exec. Director: Joan Reece
Meetings/Conferences:
Semi-annual Meetings: Summer in Los Angeles area and Winter in various locations

Leaf Tobacco Exporters Ass'n *(1939)*
3716 National Drive, Suite 114
Raleigh, NC   27612
Tel: (919)782-5151   *Fax:* (919)781-0915
Members: 45 companies
Staff: 2
Annual Budget: $100-250,000
Exec. V. President: J.T. Bunn
Historical Note
Affiliated with the Tobacco Ass'n of the U.S.
Meetings/Conferences:
Annual Meetings: May, at the Greenbrier in White Sulphur Springs, WV

Leafy Greens Council *(1976)*
33 Pheasant Lane
St. Paul, MN   55127
Tel: (651)484-3321   *Fax:* (651)484-1098
Web Site: http://leafy-greens.org
Members: 100 individuals, 100 companies
Staff: 1
Annual Budget: $25-50,000
Exec. Director: Ray L. Clark, Jr.
Historical Note
Growers, shippers, packers and sellers of spinach, cabbage, lettuce and other fresh leafy green vegetables. Founded in 1976 as the Nat'l Spinach Ass'n. Became the Leafy Greens Council in 1977.
Meetings/Conferences:
Annual Meetings: usually coincides with United Fresh Fruit and Vegetable Ass'n/February
1999 – San Diego, CA

League for Innovation in the Community College *(1968)*
26522 La Alameda Suite 370
Mission Viejo, CA   92691-6330
Tel: (714)367-2884   *Fax:* (714)367-2885
E-Mail: obanion@league.org
Web Site: http://www.league.org
Members: 600 community colleges
Staff: 12
Annual Budget: $500-1,000,000
Exec. Director: Terry O'Banion
Director: Nancy Italia
Dir., Business: Gennie Goodman
Historical Note
A national consortium of 20 districts established to stimulate innovation in community college education. Assists its members in experimenting in teaching, learning, student services and other aspects of community college operation, and in sharing the results of these experiments. Membership: $4,000-6,000/year.
Publications:
Catalyst. bi-a.
Innovator. q.
Leadership Abstracts. m.
League Connections. bi-a.
League Reports. 10/year.
Meetings/Conferences:
1999 – New Orleans, LA/June 20-23
1999 – Chicago, IL/Oct. 20-23

League of Advertising Agencies *(1951)*
Two South End Ave., Suite 4C
New York, NY   10280
Tel: (212)945-4314   *Fax:* (212)945-4992
Members: 90 agencies
Staff: 2
Annual Budget: $50-100,000
Exec. Director: Mary C. Boland
Historical Note
An organization, composed of medium-to-small-sized agencies, whose purpose is to encourage and provide a forum for the exchange of management information and creative ideas among its members through seminars and published material. Membership: $350/year, (organization).
Publications:
Manual of Agency Operations.
Meetings/Conferences:
Monthly Dinner Meetings: except in Summer

League of American Theatres and Producers *(1930)*
226 West 47th St.
New York, NY   10036-1487
Tel: (212)764-1122   *Fax:* (212)719-4389
Web Site: http://www.broadway.org
Members: 420 individuals
Staff: 24
Annual Budget: $1-2,000,000
Exec. Director: Jed Bernstein
Member Svcs./Govt. Affairs: Barbara Janowitz
Legal Counsel: Alan S. Jaffe
Historical Note
The League is a professional trade association of the tax-paying legitimate theatre. Members include producers, theatre owners and operators, and local presenters. Programs include labor relations and negotiations; marketing, economic and media research; urban environment improvement programs; government relations; institutional public relations and promotion; tourism promotion; and presentation with the American Theatre Wing of the Antoinette Perry "Tony" Awards. Membership: $650/year (individual).
Publications:
League Line. bi-m.
Stage Specs. a.
Meetings/Conferences:

League of Federal Recreation Ass'ns *(1960)*
Historical Note
Membership, concentrated in the Washington, DC area, is composed of state, county and federal government employee associations which sponsor recreational and employee benefit activities. Membership: $19/year (associate), $50-150/year (agency).

League of Historic American Theatres *(1976)*
34 Market Place, Suite 320
Baltimore, MD   21202-4034
Tel: (410)659-9533   *Fax:* (410)837-9664
Web Site: http://www.lhat.org
Members: 500 individuals
Staff: 3
Annual Budget: $100-250,000
Exec. Director: Terrance Demas
Program Coordinator: Debra Coffey
Historical Note
Members are historic and restored theatres, firms which specialize in theatre rehabilitation, operation, or other professional services, and individuals interested in historic theatre preservation. Membership: $200-550/year (theatre); $325/year (firm/supplier); $85/year (institution); $75/year (individual); $35/year (student).
Publications:
Conference Program. a. adv.
Membership Directory.
Newsletter. q. adv.
Meetings/Conferences:
1999 – Chicago, IL/July 13-17

League of Resident Theatres *(1965)*
1501 Broadway, Suite 2401
New York, NY   10036
Tel: (212)944-1501   *Fax:* (212)768-0785
Members: 69 theaters
Staff: 2
Counsel: Harry Weintraub
Historical Note
Members are professional resident theatres.
Meetings/Conferences:
Annual Meetings: Spring

Leather Apparel Ass'n *(1990)*
19 West 21st St.
Suite 403
New York, NY   10010
Tel: (212)924-8895   *Fax:* (212)727-1218
Members: 100 companies
Staff: 1
Annual Budget: $250-500,000
Managing Director: Lilli Kasdan
Historical Note
Promote the sale of leather garments through publicity, education, and business support services. Membership fee based on annual gross domestic sales.
Publications:
Member Communique. m.
Meetings/Conferences:
Annual Meetings: October

Leather Industries of America *(1917)*
1000 Thomas Jefferson St., N.W.
Suite 515
Washington, DC   20007
Tel: (202)342-8086   *Fax:* (202)342-9063
E-Mail: lia@erols.com
Members: 250 companies
Staff: 7
Annual Budget: $2-5,000,000
President: Charles S. Myers
Communication Coordinator: Jean Ann Firestone
Exhibition Coordinator: Jane P. Hardwick
Controller: Mary Agnes Gustavson
Historical Note
Formed by a merger of the Nat'l Ass'n of Tanners, the Morocco Manufacturers Nat'l Ass'n and the Patent and Enamelled Leather Manufacturers Ass'n as the Tanners' Council of America; it absorbed the Leather Industries of America in 1975 and assumed this name in 1986. LIA members are U.S. businesses involved in the tanning, finishing, manufacturing or selling of leather. General membership is availble for companies with an interest in the industry. Membership: $1,000-50,000/year.

Publications:
BLC Journal. m.
Dictionary of Leather Terminology. irreg.
Membership Directory. a.
Technical Bulletin. 8/year.
Trade Practices for Proper Packer Cattlehide Delivery. irreg. U. S.

Meetings/Conferences:
Annual Meetings: Fall

Legal Assistant Management Ass'n (1984)
1819 Peachtree St., N.E., Suite 620
Atlanta, GA   30309-1850
Tel: (404)350-7900   Fax: (404)351-3348
Members: 400 individuals
Staff: 2
Annual Budget: $100-250,000
Exec. Director: Michael J. Mazur, Jr.

Historical Note
Organized as an outgrowth of a Steering Committee of the Paralegal Manager's Conference, the LAMA is an association of persons responsible for managerial and administrative duties related to legal assistant personnel. Membership: $150/year (regular), $125/year (associate), $200/year (sustaining).

Publications:
Bibliography.
Compensation and Benefit Survey. a.
Directory of Legal Assistant Managers. a.
LAMA Manager Newsletter. bi-m.
Legal Assistant Utilization Survey. a.

Meetings/Conferences:

Lepidoptera Research Foundation (1962)
9620 Heather Road
Beverly Hills, CA   90210
Tel: (310)274-1052   Fax: (310)275-3290
E-Mail: MATTONI@UCLA.EDU
Members: 700 individuals
President and Editor: Rudolf H.T. Mattoni

Historical Note
Membership, concentrated in the western U.S., consists of professional and amateur lepidopterists. Publishes and disseminates information on the biology of butterflies and moths, as well as conservation issues relevant to lepidoptera.

Publications:
Journal of Research on the Lepidoptera. q.
Newsletter. irreg.

Lepidopterists' Soc. (1947)
Historical Note
Address unknown in 1996; presumed inactive.

Liability Insurance Research Bureau (1990)
3025 Highland Pkwy., Suite 800
Downers Grove, IL   60515-1260
Tel: (847)330-8647   Fax: (847)330-8657
Members: 160 insurance companies
Staff: 6
Annual Budget: $250-500,000
President: Wallace R. Hanson
V. President and Counsel: Paul Dispensa

Historical Note
Spun off from Property Loss Research Bureau. Provides legal research, consulting, and educational services in auto liability and CGL lines. Members are stock and mutual insurance companies.

Publications:
Homeowners Liability, Auto, Commercial and Environmental Law Reviews.

Meetings/Conferences:

Liaison Committee of Cooperating Oil and Gas Ass'ns (1957)
515 Congress Ave., Suite 1910
Austin, TX   78701
Tel: (512)477-4452   Fax: (512)476-8070
Web Site: http://www.energyconnect.com/liason
Members: 25 associations
Annual Budget: under $10,000
Secretary-Treasurer: A. Scott Anderson

Historical Note
The committee was established to facilitate communication among state and regional oil and gas associations.

Meetings/Conferences:
Annual Meetings: July or August

Library Administration and Management Ass'n (1957)
50 E. Huron St.
Chicago, IL   60611-2795
Tel: (312)280-5038   Fax: (312)944-2641
Toll Free: (800)545 - 2433
Web Site: http://www.ala.org/lama
Members: 5,138 individuals
Staff: 4
Annual Budget: $250-500,000
Exec. Director: Karen Muller

Historical Note
Formerly titled the Library Administration Division of the American Library Ass'n; it remains a division of the ALA. Membership (restricted to ALA members): $35-$50/year, based on salary (individual); $15/year (student).

Publications:
Library Administration & Management. q. adv.
Library Buildings Consultant List. bien.

Meetings/Conferences:
Annual Meetings: in conjunction with the American Library Ass'n/Summer
1999 – New Orleans, LA/June 24-July 1
2000 – Chicago, IL/July 6-13

Library and Information Technology Ass'n (1966)
50 East Huron St.
Chicago, IL   60611-2795
Tel: (312)280-4270   Fax: (312)280-3257
E-Mail: lita@ala.org
Web Site: http://www.lita.org
Members: 5,800 individuals
Staff: 4
Annual Budget: $250-500,000
Exec. Director: Jacqueline Mundell

Historical Note
LITA provides its members with a forum to discuss and learn about the development and implementation of information technology in libraries. A division of the American Library Ass'n formerly known as the Information Science and Automation Division, LITA adopted its current name in 1978. Membership: $45/year (individual); $75/year (organization).

Publications:
Information Technology and Libraries. q. adv.

Meetings/Conferences:
Semi-annual Meetings: in conjunction with the American Library Ass'n

Library Binding Institute (1935)
7401 Metro Blvd., Suite 325
Edina, MN   55439-3031
Tel: (612)835-4707   Fax: (612)835-4780
E-Mail: 71035.3504@compuserve.com
Members: 84 individuals, 80 companies
Staff: 2
Annual Budget: $100-250,000
Exec. Director: Sally M. Moyer

Historical Note
Members are firms binding books for libraries, their suppliers and certain libraries with an in-house binding capacity.

Publications:
The New Library Scene. q. adv.

Meetings/Conferences:
Semi-Annual Meetings: Spring and Fall

Library Public Relations Council (1940)
2 Jean Walling Civic Center
East Brunswick, NJ   08816
Tel: (732)390-6950   Fax: (732)390-6869
E-Mail: skarmazin@infolink.org
Web Site: http://www.ssdesign.com/librarypr
Members: 360 individuals
Annual Budget: under $10,000
Membership Chair: Sharon Karmazin

Historical Note
LPRC members are library public relations directors. Membership: $30/year.

Publications:
Membership Directory. a.

Meetings/Conferences:
Annual Meetings: in conjunction with the American Library Ass'n

Licensed Beverage Information Council (1979)
Historical Note
Reported defunct in 1997.

Licensing Executives Soc. (1965)
1800 Diagonal Rd., Suite 280
Alexandria, VA   22314-2840
Tel: (703)836-3106   Fax: (703)836-3107
E-Mail: leshq@aol.com
Web Site: http://www.usa-canada.les.org
Members: 4,500 individuals
Staff: 4
Annual Budget: $2-5,000,000
Administrative Manager: Meg Nagle Stevens

Historical Note
Membership consists of individuals concerned with licensing patents, trademarks, trade secrets, processes and other intellectual property. Membership in the United States and Canada is 3,600. Membership: $135/year (individual).

Publications:
les Nouvelles (Int'l Journal). q.
les Viewpoints (U. S.
Membership Directory. a.

Meetings/Conferences:
1999 – San Antonio, TX(Marriott River Center)/Oct. 24-27/1000
2000 – Toronto, ON, Canada(Sheraton)/Oct. 10-13/1100
2001 – Palm Desert, CA(Marriott's Desert Springs)/Oct. 25-Nov. 4
2002 – Chicago, IL(Sheraton)/Sept. 29-Oct. 2/1300

Licensing Industry Merchandisers' Ass'n (1985)
Historical Note
Became Internat'l Licensing Industry Merchandisers' Ass'n in 1996.

Life Communicators Ass'n (1933)
Historical Note
Address unknown in 1995.

Life Insurers Conference
Historical Note
Became (1997) Life Insurers Council.

Life Insurers Council (1910)
2300 Windy Ridge Pkwy., Suite 600
Atlanta, GA   30339-5671
Tel: (770)984-3740   Fax: (770)984-6405
Members: 62 companies and 38 associates

Staff: 2
Annual Budget: $100-250,000
Exec. Director: Bruce C. Dalzell, CLU, CAE

Historical Note
Established as Southern Casualty and Surety Conference, it became Southern Industrial Insurers' Conference in 1917, the Industrial Insurers Conference in 1925, Life Insurers Conference in 1948, and assumed its present name in 1997. Members are home service life insurance companies writing accident, life, and health insurance; Pre-Need funeral insurance companies; and non-life insurance company associate members which provide a service in the life insurance industry. Encourages the exchange of ideas between members, strives to maintain high standards of business conduct, and represents its members in connection with legislative, regulatory, and consumer matters.

Publications:
Communique. m.

Meetings/Conferences:
Annual Meetings: May
1999 – White Sulphur Springs, WV(Greenbrier)
2000 – Palm Beach, FL(The Breakers)

Life Office Management Ass'n (1924)
Historical Note
Known by its acronym LOMA.

Lift Manufacturers Product Section - Material Handling Institute (1990)
8720 Red Oak Blvd., Suite 201
Charlotte, NC   28217-3992
Tel: (704)676-1190   Fax: (704)676-1199
Web Site: http://www.MHIA.org
Members: 11 companies
Staff: 2
Annual Budget: $10-25,000
Managing Director: Thomas A. Carbott

Historical Note
Members are manufacturers of lift equipment. A section of the Material Handling Institute.

Light Aircraft Manufacturers Ass'n (1984)
1661 Kessler Canyon
Dallas, TX   75208
Tel: (972)386-1000   Fax: (972)490-7582
Members: 400 individuals, 100 companies
Annual Budget: $10-25,000
President: Scott Severen

Historical Note
LAMA members are manufacturers of light and ultralight aircraft and suppliers of parts. Membership: $50/year (individual); $125/year (company).

Publications:
LAMA Membership Directory. irreg.
LAMA Newsletter. irreg. adv.

Meetings/Conferences:

Lighter Ass'n (1986)
c/o Thompson, Hine and Flory, LLP
1920 N Street, N.W., Suite 800
Washington, DC   20036
Tel: (202)973-2709   Fax: (202)331-8330
Members: 10 companies
Staff: 1
Annual Budget: $100-250,000
General Counsel: David H. Baker

Historical Note
Members are manufacturers, suppliers and distributors of lighters. Membership: $4,000-48,000 (company).

Meetings/Conferences:

Lightning Protection Institute (1955)
3335 N. Arlington Heights Road, Suite E
Arlington Heights, IL   60004-7700
Tel: (847)577-7200   Fax: (847)577-7276
Web Site: www.lightning.org
Members: 100 companies
Staff: 4
Annual Budget: $25-50,000
Exec. Director: C. Andrew Larsen, CAE

Historical Note
Members are manufacturers and installers of lightning protection equipment. The LPI Professional Division has a membership of about 100 engineers and others.

Publications:
Golf Course Protection. a.
Lightning Protection.
LPI Standard of Practice. a.
Newsletter. q.
Technical Letter. q.

Meetings/Conferences:
Annual Meetings: Fall

Lignin Institute (1990)
5775 Peachtree-Dunwoody Rd., Suite 500-G
Atlanta, GA   30342
Tel: (404)252-3663   Fax: (404)252-0774
E-Mail: Li@assnhq.com
Web Site: http://www.assnhq.com/li
Staff: 3
Annual Budget: $50-100,000
President: Andrew G. Ebert, Ph.D.

Historical Note
The Institute is a trade association for manufacturers and distributors of lignin products. Lignin is co-product of the wood pulping process with applications in construction and other heavy industries.

Publications:
Dialogue Newsletter. q.

Meetings/Conferences:
Semi-Annual meetings: Atlanta, GA(Airport Facility)/May and
November

Lignite Energy Council *(1974)*
1016 East Owens Ave. Suite 200
Bismarck, ND 58502-2277
Tel: (701)258-7117   Fax: (701)258-2755
E-Mail: lec@btigate.com
Web Site: lignite-energy-council.org
Members: 207 individuals
Staff: 7
Annual Budget: $1-2,000,000
President: John W. Dwyer
Director, Communications: Lyndon Anderson
Coordinator, Membership: Renee Walz

Publications:
Buyer's Directory. a.
Inside Scoop. m.
Lignite Update. bi-m.
Member Update. bi-m.

Meetings/Conferences:
Annual Meetings: Annual/Fall
1999 – Bismarck, ND(Radison Inn)/Oct. 26-27/350
2000 – Bismarck, ND(Radisson Inn)/Oct. 25-26/350
2001 – Bismarck, ND(Doublewood Inn)/Oct. 24-25/350
2002 – Bismarck, ND(Doublewood Inn)/Oct. 23-24/350

Limousine Industry Manufacturers Organization *(1989)*
111 Park Place
Falls Church, VA 22046-4513
Tel: (703)538-1792   Fax: (703)241-5603
E-Mail: LimoHQ@aol.com
Members: 20 companies
Staff: 4
Annual Budget: $50-100,000
Exec. Director: Clay D. Tyeryar, CAE
Meetings Planner: Barbara B. Tyeryar
Member Services: Hazel Reeve

Historical Note
LIMO is the trade association of limousine manufacturing industry.
Non-voting Supplier-Service Firm and Associate Memberships are
available for companies or individuals involved in the industry in a
non-manufacturing capacity. Membership: $3,000/year
(organization/company).

Meetings/Conferences:
Annual Meetings: Winter

LIMRA Internat'l *(1916)*
P.O. Box 208
Hartford, CT 06141-0208
Tel: (860)688-3358   Fax: (860)298-9555
Toll Free: (800)235 - 4672
E-Mail: INFOCENTER@LIMRA.COM
Web Site: http://www.limra.com
Members: 700 companies
Staff: 250
Annual Budget: $10-25,000,000
President & CEO: Richard A. Wecker
Exec. V. President, Internat'l Operations: Thomas H. Kelly

Historical Note
Founded as the Life Insurance Sales Research Bureau in 1916; it
merged with the Life Officers Ass'n in 1945 to form the Life
Insurance Agency Management Ass'n and became Life Insurance
Marketing and Research Ass'n in 1974, and assumed its present
name in 1994. Street address is 8 Farm Springs, Farmington, CT.
Has an annual budget of approximately $24.4 million.

Publications:
Marketfacts. m.

Meetings/Conferences:
Annual Meetings: October/1,500

Linguistic Ass'n of Canada and the United States *(1974)*
P.O. Box 101
Lake Bluff, IL 60044
Tel: (847)234-3997
Members: 500 individuals, 200 institutions
Annual Budget: under $10,000
Exec. Director: Dr. Valerie B. Makkai

Historical Note
Established and incorporated in Illinois. LACUS is an educational
and scientific organization that promotes the objective study of
language. Has no paid officers or full-time staff. Membership:
US$35/year (U.S.), CAN$45/year (Canada).

Publications:
LACUS Forum Proceedings. a.

Meetings/Conferences:
Annual Meetings: July, August/100
1999 – Edmonton, Alberta, CN/100

Linguistic Soc. of America *(1924)*
1325 18th St., N.W., Suite 211
Washington, DC 20036-6501
Tel: (202)835-1714   Fax: (202)835-1717
E-Mail: lsa@lsadc.org
Web Site: http://www.lsadc.org
Members: 7,000 individuals
Staff: 2
Annual Budget: $250-500,000
Exec. Director: Margaret Reynolds
Exec. Assist., Meetings and Conventions: Mary Niebuhr

Historical Note
Founded December 28, 1924 at the American Museum of Natural
History in New York City and incorporated in 1940 in the District
of Columbia. A constituent member of the American Council of
Learned Societies, affiliate of Permanent Internat'l Committee of
Linguistics (CIPL), founding member of the Consortium of Social

Science Associations (COSSA). Domestic Membership: $25/year
(student); $65/year (individual); $110/year (organization). Foreign
Membership: $35/year (student); $75/year (individual);
$120/year (organization).

Publications:
Annual Meeting Handbook. adv. adv.
Language. q. adv.
LSA Bulletin. q. adv.

Meetings/Conferences:
Annual Meetings: January/1,000
1999 – Los Angeles, CA(Bonaventure)/Jan. 7-10
2000 – Chicago, IL(Palmer House)/Jan. 6-9

Lipid Nurse Task Force *(1993)*
7611 Elmwood Ave., Suite 202
Middleton, WI 53562-3161
Tel: (608)831-5683   Fax: (608)831-5122
E-Mail: lnty@tmahq.com
Web Site: http://www.lntf.org
Members: 800 individuals
Staff: 3
Annual Budget: $100-250,000
Exec. Director: Alice Holbrow

Historical Note
The LNTF is committed to developing and promoting the role of
nurses in the management of patients with lipid disorders.
Membership: $40/year (individual).

Publications:
Membership Directory. a.
The Bulletin (newsletter). q.

Meetings/Conferences:
Annual Meetings: Fall
1999 – Minneapolis, MN

Lipizzan Ass'n of North America *(1968)*
P.O. Box 1133
Anderson, IN 46015-1133
Tel: (765)644-3904
Members: 175 individuals
Staff: 9
Annual Budget: $25-50,000
Director/Administrator: Sandra Heaberlin

Historical Note
Members own and breed Lipizzan horses. Formerly (1980) the
Royal Internat'l Lipizzan Club. Formerly (1992) the Lippizan Ass'n
of America, assumed this name following a merger with the
Lippizan Soc. of North America. LANA's prime objective is to
provide members with accessible, verifiable pedigree information,
from America and oversees breeders. Membership: $45/year.

Publications:
Directory. a.
Haute Ecole. q.

Meetings/Conferences:
Semi-Annual: Spring/Fall

Liquid and Solid Industrial Control Ass'n
Historical Note
Became (1995) Environmental Management Ass'n.

Literary Managers and Dramaturgs of the Americas *(1985)*
Box 355 CASTA; CUNY Grad Center
33 West 42nd St.
New York, NY 10036
Tel: (212)642-2657   Fax: (212)642-1977
Members: 600 individuals
Annual Budget: $25-50,000
President: Jayme Koszyn

Historical Note
Formerly (1990) Literary Managers and Dramaturgs of America.
LMDA is the national network of literary managers and dramaturgs
founded in 1985 to affirm, examine and encourage these emerging
professions. Provides a job bank, script exchange, and other
programs to members. Membership: $20-45/year (individual),
$100/year (institution).

Publications:
LMDA Guide to Dramaturgy Programs.
LMDA Guide to Internships.
LMDA Review. q.
National Theatre Translation Sourcebook.
Production Diaries.
Script Exchange. 5/year.

Meetings/Conferences:

Livestock Conservation Institute *(1916)*
1910 Lyda Ave.
Bowling Green, KY 42104-5809
Tel: (502)782-9798   Fax: (502)782-0188
Web Site: http://www.lcionline.org
Members: 200 organizations
Staff: 4
Annual Budget: $250-500,000
Exec. Director: Glenn N. Slack
Manager, Project Development: Blake Aldridge
Manager, Member Services: Pamela Byrd
Editor, Publications: Joy Carter

Historical Note
Formed by a merger of the Nat'l Livestock Sanitary Committee and
the Nat'l Livestock Loss Prevention Board (founded in 1916).
Formerly (1976) Livestock Conservation, Inc. LCI provides a forum
for diverse segments of the livestock industry to discuss common
issues, build consensus, and offer solutions to the challenges facing
meat animal production in North America. Membership includes
producers, industry professionals, state and federal regulators and
the research community. The organization specializes in producing
educational materials and enhancing the industry's communication
efforts. Issues addressed by LCI include animal health, livestock
care and handling, food safety, and uniform livestock

identification.Membership: dues based on type of organization or
corporation.

Publications:
Brucellosis Progress. q.
Cattle Health Report. q.
Food Safety Digest. bi-m.
LCI News. bi-m.
Official Annual Meeting Proceedings. a.
Pseudorabies Progress. q.
Scrapie Progress Report. q.
Swine Health Epidemiology. q.

Meetings/Conferences:
1999 – Nashville, TN(Doubletree Hotel)March

Livestock Industry Institute *(1970)*
Historical Note
A division within the Livestock Marketing Ass'n.

Livestock Marketing Ass'n *(1976)*
7509 Tiffany Springs Parkway
Kansas City, MO 64153-2315
Tel: (816)891-0502   Fax: (816)891-7926
Toll Free: (800)821 - 2048
Members: 1,100 business
Staff: 30
Annual Budget: $5-10,000,000
General Manager: James Ed Frost
Director, Information: John J. McBride
V. President, Gov't & Industry Affairs: Nancy J. Robinson
Chief Financial Officer: Gary S. Smith

Historical Note
Formed by a merger (July 1, 1976) of the Competitive Livestock
Marketing Ass'n and the Nat'l Livestock Dealers Ass'n. Sponsors
the LMA Political Action Committee.

Publications:
Livestock Marketing Guide. a.
The Risk Manager. m.

Meetings/Conferences:
Annual Meetings: June
1999 – Asheville, NC(Holiday Inn)/June 17-20
2000 – Bakersfield, CA/June 15-17

Livestock Publications Council *(1974)*
910 Currie St.
Fort Worth, TX 76107
Tel: (817)336-5688   Fax: (817)336-5233
Members: 175 publications
Staff: 1
Annual Budget: $100-250,000
Exec. Director: Diane E. Johnson

Historical Note
Organized in a Texas meeting and incorporated in Colorado.
Members are magazines, newspapers and other periodicals devoting
at least 50% of their average content to the livestock industry.
Membership: $150/year.

Publications:
Actiongram (newsletter). m.
LPC Directory of Members. a.

Meetings/Conferences:
Annual Meetings: July/August
1999 – Denver, CO(Hyatt Downtown)/July 28-31/200
2000 – San Antonio, TX

Loading Dock Equipment Manufacturers
8720 Red Oak Blvd., Suite 201
Charlotte, NC 28217-3957
Tel: (704)676-1190   Fax: (704)676-1199
E-Mail: ahowie@mhia.org
Members: 6 companies
Staff: 2
Annual Budget: under $10,000
Managing Executive: Allan M. Howie

Historical Note
A product section of Material Handling Industry of America.

Meetings/Conferences:
Semi-Annual Meetings: Spring and Fall with MHIA

Locomotive Maintenance Officers' Ass'n *(1905)*
6047 S. Mobile Ave.
Chicago, IL 60638-4226
Tel: (773)586-9786   Fax: (773)586-9848
Members: 600 individuals
Staff: 1
Annual Budget: $25-50,000
Secretary-Treasurer: Ron Pondel

Historical Note
Established as the Internat'l Railway General Foremen's Ass'n, it
assumed its present name in 1938 and absorbed the Master
Boilermaker's Ass'n in 1955. Today its membership consists of
railway executives and others concerned with diesel engine
maintenance. A member group of the Committee of the Coordinated
Mechanical Ass'ns. Membership: $20/year (domestic), $30/year
(foreign).

Publications:
LMOA Newsletter. semi-a.
Locomotive Proceedings. a. adv.

Meetings/Conferences:
Annual Meetings: Always Chicago, IL(Hilton Towers)/Sept.
1999 – /Sept. 19-22

Log Homes Council *(1985)*
Historical Note
A division of Building Systems Councils of NAHB.

Log House Builders Ass'n of North America *(1967)*
22203 State Route 203
Monroe, WA 98272
Tel: (206)794-4469

Members: 16,900 companies
Staff: 4
Annual Budget: $500-1,000,000
President: DeWelle F. "Skip" Ellsworth
V. President: Robert Johnson
Exec. V. President: Mike Simmons

Historical Note
Formerly (1976) Log House Ass'n of North America.

Publications:
Log House Builders Ass'n Newsletter. irreg. adv.
Log House Builders Journal. irreg. adv.

Meetings/Conferences:

Logistics Conference
Historical Note
A conference of the Transporation Intermediaries Ass'n.

LOMA (1924)
2300 Windy Ridge Pkwy., Suite 600
Atlanta, GA   30339-8443
Tel: (770)951-1770   *Fax:* (770)984-0441
Toll Free: (800)275 - 5662
E-Mail: marketing@loma.org
Web Site: http://www.loma.org
Members: 1,161 companies
Staff: 185
Annual Budget: $10-25,000,000
President and C.E.O.: Thomas P. Donaldson, FLMI, CLU
Senior V. President, Education: William H. Rabel, PhD, FLMI,
V. President, Human Resources Services: Jean Harris Frank
Senior V. President, Research: Stephen Forbes, Ph.D., FLM
Secy./Treas., V.P. Administrative Svcs.: Aiken P. Rush, Jr., FLMI
V. President; Exec. Director, Life Insurers Council: Bruce C. Dalzell,
     CLU, CAE
Managing Director, International: Dr. Joel V. Basarich,
     FLMI,ACS,A
2nd V. President, IS: Ken Speer, ACS
AVP, Financial & Strategic Services: Carol La Porta
2nd V. President, Marketing: Jeffrey L. Hasty, FLMI, ACS
2nd V. President, Membership: Micahel B. Svwalski
AVP, Information Management, Products & Services: Ann Purr
AVP, Operations Management: Ed Burns

Historical Note
*Formerly (1996) Life Office Management Ass'n. LOMA sponsors
education, training, employee development programs, networking,
and research to promote effective management in life & health
insurance companies and other related organizations. Has an
annual budget of approximately $18 million. Membership fee
varies, based on premium income.*

Publications:
RESOURCE. m. adv.

Meetings/Conferences:
Annual Meetings: Fall
1999 – San Diego, CA(Marriott Marina)/Sept. 26-28
2000 – Orlando, FL/Sept. 24-26

Long Term Acute Care Hospital Ass'n of America (1996)
1301 K St., N.W., Suite 1100 East Tower
Washington, DC   20005
Tel: (202)296-4446   *Fax:* (202)414-9299
E-Mail: jtmarrin@rssm.com
Members: 70 individuals
Exec. Director: James T. Marrinan

Historical Note
*Established in 1996 to promote the interests of long term acute care
hospitals and their patients.*

Luggage and Leather Goods Manufacturers of America (1938)
350 Fifth Ave., Suite 2624
New York, NY   10118
Tel: (212)695-2340   *Fax:* (212)643-8021
Toll Free: (800)862 - 4224
E-Mail: aldecicco@aol.com
Web Site: http://www.llgma.org
Members: 300 individuals, 250 companies
Staff: 9
Annual Budget: $2-5,000,000
Exec. V. President: Anne DeCicco
V. President, Communications: Michele Marini Pittenger
V. President, Operations: Lois Miller

Historical Note
*LLGMA represents the manufactures and distributors of luggage,
personal leather goods, business cases, business and travel
accessories, and handbags.Membership: $1000-5000/year
(company).*

Publications:
Showcase. bi-m. adv.
Showcase International.

Meetings/Conferences:
Annual Meetings: March/5,000
1999 – Orlando, Fl

Luggage and Leather Goods Salesmen's Ass'n of America (1933)
420 W. 24th St., #3-A
New York, NY   10011-1370
Tel: (212)989-4515   *Fax:* (212)633-2752
Members: 70 individuals
Staff: 1
Annual Budget: under $10,000
Exec. Secretary: Sara Jeen Grodensky

Meetings/Conferences:
Annual Meetings: March
1999 – Orlando, FL

Lutheran Church Library Ass'n (1958)

122 W. Franklin Ave.
Minneapolis, MN   55404-2474
Tel: (612)870-3623   *Fax:* (612)870-0170
E-Mail: LCLAHQ@aol.com
Members: 125 individuals, 1,800 church libraries
Staff: 2
Annual Budget: $50-100,000
Exec. Director: Leanna D. Kloempken

Historical Note
*Founded in 1958 in Minneapolis. Membership: $28/year
(individual); $28/year (smaller churches); $40/year (medulum
churches); $55/year (larger churches).*

Publications:
Lutheran Libraries. q.

Meetings/Conferences:
Annual Meetings: Fall

Lutheran Education Ass'n (1942)
7400 Augusta, Concordia University
River Forest, IL   60305
Tel: (708)209-3343   *Fax:* (708)209-3458
E-Mail: LEA@CRF.CUIS.EDU
Web Site: http://www.lea.org
Members: 4,500 individuals
Staff: 3
Annual Budget: $50-100,000
Exec. Director: Jonathan Laabs
Director, Communications and Education: Barbara Goodwin
Director, Membership: Dorothy Freundt

Historical Note
*Teachers, administrators and board members of Lutheran schools,
as well as parish educators. LEA departments include: Theological
Educators in Associated Ministries (TEAM), Department of Early
Childhood Education (DECE), Lutheran Elementary Teachers (LET)
and Lutheran Education Administrators Department (LEAD).
Membership: $35/year.*

Publications:
Lutheran Education. 5/yr.
Monograph Series. 3-4/yr.
Shaping the Future. 5x/year.

Meetings/Conferences:
1999 – Indianapolis, IN/March 25-27

Lutheran Educational Conference of North America (1910)
1001 Connecticut Ave., N.W., Suite 504
Washington, DC   20036
Tel: (202)463-6484   *Fax:* (202)463-6609
Toll Free: (800)331 - 9650
Web Site: http://www.lutherancolleges.org
Members: 42 colleges
Staff: 2
Annual Budget: $100-250,000
Exec. Director: Donald A. Stoike
Exec. Secretary: Dabielle Mossner

Historical Note
*Members are Lutheran colleges, seminaries and boards of higher
education. Formerly (until 1967) known as the Nat'l Lutheran
Educational Conference, it is the oldest inter-Lutheran organization
in North America. Membership: $500-3,000/year, based on type
of institution.*

Publications:
Papers and Proceedings of LECNA. a.

Meetings/Conferences:
Annual Meetings: January-February
1999 – Washington, DC(Washington Monarch)/Feb. 6-9

Lutheran Hospital Ass'n of America
Historical Note
Address unknown in 1997.

Machine Knife Ass'n (1933)
30200 Detroit Road
Cleveland, OH   44145-1967
Tel: (440)899-0010   *Fax:* (440)892-1404
Members: 10 companies
Staff: 2
Annual Budget: under $10,000
Secretary-Treasurer: J. Jeffery Wherry

Historical Note
Formerly known as the Machine Knife Manufacturers Ass'n (1991)

Meetings/Conferences:
Semi-annual Meetings: March and October.
1999 – Longboat Key, FL(Longboat Key
     Club)/March 20-24/20

Machine Printers and Engravers Ass'n of the United States (1960)
690 Warren Ave.
East Providence, RI   02914
Tel: (401)438-5849
E-Mail: mpea2000@juno.com
Members: 300 individuals
Staff: 2
Annual Budget: $250-500,000
President: John J. Phillips

Historical Note
*Independent labor union formed by a merger of the Friendly Society
of Engravers and Sketchmakers (founded in 1878) and the Machine
Printers Beneficial Ass'n (founded in 1874).*

Meetings/Conferences:
Annual Meetings: Fall
1999 – Orlando, FL

Machine Vision Ass'n of SME (1984)
P.O. Box 930
One SME Drive
Dearborn, MI   48121-0930

Tel: (313)271-1500   *Fax:* (313)271-2861
Web Site: http://www.sme.org/mva.html
Members: 2,900 individuals
Staff: 2
Annual Budget: $25-50,000
Association Manager: Sandra Marshall

Historical Note
*MVA/SME is an individual member society of the Soc. of
Manufacturing Engineers with 2,900 members in 35 countries.
MVA/SME members are machine vision users in manufacturing
industries, research and education. Certification as CMfgE
(Certified Manufacturing Engineer) or CMfgT (Certified
Manufacturing Technologist) is offered through the Manufacturing
Engineer Certification Institute of SME. Membership: $72/year
(individual).*

Publications:
Machine Vision Industry Directory.
Vision. q. adv.

Meetings/Conferences:

Machinery Dealers Nat'l Ass'n (1941)
315 S. Patrick St.
Alexandria, VA   22314-3501
Tel: (703)836-9300   *Fax:* (703)836-9303
E-Mail: office@mdna.org
Web Site: http://www.mdna.org
Members: 470 individuals
Staff: 6
Annual Budget: $250-500,000
Exec. V. President: Darryl D. McEwen
Communications Director: Martha P. Deal
Controller: Theresa W. Andersson
Membership Services Director: Sam Freedenberg

Historical Note
*Represents used industrial machinery dealers. Membership:
$900/year.*

Publications:
MDNA News. m.

Meetings/Conferences:
Annual Meetings: Spring/400
1999 – Tucson, AZ(La Polma)/May 6-9/300
2000 – Boca Raton, FL(Boca Raton Club)/May 13-16/300

Machining Technology Ass'n of SME (1991)
P.O. Box 930
One SME Drive
Dearborn, MI   48121-0930
Tel: (313)271-1500   *Fax:* (313)271-2861
Web Site: http://www.sme.org/mta.html
Members: 4,300 individuals
Staff: 2
Association Manager: Kristen Dudash

Historical Note
*An individual member society of the Soc. of Manufacturing
Engineers, MTA/SME members are professionals in manufacturing
and academia concerned with material removal processes and
applications. Its mission is to monitor and assist in the identification
of technical developments, processes, and applications, and the
potential impact on industry, and to ensure that quality products
and services are delivered. Certification as CMfgE (Certified
Manufacturing Engineer) or CMfgT (Certified Manufacturing
Technologist) is offered through the Manufacturing Engineering
Certification Institute of SME. Membership: $72/year (individual).*

Publications:
Machining Technology Newsletter. q.

Meetings/Conferences:
1999 – Cincinnati, OH(Westin Hotel)

Magazine and Paperback Marketing Internat'l (1946)
Historical Note
Address unknown in 1996.

Magazine Printers Section/Printing Industries of America (1956)
100 Daingerfield Road
Alexandria, VA   22314-2888
Tel: (703)519-8141   *Fax:* (703)548-3227
Members: 28 companies
Staff: 1
Annual Budget: $25-50,000
Exec. Director: Thomas B. Basore

Historical Note
*A special industry group of Printing Industries of America. Its goal
is to find solutions to current problems unique to the magazine
printing industry. Members are officers of magazine printing firms.
Membership: $585/yr. (company).*

Meetings/Conferences:

Magazine Publishers of America (1919)
919 3rd Ave., 22nd Floor
New York, NY   10022
Tel: (212)872-3700   *Fax:* (212)888-4217
E-Mail: infocenter@magazine.org
Web Site: http://www.magazine.org
Members: 220 companies and 800 magazines
Staff: 40
Annual Budget: $5-10,000,000
President: Donald D. Kummerfeld
V. President, Marketing Promotions & Communications: Christine
     Miller
V. President, Communications: Mary McGeachey
Exec. V. President, Consumer Marketing and Meetings & Events:
     Michael Pashby
V. President, Finance & Administration: Frank Mortensen
V. President, Member Services/Franchies Development: Larry
     Kaufman

Historical Note
*Members are publishers of consumer and other magazines issued
not less than four times a year. Founded as the Nat'l Ass'n of*

Periodical Publishers, it became the Nat'l Publishers Ass'n in 1920, the Nat'l Ass'n of Magazine Publishers in 1947, the Magazine Publishers Ass'n in 1952 and assumed its present name in 1987. Affiliated with American Soc. of Magazine Editors and Media Credit Ass'n. Has an annual budget of approximately $7.9 million.

Publications:
Magazine. bi-m.
MPA Newsletter of International Publishing. 8/year.
MPA Newsletter of Research. 3/year.
MPA Washington Newsletter. m.
Newsletter of Consumer Marketing. bi-m.

Meetings/Conferences:
Annual Meetings: Fall/600-650
1999 – Boca Raton, FL(BR Resort & Country Club)/Oct. 28-31
2000 – Bermuda(Southampton Princess)/Oct. 22-25

Magic Dealers Ass'n *(1946)*
5601 Bridgeport Way, Suite A
University Place, WA   98467
Tel: (253)564-5416   *Fax:* (253)564-5416
E-Mail: gscenes@wolfenet.com
Web Site: http://www.magicdealers.com
Members: 110 companies
Annual Budget: under $10,000
Internat'l Secretary: Scott Markham

Historical Note
Incorporated in the state of Maryland in 1947. The organization exists to assist with networking magic-related businesses and provide a common bond of integrity. The members consist of retailers, wholesalers, jobbers, publishers, and inventors; who develop, manufacture and sell magic-related products. Membership: $50/year (organization/company).

Publications:
Directory. a. adv.
The Register Newsletter. q. adv.

Meetings/Conferences:
Annual Meetings: With Internat'l Brotherhood of Magicians or Soc. of American Magicians

Magnet Distributors and Fabricators Ass'n
8 South Michigan Avenue
Suite 1000
Chicago, IL   60603
Tel: (312)456-5590   *Fax:* (312)580-0165
E-Mail: mdfa@gss.net
Web Site: http://www.mdfa.org
Members: 26 companies
Staff: 2
Annual Budget: $25-50,000
Exec. Director: August L. Sisco

Historical Note
MFDA regular members are magnet distributors and fabricators. Associate membership is available for industry suppliers. Membership: $1-2,000/year (organization/company).

Publications:
Industry Technical Standards.

Meetings/Conferences:
Annual Meetings: Spring
1999 – St. Petersburg, FL(Trade Winds)

Magnetic Materials Producers Ass'n *(1959)*
8 South Michigan Avenue
Suite 1000
Chicago, IL   60603
Tel: (312)456-5590   *Fax:* (312)580-0165
E-Mail: mmpa@gss.net
Web Site: http://www.mmpa.org
Members: 35 companies
Staff: 2
Annual Budget: $25-50,000
Exec. Secretary: August L. Sisco

Historical Note
Established as the Permanent Magnet Producers Association, it assumed its present name in 1967. MMPA members are manufacturers of permanent and soft ferrite magnetic materials. Membership: $1,000-$2,000/year (corporate).

Publications:
Technical Standards.

Meetings/Conferences:
Annual Meetings: Spring, always Florida
1999 – St. Petersburg, FL(Trade Winds)

Mail Advertising Service Ass'n Internat'l *(1920)*
1421 Prince St., Suite 100
Alexandria, VA   22314-2806
Tel: (703)836-9200   *Fax:* (703)548-8204
Toll Free: (800)333 - 6272
E-Mail: masa@erols.com
Web Site: http://www.masa.org
Members: 600 companies
Staff: 10
Annual Budget: $1-2,000,000
President: David A. Weaver, CAE
Dir., Communications: Kimberly Kight
Director, Postal Affairs: Barry Brennan
Director of Conferences: Carla Corliss
Director, Finance and Accounting: Ruth Clark
General Counsel: Graeme Bush
Director, Membership: Tyler Keeney
Director, Marketing: Eric Casey

Historical Note
Members are producers of direct commercial mail, letter shops, list brokers, fulfillment operations and data processing service bureaus.

Publications:
Cost Ratio Survey. a.
Employment Points.
Membership Directory. a.
Postal Points.
Postscripts Newsletter. m.

Wage, Salary and Fringe Benefits Survey. bien.

Meetings/Conferences:
1999 – Scottsdale, AZ/Jan. 21-24
1999 – Washington, DC/Feb. 10-12
1999 – Las Vegas, NV/March 19-21
1999 – Milwaukee, WI/April 22-24
1999 – San Diego, CA/June 3-5
1999 – Charlotte, NC/Aug. 19-21
1999 – Alexandria, VA/Sept. 16-17
1999 – Salt Lake City, UT/Oct. 21-23
1999 – Baltimore, MD

Mail Order Ass'n of America *(1933)*
Patton Boggs, LLP
2550 M St., N.W., 9th Floor
Washington, DC   20037
Tel: (516)221-8257   *Fax:* (202)457-6315
Members: 5 companies
Staff: 1
Annual Budget: under $10,000
General Counsel: David C. Todd

Historical Note
Activities of the Ass'n are limited to matters pertaining to regulations issued by the Postal Rate Commission, Interstate Commerce Commission, the Department of Commerce and similar regulatory agencies and governmental offices. Members are retail firms selling by mail order.

Mail Systems Management Ass'n *(1982)*
Historical Note
Address unknown in 1997.

Maintenance Council of American Trucking Ass'ns *(1979)*
2200 Mill Road
Alexandria, VA   22314-5388
Tel: (703)838-1763   *Fax:* (703)684-4328
Web Site: www.truckline.com/insideata/councils/tmc.htm
Members: 3,500 companies
Staff: 8
Annual Budget: $1-2,000,000
Exec. Director: Carl Kirk
Director, Conventions & Exhibits: Paul Domer
Technical Director: Robert Braswell
Manager, Membership Services: Jennifer Nash

Historical Note
Trucking executives, maintenance specialists, manufacturers, and suppliers interested in the improvement of trucking equipment, its maintenance, and maintenance management. Membership: $275/year (individual); $285/year (fleet member); $385/year (associate member); $95/year (supervisor).

Publications:
Maintenance Manager. q.
Maintenance Newsletter. m.
Membership Directory.
Recommended Practices Manual. a.
The Trailblazer. 3/year.

Meetings/Conferences:
Triannual Meetings: Spring, Summer and Fall

Major League Baseball - Office of the Commissioner *(1921)*
245 Park Ave.
New York, NY   10167
Tel: (212)931-7800
Members: 28 clubs
Staff: 70
Annual Budget: $2-5,000,000
Commissioner: Bud Selig

Historical Note
Founded to provide oversight and assure the integrity of the sport, the Office of the Commissioner works to promote baseball and protect the interests of its member franchises.

Meetings/Conferences:
Annual Meetings: Winter
1999 – Quarterly meetings

Major League Baseball Players Ass'n *(1953)*
12 E. 49th Street (24th Floor)
New York, NY   10017
Tel: (212)826-0808   *Fax:* (212)752-3649
Web Site: http://www.bigleaguers.com
Members: 1,150 individuals
Staff: 30
Exec. Director: Donald Fehr

Historical Note
Independent labor union.

Meetings/Conferences:
Annual Meetings: First week in December

Major League Umpires Ass'n *(1969)*
1735 Market St., Suite 3420
Philadelphia, PA   19103
Tel: (215)979-3200   *Fax:* (215)979-3201
Web Site: http://www.majorleagueumps.com
Members: 56 individuals
Staff: 3
Annual Budget: $10-25,000
General Counsel: Richard G. Phillips

Historical Note
Merger of the Ass'n of National Baseball League Umpires (1963) and the Ass'n of American League Umpires.

Man and Cybernetics Systems Soc.
Historical Note
A subsidiary of the Institute of Electrical and Electronics Engineers. Membership in the Society, open only to IEEE members, includes subscription to a technical periodical in the field published by IEEE. All administrative support is provided by IEEE.

Managed Futures Ass'n *(1991)*
1200 19th St., N.W., Suite 300
Washington, DC   20036
Tel: (202)828-6040   *Fax:* (202)828-6041
Toll Free: (800)425 - 4632
E-Mail: rob@mfainfo.org
Web Site: http://www.mfahome.com
Members: 700 individuals
Staff: 4
Annual Budget: $2-5,000,000
President/Director, Government Affairs/General Counsel: John G. Gaine

Historical Note
Members are individuals involved in commodity/futures trading. Dedicated to protecting and advancing the broad intersts of its members by representing the industry to regulatory and legislative governing bodies and to the investing public. Member/industry services include production of investment brochures, monthly newsletters and other publications. MFA also provides industry conferences, both in the U.S. and worldwide. Membership: $150-25,000/year.

Publications:
The MFA Journal. semi-a.
The MFA Reporter. m.

Meetings/Conferences:
1999 – Palm Beach FL/Feb. 7-9

Management Ass'n for Private Photogrammetric Surveyors *(1982)*
12020 Sunrise Valley Dr., Suite 100
Reston, VA   20191
Tel: (703)391-2739   *Fax:* (703)476-2217
E-Mail: info@mapps.org
Members: 120 companies
Staff: 1
Annual Budget: $100-250,000
Exec. Director: John M. Palatiello

Historical Note
MAPPS members are companies providing photogrammetry and computer based geographic information services. Membership: $910/year.

Publications:
Capitol Coverage. bi-m.
Flightline Newsletter. bi-m.

Meetings/Conferences:
Semi-Annual Meetings: January and July
1999 – Stowe, VT(Top Notch Resort)

Manufactured Housing Ass'n for Regulatory Reform *(1985)*
1331 Pennsylvania Ave., N.W., Suite 508
Washington, DC   20004
Tel: (202)783-4087   *Fax:* (202)783-4075
Members: 34 companies
Staff: 3
Annual Budget: $250-500,000
President: Danny D. Ghorbani

Historical Note
formerly the Ass'n for Regulatory Reform. MHARR represents the interests and views of producers of manufactured housing. Dedicated to the reform of unnecessary regulation of American housing industry.

Publications:
ARR News. irreg.
ARR Washington Update. bi-m.
Deregualtor Position Papers. irreg.

Meetings/Conferences:
Annual Meetings: Varies

Manufactured Housing Institute *(1936)*
2101 Wilson Blvd., Suite 610
Arlington, VA   22201-3062
Tel: (703)558-0400   *Fax:* (703)558-0401
E-Mail: info@mfghome.org
Web Site: http://www.mfghome.org
Members: 300 companies
Staff: 20
Annual Budget: $2-5,000,000
President: Jerry C. Connors
Director, Public Affairs: Bruce A. Savage
Exec. V. President, Government Affairs: Brian Cooney
Exec. V. President, State Affairs: James R. Ayotte, CAE
V. President, Technical Affairs: Frank Walters
V. President, Finance: Joe Owens
Director, Admin. and Info: Christopher D. Busky

Historical Note
Established as Trailer Coach Manufacturers Ass'n. Became Mobile Homes Manufacturers Ass'n in 1956 and the Manufactured Housing Institute in 1975. Absorbed the Nat'l Manufactured Housing Federation in 1991 and the Nat'l Manufactured Housing Finance Ass'n in 1992. MHI members are corporations involved in the manufactured housing industry. Primary functions are governmental relations, monitoring of construction standards, public relations, community operations, site development and statistical services. Supports the MHI Political Action Committee. Membership: dues vary, based on production.

Publications:
Housing Currents. q. adv.
Manufacturing Report. m.
MHI In-Focus. m.
Quick Facts. a.

Meetings/Conferences:
Annual Meetings: October
1999 – Arlington, VA(Marriott)/Feb. 21-24
1999 – Chicago, IL/June 6-9

Manufacturers Alliance *(1933)*
1525 Wilson Blvd., Suite 900

Arlington, VA   22209
Tel: (703)841-9000   *Fax:* (703)841-9514
Members: 450 manufacturing companies
Staff: 44
Annual Budget: $5-10,000,000
President: Kenneth McLennan
Director, Public and Government Affairs: Peggy Morrissette
Director, Admin Services & Conference Plan'g: Steven Kerchner
V. President and Secretary: Francis W. Holman, Jr.
General Counsel: Frederick T. Stocker
Director, Membership Development: Kevin J. Murphy

Historical Note
*Formerly (1989) Machinery and Allied Products Institute, (1996)
Manufacturers Alliance for Productivity and Innovation. A policy
research organization whose member companies are drawn from
the producers and users of capital goods and allied products, the
Alliance includes leading companies in heavy industry, automotive,
electronics, precision instruments, telecommunications, computers,
office systems, aerospace, oil/gas, chemicals and similar high
technology industries. The Alliance conducts original research in
economics, law, and management and provides professional
analysis of issues critical to the economic performance of the private
sector. Operates 33 councils in various management disciplines,
conducts the annual Conference on Business and Economic Policies
and acts as national spokesman for policies which stimulate
technological advancement and economic growth.*

Publications:
Economic Reports.
Legal Analysis & Regulations.
Policy Reviews.

Meetings/Conferences:
Annual Meetings: June in Washington, DC/50 (Exec. Committee
    & Board of Trustees).

Manufacturers Alliance for Productivity and Innovation
Historical Note
Became Manufacturers Alliance in 1996.

Manufacturers Council of Small School Buses
Historical Note
An affiliate of the Nat'l Truck Equipment Ass'n.

Manufacturers Elevating and Work Platform Council
Historical Note
A council of the Equipment Manufacturers Institute.

Manufacturers of Aerial Devices and Digger-Derricks Council
Historical Note
A council of the Equipment Manufacturers Institute.

Manufacturers of Emission Controls Ass'n (1976)
1660 L St., N.W., Suite 1100
Washington, DC   20036
Tel: (202)296-4797   *Fax:* (202)331-1388
Members: 35 companies
Staff: 2
Exec. Director: Bruce I. Bertelsen

Meetings/Conferences:
Annual Meetings: March, in Washington, DC

Manufacturers of Telescoping and Articulating Cranes Council
Historical Note
A council of the Equipment Manufacturers Institute.

Manufacturers Representatives of America (1978)
P.O. Box 150229
Arlington, TX   76015
Tel: (817)561-7272   *Fax:* (817)561-7275
E-Mail: assnhqtrs@aol.com
Web Site: www.mra-reps.com
Members: 250 sales and marketing companies
Staff: 2
Annual Budget: $100-250,000
Exec. Director: William R. Bess

Historical Note
*Manufacturers' representatives in the paper, plastic, packaging, and
sanitary supply fields.*

Publications:
Newsline. m.
Yearbook. a. adv.

Meetings/Conferences:
1999 – Rancho Mirage(Westin Mission Hills)/April 21-24/150
2000 – Naples, FL(LaPlaya Beach Resort)/April 5-8/150

Manufacturers Standardization Soc. of the Valve and Fittings Industry (1924)
127 Park Street, N.E.
Vienna, VA   22180-4602
Tel: (703)281-6613   *Fax:* (703)281-6671
Web Site: http://www.mss-hq.com
Members: 99 companies
Staff: 4
Annual Budget: $250-500,000
Exec. Director: Olen Thornton

Historical Note
*An engineering society devoted to development and publication of
standards and specifications for the valve and fittings industry.
Membership: $1,800/year (company).*

Publications:
Standards for Valves, et. a.

Meetings/Conferences:
Annual Meetings: April-May/115
1999 – St. Petersburg, FL(Tradewinds)
2000 – Ft. Lauderdale, FL(Lago Mar)

2001 – Marco Island, FL(Marco Island Hilton)

Manufacturers' Agents for Food Service Industry (1949)
2900 Chamblee Tucker Rd.
Building 7
Atlanta, GA   30341
Tel: (770)698-8994
E-Mail: mafsi@sba.com
Members: 500 companies
Staff: 4
Annual Budget: $500-1,000,000
Exec. Director: Brad Parcells

Historical Note
*Formerly (1993) Marketing Agents for Food Service Industry.
Members are independent manufacturers representatives.*

Publications:
Annual Report. a.
Food Service Industry Marketing Agents LOCATOR. a. adv.
Outfront.
Repconnect.

Meetings/Conferences:
Annual Meetings: February, in a resort area/450

Manufacturers' Agents Nat'l Ass'n (1947)
P.O. Box 3467
23016 Mill Creek Road
Laguna Hills, CA   92654-3467
Tel: (949)859-4040   *Fax:* (949)855-2973
Members: 7,000 companies
Staff: 15
Annual Budget: $2-5,000,000
President: Lionel W. Diaz
Director, Administration: Helen Egle

Historical Note
*MANA promotes successful and profitable relationships between
multi-line sales agencies, the principals and manufacturers who
supply them with product lines, and their joint customers.
Membership: $189/year.*

Publications:
Agency Sales Magazine. m. adv.
Directory of Manufacturers' Sales Agencies. a. adv.
Newsletter bi. m.
Research Bulletins and Special Reports.

Meetings/Conferences:

Manufacturing Jewelers and Suppliers of America (1903)
One State St., 6th Floor
Providence, RI   02908
Tel: (401)274-3840   *Fax:* (401)274-0265
Toll Free: (800)444 - 6572
E-Mail: MJSA@internetmci.com
Web Site: http://www.MJSA.polygon.net
Members: 1,800 companies
Staff: 28
Annual Budget: $2-5,000,000
President and C.E.O.: James F. Marquart, CAE
V. President: Thomas Viola
C.F.O.: Thomas Daignault
Editor: Richard Youmers

Historical Note
*Established as the New England Manufacturing Jewelers' and
Silversmiths' Ass'n, it assumed its present name in 1956. MJSA is
the trade association for all segments of the American jewelry
manufacturing and supply industry. Sponsors and supports the
Jewelers Political Action Committee.*

Publications:
American Jewelry Manufacturer. m. adv.
Benchmark Newsletter. m.

Meetings/Conferences:
Annual Meetings: always Providence, RI/Oct./300

Manuscript Soc. (1948)
350 N. Niagara St.
Burbank, CA   91505-3648
E-Mail: manuscrip@aol.com
Members: 1,700 individuals
Staff: 2
Annual Budget: $50-100,000
Exec. Director: David R. Smith

Historical Note
*Formerly (1953) Nat'l Soc. of Autograph Collectors. Dealers,
curators, collectors and others interested in original manuscripts,
autographs, letters and documents. Membership: $35/year
(individual), $35/year (institution).*

Publications:
Manuscripts. q.
News. q.

Meetings/Conferences:
Annual Meetings: Spring/100
1999 – Miami, FL/100
2000 – New York, NY/120

Maple Flooring Manufacturers Ass'n (1897)
60 Revere Drive, Suite 500
Northbrook, IL   60062
Tel: (847)480-9138   *Fax:* (847)480-9282
E-Mail: dheney@maplefloor.org
Web Site: http://www.maplefloor.org
Members: 150 companies
Staff: 4
Annual Budget: $250-500,000
Exec. Director: Kevin R. Hacke
Technical Director: Daniel Heney

Historical Note
*MFMA maintains technical and general information on maple
flooring and represents manufacturing mills and allied product*

---

*manufacturers, distributors, and flooring contractors who use maple
flooring. Wood Sports Flooring Institute is an educational arm of
MFMA. Membership: $400/year (associate company), $750/year
(allied manufacturer).*

Meetings/Conferences:
Annual Meetings: Spring
1999 – Palm Springs, CA/March 21-23

Maraschino Cherry and Glace Fruit Processors (1906)
Historical Note
A section of the Ass'n of Food Industries.

Marble Institute of America (1944)
30 Eden Alley, Suite 301
Columbus, OH   43215
Tel: (614)228-6194   *Fax:* (614)461-1497
Members: 550 members
Staff: 2
Annual Budget: $500-1,000,000
Exec. V. President: Pennie L. Sabel

Historical Note
*Absorbed the National Association of Marble Dealers in 1962.
Members include producers, exporters/importers, distributors,
fabricators, finishers, installers and industry suppliers. Membership:
$500/year (domestic company), $700/year (foreign company).*

Publications:
Dimension Stone Design Manual IV. a.
Dimension Stones of the World-Vol. II ""Color Plates.

Meetings/Conferences:
Annual Meetings: Fall/600

Marina Operators Ass'n of America (1993)
Historical Note
Address unknown in 1997.

Marine Corps Reserve Officers Ass'n (1926)
110 N. Royal St., Suite 406
Alexandria, VA   22314
Tel: (703)548-7607   *Fax:* (703)519-8779
Toll Free: (800)927 - 6270
E-Mail: jvmcroa@aol.com
Members: 6,500 individuals
Staff: 3
Annual Budget: $100-250,000
Acting Exec. Director: Col. George Hofmann, Jr., USMCR

Historical Note
*The MCROA serves to support the Marine Corps, its Reserve
Component, and its Reserve Officers. Members are active and
retired Marine Corps Reserve Officers and regular officers.
Membership: $20-50/year (individual), $250-1,000/year (small
business), $1,000-10,000/year (corporate).*

Publications:
Nat'l Network Directory. a. adv.
The Word. bi-m. adv.

Meetings/Conferences:
Annual Meetings: Spring/500
1999 – Atlanta, GA/Apr. 29-May 2

Marine Fabricators Ass'n
1801 County Road B West
St. Paul, MN   55113-4052
Tel: (651)222-2508   *Fax:* (651)222-8215
Toll Free: (800)225 - 4324
E-Mail: mfa@ifai.com
Members: 300 companies
Staff: 1
Annual Budget: $10-25,000
Division Director: Star Schrodt

Historical Note
*MFA represents firms and individuals engaged in the design,
construction, and installation of marine fabric products, providing
certification and product standards. Membership: based on
company's annual sales, begins at $150/year.*

Publications:
Directory of Sources.
Fabric Specifier Guide.
Fabricator. (newsletter) bien.
Marine Fabricator. q. adv.
Membership Directory. a.

Meetings/Conferences:
Annual Meetings: Winter
1999 – Fort Myers, FL/Feb. 6-9

Marine Retailers Ass'n of America (1971)
150 E. Huron St., Suite 802
Chicago, IL   60611
Tel: (312)944-5080   *Fax:* (312)944-2716
Members: 3,000 companies
Staff: 2
Annual Budget: $500-1,000,000
President: Phil Keeter

Historical Note
*Members are manufacturers, distributors and dealers in marine
equipment. Membership: $150-5,000/year.*

Publications:
MRAA Newsletter. m.

Meetings/Conferences:
Annual Meetings: Fall

Marine Staff Officers (1960)
170 Windsor River Road, Suite W
Windsor, CA   95492-8079
Tel: (707)837-0423   *Fax:* (707)837-0423
Members: 60 individuals
Staff: 2
Secretary-Treasurer: Brandon Tynan

Historical Note
Labor union of marine nurses and pursers. Affiliated with the Seafarers Internat'l Union of North America, AFL-CIO.

Publications:
Bulletin. irreg.

Marine Technology Soc. (1963)
1828 L St., N.W., Suite 906
Washington, DC 20036-5104
Tel: (202)775-5966   Fax: (202)429-9417
E-Mail: mtsadmin@aol.com
Web Site: http://www.cms.udel.edu/mts
Members: 3,000 individuals
Staff: 4
Annual Budget: $500-1,000,000
Exec. Director: Martin J. Finerty, Jr.
Membership Manager: Emily Speight
Publication Manager: I. Clayvon Matthews

Historical Note
Founded and incorporated in New York in 1963; merged in 1971 with the American Soc. for Oceanography. Affiliated with the American Ass'n for the Advancement of Science. Concerned with such issues as coastal zone management, marine mineral and energy resources, marine environmental protection, the economic potential of the sea, and all ocean engineering matters. Membership: $55/yr. (individual); $275-650/yr. (organization); $25/yr. (student).

Publications:
Education & Training Programs in Oceanography & Related Fields. irreg.
Marine Technology Society Journal. q. adv.
MTS Conference Proceedings. a.
MTS Currents Newsletter. bi-m.
Underwater Intervention Conference Proceedings. a.

Meetings/Conferences:
Annual Meetings: Fall/2,500
1999 – Seattle, WA(Convention Center)/Sept. 13-16/2500
2000 – Providence, RI(Convention Center)/Sept. 11-14

Maritime Fire and Safety Ass'n
1275 Pennsylvania Ave., N.W., Suite 201
Washington, DC 20004
Tel: (202)467-8381
E-Mail: ourmanindc@aol.com
Annual Budget: $25-50,000
Representative: Peter Friedman

Maritime Law Ass'n of the U.S. (1899)
c/o Mosley Warren Pritchard and Parrish
501 W. Bay St.
Jacksonville, FL 32202
Tel: (904)356-1306
Members: 3,600 individuals
Annual Budget: $250-500,000
President: Howard McCormack

Historical Note
Founded to represent the U.S. in the Comite Maritime Internationale. Works to unify and improve maritime law, and to educate members in the field. Affiliated with the American Bar Ass'n. Has no paid officers or full-time staff. Membership: $95/year (individual).

Publications:
MLA Proceedings. semi-a.
MLA Reports. semi-a.

Meetings/Conferences:
Semi-Annual Meetings: first Friday in May/New York, NY and Fall/ alternates between New York, NY (even years) and other locations

Maritime Transportation Research Board (1965)
Historical Note
Operates under the Commission on Sociotechnical Systems of the Nat'l Research Council. Formed by a merger of the Maritime Cargo Transportation Conference and the Ship Hull Research Committee.

Marketing Education Ass'n (1982)
1375 King Ave., Suite 1A
P.O. Box 12278
Columbus, OH 43212-0278
Tel: (614)486-6708   Fax: (614)486-1819
Toll Free: (800)448-0398
Members: 1,100 individuals
Staff: 4
Annual Budget: $100-250,000
Project Manager: Carmel Martin

Historical Note
Formerly (1985) Marketing and Distributive Education Ass'n and (1989) Nat'l Marketing and Distributive Education Services Center. Formed by a merger of the Council of Distributive Teacher Educators (founded in 1960), the Nat'l Ass'n of Distributive Education Teachers (founded in 1957) and Nat'l Ass'n of State Supervisors of Distributive Education (founded in 1947). MEA fosters the development and expansion of education for and about marketing as a descrete, clearly defined profession. Members are high school and postsecondary marketing educators as well as university-level teacher educators and collegiate marketing teacher education students. Membership: $30/first year; $56/year (renewal); $111/year (executive membership); $250/year (institution).

Publications:
Association Perspectives. 3/yea.
Marketing Educators Journal. a.

Meetings/Conferences:
Annual Meetings: June with MarkEd Resource Center

Marketing Research Ass'n (1954)
1344 Silas Deane Hwy., Suite 306
P.O. Box 230

Rocky Hill, CT 06067-0230
Tel: (860)257-4008   Fax: (860)257-3990
E-Mail: email@mra-net.org
Web Site: www.mra-net.org
Members: 2,650 individuals
Staff: 13
Annual Budget: $1-2,000,000
Exec. Director: Betsy Peterson
Staff Manager, Professional Development: Debbie Midford
Staff Manager, Finance/Admin.: Barbara Sousa
Staff Manager, Membership/Mktg.: Kathy Null
Staff Manager, Information Technology: Paul Meliloo

Historical Note
Formerly (1971) Marketing Research Trade Ass'n. Members are companies and individuals involved in the design, administration, or analysis of market research studies. Membership: $183/year (individual), $356-947/year (company).

Publications:
Alert! Newsleter. m. adv.
Blue Book, Research Service Directory. a. adv.
The Management Notebook. q.

Meetings/Conferences:
Semi-Annual Meetings: Spring and Fall
1999 – Boston, MA/June 9-11

Marketing Research Council

Marking Device Ass'n Internat'l (1910)
222 Wisconin Ave., Suite 1
Lake Forest, IL 60045
Tel: (847)283-9810   Fax: (847)283-9808
E-Mail: mdai@mdai.com
Web Site: http://www.mdai.org
Members: 410 individualscompanies
Staff: 2
Annual Budget: $250-500,000
Exec. Director: L. Gene Griffiths

Historical Note
Formerly Internat'l Stamp Manufacturers Ass'n. Manufacturers of embossing seals, notary seals, rubber and metal stamps, plates, signs, and other hand-held marking devices. Membership: $250-995/year.

Publications:
MDAI Membership Directory. a.
MDAI Newsletter Update. bi. adv.
MDAI Seal Manual. a.
Women in Business Roster. a.

Meetings/Conferences:
Annual Meetings: Fall, with trade show/700
1999 – Orlando, FL(Hyatt Orlando)/Sept. 30-Oct. 3
2000 – Reno, NV(Nugget Hotel)/oct. 5-Oct. 8
2001 – Chicago, IL(Hyatt Regency)/Oct. 10-14

Marky Cattle Ass'n
Historical Note
See American Internat'l Marchigiana Society.

Mason Contractors Ass'n of America (1950)
1910 Highalnd Ave., Suite 101
Lombard, IL 60148-6147
Tel: (630)705-4200   Fax: (630)705-4209
E-Mail: info@masoncontractors.com
Web Site: http://www.masoncontractors.com
Members: 900 individuals
Staff: 8
Annual Budget: $500-1,000,000
Exec. Director: Michael Adelizzi
Director, Marketing and Membership: Jeff Buczkiewicz
Director, Meetings/Conventions: Rachel Young
Comptroller: Liz Fidoruk
Director, Administration: Kimberly Shifflette

Historical Note
Membership: $250-850/year.

Publications:
Masonry Magazine. bi-m. adv.
Update. bi-m. adv.

Meetings/Conferences:
Annual Meetings: late Winter/6,000
1999 – Orlando, FL

Masonry and Concrete Saw Manufacturers Institute (1981)
Historical Note
Merged with Construction Industry Manufacturers Ass'n in 1998

Masonry Heater Ass'n of North America (1986)
RR2, Box 33M
Randolph, VT 05060
Tel: (802)728-5896   Fax: (802)728-6004
E-Mail: bmarois@sovernet.com
Web Site: http://mha-net.org
Members: 47 individuals
Staff: 2
Annual Budget: $25-50,000
Administrator: Beverly J. Marois

Historical Note
MHA was founded to promote the use of masonry heaters, increase public awareness of its advantages, and encourage reasonable governmental regulation of this unique wood burning appliance. Trade association representing the United States and Canada. Membership: $100/year (affiliate); $200/year (voting).

Publications:
MHA News Newsletter. q.

Meetings/Conferences:

Masonry Soc. (1977)
3970 Broadway St., Suite 201-D
Boulder, CO 80304-1135

Tel: (303)939-9700   Fax: (303)541-9215
E-Mail: info@masonrysociety.org
Web Site: http://masonrysociety.org
Members: 1000 individuals, 50 organizations
Staff: 3
Annual Budget: $250-500,000
Exec. Director: William D. Palmer, Jr.

Historical Note
TMS is a professional/technical association dedicated to the advancement of scientific, engineering, architectural and construction knowledge of masonry. The Society stimulates research and education and disseminates information on masonry materials, design and construction. Members are architects, engineers, manufacturers of masonry products, contractors, craftsmen, building officials, educators, researchers, suppliers, students and others having an interest in masonry. Membership: $105/year (regular); $35/year (student); $295/year (company/organization).

Publications:
Masonry Soc. Journal.
Membership Directory. a.
Proceedings of the North American Masonry Conference. trien.
TMS News. bi-m.

Meetings/Conferences:
Annual Meetings: February
1999 – Orlando, FL(Country Hearth Inn)/Feb. 18-20/100
2000 – Las Vegas, NV/Feb. 17-19

Mass Finishing Job Shops Ass'n (1981)
Historical Note
Address unknown in 1995.

Mass Marketing Insurance Institute (1969)
2841 Main
Kansas City, MO 64108
Tel: (816)221-4575   Fax: (816)472-7765
Members: 300 companies
Staff: 2
Annual Budget: $50-100,000
Exec. Director: Kenneth R. Bowman
Associate Director: Sheila Curry

Historical Note
MMII provides a forum for professionals engaged in marketing, sales and administration of employee benefits such as worksite marketing, payroll deduction and other mass marketed services. Membership: $395/year (manufacturers/administrators/vendors); $95/year (producers/brokers).

Publications:
Membership Directory. a.
Membership Services Catalogue. a.
Worksite Insights. bi-m. adv.

Meetings/Conferences:
Annual Meetings: Spring
1999 – Phoenix, AZ(Pointe Squaw Peak)/April 28-30/200
2000 – Orlando, FL(Buena Vista Palace)/April 26-28/200

Master Brewers Ass'n of the Americas (1887)
2421 N. Mayfair Road, Suite 310
Wauwatosa, WI 53226-1407
Tel: (414)774-8558
Members: 3,500 individuals
Staff: 3
Annual Budget: $1-2,000,000
Senior Administrator: Connie Hanner
Director, Membership and Advertising: Veronica Rakowski

Historical Note
Founded as the Master Brewers Ass'n of America, it assumed its present name in 1979. Members are brewery executives, suppliers and technical personnel in related industries. Membership: $100/year (individual).

Publications:
MBAA Communications. q. adv.
MBAA Technical Quarterly. q. adv.

Meetings/Conferences:
Annual Meetings: Fall
1999 – Milwaukee, WI(Hilton)
2000 – Orlando, FL

Master Dairies (1965)
P.O. Box 890
Annandale, VA 22003
Tel: (703)914-1565   Fax: (703)914-1613
Members: 82 dairy companies
President and C.E.O.: William C. Tinklepaugh
Exec. Assistant/Office Manager: Betsy McCool
Comptroller: Vicki Johnson

Historical Note
Master Dairies represents U.S. and Canadian dairy companies.

Master Printers of America (1945)
100 Daingerfield Road
Alexandria, VA 22314-2888
Tel: (703)519-8130   Fax: (703)548-3227
Members: 9,000 individuals
Staff: 3
Annual Budget: $500-1,000,000
President: Brian W. Gill

Historical Note
A division of Printing Industries of America. Members are open shop printers.

Meetings/Conferences:
Annual Meetings: Spring

Mastercard Internat'l (1966)
2000 Purchase St.
Purchase, NY 10577
Tel: (914)249-2000
Web Site: http://www.mastercard.com

Members: 23,000 financial institutions
Staff: 2400
Annual Budget: Over $100,000,000
President and CEO: Robert W. Selender

Historical Note
Administers the MasterCard credit card and other MasterCard products for 29,000 member financial institutions around the world. Formerly (1979) Interbank Card Ass'n. Has an annual budget of over $150 million.

Publications:
Member News. q.

Meetings/Conferences:
1999 – Washington, DC/May 9-12

Material Handling Equipment Distributors Ass'n (1954)

201 U.S. Hwy. 45
Vernon Hills, IL   60061-2398
Tel: (847)680-3500   *Fax:* (847)362-6989
E-Mail: connect@mheda.org
Web Site: http://www.mheda.org
Members: 700 companies
Staff: 6
Annual Budget: $1-2,000,000
Exec. V President: Liz Richards

Historical Note
Membership: $415-1,550/year (company).

Publications:
The MHEDA Journal. q.

Meetings/Conferences:
Annual Meetings: Spring/750-1,000
1999 – Boca Raton, FL(Boca Raton Resort)/April 24-28/700
2000 – San Diego, CA(Hyatt Regency)/April 15-19/700

Material Handling Industry Ass'n (1945)

8720 Red Oak Blvd., Suite 201
Charlotte, NC   28217-3957
Tel: (704)676-1190   *Fax:* (704)676-1199
Web Site: http://www.mhia.org
Members: 200 companies
Staff: 20
Annual Budget: $2-5,000,000
Chief Executive Officer: Albert L. Leffler
Director, Marketing and Communication: Carol Miller
V. President, Development: Richard E. Ward, Ph.D.
C.O.O.: John Nofsinger
Director, Membership: Victoria Whaler

Historical Note
Founded as Material Handling Institute; assumed its current name in 1995. A member of the Manufacturers Alliance for Productivity and Innovation. Makers of industrial material handling equipment such as conveyors, racks, hoists and cranes, lift trucks. Membership: $1,500/year, (company).

Publications:
Membership Roster. a.
On the MHove. bi-m.
The Exhibitor. m.

Meetings/Conferences:
1999 – Amelia Island, SC(Ritz Carlton)/Oct. 1-5

Material Handling Institute

Historical Note
Became (1995) Material Handling Industry Ass'n.

Materials and Methods Standards Ass'n (1962)

P.O. Box 350
Grand Haven, MI   49417-0350
Tel: (616)842-7844   *Fax:* (616)842-1547
Members: 40 companies
Staff: 1
Annual Budget: $10-25,000
President: Harvey J. Powell

Historical Note
Incorporated in 1962 in Texas as the Mortar Manufacturers Standards Ass'n, became Methods and Materials Standards Ass'n in 1977 and assumed its present name in 1984. Membership is composed of manufacturers of ceramic tile and ceramic tile installation products. MMSA is represented on the Tile Council of America and the ANSI A108/118/136 committees. MMSA member committees develop information and ANSI standards for the industry as technology dictates. Membership: $300/year (company).

Meetings/Conferences:
Annual Meetings: Held in conjunction with the Internat'l Tile & Stone Exposition

Materials Handling and Management Soc. (1947)

8720 Red Oak Blvd., Suite 201
Charlotte, NC   28217
Tel: (704)676-1184   *Fax:* (704)676-1199
Web Site: www.mhia.org/mhms
Members: 1,500 individuals
Staff: 2
Annual Budget: $50-100,000
Exec. Director: Bobbie Curtis

Historical Note
Founded as the American Material Handling Soc. it became the Internat'l Material Management Soc. in 1966 and assumed its present name in 1991. A professional society of individuals interested in advancing the theory and practice of the management and handling of all types of material. Membership: $60/year.

Publications:
Material Handling Outlook. q.
Membership Directory. a.

Meetings/Conferences:
Semi-Annual Meetings: Spring and Fall
1999 – Chicago, IL

Materials Marketing Associates (1963)

136 S. Keowee St.
Dayton, OH   45402
Tel: (937)222-1024   *Fax:* (937)222-5794
Members: 19 companies
Staff: 7
Annual Budget: $50-100,000
Exec. Director: Kimberly Fantaci

Historical Note
Chemical distributors representing manufacturers marketing chemical raw material specialties to makers of coatings, inks, pharmaceuticals, adhesives, cosmetics, plastics, soaps, detergents, etc. Membership: $2,000/year (organization/company).

Publications:
Newsletter. m.

Meetings/Conferences:
Annual Meetings: February
1999 – Maui, HI
2000 – Boca Raton, FL

Materials Properties Council (1966)

3 Park Ave., 27th Floor
New York, NY   10016-5902
Tel: (212)705-7693   *Fax:* (212)371-9622
Members: 600 individuals, 250 companies or organizations
Staff: 3
Annual Budget: $500-1,000,000
Exec. Director: Martin Prager, Ph.D.

Historical Note
Formerly (1986) The Metal Properties Council. MPC is an outgrowth of the ASTM-ASME Joint Committee on the Effect of Temperature on the Properties of Metals which was founded in 1925 to meet the apparent need for information on the subject in the construction of central power stations. After 40 years it was apparent that a permanently staffed organization was needed to ensure the availability of valid data on materials to meet advancing technology. MPC was founded in 1966 to meet this need. Sponsored by American Soc. of Mechanical Engineers, American Soc. for Testing and Materials, American Soc. for Metals, Engineering Foundation and American Welding Soc.

Publications:
Yearbook. a.

Meetings/Conferences:
Annual Meetings: 2nd Thursday in October/25

Materials Research Soc. (1973)

506 Keystone Drive
Warrendale, PA   15086-7573
Tel: (724)779-3003   *Fax:* (724)779-8313
E-Mail: info@mrs.org
Web Site: http://www.mrs.org/
Members: 12,000 individuals
Staff: 40
Annual Budget: $2-5,000,000
Exec. Director: John B. Ballance, CAE
Director, Meeting Activities: Gail A. Oare
Director, Finance and Administration: Robert H. Pachavis
Director, Electronic Services: Robert J. Novak

Historical Note
Members are individuals adopting a multi-disciplinary approach towards the problems of research on materials. Membership: $25/year (student); $75/year (individual).

Publications:
Journal of Materials Research. m.
MRS Bulletin. m.

Meetings/Conferences:
Semi-annual Meetings: Spring in San Francisco(Marriott), Fall
        in Boston, MA(Marriott/Westin Copley Place)
1999 – /April 19-23
1999 – /Nov. 29-Dec. 3
2000 – /April 10-14
2000 – /Nov. 27-Dec. 1
2001 – /April 16-20
2001 – /Nov. 26-30
2002 – /April 1-5
2002 – /Dec. 2-6

Materials Technology Institute of the Chemical Process Industries (1977)

1215 Fern Ridge Pkwy., Suite 116
St. Louis, MO   63141-4401
Tel: (314)576-7712   *Fax:* (314)576-6078
Web Site: http://www.mti-link.org
Members: 42 companies
Staff: 8
Annual Budget: $500-1,000,000
Exec. Director: Thomas W. Gibbs, Ph.D.
Manager, Administration: Lucretia S. Humphrey

Historical Note
Established and incorporated in New York in 1977, MTI was formed to avoid duplication in investigations pertaining to materials of construction and equipment used in the process industries and to provide opportunites for the exchange of information. Membership: $5,000-26,000/yr. (based on total sales).

Publications:
Newsletter. semi-a.

Meetings/Conferences:
Annual Meetings: April
1999 – Phoenix, AZ

Mathematical Ass'n of America (1915)

1529 18th St., N.W., Suite 600
Washington, DC   20036-1358
Tel: (202)387-5200   *Fax:* (202)265-2384
Toll Free: (800)741 - 9415
E-Mail: maahg@maa.org
Web Site: http://www.maa.org
Members: 33,000 individuals

Staff: 30
Annual Budget: $2-5,000,000
Exec. Director: Marcia P. Sward, Ph.D.
Director, Finance: Neil Beskin
Director, Marketing and Membership: Caroline Hearn Fuchs
Director, Publications and Electronic Services: Donald J. Albers
Development Director: Carol Shaw

Historical Note
Founded in Columbus, Ohio in 1915 to promote the teaching of mathematics, especially on the collegiate level. A constituent member of the Conference Board of the Mathematical Sciences. Membership: $89-122/year, varies by number of journals subscribed (individual); $150/yr. (institution).

Publications:
American Mathematical Monthly. 10/yr. adv.
College Mathematics Journal. 5/yr. adv.
Focus Newsletter. bi-m. adv.
Mathematics Magazine. 5/yr. adv.

Meetings/Conferences:
Semi-annual Meetings: Winter, with the American
        Mathematical Soc. and Summer
1999 – San Antonio, TX/Jan. 16-19

Meals On Wheels Ass'n of America (1973)

1414 Prince St., Suite 202
Alexandria, VA   22314-2815
Tel: (703)548-5558   *Fax:* (703)548-8024
Members: 900 programs & corporate members
Staff: 6
Annual Budget: $250-500,000
Exec. Director: Enid A. Borden
Director, Legislative: Peggy Ingraham
Administrative Officer: Elizabeth Doyle

Historical Note
Members are organizations providing meals, particularly to the elderly, disabled and homebound. MOWAA represents these organizations by providing training/technical assistance and legislative support. MOWAA consists of organizations throughout the United States and Canada. Membership: $95/year (non-profit organizations), $200 or $300/year (corporations).

Publications:
Member Mail. q. adv.
Membership Directory. a.
MOWAA News. q. adv.

Meetings/Conferences:
1999 – Madison, WI(Concourse Hotel)/400
2000 – Redondo Beach, CA
2001 – Kansas City, MO

Measurement, Control and Automation Ass'n (1918)

P.O. Box 3698
Williamsburg, VA   23187-3698
Tel: (757)258-3100   *Fax:* (757)258-9066
E-Mail: mcaa@measure.org
Web Site: http://www.measure.org
Members: 150 companies
Staff: 2
Annual Budget: $250-500,000
President: Cynthia A. Esher

Historical Note
MCAA is a trade association representing manufacturers and distributors of instrumentation and systems used in industrial process measurement and control. MCAA disassociated from the SAMA Group of Associations in 1994. Membership: annual dues vary by sales volume (company).

Publications:
Measuring Markets - Economic Newsletter. q.
Membership Directory. a.
Messenger. irreg.

Meetings/Conferences:
1999 – Malvern, PA(Desmond Hotel)/May 17-20
2000 – Atlanta, GA(Peachtree Conference Center)/May 18-19

Meat Importers' Council of America (1962)

1901 N. Ft. Myer Drive
Arlington, VA   22209
Tel: (703)522-1910
Members: 250 companies
Staff: 4
Annual Budget: $250-500,000
Exec. Director: William Morrison

Meetings/Conferences:
Annual Meetings: Fall
1999 – Chicago, IL

Meat Industry Suppliers Ass'n (1948)

111 Park Place
Falls Church, VA   22046-4513
Tel: (703)538-1793   *Fax:* (703)241-5603
Members: 20 companies
Staff: 2
Annual Budget: $25-50,000
Exec. Director: Clay D. Tyeryar

Historical Note
Formerly (1981) Meat Industry Supply and Equipment Ass'n. Members are suppliers to the meat, poultry and seafood packing and processing industries. Absorbed the Meat Machinery Manufacturers Institute and the Food Machinery Service Institute in 1984; these are now autonomous divisions of MISA.

Publications:
Buyer's Guide. a.
Newsletters. bi-m.

Meetings/Conferences:

Meat Machinery Manufacturers Institute (1938)

Historical Note
An autonomous division of the Meat Industry Supplier Ass'n.

Mechanical Contractors Ass'n of America (1889)

1385 Piccard Drive
Rockville, MD 20850-4329
Tel: (301)869-5800 *Fax:* (301)990-9690
Web Site: http://www.mcaa.org
Members: 1,400 companies
Staff: 25
Annual Budget: $2-5,000,000
Exec. V. President: John R. Gentille

Historical Note
Founded as the Master Steam and Hot Water Fitters Ass'n. Assumed its present name in 1956. MCAA represents mechanical contractors (i.e. heating, piping, air conditioning and plumbing contractors) who employ primarily union labor. The Nat'l Certified Pipe Welding Bureau, Mechanical Service Contractors of America, and the Nat'l Plumbing Bureau are departments of MCAA.

Publications:
Membership Directory. a. adv.
The Reporter. m.

Meetings/Conferences:
Annual Meetings: February
1999 – Lake Buena Vista, FL/Feb. 21-25

Mechanical Power Transmission Ass'n (1933)

6724 Lone Oak Blvd.
Naples, FL 34109-6834
Tel: (941)514-3441 *Fax:* (941)514-3470
E-Mail: staff@mpta.org
Web Site: http://mpta.org
Members: 14 companies
Staff: 2
Annual Budget: $25-50,000
Exec. Director: Robert A. Reinfried

Historical Note
Formerly Multiple V-Belt Drive and Mechanical Power Transmission Ass'n. Membership: $500-3,850/year.

Publications:
See Web Site.

Meetings/Conferences:
Annual Meetings: April
1999 – Litchfield Park, AZ(Wigwam)/50
2000 – Litchfield Park, AZ(Wigwam)/50
2001 – Litchfield Park, AZ(Wigwam)/50
2002 – Litchfield Park, AZ(Wigwam)/50

Mechanical Service Contractors of America (1971)

1385 Piccard Drive
Rockville, MD 20850
Tel: (301)869-5800 *Fax:* (301)990-9690
Web Site: http://www.mcaa.org/msca
Members: 750 companies
Staff: 2
Annual Budget: $500-1,000,000
Exec. Director: Barbara A. Dolim

Historical Note
Formerly (1990) Nat'l Mechanical Equipment Services and Maintenance Bureau (SMB). A department of the Mechanical Contractors Ass'n of America, MSCA members are employers of United Ass'n of Journeymen and Apprentices of the Plumbing and Pipe Fitting Industry of the United States and Canada labor who are involved in service and maintenance work in the heating, ventilating, air conditioning and process piping industries. MSCA promotes the interests of service contractors by acting as a clearinghouse for information and by providing liaison between the contractor and the UA.

Publications:
Dateline MSCA.
MSCA Newsletter. q.

Meetings/Conferences:
Annual Meetings: October/300

Mechanics Educational Soc. of America (1933)

Historical Note
Address unknown in 1995.

Media Credit Ass'n (1903)

919 Third Ave., 22nd Floor
New York, NY 10022
Tel: (212)872-3700 *Fax:* (212)888-4623
Members: 850 magazines
Staff: 3
V. President: Vaughn P. Benjamin

Historical Note
Since 1903 the MCA has been the primary source of credit information to the magazine industry. The MCA provides a Credit Guideline Service to all members of the Magazine Publishers of America (MPA).

Meetings/Conferences:

Media Human Resources Ass'n (1949)

1800 Duke St.
Alexandria, VA 22314-3499
Tel: (703)535-6075 *Fax:* (703)739-0399
E-Mail: keithg@shrm.org
Web Site: http://www.shrm.org
Members: 630 individuals
Staff: 3
Annual Budget: $100-250,000
Contact: Keith J. Greene, SPHR

Historical Note
NPRA is a Professional Emphasis Group affiliated with the Soc. for Human Resources Management. Members are personnel/human resources and labor relations officers of news media organizaitons. Administrative support is provided by SHRM, whose location is the above. Membership: $270/year.

Publications:
MPRA Hot Line. bi-m.

MPRA Membership Directory. a. adv.
MPRA News. bi-m.

Meetings/Conferences:
Annual Meetings: June/7000
1999 – Atlanta, GA
2000 – Las Vegas, NV
2001 – San Fransico, CA

Media Rating Council (1964)

200 W. 57th St., Suite 204
New York, NY 10019-3211
Tel: (212)765-0200 *Fax:* (212)765-1868
Members: 53 companies
Staff: 2
Annual Budget: $250-500,000
Exec. Director: Richard Weinstein

Historical Note
Formerly (1983) Broadcast Rating Council and (1997) Electronic Media Rating Council. MRC was established by broadcast industry, trade groups and major networks to maintain industry confidence in the integrity of broadcast rating services. Conducts an accreditation system involving regular audits by professional CPA firms of all aspects of the operation of the independent companies which produce radio, TV, cable and print ratings.

Meetings/Conferences:
Annual Meetings: usually New York, NY/Summer and Fall

Media Research Directors Ass'n (1947)

Historical Note
Address unknown in 1997.

Medical Device Manufacturers Ass'n (1992)

1900 K St., N.W., Suite 300
Washington, DC 20006
Tel: (202)496-7150 *Fax:* (202)496-7756
Members: 130 companies
Staff: 4
Annual Budget: $250-500,000
Exec. Director: Stephen J. Northrup
Dep. Director: Mary-Lacey Walsh

Historical Note
Supersedes Smaller Manufacturers Medical Device Ass'n. MDMA represents manufacturers of medical devices, diagnostic products, and health care information systems. Membership fee varies, based on revenues.

Publications:
MDMA Report: Critical Issues. m. adv.

Meetings/Conferences:
Annual Meetings: May
1999 – Washington, DC/May 19-21

Medical Group Management Ass'n (1926)

104 Inverness Terrace East
Englewood, CO 80112-5306
Tel: (303)799-1111 *Fax:* (303)643-4427
Toll Free: (888)608 - 5601
E-Mail: tomadams@mgma.com
Web Site: http://www.mgma.com
Members: 19,000 individuals, 9,000 medical groups
Staff: 160
Annual Budget: $10-25,000,000
Chairman/Interim C.E.O.: W. Robert Wright
Communications Director: Dennis L. Barnhardt
Dir., Meetings and Conferences: Carol Wilke
Dep. Exec. V. President and C.O.O.: James E. Paxton, CAE
V. President and C.F.O.: Eric Cauble, CPA
V. President/C.I.O.: Gary C. Fox

Historical Note
Founded as the Ass'n of Clinic Managers, it became the Nat'l Ass'n of Clinic Managers in 1946 and assumed its present name in 1963. Affiliated with the honorary organization American College of Medical Group Administrators, and parent organization of the Center for Research in Ambulatory Health Care Administration. Members are managers of medical group practices. American College of Medical Practice Executives is a division of MGMA. Has an annual budget of over $20 million.

Publications:
MGM Journal. bi-m. adv.
MGM Update. m. adv.
MGMA Directory. a. adv.

Meetings/Conferences:
Annual Meetings: Fall
1999 – San Diego, CA(Convention Center)/Oct. 17-20
2000 – Atlanta, GA(World Congress Center)/Oct. 15-18
2001 – San Antonio, TX(Convention Center)/Oct. 21-24

Medical Library Ass'n (1898)

65 E. Wacker Place, Suite 1900
Chicago, IL 60601
Tel: (312)419-9094 *Fax:* (312)419-8950
Web Site: http://www.mlanet.org
Members: 5,000 individuals and institutions
Staff: 20
Annual Budget: $1-2,000,000
Exec. Director: Carla J. Funk
Public Relations: Evelyn Shaevel
Director, Finance and Administration: Ray Naegele
Director, Membership Development: Kate E. Corcoran

Historical Note
Originated in 1898 as the Ass'n of Medical Librarians and became the Medical Library Ass'n in 1907. Incorporated in Maryland in 1934. Membership: $110/year (individual); $175-410/year (organization).

Publications:
Bulletin of the MLA. q. adv.
Current Catalog Proof Sheets. w.
MLA Directory. a. adv.
MLA News. 10/year. adv.

Meetings/Conferences:
Annual Meetings: Spring/2,300
1999 – Chicago, IL(Hyatt)/May 14-20

Medical Marketing Ass'n (1965)

74 New Montgomery St., Suite 230
San Francisco, CA 94105-2411
Tel: (415)764-4805 *Fax:* (415)764-1023
Toll Free: (800)551 - 2173
E-Mail: info@mmanet.org
Web Site: http://www.mmanet.org
Members: 950 individuals
Annual Budget: $250-500,000
Exec. Director: Kerry G. Parker, CAE

Historical Note
Membership: $155/year (individual).

Publications:
Marketplace. q. adv.
MMA Directory. a. adv.

Meetings/Conferences:
1999 – San Diego, CA/June 2-4/300

Medical Mycological Soc. of the Americas (1966)

Bureau of Labs, Texas Dept. of Health
1100 W. 49th St.
Austin, TX 78756
Tel: (512)458-7566 *Fax:* (512)458-7697
E-Mail: jim.harris@tdh.state.tx.us
Members: 400 individuals
Annual Budget: under $10,000
Secretary-Treasurer: Dr. Jim Harris

Historical Note
Founded in 1966 to promote the development and study of medical mycology in all its aspects by scientists from the Americas. Membership: $10/year.

Publications:
Newsletter. 2/year.

Meetings/Conferences:
Annual Meetings: May, in conjunction with the American Soc. for Microbiology.
1999 – Chicago, IL/May 29-30

Medical Records Institute (1979)

P.O. Box 600770
Newtonville, MA 02460
Tel: (617)964-3923 *Fax:* (617)964-3926
E-Mail: cust_service@medrecinst.com
Web Site: http://www.tepr.com
Members: 1000 affiliates
Staff: 7
Annual Budget: $1-2,000,000
Exec. Director: C. Peter Waegemann
Manager of Industry Relations: Jack Pelrine
Conference Manager: Jana Hogan
Operations Manager/Registrar: Jason Glass

Historical Note
Formerly (1988) the Institute for Medical Record Economics. Members are medical record, computer professionals and others concerned with research and education in medical documentation.

Publications:
Toward an Electronic Patient Record. 10/yea.

Meetings/Conferences:
Annual Meetings: Spring
1999 – Orlando, Fl/May 1-6

Medical-Dental-Hospital Bureaus of America

Historical Note
Became (1996) Medical-Dental-Hospital Business Associates.

Medical-Dental-Hospital Business Associates (1939)

7315 Wisconsin Ave., Suite 424-East
Bethesda, MD 20814
Tel: (301)961-8680 *Fax:* (301)961-8681
Members: 125 companies
Staff: 4
Annual Budget: $100-250,000
Exec. Director: Sanford J. Hill
Director of Communications: Hugh Mullins
Membership Coordinator: Linda Hill

Historical Note
Founded as Medical-Dental-Hospital Bureaus of America; assumed its current name in 1996. MDHBA members are owners/general managers of collection bureaus, credit bureaus and accounts receivable management agencies. Membership: varies by company size.

Publications:
Newscope. m.

Meetings/Conferences:
Annual Meetings: Fall

Medieval Academy of America (1925)

1430 Massachusetts Ave.
Cambridge, MA 02138
Tel: (617)491-1622 *Fax:* (617)492-3303
E-Mail: maa@fas.harvard.edu
Web Site: http://www.georgetown.edu/MedievalAcademy/
Members: 3,900 individuals, 1,800 libraries & institutions
Staff: 4
Annual Budget: $250-500,000
Exec. Director: Luke Wenger
Office Manager: Sheryl Mullane-Corvi

Historical Note
Member American Council of Learned Societies. Members are scholars with an interest in the period 500-1500 AD. Membership: $55-70/year (individual); $25/year (sudent/retired); $70-80/year (organization).

Publications:
Medieval Academy News. 3/yr.

Speculum: A Journal of Medieval Studies. q. adv.

Meetings/Conferences:
Annual Meetings: Spring
1999 – Washington, DC(Georgetown
    University)/April 8-10/500
2000 – Austin, TX(University of Texas)/April 13-15/500

Meeting Professionals Internat'l (1972)
4455 LBJ Freeway, Suite 1200
Dallas, TX 75244-5903
Tel: (214)712-7718   *Fax:* (972)702-3036
Web Site: http://www.mpiweb.org
Members: 15,000 individuals
Staff: 58
Annual Budget: $10-25,000,000
Exec. V. President/C.E.O.: Edwin L. Griffin, Jr., CAE
Public Relations Manager: Cindy Walden
Director, Conferences and Meetings: Eric Johnson, CMP
Director, Education: Kimberly A. Meyer
Director, Administrative Services: Al Noland
Director, Marketing: Gary E. Boyler
Director, Publications: Linda C. Chandler

Historical Note
Formerly (1994) Meeting Planners Internat'l. A professional educational society, MPI members are meeting industry professionals who plan and/or manage meetings, conferences and trade shows for corporations, associations, and educational institutions as well as those individuals who provide goods and services to the meetings industry. MPI has 54 local chapters and one club in the U.S. and is represented in 44 countries. MPI, through its involvement in the Convention Liaison Council, supports the CLC Certified Meeting Professionals (CMP) program; also sponsors the Certified Meeting Manager (CMM) designation. Member of the Center for Exhibition Industry Research. Has an annual budget of approximately $10.5 million. Membership: $310/year (individual).

Publications:
Meeting Manager. m. adv.
Membership Directory. a.

Meetings/Conferences:
Semi-Annual Meetings: Summer and Winter
1999 – Vancouver, BC, Canada(Waterfront Hotel)
1999 – Philadelphia, PA(Marriott)

Meetings Management Ass'n
Historical Note
Became (1996) Meetings Management Soc.

Meetings Management Soc.
Historical Note
Defunct in 1997.

MEMA Information Services Council (1972)
P.O. Box 13966
Research Triangle Pk, NC 27709-3966
Tel: (919)549-4800   *Fax:* (919)549-8733
E-Mail: sales@misg.com
Web Site: http://www.affmkt.com
Members: 75 companies
Staff: 1
Annual Budget: $10-25,000
Exec. Secretary: Alan Jones
Director, Marketing: Chris Gardver

Historical Note
A peer group within the Motor and Equipment Manufacturers Ass'n, the MISC serves as a forum for industry interaction, education and idea exchange regarding matters of common interest to data processing managers and related executives in automotive manufacturing companies. Membership: $150/year (company).

Publications:
Member Company Profiles. a.
Membership Roster. a.

Meetings/Conferences:
Semi-annual Meetings: Spring and Fall

Messenger Courier Ass'n of the Americas (1987)
1101 15th St., N.W., Suite 202
Washington, DC 20005
Tel: (202)785-3298   *Fax:* (202)223-9741
E-Mail: MCAA@assnhq.com
Web Site: http://www.mcaa.com
Members: 400 companies
Staff: 3
Annual Budget: $250-500,000
Exec. Director: Robert L. DeCaprio

Historical Note
The MCAA was formed in 1987 to promote, encourage, broaden and advance the interests of those engaged in the messenger courier industry and its related services. Membership: more than 475/year (organization).

Publications:
MCAA Membership Directory and Network Guide. semi-a.
    adv.
Messenger Courier Magazine. q. adv.
On Time Newsletter. m. adv.

Meetings/Conferences:
1999 – Tucson, AZ/May 18-22

Metal Building Manufacturers Ass'n (1956)
1300 Sumner Ave.
Cleveland, OH 44115-2851
Tel: (216)241-7333   *Fax:* (216)241-0105
E-Mail: administrator@mbma.com
Web Site: http://www.mbma.com
Members: 42 manufactures, 39 associates
Staff: 2
General Manager: Charles M. Stockinger

Historical Note
A trade association representing building systems manufactures, roofing systems manufactures and suppliers to the industry. Merged with Metal Roofing Systems Ass'n in 1998.

Metal Construction Ass'n (1983)
104 S. Michigan , 15th Fl.
Chicago, IL 60603-1210
Tel: (312)201-0193   *Fax:* (312)201-0214
Members: 135 companies
Staff: 2
Annual Budget: $50-100,000
Exec. Director: James C. Stanley

Historical Note
MCA is dedicated to the promotion of the use of metal in all types of construction: residential, industrial, commercial, farm, institutional and retrofit.

Publications:
MCA News. q.
Membership Directory. a.

Meetings/Conferences:
Semi-annual Meetings: January and Trade Show in July-
August

Metal Findings Manufacturers Ass'n (1930)
25 Calhoun Ave.,
Providence, RI 02907
Tel: (401)781-3729   *Fax:* (401)941-8550
E-Mail: clint@mfma.net
Web Site: http://www.mfma.net
Members: 77 companies
Annual Budget: under $10,000
President: Clint Whitman

Historical Note
Makers of metal parts and fittings used in the assembly of jewelry. Has no paid staff or permanent address. Officers change every two years. Membership: $200/year (organization/company).

Meetings/Conferences:
Annual Meetings: May in the Providence region.

Metal Finishing Suppliers Ass'n (1951)
112-J Elden St.
Herndon, VA 20170
Tel: (703)709-5729   *Fax:* (703)709-1036
E-Mail: dtrin@erds.com
Web Site: http://www.mfsa.org
Members: 165 companies
Staff: 1
Annual Budget: $250-500,000
Exec. Director: Diana L. Tringali

Historical Note
Membership: $1,100-10,100/year (corporate).

Publications:
Newsletter. q.

Meetings/Conferences:
Semi-Annual Meetings: Spring and Fall

Metal Framing Manufacturers Ass'n (1981)
401 N. Michigan Ave.
Chicago, IL 60611
Tel: (312)644-6610   *Fax:* (312)245-1081
Members: 7 companies
Staff: 2
Annual Budget: under $10,000
Exec. Director: Jack M. Springer

Historical Note
Membership: $1,000/year.

Publications:
Guidelines for the Use of Metal Framing. a.
MFMA Standards Publication. a.

Meetings/Conferences:
Annual Meetings: None held

Metal Injection Molding Ass'n
Historical Note
A constituent association of the Metal Powder Industries Federation.

Metal Polishers, Buffers, Platers and Allied Workers Internat'l Union (1892)
Historical Note
Defunct, merged into the Internat'l Brotherhood of Boilermakers, Iron Ship Builders, Blacksmiths, Forgers and Helpers in 1997.

Metal Powder Industries Federation (1944)
105 College Rd., East
Princeton, NJ 08540-6622
Tel: (609)452-7700   *Fax:* (609)987-8523
E-Mail: info@mpif.org
Web Site: http://www.mpif.org
Members: 290 companies
Staff: 20
Annual Budget: $2-5,000,000
Exec. Director: Donald G. White
Director, Public Relations and Marketing: Peter K. Johnson, CAE
Director, Marketing and Technology: James R. Dale
Director, Conferences and Professional Development: C. James
    Trombino, CAE
Manager, Professional Development: Benny Sun

Historical Note
Represents the internat'l trade, commercial and technological interests of the metal powder producing and consuming industries. The Federation consists of the following constituent ass'ns: the Powder Metallurgy Parts Ass'n, Metal Powder Producers Ass'n, Powder Metallurgy Equipment Ass'n, Refractory Metals Ass'n, Metal Powder Technology Ass'n and Metal Injection Molding Ass'n.

Publications:
Advances in P/M and Articulate Materials. a.
P/M Science and Technology Briefs. 6/year.

Meetings/Conferences:
1999 – Vancouver, BC(Vancouver Convention
    Center)/June 20-24
2000 – New York, NY(New York Hilton)/May 30-June 3
2001 – New Orleans, LA(New Orleans Hilton
    Riverside)/May 13-17
2002 – Orlando, FL(Walt Disney World Dolphin)/June 16-21

Metal Powder Producers Ass'n
Historical Note
A constituent member of the Metal Powder Industries Federation.

Metal Powder Technology Ass'n (1985)
Historical Note
A constituent unit of the Metal Powder Industries Federation.

Metal Roofing Systems Ass'n (1994)
Historical Note
Ass'n merged with the Metal Building Manufactures Ass'n in 1998.

Metal Treating Institute (1933)
1550 Roberts Drive
Jacksonville Beach, FL 32250-3222
Tel: (904)249-0448   *Fax:* (904)249-0459
E-Mail: metaltreat@aol.com
Members: 410 companies
Staff: 4
Annual Budget: $500-1,000,000
Exec. V. President: M. Lance Miller, CAE
Director, Member Services: L.N. McIlmoil

Historical Note
Membership fee varies, approximately $1,000-$3,000/year (company).

Publications:
Open Hearth. m.

Meetings/Conferences:
Semi-Annual Meetings: Spring and Fall
1999 – Scottsdale, AZ
2000 – Hawaii

Metaphysical Soc. of America (1950)
University of Alabama in Huntsville
Huntsville, AL 35899
Tel: (256)890-6555   *Fax:* (256)895-6949
Members: 600 individuals
Staff: 1
Annual Budget: under $10,000
Secretary-Treasurer: Brian Martine

Historical Note
Promotes the consideration of fundamental philosophical issues from a wide range of historical and contemporary perspectives. A member of the American Council of Learned Societies. Membership: $15/year.

Meetings/Conferences:
Annual Meetings: March

Methacrylate Producers Ass'n (1988)
1250 Connecticut Ave.
Suite 800
Washington, DC 20036
Tel: (202)637-9040   *Fax:* (202)637-9178
Members: 4 manufacturers
Annual Budget: $250-500,000
Exec. Director: Elizabeth K. Hunt

Historical Note
Members are manufacturers of basic methacrylate monomers. MPA serves to pool health, safety and environmental information; to sponsor testing when appropriate; and to communicate the industry's views on regulatory matters.

Methods Time Measurement Ass'n for Standards and Research (1951)
Historical Note
See MTM Ass'n for Standards and Research.

Methyl Tertiary Butyl Ether Task Force (1987)
Historical Note
Task Force became defunct in 1996.

Metropolitan Symphony Managers Ass'n
Historical Note
A sub-group of the American Symphony Orchestra League without dues structure or separate headquarters.

Mexican Food and Beverage Ass'n (1989)
Historical Note
Address unknown in 1996.

Mexican-American Grocers Ass'n (1977)
405 N. San Fernando Road
Los Angeles, CA 90031
Tel: (323)227-1565   *Fax:* (323)227-6935
Members: 14,000 individuals
Staff: 6
Editor: Jerome Lloyd

Historical Note
MAGA members are food store owners who cater to the hispanic market in the United States. Membership: $100/year.

Publications:
MAGAzine. 8/yr.

Meetings/Conferences:
1999 – Palm Springs, CA/March 11-13

Micro Channel Developers Ass'n (1990)
Historical Note
Address unknown in 1998.

Microbeam Analysis Soc. (1968)
P.O. Box 3552
Gaithersburg, MD 20885
Tel: (301)540-6975
Members: 1,600 individuals, 60 companies
Staff: 2
Annual Budget: $10-25,000
Contact, Member Services: Scott Wight

Historical Note
Formerly (1973) Electron Probe Analysis Soc. of America. Society's purpose is to advance and diffuse knowledge concerning the principles and applications of microbeam instruments or related instrumentation, and to provide continuity, advanced planning, and a financing mechanism for annual meetings.

Publications:
MicroNews. 3/year.
Microscopy Microanalysis Journal. bi-m.

Meetings/Conferences:
Annual Meetings: Summer, usually August
1999 – Portland, OR/Aug. 1-5

Microcirculatory Soc. of America (1954)
444 E. Algonquin Ave.
Arlington Heights, IL 60005-4654
Tel: (847)228-8375   *Fax:* (847)228-6509
Members: 580 individuals
Annual Budget: $25-50,000
Exec. Director: Laura M. Downes

Historical Note
Incorporated in Massachusetts as the Microcirculatory Conference, it assumed its present name in 1965. Membership: $70/year.

Publications:
Directory. a.
Microcirculation. q.
Newsletter. 3/year.

Meetings/Conferences:
Annual Meetings: Prior to Federation of American Socs. for Experimental Biology

MicroComputer Investors Ass'n (1976)
902 Anderson Drive
Fredericksburg, VA 22405
Tel: (540)371-5474
Administrator: Jack Williams, Ph.D.

Historical Note
MCIA is a professional, non-profit association of persons utilizing microcomputers to assist in making and managing investments. Maintains a computer bulletin board at (540) 373-8215. Membership: $50/year (individual).

Publications:
MicroComputer Investor. semi-a.

Microneurography Soc. (1981)
Historical Note
The ass'n declined to provide updated information for this edition.

Microscopy Soc. of America (1942)
435 N. Michigan Ave., Suite 1717
Chicago, IL 60611-4067
Tel: (312)644-1527   *Fax:* (312)644-8557
Toll Free: (800)538 - 3672
Members: 4,000 individuals
Staff: 2
Annual Budget: $500-1,000,000
Managing Director: Philip Lesser, PhD, CAE

Historical Note
Formerly (1992) the Electron Microscopy Soc. of America. Established November 27, 1942 as the Electron Microscope Society of America at the Second National Chemical Exposition in Chicago and incorporated in Delaware. An affiliate of the American Institute of Physics and the American Ass'n for the Advancement of Science. Membership: $40/year (individual); $10/year (student), $350/year (organization).

Publications:
Directory. bi-a.
Journal. bi-m. adv.
Proceedings. a.

Meetings/Conferences:
Annual Meetings: August/2,000-2,500
1999 – Portland, OR(Oregon Convention Center)/Aug. 1-5
2000 – Philadelphia, PA/July
2001 – Long Beach, CA/Aug. 12-16

MicroStation Community
9238 Hwy. 20 West, Suite 117
Madison, AL 35758-9111
Tel: (205)774-0251   *Fax:* (205)774-0195
Toll Free: (800)862 - 7990
E-Mail: info@tmc.org
Web Site: http://www.tma.org
Exec. Director: Kerry F. McCain

Historical Note
Provides information, training opportunities and networking to groups and individuals interested in MicroStation technology.

Meetings/Conferences:
1999 – Philadelphia, PA/Sept. 29-Oct. 1

Microwave Theory and Techniques Soc.
Historical Note
See IEEE Microwave Theory and Techniques Soc.

Middle East Librarians' Ass'n (1972)
Cataloging, Box 352900
University of Washington
Seattle, WA 98195-2900
Tel: (206)543-1828   *Fax:* (206)685-8049
E-Mail: marys@u.washington.edu

Web Site:
     http://weber.u.washington.edu/ ~ marys/melahp.html
Members: 200 individuals, 50 institutions
Staff: 2
Annual Budget: under $10,000
Secretary-Treasurer: Mary St. Germain

Historical Note
Members are librarians and others who support the study or dissemination of information about the Middle East. Membership: $15/year.

Publications:
MELA Notes: Journal of Middle East Librarianship. bi-a. adv.

Meetings/Conferences:
Annual Meetings: November, with the Middle East Studies Ass'n
1999 – Washington, DC

Middle East Studies Ass'n of North America (1966)
1643 E. Helen St.
University of Arizona
Tucson, AZ 85721
Tel: (520)621-5850   *Fax:* (520)626-9095
E-Mail: MESANA@UU.ARIZONA.EDU
Web Site: http://www.MESA.ARIZONA.EDU
Members: 2,500 individuals
Staff: 4
Annual Budget: $250-500,000
Exec. Director: Anne Betteridge
Newsletter Editor: Sara Palmer
Meeting Planner: Mark J. Lowder
Membership Secretary: Nancy Dishaw

Historical Note
Organized by a group of U. S. and Canadian scholars concerned with the study of the Middle East, from Morocco to Pakistan, Turkey to the Sudan. Membership: $75/yr. (regular), $35/yr. (student), $500/yr. (organization).

Publications:
Graduate & Undergrad. Program & Courses i.
International Journal of Middle East Studies. q. adv.
MESA Bulletin. semi-a. adv.
Newsletter. 4/yr. adv.

Meetings/Conferences:
Annual Meetings: late October-December
1999 – Washington, DC/November 19-22
2000 – Orlando, FL/November 16-19

MIDI Manufacturers Ass'n (1984)
P.O. Box 3173
La Habra, CA 90632-3173
Tel: (714)736-9774   *Fax:* (714)736-9775
E-Mail: mma@midi.org
Web Site: http://www.midi.org
President: Tom White

Historical Note
MMA members are companies involved in the design and manufacture of MIDI (Musical Instrument Digital Interface) hardware or software and the application of audio technology to a wide variety of industries fields including stage and theater, performance, recording, multimedia computing, film and broadcast. Establishes MIDI specifications as an open standard. Sponsors the Interactive Audio Special Interest Group, an autonomous group for developers of PC and set top games and other multimedia applications. Membership: $400-$1,600/year, based on sales (company).

Publications:
Complete MIDI 1. 0 Specifications.

Meetings/Conferences:
Annual Meetings: January
1999 – Los Angeles, CA(LACC)
2000 – Anaheim, CA(ACC)
2001 – Anaheim, CA(ACC)

Midwives Alliance of North America (1982)
P.O. Box 175
Newton, KS 67114
Tel: (316)283-4543   *Fax:* (316)283-4543
Toll Free: (888)923 - 6262
E-Mail: MANAinfor@aol.com
Web Site: http://www.mana.org
Members: 1,200 individuals
Annual Budget: $10-25,000
Secretary: Singe Rogers

Historical Note
Founded to build cooperation among midwives and to promote midwifery as a standard of health care for women and childbirth. A member of the Internat'l Confederation Midwives, MANA participates in the North American Registry of Midwives. Absorbed the Nat'l Midwives Ass'n in 1985. Membership: $25/year (associate); $50-75/year (voting); $50/year (supporting groups).

Publications:
MANA News. q. adv.

Meetings/Conferences:
Annual Meetings: November
1999 – California

Military Boot Manufacturers Ass'n (1987)
c/o Dykema Gossett
1300 I St., N.W., Suite 300-W
Washington, DC 20005-3314
Tel: (202)522-8600   *Fax:* (202)522-8669
Members: 4 companies
Legal Counsel: Judy P. Jenkins

Military Chaplains Ass'n of the U.S. (1925)
P.O. Box 42660
Washington, DC 20015-0660
Tel: (202)574-2423   *Fax:* (202)574-2423
E-Mail: chaplains@erols.com
Web Site: www.wrldnet.net/ ~ mca/index.htm
Members: 1,875 individuals

Staff: 1
Annual Budget: $50-100,000
Exec. Director: David. E. White

Historical Note
A professional association of military chaplains, including active, reserve, former and retired of all religious faiths. Members include chaplains of the Veterans Administration and Civil Air Patrol as well as the Armed Forces. Membership: $25/year.

Publications:
Military Chaplain. bi-m.

Meetings/Conferences:
Annual Meetings: April/300
1999 – Atlanta, GA/April 13-16

Military Impacted Schools Ass'n (1986)
2009 Franklin St.
Bellevue, NE 68005
Tel: (402)293-4005
Toll Free: (800)291 - 6472
Web Site: http://www.esu3.org/districts/bellevue/misa/
Members: 43 school districts
Annual Budget: $100-250,000
Exec. Officer: John Deegan

Historical Note
MISA is composed of heavily impacted military school districts. Members are school districts with military personnel.

Publications:
Military Impacted Schools Legislative Newsletter. m.

Meetings/Conferences:

Military Operations Research Soc. (1966)
101 S. Whiting St., Suite 202
Alexandria, VA 22304-3483
Tel: (703)751-7290   *Fax:* (703)751-8171
E-Mail: morsone@aol.com, dick@mors.org
Web Site: http://www.mors.org
Members: 3,000 individuals
Staff: 5
Annual Budget: $500-1,000,000
Exec. V. President: Richard I. Wiles
Communications Manager: Corrina A. Ross
V. President, Administration: Natalie S. Addison

Historical Note
A professional society incorporated in the State of Virginia for the purpose of enhancing the quality and effectiveness of military operations research. Conducts a classified symposium annually and workshops as needed. Membership now requires that such symposia or other organization meetings be attended at least triennially by members.

Publications:
Military Operations Research. q.
Phalanx. q.

Meetings/Conferences:
Annual Meetings: Spring
1999 – West Point, NY(U.S. Military Academy)
2000 – Colorado Springs, CO(U.S. Air Force Academy)
2001 – Annapolis, MD(U.S. Naval Academy)

Milk Industry Foundation (1908)
1250 H St., N.W., Suite 900
Washington, DC 20005
Tel: (202)737-4332   *Fax:* (202)331-7820
Web Site: http://www.idfa.org
Members: 170 companies
Staff: 38
Annual Budget: $1-2,000,000
President and C.E.O.: E. Linwood Tipton
Director, Communications: Susan E. Ruland
Senior V. President & PAC Chairperson: Constance E. Tipton
Manager, Trade Show & Meetings: David B. Anderson
V. President, Finance and Administration: Sam J. DiCarlo
V. President & Counsel: Janet A. Nuzum
Manager, Membership Administration: Cindy F. Cavallo

Historical Note
MIF represents processors, manufacturers, distributors and marketers of fluid milk, cultured products, cream products, and other dairy products. MIF's activities range from legislative and regulatory advocacy to market research, industry training and education. Administrative support provided by Internat'l Dairy Foods Ass'n. Membership fee based on volume.

Publications:
Milk Facts and Latest Scoop. a.

Meetings/Conferences:
Annual Meetings: in conjunction with the Internat'l Dairy Foods Ass'n/Fall

Milking Machine Manufacturers Council
Historical Note
A council of the Equipment Manufacturers Institute.

Millinery Information Bureau (1955)
Historical Note
Became the Headware Information Bureau in 1997.

Million Dollar Round Table (1927)
325 W. Touhy Ave.
Park Ridge, IL 60068-4265
Tel: (847)692-6378   *Fax:* (847)518-8921
Members: 19,000 individuals
Staff: 70
Annual Budget: $5-10,000,000
Exec. V. President: John J. Prast, CAE, LLIF
Director of Public Relations: Steve Stahr
Director of Meetings & Services: Ray Kopcinski
Director, Membership: Jill Meyer, CAE, CLU
Director of Finance and Administration: Patrick Kozol

Historical Note
Members are life insurance salesmen who have sold more than $2 million of insurance in a given year. Members must qualify annually. Has an annual budget of approximately $10 million. Membership: $350/year (individual).

Publications:
Membership Directory. a.
Proceedings. a.
Round The Table. bi-m.
The Knight Letter. 3/year.

Meetings/Conferences:
Annual Meetings: June-July/5,000
1999 – New Orleans, LA/June 13-17

Mine Inspectors' Institute of America *(1912)*
Safety & Health Admin.
Laurel Rte. 1, Box 736
Hunker, PA   15639
Tel: (724)925-5150
Members: 400 individuals
Annual Budget: under $10,000
Secretary: Gerald E. Davis

Historical Note
Members are state, provincial and federal mine inspectors in the United States and Canada.

Meetings/Conferences:
Annual Meetings: Summer

Mineral Economics and Management Soc. *(1990)*
P.O. Box 721
Houghton, MI   49931
Tel: (906)487-2771   *Fax:* (906)487-2944
E-Mail: mroberts@mtu.edu
Members: 200 individuals
Annual Budget: $10-25,000
Treasurer: Mark C. Roberts

Historical Note
MEMS is a professional society for mineral, energy and natural resource economists, managers, consultants, financiers, policy analysts, geologists, engineers and others with an interest in the economics of the minerals, energy and materials industries. Membership: $45/year (individual); $20/year (student).

Publications:
Membership Directory. a.
MEMS Conference Proceedings. a.
MEMS Newsletter. 3/yr.
Resources Policy Journal.

Meetings/Conferences:
Annual Meetings: Spring
1999   Ottawa, Ontario(Sheraton Hotel)/April 14-17/125

Mineralogical Soc. of America *(1919)*
1015 18th St., N.W., Suite 601
Washington, DC   20036-5274
Tel: (202)775-4344   *Fax:* (202)775-0018
E-Mail: business@minsocam.org
Web Site: http://www.MINSOCAM.org
Members: 2,200 individuals
Staff: 4
Annual Budget: $500-1,000,000
Administrator: J. Alexander Speer, Ph.D.
Membership Coordinator: Andy Pratt

Historical Note
Established at Harvard University on December 30, 1919; Incorporated in the District of Columbia in 1937. A professional society of mineralogists, petrologists, geochemists, crystallographers and others interested in the study of minerals. A member society of the American Geological Institute. Membership: $70/year.

Publications:
American Mineralogist. bi-m.
Monographs and Textbooks. a.
Reviews in Mineralogy. a.
The Lattice. q.

Meetings/Conferences:
Annual Meetings: Fall, with Geological Soc. of America

Minerals, Metals and Materials Soc., The *(1871)*
420 Commonwealth Drive
Warrendale, PA   15086
Tel: (724)776-9000   *Fax:* (724)776-3770
E-Mail: TMSgeneral@tms.org
Web Site: http://www.tms.org
Members: 13,000 individuals
Staff: 35
Annual Budget: $2-5,000,000
Exec. Director: Alexander R. Scott
Dir., Marketing: Dan Steighner
Manager of Meeting Services: Michael Packard
Dir., Member & Educational Services: Vicki Koebnick
Director, Finance/Administration: M.R. Schlichter-Lake
Dir., Division & Meeting Services: Mark J. O'Connor
Director, Publications: Robert Makowski
Director, Information Systems: Andrew Lavella

Historical Note
The Metals Branch of the American Institute of Mining, Metallurgical and Petroleum Engineers (AIME, founded in 1871) was established in 1947. From 1957-1988, it was known as The Metallurgical Soc. The Society was separately incorporated in 1985. Membership: $80/year.

Publications:
JOM. m. adv.
Journal of Electronic Materials. m.
Metallurgical and Materials Transactions. m. adv.

Meetings/Conferences:
Annual Meetings: Winter
1999 – San Diego, CA(Convention Center)/Feb. 28-March 4

Mini-Compact Excavators Manufacturers Council

Historical Note
A council of Equipment Manufacturers Institute.

Miniature Golf Ass'n of America/Miniature Golf Develoment of America *(1989)*
P.O. Box 32353
Jacksonville, FL   32237
Tel: (904)781-4653   *Fax:* (904)781-4843
E-Mail: minigolf@minigolf.com
Web Site: http://www.minigolf.com
Members: 800 mini golf courses
Staff: 3
Annual Budget: $500-1,000,000
President: Kathy Sessions
Director, Communications: Skip Laun

Historical Note
A membership network providing resources for the family sport and fun industry comprising of a variety of components such as Miniature Golf Courses, Driving Ranges, Alternative Golf Facilities, Batting Cages/Ranges, Go-Karts, Bumper Boats, Arcades and Redemption Centers. Membership: $295/year (individual); $275/year (organization/company).

Publications:
Putting Around the 21st Century - Resource Manual.

Meetings/Conferences:
Annual Meetings: March
1999 – St. Augstine, Fl(World Golf Village)/500

Miniatures Industry Ass'n of America *(1979)*
1100-H Brandywine Blvd., P.O. Box 3388
Zanesville, OH   43702-3388
Tel: (340)452-4541   *Fax:* (340)452-2552
Toll Free: (888)878 - 6422
Members: 611 individuals and companies
Staff: 2
Annual Budget: $100-250,000
Chief Staff Officer: Walter E. Offinger
Assoc. Trade Show Manager: Jody Spencer

Historical Note
MIAA represents manufacturers, distributors, and retailers of dolls and dollhouses, collectibles, miniatures, and related product lines. Membership: $150-500/year (manufacturer-publisher-wholesaler/distributor); $150-500/year (retailer-mail order)- 75/year.

Publications:
MIAA Member News. q.
MIAA Show Directory. a. adv.

Meetings/Conferences:
Semi-Annual Meetings: February and August/1,000-1,200

Mining and Metallurgical Soc. of America *(1908)*
476 Wilson Ave.
Novato, CA   94947-4236
Tel: (415)898-4508   *Fax:* (415)899-0262
E-Mail: akburton@worldnet.att.net
Web Site: http://www.mmsa.net
Members: 350 individuals
Staff: 1
Annual Budget: $25-50,000
Exec. Director: Alan K. Burton

Historical Note
Members are individuals concerned with the conservation of the nation's mineral resources and the well-being of the mining and metallurgical industries. Membership: $75/year.

Publications:
MMSA News. q.

Meetings/Conferences:
Annual Meetings: In conjuction with the American Institute of Mining, Metallurgical and Petroleum Engineers

Minority Asset Recovery Contractors Ass'n *(1992)*
Historical Note
Address unknown in 1996.

Minority Internat'l Network for Trade *(1984)*
c/o Assist Internat'l
60 Madison Ave., 2nd Floor
New York, NY   10010
Tel: (212)725-3311   *Fax:* (212)725-3312
Members: 40 individuals, 80 companies/organizations
Annual Budget: $10-25,000
Exec. Officer: Peter Robinson

Historical Note
MINT is an organization of minority professionals involved in international trade. MINT seeks to continue the effort of developing commercial, social, cultural and governmental relationships with other nations and their people, and further the understanding of international culture and issues among the minority community of the United States. Membership: $60/year (full); $20/year (student); $125/year corporate.

Publications:
MINT Newsletter. q.

Meetings/Conferences:
Annual Meetings: May/June

Missouri Fox Trotting Horse Breed Ass'n *(1948)*
P.O. Box 1027
Ava, MO   65608
Tel: (417)683-2468   *Fax:* (417)683-6144
Members: 6,500 individuals
Staff: 6
Annual Budget: $50-100,000
Secretary: Floyd Hurst

Historical Note
Members are owners and breeders of Missouri Fox Trotting horses. Member of the Nat'l Pedigree Livestock Council. Internat'l Ass'n of Fairs & Expo. Membership: $15/year; $150 life membership.

Publications:
MFTHBA Journal. m. adv.
Show & Celebration Book. a. adv.

Meetings/Conferences:
Annual Meetings: Fourth Saturday in October on show grounds in Ava, MO.

Mobile Air Conditioning Soc. Worldwide *(1981)*
P.O. Box 100
East Greenville, PA   18041
Tel: (215)679-2220   *Fax:* (215)541-4635
E-Mail: mail@macsw.org
Web Site: http://www.macsw.org
Members: 1,600 companies
Staff: 10
Annual Budget: $500-1,000,000
President: Simon A. Oulouhojian
Senior V. President: Elvis Lynn Hoffpauir
Membership/Director of Operations: Patrice Worthington
Asst. Editor: Amy E. Kline

Historical Note
Provides technical training, information, and communication for the professionals in the automotive aftermarket specializing in car air conditioning systems. Incorporated in the Commonwealth of Pennsylvania. Membership: $180/year (service/installation/distribution); $600/year (manufacturer/supplier).

Publications:
AC Action!. bi-m.
Automotive Cooling Journal. m. adv.
MACS Service Reports. m.

Meetings/Conferences:
Annual Meetings: Winter
1999 – New Orleans, LA(Marriott)/Jan. 21-23

Mobile Industrial Caterers' Ass'n Internat'l *(1964)*
1240 N. Jefferson St., Suite G
Anaheim, CA   92807
Tel: (714)632-6800   *Fax:* (714)632-5405
Members: 185 companies
Staff: 2
Annual Budget: $50-100,000
Exec. Director: Kelly Ramirez

Historical Note
Members are companies using mobile equipment for industrial feeding.

Publications:
MICA Handbook and Roster. a.
MICA Newsletter. m.

Meetings/Conferences:
Semi-annual Meetings: Spring and Fall, and Biennial Trade Show

Model Railroad Industry Ass'n *(1967)*
303 Freeport Road
Pittsburgh, PA   15215
Tel: (412)781-2709   *Fax:* (412)781-2871
Web Site: http://www.MRIA.org
Staff: 1
Annual Budget: $25-50,000
Assoc. Exec. Director: Rose A. Ewing

Historical Note
Members are manufacturers, importers, packagers and publishers of model Railroad equipment. Affiliated with the Hobby Industry Ass'n of America, and the Radio Control Hobby Trade Ass'n and the Nat'l Model Railroad Ass'n. Membership: $125-500/year (company).

Publications:
Membership Roster. a.
Reporter. m.

Meetings/Conferences:

Modeling Ass'n of America Internat'l *(1958)*
Historical Note
Address unknown in 1996.

Modern Greek Studies Ass'n *(1968)*
P.O. Box 1826
New Haven, CT   06508
Tel: (203)392-5668   *Fax:* (203)392-5670
Members: 400 individuals
Staff: 1
Annual Budget: $25-50,000
Exec. Director: John O. Iatrides

Historical Note
MSGA defines its scope broadly to include not only post-Independence Greece but also the period of Ottoman rule and later Byzantine Empire, as well as those of early Byzantine, Hellenistic and classical times that have bearing on the modern period. Membership: $50/year, $20/year (students), $65/year (organization).

Publications:
Journal of Modern Greek Studies. semi-a. adv.
MGSA Bulletin. semi-a. adv.

Meetings/Conferences:
1999 – Princeton, NJ/Nov. 4-7/400

Modern Language Ass'n of America *(1883)*
10 Astor Place
New York, NY   10003-6981
Tel: (212)475-9500   *Fax:* (212)477-9863
Web Site: http://www.mla.org
Members: 32,000 individuals
Staff: 88
Annual Budget: $5-10,000,000
Exec. Director: Phyllis Franklin, Ph.D.
Director, Convention Programs: Maribeth T. Kraus

Historical Note
Founded at Columbia University, December 27-28, 1883 and incorporated in 1900 to elevate the study and teaching of modern languages to the status then held by the classics. Members are college-level teachers of modern languages. A member of the American Council of Learned Societies. Has an annual budget of approximately $8 million. Membership: $35 (new member, first year); $25-$125/year (reinstating member, based on income); $20/year (student member, maximum of seven years).

Publications:
ADE Bulletin. 3/year.
ADFL Bulletin. 3/year.
MLA International Bibliography. a.
MLA Newsletter. q.
Publications of the Modern Language Association (PMLA). bi-m. adv.

Meetings/Conferences:
Annual Meetings: Always December 27-30
1999 – Chicago, IL/Dec. 27-30/9000
2000 – Washington, DC/Dec. 27-30/9000

Modular Building Institute *(1983)*
413 Park St.
Charlottesville, VA   22902-4737
Tel: (804)296-3288   *Fax:* (804)296-3361
E-Mail: mbi2000@aol.com
Web Site: http://www.mbinet.org
Members: 210 individuals, 147 companies
Staff: 3
Annual Budget: $250-500,000
Exec. Director: Judy M. Smith, CMP

Historical Note
Formerly Mobile Modular Office Ass'n, assumed its current name in 1993. Members are companies involved in the manufacturing and marketing of factory-built commercial structures. MBI promotes modular commercial construction as an alternative to conventional building. Membership: $250-$7,000/year (company).

Publications:
Industry News. bi-m.
Industry Survey. a.
MBI Newsletter. 6/year.
National Industry Directory. a.

Meetings/Conferences:
Annual Meetings: late Winter
1999 – Palm Springs, CA(Riveria)/March 6-10/250
2000 – Orlando, FL(Caribe Royale)/March 11-15/250

Modular Building Systems Council *(1942)*
Historical Note
A division of the Building Systems Councils of the Nat'l Ass'n of Home Builders.

Mohair Council of America *(1966)*
P.O. Box 5337
San Angelo, TX   76902-5337
Tel: (915)655-3161   *Fax:* (915)655-4761
E-Mail: mohair@mohairusa.com
Web Site: http://wwwmohairusa.com
Members: 10,500 individuals
Staff: 2
Exec. Director: Zane Willard

Historical Note
Angora goat breeders. Street Address is: 233 W. Twohig, San Angelo.

Meetings/Conferences:
1999 – San Angelo, TX(Holiday Inn)

Molluscan Shellfish Institute *(1908)*
1901 N. Ft. Myer Drive, Suite 700
Arlington, VA   22209
Tel: (703)524-8883   *Fax:* (703)524-4619
Web Site: http://www.nfi.org
Members: 100 individuals
Staff: 3
Annual Budget: $50-100,000
Exec. Director: Roy E. Martin

Historical Note
Formerly (1970) Oyster Institute of North America and (1997) Shellfish Institute of North America, MSI is division of the Nat'l Fisheries Institute.

Meetings/Conferences:
Annual Meetings: Spring

Monorail Manufacturers Ass'n *(1933)*
8720 Red Oak Blvd., Suite 201
Charlotte, NC   28210-3992
Tel: (704)676-1190   *Fax:* (704)676-1199
E-Mail: Hal_Vandiver@mhia.org
Web Site: http://www.mhia.org
Members: 11 companies
Staff: 5
Managing Director: F. Hal Vandiver

Historical Note
A product section of the Material Handling Institute. Membership: $2500/yr.

Meetings/Conferences:
Semi-annual Meetings: With Material Handling Institute

Montadale Sheep Breeders Ass'n *(1945)*
P.O. Box 603
Plainfield, IN   46168
Tel: (317)839-6198
Web Site: http://www.montadales.com
Members: 300 individuals
Staff: 1
Annual Budget: under $10,000
Secretary-Treasurer: Mildred E. Brown

Historical Note
Members are breeders and fanciers of Montadale sheep. Membership: $10/year (senior member), $5/year (junior member).

Publications:
Montadale Mover. 3/year. adv.

Meetings/Conferences:
Semi-annual Meetings: June and November
1999 – Springfield, IL/June 17-19

Monument Builders of North America *(1906)*
3158 Des Plaines Ave., Suite 224
Des Plaines, IL   60018
Tel: (847)803-8800   *Fax:* (847)803-8823
Web Site: http://www.monumentbuilders.org
Members: 900 companies
Staff: 5
Annual Budget: $500-1,000,000
Exec. V. President: Greg Patzer

Historical Note
Formed by a merger of the Monument Builders of America (formerly Memorial Craftsmen of America, founded in 1906) and the American Historic Monument Soc. Members are makers, retailers, wholesalers and suppliers of cemetary markers and monuments. Membership: $370/year (company).

Publications:
MB News. m. adv.

Meetings/Conferences:
Annual Meetings: First week of February/1,000 1993 Louisville, KY(Galt House) 1996 Washington, DC(Capitol Hilton)
1999 – Charlotte, NC(Adams Mark)/Jan 24-27
2000 – Las Vegas, NV(Riviera)/Feb. 6-9
2001 – Birmingham, AL(Sheraton)/Jan. 21-24
2002 – Myrtle Beach, SC(Kingston Plantation)/Jan. 27-30

Mortgage Bankers Ass'n of America *(1914)*
1125 15th Street, N.W.
Washington, DC   20005
Tel: (202)861-6500   *Fax:* (202)861-0736
Web Site: http://www.mbaa.org
Members: 2,300 institutions
Staff: 135
Annual Budget: $25-50,000,000
Exec. V. President: Paul S. Reid
Sr. V.P., Communications: Jacqueline W. Grumbacher
Sr. V.P., Marketing: Brian Chappelle
Sr. V.P., Residential Finance/Govt. Agency Rels.: Robert O'Toole
Sr. V.P./Legislative Counsel: Micahel J. Ferrell
Assoc. Director of Meetings: Deborah L. Bird
Senior Dir., Meetings: Edward J. Callahan
Senior V. President, Education: Joyce Kappeler
Director, Budget/Finance: David K. Phillips, Jr.
Senior V.P./General Counsel: William E. Cumberland
Senior V.P./Chief Economist: David Lereah
Senior V.P., Commercial Real Estate: John C. Ferber
Senior V. President: Cheryl Patton Malloy

Historical Note
Formed to promote growth and excellence in the real estate finance industry. Encourages sound business practices that serve the needs of investors and borrowers. Informs members of changes in law, regulations, and pending legislation that affect the real estate and mortgage business. Members include mortgage companies, commercial banks, thrifts, life insurance companies, and other instituions. Supports the Mortgage Bankers Political Action Committee (MORPAC). Has an annual budget of approximately $30.7 million.

Publications:
MBA Economic Commentary. m.
MBA Statelines. m.
Membership Directory. a.
Mortgage Banking. m. adv.
Mortgage Banking Financial Statements and Operating Ratios. a.
Mortgage Banking Loans Closed and Servicing Volume. a.
National Delinquency Survey. q.
Real Estate Finance Today. bi-w. adv.
State and Local Report. 10/year.
Washington Report. m.

Meetings/Conferences:
Annual Meetings: October
1999 – Boston, MA/Oct. 10-13

Mortgage Insurance Companies of America *(1973)*
727 15th St., N.W., 12th Floor
Washington, DC   20005
Tel: (202)393-5566   *Fax:* (202)393-5557
Members: 10 companies
Staff: 6
Annual Budget: $1-2,000,000
Exec. V. President: Suzanne C. Hutchinson

Historical Note
MICA represents the private mortgage insurance industry.

Publications:
Fact Book & Membership Directory. a.

Meetings/Conferences:
Annual Meetings: Members only meeting

Motion Picture and Television Credit Ass'n *(1956)*
4102 W. Magnolia Blvd., Suite A
Burbank, CA   91505-2747
Tel: (818)758-6272   *Fax:* (818)758-6275
Toll Free: (800)564 - 5686
Members: 92 companies
Staff: 3
Annual Budget: $25-50,000
Exec. Director: Donna Cottone
President: Seta Kasperian
Administrator: Norma Myara

Historical Note
Established as the Motion Picture and Television Credit Managers Ass'n, it assumed its present name in 1966. Membership: $1,140/year (organization).

Publications:
Industry Credit Interchange.

Meetings/Conferences:
Monthly Luncheon: (Beverly Garland Holiday Inn)/50

Motion Picture Ass'n *(1945)*
15503 Ventura Blvd.
Encino, CA   91436
Tel: (818)995-6600   *Fax:* (818)382-1799
Members: 7 companies
Annual Budget: $5-10,000,000
Chairman and C.E.O.: Jack J. Valenti
President and C.O.O.: William Baker

Historical Note
Fomerly (1994) American Motion Picture Export Company. A Webb-Pomerene Act association affiliated with the Motion Picture Ass'n of America, MPEAA is dedicated to improving the freedom of movement of films and television in international distribution.

Motion Picture Ass'n of America *(1922)*
1600 I St., N.W.
Washington, DC   20006
Tel: (202)293-1966   *Fax:* (202)293-7674
Web Site: http://www.mpaa.org
Members: 8 companies
Staff: 142
Annual Budget: $5-10,000,000
President & C.E.O.: Jack J. Valenti
Senior V. President, Government Relations and DC General Counsel: Fritz Attaway
V. President, Congressional Affairs: Cynthia E. Merifield
V. President for Trade and Federal Affairs: Bonnie Richardson

Historical Note
Formerly (1945) Motion Picture Producers and Distributors of America. Membership includes the principal producers and distributors of films in the United States. Affiliated with the Motion Picture Ass'n.

Motion Picture Export Ass'n of America
Historical Note
Became (1995) Motion Picture Ass'n.

Motor and Equipment Manufacturers Ass'n *(1904)*
10 Laboratory Dr.
P.O. Box 13966
Research Triangle Pk, NC   27709-3966
Tel: (919)549-4800   *Fax:* (919)406-1465
Members: 700 companies
Staff: 70
Annual Budget: $10-25,000,000
President and C.E.O.: Robert R. Miller
Director, Communications: Rosemarie Kitchin
Manager, Government Relations: John Carney
V.P./Gen. Manager, Mgt. Information Systems: Alan F. Jones
V.President, Finance and Administration: Joseph A. Gristci
V.President, International Operations: Christopher Bates
V. President: James J. Conner, III
V.P./Gen. Manager, Financial Svcs.: Daniel E. Griffin

Historical Note
Serves manufacturers of automotive products used on, in or for the servicing of cars, trucks and buses; conducts market research. MEMA's TRANSNET and ANSINET Divisions provide computerized electronic data interchange services. Divisionalized by product lines, market segments and executive peer groups. Maintains offices in Washington, DC, Japan, Brussels, Sao Paulo, and Mexico City. Has an annual budget of approximately $14 million. Membership: $900-12,000/year, based on sales volume.

Publications:
Customer Credit & Sales Directory.
European Automotive Insight. m.
Heavy Duty Newsletter. 6/yr.
International Buyers Guide. bi-a.
Japan Automotive Insight. m.
Latin America Automotive Insight. 6/yr.
Market Analysis. 6/yr.
Market Research Studies.
MEMA Newsletter. bi-w.
OE Suppliers Newsletter. 6/yr.

Meetings/Conferences:
1999 – Las Vegas, NV(Mirage/Bellagio)/Nov. 2-5

Motor Freight Carriers Ass'n *(1963)*
499 South Capitol St., S.W., Suite 502-A
Washington, DC   20003
Tel: (202)554-3060   *Fax:* (202)554-3160
Web Site: http://www.mfca.org
Members: 6 carriers
Staff: 7
Annual Budget: $2-5,000,000
President and C.E.O.: Timothy P. Lynch
Director, Communications: Elisabeth Barna
V.President, Government Relations: Catherine Evans

Historical Note
Founded as Trucking Employers; became Trucking Management in 1978, and in 1997 MFCA was formed as a successor organization. MFCA is the national trade ass'n of unionized (LTC)less-than-truckload motor carriers. MFCA promotes the economic interests of motor freight carriers in public policy and through collective bargaining areans. MFCA members employ 80,000 trucking professionals.

Meetings/Conferences:

Motorcycle Industry Council *(1914)*
2 Jenner St., Suite 150
Irvine, CA   92618-3806
Tel: (949)727-4211   *Fax:* (949)727-4217

Members: 260 manufacturers
Staff: 20
Annual Budget: $2-5,000,000
President: E. Timothy Buche
V. President: Pam Amette
Vice President of Administration: Carol Kington

Historical Note
Formerly (1970) Motorcycle, Scooter and Allied Trades Ass'n. Represents motorcycle manufacturers, and members of allied trades.

Publications:
Motorcycle Statistical Annual. a.

Meetings/Conferences:
Annual Meetings: Established by Board of Directors annually during Feb.-April period.

Motorcycle Safety Foundation *(1973)*
2 Jenner St., Suite 150
Irvine, CA   92618-3806
Tel: (949)727-3227   *Fax:* (949)727-4217
Members: 6 companies
Staff: 16
Annual Budget: $2-5,000,000
President: E. Timothy Buche
V. President, Administration: Carol Kington
V. President: Thomas Yager

Historical Note
Founded by the five leading manufacturers and distributors of motorcycles for the purpose of public motorcycle safety education, licensing improvement, public information and research. Membership: dues based on marketshare.

Publications:
Safe Cycling. q.

Meetings/Conferences:
Annual Meetings: March

Motorist Information and Services Ass'n *(1988)*
P.O. Box 1584
Shawnee, OK   74802-1584
Tel: (405)214-9847   *Fax:* (405)214-9835
E-Mail: MISA@keytech.com
Members: 125 individuals
Annual Budget: $10-25,000
Exec. Director: Larry B. Hall

Historical Note
MISA represents firms and organizations involved highway information signage and other technologies developed to deliver pertinent information to motorists on the highway. Membership: $50/year (government employee); $100/year (individual); $200/year (organization/company); $250/year (multi-state operator).

Publications:
Membership Directory. a. adv.
MISA Messenger. q. adv.

Meetings/Conferences:
1999 – Portland, OR
2000 – Little Rock, AR
2001 – Tallahassee, FL

Mountain Rescue Ass'n *(1958)*
710 Tenth St., Suite 105
Golden, CO   80401
Tel: (602)205-4066
E-Mail: mra@mra.org
Web Site: http://www.mra.org
Members: 67 organizations
Annual Budget: $50-100,000

Historical Note
Since 1958, accredits mountain rescue units. MRA members are mountain rescue units in the United States and Canada and other countries. Promotes high standards, mutual aid response, research and education programs.

Publications:
Blue Book. a.
Conference Minutes. semi-a.
Rescue Forum Magazine. q. adv.

Meetings/Conferences:
Annual Meetings: Semi-annual Conference.
1999 – Tucson, AZ(Mt. Lemmon)/200
2000 – Alberta, Canada/June 22-25/200

Mounted Breakers Manufacturers Bureau
Historical Note
A bureau of the Construction Industry Manufacturers Ass'n.

Movement Disorder Soc. *(1985)*
19 Mantua Road
Mt. Royal, NJ   08061
Tel: (609)423-7220   *Fax:* (609)423-3420
Web Site: http://www.movementdisorder.org/
Members: 1,500 individuals
Annual Budget: $10-25,000,000
Exec. Director: Gregg H. Talley

Historical Note
MDS is a scholarly scientific society devoted to research in the field of movement disorders. Membership: $200/year.

Publications:
Directory of Members. a.
Movement Disorders. q.

Meetings/Conferences:
2000 – Barcelona, Spain/June 11-15/3000

MTM Ass'n for Standards and Research *(1951)*
1111 E. Touhy Ave., Suite 280
Des Plaines, IL   60018-5811
Tel: (847)299-1111   *Fax:* (847)299-3509
E-Mail: MTM@mtm.org
Web Site: http://www.mtm.org
Members: 1000 individuals

Staff: 8
Annual Budget: $1-2,000,000
Exec. Director: Dirk Rauglas

Historical Note
Membership consists of industrial psychologists, industrial engineers, academicians and corporate members. Conducts research and training on the efficiency of human motion. Also known as Methods Time Measurement Ass'n for Standards and Research. Membership: $40/year (individual), $750/year (company).

Publications:
Journal. q.
Research Reports. irreg.

Meetings/Conferences:
Annual Meetings: Chicago, IL/October

Mu Phi Epsilon *(1903)*
4202 Atlantic Ave., Suite 202
Long Beach, CA   90807-2826
Tel: (562)424-9799   *Fax:* (562)424-9778
E-Mail: mpeieo@aol.com
Members: 70,000 individuals
Staff: 2
Annual Budget: $100-250,000
Exec. Secretary Treasurer: Gerri Flynn

Historical Note
An international professional music fraternity founded November 13, 1903 at the Metropolitan College of Music, Cincinnati, Ohio. Membership is open to music majors or minors enrolled in schools where chapters exist. Concert artists, teachers, composers and other music leaders are also included. Membership: $18-$25/year.

Publications:
The Triangle of Mu Phi Epsilon. q.

Meetings/Conferences:
2001 – San Antonio, TX
2003 – Cincinnati, OH

Multi-Housing Laundry Ass'n *(1959)*
4101 Lake Boone Trail, Suite 201
Raleigh, NC   27607-6518
Tel: (919)787-5181   *Fax:* (919)787-4916
Staff: 2
Annual Budget: $100-250,000
Exec. Director: Banner Huggins

Historical Note
Formerly (until 1982) Nat'l Ass'n of Coin Laundry Equipment Operators.

Publications:
MLA News. bi-m.

Meetings/Conferences:
Annual Meetings: June
1999 – Amelia Island, FL

Multi-Level Marketing Internat'l Ass'n *(1985)*
119 Stanford Court
Irvine, CA   92612
Tel: (949)854-0484   *Fax:* (949)854-7687
E-Mail: info@mlmia.com
Web Site: http://www.mlmia.com
Members: 5,000 individuals
Staff: 2
Annual Budget: $250-500,000
President and C.E.O.: Doris Wood

Historical Note
Established and incorporated in California, MLMIA members are companies which market their products and services directly to consumers through distributors, suppliers to the industry, and distributors who interface with consumers. Maintains branch offices in England, Canada, New Zealand, and Malaysia. Membership: $1,000-10,000/year (company), $500/year (support), $50/year (distributors).

Publications:
Association News Journal. q.
Connecting Point. q.
Corporate Directory. q.
Support Directory. q.

Meetings/Conferences:
Semi-Annual Meetings: Winter and Summer
1999 – Orange Country, CA

Multicultural Publishers Education Council *(1990)*
Historical Note
Became Multicultural Publishing and Education Council in 1996.

Multicultural Publishing and Education Council *(1990)*
1215 S. Kihei Road, Suite 625
Kihei, HI   96753
E-Mail: mpec@aol.com
Web Site: http://www.mpec.org
Members: 250 individuals
President: Rennie Mau

Historical Note
Formerly (1995) Multicultural Publishers Education Council which superseded Multicultural Publishers Exchange (founded 1990). Members are publishers of multicultural books. Participates in trade shows on behalf of its members and provides other services. Has no paid officers or full-time staff. Membership: $250/year (corporate); $100/year (individual).

Publications:
MPE Newsletter. bi-m adv. adv.

Meetings/Conferences:

Multimedia Publishers Ass'n
Historical Note
A special interest group of Nat'l Ass'n of Desktop Publishers, which provides administrative support.

Multimedia Publishers Group
Historical Note
Organization defunct in 1995.

MultiMedia Telecommunications Ass'n *(1970)*
2500 Wilson Blvd., Suite 300
Arlington, VA   22201-3834
Tel: (703)907-7470   *Fax:* (703)907-7478
Toll Free: (800)799 - 6682
E-Mail: info@mmta.org
Web Site: http://www.mmta.org
Members: 250 companies
Staff: 5
Annual Budget: $2-5,000,000
President: Mary Bradshaw
Director, Membership Services: Guy Walden

Historical Note
Founded as North American Telephone Ass'n; became North American Telecommunication Ass'n in 1982, and assumed its current name in 1996. MMTA supports the convergence of communications and computing business applications as an open forum for public policy, market development, and education. Membership includes manufacturers, software developers, distributors, value-added resellers, and systems integrators. MMTA is an affiliate of the Telecommunications Industry Ass'n.

Publications:
MMT Alert. m.
MultiMedia Telecommunications Market Review and Forecast. a.
MultiMedia Telecommunications Solutions Sourcebook. a. adv.

Meetings/Conferences:
1999 – Las Vegas, NV/Apr. 17-22

Municipal Arborists and Urban Foresters Soc.
Historical Note
A special interest group within the Internat'l Soc. of Aboriculture.

Municipal Finance Industry Ass'n
1747 Pennsylvania Ave., N.W., Suite 900
Washington, DC   20006
Tel: (202)296-0784   *Fax:* (202)293-2768
General Counsel: Gregory R. Babyak

Historical Note
Address unknown in 1995.

Municipal Treasurers Ass'n of the United States and Canada *(1965)*
1229 19th St., N.W., 4th Floor
Washington, DC   20036
Tel: (202)737-0660   *Fax:* (202)833-0375
Members: 2,000 individuals
Staff: 3
Annual Budget: $250-500,000
Exec. Director: Stacey L. Crane

Historical Note
Awards the Certified Municipal Finance Adminstrator credential (CMFA). Membership: $101-301/year (city/state); $356/year (firm/associate).

Publications:
Treasury Notes. bi-m. adv.

Meetings/Conferences:
Annual Meetings: August/450
1999 – Salt Lake City, UT/Aug. 22-25

Municipal Waste Management Ass'n *(1982)*
1620 I St., N.W., 4th Floor
Washington, DC   20006
Tel: (202)293-7330   *Fax:* (202)293-2352
Web Site: http://www.usmayors.org/uscm/mwma
Members: 200 local government organizations
Staff: 2
Annual Budget: $50-100,000
Managing Director: Michael Gagliardo

Historical Note
Formerly (1991) the Nat'l Resource Recovery Ass'n. Affiliated with U. S. Conference of Mayors, members are concerned with the processing of municipal solid waste for the production of recyclable materials, heat, energy, and other purposes. Active members are local government organizations; associate members are from the private sector. Membership: $300-5,000/year, varies by population (active member), $250-750/year, varies by number of employees (associate).

Publications:
Directory of Associate Members. a.

Meetings/Conferences:
Annual Meetings: Always in Washington, DC/March-April/300
1992(Vista Internat'l)
1999 – Washington, DC

Munitions Carriers Conference *(1952)*
P.O. Box 1446
Fairfax, VA   22030
Tel: (703)273-8144   *Fax:* (703)273-8147
Members: 16 companies
Staff: 1
Annual Budget: $50-100,000
Mng. Director: Jerry Turner

Historical Note
Affiliate of American Trucking Ass'ns. Members are transporters of munitions and explosive materials.

Meetings/Conferences:
Annual Meetings: December

Musculoskeletal Tumor Soc.
6300 N. River Road, Suite 727
Rosemont, IL   60018-4226

Tel: (847)486-1120   *Fax:* (847)486-1130
Exec. Officer: Laura McLaughlan

Museum Computer Network (1967)
8720 Georgia Ave., Sutie 501
Silver Spring, MD   20910
Tel: (301)585-4413   *Fax:* (301)495-0810
Members: 800 individuals
Staff: 2
Annual Budget: $50-100,000
Exec. Director: Guy Herman
Historical Note
Membership: $60/year (individual); $150/year (institution/vendor).
Publications:
Membership Directory. a.
Spectra Newsletter. q. adv.
Meetings/Conferences:

Museum Education Roundtable (1969)
621 Pennsylvania Ave., S.E.
Washington, DC   20003-4303
Tel: (202)547-8378   *Fax:* (202)547-8344
E-Mail: meorg@erols.com
Web Site: http://www.erols.com/meorg/
Members: 600 individuals
Staff: 1
Annual Budget: $50-100,000
Office Manager: Audrey Nash
Historical Note
Members are museum educators, teachers, museums and schools. Membership: $40/year (individuals); $120/year (institution); $25/year (students);and $60(library)
Publications:
Journal of Museum Education. 3/year.
Network Newsletter. semi-a.

Museum Store Ass'n (1955)
4100 E. Mississippi Ave., Suite 800
Denver, CO   80246-3048
Tel: (303)504-9223   *Fax:* (303)504-9585
Web Site: http://www.msa.web.org
Members: 1,982 museums and 1100 exhibitor affil
Annual Budget: $100-250,000
Exec. Director: Beverly Barsook
Asst. Director, Programs and Membership: Beth Taylor
Historical Note
Affiliated professional organization of the American Ass'n of Museums.
Publications:
Directory. a. adv.
Management Insights. bi-m.
Museum Store. q. adv.
Product News. 3/year.
Meetings/Conferences:
Annual Meetings: May/1,500
1999 – Ft.Worth, TX/May 8-11

Museum Trustee Ass'n (1986)
1200 19th St., N.W., Suite 300
Washington, DC   20036-2422
Tel: (202)857-1180   *Fax:* (202)223-4579
E-Mail: mtadc@aol.com
Web Site: www.mtalhq.org
Members: 200 individuals, 212 institutions
Staff: 2
Annual Budget: $250-500,000
President: Charles F. Dambach
Historical Note
Founded as the Trustee Committee of the American Ass'n of Museums, it was separately incorporated in 1986 as the Museum Trustee Committee for Research and Development. Now the Museum Trustee Ass'n, it is the American Ass'n of Museum's affiliate for trustee affairs. Membership fee varies $100/year Minimum (individual); $200/year minimum (organization).
Publications:
Museum Trusteeship. q. adv.
Meetings/Conferences:
Semi-Annual Meetings: Spring and Fall
1999 – Pheonix, AZ

Music and Entertainment Industry Educators Ass'n (1978)
College of Fine Arts
University of Massachusettes
Lowell, MA   01854
Tel: (978)934-3882   *Fax:* (978)934-3029
E-Mail: scottfred@uml.edu
Web Site: http://www.meiea.org
Members: 350 individuals
Annual Budget: $10-25,000
President: Scott Fredrickson, Ph.D.
Historical Note
Established in Nashville, TN in 1978 as the Music Industry Educators Ass'n, it assumed its present name in April, 1986. Members are individuals, educational institutions, and companies concerned with establishing educational standards for the creative production and management aspects of the music and recording industry. Has no paid staff or permanent headquarters. Membership: $35/year (individual); $250/year (company); $50-100/year (educational institution).
Publications:
MEIEA Notes. q.
Meetings/Conferences:
Annual Meetings: Spring
1999 – Boone, NC(Appalachian State Univ.)/March 26-27

Music Box Soc. Internat'l

Historical Note
Address unknown in 1995.

Music Critics Ass'n of North America (1957)
7 Pine Ct.
Westfield, NJ   07090-3444
Tel: (908)233-8468   *Fax:* (908)233-8468
E-Mail: BRDH97A@Prodigy.com
Members: 230 individuals
Staff: 1
Annual Budget: $10-25,000
Co-Managing Director: Albert H. Cohen
Co-Managing Director: Doris LaMar
Historical Note
Added "of North America" to its name in 1994. Members are classical music critics from the various communications media. Seeks to improve the calibre of music criticism and to promote an interest in music in the U.S. and Canada. Membership: $75/year (individual); $35/year (students and retired critics).
Publications:
Critical Issues. 3/year.
Meetings/Conferences:
Annual Meetings: Usually late summer in conjunction with some significant musical event
1999 – Chicago, IL/June 9-12

Music Distributors Ass'n (1939)
38 West 21st St., Room 1106
New York, NY   10010-6906
Tel: (212)924-9175   *Fax:* (212)675-3577
E-Mail: assnhdqs@aol.com
Web Site: http://musicdistributors.org
Members: 145 companies
Staff: 2
Annual Budget: $50-100,000
Exec. V. President: Jerome Hershman
Historical Note
Formerly (1977) the Nat'l Ass'n of Musical Merchandise Wholesalers. Two-thirds of member companies are domestic, one-third overseas. Membership: $650/year (active), $325/year (international).
Publications:
Newsletter. 6-10/year.
Meetings/Conferences:
Semi-annual Meetings: following Nat'l Ass'n of Music Merchants
1999 – Hawaii(Waikoloa)(Waikoloa)
2000 – Acapulco, Mexico(Acapulco Princess)
2001 – Maui, Hawaii(Grand Wailea)

Music Educators Nat'l Conference: The Nat'l Ass'n for Music Education (1907)
1806 Robert Fulton Drive
Reston, VA   20191
Tel: (703)860-4000   *Fax:* (703)860-1531
Toll Free: (800)336 - 3768
Members: 70,000 individuals
Staff: 50
Annual Budget: $2-5,000,000
Exec. Director: John J. Mahlmann
Director of Promotion and Production: Michael Blakeslee
Director of Outreach and Special Programs: Kathleen Welling
Coordinator, Meetings and Conventions: Judith Humphrey
Director, Business Affairs/Membership: Larry Mullins
Director, Publications: Margaret A. Senko
Historical Note
Established as the Music Supervisors National Conference, it assumed its present name in 1934. A professional organization of music teachers, administrators and students. The Soc. for Research in Music Education, the Soc. for Music Teacher Education and the Soc. for General Music are councils of MENC. Affiliated with numerous other musical organizations.
Publications:
Journal of Research in Music Education. q.
Music Educators Journal. 9/year. adv.
Teaching Music Magazine.
Meetings/Conferences:
Biennial Meetings: Even years/6-8,000
2000 – Washington, DC/March 8-11

Music Industry Conference (1923)
1806 Robert Fulton Drive
Reston, VA   20191
Tel: (703)860-4000   *Fax:* (703)860-1531
Toll Free: (800)336 - 3768
Web Site: www.menc.org
Members: 450 individuals
Staff: 2
Exhibits Manager/C.S.E.: Sandra V. Friday
Conventions Coordinator: Judy Humphrey
Dir., Business Affairs: Larry Mullins
Historical Note
Formerly Music Education Exhibitors Ass'n and Music Industry Council. The auxiliary of The Music Educators Nat'l Conference, MIC represents manufacturers, publishers, retailers and other music-related organizations in support of music education. Membership fee varies; average $140/year.
Publications:
MIC Guide for Music Educators. bien.
Meetings/Conferences:
2000 – Washington, DC(Sheraton)/March 8-11
2002 – Nashville, TN/April 11-14

Music Library Ass'n (1931)
P.O. Box 487
Canton, MA   02021-0487
Tel: (781)828-8450   *Fax:* (781)828-8915
E-Mail: acadsvc@aol.com
Members: 3 individuals and institutions

Staff: 1
Annual Budget: $250-500,000
Manager: James Henderson
Historical Note
Affiliated with the Council of National Library Ass'ns.
Publications:
Music Cataloging Bulletin. m.
Music Library Ass'n Newsletter. q.
Notes. q. adv.
Meetings/Conferences:
1999 – Los Angeles, CA(Biltmore)/March 17-20
2000 – Louisville, KY/Feb. 23-26

Music Publishers' Ass'n of the United States (1895)
711 Third Ave.
New York, NY   10017
Tel: (610)648-0500
Web Site: http://www.mpa.org
Members: 75 music publishers
Staff: 5
Annual Budget: $10-25,000
President: Ron Rewe
Historical Note
Serves as a forum for publishers to deal wtih the music industry's vital issues, including copyright laws, copyright infringements, and the need for further reform. Keeps its members informed of the latest technology and production sophistication in graphics, engraving, computerization, and printing. Informs its constituents of new laws, decisions, and regulations affecting the industry. Fosters relations among the publishing industry, shools, dealers, performers, and composers.
Meetings/Conferences:

Music Teachers Nat'l Ass'n (1876)
441 Vine St., Suite 505
Cincinnati, OH   45202-2814
Tel: (513)421-1420   *Fax:* (513)421-2503
Members: 24,000 individuals
Staff: 17
Annual Budget: $1-2,000,000
Exec. Director: Gary Ingle
Foundation Director: Shirley Armitage Raut
Historical Note
Founded by Theodore Presser in Delaware, Ohio December 26, 1876 with 62 charter members, MTNA is a non-profit organization of independent and collegiate music teachers. Membership: $48/year, plus state and local dues.
Publications:
American Music Teacher. bi-m. adv.
Meetings/Conferences:
Annual Meetings: Spring
1999 – Los Angeles, CA(Bonaventure)/March 20-24
2000 – Minneapolis, MN/March 25-29
2001 – Washington, DC/March 24-28

Musicians Nat'l Hotline Ass'n (1980)
Historical Note
Organization defunct in 1995.

Mutual Advertising Agency Network (1946)
25700 Science Park Dr., Suite 200
Cleveland, OH   44122
Tel: (216)292-6609   *Fax:* (216)292-6780
E-Mail: marla@marcusad.com
Web Site: http://www.maanet.com
Members: 35 companies
Staff: 2
Annual Budget: $50-100,000
Exec. Director: Donald A. Campbell
Historical Note
Founded as the Midwestern Advertising Agency Network in Chicago, Illinois. Membership: $2,400/year (corporate).
Publications:
MAAN Matters. 3/year.
Meetings/Conferences:
1999 – Rancho Mirage, CA(Westin Mission Hills)/Feb. 27-March 2
1999 – Princeton, NJ(Nassau Inn)/June 12-15
1999 – Tulsa, OK(Doubletree Warren Place)/Oct. 16-19
2000 – Cabo San Lucas, Mexico(Westin Regina)/Feb. 26-29
2000 – Indianapolis, IN(Hyatt Regency at State Capitol)/June 24-27
2000 – Charlotte, NC(Hyatt at Southpark)/Oct. 14-17

Mutual Fund Education Alliance (1971)
100 N.W. Englewood Road, Suite 130
Kansas City, MO   64118
Tel: (816)454-9422   *Fax:* (816)454-9322
Members: 650 mutual funds
Staff: 6
Managing Director: Michelle Smith
Historical Note
Investment companies who market their shares directly to the public. Formerly No-Load Mutual Fund Ass'n; assumed its current name in 1989.
Publications:
Investor Directory. semi-a.

Mutual Fund Forum
Historical Note
Became the Forum for Investor Advice in 1997.

Mycological Soc. of America (1931)
USDA/ARS/SRRC
P.O. Box 19687
New Orleans, LA   70179
Tel: (504)286-4361   *Fax:* (504)286-4419
E-Mail: mklich@nola.srrc.usda.gov

Web Site: http://www.erin.utoronto.ca/~3msa/
Members: 1,400 individuals
Staff: 1
Annual Budget: $500-1,000,000
Secretary: Maren Klich

Historical Note
Founded in New Orleans in 1931 as an outgrowth of the Microbiological Section of the Botanical Soc. of America and incorporated in 1966 in the District of Columbia. Members are individuals interested in the study of fungi. Affiliated with the American Ass'n for the Advancement of Science and the American Institute of Biological Sciences. Membership: $60/year (individual), $150/year (organization); $30/year (student).

Publications:
Inoculum. bi-m.
Mycologia. bi-m. adv.
Mycologia Memoirs. irreg.

Meetings/Conferences:
Annual Meetings: Summer/350
1999 – St. Louis, MO/Aug. 1-7
2000 – Burlington, VT(University of Vermont)/July 30-August 3

Mystery Writers of America (1945)
17 E. 47th St., 6th Floor
New York, NY   10017
Tel: (212)888-8171   Fax: (212)888-8107
Web Site: http://www.mysterywriters.org
Members: 2,600 individuals
Staff: 1
Annual Budget: $100-250,000
Administrative Director: Mary Beth Becker

Historical Note
Professional writers of crime and mystery stories and novels. Unpublished writers are affiliate members. Publishers and agents are associate members. Membership: $65/year; $32.50/year (overseas).

Publications:
MWA Annual. a.
Third Degree. m.

Meetings/Conferences:
Annual Meetings: April in New York, NY(NY Sheraton)/700-800

NACE Internat'l (1943)
P.O. Box 218340
Houston, TX   77218-8340
Tel: (281)228-6200   Fax: (281)228-6300
E-Mail: msd@mail.nace.org
Web Site: http://www.nace.org
Members: 15,000 individuals
Staff: 63
Annual Budget: $5-10,000,000
Exec. Director: Gerald M. Shankel, CAE
Director, Conferences/Expositions: Peggy Parsons
Director, Education: Helena Alexander
Director, Administration: Robert Shields
Manager, Membership: Barbara Zlatnik
Director, Publications: Jeff Littleton

Historical Note
Formerly (1993) the Nat'l Ass'n of Corrosion Engineers. NACE advances the knowledge of corrosion engineering and science in all major industries through education, certification, standards, publications, and public awareness. Membership: $90/year (individual), $375-$2,000/year (corporate).

Publications:
Corrosion. m. adv.
Materials Performance. m. adv.

Meetings/Conferences:
Annual Meetings: Spring
1999 – San Antonio, TX(Convention Center)/April 25-30
2000 – Orlando, FL(Convention Center)/March 26-31/2000
2001 – Houston, TX(GB Brown Convention Center)/March 11-16

NADD: Ass'n for Persons with Developmental Disabilities and Mental Health Needs (1983)
132 Fair St.
Kingston, NY   12401-4802
Tel: (914)331-4336   Fax: (914)331-4569
Toll Free: (800)331 - 5362
E-Mail: nadd@ulster.net
Web Site: http://www.thenadd.org
Members: 1,143 individuals
Staff: 4
Annual Budget: $250-500,000
Exec. Director: Robert Fletcher, D.S.W.

Historical Note
Founded as Nat'l Ass'n for the Dually Diagnosed Mental Illness/Mental Retardation; assumed its current name in 1997. Membership: $78/year (individual); $350-500 (organization/company).

Meetings/Conferences:
Annual Meetings: Fall

NAFSA: Ass'n of Internat'l Educators (1948)
1307 New York Ave., N.W., Eighth Floor
Washington, DC   20005
Tel: (202)462-4811   Fax: (202)667-3419
Toll Free: (800)836 - 4994
E-Mail: inbox@nafsa.org
Web Site: http://www.nafsa.org
Members: 8,000 individuals
Staff: 50
Annual Budget: $2-5,000,000
Exec. Director: Marlene M. Johnson
Senior Director, Public Affairs: Vic Johnson
Senior Director, Product Development: Steven Kennedy
Director, Conferences & Meetings: Katherine May
Manager, Meetings/Exhibits: Berit Boegli

Director, Membership Department: Denise Jones
Historical Note
Founded (1948) as Nat'l Ass'n of Foreign Students Advisors, became (1964) Nat'l Ass'n for Foreign Student Affairs, adopted present name in 1990. Includes a division of the Council of Advisers to Foreign Students and Scholars and a section of the Administrators and Teachers in English as a Second Language. NAFSA's 7,700 members-from every state in the U.S. and more than 60 countries-make it the largest professional membership association concerned with the advancement of effecitve international educational exchange in the world. Members of NAFSA are foreign student advisers, international admissions officers, ESL teachers and administrators, study abroad administrators, overseas educational advisors, community support groups, and sponsored program administrators.

Publications:
International Educator. 4/year. adv.
NAFSA Directory. a. adv.
NAFSA Government Affairs Bulletin. 8/year.
NAFSA Newsletter. 8/year. adv.

Meetings/Conferences:
Annual Meetings: May
1999 – Denver, CO/May 23-28
2000 – San Diego, CA

NAGMR Consumer Product Brokers (1949)
401 N. Michigan Ave.
Chicago, IL   60611
Tel: (312)644-6610   Fax: (312)321-5158
E-Mail: nagmr@sba.com
Web Site: http://www.nagmr.org
Members: 110 firms
Staff: 2
Annual Budget: $500-1,000,000
Exec. Director: Jack M. Springer
Administrative Director: Kathleen M. Callahan

Historical Note
Founded as Nat'l Ass'n of Drug Manufacturer's Representatives; became (1976) Nat'l Ass'n of Diversified Manufacturers' Representatives, (1978) Nat'l Ass'n General Merchandise Representatives, and assumed its current name in 1998. Membership: $590-2,000/year.

Publications:
Membership Roster. a.
The Representative. m.

Meetings/Conferences:
Annual Meetings: Fall
1999 – San Juan, PR(El Conquistador)/Sept. 22-26/500

Nail Manufacturers Council (1989)
Historical Note
A division of the American Beauty Ass'n.

NAIOP: The Ass'n for Commercial Real Estate (1967)
Historical Note
Became the Nat'l Ass'n of Industrial and Office Properties in 1996.

NARD (1898)
Historical Note
Became Nat'l Community Pharmacists Ass'n in 1996.

Narrow Fabrics Institute
Historical Note
A division of the Industrial Fabrics Ass'n Internat'l.

NaSPA: Nat'l Systems Programmers Ass'n (1986)
Historical Note
Became NaSPA: The Ass'n for Corporate Computing Technical Professionals in 1994.

NaSPA: the Network and System Professionals Ass'n (1986)
7044 S. 13th St.
Oak Creek, WI   53154
Tel: (414)768-8000   Fax: (414)768-8001
E-Mail: sherer@naspa.net
Web Site: http://www.naspa.net
Members: 29,000 individuals, 10,000 companies
Staff: 19
Annual Budget: $2-5,000,000
President: Scott P. Sherer
V. President, Communications: Jerry Seefeldt
Director, Finance and Legal Affairs: Margaret Zizis
Director, Membership: Jeanie Bucher

Historical Note
Founded as Nat'l Systems Programmers Ass'n; became (1994) NaSPA: Nat'l Systems Programmers Ass'n and (1996) NaSPA: the Ass'n for Corporate Computing Professionals; assumed its current name in 1997. Established and incorporated in Wisconsin, NaSPA members are technical professionals in corporate computing environments. Membership: $39.95/year (individual).

Publications:
Technical Support Magazine. m. adv.

Meetings/Conferences:

Nat'l Abortion Federation (1977)
1755 Massachusetts Ave., N.W., Suite 600
Washington, DC   20036
Tel: (202)667-5881   Fax: (202)667-5890
Toll Free: (800)772 - 9100
E-Mail: naf@prochoice.org
Web Site: http://www.prochoice.org/naf
Members: 350 institutions
Staff: 15
Annual Budget: $1-2,000,000
Exec. Director: Vicki Saporta
Director, Communications: Stephanie Muler
Government Relations Director: Moreen Brutel

Historical Note
The National Abortion Federation is a professional organization of abortion providers that works to promote safe, legal abortion. NAF members include clinics, doctors and hospital surgi-centers, and provide over half of all U.S. abortions.

Publications:
Meeting Program Workbook. a. adv.
NAF News. bi-m.
NAF Report. a.

Meetings/Conferences:
Annual Meetings: Spring
1999 – Atlanta, GA

Nat'l Academic Advising Ass'n (1979)
Kansas State University
2323 Anderson Ave., Suite 225
Manhattan, KS   66502-2912
Tel: (785)532-5717   Fax: (785)532-7732
E-Mail: nacada@ksu.edu
Web Site: http://www.ksu.edu/nacada
Members: 4,600 individuals
Staff: 5
Annual Budget: $500-1,000,000
Exec. Director: Roberta D. Flaherty

Historical Note
Membership open to professionals, faculty, and students working through academic advising to ensure the educational development of students in educational institutions. Membership: $50/year (professional); $25/year (student).

Publications:
Academic Advising News. q.
NACADA Journal. semi-a. adv.

Meetings/Conferences:
Annual Meetings: October
1999 – Denver, CO(Adam's Mark)
2000 – Orlando, FL(Disney Coronado Springs)
2001 – Ottawa, ON, Canada(Conv. Cntr.)
2002 – Slat lake City, UT(Little America)
2003 – Dallas, TX

Nat'l Academies of Practice
P.O. Box 1037
Edgewood, MD   21040
Tel: (410)676-3390   Fax: (410)676-7980
Web Site: http://www.home.app.net/~nap/
Members: 700 individuals
Staff: 1
Annual Budget: $100-250,000
Exec. Director: Constance Row

Historical Note
NAP is an indisciplinary health care policy forum addressing public policy, education, research, and inquiry issues. Represents nine professions including dentistry, medicine, nursing, optometry, osteopathic medicine, posiatric medicine, psychology, social work, and veterinary medicine. Membership: $150/year (individual).

Publications:
NAP Newsletter. q.

Meetings/Conferences:
1999 – May

Nat'l Academy Museum and School Fine Arts (1825)
1083 Fifth Ave.
New York, NY   10128
Tel: (212)369 1880   Fax: (212)360-6795
Members: 600 individuals
Staff: 20
Annual Budget: $1-2,000,000
Director: Dr. Annette Blaugrund
Director, Communications: Cecilia Bonn
Director, Education: Barbara Pollard
School Administrator: Nancy Little
Director of Finance: Nancy Cafferty
Artist Membership: Deena Abu-Lughod
Chief Curator: Dr. David Dearinger
Director of Development: Anne Townsend
Director, Operations: Charles Biada

Historical Note
Founded in November 1825 as the New York Drawing Ass'n in order to furnish young artists with a place to study. In January 1826 it became the Nat'l Academy of the Arts of Design and incorporated in New York under its present title in 1828. Members are painters, sculptors, architects and print makers interested in promoting the arts. Supports a School of Fine Arts and museum. Holds changing special exhibitions of paintings, sculpture and graphic arts. Membership: $50/year, minimum (individual).

Publications:
Academy Bulletin. q.

Meetings/Conferences:
Annual Meetings: Annual Exhibition, Spring

Nat'l Academy of Arbitrators (1947)
403 Lowder Bldg.
Auburn University, AL   36849
Tel: (334)844-2817   Fax: (334)844-1498
Toll Free: (800)872 - 5617
Members: 660 individuals
Staff: 3
Annual Budget: $100-250,000
Exec. Secretary-Treasurer: William H. Holley, Jr.
Operations Manager: Brenda Ryan
Meetings Planner: Kate Planner

Historical Note
Founded in Chicago, September 14, 1947 to up-grade the professionalism of those engaged in the arbitration of labor-management disputes.

Publications:
Membership Directory. a.
The Chronicle. 3/year.

Meetings/Conferences:

Nat'l Academy of Cable Programming
Historical Note
A program of Nat'l Cable Television Ass'n, which provides administrative support.

Nat'l Academy of Clinical Biochemistry *(1976)*
2101 L St., N.W., Suite 202
Washington, DC   20037-1526
Tel: (202)659-8370   *Fax:* (202)887-5093
Web Site: http://www.nacb.org
Members: 375 individuals
Annual Budget: $50-100,000
Secretary: Barbara Goldsmith, Ph.D.

Historical Note
NACB is the official Academy of the American Ass'n for Clinical Chemistry (AACC) and membership in AACC is required. Fellows and Associate Fellows are all doctoral level scientists who are actively engaged in research, education, or service of clinical biochemistry. Fellows of the Academy are either certified by the American Board of Clinical Chemistry or another board judged to be equivalent, or have at least 10 years experience as a clinical biochemist and sufficient publications or other activities to have been judged as distinguished. Associate Fellows lack Board certification or sufficient publications to be judged distinguished, but meet all other requirements. Has no paid officers or full time staff. Membership: $45/year.

Meetings/Conferences:
Annual Meetings: Summer
1999 – New Orleans, LA/July 25-28
1999 – New Orleans, LA/July 25-28

Nat'l Academy of Conciliators *(1979)*
Historical Note
Address unknown in 1997.

Nat'l Academy of Design
Historical Note
Became (1998) Nat'l Academy and School of Fine Arts.

Nat'l Academy of Education *(1965)*
Historical Note
Address unknown in 1998.

Nat'l Academy of Elder Law Attorneys *(1987)*
1604 N. Country Club Rd.
Tucson, AZ   85716
Tel: (520)881-4005   *Fax:* (520)325-7925
Members: 3,000 individuals
Staff: 7
Annual Budget: $1-2,000,000
Exec. Director: Laury L. Adsit

Historical Note
Members are private attorneys, law professors, judges, students and Title III interest in the provision of legal services to the elderly. Attorneys with an interest in the provision of legal services to the elderly. Organization has grown from 35 to 3,000 members in 9 years. Membership: $175/year (individual).

Publications:
NAELA News. 8/year. adv.
NAELA Quarterly Journal. q. adv.
NEW. m.

Meetings/Conferences:

Nat'l Academy of Engineering of the United States of America *(1964)*
2101 Constitution Ave., N.W.
Washington, DC   20418
Tel: (202)334-3200   *Fax:* (202)334-1680
Web Site: http://www.nae.edu
Members: 1,806 individuals
Staff: 38
Annual Budget: $2-5,000,000
President: William A. Wulf, Ph.D.
Exec. Officer: William C. Salmon
Director, Administration and Finance: Carol M. Harless
Director, Membership Office: Deborah K. Brandt
Foreign Secretary: Harold K. Forsen
Home Secretary: Simon Ostrach

Historical Note
A private organization established in 1964 to share in the responsibility given the National Academy of Sciences under its Congressional charter of 1863 to examine questions of science and technology at the request of the federal government; to sponsor engineering programs aimed at meeting national needs; to encourage engineering research and to recognize distinguished engineers. Membership is by peer election only. Membership: $200/year.

Publications:
The Bridge. q.

Meetings/Conferences:
Annual Meetings: October in Washington, DC(Nat'l Academy of Sciences Bldg.)
1999 – Washington, DC/Oct. 4-5

Nat'l Academy of Neuropsychology *(1978)*
2600 S. Parker Road, Suite 1-215
Aurora, CO   80014
Tel: (303)751-1183   *Fax:* (303)751-1238
Web Site: http://www.nan.drexel.edu
Members: 3,350 individuals
Staff: 3
Annual Budget: $100-250,000
Exec. Director: J.G. Harris

Historical Note
Formerly (1989) Nat'l Academy of Neuropsychologists. NAN members are neuropsychologists and other individuals who have interests in brain-behavior relationships and neuropsychology as a science and profession. Membership: $80/year (individual); $40/year (student).

Publications:
Archives of Clinical Neuropsychology. bi-m.
Bulletin of NAN. q.
Membership Directory. bien.
Neuropsychology Review. q.

Meetings/Conferences:
Annual Meetings: November
1999 – San Antonio, TX(Hyatt)/Nov. 10-13
2000 – Orlando, FL(Sheraton)/Nov. 15-18
2001 – San Francisco, CA
2002 – Miami, FL

Nat'l Academy of Opticianry *(1963)*
8401 Corporate Dr., Suite 605
Landover, MD   20785
Tel: (301)577-4828   *Fax:* (301)577-3880
E-Mail: info@nao.org
Web Site: http://www.nao.org
Members: 5,300 individuals
Staff: 4
Annual Budget: $500-1,000,000
Exec. Director: James E. Iciek

Historical Note
An association of individual opticians who are state licensed or nationally certified, NAO's purpose is to promote continuing education through home study courses and seminars. Membership: $55/year.

Publications:
Academy Programs. q.
ARCHIVES Newsletter. m.

Meetings/Conferences:
Annual Meetings: June-September

Nat'l Academy of Recording Arts and Sciences *(1957)*
3402 Pico Blvd.
Santa Monica, CA   90405-2118
Tel: (310)392-3777   *Fax:* (310)392-2778
Web Site: http://www.grammy.com
Members: 13,000 individuals
Staff: 100
President: Michael Greene
Exec.V. President/General Manager: Rob Senn
V. President, Member Services: Kristen Madsen

Historical Note
Singers, musicians, engineers, composers, arrangers and others engaged in producing commercial recordings. Presents the annual "Grammy" awards for outstanding recordings and grants the "Grammy Lifetime Achievement" to those who have contributed to the world of music during their lifetime. Membership: $65/year (individual).

Publications:
Grammy Magazine. bi-m.
NARAS Journal. bien.
Program Book. a.
The Grammy Winner's Book. a.

Meetings/Conferences:
Annual Meetings: Spring

Nat'l Academy of Sciences *(1863)*
2101 Constitution Ave., N.W.
Washington, DC   20418
Tel: (202)334-2158   *Fax:* (202)334-1684
Web Site: http://www.nas.edu
Members: 2,158 individuals
Staff: 1100
Annual Budget: Over $100,000,000
President: Dr. Bruce Alberts
Director, Office of News and Public Information: Susan Turner-Lowe
Chief Financial Officer: Archie Turner
General Counsel: James R. Wright
Director, Office of Congressional and Government Affairs: James E. Jensen
Exec. Officer: Kenneth R. Fulton
Exec. Officer: E. William Colglazier

Historical Note
Private honorary organization of scholars in scientific and engineering research, chartered by act of Congress March 3, 1863 to serve as an advisor to the federal government on questions of science and technology. Conducts studies in all disciplines of natural and social science and engineering, with special emphasis on science advisory role in public policy issues. Affiliated with the Nat'l Academy of Engineering and the Institute of Medicine. The Nat'l Research Council is the operating arm of the NAS. Has an annual budget of approximately $190 million.

Publications:
Issues In Science and Technology. q. adv.
News Report. q.
Proceedings. bi-w.

Meetings/Conferences:
Annual Meetings: April in Washington, D.C.
1999 – Washington, DC(Nat'l Academy of Sciences Building)/April 24-27

Nat'l Academy of Televisiion Journalists *(1987)*
P.O. Box 31
Salisbury, MD   21083
Tel: (410)548-5343   *Fax:* (410)543-0658
E-Mail: NBAYNE@SHORE.INTERCOM.NET
Web Site: HTTP://ANGELFIRE.COM/MD/NATJ/INDEX.HTML
Members: 400 individuals
Staff: 6
Exec. Director: Neil F. Bayne

Historical Note
Members are television journalists and journalism students. Membership: $50/Year.

Publications:
Golden Viddy Award. a.
NATJ ON LINE.

Meetings/Conferences:
Annual Meetings: always 2nd Saturday in May.

Nat'l Academy of Television Arts and Sciences *(1947)*
111 West 57th St., Suite 1020
New York, NY   10019
Tel: (212)586-8424   *Fax:* (212)246-8129
E-Mail: trudywc@aol.com
Web Site: http://www.emmyonline.org
Members: 12,000 individuals
Staff: 10
Annual Budget: $2-5,000,000
President: John Cannon

Historical Note
Maintains an archival program library on the campus of UCLA. Members are writers, engineers, editors, musicians and others engaged in the creative aspects of the television industry. Presents the annual "Emmy" awards for excellence.

Publications:
Emmy Awards Directory. a.
NATAS News. q.
Television Quarterly. q. adv.

Meetings/Conferences:

Nat'l Account Management Ass'n *(1964)*
150 N. Wacker Dr., Suite 2222
Chicago, IL   60606-1607
Tel: (312)251-3131   *Fax:* (312)251-3132
Web Site: http://www.nams.org
Members: 1,425 individuals
Staff: 10
Annual Budget: $500-1,000,000
Exec. Director: Lisa Napolitano
Deputy Exec. Director: Maria T. Susano
Director, Meetings: Peggy Lockery
Meetings Manager: Meghan P. Miller
Dir., Membership Svcs.: Matt Fegley

Historical Note
Founded as Nat'l Account Marketing Ass'n; assumed its current name in 1993. Members are company executives concerned with sales or marketing to major national and global accounts and the special management they require. NAMA provides literature and training and conducts surveys and studies on the intricacies of large, complex account management. Incorporated in the State of Illinois. Membership: $375/year.

Publications:
Annual Survey of NAM Compensation. a.
Guidebook of Major Account Management Practices. a.
NAMA Journal. q. adv.
Velocity. q.

Meetings/Conferences:
Annual Meetings: Spring
1999 – Orlando, FL(Marriott World Center)/May 2-5/1000
2000 – San Antonio, TX

Nat'l Account Management Ass'n
Historical Note
Became (1996) Nat'l Account Management Soc.

Nat'l Accounting and Finance Council *(1941)*
2200 Mill Road
Alexandria, VA   22314
Tel: (703)838-1915   *Fax:* (703)836-6070
Web Site: http://www.trucking.org
Members: 1,100 individuals
Staff: 6
Annual Budget: $500-1,000,000
Exec. Director: Micheal Shakarun

Historical Note
NAFC is a member organization of chief financial officers within the trucking industry and is a part of the American Trucking Ass'n.

Publications:
Motor Freight Controller. bi-m.

Meetings/Conferences:
Annual Meetings: June/500
1999 – Chicago, IL/June 27-29

Nat'l Adult Education Professional Development Consortium *(1991)*
444 North Capitol St., Suite 706
Washington, DC   20001
Tel: (202)624-5250   *Fax:* (202)624-8826
Members: 55 individuals
Staff: 1
Annual Budget: $100-250,000
Exec. Director: Judith Ann Koloski

Publications:
Annual Report. a. adv.
Stateline. 8/yr.

Meetings/Conferences:
Annual Meetings: July

Nat'l Adult Vocational Education Ass'n *(1978)*
OH Dept of Ed, Div of Vocat'l/Adult Ed.
65 S. Front St., Room 915
Columbus, OH   43215-4183
Tel: (614)644-6661   *Fax:* (614)728-6176
Web Site: http://www.nhrav.org
Members: 500 individuals
Annual Budget: under $10,000
Secretary-Treasurer: Carolyn S. Gasiorek

Historical Note
A section of the American Vocational Ass'n, AVEA members are administrators, teachers and others with an interest in post secondary adult vocational education. Membership: $5/year.

Publications:
AVEA Newsletter. q.
Directory of Members. a.

Meetings/Conferences:
Annual Meetings: December, in conjunction with the American Vocational Ass'n.

Nat'l Aeronautic Ass'n (1905)
1815 N. Ft. Myer Drive, Suite 700
Arlington, VA 22209-1805
Tel: (703)527-0226   Fax: (703)527-0229
Toll Free: (800)644 - 9777
E-Mail: naa@ids2.idsonline.com
Web Site: http://www.naa.ycg.org
Members: 400,000 individuals
Staff: 7
Annual Budget: $500-1,000,000
President and C.E.O.: Donald J. Koranda
Director, Membership: James A. Way

Historical Note
Members include aerospace corporations, aero clubs, affiliates, and the major national sporting aviation organizations such as; the Academy of Model Aeronautics; the Experimental Aircraft Ass'n; the United States Parachute Ass'n; the Internat'l Aerobatic Club; the Soaring Soc. of America; the Balloon Federation of America; the Helicopter Club of America; the United States Ultralight Ass'n; and the United States Hang Gliding Ass'n. Absorbed the Aero Club of America in 1922. NAA is the U.S. representative to the Federation Aeronautique Internationale (Paris), the world organization for validating air and space records. Membership: $27/year (individual); $1,000-15,000/year (organization).

Publications:
NAA Flyer. bi-m.
National Aeronautics. bi-m.

Meetings/Conferences:

Nat'l Aerosol Ass'n (1986)
787 Windgate Dr.
Annapolis, MD 21401
Tel: (410)349-8614   Fax: (410)349-8616
E-Mail: gwbjmb@annap.infi.net
Members: 41 individuals, 41 companies
Staff: 2
Annual Budget: $100-250,000
Exec. Director: George W. Brown

Historical Note
Membership is open to individuals, firms, and agencies engaged in business related to the development, manufacture, packaging, sale or distribution of aerosol products.

Publications:
Aerosol News. q

Meetings/Conferences:
Annual Meetings: Winter

Nat'l Affordable Housing Management Ass'n
526 King St., Suite 511
Alexandria, VA 22314
Tel: (703)683-8630   Fax: (703)683-8634
Web Site: http://www.nama.org
Members: 2,500 individuals
Staff: 7
Annual Budget: $250-500,000
Exec. Director: George Caruso
Communications Coordinator: Grant Cole
Director of Education and Training: Daria Jakuowski
Director of Membership: Valerie Hairston

Historical Note
Formerly the Nat'l Assisted Housing Management Ass'n. Represents professional property managers of government assisted housing. NAHMA was formed through a merger of the former National Advisory Council of HUD Management Agents and the National Federation of Ass'ns of HUD Management Agents. Membership: $2,200/year (individual).

Publications:
NAHMA Newsletter. m. adv.

Meetings/Conferences:
Tri-annual Meetings: 2 in Washington, DC the other varies
1999 – Seattle, WA/June 26-28

Nat'l Aggregates Ass'n (1916)
900 Spring St.
Silver Spring, MD 20910
Tel: (301)587-1400   Fax: (301)585-4219
Members: 350 manufacturers
Staff: 13
Annual Budget: $1-2,000,000
President: Robert A. Gale

Historical Note
Formerly (1987) the Nat'l Sand and Gravel Ass'n. Sponsors the Nat'l Sand and Gravel Ass'n Political Action Committee.

Publications:
The NAA Insider.

Meetings/Conferences:
Annual Meetings: Jan./Feb. with The Nat'l Ready Mix Concrete Ass'nn

Nat'l Agri-Marketing Ass'n (1956)
11020 King St., Suite 205
Shawnee Mission, KS 66210-1201
Tel: (913)491-6500   Fax: (913)491-6502
E-Mail: agrimktg@nama.org
Web Site: http://www.nama.org
Members: 2,500 individuals
Staff: 10
Annual Budget: $500-1,000,000
Exec. V. President and C.E.O.: Eldon White
Director, Communications and Operations: Jenny Pickett
Director, Professionals: Dana Baith

Historical Note
Originated as the Chicago Area Agricultural Advertising Ass'n with 39 charter members. In 1963 the name was changed to the Nat'l Agricultural Advertising and Marketing Ass'n, and the present name was assumed in 1973. Membership: $100/year, average (individual).

Publications:
Leader Newsletter.
NAMA Directory of Members. a. adv.
National NAMA News. m.

Meetings/Conferences:
Annual Meetings: Spring/1,500

Nat'l Agricultural Aviation Ass'n (1967)
1005 E St., S.E.
Washington, DC 20003
Tel: (202)546-5722   Fax: (202)546-5726
E-Mail: NAAA@aol.com
Members: 1,200 cropsprayers & allied companies
Staff: 7
Annual Budget: $500-1,000,000
Exec. Director: James B. Boillot, CAE
Director, Marketing: Cary Crocker

Historical Note
Formerly (1971) Nat'l Aerial Applicators Ass'n. Membership: $350/year (operator member).

Publications:
Agricultural Aviation. 6/year.

Meetings/Conferences:
Annual Meetings: December

Nat'l Air Access Council (1995)
Historical Note
Name changed to U.S. Air Tour Ass'n in 1996.

Nat'l Air Carrier Ass'n (1962)
1730 M St., N.W., Suite 806
Washington, DC 20036
Tel: (202)833-8200   Fax: (202)659-9479
Members: 6 companies
Staff: 6
President and C.E.O.: Edward J. Driscoll

Historical Note
Members are U.S.-certificated scheduled and charter airlines.

Meetings/Conferences:
Annual Meetings: January, usually in Washington

Nat'l Air Duct Cleaners Ass'n (1989)
1518 K St., N.W., Suite 503
Washington, DC 20005
Tel: (202)737-2926   Fax: (202)347-8847
Members: 700 companies
Staff: 6
Annual Budget: $500-1,000,000
Exec. Director: Ken Sufka
Director of Communications: Shaine McMahon
Director of Membership Services: Kimberly Gorn
Director of Publications: Abbe Spada

Historical Note
NADCA, the trade association of the air duct cleaning industry, was established to raise the ethical standards and cleaning procedures within the industry and to educate the public on the need for clean indoor air. Standards for the industry and certification. Membership: $495-695/year.

Publications:
DucTales Magazine. bi-m. adv.
NADCA Update. bi-m.

Meetings/Conferences:

Nat'l Air Filtration Ass'n (1980)
1518 K St., N.W., Suite 503
Washington, DC 20005
Tel: (202)628-5328   Fax: (202)638-4833
Toll Free: (800)941 - 6274
Members: 181 companies
Annual Budget: $100-250,000
Exec. Director: Kenneth M. Sufka

Historical Note
Members are companies selling and/or servicing air filtration equipment.

Publications:
Air Media. q. adv.
Membership Directory. q.
Yearbook. As needed.

Meetings/Conferences:
Annual Meetings: early Fall

Nat'l Air Traffic Controllers Ass'n (1987)
1150 17th St. N.W., Suite 701
Washington, DC 20036
Tel: (202)223-2900   Fax: (202)659-3991
Web Site: http://home.natca.org/natca
Members: 10,000 individuals
Staff: 34
Annual Budget: $2-5,000,000
President: Michael McNally
Director, Communications: Sherrod Shim
Exec. V. President: James R. Schwitz
Legislative Director: Ken Montoya
Chief of Staff: Jack Cole

Historical Note
Membership: $50/year (associate); 1.5% base pay/year (active); $250/year (company).

Publications:
Annual Report.
NATCA Facility Representative Bulletin. bi-w.
NATCA Newsletter. m.
Quarterly Topical Publications.

Meetings/Conferences:
Biennial Conventions: even years

Nat'l Air Transportation Ass'n (1940)
4226 King St.
Alexandria, VA 22302
Tel: (703)845-9000   Fax: (703)845-8176
Toll Free: (800)808 - 6282
Web Site: http://nata.online.org
Members: 1,800 air carriers & airport svc. orgs
Staff: 16
Annual Budget: $2-5,000,000
President: James K. Coyne
Manager, Communications: Lucy Koons
Director, Marketing: Pat Neary
V. President: Andrew Cebula
Mgr., Meetings/Conventions: Connie James
V. President and C.F.O.: Alan Darrow

Historical Note
Established December, 1940 as the Nat'l Air Training Ass'n and became the Nat'l Aviation Trades Ass'n in 1946. In 1968 the Ass'n of Commuter Airlines merged with the Nat'l Air Taxi Conference and changed its name to the Nat'l Air Transportation Conferences. In 1974 the Nat'l Aviation Trades Ass'n merged with NATC and the association assumed its present name. Sponsors the Nat'l Air Transportation Foundation.

Publications:
Annual Report. a.
Annual Wage and Salary Handbook. a.
Legislative Report. 20/year.
NATAnews Newsletter. m.
Operations Bulletin. 36/year.
Regulatory Report. 20/year.

Meetings/Conferences:
Annual Meetings: Spring
1999 – Phoenix, AZ(Phoenix Civic Plaza)/April 20-22

Nat'l Aircraft Finance Ass'n (1969)
P.O. Box 85
Poolesville, MD 20837-0685
Tel: (301)349-2070   Fax: (301)972-7727
Members: 70 lending institutions
Exec. Director: Karen C. Griggs

Historical Note
NAFA members are lending institutions involved in aircraft financing.

Meetings/Conferences:
Annual Meetings: May

Nat'l Aircraft Resale Ass'n
4220 King St.
Alexandria, VA 22302-1507
Tel: (703)671-8273   Fax: (703)671-5848
Staff: 1
Exec. Director: Susan L. Sheets

Nat'l Airfreight Trucking Alliance (1987)
Historical Note
Address unknown in 1996.

Nat'l Alarm Ass'n of America (1984)
P.O. Box 3409
Dayton, OH 45401
Toll Free: (800)283 - 6285
Members: 500 companies, 200 assoc. companies
Staff: 1
Annual Budget: $10-25,000
President: Gene D. Riddlebaugh

Historical Note
Incorporated in Los Angeles, CA. Members are small alarm dealers. Membership: $100/year.

Publications:
Counterforce. a.

Meetings/Conferences:
Annual Meetings: October

Nat'l Alcohol Beverage Control Ass'n (1938)
4216 King St., West
Alexandria, VA 22302-1507
Tel: (703)578-4200   Fax: (703)820-3551
Web Site: http://www.nabca.org
Members: 18 state agencies, 175 companies
Staff: 22
Annual Budget: $1-2,000,000
Exec. Director & Treasurer: James M. Sgueo
Exec. Assistant: Dixie Jamison
Director, Administration: Patricia K. LaCava

Historical Note
Members include control jurisdictions, supplier members and industry trade associations.

Publications:
CONTACTS - Membership Directory. bien.
NABCA NewsGram. bi-m.

Meetings/Conferences:
Annual Meetings: Spring
1999 – LaQuinta, CA(LaQuinta Resort)/May 14-19

Nat'l Alliance for Media Arts and Culture (1978)
346 9th St.
San Francisco, CA 94103-3809
Tel: (415)431-1391   Fax: (415)431-1392
E-Mail: namac@namac.org
Members: 280 media arts centers
Staff: 2
Annual Budget: $100-250,000
National Director: Helen DeMichiel

Historical Note
Members are non-profit media arts centers, institutions and individuals with an interest in media arts. Formerly (1992) the

Nat'l Alliance of Media Arts Centers. Membership: $50/year (individual); company based on budget.

Publications:
MAIN Newsletter. q.
National Educational Directory. a.

Meetings/Conferences:

Nat'l Alliance for Musical Theatre (1986)
330 West 45th St., Lobby B
New York, NY   10036
Tel: (212)265-5376   *Fax:* (212)582-8730
E-Mail: NAMTheatre@aol.com
Web Site: http://www.bway.net/namt
Members: 100 theatres and organizations
Exec. Director: Helen Sneed

Historical Note
NAMT members are theatres and professional drama organizations with an interest in the development of stage musicals.

Publications:
Directory. a.

Meetings/Conferences:
1999 – Los Angeles, CA
1999 – New York, NY

Nat'l Alliance for Oral Health (1990)
1625 Massachusetts Ave., N.W., Suite 600
Washington, DC   20036-2212
Tel: (202)667-9433   *Fax:* (202)667-0642
E-Mail: magathom@erols.com
Members: 7 individuals, 20 organizations
Staff: 1
Annual Budget: $10-25,000
Treasurer: Scott Litch

Historical Note
NAOH is a coalition of organizations examining the implications on oral health of a range of human health problems and conditions. Works to include dental and oral care in comprehensive and preventive medical treatment. Membership: $25/year (individual); $100-300/year (organization).

Publications:
NAOH Reporter. q.

Meetings/Conferences:

Nat'l Alliance for Youth Sports (1980)
2050 Vista Pkwy.
West Palm Beach, FL   33411-2718
Tel: (561)684-1141   *Fax:* (561)684-2546
Toll Free: (800)729 - 2057
E-Mail: nays@nays.org
Web Site: http://www.nays.org
Members: 150,000 individuals
Staff: 25
Annual Budget: $1-2,000,000
President: Fred C. Engh
Public Relations Director: Greg Bach
V. President, Education: Michael Pfahl

Historical Note
Formerly (1997) Nat'l Youth Sport Coaches Ass'n, NAYS sponsors research and education programs to improve the quality of sports for youth. A national certification program is focused on giving coaches a clear understanding of the psychological, physical and social needs of children.

Publications:
Youth Sports Coach. q. adv.

Meetings/Conferences:
Annual Meetings: August

Nat'l Alliance of Black SalesMen and SalesWomen (1983)
Historical Note
Address unknown in 1997.

Nat'l Alliance of Black School Educators (1970)
2816 Georgia Ave., N.W.
Washington, DC   20001
Tel: (202)483-1549   *Fax:* (202)483-8323
Members: 4,000 individuals
Staff: 6
Annual Budget: $500-1,000,000
Exec. Director: Quentin Lawson

Historical Note
Formerly (until 1973) the Nat'l Alliance of Black School Superintendents. Membership: $60/year.

Publications:
NABSE News Briefs. q.
Newsletter. q.

Meetings/Conferences:
Annual Meetings: Fall

Nat'l Alliance of Independent Crop Consultants (1978)
1055 Petersburg Cove
Collierville, TN   38017
Tel: (901)861-0511   *Fax:* (901)861-0512
E-Mail: jonesnaicc@aol.com
Web Site: http://www.naicc.com
Members: 480 individuals
Staff: 2
Annual Budget: $250-500,000
Exec. V. President: Allison Jones

Historical Note
Founded in 1978, NAICC is an outgrowth of the Southern Alliance of Independent Crop Consultants. Membership: $195/year (individual), $600-2,500/year (company).

Publications:
Membership Directory. a.
Newsletter. m.

Meetings/Conferences:
1999 – Memphis, TN(Peabody)/Jan. 20-23
2000 – Portland, OR(Doubletree)January

Nat'l Alliance of Nurse Practitioners (1985)
325 Pennsylvania Ave., S.E.
Washington, DC   20003
Tel: (202)675-6350
Members: 6 organizations
Staff: 1
Annual Budget: $10-25,000
Chairperson: Ann K. Ingram, MSN, CANP

Historical Note
NANP is a coalition of national organizations with nurse practitioner constituencies. NANP promotes the public health through primary care, and promotes the visibility and unity of nurse practitioners as primary care providers. Has no paid officers or full-time staff. Membership: $750/year (organization); $500/year (associate); $1,000/year (sustaining).

Meetings/Conferences:
Semi-annual Meetings: April and November

Nat'l Alliance of Postal and Federal Employees (1913)
1628 11th St., N.W.
Washington, DC   20001
Tel: (202)939-6325   *Fax:* (202)939-6389
Members: 47,000 individuals
Staff: 51
Annual Budget: $2-5,000,000
President: James M. McGee
National Secretary: Wilbur Duncan

Historical Note
Established as the Nat'l Alliance of Postal Employees in 1913 with the immediate purpose of preventing elimination of blacks from railway mail service; became the first industrial Union in the U.S. in 1923 when it opened its membership to any postal employee who desired to join; assumed its present name in 1965 when it expanded its membership eligibility requirements to include federal employees. Supports the Nat'l Alliance for Political Action.

Publications:
National Alliance Magazine. m. adv.
Newsletter. m.
Reporter. m.

Meetings/Conferences:
Biennial Meetings: even years/Summer/1,500-2,000

Nat'l Alliance of Preservation Commissions (1983)
c/o University of Georgia
609 Caldwell Hall
Athens, GA   30602
Tel: (706)542-4731   *Fax:* (706)542-4485
E-Mail: pcassity@arches.uga.edu
Members: 400 individuals, 600 commissions
Staff: 2
Annual Budget: $50-100,000
Exec. Director: Pratt Cassity

Historical Note
Serves as a bridge between commissions and other preservation organizations. Has no paid staff. Membership fee: $15-100/year.

Publications:
Alliance Review. q.

Meetings/Conferences:
1999 – Savannah, GA(DeSoto Hilton)/Oct. 20-24/100

Nat'l Alliance of Short Story Authors (1992)
7505 S.W. 82nd St., Suite 222
Miami, FL   33143
Tel: (305)668-2283   *Fax:* (305)668-0636
Members: 135 individuals, 4 organizations
Staff: 3
Annual Budget: $50-100,000
Exec. Director: Alejandra Gonzalez-Cerda

Historical Note
Membership: $45.00/individual; $150/organization

Publications:
Today's Fiction. q. adv.
Wild Wood Reader. q.

Meetings/Conferences:
1999 – Miami, FL/200
1999 – Boston, MA/100

Nat'l Alliance of State and Territorial AIDS Directors
444 N. Capitol St., N.W., Suite 339
Washington, DC   20001-1512
Tel: (202)434-8090   *Fax:* (202)434-8092
E-Mail: nastad@aol.com
Members: 59 government agencies
Staff: 10
Annual Budget: $1-2,000,000
Exec. Director: Julie M. Scofield
Deputy Director: Joseph Kelly
Director, Government Relations: Byron J. Harris
Director, Administrator: Jason Hendrix

Historical Note
NASTAD provides support to directors of HIV/AIDS programs within the state and territorial health departments. Membership fee varies.

Publications:
NASTAD Community Planning Bulletin. m.
NASTAD HIV Prevention Update. bi-m.
NASTAD News. m.

Meetings/Conferences:
Annual Meetings: Spring/70
1999 – Washington, DC

Nat'l Alliance of Statewide Preservation Organizations (1986)
Historic Landmarks Foundation of Indiana

340 W. Michigan St.
Indianapolis, IN   46202-3204
Tel: (317)639-4534
Members: 48 organizations

Historical Note
NASPO members are state historic preservation organizations. Has no permanent office or paid staff.

Meetings/Conferences:
Semi-annual Meetings: Fall and Winter

Nat'l AMBUCS (1922)
P.O. Box 5127
High Point, NC   27262
Tel: (336)869-2166   *Fax:* (336)887-8451
E-Mail: ambucs@ambucs. com
Web Site: http://www.ambucs.com
Members: 5,500 individuals
Staff: 5
Annual Budget: $500-1,000,000
Exec. Director: J. Joseph Copeland

Historical Note
Founded as Nat'l Ass'n of American Business Clubs, AMBUCS is a national service organization dedicated to creating opportunity and independence for people with disabilities. Programs include community service projects, scholarships for therapists, and Amtryke, the therapeutic tricycle for children with disabilities.

Publications:
The AMBUC Leader. m.
The AMBUC Magazine. q. adv.

Meetings/Conferences:
Annual Meetings: Summer
1999 – Nashville, TN

Nat'l Ambucs
Historical Note
See Ambucs.

Nat'l American Indian Court Judges Ass'n (1968)
8 Annie George Dr. Ext.
P.O. Box 3126
Mashantucket, CT   06339-3126
Tel: (860)572-6156   *Fax:* (860)572-6320
E-Mail: naicja@snet.net
Web Site: see text
Members: 256 individuals
Staff: 1
President: Judge Jill Shibles

Historical Note
The mission of NAICJA, as a national representative association, is to strengthen and enhance tribal justice systems. The Web address is: http://brooks.simplenet.com/naicja/organization. html. An alternate address is 1301 Connecticut Ave., N.W. Suite 200, Washington, DC 20036

Publications:
Indian Courts Newsletter. irreg.

Nat'l American Indian Housing Council (1974)
900 2nd St., N.E., Suite 007
Washington, DC   20002
Tel: (202)789-1754   *Fax:* (202)789-1758
Toll Free: (800)284 - 9165
E-Mail: housing@naihc.net
Web Site: http://naihc.indian.com
Members: 400 agencies
Staff: 25
Annual Budget: $1-2,000,000
Exec. Director: Christoper Boesen

Historical Note
NAIHC members are tribes and tribally designated housing entities.

Publications:
Annual Report.
Native American Housing News. 9/yea.

Meetings/Conferences:
1999 – Seattle, WA/July 12-14

Nat'l American Legion Press Ass'n (1923)
P.O. Box 1184
Decatur, GA   30031-1184
Tel: (404)377-5602
E-Mail: geonaopa@mindspring.com
Members: 2,000 individuals
Staff: 1
Annual Budget: under $10,000
Exec. Director: George W. Hooten

Historical Note
Formerly (1973) American Legion Press Ass'n.

Publications:
NALPA News-Letter. bi-m.

Meetings/Conferences:
Annual Meetings: With American Legion

Nat'l Animal Control Ass'n (1978)
P.O. Box 480851
Kansas City, MO   64148-0851
Tel: (913)768-1319   *Fax:* (913)768-1378
E-Mail: naca@interserv.com
Web Site: http://www.netplace.net/naca
Members: 4,000 individuals, 5,800 animal care centers
Staff: 3
Annual Budget: $100-250,000
Exec. Director: John Mays

Historical Note
Members are animal shelters, public health organizations, government officials, humane societies, and individuals concerned with animal care and control. Membership: $35/year (individual); $125/year (organization).

Publications:
NACA News. bi-m.

Meetings/Conferences:
Annual Meetings: May

Nat'l Animal Damage Control Ass'n (1979)
RR5 Box 43F
Ardmore, OK   73401
Tel: (580)223-5810
E-Mail: jghuggins@noble.org
Members: 600 individuals
Annual Budget: $10-25,000
Treasurer: Grant Huggins

Historical Note
NADCA members are wildlife professionals and other interested persons involved in wildlife damage management. Membership: $10/year (student), $20/year (active), $40/year (sponsor), $100/year (patron).

Publications:
The Probe. m.

Meetings/Conferences:
Annual Meetings: in conjunction with other national/regional wildlife damage meetings.

Nat'l Antique and Art Dealers Ass'n of America (1954)
12 E. 56th Street
New York, NY   10022
Tel: (212)826-9707   Fax: (212)319-0471
Web Site: http://www.dir-dd.com/naadaa.html/
Members: 40 individuals, 45 companies
Annual Budget: $10-25,000
Secretary-Treasurer: Andrew H. Chait

Historical Note
A member of the Confederation Internationale des Negociants en Oeuvres d'Art. Formerly New York Antique and Art Dealers Ass'n, Inc. NAADAA works to safeguard the interests of buyers, sellers, and collectors of antiques and art. Officers change biennially in March.

Publications:
Membership Directory. bien.

Meetings/Conferences:

Nat'l Apartment Ass'n (1939)
201 N. Union St., Suite 200
Alexandria, VA   22314-2642
Tel: (703)518-6141   Fax: (703)518-6191
Web Site: http://www.naahq.org
Members: 26,600 individuals, 160 organizations
Staff: 30
Annual Budget: $2-5,000,000
Exec. V. President: Amy S. Dozier
Director, Communications: Stephanie Oetjen
Director, Meetings: Brooke Naylor
Director, Finance: James Estes
V. President, Administration: Maureen Lambe
Director, Publications: Stephanie Oetjen
Director, MIS: Gladys Romero

Historical Note
Established as Nat'l Apartment Owners Ass'n, it assumed its present name in 1967. A federation of local and state associations of owners, builders, investors and managers of rental property. Awards the CAM ("Certified Apartment Manager"), CAMT ("Certified Apartment Maintenance Technician") and CAPS ("Certified Apartment Property Supervisor") designations. Sponsors the NAA Political Action Committee and the NAA Education Foundation.

Publications:
Apartment Economics. irreg.
Income and Expense Survey. a.
Leadership Directory. a.
Units. 9/year. adv.

Meetings/Conferences:
Annual Meetings: June

Nat'l Appliance Parts Suppliers Ass'n (1966)
16420 S.E. Mcgillivray Blvd.
Suite 103-133
Vancouver, WA   98683-3461
Tel: (360)834-3805   Fax: (360)834-3507
Web Site: http://www.napsa.repairnet.com
Members: 250 companies
Staff: 4
Annual Budget: $100-250,000
Exec. Director: Suzanne Stilwill

Historical Note
Provides distributors of replacement parts for major home appliances (both non-OEM and OEM) with information and services. Sponsors industry trade show. Emphasis on supplier relations/activities to promote mutual understanding.

Publications:
NAPSA Results. q.

Meetings/Conferences:
Annual Meetings: Spring/400
1999 – Puerto Rico/October 13-17

Nat'l Appliance Service Ass'n (1949)
9247 N. Meridian St., Suite 216
Indianapolis, IN   46260
Tel: (317)844-1602   Fax: (317)844-4745
E-Mail: carrienasa@aol.com
Web Site: nasa1.org
Members: 200 companies
Staff: 1
Annual Budget: $10-25,000
Exec. Director: Carrie Giannakos

Historical Note
Members are owners of portable small appliance repair centers. Appliance manufacturers and industry suppliers also participate. Membership: $250/year (company).

Publications:
Annual Membership Directory. a. adv.
NASA Newsletter. m. adv.

Meetings/Conferences:
Annual Meetings: June
1999 – San Fransico, CA/July 31-Aug. 2

Nat'l Aquaculture Council
1901 N. Ft. Myer Dr. Suite 700
Arlington, VA   22209
Tel: (703)524-8883   Fax: (703)524-4619
Web Site: www.nfi.org
Staff: 3
Exec. Director: Roy E. Martin

Historical Note
A division of the Nat'l Fisheries Institute, NAC members are farmers, food processors, and food distributors with an interest in aquaculture.

Meetings/Conferences:
Semi-annual Meetings: April and October

Nat'l Arborist Ass'n (1938)
Meeting Pl Mall Rt 101
P.O. Box 1094
Amherst, NH   03031-1094
Tel: (603)673-3311   Fax: (603)672-2613
Toll Free: (800)733 - 2622
Members: 2,000 tree service companies
Staff: 19
Annual Budget: $2-5,000,000
Association Administrator: Pat Felix
Director, Communications: Christopher Brown
Meeting Coordinator: Carol Crossland
Director, Safety/Education: Peter Gerstenberger

Historical Note
NAA was formed to further the interests of commercial arborists. Membership: $250-$2,400/year (organization/company).

Publications:
NAA Reporter. m.
Tree Care Industry Magazine. m. adv.
Treeworker. m.

Meetings/Conferences:
Annual Meetings: February
1999 – Cancun, Mexico

Nat'l Armored Car Ass'n (1929)
1023 15th St., N.W., 7th Floor
Washington, DC   20005
Tel: (202)289-1780   Fax: (202)842-3275
Members: 85 companies
Staff: 1
Annual Budget: $100-250,000
Exec. Director: Larry Sabbath

Historical Note
Absorbed the Armored Transportation Institute in 1993. Membership: annual dues vary based on company size.

Publications:
Newsletter. q.

Meetings/Conferences:
1999 – Washington, DC(Ritz-Carlton)

Nat'l Art Education Ass'n (1947)
1916 Association Drive
Reston, VA   22091-1590
Tel: (703)860-8000   Fax: (703)860-2960
Web Site: http://www.naea-reston.org
Members: 17,000 individuals
Staff: 17
Annual Budget: $1-2,000,000
Exec. Director: Dr. Thomas A. Hatfield
Director, Membership: James E. Modrick

Historical Note
Founded in 1947 by the merger of Eastern Arts Ass'n, Pacific Arts Ass'n, Southeastern Arts Ass'n and Western Arts Ass'n with the Art Department of the Nat'l Education Ass'n. NAEA is the professional association for educators in the visual arts at all instructional levels. Its purpose is to advance art education through professional development, service, advancement of knowledge and leadership. Membership: $50/year (affiliated states).

Publications:
Art Education. bi-m. adv.
NAEA Advisory. q. adv.
NAEA News. bi-m. adv.
Studies in Art Education. q. adv.

Meetings/Conferences:
Annual Meetings: Spring
1999 – Washington, DC(Hilton)/March 24-28
2000 – Los Angeles, CA(West Bonaventure)/March 31-Apr. 4
2001 – New York, NY(Hilton)/March 14-18

Nat'l Art Materials Trade Ass'n (1950)
10115 Kincey Ave.
Suite 260
Huntersville, NC   28078
Tel: (704)948-5554   Fax: (704)948-5658
E-Mail: NAM+ANJ@aol.com
Members: 1,800 companies
Staff: 8
Annual Budget: $1-2,000,000
Exec. Director: Stephen M. Lefebvre
Sales Manager: Ron Ballok

Historical Note
International association of manufacturers, importers, publishers, manufacturer's representatives, distributors/wholesales, and retailers of fine and commercial art materials.

Publications:
Convention Program. a. adv.
Membership Directory, Who's Who in Art Materials. a. adv.

News and Views. 10/yr. adv.

Meetings/Conferences:
Annual Meetings: May
1999 – Chicago, IL/Apr. 8-11

Nat'l Artists Equity Ass'n (1947)
P.O. Box 28068, Central Stn.
Washington, DC   20038-8068
Tel: (202)628-9633   Fax: (202)628-0008
Toll Free: (800)727 - 6232
Members: 5,000 individuals
Staff: 1
Annual Budget: $100-250,000
Membership Manager: Craig Kittner

Historical Note
A society of professional visual artists working for legislation and public policy favorable to visual artists and designing services. Primary purpose is to work for improved economic conditions for artists and for the expansion and protection of artists' rights. Formerly (1984) the Artists Equity Ass'n. Membership: $40/year (at-large); $60/yr. (chapter).

Publications:
Artists Advocate. q.
Pen, Pencil, and Paint. q.

Meetings/Conferences:
Annual Meetings: Not held.

Nat'l Asphalt Pavement Ass'n (1955)
NAPA Building
5100 Forbes Boulevard
Lanham, MD   20706-4413
Tel: (301)731-4748   Fax: (301)731-4621
Members: 900 companies
Staff: 23
Annual Budget: $2-5,000,000
President: Mike Acott
Manager of Communications: Jo Bruen
Director, Marketing: Margaret Cervarich
Director, Governmental Affairs: Jay Hansen
Exec. Director: Arden Sell
Director, Finance: Carolyn Wilson
V. President: Richard Morgan

Historical Note
Founded as the National Bituminous Concrete Association, it assumed its present name in 1965. Members are producers of hot mix asphalt for paving roads, airfields and other surfaces.

Publications:
Action News. bi-w.
Focus. q. adv.
HMAT. q. adv.
Technical & Educational Publications. irreg.

Meetings/Conferences:
Annual Meetings: Winter
1999 – San Diego, CA(Hyatt Regency)/Feb 7-11

Nat'l Ass'n For Ambulatory Care (1981)
18870 Rutledge Road
Minneapolis, MN   55391
Tel: (612)476-0015   Fax: (612)476-0646
E-Mail: health1@aol.com
Web Site: http://www.nafac.com
Members: 700 individuals
Annual Budget: $500-1,000,000
President: William H. Wenmark

Historical Note
Formerly Nat'l Ass'n of Centers for Urgent Treatment and Nat'l Ass'n of Freestanding Emergency Centers and since 1984, the Nat'l Ass'n for Ambulatory Care. NAFAC represents the operational, economic, and legislative interests of 8,500 ambulatory care centers (ACC) in the United States; and provides services and information to individuals and corporations planning to open ambulatory care centers. Membership: $150/year (individual).

Meetings/Conferences:
1999 – Key West, FL/May 12-15

Nat'l Ass'n for Applied Arts and Sciences (1955)
Historical Note
Address unknown in 1996.

Nat'l Ass'n for Armenian Studies and Research (1955)
395 Concord Ave.
Belmont, MA   02478-3049
Tel: (617)489-1610   Fax: (617)484-1759
Members: 1,200 individuals
Staff: 5
Annual Budget: $100-250,000
Administrative Director: Sandra L. Jurigian

Historical Note
Founded in 1955 to sponsor and promote educational, cultural and other activities and projects to foster and promote Armenian studies, research, and publications. Membership: $50/year (individual); $40/year (senior citizen); $35/year (student); $75/year (family).

Publications:
Journal of Armenian Studies. semi-a. adv.
NAASR Book News. irreg.
NAASR Newsletter. q. adv.
NAASR Update. irreg.

Meetings/Conferences:
Annual Meetings: Fall (3rd weekend in November at Nat'l Headquarters/75-100
1999 – Belmont, MD

Nat'l Ass'n for Bank Cost and Management Accounting (1980)
Historical Note
Became the Ass'n for Management Information in Financial Services in 1997.

Nat'l Ass'n for Bilingual Education *(1975)*
1220 L St., N.W., Suite 605
Washington, DC   20005-4018
Tel: (202)898-1829   *Fax:* (202)789-2866
E-Mail: nabe@nabe.org
Web Site: http://www.nabe.org
Members: 3,500 individuals
Staff: 8
Annual Budget: $2-5,000,000
Exec. Director: James J. Lyons
Assoc. Dir., Legislation/Public Affairs: Jaime Zapata
Assoc. Dir., Legislation: Patricia Loera
Dep. Director: Nancy Zelasko
Manager, Membership: Carolyn Riddick
Information Systems Director: Jeff Spencer, Jr.

Historical Note
Professional association which represents the interests of non-English background children and families. Members are professional educators, concerned citizens and community leaders who wish to promote bilingual education. Incorporated in Washington, DC. Membership: $48/year (individual), $125/year (organization/company).

Publications:
NABE Journal. q. adv.
NABE Newsletter. 8/year. adv.

Meetings/Conferences:
Annual Meetings: Winter
1999 – Denver, CO(Convention Center)/Jan. 26-30/8000
2000 – San Antonio, TX(Convention Center)/Feb. 15-19/9000

Nat'l Ass'n for Biomedical Research *(1979)*
818 Connecticut Ave., N.W., 3rd Floor
Washington, DC   20006
Tel: (202)857-0540   *Fax:* (202)659-1902
E-Mail: info@nabr.org
Web Site: http://www.nabr.org
Members: 340 organizations
Staff: 6
Annual Budget: $500-1,000,000
President: Frankie L. Trull

Historical Note
Founded as the Reasearch Animal Alliance, it became the Ass'n for Biomedical Research in 1981. Absorbed the Nat'l Soc. for Medical Research and assumed its present name in 1985. Members are institutions, professional societies and companies that use animals in biomedical research and testing. The association's purpose is to keep members informed of legislative and regulatory activity in the field. Membership: $500-2,000 (nonprofit institutions, dependent on budget); $500-12,000 (industry, dependent on budget/sales).

Publications:
Annual Report. a.
NABR Alert. irreg.
NABR Update. irreg.
State Laws Concerning the Use of Animals in Research. bien.

Meetings/Conferences:
Annual Meetings: Fall

Nat'l Ass'n for Black Geologists and Geophysicists *(1981)*
P.O. Box 50724
New Orleans, LA   70150
Tel: (504)736-2579
Members: 250 individuals
Secretary: Alton Bates

Historical Note
NABGG members are geologists and geophysicists employed by major and independent oil companies, academics, students and others with an interest in the organization's goals.

Publications:
Newsletter. irreg.

Meetings/Conferences:
Annual Meetings: in conjunction with GSA annual meeting

Nat'l Ass'n for Business Teacher Education *(1927)*
Historical Note
A division of the Nat'l Business Education Ass'n.

Nat'l Ass'n for Campus Activities *(1960)*
13 Harbison Way
Columbia, SC   29212-3401
Tel: (803)732-6222   *Fax:* (803)749-1047
E-Mail: aland@naca.org
Web Site: http://www.naca.org
Members: 1,200 schools, 500 agencies/bureaus
Staff: 23
Annual Budget: $2-5,000,000
Exec. Director: Alan Davis
Dir., Mktg./Communications: Karen Moody
Director of Convention Services: Louis A. Ross
Dir., Educational Foundation: Dawn Blanford
Director, Finance and Administration: Jeanne M. Dunay
Director, Association Development: Marc Posner

Historical Note
NACA is an organization of colleges and universities; its purpose is to assist in marketing entertainment services to educational institutions and providing student leadership development programs and services. Membership: $230-580/year (school), $420/year (associate).

Publications:
Campus Activities Programming. m. adv.
Membership Directory. semi-a. adv.
Programming on the Road. m. adv.

Meetings/Conferences:
Annual Meetings: February/2,500
1999 – Nashville, TN(Opryland)/Feb. 13-17

Nat'l Ass'n for Check Safekeeping *(1981)*
c/o Nat'l Automated Clearing House Ass'n
13665, Suite 300 Dulles Technology Dr.
Herndon, VA   20170
Tel: (703)742-9190   *Fax:* (703)787-0996
Members: 47 banks, 25 associate suppliers
Staff: 1
Annual Budget: $50-100,000
President & CEO: Elliott C. McEntee

Historical Note
Incorporated in the District of Columbia, NACS is an affiliate of the Nat'l Automated Clearing House Ass'n, from which it receives staff support. Its members advocate fewer legislative restrictions surrounding the return of all customers' cancelled checks.

Meetings/Conferences:
Annual Meetings: Spring, with ABA National Operations and Automation Conference

Nat'l Ass'n for Chicana and Chicano Studies *(1972)*
2342 Shattuck Ave., Suite 326
Berkeley, CA   94074
Tel: (210)458-5339   *Fax:* (210)458-5366
Web Site: http://csbs3.utsa.edu/naccs/conference.htm
Director: Dr. Carlos S. Maldonado

Historical Note
Founded as Nat'l Ass'n for Chicano Studies; assumed its current name in 1995. NACCS members are academics with an interest in the study of Chicano culture. Membership: $45/year (individual); $100/year (organization).

Publications:
Noticias de NACCS. q. adv.
Proceedings. a.

Meetings/Conferences:
Annual Meetings: Spring
1999 – San Antonio, TX(Radisson)/Apr. 28-May 1

Nat'l Ass'n for College Admission Counseling *(1937)*
1631 Prince St.
Alexandria, VA   22314-2818
Tel: (703)836-2222   *Fax:* (703)836-8015
Web Site: http://www.nacac.com
Members: 2,836 individuals, 3,048 organizations
Staff: 31
Annual Budget: $2-5,000,000
Exec. Director: Joyce E. Smith
Chief Officer, Communications, Publications and Technology: Shanda T. Ivory
Director, Government Relations: Ruth Granados
Director, National Conference and Meetings: Scott Lindley
Director, Professional Development: Donna L. Raczynski
Chief Officer, Finance, Database and Operations: Desiree Jaworski
Director, Member Services, Governance and Development: Dee Dee Faulkner
Director of National College Fairs: Gregory Ferguson
Chief Officer, Programs and Services: Mark C. Milroy

Historical Note
Formerly (1995) Nat'l Ass'n of College Admissions Counselors, (1968) Ass'n of College Admissions Counselors, and (1939) Ass'n of College Representatives. Membership: $50/year (individual), $130/year (high school), $235/year (college).

Publications:
CC:NEWS.
Facts About American College. a.
Journal of College Admission. q.
NACAC Bulletin. m. adv.
NACAC Membership Directory. a.

Meetings/Conferences:
Annual Meetings: Fall
1999 – Orlando, FL
2000 – Washington, DC
2001 – San Antonio, TX
2002 – Salt Lake City, UT

Nat'l Ass'n for Community Leadership *(1979)*
200 S. Meridian St., Suite 250
Indianapolis, IN   46225
Tel: (317)637-7408   *Fax:* (317)637-7413
E-Mail: commlead@indy.net
Members: 2,200 individuals, 450 organizations
Staff: 3
Annual Budget: $250-500,000
V.President and Interim C.E.O.: Kristin L. Bakke, CAE

Historical Note
Founded in 1979 by 40 community leadership organizations as the Nat'l Ass'n of Community Leadership Organizations. Assumed its present name in 1989. Members are community leadership organizations at the state and local levels and their graduate groups. COMMUNITY LEADERSHIP is dedicated to nurturing leadership in communities throughout the U.S. Serves as an information clearinghouse develops and provides training and education in leadership, and helps members enhance their graduate capacity in serving their respective communities. Membership: $250/year minimum.

Publications:
Leadership News. q. adv.

Meetings/Conferences:
1999 – Indianapolis, IN/June 10-13/900

Nat'l Ass'n for Community Mediation *(1994)*
1527 New Hampshire Ave. N.W.
Washington, DC   20005
Tel: (202)667-9513   *Fax:* (202)667-8629
E-Mail: nafcm@nacfcm.org
Web Site: http://www.nafcm.org
Members: 525 individuals, 254 community mediation centers
Staff: 3
Annual Budget: $100-250,000
Exec. Director: Larry E. Ray

Historical Note
NAFCM supports the maintenance and growth of community-based mediation program and processes; presents a compelling voice in appropriate policy-making, legislatve, professional, and other arenas; and encourages the development and sharing of resources for these efforts. Members are community mediation programs, volunteer mediators, and other organizations and individuals that support commmunity mediation. Membership: $25/year (individual); $100-200/year (organization/company).

Publications:
Community Mediation Directory. a.
Newsletter. q.

Nat'l Ass'n for Core Curriculum *(1953)*
1640 Franklin Ave., #104
Kent, OH   44240-4324
Tel: (330)677-5008   *Fax:* (330)677-5008
E-Mail: GVarsNACC@aol.com
Members: 200 individuals
Staff: 1
Annual Budget: under $10,000
Exec. Secretary-Treasurer: Gordon F. Vars, Ph.D.

Historical Note
An outgrowth of the National Conference of Core Teachers, first held in Morgantown, West Virginia on the campus of West Virginia Univ. on October 30-31, 1953. The present name was adopted in 1966. Promotes integrative/interdisciplinary approaches to education at all levels, elementary school through college. Membership: $10/year.

Publications:
The Core Teacher. q.

Meetings/Conferences:
Annual Meetings: Fall, usually in conjuction with other educational organizations

Nat'l Ass'n for Corporate Speaker Activities *(1983)*
Historical Note
Address unknown in 1996.

Nat'l Ass'n for County Community and Economic Development *(1978)*
1200 19th St., N.W., Suite 300
Washington, DC   20036-2401
Tel: (202)857-1100   *Fax:* (202)857-1111
Web Site: http://www.nacced.org
Members: 130 individuals
Staff: 4
Exec. Director: John C. Murphy

Historical Note
NACCED members are directors and staff members of county community and economic development agencies.

Publications:
NACCED Alert. irreg.
NACCED Directory. semi-a.
NACCED Insights Newsletter. bi-m.

Meetings/Conferences:
Annual Meetings: Fall

Nat'l Ass'n for Court Management *(1985)*
Nat'l Center for State Courts
300 Newport Ave.
Williamsburg, VA   23187-8798
Tel: (757)259-1841   *Fax:* (757)259-1520
Toll Free: (800)616 - 6165
Web Site: http://www.ncsc.dni.us/nacm/nacm.htm
Members: 2,220 individuals
Association Manager: Linda D. Perkins

Historical Note
NACM members are clerks of court, court administrators and others serving in a court management capacity. NACM's purpose is to increase the proficiency of judicial administrators through the exchange of information. Membership: $75/year (individual), $300/year (organization).

Publications:
Court Communique. q.
The Court Manager. q. adv.

Meetings/Conferences:
1999 – San Jose, CA(Fairmont)/July 4-9
2000 – Atlanta, GA(Hyatt Regency)/Aug. 13-18

Nat'l Ass'n for Creative Children and Adults *(1974)*
8080 Springvalley Dr.
Cincinnati, OH   45236
Tel: (513)631-1777
Members: 750 individuals and schools
Staff: 1
Annual Budget: $25-50,000
C.E.O.: Ann Fabe Isaacs

Historical Note
Sponsors International Creative Child And Adult Month, in-service training, conferences, programs, projects, school evaluation. Invites field term applicants and interns. Members are teachers, school officials, counselors, gifted children and adults, parents, libraries and all who wish to become generally more creative. Membership: $65/year (individual), $650/year (schools/organization/company).

Publications:
It's Happening. irreg.
The Creative Child and Adult. q.

Meetings/Conferences:

Nat'l Ass'n for Developmental Education
Alabama State University
915 S. Jackson St.,
Montgomery, AL   36101
Tel: (334)229-4479
Members: 3,000 individuals
Annual Budget: $100-250,000
President: T. Clifford Bibb

Historical Note
Executives change annually. Membership: $40/year (individual); $1,000/year (organization/company).

Meetings/Conferences:
1999 - Detroit, MI/1500
2000 - Biloxi, MS/1700
2001 - Louisville, KY/1800

Nat'l Ass'n for Drama Therapy (1979)
5505 Connecticut Ave., N.W., Suite 130
Washington, DC   20015-2601
Tel: (202)966-7409   Fax: (202)966-2283
E-Mail: nadt@danielgrp.com
Members: 325 individuals
Staff: 1
Annual Budget: $25-50,000
Exec. Director: Rod Daniel

Historical Note
Established and incorporated in New York. Members are professionals trained in theatre arts, psychology and psychotherapy making use of drama/theatre processes to achieve therapeutic goals. Awards the designation R.D.T. (Registered Drama Therapist) to individuals meeting professional standards. Membership: $50-85/year.

Publications:
Dramascope Newsletter. bi-a.
Membership List. a.
Monographs on Drama Therapy. a.
Proceedings of Annual Conference. a.

Meetings/Conferences:
Annual Meetings: November

Nat'l Ass'n for Environmental Management (1990)
2025 I St., N.W., Suite 1126
Washington, DC   20006
Tel: (202)986-6616   Fax: (202)530-4408
Toll Free: (800)391 - 6236
E-Mail: NAEM@MSN.ORG
Web Site: http://www.naem.org
Members: 600 individuals
Staff: 3
Annual Budget: $250-500,000
Exec. Director: Carol Singer Neuvelt

Historical Note
NAEM is dedicated to advancing the profession of environmental management and is the only national ass'n created specifically to support the professional corporate and facility environmental manager. NAEM is composed of individuals who have responsibility for managing the environmental program of a corporation, institution, or individual facility. Primary activities include formal seminars and informal professional exchanges at the national and regional levels. NAEM focuses on information concerning emerging regulatory, technical and management issues which impact the professional environmental manager and the organizations they serve. Membership: $195/year (individual); $900-5,000/year, based on revenues (corporate); $750/year (non-profit & government).

Publications:
Network News. bi-m.

Meetings/Conferences:
Annual Meetings: Fall

Nat'l Ass'n for Equal Opportunity in Higher Education (1969)
8701 Georgia Ave., Suite 200
Silver Spring, MD   20910
Tel: (301)650-2440   Fax: (301)495-3306
Members: 117 institutions
Staff: 35
Annual Budget: $1-2,000,000
President/C.E.O.: Henry Ponder, Ph.D.
Director, Federal Relations: Bea Pace Smith
Director, Conference: Wilma Roscoe

Historical Note
Members are black colleges and universities united in an attempt to sensitize public policy makers and funders to the importance of enhancing the education of blacks. Membership: $10,000/year (organization).

Publications:
Black Excellence Magazine. bi-m. adv.
NAFEO Inroads. bi-m.
NAFEO Record-Calendar Directory. a. adv.
Proceedings of the National Conference. a.
Profiles.

Meetings/Conferences:
Annual Meetings: Spring in Washington, DC

Nat'l Ass'n for Ethnic Studies (1975)
AZ State University, Dept. of English
P.O. Box 870302
Tempe, AZ   85287-0302
Tel: (602)965-2197   Fax: (602)965-3451
E-Mail: naesi@asuvm.inre.asu.edu
Web Site: http://www.ksu.edu/ameth/naes/ethnic.htm
Members: 225 individuals, 300 institutions
Staff: 1
Annual Budget: $10-25,000
Director: Susan L. Rockwell

Historical Note
Promotes activities and scholarship in the field of ethnic studies. Formerly (1984) the Nat'l Ass'n of Interdisciplinary Ethnic Studies. Membership: $45/year (individual), $35/year (student/associate), $45/year (library), $100/year (patron).

Publications:
Ethnic Reporter. q.
Ethnic Studies in the U. S.
Ethnic Studies Review. q.

Meetings/Conferences:
1999 - Kissimmee, FL(Double Tree Resort)/March 24-28

Nat'l Ass'n for Families and Addiction Research and Education (1987)
122 S. Michigan Ave., Suite 1100
Chicago, IL   60603-6107
Tel: (312)431-8996   Fax: (312)431-8967
Members: 600 individuals
Exec. Director: Ira J. Chasnoff

Historical Note
Formerly (1996) Nat'l Ass'n for Perinatal Addiction Research and Education. Membership: $55/year (individual); $70/year (regional); $300/year (affiliate); $1,000/year (corporate).

Publications:
Update. q.

Meetings/Conferences:

Nat'l Ass'n for Family Child Care (1982)
206 6th Ave., Suite 900
Des Moines, IA   50309-4018
Tel: (515)282-8192   Fax: (515)282-9117
Members: 4,000 child care organizations
Annual Budget: $100-250,000
Business Manager: Carole Thompson, CAE

Historical Note
Formerly (1993) the Nat'l Ass'n for Family Day Care. Members are providers and users of family child care services. Operates an accreditation program for care providers. Membership: $25/year (individual); $50/year (association); $100/year (agency).

Publications:
NAFCC - Nat'l Prespective. q. adv.

Meetings/Conferences:
1999 - Denver, CO(Marriott City Center)/Aug. 13-14/600

Nat'l Ass'n for Girls and Women in Sport (1899)
1900 Association Drive
Reston, VA   20191
Tel: (703)476-3450   Fax: (703)476-9527
E-Mail: nagws@aahperd.org
Members: 7,000 individuals
Staff: 4
Annual Budget: $250-500,000
Exec. Director: Diana Everett

Historical Note
NAGWS is a member association of the American Alliance for Health, Physical Education, Recreation and Dance, and is the only national professional organization devoted exclusively to providing opportunities for girls and women in sport-related disciplines and careers. It is a non-profit, educational organization serving the needs of administrators, teachers, coaches, leaders and participants of sports programs for girls and women. Membership: $100/year.

Publications:
GWS News. 5/year. adv.
Strategies. 8/year. adv.

Meetings/Conferences:
Annual Meetings: Spring, with AAHPERD
1999 - Boston, MA(Hynes Con. Center)/April 20-24

Nat'l Ass'n for Government Training and Development
167 W. Main St., Suite 600
Lexington, KY   40507
Tel: (606)231-1904   Fax: (606)231-1928
Annual Budget: $25-50,000
Association Manager: Carol Roberts

Historical Note
Founded as Nat'l Ass'n of Government Training and Development Directors; assumed its currnet name in 1998. Membership: $150-$525/year (individual).

Publications:
NAGTADD Newletter: Government Training & Development. bi-m.

Meetings/Conferences:

Nat'l Ass'n for Health Care Recruitment (1975)
Historical Note
Address unknown in 1997.

Nat'l Ass'n for Healthcare Quality (1976)
4700 W. Lake Ave.
Glenview, IL   60025-1485
Tel: (847)375-4720   Fax: (847)375-4777
Toll Free: (800)966 - 9392
E-Mail: info@nahq.org
Web Site: http://www.nahq.org
Members: 7,000 individuals, 100 institutions
Staff: 12
Annual Budget: $1-2,000,000
Exec. Director: Diane Burgher

Historical Note
Formerly (1992) Nat'l Ass'n of Quality Assurance Professionals. NAHQ promotes continuous improvement in quality in healthcare by providing educational and developmental opportunities for professionals at all management levels and within a variety healthcare settings. Awards the CPHQ (Certified Professional in Healthcare Quality) designation to individuals who meet the requirements and pass an examiniation. Healthcare Quality Foundation and Healthcare Quality Certification Board are divisions of NAHQ. Membership: $100/year (individual); $325/year (institution).

Publications:
Directory. a.
Journal for Healthcare Quality. bi-m. adv.
NAHQ News Newsletter. q.

Meetings/Conferences:
Annual Meetings: Fall/2,500

Nat'l Ass'n for Holistic Aromatherapy (1990)
836 Hanley Industrial Court
St. Louis, MO   63144

Tel: (314)963-2071   Fax: (314)963-4454
Toll Free: (888)275 - 6242
E-Mail: info@naha.org
Web Site: http://www.naha.org
Members: 900 individuals
Annual Budget: $10-25,000
President: Cheryl Hoard

Historical Note
NAHA members are professional aromatherapists and others with an interest in the field. The organization's goals include maintaining high standards of aromatherapy education, establishing professional and ethical standards of practice, providing public education, and networking to stay abreast of current research. Membership: $35 or $50/year (individual), $100/year (company).

Publications:
Practitioner Directory. a.
Scentsitivity Quarterly. q. adv.
Source List. a.

Meetings/Conferences:
Biennial Meetings: even years/Fall

Nat'l Ass'n for Home Care (1982)
228 7th St., S.E.
Washington, DC   20003
Tel: (202)547-7424   Fax: (202)547-3540
Web Site: http://www.nahc.org
Members: 6,000 agencies
Staff: 100
Annual Budget: $10-25,000,000
President: Val J. Halamandaris
Director, Government Affairs: Dayle Berke
Deputy Dir., Government Affairs: Lucia DiVenere
Director, Meeting Services: T.J. McCabe
Director, Education: Brent Miller
Chief Operating Officer: Janet Neigh
V.P., Legal Affairs: Bill Dombi
V.P., Member Services: Ron Kolanowski
Director, Publications: Heather Dittbrenner

Historical Note
Members are concerned with the provision of health care and related services in the home and hospice services. Formerly (1982) Nat'l Ass'n of Home Health Agencies. Merged with Nat'l Homecaring Council in 1986. Sponsors and supports the NAHC Congressional Action Committee. Has an annual budget of approximately $13 million.

Publications:
Caring Magazine. m. adv.
Health Care Reform Update. irreg.
Homecare News. m.
Hospice Forum. bi-w. adv.
NAHC Report. w. adv.

Meetings/Conferences:
Annual Meetings: Fall
1999 - San Diego, CA(San Diego Convention Center)/Oct. 9-13
2000 - New Orleans, LA/Sept. 23-27

Nat'l Ass'n for Homecare (1962)
228 7th St. S.E.
Washington, DC   20003
Tel: (202)547-7424   Fax: (202)547-3540
Web Site: www.nahc.org
Staff: 5
President: Bill Halamandaris

Historical Note
A division of the Foundation for Hospice and HomeCare (same address). Agencies, other organizations and individuals concerned with ensuring quality in-home services for children, the aged and others. Conducts programs in the areas of consumer education/protection; the development of basic standards, certification of home care aids, and accreditation for home care services and training programs; and technical assistance.

Nat'l Ass'n for Humanities Education (1967)
Brigham Young University
P.O. Box 26100
Provo, UT   84602
Tel: (801)378-2212   Fax: (801)378-2284
Members: 500 individuals
Staff: 2
Annual Budget: under $10,000
Exec. Secretary-Treasurer: Michael D. Phillips

Historical Note
Growing out of a series of programs sponsored by the New York State Department of Education, NAHE is a multidisciplinary professional educational organization for teachers in colleges, schools and museums. Membership: $50/two years.

Publications:
Interdisciplinary Humanities. bi-a.

Meetings/Conferences:
Biennial Meetings: Odd years
1999 - Jacksonville, FL

Nat'l Ass'n for Independent Living (1980)
510 E. 128th St.
Des Moines, IA   50319
Tel: (515)281-5474
Members: 200 individuals

Historical Note
A division of Nat'l Rehabilitation Ass'n, which provides administrative support.

Meetings/Conferences:
1999 - Minneapolis, MN(Hyatt Regency)/Nov. 11-14

Nat'l Ass'n for Individually Guided Education (1972)
Historical Note
Organization dissolved in 1995.

Nat'l Ass'n for Industry-Education Cooperation (1949)
235 Hendricks Blvd.
Buffalo, NY 14226-3304
Tel: (716)834-7047 *Fax:* (716)834-7047
E-Mail: NAIEC@pcom.net
Web Site: http://www2.pcom.net/naiec/
Members: 950 organizations
Staff: 2
Annual Budget: $250-500,000
President and C.E.O.: Donald M. Clark, Ph.D.

Historical Note
Established as the Business-Industry Section of the National Science Teachers Association, it assumed its present name in 1964 and absorbed the Community Resources Workshop Association in 1972. Advocates improved coordination between industry and education in continuous school improvement, workforce development and human resource/economic development. Membership: $35/year. (individual), $45/year (council/chapter), $100/year (institution), and $250-1,000/year (corporate, based on net earnings).

Publications:
NAIEC Newsletter. bi-m. adv.

Meetings/Conferences:
Annual Meetings: Spring

Nat'l Ass'n for Interpretation (1988)
P.O. Box 2246
Fort Collins, CO 80522
Tel: (970)484-8283 *Fax:* (970)484-8179
Toll Free: (888)900 - 8283
E-Mail: naiexec@aol.com
Web Site: http://www.interpnet.com
Members: 3,400 individuals, 200 organizations
Staff: 14
Annual Budget: $500-1,000,000
Exec. Director: Tim Merriman
Dir., Communications: Nancy Nichols
Membership Manager: Philip B. Tedesco
Membership Manager: Heather Brooks

Historical Note
The product of a merger in 1988 of the Ass'n of Interpretive Naturalists and the Western Interpreter's Ass'n, NAI members are naturalists, historians, park rangers, educators, museum technicians and curators, administrators, recreation specialists, and others concerned with communicating the meanings and relationships between people and their natural, cultural and recreational world. Membership: $65/year (individual), $165/year (institution), $225/year (commercial), $25/year (student).

Publications:
Jobs in Interpretation. bi-w.
Journal of Interpretation Research. a.
Legacy. bi-m. adv.
NAI News. q.

Meetings/Conferences:
Annual Meetings: Fall
1999 - Syracuse, NY(Syracuse Raddison)/Oct. 14-19/1200
2000 - Tuscon, AZ(Holiday Inn)/Nov. 7-12/1500

Nat'l Ass'n for Law Placement (1971)
1666 Connecticut Ave. N.W., Suite 325
Washington, DC 20009
Tel: (202)667-1666 *Fax:* (202)265-6735
Members: 1000 law schools & employers
Staff: 7
Annual Budget: $1-2,000,000
Exec. Director: Paula A. Patton
Dep. Director: Julie Hamre

Historical Note
An incorporated not-for-profit organization of American Bar Ass'n approved law schools and employers of lawyers. Representatives include: hiring attorneys, legal administrators, law school career services officials and deans. NALP is not a placement agency for individuals jobs. It deals with issues such as career planning and ethical and effective recruiting. Membership: $435-685/year (law schools and private employers), $75-125/year (government agencies and public interest groups).

Publications:
Directory of Legal Employers. a.
Employment Report/Salary Survey. a.
Interview Training Materials.
Judicial Clerkship Directory. a.
NALP Bulletin. m. adv.
National Directory of Law Schools. a.
Survey of Legal Personnel. a.

Meetings/Conferences:
Annual Meetings: Spring
1999 - San Antonio, TX(Hyatt Regency)/April 21-24

Nat'l Ass'n for Mediation in Education (1984)
Historical Note
Became the Conflict Resolution Education Network in 1995.

Nat'l Ass'n for Medical Direction of Respiratory Care
5454 Wisconsin Ave., Suite 1270
Chevy Chase, MD 20815
Tel: (301)718-2975 *Fax:* (301)718-2976
Members: 700 individuals
Staff: 3
Annual Budget: $100-250,000
Exec. Director: Phillip Porte
Director of Marketing and Member Services: Adeline C. O'Connell

Historical Note
Formerly (1994) Nat'l Ass'n of Medical Directors of Respiratory Care. Membership: $175/year.

Publications:
Newsletter. q. adv.
Presidential Update. bien.
Washington Watch Line. m.

Nat'l Ass'n for Medical Equipment Services (1982)
625 Slaters Lane, Suite 200
Alexandria, VA 22314-1171
Tel: (703)836-6263 *Fax:* (703)836-6730
E-Mail: info@names.org
Web Site: http://names.org
Members: 1,100 companies
Staff: 23
Annual Budget: $2-5,000,000
President and C.E.O.: William D. Coughlan, CAE
Manager, Communications: Jennifer L. Gisin
V.P., Communications/Member Relations: Steve Haracznak
V.P., Government Relations: Kenneth R. Adams
V. President, Regulatory Affairs: Asela M. Cuervo
Director, Education and Meetings: Kim Kianka
V.P., Finance/Systems Management: Michael Dzatko
Director, Membership Relations: Barbara Voyiaziakas

Historical Note
NAMES was formed in May, 1982 by the merger of the Nat'l Affiliation of Durable Medical Equipment Companies and the Associated Independent Medical Equipment Suppliers. Formerly the Nat'l Ass'n of Medical Equipment Suppliers. Changed name in 1994. Trade association of home medical equipment and rehabilitation technology suppliers. Sponsors and supports the NAMES Political Action Committee. Membership: Varies based on revenue.

Publications:
Associate Member Directory. a.
Associate Member Newsletter.
Hot Wheels. m.
NAMES News Today. w.
State Lines. m.

Meetings/Conferences:
Annual Meetings: Spring
1999 - Las Vegas, NV(Bally's)

Nat'l Ass'n for Membership Development (1941)
4232 King St.
Alexandria, VA 22302-1507
Tel: (703)998-0072 *Fax:* (703)931-5624
Members: 900 individuals
Staff: 3
Annual Budget: $250-500,000
Manager: Leslie Fischer

Historical Note
Formerly (1992) the Nat'l Ass'n of Membership Directors of Chambers of Commerce. Affiliated with the American Chamber of Commerce Executives. Membership: $70/year minimum (individual).

Publications:
Compendium of Campaigns.
Compendium of Dues Formulas. a.
Compendium of Membership Letters. a.
How to Develop a Sales Training Program.
How to Write a Marketing Plan.
Membership Development Excellence: The NAMD Solution.
NAMD Newsletter. 6/year.
Nat'l Survey on Sales Programs.
Quick and Dirty Guide to Member Services.
Statistical Survey. a.
Who's Who Directory. a.

Meetings/Conferences:
Annual Meetings: September
1999 - Philadelphia, PA(Marriott)
2000 - Washington, DC(Marriott)

Nat'l Ass'n for Parish Coordinators and Directors of Religious Education
Historical Note
An affiliate of the Nat'l Catholic Educational Association which provides administrative support.

Nat'l Ass'n for Perinatal Addiction Research and Education (1987)
Historical Note
Became the Nat'l Ass'n for Family and Addiction Research and Education in 1996.

Nat'l Ass'n for PET Container Resources (1987)
2105 Water Ridge Pkwy., Suite 570
Charlotte, NC 28217
Tel: (704)423-9400 *Fax:* (704)423-9500
Web Site: http://www.napcor.com
Members: 19 companies
Staff: 9
President: Luke B. Schmidt
Director, Technical Affairs: Michael F. Schedler

Historical Note
Represents polyethylene terephthalate (PET) resin producers and container manufacturers. It facilitates the economical recovery of plastic containers with emphasis on PET plastic bottles. Assists communities in promoting PET recycling and publicizes PET as an environmentally sound packaging material.

Publications:
PET Market List. 3/year.
PET Projects.

Nat'l Ass'n for Physical Education in Higher Education (1978)
c/o Dept. of Human Performance
San Jose State University
San Jose, CA 95192-0054
Tel: (408)924-3029 *Fax:* (408)924-3053
E-Mail: grant@sjsuvm1.sjsu.edu
Members: 500 individuals
Staff: 1
Annual Budget: $25-50,000
Exec. Secretary-Treasurer: Gail G. Evans

Historical Note
The result of a merger between the National Association for Physical Education of College Women and the National College Physical Education Association for Men (founded in 1907). A professional society of physical education instructors at the college level. Has no paid staff.

Publications:
Chronicle of Physical Education in Higher Education.
Quest Journal.

Meetings/Conferences:
Annual Meetings: January

Nat'l Ass'n for Plastic Container Recovery
Historical Note
Became Nat'l Ass'n for PET Container Resources in 1998.

Nat'l Ass'n for Poetry Therapy (1981)
P.O. Box 551
Port Washington, NY 11050
Tel: (516)944-9791 *Fax:* (516)944-5818
Web Site: http://www.poetrytherapy.org
Members: 350 individuals
Staff: 1
Annual Budget: under $10,000
Administrator: Alicia Seeger

Historical Note
NAPT members represent a wide range of professional experience, schools of therapy, educational affiliations, artistic disciplines, and other fields of training in both mental and physical health. Awards the designations Certified Poetry Therapist (CPT) and Registered Poetry Therapist (RPT). Membership: $90/year (RPT); $85/year (CPT); $75/year (individual).

Publications:
Journal of Poetry Therapy. q.
Museletter. 3/year.

Meetings/Conferences:
Annual Meetings: May
1999 - Charleston, SC(Sheraton)/May 13-16

Nat'l Ass'n for Practical Nurse Education and Service (1941)
1400 Spring St., Suite 330
Silver Spring, MD 20910
Tel: (301)588-2491 *Fax:* (301)588-2839
Members: 10,000 individuals
Staff: 5
Annual Budget: $250-500,000
Exec. Director: John H. Word

Historical Note
Membership: $50/year.

Publications:
NAPNES Forum. 8/year.
The Journal of Practical Nursing. q. adv.

Meetings/Conferences:
Annual Meetings: Spring
1999 - Virginia Beach, VA(Cavalier Hotel)/April 24-29

Nat'l Ass'n for Promotional and Advertising Allowances (1989)
P.O. Box 200549
Austin, TX 78720
Tel: (512)918-9042 *Fax:* (512)335-3083
Web Site: http://www.NAPAA.ORG
Staff: 2
Annual Budget: $250-500,000
President: Roger P. Vickery
Administrator: Ari Finch-Koinuma

Historical Note
Membership: $750/year (organization/company).

Publications:
NAPAA Newsletter. q. adv.

Meetings/Conferences:
Annual Meetings: Spring.
1999 - St. Louis, MO

Nat'l Ass'n for Proton Therapy (1990)
7910 Woodmont Ave., Suite 1303
Bethesda, MD 20814
Tel: (301)913-9360 *Fax:* (301)913-0372
E-Mail: lenarzt@compuserve.com
Web Site: http://www.proton-therapy.org/
Members: 3 institutions & corporations
Staff: 1
Annual Budget: $50-100,000
Exec. Director: Leonard Arzt

Historical Note
NAPT members are medical institutions and corporations with an interest in the use of proton beam technology as a cancer therapy.

Publications:
Proton Treatment Newsletter. q.

Meetings/Conferences:

Nat'l Ass'n for Public Health Statistics and Information Systems (1933)
1220 19th St., N.W., Suite 802
Washington, DC 20036
Tel: (202)436-8500 *Fax:* (202)463-4870
E-Mail: tme.nq@naphsis.org
Web Site: http://www.NAPHSIS.org
Members: 225 individuals
Staff: 2
Annual Budget: $50-100,000
Exec. Director: Michael S. Hamm

Meetings/Conferences:
1999 - Amelia Island, FL(Ritz Carlton)/Feb. 25-27/125

Historical Note
Organized in 1933 as the American Ass'n of Registration Executives. Became American Ass'n for Vital Records and Public Health Statistics in 1958, Ass'n for Public Health Statistics and Information Systems in 1995, and assumed its current name in 1997. Has no paid officers or full-time staff. Membership: based on state population (agency based).

Publications:
The Journal. bi-m.

Meetings/Conferences:
Annual Meetings: Spring/Summer
1999 – Las Vegas, NV(Riviera)/June 6-10

Nat'l Ass'n for Pupil Transportation *(1974)*
Historical Note
Address unknown in 1996.

Nat'l Ass'n for Research and Therapy of Homosexuality *(1992)*
16633 Ventura Blvd., Suite 1340
Encino, CA 91436-1801
Tel: (818)789-4440   *Fax:* (805)373-5084
Web Site: http://www.narth.com
Members: 900 individuals
Executive Director: Joseph Nicolosi, Ph.D.

Historical Note
An organization of psychoanalysts, social workers and behavioral scientists dedicated to the research and therapy of homosexuality.

Publications:
Narth Bulletin. 3/year. adv.

Nat'l Ass'n for Research in Science Teaching *(1928)*
Ohio State University
1929 Kenny Road, Room 200-E
Columbus, OH 43210
Tel: (614)292-3339   *Fax:* (614)292-1595
Web Site: http://www.science.coe.uwf.edu/NARST
Members: 1,500 individuals
Annual Budget: $100-250,000
Exec. Secretary: Arthur L. White

Historical Note
A professional association of science educators. Affiliated with the Nat'l Science Teachers Ass'n, the American Ass'n for the Advancement of Science and the Internat'l Council of Science Ass'ns for Education. Membership: $80/yr (individual)

Publications:
Journal of Research in Science Teaching. 10/year.
Newsletter. q.
Research Matters. a.

Meetings/Conferences:
Annual Meetings: Alternately with the Nat'l Science Teachers Ass'n and the American Education Research Ass'n
1999 – Boston, MA(Boston Park Plaza)/Mar. 28-31
2000 – New Orleans, LA/Apr. 24-28

Nat'l Ass'n for Retail Merchandising Services *(1995)*
PO Box 906
Plover, WI 54467-0906
Tel: (715)342-1960   *Fax:* (715)342-1943
E-Mail: gebben@narms.com
Web Site: www.harms.com
Members: 165 individuals
Exec. Director: Gary J. Ebben

Publications:
The Retail Merchandiser. q. adv.

Meetings/Conferences:
1999 – Palm Springs, CA(Wyndam)/April 18-20/300

Nat'l Ass'n for Rural Mental Health *(1977)*
3700 W. Division St., Suite 105
St. Cloud, MN 56301-3728
Tel: (320)202-1820   *Fax:* (320)202-1833
E-Mail: narmh@facts.ksu.edu
Web Site: narmh.org
Members: 300 individuals
Staff: 1
Annual Budget: $25-50,000
Administrative Assistant: LuAnn Rice

Historical Note
Members include social workers, psychiatrists, psychologists and others who work in rural community mental health settings. Membership fee varies, based on type.

Publications:
Party-Line Newsletter. 4/year.
Rural Community Mental Health Journal. 4/year.

Meetings/Conferences:
1999 – Bloomington, MN(Double Tree Hotel)/Aug. 8-10
2000 – Portland, OR

Nat'l Ass'n for Search and Rescue *(1974)*
4500 Southgate Place, Suite 100
Chantilly, VA 20151
Tel: (703)222-6277   *Fax:* (703)222-6283
E-Mail: INFO@NASAR.ORG
Web Site: http://www.NASAR.ORG
Members: 4,000 individuals
Staff: 9
Annual Budget: $2-5,000,000
Exec. V. President: Lawrence A. Jacobson
: Judi Schmitt
: Mylea Wade
: Steve Foster
: Roni Briese,, CPA
: Larry Jacobson,, JD

Historical Note
Established as the Nat'l Ass'n of Search and Rescue Coordinators, it assumed its present name in 1975. Members belong to various

emergency medical, fire or survival rescue services. Membership: $49/year (individual), $70/year (organization).

Publications:
Briefings. q. adv.
Membership Manual. a.
Proceedings. a.
Response! The Magazine for Search, Rescue and Recovery. q.
SAR Dog Alert. bi-m.
SAR Dog Directory. a.

Meetings/Conferences:
Annual Meetings: Spring/800
1999 – Orlando, FL(Marriott; Disney Area)/May 16-19/500
2000 – Austin, TX
2002 – Hilo, HI

Nat'l Ass'n for Senior Living Industries *(1985)*
4340 East-West Hwy., Suite 401
Bethesda, MD 20814-4408
Tel: (301)656-4224   *Fax:* (301)656-0989
Members: 750 individuals, 400 companies
Staff: 10
Annual Budget: $500-1,000,000
Exec. Director: Karie Barnes

Historical Note
NASLI is a non-profit resource network of organizations, professionals and private citizens devoting efforts and resources to meeting the shelter, health, services and consumer product needs of the older populations. Membership: based on type and size of organization.

Publications:
Annual Directory and Buyer's Guide. a.
NASLI News. m.
Spectrum Magazine. bi-m. adv.

Meetings/Conferences:
Annual Meetings: Spring

Nat'l Ass'n for Sport and Physical Education *(1974)*
1900 Association Drive
Reston, VA 20191-1599
Tel: (703)476-3410   *Fax:* (703)476-8316
E-Mail: naspe@aahperd.org
Web Site: www.aahperd.org/naspe/naspe.html
Members: 20,000 individuals
Staff: 9
Annual Budget: $100-250,000
Exec. Director: Judith C. Young, Ph.D.
Communications Director: Paula Kun

Historical Note
An amalgamation of the Division of Men's Athletics and the Physical Education Division of the American Association for Health, Physical Education, Recreation and Dance, NASPE is an independent member of the American Alliance for Health, Physical Education, Recreation and Dance. Membership: $100/year.

Publications:
NASPE News. q.
Peak Performance. semi-a.
Right Moves. 3/yr.
Strategies-A Journal for Physical and Sport Educators. bi-m.

Meetings/Conferences:
Annual Meetings: in conjunction with the AAPHERD national convention
1999 – Boston, MA/April 20-24
2000 – Orlando, FL/March 21-25
2001 – Cincinnati, OH/March 27-31
2002 – San Diego, CA/April 16-20

Nat'l Ass'n for State Community Service Programs *(1968)*
444 North Capitol St., N.W., Suite 221
Washington, DC 20001
Tel: (202)624-5866   *Fax:* (202)624-8472
Members: 100 individuals
Staff: 4
Annual Budget: $500-1,000,000
Exec. Director: Marjorie J. Witherspoon

Historical Note
Members are state administrators of federal Community Service Block Grant and Low Income Weatherization Assistance programs.

Publications:
Community Services Block Grant Statistical Report. a.
Newsletter. m.

Meetings/Conferences:
Semi-Annual Meetings: March and October

Nat'l Ass'n for Stock Car Auto Racing *(1947)*
P.O. Box 2875
Daytona Beach, FL 32120-2875
Tel: (904)253-0611   *Fax:* (904)252-8804
Members: 50,000 individuals
Staff: 40
Annual Budget: $1-2,000,000
President: William C. France, Jr.

Publications:
NASCAR News. bi-m. adv.
NASCAR Yearbook. a. adv.

Meetings/Conferences:
Annual Meetings: Daytona Beach, FL/mid-February

Nat'l Ass'n for the Advancement of Black Americans in Vocational Education *(1977)*
5057 Woodward
Detroit, MI 48202
Tel: (313)494-1660   *Fax:* (313)494-1132
Members: 900 individuals
Annual Budget: under $10,000
President: Ethel O. Washington, Ph.D.

Historical Note
NAABAVE members are individuals and organizations with an interest in advancing the influence of black professionals in the field of vocational/technical education. Membership: $40/year (individual); $100/year (organization).

Publications:
Conference Proceedings. a.
NAABAVE Focus. q.

Meetings/Conferences:
Annual Meetings: in conjuntion with American Vocational Ass'n

Nat'l Ass'n for the Advancement of Psychoanalysis *(1972)*
80 8th Ave., Suite 1501
New York, NY 10011-1501
Tel: (212)741-0515   *Fax:* (212)366-4347
E-Mail: naap72@aol.com
Web Site: http://www.naap.org
Members: 1,700 individuals, 1 organization
Staff: 5
Annual Budget: $250-500,000
Executive Director: Margery Quackenbush

Historical Note
NAAP monitors educational standards for the registration of individuals as certified psychoanalysts. Membership: $165/year (individual); $95 (candidate-in-training); $250 (organization).

Publications:
NAAP News. q. adv.
National Registry of Psychoanalysts. a.

Meetings/Conferences:
Annual Meetings: Spring
1999 – New York, NY(United Nations)/April 23-24

Nat'l Ass'n for the Cottage Industry *(1982)*
Box 14850
Chicago, IL 60614
Tel: (773)472-8116   *Fax:* (773)472-8117
Members: 16,000 individuals
Staff: 2
Annual Budget: $100-250,000
Exec. Director: CoraLee Smith Kern

Historical Note
Members are owners of home-based businesses or individuals who work at flexible or remote work sites. Incorporated in the State of Illinois. Membership: $45/yr.

Publications:
The Cottage Connection. q.

Meetings/Conferences:

Nat'l Ass'n for the Dually Diagnosed Mental Illness/Mental Retardation
Historical Note
Became (1997) NADD: Ass'n for Persons with Developmental Disabilities and Mental Health Needs.

Nat'l Ass'n for the Education of Young Children *(1926)*
1509 16th St., N.W.
Washington, DC 20036-1426
Tel: (202)232-8777   *Fax:* (202)328-1846
Toll Free: (800)424 - 2460
E-Mail: naeyc@naeyc.org
Web Site: http://www.naeyc.org
Members: 103,000 individuals
Staff: 75
Annual Budget: $5-10,000,000
Exec. Director: Marilyn M. Smith, Ph.D.
Director, Public Affairs: Barbara A. Willer
C.E.O.: James D. Andrews

Historical Note
Established as the National Association for Nursery Education, it assumed its present name in 1964. Members are administrators and teachers in schools for children (birth through age 8). Membership: $25-500/year.

Publications:
Young Children. bi-m. adv.

Meetings/Conferences:
Annual Meetings: Fall

Nat'l Ass'n for the Practice of Anthropology *(1983)*
Historical Note
A section of the American Anthropological Ass'n. Represents the practice of anthropology and the interests of practicing anthropologists.

Nat'l Ass'n for the Self-Employed *(1981)*
1023 15th St., N.W., Suite 1200
Washington, DC 20005-2600
Tel: (202)466-2100   *Fax:* (202)466-2123
Toll Free: (800)232 - 6273
Web Site: http://www.nase.org
Members: 325,000 individuals
Staff: 11
Annual Budget: $10-25,000,000
President and C.E.O.: Bennie L. Thayer
V. President, Government Relations: Virginia K. Beauchamp

Historical Note
NASE promotes small business growth through education and collective purchasing. Members are small businesses, usually with 5 or fewer employees. Has an annual budget of approximately $14 million. Membership: $72/year.

Publications:
Member Benefits Guide. a.
Self-Employed America. bi-m.

Meetings/Conferences:
1999 – June

Nat'l Ass'n for the Support of Long-Term Care *(1989)*

1321 Duke St., Suite 304
Alexandria, VA 22314-3563
Tel: (703)549-8500   *Fax:* (703)549-8342
Web Site: http://www.nasl.org
Annual Budget: $500-1,000,000
Exec. V. President: Peter C. Clendenin, CAE
Historical Note
Members are health providers from the long term care industry who advocate for the industry. Membership: $2,500-25,000/year (organization).
Publications:
NASL News. q. adv.
Meetings/Conferences:
1999 – New Orleans, LA
1999 – Washington, DC

Nat'l Ass'n for Trade and Industrial Education *(1974)*
Box 1665
Leesburg, VA 20177-1655
Tel: (703)777-1740
Members: 1,500 individuals
Staff: 1
Annual Budget: $10-25,000
Exec. Director: James Wallbeoff, Jr.
Historical Note
Membership includes instructors, state supervisors, teacher educators, representatives from labor organizations, and companies concerned with vocational education and training. Affiliated with the Vocational Industrial Clubs of America, Inc., American Vocational Association, et al. Membership: $10/year (professional); $200/year (industrial).
Publications:
NATIE News Notes. q. adv.
Meetings/Conferences:
Annual Meetings: With the American Vocational Association and the Vocational Industrial Clubs of America.
1999 – Kansas City, MO/June 28-July 2

Nat'l Ass'n for Treasurers of Religious Institutes *(1981)*
8824 Cameron St.
Silver Spring, MD 20910
Tel: (301)587-7776   *Fax:* (301)589-2897
E-Mail: natri@erols.com
Members: 850 individuals
Staff: 4
Annual Budget: $500-1,000,000
Exec. Director: Carol Wester, O.P.
Associate Director, Finance: Imelda Gonzalez
Historical Note
NATRI's mission is to address the fiscal, legal and administrative responsibilities specific to religious institutes in the U.S. Membership: $300/year (individual), $475/year (organization).
Publications:
Membership Directory. a.
NATRI Newsletter. bi-m.
Service Directory. a. adv.
Meetings/Conferences:
Annual Meetings: September-October
1999 – Philadelphia, PA/Nov. 17-20
2000 – Memphis, TN(Convention Center and Plaza)/Nov. 15-18/800

Nat'l Ass'n for Uniformed Services and Soc. of Military Widows *(1968)*
5535 Hempstead Way
Springfield, VA 22151-4094
Tel: (703)750-1342   *Fax:* (703)354-4380
Toll Free: (800)842 - 3451
Web Site: http://www.naus.org
Members: 155,000 individuals
Staff: 10
Annual Budget: $1-2,000,000
President: Maj.Gen. Richard D. Murray, USAF
Director, Public Affairs: Sharon W. Barnes
Legislative Counsel: Col. Charles Partridge, USA(Ret)
Director, Membership Services: Tamea A. Boone
Historical Note
Promotes development and support of legislation to sustain the morale of the Armed Forces and provide fair and equitable consideration for all members of the uniformed services. NAUS affiliated with the Soc. of Military Widows in 1984. Sponsors the Nat'l Ass'n for Uniformed Services Political Action Committee (NAUS-PAC). Membership: $15/year, $12/year (widows).
Publications:
Uniformed Services Journal. bi-m. adv.
Meetings/Conferences:
Annual Meetings: Washington, DC area/last week of Oct.-1st week of Nov./200-300

Nat'l Ass'n for Variable Annuities *(1991)*
12030 Sunrise Valley Drive, Suite 110
Reston, VA 20191
Tel: (703)620-0674   *Fax:* (703)620-6362
Web Site: http://www.navnet.org
Members: 280 companies
Staff: 6
Annual Budget: $1-2,000,000
President and C.E.O.: Mark Mackey
V. President, Conferences and Membership: Danielle Murdock
Director, Industry Relations: Christine Underhill
Historical Note
Membership: $750/year (companies with less than 50 employees); $2,000/year (companies with more than 50 employees).
Publications:
NAVA Outlook Newsletter. bi-m.
Meetings/Conferences:
1999 – Chicago, IL(Sheridan)/Oct. 10-12

Nat'l Ass'n for Women in Education *(1916)*
Historical Note
Name changed in 1996 to NAWE: Advancing Women in Higher Education.

Nat'l Ass'n for Year-Round Education *(1972)*
P.O. Box 711386
San Diego, CA 92171-1386
Tel: (619)276-5296   *Fax:* (619)571-5754
E-Mail: info@NAYRE.org
Web Site: http://www.NAYRE.org
Members: 1,570 individuals, 130 institutions
Staff: 6
Annual Budget: $500-1,000,000
Exec. Director: Charles Ballenger, Ph.D.
Communications Coordinator: Kelly Johnson
Membership Secretary: Shirley Jensen
Historical Note
Formerly (1986) the Nat'l Council on Year-Round Education, NAYRE is a professional association of individuals with an interest in the concept of year round education. Membership: $45/year (individual); $350-$750/year, varies by enrollment (institution).
Publications:
Reference Directory of Year-Round Education Programs. a.
Year-Rounder Newsletter. q.
Meetings/Conferences:
Annual Meetings: Las Vegas, NV(Riviera Hotel)/Feb. 10-14/2,000
1999 – San Diego, CA(Town & Country)/Feb. 5-9/1900
2000 – San Diego, CA(Town & Country)/Feb. 5-9/1800

Nat'l Ass'n General Merchandise Representatives *(1949)*
Historical Note
Became Consumer Product Broker Ass'n in 1997, and NAGMR Consumer Product Brokers in 1998.

Nat'l Ass'n Medical Staff Services *(1978)*
631 E. Butterfield Road, Suite 311
Lombard, IL 60148-5647
Tel: (630)271-9814   *Fax:* (630)271-0295
E-Mail: namss@namss.org
Web Site: http://www.namss.org
Members: 4,200 individuals
Staff: 4
Annual Budget: $1-2,000,000
Coordinator, Certificate: Laurel Howard Juzkiw
Historical Note
NAMSS promotes educational opportunities to enhance the skills and general competence of practicing medical staff services professionals. Serves to increase recognition of the role of the medical staff services professional and to assist its members in understanding and succeeding in the changing health care industry. Membership: $100/year (individual).
Publications:
Synergy. m. adv.
Meetings/Conferences:
Annual Meetings: October/1,000
1999 – Nashville, TN(Opryland)
2000 – Las Vegas, NV
2001 – Chicago, IL

Nat'l Ass'n of Academic Advisors for Athletes *(1976)*
14606 Woodlake Trace
Louisville, KY 40245
Tel: (502)253-9530   *Fax:* (502)253-9533
E-Mail: kley2@juno.com
Members: 640 individuals
Annual Budget: $10-25,000
Nat'l Office Director: Kathleen Ley
Historical Note
Formerly (1997) Nat'l Ass'n of Academic Advisors for Athletics and (1985) Nat'l Academic Advisors Ass'n. An affiliate of the Nat'l Collegiate Athletic Ass'n, N4A serves professional advisors giving guidance to student athletes at the college level. Membership: $30/year (non-voting/student); $75/year (individual).
Publications:
Athletic Academic Journal. semi-a.
N4A Newsletter. 3/year.
Meetings/Conferences:
Annual Meetings: June
1999 – Cincinnati, OH(Omni Netherland Plaza)/June 11-15

Nat'l Ass'n of Academies of Science *(1926)*
2504 Griegos Road, N.W.
Albuquerque, NM 87107-2870
Tel: (505)345-3866   *Fax:* (505)345-5416
Members: 44 academies
Staff: 1
Annual Budget: $50-100,000
Past President: Dr. David Hsi
Historical Note
Before 1919 various academies were informally associated with the American Ass'n for the Advancement of Science (AAAS). In 1920 they were given the right of representation on the AAAS aouncil and became known as the Affiliated Academies. In 1926 they became a more organized group known as the Academy Conference, and in 1969 became known as the Ass'n of Academies of Science. Affiliated with AAAS. Until 1979 known as the Ass'n of Academies of Science. Membership: $250/year (maximum).
Publications:
NAAS Directory, Proceedings and Handbook. a.
Meetings/Conferences:
Annual Meetings: With American Ass'n for the Advancement of Science

Nat'l Ass'n of Accompanists and Coaches *(1984)*

Nat'l Ass'n of Activity Professionals *(1981)*
P.O. Box 23909
Jackson, MS 39225
Tel: (601)853-3722   *Fax:* (601)853-3536
E-Mail: naap1@aol.com
Web Site: http://www.naap.net
Members: 2,800 individuals
Staff: 3
Annual Budget: $250-500,000
Exec. Director: Catherine R. Selman
Historical Note
Active members are activity directors, coordinators, or consultants in long-term care facilities, senior retirement housing, senior centers, or adult day-care programs. Membership: $60/year.
Publications:
NAAP News. m. adv.
Meetings/Conferences:
Annual Meetings: April/600

Nat'l Ass'n of Addiction Treatment Providers *(1978)*
501 Randolph Dr.
Lititz, PA 17543-9049
Tel: (717)581-1901   *Fax:* (717)581-1902
E-Mail: RHunsicker@Naatp.org
Web Site: http://Naatp.org
Members: 450 organizations
Staff: 1
Annual Budget: $250-500,000
C.E.O: Dr. Ronald J. Hunsicker
Historical Note
Members are for-profit and non-profit treatment centers for alcoholism and drug dependency.
Publications:
NAATP Update. m. adv.
NAATP Vision. 10/yr. adv.
Meetings/Conferences:
Annual Meetings: May

Nat'l Ass'n of Advisors for the Health Professions *(1974)*
P.O. Box 1518
Champaign, IL 61824-1518
Tel: (217)355-0063   *Fax:* (217)355-1287
E-Mail: staff@naahp.org
Web Site: http://www.naahp.org
Members: 1,275 individuals
Staff: 5
Annual Budget: $250-500,000
Exec. Director: Julian M. Frankenberg, Ph.D.
Assoc. Exec. Director: Christine Klindworth
Historical Note
Members are college faculty who counsel students on careers in the health professions. Sponsors and supports Nat'l Prehealth Student Ass'n, which serves as an information resource for students in health professions training. Membership: $90-110/year (undergraduate institution); $250/year (health professional school).
Publications:
Between Issues Newsletter. q.
Directory. a.
The Advisor. q.
Meetings/Conferences:
Biennial Meetings: Even years/400-700
2000 – Orlando, FL(Marriott)/June 26-July 2

Nat'l Ass'n of Aeronautical Examiners *(1959)*
Historical Note
Address unknown in 1996.

Nat'l Ass'n of Affordable Housing Lenders *(1988)*
1200 19th St.,N.W., Suite 300
Washington, DC 20036
Tel: (202)429-5150   *Fax:* (202)857-1111
E-Mail: naahl@dc.sba.com
Members: 189 institutions
Staff: 2
Annual Budget: $250-500,000
President: Judith A. Kennedy
Program and Administrator: Dorothea Beckering
Historical Note
NAAHL members are financial institutions and others with an interest in affordable housing development lending. Sponsors regional conferences on lending and economic development issues, as well as other programming relevant to member needs. Membership: $250-3,000/year.
Publications:
Directions in Affordable Housing Finance. q.
Washington Update. semi-m.
Meetings/Conferences:
1999 – Washington, DC(Capitol Hilton)/Feb. 9-10
1999 – New York, NY

Nat'l Ass'n of African American Studies *(1991)*
Morehead State University
211 Rader Hall
Morehead, KY 40351-1689
Tel: (606)783-2650   *Fax:* (606)783-5046
Members: 372 individuals, 30 organizations
Staff: 4
Annual Budget: $25-50,000
Exec. Director: Lemuel Berry, Jr., Ph.D.
Historical Note
Membership: $150/year (individual); $500/year (organization).
Publications:
NAAAS Newsletter. q. adv.

Networks and Making Connections. semi-a. adv.

Meetings/Conferences:
Annual Meetings: February
1999 – Houston, TX(Adams Mark)

Nat'l Ass'n of Agricultural Fair Agencies *(1966)*
MI State Dept. of Agriculture
P.O. Box 30017
Lansing, MI 48909
Tel: (517)373-9766   *Fax:* (517)373-9146
Members: 35 agencies
Staff: 1
Annual Budget: under $10,000
Secretary-Treasurer: Carol Carlson

Historical Note
U.S. and Canadian representatives of state/provincial agencies that are responsible for the support of educational and agricultural fairs. Affiliated with the Nat'l Ass'n of State Departments of Agriculture. Has no paid officers or full-time staff. Membership: $35/year.

Publications:
Constitution and Membership Roster. a.
Newsletter. a.

Meetings/Conferences:
Semi-Annual Meetings: Summer and Winter

Nat'l Ass'n of Agricultural Journalists *(1952)*
Ohio State University
216 Kottman Hall, 2021 Coffey Road
Columbus, OH 43210
Tel: (614)292-9637   *Fax:* (614)292-2270
E-Mail: steel.7@osu.edu
Members: 130 individuals
Annual Budget: under $10,000
Exec. Secretary-Treasurer: Suzanne Steel

Historical Note
Formerly (1988) the Newspaper Farm Editors of America and the Newspaper Farm Editors Ass'n. A professional organization of agricultural newspaper and magazine editors. Has no paid staff. Membership: $50/year.

Publications:
NAAJ Newsletter. 8/year.

Meetings/Conferences:
Semi-annual Meetings: Spring/Fall (April in Washington, DC).

Nat'l Ass'n of Agriculture Employees *(1954)*
P.O. Box 99-7716
Miami, FL 33299-7716
Tel: (305)526-7204   *Fax:* (305)526-7239
Members: 750 individuals
Staff: 9
Annual Budget: $100-250,000
President: Stan Freihofer

Historical Note
Formerly (1981) the Federal Plant Quarantine Inspectors Nat'l Ass'n. NAAE is an independent federal labor union which represents employees working for the U.S. Dept. of Agriculture, Animal and Plant Health Inspection Service, Plant Protection and Quarantine. Members are professional employees with college degrees in Biological Sciences. Bargaining unit consists of federal officers enforcing federal agricultural quarantines relating to foreign and domestic programs. Membership: $15/month.

Publications:
Newsletter. q.

Meetings/Conferences:
Biennial Meetings: Even years in April

Nat'l Ass'n of Air Communications Specialists
110 N. Royal St., Suite 307
Alexandria, VA 22314
Tel: (703)836-8732   *Fax:* (703)836-8920
Web Site: http://www.naacs.org
Members: 200 individuals

Historical Note
NAACS members are air medical communicatons specialists.

Nat'l Ass'n of Air Nat'l Guard Health Technicians *(1974)*
6032 Chetwind Drive
Cicero, NY 13039
Tel: (315)458-2251
Members: 350 individuals
Annual Budget: under $10,000
Exec. Director: Timothy C. Sager

Publications:
Health Technician Newsletter. q.

Meetings/Conferences:
Annual Meetings: in conjunction with the Ass'n of Military
Surgeons of the U.S.

Nat'l Ass'n of Air Traffic Specialists *(1960)*
11303 Amherst Ave., Suite 4
Wheaton, MD 20902-4600
Tel: (301)933-6228   *Fax:* (301)933-3902
Members: 2,000 individuals
Staff: 5
Annual Budget: $500-1,000,000
Exec. Director and C.E.O.: Wally Pike

Historical Note
Supports the NAATS Political Action Fund. An independent labor union.

Publications:
NAATS News. m.

Meetings/Conferences:
Biennial Meetings: odd years in Fall

Nat'l Ass'n of Alcoholism and Drug Abuse Counselors *(1972)*

1911 North Fort Myer Dr., Suite 900
Arlington, VA 22209
Tel: (703)741-7686   *Fax:* (703)741-7698
Toll Free: (800)548 - 0497
Web Site: www.naadac.org
Members: 18,000 individuals, 47 affiliates
Staff: 16
Annual Budget: $1-2,000,000
Exec. Director: Linda P. Kaplan, CAE
Finance Manager: Jeff Crouse
Government Relations Director: Bill McColl
Director, Membership Services: Donna Croy

Historical Note
NAADAC represents alcoholism and drug abuse counselors working in hospitals, treatment centers, private practice, councils and agencies on alcoholism and drug abuse, and employee assistance programs. Incorporated in Arlington, VA. Administers certifying examinations leading to the National Certified Addiction Counselor (NCAC) designation. Membership: $40-55/year (individual), $350/year (company).

Publications:
NAADAC Newsletter. bi-m.
The Counselor Magazine. bi-m. adv.

Meetings/Conferences:
Annual Meetings: Summer
1999 – Philadelphia, PA(Windom Franklin)/May 26-29

Nat'l Ass'n of Aluminum Distributors *(1951)*
1900 Arch St.
Philadelphia, PA 19103-1498
Tel: (215)564-3484   *Fax:* (215)963-9784
Web Site: www.naad.org
Members: 100 companies
Staff: 3
Annual Budget: $500-1,000,000
Exec. V. President: Julie S. Thane

Historical Note
Membership: $3,000/year.

Publications:
Membership Directory. a.
TOPICS Newsletter. q.

Meetings/Conferences:
Annual Meetings: November/470
1999 – San Francisco, CA(Fairmont)/Oct. 27-30

Nat'l Ass'n of American Business Clubs
Historical Note
See Nat'l Ambucs.

Nat'l Ass'n of Animal Breeders *(1947)*
P.O. Box 1033
401 Bernadette Dr.
Columbia, MO 65205-1033
Tel: (573)445-4406   *Fax:* (573)446-2279
E-Mail: naab-css@naab-css.org
Web Site: http://www.naab-css.org
Members: 26 organizations
Staff: 6
Annual Budget: $1-2,000,000
President: Gordon A. Doak, Ph.D.

Historical Note
Formerly the Nat'l Ass'n of Artificial Breeders, members are farmer co-ops and others interested in livestock improvement.

Publications:
Proceedings. a. adv.
Proceedings of Technical Conference. bien.

Meetings/Conferences:
Annual Meetings: August/500-700
1999 – St. Louis, MO(Union Station Hyatt
Regency)/July 30-31/200

Nat'l Ass'n of Apnea Professionals *(1987)*
P.O. Box 37803
Honolulu, HI 96837
Toll Free: (800)392 - 2514
E-Mail: msherida@hpu.edu
Web Site: see text
Members: 250 individuals
Annual Budget: $10-25,000
Business Director: Mary S. Sheridan

Historical Note
NAAP members are professionals involved in the care of infants who have apnea or who use cardiorespiratory monitors at home. Membership: $45/year (individual). Website located at http://www.pediatrics.ucsd.edu/specialtypediatrics/pulmonology

Publications:
Directory. semi-a.
Newsletter. q.

Meetings/Conferences:
Annual Meetings: In conjunction APNEA(Annenberg Center)

Nat'l Ass'n of Architectural Metal Manufacturers *(1938)*
8 South Michigan Avenue
Suite 1000
Chicago, IL 60603
Tel: (312)332-0405   *Fax:* (312)332-0706
E-Mail: naamm@gss.net
Web Site: http://www.naamm.org
Members: 124 companies
Staff: 2
Annual Budget: $250-500,000
Exec. V. President: August L. Sisco

Historical Note
Formerly the Nat'l Ass'n of Ornamental Metal Manufacturers. Absorbed the Nat'l Steel Door and Frame Ass'n in 1962 and the Metal Lath/Steel Framing Ass'n in 1987. Comprised of six divisions: Architectural Metal Products, Flagpole, Hollow Metal

Doors and Frames, Metal Bar Grating, Metal Lath and Steel
Framing, and Modular Steel Cell. Membership: $495-2,500/year
(corporate).

Publications:
Member Directory. a.
Technical Standards.

Meetings/Conferences:
Annual Meetings: Spring
1999 – Fort Myers, FL(Sanibel Harbour Resort and
Spa)/April 17-20
1999 – Chicago, IL

Nat'l Ass'n of Area Agencies on Aging *(1974)*
1112 16th St., N.W., Suite 100
Washington, DC 20036-4823
Tel: (202)296-8130   *Fax:* (202)296-8134
Web Site: http://www.ncoa.org/lcao/members.naaaa.htm
Members: 656 agencies
Staff: 6
Annual Budget: $1-2,000,000
Exec. Director: Janice Jackson Fiegener
Conference Coordinator: Glendale V. Johnson
Fiscal Manager: Martin Kleffner

Historical Note
Members include Area Agencies on Aging, Title VI Grantees, Service Provider Organizations, Network on Aging Advisory Council Members and others with a commitment to meeting the needs of older Americans. Its mission is to promote a national policy that would allow older Americans to remain independent in their communities and homes for as long as possible. Membership: $75-$1,750/year, based on total annual budget of agency.

Publications:
Nat'l Directory for Eldercare Information and Referral. bien.
Network News. bi-m. adv.

Meetings/Conferences:
Annual Meetings: Summer

Nat'l Ass'n of Artists' Organizations *(1982)*
918 F St., N.W., Suite 611
Washington, DC 20004-1406
Tel: (202)347-6350   *Fax:* (202)347-7376
E-Mail: naao2@naao.org
Web Site: http://www.naao.org
Members: 265 individuals, 325 organizations
Staff: 2
Annual Budget: $2-5,000,000
Exec. Director: Roberto Bedoya

Historical Note
A service oriented organization which promotes and protects artists within non-profit organizations. NAAO is dedicated to the presentation of alternative visual arts, media, literature, new music, and performing arts. Membership: $35/year (individual); $175-500/year (organization).

Publications:
Directory of Artists' Organizations. bien. adv.
NAAO Bulletin. q.

Meetings/Conferences:

Nat'l Ass'n of ASCS County Office Employees
Historical Note
Became (1995) Nat'l Ass'n of FSA Committee Employees.

Nat'l Ass'n of Assistant United States Attorneys *(1992)*
8621 Silver Oak Court
Springfield, VA 22153-2129
Tel: (703)455-1753   *Fax:* (800)528-3492
Toll Free: (800)455 - 5661
E-Mail: naausa@aol.com
Web Site: http://www.naausa.org
Members: 1000 individuals
Staff: 2
Annual Budget: $100-250,000
Exec. Director: Dennis W. Boyd

Historical Note
NAAUSA is a professional association with the primary objective of promoting and protecting the career and professional interests of Assistant U.S. Attorneys. Membership: $78/year (individual).

Publications:
NAAUSA Brief. irreg.
NAAUSA Quarterly. q. adv.

Nat'l Ass'n of Athletic Development Directors *(1992)*
P.O. Box 16428
Cleveland, OH 44116
Tel: (440)892-4000   *Fax:* (440)892-4007
E-Mail: pmanak@nacda.com
Web Site: http://www.nacda.com
Members: 325 individuals
Staff: 2
Annual Budget: $10-25,000
Asst. Secretary/Treasurer: Pat Manak
Senior Staff Administrator: Bob Vecchione

Historical Note
NAADD is an affiliate of the Nat'l Ass'n of Collegiate Directors of Athletics, which provides administrative support. Membership: $50-125/year.

Meetings/Conferences:
Annual Meetings: June
1999 – Reno, NV(Hilton)/June 12-13/400

Nat'l Ass'n of Attorneys General *(1907)*
750 First St., N.E.
Washington, DC 20001
Tel: (202)326-6000   *Fax:* (202)408-7104
Web Site: http://www.naag.org
Members: 56 individuals
Staff: 30
Annual Budget: $2-5,000,000
Exec. Director/General Counsel: Christine T. Milliken

Historical Note
NAAG fosters interstate cooperation on legal and law enforcement issues, conducts policy research and analysis, provides for advocacy at all levels of government on behalf of the states' chief legal officers. Members are the Attorneys General of the 50 states and 6 territories.

Publications:
A-G Bulletin. 10/year.
Antitrust and Commerce Report. 10/year.
Consumer Protection Report. 10/year.
Membership Directory. a.
Nat'l Environmental Enforcement Journal. 11/year.
State Constitutional Law Bulletin. 10/year.

Meetings/Conferences:
Three Meetings Annually: March (Washington, DC), June, and December.

Nat'l Ass'n of Auto Trim and Restyling Shops (1953)
6255 Barfield Rd., Suite 200
Atlanta, GA 30328
Toll Free: (800)241 - 9034
Members: 8,800 auto trim shops
Staff: 7
Annual Budget: $100-250,000
Exec. Director: Angelo Varrone

Historical Note
Formerly (1995) Nat'l Ass'n of Auto Trim Shops. Members specialize in enhancing the appearance of cars and other vehicles by installation of new upholstery, convertible tops, etc.

Publications:
Auto Trim & Restyling News. m.

Meetings/Conferences:

Nat'l Ass'n of Band Instrument Manufacturers (1920)
38 West 21st St., Room 1106
New York, NY 10010-6906
Tel: (212)924-9175   *Fax:* (212)675-3577
E-Mail: assnhdqs@aol.com
Members: 29 companies
Staff: 2
Annual Budget: $25-50,000
Exec. V. President: Jerome Hershman

Historical Note
Membership fee varies by sales.

Publications:
Newsletter. bi-m.

Meetings/Conferences:
Annual Meetings: Fall
1999 – Scottsdale, AZ(The Phoenician)

Nat'l Ass'n of Bankruptcy Trustees (1981)
3008 Millwood Ave.
Columbia, SC 29205
Tel: (803)252-5646   *Fax:* (803)765-0860
Toll Free: (800)445 - 8629
Web Site: http://www.nabt.comn
Members: 1,200 individuals
Staff: 8
Annual Budget: $50-100,000
Exec. Secretary: Carol H. Davis

Historical Note
Formerly the Nat'l Ass'n of Chapter 13 Trustees. Membership: $100/yr. (basic).

Publications:
NABTalk. q. adv.

Meetings/Conferences:
1999 – Ashville, NC/Aug. 29-Sept. 1

Nat'l Ass'n of Baptist Professors of Religion (1927)
Mercer University
Macon, GA 31207
Tel: (912)752-7758   *Fax:* (912)752-2384
E-Mail: wilson_rf@mercer.edu
Members: 350 individuals
Staff: 1
Annual Budget: $10-25,000
Exec. Secretary-Treasurer: Richard F. Wilson

Historical Note
Formerly (1983) the Ass'n of Baptist Professors of Religion. Members are not required to be related to any Baptist group or denomination. Membership: varies with salary levels.

Publications:
Bibliographic Series. irreg.
Dissertation Series. irreg.
Festschriften Series. a.
Monograph Series. irreg.
NABPR News.
Perspectives in Religious Studies. q. adv.

Meetings/Conferences:
Annual Meetings: in conjunction with AAR/SBL

Nat'l Ass'n of Bar and Tavern Owners (1992)
P.O. Box 11578
Fort Lauderdale, FL 33339
Tel: (954)776-7017   *Fax:* (954)776-7017
Toll Free: (800)298 - 7665
Members: 20,000 individuals
Annual Budget: $1-2,000,000
President: Richard S. Jett
Treasurer: Dudley Johnson

Historical Note
Membership: $100/year (indvidual); $100/year (corporate).

Publications:
Newsletter. a.
Top Gun Newsletter. w.

Meetings/Conferences:
Meeting: every 12 months

1999 – Ft. Lauderdale, FL(Marriott)/700

Nat'l Ass'n of Bar Executives (1953)
541 N. Fairbanks Court
Chicago, IL 60611-3314
Tel: (312)988-5360   *Fax:* (312)988-5492
Members: 650 individuals
Staff: 3
Annual Budget: $100-250,000
Staff Director: Bryan Jordan

Historical Note
Formerly (1962) Nat'l Conference of Bar Secretaries, and (1965) Nat'l Conference of Bar Executives.

Publications:
NABE Newsletter. q.
NABE Roster. a.

Meetings/Conferences:
Semi-annual Meetings: February and August with American Bar Ass'n

Nat'l Ass'n of Bar-Related Title Insurers (1965)
1030 West Higgins Road, Suite 230
Park Ridge, IL 60068
Tel: (847)698-0500   *Fax:* (847)692-9765
Members: 10 companies
Staff: 2
Annual Budget: $25-50,000
Exec. V. President: Joanne P. Elliot

Historical Note
Formerly (until 1979) known as the Nat'l Conference of Bar-Related Title Insurers. Members are title insurance companies ''bar-related'' as registered as a service mark with the U.S. Patent Office.

Publications:
Membership Directory. a.
Newsletter. q.

Meetings/Conferences:
Annual Meetings: Usually with the American Bar Ass'n

Nat'l Ass'n of Barber Boards (1935)
2708 Pine St.,
Arkadelphia, AR 71923
Tel: (501)682-2806
Members: 50 state licensing boards
Annual Budget: $10-25,000
Exec. Officer: Charles Kirkpatrick

Historical Note
Formerly (1986) Nat'l Ass'n of Boards of Barbers Examiners of America. Members are state licensing boards for barbers. Has no full-time staff. Membership: $100/year.

Meetings/Conferences:

Nat'l Ass'n of Basketball Coaches (1927)
9300 W. 110th St., Suite 640
Overland Park, KS 66210-1486
Tel: (913)469-1001   *Fax:* (913)469-1390
Members: 5,000 individuals
Staff: 9
Annual Budget: $500-1,000,000
Exec. Director: James A. Haney
Director, Public Relations: Kevin Henderson
Director, Communications: Andrew Geerken
Director, Business Affairs: Deborah Page
Director, Membership Services: Carol Haney

Historical Note
Formerly Nat'l Ass'n of Basketball Coaches of the United States (1998). NABC lobbies on the behalf of college coaches and serves as a resource for coaches. Membership: $40-300/year (individual).

Publications:
Courtside Newspaper. 6-7/yr. adv.

Meetings/Conferences:
Annual Meetings: March/2,500-2,700
1999 – St. Petersburg, FL(Hyatt)/March 25-29/3500
2000 – Indianapolis, IN(Hyatt)/March 30-April 3/3500
2001 – Minneapolis, MN/March 29-April 2/3500
2002 – Atlanta, GA/March 28-April 1/4000

Nat'l Ass'n of Beverage Importers-Wine-Spirits-Beer (1934)
1025 Vermont Ave., N.W., Suite 1066
Washington, DC 20005
Tel: (202)638-1617   *Fax:* (202)638-3122
E-Mail: nabi-inc@msn.ciom
Members: 60 companies
Staff: 2
Annual Budget: $250-500,000
President: Robert J. Maxwell
Corporate Secretary/Assistant Treasurer: C. Jean Fellner

Historical Note
Members are required to hold a Federal Basic Importer's Permit Founded in New York City January 12, 1934 by eighteen charter members for the purpose of electing an NRA code authority. After the NRA was declared unconstitutional in 1935 the present organization was formed. Formerly (until 1979) known as the Nat'l Ass'n of Alcoholic Beverage Importers, Inc.

Publications:
Statistical Report. a.
Statistics. m.

Meetings/Conferences:
Annual Meetings: Spring

Nat'l Ass'n of Beverage Retailers (1934)
5101 River Road, Suite 108
Bethesda, MD 20816
Tel: (301)656-1494   *Fax:* (301)656-7539
Members: 13,000 individuals, 25 state ass'ns
Staff: 5
Annual Budget: $250-500,000
Exec. Director: John B. Burcham, Jr.

Historical Note
Formerly National Retail Liquor Package Stores Association and (1992) Nat'l Liquor Stores Ass'n. Members are state associations representing private-sector liquor stores and on-premise retailers of alcoholic beverages.

Publications:
News and Views. q. adv.

Meetings/Conferences:
1999 – Las Vegas, NV(Monte Carlo)/Jan. 17-20

Nat'l Ass'n of Biology Teachers (1938)
11250 Roger Bacon Drive, Suite 19
Reston, VA 20190-5202
Tel: (703)471-1134   *Fax:* (703)435-5582
Toll Free: (800)406 - 0775
E-Mail: nabter@aol.com
Web Site: http://www.nabt.org
Members: 7,500 individuals
Staff: 12
Annual Budget: $1-2,000,000
Exec. Director: Wayne W. Carley
Education Director: Kathy Frame
Membership Director: Carlotta Fischetti
Director of Publications and Marketing: Chris Chantry

Historical Note
Founded in 1938 and incorporated in Illinois in 1956. NABT members are biology educators and administrators in elementary schools, middle/junior high schools, high schools and colleges. NABT also includes representatives from biology-related industries. NABT improves biology/life science education by introducing innovative classroom strategies as well as keeping teachers informed on developments in the biological sciences. Membership: $52/year (individual); $520/year (sustaining) $125/year (organization/company).

Publications:
News and Views. q.
The American Biology Teacher. 9/year. adv.

Meetings/Conferences:
Annual Meetings: Fall/1,500
1999 – Fort Worth, TX(Worthington Hotel)/Oct. 27-30/1500
2000 – Orlando, FL(Hyatt)/Oct. 25-28/1500
2001 – PQ Canada(le Centre Sheraton)/Nov. 7-10/1500

Nat'l Ass'n of Black Accountants (1969)
7249 A Hanover Pkwy.
Greenbelt, MD 20770-3653
Tel: (301)474-6222   *Fax:* (301)474-3114
Members: 5,000 individuals
Staff: 8
Annual Budget: $500-1,000,000
Manager, Education: Charles Quinn
Manager, Membership Services: Diana Dawkins

Historical Note
Established and incorporated in New York. Absorbed the Nat'l Soc. of Certified Public Accountants. Membership: $100/year (professional); $15/year (undergraduate).

Publications:
News Plus. q.

Meetings/Conferences:
Annual Meetings: Summer
1999 – Chicago, IL(Hyatt)
2000 – Washington, DC(Sheraton)

Nat'l Ass'n of Black Consulting Engineers (1975)
1979 Beaumont Drive
Baton Rouge, LA 70806
Tel: (504)927-7240
Members: 100 companies
Annual Budget: under $10,000

Historical Note
Founded as the Nat'l Council of Minority Consulting Engineers, it represented the merging of the Western Ass'n of Minority Consulting Engineers, the American Indian Council, and the Eastern Ass'n of Black Consulting Engineers. Assumed its present name in 1978. Member firms are composed of all the consulting engineering disciplines: civil, structural, environmental, transportation, electrical, mechanical, planning, architecture, land surveying, and construction management. Has no paid officers or full-time staff. Membership: $200/year.

Meetings/Conferences:
Annual Meetings: Always Washington, DC/Sept.

Nat'l Ass'n of Black County Officials (1975)
440 First St., N.W.
Washington, DC 20001
Tel: (202)347-6953   *Fax:* (202)393-6596
E-Mail: nabco@ami.net
Web Site: http://www.nabco.org
Staff: 8
Annual Budget: $500-1,000,000
Exec. Officer: Maria D. Lopes

Historical Note
NABCO members are elected and appointed African-American county officials. The Nat'l Organization of Black County Officials is its service and business arm. Membership: $100/year (individual); $500/year (company/organization).

Publications:
County Compass. q. adv.
County-to-County. q. adv.

Meetings/Conferences:
1999 – Washington, DC/Feb. 26-March 2
1999 – Austin, TX/March 27-31
1999 – Lake Charles, LA/April 28-May 2
1999 – St. Louis, MO/July 16-20

Nat'l Ass'n of Black Hospitality Professionals (1985)
Box 8132
Columbus, GA 31908-8132
Tel: (334)298-4802

E-Mail: NABHP@aol.com
Members: 800 individuals
Staff: 4
Annual Budget: under $10,000
President: Mikoel Turner

Historical Note
Purpose is to provide a forum for black professionals in the hotel and restaurant industry, including food service and tourism professionals. Created the Nat'l Hospitality Institute for Advancement of Minorities. Provides training for people currently in low-level jobs who desire to move into supervisory or management positions. Membership: varies with length of experience.

Publications:
Updates. m.

Meetings/Conferences:

Nat'l Ass'n of Black Journalists (1975)
8701 Adelhia Rd.
Adelphia, MD   20783-1716
Tel: (301)445-7100   Fax: (301)445-7101
E-Mail: nabj@jmail.umd.edu
Web Site: http://www.nabj.org
Members: 2,800 individuals
Staff: 5
Annual Budget: $1-2,000,000
Exec. Director: Antoinette Samuel

Historical Note
Founded in 1975 by a group of journalists covering the Third Nat'l Institute for Black Elected Officials in Washington, DC. Works to strengthen ties among black journalists, reward excellence in the field, and expand job opportunities. Membership: $60/year; $35/year (associate); $20/year (student).

Publications:
NABJ Journal. 10/yr.

Meetings/Conferences:
Annual Meetings: Summer
1999 - Seattle, WA/July 7-10

Nat'l Ass'n of Black Procurement Professionals
P.O. Box 70738
Washington, DC   20024-0738
Tel: (202)554-3155   Fax: (202)554-3146
Exec. Director: Betty Wilkerson

Nat'l Ass'n of Black Real Estate Professionals (1984)
Historical Note
Address unknown in 1995; presumed inactive or defunct.

Nat'l Ass'n of Black Social Workers (1968)
8426 W. McNichols
Detroit, MI   48221
Tel: (313)862-6700   Fax: (313)862-6998
Members: 10,000 individuals
Staff: 5
Annual Budget: $500-1,000,000
President: Rudolph C. Smith
Administrator: Dr. Howard V. Brabson

Historical Note
Membership: $50/year (individual); $300/year plus $20 per capita per organization.

Publications:
Black Caucus. semi-a. adv.
Newsletter. semi-a. adv.

Meetings/Conferences:

Nat'l Ass'n of Black Women Attorneys (1972)
c/o Mabel D. Haden, Attorney
1110 Hamlin St., N.E.
Washington, DC   20017-3432
Tel: (202)526-5200   Fax: (202)526-7993
Members: 700 individuals
Staff: 1
Annual Budget: $25-50,000
President: Mabel Dole Haden

Historical Note
Formerly (until 1978) the Nat'l Ass'n of Black Women Lawyers. NABWA seeks to increase the opportunities for participation of blacks and other women at all levels of the administration of justice. Maintains a scholarship fund begun in 1978. Membership: $100/year (individual); $150/year (organization).

Publications:
NABWA News. q. adv.
Souvenir Booklet. a. adv.

Meetings/Conferences:

Nat'l Ass'n of Black Women Entrepreneurs (1978)
Historical Note
Address unknown in 1997.

Nat'l Ass'n of Black-Owned Broadcasters (1976)
1333 New Hampshire Ave., Suite 1000
Washington, DC   20036
Tel: (202)463-8970   Fax: (202)429-0657
Web Site: www.nabob@abs.net
Members: 102 individuals, 180 radio and 20 television stations
Staff: 6
Annual Budget: $100-250,000
Exec. Director: James Winston

Historical Note
Founded in September, 1976 and incorporated in the District of Columbia in 1977. Members are blacks who own radio and/or television stations, cable television systems and related businesses.

Publications:
NABOB News. m.

Meetings/Conferences:
Semi-annual Meetings: Washington, DC/Sept. and Spring
1999 - /May 14-15

Nat'l Ass'n of Blacks in Criminal Justice (1974)
P.O. Box 19788
North Carolina Central University
Durham, NC   27707-0099
Tel: (919)683-1801   Fax: (919)683-1903
E-Mail: office@nabcj.org
Web Site: nabcj.org
Members: 3 individuals
Staff: 2
Annual Budget: $100-250,000
Exec. Director: Matthew Hamidullah
Admin. Manager: Clarissa L. Grady

Historical Note
The Nat'l Ass'n of Blacks in Criminal Justice is a multiracial, nonpartisan, nonprofit association of criminal justice professionals and community leaders dedicated to improving the administration of justice. The association was founded as a vehicle by which criminal justice practitioners could initiate positive changes from within, while increasing opportunities for the average citizen to better understand the nature and the operation of our local, state, and federal criminal justice processes. Membership and participation in the activities of the association are open to all, irrespective of race, creed, or country of national origin.

Publications:
NABCJ Directory. a. adv.
NABCJ Journal. q. adv.

Meetings/Conferences:
Annual Meetings: July
1999 - Dallas, TX(Adam's Mark)/July 18-30/1200

Nat'l Ass'n of Blind Teachers (1971)
c/o American Council for the Blind
1155 15th St., N.W., Suite 720
Washington, DC   20005
Tel: (202)467-5081   Fax: (202)467-5085
Toll Free: (800)424 - 8666
Web Site: http://www.acb.org
Members: 185 individuals
Annual Budget: $10-25,000
President: Patty Slaby

Historical Note
Members are teachers who are blind. Affiliated with the American Council of the Blind, which provides administrative support. Membership: $10/year.

Publications:
The Blind Teacher. q.

Meetings/Conferences:
Annual Meetings: July

Nat'l Ass'n of Blouse Manufacturers (1933)
Historical Note
Address unknown in 1997.

Nat'l Ass'n of Boards of Education (1972)
1077 30th St., N.W., Suite 100
Washington, DC   20007-3852
Tel: (202)337-6232   Fax: (202)333-6706
Members: 4,000 individuals
Staff: 2
Annual Budget: $100-250,000
Exec. Director: Regina Haney

Historical Note
A service department of the Nat'l Catholic Educational Ass'n, which provides administrative support. NABE provides board members of Catholic organizations with information resources, networking, and pertinent education. Memberhip: $195/year.

Publications:
Issue-Gram. semi-a.

Meetings/Conferences:
Annual Meetings: With the Nat'l Catholic Educational Ass'n
1999 - New Orleans, LA(Convention Center)/April 6-9

Nat'l Ass'n of Boards of Examiners of Long Term Care Administrators (1970)
1444 I St., N.W., Suite 700
Washington, DC   20005-2210
Tel: (202)223-9750   Fax: (202)223-9569
E-Mail: NAB@Bastromdc.com
Web Site: http://www.nabweb.org
Members: 25 individuals, 51 licensing boards & 30 orgs.
Staff: 7
Annual Budget: $1-2,000,000
Exec. Director: Randy L. Lindner, CAE
Administrative Director: Susan Courtney
Education Coordinator: Mark Wright

Historical Note
Purpose is to consider questions of common interest (i.e. educational and professional standards, uniformity of laws and regulations) to the long term care administrators' examination and licensing boards and authorities of the United States. Regular members are licensing boards; associate members are individuals; subscribing members are non-profit oprganizations and educational institutions. Membership: $500/year (regular); $70/year (associate/subscribing).

Publications:
Information for Candidates Handbook. a.
NAB College Directory & LTC Licensure Requirements. bien.
NAB Newsletter. q.
NAB NHA Study Guide & CD-Rom. every 5 years.
NAB RC/AL Study Guide & CD-Rom. every 5 years.

Meetings/Conferences:
Semi-annual Meetings: June and November
1999 - Scottsdale, AZ
1999 - Baltimore, MD
2000 - Seattle, WA
2000 - Miami Beach, FL

Nat'l Ass'n of Boards of Examiners of Nursing Home Administrators (1970)
Historical Note
Became the Nat'l Ass'n of Boards of Examiners of Long Term Care Administrators in 1997.

Nat'l Ass'n of Boards of Pharmacy (1904)
700 Busse Hwy.
Park Ridge, IL   60068-2402
Tel: (847)698-6227   Fax: (847)698-0124
Members: 57 states or jurisdictions
Staff: 35
Annual Budget: $5-10,000,000
Exec. Director/Secretary: Carmen A. Catizone

Historical Note
Serves all American boards of pharmacy in matters of interstate reciprocity of licensure, uniform examination and licensing as well as other matters of mutual concern. $250/state board.

Publications:
NABP Newsletter. 10/year.
NABP Proceedings. a.
NABP Survey of Pharmacy Law. a.

Meetings/Conferences:
Annual Meetings: Spring/300
1999 - Albuquerque, NM/May 22-26

Nat'l Ass'n of Boat Manufacturers (1945)
200 E. Randolph Drive, Suite 5100
Chicago, IL   60601-6436
Tel: (312)946-6200   Fax: (312)946-0388
Members: 355 boat manufacturers
Staff: 35
Annual Budget: $100-250,000
President: Sylvan Hamburger

Historical Note
Members are makers of pleasure boats. A partner-affiliate of the Nat'l Marine Manufacturers Ass'n, which provides administrative support and with which it shares offices.

Meetings/Conferences:
Annual Meetings: Chicago in conjunction with the Marine Trade Exhibition.

Nat'l Ass'n of Bond Lawyers (1979)
1761 S. Naperville Road, Suite 105
Wheaton, IL   60187-8146
Tel: (630)690-1135   Fax: (630)690-1685
E-Mail: nabl@ntsource.com
Web Site: http://www.nabl.org
Members: 3,000 individuals
Staff: 4
Annual Budget: $1-2,000,000
Exec. Director: Patricia Appelhans

Historical Note
Members are lawyers specializing in the legal problems of debt obligations of the various states and their political subdivisions. Membership: $200/year (over 5 years of practice); $100/year (less than 5 years of practice).

Publications:
Directory. a.
Newsletter. q. adv.

Meetings/Conferences:

Nat'l Ass'n of Brick Distributors (1956)
Historical Note
Merged with Brick Institute of America in 1997 to form Brick Industry Ass'n.

Nat'l Ass'n of Broadcast Employees and Technicians (1934)
501 3rd St., N.W., Suite 880
Washington, DC   20001-2797
Tel: (202)434-1254   Fax: (202)434-1426
Web Site: http://www.nabetcwa.org
Members: 10,000 individuals
Staff: 11
Annual Budget: $5-10,000,000
Sector President: John S. Clark

Historical Note
Organized as a company union in 1934 by the National Broadcasting Company under the title, Association of Technical Employees. Broke away from NBC in 1940 and changed its name to the National Association of Broadcast Engineers and Technicians. Chartered as an industrial union in 1951 by the Congress of Industrial Organizations under the name, National Association of Broadcast Employees and Technicians. Merged with the Communications Workers of America, AFL-CIO, January 1, 1994. Membership: 1.666% of gross wages.

Publications:
NABET News. bi-m.

Meetings/Conferences:

Nat'l Ass'n of Broadcasters (1922)
1771 N St., N.W.
Washington, DC   20036-2891
Tel: (202)429-5300   Fax: (202)429-5343
Web Site: http://www.nba.org
Members: 7,500 radio, tv stations & associates
Staff: 165
Annual Budget: $25-50,000,000
President & C.E.O.: Edward O. Fritts
Senior V. President, Corporate Communications: Dennis Wharton
Exec. V. President, Corporate Communications: Rory Benson
Exec. V.P., Govt. Relations: James C. May
Senior V. Pres., Conventions & Exhibits: Haidee Calore
Senior V. President, Meetings and Special Events: Kathleen L. Muller
V. President, Science and Technology: John Marino
Exec. V. President, Operations and Business Development: John A. Knebel

Exec. V. President/C.F.O.: Kenneth D. Almgren
Exec. V.P./General Counsel: Henry L. Baumann
Sr. V.P., Finance/Controller: Mary P. Dickson

Historical Note
In 1951 NAB merged with the Television Broadcasters Ass'n and changed its name to the Nat'l Ass'n of Radio and Television Broadcasters; in 1958 the present name was reassumed. Absorbed the Daytime Broadcasters Ass'n in 1985 and the Nat'l Radio Broadcasters Ass'n in 1986. Connected with the Television and Radio Political Action Committee (TARPAC). The Television Information Office is an affliate of NAB. NAB upholds the American system of broadcasting, free from government censorship, and combats discriminatory legislative proposals against broadcasting and advertising. Has an annual budget of approximately $27 million.

Publications:
Engineering Conference Proceedings. a.
NAB Daily News. d.
RadioWeek. w. adv.
TV Today. w. adv.

Meetings/Conferences:
Semi-Annual Meetings: Spring and Fall(Radio Convention)
1999 – Las Vegas, NV/April 19-22
1999 – New Orleans, LA/Sept. 15-18
2000 – Las Vegas, NV/April 10-13
2000 – /Sept. 13-16

Nat'l Ass'n of Business and Educational Radio (1965)
Historical Note
Absorbed by Personal Communications Industry Ass'n in 1996.

Nat'l Ass'n of Business and Industrial Saleswomen (1983)
5107 N. Mesa Drive
Castle Rock, CO　80104
Tel: (303)660-3693
E-Mail: NABIS@JUNO.COM
Staff: 2
Annual Budget: $50-100,000
Exec. Director: Alan K. Lovejoy
Administrative Director: Char King

Historical Note
NABPS members are women in business and business sales. Membership: $250/year (individual); $450/year (organization/company).

Publications:
E-Zines. irreg.

Nat'l Ass'n of Business Economists (1959)
1233 20th St., N.W., Suite 505
Washington, DC　20036-2304
Tel: (202)463-6223　　　Fax: (202)463-6239
E-Mail: nabe@nabe.com
Web Site: http://www.nabe.com
Members: 3,500 individuals
Staff: 3
Annual Budget: $250-500,000
Exec. Director: Susan Doolittle

Historical Note
A professional society of persons with an active interest in business economics who are employed by private, institutional or academic concerns in the area of business. Membership: $75/year (individual); $400/year (institution).

Publications:
Business Economics. q. adv.
Employment Oportunities for Business Economists. q.
Industry Survey. q.
Membership Directory. a. adv.
NABE News. bi-m. adv.
NABE Outlook. q.
Policy Survey. semi-a.
Salary Survey. bien.

Meetings/Conferences:
Annual Meetings: Fall/300
1999 – San Francisco(Hyatt)

Nat'l Ass'n of Business Political Action Committees (1977)
2300 Clarendon Blvd., Suite 401
Arlington, VA　22201-3367
Tel: (703)516-4708　　　Fax: (703)516-9855
E-Mail: NABPAC@aol.com
Members: 130 corporate & trade ass'n PACS
Staff: 2
Annual Budget: $250-500,000
Managing Consultant: Geoff Ziebart

Historical Note
Members are companies and trade associations sponsoring political action committees for their employees and members. Provides a forum for improving PAC management, solicitation and contributions. Lobbies on campaign finance legislation. Membership: $750-4,500/year (organization).

Publications:
Membership Directory. a.
NABPAC News Memo. m.
The PAC Professional. q.

Meetings/Conferences:
1999 – Washington, DC

Nat'l Ass'n of Business Travel Agents (1980)
3255 Wilshire Blvd., Suite 1601
Los Angeles, CA　90010-1418
Tel: (213)382-3335　　　Fax: (213)480-7712
Members: 1,600 individuals
Staff: 6
Director: Stuart J. Faber

Historical Note
NABTA members are travel agents specializing in corporate and business travel.

Publications:
First Class Executive Travel. bi-m.

Nat'l Ass'n of Buying Services
Historical Note
Became United Buying Services in 1996.

Nat'l Ass'n of Canoe Liveries and Outfitters
Historical Note
Became (1996) Professional Paddlesports Ass'n.

Nat'l Ass'n of Casual Furniture Retailers
Historical Note
Became (1998) Casual Furniture Retailers.

Nat'l Ass'n of Casualty and Surety Executives (1911)
Historical Note
Became The Council of Insurance Company Executives in 1996.

Nat'l Ass'n of Catalog Showroom Merchandisers (1972)
186 Birch Hill Road
Locust Valley, NY　11560-1832
Tel: (516)676-7509　　　Fax: (516)754-4364
Members: 350 companies
Staff: 3
Annual Budget: $250-500,000
President: Jean S. Coticchio

Historical Note
Regular members are catalog showroom operators and catalog publishers and associate members are suppliers. Membership: $450/year (supplier), $190 per showroom/year (operator).

Publications:
Member Bulletin. m.
NACSM News. q.
Year Census of Catalog Showrooms. a.

Meetings/Conferences:
Annual Meetings: January/Chicago, IL(McCormick Place)/300

Nat'l Ass'n of Catastrophe Adjusters (1976)
P.O. Box 821864
North Richland Hills, TX　76182
Tel: (817)498-3466　　　Fax: (817)498-0480
E-Mail: nacatadj@aol.com
Web Site: http://www.metrongroup.com/naca/
Members: 790 individuals, 67 business associates
Staff: 1
Annual Budget: $25-50,000
Staff Assistant: Lori Ringo

Historical Note
NACA is a non-profit organization dedicated to the adjustment of losses arising from hurricane, hail, tornado, flood, earthquake and other catastrophes. NACA is concerned with improving professional standards, insuring working relations among members and promoting the general welfare of the individual members. Membership: $100/year.

Publications:
Naca News. q.
Roster. a.

Meetings/Conferences:
Annual Meetings: January
1999 – New Orleans, LA(Doubletree)/Jan. 18-21/300
2000 – Miami, FL

Nat'l Ass'n of Catering Executives (1958)
60 Revere Drive, Suite 500
Northbrook, IL　60062
Tel: (847)480-9080　　　Fax: (847)480-9282
Web Site: http://www.nace.net
Members: 3,000 individuals
Staff: 7
Annual Budget: $250-500,000
Exec. Director: John R. Waxman

Historical Note
Founded as the Banquet Managers Guild in New York City on June 3, 1958; assumed its present name in 1977. Membership: $175/year (individual); $1,750-2,750/year (company).

Publications:
The Professional Caterer. bi-m. adv.

Meetings/Conferences:

Nat'l Ass'n of Catholic Chaplains (1965)
P.O. Box 07473
3501 South Lake Drive
Milwaukee, WI　53207-0473
Tel: (414)483-4898　　　Fax: (414)483-6712
E-Mail: nacc@nacc.org
Web Site: http://www.nacc.org
Members: 3,600 individuals
Staff: 6
Annual Budget: $500-1,000,000
Exec. Director: Rev. Joseph Driscoll

Historical Note
Members are Catholic priests, sisters, permanent deacons, and laity engaged in professional health care and related institutional and parish ministries. Membership: $135/yr. (certified and non-certified).

Publications:
Vision. 10/yr.

Meetings/Conferences:
Annual Meetings: Spring, with Catholic Health Ass'n
1999 – San Diego, CA/April 22-25

Nat'l Ass'n of Catholic School Teachers (1978)
1700 Sansom St., Suite 903
Philadelphia, PA　19103
Tel: (215)665-0993　　　Fax: (215)568-8270
Members: 5,000 individuals
Staff: 1
President: Rita C. Schwartz

Historical Note
NACST members are teachers in Catholic schools. Membership: $60/year (individual).

Publications:
NACST Newsworthy. q.

Meetings/Conferences:

Nat'l Ass'n of Cellular Agents
Historical Note
Became the Wireless Dealers Ass'n in 1996.

Nat'l Ass'n of Certified Valuation Analysts (1990)
Brickyard Towers, Suite 110
1245 E. Brickyard Road
Salt Lake City, UT　84106-2563
Tel: (801)486-0600　　　Fax: (801)486-7500
Toll Free: (800)677 - 2009
E-Mail: NACVA@NACVA.COM
Web Site: http://WWW.NACVA.COM
Members: 4,000 individuals
President: Parnell Black, MBA, CPA,
Director, Technical & Research Services: Rosemarie Smith,, Ph.D.
Controller: Steve Marsten
Manager, Sales and Member Services: Sherri Lawless
Executive Director: Ross Alvord

Historical Note
NACVA member are professionals, mainly certified public accountants, who provide business valuation services. Awards to CPA's the Certified Valuation Analyst (CVA) designation upon completion of an accreditation program. Membership: $265/year.

Publications:
NACVA Membership and Resource Directory. a. adv.
Reference Guide. bi-a. adv.
Technical Support Group Directory. a.
The Valuation Examiner. bi-m. adv.

Meetings/Conferences:
1999 – Atlanta, GA/May 19-22

Nat'l Ass'n of Chain Drug Stores (1933)
413 N. Lee St.
P.O. Box 1417
Alexandria, VA　22313-1480
Tel: (703)549-3001　　　Fax: (703)836-4869
Web Site: http://www.nacds.org
Members: 135 chains and 30,000 pharmacies
Staff: 90
Annual Budget: $25-50,000,000
President & C.E.O.: Ronald L. Ziegler
Managing Director, Public Affairs: Phillip L. Schneider
V. President, Government Affairs: David F. Lambert
Sr. V. President, Pharmacy and Policy: Kurt A. Proctor, Ph.D.
Manager, Meetings: Emily T. Wheeler
Sr. V. President, Finance and Admin.: R. James Huber

Historical Note
NACDS members are retail chain drugstore companies with four or more stores. In addition, NACDS membership includes includes over 1,200 suppliers of goods and services to the chain drug industry. Sponsors and supports the NACDS Political Action Committee. Has an annual budget of approximately $17 million. Membership: $1,000-27,000/year.

Publications:
Annual Report. a.
Executive Newsletter. bi-w.
Federal Report. m.
Industry Calendar. a.
Membership Directory. a.
Sourcebook. a.
State Capitol Report. m.

Meetings/Conferences:
1999 – Palm Beach, FL(Breakers)/April 24-28

Nat'l Ass'n of Chain Manufacturers (1932)
P.O. Box 3143
York, PA　17402-0143
Tel: (717)840-1304
Members: 9 companies
Staff: 1
Annual Budget: $25-50,000
Exec. Director: William F. Westerhold

Publications:
Specifications-Tire Chains. irreg.
Specifications-Welded Chain. irreg.
Specifications-Weldless Chain. irreg.

Meetings/Conferences:
Semi-Annual Meetings: Spring and Fall, Chicago, IL

Nat'l Ass'n of Charterboat Operators (1991)
1600 Duke St., Suite 220
Alexandria, VA　22314
Tel: (703)519-1714　　　Fax: (703)519-1716
Toll Free: (800)745 - 6094
E-Mail: naco@charterboat.org
Web Site: http://www.charterboat.org
Members: 4,100 individuals
Staff: 4
Annual Budget: $100-250,000
Exec. Director: Jeffrey C. Smith
Dir., Government Affairs: Amy Taylor
Programs Director: Laura Norfolk

Historical Note
NACO members are operators of sportfishing, diving and small excursion vessels. NACO provides group charterboat insurance and a drug testing consortium. Membership: $30/year (individual).

Publications:
NACO Report. bi-m. adv.
Meetings/Conferences:
1999 – Alexandria, VA(Sheraton Suites)/Jan. 28-30/75

Nat'l Ass'n of Chemical Distributors *(1971)*
1525 Wilson Blvd., Suite 750
Arlington, VA 22209-2411
Tel: (703)527-6223 *Fax:* (703)527-7747
Web Site: http://www.nacd.com
Members: 335 companies
Staff: 13
Annual Budget: $2-5,000,000
Exec. V. President: D. Christopher Cathcart
Director of Communications: Kathee Baker
Director of Government Affairs: Geoff O'Hara
Director of Operations: Anne Marie Baranick
Historical Note
Distributors of industrial chemicals. Supports and sustains the NACD Educational Foundation. Membership: $1,175-18,750/year (company).
Publications:
The Chemical Distributor. 10/year.
Meetings/Conferences:
Annual Meetings: November-December/800

Nat'l Ass'n of Chemical Recyclers *(1979)*
1900 M St., N.W., Suite 750
Washington, DC 20036
Tel: (202)296-1725 *Fax:* (202)296-2530
Members: 30 companies
Staff: 2
Annual Budget: $250-500,000
Exec. Director: Christopher Goebel
Asst. Director, Communications: Joann Wright
Historical Note
Members are companies whose primary business is the reclamation of solvents and other chemicals from industrial waste streams and the recycling of those refined materials for industrial use. Formerly (1991) Nat'l Ass'n of Solvent Recyclers. Membership: $1,080-25,000/year (company).
Publications:
NACR News 'n' Views. m.
Meetings/Conferences:
Semi-Annual Meetings: Spring and October
1999 – Monterery, CA

Nat'l Ass'n of Chewing Gum Manufacturers *(1918)*
236 Route 38 West
Moorestown, NJ 08057
Tel: (609)231-8500 *Fax:* (609)231-4664
E-Mail: nacgm@ahint.com
Members: 20 companies
Staff: 2
Annual Budget: $250-500,000
Secretary-Treasurer: William L. MacMillan, III, CAE
Asst. Secretary/Treasurer: Robert Waller, Jr.
Meetings/Conferences:

Nat'l Ass'n of Chiefs of Police *(1962)*
3801 Biscayne Blvd.
Miami, FL 33137
Tel: (305)573-0202 *Fax:* (305)573-9819
Web Site: http://www.aphf.org
Members: 11,000 individuals
Staff: 22
Annual Budget: $500-1,000,000
President: George Vuilleevmier, Jr.
Exec. Treasurer: Debra K. Chitwood
Exec. Director: Donna M. Shepherd
Publications Editor: Jim Gordon
Historical Note
Formerly Nat'l Police Museum. Operates the American Police Academy in Washington as its educational arm. Also maintains the American Police Hall of Fame and Museum. Membership: $50/year.
Publications:
Chief of Police Magazine.
Meetings/Conferences:
Annual Meetings: With the American Federation of Police

Nat'l Ass'n of Child Advocates
1522 K St., N.W., Suite 600
Washington, DC 20005-1202
Tel: (202)289-0777 *Fax:* (202)289-0776
E-Mail: naca@childadvocacy.org
Web Site: http://www.childadvocacy.org
Members: 52 organizations
Staff: 9
Annual Budget: $1-2,000,000
President: Tamara Lucas Copeland
Chief Financial Officer: Sharon McIntosh Stokes
Director, Member Services: Morris Rodenstein
Historical Note
Membership: $500/year minumum, based on budget.
Meetings/Conferences:
Annual Meetings: January

Nat'l Ass'n of Child Care Professionals *(1984)*
304-A Roanoke St.
Christiansburg, VA 24073
Tel: (540)382-5819 *Fax:* (540)382-6529
Toll Free: (800)537-1118
E-Mail: Admin@naccp.org
Web Site: http://www.naccp.org
Members: 2,000 individuals
Staff: 5
Annual Budget: $250-500,000
Exec. Director: Donna K. Thornton

Membership Service Coordinator: Sue Self
Historical Note
Professional association for supervisors and administrators of child care facilities. Membership: $75/year (individual);$63.75/year (associate) and $35/year(student).
Publications:
Caring for Your Children Newsletter. bi-m. adv.
Professional Connections Newsletter. bi-m. adv.
Teamwork Newsletter. bi-m. adv.
Meetings/Conferences:
1999 – Austin, TX(Hyatt Regency)

Nat'l Ass'n of Child Care Resource and Referral Agencies *(1987)*
1319 F St., N.W., Suite 810
Washington, DC 20004-1106
Tel: (202)393-5501 *Fax:* (202)393-1109
E-Mail: hn5017
Members: 250 individuals, 580 organizations
Staff: 30
Annual Budget: $10-25,000,000
Exec. Director: Yasmina S. Vinci
Director, Finance: Lorraine Cyr
Historical Note
NACCRRA promotes the development, maintenance and expansion of quality community-based child care resource and referral services. Voting members are resource and referral organizations. Auxiliary members are organizations and individuals supporting NACCRRA's goals. Membership: $50-$350/year, varies by budget (voting); $50-5,000 (auxiliary).
Publications:
CCR&R Issues. q. adv.
Meetings/Conferences:
Annual Meetings: Winter

Nat'l Ass'n of Childbearing Centers *(1983)*
3123 Gottschall Road
Perkiomenville, PA 18074-9546
Tel: (215)234-8068 *Fax:* (215)234-8829
E-Mail: reachnacc@birthcenters.org
Web Site: http://www.BirthCenters.org
Members: 850 individuals, 850 birth centers
Staff: 5
Annual Budget: $250-500,000
Exec. Director: Kate Bauer
Meetings Coordinator: Tammy Pleasants
Historical Note
NACC is a not-for-profit membership organization which is a comprehensive resource on birth centers. Working on public and policy levels in government, industry and the health professions, NACC is dedicated to developing quality, holistic services for childbearing families that promote self-reliance and confidence in birth and parenting. NACC collects and disseminates information on birth centers. It sets nat'l standards for birth center operation, promotes state regulation for licensure, and nat'l accreditation by the Commission for the Accreditation of Birth Centers. Provides a Parent Information Service for consumers looking for birth centers. Membership: $20-120/year (individual); $400-1,000/year (organization/company).
Publications:
Membership Directory. a.
NACC News. q.
Meetings/Conferences:
Annual Meetings: September-October
1999 – San Diego, CA(Catamaran Resort)/Oct. 6-10
2000 – Boston, MA
2001 – Houston, TX
2002 – Orlando, FL

Nat'l Ass'n of Children's Hospitals and Related Institutions *(1968)*
401 Wythe St.
Alexandria, VA 22314
Tel: (703)684-1355 *Fax:* (703)684-1589
Members: 152 hospitals
Staff: 47
Annual Budget: $2-5,000,000
President and C.E.O.: Lawrence A. McAndrews
V. President, Public Affairs: Lisa M. Tate
V.P., Public Policy: Peters D. Willson
V. President, Operations: Mary Gorman
Asst. Dir. Member Services: Carolyn Bell
Historical Note
NACHRI promotes the well-being of children through support of children's hospitals and related institutions committed to excellence in treating, healing and nurturing children. Members are free standing hospitals providing a range of services from general acute care to specialty care. Other members include universities and medical centers specializing in the care of children.
Publications:
Children's Hospitals Today. q.
Meetings/Conferences:
1999 – Detroit, MI(Westin Rennisance)Sept.
2000 – Philadelphia, PA(Philadelphia Marriott)/Sept. 25-27
2001 – Amelia Island, FL(Amelia Island Plant)/Oct. 8-10
2002 – Seattle, WA

Nat'l Ass'n of Church and Institutional Financing Organizations *(1967)*
c/o Reliance Trust Co.
3384 Peachtree Rd., Suite 900
Atlanta, GA 30326
Tel: (440)266-0663 *Fax:* (440)365-7055
Toll Free: (800)241-5569
Members: 24 organizations
Annual Budget: $10-25,000
Secretary/Treasurer: A.J. Braswell

Historical Note
Reorganized in 1983. NACIFO assists religious and non-profit institutions in obtaining financing for their projects. Membership: $400/year (organization/company).
Meetings/Conferences:
Annual Meetings: Fall
1999 – Sarasota, FL/45

Nat'l Ass'n of Church Business Administration *(1957)*
7001 Grapevine Hwy., Suite 324
Fort Worth, TX 76180-8691
Tel: (817)284-1732 *Fax:* (817)284-1762
E-Mail: info@nacbanet.org
Web Site: http://www.nacbanet.org
Members: 2,000 individuals
Staff: 4
Annual Budget: $250-500,000
Exec. Director: Simeon May
Historical Note
Business managers of local congregations, military chapels or other religious institutions. Provides training, resources, and support for managers of all Christian churches. Also provides a certification program in church administration. Membership: $120/year.
Publications:
NACBA Gram. m.
NACBA Ledger. q.
National Church Staff Salary Survey. bien.
Meetings/Conferences:
Annual Meetings: July
1999 – Nashville, TN(Opryland)/July 2-6
2000 – Atlanta, GA(Marriott Marquis)/July 14-18
2001 – Seattle, WA(DoubleTree Hotel)/July 20-24

Nat'l Ass'n of Church Food Service *(1990)*
76 Ivy Pkwy., N.E.
Atlanta, GA 30342-4241
Tel: (404)261-1794 *Fax:* (404)266-0734
Members: 225 individuals
Exec. Director: Carolyn B. Clayton
Historical Note
NACFS members are directors of church food services. Offers certification program.
Publications:
Membership Directory.
Newsletter.
Meetings/Conferences:

Nat'l Ass'n of Church Personnel Administrators *(1971)*
100 East 8th St.
Cincinnati, OH 43202-2129
Tel: (513)421-3134 *Fax:* (513)421-3085
E-Mail: nacpa@dot-net.net
Web Site: http://www.nacpa.org
Members: 1,200 individuals
Staff: 5
Annual Budget: $500-1,000,000
Exec. Director: Ellen Doyle, OSU
Historical Note
Formed by the Nat'l Federation of Priests' Councils at the University of Notre Dame in October, 1971. Members are personnel administrators in church-related organizations. Membership: $175/year (individual), $425/year (company).
Publications:
NACPA Newsletter. bi-m. adv.
Meetings/Conferences:
Annual Meetings: Fall
1999 – Toronto, CA(Delta Chelsen Inn)/Nov. 4-7/300
2000 – Arlington, VA(Crystal Gateway Marriott)/Nov. 9-12/350
2001 – Denver, CO(Hyatt Regency)/Nov. 8-11

Nat'l Ass'n of Claims Assistance Professionals *(1991)*
Historical Note
Address unknown in 1998.

Nat'l Ass'n of Clergy Hypnotherapists *(1984)*
Historical Note
Merged with Nat'l Soc. of Hypnotherapists in 1997.

Nat'l Ass'n of Clinical Nurse Specialists *(1995)*
4700 W. Lake Ave.
Glenview, IL 60025
Tel: (847)375-4740 *Fax:* (847)375-4777
E-Mail: dburgher@amctec.com
Exec. Director: Diane Burgher
Historical Note
NACNS regular members are nurses who are masters-prepared as clinical nurse specialists, masters-prepared in related areas practicing as clinical nurse specialists, or doctorally-prepared and involved in the education of clinical nurse specialists. Membership: $98/year (individual).
Publications:
Clinical Nurse Specialists. bi-m.
Meetings/Conferences:

Nat'l Ass'n of College Admissions Counselors *(1937)*
Historical Note
Became the Nat'l Ass'n for College Admission Counseling in 1996.

Nat'l Ass'n of College and University Attorneys *(1961)*
One Dupont Circle, N.W., Suite 620
Washington, DC 20036
Tel: (202)833-8390 *Fax:* (202)296-8379
Web Site: http://www.nacua.org
Members: 660 colleges and universities
Staff: 14
Annual Budget: $1-2,000,000
Exec. Director and C.E.O.: Sheila Trice Bell

Meeting Manager: Susan Browne Shelton
Dir., Administration: Paul L. Parsons
Manager, Publications: Linda Henderson
Manager of Information Services: John R. Bishop

Historical Note
NACUA was established to improve the quality of legal assistance to colleges and universities by educating attorneys and administrators to the nature of campus legal issues. NACUA produces publications, sponsors seminars and operates a clearinghouse through which attorneys share knowledge and work-product on current legal problems. Members are accredited institutions of higher education in the U.S. and Canada; each institution may be represented by several attorneys. Membership: $270-3,155/year (organization).

Publications:
Journal of College and University Law. q.
The College Law Digest. bi-m.

Meetings/Conferences:
Annual Meetings: June/650
1999 – Nashville, TN(Opryland Hotel)/June 27-30
2000 – Washington, DC(J.W. Marriott)/June 25-28
2001 – Boston, MA(Marriott Copley Place)/June 26-29
2002 – Minneapolis, MN(Hyatt Regency Minneapolis)/June 22-25

Nat'l Ass'n of College and University Business Officers (1956)

2501 M St., N.W., Suite 400
Washington, DC   20037-1308
Tel: (202)861-2500   *Fax:* (202)861-2580
Web Site: http://www.nacubo.org
Members: 19,500 individuals, 2,600 institutions
Staff: 52
Annual Budget: $5-10,000,000
President: James E. Morley, Jr.
Director of Communications: Carla Balakgie
Dir., Public Policy/Mangement Programs: Christine Larger
V.P., Educational Svcs.: Lynn Malarz
Dir., Business Affairs/Treasurer: Zhong Wei
Membership/Publications Manager: Maryann Terrana

Historical Note
Formerly (1962) Nat'l Federation of College and University Business Officers Ass'ns. Represents accredited, non-profit institutions of higher learning approved for membership by a regional business officers association. NACUBO members represent approximately two-thirds of all institutions of higher learning in the U.S. Has an annual budget of approximately $8 million. Membership: $494-3,705/year (organization).

Publications:
Business Officer Magazine. m. adv.
Executive Strategies. q.
Federal Auditing Information. bi-m.
Financial Accounting and Reporting. bi-m.
Membership Directory. a. adv.
Special Action Report. irreg.

Meetings/Conferences:
Annual Meetings: Summer/1,200
1999 – San Antonio, TX/July 17-20
2000 – Chicago, IL/July 22-25

Nat'l Ass'n of College and University Chaplains and Directors of Religious Life (1948)

Historical Note
Address unknown in 1996.

Nat'l Ass'n of College and University Food Services (1958)

1405 S. Harrison, Suite 305
East Lansing, MI   48824-5242
Tel: (517)332-2494   *Fax:* (517)332-8144
Web Site: http://www.nacufs.org/nacufs
Members: 650 institutions, 410345 companies
Staff: 5
Annual Budget: $500-1,000,000
Exec. Director: Joseph H. Spina, Ph.D., CAE
Education Coordinator: Tracy Lee Hulin
Member Services Coordinator: Mary O'Connor

Historical Note
Membership: $210-550/year (organization).

Publications:
Campus Dining Today. q. adv.
First Monday. m.
NACUFS Annual Report. a.
NACUFS Directory. a. adv.
NACUFS Journal.

Meetings/Conferences:
Annual Meetings: Summer/750
1999 – Baltimore, MD/July 6-10

Nat'l Ass'n of College Auxiliary Services (1969)

P.O. Box 870
Staunton, VA   24402-0870
Tel: (540)885-8826   *Fax:* (540)885-8355
Web Site: http://www.nacas.org
Members: 1,400 individuals
Staff: 7
Annual Budget: $500-1,000,000
Exec. Director: Manuel R. Cunard
Asst. Exec. Dir., Educational Programs: Laura Ryman
Associate Exec. Director: Jeffery Perdue
Member Services Coordinator: Julie Arnett
Director, Publications: David Rood

Historical Note
Founded as the Ass'n of College Auxiliary Services, it assumed its present name in 1973. Members are directors of college auxiliary services such as book stores, laundries, food services, housing, vending, printing, etc. Membership: $250-350/year (organization/company).

Publications:
College Service Administration. bi-m. adv.

Meetings/Conferences:
Annual Meetings: Fall/650
1999 – Dallas, TX(Loew's Anatole)/Nov. 14-17
2000 – Las Vegas, NV(MGM Grand)/Oct. 14-18
2001 – New Orleans, LA(Hyatt)/Nov. 3-8
2002 – Vancouver, BC, Canada(Pan Pacific, Waterfront, Hyatt)/Oct. 12-16
2003 – Colorado Springs, CO(The Broadmoor)/Nov. 2-5

Nat'l Ass'n of College Broadcasters (1988)

71 George St.
Providence, RI   02912-1824
Tel: (401)863-2225   *Fax:* (401)863-2221
Members: 1000 individuals, 600 member stations
Staff: 4
Annual Budget: $250-500,000
Exec. Director: Kelley Cunningham

Historical Note
Members are student radio/TV stations and individuals with an interest in exchanging ideas, programming and information in the student media community and among students, faculty and professionals. Membership: $75/year (station); $20/year (student/faculty); $30/year (individual).

Publications:
College Broadcaster Magazine. q. adv.
Member NewsFax. m.
NACB Newsletter Poster. q. adv.
Station Handbook. a. adv.

Meetings/Conferences:
Annual Meetings: Fall/1,000

Nat'l Ass'n of College Deans, Registrars, and Admissions Officers (1925)

Albany State University
504 College Drive
Albany, GA   31705
Tel: (912)430-4638   *Fax:* (912)430-2953
Members: 315 individuals
Staff: 1
Annual Budget: $10-25,000
Registrar and Exec. Secretary: Arna Albritten

Historical Note
Deans, registrars and admissions officers of colleges with predominately black enrollments. Formerly (until 1949) known as the Nat'l Ass'n of Collegiate Deans and Registrars in Negro Schools, and (until 1970) the Nat'l Ass'n of College Deans and Registrars. Membership: $100-145/year, based on size of enrollment.

Publications:
Membership Directory. a.
NACDRAO Newsletter. semi-a.
Proceedings of Annual Meeting. a.

Meetings/Conferences:
Annual Meetings: March/125

Nat'l Ass'n of College Stores (1923)

500 East Lorain St.
Oberlin, OH   44074-1298
Tel: (440)775-7777   *Fax:* (440)775-4769
E-Mail: info@nacs.org
Web Site: http://www.nacs.org
Members: 3,019 college stores
Staff: 150
Annual Budget: $5-10,000,000
Acting Exec. Director: Cynthia D'Angelo
Director, Adv/Mktg Programs: Judith Pataky
Dir., Public Relations: Jerry Buchs
Dir., Meetings/Conferences: Viveca Kimble, CMP
Director, Exposition: Richard Chamberline
Assoc. Exec. Director/Dir., Development: Sandra L. Martin
Dir., Professional Development: Janice L. Pierce
Director of Finance: Frank Sulen
Assoc. Exec. Dir.: Larry Daniels, CSP
Associate Exec. Director, Member Relations: Pam Schuck
Associate Exec. Director, Marketing Services: Dave Moffatt
Publications Manager: Cynthia E. Ruckman

Historical Note
Organized in 1923 as an offshoot of the American Booksellers Ass'n. Originally known as the College Bookstore Ass'n. NACS is organized to provide educational and support services and products for the collegiate retail industry and to serve as a unified voice for the college store industry in all significant relationships. NACSCORP is a for-profit subsidiary of NACS which provides products and services to assist member stores. The College Stores Research and Educational Foundation (CSREF) provides management training programs, educational financial support and market research to NACS members. Campus Computer Resellers Alliance is a division of NACS. Has an annual budget of approximately $10 million + 100 million in-profit subsidary. Membership fees vary, based on store size.

Publications:
College Store. 6/yr. adv.
College Store Monthly Planner. a.
NACS Book Buyers Manual. bien.
NACS Campus Marketplace. w. adv.
NACS Directory of Colleges and College Stores. a.
NACS Directory of Publishers. a.
NACS Schedule of College & University Dates.

Meetings/Conferences:
Annual Meetings: April
1999 – Salt Lake City, UT/April 9-13
2000 – Nashville, TN(Opryland Hotel)/March 31-April 4/8000
2001 – New Orleans, LA(Convention Center)/April 6-10/8000
2002 – Los Angeles, CA(Convention Center)/April 5-9/8000

Nat'l Ass'n of College Wind and Percussion Instructors (1951)

Division of Fine Arts
Truman State Univ.
Kirksville, MO   63501
Tel: (816)785-4442   *Fax:* (816)785-7463
Members: 1,400 individuals
Staff: 1
Annual Budget: $10-25,000
Exec. Secretary-Treasurer: Richard Weerts

Historical Note
Associated with the Music Educators Nat'l Conference. Members are those responsible for teaching wind and percussion instruments in American colleges and universities. Membership: $30/year.

Publications:
Bibliography of Papers Appearing in the NACWPI Journal. a.
Holdings of the NACWPI Research Library. a.
NACWPI Journal. q. adv.

Meetings/Conferences:
Biennial Meetings: Even Years
2000 – Washington, DC/March 8-11

Nat'l Ass'n of Colleges and Employers (1956)

62 Highland Ave.
Bethlehem, PA   18017
Tel: (610)868-1421   *Fax:* (610)868-0208
Toll Free: (800)544 - 5272
E-Mail: marilyn@jobweb.org
Web Site: http://www.jobweb.org
Members: 3,300 colleges and employers
Staff: 31
Annual Budget: $2-5,000,000
Exec. Director: Marilyn F. Mackes, Ph.D.
Budget & Accounting Manager: James Mahoney
General Counsel: Rochelle Kaplan
Membership Specialist: Kathleen Katchur
Communications Director: Mimi Collins

Historical Note
Formerly (1953) Ass'n of School and College Placement and (1995) College Placement Council. NACE is a professional association for career services professionals and employers of college graduates. Membership: $360/year.

Publications:
Job Choices. a. adv.
Journal of College Placement. q. adv.
NACE Nat'l Directory: Who's Who. adv.
Salary Survey. q.
Spotlight. bi-w.

Meetings/Conferences:
2001 – Las Vegas, NV(MGM Grnad)/May 29-June 1

Nat'l Ass'n of Colleges and Teachers of Agriculture (1955)

P.O. Box 2088, Agriculture Science Dept.
Sam Houston State University
Huntsville, TX   77341-2088
Tel: (409)294-1226
Members: 1,500 individuals
Staff: 5
Annual Budget: $10-25,000
Secretary/Treasurer: Murray Brown, Ph.D.

Historical Note
NACTA is the organization and publishing organ for discussion of leading edge research on instruction in Agricultural subjects in colleges and universities. Membership: $35/year (individual); $60/year (organization/company).

Publications:
NACTA Journal. q. adv.

Meetings/Conferences:
Annual Meetings: Summer
1999 – Blacksburg, VA(Virginia Polytech Institute)/June 19-22

Nat'l Ass'n of Collegiate Directors of Athletics (1965)

P.O. Box 16428
Cleveland, OH   44116-0428
Tel: (440)892-4000   *Fax:* (440)892-4007
E-Mail: mjcleary@nacda.com
Web Site: http://www.nacda.com
Members: 6,100 individuals, 1,600 institutions
Staff: 10
Annual Budget: $1-2,000,000
Exec. Director: Michael J. Cleary
Asst. Exec. Director/Communication: Laurie Garrison
Meeting Coordinator: Dorothy A. Sikkila
Assoc. Exec. Director: Bob Vecchione
Asst. Director, Administration: Pat Manak
Business Manager: Alice Belt
Administrative Assistant: Jude Killy
Administrative Assistant: Becky Parise

Historical Note
Members are directors of athletics and athletic staff members at two- and four year institutions. Membership: $50-750/year (based on NCAA division, size of school).

Publications:
Athletics Administration. bi-m. adv.

Meetings/Conferences:
Annual Meetings: June
1999 – Reno, NV(Reno Hilton)/June 13-16/1200

Nat'l Ass'n of Collegiate Gymnastics Coaches (Men)

Historical Note
Became (1995) College Gymnastics Ass'n.

Nat'l Ass'n of Collegiate Marketing Administrators (1990)

P.O. Box 16428
Cleveland, OH   44116
Tel: (440)892-4000   *Fax:* (440)892-4007

E-Mail: mdukov@nacda.com
Web Site: http://www.nacda.com
Members: 400 individuals
Staff: 3
Exec. Director: Mike Cleary
Senior Staff Administrator: Bob Varchione

Historical Note
NACMA members are public relations and marketing professionals in college and university athletics departments. Promotes a standard of ethics and provides professional support to members. An affiliate of Nat'l Ass'n of Collegiate Directors of Athletics, which provides administrative support. Membership: $50-75/year (individual); $125/year (affiliates).

Publications:
NACMA Corner in Athletics Administration. bi-m. adv.
NACMA Ideas. q.

Meetings/Conferences:
Annual Meetings: June
1999 – Reno, NV

Nat'l Ass'n of Collegiate Women Athletic Administrators (1979)
Historical Note
Address unknown in 1997.

Nat'l Ass'n of Colored Women's Clubs (1896)
5808 16th St., N.W.
Washington, DC 20011
Tel: (202)726-2044   Fax: (202)726-0023
Members: 1000 organizations
Staff: 2
Annual Budget: $50-100,000
Exec. Secretary: Carole A. Early

Historical Note
Formed through a merger of the Nat'l Colored Women's League and the Nat'l Federation of Afro-American Women. Sponsors the National Association of Youth Clubs.

Publications:
National Notes. 2/year.

Meetings/Conferences:
Biennial Meetings: Even years
2000 – /July 25-Aug 3

Nat'l Ass'n of Commissions for Women (1970)
8630 Fenton St., #934
Silver Spring, MD 20901-3803
Tel: (301)585-8101   Fax: (301)585-3445
Toll Free: (800)338 - 9267
E-Mail: NACW2@NACW.com
Web Site: http://NACW.com
Members: 263 member commissions
Staff: 2
President: Patricia T. Hendel

Publications:
Breakthrough. q. adv.
Health. adv. adv.

Meetings/Conferences:
1999 – Boston, MA(Swissotel)/200

Nat'l Ass'n of Community Action Agencies (1968)
1100 17th Street, N.W., Suite 500
Washington, DC 20036
Tel: (202)265-7546   Fax: (202)265-8850
Web Site: http://www.nacaa.org
Members: 1,400 individuals, 700 agencies
Staff: 14
Annual Budget: $1-2,000,000
Exec. Director: John Buckstead
Dir., Communications: Bill Whoelre
Dir., Special Projects/Events: Tom Blackburn Rodriguez
Director of Membership: Avril Weisman

Historical Note
Formerly (1982) the Nat'l Community Action Agency Executive Directors Ass'n. Members are community action and limited purpose agencies. Membership: $175-925/year.

Publications:
Annual Conference Program. a. adv.
Annual Report. a.
Directory of Community Action Agencies. a.
Network. m.

Meetings/Conferences:
Annual Meetings: Fall
1999 – Chicago, IL

Nat'l Ass'n of Community Development Loan Funds
Historical Note
Became Nat'l Community Capital Ass'n in 1997.

Nat'l Ass'n of Community Health Centers (1970)
1330 New Hampshire Ave., N.W., Suite 122
Washington, DC 20036
Tel: (202)659-8008   Fax: (202)659-8519
Web Site: http://www.nachc.com
Members: 750 community health centers
Staff: 40
President and C.E.O.: Thomas Van Coverden
V.P., Policy Research/Analysis: Daniel R. Hawkins, Jr.
Director, Meetings: Jennifer B. Shehan
Director, Education and Training: Millicent Runner
V. President, Finance/Administration: Mary Hawbecker
Exec. V. President: Claudia G. Gibson
V. President, Programs and Planning: Malvise A. Scott

Historical Note
Formerly (1970) Nat'l Ass'n of Neighborhood Health Center Directors and Administrators and (1977) Nat'l Ass'n of Neighborhood Health Centers. NACHC is an organization which works to assure the continued growth and development of community-based health care programs by providing education,

training, and technical assistance to health center staff and board members. Membership: $30/yr.(individual); organizational fee based on budget.

Publications:
Link Newsletter. q. adv.
Vanguard. q. adv.
Washington Update. m.

Meetings/Conferences:
1999 – Miami, FL/Sept. 23-29

Nat'l Ass'n of Composers, USA (1932)
P.O. Box 49256, Barrington Station
Los Angeles, CA 90049
Tel: (310)541-8213   Fax: (310)373-3244
E-Mail: bbennettaucracl.ucr.edu
Web Site: http://www.thebook.com/nacusa/
Members: 600 individuals
Annual Budget: under $10,000
President: Marshall Bialosky

Historical Note
Successor (1975) to the Nat'l Ass'n of American Composers and Conductors headquartered in New York City. NACUSA members are composers, conductors and performers of music, and interested individuals. Membership: $20/year, except in New York, Los Angeles and San Fransisco; $40/year.

Publications:
Composer/USA. 3/year. adv.

Nat'l Ass'n of Computer Consultant Businesses (1987)
P.O. Box 4266
Greensboro, NC 27404
Tel: (336)273-8878   Fax: (336)273-2878
Web Site: http://www.naccb.org
Members: 375 companies
Staff: 8
Annual Budget: $100-250,000
Exec. Director: Peggy Smith

Historical Note
NACCB members are companies providing technical support services to clients such as programming, systems analysis and software/hardware engineering.

Publications:
Membership Directory. q.
NACCB Newsletter. q. adv.

Meetings/Conferences:
Annual Meetings: Fall

Nat'l Ass'n of Computerized Tax Processors (1969)
c/o Nelco Inc.
P.O. Box 10208
Green Bay, WI 54307-0208
Tel: (920)337-2801   Fax: (920)336-7253
E-Mail: email@nactp.org
Web Site: http://www.nactp.org
Members: 65 companies
Staff: 1
Annual Budget: $10-25,000
President: Cary Parker

Historical Note
Serves as a communications link with government agencies, facilitates dispersal of information affecting the industry, and coordinates solutions to industry-wide problems. Represents the computer tax industry affecting its general welfare. Members are companies developing products and services for the tax industry. Has no paid officers or full-time staff. Membership: $300/year.

Publications:
Accounting Today Supplement. a.
Bylaws. irreg.
Membership Directory. a.
Practical Accountant Supplement a.
Supplement to Accounting Today Magazine. a.
Tax Form Design Guidelines. a.

Meetings/Conferences:
Annual Meetings: August

Nat'l Ass'n of Concessionaires (1944)
35 East Wacker Drive, Suite 1816
Chicago, IL 60601
Tel: (312)236-3858   Fax: (312)236-7809
E-Mail: smcross@earthlink.net
Web Site: www.naconline.org
Members: 1000 companies
Staff: 4
Annual Budget: $500-1,000,000
Exec. Director: Charles A. Winans
Communications Director: Susan Cross
Communications Manager: Meredith Ely
Membership Coordinator: Jenetta Ross

Historical Note
Founded as the Nat'l Ass'n of Popcorn Manufacturers, it became the Internat'l Popcorn Ass'n and then the Popcorn and Concessions Ass'n before assuming its present name. Members are popcorn processors, operators of food, vending and beverage concessions and their suppliers. Membership: $175-475/year.

Publications:
Concession Profession. semi-a. adv.
Concessionworks. q.

Meetings/Conferences:
1999 – California(Disneyland Hotel)/June 7-10

Nat'l Ass'n of Conservation Districts (1946)
509 Capitol Court N.E.
Washington, DC 20002
Tel: (202)547-6223   Fax: (202)547-6450
E-Mail: nacdinfo@nacdnet.org
Web Site: http://www.nacdnet.org
Members: 3,000 districts
Staff: 45
Annual Budget: $2-5,000,000

Exec. V. President: Ernest C. Shea

Historical Note
Conservation districts are local subdivisions of state governments which work to conserve and develop land, water, forests, wildlife and related natural resources. Formerly (1970) Nat'l Ass'n of Soil and Water Conservation Districts. Membership: $35-100/year (individual).

Publications:
Conservation Briefs.
District Leader. m. adv.
Tuesday Letter. m.

Meetings/Conferences:
Annual Meetings: First week in February/1,500
1999 – San Diego, CA(Town & Country Hotel)/Jan. 31-Feb. 3

Nat'l Ass'n of Consumer Advocates (1994)
18 Tremont St., Suite 201
Boston, MA 02108
Tel: (617)723-1239   Fax: (617)742-5044
E-Mail: nacabos@share.net
Web Site: http://www.sharenegt/nacabos
Members: 450 individuals
Staff: 3
Annual Budget: $100-250,000
Exec. Director: Ron Waterman

Historical Note
Provides support to lawyers and other professionals who represent consumers seeking redress from unfair business practices. Membership: $100 and higher (individual).

Publications:
"The Consumer Advocate" Newsletter. 6x/year.

Meetings/Conferences:
1999 – San Antonio, TX/125

Nat'l Ass'n of Consumer Agency Administrators (1976)
1010 Vermont Ave., N.W., Suite 514
Washington, DC 20005
Tel: (202)347-7395   Fax: (202)347-2563
Members: 160 consumer agencies
Staff: 2
Annual Budget: $100-250,000
Exec. Director: Wendy Weinberg

Historical Note
Members are municipal, county or state supported consumer affairs agencies. Qualified individuals are eligible for associate membership. Membership: $70-450/yr. (varies with agency budget).

Publications:
NACAA News. 10/year.

Meetings/Conferences:

Nat'l Ass'n of Consumer Credit Administrators (1935)
Office of the Commissioner of Banks
P.O. Box 10709
Raleigh, NC 27605-0709
Tel: (919)733-3016   Fax: (919)733-6918
Members: 55 individuals
Annual Budget: $25-50,000
President: Reitzel Deaton

Historical Note
Formerly Ass'n of Small Loan Administrators and Nat'l Ass'n of Small Loan Supervisors. Membership: $350/yr.

Publications:
NACCA Newsletter. q.

Meetings/Conferences:
Annual Meetings: September-October/60
1999 – Orlando, FL
2000 – Palm Springs

Nat'l Ass'n of Consumer Shows
147 S.E. 102nd St.
Portland, OR 97216
Tel: (503)253-0832   Fax: (503)253-9172
Toll Free: (800)728 - 6227
Members: 250 individuals
Staff: 4
Annual Budget: $50-100,000
Exec. Director: Michael Fisher
Communication Svcs. Manager: Rob Harriman
Financial Manager: Cheryl Jorgensen

Historical Note
Membership: $200/year (individual).

Publications:
Membership Roster. a.
NACS News. bi-m.

Meetings/Conferences:
Annual Meetings: June/July
1999 – Chicago, IL/June 10-13/100

Nat'l Ass'n of Container Distributors (1925)
1900 Arch St.
Philadelphia, PA 19103-1498
Tel: (215)564-3484   Fax: (215)564-2175
E-Mail: assnhqt@netaxs.com
Web Site: http://www.fdp.com/nacd
Members: 39 companies
Staff: 2
Annual Budget: $50-100,000
Exec. Director: Maureen Brady

Historical Note
Formerly (1964) Nat'l Ass'n of Glass Containers Distributors.

Publications:
Newsletter. q.

Meetings/Conferences:
Annual Meetings: April

Nat'l Ass'n of Convenience Stores (1961)

1605 King St.
Alexandria, VA 22314-2792
Tel: (703)684-3600   *Fax:* (703)836-4564
E-Mail: kerley@cstorescentral.com
Web Site: http://www.cstorescentral.com
Members: 2,400 retail companies, 78,000 outlets
Staff: 41
Annual Budget: $10-25,000,000
President: Kerley LeBoeuf
V.P., Industry Relations/Communications: Lindsay Hutter
V.P., Government Relations: Marc Katz
V.P., Meetings & Expositions: Jane Berzan
Manager, Meetings: Kimberly P. Sumner
V. President, Education and Information: Thomas G. Monday
Manager, Education Programs: Gary James
V.P., Internet Services: Shirley Jaffe
V.P., Finance/Systems: Brian Kimmel
Sr. V.P., Research/Industry Affairs: Teri Richman

Historical Note
Retail food stores carrying a more limited selection than supermarkets and usually open longer hours. Sponsors and supports the NACS Political Action Committee. Has an annual budget of approximately $12 million. Membership: $200-10,000/year (based on sales volume).

Publications:
Compensation Survey. a.
Fact Book. a.
Membership and Services Directory. a.
NACS News Summary. w.
State of the Convenience Store Industry. a.
Washington Report. w.

Meetings/Conferences:
Annual Meetings: Fall/18,000
1999 – Chicago, IL
2000 – New Orleans, LA(Morial Convention Center)/Oct. 22-24

Nat'l Ass'n of Corporate Directors (1977)

1707 L St., N.W., Suite 560
Washington, DC 20036
Tel: (202)775-0509   *Fax:* (202)775-4857
Web Site: www.nacdonline.org
Members: 2,000 individuals
Staff: 8
Annual Budget: $1-2,000,000
President and C.E.O.: James Darazsdi
Dir., Operations: Susan A. Ostrander

Historical Note
A not-for-profit educational association dedicated to ongoing information and education for corporate directors in board practices and corporate governance; focuses on issues such as Director's and Officer's liability, shareholder concerns, and responsible board decision making. Provides publications, seminars and in-house training, as well as a Register for filling board vacancies with qualified candidacies. Membership: $425/year (individual), $375-4,200/year (full board), $225/year (deans of business schools).

Publications:
Board Practices Monographs. q.
Convention Program. a. adv.
Directors Monthly Newsletter. m.
Legislative Alerts.

Meetings/Conferences:
Annual Meetings: Fall
1999 – Washington, DC/Oct. 17-19

Nat'l Ass'n of Corporate Real Estate Executives International (1974)

440 Columbia Drive, Suite 100
West Palm Beach, FL 33409-6685
Tel: (561)683-8111   *Fax:* (561)697-4853
E-Mail: nacore@nacore.com
Web Site: www.nacore.com
Members: 3,400 individuals
Staff: 20
Annual Budget: $2-5,000,000
Exec. Director: H. Gordon Wyllie
Director of Publications: Kathleen Dempsey, & 1
Director, Education: Sally Mertens
Director, Finance and Administration: Curtis A. Addison

Historical Note
Formerly (1973) Nat'l Ass'n of Location Analysts and Negotiators and (1974) the Nat'l Ass'n of Corporate Real Estate Executives. Members are corporate executives responsible for any function related to the acquisition or management of real estate assets for corporations whose primary business is not real estate. Membership: $299/year.

Publications:
Corporate Real Estate Executive. 9/year. adv.
NACORE International Directory. a. adv.
NACORE News. q.
NACORE Placement Newsletter. m.
Who's Who in Corporate Real Estate.

Meetings/Conferences:
1999 – Atlanta, GA(Marriott Marquis)/Oct. 2-5

Nat'l Ass'n of Corporate Treasurers (1982)

11250 Roger Bacon Dr., Suite 8
Reston, VA 22090
Tel: (703)437-4377   *Fax:* (703)435-4390
Members: 825 individuals
Staff: 2
Annual Budget: $250-500,000
Exec. Director: Charles G. Hagee, CAE

Historical Note
Established in Blacksburg, Virginia and incorporated in Washington, DC; NACT members are corporate chief financial officers, treasurers, or assistant treasurers. Membership: $295/year.

Publications:
Annual Meeting Program. a. adv.
Annual Meeting Summary. a. adv.
Membership Directory. a. adv.
News & Notes. bi-m. adv.

Meetings/Conferences:
Annual Meetings: Spring, plus technical seminars in the Winter and Fall

Nat'l Ass'n of Cosmetology Schools

Historical Note
See American Ass'n of Cosmetology Schools.

Nat'l Ass'n of Counsel for Children (1977)

1825 Marion St., Suite 340
Denver, CO 80218
Toll Free: (888)828 - 6222
E-Mail: advocate@naccchildlaw.org
Web Site: http://www.naccchildlaw.org
Members: 2,000 individuals
Annual Budget: $100-250,000
Exec. Director: Marvin R. Ventrell

Historical Note
NACC members are lawyers, judges, mental health professionals, social services professionals and others with an interest in the legal status of children. Membership: $60/year (individual).

Publications:
Guardian Newsletter. q. adv.

Meetings/Conferences:
Annual Meetings: Fall
1999 – Portland, OR(Marriott)/Oct. 8-11

Nat'l Ass'n of Counselors

303 West Cypress St.
San Antonio, TX 78212-0528
Tel: (210)225-2897   *Fax:* (210)225-8450
Toll Free: (800)486 - 3676
Members: 250 individuals
Staff: 2
Annual Budget: $25-50,000
C.E.O.: Marvin T. Deane, Ph.D.

Historical Note
NAC members are individuals with an active interest in real estate, or the profession of real estate counseling. A real estate counselor is a professional representing purchasers in real estate transactions. Awards the designation Senior Real Estate Counselor (SRC) upon the successful completion of a prescribed course of study. Membership: $40/year (individual).

Publications:
Advice & Ccounsel. q.
Directory. a.

Meetings/Conferences:
Annual Meetings: Not held.

Nat'l Ass'n of Counties (1935)

440 First St., N.W., 8th Floor
Washington, DC 20001
Tel: (202)393-6226   *Fax:* (202)393-2630
Members: 1,780 counties
Staff: 79
Annual Budget: $10-25,000,000
Exec. Director: Larry E. Naake
Director, Public Affairs: G. Thomas Goodman
Director, Legislative Affairs: Edwin Rosado
Director, Finance Administration: Kathy Bosak
Director, Environmental Programs: Sandra Markwood
Deputy Exec. Director: Ed Ferguson
Director, IT: Winifred Lyday

Historical Note
Formerly Nat'l Ass'n of County Officials. Membership is by county and includes all officials within the county. Today, nearly 60% of the 3,043 counties in the United States are represented. Twenty-six associations of professionally-related county officials are affiliated with NACo. NACo represents its members before the federal government and serves as an educational agency for county officials and other appropriate audiences. Has an annual budget of approximately $15 million.

Publications:
County News. bi-w. adv.
NACo Employment and Training Update. bi-w.

Meetings/Conferences:
Annual Meetings: Summer/5,000
1999 – Clayton, MO
2000 – Charlotte, NC
2001 – Philadelphia, PA

Nat'l Ass'n of County Administrators (1961)

440 First St., N.W., 8th Floor
Washington, DC 20001
Tel: (202)393-6226   *Fax:* (202)393-2630
Web Site: www.naco.org
Members: 450 individuals
Staff: 1
Annual Budget: under $10,000
Staff Liaison: Edward Ferguson

Historical Note
An affiliate of the Nat'l Ass'n of Counties. Membership: $50/year.

Publications:
County Administrator. m. adv.

Meetings/Conferences:
Annual Meetings: With Nat'l Ass'n of Counties
1999 – St. Louis, MO/July 16-20

Nat'l Ass'n of County Aging Programs (1978)

440 First St., N.W.
8th Floor
Washington, DC 20001

Tel: (202)942-4235   *Fax:* (202)393-2630
Web Site: www.naco.org
Members: 350 individuals
Staff: 1
Annual Budget: $10-25,000
Dir., Community Services: Sandra Reinsel Markwood

Historical Note
An affiliate of the Nat'l Ass'n of Counties, which provides administrative support. Members include county elected officials and heads of county aging offices. The purpose of the Ass'n is to assist county governments effectively plan for or provide services to meet the needs of their aging population. Membership: $25/year (individual); $50/year (county); $300/year (sustaining).

Publications:
NACAP News. q.

Meetings/Conferences:
Annual Meetings: With NACo
1999 – St. Louis, MO/July 16-20

Nat'l Ass'n of County Agricultural Agents (1915)

Room B2
223 N. Live Oak Dr.
Monks Corner, SC 29461
Members: 5,000 individuals
Staff: 1
Annual Budget: $250-500,000
Secretary: Frank Fitzsimmons, III

Historical Note
Organized in Chicago in the old Livestock Record Building by a small group of county agents from 10 states. An association of associations, NACAA members are employees of the U.S. Department of Agriculture's Cooperative Extension Service and State Land Grant Universities.

Publications:
The County Agent. q.

Meetings/Conferences:
Annual Meetings: Summer/2,000
1999 – Omaha, NE/Sept. 12-16

Nat'l Ass'n of County and City Health Officials (1966)

1100 17th St., N.W., Lower 2
Washington, DC 20036-4631
Tel: (202)783-5550   *Fax:* (202)783-1583
Members: 3,000 individuals, 700 jurisdictions
Staff: 35
Annual Budget: $2-5,000,000
Exec. Director: Thomas Milne
Legislative Contact: Donna Grossman
Associate Division Director: Sarah Schnect
Director, Operations: William Locke

Historical Note
An affiliate of the Nat'l Ass'n of Counties. Incorporated in 1985. Founded as Nat'l Ass'n of County Health Officials; assumed its current name in 1994. Absorbed the United States Conference of Local Health Officers in 1997. Membership: $45-1,250/year, based on size of jurisdiction population.

Publications:
Annual Report. a.
Membership Monthly. m.
NACCHO News. bi-m.

Meetings/Conferences:
Annual Meetings: With Nat'l Ass'n of Counties in July and the American Public Health Ass'n in Fall/10,000
1999 – Detroit, MI(Ritz Carlton)/July 14-17/500
2000 – Charlotte, NC
2001 – San Francisco, CA
2002 – Madison, WI

Nat'l Ass'n of County Behavioral Health Directors

440 First St., N.W., 8th Floor
Washington, DC 20001
Tel: (202)393-6226   *Fax:* (202)393-2260
Web Site: www.naco.org
Staff Liaison: Thomas Joseph, III

Historical Note
Formerly (1997) Nat'l Ass'n of County Mental Health Directors, NACBHD is an affiliate of the Nat'l Ass'n of Counties which provides administrative support.

Meetings/Conferences:
1999 – St. Louis, MO/July 16-20

Nat'l Ass'n of County Civil Attorneys (1963)

440 First St., N.W., 8th Floor
Washington, DC 20001
Tel: (202)393-6226   *Fax:* (202)393-2630
Web Site: www.naco.org
Members: 240 individuals
Staff: 2
Annual Budget: under $10,000
Staff Liaison: Donald Murray

Historical Note
An affiliate of and supported by the Nat'l Ass'n of Counties. Has no dues structure.

Meetings/Conferences:
Annual Meetings: With NACo.
1999 – St. Louis, MO/July 16-20

Nat'l Ass'n of County Engineers (1956)

440 First St., N.W.
Washington, DC 20001
Tel: (202)393-5041   *Fax:* (202)393-2630
E-Mail: nace@naco.org
Web Site: www.naco.org/asfils/naco/index.htm
Members: 1,800 individuals
Staff: 3
Annual Budget: $250-500,000
Exec. Director: Anthony R. Giancola, P.E.

Historical Note
Members are county engineering professionals or road management authorities. NACE is an affiliate of the Nat'l Ass'n of Counties. Membership: $110/year (individual); $500-5,000/year (organization/company).

Publications:
Blading Unpaved Roads Video.
NACE Action Guides. 19 volumes.
NACE Membership Directory. a.
NACE News. m.
NACE Training Guide Series. 7 volumes.
Work Zone Safety Video.

Meetings/Conferences:
Annual Meetings: Late Winter/Early Spring
1999 – Niagra Falls, NY/April 25-29

Nat'l Ass'n of County Health Facility Administrators (1978)
1523 West US 2
Crystal Falls, MI   49920
Tel: (906)875-6671   Fax: (906)875-6573
Members: 240 individuals
Staff: 1
Annual Budget: under $10,000
President: Chester Pintarelli

Historical Note
An affiliate of the Nat'l Ass'n of Counties, which provides administrative support. NACHFA works to improve the quality of healthcare available from county nursing homes and other long-term care institutions. Membership: $10/year (individual); $100/year (organization).

Meetings/Conferences:
Semi-annual Meetings: with NACo in July and in March

Nat'l Ass'n of County Human Services Administrators (1935)
440 First St., N.W., 8th Floor
Washington, DC   20001
Tel: (202)393-6226   Fax: (202)393-2630
Web Site: www.naco.org
Members: 540 individuals
Staff: 1
Annual Budget: under $10,000
Staff Liaison: Marilina Sanz

Historical Note
An affiliate of the Nat'l Ass'n of Counties. Formerly (1981) Nat'l Ass'n of County Welfare Directors.

Meetings/Conferences:
Annual Meetings: With the Nat'l Ass'n of Counties
1999 – St. Louis, MO/July 16-20

Nat'l Ass'n of County Information Officers (1965)
440 First St., N.W.
Washington, DC   20001
Tel: (202)393-6226   Fax: (202)393-2630
Web Site: www.naco.org
Members: 300 individuals
Staff: 1
Annual Budget: under $10,000
Staff Liaison: G. Thomas Goodman

Historical Note
An affiliate of the Nat'l Ass'n of Counties, which provides administrative support. Members are county public information officers and staff. Membership: $35/year (individual), $60 (county population under 500,000), $85/year (county population over 500,000); $50/year (associate); $100/year (corporate).

Publications:
The Art of Communication. q.

Meetings/Conferences:
Annual Meetings: With Nat'l Ass'n of Counties
1999 – St. Louis, MO/July 16-20

Nat'l Ass'n of County Information Technology Administrators
440 First St., N.W.
Washington, DC   20001
Tel: (202)942-4248   Fax: (202)942-4281
Web Site: www.naco.org
Staff Liaison: Win Lyday

Historical Note
An affiliate of the Nat'l Ass'n of Counties which provides administrative support. Membership: $10/year (regular).

Meetings/Conferences:
1999 – St. Louis, MO/July 16-20

Nat'l Ass'n of County Intergovernmental Relations Officials (1966)
440 First St., N.W., 8th Floor
Washington, DC   20001
Tel: (202)393-6226   Fax: (202)393-2630
Web Site: www.naco.org
Members: 100 individuals
Staff: 1
Annual Budget: under $10,000
Staff Liaison: Jim Stabler

Historical Note
Established in 1966 as the Nat'l Ass'n of County Development Coordinators to satisfy the need for a greater exchange of ideas in coordinating federal and state aid programs at the county level; became (1975) Nat'l Ass'n of Counties Council of Intergovernmental Coordinators; assumed current name in 1991. An affiliate of the Nat'l Ass'n of Counties.

Meetings/Conferences:
Annual Meetings: Fall, in Washington, DC

Nat'l Ass'n of County Mental Health Directors

Historical Note
Became Nat'l Ass'n of County Behavioral Health Directors in 1997.

Nat'l Ass'n of County Park and Recreation Officials (1964)
440 First St., N.W.
Washington, DC   20001
Tel: (202)393-6226   Fax: (202)737-0480
Members: 250 individuals
Staff: 1
Annual Budget: under $10,000
Staff Liaison: Lou Witt

Historical Note
An affiliate of the Nat'l Ass'n of Counties, which provides administrative support. Members are professionals in the field of parks, recreation and leisure-related services. Membership: $55/year (individual).

Meetings/Conferences:
Annual Meetings: With NACo.
1999 – St. Louis, MO

Nat'l Ass'n of County Planners (1965)
440 First St., N.W., 8th Floor
Washington, DC   20001
Tel: (202)942-4237   Fax: (202)737-0480
Web Site: www.naco.org
Staff: 1
Annual Budget: $10-25,000
Staff Liaison: Lou Witt

Historical Note
Formerly organized and chartered as the Nat'l Ass'n of County Planning Directors, assumed its present name in 1991. An affiliate of and supported by the National Association of Counties. Membership: $25/year.

Publications:
Guide to County Capitol Improvement Programming.
NACP News. q. adv.

Meetings/Conferences:
Annual Meetings: Spring, with Nat'l Ass'n of Counties
1999 – St. Louis, MO/July 16-20

Nat'l Ass'n of County Recorders, Election Officials and Clerks (1948)
440 First St., N.W., 8th Floor
Washington, DC   20001
Tel: (202)393-6226   Fax: (202)737-0480
Web Site: www.naco.org
Members: 840 individuals
Staff: 1
Annual Budget: $50-100,000
Staff Liaison: John Bonkowksi

Historical Note
Formerly the Nat'l Ass'n of County Recorders and Clerks. An affiliate of and supported by the Nat'l Ass'n of Counties. Members include county officials who are responsible for adminstration of public records, courts and elections. Membership: variable, depends on the size of the county.

Publications:
The National Record. q. adv.

Meetings/Conferences:
Annual Meetings: July, with Nat'l Ass'n of Counties
1999 – St. Louis, MO/July 16-20

Nat'l Ass'n of County Surveyors
440 First St., N.W., 8th Floor
Washington, DC   20001
Tel: (202)393-6226
Web Site: www.naco.org
Staff Liaison: Angela Sides

Historical Note
An affiliate of the Nat'l Ass'n of Counties which provides administrative support.

Meetings/Conferences:
1999 – St. Louis, MO/July 16-20

Nat'l Ass'n of County Training and Employment Professionals (1974)
440 First St., N.W.
Washington, DC   20001
Tel: (202)942-4287   Fax: (202)737-0480
Web Site: www.naco.org
Members: 240 job training organizations
Annual Budget: $10-25,000
Staff Liaison: Gary Gortenburg

Historical Note
An affiliate of the National Association of Counties, which provides administrative support. Formerly (1985) the Nat'l Ass'n of County Employment and Training Admi nistrators.

Publications:
NACo Update on Job Training.

Meetings/Conferences:
Annual Meetings: Hennepin County, MN/Nov. 13-16
1999 – St. Louis, MO/July 16-20

Nat'l Ass'n of County Treasurers and Finance Officers (1950)
440 First St., N.W.
Washington, DC   20001
Tel: (202)942-4290   Fax: (202)393-2630
Members: 1,150 individuals
Staff: 1
Annual Budget: under $10,000
Staff Liaison: Ralph Tabor

Historical Note
Established as the County Treasurers Association of the United States, it assumed its present name about 1969. An affiliate of the

Nat'l Ass'n of Counties, which provides administrative support. Membership: $250/year.

Publications:
Treasury Marks. q. adv.

Meetings/Conferences:
Annual Meetings: July, usually with Nat'l Ass'n of Counties

Nat'l Ass'n of Credential Evaluation Services (1987)
P.O. Box 514070
Milwaukee, WI   53202-3470
Tel: (414)289-3400   Fax: (414)289-3411
Members: 14 firms
Annual Budget: under $10,000
Chairperson: Margit A. Schatzman

Historical Note
Members are companies specializing in the evaluation of foreign educational credentials for further education, professional licensure, employment, or immigration.

Publications:
List of Members. a.

Meetings/Conferences:
Annual Meetings: April

Nat'l Ass'n of Credit Management (1896)
8815 Centre Park Drive, Suite 200
Columbia, MD   21045-2144
Tel: (410)740-5560   Fax: (410)740-5574
Toll Free: (800)220 - 7237
Web Site: http://www.nacm.org
Staff: 35
Annual Budget: $2-5,000,000
President: Paul J. Mignini, Jr., CAE
V. President, Communications: Katherine R. Jeschke
Convention & Meetings Director: Lynne Valentic, CMP
Exec. V. President: Robin Schauseil, CMP
Controller: James E. Vanchel, CPA

Historical Note
Founded June 23, 1896 in Toledo, Ohio by 82 charter member credit executives. Provides credit reports on business customers, collection service, assistance to creditors and commercial fraud detection and prevention. Sponsors the Nat'l Institute of Credit, which is a non-profit educational organization of the NACM.

Publications:
Business Credit Magazine. 10/year.
Credit Manual of Commercial Laws. a.

Meetings/Conferences:
Annual Meetings: Spring
1999 – San Francisco, CA/May 16-19/2500
2000 – Baltimore, MD(Convention Center)/June 14-17/2300
2001 – Seattle, WA(Convention Center)/May 20-23/2500

Nat'l Ass'n of Credit Union Chairmen (1977)
P.O. Box 160
Del Mar, CA   92014-0160
Tel: (619)792-3883   Fax: (619)792-3884
Members: 250 individuals
Annual Budget: $100-250,000
Exec. Director: Katherine E. Clark

Historical Note
Formerly (1993) the Nat'l Ass'n of Credit Union Presidents. Conceived at Williamsburg in July 1976 at a conference of presidents of Southeast credit unions, the association was formally established the following year at the Hilton Inn in Albuquerque by 47 charter members representing credit unions with more than 20 million dollars in assets. It was incorporated in Alabama in 1978. Membership: $250/year.

Publications:
Directory.
Exchange. q.

Meetings/Conferences:
Annual Meetings: Fall
1999 – Nashville, TN(Loews Vanderbilt)/October 13-16/250

Nat'l Ass'n of Credit Union Service Organizations (1984)
100 South Sunrise, Suite 154
Palm Springs, CA   92262
Toll Free: (888)462 - 2870
E-Mail: info@nacuso.org
Web Site: http://www.nacuso.org
Members: 210 individuals
Annual Budget: $100-250,000
President: Robert Dorsa

Historical Note
NACUSO is a trade association for credit union service organizations (subsidiaries of credit unions). Membership: $300/year (CUSO); $500/year (CUSO sponsor company).

Publications:
NACUSO Connection. q.
Nat'l CUSO Directory. a. adv.

Meetings/Conferences:
1999 – Las Vegas, NV(Ball's)/April 27-30

Nat'l Ass'n of Crime Victim Compensation Boards (1978)
P.O. Box 16003
Alexandria, VA   22302
Tel: (703)370-2996
Members: 52 state gov't programs
Staff: 1
Annual Budget: $50-100,000
Exec. Director: Dan McLeod Eddy

Historical Note
NACVCB members are state crime victim compensation programs.

Publications:
Directory. a.
Newsletter. q.

Meetings/Conferences:
Annual Meetings: Fall

Nat'l Ass'n of Criminal Defense Lawyers (1958)
1025 Connecticut Ave., NW, Suite 901
Washington, DC 20036
Tel: (202)872-8600   Fax: (202)872-8690
E-Mail: assist@nacdl.com
Web Site: www.criminaljustice.org
Members: 10,000 individuals
Staff: 18
Annual Budget: $2-5,000,000
Exec. Director: Stuart Statler
Director, Public Affairs: Jack King
Dir., Membership & Info. Systems: Steven Frazier
Dir., Legislative Affairs: Leslie J. Hagin
Dir., Meetings & Affiliates: Cecelia Hannon
Dir., Education: Todd Wells
Dir., Finance: Brain P. Carroll
Acting Gen. Counsel/Dir., Indigent Defense: Paul Petterson
Director, Education: Todd Wells
Editor, Champion: Richard Bing

Historical Note
Formerly (1972) Nat'l Ass'n of Defense Lawyers in Criminal Cases.
Provides continuing legal education and other activities in support
of attorneys engaged in criminal defense practice. Membership:
$230/year (full member); $110/year (new lawyer/allied non-
lawyer); $90/year (public defender/judge/law professor/active
military); $20/year (student).

Publications:
Members Handbook. a.
The Champion. 10/year. adv.
Washington Digest. q.

Meetings/Conferences:
Annual Meetings: August

Nat'l Ass'n of Cruise Oriented Agencies (1985)
7600 S. Red Road, Suite 128
South Miami, FL 33143
Tel: (305)663-5626   Fax: (305)663-5625
E-Mail: drtnoc@aol.com
Web Site: http://www.nacoa.com
Members: 800 agencies
Staff: 3
Annual Budget: $250-500,000
President: Donna Esposito

Historical Note
Formerly Nat'l Ass'n of Cruise Only Agencies (1998). Members are
travel agencies specializing in cruiseship bookings. Allied
membership is available for cruise lines, supplier to the industry,
trade publications and other entities with an interest in the industry.
Membership: $150/year (individual); $3,000-10,000/year (allied
or cruise line).

Publications:
'Now Hear This' Newsletter. q. adv.

Meetings/Conferences:
1999 – Ft. Lauderdale, FL(Embassy Suites Hotel)

Nat'l Ass'n of Decorative Fabric Distributors (1969)
3008 Millwood Ave.
Columbia, SC 29205
Tel: (803)252-5646   Fax: (803)765-0860
Toll Free: (800)445 - 8629
Web Site: http://www.nadfd.com
Members: 60 companies
Annual Budget: $100-250,000
Exec. Director: MaryAnn S. Crews
Director of Communications: Nancy Cooper

Historical Note
Established in 1969 as the Nat'l Ass'n of Upholstery Fabric
Distributors, it assumed its present name in 1975.

Publications:
Swatches. irreg.

Meetings/Conferences:
1999 – Stowe, VT/Aug. 6-11

Nat'l Ass'n of Demolition Contractors (1972)
16 North Franklin St., Suite 200B
Doylestown, PA 18901-3536
Tel: (215)348-4949   Fax: (215)348-8422
Toll Free: (800)541 - 2412
E-Mail: nadc@voicenet.com
Web Site: www.demolitionassn.com
Members: 650 contractors
Staff: 3
Annual Budget: $500-1,000,000
Exec. Director: Michael R. Taylor

Historical Note
Demolition equipment manufacturers and contractors. Membership:
$300-600/year, based on revenues.

Publications:
Demolition. m. adv.
Membership List. a.

Meetings/Conferences:
Annual Meetings: March/1,500
1999 – Las Vegas, NV(Mirage)/March 14-17
2000 – Las Vegas, NV(Mirage)/March 19-22

Nat'l Ass'n of Demonstration Companies (1982)
Historical Note
Became (1996) Field Marketing Services Ass'n.

Nat'l Ass'n of Dental Assistants (1974)
900 S. Washington St., Suite G13
Falls Church, VA 22046-4020
Tel: (703)237-8616
Members: 5,000 individuals
Staff: 2
Annual Budget: $50-100,000

Membership Director: Michelle Cooper

Historical Note
Its purpose is to assist members in achieving their career goals by
keeping them informed of advances and/or changes in their chosen
professions, by offering continuing education opportunities, and by
promoting the free exchange of ideas with their peers. Membership
open to anyone employed by a dentist, including office personnel.
Membership: $30/yr.

Publications:
The Explorer. m. adv.

Meetings/Conferences:
Annual Meetings: Summer

Nat'l Ass'n of Dental Laboratories (1951)
8201 Greensboro Dr., Suite 300
McLean, VA 22102-3810
Tel: (703)610-9035   Fax: (703)610-9005
Toll Free: (800)950 - 1150
E-Mail: cbeeton@nadl.org
Web Site: http://www.nadl.org
Members: 2,000 individuals
Staff: 7
Annual Budget: $1-2,000,000
Exec. Director: Terry L. Peters, CAE
Managing Editor: Jason Polachek
Dir., Membership & Component Services: Carrie Beeton
Director, Certification Programs: Elise Lindsey
Asst. Exec. Director: Audrey J. Calomino

Historical Note
A federation of state laboratory ass'ns formed by a merger of the
Dental Laboratory Institute of America and the American Dental
Laboratory Ass'n. From 1968-71 it was known as the Nat'l Ass'n
of Certified Dental Laboratories. Affiliated with the Nat'l Board for
Certification in Dental Laboratory Technology, granting the
Certified Dental Technician (CDT) designation and the Nat'l Board
for Certification of Dental Laboratories, granting the Certified
Dental Laboratory (CDL) designation. Membership: $185/year
(active members), $225/year (affiliate members).

Publications:
Journal of Dental Technology. 10/year. adv.
NADL Leadership Newsletter. m.
NADL News. q.
Who's Who in the Dental Laboratory Industry. a. adv.

Meetings/Conferences:
Annual Meetings: June
1999 – Las Vegas, NV(Bally's)/Sept. 9-11/500
2000 – Las Vegas, NV(Bally's)

Nat'l Ass'n of Dental Plans
5001 Lyndon B. Johnson Fwy., Suite 375
Dallas, TX 75244-6104
Tel: (972)458-6998   Fax: (972)458-2258
Web Site: http://www.nadp.org
Members: 80 plans
Staff: 4
Exec. Director: Evelyn F. Ireland, CAE
Director of Government Relations: Tim Brown
Director of Education Communications: Amy Shaw
Director of Membership Sales: Kay Rose

Historical Note
NADP provides legislative action, continuing education, industry
research and other services to its members. Full membership is
available to dental HMOs and PPOs. Associate membership is
available to firms providing other dental benefit plans. Sponsors
and supports the NADP Foundation.

Publications:
Annual Statistical Profile of Industry.
NADP News. q.

Meetings/Conferences:
1999 – Rancho Miraege, CA(Las Palmas Marriott Resort)

Nat'l Ass'n of Desktop Publishers (1986)
Historical Note
Ceased operating as an association in 1997.

Nat'l Ass'n of Development Companies (1982)
6764 Old McLean Village Drive
McLean, VA 22101-3906
Tel: (703)748-2575   Fax: (703)748-2582
E-Mail: windarrow@aol.com
Members: 350 companies
Staff: 4
Annual Budget: $500-1,000,000
Exec. Director: Christopher L. Crawford

Historical Note
Organized to represent Certified Development Companies that
participate in the Small Business Administration's "504" lending
program. Through the program, CDCs provide long-term, fixed
asset financing to eligible small businesses. Affiliate membership is
open to lawyers, bankers, accountants and other participants
recommended by an active CDC. Membership: $250/year or 0.1%
of Sec. 504 debentures (up to $1,000).

Publications:
Certified News. m.

Meetings/Conferences:
Annual Meetings: Spring

Nat'l Ass'n of Development Organizations (1967)
444 North Capitol St., N.W., Suite 630
Washington, DC 20001
Tel: (202)624-7806   Fax: (202)624-8813
E-Mail: nado@sso.org
Web Site: http://www.nado.org
Members: 325 organizations
Staff: 11
Annual Budget: $1-2,000,000
Exec. Director: Aliceann Wohlbruck
Director, Legis. Affairs: Matthew Chase
Director of Administration and Meetings: Vicki Glass Smith, CMP

Director of Membership: Sandy Strother

Historical Note
Members are multi-county regional development organizations,
mainly in small metropolitan and rural areas. Primary concern is to
promote economic development in non-metropolitan regions.
Membership: $300/year (individual); $1,000/year (organization).

Publications:
Economic Development Digest. m.
Economic Development Finance Service Reporter. q.
NADO News. w.

Meetings/Conferences:
Annual Meetings: Fall

Nat'l Ass'n of Developmental Disabilities Councils (1973)
1234 Massachusetts Ave., N.W., Suite 103
Washington, DC 20005
Tel: (202)347-1234   Fax: (202)347-4023
E-Mail: naddc@igc.apc.org
Web Site: http://www.igc.apc.org/NADDC
Members: 42 councils
Staff: 4
Annual Budget: $250-500,000
Exec. Director: Susan A. Zierman
Director, Federal-State Relations: Mary M. Gennaro

Historical Note
Provides technical support to State and territorial councils on the
developmentally disabled. Known as the National Conference on
Developmental Disabilities until 1978.

Publications:
Highlights Newsletter. m.

Meetings/Conferences:

Nat'l Ass'n of Diaconate Directors (1976)
1337 W. Ohio St.
Chicago, IL 60622
Tel: (312)226-4033   Fax: (312)829-8915
E-Mail: NADDEXD@AOL.COM
Web Site: http://NADD.ORG
Members: 325 individuals
Staff: 2
Annual Budget: $100-250,000
Exec. Director: Deacon Thomas Welch

Historical Note
Founded as Nat'l Ass'n of Permanent Diaconate Directors; assumed
its current name in 1995. Members are directors and staff members
of diocesan diaconate communities responsible for the growth and
development of Catholic deacons in the U.S. Membership:
$375/year (diocesan); $60/year (full); $35/year (associate).

Publications:
NADD Newsletter. q.
Nat'l Diaconate Directory. a.
Proceedings. a.

Meetings/Conferences:
1999 – Boston, MA(Sheraton Tara)/April 21-24/200
2000 – Moraga, CA/June 19-21/200

Nat'l Ass'n of Diaper Services (1946)
994 Old Eagle School Road, Suite 1019
Wayne, PA 19087-1802
Tel: (610)971-4850   Fax: (610)971-4859
Members: 350 companies
Exec. Director: John A. Shiffert, CAE

Historical Note
Established in 1946 as the Diaper Service Institute of America.
Became the Diaper Service Industry Ass'n in 1960. Merged in 1970
with the Nat'l Institute of Diaper Services (1938), and became the
Nat'l Institute of Infant Services in 1971. It assumed its present
name in 1985. Members are diaper rental and laundry services,
whose existence is increasingly threatened by the growing use of
disposable diapers. The Diaper Service Accreditation Council is its
certification arm.

Publications:
Newsletter. m.

Meetings/Conferences:
Annual Meetings: May

Nat'l Ass'n of Diocesan Ecumenical Officers (1972)
462 N. Taylor
St. Louis, MO 63108
Tel: (314)531-9700   Fax: (314)531-2269
Members: 200 individuals
Staff: 1
President: Rev. Vincent A. Heier

Historical Note
NADEO members are officers in Roman Catholic dioceses
responsbile for promoting Christian unity and interfaith
cooperation.

Publications:
Booklet. a.
Newsletter. q.

Meetings/Conferences:

Nat'l Ass'n of Directors of Nursing Administration in Long Term Care (1986)
10999 Reed Hartman Hwy., Suite 233
Cincinnati, OH 45242
Tel: (513)791-3679   Fax: (513)791-3699
Toll Free: (800)222 - 0539
Members: 4,700 individuals
Staff: 3
Exec. Director & Founder: Joan C. Schleue-Warden, RN

Historical Note
Membership: $50/year, plus state chapter dues (individual).

Publications:
Director Journal. q. adv.

Meetings/Conferences:
Annual Meetings: June
1999 – New Orleans, LA/June 2-5

Nat'l Ass'n of Disability Evaluating Professionals (1984)

P.O. Box 35407
Richmond, VA   23235-0407
Tel: (804)378-8809
Members: 1000 individuals
Staff: 2
Annual Budget: $250-500,000
Director: Virgil Robert May, III

Historical Note
NADEP members are lawyers, medical doctors and other professionals involved in the evaluation and rehabilitation of persons with disabilities resulting from work or personal injuries. Membership: $150(individual and organization)

Publications:
Disability Guide and Rehabilitation Review. q.
NADEP-Handbook of Practice Standards and Guidelines. bi.
Newsletter. m.

Meetings/Conferences:
1999 – Orlando, FL

Nat'l Ass'n of Disability Examiners (1963)

P.O. Box 4188
Frankfort, KY   40603
Tel: (502)875-8388
Toll Free: (800)928 - 8050
Members: 2,000 individuals
Annual Budget: $50-100,000
President: Jeff Price

Historical Note
Established and incorporated in 1968 as a division of the National Rehabilitation Association, but became autonomous in late 1978. Members are doctors and examiners engaged in judging social security disability claims. Promotes disability evaluation as a science and a profession. Has no paid staff or permanent officers. Membership: $50/year (professional); $25/year (associates/retirees); $200/year (organizations); $500/year (gold corporation).

Publications:
Directory. a.
NADE Advocate. bi-m. adv.

Meetings/Conferences:
Annual Meetings: October
1999 – Denver, CO/Oct. 9-16

Nat'l Ass'n of Display Industries (1947)

Historical Note
Address unknown in 1997.

Nat'l Ass'n of Division Order Analysts (1974)

9794 Forest Lane, Suite 1012
Dallas, TX   75243
Members: 900 individuals
Annual Budget: $50-100,000
President: Sarah Tays

Historical Note
Division order analysts are petroleum and gas company employees or independent consultants responsible for royalty, working interset and overidding royalty payments. Offers a certification program providing education, training and testing for qualified applicants desiring to attain Certified Division Order Analyst credentials. Membership: $35/year (individual).

Publications:
Annual Institute Journal. a.
Directory. a.
NADOA Newsletter. bi-m.

Meetings/Conferences:

Nat'l Ass'n of Document Examiners (1979)

20 Nassau St.
Princeton, NJ   08542
Tel: (609)924-8193
Web Site: http://www.forgerynet.com
Members: 115 individuals
Annual Budget: under $10,000
Exec. Officer: Renee Martin

Historical Note
NADE was organized for the education of document examiners. Promotes the interests of forensic document examiners specializing in handwriting identification through seminars, publications, and a certification program for professional members. Membership: $150/year (individual).

Publications:
Communique Newsletter. bi-m. adv.
NADE Journal. q.

Meetings/Conferences:
Annual Meetings: October

Nat'l Ass'n of Dog Obedience Instructors (1964)

729 Grapevine Hwy., Suite 369
Hurst, TX   76054-2085
Web Site: http://www.kimberly.uidaho.edu/nadoi/
Members: 400 individuals

Historical Note
NADOI was founded to elevate the standards of the dog instructing profession, to aid both dog and human in the solution of the many problems associated with dog ownership, and to endorse its members as having attained the skills and knowledge necessary to serve those ends.

Publications:
Forward. q. adv.
NADOI News Newsletter. m.

Meetings/Conferences:
Annual Meetings: Spring

1999 – May

Nat'l Ass'n of Ecumenical and Interreligious Staff (1940)

c/o Queens Federation of Churches
86-17 105th St.
Richmond Hill, NY   11418-1597
Tel: (718)847-6764
Members: 375 individuals
Staff: 1
Annual Budget: $50-100,000
Registrar: Rev. N.J. L'Heureux, Jr.

Historical Note
A merger of Employed Council Officers Ass'n and the Ass'n of Executive Secretaries. Formerly (1971) Ass'n of Council Secretaries, and (1997) Nat'l Ass'n of Ecumenical Staff. Membership: $100/year (executive); $60/year (associate); $20/year (introductory).

Publications:
Corletter. q.

Meetings/Conferences:
Annual Meetings: Second week in July Westerville, OH/July Rock Island, IL/July

Nat'l Ass'n of Ecumenical Staff

Historical Note
Became (1997) Nat'l Ass'n of Ecumenical and Interreligious Staff.

Nat'l Ass'n of Educational Buyers (1920)

450 Wireless Blvd.
Hauppauge, NY   11788
Tel: (516)273-2600   *Fax:* (516)952-3660
Web Site: http://www.naeb.org
Members: 1,900 individuals
Staff: 10
Annual Budget: $1-2,000,000
Exec. Director: Joan S. Fox, CAE
Manager, Communications: Annette Kink
Meeting Planner: Stephanie Wnubel
Business Manager: Dennis Stoner

Historical Note
Founded as the Educational Buyers Ass'n, it assumed its present name in 1947. Members are college and university purchasing directors.

Publications:
Journal. m.
NAEB Bulletin. m.

Meetings/Conferences:
Annual Meetings: Spring
1999 – Lexington, KY(Hyatt Regency)/April 14-17
2000 – San Diego, CA(Town And Country Hotel)/April 26-29
2001 – Nashville, TN
2002 – New Orleans, LA

Nat'l Ass'n of Educational Office Professionals (1934)

P.O. Box 12619
Wichita, KS   67277-2619
Tel: (316)942-4822   *Fax:* (316)942-7100
E-Mail: naeop@naeop.org
Web Site: http://www.naeop.org
Members: 6,750 individuals
Staff: 4
Annual Budget: $250-500,000
Exec. Director: Sharon Daggett Manner

Historical Note
Formerly (1979) the Nat'l Ass'n of Educational Secretaries and (1995) Nat'l Ass'n of Office Personnel. Members are office personnel in educational institutions. Sponsors a professional standards program which awards the designation Certified Educational Office Employee. Membership: $40/year.

Publications:
The Beam. q.
The National Educational Secretary. q. adv.

Meetings/Conferences:
Annual Meetings: July
1999 – Wichita, KS
2000 – Louisville, KY
2001 – Salt Lake City, UT
2002 – Greenville, SC

Nat'l Ass'n of Electrical Distributors (1908)

1100 Corporate Square Drive, Suite 100
St. Louis, MO   63132
Tel: (314)991-9000   *Fax:* (314)991-3060
Toll Free: (888)791 - 2512
E-Mail: info@naed.org
Web Site: http://www.naed.org
Members: 667 companies, 3,500 branches
Staff: 28
Annual Budget: $2-5,000,000
President: Joel Hoiland, CAE
Dir., Marketing & Communications: Dawn Blair
Dir., Meetings & Conferences: Kathleen Eagan
Dir., NAED Education Foundation: Jim O'Hallaron
Dir., Finance & Administration: Bill Myers
Dir., Membership & Regional Services: Bernardine Purcell
Dir., Electronic Commerce: John Graham

Historical Note
NAED serves as a major resource for electrical distributors to gain business opportunities, education, industry knowledge, and information. Formerly (1928) Electrical Supply Jobbers Ass'n and (1949) Nat'l Electric Wholesalers Ass'n.

Publications:
The Electrical Distributor. m. adv.

Meetings/Conferences:
Annual Meetings: May
1999 – Boston, MA(Marriott/Westin)/May 15-17/2000
2000 – Orlando, FL(Marriott World Center)/April 29-May 3/2000

2001 – Washington, DC(Sheraton Washington)/May 5-9/2000

Nat'l Ass'n of Elementary School Principals (1921)

1615 Duke St.
Alexandria, VA   22314-3483
Tel: (703)684-3345   *Fax:* (703)549-5568
Toll Free: (800)386 - 2377
Web Site: http://www.naesp.org
Members: 28,000 individuals
Staff: 40
Annual Budget: $2-5,000,000
Exec. Director: Vincent L. Ferrandino
Deputy Exec. Director, Communications: Ted Greenleaf
Director, Govt. Relations: Sally N. McConnell
Director, Conventions: Marguerite Leishman
Senior Administrator/Asst. Exec. Director: Doris A. Belfield
Marketing Strategic Alliances: Gail Gross
Assoc. Exec. Director, Programs: Fred Brown

Historical Note
Founded in 1921 as a division of the National Education Ass'n, it became autonomous in 1972. Represents the professional interests of elementary and middle school principals in the U.S., Canada, and abroad. Serves as advocate for high-quality educational and social programs to benefit children and youth. Membership: $175/year (individual), $215/year (institution).

Publications:
Communicator. m.
Here's How. bi-m.
NAESP Research Roundup. semi-a.
Principal. 5/year. adv.
Report to Parents. 3/year.
Streamlined Seminar. bi-m.

Meetings/Conferences:
Annual Meetings: Spring
1999 – San Francisco, CA/March 20-23

Nat'l Ass'n of Elevator Contractors (1951)

1298 Wellbrook Circle
Suite A
Conyers, GA   30012
Tel: (770)760-9660   *Fax:* (770)760-9714
Members: 700 companies
Staff: 5
Annual Budget: $500-1,000,000
Exec. Director: Teresa M. Shirley

Historical Note
Members are installers and servicers of elevators and suppliers of equipment.

Publications:
MainLine Newsletter. 10/year.

Meetings/Conferences:
Annual Meetings: Fall
1999 – Atlantic City, NJ(Sheraton)

Nat'l Ass'n of Elevator Safety Authorities Internat'l (1969)

4541 N. 12th Street
Phoenix, AZ   85014-4203
Tel: (602)266-9701   *Fax:* (602)265-0093
E-Mail: naesa@pcslink.com
Web Site: http://www.pcslink.com/~naesa/
Members: 700 individuals
Staff: 5
Annual Budget: $250-500,000
Exec. Director: Floyd Rommel

Historical Note
Members are manufacturers, installers, servicers and inspectors of elevators. Membership: $75/year (individual); $500/year (organization/company).

Publications:
Progress Newsletter. m.

Meetings/Conferences:
Annual Meetings: August
1999 – Vancouver, BC/Aug. 10-12

Nat'l Ass'n of Emergency Medical Technicians (1975)

408 Monroe St.
Clinton, MS   39056
Toll Free: (800)346 - 2368
E-Mail: naemtha@aol.com
Members: 6,000 individuals
Staff: 4
Annual Budget: $250-500,000
Exec. Director: Barbara Sanders
Finance Director: Lisa Lindsay

Historical Note
Members are state certified and/or nationally registered emergency medical technicians (EMTs). The association has five divisions for its members with specialized interests: Nat'l Soc. of EMS Instructor/Coordinators; Nat'l Soc. of EMT Paramedics; Nat'l Soc. of EMS Administrators; Industrial EMS Soc.; and the Nat'l Soc. of Military EMTs. Membership: $40/year (individual); $300/year (organization).

Publications:
NAEMT News. bi-m. adv.

Meetings/Conferences:
Annual Meetings: Fall/1,500

Nat'l Ass'n of Employers on Health Care Action (1976)

Historical Note
Defunct in 1996.

Nat'l Ass'n of EMS Physicians (1983)

8310 Nieman Road
Lenexa, KS   66214-1598
Tel: (913)492-5858   *Fax:* (913)541-0156
Toll Free: (800)228 - 3677
Members: 1,500 individuals

Staff: 4
Annual Budget: $250-500,000
Exec. Director: Janelle Williams
Historical Note
NAEMSP members are designated, medically-legally responsible
medical directors of municipal and state emergency medical systems
and programs, as well as key associates, including state directors,
administrative heads, regular EMS personnel and legal experts from
the United States and Canada. NAEMSP provides a national
resource on EMS standards of care and a forum for EMS physicians
and their associates to discuss the problems and responsibilities of
EMS medical supervision, as well as to provide role models and
consensus for various aspects of EMS care. Membership:
$195/year (individual physicians); $75/year (resident medical
student); $75/year (professional/associate).
Publications:
NAEMSP News. bi-m. adv.
Prehospital Emergency Care. q. adv.
Meetings/Conferences:
Semi-Annual Meetings: Winter and Summer

Nat'l Ass'n of Energy Service Companies (1983)
1615 M Street N.W., #800
Washington, DC 20036
Tel: (202)822-0950 **Fax:** (202)822-0955
Web Site: www.naesco.org
Members: 140 companies
Staff: 6
Annual Budget: $250-500,000
Exec. Director: Terry Singer
Historical Note
A non-profit corporation formed by energy service companies to
meet the needs of the growing energy service industry. Represents
the interests of the industry before legislative and administrative
bodies; informs the public of the benefits of third party financing of
energy conservation and alternative energy programs; educates
members about the growth, development, and status of the energy
service industry.
Publications:
Financing Transaction Summaries. q.
NAESCO Bidders Sheets. a.
NAESCO News. bi-m.
Vendors Bidders Sheets. a.
Meetings/Conferences:
Semi-annual Meeting: Spring and Fall
1999 – Canada, Toronto/April 26-28
1999 – Pasadena, CA/Nov. 17-19

Nat'l Ass'n of Engineering Companies (1944)
Historical Note
Defunct in 1995.

Nat'l Ass'n of Enrolled Agents (1972)
200 Orchard Ridge Drive, Suite 302
Gaithersburg, MD 20878-1978
Tel: (301)212-9608 **Fax:** (301)990-1611
E-Mail: NAEA1@aol.com
Members: 9,600 individuals
Staff: 12
Annual Budget: $2-5,000,000
Exec. V. President: Janet B. Bray, CAE
Director, Communications: Cliff Weiss
Government Relations Director: Sharon H. Cranford
Historical Note
Membership consists of individuals who are enrolled to represent
taxpayers before the Internal Revenue Service. Formerly (until
1978) the Ass'n of Enrolled Agents. Membership: $140/year.
Publications:
E. A. adv.
Meetings/Conferences:
Annual Meetings: Summer/500
1999 – Honolulu, HI/Aug. 19-24

Nat'l Ass'n of Enrolled Federal Tax Accountants (1960)
P.O. Box 59-009
Chicago, IL 60659-0009
Tel: (773)463-5577
Members: 450 individuals
Staff: 1
Annual Budget: under $10,000
Exec. Director and Secretary: Seymour A. Rish, EFTA
Historical Note
Membership restricted to persons who have been authorized to use
the "Enrolled Federal Tax Accountant" (EFTA) Service Mark
designation and who have a Federal license as an "enrolled agent"
to practice before the Internal Revenue Service of the U.S.
Department of the Treasury, as a taxpayer's representative.
Publications:
EFTA Newsletter. irreg.
Meetings/Conferences:
Annual Meetings: late June/bi-annually

Nat'l Ass'n of Entrepreneurs (1990)
Historical Note
Became the American Cash Flow Ass'n in 1997.

Nat'l Ass'n of Environmental Professionals (1975)
6524 Ramoth Drive
Jacksonville, FL 32226-3202
Tel: (904)251-9900 **Fax:** (904)251-9901
Toll Free: (888)251 - 9902
E-Mail: naep@ilnk.com
Web Site: http://www.naep.org
Members: 2,000 individuals
Staff: 1
Annual Budget: $500-1,000,000
President: Andrew McCusker

Historical Note
Members are involved in environmental planning, assessment,
management, review and research. Awards the CEP (Certified
Environmental Professional) designation. NAEP is a
multidisciplinary, non-partisan professional ass'n dedicated to the
promotion of ethical practice in the enviromental field. NAEP's
interdisciplinary focus brings together specialists from each of the
major segments of the enviromental profession. NAEP members
represent government, consulting, industry, academe, and the
private sector in the U.S. and abroad working in all areas of air,
water, noise, waste, ecology and education, and providing access to
the latest trends in environmental research, technology, law and
policy. Membership provides access to the latest trends in research,
technology, law, and policy. Membership: $95/year (individual).
Publications:
Annual Conference Proceedings. a. adv.
NAEP News Newsletter. bi-m. adv.
Meetings/Conferences:
Annual Meetings: May/June
1999 – Kansas City, MO(Wyndam Gardens)/June 19-24

Nat'l Ass'n of Episcopal Schools (1954)
815 Second Ave., Suite 313
New York, NY 10017
Tel: (212)716-6134 **Fax:** (212)286-9366
Toll Free: (800)334 - 7626
E-Mail: info@naes.org
Members: 360 schools
Staff: 3
Annual Budget: $100-250,000
Exec. Director: Rev. Peter G. Cheney
Historical Note
Formerly (1965) Episcopal School Ass'n. Membership includes
pre-school through secondary level Episcopal schools. Membership
Fee: Based on size of school and number of students.
Publications:
Directory of Episcopal Schools. a. adv.
Network (newsletter). m.
Meetings/Conferences:
2000 – San Francisco, CA

Nat'l Ass'n of Equipment Leasing Brokers (1990)
P.O. Box 302
Wayne, PA 19087
Tel: (610)687-4129 **Fax:** (610)687-4305
Toll Free: (800)996 - 2352
E-Mail: cindy@naelb.org
Web Site: http://www.naelb.org
Members: 445 individuals
Staff: 1
Annual Budget: $100-250,000
Exec. Director: Cindy Spurdle
Administrative Coordinator: Angela Sciotto
Historical Note
Broker oriented association. Began in 1990 with conferences and
workshops covering various areas of concern to the leasing
industry. Funding sources join as non-voting members.
Membership: $295/year (broker); $450/year (funding source/
associate).
Publications:
Leaseline. q.
Leasing Logic. q.
Meetings/Conferences:
Annual Meetings: Spring
1999 – Dallas, TX(Fairmont Hotel)/April 8-11/400

Nat'l Ass'n of Estate Planning Councils (1963)
Historical Note
Address unknown in 1995.

Nat'l Ass'n of Evangelicals (1942)
P.O. Box 28
Wheaton, IL 60189
Tel: (630)665-0500 **Fax:** (630)665-8575
E-Mail: nae@nae.net
Web Site: http://www.nae.net
Staff: 11
Annual Budget: $1-2,000,000
Exec. Director: Dr. Dawn Argue
Historical Note
The National Association of Evangelicals is a voluntary association
of individuals, denominations, churches, schools and organizations
dedicated to united action without theological compromise. NAE
represents more than 50,000 local churches from 80 Protestant
denominations and serves more than 20 million people through its
subsidiary, affiliates and commissions. The Nat'l Christian
Education Ass'n is a program of NAE. The association maintains
its national offices in Carol Stream, Illinois and an office of public
affairs in Washington, D.C. Membership: $30/year (individual);
organizational fee based on size.
Publications:
NAE Washington Insight. m.
National Evangelical, Directory. bien.
United Evangelical Action. bi-m.
Meetings/Conferences:
Annual Meetings: March
1999 – Orlando, FL(Radisson Twin Towers)/Feb. 28-March 2

Nat'l Ass'n of Executive Recruiters (1984)
20 N. Wacker Dr., Suite 550
Chicago, IL 60606
Tel: (312)701-0744
Web Site: http://www.naer.org
Members: 50 companies
Staff: 2
Annual Budget: $100-250,000
President: Arnold Zimmerman

Historical Note
Incorporated in Illinois, NAER members are executive
recruitment/search firms; firms which primarily market candidates
are not eligible for membership. Membership: $650/year.
Meetings/Conferences:
Semi-Annual Meetings: Spring and Fall

Nat'l Ass'n of Executive Secretaries and Administrative Assistants (1975)
900 S. Washington St., Suite G13
Falls Church, VA 22046-4020
Tel: (703)237-8616
Members: 6,000 individuals
Staff: 3
Annual Budget: $50-100,000
Director: Ruth Ludeman
Membership Director: Susan Young
Historical Note
Formerly (1997) Nat'l Ass'n of Executive Secretaries. Membership:
$35/year.
Publications:
Executive Secretary Salary Survey Report. bien.
The Exec-U-Tary. m.
Meetings/Conferences:
Annual Meetings: Fall

Nat'l Ass'n of Export Companies (1965)
P.O. Box 1330, Murray Hill Station
New York, NY 10156
Tel: (212)490-7966 **Fax:** (718)596-5111
Web Site: nexco.org
Members: 300 companies
Staff: 1
Annual Budget: $50-100,000
Exec. Director: Nina Liebman
Historical Note
Formerly (1983) Nat'l Ass'n of Export Management Companies.
Members are export trading and export management companies,
export service vendors, and other exporting companies.
Membership: $195/year.
Meetings/Conferences:
Annual Meetings: Monthly Meetings, second Tuesday, New
York, NY

Nat'l Ass'n of Extension 4-H Agents (1946)
1605 N. Main, Room 102
Belton, TX 76513-1996
Tel: (254)933-5205
Members: 3,300 individuals
Annual Budget: $500-1,000,000
President: Tamera Beckham
Historical Note
Established as the Nat'l Ass'n of County Club Agents, it became the
Nat'l Ass'n of County 4-H Club Agents and in 1969 asssumed its
present name. NAE4-HA strives to promote, strengthen, enhance,
and advocate the 4-H youth development profession. Has no paid
staff. Administrative support is provided by the 4-H Council.
Membership: $35/year (individual).
Publications:
Journal of Extension. q.
News & Views. q. adv.
Meetings/Conferences:
Annual Meetings: Fall
1999 – Pittsburgh, PA/Oct. 24-28

Nat'l Ass'n of Extension Home Economists
Historical Note
Name changed to Nat'l Extension Ass'n of Family and Consumer
Sciences (NEAFCS) in 1996.

Nat'l Ass'n of Extradition Officials (1964)
Historical Note
Address unknown in 1996; presumed inactive or defunct.

Nat'l Ass'n of Family and Community Education (1936)
P.O. Box 835
Burlington, KY 41005
Tel: (606)586-8333 **Fax:** (606)586-8348
Web Site: http://www.nafce.org
Members: 30,000 individuals
Staff: 4
Annual Budget: $500-1,000,000
Office Manager: Kay White
Historical Note
FCE focuses on three major concerns: literacy, leadership, and the
effects of television and other media on children.
Meetings/Conferences:
1999 – Hawaii/July 26-30

Nat'l Ass'n of Farm Broadcasters (1944)
26 Exchange St. East, Suite 307
St. Paul, MN 55101
Tel: (651)224-0507 **Fax:** (651)224-1956
Web Site: http://www.nafb.com
Members: 725 individuals
Staff: 4
Annual Budget: $100-250,000
Exec. Director: Steve Pearson
Membership Manager: Mary Bock
Historical Note
Established as the Nat'l Ass'n of Radio Farm Directors, it became
the Nat'l Ass'n of Television-Radio Farm Directors in 1956 and
assumed its present name in 1964. Membership: $75 and
$100/year (individual).
Publications:
Chats. m.
NAFB Directory. a.

Meetings/Conferences:
Annual Meetings: Kansas City, MO(Crown
    Center)/November/700
1999 – Kansas City, MO/Nov. 10-14

Nat'l Ass'n of Fashion and Accessory Designers (1949)
2180 E. 93rd St.
Cleveland, OH 44106
Members: 215 individuals
Staff: 1
Annual Budget: $10-25,000
President: Elsie Reed

Historical Note
Affiliated with the Nat'l Council of Negro Women.

Publications:
Newsletter. 2/year.

Meetings/Conferences:

Nat'l Ass'n of Federal Credit Unions (1967)
3138 N. 10th St., Suite 300
Arlington, VA 22201
Tel: (703)522-4770   Fax: (703)524-1082
E-Mail: info@nafcunet.org
Web Site: http://www.nafcynet.org
Staff: 50
Annual Budget: $5-10,000,000
President: Steven K. Joiner
Director, Communications: Patrick M. Keefe
Public Relations Manager: Rosemary George
Director, Marketing: Tracey Brown
V. President, Govt. Affairs: William J. Donovan
Director, Legislative Affairs: Roland H. Myers, III
Exhibition Manager: Peter Taylor
Director, Planning/Programming: Joseph M. Boyle
Manager, Conference and meetings: Shirley Knowles
Director, Education: Sara J. Romanick
V. President, Member Services: Patricia S. Dameron
Director, Membership: Janet L. Miles

Historical Note
Originated in Los Angeles in 1966 at a meeting of 56 credit union
leaders to consider ways to shape the laws and regulations under
which federal credit unions operate and incorporated in the state of
California the next year. Supports the Nat'l Ass'n of Federal Credit
Unions Political Action Committee.

Publications:
The Federal Credit Union. bi-m.
Update. w.

Meetings/Conferences:
Annual Meetings: July/1,500
1999 – Denver, CO(Convention Center)/July 14-17/2500
2000 – Honolulu, HI(Convention Center)/July 19-22/3000

Nat'l Ass'n of Federal Education Program Administrators (1975)
1801 N. Moore St.
Arlington, VA 22209
Tel: (703)875-0729   Fax: (703)807-1849
E-Mail: smcfarland@aasa.org
Web Site: http://www.nafepa.org
Members: 5,500 individuals, 22 state affiliates
Staff: 2
Annual Budget: $100-250,000
Exec. Director: Stanley J. McFarland

Historical Note
Organized in 1975 to represent those professional educators
employed by local and intermediate school districts, state
departments of education, non-public schools, and education-
product suppliers, who have responsibility for supervising,
coordinating or administering federally funded education programs.
Formerly (1984) the Nat'l Ass'n of Administrators of State and
Federal Education Programs and (1985) the Nat'l Ass'n of
Administrators of Federal Education Programs. Membership:
$75/year (individual).

Publications:
Quarterly Newsletter. q.

Meetings/Conferences:
Annual Meetings: always Arlington, VA(Key Bridge
    Marriott)/Spring/300
1999 – /April 18-21

Nat'l Ass'n of Federal Veterinarians (1918)
1101 Vermont Ave., N.W., Suite 710
Washington, DC 20005-6308
Tel: (202)289-6334   Fax: (202)842-4360
E-Mail: nafv@erols.com
Members: 1,300 individuals
Staff: 2
Annual Budget: $100-250,000
Exec. V. President: Dale D. Boyle, D.V.M.

Historical Note
Affiliated with the American Veterinary Medical Ass'n. Supports the
Nat'l Ass'n of Federal Veterinarians Political Action Committee.
Sponsors American Academy of Veterinary Preventive Medicine.
Sponsors the NAFV Memorial Scholarship Fund. Membership:
$182/year.

Publications:
The Federal Veterinarian. m.

Meetings/Conferences:
1999 – New Orleans, LA/July 10-14
1999 – San Diego, CA(Town & Country Hotel)/Oct. 8-15

Nat'l Ass'n of Federally Impacted Schools (1973)
444 North Capitol St., N.W., Suite 419
Washington, DC 20001-1606
Tel: (202)624-5455   Fax: (202)624-5468
E-Mail: nafis@sso.org
Web Site: www.sso.org/nafis
Members: 800 school districts
Staff: 4

Annual Budget: $500-1,000,000
Exec. Director: John B. Forkenbrock

Historical Note
Association of school districts receiving federal impact aid. Serves
children in areas of military, Indian, handicapped and poverty.
Provides direct reimbursement to districts in lieu of real tax or
federal property. Membership: $300-9,000/year (based on amount
of aid received).

Publications:
Blue Book. a.
Impact!Insider. as necess.
Newsletter. m.

Meetings/Conferences:
Semi-annual Meetings: Washington, DC(Hyatt
    Regency)/Spring and Fall

Nat'l Ass'n of Federally Licensed Firearms Dealers (1973)
2455 E. Sunrise Blvd., Suite 916
Fort Lauderdale, FL 33304-3118
Tel: (954)561-3505   Fax: (954)561-4129
E-Mail: afi@amfire.com
Web Site: http://www.amfire.com
Members: 25,000 individuals
Staff: 11
President: Andrew Molchan

Historical Note
Members are individuals licensed to sell firearms. Membership:
$25/year(individual), $100/year(organization).

Publications:
AFI Buying Directory & Who's Who. a. adv.
AFI Shot Show Magazine. a.
American Firearms Industry. m. adv.

Meetings/Conferences:
1999 – Cleveland, OH(IX Center)/July 18-19/5000

Nat'l Ass'n of Fire Equipment Distributors (1962)
One E. Wacker Dr., Suite 3600
Chicago, IL 60601
Tel: (312)923-8500
Web Site: www.nafed.org
Members: 1,200 companies
Staff: 5
Annual Budget: $1-2,000,000
Exec. Director: Peter Schwartz

Historical Note
NAFED members sell, service and maintain fire equipment. It is
involved with state licensing of distributors and is working with
governmental agencies and fire services on other industry matters.

Publications:
Distributors Update. q.
Firewatch. q. adv.
Firewire. q.
Legislative Update. q.
Restaurant Systems. q.
Systems Alert. q.
Technical Update. q.

Meetings/Conferences:
Annual Meetings: May

Nat'l Ass'n of Fire Investigators (1961)
P.O. Box 957257
Hoffman Estates, IL 60195-7257
Tel: (847)885-8386   Fax: (847)885-8304
Toll Free: (888)866 - 5655
E-Mail: sysop@nafi.org
Web Site: http://www.nafi.org
Members: 3,500 individuals
Staff: 16
Annual Budget: $50-100,000
President: Patrick Kennedy
Director, Membership Services: Ann Schooley

Historical Note
Primary purposes are to increase the knowledge and improve the
skills of persons engaged in the investigation and analysis of
fires/explosions or in the litigation which ensues from such
investigations. Awards the Certified Fire and Explosion Investigator
(CFEI) and Certifed Fire Investigation Instructor (CFII)
designations. Membership: $35-$45/year.

Publications:
Nat'l Fire Investigator. irreg.

Meetings/Conferences:

Nat'l Ass'n of First Responders (1984)
Historical Note
Address unknown in 1997.

Nat'l Ass'n of Fleet Administrators (1957)
100 Wood Ave. South, Suite 310
Iselin, NJ 08830-2709
Tel: (732)494-8100   Fax: (732)494-6789
E-Mail: info@nafa.org
Web Site: http://www.nafa.org
Members: 3,200 individuals
Staff: 13
Annual Budget: $2-5,000,000
Exec. Director: David P. Lefever, CAE
Director, Communications: Michael Bevel
Director, Meetings: Pat Murtaugh

Historical Note
Individuals responsible for administration of a fleet of 25 or more
motor vehicles not for hire commercially. Organized at a luncheon
meeting at the Congress Hotel in Chicago, March 12, 1957 and
incorporated with 25 charter members in the State of Illinois, April
11, 1957. Membership: $320/year.

Publications:
NAFA Newsletter. m.
NAFA Reference Book. a. adv.

NAFA's Fleet Executive. m. adv.

Meetings/Conferences:
Annual Meetings: Spring/1,500

Nat'l Ass'n of Fleet Resale Dealers (1984)
4700 W. Lake Ave.
Glenview, IL 60025
Tel: (847)375-4729   Fax: (847)375-4777
Toll Free: (800)392 - 2536
E-Mail: info@nafrd.org
Web Site: http://www.nafrd.org
Members: 110 wholesalers
Staff: 3
Annual Budget: $100-250,000
Exec. Director: Mark T. Engle
Manager: Debra Hein
Managing Editor: Arlene Burd

Historical Note
NAFRD members are used car wholesalers who deal exclusively in
fleet vehicles. Associate membership is available for those who
provide goods or services to the industry. Industry partners are
those who are potential suppliers of vehicles to dealers.
Membership: $750/year (regular/associate); $100/year (industry
partner).

Publications:
Annual Business Survey. a.
Resource Directory. a. adv.
Tracks Newsletter. q. adv.

Meetings/Conferences:
Annual Meetings: Fall
1999 – New Orleans, LA
1999 – Miami, FL(Sheraton Bal Harbour)

Nat'l Ass'n of Flight Instructors (1966)
P.O. Box 3086
Oshkosh, WI 54903-3086
Tel: (920)426-6801   Fax: (920)426-6778
Members: 4,000 individuals
Staff: 5
Annual Budget: $100-250,000
Exec. Director: Sean Elliott

Historical Note
Members are flight instructors certified by the Federal Aviation
Administration and others who support flight instruction. Seeks to
raise the professional standards for flight instruction through
education and organization. Membership: $35/year (initial),
$35/year (renewal).

Publications:
NAFI News(published in Flight Training Mag). bi-m. adv.
NAFI Newsletter. m

Meetings/Conferences:

Nat'l Ass'n of Flood and Stormwater Management Agencies (1977)
1299 Pennsylvania Ave., N.W.
8th Floor-W
Washington, DC 20004-2400
Tel: (202)218-4122   Fax: (202)842-0621
Web Site: nasma.org
Members: 102 agencies
Staff: 4
Annual Budget: $100-250,000
Exec. Director: Susan Gilson

Historical Note
Members are state, county and municipal organizations concerned
with the management of water resources in metropolitan areas.
Formerly the Nat'l Ass'n of Urban Flood Management Agencies,
the Association assumed its present name in 1989.

Publications:
NAFSMA Monthly News Bulletin. irreg.

Meetings/Conferences:
Annual Meetings: Fall
1999 – Philadelphia, PA/Nov. 2-6

Nat'l Ass'n of Floor Covering Distributors (1971)
401 N. Michigan Ave.
Chicago, IL 60611-4703
Tel: (312)644-6610   Fax: (312)245-1085
Web Site: http://www.nafcd.org
Members: 300 individuals, 400 companies
Staff: 4
Annual Budget: $250-500,000
Exec. Director: Mariann B. Gregory

Historical Note
Membership: $520/year.

Publications:
News and Views. q.

Meetings/Conferences:

Nat'l Ass'n of Flour Distributors (1919)
c/o Compass Group, P.O. Box 610
Montville, NJ 07045
Tel: (973)402-1801   Fax: (973)316-6668
Members: 225 companies
Staff: 2
Annual Budget: $50-100,000
Ass'n Manager/Executive Secretary: Jean LaCorte

Historical Note
Members are brokers, distributors, manufacturers, and other
professionals allied with the flour industry.

Publications:
Membership Directory. a.
Newsletter. a. adv.
The Flour Distributor. 2/year.

Meetings/Conferences:
Annual Meetings: Spring
1999 – Scottsdale, AZ(Princess)/May 12-16/250
2000 – Naples, FL(Ritz Carlton)/May 17-21/250

Nat'l Ass'n of Foreign-Trade Zones (1973)
1000 Connecticut Ave., N.W., Suite 1001
Washington, DC 20036
Tel: (202)331-1950   *Fax:* (202)331-1994
E-Mail: info@naftz.org
Web Site: http://imex.com/naftz.html
Members: 620 organizations
Staff: 5
Annual Budget: $500-1,000,000
Exec. Director: Brandi B. Hanback

Historical Note
Foreign-Trade Zones are sites where foreign and domestic goods may be stored, tested, repackaged, assembled, etc. and where neither customs duty nor government excise tax is levied on exported products. Members are companies and organizations who are operators, grantees, and users of these sites. Membership: $100-950/year (company)

Publications:
Zones Report. m.

Meetings/Conferences:

Nat'l Ass'n of Forensic Economics (1986)
P.O. Box 30067
Kansas City, MO 64112-0067
Tel: (816)235-2833   *Fax:* (816)235-5263
E-Mail: nafe@cctr.umkc.edu
Web Site: http://www.haag.unkc.edu/nafe/
Members: 750 individuals, 105 organizations
Staff: 2
Annual Budget: $25-50,000
Exec. Director: Gerald Olson, Ph.D.

Historical Note
Formerly (1992) Nat'l Ass'n of Forensic Economists. NAFE fosters research and education in the application of economics to litigation. Has members in all 50 states and in 6 countries. Membership: $110/year.

Publications:
Journal of Forensic Economics. 3/year. adv.
Litigation Economics Digest. semi-a.
NAFE Membership Directory. bien.
NAFE Newsletter. q.

Meetings/Conferences:
Annual Meetings: January

Nat'l Ass'n of Foster Grandparent Program Directors (1971)
868 N. Manassas
Memphis, TN 38107
Tel: (901)577-2500
Members: 325 individuals
Annual Budget: $10-25,000
President: Jane Watkins

Historical Note
Created in 1971, NAFGPD serves as the principal advocate for Foster Grandparent Programs. The purpose of the NAFGPD is to provide a national focus for issues which directly affect both the quality of the services provided to volunteers and the children they serve, and the ability of directors to manage their programs effectively and to meet the changing needs of their communities. Professional membership is open to all directors, coordinators, and supervisors. Has no paid officers or full time staff. Membership: $75/year (individual); $125/year (organization).

Publications:
NAFGPD Update. bi-m.

Meetings/Conferences:
Semi-Annual Meetings: Washington, DC(Omni Shoreham)/Spring and Fall

Nat'l Ass'n of Franchise Companies (1969)
Historical Note
Ass'n inactive in 1997.

Nat'l Ass'n of Fraternal Insurance Counsellors (1950)
P.O. Box 357
Sheboygan, WI 53082-0357
Tel: (920)458-1996   *Fax:* (920)457-4661
Members: 2,750 individuals
Exec. Secretary: Peter Schmitt, Jr.

Historical Note
Formerly (1966) Fraternal Insurance Counsellors Ass'n. Affiliate of the Fraternal Field Managers Ass'n. Professional organization of sales personnel for fraternal benefit life insurance societies.

Publications:
The Fraternal Monitor. m.

Meetings/Conferences:
1999 – Williamsburg, VA/May 6-8

Nat'l Ass'n of Freight Payment Banks (1977)
399 Thornall St., East Tower, 5th Floor
Edison, NJ 08818
Tel: (908)906-7676   *Fax:* (908)906-5430
Members: 15 banks
Annual Budget: $100-250,000
Chairman: Harold B. Friedman

Historical Note
Incorporated in the State of Delaware, NAFPB has no paid staff or permanent address. Officers are elected annually. Members are banks offering shippers special arrangements for timely payment of freight charges.

Publications:
Membership Directory. a.

Meetings/Conferences:
Annual Meetings: Florida/April

Nat'l Ass'n of Freight Transportation Consultants (1959)
P.O. Box 53087

Albuquerque, NM 87153-3087
Tel: (505)299-0615
Web Site: http://www.naftc.com
Members: 110 companies
Staff: 1
Annual Budget: $10-25,000
Exec. Director: D.F. Behme

Publications:
The Supplement. m. adv.

Meetings/Conferences:
1999 – Orlando, FL

Nat'l Ass'n of Fruits, Flavors and Syrups (1917)
P.O. Box 545
5 Ravine Drive
Matawan, NJ 07747-0545
Tel: (732)583-8272   *Fax:* (732)583-0798
E-Mail: Bobbauer@naffs.org
Web Site: http://www.naffs.org
Members: 120 companies
Staff: 5
Annual Budget: $50-100,000
Exec. Director: Robert Bauer

Historical Note
Formerly (1974) Nat'l Fruit & Syrup Manufacturers Ass'n, Inc. Membership: $350-450/year. (company).

Publications:
NAFFS Annual Yearbook & Directory. a. adv.
NAFFS Newsletter. bi-w.

Meetings/Conferences:
Annual Meetings: Fall/120

Nat'l Ass'n of FSA County Office Employees
530 Freedom Road
Ripley, WV 25271
Tel: (304)372-8826   *Fax:* (304)372-8791
Members: 10,000 individuals
Annual Budget: $100-250,000
Secretary/Treasurer: Charlotte Saunders

Historical Note
Formerly (1995) Nat'l Ass'n of ASCS County Office Employees and (1997) Nat'l Ass'n of FSA County Office. An independent labor association. Members are county office employees of the U.S. Department of Agriculture's Farm Service Agency. Has no paid officers or full-time staff. Membership: $40/year (individual).

Publications:
NASCOE Newsletter. bi-m.

Meetings/Conferences:
Annual Meetings: August
1999 – Oklahoma City, OK(Westin)/Aug. 4-7

Nat'l Ass'n of Fund Raising Ticket Manufacturers (1983)
10 South 5th Street
Suite 810B
Minneapolis, MN 55402
Tel: (612)335-3590   *Fax:* (612)335-8244
Members: 6 manufacturers
Staff: 2
Annual Budget: $500-1,000,000
Exec. Director: Pamela A. Perri

Nat'l Ass'n of Garage Door Manufacturers
Historical Note
Merged (1996) with Door Operator and Remote Controls Manufacturers Ass'n to form Door and Access Systems Manufacturers Ass'n Internat'l.

Nat'l Ass'n of Gas Chlorinators
30575 Trabuco Canyon Road, Suite 104
Trabuco Canyon, CA 92678
Tel: (949)459-8735   *Fax:* (949)858-9607
E-Mail: AssocOfc@aol.com
Exec. Director: Lyn Paymer

Historical Note
Membership: $475/year.

Publications:
NAGC Newsletter/ bi-m. adv. adv.

Meetings/Conferences:

Nat'l Ass'n of Geology Teachers (1938)
Historical Note
Became the Nat'l Ass'n of Geoscience Teachers in 1996.

Nat'l Ass'n of Geoscience Teachers (1938)
P.O. Box 5443
Bellingham, WA 98227-5443
Tel: (360)650-3587   *Fax:* (360)650-7302
Web Site: http://www.nagt.org
Members: 1,900 individuals
Annual Budget: $50-100,000
Exec. Director: Robert A. Christman, Ph.D.

Historical Note
Founded in Rock Island, IL as the Ass'n of College Geology Teachers; dropped "College" from name in 1958; became the Nat'l Ass'n of Geology Teachers in 1958; and assumed present name in 1996. A member society of the American Geological Institute. Has no paid staff. Membership: $25/year (individual), $33/year (U.S. organization), $37/year (foreign organization).

Publications:
Journal of Geoscience Education. 5/year. adv.

Meetings/Conferences:
Annual Meetings: Fall, with Geological Soc. of America

Nat'l Ass'n of Golf Tournament Directors (1996)
8175 S. Virginia St., Suite 850-391
Reno, NV 89511
Tel: (702)852-4646   *Fax:* (702)852-0824

Toll Free: (888)899 - 2483
E-Mail: nagtd@aol.com
Web Site: www.nagtd.com
Members: 400 individuals
Staff: 4
Annual Budget: $250-500,000
Exec. Director: William R. Hoffman
Director, Conference and Education: Amanda Flangas

Historical Note
NATGD members are professionals who develop and direct national association, celebrity, charity and corporate golf tournaments. Membership $175/year (individual).

Publications:
Leaderboard Newsletter. q. adv.

Meetings/Conferences:
Annual Meetings: December 998-Miami Beach, FL(Loews)/Dec./500
1999 – Las Vegas, NV
2000 – Savannah, GA

Nat'l Ass'n of Government Archives and Records Administrators (1984)
48 Howard St.
Albany, NY 12207
Tel: (518)463-8644   *Fax:* (518)463-8656
E-Mail: nagara@capmill.com
Web Site: http://www.nagara.org
Members: 350 individuals, 48 state agencies
Annual Budget: $50-100,000
Exec. Director: Bruce W. Dearstyne

Historical Note
Incorporated in New York State, NAGARA is a nationwide association of local, state and federal records administrators and others concerned with improving administration of government records. Membership: $600/program/yr. (records management & archival agencies); $40/yr. (all others).

Publications:
The Clearinghouse. q.

Meetings/Conferences:
Annual Meetings: Summer
1999 – Columbus, OH/July 15-17

Nat'l Ass'n of Government Communicators (1976)
526 King St., Suite 423
Alexandria, VA 22314
Tel: (703)518-4369   *Fax:* (703)706-9583
Web Site: http://www.nagc.com
Members: 800 individuals
Staff: 1
Annual Budget: $100-250,000
Exec. Director: Lynn Mitchel

Historical Note
A merger of the Federal Editors Ass'n, the Government Information Organization, and the Armed Forces Writers' League. Member of the Council of Communication Societies. Membership: $85/year (individual).

Publications:
GC Newsletter q.

Meetings/Conferences:
Annual Meetings: December

Nat'l Ass'n of Government Deferred Compensation Administrators (1980)
167 W. Main St., Suite 600
Lexington, KY 40507
Tel: (606)231-1904   *Fax:* (606)231-1928
Members: 145 government & 99 industry members
Staff: 3
Annual Budget: $100-250,000
Association Manager: Carol Roberts

Historical Note
NAGDA members are state, county and municipal Section 457 plan administrators and vendor firms. Membership: $400/year (government member); $700/year (industry member).

Publications:
Conference Report. a.
Guidebook. a.
Membership Directory. a.
Newsletter. q.
Question & Answer Book. a.
Survey of 457 Plans. bien.

Meetings/Conferences:
1999 – San Antonio, TX(Hyatt Riverwalk)

Nat'l Ass'n of Government Employees (1961)
317 S. Patrick St.
Alexandria, VA 22314
Tel: (703)519-0300   *Fax:* (703)519-0311
E-Mail: nage@arols.com
Web Site: http://www.nage.org
Members: 200,000 individuals
Staff: 100
Annual Budget: $2-5,000,000
President: Kenneth T. Lyons
V. President: Susanne J. Pooler

Historical Note
NAGE, a labor union representing civilian government employees, which includes the Nat'l Ass'n of Nurses, Nat'l Ass'n of Health Care Workers, Internat'l Brotherhood of Correctional Officers, and Internat'l Brotherhood of Police Officers, became affiliated with the Service Employees Internat'l Union, AFL-CIO in 1982. Sponsors and supports the Government Employees' Political Research Institute and the Nat'l Ass'n of Government Employees Political Action Committee.

Publications:
Fednews. q.
NAGE Reporter. q.
Police Chronicle. q.

Meetings/Conferences:

Nat'l Ass'n of Government Guaranteed Lenders *(1984)*
P.O. Box 332
Stillwater, OK   74076-0332
Tel: (405)377-4022   *Fax:* (405)377-3931
E-Mail: NAGGL@aol.com
Members: 700 organizations
Staff: 8
Annual Budget: $1-2,000,000
President & C.E.O.: Anthony R. Wilkinson
Meeting Planner: Cheryl Stone
Education Director: Karen High
Chairman: Deryl Schuster
Membership Coordinator: Dena Scott
Technical Issues Director: Jackie Randle

Historical Note
NAGGL is devoted to the professional and governmental affairs interests of financial institutions and small business lenders who participate in Small Business Administration guaranteed lending and secondary market programs. Membership: $695/year (organization/company).

Publications:
NAGGL Update. m.

Meetings/Conferences:
Annual Meetings: Semi-Annual.
1999 – San Antonio, TX(Hyatt Regency Riverwalk)/May 5-7
1999 – San Diego, CA(Hotel del Coronado)/Nov. 5-7
2000 – Las Vegas, NV(MGM Grand)

Nat'l Ass'n of Government Training and Development Directors
Historical Note
Became (1998) Nat'l Ass'n for Government Training and Development.

Nat'l Ass'n of Governmental Labor Officials *(1914)*
444 N. Capitol St., N.W., Suite 401
Washington, DC   20001
Tel: (202)624-5460   *Fax:* (202)624-5452
Web Site: www.csg.org
Members: 50 individuals
Annual Budget: $25-50,000
Staff Director: David Scott

Historical Note
Founded as the Internat'l Ass'n of Governmental Labor Officials, it assumed its present name in 1979. Members are directors and commissioners of state labor departments. Has no paid staff or permanent address. Membership: $500/year.

Publications:
NAGLO Membership Directory. a.
NAGLO News. m.

Meetings/Conferences:
Annual Meetings: Summer

Nat'l Ass'n of Governors' Councils on Physical Fitness and Sports *(1979)*
201 S. Capitol Ave., Suite 560
Indianapolis, IN   46225
Tel: (317)237-5630   *Fax:* (317)237-5632
E-Mail: Govcouncil@aol.com
Web Site: http://www.fitnesslink.com/govcouncil/
Members: 40 councils
Staff: 3
Annual Budget: $250-500,000
Exec. Director: Cindy Porteous

Historical Note
Members are state and provincial governors' councils which encourage physical fitness. Membership: $150/year (council); $100/year (corporate); $50/year (community organization); $25/year (individual).

Publications:
State by State Newsletter. q.

Meetings/Conferences:
Annual Meetings: March

Nat'l Ass'n of Governors' Highway Safety Representatives *(1969)*
750 First St., N.E., Suite 720
Washington, DC   20002-4241
Tel: (202)789-0942   *Fax:* (202)789-0946
E-Mail: dmaddox@naghsr.org
Web Site: www.naghsr.org
Members: 54 states and territories
Staff: 3
Annual Budget: $250-500,000
Exec. Director: Barbara L. Harsha

Historical Note
Members are state officials who administer the Highway Safety Act.

Publications:
Newsletter. bi-m.

Meetings/Conferences:
Annual Meetings: September
1999 – San Antonio, TX/Aug. 29-Sept. 1
2000 – Biloxi, MS/Sept. 24-27

Nat'l Ass'n of Graduate Admissions Professionals *(1987)*
NYU School of Law Admissions Ofc.
110 Third St.
New York, NY   10012
Tel: (212)998-6073   *Fax:* (212)995-4527
Members: 800 individuals
President: Donald A. Resnick
Secretary: Joanne Nagy

Historical Note
The National Association of Graduate Admissions Professionals is the only professional organization devoted exclusively to the concerns of individuals working in the graduate admissions and recruitment environment. NAGAP is committed to serving the needs and interests of graduate admissions professionals in five regions of the United States (New England, Atlantic, Southern, Central and Western) plus international locations. Formerly the New England Ass'n of Graduate Admissions Professionals. Membership: $100/year (individual); $125/year (institution).

Publications:
Calendar of Grad & Professional School Fairs. a. adv.
Journal of NAGAP. q.
Membership and Resource Directory. a. adv.

Meetings/Conferences:
Annual Meetings: Annual/Spring

Nat'l Ass'n of Graphic and Product Identification Manufacturers *(1951)*
12241 Newport Ave. #100
Santa Ana, CA   92705
Tel: (714)508-4915   *Fax:* (714)508-4904
Members: 160 companies
Staff: 15
Annual Budget: $100-250,000
Exec. V. President: James A. Kinder
Media Relations: Kim Parkhurst
: George Pantos
Meeting Planner: Jessica Schwartz
Dir., Meeting Plannings: Judi Dokter
Dir., Finance: Mieka Schortez
Dir., Membership: Katie Miceer

Historical Note
Incorporated July 24, 1951 in the State of Delaware as a result of meetings by manufacturers during World War II to discuss metal shortages. Established as the Metal Etching and Fabricating Ass'n, it became Nat'l Ass'n of Metal Name Plate Manufacturers in 1967, Nat'l Ass'n of Name Plate Manufacturers in 1979, and assumed its current name in 1994. Publishes the only book of standards for the name plate industry.

Publications:
Membership Directory. a.
Newsletter. 3/year.
Standards & Practices.

Meetings/Conferences:
Semi-Annual Meetings: Spring and Fall
1999 – Scottsdale, AZ(Marriott Camelback)/April 6-11/150
2000 – Nashville(Westin)/Sept. 12-15/150

Nat'l Ass'n of Health Care Workers
Historical Note
A unit of the Nat'l Ass'n of Government Employees.

Nat'l Ass'n of Health Career Schools *(1968)*
750 First St., N.E., Suite 940
Washington, DC   20002
Members: 200 schools
Staff: 1
Annual Budget: $100-250,000
Administrator: Jeanne Russell

Historical Note
Formerly (1975) Ass'n of Accredited Medical Laboratory Schools. Membership: $300/year.

Publications:
Bulletin. q.
Newsletter. 4/year.
Washington Update. irreg.

Meetings/Conferences:
Annual Meetings: in conjunction with American Medical Technologists Ass'n

Nat'l Ass'n of Health Data Organizations *(1986)*
254-B N. Washington St.
Falls Church, VA   22046-4517
Tel: (703)532-3282   *Fax:* (703)532-3593
E-Mail: nahdo@usa.pipeline.com
Members: 250 organizations
Staff: 4
Annual Budget: $250-500,000
Exec. Director: Mark H. Epstein
Assoc. Director: Barbara Kurtzig

Historical Note
NAHDO members are federal and state health organizations, software developers, consultants, hospitals, health series researchers, insurers, managed care firms, cost containment companies, and health trade groups. Membership: $125/year (indivivual); $2,000-2,500/year (organization).

Publications:
Annual Report. a.
NAHDO News Newsletter. bi-m.
NAHDO News Update.

Meetings/Conferences:
Annual Meetings: Winter

Nat'l Ass'n of Health Services Executives *(1968)*
8630 Fenton St., Suite 126
Silver Spring, MD   20910
Tel: (301)588-0700   *Fax:* (301)588-0011
Members: 1,700 individuals
Staff: 5
Annual Budget: $250-500,000
Exec. Director: Ozzie Jenkins, CMP

Historical Note
Members are African-American health care executives. Membership: $100/year (individual), $1,100/year (organization).

Publications:
NAHSE Notes. q. adv.

Meetings/Conferences:
Annual Meetings: April-May

Nat'l Ass'n of Health Underwriters *(1930)*
200 N. 14th St., Suite 450
Arlington, VA   22201
Tel: (703)276-0220   *Fax:* (703)841-7797
E-Mail: webmaster@nahu.org
Web Site: http://www.nahu.org
Members: 14,500 individuals
Staff: 21
Annual Budget: $2-5,000,000
Exec. V. President: Kevin Corcoran
Director, Communications: Patricia Tyler
Director, Federal Legislative Affairs: Tom Bruderle
Director, State Legislative Affairs: Janet Stokes
Director of Meetings: Kathleen D. Cochran, CMP
Director, Education: Barbara Dunlavey, CMP
Director, Finance: Steve Stoupa, CPA
Director, Membership: Brian Waller

Historical Note
Formerly (1962) Nat'l Ass'n of Accident & Health Underwriters, and Internat'l Ass'n of Health Underwriters (1978). Awards the RHU (Registered Health Underwriter) and REBC (Registered Employee Benefits Consultant) designations. Membership: $105/year (individual).

Publications:
Health Insurance Underwriter. m. adv.

Meetings/Conferences:
Annual Meetings: June
1999 – Miami, FL
2000 – Cleveland, OH

Nat'l Ass'n of Health Unit Coordinators *(1980)*
1211 Locust St.
Philadelphia, PA   19107
Toll Free: (888)226 - 2482
Members: 4,000 individuals
Annual Budget: $100-250,000
Exec. Director: Tracy Trauger

Historical Note
Formerly (1990) Nat'l Ass'n of Health Unit Clerks/Coordinators. Members are coordinators of non-clinical nursing unit activities, educators, supervisors, students and graduates in the field. Membership: $30/year (new), $20/year (renewal), $195yyear (organization /company).

Publications:
NAHUC - Membership Directory. a.
The Coordinator. q. adv.

Meetings/Conferences:

Nat'l Ass'n of Healthcare Access Management *(1974)*
1200 19th St., N.W., Suite 300
Washington, DC   20036
Tel: (202)857-1125   *Fax:* (202)857-1115
Web Site: www.naham.org
Members: 1000 individuals
Staff: 3
Annual Budget: $250-500,000
Exec. Director: Sherry Meyers

Historical Note
Formerly (1990) the Nat'l Ass'n of Hospital Admitting Managers NAHAM was established and incorporated in New York. Membership: $140/year (individual); $1,000/year (corporate).

Publications:
Connections. m.
The NAHAM Management Journal q. adv. adv.

Meetings/Conferences:
Annual Meetings: May/500
1999 – Las Vegas, NV/May 16-19

Nat'l Ass'n of Healthcare Consultants *(1992)*
1255 23rd St., N.W., Suite 850
Washington, DC   20037-1174
Tel: (202)452-8282   *Fax:* (202)833-3636
Toll Free: (800)313 - 6242
E-Mail: consultants@healthcon.org
Web Site: www.healthcon.org
Members: 300 individuals
Staff: 3
Annual Budget: $250-500,000
Exec. Director: Joseph B. Morris

Historical Note
NAHCC represents consultants who provide ethical, confidential, and professional advice to the health care industry. Membership $350/year (individual).

Publications:
Hot Topics Update. q.
Photo Roster. a.
Professional Practice Today. 11/year.
Statistics of Physician Practices. a.
UPDATE Monthly. m.

Meetings/Conferences:
Annual Meetings: Spring
1999 – Boston, MA(Park Plaza)/June 23-26

Nat'l Ass'n of Hearing Officials
Historical Note
Organization defunct in 1998.

Nat'l Ass'n of Hebrew Day School Administrators *(1960)*
1114 Ave. J
Brooklyn, NY   11230
Tel: (718)258-7767   *Fax:* (718)338-1043
Members: 400 individuals
Director: Alfred Schnell, Ph.D.

Nat'l Ass'n of Hispanic and Latino Studies (1995)
Morehead State University
211 Rader Hall
Morehead, KY 40351-1689
Tel: (606)783-2650 *Fax:* (606)783-5046
Members: 176 individuals, 2 organizations
Staff: 2
Annual Budget: $25-50,000
Exec. Director: Lemuel Berry, Jr., Ph.D.
Historical Note
Membership: $150/year (individual); $500/year (organization).
Publications:
NAHLS Newsletter. q. adv.
Networks: Making Connections. semi-a. adv.
Meetings/Conferences:
1999 – Houston, TX(Adams Mark)/Feb. 9-13/2000
2000 – Houston, TX(Admas Mark)/Feb. 8-12/3000

Nat'l Ass'n of Hispanic County Officials
440 First St., N.W., 8th Floor
Washington, DC 20001
Tel: (202)942-4260 *Fax:* (202)393-2630
Web Site: www.naco.org
Annual Budget: under $10,000
Staff Liaison: Marilina Sanz
Historical Note
An affiliate of the Nat'l Ass'n of Counties which provides administrative support.
Meetings/Conferences:
1999 – St. Louis, MO/July 16-20

Nat'l Ass'n of Hispanic Federal Executives (1984)
P.O. Box 469
Herndon, VA 20172-0469
Tel: (703)787-0291 *Fax:* (703)787-4576
Members: 600 individuals
Staff: 3
Annual Budget: $50-100,000
President: Manuel Oliverez
Dir., Admin./Finance: Ana Maria Oliverez
Historical Note
NAHFE promotes the federal government as a model employer, recruits qualified Hispanics for federal service and provides quality executive development training to Federal personnel. Its goal is to increase the number of Hispanic Americans in high level policy positions in the Federal executive departments and agencies. Membership: $36/year (individual); $1,000/year (organization/company).
Publications:
Hispanic Executive. q. adv.
Project Alpha Report: Employment Analysis of Fed. Depts.
Meetings/Conferences:
1999 – Washington, DC/600
2000 – Washington, DC/650

Nat'l Ass'n of Hispanic Journalists (1982)
Nat'l Press Bldg., Suite 1193
529 14th St. N.W.
Washington, DC 20045-2100
Tel: (202)662-7145 *Fax:* (202)662-7144
E-Mail: nahj@tmn.com
Web Site: http:\\www.nahj.org
Members: 1,700 individuals
Staff: 4
Annual Budget: $1-2,000,000
Exec. Director: Patrick W. Salazar
Coordinator, Prof. Development: Nancy Tita
Historical Note
Its purposes are to increase educational and career opportunities in journalism for Hispanic Americans; to organize and provide mutual support of Hispanic journalists; and to promote fair treatment of Hispanics by the news media. Membership: $50/year (individual); $1,000/year (company).
Publications:
NAHJ Membership Newsletter. m.
National Hispanic Media Directory. a.
Meetings/Conferences:
Annual Meetings: Summer/1,200
1999 – Huntington Beach, CA(Front Water Hilton Beach)/March 3-6
2000 – Houston, TX(Westin Galleria)/June 21-24

Nat'l Ass'n of Hispanic Nurses (1974)
1501 16th St., N.W.
Washington, DC 20036
Tel: (202)387-2477 *Fax:* (202)483-7183
E-Mail: nahn@juno.com
Web Site: http://www.incacorp.com/nahn
Members: 1000 individuals, 34 chapters
Annual Budget: $50-100,000
President: Antonia M. Villarruel, RN, Ph.D.
Historical Note
NAHN strives to serve the nursing and healthcare delivery needs of the Hispanic community and the professional needs of Hispanic nurses. NAHN is designed and committed to work toward the improvement of the quality of health and nursing care for Hispanic consumers and toward providing equal access to educational, professional, and economic opportunities for Hispanic nurses. Membership: $20/year (student); $50/year (individual).
Publications:
Directory of Hispanic Nurses. a. adv.
Hispanic Nurse. q.
Meetings/Conferences:
Annual Meetings: July/110
1999 – San Juan, Puerto Rico/July 21-23
2000 – Washington, DC

Nat'l Ass'n of Hispanic Publications (1982)

652 Nat'l Press Bldg.
Washington, DC 20045
Tel: (202)662-7250 *Fax:* (202)662-7254
Members: 130 publications
Staff: 1
Annual Budget: $250-500,000
Exec. Director: Andres Tobar
Historical Note
NAHP was founded in the belief that the most effective way to reach the more than 29 million Hispanic Americans in the country is their own language. Membership open to publications which serve or cover the Hispanic and/or Spanish speaking community in the U.S. Associate membership open to individuals, corporations, or new services who support the goals of the NAHP. Membership: $100-500/yr., depending on type of publication (weekly, monthly, magazine, etc.).
Publications:
Hispanic Press. q. adv.
Marketing Hispanic Print. m. adv.
National Hispanic Media Directory. a.
Meetings/Conferences:
Annual Meetings: Winter

Nat'l Ass'n of Home and Workshop Writers (1973)
Box 12
Baker, NV 89311
Tel: (702)234-7167 *Fax:* (702)234-7361
E-Mail: dondiy@aol.com
Members: 100 individuals
Annual Budget: under $10,000
President: Don Geary
Historical Note
Writers of articles, books and video material on such subjects as home maintenance, repair and improvement, and on workshop projects. Membership: $30/year (individual); $200/year (organization).
Publications:
Directory of Members. a.
Newsletter. q.
Meetings/Conferences:
Annual Meetings: Summer
1999 – Chicago, IL

Nat'l Ass'n of Home Based Businesses (1984)
10451 Mill Run Circle
Owings Mills, MD 21117
Tel: (410)363-3698
Web Site: http:usahomebusiness.com
Staff: 10
President: Rudolph Lewis
Historical Note
Provides support and development to home based businesses.
Publications:
Business Opportunity Bulletin. q.
Home Based Business Newspaper. q. adv.
Home Business Identity Classification.
Nat'l Register of U. S. adv.
Meetings/Conferences:

Nat'l Ass'n of Home Builders of the U.S. (1942)
1201 15th St., N.W.
Washington, DC 20005-2800
Tel: (202)822-0200 *Fax:* (202)822-0559
Toll Free: (800)368 - 5242
E-Mail: info@nahb.com
Web Site: http://www.nahb.com
Members: 194,000 individuals
Staff: 285
Annual Budget: $25-50,000,000
Exec. V. President and C.E.O.: Thomas M. Downs
V.P. Public Affairs and Marketing: William Ellingsworth
V. President, Public Affairs: Elizabeth E. Christy
Senior V. President, Government Affairs: Jerry Howard
V.P. Regulatory & Legal Affairs: Bob Brown
Staff V. President, Conventions: Wayne Stetson
V.P. Of Economics, Mortgage, Finance & Housing Policy: Dave Seiders
Controller: Joe Barney
Director, Operations and Publishing: Mary A. Gallagher
V. President, Information Services: Jim Johnson
Director, Computer Technology: Jean Carmichael
Historical Note
Connected with the Builders Political Campaign Committee (BUILD-PAC). Also supports the Homeowners Warranty Corporation, the NAHB Research Center, the Home Builders Institute, the Nat'l Council of the Housing Industry, and the Nat'l Housing Endowment. The Nat'l Commercial Builders Council, Nat'l Council of the Multifamily Housing Industry, Nat'l Remodelors Council and the Nat'l Sales and Marketing Council are councils of NAHB. The Nat'l Council of Multifamily Housing is a division. Absorbed the National Association of Home Manufacturers in 1981 and the North American Log Homes Council in 1987.
Publications:
Builder. m. adv.
Forcast of Housing Activity. m.
Housing Economics. m.
Housing Market Statistics. m.
Nation's Building News. adv. adv.
Reference Guide to Homebuilding Articles. q.
Meetings/Conferences:
Annual Meetings: Winter
1999 – Dallas, TX(Convention Center)/Jan. 15-18

Nat'l Ass'n of Home Inspectors (1987)
4248 Park Glen Road
Minneapolis, MN 55416
Tel: (612)928-4641 *Fax:* (612)929-1318
Toll Free: (800)448 - 3942
E-Mail: info@nahi.org

Web Site: http://www.nahi.org
Members: 800 individuals
Annual Budget: $100-250,000
Exec. Director: Gloria Isackson
Finance Director: John Francis
Membership Administrator: Shirlene Merrill
Historical Note
NAHI is a trade association established to promote and develop the home inspection industry. Membership: $150/year (individual); $250/year (company/organization).
Publications:
Membership Directory. a.
NAHI Forum Newsletter. bi-m. adv.

Nat'l Ass'n of Homes and Servcies for Children
Historical Note
Became (1998) {Alliance for Children & Families}

Nat'l Ass'n of Homes and Services for Children (1975)
Historical Note
Merged with (1998) Family Service America.

Nat'l Ass'n of Hose and Accessories Distributors (1985)
105 Eastern Ave., Suite 104
Annapolis, MD 21403-3300
Tel: (410)263-1014 *Fax:* (410)263-1659
Toll Free: (800)624 - 2227
Members: 350 distributors, 150 manufacturers
Staff: 6
Annual Budget: $500-1,000,000
Exec. V. President: Joseph M. Thompson, Jr.
Communications/Conference Director: Kristin B. Thompson
Business Services Director: Diana J. Crumpton, CPA
Director, Membership and Resources: Wendy Blumenthal
Historical Note
NAHAD is an international association of distributors and manufacturers of industrial hose and fittings. A member of the National Association of Wholesaler Distributors. Membership: $330-580/year.
Publications:
Convention Guide. a. adv.
Membership Directory. a. adv.
NAHAD News. bi-m.
Meetings/Conferences:
1999 – San Antonio, TX(Hyatt Hill Country)/April 17-21
2000 – Monterrey, CA(Doubletree)/April 7-11

Nat'l Ass'n of Hosiery Manufacturers (1905)
200 N. Sharon Amity Road
Charlotte, NC 28211
Tel: (704)365-0913 *Fax:* (704)362-2056
Web Site: http://www.nahm.com
Members: 435 manufacturers
Staff: 15
Annual Budget: $1-2,000,000
President and CEO: Sid Smith
Director of Information Services: Virginia Prevatte
V. President and Treasurer: Sheila Simpson
Director of Finance: Jeanna Bates
V. President and Secretary: Sally Kay
Director, Meetings and Chapter Relations: Patricia Kirkman
Historical Note
Manufacturers of hosiery as well as suppliers of raw materials, machinery and packaging. Members make and distribute more than 85% of U.S. hosiery, including socks and pantyhose.
Publications:
Directory of Hosiery Manufacturers. bien (odd years). adv.
Hosiery News. m. adv.
Hosiery Statistics. a.
Meetings/Conferences:

Nat'l Ass'n of Hospital Hospitality Houses (1986)
4915 Auburn Ave., Suite 303
Bethesda, MD 20814-2636
Tel: (301)961-5264 *Fax:* (301)961-3094
Toll Free: (800)542 - 9730
E-Mail: NAHHH HQ@aol.com
Web Site: http://visit-usa.com/hhh
Members: 135 organizations
Staff: 5
Annual Budget: $100-250,000
Exec. Director: Martha J. Lockwood, CAE, APR
Manager, Development and Commuications: Kelly Rutt
Historical Note
NAHHH members are hospital hospitality house facilities providing temporary residential facilities for the use of patients and their families. Membership: $200/year (individual); $200-250/year (organization/company).
Publications:
Hospital Quarterly. q.
House Notes. bi-m.
Inside Hospitality. q.
NAHHH Newsletter. semi-a.
Nat'l Referral Directory. irreg.
Meetings/Conferences:
Annual Meetings: Spring
1999 – Bethesda, MD(Bethesda Hyatt)/June 2-5

Nat'l Ass'n of Housing and Redevelopment Officials (1933)
630 I St., N.W.
Washington, DC 20001-3736
Tel: (202)289-3500 *Fax:* (202)289-8181
Toll Free: (800)842 - 6225
E-Mail: nahro@nahro.org
Web Site: http://www.nahro.org
Members: 6,500 individuals, 2,500 agencies

Staff: 40
Annual Budget: $5-10,000,000
Exec. Director: Richard Y. Nelson, Jr.
Director, Communications/Publications: Terence Cooper
Dir., Legislation & Program Development: Julio Barreto
Director, Conferences: Midge Monello
Director, Training: Vida Nakas
Director, Technical Services: Terry Matlaga
Director, Finance and Administration: Leon Durham
Director of Member Services: Mary L. Pike
Deputy Exec. Director: Michael Nail

Historical Note
Formerly (1953) Nat'l Ass'n of Housing Officials. Members are housing and community development officials who administer local programs under the auspices of HUD. Has an annual budget of approximately $5 million.

Publications:
Journal of Housing and Community Development. bi-m. adv.
NAHRO Monitor. semi-m.

Meetings/Conferences:
1999 – Philadelphia, PA/Oct. 17-20

Nat'l Ass'n of Housing Cooperatives (1950)
1614 King St.
Alexandria, VA   22314-2719
Tel: (703)549-5201   *Fax:* (703)549-5204
Web Site: http://www.coophousing.org
Members: 1000 ass'ns, cooperatives, indiv.
Staff: 9
Annual Budget: $250-500,000
Exec. Director: Vicki Womack
Dir., Publication: Deniz Tuncer
Dir., Govt. Relations: Judy Sullivan
Dir., Educational Dev./Training: Esther Siegel

Historical Note
NAHC defines a housing cooperative as a residential community whose residents collectively own their property, vote to determine policy, and receive a limited return on invested capital. Members are housing cooperatives, management firms, attorneys, accountants, neighborhood organizations, tenant associations, government agencies and individuals interested in cooperative housing. Membership: sliding scale based on the number of co-op members.

Publications:
Cooperative Housing Bulletin. bi-m. adv.
Cooperative Housing Journal. a. adv.

Meetings/Conferences:
Annual Meetings: Fall
1999 – Toronto, Ontario, Canada(Royal York)

Nat'l Ass'n of Housing Information Managers (1992)
P.O. Box 67202
Lincoln, NE   68506-7202
Tel: (402)466-9424   *Fax:* (402)420-1770
Toll Free: (800)379 - 3807
E-Mail: NAHIMEXEC@aol.com
Web Site: http://www.nahim.org
Members: 102 public housing authorities
Annual Budget: $10-25,000
Exec. Director: John E. Mooring

Historical Note
Established to focus on information technology issues affecting public housing authorities. NAHIM members are public housing authorities. Associate membership is available for private software firms. Membership: $50-$100/year (public housing agency); $250/year (associate).

Publications:
NAHIM News Newsletter. m.

Meetings/Conferences:
1999 – Baltimore, MD

Nat'l Ass'n of Human Rights Workers (1947)
Historical Note
Address unknown in 1997.

Nat'l Ass'n of Human Service Quality Control Directors
Historical Note
Became (1998) Nat'l Ass'n of Program Information and Performance Measurement.

Nat'l Ass'n of Independent Colleges and Universities (1976)
1025 Connecticut Ave., N.W., Suite 700
Washington, DC   20036-5405
Tel: (202)785-8866   *Fax:* (202)835-0003
Members: 900 colleges and universities
Staff: 22
Annual Budget: $2-5,000,000
President: David L. Warren
V.President, Public Affairs: Roland King
V. President, Government Relations: Sarah A. Flanagan
Director, Leg. Affairs: Maureen Budetti
Director, Finance and Administration: Susan E. Luhrs
Director, Membership Services: Deborah Sykes Reilly
Director, Publications: Jeffery E. Hume-Pratuch

Historical Note
Founded as Federation of State Ass'ns of Colleges and Universities, a lobbying group for the Ass'n of American Colleges, it became the Nat'l Council of Independent Colleges and Universities in 1971 and assumed independence under its present name in 1976. Promotes private and government support for the nation's 1200 private institutions of higher learning. Membership: $500-8,000/yr. (institution).

Publications:
Week In Review. w.

Meetings/Conferences:
Annual Meetings: Winter in Washington, DC(Hyatt Regency)/600
1999 – /Feb. 3-5

Nat'l Ass'n of Independent Fee Appraisers (1961)
7501 Murdoch St.
St. Louis, MO   63119
Tel: (314)781-6688   *Fax:* (314)781-2872
E-Mail: info@naifa.com
Web Site: www.naifa.com
Members: 4,000 individuals
Staff: 18
Annual Budget: $1-2,000,000
Exec. V. President: Robert Sneed
Director, Education: Gary E. Hall
Manager, Information Systems: Roger Wolff

Historical Note
Founded in Phoenix, Arizona in 1961. Members in large part are self-employed appraisers specializing in the appraisal of real estate held in fee simple. Awards four designations: Independent Fee Appraiser (IFA), IFA Senior (IFAS), IFA Agricultural (IFAA), and IFA Counselor (IFAC). Sponsors and supports the IFA Good Government PAC and the Appraisal Foundation. Membership: $335/year.

Publications:
Appraisal Review. q.
Appraiser-Gram. m.

Meetings/Conferences:
Annual Meetings: Fall

Nat'l Ass'n of Independent Insurance Adjusters (1937)
300 W. Washington St., Suite 805
Chicago, IL   60606-2001
Tel: (312)853-0808   *Fax:* (312)853-3225
Web Site: www.naiia.com
Members: 390 companies
Staff: 3
Annual Budget: $100-250,000
Exec. V. President: David F. Mehren

Historical Note
Members are companies and individuals adjusting claims for insurance companies on a fee basis.

Publications:
Claims Professional Newsletter. q.
Membership Directory. a.
Status Report Member Newsletter. q.

Meetings/Conferences:
Annual Meetings: May
1999 – Scottsdale, AZ/May 19-22

Nat'l Ass'n of Independent Insurance Auditors and Engineers (1963)
4600 West 77th, Suite 240
Minneapolis, MN   55135
Tel: (612)844-0490   *Fax:* (612)844-0390
Toll Free: (800)243 - 0337
Members: 37 organizations
Annual Budget: $10-25,000
President: Dennis Brandanger

Historical Note
NAIIAE members are independent companies providing audits, underwriting surveys, loss control services and other related services to the insurance industry. Has no paid staff; officers change annually. Membership: $250-1,500/year.

Publications:
Directory. a.
NAI Letter. m.

Meetings/Conferences:
Annual Meetings: Always October/50

Nat'l Ass'n of Independent Insurers (1945)
2600 River Road
Des Plaines, IL   60018-3286
Tel: (847)297-7800   *Fax:* (847)297-5064
Members: 560 property & liability companies
Staff: 190
Annual Budget: $10-25,000,000
Exec. V. President and C.O.O.: Jack F. Ramirez
V. President, Public Affairs: Joanne M. Orfanos
Director, Media Relations: Joseph Annotti
Sr. V.P., Chief Adm. Office & Treasurer: June T. Holmes
Sr. V.P., General Counsel and Secretary: Michael P. Duncan
Director, Membership: Donna Callahan

Historical Note
Membership consists of property-liability companies. Supports the Nat'l Ass'n of Independent Insurers Political Action Committee. Has an annual budget of approximately $21 million. Organization was formed to promote independence in rating plans policy forms and statistical plans. NAII is also a strong defender of state regulation of insurance. Membership: depends on premium value.

Publications:
Fast Track Monitoring System. q.
Legislative Reporter. bi-w.
Update. m.
Weekly Digest. w.

Meetings/Conferences:
Annual Meetings: Fall
1999 – San Diego, CA(Marriott)/Oct. 31-Nov. 3

Nat'l Ass'n of Independent Life Brokerage Agencies (1982)
8201 Greensboro Drive, Suite 300
McLean, VA   22102
Tel: (703)610-9020   *Fax:* (703)610-9005
E-Mail: jnormandy@nailba.com
Web Site: http://www.nailba.com
Members: 300 agencies
Staff: 3
Annual Budget: $1-2,000,000
Exec. Director: Joseph Normandy
Director, Communications: Roberta Duncan

Historical Note
Membership: $975/year(agency).

Publications:
NAILBA Directory. a.
NAILBA Gram. 3/yr.
NAILBA News. 3/yr.

Meetings/Conferences:
Annual Meetings: November
1999 – Los Angeles, CA(Century Plaza)/Nov. 6-9/1400

Nat'l Ass'n of Independent Lighting Distributors (1977)
2207 Elmwood Ave.
Buffalo, NY   14216-1009
Tel: (716)875-3670   *Fax:* (716)875-0734
Web Site: http://www.naild.org
Members: 150 companies
Annual Budget: $100-250,000
Administrator: Linda Zanghi

Historical Note
NAILD members are distributors of lighting products. Associate members are manufacturers and suppliers. Membership: varies by category.

Publications:
NAILD Membership Directory. a.
Today's Lighting Distributor. bi-m. adv.

Meetings/Conferences:
1999 – Palm Springs, CA

Nat'l Ass'n of Independent Public Finance Advisors (1989)
3220 N St., N.W., Suite 175
Washington, DC   20007
Toll Free: (800)624 - 7321
Members: 71 individuals, 16 firms
Annual Budget: $25-50,000
Exec. Officer: King Forness

Historical Note
NAIPFA members are independent firms specializing in providing financial advice to public agencies regarding infrastructure financing, long-term capital improvement, marketing of debt issues, and other financial advisory engagements. Qualified employees of member firms may become Certified Independent Public Finance Advisors (Professional Members). Has no paid officers or full-time staff.

Publications:
CIPFA Newsletter. q.

Meetings/Conferences:
Semi-Annual Meetings: Spring and Fall

Nat'l Ass'n of Independent Publishers (1985)
Box 430
Highland City, FL   33846-0430
Tel: (941)648-4420   *Fax:* (941)648-4420
E-Mail: naip@aol.com
Members: 500 companies
Staff: 3
Annual Budget: $10-25,000
Exec. Director: Betsy Lampe

Historical Note
Established in Florida, NAIP members are small independent publishers and self-publishers. Purpose is to provide a clearinghouse for information about publishing and support in the field of publishing. Membership: $75/year (individual).

Publications:
Publisher's Report. q. adv.

Meetings/Conferences:
Semi-Annual Meetings: usually first weekends in April and November/100
1999 – central Florida
1999 – south Florida

Nat'l Ass'n of Independent Publishers Representatives (1989)
111 East 14th St., Suite 157
New York, NY   10003
Tel: (508)877-5328   *Fax:* (508)788-0208
E-Mail: naipr@aol.com
Members: 350 individuals, 50 companies
Annual Budget: $10-25,000
Exec. Secretary: Ralph Woodward

Historical Note
Members are individuals and companies acting as sales representatives for one or more independent publishers on contractual basis. Promotes continuing education and ethical standards for members. Has no paid officers or full-time staff. Membership: $100/year.

Publications:
Membership Directory. a.
NAIPRep Newsletter. bi-m.

Meetings/Conferences:
Semi-Annual Meetings: May and December/50

Nat'l Ass'n of Independent Record Distributors and Manufacturers
Historical Note
Became (1997) Ass'n for Independent Music.

Nat'l Ass'n of Independent Resurfacers (1973)
5806 W. 127th St.
Alsip, IL   60803
Tel: (708)371-8237
Members: 75 companies
Staff: 1
Annual Budget: $10-25,000
Exec. Secretary: Nancy Surprenant

Historical Note
Members are companies engaged in the installation and refinishing, injecting and repairing of bowling lanes.

Publications:
NAIR News. q.
Meetings/Conferences:
Annual Meetings: Fall
1999 – Tucson, AZ/Nov. 7-11

Nat'l Ass'n of Independent Schools (1962)
1620 L St., N.W., Suite 1100
Washington, DC   20036-5605
Tel: (202)973-9700   *Fax:* (202)973-9790
Members: 1,037 schools, 96 associations
Staff: 43
Annual Budget: $5-10,000,000
Exec. V. President: Ann Hicks
Director/Public Information and Resource Development: Margaret
   Goldsborough
Director, Marketing: Heather Hoerle
Director, Government Relations: Jefferson Burnett
Director, Meeting Planning: Claire Whalen
V. President, Finance and Administration: Thoai Hovanky
V. President, Promoting Independent Education: Selby Holmberg
Director, Publications: Michael Brosnan
Historical Note
*The result of a merger in 1962 of the Nat'l Council of Independent
Schools and the Independent Schools Education Board. Members
are independent elementary and secondary schools.*
Publications:
Directory. a.
Independent School Magazine. 3/yr. adv.
Meetings/Conferences:
Annual Meetings: February-March/3,000-4,500
1999 – Dallas, TX(Wyndham Anatole Hotel)/Feb. 24-27
2000 – Baltimore, MD/March 1-4
2001 – Boston, MA/Feb. 28-March 3

Nat'l Ass'n of Industrial and Office Properties (1967)
2201 Cooperative Way, 3rd Floor
Herndon, VA   20171-3024
Tel: (703)904-7100   *Fax:* (703)904-7942
Toll Free: (800)666 - 6780
Web Site: http://www.naiop.org
Members: 5,000 individuals, 4,000 companies
Staff: 22
Annual Budget: $2-5,000,000
President: Thomas J. Bisacquino
V. President, Marketing and Communications: Sheila K. Vertino
V. President, Government Affairs: Robert D. Landis
Asst. V. President of State and Local Affairs: Richard Williams
Mgr., Meeting Planning: Jennifer Goodwin
Asst. V. President, Education: Laurie Root
V. President, Finance: John T. Abbott
Senior V. President, Member Services: Shirley A. Maloney
Legislative Director: Mele Williams
Historical Note
*Formerly (1996) NAIOP: The Ass'n for Commercial Real Estate,
(1992) Nat'l Ass'n of Industrial and Office Parks and (1976) Nat'l
Ass'n of Industrial Parks. Members are professionals involved in
development, master planning, design and construction, financing,
and/or management of office and industrial properties. Sponsors
and supports the Develop America Political Action Committee.
Membership: $545/year (principal or associate).*
Publications:
Development Magazine. q. adv.
Meetings/Conferences:
Annual Meetings: October/1,000

Nat'l Ass'n of Industrial and Technical Teacher Educators (1937)
c/o EEA-SHIP, Inc.
17600 S. Williams St., Suite 6
Thornton, IL   60476-1077
Tel: (708)877-2814   *Fax:* (708)877-2819
Members: 500 individuals
Annual Budget: $25-50,000
Exec. Director: Lydia Walsh
Historical Note
*NAITTE represents trade and industrial teacher educators, business
and industrial trainers as well as persons in college and university
trade and technical teacher education. Has no paid officers or full-
time staff. Membership: $30/year.*
Publications:
Directory. a.
Journal of Industrial Teacher Education. q.
NAITTE Mailings. 3/yr.
Meetings/Conferences:
Annual Meetings: December with American Vocational Ass'n

Nat'l Ass'n of Industrial Technology (1967)
3300 Washtenaw Ave., Suite 220
Ann Arbor, MI   48104-4200
Tel: (734)677-0720   *Fax:* (734)677-2407
Web Site: http://www.nait.org
Members: 2,000 individuals
Annual Budget: $100-250,000
Exec. Director: Alvin E. Rudisill, Ph.D.
Historical Note
*Membership consists of individuals and companies active in the
field of industrial technology. Major purpose is to improve degree-
level curricula in industrial technology. Membership: $60/year
(individual), $240/year (organization).*
Publications:
Journal of Industrial Technology. q.
Program Directory - Industrial Technology. a. adv.
Meetings/Conferences:
Annual Meetings: Fall
1999 – Panama City, FL(Marriott Bay Resort)/Nov. 17-20
2000 – Pittsburgh, PA(Marriott)/Nov. 1-4

Nat'l Ass'n of Installation Developers (1978)
1730 K St., N.W., Suite 700
Washington, DC   20006
Tel: (202)822-5256   *Fax:* (202)822-8819
E-Mail: naid@urbandevelopment.com
Web Site: www.naid.org
Members: 320 individuals
Staff: 2
Annual Budget: $250-500,000
Exec. Director: Jefferey Sinkle
Editor, Newsletter: Paul Kallmiris
Historical Note
*Members are individuals, organizations and communities interested
in the industrial development of closed military bases. Ass'n is
managed by the Nat'l Council for Urban Economic Development.*
Publications:
NAID News Newsletter. bi-m. adv.
Meetings/Conferences:
1999 – Jacksonville, FL/Aug. 7-10

Nat'l Ass'n of Institutional Linen Management (1939)
2130 Lexington Road, Suite H
Richmond, KY   40475
Tel: (606)624-0177   *Fax:* (606)624-3580
Toll Free: (800)669 - 0863
Members: 1,650 individuals
Staff: 6
Annual Budget: $500-1,000,000
C.E.O.: Adrienne Grizzell
Director, Academic Affairs: Dr. Raymond Otero
Coordinator, Member Services: Barbara Withers
Historical Note
*Founded as the Nat'l Ass'n of Institutional Laundry Managers in
1939; assumed its present name in 1985. Represents a major
portion of linen service employees working in hospitals,
hotel/motels, Federal and State correctional facilities,
retirement/nursing homes, and university/educational institutions.
Mission of Ass'n is to promote the professional development of its
members and to advance and improve institutional textile
management. Membership: $120/year (individual); $290-
$410/year (institution).*
Publications:
AIDS/HIV Guide: An In-Service for Laundry and Linen
   Personnel.
NAILM News Magazine. m. adv.
Roster. a.
Meetings/Conferences:
Annual Meetings: Spring/250

Nat'l Ass'n of Insurance Brokers (1934)
701 Pennsylvania Ave., N.W., Suite 750
Washington, DC   20004-2608
Tel: (202)628-6700   *Fax:* (202)628-6707
E-Mail: NAIBStaff@naib.org
Web Site: http://www.naib.org
Members: 34 firms
Staff: 6
Annual Budget: $1-2,000,000
President: Carl A. Modecki, CAE
Director, Communications: Rick Pullen
Senior V. President and Director, Federal Affairs: Barbara Haugen
Director, State Affairs: Anne Flanagan
Historical Note
*Merged with the Council of Insurance Agents and Brokers
(1998).Represents the views and the interests of the four largest
full-service commercial insurance brokers in the world and 23 large
regional and specialty companies. Acts as the spokesman of
commercial brokers in front of the Administration, the Congress,
state insurance commissioners and legislators and other insurance
industry organizations. The members are brokers: they work for
their corporate, institutional and governmental clients. They are not
agents who work for one or more insurance companies.*
Publications:
NAIB Coverage. m.
Meetings/Conferences:

Nat'l Ass'n of Insurance Commissioners (1871)
120 W. 12th St., Suite 1100
Kansas City, MO   64105-1925
Tel: (816)842-3600   *Fax:* (816)471-7004
E-Mail: cweather@naic.org
Web Site: http://www.naic.org
Members: 55 individuals
Staff: 330
Annual Budget: $25-50,000,000
Exec. V. President: Catherine J. Weatherford
Chief Financial Officer: Darren Cook
Cheif Operations Officer: Judith Lee
Historical Note
*Members are the chief insurance regulatory officials of the 50
states, the District of Columbia, Guam, Puerto Rico and the Virgin
Islands. Formerly Nat'l Conference of Insurance Commissioners.
Has an annual budget of approximately $40 million.*
Publications:
NAIC News. m.
Proceedings. q.
Meetings/Conferences:
1999 – Washington, DC/March 6-10
1999 – Kansas City, MO/June 5-9
1999 – Atlanta, GA/Oct. 2-6
1999 – San Frnacisco, CA/Dec. 4-8

Nat'l Ass'n of Insurance Women (1940)
P.O. Box 4410
Tulsa, OK   74159-0410
Tel: (918)744-5195   *Fax:* (918)743-1968
Toll Free: (800)766 - 6249
Web Site: http://www.naiw.org

Members: 13,500 individuals
Staff: 7
Annual Budget: $1-2,000,000
Dir., Communications/Industry Rels.: Shandee J. Smith
   : Kay O'Bryant
Historical Note
*Promotes insurance education and supports the professional
advancement of its members; offers education programs through
400 local chapters in the United States, Western Canada, and
Puerto Rico. Offers the Certified Professional Insurance
Woman/Man (CPIW/CPIM) designation. Membership: $58/year
(individual); $133/year (at-large).*
Publications:
Today's Insurance Woman. bi-m. adv.
Meetings/Conferences:
Annual Meetings: June
1999 – Las Vegas, NV(The Mirage)/June 13-16
2000 – Kansas City, MO(Hyatt Crown Center)/June 7-10

Nat'l Ass'n of Intercollegiate Athletics (1940)
6120 S. Yale Ave., Suite 1450
Tulsa, OK   74136-4223
Tel: (918)494-8828   *Fax:* (918)494-8841
Web Site: http://www.naia.org
Members: 352 institutions
Staff: 25
Annual Budget: $2-5,000,000
President and C.E.O.: Steve Baker
Dir., Public Relations: Kevin Henry
Managing Director and General Counsel: James Carr
Historical Note
*Formerly (1952) Nat'l Ass'n of Intercollegiate Basketball. NAIA
members are four-year colleges and universities.*
Publications:
Football and Basketball Media Guides.
NAIA Handbook. a.
NAIA Membership Directory. a.
NAIA News. m.
NAIA Official Records Book. a.
Meetings/Conferences:
Annual Meetings: October
1999 – Lexington, KY(Hyatt-Regency)/350

Nat'l Ass'n of Investigative Specialists (1984)
P.O. Box 33244
Austin, TX   78764-6104
Tel: (512)420-9292   *Fax:* (512)719-3594
E-Mail: RThomas007@aol.com
Web Site: http://www.p.mail.com/nais
Members: 3,000 individuals, 1,400 companies
Staff: 6
Annual Budget: $100-250,000
Director: Ralph D. Thomas
Historical Note
*NAIS promotes the private investigative profession; it provides
members with case assignments from other members; provides
training manuals for the investigative profession; trains new private
investigators. Membership: $85/bien.*
Publications:
Investigator's All-in-One Directory. a. adv.
P. I. adv.
Private Investigator's Connection. bi-m. adv.
Meetings/Conferences:
1999 – Austin, TX/Apr. 22-24

Nat'l Ass'n of Investment Companies (1971)
1111 14th St. N.W., Suite 700
Washington, DC   20005
Tel: (202)289-4336   *Fax:* (202)289-4329
Members: 100 companies
Staff: 3
Annual Budget: $250-500,000
President: Marianne C. Niles
Historical Note
*NAIC is an industry association for venture capital firms that
dedicate their resources to investing in an ethnically and socially
diverse marketplace. Members include privately-owned Specialized
Small Business Investment Companies (SSBICs) licensed and
regulated by the Small Business Administration, privately-owned
venture capital firms that manage investment partnerships, and
quasi-private investment companies chartered by state and local
government for minority-focused investing. Affiliate membership
also available for individuals and for business entities with an
interest in the minority marketplace. Membership: annual dues
vary, based on committed capital for private equity funds, and on
private paid-in capital and SBA leverage for SSBICs.*
Publications:
NAIC Membership Directory. a.
Perspective. bi-m.
Meetings/Conferences:
Annual Meetings: October/125-150

Nat'l Ass'n of Jai Alai Frontons (1977)
301 East Dania Beach Blvd.
P.O. Box 96
Dania, FL   33004
Tel: (954)927-2841   *Fax:* (954)927-0149
Members: 11 frontons
Staff: 4
Annual Budget: $25-50,000
Director: Stephen F. Snyder
Historical Note
Established January 1, 1977 and incorporated in Florida.
Publications:
NAJF Notes. q.
Tournament Programs. bi-m. adv.
Meetings/Conferences:
Annual Meetings: Not held.

Nat'l Ass'n of Jewelry Appraisers (1981)

P.O. Box 6558
Annapolis, MD 21401-0558
Tel: (301)261-8270
Members: 690 individuals
Staff: 3
Annual Budget: $50-100,000
Exec. Director: James V. Jolliff

Historical Note
Purpose is to maintain professional standards and education in the field of jewelry appraisal. Members include jewelers, jewelry appraisers, importers, brokers and other professionally interested trade members. Membership: $125/year (individual) plus a $25 one time initial fee.

Publications:
Membership Directory. a.
The Jewelry Appraiser. q. adv.

Meetings/Conferences:
1999 – Tucson, AZ(Embassy Suites)/Feb. 5-6
1999 – /August. 21-25

Nat'l Ass'n of Judiciary Interpreters and Translators (1978)

551 5th Ave., Suite 3025
New York, NY 10176
Tel: (212)692-9581   Fax: (212)687-4016
E-Mail: headquarters@najit.org
Web Site: http://www.najit.org
Members: 800 individuals
Staff: 1
Annual Budget: $25-50,000
Exec. Director: Arlene Stock, CAE

Historical Note
Formerly Court Interpreters and Translators Ass'n. NAJIT members are interpreters and translators working in federal, state or local courts, or in other capacities within the legal profession. Membership: $75/year (individual); $45/year (student); $150/year (institution).

Publications:
Handbook for the Legal Profession. irreg.
Key Verbs for court Interpreters. irreg.
Language Services Guide & Interpreters/Translators Directory. a. adv.
Primer for Judiciary Interpreters. irreg.
Proteus Newsletter. q. adv.

Meetings/Conferences:
Annual Meetings: always 3rd week in May/200
1999 – San Diego, CA
2000 – Miami, FL

Nat'l Ass'n of Juvenile Correctional Agencies (1903)

55 Albin Road
Bow, NH 03304-3703
Tel: (603)224-9749   Fax: (603)226-4020
E-Mail: najcajohn@aol.com
Members: 300 individuals
Staff: 1
Annual Budget: $10-25,000
Exec. Secretary-Treasurer: John J. Sheridan

Historical Note
An affiliate of the American Correctional Ass'n. Founded as the National Ass'n of Training Schools and Juvenile Agencies, it assumed its present name in 1981. Merged with the Ass'n of State Juvenile Justice Administrators in 1984. Members are executives and staff members of residential centers and agencies for the care and treatment of adjudicated delinquent youth. Membership: $25/year (individual); $50/year (organization).

Publications:
NAJCA News. q. adv.
Proceedings. a. adv.

Meetings/Conferences:
Semi-annual Meetings: August, with the American Correctional Ass'n
1999 – Nashville, TN/Jan. 18-20
1999 – Denver, CO/Aug. 8-12

Nat'l Ass'n of Large City Directors of Vocational Education

Historical Note
Address unknown in 1996.

Nat'l Ass'n of Latino Elected and Appointed Officials (1975)

5800 S. Eastern Ave., Suite 365
Los Angeles, CA 90040
Tel: (213)720-1932   Fax: (213)720-9519
E-Mail: naleo@aol.com
Members: 5,200 individuals
Staff: 20
Annual Budget: $500-1,000,000
Nat'l Director: Arturo Vargas

Historical Note
NALEO is a non-profit, non-partisan civic affairs research organization which works to initiate public policies responsive to the Hispanic community and to inform that community of issues affecting them. While membership includes state representatives, mayors, and members of Congress, it is open to all who support its objectives. Membership: $50/year (active); $25/year (associate); $150/yr. (affiliate).

Publications:
Audit of Federal Contracting with Hispanic Firms. a.
National Directory of Citizenship Services. bi-a.
National Roster of Hispanic Elected Officials. a.
POLITICA. bim.

Meetings/Conferences:
Annual Meetings: June/500
1999 – June

Nat'l Ass'n of Leagues, Umpires and Scorers (1931)

P.O. Box 1420
Wichita, KS 67201
Tel: (316)267-3372   Fax: (316)267-3382
Toll Free: (800)677 - 4824
E-Mail: nbc@wichitawranglers.com
Web Site: http://www.wichitawranglers.com
Members: 9,500 individuals
Staff: 5
Annual Budget: $250-500,000
General Manager: Lance Deckinger
National Coordinator: Mark Chiarucci
Natioanl Commissioner: Larry Davis
Director of Administration: Dian Overaker

Historical Note
Affiliated with Nat'l Baseball Congress. Membership: $45/year (umpire); $25/year (scorekeeper); $450/year (league).

Publications:
Linedrive Newsletter. q. adv.
NBC Annual. a. adv.
Official Playing And Scoring Rules For Baseball. a. adv.

Meetings/Conferences:
Annual Meetings: August

Nat'l Ass'n of Legal Assistants (1975)

1516 S. Boston Ave., Suite 200
Tulsa, OK 74119-4013
Tel: (918)587-6828   Fax: (918)582-6772
Web Site: www.nala.org
Members: 6,000 individuals, 89 state and local associations
Staff: 7
Annual Budget: $500-1,000,000
Exec. Director: Marge Dover, CAE

Historical Note
Members are professional legal assistants. Awards the Certified Legal Assistant (CLA) designation and CLA Specialist designation. Membership: $99/year (individual); $200/year (organization/company).

Publications:
Facts and Findings. q.

Meetings/Conferences:
Annual Meetings: July
1999 – Tampa Bay, FL(Hyatt West Shore)/July 7-10/300

Nat'l Ass'n of Legal Investigators (1967)

6109 Meadowwood
Grand Blanc, MI 48439
Tel: (810)603-0608
Toll Free: (800)266 - 6254
Members: 700 individuals
Staff: 1
Annual Budget: $50-100,000
Exec. Secretary: Leonard L. Accardo

Historical Note
Members are investigators who are employed by attorneys or who are self-employed. NALI conducts a certification program for the legal investigator profession. Membership: $100/year.

Publications:
The Legal Investigator. q. adv.

Meetings/Conferences:
Semi-Annual Meetings: Winter and Summer
1999 – New Orleans, LA

Nat'l Ass'n of Legal Search Consultants (1984)

355 Lexington Ave., 17th Floor
New York, NY 10017-6603
Toll Free: (888)256 - 2732
Web Site: http://www.nalsc.org
Members: 150 firms
Staff: 3
Annual Budget: $100-250,000
Exec. Director: Willard S. Kautter, CAE

Historical Note
Originally organized to establish a code of ethics for the legal recruiting industry, NALSC now provides a forum for dialogue between firms in the field. Members are either consulting/search firms or law offices. Maintains a speakers bureau and arbitration procedure. Membership: $500/year.

Publications:
Directory of Legal Search Consultants. a.
NALSC News. q.

Meetings/Conferences:
1999 – Atlanta, GA/May 6-9

Nat'l Ass'n of Legal Secretaries (1929)

314 E. Third St., Suite 210
Tulsa, OK 74120-2409
Tel: (918)582-5188   Fax: (918)582-5907
Web Site: http://www.nals.org
Members: 6,000 individuals
Staff: 15
Annual Budget: $1-2,000,000
Exec. Director: Tammy Hailey, CAE

Historical Note
Has certification program leading to designation as a Professional Legal Secretary (PLS) and Accredited Legal Secretary (ALS). Established as the California Association of Legal Secretaries, it became Legal Secretaries, Inc. in 1940 and assumed its present name in 1950. Membership: $90/year (national).

Publications:
@LAW. q. adv.

Meetings/Conferences:
Annual Meetings: Summer/600

Nat'l Ass'n of Legal Vendors (1989)

Historical Note
Organization defunct in 1997.

Nat'l Ass'n of Letter Carriers (1889)

100 Indiana Ave., N.W.
Washington, DC 20001
Tel: (202)393-4695   Fax: (202)737-1540
Web Site: www.nalc.org
Members: 307,000 individuals
Staff: 160
Annual Budget: $50-100,000,000
President: Vincent R. Sombrotto

Historical Note
A union representing city letter carriers throughout the U.S. Formerly the Nat'l Ass'n of Letter Carriers of the United States of America, NALC was organized in Milwaukee, WI August 30, 1889 and chartered by The American Federation of Labor in 1917. Has an annual budget of approximately $82.3 million.

Publications:
NALC Bulletin. bi-w.
The Activist. q.
The Postal Record. m.
The Retiree. q.

Meetings/Conferences:
Biennial Convention: Even years

Nat'l Ass'n of Life Underwriters (1890)

1922 F St., N.W.
Washington, DC 20006-4387
Tel: (202)331-6000   Fax: (202)835-9606
Web Site: http://www.nalu.org
Members: 100,000 individuals
Staff: 105
Annual Budget: $10-25,000,000
Exec. V. President & C.E.O.: Arthur D. Kraus, CLU, ChFC
V. President, Public Relations: G. Douglas Tillett
Chief Information Officer: Ross C. Bainbridge
Dir., Public Affairs: Jay Morris
Senior V. President, Government Affairs: Michael L. Kerley
V. President, Meetings/Convention Logistics: Joanne T. Lawrence, CMP
V. President, Professional Development/Programming: John Phillips
Sr. V.P. and C.O.O.: Matthew Gertzog, CAE
Publisher: R.Afsoon Namini, ACS

Historical Note
A federation of 950-1,000 state and local ass'ns of career life insurance underwriters, NALU is a professional organization of life insurance agents, general agents and managers. Has an annual budget of approximately $15.9 million. Sponsors and supports the NALU Political Action Committee. Membership: $57/per capita.

Publications:
Life Association News. m. adv.

Meetings/Conferences:
Annual Meetings: September/3-4000
1999 – Nashville, TN
2000 – Orlando, FL

Nat'l Ass'n of Limited Edition Dealers (1976)

5235 Monticello Ave.
Dallas, TX 75206
Tel: (214)826-2002   Fax: (214)826-6673
Toll Free: (800)446 - 2533
Web Site: http://www.naled.com
Members: 860 companies
Staff: 3
Annual Budget: $250-500,000
Exec. Director: Susan K. Elliott
Membership/Finance Coordinator: Frances Knight

Historical Note
Members are dealers, vendors, artists, sales representatives, and publishers involved with limited edition collectibles and gifts. Membership: $150/year (full member), $225-$750/year (associate).

Publications:
Bulletin. bi-m.
Collectibles Now. bi-a.
Membership Directory. a.
NALED Complete Sourcebook for Collectibles & Gift Retailers. a. adv.

Meetings/Conferences:
Annual Meetings: June

Nat'l Ass'n of Litho Clubs (1946)

6550 Donjoy Drive
Cincinnati, OH 45242-7555
Tel: (513)793-2532   Fax: (513)793-2532
Members: 3,500 individuals
Staff: 1
Annual Budget: $50-100,000
Exec. V. President: Richard M. Worthington

Historical Note
NALC is a professional organization composed of litho clubs from all over the United States. Club members are supervisory personnel in lithographic plants, company owners and suppliers. Membership: $9/year (individual).

Publications:
Litho Tips. 3/year. adv.

Meetings/Conferences:
Annual Meetings: June/125-150
1999 – Las Vegas, NV/Jan. 13-17

Nat'l Ass'n of Local Boards of Health (1992)

1840 E. Gypsy Lane Road
Bowling Green, OH 43402
Tel: (419)353-7714   Fax: (419)354-6486
Toll Free: (888)649 - 8970
E-Mail: nalboh@nalboh.org
Web Site: www.nalboh.org
Members: 22,000 individuals, 370 organizations
Staff: 5
Annual Budget: $250-500,000

Exec. Director: Ned E. Baker, MPH

Historical Note
NALBOH represents local boards of health and similar organizations that oversee local public health service programs, providing members with a means of communication with each other and with the organizations who develop public health policy at the national level. Membership: $100/year (institutional); $50/year (associate); $250/year (affiliate).

Publications:
News Brief. q.

Meetings/Conferences:
Annual Meetings: Summer
1999 – Salt Lake City, UT
2000 – Charlotte, NC

Nat'l Ass'n of Local Government Auditors
6 Clouser Road
Mechanicsburg, PA   17055
Tel: (717)795-7474   *Fax:* (717)795-7473
Web Site: http://www.liberty.net/ ~ nalga
Exec. Director: Deborah A. Beamer

Historical Note
Membership: $50/year.

Meetings/Conferences:
Annual Meetings: May

Nat'l Ass'n of Local Supervisors of Vocational Home Economics *(1978)*
301 East Armor Blvd, Suite 200
Kansas City, KS   64111
Tel: (816)871-6278   *Fax:* (816)871-6414
Members: 75 individuals
President: Sharon Kauka

Historical Note
NALSVHE members are American Vocational Ass'n members who are municipal and county school district supervisors of home economic programs. Membership: $10/year.

Publications:
Newsletter. semi-a.

Meetings/Conferences:
Annual Meetings: in conjunction with the American Vocational Ass'n

Nat'l Ass'n of Managed Care Physicians *(1991)*
4435 Waterfront Dr., Suite 101
P.O. Box 4193
Glen Allen, VA   23058-4193
Tel: (804)527-1905   *Fax:* (804)747-5316
Toll Free: (800)722 - 0376
E-Mail: wmiller@namcp.com
Web Site: http://www.namcp.org
Members: 15,000 individuals
Staff: 16
Annual Budget: $500-1,000,000
President: William Clyde Williams II
Director of Communications: Whitney Miller
Director of Conference Planning: Eva Adams
Exec. V. President: Randall Killian
V. President of Marketing: Heather Millar

Historical Note
Provides continuing education and information resources to health care regarding managed care. Membership: $195/year (physicians); $250/year (other individuals); $1,500/year minimum (corporations).

Publications:
American Journal of Integrated Healthcare.
Managed Care Medicine. 6 times/year. adv.
NAMCP News. q. adv.

Meetings/Conferences:

Nat'l Ass'n of Management Consultants *(1985)*
Historical Note
Address unknown in 1997.

Nat'l Ass'n of Manufacturers *(1895)*
1331 Pennsylvania Ave., N.W.Suite 600
Washington, DC   20004-1790
Tel: (202)637-3087   *Fax:* (202)637-3182
E-Mail: manufacturing@nam.org
Web Site: http://www.nam.org
Members: 14,000 companies
Staff: 180
Annual Budget: $10-25,000,000
President: Jerry J. Jasinowski
Sr. V. Pres., Policy and Communications: Paul Huard
V. President, Communications/Media: Laura L. Brown
Senior V. President, Public Affairs: Michael E. Baroody
V.P., Trade and Technology: Howard Lewis
V. President, Resources, Environment and Regulation: H. Richard Seibert
V. President and Corp. Secretary: Joni Hodgson
Sr. V.P., Marketing/Member Services: Ladd K. Biro
V. President and General Counsel: Jan S. Amundson
V. President, Publishing: Darlene Megahan
V. President, Information Systems: Thomas J. Orlowski

Historical Note
Established in Cincinnati in 1895 to promote America's economic growth and productivity, particularly in the manufacturing sector. Headquartered in Washington, DC with eleven field offices, NAM's member companies produce more than 80% of the nation's manufactured goods. NAM is affiliated with 130 state and local business associations through its National Industrial Council, and with 200 manufacturing trade associations through its Association Council. The Manufacturing Institute is its educational affiliate. Has an annual budget of approximately $16 million.

Publications:
Associations Council Connections. m.
Briefing. w.

Congressional Directory. a.
Employer Association Group Network Notes. bi-m.
Human Resources Policy Legislative and Regulatory Update. m.
Issue Briefs. irreg.
Manufacturing Matters.
Public Affairs. q.
The Paper. m.
Washington Fax Line. m.

Meetings/Conferences:

Nat'l Ass'n of Manufacturing Opticians *(1975)*
R.R. 2, Box 35Q
Rockwall, TX   75087-9608
Tel: (972)934-8848   *Fax:* (972)771-8484
Members: 35 companies
Staff: 2
Annual Budget: $25-50,000
President: William J. Flannery, III

Historical Note
Membership is composed of individuals and businesses engaged in the manufacture and production of prescription eyewear or related ophthalmic goods and services; members must possess the ability to "full service" fabricate eyewear. One of founding associations of the Optical Product Code Council which provides the centralization and coordination of the use of the bar code system in the industry. Associate memberships available for ophthalmic manufacturers and suppliers.

Meetings/Conferences:
Semi-annual Meetings: Winter and Summer

Nat'l Ass'n of Margarine Manufacturers *(1952)*
1101 15th St., N.W., Suite 202
Washington, DC   20005
Tel: (202)785-3232   *Fax:* (202)223-9741
Members: 30 companies
Staff: 6
Annual Budget: $100-250,000
Exec. Director: Richard E. Cristol

Historical Note
Members are manufacturers and distributors of margarine industry products and ingredient suppliers.

Meetings/Conferences:
1999 – Key Largo, FL(Ocean Reef Club)/April 21-24

Nat'l Ass'n of Marine Products and Services *(1972)*
200 E. Randolph Dr.
Suite 5100
Chicago, IL   60601
Tel: (312)946-6200   *Fax:* (312)946-6263
Members: 800 firms
Staff: 4
Annual Budget: $2-5,000,000
Contact: Tammy Rossow

Historical Note
Formerly (1979) the Marine Accessories and Services Ass'n, it absorbed the Trailer Manufacturers Ass'n in 1980. Members are manufacturers of marine recreational equipment and accessories. A partner-affiliate of the Nat'l Marine Manufacturers Ass'n, which provides administrative support and with which it shares offices. Membership: $800-$2,000.

Meetings/Conferences:
Annual Meetings: Chicago, in conjunction with the Marine Trade Exhibition

Nat'l Ass'n of Marine Services *(1951)*
5458 Wagonmaster Drive
Colorado Springs, CO   80917
Tel: (719)573-5946   *Fax:* (719)573-5952
E-Mail: nams@citystar.com
Members: 80 firms
Staff: 2
Annual Budget: $100-250,000
Exec. Director: William L. Robinson

Historical Note
Established as Associated Ship Chandlers, it became the National Associated Marine Suppliers in 1951 and assumed its present name in 1969. Members are purveyors of supplies and equipment to ocean-going commercial vessels.

Publications:
Directory of American Ship Services. a. adv.
NAMS News. q.

Meetings/Conferences:
Annual Meetings: May
1999 – Houston, TX

Nat'l Ass'n of Marine Surveyors *(1960)*
P.O. Box 9306
Chesapeake, VA   23321-9306
Tel: (757)488-9538   *Fax:* (757)488-0584
Toll Free: (800)822 - 6267
E-Mail: NAMSOFFICE@JUNO.ORG
Web Site: http://www.namsurveyors.org
Members: 400 individuals
Staff: 2
Annual Budget: $50-100,000

Historical Note
Incorporated in the State of New York, September, 1962. Originally Corresponding Surveyors to the Yacht Safety Bureau. Founded to create an organization that would establish professional qualifications and generate an exchange of current information on approved and recommended practices relating to marine surveying. Offers Certified Marine Surveyor (CMS) distinction. Membership: $300/year.

Publications:
Conference Proceedings. a.
Membership List. a.
NAMS News. semi-a.

Meetings/Conferences:
Meetings: Holds one national and one western area meeting/100-200
1999 – Cleerwater, FL/March 11-13

Nat'l Ass'n of Maritime Educators *(1987)*
Historical Note
Address unknown in 1998.

Nat'l Ass'n of Market Developers *(1953)*
Historical Note
Address unknown in 1995.

Nat'l Ass'n of Master Appraisers *(1982)*
P.O. Box 12528
303 West Cypress St.
San Antonio, TX   78212-0528
Tel: (210)271-0781   *Fax:* (210)225-8450
Toll Free: (800)229 - 6262
E-Mail: lincolncenter@worldnet.att.net
Web Site: http://www.masterappraisers.org
Members: 5,000 individuals
Staff: 20
Annual Budget: $500-1,000,000
C.E.O.: Marvin T. Deane, Ph.D.
Exec. Director: Deborah J. Deane

Historical Note
NAMA members are professional real estate appraisers. Awards the designations Master Senior Appraiser (MSA), Master Farm & Land Appraiser (MFLA) and Master Residential Appraiser (MRA). Membership: $150/year (individual).

Publications:
Master Appraiser. m.
Membership Directory. a.
NAMA Alert. q.

Meetings/Conferences:
1999 – San Antonio, TX(Gunter Hotel)/March 12-13

Nat'l Ass'n of Meat Purveyors *(1942)*
Historical Note
Became North American Meat Processors Ass'n in 1996.

Nat'l Ass'n of Media Brokers *(1979)*
c/o Pepper & Corazzini
1776 K St., N.W., Suite 200
Washington, DC   20006
Tel: (202)296-0600   *Fax:* (202)296-5572
Members: 60 firms
Annual Budget: $50-100,000
General Counsel: Vincent Pepper

Historical Note
Members are media brokerage firms.

Publications:
Membership Directory & Organization Brochure. a.

Meetings/Conferences:

Nat'l Ass'n of Medicaid Directors
810 First St., N.E., Suite 500
Washington, DC   20002-4267
Tel: (202)682-0100   *Fax:* (202)289-6555
Members: 54 individuals
Annual Budget: $250-500,000
Director: Lee Partridge

Historical Note
Formerly (1996) State Medicaid Directors Ass'n. Members are directors of state and territorial medical assistance programs. An affiliate of the American Public Welfare Ass'n. Has no independent paid staff.

Publications:
MMI Bulletin.

Meetings/Conferences:
Semi-annual Meetings: Spring and Fall

Nat'l Ass'n of Medical Directors of Respiratory Care
Historical Note
Became (1994) Nat'l Ass'n for Medical Direction of Respiratory Care.

Nat'l Ass'n of Medical Examiners *(1966)*
1402 S. Grand Blvd., Room C-305
St. Louis, MO   63104
Tel: (314)577-8298   *Fax:* (314)268-5124
Web Site: http://www.thename.org
Members: 800 individuals
Staff: 2
Annual Budget: $100-250,000
Secretary-Treasurer: Michael Graham, M.D.
Meetings Planner: Mary Fran Ernst

Historical Note
Membership: $170/year for physicians, $65/year for affiliates.

Publications:
Journal of Forensic Medicine & Pathology. q. adv.

Meetings/Conferences:
Annual Meetings: Fall

Nat'l Ass'n of Medical Minority Educators *(1975)*
UCSF School of Dentistry
513 Parnassus Ave., Suite 630
San Francisco, CA   94143-0430
Tel: (415)476-2712   *Fax:* (415)476-4226
Annual Budget: $50-100,000
President: Dr. Charles J. Alexander

Historical Note
Membership: $125/year (individual); $1,000/year (company).

Publications:
NAMME Edition Newsletter.

Meetings/Conferences:
Annual Meetings: Fall
1999 – Dallas, TX(Hyatt Reunion)/300
1999 – Dallas, TX(Hyatt Reunion)/Sept. 16-22

Nat'l Ass'n of Men's Sportswear Buyers (1954)
60 E. 42nd St., Rm. 2430
New York, NY 10165-2430
Tel: (212)856-9644   Fax: (212)856-0825
Members: 1000 individuals
Staff: 3
Exec. Director: Jack Herschlag

Historical Note
Formed in 1954 by men's wear retailers to provide industry services and to sponsor a trade show for men's wear; now produces four such shows each year in New York City. Membership: $10/year.

Publications:
NAMSB New York, the Show Week Directory. q. adv.
NAMSB Newsletter. m.

Meetings/Conferences:
Quarterly Trade Shows: New York, NY(Jacob Javits
Convention Center) January, March, June and October

Nat'l Ass'n of Metal Finishers (1955)
112-J Elden St.
Herndon, VA 20170-4809
Tel: (703)709-8299   Fax: (703)709-1036
E-Mail: namf@erols.com
Web Site: www.namf.org
Members: 950 companies
Staff: 5
Annual Budget: $500-1,000,000
Exec. Director: David W. Barrack
Deputy Director: Steve Vernon
Vice President Legislative Affairs: Christian Richter
Vice President Regulatory Affairs: Al Collins
Meetings Coordinator: Diana Tringali
Finance: Enid Palazzolo
Membership Coordinator: Sarah Jane Ziaya

Historical Note
Merger of the National Federation of Metal Finishers and the National Association of Plating. Members are executives of firms engaged in all methods of finishing metal, plastic and organic surfaces. Memebership: $695/year (company).

Publications:
(SFMRB)Statistics of the Metal Finishing Industry Report.
Crisis Management Manual.
Directory. a.
Finishing Line. m.
Legislative Line. q.
Management Manual.
Products Finishing Magazine. m. adv.
Regulatory Compliance Manual.

Meetings/Conferences:
1999 – San Juan, PR(Celebrity Cruise)/Feb. 27-March 6
2000 – Hawaii

Nat'l Ass'n of Milliners, Dressmakers and Tailors (1966)
Historical Note
Address unknown in 1996.

Nat'l Ass'n of Minorities in Cable (1980)
c/o Reid Dugger Consulting Group
One Centerpointe Dr., Suite 410
La Palma, CA 90623
Tel: (714)736-9600   Fax: (714)736-9699
E-Mail: kathy.johnson@rdgc.com
Web Site: http://www.namic.com
Exec. Director: Kathy A. Johnson

Historical Note
NAMIC educates members and the industry at large on marketing approaches programming interest and operating strategies relevant to the urban cable marketplace.

Publications:
Spectrum Newsletter.

Meetings/Conferences:

Nat'l Ass'n of Minority Automobile Dealers (1980)
1111 14th St., N.W., Suite 720
Washington, DC 20005
Tel: (202)789-3140   Fax: (202)789-3133
E-Mail: namad-dc@email.msn.com
Web Site: http://www.namad.com
Members: 425 individuals
Staff: 2
Annual Budget: $250-500,000
Exec. Director: Sheila Vaden-Williams

Historical Note
NAMAD is committed to increasing opportunities for minorities in the automobile industry. Membership: $250/year (individual).

Publications:
Newsletter. q. adv.
Resource Guide. a. adv.

Meetings/Conferences:

Nat'l Ass'n of Minority Contractors (1969)
666 11th St., N.W., Suite 520
Washington, DC 20001-4542
Tel: (202)347-8259   Fax: (202)628-1876
Toll Free: (800)758 - 0883
Members: 5,000 individuals
Staff: 5
Annual Budget: $1-2,000,000
Exec. Director: Samuel A. Carradine, Jr.
Project Director: Ellie Anderson

Historical Note
Established in Washington, DC in 1969 and incorporated the same year. Membership consists of, but is not limited to, general contractors, subcontractors, construction managers, manufacturers, suppliers, local minority contractor associations, funded technical assistance organizations, state and local government agencies, attorneys and accountants. Regular Membership: $300/year; $3,000/year (corporate).

Publications:
Building Concerns. q. adv.

Meetings/Conferences:

Nat'l Ass'n of Minority Engineering Program Administrators (1979)
1133 W. Morse Blvd., Suite 201
Winter Park, FL 32789
Tel: (407)647-8839   Fax: (407)629-2502
E-Mail: NAMEPA@nampea.org
Web Site: http://www.namepa.org
Members: 575 individuals
Staff: 12
Annual Budget: $250-500,000
Exec. Manager: Brenda Thomas

Historical Note
NAMEPA was established to provide a communication network among college level administrators of minority engineering programs and to provide a cohesive voice in the national minority engineering effort. Membership: $105/year (individual); $255/year (institution); $655/year (corporate).

Publications:
Brochure. a.
NAMEPA Newsletter. q. adv.
Report. semi-a.

Meetings/Conferences:
Annual Meetings: January-February
1999 – Atlanta, GA(Sheraton Colony Square)/Jan. 30-Feb. 2/250

Nat'l Ass'n of Minority Media Executives (1990)
1921 Gallows Road
Vienna, VA 22182-3900
Toll Free: (888)968 - 7658
Web Site: http://www.namme.com
Members: 238 individuals
Exec. Director: Randy Chorney

Historical Note
NAMME members are minority media executives. Membership: $200/year (individual); $150/year (affiliate); $50/year (associate); $750-$2,500/year (corporate).

Publications:
NAMME Membership Directory. bien.
NAMME Newsletter. m.

Meetings/Conferences:

Nat'l Ass'n of Mirror Manufacturers (1957)
Historical Note
Became (1997) North American Ass'n of Mirror Manufacturers.

Nat'l Ass'n of Miscellaneous, Ornamental and Architectural Products Contractors (1969)
10382 Main St., Box 280, Suite 200
Fairfax, VA 22030
Tel: (703)591-1870   Fax: (703)591-1895
Members: 950 companies
Staff: 3
Annual Budget: $100-250,000
Exec. V. President: Fred H. Codding

Historical Note
Members are companies fabricating and installing decking systems, ornamental iron, steel and aluminum sheathing and architectural motifs on building exteriors.

Publications:
Membership Roster. irreg.
Newsletter. m.

Meetings/Conferences:

Nat'l Ass'n of Mortgage Brokers (1973)
8201 Greensboro Drive, Suite 300
McLean, VA 22102
Tel: (703)610-9000   Fax: (703)610-9005
Web Site: http://www.namb.org
Members: 5,300 individuals
Annual Budget: $2-5,000,000
Exec. V. President: Brian J. Kinsella
Dir., Conferences/Certification: Julie Howard
Meetings Manager: Amber T. Johnson
General Manager: James Hirt
Dir., Member Services: Robert Bergeron
Director, Legislative & Public Affairs: Channing Nuss
Exec. Assistant: Amy L. Comer
Membership Coordinator: Peter Doherty
Administrative Assistant: Stephanie J. Baer

Historical Note
Formed to provide a focal point for mortgage brokers and a communications link with mortgage bankers and underwriters. Membership: $95/year, plus a $25 one-time application fee.

Publications:
Capitol Comment. m.
National Mortgage Broker. m. adv.

Meetings/Conferences:
1999 – Phoenix, AZ(Hyatt Downtown & Conv.
Cneter)/June 5-9
2000 – New Orleans, LA(Morial Center)/June 24-28

Nat'l Ass'n of Music Education (1983)
c/o Music Educators Nat'l Conference
1806 Robert Fulton Dr.
Reston, VA 20191
Tel: (703)860-4000   Fax: (703)860-1531
Toll Free: (800)336 - 3768
E-Mail: PSENKO@aol.com
Web Site: http://www.menc.org
Members: 1,200 individuals
Exec. Director: John J. Mahlmann

Historical Note
Formerly (1998) the Society for Music Teacher Education, NAME was formed in response to a need felt by college instructors within the Music Educators Nat'l Conference for more specific meetings and programs aimed at their instruction and curriculum.

Publications:
Journal of Music Teacher Education. semi-a.

Meetings/Conferences:
Biennial Meetings: even years with Music Educators Nat'l Conference

Nat'l Ass'n of Music Executives in State Universities (1935)
Historical Note
Address unknown in 1995; presumed inactive.

Nat'l Ass'n of Music Merchants
Historical Note
Became (1997) Internat'l Music Products Ass'n.

Nat'l Ass'n of Mutual Insurance Companies (1895)
P.O. Box 68700
3601 Vincennes Road
Indianapolis, IN 46268
Tel: (317)875-5250   Fax: (317)879-8408
E-Mail: LForrester@namic.org
Web Site: www.namic.org
Members: 1,288 companies
Staff: 62
Annual Budget: $5-10,000,000
President: Larry L. Forrester, CAE
V. President, Public Affairs: Charles M. Chamness
V. President, Regulatory Affairs: Steven C. Elliot
V. President, Finance and C.F.O.: Beverly M. Sokolek
Asst. V. President Administration: Robert Larry Baile, CAE
Director, Finance: Jennifer Schuessler
General Counsel: Robert Spolyar
V. President, Member Services: Gary W. Eberhart, CAE
Director, Information Systems/Manager of MIS: Mike Ulmer

Historical Note
Founded in 1895, NAMIC is America's largest trade ass'n for property and casualty insurance companies. The Ass'n represents over 1,200 members which comprise over 30 percent of all property and casualty insurance premiums in the United States. NAMIC benefits member companies through government relations, educational services, and insurance and employee benefits programs. Membership consists of property and casualty mutual insurance companies. Sponsors and supports the NAMIC Political Action Comittee.

Publications:
NAMIC Forum. m.
NAMIC Government Affairs Insider. bi-w.
NAMIC Magazine. bi-m. adv.

Meetings/Conferences:
Annual Meetings: Fall
1999 – San Antonio, TX/Sept. 19-22

Nat'l Ass'n of Name Plate Manufacturers
Historical Note
Became (1994) Nat'l Ass'n of Graphic and Product Identification Manufacturers.

Nat'l Ass'n of Negro Business and Professional Women's Clubs (1935)
1806 New Hampshire Ave., N.W.
Washington, DC 20009
Tel: (202)483-4206   Fax: (202)462-7253
Web Site: www.nanbtwc.org
Members: 10,000 individuals, 380 clubs
Staff: 4
Annual Budget: $100-250,000
Exec. Director: Glo Ivory
Convention Coordinator: Sherelle Carper
Dir., Education: Denise Taylor
Coordinator, Membership Services: Janice S. Reuben

Historical Note
Membership: $75/year.

Publications:
Responsibility. q.

Meetings/Conferences:
Annual Meetings: Summer
1999 – Norfolk, VA/July 19-25

Nat'l Ass'n of Neighborhoods (1975)
1651 Fuller St., N.W.
Washington, DC 20009
Tel: (202)332-7766   Fax: (202)332-2314
Members: 2,400 organizations
Staff: 4
Annual Budget: $250-500,000
Exec. Director: Ricardo Byrd

Historical Note
Urban and rural organizations and coalitions working to strengthen neighborhood rights and responsibilities. Membership: $25/year (individual), $100/year (organization).

Publications:
NAN Bulletin. q.

Meetings/Conferences:
Annual Meetings: Fall

Nat'l Ass'n of Neonatal Nurses
1304 Southpoint Blvd., Suite 280

Petaluma, CA 94954-6861
Tel: (707)762-5588   *Fax:* (707)762-0401
Web Site: http://www.nann.org
Members: 12,000 individuals
Staff: 10
Annual Budget: $1-2,000,000
Exec. Director: Barbara Morrison, Ph.D., CAE
Program Manager: Dee Stewart
Membership Director: Jennifer Crist

Historical Note
NANN regular members are nurses specializing in neonatal care. Sponsors and supports a specialty interest group for advanced practice and management issues. Membership: $65/year (regular); $10/year, plus NANN dues (specialty).

Publications:
Central Lines Newsletter. q.
Neonatal Network Journal. 8/yr.

Meetings/Conferences:
Annual Meetings: September/1,000
1999 – Orlando, FL(Coronado Springs Resort)/Sept. 15-19
2000 – San Antonio, TX(Convention
         Center/Marriott)/Sept. 27-Oct. 1

Nat'l Ass'n of Nephrology Technologists and Technicians *(1982)*
P.O. Box 2307
Dayton, OH 45401-2307
Tel: (937)586-3705   *Fax:* (937)586-3699
E-Mail: nant@nant.meinet.com
Members: 1000 individuals
Annual Budget: $250-500,000
Exec. Director: Francine W. Rickenbach, C.A.E.

Historical Note
Added Technicians to their title in 1993. Membership: $50/year (individual).

Publications:
Annual Symposium Proceedings. a. adv.
Newsletter. bi-m.

Meetings/Conferences:
Annual Meetings: May-June
1999 – Baltimore, MD/400
2000 – Nashville, TN(Opryland)

Nat'l Ass'n of Noise Control Officials *(1978)*
53 Cubberley Road
Trenton, NJ 08690
Tel: (609)586-2684
Members: 70 individuals
Annual Budget: under $10,000
Administrator: Edward J. Di Polvere

Historical Note
Incorporated in the State of New Jersey. Members are employees of the federal or state governments, consultants, scientists and students concerned with acoustical control of the environment. Membership: $30/yr.

Publications:
Vibrations. m. adv.

Meetings/Conferences:
Annual Meetings: Fall, with the Nat'l Environmental Health
         Ass'n

Nat'l Ass'n of Nurse Massage Therapists
Historical Note
Organization dissolved in 1997; superseded by Nursing Touch and Massage Therapy Ass'n Internat'l.

Nat'l Ass'n of Nurse Practitioners in Reproductive Health *(1980)*
503 Capital Ct., N.E., Suite 300
Washington, DC 20005-4905
Tel: (202)543-9693   *Fax:* (202)543-9858
E-Mail: nanprh@aol.com
Members: 2,500 individuals
Staff: 2
Annual Budget: $100-250,000
President: Susan Wysocki

Historical Note
Membership: $75/year (individual); $75-1,000/year (organization).

Publications:
Reprocussions. 3/year. adv.

Meetings/Conferences:
Annual Meetings: always January or February
1999 – /Oct. 14-16

Nat'l Ass'n of Nurses
Historical Note
A unit of the Nat'l Ass'n of Government Employees.

Nat'l Ass'n of Nutrition and Aging Services Programs *(1976)*
1621 44th St., S.W., Suite 300
Grand Rapids, MI 49509-4387
Toll Free: (800)999 - 6262
Members: 1000 individuals
Staff: 3
Annual Budget: $250-500,000
Exec. Director: Connie Benton Wolfe

Historical Note
Incorporated in Delaware, NANASP members are individuals and organizations involved with direct service provision under the Older Americans Act. Associate membership is open to individuals or group supportive of NANASP's work. Affiliate membership is open to project staff whose agency holds a regular membership. Membership: $125/yr. (regular); $200/year (corporate).

Publications:
NANASP News. q. adv.

Meetings/Conferences:
Annual Meetings: June

Nat'l Ass'n of Off-Track Betting *(1973)*
Park Place
Pomona, NY 10970
Tel: (914)362-0400   *Fax:* (914)362-0419
Web Site: http://www.interbets.com
Members: 12 companies
Staff: 3
President: Donald Groth

Historical Note
Members are legal off-track betting companies.

Meetings/Conferences:

Nat'l Ass'n of Office Furniture Dealers *(1963)*
10357 Cruzenshire Cove
Collierville, TN 38017
Tel: (901)853-1716   *Fax:* (901)853-1826
E-Mail: npgroup@earthlink.net
Members: 85 companies
Staff: 3
Annual Budget: $1-2,000,000
President and C.E.O.: G.E. Russell

Historical Note
Incorporated in Ohio as MIV (More in Value) Inc., NAOFD is a marketing group providing advertising, catalogues and related services to its member dealers. Membership: $1,200-2,400/year.

Publications:
The Informer. q.

Meetings/Conferences:
Annual Meetings: first Quarter
1999 – Orlando, FL

Nat'l Ass'n of Oil Heating Service Managers *(1952)*
P.O. Box 309
Rutherford, NJ 07070-0309
Tel: (201)939-0963   *Fax:* (201)939-1004
E-Mail: info@naohsm.org
Web Site: http://www.naohsm.org
Members: 1,200 individuals
Staff: 2
Annual Budget: $100-250,000
Exec. Administrator: Louis P. Minigiello

Historical Note
Members are oil heat service managers. NAOHSM provides members with technical tapes, books and speakers to train their employee technicians. Membership: $40/year.

Publications:
Newsletter. 3/year.

Meetings/Conferences:
1999 – Hershey, PA(Hershey Park)/May 23-27

Nat'l Ass'n of Older Worker Employment Services *(1980)*
Historical Note
A special interest group of the Nat'l Council on the Aging concerned with employment opportunities for older workers.

Nat'l Ass'n of Optometrists and Opticians *(1959)*
P.O. Box 479
Marble Head, OH 4344
Tel: (419)798-4071   *Fax:* (419)798-5548
Members: 15,500 individuals
Staff: 4
Annual Budget: $100-250,000
Treasurer: Frank Rozak

Historical Note
Formerly the National Optical Association. NAOO carries out continuing educational and public affairs programs of mutual importance to members and serves as a clearing house for retail optical information. Membership: $500/year (individual); $1,000 minimum/year (organization/company).

Meetings/Conferences:
Semi-annual Meetings: Spring and Fall

Nat'l Ass'n of Orthopaedic Nurses *(1980)*
East Holly Ave., Box 56
Pitman, NJ 08071-0056
Tel: (609)256-2310   *Fax:* (609)589-7463
E-Mail: naon@mail.ajj.com
Web Site: http://www.inurse.com/~naon
Members: 7,000 individuals
Annual Budget: $2-5,000,000
Chief Staff Executive: Anthony J. Jannetti
Staff Executive: Cynthia R. Nowicki, Ed.D., RN,
Membership Services Secretary: Fran Chiraelli

Historical Note
Members are licensed registered nurses, LVN's or LPN's, and students associated with all facets of orthopaedic patient care. Membership: $60/year (individual); $1,500/year (organization/company).

Publications:
NAON News. bi-m.
Orthopaedic Nursing. bi-m.

Meetings/Conferences:
Annual Meetings: Spring/2,500
1999 – Atlanta, GA(Marriott Marquis)/May 22-26

Nat'l Ass'n of Orthopaedic Technologists *(1982)*
P.O. Box 14148
Research Triangle Pk, NC 27709-4148
Tel: (919)572-6821   *Fax:* (919)361-2426
E-Mail: rmckinno@intrex.net
Web Site: http://wwwrealsolutions.org/naot.htm
Members: 2,500 individuals, 30 companies and organizations
Staff: 2
Annual Budget: $100-250,000

Exec. Director: Rhonda McKinnon
Historical Note
Membership: $50/yr. (individual), and $850/yr. (organization).

Publications:
NAOT News. q.
Online: Advancements in Orthopaedic Technology. bien. adv.

Meetings/Conferences:
1999 – Long Beach, CA(Hyatt)/Aug. 10-14

Nat'l Ass'n of Paralegal Personnel *(1975)*
Historical Note
Address unknown in 1997.

Nat'l Ass'n of Parish Coordinators/Directors of Religious Education
Historical Note
A division of the Nat'l Catholic Educational Ass'n.

Nat'l Ass'n of Parliamentarians *(1930)*
213 S. Main St.
Independence, MO 64050-3850
Tel: (816)833-3892   *Fax:* (816)833-3992
Toll Free: (888)627 - 2929
E-Mail: nap2@prodigy.net
Web Site: www.parliamentarians.org
Members: 4,000 individuals
Staff: 4
Annual Budget: $250-500,000
Exec. Director: Sarah Niett

Historical Note
Organized in 1930 for the purposes of studying, teaching and promoting the rules of deliberative assemblies.

Publications:
National Parliamentarian. q.

Meetings/Conferences:
Annual Meetings: Biennial.
1999 – Kansas City, MO(Westin Crown Center)/Sept. 29-Oct.
         6/400

Nat'l Ass'n of Pastoral Musicians *(1976)*
225 Sheridan St., N.W.
Washington, DC 20011
Tel: (202)723-5800   *Fax:* (202)723-2262
E-Mail: NPMSING@NPM.org
Members: 9,300 individuals
Staff: 10
Annual Budget: $1-2,000,000
President: Rev. Virgil C. Funk
Membership Director: Margie Kitty
Editor: Dr. Gordon E. Truitt

Historical Note
NPM is a national membership organization for parish musicians and parish clergy. Membership: $66/year.

Publications:
Catholic Music Educator. 5/yr.
Pastoral Music. 6/yr. adv.
Pastoral Music Notebook. 6/yr.

Meetings/Conferences:
Annual Meetings: Biennial Meetings/odd years

Nat'l Ass'n of Pediatric Nurse Associates and Practitioners *(1973)*
1101 North Kings Highway, Suite 206
Cherry Hill, NJ 08034-1912
Tel: (609)667-1773   *Fax:* (609)667-7187
E-Mail: napnap1@aol.com
Web Site: http://www.napnap.org
Members: 5,500 individuals
Staff: 9
Annual Budget: $500-1,000,000
Exec. Director: Mavis McGuire
Dir., Membership/Communications: Joseph G. Casey
Director of Education: Dolores C. Jones

Historical Note
The goals of NAPNAP are to provide continuing education and standards for pediatric nurse practitioners and to support certification for practice; and to support legislation designed to improve the quality of infant, child and adolescent health. Membership: $120/year.

Publications:
The Journal of Pediatric Health Care. bi-m. adv.
The Pediatric Nurse Practitioner. bi-m.

Meetings/Conferences:
Annual Meetings: Spring
1999 – San Antonio, TX(Marriott
         Rivercenter)/April 7-10/1250
2000 – Atlanta, GA(Hyatt Regency)/March 29-April 1/1250

Nat'l Ass'n of Performing Arts Managers and Agents *(1977)*
459 Columbus Ave., Suite 144
New York, NY 10029
Tel: (212)799-5308   *Fax:* (212)580-5438
E-Mail: bcolton@napama.org
Members: 125 individualscompanies
Annual Budget: $25-50,000
Exec. Director: Barbara Colton

Historical Note
Incorporated in New York, NY. Organization of professionals who serve artists in the development of their performing careers. Members are professional managers, agents, or personal representatives, and businesses and individual related to the industry. Membership $100/year (individual); $250-300/year (company).

Publications:
NAPAMA News. 3/yr.
Notes from NAPAMA. m.

Meetings/Conferences:
Annual Meetings: New York, NY/December
1999 – New York, NY(Hilton)

Nat'l Ass'n of Permanent Diaconate Directors
Historical Note
Became (1995) Nat'l Ass'n of Diaconate Directors.

Nat'l Ass'n of Personal Financial Advisors (1983)
355 West Dundee Rd., Suite 200
Buffalo Grove, IL   60089-3500
Tel: (847)537-7722   *Fax:* (847)537-7740
Toll Free: (888)333 - 6659
E-Mail: info@napfa.org
Web Site: http://www.napfa.org
Members: 525 companies
Staff: 6
Annual Budget: $1-2,000,000
President & C.E.O.: Carole Z. Badger, JD, CAE
Communications & Technical Manager: Ellen Turf
Exec. Director: Margery Wasserman
Historical Note
Members are financial planners who are compensated only by fees. NAPFA members are prohibited from receiving any type of product-related compensation, such as sales commissions. Members do not sell products nor do they direct sales to parties with whom they have financial interests. Membership: $250/year.
Publications:
NAPFA Advisor Magazine. m. adv.
NAPFA Membership Directory. a.
Meetings/Conferences:
1999 – Washington, DC(Omni Shoreham)/800

Nat'l Ass'n of Personnel Services (1917)
3133 Mt. Vernon Ave.
Alexandria, VA   22305
Tel: (703)684-0180   *Fax:* (703)684-0071
Web Site: http://www.napsweb.org
Members: 1,520 individuals
Staff: 8
Annual Budget: $1-2,000,000
President: Diane B. Callis
Editor: Beth Rogers
Director, Ass'n Services: Scott Kennaugh
Program Manager: Marjorie Bowman
Historical Note
Formerly (1992) the Nat'l Ass'n of Personnel Consultants. Founded as the Nat'l Employment Board. Merged (1960) with Employment Agencies Ass'n (1923) and Nat'l Ass'n of Employment Agencies (1956) to become the Nat'l Employment Ass'n, then the Nat'l Ass'n of Personnel Consultants (1978). Membership: $400/year minimum. Awards the Certified Personnel Consultant (CPC) designation.
Publications:
Inside NAPS. 10/year.
National Directory of Personnel Consultants. a. adv.
Meetings/Conferences:
Annual Meetings: Fall/1,200
1999 – New York, NY(Marriott Marquee)/Sept. 23-36

Nat'l Ass'n of Personnel Workers (1954)
Historical Note
Became Nat'l Ass'n of Student Affairs Professionals in 1994.

Nat'l Ass'n of Pet Sitters
Historical Note
Became Nat'l Ass'n of Professional Pet Sitters in 1994.

Nat'l Ass'n of Pharmaceutical Manufacturers (1955)
320 Old Country Road, Room 205
Garden City, NY   11530-1752
Tel: (516)741-3699   *Fax:* (516)741-3696
E-Mail: NAPMGENRX@aol.com
Web Site: www.napmnet.org
Members: 46 manufacturers
Staff: 3
Annual Budget: $500-1,000,000
President: Robert S. Milanese
Office Manager: Maureen D'Agostino
Historical Note
Formerly (1968) Drug and Allied Products Guild. NAPM is the trade organization of the generic drug industry representing generic pharmaceutical manufacturers. Associate members are distributors, repackagers, and suppliers of products and services to the industry. Technical membership is open to all research and development, manufacturing and drug regulatory staffs of generic pharmaceutical companies. Membership: varies.
Publications:
NAPM News Bulletin. m.
Meetings/Conferences:

Nat'l Ass'n of Photo Equipment Technicians (1973)
3000 Picture Place
Jackson, MI   49201
Tel: (517)788-8100   *Fax:* (517)788-8371
E-Mail: bcovey@pmai.org
Web Site: http://www.pmai.org
Members: 250 individuals
Staff: 1
Annual Budget: $10-25,000
Exec. Liaison: Bill Covey
Historical Note
A division (1976) of the Photo Marketing Ass'n Internat'l. Provides information on the photographic industry to those engaged in photographic repair. Membership $25/year (individual), $95/year (company).
Publications:
NAPET News. q.

Who's Who in Photographic Management. semi-a.
Meetings/Conferences:
Annual Meetings: February
1999 – Las Vegas, NV

Nat'l Ass'n of Photographic Manufacturers
Historical Note
Became (1997) Photographic and Imaging Manufacturers Ass'n.

Nat'l Ass'n of Physician Nurses (1973)
900 S. Washington St., Suite G13
Falls Church, VA   22046-4020
Tel: (703)237-8616
Members: 3,000 individuals
Staff: 2
Annual Budget: $100-250,000
Membership Director: S. Young
Historical Note
Membership: $30/year.
Publications:
The Nightingale. m.
Meetings/Conferences:
Annual Meetings: Spring/Summer

Nat'l Ass'n of Physician Recruiters (1984)
P.O. Box 150127
Altamonte Springs, FL   32715-0127
Tel: (407)774-7880   *Fax:* (407)774-6440
E-Mail: WKautter@napr.org
Web Site: http://napr.org
Members: 275 companies
Staff: 3
Annual Budget: $250-500,000
Exec. V. President: Willard S. Kautter, CAE
Historical Note
Membership: $300-975/year.
Publications:
NAPR Business Report. q.
Newsletter. bi-m. adv.
Meetings/Conferences:
1999 – Scottsdale, AZ or Miami, FL

Nat'l Ass'n of Pipe Coating Applicators (1965)
Deposit Guaranty Bank Building
333 Texas St., Suite 717
Shreveport, LA   71101-3673
Tel: (318)227-2769   *Fax:* (318)222-0482
Web Site: http://www.napca.com
Members: 145 companies
Staff: 2
Annual Budget: $100-250,000
Managing Director: Merritt B. Chastain, Jr.
Historical Note
Members apply exterior and interior protective pipe coatings to steel pipe in permanently established facilities. NAPCA is the trade ass'n for the plant pipe coating industry throughout the world. Membership: $1,500/year (full member), $300/year (associate); $500/year (foreign), $150/year (foreign associate).
Publications:
Application Specifications.
Membership Roster. a. adv.
Newsletter. q.
Meetings/Conferences:
Annual Meetings: March/April
1999 – Naples, FL(Registry Resort)/April 10-14/260
2000 – Tucson, AZ/April 12-16/260

Nat'l Ass'n of Pipe Fabricators (1977)
3132 Birch Bark Lane
Oklahoma City, OK   73120
Tel: (405)721-9486   *Fax:* (405)755-5033
Toll Free: (888)798 - 1924
E-Mail: twright@napf.com
Web Site: http://www.napf.com
Annual Budget: $100-250,000
Exec. Director: Ted Wright
Historical Note
NAPF members are independent fabricators of ductile iron pipe. Members must be in compliance with all phases of the the NAPF Quality Certification Program. Membership: $2,500/year (company).
Publications:
NAPF Pipeline. q.
Meetings/Conferences:
1999 – Mesa, AZ(Arizona Golf Resort)/70

Nat'l Ass'n of Pizza Operators (1982)
P.O. Box 1347
New Albany, IN   47151-1347
Tel: (812)949-0909   *Fax:* (812)941-9711
Toll Free: (800)489 - 8324
Web Site: http://www.pizzatoday.com
Members: 40,000 individuals
Staff: 35
Annual Budget: $1-2,000,000
Exec. Director: Gerry Durnell
Show Manager: Gerry Dernell
Director, Membership: Robert T. Jordan
Historical Note
Pizza equipment manufacturers, industry suppliers, franchise and independent pizza operators and frozen pizza producers. Provides liaison between pizza industry and governmental agencies. Researches industry data and statistics. Membership: $29.95/year.
Publications:
Pizza Today. m. adv.
Meetings/Conferences:
Annual Meetings: January-March/4,000

1999 – Las Vegas, NV/Feb. 8-11

Nat'l Ass'n of Plant Patent Owners (1939)
1250 I St., N.W., Suite 500
Washington, DC   20005
Tel: (202)789-2900   *Fax:* (202)789-1893
Members: 70 individuals
Staff: 1
Annual Budget: $10-25,000
Exec. V. President: Robert J. Dolibois, CAE
Historical Note
Owners of patents on newly propagated flowers, trees and plants. Affiliated with American Nursery and Landscape Ass'n.
Meetings/Conferences:
Annual Meetings: July, with American Ass'n of Nurserymen

Nat'l Ass'n of Plumbing Specialty Distributors (1983)
Historical Note
Address unknown in 1997.

Nat'l Ass'n of Plumbing-Heating-Cooling Contractors
Historical Note
Became (1997) Plumbing-Heating-Cooling Contractors - Nat'l Ass'n.

Nat'l Ass'n of Police Equipment Distributors
8421 Frost Way
Annandale, VA   22003
Tel: (703)280-4622   *Fax:* (703)280-0942
Exec. Director: Fred Cannon
Representative: Kenton Pattie
Historical Note
Members are dealers and distributors of police equipment who sell to local, state, Federal law enforcement, police and security organizations.
Meetings/Conferences:
Annual Meetings: Fall

Nat'l Ass'n of Police Organizations (1979)
750 First Street, N.E., Suite 920
Washington, DC   20002-4241
Tel: (202)842-4420   *Fax:* (202)482-4396
Toll Free: (800)322 - 6276
E-Mail: NAPO2erols.com
Web Site: http://www.napo.org
Members: 220,000 individuals
Staff: 7
Exec. Director: Robert T. Scully
Director, Communications & Development: Jody Hedeman
General Counsel: Steve McSpadden
Historical Note
Members are bonefide sworn law enforcement officers.
Publications:
Newsletter. m.
Meetings/Conferences:
Annual Meetings: August
1999 – Denver, CO(Hyatt)/Aug. 12-16
2000 – Washington, DC(Hyatt)/Aug. 3-8

Nat'l Ass'n of Postal Supervisors (1908)
1727 King St., Suite 400
Alexandria, VA   22314-2753
Tel: (703)836-9660   *Fax:* (703)836-9665
Members: 35,500 individuals
Staff: 9
Annual Budget: $2-5,000,000
President: Vincent Palladino
National Secretary/Treasurer: Adolph Ruiz
Historical Note
An independent professional association founded in Louisville, KY. Sponsors the Supervisors Political Action Committee. Membership: $72/year (individual).
Publications:
The Postal Supervisor Newsletter.
Meetings/Conferences:
Biennial Meetings: even years in August/September
2000 – Anchorage, AK
2002 – Greensboro, NC

Nat'l Ass'n of Postmasters of the U.S. (1898)
8 Herbert St.
Alexandria, VA   22305-2600
Tel: (703)683-9027   *Fax:* (703)683-6820
Web Site: http://www.napus.org
Members: 43,000 individuals
Staff: 9
Annual Budget: $2-5,000,000
Exec. Director: Edward J. Baer
Meeting Planner: Geraldine Swarm
Historical Note
NAPUS members are active and retired postmasters. Sponsors and supports the Political Education for Postmasters Political Action Committee. Membership: $36-$293/year (active individual).
Publications:
Postmaster's Gazette. 11/yr. adv.
Update Newsletter. m.
Meetings/Conferences:
Annual Meetings: August-September/5,000
1999 – Charlotte, NC/Aug. 14-20
2000 – Minneapolis, MN
2000 – New Orleans, LA
2001 – Las Vegas, NV

Nat'l Ass'n of Power Engineers (1879)
1 Springfield St.
Chicopee, MA   01013-2624
Tel: (413)592-6273   *Fax:* (413)592-1998
Members: 3,000 individuals

Staff: 3
Annual Budget: $250-500,000
Office Manager: William Judd

Historical Note
Members include those in power plant operation and maintenance responsible for supplying industry and service establishments with process power, heat, air conditioning, lighting, ventilation and related building and plant services. Membership: $50/year (individual), $500/year (corporation).

Publications:
National Engineer. m. adv.

Meetings/Conferences:
Annual Meetings: Summer
1999 – Tampa, Fl(Cruise)

Nat'l Ass'n of Principals of Schools for Girls *(1921)*
41 Van Brunt Manor Road
East Setauket, NY   11733
Tel: (516)751-0850   *Fax:* (516)689-7311
Members: 600 individuals
Staff: 1
Annual Budget: $100-250,000
Exec. Director: Carol M. Lane

Historical Note
NASPG addresses common concerns of administrators of American and Canadian independent schools and colleges which enroll women. Membership: $50/yr. (college), $100/yr. (school).

Publications:
Proceedings. a.

Meetings/Conferences:
Annual Meetings: Late Winter

Nat'l Ass'n of Printers and Lithographers *(1933)*
75 West Century Rd.
Paramus, NJ   07652
Tel: (201)342-0700   *Fax:* (201)634-0325
Toll Free: (800)642 - 6275
Web Site: http://www.napl.org
Members: 2,000 companies
Staff: 45
Annual Budget: $5-10,000,000
President: I. Gregg Van Wert
Director, Ctr. for Continuing Education: Fern Dickey
Dir., Finance: Dean D'Ambrosi
Exec. V. President: Joseph P. Truncale, CAE
Dir., Member Rels.: Mike Speath
Editorial Director: Dawn Lospaluto
Interactive Media Svcs. Mgr.: Marie Letarte

Historical Note
Established as the Nat'l Ass'n of Photo-Lithographers in 1933, it assumed its present name in 1972. NAPL works toward increasing printers' profitability via a full range of management and educational services for its worldwide membership. Services cover every aspect of profitable printing management including cost and finance, human resources, sales and marketing, quality, desktop, economics, the environment and more. Membership: $300-2,270/year (company, based on annual sales/annual payroll); $155/year (educational members).

Publications:
Cyber Ink. q.
Desktop for Profit. m.
Leadership Excellence.
Prepress Market Watch. q.
Printing Business Report. q.
Printing Manager. q.
Quality Improvement Quarterly. q.
Sheetfed Operations Quarterly. q.
Tech Trends. q.

Meetings/Conferences:
1999 – Santa Barbara, CA

Nat'l Ass'n of Printing Ink Manufacturers *(1914)*
581 Main St.
Woodbridge, NJ   07905
Tel: (732)855-1525   *Fax:* (732)855-1838
Web Site: http://www.napim@napim.org
Members: 77 ink companies, 90 suppliers
Staff: 2
Annual Budget: $500-1,000,000
Exec. Director: James E. Coleman

Historical Note
Established as the Nat'l Ass'n of Printing Ink Makers, it assumed its present name in 1967. Sponsors the Nat'l Printing Ink Research Institute.

Publications:
American Ink-Maker. m. adv.
NAPIM News. q.
Pilt. bi-m.

Meetings/Conferences:
Annual Meetings: Spring/350
1999 – Miami, FL(Doral Hotel)

Nat'l Ass'n of Private Enterprise *(1983)*
7819 Shelburne Cir.
Spring, TX   77379-4687
Tel: (281)655-5412   *Fax:* (281)257-3244
Toll Free: (800)223 - 6273
E-Mail: jlsq@aol.com
Members: 1,200 individuals
Staff: 3
Annual Budget: $100-250,000
V. President: Laura Squiers
Marketing Director: Barbara Sproull

Historical Note
Founded to promote the survival and growth of private enterprise and small businesses in the U.S. Programs include insurance coverage, cooperative buying services, legislative action, and continuing education scholarships. Membership: $120/year.

Publications:
NAPE News. q.

Nat'l Ass'n of Private Industry Councils *(1979)*
1201 New York Ave., N.W., Suite 350
Washington, DC   20005
Tel: (202)289-2950   *Fax:* (202)289-2846
Web Site: http://www.work-web.com/napic
Members: 500 councils
Staff: 5
Annual Budget: $250-500,000
President: Robert F. Knight

Historical Note
Private industry councils and private employers concerned with employment and training policies in the context of economic development and education. Membership: $150-600/year.

Publications:
NAPIC Reports To.
Workforce Advisor. q.

Meetings/Conferences:
Annual Meetings: February
1999 – Washington, DC(Renaissance Hotel)/Feb. 28-Mar. 2

Nat'l Ass'n of Private Process Servers *(1980)*
Historical Note
Address unknown in 1997.

Nat'l Ass'n of Private Schools for Exceptional Children *(1971)*
1522 K St., N.W., Suite 1032
Washington, DC   20005-1202
Tel: (202)408-3338   *Fax:* (202)408-3340
E-Mail: napsec@aol.com
Web Site: http://www.napsec.com
Members: 230 schools
Staff: 4
Annual Budget: $250-500,000
Exec. Director and C.E.O.: Sherry L. Kolbe
Office Administrator: Pamela A.P. Cowen

Historical Note
Founded to improve educational opportunities for children with disabilities, promote private special education as a vital component of the nation's educational system, and educate the public about the services provided and needed for these students. Members are private facilities serving children with disabilities in an educational/therapeutic setting, as well as organizations and individuals supporting such institutions. Membership: $250/year (affiliate); $775-$1,675/year (private school); $750-$2,750(Council of State Affiliated Ass'ns).

Publications:
Directory. bi-a.
National Issues Service. m.
The NAPSEC News. 3/yr. adv.

Meetings/Conferences:
Annual Meetings: January Sanibel Island, FL(Sun Dial)/Jan. 17-22/200
1999 – Captiva, Island, FL(South Seas Plantation)
2000 – Captiva Island, FL(South Seas Plantation)

Nat'l Ass'n of Private, Nontraditional Schools and Colleges
Historical Note
Became (1998) Nat'l Ass'n of Private, Nontraditional Schools and Colleges with Accrediting Commission for Higher Education.

Nat'l Ass'n of Private, Nontraditional Schools and Colleges with Accrediting Commission for Higher Education *(1974)*
182 Thompson Road
Grand Junction, CO   81503
Tel: (970)243-5441   *Fax:* (970)242-4392
E-Mail: director@napnsc.org
Web Site: http://www.napnsc.org
Members: 8 institutions
Staff: 3
Annual Budget: $100-250,000
Exec. Director: H. Earl Heusser, Ed.D.

Historical Note
Formerly (1977) Nat'l Ass'n of Schools and Colleges. Later (1998) Nat'l Ass'n of Private, Nontraditional schools and Colleges. It's Accrediting Commission for Higher Education is the only national, institutional accrediting body which has developed criteria, standards and guidelines expressly for private, nontraditional or alternative education at all postsecondary levels.

Publications:
A Summary of NAPNSC Accrediting History. a.
Accreditation Brochure. a.
Accreditation Fact Sheet. q.
Comparisons of Traditional & Nontraditional Education. a.
Founding History of the NAPNSC Accrediting Commission. a.
General Information Brochure. a.

Meetings/Conferences:
Annual Meetings: Winter or Spring

Nat'l Ass'n of Produce Market Managers *(1946)*
c/o Ontario Food Terminal Board
165 The Queen's Way
Toronto, ON   M8Y 1-H8
Tel: (716)424-4600   *Fax:* (716)427-2690
Members: 110 individuals
President: William Mulligan, Jr.

Historical Note
Produce market managers and industrial produce dealers. Has no paid officers or full-time staff.

Publications:
Convention Proceedings. a.
Green Sheet. q.

Meetings/Conferences:
Annual Meetings: April

Nat'l Ass'n of Professional Band Instrument Repair Technicians *(1976)*
P.O. Box 51
Normal, IL   61761-0051
Tel: (309)452-4257   *Fax:* (309)452-4825
E-Mail: changler@napbrit.org
Web Site: http://www.napbirt.org
Members: 1,200 individuals
Staff: 1
Annual Budget: $100-250,000
Exec. Director: Chuck Hagler

Historical Note
Dedicated to integrity and professionalism in the craft of repair, restoration, and maintenance of band instruments. Membership: $85/year.

Publications:
Directory. a.
Newsletter. q.
Techni-Com. bi-m. adv.

Meetings/Conferences:
Annual Meetings: April
1999 – Anchorage, AK/April 8-11
2000 – New Orleans, LA

Nat'l Ass'n of Professional Baseball Leagues *(1901)*
P.O. Box A
201 Bayshore Dr. SE
St. Petersburg, FL   33731
Tel: (813)822-6937   *Fax:* (813)821-5819
Members: 19 minor leagues
Staff: 20
Annual Budget: $1-2,000,000
President: Mike Moore
C.O.O.: Robert Dlugozima

Historical Note
Oversees the activity of minor league baseball.

Publications:
Annual Trade Show Publications.
Newsletter. m. adv.
Orange Book. a. adv.

Meetings/Conferences:
Annual Meetings: First week in December/2,000

Nat'l Ass'n of Professional Educators *(1972)*
P.O. Box 2206
Reston, VA   22090
Tel: (602)584-4920
Exec. Secretary: Philip Strittmatter

Historical Note
Members are associations representing professional educators opposed to the unionist policies. Operates from a legislative consultant's office in Washington. Has voluntary dues.

Publications:
Professional Educator Newsletter. 7/yr.

Nat'l Ass'n of Professional Employer Organizations *(1984)*
901 N. Pitt St., Suite 150
Alexandria, VA   22314
Tel: (703)836-0466   *Fax:* (703)836-0976
E-Mail: info@napeo.org
Web Site: http://napeo.org
Members: 600 companies
Staff: 12
Annual Budget: $2-5,000,000
Exec. V. President: Milan P. Yager
Manager, Meetings: Michelle Meyer
Assoc. Director: Bari Moorefield
Director of Membership Services: Melissa A. Viscovich

Historical Note
Formerly (1993) Nat'l Staff Leasing Ass'n. Established in California and incorporated in Virginia, NAPEO members are firms providing professional employer services. Membership: $750-25,000/year (based on volume).

Publications:
NAPEO Convention Program. a. adv.
NAPEO Directory. q. adv.
NAPEO In Touch. q.
NAPEO PEO Insider Magazine. m. adv.

Meetings/Conferences:
Semi-Annual Meetings: May and October
1999 – New Orleans, LA

Nat'l Ass'n of Professional Environmental Communicators *(1990)*
Historical Note
Address unknown in 1997.

Nat'l Ass'n of Professional Geriatric Care Managers *(1987)*
1604 N. Country Club Road
Tucson, AZ   85716
Tel: (520)881-8008   *Fax:* (520)325-7925
Members: 1,150 individuals
Staff: 16
Annual Budget: $100-250,000
Exec. Director: Laury L. Adsit
Communications Director: Jihane K. Rohrbacker
Finance Coordinator: Janet Tite
Membership Director: Jenifer Mowery

Historical Note
Formerly (1994) the Nat'l Ass'n of Private Geriatric Care Managers. GCM is an organization of practitioners whose goal is the advancement of dignified care for the elderly and their families. Emphasizes the autonomy of the elderly patient along with

principles of appropriate and effective care. Membership: $150/year.

Publications:
GCM Journal. q.
Geriatric Care Management Insurance. q. adv.
Inside GCM. q. adv.

Meetings/Conferences:
1999 – San Diego, CA

Nat'l Ass'n of Professional Insurance Agents (1931)
400 N. Washington St.
Alexandria, VA 22314-2312
Tel: (703)836-9340   *Fax:* (703)836-1279
E-Mail: piaweb@pianet.org
Web Site: http://www.pianet.com
Members: 160,000 individuals
Staff: 65
Annual Budget: $10-25,000,000
Exec. V. President: Douglas S. Culkin, CIC, CAE
Director, Public Relations: Ted Besesparis, Jr.
Manager, Meetings and Conventions: Laurie Burke
V.President, Research and Technical Affairs: Patricia A. Borowski, CAE
Director, Education: Connie Paradise
Senior V. President: Jeffrey D. Morgan, CAE
V. President, Finance: William F. Deichler
V. President Member Services and Products: Bruce N. Scholnick

Historical Note
Formerly (1976) the Nat'l Ass'n of Mutual Insurance Agents. Members are independent insurance agents/brokers and their employees representing over 160,000 individuals. Supports the Professional Insurance Agents Political Action Committee. Has an annual budget of approximately $14 million.

Publications:
Action. m.
Professional Agent. m. adv.

Meetings/Conferences:
Annual Meetings: Fall/2,000
1999 – Denver, CO/Aug. 7-11

Nat'l Ass'n of Professional Mortgage Women (1964)
23607 Hwy. 99, Suite 2-C
P.O. Box 2016
Edmonds, WA 98020-9516
Tel: (425)778-6162   *Fax:* (425)771-9588
Toll Free: (800)827 - 3034
E-Mail: napmw@aol.com
Web Site: http://www.napmw.org
Members: 4,500 individuals
Staff: 2
Annual Budget: $250-500,000
Exec. Director: Patricia Hull

Historical Note
NAPMW is a network of more than 80 local associations in 21 states. Members are individuals employed in mortgage banking and related fields. Nat'l Membership: $35/year (individual).

Publications:
National Mortgage Notes & Deeds. q. adv.

Meetings/Conferences:
Annual Meetings: May
1999 – Louisville, KY/May 12-16/500
2000 – Chicago, IL/May 17-21/500
2001 – Norfolk, VA/May 16-20/500

Nat'l Ass'n of Professional Organizers (1985)
1033 La Posada Drive, Suite 220
Austin, TX 78752-3880
Tel: (512)454-8626   *Fax:* (512)454-3036
E-Mail: napo@assnmgmt.com
Web Site:
          http://www.ccsi.com/ ~ asmi/GROUPS/NAPO/napo.html
Members: 960 individuals
Annual Budget: $100-250,000
Exec. Director: Phyllis Pilger

Historical Note
Formerly (1986) Ass'n of Professional Organizers. NAPO members are time, productivity, and organization management consultants. Membership: $150/year (individual); $450/year (organization).

Publications:
NAPO Membership Directory. a. adv.
NAPO News Newsletter. q. adv.
Resource Directory. irreg.

Meetings/Conferences:
Annual Meetings: Spring
1999 – Philadelphia, PA
2000 – Los Angeles, CA
2001 – Atlanta, GA

Nat'l Ass'n of Professional Pet Sitters (1989)
1030 15th St., N.W. Suite 870
Washington, DC 20005
Tel: (202)393-3317   *Fax:* (202)393-0336
Toll Free: (800)296 - 7387
Members: 1000 companies
Staff: 5
Annual Budget: $100-250,000
Exec. Director: Marianne McDermott

Historical Note
Formerly (1994) Nat'l Ass'n of Pet Sitters. Members are owners of pet-care services offering in-home pet care. Membership: $130/year.

Publications:
NAPS Network. bi-m.

Meetings/Conferences:

Nat'l Ass'n of Professional Process Servers (1982)
P.O. Box 4547

Portland, OR 97208
Tel: (503)222-4180   *Fax:* (503)222-3950
Toll Free: (800)477 - 8211
E-Mail: administration@napps.org
Web Site: http://www.napps.org
Members: 1,300 individuals
Annual Budget: $100-250,000
Administrator: Alan H. Crowe

Historical Note
Members are individuals and companies serving summonses, complaints, subpoenas, and other documents of the courts. Provides services to members including E&O and professional liability insurance. Membership: $150/year.

Publications:
Docket Sheet Newsletter. bi-m. adv.
Membership Directory. semi-a.

Meetings/Conferences:
1999 – Chicago, IL(Windham NW Chicago)/April 29-May 2
2000 – Las Vegas, NV(LV Hilton)
2000 – Las Vegas, NV(Hilton)April

Nat'l Ass'n of Professional Surplus Lines Offices (1975)
6405 N. Cosby Ave., Suite 201
Kansas City, MO 64151-3963
Tel: (816)741-3910   *Fax:* (816)741-5409
E-Mail: NAPSLO@microlink.net
Web Site: http://www.napslo.org
Members: 800 firms
Staff: 5
Annual Budget: $2-5,000,000
Exec. Director: Richard M. Bouhan
Communications Corrdinator: Mike Ardis
Meetings Coordinator: Debbie Hill

Historical Note
Members are brokerage firms and companies writing excess and surplus insurance lines. Founded and incorporated in the State of New York. Membership: $2,500-5,000/year (company); $700/year (broker).

Publications:
NAPSLO News. bi-m.
Security & Review. a.

Meetings/Conferences:
Annual Meetings: Fall/2,000
1999 – New York, NY
2000 – Chicago, IL

Nat'l Ass'n of Professional Word Processing Technicians (1980)

Historical Note
Purpose is to test, certify and document word processing hardware, software companies and competent word processors. Biennial scholarship offered to undergraduate and graduates. Membership: registration of $20.

Nat'l Ass'n of Professionals in Women's Health (1987)
175 W. Jackson Blvd., Suite A1711
Chicago, IL 60604-2801
Tel: (312)786-1468   *Fax:* (312)786-0376
Web Site: http://www.napwh.org
Members: 825 individuals
Staff: 3
Annual Budget: $250-500,000
Acting Exec. Director: Patty Looker
Program Director: Missy Hession
Marketing and Membership Director: Serena Chaudhry

Historical Note
Formerly (1997) the Nat'l Ass'n of Women's Health Professionals, NAPWH was founded in 1987 and incorporated in 1990 as a non-profit, non-partisan professional membership ass'n. It's mission is to promote excellence and provide leadership, resources, and collegial support to professionals who influence and champion quality health care for women and their communities. Members are a growing constituency of women's health professionals - clinicians, administrators, educators, social workers, marketing professionals, research specialists, policy analysts, and others - all with a common interest in improving health outcomes for women. Membership: $185/year (individual).

Publications:
FOCUS Newsletter. q. adv.
Membership Directory. a.
Women's HealthBeat (fax update). q. adv.

Meetings/Conferences:
Annual Meetings: Fall
1999 – Philadelphia, PA/Oct. 24-27

Nat'l Ass'n of Professors of Hebrew in American Institutions of Higher Learning (1950)
1346 Van Hise Hall, 1220 Linden Drive
Univ. of Wisconsin
Madison, WI 53706-1558
Tel: (608)262-2968
Members: 400 individuals
Annual Budget: under $10,000
Exec. V. President: Gilead Morahg

Historical Note
A service and information organization comprised of professors in colleges, universities and seminaries who specialize in the area of Hebrew Language (from Biblical to Modern) and related subjects and non-academic associate members whose occupations or interests are related to Hebrew studies. Membership: $35/year.

Publications:
Bulletin of Higher Hebrew Education. a.
Hebrew Studies. a.
Iggeret. semi-a.

Meetings/Conferences:
Annual Meetings: With the Soc. for Biblical Literature

Nat'l Ass'n of Program Information and Performance Measurement
810 First St., N.E., Suite 500
Washington, DC 20002-4265
Tel: (202)682-0100   *Fax:* (202)289-6555
Contact: Larry Goolsby

Historical Note
Formerly (1998) Nat'l Ass'n of Human Service Quality Control Directors. An affiliate unit of the Ass'n of Public Welfare Ass'n which provides administrative support.

Meetings/Conferences:

Nat'l Ass'n of Property Inspectors (1993)
303 W. Cypress
P.O. Box 12528
San Antonio, TX 78212-0528
Tel: (210)225-2897   *Fax:* (210)225-8450
Toll Free: (800)486 - 3676
E-Mail: lincolncenter@worldnet.att.net
Web Site: masterappraisers.org
Members: 800 individuals
Staff: 6
Annual Budget: $50-100,000
President: Marvin T. Deane, Ph.D.
Exec. Director: Deborah J. Deane

Historical Note
Members are professionals in real estate inspection. Promotes ethical standards and provides continuing education opportunities to members. Maintains a certification program granting three distinct designations. Membership: $125/year.

Publications:
Membership Directory. a. adv.
Property Inspector News. q.

Meetings/Conferences:
1999 – San Antonio, TX(Gunter Hotel)/March 12-13

Nat'l Ass'n of Protection and Advocacy Systems (1978)
900 2nd St., N.E., Suite 211
Washington, DC 20002
Tel: (202)408-9514   *Fax:* (202)408-9520
E-Mail: napa5@earthlink.net
Members: 96 programs
Staff: 14
Annual Budget: $1-2,000,000
Exec. Director: Curtis L. Decker

Historical Note
NAPAS members are disability rights agencies, protection and advocacy systems (P&As), and client assistance programs (CAPs) assisting the disabled and mentally ill

Publications:
Protection and Advocacy News. q.
State Protection and Advocacy Agencies Directory. a.

Meetings/Conferences:
1999 – Washington, DC

Nat'l Ass'n of Psychiatric Health Systems (1933)
1317 F St., N.W., Suite 301
Washington, DC 20004-1105
Tel: (202)393-6700   *Fax:* (202)783-6041
Web Site: http://www.naphs.org
Members: 400 behavioral systems of care
Staff: 6
Annual Budget: $1-2,000,000
Exec. Director: Mark J. Covall
Director of Communications: Carole Szpak
Dir., Legislative/Regulatory Affairs: Cidette Perrin
Dir., Clinical Svcs.: Kathleen McCann, RN

Historical Note
Formerly (1993) Nat'l Ass'n of Private Psychiatric Hospitals. An association of specialty psychiatric healthcare organizations for the treatment of mental illness, alcohol, and drug dependencies. Sponsors the Nat'l Ass'n of Psychiatric Health Systems Political Action Committee. Membership: $300/year (individual); organization dues are based on net revenues.

Publications:
Membership Directory. a. adv.

Meetings/Conferences:
Annual Meetings: January/850
1999 – Washington, DC/April 8-9

Nat'l Ass'n of Psychiatric Treatment Centers for Children (1983)

Historical Note
NAPTCC is a trade association representing psychiatric treatment centers for children. Members serve as multi-service agencies with residential, in-home, day and partial hospitalization treatment, foster care, and the wide variety of related services necessary to treat and attend to the needs of children, adolescents and young adults requiring a 24-hour therapeutically planned environment and mileu. Membership: $750/year (corresponding); $3,200-$3,950/year (organization/company).

Nat'l Ass'n of Public Child Welfare Administrators
810 1st St., N.E., Suite 500
Washington, DC 20002-4267
Tel: (202)682-0100   *Fax:* (202)289-6555
E-Mail: gtest@aphsa.org
Web Site: http://www.aphsa.org
Members: 280 individuals
Staff: 1
Annual Budget: $100-250,000
Project Manager: Gretchen Test

Historical Note
A constituent unit of the American Public Human Services Ass'n. Members are primarily state or local administrators responsible for public child welfare agencies that provide child protective services, foster care, adoption, and family preservation services. Membership: $75/year (individual);$1,000-$3,000-organization.

Publications:
NETWORK. q.

Meetings/Conferences:
Annual Meetings: Held 3 times/year, usually in Washington, DC

Nat'l Ass'n of Public Hospitals

Historical Note
Became (1996) Nat'l Ass'n of Public Hospitals and Health Systems.

Nat'l Ass'n of Public Hospitals and Health Systems (1980)

1212 New York Ave., N.W., Suite 800
Washington, DC   20005
Tel: (202)408-0223   Fax: (202)408-0235
Web Site: www.naph.org
Members: 110 hospitals and hospital systems
Staff: 12
Annual Budget: $1-2,000,000
Exec. Director: Christine C. Burch
Public Relations Coordinator: Kathleen Song
Office Manager: Pam Bradley

Historical Note
Formerly (1996) Nat'l Ass'n of Public Hospitals. Members provide primary care and public health services. Membership: $17,500/year (institution).

Publications:
Safety Net. q.

Meetings/Conferences:
1999 – Welches, OR/June 16-19

Nat'l Ass'n of Public Insurance Adjusters (1951)

112J Elden St.
Herndon, VA   20170-4809
Tel: (703)709-8254   Fax: (703)709-1036
E-Mail: napia@erols.com
Web Site: http://www.napia.com
Members: 95 companies
Staff: 4
Annual Budget: $50-100,000
Administrator: David W. Barrack

Historical Note
Dedicated to improving and maintaining the professional standards of the public insurance adjuster through a rigid code of professional conducts and ethics.

Publications:
NAPIA Bulletin. m.

Meetings/Conferences:
Semi-Annual Meetings: June and December
1999 – Vancouver, BC(Pan Pacific Hotel)/June 16-20

Nat'l Ass'n of Public Sector Equal Opportunity Officers

c/o Tallahassee Equal Opportunity Dept.
300 S. Adams St.
Tallahassee, FL   32301
Tel: (850)891-8290   Fax: (850)891-8733
Contact: Sharon Ofuani

Historical Note
NAPSEO members are equal opportunity professionals and other public sector professional with an interest in the field. Has no paid officers or full-time staff. Membership: $75/year (active/associate); $100/year (affiliate).

Meetings/Conferences:
Annual Meetings: August-September

Nat'l Ass'n of Publishers' Representatives (1952)

P.O. Box 3139, Grand Central Stn.
New York, NY   10163-3139
Tel: (212)685-3254   Fax: (212)644-0296
E-Mail: jwpgroup@aol.com
Members: 265 individuals
Staff: 2
Annual Budget: $25-50,000
Exec. Director: James W. Prendergast

Historical Note
Members are independent magazine advertising salespeople who have their own firms. Formerly (1982) the Ass'n of Publishers' Representatives. Membership: $125/year.

Publications:
NAPR Bulletin. 8/year. adv.

Meetings/Conferences:
Monthly Meetings: Chicago and New York City in various locations

Nat'l Ass'n of Punch Manufacturers (1963)

Historical Note
Became the North American Punch Manufacturers Ass'n in 1996.

Nat'l Ass'n of Pupil Services Administrators (1966)

Univ. of Mass.-Bocton
100 Morrissey Blvd
Boston, MA   02125-3393
Tel: (617)287-7258   Fax: (617)287-7249
E-Mail: napsa@umbsky.cc.umb.edu
Web Site: http://www.napsa.com
Members: 800 individuals
Staff: 1
Annual Budget: $100-250,000
Exec. Director: Robert E. Boyd, Ph.D.

Historical Note
Members are public and private school administrative personnel with district or statewide responsibility for the development and supervision of student support programs and personnel including attendance and student accounting, guidance, nursing, school psychology, school social work, exceptional or special education, pupil appraisal, at-risk programs, Discipline, gifted programs, and federal or state grants. Associate members are other professional administrators whose interests are compatible with the purposes of NAPSA. Formerly the Nat'l Ass'n of Pupil Personnel

Administrators, the group assumed its present name in 1989. Membership: $75/year; $55/year (associate); $37/year (student).

Publications:
NAPSA News. q.
NAPSA Notes. q.

Meetings/Conferences:
Annual Meetings: October
1999 – Clearwater Beach, FL(Sheraton Sand Key)/Oct. 23-27

Nat'l Ass'n of Purchasing Management (1915)

2055 East Centennial Circle
P.O. Box 22160
Tempe, AZ   85285-2160
Tel: (602)752-6276   Fax: (602)752-7890
Toll Free: (800)888 - 6276
Web Site: http://www.napm.org
Members: 43,000 individuals
Staff: 52
Annual Budget: $10-25,000,000
Exec. V. President and C.O.O.: Paul Novak, CPM
Sr. V. President: Holly LaCroix Johnson
Sr. V. President: Deborah Webber
V. President, Marketing: Nora Neibergall

Historical Note
Established as the Nat'l Ass'n of Purchasing Agents, it assumed its present name in 1968. Sponsors the Certified Purchasing Manager (CPM) and Accredited Purchasing Practioner (APP) programs of professional competency. Has an annual budget of approximately $15 million. Membership: $90/year, plus affiliate dues.

Publications:
Internat'l Journal of Purchasing and Materials Management. q.
NAPM Info Edge. m.
Purchasing Today. m.
Report on Business. m.

Meetings/Conferences:
Annual Meetings: May/3,000
1999 – San Diego, CA(Marriott)/May 23-26
2000 – New Orleans, LA(Hilton)/April 30-May 3
2001 – Orlando, FL(Marriott)/April 29-May 2

Nat'l Ass'n of Quick Printers

Historical Note
Became PrintImage Internat'l in 1998.

Nat'l Ass'n of Radio and Telecommunications Engineers (1982)

P.O. Box 678
Medway, MA   02053-0678
Tel: (508)533-8333   Fax: (508)533-3815
Toll Free: (800)896 - 2783
E-Mail: narte@110.net
Web Site: http://www.narte.org
Members: 8,000 individuals
Staff: 5
Annual Budget: $250-500,000
Exec. Director: John B. Holmberg

Historical Note
A non-profit certification agency, founded in 1982 by telecommunication industry leaders concerned over potential proliferation of pseudo qualified engineers and technicians that could result as a by-product of Federal deregulation. Expanded in 1988 to include the field of Electromagnetic Compatibility at the request of the NAVAIR of the US Navy. Certifies engineers and technicians in Electro Static Discharge Control. Certified as a Commercial Operators license Examination manager by the Federal Communications Commission in August, 1993. Also established the Association of Access Engineering Specialist. Membership: $20-65/year.

Publications:
NARTE Newsletter. q. adv.

Meetings/Conferences:

Nat'l Ass'n of Radio Reading Services (1978)

2100 Wharton St., Suite 140
Pittsburgh, PA   15203
Tel: (412)488-3944   Fax: (412)488-3953
Toll Free: (800)280 - 5325
Members: 140 reading services
Annual Budget: $10-25,000
President: David Noble

Historical Note
In the late 1970's, the 15 reading services on the air formed the Ass'n of Radio Reading Services; numbers grew rapidly afterwards, and today 157 transmittal sites exist in all states. Membership open to radio reading services for the blind and other print-handicapped persons. Assumed its current name in 1993. Has no paid officers or full-time staff. Membership: $200/year.

Publications:
Directory of Radio Reading Services. a.
Hearrsay. q.

Meetings/Conferences:
Annual Meetings: Spring
1999 – Rochester, NY

Nat'l Ass'n of Rail Shippers (1937)

2115 Portsmouth Drive
Richardson, TX   75082
Tel: (214)344-0254   Fax: (972)644-8208
Members: 1,500 individuals, 6 regional associations
Staff: 1
Annual Budget: $50-100,000
Exec. Director: E. Leo Mountjoy

Historical Note
Members are industrial traffic executives using rail transportation. An umbrella association for six regional associations. NARS has no dues. Administrative support provided by Ass'n of American Railroads. Formerly (1984) the Nat'l Ass'n of Shippers Advisory

Boards and the Nat'l Ass'n of Rail Shippers Advisory Board (1985).

Meetings/Conferences:
Transportation Seminar: May

Nat'l Ass'n of Railroad Property Tax Representatives (1963)

P.O. Box 70
Boise, ID   83707
Tel: (208)388-2328
Members: 40 individuals
Annual Budget: under $10,000
Contact: Katrina Basye

Historical Note
Formerly the Western Ass'n of Railway Tax Commissioners, the Nat'l Ass'n of Railway Tax Commissioners and (1987) the Nat'l Ass'n of Railroad Tax Representatives. Has no paid staff or permanent address; officers change annually. Membership: $20/yr.

Publications:
None.

Meetings/Conferences:
Annual Meetings: Fall

Nat'l Ass'n of Railroad Trial Counsel (1954)

881 Alma Real Drive, Suite 218
Pacific Palisades, CA   90272-3733
Tel: (310)459-7659   Fax: (310)459-6603
Members: 1,100 individuals
Staff: 4
Annual Budget: $250-500,000
Exec. Director: Henry M. Moffat
Assistant Executive Director: Mary Goff

Historical Note
Membership: $240/year.

Publications:
NARTC Newsletter. irreg.

Meetings/Conferences:
Meetings: Winter/350, Spring/200, and Summer/400

Nat'l Ass'n of Railway Business Women (1941)

6327 Wesleyan Rd.
Jacksonville, FL   32217
Tel: (904)733-6836
Toll Free: (800)676 - 2729
E-Mail: ruthspears@csx.com
Web Site: http://www.narbw.org
Members: 1,700 individuals
Staff: 1
Annual Budget: $25-50,000
President: Ruth Spears

Historical Note
Established as the Railway Business Women's Ass'n, it assumed its present name in 1954. Founded originally to foster friendship between women employees of various railroads nationwide, to support the railroad industry, and to build and maintain a retirement residence for women. NARBW now also awards scholarship grants and supports a benevolent fund. Has no paid officers or full-time staff; the presidency changes every two years. Membership fee set by each local chapter for its members.

Publications:
Capsule. m.

Meetings/Conferences:
Annual Meetings: Spring/200
1999 – Saratoga Springs, NY

Nat'l Ass'n of Real Estate Appraisers (1966)

1224 N. Nokomis, N.E.
Alexandria, MN   56308
Tel: (320)763-7626   Fax: (320)763-9290
Members: 23,500 individuals
Staff: 23
Annual Budget: $2-5,000,000
Managing Director: Joan Powell

Historical Note
Established in New York, members primarily specialize in residential appraisals. New members must have two years of experience in the field, submit two appraisal reports and pass an appraisal certification examination. Awards the Certified Real Estate Appraiser (CREA) and Certified Commercial Real Estate Appraiser (CCRA) designations. Mandatory continuing education/recertification of 60 hours every 5 years required. Membership: $195/year.

Publications:
Annual Membership Directory. a.
Appraisal Guidelines. m.
Appraisal Report. 3/year. adv.
Real Estate Appraisal Newsletter. bi-m. adv.

Meetings/Conferences:
Semi-annual Meetings: March-April in Atlantic City, NJ and Sept.-Oct. in Las Vegas, NV

Nat'l Ass'n of Real Estate Brokers (1947)

1629 K St., N.W., Suite 602
Washington, DC   20006
Tel: (202)785-4477   Fax: (202)785-1244
Members: 13,000 individuals
Staff: 1
Annual Budget: $250-500,000
President: H. Bernie Jackson
Office Manager: Stephanie Haley

Historical Note
Membership consists principally of minority real estate brokers. Certifies qualified members to use the title, "Realtists." The Nat'l Soc. of Real Estate Appraisers, Real Estate Management Brokers Institute and United Developers Council are affiliates of NAREB. Membership: $100 initial fee and then $200/year (member-broker).

Publications:
Communicator. q. adv.
The Realtist Today Newsletter. q.
Meetings/Conferences:
Annual Meetings: August/800-900

Nat'l Ass'n of Real Estate Buyer Brokers (1982)
1660 S. Amphlett Blvd., Suite 118
San Mateo, CA 94402-2507
Tel: (650)655-2500   Fax: (650)655-2294
E-Mail: stoklosa@earthlink.net
Members: 2,600 individuals
Staff: 5
Annual Budget: $50-100,000
President: Raymond J. Stoklosa
Historical Note
Dedicated to foster professionalism among real estate brokers and
to protect consumers of real estate services through education,
communication and improved understanding of agency
relationships and responsibilities. NAREBB members represent the
buyers only in real estate transactions. Membership: $90/year
(individual); $200/year (organization/company).
Publications:
Newsletter. q.
Meetings/Conferences:
Annual Meetings: September-October

Nat'l Ass'n of Real Estate Companies (1977)
P.O. Box 958
Columbia, MD 21044-0958
Tel: (410)992-6476   Fax: (410)992-6363
E-Mail: cisenhour@therousecompany.com
Web Site: http://www.narec.inter.net
Members: 205 individuals
Staff: 1
President: Lawrence A. Gerlach
Exec. Assistant: Cynthia S. Isenhour
Historical Note
NAREC members are individuals concerned with the financial
management and accounting practices of real estate companies.
Membership: $175/year (individual); $500/year (company).
Publications:
NAREC Newsletter. q.
Meetings/Conferences:

Nat'l Ass'n of Real Estate Editors (1929)
1003 N.W. 6th Terrace
Boca Raton, FL 33486-3455
Tel: (561)391-3599   Fax: (561)391-0099
E-Mail: madkimba@aol.com
Web Site: http://www.naree.org
Members: 650 individuals
Staff: 1
Annual Budget: $100-250,000
Exec. Director: Mary Doyle-Kimball
Historical Note
Founded as Nat'l Conference of Real Estate Editors; assumed its
current name in 1936.Serves the interest of real estate journalist,
including writers and editors, from all forms of media. Membership:
$75/year (active); $110/year (associate).
Publications:
Directory. a. adv.
NAREE Network. a.
NAREE News. bi-m. adv.
NAREE Sourcebook for Real Estate and Housing Journalists.
    bien. adv.
Meetings/Conferences:
1999 – Chicago, IL(Hotel International)/June 3-6
2000 – Seattle, WA

Nat'l Ass'n of Real Estate Investment Managers (1990)
11755 Wilshire Blvd., Suite 1380
Los Angeles, CA 90025-1506
Tel: (310)479-2219   Fax: (310)445-2565
Web Site: naveim.org
Members: 65 corporate members
Staff: 2
Annual Budget: $250-500,000
President: Fredric Halperin
Historical Note
Membership: $7,000/year (organization/company).
Meetings/Conferences:
1999 – Palm Beach, FL(Ritz Carlton)

Nat'l Ass'n of Real Estate Investment Trusts (1960)
1875 Eye St. N.W., Suite 600
Washington, DC 20006
Tel: (202)739-9400   Fax: (202)739-9401
Web Site: http://www.nareit.com
Members: 1,850 REITS & affiliated organizations
Staff: 27
Annual Budget: $2-5,000,000
President and C.E.O.: Steven A. Wechsler
V. President, Communications: Victoria J. Baker
V.P., Govt. Relations: Martin Depoy
Director, Meetings and Conventions: Janet E. Rowson
Meetings Manager: Catherine Kaempffer
V. President/General Counsel: Tony M. Edwards
Director, Membership Services and Marketing: Suzanne Karpick
Director, Publications: Karen White
Historical Note
Formerly Nat'l Ass'n of Real Estate Investment Funds, it assumed
its present name in 1972. Membership is open to qualified REITs
and other organizations and individuals in related fields such as
law, accounting, financial advising, mortgage and investment
banking, teaching and real estate services. NAREIT's primary
purpose is to represent the REIT industry before Congress and the
Executive branch; it also provides education and information for the
industry and the financial media and holds three major conferences

each year. Membership: $695/year (associate), REIT fee
determined by assets; $100/year (academic and other institutions).
Publications:
Compendium. bien.
Executive Compensation. a.
Insurance Issues. q.
REIT Handbook Directory. a.
REIT Watch. m.
The REIT Report. q.
Meetings/Conferences:
Three Meetings Annually: CEO Conference/Spring, Law and
        Accounting Conference/May and Annual
        Conference/October
1999 – Los Angeles, CA(Century Plaza Hotel)/Oct. 27-29

Nat'l Ass'n of REALTORS (1908)
225 Hillcrest Dr.
Suite 100
Thousand Oaks, CA 91360
Tel: (805)557-2300   Fax: (818)557-2680
Web Site: http://www.realtor.com
Members: 735,000 individuals
Staff: 450
Annual Budget: $50-100,000,000
Exec. V. President: Terrence M. McDermott
C.F.O./V. President, Controller: Dale Alexander Stinton, CAE
Director, Professional Standards: Lorraine Connors Cates
Legal Counsel: Laurene K. Janik
Historical Note
Founded in Chicago as the Nat'l Ass'n of Real Estate Exchanges by
120 representatives from 19 local boards and one state association.
Became the Nat'l Ass'n of Real Estate Boards in 1916 and assumed
its present name in 1974. Today it is a federation of about 1,800
local boards and 50 state associations. Supports the Nat'l Realtors
Political Action Committee and a number of state political action
groups. Has a budget of approximately $54.1 million.
Publications:
Today's Realtor. m.
Meetings/Conferences:
Annual Meetings: Mid-November

Nat'l Ass'n of Recording Merchandisers (1958)
9 Eves Drive, Suite 120
Marlton, NJ 08053-3138
Tel: (609)596-2221   Fax: (609)596-3268
E-Mail: wooton@narm.com
Web Site: http://www.narm.com
Members: 1,220 companies
Staff: 17
Annual Budget: $1-2,000,000
President: Pamela Horovitz
V. President, Communications: Jim Donio
Director, Meetings and Conventions: Linda Still
V.P., Admin./Operations: Yale Hoffstein
Director, Membership: Holly Rosum
Historical Note
General members include all categories of phonograph record, CD,
and video tape merchandisers: retailers, rack-jobbers, one-stops,
independent distributors and wholesalers; associates are
manufacturers and suppliers to the industry. Membership fee based
on annual sales volume.
Publications:
NARM Sounding Board. m.
Meetings/Conferences:
Annual Meetings: Late Winter
1999 – Las Vegas, NV(Hilton)/March 8-11

Nat'l Ass'n of Recreation Resource Planners (1981)
Texas Parks and Wildlife Dept.
4200 Smith School Road
Austin, TX 78744
Tel: (512)912-7109
Members: 150 individuals
Annual Budget: $25-50,000
Treasurer: Timothy Bradle
Historical Note
Formerly known as the Nat'l Ass'n of State Recreation Planners
(1994). Established to promote the professionalization of outdoor
recreation resource planning at the state and regional level. Has no
permanent staff or address; officers change annually in the spring.
Membership: $50/year (individual); $145/year
(institutional/affiliate); $25/year (student).
Publications:
Membership Directory. irreg.
NASRP Newsletter. q.
Meetings/Conferences:
Annual Meetings: Spring/100-125

Nat'l Ass'n of Regional Councils (1967)
1700 K St., N.W., Suite 1300
Washington, DC 20006-3817
Tel: (202)457-0710   Fax: (202)296-9352
E-Mail: narc@clark.net
Web Site: http://www.narc.org
Members: 275 councils
Staff: 14
Annual Budget: $1-2,000,000
Exec. Director: William R. Dodge
Director of Operations: Patsy Chappelear
Director, Communications: Beverly Mykwest
General Counsel: John Bosley
Historical Note
Established in 1967 by the Nat'l League of Cities and the Nat'l
Ass'n of Counties. Incorporated as a membership organization in
1968. Members are regional councils of local governments and
governmental agencies. Annual dues vary, based on council
salaries.
Publications:
Directory of Regional Councils. a. adv.

Metropolitan Planning Organizations Directory.
Regional Reporter. m.
Special Report. irreg.
Meetings/Conferences:
Annual Meetings: Spring
1999 – Monterey, CA(Doubletree)/June 12-15

Nat'l Ass'n of Regional Media Centers (1979)
1382 4th Ave., NE.
Sioux Center, IA 51250
Tel: (712)722-4378
Members: 260 individuals
Annual Budget: $25-50,000
President: Don Whitmarsh
Historical Note
NARMC members are regional, K-12 and higher education media
centers which serve K-12, as well as commercial media and
technology vendors. Has no paid officers or full-time staff.
Membership: $55/year (individual); $250/year (institutional).
Publications:
Directory. a.
NARMC Press. m.
NARMC'etin q.
Meetings/Conferences:
Semi-annual Meetings: with AECT/February

Nat'l Ass'n of Registered Lobbyists (1994)
Historical Note
Defunct in 1996.

Nat'l Ass'n of Regulatory Utility Commissioners (1889)
P.O. Box 684
1100 Pennsylvania Ave. NW., Suite 603
Washington, DC 20044-0684
Tel: (202)898-2200   Fax: (202)898-2213
Members: 360 individuals
Staff: 15
Annual Budget: $1-2,000,000
Exec. Director: Margaret A. Welsh
Director, Congressional and Public Relations: Chris Mele
General Counsel: Charles D. Gray
Historical Note
State and Federal regulatory commissioners. Formerly (1918) Nat'l
Ass'n of Railway Commissioners; (1923) Nat'l Ass'n of Railroad
and Utilities Commissioners and (1967) Nat'l Ass'n of Regulatory
Utility Commissioners.
Publications:
Annual Report on Utility and Carrier Regulations a.
Blue Bulletin. w.
Proceedings. a.
Meetings/Conferences:
Annual Meetings: Fall/2,000
1999 – San Antonio, TX(Marriott Rivercenter)/Nov. 7-10
2000 – San Diego, CA(Marriott Hotel & Marina)/Nov. 12-15
2001 – Philadelphia, PA(Marriott)/Nov. 11-14
2002 – New York, NY(Marriott Marquis)/Nov. 16-19

Nat'l Ass'n of Rehabilitation Agencies (1978)
11250-8 Roger Bacon Drive, Suite 8
Reston, VA 20190
Tel: (703)437-4377   Fax: (703)435-4390
E-Mail: rick@naranet.org
Web Site: http://www.naranet.org/nara/
Members: 280 agencies
Staff: 2
Annual Budget: $100-250,000
Exec. Director: Richard A. Guggolz
Historical Note
Members are government-certified rehabilitation agencies, non-
certified rehabilitation agencies, multidisciplinary rehabilitation
companies, and rehabilitation vendors. Membership: $750/year
(providers); $450/year (vendors).
Publications:
NARA News. adv. adv.
Meetings/Conferences:
Semi-annual Meetings: Spring and Fall
1999 – Washington, DC(Marriott)/May 13-15
1999 – San Antonio, TX(Adam's Mark)

Nat'l Ass'n of Rehabilitation Facilities (1969)
Historical Note
Became the American Rehabilitation Ass'n in 1994.

Nat'l Ass'n of Rehabilitation Instructors
1305 37th St. East
Tuscaloosa, AL 35405
Tel: (205)554-1300   Fax: (205)554-1369
Toll Free: (800)671 - 6837
Members: 325 individuals
President: Julie Brock
Secretary-Treasurer: Jane Shirley
Historical Note
A professional division of the Nat'l Rehabilitation Ass'n; NRA may
also be contacted for information on NARI. Members include
special education teachers; other special instructors, such as
mobility and orientation instructors; occupational therapists;
physical therapists; speech, hearing and visual therapists; and
home health nurses. NARI provides opportunites for the
professional growth and development of rehabilitation instructors.
Membership: $7/year, plus NRA membership (individual).
Publications:
Bulletin.
Meetings/Conferences:
1999 – Minnesota, MN

Nat'l Ass'n of Rehabilitation Professionals in the Private Sector (1977)
1661 Worcester Road, Suite 203

Framingham, MA   01701
Tel: (508)820-8889   *Fax:* (508)820-4337
E-Mail: narpps@ix.netcom.com
Web Site: www.narpps.org
Members: 3,200 individuals
Staff: 4
Annual Budget: $500-1,000,000
Exec. Director: Robert Teplansky
Program Director: Judy Benjamin

Historical Note
Incorporated in Pennsylvania. Members are individuals in private sector companies or non-profit organizations that provide rehabilitation services. Membership: $155/year (individual).

Publications:
NARPPS National Directory. a. adv.
Rehabilitation Professional. bi-m. adv.

Meetings/Conferences:
1999 – Boston, MA(Westin Copley Place)/March 12-15

Nat'l Ass'n of Rehabilitation Secretaries *(1971)*
P.O. Box 3781
Little Rock, AR   72203
Tel: (501)296-1611   *Fax:* (501)296-1655
Members: 1,200 individuals
Staff: 1
Annual Budget: under $10,000
President: Mary Linn

Historical Note
A professional division of the Nat'l Rehabilitation Ass'n; NRA may also be contacted for information on NARS. Members are secretaries, stenographers, clerical assistants and other office support staff who work in the field of rehabilitation, either in the public or private sectors. Officers change annually. Membership: $10/year, plus NRA dues (individual).

Publications:
NARS Newsletter. q.

Meetings/Conferences:
Annual Meetings: Fall, with Nat'l Rehabilitation Ass'n

Nat'l Ass'n of Reimbursement Officers *(1954)*
Historical Note
Address unknown in 1996.

Nat'l Ass'n of Reinforcing Steel Contractors *(1969)*
10382 Main St., Box 280, Suite 200
Fairfax, VA   22030
Tel: (703)591-1870   *Fax:* (703)591-1895
Members: 425 companies
Staff: 3
Annual Budget: $100-250,000
Exec. Director: Fred H. Codding

Historical Note
NARSC members are involved with the placing and installation of reinforcing steel end post-tensioning in commercial, bridge, highway, industrial and public projects.

Publications:
Membership Roster. irreg.
Newsletter. m.

Meetings/Conferences:
Annual Meetings: Winter
1999 – Aruba(Wyndham)/Jan. 28-Feb. 5

Nat'l Ass'n of Relay Manufacturers *(1947)*
9459 N. Broadmoor Rd.
Milwaukee, WI   53217-1310
Tel: (414)351-4548   *Fax:* (414)351-4897
E-Mail: narm@execpc.com
Web Site: http://www.industry.net/c/orgindex/narm
Members: 45 manufacturers
Staff: 2
Annual Budget: $100-250,000
Exec. Director: Donald E. Dangott

Historical Note
NARM is a trade association for the electro-mechanical and solid state relays and associated switching devices industry. NARM holds National Relay Conference annually in April in conjunction with Electronic Industries Ass'n in Washington, D.C. Membership: $2,000/year.

Publications:
Engineers' Relay Hand Book, Fifth Edition.
Proceedings. a.

Meetings/Conferences:
Annual Meetings: Semi-Annual.

Nat'l Ass'n of Resale and Thrift Shops *(1984)*
P.O. Box 80707
St. Clair Shores, MI   48080-5707
Tel: (810)294-6700   *Fax:* (810)294-6776
Toll Free: (800)544 - 0751
E-Mail: webmaster@narts.org
Web Site: http://www.narts.org
Members: 2,065 individuals
Staff: 3
Annual Budget: $250-500,000
Ass'n Manager and Meeting Planner: Adele R. Meyer
Membership Services Coordinator: Gail A. Siegel

Historical Note
Members are owners, managers, professionals and other individuals who represent both profit and non-profit resale and thrift shops. Membership: $120/year.

Publications:
Membership Directory.
Your NARTS Network. m. adv.

Meetings/Conferences:
Annual Meetings: June/250-300

Nat'l Ass'n of Resident Management Corporations *(1988)*

4524 Douglas St., N.E.
Washington, DC   20019-2003
Tel: (202)397-7002   *Fax:* (202)399-1625
Toll Free: (800)572 - 6673
Members: 248 individuals
Staff: 5
Annual Budget: $250-500,000
Program Coordinator: Debra Crawford

Historical Note
Membership: $25/year (individual); corporate fee varies, maximum $1,500/year.

Publications:
Newsletter. q. adv.

Meetings/Conferences:
Annual Meetings: Summer

Nat'l Ass'n of Residential Care Facilities *(1984)*
Historical Note
Merged with ALFA in 1998.

Nat'l Ass'n of Residential Property Managers *(1988)*
35 E. Wacker Dr., Suite 500
Chicago, IL   60601-2102
Tel: (312)782-5252   *Fax:* (312)236-1140
Toll Free: (800)782 - 3452
E-Mail: narpminfor@narpm.org
Web Site: http://www.narpm.org
Members: 1,400 individuals
Conv./Trade Show Manager: Allison Walvoord

Historical Note
Founded to promote professionalism through education and publications for the single-family residential property manager. NARPM awards three professional designations to licensed real estate professionals. Membership $150/year.

Publications:
Membership Director. a. adv.
Residential Resource. m. adv.

Meetings/Conferences:

Nat'l Ass'n of Retail Collection Attorneys *(1993)*
1515 N. Warson Road, Suite 141
St. Louis, MO   63132
Tel: (314)428-6190   *Fax:* (314)428-0810
Toll Free: (800)633 - 6069
E-Mail: narca@primary.net
Members: 700 law firms
Staff: 3
Annual Budget: $100-250,000
Exec. Director: Marti Revor

Historical Note
NARCA members are law firms which engage in the collection of consumer accounts. Membership: $325/year (firms in large cities); $250/year (firms in small cities).

Publications:
Membership Directory. a. adv.
NARCA Newsletter. q. adv.

Meetings/Conferences:
1999 – Washington, DC(Loews L'Enfant)/Oct. 22-25/300
1999 – Orlando, FL(Buena Vista Palace)/Nov. 4-7/300

Nat'l Ass'n of Retail Dealers of America *(1943)*
Historical Note
Became North American Retail Dealers Ass'n in 1994.

Nat'l Ass'n of Retired Federal Employees *(1921)*
606 N. Washington St.
Alexandria, VA   22314
Tel: (703)838-7760   *Fax:* (703)838-7785
Members: 450,000 individuals
Staff: 70
Annual Budget: $5-10,000,000
National President: Frank G. Atwater
Manager, Marketing and Meetings: Juliet Harding
Director, Legislation: Judy Park
Director, Office Operations: Wilbur Speer
Manager, Membership: Samuel H. Rosenberg
Member Relations: Lee Jones

Historical Note
Formerly (1971) Nat'l Ass'n of Retired Civil Employees. Sponsors and supports the National Ass'n of Retired Federal Employees Political Action Committee. Has an annual budget of over $7 million. Membership: $20/year, plus chapter dues.

Publications:
Retirement Life. m. adv.

Meetings/Conferences:
Biennial Meetings: Even years/2,800

Nat'l Ass'n of Retired Senior Volunteer Program Directors *(1976)*
739 Thimble Shoals BLVD., Suite 400
Newport News, VA   23606
Tel: (757)873-9328   *Fax:* (757)873-9329
E-Mail: foxnraven@Livenet.net
Members: 600 individuals
Annual Budget: $100-250,000
President: Nan York

Historical Note
NARSVPD members are directors of programs sponsored by the Retired Senior Volunteer Program (RSVP). Membership: $35 (assoc. member); $75 (professional); $100 (organization).

Publications:
Newsletter. semi-a. adv.

Meetings/Conferences:
Semi-annual Meetings: Spring and Fall

Nat'l Ass'n of Reunion Managers *(1986)*
P.O. Box 23211

Tampa, FL   33623
Toll Free: (800)654 - 2776
Members: 60 companies
Annual Budget: $10-25,000
President: Katy Anderson

Historical Note
Formerly (1994) Nat'l Ass'n of Reunion Planners. NARM members are individually owned, locally operated companies providing comprehensive reunion planning services for high schools, sororities, fraternities, military units and families. Has no paid officers or full-time staff. Membership: $250/year (initial); $200/year (renewal).

Publications:
Reunion Reporter. q. adv.

Meetings/Conferences:
Annual Meetings: Winter/60
1999 – New Orleans, LA(Westin)/Jan. 14-16
2000 – Las Vegas, NV

Nat'l Ass'n of Reunion Planners
Historical Note
Became Nat'l Ass'n of Reunion Managers in 1994.

Nat'l Ass'n of Review Appraisers and Mortgage Underwriters *(1975)*
1224 No. Nokomis N.E.
Alexandria, MN   56308
Tel: (320)763-6870   *Fax:* (320)763-9290
Members: 8,000 individuals
Staff: 12
Annual Budget: $1-2,000,000
Exec. Director: Robert G. Johnson
Director, Education and Publications: James Field

Historical Note
Members, mainly from financial institutions, are responsible for overseeing, reviewing or supervising the work of appraisers. Awards the CRA (Certified Review Appraisal) designation. Membership: $195/year.

Publications:
Appraisal Review and Mortgage Underwriting Journal. q. adv.
NARA Newsletter. 6/yr. adv.

Meetings/Conferences:
Annual Meetings: Fall/350

Nat'l Ass'n of Royalty Owners *(1980)*
119 N. Broadway
Ada, OK   74820
Tel: (580)436-0034   *Fax:* (580)436-1535
E-Mail: naro@chickasaw.com
Web Site: http://www.naro-us.org
Members: 5,000 individuals
Staff: 3
Annual Budget: $100-250,000
President: James L. Stafford
Director of Member Services: Sandra R. Stafford

Historical Note
Organized in Oklahoma City in June 1980 after the passage of the Windfall Profits Tax, members are mineral, surface and royalty (producing sub-surface interests) owners concerned with the tax aspects of federal and state legislation, and with the effective management of their mineral properties. Incorporated in the State of Oklahoma. Membership: $65/year (individual); $200/year (corporate).

Publications:
Royalty Owners Action Report (ROAR). m.

Meetings/Conferences:
1999 – Austin, TX(Hyatt)/Nov. 3-7/700

Nat'l Ass'n of RV Parks and Campgrounds *(1966)*
8605 Westwood Center Drive, Suite 201
Vienna, VA   22182-2231
Tel: (703)734-3000   *Fax:* (703)734-3004
E-Mail: arvc@erols.com
Web Site: http://www.gocampingamerica.com
Members: 3,100 businesses
Staff: 5
Annual Budget: $500-1,000,000
President and C.E.O.: David Gorin
Mgr., Mktg./Communications: Rick Carbo
V. President: Jane L. Nordstrom
Dir., Member Services: Denise Morgan

Historical Note
Formerly (1992) the Nat'l Campground Owners Ass'n, ARVC is only trade association exclusively representing the U.S. commercial RV park and campground industry. Members are campground owners and operators, manufactures and suppliers of campground products and services. The RV Park & Campground Industry Education Foundation is the non-profit educational arm of ARVC. The Nat'l Campground Institute is the promotional arm of the ass'n.

Publications:
ARVC Direct Line. m. adv.
Outdoor Hospitality. q.
RV Park & Campground Report. m. adv.

Meetings/Conferences:
Annual Meetings: late Fall

Nat'l Ass'n of Sailing Instructors and Sailing Schools *(1980)*
15 Renier Court
Middletown, NJ   07748-1612
Tel: (732)671-6190
E-Mail: nasiss@aol.com
Members: 50 schools and individuals
Staff: 1
Annual Budget: under $10,000
Exec. Director: Richard A. Herbst

Historical Note
Primary functions are to accredit sailing schools, certify and provide advice and counsel in the administrative operation of schools and their ancillary business activities. NASISS also provides commercial insurance for school and charter operators. Membership: $15-250/year.

Publications:
Directory of American Sailing Schools. q.
NASISS Newsletter. q.

Meetings/Conferences:
Annual Meetings: Not held.

Nat'l Ass'n of School Music Dealers *(1962)*
4020 McEwen, Suite 105
Dallas, TX   75244-5019
Tel: (972)233-9107   *Fax:* (972)490-4219
Web Site: www.nasmd.com
Members: 300 dealers & manufacturers
Staff: 1
Annual Budget: $25-50,000
Executive Secretary: Madeleine Crouch

Historical Note
Formed by a charter group of music dealers during the 1962 Trade Show in Chicago. Has no paid staff. Membership: $200/yr.

Publications:
NASMD Newsletter. q.

Meetings/Conferences:
Annual Meetings: Winter
1999 – Dana Point, CA

Nat'l Ass'n of School Nurses *(1968)*
P.O. Box 1300
Scarborough, ME   04074-1300
Tel: (207)883-2117   *Fax:* (207)883-2683
E-Mail: NASN@aol.com
Members: 10,000 individuals
Staff: 6
Annual Budget: $1-2,000,000
Exec. Director: Judith Robinson
Administrator: Gloria Durgin

Historical Note
Originally established as a department of the National Education Ass'n, NASN set up its own office in 1978 and is now an affiliate of NEA. Membership: $70/year (individual), $110/year (organization).

Publications:
Journal of School Nursing.
NASN Newsletter. q.

Meetings/Conferences:
Annual Meetings: Last week of June
1999 – Providence, RI/June 26-29
2000 – Milwaukee, WI

Nat'l Ass'n of School Psychologists *(1969)*
4340 East West Hwy., Suite 402
Bethesda, MD   20814
Tel: (301)657-0270   *Fax:* (301)657-0275
E-Mail: NASP8455@aol.com
Web Site: www.naspweb.org
Members: 21,000 individuals
Staff: 20
Annual Budget: $2-5,000,000
Exec. Director: Susan Gorin, CAE
Director, Professional Information & Communication: Victoria
    Stanhope
Dir., Public Policy: Libby Kuffner
Director, Meetings & Conventions: Jacqueline Williams
Director, Certification: Anne Rood
Director, Financial Operations: Holly Sullivan
Dep. Exec. Director: Marilyn Brazier
Director, Membership & MIS: Alexander Hyman
Asst. Exec. Director, Professional Relations: Larry Sullivan
Dir., Publications: Gina Grieb
Director, Leadership Activities: Rosemary O'Donnell

Historical Note
Promotes educationally and psychologically healthy environments for all children and youth by implementing research-based, effective programs that prevent problems, enhance independence, and promote optimal learning. Membership: $110/year.

Publications:
Communique. 8/year. adv.
Convention Program and Abstracts. a. adv.
School Psychology Review. q. adv.

Meetings/Conferences:
Annual Meetings: Spring
1999 – Las Vegas, NV(Bally's Hotel & Resort)/April 6-10
2000 – New Orleans, LA(Sheraton)/March 28-April 1
2001 – Washington, DC(Marriott Wardman Park)/April 17-21
2002 – Chicago, IL(Hyatt Regency Chicago)/March 5-9
2003 – Toronto, On, Canada(Sheraton Centre
    Toronto)/April 8-12

Nat'l Ass'n of School Resource Officers *(1989)*
2714 S.W. 5th St.
Boynton Beach, FL   33435
Tel: (561)736-1736   *Fax:* (561)736-1736
Toll Free: (888)316 - 2776
E-Mail: RESOURCER@AOL.COM
Members: 5,000 individuals
Staff: 3
Annual Budget: $50-100,000
Executive Director: Curtis Lavarello
News Editor: Kathy Shirling
Staff Attorney: Paul Marino, Esq.

Historical Note
NASRO members are school police, security officers, administrators and others law enforcement professionals with an interest in the police-student relations. Membership fee: $20

Publications:
Resourcer. q.

Meetings/Conferences:
Annual Meetings: July or August
1999 – Palm Beach, FL(PGA National Resort)/July 11-17/500

Nat'l Ass'n of School Safety and Law Enforcement Officers *(1970)*
P.O. Box 118
Catlett, VA   20119-0118
Tel: (540)788-4966   *Fax:* (540)788-4966
E-Mail: Regriff@erols.com
Web Site: http://www.nassleo.org
Members: 350 individuals
Annual Budget: $25-50,000
Exec. Secretary: Ralph E. Griffith

Historical Note
Founded (1970) as the Nat'l Ass'n of School Security Directors. Persons engaged in school security and school policy operations. Committed to reduce personal risk and tax dollar losses from vandalism, burglary, theft, assault, and other disturbances. Membership: $50/year (individual); $50/year (organization).

Publications:
Membership Directory. a.
Quarterly. 3-4/yr. adv.

Meetings/Conferences:
Annual Meetings: July
1999 – Atlanta, GA
2000 – Las Vegas, NV

Nat'l Ass'n of Schools and Colleges of the United Methodist Church *(1940)*
P.O. Box 871
Nashville, TN   37202
Tel: (615)340-7399   *Fax:* (615)340-7379
Members: 123 schools and colleges
Staff: 2
Annual Budget: $50-100,000
Secretary-Treasurer: Ken Yamada, Ph.D.

Historical Note
Membership: $550/year(universities), $450/year (2 & 4 year colleges); $150/year (secondary schools).

Publications:
Directory of Chief Executives Officers. a.
United Methodist-Related Schools Colleges.
Universities and Theological Schools.

Meetings/Conferences:
Semi-annual Meetings: Winter and Summer
1999 – Washington, DC(Hyatt Regency)/Feb. 2-3/80
1999 – Sante Fe, NM(Hilton)/July 25-29/100
2000 – Washington, DC(Hyatt Regency)/Feb. 1-2/80
2000 – Hilton Head, SC(Hilton)/July 23-27/100

Nat'l Ass'n of Schools of Art and Design *(1944)*
11250 Roger Bacon Drive, Suite 21
Reston, VA   20190-5202
Tel: (703)437-0700   *Fax:* (703)437-6312
E-Mail: info@arts-accredit.org
Web Site: http://www.arts-accredit.org
Members: 200 schools
Staff: 9
Annual Budget: $250-500,000
Exec. Director: Samuel Hope

Historical Note
Established as the Nat'l Conference of Schools of Design, it became the Nat'l Ass'n of Schools of Design in 1948, the Nat'l Ass'n of Schools of Art in 1961, and assumed its present name in 1981. Membership: $40/year (individual).

Publications:
Directory. a.
Handbook. bien.

Meetings/Conferences:
Annual Meetings: October/250
1999 – Los Angeles, CA(Hotel Inter-
    Continental)/Oct. 14-17/250

Nat'l Ass'n of Schools of Dance *(1980)*
11250 Roger Bacon Drive, Suite 21
Reston, VA   20190-5202
Tel: (703)437-0700   *Fax:* (703)437-6312
E-Mail: info@arts-accredit.org
Web Site: http://www.arts-accredit.org
Members: 49 schools
Staff: 9
Annual Budget: $50-100,000
Exec. Director: Samuel Hope

Historical Note
An outgrowth of the Joint Commission on Dance and Theatre Accreditation. NASD is the recognized accrediting agency for education programs in dance. Membership: $75/year (individual).

Publications:
Directory. a.
Handbook. bien.

Meetings/Conferences:
Annual Meetings: September
1999 – Palm Beach, FL(Ritz-Carlton)/Sept. 16-19/100

Nat'l Ass'n of Schools of Music *(1924)*
11250 Roger Bacon Drive, Suite 21
Reston, VA   20190-5202
Tel: (703)437-0700   *Fax:* (703)437-6312
E-Mail: info@arts-accredit.org
Web Site: http://www.arts-accredit.org
Members: 570 schools
Staff: 9
Annual Budget: $1-2,000,000
Exec. Director: Samuel Hope

Historical Note
The accrediting agency for educational programs in music in the U.S. Membership: $45/year (individual).

Publications:
Directory. a.
Handbook. bien.
Proceedings of the Annual Meeting. a.

Meetings/Conferences:
Annual Meetings: November
1999 – Chicago, IL(Fairmont Hotel)/Nov. 20-23/600
2000 – San Diego, IL(Hyatt Regency)/Nov. 18-21/600

Nat'l Ass'n of Schools of Public Affairs and Administration *(1970)*
1120 G St., N.W., Suite 730
Washington, DC   20005
Tel: (202)628-8965   *Fax:* (202)626-4978
E-Mail: NASPAA@NASPAA.org
Web Site: http://www.naspaa.org
Members: 239 institutions
Staff: 4
Annual Budget: $500-1,000,000
Exec. Director: Michael A. Brintnall
Coordinator, Meetings & Asst. Exec. Director: Alma Beals

Historical Note
Concerned with public service education and research in public policy and administration Membership: $590-$2,380/year (institution, based on total enrollment).

Publications:
Journal of Public Affairs Education.
The Guide To Graduate Education in Public Affairs.

Meetings/Conferences:
Annual Meetings: Fall
1999 – Miami, FL/Oct. 13-16

Nat'l Ass'n of Schools of Theatre *(1969)*
11250 Roger Bacon Drive, Suite 21
Reston, VA   20190-5202
Tel: (703)437-0700   *Fax:* (703)437-6312
Web Site: www.arts-accredit.org
Members: 110 schools
Staff: 9
Annual Budget: $100-250,000
Exec. Director: Samuel Hope

Historical Note
The outgrowth of a study committee set up by the American Theatre Ass'n, NAST was established as a division of ATA but is now autonomous. Its primary purpose is accreditation. NAST is the recognized accrediting agency for educational programs in theatre. Membership: $35/year (individual).

Publications:
Directory of Member Institutions. a.
Handbook of Accreditation Standards. a.

Meetings/Conferences:
Annual Meetings: Spring
1999 – Pittsburg, PA(Westin William Penn)/Apr. 8-11/110

Nat'l Ass'n of Science Writers *(1934)*
P.O. Box 294
Greenlawn, NY   11740
Tel: (516)757-5664
E-Mail: diane@nasw.org
Web Site: http://www.NASW.ORG
Members: 2,000 individuals
Staff: 1
Annual Budget: $100-250,000
Administrative Secretary: Diane McGurgan

Historical Note
Journalists and others who convey information about scientific developments to the public. Organized September 14, 1934, by twelve science reporters. Incorporated in the State of New York in 1955. Membership: $60/year.

Publications:
NASW Newsletter. q.

Meetings/Conferences:
Annual Meetings: With the American Ass'n for the
    Advancement of Science
1999 – Anaheim, CA(Hilton)/Jan. 21-26
2000 – Washington, DC(Sheraton)/Feb. 12-18
2001 – San Francisco, CA(Hilton)/Feb. 13-18

Nat'l Ass'n of Scientific Materials Managers *(1973)*
Third Wave Technologies
502 S. Rosa Rd.
Madison, WI   53719
Tel: (608)663-7026   *Fax:* (608)663-7027
Web Site: http://www.denison.edu/naosmm
Members: 380 individuals, 97 corporations
Staff: 1
Annual Budget: $25-50,000
President: Joe Chase

Historical Note
Members are stockroom managers, supervisors and other support personnel, mainly in university, industry, and commercial research laboratories, who purchase scientific equipment. Membership: $25/year (individual); $50/year (organization/company).

Publications:
Directory. a.
Newsline. q. adv.

Meetings/Conferences:
Annual Meetings: End of July-first of August.
1999 – Denver, CO

Nat'l Ass'n of Scissors and Shears Manufacturers *(1925)*

Historical Note
Organization inactive in 1998.

Nat'l Ass'n of Secondary School Principals (1916)
1904 Association Drive
Reston, VA 20191-1537
Tel: (703)860-0200   *Fax:* (703)476-9321
Toll Free: (800)253 - 7746
E-Mail: nassp@nassp.org
Web Site: http://nassp.org/
Members: 41,000 individuals
Staff: 110
Annual Budget: $10-25,000,000
Exec. Director: Dr. Tom Korner
Director, Communications: Robert V. Mahaffey
Manager, Conference Prog.: Donna Clark
Controller and Human Resources Director: Barbara Beasley
Deputy Exec. Director: Thomas F. Koerner
Director, Urban Svcs.: Gwendolyn Cooke
Legal Counsel: Steven R. Yurek
Manager, Membership Services: Kathy Behl

Historical Note
Administers 4 non-profit organizations: Nat'l Ass'n of Student Councils, Nat'l Ass'n of Student Activity Advisers, Nat'l Honor Soc., and Nat'l Junior Honor Soc. Membership: $165/year (individual); $215/year (institution); $49/year (student/teacher); $25/year (retired).

Publications:
Bulletin. 9/year.
Cases in Point. 9/year.
Curriculum Report. 5/year.
High School Magazine. q.
Leadership for Student Activities. 9/year.
Legal Memorandum. 5/year.
NewsLeader. m.
Practitioner. 5/year.
Schools in the Middle. q.
Tips for Principals. 9/year.

Meetings/Conferences:
Annual Meetings: Winter
1999 – New Orleans, LA(Convention Center)/Feb. 26-March 2/6500
2000 – San Antonio, TX(Convention Center)/Feb. 4-8/7000

Nat'l Ass'n of Secrectarial Services
Historical Note
Became (1997) Ass'n of Business Support Services Internat'l.

Nat'l Ass'n of Secretaries of State (1904)
501 Darby Creek Rd., Suite 51 A
Lexington, KY 40509-2610
Tel: (606)264-9257   *Fax:* (606)263-8601
E-Mail: bsinclair@uky.campus.mci.net
Web Site: http://www.nass.org
Members: 55 individuals
Staff: 1
Annual Budget: $250-500,000
Exec. Director: Bertie Sinclair

Historical Note
Established at the St. Louis World's Fair in 1904 as the Ass'n of American Secretaries of State, it is the oldest organization of major public officials in the U.S.; assumed its present name in 1921. An affiliate organization of the Council of State Governments which provides administrative support. Membership: assessed by state population and tied to the CPI.

Publications:
NASS Handbook. a.
NASS News. q.
Office and Duties of the Secretary of State. irreg.

Meetings/Conferences:
1999 – St. Louis, MO/June 25-30

Nat'l Ass'n of Securities and Commercial Law Attorneys (1988)
317 Massachusetts Ave., N.E., Suite 300
Washington, DC 20002-5701
Tel: (202)789-3963   *Fax:* (202)789-1814
Staff: 2
Exec. Director: Jon Koneo

Nat'l Ass'n of Securities Dealers (1938)
1735 K St., N.W.
Washington, DC 20006
Tel: (202)728-8000   *Fax:* (301)590-6506
Web Site: http://www.nasdaq.com
Members: 505,600 individuals, 5,400 firms
Staff: 2600
Annual Budget: Over $100,000,000
President and C.E.O.: Frank G. Zarb
Senior V. President, Corporate Communications: Robert D. Leahy
Sr. V.P. and Treasurer: James R. Allen
C.F.O.: Salvatore F. Sodano
Senior V. President and General Counsel: T. Grant Callery
Corp. Secretary: Joan C. Conley
Exec. V.P., Member Regulation: John E. Pinto
Exec. V.P., Enforcement: Barry Goldsmith
Exec. V. President and C.O.O.: Richard G. Ketchum
President, Nasdaq Stock Market: Alfred R. Berkeley, III
Exec. V. President, Dispute Resolution & Chief Hearing Officer: Linda D. Fienberg
President, NASD Regulation: Mary L. Schapiro

Historical Note
Established as the Investment Bankers Conference, it assumed its present name in 1939. NASD is the self-regulatory organization of the securities industry responsible for the regulation of the NASDAQ securities exchange and other over-the counter securities market and related financial products. in 1998, NASD merged with the American Stock Exchange to form the NASDAQ-AmEx Market Group, under which the two stock exchanges operate. Has an annual budget of approximately $500 million.

Publications:
Annual Report. a.

NASD Subsription Services. irreg.
NASDAQ Fact Book & Company Directory. a.
Notice to Members. m.
Regulatory and Compliance Alert. q.
Subscriber Bulletin. bi-m.

Nat'l Ass'n of Securities Professionals (1985)
1212 New York Ave., N.W., Suite 210
Washington, DC 20005
Tel: (202)371-5535   *Fax:* (202)371-5536
Members: 470 individuals
Staff: 2
Annual Budget: $500-1,000,000
Exec. Director: Dr. Terri Y. Adams

Historical Note
NASP members are minority securities professionals. Membership: $250/year (individual).

Publications:
Bullseye. q. adv.

Meetings/Conferences:

Nat'l Ass'n of Security and Data Vaults (1981)
Historical Note
Organization defunct in 1994.

Nat'l Ass'n of Security Companies (1972)
2670 Union Ave. Extended, Suite 710
Memphis, TN 38112-4428
Tel: (901)323-0173   *Fax:* (901)458-4428
Members: 18 companies
Staff: 2
Annual Budget: $100-250,000
Exec. Director and General Counsel: Gail M. Simonton

Historical Note
Formerly (1993) the Committee of Nat'l Security Companies. Incorporated in New York, CONSCO members are major contract security guard firms concerned with industry standards, legislation and public education. Membership Fee varies, based on revenues.

Nat'l Ass'n of Self-Instructional Language Programs (1971)
Critical Language Center, U of AZ
1717 E. Speedway, Ste. 3312, Box 210151
Tucson, AZ 85721-0151
Tel: (520)626-5258   *Fax:* (520)626-8205
E-Mail: Adunkel@u.arizona.edu
Members: 120 academic institutions
Staff: 3
Annual Budget: $10-25,000
Exec. Director: Dr. Alexander Dunkel
Director, Communications: Phetsamone Darakhan

Historical Note
North America's only professional organization specifically devoted to the fostering of self-instructional academic programs in foreign language skills acquisition. At the secondary, college and university levels, NASILP provides ongoing assistance in materials selection and utilization, testing standardization, program design and operation, and multi-media orientation for coordinators, drillers, examiners and students. Membership: $250/year.

Publications:
NASILP Journal.

Meetings/Conferences:
Annual Meetings: Fall
1999 – Washington, DC/Oct. 29-30/120
2000 – Washington, DC/Nov. 3-4/120

Nat'l Ass'n of Senior Companions Project Directors (1978)
2001 South State St., Suite 51500
Salt Lake City, UT 84190-2300
Tel: (801)468-2775   *Fax:* (801)468-2852
Members: 150 individuals
Annual Budget: $10-25,000
President: Dwight Rasmussen

Historical Note
NASCPD members are directors of Corporation for National Service's senior companion program. Established in 1973 the Senior Companion Program provides stipended volunteer opportunities for low-income seniors who work with those over the age of 21, but particularly with the frail, home-bound were matched with over 36,000 clients in 144 federally-funded and 37 locally-funded projects nationwide. Associate members are other SCP staff and interested individuals. Membership: $50/year (individual); $25/year (associate).

Publications:
Membership Briefing. m.

Meetings/Conferences:
Annual Meetings: Washington, DC/12-15 attendees

Nat'l Ass'n of Service and Conservation Corps (1985)
666 11th St., N.W., Suite 1000
Washington, DC 20001-4542
Tel: (202)737-6272   *Fax:* (202)737-6277
E-Mail: nascc@nascc.org
Web Site: www.nascc.org
Members: 50 individuals, 120 organizations
Staff: 10
Annual Budget: $1-2,000,000
President: Kathleen Selz
V. President, Government Affairs: Andrew Moore
Manager, Administration: Michael A. Butler
Director, Member Services: Leslie Wilkoff

Historical Note
NASCC serves youth corps programs as a national advocate and information exchange network, and provides technical assistance and training to strengthen and expand new and existing youth corps programs. Membership: $100/year (individual); $600-$2400/year (organization)

Publications:
Crew Supervisor Training Manual.
NASCC News Newsletter. q.
Youth Corps Profiles. a.
Youth Corps Wellness Guide.

Meetings/Conferences:
Annual Meetings: late Summer-Fall

Nat'l Ass'n of Service Dealers
Historical Note
A division of the North American Retail Dealers Ass'n.

Nat'l Ass'n of Service Managers (1955)
P.O. Box 712500
Santee, CA 92072
Tel: (619)562-7004   *Fax:* (619)562-7153
Toll Free: (888)562 - 7004
E-Mail: nasm@nasm.com
Web Site: http://www.nasm.com
Members: 1000 individuals
Staff: 3
Annual Budget: $250-500,000
Managing Director: Caryn Worcester

Historical Note
Committed to the educational and professional advancement of service managers in all industries. Maintains a Product Safety and Liability Special Interst Group. Administers a certification board awarding the ASE (Associate Service Executive) and CSE (Certified Sevice Executive) designations. Membership: $225/year (individual), $1,800/year (company).

Publications:
Membership Directory. a. adv.
NASM Service Management. m. adv.
Proceedings Manual. a. adv.

Meetings/Conferences:
1999 – Scottsdale, AZ(Radisson)/Sept. 19-22

Nat'l Ass'n of Service Merchandising (1979)
Historical Note
Absorbed by American Wholesale Marketers Ass'n in 1994.

Nat'l Ass'n of Service Providers in Private Rehabilitation (1989)
633 South Washington St.
Alexandria, VA 22314-4109
Tel: (208)336-5947
Web Site: www.nationalrehab.org
Members: 600 individuals
Annual Budget: $10-25,000
President: Mary Barros

Historical Note
A professional division of the Nat'l Rehabilitation Ass'n; NRA may also be contacted for information on NASPPR. NASPPR members provide a wide variety of medical, rehabilitation, insurance and legal services in highly diverse settings. NASPPR provides a forum where professionals from many disciplines can work more closely together to enhance the delivery of services to persons with disabilities. Membership is open to any profit or non-profit service provider in private rehabilitation and others interested in such services. Membership: $20/year, plus NRA dues.

Publications:
Rehabilitation. q. adv.

Meetings/Conferences:
Annual Meetings: usually with Nat'l Rehabilitation Ass'n meeting
1999 – Minnesota

Nat'l Ass'n of Settlement Purchasers (1995)
1200 19th St., N.W., Suite 300
Washington, DC 20036
Tel: (202)828-6050   *Fax:* (202)429-5113
Toll Free: (888)311 - 6277
Annual Budget: $100-250,000
Exec. Director: William E. Kelley, CAE

Historical Note
Members are companies who purchase structured settlements, lottery annuities, and similar periodic payment plans from their beneficiaries. Membership: $40,000/year (premier); $10,000/year (master); $400/year (associate).

Nat'l Ass'n of Seventh-Day Adventist Dentists (1944)
P.O. Box 101
Loma Linda, CA 92354
Tel: (909)794-8025
Members: 600 individuals
Staff: 1
Annual Budget: $25-50,000
Exec. Director: Karen Sutton

Historical Note
Affiliated with the American Dental Ass'n. Membership: $80/year.

Publications:
SDA Dentist Directory. a.

Meetings/Conferences:
Annual Meetings: Fall

Nat'l Ass'n of Sewer Service Companies (1976)
140 Circle Dr., Suite 103
Maitland, FL 32751-6466
Tel: (407)740-6634   *Fax:* (407)740-6637
Members: 250 companies
Staff: 2
Annual Budget: $100-250,000
Exec. Director: Allen Thomas

Historical Note
Members clean, inspect and rehabilitate sewer pipes and structures are manufacturers or dealers in products utilized or others interested in pipeline rehabilitation (e.g. municipalities, consulting engineers, etc.) Membership: $650/year (contractors); $300/year

(dealers); $550/year (manufacturers); $200/yr (municipalities & others)

Publications:
Inspector Handbook for Sewer Rehabilitation.
Manual of Practices.
Safety Training for Sewer Workers.
Sewer Rehabilitation Specification Guidelines.

Meetings/Conferences:
Annual Meetings: February-March
1999 – San Diego, CA/Jan. 31-Feb. 3

Nat'l Ass'n of Sign Supply Distributors *(1991)*
5024-R Campbell Blvd.
Baltimore, MD   21236-5974
Tel: (410)931-8100   *Fax:* (410)931-8111
E-Mail: nassd@aol.com
Web Site: http://www.nassd.org
Members: 23 distributors, 35 manufacturers
Staff: 2
Annual Budget: $100-250,000
Exec. Director: Celeste Powers, CAE

Historical Note
Members are full line sign supply distributors and manufacturers of commercial, neon, and electrical products.

Publications:
NASSD News. 3/year.

Meetings/Conferences:
Annual Meetings: October

Nat'l Ass'n of Small Business Internat'l Trade Educators *(1988)*
c/o Richland College Business Division
12800 Abrams Road
Dallas, TX   75243-2199
Tel: (214)238-6943   *Fax:* (214)238-6092
Members: 300 individuals and organizations
Staff: 1
Annual Budget: $50-100,000
Exec. Director: Martha Camarillo

Historical Note
The Nat'l Ass'n of Small Business Internat'l Trade Educators was formed in 1988 to promote and enhance the involvement and competitiveness of small businesses in internat'l trade. It's mission is to improve global competitiveness through effective education and training. NASBITE members include U.S. Dept. of Education, Commerce, State and U.S. Small Business Administration officials. Membership: $75/year (individual), $225/year (institutional).

Publications:
Membership Directory. a.
Resource Directory. a.

Meetings/Conferences:

Nat'l Ass'n of Small Business Investment Companies *(1958)*
666 11th St., N.W., Suite 750
Washington, DC   20001
Tel: (202)628-5055   *Fax:* (202)628-5080
E-Mail: nasbic@nasbic.org
Web Site: http://www.nasbic.org
Members: 300 companies
Staff: 6
Annual Budget: $1-2,000,000
President: Lee W. Mercer
V. President: Jeanette D. Paschal
Director, Member Services: Jamie G. Blake

Historical Note
Members are companies licensed under the Small Business Investment Act of 1958. Sponsors the Nat'l Ass'n of Small Business Investment Companies Political Action Committee.

Publications:
Membership Directory. a.
NASBIC News. m.

Meetings/Conferences:
Annual Meetings: Fall
1999 – West Palm Beach, FL(The Breakers)

Nat'l Ass'n of Social Workers *(1955)*
750 First St., N.E., Suite 700
Washington, DC   20002-4241
Tel: (202)408-8600   *Fax:* (202)336-8311
Toll Free: (800)638 - 8799
Members: 155,000 individuals
Staff: 120
Annual Budget: $10-25,000,000
Exec. Director: Josephine Nieves
Manager, Marketing and Membership: Margaret F. O'Hare
Manager, Office of Continuing Education: Georgianna Carrington
Director, Professional Development and Advocacy: Toby Weismiller
Director, Management and Administrative Services: Floyd Lewis
General Counsel: Carolyn Polovy
Director, Chapter Services and Continuing Education: Lorraine Zito
Director, Member Services and Publications: Jane Browning

Historical Note
A professional association of social workers formed Oct. 1, 1955 through the merger of the American Ass'n of Group Workers, the American Ass'n of Medical Social Workers, the American Ass'n of Psychiatric Social Workers, the American Ass'n of Social Workers, Ass'n for the Study of Community Organization, the Nat'l Ass'n of School Social Workers and the Social Work Research Group. Administers the Academy of Certified Social Workers and awards the ACSW designation. 55 chapters. Supports PACE (a political action committee). Membership: $157.50/year (regular); $39.50/year (student); $47.75/year (retired/doctoral candidate); $126.00/year (associate). Has an annual budget of approximately $15.6 million.

Publications:
Health and Social Work. q. adv.
NASW News. m. adv.

NASW Register of Clinical Social Workers. bien.
Social Work. bi-m. adv.
Social Work Abstracts. q. adv.
Social Work in Education. q. adv.
Social Work Research. q. adv.

Meetings/Conferences:

Nat'l Ass'n of Software Consultants and Programmers

Historical Note
Address unknown in 1996.

Nat'l Ass'n of Solar Contractors *(1977)*
P.O. Box 15240
Phoenix, AZ   85060-5240
Tel: (602)957-2365
Members: 500 individuals
Staff: 2
Annual Budget: $50-100,000
President: Edward A. Schein

Historical Note
Members are contractors, architects, engineers, manufacturers and others involved in the installation of solar equipment. Serves as a clearinghouse for technical information, and represents the industry before Congress and the Department of Energy. Absorbed the American Solar Energy Ass'n in 1978.

Publications:
NASC News. bi-m.
Tech Bulletin q. adv. adv.

Nat'l Ass'n of Special Needs State Administrators *(1983)*
40 Illinois State Board of Education
100 N. First St., #C-421
Springfield, IL   62777
Tel: (217)782-3370   *Fax:* (217)782-9224
Members: 30 individuals
Annual Budget: under $10,000
Exec. Officer: Sharon Full

Historical Note
NASNSA is a very small organization whose members are state administrators of programs for special populations and vocational education. Officers and address change annually. Membership: $15/year.

Publications:
Newsletter. 3/year.

Meetings/Conferences:
Annual Meetings: September

Nat'l Ass'n of Specialty Food and Confection Brokers *(1966)*
Exclusively Gourmet
1350 N. Wells St., G-408
Chicago, IL   60610
Tel: (312)397-9494   *Fax:* (312)397-0368
E-Mail: exgourmet@aol.com
Members: 300 individuals, 100 broker companies
Staff: 1
Annual Budget: under $10,000
Publicity Chair: Brian Schwenger

Historical Note
NASFCB members are brokers of gourmet, specialty food and confections to the distribution, wholesale and retail trades. Members: $75/year.

Publications:
Directory of Members. a.
Newsletter. semi-a. adv.

Meetings/Conferences:
Semi-Annual Meetings: in conjunction with Nat'l Fancy Food Show
1999 – New York, NY
2000 – San Francisco, CA
2001 – New York, NY

Nat'l Ass'n of Sporting Goods Wholesalers *(1953)*
400 E. Randolph St., #700
Chicago, IL   60601
Tel: (312)565-0233
Members: 80 wholesalers, 300 manufacturers
Staff: 1
Annual Budget: $250-500,000
Exec. Director: Rebecca A. Maddy

Historical Note
Formerly the Sporting Goods Jobbers Ass'n. Membership includes 80 wholesalers of primarily fishing and shooting sports equipment and approximately 300 manufacturers of this equipment. Membership: $300/yr. (wholesalers), $150/yr. (manufacturers).

Publications:
Membership Directory. a.

Meetings/Conferences:
Annual Meetings: November

Nat'l Ass'n of Sports Officials *(1980)*
2017 Lathrop Ave.
Racine, WI   53405
Tel: (414)632-5448   *Fax:* (414)632-5460
E-Mail: naso@naso.com
Web Site: naso.org
Members: 18 individuals
Staff: 16
Annual Budget: $250-500,000
Ass'n Events Manager: Bonnie Schwartz
Administration: Marylou Clayton
Coordinator, NASO: Bob Still

Historical Note
A non-profit organization providing services and benefits to amateur sports officials and umpires. Membership: $69/year.

Publications:
NASO Newsletter. m.

Referee. m. adv.

Meetings/Conferences:
Annual Meetings: Summer

Nat'l Ass'n of State Administrators and Supervisors of Private Schools *(1971)*
Maryland Higher Education Commission
16 Francis St.
Annapolis, MD   21401
Tel: (410)974-2971
Members: 50 individuals
Annual Budget: under $10,000
President: Judy Hendrickson

Historical Note
Members are state licensure staff for private, post-secondary vocational schools Has no paid staff or permanent office. Membership: $25/year.

Publications:
None.

Meetings/Conferences:
Annual Meetings: May-June

Nat'l Ass'n of State Administrators for Family and Consumer Sciences
Ohio Dept. of Education
65 S. Front St., Room 909
Columbus, OH   43215-4183
Tel: (614)644-6818   *Fax:* (614)728-0484
Members: 125 individuals
Annual Budget: under $10,000
President: Barbara Woods

Historical Note
Founded as Nat'l Ass'n of State Supervisors of Vocational Home Economics; assumed its current name in 1997.

Publications:
Membership Directory. a.
Newsletter. 2-3/yr.

Meetings/Conferences:
Annual Meetings: in conjunction with the American Vocational Ass'n

Nat'l Ass'n of State Agencies for Surplus Property *(1947)*
14410 Spellman Court
Spring Hill, FL   34610
Tel: (813)856-7212   *Fax:* (813)857-0196
Members: 56 individuals1,300 associate
Annual Budget: $50-100,000
Program Administrator: W.D. Carpenter

Historical Note
Members are surplus property agencies in the states and territories.

Publications:
Surplus Makes Sense Newsletter. q.

Meetings/Conferences:
Annual Meetings: August

Nat'l Ass'n of State Alcohol and Drug Abuse Directors *(1972)*
808 17th St., N.W., Suite 410
Washington, DC   20006
Tel: (202)293-0090   *Fax:* (202)293-1250
E-Mail: dcoffice@nasadad.org
Web Site: http://www.nasadad.org
Members: 57 state territorial agencies
Staff: 17
Annual Budget: $2-5,000,000
Exec. Director: Jack Gustafson
Director of Public Policy: Kathleen Sheehan
Director, Meetings and Projects: Jo Lynn
Exec. Secretary: Virginia Person
Dir., Finance/Support Services: Hollis McMullen
Director, Prevention Services: Stephanie McGencey

Historical Note
Formerly (until 1978) known as the Nat'l Ass'n of State Drug Abuse Program Coordinators. Composed of directors of State and Territorial Alcoholism and Drug Abuse Agencies. Basic purpose is to foster, support and share information on the development of effective alcohol and drug abuse prevention and treatment services; serves as a focal point for public and private agency contacts. Membership: dues based on size of state.

Publications:
NASADAD Alcohol and Drug Abuse Special Report. bi-m.
State Alcohol and Drug Abuse Profile (SADAP). a.
State Substance Abuse Quarterly. q.

Meetings/Conferences:
Annual Meetings: early June/location alternates between eastern and western U.S.
1999 – Florida

Nat'l Ass'n of State Approving Agencies *(1944)*
Historical Note
Address unknown in 1995.

Nat'l Ass'n of State Archaeologists *(1978)*
c/o Massachusetts Historical Commission
220 Morrissey Blvd.
Boston, MA   02125
Tel: (617)727-8470   *Fax:* (617)727-5128
E-Mail: bsimon@mhc.sec.state.ma.us
Web Site: http://nasa.uconn.edu/
Members: 58 individuals
Annual Budget: under $10,000
President: Brona Simon

Historical Note
Membership in NASA is limited to the official State Archaeologist of each state in the U.S. Has no paid officers or full-time staff. Membership: $25/year (individual).

Publications:
NASA Directory.
NASA Newsletter. q.
Meetings/Conferences:
Annual Meetings: Spring, with the Society for American
  Archaeology.
1999 – Chicago, IL

Nat'l Ass'n of State Auditors, Comptrollers and Treasurers *(1916)*
2401 Regency Road, Suite 302
Lexington, KY 40503
Tel: (606)276-1147   *Fax:* (606)278-0507
Members: 170 individuals
Staff: 11
Annual Budget: $1-2,000,000
Exec. Director: Relmond P. Van Daniker

Historical Note
*Membership consists of 3 individuals from each state who serve in
the capacity of auditors, comptrollers and treasurers of each state.*
Publications:
Directory. a.
Newsletter. bi-m.
Meetings/Conferences:

Nat'l Ass'n of State Aviation Officials *(1931)*
8401 Colesville Road, Suite 505
Silver Spring, MD 20910
Tel: (301)588-0587   *Fax:* (301)585-1803
Web Site: www.nasao.org
Members: 52 states and territories
Staff: 6
Annual Budget: $250-500,000
President: Henry M. Ogrodzinski
Director, Aviation Programs: Lori P. Lehnerd

Historical Note
*Incorporated an affiliated research arm in 1986, the NASAO Center
for Aviation Research and Education.*
Publications:
Directory. a.
NASAO Newsletter. m.
Meetings/Conferences:
Annual Meetings: Fall/250
1999 – Williamsburg, VA(Colonial Williamsburg
  Hotel)/Sept. 17-22

Nat'l Ass'n of State Boards of Accountancy *(1908)*
150 4th Ave. North
Nashville, TN 37219-2415
Tel: (615)880-4200   *Fax:* (615)880-4200
Web Site: http://www.nasba.org
Members: 54 state boards
Staff: 30
Annual Budget: $5-10,000,000
President and Exec. Director: David A. Costello
Director of Communications: Lisa Axisa
Meetings Manager: Thomas Kenny
Exec. V. President and C.O.O.: Lorraine P. Sachs
C.F.O.: Gene Brosky
Manager, Member Services: Louise Dratler Haberman

Historical Note
*Formerly (1967) Ass'n of Certified Public Accountant Examiners.
Has an annual budget of approximately $8.5 million. Membership:
$100/year (individual), $100/year (organization).*
Publications:
CPA Candidate Performance on the Uniform CPA
  Examination. a.
The State Board Report. m.
Meetings/Conferences:
Annual Meetings: September/October
1999 – Nashville, TN

Nat'l Ass'n of State Boards of Education *(1959)*
1012 Cameron St.
Alexandria, VA 22314
Tel: (703)684-4000   *Fax:* (703)836-2313
Web Site: www.nasbe.org
Members: 650 boards
Staff: 16
Annual Budget: $2-5,000,000
Exec. Director: Brenda Welburn
Dir., Public Relations and Publications: David Kysilko
Director of Conventions and Meetings: Doris J. Cruel
Director of Government Affairs: David Griffith
Director, Finance: Dee Elenhan

Historical Note
*Composed of state board of education members from the U.S. and
Canada.*
Publications:
Issues in Brief. q.
State Board Connection. q.
Meetings/Conferences:
Annual Meetings: Third week in October
1999 – New Orleans, LA/Oct. 14-16

Nat'l Ass'n of State Boards of Geology *(1991)*
P.O. Box 11591
Columbia, SC 29211-1591
Tel: (803)799-1047   *Fax:* (803)252-3432
E-Mail: 102667.2674@compuserve.com
Members: 12 boards
Exec. Director: Sam Swinehart

Historical Note
NASBG members are state boards of geology.
Meetings/Conferences:

Nat'l Ass'n of State Boating Law Administrators *(1961)*
P.O. Box 11099

Lexington, KY 40512-1099
Tel: (606)225-9487   *Fax:* (606)231-6403
Web Site: http://www.uscgboating.org/index1.html
Members: 56 state/territories, 90 assoc.
Staff: 6
Annual Budget: $500-1,000,000
Exec. Secretary: John M. Johnson

Historical Note
*NASBLA is a professional association of state, commonwealth, and
provincial officials having responsibility for administering and/or
enforcing state boating laws. Non-voting membership is open to
others on an associate basis. Membership: $100/yr. (reg.
individual); $975/yr. (state territories); $200/yr (501c3's).*
Publications:
Directory. a.
Policy Manual. a.
Reference Guide to State Boating Laws. a.
Small Craft Advisory. bi-m.
Meetings/Conferences:
Annual Meetings: Fall/250-350
1999 – Hot Springs, AR(Arlington)/Sept. 18-22/300
2000 – Machinac Island, MI(Mission Point)/Sept. 9-13/300
2001 – Anchorage, AK

Nat'l Ass'n of State Budget Officers *(1945)*
444 North Capitol St., N.W., Suite 642
Washington, DC 20001
Tel: (202)624-5382   *Fax:* (202)624-7745
Web Site: www.nasbo.org
Members: 125 individuals
Staff: 2
Annual Budget: $250-500,000
Exec. Director: Gloria Timmer

Historical Note
*Membership limited to three budget officers per state. Affiliated with
the Nat'l Governors Ass'n.*
Publications:
Fiscal Survey of the States. semi-a.

Nat'l Ass'n of State Cable Agencies *(1978)*
Historical Note
Address unknown in 1997.

Nat'l Ass'n of State Catholic Conference Directors *(1967)*
c/o Illinois Catholic Conference
65 E. Wacker Pl., #1620
Chicago, IL 60601-7296
Tel: (312)368-1066   *Fax:* (312)368-1090
E-Mail: jenatcci@aol.com
Members: 37 individuals
Staff: 1
Annual Budget: under $10,000
Exec. Director: Doug Delaney

Historical Note
Directors of State Catholic Conferences.
Meetings/Conferences:
Semi-annual Meetings: Summer and Winter
1999 – Chicago, IL

Nat'l Ass'n of State Charity Officials *(1978)*
c/o Office of the Attorney General
State Capitol, 33 Capitol St.
Concord, NH 03301
Tel: (603)271-3591   *Fax:* (603)271-2110
Members: 100 individuals
Annual Budget: under $10,000
President: Michael DeLucia

Historical Note
*NASCO members are state government officers responsible for the
regulation of charities.*
Meetings/Conferences:
Annual Meetings: Fall, in conjunction with the Nat'l Ass'n of
  Attorneys General
1999 – Charleston, SC

Nat'l Ass'n of State Chartered Credit Unions
Historical Note
Address unknown in 1996.

Nat'l Ass'n of State Controlled Substances Authorities *(1984)*
120 Woodcock Trail
West Columbia, SC 29169-3754
Tel: (803)939-9219   *Fax:* (803)939-0070
E-Mail: NASCSA@juno.com
Staff: 1
Annual Budget: $10-25,000
Exec. Director: Thomas D. Wyatt, Jr.

Historical Note
*NASCSA members are state, commonwealth and territory
government agencies responsible for implementing and
administering controlled substance scheduling, regulation and
diversion control. Membership: $150/year (state agency).*
Publications:
Controlled Substances Authorities. 3x/year.
Meetings/Conferences:
1999 – Coeur d'Alene, ID(Coeur d'Alene Inn)/Oct. 26-30/150

Nat'l Ass'n of State Credit Union Supervisors *(1966)*
1901 N. Moore St., Suite 203
Arlington, VA 22209
Tel: (703)528-8351   *Fax:* (703)528-3248
Web Site: www.nascus.org
Members: 615 individuals
Staff: 6
Annual Budget: $1-2,000,000
President and C.E.O.: Douglas Duerr

Management of regulatory & Research Services: Brian D. Knight
Manager of Communications: Ronda Combs
V. President, Accreditation and Communication: Mary Martha
  Fortney
Manager, Corporate Affairs: Leish Bell
Dir., Education & State Programs Coordinator: Jennifer Slavin

Historical Note
*State chartered credit unions and state credit union supervisors.
Membership: $100-$3,600/year.*
Publications:
Annual Report. a.
Fax from Washington.
Stateline. m.
Meetings/Conferences:
Annual Meetings: Autumn
1999 – Scottsdale, AZ(Marriott)
2000 – Dane Point, CA(Marriott)
2001 – Key West, Fl(Marriott)

Nat'l Ass'n of State Departments of Agriculture *(1915)*
1156 15th St., N.W., Suite 1020
Washington, DC 20005
Tel: (202)296-9680   *Fax:* (202)296-9686
E-Mail: nasda@patriot.net
Web Site: http://www.nasda-hq.org
Members: 54 departments
Staff: 9
Annual Budget: $500-1,000,000
Executive V. President and CEO: Richard W. Kirchhoff
Manager, Legislative & Regulatory Affairs: Charles Ingram
Manager, Legislative and Regulatory Affairs: Kim C. Putens
Chief Financial Officer: Curtis M. Anderson

Historical Note
*NASDA is a nonpartisan association of public officials comprised of
the executive heads of the fifty state Departments of Agriculture and
those from the territories of Puerto Rico, Guam, American Samoa
and the Virgin Islands. NASDA's mission is to support and promote
the American agriculture industry, while protecting the
environment, through the development , implementation and
communication of sound policy and programs.*
Publications:
AG in Perspective. q.
NASDA News. w.
Meetings/Conferences:
1999 – St. George, UT(Holiday Inn)/Sept. 25-29

Nat'l Ass'n of State Development Agencies *(1946)*
750 First St., N.E., Suite 710
Washington, DC 20002
Tel: (202)898-1302   *Fax:* (202)898-1312
Members: 50 state agencies
Staff: 15
Annual Budget: $500-1,000,000
Exec. Director: Miles Friedman

Historical Note
*Formerly (1970) Ass'n of State Planning & Development Agencies.
Membership: $1,000-8,500/year.*
Publications:
Directory of Incentives for Business Investment in the U. S.
Expenditure & Salary Survey. bien.
The NASDA Newsletter. 8-10/year.
Meetings/Conferences:

Nat'l Ass'n of State Directors of Administration and General Services *(1976)*
167 W. Main St, Suite 600
Lexington, KY 40507-1324
Tel: (606)231-1877   *Fax:* (606)231-1928
Members: 75 individuals
Staff: 2
Annual Budget: $50-100,000
Association Manager: Dana A. Carter

Historical Note
*Formerly (1988) Nat'l Conference of State General Services
Officials, NASDAGS members are directors of state agencies
charged with the administration of state general services.
Membership: $1,000-2,250/year.*
Publications:
NASDAGS News: Managing Administrative Services. q.
Profiles of Administration and General Services, Departments
  and Leaders.
Meetings/Conferences:
Annual Meetings: Fall
1999 – Salt Lake City, UT

Nat'l Ass'n of State Directors of Developmental Disability Services *(1963)*
113 Oronoco St.
Alexandria, VA 22314
Tel: (703)683-4202   *Fax:* (703)684-1395
Members: 53 individuals
Staff: 7
Annual Budget: $250-500,000
Exec. Director: Robert M. Gettings

Historical Note
*Formerly the Nat'l Ass'n of State Mental Retardation Program
Directors.*
Publications:
Community Service Reporter. m. adv.
Perspectives. m. adv.
Meetings/Conferences:
Annual Meetings: Washington, DC/December
1999 – Alexandria, VA/100

Nat'l Ass'n of State Directors of Migrant Education *(1968)*
North carolina Education Bldg.

301 N. Wilmington St.
Raleigh, NC 27601-2825
Tel: (919)715-1356
Members: 51 individuals
Annual Budget: $250-500,000
President: Bill McGrady

Historical Note
Members are the person in each state education agency who has responsibility for Chapter One Migrant Education Program operation. NASDME promotes interstate coordination and cooperation to further the education of children whose parents are migrant agriculture or maritime workers.

Publications:
Chapter I Migrant Education Program State Directors. a.

Meetings/Conferences:
Annual Meetings: Spring/1,500
1999 – Little Rock, AR(Excelsior/Doubletree)

Nat'l Ass'n of State Directors of Special Education *(1938)*
1800 Diagonal Road, Suite 320
Alexandria, VA 22314-2840
Tel: (703)519-3800   *Fax:* (703)519-3808
E-Mail: nasdse@nasdse.org
Members: 2,500 individuals
Staff: 20
Annual Budget: $2-5,000,000
Exec. Director: Martha J. Fields
Director, Governmental Relations: Myrna Mandlawitz
Deputy Exec. Director: Bill East
General Counsel: Sheldon Cohen

Historical Note
Represents state personnel responsible for education of handicapped students with disabilities. Provides training and technical assistance to state education agency staff.

Publications:
Counterpoint. q.
Liaison Bulletin. irreg.

Meetings/Conferences:
Annual Meetings: October
1999 – Lake Tahoe, NV

Nat'l Ass'n of State Directors of Teacher Education and Certification *(1922)*
P.O. Box 256
Bedford, MA 01730-0256
Tel: (781)275-8839   *Fax:* (781)271-1573
Members: 60 government agencies
Staff: 2
Annual Budget: $250-500,000
Exec. Director: Roy Einreinhofer

Historical Note
Purpose is to exercise leadership in matters related to the preparation and certification of professional school personnel. Membership: $3,500/year (state); $200/year (associate).

Publications:
Certification Manual. a.
Directory. a.

Meetings/Conferences:
Annual Meetings: June
1999 – Santa Rosa, CA(Flamingo Resort Hotel)
1999 – Bellevue, WA(Hyatt Regency)
2000 – Portland, ME/175

Nat'l Ass'n of State Directors of Veterans Affairs *(1946)*
c/o Delaware Commn. of Veterans Affairs
500 E. Capital Ave.
Pierre, SD 57501
Tel: (605)773-3269   *Fax:* (605)773-5380
Members: 51 individuals
Staff: 1
Annual Budget: under $10,000
President: Antonio Davila

Historical Note
Membership: $200/yr.

Meetings/Conferences:
Semi-Annual Meetings: Spring and Fall
1999 – Washington, DC
1999 – Orlando, FL

Nat'l Ass'n of State Directors of Vocational-Technical Education *(1920)*
444 North Capitol St., N.W., Suite 830
Washington, DC 20001
Tel: (202)737-0303   *Fax:* (202)737-1106
E-Mail: nasdvtec@iris.org
Web Site: http:www.iris.org/~nasdvtec
Members: 250 individuals, 50 states
Staff: 2
Annual Budget: $250-500,000
Exec. Director: Kimberly A. Green

Historical Note
Formerly the Nat'l Ass'n of State Directors of Vocational Education, the consortium adopted its present name in 1989. NASDVTEC is the professional leadership association for 59 state occupational education agency heads committed to outstanding performance in vocational-technical education. Membership also includes business, labor and education officials who share this committment to quality occupational education at the secondary, post-secondary and adult levels. Membership: $60/year (individual), $2,500 and above/year (organization).

Publications:
Conference Programs. 3/year. adv.
Congressional Testimony. irreg.
Directory of State Directors of Vocational-Technical
  Educators. irreg.
Position Papers. irreg.
Washington Watch. bi-m. adv.

Meetings/Conferences:
1999 – Washington, DC
1999 – St. George, UT
1999 – Orlando, FL

Nat'l Ass'n of State Election Directors
444 N. Capitol St., N.W., Suite 401
Washington, DC 20001
Tel: (202)624-5460   *Fax:* (202)624-5452
Web Site: www.csq.org
Members: 50 individuals
Staff: 1
Manager: David Scott

Historical Note
NASED members are state, commonwealth or territorial election directors or directors of voter registration. Administrative support provided by the Council of State Governments.

Nat'l Ass'n of State Emergency Medical Services Directors *(1980)*
111 Park Place
Falls Church, VA 22046-4513
Tel: (703)538-1799   *Fax:* (703)241-5603
E-Mail: nasemsd@aol.com
Members: 56 individuals
Staff: 2
Annual Budget: $100-250,000
Exec. Director: Elizabeth B. Armstrong, CAE

Historical Note
Members are directors of state emergency medical services. Membership: $450/year.

Publications:
NASEMSD Scanner. q.

Meetings/Conferences:
Annual Meetings: Third week in October
1999 – South Dakota/Oct. 18-23

Nat'l Ass'n of State Energy Officials
1414 Prince St., Suite 200
Alexandria, VA 22314-2853
Tel: (703)299-8800   *Fax:* (703)299-6208
Web Site: http://www.naseo.org
Staff: 4
Exec. Director: Frank Bishop

Publications:
Energy Forum. q.
NASEO newsfax. m.

Meetings/Conferences:
Annual Meetings: Winter
1999 – Indianapolis, IN(Omni)/Sept. 19-21

Nat'l Ass'n of State Facilities Administrators *(1987)*
P.O. Box 11910
2760 Research Park Drive
Lexington, KY 40578-1910
Tel: (606)244-8181   *Fax:* (606)244-8015
E-Mail: nasfa@csg.org
Web Site: http://www.csg.org/nasfa.html
Members: 600 individuals, 50 states, 15 corporate affiliates
Staff: 3
Annual Budget: $100-250,000
Ass'n Director: Marcia Stone

Historical Note
NASFA is a professional organization whose mission is to provide a forum for sharing information on effective state facility administration and to give state officials an opportunity to discuss the problems and solutions that demand the attention of the professional administrator. NASFA members are state administrators of facilities and properties.

Publications:
NASFA Representatives Directory.
NASFA Resource Guide.
NASFA Roster. semi-a.
State Facilities. q.

Meetings/Conferences:
Annual Meetings: Summer
1999 – Jackson Hole, WY(Snow King Resort)/June 12-16
2000 – Burlington, VA/June 24-28

Nat'l Ass'n of State Fire Marshals
721 S. Kirkman Road
Orlando, FL 32811
Tel: (407)299-8743   *Fax:* (407)299-8458
Toll Free: (800)437 - 1016
Web Site: www.firemarshals.org
Executive Director: Michael Minieri

Historical Note
NASFM members are all the state fire marshals and private industry supporters. Membership: $100/year (individual), $2500/year (oganization/company).

Publications:
State Fire Marshal Magazine. bi-m. adv.

Meetings/Conferences:

Nat'l Ass'n of State Foresters *(1920)*
444 North Capitol St., N.W., Suite 540
Washington, DC 20001
Tel: (202)624-5415   *Fax:* (202)624-5407
E-Mail: nasf@sso.org
Web Site: http://sso.org.nasf/nasf.html
Members: 50 states, 3 U.S. territories & DC
Staff: 2
Annual Budget: $100-250,000
Washington Representative: William G. Imbergamo

Historical Note
Founded as the Ass'n of State Foresters in 1920, nationwide successor to the Ass'n of Eastern Forester (1911), NASF assumed its present name in 1964. Has no staff or permanent office other

than the above. Officers are elected annually. Membership: $3,500/yr. (state).

Publications:
Directory. a.
NASF State Forestry Statistics. a.
NASF Washington Update. m.

Meetings/Conferences:
Annual Meetings: Fall
1999 – Harrisburg, PA

Nat'l Ass'n of State Information Resource Executives *(1969)*
167 W. Main St., Suite 600
Lexington, KY 40507
Tel: (606)231-1875   *Fax:* (606)231-1928
Members: 50 states
Staff: 2
Annual Budget: $100-250,000
Ass'n Manager: Elizabeth Miller

Historical Note
Formerly (1989) Nat'l Ass'n for State Information Systems. NASIRE represents information resource executives and managers from the fifty states, six U.S. territories, and the District of Columbia. NASIRE provides a forum to exchange information and to address the opportunities and challenges related to information technology, while also providing a vehicle to identify information technology issues.

Publications:
Information Systems Technology in State Government. bi-a.
NASIRE Newsletter. q.

Meetings/Conferences:
Semi-Annual Meetings: usually Spring and Fall

Nat'l Ass'n of State Land Reclamationists *(1973)*
Office of Mines & Minerals
IL Dept of Nat Resources, 524 S. 2nd St.
Springfield, IL 62701-1787
Tel: (217)782-4970
Members: 140 individuals
Annual Budget: under $10,000
Secretary/Treasurer: Dean Spindler

Historical Note
Organized to bring together State reclamation officials for activities of mutual interest and to promote cooperation between the states, private mining groups and the federal government on matters affecting the reclamation of mined lands. The Interstate Mining Compact Commission serves as the executive secretariate for NASLR. Membership: $10/year (individual), $100/year (corporate), $200/year (state).

Publications:
NASLR Newsletter. q.

Meetings/Conferences:
Annual Meetings: Spring or Fall

Nat'l Ass'n of State Mental Health Program Directors *(1963)*
66 Canal Center Plaza, Suite 302
Alexandria, VA 22314-1591
Tel: (703)739-9333   *Fax:* (703)548-9517
Web Site: http://www.nasmpd.org
Members: 55 state & territorial agencies
Staff: 22
Annual Budget: $1-2,000,000
Exec. Director: Robert W. Glover, Ph.D.

Historical Note
State commissioners in charge of the state government programs for persons with mental illness. Promotes cooperation and exchange of ideas in the administration of public mental health programs. A cooperating agency of the Nat'l Governors' Ass'n and the Council of State Governments.

Publications:
Aging Issues.
Children & Youth Update.
Federal Agencies Report.
Forensic Issues.
Human Resource Development Issues.
Legal Issues.
State Report.
Studies on State Mental Health Systems.
U. S.

Meetings/Conferences:
Semi-annual meetings: Winter & Summer/100
1999 – Washington, DC

Nat'l Ass'n of State Outdoor Recreation Liaison Officers *(1967)*
126 Mill Branch Road
Tallahassee, FL 32312
Tel: (850)893-4959
Members: 56 state/territorial representative
Annual Budget: $25-50,000
Exec. Director: Ney C. Landrum

Historical Note
NASORLO members are governor-appointed state administrators of outdoor recreational grant programs funded under the federal Land and Water Conservation Act. Membership: $750/year (organization/company).

Meetings/Conferences:
1999 – Saratoga Springs, NY

Nat'l Ass'n of State Park Directors *(1962)*
9894 E. Holden Place
Tucson, AZ 85748
Tel: (520)298-4924   *Fax:* (520)298-6515
E-Mail: naspdglen@dakotacom.net
Web Site: www.indiana.edu/~naspd
Members: 50 states
Annual Budget: $50-100,000

Exec. Director: Glen Alexander
Historical Note
Members are chief administrative officers of each state park agency. Officers are elected biennially. Membership: $1,400/year (state).
Publications:
Annual Information Exchange. a.
Directory of State Park Directors. a.
State Parks Newsletter. a.
Meetings/Conferences:
Annual Meetings: September/200
1999 – Jackson, WY(Jackson Lake Lodge)/Sept. 7-11/250
2000 – Lone Wolf, OK(Quartz Mtn. Lodge)/Sept. 6-10/200

Nat'l Ass'n of State Personnel Executives *(1976)*
P.O. Box 11910
2760 Research Park Drive
Lexington, KY 40578-1910
Tel: (606)244-8181   *Fax:* (606)244-8015
E-Mail: naspe@csg.org
Web Site: http://www.csg.org/naspe.html
Members: 150 individuals
Staff: 3
Annual Budget: $50-100,000
Ass'n Director: Marcia Stone
Historical Note
An affiliate of the Council of State Governments which provides administrative support, NASPE members are the chief personnel executives in each of the United States; the territories of Guam, Virgin Islands and American Somoa; the Commonwealth of Puerto Rico and the District of Columbia. To provide a forum for state personnel executives to share information on human resource issues and to collectively influence those issues through the conduct of professional research and the participation in various regional and national committees, forums and meetings so that members can better achieve their state's mission and business objectives. Membership: $1,500/year (state).
Publications:
State Personnel Representatives Directory. bien.
State Personnel Roles and Functions. trien.
State Personnel View. q. adv.
Meetings/Conferences:
Annual Meetings: Summer
1999 – Columbus, OH(Hyatt Capitol Square)/Aug. 14-18
2000 – Princeton, NJ/200

Nat'l Ass'n of State Public Health Veterinarians *(1953)*
Historical Note
Address unknown in 1997.

Nat'l Ass'n of State Purchasing Officials *(1947)*
167 W. Main St., Suite 600
Lexington, KY 40507
Tel: (606)231-1877   *Fax:* (606)231-1928
E-Mail: DCARTER@islou.com
Web Site: www.NASPO.org
Members: 80 individuals
Staff: 125
Annual Budget: $100-250,000
Association Manager: Dana A. Carter
Historical Note
NASPO was established to address purchasing of goods and services by state governments. Membership: $850/year.
Publications:
Contract Cookbook for Purchase of Services.
How To Do Business With the States: A Guide for Vendors.
Issues in Public Purchasing/Survey of Principles & Practices.
NASPO Newsletter. q. adv.
State and Local Government Purchasing.
Meetings/Conferences:
Annual Meetings: Fall
1999 – Madison, WI

Nat'l Ass'n of State Radio Networks *(1973)*
c/o Arkansas Radio Network
4021 West 8th St.
Little Rock, AR 72204
Tel: (501)661-7500
Members: 26 companies
Annual Budget: $250-500,000
President: Neal Gladner
Historical Note
Members are companies that broadcast news and other informational programming to affiliated radio stations via satelite transmission. Member networks serve over 1,600 such stations.
Publications:
State Network Newsletter. m.
Meetings/Conferences:
1999 – North Carolina

Nat'l Ass'n of State Recreation Planners *(1981)*
Historical Note
Became the Nat'l Ass'n of Recreation Resource Planners in 1994.

Nat'l Ass'n of State Retirement Administrators *(1956)*
P.O. Box 2360
Carson City, NV 89702-2360
Tel: (702)882-6500   *Fax:* (702)882-1045
E-Mail: will@nasra.org
Web Site: http://www.nasra.org
Members: 55 individuals, 165 associate members
Staff: 1
Annual Budget: $500-1,000,000
Administrative Officer: Will Keating
Historical Note
Represents the administrators of various public-sector retirement programs, providing legislative advocacy and public and professional education Membership: $600/year (administrator), $1,250/year (associate).

Publications:
Newsletter. irreg.
Survey of State and Local Government Retirement Systems. a.
Meetings/Conferences:
1999 – Squaw Valley, CA/Aug. 6-11

Nat'l Ass'n of State Supervisors of Home Economics Education
Historical Note
A division of the American Vocational Ass'n.

Nat'l Ass'n of State Supervisors of Music *(1940)*
Florida Dept. of Education
325 W. Gaines St., Suite 444
Tallahassee, FL 32399
Tel: (850)488-6047   *Fax:* (850)922-0028
Members: 37 individuals
Staff: 6
Annual Budget: under $10,000
Contact: June Hinckley
Historical Note
Established as the Nat'l Council of State Supervisors of Music, members are supervisors of music in state departments of education. Affiliated with the Music Educators Nat'l Conference. Has no permanent address.
Publications:
Directory of State Supervisors of Music. a.
Meetings/Conferences:
Biennial: even years, with the Music Educators Nat'l
Conference

Nat'l Ass'n of State Supervisors of Trade and Industrial Education *(1925)*
State Board for Vocational-Technical Ed.
Capitol Bldg 15th Flr, 600 E Blvd Ave
Bismarck, ND 58505
Tel: (701)328-3183   *Fax:* (701)328-1255
Members: 100 individuals
Staff: 1
Annual Budget: under $10,000
President: Donald Roloff
Historical Note
Has no paid officers or full-time staff. Membership: $20/year (individual).
Meetings/Conferences:
Annual Meetings: December and June Kansas City, MO/June

Nat'l Ass'n of State Supervisors of Vocational Home Economics
Historical Note
Became (1997) Nat'l Ass'n of State Administrators for Family and Consumer Sciences.

Nat'l Ass'n of State Telecommunications Directors *(1978)*
P.O. Box 11910
2760 Research Park Drive
Lexington, KY 40578-1910
Tel: (606)244-8187   *Fax:* (606)244-8015
Web Site: http://www.nastd.org
Members: 120 individuals
Staff: 4
Annual Budget: $250-500,000
Staff Professional: Jack J. Gallt
Program Coordinator: Wayne W. Hall
Program Coordinator: Karen Britten
Historical Note
With directors representing all fifty states, NASTD is concerned with providing a forum for the exchange of ideas and practices; the development of a unified position on matters of national telecommunications policy and regulatory issues; and the improvement of state telecommunications systems. Administrative support is provided by the Council of State Governments. Membership: $1000/year (state); $1,500/year (corporation).
Publications:
Monitor - electronic. w.
Monitor Regulatory Bulletin. m.
State Telecommunications Reports. a.
Meetings/Conferences:
Annual Meetings: Fall/250
1999 – Kansas City, MO/Sept. 14-19

Nat'l Ass'n of State Textbook Administrators
Dept. of Education
4 Capitol Mall, Rm 110 B
Litte Rock, AR 72201
Tel: (501)682-4593   *Fax:* (501)682-4487
E-Mail: smckenzi@arkedu.k.12.ar.us
Members: 23 individuals
Annual Budget: under $10,000
President: Sue McKenzie
Historical Note
Membership: $25/year (individual).
Publications:
Newsletter. a.
Meetings/Conferences:
Semi-Annual Meetings: Winter and Summer

Nat'l Ass'n of State Treasurers *(1976)*
P.O. Box 11910
2760 Research Park Drive
Lexington, KY 40578-1910
Tel: (606)244-8175   *Fax:* (606)244-8053
Web Site: nast.net
Members: 53 individuals
Staff: 7
Annual Budget: $500-1,000,000
Director: Pamela Taylor

Historical Note
Membership consists of State Treasurers, their deputies and staffs. Officers change annually; permanent staff is provided by the Council of State Governments. Membership: $1,000/year (state); $1,000-3,000/year (corporate).
Publications:
NAST Review. q.
State Treasury Activities and Functions.
State Treasury Profiles. bien.
Meetings/Conferences:
Annual Meetings: July/over 450
1999 – Portland, OR

Nat'l Ass'n of State Units on Aging *(1964)*
1225 I St., N.W., Suite 725
Washington, DC 20005
Tel: (202)898-2578   *Fax:* (202)898-2583
E-Mail: ncea@nasua.org
Web Site: http://www.nasua.org
Members: 57 individuals, 57 state and territorial agencies
Staff: 16
Annual Budget: $1-2,000,000
Exec. Director: Daniel A. Quirk, Ph.D.
Director, Communications & Developm't: Theresa N. Lambert
Deputy Director: Diane Justice
Director of Finance and Administration: Deborah White-Martin
Director, Elder Rights: Sara Aravanis
Director of Management Forum in Aging: James Whaley
Historical Note
Members are the state agencies on aging of the fifty states, the District of Columbia,and U.S. territories. Provides general and specialized information, technical assistance and professional development support to state units on aging. Serves as organized channel for officially designated state leadership in aging to exchange information and mutual experiences and to join together for appropriate action on behalf of the elderly.
Meetings/Conferences:
Annual Meetings: Washington, DC/Spring

Nat'l Ass'n of State Universities and Land Grant Colleges *(1887)*
1307 New York Ave., N.W., #400
Washington, DC 20005-4701
Tel: (202)478-6040   *Fax:* (202)478-6046
E-Mail: hiebertr@nasulgc.nche.edu
Web Site: http://www.nasculgc.nche.edu
Members: 195 institutions
Staff: 35
Annual Budget: $2-5,000,000
President: C. Peter Magrath
Director of Public Affairs: Roz Hiebert
Director, Federal Relations/Higher Ed.: Jerold Roschwalb
Finance and Administration Director: Ruth N. Smith
Historical Note
The association's overriding mission is to support high quality public higher education and its member institutions as they perform their traditional teaching, research and public service roles. NASULGC provides a forum for the discussion and development of policies affecting higher education and the public interest.
Publications:
Newsline. 10/year.
Meetings/Conferences:
Annual Meetings: November

Nat'l Ass'n of State Utility Consumer Advocates *(1979)*
1133 15th St., N.W., Suite 550
Washington, DC 20005
Tel: (202)727-3908   *Fax:* (202)727-3911
E-Mail: nasuca@nasuca.org
Web Site: http://www.nasuca.org
Members: 41 state offices, 7 affil, 2 assocs
Staff: 3
Annual Budget: $100-250,000
Exec. Director: Charles A. Acquard
Historical Note
Represents utility consumer advocacy agencies which operate independently from the regulatory commissions in their states. Officers change every two years.
Publications:
Consultants Directory. a.
Membership Directory. a.
NASUCA News. m. adv.
Washington Report. m.
Meetings/Conferences:
Semi-Annual Meetings: June and November
1999 – Baltimore, MD(Tremont Plaza Hotel)/June 13-17
2000 – San Diego, CA(Clarrion Hotel Bay View)/Nov. 12-16
2001 – Chicago, IL/Nov. 17-21

Nat'l Ass'n of State Veterans Homes *(1953)*
Idaho State Veterans Home
P.O. Box 7765
Boise, ID 83707
Tel: (208)334-5000   *Fax:* (208)334-4753
Members: 87 facilities
Annual Budget: $50-100,000
Secretary-Treasurer: David Riggs
Historical Note
Encourages continued federal support for building state facilities and to provide care for veterans currently living in state homes. Has no paid officers or full-time staff.
Publications:
LINK. q.
Nat'l Ass'n of State Veterans Homes Directory. a.
Nat'l Ass'n of State Veterans Homes Newsletter. 3/yr.
Meetings/Conferences:
1999 – Washington, DC/Feb. 27-March 3
2000 – Orlando, FL/Aug. 1-4

Nat'l Ass'n of Steel Pipe Distributors (1975)
14760 Memorial Dr., # 302
Houston, TX 77079-5234
Tel: (713)531-7473 *Fax:* (713)531-7475
Members: 250 companies
Staff: 3
Annual Budget: $100-250,000
Exec. Director: Susannah F. Porr
Administrative Office Manager: Nancy Strickland

Historical Note
Trade Ass'n organized in San Antonio, TX, April 1975, and incorporated in the same state. Members are distributors and manufacturers of steel pipes and tubing, and allied businesses. Membership: $750-1,200/year, dependent on type and size of company.

Publications:
Membership Directory. a. adv.
OSHA Compliance Manual.
Pipeline. m. adv.
Tubular Products Manual. a.

Meetings/Conferences:
Three Meetings Annually: February, May, and October
1999 – San Diego, CA(N.S. Grant Hotel)/March 4-7
1999 – Cancun, MX(Ritz Carleton)/Sept. 23-26
1999 – Montreal, Canada(Ritz Carleton)/June 17-20

Nat'l Ass'n of Stock Plan Professionals (1993)
P.O. Box 21639
Concord, CA 94521-0639
Tel: (925)685-9271 *Fax:* (925)685-5402
Members: 4,000 individuals
Exec. Director: Sandra L. Sussman

Historical Note
NASPP is dedicated to providing its members, including compensation and human resource professionals, stock plan administrators and brokers, opportunities for professional growth and education advancement. Membership: $295/year (individual); $395/year (corporate).

Meetings/Conferences:
1999 – Washington, DC(Omni Sheraham)

Nat'l Ass'n of Store Fixture Manufacturers (1956)
3595 Sheridan St., Suite 200
Hollywood, FL 33021
Tel: (954)893-7300 *Fax:* (954)893-7500
E-Mail: nasfm@nasfm.org
Web Site: http://www.nasfm.org
Members: 150 manufacturers, 200 suppliers
Staff: 8
Annual Budget: $1-2,000,000
Exec. Director: Klein S. Merriman
Director of Communications: Karen Budlong
Director of Marekting/Member Services: Karen Doodeman
Director, Member Services: Catharine MsSwegin

Historical Note
Manufacturers of store fixtures and displays. Membership: $850/year.

Publications:
NASFM Directory. a. adv.
NASFM Magazine. bi-m. adv.
Store Fixture Buyers' Guide. a. adv.

Meetings/Conferences:
Annual Meetings: March/150

Nat'l Ass'n of Student Activity Advisors (1971)
1904 Association Drive
Reston, VA 20191
Tel: (703)860-0200 *Fax:* (703)860-4597
Members: 280,000 individuals
Staff: 10
Director: Rocco Marano

Historical Note
Administrative support is provided by the Division of Student Activities of the Nat'l Ass'n of Secondary School Principals. Members are education professionals involved with student activity programs.

Publications:
Leadership for Student Activities. m.
Monographs. irreg.

Meetings/Conferences:
Regional Fly-ins: Five to Six times each year
1999 – Chicago, IL/Nov. 4-6

Nat'l Ass'n of Student Affairs Professionals (1954)
Office of Admissions, Box 9217
Albany State University
Albany, GA 31705
Tel: (912)430-5118 *Fax:* (912)430-3936
E-Mail: dfrink@flg94.alsnet.peachnet.edu
Treasurer: Diane Frink

Historical Note
Black counterpart of the Nat'l Ass'n of Student Personnel Administrators. Formerly (1994) Nat'l Ass'n of Personnel Workers. Members are student affairs personnel in the fields of teaching, housing, financial aid and social services.

Meetings/Conferences:
Annual Meetings: In February at a college or university setting.

Nat'l Ass'n of Student Anthropolgists
Historical Note
A section of the American Anthropological Soc.

Nat'l Ass'n of Student Assistance Professional (1987)
4200 Wisconsin Ave., N.W. Suite 116-118
Washington, DC 20016
Toll Free: (800)257 - 6310
E-Mail: info@nasap.org
Web Site: http://www.nasap.org

Members: 500 individuals and institutions
Annual Budget: $50-100,000
Exec. Director: Lee Rush

Historical Note
Formerly Nat'l Ass'n of Leadership for Student Assistance Programs (1998). NASAP members represent a full spectrum of individuals and organizations involved with student assistance programs for students at risk. Members include teachers, counselors, psychologists, social workers, nurses, program coordinators, administrators and others with an interest in student assistance programs. Membership: $85/year (individual).

Publications:
Legislative Update. 3/year.
NASAP Membership Directory. a.
Student Assistance Journal. 5/yea.
Student Assistance Today Newsletter. 2/year.

Meetings/Conferences:
1999 – Newport Beach, CA(Marriott)/March 7-10/900

Nat'l Ass'n of Student Councils (1932)
Historical Note
An activity administered by the Office of Student Activities of the Nat'l Ass'n of Secondary School Principals. Now includes more than 7,000 student councils and their advisers.

Nat'l Ass'n of Student Employment Administrators
Historical Note
Became (1998) Nat'l Student Employment Ass'n.

Nat'l Ass'n of Student Financial Aid Administrators (1966)
1129 20th St. N.W.Suite 200
Washington, DC 20036
Tel: (202)785-0453 *Fax:* (202)785-1487
Web Site: http://www.nasfaa.org
Members: 3,200 institutions
Staff: 32
Annual Budget: $2-5,000,000
President: A. Dallas Martin, Ph.D.
Director of Communications: Jeffrey Sheppard
Director of Government Relations: Marty Guthrie

Publications:
Encyclopedia of Financial Aid. as needed.
Journal of Student Financial Aid. 3/year.
NASFAA Directory. a. adv.
NASFAA Newsletter. bi-w.
Student Aid Transcript. q.

Meetings/Conferences:
1999 – Las Vegas, NV(Bally's)/July 12-15
2000 – Washington, DC(Sheraton)/July 9-12

Nat'l Ass'n of Student Personnel Administrators (1919)
1875 Connecticut Ave., N.W., Suite 418
Washington, DC 20009
Tel: (202)265-7500 *Fax:* (202)797-1157
E-Mail: office@naspa.org
Web Site: http://www.naspa.org
Members: 7,500 individuals, 1,160 institutions
Staff: 14
Annual Budget: $1-2,000,000
Exec. Director: Gwendolyn Jordan Dungy
Assoc. Exec. Director: Kevin Kruger

Historical Note
Established in 1919 as the Nat'l Ass'n of Deans and Advisers of Men by a group of midwestern deans. The name was changed to the Nat'l Ass'n of Student Personnel Administrators in 1951. Works to improve practices in student affairs administration. Membership: $54-$162/year (individual); $275-$1,266/year (institution).

Publications:
Membership Handbook.
NASPA Forum. 10/yr. adv.
NASPA Journal. q.
NASPA Monograph Series. bi-a.
NASPA Newsletters. irreg.
Net Results. q.

Meetings/Conferences:
Annual Meetings: Spring
1999 – New Orleans, LA(Hyatt)/March 27-30

Nat'l Ass'n of Substance Abuse Trainers and Educators (1983)
1521 Hillary St.
New Orleans, LA 70118
Tel: (504)286-5234
Members: 41 colleges and universities
Annual Budget: under $10,000
President: Dr. Thomas Lief

Historical Note
Participating institutions of higher education are accredited colleges, universities and professional schools which offer twelve or more hours of substance abuse or alcoholism courses.

Publications:
Directory of the NASATE. a.

Nat'l Ass'n of Superintendents of U.S. Naval Shore Establishments (1912)
Historical Note
Address unknown in 1997.

Nat'l Ass'n of Supervisors and Administrators of Health Occupations Education
c/o Virginia Dept. of Education
P.O. Box 2120
Richmond, VA 23218-2120
Tel: (804)225-2842 *Fax:* (804)371-2456
E-Mail: jwakelyn@pen.k12.va.us.
Members: 35 individuals

Annual Budget: under $10,000
President: Jo Ann Wakelyn

Historical Note
An affiliate of American Vocational Ass'n. NASAHOE members are state supervisors of health occupations education, as well as municipal-government managers in the field. Has no paid officers or full-time staff. Membership: 20/year, plus AVA dues.

Publications:
NASAHOE News. q. adv.

Meetings/Conferences:
Annual Meetings: in conjunction with the American Vocational Ass'n.

Nat'l Ass'n of Supervisors of Agricultural Education (1962)
Historical Note
Address unknown in 1997.

Nat'l Ass'n of Supervisors of Business Education (1955)
Historical Note
Address unknown in 1996.

Nat'l Ass'n of Supervisors of Business Education (1965)
Nebraska Dept. of Education
P.O. Box 94987
Lincoln, NE 68509
Tel: (402)471-4818 *Fax:* (402)471-0117
E-Mail: bsibert@nde4.nde.state.ne.us
Members: 125 individuals
Annual Budget: under $10,000
President: Bonnie Sibert

Historical Note
Formerly (1981) Nat'l Ass'n of State Supervisors of Business and Office Education. NABESS members are state supervisors of business education programs. Membership: $15/year (individual).

Publications:
NABESS Directory. a.
NASBE Newsletter. 3/yr.

Meetings/Conferences:
Semi-Annual: Spring in conjunction with Nat'l Business Education Ass'n and Winter with the American Vocational Ass'n

Nat'l Ass'n of Surety Bond Producers (1942)
5225 Wisconsin Ave., N.W., Suite 600
Washington, DC 20015-2014
Tel: (202)686-3700 *Fax:* (202)686-3656
E-Mail: bjohnsm@nasbp.org
Members: 550 bond producers
Staff: 12
Annual Budget: $1-2,000,000
Director, Member Services & Meetings: Robert A. Johnson
Director, Education: Nancy C. Gober
Director, Finance: Koula K. Donohoe

Publications:
Pipeline. m.

Meetings/Conferences:
Annual Meetings: Spring/900
1999 – Vancouver, BC(Waterfront Centre & Pan Pacific)/May 23-26
2000 – Palm Beach, FL(Breakers)/April 9-12

Nat'l Ass'n of Swine Records (1954)
1769 U.S. Hwy. 52 West
P.O. 2417
West Lafayette, IN 47996-2417
Tel: (765)463-3593 *Fax:* (765)497-2959
Members: 8 companies and 8 associations
Staff: 2
Annual Budget: $100-250,000
Secretary/Treasurer: Mike Paul

Nat'l Ass'n of Tax Consultants (1970)
Historical Note
Address unknown in 1996.

Nat'l Ass'n of Tax Practitioners (1979)
720 Association Drive
Appleton, WI 54914-1483
Tel: (414)749-1040 *Fax:* (414)749-1062
Web Site: http://www.natptax.com
Members: 14,500 individuals
Staff: 34
Annual Budget: $2-5,000,000
Exec. Director: Alan S. Prahl
Dir., of Administration/Finance: Mary Jo Delfosse
Dir., Membership Services: Kathy Stanek

Historical Note
Membership is open to any individual, group or business interested in the betterment of those engaged in the practice of preparing federal or state tax returns. Provides a tax research center and over 200 tax workshops. Membership: $105/year (new member); $90/year (renewal).

Publications:
1040 Report Newsletter. m.
Annual Tax Software Survey.
NATP Tax Journal. q.
Who's Who in Tax Preparation (membership directory). a. adv.

Meetings/Conferences:
Annual Meetings: August
1999 – Reno, NV(Hilton)/July 13-17

Nat'l Ass'n of Tax Reducing Income Plans
562 Lynnhaven Pkwy.
Virginia Beach, VA 23452

Tel: (757)431-6447   *Fax:* (757)431-8396
President: John L. Ames, Jr.

Nat'l Ass'n of Teacher Educators for Business Education *(1970)*

Historical Note
Address unknown in 1998.

Nat'l Ass'n of Teacher Educators for Family and Consumer Sciences *(1949)*

Family/Consumer Sci., Tennessee State U.
3500 John A. Merritt Blvd.
Nashville, TN   37209-1561
Tel: (615)963-5617
Members: 150 individuals
Staff: 1
Annual Budget: under $10,000
President: Geraldine Johnson

Historical Note
Formerly (1995) Nat'l Ass'n of Teacher Educators for Vocational Home Economics. NATEFACS members are teacher educators in family and consumer sciences. Has no paid officers or full-time staff.

Publications:
Directory. a.
Journal of Family and Consumer Sciences Education. semi-a.

Meetings/Conferences:
Annual Meetings: December

Nat'l Ass'n of Teacher Educators for Vocational Home Economics

Historical Note
Became (1995) Nat'l Ass'n of Teacher Educators for Family and Consumer Sciences.

Nat'l Ass'n of Teachers of Singing *(1944)*

2800 University Blvd. North
Jacksonville, FL   32211
Tel: (904)744-9022   *Fax:* (904)744-9033
E-Mail: wmvessels@aol.com
Members: 5,300 individuals
Staff: 4
Annual Budget: $250-500,000
Exec. Director: William A. Vessels, Ph.D.

Historical Note
Teachers of singing and vocal instruction in private studios, conservatories, schools, colleges and community life. Membership: $65/year.

Publications:
Inter Nos Newsletter. 3/yr.
Journal of Singing. 5/y.

Meetings/Conferences:
Meetings every 2 years: July
2000 – Philadelphia, PA(Marriott)/600

Nat'l Ass'n of Teachers' Agencies *(1914)*

524 South Ave. East
Cranford, NJ   07016-3209
Tel: (908)272-2080   *Fax:* (908)272-2962
Web Site: jobsforteachers.com
Members: 22 agencies
Annual Budget: under $10,000
Treasurer/Secretary: Eugene Alexander

Historical Note
Members are private employment agencies concentrating on the placement of teachers and administrators serving public and private schools. Absorbed the Ass'n of Southern Teacher Agencies (1909). Membership: $225/year (organization).

Publications:
Membership List. a.
N. A.

Meetings/Conferences:
Annual meetings in Fall

Nat'l Ass'n of Telecommunications Officers and Advisers *(1980)*

1650 Tysons Blvd., Suite 200
McLean, VA   22102
Tel: (703)506-3275   *Fax:* (703)506-3266
Web Site: http://www.natoa.org
Members: 800 agencies and individuals
Staff: 2
Annual Budget: $500-1,000,000
Exec. Director: Lee Ruck
Manager Association Services: Stacy Stryjewski

Historical Note
NATOA is a professional organization serving citizens through city and county governments and regional authorities in the development, regulation, and administration of cable television and other telecommunication systems.

Publications:
NATOA News Quarterly. q.

Meetings/Conferences:

Nat'l Ass'n of Television Program Executives *(1963)*

2425 Olympic Blvd., Suite 550-E
Santa Monica, CA   90404-4030
Tel: (310)453-4440   *Fax:* (310)453-5258
Toll Free: (800)628 - 7346
Web Site: http://www.natpe.org
Members: 2,800 corporations
Staff: 23
President/C.E.O.: Bruce Johansen
Sr. V. President of Conferences and Special Events: Nick Orfanopoulos
V. President of Finance: Jon Dobkin
V.President, Finance: Jon Dobkin

Legal Counsel: Mickey Gardner
Manager, Members Services: Brigette Parise
Manager, Member Services: Brigette Parise
V. President of Creative Services: Beth Braen

Historical Note
NATPE is dedicated to furthering excellence in television programming around the world. NATPE represents executives involved in all sectors of the television industry. Sponsors and supports the NAPTE Educational Foundation. Membership: $475/year (organization/company/individual).

Publications:
NATPE Daily. a. adv.
NATPE Monthly Newsletter. m.
Pocket Reps, Groups, and Distributors Guide. semi-a.
Pocket Station Listing Guide. q. adv.
Programmers Guide. a. adv.

Meetings/Conferences:
Annual Meetings: Winter/8,000
1999 – New Orleans, LA(Morial Convention Center)/Jan. 25-28/20000
2000 – New Orleans, LA(Morial Convention Center)/Jan. 24-27/20000
2001 – Las Vegas, NV/Jan. 22-25/20000
2002 – Las Vegas, NV/Jan. 22-24/20000

Nat'l Ass'n of Temple Administrators *(1941)*

c/o Brock and Assocs.
6114 LaSalle Ave., Box 731
Oakland, CA   94611
Toll Free: (800)966 - 6282
Web Site: http://www.shamash.org/reform/nata
Members: 325 individuals
Annual Budget: $100-250,000
President: Fern M. Kamen

Historical Note
Members are synagogue executive directors in the Reform Jewish movement. Affiliated with the Union of American Hebrew Congregations. Established as the Nat'l Ass'n of Temple Secretaries, it assumed its present name in 1959. Has no paid officers or full-time staff.

Publications:
NATA Journal. q.
Temple Management Manual. irreg.

Meetings/Conferences:
1999 – Orlando, FL(Peabody Hotel)/Dec. 11-15
2000 – San Antonio, TX/Oct. 28-Nov. 1
2001 – Boston, MA/Dec. 1-5
2002 – Israel

Nat'l Ass'n of Temple Educators *(1955)*

10425 Old Olive St. Road, Suite 2
St. Louis, MO   63141-5940
Tel: (314)692-2224   *Fax:* (314)692-2225
E-Mail: nateoff@aol.com
Members: 950 individuals
Staff: 2
Annual Budget: $100-250,000
Exec. V. President: Lori Serbin Lasday

Historical Note
Affiliated with the Union of American Hebrew Congregations. Members are educational administrators associated with Reform Jewish movement in the United States, Canada, England, Israel, Australia and South Africa.

Publications:
NATE News. m.

Meetings/Conferences:
2000 – St. Louis, MO/100
2000 – Israel/June 26-July 9/200
2000 – San Francisco, CA/Dec. 24-27/200

Nat'l Ass'n of Temporary and Staffing Services *(1966)*

119 S. Saint Asaph St.
Alexandria, VA   22314
Tel: (703)549-6287   *Fax:* (703)549-4808
Toll Free: (800)315 - 3736
Web Site: http://www.natss.com/staffing/
Members: 1,640 companies
Staff: 21
Annual Budget: $2-5,000,000
Exec. V. President: Richard Wahlquist
Asst. VP of Publishing & Promotion: Louise Gates Seghers
V. President, Communications: Steve Birchim
Senior V. President, Public Affairs and General Counsel: Edward A. Lenz
Director, Membership: Suzy Brown, CMP
Associate V. President of Membership and Meetings: Kelly Verberg

Historical Note
Formerly (1971) Institute of Temporary Services and (1994) Nat'l Ass'n of Temporary Services. Members are companies providing the full range of staffing services, including temporary help, placement services, managed services and employee leasing to business and government. Sponsors and supports the National Association of Temporary Services Political Action Committee. Membership: $450/yr. (associate), $240-60,000/yr. (company).

Publications:
Contemporary Times Magazine. q.
Directory. a.
In Touch. bi-m.
Legislative Lookout. q.
P. R.
Souvenir Journal. a.

Meetings/Conferences:
Annual Meetings: Fall/850
1999 – Dallas, TX(Loew's Anatole)/Sept. 26-29
2000 – Las Vegas, NV(Mirage)/Oct. 15-18
2001 – New York, NY(Hilton)/Oct. 3-6

Nat'l Ass'n of Test Directors *(1985)*

549 North Stapely Dr.

Mesa, AZ   85203-7297
Tel: (602)472-0241   *Fax:* (602)890-7065
Web Site: http://www.NATO.org
Members: 250 individuals
Annual Budget: under $10,000
President: Mary Ellen Donahue

Historical Note
NATD members are individuals administering educational testing programs (primarily in the public schools). Has no paid officers or full-time staff. Membership: $20/year(individual).

Publications:
Membership List. a.
NATD Newsletter. q.
Symposia Papers. a.

Meetings/Conferences:
Annual Meetings: in conjunction with AERA & NCME
1999 – Montreal, Canada/Apr. 19-24

Nat'l Ass'n of Textile Supervisors *(1883)*

U. Mass./Dartmouth Textile Science Dept.
285 Old Westport Road
North Dartmouth, MA   02747-2300
Tel: (508)999-8453   *Fax:* (508)999-9139
Members: 150 individuals
Annual Budget: under $10,000
Secretary: Alton R. Wilson

Historical Note
Formerly (1976) the Nat'l Ass'n of Woolen and Worsted Overseers. Members are superintendents, designers, production personnel and allied trade personnel in the textiles industry. Membership: $20/year (individual).

Publications:
NATS Yearbook. a. adv.

Meetings/Conferences:
Semi-annual Meetings: May and November

Nat'l Ass'n of the Remodeling Industry *(1982)*

4900 Seminary Road, Suite 320
Alexandria, VA   22311-1811
Tel: (703)575-1100   *Fax:* (703)575-1121
Web Site: http://www.nari.org
Members: 5,900 companies and 75 chapters
Staff: 22
Annual Budget: $2-5,000,000
Exec. V. President: Randall W. Scott, CAE, CMP
Public Affairs Director: Patti Burgio
Director, Conventions: Tracy Purcell, CMP
Asst. Director, Meetings: Karen Dunham
Director, Education: Suzanne Clements
Controller: Jeffrey Olszweski
General Counsel: Sherman Pogrund
Asst. Director, Publications: Brett Martin

Historical Note
Manufacturers of building products, remodeling contractors, lending institutions and other firms in the home improvement industry. The result of a merger (1982) between the Nat'l Remodelers Ass'n and the Nat'l Home Improvement Council. Membership: $125/year, plus local chapter dues, when within 50-mile radius.

Publications:
Remodeler's Journal. 9/year. adv.

Meetings/Conferences:
Annual Meetings: March/12,000
1999 – Atlantic City, NJ
2000 – Atlantic City, NY(Convention Center)
2001 – Chicago, IL(McCormick Place)

Nat'l Ass'n of Theatre Owners *(1920)*

4605 Lankershim Blvd., Suite 340
North Hollywood, CA   91602-1891
Tel: (818)506-1778   *Fax:* (818)506-0269
Members: 19,000 screens
Staff: 8
Exec. Director and Vice President: Mary Ann Grasso

Historical Note
Theatre Owners of America (1966). Merged with Allied Theatre Owners of America.

Publications:
Encyclopedia of Exhibition. a. adv.
NATO News. m.

Meetings/Conferences:
Semi-Annual Meetings: Fall(West Coast) and Spring(East Coast)

Nat'l Ass'n of Ticket Brokers *(1994)*

One E. Wacker Dr.
Chicago, IL   60614
Tel: (312)923-8500   *Fax:* (312)923-8509
Members: 140 companies
Staff: 2
Annual Budget: $100-250,000
Management Exec.: Peter Schwartz

Historical Note
NATB represents businesses engaged in the reselling of tickets to entertainment and sporting events. Members must have a permanent business location and abide by the NATB code of ethics. Membership: $750-2,500/year.

Publications:
Newsletter. q.

Meetings/Conferences:

Nat'l Ass'n of Towns and Townships *(1963)*

444 North Capitol St., N.W., Suite 208
Washington, DC   20001
Tel: (202)624-3550   *Fax:* (202)624-3554
Members: 13,000 local governments
Staff: 4
Annual Budget: $500-1,000,000

Exec. Director: Tom Halicki

Historical Note
Established as the Nat'l Ass'n of Town and Township Officials. Assumed its present name and opened a Washington office in 1977. NATaT is a non-profit membership organization offering technical assistance, educational services and public policy support to local government officials from 13,000 small communities across the U.S. Absorbed the Nat'l Ass'n of Smaller Communities in 1983; created the Nat'l Center for Small Communities in 1984. Membership: $100(individual), $250 (organization).

Publications:
NATaT's Washington Report. bi-m.
Small Community Quarterly. q. adv.

Meetings/Conferences:
Annual Meetings: Washington, DC(Hyatt
        Regency)/September/800
1999 – Washington, DC(Hyatt-Capitol Hill)

Nat'l Ass'n of Trade and Industrial Instructors *(1969)*

Historical Note
Became the American Ass'n of Trade and Industrial Instructors in 1996.

Nat'l Ass'n of Traffic Accident Reconstructionists and Investigators *(1984)*
P.O. Box 361
Jamison, PA   18929-0361
Tel: (215)672-4784
Members: 200 individuals
Annual Budget: $25-50,000
President: Charles Sulzbach

Historical Note
Established to foster the exchange of information between professionals involved in motor vehicle traffic collision analysis. Membership: $50/year.

Publications:
Accident Investigation Formula Book. irreg.
NATARI Newsletter. q. adv.

Meetings/Conferences:
Annual Meetings: October

Nat'l Ass'n of Trailer Manufacturers *(1988)*
2945 S.W. Wanamaker Dr., Suite A
Topeka, KS   66614-5321
Tel: (785)271-0208   *Fax:* (785)271-0166
E-Mail: natm@natm.com
Web Site: http://208.161.58.11
Members: 93 individuals, 136 companies
Staff: 2
Annual Budget: $50-100,000
Exec. Director: William J. Birch

Historical Note
Formerly (1992) Nat'l Ass'n of Livestock Trailer Manufacturers. Membership: $400/year.

Publications:
Membership Directory and Buyer's Guide. a. adv.
Recommended Minimun Mft. Guidelines for Trai.
Tracks. bi-m. adv.

Meetings/Conferences:
1999 – Dallas, TX
2000 – Nashville, TN

Nat'l Ass'n of Tribal Court Personnel *(1980)*
P.O. Box 221
Jicarilla Apache Tribal Court
Dulce, NM   87528
Tel: (505)759-3366   *Fax:* (505)759-3721
Members: 257 individuals
Staff: 2
Annual Budget: $10-25,000
President: Robert Miller

Historical Note
Formerly(1998) Nat'l American Indian Court Clerks Ass'n. A national professional association dedicated to improving the American Indian court system throughout the U.S. through research, professional advancement and continuing education. Has no paid staff.

Nat'l Ass'n of Tutoring

Historical Note
Became the Nat'l Tutoring Ass'n in 1995.

Nat'l Ass'n of Unclaimed Property Administrators *(1962)*
P.O. Box 7156
Bismarck, ND   58507-7156
Tel: (701)258-8667   *Fax:* (701)221-9151
Members: 51 states and D.C.
Staff: 1
Annual Budget: $100-250,000
Exec. Director: Valerie Jundt

Historical Note
NAUPA members are state officials who administer escheat and unclaimed property programs. Facilitates transfer of unclaimed properties to their appropriate jurisdictions. Formerly (1980) the Ass'n of Unclaimed Property Administrators. Membership: $200/year.

Publications:
NAUPA News Newsletter. q.
Quick Reference Packet. a.

Meetings/Conferences:
Annual Meetings: Fall
1999 – Des Moines, IA/Aug. 29-Sept. 2

Nat'l Ass'n of Underwater Instructors *(1960)*
9942 Currie Davis Dr., Suite H
Tampa, FL   33619-2667
Tel: (813)628-6284   *Fax:* (813)628-8253

Toll Free: (800)553 - 6284
Web Site: http://www.naui.org/
Members: 10,500 individuals
Staff: 30
Annual Budget: $2-5,000,000
President: Jim Bram

Historical Note
Certified instructors of basic, advanced, and specialized courses in underwater diving. Offers instructor certification programs and training programs. Affiliated with the Nat'l Safety Council, Nat'l Boating Council, American Red Cross and Underwater Soc. of America. Membership: $120/year (individual).

Publications:
Sources: The Journal of Underwater Education. q. adv.

Meetings/Conferences:
Semi-annual Meetings: Spring and Fall

Nat'l Ass'n of Uniform Manufacturers and Distributors *(1932)*
1156 Ave. of the Americas, Suite 700
New York, NY   10036
Tel: (212)869-0670   *Fax:* (212)575-2847
Web Site: http://www.naumid.com
Members: 475 companies
Staff: 4
Annual Budget: $250-500,000
Exec. Director: Bernard J. Lepper

Historical Note
Membership: $350-2,650/year (organization, depending on size).

Publications:
NAUMD News. m.

Meetings/Conferences:
Annual Meetings: February
1999 – San Diego, CA(Sheraton)/Feb. 26-March 3

Nat'l Ass'n of University Fisheries and Wildlife Programs
Dept. of Wildlife & Fisheries Sciences
South Dakota State Univ. Box 2140B
Brookings, SD   57007-1696
Tel: (605)688-6121
Toll Free: (605)688 - 4515
Members: 55 university programs
Annual Budget: $25-50,000
President: Charles G. Scalet, Ph.D.

Historical Note
NAUFWP members are administrators of fisheries and wildlife programs in colleges/universities. NAUFWP aims to strengthen fisheries and wildlife education, research, public service and outreach, and international programs at the university level. Has no paid officers or full-time staff. Membershp: $500/year.

Meetings/Conferences:
Semi-Annual Meetings: Spring and Fall

Nat'l Ass'n of Urban Bankers *(1975)*
1801 K St., N.W., Suite 200-A
Washington, DC   20006-1301
Tel: (202)861-0000   *Fax:* (202)861-1252
E-Mail: naub340@aol.com
Members: 3,000 individuals, 50 chapters
Staff: 2
Annual Budget: $100-250,000
Exec. Director: Karen M. Bose

Historical Note
Members, primarily from large institutions in major metropolitan areas, are minority professionals in the banking industry and related fields. Membership: annual dues vary by chapter (individual); $5,000-10,000/year, varies by assets (corporate).

Publications:
Monthly News from National. m.
NAUB Conference Journal. a.
The Urban Banker Newsletter. q.

Meetings/Conferences:
Annual Meetings: June

Nat'l Ass'n of Urban Critical Access Hospitals
1212 New York Ave., N.W., Suite 310
Washington, DC   20005
Tel: (202)371-0916   *Fax:* (202)898-0458
Exec. Director: Charles L. DeBrunner
Assoc. Director: Ellen Finkelstein Kugler

Nat'l Ass'n of Used Fitness and Rehabilitation Equipment Dealers *(1993)*
P.O. Box361
Gillette, NJ   07933
Tel: (908)604-0799   *Fax:* (908)756-2788
Members: 75 individuals
Staff: 2
Annual Budget: under $10,000
Exec. Director: Michael Zarrillo

Historical Note
Members are independent retailers of used fitness and rehabilitation equipment. Membership: $125/year (individual); $500/year (corporate).

Publications:
Fitness & Rehab Trader Newsletter. bi-m.

Nat'l Ass'n of VA Physicians and Dentists *(1975)*
1414 Prince St., Suite 202
Alexandria, VA   22314
Tel: (703)548-0280   *Fax:* (703)548-8024
E-Mail: navapd@dgsys.com
Web Site: http://www.navapd.org
Members: 2,000 individuals
Annual Budget: $250-500,000
President: Robert M. Conroy, M.D.
Director, Policy and Legislation: Margaret B. Ingraham

Historical Note
Membership: $150/year.

Publications:
NAVAPD News. bi-m. adv.
NAVAPD Notes. bi-m.

Meetings/Conferences:
Annual Meetings: May

Nat'l Ass'n of Vertical Transportation Professionals *(1990)*
1713-19 Ralph Ave.
Brooklyn, NY   11236-3538
Members: 60 individuals
Annual Budget: $10-25,000
Exec. Director: Hubert H. Hayes, Jr.

Historical Note
NAVTP members are engineers and other professionals specializing in elevator and escalator design. Membership: $150/year.

Publications:
Newsletter. a.

Meetings/Conferences:

Nat'l Ass'n of Veterans Program Administrators *(1975)*
2020 Pennsylvania Ave., NW
Washington, DC   20006
Tel: (509)335-1649   *Fax:* (509)335-7823
Web Site: www.va.ucf.edu/navpa/
Members: 500 individuals, 550 universities and colleges
Annual Budget: $25-50,000
President: David Guzman
Secretary, Exec. Board: Kathy Borelli
V. President, Exec. Board: John Vickroy
Conference Chair: Faith Stellitano
Treasurer, Exec. Board: Patrick Sutlitt
Director of Membership: Jack Mordente
Chair, Membership: Giacomo Mordente
Chair, Technology/DIS: Scott Shorr

Historical Note
Members are coordinators of veterans programs on college campuses. Concerned with administering and preserving the educational benefits promised by the military to service persons upon their enlistment. Membership: $30/year (individual and associate) $50/year (organization).

Publications:
NAVPA Newsletter. Semi-a.

Meetings/Conferences:
Annual Meetings: Last week in October/250
1999 – Nashville, TN
2000 – Washington, DC

Nat'l Ass'n of Veterans' Research and Education Foundations *(1992)*
5018 Sangamore Rd., Suite 300
Bethesda, MD   20816
Tel: (301)229-1048   *Fax:* (301)229-0442
Members: 85 organizations
Staff: 1
Annual Budget: $100-250,000
Exec. Director: Barbara F. West

Historical Note
NAVREF is the national association representing nonprofit research foundations conducting programs under the U.S. Department of Veterans Affairs (DVA). Membership: 0.5% of annual revenues (organization).

Publications:
NAVREF Newsletter. q. adv.

Meetings/Conferences:
1999 – Washignton, DC

Nat'l Ass'n of Video Distributors *(1981)*
700 Frederica St., Suite 205
Owensboro, KY   42301
Tel: (502)926-6002   *Fax:* (502)685-6080
Members: 35 companies
Staff: 2
Annual Budget: $500-1,000,000
Exec. Director: Bill Burton

Historical Note
Members are wholesale distributors of home video software; associate members are manufacturers of such goods.

Meetings/Conferences:
Annual Meetings: April-May/300

Nat'l Ass'n of Vision Professionals *(1976)*
1775 Church St., N.W.
Washington, DC   20036
Tel: (202)234-1010   *Fax:* (202)234-1020
E-Mail: prvblind@erols.com
Members: 200 individuals
Staff: 1
Annual Budget: $25-50,000
Exec. Officer: Dr. Arnold Simonse

Historical Note
Formerly (1985) Nat'l Ass'n of Vision Program Consultants. Professionals in the field of eye health and safety. Has no paid staff. Membership: $25/year.

Publications:
Newsletter. q.

Meetings/Conferences:
Annual Meetings: August
1999 – New Orleans, LA

Nat'l Ass'n of Vocational Education Special Needs Personnel *(1973)*
Special Vocational Services
101 Ostermayer, Penn State
McKeesport, PA   15132-7698

Tel: (412)675-9065   Fax: (412)675-9067
Members: 2,200 individuals
Annual Budget: $25-50,000
Exec. Officer: Eleanor Bicanich

Historical Note
NAVESNP serves personnel interested in or responsible for the development or operation of programs for learners with special vocational education needs in the U.S.

Publications:
Journal for Vocational Special Needs Education. 3/yr.
Newsnotes Newsletter. q.
Vocational Special Needs Teacher Education Directory. bien.

Meetings/Conferences:

Nat'l Ass'n of Vocational-Technical Education Communicators (1974)
1500 West 7th Street
Stillwater, OK 74074
Tel: (405)743-5108   Fax: (405)743-5541
Members: 200 individuals
Annual Budget: under $10,000
Contact: Ronald Wilkerson

Historical Note
Membership: $25/year (individual).

Publications:
NAVTEC Communicator. 3/year.

Meetings/Conferences:

Nat'l Ass'n of Waste Transporters (1983)
26 East Exchange St., Fifth Floor
St. Paul, MN 55101
Tel: (651)265-7846   Fax: (651)290-2266
Toll Free: (800)236 - 6298
Members: 3,000 individuals
Staff: 3
Annual Budget: $50-100,000
Contact: David Ewald

Historical Note
Membership: $100/year (individual); $500/year (organization/company).

Publications:
NAWT News. m. adv.

Meetings/Conferences:
Annual Meetings: Winter

Nat'l Ass'n of Water Companies (1895)
1725 K St., N.W., Suite 1212
Washington, DC 20006
Tel: (202)833-8383   Fax: (202)331-7442
Members: 332 companies
Staff: 10
Annual Budget: $1-2,000,000
Exec. Director: Peter L. Cook
Dep. Exec. Director, Federal Relations: Robert J. Lewis
Director, Federal Relations: Louis J. Jenny
Dep. Exec. Director, state Relations & Administration: Sharon L. Gascon
Administrative Manager: Betty Jean Lewis
Finance Manager: Bonnie Hayden
Director, Administration and Membership: Michael J. Horner

Historical Note
Established July 30, 1895 at a meeting in Cresson Springs, Pennsylvania, as the Pennsylvania Water Works Ass'n. Became the Eastern Water Company Conference in 1959, and in 1963 the Nat'l Water Company Conference. Adopted its present name in 1971. Sponsors the Nat'l Ass'n of Water Companies Political Action Committee (NAWC/PAC). Membership: dues vary by company GWR; $200/year (associate).

Publications:
Newsflow Water Magazine. q.

Meetings/Conferences:
Annual Meetings: October
1999 – Charleston, SC(The Omni Hotel at Charleston Place)/Oct. 17-21
2000 – Boston, MA(The Westin Hotel)/Sept. 24-28
2001 – Palm Springs, CA(La Quinta Resort & Club)/Oct. 7-11

Nat'l Ass'n of Waterfront Employers (1933)
2011 Pennsylvania Ave., N.W., Suite 301
Washington, DC 20006
Tel: (202)296-2810   Fax: (202)331-7479
Members: 32 companies
Staff: 3
Annual Budget: $250-500,000
Exec. Director/General Counsel: Charles T. Carroll, Jr.
Meeting Manager: Elaine Tendler

Historical Note
Formerly (1993) Nat'l Ass'n of Stevedores. Privately owned stevedore contractors, marine terminal operators, and other waterfront-activity employers.

Publications:
NAS Bulletins. as needed.
NAS Legal Report. q.
NAS Legislative Update. m.
NAS Newsletter. m.

Meetings/Conferences:

Nat'l Ass'n of Waterproofing Contractors
25550 Shagrin
Suite 403
Cleveland, OH 44122
Tel: (216)464-2484   Fax: (216)595-8230
Toll Free: (800)245 - 6292
Web Site: www.apk.net.nawc
Members: 150 contractors
Staff: 2
Annual Budget: $25-50,000
Exec. Director: Avery H. Fromet

Historical Note
NAWC was established to promote ethical business standards and to improve communication in the waterproofing industry. Membership $350/yr.(organization or company)

Publications:
NAWC Foundation News.

Meetings/Conferences:
Annual Meetings: Fall
1999 – Las Vegas, NV

Nat'l Ass'n of Wheat Growers (1950)
415 Second Street, N.E., Suite 300
Washington, DC 20002
Tel: (202)547-7800   Fax: (202)546-2638
E-Mail: nawg1@aol.com
Web Site: www.wheatworld.org
Members: 28,000 individuals
Staff: 8
Annual Budget: $1-2,000,000
C.E.O.: Jack E. Eberspacher
Director, Communications: Gina Hoback
V. President, Government Affairs: Jim Miller
Director of Meetings: Annie Leftwood
Fiscal Administrator: Kevin Kezer

Historical Note
A non-profit federation of state wheat organizations. Sponsors and supports the Nat'l Ass'n of Wheat Growers Foundation and the NAWG Political Action Committee (Wheat-PAC). Membership: $50/year (individual), $2,000/year (company).

Publications:
Report from Washington. w.

Meetings/Conferences:
Annual Meetings: January
1999 – Nashville, TN(Convention Center)/Feb. 3-6
2000 – Las Vegas, NV

Nat'l Ass'n of Wholesale Independent Distributors (1961)

Historical Note
Formerly the Nat'l Ass'n of Writing Instrument Dealers (1991). Merged with the Wholesale Stationers Ass'n to form the Office Products Wholesalers Ass'n in 1995.

Nat'l Ass'n of Wholesaler-Distributors (1946)
1725 K St., N.W., 3rd Floor
Washington, DC 20006
Tel: (202)872-0885   Fax: (202)785-0586
Staff: 40
Annual Budget: $5-10,000,000
President: Dirk Van Dongen
Chief Information Officer: Ed Jones
V. President, Strategic Directions and Communications: Ron Schreibman, CAE
Sr. V. President, Government Relations: Alan Kranowitz
Director, Meetings: Laura Howard
Senior Dir. Publications: Rick Ludwick
Director, Information Systems: Patrick Burns

Historical Note
Established as the Nat'l Ass'n of Wholesalers by a group of leading wholesaler-distributor trade associations that specialized in a particular product such as auto parts, drugs, lumber, food, or tobacco. Assumed its present name in 1970. A federation of national, state and local wholesaler associations, together with individual wholesalers. Supports the Wholesaler-Distributor Political Action Committe (WDPAC). Maintains the Distribution Research and Education Foundation and the NAW Service Corporation. Has an annual budget of approximately $6.0 million

Publications:
NAW Report. 8/year.

Meetings/Conferences:
Annual Meetings: Winter
1999 – Washington, DC/Feb. 1-3

Nat'l Ass'n of WIC Directors
2001 S St., N.W., Suite 580
Washington, DC 20009-3405
Tel: (202)232-5492   Fax: (202)387-5281
Web Site: www.wicdirectors.org
Members: 1,500 individuals
Staff: 6
Annual Budget: $500-1,000,000
Exec. Director: Douglas A. Greenaway
Communications & Marketing Director: Doug Gunster
Legislative Assistant: Ella McDowell
Adminstrative Assistant: Malina Anderson
Director, Membership and Special Events: Jessica Beach
Director, Nutrition Programs: Cecilia Richardson, MS, RD, LD

Historical Note
NAWD members are state and local agency directors and nutrition coordinators of the Special Supplemental Nutrition Program for Women, Infants and Children.

Publications:
Legislative Alert.
Monday Morning Report. w.
NAWD Focus. q.
Nutrition Link. m.
Washington Update.

Meetings/Conferences:
1999 – New Orleans, LA

Nat'l Ass'n of Women Artists (1889)
41 Union Square W., Room 906
New York, NY 10003
Tel: (212)675-1616   Fax: (212)675-1616
E-Mail: NAWOMENA@MSN.COM
Members: 750 individuals
Staff: 1
Annual Budget: $10-25,000
Exec. Secretary: Ann Hermanson Chennault

Historical Note
Established in 1889 as the Women's Art Club of the City of New York. NAWA is a non-profit, non-political member-supported art association for women in the fine arts. Its purpose is to serve as a forum for members by seeking exhibition space and creating opportunities for its painters, printmakers and sculptors. Provides free cultural/educational programs to the public. Holds an annual exhibition of members' works in New York City in Spring. Sponsors group traveling art shows of works by members, shown both in the U.S. and abroad. Membership: $45/year (individual).

Publications:
Exhibition Catalog. a. adv.
Newsletter. 2/year.

Meetings/Conferences:
Semi-annual Meetings: May and November/75

Nat'l Ass'n of Women Business Owners (1974)
1100 Wayne Ave., Suite 830
Silver Spring, MD 20910
Tel: (301)608-2590   Fax: (301)608-2596
E-Mail: NAWBOHQ@aol.com
Web Site: http://www.nawbo.org
Members: 7,000 individuals
Staff: 2
Annual Budget: $250-500,000
Director, Operations: Debbie Hickerson
Communications/P.R. Manager: Bruce G. Rosenthal

Historical Note
Established in Washington D.C. as the Ass'n of Women Business Owners, NAWBO assumed its present name in 1976 and exists to provide education and training to its members, promote business ownership by women and serve as a forum through which women can establish themselves in the business world. An affiliate, Nat'l Foundation for Women Business Owners (same address), provides research, consulting, and leadership development programs. Membership: $75/year, plus chapter dues.

Publications:
NAWBO Time. m.

Meetings/Conferences:
Annual Meetings: Summer/300

Nat'l Ass'n of Women Highway Safety Leaders (1967)
7206 Robin Hood Drive
Upper Marlboro, MD 20772
Tel: (301)868-7583   Fax: (301)868-1829
Members: 100,000 individuals
Staff: 2
Annual Budget: $100-250,000
Exec. Director: Agnes Beaton

Historical Note
Promotes safety belt usage, alcohol and drug education, child passenger seats, car care, gasoline saving tips, motorcycle safety, police enforcement, highway environment, traffic court improvement, mature driver safety, and high school driver education.

Publications:
National News. q.
NAWHSL Newsletter. q.
News from NAWHSL. q.
Presient's Newsletter. q.
Regional Director's Newsletter. m.
Serving Safety. q.
State Representatives Newsletter. irreg.

Meetings/Conferences:
1999 – San Antonio, TXAugust /250

Nat'l Ass'n of Women in Chambers of Commerce (1985)

Historical Note
Organization defunct in 1997.

Nat'l Ass'n of Women in Construction (1955)
327 South Adams St.
Fort Worth, TX 76104-1002
Tel: (817)877-5551   Fax: (817)877-0324
Toll Free: (800)552 - 3506
E-Mail: nawic@onramp.net
Web Site: http://www.nawic.org
Members: 6,200 individuals, 200 chapters
Staff: 6
Annual Budget: $500-1,000,000
Exec. V. President: Delia A. Hughes
Director, PR/Communications: Rachel Fox
Director, Conventions and Expos: Shelly Reeves
Membership Director: Lisa Simonds

Historical Note
NAWIC members hold diverse positions within the construction industry including architects, owners, estimators, accountants and tradeswomen. Members encourage continuing education within the industry and for students to promote interest. Membership: $90 (national dues plus additional chapter dues).

Publications:
NAWIC Image. bi-m. adv.

Meetings/Conferences:
Annual Meetings: September
1999 – Anaheim, CA(Hilton)/Sept. 1-4
2000 – Salt Lake City, UT(Little America)/Aug. 30-Sept. 2
2001 – Anchorage, AK(Hilton)/Sept. 26-29

Nat'l Ass'n of Women Judges (1979)
815 15th St., N.W., Suite 601
Washington, DC 20005
Tel: (202)393-0222   Fax: (202)393-0125
Members: 1 individuals
Staff: 3
Annual Budget: $250-500,000
Exec. Director: Darlene Averick

Historical Note
Organized in Los Angeles, October 28, 1979. Membership: $100/year.

Publications:
NAWJ Counterbalance. 3/year.

Meetings/Conferences:
Annual Meetings: October/250
1999 – Miami, FL/Oct. 13-17

Nat'l Ass'n of Women Lawyers (1899)
750 N. Lake Shore Drive
Chicago, IL 60611
Tel: (312)988-6186   Fax: (312)988-6281
Staff: 1
Exec. Director: Peggy L. Golden

Historical Note
Founded in 1899 as the Women Lawyers Club. Re-organized in 1911 as the Nat'l Ass'n of Women Lawyers. Membership: $35-80/year (individual); $20/year (student).

Publications:
President's Newsletter. q.
Women Lawyers Journal. q. adv.

Meetings/Conferences:
Semi-Annual Meetings: February and August, with American Bar Ass'n

Nat'l Ass'n of Women's Health Professionals (1987)
Historical Note
Became Nat'l Ass'n of Professionals in Women's Health in 1997.

Nat'l Ass'n of Workforce Development Professionals (1989)
1620 I St., N.W., Suite LL-30
Washington, DC 20006-4005
Tel: (202)887-6120   Fax: (202)887-8216
E-Mail: nawdp@aol.com
Web Site: http://www.nawdp.org
Members: 1,800 individuals
Staff: 2
Annual Budget: $250-500,000
Exec. Director: C. Paul Mendez
Director, Member Services: Vernetta Lindsey

Historical Note
NAWDP is an nat'l ass'n for individual practitioners who work in workforce development programs. It's mission is to be the national voice for the profession and meet the individual professional development needs of it's membership. Membership: $50/year (individual).

Publications:
NAWDP Advantage. m. adv.

Meetings/Conferences:
Annual Meetings: Spring

Nat'l Ass'n of Youth Clubs (1930)
5808 16th St., N.W.
Washington, DC 20011
Tel: (202)726-2044   Fax: (202)726-0023
Members: 250 clubs
Staff: 2
Annual Budget: $10-25,000
Exec. Secretary: Carole A. Early

Historical Note
Formerly (1992) Nat'l Ass'n of Girls Clubs. Membership consists of African Americans aged 6-18. Sponsored by the National Association of Colored Women's Clubs. Aims are to begin training toward moral, mental and material development of its members and to give girls the right conceptions of health, beauty, love, home and service. Formerly (1976) National Association of Colored Girls Clubs.

Meetings/Conferences:
Biennial Meetings: Even years in July with the Nat'l Ass'n of Colored Women's Clubs.
2000 – /July 25-Aug 3

Nat'l Assembly of Local Arts Agencies (1978)
Historical Note
Merged with American Council for the Arts in 1996 to form Americans for the Arts.

Nat'l Assembly of Nat'l Voluntary Health and Social Welfare Organizations (1923)
1319 F St., N.W., Suite 601
Washington, DC 20004
Tel: (202)347-2080   Fax: (202)393-4517
E-Mail: nassembly@nassembly.org
Web Site: http://www.nassembly.org
Members: 52 organizations
Staff: 7
Annual Budget: $250-500,000
President and C.E.O.: Gordon A. Raley

Historical Note
Established as the Nat'l Social Work Council, it became the Nat'l Social Welfare Assembly in 1945, the Nat'l Assembly for Social Policy and Development in 1967 and assumed its present name in 1974. Advances the effectiveness of each member and provides collective leadership in the areas of health and human services. As members face organizational challenges, the Nat'l Assembly provides a forum for them to focus on both operational and policy issues and work toward mutual goals.

Publications:
Assembly Line. semi-a.

Meetings/Conferences:

Nat'l Assembly of State Arts Agencies (1974)
1029 Vermont Ave., N.W., Second Floor
Washington, DC 20005-4902
Tel: (202)347-6352   Fax: (202)737-0526
Web Site: http://www.nasaa.arts.org

Members: 54 agencies
Staff: 12
Annual Budget: $500-1,000,000
C.E.O.: Jonathan Katz
Manager, Communications: Kimber Craine
Program Associate: Beth Rather
Managing Director: Dennis Dewey
Director, Member Services: Johanna Boyer

Historical Note
Founded June 1968 as the North American Assembly of State and Provincial Arts Agencies and affiliated with the Associated Councils of the Arts. The organization became independent and assumed its present name in 1976. Members are state agencies receiving appropriations from their states and designated by federal legislation to receive funding from the National Endowment for the Arts.

Publications:
Legislative Appropriations Survey. a.
Legislative Resource Manual. a.
NASAA Membership Directory. m.

Meetings/Conferences:
Annual Meetings: Fall/500
1999 – Louisville, KY

Nat'l Assisted Housing Management Ass'n
Historical Note
Name changed to Nat'l Affordable Housing Management Ass'n in 1996.

Nat'l Athletic Trainers' Ass'n (1950)
2952 North Stemmons Freeway, Suite 200
Dallas, TX 75247-6916
Tel: (214)637-6282   Fax: (214)637-2206
Web Site: http://www.nata.org
Members: 23,000 individuals
Staff: 30
Annual Budget: $2-5,000,000
Exec. Director: Eve Becker-Doyle, CAE
Director, Marketing: Teresa Foster Welch
Director, Government Relations: Laura Jetton
Manager of Government Relations: Rich Rogers
Director, Meeting Management: Lewayne Putman
Director, Accounting: Linda Tilley
Dir., Membership/MIS: Sandy Ward

Historical Note
NATA members are athletic trainers working in high schools, colleges, clinics, industry, hospitals and professional sports teams. Membership is also open to those individuals whose interests are related to sports medicine, such as doctors, and to corporations and businesses that sell or manufacture sports medicine products. Membership: $110/year, plus district; $60/year (student).

Publications:
Journal of Athletic Training. q. adv.
NATA News. m. adv.

Meetings/Conferences:
Annual Meetings: During last two weeks in June
1999 – Kansas City, MO/June 16-19/6000
2000 – Nashville, TN/June 29-July 2/6000
2001 – Los Angeles, CA/June 20-23/6000

Nat'l Auctioneers Ass'n (1949)
8880 Ballentine St.
Overland Park, KS 66214-1985
Tel: (913)541-8084   Fax: (913)894-5281
E-Mail: NAAHQ@aol.com
Web Site: http://www.auctioneers.org
Members: 5,600 individuals
Staff: 7
Annual Budget: $500-1,000,000
Exec. V. President: Joseph G. Keefhaver
Director of Publications: Holly Neuman
Director, Membership: Tammy Bolline

Historical Note
Membership: $100/year.

Publications:
The Auctioneer. m. adv.

Meetings/Conferences:
Annual Meetings: July
1999 – Grand Rapids, MI(Amway Grand Plaza)/July 20-24/1100
2000 – Norfolk, VA(Marriott/Sheraton)/July 18-22/1100
2001 – Boise, ID(Grove Hotel/Boise Center)/July 17-21/1100
2002 – Orlando, FL(Walt Disney Village)/July 16-20/1100

Nat'l Auto Auction Ass'n (1945)
5320-D Spectrum Dr.
Frederick, MD 21703
Tel: (301)696-0400   Fax: (301)631-1359
E-Mail: naaa@earthlink.net
Web Site: http://www.naaa.com
Members: 274 companies
Staff: 5
Annual Budget: $1-2,000,000
Exec. Director: Peter Lukasiak
Manager, Membership Services & Meetings: Erin Betz
Controller: Janis R. Bunch

Historical Note
NAAA represents dealers wholesale auto auctions, held in a permanent location on a regular weekly schedule. Promotes exchange of ideas and works in public relations in the used car merchandising industry. Members are from nine countries and handle approximately 15 million vehicles per year. Membership: $700-1,700/year (organization/company).

Publications:
Membership Directory. a.
On the Block. q.

Meetings/Conferences:
Annual Meetings: September/October
1999 – Chicago, IL/Sept. 1-5

Nat'l Automated Clearing House Ass'n (1974)
607 Herndon Parkway, Suite 200
Herndon, VA 20171
Tel: (703)742-9190   Fax: (703)787-0996
Web Site: http://www.nacha.org
Members: 14,000 financial inst. & 30 ass'ns
Staff: 48
Annual Budget: $5-10,000,000
President and C.E.O.: Elliott C. McEntee
Dir., Public Relations: Michael Herd
Senior Director, Gov't Relations: Ian Macoy
Sr. Director, Conference and Meetings: Thom Bliss
Senior Director, Network Services: Deborah Shaw, AAP
Exec. V. President: William B. Nelson
Director, Administration: Kerry Weathington
Senior Director, Network Products: Scott Lang
Sr. Director, Electronic Benefits Transfer: Helena Sims
General Counsel: Jane Larimer

Historical Note
NACHA is a trade association that forms the cooperative foundation for the automated clearing house (ACH) payments system through a network of 35 ACH associations nationwide. NACHA is responsible for establishing the rules for the exchange of ACH transactions between financial institutions. It also provides marketing and educational support to the banking industry.

Publications:
Affiliate Forum. 3/year.
NACHA Operating Rules & Guidelines. a.
Payments System Report. m. adv.

Meetings/Conferences:
Annual Meetings: Spring/1,000
1999 – Atlanta, GA(Atlanta Marriott Marquis)/April 11-14
2000 – Los Angeles, CA(Century Plaza Hotel)/April 9-12

Nat'l Automatic Merchandising Ass'n (1936)
20 North Wacker Drive, Suite 3500
Chicago, IL 60606-3102
Tel: (312)346-0370   Fax: (312)704-4140
Web Site: http://www.vending.org
Members: 2,500 companies
Staff: 25
Annual Budget: $2-5,000,000
President & C.E.O.: Richard M. Geerdes
Director, Government Affairs: Brian B. Allan
Director, Meeting Services: Lynae Schleyer
Director, Finance: Patrick Caffarelli
Director, Trade Shows: Stuart Aizenberg
Director, Health, Safety and Technical Standards: Larry M. Eils
Midwest Manager & Counsel: William F. Hurley

Historical Note
Members are makers and operators of automatic vending equipment, contract food service management, and office coffee service industry in collaboration with the providers of products and services to the vending industry. Programs in health, safety and standards, public relations, employee relations and training, education, accounting, and statistics comprise some of NAMA's other services. Sponsors and supports the NAMA Political Action Committee.

Publications:
Directory of Members. a.
In Touch Newsletter. bi-m.
Quarterly Labor Relations Report. q.

Meetings/Conferences:
Semi-annual meetings: Spring and Fall
1999 – Anaheim, CA(Convention Center)/April 15-17/4800

Nat'l Automobile Transporters Ass'n (1934)
535 Griswold, 902 Buhl Bldg.
Detroit, MI 48226
Tel: (313)965-6533   Fax: (313)965-6950
Members: 75 companies
Staff: 3
Annual Budget: $250-500,000
President: Robert P. Farrell

Historical Note
Affiliate of American Trucking Ass'ns, Inc. Members transport motor vehicles from assembly plants, railheads and seaports to dealers in U.S.A. and Canada by both "truckaway" and "driveaway".

Publications:
Membership Directory. a.
Newsletter. bi-w.

Meetings/Conferences:
Annual Meetings: Always in Detroit metropolitan area.
1999 – (Ritz-Carlton)/May 10-11

Nat'l Automotive Radiator Service Ass'n (1954)
P.O. Box 97
East Greenville, PA 18041
Tel: (215)541-4500   Fax: (215)679-4977
E-Mail: narsa@narsa.org
Web Site: http://www.narsa.org
Members: 2,000 individuals
Staff: 9
Annual Budget: $1-2,000,000
Exec. Director: Wayne H. Juchno
Communications Director: Richard Krisher
Meetings Specialist: Eileen O'Shea

Historical Note
Founded to promote the interests of radiator repair shop owners, NARSA acts as an educational industry forum for cooling system specialists, shops, and allied industries. Headquarters street address: 2767 Geryville Pike, Pennsburg, PA 18073. Membership: $500-$2000/year (associate) $215(shop member); $35/year (retired).

Publications:
Automotive Cooling Journal. m. adv.
NARSA Legal Reports. q.
NARSA Nat'l Newsletter. bi-m.

NARSA Service Reports. bi-m.
Meetings/Conferences:
Annual Meetings: Spring/2,000
1999 – Dearborn, MI(Dearborn Hyatt)/April 21-24
2000 – Orlando, FL(Disney's Coronado Springs Resort)/March 15-18

Nat'l Avionics Soc. *(1973)*
Historical Note
Address unknown in 1995.

Nat'l Ballroom and Entertainment Ass'n *(1947)*
2799 Locust Road
Decorah, IA   52101-9612
Tel: (319)382-3871
Members: 650 member
Staff: 1
Annual Budget: $10-25,000
Exec. Director: John Matter
Historical Note
Origins go back to the late 1930s when a state organization was formed to work out mutual problems of the ballroom industry. In 1941 this became the Midwestern Ballroom Operators Association and, in 1948, the National Ballroom Operators Association. In 1970 the name was changed to the Entertainment Operators of America and the present name was adopted in 1976. Membership is open to anyone operating a ballroom or dance establishment featuring live music for public dancing. Members include band leaders, agents, and dance instructors. Membership: $15-25/year (individual); $100-125/year (organization/company).
Publications:
NBEA Newsletter. q. adv.
Meetings/Conferences:

Nat'l Band Ass'n *(1960)*
P.O. Box 121292
Nashville, TN   37212
Tel: (615)385-2650   *Fax:* (615)385-2650
E-Mail: NBASSOC@BELLSOUTH.NET
Members: 3,000 individuals
Staff: 1
Annual Budget: $50-100,000
Exec. Secretary: Edward Lisk
Historical Note
Members are band directors, music teachers, musical instrument makers and others interested in band development. Affiliated with the Music Educators Nat'l Conference. Membership: $40/year (individual), $50/year (institution & internat'l); $60/year (companies).
Publications:
Journal. 3 times/year.
NBA Membership Directory. bien. adv.
NBA Newsletter. 3 times/year.
Selective Music List For Bands. every 4 years. adv.
Meetings/Conferences:
Biennial Meetings: Even years

Nat'l Bankers Ass'n *(1927)*
1513 P St., N.W.
Washington, DC   20005-1909
Tel: (202)588-5432   *Fax:* (202)588-5443
Web Site: http://www.nationalbanks.org
Members: 49 banks
Staff: 4
Annual Budget: $500-1,000,000
President: Norma Hart
Historical Note
Formerly (1951) Nat'l Negro Bankers Ass'n. Members are minority and women's banking institutions, minority individuals employed by majority banks and majority institutions. Membership: Institutional (minority bank) based on assets, Associate (minority individual employed in a majority bank) $150/yr., Affiliate (majority institution) $2,000/yr.
Publications:
NBA Monitor. q.
NBA Today. a. adv.
Meetings/Conferences:
Annual Meetings: Fall

Nat'l Bar Ass'n *(1925)*
1225 11th St., N.W.
Washington, DC   20001-4217
Tel: (202)842-3900   *Fax:* (202)289-6170
Web Site: www.nationalbar.org
Members: 1,700 individuals
Staff: 10
Annual Budget: $1-2,000,000
Exec. Director: John L. Crump, CMP, CAE
Director, Special Project: Maurice Foster, CMP
Historical Note
Membership consists principally of black lawyers. Oldest ass'n of minority attorneys in the U.S. Membership: $75-200/yr.
Publications:
NBA Magazine. bi-m. adv.
Meetings/Conferences:
1999 – Philadelphia, PA(Marriott)/July 27-Aug. 3/2000
2000 – Washington, DC/Aug. 9-15/2000
2001 – Dallas, TX

Nat'l Barbecue Ass'n *(1991)*
P.O. Box 9685
Kansas City, MO   64134
Tel: (816)767-8311   *Fax:* (816)765-5860
Web Site: http://www.nbbga.org
Members: 260 individuals, 700 companies
Staff: 2
Annual Budget: $100-250,000
Exec. V. President: Carolyn S. Wells

Historical Note
Represents manufacturers of barbecue equipment, products, and supplies, as well as professional barbecuers, food industry professionals in barbecue, and barbecue enthusiasts. Membership: $35/year (individual); $150/year (company).
Publications:
Barbecue Buyers Guide. a. adv.
Barbecue Today. m. adv.
Meetings/Conferences:
Annual Meetings: Spring
1999 – Orlando, FL(Marriott)

Nat'l Bareboat Charter Ass'n *(1992)*
6553 46th St. N., Suite 905
Pinellas Park, FL   33781-0913
Tel: (727)520-1555   *Fax:* (727)520-8765
Annual Budget: $10-25,000
Exec. Director: Michael A. Fryer
Historical Note
Originally formed to provide legislative advocacy on behalf of the charter boat rental industry, NBCA now provides a range of services to members, including Coast Guard compliance. Membership: $35/year.
Publications:
Legislative Bulletin. irreg.
Newsletter. q. adv.
Meetings/Conferences:

Nat'l Bark and Soil Producers Ass'n *(1971)*
10210 Leatherleaf Court
Manassas, VA   20111-4245
Tel: (703)257-0111   *Fax:* (703)257-0213
E-Mail: assnctr@earthlink.net
Members: 90 companies
Annual Budget: $100-250,000
Exec. Director: Robert C. LaGasse, CAE
Historical Note
Formerly (1988) Nat'l Bark Producers Ass'n. Members are manufacturers of bark and soil products and industry suppliers.
Publications:
Bark Producers Report. q.
Capitol Hill Report. m.
Special Regional Releases. irreg.
Meetings/Conferences:
Annual Meetings: Fall

Nat'l Basketball Ass'n *(1946)*
645 Fifth Avenue, 15th Floor
New York, NY   10022
Tel: (212)407-8000   *Fax:* (212)826-0579
Web Site: http://www.nba.com
Members: 29 clubs
Staff: 800
Annual Budget: $5-10,000,000
Commissioner: David Stern
Historical Note
The association which administers the principal professional basketball league in the United States.
Publications:
Guide. a.
Hoop. m.
NBA Encyclopedia. Every three years.
Register. a.
Meetings/Conferences:
Annual Meetings: September

Nat'l Basketball Players Ass'n *(1954)*
1700 Broadway, Suite 1400
New York, NY   10019
Tel: (212)655-0880   *Fax:* (212)956-5687
Members: 406 individuals, 29 clubs
Staff: 20
Annual Budget: $2-5,000,000
Exec. Director: G. William Hunter
Historical Note
Independent labor union. Membership: $5,000/year.
Publications:
Time out. q.
Meetings/Conferences:
Semi-Annual Meetings: February and September

Nat'l Basketball Referees Ass'n *(1977)*
P.O. Box 6693
Huntington Beach, CA   92615-6693
Tel: (714)894-9564   *Fax:* (714)895-2107
Members: 60 individuals
Staff: 5
Annual Budget: $10-25,000
Treasurer: Greg Willard
Historical Note
Formerly (1993) Nat'l Ass'n of Basketball Referees. An independent union of professional basketball referees. Conducts basketball camps.

Nat'l Basketball Trainers' Ass'n *(1974)*
400 Colony Square, Suite 1750
Atlanta, GA   30361
Tel: (404)875-4000   *Fax:* (404)892-8560
Members: 30 individuals
Annual Budget: $50-100,000
General Counsel: Rollin E. Mallernee, II
Historical Note
A satellite of the Nat'l Athletic Trainers' Ass'n. NBTA is a professional association composed of all athletic trainers in the NBA. Membership: $300/yr.
Publications:
NBTA Media Guide. a.

Meetings/Conferences:
Annual Meetings: always Chicago, IL/June in conjunction with NBA combine

Nat'l Beauty Culturists' League *(1919)*
25 Logan Circle, N.W.
Washington, DC   20005
Tel: (202)332-2695   *Fax:* (202)332-0940
Members: 10,000 individuals
Staff: 5
President: Dr. Wanda J. Nelson
Historical Note
Established as the Nat'l Hair System Culture League, it assumed its present name in 1920. Members are black beauticians and cosmetologists.
Meetings/Conferences:
Annual Meetings: Summer
1999 – St. Louis, MO(Renaissance Airport Hotel)/July 31-August 2

Nat'l Bed and Breakfast Ass'n *(1981)*
P.O. Box 332
Norwalk, CT   06852
Tel: (203)847-6196   *Fax:* (203)847-0469
Web Site: http://www.nbba.com
Members: 2,000 facilities
Staff: 11
Annual Budget: $10-25,000
President: Phyllis Featherston
Historical Note
Membership includes individual B & B homes and inns in the U.S., Canada, Bermuda, Puerto Rico, and the U.S. Virgin Islands.
Publications:
Official Bed and Breakfast Guide. bien. adv.
Meetings/Conferences:
Annual Meetings: None held.

Nat'l Beefmaster Ass'n *(1976)*
Historical Note
Address unknown in 1996.

Nat'l Beer Wholesalers Ass'n *(1938)*
1100 S. Washington St.
Alexandria, VA   22314-4494
Tel: (703)683-4300   *Fax:* (703)683-8965
Members: 1,800 beer wholesalers
Staff: 26
Annual Budget: $2-5,000,000
President: Ronald A. Sarasin
Director, Public Affairs: Tamara Tyrell
V. President, Government Affairs: David K. Rehr
Director, Conventions and Meetings: Patricia Rouzie
Director, Finance: Paul McGuire
Director, Administration: Vernette A. Kukolich
Director, Industry Affairs: Craig Purser
Historical Note
Represents the independent wholesaling segment of the U.S. malt beverage industry. Sponsors and supports the Nat'l Beer Wholesalers Ass'n Political Action Committee. Membership: fees proportional to member company's annual sales.
Publications:
Compensation & Benefits Study.
Distributor Productivity Report. a.
NBWA Beer Perspectives. w.
NBWA Handbook (members only). a.
Meetings/Conferences:
Annual Meetings: Fall
1999 – Las Vegas, NV(Bally's)/Oct. 3-6/3000

Nat'l Beverage Dispensing Equipment Ass'n
Historical Note
Became (1996) Internat'l Beverage Dispensing Equipment Ass'n.

Nat'l Beverage Packaging Ass'n *(1947)*
200 Daingerfield Road
Alexandria, VA   22314-2800
Tel: (703)684-1080   *Fax:* (703)548-6563
Toll Free: (800)331 - 8816
Members: 800 individuals, 8 regional chapters
Staff: 1
Annual Budget: $50-100,000
Exec. Director: Ronald F. McNally, CAE
Historical Note
NBPA members represent all facets of the beverage packaging industry including soft drink, beer, bottled water and juice.
Publications:
Membership Directory. a.
NBPA's Voice. q.
Meetings/Conferences:
Biennial Meeting: concurrent with FPM&SA's Internat'l Exposition

Nat'l Bicycle Dealers Ass'n *(1946)*
2240 University Drive, #130
Newport Beach, CA   92660-3319
Tel: (949)722-6909   *Fax:* (949)722-1747
E-Mail: bikeshops@aol.com
Web Site: http://wwwNBDA.com
Members: 1,200 dealers
Staff: 2
Exec. Director: Fred Clements
Historical Note
Trade association of independent bicycle dealers. Manufacturers and distributors are eligible for associate membership. Membership: $100/year (dealer), $225/year (associate).
Publications:
Outspokin'. m.

Meetings/Conferences:
1999 – Las Vegas, NV

Nat'l Bio-Energy Industries Ass'n *(1979)*

122 C St., N.W., Fourth Floor
Washington, DC   20001-2109
Tel: (202)383-2540   *Fax:* (202)383-2651
E-Mail: kef@seia.org
Members: 90 companies
Staff: 2
Annual Budget: $250-500,000
Exec. Director: Scott Sklar
Administrative Director: Karen Seho

Historical Note
Formerly (1994) Nat'l Wood Energy Ass'n. Founded in Bloomfield Hills, MI; incorporated in the District of Columbia. Represents the commercial/industrial/utility biomass energy industry. Provides legislative and regulatory advocacy, statistical research and publications. Membership: $75/year (individual), $350-5,000/year (company).

Publications:
Bio Bulletin. m.
Biologue. q. adv.

Meetings/Conferences:
Annual Meetings: Fall

Nat'l Biotherapy Study Group

Historical Note
Became (1997) Cancer Biotherapy Research Group.

Nat'l Bison Ass'n

4701 Marion St., Suite 100
Denver, CO   80216-2140
Tel: (303)292-2833   *Fax:* (303)292-2564
E-Mail: info@nbabison.org
Web Site: http://www.nbabison.org
Members: 2,200 individuals
Staff: 5
Annual Budget: $500-1,000,000
Exec. Director: Samuel Albrecht

Historical Note
Formerly (1965) the National Buffalo Ass'n and (1975) American Bison Ass'n. Members are producers and marketers of buffalo products; their purpose is to promote and preserve the American Bison. Absorbed Nat'l Buffalo Ass'n in 1994. Membership: $100/year (full member), $75/year (associate).

Publications:
Bison World Magazine. q.

Meetings/Conferences:
Annual Meetings: Winter
1999 – Denver, CO

Nat'l Black American Paralegal Ass'n *(1994)*

P.O. Box 871706
New Orleans, LA   70187-1706
Tel: (202)452-7485
Annual Budget: under $10,000
President: Charsie LeDuff

Historical Note
The NBAPA was formed in 1994 as a volunteer organization by a group of African-American paralegal professionals from all over the U.S. to cultivate, promote and recognize Black paralegal professionals. It was formed in response to the growing need for an organized professional association for Black paralegals to address the issues and concerns that were predominant among Black legal professionals. Today NBAPA provides support to the growing number of Black Americans in the paralegal profession, and promotes diversity within the legal community. Has no paid officers or full-time staff. Membership: $50/year (voting); $100/year (sustaining); $40/year (associate), $25/year (student).

Publications:
NBAPA Review. q. adv.

Meetings/Conferences:

Nat'l Black Ass'n for Speech, Language and Hearing *(1978)*

P.O. Box 50605
Washington, DC   20091-0605
Tel: (202)274-6162   *Fax:* (202)274-6350
Members: 400 individuals
Annual Budget: $50-100,000
Exec. Director: M. Eugene Wiggins

Historical Note
Addresses the specific needs, concerns, and interests of African American students studying in the profession, practicing professionals, and consumers with communication disorders. Membership: $60/year (individual).

Publications:
Echo Magazine. semi-a. adv.

Meetings/Conferences:
1999 – St Louis, MI(Marriot Pavilion)/April 22-25

Nat'l Black Caucus of Local Elected Officials *(1970)*

1301 Pennsylvania Ave., N.W., Suite 550
Washington, DC   20004
Tel: (202)626-3120   *Fax:* (202)626-3043
Web Site: www.nlc.org/nbc-leo
Members: 1,500 individuals
Staff: 1
Contact: Mary France Gordon

Meetings/Conferences:
1999 – Washington, DC/Mar. 7-10

Nat'l Black Caucus of State Legislators *(1977)*

444 North Capitol St., N.W., Suite 622
Washington, DC   20001
Tel: (202)624-5457   *Fax:* (202)508-3826
Members: 540 individuals

Staff: 6
Annual Budget: $500-1,000,000
Exec. Director: Ivan Lanier

Historical Note
Promotes and sponsors training and education for its members on issues and potential legislation which may affect African-American constituencies within their jurisdictions. Membership includes individuals in the Virgin Islands and the District of Columbia. Membership: $100/year.

Publications:
Directory of Black State Legislators. bien.
NBCSL Public Policy Document. a.
Newsletter. q.

Meetings/Conferences:
Annual Meetings: Nov/Dec

Nat'l Black Chamber of Commerce *(1993)*

2000 L St., N.W., Suite 200
Washington, DC   20036
Tel: (202)416-1622   *Fax:* (202)416-1722
Web Site: http://www.nbcc-net.com
Members: 62,000 individuals, 175 chapters and affiliates
Exec. V. President: Kay DeBow
Planning Manager: Michelle Darden

Historical Note
NBCC is dedicated to the economic development of African American communities.

Nat'l Black Coalition of Federal Aviation Employees *(1976)*

P.O. Box 44392
Washington, DC   20026-4392
Tel: (202)267-7911   *Fax:* (202)267-5632
Toll Free: (800)622 - 9848
Members: 900 individuals
Annual Budget: $100-250,000
President: Alfredia Brooks

Historical Note
Represents the concerns of minority FAA employees. Recruits minorities and women for aviation careers in the FAA and addresses minority concerns for equal employment opportunities in the FAA. Membership: 0.75% of base salary/year (individuals); $500/year (corporate); $250/year (associate corporate).

Publications:
Conference Journals. a. adv.
Update. semi-a.
Visions. bi-m.

Meetings/Conferences:
Annual Meetings: September-October

Nat'l Black MBA Ass'n *(1974)*

180 North Michigan Ave., Suite 1515
Chicago, IL   60601
Tel: (312)236-2622   *Fax:* (312)236-4131
Members: 4,000 individuals
Staff: 20
Annual Budget: $2-5,000,000
Exec. Director: Antoinette Malveaux
Program Manager, Education: Marcus Cato
Nat'l Membership Manager: Wayne Josey

Historical Note
Composed of minority MBAs in both the private and public sectors, the NBMBAA seeks to improve the professional skills of the membership body and to focus its combined leverage towards achieving meaningful gains for minority MBA students and professionals. Membership: $100/yr. (individual), $2,500-12,500/yr. (organization).

Publications:
NBMBAA Newsletter. q. adv.

Meetings/Conferences:
Annual Meetings: Fall

Nat'l Black Nurses Ass'n *(1971)*

1511 K St., N.W., Suite 415
Washington, DC   20005-1401
Tel: (202)393-6870   *Fax:* (202)347-3808
Members: 3,000 individuals
Staff: 3
Annual Budget: $250-500,000
Exec. Director: Millicent Gorham

Historical Note
Functions as a non-profit membership ass'n and as an advocate for the Black community and their health care. Assists Blacks and minorities interested in pursuing a nursing career. Membership: $150/year (RN/LVN/LPN); $35/year (student).

Publications:
Journal NBNA. semi-a. adv.
NBNA Newsletter. q. adv.

Meetings/Conferences:
Annual Meetings: August
1999 – Atlanta, GA(Hyatt Regency)/Aug. 11-15
2000 – Washington, DC(Grand Hyatt)/Aug. 16-20

Nat'l Black Police Ass'n *(1972)*

3251 Mount Pleasant St., N.W., 2nd Floor
Washington, DC   20010-2103
Tel: (202)986-2070   *Fax:* (202)986-0410
Members: 130 associations
Staff: 2
Annual Budget: $100-250,000
Exec. Director: Ronald E. Hampton

Historical Note
Established in November 1972 by 13 charter police associations and incorporated in the District of Columbia. A federation of police associations with about 35,000 individual members. NBPA serves as an advocate for minority police officers and provides training and education programs. Membership: $75/year (individual); $200/year (organization).

Publications:
NBPA Advocate Newsletter. q. adv.

Meetings/Conferences:
Annual Meetings: Summer/400
1999 – Milwaukee, WI(Hilton)/Aug. 15-22
2000 – Toronto, Canada(Inn on the Park)
2001 – Miami, FL(Doral Hotel)

Nat'l Black Public Relations Soc. *(1982)*

6565 Sunset Blvd., Suite 301
Hollywood, CA   90028
Tel: (213)466-8221   *Fax:* (213)856-9510
Web Site: http://www.tobinpr@aol.com
Members: 2,500 individuals, 5 chapters
Annual Budget: under $10,000
President: Patricia L. Tobin

Historical Note
Established in Chicago, IL in 1982, NBPRS was formed to promote and expand the opportunites for minorities in public relations. Chapters located in Chicago, New York, Washington and Atlanta. Membership: $75/year.

Publications:
Beepers Newsletter. q.

Meetings/Conferences:

Nat'l Blacksmiths and Weldors Ass'n *(1875)*

P.O. Box 123
Arnold, NE   69120-0123
Tel: (308)848-2913
Members: 250 individuals
Staff: 1
Annual Budget: under $10,000
Information Director: James E. Holman

Historical Note
Blacksmiths, weldors, manufacturing machine shops and general repair shops. Has no paid staff or permanent headquarters; officers change annually. Membership principally in the Midwest. Membership: $30/year.

Publications:
Black Smithing Today. q. adv.

Meetings/Conferences:
Annual Meetings: First week of December.
1999 – Nebraska

Nat'l Block and Bridle Club *(1919)*

c/o Dept of Animal Science,
Colorado State University
Fort Collins, CO   80523-1171
Tel: (970)491-7777   *Fax:* (970)491-5326
E-Mail: RDGGENE@LAMAR.COLOSTATE.EDU
Web Site: http://www.asas.uiuc.edu/bandb/
Members: 87 active chapters
Annual Budget: $100-250,000
President: Ronnie Green, D.V.M.

Historical Note
Professional fraternity of men and women working in animal husbandry and affiliated with the American Soc. of Animal Science.

Publications:
Annual Report. a.
Newsletter. bien.

Meetings/Conferences:
1999 – Ft.Worth, TX/Jan. 27-31

Nat'l Blue Crab Industry Ass'n *(1977)*

1901 N. Ft. Myer Dr., Suite 700
Arlington, VA   22209
Tel: (703)524-8883   *Fax:* (703)524-4619
Members: 25 individuals
Staff: 2
Exec. Director: Robert Collette

Historical Note
NBCIA represents harvesters, processors and importers of blue crabs. In 1983 became a division of the Nat'l Fisheries Institute.

Meetings/Conferences:

Nat'l Board for Certified Clinical Hypnotherapists

8750 Georgia Ave., Suite 142E
Silver Spring, MD   20910
Tel: (301)608-0123   *Fax:* (301)588-9535
Toll Free: (800)449 - 8144
Members: 2,000 individuals
Staff: 5
Annual Budget: $100-250,000
Exec. Director, Certification: Frank Gunzburg, Ph.D.
Exec. Director, Administration: Ron Klein, CAAC

Historical Note
NBCCH provides professional credentials to mental health and counseling professionals who utilize hypnotherapy as a subspecialty. Provides two certification categories: NBCCH (Nat'l Board Certified Clinical Hypnotherapist) and NBCCH-PS (Nat'l Board Certified Clinical Hypnotherapist in Public Service). Requires a minimum of a master's degree in a mental health field, training and experience in hypnosis. Membership: $65/year.

Publications:
Interlink Newsletter. q.

Meetings/Conferences:
Annual Meetings: Fall

Nat'l Board of Boiler and Pressure Vessel Inspectors *(1919)*

1055 Crupper Ave.
Columbus, OH   43229
Tel: (614)888-8320   *Fax:* (614)888-0750
Web Site: www.nationalboard.org
Members: 60 individuals
Staff: 709
Annual Budget: $5-10,000,000
Exec. Director: Albert J. Justin

Director of Communications: Paul D. Brennan
Comptroller: Marsha Harvey

Historical Note
Membership is composed of chief boiler inspectors of states, major U.S. cities and provinces of Canada having boiler laws.

Publications:
Bulletin. q.
Nat'l Board Inspection Code. trien.
Pressure Relief Device Certifications. a.
Proceedings. a.
The Directory of Manufacturers and Repair Certificate
   Holders. a.

Meetings/Conferences:
Annual Meetings: April-May

Nat'l Board of Fur Farm Organizations

Historical Note
Became Fur Commission USA in 1995.

Nat'l Book Critics Circle *(1974)*
582 30th St.
San Francisco, CA 94131
Web Site: http://www.bookwire.com/nbcc/
Members: 700 individuals
Contact: Patricia Holt

Historical Note
NBCC encourages the advancement of book criticism in all media. Full membership is open to professional book reviewers and book review editors; associate membership is available to other professionals in publishing. Presents annual awards to recognize achievement in fiction, poetry, non-fiction, biography, and criticism. Has no paid officers or full-time staff. Membership: $35/year.

Publications:
NBCC Journal.

Meetings/Conferences:
Annual Meetings: usually New York, NY/March

Nat'l Border Patrol Council *(1965)*
P.O. Box 678
Campo, CA 91906-0678
Tel: (619)478-5145   Fax: (619)478-5716
Members: 4,000 individuals
Staff: 1
Annual Budget: $100-250,000
President: T.J. Bonner

Historical Note
A labor union representing employees of the U.S. Border Patrol, affiliated with the AFL-CIO and the American Federation of Government Employees.

Publications:
The Educator. bi-m.

Meetings/Conferences:
Biennial Meetings: odd years

Nat'l Bowling Council

Historical Note
Became (1995) Bowling, Inc.

Nat'l Broadcast Ass'n for Community Affairs *(1974)*
1200 19th St., N.W., Suite 300
Washington, DC 20036-2401
Tel: (202)857-1155   Fax: (202)223-4579
Web Site: http://www.sba.com/nbaca
Members: 300 companies/organizations
Annual Budget: $50-100,000

Historical Note
NBACA is an organization for broadcast professionals dedicated to strengthening community affairs programming. NBACA acts as an advocate and resource for community affairs broadcasters seeking professional development.

Publications:
NBACA Membership Directory. a. adv.
NBACA News. q. adv.

Meetings/Conferences:
Annual Meetings: Fall.

Nat'l Broiler Council *(1954)*
1015 15th St., N.W., Suite 530
Washington, DC 20005
Tel: (202)296-2622   Fax: (202)293-4005
Members: 225 companies
Staff: 11
Annual Budget: $2-5,000,000
President: George B. Watts
Director, Government Relations: Mary Colville
Director, Science & Technology: Stephen Pretanik

Historical Note
Organized at a meeting in Atlanta, Georgia, sponsored by the Broiler Institute in May, 1954 and incorporated in 1955. Members are producers and processors of broiler chickens, and their suppliers. Absorbed the Nat'l Broiler Ass'n in 1956. Supports the NBC Political Action Committee. Membership: Processors - fee based on liveweight production; Allied - supplies to broiler trade industry $1,250-11,000; Distributor - $200/year.

Publications:
Broiler Marketing Practices Survey. bien.
NBC Washington Report. w.
What's Happening in Consumer Education. q.

Meetings/Conferences:
Annual Meetings: Washington, DC/October

Nat'l Building Granite Quarries Ass'n *(1917)*
1220 L St., N.W., Suite 100-167
Washington, DC 20005
Toll Free: (800)557 - 2848
Web Site: http://nbgqa.com
Members: 10 companies

Staff: 1
Annual Budget: $10-25,000
Secretary: Kurt Swenson
Specifications Specialist: Charles Muellebauer

Historical Note
Annual dues based on sales volume.

Publications:
Specifications for Architectural Granite. a.

Meetings/Conferences:
Annual Meetings: April

Nat'l Bulk Vendors Ass'n *(1949)*
200 N. LaSalle St., Suite 2100
Chicago, IL 60601-1095
Tel: (312)612-1400   Fax: (312)621-1750
E-Mail: mmuch@muchlaw.com
Web Site: www.NBVA.org
Staff: 1
Annual Budget: $100-250,000
Counsel: Morrie Much

Historical Note
Founded as the Nat'l Vendors Ass'n, it assumed its present name in 1977. Members are makers and operators of bulk vending equipment and supplies. Membership: $100/year (company).

Publications:
Bulletin. bi-m.

Meetings/Conferences:
Annual Meetings: Spring

Nat'l Bureau of Certified Consultants *(1989)*
Management Consulting Center
2728 5th Avenue
San Diego, CA 92103-6329
Tel: (619)297-2210   Fax: (619)296-3580
Members: 2,200 individuals
Staff: 6
Annual Budget: $250-500,000
Chairman: Vito A. Tanzi
Director of Professional Services: James R. Bickmann

Historical Note
Formerly Nat'l Bureau of Professional Management Consultants (1998). A national organization with an objective to secure legislative Certification in order to recognize the appellation of CPCM (Certified Professional Consultant to Management). NBPMC is also working with the academic community to introduce MBA graduate courses in consultancy in the United States. The American Ass'n of Professional Consultants became a professional division of NBPMC after merging in 1992. Membership: $200/year (individual).

Publications:
Consultant's Bulletin/NBPMC. bi-m.

Meetings/Conferences:

Nat'l Bureau of Document Examiners *(1984)*

Historical Note
Organization defunct in 1997.

Nat'l Burglar and Fire Alarm Ass'n *(1948)*
7101 Wisconsin Ave., Suite 901
Bethesda, MD 20814-4805
Tel: (301)907-3202   Fax: (301)907-7897
E-Mail: staff@alarm.org
Web Site: http://www.alarm.org
Members: 3,900 companies
Staff: 16
Annual Budget: $2-5,000,000
Exec. Director: Brad Shipp
Director, Communications: David Saddler
Director, Government Affairs: Matt Wald
Director, State and Customer Relations: Sue Andres
Director, Training: David Newweiler

Historical Note
Members provide installation, repair, and/or monitoring of burglar alarms, fire alarms, and other secutiry systems. Houses the Alarm Industry Research and Education Foundation (AIREF), which sponsors industry and safety research programs. Membership: $125-33,800/year, based on number of employees and branch offices.

Publications:
National Newsline. m. adv.
NBFAA Directory of Members. a. adv.
NBFAA Leadership Today. m.

Meetings/Conferences:
Annual Meetings: Spring/Summer
1999 – Washington, DC(Loews Plaza)
1999 – San Juan, Puerto Rico/March 4-8

Nat'l Business Aircraft Ass'n *(1947)*

Historical Note
Became the Nat'l Business Aviation Ass'n in 1997.

Nat'l Business Ass'n *(1982)*
5151 Beltline Road, Suite 1150
Dallas, TX 75240-6739
Tel: (972)458-0900   Fax: (972)960-9149
Toll Free: (800)456 - 0440
E-Mail: NbaIZ@airmail.net
Web Site: www.nationalbusiness.org
Members: 50,000 individuals
Staff: 11
Annual Budget: $2-5,000,000
President: Pat Archibald

Historical Note
NBA is a national non-profit that assists the Sel-Employed and Small Business community. Members are small-business owners, entrepreneurs, and professionals. Membership:$144 (individual).

Publications:
Nat'l Business News. bi-m.

Nat'l Business Circulation Ass'n *(1948)*

Historical Note
Address unknown in 1997.

Nat'l Business Education Ass'n *(1946)*
1914 Association Drive
Reston, VA 20191-1596
Tel: (703)860-8300   Fax: (703)620-4483
E-Mail: nbea@nbea.org
Members: 15,000 individuals
Staff: 9
Annual Budget: $500-1,000,000
Exec. Director: Janet M. Treichel
Director, Communications and Marketing: Noelle C. Sotack

Historical Note
Formed in Buffalo, NY as the United Business Education Ass'n through a merger of the Dept. of Business Education of the Nat'l Education Ass'n (founded in 1892) and the Nat'l Council for Business Education. Absorbed the Nat'l Business Teachers Ass'n (formerly the Nat'l Commercial Teachers Federation) and assumed its present name in 1962. The Nat'l Ass'n for Business Teacher Education is a division. Membership: $50/year.

Publications:
Business Education Forum. q. adv.
Keying In Newsletter. q.
NBEA Yearbook. a.

Meetings/Conferences:
Annual Meetings: Spring/2,000
1999 – Chicago, IL(Marriott)/March 31-April 3

Nat'l Business Forms Ass'n *(1945)*

Historical Note
Became Document Mnagement Industries Ass'n in 1996.

Nat'l Business Incubation Ass'n *(1985)*
20 E. Circle Drive, Suite 190
Athens, OH 45701
Tel: (614)593-4331   Fax: (614)593-1996
E-Mail: dadkins@nbia.org
Web Site: http://www.nbia.org
Members: 900 individuals
Staff: 13
Annual Budget: $500-1,000,000
Exec. Director: Dinah Adkins
Director, Education: JoAnn Rollins
Director of Business Administration: Cheryl Brink
Member Services Director: Susanne McKinnon
Director of Publications: Sally Hayholo
Director of Development: Sallie Traxler

Historical Note
An organization of small business incubator managers and developers, as well as those interested in tracking the industry. Business incubators are business assistance programs that provide support/business development services. Membership: $195/year (individual); $320/year (organization).

Publications:
NBIA Review. bi-m. adv.

Meetings/Conferences:
Annual Meetings: Spring
1999 – Chicago, IL/March 21-24

Nat'l Business League *(1900)*

Historical Note
Address unknown in 1997.

Nat'l Business Owners Ass'n *(1987)*

Historical Note
Address unknown in 1997.

Nat'l Business Travel Ass'n *(1968)*
1650 King St., Suite 401
Alexandria, VA 22314-2747
Tel: (703)684-0836   Fax: (703)684-0263
E-Mail: Info@NBTA.org
Web Site: http://www.NBTA.org
Members: 1,800 individuals
Staff: 13
Annual Budget: $2-5,000,000
Exec. Director: Norman R. Sherlock
Communications Director: Marianne McInerney
Director, Meetings & Conventions: Henry J. Roeder
Director, Education: Katherine Parramore, Ed.D., CAE

Historical Note
The voice of business travel management, a professional non-profit association of business travel managers and business travel service/product suppliers. Formerly (1989) Nat'l Passenger Traffic Ass'n. Membership: $310/first year, $260/year thereafter (travel managers); $1,260/first year, $260/year thereafter (suppliers).

Publications:
Conference Journal. a. adv.
Membership Directory. a. adv.

Meetings/Conferences:
Annual Meetings: July/2,700
1999 – Minneapolis, MN/July 18-21
2000 – Los Angeles, CA/July 30-Aug. 2
2001 – Atlanta, GA/July 29-Aug. 1

Nat'l Cable Television Ass'n *(1952)*
1724 Massachusetts Ave., N.W.
Washington, DC 20036-1969
Tel: (202)775-3550   Fax: (202)775-3696
Web Site: http://www.aescon.com/nctahome.htm
Members: 2,713 cable systems, 476 associates
Staff: 85
Annual Budget: $25-50,000,000
President: S. Decker Anstrom
Director, Technical Services: Katherine Rutkowski

Historical Note
Formerly (1968) Nat'l Community Television Ass'n. Members are cable TV systems; associate members are manufacturers, distributors, suppliers of hardware, programmers and other services. Has an annual budget of approximately $29.7 million. Sponsors and supports the Cable Television Political Action Committee (Cable-PAC).

Publications:
Convention Newsletter. a.
Linking Up. m.
Tech Line. m.

Meetings/Conferences:
Annual Meetings: Spring

Nat'l Campground Institute *(1974)*

Historical Note
Promotional arm of the Nat'l Ass'n of RV Parks and Campgrounds.

Nat'l Campus Ministries Ass'n *(1965)*

Historical Note
Address unknown in 1997.

Nat'l Cancer Registrar's Ass'n *(1974)*

8310 Nieman Road
Lenexa, KS 66214
Tel: (913)438-6272   *Fax:* (913)541-0156
Members: 2,700 individuals
Staff: 11
Annual Budget: $100-250,000
Exec. Director: Dede Lisa Panjada

Historical Note
Members are persons involved with hospital, state or regional data banks that maintain statistics on cancer. Formerly (1993) Nat'l Tumor Registrars Ass'n. Membership: $80/year (individual), $150/year (organization).

Publications:
Journal of Registry Management. tri-a. adv.
The Connection. q. adv.

Meetings/Conferences:
Annual Meetings: May/June
1999 – Dallas, TX/May 25-28

Nat'l Candle Ass'n *(1974)*

1030 15th St., N.W., Suite 870
Washington, DC 20005
Tel: (202)393-2210   *Fax:* (202)393-0336
Members: 100 companies
Staff: 4
Annual Budget: $100-250,000
Exec. V. President: Marianne McDermott

Historical Note
Established as the Candle Manufacturers Ass'n in 1933, NCA assumed its present name in 1974. Maintains a Technical Committee, providing research to the industry.

Publications:
Illuminations. q.

Meetings/Conferences:
Annual Meetings: Fall, usually held in Washington, DC

Nat'l Candy Brokers Ass'n *(1981)*

710 E. Ogden Ave., Suite 600
Naperville, IL 60563
Tel: (630)369-2406
Members: 450 individuals, 250 companies
Staff: 2
Annual Budget: $100-250,000
Exec. V. President: Michael D. Hansen

Historical Note
Established as the Candy Brokers Ass'n of America, it became the Nat'l Candy Brokers and Sales Ass'n in 1981 and assumed its present name in 1982. Membership: $225/year.

Publications:
Membership Roster. a.
The Candy Dish. bi-m.

Meetings/Conferences:
Semi-Annual Meetings: February and July

Nat'l Career Development Ass'n *(1913)*

317 Kertess Avenue
Worthington, OH 43085
Members: 5,500 individuals
Staff: 2
Annual Budget: $250-500,000
Exec. Director: Juliet Miller

Historical Note
Founded as the Nat'l Vocational Guidance Ass'n, NCDA assumed its present name in 1985. Members are counselors and career development professionals who work in education, business/industry, community agencies, military installations and private practice. NCDA is a division of the American Counseling Ass'n. Membership: $27/year (professional); $35/year (general).

Publications:
Career Development Newsletter. 5/yr. adv.
Career Development Quarterly. q. adv.

Meetings/Conferences:

Nat'l Cargo Bureau *(1952)*

30 Vesey St.
New York, NY 10007-2914
Tel: (212)571-5000   *Fax:* (212)571-5005
Members: 215 businesses
Staff: 105
Annual Budget: $10-25,000,000
President: Captain James J. McNamara
V. President, Corporate Secretary/General Counsel: Charles S. Cumming

Historical Note
Formed by the merger of the Bureau of Inspection of the Board of Underwriters of New York (founded in 1820) and the Board of Marine Underwriters of San Francisco (founded in 1886). Promotes the safe loading, stowage, securing and unloading of cargo on all vessels. Has an annual budget of approximately $10 million.

Publications:
Correspondence Course: Hazardous Cargo.
Correspondence Course: Ship's Stability.
Correspondence Course: Stability for Fishermen.

Meetings/Conferences:
Annual Meetings: New York, NY/first Monday in March

Nat'l Cargo Security Council *(1983)*

526 King St., Suite 423
Alexandria, VA 22314-3143
Tel: (703)706-5311   *Fax:* (703)706-9583
Web Site: http://www.cargosecurity.com
Members: 1000 companies and individuals
Annual Budget: $25-50,000
Managing Director: Mary Jane Kolar, CAE

Historical Note
NCSC members are drawn from the full spectrum of the air, truck/rail, and maritime cargo security industry.

Publications:
Cargo Security Report Newsletter. q. adv.

Meetings/Conferences:
Quarterly Meetings: Feb/May/Aug/Sept
1999 – Los Angeles, CA

Nat'l Cartoonists Soc. *(1946)*

4101 Lake Boone Trail, Suite 201
Raleigh, NC 27607
Tel: (919)787-5181   *Fax:* (919)787-4916
Members: 600 individuals
Administration Coordinator: Shannon Parham

Historical Note
A professional organization of cartoonists. Editors, writers and others interested in cartooning are accepted as associate members.

Publications:
NCS Album.
The Cartoonist. q.

Meetings/Conferences:
1999 – San Antonio, TX/May 6-9

Nat'l Casino Executives Ass'n

Nat'l Catalog Managers Ass'n *(1974)*

EIS Brake Parts
129 Worthington Ridge
Berlin, CT 06037
Tel: (860)828-8290   *Fax:* (860)828-0832
Members: 143 individuals
Annual Budget: $25-50,000
President: Joyce Tobias

Historical Note
Members are producers of automotive products catalogues. Has no paid staff or function beyond standardizing the publications its members prepare. Affiliated with the Automotive Service Industry Ass'n. Membership: $150/year (individual); $175 (new).

Publications:
Membership Book. adv. adv.
Newsletter. q.

Meetings/Conferences:
Annual Meetings: April/May

Nat'l Caterers Roundtable Ass'n *(1981)*

Historical Note
Address unknown in 1995.

Nat'l Catholic Ass'n for Communicators *(1972)*

Historical Note
Became UNDA-USA, Nat'l Catholic Ass'n for Communicators in 1995.

Nat'l Catholic Band Ass'n *(1953)*

1452 Glenlake Drive
South Bend, IN 46614
Tel: (219)291-3391
Members: 275 individuals
Annual Budget: under $10,000
Secretary-Treasurer: Robert F. O'Brien

Historical Note
Formerly (1993) Nat'l Catholic Bandmasters' Ass'n. Active membership open to any qualified band director who teaches in a Catholic grammar school, high school or college, and to woodwind, brass or percussion instructors in a Catholic band program. Membership: $40/year (individual/retail); $50/year (commercial).

Publications:
Directory. a.
Newsletter. bi-m.
Proceedings. a.
Update. irreg.

Meetings/Conferences:
Annual Meetings: July or August Chicago, IL/December/Board of Directors Meeting
1999 – Notre Dame, IN

Nat'l Catholic Business Education Ass'n *(1945)*

Historical Note
Address unknown in 1996.

Nat'l Catholic Cemetery Conference *(1949)*

710 North River Rd.
Des Plaines, IL 60016
Tel: (847)824-8131   *Fax:* (847)824-9608
E-Mail: nat.cat.cem.con.@worldnet.att.net

Members: 1,800 businesses
Staff: 4
Annual Budget: $500-1,000,000
Exec. Director: Irene K. Pesce, CAE

Publications:
Membership Directory. a.
The Catholic Cemetery. m. adv.

Meetings/Conferences:
Annual Meetings: Fall/500
1999 – Chicago, IL(Hilton & Towers)/Sept. 11-16
2000 – Greensboro, NC(Holiday Inn Four Seasons)/Sept. 22-25
2001 – Anaheim, CA(Disneyland Hotel)/Sept. 17-20

Nat'l Catholic Conference of Airport Chaplains *(1986)*

P.O. Box 2220
Newark, NJ 07114
Tel: (973)961-0260   *Fax:* (973)961-0260
Members: 35 individuals
President: Rev. David J. Baratelli

Historical Note
Members are Roman Catholic clergy ministering to air travelers. Membership: $25/year.

Publications:
NCCAC Newsletter. bi-m.
Proceedings. a.

Meetings/Conferences:
1999 – North Palm Beach, FL(Our Lady of FL Center)/Jan. 26-29

Nat'l Catholic Development Conference *(1968)*

86 Front St.
Hempstead, NY 11550-3667
Tel: (516)481-6000   *Fax:* (516)489-9287
Web Site: http://www.amm.org/ncdc.htm
Members: 500 organizations
Staff: 9
Annual Budget: $500-1,000,000
President: George T. Holloway
Coordinator, Public Relations: Richard A. Reale
Coordinator, Membership Services: James R. Renert

Historical Note
NCDC members are religious fund raising organizations including development officers and key fund raisers of charitable institutions and agencies, religious orders, dioceses, hospitals and educational institutions. While active membership is restricted to Catholic organizations, non-Catholic groups may apply for associate memberships. Active and associate membership dues based on gross philanthropic income. Corporate membership: $1,000/year.

Publications:
Corporate Member Bulletin. q.
Dimensions. m. adv.
Member Resource Directory. a. adv.
Monitor. 8/year.
Resource Guide. a.

Meetings/Conferences:
Annual Meetings: Fall/600
1999 – Chicago, IL(Marriott Downtown)/Sept. 19-22
2000 – Palm Desert, CA(Marriott Desert Springs)/Sept. 10-13

Nat'l Catholic Educational Ass'n *(1904)*

1077 30th St., N.W., Suite 100
Washington, DC 20007-3852
Tel: (202)337-6232   *Fax:* (202)333-6706
E-Mail: nceaadmin@ncea.org
Web Site: http://www.ncea.org
Members: 24,000 individuals and institutions
Staff: 52
Annual Budget: $5-10,000,000
President: Leonard DeFiore, Ph.D.
Director, Communications: Patricia Feistritzer
Director, Public Relations: Barbara Keebler
Exec. Assistant to the President: Sister Patrice Hughes
Director, Public Policy and Educational Research: Sr. Dale McDonald
Director, Convention/Expo: Nancy A. Brewer
Director of Administrative Services: James A. McDaniel
Comptroller: George W. Kirby
Membership Manager: Marlene S. Sanchez

Historical Note
Founded in St. Louis June 12-14, 1904 as the Catholic Education Association through the merger of the Association of Catholic Colleges (1899), the Parish School Conference (1902) and the Educational Conference of Seminary Faculties (1898). Within NCEA are several entities including the Ass'n of Catholic Colleges and Universities (ACCU); Chief Administrators of Catholic Education and the National Association for Parish Coordinators and Directors of Religion Education (NPCD). Members are Catholic educators involved at all levels from preschool through universities and seminaries. Membership: $105-115/year (individual); $100-4,590/year (institution).

Publications:
Accent.
ACCU Update.
Beginnings.
Current Issues in Higher Education.
Development Sharing.
Issue-Gram.
Momentum. q. adv.
NCEA Notes.
Seminary Notes.
The NCEA Pastors Education Digest.

Meetings/Conferences:
Annual Meetings: Week after Easter

Nat'l Catholic Educational Exhibitors *(1950)*

330 Progress Road
Dayton, OH 45449
Tel: (937)847-5900   *Fax:* (937)847-5910
Members: 500 individuals, 350 companies

Staff: 2
Annual Budget: $25-50,000
Exec. Director: Peter Li
Director of Communications: Cyndi Morris

Historical Note
Members are companies and individuals who exhibit at Catholic shows. Associate members are 150 Catholic school superintendents and administrators. Membership: $25/year (individual); $135/year (organization).

Publications:
Membership Directory. a.
NCEE Bulletin. q.

Meetings/Conferences:
Annual Meetings: always the week after Easter with the Nat'l
   Catholic Educational Ass'n
1999 – New Orleans, LA

Nat'l Catholic Pharmacists Guild of the United States (1962)
1012 Surrey Hills Dr.
St. Louis, MO   63117-1438
Tel: (314)645-0085
Members: 375 individuals
Staff: 1
Annual Budget: under $10,000
Co-President & Exec. Director: John Paul Winkelmann

Historical Note
Founded on September 19, 1962 in New York City through the auspices of the Nat'l Catholic Welfare Conference (currently known as the United States Catholic Conference.) Affiliated with the Nat'l Council of Catholic Laity and the Internat'l Federation of Catholic Pharmacists. Membership: $20/year.

Publications:
The Catholic Pharmacist. q. adv.

Meetings/Conferences:
Biennial meetings: odd years

Nat'l Cattlemen's Ass'n (1977)
Historical Note
Became the Nat'l Cattlemen's Beef Ass'n in 1996.

Nat'l Cattlemen's Beef Ass'n (1896)
P.O. Box 3469, 5420 South Quebec St.
Englewood, CO   80155
Tel: (303)694-0305   Fax: (303)694-2851
Web Site: http://www.beef.org
Members: 40,000 individuals, 130 associations
Staff: 150
Annual Budget: $10-25,000,000
C.E.O.: Charles P. Schroeder
V.P., Communications/Public Relations: Kendal Frazier
Director, Conventions and Meetings: Debbie Kaylor
V.P., Quality: Dr. Jim Gibb
V.P., Finance and Administration: Jay H. Wardell
V.P., Ass'n Services: Marvin Kokes

Historical Note
Formed as Nat'l Cattlemen's Ass'n as the result of a merger of American Nat'l Cattlemen's Ass'n (founded 1898) and Nat'l Livestock Feeders Ass'n (founded 1943). Absorbed Nat'l Livestock Tax Committee in 1978; consolidated with Nat'l Live Stock and Meat Board and Beef Industry Council and assumed its current name in 1995. NCBA provides unified efforts on behalf of the beef industry to increase market share and provide quality meat. Supports the Public Lands Council and sponsors the NCBA Political Action Committee. Has an annual budget of approximately $11.5 million. Membership: $60/year (individual).

Publications:
Beef Business Bulletin. w.
National Cattlemen. m. adv.

Meetings/Conferences:
Annual Meetings: Winter/5,500-6,000
1999 – Charlotte, NC/Feb. 10-14

Nat'l Caves Ass'n (1965)
4138 Dark Hollow Road
McMinnville, TN   37110-8629
Tel: (931)668-3925   Fax: (931)668-3988
Web Site: http://www.cavern.com
Members: 93 cave operators
Staff: 1
Annual Budget: $25-50,000
Secretary-Treasurer: Barbara Munson

Historical Note
NCA is a non-profit organization which sets and maintains standards for show caves throughout the country. NCA's Legislative Program is designed to protect caves being operated as attractions. Membership: $240-490/year.

Publications:
Caves and Caverns Directory. a.
NCA Cave Talk Newsletter. bi-m.

Meetings/Conferences:
Annual Meetings: Fall/110-125

Nat'l Cellular Resellers Ass'n (1987)
Historical Note
Became Nat'l Wireless Resellers Ass'n in 1997.

Nat'l Center for Advanced Technologies
Historical Note
The non-profit foundation of the Aerospace Industries Ass'n.

Nat'l Center for Homeopathy (1974)
801 N. Fairfax St., Suite 306
Alexandria, VA   22314-1757
Tel: (703)548-7790   Fax: (703)548-7792
Web Site: http://www.homeopathic.org
Members: 7,000 individuals
Staff: 6

Annual Budget: $250-500,000
Exec. Director: Sharon Stevenson

Historical Note
Formerly associated with the American Foundation for Homoeopathy, but now independent. Membership: $40/year.

Publications:
Directory of Homeopathy Practitioners. bien.
Homoeopathy Today. m.

Meetings/Conferences:
Annual Meetings: Spring
1999 – Fort Lauderdale, FL/Apr. 16-20

Nat'l Center on Rural Aging (1978)
Historical Note
A special interest group of the Nat'l Council on the Aging concerned with the interests of older persons living in rural America.

Nat'l Certification Commission (1993)
P.O. Box 15282
Chevy Chase, MD   20825-5282
Tel: (301)588-1212   Fax: (301)588-1212
Members: 30 individuals, 150 organizations
Staff: 3
Annual Budget: $50-100,000
Exec. Director: Richard C. Jaffeson, AICP, ACA

Historical Note
Members are associations and individuals with interests in certification program development and implementation. Operates the Approved Certification Administrator (ACA), Basic Certification Administrator (BCA), Certification Committee Administrator (CCA) and Distinguished Certification Administrator (DCA) programs, national registration for certification programs, and offers educational seminars on development and legal issues. Membership: $50/year, initial/$25/year, renewal (ACA and CCA); $40/year, initial/$25/year, renewal (BCA); $100/year, national registration.

Publications:
Career Captions. w.
Certification Communications. m.
Program Profiles. w.

Meetings/Conferences:
Annual Meetings: always in Bethesda, MD/Fall
1999 – Bethedsa, MD(Marriott)
2000 – Bethesda, MD(Marriott)
2001 – Bethesda, MD(Marriott)

Nat'l Certification Council for Activity Professionals (1986)
P.O. Box 62589
Virginia Beach, VA   23466-2589
Tel: (757)552-0653   Fax: (757)552-0491
Members: 6,500 individuals
Staff: 3
Annual Budget: $250-500,000
Exec. Director: Karen Land

Historical Note
NCCAP is the only national organization that exclusively certifes activity professionals who work with the elderly. Certifications are: Activity Assistant Certified (AAC), Activity Director Provisionally Certified (ADPC); Activity Director Certified (ADC); and Activity Consultant Certified (ACC).

Publications:
NCCAP Newsletter. semi-a.

Meetings/Conferences:
Annual Meetings: in conjunction with the Nat'l Ass'n of Activity
   Professionals

Nat'l Certified Pipe Welding Bureau (1944)
1385 Piccard Drive
Rockville, MD   20850
Tel: (301)869-5800   Fax: (301)990-9690
E-Mail: nick@mcaa.org
Members: 600 companies
Staff: 2
Annual Budget: $250-500,000
Exec. Director: Darush Nirpourfard

Historical Note
A department of the Mechanical Contractors Ass'n of America. Membership: $400/year.

Publications:
Membership Directory. a. adv.
NCPWB Newsletter. semi-a.

Meetings/Conferences:
Annual Meetings: Spring/60

Nat'l Cheese Institute (1927)
1250 H St., N.W., Suite 900
Washington, DC   20005
Tel: (202)737-4332   Fax: (202)331-7820
Members: 100 manuf., distributors, & proc.
Staff: 45
Annual Budget: $250-500,000
President and C.E.O.: E. Linwood Tipton
Dirctor, Communications: Susan E. Ruland
Senior V. President & PAC Chairperson: Constance E. Tipton
Senior V. President: Jerome J. Kozak
Director, Finance: Sam J. DiCarlo
V. President and Counsel: Janet A. Nuzum
V. President: Thomas M. Balmer

Historical Note
NCI is a trade association representing manufacturers, processors and distributors of natural and process cheese and cheese products. NCI's activities range from legislative and regulatory advocacy to market research, industry training and education. Administrative support provided by Internat'l Dairy Foods Ass'n. Membership: annual dues based on volume.

Publications:
Cheese Facts.

Meetings/Conferences:
Annual Meetings: in conjunction with Internat'l Dairy Foods
   Ass'n/Fall

Nat'l Chemical Credit Ass'n (1936)
Historical Note
Address unknown in 1996.

Nat'l Cherry Growers and Industries Foundation (1946)
P.O. Box 946
Hood River, OR   97031
Tel: (541)386-7710   Fax: (541)386-1177
Members: 1,500 growers and industries
Staff: 2
Annual Budget: $100-250,000
Manager: George Ing

Historical Note
NCGIF members are growers and processors of canned, frozen and brined cherries. Provides funds for promotional campaigns on behalf of the cherry industry.

Publications:
NCGIF Statistical Summary. a.

Meetings/Conferences:
Annual Meetings: November

Nat'l Child Care Ass'n (1988)
1016 Rosser St.
Conyers, GA   30012
Tel: (770)922-8198   Fax: (770)388-7772
Toll Free: (800)543 - 7161
E-Mail: nccallw@mindspring.com
Web Site: http://www.mccanet.org
Members: 6,000 individuals
Staff: 5
Annual Budget: $250-500,000
Exec. Director: Lynn White

Historical Note
NCCA is a professional trade association representing licensed private child care centers. Membership: $30/year.

Publications:
NCCA's National Focus. q.

Meetings/Conferences:
Annual Meetings: Annual/March
1999 – Orlando, FL/March 12-14

Nat'l Child Support Enforcement Ass'n (1952)
444 North Capitol St., N.W., Suite 414
Washington, DC   20001-1512
Tel: (202)624-8180   Fax: (202)624-8828
Members: 1,800 individuals, 172 state and county agencies
Staff: 8
Annual Budget: $500-1,000,000
Exec. Director: Joel Bankes
Communications Director: Jane Toblin
Governmental Relations Director: Kelly Thompson
Membership Director: Heather Tonks
Business Manager: Linda Adams

Historical Note
Formerly the Nat'l Conference on Uniform Reciprocal Enforcement of Support and (1984) the Nat'l Reciprocal and Family Support Enforcement Ass'n. Assumed its present name in August of 1984. Members are child support professionals at all levels of government. Membership: $50/year (individual); $300/year local agency, and $300-1,500/year, varies based on population (state agency); $600-5,000/year (private sector corporate membership).

Publications:
Nat'l Child Support Enforcement Interstate Roster & Referral
   Guide.
NCSEA News. q. adv.

Meetings/Conferences:
Annual Meetings: August/1,500
1999 – Chicago, IL(Palmer House Hilton)/Aug. 8-12
2000 – San Diego, CA(Town and Country)/July 30-Aug. 3

Nat'l Child Transport Ass'n (1995)
c/o Cruisin Kids Carpool
4801 S. Union Dr. #305E
Naples, FL   34113-7621
Tel: (954)252-9966   Fax: (954)252-9966
E-Mail: crsnk@aol.com
Web Site: www.naples.net/clubs/ncta
Members: 75 individuals
Staff: 1
Annual Budget: $25-50,000
Treasurer: Mike Lopeman

Historical Note
NCTA is a network of transportation providers, child care facilities, schools, and other organizations with an ongoing interest in improved child transport. Membership: $175/year (associate); $250/year (primary); $1,200 (corporate).

Publications:
NCTA Update. bi-m. adv.

Meetings/Conferences:
Annual Meetings: June

Nat'l Chimney Sweep Guild (1976)
8752 Robbins Rd.
Indianapolis, IN   46268-1021
Tel: (317)871-0030   Fax: (317)871-0030
E-Mail: office@ncsg.org
Web Site: http://www.csia.org
Members: 1000 service companies, 45 additional
Staff: 6
Annual Budget: $250-500,000
Exec. Director: Jo Anne Calderone

Director of Communications: Theresa Joycedt
Director of Finance: Sandy Cosner
Historical Note
Members are professional chimney service companies and their suppliers. Membership: $295/year (company); $495/year (supplier).
Publications:
News/Link. m.
Sweeping Magazine. m. adv.
Meetings/Conferences:
1999 – Milwakee, WI/Feb 16-20

Nat'l Christian College Athletic Ass'n (1966)
P.O. Box 1312
Marion, IN 46952
Tel: (765)674-8401 *Fax:* (765)674-1364
E-Mail: thenccaa@comtec.com
Members: 109 colleges
Staff: 4
Annual Budget: $250-500,000
Interim Exec. Director: Rob Miller
Historical Note
NCCAA members are evangelical Christian colleges.
Publications:
NCCAA Directory. a.
NCCAA News Update. q. adv.
NCCAA Official Handbook. a.
Meetings/Conferences:
1999 – Nashville, TN/May 20-22

Nat'l Christian Education Ass'n (1942)
Historical Note
A program of the Nat'l Ass'n of Evangelicals.

Nat'l Christmas Tree Ass'n (1955)
1000 Executive Pkwy., Suite 220
St. Louis, MO 63141
Tel: (314)205-0944 *Fax:* (314)576-7983
E-Mail: info@christree.org
Web Site: http://www.christree.org
Members: 2,000 individuals
Staff: 4
Annual Budget: $250-500,000
Exec. Director: Don Evashenko
Historical Note
Formerly (1974) the National Christmas Tree Growers' Ass'n. Membership: $125/year.
Publications:
American Christmas Tree Journal. q. adv.
Christmas Tree Times. q. adv.
Membership Directory. bien. adv.
Meetings/Conferences:
Semi-Annual Meetings: Summer and Winter

Nat'l Church Goods Ass'n (1904)
P.O. Box 489
Milford, PA 18337
Tel: (717)296-8818 *Fax:* (717)296-2236
Members: 300 companies
Staff: 1
Annual Budget: $100-250,000
Exec. Secretary: David R. Malhame
Historical Note
Membership fee varies, based on sales volume.
Publications:
Association News. 3/year.
Meetings/Conferences:
Annual Meetings: usually January/200
1999 – Las Vegas, NV

Nat'l Classification Management Soc. (1964)
994 Old Eagle School Road, Suite 1019
Wayne, PA 19087-1802
Tel: (610)971-4856 *Fax:* (610)971-4859
Members: 1,600 individuals
Annual Budget: $100-250,000
Exec. Secretary: Sharon K. Tannahill
Historical Note
Members consist of information security professionals concerned with identifying and assigning a security classification to information and materials needing protection in the national interest. Membership: $60/year, plus $25 entrance fee.
Publications:
C M Bulletin. bi-m.
Directory. a.
Meetings/Conferences:
Annual Meetings: Summer/300-400
1999 – Minneapolis, MN
2000 – Washington, DC

Nat'l Clay Pipe Institute (1942)
253-80 Center St.
P.O. Box 759
Lake Geneva, WI 53147
Tel: (414)248-9094
Members: 6 companies
Staff: 6
Annual Budget: $100-250,000
President: Edward J. Sikora
Historical Note
Formerly Nat'l Clay Pipe Manufacturers. Makers of vitrified clay sewer pipes and fittings.
Publications:
Sewer Sense. q.

Nat'l Clay Pot Manufacturers Ass'n (1956)
Drawer 485

Jackson, MO 63755-0485
Tel: (573)243-3138 *Fax:* (573)243-3130
Members: 8 companies
Staff: 1
Annual Budget: under $10,000
President: Stone Manes
Historical Note
The National Clay Pot Manufacturers acts to stimulate the professional and public interest in the uses and advantages of clay flower pots and in the modern techniques employed in their manufacture and production. Members are makers of flower pots. NCPMA is a small organization with no headquarters or paid staff; the present president, who runs the organization, has held this office for some years. Membership: $400/year (organization/company).
Meetings/Conferences:
1999 – Cruise, Vancouver to Alaska/July 25-31/35

Nat'l Club Ass'n (1961)
One Lafayette Ctr
1120 20th St. N.W., Suite 725
Washington, DC 20036-3406
Tel: (202)822-9822 *Fax:* (202)822-9808
Members: 1000 private clubs
Staff: 9
Annual Budget: $1-2,000,000
Exec. V. President: Susanne R. Wegrzyn
V. President, Legal & Gov't Relations: Elizabeth Kirby Hart
Director, Publishing Services: Mary Barnes Embody
Historical Note
Members are private golf, country, city, tennis, and yacht clubs. Membership: $500-2,500/year, dues vary with membership size.
Publications:
Club Director. 6/yr. adv.
Clubhouse. 6/yr. adv.
Reference Series. m.
Meetings/Conferences:
Annual Meetings: Not held.

Nat'l Coaches Council (1974)
Historical Note
Organization defunct in 1997.

Nat'l Coal Ass'n (1917)
Historical Note
Merged with the American Mining Congress in 1995 to form the Nat'l Mining Ass'n.

Nat'l Coalition for Advanced Manufacturing (1989)
1201 New York Ave., N.W., Suite 725
Washington, DC 20005-3917
Tel: (202)216-2740 *Fax:* (202)289-7618
E-Mail: NACFAM@aol.com
Web Site: http://nacfam. org
Members: 300 companies and organizations
Staff: 10
Annual Budget: $500-1,000,000
President: Leo Reddy
Director, Communications: Leesa Gerst
Exec. V. President: Egils Milbergs
Historical Note
NACFAM members are manufacturers, non-profit organizations and educational institutions with an interest in advanced manufacturing technology. NACFAM promotes the interests of United States manufacturers by improving their product quality, market share and productivity through the deployment of advanced manufacturing processes, related management strategies, and technical training. Membership: $500-15,000/year, varies by type and size of organization.
Publications:
Directory of Advanced Manufacturing Resource Centers.
NACFAM Weekly. w.
NACFAM White Paper.
Meetings/Conferences:
Annual Meetings: Spring
1999 – Washington, DC(Hyatt Regency-Capitol Hill)/March 24-26

Nat'l Coalition of Abortion Providers
206 King St.
Alexandria, VA 22314
Tel: (703)684-0055 *Fax:* (703)684-5051
Web Site: www.ncap.com
Members: 200 clinics
Annual Budget: $100-250,000
Exec. Director: Ron Fitzsimmons
Historical Note
Members are independtly-owned clinics providing abortion services. Membership: $2,000/year.
Publications:
Newsletter. bi-m.

Nat'l Coalition of Alternative Community Schools (1978)
P.O. Box 15036
Santa Fe, NM 87506
Tel: (505)474-4312
Members: 400 schools
Staff: 1
Annual Budget: $10-25,000
National Office Manager: Ed Nagel
Historical Note
NCACS is composed of individuals, schools, home schools, foreign schools and resources supporting alternatives to traditional educational systems including educating children at home and developing tools and skills to work for social justice. Programs include teacher education. Membership: $40/year (individual); $50-$200/year, varies by enrollment (school).

Publications:
Nat'l Coalition News Newsletter. q. adv.
Nat'l Directory of Alternative Schools. bien. adv.
Meetings/Conferences:
Annual Meetings: Spring
1999 – Evergreen, CO/Apr. 21-25

Nat'l Coalition of Arts Therapies Ass'ns (1979)
Historical Note
Address unknown in 1997.

Nat'l Coalition of Black Meeting Planners (1982)
8630 Fenton St., Suite 126
Silver Spring, MD 20910-3803
Tel: (202)628-3952 *Fax:* (301)588-0011
Members: 625 individuals
Staff: 4
Annual Budget: $50-100,000
Exec. Director: Ozzie Jenkins, CMP
Historical Note
Formerly (1984) the Nat'l Black Meeting Planners Coalition. Fax number at a Baltimore location, (410) 992-1404. Membership: $125/year (meeting planners), $250/year (suppliers).
Publications:
NCBMP Newsletter. q. adv.
Meetings/Conferences:
Semi-annual Meetings: Spring and Fall/350

Nat'l Coalition of Girls Schools (1991)
228 Main St.
Concord, MA 01742
Tel: (978)287-4485 *Fax:* (978)287-6014
E-Mail: ncgs@ncgs.org
Web Site: http://www.ncgs.org
Members: 90 schools
Staff: 3
Annual Budget: $100-250,000
Exec. Director: Whitney Ransome
Co Exec. Director: Meg Moulton
Historical Note
Represents boarding, day, public and private schools for girls in the U.S., Canada, and Australia. Membership: $1,500-5,200/year.
Meetings/Conferences:
1999 – Baltimore, MD

Nat'l Coalition of Hispanic Health and Human Services Organizations (1973)
1501 16th St., N.W.
Washington, DC 20036-1401
Tel: (202)387-5000 *Fax:* (202)797-4353
E-Mail: info@cossmho.org
Web Site: http://www.cossmho.org
Members: 1,200 organizations and individuals
Staff: 30
Annual Budget: $2-5,000,000
President and C.E.O.: Jane L. Delgado, Ph.D.
C.F.O.: Hazel Moss, C.P.A.
General Counsel: Raphael Metzger
Director, Program Planning and Review: Ligia Serrano
Historical Note
Formerly (1986) Nat'l Coalition of Hispanic Mental Health and Human Services Organizations. Formed to expand and improve services, research, and training opportunities for the advancement of health status and quality of life of Hispanic families, youth, aged, handicapped and special Membership: $40/year (individual), $50-250/year (organization).
Publications:
The COSSMHO Reporter. q. adv.
Meetings/Conferences:
Biennial Meetings: even years

Nat'l Coffee Ass'n of the U.S.A. (1911)
110 Wall St.
New York, NY 10005
Tel: (212)344-5596 *Fax:* (212)425-7059
Web Site: http://www.coffeescience.org
Members: 161 manufacturers
Staff: 6
Annual Budget: $1-2,000,000
President and C.E.O.: Robert F. Nelson
Communications Manager: Gary Goldstein
Dir., Membership Development/Mktg.: Melissa Angerman, CAE
Historical Note
Formerly (1939) Associated Coffee Industries of America.
Publications:
Coffee Reporter Newsletter. m.
CoffeeTrax.
Winter Coffee Drinking Study. a.
Meetings/Conferences:
1999 – Aventura, FL/Feb. 25-28

Nat'l Coffee Service Ass'n (1972)
1899 Preston White Dr.
Reston, VA 20191-5435
Tel: (703)273-9008 *Fax:* (703)273-9011
Toll Free: (800)683 - 6272
Members: 650 companies
Staff: 8
Annual Budget: $500-1,000,000
Exec. Director: Terry L. Peters, CAE
Historical Note
Firms engaged in furnishing office and food services including coffee, refreshment, snack and vending services.
Publications:
Membership Directory. a. adv.
What's Brewing. m.

Meetings/Conferences:
Annual Meetings: Summer/1,600

Nat'l Coil Coaters Ass'n (1962)
401 N. Michigan Ave.
Chicago, IL   60611-4267
Tel: (312)321-6894   Fax: (312)527-6640
E-Mail: NCCA@sba.com
Web Site: http://www.ncca.org
Members: 180 companies
Staff: 3
Annual Budget: $1-2,000,000
Exec. Director: Glen R. Anderson

Historical Note
Manufacturers of continuously coated metal coil and suppliers of materials or services used in coil coating.

Publications:
Coil Lines. q.
Membership Directory. a.
Proceedings. a.
Product Capability Directory. bien.

Meetings/Conferences:
Semi-Annual Meetings: April and October/800
1999 – Indian Wells, CA(Stouffer Renaissance)/April 17-20
1999 – Rosemont, IL(Westin Hotel O'Hare)/October 6-8
2000 – Boca Raton, FL(Boca Raton Resort)/April 29-May 2

Nat'l Coin Machine Institute
Historical Note
Probably defunct.

Nat'l College of Foot Surgeons (1960)
Historical Note
Address unknown in 1998.

Nat'l Collegiate Athletic Ass'n (1906)
6201 College Blvd.
Overland Park, KS   66211-2422
Tel: (913)339-1906   Fax: (913)339-1950
Web Site: http://www.ncaa.org
Members: 1,202 institutions and organizations
Staff: 300
Annual Budget: Over $100,000,000
Exec. Director: Cedric Dempsey
Director, Federal Relations: Doris L. Dixon

Historical Note
NCAA members are colleges, universities and related educational athletic organizations. Annual Budget: $160 million.

Publications:
NCAA Annual Report. a.
NCAA Convention Proceedings. a.
NCAA Directory. a.
NCAA Manual. a.
NCAA News. 46/yr.

Meetings/Conferences:
Annual Meetings: January

Nat'l Collegiate Baseball Writers Ass'n (1960)
Historical Note
Address unknown in 1996.

Nat'l Collegiate Honors Council (1966)
Radford University, Boc 7017
Radford, VA   24142-7017
Tel: (540)831-6100   Fax: (540)831-5004
E-Mail: nchc@runet.edu
Web Site: http://www.honors.indiana.edu/nchc/index.html
Members: 588 individuals, 710 institutions; 119 students
Staff: 3
Annual Budget: $250-500,000
Exec. Secretary/Treasurer: Earl B. Brown, Jr.

Historical Note
An outgrowth of the Inter-University Committee on the Superior Student (ICSS) which was funded by the Carnegie Foundation from 1958 to 1965. A professional organization composed of faculty, administrators, and students dedicated to the encouragement of undergraduate honors learning; includes both public and private universities and colleges. Membership: $50/year (individual); $250/year (institution); $125/year (non-members); $35/year (student).

Publications:
Nat'l Honors Report. q.

Meetings/Conferences:
Annual Meetings: Fall
1999 – Orlando, FL(Stouffer)/Oct. 26-31
2000 – Washington, DC(Hilton & Towers)/Oct. 24-29
2001 – Minneapolis, MN(Hilton)/Oct. 31-Nov. 5

Nat'l Comedians' Ass'n (1984)
Historical Note
Address unknown in 1995.

Nat'l Commercial Builders Council
Historical Note
A council of the Nat'l Ass'n of Home Builders of the United States.

Nat'l Commercial Refrigeration Sales Ass'n
Historical Note
Became (1995) Nat'l Refrigeration Contractors Ass'n.

Nat'l Commission for Certifying Agencies
Historical Note
The accrediting division of Nat'l Organization for Competency Assurance, NCCA supersedes the commission for Health Certifying Agencies and exists to provide standards of excellence to NOCA member organizations.

Nat'l Committee for Clinical Laboratory Standards (1968)
940 West Valley Rd., Suite 1400
Wayne, PA   19087-1832
Tel: (610)688-0100   Fax: (610)688-0700
E-Mail: exoffice@nccls.com
Web Site: http://www.nccls.org
Members: 2,000 organizations
Staff: 26
Annual Budget: $2-5,000,000
Exec. Director: John V. Bergen, Ph.D
Director, Office Operations: Helen Gallagher
Director, Education: Karen M. Gerace

Historical Note
Became NCCLS in 1994. Members of the committee are from the medical community and are committed to improving the quality of laboratory practices, medical testing and healthcare services.

Publications:
Membership Report/Directory. a.
Update/Standards Status. m.

Meetings/Conferences:
1999 – Baltimore, MD(Renaissance
        Harborplace)/April 27-May 1/200

Nat'l Committee for Motor Fleet Supervisor Training
Historical Note
Became (1997) North American Transportation Management Institute.

Nat'l Committee for Quality Assurance (1979)
2000 L St., N.W., Suite 500
Washington, DC   20036
Tel: (202)955-3500   Fax: (202)955-3599
Web Site: http://www.NCQA.org
Staff: 145
Annual Budget: $10-25,000,000
President: Margaret O'Kane
Director, Communications: Barry Scholl
Asst. V. President, Public Policy: Steve Lamb
Director, Education: Donna Bruce
Education Program Coordinator: Eric Fennel
C.O.O.: Janet Marchibroda
Exec. V. President: Cary Jennett, M.D., Ph.D
C.F.O.: Scott Hartranft

Historical Note
Founded as a subdivision of Group Health Ass'n of America; became an autonomous organization in 1990. Reviews performance and qualifications of health maintenance organizations and other managed health care providers in the U.S., and confers accreditation on organizations meeting standards in several categories.

Nat'l Committee on Planned Giving (1988)
233 McCrea St., Suite 400
Indianapolis, IN   46225-1030
Tel: (317)269-6274   Fax: (317)269-6276
E-Mail: ncpg@iupui.edu
Web Site: http://www.ncpg.org
Members: 11,500 individuals
Staff: 16
Annual Budget: $1-2,000,000
Exec. Director: Tanya Howe Johnson, CAE
Communications Manager: Ron Tellmann
Manager, Education, Government Relations and Journal Editor:
        Sandra Kerr
Manager, Education: Kirt Reusre
Finance Manager: Staci Tingley
Business and Membership Manager: Barbara Owens
Administrative Manager: Kay Ramsay
Director of Operations: Barbara Yeager

Historical Note
Members are professionals involved in the process planning and cultivating charitable gifts.

Publications:
Directory of Council Members. a.
Guide to Starting a Planned Giving Program.
Journal of Gift Planning. q.
Planned Giving Newsletter. m.
Proceedings of the Nat'l Conference on Planned Giving. a.
Research Reports. irreg.
Workbook for Gift Planners (1997). irreg.

Meetings/Conferences:
1999 – Anaheim, CA(Disneyland)/Oct. 13-16/1900

Nat'l Communication Ass'n (1914)
5105 Backlick Road, Bldg. E
Annandale, VA   22003
Tel: (703)683-0533   Fax: (703)914-9471
Members: 7,000 individuals
Staff: 15
Annual Budget: $1-2,000,000
Exec. Director: James L. Gaudino, Ph.D.

Historical Note
Founded in 1914 as the Nat'l Ass'n of Academic Teachers of Public Speaking. Became the Nat'l Ass'n of Teachers of Speech in 1923, the Speech Ass'n of America in 1946, the Speech Communication Ass'n in 1970, and the National Communication Ass'n in 1998. Incorporated in Missouri in 1950. A constituent of the American Council on Education. Members are teachers at all levels and in all aspects of communication arts and sciences; media and communications consultants; students; libraries; and persons in theatre production. SCA promotes the study, criticism, research, educating, and application of the artistic, humanistic, and scientific principles of communication. Membership: $110/year (individual); $150/year (organization).

Publications:
Communication Education. q. adv.
Communication Monographs. q.
Critical Studies in Mass Communication. q.

Journal of Applied Communication Research.
Quarterly Journal of Speech. q.
Text and Performance Quarterly.

Meetings/Conferences:
Annual Meetings: November
1999 – Chicago, IL(Chicago Hilton)/Nov. 4-7/4500

Nat'l Communications Ass'n (1955)
16 E. 34th St., 15th Floor
New York, NY   10016
Tel: (212)683-8585   Fax: (212)532-7144
Members: 75 companies
Staff: 12
President: George Schoenberg

Historical Note
Companies making and selling privately-marketed communications equipment such as intercoms, pagers, security and fire alarms.

Publications:
NCA News. 3/year.

Nat'l Community Capital Ass'n (1986)
924 Cherry St., Second Floor
Philadelphia, PA   19107-2411
Tel: (215)923-4754   Fax: (215)923-4755
Members: 46 funds
Staff: 13
Annual Budget: $500-1,000,000
Exec. Director: Mark Pinsky
Director, Administration and Finance: Nita Melancon

Historical Note
Founded as Nat'l Ass'n of Community Development Loan Funds; assumed its current name in 1997. NCCA provides support for non-profit revolving loan funds that lend capital and provide technical assistance and training in distressed and disenfranchised communities.

Publications:
Community Investment Monitor Newsletter. semi-a.

Meetings/Conferences:
1999 – Denver, Co

Nat'l Community Development Ass'n (1973)
522 21st St., N.W., Suite 120
Washington, DC   20006
Tel: (202)293-7587   Fax: (202)887-5546
Web Site: http://www.ncdsonline.org
Members: 500 individuals
Staff: 5
Exec. Secretary: John A. Sasso

Historical Note
Formerly (1977) Nat'l Model Cities Community Development Directors Ass'n. NCDA members are community development program administrators.

Meetings/Conferences:
1999 – Washington, DC/Jan. 28-30

Nat'l Community Education Ass'n (1966)
3929 Old Lee Hwy., Suite 91-A
Fairfax, VA   22030-2401
Tel: (703)359-8973   Fax: (703)359-0972
E-Mail: ncea@ncea.com
Web Site: www.ncea.com
Members: 1,400 individuals
Staff: 4
Annual Budget: $500-1,000,000
Exec. Director: Starla Jewell-Kelly
Director of Communications: Ursula Ellis
Policy Analyst: Susan Burk
: Starla Jewell-Kelly
Dir., Membership: Diane Kurtz

Historical Note
Established as the Nat'l Community School Education Ass'n, it assumed its present name in 1974. Members are primarily school administrators. NCEA sponsors and supports community involvement in public education and lifelong learning opportunities. Membership: $125/year (individual); $300/year (organization).

Publications:
Community Education Journal. q. adv.
Community Education Today. m.

Meetings/Conferences:
Annual Meetings: Early December/1,500
1999 – Orlando, FL(Hyatt)
2000 – Reno, NV(The Nugget)
2001 – Charleston, SC(Charleston Place)

Nat'l Community Pharmacists Ass'n (1898)
205 Daingerfield Road
Alexandria, VA   22314
Tel: (703)683-8200   Fax: (703)683-3619
Toll Free: (800)544 - 7447
E-Mail: info@ncpanet.org
Web Site: http://www.ncpanet.org
Members: 35,000 individuals
Staff: 40
Annual Budget: $5-10,000,000
Exec. V. President: Calvin J. Anthony Ph.D.
V. President, Communications: Todd Dankmeyer
V.P., Government Affairs/General Counsel: John Rector
Assoc. Dir, Meetings: Lois Davis
V. President, Professional Affairs Covention: Kathryn Kuhn
Director, Finance: Bob R. Lebowski
V. President, Industry Affairs: Terry W. Hall

Historical Note
Formerly the Nat'l Ass'n of Retail Druggists, adopted its acronym (NARD) as its official name in 1987, and assumed it current name in 1996. NCPA promotes the needs of the independent pharmacist. Sponsors and supports the NCPA Political Action Committee.

Publications:
American Journal. m. adv.
Newsletter. m.

Pharmacists. m.

Meetings/Conferences:
Annual Meetings: Fall
1999 – Las Vegas, NV/Oct. 21-25

Nat'l Computer Dealer Forum

Historical Note
A forum of the Business Products Industry Ass'n.

Nat'l Computer Graphics Ass'n (1979)

Historical Note
NCGA members are individuals and comapnies interested in the development and promotion of the computer graphics industry and the improvement of computer graphics applications in business, industry, government, science and the arts. The Ass'n for the Development of electronic Publishing Technique (ADEPT) became a division of NCGA in 1993. Memebership: $75/year.

Nat'l Computer Security Ass'n (1989)

1200 Walnut Bottom Road, Suite 3
Carlisle, PA   17013-7635
Tel: (717)258-1816   Fax: (717)243-8642
Toll Free: (800)488 - 4595
E-Mail: office @ncsa.com
Web Site: http://www.icsa.net
Members: 2,500 companies and individuals
Staff: 87
Annual Budget: $1-2,000,000
President & C.E.O.: Peter S. Tippett
Director of Education: Dr. Michel E. Kabay, Ph.D.
Senior V. President, Research Outreach and Strategy: Pamela C.
   Martin
Exec. V. President: Robert C. Bales
Membership Director: Bob Daman

Historical Note
NCSA is an independent, international organization which facilitates interchange among end users, industry experts and vendors on information security, ethics and reliability. Membership: $95/year (individual).

Publications:
Information Security. m. adv.
NCSA Info Security Catalogue. semi-a. adv.

Meetings/Conferences:
Annual Meetings: Spring

Nat'l Concrete Burial Vault Ass'n (1929)

926 Great Pond Drive, Suite 1003
Altamonte Springs, FL   32714-7244
Tel: (407)788-1996   Fax: (407)774-6751
Toll Free: (800)538 - 1423
E-Mail: camco@iag.net
Web Site: http://www.ncbva.org
Members: 350 companies
Staff: 3
Annual Budget: $50-100,000
Exec. Director: Thomas A. Monahan, CAE

Historical Note
Members are companies seeking recognition and uniformity in the industry. Membership: $125-500/year (organization).

Publications:
Newsletter. bi-m.

Meetings/Conferences:
Annual Meetings: June/200
1999 – Cincinnati, OH(Hyatt Regency)/June 17-19

Nat'l Concrete Masonry Ass'n (1920)

2302 Horse Pen Road
Herndon, VA   20171
Tel: (703)713-1900   Fax: (703)713-1910
E-Mail: ncma@ncma.org
Web Site: http://www.ncma.org
Members: 500 companies
Staff: 30
Annual Budget: $2-5,000,000
President: Mark Hogan
Dir., Marketing/Communications: Charles W.L. Deale, CAE
Mgr., Communications: Randi Hertzberg
Director, Government Relations: Randall Pence
Director, Meetings and Conventions: Deborah W. Morris
Director, Administration: Jim Miller
Director of Engineering: Bob Thomas

Historical Note
Membership consists of manufacturers of concrete masonry products, and suppliers to the industry. Sponsors the NCMA Political Action Committee.

Publications:
C/M Architecture.
C/M News. m. adv.
CM Landscape Products.
Market Planning Statistical Survey. a.
Wage and Benefit Survey.

Meetings/Conferences:
Annual Meetings: Winter/2,800

Nat'l Confectioners Ass'n of the United States (1883)

7900 Westpark Drive, Suite A320
McLean, VA   22102-4203
Tel: (703)790-5750   Fax: (703)790-5752
Web Site: http://www.candyusa.org
Members: 300 manufacturers and suppliers
Staff: 16
Annual Budget: $2-5,000,000
President: Lawrence T. Graham
Senior V. Preisdent, Public and Legislative Affairs: Susan Snyder
   Smith
Director, Legislative Affairs: Stephen G. Lodge
V. President, Scientific Affairs: Carol Knight, Ph.D.
Mgr., Administration: Ruth A. Dickerson
Dir., Trade Relations: Jim Corcoran

Historical Note
Manufacturers of confectionery products and their suppliers. NCA is connected with the Nat'l Confectioners Ass'n of the United States Political Action Committee.

Publications:
All Sweet Journal. bi-m.
Membership Directory. a.
Short & Sweet Fax. bi-w.

Meetings/Conferences:

Nat'l Confectionery Sales Ass'n of America (1899)

10225 Berea Road, Suite C
Cleveland, OH   44102
Tel: (216)631-8200   Fax: (216)631-8210
E-Mail: propress1@aol.com
Web Site: http://www.candyhalloffame.com
Members: 318 individuals
Staff: 2
Annual Budget: under $10,000
Exec. Director: Teresa Tarantino

Historical Note
Formerly known as the Nat'l Confectionery Salesmen's Ass'n of America (1992). Founded in 1899 and incorporated in 1912. Sponsors the Candy Hall of Fame, established in 1971. Membership: $40/year (individual).

Publications:
NCSAA Journal. a adv. adv.

Meetings/Conferences:
1999 – Hershey, PA(Hershey Lodge)/April 29-May 2/500

Nat'l Conference of Appellate Court Clerks (1974)

Nat'l Center for State Courts
300 Newport Ave., P.O. Box 8798
Williamsburg, VA   23187-8798
Tel: (757)259-1841   Fax: (757)259-1520
Members: 230 individuals
Staff: 1
Annual Budget: under $10,000
Ass'n Management Specialist: Shelley Rockwell

Historical Note
To improve the appellate process. Officers are elected annually, administrative support provided by the Nat'l Center for State Courts. Membership: $50/yr. (individual).

Publications:
NCACC Newsletter. q.

Meetings/Conferences:
Annual Meetings: August
1999 – Skamania, WA

Nat'l Conference of Bankruptcy Judges (1926)

235 Secret Cove Drive
Lexington, SC   29072-8854
Tel: (803)957-6225   Fax: (803)957-8890
Members: 350 individuals
Staff: 1
Exec. Director: Christine Molick

Historical Note
An organization of bankruptcy judges and former judges organized to further the administration of bankruptcy laws. Established as the Nat'l Ass'n of Referees in Bankruptcy, it became the Nat'l Conference of Referees in Bankruptcy in 1969 and assumed its present name in 1973. Has no permanent address or paid staff.

Publications:
American Bankruptcy Law Journal. q.

Meetings/Conferences:
Annual Meetings: Fall
1999 – San Francisco, CA(Marriott)
2000 – Boston, MA(Marriott)
2001 – Orlando, FL(Marriott)
2002 – Chicago, IL(Hyatt)
2003 – San Diego, CA(Marriott)
2004 – Nashville, TN(Opryland)

Nat'l Conference of Bar Examiners (1931)

333 North Michigan Ave., Suite 1025
Chicago, IL   60601
Tel: (312)641-0963   Fax: (312)641-2052
Staff: 30
Annual Budget: $500-1,000,000
President: Erica Moeser

Historical Note
Conducts character investigations pertinent to admission to the practice of law at the request of state bar examiners boards, principally in cases of lawyers moving across state lines. An affiliated organization of the American Bar Ass'n.

Publications:
The Bar Examiner. q.

Meetings/Conferences:
Annual Meetings: With American Bar Ass'n in August

Nat'l Conference of Bar Foundations (1977)

c/o American Bar Ass'n, Div of Bar Svcs
541 North Fairbanks Ct., 14th Floor
Chicago, IL   60611-3314
Tel: (312)988-5354   Fax: (312)988-5492
Web Site: http://www.abanet.org
Members: 80 bar foundations
Staff: 2
Annual Budget: $25-50,000
President: Kathleen Schoene

Historical Note
NCBF assists its members by providing a medium for the exchange of ideas and information related to foundation management, raising and allocating funds, developing public service programs and accomplishing law-related service objectives. Bar foundations and other educational and charitable foundations affiliated with local, state or national bar associations, and foreign law foundations.

Membership: $25/year (individual), $150/year (foundation), $10/year/person/Board (must be a foundation member).

Publications:
NCBF Bar Foundation Activities Survey. bien.
Newsletter. q.
Roster. a.

Meetings/Conferences:
Semi-annual Meetings: with the American Bar Ass'n
1999 – Los Angeles, CA
1999 – Atlanta, GA

Nat'l Conference of Bar Presidents (1950)

541 N. Fairbanks Court
Chicago, IL   60611-3314
Tel: (312)988-5353   Fax: (312)988-5492
Members: 250 individuals, 170 membership bar ass'ns
Staff: 2
Annual Budget: $100-250,000
President: Stephen Zack
Assoc. Director, ABA Division for Bar Services: Pamela E. Robinson

Historical Note
Officers change annually. Composed of presidents and past presidents of local, state and national bar associations. Affiliated with American Bar Ass'n. Membership: $25/year (individual); $100-200/year (organization/company, depending on bar ass'ns member size).

Publications:
Best Projects.
Conference Call Newsletter.

Meetings/Conferences:
Semi-Annual Meetings: February, and August, with American
   Bar Ass'n
1999 – Los Angeles, CA/Feb. 4-6
1999 – Atlanta, GA/Aug. 5-7

Nat'l Conference of Black Lawyers (1968)

2 W. 125th St.
New York, NY   10027-4500
Tel: (212)864-4000   Fax: (212)222-2680
Members: 1,500 individuals
Staff: 2
Annual Budget: $100-250,000
Co-Chair: Marlene Archer

Historical Note
Membership in the U.S., Canada, and the Virgin Islands. A progressive organization of lawyers, law students, judges and lay people committed to utilizing legal remedies to eliminate institutional racism and aid in the development of the black community. Membership: $25-100/year (individual); $50/year (organization/company).

Publications:
Community Organization Legal Assistance Project (COLA)
   Notes. q.
NCBL Notes. q.
Various Section Newletters.

Meetings/Conferences:

Nat'l Conference of Black Mayors (1974)

1422 West Peachtree St., N.W., Suite 800
Atlanta, GA   30309
Tel: (404)892-0127   Fax: (404)876-4597
E-Mail: ncbm@aol.com
Members: 422 individuals
Staff: 4
Annual Budget: $500-1,000,000
Exec. Director: Michelle D. Kourouma
Dep. Director, Convention Coordinator: Carol Crawford

Historical Note
Organized in 1974 as the Southern Conference of Black Mayors. Changed to its present name in January, 1977. Membership fee based on sliding scale according to population.

Publications:
Convention Program and Journal. a.
Membership Roster. a.
Municipal Watch Newsletter. q.

Meetings/Conferences:
Annual Meetings: April
1999 – Denver, CO/April 20-25

Nat'l Conference of Black Political Scientists (1969)

c/o K.C. Morrison, Dept. Pol. Science
University of Missouri, Columbia
Columbia, MO   65211
Tel: (573)882-0125   Fax: (573)884-5131
E-Mail: polskcm@showme.missouri.edu
Web Site: http://www.power.ncat.edu/ncobps/default.htm
Members: 400 individuals
Staff: 1
President: K.C. Morrison

Historical Note
The NCOBPS is a professional organization of political scientists and other scholars committed to the study and research of those aspects of political science and political institutions which clarify the problem of black people, suggest useful remedies for solutions and mobilize needed resources. Membership: $65/year (professional)$35/year (student); $150/year (institutional).

Publications:
Nat'l Political Science Review. a.
NCOBPS Newsletter. q.
Roster of Black Political Scientists. irreg.

Meetings/Conferences:
Annual Meetings: Spring

Nat'l Conference of Brewery and Soft Drink Workers - United States and Canada (1886)

25 Louisiana Ave., N.W.
Washington, DC   20001
Tel: (202)624-6921   Fax: (202)624-6925

Members: 75 individuals
Director: David W. Laughton

Historical Note
Formerly the Internat'l Union of United Brewery, Flour, Cereal, Soft Drink and Distillery Workers of America, it became a conference of the Internat'l Brotherhood of Teamsters in 1976.

Publications:
Quadrennial Meeting: 1977.

Nat'l Conference of Catechetical Leadership *(1905)*
3021 Fourth St., N.E.
Washington, DC 20017-1102
Tel: (202)636-3826   *Fax:* (202)832-2712
E-Mail: nccl@clark.net
Web Site: http://nccl.org
Members: 1,400 individuals
Staff: 4
Annual Budget: $100-250,000
Exec. Director: Neil Parent
Assoc. Director: Christopher Anderson

Historical Note
Formerly (1966) Confraternity of Christian Doctrine. Members are directors of religious education for Catholic Dioceses. Formerly (1992) the Nat'l Conference of Diocesan Directors of Religious Education (CCD). Membership has been expanded to include academicians in religious education, publishers, and those in ministry or religious education. Membership: $50/year (individual); $250-650/year (organization).

Publications:
Directory. a.
Newsletter. 5/year.

Meetings/Conferences:
1999 – Indianapolis, IN(Adam's Mark)/April 18-22

Nat'l Conference of Catholic Bishops/U.S. Catholic Conference *(1966)*
3211 Fourth St., N.E.
Washington, DC 20017
Tel: (202)541-3000   *Fax:* (202)541-3166
Web Site: http://nccbuscc.org
Members: 400 individuals
Staff: 350
Annual Budget: $25-50,000,000
Gen. Secretary: Msgr. Dennis M. Schnurr
Secretary, Communications: Msgr. Francis W. Maniscalco
Director, Govt. Liaison: Frank Monahan
Director, Finance: Kenneth Korotky
General Counsel: Mark Chopko

Historical Note
Affiliated with the United States Catholic Conference, with which it shares staff. Founded in 1917 as the Nat'l Catholic War Council. Has an annual budget of approximately $41 million.

Publications:
NCCB/USCC Report. m.

Meetings/Conferences:
Annual Meetings: November in Washington, DC

Nat'l Conference of Commissioners on Uniform State Laws *(1892)*
211 E. Ontario St., Suite 1300
Chicago, IL 60611
Tel: (312)915-0195   *Fax:* (312)915-0187
E-Mail: nccusl@nccusl.org
Web Site: http://www.nccusl.org
Members: 335 individuals
Staff: 5
Annual Budget: $500-1,000,000
Chief Administrative Officer: Ellyce Anapolsky
Communications: Rachel R. Robinson
Director, Legislation: John McCabe

Historical Note
The Conference, one of the oldest of state organizations designed to encourage interstate cooperation, was organized in 1892 to promote uniformity by voluntary action of each state government. Since its organization, the Conference has drafted over two hundred uniform laws on numerous subjects in various fields of law, many of which have been widely enacted.

Publications:
Handbook and Proceedings. a.

Meetings/Conferences:
Annual Meetings: Last week in July
1999 – Denver, CO(Hyatt Regency Tech Center)/July 23-30

Nat'l Conference of CPA Practitioners *(1979)*
3000 Marcus Ave., Suite LL-09
Lake Success, NY 11042-1012
Tel: (516)488-5400   *Fax:* (516)488-5549
Toll Free: (888)488 - 5400
Web Site: www.nccpap.org
Members: 1,200 firms
Staff: 2
Annual Budget: $250-500,000
Exec. Director: Brenda Mahler

Historical Note
NCCPAP represents independent, medium sized regional and local CPA firms. Membership: $160-$500/year (depending on number of professional personnel in firm).

Publications:
NCCAP News & Views. m. adv.

Meetings/Conferences:
Annual Meetings: October
1999 – Boca Raton, FL/Jan. 4-5
1999 – Washington, DC
1999 – New York, NY(Laguardia Airport)
1999 – Boston, MA

Nat'l Conference of Diocesan Vocation Directors *(1971)*

P.O. Box 1570
Little River, SC 29566
Tel: (803)280-7191   *Fax:* (803)280-0681
E-Mail: Ncvocdir@aol.com
Web Site: www.catholic-forum.com/ncdud
Members: 500 individuals, 188 organizations
Staff: 2
Annual Budget: $50-100,000
Exec. Director: Dorothy Foss

Historical Note
NCDVD is a professional conference of Roman Catholic diocesan vocation directors whose mission is to provide service, training and development, vocation awareness materials, network relationships and support. Membership: $395-595/year (organization/company).

Publications:
Directory of Diocesan Vocation Office Personnel. a.
NCDVD News. 5/yr.

Meetings/Conferences:
1999 – St. Louis, MO

Nat'l Conference of Directors of Religious Education

Historical Note
A division of the Nat'l Catholic Educational Ass'n.

Nat'l Conference of Editorial Writers *(1947)*
6223 Executive Blvd.
Rockville, MD 20852-3906
Tel: (301)984-3015   *Fax:* (301)231-0026
Web Site: http://www.ncew.org
Members: 600 individuals
Staff: 5
Annual Budget: $50-100,000
Exec. Secretary: Cora B. Everett

Historical Note
Members are active editorial writers or others who devote a substantial part of their time to the preparation of editorial copy, columns, or broadcast commentary, or to the determination of editorial policy; active members of the faculty of recognized colleges, schools or departments of journalism who teach courses in editorial writing and related areas, or supervise the editorial page of student of student publications; and others who are able to satisfy the membership committee that they play an active role in editorial page or broadcast editorial operations. Membership: $85-$150/year (individual).

Publications:
The Masthead. q.

Meetings/Conferences:
Annual Meetings: September, by invitation of a host member or newspaper
1999 – Denver, CO(Westin Tabor Center)/Sept. 14-18
2000 – Seattle, WA(Cavanaugh's Inn)/Sept. 13-16
2001 – Pittsburgh, PA(Pittsburgh Marriott)/Sept. 12-15
2002 – Nashville, TN

Nat'l Conference of Executives of the Arc *(1964)*
500 E. Border St., Suite 300
Arlington, TX 76010
Tel: (817)261-6003   *Fax:* (817)277-3491
Toll Free: (800)433 - 5255
E-Mail: NCEarc@aol.com
Web Site: http://Thearc.org/nce/nce.html
Members: 425 individuals
Staff: 1
Annual Budget: $100-250,000
President: Marsha Blanco

Historical Note
Formerly the Nat'l conference of Executives of Ass'ns for Retarded Citizens. Membership: $75-175/year (individual).

Publications:
Employment Registry. irreg.
Executive. bi-m. adv.
Membership Directory. a.
Salary & Benefits Survey. a.

Meetings/Conferences:
Annual Meetings: Fall

Nat'l Conference of Federal Trial Judges *(1972)*
c/o American Bar Ass'n
541 N. Fairbanks Court
Chicago, IL 60611
Tel: (312)988-5705   *Fax:* (312)988-5709
Members: 400 individuals
Staff: 1
Annual Budget: $25-50,000
Div. Director: Luke Bierman

Historical Note
Holds one conference within the Judicial Division of the American Bar Ass'n.

Meetings/Conferences:
1999 – Los Angeles, CA/Feb. 3-9
1999 – Atlanta, GA/Aug. 5-11

Nat'l Conference of Firemen and Oilers *(1898)*
1900 L. St., N.W., Suite 502
Washington, DC 20036
Tel: (202)872-3600   *Fax:* (202)872-1222
Members: 25,000 individuals
Staff: 10
Annual Budget: $1-2,000,000
Int'l President: George G. Francisco, Jr.
Internat'l Secretary-Treasurer: Daniel S. Anderson, Jr.

Historical Note
Formerly (1995) Internat'l Brotherhood of Firemen and Oilers. Organized in Kansas City December 18, 1898 as the Internat'l Brotherhood of Stationary Firemen and chartered by the American Federation of Labor the following year. In 1919 the charter was expanded to include oilers and boiler room helpers and the name

was changed to its present form. Sponsors and supports the Internat'l Brotherhood of Firemen and Oilers Political League.

Meetings/Conferences:
Annual Meetings: Every 5 years (2001)

Nat'l Conference of Insurance Legislators *(1969)*
122 S. Swan St.
Albany, NY 12210-1715
Tel: (518)449-3210   *Fax:* (518)432-5651
E-Mail: info@ncoil.org
Web Site: http://www.ncoil.org
Members: 34 states
Staff: 7
Annual Budget: $50-100,000
Exec. Director: Robert E. Mackin
Meeting Director: Susan F. Nolan

Historical Note
A national organization of state legislators working toward a better understanding of insurance, state insurance regulation and legislation and against federal intervention into the rights of states to regulate and legislate insurance matters. Added "National" to its name in 1987. Liasons with the Nat'l Ass'n of Insurance Commissioners. Membership: $3,000/year (state).

Publications:
NCOIL Legislative Fact Book and Almanac. a.
NCOILetter. m.

Meetings/Conferences:
Annual Meetings: November/400

Nat'l Conference of Lieutenant Governors *(1962)*
P.O. Box 11910
Lexington, KY 40578-1910
Tel: (606)244-8171   *Fax:* (606)244-8001
E-Mail: gmanning@csg.org
Members: 55 individuals
Staff: 1
Annual Budget: $100-250,000
Director: Gail B. Manning

Historical Note
Affiliated with the Council of State Governments. Promotes the exchange of information; fosters interstate cooperation; and seeks to improve the efficiency and the effectiveness of the office of the lieutenant governor. Membership: $600-800/year (state).

Publications:
NCLG Focus. q.

Meetings/Conferences:
Semi-annual Meetings: Late Summer & State-Fed/Washington, DC/Feb-March

Nat'l Conference of Local Environmental Health Administrators *(1938)*
c/o NEHA, 720 S. Colorado Blvd.,
South Tower, Suite 970
Denver, CO 80222
Tel: (303)756-9090   *Fax:* (303)691-9490
E-Mail: lthack@aol.com
Members: 300 individuals
Staff: 1
Annual Budget: under $10,000
Exec. Director: Nelson E. Fabian

Historical Note
Formerly (1966) the Conference of Municipal Public Health Engineers and (1983) Conference of Local Environmental Health Administrators. An organization of environmental health administrators employed at the local level, at universities, and in industry. Purpose is to promote efficient and effective local environmental health programs. Affiliated with the National Environmental Health Association. Membership: $15/year.

Publications:
Newsletter. 3/year. adv.

Meetings/Conferences:
Annual Meetings: June, with the Nat'l Environmental Health Ass'n
1999 – Nashville, TN(Renaissance)/July 5-9
2000 – Denver, CO(Adams Mark)

Nat'l Conference of Personal Managers *(1967)*
46-19 220 Place
Bayside, NY 11361
Tel: (212)421-2670   *Fax:* (212)838-5105
Members: 180 individuals
Annual Budget: under $10,000
President: Gerard W. Purcell

Historical Note
Members are personal managers for artists in the entertainment industry.

Publications:
NCOPM Newsletter. q.

Nat'l Conference of Regulatory Utility Commission Engineers *(1922)*
c/o IN Utility Regulatory Commission
302 W. Washington, Suite E-306
Indianapolis, IN 46204
Tel: (317)232-2523   *Fax:* (317)233-1981
Web Site: http://www.ai.org/iurc
Members: 125 individuals
Annual Budget: $10-25,000
Secretary: Sandy Ilbaugh

Historical Note
Formerly (1972) Conference of State Utility Commission Engineers. Affiliated with the Nat'l Ass'n of Regulatory Utility Commissioners.

Publications:
Proceedings. a.

Meetings/Conferences:
Annual Meetings: June

Nat'l Conference of Special Court Judges (1969)

541 North Fairbanks Court
13th Floor
Chicago, IL 60611
Tel: (312)988-5697   *Fax:* (312)988-5709
Members: 900 individuals
Staff: 1

Historical Note
A conference of the American Bar Ass'n, NCSCJ members are judges sitting on limited jurisdiction courts.

Publications:
Special Court News. q.

Meetings/Conferences:
Annual Meetings: In conjunction with the American Bar Ass'n

Nat'l Conference of Standards Laboratories (1961)

1800 30th St., Suite 305B
Boulder, CO 80301
Tel: (303)440-3339   *Fax:* (303)440-3384
E-Mail: ncsl-staff@ncsl-hq.org
Web Site: http://www.ncsl.hq.org
Members: 1,400 laboratories
Staff: 3
Annual Budget: $250-500,000
Business Manager: Wilbur Anson

Historical Note
NCSL is an independent non-profit association of academic, scientific, industrial, commercial and governmental laboratories concerned with the measurement of physical quantities, the callibration of standards and instruments, and the development of standards of practice. Membership: $225/year.

Publications:
Conference Proceedings. a.
NCSL Directory of Standards Laboratories. bien.
NCSL Newsletter. q.

Meetings/Conferences:
Annual Meetings: Summer
1999 – Charlotte, NC/July 11-15

Nat'l Conference of State Fleet Administrators (1986)

P.O. Box 1012
Versailles, KY 40383-5012
Tel: (606)873-2981   *Fax:* (606)231-1887
E-Mail: ncsfa@iglou.com
Web Site: http://www.ncsfa.org
Members: 150 individuals
Staff: 1
Annual Budget: $100-250,000
Exec. Director: Gaye Horton

Historical Note
NCFSA members are state goverment administrators responsible for vehicle fleet management. Associate membership is available to municipal or local government entities. Auxiliary membership is available for private sector representatives. Membership: $480/year (1st member from state agency); $240/year (2nd member from state agency/associate); $1,000/year (auxiliary).

Publications:
Annual Survey Report. a.
Fleet Administration News Newsletter. q.
NCSFA Roster. irreg.

Meetings/Conferences:
Annual Meetings: Fall/150

Nat'l Conference of State Historic Preservation Officers (1969)

444 N. Capitol St., N.W., Suite 342
Washington, DC 20001
Tel: (202)624-5465   *Fax:* (202)624-5419
Members: 59 states and territories
Staff: 3
Annual Budget: $250-500,000
Exec. Director: Eric Hertfelder

Historical Note
Professional organization of the gubernatorially appointed State Historic Preservation Officers who carry out the national preservation program for the Secretary of the Interior under the National Historic Preservation Act.

Meetings/Conferences:
Annual Meetings: Always Washington, DC in March.
1999 – Washington, DC(Marriott Metro
     Center)/March 20-23/150

Nat'l Conference of State Legislatures (1975)

1560 Broadway, Suite 700
Denver, CO 80202
Tel: (303)830-2200   *Fax:* (303)863-8003
Web Site: www.ncsl.org
Members: 31,993 individuals, 50 state legislatures
Staff: 150
Annual Budget: $10-25,000,000
Exec. Director: William T. Pound
Director, Legislative Programs: Rich Jones
Director, Finance: N. Douglas Webb
Operations Director: Diane Chaffin
Director, Economic, Fiscal and Human Resources: Ronald Snell
State Services Director: Karl Kurtz

Historical Note
Formed by a merger of the National Legislative Conference (founded in 1947), the National Conference of State Legislative Leaders (founded 1959) and the National Society of State Legislators (founded in 1965). An organization of state legislators, legislative staffs, territories, and commonwealths. Supported by state dues; the Foundation for State Legislatures, a center for public/private sector interaction; private foundations, grants and contracts. Affiliated with the Council of State Governments and the National Governors' Association. Has an annual budget of $13 million.

Publications:
Fiscal Letter. bi-m.

LegisBrief. 48/yr.
State Legislatures Magazine. 10/yr.

Meetings/Conferences:
Annual Meetings: Summer

Nat'l Conference of State Liquor Administrators (1934)

New Jersery Dept. of Law & Public Safety
Div. of ABC, P.O. Box 087
Trenton, NJ 08625-0087
Tel: (609)984-2598   *Fax:* (609)633-6078
Members: 41 government and state agencies
Annual Budget: $50-100,000
Exec. Secretary-Treasurer: Charles D. Sapienza

Historical Note
NCSLA was formed to provide opportunities for state-licensed administrators to meet and exchange ideas and information and to formulate uniform regulations, statute and laws affecting the sales of alcoholic beverages. Has no paid officers or full-time staff. Membership: $225/year (state).

Publications:
Directory. a.

Meetings/Conferences:
Annual Meetings: June/350
1999 – Atlantic City, NJ(Taj Mahal)/June 20-25

Nat'l Conference of State Retail Ass'ns (1968)

Historical Note
A federation of 50 state retail associations meeting annually in Washington in May under the auspices of the Nat'l Retail Federation.

Nat'l Conference of State Social Security Administrators (1952)

P.O. Box 557
Frankfort, KY 40602-0557
Tel: (502)564-3952   *Fax:* (502)564-2124
Members: 115 individuals
Staff: 1
Annual Budget: $10-25,000
Membership Chairperson: Daryl Dunagan

Historical Note
Founded in January 1952 in Bloomington, Indiana. Formerly (1963) Conference of State Social Security Administrators. NCSSSA acts as the administrator for state government and political subdivisions within each state. Membership: $125/year (organization).

Publications:
Newsletter. q.
Proceedings. a.

Meetings/Conferences:
Annual Meetings: Fall
2000 – Baltimore, MD

Nat'l Conference of State Transportation Specialists (1958)

Historical Note
Address unknown in 1997.

Nat'l Conference of States on Building Codes and Standards (1967)

505 Huntmar Park Drive, Suite 210
Herndon, VA 20170
Tel: (703)437-0100   *Fax:* (703)481-3596
Members: 290 individuals and organizations
Staff: 50
Annual Budget: $250-500,000
Exec. Director: Robert C. Wible
Director, Technical Services: Mari CotÈ

Historical Note
Serves the building code and public safety interests of the 50 states and territories. Provides a forum for the discussion and solution of problems of state building codes and regulations and coordinates intergovernmental reforms in the area of building codes and standards. Executive branch agreement with the Nat'l Governors' Ass'n. Works closely with the Center for Building Technology of the Nat'l Institute of Standards and Technology. Membership: $75/year (associate); $300/year (organization); $75/year (affiliate); $50/year (state).

Publications:
Directory of Building Codes & Regulations. a.
Newsletter. q.

Meetings/Conferences:
Annual Meetings: October

Nat'l Conference of Women's Bar Ass'ns (1981)

P.O. Box 82366
Portland, OR 97282-0366
Tel: (503)775-4396   *Fax:* (503)775-9605
E-Mail: ncwba@aol.com
Members: 300 individuals, 100 women's bar ass'ns
Staff: 1
Exec. Director: Diane Ryherson

Historical Note
Members are state and local women's bar associations, sections, special interest groups and individuals serving as a resource for members and offering them support, guidance and information. Membership: $50/year (individual), $75-350/year (based upon bar association).

Publications:
NCWBA Newsletter. q.

Meetings/Conferences:
Semi-annual Meetings: in conjuction with the American Bar
     Ass'n
1999 – Los Angeles, CA/Feb. 5-6
1999 – Atlanta, GA/Aug. 5-8

Nat'l Conference of Yeshiva Principals (1947)

160 Broadway
New York, NY 10038
Tel: (212)227-1000   *Fax:* (212)406-6934
Members: 380 individuals
Staff: 2
Annual Budget: $25-50,000
Exec. V. President: Rabbi A. Moshe Possick

Historical Note
Affiliated with the Nat'l Soc. for Hebrew Day Schools.

Publications:
Hamenahel-The Principal. 8/year.

Meetings/Conferences:
Annual Meetings: May in New York, NY

Nat'l Conference on Public Employee Retirement Systems (1941)

1620 I St., N.W., Suite 220
Washington, DC 20006-4005
Tel: (202)429-2230   *Fax:* (202)223-8323
Web Site: http://www.ncpers.org
Members: 1,300 individuals, 550 organizations
Staff: 3
Annual Budget: $250-500,000
President: Jay W. Bixby
Legislative Coordinator: Ed Braman
Conference Facilitator: Kristen Sirovatka
Exec. Secretary: Carlos Resendez

Historical Note
NCPERS represents administrators and trustees of public pension funds. Membership: $100-400/year (individual); $6,000/year (organization)

Publications:
Legislative Alert. w.
Monthly Monitor. m.
Persist Newsletter. q.
Proceedings. a.
Sponsoring Member Services Directory. a.

Meetings/Conferences:
1999 – Atlanta, GA/1300
2000 – Honolulu, HI

Nat'l Conference on Research in English (1937)

Historical Note
Became Nat'l Conference on Research of Language and Literacy in 1996.

Nat'l Conference on Research in Language and Literacy (1937)

Box 330, George Peabody College
Vanderbilt Univ.
Nashville, TN 37203
Tel: (615)322-8044   *Fax:* (615)322-8999
Members: 450 individuals
Annual Budget: $25-50,000
Secretary: Deborah Rowe

Historical Note
Formerly the Nat'l Conference on Research in English(1996). Members are teachers and researchers in English. Has no paid officers or full-time staff; the secretariat changes bienially. Membership by invitation only. Membership: $10/year.

Publications:
Directory.
Newsletter. semi-a.

Meetings/Conferences:
Annual Meetings: Spring, with Internat'l Reading Ass'n and Fall,
     with Nat'l Council of Teachers of English
1999 – San Diego, CA/May 2-7
1999 – Denver, CO/Nov. 18-23

Nat'l Conference on Weights and Measures (1905)

15245 Shady Grove Road, Suite 130
Rockville, MD 20850-3222
Tel: (301)975-4004   *Fax:* (301)926-0647
Members: 3,300 individuals
Staff: 2
Annual Budget: $100-250,000
Exec. Secretary: Beth W. Palys, CAE

Historical Note
Members are weights and measures enforcement officials from Federal, state, county and local governments; associate members from industry. Sponsored by the National Institute of Standards & Technology. Membership: $35/year (state or government); $50/year (associate member).

Publications:
Annual Report. a.
Directory of Weights and Measures Officials. a.
Handbook 130. a.
Handbook 44. a.
Proceedings of Annual Meeting. a.

Meetings/Conferences:
Annual Meetings: July/450

Nat'l Congress for Community Economic Development

1875 Connecticut Ave., N.W. Suite 524
Washington, DC 20009
Tel: (202)234-5009   *Fax:* (202)234-4510
V.P., Administration: Kim Honor

Nat'l Congress of Animal Trainers and Breeders (1975)

23675 W. Chardon Road
Grayslake, IL 60030
Tel: (847)546-0717   *Fax:* (847)546-3454
Members: 300 individuals
Staff: 2
President: John F. Cuneo, Jr.

Historical Note
NCATB members are individuals and organizations involved in the breeding and training of rare animals for display in circuses, fairs and parks.

Nat'l Consortium of Chemical Dependency Nurses (1987)
1720 Willow Creek Circle, Suite 519
Eugene, OR 97402-9152
Tel: (541)485-4421   *Fax:* (541)485-7372
Toll Free: (800)876 - 2236
Members: 1000 individuals
Annual Budget: $100-250,000
Exec. Director: Randy Bryson, R.N.

Historical Note
NCCDN members are registered and licensed practical nurses specializing in the treatment of chemical dependency. Provides certification for members. Membership: $55/year.

Publications:
CD Nurse Briefing Newsletter. q. adv.

Meetings/Conferences:
Annual Meetings: Fall

Nat'l Constables Ass'n (1976)
16 Stonybrook Drive
Levittown, PA 19055-2217
Tel: (215)547-6400   *Fax:* (215)943-0979
Toll Free: (800)272 - 1775
E-Mail: LEFCOURTAPR@juno.com
Members: 15,000 individuals
Staff: 2
Annual Budget: $50-100,000
Exec. Director: Hal Lefcourt, APR
Exec. Secretary: Roz Liberatore
Treasurer: Lou Tabat
Project Director: Peggy Irons

Historical Note
Founded in New Jersey in 1973 as the Nat'l Police Constables Ass'n and incorporated in Pennsylvania in 1976. The present name was assumed in 1981. A non-profit, professional fraternal organization of constables, geared to a rebirth of the constable system and dedicated to upgrading their quality of performance. Membership: $25/year.

Publications:
All Points Bulletin. q. adv.
Buyer's Guide. semi-a. adv.
Constable News. q. adv.
NCA Program Booklet. a. adv.
Newsletter. q. adv.

Meetings/Conferences:
Annual Meetings: March
1999 – Biloxi, MS(Beaurivage Hotel)/March 4-7/100

Nat'l Constructors Ass'n (1947)
1730 M St., N.W., Suite 503
Washington, DC 20036-4508
Tel: (202)466-8880   *Fax:* (202)466-7512
Members: 14 companies
Staff: 4
Annual Budget: $250-500,000
Senior V. President: Nicholas A. Fiore

Historical Note
Large, unionized engineering and construction companies. Deals in labor relations, safety issues, and government relations. Membership: $27,000/year (company).

Publications:
Directory. a.
NCA Newsletter. bi-m.

Meetings/Conferences:

Nat'l Consumers League (1899)
1701 K St., N.W., #1200
Washington, DC 20006
Tel: (202)835-3323   *Fax:* (202)835-0747
E-Mail: nclncl@aol.com
Web Site: http://www.nclnet.org
Members: 8,000 affiliates
Staff: 20
Annual Budget: $1-2,000,000
President: Linda F. Golodner
V. President, Public Affairs: Cleo Manuel
V. President, Public Policy: Susan Grant
V. President, Public Policy: Darlene Adkins
Special Events Coordinator: Janet Coco
Exec. V. President: Sara Cooper
V. President, Development: Larry Bostian

Historical Note
A non-profit membership organization, the League's mission is to identify, protect, represent, and advance the economic and social interests of consumers and workers. Absorbed the Nat'l Consumers Congress in 1978. Membership: $20/year (individual); $25-250/year (organization).

Publications:
AAFT Quarterly. q.
Bulletin. bi-m.
Child Labor Monitor. q.
Community Credit Link. q.
Focus on Fraud. q.

Meetings/Conferences:
Annual Meetings: April or May
1999 – Washington, DC(Hyatt Regency-Capital Hill)/May 15-19/300
2000 – Milwaukee, WI

Nat'l Contact Lens Examiners (1976)
10341 Democracy Lane
Fairfax, VA 22030
Tel: (703)691-1061   *Fax:* (703)691-3929
Web Site: http://www.opticians.org.

Members: 7,500 individuals
Staff: 8
Annual Budget: $250-500,000
Exec. Director: Candace Purdun

Nat'l Contract Management Ass'n (1959)
1912 Woodford Road
Vienna, VA 22182-3728
Tel: (703)448-9231   *Fax:* (703)448-0939
Toll Free: (800)344 - 8096
Web Site: http://www.ncmahq.com
Members: 21,500 individuals
Staff: 28
Annual Budget: $2-5,000,000
Exec. V. President: James W. Goggins, CPCM, CAE
Communications Manager: Terry Hoskins
Director, Finance/Information Services: Marian Kann
Director, Member Services: Stan Barrett
Director, Programs: Andrea Papilion

Historical Note
Members are concerned with various forms of contracting with federal, state and local governments and industry. Formerly (1965) Nat'l Ass'n of Professional Contracts Administrators. Absorbed Gov't Contract Management Ass'n of America in 1965. Membership: $65/year.

Publications:
Contract Management Magazine. m. adv.
National Contract Management Journal. semi-a.
Topical Issues in Procurement Series Newsletter.

Meetings/Conferences:
1999 – Washington, DC/Apr. 9-12

Nat'l Contract Sweepers Institute
Historical Note
Became (1995) Contract Sweepers Institute. A division of American Public Works Ass'n, which provides administrative support.

Nat'l Cooperative Business Ass'n (1916)
1401 New York Ave., N.W., Suite 1100
Washington, DC 20005-2160
Tel: (202)638-6222   *Fax:* (202)638-1374
Web Site: http://www.cooperative.org
Members: 385 individuals, 261 companies
Staff: 35
Annual Budget: $5-10,000,000
President and C.E.O.: Paul Hazen
Director of Communications: Leta M. Mach
V. President, Government Relations: Alan Zepp
V. President, Finance and Administration: Constance L. Moser
Director, Human Resources: Peggy Spangler

Historical Note
Founded as the Cooperative League of the U.S.A., NCBA assumed its present name in 1985. Represents American cooperatives in Internat'l Cooperative Alliance. Supports and represents all types of cooperatives. Sponsors and supports the Cooperative Action for Congressional Trust (CO-ACT). Has an annual budget of approximately $9.3 million. Membership: $50/year (individual); varies for organizations.

Publications:
Cooperative Business Journal. 10/year.

Meetings/Conferences:
Annual Meetings: Spring in Washington, DC

Nat'l Coordinating Council on Emergency Management
Historical Note
Became Internat'l Ass'n of Emergency Managers in 1998.

Nat'l Corn Growers Ass'n (1957)
1000 Executive Pkwy., Suite 105
St. Louis, MO 63141
Tel: (314)275-9915   *Fax:* (314)275-7061
E-Mail: corninfo@ncga.com
Web Site: http://www.ncga.com
Members: 30,000 individuals, 25 state ass'ns; 19 state boards
Staff: 30
Annual Budget: $2-5,000,000
C.E.O. and Exec. V. President: Christine Wehrman
Director, Communications: Kevin Aandahl
Director, State Relations: Brian Stockman
Director, Conventions and Trade Shows: Peggy Findley
Director, Finance: Wanda Salzman

Historical Note
NCGA represents U.S. corn growers. Membership: $20-50/yr. (varies by state).

Publications:
Corn Grower Newsletter. m.

Meetings/Conferences:

Nat'l Correctional Recreational Ass'n (1966)
Historical Note
Address unknown in 1995; presumed inactive.

Nat'l Corrugated Steel Pipe Ass'n (1955)
1255 23rd St., N.W.
Washington, DC 20037-1174
Tel: (202)452-1700   *Fax:* (202)833-3636
E-Mail: csp@ncspa.org
Web Site: http://www.ncspa.org
Members: 90 manufacturers
Staff: 3
Annual Budget: $500-1,000,000
Exec. V. President: Joseph B. Morris

Historical Note
Formerly Nat'l Corrugated Metal Pipe Ass'n. Membership: $550-$1,300/year (company).

Publications:
Corrugations. bi-m.
Membership Directory. a.

NCSPA News. q.
Pipeline. q.
Meetings/Conferences:
Annual Meetings: March
1999 – Southampton, Bermuda(Sonesta)

Nat'l Cosmetology Ass'n (1921)
401 N. Michigan Ave.
Chicago, IL 60611-4255
Tel: (314)534-7980   *Fax:* (314)534-8618
Members: 40,000 individuals
Staff: 20
Annual Budget: $2-5,000,000
Exec. Director: Paul Bykxtra
Coordinator, Public Relations: Julie Becker

Historical Note
Owners and operators of hair, skin and nail salons. Formerly (1986) Nat'l Hairdressers and Cosmetologists Ass'n. Sponsors and supports the NCA Political Action Committee. Membership: $45-$125/year (individual).

Publications:
American Looks. semi-a.
CB Journal.
Leadership Newsletter. q.
Salon Ovations Magazine. m. adv.

Meetings/Conferences:
Semi-Annual Meetings: Winter and Summer
1999 – Boston, MA(Sheraton)
2000 – St. Louis, MO(Adams Mark)

Nat'l Costumers Ass'n (1923)
3038 Hayes Ave.
Fremont, OH 43420
Tel: (419)334-4098
Members: 400 theatrical costumers & suppliers
Staff: 2
Annual Budget: $50-100,000
Secretary-Treasurer: La Mar C. Kerns

Historical Note
Membership: $150/year (organization/company).

Publications:
The Costumers Magazine. bi-m. adv.

Meetings/Conferences:
Annual Meetings: July
1999 – Los Angeles, CA(Biltmore Hotel)/July 16-22/400
2000 – Pittsburgh, PA/400
2001 – Portland, OR/400

Nat'l Cotton Batting Institute (1954)
P.O. Box 820287
Memphis, TN 38112
Tel: (901)274-9030   *Fax:* (901)725-0510
Members: 40 individuals, 53 companies
Staff: 2
Annual Budget: $10-25,000
Exec. Secretary: Tommy Horton

Historical Note
Administrative support provided by Nat'l Cotton Council.

Publications:
NCBI Newsletter. bi-m.

Meetings/Conferences:
Annual Meetings: Spring

Nat'l Cotton Council of America (1938)
Box 820285, 1918 North Pkwy.
1918 North Pkwy
Memphis, TN 38182-0285
Tel: (901)274-9030   *Fax:* (901)725-0510
E-Mail: info@cotton.org
Web Site: http://www.cotton.org
Staff: 95
Annual Budget: $5-10,000,000
Exec. V. President: Phillip C. Burnett
Director, Communications: Fred Middleton
Meeting Planner: Ellen Carpenter

Historical Note
Membership consists of approximately 300 delegates named by cotton interests in the cotton-producing states. Seeks to increase the consumption of cotton and cottonseed products. Supports the Committee for the Advancement of Cotton (political action). Has an annual budget of approximately $8.2 million.

Publications:
Cotton Commentary. q.
Cotton Economic Review. m.
Cotton Physiology Today. m.
Cotton's Week. w.

Meetings/Conferences:
Annual Meetings: Winter
1999 – Memphis, TN(Peabody)/Feb. 4-8/1200
2000 – Washington, DC/Feb. 3-7
2001 – San Diego, CA(Hyatt Regency)/Jan. 27-31

Nat'l Cotton Ginners' Ass'n (1937)
P.O. Box 820285
Memphis, TN 38182-0285
Tel: (901)274-9030   *Fax:* (901)725-0510
Web Site: www.cotton.org
Members: 23 organizations
Staff: 2
Annual Budget: $10-25,000
Exec. V. President: Phillip C. Burnett

Historical Note
Members are state societies and associations representing cotton ginners and processors. Administrative support provided by Nat'l Cotton Council.

Meetings/Conferences:
Annual Meetings: Winter with Nat'l Cotton Council
1999 – Memphis, TN(Peabody)/Feb. 4-8

Nat'l Cottonseed Products Ass'n (1897)

P.O. Box 172267
Memphis, TN 38187-2267
Tel: (901)682-0800   Fax: (901)682-2856
E-Mail: info@cottonseed.com
Web Site: http://www.cottonseed.com
Members: 300 businesses
Staff: 6
Annual Budget: $500-1,000,000
Exec. V. President: Lynn A. Jones
Secretary/Treasurer: J. Ben Morgan
Director Research & Education: D.H. Kinard

Historical Note
Founded as the Interstate Cottonseed Crushers Ass'n, it assumed its present name in 1929. NCPA is the trade association of the cottonseed processing industry in the United States and represents the industry's interests in many fora. Major services include administration of a set of trading rules, a research program helping to add value to cottonseed products, providing information to individuals and groups, and promoting the culinary value of cottonseed oil and the animal feed value of cottonseed meal.

Publications:
Newsletter. bi-w.
Proceedings. a.
Statistical Handbook. a.
Trading Rules. a.

Meetings/Conferences:
Annual Meetings: May
1999 – Hilton Head, SC(Westin Resort)/May 16-18

Nat'l Council for Agricultural Education (1983)

1410 King St., Suite 400
Alexandria, VA 22314
Tel: (703)838-5881   Fax: (703)838-5888
E-Mail: council@teamaged.org
Web Site: www.teamaged.org
Staff: 7
Exec. Director: Rosco Vaughn
Proect Director: Bryan Daniel
Project Director: Gordon Mengel
Project Director: Melissa Lewis

Publications:
AG ED Connection. q.

Meetings/Conferences:
1999 – Alexandria, VA(Embassy Suites)/March 24-27/25

Nat'l Council for Community Behavioral Healthcare (1970)

12300 Twinbrook Pkwy, Suite 320
Rockville, MD 20852
Tel: (301)984-6200
Members: 850 individuals
Staff: 20
Annual Budget: $1-2,000,000
C.E.O.: Charles G. Ray
Vice President, Government Relations: Pope Simmons
Vice President of Administration: Thomas R. Willis
V. President, Membership and Educational Services: Jeannie Campbell

Historical Note
Founded as Nat'l Council of Community Mental Health Centers; became Nat'l Community Mental Healthcare Council in 1993, and assumed its current name in 1997. Absorbed Ass'n of Mental Health Administrators in 1998. Promotes a unified network of community behavioral health care providers, authorities, state ass'ns, integrated service networks on the national, state and local level. Membership fee based on budget.

Publications:
National Council News. m. adv.

Meetings/Conferences:
Annual Meetings: Spring
1999 – Atlanta, GA(Marriott)/March 28-30

Nat'l Council for Geographic Education (1915)

Leonard 16 A
Indiana Univ. of Pennsylvania
Indiana, PA 15705
Tel: (412)357-6290   Fax: (412)357-7708
E-Mail: NCGE-ORG@GROVE.IUP.EDU
Web Site: http://www.ncge.org
Members: 4,000 individuals
Staff: 2
Annual Budget: $250-500,000
Exec. Director: Ruth I. Shirey

Historical Note
Formerly Nat'l Council of Geography Teachers. Seeks to enhance the status, quality, and effectiveness of geography teaching in North America. Membership: $40/year (individual), $60/year (institution).

Publications:
Journal of Geography. bi-m. adv.
Perspective. bi-m.

Meetings/Conferences:
Annual Meetings: Fall/850
1999 – Boston, MA/Nov. 3-6
2000 – Chicago, IL/Aug. 2-5
2001 – Vancouver, BC, Canada/Aug. 1-4

Nat'l Council for Marketing and Public Relations (1974)

4602 W. 21st St. Cir.
Greeley, CO 80634-3277
Tel: (970)330-0771   Fax: (970)330-0769
Members: 1,500 individuals
Staff: 1
Annual Budget: $100-250,000
Exec. Director: Rebecca Olson

Historical Note
Formerly (1988) the Nat'l Council for Community Relations. Affiliated with the American Ass'n of Community Colleges. Organization created to focus on the responsibilities of officers of junior community and technical colleges as communicators. Membership: $100/year (individual), $250/year (college institution), $375/year (associate college), $250/year (educational institutions).

Publications:
Counsel. q.

Meetings/Conferences:
Annual Meetings: Spring
1999 – Chicago, IL/March 7-10

Nat'l Council for Occupational Education

Central Community College
P.O. Box 1027
Columbus, NE 68601-1027
Tel: (815)773-6629   Fax: (815)729-4256
Web Site: http://www.unt.edu/ncoe/
Members: 1000 individuals
President: Richard Shank

Historical Note
NCOE members are occupational, vocational, technical and career educators; economic development professionals; and business, labor, military and government representatives. An affiliate council of the American Ass'n of Community Colleges, NCOE provides a national forum for workforce and economic development professionals to affect and direct the future of work-related education. Alternate address is 1161 Francisco Road, Columbus, OH 43220-2654. Membership: $80/year (individual); $225/year (institution).

Publications:
Membership Directory. a.
Workplace Newsletter. q.

Meetings/Conferences:

Nat'l Council for Prescription Drug Programs (1977)

4201 N. 24th St., Suite 365
Phoenix, AZ 85016-6268
Tel: (602)957-9105   Fax: (602)955-0749
E-Mail: ncpdp@ncpdp.org
Web Site: http://www.ncpdp.org
Members: 1,300 individuals, 1,300 organizations and individuals
Staff: 18
Annual Budget: $1-2,000,000
President: Lee Ann C. Stember
Exec. V.P., External Affairs: Daniel J. Staniec, R.Ph.
General Manager: David M. Goodspeed
Coordinator, Membership: Ronnie Lemoine
Dir., Standards Development: Joanne Longie
Dir., Information Technology: Brian D. Tayloe

Historical Note
NCPDP members are chain and independent pharmacies, consulting companies, pharmacists, database management organizations, federal/state agencies, health insurers, health maintenance organizations, mail service pharmacy companies, pharmaceutical manufacturers, pharmaceutical services administration organizations, presciption service organizations, pharmacy benefit management companies, professional and trade associations, telecommunications and systems vendors, wholesale drug distributors, and other parties interested in electronic standardization within the pharmacy services sector of the health care industry. Membership: $450/year (individual).

Publications:
Council Connection. bi-m. adv.
Council Connection. bi-m. adv.

Meetings/Conferences:
1999 – Scottsdale, AZ(DoubleTree Valley Resort)/Feb. 28-March 3
2000 – /Feb. 27-March 1
2001 – /Feb. 25-28
2002 – /March 3-6

Nat'l Council for Resource Development (1972)

One Dupont Circle, N.W., Suite 410
Washington, DC 20036-1176
Tel: (202)822-0750   Fax: (202)822-5014
Members: 1000 individuals
Staff: 1
Annual Budget: $250-500,000
Exec. Director: Joy Rafey

Historical Note
A council of the American Ass'n of Community Colleges, NCRD members are presidents and development administrators of two-year colleges. Membership: $140/year.

Publications:
Dispatch Express (fax broadcast newsletter).
Dispatch Newsletter. q.
Federal Funding to Two-Year Colleges. a.
Membership Directory. a.

Meetings/Conferences:
Annual Meetings: always Washington, DC in Fall

Nat'l Council for Textile Education (1933)

Auburn Univ., Textile Engineering Dept.
115 Textile Building
Auburn, GA 36849-5327
Tel: (334)844-4123   Fax: (334)844-4068
E-Mail: walshwk@mail.auburn.edu
Members: 30 individuals
Annual Budget: under $10,000
President: William K. Walsh, Ph.D.

Historical Note
Founded as The Nat'l Council of Textile School Deans, it assumed its present name in 1953. Members are administrator of college textile departments whose curriculum comprise science-based programs with substantial laboratory and plant experience.

Meetings/Conferences:
Semi-annual Meetings: Fall, with the American Textile Manufacturers Institute, and Spring

Nat'l Council for the Social Studies (1921)

3501 Newark St., N.W.
Washington, DC 20016-3199
Tel: (202)966-7840   Fax: (202)966-2061
E-Mail: ncss@ncss.org
Web Site: http://www.ncss.org
Members: 23,000 individuals
Staff: 20
Annual Budget: $2-5,000,000
Exec. Director: Martharose Laffey
Dir., Communications & Gov't Relations: Janet Lieberman
Director of Meetings: Jaime E. Hitchcock
Director of Finance: Timothy McGettigan
Director, Membership Processing: Cassandra Roberts
Director, Council Services & Membership: Susan Griffin
Director of Publications: Michael Simpson

Historical Note
Formed by a group of college and public school educators in 1921 in Atlantic City, NJ as the Nat'l Council of Teachers of the Social Studies, it was transformed into the Nat'l Council for the Social Studies a year later with a new constitution. This subsequently became a department of the Nat'l Education Ass'n in 1925 and completely independent in 1973. NCSS includes elementary and secondary teachers of history, geography, economics, political science, sociology, psychology, anthropology and law-related education, as well as college and university professors involved in teacher education and social studies research. NCSS provides leadership in the field of social studies education, assists in the professional development for social studies educators, and fosters and strengthens the advancement of social studies education. Membership: $50/year (individual); $79/year (institution).

Publications:
NCSS Bulletin. irreg.
Social Education. 7/yr. adv.
Social Studies and the Young Learner. q. adv.
Social Studies Professional. bi-m. adv.
Theory and Research in Social Education. q.

Meetings/Conferences:
Annual Meetings: November
1999 – Orlando, FL/Nov. 18-21

Nat'l Council for Therapeutic Recreation Certification (1981)

7 Elmwood Dr.
New City, NY 10956-5136
Tel: (914)639-1439   Fax: (914)639-1471
E-Mail: nctrc@ix.netcom.com
Members: 15,000 individuals
Staff: 12
Annual Budget: $1-2,000,000
Exec. Director: Peg Connolly, Ph.D.

Historical Note
Founded in 1981 NCTRC is the recognized certifying body for recreation therapy personnel in the United States, awarding the Certified Therapeutic Recreation Specialist (CTRS) designation. Certification renewal; $40.

Publications:
Educator's Link. semi-a.
NCTRC Newsletter. 2/year.

Meetings/Conferences:
Semi-Annual: April and November in New York City, NY

Nat'l Council for Uniform Interest Compensation

13665 Dulles Technology Drive, Suite 300
Herndon, VA 20170
Tel: (703)742-9190   Fax: (703)787-0996
Web Site: http://www.ncuic.org
Members: 300 individuals
Staff: 2
Annual Budget: $25-50,000
Exec. Director: Ian Macoy

Historical Note
NCUIC members are bank clearing houses and individual financial institutions. The association establishes and administers the procedures for determining interbank liability for errors in wire transfer, check, securities, and other payments. Administrative and support services are provided by the Nat'l Automated Clearing House Ass'n. Membership: $250/year(clearing house); $350 (company).

Meetings/Conferences:
Annual Meetings: Semi-Annual
1999 – Atlanta, GA

Nat'l Council of Acoustical Consultants (1962)

66 Morris Ave., Suite 1A
Springfield, NJ 07081-1409
Tel: (973)564-5859   Fax: (973)564-7480
E-Mail: info@ncac.com
Web Site: http://www.2000.com
Members: 116 companies
Staff: 2
Annual Budget: $10-25,000
Exec. Secretary: Peter Allen

Historical Note
Dedicated to management and related concerns of professional acoustical consulting firms and to safeguarding the interests of the clients and public which they serve. Membership: $180/year (one person firm).

Publications:
Directory. a.
NCAC Newsletter. q. adv.

Meetings/Conferences:
Semi-annual Meetings: May/November
1999 – Berlin, Germany
1999 – Columbus, OH

Nat'l Council of Administrative Women in Education
(1915)
Lakeside Union School District
P.O. Box 578
Lakeside, CA   92040
Tel: (619)390-2606   *Fax:* (619)561-7929
E-Mail: DCleighty@sdcoe.k12.ca.us
Members: 1,500 individuals
Annual Budget: $10-25,000
President: Carol Leighty

Historical Note
*Founded in 1915 at the Nat'l Education Ass'n convention in
Oakland, California. Became an accredited department of the NEA
in 1932, and an autonomous organization in 1973. Main purpose
is to encourage women to prepare for and accept administrative and
executive positions in education. Has no paid officers or full-time
staff; officers change annually in June. Membership: $15/year.*

Publications:
Leadership in Education Journal. bien.
NCAWE News. 2/year. adv.

Meetings/Conferences:
Annual Meetings: Spring

Nat'l Council of Agricultural Employers *(1964)*
1112 16th St., N.W., Suite 920
Washington, DC   20036-4823
Tel: (202)728-0300   *Fax:* (202)728-0303
E-Mail: ncae@erols.com
Members: 300 individuals
Staff: 2
Annual Budget: $250-500,000
Exec. V. President: Sharon M. Hughes, CAE
Executive Assistant: Celenda A. Stanford

Historical Note
*Members are growers and producers who employ agricultural
laborers, as well as processors and organizations related to the
agriculture business. Strictly an information and government
relations center; does not negotiate contracts. Membership:
$300/year minimum.*

Publications:
NCAE Newsletter. m.

Meetings/Conferences:
Annual Meetings: February
1999 – Washington, DC(Hyatt Regency
    Washington)/Jan. 27-29

Nat'l Council of Architectural Registration Boards
(1919)
1735 New York Ave., N.W., Suite 700
Washington, DC   20006
Tel: (202)783-6500   *Fax:* (202)783-0290
Web Site: http://www.ncarb.com
Members: 55 state registration boards
Staff: 54
Annual Budget: $10-25,000,000
Exec. V. President: Lenore M. Lucey, FAIA
Exec. Director, Professional Development: Jeffrey F. Kenney
Director, Corporate Affairs: Susan L. Wise
Director, Finance and Administration: Dennis J. Flynn
Director, Operations and Services: Michiel M. Bourdrez

Historical Note
*Assists state regulatory agencies in developing regulations for the
practice of architecture and the licensing of persons wishing to
practice. Membership: $3,000/year (state regulatory boards).*

Publications:
Annual and Pre-Annual Reports. a.
Examination Handbooks. a.

Meetings/Conferences:
Annual Meetings: June/400
1999 – Charleston, SC
2000 – Chicago, IL
2001 – Seattle, WA

Nat'l Council of Area and Regional Travel Organizations
Historical Note
*A division of the Travel Industry Association of America, which
provides administrative support.*

Nat'l Council of Athletic Training *(1976)*
1900 Association Drive
Reston, VA   20191
Tel: (703)476-3417   *Fax:* (703)476-8316
Toll Free: (800)213 - 7193
Members: 3,500 individuals
Staff: 1
NCAT Liaison: Christine Bolger

Historical Note
*Formerly (1976) NAGWS Athletic Training Committee amd (1986)
Athletic Training Council. Members are members of the Nat'l Ass'n
for Girls and Women in Sport and the Nat'l Ass'n for Sport and
Physical Education who have an interest in the profession of
athletic trainer. Administrative support is provided by the Nat'l
Ass'n for Sport and Physical Education. Membership: $100/year
(individual).*

Meetings/Conferences:
Annual Meetings: in conjunction with AAHPERD Nat'l
    Convention
1999 – Boston, MA

Nat'l Council of Black Engineers and Scientists *(1977)*
1525 Aviation Blvd., Suite C424
Redondo Beach, CA   90278
Tel: (213)896-9779
Annual Budget: $100-250,000
Secretary: John R. Zeigler

Historical Note
*Created to establish a link between individual technical
organizations in order to maintain communications between such
groups and improve the ability of these organizations to voice their
concerns on a national level. Membership: $50/year (national
dues).*

Publications:
NCBES Magazine. a. adv.
Technet Conference Program Book. a. adv.
Technews. q. adv.

Meetings/Conferences:
Annual Meetings: October
1999 – Los Angeles, CA/Oct. 21-24

Nat'l Council of Catholic Women *(1920)*
1275 K St., N.W.
Washington, DC   20005
Tel: (202)682-0334   *Fax:* (202)682-0338
Members: 7,800 organizations
Staff: 6
Annual Budget: $500-1,000,000
Exec. Director: Annette Kane
Director of Meetings: Jeanne Murphy

Historical Note
*A federation of national, state, diocesan, inter-parochial, and
parochial organizations of Catholic women. Membership fee based
upon type of organization.*

Publications:
Catholic Woman. bi-m.

Meetings/Conferences:
Annual Meetings: Fall

Nat'l Council of Chain Restaurants *(1965)*
325 7th St., N.W., Suite 1000
Washington, DC   20004
Tel: (202)626-8183   *Fax:* (202)626-8185
Members: 40 companies
Staff: 2
Annual Budget: $250-500,000
Exec. Director: Terrie Dort

Historical Note
*Formerly (1973) American Restaurant Institute and (1990)
Foodservice and Lodging Institute. Membership limited to major
multi-unit, multi-state operators. The principal objective of NCCR
is to monitor and lobby the government on legislative and
regulatory initiatives of general significance to its membership.
NCCR also litigates issues of common interest to the majority of its
membership. Membership fees vary, based on sales.*

Publications:
Washington Report. q.

Meetings/Conferences:
Three Meetings Annually: two in Washington, DC, one
    elsewhere

Nat'l Council of Coal Lessors *(1951)*
1050 One Valley Square
Charleston, WV   25301
Tel: (304)346-0569   *Fax:* (304)346-6516
Members: 75 companies
Staff: 2
Asst. Secretary: Lynn Lawson

Historical Note
*Supports the Nat'l Council of Coal Lessors Political Action
Committee. Members are owners of coal-bearing land concerned
with taxes, depletion allowances, black lung payments, etc.*

Nat'l Council of Commercial Plant Breeders *(1954)*
601 13th St., N.W., Suite 570 South
Washington, DC   20005-3807
Tel: (202)638-3128   *Fax:* (202)638-3171
Members: 63 companies
Staff: 2
Annual Budget: $25-50,000
Exec. V. President: Dean Urmston
Secretary-Treasurer: Robert J. Falasca

Historical Note
*Founded in 1954 by representatives of thirteen commercial firms as
a non-profit organization to promote the achievement and interest
of American plant breeders both in the United States and abroad.*

Publications:
Membership List. a.

Meetings/Conferences:
Annual Meetings: June/100
1999 – Palm Spring, CA(Renaissance Esmeralda
    Resort)/June 20-24

Nat'l Council of Community Hospitals *(1974)*
1700 K St., N.W., Suite 906
Washington, DC   20006
Tel: (202)728-0830   *Fax:* (202)296-7689
Members: 125 institutions
Staff: 6
Annual Budget: $500-1,000,000
V. President: Mary M. McGeein

Historical Note
*Primary purpose is to ensure that the point of view of its members is
adequately represented to the Federal Government. Membership:
$500/year (individual), $4,500-9,000/year (organization).*

Meetings/Conferences:
Semi-annual Meetings: Spring in the East, Fall in the West.

Nat'l Council of County Ass'n Executives *(1948)*
440 First St., N.W.
Washington, DC   20001
Tel: (202)393-6226   *Fax:* (202)393-2360
Web Site: http://www.naco.org
Members: 50 individuals
Staff: 1

Annual Budget: under $10,000
Staff Liaison: Dotty Byars

Historical Note
*An affiliate of the Nat'l Ass'n of Counties. Formerly (1973)
Conference of Executives of State Ass'ns of Counties.*

Meetings/Conferences:
Annual Meetings: With Nat'l Ass'n of Counties
1999 – St. Louis, MO/July 16-20

Nat'l Council of Educational Opportunity Ass'ns *(1981)*
1025 Vermont Ave., N.W., Suite 900
Washington, DC   20005-3516
Tel: (202)347-7430   *Fax:* (202)347-0786
Web Site: http://www.trioprograms.org
Members: 500 institutions, 10 regional orgs.
Staff: 20
Annual Budget: $1-2,000,000
Exec. Director: Arnold Mitchem, Ph.D.
V. President, Business/Finance: Susan M. Dorsey

Historical Note
*NCEOA members are regional organizations, institutions of higher
education and agencies concerned with equality of educational
opportunity and access. Membership: $1,000/year (organization).*

Publications:
Equality Newsletter. bi-m. adv.
Journal. bi-a.
NCEOA Nat'l Trio Directory of Funded Programs. bien.

Meetings/Conferences:
Annual Meetings: September

Nat'l Council of Erectors, Fabricators and Riggers
(1969)
P.O. Box 280
10382 Main Street
Fairfax, VA   22030-0280
Tel: (703)591-1870   *Fax:* (703)591-1895
Members: 3 organizations
Staff: 33
Annual Budget: $50-100,000
Exec. V. President: Fred H. Codding

Historical Note
*Members are the Specialized Carriers and Rigging Ass'n, the Nat'l
Ass'n of Reinforcing Steel Contractors and the Nat'l Ass'n of
Miscellaneous Ornamental and Architectural Products Contractors.
Serves as interface with the labor unions.*

Nat'l Council of Examiners for Engineering and Surveying *(1920)*
P.O. Box 1686
Clemson, SC   29633-1686
Tel: (864)654-6824   *Fax:* (864)654-6033
Web Site: http://www.ncees.org
Members: 70 member boards
Staff: 26
Annual Budget: $5-10,000,000
Exec. Director: Frances Elizabeth Browne
Director, Communications: Joseph Phaneuf
Meeting Planner: Diane Quarles
Director, Finance: Jeannine VanderZalm
Managing Editor: Ashley Farmer
Director, Information Technology: Phyllis Fenno

Historical Note
*Formerly (1967) Nat'l Council of State Boards of Engineering
Examiners, and (1989) Nat'l Council of Engineering Examiners.
Coordinates examination and registration of professional engineers
and land surveyors. Has an annual budget of approximately $5.2
million. Membership: $2,250/year (company).*

Publications:
Convention Reports. a.
Licensure Exchange. q.

Meetings/Conferences:
Annual Meetings: August/350
1999 – Buffalo, NY/Aug. 4-7
2000 – Chicago, IL/Aug. 9-12

Nat'l Council of Exchangors *(1975)*
430 Quintana Road, Suite 150
Morro Bay, CA   93442-1948
Toll Free: (800)324 - 1031
E-Mail: nce@infoville.com
Web Site: http://www.infoville.com/nce
Members: 400 individuals
Staff: 2
Annual Budget: $50-100,000
President: Robert Cooke

Historical Note
*The Nat'l Council of Exchangors, a non-profit ass'n, is a
nationwide network of real estate professionals who specialize in
marketing real estate equities primarily through the medium of the
real estate exchange. This network is comprised of local Groups
organized into Regional Chapters. Membership: $150/year
(indvidual).*

Publications:
Journal of Equity Marketing. bi-m. adv.
NCE MarketPlace Magazine.
NCE Membership Networking Directory. a.
NCE UPDATE (newsletter).
Transaction Makers Digest. q.

Meetings/Conferences:

Nat'l Council of Farmer Cooperatives *(1929)*
50 F St., N.W., 9th Floor
Washington, DC   20001-1530
Tel: (202)626-8700   *Fax:* (202)626-8722
E-Mail: info@ncfc.org
Web Site: http://access.digex.net/ncfc
Members: 100 co-ops and 31 farmer councils
Staff: 26
Annual Budget: $2-5,000,000

President and C.E.O.: David R. Graves
V.P., Communications/ Member Rels.: Lisa Keller Smith
Sr. V.P., Govt./Public Affairs: Randy Jones
Dir., Meetings/Conventions: Gail Tannenbaum
V.P., Education: Thomas Little
V.P., Finance/Administration: Joseph Smolskis
Sr. V.P./General Counsel: James S. Krzyminski

Historical Note
NCFC is a nationwide association of cooperative businesses which are owned and controlled by farmers. Members include major agricultural marketing, supply and credit cooperatives, plus 32 state councils of farmer cooperatives. Absorbed Nat'l Federation of Grain Cooperatives (1973) and American Institute of Cooperation (1991). Sponsors and supports the National Council of Farmer Cooperatives Political Action Committee (Co-op PAC). Affiliated with Farm Credit Council and the Agricultural Cooperative Development Internat'l.

Publications:
American Cooperation. a.
Journal of Agricultural Cooperation. a.
Washington Cooperator. q.
Washington Councilor. w.

Meetings/Conferences:
1999 – San Antonio, TX(RiverCenter/Riverwalk)/Jan. 17-20

Nat'l Council of Forestry Ass'n Executives (1949)

Historical Note
Address unknown in 1997.

Nat'l Council of Health Facilities Finance Authorities
P.O. Box 200506
Helena, MT 59620-0506
Tel: (406)444-5435   *Fax:* (406)449-6579
E-Mail: jhoover@mt.gov
Annual Budget: $100-250,000
President: Jerry Hoover

Historical Note
Membership: $2,000-6,000/year.

Publications:
Council Report. bien.
Nat'l Council of Health Facilities Finance Authorities. q.

Meetings/Conferences:
Annual Meetings: Fall
1999 – Seattle, WA(Sheraton Seattle)/Sept. 15-18/250
2000 – Boise, ID(DoubleTree Hotel)/Sept. 13-16/250
2001 – Orlando, FL(Buena Vista Palace)/Sept. 12-15/250
2002 – Big Sky, MT/200

Nat'l Council of Higher Education Loan Programs
(1961)
1100 Connecticut Ave., N.W., Suite 1200
Washington, DC 20036-4110
Tel: (202)822-2106
Web Site: http://www.nchelp.org
Members: 175 organizations
Staff: 7
Annual Budget: $500-1,000,000
President: Brett E. Lief
V.P., Govt. Relations: Lisa Ross
Meetings Manager: Avis G. Ali
Exec. V.P. and General Counsel: Jean S. Frolicher
Dir., Info. Technology: Karen S. Haney

Historical Note
Formerly (1969) Nat'l Conference of Executives of Higher Education Loan Plans. Members are private and state non-profit corporations that guarantee student loans under the Higher Education Act of 1965, secondary markets, lenders, servicers, collectors, institutions of higher education and other organizations involved in the administration of the Federal Family Education Loan Program.

Meetings/Conferences:
Semi-Annual Meetings: Spring and Fall

Nat'l Council of Industrial Naval Air Stations (1957)
Route 2, Box 1147-H
Lawtey, FL 32058
Tel: (904)542-2617
Members: 6 organizations
Staff: 2
Annual Budget: $10-25,000
President: Barry K. Adams

Historical Note
Formerly (1980) Nat'l Council of Naval Air Station Employee Organizations. NCINAS is an umbrella organization composed of regional organizations representing 20,000 civilian employees of naval air stations.

Meetings/Conferences:

Nat'l Council of Intellectual Property Law Ass'ns
(1934)
1255 23rd St., N.W., Suite 850
Washington, DC 20037
Tel: (202)466-2396   *Fax:* (202)466-2893
Members: 49 associations
Annual Budget: $10-25,000
Exec. Director: Herbert C. Wamsley

Historical Note
NCIPLA is an organization of local, regional and national intellectual property law associations. Its aim is to assist member associations to act as an effective force for the advancement of the United States system for the ownership and development of intellectual property. NCIPLA monitors legislative and executive actions which could affect the nation's intellectual property system.

Publications:
NCIPLA Chariman's Letter. m.
NCIPLA Legislative Letter. m.
NCIPLA Newsletter. q.

Meetings/Conferences:
Semi-annual Meetings: Spring and Fall

Nat'l Council of Investigation and Security Services
(1975)
908 21st St.
Sacramento, CA 95814
Tel: (916)441-2616   *Fax:* (916)441-2617
Toll Free: (800)445 - 8408
Members: 525 state ass'ns and firms
Staff: 1
Annual Budget: $50-100,000
Exec. Director: Sharon Hilke

Historical Note
State associations and firms providing contract security services and investigative services. Membership: $125/year (organization/company).

Publications:
NCISS Report. q.

Meetings/Conferences:
1999 – Tucson, AZ(Westword)

Nat'l Council of Juvenile and Family Court Judges
(1937)
P.O. Box 8970
1010 N. Virginia St.
Reno, NV 89507
Tel: (702)784-6012   *Fax:* (702)784-1084
Web Site: http://ncjfcj.unr.edu
Members: 2,500 individuals
Staff: 55
Annual Budget: $5-10,000,000
Exec. Director: Louis W. McHardy
Director, Public Relations: Steven G. Riddell
Senior Attorney: Arne Schoeller
Conference Coordinator: Diane Barnette
Assoc. Director, Continuing Education: M. James Toner
Comptroller: Carol Guarino
Assoc. Director for Administration: Marie Mildon
Dir., Family Violence Project: Merry Hofford

Historical Note
Located on the campus of Univ. of Nevada at Reno. Supports the judicial officers of the juvenile justice system and promotes the development of treatment programs for children with special needs in the system. Operates the Nat'l College of Juvenile and Family Law at Reno and the Nat'l Center for Juvenile Justice, a research center, in Pittsburgh, PA. Sponsors and supports the Nat'l Juvenile Court Services Ass'n, serving non-judge professionals of the courts. Has an annual budget of approximately $5.3 million. Membership: $125/year (regular); $77/year (associate); $35/year (student).

Publications:
Juvenile and Family Court Journal. q.
Juvenile and Family Court Today. 6/year.
Juvenile and Family Law Digest. m.

Meetings/Conferences:
Annual Meetings: July
1999 – Chicago, IL/July 18-21

Nat'l Council of Legislators from Gaming States (1985)
122 S. Swan St.
Albany, NY 12210-1715
Tel: (518)449-4699   *Fax:* (518)432-5651
E-Mail: mackinco@albany.net
Exec. Director: Robert E. Mackin

Historical Note
NCLGS members are states that allow gaming. NCLGS exists to educate legislators and policy makers on issues relevant to the gaming industry, and monitors regulations which affect gaming in the U.S.

Nat'l Council of Local Administrators for Vocational Technical Education (1942)

Historical Note
Address unknown in 1996.

Nat'l Council of Local Public Welfare Administrators
(1940)
810 1st St., N.E., Suite 500
Washington, DC 20002-4205
Tel: (202)682-0100   *Fax:* (202)289-6555
Members: 100 individuals
Staff: 1
Annual Budget: under $10,000
Contact: Elaine Ryan

Historical Note
A council of the American Public Welfare Ass'n. NCLPWA represent local agencies and their policy concerns.

Meetings/Conferences:

Nat'l Council of Multifamily Housing

Historical Note
A division of the Nat'l Ass'n of Home Builders of the U.S.

Nat'l Council of Music Importers and Exporters (1966)
38 West 21st St., Room 1106
New York, NY 10010-6906
Tel: (212)924-9175   *Fax:* (212)675-3577
E-Mail: assnhdqs@aol.com
Members: 75 companies
Staff: 2
Annual Budget: $10-25,000
Exec. V. President: Jerome Hershman

Historical Note
Formerly Nat'l Ass'n of Music Importers Membership: $250/year (company).

Publications:
Newsletter. bi-m.

Meetings/Conferences:
1999 – Los Angeles, CA(Bonaventure)

Nat'l Council of Nonprofit Ass'ns (1989)
1900 L St. N.W., Suite 605
Washington, DC 20036
Tel: (202)467-6262   *Fax:* (202)833-5747
E-Mail: amsackey@ncna.org
Web Site: http://www.ncna.org
Members: 35 state ass'ns of non-profits
Staff: 4
Annual Budget: $250-500,000
Exec. Director: Ann Mitchell
Director, Membership Services: David DeVito
Director, Public Policy: Jane Robinson Ward

Historical Note
NCNA is an alliance of state/regional ass'ns of nonprofits. Represents 20,000 individual organizations addressing quality of life issues at the local level. Current programming initiatives include ethics and accountability, public policy and public education on the nonprofit sector. Membership: $600/year (regular member); $300/year (supporter member).

Publications:
NCNA Forum. q. adv.
Public Policy Update. q.
State Tax Trends. q.

Meetings/Conferences:
Annual Meetings: Fall
1999 – Atlanta, GA(Swissotel)

Nat'l Council of Postal Credit Unions (1984)
P.O. Box 160
Del Mar, CA 92014-0160
Tel: (619)792-3883   *Fax:* (619)792-3884
Members: 160 credit unions
Staff: 2
Exec. Director: Robert P. Spindler

Publications:
Directory.
Postal Courier. q.

Meetings/Conferences:
1999 – Dever, CO(Westin Tabor Center)/April 24-27

Nat'l Council of Preservation Executives (1982)
c/o State Historic Preservation Office
109 E. Jones St.
Raleigh, NC 27601-2807
Tel: (919)733-4763   *Fax:* (919)733-8653
Members: 106 individuals
Annual Budget: under $10,000
Treasurer: David Brook

Historical Note
Founded to promote better working conditions and professional standards. NCOPE provides an information exchange for the executives of non-profit historic preservation organizations. Has no paid officers or full-time staff. Membership: $25/year.

Meetings/Conferences:
Annual Meetings: Fall, with the Nat'l Trust for Historic Preservation
1999 – Washington, DC(Mayflower)/Oct. 19-24
2000 – Los Angeles, CA(Biltmore)Oct.
2001 – Providence, RI/Oct. 16-21
2002 – Cleveland, OH

Nat'l Council of Real Estate Investment Fiduciaries
(1982)
180 N. Stetson Ave., Suite 2515
Chicago, IL 60601
Tel: (312)819-5890   *Fax:* (312)819-5891
Web Site: www.nacreif.com
Members: 300 companies
Staff: 4
Annual Budget: $500-1,000,000
Exec. Director: Richard B. Gaskins
Sr. Director, Meetings: Stacy A. Gaskins, CMP

Historical Note
Members are real estate investment managers, including insurance companies, banks and independent investment advisors, serving the pension fund real estate industry. Membership: $4,500/year (voting membership), $3,500/year (professional membership), $250/year (academic). Subscriptions for NCREIF Report available to non-members for $1,000/year.

Publications:
NCREIF Real Estate Performance Report. q.

Meetings/Conferences:
Three Meetings Annually: March, June and October
1999 – Naples, FL/Oct. 6-8

Nat'l Council of Salesmen's Organizations (1946)

Historical Note
Organization defunct in 1995.

Nat'l Council of Self-Insurers (1945)
1253 Springfield Ave, Suite 345
New Providence, NJ 07974
Tel: (908)665-2152   *Fax:* (908)665-4020
Members: 350 individuals
Staff: 2
Annual Budget: $50-100,000
Exec. Director: Lawrence J. Holt

Historical Note
Formerly (1973) Nat'l Council of State Self-insurers Ass'ns. Organizations and individuals concerned with self-insurance under the workmen's compensation laws. The above address is the law firm of Stevenson, Rusin & Friedman. Membership: $150/year (individual); $475/year (organization/company).

Publications:
Membership Directory. a.
State Self-Insurance Requirements. 3/year.

Meetings/Conferences:
Annual Meetings: Spring
1999 – Lake Taho, NV

Nat'l Council of Social Security Management Ass'ns *(1970)*
528 N. Monroe Ave.,
Greenbay, WI 54301
Tel: (920)433-3920 *Fax:* (920)433-3873
Members: 3,000 individuals, 10 associations
Annual Budget: $100-250,000
President: Donald E. Seatter

Historical Note
Members are managers and supervisors of Social Security field offices and teleservice centers in the U.S. and Puerto Rico. Has no paid officers or full-time staff. Membership: $52–104/year (individual).

Publications:
Mass Media. q.

Meetings/Conferences:
1999 – Charleston, SC

Nat'l Council of State Agencies for the Blind
1213 29th St., N.W.
Washington, DC 20007
Tel: (202)298-8468 *Fax:* (202)333-5881
Members: 54 agencies
Annual Budget: $50-100,000
Counsel: Jack Duncan

Nat'l Council of State Boards of Nursing *(1978)*
676 North St. Clair, Suite 550
Chicago, IL 60611-2921
Tel: (312)787-6555 *Fax:* (312)787-6898
Web Site: http://www.ncsbn.org
Members: 61 boards
Staff: 60
Annual Budget: $10-25,000,000
Exec. Director: Elisoe Cathcart
Director of Communications: Susan Woodward
Senior Policy Advisor: Carolyn Hutcherson
Manager, Meetings: Susan Davids
Director, Administrative Services: Thomas Vicek
Director, Information Technology: Angela Diaz-Kay

Historical Note
Members are state boards of nursing. Provides members with programs and services related to the regulation of nursing practice, including research, the collection and analysis of data, communications, and consulting services. The National Council has developed licensure examinations used by its members to test the entry-level nursing competence of candidates for licensure as registered nurses, practical nurses and nurse aides. Has an annual budget of approximately $6 million. Membership: $3,000/year.

Publications:
Insight: NACEP News and Notes. 3/yr.
Issues. q.
Newsletter (for members only). bi-w.
State Nursing Legislation Quarterly. (for members only).

Meetings/Conferences:
Annual Meetings: August
1999 – Atlanta, GA(Marriott)
2000 – Minneapolis, MN

Nat'l Council of State Directors of Community Junior Colleges *(1969)*
c/o American Ass'n of Community Colleges
1 Dupont Circle, Suite 410
Washington, DC 20036-1176
Tel: (202)728-0200 *Fax:* (202)833-2467
Members: 35 individuals
Annual Budget: $10-25,000
Contact: David Buonora

Historical Note
Affiliated with American Ass'n of Community and Junior Colleges. Membership: $20/yr.

Meetings/Conferences:
Semi-annual Meetings: April and October, and Workshop in July

Nat'l Council of State Education Ass'ns *(1966)*
1201 16th St., N.W.
Washington, DC 20036
Tel: (202)822-7745 *Fax:* (202)822-7624
Members: 198 individuals, 52 associations
Staff: 6
Annual Budget: $100-250,000
Exec. Director: Larry Diebold

Historical Note
Merger in 1966 of the Nat'l Ass'n of Secretaries of State Teachers Ass'ns (1924) and the Nat'l Council of State Ass'n Presidents (1961). Members are secretaries and presidents of state education associations. Members are executive directors, meetings, vice presidents, presidents-elect and treasurers of state education ass'ns.

Publications:
Information Service Reports. irreg.
NCSEA Newsletter. q.
Profiles of State Associations. a.

Meetings/Conferences:
Three Meetings Annually: July, September and November

Nat'l Council of State Emergency Medical Services Training Coordinators *(1977)*
1685 S. Colorado Blvd.
Denver, CO 80222
Tel: (888)595-2668 *Fax:* (888)595-2668
E-Mail: ncsemstc@csn.net
Web Site: http://www.ncsemstc.org/ncsemstc
Members: 75 individuals
Staff: 1

Annual Budget: $10-25,000
Chair: Larry Weber

Historical Note
Members are supervisors or coordinators of state EMS training programs (limited to three members from each state). Affiliated with the American College of Emergency Physicians, Nat'l Ass'n of State Emergency Medical Service Directors, Nat'l Ass'n of Emergency Technicians, and the Nat'l Registry of Emergency Medical Technicians. Purpose is to improve EMS education and promote standardized training and licensure. No membership fee.

Publications:
Minutes of the Annual Meeting. a.

Meetings/Conferences:
Annual Meetings: Fall
1999 – Savannah, GA
2000 – Charleston, SC

Nat'l Council of State Garden Clubs *(1929)*
4401 Magnolia Ave.
St. Louis, MO 63110-3492
Tel: (314)776-7574 *Fax:* (314)776-5108
Web Site: http://www.gardenclub.org
Members: 264,440 individuals, 8,488 clubs
Staff: 15
Exec. Director: Francis Mantler

Historical Note
A federation of garden clubs united to protect and conserve natural resources through teacher training and environmental workshops. Supported by dues of 25 cents per person from its member clubs. Sponsors the National Garden Week.

Publications:
The National Gardener. bi-m. adv.

Meetings/Conferences:
Annual Meetings: May/1,000
1999 – Atlanta, GA/May 18-20
2001 – Chicago, IL/May 4-6

Nat'l Council of State Housing Agencies *(1970)*
444 North Capitol St., N.W., Suite 438
Washington, DC 20001
Tel: (202)624-7710 *Fax:* (202)624-5899
E-Mail: ncsha1@sso.org
Web Site: http://www.nchsa.org
Members: 58 agencies, 348 affiliates
Staff: 20
Annual Budget: $1-2,000,000
Exec. Director: John T. McEvoy
Manager, Communications: Amy M. Meyer
Dir., Policy/Govt. Affairs: Barbara J. Thompson
Director, Project Mgmt./Meetings: Kathryn Oates Domenick
Dir., Admin./Member Services: Ann M. Dorman

Historical Note
Formerly (1987) the Council of State Housing Agencies. Members are the housing finance agencies of the fifty states, the District of Columbia, Virgin Islands, Puerto Rico, and New York City. Sponsors workshops and other opportunities for members.

Publications:
Dir. of State Housing Fi.
State Housing Finance. q.
Survey of State Housing Finance Agencies. a.

Meetings/Conferences:
Annual Meetings: October
1999 – Chicago, IL/Oct. 24-26

Nat'l Council of State Human Service Administrators *(1939)*
810 1st St., N.E., Suite 500
Washington, DC 20002-4267
Tel: (202)682-0100 *Fax:* (202)289-6555
Members: 200 individuals
Staff: 10
Contact: Elaine Ryan

Historical Note
Formerly (1984) Nat'l Council of State Public Welfare Administrators. A constituent unit of the American Public Welfare Ass'n.

Publications:
Public Welfare. q.
The Public Welfare Directory. a.
This Week in Washington. w.
W-Memo. 10/yr.

Meetings/Conferences:
Annual Meetings: Spring and Fall

Nat'l Council of State Pharmacy Ass'n Executives *(1929)*
8515 Douglas Ave., Suite 16
Des Moines, IA 50322-0151
Tel: (515)270-0713 *Fax:* (515)270-2979
E-Mail: ttemple@iarx.org
Web Site: http://www.iarx.org
Members: 52 individuals
Staff: 1
Annual Budget: $10-25,000
Secretary-Treasurer: Thomas Temple

Historical Note
Formerly (1993) Nat'l Council of State Pharmaceutical Ass'n Executives. Membership: $100-$300/year.

Meetings/Conferences:
Annual Meetings: With American Pharmaceutical Ass'n and Nat'l Ass'n of Retail Druggists

Nat'l Council of State Supervisors of Foreign Languages *(1960)*
Foreign Lang. Ed., State Dept. of Ed.
205 E. Butler St., Suite 1762
Atlanta, GA 30334-5040
Tel: (404)651-7275 *Fax:* (404)651-8582

Members: 75 individuals
Annual Budget: under $10,000
President: Marcia Spielberger

Historical Note
Provides support for foreign language programs at the state level and liaison with other agencies and federal and local government. The President is elected on biennial, even years, the Vice President and Secretary/Treasurer on biennial, odd years. Membership: $30/year (regular), $15/year (retired).

Publications:
President's Quarterly Update. q.

Meetings/Conferences:
Annual Meetings: November, with the American Council on the Teaching of Foreign Languages/50
1999 – Dallas, TX/Nov. 17-18

Nat'l Council of State Tourism Directors *(1969)*
c/o Travel Industry Ass'n
1100 New York Ave., Suite 450
Washington, DC 20005
Tel: (202)408-8422 *Fax:* (202)408-1255
Members: 56 individuals
Staff: 2
Annual Budget: under $10,000
Exec. Director: Patty H. Hubbard

Historical Note
A council of the Travel Industry Ass'n of America, which provides administrative support. Members are state and territorial government travel offices. Formerly (1978) the Council of Regional Travel Executives (CORTE). Membership: $1,000/year.

Publications:
Stateside. q.

Meetings/Conferences:
1999 – Roanoke, VA(Hotel Roanoke and Conference Center)/July 10-15

Nat'l Council of Supervisors of Mathematics *(1968)*
P.O. Box 10667
Golden, CO 80401-0600
Tel: (303)274-5932 *Fax:* (303)274-5932
E-Mail: ncsm@forum.swarthmore.edu
Web Site: forum.swarthmore.edu/ncsm
Members: 2,900 individuals
Staff: 1
Annual Budget: $100-250,000
President: Bonnie Walker
Membership Services: Mo Nelson

Historical Note
Members are leaders in mathematics education at all levels of the educational system. Membership: $40/year (individual), or $100/three years.

Publications:
Membership Directory. a.
NCSM Journal of Mathematics Education Leadership. q.
NCSM Newsletter. q.
Sourcebook. a.

Meetings/Conferences:
Annual Meetings: Early Spring/1,500
1999 – San Francisco, CA/April 20-21
2000 – Chicago, IL/April 11-12
2001 – Orlando, FL/April 3-4

Nat'l Council of Teachers of English *(1911)*
1111 W. Kenyon Road
Urbana, IL 61801-1096
Tel: (217)328-3870 *Fax:* (217)328-0977
Toll Free: (800)369 - 6283
Web Site: http://www.ncte.org
Members: 80,000 individuals, 20,000 institutions
Staff: 90
Annual Budget: $2-5,000,000
Exec. Director: Faith Z. Schullstrom
Public Affairs Assistant: Lori Bianchini
Convention Center: Jacqui Joseph-Biddle
Dir., Finance: Bill Subick
Assoc. Exec. Dir., Business: Kent Williamson
Dir., Instructional Technology: Tim Barker

Historical Note
An educational association devoted to improving the teaching of English and language arts, serves as a forum for the profession providing opportunities for teachers to continue their professional growth and is a forum for dealing with relevant issues. Publishes 20-25 books for teachers of English and the language arts at the elementary, secondary and college levels. Membership: $30/year (individual); $50/year (organization).

Publications:
College Composition and Communication. q. adv.
College English. 6/year. adv.
Council Chronicle Newspaper. 5/yr. adv.
English Education. q. adv.
English Journal. 6/year. adv.
English Leadership Quarterly. q. adv.
Language Arts. 6/yr. adv.
Primary Voices, K-6. q. adv.
Quarterly Review of Doublespeak. q.
Research in the Teaching of English. q. adv.
SLATE Newsletter. 3/year.
Talking Points. 2/yr.
Teaching English in the Two-Year College. q. adv.
Voices from the Middle. q. adv.

Meetings/Conferences:
Annual Meetings: November
1999 – Cincinnati, OH/March 4-6
1999 – Denver, CO(Adams Mark)/Nov. 18-23
2000 – New York, NY/March 16-18
2000 – Milwaukee, WI/Nov. 16-21

Nat'l Council of Teachers of Mathematics *(1920)*
1906 Association Dr.

Reston, VA 20191-1593
Tel: (703)620-9840   Fax: (703)476-2970
E-Mail: nctm@nctm.org
Web Site: http://www.nctm.org
Members: 110,000 individuals, 260 affiliated groups
Staff: 75
Annual Budget: $5-10,000,000
Exec. Director: John A. Thorpe, Ph.D.
External/Media Relations Manager: L. Eileen Erickson
Dir., Member Programs and Services: Susan Bayley
Manager, Conventions: Mark E. Workman
Director, Administration/Finance: David Shayka
Director, Marketing/Information: Cynthia Rosso
Director of Publications: Harry Tunis

Historical Note
Dedicated to the improvement of mathematics education and to meeting the needs of mathematics teachers at all levels, NCTM serves as a forum for discussing developments within the discipline and sharing innovative classroom techniques. Membership: $57/year (individual), $62/year (institution).

Publications:
Journal for Research in Mathematics Education. 5/year. adv.
Mathematics Teacher. 9/year. adv.
Mathematics Teaching in the Middle School. 5/year.
NCTM News Bulletin. 5/year.
Teaching Children Mathematics. 9/year. adv.

Meetings/Conferences:
Annual Meetings: Spring
1999 – San Francisco, CA/April 22-25
2000 – Chicago, IL/April 13-16
2001 – Orlando, FL/April 5-8

Nat'l Council of the Churches of Christ in the U.S.A. *(1950)*
475 Riverside Drive, Room 880
New York, NY 10115-0050
Tel: (212)870-2141   Fax: (212)870-2817
Members: 34 communions
Staff: 340
Annual Budget: $50-100,000,000
General Secretary: Rev. Dr. Joan Brown Campbell
Dir., Communications: Randy Naylor
Assoc. General Secretary: Eileen W. Lindner
Deputy General Secretary/NMU: Staccato Powell
Deputy General Secretary/CWSW: Rodney Page

Historical Note
Founded in 1950 by representatives of 29 major Protestant and Orthodox denominations who met to unite 12 nationwide interchurch agencies and form the Nat'l Council of Churches, NCC is now the primary expression of the ecumenical movement in the United States with 34 communions - Protestant, Orthodox and Anglican church bodies with a combined membership of 52 million Christians. Has an annual budget of over $50 million.

Publications:
Eeu Link. q.
Yearbook of American and Canadian Churches. a.

Meetings/Conferences:
Annual Meetings: Annual General Board Meeting in November
1999 – Cleveland, OH/Nov. 7-12

Nat'l Council of the Housing Industry
Historical Note
A subsidiary of the Nat'l Ass'n of Home Builders of the U.S.

Nat'l Council of the Multifamily Housing Industry
Historical Note
A council of the Nat'l Ass'n of Home Builders of the United States.

Nat'l Council of the Paper Industry for Air and Stream Improvement *(1943)*
P.O. Box 13318
Research Triangle Pk, NC 27709
Tel: (919)558-1999   Fax: (919)558-1998
Members: 100 companies
Staff: 100
Annual Budget: $10-25,000,000
President: Ronald Yeske, Ph.D.
Exec. Secretary: Carol Knight
Manager, Publications: Pamela Bruns

Historical Note
A technical organization devoted to finding solutions to environmental protection problems related to the manufacture of pulp, paper and wood products and industrial forestry. Formerly (1968) Nat'l Council for Stream Improvement. Annual budget: over $10 million. Membership dues based on production.

Publications:
Bulletin Board. bi-w.
Forestry Environmental Program News. bi-w.
Technical Bulletins. irreg.

Meetings/Conferences:

Nat'l Council of Travel Attractions
Historical Note
A division of the Travel Industry Association of America, which provides administrative support.

Nat'l Council of University Research Administrators *(1959)*
One Dupont Circle, N.W., Suite 220
Washington, DC 20036
Tel: (202)466-3894   Fax: (202)223-5573
Web Site: http://ncura.edu
Members: 3,100 individuals
Staff: 6
Annual Budget: $250-500,000
Exec. Director: Kathleen Larmett
Exec. Director: Kathleen M. Larmett
Assistant Executive Director: Tara Bishop

Historical Note
Individuals with professional interests in problems and policies relating to the administration of sponsored research, education and training activities at colleges and universities. Membership: $120/year.

Publications:
Clinical Trials Handbook.
NCURA Directory. a.
NCURA Newsletter. 5/year.
Research Management Review. semi-a.

Meetings/Conferences:
1999 – Washington, DC(Hilton & Towers)/Nov. 1-4
2000 – Washington, DC(Hilton & Towers)/Nov. 1-4

Nat'l Council of Urban Tourism Organizations
Historical Note
A division of the Travel Industry Association of America, which provides administrative support.

Nat'l Council of World Affaris Organizations
Historical Note
Became (1997) World Affairs Councils of America.

Nat'l Council of Writing Program Administrators *(1975)*
Department of English
Miami University
Oxford, OH 45056
Tel: (513)529-7340   Fax: (513)529-1392
Members: 600 individuals, 100 institutions
Annual Budget: $10-25,000
Secretary-Treasurer: Robert R. Johnson

Historical Note
Also known as Council of Writing Program Administrators. A national organization that fosters professional development, communication and community among college and university writing program administrators and other interested faculty. WPA provides institutions with consultant-evaluators to assess activities. Affiliated with Ass'n of American Colleges. Membership: $30/year (individual), $40/year (institution).

Publications:
WPA News. q.
WPA: Writing Program Administration. semi-a.

Meetings/Conferences:

Nat'l Council on Compensation Insurance *(1922)*
750 Park of Commerce Drive
Boca Raton, FL 33487
Tel: (561)997-1000   Fax: (561)997-4233
Members: 750 insurance companies and carriers
Staff: 1400
Annual Budget: $50-100,000,000
President: David Kocher

Historical Note
NCCI is a voluntary, non-profit, statistical research and ratemaking organization. Supported by the insurance industry, NCCI's primary functions are the preparation and administration of rates, rating plans and systems for worker's compensation insurance in 32 states and providing similar assistance in about one-half of the remaining states. Members include stock companies, mutual companies, competitive state funds and reciprocals. Membership: based on sliding scale. Has an annual budget of approximately $94.5 million.

Publications:
Annual Statistical Bulletin. a.
Cost Containment & Reform Activity Report. bi-m.
Issues Report. a.
NCCI Digest. bien.
NCCI Update. q.
Safe Workplace. q.
Scopes. a.

Meetings/Conferences:
Annual Meetings: April

Nat'l Council on Crime and Delinquency *(1907)*
685 Market St., Suite 620
San Francisco, CA 94105
Tel: (415)896-6223   Fax: (415)896-5109
E-Mail: pat@nccdsf.attmail.com
Members: 500 individuals
Staff: 25
Annual Budget: $2-5,000,000
President: Dr. Barry Krisberg

Historical Note
Established in 1907 as the Nat'l Probation Ass'n. Is concerned with upgrading criminal justice practices. Membership: $200/year (institutional); $50/year (charter), $130/year (advocate); $40/year (subscribers).

Publications:
NCCD FOCUS. q.
NCCD Policy Papers. semi-a.

Meetings/Conferences:
Meetings: three or four per year

Nat'l Council on Education for the Ceramic Arts *(1967)*
P.O. Box 158
Bandon, OR 97411
Toll Free: (800)996 - 2322
Web Site: www.arts.edu/nceca/
Members: 2,500 individuals
Staff: 3
Exec. Secretary: Regina Brown

Historical Note
Members are teachers, professional studio artists, students and others concerned with the ceramic arts. NCECA became an independent organization in 1967 after several years of affiliation with the Ceramic Educational Council of the American Ceramic Society. Purpose is to promote and improve education in the ceramic arts. Membership: $40/year (United States and Canada), $55/year (overseas), $25/year (student).

Publications:
NCECA Journals. a.
NCECA Newsletter. q.

Meetings/Conferences:
1999 – Columbus, OH/March 17-20

Nat'l Council on Family Relations *(1938)*
3989 Central Ave., N.E., Suite 550
Minneapolis, MN 55421
Tel: (612)781-9331   Fax: (612)781-9348
Toll Free: (888)781 - 9331
E-Mail: ncfr3989@ncfr.com
Web Site: www.ncfr.com
Members: 4,000 individuals
Staff: 12
Annual Budget: $1-2,000,000
Exec. Director: Mary Jo Czaplewski, Ph.D.
Conference Coordinator: Cynthia Winter

Historical Note
Professionals, academics and others interested in education and research about the family, development of community services for and government policies concerning families, and related issues. Provides a forum for family researchers, educators, practitioners and policy makers to share in the development and dissemination of knowledge about families and family relationships, establishes professional standards, and works to promote family well-being. Membership: $90/year (colleague); $125/year (organization); $130/year (benefactor); $50-$75/year (student).

Publications:
Family Relations. q. adv.
Journal of Marriage and the Family. q. adv.
Newsletter q. adv. adv.

Meetings/Conferences:
Annual Meetings: Fall
1999 – Irvine, CA(Hyatt)/Nov. 10-15
2000 – Minneapolis, MN/Nov. 9-14

Nat'l Council on Internat'l Trade Development *(1967)*
1620 I St., N.W., Suite 615
Washington, DC 20006
Members: 100 individuals, 60 companies
Staff: 1
Annual Budget: $250-500,000
Chairman: James Wheeler

Historical Note
Formerly (1988) Nat'l Council on Internat'l Trade Documentation and (1995) NCITD-Internat'l Trade Facilitation Council. Members are exporters and importers and other professionals serving the international trade industry. Emphasis is on improved documentation of international trading, electronic recordkeeping, and procudures to increase the efficiency of trade. Membership: $250/year (individual), $500/year (corporate minimum).

Publications:
NCITD Newsletter. m.

Meetings/Conferences:
Annual Meetings: April-June

Nat'l Council on Measurement in Education *(1938)*
1230 17th St., N.W.
Washington, DC 20036-3078
Tel: (202)223-9318   Fax: (202)775-1824
Members: 2,100 individuals
Annual Budget: $100-250,000
Exec. Director: William J. Russell, Ph.D.

Historical Note
Founded as the National Council on Measurements used in Education, it assumed its present name in 1960. Has no paid officers or full-time staff. Membership: $45/year.

Publications:
Educational Measurement: Issues and Practice. q.
Journal of Educational Measurement. q. adv.

Meetings/Conferences:
Annual Meetings: With American Educational Research Association in Spring

Nat'l Council on Public History *(1979)*
327 Cavanaugh Hall - IUPUI
425 University Blvd.
Indianapolis, IN 46202-5140
Tel: (317)274-2716   Fax: (317)274-2347
E-Mail: neph@iupui.edu
Web Site: http://www.iupui.edu/it/ncph/ncph.html
Members: 1,500 individuals
Staff: 2
Annual Budget: $25-50,000
Exec. Director: David G. Vanderstel

Historical Note
NCPH members are professionals and others concerned with the presentation of history in non-academic settings. Membership: $47/year (individual); $21/year (student); $79/year (institution).

Publications:
Guide to Graduate Programs in Public History. irreg.
Public Historian. q.
Public History News Newsletter. q.

Meetings/Conferences:
Annual Meetings: Spring
1999 – Lowell, MA/April 29-May 1
2000 – St. Louis, MO

Nat'l Council on Public Polls *(1969)*
1375 Kings Highway East, Suite 300
Fairfield, CT 06430
Toll Free: (800)239 - 0909
Members: 26 companies
Annual Budget: under $10,000

President: Sheldon R. Gawiser

Historical Note
Formerly Nat'l Committee on Public Polls. Members are public opinion polling organizations. Has no paid staff.

Meetings/Conferences:
Annual Meetings: No set pattern.

Nat'l Council on Radiation Protection and Measurements *(1964)*
7910 Woodmont Ave., Suite 800
Bethesda, MD   20814-3095
Tel: (301)657-2652
Toll Free: (800)229 - 2652   *Fax:* (301)907-8768
E-Mail: ncrp@ncrp.com
Web Site: http://www.ncrp.com
Members: 80 individuals
Staff: 16
Annual Budget: $1-2,000,000
Exec. Director: William M. Beckner

Historical Note
Formerly (1929) Advisory Committee on X-ray and Radium Protection; (1947) Nat'l Committee on Radiation Protection; (1957) Nat'l Committee on Radiation Protection and Measurements.

Publications:
Annual Report. a.
Commentaries. irreg.
NCRP Reports. irreg.
Proceedings. a.
Statements. irreg.

Meetings/Conferences:
Annual Meetings: Washington, DC/Spring
1999 - Alexandria, VA(Crystal City Marriott)/April 7-8

Nat'l Council on Rehabilitation Education *(1961)*
Dept. of Special Education and Rehab.
Utah State University
Logan, UT   84322-2870
Tel: (435)797-3241   *Fax:* (435)797-3572
Members: 540 individuals
Staff: 1
Annual Budget: $50-100,000
Administrative Secretary: Dr. Garth M. Eldredge

Historical Note
Members are professional educators and researchers with expertise in numerous facets of vocational rehabilitation and eduational institutions offering academic training programs and conducting research related to rehabilitation education and improved services to consumers. Membership: $50/year (individual); $350/year (organization).

Publications:
Membership Directory. a.
Rehabilitation Education Journal. q.
Report Newsletter. q.

Meetings/Conferences:
Annual Meetings: Semi-Annual Meetings

Nat'l Council on Student Development *(1960)*
c/o Arkansas Ass'n of Two-Year Colleges
114 E. Capitol Ave.
Little Rock, AR   72201
Tel: (501)371-2014   *Fax:* (501)371-2084
E-Mail: edf@adhe.arknet.edu
Members: 700 individuals
Annual Budget: $10-25,000
President: Ed Franklin

Historical Note
A council of the American Ass'n of Community Colleges. Members are student affairs, student development and personnel management professionals at two-year colleges. Has no paid officers or full-time staff. Membership: $35/year (individual), $125/year (organization).

Meetings/Conferences:
Annual Meetings: April, with American Ass'n of Community and Junior Colleges

Nat'l Council on Teacher Retirement *(1924)*
P.O. Box 202243
Austin, TX   78720
Tel: (512)335-0055   *Fax:* (512)335-8823
Web Site: http://www.nctr.org
Members: 284 organizations
Staff: 1
Annual Budget: $250-500,000
Exec. Director: Bruce Hineman

Historical Note
Members are 50 state and 12 local retirement systems, 20 education associations, 10 state departments and agencies and 192 commercial firms.

Publications:
Newsletter. m.
Proceedings and Membership Directory. a.

Meetings/Conferences:
Annual Meetings: Fall
1999 - Nashville, TN(Opryland)/Oct. 3-7
2000 - Boston, MA(Westin Copley Plaza)/Oct. 1-5

Nat'l Council on the Aging *(1950)*
409 3rd St., S.W.
Washington, DC   20024
Tel: (202)479-1200   *Fax:* (202)479-0735
E-Mail: info@ncoa.org
Web Site: http://www.ncoa.org
Members: 7,500 individuals
Staff: 90
Annual Budget: $25-50,000,000
President and C.E.O.: James Firman
Director, Communications: Michael Reinemer
V.P., Public Policy: Howard Bedlin

V.P., Membership: Joyce Welsh

Historical Note
A nonprofit voluntary organization in the field of aging, NCOA is also a central national resource for planning information, technical consultation, advocacy, and materials for professionals in the field. Supports the Health Promotion Institute; the Nat'l Ass'n of Older Worker Employment Services; the Nat'l Center on Rural Aging; the Nat'l Institute of Senior Centers; the Nat'l Institute of Senior Housing; the Nat'l Adult Day Services Ass'n; the Nat'l Institute on Community-Based Long-Term Care; the Nat'l Institute on Financial Issues and Services for Elders; and Nat'l Interfaith Coalition on Aging. Membership: $75/year (individual).

Publications:
Innovations in Aging. q.
NCOA Networks. bi-m.

Meetings/Conferences:
Annual Meetings: Spring/1,800

Nat'l Counter Intelligence Corps Ass'n *(1947)*
613 S. Fine Points Rd.
Westchester, PA   19382
Tel: (610)429-3943
Members: 1,600 individuals
Staff: 1
Annual Budget: under $10,000
Chairman: James Marion

Historical Note
Members are former counter intelligence agents of the U.S. Armed Forces. Membership: $10/year; $150 life member.

Publications:
Golden Sphinx. q.

Meetings/Conferences:
Annual Meetings: Fall

Nat'l Court Reporters Ass'n *(1899)*
8224 Old Courthouse Road
Vienna, VA   22182-3808
Tel: (703)556-6272   *Fax:* (703)556-6291
Toll Free: (800)272 - 6272
Web Site: http://www.verbatimreporters.com
Members: 35,000 individuals
Staff: 57
Annual Budget: $5-10,000,000
Director of Communications: Marshall S. Jorpeland
Manager of State Relations: Dave Wenhold
Director of Professional Development: Karen S. Jacoby
Director of Finance: Nellie Sarkissian
Director of Membership and Marketing: Irene Cahill
Adimistrative Assistant: Melanie Richardson
Manager, Information Systems & Technology: Shakila Anwari

Historical Note
Formerly (1991) Nat'l Shorthand Reporters Ass'n. Merged (1970) with Associated Stenotypists of America. Sponsors and supports the Nat'l Court Reporters Ass'n Political Action Committee. Members are individuals "skilled in the art of verbatim reporting of proceedings by the use of shorthand symbols, manually or by machine". Membership: $150/year. Has an annual budget of $8.4 million.

Publications:
Annual Report & Convention Proceedings. a.
Court Reporter Source Book/Membership Directory. a. adv.
Journal of Court Reporting. 10/year. adv.

Meetings/Conferences:
Annual Meetings: August/1,700
1999 - Boston, MA(Marriott/Westin)/Aug. 4-7
2000 - San Diego, CA(Marriott Hotel & Marina)/July 20-23

Nat'l CPA Health Care Advisors Ass'n *(1992)*
111 E. Wacker Dr., Suite 990
Chicago, IL   60601
Tel: (312)729-9900   *Fax:* (312)729-9800
Toll Free: (800)869 - 0491
E-Mail: info@pencormazur.com
Web Site: http://www.hcaa.com
Members: 58 firms
Staff: 10
Director of Communications: Michelle Durham

Historical Note
HCAA is an association of CPA firms that provide services to health care providers beyond traditional compliance work. Members are admitted on a territorial exclusive basis with a limit of one member in each Metropolitan Statistical Area.

Publications:
Health Care Management Survey Report (Client Newsletter).
Members' Bulletin.
Practice Management Advisor. q.

Meetings/Conferences:
1999 - New Orleans, LA
1999 - Fall

Nat'l Credit Union Management Ass'n *(1949)*
4989 Rebel Trail, N.W.
Atlanta, GA   30327
Tel: (404)255-6828   *Fax:* (404)851-1752
Members: 7,200 international credit unions
Annual Budget: $250-500,000
President: Jerry K. Anchors

Historical Note
Members are credit unions whose assets total more than $5 million.

Meetings/Conferences:
Annual Meetings: September or October
1999 - Montreal, QB, Canada/July 3-7
1999 - Maui, HI/Sept. 25-29

Nat'l Crime Prevention Institute *(1971)*

Historical Note
Merged with Internat'l Soc. of Crime Prevention Practitioners in 1997.

Nat'l Criminal Justice Ass'n *(1971)*
444 North Capitol St., N.W., Suite 618
Washington, DC   20001
Tel: (202)624-1440   *Fax:* (202)508-3859
E-Mail: incja@sso.orh
Web Site: www.sso.org/ncga/
Members: 1,200 individuals
Staff: 8
Annual Budget: $500-1,000,000
Exec. Director: Cabell C. Cropper
Director, Administration: Paul E. Lawrence

Historical Note
Membership open to all criminal justice system practitioners and others with interest in crime prevention and control, law enforcement, the courts, corrections or other aspects of the administration of justice. Incorporated in the District of Columbia in 1974. Formerly (until 1979) known as the Nat'l Conference of State Criminal Justice Planning Administrators. Membership: $65/year.

Publications:
Justice Bulletin. m.

Meetings/Conferences:
Annual Meetings: Spring
1999 - Pittsburgh, PA/July 17-21

Nat'l Crop Insurance Services *(1948)*
7201 W. 129th St., Suite 200
Overland Park, KS   66213
Tel: (913)685-2767   *Fax:* (913)685-3080
Web Site: http://www.ag.rsk.org
Members: 135 companies
Staff: 45
Annual Budget: $2-5,000,000
President: Robert W. Parkerson
Director, Public Relations: Laura A. Langstraat

Historical Note
Formed in 1989 by the merger of the Crop Hail Insurance Actuarial Ass'n and the Nat'l Crop Insurance Ass'n. NCIS is an association of insurance companies writing insurance for damage by hail, fire and other weather perils to growing crops. Membership: dues based upon crop insurance writings. Has an annual budget of $5.5 million.

Publications:
Crop Insurance Today. q.
CropTalk. m.

Meetings/Conferences:
Annual Meetings: February/March

Nat'l Customs Brokers and Forwarders Ass'n of America *(1897)*
1200 18th St., N.W., Suite 901
Washington, DC   20036
Tel: (202)466-0222   *Fax:* (202)466-0226
E-Mail: staff@ncbfaa.org
Web Site: http://www.ncbfaa.org/ncbfaa
Members: 700 firms
Staff: 5
Annual Budget: $1-2,000,000
Exec. V. President: Barbara Reily
Director of Communications: Marilyn Kornfeld

Historical Note
Founded (1897) as the Customs-Clerks Ass'n of the Port of New York. Became the New York Customs Brokers Ass'n (1922) and was incorporated under the same name in 1933. Accepted national membership in 1945, and was incorporated as the Customs Brokers and Forwarders Ass'n of America, Inc., in 1948. Name changed to Nat'l Customs Brokers and Forwarders Ass'n of America, Inc., in 1962. NCBFAA represents licensed customs brokers, international freight forwarders, international air cargo agents and non-vessel operating common carriers (NVOCCs) located throughout the United States. Internationally, NCBFAA represents its membership at the International Federation of Customs Brokers Ass'n, which represents many foreign countries and maintains ties APEC and the World Customs Organization. Membership dues vary, based on the size of the firm.

Publications:
Membership Directory. a. adv.
Monday Morning Briefing. w.
NCBFAA Bulletin Newsletter. m. adv.

Meetings/Conferences:
Annual Meetings: March

Nat'l Cutting Horse Ass'n *(1946)*
4704 Hwy. 377, South
Fort Worth, TX   76116-8805
Tel: (817)244-6188   *Fax:* (817)244-2015
Web Site: www.nchacutting.com
Members: 12,345 individuals, 112 affiliated organizations
Staff: 29
Annual Budget: $2-5,000,000
Exec. Director: Henry Conley
Dir., Media and Marketing: Darrell Burnett

Historical Note
Members are individuals, firms, organizations and riding clubs interested in the development of superior horses and the refinement of true cutting horse competition. Membership: $50/yr.

Publications:
Annual Yearbook. a.
NCHA Rule Book.
The Cutting Horse Chatter. m. adv.

Meetings/Conferences:
1999 - Fort Worth, TX/June 11-13
2000 - Las Vegas, NV
2001 - Denver or Colorado Springs, CO
2001 - Atlanta, GA

Nat'l Dairy Council *(1915)*
10255 W. Higgins Road, Suite 900

Rosemont, IL   60018-5616
Tel: (847)803-2000   Fax: (847)803-2077
Web Site: http://www.dairyinfo.com.
Members: 300 individuals, 22 organizations
Staff: 60
Annual Budget: $2-5,000,000
Chief Exec. Officer: Thomas P. Gallagher
Sr. V.P., Finance and Administration: Daniel J. Chavka

Historical Note
Supported by all segments of the dairy industry in its promotion of
nutrition research and nutrition education. Funds are channelled
through the United Dairy Industry Ass'n to the Nat'l Dairy
Council.

Publications:
Catalog of Nutrition Education Materials. a.
Dairy Council Digest. bi-m.
Nutrition News. q.

Meetings/Conferences:
Annual Meetings: September, with the United Dairy Industry
Ass'n

Nat'l Dairy Herd Improvement Ass'n
3021 E. Dublin-Granville Road, Suite 102
Columbus, OH   43231-4031
Tel: (614)890-3630   Fax: (614)890-3667
E-Mail: dnia@compuserv.com
Web Site: http://www.dhia.org
Members: 4,500 individuals
Staff: 2
Annual Budget: $250-500,000
Acting Manager: Paul Miller
Meeting/Accounting Coordinator: Diane Ross

Historical Note
Dairy industry association provides sample analysis data
processing and communications services to 48% of U.S. dairy
farmers.

Publications:
DHIA Connection. 10/year.

Meetings/Conferences:
1999 – Las Vegas, NV

Nat'l Dance Ass'n (1932)
1900 Association Drive
Reston, VA   20191-1599
Tel: (703)476-3421   Fax: (703)476-9527
E-Mail: nda@aahperd.org
Web Site: http://www.aahperd.org/nda/nda.html
Members: 2,000 individuals
Staff: 1
Annual Budget: $100-250,000
Exec. Director: Jane Bonbright
Program Administrator: Judy Oberle

Historical Note
Until 1974 a division of the American Ass'n for Health, Physical
Education and Recreation. It is now an ass'n of the American
Alliance for Health, Physical Education, Recreation and Dance
(AAHPERD). NDA is dedicated to promoting the development and
implementation of sound philosophies and policies in all forms of
dance and in dance education at all levels. In cooperation with
other arts and education organizations, NDA strives to cultivate,
facilitate, and promote the understanding and the practice of dance.
Membership in NDA includes dancers, choreographers, dance
educators, therapists, dance science and medicine specialists, and
arts administrators. Membership: $100/year.

Publications:
Journal of Physical Education, Recreation and Dance. 9/year.
   adv.
Spotlight on Dance. q.

Meetings/Conferences:
Annual Meetings: Spring, with AAHPERD
1999 – Boston, MA/April 20-24
2000 – Orlando, FL/March 21-25
2001 – Cincinnati, OH/March 27-31
2002 – San Diego, CA/April 9-13

Nat'l Dance Council of America (1948)
Historical Note
Address unknown in 1998.

Nat'l Dance-Exercise Instructor's Training Ass'n (1980)
1503 S. Washington Ave., Suite 208
Minneapolis, MN   55454
Tel: (612)340-1306   Fax: (612)340-1619
Toll Free: (800)237 - 6242
Web Site: http://www.ndeita.com
Members: 80,000 individuals
Staff: 30
Exec. Director: Michael Wollman

Historical Note
Members are aerobic exercise instructors and personal trainers.

Publications:
Aerobic Instructor/Personal Trainer Fitness Training Manual.
   semi-a.

Nat'l Decorating Products Ass'n (1947)
Historical Note
Became Paint and Decorating Retailers Ass'n in 1996.

Nat'l Defense Industrial Ass'n (1919)
2111 Wilson Blvd., Suite 400
Arlington, VA   22201-3061
Tel: (703)522-1820   Fax: (703)522-1885
Web Site: www.ndia.org
Members: 27,000 individuals, 900 companies
Staff: 65
Annual Budget: $10-25,000,000
President: Lt.Gen. Lawrence F. Skibbie, USAF(Ret.)
Public Relations Director: Fred Lash
V.P., Government Policy: Pete Scrivner

V. President, Operations: Maj. Gen. Paul Greenberg
V. P., Membership: Maj.Gen. Jim McInerney, USAF(Ret.)

Historical Note
NDIA was formed from the merger of the Nat'l Security Industrial
Ass'n and the American Defense Preparedness Ass'n in 1997.
Members are industrial, research, legal and educational
organizations of all sizes and drawn from all segments of the
industrial community interested in and related to the national
security. Fosters an effective working relationship between
government and industry in the interest of national security.
Membership: $700-15,525/year, based on sales to the federal
government.

Publications:
National Defense Magazine.

Meetings/Conferences:
Annual Meetings: Washington, DC(Sheraton Washington)/3rd
   week in Sept./500

Nat'l Defense Transportation Ass'n (1944)
50 S. Pickett St., Suite 220
Alexandria, VA   22304-7296
Tel: (703)751-5011   Fax: (703)823-8761
E-Mail: ndta@pop.erols.com
Web Site: http://ndta.volpe.dot.gov
Members: 8,300 individuals, 165 corporations
Staff: 8
Annual Budget: $500-1,000,000
President: Lt.Gen. Edward Honor, USA(Ret.)

Historical Note
Established October 11, 1944 as the Army Transport Ass'n by
seven officers from the Army Transportation Corps, it assumed its
present name in 1949. Originally intended as a liaison between
government and private transportation officials, it has evolved into
a major facilitator of interaction between government and
commercial transportation interests. Sustaining members are air,
sea and land transportation industry and private enterprise.
Membership: $35/year (individual), $1,100/year (company).

Publications:
Defense Transportation Journal. bi-m. adv.
NDTA Gram. m.

Meetings/Conferences:
Annual Meetings: September-October
1999 – Anchorage, AK/Oct. 2-8
2000 – Albuquerque, NM/Oct. 1-5
2001 – Milwaukee, WI/Sept. 29-Oct. 3

Nat'l Defined Contribution Council (1995)
9101 E. Kenyon Ave., Suite 3000
Denver, CO   80237
Tel: (303)770-2220   Fax: (303)770-1812
E-Mail: NDCC@GWami.com
Annual Budget: $100-250,000
Exec. Director: Anita J. Hutner

Historical Note
NDCC is dedicated to the promotion and protection of the defined
contribution industry and the public it serves. The Council
specifically addresses the legislative needs of the defined
contribution industry's plan service providers. Membership:
$5,000/year (organization/company); $2,500/year (associate
member)

Publications:
DC Advocate. q.

Meetings/Conferences:
Annual Meetings: Symposiums twice a year in Spring and Fall.
1999 – Atlanta, GA(JW Marriott)/May 19-20

Nat'l Dental Ass'n (1913)
3517 16th St., NW
Washington, DC   20010
Tel: (202)588-1697   Fax: (202)588-1244
Web Site: www.natdent.org
Members: 7,000 individuals
Staff: 7
Annual Budget: $250-500,000
Exec. Director: Robert Johns

Historical Note
Founded in Hampton, VA. Members are minority dentists dedicated
to providing quality dental care to the unserved and underserved.
Membership: $250/yr.

Publications:
Flossline Newsletter. q.
National Dental Ass'n Journal. q. adv.

Meetings/Conferences:
Annual Meetings: Summer/1,000
1999 – Atlanta, GA(Hyatt)/July 31-Aug. 4

Nat'l Dental Assistants Ass'n (1964)
c/o Nat'l Dental Ass'n
3517 16th St., N.W.
Washington, DC   20010-3041
Tel: (202)244-7555   Fax: (202)244-5992
Members: 50,000 individuals
President: Martha Cline

Historical Note
An auxiliary of the Nat'l Dental Ass'n.

Publications:
Newsletter. q.

Meetings/Conferences:

Nat'l Dental Hygienists' Ass'n (1932)
3517 16th St., N.W.
Washington, DC   20010-3041
Tel: (202)588-1697   Fax: (202)588-1244
Web Site: www.natdent.org
Members: 200 individuals
Staff: 7
President: Darchelle Strickland

Historical Note
Members are minority dental hygienists. An affiliate of Nat'l Dental
Ass'n, which provides administrative support.

Publications:
Newsletter. q.

Meetings/Conferences:
Annual Meetings: In conjunction with the Nat'l Dental Ass'n

Nat'l Denturist Ass'n (1976)
Box 637
Poulsbod, WA   98370
Tel: (360)779-5326   Fax: (360)779-1566
Web Site: wandaa@tscnet.com
Members: 150 companies
Staff: 2
Annual Budget: $25-50,000
Exec. Director: Wanda Anderson

Historical Note
Members are denturists (makers of dentures, either with or without
the aid of a dentist) in the U.S. and Canada. Membership:
$100/year.

Publications:
NDA Newsletter. q. adv.

Meetings/Conferences:
1999 – Portland, OR/May 18-23

Nat'l Dimension Manufacturers Ass'n (1929)
Historical Note
Became the Wood Component Manufacturers Ass'n in 1996.

Nat'l Directory Publishing Ass'n (1987)
4201 Connecticut Ave., N.W. Suite 610
Washington, DC   20008
Tel: (202)342-0250   Fax: (202)686-3228
E-Mail: info@idpa.org
Web Site: http://www.idpa.org
Annual Budget: $10-25,000
President: William Wade
Treasurer: Tom Johnson
Membership Chair: Michael Taliaferro

Historical Note
Formerly the Washington Directory Ass'n, NDPA members are
professionals involved in the publishing of directories and
information products. Membership: $35/year (individual);
$75/year (corporate).

Publications:
Membership Directory. a.
Newsletter. m.

Nat'l Dissemination Ass'n
4732 N. Oracle Road, Suite 217
Tucson, AZ   85705
Tel: (520)888-2838   Fax: (520)888-2621
Annual Budget: $50-100,000
Exec. Director: Max McConkey

Historical Note
Represents educators who disseminate exemplary programs
nationwide.

Publications:
Dissemination Perspective.

Meetings/Conferences:

Nat'l District Attorneys Ass'n (1950)
99 Canal Center Plaza, Suite 510
Alexandria, VA   22314
Tel: (703)549-9222   Fax: (703)836-3195
E-Mail: newmanf@erols.com
Members: 7,800 individuals
Staff: 48
Annual Budget: $2-5,000,000
Exec. Director: Newman Flanagan
Director, Government Affairs: James D. Polley, IV
Meeting Director: Shirley Sarni
Comptroller: Scottie Teich
Membership Director: Cathy Yates

Historical Note
Established as the Nat'l Ass'n of County and Prosecuting
Attorneys, it assumed its present name in 1959. Membership: $25-
975/year, varies by size of jurisdiction (individual).

Publications:
Case Commentaries & Briefs. m.
The Prosecutor. q. adv.

Meetings/Conferences:
Annual Meetings: July
1999 – Palm Beach, FL(Breakers)/July 18-22/300
2000 – Spokane, WA

Nat'l Dog Groomers Ass'n of America (1969)
P.O. Box 101
Clark, PA   16113
Tel: (724)962-2711
E-Mail: ndgaa@nauti.com
Web Site: http://www.mauticom.net/www/ndga
Members: 2,500 individuals, 500 certified master groomers
Staff: 2
Annual Budget: $100-250,000
Exec. Director: Jeffrey L. Reynolds

Historical Note
Established to provide professional indentification and continuing
education; awards the designation NCMG (Nat'l Certified Master
Groomer). Holds 20 certification workshops every year throughout
the U.S. Membership: $65/first year; $40/year (renewal).

Publications:
Groomers Voice. q. adv.

Meetings/Conferences:
1999 – Lexington, KY
1999 – Orlando, FL

Nat'l Drilling Ass'n *(1977)*

3008 Millwood Ave.
Columbia, SC   29205
Tel: (803)252-5646   *Fax:* (803)765-0860
Toll Free: (800)445 - 8629
Members: 195 companies
Annual Budget: $50-100,000
Exec. Director: MaryAnn S. Crews

Historical Note
Formerly Nat'l Drilling Contractors Ass'n; merged with Drilling Equipment Manufacturers Ass'n and Internat'l Drilling Federation and assumed its current name in 1995. Members are exploratory, ground water monitoring well, and ground water recovery well drillers. Incorporated in the State of Pennsylvania.

Publications:
Drillbits. q.

Meetings/Conferences:
Annual Meetings: Fall

Nat'l Drilling Contractors Ass'n

Historical Note
Merged with the Drilling Equipment Manufacturers Ass'n and the Internat'l Drilling Federation to form the Nat'l Drilling Ass'n in 1995.

Nat'l Dry Bean Council *(1950)*

6707 Old Dominion Dr., Suite 315
McLean, VA   22101
Tel: (703)556-9304   *Fax:* (703)556-9301
Members: 11 associations
Staff: 3
Annual Budget: $100-250,000
Exec. Director: Philip H. Kimball

Historical Note
Formerly Nat'l Dried Bean Council. Conducts export development programs on behalf of the U.S. dry bean industry. Officers change biennially.

Meetings/Conferences:

Nat'l Early Care and Education Ass'n

Historical Note
Address unknown in 1996.

Nat'l Earth Science Teachers Ass'n *(1982)*

2000 Florida Ave., N.W.
Washington, DC   20009
Tel: (202)462-6910   *Fax:* (202)328-0566
E-Mail: fireton@agu.org
Members: 1000 individuals
Annual Budget: $10-25,000
Exec. Advisor: Frank Watt Ireton

Historical Note
NESTA members are earth science teachers concerned with teaching in grades K-12. NESTA is affiliated or associated with the Nat'l Science Teachers Ass'n, Triangle Coalition, Geological Soc. of America, American Geophysical Union, and the American Geological Institute. Membership: $15/year (individual).

Publications:
Earth Scientist. q. adv.
Summer School Oportunities. a.

Meetings/Conferences:
Annual Meetings: in conjunction with the Nat'l Science
    Teachers Ass'n

Nat'l Economic Ass'n *(1969)*

School of Business
University of Michigan
Ann Arbor, MI   48109-1234
Tel: (313)763-0121   *Fax:* (313)647-7930
Members: 150 individuals
Annual Budget: under $10,000
Secretary-Treasurer: Alfred L. Edwards

Historical Note
Formerly (1975) Caucus of Black Economists. NEA promotes black representation in the economics profession, acts as a job clearing house and gives financial assistance to black students of economics. Membership: $40/year; $15/year (student).

Publications:
Review of Black Political Economy. q.

Meetings/Conferences:
Annual Meetings: In conjunction with the American Economic
    Ass'n

Nat'l Education Ass'n of the U.S. *(1857)*

1201 16th St., N.W.
Washington, DC   20036
Tel: (202)833-4000   *Fax:* (202)822-7974
Web Site: http://www.nea.org
Members: 2,300,000 individuals
Staff: 600
Annual Budget: Over $100,000,000
Exec. Director: Don Cameron
Director, Government Relations: Mary Elizabeth Teasley
General Counsel: Robert Chanin
Mgr., Membership Support: Linda Riddle
Manager, Publishing Systems: Lorraine Wilson

Historical Note
Formerly (1870) Nat'l Teachers Ass'n. Merged with American Teachers Ass'n in 1966. Supports the Nat'l Education Ass'n Political Action Committee. Strives to enhance and strengthen public education in America in order to further equity and excellence for all Americans. Also works to advance human and civil rights. Has an annual budget of approximately $190 million. Membership: $107/year.

Publications:
Almanac of Higher Education. a.
ESP Progress. q.

NEA Addresses and Proceedings. a.
NEA Advocate. q.
NEA Handbook. a.
NEA Now. w.
NEA Today. 10/year.
The Best Years. q.
Today's Education. a.

Meetings/Conferences:
Annual Meetings: June/July
1999 – Orlando, FL/July 1-6

Nat'l Education Knowledge Industry Ass'n *(1971)*

1200 19th St., N.W., Suite 300
Washington, DC   20036
Tel: (202)429-5101   *Fax:* (202)785-3849
Web Site: http://www.nekia.org
Members: 15 companies
Staff: 6
Annual Budget: $250-500,000
Acting Exec. Director: Roy Forbes

Historical Note
Founded as Council for Educational Development and Research; assumed its current name in 1997. Members are companies and institutions interested in continuing research and development that contributes to cost-effective education innovation.

Publications:
Directory. a.
R & D Preview. bi-m.

Meetings/Conferences:
Annual Meetings: Fall

Nat'l Educational Telecommunications Ass'n *(1967)*

939 S. Stadium Road
P.O. Box 50008
Columbia, SC   29505
Tel: (803)799-5517   *Fax:* (803)771-4831
Web Site: http://www.netaonline.org
Members: 86 individuals
Exec. Director: Wilbur H. "Skip" Hinton

Historical Note
Founded as Southern Educational Communications Ass'n; assumed its current name in 1997 to reflect its national constituency. Members are public television licensees.

Meetings/Conferences:
1999 – Albuquerque, NM/Oct. 31-Nov. 3

Nat'l Electric Sign Ass'n *(1944)*

Historical Note
Became the Internat'l Sign Ass'n in 1995.

Nat'l Electrical Contractors Ass'n *(1901)*

3 Bethesda Metro Center, Suite 1100
Bethesda, MD   20814-5330
Tel: (301)657-3110   *Fax:* (301)215-4500
E-Mail: webmaster@necanet.org
Web Site: http://www.necanet.org
Members: 4,000 companies and 118 local chapters
Staff: 80
Annual Budget: $10-25,000,000
Exec. V. President and C.E.O.: John M. Grau
Publisher: Joseph A. Salimando
Director, Public Relations: Thomas Naber
Government Affairs: George White
Legislative Representative: Kate Widmayer
Convention/Expostion Director: Stephen Schultz
Director, Management Development: William J. Normand
Secretary-Treasurer: J. Michael Thompson
Senior Executive Director: Daniel G. Walter
Editor: Bonnie N. Duncan

Historical Note
Members are electrical contruction companies. Sponsors and supports the Electrical Construction Political Action Committee (ECPAC). Has an annual budget of approximately $12.5 million.

Publications:
Electrical Contractor. m. adv.
NECA News. w.

Meetings/Conferences:
Annual Meetings: October/8,000
1999 – New Orleans, LA/Oct. 24-26

Nat'l Electrical Engineering Department Heads Ass'n *(1985)*

549 W. Randolph St., Suite 600
Chicago, IL   60661-2208
Tel: (312)559-3724   *Fax:* (312)559-4111
Web Site: www.needha.org
Members: 250 individuals
Staff: 50
Exec. Director: Robert M. Janowiak

Historical Note
Members are educators chairing collegiate electrical engineering programs.

Publications:
Annual Review of Communications. a.
Directory of Electrical & Computer Engineering Departments. a.

Meetings/Conferences:
Annual Meetings: March
1999 – Destin, FL(San Destin Hilton)/March 5-9/170

Nat'l Electrical Manufacturers Ass'n *(1926)*

1300 N. 17th St., Suite 1847
Rosslyn, VA   22209
Tel: (703)841-3200   *Fax:* (703)841-3351
E-Mail: webmaster@nema.org
Web Site: http://www.nema.org
Members: 630 companies
Staff: 95

Annual Budget: $5-10,000,000
President: Malcolm E. O'Hagan, Ph.D.
Director, Communications and Publications: Rae Mark Hamilton
V. President, Gov't Affairs: Timothy Feldman
V.P., Administration: Thomas E. Hixon
Counsel: Clark R. Silcox
Senior Editor: Natalie Fern
V. President and Chief Economist: Donald Leavens
Dir., Information Systems: Paul Hou

Historical Note
The largest trade organization for manufacturers of electrical products in the U.S. Organized in 1926 through the merger of several organizations, the oldest of which, Electrical Manufacturers Club, was formed in 1905. Has an annual budget of approximately $8.4 million.

Publications:
Electroindustry.

Meetings/Conferences:
1999 – Washington, DC/Nov. 7-8
2000 – Chicago, IL/Nov. 12-13

Nat'l Electrical Manufacturers Representatives Ass'n *(1969)*

200 Business Park Drive, Suite 301
Armonk, NY   10504
Tel: (914)273-6780   *Fax:* (914)273-6785
E-Mail: nemra@nemra.org
Web Site: http://www.NGMRA.org
Members: 1,150 companies
Staff: 11
Annual Budget: $1-2,000,000
President: Henry P. Bergson
V. President, Operations: Nancy J. Sciotto

Historical Note
Members are independent electrical sales representatives. Membership: $800/yr.

Publications:
NEMRA Locator. a. adv.
Repconnections. m.
The Insider. irreg.

Meetings/Conferences:
Annual Meetings: Spring
1999 – San Francisco, CA(Marriott)/Feb. 23-March 1/2000
2000 – New Orleans, LA(Marriott)
2001 – Boston, MA(Marriott Westin)/March 20-26
2002 – Dallas, TX(Wyndham Anatole)/Mar. 5-11/2000

Nat'l Electronic Distributors Ass'n *(1937)*

1111 Alderman Dr., Suite 400
Alpharetta, GA   30005-4143
Tel: (678)393-9990   *Fax:* (678)393-9998
Web Site: NEDASSOC.ORG
Members: 400 distributors and manufacturers
Staff: 10
Annual Budget: $1-2,000,000
Exec. V. President: Robin B. Gray, Jr.
Director, Communications: Carolyn M. Kulawiak
Director, Program Development: Greg Younghans
Dir., Administration: Janet Wood

Historical Note
Formerly National Radio Parts Distributors Ass'n. Members are distributors and manufacturers of electronics and high technology components and systems to industry.

Publications:
MRO Quarterly Newsletter. q.
NEDA Membership Directory. a. adv.
NEDA News. m.

Meetings/Conferences:
Semi-Annual Meetings: Spring and Fall
1999 – Las Vegas, NV(Hilton)/May 17-21
1999 – Chicago, IL(Renaissance)/Nov. 7-9/390

Nat'l Electronic Service Dealers Ass'n *(1963)*

2708 West Berry
Fort Worth, TX   76109-2356
Tel: (817)921-9061   *Fax:* (817)921-3741
E-Mail: clydenesda@aol.com
Web Site: http://www.nesda.com
Members: 800 individuals
Staff: 11
Annual Budget: $500-1,000,000
Exec. Director: Clyde W. Nabors
Director, Communications: Wallace S. Harrison
Manager, Marketing: Laura Troyer
Director, Member Services: Alice Brown

Historical Note
Formerly Nat'l Electronic Ass'n; became (1974) Nat'l Electronic Service Dealers Ass'n and (1983) Nat'l Electronic Sales and Service Dealers Ass'n; again became Nat'l Electronic Service Dealers Ass'n in 1992. Absorbed Nat'l Ass'n of Television and Electronic Servicers of America in 1986. Members are electronics service centers. Sponsors Internat'l Soc. of Certified Electronics Technicians. Membership: $120/year.

Publications:
Newsletter.
ProService. m. adv.
ProService Yearbook. a. adv.

Meetings/Conferences:
1999 – Dallas, TX(Inter-Continental)/Aug. 2-7/900

Nat'l Elevator Industry *(1934)*

185 Bridge Plaza North, Suite 310
Ft. Lee, NJ   07024
Tel: (201)944-3211   *Fax:* (201)944-5483
Members: 35 companies
Staff: 3
Annual Budget: $500-1,000,000
Exec. Director: E. James Walker, Jr.

Historical Note
*Formerly (1969) Nat'l Elevator Manufacturing Industry, Inc.
Membership: fees based on hours worked*
Meetings/Conferences:
1999 – Emilia Island, FL(Emilia Island Plantation)

Nat'l Emergency Equipment Dealers Ass'n *(1996)*
8421 Frost Way
Annandale, VA 22003
Tel: (703)280-4622   *Fax:* (703)280-0942
E-Mail: KentonP1@aol.com
Web Site: http://www.needa.org
Members: 110 individuals
Annual Budget: $25-50,000
Exec. Officer: Kenton Pattie
Historical Note
*This association represents dealers and distributors who sell fire
trucks, ambulances, rescue vehicles and all equipment, parts,
maintenance and repair. Membership: $400/year(company).*
Publications:
Congressional Directory. a.
Needa News. q.
Meetings/Conferences:
Annual Meetings: January
1999 – Orlando, FL(Grovesnor Resort)/50
2000 – San Diego, CA(Catamaran Resort)/50

Nat'l Emergency Management Ass'n *(1950)*
P.O. Box 11910
Lexington, KY 40578-1910
Tel: (606)244-8000   *Fax:* (606)244-8239
Web Site: http://www.csg.org/nemaweb/
Members: 250 individuals
Staff: 3
Annual Budget: $10-25,000
Exec. Director: Trina Hembree
Historical Note
*Founded as the Nat'l Ass'n of State Civil Defense Directors, it
became the Nat'l Ass'n of State Directors for Disaster Preparedness
in 1974 and assumed its present name in 1980. Members include
State Directors of Emergency Management, while associate
members include, federal agencies, local emergency management
representatives and interested individuals, associations, and
corporations. Affiliated with the Council of State Governments in
1990. Officers change annually. Membership: $50/year
(individual), $200/year (association), $600/year (state), and
$1000/year (corporate).*
Publications:
NEMA News. q. adv.
Meetings/Conferences:
Semi-annual Meetings: Washington, DC/Spring and Fall
1999 – Washington, DC(Mayflower Hotel)/Feb. 7-10
1999 – Des Moines, IA/Sept. 20-25

Nat'l Employee Benefits Institute *(1977)*
1350 Connecticut Ave., N.W., Suite 600
Washington, DC 20036
Toll Free: (888)822 - 1344
Members: 100 companies
Staff: 4
Annual Budget: $100-250,000
Exec. Director: Joseph Semo
Historical Note
*NEBI was established to represent the employee benefit interests of
large, multistate employers before Congress and Federal regulatory
agencies. Membership: $3,600/year.*
Publications:
Benefits Developments This Week. w.
Employee Benefits Update. m.
Legislative Alerts. irreg.
Meetings/Conferences:
Semi-annual Meetings: Washington, DC

Nat'l Employee Services and Recreation Ass'n *(1941)*
2211 York Road, Suite 207
Oak Brook, IL 60521-2371
Tel: (630)368-1280   *Fax:* (630)368-1286
E-Mail: nesrahq@aol.com
Web Site: http://www.nesra.org
Members: 4,000 companies; 50 local chapters
Staff: 6
Annual Budget: $250-500,000
Exec. Director: Patrick B. Stinson
Director of Communications: Cynthia M. Helson
Member Services Director: Kenneth F. Cammarata
Historical Note
*A professional association for employee services and recreation
management. Founded as the Nat'l Industrial Recreation Ass'n, it
assumed its present name in 1982. Members include managers of
such programs as employee assistance, pre-retirement planning,
fitness, child care, sports, travel and educational and cultural
programs in business, the government and military. Membership:
$135/year (company).*
Publications:
Employee Services Management. 10/year. adv.
Meetings/Conferences:
Annual Meetings: Spring
1999 – Las Vegas, NV(Rio Suite Hotel Casino)/April 25-29

Nat'l Employment and Training Ass'n *(1966)*
Historical Note
Address unknown in 1997.

Nat'l Employment Counseling Ass'n *(1964)*
5999 Stevenson Ave.
Alexandria, VA 22304-3300
Tel: (703)823-9800   *Fax:* (703)823-0252
Members: 1,213 individuals

Staff: 2
Annual Budget: $25-50,000
Interim Exec. Director: Richard Yep
Historical Note
*Formerly (1992) Nat'l Employment Counseling Ass'n. NECA is
committed to offering professional leadership to people who counsel
within employment and /or career development settings. A division
of the American Counseling Ass'n. Membership: $24/year
(professional); $12/year (student/retired).*
Publications:
Journal of Employment Counseling. q. adv.
NECA Newletter.
Meetings/Conferences:
Annual Meetings: Spring, with American Counseling Ass'n
1999 – San Diego, CA/April 14-17
2000 – Washington, DC/March 22-24
2001 – San Antonio, TX
2002 – New Orleans, TX

Nat'l Employment Lawyers Ass'n *(1985)*
600 Harrison St., Suite 535
San Francisco, CA 94107-1370
Tel: (415)227-4655   *Fax:* (415)495-7465
E-Mail: NELAHQ@nela.org
Web Site: http://www.nela.org
Members: 3,400 individuals
Staff: 5
Annual Budget: $500-1,000,000
Exec. Director: Terisa E. Chaw
Historical Note
*Founded to provide assistance and support to lawyers in protecting
the rights of employees against the greater resources of their
employers and the defense bar. NELA is the country's only
professional organization that is exclusively comprised of lawyers
who represent individual employees in cases involving employment
discrimination, wrongful termination, employee benefits and other
employment-related matters. Membership: $175/year.*
Publications:
Employee Advocate Newsletter. q. adv.
Employee Rights Litigation: Pleading & Practice.
Membership Directory. a.
Meetings/Conferences:
Annual Meetings: June/350-400
1999 – New Orleans, LA/June 30-July 3

Nat'l EMS Pilots Ass'n *(1985)*
110 N. Royal St., Suite 307
Alexandria, VA 22314
Tel: (703)836-8930   *Fax:* (703)836-8920
E-Mail: natloffice@nemspa.org
Web Site: http://www.nemspa.org
Members: 250 individuals
Staff: 4
Annual Budget: $100-250,000
Exec. Director: Dawn Mancuso, CAE
Historical Note
*NEMSPA is a professional organization serving both helicopter and
fixed-wing aircraft pilots involved in emergency medical service.
Membership: $38/year (active/affiliate); $250/year (corporate
sponsor).*
Publications:
Air Medical Journal. q.
AirMed Journal. bi-m.
AirNet Newsletter. q.
Meetings/Conferences:
Annual Meetings: Fall

Nat'l Energy Assistance Directors Ass'n *(1983)*
P.O. Box 42655
Washington, DC 20036-0655
Tel: (202)237-5199   *Fax:* (202)237-7316
E-Mail: eastham@clark.net
Web Site: see text
Exec. Director: Mark Wolfe
Historical Note
*NEADA support states in the development of Low-Income Home
Energy Assistance(LIHEAP) policies. The association coordinates
and cooperates in the collection and dissemination of information
and proposes energy policies. The Internet address is
http://userweb.interactive.net/~swayze/energy/neada.html*

Nat'l Energy Services Ass'n
7600 West Tidwell, Suite 804
Houston, TX 77040
Tel: (713)939-9200   *Fax:* (713)690-7969
Web Site: http://www.nesanet.org
Members: 2,200 industries
Staff: 3
Annual Budget: $1-2,000,000
President: William T. Harper, Jr.
Director, Conventions and Expo.: Tracy L. Cummins
Historical Note
*Formerly the Nat'l Gas Transportation Ass'n (NGTA). Assumed its
current name in 1996. Membership: $90/year (individual).*
Publications:
NESA Directory. a.
Newsletter. bi-m.
Meetings/Conferences:
Annual Meetings: September
1999 – Houston, TX/Feb. 17-19
1999 – San Francisco, CA/Sept. 7-10

Nat'l Engine Parts Manufacturers Ass'n *(1944)*
42 Park Drive
Port Clinton, OH 43452
Tel: (419)734-2501   *Fax:* (419)732-3780
Members: 25 companies
Staff: 2
Annual Budget: $50-100,000

Exec. V. President: W.E. Herring
Legal and Government Relations: George Keeley
Historical Note
*Founded as Piston Ring Manufacturers Group; merged with Piston
and Pin Standardization Group and Automotive Engine Bearings
Group and assumed its current name in 1972. Membership:
$2,500/year (organization/company).*
Meetings/Conferences:
1999 – Longboat Key, FL(Long Boat Key Club)

Nat'l Environmental Balancing Bureau *(1971)*
8575 Grovemont Circle
Gaithersburg, MD 20877-4121
Tel: (301)977-3698   *Fax:* (301)977-9589
E-Mail: MrNEBB@AOL.COM
Web Site: http://www.nebb.org
Members: 550 companies
Staff: 4
Annual Budget: $500-1,000,000
Exec. V. President: Michael P. Dolim
Historical Note
*The National Environmental Balancing Bureau(NEBB) is a
nonprofit organization, founded in 1971 by contractors in heating,
ventilating and air conditioning (HVAC) industry. NEBB exists to
help architects, building owners, and contractors produce great
buildings with HVAC systems that performed in ways they have
been visualized and designed. NEBB establishes and maintains
industry standards, procedures and specifications for work in its
various disciplines. Membership: $500/year.*
Publications:
The Balance Sheet Newsletter. q.
Meetings/Conferences:
Annual Meetings: Fall

Nat'l Environmental Development Ass'n *(1973)*
818 Connecticut Ave., N.W., 2nd Floor
Washington, DC 20006
Tel: (202)289-0966   *Fax:* (202)289-1327
Members: 40 companies and organizations
Staff: 3
Annual Budget: $50-100,000
Exec. Director: Steve Hellem
Historical Note
*NEDA members are companies and other organiztions concerned
with balancing environmental and economic interests to obtain both
a clean environment and a strong economy.*
Meetings/Conferences:
Annual Meetings: Always Washington, DC

Nat'l Environmental Health Ass'n *(1937)*
720 S. Colorado Blvd.
South Tower, Suite 970
Denver, CO 80246-1925
Tel: (303)756-9090   *Fax:* (303)691-9490
E-Mail: staff@neha.org
Web Site: http://www.neha.org
Members: 5,700 individuals
Staff: 12
Annual Budget: $2-5,000,000
Exec. Director: Nelson E. Fabian
Manager, Education: Reggie Moore
Manager, Operations: Becky Roland
Manager, Research & Development: Larry Marcum
Historical Note
*Incorporated in California in 1937 as the Nat'l Ass'n of
Sanitarians. Became the Nat'l Environmental Health Ass'n in
1970. NEHA members represent virtually all environmental health
and protection professionals. NEHA administers certification
programs concerning environmental health, hazardous waste and
food protection. NEHA also conducts continuing education
programs and special seminars. Membership: $75/year
(individual); $25/year (student/retired); $175/year (institution),
$350/year (company).*
Publications:
Environmental News Digest. q.
Journal of Environmental Health. 10/year. adv.
Membership Directory. a.
Publications Catalog. a.
Meetings/Conferences:
Annual Meetings: June/1,500
1999 – Nashville, TN(Renaissance)/July 5-9
2000 – Denver, CO(Adam's Mark)/June 14-18/2000

Nat'l Environmental Training Ass'n *(1977)*
3020 E. Camelback Road, Suite 399
Phoenix, AZ 85016
Tel: (602)956-6099   *Fax:* (602)956-6399
E-Mail: neta@ehs-training.org
Web Site: http://www.ehs-training.org
Members: 1,500 individuals
Staff: 6
Annual Budget: $500-1,000,000
Exec. Director: Charles L. Richardson
Manager, Ass'n Services: Joan J. Jennings
Manager, Membership Services: Suzanne Lanctot
Historical Note
*Trainers of personnel in the field of air and noise pollution, solid
and hazardous waste control, water supply and waste-water
treatment, and occupational safety and health. Membership:
$70/year (individual), $280/year (organization/company).*
Publications:
Green Pages Environmental Training Referral Directory. a.
NETAnews. q. adv.
Who's Who in Environmental Training. a
Meetings/Conferences:
Annual Meetings: April/150
1999 – Nashville, TN/April 24-28

Nat'l Equipment Leasing Ass'n *(1975)*

Historical Note
Became the United Ass'n of Equipment Leasing in 1995.

Nat'l Erectors Ass'n *(1969)*
1501 Lee Highway, Suite 202
Arlington, VA 22209
Tel: (703)524-3336   *Fax:* (703)524-3364
Members: 139 companies
Staff: 8
Annual Budget: $250-500,000
Exec. V. President: Noel C. Borck
V. President, Operations: William J. Charron
V. President, Membership Services: Eric S. Waterman

Historical Note
A construction employers trade association consisting of steel
erectors, general contractors, and industrial maintenance firms.
Primary functions are labor relations and safety/information
services. Formerly Nat'l Steel Erectors Ass'n.

Publications:
NEA Craft Jurisdiction Guide.
NEA Notes. m.

Meetings/Conferences:
Annual Meetings. Spring
1999 – Carlsbad, CA(Lacasta Resort)/March 24-28

Nat'l Exchange Carrier Ass'n *(1983)*
100 S. Jefferson Road
Whippany, NJ 07981
Tel: (973)884-8000   *Fax:* (973)884-8469
Web Site: http://www.neca.org
Members: 1,250 local telephone companies
President: Bob Anderson
Manager, Government Relations: Lora Magruder

Historical Note
NECA members are local telephone companies.

Nat'l Executive Housekeepers Ass'n *(1930)*
Historical Note
Became Internat'l Executive Housekeepers Ass'n in 1996.

Nat'l Executive Service Corps *(1977)*
120 Wall St., 16th Floor
New York, NY 10005-4001
Tel: (212)269-1234   *Fax:* (212)228-3958
Members: 5,000 individuals
Staff: 20
Annual Budget: $1-2,000,000
President: Don Stewart

Nat'l Extension Ass'n of Family and Consumer Sciences *(1933)*
736 E. Flynn Lane
Phoenix, AZ 85014-1031
Tel: (602)212-0453   *Fax:* (602)212-9692
Web Site: http://www.neafcs.org
Members: 3,300 individuals
Staff: 3
Annual Budget: $250-500,000
Exec. Administrator: Ruth Helein

Historical Note
Formerly Nat'l Home Demonstration Agents' Ass'n and Nat'l Ass'n
of Extension Home Economists; assumed its current name in 1996.
Extension Family and Consumer Sciences Educators are employees
of the Cooperative Extension Service, a joint venture of the U.S.
Department of Agriculture, county government and State Land
Grand Universities. NEAFCS is a professional organization
providing encouragement and opportunities for members to improve
their skills as extension educators. Membership: $40/year
(individual).

Publications:
Communique. q.
The Reporter. bi-m.

Meetings/Conferences:
Annual Meetings: September-October
1999 – Greensboro, NC/Oct. 31-Nov. 4
2000 – Baltimore, MD/Oct. 15-19

Nat'l Eye Research Foundation *(1956)*
910 Skokie Blvd., Suite 207A
Northbrook, IL 60062
Tel: (847)564-4652   *Fax:* (847)564-0807
Toll Free: (800)621 - 2258
Web Site: http://www.nerf.org
Members: 250 individuals
Staff: 6
Annual Budget: $250-500,000
President: Andrew K. Kim
V.President, Foundation: Morgan N. Wesley

Historical Note
Membership: varies by section.

Publications:
Contacto. q. adv.
Pinnacle. m.

Meetings/Conferences:
1999 – /April 22-25

Nat'l Family Business Ass'n *(1985)*
Historical Note
Address unknown in 1995.

Nat'l Family Business Council *(1969)*
1640 W. Kennedy Road
Lake Forest, IL 60045
Tel: (847)295-1040   *Fax:* (847)295-1898
Members: 10,000 family businesses
Staff: 4
Annual Budget: $1-2,000,000
Director & Principal Consultant: John E. Messervey

Historical Note
NFBC serves as the resource center for closely held and family
owned businesses. The Council was formed in 1969 by a group of
concerned successors to family business as the Sons of Bosses
(SOB's) and assumed it present name in 1976. Provides research,
consulting, and other services to client members.

Publications:
Conference Proceedings & Audio Tapes. a.
Family Business Letter. q.

Meetings/Conferences:
Semi-Annual Meetings: Spring and Winter

Nat'l Family Caregivers Ass'n *(1992)*
10605 Concord St.
Suite 501
Kensington, MD 20895-2504
Tel: (301)942-6430   *Fax:* (301)942-2302
Toll Free: (800)896 - 3650
E-Mail: info@nfcacares.org
Web Site: http://www.nfcacares.org
Members: 2,500 individuals
Staff: 2
Annual Budget: $100-250,000
President: Suzanne Mintz
Administrative Manager: Diane Walden
Director, Finance: Mary Ellen Curto

Historical Note
NFCA members are health professionals and caregivers with an
interest in the provision of home health care. Membership:
$20/year (individual); $30/year (professional); $50/year (non-
profit group); $100/year (medical practice); $200/year (insitution).

Publications:
Take Care! Newsletter. q. adv.

Nat'l Family Planning and Reproductive Health Ass'n *(1971)*
122 C St., N.W., Suite 380
Washington, DC 20001-2109
Tel: (202)628-3535   *Fax:* (202)737-2690
Web Site: http://www.nfprha.org
Members: 1000 organizations and individuals
Staff: 9
Annual Budget: $500-1,000,000
President and C.E.O.: Judith M. DeSarno
Director, Public Policy and Service Delivery: Marilyn Keefe
Director, Membership and Meetings: Shauna Walden
Director, Finance and Administration: Megan Jackson
Director, Development: Debra Dillon

Historical Note
A professional membership group concerned with the delivery and
availability of family planning services in the United States. Its
members are primarily government-funded agencies involved in the
provision of family planning and related health services. NFPRHA
follows legislative and administrative developments affecting
reproductive health issues, conducts policy research analysis and
provides technical assistance. Funding sources include private
donations, membership dues and foundation grants. Until 1979
known as the National Family Planning Forum. Membership:
$150/year (individual), $3,000/year (organization).

Publications:
NFPRHA ALERT. irreg.
NFPRHA Annual Report. a.
NRPRHA REPORT. bi-w.

Meetings/Conferences:
Annual Meetings: Washington, DC/February/300-500
1999 – Washington, DC

Nat'l Farmers Organization *(1955)*
2505 Elwood Drive
Ames, IA 50010-2000
Tel: (515)292-2000   *Fax:* (515)292-7106
E-Mail: nfo.netins.net
Web Site: http://www.nfo.org
Staff: 250
President: Gene Paul

Historical Note
An agricultural marketing company utilizing group marketing
concepts to achieve higher returns for its member producers.

Publications:
NFO Reporter.

Meetings/Conferences:
Annual Meetings: December/2,000
1999 – St. Louis, MO/Jan. 18-21

Nat'l Farmers Union
Historical Note
Official name is the Farmers Educational and Co-operative Union
of America.

Nat'l Fashion Accessories Ass'n *(1916)*
330 5th Ave., Suite 205
New York, NY 10001
Tel: (212)947-3424   *Fax:* (212)629-0361
Web Site: http://www.accessoryweb.com
Members: 100 individuals
Staff: 4
Annual Budget: $100-250,000
Exec. Director: Harold Sachs

Historical Note
Formerly (1966) Nat'l Authority for the Ladies Handbag Industry.
Added the title Nat'l Fashion Accessories Ass'n, in 1986. Formerly
(1987) Nat'l Ass'n of Handbag Makers/Nat'l Fashion Accessories
Ass'n.

Publications:
Newsletter. m.

Meetings/Conferences:
Annual Meetings: None held.

Nat'l Fastener Distributors Ass'n *(1968)*
1717 E. Ninth St., Suite 1185
Cleveland, OH 44114-2803
Tel: (216)579-1571   *Fax:* (216)579-1531
Members: 247 companies
Staff: 2
Annual Budget: $250-500,000
Exec. V. President: Dave Merrifield

Historical Note
Absorbed the Southern Ass'n of Industrial Fastener Distributors in
1972. Membership: $925/year, plus $1000 initiation
(organization).

Publications:
NFDA Now. q.
Roster/Source Guide.

Meetings/Conferences:
Semi-Annual Meetings: Spring and Fall/300
1999 – Acapulco, Mexico(Acapulco Princess)/April 12-17
2000 – Palm Springs, CA(Westin Mission Hills
      Resort)/April 11-16

Nat'l Federation for Specialty Nursing Organizations *(1972)*
East Holly Ave., P.O. Box 56
Pitman, NJ 08071-0056
Tel: (609)256-2333   *Fax:* (609)589-7463
Web Site: http://www.nfsno.inurse.com
Members: 37 organizations
Annual Budget: $100-250,000
Exec. Director: Cynthia Nowicki

Historical Note
Umbrella organization for 43 nursing specialties representing over
400,000 nurses. Formerly (1981) Federation of Specialty Nursing
Organizations. Membership: $575-2,300/year.

Publications:
Focus on the Federation. q.

Meetings/Conferences:
Annual Meetings: July
1999 – Washington, DC

Nat'l Federation Interscholastic Coaches Ass'n *(1981)*
P.O. Box 20626
11724 Plaza Circle
Kansas City, MO 64195
Tel: (816)464-5400   *Fax:* (816)464-5571
Web Site: http://www.nfhs.org
Members: 30,000 individuals
Staff: 2
Annual Budget: $500-1,000,000
Director: Tim Flanner

Historical Note
Formed through the Nat'l Federation of State High School Ass'ns,
NFICA members are secondary school athletic coaches.

Publications:
Nat'l Federation News. 5/yr. adv.

Meetings/Conferences:
Annual Meetings: in conjunction with Nat'l Federation
      Interscholastic Officials Ass'n

Nat'l Federation Interscholastic Music Ass'n *(1983)*
P.O. Box 20626
11724 N.W. Plaza Circle
Kansas City, MO 64195-0626
Tel: (816)464-5400   *Fax:* (816)464-5571
E-Mail: tkdayton@nfhsmail.org
Web Site: http://www.nfhs.org
Members: 725 individuals
Staff: 2
Annual Budget: under $10,000
Asst. Director: Treva Dayton
Director, Membership: Teresa Hon

Historical Note
NFIMA members are secondary school and college music directors.
Membership: $10/year (individual).

Publications:
NFIMA Journal. semi-a.

Nat'l Federation Interscholastic Officials Ass'n *(1981)*
P.O. Box 20626
11724 Plaza Circle
Kansas City, MO 64195
Tel: (816)464-5400   *Fax:* (816)464-5571
Web Site: nfhs.org
Members: 118,000 individuals
Staff: 5
Annual Budget: $500-1,000,000
Director: Tim Flanner

Historical Note
Formed through the Nat'l Federation of State High School Ass'ns,
NFIOA members are secondary school, college and youth league
sports officials. Membership: $12/year (individual).

Publications:
Nat'l Federation News. 5/yr. adv.

Meetings/Conferences:
Annual Meetings: in conjunction with Nat'l Federation
      Interscholastic Coaches Ass'n

Nat'l Federation Interscholastic Speech and Debate Ass'n *(1986)*
11724 N.W. Plaza Circle
P.O. Box 20626
Kansas City, MO 64195-0626
Tel: (816)464-5400   *Fax:* (816)464-5571
E-Mail: tkdayton@nfhsmail.org
Web Site: http://www.nfhs.org
Members: 1,125 individuals
Staff: 2

Annual Budget: under $10,000
Assistant Director: Treva Dayton

Historical Note
NFISDA members are secondary and post-secondary speech, drama and debate coaches. Affiliated with the Nat'l Federation of State High School Ass'ns. Membership:$ 10/year (individual).

Publications:
Forensic Educator. bien.
Nat'l Federation News. m.

Nat'l Federation of Abstracting and Information Services (1958)
1518 Walnut St., Suite 307
Philadelphia, PA 19102-3403
Tel: (215)893-1561   *Fax:* (215)893-1564
E-Mail: nfais@nfais.org
Web Site: http://www.pa.utulsa.edu/nfais.html
Members: 60 organizations
Staff: 5
Annual Budget: $250-500,000
Exec. Director: Richard Kaser
Asst. Director: Marian H. Gloninger

Historical Note
Formerly (1972) Nat'l Federation of Science Abstracting and Indexing Services and (1982) Nat'l Federation of Abstracting and Indexing Services. Cooperates with the American Soc. for Information Science, the American Library Ass'n and other national and international organizations concerned with information science. Members are private organizations and government offices here and abroad which abstract and index popular and professional literature in print and machine-readable form, plus online vendors, CD-ROM vendors and others in related fields. Membership fee varies with revenues.

Publications:
Membership Directory. a.
NFAIS Newsletter. m.
NFAIS Report Series. 3/year.

Meetings/Conferences:
Annual Meetings: February
1999 – Philadelphia, PA/Feb. 21-24

Nat'l Federation of Black Women Business Owners (1984)
1500 Massachusetts Ave., N.W., Suite 34
Washington, DC 20005
Tel: (202)833-3450   *Fax:* (202)331-7822
President: Mary Walker

Historical Note
NFBWBO focuses on federal, state, county, and corporate policies that affect purchasing and contracting opportunities for women owned businesses. Membership:$25/year (women interested in business); $10/year (college students); $100/year (business owners); $300/year (organizations); $500/year (small business); $5,000/year (corporate sponsors).

Nat'l Federation of Catholic Physicians' Guilds (1932)
850 Elm Grove Rd.
Elm Grove, WI 53122
Tel: (414)784-3435   *Fax:* (414)782-8788
Members: 3,500 individuals
Staff: 4
Annual Budget: $50-100,000
Exec. Secretary: Michael Herzog

Historical Note
Formed in 1932 and incorporated in Washington, DC in 1964, NFCPG coordinates the activities of local guilds, upholds the principles of the Catholic faith and morality as related to the science and practice of medicine, communicates Catholic medical ethics to the medical profession and the community-at-large, supports Catholic hospitals in the application of Catholic moral principles, and enables Catholic physicians to work together with deeper mutual support and understanding. Membership: $110/year, active or associate (individual).

Publications:
The Linacre. q.

Meetings/Conferences:
Annual Meetings: Fall

Nat'l Federation of Community Broadcasters (1975)
Ft. Mason Center, Bldg. D
San Francisco, CA 94123
Tel: (415)771-4343
E-Mail: NFCB@aol.com
Web Site: http://www.nfcb.org
Members: 175 stations
Staff: 4
Annual Budget: $250-500,000
President: Lynn Chadwick

Historical Note
Members are non-commercial public radio stations licensed to community organizations, as well as university and other licensees, independent producers and production groups. NFCB's purpose is to advance community-oriented non-commercial broadcasting; provide programming, services, and resources to community licensees; foster cooperation among local broadcasting organizations; and participate at the national level in the development of public broadcasting policy. Membership: $75/year (individual); $400-2,500/year (company).

Publications:
Community Radio News. m.

Meetings/Conferences:
Annual Meetings: Spring

Nat'l Federation of Community Development Credit Unions (1974)
120 Wall St., 10th Floor
New York, NY 10005-3902
Tel: (212)809-1850   *Fax:* (212)809-3274

Web Site: http://www.netfed.org
Members: 200 credit unions
Staff: 10
Annual Budget: $1-2,000,000
Exec. Director: Clifford N. Rosenthal

Historical Note
Established in 1974 to serve and represent financial cooperatives in low-income communities. Members are community-based credit unions. The Federation provides training and management support to CDCU's and assists groups in organizing new credit unions. NFCDCU has an annual budget of $1.5 million. Membership: $50-$3,500/year depending on assets.

Meetings/Conferences:
Annual Meetings: Spring
1999 – New York, NY(Marriott)/June 15-19

Nat'l Federation of Federal Employees (1917)
1016 16th St., N.W., Third Floor
Washington, DC 20036
Tel: (202)862-4400   *Fax:* (202)862-4432
Web Site: http://www.nffehq@erols.com
Members: 30,000 individuals
Staff: 55
Annual Budget: $2-5,000,000
President: Richard Brown

Historical Note
Chartered by the American Federation of Labor in 1917, NFFE withdrew from the AFL in 1931 objecting to the AFL's position that civil service classification should not be extended to skilled crafts. It is now an independent labor union in competition with the American Federation of Government Employees (AFL-CIO). Sponsors the Public Affairs Council (NFFE), a political action committee.

Publications:
The Federal Employee. m.

Meetings/Conferences:
Biennial meetings: Even years

Nat'l Federation of Grange Mutual Insurance Companies (1934)
769 Hebron Ave., Box 6517
Glastonbury, CT 06033-6517
Tel: (860)633-4678   *Fax:* (860)633-3942
Toll Free: (800)800 - 0863
Members: 8 companies
Staff: 1
Annual Budget: under $10,000
Secretary: Alden A. Ives

Historical Note
Membership: $100/year.

Meetings/Conferences:
Annual Meetings: Fall, with Nat'l Ass'n of Mutual Insurance Companies/50
1999 – San Antonio, TX

Nat'l Federation of Hispanic Owned Newspapers (1982)
853 Broadway, Suite 811
New York, NY 10003
Tel: (212)420-0009   *Fax:* (212)674-6861
Members: 75 individuals
Annual Budget: $50-100,000
President: Carlos G. Carillo

Historical Note
NFHON is a network of Hispanic newspapers in the U.S. and Puerto Rico. Membership: $125/year (individual).

Publications:
Hispanic Print Media Directory. a.
Ultima Hora Newsletter. q. adv.

Meetings/Conferences:
Annual Meetings: Fall
1999 – Chicago, IL
2000 – Washington, DC

Nat'l Federation of Hispanics in Communication (1985)
P.O. Box 2976, Hollywood Station
Los Angeles, CA 90078-2976
Tel: (323)469-4698
Members: 50 individuals
Annual Budget: under $10,000
Chair: Carlos Gaivar

Historical Note
An unmbrela organization supporting Latinos working in all facets of communications media. Has no paid officers or full-time staff. Membership: $50/year (regular).

Nat'l Federation of Housestaff Organizations (1984)
Historical Note
Organization defunct in 1998.

Nat'l Federation of Housing Counselors (1973)
P.O. Box 5607
Savannah, GA 31414
Tel: (912)236-9670   *Fax:* (912)238-2977
Members: 1,600 individuals
Staff: 1
Annual Budget: $50-100,000
President: Terry Tolbert

Historical Note
Members are individuals who assist families with the acquisition and management of rented or privately owned homes. NFHC maintains a certification program to develop standards of competency and efficiency, provides technical assistance in the development of counseling programs, provides legislative representation, and operates a clearinghouse for housing information. Membership: $35/year (individual); $50/year (organization/company).

Publications:
Housing Pipeline. q. adv.
Training Manual. a. adv.

Meetings/Conferences:
Annual Meetings: 3rd week in June

Nat'l Federation of Independent Business (1943)
600 Maryland Ave., S.W., Suite 700
Washington, DC 20024
Tel: (202)554-9000   *Fax:* (202)554-0496
Toll Free: (800)552 - 6342
Web Site: http://www.nfibonline.com
Members: 600,000 individuals
Staff: 1000
Annual Budget: $50-100,000,000
President & CEO: S. Jackson Faris
V. President, Public Affairs: David Cullen
V. President Federal Government Relations & Political Affairs: Donald Danner
Exec. V. President, C.O.O.: Larry Larkin
V. President, C.F.O.: Fred Holladay, CPA
V. President, Corporate Partner Sales: David Perdue
V. President, State Government Relations: Steve Woods
V. President, Human Resources: Martha Olsen

Historical Note
Established as the National Federation of Small Business, it assumed its present name about 1950. In addition to the Washington office, it maintains offices in all 50 state capitals. Its principal focus is legislative relations and research. Sponsors the NFIB Safe Trust and NFIB Foundation. Has an annual budget of approximately $70 million. Membership: $100-1,000/year.

Publications:
Action Report. a.
Capitol Coverage. bi-m.
How Congress Voted. a.
IB Magazine. bi-m. adv.
Small Business Economic Trends. m.
State Reports.
The Mandate. bi-m.

Meetings/Conferences:
Quadrennial Meetings: (1999)

Nat'l Federation of Independent Unions (1963)
1166 South 11th St.
Philadelphia, PA 19147
Tel: (215)336-3300
Members: 57,000 individuals
Staff: ?
Annual Budget: $25-50,000
President: F.J. Chiappardi

Historical Note
Independent labor federation. Merger of Nat'l Independent Union Council and Confederated Unions of America.

Meetings/Conferences:
Semi-annual Meetings: March and September

Nat'l Federation of Licensed Practical Nurses (1949)
893 U.S. Hwy. 70 West
Suite 202
Garner, NC 27592-4547
Tel: (919)779-0046   *Fax:* (919)779-5642
Toll Free: (800)948 - 2511
Web Site: http://www.nflpn.org
Members: 6,000 individuals
Staff: 3
Annual Budget: $250-500,000
Administrator: Charlene Barbour
Member Service Director: Jennifer Beal

Historical Note
Independent professional association. Membership: $50/year.

Publications:
Practical Nurses Today. q.

Meetings/Conferences:
Annual Meetings: Fall/500
1999 – Louisville, KY/Sept. 16-22

Nat'l Federation of Modern Language Teachers Ass'ns (1916)
1933 N. Fountain Park Ave.
Tucson, AZ 85715
Tel: (520)885-2663   *Fax:* (520)885-2663
E-Mail: 76703.2063@compuserve.com
Members: 15 associations
Annual Budget: $100-250,000
Treasurer: Gerard L. Ervin, Ph.D.

Historical Note
Provides a forum for the exchange of information of interest to organizations of modern language teachers.

Publications:
The Modern Language Journal. q. adv.

Meetings/Conferences:
Annual Meetings: With the American Council on the Teaching of Foreign Languages

Nat'l Federation of Municipal Analysts (1983)
P.O. Box 14893
Pittsburgh, PA 15234-0893
Tel: (304)242-2503   *Fax:* (304)242-2682
Web Site: http://www.nsma.org
Members: 1000 individuals
Exec. Director: Lisa S. Good

Historical Note
Founded by four regional organizations of municipal analysts, NFMA now promotes the profession of municipal credit analyst, through educational programs, industry communications, and related programming. Membership: $20-35/year.

Publications:
Municipal Analysts Bulletin. 3-4/year.

Meetings/Conferences:
Annual Meetings: Spring/175
1999 – Boston, MA/May 4-7

Nat'l Federation of Music Clubs (1898)
1336 North Delaware St.
Indianapolis, IN 46202-2481
Tel: (317)638-4003   Fax: (317)638-0503
Members: 200,000 individuals, 5,300 organizations
Staff: 2
Annual Budget: $100-250,000
Exec. Director: Melinda S. Ullrich

Historical Note
NFMC supports professional and amateur musicians and
composers. Through its own programming and the programs of its
member clubs, it strives to recognize musical talent, promote
American music, and enhance music education and music therapy
programs.

Publications:
Junior Keynotes. q. adv.
Music Clubs Magazine. q. adv.

Meetings/Conferences:
Biennial Meetings: odd years

Nat'l Federation of Non-Profits (1982)
815 15th St., N.W., Suite 822
Washington, DC 20005-2201
Tel: (202)628-4380   Fax: (202)628-4383
E-Mail: NFNDC@AOL.COM
Members: 400 organizations
Staff: 3
Annual Budget: $250-500,000
Exec. Director: Lee M. Cassidy
Office Manager: Ayoka Blandford

Historical Note
Formerly known as the Nonprofit Mailers Federation. Members are
nonprofit groups using direct mail to fund their activities or
disseminate information.

Publications:
Action Alert. irreg.
Federation Folio. q.
Legislative Alert. irreg.
News Update. bi-w.

Meetings/Conferences:
1999 – Washington, DC

Nat'l Federation of Nonpublic School State Accrediting Ass'ns
4140 Lindell Blvd.
St. Louis, MO 63108
Tel: (314)371-4980   Fax: (314)371-0267
Members: 6 state chapters
Annual Budget: under $10,000
V. President: Al Winkleman

Historical Note
A federation of state accrediting associations serving non-public
schools. Through its state chapters, NF accredits over 800
elementary and secondary schools in the U.S. Has no paid officers
or full-time staff. Membership: $200/year.

Meetings/Conferences:

Nat'l Federation of Paralegal Ass'ns (1974)
P.O. Box 33108
Kansas City, MO 64114-0108
Tel: (816)941-4000   Fax: (816)941-2725
E-Mail: info@paralegals.org
Web Site: http://www.paralegals.org
Members: 63 state and local associations
Staff: 3
Annual Budget: $500-1,000,000
Managing Director: Lu Hangley

Historical Note
Founded in Washington, DC by eight charter member paralegal
associations. Members of the Federation now represent over 17,500
individual paralegals. Offers a forum for paralegals practicing in all
sectors, including private and public law firms, legal services,
financial institutions, the courts, trade associations and federal,
state and local government. Maintains an Internet address:
http://www.paralegals.org. Membership: $75-150/year
(sustaining individual/organization); $20 per member/year
(association).

Publications:
National Paralegal Reporter. q. adv.

Meetings/Conferences:
1999 – Atlanta, GA
1999 – New Orleans, LA
2000 – Hawaii

Nat'l Federation of Press Women (1937)
P.O. Box 5556
Arlington, VA 22205-282
Tel: (703)534-5751   Fax: (703)534-5750
Toll Free: (800)780 - 2715
E-Mail: presswoman@aol.com
Web Site: http://www.nfpw.org
Members: 3,000 individuals
Annual Budget: $100-250,000
Exec. Director: Carol Pierce

Historical Note
NFPW members are writers, editors and other communications
professionals for newspapers, magazines, radio-TV, corporations,
wire services, agencies and freelance. Organized at the Chicago
Women's Club, May 6, 1937 under the leadership of Helen Miller
Malloch as a federation of state affiliates of working press women.
Membership: $50/year, plus affiliate dues.

Publications:
NFPW Agenda. 6/yr. adv.

Meetings/Conferences:
Annual Meetings: Summer
1999 – Nashville, TN/June 23-27
2000 – Anchorage, Alaska

Nat'l Federation of Priests' Councils (1968)
1337 W. Ohio
Chicago, IL 60622-6490
Tel: (312)226-3334   Fax: (312)829-8915
Members: 110 councils
Staff: 3
Annual Budget: $250-500,000
Exec. Director: Bernard F. Stratman, SM

Historical Note
Members are priest's councils, no individual membership.

Publications:
Touchstone Newsletter. q.

Meetings/Conferences:
Annual Meetings: April/250-275
1999 – San Antonio, TX/Apr. 21-25

Nat'l Federation of Socs. for Clinical Social Work (1971)

Historical Note
Became the Clinical Social Work Federation in 1997.

Nat'l Federation of State High School Ass'ns (1920)
11724 N.W. Plaza Circle
Kansas City, MO 64153
Tel: (816)464-5400   Fax: (816)464-5571
Members: 51 state ass'ns/18,000 high schools
Staff: 48
Annual Budget: $2-5,000,000
Exec. Director: Robert F. Kanaby
Communications Director: Bruce Howard
Assistant Director: Frank Kovakefsky

Historical Note
Established as the Nat'l Federation of State High School Athletic
Ass'ns, it assumed its present name in 1970. The governing body
for the interscholastic athletic activity of more than 18,000 high
schools in the United States, Canada, the Philippines, Bermuda,
Guam and the Virgin Islands.

Publications:
Interscholastic Athletic Administration Magazine. q.
Nat'l Athletic Director Conference Proceedings. a.
National Federation News. 9/year.

Meetings/Conferences:
Annual Meetings: June/July

Nat'l Feeder Pig Marketing Ass'n (1966)
Historical Note
Formerly Nat'l Feeder Pig Dealers Ass'n.

Nat'l Fellowship of Child Care Executives (1954)
c/o Children's Aid Home & Society of
Somerset County, Inc.
Somerset, PA 15501
Tel: (814)443-1637   Fax: (814)445-8481
Members: 80 individuals
Annual Budget: under $10,000
Exec. Secretary: Patricia Stone

Historical Note
Members are administrators of homes maintaining group residential
care for children. Established as the Nat'l Ass'n of Homes for Boys,
it assumed its present name in 1981. Membership: $100/year.

Publications:
Book of Proceedings. a.

Nat'l FFA Organization (1928)
6060 FFA Drive
Indianapolis, IN 46268
Tel: (317)838-5889   Fax: (317)838-5888
Toll Free: (800)772 - 0939
E-Mail: larry_case@ffa.org
Web Site: http://www.ffa.org
Members: 452,734 individuals
Staff: 60
Annual Budget: $2-5,000,000
Nat'l Advisor and C.E.O.: Larry D. Case, Ed.D.
Communications Resources: William Stagg
Nat'l Exec. Secretary: C. Coleman Harris
Finance: Sue Springirth
Chief Operating Officer: Bernie Staller
Technology: Mark Cavell
Membership: Janet Lewis

Historical Note
Formerly the Future Farmers of America, the organization adopted
its present name in 1989. A vocational student organization
organized under the National Vocational Education Act to foster
character, leadership and good citizenship. Absorbed the New
Farmers of America in 1965. Membership: $5.00/year.

Publications:
FFA New Horizons. bi-m. adv.
Update. m.

Meetings/Conferences:
Annual Meetings: November in Kansas City, MO (Municipal
    Auditorium)/30,000
1999 – Louisville, KY(Convention Center)/Oct. 28-30

Nat'l Field Selling Ass'n (1987)
1900 Arch St.
Philadelphia, PA 19103-1498
Tel: (215)564-1627   Fax: (215)564-2175
E-Mail: assnhot@netaxs.com
Web Site: http://www.nfsa.com
Staff: 3
Annual Budget: $100-250,000
Exec. Director: John D. McGreevey, Jr.

Admin. Director: Ellen R. Buckley
Historical Note
Promotes professional excellence in the door-to-door direct selling
industry.

Meetings/Conferences:
1999 – Bloomindale, IL(Indian Lakes Resort)/June 7-10

Nat'l Finance Adjusters (1947)
1370 W. North Ave.
Baltimore, MD 21217
Tel: (410)728-2400   Fax: (410)523-8336
Web Site: http://www.nfa.org/index.html
Members: 210 individuals
Exec. Director: Jack S. Barnes

Historical Note
The NFA is the largest association of professional collateral
recovery specialists.

Publications:
NFA Newsletter. irreg.

Meetings/Conferences:
1999 – Chicago, IL

Nat'l Fire Protection Ass'n (1896)
P.O. Box 9101
1 Battery March Park
Quincy, MA 02269-9101
Tel: (617)770-3000   Fax: (617)770-0200
Web Site: http://www.nfpa.org & www.sparky.org
Members: 2,464 individuals and organizations
Staff: 300
Annual Budget: $50-100,000,000
President and C.E.O.: George D. Miller
Director, Public Affairs: Julie Reynolds
V.P., Public Education: Meredith K. Appy
V. President, Finance; C.F.O.: Richard J. McCrossan
Senior V. President, Administration and General Counsel: James E.
    Shannon
Asst. V. President, Support Services: Albert B. Sears
Sr. V. President, Operations: Arthur E. Cote

Historical Note
Founded in 1896 and incorporated in Massachusetts in 1930.
NFPA promotes fire protection through the promulgation of codes
and standards, research, technical advisory sources and public
education. Has an annual budget of approximately $52 million.
Membership: $95/year.

Publications:
Buyers' Guide. a. adv.
Fire Technology. q.
National Fire Codes. a.
NFPA Journal. bi-m. adv.
NFPA Update. bi-m.

Meetings/Conferences:
Semi-annual Meetings: Spring and Fall
1999 – Baltimore, MD

Nat'l Fire Sprinkler Ass'n (1905)
Rte. 22 and Robin Hill Park, Box 1000
Patterson, NY 12563
Tel: (914)878-4200   Fax: (914)878-4215
Web Site: www.nfsa.org
Members: 1,200 individuals, 400 companies
Staff: 30
Annual Budget: $2-5,000,000
President: John A. Viniello
Membership/Communications Mgr.: David J. Vandeyar
Dir., Training/Education: Mark Riffey
Senior V. President: Richard D. Sullivan
V. President, Engineering: Russell P. Fleming
Director, Codes: Gene Endthoff

Historical Note
Founded as the Nat'l Automatic Sprinkler Ass'n, it became the Nat'l
Automatic Sprinkler and Fire Control Ass'n (1958) and assumed its
present name in 1983. Members are makers and installers of
automatic fire sprinklers and related equipment. Membership: $75-
150/year (individual); $850/year (minimum, company).

Publications:
Code Watch. q.
Labor Line. bi-m.
NFSA Grassroots. m.
Sprinkler Quarterly. q. adv.
Sprinkler Scene. bi-m.
Sprinkler Technotes. bi-m.

Meetings/Conferences:
1999 – Chicago, IL(Fairmont)/Sept. 16-19

Nat'l Fish Meal and Oil Ass'n (1950)
Historical Note
Defunct in 1997.

Nat'l Fisheries Institute (1945)
1901 Fort Myer Dr., Suite 700
Arlington, VA 22209
Tel: (703)524-8880   Fax: (703)524-4619
E-Mail: office@nfi.org
Web Site: http://www.nfi.org
Members: 1000 companies
Staff: 20
Annual Budget: $2-5,000,000
Exec. V. President: Richard E. Gutting, Jr.
V. President, Communications: Linda Candler
Sr. V. President, Science and Technology: Roy E. Martin

Historical Note
Absorbed (1970) American Seafood Distributors Ass'n, (1983) the
Shellfish Institute of North American and (1983) the National Blue
Crab Industry Association. Divisions include Nat'l Aquaculture
Council, Molluscan Shellfish Institute and Shrimp Council.
Sponsors the NFI Political Action Committee.

Five Directories

PUBLISHED BY Columbia Books, Inc.

Updated annually for maximum ACCURACY ...

Designed for CONVENIENCE ...

Priced to be AFFORDABLE

National Directory of Corporate Public Affairs

Tracks the public/government affairs programs of about 1,900 major U.S. corporations and lists the 14,000 people who run them. Also lists: Washington area offices, corporate foundations/giving programs, corporate PACs, federal and state lobbyists, outside contract lobbyists. Indexed by subject and geographic area. Includes membership directory of the Public Affairs Council.

$99 for 1999 edition

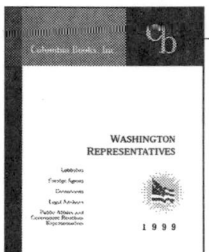

Washington Representatives

Includes over 17,000 lobbyists, public and government affairs representatives, and special interest advocates in the nation's capital, and the causes they represent. Includes contact information and foreign agent and federal lobbyist indicators. Listings organized by client and by representative. Indexed by subject/industry and foreign interest. Also includes a new index of PACS by industry.

$99 for 1999 edition

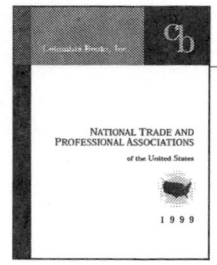

National Trade and Professional Associations of the United States

Lists 7,600 national trade associations, professional societies and labor unions. Five convenient indexes enable you to look up associations by subject, budget, geographic area, acronym and executive director. Other features include: contact information, serial publications, upcoming convention schedule, membership/staff size, budget figures, and background information.

$99 for 1999 edition

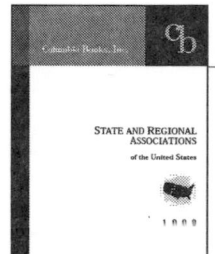

State and Regional Associations of the United States

Lists 7,200 of the largest and most significant state and regional trade and professional organizations in the U.S. Look up associations by subject, budget, state, acronym, or chief executive. Also lists contact information, serial publications, upcoming convention schedule, membership/staff size, budget figures, and background information.

$79 for 1999 edition

Washington

A guide to 4,500 major organizations and institutions in the nation's capital and the 22,000 key individuals who run them. Chapters include: government, business, education, medicine/health, community affairs, arts/culture, etc. Combined index cross-references each individual's multiple affiliations.

$85 for 1999 edition

✓ Yes, I would like to order:

___ copies of National Trade and Professional Associations 1999	@ $99 each	$_____
___ copies of State and Regional Associations of the U.S. 1999	@ $79 each	$_____
___ copies of National Directory of Corporate Public Affairs 1999	@ $99 each	$_____
___ copies of Washington Representatives 1999	@ $99 each	$_____
___ copies of Washington 1999	@ $85 each	$_____
	Tax (if D.C. resident):	$_____
	TOTAL:	$_____

METHOD OF PAYMENT (D.C. residents add 5.75% sales tax):

☐ **Check enclosed.** (CBI pays postage)

☐ **Bill me.** (Add $6 shipping and handling for the first book, $1 per each additional book)

☐ **Credit Card:** (CBI pays postage) ☐ MasterCard ☐ VISA ☐ AMEX

Credit Card #:_____ Expiration Date:_____

NAME

TITLE

ORGANIZATION

ADDRESS

CITY/STATE/ZIP

TELEPHONE (required)   FAX

SIGNATURE (required)   DATE

BC99

TO ORDER: **MAIL** this form to Columbia Books, Inc., PO Box 69, Spencerville, MD 20868-0069, **FAX** this form to (301) 559-5167, or **PHONE** Toll-Free 888-265-0600. FOR MAIL LIST INFORMATION call (202) 898-0662, or see the form in the back of this book.

Columbia Books Directories "THE REFERENCE PREFERENCE"

Five outstanding reference guides that are:

Relevant…focused on subjects of interest and importance

Timely…updated every year and throughout the year

Accurate…compiled from reliable sources, confirmed with each organization listed via questionnaire and/or phone interview

Concise…providing the significant, omitting the trivial

Convenient…attractively bound in volumes of manageable size and weight. Take them with you anywhere.

Affordable…reasonably priced with the individual as well as the institution in mind.

But don't just take our word for it! Here's what others have said:

Washington Representatives

"…whether checking on our clients or competitors, we rate the directory as priceless."

—Hon. Norman F. Lent
Lent & Scrivner

National Directory of Corporate Public Affairs

"…a vital resource that provides me with much-needed, up to date information…"

—Stephen E. Chaudet
Lockheed Martin
Corp.

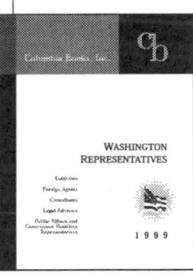

State and Regional Associations of the U.S.

"…a valuable reference for companies needing prime and direct contacts in the states"

—Association Trends

National Trade and Professional Ass'ns

"…NTPA is one of the most used books in our library… it has the information needed by business people."

—Ken Davis, Manager
Los Angeles SBA
Business Information
Center

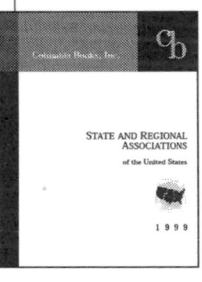

Washington

"Highly recommended as a primary ready reference tool…"

—American Reference
Book Annual

Publications:
Fisheries Blue Book. a. adv.
NFI Flashes. m.
NFInsider. w.
Sea Food Source. q.
Meetings/Conferences:
Annual Meetings: Fall
1999 – Miami, FL(Internat'l Hotel)/Sept. 28-Oct. 2

Nat'l Flight Nurses Ass'n (1980)
216 Higgins Road
Park Ridge, IL 60068-5736
Tel: (847)698-1733   *Fax:* (847)698-9407
Web Site: http://www.nfna.org
Members: 1,800 individuals
Staff: 2
Annual Budget: $100-250,000
Exec. Director: Susan Oster

Historical Note
Membership: $65/year (active); $60/year (inactive and affiliate).
Publications:
Across the Board. bi-m.
Air Medical Journal.
Meetings/Conferences:
Annual Meetings: Fall

Nat'l Flight Paramedics Ass'n (1986)
383 F St.
Salt Lake City, UT 84103-2756
Toll Free: (800)381 - 6372
Web Site: http://www.nfpa.rotor.com
Members: 800 individuals
Annual Budget: $25-50,000
Acct. Executive: Pat Petersen

Historical Note
A professional association for flight paramedics involved with the air-medical industry. Membership: $45/year (individual, active or associate).
Publications:
Air Med. bi-m.
Air Medical Journal. bi-m.
Flight Paramedic News. q.
Meetings/Conferences:
1999 – Nassau, Bahamas(Carnival Cruise)/April 28-May 2

Nat'l Florist Ass'n (1953)
1175 Elizabeth Ave.
Elizabeth, NJ 07201
Tel: (908)289-5855
Members: 1,100 individuals
President: Marti Hall

Historical Note
Formerly (1963) Internat'l Flower Ass'n and (1988) Internat'l Florists Ass'n. NFA members are black retail florists.

Nat'l Fluid Power Ass'n (1953)
3333 N. Mayfair Road, Suite 311
Milwaukee, WI 53222-3219
Tel: (414)778-3344   *Fax:* (414)778-3361
E-Mail: nfpa@nfpa.com
Web Site: http://www.nfpa.com
Members: 195 companies
Staff: 17
Annual Budget: $1-2,000,000
Exec. Director: Dennis P. McGuirk
Director, Expositions: Bill Prueser
Internat'l Standards Development Manager: Karen Boehme
Industry/Nat'l Standards Development Mgr: Shirley Seal
Controller and Secretary: Janet Weitkunat
Director, Ass'n Services & Development: Linda Western
Statistical Services Manager: Steve Latin-Kasper

Historical Note
Companies which have designed, manufactured and nationally marketed a fluid power component for at least two years in the United States.
Publications:
NFPA Membership Directory. a.
NFPA Publications Catalog.
NFPA Reporter. m.
Meetings/Conferences:
Semi-Annual Meetings: Spring and Fall; International Fluid Power Exhibition held quadrennially - next 1996
1999 – Orlando, FL(Boardwalk Inn)/Feb. 28-March 3

Nat'l Flute Ass'n (1972)
26951 Reuther Ave., Suite H
Santa Clarita, CA 91351
Tel: (805)250-8920   *Fax:* (805)299-6681
Members: 5,000 individuals, 100 organizations
Staff: 1
Annual Budget: $100-250,000
Exec. Coordinator: Phyllis Pemberton

Historical Note
Members are flutists and individuals interested in the flute. Membership: $45/year.
Publications:
Flutist Quarterly Newsletter. q.
Membership Roster. a.
Meetings/Conferences:
Annual Meetings: August
1999 – Atalanta, GA/Aug. 19-22
2000 – Columbus, OH/August 17-20
2001 – Dallas, TX/Aug. 16-19

Nat'l Food and Energy Council (1957)
601 Business Loop 70-W, Suite 216-D
Columbia, MO 65203-2546
Tel: (573)875-7155   *Fax:* (573)449-5322

Members: 250 companies
Staff: 2
Annual Budget: $100-250,000
President/Exec. Manager: Richard S. Hiatt

Historical Note
Formerly (1957) Inter-Industry Farm Electric Utilization Council, (1962) Farm Electrification Council and (1977) the Food and Energy Council, it assumed its present name in 1982. Members are electric utilities, agricultural cooperatives and related organizations.
Publications:
Current Marketing. bi-m.
Meetings/Conferences:

Nat'l Food Brokers Ass'n (1904)
Historical Note
Became the Ass'n of Sales and Marketing Companies in 1997.

Nat'l Food Distributors Ass'n (1927)
401 N. Michigan Ave.
Chicago, IL 60611-4267
Tel: (312)644-6610   *Fax:* (312)321-6869
Members: 600 distributors and suppliers
Staff: 5
Annual Budget: $1-2,000,000
Managing Director: Arthur H. Klawans

Historical Note
NFDA represents independent specialty food full service distributors and suppliers delivering specialty products to chains or retail outlets.
Publications:
NFDA Newsletter.
Meetings/Conferences:
Semi-Annual Meetings: Mid-winter conference and summer convention
1999 – Orlando, FL/Jan. 9-11
2000 – Palm Springs, CA/Jan. 10-12

Nat'l Food Processors Ass'n (1907)
1350 I St. N.W., Suite 300
Washington, DC 20005
Tel: (202)639-5963   *Fax:* (202)637-8464
Members: 450 companies
Staff: 150
Annual Budget: $10-25,000,000
President and C.E.O: John R. Cady
Director, Media Relations and External Affairs: Jason Whiting
Exec. V. President, Government Affairs and Communications: Kelly D. Johnston
V. President, Federal Affairs: Brian B. Folkerts
Exec. V. President, Scientific and Technical Regulatory Affairs: Dr. Rhona Applebaum
Senior V. President/C.F.O.: Greg Cofoid
Director, Membership: Steven Langley
Director, Publications: Michelle P. Spring

Historical Note
Founded in 1907 through a merger of the Atlantic State Canners Ass'n and the Western Packers Ass'n. Members are commercial packers of canned, frozen and dehydrated foods. Established scientific research facilities in 1913, currently located in Dublin, California, Seattle, Washington and at its headquarters in Washington, DC. Acts as liaison for the food industry to regulatory and legislative bodies on scientific and technical issues. The Nat'l Food Laboratory is its wholly-owned subsidiary to conduct contract research on a proprietary basis. The Food Processors Institute is its educational and training arm. Formerly (1977) the Nat'l Canners Ass'n. Sponsors the Nat'l Food Processors Ass'n Political Action Committee and provides administrative support for the Council of Food Processors Ass'n Executives.
Publications:
Annual Report. a.
Information Letter. bi-w.
Lab Annual Report. a.
NFPA Journal. m.
State Legislative Update. bi-w.
Meetings/Conferences:
Annual Meetings: Winter/3,000
1999 – Chicago, IL/Oct. 28-30

Nat'l Food Processors Institute (1973)
Historical Note
An educational organization established and managed by the National Food Processors Association. Also known as the Food Processors Institute.

Nat'l Football League (1920)
280 Park Ave., Suite 12-West
New York, NY 10017-1216
Tel: (212)450-2000   *Fax:* (212)681-7559
Web Site: http://www.nfl.com
Members: 30 teams
Staff: 100
Annual Budget: $5-10,000,000
Commissioner: Paul Tagliabue
Senior V. President, Communications and Government Affairs: Joe Browne
Exec. V. President, Labor: Harold Henderson

Historical Note
Founded as the American Professional Football Ass'n on September 17, 1920 in the showroom of the Huppmobile agency in Canton, Ohio with Jim Thorpe as President. Assumed its present name in 1922 and merged with the American Football League on February 1, 1970.
Publications:
NFL Record and Fact Book. a.
Meetings/Conferences:
Annual Meetings: March
1999 – Phoenix, AZ/March 14-18

Nat'l Football League Players Ass'n (1970)
2021 L St., N.W., Suite 600
Washington, DC 20036
Tel: (202)463-2200   *Fax:* (202)857-0673
Web Site: http://www.nflplayers.com
Members: 1,800 individuals3500 retired player members
Staff: 65
Annual Budget: $1-2,000,000
Exec. Director: Gene Upshaw
Director of Communications: Carl Francis
Controller: William Garner
Director, Membership Services: Anne Selby
Director, Information Systems: Laura Taglienti

Historical Note
The result of a merger on January 8, 1970 of the Nat'l Football League Players Ass'n (formed in 1956) and the American Football League Players Ass'n (formed about 1959). Originally a labor union affiliated with AFL/CIO under the umbrella of the Federation of Professional Athletes, NFLPA decertified itself in 1989 and acted solely as a professional association representing players in such areas as group licensing, insurance services and salary information. In 1993, NFPLA was again certified as the players' collective bargaining agent with the Nat'l Football League.
Publications:
The Playbook. w.
Meetings/Conferences:
Annual Meetings: March

Nat'l Foreign Trade Council (1914)
1625 K St. N.W., Suite 1090
Washington, DC 20006
Tel: (202)887-0278   *Fax:* (202)452-8160
Members: 560 companies
Staff: 20
Annual Budget: $1-2,000,000
President: Frank D. Kittredge

Historical Note
Established in New York City pursuant to a resolution of the First National Foreign Trade Convention in 1914 as a private non-profit organization for the promotion and protection of U.S. international trade and investment.
Publications:
COUNCIL HIGHLIGHTS. m.
Meetings/Conferences:
Annual Meetings: None held

Nat'l Forensic Ass'n (1972)
Historical Note
Address unknown in 1996.

Nat'l Forest Recreation Ass'n (1948)
325 Pennsylvania Ave., S.E.
Washington, DC 20003
Tel: (202)546-8527   *Fax:* (202)546-8528
E-Mail: info@nfra.org
Web Site: http://www.nfra.org
Members: 300 individuals
Staff: 2
Annual Budget: $50-100,000
Exec. Director: Pat O'Brien

Historical Note
NFRA is an organization assisting owners and operators of recreational and commercial facilities on National Forest, and Bureau of Land Management lands, principally in the West in their relationship with their respective agency(ies). Members include ski resorts, guest ranches, organization camps, marinas, stores, restaurants, campgrounds, packers and outfitters, river float outfitters and recreational residents. Membership: $100-500/year, (based upon a revenue scale of $100,000-500,000 of the applicant).
Publications:
NFRA Report. q. adv.
Meetings/Conferences:
Annual Meetings: April
1999 – Reno, NV(Silver Legacy)/March 23-26/150

Nat'l Forum for Black Public Administrators (1983)
777 North Capitol St., N.E., Suite 807
Washington, DC 20002
Tel: (202)408-9300   *Fax:* (202)408-8558
E-Mail: nfvpa@erols.com
Web Site: http://www.nfvpa.org
Members: 2,800 individuals
Staff: 5
Annual Budget: $1-2,000,000
Exec. Director: John E. Saunders, III

Historical Note
NFBPA members are city and county managers; chief administrative officers; agency and department directors; rank-and-file professionals; and deans, faculty members and graduate students at schools of public administration. NFBPA was established to strengthen the position of blacks in the field of public administration, to correct the inequity which exists with respect to the representation of blacks at the executive level, and to groom younger, aspiring administrators for top level public administrative posts. Membership: $150/year (individual); $1000-$5000 (organization/company).
Publications:
Forum Newsletter. q.
Membership Directory. bi-a.
Meetings/Conferences:
Annual Meetings: April/1,400
1999 – Austin, TX/March 27-31

Nat'l Foundation for Consumer Credit (1942)
8611 2nd Ave., Suite 100
Silver Spring, MD 20910-3372
Tel: (301)589-5600   *Fax:* (301)495-5623

Web Site: http://www.nfcc.org
Members: 1,100 consumer credit counseling svcs.
Staff: 20
Annual Budget: $1-2,000,000
President and C.E.O.: Durant S. Abernethy
Director, Communications: William Furmanski
Exec. V. President and C.O.O.: Jay Thormodsgard

Historical Note
Members are non-profit community Consumer Credit Counseling Services and creditors. The purpose is to educate the public to the proper and wise use of credit and to provide budget and debt management counseling to families in financial difficulty. Absorbed the Retail Credit Institute of America in 1951.

Publications:
Magazine. q.
Newsletter. m.

Meetings/Conferences:
Annual Meetings: Fall
1999 – Dallas, TX

Nat'l Foundation for Women Business Owners

Historical Note
NFWBO is a research and development affiliate of Nat'l Ass'n of Women Business Owners.

Nat'l Frame Builders Ass'n (1970)

4840 W. 15th St., Suite 1000
Lawrence, KS 66049-3876
Tel: (785)843-2444   *Fax:* (785)843-7555
Members: 524 companies
Staff: 12
Annual Budget: $250-500,000
Management Exec.: James T. Knight

Historical Note
Building contractors, suppliers, design and code professionals and academic personnel specializing in the post-frame construction industry comprise NFBA's membership. The largest portion of membership consists of post-frame building contractors. Membership fee varies for each membership type.

Publications:
Builders Newsletter. m. adv.
Frame Building News Magazine. 8/yr.
Membership Directory. a. adv.
Suppliers Newsletter. q.

Meetings/Conferences:

Nat'l Fraternal Congress of America (1913)

1280 Iruquois Drive, Suite 300
P.O. Box 3087
Naperville, IL 60566-7087
Tel: (630)355-6633
Web Site: www.nfcanet.org
Members: 92 societies
Staff: 10
Annual Budget: $500-1,000,000
Exec. V. President: David A. Tetzlaff, FLMI

Historical Note
Membership open to any fraternal organization which is without capital stock, is carried on solely for the mutual benefit of its members and their beneficiaries, having a lodge system and a representative form of government which provides for the payment of death, sickness or disability benefits. Formed by a merger of the National Fraternal Congress (founded in 1886) and the Associated Fraternities of America (founded in 1901).

Publications:
Manual and Directory. a.
Report of Annual Meeting. a.
Statistics of Fraternal Benefit Societies. a.

Meetings/Conferences:
Annual Meetings: September/700
1999 – Arlington, VA(Hyatt Regency Crystal City)/Sept. 15-18
2000 – Chicago, IL(Sheraton Chicago Hotel & Towers)/Sept. 27-30
2001 – Lake Buena Vista, FL(Hilton at Disney World Village)/Sept. 19-22

Nat'l Fraternal Order of Police (1915)

1410 Donelson Pike, Suite A-17
Nashville, TN 37217-2933
Tel: (615)399-0900   *Fax:* (615)399-0400
Toll Free: (800)451 - 2711
E-Mail: jlfop@grandlodgefop.org
Members: 230,000 individuals
Staff: 13
Annual Budget: $500-1,000,000
Nat'l Secretary: Jerry Atnip

Historical Note
Formerly (1988) the Fraternal Order of Police. Full time law enforcement officers seeking economic benefits and professional advancement. Membership: $3.50/year.

Publications:
Collective Bargaining and Dispute Resolution.
Corporate and Tax Affairs of a Lodge.
Fair Labor Standards Handbook and FLSA Update. a.
National FOP Journal. q. adv.

Meetings/Conferences:
Biennial Meetings: odd years in Summer
1999 – Mobile, AL

Nat'l Fraternity of Student Musicians (1927)

Historical Note
NFSM is a division of the American College of Musicians, representing students whose teachers are members of the Nat'l Guild of Piano Teachers, another division of ACM. For more information see American College of Musicians.

Nat'l Freight Claim and Security Council of the American Trucking Ass'ns

Historical Note
Became (1995) Transportation Loss Claim and Security Council of the American Trucking Ass'ns.

Nat'l Freight Transportation Ass'n (1905)

Historical Note
Declined to provide updated information for this edition.

Nat'l Frozen Dessert and Fast Food Ass'n (1961)

P.O. Box 1116
Millbrook, NY 12545
Tel: (914)677-9301   *Fax:* (914)677-3387
Toll Free: (800)535 - 7748
E-Mail: thermrsandme@worldnet.att.net
Members: 304 stores
Staff: 2
Annual Budget: $25-50,000
Exec. Director: Dave Roberts

Historical Note
Formerly (1996) Nat'l Soft Serve and Fast Food Ass'n. NFD & FFA was established as a medium through which operators and suppliers of frozen desserts and fast food establishments may promote their industry and speak with a unified voice. Membership: $75/year (operator); $85/year (distributor); $125/year (supplier).

Publications:
NSS&FFA News. bi-m. adv.
Tidbits. bi-m. adv.

Meetings/Conferences:
Annual Meetings: January
1999 – Orlando, FL(Clarion Plaza)/Jan. 13-16/250

Nat'l Frozen Food Ass'n (1945)

P.O. Box 6069
4755 Linglestown Rd., Suite 300
Harrisburg, PA 17112-0069
Tel: (717)657-8601   *Fax:* (717)657-9862
E-Mail: nffa.org
Web Site: http://www.nffa.org
Members: 810 companies
Staff: 9
Annual Budget: $1-2,000,000
President: Nevin B. Montgomery
Exec. V. President: H.V. Skip Shaw
Director, Finance: Winifred E. Ethridge
Vice President of Foodservice and Membership: Marlene Redden
V.P., Publications/New Media: Lori B. Pohlman

Historical Note
Supports the Nat'l Frozen Food Ass'n. Sponsors Nat'l Frozen Food Month. Membership fee based on volume of frozen food sales.

Publications:
Frozen Food Executive. m. adv.
National Frozen Food Association Directory. a. adv.

Meetings/Conferences:
Annual Meetings: Fall/1,200
1999 – Boston, MA(Marriott/Westin)/Oct. 3-6
2000 – San Francisco, CA(Hilton)/Oct. 15-18/1250
2001 – San Antonio, TX(Marriott River Center)/Oct. 7-10/1250
2002 – Orlando, FL(Dolphin)/Oct. 13-16/1250

Nat'l Frozen Pizza Institute (1975)

2000 Corporate Ridge
Suite 1000
McLean, VA 22102
Tel: (703)821-0770   *Fax:* (703)821-1350
Staff: 3
Exec. Director: Heather Schreoder

Historical Note
Managed by American Frozen Food Institute.

Meetings/Conferences:
Annual Meetings: Fall in either Washington, DC or Chicago, IL

Nat'l Funeral Directors and Morticians Ass'n (1938)

3951 Snapfinger Pkwy.
Decatur, GA 30035
Tel: (404)286-6680   *Fax:* (404)286-6573
E-Mail: nfdma@mindspring.com
Members: 1,500 individuals
Staff: 2
Annual Budget: $100-250,000
Exec. Director: Sharon L. Seay

Historical Note
Membership in respective state association required.

Publications:
Directory. bien. adv.

Meetings/Conferences:
Annual Meetings: August

Nat'l Funeral Directors Ass'n (1882)

13625 Bishop's Drive
Brookfield, WI 53005
Tel: (414)789-1880   *Fax:* (414)789-6977
E-Mail: nfda@nfda.org
Web Site: http://www.nfda.org
Members: 14,000 individuals
Staff: 45
Annual Budget: $5-10,000,000
Exec. Director: Robert E. Harden, CAE
Manager, Meetings and Conventions: DeAnn L. Scrabeck, CMP
Director, Marketing Services/Education: Connie Crabb
Asst. Exec. Director, Finance & Operations: Christine Reichelt-Pepper

Historical Note
NFDA sponsors and supports the NFDA Political Action Committee. Members are licensed funeral directors. Membership: $225/year (individual-Category I); $95/year (individual-Category II).

Publications:
Capitol Reports. q.

Directory of Members/Resource Guide. a. adv.
Leadership Bulletin Newsletter. m.
The Director. m. adv.

Meetings/Conferences:
Annual Meetings: October-early November
1999 – Kansas City, MO/Nov. 1-3
2000 – Baltimore, MD/Oct. 16-18

Nat'l Furniture Traffic Conference (1927)

P.O. Box 889
Gardner, MA 01440
Tel: (978)632-1913   *Fax:* (978)630-2917
Members: 170 businesses
Staff: 2
Annual Budget: $50-100,000
Managing Director: Raynard F. Bohman, Jr.

Historical Note
Members are furniture manufacturers, wholesalers, warehouses, retailers and makers of allied products. Represents furniture interests before the Interstate Commerce Commission and other rate and classification bodies.

Publications:
National Directory of Specialized Furniture Carriers. bi-a.
Ocean Shipping News Summary. m.
The Furniture Transporter. m.
Traffic Newsletter. m.

Meetings/Conferences:
Annual Meetings: Spring
1999 – Fort Lauderdale, FL(Lago Mar Hotel)/April 28-30

Nat'l Futures Ass'n (1982)

200 W. Madison St., Suite 1600
Chicago, IL 60606-3447
Tel: (312)781-1300   *Fax:* (312)781-1467
Toll Free: (800)621 - 3570
E-Mail: public-affairs@NFA.futures.org
Web Site: http://www.nfa.futures.org
Members: 3,882 firms
Staff: 300
Annual Budget: $25-50,000,000
President and C.E.O.: Robert K. Wilmouth
V.P., Information Systems: Ken Haase
Dir., Communication & Education Dept.: Laura M. Oatney
Director, Public Affairs & Education: Larry Dyekman
V. President, Treasurers Office: Judith Lyons
V. President, Administration: Jean W. Tippins
V.P., General Counsel, and Secretary: Daniel J. Roth
V. President, Membership/Registration: Gregory C. Prusik
V. President, Compliance: Daniel A. Driscoll

Historical Note
Registered as a futures association under the Commodity Exchange Act in the fall of 1981 and began operations October 1, 1982 as an industry-wide self-regulatory organization for the futures industry. Members are futures commission merchants (FCMs), commodity trading advisors (CTAs), commodity pool operators (CPOs), introducing brokers (IBs), exchanges and associated personnel. Maintains a separate toll-free number for Illinois residents: (800) 572-9400. Has an annual budget of approximately $28 million. Membership: $1,000-5,000/year (FCM), $500/year (CPO, CTA, or IB).

Publications:
Annual Review. a.
Report of Quarterly Actions.

Meetings/Conferences:
Annual Meetings: Third or Fourth Thursday in February

Nat'l Gas Measurement Ass'n (1965)

Historical Note
Organization inactive in 1996.

Nat'l Gas Transportation Ass'n

Historical Note
Name changed to Nat'l Energy Services Ass'n (NESA) in 1996.

Nat'l Genealogical Soc. (1903)

4527 17th St., North
Arlington, VA 22207-2399
Tel: (703)525-0050   *Fax:* (703)525-0052
Toll Free: (800)473 - 0060
E-Mail: shane@nqsgenealogy.org
Web Site: http://www.ngsgenealogy.org
Members: 18,300 individuals
Staff: 12
Annual Budget: $1-2,000,000
Exec. Director: Francis J. Shane
Manager, Education: Suzanne Murray
President: Shirley Wilcox
Membership Manager: Elizabeth Auins
Manager, Publications: Russell L. Henderson
Librarian: Dereka Smith

Historical Note
Established April 24, 1903 at 920 S St., N.W. Washington, DC by Newton L. Collamer and other genealogists. Absorbed the Ass'n for Genealogical Education in 1981. Incorporated as a nonprofit organization under the laws of the District of Columbia in 1904 to collect and preserve genealogical, historical and heraldic data, to inculcate and promote interest in research, to foster careful documentation and promote scholarly writing, to issue publications relating to the field of genealogy. Membership: $35/year.

Publications:
National Genealogical Society Quarterly. q. adv.
Newsletter. bi-m. adv.

Meetings/Conferences:
Annual Meetings: Spring
1999 – Richmond, VA
2000 – Providence, RI
2001 – Portland, OR
2002 – Milwaukee, WI

Nat'l Gerontological Nursing Ass'n *(1984)*
7794 Grow Dr.
Pensacola, FL   32514
Tel: (850)484-9987   *Fax:* (850)484-8762
Toll Free: (800)486 - 9927
Members: 1,600 individuals, 6 companies
Staff: 2
Annual Budget: $50-100,000
Exec. Director: Belinda Puetz

Historical Note
NGNA is a professional organization of registered nurses, licensed practical nurses and allied health professionals working in, or with an interest in, the field of gerontology. Membership: $60/year (individual); $150/year (corporate); 5 individuals at $250, 10 individuals at $450.

Publications:
Geriatric Nursing Magazine. bi-m. adv.
New Horizons Newsletter. bi-m.

Meetings/Conferences:
Annual Meetings: October

Nat'l Glass Ass'n *(1948)*
8200 Greensboro Drive, Suite 302
McLean, VA   22102
Tel: (703)442-4890   *Fax:* (703)442-0630
E-Mail: NGA@GLASS.ORG
Members: 1,900 individuals, 4,500 companies
Staff: 30
Annual Budget: $5-10,000,000
President and C.E.O.: Philip J. James, CAE
Dir., Meetings & Expositions: Denise Sheehan
Dir., Education & Training: Susan Pferchy
Dir., Publications: Nicole Harris

Historical Note
Formerly the Nat'l Auto & Flat Glass Dealers Ass'n and the Nat'l Glass Dealers Ass'n (until 1984). Incorporated in the State of Michigan in 1948. Reincorporated in the District of Columbia in 1978. Members are architectural and automobile glass manufacturers, wholesalers, fabricators, distributors, installers and related industries such as windows, mirrors, sealants, tools, and material handling equipment. Absorbed the Auto Glass Industry Council in 1990. Sponsors the Glass Industry Political Action Committee (GLASPAC). Parent association for the Nat'l Glass Foundation and Glassco Insurance Services, Inc.

Publications:
Auto Glass Magazine. m. adv.
Glass Magazine. m. adv.
Glass Magazine, Latin American Edition. q. adv.
Membership Directory. a.
NGA Catalogue of Products and Services. a.
NGA Chapter Focus. q.
NGA Members Services Update. m.
Window & Door Fabricator. bi-m adv. adv.

Meetings/Conferences:
Annual Meetings: The NGA Show
1999 – Palm Beach, FL/Sept. 22-25
1999 – Atlanta, GA/Apr. 7-9
2000 – Las Vegas, NV/Mar. 15-17
2000 – Palm Springs, CA/Sept. 13-16
2001 – Atlanta, GA/Mar. 15-17
2002 – Houston, TX/March 19-22

Nat'l Golf Car Manufacturers Ass'n *(1984)*
Two Ravinia Drive, Suite 310
Atlanta, GA   30346
Tel: (770)394-7200   *Fax:* (770)395-7698
President: Fred L. Somers, Jr.

Nat'l Golf Course Owners Ass'n *(1976)*
1470 Ben Sawyer Blvd., Suite 18
Mt. Pleasant, SC   29464
Tel: (843)881-7572   *Fax:* (843)881-9958
E-Mail: ngcoa@ngcoa.com
Members: 3,000 clubs
Staff: 4
Annual Budget: $1-2,000,000
Exec. Director: Mike Hughes

Historical Note
Established as the Nat'l Ass'n of Public Golf Courses under the aegis of the Nat'l Golf Foundation, it became fully independent as Golf Course Ass'n in 1982 and assumed its present name in 1991. Members are privately-owned golf courses. Membership: $325/year.

Publications:
Golf Business Magazine. m. adv.

Meetings/Conferences:
Annual Meetings: Winter
1999 – Monterey, CA

Nat'l Golf Foundation *(1936)*
1150 South U.S. Hwy. 1, Suite 401
Jupiter, FL   33477
Tel: (561)744-6006   *Fax:* (561)744-6107
E-Mail: ngf@ngf.org
Web Site: http://www.ngf.org
Members: 6,000 organizations
Staff: 45
Annual Budget: $2-5,000,000
President and C.E.O.: Dr. Joseph Beditz
V. President, Marketing & Communications: Bruce Florine
V. President, Membership Services: Barry Frank
V. President Finance: Gloria Rex
V. President, Operations: Rick Norton

Historical Note
Since its formation in 1936, the NGF has forged a worldwide reputation as the U.S. golf industry's umbrella organization. NGF is the primary source of research and information on the business of golf. More recently the NGF has become a leading proponent of golf course development and a driving force in industry planning. Its

membership includes virtually every major equipment manufacturer and golf association, as well as architects, consultants, builders, and developers and golf course owners and operators. Membership: $150/year (individual), $250 and up/year (organization).

Publications:
Directory of Golf. a.
Golf Market Today. bi-m.
NGF Catalogue. bi-a.
NGF Research Publications. a.

Meetings/Conferences:

Nat'l Goose Council *(1971)*
7 Oak St. West, Box 267
Sisseton, SD   57262-0267
Tel: (605)698-7651   *Fax:* (605)698-7112
Members: 2 companies
Staff: 3
Annual Budget: $25-50,000
President: Marlin Schiltz

Historical Note
Members are breeders of market geese and their suppliers. Membership: $5,000-15,000/year (company).

Meetings/Conferences:

Nat'l Governors' Ass'n *(1908)*
444 North Capitol St., N.W., Suite 267
Washington, DC   20001-1512
Tel: (202)624-5300   *Fax:* (202)624-5313
Web Site: http://www.nga.org
Members: 55 governors
Staff: 87
Annual Budget: $10-25,000,000
Exec. Director: Raymond C. Scheppach, Ph.D.
Dir., Public Affairs: Noel Milan
Director, State-Federal Relations: James L. Martin
Dir., Conference/Office Svcs.: Susan Dotchin
Director, Administration and Finance: Laura W. Shiflett

Historical Note
Formerly (1977) Nat'l Governors Conference. Members are the Governors of the 50 states and five territories of the U.S. Funded by individual states and grants, NGA informs members of federal legislation that will have an impact on their states. Influences the development of national policy. Includes an Office of Management Services which offers technical and consultant services, as well as a Center for Best Practices, which handles demonstration projects.

Publications:
Current Developments in Employment & Training.
Dir. of Governors of Ame.
Fiscal Survey of the States. semi-a.
Governors Executive Report.
Governors' Bulletin. semi-m.
Governors' Staff Directory. semi-a.
Labor Notes. m.
LegisLine.
Regsline.

Meetings/Conferences:
Semi-annual Meetings: Winter and Summer
1999 – Washington, DC(Marriott)/Feb. 20-23
1999 – St. Louis, MO/Aug. 7-10

Nat'l Grain and Feed Ass'n *(1896)*
1201 New York Ave., N.W., Suite 830
Washington, DC   20005-3917
Tel: (202)289-0873   *Fax:* (202)289-5388
Web Site: http://www.ngfa.org
Members: 1000 companies
Staff: 14
Annual Budget: $1-2,000,000
President: Kendell W. Keith
V.P., Communications & Govt. Relations: Randall C. Gordon
General Counsel: David C. Barrett, Jr.
Director, Membership and Marketing: David Poulos

Historical Note
Formerly (1970) Grain and Feed Dealers Nat'l Ass'n. Represents firms that store, handle, merchandise, mill, process, and/or export grains and oilseeds for domestic and international markets.

Publications:
Directory of River Barge Shipping Points. irreg.
Feed Quality Assurance Manual.
NGFA Directory Yearbook. a. adv.
NGFA Newsletter. bi-w.

Meetings/Conferences:

Nat'l Grain Sorghum Producers *(1985)*
P.O. Box 560
Abernathy, TX   79311-0530
Tel: (806)298-4501   *Fax:* (806)298-4234
Web Site: http://www.sorghumgrowers.com
Members: 4,000 individuals
Staff: 6
Annual Budget: $250-500,000
Exec. Director: Tim Lust
Communications Director: Frances Thompson

Historical Note
Founded as the Grain Sorghum Producers Ass'n in 1955; assumed its present name in 1985. Affiliated with the Texas Grain Sorghum Producers Board and the U.S. Feed Grains Council. Membership: $40/year.

Publications:
Grain Sorghum News. m.
Utilization Conference Proceedings. bien.

Meetings/Conferences:
Annual Meetings: February
1999 – Tucson, AZ/Feb. 18-23

Nat'l Grain Trade Council *(1936)*
1300 L St., N.W., Suite 925
Washington, DC   20005-4113
Tel: (202)842-0400   *Fax:* (202)789-7223

E-Mail: ngtcwash@aol.com
Members: 57 companies and organizations
Staff: 3
Annual Budget: $100-250,000
President: Robert R. Petersen
Legal Counsel: J.J. Weiland

Historical Note
NGTC Members are commodity exchanges, boards of trade, national grain marketing ass'ns and grain related businesses.

Meetings/Conferences:
Annual Meetings: May

Nat'l Grange *(1867)*
1616 H St., N.W.
Washington, DC   20006
Tel: (202)628-3507   *Fax:* (202)347-1091
Toll Free: (888)447 - 2643
Members: 300,000 individuals
Staff: 20
National Master: Kermit W. Richardson
Dir., Internal Information: Barbara Jones
Membership Director: Roger Halbert

Historical Note
Fraternal organization of rural families.

Publications:
Grange Today. bi-m.
Journal of Proceedings. a.
Legislative Policies. a.
View from the Hill Newsletter. m.

Meetings/Conferences:
1999 – Portland, ME/Nov. 8-14

Nat'l Grants Management Ass'n *(1978)*
Historical Note
Address unknown in 1995.

Nat'l Grape Growers Cooperative
1223 Potomac St., N.W.
Washington, DC   20007-3212
Tel: (202)333-8190   *Fax:* (202)337-3809
Washington Representative: Nicholas A. Pyle

Nat'l Greenhouse Manufacturers Ass'n *(1958)*
7800 S. Elati, Suite 113
Littleton, CO   80120
Toll Free: (800)792 - 6462
Members: 80 companies
Staff: 2
Annual Budget: $100-250,000
Exec. Director: Melanie K. Hughes

Historical Note
Founded to foster and advance the interests of the greenhouse industry. Serves various segments of the industry: growers, consumers, manufacturers or suppliers of materials and equipment, or related services. Membership: $600-800/year.

Meetings/Conferences:
Semi-Annual Meetings: Spring and Fall

Nat'l Grocers Ass'n *(1982)*
1825 Samuel Morse Drive
Reston, VA   20190-5317
Tel: (703)437-5300   *Fax:* (703)437-7768
Members: 2,000 retailers and wholesalers
Staff: 32
Annual Budget: $2-5,000,000
President and C.E.O.: Thomas K. Zaucha
Sr. V. President & General Counsel: Thomas F. Wenning
Manager, Membership Development: Larry Gibson

Historical Note
The Nat'l Grocers Ass'n was formed in 1982 as the result of a merger between the Nat'l Ass'n of Retail Grocers of the U.S. (founded in 1893) and the Cooperative Food distributors of America (founded in 1937). It is the only nat'l trade ass'n representing the retail and wholesale grocers who comprise the independent sector of the food industry which accounts for nearly one-half of all food store sales in the U.S. Retail and wholesale grocers hold membership in NGA as state and local ass'ns and manufacturers/service suppliers. NGA services include legislative and regulatory advocacy, trade relations and labor relations; as well as educational programs and operational research through the Grocers Research and Education Foundation (GREF); and central buying and marketing through its subsidary, the NGA Service Corporation (NGASC).

Publications:
Advocate. m.
Employee & Labor Relations. q.
Express Lane. m.
National Grocer. q. adv.
Scan. bi-m.
Share Gram. bi-m.
Shelf Talk. bi-m.

Meetings/Conferences:
Annual Meetings: Winter/6,000
1999 – San Francisco, CA(Mariott)/Jan. 27-31

Nat'l Ground Water Ass'n *(1948)*
601 Dempsey Road
Westerville, OH   43081-8978
Tel: (614)898-7791   *Fax:* (614)898-7786
Toll Free: (800)551 - 7379
E-Mail: ngwa@ngwa.org
Web Site: http://www.ngwa.org
Members: 16,000 individuals and companies
Staff: 41
Annual Budget: $5-10,000,000
Exec. Director: Kevin McCray
Director, Marketing: Jim Davis
Government Affairs: Chris Reimer
Expositions Director: Kathy Butcher

Director, Finance: Paul Humes
Historical Note
Formerly (1991) the Nat'l Water Well Ass'n. Members are ground water contractors, makers and suppliers of well drilling/water systems equipment, and scientists/engineers interested in the problems of locating, using and protecting underground water. The Ass'n of Ground Water Scientists and Engineers and the Maufacturers and Suppliers are divisions of NGWA. Provides education, information, and leadership to an international membership. Sponsors the National Ground Water Information Center. Membership: $95-275/year (individual), $115-1,100/year (company/organization).
Publications:
Ass'n of Ground Water Scientists and Engineers Newsletter. bi-m.
Ground Water Monitoring & Remediation. q. adv.
Journal of Ground Water. bi-m. adv.
Membership Directory. trien.
Standards Update. bi-m.
Tailgate Talk. q.
The Well Log. m.
Water Well Journal. m. adv.
Meetings/Conferences:
Annual Meetings: Fall/4,000
1999 – Nashville, TN
2000 – Las Vegas, NV

Nat'l Guard Ass'n of the U.S. *(1878)*
One Massachusetts Ave., N.W., Suite 200
Washington, DC   20001
Tel: (202)789-0031   *Fax:* (202)682-9358
Toll Free: (888)226 - 4287
Members: 58,000 individuals
Staff: 25
Annual Budget: $2-5,000,000
Exec. Director: Maj.Gen. Edward J. Philbin, (Ret.)
Historical Note
Founded at Richmond, Virginia in 1878. Membership is open to any officer or warrant-officer who serves or has served in the Army or Air Nat'l Guard and ass'n members. Membership Fee: Scaled according to rank.
Publications:
The National Guard. m. adv.
Meetings/Conferences:
1999 – Atlanta, GA

Nat'l Guard Executive Directors Ass'n
P.O. Box 10045
3706 Crawford
Austin, TX   78766-1045
Tel: (512)454-7300   *Fax:* 512/467-6803
Web Site: http://www.ngeda.org
Members: 200 individuals
Staff: 7
Annual Budget: $25-50,000
Secretary-Treasurer: Dale M. Pyeatt
Historical Note
Membership: $50/year (individual).
Publications:
Directory. a. adv.
Meetings/Conferences:
1999 – Atlanta, GA/Jan. 22-26

Nat'l Guardianship Ass'n *(1988)*
1604 N. Country Club Road
Tucson, AZ   85716
Tel: (520)881-6561   *Fax:* (520)325-7925
Web Site: http://www.guardianship.org
Members: 750 individuals
Staff: 16
Annual Budget: $10-25,000
Exec. Director: Laury L. Adsit
Communications Director: Jihane K. Rohrbacker
Finance Coordinator: Janet Tite
Membership Director: Jenifer Mowery
Historical Note
Membership: $50/year (family), $125/year (professional).
Publications:
Membership Directory. a. adv.
National Guardian. q. adv.
Meetings/Conferences:
Annual Meetings: October
1999 – Chicago, IL

Nat'l Guild of Community Schools of the Arts *(1937)*
P.O. Box 8018
Englewood, NJ   07631
Tel: (201)871-3337   *Fax:* (201)871-7639
E-Mail: Almayadas@worldnet.att.net
Web Site: http://www.natguild.org
Members: 240 institutions
Staff: 4
Annual Budget: $500-1,000,000
Exec. Director: Lolita Mayadas
Director of Programs and Information Services: Jonathan Herman
Managing Director: Azim L. Mayadas
Historical Note
Non-profit, non-degree-granting association of schools teaching music, dance, drama and the visual arts. Incorporated in 1954. Membership: $60-200/year (business affiliate); $150-800/year (institution).
Publications:
Annual Report.
Employment Opportunities. m.
Guildnotes. bi-m.
Membership Directory. a.

Meetings/Conferences:

Nat'l Guild of Piano Teachers *(1929)*
808 Rio Grande St., Box 1807
Austin, TX   78767-1807
Tel: (512)478-5775
Members: 115,000 individuals
Staff: 11
Annual Budget: $1-2,000,000
President: Richard Allison
Historical Note
A division of the American College of Musicians. Professional society of piano teachers and music faculty members. Sponsors national examinations.
Publications:
Piano Guild Notes. bi-m. adv.

Nat'l Guild of Professional Paperhangers *(1974)*
910 Charles St.
Fredericksburg, VA   22401
Tel: (540)370-0012   *Fax:* (540)370-0015
Web Site: http://www.ngpp.org
Members: 1000 individuals
Staff: 7
Annual Budget: $250-500,000
Exec. V. President: Peggy McElgunn
Historical Note
Founded at Hicksville, NY in 1974, incorporated in Pennsylvania in 1982. Membership: $125/year (individual), $250/year (organization/company).
Publications:
National Membership Directory. a. adv.
NGPP Wallcovering Installer. bi-m. adv.
Meetings/Conferences:
Annual Meetings: Summer
1999 – Atlanta, GA(Renaissance and Waverly)
2000 – San Francisco, CA

Nat'l Gymnastics Judges Ass'n *(1969)*
250 Mabel Lee Hall
Univ. of Nebraska
Lincoln, NE   68588-0229
Tel: (402)472-1704   *Fax:* (402)472-4305
E-Mail: jscheer@unl.edu
Web Site: http://www.NGJA.org
Members: 800 individuals
Annual Budget: $25-50,000
President: John Scheer
Historical Note
Founded in 1969 and incorporated in 1980, the NGJA acts as a professional service organization, providing technical and educational knowledge, training and certification for men's gymnastics officials. Affiliated with USA Gymnastics. Assigns officials for men's gymnastic competitions at junior, national and international levels. NGJA President serves on the USA Gymnastics Board of Directors. Provides officials for men's gymnastic competitions. Organization has National Hall of Fame. Officials certify at three levels: JO, National and FIG (international). Officials take national examiniation annually. Membership: $25/year.
Publications:
Men's Rules Interpretations Book. quadren. adv.
Men's Rules Interpretations Book Update. a. adv.
NGJA Directory. a.
NGJA Newsletter. a.
Meetings/Conferences:
Semi-annual Meetings: Fall, with USA Gymnastics and Spring, in conjunction with major gymnastics championships

Nat'l Hardwood Lumber Ass'n *(1898)*
P.O. Box 34518
Memphis, TN   38184-0518
Tel: (901)377-1818   *Fax:* (901)382-6419
E-Mail: NHLA@natlhardwood.org
Members: 1,200 companies
Staff: 35
Annual Budget: $2-5,000,000
Exec. Manager: Paul Houghland, Jr., CAE
Director, Public Affairs: Shelly Hicks
Meetings/Publications Manager: Cathy Gregory
General Counsel: Grattan Brown
Historical Note
Trade association of the hardwood lumber industry. Establishes offical grading rules for hardwood lumber, provides lumber inspection service in the U.S. and Canada, and conducts the Hardwood Institute promotion program and Hardwood Research Council. Operates school for teaching hardwood lumber grading rules. Helps maintain order, structure and ethics in the hardwood market place.
Publications:
Exporter's Directory. a. adv.
Hardwood Forestry Bulletin. m.
Membership Directory. a. adv.
NHLA GreenSpeak. m.
NHLA News. m.
Meetings/Conferences:
Annual Meetings: Fall/1,500

Nat'l Hay Ass'n *(1895)*
102 Treasure Island Causeway, Suite 201
Treasure Island, FL   33706-4716
Tel: (813)367-9702   *Fax:* (813)367-9608
Toll Free: (800)707 - 0014
E-Mail: naynha@aol.com
Web Site: http://www.haynha.org
Members: 550 individuals
Staff: 2
Annual Budget: $50-100,000
Exec. Director: Donald Kieffer

Historical Note
Represents the interests of both companies and individuals which make up the hay industry as it moves hay and straw from surplus to deficit areas. Membership: $260/year.
Publications:
Hay There. m. adv.
Yearbook and Membership Directory. a. adv.
Meetings/Conferences:
Annual Meetings: Fall

Nat'l Head Start Ass'n *(1973)*
1651 Prince St.
Alexandria, VA   22314-2818
Tel: (703)739-0875   *Fax:* (703)739-0878
Web Site: http://www.nhsa.org
Members: 8,000 individuals, 800 programs
Staff: 22
Annual Budget: $250-500,000
C.E.O.: Sarah M. Greene
Director, Public Relations/Marketing: Marlene Karwoski
Director, Government Affairs: James Delaney
Conference Coordinator: A. Renee Battle
Director, Fiscal Operations: Paul Forst
Director, Research and Evaluations: Gregg Powell
Director, Technology Services: Sheila Boyd
Director, Partnership Project: Maggie Holmes
Historical Note
NHSA members include staff, parents, directors, agencies and other organizations concerned with the Head Start program. NHSA provides professional, statistical and technical assistance to encourage and promote the development of children, youth, families and communities. Membership: $30/year (individual); $100/year (affiliate); $200-800/year (agency); $350/year (corporation).
Publications:
NHSA Conference Program. a. adv.
NHSA Journal. q. adv.
NHSA PCLI Parent Conference Program. a. adv.
Meetings/Conferences:

Nat'l Health Care Anti-Fraud Ass'n *(1985)*
1255 23rd St., N.W., Suite 850
Washington, DC   20037-1174
Tel: (202)659-5955   *Fax:* (202)833-3636
Members: 650 individuals
Staff: 5
Annual Budget: $500-1,000,000
Exec. Director: William J. Mahon
Historical Note
NHCAA's mission is to improve the indentification, detection and prosecution, both civil and criminal, of health care fraud offenders. It seeks to help control health care costs through an aggressive and coordinated anti-fraud effort employing public awareness, national communications, information systems and private/public sector cooperation. Membership: $60/year (individual), $2,500-25,000/year (organization/company).
Publications:
Membership Directory. semi-a.
NHCAA Newsletter. q.
Meetings/Conferences:
Annual Meetings: November

Nat'l Health Club Ass'n *(1988)*
12596 W. Bayaud Ave., 1st Floor
Denver, CO   80228
Tel: (303)753-6422   *Fax:* (303)986-6813
Members: 3,000 health clubs
Staff: 20
Exec. V. President: Robert Riches
Historical Note
Absorbed the Fitness Trade Ass'n in 1990. NHCA members are fitness centers.
Publications:
Nat'l Fitness Trade Journal. bi-m. adv.
Meetings/Conferences:
Annual Meetings: always Las Vegas, NV/September

Nat'l Health Council *(1920)*
1730 M St., N.W., Suite 500
Washington, DC   20036
Tel: (202)785-3910   *Fax:* (202)785-5923
Web Site: http://www.nhcouncil.org
Members: 109 national organizations
Staff: 10
Annual Budget: $500-1,000,000
President: Myrl Weinberg, CAE
Director, Govt. Affairs: Stephanie Marshall
Director, Finance: Nancy Reich
V. President, Operations and Membership: Robert J. Goldberg
Historical Note
A federation of voluntary health agencies, professional societies, business groups, government bodies and other organizations concerned with the nation's health. Membership: $1,000-30,000/year, dues vary as a percentage of total income (voluntary health agencies); $500-5,000/year, dues vary by gross income (professional and membership associations); $500-1,000/year, dues vary by total income (nonprofit organizations), $5,000/year (companies); $500/year (federal government agencies).
Publications:
Council Currents. bi-m.
NHC Washington Report. q.
Report on Voluntary Health Agency Revenue and Expenses. a.
Standards of Accounting & Financial Reporting for Vol. H&W Orgs.
Washington Health Groups Directory. a.
Meetings/Conferences:
Annual Meetings: Spring

Nat'l Hearing Conservation Ass'n *(1976)*

9101 E. Kenyon Ave., Suite 3000
Denver, CO   80237-1855
Tel: (303)224-9022   *Fax:* (303)770-1812
E-Mail: nhca@gwami.com
Web Site: http://www.hearingconservation.org
Members: 650 companies and individuals
Staff: 2
Annual Budget: $50-100,000
Exec. Director: Karen Wojdyla

Historical Note
*Established and incorporated in Florida. Reincorporated in Iowa.
Members are groups providing hearing conservation program
services; companies manufacturing occupational noise or hearing
loss products; and individuals holding advanced degress in
disciplines dealing with hearing and hearing loss. Membership:
$95/year (individual), $65/year (associate), $225/year (service
organization), $635/year (commercial), $25/year (student).*

Publications:
Membership Directory. a.
PSO Directory. a.
Spectrum. q. adv.

Meetings/Conferences:
Annual Meetings: February-March
1999 – Atlanta, GA(Hyatt Regency Downtown)/Feb. 25-27

Nat'l Hemophilia Foundation *(1948)*
116 W. 32nd St., Floor 11
New York, NY   10001-3212
Tel: (212)328-3700   *Fax:* (212)328-3777
E-Mail: info@hemophilia.org
Web Site: http://www.hemophilia.org
Members: 13,500 individuals
Staff: 40
Annual Budget: $5-10,000,000
Exec. Director: Stephen E. Bajardi

Historical Note
*The National Hemophilia Foundation is dedicated to finding the
cures for inherited bleeding disorders and to preventing and treating
the complications of these diseases-through education, advocacy,
and research.*

Publications:
Community Alert. q.
HIV Treatment Exchange. a.
Mandiquarterly.

Meetings/Conferences:
Annual Meetings: Fall
1999 – San Francisco, CA

Nat'l Hereford Hog Record Ass'n *(1933)*
Route 1, Box 37
Flandreau, SD   57028-0037
Tel: (605)997-2116   *Fax:* (605)997-2116
Members: 150 individuals
Staff: 1
Annual Budget: under $10,000
Secretary-Treasurer: Ruby Schrecengost

Historical Note
*Established and incorporated in Iowa. Maintains registry of
pedigrees. Membership: $10/lifetime (individual); $100/lifetime
(organization/company)*

Publications:
Advertiser. q. adv.
Newsletter. a.

Meetings/Conferences:
Annual Meetings: September
1999 – Greencastle, IN/Sept. 10-11

Nat'l High School Athletic Coaches Ass'n *(1965)*
P.O. Box 2569
Gig Harbor, WA   98335-4569
Tel: (253)853-6777   *Fax:* (253)853-6788
Members: 55,000 individuals
Staff: 4
Annual Budget: $500-1,000,000

Historical Note
*NHSACA sponsors programs of recognition (High School Coach of
the Year Awards for 16 different sports), education and competition.
It is involved in varied activities in the commmercial, educational,
governmental and communications fields and serves as a source of
information and counsel to individuals and organizations. Members
number 55,000 men and women coaches and athletic directors
from 40 affiliated state coaches organizations. Membership:
$35/year (individual).*

Publications:
National Coach. 3/year. adv.

Meetings/Conferences:
Annual Meetings: June/1,000
1999 – San Diego, CA(Town & Country)/June 19-26

Nat'l Hockey League *(1917)*
1251 Ave. of the Americas
New York, NY   10020-1104
Tel: (212)789-2000   *Fax:* (212)789-2020
Members: 27 teams
Staff: 160
Annual Budget: $5-10,000,000
Commissioner: Gary B. Bettman
V.P. Communications: Bernadette Mansur
V. President, Public Relations: Arthur Pincus
Group V.P. and C.F.O.: Craig Harnett
Senior V. President, C.O.O.: Stephen Solomon
Sr. V.P./Director, Hockey Operations: Colin Campbell
Sr. V.P. and General Counsel: William Daly
V. President, Media Relations: Frank Brown

Historical Note
*Professional ice hockey league based in Canada and the United
States.*

Publications:
All-Star Magazine. a.

Club Media Guides. a.
NHL This Week. w.
Official Guide and Record Book. a.
Rule Book. a.

Meetings/Conferences:
Annual Meetings: Summer

Nat'l Hockey League Player's Ass'n *(1967)*
777 Bay St., Suite 2400
P.O. Box 121
Toronto, ON   M5G 2-C8
Tel: (416)408-4040   *Fax:* (416)408-3685
Web Site: http://www.nhlpa.com
Members: 575 individuals
Staff: 20
Annual Budget: $2-5,000,000
Exec. Director: Robert W. Goodenow

Historical Note
*Independent labor union established in Montreal in June, 1967.
Membership: $2,880/year.*

Publications:
Goals. 4/year.

Meetings/Conferences:
Annual Meetings: Summer

Nat'l Home Equity Mortgage Ass'n *(1974)*
3833 Schaefer Ave., Suite K
Chino, CA   91710-5456
Tel: (909)590-8133   *Fax:* (909)590-8128
Toll Free: (800)342 - 1121
E-Mail: nhema@mindspring.com
Web Site: http://www.nhema.org
Members: 215 companies
Staff: 2
Annual Budget: $1-2,000,000
Exec. Director: Jeffrey L. Zeltzer
Director, Meetings: Joan Joffe
Membership Director: Jennifer Zeltzer

Historical Note
*Formerly (1995) Nat'l Second Mortgage Ass'n. Active members
include banks, bank holding companies, national and regional
finance companies, savings associations, mortgage bankers and
brokers, and a full array of mortgage product and service providers.
Membership: $1,500/year.*

Publications:
Annual Statistical Report. a.
Equity: The Journal of the Home Equity Mortgage
    Professional. q. adv.
Federal Regulation of Second Mortgage Lending. a.
Member Company Profile. semi-a.
Membership Roster. semi-a.

Meetings/Conferences:
Annual Meetings: April/330
1999 – Rancho Mirage, CA(Westin Mission Hills
    Resort)/March 17-21

Nat'l Home Furnishings Ass'n *(1920)*
P.O. Box 2396
High Point, NC   27261
Tel: (910)883-1650   *Fax:* (910)883-2892
Toll Free: (800)888 - 9590
Members: 3,000 corporations
Staff: 40
Annual Budget: $2-5,000,000
Exec. V. President: Patricia N. Bowling
Director of Education and Meetings: Karin Mayfield
Director, Education/Meetings: Karin Mayfield, CMP
Director of Marketing and Membership: Carolyn McManus
V. President, Operations: David Parker

Historical Note
*Formerly (1970) Nat'l Retail Furniture Ass'n. NHFA's corporate
members represent 13,000 retail stores. Membership fee determined
by volume.*

Publications:
Home Furnishings Executive. m. adv.

Meetings/Conferences:
Biennial Meetings: odd years(fall)/600

Nat'l Home Study Council
Historical Note
Became (1995) Distance Education and Training Council.

Nat'l Honey Packers and Dealers Ass'n *(1952)*
P.O. Box 545
5 Ravine Drive
Matawan, NJ   07747-0545
Tel: (732)583-8188   *Fax:* (732)583-0798
Members: 35 companies
Staff: 5
Annual Budget: $50-100,000
Exec. V. President: Richard J. Sullivan, CAE
V. President: Robert Bauer
Assistant to the President: Gregory Eckhardt
Accountant: Joyce Beckerman
Lawyer: Robert Ward

Historical Note
*NHPDA is a section of the Ass'n of Food Industries, Inc. with its
own officers and directors. It is committed to an industry quality
assurance program; the development of the honey market in the
U.S.; and the welfare of packers and importers of honey.*

Publications:
AFI Annual. a. adv.
AFI Newsletter. bi-m.
NHPDA Bulletins. 2-4/month.

Meetings/Conferences:
Annual Meetings: Winter

Nat'l Hospice Organization *(1978)*

1901 N. Moore St., Suite 901
Arlington, VA   22209-1714
Tel: (703)243-5900   *Fax:* (703)525-5762
Toll Free: (800)658 - 8898
Web Site: http://www.nho.org
Members: 4,100 individuals, 2,100 provider members
Staff: 16
Annual Budget: $2-5,000,000
President: Karen A. Davie
Dir., Conference Services: Sandra Kyles, CMP
Director, Operation: Eileen M. Carr

Historical Note
*The hospice concept cares for terminally ill people and their families
by centering the caring process in the home backed up by in-patient
facilities when needed and appropriate.*

Publications:
Hospice Magazine. q.
NHO Newsline. m.
The Hospice Professional. q.

Meetings/Conferences:
Annual Meetings: Fall

Nat'l Housewares Manufacturers Ass'n *(1938)*
6400 Shafer Court, Suite 650
Rosemont, IL   60018-4929
Tel: (847)292-4200   *Fax:* (847)292-4211
Web Site: http://www.housewares.org
Members: 2,000 companies
Staff: 21
Annual Budget: $2-5,000,000
Exec. Director: Philip J. Brandl
Mgr., Media Rels/Communications: Debbie Teschke
Director, Meetings and Trade Show: Mia Rampersad
Director, Finance & Administation: Dean Kurtis
Manager, Membership Services: Judy Colitz
Director, International Services: Helen Chantos

Historical Note
*Serves manufacturers of kitchen tools and gadgets, cookware and
bakeware items, serving and buffet products, glassware and china,
bath and closet accessories, small electrical appliances, outdoor
products and accessories, decorative accessories, pet supplies,
hardware, cleaning products and tabletop products. Membership:
$250/year (regular); $350/year (associate).*

Publications:
Housewares Around the World Directory. a.
Housewares Indexes. q.
NHMA Internat'l Housewares Membership Directory. a.
NHMA Reports. bi-m.
NHMA State of the Industry Report. a.
Show Directory. a.

Meetings/Conferences:
Annual Meetings: January

Nat'l Housing and Rehabilitation Ass'n *(1971)*
1625 Massachusetts Ave., N.W.
Suite 601
Washington, DC   20036-2244
Tel: (202)939-1750   *Fax:* (202)265-4435
Web Site: http://www.housingonline.com
Members: 300 individuals
Staff: 7
Annual Budget: $250-500,000
Exec. Director: Peter H. Bell
Director, Communications: Glenn Petherick
Administrator: Emma Jean Johnson

Historical Note
*Formerly (1985) Nat'l Housing Rehabilitation Ass'n. NHRA
promoted partnerships among professionals with an interest in
affordable multi-family housing. Members include organizations
and individuals in construction, finance, property management and
real estate development. Membership: $1,250/year (full);
$750/year (associate); $350/year (public).*

Publications:
First of the Month Bulletin. m.
Multifamily Advisor Newlsetter. q.

Meetings/Conferences:
Annual Meetings: March
1999 – San Juan, Puerto(Ritz Carlton)/March 11-14

Nat'l Housing Conference *(1931)*
815 15th St., N.W., Suite 538
Washington, DC   20005-2201
Tel: (202)393-5772   *Fax:* (202)393-5656
Web Site: http://www.nhc.org
Members: 700 individuals and companies
Staff: 10
Annual Budget: $1-2,000,000
Exec. Director: Robert J. Reid
Dep. Director, Policy Development: Conrad E. Egan
Deputy Director, Operations: Maria J. Sayers

Historical Note
*Formerly the National Public Housing Conference, NHC is an
affordable housing advocacy organization representing the breadth
of the housing community in the U.S. Membership: $500-
$3,000/year (organization).*

Publications:
NHC News. q.
Washington Wire Weekly Fax Service. w.

Meetings/Conferences:
Annual Meetings: Spring

Nat'l Human Resources Ass'n *(1950)*
6767 W. Greenfield Ave.
Milwaukee, WI   53214-4967
Tel: (414)453-7499   *Fax:* (414)475-5959
Web Site: http://www.humanresources.org
Members: 2,000 individuals
Staff: 1
Annual Budget: $100-250,000

Ass'n Manager: Judy Huschka

Historical Note
Formerly (1992) Internat'l Ass'n for Personnel Women. Membership: $70/year.

Publications:
Annual Roster. a.
Connections. q.
Human Resources: Journal of IAPW. q. adv.

Meetings/Conferences:
Annual Meetings: Spring
1999 – Philadelphia, PA/June 3-4

Nat'l Humanities Alliance (1981)
21 Dupont Circle, N.W., Suite 604
Washington, DC   20036
Tel: (202)296-4994   *Fax:* (202)872-0884
E-Mail: jhammer@cni.org
Web Site: http://www.nhalliance.org
Members: 82 associations
Staff: 2
Annual Budget: $100-250,000
Director: John H. Hammer

Historical Note
NHA, made up of associations, organizations and institutes in the humanities, is a representation of the interests in the humanities - scholarly, higher education, museums, libraries, state and local organizations. NHA also speaks on behalf of the interests of individuals engaged in research, writing, teaching, and public presentations of the humanities. Membership: $1,000-$25,000 (active); $500-$999 (associate).

Meetings/Conferences:
Annual Meetings: April
1999 – Philadelphia, PA(Sheraton Society Hill)

Nat'l Hydrogen Ass'n (1989)
1800 M St., N.W., Suite 300
Washington, DC   20036
Tel: (202)223-5547   *Fax:* (202)223-5537
E-Mail: nha@ttcorp.com
Web Site: http://www.ttcorp.com/nha/
Members: 70 companies and universities
Annual Budget: $250-500,000
President: Jeffrey A. Serfass
Program Manager: Karen Miller
Exec. V. President: Bob Mauro

Historical Note
NHA members are industrial companies, university and other research organizations with an interest in hydrogen production, storage, transport or utilization. NHA was established to foster the development of hydrogen technologies and their utilization in industrial and commercial applications and promote the transition role of hydrogen in the energy field. $1,500/year (small business); $600/year (univesity/research). Membership: $7,500/year (sustaining); $3,000/year (industry).

Publications:
Annual U. S.
H2 Digest. bi-m.
H2 Legislative Update. q.
NHA News. q.

Meetings/Conferences:
Annual Meetings: March

Nat'l Hydropower Ass'n (1983)
122 C St., N.W., 4th Floor
Washington, DC   20001
Tel: (202)383-2530   *Fax:* (202)383-2531
E-Mail: hydroinfo@aol.com
Web Site: http://www.hydro.org
Members: 150 companies
Staff: 5
Annual Budget: $500-1,000,000
Exec. Director: Linda Church Ciocci
Manager, Finance and Administration: Betty Carreiro

Historical Note
Provides regulatory and legislative advocacy for hydropower industry. Members include all segments of industry, public and private utilities, developers, equipment manufacturers, engineering and design firms, environmental and hydro licensing consultants, legal and financial firms. Membership: $600/year, (individual); corporate membership fee based on megawatts produced.

Publications:
Internat'l Update. m.
NHA News. m.
NHA Online. bi-m.
NHA Regline. m.
NHA Today. bi-m.

Meetings/Conferences:
Annual Meetings: Spring/400
1999 – Washington, DC(Capitol Hilton)/Feb. 27-March 5

Nat'l Ice Cream and Yogurt Retailers Ass'n (1933)
1429 King Ave., Suite 210
Columbus, OH   43212-2108
Tel: (614)486-1444   *Fax:* (614)486-4711
E-Mail: nicyra@aol.com
Web Site: http://www.nicyra.org
Members: 400 companies
Staff: 2
Annual Budget: $100-250,000
Exec. Director: Don Buckley

Historical Note
Established as the Nat'l Ass'n of Retail Ice Cream Manufacturers, it became Nat'l Ice Cream Retailers Ass'n in the mid-1960s and assumed its present name in 1989. Membership: $125-450/year (company, based on number of retail locations operated).

Publications:
Bulletin. m.
NICYRA Yearbook. a. adv.

Meetings/Conferences:
Annual Meetings: Fall/250
1999 – Orlando, FL(Royal Plaza)/Oct. 19-23/300

Nat'l Ice Cream Mix Ass'n (1945)
Historical Note
NICMA declined to provide updated information for this edition.

Nat'l Independent Automobile Dealers Ass'n (1946)
2521 Brown Blvd., Suite 100
Arlington, TX   76006-5203
Tel: (817)640-3838   *Fax:* (817)649-5866
Members: 13,000 companies
Staff: 11
Annual Budget: $1-2,000,000
Exec. V. President: R.B. Grisham
Administrative Director: Lou Ann Davis

Historical Note
Founded as the Nat'l Used Car Dealers Ass'n, it assumed its present name in 1955. Regular membership is open to any organization, company or corporation licensed through the state to buy, sell or auction used motor vehicles, and who are members of the affiliated state association. Regular membership: through affiliated state association, or $60/year in states without an affiliated state association.

Publications:
Used Car Dealer. m. adv.

Meetings/Conferences:
Semi-Annual Meetings: February and August

Nat'l Independent Bank Equipment and Systems Ass'n (1973)
1411 Peterson
Park Ridge, IL   60068
Tel: (847)825-8419   *Fax:* (847)825-8445
Toll Free: (800)843 - 6082
Members: 250 dealers and manufacturers
Staff: 2
Annual Budget: $100-250,000
Exec. Director: Ann Walk

Historical Note
Established as the Nat'l Independent Bank Equipment and Suppliers Ass'n, it assumed its present name in 1977. Membership: $395/year.

Publications:
Newsletter. m.

Meetings/Conferences:
Annual Meetings: Spring/300
1999 – San Antonio, TX(Adam's Mark)/May 18-23/200

Nat'l Independent Dairy-Foods Ass'n (1957)
Historical Note
Organization defunct in 1997.

Nat'l Independent Energy Producers (1987)
Historical Note
Merged with Electric Generation Ass'n in 1997 to form Electric Power Supply Ass'n.

Nat'l Independent Flag Dealers Ass'n
136 S. Keowee St.
Dayton, OH   45402
Tel: (937)222-1024   *Fax:* (937)222-5794
Toll Free: (800)458 - 4838
E-Mail: flaginfo@erinet.com
Web Site: http://www.flaginfo.com
Members: 80 flag dealers and manufacturers
Annual Budget: $100-250,000
Exec. Director: Daniel Lea

Historical Note
Membership: $400/year.

Publications:
NIFDA News. bi-m. adv.

Meetings/Conferences:

Nat'l Independent Nursery Furniture Retailers Ass'n (1975)
Historical Note
Address unknown in 1996.

Nat'l Independent Textiles Retailers Organization (1995)
355 Lexington Ave., 17th Floor
New York, NY   10017-6603
Tel: (212)661-4261   *Fax:* (212)370-9047
Members: 60 companies
Staff: 1
Annual Budget: $10-25,000
Exec. Director: Holly J. Munter-Koenig

Historical Note
NITRO is an association of privately held home fashion retailers committed to the continued growth of our members. Our mission is to provide education, information and industry representation to a network of like-minded entrepreneurs, thereby promoting the benefits of independent retailing to the consuming public.

Publications:
Newsletter. q.

Nat'l Indian Counselors Ass'n (1980)
Univ. of Nebraska Multi-Cultural Affairs
220 Administration Bldg.
Lincoln, NE   68588
Tel: (402)472-9338
Members: 75 individuals
Annual Budget: under $10,000
President: Helen Long Soldier

Publications:
NICA Newsletter. semi-a.

Meetings/Conferences:
Annual Meetings: in conjunction with the Nat'l Indian Education Ass'n

Nat'l Indian Education Ass'n (1970)
700 N. Fairfax St., Suite 210
Alexandria, VA   22314-2040
Tel: (703)838-2870   *Fax:* (703)838-1620
E-Mail: niea@mindspring.com
Web Site: http://www.niea.org
Members: 3,000 individuals
Staff: 3
Annual Budget: $50-100,000
Exec. Director: Lorraine P. Edmo

Historical Note
American Indian teachers and school administrators. Membership: $75/year (professional), $20/year (student).

Publications:
NIEA Newsletter. q.

Meetings/Conferences:
Annual Meetings: Fall
1999 – Oklahoma City, OK(Myrad Convention Center)/Oct. 17-20
2000 – Sioux Falls, SD
2001 – Billings, MT
2002 – Albuquerque, NM

Nat'l Indian Gaming Ass'n (1985)
224 2nd St., S.E.
Washington, DC   20003-1943
Tel: (202)546-7711   *Fax:* (202)546-1755
Toll Free: (800)286 - 6442
E-Mail: niga@dgsys.com
Web Site: http://www.indiangaming.org
Members: 165 Tribes 63 Associate Members
Staff: 10
Annual Budget: $1-2,000,000
Exec. Director: Jacob L. Coin
Communications Director: Gay Kingman
Meeting Manager: Dianne Wyss
Seminar Institute Director: Gay Kingman
Business Manager: Amy Christianson
Policy Analyst: Charles Robertson

Historical Note
NIGA is an organization representing Indian Nations, with other non-voting associate members representing organizations, tribes and businesses engaged in tribal gaming enterprises from around the country. NIGA operates as a clearinghouse and educational, legislative and public policy resource for tribes, policymakers and the public on Indian gaming issues and tribal community development.

Publications:
Indian Gaming Insider. bi-m. adv.
Seminar Manuals. a. adv.

Meetings/Conferences:
1999 – Tucson, AZ(Tucson Convention Center)

Nat'l Industrial Belting Ass'n (1920)
235 N. Executive Dr., Suite 100
Brookfield, WI   53005
Tel: (414)797-7580   *Fax:* (414)797-7591
Web Site: http://www.niba.org
Members: 250 companies
Staff: 2
Annual Budget: $100-250,000
Exec. V. President: Charles J. Blanchard, CAE
Coordinator, Conventions/Meetings: Cie Motelet

Historical Note
Founded as the American Leather Belting Association, it became the National Industrial Leather Association in 1926 and assumed its present name in 1977. Composed of distributors and manufacturers of flat industrial belting used for conveying, elevating and power transmission. Membership: $550/year.

Publications:
Beltline. q.
Tech Notes. irreg.

Meetings/Conferences:
Annual Meetings: Fall/450
1999 – Orlando, FL(Swan Hotel)/Sept. 15-18

Nat'l Industrial Council - Employer Ass'n Group (1907)
1331 Pennsylvania Ave., N.W., 6th Floor
Washington, DC   20004-1703
Tel: (202)637-3052   *Fax:* (202)637-3182
Members: 75 organizations
Staff: 2
Annual Budget: $100-250,000
Exec. Director: Mark Stuart

Historical Note
A federation of state and local manufacturers' associations. Affiliated with Nat'l Ass'n of Manufacturers. Founded as the Nat' Council for Industrial Defense by the Nat'l Ass'n of Manufacturers in 1907; became the Nat'l Industrial Council in 1918. Known as the Nat'l Industrial Council - Industrial Relations Group until 1990. Composed of two groups of employer associations, each with its own executive director: the Employer Ass'n Group and the State Associations Group (see separate entry). Primarily interested in labor relations and employment law issues. Membership: $300-1,500/yr. (association).

Publications:
Annual Executive Compensation Survey. a.
Annual Succesful Programs/Services Survey. a.
EAG Network Notes. bi-m.

Meetings/Conferences:
Semi-annual Meetings: Spring and Fall

Nat'l Industrial Council - State Ass'ns Group (1907)

1331 Pennsylvania Ave., N.W., 6th Floor
Washington, DC   20004-1703
Tel: (202)637-3054   *Fax:* (202)637-3182
Members: 46 state associations
Staff: 3
Annual Budget: $100-250,000
Exec. Director: Barry Buzby

Historical Note
The NIC is composed of two groups of industrial employer associations: NIC State Ass'ns Group and NIC Employer Ass'n Group (see listing). Forty-four states plus the Commonwealth of Puerto Rico are represented in the SAG. While ass'ns vary in size, structure and primary activities, their goals are to maintain and strengthen the private enterprise system in the US so as to encourage individual initiative, progress and freedom. SAG association not only represent a business constituency interested in federal and state legislation, but also many association executives have personal ties with members of Congress, particularly those who previously had served in state or local government. Membership: $350-$2,000/year (organization).

Publications:
Nat'l Industrial Council Member Directory. a.

Meetings/Conferences:
Annual Meetings: May

Nat'l Industrial Glove Distributors Ass'n *(1959)*
1900 Arch St.
Philadelphia, PA   19103-1498
Tel: (215)564-3484   *Fax:* (215)564-2175
E-Mail: assnhqt@netaxs.com
Web Site: http://www.nigda.org
Members: 150 companies
Staff: 3
Annual Budget: $100-250,000
Exec. Director: John D. McGreevey, Jr.

Publications:
NIGDA News. q.

Meetings/Conferences:
Annual Meetings: Spring/150 and Fall
1999 – Marco Island, FL(Mariott Marco)/June 19-23/150

Nat'l Industrial Sand Ass'n *(1936)*
4041 Powder Mill Road, Suite 402
Calverton, MD   20705
Tel: (301)595-5550   *Fax:* (301)595-3303
Members: 35 businesses
Staff: 3
Annual Budget: $500-1,000,000
President: Robert E. Glenn
V. President: Gerald C. Hurley

Historical Note
NISA provides member companies with programs including silicosis prevention and other safety and health initiatives, government relations, and technical support. Membership fee varies, based on sales.

Meetings/Conferences:
Annual Meetings: Spring/80
1999 – Sea Island, GAA(Cloisters)/April 10-14

Nat'l Industrial Transportation League *(1907)*
1700 North Moore St., Suite 1900
Arlington, VA   22209 1904
Tel: (703)524-5011   *Fax:* (703)524-5017
E-Mail: info@nitl.org
Web Site: http://www.nitl.org
Members: 1,500 individuals
Staff: 10
Annual Budget: $2-5,000,000
President and C.O.O.: Edward M. Emmett
Communications Manager: William J. Clapper
Director, Government Affairs: Kathy Luhn
Director, Policy Development: Peter J. Gatti
Director, Policy Development: Edward Rastatter
Meetings Manager: Virginia Roberts
Dir., Finance: Ellie Gilanshah
Membership Secretary: Kira Calm

Historical Note
Founded as Nat'l Industrial Traffic League, it assumed its current name in 1982. Represents industrial and commercial shippers, boards of trade, chambers of commerce, and similar groups. Its members use all modes of transportation, and directly or indirectly represent an estimated 80 per cent of the nation's commercial freight. Membership: $400-3,500/year (regular), $350-2,000/year (associate).

Publications:
Notice. w.
Reporter. irreg.

Meetings/Conferences:
Annual Meetings: November/3,000
1999 – San Antonio, TX/Nov. 14-17
2000 – Ft. Lauderdale, FL/Nov. 12-15
2001 – Charlotte, NC/Nov. 11-14

Nat'l Industrial Workers Union *(1955)*
Historical Note
Address unknown in 1996.

Nat'l Industrial Zoning Committee *(1948)*
1858 Chatfield Road
Columbus, OH   43221-3819
Tel: (614)488-9001
Members: 8 national organizations
Annual Budget: under $10,000
Secretary: James M. Jennings

Historical Note
An umbrella group founded by the American Soc. of Planning Officials, American Institute of Planners, American Industrial Development Council, American Railway Development Ass'n, American Soc. of Civil Engineers, Ass'n of State Planning and

Development Agencies, Soc. of Industrial Realtors and Urban Land Institute. NIZC is concerned with improving the techniques and practices for zoning land for industry as a part of comprehensive community planning.

Meetings/Conferences:
Annual Meetings: Infrequent

Nat'l Industries for the Blind *(1938)*
1901 North Beauregard St., Suite 200
Alexandria, VA   22311-1727
Tel: (703)998-0770   *Fax:* (703)948-8268
Members: 118 agencies
Staff: 100
Annual Budget: $5-10,000,000
President and C.E.O.: James Gibbons
Dir., Public Policy: Patricia M. Beattie
Director, Rehabilitation Services: Robert Hanye
V. President, Finance: Guy DeRossi
V. President, Strategic Business Issues: Arun Shimpi
Director, Government and Commercial Business: Kevin Lynch

Historical Note
Congress passed the Wagner-O'Day Act in 1938 directing the Federal Government to purchase, under certain conditions, products from agencies employing people who are blind. To carry the provisions of the Act, the Committee for Purchase from the Blind (now known as the Committee for Purchase From People who are Blind or Severly Disabled) was established; it designated Nat'l Industries for the Blind as a central non-profit agency to facilitate equitable distribution of Federal Government contracts to its associated agencies throughout the country. In 1971, the Act was amended to include the purchase of services as well as products from industries employing people who are blind. It also provided that agencies employing people who are severly disabled participate in the Act, which became known as the Javits-Wagner-O'Day Act. Has an annual budget of $9 million.

Publications:
Annual Report. a.
Opportunity. q.

Meetings/Conferences:
Semi-annual Meetings: Spring and Fall

Nat'l Infomercial Marketing Ass'n
Historical Note
Became NIMA Internat'l in 1994.

Nat'l Information Standards Organization *(1939)*
4733 Bethesda Ave., Suite 300
Bethesda, MD   20814-5248
Tel: (301)654-2512   *Fax:* (301)654-1721
E-Mail: nisohq@niso.org
Web Site: http://www.niso.org
Members: 70 organizations
Staff: 3
Annual Budget: $500-1,000,000
Exec. Director: Patricia R. Harris

Historical Note
Originally Committee Z39 of the American Nat'l Standards Institute, NISO was incorporated in the District of Columbia in 1983 and assumed its present name the following year. NISO is a non-profit association concerned with developing voluntary consensus technical standards used in libraries, information services and publishing. Three of the best known NISO standards are the International Standard Serial Number (ISSN), the International Standard Book Number (ISBN) identifying publications and Z39.50 the information retrieval protocol. NISO Voting Members are organizations, national in scope, which have an interest in the standards and activities promoted by NISO. NISO is accredited by the American Nat'l Standards Institute and serves as the U.S. Technical Advisory Group on the work of Technical Committe 46 of the Internat'l Organization for Standardization.

Publications:
Information Standards Quarterly. q.

Meetings/Conferences:
1999 – Philadelphia, PA/75

Nat'l Institute for Architectural Education *(1894)*
30 West 22nd St., 6th Floor
New York, NY   10010
Tel: (212)924-7000   *Fax:* (212)366-5836
E-Mail: vanalen@vanalen.org
Web Site: http://www.vanalen.org
Members: 250 individuals
Staff: 3
Annual Budget: $250-500,000
Exec. Director: Raymond Gastil

Historical Note
Established as the Society of Beaux-Arts Architects, it became the Beaux-Arts Institute of Design in 1916 and assumed its present name in 1956. NIAE is devoted to promoting excellece in architectural Education and to bridging the gap between the academic and professional sectors. NIAE's New York headquarters are an active center for exhibitions, lectures, and other events of interest to the architectural community. Membership: $50/year (active); $25 (intern architect); $30/year (supporting); $15/year (student).

Publications:
Competition Jury Reports. a.

Meetings/Conferences:
Annual Meetings: Always in October at the Institute's headquarters

Nat'l Institute for Dispute Resolution *(1981)*
1527 New Hampsher Ave. N.W.
Washington, DC   20005
Tel: (202)667-9700
E-Mail: nidr@igc.apc.org
Staff: 10
President: Margery Baker
Director, Communications: Doug Harbit

Historical Note
Promotes the settling of disputes without litigation through methods such as arbitration and mediation. Promotes research, development, testing and discussion on innovative techniques and practices of dispute resolution; seeks to enhance the fairness, effectiveness, and efficiency of the ways disputes are resolved. The Conflict Resolution Education Network is a program of NIDR. Membership: $75/year (individual); $150/year (organization); $35/year (student).

Publications:
Forum. trien.
Fourth R. bi-m.
NIDR News. bi-m.

Nat'l Institute for Electromedical Information *(1984)*
Historical Note
Address unknown in 1998.

Nat'l Institute for Farm Safety *(1962)*
2-54 Agriculture Building
Columbia, MO   65211
Tel: (573)882-6385   *Fax:* (573)884-7993
Members: 200 individuals
Staff: 2
Annual Budget: $10-25,000
Interim Executive Secretary: David E. Baker

Historical Note
Members professionals concerned with agricultural safety. Membership: $50-75/year (individual), $100 + /year (organization /company).

Publications:
Newsletter. q.

Meetings/Conferences:
1999 – Deleware/200

Nat'l Institute of American Doll Artists *(1963)*
P.O. Box 87
Bybee, TN   37713
Tel: (423)625-1160
Members: 200 individuals
Staff: 1
Annual Budget: $25-50,000
President: Akira Blount

Historical Note
Professional doll artists creating original dolls. Has no paid officers or full-time staff. Membership is by election. Membership: $50/year.

Publications:
Directory.
Newsletter. q.
Yearbook. a. adv.

Meetings/Conferences:
1999 – Bethesda, MD(Hyatt)/July 28-Aug. 1

Nat'l Institute of Building Sciences *(1976)*
1090 Vermont Ave., Suite 700
Washington, DC   20005-4905
Tel: (202)289-7800   *Fax:* (202)289-1092
E-Mail: nibs@nibs.org
Web Site: http://www.nibs.org/nibshome.htm
Members: 1,100 individuals and organizations
Staff: 35
Annual Budget: $10-25,000,000
President: David A. Harris, FAIA
Director, Communications: Neil W. Sandler
V.P., Councils & Tech. Programs: Bruce Vogelsinger, P.E.
V.P., Finance/Administration: John Lloyd
Director, Marketing and Administration: Pamela R. Towns
V.P., Development and Director, NCEF: William Brenner, AIA
Mgr., Publications/Membership: Pamela Williams
V.P., Construction Criteria Base: Earle Kennett

Historical Note
A public-private partnership created by Congress to improve regulation of the building process, facilitate the introduction of new and innovative building technology, and disseminate technical and regulatory information. Affiliated councils include: Building Environment and Thermal Envelope Council (BETEC), Building Seismic Safety Council (BSSC), Construction Metrication Council (CMC) and CADD Council. Membership includes individuals, companies, associations, government bodies and unions. Membership: $75-150/year (individual), $1,000-$25,000/year (company).

Publications:
Annual Report to the President of the U. S.
Building Sciences Newsletter. bi-m.
CCB Bulletin Newsletter. q.
Construction Criteria Base on CD-ROM. q.
Membership Directory. a.
Metrication Construction Newsletter. bi-m.
SPECTEXT Guide Specifications. a.

Nat'l Institute of Ceramic Engineers *(1938)*
735 Ceramic Place
Westerville, OH   43081-8720
Tel: (614)890-4700   *Fax:* (614)899-6109
Members: 2,018 individuals
Annual Budget: $50-100,000
Exec. Director: W. Paul Holbrook

Historical Note
Professional society of ceramic engineers, dedicated to the development, promotion and advancement of ceramic engineering interests. Founded by the American Ceramic Soc. of which it remains a class. Also affiliated with the American Ass'n of Engineering Socs., the Accreditation Board for Engineering and Technology, the Nat'l Soc. of Professional Engineers and the Nat'l Council of Engineering Examiners. Membership: $20/year. (Applicants must be members of the ACerS and approved for admission.) ACerS provides administrative support.

Publications:
Newsletter. 3/yr.

Meetings/Conferences:
Annual Meetings: Spring, with ACerS

Nat'l Institute of Certified Moving Consultants (1974)
1611 Duke St.
Alexandria, VA   22314
Tel: (703)683-7410   *Fax:* (703)683-7527
Toll Free: (800)538 - 6672
Members: 1,760 individuals, 26 sponsoring industries
Staff: 2
Annual Budget: $100-250,000
Director: Judy Stuchell

Historical Note
Established by the Nat'l Moving and Storage Ass'n as a separate educational membership organization. Awards the CMC (Certified Moving Consultant) designation to those who have passed an exam testing their ability ""to give sound moving advice, accurate estimates and coordinate moving services." Membership: $50-$250/year.

Publications:
CMC Forum Newsletter. q.
Moving Consultants Certification Manual.
Office and Industrial Moves Manual.

Nat'l Institute of Fire Restoration (1968)
Historical Note
A division of the Ass'n of Specialists in Cleaning and Restoration.

Nat'l Institute of Governmental Purchasing (1944)
151
Spring St., Suite 300
Herndon, VA   20170
Tel: (703)736-8900   *Fax:* (703)736-0644
Toll Free: (800)367 - 6447
Web Site: http://www.nigp.org
Members: 2,000 agencies
Staff: 23
Annual Budget: $2-5,000,000
Exec. V. President: Rick Grimm
Manager, Communications: Ann Deatherage
Manager, Education: Jennifer Greenfield
Deputy Executive Vice President, Administration: Anne Deatherage
Manager, Membership Operations: Cyndi Cooksey

Historical Note
Members are government buying agencies at local, state and federal levels in the U.S. and Canada. Promotes professional development, uniform purchasing laws and procedures. Affiliated with the United States Conference of Mayors, the Chartered Institute of Purchasing & Supply of Great Britain and the Internat'l Federation of Purchasing and Materials Management. Conducts a two-tier certification program awarding CPPO (Certified Public Purchasing Officer) and CPPB (Certified Professional Public Buyer) designations. Conducts seminars in public purchasing. Membership: $135-$650/year (agency).

Publications:
Government PROcurement. q. adv.
NIGP Technical Bulletin. bi-m.

Meetings/Conferences:
Annual Meetings: Summer
1999 – Halifax, NS, Canada/July 23-28
2000 – Baltimore, MD/Aug. 11-15
2001 – Columbus, OH/Aug. 17-21

Nat'l Institute of Management Counsellors (1954)
P.O. Box 193
Great Neck, NY   11022-0193
Tel: (516)482-5683
Members: 250 individuals
Staff: 2
Exec. Director: Willard Warren

Nat'l Institute of Municipal Law Officers (1935)
Historical Note
Became the Internat'l Municipal Lawyers Ass'n in 1996.

Nat'l Institute of Oilseed Products (1934)
1101 15th St., N.W., Suite 202
Washington, DC   20005
Tel: (202)785-3232   *Fax:* (202)223-9741
E-Mail: niop@assnhq.com
Members: 300 companies
Staff: 5
Annual Budget: $100-250,000
Exec. Director: Richard E. Cristol
Exec. Secretary: Belva Jones

Historical Note
Members are importers, exporters, storage tank operators, and brokers in copra, palm, coconut, and other edible oils and related raw material.

Publications:
Trading Rules. a.
Washington Correspondence. w.

Meetings/Conferences:
Annual Meetings: March
1999 – Palm Springs, CA(Westin Mission Hills)/March 24-27
2000 – Tucson, AZ(Westin La Paloma)/March 15-18

Nat'l Institute of Packaging, Handling and Logistics Engineers (1956)
6902 Lyle Street
Lanham, MD   20706-3454
Tel: (301)459-9105   *Fax:* (301)459-4925
Web Site: http://www.earls.com/niphle
Members: 700 individuals
Staff: 1
Annual Budget: under $10,000
Exec. Director: James A. Russell

Historical Note
Originally the DC chapter of the Soc. of Packaging and Handling Engineers, the Institute became independent in an effort to give more emphasis to the government liaison responsibilities of its members. The majority of its membership still is to be found in the greater metropolitan Washington area. Membership: $50/year (individual), $135 & 325/year, varies by number of members (company).

Publications:
Annual Report. adv. adv.
Membership Directory. a. adv.
PHL Bulletin. m. adv.

Meetings/Conferences:
Semi-annual meetings: Spring and Fall
1999 – San Antonio, TX(St. Anthony Hotel)/Feb. 21-25

Nat'l Institute of Pension Administrators (1983)
401 N. Michigan Ave.
Chicago, IL   60611-4267
Toll Free: (800)999 - 6472
E-Mail: nipa@sba.com
Web Site: http://www.nipa.org
Members: 460 individuals, 50 companies
Staff: 2
Annual Budget: $250-500,000
Exec. Director: Jody Schermerhorn

Historical Note
The Institute is responsible for the formation of professional standards, an ongoing education program consisting of workwhops and home study courses, and awards the APA (Accredited Pension Adminstrator) and the APR (Accredited Pension Rrepresentative) designations by examination and experience. Membership: $200/year (individual); $500-1,000/year (firm).

Publications:
Plan Horizons. q. adv.

Meetings/Conferences:
Annual Meetings: May
1999 – Scottsdale, AZ(Radisson Resort & Spa)/May 1-5/350

Nat'l Institute of Rug Cleaning (1945)
Historical Note
A division of the Ass'n of Specialists in Cleaning and Restoration.

Nat'l Institute of Senior Centers (1970)
409 3rd St., S.W., 2nd Floor
Washington, DC   20024
Tel: (202)479-6683   *Fax:* (202)479-0735
Web Site: http://www.ncoa.org
Members: 2,500 centers
Staff: 1
Exec. Director: Deborah Broughten

Historical Note
Originally (1962) the Nat'l Advisory Committee on Senior Centers of the Nat'l Council on the Aging. NISC is a special interest group of the Nat'l Council on the Aging.

Publications:
Perspective on Aging. bi-m.

Meetings/Conferences:
Annual Meetings: in conjunction with Nat'l Council on the Aging

Nat'l Institute of Senior Housing (1979)
Historical Note
A special interest group of the Nat'l Council on the Aging.

Nat'l Institute of Steel Detailing (1969)
P.O. Box 121484
Arlington, TX   76012
Tel: (817)860-9890   *Fax:* (817)860-9891
Members: 250 firms
Annual Budget: $50-100,000
President: Don Pope

Historical Note
Steel detailing is the production, from architectural and engineering drawings, of fabrication drawings that can be read by workers in a fabrication shop, where designs for steel skeletons of buildings are created. Founded May 10, 1969 in Houston by thirty-eight detailing firms. Membership: $345-375/year (organization/company).

Publications:
The Connection. q.

Meetings/Conferences:
Annual Meetings: June

Nat'l Institute on Adult Daycare (1979)
Historical Note
A special interest group of the Nat'l Council on the Aging concerned with meeting the needs of day care practitioners.

Nat'l Institute on Age, Work and Retirement (1967)
Historical Note
Formerly (1978) Nat'l Institute of Industrial Gerontology. The research arm of the Nat'l Council on the Aging. Not a membership organization.

Nat'l Institute on Community-based Long-term Care (1983)
409 3rd St., S.W., 2nd Floor
Washington, DC   20024
Tel: (202)479-1200   *Fax:* (202)479-0735
Members: 1,100 individuals
Staff: 1
Program Manager: Carol McClendon

Historical Note
A special interest group of the Nat'l Council on the Aging providing a focal point for all long-term care planners and practitioners in

public and private agencies. Membership: $75/year (core membership); $75/year (constituents units).

Publications:
NCOA NETWORKS. bi-m. adv.
Perspective on Aging. q. adv.

Meetings/Conferences:
Annual Meetings: in conjunction with the Nat'l Council on the Aging

Nat'l Institute on Park and Grounds Management (1975)
730 W. Frances St.
Appleton, WI   54914-2365
Tel: (920)733-2301   *Fax:* (920)733-2301
E-Mail: nipgm@tpo.org
Members: 1,050 individuals
Staff: 2
Annual Budget: $50-100,000
Exec. Director: Erik L. Madisen, Jr.
Executive Secretary: Barbara Walters

Historical Note
Seeks to improve grounds management through education and exchange of information within its membership. Members include managers of parks, campuses and other large outdoor areas. Membership: $115/year (individual); $130/year (company).

Publications:
Clearing House Newsletter. 10/year. adv.
Roster (members only). a. adv.

Meetings/Conferences:
Annual Meetings: Fall
1999 – Kansas City, MO(Hyatt Regency)/Nov. 7-10/400

Nat'l Institutes for Water Resources (1974)
Blaisdell House, University of Mass.
Amherst, MA   01003
Tel: (413)545-2842   *Fax:* (413)545-2304
E-Mail: godfrey@tei.umass.edu
Members: 54 individuals
Annual Budget: $10-25,000
Treasurer: Paul Joseph Godfrey, Ph.D.

Historical Note
Formed in 1974 to coordinate the institute program both internally and externally. Membership consists of the directors of 54 institutes. Has no paid staff. Formerly (1992) the Nat'l Ass'n of Water Institute Directors. Membership: $2,700/year.

Publications:
Annual Research Program Report. a.
Directory of Institute Programs. bi-a.
NIWR Publications: An Electronic Database. bi-a.

Meetings/Conferences:
Annual Meetings: Spring in Washington, DC/50

Nat'l Insulation and Abatement Contractors Ass'n
Historical Note
Became Nat'l Insulation Ass'n in 1995.

Nat'l Insulation Ass'n (1954)
99 Canal Center Plaza, Suite 222
Alexandria, VA   22314-1538
Tel: (703)683-6422   *Fax:* (703)549-4838
Web Site: http://www.insulation.org
Members: 450 headquarter company members
Staff: 10
Annual Budget: $1-2,000,000
Exec. V. President: William Pitkin
Director, Marketing/Operations: Michele M. Jones, CMP

Historical Note
Formerly (1970) Insulation Distributor-Contractors Nat'l Ass'n , (1989) Nat'l Insulation Contractors Ass'n and (1995) Nat'l Insulation and Abatement Contractors Ass'n. Members are industrial and commercial insulation contractors, manufacturers and distributors. Membership fee based on volume of business.

Publications:
Industry Directory and Buyers Guide. a. adv.
Insulation Industry File. bi-a. adv.
Insulation Outlook. m. adv.

Meetings/Conferences:
Annual Meetings: Spring
1999 – San Antonio, TX/April 7-10

Nat'l Insurance Ass'n (1921)
1133 Desert Shale Ave.
Las Vegas, NV   89123
Tel: (702)269-2445   *Fax:* (702)269-2446
Members: 13 companies
Staff: 2
Annual Budget: $50-100,000
Exec. Director: Josephine King

Historical Note
Formerly (1954) Nat'l Negro Insurance Ass'n. NIA is an organization of black-owned and operated life insurance companies cooperating to raise standards and promote efficiency in practices among participating members, to contribute to the total health and insurance education of the nation, and to build confidence in insurance companies owned and controlled by its members. Membership: $700/year, minimum (company).

Publications:
Membership Roster. a.

Meetings/Conferences:
Annual Meetings: June
1999 – New Orleans, LA/June 10-13

Nat'l Insurance Crime Bureau (1992)
10330 S. Roberts Rd.
Palos Hills, IL   60465-1971
Tel: (708)430-2430   *Fax:* (708)430-2446
Toll Free: (800)447 - 6282
Web Site: http://www.nich.org

Members: 1000 insurance companies
Staff: 380
Annual Budget: $25-50,000,000
President and C.E.O.: John G. Di Liberto
Director, Corporate Communications: Jeff Benzing
Associate V.P. & Director, Government Affairs: Judy Fitzgerald
National Membership Director: Marcy Shuld
Treasurer and Chief Financial Officer: Robert Jachnicki
Director, Human Resources: Christine Harvey
V.P. General Counsel: Robert Mason

Historical Note
Formed in 1992 by the merger of Insurance Crime Prevention Institute (founded 1970) and Nat'l Automobile Theft Bureau (founded 1912). Members are insurance companies interested in the detection, prevention and prosecution of fraud.

Publications:
Spotlight on Insurance Crime. q.

Meetings/Conferences:
1999 - Rosemont, IL(O'Hare Marriott)/May 11-13/1000

Nat'l Intercollegiate Soccer Officials Ass'n *(1964)*
541 Woodview Drive
Longwood, FL 32779-2614
Tel: (407)862-3305   *Fax:* (407)862-8545
Members: 4,000 individuals
Annual Budget: $100-250,000
Exec. Director: Raymond Bernabei

Historical Note
NISOA has a nationwide volunteer staff of approximately 225 individuals. Membership: $50/year.

Publications:
Newsletter. 3/yr. adv.

Meetings/Conferences:
Annual Meetings: Summer
1999 - Pittsburgh, PA(Embassy Suites)/July 20-24

Nat'l Interfaith Coalition on Aging *(1972)*
Historical Note
A special interest group of the Nat'l Council on the Aging.

Nat'l Interfraternity Conference *(1909)*
3901 West 86th St., Suite 390
Indianapolis, IN 46268-1791
Tel: (317)872-1112   *Fax:* (317)872-1134
Web Site: http://www.nicindy.org
Members: 67 fraternities
Staff: 10
Annual Budget: $500-1,000,000
Exec. V. President: Jonathan J. Brant, CAE

Historical Note
An association of men's national social fraternities whose members convened originally November 27, 1909 at the University Club in New York City. Membership: $400/year (organization).

Publications:
Campus Commentary.
Foundation Focus. 3/yea.
Interfraternity Directory.

Meetings/Conferences:
Annual Meetings: Always week after Thanksgiving.
1999 - Denver, CO/Dec. 3-6

Nat'l Interscholastic Athletic Administrators Ass'n *(1977)*
P.O. Box 20626
Kansas City, MO 64195-0626
Tel: (816)464-5400   *Fax:* (816)464-5571
Web Site: http://www.nfhs.org/niaa.htm
Members: 5,000 individuals
Staff: 2
Annual Budget: $100-250,000
Exec. Officer: Frank Kovaleski

Historical Note
Members are high school athletic administrators. Membership: $37/year (individual); $25-125/year (organizational).

Publications:
Interscholastic Athletic Administration. q. adv.
Nat'l Conference Proceedings. a.
State Athletic Director Ass'n Directory. a.

Meetings/Conferences:

Nat'l Interscholastic Swimming Coaches Ass'n *(1934)*
Glenbrook South High School
4000 W. Lake Ave.
Glenview, IL 60025
Tel: (847)486-4426   *Fax:* (847)486-4428
E-Mail: dallen@glenbrook.k12.il.us
Web Site:
      http://wwww.glenbrook.k12.il.us/gbsath/nisca.html
Members: 1,500 individuals
Secretary: Donald R. Allen

Historical Note
NISCA represents interscholastic swimming, driving and water polo coaches.

Publications:
High School Academic All-America. a.
High School Diving All-America. a.
High School Swimming All-America. a.
High School Water Polo All-America. a.
NISCA Journal. bi-m. adv.
NISCA Newsletter. q. adv.

Nat'l Interstate Council of State Boards of Cosmetology *(1936)*
7 South School Ave.
Fayetteville, AR 72701
Tel: (501)521-2615   *Fax:* (501)521-4378
Members: 250 individuals, 50 boards
Annual Budget: $50-100,000

President: Ray Gambrell

Historical Note
Merger (1956) of Nat'l Council of State Boards of Cosmetology and Interstate Council of State Boards of Cosmetology. Persons commissioned by state governments to administer cosmetology laws and examine applicants for cosmetology licenses.

Publications:
NIC Bulletin. bi-m.
NIC Directory. a.

Meetings/Conferences:

Nat'l Intramural-Recreational Sports Ass'n *(1950)*
4185 S.W. Research Way
Corvallis, OR 97333-1067
Tel: (541)766-8211   *Fax:* (541)766-8284
E-Mail: nirsa@nirsa.org
Web Site: http://nirsa.org
Members: 2,500 individuals, 700 institutions
Staff: 15
Annual Budget: $1-2,000,000
Exec. Director: Kent J. Blumenthal
Communications Administrator: Todd M. Cotton
Exposition Manager: Carole Holbrook
Education Director: Joell Brown

Historical Note
Formerly (1973) Nat'l Intramural Ass'n. NIRSA members include recreational sports professionals, institutions, and students. Promotes the advancement of recreational sports programs and the professional growth of individuals. Membership: $95/year (individual).

Publications:
Flag & Touch Football Rules & Official's Manual. bien. adv.
NIRSA Journal. 3/yr. adv.
NIRSA Newsletter. q.
NIRSA Proceedings. a.
Recreational Sports Directory. a.

Meetings/Conferences:
Annual Meetings: April
1999 - Milwaukee, WI(Convention Center)/April 16-20/1800

Nat'l Investment Company Service Ass'n *(1962)*
36 Washington St., Suite 70
Wellesley Hills, MA 02181-1904
Tel: (617)277-1855   *Fax:* (617)277-1588
Web Site: http://nicsa.org
Members: 380 firms
Staff: 7
Annual Budget: $1-2,000,000
President: Robert L. Goldberg
Marketing and Communications Manager: Ellen Weintraub
Operations and Meetings Manager: Elizabeth Twombly

Historical Note
NICSA works to facilitate and promote leadership and innovation within the operations sector of the mutual fund industry. Membership: $1,000/year.

Publications:
Inside NICSA. q.
Membership Directory. a.
Surveys and White Papers. irreg.

Meetings/Conferences:
1999 - Tarpon Springs, FL(Westin Innisbrook)/Feb. 20-24
2000 - Tarpon Springs, FL(Westin Innisbrook)/Feb. 12-16

Nat'l Investor Relations Institute *(1969)*
8045 Leesburg Pike, Suite 600
Vienna, VA 22182
Tel: (703)506-3570   *Fax:* (703)506-3571
Web Site: http://www.niri.com
Members: 3,000 individuals
Staff: 10
Annual Budget: $1-2,000,000
President and C.E.O.: Louis M. Thompson, Jr.
V. President, Operations/External Affairs: Beth Carty
Director, Administration and Treasurer: Carolyn R. Wheatly
V. President, Member Services: Susan Nunn

Historical Note
A professional association of corporate officers and investor relations consultants. Membership: $375/year.

Publications:
Director of Meeting Information. a.
Emerging Trends in Investor Relations. trien.
Investor Relations Job Descriptions. a.
Investor Relations Resource Guide. a.
Investor Relations Update. m.
IR Bibliography. irreg.
Legislative Bulletin. irreg.
Practice Guides. irreg.
Who's Who in Investor Relations. a.

Meetings/Conferences:
Annual Meetings: Spring

Nat'l Iridology Research Ass'n *(1982)*
P.O. Box 31013
Seattle, WA 98103
Tel: (206)282-6604   *Fax:* (206)282-9631
Toll Free: (888)682 - 2208
President: William Caradonna

Historical Note
Promotes the art and science of iridology, providing for the exchange of research and information leading to the development of a national standard for the industry.

Publications:
Iridology Review.
NIRA News Newsletter.

Nat'l Judges Ass'n *(1979)*
9591 Hwy. 96
Westcliffe, CO 81252

Tel: (719)783-3072   *Fax:* (719)783-9362
Toll Free: (888)366 - 3652
Members: 400 individuals
Staff: 1
Annual Budget: $10-25,000
Exec. Director/Treasurer: Harold D. Taylor

Historical Note
Incorporated in Nevada, NJA members are non-lawyer judges and judicial officers. Works to publicize the contributions of non-lawyer judges to the court system, fosters the exchange of information among members, and encourages further education to enhance members' judicial performance. Conducts a judicial training program. Membership: $35-50/year, based on salary.

Publications:
The Gavel. q. adv.

Meetings/Conferences:
Annual Meetings: Spring/200
1999 - St. Johnsbury, VT
2000 - Reno, NV

Nat'l Juice Products Ass'n *(1957)*
400 N. Tampa St.
PO Box 1531
Tampa, FL 33601-1531
Tel: (813)273-6572   *Fax:* (813)273-4396
Web Site: http://www.njpa.com
Members: 91 regular, 63 associates
Staff: 1
Annual Budget: $250-500,000
Exec. Director: David C.G. Kerr
Exec. Secretary: Tammy G. Andis

Historical Note
Established by a group of citrus juice processors in Dallas, TX in Jan., 1957 as the Nat'l Ass'n of Citrus Juice Processors and incorporated in Florida in June of that year; became the Nat'l Orange Juice Ass'n in 1960; and assumed its present name in 1966. Its objectives are the promulgation of uniform standards and uniform advertising and labeling practices; the promotion of high standards of quality; liaison between Federal and state regulatory agencies; and promotion of research, technology and distribution of chilled fruit juices. Membership: $3,500/year.

Publications:
Membership Directory. a.
Newsletter. 3/month. adv.

Meetings/Conferences:
Annual Meetings: Spring/400
1999 - Pebble Beach, CA(Inn at Spanish Bay)/May 3-9/400

Nat'l Junior College Athletic Ass'n *(1938)*
P.O. Box 7305
Colorado Springs, CO 80933-7305
Tel: (719)590-9788   *Fax:* (719)590-7324
E-Mail: njcaa@ix.netcom.com
Web Site: http://www.njcaa.org
Members: 540 junior colleges
Staff: 7
Annual Budget: $500-1,000,000
Exec. Director: George E. Killian

Historical Note
NJCAA members are two year institutions recognized by the American Ass'n of Community and Junior Colleges.

Publications:
Eligibility Rules of NJCAA. a.
Juco Review Magazine. 9/yr. adv.
NJCAA Handbook & Casebook. a. adv.

Meetings/Conferences:
Annual Meetings: March-April

Nat'l Juvenile Court Services Ass'n *(1970)*
1041 North Virginia St., 3rd Floor
P.O. Box 8970
Reno, NV 89557-8970
Tel: (702)784-6012   *Fax:* (702)784-6628
Members: 600 individuals
Staff: 2
Annual Budget: $10-25,000
Staff Liason: David Gamble

Historical Note
Formed in 1970 and chartered in 1972, NJCSA members are individuals operating in the juvenile justice systems of the United States and Canada. In 1992 NJCSA absorbed the membership from the Internat'l Conference of Administrators of Residential Agencies. Administrative support provided by Nat'l Council of Juvenile and Family Court Judges (same address). Membership: $30-92/year (individual); $138-200(organization).

Publications:
Rapport Newsletter. q. adv.

Meetings/Conferences:
Semi-annual Meetings: Spring and Summer
1999 - Las Vegas, NV(Tropicana)/May 23-26/300
2000 - Tucson, AZ/300
2001 - Norfolk, VA(Waterside Marriott)/300

Nat'l Juvenile Detention Ass'n *(1968)*
Eastern Kentucky University
521 Lancaster Ave.
Richmond, KY 40475-3127
Tel: (606)622-6259   *Fax:* (606)622-2333
E-Mail: njdadeku@aol.com
Members: 600 individuals
Staff: 6
Annual Budget: $50-100,000
Exec. Director: Earl Dunlap
Dir., Conferences & Communications: Sherry L. Scott
Director, Finance: Mary Frances Johnson
Asst. Exec. Director: Michael A. Jones

Historical Note
An affiliate of the Amercian Correctional Ass'n, NJDA was incorporated in Illinois in 1971. Members include professionals

from detention facilities, the justice system, detention education, and other programs and services related to promoting adequate detention services for juveniles. NJDA reviews standards and practices, encourages training programs for detention staffs, conducts research, and provides a forum for the exchange of ideas between members as well as with other organizations interested in the field of juvenile detention. Membership: $20-250/year.

Publications:
Directory.
Journal for Juvenile Justice and Detention Services. bi-a. adv.
NJDA News. q. adv.

Meetings/Conferences:
Semi-Annual Meetings: June and October/300-500

Nat'l Kerosene Heater Ass'n (1981)
1816 Old Natchez Trace
Franklin, TN 37069-4785
Tel: (615)790-0770   *Fax:* (615)790-6700
E-Mail: thomsmyth@aol.com
Members: 6 companies
Staff: 5
Annual Budget: $250-500,000
General Counsel: J. Thomas Smith

Historical Note
Members are individuals, partnerships and corporations involved in the manufacturing and marketing of kerosene heaters.

Publications:
Bulletins. irreg.

Meetings/Conferences:
Semi-Annual Meetings: usually in greater New York City.

Nat'l Kidney Foundation (1950)
30 East 33rd St., 11th Floor
New York, NY 10016
Tel: (212)889-2210   *Fax:* (212)689-9261
Toll Free: (800)622 - 9010
Web Site: http://www.kidney.org
Members: 52 affiliates, 200 chapters
Staff: 36
Annual Budget: $25-50,000,000
Exec. Director: John Davis

Historical Note
The Nat'l Kidney Foundation, Inc. is the major voluntary health agency seeking the total answer to diseases of the kidney and urinary tract through research, patient serviies, nation-wide organ donor program, professional education and public information. Physician and Scientist Members may join one or more NKF Scientific Councils (Diabetic Kidney Disease, Dialysis, Glomerulonephritis, Hypertension, Pediatric Nephrology and Urology, Polycystic Kidney Disease, Transplantation, and Urology). Professional Members may join one of three NKF Professional Councils (Nephrology Nurses and Technicians, Nephrology Social Workers, or Renal Nutrition). Formerly (1958) Nat'l Nephrosis Foundation and (1964) Nat'l Kidney Disease Foundation. Has an annual budget of over $35 million. Membership: $155/year (physician/scientist); $55/year (professional).

Publications:
Advances in Renal Replacement Therapy Journal.
American Journal of Kidney Diseases. q.
Council of Nephrology Social Workers Newsletters. q.
For Those Who Give - Grieve. q.
Journal of Renal Nutrition. q.
NKF Family Focus. q.
Parent Connection. q.
Perspectives: Journal of the Council of Nephrology Social
       Workers. a.
Straight Talk. q.
The Kidney. m.
Transplant Chronicles. q.

Meetings/Conferences:
Annual Meetings: Late Fall

Nat'l Kitchen and Bath Ass'n (1963)
687 Willow Grove St.
Hackettstown, NJ 07840
Tel: (908)852-0033   *Fax:* (908)852-1695
Members: 6,600 companies
Staff: 35
Annual Budget: $5-10,000,000
C.O.O.: Cecelia Balazs
Manager, Public Relations and Communications: Rhonda Moritz
Dir., Conferences: Linda Schonwald
Director, Planning and Research: Henrianne Wakefield
Director, Professional Programs: John S. Spitz, CKD, CBD,N
Director, Marketing and Membership: Larry Spangler

Historical Note
Kitchen equipment manufacturers, suppliers, wholesalers, retail dealers, distributors and designers. Awards the designations Certified Kitchen Designer (CKD), Certified Bath Designer (CBD), and Certified Kitchen and Bath Installer. Formerly (1982) the American Institute of Kitchen Dealers. Membership: $300/year.

Publications:
Directory. a.
Newsletter. m.
Perspectives. m. adv.

Meetings/Conferences:
1999 – Orlando, FL/April 16-18

Nat'l Knitwear and Sportswear Ass'n (1918)
386 Park Ave. South
New York, NY 10016-8897
Tel: (212)683-7520   *Fax:* (212)532-0766
Web Site: http://www.nksapop.internet.net
Members: 600 manufacturers
Staff: 20
Annual Budget: $100-250,000
Exec. Director: Seth M. Bodner

Historical Note
Until 1980 known as the Nat'l Knitted Outerwear Ass'n.

Publications:
American Sportswear & Knitting Times. m.
AW Buyers Guide. a.

Meetings/Conferences:
Annual Meetings: November

Nat'l Labor Relations Board Professional Ass'n (1962)
1099 14th St., N.W., Suite 8824
Washington, DC 20570
Tel: (202)273-3771   *Fax:* (202)273-4283
Members: 160 individuals
Annual Budget: $10-25,000
President: Norman Graber
V. President: David Seddelmeyer

Historical Note
Independent union of lawyers working for the N.L.R.B. in Washington. In additon to representing attorneys, the association also represents law clerks and law students employed by the Board's Division of Administrative Law Judges. Has no headquarters or paid staff. Officers are elected annually. Membership: $78/year.

Nat'l Lamb Feeders Ass'n (1950)
P.O. Box 238
Bristol, IL 60512-0238
Tel: (630)553-5512
Members: 300 individuals
Staff: 1
Annual Budget: $50-100,000
Treasurer: Howard Wyman

Publications:
Newsletter. bi-m.

Meetings/Conferences:
Semi-annual meetings: February and July
1999 – San Diego, CA(Havalei)/Jan. 21-24/150

Nat'l Land Improvement Contractors of America (1952)
3060 Ogden Ave.
Lisle, IL 60532
Tel: (630)548-1984
Members: 2,500 companies
Staff: 3
Annual Budget: $500-1,000,000
Exec. V. President: Wayne Maresch

Historical Note
Dedicated to the professional conservation of soil and clean water. Membership fee varies by state. Has 30 state chapters.

Publications:
Directory/Buyers Guide. a. adv.
LICA News. bi-m. adv.

Meetings/Conferences:
1999 – San Antonio, TX/Feb. 17-20
2000 – Savannah, GA

Nat'l Landscape Ass'n

Historical Note
A division of American Nursery and Landscape Ass'n.

Nat'l Law Firm Marketing Ass'n (1986)
401 N. Michigan Ave.
Chicago, IL 60611
Tel: (312)245-1592   *Fax:* (312)321-5194
Web Site: http://www.legalmarketing.org
Members: 1000 individuals
Annual Budget: $500-1,000,000
Exec. Director: Kathleen M. Bell, CAE

Historical Note
Formerly the Nat'l Ass'n of Law Firm Marketing Administrators; assumed its present name in 1990. NALFMA serves the needs and maintains professional standards for those involved in marketing for the legal profession. Membership: $240/year, plus $100 initiation fee.

Publications:
Law Marketing Exchange. m. adv.
Membership Directory.

Meetings/Conferences:
1999 – Miami, FL(Hotel InterContinental)/Apr. 14-17

Nat'l Lawn and Garden Distributors Ass'n

Historical Note
Became (1997) Lawn and Garden Marketing and Distribution Ass'n.

Nat'l Lawyers Guild (1937)
126 University Place
New York, NY 10003
Tel: (212)627-2656   *Fax:* (212)627-2404
E-Mail: nlgno@igc.apc.org
Members: 6,000 individuals
Staff: 5
Annual Budget: $250-500,000
President: Karen Jo Koonan
Director, Membership: Kevi Brannery

Historical Note
Funded as a progressive, anti-racist alternative to the American Bar Association. The Guild is open to lawyers, law students, legal workers and jailhouse lawyers, supporting the movement for social change in the U.S. Progressive membership fee schedule.

Publications:
Guild Notes. q. adv.
Guild Practitioner. q.
Referral Directory. a.

Meetings/Conferences:
Annual Meetings: late Summer-Fall
1999 – San Francisco, CA

Nat'l Lead Burning Ass'n (1945)

c/o New England Lead Burning Co. - NELCO
98 Baldwin Ave., Box 607
Woburn, MA 01801
Tel: (781)933-1940   *Fax:* (781)933-4763
Members: 6 companies
Annual Budget: under $10,000
President: Karl E. Weiss

Historical Note
Fabricators of lead-lined equipment for handling corrosive chemicals and radiation shielding. Primarily exists to negotiate labor agreements on behalf of member companies.

Meetings/Conferences:
Annual Meetings: New York, NY in Spring
1999 – Washington, DC

Nat'l League for Nursing (1952)
61 Broadway
New York, NY 10014
Tel: (212)363-5555   *Fax:* (212)812-0393
Toll Free: (800)669 - 9656
Web Site: http://www.nln.org
Members: 18,000 individuals, 1,569 organizations
Staff: 100
Annual Budget: $10-25,000,000
V. President, Finance and Administration: Steve Cerane
V. President, Communications: Glenn Peterson
Director, Web Site: Javier Broch

Historical Note
Founded and incorporated in Washington, DC in 1952 as a merger of the Nat'l League of Nursing Education, Nat'l Organization for Public Health Nursing, Ass'n of Collegiate Schools of Nursing, Joint Committee on Practical Nurses and Auxiliary Workers in Nursing, Services, Joint Committee on Careers in Nursing, Nat'l Committee for the Improvement of Nursing Services, and the Nat'l Nursing Accrediting Service. Has an annual budget of approximately $15 million. Membership: $110/year (individual), $65/year (graduate), $35/year (student).

Publications:
Connections. q.
Nursing and Health Care. m. adv.
Open Mind. q.

Meetings/Conferences:
Biennial Meetings: Odd years/4,000
1999 – Miami, FL

Nat'l League of American Pen Women (1897)
1300 17th St., N.W.
Washington, DC 20036-1973
Tel: (202)785-1997   *Fax:* (202)452-6868
Web Site: http://members.aol.com/penwomen/pen.htm
Members: 5,000 individuals
Staff: 2
Annual Budget: $100-250,000
President: Judith LaFourest

Historical Note
Organized June 26, 1897 in Washington, DC as the League of American Pen Women; assumed its present name and was incorporated in 1926. Promotes the development of the creative talents of professional women artists, writers, dramatists, lecturers and composers. Membership: $30/year (individual).

Publications:
Roster for Membership and Bylaws. bien.
The Pen Woman. bi-m. adv.

Meetings/Conferences:
Biennial Meetings: Even years

Nat'l League of Cities (1924)
1301 Pennsylvania Ave., N.W., Suite 550
Washington, DC 20004-1701
Tel: (202)626-3000   *Fax:* (202)626-3043
E-Mail: borut@nlc.org
Web Site: http://www.nlc.org
Members: 1,400 municipalities, 49 leagues
Staff: 95
Annual Budget: $10-25,000,000
Exec. Director: Donald J. Borut
Director, Public Affairs: Jeff Fletcher
Director, Policy and Federal Relations: Frank Shafroth
Director, Conference Planning/Management: Fonda Richardson
Director, Education/Information Resource: Sharon Anderson
Director, Finance: Carlsen Griffith
Dep. Exec. Director: Christine Becker
Director, Human Resources: Elisabeth McClain
Director, Research: Bill Barnes

Historical Note
Known until 1964 as the American Municipal Ass'n, the Nat'l League of Cities was founded in 1924 by reform-minded state municipal leagues to represent the interests of its members to the federal and state governments. Has an annual budget of approximately $11 million. Membership: $725-60,000/year (city), based on city population.

Publications:
Nation's Cities Weekly. w. adv.

Meetings/Conferences:
Annual Meetings: Winter - Annual Congress, Business Meeting,
      and Exhibition Spring - Annual Congressional
      Conference
1999 – Los Angeles, CA/Nov. 30-Dec. 4
2000 – Boston, MA/Dec. 5-9
2001 – Atlanta, GA/Nov. 27-Dec. 1
2002 – Salt Lake City, UT/Dec. 3-7

Nat'l League of Postmasters of the U.S. (1887)
1023 N. Royal St.
Alexandria, VA 22314-1569
Tel: (703)548-5922   *Fax:* (703)836-8937
Toll Free: (800)544 - 7111
Members: 30,000 individuals
Staff: 85
Annual Budget: $2-5,000,000

President: Joseph W. Cinadr
Director, Conventions & Meetings: Barbara Veech
Exec. Director and Controller: Richard A. Weinberg
Director, League Administration: Brenda Tanner
Director, Information Systems: Frank Auqustosky

Historical Note
*Organized in Wasington, DC December 13-15, 1887 by about 200
Third and Fourth Class Postmasters to represent the interests of
professional postmasters. Sponsor of Postmasters Benefit Plan, a
health insurance program operated under the Federal Employees
Health Benefits Program. Membership fee varies according to level
of Postmaster.*

Publications:
Postmasters Advocate.
Postmasters Advocate Express.

Meetings/Conferences:
1999 – Tucson, AZ
2000 – New Orleans, LA/1600

Nat'l League of Professional Baseball Clubs *(1876)*
350 Park Ave., 18th Floor
New York, NY   10022
Tel: (212)339-7700   *Fax:* (212)935-5069
Members: 16 clubs
Staff: 10
Annual Budget: $2-5,000,000
President: Leonard Coleman

Historical Note
*Established February 2, 1876 at the Grand Central Hotel in New
York City.*

Publications:
Green Book. a.

Nat'l Leased Housing Ass'n *(1972)*
1300 19th St., N.W., Suite 410
Washington, DC   20036
Tel: (202)785-8888   *Fax:* (202)785-2008
Web Site: http://www.worldweb.net/~hudnlha
Members: 575 companies and individuals
Staff: 5
Annual Budget: $250-500,000
Exec. Director: Denise Muha
Meeting Coordinator: Cynthia Melton-Bitterman

Historical Note
*Founded by developers and financers of federally funded housing
under the government's Section 8 rent subsidy program for the
poor. With the demise of the Section 8 new
construction/substantial rehabilitation program, NLHA has
broadened its purview to all government related rental housing
programs. Membership: $300-550/year (organization).*

Publications:
Membership Directory. a.
NLHA Bulletin. m.

Meetings/Conferences:
1999 – Washington, DC/June 16-18

Nat'l Legal Aid and Defender Ass'n *(1911)*
1625 K St., N.W., Suite 800
Washington, DC   20006-1604
Tel: (202)452-0620   *Fax:* (202)872-1031
E-Mail: info@nlada.org
Web Site: http://www.nlada.org
Members: 1,200 individuals, 3,500 organizations and
         associates
Staff: 25
Annual Budget: $1-2,000,000
Exec. Director: Clinton Lyons
Manager, Membership/Training: Steven C. Kemp

Historical Note
*Organized in 1911 by fifteen legal assistance programs as the Nat'l
Alliance of Legal Aid Socs., it became the Nat'l Ass'n of Legal Aid
Organizations in 1949 and assumed its present name in 1958. The
only private, non-profit organization devoting all its resources to
the support and development of quality legal assistance to the poor.
Membership: $60/year (individual); .137%/budget/year
(organization).*

Publications:
Capital Report. bi-m.
Cornerstone. q. adv.
Directory of Legal Aid and Defender Services. bien.
Indigent Defense. 6x/year.

Meetings/Conferences:
Annual Meetings: Fall/800

Nat'l Lesbian and Gay Journalists Ass'n
1718 M St., N.W., Suite 245
Washington, DC   20036
Tel: (202)588-9888   *Fax:* (202)588-1818
E-Mail: nlga@aol.com
Web Site: http://www.nlgja.org
Members: 1,200 individuals
Annual Budget: $500-1,000,000
Exec. Director: Michael L. Frederickson

Historical Note
Membership : $55/year (individual); $750/year (organization)

Publications:
Alternatives. q. adv.

Meetings/Conferences:

Nat'l Lesbian and Gay Lawyers Ass'n
P.O. Box 57225
Washington, DC   20036
Tel: (202)543-7408
Co-Chair: Natalie Butto

Nat'l Librarians Ass'n *(1975)*
Historical Note
Organization defunct in 1997.

Nat'l Licensed Beverage Ass'n *(1950)*
20 S. Quaker Ln., #230
Alexandria, VA   22314
Tel: (703)751-9730   *Fax:* (703)751-9448
Toll Free: (800)441 - 9894
E-Mail: nlba@msn.com
Web Site: http://www.nlba.org
Members: 16,000 individuals
Staff: 4
Annual Budget: $500-1,000,000
Exec. Director: Debra A. Leach
Director, Communications: Amy Russ
Director, Membership: Tracy Reynolds

Historical Note
*NLBA represents the interests of licensed beverage retailers,
including owners of bars, restaurants, taverns adn liquor stores.*

Publications:
NLBA Industry Directory. a.
NLBA News. q.
NLBA Report. m.

Meetings/Conferences:
Annual Meetings: January
1999 – Las Vegas, NV(Monte Carlo Resort)/Jan. 17-21

Nat'l Lime Ass'n *(1902)*
200 N. Glebe Road, Suite 800
Arlington, VA   22203-3728
Tel: (703)243-5463   *Fax:* (703)243-5489
E-Mail: natlime@aol.com
Web Site: http://www.lime.org
Members: 24 manufacturers
Staff: 8
Annual Budget: $500-1,000,000
Exec. Director: Arline Seeger
Director, Government Affairs: Hunter Prillaman
Director, Regulatory Issues: Eric Males

Historical Note
*Members are manfacturers of quicklime and hydrated lime for
environmental, industrial, construction, and other purposes.*

Publications:
Lime-Lites. q.

Meetings/Conferences:

Nat'l Limousine Ass'n *(1985)*
901 N. Pitt St., Suite 220
Alexandria, VA   22314-1536
Tel: (703)838-2933   *Fax:* (703)838-2936
Members: 800 individuals
Staff: 3
Annual Budget: $100-250,000
Exec. Director: Wayne J. Smith

Historical Note
Members are manufacturers, owners and operators of limousines.

Publications:
Limo Scene. m.
Membership Directory. a.

Meetings/Conferences:

Nat'l Lincoln Sheep Breeders Ass'n *(1889)*
R.R. #6, Box 24
Decatur, IL   62521
Tel: (217)864-3601
Members: 75 individuals
Staff: 1
Annual Budget: under $10,000
Secretary: Teresa M. Kruse

Historical Note
*Breeders and fanciers of Lincoln sheep. Membership: $10/year, plus
$10 initiation fee.*

Nat'l Litigation Support Services Ass'n *(1991)*
111 E. Wacker Dr., Suite 990
Chicago, IL   60601
Tel: (312)729-9900   *Fax:* (312)729-9800
Toll Free: (800)869 - 0491
E-Mail: info@pencormazur.com
Web Site: http://www.nlssa.com
Members: 36 firms
Staff: 10
Exec. Director: George A. Buckley, Jr., CAE

Historical Note
*NLSSA is a not-for-profit and business valuation of CPA firms that
provide litigation support services. Member firms are accepted on a
territorial exclusive basis.*

Publications:
Members Bulletin. q.
The Expert. q.

Meetings/Conferences:
1999 – New Orleans, LA/Jan. 20-22

Nat'l Live Stock and Meat Board *(1922)*
Historical Note
*The Meat Board consolidated with the Nat'l Cattlemen's Ass'n to
form a new organization, the Nat'l Cattlemen's Beef Ass'n, in early
1996.*

Nat'l Live Stock Producers Ass'n *(1922)*
660 Southpointe Court, Suite 314
Colorado Springs, CO   80906-3874
Tel: (719)538-8843   *Fax:* (719)538-8847
Web Site: http://www.nlpa.org
Members: 28,392 livestock producers
Staff: 3
Annual Budget: $250-500,000
President and C.E.O.: Scott Stewart

Historical Note
*Formerly (1943) Nat'l Live Stock Marketing Ass'n. A federation of
cooperative livestock marketing agencies and regional credit
corporations.*

Publications:
Annual Report. a.
Yearbook. a.

Meetings/Conferences:
Annual Meetings: Fourth Tuesday in March.

Nat'l Locksmith Suppliers Ass'n
Historical Note
Became (1997) Security Hardware Distributors Ass'n.

Nat'l Lubricating Grease Institute *(1933)*
4635 Wyandotte St.
Kansas City, MO   64112-1542
Tel: (816)931-9480   *Fax:* (816)753-5026
Web Site: http://www.nlgi.org
Members: 280 companies
Staff: 2
Annual Budget: $250-500,000
General Manager: Chuck Hichcock

Historical Note
*Incorporated as the Nat'l Ass'n of Lubricating Grease
Manufacturers. Assumed its present name in 1937. Members are
companies who manufacture and market all types of lubricating
greases, additive or equipment suppliers, and research and
educational groups whose interests are primarily technical.*

Publications:
NLGI Spokesman. m. adv.

Meetings/Conferences:
Annual Meetings: Fall
1999 – Tucson, AZ(El Conquistador)/Oct. 24-27/500

Nat'l Luggage Dealers Ass'n *(1925)*
3338 Westlake Ave.
Glenview, IL   60025
Tel: (847)998-6869   *Fax:* (847)998-6884
Members: 75 individuals
Staff: 13
Annual Budget: $500-1,000,000
Exec. Administrator: Marrilyn Murray

Historical Note
*Members are retailers of luggage, leather goods, gifts and handbags
with over 300 stores nationally. NLDA acts as a purchasing office
for membership. Membership fee based on retail volume.*

Publications:
Retail Christmas Catalogue. a.

Meetings/Conferences:
Semi-annual Meetings: March and June

Nat'l Lumber and Building Material Dealers Ass'n *(1916)*
40 Ivy St. SE
Washington, DC   20003-4006
Tel: (202)547-2230   *Fax:* (202)547-7640
Web Site: http://www.dealers.org
Members: 9,000 companies
Staff: 8
Annual Budget: $1-2,000,000
President: Gary W. Donnelly, CAE
Director, Public Affairs: Vicki L. Worden
V. President, Government Affairs: Allynn L. Howe
Director, Member Services: JoAnn Buckley

Historical Note
*Formerly the Nat'l Retail Lumber Dealers Ass'n, it absorbed the
Lumber Dealers Research Council (founded in 1966). Supports the
Lumber Dealers Political Action Committee (LUDPAC).*

Publications:
Building Material Dealer Newsletter. m. adv.
Wood-Fax. w.

Meetings/Conferences:
Annual Meetings: Fall
1999 – Hilton Head, SC(Hyatt)/Oct. 13-16

Nat'l Machine Embellishment Instructors and Artists *(1983)*
P.O. Box 46127
Seattle, WA   98146-0127
Tel: (206)763-0428
Members: 200 individuals
Annual Budget: $50-100,000
President: Jeanne Martenson

Historical Note
*Formerly (1994) Nat'l Machine Embroidery Instructors Ass'n.
NMEIA was established to provide a meeting ground for sewing
machine art instructors, to upgrade sewing art through education
and communication, to conduct educational workshops and
seminars and to encourage high ethical standards and a
professional approach. Membership: $30/year, plus Initiation fee.*

Publications:
Machine Artist's Magazine. q. adv.

Meetings/Conferences:
Annual Meetings: Summer
1999 – Oklahoma City, OK(Clarion Hotel & Convention
Center)/July 13-20

Nat'l Magazine and Film Carriers *(1932)*
Historical Note
*Name changed to Nat'l Magazine, Book, and Film Carriers
Conference in 1996.*

Nat'l Magazine, Book, and Film Carriers Conference *(1932)*
2200 Mill Road
Alexandria, VA   22314

Tel: (703)838-7985   *Fax:* (703)519-1866
Members: 46 companies
Staff: 2
Annual Budget: $50-100,000
Exec. Director: Kent Van Amburg
Historical Note
Founded as Nat'l Film Carriers Corporation, it became affiliated with American Trucking Ass'ns as the Film Carriers Conference in 1935. Merged in 1969 with the Air Freight Motor Carriers Conference (1964) and became the Nat'l Film Carriers as part of the Film, Air and Package Carriers Conference, which provides administrative support. Assumed its present name in 1992. Membership includes film carriers, and truckers of magazines and newspapers. Membership fee: based on annual gross revenue.
Meetings/Conferences:
Annual Meetings: May

Nat'l Mail Order Ass'n *(1972)*
2807 Polk St., N.E.
Minneapolis, MN 55418-2954
Tel: (612)788-1673   *Fax:* (612)788-1147
E-Mail: schulte@nmoa.org
Web Site: http://www.nmoa.org
Annual Budget: $100-250,000
Chief Manager: John Schulte
Director, Membership: Carole Williams
Director, Publications: George Knotek
Historical Note
Founded to help small-to-midsize firms in mail order and other direct marketing areas. Membership: $99/year (individual); $100-$999 (organization).
Publications:
Mail Order Digest. m.
NMOA Contact Directory. a. adv.
Washington Newsletter. m.

Nat'l Management Ass'n *(1925)*
2210 Arbor Blvd.
Dayton, OH 45439
Tel: (937)294-0421   *Fax:* (937)294-2374
E-Mail: sue@nma1.org
Web Site: http://www.nma.org
Members: 35,000 individuals
Staff: 18
Annual Budget: $2-5,000,000
President: K. Stephen Bailey
V. President: Sue Kappeler
V. President: Douglas Shaw
V. President: Karen Tobias
Historical Note
Formerly (1956) Nat'l Ass'n of Foremen. Members are middle level and supervisory management personnel united to professionalize management and promote American competitive enterprise. Membership: $35/year (individual), $30/year (chapter member).
Publications:
Manage. q. adv.
Meetings/Conferences:
Annual Meetings: Fall
1999 – San Diego, CA

Nat'l Marine Bankers Ass'n *(1979)*
200 E. Randolph Drive, Suite 5100
Chicago, IL 60601-6436
Tel: (312)946-6250
Members: 65 companies
Annual Budget: $25-50,000
Exec. Director: Gregory Proteau
Historical Note
Any bank, savings institution or credit union which holds marine loans directly in its portfolio is elighile for membership. Membership: $325/year, plus $100 initiation fee.
Publications:
The Business of Pleasure Boats. q.
Meetings/Conferences:
Annual Meetings: Fall

Nat'l Marine Distributors Ass'n *(1965)*
1810 S. Rittenhouse Sq., Suite 411
Philadelphia, PA 19103
Tel: (215)735-3303
Members: 100 wholesalers
Staff: 2
Annual Budget: $100-250,000
Exec. Director: Elizabeth A. Kelly
Historical Note
Wholesalers of marine accessories and hardware.
Publications:
The Journal. bi-m.
Meetings/Conferences:
Annual Meetings: Spring

Nat'l Marine Educators Ass'n *(1976)*
P.O. Box 1470
Ocean Springs, MS 39566-1470
Tel: (601)374-7557
Web Site: http://www.marine-ed.org
Members: 1,200 individuals
Staff: 1
Annual Budget: $25-50,000
Contact: Tina Shoemaker
Historical Note
Members are interested in all types of marine education at K-12 and college levels as well as continuing education and informal instruction in the marine environment. The association's primary goal is to promote a "marine literate" society. Membership: $40/year.
Publications:
Current. q. adv.

NMEA News. q.
Meetings/Conferences:
Annual Meetings: July-August
1999 – Charleston, SC/Aug. 6-11

Nat'l Marine Electronics Ass'n *(1957)*
P.O. Box 3435
New Bern, NC 28564-3435
Tel: (252)638-2626   *Fax:* (252)638-4885
E-Mail: nmea@coastalnet.com
Web Site: http://www.nmea.org/
Members: 350 companies
Staff: 2
Annual Budget: $250-500,000
Exec. Director: Cindy G. Ensley
Historical Note
A national trade association for manufacturers and dealer/distributors in the marine electronics industry. Supports education, industry standards and government regulations for the industry and acts as an information clearinghouse. Membership: $100/year (individual); $200-$800/year (organization/company).
Publications:
Marine Electronics Journal. bi-m. adv.
NMEA News Newsletter. bi-m.
Meetings/Conferences:

Nat'l Marine Engineers Beneficial Ass'n *(1875)*
1150 17th St., N.W., Suite 700
Washington, DC 20036
Tel: (202)466-7060   *Fax:* (202)872-0912
Members: 50,000 individuals
Staff: 11
Annual Budget: $5-10,000,000
General Counsel: Larry Brundick
President: Rene Lioeanjai
Historical Note
NMU was founded May 3, 1937 in New York City and affiliated with the AFL-CIO. MEBA/NMU is the product of a merger of Marine Engineers Beneficial Ass'n (founded 1875) with Nat'l Maritime Union of America in 1988. Professional Airways Systems Specialists is a division of MEBA/NMU. Has a budget of about $7 million.
Publications:
American Marine Engineer. q.
ITPE News. m.
Marine Journal. q.
NMU Government Operations News. q.
The NMU Pilot. m.

Nat'l Marine Manufacturers Ass'n *(1979)*
200 E. Randolph Drive, Suite 5100
Chicago, IL 60601-6436
Tel: (312)946-6200   *Fax:* (312)946-0388
Members: 1,200 companies
Staff: 40
Annual Budget: $500-1,000,000
President: Jeffrey W. Napier
C.F.O.: Robert E. Harris
Membership Development Director: Tammy Rossow
Historical Note
Manufacturers of pleasure boats, boating supplies and marine engines. Formed by the merger of Boating Industry Ass'ns and the Nat'l Ass'n of Engine and Boat Manufacturers, Inc., NMMA is now an umbrella support organization for three affiliates - the Nat'l Ass'n of Marine Products and Services, the Ass'n of Marine Engine Manufacturers and the Nat'l Ass'n of Boat Manufacturers. The Nat'l Sailing Industry Ass'n is a promotional council within NMMA. Sponsors the Nat'l Marine Manufacturers Ass'n Political Action Committee. Maintains New York, Miami, and Washington, DC offices.
Publications:
Boating News. w. adv.
Inter/port. w.
Meetings/Conferences:
Annual Meetings: Fall

Nat'l Marine Representatives Ass'n *(1960)*
P.O. Box 969
Camden, TN 38320-0969
Tel: (901)584-0203   *Fax:* (901)584-0420
E-Mail: NMRA95@aol.com
Web Site: http://www.nmra.com
Members: 560 individuals
Staff: 1
Annual Budget: $50-100,000
Exec. Director: David McCloskey
Historical Note
Members are independent boat and marine accessory sales representatives. Membership: $275/year, plus $100 initiation fee (individual); $60/year, plus $15 initiation fee (associate); $100/year (manufacturer affiliates).
Publications:
NMRA Association Information. bi-m.
NMRA Membership Directory. a. adv.
Tidings. q. adv.
Meetings/Conferences:
Annual Meetings: With International Marine Trades Exhibit & Conference in Chicago, IL/ Fall

Nat'l Maritime Alliance *(1988)*
Historical Note
Adress unknown in 1997.

Nat'l Marrow Donor Program *(1986)*
3433 Broadway St., N.E., Suite 500
Minneapolis, MN 55413
Tel: (612)627-5800   *Fax:* (612)627-8125
Toll Free: (800)526 - 7809
E-Mail: chowe@nmdp.org

Web Site: http://www.marrow.org
Members: 300 medical centers
Staff: 200
Annual Budget: $50-100,000,000
C.E.O.: Craig W.S. Howe, M.D., Ph.D
Dir., Meetings/Education: Robert Pinderhughes
Meetings/Membership: Pam Robinett
Historical Note
NMDP is a national registry of volunteer marrow donors, and the coordinating body for medical centers performing marrow transplants. Maintains database on transplant outcomes.
Publications:
Marrow Matters. q.
Marrow Messenger. a.
The Networker.
Meetings/Conferences:
1999 – Minneapolis, MN(Marriott)/Oct. 8-10/800

Nat'l Mastitis Council *(1961)*
2820 Walton Commons West, Suite 131
Madison, WI 53718
Tel: (608)224-0622
E-Mail: nmc@nmconline.org
Web Site: http://www.nmconline.org
Members: 2,000 individuals
Staff: 1
Annual Budget: $100-250,000
Exec. Director: Anne Saeman
Historical Note
Members are dairy industry professionals. Membership: $35/year (individual); $150-550/year (organization).
Publications:
Annual Meeting Proceedings. a.
Udder Topics Newsletter. bi-m.
Meetings/Conferences:
Annual Meetings: February
1999 – Arlington, VA

Nat'l Meat Ass'n *(1946)*
1970 Broadway, Suite 825
Oakland, CA 94612
Tel: (510)763-1533   *Fax:* (510)763-6186
E-Mail: nma@hooked.net
Web Site: http://www.nmaonline.org
Members: 600 companies
Staff: 6
Annual Budget: $500-1,000,000
Exec. Director: Rosemary M. Mucklow
Historical Note
Originally the Western States Meat Ass'n formed in 1982 by a merger of the Western States Meat Packers Ass'n and the Pacific Coast Meat Ass'n; assumed its current name to reflect its national membership in 1995. General members are persons or companies engaged in the slaughtering of livestock or the processing, sale and distribution of meat and meat products. Allied members are persons or firms engaged primarily in buying and selling meat and poultry products; associate members are persons or companies supplying non-meat supplies and equipment to the meat processing industry. Membership fee varies, based on classification: $500-$15,000/year.
Publications:
Herd on the Hill. w.
Lean Trimmings Bulletin. w.
NMA Membership Directory. a. adv.
NMA Resource. m.
Meetings/Conferences:
Annual Meetings: late February; plus Biennial Exposition (1999)
1999 – Monterey, CA(Marriott)/Feb. 18-20

Nat'l Meat Canners Ass'n *(1923)*
1700 N. Moore St., Suite 1600
Arlington, VA 22209
Tel: (703)841-3680   *Fax:* (703)841-9656
Web Site: http://www.meatpmi.org
Members: 35 companies
Staff: 4
Annual Budget: $10-25,000
Exec. Secretary: J. Patrick Boyle
Regulatory Advisor: Bill Dennis
Historical Note
Promotes the interests of packers of commercially sterile canned meats, and encourages scientific and practial research. Affiliated with the American Meat Institute. Membership: $725/year.
Meetings/Conferences:
Annual Meetings: Spring
1999 – Sanibel, FL(Sanibel Island Resort)/March 6-10/50

Nat'l Medical Ass'n *(1895)*
1012 10th St., N.W.
Washington, DC 20001
Tel: (202)347-1895   *Fax:* (202)842-3293
Web Site: www.mna.ent.org
Members: 16,000 individuals
Staff: 23
Annual Budget: $1-2,000,000
Exec. Director: Lorraine Cole, Ph.D.
Historical Note
Professional society of black physicians. Membership: $445/year.
Publications:
Journal of the National Medical Association. m. adv.
National Medical Association News. bi-m. adv.
National Medical Association Newsletter. q.
Meetings/Conferences:
Annual Meetings: Summer
1999 – Las Vegas, NV(Hilton)/Aug. 8-13

Nat'l Mental Health Ass'n *(1909)*
1021 Prince St.

Alexandria, VA 22314-2971
Tel: (703)684-7722   Fax: (703)684-5968
Toll Free: (800)969 - 6642
E-Mail: nmhainfo@aol.com
Web Site: http://www.nmha.org
Members: 345 affiliates
Staff: 50
Annual Budget: $2-5,000,000
President and C.E.O.: Michael M. Faenza
V. President, Development: Kathleen Wiedemer
Sr. Director, Public Education: Shela Halper
Director, Media Relations: Patrick Cody
V. President, Government Affairs: Al Guida
V. President, Affiliate Services: Judy Leaver
Senior V. President: Rob Gabriel
Director, Finance: Cathy Stewart
Sr. Director, Marketing: Mary Nokes
Sr. Advisor to the President: Sandra McElhaney
Sr. Director of State Affairs: Mary Graham

Historical Note
Formed by a merger of the Nat'l Committee for Mental Hygiene, the
Nat'l Mental Health Foundation and the Psychiatric Foundation.
Absorbed the Nat'l Organization for Mentally Ill Children. Formerly
(1978) the National Association for Mental Health and (1980) the
Nat'l Mental Health Association.

Publications:
Advocacy Update. q.
Bell. m.

Meetings/Conferences:
1999 – Washington, DC(Lowes L'Enfant Plaza)/June 9-12

Nat'l Metal Decorators Ass'n (1936)
9616 Deereco Road
Timonium, MD 21093
Tel: (410)252-5205   Fax: (410)628-8079
Web Site: http://www.nmda.org
Members: 850 individuals
Staff: 2
Annual Budget: $250-500,000
Exec. Director: Michael Masenior

Historical Note
Members are individuals in firms that apply decoration and supplies
and services to metal surfaces through lithography or rollercoating.
Membership: $65/year.

Publications:
Internat'l Metal Decorator. q. adv.

Meetings/Conferences:
Annual Meetings: Fall/700
1999 – Accapulco, Mexico(Prince Hotel)/Oct. 16-19

Nat'l Metal Spinners Ass'n (1933)
P.O. Box 358
Farmingdale, NY 11735
Tel: (516)249-2468   Fax: (516)249-2599
Members: 17 companies
Secretary: Richard F. Goldhaber

Historical Note
NMSA members are metal spinning and stamping companies.
Membership concentrated in metropolitan New York.

Nat'l Middle School Ass'n (1973)
2600 Corporate Exchange Dr., Suite 370
Columbus, OH 43231-1672
Tel: (614)895-4730   Fax: (614)895-4750
Members: 13,000 individuals
Staff: 21
Annual Budget: $1-2,000,000
Exec. Director: Sue Swaim
Director of Professional Development: Lynn Wallich
Director, Membership: Jack Berckmeyer

Historical Note
Formerly (1973) Midwest Middle School Ass'n. Educators and
parents involved in middle school education. Membership: $45-
55/year (individual); $175/year (organization).

Publications:
Middle Ground. 2/year.
Middle School Journal. 5/year. adv.
Target. 4/year.

Meetings/Conferences:
Annual Meetings: Fall/8,000-10,000

Nat'l Military Intelligence Ass'n (1974)
9200 Centerway Road
Gaithersburg, MD 20879
Tel: (301)840-6642   Fax: (301)840-8502
E-Mail: zhi@tiac.net
Web Site: http://www.nmia.org
Members: 2,500 individuals
Staff: 1
Annual Budget: $100-250,000
Exec. Director: Zhi Marie Hamby-Nye

Historical Note
NMIA is a professional association focusing on devense
intelligence, including strategic, tactical and counter intelligence
affecting the security of the United States. Members are current and
former U.S. intelligence professionals and U.S. citizens interested in
supporting defense intelligence through educational efforts.
Membership: $15-35/year (individual, based on rank), $600-
$1,200/year (corporate).

Publications:
American Intelligence Journal. semi-a. adv.
NMIA Newsletter. 3/yr. adv.
NMIA Z-GRAM. 5/wk. adv.

Meetings/Conferences:
Awards Banquet: June

Nat'l Milk Producers Federation (1916)
2101 Wilson Blvd., Suite 400
Arlington, VA 22201

Tel: (703)243-6111   Fax: (703)841-9328
Web Site: http://www.nmpf.org
Members: 28 dairy cooperatives
Staff: 18
Annual Budget: $2-5,000,000
C.E.O.: Jerome J. Kozak
V.P., Govt. Relations: Roger Eldridge
Senior V. President: Tom Balmer
Senior Policy Advisor: Ed Coughlin

Historical Note
Established as the Nat'l Cooperative Milk Producers Federation, it
assumed its present name in 1966 and absorbed the Nat'l
Creameries Ass'n in 1966. Membership fee varies based on
production.

Publications:
Dairy Market Report. m.
News for Dairy Co-ops. w.

Meetings/Conferences:
Annual Meetings: November/1,200

Nat'l Miniature Donkey Ass'n (1990)
6450 Dewey Road
Rome, NY 13440
Tel: (315)336-0154   Fax: (315)339-4414
Web Site: http://www.matrixdm.com/nmda
Exec. Director: Lynn Gattari

Historical Note
Established to protect and promote the miniature donkey breed.
Membership: $25/year (domestic), $35/year (internat'l).

Publications:
Asset. q.

Nat'l Mining Ass'n (1995)
1130 17th St., N.W.
Washington, DC 20036-4677
Tel: (202)463-2651   Fax: (202)857-0135
Web Site: http://www.nma.org
Members: 400 companies
Staff: 80
Annual Budget: $10-25,000,000
President and C.E.O.: Gen. Richard L. Lawson, USAF (Ret.
Sr. V.P., Public/Constituent Relations: Daniel R. Gerkin
V.P., External Communications: John Grasser
Sr. V.P., Government Affairs: Thomas H. Altmeyer
Sr. V.P., Policy Analysis: Constance D. Holmes
Dir., Conventions/Conferences/Membership Development: Francis
     M. Eckert
V.P., Finance and Administration: Nori Jones
Sr. V.P. and General Counsel: Harold P. Quinn, Jr.
Director, Editorial Services: E. Joyce Morgan
Manufacturers Service Division: Joseph E. Lema

Historical Note
Product of the merger of the American Mining Congress and the
Nat'l Coal Ass'n in 1995. NMA is an industry association that
encompasses producers of most of America's metals, coal,
industrial and agricultural minerals; manufacturers of mining and
mineral processing machinery, equipment and supplies; and
engineering and consulting firms and financial institutions that
serve the mining industry. The NMA is both a clearinghouse for
information and coordinator for action on behalf of the mining
industry. The political action committees of the NMA are CoalPAC
and MinePAC. Has an annual budget of approximately $12 million.
Membership fee is based upon a rolling three-year average of sales
or production of mineral commodities, minimum: $500/year.

Publications:
Mining Voice. bi-m. adv.
Mining Week. w.

Meetings/Conferences:
Annual Meetings: Winter, Spring and Fall
1999 – Rancho Mirage, CA/Jan. 27-29
1999 – White Sulphur Springs, WV/May 20-22
1999 – St. Louis, MO/Oct. 10-13

Nat'l Minority Business Council (1972)
235 E. 42nd St.
New York, NY 10017
Tel: (212)573-2385   Fax: (212)573-4462
E-Mail: mnbc@msn.com
Web Site: http://www.nmbc.org
Members: 350 firms
Annual Budget: $250-500,000
President and C.E.O.: John F. Robinson
V.President, Administration and Special Projects: Elsie McCarthy
Membership Administrator: Ian Stevenson

Historical Note
NMBC is dedicated to providing business assistance, educational
opportunities, seminars, purchasing exchanges, mentoring,
business listings and related services to small, minority and
women-owned businesses.

Publications:
NMBC Business Report. q.

Meetings/Conferences:
Annual Luncheon: always February

Nat'l Minority Supplier Development Council (1972)
15 W. 39th St., 9th Floor
New York, NY 10018
Tel: (212)944-2430   Fax: (212)719-9611
Web Site: http://www.nmsdc.org
Members: 170 companies
Staff: 15
Annual Budget: $2-5,000,000
President: Harriet R. Michel
V. President, Finance and Administration: Casilda Del Valle

Historical Note
Formerly (1980) known as the Nat'l Minority Purchasing Council.
Founded to expand business opportunities for minority-owned
companies and to encourage mutually beneficial economic links
between minority suppliers and the public and private sector.

Network includes 45 Regional Councils across the country. There
are 3,500 corporate members throughout the network, including
more than 170 of the top Fortune 500. Regional councils certify
and match more than 15,000 minority-owned businesses with
member corporations which want to purchase goods and services.
Membership fee based on a sliding scale.

Publications:
Annual Report. a.
Bottom Line. 2/year.
Minority Supplier News. q.

Meetings/Conferences:
Annual Meetings: Fall
1999 – Phoenix, AZ/Oct. 27-29

Nat'l Mobility Equipment Dealers Ass'n
909 E. Skagway Ave.
Tampa, FL 33604-1747
Tel: (813)932-8566   Fax: (813)931-4683
Toll Free: (800)833 - 0427
Web Site: http://www.nmeda.org
Exec. Director: Rebecca D. Plank

Historical Note
A trade association of dealers and merchants who convert vehicles
for use by the handicapped.

Publications:
Circuit Breaker. q.

Meetings/Conferences:
1999 – Daytona Beach, FL/Feb. 3-6

Nat'l Motor Freight Traffic Ass'n (1956)
2200 Mill Road
Alexandria, VA 22314
Tel: (703)838-1810   Fax: (703)683-1094
Web Site: www.erols.com/nmfta
Members: 1,700 individuals
Staff: 18
Annual Budget: $2-5,000,000
Exec. Director and Secretary: Martin E. Foley
General Counsel: William W. Pugh

Historical Note
NMFTA is a trade association representing motor common carriers
(trucking companies) of every kind of product which moves via less
than truckload service. Membership: $265-$13,314/year.

Publications:
Continental Directory of Standard Point Location Codes. a.
Directory of Standard Carrier Agent Codes. a.
National Motor Freight Classification Tariff. a.

Meetings/Conferences:
1999 – Palm Springs, CA(Marquis)/Feb. 8-9/150

Nat'l Motorsports Press Ass'n (1959)
P.O. Box 500
Darlington, SC 29540
Tel: (843)395-8900   Fax: (843)393-3911
Members: 350 individuals
Staff: 1
Exec. Secretary: Bridget Blackwell

Historical Note
Formerly Southern Motorsports Press Ass'n. Membership:
$35/year (full member); $75/year (associate).

Meetings/Conferences:

Nat'l Movement Theatre Ass'n (1984)
615 15th St.
Minneapolis, MN 55407
Tel: (612)339-4709
E-Mail: margobroco@aol.com
Members: 200 individuals
Annual Budget: under $10,000
President: Kari Margolis

Historical Note
Formerly (1990) Nat'l Mime Ass'n. Members are mimes and other
performance and movement artists. Has no paid officers or full-time
staff. Membership: $50/year (company); $30/year (individual);
$20/year (student); $100/year (benefactor); $250/year (patron).

Publications:
Directory of Educational Programs.
Membership Directory.
Movement Theater Quarterly. q. adv.

Meetings/Conferences:

Nat'l Moving and Storage Ass'n (1920)

Historical Note
Merged with American Movers Conference in 1998 to form
American Moving and Storage Ass'n.

Nat'l Multi Housing Council (1978)
1850 M St., N.W., Suite 540
Washington, DC 20036-5803
Tel: (202)974-2300   Fax: (202)775-0112
E-Mail: info@nmhc.org
Web Site: http://www.nmhc.org
Members: 700 individuals, 725 companies
Staff: 27
Annual Budget: $2-5,000,000
President: Jonathan L. Kempner
Director, Communications: Kimberly Duty
Sr. V.P., Government Affairs: Clarine Nardi Riddle
V. President, Research: John L. Goodman, Jr.
V.P., Operations: Jayne Somes-Schloesser
Manager, Membership: Charles A. Papa
V.P., Environment: Eileen Lee

Historical Note
Land developers, realtors, apartment owners, builders and
developers, property managers, financiers, and others concerned
with issues relating to rent, rent control, multifamily housing,
condominium conversions, and tax legislation. Formerly (until
1980) known as the National Rental Housing Council. Sponsors

and supports the National Multi Housing Council Political Action Committee. Membership: $1,000-20,000/year (company).

Publications:
Building Codes Update. q.
Environmental Update. q.
Market Trends. q.
Research Notes. q.
Seniors Housing Update. q.
Tax Update. q.
Technology Update. q.
Washington Update. semi-m.

Meetings/Conferences:
Annual Meetings: January
1999 – Rancho Mirage, CA(Westin Mission
    Hills)/Jan. 13-15/1000
2000 – Palm Beach, FL(The Breakers)/Jan. 12-14/1000
2001 – Phoenix, AZ(Arizona Biltmore)/Jan. 10-12/1000
2002 – Naples, FL(Ritz-Carlton)/Jan. 9-11/1000

Nat'l Multimedia Ass'n of America *(1994)*

Historical Note
Address unknown in 1998.

Nat'l Multiple Sclerosis Soc. *(1946)*
733 Third Ave.
New York, NY   10017
Tel: (212)986-3240   *Fax:* (212)986-7981
Toll Free: (800)344 - 4867
E-Mail: net@nmss.org
Web Site: http://www.nmss.org
Members: 700,000 individuals, 2,000 volunteers
Staff: 130
Annual Budget: $25-50,000,000
President and CEO: Gen. Michael J. Dugan, USAF(Ret.)
V. President, Communications: Diann Rohde
Director, Communications and Government Relations: Susan
    Sanabria
Director, Finance and Administration: Joseph C. DeSapio

Historical Note
Until 1947 known as the Ass'n for the Advancement of Research on Multiple Sclerosis. Promotes research into the cause, prevention, treatment and cure of multiple sclerosis, a neurological disorder and provides services to persons with MS and their families. Also supplies information and medical/scientific opinion to individuals with MS, their families, the general public, and the scientific community. Has an annual budget of $30 million. Membership: $20/year.

Publications:
Inside MS. q. adv.

Meetings/Conferences:

Nat'l Music Council *(1940)*
425 Park St.
Upper Montclair, NJ   07043
Tel: (973)655-7974   *Fax:* (973)655-5432
Web Site: http://www.musiccouncil.org
Members: 50 organizations
Staff: 1
Annual Budget: $25-50,000
Director: David Sanders, Ph.D.

Historical Note
Association of music organizations chartered by the U.S. Congress as a forum for discussion of national music problems. Composed of organizations of national scope and activity which are interested in the development of music and in the purposes for which the Nat'l Music Council was formed. Council has no individual members; however, individuals associated with member organizations are encourage to attend the Council's Music Leadership Meetings and Symposia.

Publications:
Membership Directory. a.

Meetings/Conferences:
Annual Meetings: New York/June

Nat'l Music Publishers' Ass'n *(1917)*
711 Third Ave., 8th Floor
New York, NY   10017-4014
Tel: (212)370-5330   *Fax:* (212)953-2384
Web Site: http://www.nmpa.org
Members: 700 companies
Staff: 6
Annual Budget: $1-2,000,000
President and C.E.O.: Edward P. Murphy
VP: Margaret A. Drum
V. President, Finance: Sylvar Stener
Senior V.P., International/HFA: Yoshio Inomata
Exec. V.P., Chief Operations Officer: Robert Shaw

Historical Note
Established as the Music Publishers Protective Ass'n; assumed its present name in 1966. Members are publishers of music concentrated principally around New York, Los Angeles and Nashville. A separate staff presides over subsidiary, the Harry Fox Agency, a licensing group for the members' product. Membership: $50/year.

Publications:
NMPA News & Views. q.

Meetings/Conferences:
Annual Meetings: June-July
1999 – New York, NY

Nat'l Naval Officers Ass'n *(1972)*

Historical Note
Membership: $50/year (indiviudal); $500/year (organization/individual)

Nat'l Needlework Ass'n *(1974)*
P.O. Box 3388

Zanesville, OH   43702-2188
Tel: (740)455-6773   *Fax:* (740)452-4541
Toll Free: (800)889 - 8662
E-Mail: tnna.info@offinger.com
Web Site: http://www.creative-industries.com/tnna
Members: 1,300 businesses
Staff: 5
Annual Budget: $500-1,000,000
Exec. Director: Patty Parrish
Assistant Trade Show Manager: Connie Stoneburner

Historical Note
In the spring of 1974, 34 companies met to form TNNA for the purposes of advancing needlework quality, understanding and marketing in the United States. Members are needlework manufacturers, retailers, and distributors. Holds both national and regional shows. Membership: $35/year (buyers); $250-750/year (exhibitors).

Publications:
Membership Directory. a.
Show Directory. a.
TNNA Today. 6/year.

Meetings/Conferences:
1999 – San Diego, CA(Town and Country)/Jan. 23-25/1000
1999 – Columbus, OH(Greater Columbus Convention
    Center)/June 19-21

Nat'l Network for Social Work Managers *(1985)*
1316 New Hampshire Ave., N.W., Suite 602
Washington, DC   20036
Tel: (202)785-2814   *Fax:* (202)785-2904
E-Mail: brotmandc@aol.com
Members: 800 individuals
Staff: 2
Annual Budget: $100-250,000
Exec. Director: Judith Brotman, CSWM

Historical Note
NNSWM members are administrators and managers of human services with degrees in social work. NNSWM works to improve the management of social programs by connecting social work-degreed professionals engaged in or interested in management; by positioning and enhancing social work managers' careers, and by acting as a professional forum for social work manager concerns. Awards the designation CSWM (Certified Social Work Manager). Membership: $85/year (individual); $765/year (organization); $2000/year (council of 100).

Publications:
Administration in Social Work. q.
Membership Directory. a.
Monographs. a.
Social Work Executive. q.

Meetings/Conferences:

Nat'l Network of Commercial Real Estate Women *(1989)*
1201 Wakarusa Dr., Suite 11
Lawrence, KS   66049-3107
Tel: (785)832-1808   *Fax:* (785)832-1551
E-Mail: lindah@nncrew.org
Web Site: http://www.nncrew.org
Members: 4,000 individuals, 24 organizations
Staff: 5
Annual Budget: $100-250,000
Exec. Director: Linda Holleman

Historical Note
Product of a merger in 1989 of Women in Commercial Real Estate Nat'l Network and Commercial Real Estate Women - Nat'l, the Nat'l Network provides a national communication network for women involved in all fields of commercial real estate and assists in the formation of new local groups in cities not currently represented in the Nat'l Network. Member organizations are existing, independent, local groups with goals similar to those of the Nat'l Network. Membership: $70/year (individual).

Publications:
Directory. a. adv.
National Network Newsletter. q. adv.

Meetings/Conferences:
Annual Meetings: Fall
1999 – Washington, DC/Sept. 30-Oct. 2

Nat'l Network of Estate Planning Attorneys *(1989)*
410 17th St., Suite 1260
Denver, CO   80202
Tel: (303)446-6100   *Fax:* (303)446-6060
Web Site: http://www.netplanning.com
Members: 1,200 individuals
Staff: 20
Annual Budget: $2-5,000,000
Exec. Director: A. Dennis Zehnle
Executive Director, Membership: Richard Randall, JD
Senior V. President, Publishing: Eileen Sacco
Executive Director, Operations: Dr. Neal McBride

Historical Note
An interactive alliance of over 500 estate planning attorneys nationwide which provides leadership in innovative estate planning techniques to assist families from various income levels in preserving their assets and perpetuating philanthropy.

Meetings/Conferences:

Nat'l Network of Grantmakers *(1980)*
1717 Kettner Blvd., Suite 110
San Diego, CA   92101
Tel: (619)231-1348   *Fax:* (619)231-1349
E-Mail: NNG@nng.org
Web Site: http://www.nng.org
Members: 450 individuals
Annual Budget: $500-1,000,000
Exec. Director: Teresa Odendahl
Assoc. Director: Joan Garner

Historical Note
NNG members are staff or trustees of private, public and corporate philanthropic organizations dedicated to social and economic justice. Membership:$100(individual); $1000(organization).

Publications:
Grantmakers Directory. a.
Network Newsletter. q.

Meetings/Conferences:

Nat'l Newspaper Ass'n *(1885)*
1010 N. Glebe Rd., Suite 450
Arlington, VA   22201-4749
Tel: (703)907-7900   *Fax:* (703)907-7901
E-Mail: TheNNA@aol.com
Web Site: http://www.nna.org
Members: 4,000 newspapers
Staff: 18
Annual Budget: $1-2,000,000
President and C.E.O.: Kenneth B. Allen
Communications Manager: Adam Wachter
Director, Government Relations: Xenia "Sonny" Boone

Historical Note
Founded as the Nat'l Editorial Ass'n and assumed its present name in 1960. Members comprise about 45% of the country's weeklies and one-third of the nation's dailies. In addition to its National Convention, NNA sponsors a Government Affairs Conference in the spring. Membership fee based on individual paper plus circulation.

Publications:
Publishers' Auxiliary. bi-w. adv.

Meetings/Conferences:
Semi-annual Meetings: Spring and Fall

Nat'l Newspaper Publishers Ass'n *(1940)*
3200 13th St., N.W.
Washington, DC   20010-2410
Tel: (202)588-8764   *Fax:* (202)588-5029
E-Mail: nnpadc@nnp2.org
Web Site: http://www.nnpa.org
Members: 215 newspaper publishers
Staff: 6
Annual Budget: $500-1,000,000
Executive Director: Yvonne Cooper

Historical Note
Formerly Nat'l Negro Publishers Ass'n. Membership: $150-660/year (based on circulation).

Publications:
Convention Journal. a.

Meetings/Conferences:
1999 – New York, NY/300
2000 – Chicago, IL/350

Nat'l Notary Ass'n *(1957)*
9350 DeSoto Ave.
Chatsworth, CA   91311
Tel: (818)739-4000   *Fax:* (818)700-0920
Toll Free: (800)876 - 6827
E-Mail: nna@nationalnotary.org
Web Site: http://www.nationalnotary.org
Members: 150,000 individuals
Staff: 70
Annual Budget: $2-5,000,000
Exec. Director: Deborah M. Thaw
Director, Strategic Planning: Gaia Winter
Public Affairs Coordinator: Carol Eisman
V. President, Legislation: Charles Faerber
Conference Coordinator: Hilary Mahon

Historical Note
Established in 1957 as the California Notary Ass'n; assumed its present name in 1965. Membership: $34/year.

Publications:
National Notary Magazine. bi-m.
Notary Bulletin Newspaper. bi-m.

Meetings/Conferences:
1999 – Denver, CO(Renaissance)/June 9-12

Nat'l Nurses Soc. on Addictions *(1974)*
4101 Lake Boone Trail, Suite 201
Raleigh, NC   27607
Tel: (919)783-5871   *Fax:* (919)787-4916
Members: 1,200 individuals
Staff: 4
Annual Budget: $100-250,000
Exec. Director: Mary Evelyn Zachar

Historical Note
Formerly (1983) Nat'l Nurses Soc. on Alcoholism. A national specialty nursing organization for nurses whose field of practice is substance abuse/addictions nursing, including clinicians, educators, managers and researchers. Incorporated the Drug and Alcohol Nursing Ass'n. Membership: $100/year (individual).

Publications:
Perspectives on Addictions Nursing. bi-m. adv.

Meetings/Conferences:
Annual Meetings: Fall

Nat'l Nursing Staff Development Organization *(1989)*
7794 Grow Dr.
Pensacola, FL   32514
Tel: (850)474-0995   *Fax:* (850)484-8762
Toll Free: (800)489 - 1995
E-Mail: NNSDO@aol.com
Members: 3,000 individuals
Staff: 13
Annual Budget: $250-500,000
Exec. Director: Belinda E. Puetz, Ph.D.
Director, Education: Janice Ward
Manager, Publications: Shay Stephens

Historical Note
NNSDO provides training and networking opportunities for professionals specializing in staff development in a variety of medical settings. Membership: $50/year.

Publications:
Journal for Nurses in Staff Development. bi-m. adv.
Trendlines. bi-m. adv.

Meetings/Conferences:
Annual Meetings: Boston, MA(Westin Copley Square)/July 18-21/700
1999 – Washington, DC(Crystal Gateway Marriott)/July 15-18

Nat'l Nutritional Foods Ass'n *(1936)*
3931 MacArthur Blvd., Suite 101
Newport Beach, CA   92660-3013
Tel: (949)622-6272   *Fax:* (949)622-6266
Toll Free: (800)966 - 6632
E-Mail: nnfa@nnfa.org
Web Site: http://www.nnfa.org
Members: 4,000 retailers and manufacturers
Staff: 16
Annual Budget: $2-5,000,000
Exec. Director: Michael Q. Ford
Dir., Public Affairs/Communications: Chris Jorgenson
Director, Conventions and Meetings: Sheldon Metz
Dir., Finance & Administration: Brent Weickert

Historical Note
Organized in 1936 as the Nat'l Dietary Foods Ass'n. Absorbed the American Dietary Retailers Ass'n in 1969 and assumed its present name in 1970. Natural, nutritional and dietary food retailers, distributors and producers. Supports the Nat'l Nutritional Foods Political Action Committee.

Publications:
NNFA Today. m.

Meetings/Conferences:
Annual Meetings: Summer/10,000

Nat'l Oak Flooring Manufacturers Ass'n *(1909)*
P.O. Box 3009
Memphis, TN   38173-0009
Tel: (901)526-5016   *Fax:* (901)526-7022
E-Mail: info@nofma.org
Web Site: http://www.nofma.org
Members: 25 manufacturers
Staff: 6
Annual Budget: $50-100,000
Exec. V. President: Stan Elberg

Historical Note
Main purpose is to establish manufacturing and grading standards for the industry and to see that these standards are observed by a continuous inspection service. Open to manufacturers in the U.S. who make solid hardwood flooring. Formerly the Oak Flooring Manufacturers of the United States and Southern Oak Flooring Industries. NOFMA sponsors the Hardwood Flooring Installation School (since 1979) with the American Parquet Ass'n, the Maple Flooring Manufacturers Ass'n and the National Wood Flooring Ass'n. The Oak Flooring Institute is the promotional arm of NOFMA.

Meetings/Conferences:
Semi-Annual Meetings: Summer & first week of December Memphis, TN(Peabody)
1999 – Memphis, TN(Peabody)/Nov. 20-21

Nat'l Ocean Industries Ass'n *(1972)*
1120 G St., N.W., Suite 900
Washington, DC   20005
Tel: (202)347-6900   *Fax:* (202)347-8650
E-Mail: noiaenoia.org
Members: 280 companies
Staff: 7
Annual Budget: $1-2,000,000
President: Robert B. Stewart
Director, Public Affairs: Laura Smith
Director, Admin. and Member Services: Franki K. Stuntz

Historical Note
Oil and gas companies, their suppliers, and support companies drilling and exploring on the outer continental shelf.

Publications:
NOIA Leaders. a.
NOIA Membership Directory. a.
Washington Report. bi-w.

Meetings/Conferences:
Semi-annual Meetings: Spring (always in Washington, DC) and Fall
1999 – Washington, DC(Grand Hyatt)/March 25-28/300

Nat'l Office Products Ass'n
Historical Note
Became the Business Products Industry Ass'n in 1994.

Nat'l Office Systems Ass'n *(1983)*
Historical Note
Organization is defunct.

Nat'l Officers Ass'n *(1981)*
1765 Business Center Drive., Suite 100
Reston, VA   20190-5326
Tel: (703)438-3060   *Fax:* (703)438-3072
Toll Free: (800)248 - 9632
E-Mail: mod@megascorp.com
Web Site: http://www.memserv.com
Members: 25,000 individuals
Staff: 5
Annual Budget: $100-250,000
Director of Operations: Bruce A. Pifel

Historical Note
A benefits-oriented association serving officers of the U.S. uniformed services, service retirees, and their dependents with a broad array or programs. Membership: $18/year.

Publications:
Officers Call. q. adv.

Nat'l Oil Recyclers Ass'n *(1984)*
12429 Cedar Road, Suite 26
Cleveland, OH   44106-3172
Tel: (216)791-7316   *Fax:* (216)791-6047
E-Mail: noraoil.com
Members: 140 companies
Staff: 4
Annual Budget: $250-500,000
Exec. Director: Kathryn McWilliams
Administrative Manager: Martha Peckinpaugh

Historical Note
NORA is a trade association representing the interests of companies in the United States engaged in the safe recycling of used oil, antifreeze, waste water and oil filters. Membership: $1,000-5,000/year (company).

Publications:
NORA News. q. adv.

Meetings/Conferences:
Annual Meetings: Semi-Annual, May and November
1999 – Washington, DC/125
1999 – Palm Springs, CA/300

Nat'l Oilseed Processors Ass'n *(1929)*
1255 23rd St., N.W., Suite 220
Washington, DC   20037-1174
Tel: (202)452-8040   *Fax:* (202)835-0400
E-Mail: nopa@nopa.org
Members: 14 companies
Annual Budget: $1-2,000,000
President: Allen F. Johnson

Historical Note
Formerly (1988) Nat'l Soybean Processors Ass'n.

Publications:
NOPA Yearbook and Trading Rules. a.

Meetings/Conferences:
Annual Meetings: June/200
1999 – Lake Tahoe, NV(Hyatt regency)/June 25-29/200
2000 – Santa Barbara, CA(Four Seasons Biltmore)/June 23-27/200

Nat'l Onion Ass'n *(1913)*
822 7th St., Suite 510
Greeley, CO   80631
Tel: (970)353-5895   *Fax:* (970)353-5897
E-Mail: wmininger@onions-usa.org
Web Site: http://www.onions-usa.org
Members: 750 individuals and companies
Staff: 3
Annual Budget: $250-500,000
Exec. V. President: Wayne Mininger
Promotion Director/Membership Coord'r: Nancy Teksten
Director, Publicity and Industry Relations: Tanya Fell

Historical Note
Represents interests of U.S. onion producers. Informational, lobbying, and generic promotional headquarters for fresh dry bulb onion growers in this country. Provides conventions for networking and education exchange. Voluntary contributions (dues/assessments) are sole means of support.

Publications:
Legislative Outlook. a.
Membership Directory. a.
News Letter. m.
Statistical Report. m.

Meetings/Conferences:
Semi-Annual Meetings: Summer and Fall
1999 – Portland, OR

Nat'l Onsite Wastewater Recycling Ass'n
P.O. Box 647
Northbrook, IL   60065-0647
Tel: (847)509-9233   *Fax:* (847)559-9235
Web Site: http://www.nowra.org
Members: 1,600 individuals
Exec. Director: Pamela W. Franzen

Publications:
Onsite Insight. m.

Meetings/Conferences:
1999 – Jekyll Island, GA(Comfort Inn)/Nov. 3-6/500
2000 – Lansing, MI(Holiday Inn)

Nat'l Opera Ass'n *(1955)*
6805 Tennyson Drive
McLean, VA   22101
Tel: (703)790-3393   *Fax:* (703)790-3393
E-Mail: arvidius@aol.com
Web Site: http://www.noa.org
Members: 550 individuals
Staff: 1
Annual Budget: $50-100,000
Exec. Secretary: Arvid Knutsen

Historical Note
Members are opera companies, schools of music, opera directors, composers, conductors, librettists, teachers, and other professionals whose work is opera-related. Sponsors the nationwide Opera Production Competition, the New Opera Competition, and the NOA Voice Competition. Membership: $45/year (individual); $60/year (organization); $30/year (libraries). Has 160 library subscription members in addition to regular members.

Publications:
Membership Directory. a. adv.
NOA Newsletter. q. adv.

Opera Journal. q. adv.

Meetings/Conferences:

Nat'l Options and Futures Soc. *(1979)*
Historical Note
Organization defunct in 1997.

Nat'l Optometric Ass'n *(1969)*
1489 Livingston Ave.
Columbus, OH   43205
Tel: (614)253-5593   *Fax:* (614)253-6069
E-Mail: cnhicks@compuserve.com
Members: 600 individuals
Staff: 1
Annual Budget: $50-100,000
Meeting Planner: Dr. Clayton Hicks

Historical Note
Established and incorporated in Atlanta, NOA is a professional society of predominantly minority optometrists especially concerned with the delivery of vision/eye health care to the minority community. Affiliated with the American Optometric Ass'n, American Public Health Ass'n, Ass'n of Schools and Colleges of Optometry and Nat'l Health Council. Membership: $150/year.

Publications:
NOA Newsletter. q. adv.

Meetings/Conferences:
Annual Meetings: July-August
1999 – San Antonio, TX(Hyatt)/July 8-12/300
2000 – Washington, DC.July

Nat'l Order of Women Legislators/Nat'l Foundation for Women Legislators *(1938)*
910 16th St., N.W., Suite 100
Washington, DC   20006-2903
Tel: (202)337-2765   *Fax:* (202)337-3566
E-Mail: nfwl@erols.com
Web Site: http://womenlegislators.org
Members: 3,300 individuals
Staff: 9
Annual Budget: $500-1,000,000
President NFWL/Exec. Director NOWL: Robin Read
Director, Events: Elsa Keshishian
Director, Finance: Kwame Frimpong
Director of Development: Rebecca Johnson
Dir., Programs: Nensi Fiorenini

Historical Note
NOWL/NFWL is a non-partisan, nonprofit educational foundation consisting of members of Nat'l Order of Women Legislators (current and former women state legislators), and corporate and associate members (women and men) who, with funds and participation, support women state legislators. Mission of the foundation is to provide a stepping stone for women state legislators as they become comfortable in the positions of leadership and authority to climb into higher state or federal office, commissions, or appointed positions on the political ladder. Membership: $25/year.

Publications:
Connection. q. adv.
Newsletter. 6/year.

Meetings/Conferences:
Annual Meetings: Fall

Nat'l Organization for Associate Degree Nursing *(1984)*
11250 Roger Bacon Drive, Suite 8
Reston, VA   20190-5202
Tel: (703)437-4377   *Fax:* (703)435-4390
E-Mail: noadn@aol.com
Web Site: http://www.noadn.org/adnursing/
Members: 1,750 individuals
Staff: 5
Annual Budget: $250-500,000
Exec. Director: Randall C. Price, CAE
Director of Communications: Peggy Gartner
Comptroller: Allen Beam
Administrator: Maureen Thompson

Historical Note
NOADN is a professional network and forum for ideas concerning associate degree nursing recruitment, education and practice. Membership: $75/year (individual); $225/year (organization/company).

Publications:
NOADN Newsletter. q. adv.

Meetings/Conferences:
Annual Meetings: Fall
1999 – Biloxi, MS

Nat'l Organization for Competency Assurance *(1987)*
1200 19th St., N.W., Suite 300
Washington, DC   20036-2401
Tel: (202)857-1165   *Fax:* (202)223-4579
Members: 160 organizations
Staff: 2
Annual Budget: $250-500,000
Exec. Director: Bonnie M. Aubin

Historical Note
Established and incorporated in the District of Columbia, NOCA members are primarily organizations interested in encouraging the establishment and implementation of methods to insure the competency of practitioners whose services directly affect public health, safety, and welfare. Many members are certifying programs that have been accredited by the Nat'l Commission for Certifying Agencies, an accreditation division of NOCA. Membership: $500-$3,000/year.

Publications:
Professional Regulation News. m.

Meetings/Conferences:
Annual Meetings: November

Nat'l Organization for Human Service Education *(1975)*
Tacoma Community College
6501 South 19th Street
Tacoma, WA 98466
Tel: (253)566-5214   *Fax:* (253)566-5365
Members: 600 individuals
Annual Budget: $25-50,000
President: James Carroll

Historical Note
NOHSE members are drawn from diverse educational and professional backgrounds including educators, students, direct care professionals, administrators as well as organizations in both the U.S. and Canada. NOHSE's focus includes supporting and promoting improvements in direct service, public education, program development, planning and evaluation, administration and public policy. Membership: $50/year (individual); $100/year (organization); $15/year (student).

Publications:
Journal of Human Service Education. a. adv.
Membership Directory. bien.
The Link Newsletter. q. adv.

Meetings/Conferences:
Annual Meetings: October

Nat'l Organization for the Professional Advancement of Black Chemists and Chemical Engineers *(1972)*
Historical Note
Address unknown in 1997.

Nat'l Organization of Bar Counsel *(1964)*
Bd. of Professional Resp., Supreme Court
Oaks Tower Suite 730, 1101 Kermit Dr.
Nashville, TN 37217
Tel: (615)361-7500   *Fax:* (615)367-2480
Members: 450 individuals
Annual Budget: $25-50,000
President: Laura L. Chastian

Historical Note
Attorneys representing bar associations and disciplinary agencies on the state, local and national levels. Officially affiliated with the American Bar Ass'n as of August 1991. Has no permanent office or staff. Officers are elected annually. Membership: $150/year (individual).

Meetings/Conferences:
Annual Meetings: February and August, with the American Bar Ass'n

Nat'l Organization of Black County Officials *(1975)*
440 First St., N.W., Suite 410
Washington, DC 20001
Tel: (202)347-6953   *Fax:* (202)393-6596
E-Mail: nobco@ami.net
Members: 2,000 individuals
Staff: 4
Annual Budget: $500-1,000,000
Exec. Director: Maria D. Lopes

Historical Note
NOBCO is an education services organization and serves as the business arm of the Nat'l Ass'n of Black County Officials, and is a member of the Nat'l Policy Institute. Coordinates and facilitates county-related activities for its members and serves as a clearinghouse for technical information. Membership: $100/year (individual); $500/year (organization/company).

Publications:
County Compass Newsletter. q. adv.
County to County. bi-m.

Meetings/Conferences:
1999 – Lake Charles, LA/April 28-May 2

Nat'l Organization of Black Law Enforcement Executives *(1976)*
4609 Pinecrest Office Park Drive
2nd Floor, Suite F
Alexandria, VA 22312
Tel: (703)658-1529   *Fax:* (703)658-9479
E-Mail: noble@nobleatl.org
Web Site: http://www.nobleat.org
Members: 2,300 individuals
Staff: 17
Annual Budget: $1-2,000,000
Exec. Director: Robert Stewart
Communications Director: Chester White
Education Director: Doris Bey
Business Director: James Mcluer

Historical Note
NOBLE members are minority law enforcement executives including police chiefs, command-level officers and others. Membership: $75/year (individual).

Publications:
NOBLE Actions. bi-m. adv.
NOBLE National. q. adv.

Meetings/Conferences:
Annual Meetings: Biluxi, MS/2,000
1999 – Portland, OR(Doubletree)/1500

Nat'l Organization of Industrial Trade Unions *(1954)*
148-06 Hillside Ave.
Jamaica, NY 11435
Tel: (718)291-3434   *Fax:* (718)526-2920
Members: 10,000 individuals
Staff: 40
Annual Budget: $250-500,000
Secretary-Treasurer: Phillip Siegel

Historical Note
Independent labor union.

Publications:
NOITU Reporter. q.

Meetings/Conferences:
Annual Meetings: December, usually New York, NY

Nat'l Organization of Legal Services Workers *(1972)*
113 University Pl., 5th Floor
New York, NY 10003
Tel: (212)228-0992   *Fax:* (212)228-0097
E-Mail: loines@worldnet.att.net
Members: 4,800 individuals
Staff: 7
President: Dwight Loines

Historical Note
Labor union affiliated with the AFL-CIO.

Publications:
Newsletter. irreg.

Nat'l Organization of Life and Health Insurance Guaranty Ass'ns *(1983)*
13873 Park Center Road, Suite 329
Herndon, VA 20171
Tel: (703)481-5206   *Fax:* (703)481-5209
Members: 52 associations
Staff: 21
Annual Budget: $2-5,000,000
President: Brian J. Donnelly
Manager, Communications: Peter J. Marigliano
Exec. V. President, Insurance Services: Richard Klipstein
Vice President, Administrative Services: Holly Wilding
Exec. V. President & General Counsel: Anthony Buonaguro
Systems Manager: Beth E. Watson

Historical Note
NOLHGA members are state life and health insurance guaranty associations. NOLHGA is located in 50 states as well as Washington D.C. and Puerto Rico. Membership: $16,000-$33,000 (association).

Publications:
NOLHGA Journal. bi-a.
Weekly Wire. 52/year.

Meetings/Conferences:
Annual Meetings: Fall

Nat'l Organization of Minority Architects *(1971)*
666 11th st., NW
Suite 250
Washington, DC 20001
Tel: (202)638-1938
Web Site: http://www.homa.net
Members: 750 individuals
Staff: 1
Annual Budget: $100-250,000
President: William Davis
Exec. Director: Sam Carradine

Historical Note
Formerly (1973) Nat'l Organization of Black Architects. Membership: $175/year (individual).

Publications:
Newsletter. q.
Roster of Minority Firms. irreg.

Meetings/Conferences:
Annual Meetings: October
1999 – Charlotte, NC

Nat'l Organization of Nurse Practitioner Faculties
1 Dupont Circle, N.W., Suite 530
Washington, DC 20036
Tel: (202)452-1405   *Fax:* (202)452 1406
E-Mail: NONPF@aacn.nche.edu
Web Site: http://www.nonpf.com
Members: 900 individuals, 780 organizations
Staff: 2
Annual Budget: $100-250,000
Administrative Director: Kathryn E. Werner

Historical Note
NONPF is committed to leadership in the development, implementation and evaluation of nurse practitioner education at the regional, national and international levels. Membership: $75/year (organization).

Publications:
Directory of Nurse Practitioner Programs. bien.
NONPF Quarterly Newsletter. q. adv.

Meetings/Conferences:
Annual Meetings: April
1999 – San Francisco, CA(Hyatt Regency on Union Square)/Arpil 15-18/400

Nat'l Organization of Social Security Claimants' Representatives *(1979)*
6 Prospect St.
Midland Park, NJ 07432-1634
Tel: (201)444-1415   *Fax:* (201)444-1823
E-Mail: nosscr@worldnet.att.net
Web Site: http://www.nosscr.org
Members: 3,500 individuals
Staff: 6
Annual Budget: $50-100,000
Exec. Director: Nancy G. Shor

Historical Note
Composed mostly of lawyers.

Publications:
NOSSCR Forum. m.

Meetings/Conferences:
Semi-annual Meetings: Spring and Fall

Nat'l Organization of Test, Research and Training Reactors *(1982)*

Historical Note
Address unknown in 1997.

Nat'l Organization on Legal Problems of Education
Historical Note
Became (1996) Education Law Ass'n.

Nat'l Orientation Directors Ass'n *(1947)*
Maxwell Hall, Room 122
Indiana University at Bloomington
Bloomington, IN 47405
Tel: (812)855-3907   *Fax:* (812)855-1319
E-Mail: noda1@indiana.edu/tildanoda1
Web Site: www.indiana.edu/tildanoda1
Members: 1,200 individuals
Staff: 2
Annual Budget: $50-100,000
Exec. Secretary-Treasurer: Christina E. Cook

Historical Note
NODA members are college personnel professionals, graduate and undergraduate students who are responsible for student orientation programs. Membership $50/year.

Publications:
NODA Data Bank. bien.
NODA First Timers Handbook. a.
NODA Membership Directory. a.
Orientation Director's Manual. bien.
Orientation Review Newsletter. q.

Meetings/Conferences:
Annual Meetings: October
1999 – Tampa, FL/Nov. 6-9

Nat'l Ornament and Electric Lights Christmas Ass'n *(1975)*
236 Route 38 West, Suite 100
Moorestown, NJ 08057
Tel: (609)231-8500   *Fax:* (609)231-4664
Members: 60 companies
Staff: 2
Annual Budget: $10-25,000
Exec. Director: Bill Pawlucy

Historical Note
Formed in 1975 to promote the general welfare and common interests in the trim-a-tree industry, NOEL serves as the spokesperson for the Christmas products and related industries. The bulk of the members are in the New York area. Membership: $550/year (sales under $1 milion), $1,100/year (sales over $1 million).

Publications:
Membership Directory. irreg.
NOEL Notable. newsletter.

Meetings/Conferences:
Annual Meetings: February, in New York City.

Nat'l Ornamental and Miscellaneous Metals Ass'n *(1958)*
804 Main St., Suite F
Forest Park, GA 30297
Tel: (404)363-4009   *Fax:* (404)366-1852
E-Mail: nommainfo@aol.com
Web Site: http://www.nomma.org/nomma/
Members: 850 individuals, 730 companies
Staff: 5
Annual Budget: $500-1,000,000
Exec. Director: Barbara H. Cook
Publications Manager: J. Todd Daniel
Meetings & Exposition Manager: Martha Pennington

Historical Note
Organized at the Claridge Hotel, Memphis, Tennessee in January, 1958 as the Nat'l Ornamental Iron Manufacturers Ass'n. In 1961 the name was changed to Nat'l Ornamental Metal Manufacturers Ass'n. The present name was adopted in 1977. Membership: $275/year (company).

Publications:
NOMMA Newsletter. bi-m.
NOMMA Ornamental/Miscellaneous Metal Fabricator. bi-m. adv.

Meetings/Conferences:
Annual Meetings: Winter
1999 – Nashville, TN(Opryland)/March 9-13
2000 – Reno, NV(John Asqnaga's Resort)

Nat'l Ornamental Goldfish Growers Ass'n *(1981)*
6916 Black's Mill Road
Thurmont, MD 21788
Tel: (301)271-7475   *Fax:* (301)271-7059
Members: 6 companies
Annual Budget: under $10,000
Exec. Secretary: Raymond W. Klinger

Historical Note
NOGGA was established by the existing full-time goldfish growers in the U.S. to fund research on goldfish, principally disease research.

Meetings/Conferences:
Annual Meetings: Winter

Nat'l Osteopathic Women Physicians Ass'n *(1904)*
Historical Note
Address unknown in 1996.

Nat'l Paint and Coatings Ass'n *(1933)*
1500 Rhode Island Ave., N.W.
Washington, DC 20005-5503
Tel: (202)462-6272   *Fax:* (202)462-8549
Members: 400 manufacturers
Staff: 40
Annual Budget: $5-10,000,000
President: J. Andrew Doyle

Director, Public Affairs: Kristina C. Cook
Director, Meetings and Conventions: Cheryl Matthews
Secretary and V. President, Administration: Allan W. Gates
Director, Member Relations: Joe Grimes

Historical Note
Manufacturers of paints and industrial coatings, and suppliers to the industry. Formed in 1933 as the Nat'l Paint, Varnish and Lacquer Ass'n through a merger of the American Paint Manufacturers Ass'n and the Nat'l Paint, Oil and Varnish Ass'n, the name was changed to the Nat'l Paint and Coatings Ass'n in 1972.

Publications:
Coatings. 10/yr.
Member/Services Directory. a. adv.
Trade Mark Directory. irreg.

Meetings/Conferences:
Annual Meetings: Fall
1999 – Dallas, TX/Oct. 17-19

Nat'l Pan Hellenic Council (1930)
Memorial Hall West 108
Bloomington, IN 47405
Tel: (812)855-8820 *Fax:* (812)855-4869
E-Mail: gordon@indiana.edu
Members: 9 fraternities & sororities
Staff: 2
Annual Budget: $25-50,000
Exec. Director: Michael Gordon, Ph.D.

Historical Note
NPHC is the umbrella organization coordinating activities among eight predominately national black fraternities and sororities. Membership: $100/year (organization).

Publications:
Directory of Members. a.
Summit Newsletter. q. adv.

Meetings/Conferences:
Biennial Meetings: odd years in Oct.
1999 – Atlanta, GA/Feb. 18-21

Nat'l Panhellenic Conference (1902)
3901 West 86th Street, Suite 380
Indianapolis, IN 46268
Tel: (317)872-3185 *Fax:* (317)872-3192
E-Mail: NPCCENTRAL@aol.com
Web Site: http://www.greeklife.org/npc
Members: 26 national sororities
Staff: 2
Annual Budget: $50-100,000
Administrative Assistant: Crystal Danielson
Coord., Education Programs: Merritt Olsen

Historical Note
Organized in Chicago, May 24, 1902.

Publications:
Chapter & Campus Listing. a.
NPC Directory. a.
PH Factor. bien.

Meetings/Conferences:
1999 – Florida

Nat'l Paper Trade Ass'n (1903)
111 Great Neck Road
Great Neck, NY 11021
Tel: (516)829-3070 *Fax:* (516)829-3074
Web Site: http://www.papertrade.com
Members: 850 wholesalers
Staff: 20
Annual Budget: $2-5,000,000
President: John J. Buckley
Exec. V. President: William H. Frohlich

Historical Note
NTPA serves the paper, packaging and allied products distribution channel.

Publications:
Distribution Sales and Management. m.

Meetings/Conferences:
Annual Meetings: Fall
1999 – Chicago, IL/April 23-26
2000 – Boston, MA/April 14-17

Nat'l Paperbox Ass'n (1918)
801 N. Fairfax St., Suite 211
Alexandria, VA 22314-1757
Tel: (703)684-2212 *Fax:* (703)683-6920
E-Mail: Boxmaker@paperbox.org
Web Site: http://www.paperbox.org
Members: 300 companies
Staff: 4
Annual Budget: $500-1,000,000
President: R. Mickey Gorman, CAE
Meetings & Conventions: Joan Griffith
Membership/Exec. V. President: Scott Miller

Historical Note
Formed in 1918 as the Nat'l Federation of Paper Box Manufacturers; developed into the Nat'l Paper Box Manufacturers Ass'n in 1919; changed name to the Nat'l Paper Box Ass'n in 1972; the Nat'l Paperbox and Packaging Ass'n in 1981; and assumed its present name in 1992. In 1982 NPPA opened membership to all independent manufacturers of packaging including rigid paper boxes, folding cartons and thermoform materials and their suppliers. Membership: fee based upon sales volume.

Publications:
Benefits & Wage Rates of the Rigid Box and Folding Carton Industries.
Key Ratios of the Folding Carton Industry. bien.
Key Ratios of the Rigid Box Industry.
Membership Directory. a.
Monthly Billing Reports for Rigid Box and Folding Carton Industries.

Packet Magazine. q.
Packet Update. m.

Meetings/Conferences:
Annual Meetings: April-May/300
1999 – Orlando. Fl(Disney Yacht Club)/April 28-May 2/300
2000 – Banff, Canada(Banff Springs Resort)/June 21-25/400
2001 – Palm Desset, CA(La Quinta Resort)/300

Nat'l Paralegal Ass'n (1982)
P.O. Box 406
Solebury, PA 18963-0406
Tel: (215)297-8333 *Fax:* (215)297-8358
E-Mail: admin@nationalparalegal.org
Members: 24,500 individuals, schools and firms
Staff: 6
Exec. Director: H. Jeffrey Valentine

Historical Note
Members are paralegals, paralegal educators, independent paralegals, paralegal schools, corporate law departments, law libraries, law firms, paralegal students, and others with an interest in the advancement of the profession. Membership: $70/first year, $45/year (full member), $70/year (associate); $30/year (student); $20/year (pre-student).

Publications:
Annual Nat'l Salary & Employment Survey. a. adv.
Directory of Corporate Legal Departments.
Directory of Local Paralegal Clubs. a. adv.
Legal Publishers Directory. adv. adv.
Nat'l School & Institute Directory. a. adv.
National Legal Placement Agency Directory. adv. adv.
NPA News. m.
Paralegal Career Booklet. a. adv.
The Paralegal. irregular, adv. adv.

Nat'l Park Hospitality Ass'n (1919)
1225 New York Ave., N.W., Suite 450
Washington, DC 20005
Tel: (202)682-9507 *Fax:* (202)682-9509
Members: 125 companies and individuals
Staff: 1
Annual Budget: $250-500,000
Exec. Officer: Allan T. Howe

Historical Note
Individuals and companies holding contracts with the Department of the Interior to provide goods and services to visitors to U.S. national parks. Established in 1919. Incorporated in 1975. Supports the Concessioners Political Action Committee. Formerly the Conference of Nat'l Park Concessioners. Membership: $200 plus % of Annual Budget.

Publications:
Membership Roster. semi-a.
National Parks Visitor Facilities & Services Guide.

Meetings/Conferences:
Semi-annual Meetings: Washington, DC/March & National Park/Oct.

Nat'l Parking Ass'n (1951)
1112 16th St., N.W., Suite 300
Washington, DC 20036
Tel: (202)296-4336 *Fax:* (202)331-8523
Toll Free: (800)647 - 7275
Web Site: http://www.npapark.org
Members: 1,100 individuals, 500 organizations
Staff: 5
Annual Budget: $1-2,000,000
Exec. Director: Barbara O'Dell, CEM

Historical Note
Sponsors the Nat'l Parking Ass'n Political Action Committee and the Parking Industry Institute. Membership: $250/year associate (individual), $250-13,000 (organizations).

Publications:
Legislative Updates. 10/yea.
Membership Directory. a.
Parking Magazine. 10/year. adv.

Meetings/Conferences:
1999 – Nashville, TN(Opryland Hotel)/Oct. 3-7

Nat'l Parks and Conservation Ass'n (1919)
1776 Massachusetts Ave., N.W., Suite 200
Washington, DC 20036
Tel: (202)223-6722 *Fax:* (202)659-0650
E-Mail: npca@npca.org
Web Site: http://www.npca.org
Members: 500,000 individuals
Staff: 82
Annual Budget: $10-25,000,000
President: Tom Kiernan
Director, Communications: Kathy Westra
Director, Conservation Programs: William Chandler
Exec. Board Liaison: Jennifer Robertson
Chief Financial Officer: Davinder S. Khanna
C.O.O.: Lazaro Garcia
Staff Counsel: Libby Fayad
Director, Membership: Terry Vines

Historical Note
Established as the Nat'l Parks Ass'n, it assumed its present name in 1970. Members are individuals interested in conservation, protection of national Parks, wildlife and the wilderness. Varying membership fees available; $25/year (individual). Has an annual budget of $16 million.

Publications:
National Parks Magazine. bi-m. adv.

Nat'l Particleboard Ass'n (1960)
Historical Note
Became the Composite Panel Ass'n in 1997.

Nat'l Party Boat Owners Alliance (1952)
181 Thames St.

Groton, CT 06340
Tel: (860)535-2066 *Fax:* (860)535-8389
Members: 500 individuals
Annual Budget: under $10,000
Exec. Director: Bradley J. Glas

Historical Note
Established in 1952 in response to increased federal legislation affecting the industry, NPBOA members are Coast Guard licensed Operators or Masters of passenger-for-hire charter/party boats. NPBOA's principal activity is monitoring proposed and new laws or regulations that might be detrimental to its segment of the maritime industry. Membership: $30/year (individual).

Publications:
Newsletter. 6 + /yr.

Nat'l Pasta Ass'n (1904)
2101 Wilson Blvd., Suite 920
Arlington, VA 22201
Tel: (703)841-0818 *Fax:* (703)528-6507
E-Mail: NPA@ibm.net
Web Site: http://www.ilovepasta.org
Members: 80 businesses
Staff: 2
Annual Budget: $1-2,000,000
President: Jula J. Kinnaird

Historical Note
Established as the Nat'l Macaroni Manufacturers Ass'n, it absorbed the Nat'l Macaroni Institute in 1979 and assumed its present name in 1981. NPA member manufacturers provide a wide variety of pasta products for the retail and foodservice markets.

Publications:
NPA Newsletter. bi-w.
PASTA Journal. bi-m. adv.

Meetings/Conferences:
Annual Meetings: Spring
1999 – Phoenix, AZ(Hilton Tapako Cliffs)

Nat'l Patio Enclosure Ass'n (1952)
12625 Frederick St.
Moreno Valley, CA 92553
Tel: (909)485-8881 *Fax:* (909)924-3078
Members: 43 companies
Staff: 3
Annual Budget: $10-25,000
Exec. Director: Tom Brandon

Historical Note
Formerly (1990) Western Awning Ass'n. Sellers and manufacturers of patio structures, screen enclosures and sun rooms. Member of The Internat'l Conference of Building Officials.

Publications:
News Bulletin. q.

Nat'l Pawnbrokers Ass'n (1989)
P.O. Box 420028
Dallas, TX 75342-0028
Tel: (214)745-4746 *Fax:* (214)745-1459
E-Mail: natpawn@ix.netcom.com
Members: 3,000 individuals
Staff: 4
Annual Budget: $500-1,000,000
Exec. Director: Tom Horne
Director, Marketing: Yvette Horgsberg
Director, Membership: Paige Prosser

Historical Note
NPA was founded to unite all pawnbrokers in their common efforts to improve the image of the industry, educate the public, and disseminate professional information and assistance. Provides numerous membership benefits. Membership: $160/year (individual).

Publications:
National Pawnbroker Magazine. q. adv.
Pawnbroker News and Fraud Alert. 8/year. adv.

Meetings/Conferences:
1999 – Orlando, FL/June 10-12

Nat'l Peach Council (1942)
12 Nicklaus Lane, Suite 101
Columbia, SC 29229
Tel: (803)788-7101
E-Mail: charleswalker@worldnet.att.net
Members: 2,400 individuals
Staff: 2
Annual Budget: $50-100,000
Managing Director: Charles Walker

Historical Note
Formed in 1942 and incorporated in 1945 in West Virginia. A federation of state associations of peach growers and allied industry members. Membership: $20/year (individual).

Publications:
Peach Times Newsletter. q. adv.

Meetings/Conferences:
Annual Meetings: January/4-500
1999 – Myrtle Beach, SC

Nat'l Pecan Growers Council (1946)
Historical Note
Organization defunct in 1997.

Nat'l Pecan Shellers Ass'n (1960)
5775 Peachtree-Dunwoody Rd., Suite 500-G
Atlanta, GA 30342-1558
Tel: (404)252-3663 *Fax:* (404)252-0774
E-Mail: npsa@assnhq.com
Members: 60 companies
Staff: 4
Annual Budget: $50-100,000
Exec. Director: Russell A. Lemieux
Manager, Client Services: Nancy Marlin

Historical Note
Formerly (1985) the Nat'l Pecan Shellers and Processors Ass'n. NPSA members are pecan shellers and processors; brokers; accumulators; growers; and packaging, equipment and ingredient suppliers to the industry.

Publications:
Perfect Performance with Pecans.

Meetings/Conferences:
Semi-Annual Meetings: Winter and Fall

Nat'l Pedigreed Livestock Council (1911)
272 Meetinghouse Lane
West Brattleboro, VT 05301
Tel: (802)257-9396   Fax: (802)254-6290
Web Site: http://www.nplczva.sover.net
Members: 60 registry associations
Staff: 1
Annual Budget: $25-50,000
Secretary-Treasurer: Zane Akins

Historical Note
A federation of cattle, horse, swine, goat and sheep breeders having a common interest in purebred stock as a means of livestock improvement. Formerly (1985) the Nat'l Soc. of Livestock Record Ass'ns. The American Berkshire Ass'n is a member society. Membership: $150/year (organization/company).

Publications:
Annual Report. a.
Directory. a. adv.

Meetings/Conferences:
Annual Meetings: Second week in May/50
1999 – Columbus, OH/May 6-9
2000 – Coeur d'Alene, ID(Couer d'Alene Inn)/May 3-6

Nat'l Perinatal Ass'n (1976)
3500 E. Fletcher Ave., Suite 209
Tampa, FL 33613-4712
Tel: (813)971-1008   Fax: (813)971-9306
E-Mail: npaonline@aol.com
Web Site: http://www.nationalperinatal.org
Members: 1,100 individuals
Staff: 3
Annual Budget: $250-500,000
Exec. Director: Judith Burke
Director, Operations: Lorie Craft

Historical Note
Members are individuals providing health care with particular emphasis on care for the pregnant woman, fetus and newborn. Membership: $75/year (individual), $200/year (organization), $5,000/year (corporate).

Publications:
Journal of Perinatology. bi-m. adv.
NPA Bulletin. q. adv.

Meetings/Conferences:
Annual Meetings: Fall
1999 – Milwaukee, WI(Hilton & Wisconsin Center)/Oct. 21-24/300
2000 – Charlotte, NC(Hilton)/Nov. 16-19/300

Nat'l Perishable Logistics Ass'n (1975)
P.O. Box 3267
Missoula, MT 59806-3267
Tel: (406)721-0720
Members: 200 executives and manufacturers
Annual Budget: $50-100,000
Counsel: William H. Towle

Historical Note
Founded as the Nat'l Perishable Traffic Ass'n, it assumed its present name in 1979. Formerly (1992) the Nat'l Perishable Transportation Ass'n. Members are executives of motor carriers, shippers and receivers of perishable commodities interested in the transportation of perishable goods. Membership: $200/year (individual).

Meetings/Conferences:
Annual Meetings: First week after Labor Day
1999 – Carlsbad, NM(La Costa Resort)/Aug. 15-17/150

Nat'l Pest Control Ass'n (1933)
8100 Oak St.
Dunn Loring, VA 22027
Tel: (703)573-8330   Fax: (703)573-4116
Members: 2,500 companies
Staff: 15
Annual Budget: $2-5,000,000
Exec. V. President: Robert F Lederer, Jr.
Director, Government Affairs: Robert Rosenberg
Director, Field Services: Greg Baumann
Director, Finance: Gary McKenzie, CFO
Director, Marketing: Bryan Jernigan

Historical Note
Formerly (1937) Nat'l Ass'n of Exterminators and Fumigators. Members are companies engaged in the integrated management of insects, rodents, birds and other pests which inhabit buildings or structures of any kind. Produces educational and training materials and conducts workshops. Supports the Nat'l Pest Control Ass'n Political Action Committee (NPCA-PAC).

Publications:
Convention Workbook. a. adv.
Who's Who in Professional Pest Control. a. adv.

Meetings/Conferences:
Annual Meetings: Late October

Nat'l Petroleum Council (1946)
1625 K St., N.W., Suite 600
Washington, DC 20006
Tel: (202)393-6100   Fax: (202)331-8539
Members: 175 individuals
Staff: 12
Annual Budget: $1-2,000,000
Exec. Director: Marshall W. Nichols
Information Coordinator: Carla Scali Byrd

Dep. Exec. Director: John H. Guy,, IV
Dir., Administration: James A. Hough
Committee Coordinator: Benjamin A. Oliver,, Jr.

Historical Note
Self-supporting federal advisory body to the Secretary of Energy established in 1946 at the request of President Truman.

Meetings/Conferences:
Semi-annual Meetings: always Washington, DC

Nat'l Petroleum Refiners Ass'n (1902)
1899 L St., N.W., Suite 1000
Washington, DC 20036
Tel: (202)457-0480   Fax: (202)457-0486
Members: 490 companies
Staff: 28
Annual Budget: $1-2,000,000
President: Urvan R. Sternfels
Director, Government Relations: June M. Whelan
Dir., Federal Affairs: Kevin Anderson
Dir., Congressional Realtions: Sharon Kirk
Convention Services Director & Safety Programs: Helen Kutska
Asst. Treasurer and Technical Director: Terrence S. Higgins
Director, Administration: Elizabeth Connelly
Secretary and Attorney: Maurice H. McBride, CAE
Director, Environmental Affairs: Norbert Dee, Ph.D.
Dir., Lubricants & Waxes, Computer Applications: Jeff Hazle

Historical Note
Merger in 1961 of the Nat'l Petroleum Ass'n (1902) and the Western Petroleum Refiners Ass'n (1912). Members are petroleum, petrochemical, and refining companies.

Publications:
The Exchanger. q.
Washington Bulletin. m.

Meetings/Conferences:
Annual Meetings: Spring/4,000

Nat'l Pharmaceutical Alliance
421 King St., Suite 222
Alexandria, VA 22314
Tel: (703)836-8816   Fax: (703)549-4749
Web Site: http://www.n-p-a.org
Members: 165 companies
Annual Budget: $250-500,000
President: Christina Sizemore

Historical Note
The National Pharmaceutical Alliance is an association representing the interests of small pharmaceutical companies and allied industries. Members of NPA are bound by several common, basic objectives. Among these are the development of bioequivalent versions of major branded products, the creation of products having alternate combinations, strengths, and/or dosage forms, and the marketing of products which are not of interest to the major traditional companies and would not otherwise be available. The success of small pharmaceutical companies in providing lowcost, safe, and effective choices ensures price competition and the availability of an extensive array of consumer products. NPA's mission is to support and advance the substantial common interests of its members. To this end, NPA provides a forum for discussion and agreement of mutually beneficial goals. It establishes a vehicle for the organization and direction of grass roots lobbying activity and other actions directed towards obtaining legislative and regulatory relief for its member companies.

Publications:
NPA & News Washington Report. bi-m.

Meetings/Conferences:
1999 – San Antonio, TX/Feb. 17-19

Nat'l Pharmaceutical Ass'n (1947)
107 Kilmayne Dr., Suite C
Cary, NC 27511
Toll Free: (800)944 - 6742
Members: 350 individuals
Staff: 1
Annual Budget: under $10,000
Exec. Consultant: Terrence V. Burroughs

Historical Note
Members are black pharmacists and pharmacy students. Membership: $100/year (individual).

Publications:
Newsletter. q.

Meetings/Conferences:
Annual Meetings: Summer/350
1999 – Orlando, FL(Hotel Royal Plaza)/July 23-27

Nat'l Pharmaceutical Council (1953)
1894 Preston White Drive
Reston, VA 22091
Tel: (703)620-6390   Fax: (703)476-0904
Members: 29 companies
Staff: 15
Annual Budget: $2-5,000,000
President: Karen Williams, &1
Meeting Planner: Kathryn Gleason
V. President: Patricia L. Adams
V. President, Health Care Systems: Gary S. Persinger
V.P., Scientific Affairs: Richard A. Levy

Historical Note
Members are research-intensive companies producing brand name prescription medicines. NPC conducts and disseminates research on the appropriate use of pharmaceuticals and prepares educational and informative resources on behalf of the pharmaceutical research industry.

Publications:
Pharmaceutical Benefits Under State Medical Assistance Programs. a.

Meetings/Conferences:
1999 – Palm Beach(Ritz Carlton)/Oct. 24-26

Nat'l Phlebotomy Ass'n (1978)
1901 Brightseat Road
Landover, MD 20785
Tel: (301)386-4200   Fax: (301)386-4203
Members: 15,000 individuals
Staff: 9
Annual Budget: $250-500,000
Chief Exec. Officer: Diane C. Crawford

Historical Note
NPA's primary focus is on education and research in phlebotomy; it provides certification to individuals through school programs. Accreditation mechanism for phlebotomy training programs. Membership: $95(certification); $60/year (renewal fee).

Publications:
The Tourniquet. semi-a. adv.

Meetings/Conferences:
Annual Meetings: August

Nat'l Plant Board (1925)
c/o Nebraska Dept. Agriculture
P.O. Box 99756
Lincoln, NE 68509
Tel: (402)471-2394   Fax: (402)423-5621
E-Mail: stephenj@agr.state.ne.us
Web Site: http://www.aphis.usda.gov/ppq/NPB
Members: 51 individuals
Annual Budget: $10-25,000
President: Stephen V. Johnson

Historical Note
Representatives from each state and Puerto Rico interested in protecting agriculture, forestry and horticulture throughout the U.S. by pest control and plant quarantine. Affiliated with the Nat'l Ass'n of State Departments of Agriculture. Has no paid staff. Membership: $125/year (state).

Publications:
Minutes of Annual Meeting. a.

Meetings/Conferences:
Annual Meetings: Third week of August/75
1999 – Portland, OR

Nat'l Plastercraft Ass'n (1972)
c/o Chris-Crafts
3417 Apple Dr.
St. Charles, MO 63301-3212
Members: 100 companies
Annual Budget: under $10,000
President: Vincent Chris

Historical Note
Formerly (1980) Plastercraft Ass'n. Makers and dealers in plaster and plaster products and molds for the hobby industry. Affiliated with the Hobby Industry Ass'n of America. Has no paid officers or full-time staff. Membership: $50/year.

Publications:
Membership Directory. a. adv.
The Plastercrafter. q. adv.

Meetings/Conferences:
Annual Meetings: June/300-400

Nat'l Plasterers Council
30575 Trabuco Canyon Road, Suite 104
Trabuco Canyon, CA 92678-3002
Tel: (949)459-8735   Fax: (949)858-9607
Exec. Director: Lyn Paymer

Meetings/Conferences:
1999 – Newport Beach, CA

Nat'l Plumbing Bureau (1989)
1385 Piccard Drive
Rockville, MD 20850
Tel: (301)869-5800   Fax: (301)990-9690
E-Mail: npb@ncaa.org
Web Site: http://www.ncaa.org/npb.htm
Members: 1,300 firms
Annual Budget: $2-5,000,000
Chairman: Robert A. Rimel
Exec. V. President: John Gentille
Director of Member Services: Patricia Fink

Historical Note
A department of the Mechanical Contractors Ass'n of America, NPB assists plumbing contractors in becoming better equipped to conduct business.

Publications:
Plumbing Bulletin. q.
Reporter. m.

Meetings/Conferences:
Annual Meetings: In conjunction with the MCAA national convention.
1999 – Orlando, FL(Disney Yacht Club)/Feb. 20-25
2000 – San Diego, CA(Marriott)/Feb. 19-24
2001 – Wailea, HI(Grand Wailea Resort)/Feb. 10-15

Nat'l Podiatric Medical Ass'n (1971)
1706 E. 87th St.
Chicago, IL 60617-2740
Tel: (773)374-1616   Fax: (773)374-5860
Members: 200 individuals
Annual Budget: $10-25,000
President: Dr. Neil Horsley, DPM

Historical Note
Formerly (1987) Nat'l Podiatry Ass'n. Members are minority podiatrists.

Publications:
Newsletter. a.

Meetings/Conferences:
Annual Meetings: March-April

Nat'l Police Officers Ass'n of America (1955)

7811 Old Tree Run
Louisville, KY 40222
Tel: (502)425-9215   *Fax:* (502)326-3705
Members: 6,200 individuals
Staff: 2
Annual Budget: $50-100,000
Nat'l Exec. Director and Editor: John R. & Moore

Historical Note
NPOA active members are law enforcement, corrections, security, and military officers. Promotes training through scholarships, seminars, and a yearly conference. Membership: $18/year (individual); $75/year (organization).

Publications:
Nat'l Police Review. q. adv.

Meetings/Conferences:

Nat'l Policy Ass'n *(1934)*
1424 16th St., N.W., Suite 700
Washington, DC 20036
Tel: (202)265-7685   *Fax:* (202)797-5516
Members: 750 orgs, institutions & individuals
Staff: 20
Annual Budget: $1-2,000,000
President and C.E.O.: Malcolm R. Lovell, Jr.
Coordinator, Meetings: Joan Anderson
Senior, V. President: James A. Auerbach

Historical Note
Founded during the Great Depression of the 1930's as the Nat'l Economic and Social Planning Ass'n; became Nat'l Planning Ass'n in 1941, and assumed its present name in 1997. NPA is a private, non-profit, non-political organization that brings together leaders from business, labor, agriculture, and the applied and academic professions to identify emerging problems confronting the nation and agree upon policies and programs to cope with them. Membership:$100 (individual); varies(organization).

Publications:
Looking Ahead. q.

Meetings/Conferences:
Annual Meetings: None held.

Nat'l Pork Producers Council *(1954)*
P.O. Box 10383
Des Moines, IA 50306
Tel: (515)223-2600   *Fax:* (515)223-2646
Web Site: http://www.nppc.org/
Members: 85,000 individuals
Staff: 100
Annual Budget: $25-50,000,000
C.E.O.: Alan Tank
Vice President, Communications: Charles Harness
Manager, Meeting Services: Kathy Codner
Senior V. President, Programs: Neil Dierks
V. President, Eduaction, Environment, & Production Research: Earl Dotson
Senior V. President, Administrative Services: Jim Meimann
C.F.O.: Jim Stavneak

Historical Note
Established as the National Swine Growers Council, NPPC assumed its present name in 1967 and is now a federation of 44 state associations.

Publications:
Pork Report. 9/yr.

Meetings/Conferences:
Annual Meetings: March, during the Nat'l Pork Industry Forum
1999 – Nashville, TN/March 4-6

Nat'l Postal Mail Handlers Union
1101 Connecticut Ave., N.W., Suite 500
Washington, DC 20036-4303
Tel: (202)833-9095   *Fax:* (202)833-0008
Web Site: http://npmhu.org
Members: 52,000 individuals
President: William H. Quinn

Historical Note
A division of the Laborers' Internat'l Union of North America, AFL-CIO.

Publications:
Mail Handler Exchange Magazine. q. adv.
Mail Handlers Newspaper. m.

Meetings/Conferences:
Quadrennial Meetings: (2000)

Nat'l Postsecondary Agriculture Student Organization *(1979)*
P.O. Box 221897
Sacramento, CA 95822
Tel: (916)395-5697   *Fax:* (916)395-5699
E-Mail: kperry@ednet.cc.ca.us
Web Site: www.ffa.org
Members: 1,200 individuals, 59 institutions
Staff: 1
Annual Budget: $100-250,000
Exec. Director: Kimberly A. Perry

Historical Note
Members are institutions educating agricultural students on the college level. Membership: $15/year (individual); $50/year (institution).

Publications:
Newsletter. 3/year.

Meetings/Conferences:
Annual Meetings: March
1999 – Joplin, MO/March 10-13
2000 – Des Moines, IA/March 15-18

Nat'l Potato Council *(1948)*
5690 DTC Blvd., Suite 230 E
Englewood, CO 80111-3200
Tel: (303)773-9295   *Fax:* (303)773-9296

E-Mail: npcspud@ix.netcom.com
Web Site: http://www.npcspud.com
Members: 10,500 individuals
Staff: 5
Annual Budget: $10-25,000,000
Exec. Director: Alan R. Middaugh
Grower Relations/Communications Assistant: Kristen F. Damazio
Finance Assistant: Carol L. Mitchell
Industry Relations Director: David R. Lavway

Historical Note
Represents all U.S. potato growers on federal legislative and regulatory issues. Membership: $50/year (individual).

Publications:
Insider. w.
Potato Statistical Year Book. a. adv.
Spudletter. 1-3/yea.

Meetings/Conferences:
Annual Meetings: January San Diego, CA(Catamaran Resort)/Jan. 16-20
1999 – Maui, HI(Westin Maui)/Jan. 12-15
2000 – Orlando, FL(Coronado Springs Resort)/Jan. 11-15

Nat'l Potato Promotion Board *(1972)*
7555 E. Hampden Ave., Suite 412
Denver, CO 80231-4835
Tel: (303)369-7783   *Fax:* (303)369-7718
Members: 8,000 individuals
Staff: 14
Annual Budget: $5-10,000,000
President/C.E.O.: Douglas W. Slothower
V. President, Finance and Administration: Lonnie Hart
Administrator, Exec. Office: Karen Trouly
V. President, Marketing: Linda McCashion

Historical Note
Also known as The Potato Board. Founded in 1972 by federal law and a grower referendum. The Board was organized to operate a national promotion plan for potatoes, to position it as a low-calorie, nutritious vegetable and to facilitate market expansion into such areas as domestic and export sales.

Publications:
Tuber News.

Meetings/Conferences:
1999 – Denver, CO(Westin Tabor Center)/March 19-20

Nat'l Poultry and Food Distributors Ass'n *(1967)*
958 McEver Road Ext., Suite B-5
Gainesville, GA 30504
Tel: (770)535-9901   *Fax:* (770)535-7385
E-Mail: NPFDA@aol.com
Web Site: http://www.INTERXCHANGE.COM/NPFDA
Members: 250 companies
Staff: 2
Annual Budget: $100-250,000
Exec. Director: Kristin McWhorter

Historical Note
Formerly (1992) the Nat'l Independent Poultry and Food Distributors Ass'n. Established to represent the varied voices of independent poultry distributors, processors, marketing firms and allied suppliers. Provides members with cost saving programs. Membership: $450/year (corporate).

Publications:
NIPFDA Handbook/Directory. a. adv.
NPFDA News Newsletter. m. adv.

Meetings/Conferences:
1999 – Atlanta, GA(Hyatt Regency)/Jan. 17-21/700
1999 – Scottsdale, AZ(Radisson)/April 8-11/125
2000 – Atlanta, GA(Hyatt Regency)/Jan. 18-21/800
2000 – Biloxi, MS(Beau Rivage Resort)/April 6-9/125
2001 – San Destin, FL/April 19-22/125

Nat'l Precast Concrete Ass'n *(1965)*
10333 North Meridian Street, Suite 272
Indianapolis, IN 46290-1081
Tel: (317)571-9500   *Fax:* (317)571-0041
Toll Free: (800)366 - 7731
E-Mail: npca@precast.org
Web Site: www.precast.org
Members: 700 companies
Staff: 12
Annual Budget: $2-5,000,000
President: Ty E. Gable, CAE
Director of Marketing: Rick Del Vecchio
Director of Membership: Brenda Malayeri
Director of Administration: Daryl Shannon
Director of Technical Services: John Talbot

Historical Note
Membership: $595-$1,650/year (company).

Publications:
MC Magazine.

Meetings/Conferences:
Annual Meetings: February-March
1999 – Orlando, FL/Feb. 19-24/2400
2000 – Kansas City, MO/March 3-8

Nat'l Prehealth Student Ass'n

Historical Note
The student support division of Nat'l Ass'n of Advisors for the Health Professions, which provides administrative support.

Nat'l Prepared Food Ass'n *(1953)*
485 Kinderkamack Road
Second Floor
Oradell, NJ 07649
Tel: (201)634-1870   *Fax:* (201)634-1871
E-Mail: 1870@aol.com
Members: 170 businesses
Staff: 4
President: Michael L. Isaacs

Historical Note
Formerly (1981) Nat'l Prepared Frozen Food Processors Ass'n and (1994) Nat'l Prepared Frozen Food Ass'n. Promotes the common interests of those engaged in the prepared frozen foods industry and educates processors, distributors, merchandisers, and the public to the necessity and advantages of the proper handling and use of prepared frozen foods. Membership: $295/year.

Publications:
NPFA Executive Bulletin. q. adv.

Meetings/Conferences:
1999 – Ft. Lee, NJ(Harbor House)

Nat'l Press Photographers Ass'n *(1946)*
3200 Croasdaile Drive, Suite 306
Durham, NC 27705-2588
Tel: (919)383-7246   *Fax:* (919)383-7261
E-Mail: npp2@mindspring.com
Web Site: http://www.sunsite.unc.edu/nppa
Members: 11,500 individuals
Staff: 7
Annual Budget: $1-2,000,000
Exec. Director: Allen Dew

Historical Note
Membership: $40/year (student); $75/year (professional).

Publications:
News Photographer. m. adv.
NPPA Membership Directory. a. adv.

Meetings/Conferences:
Annual Meetings: Summer
1999 – Denver, CO(Adam's Mark)/June 30-July 3/200

Nat'l Prison Hospice Ass'n *(1991)*
P.O. Box 3769
Boulder, CO 80307-3769
Tel: (303)543-8913   *Fax:* (303)554-6011
E-Mail: lizcnpha.org
Members: 10 hospice care organizations
Staff: 1
Annual Budget: $25-50,000
Exec. Director: Elizabeth L. Craig

Historical Note
Mission is to promote hospice care for terminally ill inmates and those facing the prospect of dying in prison. Goal is assist and support corrections professionals in their continuing efforts to develop high-quality patient care procedures and management programs.

Publications:
NPHA Newsletter. q.

Nat'l Private Truck Council *(1988)*
66 Canal Center Plaza, Suite 600
Alexandria, VA 22314
Tel: (703)683-1300   *Fax:* (703)683-1217
Members: 1,300 companies
Staff: 18
Annual Budget: $2-5,000,000
President and C.E.O.: John A. McQuaid
Director, Communications: James Galligan
Director of Meetings, Conventions & Membership: Wendy Davison
Dir., Finance and Human Resources: Nancey Jo Tolliver
Director, Safety: Jim York
Director, Research and ITS Programs: Dave Barry
Dir., Fleet Management Services: Lisa Carol Deyo

Historical Note
Formed in 1988 in consolidation of Private Carrier Conference with Private Truck Council of America. In 1990, NPTC formed the Private Fleet Management Institute, a research, education, and certification subsidiary. Coordinates activities with Private Motor Truck Council of Canada, and the North American Private Truck Council, formed in 1993.

Publications:
PFMI Review. q.
Private Carrier. m. adv.
Private Line Newsletter. m.
Safety & Compliance News. m.

Meetings/Conferences:
Annual Meetings: Spring

Nat'l Professional Soccer League *(1984)*
115 Dewalt Ave. NW, Fifth Floor
Canton, OH 44702
Tel: (330)455-4625   *Fax:* (330)455-3885
E-Mail: NPSL1@AOL.com
Web Site: www.NPSL.com
Members: 15 clubs
Staff: 6
Commissioner: Steve Paxos
Director of Media Relations: Bob Young
Director of Operations: Paul Luchowski

Historical Note
NPSL is an indoor league dedicated to North American players and its fans. NPSL consists of 13 teams that are divided into four divisions. NPSL actively pursues corporate sponsorships and provides a variety of promotional opportunities at the local, regional, and nat'l levels.

Publications:
NPSL Guide and Record Book. a. adv.
NPSL News Weekly. w.
NPSL Shootout Magazine. 3 times/year. adv.

Nat'l Propane Gas Ass'n *(1931)*
1600 Eisenhower Lane, Suite 100
Lisle, IL 60532
Tel: (630)515-0600   *Fax:* (630)515-8774
E-Mail: npga@propanegas.com
Web Site: http://www.propanegas.com/npga
Members: 3,500 marketers, producers & suppliers
Staff: 32
Annual Budget: $2-5,000,000

Exec. V. President & General Manager: Daniel N. Myers
V. President, Technical Services: Bruce J. Swiecicki
V. President, Marketing & Member Services: Rita Rubidge
     Pecilunas
Director of Education and Safety: Susan Spear
V. President, Administration and Finance: M. A. Spear
Dir. of Member Services: Jeanne Farrell

Historical Note
Formerly (1988) Nat'l LP-Gas Ass'n. Formed by a merger of the
Nat'l Liquified Petroleum Gas Ass'n and the Nat'l LP Gas Council.
Members are producers and distributors of liquefied petroleum gas
and manufacturers of equipment for its use. Supports the Propane
Industry Political Action Committee and the Nat'l Propane Gas
Foundation. The Propane Vehicle Council (Washington, DC) is a
division of NPGA.

Publications:
NPGA Reports. w.

Meetings/Conferences:
Annual Meetings: Spring/3,000
1999 – Keystone, CO/June 7-9

Nat'l Property Management Ass'n (1970)
1108 Pinehurst Road
Dunedin, FL   34698
Tel: (727)736-3788   Fax: (727)736-6707
E-Mail: NPMA@GTE.NET
Web Site: HTTP://WWW.NPMA.ORG
Members: 2,400 individuals
Staff: 2
Annual Budget: $250-500,000
Exec. Director: Pam Gahr

Historical Note
Formed by a merger of the Nat'l Industrial Property Management
Ass'n and the Property Administration Ass'n. NPMA members
specialize in asset management for federal, state and local
government agencies; industry; educational institutions and non-
profit organizations. Membership: $60/year (individual).

Publications:
Property Professional. bi-m. adv.

Meetings/Conferences:
Annual Meetings: Summer
1999 – Orlando, FL

Nat'l Psychological Ass'n for Psychoanalysis (1948)
150 West 13th St.
New York, NY   10011-7891
Tel: (212)924-7440
E-Mail: info@npap.org
Web Site: http://www.npap.org
Members: 362 individuals
Staff: 2
Exec. Director: Annabella B. Nelken

Historical Note
Founded in 1948 by Dr. Theodor Reik.

Publications:
News and Reviews. 3/year.
The Psychoanalytic Review. bi-m. adv.

Meetings/Conferences:
Annual Meetings: December

Nat'l Public Employer Labor Relations Ass'n (1971)
1620 I St., N.W., 4th Floor
Washington, DC   20006
Tel: (202)296-2230   Fax: (202)293-2352
Members: 2,300 individuals
Staff: 4
Annual Budget: $250-500,000
Exec. Director: Roger E. Dahl

Historical Note
Members are federal, state, county and municipal labor and
employee relations professionals. Membership: $125/year
(individual).

Publications:
NPELRA Newsletter. 11/yr.

Meetings/Conferences:
Annual Meetings: March-April

Nat'l Purchasing Institute (1968)
P.O. Box 2777
Reno, NV   89505
Tel: (702)332-1674   Fax: (702)333-0648
Web Site: http://npi.purchasing.co.harris.tx.us
Members: 600 individuals
Staff: 1
Annual Budget: $100-250,000
Exec. Director: Richard Schlegel

Historical Note
Established in 1968 in Galveston, Texas as The Southern
Purchasing Institute; assumed its present name in 1973. Members
are educational, government, and institutional purchasing
administrators. Membership: $150/year (individual).

Publications:
Conference Program. a. adv.
Membership Directory. a. adv.
Purchasing News. bi-m.

Meetings/Conferences:

Nat'l Quartz Producers Council (1967)
P.O. Box 1719
Wheat Ridge, CO   80034-1719
Tel: (303)430-1307   Fax: (303)430-1426
Members: 6 producers
Staff: 1
Annual Budget: under $10,000
V. President: Marc R. Busley

Historical Note
Members are producers of crushed quartz for use in decorative
architectural concrete.

Nat'l Railroad Construction and Maintenance Ass'n (1967)
122 C St., N.W., Suite 850
Washington, DC   20001-2109
Tel: (202)638-7790   Fax: (202)638-1045
Toll Free: (800)883 - 1557
Web Site: http://www.nrcma.org
Members: 250 companies
Staff: 2
Annual Budget: $100-250,000
President: Kimberly Madigan
V.P., Admin./Member Services: Danielle G. Farley

Historical Note
Originated in 1967 with labor negotiations with the Laborers'
Internat'l Union of North America and the Internat'l Union of
Operating Engineers for a national agreement on railroad
construction and maintenance. Members are railroad construction
and maintenance contractors, manufacturing, supply and service
firms. Formerly (until 1978), Railroad Construction and
Maintenance Ass'n. Membership: $600-2,500/year (contractors);
$750/year (suppliers).

Publications:
Directory. a. adv.
Medical Contractor Safety Program. a.
On Track Newsletter. bi-w.

Meetings/Conferences:
Annual Meetings: Winter
1999 – Palm Springs, CA(Westin Mission Hills)/Jan. 8-12
2000 – Coral Gables, FL(The Biltmore Hotel)/Jan. 7-11

Nat'l Railroad Freight Committee

Historical Note
Membership: $150-$500/year (organization/company).

Nat'l Reading Conference (1950)
122 S. Michigan Ave., Suite 1776
Chicago, IL   60603
Tel: (312)431-0013   Fax: (312)431-8697
E-Mail: nrc@fmtp.vmai.momapplei.com
Members: 1,100 individuals
Staff: 5
Annual Budget: $100-250,000
Exec. Director: Judith C. Burnison

Historical Note
Teachers involved in college and adult education literacy programs
and research. Membership: $70/year (regular); $115/year (family);
$35/year (student); $50/year (emeritus).

Publications:
Journal of Literacy Research. q. adv.
NRC Yearbook. a.

Meetings/Conferences:
Annual Meetings: Winter
1999 – Orlando, FL/Dec. 1-4

Nat'l Ready Mixed Concrete Ass'n (1930)
900 Spring St.
Silver Spring, MD   20910
Tel: (301)587-1400   Fax: (301)585-4219
Web Site: http://www.nrmca.org
Members: 1,200 producers
Staff: 20
Annual Budget: $2-5,000,000
President: Robert A. Garbini

Historical Note
Affiliated with the Nat'l Aggregates Ass'n. Sponsors the Nat'l
Ready Mixed Concrete Ass'n Political Action Committee.

Meetings/Conferences:
Annual Meetings: January

Nat'l Real Estate Forum (1978)
352 Hungerford Dr.
Rockville, MD   20850-4117
Tel: (301)251-5220   Fax: (301)762-3456
Members: 200 individuals
Staff: 5
Exec. V. President: Lewis O. Kerwood

Historical Note
Formerly (1998) Nat'l Society for Real Estate Finance. Incorporated
in Delaware in 1978 as the Nat'l Ass'n of Certified Mortgage
Bankers, it began functioning in the spring of 1979 and was
rechartered under its present name in 1982. Membership consists
of individuals who have achieved distinction in some aspect of real
estate/real estate finance.

Nat'l Real Estate Investors Ass'n (1985)

Historical Note
Address unknown in 1998.

Nat'l Realty Committee (1969)
1420 New York Ave., N.W., Suite 1100
Washington, DC   20005
Tel: (202)639-8400   Fax: (202)639-8442
E-Mail: email@nrc.org
Members: 220 firms
Staff: 11
Annual Budget: $2-5,000,000
President and C.E.O.: Jeffrey D. DeBoer
V.P., Communications: Audra S. Capas
Director, Meetings: Kate Gilman
V. President and Counsel: Roger Platt
V. President, Membership: Clifton E. Rodgers, Jr.

Historical Note
NRC serves as the real estate industry's roundtable for national
policy issues affecting the income-producing real estate sector,
including capital, credit, taxes, the environment,
telecommunications, technology and investment-related issues.
Members are real estate owners, advisors, builders, investors,
lenders and managers. Members are top business leaders from more

than 200 U.S. public and private companies from the commercial
real estate industry. Supports the REALPAC Political Action
Committee.

Publications:
Alerts. irreg.
Bulletins.
Cornerstone. bi-m.
Perspective issue papers. irreg.

Meetings/Conferences:
Annual Meetings: Held in Washington, DC.

Nat'l Recovery and Collection Ass'n (1974)

Historical Note
Address unknown in 1996.

Nat'l Recreation and Park Ass'n (1965)
22377 Belmont Ridge Road
Ashburn, VA   20148
Tel: (703)858-0784   Fax: (703)858-0794
Web Site: http://www.nrpa.org/nrpa
Members: 24,000 individuals
Staff: 52
Annual Budget: $5-10,000,000
Exec. Director: R. Dean Tice
Dir., Marketing and Communications: Michael Corwin
Director of Public Policy: Barry Tindall
Director of Resource Development: Chris Bresnan
Director of Professional Services: Van Anderson
Director of Operations: Elaine S. Lynch
Membership Director: Patricia Cartwright

Historical Note
Formed by a merger of the American Ass'n of Zoological Parks and
Aquariums (founded in 1924), the American Institute of Park
Executives (formed in 1898), the American Recreation Soc. (formed
in 1938), the Nat'l of State Parks (founded in 1921) and the Nat'l
Recreation Ass'n (founded in 1906). Has an annual budget of
approximately $7.6 million.

Publications:
Journal of Leisure Research. q.
National Job Bulletin. bi-m.
Park Practice. q.
Parks and Recreation. m. adv.
Programmers Information Network. q.
Recreation and Parks Law Reporter. q.
Therapeutic Research Journal. q.

Meetings/Conferences:
Annual Meetings: Fall/4,000
1999 – Nashville, TN

Nat'l Refrigeration Contractors Ass'n (1946)
1900 Arch St.
Philadelphia, PA   19103-1498
Tel: (215)564-3484   Fax: (215)963-9785
E-Mail: assnhqt@netaxs.com
Members: 65 companies
Staff: 2
Annual Budget: $50-100,000
Exec. Director: Elizabeth Barnett-Franks

Historical Note
Formerly (1995) Nat'l Commercial Refrigeration Sales Ass'n.
Members are installing contractors, manufacturers and distributors
of commercial refrigeration equipment. Membership: $300-550/yr.

Publications:
Membership Directory.
Refrigeration News (newsletter). m.

Meetings/Conferences:
Annual Meetings: March
1999 – Key Largo, FL(Marriott Beach Resort)/Feb. 13-16

Nat'l Register of Health Service Providers in Psychology (1974)
1120 G St., N.W., Suite 330
Washington, DC   20005-3801
Tel: (202)783-7663   Fax: (202)347-0550
E-Mail: natlregister@aol.com
Web Site: http://www.nationalregister.com
Members: 16,000 individuals
Staff: 19
Annual Budget: $1-2,000,000
Exec. Officer: Judy E. Hall, Ph.D.
Marketing Coordinator: Marilyn Humm

Historical Note
Established to identify licensed psychotherapists who are qualified
to deliver health care services. Provides credential verification to the
health care industry through its subsidiary, HSP Verified.
Membership: $95/year.

Publications:
Legal Update. 3-4/year.
Nat'l Register of Health Service Providers in Psychology. a.
Register Report. 3-4/year.

Meetings/Conferences:
Annual Meetings: None held.

Nat'l Registry of Environmental Professionals (1983)
P.O. Box 2099
Glenview, IL   60025
Tel: (847)724-6631   Fax: (847)724-4223
E-Mail: nrep@aol.com
Members: 10,000 individuals
Staff: 8
Annual Budget: $500-1,000,000
Exec. Director: Richard A. Young
Director of Communications: Alan Richards
V. President, Training: Valcar Bowman, Ph.D.
Senior Director: Edward Beck, Ph.D.
Director, Membership: Carol Schellinger

Historical Note
Membership: $90/yr.

Publications:
Code of Professional Practice.
Registry Report. bi-m. adv.
Meetings/Conferences:
Annual Meetings: Semi-Annual meetings
1999 – Las Vegas, NV

Nat'l Rehabilitation Administration Ass'n
1020 W. 5th St.
Dickinson, ND   58601
Tel: (701)227-7415   *Fax:* (701)227-7418
Members: 1000 individuals
President: Dale Sattler
Historical Note
*A professional division of the Nat'l Rehabilitation Ass'n;
information on NRAA may also be obtained from NRA. Members
are non-profit rehabilitation administrators, state agency vocational
rehabilitation administrators and private rehabilitation
administrators. NRAA supports professional training sessions on
the state and regional levels and encourages professional
development of rehabilitation administrators. Membership:
$50/year, plus NRA dues (professional); $25/year, plus NRA dues
(affiliate).*
Publications:
Journal of Rehabilitation Administration.
NRAA Newsletter.

Nat'l Rehabilitation Ass'n *(1925)*
633 South Washington St.
Alexandria, VA   22314-4109
Tel: (703)836-0850   *Fax:* (703)836-0848
E-Mail: info@nationalrehab.org
Web Site: http://www.nationalrehab.org
Members: 11,000 individuals
Staff: 10
Annual Budget: $1-2,000,000
Exec. Director: Michelle Vaughan
Director, Program Services: Carol Jaafar
Director, Governmental Affairs: Thomas Stewart
Historical Note
*Founded in 1925 and incorporated in the District of Columbia in
1963. Membership consists of those concerned with the
rehabilitation of the physically and mentally impaired. Professional
divisions include: Nat'l Ass'n for Independent Living, Nat'l Ass'n of
Rehabilitation Instructors, Nat'l Ass'n of Rehabilitation Secretaries,
Nat'l Ass'n of Service Providers in Private Rehabilitation, Nat'l
Ass'n on Multi-cultural Rehabilitation Concerns, Nat'l
Rehabilitation Administration Ass'n, Nat'l Rehabilitation
Counseling Ass'n, and Vocational Evaluation and Work Adjustment
Ass'n (see separate listings). Membership: $91/year (individual).*
Publications:
Contemporary Rehabilitation. 6/year. adv.
Guide for Accessibility.
Journal of Rehabilitation. q. adv.
Mary Switzer Monograph. a. adv.
Meetings/Conferences:
Annual Meetings: Fall/800

Nat'l Rehabilitation Counseling Ass'n *(1958)*
8807 Sudley Road, Suite 102
Manassas, VA   20110-4719
Tel: (703)361-2077   *Fax:* (703)361-2489
Members: 4,000 individuals
Staff: 2
Annual Budget: $100-250,000
Administrator: Richard Coelho, Ph.D.
Historical Note
*A professional division of the Nat'l Rehabilitation Ass'n.
Membership: $50/year, plus NRA dues.*
Publications:
Journal of Applied Rehabilitation Counseling. q. adv.
With One Voice. bi-m.
Meetings/Conferences:
Annual Meetings: September, with Nat'l Rehabilitation Ass'n.
1999 – Dallas, TX(Sheridan)/March 5-7

Nat'l Reining Horse Ass'n
3000 N.W. 10th St.
Oklahoma City, OK   73107-5302
Tel: (405)946-7400   *Fax:* (405)946-8410
Web Site: www.nrha.com
Members: 9,000 individuals
Staff: 13
Annual Budget: $250-500,000
Historical Note
Membership: $40/year.
Publications:
Reiner. 11/year. adv.
Meetings/Conferences:
Annual Meetings: June/100

Nat'l Religious Broadcasters *(1944)*
7839 Ashton Ave.
Manassas, VA   20109
Tel: (703)330-7000   *Fax:* (703)330-7100
E-Mail: bgustavson@nrb.org
Web Site: http://www.nrb.org
Members: 800 stations, 150 associates
Staff: 15
Annual Budget: $1-2,000,000
President: E. Brandt Gustavson, Ph.D.
Director, Communication: Karl Stoll
V. President, Expositions: Michael Glenn
Director, Finance & Business: Mike Kisha
Director, Membership: Anne Tower
Historical Note
*The oldest and most comprehensive ass'n in the field of religious
broadcasting, representing about 75% of those in the field. Strives
to maintain free access to the U.S. airwaves by religious*

broadcasters and to improve quality of religious media. Individual
members are program producers. Membership Fee: Based on
income.*
Publications:
Directory of Religious Media. a. adv.
Membership Newsletter.
NRB Convention Program/News. a.
Religious Broadcasting. m. adv.
Meetings/Conferences:
1999 – Nashville, TN(Opryland Hotel)/Jan. 30-Feb. 2/6000

Nat'l Reloading Manufacturers Ass'n *(1958)*
1 Centerpointe Dr., Suite 300
Lake Oswego, OR   97035-8613
Members: 25 individuals, 20 companies
Staff: 3
Annual Budget: $10-25,000
Exec. Secretary: William J. Chevalier
Historical Note
Manufacturers of tools and components for reloading ammunition.

Nat'l Remodelers Council
Historical Note
A division of the Nat'l Ass'n of Home Builders of the United States.

Nat'l Remotivation Therapy Organization *(1972)*
P.O. Box 440
York Harbor, ME   03911
Tel: (207)363-7577
Members: 400 individuals
Staff: 1
Annual Budget: $10-25,000
Exec. Director: Michael L. Stotts
Historical Note
*Established in Philadelphia. NRTO members are certified
remotivation therapists. Recertification is every two years.
Membership: $30/year (individual).*
Publications:
Remotivator Newsletter. q. adv.
Meetings/Conferences:
Annual Meetings: Fall
1999 – Boston, MA

Nat'l Renal Administrators Ass'n *(1977)*
11250 Roger Bacon Drive, Suite 8
Reston, VA   22090
Tel: (703)437-4377   *Fax:* (703)435-4390
Web Site: http://www.nraa.org/renal/
Members: 800 individuals, 25 companies
Staff: 3
Annual Budget: $500-1,000,000
Exec. Director: William M. Drohan, CAE
Historical Note
*NRAA was formed to provide a vehicle for the development of
educational and informational services for administrative personnel
involved in the ESRD program. Membership: $250/year
(professional); $1,000/year (corporate).*
Publications:
NRAA Journal. a. adv.
NRAA Membership Directory. a.
President's Letter. m.
Meetings/Conferences:
Semi-Annual Meetings: Fall and Spring(Administrators
   Workshop)
1999 – San Francisco, CA(Hyatt Regency)
2000 – Washington, DC(Marriot Renaissance)

Nat'l Renderers Ass'n *(1933)*
801 N. Fairfax St., Suite 207
Alexandria, VA   22314
Tel: (703)683-0155   *Fax:* (703)683-2626
Members: 260 companies and plants
Staff: 12
Annual Budget: $2-5,000,000
Exec. Director and C.E.O.: Tom Cook
Convention Coordinator: Marty Covert
Historical Note
*NRA is a trade organization representing companies which are
producers of animal byproducts and supplier firms servicing the
industry. Membership: varies*
Publications:
Render. bi-m. adv.
Renditions. m.
Meetings/Conferences:
Annual Meetings: October-November/600
1999 – Phoenix, AZ/Oct. 19-23

Nat'l Rep/Wholesaler Ass'n *(1979)*
2215 Southridge Dr.
Sachse, TX   75048-4217
Tel: (972)496-1689   *Fax:* (972)496-2434
Members: 75 wholesalers/reps
Annual Budget: $50-100,000
Exec. Officer: Don B. Akerman
Historical Note
*Office furniture representatives that have wholesale outlets.
Affiliated with the Nat'l Office Products Ass'n. Membership:
$1,500/year (organization/company).*
Meetings/Conferences:
Semi-annual Meetings: June and October

Nat'l Research Council *(1916)*
Historical Note
*Established by the National Academy of Sciences in 1916 and
perpetuated at the request of the President of the United States to
serve as the operating arm of the National Academy of Sciences and
the National Academy of Engineering for providing scientific and*

technical advice to the government, the public and the scientific and
engineering communities. Administered by the National Academy of
Sciences, the National Academy of Engineering and the Institue of
Medicine. Not a membership organization.*

Nat'l Restaurant Ass'n *(1919)*
1200 17th St., N.W.
Washington, DC   20036-3097
Tel: (202)331-5900   *Fax:* (202)331-2429
E-Mail: info@dineout.org
Web Site: http://www.restaurant.org
Staff: 225
Annual Budget: $10-25,000,000
President and C.E.O.: Herman Cain
Sr. V.P., Communications: Eric Ruff
Sr. V.P., Government Affairs: Elaine Z. Graham
V.P., Federal Relations: R. Lee Culpepper
V.P., State Relations: Don Thoren
Sr. V.P./Convention Director: Richard J. Gaven
V.P./Corp. Secretary: LaVerne Warlick
V. President/Controller: George Margula
Director, Research: Susan Mills
Sr. V.P./General Counsel: Peter G. Kilgore
V.P., Membership: Frank M. Doyle
Director, Information Services and Tech.: Laurence Himelfarb
Historical Note
*NRA is the foodservice industry's leading trade group with a
membership representing more than 175,000 establishments.
Maintains a Chicago office. Sponsors the National Restaurant
Association Political Action Committee (NRA PAC). Has an annual
budget of approximately $40 million. Membership: $125-
20,000/year (company, based on sales volume).*
Publications:
Restaurants U. S.
Washington Weekly. w.
Meetings/Conferences:
Annual Meetings: Chicago, IL/Spring
1999 – Chicago, IL(McCormick Place)/May 22-25

Nat'l Retail Federation *(1911)*
Liberty Place
325 7th St., N.W., Suite 1000
Washington, DC   20004-2608
Tel: (202)783-7971   *Fax:* (202)737-2849
Toll Free: (800)673 - 4692
Web Site: http://www.nrf.com
Staff: 65
Annual Budget: $5-10,000,000
President: Tracy Mullin
V. President, Marketing and Public Relations: Mike Gatti
Senior V. President, Government Affairs: John Motley
V. President, Director of Political Affairs: Steve Pfister
V. President, International Trade Counsel: Robert P. Hall, III
V. President, State and Federal Relations: Bill Manteria
V. President, Conferences and Exhibitions: Kim Sackett
V. President, Research and Education: Katherine Mance
V. President and General Counsel: Mallory B. Duncan
V. President, Member Services: Christine Jobes
Senior V. President, Member Services: Sandra Kennedy
V. President, Member Services: Bruce Van Kleeck
V. President, Membership: Karen Thiebert-Knobloch
V. President/Publisher/Editor, STORES Magazine: Rick Gallagher
Senior V. President, Information Technology: Don Gilbert
Historical Note
*Founded as Nat'l Retail Dry Good Ass'n, it became the Nat'l Retail
Merchants Ass'n in 1958. Assumed its present name after merging
with the American Retail Federation in 1990. Absorbed the Apparel
Retailers of America in 1995. NRF is the world's largest retail trade
association, with membership that includes the leading department,
specialty, discount, mass merchandise and independent stores, as
well as 32 national and 50 state associations. NRF members
represent an industry that encompasses over 1.4 million U.S. retail
establishments, employs more than 20 million people, 1 in 5
American workers, and registered 1996 sales of more than $2.6
trillion. NRF's international members operate stores in more than
50 nations.*
Publications:
NRF Weekly Tax Update. w.
Retail Sales Outlook. q.
Retail Trade Bulletin. m.
Stores. m. adv.
Washington Retail Insight. w.
Meetings/Conferences:
Annual Meetings: usually New York, NY/January
1999 – (Javits Convention Center)/Jan. 17-20
2000 – (Javits Convention Center)/Jan. 16-19
2001 – (Javits Convention Center)/Jan. 14-17

Nat'l Retail Hardware Ass'n *(1900)*
5822 West 74th St.
Indianapolis, IN   46278-1756
Tel: (317)290-0338   *Fax:* (317)328-4354
Members: 15,000 individuals
Staff: 47
Annual Budget: $50-100,000
Managing Director: John Hammond
Director of Communications: Ellen Hackney
Conventions/Meeting Director: Dianne Allen
Controller: Thomas W. Smith
Historical Note
*Founded in 1900, the organization serves more than 15,000
hardware retailers through its 15 state and regional affiliates in the
U.S. and Canada. Has an annual budget of approximately $6
million. Services include more than 100 educational products,
business consultation, industry research and statistics, and a wide
range of store management aids. Membership: $140/year
(company average).*
Publications:
Do-It-Yourself Retailing. m. adv.

Meetings/Conferences:

Nat'l Retail Hobby Store Ass'n
5440 W. St. Charles Road, Suite 103
Berkeley, IL   60163
Tel: (708)544-3240   *Fax:* (708)544-3253
Web Site: http://www.hobbystores.org
Publications:
Newsletter.
The Hobby Shop Owners Guide. a.
Meetings/Conferences:
Annual Meetings: Quarterly Meetings.

Nat'l Rifle Ass'n of America *(1871)*
11250 Waples Mill Road
Fairfax, VA   22030
Tel: (703)267-1000   *Fax:* (703)267-3918
E-Mail: nra-contact@nra.org
Web Site: http://www.nra.org
Members: 2,800,000 individuals
Staff: 410
Annual Budget: Over $100,000,000
Exec. V. President: Wayne R. LaPierre, Jr.
Historical Note
Formed August 19, 1871 in New York City "to promote and encourage rifle shooting on a scientific basis" and incorporated in the State of New York November 20, 1871 with General Ambrose Burnside as first President. It is the oldest sportsmen's organization in the U.S. Maintains the NRA Political Victory Fund and supports the Institute for Legislative Action (founded in 1975), its political action arm. Has an annual budget over $140 million. Membership: $35/year.
Publications:
American Guardian. m. adv.
American Rifleman. m. adv.
InSights. m. adv.
Shooting Education Update. q. adv.
Shooting Sports USA. m. adv.
The American Hunter. m. adv.
Meetings/Conferences:
1999 – Denver, CO/April 30-May 4/30000

Nat'l Risk Retention Ass'n *(1987)*
4248 Park Glen Road
Minneapolis, MN   55416
Tel: (612)927-9220   *Fax:* (612)929-1318
Toll Free: (800)999 - 4505
Members: 125 individuals
Annual Budget: $100-250,000
Exec. Director: Judith A. Harrington
Publications:
Membership Directory. a. adv.
NRRA Newsletter. bi-m. adv.
Meetings/Conferences:

Nat'l Roadside Vegetation Management Ass'n *(1984)*
218 Rhett Drive, Adams Run
Newark, DE   19702
Tel: (302)832-2960
Web Site: http://www.nrvma.com
Members: 750 individuals
Annual Budget: $25-50,000
Exec. Director: Turney J. Hernandez
Historical Note
NRVMA members are individuals concerned with the management, beautification, and maintenance of roadside vegetation. Membership: $110/year (individual).
Publications:
Newsletter. q.
Proceedings. a.
Meetings/Conferences:
1999 – Louisville, KY(Galt House)/350
1999 – Louisville, KY(Galt House)/Sept. 19-22

Nat'l Roof Deck Contractors Ass'n *(1959)*
104 S. Michigan Ave., Suite 1500
Chicago, IL   60603-1210
Tel: (312)201-0101   *Fax:* (312)201-0214
Members: 60 companies
Staff: 2
Annual Budget: $10-25,000
Exec. Director: George M. Otto, Sr.
Historical Note
Members are contractors installing poured gypsum, lightweight insulating concrete and cementitious wood fibre structural roof deck systems. Formerly (until 1980) known as the Gypsum Roof Deck Foundation.
Meetings/Conferences:
Annual Meetings: January

Nat'l Roofing Contractors Ass'n *(1886)*
O'Hare International Center
10255 W. Higgins Road, Suite 600
Rosemont, IL   60018-5607
Tel: (847)299-9070   *Fax:* (847)299-1183
Web Site: http://www.roofonline.org
Members: 4,000 firms
Staff: 58
Annual Budget: $5-10,000,000
Exec. V. President: William A. Good, CAE
Dir., Meetings/Conventions: Bennett Judson, CMP
Director, Education: Amy Staska
Exec. Director, Nat'l Roofing Foundation: Chris Seidel
Assoc. Exec. Director, Technical Services: Mark Graham
Assoc. Exec. Director, Finance: Harry Ryder
Director, Member Services: Carl Good
Assoc. Exec. Director, Membership: Alison L. LaValley, CAE
Assoc. Exec. Director, Risk Management: Thomas Shanahan, CAE

Historical Note
Installers of all types of roofs and roofing materials. Sponsors and supports the NRCA Political Action Committee. Has an annual budget of approximately $7.3 million. Membership: $395-1300/year (company).
Publications:
Material Reference Guide.
NRCA Annual Membership Directory. a.
Professional Roofing. m. adv.
Meetings/Conferences:
Annual Meetings: Late Winter
1999 – Phoenix, AZ/Feb. 7-10
2000 – Atlanta, GA

Nat'l Rural Education Ass'n *(1907)*
230 Education Bldg.
Colorado State University
Fort Collins, CO   80523-0002
Tel: (970)491-7022   *Fax:* (970)491-1317
E-Mail: jnewlin@lamar.colostate.edu
Web Site: http://www.colostate.edu/Orgs/NREA
Members: 1000 individuals and organizations
Staff: 6
Annual Budget: $50-100,000
Exec. Director: Joseph T. Newlin
Historical Note
Established as the Department of Rural and Agricultural Education of the Nat'l Education Ass'n, it became the Rural Education Ass'n in 1959, the Rural Regional Education Ass'n in 1975, the Rural Education Ass'n in 1986 and assumed its present name in 1987. Purpose is to improve and expand public education in rural areas. Membership: $85/year (individual), $35/year (teachers), $30/year (libraries), $225/year (institution), and $250/year (affiliate).
Publications:
The NREA News. 4/yr. adv.
The Rural Educator. 3/yr. adv.
Meetings/Conferences:
Annual Meetings: Fall

Nat'l Rural Electric Cooperative Ass'n *(1942)*
4301 Wilson Blvd.
Arlington, VA   22203-1860
Tel: (703)907-5500
Web Site: http://www.nreca.org
Members: 1000 cooperatives
Staff: 500
Annual Budget: Over $100,000,000
C.E.O.: Glenn L. English
Manager, Media and Public Relations: Eleanor C. Miller
Director, Communications: Warren Dunn
Director, Govt. Relations: Wallace Rustad
Manager, Annual and Regional Meetings: Russell McKinnon
Exec. V. President, Internal Services: Patrick Gioffre
Chief Counsel and Director, Energy Policy: Wallace F. Tillman
Newspaper Editor: Martin King
Historical Note
Membership consists of cooperative systems, public power and public utility districts. Has an annual budget of approximately $140 million. Sponsors and supports the Action for Rural Electrification Political Action Committee (ACRE PAC).
Publications:
Electric Co-Op Today. w.
Rural Electrification Magazine. m. adv.
Meetings/Conferences:
Annual Meetings: Late Winter/14,000

Nat'l Rural Health Ass'n *(1978)*
1 West Armour Blvd., Suite 203
Kansas City, MO   64111
Tel: (816)756-3140   *Fax:* (816)756-3144
E-Mail: mail@nrharural.org
Web Site: http://www.NRHArural.org
Members: 1,025 individuals, 976 organizations
Staff: 18
Annual Budget: $2-5,000,000
Exec. V. President: Donna M. Williams
Director, Communications: Tammy Houck Talbott
Director, Finance: Robert McVay
Director, Marketing and Membership Services: Michelle Cheney
Director, Development: J. Stuart Hoffman
Historical Note
Formerly (1984) Nat'l Rural Primary Care Ass'n and (1987) Nat'l Rural Health Care Ass'n. Absorbed the American Rural Health Ass'n and the American Small and Rural Hospital Ass'n in 1986. Members are rural health professionals and institutions involved in rural health care. Membership: $125/year (individual), $330-1,190/year (organization), $1,470 /year (supporting), and $40/year (student).
Publications:
Journal of Rural Health. q. adv.
Rural Clinician Quarterly. q.
Rural Health FYI Magazine. bi-m. adv.
Meetings/Conferences:
1999 – San Diego, CA(Sheraton)/May 27-30/1000
2000 – New Orleans, LA/1000
2001 – Dallas, TX/1000
2002 – Kansas City, MO(Hyatt Regency)/1000

Nat'l Rural Letter Carriers' Ass'n *(1903)*
1630 Duke St., Fourth Floor
Alexandria, VA   22314-3465
Tel: (703)684-5545   *Fax:* (703)548-8735
Members: 97,195 individuals
Staff: 20
Annual Budget: $5-10,000,000
President: Steven R. Smith
V.P., Govt. Affairs: Ken Parmelee
Managing Editor: Kathleen N. O'Connor

Historical Note
Independent labor union organized in Chicago in 1903 and composed of 47 state associations. NRLCA is the exclusive bargaining representative for rural carriers. Sponsors and supports the Nat'l Rural Letter Carriers Ass'n Political Action Committee. Membership: $103/year.
Publications:
The National Rural Letter Carrier. bi-w. adv.
Meetings/Conferences:
Annual Meetings: First full week in August/3,000
1999 – Nashville, TN
2000 – Madison, WI
2001 – Atlantic City, NJ
2002 – Portland, ME
2003 – Chicago, IL

Nat'l Rural Water Ass'n *(1976)*
2915 S. 13th St.
Duncan, OK   73533
Tel: (580)252-0629   *Fax:* (580)255-4476
Members: 900 individuals, 120 associate members
Staff: 48
Annual Budget: $10-25,000,000
Exec. Director: Robert K. Johnson
Historical Note
NRWA is a water, wastewater and groundwater public utility membership organization representing over 16,000 utilities through state rural water affiliates. The association provides training, technical assistance, retirement and legislative representation services. Sponsors and supports the NRWA Political Action Committee (Water PAC). Has an annual budget of approximately $20 million. Membership: $25/year (individual).
Publications:
Educational Materials. irreg.
NRWA Bottom Line. m.
Rural Water Magazine. q. adv.
Meetings/Conferences:
Annual Meetings: October-November
1999 – Albuquerque, NM/Oct. 18-20/2200

Nat'l Safety Council *(1913)*
1121 Spring Lake Drive
Itasca, IL   60143-3201
Tel: (630)285-1121   *Fax:* (630)285-1315
Web Site: http://www.nsc.org
Members: 17,500 individuals
Staff: 325
Annual Budget: $25-50,000,000
President: Gerard F. Scannell
Director, Conventions/Meetings: William Fox
Director, Training Group: Neil Boot
Publisher: John Kennedy
Historical Note
Founded September 24, 1913 in Chicago as the Nat'l Council for Industrial Safety. Became the Nat'l Safety Council in 1914 and was granted a charter by Congress August 13, 1953 to arouse and maintain the interest in safety and accident prevention, and to encourage the adoption and institution of safety methods by all persons, corporations and other organizations. Has an annual budget of $46 million.
Publications:
Family Safety and Health. q.
Journal of Safety Research. q.
Safe Driver. m.
Safe Worker. m.
Safety and Health. m. adv.
Today's Supervisor. m.
Traffic Safety. m. adv.
Meetings/Conferences:
Annual Meetings: Fall, Nat'l Safety Congress & Exposition/20,000

Nat'l Safety Management Soc. *(1966)*
123 KyFields
Weaverville, NC   28787-9469
Tel: (828)645-5229   *Fax:* (828)645-5229
Members: 800 individuals
Annual Budget: $25-50,000
President: Carl Griffith
Business Manager: Robert E. LeClerg
Historical Note
A professional society dedicated to the advancement of new concepts of accident prevention and loss control, promoting the role of safety management as an indispensable tool for management improvement, and providing the individual member an opportunity for professional growth. Membership is open to anyone with management responsibilities. Membership: $60/year.
Publications:
Focus. q.
Journal of Safety Management. q.
The Communique. m.
Meetings/Conferences:
Annual Meetings: October, in conjunction with the Nat'l Safety Congress.

Nat'l Sailing Industry Ass'n
Historical Note
A promotional council comprised of Nat'l Marine Manufacturers Ass'n members interested in promoting amateur sailing.

Nat'l Sales and Marketing Council
Historical Note
A council of the Nat'l Ass'n of Home Builders of the United States.

Nat'l Sash and Door Jobbers Ass'n *(1935)*
10225 Robert Trent Jones Pkwy.
New Port Richey, FL   34655-4649
Tel: (727)372-3665
Members: 1,050 companies

Staff: 6
Annual Budget: $2-5,000,000
Exec. V. President, C.E.O.-C.O.O.: Robert T. O'Keefe

Historical Note
Formed by a merger of the Northern and Southern Sash and Door Jobbers Associations (both founded in 1935). Membership:$750-$1300 (organization).

Publications:
Business Math Home Study. a.
Membership Directory and Products Guide. a.
Millwork Home Study. a.
Millwork Product Guide. a.
Millwork Sales Manual.
NSDJA News. m.

Meetings/Conferences:
Annual Meetings: October/3,000
1999 – Nashville, TN/Oct. 2-6
2000 – Philadelphia, PA/Oct. 14-18
2001 – Reno, NV/Oct. 27-31
2002 – San Antonio, TX/Oct. 12-16
2003 – Orlando, FL/Oct. 12-16

Nat'l Scholastic Press Ass'n

Historical Note
See Associated Collegiate Press, Nat'l Scholastic Press Ass'n.

Nat'l School Boards Ass'n *(1940)*
1680 Duke St.
Alexandria, VA 22314-3407
Tel: (703)838-6722   *Fax:* (703)548-5613
E-Mail: abryant@nsba.org
Web Site: http://nsba.org
Members: 54 state level organizations
Staff: 125
Annual Budget: $10-25,000,000
Exec. Director: Anne L. Bryant, Ed.D., CAE
Director, Public Relations: John Butler
Director, Federal Programs: Michelle Richards
Senior Assoc. Exec. Director: Michael Resnick
Director, Education: Donna Haines
Director, Training/Research/Membership Services Department: Adria L. Thomas, CAE
Director, Council of School Attorneys: Susan R. Butler, CAE
General Counsel: Julie Underwood
Director, School Board Members: Ellie Ashford
Dep. Exec. Director: Harold P. Seamon, CAE

Historical Note
Formerly (1940) Nat'l Council of State School Boards Assn's. The Institute for the Transfer of Technology to Education is a division of NSBA. Has an annual budget of approximately $18.0 million.

Publications:
American School Board Journal. m. adv.
School Board News. bi-w. adv.

Meetings/Conferences:
Annual Meetings: Spring/20,000
1999 – San Francisco, CA/April 10-13

Nat'l School Orchestra Ass'n *(1958)*

Historical Note
An affiliate of Music Educators Nat'l Conference, which provides administrative support.

Nat'l School Public Relations Ass'n *(1935)*
15948 Derwood Road
Rockville, MD 20855-2123
Tel: (301)519-0496   *Fax:* (301)519-0494
E-Mail: nspra@nspra.org
Web Site: http://www.nspra.org
Members: 1,700 individuals
Staff: 7
Annual Budget: $500-1,000,000
Exec. Director: Richard Bagin
Associate Director: Karen Kleine
Editorial Coordinator: Andy Grunig
Business Coordinator: Tom Jones

Historical Note
Formerly (1950) School Public Relations Ass'n. Individuals from school districts, national state and local ass'ns, state education agencies, school-community relations programs, and information agencies. Membership: $180/year (professional), $450/year (institutional).

Publications:
It Starts on the Frontline. m.
NSPRA Network. m.

Meetings/Conferences:
Annual Meetings: July/500
1999 – Baltimore, MD(Omni Inner Harbor)
2000 – San Antonio, TX(Hilton Palacio del Rio)
2001 – Minneapolis, MN(Marriott)

Nat'l School Supply and Equipment Ass'n *(1916)*
8300 Colesville Road, Suite 250
Silver Spring, MD 20910
Tel: (301)495-0240   *Fax:* (301)495-3330
Toll Free: (800)395 - 5550
E-Mail: NSSEA@nssea.org
Web Site: http://www.nssea.org
Members: 1,600 companies
Staff: 13
Annual Budget: $1-2,000,000
President: Tim Holt
V. President, Marketing and Communications: Adrienne Watts
Dir., Meetings & Conventions: Monique Ferguson
V. President of Operations: William T. Duffy
Database/Marketing Manager: Emily Haftl

Historical Note
Formerly (1958) Nat'l School Service Institute. Members are manufacturers, distributors, retailers and independent manufacturers representatives of school supplies, instructional materials and equipment. Absorbed the Education Industries Ass'n in 1978.

Publications:
Membership Directory.
State of the School Market.
Tidings. m.

Meetings/Conferences:
Semi-Annual Meeting: Spring and Fall/1,500-2,300

Nat'l School Transportation Ass'n *(1964)*
6213 Old Keene Mill Court
P.O. Box 2639
Springfield, VA 22152
Tel: (703)644-0700   *Fax:* (703)644-9385
E-Mail: info@schooltrans.com
Web Site: http://www.schooltrans.com
Members: 1,500 companies and individuals
Staff: 2
Annual Budget: $250-500,000
Exec. Director: Karen E. Finkel

Historical Note
Formerly (1975) Nat'l Ass'n of School Bus Contract-Operators. Founded in 1964 to represent the interests of school bus contractors, NSTA works with government officials, parents, teachers and all others interested in school bus safety. Supports the Non-Partisan Transportation Action Committee (political action). Membership: $115-7,600/year ($18.50 per vehicle/year).

Publications:
NSTA Newsletter. bi-w.
NSTA Washington Update Fax. bi-w.

Meetings/Conferences:
Annual Meetings: July/400

Nat'l Science Education Leadership Ass'n *(1960)*
P.O. Box 99381
Raleigh, NC 27624-9381
Tel: (919)848-8171   *Fax:* (919)848-0496
E-Mail: pholliday@intercenter.net
Web Site: http://.coe.uwf.edu/NSELA/NSELA.html
Members: 1,230 individuals
Staff: 1
Annual Budget: $25-50,000
Exec. Director: Peggy W. Holliday

Historical Note
Formerly (1994) Nat'l Science Supervisors Ass'n. An affiliate of the Nat'l Science Teachers Ass'n and the American Ass'n for the Advancement of Science, NSELA members include department heads, supervisors, consultants, administrators, coordinators and directors of science programs in public and private educational institutions. Membership: $25/year (individual).

Publications:
Membership Directory. a.
Science Educator Journal. a.
The Navigator. q.

Meetings/Conferences:
Annual Meetings: usually in conjunction with Nat'l Science Teachers Ass'n meeting

Nat'l Science Teachers Ass'n
1840 Wilson Blvd.
Arlington, VA 22201-3000
Tel: (703)243-7100   *Fax:* (703)841-5114
Toll Free: (800)722 - 6782
Web Site: http://www.nsta.org
Members: 53,000 individuals
Staff: 110
Annual Budget: $10-25,000,000
Exec. Director: Gerald F. Wheeler, Ph.D.
Manager, Public Relations: Cynthia S. Workosky
Director, Marketing: Karen B. Baker
Assoc. Director, Business & Finance: Moira Fathy
Assoc. Exec. Director, Administration: Marily DeWall
Assoc. Director, Membership/Programs: Wendell Mohling
Assoc. Director, Publications: Phyllis Marcuccio

Historical Note
NSTA is committed to promoting excellence and innovation in science teaching and learning for all. The association provides many programs and services to science educators, including awards and professional development workshops. NSTA also serves as an advocate for science educators through its programs and legislative campaigns. Membership includes science teachers, scientists, and others involved in science education.

Publications:
Dragonfly. 6/year.
Journal of College Science Teaching. 6/yr. adv.
NSTA Reports. 6/yr. adv.
Quantum. 6/year.
Science and Children. 8/yr. adv.
Science Scope. 8/yr. adv.
The Science Teacher. 9/yr.

Meetings/Conferences:
Annual Meetings: Spring
1999 – Boston, MA/March 25-28
2000 – Orlando, FL/April 6-9
2001 – St. Louis, MO/March 22-25

Nat'l Scoiety for Real Estate Finance

Historical Note
Became (1998) Nat'l Real Estate Forum.

Nat'l Screw Machine Products Ass'n

Historical Note
Became Precision Machined Products Ass'n in 1996.

Nat'l Sculpture Soc. *(1893)*
1177 Avenue of the Americas
New York, NY 10036
Tel: (212)764-5645
Web Site: http://www.sculpturereview.com

Members: 4,000 individuals
Staff: 4
Annual Budget: $250-500,000
Exec. Director: Gwen Pier

Historical Note
Mission is to promote excellence in figurative sculpture throughout the United States, to which end its programs are directed. Members are professional sculptors united to promote the development and appreciation of sculpture. Membership: $40/year (individual).

Publications:
News Bulletin. bi-m.
Sculptors Bookshelf. bien.
Sculpture Review. q. adv.

Meetings/Conferences:
Annual Meetings: always at headquarters New York, NY/January/65-80

Nat'l Seasoning Manufacturers Ass'n *(1972)*
8905 Maxwell Dr., Suite 200
Potomac, MD 20854-3125
Tel: (301)765-9675   *Fax:* (301)299-7523
Members: 25 companies
Staff: 1
Annual Budget: $10-25,000
Exec. Director: Dr. Richard Alsmeyer

Historical Note
Established as the Industrial Meat Seasoning Manufacturers Ass'n, it became the Nat'l Ass'n of Meat Seasoning Manufacturers. In 1981 it became the Nat'l Ass'n of Meat and Food Seasoning Manufacturers and assumed its present name in 1984. Promotes scientific study and research in the seasoning industry. Membership: $500/year (company); $500/year (associate: non-voting).

Meetings/Conferences:
Annual Meetings: With the Institute of Food Technologists in the Summer
1999 – Chicago, IL(McCormick Place)/July 25-28

Nat'l Second Mortgage Ass'n

Historical Note
Became the Nat'l Home Equity Mortgage Ass'n in 1995.

Nat'l Security Industrial Ass'n *(1944)*

Historical Note
Merged with the American Defense Preparedness Ass'n to form the Nat'l Defense Industrial Ass'n in 1997.

Nat'l Selected Morticians *(1917)*
5 Revere Drive, Suite 340
Northbrook, IL 60062-8009
Tel: (847)559-9569   *Fax:* (847)559-9571
Web Site: http://www.nsm.org
Members: 950 firms
Staff: 10
Annual Budget: $500-1,000,000
Exec. Director: George Clarke

Publications:
NSM Bulletin. m.

Meetings/Conferences:
Annual Meetings: Fall/900
1999 – New Orleans, LA/Oct. 5-10

Nat'l Shellfisheries Ass'n *(1909)*
c/o Academy of Natural Sciences
10545 Mackall Rd.
St. Leonard, MD 20685
Tel: (410)586-9709
Web Site: http://www.shellfish.org
Members: 900 individuals
Annual Budget: $50-100,000
Secretary: George Abbe

Historical Note
Organized as Nat'l Ass'n of Shellfish Commissioners, it assumed its present name in 1930 and was incorporated in Maryland in 1968. Members are individuals interested in research on that group of mollusks and crustaceans of economic importance known as shellfish. Has no paid officers or full-time staff. Membership: $40/year (full member), $25/year (student).

Publications:
Journal of Shellfish Research. semi-a.
Newsletter. q.

Meetings/Conferences:
Annual Meetings: late Spring
1999 – Halifax, Nova Scotia/Apr. 18-22

Nat'l Sheriffs' Ass'n *(1940)*
1450 Duke St.
Alexandria, VA 22314-3490
Tel: (703)836-7827   *Fax:* (703)683-6541
Toll Free: (800)424 - 7827
Web Site: http://www.sheriffs.org
Members: 22,000 individuals
Staff: 30
Annual Budget: $2-5,000,000
Exec. Director: A. N. "Bubby" Moser, Jr.
Exec. Secretary: Miriam Kendall
Legislative Liaison: Dean Kueter, Jr.
Director, Meetings: Ross F. Mirmelstein
Director, Membership: Heather Rovston
Publications Director: Janet Hawkins

Historical Note
The NSA is dedicated to assisting sheriffs and other law enforcement practitioners to perform their duties in the most professional manner possible. Membership: $25-100/year (individual); $1,000/year (organization).

Publications:
Sheriff Magazine. bi-m. adv.

Meetings/Conferences:
Annual Meetings: June/3,500
1999 – Columbus, OH/June 26-30

Nat'l Shipyard Ass'n *(1976)*
1600 Wilson Blvd., Suite 1000
Arlington, VA   22209
Tel: (703)351-6734   *Fax:* (703)351-6736
E-Mail: NSA@vesselsalliance.com
Web Site: http://www.nsashipyards.com
Members: 50 shipyards
Staff: 2
Annual Budget: $250-500,000
Exec. Director: Allen Walker
Manager, Government Affairs and Member Services: Susan Swatski

Historical Note
Formerly (1997) the American Waterways Shipyard Conference, NSA is a national trade association representing U.S. shipyards engaged in building, repairing and cleaning commercial and government vessels. Membership: annual dues vary, based on number of employees.

Publications:
Injury & Illness Survey.
NSA Newsline. m.
Wage & Benefit Survey.

Meetings/Conferences:
Annual Meetings: Quarterly Meetings

Nat'l Shoe Retailers Ass'n *(1912)*
9861 Broken Land Pkwy., Suite 255
Columbia, MD   21046-1151
Tel: (410)381-8282   *Fax:* (410)381-1167
Toll Free: (800)673 - 8446
Members: 1,800 individuals
Staff: 12
Annual Budget: $500-1,000,000
President: William Boettge
Director, Marketing: Nancy Hultquist
Manager, Meetings & Conventions: Jeanne Williams
Director of Administration: Dawn Connolly
V. President: Phyllis Endrich

Historical Note
NSRA members are owners of independent shoe stores and managers of multi-store operations, department store shoe sections and leased departments.

Publications:
Business Performance Report. bien.
Shoe Retailing Today Newsletter. bi-m.
Software Directory. bien.

Meetings/Conferences:
Semi-Annual Meetings: Las Vegas, NV/February and
   August/300

Nat'l Shoe Travelers Ass'n *(1910)*
313 Adams St., Suite 101
Abington, MA   02351
Tel: (781)982-8940   *Fax:* (781)871-8033
Toll Free: (800)200 - 6782
Members: 3,200 individuals
Staff: 2
Annual Budget: $50-100,000
Exec. Secretary: Suzanne Flannery

Historical Note
NSTA offers a placement program and other services to members. Membership: $50/year (individual).

Publications:
Open Line. q.

Meetings/Conferences:
Semi-Annual Meetings: Spring and Fall/30

Nat'l Shooting Sports Foundation *(1961)*
11 Mile Hill Road
Newtown, CT   06470-2359
Tel: (203)426-1320
Members: 1,200 businesses
Staff: 25
Annual Budget: $5-10,000,000
President: Robert T. Delfay

Historical Note
Absorbed (1963) Sportmen's Service Bureau. Manufacturers of hunting and shooting equipment and accessories. Supported by about 1150 firms involved in all aspects of the shooting industry, as well as dealers, distributors and sales reps. Annual Budget: $7 million.

Publications:
Shot Business.

Meetings/Conferences:
Annual Meetings: January

Nat'l Show Horse Registry *(1981)*
11700 Commonwealth Dr.
Louisville, KY   40299-2344
Tel: (502)266-5100   *Fax:* (502)266-5806
Members: 1000 individuals, 14 organizations
Staff: 3
Annual Budget: $500-1,000,000
Exec. Director: Robert Peebles

Historical Note
The purpose of the Registry is to create a high performance, low maintenance show horse and to encourage the amateur as well as the professional competitor. Membership: $60/year.

Publications:
National Show Horse Connection. m. adv.

Meetings/Conferences:
Annual Meetings: September/October

Nat'l Shrimp Processors Ass'n *(1957)*
2800 One Atlantic Center

1201 W. Peachtree St.
Atlanta, GA   30309-3450
Tel: (404)873-8500   *Fax:* (404)873-8645
Members: 40 processors
Staff: 2
Annual Budget: $10-25,000
Coordinator: Allene M. Scoma

Historical Note
Formerly (1984) the Nat'l Shrimp Breaders and Processors Ass'n. Membership: $500/year (corporate).

Publications:
Newsnet. q.

Meetings/Conferences:
Annual Meetings: February/100

Nat'l Ski and Snowboard Retailers Ass'n *(1987)*
1699 Wall St.
Mount Prospect, IL   60056-5780
Tel: (847)439-4293   *Fax:* (847)439-0111
Members: 400 companies
Staff: 1
Annual Budget: $10-25,000
President: Thomas B. Doyle

Historical Note
Formerly Nat'l Ski Retailers Ass'n (1996). Retail association providing ski and snowboard shops with business-related services and representation. Administrative support for NSSRA is provided by ASMI, a subsidiary of Nat'l Sporting Goods Ass'n (same location). Membership: $100-300/year.

Publications:
NSSRA Cost of Doing Business Survey. bi-a.
NSSRA Newsletter. q.

Meetings/Conferences:
Annual Meetings: Las Vegas, NV(Convention Center)/March
1999 – Las Vegas, NV(Las Vegas Convention Center)/50

Nat'l Ski Areas Ass'n *(1962)*
133 South Van Gordon St., Suite 300
Lakewood, CO   80228
Tel: (303)987-1111   *Fax:* (303)986-2345
Web Site: http://www.nsaa.org
Members: 330 ski areas and 440 suppliers
Staff: 13
Annual Budget: $1-2,000,000
President: Michael Berry
Markeing Director: Rob Linde
Director of Public Policy: Geraldine Hughes
Director of Conventions and Meetings: Tom Moore
Director of Education: Tim White
Membership Services: Kate Powers

Historical Note
NSAA is a trade ass'n for ski area owners and operators. The association's member areas represent about 90 percent of the skier visits nationwide. For its members, NSAA develops educational programs and employee training materials, and provide information on important industry issues including: OSHA, ADA, NEPA, environmental laws, state regulatory industries, aerial tramway safety and area operations. NSAA also analyzes and provides industry statistics for members and participates in state and federal lobbying efforts.

Publications:
NSAA Member Update.

Meetings/Conferences:
1999 – San Francisco, CA(Marriott Mosgone
   Center)/May 23-26

Nat'l Ski Patrol System *(1938)*
133 S. Van Gordon St., Suite 100
Lakewood, CO   80228-1706
Tel: (303)988-1111   *Fax:* (303)988-3005
Members: 24,500 individuals
Staff: 20
Annual Budget: $500-1,000,000
Exec. Director: Stephen M. Over
Communications Director: Rebecca Ayers
Administrative Director: Frankie Jean Barr
Director, Education: Judith M. Outlaw

Historical Note
Started in 1938 by Minot Dole. Chartered in 1980 by Act of Congress to promote ski safety, the sport of skiing and under the direction of ski area management render immediate first aid to injured skiers and evacuate them from slopes for further attention. Members are trained in all phases of ski patrolling, including W.E.C. first aid, ski mountaineering, avalanche patrol and lift evacuation.

Publications:
Ski Patrol Magazine. q.

Meetings/Conferences:
Annual Meetings: June

Nat'l Slag Ass'n *(1918)*
100 W. Lancaster Ave., Suite 2
Wayne, PA   19087-4043
Tel: (610)971-4840   *Fax:* (610)971-4841
Members: 35 processors
Staff: 2
Annual Budget: $100-250,000
President: Robert W. Twitmyer

Historical Note
Members are processors of steel industry slags for use as a mineral aggregate in construction and manufacturing applications.

Publications:
NSA Bulletin. m.
The Slag Runner. 10/year.

Meetings/Conferences:

Nat'l Small Business Government Contractors Ass'n
   (1982)

Historical Note
Reportedly defunct in 1986.

Nat'l Small Business United *(1937)*
1156 15th St., N.W., Suite 1100
Washington, DC   20005
Tel: (202)293-8830   *Fax:* (202)872-8543
E-Mail: nsbu@nsbu.org
Web Site: http://www.nsbu.org
Staff: 16
Annual Budget: $2-5,000,000
President: Todd O. McCracken
Dir., Govt./Public Affairs: David D'Onofrio
Director, Administration: Rosa Wright
V.P., Member Relations: Jeane Warkentin

Historical Note
Founded and incorporated in Ohio in 1937 as the Nat'l Small Business Men's Ass'n. Became the Nat'l Small Business Ass'n in 1962, the same year in which the American Ass'n of Small Business was absorbed. Mission is "to foster the birth and vigorous development of independent small business." Merged with Small Business United in 1986 and changed its name to Nat'l Small Business United. Sponsors and supports the NSBU Political Action Committee. Acts as an advocate for the small business community.

Publications:
SBU net. w.
Small Business USA. bi-m. adv.

Meetings/Conferences:
Semi-Annual Meetings: Winter and Spring

Nat'l Small College Athletic Ass'n *(1966)*
Historical Note
Address unknown in 1996.

Nat'l Small Shipments Traffic Conference *(1952)*
1750 Pennsylvania Ave., N.W., Suite 1111
Washington, DC   20006
Tel: (202)393-5505   *Fax:* (202)347-8978
Members: 525 companies
Staff: 2
Annual Budget: $500-1,000,000
Exec. Director: Joseph F.H. Cutrona

Historical Note
Founded in 1952 by former members of The National Industrial Traffic League, making LTL ("less than truckload") shipments. Members are truck, air, rail and sea shippers of freight weighing less than 10,000 pounds. Membership fee based on gross annual sales.

Publications:
Package Guidelines. bi-a.
The Small Shipment. bi-w.

Meetings/Conferences:
Semi-annual meetings: Spring and Fall/175
1999 – Naples, FL(Registry)/Apr. 5-8/220
1999 – Washington, DC(Madison Hotel)/Sept. 12-14

Nat'l Soc. for Experiential Education *(1971)*
3509 Haworth Drive, Suite 207
Raleigh, NC   27609-7229
Tel: (919)787-3263   *Fax:* (919)787-3381
E-Mail: info@nsee.org
Web Site: http://www.nsee.org
Members: 1,800 individuals
Staff: 8
Annual Budget: $500-1,000,000
Exec. Director: Sally Migliore

Historical Note
NSEE is an education membership association and acts as a clearinghouse for information on experiential and service learning. Members are college and K-12 faculty; directors of internship, service-learning, school to work, and cooperative education programs; principals, superintendents, and deans; career counselors; and employers who sponsor interns who all have an interest in fostering the effective use of experience as an integral part of education. Experiential Education includes internships, service-learning, school-to-work, cooperative education, field studies, cross-cultural education, leadership development, and active learning in the classroom. Formerly (1992) the Nat'l Soc. For Internships and Experiential Education. Membership: $85/year (individual), $325-750/year (institution).

Publications:
Combining Service and Learning. irreg.
Critical Issues in K-12 Service-Learning: Case Studies. irreg.
Internship as Partnership:Handbook for Campus-based
   Coordinator. irre.
Internship as Partnership:Handbook for Site Supervisors.
   irreg.
Nat'l Directory of Internships. bien.
NSEE Membership Directory. a.
NSEE Quarterly. q.
Program Evaluation Handbook. irreg.
Service Learning in Ed Reform. irreg.
Service-Learning Reader: Reflections and Perspectives. irreg.
Strengthening Experiential Education Within Your
   Instititution. irreg.

Meetings/Conferences:
Annual Meetings: Fall
1999 – San Diego, CA(Princess Resort)

Nat'l Soc. for Graphology *(1972)*
250 W. 57th St.
Room 1228A
New York, NY   10107
Tel: (212)265-1148   *Fax:* (212)307-5671
Members: 300 individuals
Annual Budget: under $10,000
President: Roger Rubin
V. President, Meetings: Irene Lawrence
Treasurer/Accreditations: Janice Klein

Historical Note
Members are professional graphologists and individuals interested in graphology. NSG promotes the study and practice of gestalt graphology. Membership $65/year (individual).
Publications:
"Write-Up" Newsletter. bi-m.
Meetings/Conferences:
Eight Meetings Annually: Jan.-June, Oct, Nov.

Nat'l Soc. for Healthcare Foodservice Management (1990)
204 E St., N.E.
Washington, DC 20002
Tel: (202)546-7236   Fax: (202)547-6348
E-Mail: hfm1mg@aol.com
Web Site: http://www.hfm.org
Members: 2,600 individuals, 175 companies
Staff: 4
Annual Budget: $250-500,000
Exec. Director: Michael J. Giuffrida
Historical Note
HFM members are independent, self-operated healthcare foodservice managers and suppliers to the industry. Membership: $125/year (individual); $650/year (corporate); $50/year (student); $100/year (educational institution).
Publications:
Innovator. q. adv.
Membership & Networking Directory. a. adv.
Meetings/Conferences:
1999 – /Sept. 14-18

Nat'l Soc. for Hebrew Day Schools (1944)
160 Broadway
New York, NY 10038
Tel: (212)227-1000   Fax: (212)406-6934
Members: 600 organizations
Staff: 25
Annual Budget: $500-1,000,000
Exec. V. President: Rabbi Joshua Fishman
Historical Note
Torah Umesorah was originally organized by Rabbinical leaders of Eastern Europe who found haven in America and who wished to re-establish Jewish centers of learning on this continent. NSHDS is the North American organization for Torah Umesorah, supporting the religious and secular learning traditions of the Hebrew Day School. Provides a range of services to member schools.
Meetings/Conferences:
1999 – New York, NY

Nat'l Soc. for Histotechnology (1973)
4201 Northview Dr., Suite 502
Bowie, MD 20716-2604
Tel: (301)262-6221   Fax: (301)262-9188
E-Mail: histo@nsh.org
Web Site: http://www.nsh.org
Members: 4,500 individuals
Staff: 2
Annual Budget: $250-500,000
Exec. Secretary: Roberta Mosedale
Historical Note
Members are laboratory personnel who study tissues and prepare slides for diagnosis by a pathologist. Membership: $40/year (individual), $250/year (organization/company).
Publications:
Journal of Histotechnology. q. adv.
NSH in Action. q.
Meetings/Conferences:
Annual Meetings: Fall
1999 – Providence, RI(Convention Center)/Oct. 16-20/1500
2000 – Milwaukee, WI(Convention Center)/Sept. 16-20/1500
2001 – Charlotte, NC/Sept. 22-27
2002 – Long Beach, CA/Sept. 28-Oct. 3

Nat'l Soc. for Park Resources (1921)
22377 Belmont Ridge Road
Ashburn, VA 20148-4501
Tel: (703)858-2170   Fax: (703)858-0794
Members: 1,200 individuals
Staff: 3
Annual Budget: $10-25,000
Staff Liaison: Chris Bresnan
Historical Note
A division of the Nat'l Recreation and Park Ass'n, NSPR members are professionals concerned with development and management of outdoor facilities.
Publications:
NSPR Tidbits.
Park Practice Program: Design. q.
Park Practice Program: Grist. irreg.
Park Practice Program: Trends. q.
Parks & Recreation Magazine. m.
Parks & Recreation Opportunities Job Bulletin. m.
Recreation & Parks Law Reporter. q.
Meetings/Conferences:
1999 – Nashville, TN/Oct. 20-24
2000 – Phoenix, AZ/Oct. 11-15

Nat'l Soc. for Patient Representation and Consumer Affairs (1972)
Historical Note
Became the Soc. for Healthcare Consumer Advocacy in 1997.

Nat'l Soc. for the Study of Education (1901)
5835 South Kimbark Ave.
Chicago, IL 60637
Members: 1,500 individuals
Staff: 1
Annual Budget: $100-250,000

Secretary-Treasurer: Kenneth J. Rehage
Historical Note
A professional society of professors, administrators, and teachers established as the Nat'l Herbart Soc. for the Scientific Study of Education, it assumed its present name in 1910. Membership: $30/year (regular).
Publications:
Yearbooks of The N. S.
Meetings/Conferences:
Annual Meetings: With one or more of the nat'l educational ass'ns.

Nat'l Soc. of Accountants (1945)
1010 N. Fairfax St.
Alexandria, VA 22314-1574
Tel: (703)549-6400   Fax: (703)549-2984
Toll Free: (800)966 - 6679
Web Site: www.nsacct.org
Members: 17,000 individuals
Staff: 32
Annual Budget: $2-5,000,000
Exec. V. President: William R. Mathisen
Financial Director: John Mericsko
Directo of Member Services: Sandy Herring
Director, Member Services: Jeffrey Thurmond
Special Projects: Arlene Richmond
Historical Note
Formerly (1996) Nat'l Soc. of Public Accountants. NSA is a professional society of practicing accountants and tax practitioners. Sponsors the Accreditation Council for Accountancy and Taxation. Supports the Nat'l Soc. of Public Accountants Political Action Committee and NSPA Scholarship Foundation. Membership: $138/year (individual).
Publications:
The National Public Accountant. m. adv.
The Practitioner. semi-m.
Meetings/Conferences:
Annual: August/1000
1999 – Scottsdale, AZ/Aug. 19-24

Nat'l Soc. of Accountants for Cooperatives (1936)
6320 Augusta Drive, Suite 800
Springfield, VA 22150
Tel: (703)569-3088   Fax: (703)569-0235
E-Mail: bhickey@nsacoop.org
Web Site: nsacoop.org
Members: 2,200 individuals
Staff: 3
Annual Budget: $250-500,000
Exec. Director: Barbra C. Hickey
Historical Note
Members are accountants, attorneys, financial officers and other professionals actively involved in the financial planning and management of cooperative businesses. Membership: $95/year (individual).
Publications:
The Cooperative Accountant. q.
Meetings/Conferences:
Annual Meetings: August/800
1999 – Montreal, Canada
2000 – San Antonio, TX

Nat'l Soc. of Appraiser Specialists (1969)
303 W. Cypress
P.O. Box 12528
San Antonio, TX 78212-0528
Tel: (210)271-0781   Fax: (210)225-8450
Toll Free: (800)486 - 3676
Web Site: http://mfdhousing.com/lgc
Members: 800 individuals
Staff: 4
Annual Budget: $25-50,000
Exec. Director: Gary T. Deane
Historical Note
Founded as Real Estate Law Institute; assumed its current name in 1995. NSAS members are real estate professionals. Offers certification in three specializations: Business Appraisal, Manufactured Housing Valuation, and Real Estate Litigation Management. Membership: $120/year (new member); $55/year (renewal).
Publications:
1998 Directory of Board Certified Specialists.
Agenda. q.
Meetings/Conferences:
Semi-Annual Meetings: Spring and Summer

Nat'l Soc. of Architectural Administrators (1965)
Historical Note
Address unknown in 1996.

Nat'l Soc. of Architectural Engineers (1984)
700 S.W. Jackson St., Suite 702
Topeka, KS 66603-3758
Tel: (913)232-5707   Fax: (913)357-6629
Web Site: http://www.arce.ukans.edu/main.htm
Members: 1,250 individuals
Staff: 8
Annual Budget: $25-50,000
Exec. Director: Jean Barbee
Historical Note
Members are architectural engineers involved in engineering design and/or construction.
Publications:
Membership Directory. a.
NSAE Times. q.
Meetings/Conferences:
Annual Meetings: Fall

Nat'l Soc. of Black Physicists (1977)
North Carolina A&T State Univ.
1601 E. Market St., Marteena Hall 101
Greensboro, NC 27411
Tel: (910)334-7646   Fax: (910)334-7283
E-Mail: mtingwas@athena.ncat.edu
Web Site: http://www.nsbp.org
Members: 300 individuals
Annual Budget: under $10,000
Exec. Officer: Dr. Floyd James
Historical Note
NSBP recognizes the contributions of African-Americans to advances in the sciences in general and particulary in the field of physics. Promotes education in the sciences. Has no paid officers or full-time staff. Membership: $45/year (individual); $15/year (student); $2,500/year (organization).
Publications:
Newsletter. irreg.
Meetings/Conferences:
Annual Meetings: April

Nat'l Soc. of Compliance Professionals (1987)
P.O. Box 351
Lakeville, CT 06039
Tel: (860)435-0843   Fax: (860)435-3005
E-Mail: NSCP@MSN.COM
Members: 1000 individuals
Staff: 4
Annual Budget: $1-2,000,000
Exec. Director: Joan Hinchman
Membership Coordinator: Maggie Wells
Historical Note
NSCP members are individuals responsible for insuring their company's compliance with government regulations. Membership: $345/year (individual).
Publications:
Hotline Memo. m.
NSCP Currents. bi-m.
Meetings/Conferences:
Annual Meetings: Fall
1999 – Washington, DC(J.W. Marriott)/Oct. 13-15

Nat'l Soc. of EMS Administrators
Historical Note
A division of the National Ass'n of Emergency Medical Technicians.

Nat'l Soc. of EMS Instructor/Coordinators
Historical Note
A division of the National Ass'n of Emergency Medical Technicians.

Nat'l Soc. of EMT Paramedics
Historical Note
A division of the National Ass'n of Emergency Medical Technicians.

Nat'l Soc. of Environmental Consultants (1992)
303 W. Cypress
P.O. Box 15258
San Antonio, TX 78212-0258
Tel: (210)271-0781   Fax: (210)225-8450
Toll Free: (800)486 - 3676
Members: 1000 individuals
Staff: 4
Annual Budget: $50-100,000
Exec. Director: Gary T. Deane
Historical Note
NSEC members are predominantly real estate professionals concerned with assessment of enviromental risks in property acquisition. Offers certification leading to the designations Environmental Screening Consultant and Environmental Assessment Consultant. Membership: $75/year.
Publications:
Environmental Consultant. q.
Membership Directory. a. adv.
Meetings/Conferences:
Annual Meetings: Spring/150
1999 – San Antonio, TX(Gunter Hotel)

Nat'l Soc. of Fund Raising Executives (1960)
1101 King St., Suite 700
Alexandria, VA 22314-2967
Tel: (703)684-0410   Fax: (703)684-0540
Toll Free: (800)666 - 3863
E-Mail: nsfre@nsfre.org
Web Site: http://www.nsfre.org
Members: 20,000 individuals
Staff: 40
Annual Budget: $5-10,000,000
President & C.E.O.: Paulette V. Maehara, CFRE
Coordinator, Marketing & Communications: Alison Bohn
Coordinator, Public Affairs: Michael Nilsen
Dir., Meetings/Conferences: Lynn Smith
V. President, Professional Advancement: Marie A. Reed, Ed.D., CNA
Director, Education and Research: Cathlene Williams, Ph.D.
Dir., Membership & Marketing: Jim Fleckenstein, CAE
Dir., Information Systems: Lori Gusdorf
Historical Note
Individual fund raisers with experience in directing, managing or counseling fund raising programs. Formerly the Ass'n of Fund-Raising Directors, and (1978) the Nat'l Soc. of Fund Raisers. Annual Budget: over $6 million. Membership: $175/year, plus local fees (individual).
Publications:
Advancing Philanthropy. (NSFRE Journal) q. adv.
Directory. a.
NSFRE News. 10/year.

Meetings/Conferences:
1999 – Miami Beach, FL/April 25-28
2000 – New Orleans, LA/March 8-15
2001 – San Diego, CA/March 7-15

Nat'l Soc. of Genetic Counselors (1978)
233 Canterbury Drive
Wallingford, PA   19086-6617
Tel: (610)872-7608   *Fax:* (610)872-1192
E-Mail: nsgc@aol.com
Web Site: http://www.nsgc.org
Members: 1,500 individuals
Staff: 1
Annual Budget: $250-500,000
Exec. Director: Bea Leopold

Historical Note
Incorporated in New York, NSGC was formed to further the professional interests of those with advanced education and experience in the areas of medical genetics and counseling separate from the concerns of any particular genetic disorder. Membership: $100/year (regular); $90/year (associate); $50/year (student).

Publications:
Journal of Genetic Cunseling. q.
Membership Directory. a.
Perspectives in Genetic Counseling. q.

Meetings/Conferences:
Annual Meetings: Fall
1999 – Oakland, CA/Oct. 16-19

Nat'l Soc. of Hispanic MBAs (1988)
8204 Elmbrook Dr., #235
Dallas, TX   75247-4067
Tel: (214)267-1622   *Fax:* (214)267-1626
E-Mail: nshmba@sprintmail.com
Web Site: http://www.nshmba.org
Members: 1,600 individuals
Annual Budget: $1-2,000,000
Exec. Director: John Honaman
Director, Communications: Cathy Crowson
Manager, Conference Services: Rafael Rivera
Education Program Specialist: Jenna Lee McMillen
Membership Services: Rose Duke

Historical Note
Formed by a group of Hispanic MBAs in order to address the declining enrollment of Hispanics in graduate business programs and to promote the growth of Hispanic MBAs in the private and public environments. Membership: $50/year (individual), $15/year (student).

Publications:
Bottom Line. m. adv.

Meetings/Conferences:
1999 – Denver, CO(Adam's Mark)/Oct. 28-30
2000 – Orlando, FL(Disney's Coronado Springs)
2001 – San Antonio, TX
2002 – Phoenix, AZ

Nat'l Soc. of Hypnotherapists (1984)
Historical Note
Address unknown in 1997.

Nat'l Soc. of Insurance Premium Auditors (1975)
5800 Foxridge Dr., # 115
Mission, KS   66202-2333
Tel: (913)262-0163   *Fax:* (913)262-0174
Toll Free: (888)846 - 7472
E-Mail: nsipa@idir.net
Web Site: http://nsipa.org
Members: 800 individuals
Staff: 5
Annual Budget: $50-100,000
Exec. Secretary: Jane Male, CAE

Historical Note
A professional society of auditors from insurance or fee service insurance auditing companies. Membership: $75/year.

Publications:
National Auditor. bi-m.
Premium Audit Ledger. 3/yr.

Meetings/Conferences:

Nat'l Soc. of Military EMTs
Historical Note
A division of the Nat'l Ass'n of Emergency Medical Technicians.

Nat'l Soc. of Mural Painters (1895)
c/o American Fine Arts Soc.
215 W. 57th St.
New York, NY   10019
Tel: (212)777-8570   *Fax:* (212)473-8268
E-Mail: reginas@anny.org
Web Site: http://www.anny.org/nsmp
Members: 120 individuals
Annual Budget: under $10,000
President: Jack Stewart, Ph.D., NA

Historical Note
Founded in 1895 NSMP members are muralists from all over the world chosen by a majority vote of the organization after a review of slides and biographical material. Membership: $25/year; $40 + /year (patron).

Publications:
National Society of Mural Newsletter. q.

Meetings/Conferences:
Annual Meetings: usually Spring/New York, NY

Nat'l Soc. of Newspaper Columnists (1978)
P.O. Box 1203
Keller, TX   76244
Web Site: http://www.columnists.com
Members: 300 individuals

Annual Budget: under $10,000
Treasurer: Vicki Maloney

Historical Note
Members are columnists on daily newspapers. Membership: $30/year (individual), $50/year (corporation).

Meetings/Conferences:
Annual Meetings: June
1999 – Louisville, KY/June 18-21

Nat'l Soc. of Painters in Casein and Acrylic (1952)
969 Catasauqua Road
Whitehall, PA   18052
Annual Budget: $10-25,000
President: Douglas Wiltraut

Historical Note
Established to give artists opportunity to exhibit works regardless of style, school, or subject matter. Membership limited to 150 professional artists (by invitation). Sponsors exhibitions and demonstrations of painting in casein, acrylic and polymer watercolor. Has no paid staff. Membership: $40/yr. (individual).

Publications:
Catalog. bien.

Nat'l Soc. of Performance and Instruction
Historical Note
Became (1995) Internat'l Soc. for Performance Improvement.

Nat'l Soc. of Pharmaceutical Sales Trainers (1971)
5 Homestead Lane
Avon, CT   06001-2933
Tel: (860)675-1824   *Fax:* (860)673-1445
Web Site: http://www.nspst.com
Members: 500 individuals
Staff: 4
Annual Budget: $250-500,000
Business Manager: Bob Rodman

Historical Note
Members are training personnel employed by pharmaceutical and medical companies. Membership: $175/year (individual).

Publications:
Directory. a. adv.
Newspost Journal. q. adv.

Meetings/Conferences:
Annual Meetings: May or June
1999 – San Francisco, CA(Hyatt Embarcadero)/June 6-9/390
2000 – Dallas, TX(Wyndham)/May 7-10/450

Nat'l Soc. of Professional Engineers (1934)
1420 King St.
Alexandria, VA   22314-2794
Tel: (703)684-2800   *Fax:* (703)836-4875
Toll Free: (888)285 - 6773
E-Mail: customer.service@nspe.org
Web Site: http://www.nspe.org
Members: 63,000 individuals
Staff: 47
Annual Budget: $5-10,000,000
Exec. Director: Arthur D. Schwartz
Director, Communications: Mary Paris
Director, Government Relations: Larry Bory
Director, Meetings: Polly P. Collins
Director, Education Services: Marla Berman
Assoc. Exec. Director: Walter Marlowe, P.E.
Director of Membership Development & Membership Services:
    Richard Thomas
Director, Publications: Stefan Jaeger
Director, Information Systems: David L. Krosnick

Historical Note
Founded in New York City in 1934 and incorporated the same year in South Carolina. Consists of 54 state societies and more than 500 chapters. The Nat'l Institute for Certification in Engineering Technologies is a part of NSPE. Affiliated with the Accreditation Board for Engineering and Technology. Sponsors and supports the NSPE Political Action Committee, the NSPE Education Foundation, and the Nat'l Institute for Engineering Ethics.

Publications:
Engineering Times. 11/year. adv.

Meetings/Conferences:
Semi-Annual Meetings: Winter and Summer

Nat'l Soc. of Professional Surveyors (1981)
5410 Grosvenor Lane
Bethesda, MD   20814
Tel: (301)493-0200   *Fax:* (301)493-8245
E-Mail: nsps@mindspring.com
Web Site: http://www.survmap.org
Members: 6,000 individuals
Staff: 2
Annual Budget: $100-250,000
Exec. Administrator: Pat Canfield

Historical Note
A member organization of the American Congress on Surveying and Mapping. Membership is concurrent. Called the Land Surveys Division of ACSM until 1981 when it became a self-governing organization as the American Soc. of Professional Surveyors. It assumed its present name in 1983.

Publications:
Membership Directory. irreg.
Survey and Mapping. q.

Meetings/Conferences:
Annual Meetings: With the American Congress on Surveying
    and Mapping.
1999 – Portland, OR/March 13-18

Nat'l Soc. of Public Accountants (1945)
Historical Note
Became the Nat'l Soc. of Accountants in 1996.

Nat'l Soc. of Real Estate Appraisers
Historical Note
An affiliate of the Nat'l Ass'n of Real Estate Brokers.

Nat'l Soc. to Prevent Blindness/Prevent Blindness America (1908)
500 E. Remington Road
Schaumburg, IL   60173-4557
Tel: (847)843-2020   *Fax:* (847)843-8458
Toll Free: (800)331 - 2020
E-Mail: info@preventblindness.org
Web Site: http://www.preventblindness.org
Members: 18,928 individuals and companies
Staff: 150
Annual Budget: $10-25,000,000
President & C.E.O.: Richard T. Hellner
Mgr., Meetings & Conferences: Sally Magallanes, CMP
Sr. V. President: Suzanne Gedance
Vice President, Program & Information Services: Tod Turriff

Historical Note
Formerly (1927) Nat'l Committee for the Prevention of Blindness, (1979) Nat'l Soc. for the Prevention of Blindness, and (1993) Nat'l Soc. to Prevent Blindness. Absorbed (1961) Ophthalmological Foundation. Has an annual budget of approximately $10 million. Membership: $25/year (individual); $500/year (organization/company).

Publications:
Annual Report. a.
Catalogue of Publications.
Prevent Blindness News. q.
Wise Owl News. q.

Meetings/Conferences:
Annual Meetings: Fall/400
1999 – Chicago, IL(Inter-Continental)/Nov. 13-15

Nat'l Soccer Coaches Ass'n of America (1941)
6700 Squibb Road, Suite 215
Mission, KS   66202
Tel: (913)362-1747   *Fax:* (913)362-3439
Toll Free: (800)458 - 0678
Web Site: http://www.nscaa.com
Members: 15,000 individuals
Staff: 6
Annual Budget: $1-2,000,000
Exec. Director: Jim Sheldon
Communications Director: Mike McFarland
Membership Coordinator: Sandy Williamson
Program Director: Steve Veal

Historical Note
The purpose of NSCAA is to educate coaches and promote the game of soccer. Has an annual budget of approximately $1.8 million. Membership: $60/year (regular), $40/year (youth coach).

Publications:
Soccer Journal. bi-m. adv.

Meetings/Conferences:
Annual Meetings: January/3,000
1999 – Philadelphia, PA(Marriott/Penn. Con.
    Center)/Jan. 12-17/5000
2000 – Baltimore, MD(Hyatt/Convention
    Center)/Jan. 12-16/5000

Nat'l Soft Drink Ass'n (1919)
1101 16th St., N.W.
Washington, DC   20036-4803
Tel: (202)463-6732   *Fax:* (202)463-8172
Web Site: http://www.nsda.org
Members: 300 firms
Staff: 40
Annual Budget: $5-10,000,000
President: William L. Ball, III
Sr. V.P., Public Affairs: Jim Finkelstein
Sr. V.P., Scientific & Technical Affairs: Richard H. Adamson, Ph.D.
V.P., State & Local Affairs: Judith Thorman
V.P., Environmental Affairs: E. Gifford Stack
V. President, Federal Affairs: Drew M. Davis
Chief Financial Officer: Mark N. Hammond
V. President, Administration: Denise M. Burke
General Counsel: Patricia M. Vaughan
Director, Membership and MIS: Tara Spence

Historical Note
Established as the American Bottlers of Carbonated Beverages, it assumed its present name in 1967. Absorbed the Nat'l Bottlers Ass'n and the Nat'l Bottlers Protective Ass'n. Members are soft drink makers and their suppliers. Has an annual budget of approximately $5.0 million.

Publications:
Soft Drink Recycler. q.

Meetings/Conferences:
Annual Meetings: Fall/25,000

Nat'l Soft Serve and Fast Food Ass'n
Historical Note
Became (1997) Nat'l Frozen Dessert and Fast Food Ass'n.

Nat'l Solid Waste Management Environmental (1982)
4301 Connecticut Ave., N.W., Suite 300
Washington, DC   20008
Tel: (202)244-4700   *Fax:* (202)966-4818
Toll Free: (800)424 - 2869
Members: 40 companies
Staff: 3
Annual Budget: $250-500,000
Exec. V. President: Jaclyn Wolfe

Historical Note
A constituent group of the Environmental Industry Ass'ns. The Chemical Waste Transportation Institute, Institute of Chemical Waste Management, and the Remedial Contractors Institute are divisions of HWMA. Membership: dues vary by size of company.

Publications:
HWMA Directory. a.
Information Packets. m.

Meetings/Conferences:
Annual Meetings: With Environmental Industry Ass'ns

Nat'l Solid Wastes Management Ass'n
4301 Connecticut Ave., N.W., Suite 300
Washington, DC   20008
Tel: (202)244-4700   Fax: (202)966-4818
Toll Free: (800)424 - 2869
Exec. V. President: Sheila M. Prindiville

Historical Note
A constituent group of the Environmental Industries Ass'ns.

Meetings/Conferences:
Annual Meetings: with the Environment Industry Ass'ns.

Nat'l Spa and Pool Institute (1956)
2111 Eisenhower Ave.
Alexandria, VA   22314
Tel: (703)838-0083   Fax: (703)549-0493
Web Site: http://www.poolspaworld.com
Members: 5,000 companies
Staff: 31
Annual Budget: $5-10,000,000
C.E.O.: Roger Galvin
Director, Communications: John J. Cergol, Jr.
Director, Government Relations & Counsel: David L. Karmol
Director, Conventions and Expositions: Molly Finney
Technical Director: Carvin DiGiovanni
Controller: Carol Citron
Dir., Marketing and Member Services: Cary Gray

Historical Note
Founded in Chicago, IL. Formerly (until 1980) known as the Nat'l Swimming Pool Institute. Absorbed the Internat'l Spa and Tub Institute in 1983. Represents all segments of the spa and pool industry. Has an annual budget of approximately $6 million.

Publications:
Swimming Pool and Spa Industry Market Report. a.
Team NSPI News. m.
Who's Who in the Swimming Pool Industry. a.

Meetings/Conferences:
Annual Meetings: Fall
1999 – Las Vegas, NV/Dec. 1-3

Nat'l Speakers Ass'n (1973)
1500 S. Priest Drive
Tempe, AZ   05201
Tel: (602)968-2552   Fax: (602)968-0911
E-Mail: information@nsaspeaker.com
Web Site: http://www.nsaspeaker.org
Members: 3,600 individuals
Staff: 17
Annual Budget: $2-5,000,000
Interim Exec. V. President: Stacy Tetschner
Manager of Meetings: Dawn Milner, CMP
Manager of Accounting: Carol Sheehy
Manager of Membership: Beverly Babb

Historical Note
Provides a common platform for those interested in increasing the quality, integrity and visibility of the speaking profession. Membership: $325/year.

Publications:
Journal of Professional Speaking. m. adv.
Meeting Planners Guide to Professional Speakers. a. adv.
Who's Who in Professional Speaking. a. adv.

Meetings/Conferences:
Annual Meetings: Summer
1999 – San Antonio, TX(Marriott)/2300
2000 – Washington, DC(Sheraton)/2300
2001 – Dallas, TX/2300

Nat'l Speleological Soc. (1941)
2813 Cave Ave.
Huntsville, AL   35810-4431
Tel: (256)852-1300   Fax: (256)851-9241
E-Mail: nss@caves.org
Web Site: http://www.caves.org/~nss
Members: 11,600 individuals
Staff: 3
Annual Budget: $100-250,000
Operations Manager: Camille Mueller

Historical Note
Founded and incorporated in the District of Columbia in January 1941. Affiliated with the American Ass'n for the Advancement of Science, the Nat'l Parks and Conservation Ass'n and the Internat'l Union of Speleology. Dedicated to the exploration, study and conservation of caves and caverns. Membership: $30/year (individual); $60/year (company).

Publications:
Journal of Cave and Karst Studies. 3x/year.
NSS News. m. adv.

Meetings/Conferences:
1999 – Filer, ID/July 12-16
2000 – Daily, WV

Nat'l Spinal Cord Injury Ass'n (1948)
8300 Colesville Road, Suite 551
Silver Spring, MD   20910-3243
Tel: (301)588-6959   Fax: (301)588-9414
Toll Free: (800)462 - 9629
E-Mail: nscia2@aol.com
Web Site: http://www.spinalcord.org
Members: 8,000 individuals
Staff: 4
Annual Budget: $250-500,000
Exec. Director: Thomas Countee
Finance/Administration: Mary Gonzales

Historical Note
Founded by the Paralyzed Veterans of America in response to the medical and social problems arising from spinal cord injury. Focuses on information, referral and health maintenance. Members are individuals with spinal cord injuries, their families, health professionals, and others. Membership: $25/year (individual), $50/year (professional), $100/year, minimum (organization).

Publications:
National Resource Directory.
SCI Life. q. adv.

Meetings/Conferences:
Annual Meetings: late Summer

Nat'l Sporting Goods Ass'n (1929)
1699 Wall St., Suite 700
Mount Prospect, IL   60056-5780
Tel: (847)439-4000   Fax: (847)439-0111
E-Mail: NSGA1699@aol.com
Web Site: http://www.nsga.com
Members: 22,000 retail outlets & 3000 suppliers
Staff: 32
Annual Budget: $5-10,000,000
President and C.E.O.: James L. Faltinek, Ph.D., CAE
Director of Communications: Larry Weindruch
V. President, Sales and Marketing: Thomas G. Drake, CAE
V. President of Trade Show Services: Paul M. Prince
V. President, Information and Reserach: Thomas B. Doyle
V. President, Internal Operations: William H. Webb, Jr.
Dir., Membership: Rhonda Haenszel
V. President Administration: Susan L. Wenderski

Historical Note
NSGA membership consists of suppliers, retailers, wholesalers, sales agents and media in the sporting goods industry. It is the largest sporting goods trade association in the world. The Athletic Goods Team Distributors division of NSGA is comprised of members who specialize in supplying equipment to high schools, colleges and organized teams. The Sports Foundation, Inc. is a non-profit membership organizations founded in 1965 to promote interest in active sports participation and Ass'n and Show Management, Inc. (ASMI) is a trade show and association management subsidiary. Sponsor of NSGA World Sports EXPO (R) and World Sports, held annually in Chicago, and the NSGA Annual Management Conference. Has an annual budget of approximately $8 million. Membership fee: $100-450/year (company).

Publications:
Fitness in America. semi-a.
NSGA Buying Guide. a.
NSGA Cost of Doing Business Survey. bi-a.
NSGA Retail Focus. m. adv.
NSGA Sports Participation Study. a.
Sporting Goods Market. a.

Meetings/Conferences:
Annual Meetings: Internat'l Convention & Show/Chicago,
    IL(McCormick Place)/Summer
1999 – Chicago, IL/July 9-11

Nat'l Sportscasters and Sportswriters Ass'n (1959)
P.O. Box 559
Salisbury, NC   28145
Tel: (704)633-4275   Fax: (704)639-1200
Members: 1000 individuals
Staff: 1
Annual Budget: $50-100,000
Program Coordinator: Barbara Lockert

Historical Note
Membership: $25/year.

Publications:
NSSA News. semi-a.

Meetings/Conferences:
Annual Meetings: Always Salisbury, NC/April

Nat'l Spotted Saddle Horse Ass'n (1979)
Box 898, 108 N. Spring
Murfreesboro, TN   37133-0898
Tel: (615)890-2864   Fax: (615)890-2864
E-Mail: NSSHA898@AOL.COM
Web Site: http://www.DNJ.COM/SPOTHORSE
Members: 4,000 individuals
Staff: 2
Annual Budget: $100-250,000
Manager: Donna D. West

Historical Note
NSSHA, Inc. is a Breed Registry for spotted, gaited horses.

Publications:
Nat'l Spotted Saddle Horse Journal. q. adv.
Newsletter. m. adv.

Meetings/Conferences:
Annual Meetings: Always held in Murfreesboro, TN on the last
    Saturday in January

Nat'l Spotted Swine Record (1914)
P.O. Box 9758
Peoria, IL   61612-9758
Tel: (309)693-6301   Fax: (309)691-0168
Members: 565 individuals
Staff: 3
Annual Budget: $100-250,000
Dir., Promotions: Jack Wall

Historical Note
Breeders and fanciers of spotted swine. Member of the National Society of Livestock Record Associations. Affiliated with the National Association of Swine Records. Maintains a registry of purebred spotted swine. Membership: $30/year.

Publications:
Spotted News. 10/year. adv.

Meetings/Conferences:
Annual Meetings: July

Nat'l Spray Equipment Manufacturers Ass'n (1922)
550 Randall Road
Elyria, OH   44035
Tel: (440)366-6808
Members: 16 companies
Staff: 1
Annual Budget: under $10,000
Exec. Secretary: Don R. Scarbrough

Historical Note
Established as the Nat'l Spray Painting and Finishing Equipment Ass'n, it assumed its present name in 1974. Serves as a technical forum for safety and environmental matters pertaining to the spray finishing industry. Membership: $800/year (company).

Publications:
None.

Meetings/Conferences:
Annual Meetings: June
1999 – Stow, VT

Nat'l Staff Development and Training Ass'n (1984)
810 First St., N.E., Suite 500
Washington, DC   20002-4267
Tel: (202)682-0100   Fax: (202)289-6555
Members: 500 individuals
Contact: Doris Pollard

Historical Note
An affiliate unit of the American Public Welfare Ass'n which provides administrative support. NSDTA members are social workers involved with staff development and training.

Publications:
NSDTA Directory.

Meetings/Conferences:

Nat'l Staff Development Council (1980)
P.O. Box 240
Oxford, OH   45056
Tel: (513)523-6029   Fax: (513)523-0638
Members: 7,200 individuals
Staff: 10
Annual Budget: $500-1,000,000
Exec. Director: Dennis Sparks, Ph.D.

Historical Note
NSDC members are local school district administrators responsible for staff development. Membership fees vary, based on number of publications received: $69 or $109/year (individual); $149/year (organization).

Publications:
Journal of Staff Development. q. adv.
Resolve. 8/yr.
Tools for Schools. 8/year.

Meetings/Conferences:
Annual Meetings: December/1,500-2,000
1999 – Dallas, TX/Dec. 4-8

Nat'l Star Route Mail Contractors Ass'n (1933)
324 East Capitol St.
Washington, DC   20003-3897
Tel: (202)543-1661   Fax: (202)543-8863
Members: 4,500 individuals
Staff: 4
Annual Budget: $250-500,000
Exec. Director: John V. "Skip" Maraney

Historical Note
Members have mail delivery contracts with the U.S. Postal Service to transport mail over the highways on authorized schedules. Formerly (1982) known as the Nat'l Star Route Mail Carriers Ass'n.

Publications:
Star Carrier. m.

Meetings/Conferences:
Annual Meetings: August
1999 – Hershey, PA(Hershey Lodge)/July 31-Aug. 5
2000 – Orlando, FL(Coranado Springs)

Nat'l State Printing Ass'n

Historical Note
Became Nat'l State Publishing Ass'n in 1998.

Nat'l State Publishing Ass'n (1977)
48 Liberty Pl., Suite 2
Box 15215
Hattiesburg, MS   39404
Tel: (601)264-3442   Fax: (601)264-3442
Members: 125 jurisdictions
Staff: 2
Annual Budget: $50-100,000
Exec. Director: F. Lamar Evans

Historical Note
An association of various states and other related political jurisdictions, NSPA is concerned with improving the management of printing programs, exchanging information, cooperating for more effective production and procurement of printing products. Membership: $400/year (individual); $750/year (company); $225/year (associate).

Publications:
NSPA Newsletter. q.

Meetings/Conferences:
Annual Meetings: Fall
1999 – Bismark, ND

Nat'l Stone Ass'n (1985)
1415 Elliot Place, N.W.
Washington, DC   20007-2599
Tel: (202)342-1100   Fax: (202)342-0702
Toll Free: (800)342 - 1415
Web Site: http://www.aggregates.org
Members: 670 companies

Staff: 22
Annual Budget: $2-5,000,000
President: Jennifer Joy Wilson
V. President, Communications/Public Affairs: R. A. Edwards
V. President, Government Affairs: William D. Kelleher
V. President, Special Events and Services: David McConnell
Sr. V. President: William C. Ford

Historical Note
The result of a merger in 1984 between the Nat'l Crushed Stone Ass'n (1918) and the Nat'l Limestone Institute (1945). In 1992 absorbed the Pulverized Limestone Ass'n, which is now a division of the NSA. Quarry owners and operators, equipment manufacturers and service organizations connected with the construction aggregates industry. Supports the Nat'l Stone Ass'n Political Action Committee.

Publications:
Digest Newsletter. bi-w.
Stone Review Magazine. bi-m.

Meetings/Conferences:
Annual Meetings: Winter
1999 – Las Vegas, NV/March 23-27

Nat'l Strength and Conditioning Ass'n *(1978)*
P.O. Box 38909
Colorado Springs, CO   80937-8909
Tel: (719)632-6722   *Fax:* (719)632-6367
Members: 15,600 individuals
Staff: 15
Annual Budget: $1-2,000,000
Exec. Director: Harvey Newton

Historical Note
Formerly (1981) Nat'l Strength Coaches Ass'n. Members are professionals involved in all aspects of the strength training. Provides certification and other opportunities to members. Membership: $75/year (professional level).

Publications:
Journal of Strength & Conditioning Research. q. adv.
NSCA Bulletin. bi-m. adv.
Strength and Conditioning Journal. bi-m. adv.

Meetings/Conferences:
Annual Meetings: Summer
1999 – Kansas City, KS/June 23-26

Nat'l Stripper Well Ass'n *(1934)*
c/oEquinox, Oil Inc.
10077 Grogan Mill Rd., Suite 200
The Woodlands, TX   77380
Tel: (281)364-7037   *Fax:* (281)364-8480
Members: 300 owners
Annual Budget: $25-50,000
President: Stephen P. Layton

Historical Note
A stripper oil well produces a daily average of 10 barrels or less of crude petroleum. Suggested Membership: $100/year.

Publications:
National Stripper Well Survey. a.
Newsletter. q.

Meetings/Conferences:
Semi-annual Meetings: with the Independent Petroleum Ass'n of America

Nat'l Stroke Ass'n *(1984)*
9707 Easter Lane
Englewood, CO   80012
Tel: (303)649-9299   *Fax:* (303)649-1328
Toll Free: (800)787 - 6537
E-Mail: info@stroke.org
Web Site: http://www.stroke.org
Members: 10,000 individuals
Staff: 43
Annual Budget: $2-5,000,000
President: Pete Todd
Director, Communications: Rachelle Trujillo
Director, Meetings and Exhibits: Thelma J. Edwards
Director, Chapter Development: Brenna McCraken

Historical Note
NSA is a national voluntary health care organization focusing exclusively on stroke prevention, treatment, rehabilitation, research and support of stroke survivors and their families. NSA's professional society is open to all health care professionals, including physicians, therapists, nurses and others involved in preventing and treating stroke. Membership: $50/year (professional); $200/year(organization).

Publications:
Journal of Stroke and Cardiovascular Disease. q.
Newsletter-"Be Stroke Smart. " m.
Newsletter-Stroke Clinical Update. q.

Meetings/Conferences:

Nat'l Structured Settlements Trade Ass'n *(1985)*
1420 16th St., N.W.
Washington, DC   20036
Tel: (202)797-5108   *Fax:* (202)332-2301
Members: 700 individuals, 85 companies
Staff: 5
Annual Budget: $500-1,000,000
Exec. V. President: Randy Dyer, CAE

Historical Note
Provides long-term periodic payment of settlements on personal injury lawsuits. Membership fee varies by category.

Publications:
NSSTA Newsletter. bi-m.

Meetings/Conferences:
Annual Meetings: Spring/300
1999 – Tempe, AZ(Buttes)/May 2-5

Nat'l Student Employment Ass'n *(1976)*
2852 Willamette 202

Eugene, OR   97405
Tel: (541)744-3978   *Fax:* (541)322-5573
Members: 600 individuals
Staff: 1
Annual Budget: $100-250,000
Treasurer: Joan Adams

Historical Note
Formerly (1975) Nat'l Ass'n on Work and the College Student and (1997) Nat'l Ass'n of Student Employment Administrators. Currently the Nat'l Student Employment Ass'n. NSEA members are professionals involved with programs for students who work while attending college. Membership: $75/year (individual); $250/year (organization, minimum); $750/year (company).

Publications:
Annual Report. a.
Bibliography. a.
Membership Directory. a.
NASEA News. q.
Student Employment Journal. a.
Workbook.

Meetings/Conferences:
Annual Meetings: Fall/200-250
1999 – San Diego, CA/Oct. 26-29

Nat'l Student Nurses Ass'n *(1952)*
555 West 57th St.
Suite 1327
New York, NY   10019
Tel: (212)581-2211   *Fax:* (212)581-2368
E-Mail: NSNA@NSNA.ORG
Members: 40,000 individuals
Staff: 12
Annual Budget: $2-5,000,000
Exec. Director: Diane J. Mancino, Ed.D., RN,
Director, Communications: Caroline Jaffe
Director of Program: Judy Tyler, CAE
Dep. Exec. Director: Carlos Rivera

Historical Note
Provides education, representation, and a forum in which to further the current professional interests and concerns of student nurses. Membership: $30/year (individual); $250-2000/year (organization/company).

Publications:
Imprint. 5/yr. adv.
NSNA News. bi-m. adv.
Pieces. a.

Meetings/Conferences:
Annual Meetings: April
1999 – Pittsburgh, PA(Convention Center)/April 21-25/3000
2000 – Salt Lake City, UT/April 12-16/3000
2001 – Nashville, TN/April 4-8/3000
2002 – Philadelphia, PA(Convention Center)/April 3-7/3000

Nat'l Student Osteopathic Medical Ass'n *(1970)*
142 E. Ontario St.
Chicago, IL   60611
Tel: (312)202-8193   *Fax:* (312)202-8220
E-Mail: somanat@aol.com
Members: 5,000 individuals
Staff: 1
Annual Budget: $50-100,000
Administrator: Marie Perone

Historical Note
Affiliated with the American Osteopathic Ass'n (Chicago, IL), SOMA was founded in 1970 and is a professional association of osteopathic medical students from the 19 colleges of osteopathic medicine. Membership: $50/year.

Publications:
Student Doctor Journal. 5/year. adv.

Meetings/Conferences:
1999 – Philadelphia, PA

Nat'l Student Speech Language Hearing Ass'n *(1972)*
10801 Rockville Pike
Rockville, MD   20852
Tel: (301)897-5700   *Fax:* (301)571-0457
Members: 18,500 individuals
Staff: 2
Annual Budget: $500-1,000,000
Chief Administrative & Financial Officer: Brian B. Shulman
Director of Operations: Jenny Martinez

Historical Note
Formed as Nat'l Student Speech and Hearing Ass'n through a merger of Sigma Alpha Eta and the Student Journal Group of American Speech and Hearing Ass'n; assumed its present name in 1980. Members are undergraduates and master's degree candidates working in the field of speech-language pathology and audiology. Recognized by the American Speech-Language-Hearing Ass'n as the only official national student association in speech and hearing. Membership: $35/year.

Publications:
Clinical Series. bien.
NSSLHA Journal. a.

Meetings/Conferences:
Annual Meetings: With the American Speech-Language-Hearing Ass'n.

Nat'l Subacute Care Ass'n *(1992)*
7315 Wisconsin Ave., Suite 424-East
Bethesda, MD   20814-3202
Tel: (301)961-8680   *Fax:* (301)961-8681
Members: 1,200 individuals
Staff: 5
Annual Budget: $250-500,000
Exec. Director: Sanford J. Hill
V. President, Membership: Anthony Simone

Historical Note
Seeks to develop standards for the subacute and transitional healthcare industry so that the public, payers and healthcare

personnel can clearly identify quality providers. Represents the industry to the federal government. Provides education and information to those interested in subacute healthcare. Supersedes Ass'n for Advancement of Rehabilitation, which disbanded in 1991. Membership: $300/year (individual), $750-$7,500 (organization).

Publications:
InfoFAX. irreg.
NSCA News. m.

Meetings/Conferences:
Annual Meetings: Spring/800
1999 – Denver, CO(Adams Mark)/May 11-14

Nat'l Suffolk Sheep Ass'n *(1935)*
1120 Wilkes Blvd.
Columbia, MO   65201
Tel: (573)442-4103   *Fax:* (573)443-3632
Members: 4,000 individuals
Staff: 6
Annual Budget: $100-250,000
Exec. Secretary: David Kloostra

Historical Note
Maintains pedigree registry and promotes the Suffolk breed. Merged with American Suffolk Sheep Ass'n in 1998. Member of the Nat'l Pedigree Livestock Council. NSSA also oversees the Nat'l Junior Suffolk Sheep Ass'n. Membership: $20/year (individual).

Publications:
The Suffolk News. q. adv.

Meetings/Conferences:
Annual Meetings: November

Nat'l Sugar Brokers Ass'n *(1903)*
90 West St., Suite 706
New York, NY   10006-1039
Tel: (212)349-6063   *Fax:* (212)233-6815
Members: 100 sugar brokers
Staff: 1
Annual Budget: under $10,000
Exec. Secretary: Gwen Cody

Historical Note
Members are brokers of refined sugar.

Publications:
Bulletin. q.

Meetings/Conferences:
Annual Meetings: January in New York, NY
1999 – Chicago, IL

Nat'l Sunflower Ass'n *(1975)*
4023 State St.
Bismarck, ND   58501-0690
Tel: (701)328-5100   *Fax:* (701)328-5101
Web Site: http://www.sunflowernsa.com
Members: 22,000 individuals, 100 organizations
Staff: 6
Annual Budget: $250-500,000
Exec. Director: Larry Kleingartner
Director, Communications: Ruth Isaak
Marketing Director: John SandBakken
Office Manager: Lerrene Kroh

Historical Note
Companies associated with sunflower products, including growers' councils, seed companies, processors, exporters, researchers, chemical firms, shippers, commission firms and merchandisers. Established as the Sunflower Association of America, it assumed its present name in 1981. Membership: $40/year (individual); $325-500/year (company).

Publications:
Sunflower Directory. bien. adv.
Sunflower Week in Review. bi-w.
The Sunflower Magazine. bi-m. adv.

Meetings/Conferences:

Nat'l Sunroom Ass'n
2945 Wanamaker Dr., Suite A
Topeka, KS   66141-5321
Tel: (785)271-0208   *Fax:* (785)271-0166
E-Mail: nsa@glasswebsite.com
Web Site: http://www.glasswebsite.com/nsa
Exec. Director: William J. Birch

Historical Note
Established in 1997, members are manufactures and producers of sunrooms, patio rooms, solariums and related structures.

Meetings/Conferences:
Semi-annual Meetings: Spring and Fall

Nat'l Supply Distributors Ass'n *(1933)*
Historical Note
Address unknown in 1996.

Nat'l Surgical Assistant Ass'n *(1983)*
736 E. Flynn Lane
Phoenix, AZ   85014-1031
Tel: (602)212-0479   *Fax:* (602)212-9692
Web Site: www.neafcs.org
Annual Budget: $50-100,000
Exec. Director: Ruth Helein

Publications:
Newsletter. q. adv.

Meetings/Conferences:
Annual Meetings: October
1999 – Orlando, FL

Nat'l Swim and Recreation Ass'n
Historical Note
Became (1998) Club Pool Ass'n.

Nat'l Swim School Ass'n *(1988)*

776 21st Ave. North
St. Petersburg, FL 33704-3348
Tel: (813)896-7946   *Fax:* (813)896-3933
E-Mail: NSSA@shamrockgroup.com
Web Site: http://shamrockgroup.com
Members: 200 swim schools
Staff: 1
Annual Budget: $100-250,000
Exec. Director: Stephen W. Graves

Historical Note
Membership: $45/year (individual); $245-495/year (organization/company).

Publications:
Swim School Scene. m. adv.

Meetings/Conferences:
1999 – Colorado Springs, CO

Nat'l Swine Improvement Federation (1975)
NC State University, Box 7621
203 Polk Hall
Raleigh, NC 27695-7621
Tel: (919)851-6222   *Fax:* (919)515-6316
Members: 60 individuals
Annual Budget: under $10,000
Secretary-Treasurer: Charles Stanislaw, Ph.D.

Historical Note
Established in Kansas City, MO and incorporated in Nebraska. Members are central testing stations, field performance testing programs, purebred breed associations and the Nat'l Pork Producers Council. Membership: $100/yr.

Publications:
Guidelines for Uniform Swine Improvement Programs.
Proceedings of the Annual Conference. a.
Swine Genetics Handbook.

Meetings/Conferences:
Annual Meetings: December

Nat'l Swine Registry
P.O. Box 2417
1769 U.S. 52 West
West Lafayette, IN 47996-2417
Tel: (765)463-3593   *Fax:* (765)497-2959
Annual Budget: $1-2,000,000
C.E.O.: Darrell D. Anderson

Historical Note
Product of the merger of the American Yorkshire Club, the Hampshire Swine Registry and the United Duroc Swine Registry in 1996. Membership: $50/year (individual).

Publications:
Seedstock Edge. m. adv.

Nat'l Systems Contractors Ass'n (1980)
419 First Street, S.E.
Cedar Rapids, IA 52401
Tel: (319)366-6722   *Fax:* (319)366-4164
Toll Free: (800)446 - 6722
Web Site: http://www.nsca.org
Members: 2,800 companies
Staff: 9
Annual Budget: $1-2,000,000
Exec. Director: Chuck Wilson
V. President, Events and Conference: Dennis Milan

Historical Note
Formerly (1994) Nat'l Sound and Communications Ass'n. Members are installers and servicers of electronic communications equipment.

Meetings/Conferences:
1999 – Nashville, TN(Opryland)/Apr. 29-May 1

Nat'l Tabletop and Giftware Ass'n (1984)
355 Lexington Ave., 17th Floor
New York, NY 10017-6603
Tel: (212)661-4261   *Fax:* (212)370-9047
E-Mail: assocmgmt@aol.com
Members: 80 companies
Staff: 3
Annual Budget: $50-100,000
Exec. Director: Peter S. Rush
Program Director: Maria Ungaro

Historical Note
Established and incorporated in New York as Nat'l Tabletop Ass'n; assumed its current name in 1995. Members are manufacturers of dinnerware, crystal, silver and giftware as well as companies providing services to the tabletop industry.

Publications:
Nat'l Bridal Directory. a.
Newsletter. q.

Meetings/Conferences:
Annual Meetings: always Sept. in New York, NY

Nat'l Tabletop Ass'n
Historical Note
Became (1995) Nat'l Tabletop and Giftware Ass'n.

Nat'l Tank Truck Carriers (1945)
2200 Mill Road
Alexandria, VA 22314-4677
Tel: (703)838-1960   *Fax:* (703)684-5753
E-Mail: NTTC@JUNO.COM
Members: 240 carriers
Staff: 6
Annual Budget: $250-500,000
President: Clifford J. Harvison
V. President: John Conley

Historical Note
Represents the for-hire tank truck industry. Membership: $500-6,600/year; $600/year (associate).

Publications:
Directory. a. adv.
Newsletter. m.
Regulations. a.

Meetings/Conferences:
Annual Meetings: May
1999 – Atlanta, GA(Westin Peachtree)/May 16-19/550
2000 – Chicago, IL(Fairmont Hotel)/May 15-18/550
2001 – Boston, MA(Westin Copley Place)/May 6-8/600

Nat'l Tax Ass'n-Tax Institute of America (1907)
725 15th St., N.W., Suite 600
Washington, DC 20005-2109
Tel: (202)737-3325   *Fax:* (202)737-7308
Members: 1,600 individuals and institutions
Staff: 2
Annual Budget: $250-500,000
Exec. Director: Robert Ebel, Ph.D.

Historical Note
Merged in 1973 with the Tax Institute of America (1932). Provides the taxpayer, tax administrator, practitioner, educator, and student with a vehicle for national research, discussion, and dissemination of information. Membership: $70-120/year (individual); $300/year (organization).

Publications:
National Tax Journal. q.
NTA Forum. q.
Proceedings. a.

Meetings/Conferences:
Annual Meetings: Fall/350
1999 – Atlanta, GA/Oct. 24-26

Nat'l Tax Lien Ass'n (1997)
1919 Pennsylvania Ave., N.W., Suite 800
Washington, DC 20006
Tel: (202)887-1434   *Fax:* (202)466-2198
Members: 75 individuals
Staff: 3
Executive Director: Bruce McLellan

Nat'l Taxidermists Ass'n (1970)
108 Branch Drive
Slidell, LA 70461
Tel: (504)641-4682   *Fax:* (504)641-0191
Members: 2,500 individuals
Staff: 5
Annual Budget: $100-250,000
Exec. Director: Greg Crain

Historical Note
Membership: $40/year (individual).

Publications:
Annual Directory of Membership. a. adv.
Outlook Magazine. bi-m.

Meetings/Conferences:
1999 – Billings, MT

Nat'l Tay-Sachs and Allied Diseases Ass'n (1957)
2001 Beacon St.
Brighton, MA 02135
Tel: (617)277-4463   *Fax:* (617)277-0134
Web Site:
      http://www.mcrcr2.med.nyu.edu/murphpol/taysachs.
      htm
Members: 14,000 individuals
Staff: 3
Annual Budget: $250-500,000
Exec. Director: Debra Dunkless

Historical Note
Tay-Sachs disease is an inherited genetic disorder, caused by the absence of a vital enzyme and resulting in the destruction of the nervous system; most reported cases are of eastern-central European ancestry. NTSAD's purpose is public and professional education, prevention, services to families, detection and research of Tay-Sachs and allied diseases. Membership: $25/year.

Meetings/Conferences:
Annual Meetings: May/175
1999 – White Plains, NY/May 1-3

Nat'l Technical Ass'n of Scientists
6919 N. 19th
Philadelphia, PA 19126
Tel: (215)549-5743   *Fax:* (215)549-6509
E-Mail: ntamfj1@aol.com
Web Site: http://www.huenet/com/nta
Exec. Director: Mildred Fitzgerald Johnson

Meetings/Conferences:
1999 – Atlanta, GA

Nat'l Technical Services Ass'n (1966)
325 South Patrick Street, Suite 104
Alexandria, VA 22314-3501
Tel: (703)684-4722   *Fax:* (703)684-7627
E-Mail: ntsa@ntsa.com
Web Site: http://www.ntsa.com/ntsa
Members: 300 firms
Staff: 4
Annual Budget: $500-1,000,000
Exec. Director: Carolyn Kelley
Director, Gov. Relations/Public Relations: Robert Drummer

Historical Note
Formerly the Technical Services Industry Ass'n. Trade association of contract technical services firms (engineering, designing and drafting, and information service companies).

Publications:
NTSA Reporter. m. adv.
Weekly Fast Facts. w.

Meetings/Conferences:
Annual Meetings: September
1999 – Nashville, TN/Sept. 7-9

Nat'l Telephone Cooperative Ass'n (1954)
2626 Pennsylvania Ave., N.W.
Washington, DC 20037-1695
Tel: (202)298-2300   *Fax:* (202)298-8749
Members: 474 phone cos., 56 ass'ns
Staff: 120
Annual Budget: $10-25,000,000
Exec. V. President: Michael E. Brunner, CAE
Director, Communications: Paul Shultz
V. President, Government Affairs: Shirley Bloomfield
Education Manager: Ronald D. Precourt, CAE
V. President, Finance: Lisa T. Schweitzer
Manager, Membership Affairs: Dianne Savoy
Publications Manager: Jill O'Rourke

Historical Note
Represents both cooperative and commercial, independent rural phone companies. Has an annual budget of approximately $11.0 million.

Publications:
Compensation & Benefits in the Independent Telephone
      Industry. a.
NTCA Exchange. bi-m.
Rural Telecommunications. bi-m. adv.
Washington Report. w.

Meetings/Conferences:
Annual Meetings: First Quarter/2,500 and Conference/Fall
1999 – San Antonio, TX(Marriott & Hyatt)/Feb. 7-11
1999 – Chicago, IL(Sheraton)/Sept. 19-22
2000 – New Orleans, LA(Hilton Riverside & Crowne
      Plaza)/Feb. 13-17
2000 – Nashville, TN(Opryland)/Sept. 17-20
2001 – Lake Buena Vista, FL(Disney Dolphin &
      Swan)/Feb. 4-8
2001 – Baltimore, MD(Hyatt Regency &
      Renaissance)/Sept. 23-26
2002 – Anaheim, CA(Marriott & Inn at the Park)/Feb. 10-14
2002 – Las Vegas, NV(Mirage)/Sept. 23-26
2003 – Phoenix, AZ(Hyatt Regency & Crowne Plaza)/Feb. 2-6

Nat'l Terrazzo and Mosaic Ass'n (1924)
110 E. Market St., Suite 200-A
Leesburg, VA 20176-3122
Tel: (703)779-1022   *Fax:* (703)779-1026
Toll Free: (800)323 - 9736
Members: 200 individuals
Staff: 2
Annual Budget: $250-500,000
Exec. Director: Derrick Hardy
Director, Member Services: George D. Hardy

Historical Note
Membership: $1,932/year.

Publications:
Catalog - Terrazzo Systems.
Convention Program Journal. a. adv.
NTMA Newsletter. q.
Technical Brochures on Terrazzo Systems.
Terrazo Design Guide.
Terrazzo Information Guide.

Meetings/Conferences:
Annual Meetings: March/April
1999 – San Antonio, TX(La Mansion Del Rio)/March 14-17

Nat'l Therapeutic Recreation Soc. (1966)
22377 Belmont Ridge Rd.
Ashburn, VA 20148-4501
Tel: (703)858-2151   *Fax:* (703)858-0794
Toll Free: (800)626 - 6772
E-Mail: ntrsnrpa@aol.com
Web Site: http://www.nrpa.org/branches/ntrs.htm
Members: 2,700 individuals
Staff: 2
Annual Budget: $100-250,000
Exec. Director: Rikki Epstein

Historical Note
A branch of the Nat'l Recreation and Park Ass'n. Formed (1966) by a merger of Nat'l Ass'n of Recreation Therapists and the Hospital Section of the American Recreation Soc. NTRS promotes therapeutic recreation services in clinical, residential, and community settings. Membership: $45-$210/year, based on annual salary (individual); $230/year (commercial firm); $175/year (non-profit organization).

Publications:
NTRS Report Newsletter. q.
Parks and Recreation Magazine. m. adv.
Therapeutic Recreation Journal. q.

Meetings/Conferences:
Annual Meetings: October, with Nat'l Recreation and Park Ass'n
1999 – Nashville, TN(Convention Center)/Oct. 20-24

Nat'l Tile Contractors Ass'n (1947)
P.O. Box 13629
Jackson, MS 39236
Tel: (601)939-2071   *Fax:* (601)932-6117
Members: 700 companies
Staff: 4
Annual Budget: $500-1,000,000
Exec. Director: Joe A. Tarver

Historical Note
Formerly (1988) the Ass'n of Tile Terrazzo, Marble Contractors and Affiliates and the Southern Tile, Terrazzo, Marble Contractors Ass'n. Membership limited to individuals, firms, and corporations engaged in the installation, manufacture, or sale of ceramic tile, terrazzo, marble and allied products. Street address is 626 Lakeland East Dr., Jackson, MS 39208. Membership: $275/year.

Publications:
Tileletter. m. adv.

Meetings/Conferences:
Annual Meetings: in conjunction with the Internat'l Tile
      Exposition

Nat'l Tile Roofing Manufacturers Ass'n (1976)
P.O. Box 40337
Eugene, OR 97404
Tel: (541)689-0366   Fax: (541)689-5530
Web Site: http://www.ntrma.com
Members: 91 individuals, 40 companies
Annual Budget: $250-500,000
President: Richard K. Olson

Historical Note
Manufacturers of clay and concrete roof tiles. Emphasis is on technical issues and codes that involve tile. Has no paid officers or full-time staff. Membership: $3,500-$100,000/year (company, depending on production output).

Publications:
Newsletter. bi-m.

Meetings/Conferences:

Nat'l Time Equipment Ass'n (1977)
P.O. Box 1447
Norcross, GA 30091-1447
Toll Free: (800)235 - 6832
Members: 350 manufacturers
Staff: 1
Annual Budget: $50-100,000
Exec. Secretary: Norman H. Gage, Jr.

Historical Note
NTEA members are manufacturers and distributors of time keeping devices such as time clocks, computerized time systems and peripherals.

Publications:
NTEA Members Handbook & Directory. a.
Times Newsletter. m.

Meetings/Conferences:
1999 – Sacremento, CA

Nat'l Tire Dealers and Retreaders Ass'n
Historical Note
Became (1997) Tire Ass'n of North America.

Nat'l Tooling and Machining Ass'n (1943)
9300 Livingston Road
Fort Washington, MD 20744
Tel: (301)248-6200   Fax: (301)248-7104
Web Site: http://www.ntma.org
Members: 2,700 companies
Staff: 31
Annual Budget: $2-5,000,000
President & C.O.O.: Matthew B. Coffey

Historical Note
Established as the Nat'l Tool and Die Manufacturers Ass'n, it became the Nat'l Tool, Die and Precision Machining Ass'n in 1960 and assumed its present name in 1980. Members are makers of jigs, molds, tools, gages, dies and fixtures for companies doing precision machining. Supports the NTMA - Committee for A Strong Economy (CFASE).

Publications:
Business and Customer Market Forecast Reports. q.
Membership Directory. a.
The Record. m. adv.

Meetings/Conferences:
Annual Meetings: January
1999 – Coronado, CA(Hotel Del Coronado)

Nat'l Tour Ass'n (1951)
P.O. Box 3071
546 East Main St.
Lexington, KY 40596-3071
Tel: (606)226-4444   Fax: (606)226-4414
Toll Free: (800)682 - 8886
E-Mail: ntahci@aol.com
Members: 3,900 companies
Staff: 42
Annual Budget: $5-10,000,000
Exec. Director: Hank Phillips
Director, Marketing/Media Relations: Kim G. Griffin
Director of Conventions: Denise Stenzel
Director, TTRA: Lisa Carey
V. President, Finance: Bob Livesay
V. President: Lisa Simon
Director, Nat'l Tour Foundation: Keith Howard

Historical Note
Founded as Nat'l Tour Brokers Ass'n, it assumed its present name in 1983. A non-profit organization of package travel companies and allied suppliers, it sponsors the Nat'l Tour Ass'n Political Action Committee (TourPAC); the Nat'l Tour Foundation, a 501(c) foundation; and Nat'l Tour Marketing Services, Inc., a for-profit subsidiary. Has an annual budget of approximately $5.5 million.

Publications:
NTA Courier. m. adv.
Tour Operator Directory. a.
Tour Supplier/Destination Marketing Organization Directory. a.
Tuesday. bi-w.

Meetings/Conferences:
Annual Meetings: November/3,000
1999 – Nashville, TN/Nov. 5-10

Nat'l Tractor Pullers Ass'n (1970)
6969 Worthington-Galena Road, Suite L
Worthington, OH 43085
Tel: (614)436-1761   Fax: (614)436-0964
Members: 5,600 individuals
Annual Budget: $500-1,000,000
Exec. Director: David P. Schreier

Historical Note
Members are competitors and others in the sport of tractor pulling.

Publications:
Media Guide. irreg.
Pull! Program & Yearbook. a. adv.
Puller Magazine. m. adv.
Pulling Rules: Official Rule Book. a. adv.
Tire Tracks Newsletter. q. adv.

Meetings/Conferences:

Nat'l Trailer Dealers Ass'n (1989)
4090 W. Main Ave.
P.O. Box 7310
Fargo, ND 58106
Toll Free: (800)800 - 4552
Web Site: http://www.ntda.org
Members: 400 individuals
Staff: 2
Annual Budget: $50-100,000
Exec. Director: Sue Dorso

Historical Note
NTDA members are companies with interests in all aspects of the semi-trailer industry. Membership: $250-300/year.

Publications:
Trailer Talk Hotline. q. adv.
Trailer Talk Newsletter. m.

Meetings/Conferences:
Annual Meetings: Fall/160
1999 – San Antonio, TX

Nat'l Training Systems Ass'n (1988)
2111 Wilson Blvd., Suite 400
Arlington, VA 22201-3061
Tel: (703)522-1820   Fax: (703)243-1659
Members: 150 individuals, 150 companies
Staff: 3
Annual Budget: $500-1,000,000
Exec. Director: Frederick L. Lewis
Director, Member Services: Barbara McDaniel

Historical Note
Represents companies in the simulation and training industry and training support services. Provides industry forums, market surveys, business development information and other services to members. Membership: $500-$5,000/year(companies), $125/year(individuals).

Publications:
Directory. a.
NTSA Newsletter. bi-m.
Training Survey - NTSA Training 2000.

Meetings/Conferences:
Annual Meetings: November in Orlando, FL/3-4000

Nat'l Translator Ass'n (1962)
5611 Kendell Court
Arvada, CO 80002
Tel: (303)465-5742   Fax: (303)465-4067
Members: 250 translator stations
Annual Budget: $100-250,000
President: Byron St. Clair

Historical Note
Translator FM and TV stations boost normal signals over mountains into rural areas. Membership: $125/year (individual or organization/company).

Publications:
The Translator. q. adv.

Meetings/Conferences:
Annual Meetings: Spring
1999 – Albuquerque, NM/150

Nat'l Trappers Ass'n (1959)
P.O. Box 3667
Bloomington, IL 61702
Tel: (309)829-2422   Fax: (309)829-7615
E-Mail: trappers@ov-net.com
Members: 20,000 individuals
Staff: 7
Annual Budget: $250-500,000
President: Craig Spoores

Historical Note
Formerly (1969) Nat'l Trappers Ass'n of America. Promotes wildlife management programs, education for trappers and the general public, helps maintain trapper rights and preserve their heritage, and provides youth scholarships. Membership: $25/year.

Publications:
American Trapper. bi-m. adv.

Meetings/Conferences:
1999 – Syracuse, NY
2000 – York, PA

Nat'l Treasury Employees Union (1938)
901 E St., N.W., Suite 600
Washington, DC 20004-1475
Tel: (202)783-4444   Fax: (202)783-4085
Members: 150,000 individuals
Staff: 130
Annual Budget: $10-25,000,000
Nat'l President: Robert M. Tobias

Historical Note
Formerly (1957) Nat'l Ass'n of Collectors of Internal Revenue and (1973) Nat'l Ass'n of Internal Revenue Service Employees. Absorbed (1970) Nat'l Ass'n of Alcohol and Tobacco Tax Officers (1935). An independent labor union. Absorbed the Nat'l Custom Service Ass'n in 1975. Sponsors and supports the Nat'l Treasury Employees Union Political Action Committee. Has an annual budget of approximately $10 million.

Publications:
Capitol Report. m.
NTEU Bulletin. every 3 wks.
Stewards Update. m.

Meetings/Conferences:
Biennial Meetings: odd years in August
1999 – Las Vegas, NV

Nat'l Troubleshooting Ass'n
P.O. Box 510020
St. Louis, MO 63151
Tel: (314)846-0640   Fax: (314)846-9950
Staff: 2
Annual Budget: under $10,000
President: Ronald J. Montplaisir

Historical Note
Members are industrial machinery manufacturers, users of industrial machinery systems, and other interested individuals and companies. NTA develops standards and conducts programs on troubleshooting industrial machinery. Membership: $195/year (individual); $495/year (organization/company).

Publications:
Troubleshooting Readiness. m.

Nat'l Truck and Heavy Equipment Claims Council (1961)
18504 Bothell Way, N.E.
Bothell, WA 98011
Tel: (425)481-2800   Fax: (425)481-0817
E-Mail: glenke@alliedpacific.com
Web Site: http://www.nhcc.org
Members: 55 individuals, 18 companies
Staff: 1
Annual Budget: $10-25,000
Administrator: Greg Lenke

Historical Note
Formerly (1995) Truck and Heavy Equipment Claims Council. Established Oct. 3, 1961, in Chicago, to consider common problems of the members in the handling of insurance claims in trucks and heavy equipment. Membership: $150/year.

Publications:
T. H.

Meetings/Conferences:
Annual Meetings: October/250
1999 – Boston, MA/Oct. 9-11

Nat'l Truck Equipment Ass'n (1964)
37400 Hills Tech Dr.
Farmington Hills, MI 48331-3414
Tel: (810)489-7090   Fax: (810)489-8590
Toll Free: (800)441 - 6832
E-Mail: info@ntea.com
Members: 1,550 companies
Staff: 20
Annual Budget: $1-2,000,000
Exec. Director: James D. Carney
Director, Communications: Joan M. Christophersen
Director, Meetings and Member Services: Steve Carey
Director, Technical Services: Louis Kleinstiver
Membership & Advertising Sales Manager: Kathy Schwartzentrover
Director, Information Technology: David C. Lee
Director, Technical Services: Louis Kleinstiver

Historical Note
Formerly (1979) Truck Equipment and Body Distributors Ass'n. Members are companies engaged in the manufacture, distribution and repair of commercial trucks, truck bodies, accessories and equipment. NTEA affiliates include the Ambulance Manufacturers Division, American Institute of Service Body Manufacturers, Articulating Crane Council of North America, Body and Hoist Manufacturers Committee, Manufacturers Council of Small School Buses, Snow Control Equipment Manufacturers Committee, Towing Equipment Manufacturers Ass'n, and Van Body Manufacturers Division. Sponsors and supports the Truck Equipment Political Action Committee (TREQPAC). Membership: $450-1,600/year, based on sales volume.

Publications:
Early Warning Truck Sales Forecast. q.
Excise Tax Quarterly. q.
Membership Roster and Product Directory. a. adv.
Previews Pre-Convention Magazine. a. adv.
Technical Report. irreg.
TENEWS. m.
Washington Update. m.

Meetings/Conferences:
Annual Meetings: Spring
1999 – Indianapolis, IN(Convention Center)/Feb. 24-27/3000
2000 – St. Louis, MO(Convention Center)/Feb. 23-26/5000

Nat'l Truck Leasing System (1944)
1 South 450 Summit Ave., Suite 300
Oak Brook Terrace, IL 60181-3976
Tel: (630)953-8878   Fax: (630)953-0040
Web Site: http://www.ntls.com
Members: 124 companies
Staff: 29
Annual Budget: $1-2,000,000
President: William J. Ford
Director, Franchise Services: Penny Davoran
Corporate Controller: Murray Messner

Historical Note
Members are independent truck leasing companies. Membership: based on size of company.

Publications:
NationaLease Newsletter. w.

Meetings/Conferences:
Annual Meetings: Fall

Nat'l Trucking Industrial Relations Ass'n (1987)
Historical Note
Became North American Trucking Industrial Relations Ass'n in 1997.

Nat'l Tunis Sheep Registry (1929)

Historical Note
Address unknown in 1997.

Nat'l Turf Writers Ass'n (1960)

1314 Bentwood Way
Louisville, KY 40223
Tel: (502)875-4864 *Fax:* (502)244-3895
Toll Free: (800)866 - 2361
Members: 250 individuals
Staff: 1
Annual Budget: $10-25,000
Secretary-Treasurer: Dan Liebman

Publications:
NTWA Awards Dinner Journal. a.
NTWA News Newsletter. m.
Roster of Membership. a.

Meetings/Conferences:
Semi-Annual Meetings: usually in conjunction with the
  Kentucky Derby and the Breeders' Cup

Nat'l Turkey Federation (1939)

1225 New York Ave., N.W., Suite 400
Washington, DC 20005-6156
Tel: (202)898-0100 *Fax:* (202)898-0203
Members: 4,000 individuals
Staff: 11
Annual Budget: $1-2,000,000
President: Stuart E. Proctor, Jr.
Dir., Public Relations: Sherrie Rosenblatt
V. President, Legislative Affairs: Joel Brandenberger
Manager, Member Services: Laurel Cunningham
Dir., Scientific & Regulatory: Alice Hurlburt
Director, Administration: Kathy Henderson

Historical Note
*Provides support to the U.S. turkey industry in marketing and
government relations.*

Publications:
NTF Newsletter. m.

Meetings/Conferences:
Annual Meetings: January
1999 – Washington, DC/July 20-22
1999 – Phoenix, AZ/Jan. 10-13

Nat'l Tutoring Ass'n (1991)

Division of Learning Support Programs
GA State U., Suite 700, 1 Park Place S.
Atlanta, GA 30303-3083
Toll Free: (800)621 - 2930
E-Mail: jtrueschel@po-box.esu.edu
Members: 400 individuals
Annual Budget: $10-25,000
President: Jack Trueschel

Historical Note
*Founded as Nat'l Organization of Tutoring and Mentoring Centers;
became Nat'l Ass'n of Tutoring in 1993, and assumed its current
name in 1995. NTA members are individuals who are actively
engaged in tutoring or in tutoring program administration, and
others with an interest in the field. Has no paid officers or full-time
staff. Membership: $25/year (individual); $50/year (program);
$5/year (student/tutor).*

Publications:
Journal. irreg.
NTA Newsletter. 3/year.

Meetings/Conferences:
Annual Meetings: Spring

Nat'l U.S.-Arab Chamber of Commerce (1987)

1100 New York Ave., N.W., Suite 550 East
Washington, DC 20005-3934
Tel: (202)289-5920 *Fax:* (202)289-5938
Web Site: http://www.nusacc.org
Members: 410 companies and individuals
Staff: 32
Annual Budget: $2-5,000,000
President: Richard P. Holmes
E.Dir., Marketing/Strategic Dev.: Reema Jweied
Exec. V. President: Mazhar Samman

Historical Note
*A trade ass'n chartered in Washington DC with branch offices in
Houston, New York, and Chicago. Membership includes
corporations, associations, and individuals with interests in US-
Arab business. Extensive research, programs, and information
services. Membership: $250/year (individual); $500-1,000/year
(corporation).*

Publications:
Economic and Commercial Directory. a. adv.
National U. S. adv.
Newsletter. q. adv.
Proceedings, Country Profiles, Fact Sheets, etc. irreg.
Quarterly. q. adv.
Trade Opportunities Bulletin. m. adv.
U. S. adv.

Meetings/Conferences:
Annual Meetings: May, in Washington, DC

Nat'l United Affiliated Beverage Ass'n (1979)

P.O. Box 9308
Philadelphia, PA 19139
Tel: (215)724-7585
Chairman: Jeff Jamison

Historical Note
*Members are minority beverage distributors. Street address is: 6216
Woodland Ave., Philadelphia, 19142.*

Publications:
Corkscrew. m.

Meetings/Conferences:
Annual Meetings: Summer

Nat'l United Licensees Beverage Ass'n (1964)

Historical Note
Address unknown in 1996.

Nat'l University Continuing Education Ass'n (1915)

Historical Note
Became University Continuing Education Ass'n in 1996.

Nat'l Used Truck Ass'n (1988)

Historical Note
Became Used Truck Ass'n in 1996.

Nat'l Utility Contractors Ass'n (1964)

4301 N. Fairfax Drive, Suite 360
Arlington, VA 22203-1627
Tel: (703)358-9300 *Fax:* (703)358-9307
Web Site: www.nuca.com
Members: 2,000 companies
Staff: 19
Annual Budget: $2-5,000,000
Exec. V. President: William G. Harley
Director of Communications: Anne Luzier
Director of Government Relations: Bill Hillman
Director of Safety: George Kennedy, CSP
Exec. Director: Peggie Woodward
Director of Membership: Shelly Good
Director of Marketing: Lynn Harrington

Historical Note
*NUCA is comprised of 2000 member Companies And 40 groups of
local underground utility construction contractors and suppliers
throughout the United States. Membership: $750/year (contractor);
$450/year (associate).*

Publications:
Directory of Members. a. adv.
NUCA News. m.
NUCA Safety News. bi-m.
Utility Contractor. m. adv.

Meetings/Conferences:
Annual Meetings: late Winter
1999 – Long Beach, CA(Sheraton)/Feb. 10-14
2000 – Phoenix, AZ(Phoenix Civic Plaza)/March 22-26

Nat'l Vehicle Conversion Ass'n (1991)

Historical Note
Organization defunct in 1997.

Nat'l Vehicle Leasing Ass'n (1968)

P.O. Box 281230
San Francisco, CA 94128-1230
Tel: (650)548-9135 *Fax:* (650)548-9155
E-Mail: nvla@ix.netcom.com
Web Site: http://www.nvla.org
Members: 500 companies
Staff: 4
Annual Budget: $250-500,000
Exec. Director: Rodney J. Couts
Deputy Director: Katherine Sparacino, CAE

Historical Note
*Founded as an amalgamation of two separate groups of pioneer
lessors in 1968 in San Francisco as the Automotive Leasing Ass'n;
merged with the Southern California Leasing Ass'n to become the
California Vehicle Leasing Ass'n; expanded its membership in 1981
to become the Western Vehicle Leasing Ass'n; and in 1984 voted to
act as a national body under the name Nat'l Vehicle Leasing Ass'n.
As the central representative body for all members of the vehicle
leasing industry in the U.S., NVLA's activities include:
governmental affairs, education, publishing, conferences, legal and
other member services, industry relations and certification.
Membership: $550-$2,000/year (organization).*

Publications:
A Consumer Education Guide to Leasing vs. Buying.
Leasing News. q.
Lifeline. q.
Vehicle Leasing Today. q. adv.

Meetings/Conferences:
Annual Meetings: May Lake Buena Vista, FL(Disney's Coronado
  Springs)/May 3-6/500
1999 – Monterey, CA(Marriott)/May 19-22/500
2001 – Colorado Springs, CO(The Broadmoor)/May 9-12/500

Nat'l Venture Capital Ass'n (1973)

1655 N. Fort Myer Drive, Suite 850
Arlington, VA 22209
Tel: (703)524-2549 *Fax:* (703)524-3940
Web Site: www.nvca.org
Members: 230 companies
Staff: 9
Annual Budget: $1-2,000,000
Exec. Director: Daniel T. Kingsley
Director of Administration/Program Development: Molly M. Myers
Director, Research: John S. Taylor, Sr.

Historical Note
*Membership by invitation. Members consist of corporations,
corporate financiers and private individuals who are responsible for
investing private capital in young companies on a professional
basis. Sponsors and Supports the NVCA Political Action
Committee.*

Publications:
Membership Directory.
NVCA Today. bi-m.

Meetings/Conferences:
Annual Meetings: Spring

Nat'l Verbatim Reporters Ass'n

2729 Drake St., Suite 130
Fayetteville, AR 72703

Tel: (501)582-2200 *Fax:* (501)521-7459
E-Mail: nvra@aol.com
Web Site: nvra.org
Annual Budget: $100-250,000
Exec. Director: Jan Cooper

Historical Note
Membership: $100/year (individual).

Publications:
Stenomask Reporter. 5/year.

Meetings/Conferences:
1999 – Willmington, DL/Aug 18-22

Nat'l Viatical Ass'n (1993)

1030 15th St., N.W. Suite 870
Washington, DC 20005
Tel: (202)347-7361 *Fax:* (202)393-0336
Toll Free: (800)741 - 9465
Members: 40 individuals, 20 companies
Staff: 2
Annual Budget: $50-100,000
Exec. Director: Valerie Cooper

Historical Note
*NVA is an association of firms which purchase life insurance
policies from people diagnosed with terminal illnesses in order that
they might have access to these funds before they die. Membership:
$75/year (individual); $500/year (company).*

Publications:
Viatical Association News. q.

Meetings/Conferences:
Semi-Annual Meetings: Spring and Fall
1999 – Miami, FL
1999 – Cincinnati, OH

Nat'l Vocational Agricultural Educators Ass'n (1948)

1410 King St., Suite 400
Alexandria, VA 22314-2749
Tel: (703)838-5885 *Fax:* (703)838-5888
E-Mail: naae@teamaged.org
Web Site: www.teamaged.org
Members: 7,250 individuals
Staff: 3
Annual Budget: $100-250,000
Exec. Director: Wm. Jay Jackman, Ph.D.

Historical Note
*Formerly (1998) Nat'l Vocational Agricultural Educators Ass'n,
NVAEA is a federation of fifty affiliated state voactional agricultural
teacher associations. NVATA was organized in 1948 in Milwaukee,
WI. A member of the Agricultural Education Division of the
American Vocational Ass'n. Membership: $35/yr. (individual),
$17.50/yr. (associate), $330/yr.(life), $175/year (associate life),
$3/year (student).*

Publications:
NAAE News and Views. q.

Meetings/Conferences:
Annual Meetings: December, with the American Vocational
  Ass'n
1999 – Orlando, FL/Dec. 10-14

Nat'l Vocational Agricultural Teachers Ass'n

Historical Note
Became (1998) National Vocational Agricultural Educators Ass'n.

Nat'l Voluntary Organizations for Independent Living for the Aging (1971)

Historical Note
A special interest group of the Nat'l Council of the Aging.

Nat'l Volunteer Fire Council (1976)

1050 17th St., N.W., Suite 1212
Washington, DC 20036
Tel: (202)887-5700 *Fax:* (202)887-5291
E-Mail: nvfcoffice.org
Web Site: http://www.nvfc.org
Members: 1000 individuals, 2 fire departments & 48 ass'ns
Staff: 3
Annual Budget: $250-500,000
Exec. Manager: Heather Schafer
Government Affairs Representative: Anne Wilson

Historical Note
*NVFC members include state level organizations that represent
volunteer firefighters and EMS personnel, volunteer fire
departments, individual firefighters, corporate members, and a
number of allied organizations. Membership: $300/year
(organization); $25/year (individual).*

Publications:
Dispatch. m.

Meetings/Conferences:
Semi-annual Meetings: spring and fall.

Nat'l Water Resources Ass'n (1932)

3800 N. Fairfax Drive, Suite 4
Arlington, VA 22203-1703
Tel: (703)524-1544 *Fax:* (703)524-1548
E-Mail: nwra@erols.com
Web Site: http://www.nwra.org
Members: 5,000 individuals
Staff: 5
Annual Budget: $250-500,000
Exec. V. President: Thomas F. Donnelly
Dir., Govt. Relations: Kris D. Polly
Administrative Assistant: Jess Baldwin

Historical Note
*Formerly (1970) Nat'l Reclamation Ass'n. Operates in 16 western
states. Members are directors of water resource development
projects such as irrigation districts, canal companies, conservancy
districts and water users in general. Memberships available through
state ass'ns and the Professional Services Council. Membership:
$150/year.*

Publications:
Ground Water Report. m.
Municipal Caucus News. m.
Nat'l Water Line. m. adv.
Water Report. bi-m.
Meetings/Conferences:
Annual Meetings: Fall

Nat'l Watercolor Soc. (1920)
215 Paseo Del Mar
San Pedro, CA 90732
Toll Free: (800)486 - 8670
Web Site: http://www.nws-online.org
Members: 1,300 individuals830 associates
Annual Budget: $50-100,000
Newsletter Editor: Lowri Sprung
Historical Note
NWS is dedicated to the exhibition and promotion of excellence in
water media painting. Membership: $30/year (signature juried
member), $25/year (associate).
Publications:
Newsletter. q. adv.
NWS Catalogue. a.
Meetings/Conferences:
Annual Meetings: January, with an Exhibition in Fall or early
     Winter

Nat'l Waterfowl Council (1952)
Historical Note
Defunct in 1995.

Nat'l Watermelon Ass'n (1914)
P.O. Box 38
Morven, GA 31638
Tel: (912)775-2130   Fax: (912)775-2344
Members: 700 individuals
Staff: 3
Annual Budget: $250-500,000
Exec. Secretary/Treasurer: Nancy Childers
Historical Note
NWA members are producers, distributors and sellers of
watermelons and related support industries.
Membership:$100(individual).
Publications:
Bulletin. semi-a. adv.
Convention Proceedings. a.
Meetings/Conferences:
1999 – Washington, DC(Ritz Carlton)/350
1999 – Washington, DC(Ritz-Carlton)/Feb. 25-28

Nat'l Waterways Conference (1960)
1130 17th St., N.W.
Washington, DC 20036-4676
Tel: (202)296-4415   Fax: (202)835-3861
Web Site: http://www.waterways.org
Members: 350 businesses
Staff: 4
Annual Budget: $250-500,000
President: Harry N. Cook
Convention Coordinator: Medina S. Moran
Historical Note
An umbrella group of shippers, barge lines and local port
authorities working to promote a better understanding of the public
value of the American waterways system. Membership: $100/year
(individual); $600/year (organization/company).
Publications:
Washington Watch. m.
Meetings/Conferences:
Annual Meetings: September/350
1999 – Nashville, TN(Sheraton Music City Hotel)/Sept. 15-17
2000 – St. Louis, MO

Nat'l Weather Ass'n (1975)
6704 Wolke Ct.
Montgomery, AL 36116-2134
Tel: (334)213-0388   Fax: (334)213-0388
E-Mail: natweaasoc@aol.com
Web Site: http://WWW.NWAS.ORG
Members: 2,500 individuals
Staff: 1
Annual Budget: $100-250,000
Exec. Director: J. Kevin Lavin
Historical Note
Individuals and groups interested in practical meteorology on a
professional basis. Awards the Radio-Television Weathercaster Seal
of Approval. Membership: $28/year (individual); $75/year
(organization/company).
Publications:
Meeting Program. a. adv.
National Weather Digest. q. adv.
Newsletter. 12/year.
Meetings/Conferences:
Annual Meetings: late October-early December/200-250

Nat'l Weather Service Employees Organization (1976)
601 Pennsylvania Ave., N.W., #900
Washington, DC 20004-2612
Tel: (703)293-9651
Members: 1,200 individuals
Staff: 2
Annual Budget: $250-500,000
Contact: Peter Nuhn
Publications:
Four Winds. q.
Meetings/Conferences:
Annual Meetings: Fall

Nat'l Welding Supply Ass'n (1945)

1900 Arch St.
Philadelphia, PA 19103-1498
Tel: (215)564-3484   Fax: (215)564-2175
E-Mail: nwsa@nwsa.com
Web Site: http://www.nwsa.com
Members: 1,200 companies
Staff: 6
Annual Budget: $2-5,000,000
Exec. Director: John P. Derrickson
Conference Coordinator: Jennifer Miller
Coordinator, Member Services and Convention: Sheree Mazzella
Publications:
Spatter. 4/year.
Meetings/Conferences:
Annual Meetings: Fall

Nat'l Wellness Ass'n (1985)
1300 College Ct.
P.O. Box 827
Stevens Point, WI 54481-0827
Tel: (715)342-2969   Fax: (715)342-2979
Web Site: http://www.wellnessnwi.org
Members: 2,000 individuals
Staff: 3
Annual Budget: $250-500,000
Exec. Director: Linda R. Chapin, D.D.S., MS
Director, Membership Services: Anne Hellmke
Historical Note
Organized under the Nat'l Wellness Institute, NWA is composed of
professionals working in all areas of health and wellness promotion.
Its mission is to meet the growing need of these professionals for
information, services and networking. Membership: $120/year
(professional individual); $280/year (professional organization);
$58/year (associate individual); $135/year (associate
organization).
Publications:
Wellness Management (newsletter). q.
Meetings/Conferences:
Annual Meetings: With Nat'l Wellness Conference in July at
     Univ. of WI - Stevens Pt.

Nat'l Wheel and Rim Ass'n (1924)
5121 Bowden Rd., Suite 303
Jacksonville, FL 32216-5950
Tel: (904)737-2900   Fax: (904)636-9881
Members: 36 with over 210 locations
Staff: 3
Annual Budget: $250-500,000
Exec. V. President: Angelo Volpe
Historical Note
Organized in Chicago in 1924 at the Metropole Hotel. Warehouse
distributors of wheels, rims and related parts. Affiliated with the
Nat'l Ass'n of Wholesaler-Distributors.
Publications:
Membership Directory/Roster. a.
Wheel and Rim Manual.
Meetings/Conferences:
Annual Meetings: September/200
1999 – Sea Island, GA(The Cloister)/Sept. 19-24/200
2000 – Colorado Springs, CO(Broadmoor)/Sept. 17-22/200

Nat'l Wholesale Druggists' Ass'n (1876)
1821 Michael Faraday Drive, Suite 400
Reston, VA 20190-5348
Tel: (703)787-0000   Fax: (703)787-6930
Web Site: http://www.nwda.org
Members: 400 companies
Staff: 42
Annual Budget: $5-10,000,000
President and C.E.O.: Ronald J. Streck
V. President, Mktg./Communications: Bruce Kneeland
V. President, Information Services: Marsha Friedman
Director, Communications: Mark W. Doyon
V. President, Government & Public Affairs: Sherry J. Haber
Director, Congressional Affairs: Robert Falb
Director, Reg. Affairs: Diane Goyette
V. President, Meetings & Media Services: Linda Thomas
Executive V. President, Finance/Administration: Nancy E. Hanagan
Director, Technical Services: Robert A. Borger
Director, Information Systems: Heidi W. Byerly
Historical Note
Established as Western Wholesale Druggists, it assumed its present
name in 1881. Sponsors and supports the NWDA Political Action
Committee. Absorbed the Druggists Service Council in 1971.
Merged (1984) with Drug Wholesalers Ass'n. Has an annual
budget of approximately $8 million. Membership fee varies, based
on sales volume.
Publications:
Business Systems Update. irreg
EDItion. irreg.
Fact Book. a.
Government Update. m.
Human Resource Letter. irreg.
Marketing Bulletins. irreg.
NWDA Industry Analysis Report. a.
NWDA Industry Trend Report. a.
NWDA Membership Directory. a.
Operating Survey. a.
Operations Bulletin. irreg.
The Vital Link. m.
Meetings/Conferences:
Annual Meetings: Fall

Nat'l Wildlife Rehabilitators Ass'n (1982)
14 North 7th Ave.
St. Cloud, MN 56303-4766
Tel: (320)259-4086
E-Mail: nwra@cloudnet.com
Members: 1,500 individuals, 200 organizations
Staff: 2

Annual Budget: $100-250,000
President: Elaine M. Thrune
Historical Note
NWRA members are professional wildlife rehabilitators and others
with an interest in wild animal care. NWRA provides information,
education and training to persons involved with helping injured,
orphaned and displaced wild animals grow, heal and return to the
wild. Membership: $30/year (individual); $15/year (student);
$50/year (family); $1000 + (life membership).
Publications:
NWRA Membership Directory. a.
Quarterly Journal. q. adv.
Training Opportunities in Wildlife Rehabilitation. bien.
Wildlife Rehabilitation. a.
Meetings/Conferences:
Annual Meetings: Spring
1999 – Greensboro, NC(Hilton)/March 9-13

Nat'l Wine Coalition (1989)
Historical Note
Reported ceased operations in 1997.

Nat'l Wireless Resellers Ass'n (1987)
1825 I St., N.W., Suite 400
Washington, DC 20006
Tel: (202)835-9898
Members: 10 companies
Staff: 3
Annual Budget: $250-500,000
Exec. Director: David Gusky
Historical Note
Formerly (1997) Nat'l Cellular Resellers Ass'n, NWRA members
are non-affiliated resellers of cellular telephone service in the U.S.
NWRA is charged with establishing and promoting the resale of
cellular telephone service to create and ensure a more competitive
marketplace.
Meetings/Conferences:
Annual Meetings: Autumn, in Washington, DC

Nat'l Women's Economic Alliance Foundation (1984)
808 17th St., N.W., Suite 600
Washington, DC 20006
Tel: (202)863-8689   Fax: (301)977-4400
Staff: 5
Annual Budget: $100-250,000
Exec. Director: Elise W. Garfinkel
Historical Note
Formerly (1990) Nat'l Women's Economic Alliance.
Publications:
Outlook. 2/year.
Women Directors of the Top 1,000 Corporations. a.
Meetings/Conferences:
Annual Meetings: December in Washington, DC

Nat'l Women's Neckwear and Scarf Ass'n (1933)
Historical Note
Organization defunct in 1997.

Nat'l Women's Studies Ass'n (1977)
7100 Baltimore Ave., Suite 500
College Park, MD 20740
Tel: (301)403-0525   Fax: (301)403-4137
Members: 3,000 individuals
Annual Budget: $100-250,000
Nat'l Exec. Administrator: Loretta Younger
Historical Note
NWSA members are teachers, students, independent scholars,
program administrators, and community activists. Membership:
$75/year (individual); $185/year (institution).
Publications:
NWSA Journal. q. adv.
NWSAction Newsletter.
Women's Studies Program Directory. bien.
Meetings/Conferences:
Annual Meetings: June
1999 – Albuquerque, NM(Radisson)/June 17-20

Nat'l Wood Flooring Ass'n (1986)
16388 Westwoods Business Pk.
Ellisville, MO 63021-4522
Tel: (314)391-5161   Fax: (314)391-6137
Toll Free: (800)422 - 4556
E-Mail: natlwood@aol.com
Web Site: http://www.woodfloors.org
Members: 1,800 companies
Staff: 8
Annual Budget: $1-2,000,000
Exec. Director: Edward S. Korczak, CAE
Director, Education: Bonnie J. Holmes
Director, Technical Services: Daniel Boone
Membership/Marketing: Karen Gentles
Historical Note
Membership includes all segments of the wood flooring industry:
distributors, manufacturers, retailers/contractors, etc. NWFA's
purposes include advertising and promotion, education and
training, the development of standards and grade levels and intra-
industry communications. Membership: $375/yr (corporate).
Publications:
Hardwood Floors Magazine. bi-m. adv.
The Log. bi-m.
Meetings/Conferences:
Annual Meetings: Spring
1999 – Reno, NV(The Nugget Hotel)/April 22-24/2000
2000 – Dallas, TX(Adam's Mark)/2100
2001 – Palm Springs, FL/2200

Nat'l Wood Tank Institute (1942)
P.O. Box 2755

Philadelphia, PA   19120
Tel: (215)329-9022   *Fax:* (215)329-1177
Members: 8 companies
Secretary: Harrison W. Rippen
Historical Note
NWTI members are companies and individuals in the U.S. and Canada involved in the manufacture of wood tanks, vats and pipes.

Nat'l Wood Window and Door Ass'n *(1926)*
1400 East Touhy Ave., Suite 470
Des Plaines, IL   60018-3305
Tel: (847)299-5200   *Fax:* (847)299-1286
Toll Free: (800)223 - 2301
Web Site: http://www.nwwda.org
Members: 140 companies
Staff: 6
Annual Budget: $1-2,000,000
President: Alan J. Campbell, CAE
Historical Note
Founded as the Nat'l Door Manufacturers Ass'n and became the Nat'l Woodwork Manufacturers Ass'n, Inc. in 1950; assumed its present title in 1985. Absorbed the Ponderosa Pine Woodwork Ass'n in 1975. Members are makers of standard building products such as doors, windows, and frames.
Publications:
Membership Directory. a.
Millwork Sources of Supply. a.
NWWDA Newsletter. m.
Meetings/Conferences:
Annual Meetings: Febraury/250
1999 – Marco Island, FL(Marriott)/Feb. 6-10
2000 – Tucson, AZ(Westin La Paloma)/Feb. 12-16

Nat'l Wooden Pallet and Container Ass'n *(1947)*
1800 N. Kent St., Suite 911
Arlington, VA   22209-2109
Tel: (703)527-7667   *Fax:* (703)527-7717
E-Mail: palletassn@aol.com
Web Site: http://www.nwpca.com
Members: 550 companies
Staff: 9
Annual Budget: $1-2,000,000
Exec. V. President/C.E.O.: John J. Healy, CAE
Meetings Manager: Jeni Kraich
Membership and Member Services Director: Judith A. Peck
Industry Promotion and Marketing Director: Kathy Conroy, CAE
Historical Note
Represents manufacturers, recyclers and distributors of pallets, containers and reels and companies that supply products, equipment, and services to the industry. Membership fee varies, based on annual volume of sales.
Publications:
Buyers Guide. a.
Directory. a.
NWPCA Newsletter. bi-w.
Meetings/Conferences:
Annual Meetings: February
1999 – La Jolla, CA(Sheraton Torrey Pines)

Nat'l Woodland Owners Ass'n *(1983)*
374 Maple Ave. East, Suite 310
Vienna, VA   22180-4751
Tel: (703)255-2700
Toll Free: (800)476 - 8733
Members: 39,000 individuals
Staff: 4
Annual Budget: $250-500,000
President: Keith A. Argow
Historical Note
Founded with the purpose of uniting non-industrial private woodland owners in America; membership includes landowners in all 50 states. Although independent of the forest products industry and public agencies, NWOA works with all organizations to promote non-industrial forestry and the interests of woodland owners. Has 34 state affiliates. Membership: $25/year (individual), $75-500/year (state ass'n).
Publications:
Conservation News Digest. q.
National Woodlands Magazine. q.
Woodland Report. 8/year.
Meetings/Conferences:
Annual Meetings: Not held.

Nat'l Wool Marketing Corporation *(1929)*
9449 Basil Western Road, N.W.
Canal Winchester, OH   43110-9278
Tel: (614)834-1957   *Fax:* (614)834-2008
Members: 3 state associations
Staff: 1
Annual Budget: $100-250,000
President: Duncan McCormick
Historical Note
A wool marketing agency for a number of state associations of sheep growers.
Meetings/Conferences:
Annual Meetings: February and September

Nat'l Wrestling Coaches Ass'n *(1946)*
Historical Note
Address unknown in 1996.

Nat'l Writers Ass'n *(1937)*
3140 S. Peoria St., Suite 295
Aurora, CO   80014-3155
Tel: (303)841-0246   *Fax:* (303)751-8593
Web Site: http://www.nationalwriters.com
Members: 3,000 individuals
Staff: 2
Annual Budget: $100-250,000

Exec. Director: Sandy Whelchel
Historical Note
Founded in 1937 by David Raffelock to serve freelance writers. Membership: $60/yr.
Publications:
Authorship. bi-m. adv.
Flash Market News. 6/year.
Professional Freelance Writers Directory. a.
Meetings/Conferences:
Annual Meetings: June, with the Associated Business Writers of America

Nat'l Writers Union *(1983)*
113 University Place, 6th Floor
New York, NY   10003
Tel: (212)254-0279   *Fax:* (212)254-0673
E-Mail: nwu@nwu.org
Web Site: http://www.nwu.org/nwu/
Members: 4,600 individuals
Staff: 8
Annual Budget: $500-1,000,000
President: Jonathan Tasini
Historical Note
An independent union established to improve the working conditions of freelance writers through the collective strength of its members. NWU members include journalists, novelists, biographers, historians, poets, children's book authors, textbook authors, commercial writers, technical writers and cartoonists. Originated in New York City in October, 1981 in connection with the American Writers Congress. Membership: $90-$195/year *(based on income).*
Publications:
The American Writer. q. adv.
Meetings/Conferences:
Monthly Meetings: based on local area

Nat'l Writing Centers Ass'n *(1983)*
University of Toledo
2801 West Bancroft
Toledo, OH   43606-3390
Tel: (419)530-4913   *Fax:* (419)530-4752
E-Mail: jmullin@uoft02.utoledo.edu
Members: 900 individuals
Staff: 4
Editor: Joan Mullin
Historical Note
NWCA was founded to foster communication among writing centers and to provide a forum for concerns. Members are writing center directors and staff members. Membership: $10/year *(individual);* $20/year (w/WCJ); $35/year (w/WCJ and WLN).
Publications:
Writing Center Journal (WCJ). bi-a. adv.
Writing Lab Newsletter (WLN). m. adv.

Nat'l Yogurt Ass'n *(1987)*
2000 Corporate Ridge
Suite 1000
McLean, VA   22102
Tel: (703)821-0770   *Fax:* (703)821-1350
Members: 15 companies
Staff: 4
Annual Budget: $250-500,000
President and C.E.O.: Leslie G. Sarasin
Historical Note
Members are manufacturers and marketers of live and active culture yogurt products, and the suppliers to the industry.
Publications:
NYA News. q.
Meetings/Conferences:

Nat'l Youth Sport Coaches Ass'n *(1990)*
Historical Note
Became the Nat'l Alliance for Youth Sports in 1997.

Nat'l-American Wholesale Grocers' Ass'n *(1906)*
Historical Note
Became Food Distributors Internat'l in 1996.

Nationwide Alternate Delivery Alliance
P.O. Box 71142
Washington, DC   20024
Tel: (202)678-8350   *Fax:* (202)889-9209
Toll Free: (800)969 - 2258
President: Clyde Northrop
Historical Note
Members are private, regional delivery companies united to provide publishers with an alternative to postal delivery.

Natl Health Lawyers Ass'n/American Academy of Healthcare Attorneys
155 E. 55th St., Suite 302-B
New York, NY   10022
Tel: (212)832-4939   *Fax:* (212)832-4939
Historical Note
Became the American Health Lawyers Ass'n in 1998.

NATSO, Representing America's Travel Plaza and Truckstops *(1960)*
1199 N. Fairfax St., Suite 801
Alexandria, VA   22314
Tel: (703)549-2100   *Fax:* (703)684-4525
E-Mail: natsoinc@aol.com
Web Site: http://www.natso.com
Members: 1,050 locations
Staff: 21
Annual Budget: $2-5,000,000
President: W. Dewey Clower

V. President, Communications: Paul Savary
V. President, Government Affairs: Scot Imus
V. President, Operations: Barbara Tulipane
Historical Note
Formerly (1993) the Nat'l Ass'n of Truck Stop Operators. Owners and operators of large fully-equipped truck stops. Allied members are oil companies and other suppliers. Sponsors the Political Action Committee (NATSO/PAC). Headquarters for the American Truck Stop Foundation, dba The Natso Foundation.
Publications:
Allied News. q.
Checklink Directory. m.
Membership Directory. a.
NATSO Truckers News. m. adv.
Stopwatch Newsletter. m.
Meetings/Conferences:
Annual Meetings: February
1999 – Phoenix, AZ/Jan. 26-30
2000 – Memphis, TN/Feb. 17-20
2001 – Los Angeles, CA/Feb. 20-24

Natural Colored Wool Growers Ass'n *(1977)*
429 W. U.S. Highway 30
Valparaiso, IN   46385-9207
Tel: (219)759-9665
Members: 500 individuals
Annual Budget: $10-25,000
Registrar: Barbara Kloese
Historical Note
NCWGA members are breeders and owners of colored sheep as well as those who use or otherwise have an interest in colored wool. In addition to assisting members in the development, improvement and promotion of colored sheep and colored wool, the NCWGA maintains a registration program. Membership: $20/year *(individual);* $15/year (organization/company); $5/year (junior).
Publications:
Marker. q. adv.

Natural Gas Supply Ass'n *(1965)*
805 15th St., N.W., Suite 510
Washington, DC   20005
Tel: (202)326-9300   *Fax:* (202)326-9330
Web Site: http://www.ngsa.org
Members: 90 companies
Staff: 10
Annual Budget: $2-5,000,000
President: Nicholas J. Bush
Dir. Industry/Public Relations: Charlotte Le Gates
Historical Note
Members are domestic natural gas producers. Formerly (1979) known as the Natural Gas Supply Committee.
Meetings/Conferences:
Annual Meetings: First Quarter of the Year

Natural Gas Vehicle Coalition *(1988)*
1515 Wilson Blvd., Suite 1030
Arlington, VA   22209
Tel: (703)527-3022   *Fax:* (703)527-3025
E-Mail: rkolodziej@ngvc.org
Web Site: http://www.ngvc.org
Members: 200 companies
Staff: 9
Annual Budget: $1-2,000,000
President: Richard R. Kolodziej
Director, Government Relations: Paul Kerkhoven
Historical Note
NGVC members are organizations with an interest in encouraging the development of natural gas powered vehicles. Membership fee varies, $500-$25,200/year, *based on type of company and business volume.*
Publications:
Member Business Guide. a. adv.
NGVCommunications. w.
Meetings/Conferences:
1999 – Minneapolis, MN(Convention Center)/Oct. 3-5

Natural Product Broker Ass'n *(1978)*
3933 N. Hoyne St.
Chicago, IL   60618
Tel: (773)525-5887   *Fax:* (773)525-6688
Web Site: http://www.naturalbrokers.com
Members: 34 companies
Annual Budget: under $10,000
President: Ray Flores
Historical Note
Purpose is to open channels between manufacturers/distributors and brokers of natural food and nonfood products. Has no paid officers or full-time staff. Membership: $300/year.
Meetings/Conferences:
Semi-Annual Meetings: Spring and Summer/50

Natural-Source Vitamin E Ass'n *(1984)*
Historical Note
Address unknown in 1997.

Naval Enlisted Reserve Ass'n *(1957)*
6703 Farragut Ave.
Falls Church, VA   22042-2189
Tel: (703)534-1329   *Fax:* (703)534-3617
Toll Free: (800)776 - 9020
E-Mail: NERABob@nera.org
Web Site: http://www.cais.com/nera
Members: 15,500 individuals
Staff: 3
Annual Budget: $250-500,000
National Exec. Secretary: Robert H. Lyman

Historical Note
Members are the enlisted personnel in the Navy, Marine Corps and Coast Guard Reserve. Membership: $20/year (individual).

Publications:
Mariner. bi-m. adv.
Roster of Nat'l and Regional Officers and Chapter Presidents. a.

Meetings/Conferences:
Annual Meetings: October

Naval Reserve Ass'n *(1954)*
1619 King St.
Alexandria, VA   22314
Tel: (703)548-5800   *Fax:* (703)683-3647
E-Mail: exec.dir@navy-reserve.org
Web Site: http://www.navy-reserve.org
Members: 2,200 individuals
Staff: 5
Annual Budget: $500-1,000,000
Exec. Director: R.Adm. Thomas Hall, USN(Ret.)
Meetings: Al Rieder
Asst. Exec. Director and Director, Legislation: Captain John Godley, USNR
Finance: Dick Martin
Membership: Mark Deville

Historical Note
NRA is a professional organization of officers joined together to support the Navy and to provide services to Naval Reserve Officers. Membership: $35/year (individual).

Publications:
Naval Reserve Association News. m. adv.

Meetings/Conferences:
1999 – San Diego, CA/March 3-6
1999 – Falls Church, VA/Sept. 29-Oct. 2

NAWE: Advancing Women in Higher Education *(1916)*
1325 18th Street, N.W., Suite 210
Washington, DC   20036-6511
Tel: (202)659-9330   *Fax:* (202)457-0946
E-Mail: nawe@nawe.org
Web Site: http://www.nawe.org
Members: 1,400 individuals
Staff: 5
Annual Budget: $250-500,000
Exec. Director: Lynn M. Gangone

Historical Note
Formerly (1956) Nat'l Ass'n of Deans of Women, (1973) Nat'l Ass'n of Women Deans and Counselors, (1991) Nat'l Ass'n for Women Deans, Administrators, and Counselors, and (1996) Nat'l Ass'n for Women in Education. Provides professional support for women educators through programs, services, advocacy, and scholarly publications. Committed to lifelong learning and to furthering educational opportunites for women students and professionals at all levels of learning, growth, and development. Membership: $75/year (individual); $35/year (student); $55/year (new member).

Publications:
About Women on Campus. adv. adv.
Directory. a.
Initiatives.
Journal. q. adv.
Newsletter. q.

Meetings/Conferences:
1999 – Denver, CO(Adam's Mark)/Feb. 24-27
2000 – Boston, MA(Swissotel)/Feb. 23-26

NBFA: the Ass'n for Independent Marketers of Business Printing and Information Systems
Historical Note
Became Document Management Industries Ass'n in 1996.

NCCLS *(1968)*
940 West Valley Road
Suite 1400
Wayne, PA   19087-1898
Tel: (610)688-0100   *Fax:* (610)688-0700
E-Mail: exoffice@NCCLS.ORG
Web Site: http://www.NCCLS.ORG
Members: 2,000 organizations
Staff: 27
Annual Budget: $2-5,000,000
Exec. Director: John V. Bergen, Ph.D.
Communications Coordinator: Fiona Keating
Director of Office Operations: Helen Gallagher
Assistant Executive Director for Standards Application: Geraldine L. Barnes
Assistant Exec. Director for Business Services: Lola Pugliese
Assistant Exec. Director for Marketing: Louise A. Ciccarelli

Historical Note
Formerly (1994) Nat'l Committee for Clinical Laboratory Standards Organization. Develops voluntary consensus standards for patient testing. Affiliated with the American National Standards Institute.

Publications:
Standards. irreg.
Update Standards Status. m.

Meetings/Conferences:
Annual Meetings: Spring/250
1999 – Baltimore, MD(Renaissance)/April 27-May 1/200

NCITD - Internat'l Trade Facilitation Council *(1967)*
Historical Note
Became Nat'l Council on Internat'l Trade Development in 1995.

Neckwear Ass'n of America *(1946)*
151 Lexington Ave., #2F
New York, NY   10016
Tel: (212)683-8454   *Fax:* (212)686-7382
Members: 110 companies

Staff: 2
Annual Budget: $100-250,000
Exec. Director: Gerald Andersen, CAE

Historical Note
Formerly (1979) known as the Men's Tie Foundation, Inc.

Publications:
Neckwear Industry Directory. bien.

Meetings/Conferences:
Semi-annual Meetings: June and October in New York, NY

Neighborhood Cleaners Ass'n-Internat'l *(1946)*
252 W. 29th St., 2nd Floor
New York, NY   10001-5201
Tel: (212)967-3002   *Fax:* (212)967-2240
Members: 4,200 companies
Staff: 26
Annual Budget: $1-2,000,000
Exec. Director: William Seitz
Field Supervisor: Vincent Beazer

Historical Note
Membership: $276-505/year, based on number of employees.

Publications:
NCA Bulletin. m. adv.

Meetings/Conferences:
1999 – Newark, NJ(Convention Center)/Oct. 16-17

Netherlands Chamber of Commerce in the United States *(1903)*
One Rockefeller Plaza, Suite 1420
New York, NY   10020
Tel: (212)265-6460   *Fax:* (212)265-6402
Web Site: http://www.netherlands.org
Members: 1000 businesses
Staff: 20
Annual Budget: $2-5,000,000
Managing Director: Kersen J. De Jong

Historical Note
Membership: $500/year (corporate), $1,000/year (sustaining).

Publications:
Annual Report. a.
Holland-USA. q.
Orange Report. bi-m.

Meetings/Conferences:
Annual Meetings: November/New York, NY

Network of Ingredient Marketing Specialists *(1981)*
P.O. Box 76422
Atlanta, GA   30358
Tel: (770)977-1476   *Fax:* (770)973-6662
E-Mail: kwr@nims.com
Web Site: http://www.nims.com
Members: 18 companies
Staff: 1
Annual Budget: $50-100,000
Exec. Director: Kenneth W. Reynolds

Historical Note
Founded as NorthAmerican Ingredient Marketing Specialists; assumed its current name in 1998. NIMS members are food ingredient brokers.

Meetings/Conferences:
Semi-Annual Meetings: Summer and Winter

Neural Networks Council
Historical Note
A subsidiary of the Institute of Electrical and Electronics Engineers (IEEE). Membership in the Council, open only to IEEE members, includes subscription to a technical periodical in the field published by IEEE. Administrative support is provided by IEEE.

Neurodevelopmental Treatment Ass'n *(1967)*
1550 S. Coast Hwy., Suite 201
Laguna Beach, CA   92651
Tel: (714)497-9007   *Fax:* (714)376-3456
Toll Free: (800)869 - 9295
E-Mail: Webmaster@NDTA.org
Web Site: http://www.ndta.org
Members: 4,000 individuals
Annual Budget: $100-250,000
Exec. Director: Fred Droz

Historical Note
NDTA members include physical therapists, occupational therapists, speech-language pathologists, special education professionals, physicians and others using an interdisciplinary approach in treating individuals with central nervous system dysfunction. Membership: $60/year (individual); $26/year (student/retired); $240/year (organization/company).

Publications:
Membership Directory. a.
NDTA Network Newsletter. bi-m. adv.

Meetings/Conferences:
Annual Meetings: October

Neurosurgical Soc. of America *(1948)*
Univ. of Tex, Div. of Neurosurgery
7703 Floyd Curl Drive
San Antonio, TX   78284-7843
Tel: (210)567-5625   *Fax:* (210)567-6066
Members: 205 individuals
Annual Budget: $50-100,000
General Secretary: Dr. Paul Nelson

Historical Note
Membership by invitation only.

Meetings/Conferences:

Neurotrauma Soc.
Historical Note
Address unknown in 1996.

New Alternatives for Publishers, Retailers and Artists *(1986)*
6 Eastsound Square
P.O. Box 9
Eastsound, WA   98245-0009
Tel: (360)376-2702   *Fax:* (360)376-2704
E-Mail: napra@napra.com
Web Site: http://www.napra.com
Members: 600 individuals, 450 companies
Staff: 10
Annual Budget: $250-500,000
President: Marilyn McGuire
Exec. Director: Suzanne M. Humes

Historical Note
Formerly New Age Publishing and Retailing Alliance (1998). NAPRA is a trade association representing publishers, retailers, producers, manufacturers, authors, editors and others who are creating or selling books, music and other products that promote spritual growth and positive social change. Member benefits include, subscription to NAPRA Review, trade exhibit discounts, a quarterly newsletter, and opportunities for networking with colleagues in retailing and publishing, along with other services.

Publications:
NAPRA ReVIEW. bi-m. adv.

Meetings/Conferences:
1999 – Los Angeles, CA(Marriott)/April 30-May 2

New York Academy of Sciences *(1817)*
2 E. 63rd St.
New York, NY   10021
Tel: (212)838-0230   *Fax:* (212)888-2894
Toll Free: (800)843 - 6927
E-Mail: rnichols@nyas.org
Web Site: http://www.nyas.org
Members: 40,000 individuals
Staff: 76
Annual Budget: $10-25,000,000
President and C.E.O.: Rodney W. Nichols
Director, Communications: Diane McNulty
Director, Membership and Marketing: Katherine T. Goldring
Director, Science and Technology Meetings: Rashid Shaikh, Ph.D.
Director, Education: Lori Skopp
Director, Policy and Programs: Alison C. deCerreno
V. President, Institutional Advancement: Peter Kohn
Director, Human Rights of Scientists: Svetlana Stone

Historical Note
The Academy, founded in 1817, is the oldest scientific organization in New York and the third oldest in the nation. Its initiatives include disseminating scientific information, advancing science education, protecting the human rights of scientists, and applying science and technology to achieve economic and social goals. Has an annual budget of $11 million. Membership: $95/year (domestic); $115/year (overseas).

Publications:
Academy Update. q.
Science in Society Policy Reports. 6/year.
The Annals. 32/year.
The Sciences. bi-m. adv.

Meetings/Conferences:
1999 – New York, NY

New York Board of Trade *(1870)*
4 World Trade Center
New York, NY   10048
Tel: (212)742-5000   *Fax:* (212)742-5120
Toll Free: (800)692 - 6886
Web Site: http://www.nyce.com
Members: 450 individuals
Staff: 115
Annual Budget: $10-25,000,000
President: James J. Bowe
Director of Market and Product Development: Janet E. Troy
Senior V. President, Finance and Administration: Bruce Cooperman

Historical Note
Formerly (1998) the New York Cotton Exchange. Oldest of the New York commodity futures exchanges. Formed Citrus Associates in 1966 and Finex Division in 1985. Purchased the New York Futures Exchange, a wholly-owned subsidiary, in 1993. Membership: $500/year. Has an annual budget of $10 million.

Publications:
Daily Market Report. d.
Weekly Trade Report. w.

New York Cotton Exchange
Historical Note
Became the New York Board of Trade in 1998.

New York Mercantile Exchange *(1872)*
4 World Trade Center
New York, NY   10048
Tel: (212)748-3000   *Fax:* (212)742-5258
Members: 816 individuals
Staff: 245
Annual Budget: $10-25,000,000
President: Patrick Thompson

Historical Note
Formerly (1880) Butter, Cheese, and Egg Exchange of the City of New York. Concerned with the trading of futures in heating and crude oil, unleaded gasoline and heating options, platinum, and palladium. Also known as the Commodity Exchange. Has an annual budget of approximately $10 million.

Publications:
Energy in the News. q.
Membership Directory. a.
Metals in the News. bi-a.

New York Stock Exchange *(1792)*
11 Wall St.
New York, NY   10005

Tel: (212)656-3000   *Fax:* (212)656-2294
Web Site: http://www.nyse.com
Members: 13,660 individuals
Staff: 1450
Annual Budget: $5-10,000,000
Chairman: Richard A. Grasso
Senior V. President, Communications: Robert T. Zito

Historical Note
The Exchange member organizations number 504 with a total of 11,662 sales offices in the U.S. and foreign countries. The NYSE is the premier marketplace for the securities of more than 2,500 major U.S. and foreign corporations and also provides a marketplace to trade options on the NYSE composite index, NYSE utility index, and more than 160 stock options.

Newsletter Publishers Ass'n (1964)
1501 Wilson Blvd., Suite 509
Arlington, VA   22209-2403
Tel: (703)527-2333   *Fax:* (703)841-0629
Members: 700 publishers
Staff: 5
Annual Budget: $500-1,000,000
Exec. Director: Patricia Wysocki

Historical Note
Founded as the Independent Newsletter Ass'n, it became the Newsletter Ass'n of America in 1977 and was incorporated in the District of Columbia. Merged with the Nat'l Ass'n of Investment Advisory Publishers in 1979. It became the Newsletter Ass'n in 1983 and assumed its present name in 1991. NPA represents nearly 700 publishers producing more than 2,000 newsletters and other information services. The membership fee is based on newsletter revenue.

Publications:
Directory of Members & Industry Suppliers. a.
Hotline. bi-w.

Meetings/Conferences:
Semi-Annual Meetings: Washington, DC/June and Fall
1999 – Washington, DC(Mayflower Hotel)/June 6-8

Newspaper Advertising Sales Ass'n (1907)
Historical Note
Address unknown in 1998.

Newspaper Ass'n Managers (1923)
c/o New England Newspaper Ass'n
70 Washington St.
Salem, MA   01970
Tel: (978)744-8940   *Fax:* (978)744-0333
Members: 70 individuals
Staff: 1
Annual Budget: $25-50,000
Exec. Director: Morley Piper

Historical Note
An association of managers of state, regional, national and international press associations.

Publications:
The Round-Table. bi-m.

Meetings/Conferences:
Annual Meetings: August, and Legislative Conference in December
1999 – Arlington, VA/Dec. 6-8

Newspaper Ass'n of America (1992)
1921 Gallows Road, Suite 600
Vienna, VA   22182
Tel: (703)902-1600   *Fax:* (703)917-0636
Web Site: http://www.naa.org
Members: 1,700 individuals, 1,496 newspapers
Staff: 180
Annual Budget: $25-50,000,000
President and C.E.O.: John F. Sturm
Senior V. President, Communications: Judith A. Burrell
Senior V. President, Technology: Eric Wolferman
Senior V. President/C.F.O.: Margaret Vassilikos
Senior V. President & Chief Marketing Officer: John Kimball
Senior V. President, Membership Services: Reggie R. Hall
Senior V. President for Diversity and the NAA Foundation: Toni F. Laws

Historical Note
Formed in 1992 by the American Newspaper Publishers Ass'n, Ass'n of Newspaper Classified Advertising Managers, Internat'l Circulation Managers Ass'n, Internat'l Newspaper Advertising and Marketing Executives, Newspaper Advertising Bureau, Newspaper Advertising Co-op Network and the Newspaper Research Council. Members include 1,700 newspapers in the United States and Canada and 63 international newspapers. Has an annual budget of approximately $30 million.

Publications:
Facts About Newspapers. a.
Presstime Journal. m.
Tech News. bi-m.
Update Newsletter. m.

Meetings/Conferences:
Annual Meetings: Spring
1999 – San Diego, CA(Hotel del Coronado)/April 25-28
2000 – New York, NY(Hilton Waldorf)/May 7-10
2001 – Toronto, ON, Canada

Newspaper Features Council (1955)
22 Byfield Lane
Greenwich, CT   06830-3446
Tel: (203)661-3386   *Fax:* (203)661-7337
Members: 130 newspapers and writers
Staff: 1
Annual Budget: $25-50,000
Exec. Director: Corinta N.C. Kotula

Historical Note
Formerly (1984) Newspaper Comics Council. NFC is a forum for newspapers, editors, writers, columnists, cartoonists and syndicates

to exchange views and improve the content of newspapers for the betterment of the general public and the industry. Membership: $75-1,250/year.

Publications:
NFC. a.

Meetings/Conferences:
Annual Meetings: Fall
1999 – Vancouver, BC, Canada
2000 – New York, NY

Newspaper Food Editors and Writers Ass'n (1974)
Historical Note
Became Ass'n of Food Journalists in 1994.

Newspaper Guild (1933)
501 Third St., N.W., 2nd Floor
Washington, DC   20001-2760
Tel: (202)434-7177   *Fax:* (202)434-1472
Web Site: www.newsguild.org
Members: 34,000 individuals
Staff: 32
Annual Budget: $2-5,000,000
President: Linda Foley
Editor, Guild Reporter: Andrew Zipser

Historical Note
A labor union representing editorial and commercial department employees of newspapers, wire and news services, magazines and related enterprises in the U.S., Canada and Puerto Rico. Established as the American Newspaper Guild in Washington, DC, December 15, 1933. Assumed its present name in 1971. Affiliated with AFL-CIO, the Canadian Labour Congress, and the Internat'l Federation of Journalists. Membership: 6% of 1 weeks pay/month.

Publications:
Guild Reporter. m.

Meetings/Conferences:
Annual Meetings: June-July/350
1999 – Ottawa, ON, Canada/April 29-May 2

Newspaper Purchasing Management Ass'n (1957)
Historical Note
Address unknown in 1997.

Newspaper Systems Group (1967)
Atlanta Journal Constitution
72 Marietta St. NW
Atlanta, GA   30303
Tel: (404)526-5101   *Fax:* (404)526-5167
Web Site: http://www.accessatlanta.com
Members: 40 individuals
Director: Edward F. Baer

Historical Note
Members are concerned with computer systems applications in newspapers and related organizations.

NGV Producers Ass'n
901 N. Pitt St., Suite 220
Alexandria, VA   22314-1536
Tel: (703)838-2933   *Fax:* (703)838-2936
Managing Director: Wayne J. Smith

Nigerian-American Chamber of Commerce
Historical Note
Organization inactive in 1997.

NIMA Internat'l
Historical Note
Became (1998) Electronic Retailing Ass'n.

Nine to Five, Nat'l Ass'n of Working Women (1973)
231 W. Wisconsin Ave., Suite 900
Milwaukee, WI   53203-2306
Tel: (414)274-0925   *Fax:* (414)272-2870
Toll Free: (800)522 - 0925
Members: 15,000 individuals
Staff: 25
Annual Budget: $1-2,000,000
Co-Director: Ellen Bravo
Co-Director: Gloria Santa Anna
Development Director: Jen Benka

Historical Note
Established in Boston. 9 to 5 is a research and advocacy group concerned with working women's issues. Membership: $25/year (individuals); $40/year (institutions).

Publications:
Newsline. 5/year. adv.

Meetings/Conferences:

Nitrogen Fixing Tree Ass'n
Historical Note
Became Forest Farm and Community Tree Network in 1996.

Noah Worcester Dermatological Soc. (1958)
1299 Trapp Lane
Winnetka, IL   60093
Tel: (847)446-0314   *Fax:* (847)446-0315
Members: 180 individuals
Annual Budget: $100-250,000
Secretary/Treasurer: Dr. Alan Lasser

Historical Note
Named for Noah Worcester, author of the first American text on dermatology, published in 1845. Officers remain for five-year terms.

Meetings/Conferences:
1999 – St. Petersburg, FL(Vinoy)

Noise Control Ass'n (1976)

Historical Note
Organization inactive in 1998.

Noise Control Products and Materials Ass'n (1976)

Non Commissioned Officers Ass'n of the U.S.A. (1960)
Box 33610
San Antonio, TX   78265
Tel: (210)653-6161   *Fax:* (210)637-3337
Web Site: http://www.ncoausa.org
Members: 160,000 individuals
Staff: 47
Annual Budget: $2-5,000,000
President and C.E.O.: Roger Putnam
V.P., Operations: Dave Sommers
Director, Chapter/Community Activities: Robert W. Guthrie
Exec. V. President: Wayne M. Smith

Historical Note
Individuals who serve or have served in U.S. Military forces in grades E1 through E9. Membership: $25/year (full member), $20 (auxiliary), $15/year (apprentice).

Publications:
NCOA Inside Update. m.
NCOA Journal. m. adv.
NCOA Newsbrief. bi-w.

Meetings/Conferences:
Annual Meetings: Annual/Summer
1999 – Las Vegas, NV(Bally's)/July 8-11
2000 – Atlanta, GA(Atlanta Marriott)/July 6-9

Non Destructive Testing Management Ass'n
Historical Note
A professional/technical organization formed to assist companies engaged in non-destructive testing manage their business. Membership: $175/year (company).

Non-Ferrous Founders' Soc. (1943)
455 State St., Suite 100
Des Plaines, IL   60016
Tel: (847)299-0950   *Fax:* (847)299-3598
E-Mail: staff@nffs.org
Web Site: http://www.nffs.org
Members: 215 companies
Staff: 4
Annual Budget: $500-1,000,000
Exec. Director: James L. Mallory, CAE
Manager, Member Services: Ryan J. Moore

Historical Note
Members are manufacturers of bronze, brass and aluminum castings. Absorbed the Cast Bronze Institute in 1988. Introduced NQS 9000 Quality System for Metalcasting in 1996. Membership: $700-3,200/yr. (company).

Publications:
Crucible. bi-m. adv.
NFFS Notes. m.
NFFScene. bi-m.

Meetings/Conferences:
Annual Meetings: Fall
1999 – Washington, DC(ANA Hotel)/Oct. 3-6/150
2000 – Oak Brook, IL(Oak Brook Hills Resort)/Sept. 24-27/150

Non-Ferrous Metals Producers Committee (1957)
c/o Economic Consulting Services
2030 M St., N.W., Suite 800
Washington, DC   20036
Tel: (202)466-7720   *Fax:* (202)466-2710
Staff: 35
Exec. Secretary: Kenneth Button

Historical Note
Formerly (1987) Lead-Zinc Producers Committee. Founded as the Emergency Lead-Zinc Committee. Major interests are tariffs, investment, and international trade.

Non-Heatset Web Section
100 Daingerfield Road
Alexandria, VA   22314-2888
Tel: (703)519-8156   *Fax:* (703)519-7109
E-Mail: tbasore@printing.org
Web Site: www.printing.org
Members: 650 individuals
Staff: 4
Annual Budget: $100-250,000
Exec. Director: Thomas B. Basore
Director of Programs & Publications: Betti Parrott

Historical Note
A special industry group of Printing Industries of America.

Publications:
Future of NWS Printers.
Market Outlook.
Non-Heatseat Web Offset Directory. bien.
Web Offset Product Catalogue. bien.

Meetings/Conferences:

Non-Powder Gun Products Ass'n (1975)
200 Castlewood Drive
North Palm Beach, FL   33408
Tel: (561)842-4100   *Fax:* (561)863-8984
E-Mail: slsgma@aol.com
Members: 9 companies
Staff: 2
Exec. Director: Sharon Lincoln

Historical Note
Members are manufacturers and distributors of air guns and ammunition. Affiliated with the Sporting Goods Manufacturers Association which provides administrative support.

Meetings/Conferences:
Annual Meetings: January with The "SHOT" Show (Shooting, Hunting, Outdoors show).

Non-Profit Ass'n of North America *(1992)*
Historical Note
Address unknown in 1995.

Nonprescription Drug Manufacturers Ass'n *(1881)*
1150 Connecticut Ave., N.W., Suite 1200
Washington, DC   20036-4104
Tel: (202)429-9260   *Fax:* (202)223-6835
Members: 75 active, 150 associate
Staff: 39
Annual Budget: $5-10,000,000
President: James D. Cope
Sr. V.P./Dir., Public Affairs: Joseph K. Doss
V.P./Dir., Fed. Government Rels.: J. Robert Brouse
Director, Government Affairs: Kevin Kraushaar
Dir., Meetings: Kass Kassouf
V. President, Finance/Treas.: Thomas E. Hixon
Sr. V.P./General Counsel: Eve Bachrach
Dir., Member Services: Phyllis M. Taylor

Historical Note
Organized in New York City on November 26, 1881 as the Proprietary Medicine Manufacturers and Dealers Ass'n; assumed its present name in 1989. Members are producers of medicines for self-care sold over the counter without a prescription. Has an annual budget of approximately $6.7 million. Membership fee based on sales volume.

Publications:
Executive Newsletter. semi-m.
Legislative News Bulletins. irreg.
Membership Directory. a.

Meetings/Conferences:
Annual Meetings: Spring/700
1999 – Boca Raton, FL(Resort and Club)/March 11-14/700

Nonprofit Management Ass'n
Historical Note
Became (1998) Alliance for Nonprofit Management.

North American Advertising Agency Network *(1932)*
Historical Note
Address unknown in 1997.

North American Agricultural Marketing Officials *(1920)*
Utah Dept. of Agric., 350 N. Redwood Rd.
P.O. Box 146500
Salt Lake City, UT   84114-6500
Tel: (801)538-7108   *Fax:* (801)538-9436
E-Mail: agmainagmoker@email.state.ut.us
Web Site: www.ag.ftate.ut.us
Members: 45 individuals
Annual Budget: $10-25,000
Secretary-Treasurer: Randy Parker

Historical Note
Formerly (1977) Nat'l Ass'n of Marketing Officials and (1992) Nat'l Agricultural Marketing Officials. Has no paid staff or permanent address. Officers change annually. Members are state and provincial officials responsible for agricultural products marketing programs in the United States, Canada and ultimately Mexico. Membership: $150/year (individual); $30/year (associate).

Publications:
Directory and Report. a.
Newsletter. irreg.

Meetings/Conferences:
Annual Meetings: mid-July
1999 – Wisconsin

North American Ass'n for Environmental Education *(1971)*
1255 23rd St., N.W., Suite 400
Washington, DC   20037
Tel: (202)884-8912   *Fax:* (202)884-8701
Members: 2,500 individuals
Staff: 12
Annual Budget: $500-1,000,000
Exec. Director: Edward J. McCrea
Director of Communications: Andrea Shotkin

Historical Note
Formerly (1985) the Nat'l Ass'n for Environmental Education. Merged with the Conservation Education Ass'n in 1990. Purpose is to assist and support the work of individuals and groups engaged in environmental education, research and service. NAAEE is organized into four interactive sections: Elementary and Secondary Education Section; Environmental Studies Section; the Non-Formal Section; and the Conservation Education Section. Membership: $45/year (individual), $200/year (institution).

Publications:
Conference Proceedings. a.
Environmental Communicator. bi-m.
Monographs. 1-3/year.

Meetings/Conferences:
Annual Meetings: Fall
1999 – Cincinnati, OH

North American Ass'n of Christians in Social Work *(1954)*
P.O. Box 121
Botsford, CT   06404-0121
Tel: (203)270-8780   *Fax:* (203)270-8780
Toll Free: (888)426 - 4712
E-Mail: NACSW@aol.com
Web Site: http://www.nacsw.org
Members: 1,200 individuals
Staff: 1
Annual Budget: $100-250,000
Exec. Director: Rick Chamiec-Case

Historical Note
NACSW assists its members in integrating their Christian faith with their social work practice and in representing a Christian presence in the social work profession and a social work presence in the Christian church. Membership: $65/year (individual); $20/year (student).

Publications:
Catalyst. bi-m. adv.
Practice Monograph Series. irreg.
Social Work and Christianity. semi-a. adv.

Meetings/Conferences:
Annual Meetings: Fall
1999 – St. Louis, MO
2000 – Columbus, OH

North American Ass'n of Educational Negotiators *(1970)*
122 White Pine Drive
Springfield, IL   62707
Tel: (217)529-7902   *Fax:* (217)529-7904
E-Mail: naen@aol.com
Web Site: http://www.naen.org
Members: 500 individuals
Staff: 1
Annual Budget: $50-100,000
Exec. Secretary: Lyn D. King

Historical Note
NAAEN members are individuals who negotiate on the behalf of college and school administrations, and school boards. Established as the Ass'n of Educational Negotiators, it became the Nat'l Ass'n of Educational Negotiators and assumed its present name in 1991. Membership: $55/year (individual), $125/year (institution).

Publications:
The NAEN Bulletin. 8/yr. adv.

Meetings/Conferences:
1999 – San Antonio, TX(Menger Hotel)/March 14-17

North American Ass'n of Food Equipment Manufacturers *(1948)*
401 N. Michigan Ave.
Chicago, IL   60611-4267
Tel: (312)644-6610   *Fax:* (312)527-6658
E-Mail: nafem_hq@sba.com
Web Site: http://www.nafem.org
Members: 700 manufacturers
Staff: 15
Annual Budget: $2-5,000,000
Exec. V. President: Maxine Lee Couture

Historical Note
Formerly (1994) Nat'l Ass'n of Food Equipment Manufacturers. Membership: dues vary, based on company sales volume.

Publications:
NAFEM News. bi-m.

Meetings/Conferences:
Annual Meetings: and biennial Trade Show
1999 – Dallas, TX(Convention Center)/Oct. 1-3/20000

North American Ass'n of Inventory Services *(1982)*
Historical Note
Address unknown in 1994.

North American Ass'n of Jewish Homes and Housing for the Aging *(1960)*
Historical Note
Became the Ass'n of Jewish Aging Services in 1997.

North American Ass'n of Mirror Manufacturers *(1958)*
2945 S.W. Wanamaker Dr., Suite A
Topeka, KS   66614-5321
Tel: (785)271-0208   *Fax:* (785)271-0166
E-Mail: naamm@glasswebsite.com
Web Site: http://www.glasswebsite.com/naamm
Members: 14 companies
Exec. Director: William J. Birch

Historical Note
Founded as Nat'l Ass'n of Mirror Manufacturers; assumed its current name in 1997.

Publications:
Membership Directory. a.

Meetings/Conferences:
Semi-annual Meetings: Spring and Fall

North American Ass'n of Professors of Christian Education *(1947)*
4050 Lee Vance View
Colorado Springs, CO   80918
Tel: (502)897-4813   *Fax:* (502)897-4004
E-Mail: celead@sbts.edu
Web Site: http://www.sbts.edu/celead/napce/napce.html
Members: 200 individuals
Annual Budget: $10-25,000
Exec. Administrator: Dennis E. Williams, Ph.D.

Historical Note
Formerly (1992) Nat'l Ass'n of Professors of Christian Education. NAPCE is a professional society for teachers of Christian education in post-secondary institutions. The above address handles all written communication for NAPCE; the administrator's office can be contacted directly at (502) 897-4813. Membership: $40/year.

Publications:
Christian Education Journal. semi-a.
NAPCE Newsletter. 3/year.

Meetings/Conferences:
Annual Meetings: third weekend in October
1999 – San Diego, CA(Hanalei Hotel)/Oct. 28-31
2000 – Midwest/Oct. 26-29

North American Ass'n of State and Provincial Lotteries *(1971)*
1700 E. 13th St., Suite 4PE
Cleveland, OH   44114
Tel: (216)241-2310   *Fax:* (216)241-4350
E-Mail: nasplhq@aol.com
Members: 46 organizations
Staff: 3
Annual Budget: $500-1,000,000
Exec. Director: David B. Gale
Director of Administration: Thomas C. Tulloch
Administrative Assistant: Bebe C. Crone

Historical Note
NASPL evolved from an informal exchange of information among three pioneering lottery directors and has now grown into an active ass'n of state and provincial lotteries representing 46 lottery organizations throughout North America. The Ass'n works to assemble and disseminate information and benefits of state and provincial lottery organizations through education and communications and where appropriate publicly advocate the positions of the Ass'n on matters of general policy. Membership: $5,000/year.

Publications:
Annual Report. a.

Meetings/Conferences:
Semi-annual Meetings: Spring and Fall
1999 – Halifax, NS, Canada(Convention
          Center)/Sept. 20-25/1000
2000 – Dallas, TX(Convention Center)/Sept. 26-Oct. 1/1000
2001 – Albuquerque, NM

North American Ass'n of Summer Sessions *(1964)*
43 Belanger Drive
Dover, NH   03820-4602
Tel: (603)740-9880   *Fax:* (603)742-7085
E-Mail: naass@aol.com
Members: 450 schools
Staff: 1
Annual Budget: $50-100,000
Exec. Secretary: Michael U. Nelson

Historical Note
Established as the National Association of College and University Summer Sessions, it became the National Association of Summer Sessions in 1968, and assumed its present name in 1975. Membership: $35/year (individual), $100/year (institution).

Publications:
Joint Statistical Report.
Membership Directory.
Newsletter. q.
Proceedings.
Summer Academe.

Meetings/Conferences:
Annual Meetings: Fall

North American Ass'n of Synagogue Executives *(1948)*
Historical Note
Address unknown in 1996.

North American Ass'n of Wardens and Superintendents *(1970)*
c/o US Medical Ctr. for Federal Prisons
P.O. Box 4000
Springfield, MO   65801-4000
Tel: (417)865-8455   *Fax:* (417)837-1717
Members: 350 individuals
Annual Budget: under $10,000
Presdient: Patrick Keohane

Historical Note
Formerly (1971) Wardens' Ass'n of America and (1980) American Ass'n of Wardens and Superintendents. Has no paid officers or full-time staff. An affiliate of the American Correctional Ass'n. Membership: $25/year.

Publications:
The Grapevine. q.

Meetings/Conferences:
Semi-Annual Meetings: January, and August, with ACA
1999 – Lake Ozark, MO(Lodge of the Four
          Seasons)/May 23-26

North American Benthological Soc. *(1953)*
Department of Biological Sciences
University of Windsor
Windsor, ON   N9B 3-P4
Tel: (519)253-4232   *Fax:* (519)971-3609
Web Site: http://www.benthos.org
Members: 1,500 individuals
Secretary: Lynda Corkum

Historical Note
Founded as Midwest Benthological Soc., NABS now serves an international membership. Members are scientists concerned with freshwater-habitat ecology. Has no paid officers or full-time staff. Membership: $25/year (individual), $10/year (student). (Subscription to Journal of NABS not included in dues.)

Publications:
Bibliography. a.
Bulletin of NABS. 3/yr.
Journal of NABS. q.

Meetings/Conferences:
1999 – Duluth, MN/May 25-28

North American Blueberry Council *(1965)*
4995 Golden Foothill Pkwy., Suite 2
El Dorado Hills, CA   95762
Tel: (916)933-9399   *Fax:* (916)933-9777
E-Mail: nvnabc@compuserve.com
Web Site: http://www.blueberry.org
Members: 45 growers/organizations
Staff: 2

Annual Budget: $250-500,000
Exec. Director: Mark Villata
Historical Note
Blueberry growers and marketers from the U.S. and Canada.
Membership fee varies, based on annual production (full member);
$700/year (associate).
Publications:
Calyx. bi-m.
Proceedings. a.
Meetings/Conferences:
Annual Meetings: Winter
1999 – Las Vegas, NV/Feb. 1-4
2000 – Nashville, TN/Jan. 30-Feb. 2

North American Building Material Distribution Ass'n
(1952)
401 N. Michigan Ave.
Chicago, IL 60611-4274
Tel: (312)321-6845   Fax: (312)644-0310
Toll Free: (888)747 - 7862
E-Mail: nbmda@sba.com
Web Site: http://www.nbmda.org
Members: 500 companies
Staff: 7
Annual Budget: $1-2,000,000
Exec. V. President: Kevin Gammonley
Communications Manager: Lori Seaberg
Opertions Manager: Judi Nosal
Marketing Director: Daniel Grant
Historical Note
Absorbed (1964) Nat'l Plywood Distributors Ass'n. Formerly
(1994) Nat'l Building Material Distributors Ass'n. Merged (1994)
with the Canadian Nat'l Building Materials Distributors Ass'n.
NBMDA is one of the largest ass'n of building products distributors
and manufacturers in North America representing over 1,200
locations with distributor sales in excess of $10 billion.
Membership: dues vary, based on annual sales.
Publications:
Journal. m. adv.
Membership Directory. a. adv.
Sales Trainer. m.
Meetings/Conferences:
1999 – Reno, NV(Reno Hilton)/Nov. 4-6/700
2000 – Dallas, TX(Hyatt Regency)/Nov. 2-4/700

North American Canon Law Soc. *(1986)*
2123 W. Fifth St., Suite 2
Duluth, MN 55806-1812
Tel: (218)733-9676   Fax: (218)733-0349
Members: 30 individuals
Annual Budget: under $10,000
Canonical Auditor and Registrar: Aron J. Kjera, AA, CLA
Historical Note
Established in Indiana as a professional organization dedicated to
canon and church lawyers trained in the canon laws accepted by
the Orthodox Catholic Church. Membership: $175/year.
Publications:
Legal Notes. q.
Orthodox Christian Herald. bi-m. adv.
Meetings/Conferences:
Biennial Meetings: Fall

North American Cartographic Information Soc. *(1980)*
American Geographic Soc. Collection
P.O. Box 399
Milwaukee, WI 53201
Tel: (414)229-6282   Fax: (414)229-3624
Toll Free: (800)558 - 8993
Members: 450 individuals
Annual Budget: under $10,000
Exec. Director: Chris Baruth
Historical Note
Incorporated in Wisconsin. Members are cartographers and others
interested in the creation and use of accurate maps. Membership:
$42/year (individual); $20/year (student); $72/year
(organization).
Publications:
Cartographic Perspectives. 3/year.
Meetings/Conferences:
Annual Meetings: October/100
1999 – Williamsburg, VA(Ft. Magruder Inn)/Oct. 20-24/150
2000 – Knoxville, TN(Hilton)/Oct. 11-15/150

North American Case Research Ass'n *(1958)*
1117 N. 13th St.
Columbus, GA 31901
Tel: (706)324-5515
E-Mail: RCarter211@aol.com
Members: 350 individuals
Staff: 1
Secretary-Treasurer: Robert N. Carter, Ph.D.
Historical Note
Founded as Souther Case Writers; became Southern Case Research
Ass'n in 1971, and assumed its current name in 1981. Sponsors
and supports case research in a number of areas in business,
management, and academia. Membership: $50/year.
Publications:
Case Research Journal. q. adv.
Newsletter. 2-3/year.
Meetings/Conferences:
Annual Meetings: Fall
1999 – San Francisco, CA area

North American Catalysis Soc. *(1955)*
DuPont Experimental Station
P.O. Box 80262
Wilmington, DE 19880-0262
Tel: (302)695-2488   Fax: (302)695-8347

E-Mail: michael.b.damore@usa.dupont.com
Web Site: www.dupont.com/nacs
Members: 2,000 individuals
Annual Budget: $10-25,000
Editor: Michael D'Amore, Ph.D.
Historical Note
Formerly (1995) The Catalysis Soc. (North America). Fosters an
interest in heterogeneous and homogeneous catalysis in the U.S.,
Mexico, and Canada. Organizes national meetings for the purpose
of discussing the latest developments in the field. Members are
chemists and chemical engineers engaged in the study and use of
reactions involving catalysts, substances used to accelerate
reactions and which may be recovered virtually unchanged.
Membership: $5/year and a prerequisite of local affiliate
membership.
Publications:
Catalysis Soc. Newsletter.
Meetings/Conferences:
Biennial Meetings: Spring
1999 – Boston, MA

North American Clinical Dermatological Soc. *(1959)*
4500 San Pablo Road
Jacksonville, FL 32224
Tel: (904)953-2219   Fax: (904)953-2510
Members: 185 individuals
Annual Budget: $100-250,000
Secretary-General: John W. White, Jr.
Publications:
Cutis. a.
Program. a.
Meetings/Conferences:
Annual Meetings: Spring, for members only
1999 – Canada
2000 – Scandanavia

North American Clun Forest Ass'n *(1973)*
Historical Note
Address unknown in 1997.

North American Computer Service Ass'n *(1982)*
One S. Orange Ave., Fifth Floor
Orlando, FL 32801-2627
Tel: (407)206-1111   Fax: (407)206-1114
Toll Free: (888)666 - 1160
Members: 1000 individuals
Staff: 10
Annual Budget: $250-500,000
Director: David G. Glascock
Historical Note
Membership is composed of computer service and repair companies,
suppliers, consultants, schools and professional educators.
Membership: $50-250/year (individual); $1,000-4,000/year
(company).
Publications:
Read Out. m. adv.
Meetings/Conferences:
Annual Meetings: 1st weekend in November
1999 – Orlando, FL

North American Concert Promoters Ass'n *(1988)*
P.O. Box 753
McLean, VA 22101-0753
Tel: (703)538-3575   Fax: (703)538-3876
Members: 21 companies
Staff: 2
Exec. Director: Cynthia Wallace
Historical Note
Members must promote a minimum of 40 concerts per year.
Publications:
Business Briefs. m. adv.
Meetings/Conferences:
Quarterly Meetings: various locations

North American Conference on British Studies *(1950)*
Dept. of Liberal Studies
California State Polytechnic Univ.
Pomona, CA 91768
Tel: (909)869-3567   Fax: (909)869-4311
Members: 1,100 individuals
Assoc. Exec. Secretary: Joseph Block
Historical Note
NACBS welcomes scholars from all fields dealing with the history
and culture of the British Isles. Membership: $25-50/year
(regular), $12-29.50/year (student), $25-52.50/year (foreign),
$12-32/year (foreign/student), $75/year (sustaining), $400/year
(life member).
Publications:
Albion. q. adv.
British Studies Intelligencer Newsletter. semi-a.
Current Research in British History in the US & Canada.
        quadrennial.
Journal of British Studies. q. adv.
Meetings/Conferences:
Annual Meetings: October-November

North American Corriente Ass'n *(1982)*
P.O. Box 12359
Kansas City, MO 64116
Tel: (816)421-1992   Fax: (816)421-1991
E-Mail: JSpawn321@aol.com
Members: 625 individuals
Staff: 2
Annual Budget: $100-250,000
Exec. Officer: James A. Spawn
Historical Note
The NACA promotes the use of Corriente cattle and has instituted
and proceeds to monitor a registered breeding program to preserve

the true breed and make it available for the fast growing rodeo
circuit. Membership: $350/life; $35/year (active member);
$15/year (associate).
Publications:
The Corresponder. q. adv.
Meetings/Conferences:
Annual Meetings: Spring

North American Council of Automotive Teachers
(1974)
11956 Bernardo Plaza Drive, Dept. 436
San Diego, CA 92128-9713
Tel: (619)487-8126   Fax: (619)487-3617
E-Mail: nacat@cts.com
Members: 750 individuals, 50 companies
Staff: 1
Annual Budget: under $10,000
Exec. Manager: Al Goodyear
Historical Note
Formerly (1991) Nat'l Ass'n of College Automotive Teachers.
NACAT is an organization of automotive teachers and supporting
companies in the automotive industry. The purpose of the
organization is to advance all levels of automotive education.
Operates the NACAT Foundation to provide funding for scholarships
and other worthy causes. Membership: $40/year.
Publications:
NACAT News. 3/year. adv.
Meetings/Conferences:
Annual Meetings: Third week in July.
1999 – Charleston, SC(Trident College)
2000 – Big Rapids, MI(Ferris College)
2001 – Winnipeg, SK, Canada(Red River College)

North American Dairy Sheep Ass'n *(1987)*
23896 740th Ave.
Renville, MN 56284-2058
Tel: (507)256-4788
E-Mail: mnrog@aol.com
Members: 100 individuals
Annual Budget: under $10,000
President: Roger Steinkamp
Historical Note
Membership: $15/year (individual); $20/year (family).
Publications:
Dairy Shepherd Newsletter. bi-a. adv.

North American Deer Farmers Ass'n *(1983)*
9301 Annapolis Road, Suite 206
Lanham, MD 20706-3115
Tel: (301)459-7708   Fax: (301)159 7861
E-Mail: info@nadefa.org
Members: 600 individuals
Staff: 2
Annual Budget: $100-250,000
Exec. Director: Barbara Ramey Fox
Historical Note
NADeFA members are commercial deer farmers, producing venison
for public consumption. Membership: $75-$195/year (individual);
$195/year (organization).
Publications:
Newsletter. q. adv.
North American Deer Farmer Journal. q. adv.
Meetings/Conferences:
Annual Meetings: Spring
1999 – San Antonio(Hilton)

North American Die Casting Ass'n *(1989)*
9701 W. Higgins Road, Suite 880
Rosemont, IL 60018-4921
Tel: (847)292-3600   Fax: (847)292-3620
E-Mail: nadca@diecasting.org
Web Site: http://www.diecasting.org
Members: 3,700 individuals
Staff: 19
Annual Budget: $2-5,000,000
Exec. V. President: Daniel Twarog
Dir., Research/Education/Technology: Steven P. Udvardy
Historical Note
The mission of the North American Die Casting Associaton is to be
the world wide leader of and resource for stimulating continuous
improvement in the die casting industry. Membership: $85/year,
renewal (individual); $1,975/year, minimum (corporate).
Publications:
Die Casting Engineer. bi-m. adv.
Meetings/Conferences:
Biennial Meetings: Odd years in Fall
1999 – Cleveland, OH/Nov. 1-4
2001 – Cincinnati, OH/Oct. 29-Nov. 1

North American Electric Reliability Council *(1968)*
116-390 Village Blvd.
Princeton, NJ 08540-5731
Tel: (609)452-8060   Fax: (609)452-9550
E-Mail: info@nerc.com
Web Site: http://www.nerc.com
Members: 10 regional councils, 1 affiliate
Staff: 20
Annual Budget: $1-2,000,000
President: Michehl R. Gent
Director, Communications: Eugene F. Gorzelnik
Historical Note
Founded in 1968 as the Nat'l Electric Reliability Council, it
assumed its current name in 1981. NERC is the principal
organization for coordinating, promoting, and communicating
about North America's electrical supplies, demands and reliability
issues.
Publications:
Annual Report. a.

Generating Availability Report. a.
Reliability Assessment. a.
Summer Assessment. a.
System Disturbances. a.
Winter Assesment. a.
Meetings/Conferences:
1999 – Texas

North American Elk Breeders Ass'n
1708 N. Prairie View Rd.
Platte City, MO   64079-1640
Tel: (816)431-3605   *Fax:* (816)431-2705
Web Site: http://www.naelk.org
Exec. Director: Ben Copland
Director, Operations: Angie Cox
Publications:
NAEBA Newsletter. bi-m. adv.
North American Elk Journal. q. adv.
Meetings/Conferences:
1999 – Orlando, FL/Feb. 3-6

North American Equipment Dealers Ass'n *(1900)*
10877 Watson Rd.
St. Louis, MO   63127-1081
Tel: (314)821-7220   *Fax:* (314)821-0674
Web Site: http://www.naeda.com
Members: 6,200 retail dealers
Staff: 27
Annual Budget: $250-500,000
Exec. V. President and C.E.O.: David G. Ottaway, CAE, CMP
Director, Communications: Mike Kraemer
Director, Education: Ronald Walberg

Historical Note
Founded as the Nat'l Retail Farm Equipment Ass'n, it became the Nat'l Farm and Power Equipment Dealers Ass'n in 1962 and assumed its present name in 1988. Members are retail dealers of agricultural, industrial and outdoor power equipment in the U.S. and Canada.
Publications:
Cost of Doing Business Study. a.
Equipment Dealer. m. adv.
Official Guide - Tractors and Farm Equipment. q.
Official Industrial Equipment Guide. semi-a.
Outdoor Power Equipment Official Guide. a.
Meetings/Conferences:
Annual Meetings: August
1999 – San Antonio, TX/Jan. 7-10/350
2000 – Maui, HI

North American Export Grain Ass'n *(1920)*
1300 L St., N.W., Suite 900
Washington, DC   20005
Tel: (202)682-4030   *Fax:* (202)682-4033
E-Mail: naega@cwixmail.com
Members: 41 companies
Staff: 4
Annual Budget: $500-1,000,000
President: Daniel G. Amstutz
Director, International Program: W. Kirk Miller

Historical Note
Incorporated in 1920, NAEGA represents North American grain and oilseed exporters.
Publications:
Bulletins. irreg.
Meetings/Conferences:
1999 – Rancho Mirage, CA(Westin Mission Hills Resort)/Feb. 11-13/100

North American Farm Show Council *(1972)*
590 Woody Hayes Drive
Columbus, OH   43210-6131
Tel: (614)292-4278   *Fax:* (614)292-9448
Web Site: http://www.ag.ohio-state.edu/farmshow
Members: 25 member shows, 12 associates
Staff: 1
Annual Budget: $25-50,000
Exec. Coordinator: Craig Fendrick

Historical Note
Established in Chicago and incorporated in Ohio, NAFSC members are agricultural trade shows. Suppliers of services to shows can obtain an associate membership. Membership: $700/year (regular); $100/year (associate).
Meetings/Conferences:
Annual Meetings: May
1999 – Niagara Fall, Canada

North American Flowerbulb Wholesalers Ass'n *(1984)*
208 W. Main St.
Ninety-Six, SC   29666
Tel: (864)543-2128   *Fax:* (864)543-4480
Members: 50 companies
Staff: 1
Annual Budget: $10-25,000
Secretary-Treasurer: Jack DeVroomen

Historical Note
Absorbed the Horticultural Dealers Ass'n in 1984.
Publications:
NAFWA News. q.
Meetings/Conferences:
1999 – Memphis, TN(Marriot)/Feb. 5-6
2000 – Ithaca, NY(Cornell University)/April 7-8

North American Folk Music and Dance Alliance *(1989)*
1001 Connecticut Ave., N.W., Suite 501
Washington, DC   20036-5504
Tel: (202)835-3655   *Fax:* (202)835-3656
E-Mail: fa@folk.org
Web Site: http://www.folk.org

Members: 1,750 individuals, 250 organizations
Staff: 3
Annual Budget: $500-1,000,000
Exec. Director: Phyllis Barney
Admin. Director: Margaret Loomis

Historical Note
The Folk Alliance fosters and promotes multi-cultural, traditional and contemporary folk music, dance and related performing arts in the United States and Canada. Membership: $40/year (individual), $100-400/year (organization/ company).
Publications:
Annual Report. a.
Membership Directory. a. adv.
Newsletter. bi-m. adv.
Meetings/Conferences:
Annual Meetings: February/1,500
1999 – Albuquerque, NM(Convention Center)/Feb. 25-28
2000 – Cleveland, OH(Convention Center)/Feb. 8-13
2001 – Vancouver, BC/Feb. 15-18
2002 – Pittsburgh, PA/Feb. 21-24

North American Free Trade Ass'n *(1991)*
1130 Connecticut Ave., N.W., Suite 500
Washington, DC   20036
Tel: (202)296-3019   *Fax:* (202)296-3037
Members: 80 organizations and individuals
Staff: 5
Annual Budget: $500-1,000,000
President: G.J. Van Heuven
V. President, Public Affairs: Brian Marshall

Historical Note
NAFTA informs and assists members seeking opportunities arising from trade liberalization in North America. Membership: $300/year (individual); $750/year (firms with revenues under $20 million); $1,500/year (firms with revenues over $20 million); $3,000/year (founding member).
Publications:
Issue Report. bi-m.
Special Report. irreg.
Trade & Investment Report. bi-m.

North American Fuzzy Information Processing Soc. *(1981)*
Kennesaw State University
1000 Chastain Road
Marietta, GA   30144-5591
Tel: (770)423-6042   *Fax:* (770)423-6539
E-Mail: nhall@ksumail.kennesaw.edu
Web Site: http://khorshid.ut.ac.ir/ISG/nafips.html
Members: 120 individuals
Annual Budget: under $10,000
Treasurer: Nancy Hall

Historical Note
Affiliated with the Internat'l Fuzzy Systems Ass'n, NAFIPS was established to promote and disseminate studies related to theories of fuzzy sets and related topics and to the study of their application in such fields as artificial intelligence, medicine, image processing, speech, linguistics, control theory, operations research, economics, and decision theory. Membership: $19/year (individual).
Publications:
Internat'l Journal of Approximate Reasoning. bi-m. adv.
Meetings/Conferences:
1999 – /June 10-12

North American Gamebird Ass'n *(1931)*
1214 Brooks Ave.
Raleigh, NC   27607
Tel: (919)782-6758
E-Mail: gamebird@naga.org
Web Site: http://www.naga.org
Members: 1,900 individuals
Staff: 2
Annual Budget: $25-50,000
Exec. Director: Dr. Gary S. Davis

Historical Note
Formerly (1981) North American Game Breeders and Shooting Preserve Operators Ass'n. Membership: $45/year (U.S.), $55/year (Canada & Mexico), $60/year (foreign).
Publications:
Membership Directory.
NAGA Hunting Preserve Directory.
Wildlife Harvest. q. adv.
Meetings/Conferences:
Annual Meetings: Winter

North American Gaming Regulators Ass'n *(1984)*
P.O. Box 21886
Lincoln, NE   68542-1886
Tel: (402)474-4261   *Fax:* (402)474-2426
Members: 105 agencies
Annual Budget: $100-250,000
Administrator: Susan Ugai

Historical Note
Members are government entities involved in local, state, federal, and provincial regulation of gambling activities. Membership: $350-525/year (organization).
Publications:
NAGRA News. q.
Meetings/Conferences:
Semi-Annual Meetings: Spring and Fall
1999 – Albuquerque, NM

North American Graphic Arts Suppliers Ass'n *(1993)*
1604 New Hampshire Ave., N.W.
Washington, DC   20009-2512
Tel: (202)328-8441   *Fax:* (202)328-8513
E-Mail: nagasa@smart.net
Web Site: http://www.nagasa.org

Members: 400 individuals, 400 companies
Staff: 3
Annual Budget: $500-1,000,000
President and C.E.O.: David J. Steinhardt
Membership Director: Vickie Braxton Schulz

Historical Note
This organization was formed in 1993 following the merger of the Graphic Arts Suppliers Ass'n with the Nat'l Graphic Arts Distributors Ass'n. Membership: dues vary by sales volume.
Publications:
Compass. q. adv.
Eagle. q.
Meetings/Conferences:
1999 – Phoenix, AZ(Pointe Hilton at Squaw Peak)/April 25-27/300
2000 – San Antonio, TX(Hilton Palacio Del Rio)/Apr. 8-12/400

North American Hernia Soc.
Historical Note
Defunct in 1997.

North American Horticultural Supply Ass'n *(1988)*
1900 Arch St.
Philadelphia, PA   19103-1498
Tel: (215)564-3484   *Fax:* (215)564-2175
E-Mail: assnhqt@netaxs.com
Web Site: www.nahsa.org
Members: 80 manufacturers, 45 suppliers
Staff: 3
Annual Budget: $50-100,000
Exec. Director: Julie S. Thane

Historical Note
NAHSA promotes the role of the full service distributors in the greenhouse and nursery hard good supply market. NAHSA serves as liaison between industry distributors and manufacturers.
Publications:
Membership Directory. a.
NAHSA Newsletter. q.
Meetings/Conferences:
1999 – Nashville, TN(Opryland Hotel)/June 13-16

North American Hyperthermia Soc. *(1986)*
820 Jorie Blvd.
Oak Brook, IL   60561
Tel: (630)571-2904   *Fax:* (630)571-7837
E-Mail: swanson@rsn.org
Members: 340 individuals
Exec. Secretary: Lise Swanson
Assoc. Exec. Secretary: Mark Lichtenberger

Historical Note
NAHS members are professionals from the physical, engineering, biological, chemical, and clinical and medical sciences with an interest in the field of hyperthermia.
Publications:
Internat'l Journal of Hyperthermia. bi-m.
Membership Directory. bien.
NAHS Newsletter. irreg.
Meetings/Conferences:
Annual Meetings: in conjunction with the Radiation Research Soc.
1999 – Philadelphia, PA/Apr. 8-10

North American Indian Museums Ass'n *(1979)*
c/o North Dean Realty Corp.
P.O. Box 348
Englewood, NJ   07631-0348
Members: 50 individuals
Staff: 1
Chairperson: George H.J. Abrams

Historical Note
NAIMA members are museums, institutions and individual professionals specializing in the preservation and display of native American artifacts.
Publications:
Directory of Indian Museums. a.
Newsletter. irreg.
Meetings/Conferences:
Annual Meetings: in conjunction with the American Ass'n of Museums

North American Insulation Manufacturers Ass'n *(1933)*
44 Canal Center Plaza, Suite 310
Alexandria, VA   22314
Tel: (703)684-0084   *Fax:* (703)684-0427
E-Mail: insulation@naima.org
Web Site: http://naima.org
Members: 16 companies
Staff: 9
Annual Budget: $2-5,000,000
Exec. V. President: Kenneth D. Mentzer
General Counsel: Angus Crane
Manager, Administration: Michelle Bunch

Historical Note
Formerly the National Rock and Slag Wool Association, the National Mineral Wool Association, (1980) the National Mineral Wool Insulation Association, and (1992) the Mineral Insulation Manufacturers Ass'n.
Meetings/Conferences:
Annual Meetings: Fall

North American Lake Management Soc. *(1980)*
P.O. 5443
Madison, WI   53705-5443
Tel: (608)233-2836   *Fax:* (608)233-3186
E-Mail: nalms@nalms.org
Web Site: http://www.nalms.org

Members: 2,500 individuals
Staff: 1
Office Manager: Barbare Timmel
Conference Coordinator: Terry Thiessen

Historical Note
Members are academics, lake managers and others having an interest in furthering the understanding of lake ecology. Awards the CLM (Certified Lake Manager) designation to members meeting program requirements. Membership: $25/year (student); $35/year (individual); $45/year (non-profit organizations/company); $75/year (library); $300/year (corporate).

Publications:
Lake & Reservoir Management.
LakeLine Newsletter. q. adv.
NALMS Membership Directory. a.
Products and Services Directory.

Meetings/Conferences:
1999 – Reno, NV/Dec. 1-4

North American Limousin Foundation *(1968)*
7383 S. Alton Way, Suite 100
P.O. Box 4467
Englewood, CO 80155
Tel: (303)220-1693   *Fax:* (303)220-1884
E-Mail: Limousin@nalf.org. or NALlimousin@aol.com
Web Site: http://www.nalf.org
Members: 12,000 individuals
Staff: 16
Annual Budget: $1-2,000,000
Exec. V. President: John W. Edwards
Director, Communications: Casey Kelley
Director, Commerical Programs: Benjie Lemon
Director of Education and Research: Kent Andersen
Director of Operations: Gina Egbert

Historical Note
Registers, promotes and develops limousin beef cattle, a French breed introduced into the U.S.A. in 1968. Lifetime Membership: $200

Publications:
Limousin World. m. adv.

Meetings/Conferences:
1999 – Denver, CO(Renaissance Denver)/500

North American Manufacturing Research Institution of SME *(1981)*
P.O. Box 930
One SME Drive
Dearborn, MI 48121-0930
Tel: (313)271-1500   *Fax:* (313)271-2861
Web Site: http://www.sme.org/namri
Members: 180 individuals
Staff: 2
Annual Budget: $10-25,000
Manager: Kristen Dudash

Historical Note
Founded and supported by the Soc. of Manufacturing Engineers. Members are individuals engaged in manufacturing research and technology development. Membership: $60/year, plus $15 initial fee.

Publications:
Manufacturing Engineering. m.
Transactions of NAMRI/SME. a.

Meetings/Conferences:
Annual Meetings: May
1999 – Berkeley, CA(University of California-Berkeley)
2000 – Louisville, KY(University of Kentucky)
2001 – West Lafayette, IN(Purdue University)

North American Maple Syrup Council *(1959)*
25 Stowell St.
St. Albans, VT 05478-2212
Tel: (414)779-6672   *Fax:* (414)779-6672
E-Mail: reynolds@dataex.com
Members: 16 associations
Staff: 1
Annual Budget: under $10,000
Past President: Lynn H. Reynolds

Historical Note
Members are state and provincial maple syrup associations.

Publications:
Maple Syrup Digest. q. adv.

Meetings/Conferences:
Annual Meetings: October
1999 – Maine
2000 – Vermont

North American Meat Processors Ass'n *(1942)*
1920 Association Dr., Suite 400
Reston, VA 20191-1547
Tel: (703)758-1900   *Fax:* (703)758-8001
Toll Free: (800)368 - 3043
Members: 400 purveyors
Staff: 4
Annual Budget: $1-2,000,000
Exec. V. President/Secretary: Deven L. Scott

Historical Note
Formerly (1966) Nat'l Ass'n of Hotel & Restaurant Meat Purveyors and (1996) Nat'l Ass'n of Meat Purveyors. Represents processors and distributors of meat, poultry, seafood, and game to the food-service industry. Membership: $450–$1,900/year, varies according to sales.

Publications:
Newsletter. w.
The Meat Buyers Guide. a. adv.

Meetings/Conferences:
1999 – Maui, HI(Four Seasons)/Sept. 23-26

North American Membrane Soc. *(1985)*
Chemical Engineering Dept.
University of Texas
Austin, TX 78712-1062
Tel: (512)471-5866   *Fax:* (512)471-9643
Members: 600 individuals
Annual Budget: $50-100,000
Secretary: William J. Koros

Historical Note
NAMS members are scientists, engineers, academics and businessmen interested in promoting research and development in the membrane separations area. Membership: $50/year (individual); $20/year for students; $60/year for students outside of North America.

Publications:
Membrane Quarterly. q. adv.

Meetings/Conferences:
1999 – Toronto, Canada/June 12-18

North American Menopause Soc. *(1989)*
Univ. Hosp. of Cleveland, OB/GYN Dept.
11100 Euclid Ave., Suite 7024
Cleveland, OH 44106
Tel: (216)844-8748   *Fax:* (216)844-8708
E-Mail: info@menopause.org
Web Site: http://www.menopause.org
Members: 2,000 individuals
Staff: 3
Annual Budget: $1-2,000,000
Exec. Director: Wulf H. Utian, M.D., Ph.D
Director of Education and Development: Pamela Boggs
Administrative Director: Carolyn Develen

Historical Note
Members are health professionals interested in human female menopause. NAMS promotes the understanding of menopause among professionals and the general public. Membership: $170/year.

Publications:
Flashes Newsletter. q.
Menopause - The Journal of NAMS. q. adv.
Menopause Management. 6 times/year. adv.

Meetings/Conferences:
Annual Meetings: September
1999 – New York, NY(Hilton)/Sept. 23-25/1600
2000 – Orlando, FL(Walt Disney Dolphin)/Sept. 7-9
2001 – New Orleans, LA/Oct. 4-6

North American Millers Ass'n *(1902)*
600 Maryland Ave., S.W., Suite 305-W
Washington, DC 20024-2520
Tel: (202)484-2200   *Fax:* (202)488-7416
Members: 38 companies
Staff: 2
Annual Budget: $500-1,000,000
President: Betsy Faga

Historical Note
Formerly (1998) Millers' Nat'l Federation. Represents mills grinding 91% of U.S. wheat, rye and durum flour. Absorbed the Nat'l Soft Wheat Ass'n in 1976, and the Durum Wheat Institute in 1982. Membership fee based on hundredweights of production.

Publications:
Handbook. a
Newsletter. w.

Meetings/Conferences:
Annual Meetings: Spring/200
1999 – Amelia Island, FL(The Ritz-Carlton)/May 16-18

North American Morab Horse Ass'n/Registry *(1984)*
W3174 Faro Springs Road
Hilbert, WI 54129
Tel: (920)853-3086   *Fax:* (920)853-3114
E-Mail: pmha@morab.org
Web Site: www.morab.org and www.morabnet.com
Members: 150 individuals
Staff: 1
Annual Budget: under $10,000
Exec. Director: Patricia Fochs

Historical Note
Members are owners and breeders of Morab horses, a crossbreed of Arabian and Morgan horses. Absorbed the Hearst Memorial Morab Horse Registry in 1985. Membership: $15/year.

Publications:
Morab World. q.

Meetings/Conferences:
Annual Meetings: October

North American Mycological Ass'n *(1959)*
10 Lynn Brooke Pl.
Charleston, WV 25312-9521
Tel: (304)744-1654
E-Mail: joemiller@citynet.net
Web Site: http://www.namyco.org
Members: 2,000 individuals & local clubs
Staff: 1
Annual Budget: $25-50,000
Exec. Secretary: Joseph J. Miller

Historical Note
Originated at Ohio State University in November 1959 as the Committee on Fungi and was incorporated in Ohio as the North American Mycological Ass'n in 1967. Membership: $20/year (individual), $30/year (organization).

Publications:
McIlvainea. a.
The Mycophile. bi-m.

Meetings/Conferences:
Annual Meetings: July-November
1999 – Cape Giradeau, MO/Aug. 12-15/350

North American Natural Casing Ass'n *(1990)*
111 Park Place
Falls Church, VA 22046-4513
Tel: (703)538-1794   *Fax:* (703)241-5603
E-Mail: nancahq@aol.com
Members: 25 companies
Annual Budget: $50-100,000
Exec. V. President: Susan A. Denston
Director of Government Affairs: Clay D. Tyeryar

Historical Note
An outgrowth of the Internat'l Natural Sausage Casing Ass'n, NANCA was formed to confront trade issues that affect North American suppliers, producers and distributors of natural casings.

Publications:
NANCA News Newsletter. semi-a.

Meetings/Conferences:
1999 – New York, NY(The Roosevelt Hotel)/April 15-16/40

North American Nature Photography Ass'n *(1993)*
10200 West 44th Ave., Suite 304
Wheat Ridge, CO 80033-2840
Tel: (303)422-8527   *Fax:* (303)422-8894
E-Mail: nanpa@resourcenter.com
Web Site: http://www.nanpa.org
Members: 2,000 individuals
Staff: 16
Annual Budget: $500-1,000,000
Exec. Director: Francine Butler, Ph.D., CAE
Director, Communications: Michael P. Thompson
Director, Meetings: Kate Holland, CMP
Exec. Director: Jerry Bowman, CAE

Historical Note
NANPA represents photographers, editors, publishers, educators, and students interested in photography of nature and the environment. Provides educational opportunities and promotes standards of ethical conduct. Membership: $75/year (general), $25/year (student); $100/year (joint); $250-3,000/year (corporate).

Publications:
Currents. Newsletter.
Membership Directory. a. adv.

Meetings/Conferences:
Annual Meetings: January
1999 – San Diego, CA(Town and Country)/Feb. 3-7/700

North American Normande Ass'n *(1982)*
Historical Note
Organization dissolved in 1995.

North American Nursing Diagnosis Ass'n *(1972)*
1211 Locust St.
Philadelphia, PA 19107
Tel: (215)545-8105   *Fax:* (215)545-8107
Toll Free: (888)226 - 2482
E-Mail: 73764.123@compuserve.com.
Members: 800 individuals
Exec. Director: Joseph Braden
Dir., Management Services: Joseph Braden

Historical Note
NANDA members are registered nurses and other health professionals with an interest in nursing diagnosis. Has no paid staff. Membership,(includes subscription to quarterly journal, "Nursing Diagnosis"): $85/year.

Publications:
NANDA Book. bien.
NANDA Nursing Diagnosis Journal. q.
Proceedings. bien. adv.

Meetings/Conferences:
1999 – New Orleans, LO(Radisson Hotel)/April 13-18/300
2000 – Orlando, FL(Sheraton World Resort)/April 4-9/300

North American Plant Preservation Council *(1990)*
HC 67, Box 539-B
Renick, WV 24966
Tel: (304)497-3163   *Fax:* (304)497-2698
E-Mail: barryg@slip.net
Web Site:
    http://www.gardenweb.com/orgs/nappc/nappc.html
Members: 3,500 individuals, 65 organizations
Annual Budget: $25-50,000
Exec. Director: Barry Glick

Historical Note
NAPPC is dedicated to establishing plant collections in a range of areas and climate zones on the North American continent. These collections will be used to preserve plants in danger of extinction, for research, for horticultural study, education and dissemination. Membership $10/year (individual).

Publications:
Directory of Collections. a.

Meetings/Conferences:
1999 – Detroit, MI/Aug. 1-7

North American Private Truck Council
Historical Note
NAPTC is an umbrella organization supported by the Nat'l Private Truck Council to coordinate activities between NPTC and Private Motor Truck Council of Canada, NPTC's Canadian counterpart.

North American Professional Driver Education Ass'n *(1958)*
5180 N. Elston Ave.
Chicago, IL 60630-1682
Tel: (773)777-9605
Members: 280 schools
Staff: 2
Annual Budget: $50-100,000
President: Charles Rumsfield

Historical Note
Formerly (1970) Nat'l Professional Driver Education Ass'n, Inc., and (1960) Nat'l Ass'n of Driving Schools. Members are individuals and companies involved in driver education. Awards the "Qualified Driving School" designation. Membership: $200/year (full member), $50/year (associate).

Publications:
Driver Training Bulletin.
NAPDEA News. q. adv.

Meetings/Conferences:
Annual Meetings: Spring

North American Professors of Christian Education (1942)

4050 Lee Vance View
Colorado Springs, CO   80918
Tel: (502)897-4813   Fax: (502)897-4004
E-Mail: Celead@sbts.edu
Web Site: http://www.sbts/edu/celead/napce/napce.html
Members: 260 individuals
Staff: 14
Exec. Administrator: Dr. Dennis E. Williams

Historical Note
NAPCE cultivates the personal and professional development of Christian educators through educational, research and fellowship opportunities.

Publications:
NAPCE Newsletter 3/year.

Meetings/Conferences:
1999 – San Diego, CA/October 28-31

North American Public Relations Network

Historical Note
Address unknown in 1998.

North American Punch Manufacturers Ass'n (1963)

7402 Chestnut Ridge Road
Lockport, NY   14094
Tel: (716)433-2917
Members: 21 companies
Staff: 1
Annual Budget: $10-25,000
Exec. Secretary: Alan M. Hamilton

Historical Note
Formerly (1996) the Nat'l Ass'n of Punch Manufacturers. Membership: $1,000/year (full membership) and $350/year (associate membership).

Meetings/Conferences:
Annual Meetings: March

North American Retail Dealers Ass'n (1943)

10 E. 22nd St., Suite 310
Lombard, IL   60148
Tel: (630)953-8950   Fax: (630)953-8957
Toll Free: (800)621 - 0298
Web Site: http://www.narda.com
Members: 3,500 dealers
Staff: 25
Annual Budget: $2-5,000,000
Exec. Director: Elly S. Valas
Director, Operations: Rosemary Wemstrom
Editor: Russ Gager

Historical Note
Formerly (until 1979) the Nat'l Appliance and Radio TV Dealers Ass'n and (1994) Nat'l Ass'n of Retail Dealers of America. The Nat'l Ass'n of Service Dealers is a division. Membership: $150/year (individual).

Publications:
Membership Directory.
NARDA News. m. adv.
NARDA Retailer.

Meetings/Conferences:
Annual Meetings: None held. Norman,OK/March 14-17
    Leesburg,VA/August 14-18 Atlanta,GA/Oct.17-20

North American Rhea Ass'n (1991)

Historical Note
Address unknown in 1998.

North American Saxophone Alliance

Northwestern University
School of Music
Evanston, IL   60208
Tel: (847)491-7228
E-Mail: jah@nwu.edu
Web Site: www.indstate.edu/nasa
Members: 900 individuals
Annual Budget: $10-25,000
Membership Director: Jonathan Helton

Historical Note
NASA members are professional musicians, teachers and amateur players of the saxophone. Membership: $35/year.

Publications:
NASA Update Newsletter. bi-m. adv.
Saxophone Symposium. a. adv.

Meetings/Conferences:
1999 – Ten regional conferences throughout the US and Canada.
2000 – Montreal, Canada

North American Securities Administrators Ass'n (1917)

10 G Street, N.E., Suite 710
Washington, DC   20002
Tel: (202)737-0900   Fax: (202)783-3571
Members: 65 individuals
Staff: 8
Annual Budget: $2-5,000,000

Exec. Director: Philip A. Feigin
Director, Government Affairs: Deborah A. Fischione
Director, Finance and Administration: John Lynch
General Counsel: Karen M. O'Brien
Director, Membership Services: Donna M. Holt

Historical Note
Formerly (1945) Nat'l Ass'n of Securities Administrators. NASAA members are the 65 state, provincial and territorial securities administrators in the United States, Canada, Mexico and Puerto Rico. In the U.S., NASAA is the national voice of the fifty state agencies responsible for investor protection and regulatory oversight of the securities industry. The jurisdiction of state governments over securities regulation is co-extensive with that of the U.S. Securities and Exchange Commission. As industry co-regulators, state securities commissioners play a key role in assuring fairness in the securities markets, particularly in regard to the treatment of individual small investors. Membership: $600/year.

Publications:
Investor Alert. q.
NASAA Investor Bulletin. q.
NASAA Reports. m.

Meetings/Conferences:
Annual Meetings: Fall

North American Serials Interest Group (1985)

2103 N. Decatur Road, #214
Decatur, GA   30033
E-Mail: nasiginfo@nasig.ils.unc.edu
Web Site: http://nasig.ils.unc.edu/
Members: 1000 individuals
Annual Budget: $100-250,000
President: Steve Orberg

Historical Note
NASIG promotes communication and sharing of ideas among all members of the serials information chain, anyone working with or concerned about serial publication.

Publications:
NASIG Newsletter. bi-m.
Proceedings. a.

Meetings/Conferences:
Annual Meetings: June

North American Shippers Ass'n (1987)

Historical Note
Organization defunct in 1998.

North American Simulation and Gaming Ass'n (1961)

1128 East Bluff Drive
Penn Yan, NY   14527
Tel: (315)536-7895
Web Site: http://www.nasaga.org
Members: 200 individuals
Annual Budget: under $10,000
Membership Coordinator: Barbara Steinwachs

Historical Note
Established as Nat'l Gaming Council, it assumed its present name in 1974. Members are teachers, trainers and others interested in the concept of using simulated situations and games as educational and planning tools. Has no paid staff. Membership: $55/year.

Publications:
Simages Newsletter. irreg.
Simulation and Gaming: An Internat'l Journal. q. adv.

Meetings/Conferences:
Annual Meetings: Fall
1999 – San Francisco, CA/Oct. 13-16

North American Skull Base Soc. (1989)

4815 Rugby Ave., Suite 203
Bethesda, MD   20814-3033
Tel: (301)654-6802   Fax: (301)718-8692
Web Site: nasbs.org
Annual Budget: $250-500,000
Exec. Director: Lawrence Leong, CMP

Historical Note
NASBS is a medical subspecialty society with representation from many disciplines with an interest in diseases involving the base of the skull. Members include neurosurgeons, otolaryngologists, plastic surgeons, ophthalmologists, pathologists, anesthesiologists and radiologists. Membership: $220/year (individual).

Publications:
Petrous Pulse Newsletter. semi-a. adv.
Skull Base Surgery. q. adv.

Meetings/Conferences:
1999 – Chicago, IL(Chicago Marriott)/May 28-31

North American Snowsports Journalists Ass'n (1963)

P.O. 74563
Vancouver, BC   V6K 4-P4
Tel: (604)877-1141
E-Mail: stevet@infoserve.net
Web Site: http://nasja.org
Members: 400 individuals, 120 corporate
Annual Budget: $25-50,000
Exec. Secretary: Steve Threndyle

Historical Note
Founded as United States Ski Writers Ass'n; became North American Ski Journalists Ass'n in 1990, and assumed its current name in 1998. NASJA is a professional group of writers, photographers, film-makers and broadcasters who present ski-related news, information and features throughout the United States and Canada, via the various media. Corporate members include media contacts, employees of ski-related businesses, and others who have a commercial interest in the journalistic coverage of the sport. Membership: $75 initiation, $25/year (individual); $100/year (coprorate).

Publications:
Inside Edge Newsletter. q.

NASJA Directory. a. adv.

Meetings/Conferences:
Annual Meetings: March-April/300-400
1999 – Mammoth Mountain, CA/April 7-11

North American Soc. for Cardiac Imaging (1973)

P.O. Box 411106
San Francisco, CA   94141-1106
Tel: (415)487-9802   Fax: (415)487-9803
E-Mail: info@nasci.org
Web Site: http://www.nasci.org
Members: 170 individuals
Annual Budget: $50-100,000
Exec. Director: Joan Saluzzi

Historical Note
NASCI members are radiologists with an interest in cardiac imaging and the application of imaging methods to the study of heart disease in both research laboratory and clinical settings. Membership: $100/year (individual).

Meetings/Conferences:
1999 – Vienna, Austria

North American Soc. for Dialysis and Transplantation (1981)

6550 Fannin, Suite 1273
Houston, TX   77030
Tel: (713)790-3275   Fax: (713)790-5055
Members: 200 individuals
Secretary-Treasurer: Wadi Suki, M.D.

Historical Note
NASDT members are health professional concerned with kidney dialysis and transplantation procedures.

Meetings/Conferences:
1999 – Maui, HI/July 18-22

North American Soc. for Pediatric Gastroenterology and Nutrition (1971)

6900 Grove Road
Thorofare, NJ   08086-9447
Tel: (609)848-1000   Fax: (609)848-5274
E-Mail: naspgn@slackinc.com
Web Site: www.naspgn.org
Members: 480 individuals
Staff: 1
Annual Budget: $100-250,000
Exec. Director: Margaret Stallings
Meetings Manager: Rhonda Simmons

Historical Note
Formerly (1988) North American Soc. for Pediatric Gastroenterology. NASPGN promotes excellence in training, education, research and patient care in the area of pediatric intestinal and liver disease. Membership: $170/yr. (individual).

Publications:
Journal Pediatric Gastroenterology and Nutrition.
NASPG Membership Directory. a.
Newsletter. q.

Meetings/Conferences:
1999 – Denver, CO(Adam's Mark Hotel)/October 21-24

North American Soc. for Social Philosophy (1983)

Dept. of Philosophy
Villanova University
Villanova, PA   19085-1699
Tel: (610)519-4708   Fax: (610)519-4639
Members: 600 individuals
President: Dr. Joseph Betz

Historical Note
NASSP members are academics drawn from a wide range of disciplines with an interest in social philosophy. Has no paid officers or full-time staff. Membership: $30/year (individual).

Publications:
Journal of Social Philosophy. 3/yr.
Proceedings published every 1-2 years.

Meetings/Conferences:
Annual Meetings: Summer
1999 – Villanova, PA

North American Soc. for Sport History (1972)

P.O. Box 1026
Lemont, PA   16851-1026
Tel: (814)238-1288   Fax: (814)238-1288
E-Mail: ronsmith22@juno.com
Web Site: http://nassh.uwo.ca/
Members: 950 individuals
Annual Budget: $25-50,000
Secretary-Treasurer: Ronald A. Smith

Historical Note
Has no paid officers or full-time staff. Membership: $5/year(foreign); $50/year (individual); $20/year (student); $55/year (institution).

Publications:
Directory of Scholars Identifying with the History of Sport.
    irreg.
Journal of Sport History. 3/yr.
Newsletter. irreg.
Proceedings. a.

Meetings/Conferences:
Annual Meetings: May, usually in a university setting

North American Soc. for Sport Management (1985)

Univ. of New Brunswick, Kinesiology Fac.
Fredericton, NB   E3B 5-A3
Tel: (506)453-5010   Fax: (506)453-3511
Web Site: http://www.unb.ca/sportmanagement/
Members: 475 individuals
Contact: Garth Paton, Ph.D.

Historical Note
NASSM members are academics with an interest in sport management.
Publications:
Journal of Sport Management. q.
Meetings/Conferences:
Annual Meetings: Spring
1999 – Vancouver, BC(Univ. of British Columbia)/June 2-5

North American Soc. for the Psychology of Sport and Physical Activity *(1966)*
Historical Note
Address unknown in 1997.

North American Soc. for the Sociology of Sport *(1980)*
Dept. of Sociology & Anthropology
Northeastern University
Boston, MA   02115
Tel: (414)229-6080   *Fax:* (414)229-5100
Members: 280 individuals
Annual Budget: $10-25,000
President: Allen Klein
Historical Note
NASSS members are academics concerned with the sociology of sport. Membership: $60/year (individual) and $150/year (company).
Publications:
Newsletter. 3/yr.
Sociology of Sport Journal. q. adv.
Meetings/Conferences:
Annual Meetings: early November
1999 – Cleveland, OH
2000 – Colorado Springs, CO

North American Soc. for Trenchless Technology *(1990)*
1655 Fort Myer Dr., Suite 700
Arlington, VA   22209-3199
Tel: (703)351-5252   *Fax:* (703)357-5261
E-Mail: dmartin@nastt.org or nastt@erols.com
Web Site: www.nastt.org.irap.nrc.ca/nodig
Members: 1,050 individuals and companies
Staff: 3
Annual Budget: $500-1,000,000
Exec. Director: Daivd Martin
Deputy, Operations: John Hemphill
Office Manager: Debby Shields
Historical Note
Members are individuals and organizations interested in the construction, maintenance and rehabilitation of utility service lines without the use of trenches. An affiliate of the Internat'l Soc. for Trenchless Technology. Membership: $150/year (individual); $500/year (company); $300/year (governmental/educational institutions).
Publications:
Conference Proceedings. a. adv.
Membership Directory. a. adv.
Newsletter. q. adv.
Meetings/Conferences:
Annual Meetings: Spring
1999 – Orlando, FL(Convention Center/Clarion)/May 23-26
2000 – Anaheim, CA/April 9-12
2001 – Nashville, TN

North American Soc. of Adlerian Psychology *(1952)*
65 E. Wacker Place, Suite 1710
Chicago, IL   60601-7203
Tel: (312)629-8801   *Fax:* (312)201-5917
E-Mail: nasap@msn.com
Members: 1,100 individuals
Staff: 2
Annual Budget: $100-250,000
Exec. Director: Lee Ann Deal
Historical Note
Formerly (1976) American Soc. of Adlerian Psychology. Members are individuals interested in the teachings of the Austrian psychiatrist, Alfred Adler (1870-1937). His system emphasizes the uniqueness of each individual and that individual's relationships with society. Membership: $100/year.
Publications:
Journal of Individual Psychology. q.
Membership Directory. bien. adv.
NASAP Newsletter. 9/yr.
Meetings/Conferences:
Annual Meetings: May
1999 – Atlanta, GA(Grand Hyatt)/May 27-30
2000 – St. Paul, MN
2000 – Chicago, IL
2001 – Arizona

North American Soc. of Pacing and Electrophysiology *(1979)*
Natick Executive Park
2 Vision Drive
Natick, MA   01760-2059
Tel: (508)647-0100   *Fax:* (508)647-0124
E-Mail: info@naspe.org
Web Site: http://www.naspe.org
Members: 2,500 individuals
Staff: 34
Annual Budget: $2-5,000,000
Exec. Director: Carol J. McGlinchey
Meeting Manager: Victoria Cook
CME Director: Barbara K. Krause
Membership Manager: Betsy Bogdansky
Historical Note
Members are physicians and associated professionals involved in cardiac pacing and cardiac electrophysiology and the diagnosis and treatment of cardiac arrythmias. Membership: $260/year.

Publications:
Journal of Cardiovascular Electrophysiology. m.
Membership Directory. a.
NASPE News. q.
NASPETAPES– Audio Journal.
PACE Journal m. adv. adv.
Meetings/Conferences:
Annual Meetings: Spring/5,000
1999 – Toronto, Ontario(Convention Center)/May 12-15
2000 – Washington, DC/May 17-20

North American Soc. of Scaffold Professionals
20335 Ventura Blvd., Suite 310
Woodland Hills, CA   91364-2144
Tel: (818)610-0320   *Fax:* (818)610-0323
Annual Budget: under $10,000
Exec. Director: Gary W. Larson
Historical Note
Membership: $200-$650/year.
Meetings/Conferences:

North American Soc. of Teachers of the Alexander Technique *(1987)*
3010 Hennepin Ave. South, Suite 10
Minneapolis, MN   55408
Tel: (612)824-5066   *Fax:* (612)822-7224
Toll Free: (800)473 – 0620
E-Mail: nastat@ix.netcom.com
Web Site: www.alexandertech.com
Members: 500 individuals
Administrator: Brian McCullough
Historical Note
Members are practitioners and trainees in the Alexander technique, an instructive kinesiotherapy designed to reduce harmful repetitive movement, thus reducing body fatigue and strain.
Publications:
List of Certified Training Courses. semi-a.
NASTAT News. q. adv.
Teaching Members List. semi-a.

North American South Devon Ass'n *(1974)*
7383 S. Alton Way, #103
Englewood, CO   80112-2302
Tel: (303)770-3130   *Fax:* (816)842-6931
Members: 220 individuals
Staff: 3
Annual Budget: $100-250,000
Historical Note
Members are owners and breeders of purebred South Devon cattle, a breed originating in England and now used as a maternal beef bloodstock. Maintains breed registry. Membership: $75 + $25/year (active member), $25/year (associate), $15 (junior member).
Publications:
North American South Devon. q.
Sire Summary. a.
Meetings/Conferences:
Annual Meetings: Always in conjunction with Nat'l Western Stock Show/Denver, CO

North American Spine Soc. *(1985)*
6300 N. River Road, Suite 500
Rosemont, Il   60018-4231
Tel: (847)698-1630   *Fax:* (847)823-8668
E-Mail: nassman@aol.com
Web Site: http://www.spine.org
Members: 2,050 individuals
Staff: 10
Annual Budget: $1-2,000,000
Exec. Director: Eric J. Muehlbauer
Mgr., Health Policy/Communications: Pamela M. Hayden
Mgr., Education: Patricia Fuller
Historical Note
Formed by the merger of the American College of Spine Surgeons and the North American Lumbar Spine Ass'n, NASS members are physicians, orthopedists, osteopaths and other health professionals with an interest in the treatment of the spine. Membership: $250/year (individual).
Publications:
NASS News Newsletter. q.
Spine Journal. m.
Meetings/Conferences:
2000 – New Orleans
2001 – Seattle, WA

North American Strawberry Growers Ass'n *(1978)*
324 Lake St.
Grimsby, ON   L3M 1-Z4
Tel: (905)945-9057   *Fax:* (905)945-8643
Members: 400 individuals
Staff: 2
Annual Budget: $50-100,000
Exec. Secretary: Bob Cobbledick
Historical Note
NASGA members are growers, nurserymen and academics interested in strawberry production and development. Membership: $55/year (professional); $175/year (grower/organization/company). Website located at: http://www.fvs.cornell.edu/growerOrganization/NASGA/welcome.htm
Publications:
Advances in Strawberry Production. a.
Proceedings. a.
Quarterly Newsletter. 5/yr.
Meetings/Conferences:
Annual Meetings: February
1999 – Orlando, FL(Adams Mark Hotel)/Feb. 9-12/400
2000 – Las Vegas, NV

2001 – Raleigh, NC(North Carolina State University/Small Fruit Ctr.)

North American Technician Excellence *(1997)*
8201 Greensboro Dr., Suite 300
McLean, VA   22102
Tel: (703)610-9033   *Fax:* (703)610-9005
Staff: 5
Annual Budget: $1-2,000,000
President: Rex P. Boynton
Historical Note
In order to develop and promote excellence in the installation and service of HVACR equipment, NATE provides a national certification program with broad based industry support to recognize high quality industry technicians through voluntary testing and certification.

North American Telecommunications Ass'n *(1970)*
Historical Note
Became MultiMedia Telecommunications Ass'n in 1996.

North American Thermal Analysis Soc. *(1968)*
Historical Note
Address unknown in 1992.

North American Thermal Soil Recycling Ass'n *(1993)*
Historical Note
Address unknown in 1997.

North American Trakehner Ass'n *(1977)*
P.O. Box 12172
Lexington, KY   40581-2172
Tel: (502)867-0375   *Fax:* (502)867-1820
Members: 400 individuals
Staff: 2
Annual Budget: $10-25,000
Exec. Director: Katherine Gilbertson-Smock
Historical Note
Members are owners and breeders of Trakehner horses. Maintains breed registry. Membership: $50/year (individuals).
Publications:
Handbook. a.
Trakehner Tails Newsletter. bi-m.
Meetings/Conferences:
Annual Meetings: Fall

North American Transplant Coordinators Organization *(1900)*
8310 Nieman Road
Lenexa, KS   66214
Tel: (913)492-3600   *Fax:* (913)541-0156
E-Mail: natco-info@applmeapro.com
Web Site: www.applmeapro.com/natco
Members: 1,700 individuals
Staff: 3
Annual Budget: $500-1,000,000
Exec. Director: Deidre Gish Panjada
Historical Note
Health professionals, involved in obtaining and distributing human organs and tissues for transplant, or working with recipients. Membership: $150/year.
Publications:
Journal of Transplant Coordination. q. adv.
NATCO Newsletter. bi-m. adv.
Meetings/Conferences:
Annual Meetings: July-August
1999 – Albuquerque, NM(Double Tree/Hilton)/July 25-28/500
2000 – Orlando, FL

North American Transportation Management Institute *(1945)*
2200 Mill Road
Alexandria, VA   22314
Tel: (703)838-7952   *Fax:* (703)683-9752
Members: 1,050 individuals and organizations
Staff: 5
Annual Budget: $250-500,000
Exec. Director: Jay Kundu
Director: Jeff Arnold
Mgr., Membership/Meetings: Erica Wong, CMP
Historical Note
Founded as Nat'l Committee for Motor Fleet Supervisor Training; assumed its current name in 1997. Provides certification which designates competence in the fleet industry's universal standards. Members are those in the industry and related organizations concerned with training and certification. Membership: $225/year.
Publications:
Guardrail Magazine. q. adv.
Motor Fleet Monthly. m.
Meetings/Conferences:
Annual Meetings: Spring
1999 – Atlanta, GA.

North American Trucking Industrial Relations Ass'n *(1987)*
908 King St., Suite 300
Alexandria, VA   22314-3019
Tel: (703)836-9400   *Fax:* (703)836-9409
Members: 128 individuals
Staff: 2
Annual Budget: $25-50,000
Exec. Director: Herve Aitken
Administrative Assistant: Connie Webb
Bookkeeper: Kimberley B. Sorrell

Historical Note
Formerly (1997) Nat'l Trucking Industrial Relations Ass'n, NATIRA members are trucking executives and lawyers concerned with personnel and labor relations issues.

Publications:
Newsletter. q.

Meetings/Conferences:

North American Wholesale Lumber Ass'n *(1893)*
3601 Algonquin Rd., Suite 400
Rolling Meadows, IL   60008-3108
Tel: (847)870-7470   *Fax:* (847)870-0201
Web Site: http://www.lumber.org
Members: 630 companies
Staff: 6
Annual Budget: $1-2,000,000
Exec. V. President: Nicholas R. Kent
Director, Membership & Communications: Allison Hayes
Manager, Meeting Services: Pam Baker
Director of Education: Sherman D. Leibow

Historical Note
Formerly (1972) Nat'l American Wholesale Lumber Ass'n. Membership: $865-1,650/year (organization/company), depending on membership category and size.

Publications:
Annual Directory of Membership. a.
NAWLA Bulletin. m.

Meetings/Conferences:
Annual Meetings: Spring/500
1999 – Tucson, AZ(Loew's Ventura Canyon)/May 1-4

North American-Chilean Chamber of Commerce
50 Riverside Dr.
New York, NY   10024
Tel: (212)787-4321
Members: 120 businesses
Staff: 1
Annual Budget: $10-25,000
Exec. Director: Lester Ziffren

Historical Note
Founded in 1980 by the merger of Chile-American Ass'n with North American-Chile Chamber of Commerce. Members are United States, Canadian and Chilean executives interested in fostering improved trade and commerce between their repective countries. Membership: $50/year (individual); $150/year (corporate).

Meetings/Conferences:
Annual Meetings: January in New York

North-American Ass'n of Telecommunications Dealers *(1987)*
1045 E. Atlantic Ave., Suite 206
Delray Beach, FL   33483
Tel: (561)266-9440   *Fax:* (561)266-9017
E-Mail: jmarien@ix.netcom.com
Web Site: http://www.natd.com
Members: 110 companies
Staff: 3
Annual Budget: $100-250,000
Exec. Director: Joseph Marion
Conventions Director: Ruth Stramberg

Historical Note
Formerly (1994) the Nat'l Ass'n of Telecommunications Dealers, NAATD members are secondary marketers of telecommunications equipment and major PBX installations. Membership: $600-2,000/year.

Publications:
NATD-Network. q.

Meetings/Conferences:
Semi-Annual Meetings: January and June/300

Northamerican Heating and Airconditioning Wholesalers Ass'n
Historical Note
Became (1994) Northamerican Heating, Refrigeration and Airconditioning Ass'n.

Northamerican Heating, Refrigeration and Airconditioning Wholesalers Ass'n *(1947)*
P.O. Box 16790
Columbus, OH   43216
Tel: (614)488-1835   *Fax:* (614)488-0482
Web Site: www.nhraw.org
Members: 400 wholesalers
Staff: 10
Annual Budget: $1-2,000,000
Exec. V. President: James D. Wilder
Dir., Education: James Healy

Historical Note
Affiliated with the Nat'l Ass'n of Wholesaler-Distributors. Formerly Nat'l Heat Wholesalers Ass'n; Nat'l Heating and Air Conditioning Wholesalers; and Northamerican Heating and Airconditioning Wholesalers Ass'n; assumed its current name in 1994. Absorbed (1969) Northamerican Ass'n of Sheet Metal Distributors. Street address is 1389 Dublin Rd., Columbus, OH.

Publications:
NHAW Scene. semi-a.

Meetings/Conferences:
Semi-Annual Meetings: June and December

Northamerican Industrial Representatives Ass'n
400 E. Randolph St., Suite 500-6
Chicago, IL   60601-7329
Tel: (312)240-0820   *Fax:* (312)240-1005
E-Mail: info@nira.org
Web Site: http://www.nira.org
Members: 240 companies
Staff: 2
Annual Budget: $50-100,000

Exec. Director: William Weiner

Historical Note
Formerly (1994) Nat'l Ass'n of Industrial Agents. Members are independent manufacturers representatives in the industrial market. Membership: $295/year(organization).

Publications:
The Locator/Directory. a. adv.
The Reporter. q.

Meetings/Conferences:
1999 – Las Vegas, NV(Luxor)/200
1999 – Las Vegas, NV(Luxor)/Feb. 22-25

NorthAmerican Ingredient Marketing Specialists
Historical Note
Became (1998) Network of Ingredient Marketing Specialists.

Northeastern Weed Science Soc. *(1947)*
3059 Sound Ave.
Riverhead, NY   11901
Tel: (516)727-3595   *Fax:* (516)727-3611
E-Mail: afsd@cornell.edu
Members: 336 individuals
Staff: 1
Annual Budget: $10-25,000
Secretary-Treasurer: Andy Senesac

Historical Note
Membership: $20/year (individual), $125/year (organization/company).

Publications:
Annual Meetings Program. a.
NEWSS Newsletter. q.
NEWSS Proceedings and Supplement. a.

Meetings/Conferences:
Annual Meetings: January
1999 – Cambridge, MA(Marriott)/Jan. 4-7

Northern Nut Growers Ass'n *(1910)*
R.R. 1
Niagara-on-the-Lake
Ontario, ON   L0S 1-J0
Tel: (905)262-4927
Members: 2,050 individuals
Staff: 1
Annual Budget: $25-50,000
Meetings Chairman: Doug Campbell

Historical Note
Promotes interest in nut-bearing trees, their culture and products. Mainly concerned with 14 different species of nut trees grown in the northern U.S. and southern Canada. Has no paid staff.

Publications:
Nutshell. q. adv.
Proceedings. a. adv.

Meetings/Conferences:
Annual Meetings: August
1999 – Lincoln, NE
2000 – Pennsylvania
2001 – New York, NY
2002 – Meadowview, VA
2003 – Washington State
2004 – Columbia, MO

Northern Textile Ass'n *(1854)*
230 Congress St., 3rd Floor
Boston, MA   02110
Tel: (617)542-8220   *Fax:* (617)542-2199
E-Mail: textilenta@aol.com
Web Site: www.textilenta.org
Members: 280 mills
Staff: 6
Annual Budget: $250-500,000
President: Karl H. Spilhaus

Historical Note
Originally established as the New England Cotton Manufacturers Ass'n, it changed its name to the Nat'l Ass'n of Cotton Manufacturers around 1890 and assumed its present name in 1956. Its core membership today consists of makers of cotton and synthetic yarns, but it also provides staff support for and includes four semi-autonomous councils: Wool Manufacturers (absorbed in 1956); Felt Manufacturers (absorbed in 1961); Elastic Fabric Manufacturers (formerly the Elastic Fabric Manufacturers Institute, absorbed in 1970); and the American Flock Ass'n. Sponsors the Northern Textile Ass'n Political Action Committee.

Meetings/Conferences:
1999 – South Carolina(Wild Dunes Resort)/Oct. 17-19

Northwest Fruit Exporters *(1980)*
105 South 18th St., Suite 227
Yakima, WA   98901
Tel: (509)576-8004   *Fax:* (509)576-3646
E-Mail: nfe@wolfenet.com
Members: 17 companies
Staff: 3
Annual Budget: $250-500,000
Manager: Jim Archer

Historical Note
A Webb-Pomerene Act association. Membership: $1500 (organization/company).

Norwegian Fjord Ass'n of North America *(1977)*
Historical Note
Address unknown in 1998.

Norwegian-American Chamber of Commerce *(1915)*
c/o Norwegian Trade Council
800 Third Ave., 23rd Floor
New York, NY   10022
Tel: (212)421-1653   *Fax:* (212)838-0374
Web Site: http://www.norway.org

Members: 1000 companies
Staff: 2
Annual Budget: $50-100,000
General Manager: Inger M. Tallaksen

Historical Note
Membership: $350/yr. (regular corporate); $3000/yr. (patron corporate)

Meetings/Conferences:
Annual Meetings: New York City, in March/150-200

Not-for-Profit Services Ass'n *(1995)*
111 E. Wacker Dr., Suite 990
Chicago, IL   60601
Tel: (312)729-9900   *Fax:* (312)729-9800
Toll Free: (800)869 - 0491
E-Mail: info@pencormazur.com
Web Site: www.cpaselect.com/nsa
Members: 22 firms
Staff: 10
Exec. Director/Administrator: George A. Buckley, Jr., CAE
Director, Communications: Michelle Durham

Historical Note
NSA members are primarily CPA firms who provide services to not-for-profit organizations, particularly firms who specialize in providing financial services beyond traditional compliance accounting and firms who are expanding the range of services they provide to not-for-profit clients.

Publications:
Members' Bulletin. q.
Non-Profit Observer. q.

Meetings/Conferences:

NPES, the Ass'n for Suppliers of Printing and Publishing Technologies *(1933)*
1899 Preston White Drive
Reston, VA   20191-4367
Tel: (703)264-7200   *Fax:* (703)620-0994
E-Mail: npes@npes.org
Web Site: http://www.npes.org
Members: 350 suppliers
Staff: 25
Annual Budget: $2-5,000,000
President: Regis J. Delmontagne
Director, Communications & Marketing: Carol J. Hurlburt
Director, Government Affairs: Mark J. Nuzzaco
V. President, Member Services: William K. Smythe

Historical Note
Established as the Nat'l Printing Equipment Ass'n, became the Nat'l Printing Equipment and Supply Ass'n in 1979 and assumed its present name in 1991. Members are manufacturers and distributors of graphic arts equipment, systems, software, and supplies. The purpose of the association is to strengthen the entire industry and aid member firms in the areas of statistics and marketing, safety and industry standards, international trade, and government relations.

Publications:
NPES Directory-Internat'l Suppliers of Printing and Publishing
     Technologies. a.
NPES Guide. a.
NPES Internat'l News. q.
NPES News. m.
NPES Safety News. q.

Meetings/Conferences:
Annual Meetings: Fall/100 and Spring

Nuclear and Plasma Sciences Soc. *(1963)*
Historical Note
A technical society of the Institute of Eletrical and Electronics Engineers (IEEE). Membership in the Society, open only to IEEE members, includes subscription to technical periodicals in the field published by IEEE. All administrative support provided by IEEE.

Nuclear Energy Institute *(1981)*
1776 I St., N.W., Suite 400
Washington, DC   20006-3708
Tel: (202)739-8000   *Fax:* (202)785-4019
Web Site: http:\\www.nei.org
Members: 370 organizations
Staff: 140
Annual Budget: $25-50,000,000
C.E.O.: Joe F. Colvin
Sr. V.P., Industry Communications: Angelina S. Howard
V. President, Governmental Affairs: John E. Kane
Sr. Dir., Finance and Administration: Linda Nahin
Controller: Walter S. Harris
V. President, Legal: Robert Bishop
Dir., Member Services: Lisa Steward
V.P., Suppliers, Internat'l Progs. and Nuclear Infrastructure: Marvin Fertel
Senior V. President & Chief Nuclear Officer for Nuclear Generation: Ralph Beedle

Historical Note
Established as the U.S. Committee for Energy Awareness, it became the U.S. Council for Energy Awareness in 1987. Absorbed the American Nuclear Energy Council and the Nuclear Management and Resources Council and assumed its present name in 1994. In July 1987, the Atomic Industrial Forum was merged with the Council. Members consist of utilities, manufacturers of electrical generating equipment, researchers, architects, engineers, labor unions, milling and mining companies, constructors, laboratories, educational institutions and government agencies with interest in the generation of electricity by nuclear power. Has an annual budget of approximately $27 million. Membership dues vary, based on type of company.

Publications:
Nuclear Energy Insight.

Meetings/Conferences:
Annual Meetings: May/500

Nuclear Information and Records Management Ass'n (1978)

210 Fifth Ave.
New York, NY 10010
Tel: (603)432-6476
Members: 400 individuals
Staff: 1
Annual Budget: $50-100,000
Administrative Assistant: Jane Hannum

Historical Note
Purpose is to improve the management of corporate information and records relating to nuclear facilities. Membership includes utility company employees, architectural engineers and industrial consultants. Formerly (1985) the Nuclear Records Management Ass'n. Membership: $60/year.

Publications:
Newsletter. q.

Meetings/Conferences:
Annual Meetings: Fall
1999 – Kansas City, MO(Hyatt Regency Kansas City)/Aug. 1-4/300
2000 – Dallas, TX(Hyatt Regency Dallas)/Aug. 20-23/300
2001 – Orlando, FL(Hyatt Orlando)/Aug. 26-29/300

Nuclear Suppliers Ass'n (1984)

P.O. Box 2038
Springfield, VA 22152
Tel: (703)451-1912   *Fax:* (703)451-2334
E-Mail: NSA NEWS@aol.com
Members: 78 companies
Annual Budget: $50-100,000
Director, Meetings: R. Travis

Historical Note
Members are companies which specialize in the manufacture and distribution of products and services for the nuclear industry. Membership: $150/year (organization).

Meetings/Conferences:
1999 – Orlando, FL(Orlando Marriott)/Feb. 1-3
1999 – Hutchison Island, FL(Indian River Marriott)/June 20-23

Nurse Healers - Professional Associates Internat'l (1978)

1211 Locust St.
Philadelphia, PA 19107-5409
Tel: (215)545-8079   *Fax:* (215)545-8107
Members: 1,500 individuals
Annual Budget: $25-50,000
Exec. Officer: Joseph Braden

Historical Note
A cooperative of health care and human service professionals organized for the promotion of healing through complimentary techniques such as therapeutic touch, biofeedback, guided imagery, acupuncture and homeopathy. Membership: $75/year.

Publications:
Cooperative Connection. a. adv.

Meetings/Conferences:
Annual Meetings: October

Nursery Ass'n Executives of North America (1947)

HC 32, Box 121 A
Owls Head, ME 04854
Tel: (207)594-5657   *Fax:* (207)594-5657
E-Mail: JHBRAGG@MIDCOAST.COM
Members: 54 associations
Staff: 1
Annual Budget: $10-25,000
Exec. Director: John H. Bragg

Historical Note
Chief executives of nursery ass'ns of the U.S. and Canada. Formerly (1972) Nursery Ass'n Secretaries and (1987) Nursery Ass'n Executives. The association was formed primarily for educational purposes.

Publications:
Newsletter. q.

Meetings/Conferences:
Semi-annual Meetings: Winter and Summer, with American Ass'n of Nurserymen

Nurses Organization of Veterans Affairs (1980)

1726 M St., N.W., Suite 1101
Washington, DC 20036
Tel: (202)296-0888   *Fax:* (202)833-1577
Members: 2,600 individuals
Staff: 2
Annual Budget: $250-500,000
Exec. Director: Deborah Beck
Director of Administration: Isabel Regina Borkoski

Historical Note
Formerly (1989) Nurses Organization of the Veterans Administration. Membership: $75/year.

Publications:
Legislatively Speakings.
News from NOVA. q. adv.

Meetings/Conferences:
Annual Meetings: April
1999 – Washington, DC/March 10-13
2000 – Orlando, FL(Adams Mark Hotel)/April 26-29

Nursing Touch and Massage Therapy Ass'n Internat'l (1990)

1438 Shortcut East
Slidell, LA 70458
Tel: (504)893-8002   *Fax:* (504)892-3493
E-Mail: NTMTA@aol.com
Web Site: http://members.aol.com/NTMTA
Members: 1000 individuals

Annual Budget: $50-100,000
Exec. Director: Sue Berger-deRada, R.N., LMT

Historical Note
Founded as Nat'l Ass'n of Nurse Massage Therapists; assumed its current name after reorganization in 1997. NTMTAI members are licensed nurses who practice touch/massage therapy. Promotes the recognition of therapeutic touch within nursing practice, and acts as a source of information for members and the nursing profession. Membership: $80/year (active individual); $60/year (student/retired); $125/year (corporate).

Publications:
NTMTA Membership Directory. a.
Nurses Touch Journal.

Meetings/Conferences:

Occupational Medical Administrators' Ass'n (1959)

Historical Note
Address unknown in 1996.

Occupational Program Consultants Ass'n (1974)

3110 Fairview Park Dr.
Falls Church, VA 22042
Tel: (703)205-6796
Members: 150 individuals
Annual Budget: under $10,000
President: Chuck Taylor

Historical Note
The OPCA is a non-profit professional organization for consultants who initiate and guide the planning for implementation of Employee Assistance Programs. Its purpose is to provide a forum through which consultants can address common concerns, enhance their skills and obtain the group identity necessary for professional recognition. Has no paid staff. Membership: $25/year (individual); $50/year (organization).

Publications:
Conference Announcement. a.
OPCA Directory. a.
OPCA Newsletter. q.

Meetings/Conferences:
Annual Meetings: Fall
1999 – Orlando, FL
2000 – New York, NY

Oceanic Engineering Soc.

Historical Note
A technical society of the Institute of Electrical and Electronics Engineers (IEEE). Membership in the Society, open only to IEEE members, include a subscription to a technical periodical in the field published by IEEE. All administrative support provided by IEEE.

Oceanography Soc. (1988)

4052 Timber Ridge Drive
Virginia Beach, VA 23455-7017
Tel: (757)464-0131   *Fax:* (757)464-1759
E-Mail: rhodesj@exis.net
Web Site: http://www.tos.org
Exec. Director: Judi Rhodes

Historical Note
TOS members are oceanographers, scientists and engineers with a professional interest in oceanography and related fields. Membership: $50/year (individual); $25/year (student); $125/year (library); $500/year (corporate/institution).

Publications:
Oceanography Magazine. 3/yr.
TOS Newsletter. irreg.

Meetings/Conferences:
1999 – Reno, NV

Office and Professional Employees Internat'l Union (1945)

265 W. 14th St., Suite 610
New York, NY 10011
Tel: (212)675-3210   *Fax:* (212)727-3466
Members: 140,000 individuals
Staff: 50
Annual Budget: $2-5,000,000
President: Michael Goodwin

Historical Note
Organized in Cincinnati, Ohio January 8, 1945 as the Office Employees International Union and chartered by the American Federation of Labor at the same time. Absorbed the Associated Unions of America in 1972. Sponsors and supports the Voice of the Electorate Political Action Committee. Absorbed the Leather Workers Internat'l Union (previously in Peabody, MA) in 1992. Membership fee varies by local union.

Publications:
Research News. q.
White Collar. q.

Meetings/Conferences:
Triennial Meetings: June (1998)

Office Automation Soc. Internat'l (1982)

Historical Note
Merged (1995) with Office Systems Research Ass'n.

Office Furniture Dealers Alliance

Historical Note
An alliance of the Business Products Industry Ass'n.

Office Furniture Distribution Ass'n (1976)

P.O. Box 326
Petersham, MA 01366-0326
Tel: (508)724-3267   *Fax:* (508)724-3507
Members: 50 individuals
Staff: 3
Managing Director: Kenneth E. Miller

Historical Note
Membership: $200/year (individual).

Publications:
Freight Traffic Newsletter. m.

Office Planners and Users Group (1969)

Box 11182
Philadelphia, PA 19136
Tel: (215)335-9400
Members: 155 individuals
Staff: 1
Annual Budget: $25-50,000
Exec. Director: Frank J. Carberry

Historical Note
Formerly (1987) Office Landscape Users Group. OPUG members are architects, designers, space planners, office administrators and other professionals with an interest in office planning and management.

Meetings/Conferences:
1999 – Phoenix, AZ/May 3-5
1999 – Toronto, Canada

Office Products Dealers Alliance (1983)

Historical Note
A subsidiary of Business Products Industry Ass'n.

Office Products Manufacturers Ass'n (1970)

Historical Note
An alliance of the Business Products Industry Ass'n.

Office Products Representatives Ass'n (1973)

Historical Note
An alliance of the Business Products Industry Ass'n.

Office Products Wholesalers Ass'n (1995)

5024-R Campbell Blvd.
Baltimore, MD 21236-5974
Tel: (410)931-8100   *Fax:* (410)931-8111
E-Mail: opwa@aol.com
Web Site: http://www.opwa.org
Members: 32 wholesalers, 105 manufacturers
Staff: 3
Annual Budget: $500-1,000,000
Exec. V. President: Calvin K. Clemons, CAE, CMP

Historical Note
Successor organization after the consolidation (1995) of Nat'l Ass'n of Wholesale Independent Distributors (formerly Nat'l Ass'n of Writing Instrument Distributors) and Wholesale Stationers Ass'n. OPWA members are chief executives of office product wholesalers and manufacturers who affirm the concept of wholesale distribution in the office products industry.

Publications:
OPWA Magazine. a.
OPWA Record. q.

Meetings/Conferences:
1999 – Miami Beach, FL/March 6-10

Office Systems Research Ass'n (1981)

Univ. of Nebraska, 529-A Nebraska Hall
Lincoln, NE 68588
Tel: (402)472-4789   *Fax:* (402)472-5907
E-Mail: info@osra.org
Web Site: http://www.osra.com
Members: 225 individuals
Staff: 1
Annual Budget: $10-25,000
Exec. Director: Donna McAlister-Kizzier

Historical Note
Organized in Washington, DC in the fall of 1980 and officially chartered in the State of Ohio in June 1981. Members are individuals from business, government or education interested in a professional approach to the planning of office systems. Absorbed (1995) Office Automation Soc. Internat'l. Membership: $55/year (individual); $300/year (corporate).

Publications:
Newsletter. q.
Office Systems Research Journal. semi-a.

Meetings/Conferences:
1999 – Atlanta, GA(Terrace Gorden)/Feb. 26-28/100
2000 – Toronto, ON, Canada/100

Offshore Marine Service Ass'n (1957)

990 N Corporate Dr., Suite 210
Harahan, LA 70123-3324
Tel: (504)734-7622   *Fax:* (504)734-7134
Members: 270 corporations
Staff: 4
Annual Budget: $10-25,000
President: Robert Alario
Exec. Secretary: Lillie Eden
V. President: Christopher Sullivan
Manager, Administration/Finance: Mitzi Ray

Historical Note
Members are owners and operators of offshore installations or of vessels servicing such installations, and suppliers to the industry. Provides regulatory input on issues of concern to the offshore business community. Membership: $750-40,000/year (company).

Publications:
OMSA Newsletter. q.

Meetings/Conferences:
Quarterly Meetings: usually New Orleans, LA/300

Offshore Valve Ass'n (1979)

1620 I St., N.W., Suite 220
Washington, DC 20006
Tel: (202)452-8811   *Fax:* (202)659-5427
Members: 10 individuals, 20 companies
Staff: 2

Annual Budget: $50-100,000
Exec. V. President: George G. Pagonis

Historical Note
Membership fee: $300-3,000/year.

Publications:
Newsletter. q.

Oil, Chemical and Atomic Workers Internat'l Union *(1955)*
Box 281200
Lakewood, CO   80228-8200
Tel: (303)987-2229   *Fax:* (303)987-1967
Members: 90,000 individuals
Staff: 90
Annual Budget: $10-25,000,000
President: Robert E. Wages
Communications Director: Lynne Baker
Secretary-Treasurer: R.J. Christie
Research and Educational Director: John Varjonack
General Counsel: Kathleen Hostetler

Historical Note
Merged with United Paperworks Int'l Union in 1999. Also the product of a merger in 1955 of the Oil Workers International Union (founded in 1918) and the United Gas, Coke and Chemical Workers International Union (founded in 1942). Has a budget of about $14 million. Sponsors and supports the Oil, Chemical and Atomic Workers Committee on Political Education Fund.

Publications:
OCAW Reporter.

Meetings/Conferences:
Triennial Meetings: Summer

Ombudsman Ass'n, The *(1982)*
5521 Greenville Ave., Suite 104-265
Dallas, TX   75206
Tel: (214)553-0043   *Fax:* (214)348-6621
E-Mail: 73772.1763@compuserve.com
Members: 310 individuals
Annual Budget: $100-250,000
Exec. Director: Carole M. Trocchio

Historical Note
Formerly (1992) the Corporate Ombudsman Ass'n. Incorporated as an association of individuals actively engaged in the practice of ombudsmanry, as designated neutrals. TOA works to enhance the quality and value of the ombudsman profession. Membership: $175.

Publications:
Booklets. irreg.
Bulletin. irreg.
Ombuds News Newsletter. q. adv.
Ombudsman Handbook. irreg.

Meetings/Conferences:
Annual Meetings: May
1999 – Phoeniz, AZ/150

Omega Tau Sigma *(1907)*
239 Sisson Hall
1900 Coffey Road
Columbus, OH   43210
Tel: (614)292-1206
Members: 5,500 individuals
Staff: 1
Annual Budget: under $10,000
President: John Gordan, D.V.M.

Historical Note
Professional veterinary medical fraternity, established at the University of Pennsylvania School of Veterinary Medicine. Member of the Professional Fraternity Ass'n.

Publications:
Inner Square. semi-a.
OTS Directory. irreg.

Meetings/Conferences:
Annual Meetings: Fall, on a college campus hosted by local chapter/100

Omicron Kappa Upsilon *(1914)*
College of Dentistry, Room 105
Lincoln, NE   68583-0740
Tel: (402)472-1339
Members: 17,000 individuals
Staff: 2
Annual Budget: $10-25,000
Corresponding Secretary: Jan John

Historical Note
Honorary dental society. Organized May 21, 1914 by the faculty of Northwestern University Dental School.

Publications:
OKU Bulletin. a.

Meetings/Conferences:
Annual Meetings: Spring, in conjunction with the American Ass'n of Dental Schools

Oncology Nursing Soc. *(1975)*
501 Holiday Drive
Pittsburgh, PA   15220-2749
Tel: (412)921-7373   *Fax:* (412)921-6565
E-Mail: member@ons.org
Web Site: http://www.ons.org
Members: 27,000 individuals
Staff: 83
Annual Budget: $5-10,000,000
Exec. Director: Pearl Moore, R.N.
Director, Meeting Services: Nancy Berkowitz
Project Coordinator, Education Cancer Care Issues: Linda Worrall
Director, Finance and Administration: Layla Ballon

Historical Note
Members are nurses involved in the treatment and care of cancer patients. Has an annual budget of approximately $6 million. Membership: $71/year (individual); $1,000/year (organization).

Publications:
Oncology Nursing Forum. 10/yr. adv.
ONS News. m. adv.

Meetings/Conferences:
Annual Meetings: Spring/5,000
1999 – Atlanta, GA(Convention Center)/April 28-May 1/5000
2000 – San Antonio, TX(Convention Center)/May 11-14/5000
2001 – San Diego, CA(Convention Center)/May 17-20/5000

Online Audiovisual Catalogers *(1980)*
Univ. of N. Florida, Carpenter Library
4567 St. Johns Bluff Rd., South
Jacksonville, FL   32224-2645
Tel: (904)620-2550   *Fax:* (904)620-2719
Members: 700 individuals
Annual Budget: under $10,000
Archivist: Verna Urbanski

Historical Note
Representing catalogers of audiovisual materials and computer files, OLAC provides a means of exchange of information, opportunities for continuing education, a unified voice for its members and works toward a common understanding of practices and standards. Membership: $12/year (individual, US); $18/year (institution, US).

Publications:
OLAC Newsletter. q.

Meetings/Conferences:
Annual Meetings: Semi-annual meetings in conjunction with the American Library Ass'n Biennial Conference.
1999 – New Orleans, LA/June 24-July 1
1999 – Philadelphia, PA/Jan. 22-28
2000 – Chicago, IL/July 6-13

Open Applications Group *(1995)*
401 N. Michigan Ave.
Chicago, IL   60611-4267
Tel: (312)527-6799   *Fax:* (312)245-1081
E-Mail: openapplications@sba.com
Web Site: http://www.openapplications.com
President and Chief Technology Officer: David Connelly

Historical Note
The OAGI sets specifications that define the business object interoperability between enterprise business applications. Members are enterprise application software developers. Membership: $25,000/year (corporate); $12,000/year (associate).

Open Pit Mining Ass'n *(1944)*
Historical Note
Address unknown in 1996.

OPERA America *(1970)*
1156 15th St. N.W.
Suite 810
Washington, DC   20005-1704
Tel: (202)293-4466   *Fax:* (202)393-0735
E-Mail: frontdesk@operaam.org
Web Site: http://www.operaam.org
Members: 1,500 individuals, 150 opera companies, 210 affiliates
Staff: 20
Annual Budget: $2-5,000,000
President: Marc A. Scorca
Information Service Director: Elizabeth Cecchetti
Director, Media & Audience Relations: Samuel Smith
Managing Director/Artistic & Audience Initiative: Jamie Driver
Director, Finance and Administration: Harris Povich
Membership Coordinator: Elizabeth Stager
Development Director: Jane Nelson
Director, Operations: Eve Smith

Historical Note
Established to facilitate communication and cooperation among opera producing companies in the U.S., Canada, and abroad. Purpose is to: promote the growth and expansion of opera; assist in development of resident professional opera companies through cooperative artistic management services to its members; assist improvement of operatic presentations; encourage the appreciation and enjoyment of opera by all segments of society; and to foster the education, training and development of operatic composers, singers and allied talents. Membership: sliding scale based on budget (professional companies); $150/year (affiliate organizations); $40-150/year (individuals); $250/year (businesses); $35/year (singer).

Publications:
Annual Field Report. a.
Career Guide for Singers. bien.
Career Guide Update. bi-m.
Directory of Production Materials for Rent. bien.
Encore - North American Operatic Works. semi-a.
In the Works-Works-in-Progress Update. semi-a.
Membership List. a.
OPERA America Newsline. 10/year.
Opera-In-Trust. 3/year.
Season Performance Schedule. a.
Voices. 3/year.

Meetings/Conferences:
1999 – Vancouver, BC/May 5-8

Operations Management Soc.
Historical Note
Organization defunct in 1997.

Operations Research Soc. of America
Historical Note
Merged with Institute of Management Sciences to form Institute for Operations Research and the Management Sciences in 1994.

Operations Security Professionals Soc. *(1990)*
9200 Centerway Road
Gaithersburg, MD   20879
Tel: (301)840-6770   *Fax:* (301)840-8502
E-Mail: zhi@tiac.net
Web Site: http://www.opsec.org
Members: 780 individuals
Annual Budget: $100-250,000
Exec. Director: Zhi Marie Hamby-Nye

Historical Note
Also known as OPSEC Professionals Soc. OPS members are are operations security professionals from both government and the private sector. Awards the designation OCP (OPSEC Certified Professional). Membership: $40/year (individual); $200/year (corporate).

Publications:
Operations Security Journal. irreg. adv.
OPS News Newsletter. q.
OPS ZGram. d.

Meetings/Conferences:

Operative Plasterers' and Cement Masons' Internat'l Ass'n of the United States and Canada *(1864)*
14405 Laurel Place
Laurel, MD   20707
Tel: (301)470-4200   *Fax:* (301)470-2502
Members: 54,000 individuals
Staff: 43
Annual Budget: $2-5,000,000
President: John J. Dougherty

Historical Note
Founded in 1864 as the Nat'l Plasterers' Organization of the United States, it was renamed the Operative Plasterers International the United States and Canada in 1889. Affiliated with the American Federation of Labor in 1908, it absorbed the cement finishers of the United Brotherhood of Cement Workers in 1915 and changed its name to the Operative Plasterers' and Cement Finishers' Internat'l Ass'n of the United States and Canada. The present name was adopted in 1950. Sponsors and supports the Plasterers' and Cement Masons' Political Action Committee.

Publications:
The Plasterer and Cement Mason. bi-m.

Meetings/Conferences:

Ophthalmic Photographers' Soc. *(1969)*
213 Lorene St.
Nixa, MO   65714-9230
Tel: (417)725-0181   *Fax:* (417)724-8450
Toll Free: (800)403 - 1677
E-Mail: OPSMember@aol.com
Members: 1,200 individuals
Staff: 1
Annual Budget: $50-100,000
Manager: Barbara McCalley

Historical Note
OPS members are health professionals actively engaged in ophthalmic photography includinjg ophthalmic photographers, ophthamologists, ophthalmic technicians, and basic scientific researchers. Provides continuing education opportunities and certification as Certified Retinal Angiographer (CRA). Membership: $75/year (individual); $250/year (sustaining membership).

Publications:
Journal of Ophthalmic Photography. semi-a. adv.
OPS Directory. a.
OPS Newsletter. bi-m.

Meetings/Conferences:
Annual Meetings: Fall/450
1999 – Orlando, FL/Oct. 23-27
2000 – Dallas, TX/Nov. 11-15
2001 – New Orleans, LA/Nov. 10-14

OPSEC Professionals Soc. *(1990)*
Historical Note
See Operations Security Professionals Soc.

Optical Industry Ass'n: OMA *(1916)*
6055-A Arlington Blvd.
Falls Church, VA   22044
Tel: (703)237-8433   *Fax:* (703)237-0643
E-Mail: OMAassoc@aol.com
Members: 61 companies
Staff: 5
Annual Budget: $1-2,000,000
Exec. V. President: William C. Thomas

Historical Note
Formerly (1992) Optical Manufacturers Ass'n. Members are makers and importers of spectacle frames, lenses, cases, contact lenses, technical instruments, machinery, and solutions. Membership: annual dues vary based on sales.

Publications:
Barometer. m.
Credit Reporting Service. m.
Optical Product Code Report. m.
Sales/Shipments Reports. m.
Synoptic. bi-m.

Meetings/Conferences:

Optical Laboratories Ass'n *(1894)*
11096-B Lee Hwy., Suite 102
Fairfax, VA   22030-5014
Tel: (703)359-2830   *Fax:* (703)359-2834
Web Site: http://www.ola-labs.org
Members: 360 companies
Staff: 8
Annual Budget: $1-2,000,000
Exec. Director: Robert L. Dziuban, CAE
Manager, Membership & Communications: Phyllis R. Himmelfarb, CAE

Director, Administration: Arlene J. Hiller

Historical Note
Formerly the Optical Wholesalers Ass'n, it adopted its present name in 1977. Independent ophthalmic laboratories and supply houses making prescription glasses to requirements of ophthalmologists, optometrists and opticians.

Publications:
Clear Visions. q.
Special Bulletin. irreg.
Swap Shop.
Technical Topics.

Meetings/Conferences:
Annual Meetings: November/2,400
1999 – Nashville, TN(Opryland Hotel)/Nov. 18-20/2400
2000 – San Diego, CA(Convention Center)/Nov. 3-5/2500

Optical Publishing Ass'n *(1988)*
Historical Note
Address unknown in 1998.

Optical Soc. of America *(1916)*
2010 Massachusetts Ave., N.W.
Washington, DC 20036
Tel: (202)223-8130   *Fax:* (202)223-1096
E-Mail: info@osa.org
Web Site: http://www.osa.org
Members: 12,000 individuals
Staff: 90
Annual Budget: $10-25,000,000
Exec. Director: John A. Thorner
Director, Communications: Andrea Pendleton
Public Policy Manager: Elizabeth A. Baldwin
Director, Conference Services: Cynthia Gady
Director, Program Development: Barbara Hicks
Education Coordinator: Tracye Flowers
Administrative Director: Adrienne Garritson
Director of Finance: Elizabeth Rogan
Director, Corporate services/marketing: Dorothy Bomberger
Director, Publications: Ghassan Rassan

Historical Note
OSA is a professional society of optical engineers and scientists concerned with the fields of optics and photonics. A member of the American Institute of Physics. Has an annual budget of $10 million. Membership: $75/year (regular), $30/year (student), $550/year (corporation), $24/year (teachers).

Publications:
Applied Optics. 3/m. adv.
Journal of Lightwave Technology. m.
Journal of Optical Technology. m.
Journal of the Optical Soc. of America A.
Journal of the Optical Soc. of America B.
Optics & Photonics News. m. adv.
Optics and Spectroscopy. m.
Optics Letters. bi-w.

Meetings/Conferences:
1999 – Santa Clara, CA/Sept. 26-Oct. 1

Optical Video Disc Ass'n *(1980)*
P.O. Box 641667
Los Angeles, CA 90064-1667
Tel: (310)319-9119
Web Site: http://www.ovda.org
Annual Budget: $100-250,000
Exec.Director: Judy Anderson

Historical Note
Founded as Laser Disc Ass'n; assumed its current name in 1997. OVDA works to foster a positive and dynamic image of the disc industry and to keep members and the public apprised of new technologies that may have an impact on the business.

Meetings/Conferences:

Opticians Ass'n of America *(1926)*
10341 Democracy Lane
Fairfax, VA 22030-2505
Tel: (703)691-8355   *Fax:* (703)691-3929
E-Mail: oaa@opticians.org
Web Site: http://www.opticians.org
Members: 7,500 individuals, 500 retail optical companies
Staff: 15
Annual Budget: $1-2,000,000
Exec. Director: David A. Digby, FOAA
Director, Communications: Jacqueline E. Fairbairns
Government Affairs Director: James Boxall
Membership/Education Director: Cathy Browning

Historical Note
Formerly (1972) Guild of Prescription Opticians of America, Inc. Membership: $50/yr. (individual), company memberships vary in price depending on number of locations.

Publications:
American Optician.
Guild Quarterly. q.
Membership Directory. a.
OAA News.
State Leaders Bulletin.

Meetings/Conferences:
Annual Meetings: Summer/1,000
1999 – Dallas, TX(Fairmont)
2000 – New Orleans, LA(Fairmont)

Opto-Precision Instruments Ass'n
225 Reinekers Lane, Suite 625
Alexandria, VA 22314
Tel: (703)836-1360   *Fax:* (703)836-6644
Members: 25 companies
Staff: 1
Annual Budget: $50-100,000
Exec. Director: William C. Strackbein

Historical Note
OPIA is an affiliate of the SAMA Group of Ass'ns.

Optometric Editors Ass'n *(1965)*
1921 E. Carnageie Ave., Suite 3L
Santa Ana, CA 92705-5510
Tel: (949)250-8070   *Fax:* (949)250-8157
Members: 30 associations and publications
Annual Budget: under $10,000
Secretary: Sally Marshall Corngold

Historical Note
Members are editors of optometric publications.

Publications:
Optometric Editors Ass'n - Proceedings. a.
Report. q.

Meetings/Conferences:
Annual Meetings: June

Oral History Ass'n *(1966)*
P.O. Box 97234
Baylor University
Waco, TX 76798-7234
Tel: (254)710-2764   *Fax:* (254)710-1571
E-Mail: oha_support@baylor.edu
Web Site: http://www.baylor.edu/~OHA/
Members: 1,400 individuals
Staff: 1
Annual Budget: $50-100,000
Exec. Secretary: Rebecca Sharpless

Historical Note
Historians and others involved in recording, transcribing, and preserving conversations with persons who have participated in seminal developments of history. Membership: $500 (lifetime individual), $50/year (regular individual), $75-120/year (institutional), $50/year (library), $25/year (student).

Publications:
Annual Report & Membership Directory. a.
Oral History Association Newsletter. 3/year.
Oral History Evaluation Guidelines.
Oral History Review. 2/year. adv.
Pamphlet Series. irreg.

Meetings/Conferences:
Annual Meetings: Fall
1999 – Anchorage, AK(Anchorage Hilton)/Oct. 6-10

Order Selection, Staging and Storage Council *(1986)*
8720 Red Oak Blvd., Suite 201
Charlotte, NC 28217-3957
Tel: (704)676-1190   *Fax:* (704)676-1199
E-Mail: jnfosinger@mhia.org
Web Site: http://www.mhia.org
Members: 60 associations
Staff: 2
Annual Budget: $50-100,000
Managing Director: John B. Nofsinger

Historical Note
Members are storage industry manufacturers.

Meetings/Conferences:
Annual Meetings: with the Materials Handling Industry Ass'n
1999 – Charlotte, NC
1999 – Amelia Island, FL

Organic Crop Improvement Ass'n Internat'l *(1985)*
1001 Y St., Suite B
Lincoln, NE 68508-1172
Tel: (402)477-2323   *Fax:* (402)477-4325
E-Mail: info@ocia.org
Web Site: http://ocia.org
Staff: 20
Annual Budget: $1-2,000,000
Chief Operating Officer: John R. Moore

Historical Note
OCIA members are farmers, processors, manufacturers and traders of organic crops from different parts of the world. The association aims to expand organic cultivation by ensuring organic production is economically and environmentally viable. Membership:$250 (member); $15(chapter member).

Publications:
Organic Crop Improvement Newsletter. bi-m. adv.

Meetings/Conferences:
1999 – Lincoln, NE

Organic Growers and Buyers Ass'n *(1977)*
8525 Edinbrook Crossing, Suite 3
Brooklyn Park, MN 55443
Tel: (612)424-2450   *Fax:* (612)315-2733
E-Mail: ogba@mwt.net
Members: 180 individuals
Staff: 3
Annual Budget: $100-250,000
Exec. Director: Sue Cristan

Organic Reactions Catalysis Soc. *(1966)*
Historical Note
Society inactive in 1997.

Organic Trade Ass'n *(1984)*
P.O. Box 1078
Greenfield, MA 01302-1078
Tel: (413)774-7511   *Fax:* (413)774-6432
E-Mail: ota@igc.apc.org
Web Site: http://www.ota.com
Members: 837 individuals
Staff: 5
Annual Budget: $500-1,000,000
Exec. Director: Katherine Dimatteo
Director, Communications: Holly Givens

Historical Note
Formerly (1994) Organic Foods Production Ass'n of America. Members are businesses involved in the organic products industry. The association seeks to promote the industry and establish

production and marketing standards. Absorbed (1991) Organic Food Alliance. Membership: begins at $75/year (business); increases based on annual sales.

Publications:
Organic Pages-Resources Directory. a. adv.
Organic Production Guidelines.
Position Paper on Analytical Testing.
The Organic Report.

Meetings/Conferences:
1999 – Baltimore, MD(Convention Center)

Organization Development Institute *(1968)*
11234 Walnut Ridge Road
Chesterland, OH 44026-1299
Tel: (440)729-7419   *Fax:* (440)729-9319
E-Mail: DonWCole@aol.com
Web Site: http://members.aol.com/odinst
Members: 455 individuals
Staff: 1
Annual Budget: $25-50,000
President: Donald W. Cole, Ph.D., ROD

Historical Note
International, educational association organized to disseminate information about organization development, training in conflict resolution technologies for effective management. Wants to build the field of organization development into a respected profession and establish a worldwide network of organization development professionals and networks. Awards the RODC (Registered Organization Development Consultant) to professional consultant members who demonstrate minimum experience and educational credentials and pass the Institute's written exam. Membership: $110/year (regular), $150/year (professional/consultant), $60/year (students).

Publications:
Internat'l Registry of O. D.
Organizations and Change. m. adv.
The Organization Development Journal. q. adv.

Meetings/Conferences:
Semi-annual Meetings: Spring in the U.S. and Summer or Fall abroad.
1999 – San Antonio, TX(Trinity University)/May 18-21
1999 – Harare, Zimbabwe(Cresta Oasis Hotel)/July 12-17

Organization Development Network *(1964)*
71 Valley St. #301
South Orange, NJ 07079-2825
Tel: (973)763-7337   *Fax:* (973)763-7488
E-Mail: runge16469@aol.com
Members: 3,000 individuals
Staff: 6
Annual Budget: $500-1,000,000
Exec. Director: Richard A. Ungerer

Historical Note
Members are scholars, practitioners and others with an interest in human, organization, and systems development. Membership: $110/year (individual).

Publications:
Education Resource Directory. a.
OD Practitioner. q.
ODN News.
Roster. a.

Meetings/Conferences:
1999 – San Diego, CA(Sheraton Hotel & Marina)/Oct. 9-13

Organization for Internat'l Investment *(1991)*
1901 Pennsylvania Ave., N.W., Suite 807
Washington, DC 20006
Tel: (202)659-1903   *Fax:* (202)659-2293
Web Site: www.ofii.org
Members: 60 companies
Staff: 4
Exec. Director: Todd M. Malan

Historical Note
The Organization for Internat'l Investment (OFII) is a Washington, DC-based ass'n representing the US subsidiaries of foreign parent companies. OFII's member companies range from medium-sized enterprises to some of the largest firms in the United States. OFII's members employ hundreds of thousands of workers in thousands of plants and locations throughout America. OFII is dedicated to ensuring that US subsidiaries receive nondiscriminatory treatment under US federal and state law.

Meetings/Conferences:
Annual Meetings: November

Organization for the Promotion and Advancement of Small Telecommunications Companies *(1963)*
21 Dupont Circle, N.W., Suite 700
Washington, DC 20036-1109
Tel: (202)659-5990   *Fax:* (202)659-4619
Web Site: http://www.opastco.org
Members: 500 companies, 175 associate members
Staff: 22
Annual Budget: $10-25,000,000
President: John N. Rose
Director, Public Relations: Martha Silver
Meeting Planner: Robert Meisnere
Director, Education: Suzanne Bagshaw
Financial Controller: Richard F. Scarino
Director, Membership Relations: Ellen Iversen

Historical Note
Formerly (1996) the Organization for the Protection and Advancement of Small Telephone Comapnies. OPASTCO protects the interests of small, rural, independent commercial telephone companies and cooperatives that have less than 50,000 access lines. Has an annual budget of $17 million.

Publications:
Annual Report. a.
Convention Wrap-up. semi-a. adv.
Membership Directory. a. adv.

OPASTCO Roundtable. q. adv.
The Washington Weekly Report. w.
Meetings/Conferences:
Semi-Annual Meetings: January and July

Organization for the Protection and Advancement of Small Telephone Companies (1963)
Historical Note
Became the Organization for the Promotion and Advancement of Small Telecommunications Companies in 1996.

Organization for Tropical Studies (1963)
410 Swift Ave.
Box 90630, Duke University
Durham, NC 27708-0360
Tel: (919)684-5774   Fax: (919)684-5661
E-Mail: nao@acpub.duke.edu
Web Site: http://www.ots.duke.edu
Members: 55 institutions
Staff: 30
Annual Budget: $5-10,000,000
Exec. Director: Gary S. Hartshorn
Academic Director: Norma Bynum
Historical Note
Universities and research institutions with graduate and undergraduate programs in tropical studies. Maintains an office and research stations in Costa Rica. Membership: $35/year (individual), $8,800/year (organization).
Publications:
LIANA. 2/year.
OTS Newsletter. q.
Meetings/Conferences:
Annual Meetings: Spring/Summer in San Jose, Costa
    Rica/March/100

Organization of American Historians (1907)
112 N. Bryan St.
Bloomington, IN 47408-4199
Tel: (812)855-7311   Fax: (812)855-0696
E-Mail: oah@indiana.edu
Web Site: http://www.indiana.edu/~oah
Members: 9,200 individuals, 3,000 institutions
Staff: 10
Annual Budget: $1-2,000,000
Exec. Director: Arnita A. Jones
Advertising Coordinator: Tamzen Meyer
Historical Note
Formerly (1964) Mississippi Valley Historical Ass'n. Members are specialists in United States history and others concerned with the promotion of historical study and research in American history. Membership Fee: $35-130/year, varies by income (individual historian); $120/year (institution); $45/year (associate non-historian).
Publications:
Journal of American History. q. adv.
OAH Annual Program. a. adv.
OAH Magazine of History. q. adv.
OAH Newsletter. q. adv.
Meetings/Conferences:
Annual Meetings: April/2,000-2,500
1999 – Toronto, Canada(Sheraton Centre)/April 22-25
2000 – St. Louis, MO/March 30-April 2
2001 – Los Angeles, CA(Westin Bonaventure)/April 26-29
2002 – Washington, DC

Organization of American Kodaly Educators (1976)
P.O. Box 9804
Fargo, ND 58106-9804
Tel: (701)235-0366   Fax: (701)241-7051
E-Mail: wignesg@fargo.k12.nd.us
Web Site: http://www.music.indiana.edu/kodaly/kodaly.htm
Members: 1,700 individuals
Staff: 1
Annual Budget: $100-250,000
Exec. Director: Glenys Wignes
Historical Note
Members are music teachers interested in the Kodaly approach to music education. Membership: $40/year.
Publications:
Kodaly Envoy. q. adv.
Meetings/Conferences:
Annual Meetings: early Spring
1999 – Columbus, OH

Organization of Black Airline Pilots (1976)
P.O. Box 5793
Englewood, NJ 07631
Tel: (201)568-8145
Members: 1000 individuals, 5 regions
Staff: 3
Annual Budget: under $10,000
General Counsel: Eddie R. Hadden
Historical Note
Seeks to enhance the participation of minorities in the aerospace industry. Provides a communication network and job search assistance. Regular membership is open to cockpit crewmembers of commercial air carriers including corporate pilots. Sponsors a summer flight academy for youth at Tuskegee, Alabama. Membership: $100/year (individual), $1,000/year (organization).
Publications:
OBAP Newsletter. q.
Meetings/Conferences:
Semi-annual Meetings: Spring and August

Organization of Black Designers (1990)
300 M St., S.W., Suite N-110
Washington, DC 20024
Tel: (202)659-3918   Fax: (202)488-3838

E-Mail: OBDesign@aol.com
Web Site: http://www.core77.com/OBD
Members: 4,100 individuals
Staff: 6
Annual Budget: $250-500,000
Exec. Director: Shauna D. Stallworth
Director, Membership Development: Kathy Johnson
Director, Member Services: Bill Browne
Chairman: D.H. Rice
Historical Note
OBD members are African-Americans working as fashion, graphic, product, interior or industrial designers. Membership: $175/year (professional); $150/year (affiliate); $75/year (student); $500/year (corporate).
Publications:
DesigNation Journal.
Newsletter.
Meetings/Conferences:
Annual Meetings: Annual meetings.
1999 – Atlanta, GA
2000 – New York, NYOct. /10000

Organization of Flying Adjusters (1958)
5940 Bafil St., N.E.
Salem, OR 97301-1318
Tel: (503)585-1318   Fax: (503)585-3776
Members: 50 companies and individuals
Staff: 1
Annual Budget: $10-25,000
Exec. Secretary: Larry Larson, Sr.
Historical Note
Aircraft insurance adjusters who process aviation insurance claims and investigate causes of aircraft accidents. Membership: $175/year (regular); $125/year (associate).
Publications:
Membership Directory. a.
OFA Newsletter. q.
Meetings/Conferences:
Annual Meetings: October/by invitation only
1999 – Portland, MN

Organization of News Ombudsmen (1980)
6307 Surfside Way
Sacramento, CA 95831
Tel: (916)391-1314
E-Mail: Artnauman@aol.com
Web Site: http://www5.infi.net/ono
Members: 80 individuals
Annual Budget: $10-25,000
Secretary: Art Nauman
Historical Note
Formerly (1983) Organization of Newspaper Ombudsmen. ONO members are ombudsmen from both the print and broadcast news media. Has no paid officers or full-time staff. Membership: $75/year (individual).
Publications:
ONO Newsletter. m.
Meetings/Conferences:
Annual Meetings: Spring

Organization of Professional Acting Coaches and Teachers (1980)
3968 Eureka Drive
Studio City, CA 91604
Tel: (213)877-4988
Members: 12 individuals
Annual Budget: under $10,000
President: Lilyan Chauvin
Publications:
An Actors Guide to Professional Training.
Find Yourself in Hollywood.
Speak the French You Already Know.

Organization of Professional Employees of the U.S. Department of Agriculture (1929)
Box 381
Washington, DC 20044
Tel: (202)720-4898   Fax: (202)720-2799
Members: 7,500 individuals
Staff: 2
Annual Budget: $100-250,000
Exec. Director: Otis N. Thompson
Historical Note
OPEDA works for the economic and professional interests of its members. Membership: $52/year (active employees); $25/year (retired).
Publications:
OPEDA Journal. 3/year.
OPEDA News. m.
Meetings/Conferences:
Annual Meetings: May

Organization of Teachers of Oral Diagnosis (1963)
800 Fletcher Road
Hillsborough, NC 27278
Tel: (919)966-6114   Fax: (919)966-7007
E-Mail: Sam_Nesbit@dentistry.unc.edu
Members: 1,100 individuals
Annual Budget: under $10,000
Secretary-Treasurer: Dr. Sam Nesbit
Historical Note
Conceived at a workshop for oral diagnosis teachers in 1963 at Iowa State University. Has no paid officers or full-time staff. Membership: $90/year.
Publications:
OTOD Newsletter. q.

Meetings/Conferences:
Annual Meetings: March, with American Ass'n of Dental
    Schools
1999 – Vancouver, BC/March 8-12

Organization of Wildlife Planners (1978)
S.C. Dept of Wildlife & Marine Resources
P.O. Box 167
Columbia, SC 29202
Tel: (803)734-4008   Fax: (803)734-6310
Members: 100 individuals, 35 companies
Annual Budget: $10-25,000
President: Larry Cartee
Historical Note
Provides resources to improve management of fish and wildlife resources. Has no paid officers or full-time staff. Membership: $25/year (individual), $50/year (company).
Publications:
OWP Annual Proceedings. a.
President's Report. q.
Tomorrow's Management. semi-a.
Meetings/Conferences:
Annual Meetings: May-June
1999 – Shepardstown, WV/May 13-19

Organization of Women in Internat'l Trade (1989)
1413 K St. N.W., First Floor, Suite 857
Washington, DC 20005-3405
Tel: (202)785-9842
E-Mail: DURKE1901@AOL.COM
Web Site: http://www.owit.org
Members: 19 chapters
Annual Budget: $10-25,000
President: Donna Murray
Historical Note
The Organization of Women in Internat'l Trade is a federation of nineteen organizations of women in international trade whose purpose is to enhance the role of women in the profession. Has no paid officers or full-time staff. Membership: $250/year (organization).
Publications:
Directory Report. a. adv.
Meetings/Conferences:
Annual Meetings: Fall
1999 – Washington, DC

Organizational Behavior Teaching Soc. (1973)
Management Dept. Colorado State Univ.
Rockwell Hall
Fort Collins, CO 80523-1275
Tel: (970)491-6876   Fax: (970)491-3522
E-Mail: mccarthy@lamarcolostate.edu
Web Site: pitzer.edu
Contact: Anne M. McCarthy
Historical Note
Members are academics, consultants and other teaching professionals with an interest in organizational behavior. Membership: $38/year.
Publications:
Journal of Management Education. 6/yea.
Meetings/Conferences:
Annual Meetings: May-June
1999 – Las Cruces, NM(New Mexico State University)

Oriental Rug Importers Ass'n of America (1928)
100 Park Plaza Dr.
Secaucus, NJ 07094-3606
Tel: (201)866-5054   Fax: (201)866-6169
Web Site: http://www.oria.org
Members: 100 companies
Annual Budget: $10-25,000
Exec. Director: Lucille J. Laufer
Historical Note
Membership is concentrated in the New York area.
Publications:
Oriental Rug Magazine. q. adv.
Meetings/Conferences:
Quarterly Meetings: New York, NY

Oriental Rug Retailers of America (1970)
P.O. Box 1643
Gordonsville, VA 22942-1643
Tel: (540)832-3353   Fax: (540)832-5379
E-Mail: orra@orrainc.com
Web Site: http://www.orrainc.com
Members: 338 individuals
Staff: 4
Annual Budget: $250-500,000
Exec. Director: Frank S. Eways
Administrator: Gay A. Young
Historical Note
Members represents over 500 store locations. Membership: $250/year.
Publications:
Membership Directory.
Newletter. q. adv.
Meetings/Conferences:
Annual Meetings: Summer
1999 – Atlanta, GA(Ritz Carlton)/Jan. 14-17/300

Original Equipment Suppliers Association - MEMA
2950 W. Square Lake Road
Suite 101
Troy, MI 48098-5724
Tel: (248)952-6401   Fax: (248)952-6404
Staff: 2
Managing Director: Neil De KoKoker

Historical Note
A market division of Motor and Equipment Manufacturers Ass'n. Represents manufacturers who specialize in original equipment parts and accessories for motor vehicles.

Ornamental Concrete Producers Ass'n *(1991)*
502 Kay Ave., S.E.
Bemidji, MN   56601-3637
Tel: (218)751-1982   *Fax:* (218)751-2186
E-Mail: delpreus@paulbunyan.net
Web Site: www.ornamentalconcrete.org
Members: 700 individuals
Annual Budget: $250-500,000
Exec. Director: Del R. Preuss

Historical Note
Primarily concerned with Education. Membership: $50/year (individual or company), $100/year (supplier to industry).

Publications:
Ornamental Observer. bi-m. adv.

Meetings/Conferences:
1999 – Tulsa, OK(Adams Mark)
2000 – Pigeon Forge, TN(The Grand)

Orthodox Theological Soc. in America *(1968)*
44 Midland St.
Worcester, MA   01602-2417
Members: 110 individuals
Annual Budget: under $10,000
Treasurer: Rev.Dr. Anthony Nicklas

Historical Note
Members are Orthodox Christian theologians. Has no paid staff. Membership: $30/year.

Publications:
Bulletin. semi-a.
Directory. a.

Meetings/Conferences:
Annual Meetings: Spring Alternate between Hellenic College-Holy Cross Greek Orthodox Seminary in Brookline, MA and St.Vladimir's Orthodox Seminary in Crestwood, NY.

Orthopaedic Research Soc. *(1954)*
6300 N. River Rd., Suite 727
Rosemont, IL   60018-4226
Tel: (847)698-1625   *Fax:* (847)823-0536
E-Mail: ors@aaos.org
Web Site: http://www.ors.org
Members: 1,700 individuals
Staff: 4
Annual Budget: $250-500,000
Exec. Director: Colette Hohimer

Historical Note
An international society of orthopedic researchers. Membership: $220/year.

Publications:
Journal of Orthopaedic Research. q. adv.
Transaction Book of the Annual Meeting. a.

Meetings/Conferences:
Annual Meetings: Winter
1999 – Anaheim, CA/Jan. 31-Feb. 4
2000 – Orlando, FL/March 12-15
2001 – San Francisco, CA/Feb. 25-28
2002 – Dallas, TX/Feb. 10-13

Orthopaedic Section - American Physical Therapy Ass'n *(1974)*
2920 East Ave. South
Suite 200
La Crosse, WI   54601-7202
Tel: (608)788-3982   *Fax:* (608)788-3965
E-Mail: tdeflorian@centuryinter.net
Web Site: http://orthopt.org
Members: 13,000 individuals
Staff: 8
Annual Budget: $1-2,000,000
Exec. Director: Terri A. DeFlorian

Historical Note
Members are orthopaedic physical therapists. Membership: $50/year.

Publications:
Journal of Orthopaedic and Sports Physical Therapy. m.
Orthopaedic Physical Therapy Practice. q.

Orthopaedic Trauma Ass'n
6300 N. River Road, Suite 727
Rosemont, IL   60018-4226
Tel: (847)698-1631   *Fax:* (847)823-0536
Exec. Officer: Nancy Franzon

Orthopedic Surgical Manufacturers Ass'n *(1955)*
1962 Deep Valley Cove
Germantown, TN   38138
Tel: (901)754-8097   *Fax:* (901)754-8097
Members: 24 companies
Staff: 1
Annual Budget: $25-50,000
Exec. Secretary: Robert Games

Historical Note
OSMA member companies are manufacturers and distributors of orthopedic devices, instrumentation and biological materials used to treat orthopedic conditions. Meetings are attended primarily by regulatory affairs professionals to interface with government agencies and professional health associations, develop guidelines and standardize orthopedic device materials and sizes, foster research, and promote ethical conduct in all phases of the surgical supply industry. Membership: $800-$5,000/year, varies by size (corporate).

Orton Dyslexia Soc., The *(1949)*
Historical Note
Became the Internat'l Dyslexia Ass'n in 1997.

Osborne Ass'n *(1932)*
135 East 15th St.
New York, NY   10003
Tel: (212)673-6633   *Fax:* (212)979-7652
E-Mail: egaynes@osborne.ny.org
Staff: 100
Annual Budget: $5-10,000,000
Exec. Director: Elizabeth Gaynes

Historical Note
Formed by merger of the National Society of Penal Information and the Welfare League Association of New York. Named after Thomas Mott Osborne (1859-1926), pioneer prison reformer and founder of the Welfare League Ass'n to assist persons discharged from prison. The Ass'n relies on government funding and private donors for a variety of programs including: El Rio, an intensive all-day treatment program for substance abusers involved with the criminal justice system; LIVING-Well, HIV/AIDS services; social work advocacy programs through which staff work with defendants attorneys to develop non-prison alternatives; job placement; and FamilyWorks, a model parenting program. Has an annual budget of approximately $5.3 million.

Publications:
Newsletter. q.

Meetings/Conferences:
Annual Meetings: July

OsteoArthritis Research Soc. Internat'l *(1990)*
1200 19th St., N.W., Suite 300
Washington, DC   20036-2401
Tel: (202)857-5323   *Fax:* (202)857-1115
E-Mail: oarsi@dc.sba.com
Web Site: http://oarsi.neology.com/oarsi
Members: 350 individuals
Staff: 1
Exec. Director: James Zaniello

Otosclerosis Study Group *(1947)*
Historical Note
Organization defunct in 1995.

Outdoor Advertising Ass'n of America *(1891)*
1850 M St., N.W., Suite 1040
Washington, DC   20036-5803
Tel: (202)833-5566   *Fax:* (202)833-1522
E-Mail: info@oaaa.org
Web Site: http://www.oaaa.org
Members: 600 companies
Staff: 14
Annual Budget: $2-5,000,000
President and C.E.O.: Nancy J. Fletcher
Director, Communications: Sheila Hayes
Director, Regulatory Affairs and Operations: Myron Liable
V.P., Admin./Membership: Sherry Crittenden
Exec. V. President: Ruth L. Segal

Historical Note
OAAA protects and promotes outdoor advertising. Recommends standards for outdoor display structures and disseminates information on the industry. Sponsors and supports the Outdoor Advertising Political Action Committee (OA-PAC).

Publications:
Outlook. m.

Meetings/Conferences:
Biennial meetings: odd years
1999 – San Francisco, CA

Outdoor Amusement Business Ass'n *(1965)*
4600 West 77th St., Suite 270
Minneapolis, MN   55435-4909
Tel: (612)831-4643   *Fax:* (612)831-4642
Toll Free: (800)517 - 6222
E-Mail: oaba@aol.com
Web Site: www.oaba.org
Members: 5,000 companies
Staff: 5
Annual Budget: $500-1,000,000
Exec. Director: Robert W. Johnson

Historical Note
Membership consists of road shows, food and beverage and games suppliers, carnivals and equipment suppliers. Sponsors the OABA Political Action Committee and trade show "Amusement Industry Expo". Membership: $30/year (individual); $1,500/year (organization/company).

Publications:
Newsletter. m. adv.
OABA Annual. a. adv.

Meetings/Conferences:
Semi-Annual Meetings: Tampa, FL/February and Las Vegas, NV/November

Outdoor Power Equipment Aftermarket Ass'n *(1986)*
1726 M St., N.W., Suite 1101
Washington, DC   20036
Tel: (202)775-8605   *Fax:* (202)833-1577
E-Mail: opedd@opedd.org
Members: 75 companies
Staff: 3
Annual Budget: $100-250,000
Exec. V. President: William S. Bergman, CAE
Director, Administration: I. Regina Borkoski

Historical Note
OPEAA is a group of small to medium-sized businessmen dedicated to promoting the use of aftermarket (spare) parts in outdoor power equipment (lawnmowers, chain saws, etc.), as well as to ensuring

an atmosphere of free and unrestrained trade in the industry. Membership: $395(indivdual).

Publications:
Cutting Edge. q. adv.

Meetings/Conferences:
Annual Meetings: February
1999 – Cancun, Mexico(Inter-Continental)/Feb. 13-16/150
2000 – Bermuda

Outdoor Power Equipment Distributors Ass'n *(1980)*
1900 Arch St.
Philadelphia, PA   19103-1499
Tel: (215)564-3484   *Fax:* (215)564-2175
E-Mail: assnhqt@netaxs.com
Members: 150 companies
Staff: 3
Annual Budget: $100-250,000
Exec. Director: Julie S. Thane

Historical Note
OPEDA members are distributors of outdoor power equipment to retailers with a minimum of $1 million gross sales. Associate membership is available for suppliers and finance companies associated with the industry.

Publications:
Membership Directory. a.
OPEDA Outlook. q.

Meetings/Conferences:
Annual Meetings: February

Outdoor Power Equipment Institute *(1952)*
341 South Patrick St.
Alexandria, VA   22314
Tel: (703)549-7600   *Fax:* (703)549-7604
E-Mail: opeimow@aol.com
Web Site: http://opei.mow.org
Members: 83 companies
Staff: 8
Annual Budget: $2-5,000,000
President and C.E.O.: Dennis C. Dix, CAE
Director, Public Relations: Peggy A. Douglas
Director, Finance and Administration: Jean Hawes

Historical Note
Established as the Lawn Mower Institute, OPEI assumed its present name in 1960. Members are manufacturers of all types of mechanized lawn and garden equipment and industry suppliers of major components.

Publications:
Executive Update. m.

Meetings/Conferences:
Annual Meetings: June
1999 – Amelia Island, FL(Ritz-Carlton)/June 24-27/180
2000 – Napa, CA(Silverado)/June 22-25/180

Outdoor Writers Ass'n of America *(1927)*
2155 E. College Ave.
State College, PA   16801-7204
Tel: (814)234-1011   *Fax:* (814)234-9692
E-Mail: eking40waa@compuserve.com
Members: 1,980 individuals, 420 organizations
Staff: 3
Annual Budget: $100-250,000
Exec. Director: Steve Wagner
Meeting Planner: Eileen N. King

Historical Note
OWAA was formed at a meeting April 9, 1927 in Chicago by a group of writers attending an Izaak Walton League of America convention. Members are broadcasters, writers and editors, authors, photographers and artists who communicate about outdoor recreation and related topics. Sponsors the North American Outdoor Film/Video Awards annually. Membership: $100/year (individual); $300/year (organization).

Publications:
Outdoors Unlimited. m.

Meetings/Conferences:
Annual Meetings: June
1999 – Sioux Falls, SD/June 20-24/900
2000 – Greensboro, NC(Holiday Inn)/June 23-26

Outpatient Intravenous Infusion Therapy Ass'n *(1992)*
240 Stadium Way South
Tacoma, WA   98402
Tel: (253)627-1850   *Fax:* (253)274-0877
Web Site: http://www.optivita.com
Staff: 1
Exec. Director: Alan Tice

Outpatient Ophthalmic Surgery Soc. *(1981)*
P.O. Box 23220
San Diego, CA   92193
Tel: (619)692-4426
E-Mail: ooss@ama.inc.com
Web Site: http://www.ama.inc.com
Members: 560 individuals
Staff: 3
Exec. Director: Karen Morgan

Historical Note
OOSS members are ophthalmic surgeons.

Publications:
Journal. a.
Newsletter. q.

Meetings/Conferences:

Overseas Automotive Council *(1923)*
Historical Note
Name changed to Overseas Automotive Council, Internat'l Aftermarket Division - Motor Equipment Manufacturers Ass'n in 1996.

Overseas Automotive Council, Internat'l Aftermarket Division - Motor and Equipment Manufacturers Ass'n *(1923)*
P.O. Box 13966
Research Triangle Pk, NC   27709-3966
Tel: (919)406-8810   *Fax:* (919)549-4824
E-Mail: aac@mema.org
Members: 700 individuals
Staff: 2
Annual Budget: $100-250,000
Exec. Secretary: Anthony Cardez

Historical Note
Formerly the Overseas Automotive Club (1996). An international organization whose membership is about half from the United States and half from overseas. Members export U.S. automotive parts, chemicals, tools, accessories and other automotive products. Internat'l members are importers of these products into their countries. Membership: $300/year (domestic); $150/year (international).

Publications:
OAC Roster. a.
OAC Update Newsletter. m.
Personal Insight. m.

Meetings/Conferences:
1999 – Miami, FL/100

Overseas Education Ass'n *(1956)*

Historical Note
Name changed to Federal Education Ass'n in 1996.

Overseas Press Club of America *(1939)*
320 East 42nd St., Mezzanine
New York, NY   10017
Tel: (212)983-4655   *Fax:* (212)983-4692
Members: 500 individuals
Staff: 2
Exec. Director: Sonya K. Fry

Historical Note
Members are professional journalists. Membership: $300/year (resident members); $100/year (non-resident members).

Publications:
Dateline. a. adv.
Overseas Press Club Bulletin. m. adv.

Meetings/Conferences:
Annual Meetings: Awards Dinner in April (NYC)

Overseas Sales and Marketing Ass'n of America *(1964)*
1020 W. 31st Street
P.O. Box 1590
Downers Grove, IL   60515-0790
Tel: (630)963-7800   *Fax:* (630)963-7123
E-Mail: Engreqmt@aol.com
Members: 30 individuals, 30 companies
Staff: 2
Annual Budget: under $10,000
President: Frank Cullen

Historical Note
Members are export management and trading companies. Has no office or paid staff. Correspondence is handled by ITA–International Trade Ass'n of Greater Chicago, whose members can become members of OSMA if they qualify as independent exporters on a complimentary basis. Membership: $30/year.

Publications:
Directory. bien.

Meetings/Conferences:
Annual Meetings: Chicago Suburbs

Owner Operators of America *(1982)*
P.O. Box 582
Orchard Park, NY   14127-0582
Tel: (716)662-0597
Members: 250 individuals
Staff: 1
Annual Budget: $50-100,000
Exec. Secretary: Chuck DeVaul

Historical Note
Provides business and legislative information to self-employed truckers; represents self-employed truckers on Capitol Hill; Discounts on services and supplies for self-employed members.

Publications:
Owner Operators News. q.

Meetings/Conferences:
Annual Meetings: Not held.

Owner-Operator Independent Drivers Ass'n *(1973)*
311 R.D. Mize Rd.
Grain Valley, MO   64029
Iel: (816)229-5791   *Fax:* (816)229-0518
Toll Free: (800)444 – 5791
E-Mail: ooida@Aol.com
Web Site: www.ooida.com
Members: 39,000 individuals
Staff: 107
Annual Budget: $2-5,000,000
President: James J. Johnston
Executive V. President: Todd Spencer
Communications Director: Rick Craig

Historical Note
Membership: $45/yr. (driver), $45/yr. plus $10/truck (owner/operator). A national association lobbying on behalf of the interests of small business truckers.

Publications:
Land*Line Magazine. bi-m. adv.
OOIDA News Update. q.

Meetings/Conferences:
Annual Meetings: Open Board of Directors Meeting

Oxygen Soc., The *(1988)*
74 New Montgomery, Suite 230
San Francisco, CA   94105
Tel: (415)546-3124   *Fax:* (415)764-4915
E-Mail: 105472.24@compuserve.comm
Web Site: http://www.biophysics.mcw.edu/oxsoc/
Members: 1000 individuals
Staff: 2
Annual Budget: $250-500,000
Exec. Director: Kent A. Lindeman, CMP
Administrative Manager: Justine Abel

Historical Note
The Oxygen Soc. promotes interaction between the various disciplines involved in oxygen related research. Membership: $125/year (individual); $85/year (postdoctorial); $20/year (student).

Publications:
Free Radical Biology & Medicine. m. adv.

Meetings/Conferences:
1999 – New Orleans, LA(Marriott)/Nov. 18-22
2000 – San Diego, CA(Paradise Point Resort)/Nov. 16-20

Oxygenated Fuels Ass'n *(1983)*
1300 17th St. North, Suite 1850
Arlington, VA   22209-3801
Tel: (703)841-7100   *Fax:* (703)841-7720
E-Mail: twiggs@bellatlantic.com
Web Site: http://www.ofa.net
Members: 12 companies
Staff: 6
Annual Budget: $2-5,000,000
Exec. Director: Ms. Terry Wigglesworth
Dir., Communications: Eric Bolton
Director, Government Affairs: Charles Drevna
Health Sciences Director: John Kneiss
Dir., Administration: Julia Conroy

Historical Note
Members are producers and marketers of oxygenated fuel additives, typically used in motor fuels for emissions abatement.

Publications:
OFA News. bi-w.

Meetings/Conferences:
Annual Meetings: November

Package Design Council Int'l *(1952)*
481 Carlisle Drive
Herndon, VA   20170
Tel: (703)318-7225   *Fax:* (703)318-0310
Members: 250 individuals
Staff: 1
Annual Budget: $50-100,000
Exec. Director: William C. Pflaum

Historical Note
Formerly (1987) the Package Designers Council. A non-profit membership association of design and marketing specialists engaged in package design and brand identity development and management. Represents members in the U.S. and abroad.

Publications:
Forum. q.
Update. m.

Meetings/Conferences:
Annual Meetings: Fall/125

Packaged Ice Ass'n *(1917)*
P.O. Box 1199
Tampa, FL   33601-1199
Tel: (813)258-1690   *Fax:* (813)251-2783
Web Site: http://www.packagedice.com
Members: 150 companies
Staff: 5
Annual Budget: $250-500,000
Exec. Director: Jane W. McEwen

Historical Note
Manufacturers and distributors of ice and their suppliers. Founded as the Nat'l Ass'n of Ice Industries, it became the Nat'l Ice Ass'n in 1958 and assumed its present name in December, 1980.

Publications:
Ice News. bi-m. adv.
Membership Directory. a. adv.

Meetings/Conferences:
Annual Meetings: Fall
1999 – Orlando, FL(Coronado Springs)/Nov. 10-13
2000 – Scottsdale, AZ(Princess)/Nov. 27-Dec. 1

Packaging Machinery Manufacturers Institute *(1932)*
4350 N. Fairfax Drive, Suite 600
Arlington, VA   22203
Tel: (703)243-8555   *Fax:* (703)243-8556
Web Site: http://www.packexpo.com
Members: 400 individuals
Staff: 21
Annual Budget: $2-5,000,000
President: Charles D. Yuska
Director, Communications: Matt Croson
Exposition Director: Bonnie Kilduff
Director, Meetings: Patricia Fee
Director, Education: Debra Rapone
Director, Technical Services: Timothy O'Rourke
Director, Finance and Administration: Craig Silverio
General Counsel: Hugh Webster
V. President, Member Services: Jerry Welcome

Historical Note
PMMI members are manufacturers of packaging and packaging-related converting equipment. Owns and manages PACK EXPO and PACKEXPO West, expositions of packaging machinery and materials. Membership: $1,000/year (company).

Publications:
Packaging Machinery Directory. bi-a.

PMMI Reports Newsletter. m.

Meetings/Conferences:
Semi-Annual Meetings: Spring and Fall
1999 – Las Vegas, NV/Oct. 18-20

Paint and Decorating Retailers Ass'n *(1947)*
403 Axminster Drive
St. Louis, MO   63026-2941
Tel: (314)326-2636   *Fax:* (314)326-1823
E-Mail: info@pdra.org
Web Site: http://www.pdra.org
Members: 3,500 individuals, 6,500 companies
Staff: 20
Annual Budget: $10-25,000,000
Exec. V. President: Ernest W. Stewart
Education, Membership: Margi Barnes
V. President, Sales: Nicholas R. Cichielo

Historical Note
Formerly Retail Paint & Wallpaper Distributors of America, (1972) Paint and Wallpaper Ass'n of America, and (1996) Nat'l Decorating Products Ass'n. Members are independent dealers and interior designers selling decorating products. Has an annual budget of approximately $10 million. Membership: $125/year (company).

Publications:
Paint & Decorating Retailer Gold Book directory. a. adv.
Paint & Decorating Retailer Magazine. m. adv.
Paint & Decorating Retailer's Registry directory. a.

Meetings/Conferences:
1999 – Chicago, IL(Lakeside Center)/Nov. 20-21

Paint, Body and Equipment Ass'n *(1975)*
9600 Delmar
Overland Park, KS   66207
Tel: (913)383-1713   *Fax:* (913)383-9299
E-Mail: sainte@kcnet.com
Web Site: http://www.pbea.org
Members: 250 companies
Staff: 2
Annual Budget: $100-250,000
Exec. Director: Barbara St. Aubin

Historical Note
Represents distributors, manufacturers, reps and jobbers of automotive paint and other repair products through its PBEA Councils, which include Autobody Representatives Council. Membership fee varies, based on type of company, $250-600/year.

Publications:
Membership Directory. a. adv.
PBEA Extra. 6/year.

Meetings/Conferences:
1999 – Dallas, TX(Westin Galleria)/Sept. 23-28/225

Painting and Decorating Contractors of America *(1884)*
3913 Old Lee Hwy., Suite 33B
Fairfax, VA   22030
Tel: (703)359-0826   *Fax:* (703)359-2576
Toll Free: (800)332 – 7322
Web Site: http://www.pdca.com
Members: 3,000 individuals
Staff: 12
Annual Budget: $1-2,000,000
Exec. V. President: Gene S. Bartlow, CAE
Director of Government Affairs: Marc D. Freedman
Director, Meetings & Expositions: Mary De Persig
Director of Education and Certification: Jerry Howell
Director, Membership and Development: Anita R. Dallas

Historical Note
PDCA is the trade association of the coatings applications industry. Members are professional painting and decorating contractors. Membership: $235-500/year, varies by sales volume; plus council and chapter dues.

Publications:
Membership Directory. a. adv.
Painting and Wallcovering Contractor Magazine. bi-m. adv.
PDCA Briefer Newsletter. m.

Meetings/Conferences:
Annual Meetings: March
1999 – Reno, NV(Nugget)/March 17-20
2000 – Tampa, FL/March 15-18/2000
2001 – Honolulu, HI

Paleontological Research Institution *(1932)*
1259 Trumansburg Road
Ithaca, NY   14850
Tel: (607)273-6623   *Fax:* (607)273-6620
Web Site: http://www.englib.cornell.edu/PRI
Members: 1,100 individuals
Staff: 9
Annual Budget: $250-500,000
Director: Dr. Warren D. Allmon

Historical Note
Founded in Ithaca in 1932 and incorporated in New York in 1933. Affiliated with the American Ass'n for the Advancement of Science and the Ass'n of Systematics Collections.

Publications:
Bulletins of American Paleontology. 2-5/year.
Paleontographica Americana. irreg.

Meetings/Conferences:
Annual Meetings: Always Ithaca, NY/May

Paleontological Soc. *(1908)*
Box 28200-16
Lakewood, CO   80228-3108
Tel: (303)987-9293
E-Mail: twhenry@usa.net
Web Site: http://www.uic.edu/orgs/paleo/homepage.html
Members: 1,700 individuals
Staff: 1

Annual Budget: $250-500,000
Secretary: Thomas W. Henry

Historical Note
Affiliated with the Geological Society of America. The Secretary also maintains an E-Mail address: twhenry@greenwood.cr.usgs.gov. Membership: $59/year.

Publications:
Journal of Paleontology. bi-m.
Memoirs of The Paleontological Society. irreg.
Paleobiology. q.
Papers and Palentology. irreg.
Priscum. semi-a.
Short Course Notes. a.

Meetings/Conferences:
Annual Meetings: Fall, with the Geological Soc. of America.

Palmeto Baptist Medical Center *(1975)*
c/o Baptist Health Care System of S.C.
Tyler @ Marion Sts.
Columbia, SC   29220
Tel: (803)771-5046
Web Site: palmettobaptist.org
Members: 75 hospitals
Annual Budget: under $10,000
Administrator: Charles Beaman, Jr.

Historical Note
Fomerly (1998) Baptist Hospital Association. A very loosely structured grouping of Baptist hospitals and medical centers.

Palomino Horse Ass'n *(1936)*
Box 24, Star Route
Dornside, PA   17823
Tel: (717)758-3067
Members: 400 individuals
Staff: 2
Annual Budget: under $10,000
President: Steven D. Rebuck

Historical Note
PHA is the original registry for the Palomino horse. Members are owners and breeders of Palomino horses. Membership: $15/year (individual).

Publications:
Palomino Parade. m. adv.

Meetings/Conferences:

Palomino Horse Breeders of America *(1941)*
15253 E. Skelly Dr.
Tulsa, OK   74116-2637
Tel: (918)438-1234   *Fax:* (918)438-1232
E-Mail: yellahrses@aol.com
Web Site: http://www.palominohba.com
Members: 12,011 individuals
Staff: 7
General Manager: Cindy Chilton

Historical Note
Members are owners and breeders of Palomino horses. Maintains a registry as well as show records. Membership: $40/year.

Publications:
Palomino Horses. m. adv.

Meetings/Conferences:
Semi-Annual Meetings: June at varying locations & July in Tulsa, OK

Panelized Building Systems Council *(1942)*
Historical Note
A division of the Building Systems Councils of the Nat'l Ass'n of Home Builders.

Paper and Plastic Representatives Management Council *(1995)*
7208 Forestburg Dr.
Arlington, TX   76001-4841
Tel: (817)561-7272   *Fax:* (817)561-7275
E-Mail: assnhqtrs@aol.com
Web Site: www.pprmc.com
Members: 20 individuals
Staff: 2
Annual Budget: $25-50,000
Exec. Director: William R. Bess

Historical Note
Membership: $1,800/year.

Paper Bag Institute *(1935)*
Historical Note
Organization is defunct in 1996.

Paper Distribution Council *(1958)*
c/o Nat'l Paper Trade Ass'n
111 great Neck Road
Great Neck, NY   11021
Tel: (516)829-3070   *Fax:* (516)829-3074
Web Site: http://www.papertrade.com
Members: 40 companies
Staff: 1
Annual Budget: under $10,000
Secretary: John J. Buckley

Historical Note
Members are manufacturers and distributors concerned with the problems of wholesale paper distribution. Affiliated with the American Paper Institute and the Nat'l Paper Trade Ass'n, which provides administrative support.

Meetings/Conferences:
1999 – Captiva Island, FL(Southseas Plantation)/Jan. 20-22

Paper Industry Management Ass'n *(1919)*
1699 Wall St., Suite 212
Mount Prospect, IL   60056
Tel: (847)956-0250   *Fax:* (847)956-0520

E-Mail: pimastaf@wwa.com
Web Site: http://www.pima-online.org
Members: 5,000 individuals
Staff: 14
Annual Budget: $2-5,000,000
Exec. V. President/C.O.O.: Scott A. Baumruck
Director, Communications: Alan Rooks
Manager, Conferences and Education Services: Barbara S. Schell, CAE
Director, Finance/Administration: Ronald J. Bordui
Mgr., Marketing/Membership: Bill Gentes

Historical Note
Founded as the American Pulp and Paper Mill Superintendents Ass'n, it assumed its present name in 1959. PIMA provides networking and education opportunities to its members, who are typically managers in paper mills.

Publications:
PIMA Membership Directory. a. adv.
PIMA's Papermaker. m. adv.

Meetings/Conferences:
Annual Meetings: June
1999 – Arlington, VA(Marriott Crystal Gateway)/June 23-25
2000 – San Diego, CA(Sheraton Hotel & Marina)/June 14-16
2001 – Baltimore, MD(Renaissance Harborplace)/June 27-29

Paper Machine Clothing Council *(1924)*
c/o Conlon, Frantz
1818 N St., N.W., Suite 700
Washington, DC   20036
Tel: (202)331-7050
Members: 7 companies
Staff: 2
Annual Budget: $50-100,000
Secretary-Treasurer/General Counsel: David Frantz
Exec. V. President: Walter L. Frankland, Jr.

Historical Note
Formerly Paper Mill Fourdrinier Wire Cloth Manufacturers Ass'n (1965) and Fourdrinier Wire Council (1996). Fourdrinier machines manufacture paper through a process requiring machine clothing, which is manufactured by members PMCC.

Publications:
None.

Meetings/Conferences:
Annual Meetings: None held.

Paper Shipping Sack Manufacturers Ass'n *(1933)*
505 White Plains Road, Suite 206
Tarrytown, NY   10591-5108
Tel: (914)631-0909   *Fax:* (914)631-0333
Members: 45 companies
Staff: 2
Annual Budget: $250-500,000
President: Brent C. Dixon

Publications:
Industry Reference Guide. irreg.

Meetings/Conferences:
Annual Meetings: October

Paperboard Packaging Council *(1967)*
201 N. Union St., Suite 220
Alexandria, VA   22314-2642
Tel: (703)836-3300   *Fax:* (703)836-3290
E-Mail: ppcmail@erols.com
Web Site: http://www.ppcnet.org
Members: 50 companies
Staff: 8
Annual Budget: $2-5,000,000
President: Marla Donahue
Director, Marketing and Communications: Mark Serepca
Director, Public Affairs: Peter Eberle
Director, Meetings/Membership Services: Rochelle A. Nezin
Director, Industry Information: Liz Hill

Historical Note
Formed by a merger of the Folding Paper Box Association of America (founded in 1929) and the Institute for Better Packaging (founded in 1929). Members are companies making folding cartons. Provides a range of publications and instructional materials on aspects of the paper industry, recycling, and other pertinent issues. Membership fee varies, based on annual sales.

Publications:
Business Activity Report. q.
Directory of Members. a.
PPC Today. bi-m.
The Trendicator. irreg.

Meetings/Conferences:
Semi-Annual Meetings: Spring and Fall

Parapsychological Ass'n *(1957)*
Rhine Research Center
402 N. Buchanan Blvd.
Durham, NC   27701-0700
Tel: (919)688-8241   *Fax:* (919)683-4338
Web Site: http://www.rhine.org
Members: 350 individuals
Staff: 1
Annual Budget: $10-25,000
Contact: Barbara Gruber

Historical Note
Membership open to persons doing research or scholarly work of publishable quality in the field, also professionals and students in other academic disciplines with a serious interest in this field. Affiliated with the American Ass'n for the Advancement of Science, PA strives to promote and advance rigorous scientific inquiry into anomalous areas of human communication processes, disseminate such information to the wider scientific community, and integrate this information with findings from other scientific disciplines. Membership: $55/year.

Publications:
PSI News. q.

Research in Parapsychology. a.

Meetings/Conferences:
Annual Meetings: August
1999 – San Francisco, CA
2000 – Freiburg, Germany

Parcel Shippers Ass'n *(1953)*
1211 Connecticut Ave., N.W., Suite 610
Washington, DC   20036-2701
Tel: (202)296-3690   *Fax:* (202)296-0343
Web Site: http://www.parcelshippers.org
Members: 200 companies
Staff: 2
Annual Budget: $100-250,000
Exec. V. President: James V. Jellison
Administration: Helen J. Piatt

Historical Note
Formerly (1977) the Parcel Post Ass'n. Sponsors and supports the Parcel Shippers Association Political Action Committee.

Publications:
Newsletter. m.

Meetings/Conferences:
Annual Meetings: Spring and Biennial Operations Workshop

Parenteral Drug Ass'n *(1946)*
7500 Old Georgetown Road, Suite 620
Bethesda, MD   20814-6133
Tel: (301)986-0293   *Fax:* (301)986-0296
E-Mail: info@pda.org
Web Site: http://www.pda.org
Members: 9,100 individuals, 250 corporations
Staff: 21
Annual Budget: $2-5,000,000
President: Edmund M. Fry
Director, Marketing and Member Services: Margaret A. Wanca
V. President, Regulatory & External Affairs: James C. Lyda
Program Director: Angie Fischer
Director, Finance/Admin.: Kenneth R. Dickerson
V. President, Scientific Affairs: Russell Madsen

Historical Note
Members are makers of parenteral (injectable) drugs and other pharmaceuticals, as well as suppliers, academia, regulatory and compendial bodies, and other interested parties. Membership: $150/year (individual)

Publications:
Journal of Pharmaceutical Science and Technology. bi-m. adv.
PDA Letter. m. adv.

Meetings/Conferences:
1999 – Washington, DC(Marriott Wardman Park)/Nov. 29-Dec. 3

Parenting Publications of America *(1988)*
1846 Lockhill-Selma Road, Suite 102
San Antonio, TX   78213-1551
Tel: (210)348-8396   *Fax:* (210)348-8397
E-Mail: parpubs@family.com
Members: 155 publishers
Staff: 1
Annual Budget: $100-250,000
Exec. Director: Kathy H. Mittler

Historical Note
PPA members are regional free controlled-circulation periodicals,published monthly or bi-monthly that serve as resource guides for parents and children and provide information on trends and issues relevant to contemporary parenting. Member publications have a combined circulation of over 6.7 million. Membership: $550/year (initial); varies based on total revenues (renewal).

Publications:
PPA Directory. a.
PPA Newsletter. m. adv.

Meetings/Conferences:
Annual Meetings: late January-early February
1999 – San Diego, CA(Westin Horton Plaza)

Parliamentary Associates *(1990)*
P.O. Box 1102
Independence, MO   64051-0602
Tel: (816)461-4435   *Fax:* (816)461-4435
Toll Free: (800)572 - 8328
Web Site: http://www.parliassoc.com
Members: 40 individuals
Staff: 2
Annual Budget: $10-25,000
Headquarters Director: Lorraine Buckley

Historical Note
Members are accredited professional parliamentarians.

Meetings/Conferences:
1999 – Independence, MO/Jan. 29-Feb. 1

Parole and Probation Compact Administrators Ass'n *(1946)*
Historical Note
Formerly the Ass'n of Administrators of the Interstate Compact for the Supervision of Parolees and Probationers, PPCAA members are officials responsible for the administration of the compact which allows parolees and proationers to transfer supervision to another state. Affiliated with the American Probation and Parole Ass'n and the American Correctional Ass'n.

Parthenais Cattle Breeders of America
Historical Note
Address unknown in 1998.

Paso Fino Horse Ass'n *(1972)*
101 N. Collins St.
Plant City, FL   33566-3311
Tel: (813)719-7777   *Fax:* (813)719-7872

Web Site: http://www.pasofino.org
Members: 6,946 individuals
Staff: 11
Annual Budget: $1-2,000,000
Exec. Director: C.J. Marcello, Jr.
Show Manager: Karen Dennis

Historical Note
Formerly (1986) Paso Fino Owners and Breeders Ass'n. Members are owners and breeders of Paso Fino horses. Incorporated in Tennessee. Membership fee varies.

Publications:
Paso Fino Horse World. m. adv.

Meetings/Conferences:
Annual Meetings: Winter/200
1999 – Las Vegas, NV

Passenger Vessel Ass'n *(1971)*
1600 Wilson Blvd., Suite 1000-A
Arlington, VA   22209
Tel: (703)807-0100   *Fax:* (703)807-0103
Web Site: www.passangervessel.com
Members: 4 individuals, 500 companies
Staff: 4
Annual Budget: $500-1,000,000
Exec. Director: John Groundwater
Director, Membership: Jennifer Williams

Historical Note
Formerly (1993) the Nat'l Ass'n of Passenger Vessel Owners. PVA represents operators of tours, excursions, ferries, charter vessels, dinner boats, and other small passenger vessels.

Publications:
Foghorn Newsletter. m. adv.
Passenger Vessel Directory. a.

Meetings/Conferences:
Annual Meetings: January
1999 – Long Beach, CA(Long Beach Convention Center)/Feb. 20-23

Passive Solar Industries Council *(1980)*
1331 H St., N.W., Suite 1000
Washington, DC   20005
Tel: (202)628-7400   *Fax:* (202)393-5043
E-Mail: psicouncil@aol.com
Web Site: www.psic.org
Members: 70 companies
Staff: 8
Annual Budget: $100-250,000
Exec. Director: Helen English

Historical Note
Founded in 1980, PSIC formed by the leading organizations in the building industry. Membership is comprised mainly of trade associations, manufacturers and suppliers interested in the construction of buildings that, by their design, use and store solar energy. Membership: $100/year (individual); $350/year (small business); $750/year (regular).

Publications:
Buildings Inside and Out. semi-a.

Meetings/Conferences:
Semi-annual: Spring and Fall in Washington, DC/25-50
1999 – Washington, DC

Passive Solar Products Ass'n *(1979)*
Historical Note
A division of the Industrial Fabrics Association International. Members are makers of screens, awnings, movable insulation, window glazings and thermal storage units.

Patent and Trademark Office Soc. *(1917)*
P.O. Box 2089, Eads Station
Arlington, VA   22202-0089
Tel: (703)306-4115
Members: 1,800 individuals
Staff: 8
Annual Budget: $100-250,000
Administrator, Communications: Judy Swann

Historical Note
Formerly (1986) Patent Office Soc. Members are past and present examiners in the U.S. Patent and Trademark Office, together with registered patent attorneys and agents, trademark practitioners, patent practitioners for federal agencies, judges and other patent professionals. Membership: $39/year.

Publications:
Journal of Patent and Trademark Office Society. m. adv.

Meetings/Conferences:
Annual Meetings: February in Arlington, VA(Marriott-Crystal City)

Patent Office Professional Ass'n *(1962)*
Box 15848
Arlington, VA   22215
Tel: (703)308-0818   *Fax:* (703)308-0818
Members: 2,800 individuals
Staff: 7
Annual Budget: $100-250,000
President: Ronald J. Stern

Historical Note
Independent labor union representing all non-managerial professionals (other than trademark professionals) in the U.S. Patent and Trademark Office. Affiliated with Public Employees Roundtable, Federal Employees Coordinating Committee and Fund for Assuming an Independent Retirement Membership: $104/year.

Publications:
POPA Newsletter. m.

Meetings/Conferences:
Annual Meetings: First Thursday in December near Washington, DC

Pattern Recognition Soc. *(1966)*

Georgetown Univ. Medical Center
3900 Reservoir Road, N.W., Rm. LR-3
Washington, DC   20007
Tel: (202)687-2121   *Fax:* (202)687-1662
Web Site: www.nvrf.georgetown.edu/pir
Members: 300 individuals
Staff: 2
Annual Budget: $10-25,000
Exec. Director: Dr. Robert S. Ledley

Historical Note
Members are scientists and engineers interested and working in the field of pattern recognition in the broad sense. Membership: $75/year.

Publications:
Pattern Recognition. m.

Meetings/Conferences:
Annual Meetings: Not held

Pattern, Model and Plastic Toolbuilders Ass'n *(1962)*
328 S. East St.
Galion, OH   44833
Tel: (419)468-1761   *Fax:* (419)468-3989
Nat'l Coordinator: Terry Williams

Historical Note
Organization reported defunct in 1994.

PCPCI - The Transformer Ass'n *(1974)*
P.O. Box 378
4 Hollis St.
Sherborn, MA   01770-0378
Tel: (508)655-4409   *Fax:* (508)651-3920
Members: 50 companies
Staff: 2
Annual Budget: $50-100,000
Exec. Director: Elizabeth Bevington-Chambers
Operations Director: W.H. Chambers

Historical Note
Formerly (1994) Power Conversion Products Council, Internat'l. Members are manufacturers and suppliers to the wall plug-in transformer/transformer charger/converter industry.

Publications:
Directory.

Meetings/Conferences:
1999 – Dallas, TX(Hampton Inn)/March 11-12

Peanut and Tree Nut Processors Ass'n *(1969)*
P.O. Box 59811
Potomac, MD   20859-9811
Tel: (301)365-2521   *Fax:* (301)365-7705
Members: 156 companies
Staff: 3
Annual Budget: $100-250,000
Exec. V. President: Russell E. Barker

Historical Note
Formed by a merger of The Peanut Butter Manufacturers Ass'n (1939) and The Peanut and Nut Salters Ass'n (1941). Absorbed the Peanut Butter Sandwich and Cookie Manufacturers Ass'n. Formerly (1978) Peanut Butter Manufacturers and Nut Salters Ass'n, and (1995) Peanut Butter and Nut Processors Ass'n. Sponsors and supports the Peanut Butter and Nut Processors Association Political Action Committee.

Meetings/Conferences:
Annual Meetings: January

Peanut Butter and Nut Processors Ass'n
Historical Note
Became (1995) Peanut and Tree Nut Processors Ass'n.

Pecan Marketing Board *(1979)*
Historical Note
Address unknown in 1996.

Pediatric Orthopedic Soc. of North America *(1982)*
6300 N. River Road, Suite 727
Rosemont, IL   60018-4226
Tel: (847)698-1692   *Fax:* (847)823-0536
Members: 669 individuals
Staff: 2
Annual Budget: $250-500,000
Executive Director: Sharon T. Goldberg
Assistant: Teri Stech

Historical Note
Formerly (1985) the Soc. of Pediatric Orthopedics. POSNA members are pediatric orthopedic surgeons who support the highest quality of education to assure the best possile care of children with musculoskeletal disorders. Membership: $250/year (individual).

Publications:
Abstracts of Annual Meeting.
Membership Directory. a.
Newsletter. q.

Meetings/Conferences:
1999 – Orlando, FL(Buena Vista Palace)/May 17-19
2000 – Vancouver, BC(Hotel Vancouver)/May 2-4
2001 – Cancun, Mexico

Pedorthic Footwear Ass'n *(1958)*
9861 Broken Land Pkwy., Suite 255
Columbia, MD   21046-1151
Tel: (410)381-7278   *Fax:* (410)381-1167
Toll Free: (800)673 - 8447
Members: 1,400 individuals, 1,400 companies and individuals
Staff: 9
Annual Budget: $1-2,000,000
Exec. Director: William Boettge
Director, Government Relations: Janis Gregory
Director, Education: Carole Miller
Deputy Exec. Director, Membership and Editor: Cynthia Mullaly
Director, MIS: Dawn Jones

Historical Note
PFA is the membership organization for people engaged in pedorthics: the design, manufacture, modification and fit of footwear, including foot orthoses, to alleviate foot problems caused by disease, overuse or injury. Members include individuals and companies. PFA provides educational programs, publications, legislative monitoring, marketing materials, professional liaison and business operations services to members. Membership: $225/year (individual); $595/year (company).

Publications:
Current Pedorthic.

Meetings/Conferences:
Annual Meetings: Late Fall/400
1999 – New Orleans, LA
2000 – San Diego, CA

Pellet Fuels Institute *(1982)*
1601 N. Kent St., Suite 1001
Arlington, VA   22209-2105
Tel: (703)522-6778   *Fax:* (703)522-0548
Members: 100 companies
Staff: 2
Annual Budget: $1-2,000,000
Technical Director: Michael Van Buren

Historical Note
Formerly Fiber Fuels Institute, Institute members are maufacturers of pellet and briquette fuel, suppliers and others with an interest in the industry. Membership: $200/year (individual); $500-$4,500/year (organization/company).

Publications:
PFI Newsletter. bi-m. adv.

Meetings/Conferences:

Pencil Makers Ass'n *(1918)*
Historical Note
Became inactive in 1994 and later merged with Writing Instrument Manufacturers Ass'n.

Pennsylvania Grade Crude Oil Ass'n *(1923)*
Historical Note
Defunct in 1996.

Pension Real Estate Ass'n *(1979)*
95 Glastonbury Blvd.
Glastonbury, CT   06033
Tel: (860)657-2612   *Fax:* (860)659-4784
E-Mail: ghaynes@prea.org
Web Site: http://www.prea.org
Members: 1,060 firms and organizations
Staff: 8
Annual Budget: $1-2,000,000
President: Gail C. Haynes

Historical Note
Industry trade association whose members share a interest in investment practices for pension funds (public, private and Taft-Hartley) participating in real estate capital markets. Membership open to qualified pension funds, plan sponsors, asset managers and other supportive firms. Represents the industry before Congress and the Executive branch. Membership: fee varies.

Publications:
Membership Directory. a.
PREA Magazine. q.
Research Review. semi-a.

Meetings/Conferences:
Semi-Annual: Conferences

Percheron Horse Ass'n of America *(1876)*
10330 Quaker Road
Fredericktown, OH   43019
Tel: (614)694-3602
Members: 900 individuals
Staff: 3
Annual Budget: $50-100,000
Secretary-Treasurer: Alex T. Christian

Historical Note
Formerly Percheron Soc. of America, it assumed its present name in 1934. Members are owners and breeders of Percheron horses. Membership: $20/yr.

Publications:
Percheron News. q. adv.

Meetings/Conferences:
Annual Meetings: First Saturday in November

Percussive Arts Soc. *(1961)*
701 N.W. Ferris Ave.
Lawton, OK   73507
Tel: (580)353-1455   *Fax:* (580)353-1456
E-Mail: percarts@pas.org
Web Site: http://www.pas.org
Members: 6,000 individuals
Staff: 7
Annual Budget: $250-500,000
Exec. Director: Randall A. Eyles, Ph.D.
Manager, Publications/Marketing: Teresa Peterson

Historical Note
Members are teachers and performers on drums and other percussion instruments. Membership: $55/year (professional); $35/year (student/senior citizen).

Publications:
Percussion News. bi-m.
Percussive Notes. bi-m.

Meetings/Conferences:
Annual Meetings: Fall
1999 – Columbus, OH(Convention Center)/Oct. 26-31

Perennial Plant Ass'n *(1983)*
3383 Schirtzinger Rd.
Hilliard, OH   43026

Tel: (614)771-8431
E-Mail: ppa@perennialplant.org
Web Site: http://www.perennialplant.org
Members: 2,000 firms and individuals
Staff: 1
Annual Budget: $100-250,000
Exec. Secretary: Steven M. Still, Ph.D.

Historical Note
Voting membership in PPA is open to firms or individuals who are actively engaged in the growing, landscape planting, landscape designing or merchandising of perennials. Membership: Based upon gross volume of business in perennials.

Publications:
Newsletter. q. adv.
Proceedings of Herbaceous Perennial Plant Symposium. a. adv.

Meetings/Conferences:
Annual Meetings: August
1999 – Lansing, MI/July 26-31

Performance Warehouse Ass'n (1971)
21311 Hawthorne Blvd., Suite 103
Torrance, CA   90503-5610
Tel: (310)543-1523   Fax: (310)543-9623
Members: 650 individuals
Staff: 3
Annual Budget: $250-500,000
Exec. Director: John M. Towle

Historical Note
PWA members are distributors of specialty automotive parts and suppliers.

Publications:
PWA Membership Directory. a.
PWA Newsletter. q. adv.

Meetings/Conferences:
1999 – Arizona

Periodical and Book Ass'n of America (1965)
475 Park Ave. South, Suite 8484
New York, NY   10016
Tel: (212)689-4952   Fax: (212)545-8328
Members: 80 individuals
Staff: 1
Annual Budget: $100-250,000
Exec. Director: Richard Browne

Historical Note
Publishers who have newsstand sales. Membership: $2,000/year (publishers); $333/year (consultants), $2,000/year (associate membership for suppliers).

Meetings/Conferences:
Annual Meetings: Regular member meetings held in New York City
1999 – Atlantic City, NJ(Trump Plaza Hotel & Casino)/June 6-8

Perishable Agricultural and Foodstuffs Conference
Historical Note
A conference of the Transporation Intermediaries Ass'n.

Perlite Institute (1949)
88 New Dorp Plaza
Staten Island, NY   10306-2994
Tel: (718)351-5723   Fax: (718)351-5725
E-Mail: WCH@perlite.org
Web Site: http://www.perlite.org
Members: 80 companies
Staff: 2
Annual Budget: $250-500,000
Managing Director: William C. Hall

Historical Note
Members include mining firms; processors of expanded perlite; roof deck applicators; furnace manufacturers; other processors of perlite, a volcanic rock used for horticultural applications, building and industrial insulation, plaster and concrete aggregate, and in fillers and filter aid applications. Membership: $3,400/year (organization/company).

Meetings/Conferences:
Annual Meetings: Spring and Fall
1999 – Colorado Springs, CO(Antlers DoubleTree)/90

Personal Communications Industry Ass'n (1949)
500 Montgomery St., Suite 700
Alexandria, VA   22314-1561
Tel: (703)739-0300   Fax: (703)836-1608
Web Site: http://www.pcia.com
Members: 3,000 companies
Staff: 95
Annual Budget: $5-10,000,000
President: Emmett B. "Jay" Kitchen, Jr.
Director, Communication: Brenda Maxfield
V. President, Marketing and Communications: Beth T. Hampton
Senior V. President, Gov't Relations and Chief of Staff: Mary McDermott
Senior V. President, Regulatory Relations: Robert L. Hoggarth
Director, Conventions and Education: Nancy Palleschi
Director, Training and Development: Jill Rogers
Senior V. President, Finance and C.F.O.: Carleen Kohut
Director, Financial Analysis: Leigh Veshosky
V. President, Membership: Sharon A. Ferraro

Historical Note
PCIA is an international trade association representing the wireless communications industry, particularly in the areas of regulatory policy, legislation, and technological standards. PCIA members include PCS licensees and those in paging, ESMR, SMR, mobile data, manufacturing, cable, cellular, computer and local and interexchange sectors of the wireless communications industry. Absorbed (1996) Nat'l Ass'n of Business and Educational Radio.

Publications:
Bulletin. w.

Inside PCIA. q.

Meetings/Conferences:
1999 – New Orleans, LA

Personal Computer Memory Card Internat'l Ass'n (1989)
2635 N. First St., Suite 209
San Jose, CA   95131
Tel: (408)433-2273   Fax: (408)433-9558
E-Mail: office@pcmcia.org
Web Site: http://www.pc-card.com
Members: 350 companies
Staff: 8
Annual Budget: $2-5,000,000
Membership Services Manager: Patrick Maher

Historical Note
Members are manufacturers, distributors, and suppliers of laptop personal computers and software and other products for laptops. Promotes standards and specifications for laptop peripherals and other computer hardware items. PCMCIA establishes standards and promotes interoperability of PC cards in mobile and a variety of other products. Membership: $1,500/year (affiliate); $3,500/year (associate); $10,000/year (executive).

Publications:
PC Card Resource Directory. a.
PC Card Standard. bi-m.

Meetings/Conferences:

Personal Protective Armor Ass'n (1977)
Historical Note
Address unknown in 1997.

Personal Watercraft Industry Ass'n (1987)
1819 L St., N.W.
Washington, DC   20036
Tel: (312)746-6207   Fax: (312)946-0388
Members: 7 companies
Staff: 1
Annual Budget: $500-1,000,000
Exec. Director: John L. Birkinbine

Historical Note
An affiliate of the Nat'l Marine Manufacturers Ass'n, PWIA members are manufacturers of jet drive watercraft.

Meetings/Conferences:
Annual Meetings: Not held.

Personalization and Identification Ass'n (1994)
5342 N. Reuse Ave.
Fresno, CA   93722
Tel: (209)276-8494   Fax: (209)276-8496
Toll Free: (800)276 - 8428
Members: 1,200 companies
Staff: 4
Director: Michael R. Neer

Historical Note
PIA represents the personalized products industry which inludes, embroidery, engraving, transfers, etching, printing(screen pad), lettering and stamping. Sponsors several meetings throughout the year. Membership: $80/year (company).

Publications:
P&I Sourcebook. a. adv.
Personalization & Identification News. m. adv.

Meetings/Conferences:

Peruvian Paso Horse Registry of North America (1970)
3077 Wiljan Court, Suite A
Santa Rosa, CA   95407-5702
Tel: (707)579-4394
Members: 1,400 individuals
Staff: 4
Annual Budget: $100-250,000
Registrar: Janetta Michael

Historical Note
Members breed and own Peruvian Paso horses. Maintains the stud book for purebred Peruvian Pasos, formulates rules and regulations for showing, promotes shows and exhibitions. Membership: $45/year (individual).

Publications:
Membership Directory.
Nuestro Caballo (newsletter). bi-m.

Meetings/Conferences:
1999 – Las Vegas, NV(Rio)/Feb. 11-13

Pet Food Institute (1958)
1200 19th St., N.W., Suite 300
Washington, DC   20036-2401
Tel: (202)857-1120   Fax: (202)223-4579
Web Site: www.pfionline.org
Members: 100 companies
Staff: 5
Annual Budget: $250-500,000
Exec. Director: Duane Ekedahl
Director, Technical/Regulatory Affairs: Nancy K. Cook

Historical Note
PFI represents dog and cat food manufacturers.

Publications:
PFI Monitor. q.

Meetings/Conferences:
Annual Meetings: Fall
1999 – Chicago, IL/Oct. 17-19

Pet Industry Distributors Ass'n (1968)
5024-R Campbell Blvd.
Baltimore, MD   21236
Tel: (410)931-8100   Fax: (410)931-8111
E-Mail: sking@unidial.com
Web Site: http://www.pida.org

Members: 300 companies
Staff: 2
Annual Budget: $500-1,000,000
Exec. V. President: Steven T. King, CAE

Historical Note
Affiliated with the Nat'l Ass'n of Wholesaler-Distributors and the Pet Industry Joint Advisory Council. Membership: $500-1,200/year (company).

Publications:
PIDA News Bulletin. bi-m.
Profit Report. a.

Meetings/Conferences:
Annual Meetings: Winter
1999 – Puerto Vallarta, Mexico(Westin Regina)/250
2000 – Key Biscayne, FL(Sonesta)/Jan. 15-19/250

Pet Industry Joint Advisory Council (1971)
1220 19th St., N.W., Suite 400
Washington, DC   20036
Tel: (202)452-1525   Fax: (202)293-4377
Toll Free: (800)553 - 7387
Members: 2,000 firms & associations
Staff: 7
Annual Budget: $1-2,000,000
Exec. V. President/General Counsel: N. Marshall Meyers

Historical Note
Monitors federal and state legislation affecting the industry; sponsors research; publishes management and training manuals for pet shops; and disseminates information on pet ownership responsibility, and on the pet industry. Members are pet shop retailers, companion animal breeders and importers, product manufacturers, and distributors.

Publications:
Pet Alert. irreg.
Pet Letter. m.

Meetings/Conferences:

Pet Sitters Internat'l (1994)
418 E. King St.
King, NC   27021-9163
Tel: (336)983-9222   Fax: (336)983-3755
E-Mail: petsit@ols.net
Web Site: http://www.petsit.com
Members: 2,500 companies
Staff: 10
Annual Budget: $100-250,000
President: Patti J. Moran

Historical Note
PSI is an educational organization for professional pet sitters. It awards the Pet Sitting Technician, Advanced Pet Sitting Technician and Master Pet Sitting Technician designations to individuals and Accredited Pet Sitting Service to firms. Membership: $75/year (individual); $250/year, minimum (corporate).

Publications:
World of Professional Pet Sitting. bi-m.

Meetings/Conferences:
Annual Meetings: mid-September to mid-October

Petroleum Equipment Institute (1951)
6514 East 69th St.
Tulsa, OK   74133-1719
Tel: (918)494-9696   Fax: (918)491-9895
Web Site: www.pei.org
Members: 1,630 companies
Staff: 12
Annual Budget: $1-2,000,000
Exec. V. President: Robert N. Renkes
Administrative Director: Connie Dooley
Membership Director: Carlette Denison

Historical Note
Established as the Nat'l Ass'n of Oil Equipment Jobbers, it assumed its present name in 1966. Members are makers and distributors of equipment used in service stations, bulk plants and other petroleum marketing facilities.

Publications:
Petroleum Equipment Directory. a. adv.
Tulsa Letter. semi-m.

Meetings/Conferences:
1999 – Toronto, Ontario(Convention Center)/Oct. 5-7
2000 – San Diego, CA(Convention Center)/Oct. 2-4

Petroleum Equipment Suppliers Ass'n (1933)
9225 Katy Freeway, Suite 310
Houston, TX   77024-1586
Tel: (713)932-0168   Fax: (713)932-0497
Members: 175 individuals, 205 companies
Staff: 36
Annual Budget: $500-1,000,000
President: Sherry A. Stephens
Exec. Administration: Juanita Andrews
Editor: Ted Venker

Historical Note
Founded as American Petroleum Equipment Suppliers; assumed its current name in 1938. Members are makers of oil field production and drilling equipment, well site services and supplies.

Publications:
Annual Report. a.
PESA News.
Service Point Directory.

Meetings/Conferences:
Annual Meetings: April
1999 – Tuscon, AZ(Loews Ventarra)/April 21-23/200
2000 – San Antonio, TX(Westin La Cantena)/April 11-15/200

Petroleum Industry Security Council (1982)
5161 San Felipe St., Suite 320
Houston, TX   77056-3634
Tel: (281)397-7464   Fax: (713)623-0160

Members: 350 companies
Staff: 2
Annual Budget: $100-250,000
Exec. Director: Betty Burdett
Historical Note
Founded in April 1982 by a group of Texans to combat the growing problem of crimes affecting the oil industry. Membership: $150/year, $300/year (company), $1,000/year (corporate).
Publications:
Monthly Security Report. m. adv.
National Membership Directory. a. adv.
Meetings/Conferences:
Annual Meetings: Summer

Petroleum Marketers Ass'n of America (1941)
1901 N. Fort Myer Dr., Suite 1200
Arlington, VA 22209-1604
Tel: (703)351-8000   *Fax:* (703)351-9160
Toll Free: (800)300 - 7622
Web Site: www.pmaa.org
Members: 44 associations
Staff: 14
Annual Budget: $2-5,000,000
Exec. V. President: Daniel Gilligan, CAE
V.P., Communications/Bus. Programs: Sherry Syence
Director, Finance and Administration: Anita Gonzales
Historical Note
A federation of state and regional petroleum marketing association comprising about 10,000 independent petroleum marketers. Formerly (1941) Council of Independent Petroleum Marketers; (1948) Nat'l Council of Independent Petroleum Ass'ns; and (1984) Nat'l Oil Jobbers Council. Absorbed the Nat'l Oil Fuel Institute in 1974. Maintains the Petroleum Marketers Small Businessmen's Committee.
Publications:
Directory. a.
Journal of Petroleum Marketing. m.
Weekly Review.
Meetings/Conferences:
Annual Meetings: Fall (Conference and Trade Show)

Petroleum Packaging Council (1989)
c/o Kreer & Associates
35 E. Wacker Drive
Chicago, IL 60601
Tel: (312)346-7784   *Fax:* (312)372-7860
E-Mail: ppc@ameritech.net
Web Site: http://www.ppcouncil.org
Members: 440 individuals
Administrator: Irene Overman Kreer
Historical Note
PPC is formed to provide technical leadership and education to the Petroleum Packaging Industry. Various forums are used to disseminate information and technical knowledge to members. Membership: $350/year (individual), $1,500/year (corporate).
Publications:
PPC Newsletter. semi-a.
PPC Newsletter. m.
Meetings/Conferences:
Semi-Annual: Spring and Fall

Petroleum Product Stewardship Council
Historical Note
An affiliate of the Synthetic Organic Chemical Manufacturers Ass'n which provides administrative support.

Petroleum Technology Transfer Council (1994)
1101 16th St., N.W., Suite 1-C
Washington, DC 20036
Tel: (202)785-2225   *Fax:* (202)785-2240
Toll Free: (888)843 - 7882
E-Mail: hq@pttc.org
Web Site: http://www.pttc.org
Annual Budget: $2-5,000,000
Exec. Director: Deborah Rowell
Communications & Marketing Manager: Jeff Leonard
Financial/Contracts Manager: Kathryn Chapman
Project Manager: Lance Cole
Historical Note
PTTC is a national non-profit organization formed to foster the effective transfer of exploration and production technology to U.S. petroleum producers. The technical information that the PTTC transfers to producers comes from the research and development community and intermediary providers of technology including: government, universities, professional and trade societies, national labs, major companies, the service industry, etc. Although the PTTC is not involved directly with any research and development efforts, it identifies the best mechanisms for improving near-term and long-term technology transfer to domestic operators.

PGA TOUR Tournaments Ass'n (1970)
13000 Sawgrass Village Cir., Suite 36
Ponte Vedra Beach, FL 32082-5023
Tel: (904)285-4222   *Fax:* (904)273-5726
E-Mail: pgatourta@aol.com
Members: 50 individuals
Staff: 3
Annual Budget: $250-500,000
Exec. Director: Barry J. Palm
Historical Note
AGSA members are sponsors of Professional Golf Ass'n tournaments. Formerly (1970) Internat'l Golf Sponsors Ass'n and (1997) American Golf Sponsors Ass'n. Membership: $3000/year (organization).
Publications:
AGS Quarterly. q.
Meetings/Conferences:
Annual Meetings: November

1999 – Las Vegas, NV(Bellagio)/Dec. 5-10/350
2000 – Los Angeles(Universal City Hilton)/Nov. 14-19/350

Pharmaceutical Advertising Council
Historical Note
Became (1995) Healthcare Marketing and Communications Council

Pharmaceutical Care Management Ass'n (1975)
2300 Ninth St. South, Suite 210
Arlington, VA 22204-2320
Tel: (703)920-8480   *Fax:* (703)920-8491
Members: 138 companies
Staff: 13
Annual Budget: $1-2,000,000
President & C.E.O.: Delbert D. Konnor
V. President for Regulatory & Government Affairs: Margaret J. Hardy
Director of Meetings: Jennyfer M. Borrero, CMT
Director, Membership Services: Phyllis A. Biermann
Vice President for Administration: M. John Coburn, Pharmms
Historical Note
Formerly (1996) American Managed Care Pharmacy Ass'n and (1989) Nat'l Ass'n of Mail Service Pharmacies. PCMA and its members strive to maintain the highest standards of professional pharmacy practice. The Ass'ns goals are to assure quality standards throughout the industry, to reduce healthcare costs to providers and consumers, and to promote managed care pharmacy as a quality cost-effective method of prescription drug delivery. The association serves its members in the areas of legislation, practice standards, education, and research.
Publications:
Directory of Managed Care Providers. a. adv.
Legislative Desk Reference. irreg.
Meetings/Conferences:
Annual Meetings: October

Pharmaceutical Manufacturers Ass'n (1958)
Historical Note
Became Pharmaceutical Research and Manufacturers of America in 1994.

Pharmaceutical Research and Manufacturers of America (1958)
1100 15th St., N.W., 9th Fl
Washington, DC 20005
Tel: (202)835-3400   *Fax:* (202)835-3414
Web Site: http://www.phrma.org
Members: 100 companies
Staff: 75
Annual Budget: $5-10,000,000
President: Alan F. Holmer
Asst. V.P., Communications: Mark Grayson
V. President, Public Affairs: Alixe R. Glen
V. President, Federal Affairs: Barry H. Caldwell
V.P., State Govt. Affairs: Kurt Malmgren
V. President, Finance and Operations: Del Persinger
Exec. V. President: Judy Bello
Comptroller: Joy A. Garish
Senior V. President and General Counsel: Russel A. Bantham
Historical Note
Formed by merger of the American Drug Manufacturers Ass'n and the American Pharmaceutical Manufacturers Ass'n. Formerly (1994) Pharmaceutical Manufacturers Ass'n. Non-profit trade association of over 100 research-based pharmaceutical companies. To qualify for membership, a company must manufacture market finished dosage-form pharamaceuticals under their own brand name. In addition, they must conduct a significant amount of R&D within the United States. Together, PhRMA member companies account for 90 percent of sales within the United States and a substantial portion of the world's supply.
Meetings/Conferences:
Annual Meetings: Spring

Pharmacists in Ophthalmic Practice (1984)
Wills Eye Hospital
900 Walnut St.
Philadelphia, PA 19107
Tel: (215)928-3334
Members: 25 individuals
Annual Budget: under $10,000
Board Chairman: Clement A. Weisbecker
Historical Note
PIOP members are directors of pharmacy departments in ophthalmic teaching institutions.
Publications:
Directory of Pharmacists in Ophthalmic Institutions. irreg.

Phi Alpha Delta (1902)
10722 White Oak Ave., Box 3217
Granada Hills, CA 91394-0217
Tel: (818)360-1941   *Fax:* (818)363-5851
Members: 150,000 individuals
Staff: 6
Annual Budget: $500-1,000,000
Exec. Director: Frank Patek
Historical Note
Professional and international law fraternity formed in Chicago, Nov. 8, 1902. Absorbed Phi Delta Delta, a women's professional law sorority, in 1972. Membership: $70/year (individual).
Publications:
The Reporter. q. adv.
Meetings/Conferences:
Biennial Meetings: August, even years

Phi Alpha Theta (1921)
50 College Drive
Allentown, PA 18104-6100
Tel: (610)433-4140   *Fax:* (610)433-4661
Toll Free: (800)394 - 8195
E-Mail: phialpha@ptd.net

Members: 220,000 individuals
Staff: 5
Annual Budget: $500-1,000,000
Exec. Director: Graydon A. Tunstall, Jr.
Historical Note
Phi Alpha Theta is the college level honor society promoting the study of history through the encouragement of research, teaching, publication, and the exchange of learning and ideas among historians. Membership: $30/life (individual).
Publications:
Historian. q. adv.
News Letter. 3/yr.
Meetings/Conferences:
Biennial Convention: (odd years)
1999 – Tampa, FL

Phi Beta (1912)
5481-D Millwood Lane
Willoughby, OH 44094
Tel: (440)942-7337
E-Mail: ringleader@compuserve.com
Members: 400 individuals, 3 collegiate and 10 alumni chaptrs
Exec. Director: Nancy Schumann, Ph.D.
Historical Note
Professional fraternity in the creative and performing arts. Membership: $25/year (individual).
Publications:
Baton. semi-a. adv.
Meetings/Conferences:
Biennial Meetings: even years

Phi Beta Lambda
Historical Note
See Future Business Leaders of America

Phi Chi Theta (1924)
1704 hanks Street
Lufkin, TX 75904
Tel: (409)637-0966
E-Mail: phichi@lcc.net
Web Site: http://www.phichitheta.org
Members: 47,000 individuals
Staff: 1
Annual Budget: $100-250,000
Exec. Director: Leslie A. Trout
Historical Note
A co-ed professional fraternity in business and economics which seeks to promote the cause of higher business education and training for all individuals . Membership: $50/year (individual).
Publications:
Iris. semi-a.
Meetings/Conferences:

Phi Delta Chi (1883)
P.O. Box 1883
Athens, GA 30603-1883
Tel: (706)613-0300   *Fax:* (706)613-0200
E-Mail: phidexnatl@aol.com
Web Site:
     http://www.umich.edu/~ jbonasso/pdcnew/home.htm
Members: 40,500 individuals
Annual Budget: $100-250,000
Exec. Director: Anthony D. Chaffee
Historical Note
A professional fraternity in pharmacy. Membership: $50/year.
Publications:
The Brotherhood Directory. bien.
The Communicator. q. adv.
Who's Who in Phi Delta Chi. a.
Meetings/Conferences:
Biennial Meetings: August
1999 – San Diego, CA(U.S. Grant)/August 3-8
2000 – Ann Arbor, MI(University of Michigan Conf. Center)
2001 – Boston, MA

Phi Delta Epsilon Medical Fraternity (1904)
11595 N. Meridian St., Suite 300
Carmel, IN 46032
Tel: (317)573-2961   *Fax:* (317)573-2994
Toll Free: (800)347 - 3713
E-Mail: phide@phide.org
Members: 25,000 individuals
Staff: 1
Exec. Director: S.M. Greenstone
Historical Note
Professional fraternity serving the medical profession.
Publications:
Phi Delta Epsilon News & Scientific Journal. q.

Phi Delta Kappa (1906)
408 N. Union Ave.
P.O. Box 789
Bloomington, IN 47402-0789
Tel: (812)339-1156   *Fax:* (812)339-0018
Toll Free: (800)766 - 1156
E-Mail: headquarters@pdkinpl.org
Web Site: www.pakintl.org
Members: 150,000 individuals
Staff: 70
Annual Budget: $2-5,000,000
Exec. Director: Dr. Ron Joekel
Historical Note
Phi Delta Kappa is a professional education fraternity concerned with providing leadership and research in the field. Members include classroom teachers, school administrators, college and university professors, and educational specialists of many types. The primary focus of the fraternity is to promote quality publicly-supported education. Membership is by invitation only.

Membership: $30/year (international dues) + local dues and initiation fee.
Publications:
News, Notes & Quotes. q.
Phi Delta Kappan. 10/yr.
Meetings/Conferences:
Biennial Meetings: (International)
1999 – Bloomington, IN/Oct. 21-24

Phi Delta Phi (1869)
1750 N St., N.W.
Washington, DC   20036-2089
Tel: (202)628-0148   *Fax:* (202)296-7619
Toll Free: (800)365 - 5606
Web Site: phideltaphi.org
Members: 170,000 individuals
Staff: 3
Annual Budget: $1-2,000,000
Exec. Director: Sam S. Crutchfield
Historical Note
Professional international legal fraternity. Membership: $70 initiation fee; voluntary alumni dues.
Publications:
The Headnoter. q.
Meetings/Conferences:
Biennial Meetings: odd years in August
1999 – Philadelphia, PA/Aug. 11-14

Phi Epsilon Kappa (1913)
901 W. New York St.
Indianapolis, IN   46202
Tel: (317)637-8431
Members: 3,000 individuals
Staff: 1
Annual Budget: $50-100,000
Exec. Secretary: Jeffery Vessely, Ed.D.
Historical Note
A professional fraternity in physical education. Membership: $20/year.
Publications:
Black and Gold Bulletin. semi-a.
Physical Educator. q.
Meetings/Conferences:
Triennial Meetings: (1999)

Phi Gamma Nu (1924)
Historical Note
Address unknown in 1997.

Phi Lambda Kappa Medical Fraternity (1907)
60 Fountain Road
Levittown, PA   19056-1915
Tel: (215)949-8700
Members: 4,800 individuals
Annual Budget: under $10,000
Exec. Director: Eleanor G. Halprin
Historical Note
Provides a fraternal and professional network for current and future medical practitioners. Membership: $40/year.
Publications:
PLK-MSAS Quarterly. q. adv.
Meetings/Conferences:
Annual Meetings: Spring

Phi Mu Alpha - Sinfonia (1898)
Lyrecrest
10600 Old State Road
Evansville, IN   47711
Tel: (812)867-2433   *Fax:* (812)867-0633
Toll Free: (800)473 - 2649
E-Mail: lyrecrest@sinfonia.org
Members: 125,000 individuals
Staff: 5
Annual Budget: $250-500,000
Exec. Director: James P. Morris
Historical Note
A professional fraternity in music. Formerly (1934) The Sinfonia Fraternity. Membership: $100/year (individual).
Publications:
National Directory. a.
Sinfonian Magzine. q.
The Red and Black Newsletter. bi-m.
Meetings/Conferences:

Phi Rho Sigma Medical Soc. (1890)
P.O. Box 90264
Indianapolis, IN   46290
Tel: (317)255-4379   *Fax:* (317)253-5067
Members: 31,000 individuals
Staff: 1
Annual Budget: $50-100,000
Central Office Director: Harriet Rodenberg
Historical Note
A professional fraternity in medicine, stressing professional development, high scholarship and community service. Membership: $35/year (voluntary dues).
Publications:
Journal of Phi Rho Sigma. q.
Meetings/Conferences:
Annual Meetings: Fall

Philippine-American Chamber of Commerce (1920)
711 Third Ave., 17th Floor
New York, NY   10017-4046
Tel: (212)972-9326   *Fax:* (212)867-9882
Members: 105 individuals
Staff: 4

Annual Budget: $100-250,000
President: John Howley
Historical Note
Non-profit organization working with the public and private sector in the United States and the Philippines to promote trade and investment between the two countries. Assists U.S. companies seeking business opportunities in the Philippines and Philippine companies seeking U.S. markets.
Publications:
PHILAMCHAM News Briefs. q.
Philippine Business. m.
Meetings/Conferences:

Philosophy of Education Soc. (1941)
116-M Erickson Hall Michigan State Univ.
East Lansing, MI   48824
Tel: (517)355-3486
E-Mail: floden@msu.edu
Members: 500 individuals
Annual Budget: $25-50,000
Exec. Secretary: Robert Floden
Historical Note
The Society addresses philosophic issues in education, particularly those which focus on professional ethics. Has no paid staff. Membership: $65/year.
Publications:
Educational Theory. q.
Newsletter. irreg.
Philosophy of Education (Yearbook). a.
Meetings/Conferences:
Annual Meetings: Spring
1999 – New Orleans, LA/March 26-29

Philosophy of Science Ass'n (1934)
U of MO-Kansas City, Dept of Philosophy
5100 Rockhill Road
Kansas City, MO   64110-2499
Tel: (816)235-2816   *Fax:* (816)235-2819
E-Mail: admin@scistud.umkc.edu
Web Site: http://scistud.umkc.edu/psa/
Members: 950 individuals
Staff: 1
Annual Budget: $50-100,000
Exec. Secretary: George D. Gale, Ph.D.
Historical Note
Member of the Internat'l Union of History and Philosophy of Science and affiliate of the American Ass'n for the Advancement of Science. Membership: $40-300/year based on income,
Publications:
Newsletter. q.
Philosophy of Science. q. adv.
Proceedings of Biennial Meetings. bi-a.
Meetings/Conferences:
Biennial Meetings: even years in Fall

Phlebology Soc. of America (1962)
5 Daremy Court
Nesconset, NY   11767-1547
Tel: (516)366-1429   *Fax:* (516)366-3609
Members: 260 individuals
Staff: 1
Annual Budget: $100-250,000
Exec. Director: Denise Rosignol
Historical Note
Established and incorporated in New York in 1962 as a professional membership society for the purpose of exchanging scientific information, nationally, in the field of peripheral vascular disease. Members are designated as Fellows, Associate Fellows, and Clinical Members, depending upon the extent of their involvement in the research or clinical practice in phlebology. Membership: $150/year.
Publications:
Internat'l Journal of Angiology. q.
Proceedings of the Annual Meeting. a. adv.
Meetings/Conferences:
Annual Meetings: Spring/200
1999 – Denver, CO/Apr. 18-21

Phosphate Chemicals Export Ass'n (1975)
c/o IMC Global Operations
2345 Waukegan Road, Suite E-200
Bannockburn, IL   60015-1580
Tel: (847)607-3000   *Fax:* (847)607-3390
Members: 3 companies
Annual Budget: $2-5,000,000
Exec. V. President/Asst. Secretary: Richard Blattner
Historical Note
A Webb-Pomerene Act association.

Phosphate Rock Export Ass'n (1970)
Historical Note
Organization defunct in 1996.

Phosphonates Task Force
Historical Note
An affiliate of the Synthetic Organic Chemical Manufacturers Ass'n which provides administrative support.

Photo Chemical Machining Institute (1968)
P.O. Box 3549
San Clemente, CA   92674
Tel: (714)493-5702   *Fax:* (714)493-2043
Members: 150 companies
Annual Budget: $100-250,000
Exec. Director: Richard H. Shute
Historical Note
PCMI members are companies producing metal products through photo chemical machining. In addition the Institute includes

companies that service the PCM industry and supply its needs.
Membership: $500/year (organization).
Publications:
Journal. q. adv.
Membership Directory. a.
Meetings/Conferences:
Semi-annual Meetings: February and September

Photo Marketing Ass'n-Internat'l (1924)
3000 Picture Place
Jackson, MI   49201-8853
Tel: (517)788-8100   *Fax:* (517)788-8371
E-Mail: PMA_Information_Central@pmai.org
Web Site: http://www.pmai.org
Members: 17,000 individuals
Staff: 85
Annual Budget: $5-10,000,000
Exec. Director: Roy S. Pung
Group Exec., Convention Activities: Ronald F. Rowley
Group Exec., Education: Mary Anne LaMarre
Group Exec., Staff Services Unit: George Olsen
Group Exec., International Activities: Bob Leidlein
Group Exec., Environment Unit: Ron Willson
Director of Membership: William Covey
Asst. Exec. Director: Craig Halverson
Historical Note
Merger of Nat'l Photo Dealers Ass'n (1946) and Master Photo Finishers of America. Formerly (1974) Master Photo Dealers and Finishers' Ass'n. Maintains branches in Australia, Brazil, Canada, Europe, Italy, New Zealand, and in the United Kingdom. The Ass'n of Photo CD Imagers, the Ass'n of Professional Color Laboratories, the Digital Imaging Marketing Ass'n and the Professional School Photographers are sections of PMA-I. Has an annual budget of approximately $8.1 million.
Publications:
Newsline. w.
Photo Marketing Magazine. m. adv.
Meetings/Conferences:
Semi-Annual Meetings: Spring and Fall
1999 – Las Vegas, NV(Las Vegas Convention Center)/Feb. 18-21/2200
1999 – Miami, FL(Fountainebleau Hilton)/Sept. 30-Oct. 3/3000

Photographic and Imaging Manufacturers Ass'n (1946)
550 Mamaroneck Ave., Suite 307
Harrison, NY   10528-1612
Tel: (914)698-7603   *Fax:* (914)698-7609
E-Mail: pima@pima.net
Web Site: pima.net
Members: 56 companies
Staff: 6
Annual Budget: $500-1,000,000
Exec. V. President: Thomas J. Dufficy
Director of Standards: James A. Peyton
Historical Note
Formerly (1997) Nat'l Ass'n of Photographic Manufacturers. Membership fee varies, based on annual sales.
Publications:
Membership Directory. a.
PIMA News. q.
Proceedings. a.
Meetings/Conferences:
Annual Meetings: November

Photographic Manufacturers and Distributors Ass'n (1939)
1120 Ave. of the Americas, 4th Fl.
New York, NY   10036
Tel: (732)679-3460   *Fax:* (732)679-2294
E-Mail: bclarkpmda@aol.com
Members: 78 companies
Staff: 1
Annual Budget: $250-500,000
Exec. Manager: Willard Clark
Historical Note
Formerly Photographic Merchandising and Distributing Ass'n. Membership: $500/year (associate members); $1,000/year (voting members).
Publications:
Membership Directory. a.
PMDA Today-Newsletter. 6/yea.
Meetings/Conferences:
1999 – Las Vegas, NV(Bellagio)/375

Phycological Soc. of America (1946)
Center for Marine Studies, UCSD
Earth and Marine Sciences Bldg.
Santa Cruz, CA   95064
Tel: (408)459-2832
E-Mail: goff@biology.ucsd.edu
Members: 1,200 individuals
Annual Budget: $250-500,000
President: Linda Goff, Ph.D.
Historical Note
Established in 1946 to promote basic and applied research of algae. Affiliated with the American Ass'n for the Advancement of Science and the American Institute of Biological Sciences. Has no paid officers or full-time staff. Membership: $65/year (individual), $195/year (institution).
Publications:
Applied Phycology Forum. 3/yr.
Journal of Phycology. bi-m.
Phycological Newsletter. 3/yr.
Meetings/Conferences:
Annual Meetings: Summer, at a university environment.

Physician Insurers Ass'n of America *(1977)*
2275 Research Blvd., Suite 250
Rockville, MD 20850-3268
Tel: (301)947-9000   *Fax:* (301)947-9090
Web Site: www.thepiaa.org
Members: 63 companies
Staff: 14
Annual Budget: $2-5,000,000
President: Lawrence Smarr
Director of Communications: Jack E. Pope
Dir., Gov't Relations: Bruce A. Wilson
Director, Meeting Services: Rosemarie Rauzino-Heller
Education Coordinator: Lynn S. Powell
Director, Administrative Services: Paul W. Waldron
Director, Loss Prevention & Research: Lori A. Bartholomew

Historical Note
Represents domestic and international medical and dental malpractice insurance companies which are practitioner-owned or controlled. Membership fee varies, approximately $20,000/year (company).

Publications:
Physician Insurer. q.

Meetings/Conferences:
Annual Meetings: May-June/1,200
1999 – Palm Desert, CA(Marriott Desert
    Springs)/May 26-29/1200
2000 – Washington, DC(Willard & JW Marriott)/May 31-June
    3/1200
2001 – San Antonio, TX(Marriott Rivercenter)/May 20-June
    2/1200
2002 – Denver, CO(Adam's Mark)/May 15-18/1200

Pi Lambda Theta *(1910)*
4101 East Third St.
P.O. Box 6626
Bloomington, IN 47407-6626
Tel: (812)339-3411   *Fax:* (812)339-3462
Toll Free: (800)487 - 3411
E-Mail: member@pilambda.org
Web Site: http://www.pilambda.org
Members: 13,000 individuals
Staff: 6
Annual Budget: $500-1,000,000
Exec. Director: J. Ogden Hamilton, Ph.D.

Historical Note
An honor society and professional ass'n in the field of education. Purpose is to recognize individuals of superior scholastic achievement and high potential for professional leadership while stimulating independent-thinking educators who can ask critical questions to improve educational decision making. Established November 1910 at the University of Missouri. Founded as a women's organization, PLT opened its membership to men in 1974. Incorporated in the State of Indiana in 1976. Professionals who have achieved certification by the National Board for Professional Teaching Standards are welcomed as members. Membership: $35/year (professional); $25/year (student).

Publications:
Educational Horizons. q.
Pi Lambda Theta Newsletter. bi-m.

Meetings/Conferences:
Biennial meetings: uneven years in summer.
1999 – Atlanta, GA/600

Pi Sigma Epsilon

Historical Note
Professional fraternity affiliated with Sales and Marketing Executives, International, Inc.

Piano Manufacturers Ass'n Internat'l *(1896)*
4020 McEwen, Suite 105
Dallas, TX 75244-5019
Tel: (972)233-9107   *Fax:* (972)490-4219
Members: 20 piano manufacturers
Annual Budget: $500-1,000,000
Exec. Director: Donald W. Dillon

Historical Note
Formerly (1986) the Nat'l Piano Manufacturers Ass'n. Supports the Nat'l Piano Foundation (same address) as its educational arm.

Publications:
NPF Piano Notes. q.

Meetings/Conferences:
Semi-annual Mtgs: Winter & Summer with Nat'l Ass'n of
    Music Merchants
1999 – Los Angeles, CA(Convention Center)
2000 – Anaheim, CA(Convention Center)
2001 – Anaheim, CA(Convention Center)

Piano Technicians Guild *(1957)*
3930 Washington St.
Kansas City, MO 64111
Tel: (816)753-7747   *Fax:* (816)531-0070
E-Mail: ptg@ptg.org
Web Site: http://www.ptg.org
Members: 3,900 individuals
Staff: 6
Annual Budget: $500-1,000,000
Exec. Director: David K. Hanzlick

Historical Note
Formed in 1957 by consolidation of the American Soc. of Piano Technicians and the Nat'l Ass'n of Piano Tuners. Membership as Registered Technician acquired by examination. Membership: $147/year.

Publications:
Membership Directory. a.
The Piano Technician's Journal. m. adv.

Meetings/Conferences:
1999 – Kansas City, MO
2000 – Arlington, VA

2001 – Reno, NV

Pickle Packers Internat'l *(1893)*
P.O. Box 606
108 1/2 E. Main St.
St. Charles, IL 60174
Tel: (630)584-8950   *Fax:* (630)584-0759
Members: 160 companies
Staff: 2
Annual Budget: $250-500,000
Exec. V. President: Richard Hentschel
Bookkeeper: Barbara Trupp

Historical Note
Formerly (1963) Nat'l Pickle Packers Ass'n. Members are manufacturers of pickles and other fermented or acidified vegetables, suppliers of salt, salt stock brokers, and other suppliers to the industry. The objectives of the PPI are to perfect the pickling process from seed to finished product and to increase consumption of pickled vegetables. Membership: annual dues vary.

Meetings/Conferences:
1999 – Nashville, TN
2000 – San Antonio, TX

Picture Agency Council of America
P.O. Box 308
Northfield, MN 55057
Toll Free: (800)457 - 7222
E-Mail: paca@earthlink.net
Web Site: http://www.pacaoffice.org
Members: 145 firms
Annual Budget: $250-500,000
Exec. Administrator: Lonnie Tuttle Schroeder

Historical Note
PACA is the trade association for stock picture agencies in North America. Membership: dues vary by staff size and membership category.

Publications:
PACA Membership Directory. a. adv.
PACA News. q. adv.
PACA update. w.

Meetings/Conferences:
Annual Meetings: May Newport Beach, CA(Marriott Tennis
    Club)/May 4-7/100
1999 – Tarrytown, NY/Apr. 28-May 1

Piedmontese Ass'n of the United States *(1984)*
108 Livestock Exchange Building
Denver, CO 80216
Tel: (303)295-7287   *Fax:* (303)295-7935
Members: 330 individuals
Staff: 1
Annual Budget: $50-100,000
Exec. Director: Mary Jo McCormick

Historical Note
PAUS members are breeders of Piedmontese cattle. Membership: $50/year.

Publications:
Magazine. q. adv.

Meetings/Conferences:
Annual Meetings: January/150
1999 – Springfield, IL/150

Pierre Fauchard Academy *(1936)*
P.O. Box 80330
Las Vegas, NV 89180-0330
Tel: (702)365-9454   *Fax:* (702)365-8002
Toll Free: (800)232 - 0099
Members: 6,000 individuals, 50 state organizations
Staff: 2
Annual Budget: $100-250,000
Exec. Director: Dr. Richard A. Kozal

Historical Note
Academy members are dentists. Membership: $80/year, plus $35 initiation fee (individual).

Publications:
Dental Abstracts. bi-m. adv.
Dental World. bi-m.
Membership Roster. irreg.

Meetings/Conferences:
1999 – Las Vegas, NV/Oct. 16-21
2000 – Chicago, IL/Oct. 28-Nov. 2
2001 – Honolulu, HI/Oct. 13-18

Pile Driving Contractors Ass'n *(1996)*
P.O. Box 410260
St. Louis, MO 63141
Tel: (314)275-7453   *Fax:* (314)576-7989
Members: 120 companies
Annual Budget: $25-50,000
Exec. Director: Pam Helmsing

Historical Note
PDCA is an organization of pile driving contractors that seeks to increase the use of driven piles for deep foundations and earth retention systems. Membership: $550/year (company).

Publications:
Pile Driver. q.

Meetings/Conferences:
1999 – San Diego, CA

Pilots Internat'l Ass'n *(1965)*

Historical Note
Organization defunct in 1997.

Pin, Clip and Fastener Services *(1933)*

Historical Note
Organization defunct in 1995.

Pine Chemicals Ass'n *(1947)*
15 Technology Park South, Suite 250
Norcross, GA 30092
Tel: (770)446-1290   *Fax:* (770)446-1487
E-Mail: jlazakus@tappi.org
Web Site: http://www.pinechemicals.org/
Members: 30 companies
Staff: 2
Annual Budget: $250-500,000
Exec. Director: Charles T. Bohanan, CAE

Historical Note
Membership consists of international manufacturers of chemical products (other than pulp and paper) produced by or from products of the wood pulp industry.

Publications:
Conference Proceedings. bien.
PCA Newsletter. q.

Meetings/Conferences:
Annual Meetings: Fall/300

Pinto Horse Ass'n of America *(1956)*
1900 Samuels Ave.
Fort Worth, TX 76102-1141
Tel: (817)336-7842   *Fax:* (817)336-7416
E-Mail: pinto@airmail.net
Web Site: www.pinto.org
Members: 7,500 membership units
Staff: 10
Annual Budget: $500-1,000,000
Exec. Manager: Joe Grissom

Historical Note
Members are breeders and owners of Pinto horses. Maintains the registry for the Pinto breed, sets standards for conformation, color, and performance, and encourages the showing of the Pinto breed. Membership: $20/year.

Publications:
The Pinto Horse Magazine. q. adv.

Meetings/Conferences:
Annual Meetings: Late Fall

Pipe Fabrication Institute *(1913)*
Box 173
612 Lenore Ave.
Springdale, PA 15144-1518
Tel: (514)634-3444   *Fax:* (514)634-9736
Members: 48 companies
Staff: 1
Annual Budget: $50-100,000
Exec. Director: Lois A. Moore

Historical Note
PFI members are companies producing sophisticated high-temperature, high-pressure piping systems installed throughout the U.S. and Canada. PFI member companies employ specialists from the ranks of the United Ass'n of Journeymen and Apprentices of the Plumbing and Pipe Fitting Industry and are signatories to the Pipe Fabrication Agreement with the United Association.

Meetings/Conferences:

Pipe Line Contractors Ass'n *(1948)*
1700 Pacific Ave., Suite 4100
Dallas, TX 75201
Tel: (214)969-2700   *Fax:* (214)969-2705
Members: 136 companies
Staff: 1
Managing Director/General Counsel: J. Patrick Tielborg

Historical Note
Members are builders of cross-country pipelines and their suppliers.

Publications:
Newsletter. w.

Meetings/Conferences:
Annual Meetings: February
1999 – Scottsdale, AZ(Hyatt Regency)

Pipe Tobacco Council *(1988)*
1100 17th St., N.W., Suite 504
Washington, DC 20036
Tel: (202)223-8207   *Fax:* (202)833-0379
Members: 17 businesses
Staff: 3
Annual Budget: $100-250,000
President: Norman F. Sharp

Historical Note
Formed in 1988 "to advance and foster the economic interests of its members, the general welfare of the pipe and smoking tobacco industry, and the nation's economy and society."

Meetings/Conferences:
Annual Meetings: Fall

Planning Forum

Historical Note
Became (1995) Strategic Leadership Forum.

Plant Growth Regulator Soc. of America *(1973)*

Historical Note
Address unknown in 1998.

Plastic and Metal Products Manufacturers Ass'n *(1937)*
145 W. 45th St., Suite 800
New York, NY 10036
Tel: (212)398-5700   *Fax:* (212)398-7818
Members: 175 companies
Staff: 6
Annual Budget: $100-250,000
Exec. Director: Sheldon M. Edelman

Historical Note
Formerly (1970) Plastic Products Manufacturers Ass'n, Inc.

Plastic Bottle Institute

Historical Note
Organization defunct in 1995.

Plastic Drum Institute

Historical Note
Merged with (1998) Society of Plastics Industry.

Plastic Pipe and Fittings Ass'n *(1978)*

800 Roosevelt Road, Bldg. C, Suite 20
Glen Ellyn, IL   60137-5833
Tel: (630)858-6540   *Fax:* (630)790-3095
Members: 82 companies
Staff: 4
Annual Budget: $500-1,000,000
Exec. Director: Richard W. Church
Field Representative: Mike Gillespie

Historical Note
PPFA is the national trade association of manufacturers of plastic piping products used for plumbing applications. Members include pipe and fitting processors, prime resin suppliers, equipment suppliers, solvent cement manufacturers and suppliers of compounding ingredients.

Meetings/Conferences:
Semi-annual meetings: March and October/120
1999 – LaQuinta, CA/Feb. 21-24
1999 – Asheville, NC/Oct. 3-6

Plastic Shipping Container Institute *(1976)*

1920 N. St. N.W.
Washington, DC   20036
Tel: (202)973-2709   *Fax:* (202)331-8330
Members: 45 companies
Staff: 1
Annual Budget: $100-250,000
General Council: David Baker

Historical Note
Members are manufacturers of open head plastic shipping containers. Associate members are companies producing virgin high density polyethylene, component parts for shipping containers and companies manufacturing machines capable of producing a finished plastic shipping container, and all companies which provide a performance evaluation service on the finished plastic shipping container. Membership: $4,000/year, plus additional for plants over one; $1,250/year (associate).

Meetings/Conferences:
Semi-annual Meetings: Winter and Fall
1999 – Fort Lauderdale, FL/March 14-16
1999 – Washington, DC(L'Enfant Plaza Hotel)/Sept. 23-24

Plastic Soft Materials Manufacturers Ass'n *(1937)*

145 W. 45th St., Suite 800
New York, NY   10036
Tel: (212)398-5700   *Fax:* (212)398-7818
Members: 45 companies
Staff: 2
Annual Budget: $50-100,000
Exec. Director: Sheldon M. Edelman

Plastic Surgery Admininstrative Ass'n

444 F. Algonquin Ave.
Arlington Heights, IL   60005-4654
Tel: (847)228-8375   *Fax:* (847)228-6509
Members: 500 individuals
Annual Budget: $50-100,000
Exec. Director: Cathy Hay

Historical Note
Membership: $110/year (individual).

Publications:
Administrative Review. q. adv.

Meetings/Conferences:
Annual Meetings: Spring
1999 – Dallas, TX

Plastic Surgery Research Council *(1955)*

444 E. Algonquin Ave.
Arlington Heights, IL   60005-4564
Tel: (847)228-8375   *Fax:* (847)228-6509
Members: 243 individuals
Staff: 1
Annual Budget: $10-25,000
Secretary-Treasurer: Peter C. Johnson

Historical Note
To promote basic research in plastic and reconstructive surgery. Membership: $100/year.

Meetings/Conferences:
Annual Meetings: Spring/200
1999 – Pittsburgh, PA/May 22-25

Plastics Pipe Institute *(1950)*

1801 K St., N.W., Suite 600-K
Washington, DC   20006
Tel: (202)974-5201   *Fax:* (202)293-0048
Members: 44 companies/consultants
Staff: 4
Annual Budget: $500-1,000,000
Exec. Director: Rich Gottwald

Historical Note
A division of Soc. of the Plastics Industry, PPI promotes the effective use of plastic piping systems, contributes to the development of standards, publishes technical reports and statistics, educates designers, installers, users and officials and maintains liaison with other groups. Membership: varies by sales level (corporate).

Meetings/Conferences:
Semi-annual Meetings: Spring and Fall

Pleaters, Stitchers and Embroiderers Ass'n *(1920)*

145 W. 45th St., Suite 800

New York, NY   10036
Tel: (212)398-5700   *Fax:* (212)398-7818
Members: 110 companies
Staff: 6
Exec. Director: Sheldon M. Edelman

Historical Note
Absorbed (1988) Nat'l Hand Embroidery and Novelty Manufacturers Ass'n, and (1996) Artificial Flower Manufacturers Board of Trade. Major activity is labor negotiations with the Internat'l Ladies Garment Workers Union.

Plumbing and Drainage Institute *(1928)*

45 Bristol Drive, Suite 101
South Easton, MA   02375
Tel: (508)230-3516   *Fax:* (508)230-3529
Toll Free: (800)589 - 8956
E-Mail: pdiww@tiac.net
Web Site: http://www.pdionline.org
Members: 14 companies, 5 licensees
Staff: 1
Annual Budget: $100-250,000
Exec. Secretary: William C. Whitehead

Historical Note
Formerly (1949) Plumbing and Drainage Manufacturers Ass'n. Incorporated in 1954 in the State of Illinois. Members are manufacturers of engineered plumbing products, including drains, cleanouts, backwater valves, and other drainage specialties. PDI is active in the development and implementation of engineering standards for the industry.

Meetings/Conferences:
Annual Meetings: April
1999 – Dallas, TX

Plumbing Manufacturers Institute *(1956)*

1340 Remington Road, Suite A
Schaumburg, IL   60137
Tel: (847)884-9764   *Fax:* (847)884-9772
E-Mail: bhiggens@pmihome.org
Web Site: http://www.pmihome.org
Members: 44 companies
Staff: 4
Annual Budget: $500-1,000,000
Exec. Director: Barbara C. Higgens
V. President, Government Affairs: CeCe Kremer

Historical Note
The national trade association of plumbing products manufacturers. It has been, successively, the Sanitary Brass Institute, the Brass Gas Stop Institute, the Tubular Brass Institute and, most recently, in 1975, the Plumbing Brass Institute

Publications:
PMI News. m.

Meetings/Conferences:
Semi-Annual Meetings: Fall and Winter
1999 – Marco Island
2000 – Washington, DC(Williard)

Plumbing-Heating-Cooling Contractors - Nat'l Ass'n *(1883)*

180 S. Washington St., Box 6808
Falls Church, VA   22046-1148
Tel: (703)237-8100   *Fax:* (703)237-7442
Toll Free: (800)533 - 7694
E-Mail: naphcc@naphcc.org
Web Site: http://www.naphcc.org
Members: 5,500 individuals
Staff: 22
Annual Budget: $2-5,000,000
C.E.O.: Allen R. Inlow
Marketing/Communications Director: Charlotte Perham
Govt. Relations Director: Claudia Harris
Dir., Conventions/Meetings: Karen Weeks
V.P., Operations: John Weaver
Exec. Financial Officer: Laura Curtis
Membership Director: Pat Brookover
Editor: Julie A. Turner

Historical Note
Established as the Nat'l Ass'n of Master Plumbers, it became the Nat'l Ass'n of Plumbing Contractors in 1953, Nat'l Ass'n of Plumbing-Heating-Cooling Contractors in 1962, and assumed its present name in 1997. Sponsors and supports the PHCC-NA Political Action Committee, Education Techshow, Foundation, Scholarship Trust, and Legal Action Trust. Membership: $255/year.

Publications:
Connection. m. adv.
Execugram. m.
Techshow Exposition Buyers Guide. a. adv.
Who's Who in PHCC. a. adv.

Meetings/Conferences:
Annual Meetings: Fall

Plumbing-Heating-Cooling Information Bureau *(1919)*

200 E. Randolph
Suite 5000
Chicago, IL   60601-6401
Tel: (312)372-7331   *Fax:* (312)946-6100
Web Site: http://www.phcib.org
Members: 1000 individuals
Staff: 3
Assoc. Director: Frank Morasky

Historical Note
Formed by a merger of the Plumbing and Heating Modernization Committee (1955) and the Plumbing and Heating Industries Bureau (1919).

Meetings/Conferences:
Annual Meetings: Not held.

Poetry Soc. of America *(1910)*

15 Gramercy Park South

New York, NY   10003
Tel: (212)254-9628   *Fax:* (212)673-2352
Toll Free: (888)872 - 7636
Web Site: http://www.poetrysociety.org
Members: 3,000 individuals
Staff: 6
Annual Budget: $250-500,000
Exec. Director: Elise Paschen
Managing Director: Timothy Donnelly
Coordinator, Poetry in Motion: Andrew Zawacki
Director, Development: Bill Lynch

Historical Note
A non-profit cultural organization in support of poetry and poets, PSA's mission is to secure a wider recognition for poetry as one of the important forces making for a higher cultural life, to kindle a more intelligent appreciation of poetry, and to assist poets. PSA offers readings, lectures and symposia open to the public and conducts an extensive awards program. Membership: $40/year (individual).

Publications:
Poetry Society of America Journal. semi-a. adv.

Point-of-Purchase Advertising Institute *(1938)*

1660 L St., N.W., 10th Floor
Washington, DC   20036-5603
Tel: (202)530-3000   *Fax:* (202)530-3030
Web Site: http://www.popai.com
Members: 1,500 companies
Staff: 19
Annual Budget: $5-10,000,000
President: Richard K. Blatt
Director, Trade Show: Richard Walsh

Historical Note
Members are producers, buyers and users of signs and displays at retail.

Publications:
POPAI Merchandising Awards. a.
Research Bulletins. bi-m.
The POPAI Post. m.

Meetings/Conferences:
Annual Meetings: Annual Meeting in April and Annual
    Marketplace in October-November
1999 – Chicago, IL/March 27-29

Poland China Record Ass'n *(1876)*

P.O. Box 9758
Peoria, IL   61612-9758
Tel: (309)691-6301   *Fax:* (309)691-0168
Members: 275 individuals
Staff: 3
Annual Budget: under $10,000
Dir., Promotions: Jack Wall

Historical Note
Breeders and fanciers of Poland China swine. Member of the Nat'l Soc. of Livestock Record Ass'ns. Membership: $10 (first year); $75/year (thereafter - includes magazine subscription, listing in breeders directory, and maintenance fee).

Publications:
Purebred Picture. 10/year. adv.

Meetings/Conferences:
Annual Meetings: Semi-annual Meetings

Polaris Internat'l *(1969)*

3700 Crestwood Pkwy., Suite 350
Duluth, GA   30096
Tel: (770)279-4560   *Fax:* (770)279-4566
E-Mail: greene@america.net
Web Site: http://www.araf.com
Members: 63 firms
Staff: 13
President: Rudolf Beilfuss

Historical Note
Formerly (1998) Associated Regional Accounting Firms. Polaris is an association of independently owned and operated accounting and consulting firms with offices throughout North America.

Publications:
Management Services Update.
Marketing Services Update.
Membership Directory. a.
Pictorial Directory.
Resource Directory. a.
Resource Guide.
Technical Services Update.

Police Executive Research Forum *(1977)*

1120 Connecticut Ave., N.W., Suite 930
Washington, DC   20036
Tel: (202)466-7820   *Fax:* (202)466-7826
Web Site: http://www.policeForum.org
Members: 800 individuals
Staff: 29
Annual Budget: $2-5,000,000
Exec. Director: Chuck Wexler
Dir., Communications: Martha Plotkin
Membership/Meeting Coordinator: Dawn Blackburn
Dir., Finance: Ken Hartwick
Dir., Operations: Jim Burack
Dir., Research: Dennis Kenney
Dir., Management Services: Craig Fraser

Historical Note
A national organization of chief executives of city, county, and state police agencies. Membership is limited to nominated leaders of large police departments -- those with more than one hundred members or which are the principal police agency for a jurisdiction of at least 50,000 people. Originated in January, 1975; officially established in July, 1976; and incorporated in the District of Columbia in May, 1977. Membership: $250/year.

Publications:
Problem Solving Quarterly. q.

Subject of Debate. m.
Meetings/Conferences:
Annual Meetings: Spring/200
1999 – San Francisco, CA(Holiday Inn)

Polish-United States Economic Council *(1974)*
Historical Note
Became (1997) American Business Alliance for the Transition Economies of Eurasia.

Political Products Manufacturers Ass'n *(1972)*
60 State Rd.
Liberty, NY 12754
Tel: (914)292-7677   *Fax:* (914)292-2695
Members: 14 companies
Staff: 1
President: David Ross
Historical Note
Monitors laws pertaining to campaign spending as they affect the political products field.

Pollution Liability Insurance Ass'n *(1982)*
1333 Butterfield Road, Suite 408
Downers Grove, IL 60515-5609
Tel: (630)969-5300   *Fax:* (630)969-9404
Members: 20 companies
Staff: 2
Annual Budget: $5-10,000,000
President and C.E.O.: Thomas E. Knowlton
Historical Note
PLIA is a reciprocal pool, reinsuring pollution liability policies written by member companies.
Meetings/Conferences:
Annual Meetings: Spring

Polycrystalline Products Ass'n *(1992)*
Historical Note
Defunct in 1997.

Polyisocyanurate Insulation Manufacturers Ass'n *(1986)*
1001 Pennsylvania Ave., N.W.
5th Floor North
Washington, DC 20004
Tel: (202)624-2709   *Fax:* (202)628-3856
E-Mail: pima@pima.org
Web Site: http://www.pima.org
Members: 27 companies
Staff: 3
Annual Budget: $1-2,000,000
President: Jared O. Blum
Director, Administration: Alysa Lebeau
Membership Services: Rebecca Lloyd
Historical Note
Formerly (1986) Roof Insulation Council. Incorporated in Delaware, PIMA represents the interests of polyisocyanurate (polyiso) manufacturers and suppliers to the industry. PIMA's efforts center around four principal activities: product education, environmental responsibility, government partnerships, and energy conservation.
Publications:
PIMA Pages.
Meetings/Conferences:

Polymer Particulate Inhalation Group *(1997)*
1250 Connecticut Ave., N.W., Suite 700
Washington, DC 20036
Tel: (202)637-9040   *Fax:* (202)637-9178
Members: 12 manufacturers
Annual Budget: $25-50,000
Exec. Director: Elizabeth K. Hunt

Polystyrene Packaging Council *(1988)*
1801 K St., N.W., #600K
Washington, DC 20006
Tel: (202)974-5209   *Fax:* (202)296-7354
E-Mail: pspc@socplas.org
Web Site: http://www.polystyrene.org
Members: 12 companies
Staff: 4
Annual Budget: $1-2,000,000
Exec. Director: Michael Levy
Director of Communications: Laurie Keisek
Director, Environmental Affairs: Raymond Ehrlich
Publications:
Polystyrene News. q.

Polyurethane Foam Ass'n *(1980)*
P.O. Box 1459
Wayne, NJ 07474-1459
Tel: (973)633-9044   *Fax:* (973)628-8986
E-Mail: http://www.pfa.org
Members: 63 companies
Staff: 1
Annual Budget: $250-500,000
Exec. Director: Louis H. Peters
Historical Note
Formerly (1981) Flexible Polyurethane Foam Manufacturers Ass'n. Members are manufacturers of flexible polyurethane foam. Suppliers of raw material and equipment to the industry are eligible for associate membership.
Publications:
INTOUCH Bulletin. irreg.
Meetings/Conferences:
1999 – Arlington, VA/250
1999 – San Diego, CA/250
2000 – Arlington, VA/250
2000 – Newport, RI/250

Polyurethane Manufacturers Ass'n *(1971)*
800 Roosevelt Road, Bldg. C, Suite 20
Glen Ellyn, IL 60137-5833
Tel: (630)858-2670   *Fax:* (630)790-3095
E-Mail: info@pmahome.org
Web Site: http://www.pmahome.org
Members: 116 companies
Annual Budget: $250-500,000
Exec. Director: Richard W. Church
Exec. Secretary: Jerilyn Church
Ass'n Manager: Linda W. Kolling
Publications Editor: Janet Arden
Historical Note
Membership includes processors of solid cast, microcellular, RIM and thermoplastic urethane elastomers; manufacturers, suppliers, distributors and sales agents of raw materials, additives or processing equipment; and individuals or companies providing publishing, education, research, or consulting services to the industry. Membership: $1,000-4,000/year, based on sales volume (company).
Publications:
Membership Directory. a.
Polytopics. bi-m.
Meetings/Conferences:
Semi-Annual Meetings: Spring and Fall/200
1999 – Hilton Head, SC(Hyatt Regency)/March 20-24
1999 – New Orleans, LA/Nov. 6-10

Pony of the Americas Club
5240 Elmwood Ave.
Indianapolis, IN 46203
Tel: (317)788-0107   *Fax:* (317)788-8974
E-Mail: poac@iquest.net
Web Site: http://www.poac.org
Members: 2,300 individuals
Staff: 4
Annual Budget: $250-500,000
Exec. Secretary Protem: Jean Kelley
Historical Note
Members are breeders and fanciers of the Pony of the Americas breed, an Appaloosa-type pony used in pleasure, performance, and halter competitions. Membership: $20/year.
Publications:
PoA. a. adv.
Meetings/Conferences:
Annual Meetings: Februray/200
1999 – Orlando, FL(Disney)

Popcorn Institute *(1943)*
401 N. Michigan Ave.
Chicago, IL 60611-4267
Tel: (312)644-6610   *Fax:* (312)245-1085
Web Site: http://www.popcorn.org
Members: 37 companies
Staff: 2
Annual Budget: $250-500,000
Exec. Director: William E. Smith
Mktg./Communications Director: Deirdre Flynn
Historical Note
Official trade association of the popcorn industry. Compiles and publishes statistics on popcorn production and distribution, sponsors consumer education programs, and supports responsible crop technology. Absorbed the Popcorn Processors Ass'n in 1960.
Meetings/Conferences:
1999 – Chicago, IL

Popular Culture Ass'n *(1967)*
Bowling Green University
Bowling Green, OH 43403-0177
Tel: (419)372-7861   *Fax:* (419)372-8095
Members: 3,000 individuals
Staff: 2
Annual Budget: $50-100,000
Secretary-Treasurer: Ray B. Browne, Ph.D.
Historical Note
Educators interested in various aspects of popular culture, i.e., cartoons, folklore, protest music, soap operas, black culture, motion pictures, etc. Membership: varies by number of publication volumes.
Publications:
Journal of Popular Culture. q. adv.
Popular Culture Newsletter. q.
Meetings/Conferences:
Annual Meetings: Spring
1999 – San Diego, CA/March 31-April 3/1500
2000 – New Orleans, LA(Marriott)

Population Ass'n of America *(1931)*
721 Ellsworth Dr., Suite 303
Silver Spring, MD 20910-4436
Tel: (301)565-6710   *Fax:* (301)565-7850
E-Mail: info@popassoc.org
Web Site: http://www.popassoc.org
Members: 3,000 individuals
Staff: 2
Annual Budget: $500-1,000,000
Exec. Administrator: Stephanie D. Dudley
Historical Note
Established in 1931 and incorporated in New York in 1937. Promotes research in human population. Membership: $70/year (individual), $205/year (company).
Publications:
Applied Demography. q.
Demography. q. adv.
PAA Affairs. q.
Meetings/Conferences:
Annual Meetings: Spring/1,400
1999 – New York, NY(Marriott Marquis)/March 25-27/1400
2000 – Los Angeles, CA(Bonaventure)/March 23-25/1400

2001 – Washington, DC(Grand Hyatt)/March 29-31/1600
2002 – Atlanta, GA(Hilton)/May 9-11/1400

Porcelain Enamel Institute *(1930)*
4004 Hillsboro Pike, Suite 224-B
Nashville, TN 37215
Tel: (615)385-5357   *Fax:* (615)385-5463
E-Mail: penamel@aol.com
Members: 90 companies
Staff: 3
Annual Budget: $250-500,000
Exec. V. President: Tom Sanford
Historical Note
PEI broke away from the American Ceramic Soc. in 1930. From then until 1994, it represented the porcelain enamel industry in the United States, when it expanded its scope to include suppliers and makers of porcelain enamel products and raw materials in all of North America. Membership: annual dues based on sales volume.
Publications:
First Firing. m.
Newsletter. bi-m. adv.
Proceedings. a.
Meetings/Conferences:
Annual Meetings: Fall/100
1999 – Naples, FL

Portable and Stationary Crushing Bureau
Historical Note
A bureau of the Construction Industry Manufacturers Ass'n.

Portable Computer and Communications Ass'n
P.O. Box 2460
Boulder Creek, CA 95006-2460
Tel: (831)338-0924   *Fax:* (831)338-7806
E-Mail: pcca@pcca.org
Web Site: http://www.pcca.org
Members: 75 firms and organizations
Staff: 2
Annual Budget: $50-100,000
Exec. Director: Bob Venter
Historical Note
Representing firms, organizations, and individuals interested in mobile communications, PCCA publishes and disseminates information, standards, software, and other materials to facilitate the synthesis of computing and communications technologies.

Portable Power Equipment Manufacturers Ass'n *(1959)*
4340 East-West Hwy. Suite 912
Bethesda, MD 20814
Tel: (301)652-0774   *Fax:* (301)654-6138
E-Mail: ppema1@msn.com
Members: 15 companies
Staff: 3
Annual Budget: $500-1,000,000
President: Donald E. Purcell
Director, Public Affairs: Karen Hutchison
Historical Note
Formerly (1977) Power Saw Manufacturers Ass'n and until 1984, the Chain Saw Manufacturers Ass'n.
Publications:
PPEMA Perspectives. 3/year.
Meetings/Conferences:
Annual Meetings: June

Portable Rechargeable Battery Ass'n *(1991)*
1000 Parkwood Circle, Suite 430
Atlanta, GA 30339
Tel: (770)612-8826   *Fax:* (770)612-8841
Members: 130 companies
Staff: 2
Annual Budget: $1-2,000,000
President and C.E.O.: Norm England
Historical Note
Incorporated in the District of Columbia in 1991. Members are manufacturers, distributors, users, and sellers of small rechargeable batteries and battery-powered products. Works to facilitate the collection and recycling of small sealed rechargeable batteries. Membership fee varies, based on sales volume.
Publications:
Recharger Newsletter. q.
Recharger Update. irreg.
Meetings/Conferences:
1999 – Orlando, FL/Apr. 21-22

Portable Sanitation Ass'n Internat'l *(1971)*
7800 Metro Pkwy., Suite 104
Bloomington, MN 55425
Tel: (612)854-8300   *Fax:* (612)854-7560
Toll Free: (800)822 - 3020
Members: 584 companies
Staff: 3
Annual Budget: $250-500,000
Exec. Director: William F. Carroll
Historical Note
PSAI members are makers of chemical toilets, supplies and services and companies that rent and service them. Representation is expanding to include site services on constuction and special events. Membership: $300/yr. (company, average).
Publications:
Industry Catalog. a.
PSA In Action. m. adv.
Meetings/Conferences:
Annual Meetings: November/300-400 Virginia Beach,
    VA(Pavilion Towers & Resort)/Nov./400
1999 – Pasadena, CA(Holiday Inn)/400

Portland Cement Ass'n *(1916)*

5420 Old Orchard Road
Skokie, IL 60077-1083
Tel: (847)966-6200   *Fax:* (847)966-8389
Web Site: http://www.portcement.org
Members: 45 companies
Staff: 250
Annual Budget: $25-50,000,000
President: John P. Gleason, Jr.
Communications Director: Bruce D. McIntosh
V. President, Market Development: George B. Barney
Corporation Secretary: Jan Farnsworth
V. President, Research and Technical Services: Anthony E. Fiorato
Manager, Education and Training: Richard Bohan
V. President, Finance and Treasurer: William C. Kramer
Director, MIS: Kim L. Martin

Historical Note
Has an annual budget of approximately $30 million.

Publications:
Executive Report. bi-w.

Meetings/Conferences:
Annual Meetings: November
1999 – Boca Raton, FL(Boca Raton Club)/Nov. 14-16/125
2000 – Pebble Beach, CA(Spanish Inn)/Nov. 12-14/125
2001 – Washington, DC(Four Seasons)/Nov. 11-13/125

Portugal-United States Chamber of Commerce (1979)
590 Fifth Ave., Third Floor
New York, NY 10036
Tel: (212)354-4627   *Fax:* (212)575-4737
Members: 150 businesses
Staff: 1
Annual Budget: $100-250,000
Exec. Director: Ana M. Osorio

Historical Note
A bilateral Chamber of Commerce, PUSCC exists to promote trade, investment and joint ventures between the two countries. Membership: $200/year (individual); $500/year (corporation); $1,000/year (sustaining).

Publications:
Directory. a. adv.
Newsletter. w.

Post Card Distributors Ass'n of North America (1973)
5024-R Campbell Blvd.
Baltimore, MD 21236
Tel: (410)931-8100   *Fax:* (410)931-8111
E-Mail: sking@unidial.com
Members: 110 companies
Staff: 2
Annual Budget: $100-250,000
Exec. Director: Steven T. King, CAE

Historical Note
PCDANA members are companies distributing local view scenic post cards and souvenirs in North America and the Caribbean. Membership: $250-300/year (company).

Publications:
Post Card Letter. 4/year. adv.

Meetings/Conferences:

Post-Tensioning Institute (1976)
1717 West Northern Ave., Suite 114
Phoenix, AZ 85021-5470
Tel: (602)870-7540   *Fax:* (602)870-7541
Web Site: PTI-USA.ORG
Members: 900 individuals
Staff: 3
Annual Budget: $500-1,000,000
Exec. Director: Gerard J. McGuire

Historical Note
PTI provides research, technical development, marketing and promotional activities for companies engaged in post-tensioned prestressed construction. Members of the institute include major post-tension materials fabricators and manufacturers of prestressing materials. Membership: $80/year (individual); corporate dues vary.

Publications:
PTI Newsletter. q.
Technical Notes. q.

Meetings/Conferences:
Semi-annual Meetings: Fall and Spring

Potash and Phosphate Institute (1935)
655 Engineering Drive, Suite 110
Norcross, GA 30092-2821
Tel: (770)447-0335   *Fax:* (770)448-0439
Members: 9 companies
Staff: 35
Annual Budget: $5-10,000,000
President: David W. Dibb
Exec. V. President: B.C. Darst
V. President: R.T. Roberts

Historical Note
Formerly (1971) American Potash Institute, Inc., (1975) Potash Institute of North America and (1977) Potash and Phosphate Institute.

Publications:
Better Crops with Plant Food. q.

Meetings/Conferences:
Annual Meetings: October

Potato Ass'n of America (1913)
Univ. of Maine, 5715 Coburn Hall, Rm. 6
Orono, ME 04469-5715
Tel: (207)581-3042   *Fax:* (207)581-3015
E-Mail: umpotato@maine.maine.edu
Web Site: http://www.potato.tamu.edu/variety/paa.html
Members: 1,833 individuals
Staff: 4

Annual Budget: $50-100,000
Secretary: John Ojala, Ph.D.

Historical Note
Founded in New York, NY in 1912 as the Nat'l Potato Ass'n of America and incorporated in New Jersey in 1913; became the Potato Ass'n of America, Inc. in 1917. PAA is a professional society for potato research, extension, utilization and technical workers in all aspects of the American potato industry. Membership: $40/year (individual), $65/year (organization), $15/year (student), $300/year (sustaining).

Publications:
American Journal of Potato Research. bi-m.

Meetings/Conferences:
Annual Meetings: Summer
1999 – Trenton, NJ/Aug. 1-5

Potato Board (1972)
Historical Note
Common name for the Nat'l Potato Promotion Board.

Poultry Science Ass'n (1908)
1111 N. Dunlap Ave.
Savoy, IL 61874
Tel: (217)356-3182   *Fax:* (217)398-4119
E-Mail: psa@assochq.org
Web Site: http://www.psa.uiuc.edu
Members: 2,000 individuals
Staff: 1
Annual Budget: $500-1,000,000
Business Manager: Gregory P. Martin

Historical Note
Originated in 1908 as the Internat'l Ass'n of Instructors and Investigators in Poultry Husbandry. Became the American Ass'n of Instructors and Investigators in Poultry Husbandry in 1912 and the Poultry Science Ass'n, Inc. 1926. Members are university and industry researchers involved in poultry, avian science, and related disciplines. Membership: $55/year (individual); $500-1,000/year (company).

Publications:
Abstracts. a. adv.
Poultry Science. m. adv.
PSA Newsletter. q.

Meetings/Conferences:
Annual Meetings: Summer
1999 – Fayetteville, NC(Univ. of Arkansas)/July 25-28

Powder Actuated Tool Manufacturers Institute (1952)
1603 Boonslick Road
St. Charles, MO 63301
Tel: (314)947-6610   *Fax:* (314)946-3336
Members: 7 companies
Staff: 2
Annual Budget: $50-100,000
Exec. Director: James A. Borchers

Historical Note
Represents manufacturers of construction tools used to fasten to and into steel and concrete. PATMI is a member of the Nat'l Safety Council and the American Nat'l Standards Institute. Membership: $5,000/year.

Publications:
PATMI Basic Training Manual.

Meetings/Conferences:

Powder Coating Institute (1981)
2121 Eisenhower Ave., Suite 401
Alexandria, VA 22314
Tel: (703)684-1770   *Fax:* (703)684-1771
Web Site: http://www.powdercoating.org
Members: 140 individuals, 290 companies
Staff: 4
Annual Budget: $1-2,000,000
Exec. Director: Gregory J. Bocchi
Dir., Communications: Jeff Palmer
Director, Programs: Clark Mulligan

Historical Note
Members are companies producing powder coatings and related application equipment used to coat and protect metals.

Publications:
PCI Newsletter. bi-m.

Meetings/Conferences:
1999 – Dallas, TX(Dallas Conv. Centr.)/Sept. 21-23

Powder Metallurgy Equipment Ass'n (1958)
Historical Note
A constituent part of the Metal Powder Industries Federation. Equipment suppliers for powder metallurgy parts and products.

Powder Metallurgy Parts Ass'n (1957)
Historical Note
A constituent part of the Metal Powder Industries Federation. Manufacturers of powder metallurgy parts and products. Formerly (1967) Powder Metallurgy Parts Manufacturers Ass'n.

Power and Communication Contractors Ass'n (1945)
6301 Stevenson Ave., Suite One
Alexandria, VA 22304
Tel: (703)823-1555   *Fax:* (703)823-5064
Web Site: http://www.pccaweb.org
Members: 550 companies
Staff: 5
Annual Budget: $500-1,000,000
Exec. V. President: Michael E. Strother

Historical Note
Contractors and suppliers specializing in electric power line, telephone, cable television construction, directional drilling and their suppliers. Formerly (1950) Rural Electrical Contractors Ass'n. Membership: $500/year (company).

Publications:
Reporter. m. adv.

Meetings/Conferences:
1999 – Maui, HI(Four Seasons Resort)/Feb. 27-March 3

Power Crane and Shovel Ass'n (1945)
Historical Note
A bureau of the Construction Industry Manufacturers Association.

Power Electronics Soc. (1987)
Historical Note
See IEEE Power Electronics Soc.

Power Engineering Soc.
Historical Note
See IEEE Power Engineering Soc.

Power Sources Manufacturers Ass'n (1985)
14 Ridgedale Ave., Suite 125
Cedar Knolls, NJ 07927
Tel: (973)538-9170   *Fax:* (973)326-8943
E-Mail: power@psma.com
Web Site: http://www.psma.com
Members: 80 companies
Staff: 3
Annual Budget: $50-100,000
Exec. Director: J.M. Fletcher

Historical Note
Worldwide membership consists of manufacturers and users of AC and DC power source systems and related components. Publishes technical standards and other information for the industry. Co-sponsors the Applied Power Electronics Conference annually each Spring. Regular membership: $750-2,500/year, based on number of employees.

Publications:
Handbook of Terminology.
Research & Development Handbook.
Technical Journals & Proceedings. irreg.
Update Newsletter. q.

Meetings/Conferences:
Annual Meetings: February-March/600
1999 – Dallas, TX(Adams Mark)/March 14-18

Power Tool Institute (1937)
1300 Sumner Ave.
Cleveland, OH 44115-2851
Tel: (216)241-7333   *Fax:* (216)241-0105
E-Mail: pti@taol.com
Web Site: http://www.taol.com/pti
Members: 12 companies
Staff: 2
Exec. Manager: Charles M. Stockinger

Historical Note
Formerly (1969) Electric Tool Institute. PTI works to harmonize global product listing standards and develops educational programs on the safe use of power tools.

Publications:
Directory. a.

Meetings/Conferences:
Annual Meetings: second or third week of October, alternating west coast-east coast.

Power Transmission Distributors Ass'n (1960)
6400 Shafer Court, Suite 670
Rosemont, IL 60018-4909
Tel: (847)825-2000   *Fax:* (847)825-0953
E-Mail: ptda@ptda.org
Web Site: http://ptda.org
Members: 496 companies
Staff: 7
Annual Budget: $1-2,000,000
Exec. V. President: Mary Sue Lyon
Meeting Manager: Beth Silos

Historical Note
Established as Mechanical Power Transmission Equipment Distributors Ass'n, it assumed its present name in 1966. Members are industrial power transmission/motion control distributor firms representing locations throughout North America and several other countries, and manufacturing firms. Membership: based on annual sales volume.

Publications:
Convention Guide. a.
Membership Directory. a.
Transmissions. q.

Meetings/Conferences:
Annual Meetings: Fall/1,000
1999 – Toronto, ON, Canada(Sheraton Centre)/Oct. 13-16
2000 – Hawaii(Hilton Waikoloa)/Oct. 25-28
2001 – Atlanta, GA(Marriott Marquis)/Oct. 3-6
2002 – Palm Desert, CA(Marriott Desert Springs)/Oct. 9-12

Power Transmission Representatives Ass'n (1972)
Historical Note
Organization changed name to Power-Motion Technology Representatives Ass'n in 1994.

Power Washers of North America
Two Wisconsin Circle, Suite 700
Chevy Chase, MD 20815
Tel: (301)961-1528
Toll Free: (800)393 - 7962
E-Mail: pwnamail@aol.com
Web Site: http://www.pwna.org
Members: 300 companies
Staff: 4
Annual Budget: $250-500,000
Exec. Director: Glenn Fellman
Dir., Communications: Andrew Avery

Historical Note
Membership: $200-400/year (company).

Publications:
PWNA Talks. m.
Waterworks. bi-m. adv.

Meetings/Conferences:

Power-Motion Technology Representatives Ass'n *(1972)*
330 S. Wells St., Suite 1422
Chicago, IL 60606-7105
Tel: (312)360-0389 *Fax:* (312)360-0388
Toll Free: (888)737 - 7872
E-Mail: REP-PTRA@worldnet.att.net
Members: 165 companies, 75 allied
Staff: 2
Annual Budget: $100-250,000
Exec. Director: Barbara Boden
Ass'n Counsel: Mitchell Kramer

Historical Note
Formerly Power Transmission Representatives Ass'n(1994). The purpose of this organization is three-fold: 1)to promote science of power transmission/motion control engineering, 2)to promote educational programs and activities and 3)to promote representatives placed in the industry.

Publications:
Focus Newsletter. q.
Locator Membership Directory. a.

Meetings/Conferences:
Annual Meetings: Spring/300
1999 – Monterey, CA(Doubletree)/April 14-18/400

Practising Law Institute *(1933)*
810 Seventh Ave.
New York, NY 10019
Tel: (212)824-5700 *Fax:* (800)321-0093
Toll Free: (800)260 - 4754
Web Site: http://www.pli.edu
Members: 60,000 individuals
Staff: 100
Annual Budget: $10-25,000,000
Exec. Director: Victor J. Rubino
Manager, Public Information: Ann Tracy

Historical Note
Has an annual budget of approximately $16 million. Membership: $100-$975/year, on a sliding scale based on the number of practicing attorneys in the firm.

Publications:
Business Accounting for Lawyers. 8/year.
PLI News. 2/week.

Meetings/Conferences:

Pre-Arrangement Ass'n of America *(1956)*
Historical Note
Became a part of the Internat'l Cemetery and Funeral Ass'n in 1996.

Precast/Prestressed Concrete Institute *(1954)*
175 W. Jackson Blvd., Suite 1859
Chicago, IL 60604
Tel: (312)786-0300 *Fax:* (312)786-0353
E-Mail: info@pci.org
Web Site: http://www.pci.org
Members: 2,550 firms, engineers & architects
Staff: 23
Annual Budget: $2-5,000,000
President: Thomas B. Battles
Nat'l Marketing Director: Brian D. Goodmiller
Director, Administration & Finance: Gary Munstermann

Historical Note
PCI is a non-profit association for the advancement of the design, manufacture and use of precast prestressed concrete, plant-produced building and bridge components. Members are producer companies, suppliers, engineers and architects. Formerly (1989) Prestressed Concrete Institute.

Publications:
Ascent. q.
Membership Directory. a. adv.
PCI Journal. bi-m. adv.
Publications Catalog. a.

Meetings/Conferences:
Annual Meetings: October/750

Precious Metals Producers Group
Historical Note
Address unknown in 1997.

Precision Chiropractic Research Soc. *(1976)*
Historical Note
Address unknown in 1998.

Precision Machined Products Ass'n *(1933)*
6700 W. Snowville Road
Brecksville, OH 44141-3292
Tel: (440)526-0300 *Fax:* (440)526-5803
E-Mail: jmcnaughton@pmpa.org
Web Site: http://www.pmpa.org
Members: 600 companies
Staff: 16
Annual Budget: $1-2,000,000
Exec. V. President: Jack D. McNaughton, CAE
Dir., Human Resources/Govt. Affairs: David Burch
Dir., Marketing/Training: Scott D. Giesler
Director, Membership Services: Robert C. Kiener

Historical Note
Formerly (1995) Nat'l Screw Machine Products Ass'n. PMPA member companies are producers of high precision component products. Produces several educational opportunities for members,

emphasizing quality assurance and emerging technologies. Sponsors the PMPA Political Action Committee.

Publications:
PMPA Reports. m.

Meetings/Conferences:
Annual Meetings: Fall/250
1999 – Acapulco, Mexico(Princess)/Oct. 24-27
2000 – San Diego, CA(Rancho Bernando)/Oct. 21-25
2001 – Marco Island, FL(Marriott)Sept.

Precision Measurements Ass'n *(1958)*
Historical Note
Address unknown in 1995.

Precision Metalforming Ass'n *(1942)*
6363 Oak Tree Blvd.
Independence, OH 44131-2500
Tel: (216)901-8800 *Fax:* (216)901-9190
E-Mail: pma@pma.org
Web Site: http://www.metalforming.com
Members: 1,500 companies
Staff: 38
Annual Budget: $5-10,000,000
President: Jon E. Jenson, CAE
Coordinator, Communications: Marlene O'Brien
Manager, Meetings: Janine M. Langer
Exposition Manager: Cathy Ledenican
Manager, Training and Education: David C. Sansone, CAE
Program Dir., PMA Educational Foundation: Charlie Brinkman
Exec. V. President: William E. Gaskin, CAE
Regulatory Issues Manager: Laura A. Nakoneczny
Manager, Administrative Services: Ariana R. Molina
Controller: Marcia C. Daniels
Membership Development Manager: Michael Young, Sr.
Membership Development Coordinator: Janet Krall
Editor: Donald B. Dibbons
Associate Publisher: Kathy M. Delollis
Government Relations Manager: Christopher E. Howell
V. President: Daniel E. Ellashek, CAE

Historical Note
Established in 1942 as the Pressed Metal Institute, it became the American Metal Stamping Ass'n in 1961, and assumed its present name in 1987. Custom Roll Forming Institute was merged into PMA in August, 1992. PMA is the trade association representing the metalforming industry of North America. Members include producers of metal stampings, spinnings, washers and precision sheet metal fabrications as well as suppliers of equipment, materials and services to the metalforming industry. Sponsors and supports the PMA Voice of the Industry Committee. Membership: dues based on member company's annual sales.

Publications:
Metal Forming Magazine. m. adv.
Update. bi-m.

Meetings/Conferences:
1999 – Chicago, IL(Rosemont Convention Center)/April 11-15/13000

Preferred Funeral Directors Internat'l *(1937)*
347 Main St.
Placerville, CA 95667
Tel: (530)626-7255 *Fax:* (530)626-5420
Members: 100 companies
Staff: 2
Annual Budget: $100-250,000
Exec. Director: Roger L. Duerksen

Historical Note
Established as the Advertising Funeral Directors of America, it assumed its present name in the mid-50s. Members are larger-volume independent funeral homes.

Publications:
P. F.

Meetings/Conferences:
Semi-Annual Meetings: Spring and Fall.
1999 – Death Valley, CA

Preferred Hotels and Resorts Worldwide *(1968)*
311 S. Wacker Dr., Suite 1900
Chicago, IL 60606-6618
Tel: (312)913-0400 *Fax:* (312)913-0444
Web Site: http://www.preferredhotels.com
Members: 100 hotels
Staff: 30
Annual Budget: $5-10,000,000
President and C.E.O.: Peter Cass
Director, Public Relations/Advertising: Robert Dirkes

Historical Note
An exclusive group of luxury hotels and resorts worldwide. Founded to give independent hotels a way to compete with hotel chains in marketing and reservation programs. Formerly (1992) the Preferred Hotels Ass'n. Membership dues computed on a per-room basis.

Publications:
Directory. a.
Inside Preferred Hotels.

Meetings/Conferences:
1999 – Hong Kong, Japan/July 23-28

Prepaid Communications Ass'n *(1994)*
Historical Note
Organization defunct in 1996.

Presbyterian Health, Education and Welfare Ass'n *(1956)*
Presbyterian Center Room 3041
100 Witherspoon St.
Louisville, KY 40202-1396
Tel: (502)569-5794 *Fax:* (502)569-8034
E-Mail: helenl@crt.pcusa.org
Members: 1,500 individuals
Staff: 2

Annual Budget: $50-100,000
Exec. Director: Rev. Helen Locklear

Historical Note
Formerly Nat'l Presbyterian Health and Welfare Ass'n. Became the United Presbyterian Health, Education and Welfare Ass'n in 1969 and assumed its present name in 1989. PHEWA is an organization for Presbyterians dedicated professionally and personally to the enactment of social justice. Eight networks are organized under the PHEWA aegis: Community Ministries and Neighborhood Organizations, Presbyterian AIDS Network, Presbyterians Affirming Reproductive Options, Presbyterian Ass'n of Specialized Pastoral Ministries, Presbyterians for Disability Concerns, Presbyterian Health Network, Presbyterian Network on Alcohol and Other Drug Abuse, and Presbyterian Serious Mental Illness Network. Membership: $35/year (individual); $100-250/year (organization).

Publications:
Newsletter. q.

Meetings/Conferences:
Biennial Meetings: Uneven years
1999 – San Diego, CA(Four Point Sheraton)/Jan. 28-31

Pressure Sensitive Tape Council *(1953)*
401 N. Michigan Ave., Suite 2200
Chicago, IL 60611-4267
Tel: (312)644-6610 *Fax:* (312)527-6640
E-Mail: pstc@sba.com
Members: 27 companies
Staff: 3
Annual Budget: $250-500,000
Exec. V. President: Glen R. Anderson

Historical Note
Members are manufacturers of pressure sensitive tape located in North America. Membership: dues based on volume of tape sales.

Publications:
Pressure Sensitive Tape Products Directory. a.
Technical Seminar Proceedings. a.
Test Methods For Pressure Sensitive Adhesive Tape. irreg.

Meetings/Conferences:

Pressure Vessel Manufacturers Ass'n *(1975)*
8 South Michigan Avenue
Suite 1000
Chicago, IL 60603
Tel: (312)456-5590 *Fax:* (312)580-0165
E-Mail: pvma@gss.net
Web Site: http://www.pvma.org
Members: 27 companies
Staff: 2
Annual Budget: $50-100,000
Exec. Director: August L. Sisco

Historical Note
Members are manufacturers and suppliers for the pressure vessel fabricating industry. Membership: $900-3,600/yr. (based on sales).

Meetings/Conferences:
Annual Meetings: Spring

Pressure Washer Manufacturers Ass'n *(1997)*
1300 Sumner Ave.
Cleveland, OH 44115-2851
Tel: (216)241-7333 *Fax:* (216)241-0105
E-Mail: pwma@taol.com
Web Site: http://www.taol.com/pwma
Members: 4 individuals
Staff: 3
Annual Budget: $50-100,000
Secretary/Treasurer: John H. Addington

Primary Glass Manufacturers Council
2945 S.W. Wanamaker Dr., Suite A
Topeka, KS 66614-5321
Tel: (785)271-0208 *Fax:* (785)271-0166
E-Mail: pgmc@glasswebsite.com
Web Site: http://www.glasswebsite.com/pgmc
Members: 5 companies
Staff: 8
Annual Budget: $250-500,000
Exec. V. President: William J. Birch
Technical Director: James Benney

Historical Note
Represents manufacturers of architectural glass products, providing standards development and other technical services. Membership: $60,000/year.

Publications:
Specifiers Guide to Architectural Glass. a.

Meetings/Conferences:

Print Council of America *(1956)*
Spencer Museum of Art
University of Kansas
Lawrence, KS 66045
Tel: (785)864-4710 *Fax:* (785)864-3112
Members: 170 individuals
Annual Budget: under $10,000
President: Stephen Goddard

Historical Note
Professional organization of museum curators of prints, drawings, and photographs. Has no paid staff. Membership: $40/year.

Publications:
Newsletter. a.

Meetings/Conferences:
Annual Meetings: Spring
1999 – New York, NY
2000 – Los Angeles, CA

Print Information Center

Historical Note
A special industry group of Printing Industries of America.

PrintImage Internat'l *(1975)*
401 N. Michigan Ave., Suite 2100
Chicago, IL 60611-4390
Tel: (312)321-6886   *Fax:* (312)527-6789
Web Site: http://www.printimage.org
Members: 3,000 companies
Staff: 8
Annual Budget: $2-5,000,000
Exec. Director: David J. Steinhardt
Director, Marketing Communications: Kyle Donnelly
Director, Membership: Jeff Wilson

Historical Note
Founded as Nat'l Ass'n of Quick Printers; assumed its current name in 1998. Members are owners and managers of businesses that provide printing and print-related services on a quick turn-around basis. Membership: $349-695/year.

Publications:
Annual Resource Guide and Directory. a. adv.
PrintImage Network Newsletter. m. adv.

Meetings/Conferences:
Semi-Annual Meetings: February and July
1999 - Beverly Hills, CA(Beverly Hilton)/Feb. 16-20/300
1999 - Chicago, IL(Hyatt Regency)

Printing Brokerage Buyers Ass'n *(1985)*
P.O. Box 744
Palm Beach, FL 33480
Tel: (561)844-9834   *Fax:* (561)845-7130
Toll Free: (800)448 - 8952
Members: 1000 individuals, 700 companies, 100 internat'l
Staff: 5
Annual Budget: $500-1,000,000
Exec. Director: Vincent Mallardi

Historical Note
Formerly (1993) Printing Brokerage Ass'n. PBBA promotes business relationships between brokers, buying groups, manufacturers and related companies in the printing industry; sets standards and codes of ethical conduct and acts as a source of information and referral. Membership: $545/year (individual); $5,000/year (organization).

Publications:
Broker Age. m
Directory and Sourcebook. a.

Meetings/Conferences:
Annual Meetings: Spring

Printing Industries of America *(1887)*
100 Daingerfield Road
Alexandria, VA 22314
Tel: (703)519-8100   *Fax:* (703)548-3227
E-Mail: rroper@printing.com
Web Site: http://www.printing.org
Members: 14,000 companies
Staff: 75
Annual Budget: $10-25,000,000
President & C.E.O.: Ray W. Roper, CAE
Manager, Public Relations: Dorothy Thompson
Senior V. President, Government Affairs: Benjamin Y. Cooper
Director, Political Affairs: Wendy Lechner
Director, Education and Training: Mary Garnett
Senior V. President, Education and Human Relations: Brian W. Gill
Sr. V. President, Finance and Administration: Dan E. Robertson
Director, Marketing and Publications: Lucy Seal
Director, Information Systems: Stacey Kuhlman

Historical Note
The umbrella organization of the graphic arts industry. PIA is a federation of national, regional, state, and city associations incorporated under the laws of the District of Columbia. Established as United Typothetae of America, it became Printing Industry of America in 1945 and assumed its present name in 1965. Sections include Binding Industries of America, Graphic Arts Marketing Information Service, Graphic Communications Ass'n, Internat'l Thermographers Ass'n, Label Printing Industries of America, Magazine Printers Section, Non-Heatset Web Section, Printing Industry Financial Executives, Print Information Center, and Web Offset Ass'n. Supports the Printing Industries of America Political Action Committee (PRINT-PAC). Has an annual budget of approximately $12.0 million.

Publications:
Benchmark Technologies.
Digits.
PIA Ratios.
Printer's Resource Catalog.
The Capital Letter. w.
The Managment Portfolio. m.

Meetings/Conferences:
Annual Meetings: Fall
1999 - San Antonio, TX(Hyatt Hill Country)

Printing Industry Credit Executives *(1977)*
150 Broadway, Suite 1113
New York, NY 10038
Tel: (212)964-8600   *Fax:* (212)964-0527
Web Site: http://www.piceservices.com
Members: 130 individuals
Staff: 4
Annual Budget: $100-250,000
Administrator: Lee Berkowitz

Historical Note
Membership: $825/year (organization).

Publications:
Price Update Newsletter. semi-a.

Meetings/Conferences:
Semi-annual Meetings: always March and September

Printing Industry Financial Executives

Historical Note
A special industry group of Printing Industries of America.

Private Art Dealers Ass'n *(1990)*
P.O. Box 872, Lenox Hill Station
New York, NY 10021
Tel: (212)572-0772   *Fax:* (212)572-8398
Members: 60 individuals

Historical Note
PADA represents a select group of private art dealers. Services include appraisals for estate purposes and donations. Membership (by invitiation only): $650/year (individual).

Publications:
Directory of PADA Dealer Members. a.

Private Label Manufacturers Ass'n *(1979)*
369 Lexington Ave., Third Floor
New York, NY 10017
Tel: (212)972-3131   *Fax:* (212)983-1382
Web Site: http://www.plma.com
Members: 2,500 companies
Staff: 45
Annual Budget: $5-10,000,000
President: Brian Sharoff
V. President, Administration: Myra Rosen
V.P., Sales and Marketing: Lewis Sterler

Historical Note
Promotes the purchase of private label or store brand products by consumers. Has an annual budget of approximately $6 million.

Publications:
Newsletter. q.

Meetings/Conferences:
1999 - Rosemont, IL(Convention Center)/Nov. 14-17

Process Equipment Manufacturers' Ass'n *(1960)*
111 Park Place
Falls Church, VA 22046-4513
Tel: (703)533-0286   *Fax:* (703)241-5603
E-Mail: pemahq@aol.com
Members: 50 companies
Staff: 12
Annual Budget: $100-250,000
Exec. Director: Harry W. Buzzerd, Jr. CAE
Meetings & Travel Manager: Judith O. Buzzerd
Members Services: Sue Denston

Historical Note
Companies engaged in the manufacture and supply of equipment for food, chemical, pulp & paper, water and wastewater processing, air pollution control, liquids-solids separation, etc.

Publications:
PEMA Press. bi-m.

Meetings/Conferences:
Biennial Meetings: odd years in February
1999 - Delray Beach, FL(Marriott)/Feb. 18-21/100

Processed Apples Institute *(1951)*
5775 Peachtree-Dunwoody Rd., Suite 500-G
Atlanta, GA 30342-1558
Tel: (404)252-3663   *Fax:* (404)252-0774
E-Mail: pai@assnhq.com
Web Site: http://www.appleproducts.org
Members: 80 companies
Staff: 5
Annual Budget: $100-250,000
President: Andrew G. Ebert, Ph.D.
Director, Client Services: Nancy Marlin

Historical Note
Members are producers of processed apple products; suppliers of equipment, packaging or ingredients to the apple processing industry; brokers and concentrate manufacturers.

Publications:
Reference Manual for the Processed Apples Industry.

Meetings/Conferences:
Annual Meetings: Spring
1999 - Rahono, CA(La Costa)/April 17-20

Procurement Round Table *(1984)*
Historical Note
Address unknown in 1997.

Produce Marketing Ass'n *(1949)*
1500 Casho Mill Rd., P.O. Box 6036
Newark, DE 19714-6036
Tel: (302)738-7100   *Fax:* (302)731-2409
E-Mail: PMA@mail.pma.com
Web Site: http://www.pma.com
Members: 2,500 companies & individuals
Staff: 64
Annual Budget: $5-10,000,000
President: Bryan E. Silbermann, CAE
Director, Information and Communications: Julie Stewart
V. President, Communications/Membership: Kathy Means, CAE
V. President, Industry Programs: Duane Eaton, CEM, CAE
Director, Conventions and Meetings: Patricia F. Quinlan
Director, Trade Shows: Connie Akin
V.P., International Development: Nancy Tucker, CAE
V. President, Administration and Finance: Rita Beasley, CAE
Director, Membership: Julia Bowers Koch
V. President, Division Programs: Terry Humfeld

Historical Note
Founded as Produce Prepackaging Ass'n; became Produce Packaging Ass'n in 1956, Produce Packaging and Marketing Ass'n in 1967, and assumed its current name in 1971. Members are companies, corporations, organizations or individuals engaged in any facet of marketing fresh produce and floral products, or providing equipment, supplies, transportation, or other services to the fresh produce and floral industry. Sponsors and supports the Produce for Better Health Foundation.

Publications:
Floraline.
Freshline. m.
PMA Floral Marketing Directory and Buyer's Guide. a. adv.
PMA Membership Directory. a. adv.

Meetings/Conferences:
Annual Meetings: October
1999 - Atlanta, GA(World Congress Center)/Oct. 23-26
2000 - Anaheim, CA(Convention Center)/Oct. 28-31
2001 - Philadelphia, PA(Convention Center and Area Hotels)/Oct. 27-30
2002 - New Orleans, LA(Convention Center and Area Hotels)/Oct. 19-22
2003 - Orlando, FL(Convention Center and Area Hotels)/Oct. 17-20
2004 - Anaheim, CA(Convention Center & Area Hotels)/Oct. 14-18

Producer's Guild of America *(1950)*
400 S. Beverly Drive, Suite 211
Beverly Hills, CA 90212-4404
Tel: (310)557-0807   *Fax:* (310)557-0436
E-Mail: thepaga@pacbell.net
Web Site: http://www.producersguild.com
Exec. Director: Charles B. FitzSimons

Historical Note
Formerly (1967) Pre-Screen Producers Guild. Members are producers of motion pictures and television shows. Membership: $300/year. (individual).

Publications:
POV Magazine. a. adv.

Product Development and Management Ass'n *(1976)*
401 N. Michigan Ave.
Chicago, IL 60611-4267
Tel: (312)527-6644   *Fax:* (312)527-6729
Toll Free: (800)232 - 5241
Members: 2,600 individuals
Annual Budget: $1-2,000,000
Admin. Director: Pamela Holman

Historical Note
International association designed to serve people with a professional interest in improving the management of product innovation. Membership: $225/year; $400/2years (general); $135/year; $250/2years (academic/nonprofit).

Publications:
Directory. a.
Journal of Product Innovation Management. 5/yr.
Newsletter. q.

Meetings/Conferences:
Annual Meetings: Fall Atlanta, GA/Oct.

Production and Operations Management Soc. *(1989)*
PC Building, Room 543
Florida International University
Miami, FL 33199
Tel: (305)348-1413   *Fax:* (305)348-1908
E-Mail: POMS@FIU.EDU
Web Site: http://www.poms.org
Members: 1,200 individuals
Annual Budget: $100-250,000
Exec. Director: Sushil K. Gupta, Ph.D.

Historical Note
POMS members are professionals and academics with an interest in production and operations management. Membership. $60/year (individual).

Publications:
POM Chronicle Newsletter. q.
Production & Operations Management Journal. q.

Meetings/Conferences:

Production Engine Remanufacturers Ass'n *(1946)*
415 W. Golf Road, Suite 43
Arlington Heights, IL 60005-3923
Tel: (847)439-0491   *Fax:* (847)439-7294
E-Mail: jpolich@pera.org
Web Site: http://www.pera.org
Members: 251 companies
Staff: 2
Annual Budget: $250-500,000
Exec. V. President: Joe Polich

Historical Note
Formerly (1970) Western Engine Rebuilders Ass'n and (1973) Production Engine Rebuilders Ass'n. Members are manufacturers, remanufacturers and parts suppliers to the production line combustion engine industry. Membership: $575-805/year.

Publications:
Current Concerns. m.
Membership Directory. a.

Meetings/Conferences:
Annual Meetings: Fall/500
1999 - San Diego, CA(Hyatt Islandia)/Sept. 22-26/380
2000 - Point Clear, AL(Marriott's Grand Hotel)Sept. /400

Production Equipment Rental Ass'n *(1992)*
P.O. Box 55515
Sherman Oaks, CA 91413-0515
Tel: (818)906-2467   *Fax:* (818)906-1720
E-Mail: peraman@aol.com
Web Site: http://wwww.productionequipment.com
Members: 200 companies
Staff: 1
Annual Budget: $50-100,000
Exec. Director: Edwin S. Clare

Historical Note
Members are rental companies who supply production equipment to the entertainment industry. Membership is international, with roughly half concentrated in southern California. Membership: $265-1,600/year (company).

Publications:
PERA Scope. m.
Rental Resource Guide. a.

Meetings/Conferences:
Annual Meetings: None held.

Production Music Library Ass'n *(1982)*
747 Chestnut Ridge Road
Chestnut Ridge, NY 10977
Tel: (914)356-0800   *Fax:* (914)356-0895
Members: 17 libraries
Annual Budget: under $10,000
President: Michael Nurko

Historical Note
Members are music libraries supplying and licensing producers with music.

Production Service Sales District Council
100 Livingston St.
Brooklyn, NY 11201
Tel: (718)858-4900   *Fax:* (718)802-0997
Members: 21,000 individuals
Staff: 18
Annual Budget: $500-1,000,000
President: Robert J. Rao

Historical Note
An independent labor union for hotel workers. Formerly known as the Internat'l Production, Service and Sales Union.

Meetings/Conferences:
Quinquennial Meetings: (1995)

Professional Aeromedical Transport Ass'n *(1986)*
2095 E. 32nd St.
Dyuma, AZ 85365
Toll Free: (800)327 - 0906
Members: 40 individuals, 30 companies, 100 associates
Staff: 1
Annual Budget: $25-50,000
President: John Ewing

Historical Note
PATA's primary purpose is to standardize and upgrade services of aeromedical transport operations. Membership is open to companies which provide such services or are suppliers to the industry and to individuals with an interest in the industry. Membership: $100/year (individual), $500/year (company), $25/year (associate).

Publications:
Lifeguard Newsletter. q. adv.

Meetings/Conferences:
1999 – Oklahoma City, OK

Professional Airways Systems Specialists *(1977)*

Historical Note
PASS is a division of the Nat'l Marine Engineers Beneficial Ass'n/Nat'l Maritime Union of America.

Professional and Organizational Development Network in Higher Education *(1975)*
115 Slater St.
Valdosta State University
Valdosta, GA 31698
Tel: (912)293-6178   *Fax:* (912)293-6179
Web Site: www.podnetwork.org
Members: 1,100 individuals
Staff: 1
Annual Budget: $100-250,000
Manager of Administrative Services: David Graf, Ph.D.

Historical Note
POD Network members are academics and other educational professionals with an interest the restructuring of postsecondary education. Membership: $50/year (individual); $125/year (organization); $60/year (international).

Publications:
Teaching Excellence. 8/yr.
To Improve the Academy Handbook. a.

Meetings/Conferences:
Annual Meetings: Fall
1999 – St. Louis, MO/Jan. 18-21

Professional and Technical Consultants Ass'n *(1975)*
849-B Independence Ave.
Mountain View, CA 94043
Tel: (650)903-8305   *Fax:* (650)967-0995
Toll Free: (800)747 - 2822
E-Mail: info@patca.org
Web Site: http://www.patca.org
Members: 400 individuals
Staff: 3
Annual Budget: $100-250,000
Exec. Director: Catherine Tornbom
Membership Director: Jeff Shelton

Historical Note
PATCA members are independent technical consultants and small consulting firms. Members are concentrated in northern California. Membership: $345/year.

Publications:
PATCA Directory of Consultants. a.
PATCA Newsletter. m. adv.
PATCA Survey of Rates and Business Practices. bien.

Professional Apparel Ass'n
994 Old Eagle School Road, Suite 1019
Wayne, PA 19087-1802
Tel: (610)971-4850   *Fax:* (610)971-4859
Toll Free: (800)722 - 7712
E-Mail: info@proapparel.com
Web Site: http://www.proapparel.com
Members: 34 companies

Staff: 4
Annual Budget: $100-250,000
Exec. Director: Hope Silverman

Historical Note
PAA is a trade association representing manufacturers of uniforms, shoes and accessories for the medical and hospitality industries. Members also manufacture career apparel and school uniforms. Membership: $1,000-$5,000/year.

Publications:
Uniformer Newsletter. bi-m.

Meetings/Conferences:
Annual Meetings: Fall
1999 – Las Vegas, NV(Ballys)/Oct. 21-23
2000 – Kissimmee, FL(Hyatt Orlando)/Nov. 2-4

Professional Archers Ass'n *(1961)*

Historical Note
Address unknown in 1996.

Professional Ass'n for Childhood Education *(1955)*
74 New Montgomery, Suite 230
San Francisco, CA 94105
Tel: (415)764-4805   *Fax:* (415)764-4915
Members: 600 child care centers
Annual Budget: $100-250,000
Exec. Director: Ken Miles

Publications:
Pacesetter. q. adv.

Meetings/Conferences:
Semi-Annual Meetings: Spring and Fall
1999 – San Ramon, CA(Marriott)/600

Professional Ass'n of Christian Educators *(1959)*
P.O. Box 140284
Dallas, TX 75214
Tel: (214)841-3566   *Fax:* (214)841-3773
Toll Free: (800)829 - 9410
Web Site: http://www.gospelcom.net/paceinc/
Members: 200 individuals
Annual Budget: $100-250,000
President: Dr. Michael S. Lawson

Historical Note
Formerly (1959) Nat'l Ass'n of Directors of Chirstian Education. PACE members are Christian educators. Membership: $50/year.

Professional Ass'n of Comics Entertainment Retailers
531 Washington Ave.
Brooklyn, NY 11238-2724
President: Susan Hyacinth

Historical Note
Memebrship: $250/year.

Professional Ass'n of Custom Clothiers *(1991)*
P.O. Box 8071
Medford, OR 97504
Tel: (541)772-4119   *Fax:* (541)770-7041
E-Mail: www.paccprofessionals.org
Web Site: http://www.paccprofessional.org
Members: 730 individuals
Annual Budget: $50-100,000
National Administrator: Jean Fristensky

Historical Note
PACC serves the needs of professionals in a home-based business or commercial setting through elevating the professional status of custom clothiers, setting professional standards, keeping members informed of industry developments, offering opportunities for continuing education and promoting the general use of custom clothing services. Membership: $50/year (individual).

Publications:
PACC News. q. adv.

Meetings/Conferences:
Annual Meetings: Spring
1999 – New Jersey

Professional Ass'n of Diving Instructors *(1966)*
30151 Tomas St.
Rancho Santa Margarito, CA 92688-2125
Tel: (949)858-7234   *Fax:* (949)858-7264
Toll Free: (800)729 - 7234
E-Mail: jcceo@padi.com
Web Site: http://www.padi.com
Members: 80,000 individuals, 3,000 dive stores
Staff: 220
Annual Budget: $25-50,000,000
C.E.O.: John Cronin
Sr. V.P., Education/Membership: Drew Richardson
C.F.O.: Gary Prenovost

Historical Note
PADI is a professional diving organization that certifies scuba diving instructors. Over 80,000 PADI instructor members and 3,000 dive store members (PADI Dive Centers) conduct training in over 175 countries. PADI provides educational/training materials and retail support to its members.

Publications:
Undersea Journal. q. adv.

Meetings/Conferences:
1999 – New Orleans, LA/Jan. 13-16
2000 – Las Vegas, NV/Jan. 25-28

Professional Ass'n of Health Care Office Managers *(1988)*
461 E. Ten Mile Road
Pensacola, FL 32534-9712
Tel: (202)216-9220   *Fax:* (850)474-6352
Toll Free: (800)451 - 9311
E-Mail: pahcom@pahcom.com
Web Site: http://www.pahcom.com
Members: 3,300 individuals, 100 companies

Staff: 8
Annual Budget: $500-1,000,000
Exec. Director: Rose Chambers
Professional Development Coordinator/Business Manager: Roger Landers
Marketing Director/Chapter Coordinator: Kathy Barnes
Member Benefits Advisor: Sean Warden
Membership Coordinator: Karen Williams
Strategic Support Services: Richard Blanchette
Special Projects: Carol Potter

Historical Note
PAHCOM was founded in January 1988 with the explicit purpose of providing a networking system to managers of medical practices. Offers a certification exam leading to the designation CCM. Membership: $125/year (individual); $250/year (company).

Publications:
Medical Office Management Newsletter. bi-m. adv.

Meetings/Conferences:
Annual Meetings: May
1999 – Savannah, GA(Hyatt)/Sept. 15-18/350
1999 – San Diego, CA/400

Professional Ass'n of Innkeepers Internat'l
P.O. Box 90710
Santa Barbara, CA 93190
Tel: (805)569-1853   *Fax:* (805)682-1016
E-Mail: jmb@paii.org
Web Site: http://www.paii.org
Members: 3,500 individuals
Staff: 10
Annual Budget: $500-1,000,000
Co-Director: Pat Hardy
Co-Exec. Director: J.M. Bell

Historical Note
North American trade association for bed and breakfast/country inns. Membership: $165/year.

Publications:
Innkeeping, Newsletter. m. adv.

Meetings/Conferences:
2000 – Hilton Head, SC(Hyatt)/March 26-29

Professional Ass'n of Lumbermen - World Lumber Standards
8235 S.W. Peninsula Dr.
Crooked River Ranch, OR 97760-9258
Tel: (503)245-7338
Members: 4 companies
Annual Budget: $50-100,000
President: Carl Edward Massie

Historical Note
A division of World Lumber Standards.

Publications:
World Lumber Standards. a.

Meetings/Conferences:
Annual Meetings: September

Professional Ass'n of Pet Industries *(1972)*

Historical Note
Organization defunct in 1996.

Professional Ass'n of Resume Writers *(1990)*
3637 4th St. North, Suite 330
St. Petersburg, FL 33704
Tel: (813)821-2274   *Fax:* (813)894-1277
Toll Free: (800)822 - 7299
E-Mail: PARWHQ@aol.com
Web Site: http://www.parw.com
Members: 950 companies
Staff: 4
Annual Budget: $250-500,000
Exec. Director: Frank X. Fox

Historical Note
PARW members are companies offering resume writing services. Membership: $125/year.

Publications:
Membership Directory. a.
Spotlight. m.

Meetings/Conferences:
1999 – Colorado Springs, CO

Professional Audio-Video Retailers Ass'n *(1979)*
10 East 22nd Street, Suite 310
Lombard, IL 60148
Tel: (630)268-1500   *Fax:* (630)953-8957
Web Site: http://www.paralink.org
Members: 375 companies
Staff: 2
Annual Budget: $250-500,000

Historical Note
An organization formed to assist the owners and operators of independently owned, high-end audio/video stores to work toward the mutually compatible goal of providing services to members which would be unattainable by retailers working separately. Also includes manufactures of high-end audio/video equipment. Membership: $350-$1,800/year.

Publications:
Parascope. q.

Meetings/Conferences:
Annual Meetings: March/April

Professional Aviation Maintenance Ass'n *(1972)*
636 Eye St., N.W. Suite 300
Washington, DC 20001-3736
Tel: (202)216-9220   *Fax:* (202)216-9224
E-Mail: hq@pama.org
Web Site: http://www.pama.org
Members: 4,500 individuals, 250 companies
Staff: 6

Annual Budget: $500-1,000,000
President: Stanislaus Mackiewicz
Manager, Communications: Anne Culver
Manager, Administration: Uve Hodgins

Historical Note
Members are technicians holding an A&P (AirFrame and PowerPlant) license, aviation maintenance companies and institutions. Membership: $20/year (student and active military), $35/year (individual); $325/year (company); $200/year (education).

Publications:
Membership Directory and Information Guide. a.
The PAMA News. m. adv.

Meetings/Conferences:
Annual Meetings: May
1999 – Phoenix, AZ(Phoenix Civic Plaza)/April 20-22

Professional Bail Agents of the United States *(1981)*
1155 Connecticut Ave., N.W., Suite 400
Washington, DC   20036-4306
Tel: (202)429-6465   *Fax:* (202)296-8128
Toll Free: (800)883 - 7287
E-Mail: S.Kreimer@HuskyNet.com
Web Site: http://PBUS.com
Members: 800 individuals
Staff: 3
Annual Budget: $100-250,000
Exec. Director: Stephen H. Kreimer

Historical Note
PBUS promotes the bail bond industry throughout the United States, educates members of changes, serves as a forum for the interchange of ideas, and serves as industry spokesman. Membership: $200/year (individual), $450/year (organization/company).

Publications:
Bail Agent's Prespective Newsletter. q. adv.

Meetings/Conferences:
Semi-annual Meetings: January and June
1999 – Las Vegas, NV(Luxor)
1999 – Las Vegas, NV(Luxor)/Feb. 15-19

Professional Baseball Athletic Trainers' Ass'n *(1983)*
400 Colony Square, Suite 1750
Atlanta, GA   30361
Tel. (404)875-4000   *Fax:* (404)892-8560
Members: 56 individuals
Annual Budget: $50-100,000
General Counsel: Rollin E. Mallernee, II

Historical Note
A satellite organization of the Nat'l Athletic Trainers' Ass'n. PBATS is professional society composed of all athletic trainers in major league baseball. Membership: $100/year.

Publications:
Media Guide. a.
PBATS Newsletter. semi-a.

Meetings/Conferences:
Annual Meetings: First weekend in Dec., in conjunction with Baseball Winter Meeting

Professional Basketball Writers' Ass'n *(1972)*
Club Side Rd.
Lyndhurst, OH   65025
Tel: (248)542-0805
Members: 175 individuals
Staff: 1
Annual Budget: under $10,000
Secretary-Treasurer: Mary Schmitt-Boyer

Historical Note
Members are sports editors and reporters who cover professional basketball. Membership: $35/year.

Publications:
Newsletter. 8/yr.

Meetings/Conferences:
Annual Meetings: During the NBA All-Star Game.

Professional Bowlers Ass'n of America *(1958)*
P.O. Box 5118
1720 Merriman Road
Akron, OH   44334-0118
Tel: (330)836-5568   *Fax:* (330)836-2107
Web Site: http://www.pbatour.org
Members: 3,700 individuals
Staff: 20
Annual Budget: $5-10,000,000
Commissioner: Mark Gerberich
Public Relations Director: Dave Schroeder
Financial Director: Tom Menyes
Assistant Commisioner: Kevin Shippy
Director of Operations: Bobby Dinkins

Historical Note
Members must have a minimum average of 200 established for 66 or more games per season for the 2 most recent seasons prior to applying for membership. Hosts regional, national, and senior tournaments throughout the year. Has an annual budget of approximately $9.5 million. Membership: $200/year (regional membership).

Publications:
Newsletter. q.
Press-Radio-TV Guide. a.
Senior Tour Program. a.
Tournament Annual. a. adv.

Meetings/Conferences:
Annual Meetings: Held in conjunction with tournaments/60.

Professional Cartridge Remanufacturers Institute
Historical Note
Became (1996) Imaging Products Remanufacturing Ass'n.

Professional Communications Soc. *(1957)*
Historical Note
A technical society of the Institute of Electrical and Electronics Engineers (IEEE). Membership in the Society, open only to IEEE members, includes a subscription to a technical periodical in the field published by IEEE. All administrative support is provied by IEEE.

Professional Construction Estimators Ass'n of America *(1956)*
P.O. Box 11626
Charlotte, NC   28220-1626
Tel: (704)522-6376   *Fax:* (704)522-7013
Web Site: http://www.pcea.org
Members: 1,200 individuals
Staff: 1
Annual Budget: $100-250,000

Historical Note
PCEA's goal is to promote construction estimating as a profession by upholding the code of ethics, expanding public awareness through charity projects and supporting education programs and scholarships.

Publications:
Nat'l Estimator. q.
PCEA Nat'l Director. a. adv.

Meetings/Conferences:
Annual Meetings: Spring
1999 – Savannah, GA(Marriott Riverfront)

Professional Convention Management Ass'n *(1958)*
100 Vestavia Pkwy., Suite 220
Birmingham, AL   35216
Tel: (205)823-7262   *Fax:* (205)822-3891
Members: 4,000 individuals
Annual Budget: $5-10,000,000
Exec. V. President/CEO: Roy B. Evans, Jr., CAE
Director, Meeting Services: Pamela K. McDonald
Manager, Meetings: Nancy Cisseon, LES
Director, Education: Phillip Mogle
Controller: Dan Carre
V. President, Membership: Gerald Donohue, Jr., CAE

Historical Note
Incorporated in Illinois February 28, 1958. Membership consists of convention managers, CEOs, meeting planners, and suppliers representing 1,000 organizations. Member of the Center for Exhibition Industry Research. Membership: $280-430/year.

Publications:
Convene. 11/year.
Membership Directory. a.
PCMA Member Digest. 5x/yea.

Meetings/Conferences:
Annual Meetings: Winter
1999 – Orlando, FL/Jan. 10-13
2000 – San Fransisco, CA/Jan. 15-18

Professional Currency Dealers Ass'n *(1985)*
P.O. Box 7157
Westchester, IL   60154
Tel: (708)345-8207
Members: 75 individuals
Staff: 1
Annual Budget: $25-50,000
Secretary-Treasurer: James Simek

Historical Note
A trade association composed of the leading dealers in rare currency, the PCDA's primary objective is to promote interest in the collecting of rare currency. Membership: $250/year.

Meetings/Conferences:
Annual Meetings: Fall.

Professional Dance Teachers Ass'n
Historical Note
Organization defunct in 1998.

Professional Engineers in Private Practice *(1955)*
1420 King St.
Alexandria, VA   22314-2794
Tel: (703)684-2862   *Fax:* (703)836-4875
Members: 24,000 individuals
Staff: 3
Annual Budget: $1-2,000,000
Director: James F. Pierce

Historical Note
Formed in 1955 as an autonomous division of the Nat'l Soc. of Professional Engineers to address concerns of individual consulting professional engineers; reorganized in 1965 with independent dues structure. Provides information and lobbying efforts on practice management, professional liability, and career development interests of members. Membership: $60/year.

Publications:
Directory of Engineers in Private Practice. bien.
Private Practice News. m.

Meetings/Conferences:

Professional Film and Video Equipment Ass'n *(1973)*
Historical Note
Organization defunct in 1995.

Professional Football Athletic Trainers Soc. *(1982)*
400 Colony Square, Suite 1750
Atlanta, GA   30361
Tel: (404)875-4000   *Fax:* (404)892-8560
Members: 65 individuals
Annual Budget: $50-100,000
General Counsel: Rollin E. Mallernee, II

Historical Note
An affiliate organization to the National Athletic Trainers Ass'n. PFATS is a professional society composed of all the athletic trainers in the NFL. Promotes the professional interests of NFL athletic trainers

Publications:
Media Guide. a.
Pro Football Athletic Trainer. semi-a.

Meetings/Conferences:
Annual Meetings: June, in conjunction with NATA's national convention

Professional Football Writers of America *(1962)*
12030 Cedar Lake Court
Maryland Heights, MO   63043-4102
Tel: (314)453-0755
Members: 400 individuals
Annual Budget: under $10,000
Secretary-Treasurer: Howard Balzer

Historical Note
Members are sportswriters and columnists who cover professional football regularly. Promotes good working relationships between writers and leagues, clubs and players' associations. Membership: $25/year.

Publications:
Newsletter. bi-m.

Meetings/Conferences:
Annual Meetings: Friday preceeding Super Bowl.
1999 – Miami, FL

Professional Fraternity Ass'n *(1977)*
P.O. Box 90264
Indianapolis, IN   46290
Tel: (317)257-5235   *Fax:* (317)253-5067
Members: 37 fraternities & sororities
Staff: 1
Annual Budget: $10-25,000
Exec. Secretary: Harriet Rodenberg

Historical Note
Established October 22, 1977, through merger of the Professional Panhellenic Ass'n (established 1925) and the Professional Interfraternity Conference (established 1928). Membership: $200/year. (organization).

Publications:
Membership Directory. a.
PFA Newsletter. 4-6/year.

Meetings/Conferences:
Annual Meetings: late September
1999 – Oxford, OH(Miami University)
2000 – San Diego, CA(Hilton)

Professional Golf Club Repairmen's Ass'n *(1977)*
Historical Note
Persons engaged in golf club repair and/or custom golf club making and golf professionals whose jobs include repair work. Membership: $20/yr., $24/yr. (outside U.S.).

Professional Golfers Ass'n of America *(1916)*
100 Avenue of Champions
PO Box 109601
Palm Beach Gardens, FL   33410-9601
Tel: (561)624-8401   *Fax:* (561)624-8410
Members: 24,000 individuals
Staff: 115
Annual Budget: $2-5,000,000
C.E.O.: Jim Awtrey
Senior Director, Communications and Broadcasting: Joe Steranka
Director, Education: Jan Gilpin
Senior Director of Operations, Learning Center: Marty Kavanaugh
C.F.O.: Jesse A. Holhouser, III
C.O.O.: Paul Bogin
Senior Director, Membership Programs: Chris Hunkler
Senior Director, Licensing: John Zurek

Historical Note
Founded in New York City in 1916. Runs local, national and international tournaments. Most members are golf professionals managing golf courses.

Publications:
PGA Magazine. m. adv.

Meetings/Conferences:

Professional Grounds Management Soc. *(1911)*
120 Cockeysville Road, Suite 104
Hunt Valley, MD   21030-2133
Tel: (410)584-9754   *Fax:* (410)584-9756
Toll Free: (800)609 - 7467
Members: 1,500 individuals
Staff: 4
Annual Budget: $250-500,000
Exec. Director: John T. Gillan

Historical Note
Formerly (1971) Nat'l Ass'n of Professional Gardeners. Members are professionals involved in the care and maintenance of schools, universities, parks, office parks, shopping malls, municipalities, sports grounds, etc. Awards the CGM (Certified Grounds Manager) designation. Membership: $150/year (individual); $400/year (organization/company).

Publications:
Grounds Maintenance Estimating Guidelines. bi-a.
Grounds Maintenance Management Guidelines. bi-a.
Grounds Management Forms and Job Descriptions Guide. bi-a.
Grounds Management Forum. bi-m. adv.
PGMS Membership Directory. a. adv.

Meetings/Conferences:
Annual Meetings: Fall
1999 – Baltimore, MD(Marriott Inner Harbor)Nov.

Professional Handlers Ass'n (1926)
15810 Mount Everest Lane
Silver Spring, MD   20906
Tel: (301)924-0089
Members: 250 individuals
Contact: Kathy Bowser

Historical Note
Members are individuals who show purebred dogs professionally as well as others interested in improving the stature of professional dog handling.

Publications:
Newsletter. q.

Professional Hockey Writers' Ass'n (1967)
1480 Pleasant Valley Way, #44
West Orange, NJ   07052
Tel: (973)669-8607
Members: 350 individuals
Staff: 5
Annual Budget: under $10,000
Secretary-Treasurer: Sherry L. Ross

Historical Note
Formerly (1971) Nat'l Hockey League Writers' Ass'n. PHWA members are journalists covering the teams of the Nat'l Hockey League. Membership: $15/year (individual).

Publications:
PHWA Newsletter. q.

Meetings/Conferences:
Annual Meetings: January and June

Professional Housing Management Ass'n (1973)
P.O. Box 4251
Leesburg, VA   20177-8369
Tel: (703)327-6873   *Fax:* (703)327-4005
Toll Free: (800)543 - 7188
E-Mail: jon12141@aol.com
Members: 3,000 individuals, 120 organizations
Staff: 4
Annual Budget: $500-1,000,000
Exec. Director: Jon Moore

Historical Note
PHMA members are federal government employees, civilian or military, who are directly involved in the profession of housing management; or whose responsibility provides direct support to the field of housing management. Membership: $30/year.

Publications:
Defense Communities. bi-m. adv.

Meetings/Conferences:
Annual Meetings: Winter
1999 – Louisville, KY(Gault House)
1999 – Louisville, KY(Galt House)/Feb. 14-18

Professional Insurance Communicators of America (1955)
Box 68700
Indianapolis, IN   46268
Tel: (317)875-5250   *Fax:* (317)879-8408
Members: 70 individuals
Staff: 1
Annual Budget: under $10,000
Secretary-Treasurer: Janet E.H. Wright

Historical Note
Founded as the Mutual Insurance Council of Editors, it became the Mutual Insurance Communicators in 1969 and assumed its present name in 1981. An affiliate of the Nat'l Ass'n of Mutual Insurance Companies. Members are editors of insurance company newsletters.

Publications:
Communique. q.

Meetings/Conferences:
Annual Meetings: Spring

Professional Insurance Mass-Marketing Ass'n (1975)
4733 Bethesda Ave., Suite 330
Bethesda, MD   20814-5228
Tel: (301)951-1260   *Fax:* (301)951-1264
Web Site: wcsummers@pima-assn.org
Members: 500 individuals
Staff: 2
Annual Budget: $500-1,000,000
Exec. Director: William C. Summers
Manager of Communications: Marci Y. Vanim
Director of Meetings and Administration: Debra E. Kaufman, CMP
Manager of Membership Services: Jean McNeil

Historical Note
Formerly (1982) the Professional Independent Mass-Marketing Administrators. PIMA is the national association of leading third-party administrators and companies active in mass marketing all lines of insurance. The association was formed in 1975 to protect the interests of consumers and advance the professional quality of the independent mass marketer in business today. Membership dues for companies and agencies are based upon annual mass-marketed premium volume. Membership: $600 to 3,300/year (agency); $4,500 to $7,750/year (company); $150/year (employees of agency members); $1,200/year (allied members).

Publications:
PIMA Membership Directory. a.
PIMA News. m.

Meetings/Conferences:
Annual Meetings: Semi-Annual Meetings
1999 – Dana Point, CA(Ritz-Carlton)/Feb. 7-10
1999 – Bermuda(Southampton Princess)/Aug. 1-4
2000 – Phoenix, AZ(Scottsdale Princess)/Jan. 30-Feb 2

Professional Internat'l Network Soc. (1993)
Historical Note
Organization defunct in 1997.

Professional Knitwear Designers Guild
W 3090 Cty. Road Y
Lomira, WI   53048
Tel: (920)583-4298
Membership Chair: Diane Zangl

Historical Note
PKDG provides networking, professional accreditation, and other services to freelance knitwear designers. Also sponsors seminars and maintains a resource library. Has no paid officers or full-time staff. Membership: $25/year.

Publications:
PKDG Newsletter. 4-6/year.
PKDG Teachers Directory.

Professional Lawn Care Ass'n of America (1979)
1000 Johnson Ferry Rd. N.E., Suite C-135
Marietta, GA   30068-2112
Tel: (770)977-5222   *Fax:* (770)578-6071
Toll Free: (800)458 - 3466
E-Mail: PLCAA@atlcom.net
Web Site: http://www.plcaa.org
Members: 1,200 companies
Staff: 9
Annual Budget: $1-2,000,000
Exec. V. President: Thomas J. Delaney
Director, Communications: Karen Weber
Coordinator, Membership: Heath D. Moore

Historical Note
Lawn care operators and manufacturers/suppliers of associated products. Membership Fee: Based on gross sales volume.

Publications:
ProSource Newsletter. bi-m.

Meetings/Conferences:
Annual Meetings: Fall

Professional Liability Underwriting Soc. (1988)
4248 Park Glen Road
Minneapolis, MN   55416
Tel: (612)928-4644   *Fax:* (612)929-1318
Toll Free: (800)845 - 0778
Members: 2,500 individuals
Staff: 6
Annual Budget: $1-2,000,000
Exec. Director: Derek Hazeltine

Historical Note
Membership: $150/year (individual); $1,000/year (organization/company).

Publications:
Educational Program.
Monthly Newsletter. m.
Resource Directory. a.

Meetings/Conferences:
Annual Meetings: Fall
1999 – New York, NY/Nov. 10-12
2000 – San Antonio, TX/Nov. 14-16
2001 – Chicago, IL/Nov. 14-16

Professional Managers Ass'n (1981)
L'Enfant Plaza Station
P.O. Box 45070
Washington, DC   20026
Tel: (202)401-6737   *Fax:* (202)401-4277
E-Mail: PMAoffice@aol.com
Staff: 5
Annual Budget: $100-250,000
National President: Ray Woolner
Legislative/Communications Director: Hydi Miller

Historical Note
Members are federal employees in management positions and management officials. Chapters established throughout the country. Membership: $65/year.

Publications:
Capitol Digest. w.
The Professional Manager. q.

Professional Numismatists Guild (1950)
3950 Concordia Lane
Fallbrook, CA   92028
Tel: (760)728-1300   *Fax:* (760)728-8507
E-Mail: info@pngdealers.com
Web Site: http://www.pngdealers.com
Members: 300 individuals
Staff: 2
Annual Budget: $250-500,000
Exec. Director: Robert Brueggeman

Historical Note
Members are individuals who have been full-time coin dealers for at least five years. Associate members have been full-time for 2 years. Promotes high standards of ethics in the hobby of numismatics. Affiliated with the American Numismatic Ass'n and the American Numismatic Soc. Incorporated in 1955 as the Professional Numismatists Guild. Membership: $1,000/yr. (regular); $300/yr. (associate).

Publications:
Consumer Alert Brochure.
Membership Directory. a.
The Guild. bi-m. adv.

Meetings/Conferences:
1999 – Milwaukee, WI
1999 – Chicago, IL

Professional Paddlesports Ass'n (1979)
P.O. Box 248
Butler, KY   41006-0248
Tel: (606)472-2205   *Fax:* (606)472-2030
E-Mail: paddlespt@unidial.com
Web Site: http://www.propaddle.com
Members: 450 companies

Staff: 3
Annual Budget: $100-250,000
Exec. Director: Jim Thaxton

Historical Note
Established as Nat'l Ass'n of Canoe Liveries and Outfitters; assumed its current name in 1996. Incorporated in the state of Michigan. Promotes canoeing and related sports, works to preserve waterways for human-powered recreation, and protects the interests of professional outfitters and outfitting firms. Membership: $149-499/year.

Publications:
Let's Go Paddling. a. adv.
Paddler Magazine.
Pen and Paddle. m. adv.

Meetings/Conferences:
Annual Meetings: December/500

Professional Photographers of America (1880)
229 Peachtree St., Suite 2200
Atlanta, GA   30303
Tel: (404)522-8600   *Fax:* (404)614-6400
E-Mail: jhopper594@aol.com
Web Site: http://www.ppa-world.org
Members: 14,000 individuals
Staff: 40
Annual Budget: $5-10,000,000
Dir., Marketing & Communications: David Trust
Dir., Events & Publications/Interim Exec. Director: Donna R. McMahon
Director, Finance: Scott Kurkian
Director, Membership: J. Alexander Hopper

Historical Note
Professional society of portrait, commercial, wedding, industrial and specialized photographers and photographic artists. Grants the Master of Photography, Photographic Craftsman, Master of Electronic Imaging and Photographic Artist degrees in recognition of exceptional ability and service. Sponsors the Winona International School of Professional Photography. Formerly (1958) the Photographers' Ass'n of America. Annual Budget: $7 million.

Publications:
Marketing Guide. q.
Photo Electronic Imaging. m. adv.
PPA Today. m.
Professional Photographer Storytellers. m. adv.
Who's Who in Professional Imaging. a. adv.

Meetings/Conferences:
Annual Meetings: Summer
1999 – Atlanta, GA/July 23-28
2000 – Las Vegas, NV

Professional Picture Framers Ass'n (1971)
4305 Sarellen Road
Richmond, VA   23231
Tel: (804)226-0430   *Fax:* (804)222-2175
E-Mail: ppfa@ppfa.com
Members: 5,000 retailers, suppliers & instit.
Staff: 12
Annual Budget: $1-2,000,000
Exec. Director: Julie A. Freeman
Director, Programs: John Redmond
Director, Membership Services: Betty Ann Watson

Historical Note
A trade association of manufacturers, wholesalers, print publishers, importers and retailers selling art, framing, and related supplies. Membership: $180-1,350/year.

Publications:
For Members Only. m.
Leaders. q.
Who's Who Directory. a.

Meetings/Conferences:
1999 – Orlando, FL/Jan. 15-18/1500

Professional Putters Ass'n (1959)
P.O. Box 35237
Fayetteville, NC   28303
Tel: (910)485-7131   *Fax:* (910)485-1122
Web Site: http://www.putt-putt.com
Members: 1,117 individuals
Staff: 25
Annual Budget: $100-250,000

Historical Note
Members are individuals over the age of 18 who compete in national putting tournaments as well as golf course owners, managers and suppliers. Membership: $20/year.

Publications:
Facts and Membership. a.
Official Rules and Regulations of the PPA.
Putt-Putt World. q.

Meetings/Conferences:
Annual Meetings: Not held.

Professional Reactor Operator Soc. (1981)
P.O. Box 484
Byron, IL   61010-0484
Tel: (815)234-4174
Toll Free: (800)422 - 2725
Members: 800 individuals
Annual Budget: $25-50,000
President: Mike Jacobson
National Meeting Coordinator: Glenn W. Hoppe

Historical Note
Members are operators of nuclear power facilities. Membership: $35/year (individual).

Publications:
The Communicator. q. adv.

Meetings/Conferences:
Annual Meetings: Summer
1999 – June 3rd

Professional Records and Information Services Management Internat'l (1980)

16 E. Rowan St., Suite 400
Raleigh, NC   27609
Tel: (919)881-0677   *Fax:* (919)881-0339
Toll Free: (800)336 - 9793
Web Site: http://www.prismintl.org
Members: 500 individuals
Staff: 4
Annual Budget: $250-500,000
Exec. Director: April Ryan
Dir., Communications: Jean Yount

Historical Note
PRISM Internat'l is a trade association providing educational and advocacy resources to promote smart records and information management solutions for its members and the business public.

Publications:
In Focus. q.

Meetings/Conferences:
Annual Meetings: Spring
1999 – Atlanta, GA/April 27-May 1

Professional Rodeo Cowboys Ass'n (1936)

101 Prorodeo Drive
Colorado Springs, CO   80919-9989
Tel: (719)593-8840   *Fax:* (719)548-4876
E-Mail: www.prorodeo.com
Web Site: http://www.prorodeo.com
Members: 11,375 individuals
Staff: 90
Annual Budget: $25-50,000,000
Comissioner: Steven J. Hatchell
Director, Rodeo Administration: T.J. Walker

Historical Note
Founded as Cowboys Turtle Ass'n. Became Rodeo Cowboys Ass'n in 1945 and Professional Rodeo Cowboys Ass'n in 1975.

Publications:
Media Guide. a.
Prorodeo Sports News. bi-w. adv.

Meetings/Conferences:
1999 – Las Vegas, NV(National Finals Rodeo)/Dec. 4-13

Professional Sales Ass'n

c/o Miller Puthuff
2873 Daley
Troy, MI   48083
Members: 25 companies
Exec. Officer: Ed Puthuff

Historical Note
An organization of manufacturers representative firms which sell hardware, housewares, lawn and garden products, and traffic appliances to the retail trade. Has no paid officers or full-time staff.

Meetings/Conferences:

Professional School Photographers (1951)

Historical Note
PSP is a section of Photo Marketing Ass'n-Internat'l.

Professional Secretaries Internat'l

Historical Note
Became (1998) Internat'l Ass'n of Administrative Professionals.

Professional Service Ass'n (1989)

71 Columbia St.
Cohoes, NY   12047
Tel: (518)237-7777   *Fax:* (518)237-0418
Members: 1,105 companies
Staff: 2
Annual Budget: $50-100,000
President: Ron Sawyer

Historical Note
PSA members are companies servicing and repairing electonics and appliances. Membership: $75/year.

Publications:
Professional Service Ass'n News. q. adv.
PSA Update. m.

Meetings/Conferences:

Professional Services Council (1972)

2101 Wilson Blvd., Suite 750
Arlington, VA   22201-3062
Tel: (703)875-8059   *Fax:* (703)875-1922
Members: 130 companies, 8 associations
Staff: 7
Annual Budget: $500-1,000,000
President: Bert M. Concklin
V. President, Communications: Heather Beldon Rosenker
V.P., Government Relations: Charles H. Cantus
Director, Finance: Diana F. Little

Historical Note
Formerly (until 1982) the Nat'l Council of Professional Services Firms. Members are companies that provide professional and technical services to the government and private industry. Sponsors and supports the Professional Services Council Political Action Committee. Membership: $100/year (trade ass'ns); $750-15,900/year (company); $5,000/year (associate).

Publications:
Executive Report. m.
Membership Directory. a.

Meetings/Conferences:
Annual Meetings: Fall
1999 – Hot Springs, VA(Homestead)/Oct. 3-6

Professional Services Management Ass'n (1975)

4101 Lake Boone Trail
Suite 201
Raleigh, NC   27607

Tel: (919)571-2562   *Fax:* (919)787-4916
Web Site: http://psma.org
Members: 600 individuals
Staff: 3
Annual Budget: $250-500,000
Exec. Director: Susan Van der Weert

Historical Note
Members are business managers, owners and principals of professional service firms (i.e. engineering, architecture, landscape architecture, interior design, management consultants, etc.) seeking to promote the exchange of ideas and information and to establish guidelines in the field of professional service firm management. Membership: $295/year.

Publications:
Ascent. bi-m. adv.
Focus on Finance. bi-m.
Focus on General Management. bi-m.
Focus on Human Resources. bi-m.
Focus on Marketing. bi-m.
Focus on Operations. bi-m.
Management Reports. 3-4/yr.
PSMA Member Directory. a. adv.

Meetings/Conferences:
Annual Meetings: Fall
1999 – Scottsdale, AZ(Scottsdale Plaza Hotel)/Sept. 22-25

Professional Show Managers Ass'n

One Regency Drive, P.O. Box 30
Bloomfield, CT   06002
Tel: (860)243-3977   *Fax:* (860)286-0787
Web Site: http://www.psma-shows.org
Members: 180 individuals
Staff: 1
Exec. Director: Mitch Sorensen

Meetings/Conferences:
1999 – October

Professional Skaters Ass'n (1938)

1821 2nd St., S.W.
Rochester, MN   55902
Tel: (507)281-5122   *Fax:* (507)281-5491
E-Mail: skatepsa@aol.com
Web Site: http://members.aol.com/skatepsa/homepage.html
Members: 4,000 individuals
Annual Budget: $500-1,000,000
Exec. Director: Carole K. Shulman

Historical Note
PSA members are ice skaters, coaches, judges and others interested in the sport. Membership: $25-100/year.

Publications:
Coaches Manual. irreg.
Professional Skater Magazine. bi-m. adv.
PSA Membership Directory. a.
PSA Ratings Systems Manual. irreg.

Meetings/Conferences:
Annual Meetings: May
1999 – Colorado Springs, CO/May 26-29
2000 – Orlando, FL(Peabody)/May 24-27

Professional Ski Instructors of America (1961)

133 S. Van Gordon St., Suite 101
Lakewood, CO   80228-1700
Tel: (303)987-9390   *Fax:* (303)988-3005
Toll Free: (800)222 - 4754
E-Mail: psia@psia.org
Web Site: http://www.psia.org
Members: 20,000 individuals, 350 ski schools, 35 companies
Staff: 14
Annual Budget: $500-1,000,000
Exec. Director: Stephen M. Over
Director, Communications: Rebecca Ayers
Director, Marketing: Mark Dorsey
Director, Meeting and Conventions: Karen Hagaman

Historical Note
Provides on-going education for certified ski instructors and international educational training.

Publications:
Convention Proceedings. a.
The Professional Skier. q. adv.

Meetings/Conferences:
Semi-annual Meetings: Spring and Fall

Professional Soc. for Sales and Marketing Training (1940)

1900 Arch St.
Philadelphia, PA   19103-1498
Tel: (215)564-3484   *Fax:* (215)564-2175
Members: 170 individuals
Staff: 1
Annual Budget: $250-500,000
Exec. Director: Charlene Mayfield
Director, Administrative: Kim Soldavin

Historical Note
Formerly (1993) Nat'l Soc. of Sales Training Executives.

Meetings/Conferences:
1999 – Palm Springs, CA(Hyatt Grand Champions)/Dec. 4-8

Professional Soccer Reporters Ass'n (1975)

6700 Squibb Road, Suite 215
Mission, KS   66202
Tel: (913)362-1747   *Fax:* (913)362-3439
Members: 100 individuals
Annual Budget: under $10,000
Secretary: Mike McFarland

Historical Note
Formed to further and foster better working conditions for those covering soccer in North America. Has no paid staff or permanent headquarters. Membership: $15/year.

Publications:
Membership Directory. a.
Newsletter.

Meetings/Conferences:
Annual Meetings: Winter, in conjunction with the Major Soccer League All-Star Game

Professional Speakers Network

8502 E. Chapman Ave., Suite 184
Orange, CA   92869
Tel: (714)731-0288   *Fax:* (714)731-0288
Members: 1000 individuals
Staff: 4
Exec. Director: R. Gregory Alonzo

Historical Note
Membership: $100/year (individual); $150/year (company).

Publications:
Speakers Corner. m.

Meetings/Conferences:
Annual Meetings: Fall

Professional Squash Ass'n (1928)

56 Spooner Road
Chestnut Hill, MA   02167
Tel: (617)731-6874   *Fax:* (617)277-1457
Members: 550 individuals
Staff: 6
Annual Budget: $1-2,000,000
Exec. Director: John Nimick

Historical Note
Conducts a squash tour consisting of 30 tournaments and provides a network of teaching programs. Formerly (1977) North American Professional Squash Racquets Ass'n, (1992) World Professional Squash Ass'n. Became PSA after merging with Internat'l Squash Players Ass'n in 1992. Membership: $500/year (full member), $75/year (teaching pro), $250/year (provisional member), $250/year (hardball member).

Publications:
Professional Squash Ass'n Newsmagazine. q.

Meetings/Conferences:
1999 – Egypt, Cairo

Professional Tattoo Artists Guild (1975)

P.O. Box 1374
27 Mt. Vernon Ave.
Mt. Vernon, NY   10550-1374
Tel: (914)668-2300   *Fax:* (914)668-5200
Members: 2,500 individuals
President: Joe Kaplan

Meetings/Conferences:
1999 – Schenectady, NY/Jan. 6-9

Professional Travelogue Sponsors (1967)

337 S. Madison
Adrian, MI   49221
Tel: (517)263-2867
E-Mail: awilson@pc3net.com
Members: 55 individuals
Annual Budget: under $10,000
President: Edmond Wilson

Historical Note
Formerly (1971) Professional Travel Film Managers Ass'n and (1987) Professional Travel Film Directors Ass'n. Promotes communication between sponsors, speakers and managers. Membership: $35-65/year.

Publications:
Bulletin. q.
Newsletter. irreg.

Meetings/Conferences:
Annual Meetings: Winter

Professional Trucking Services Ass'n (1984)

c/o United Truckers Service
1385 Iris Drive
Conyers, GA   30208
Tel: (770)922-6200
Web Site: info@utsvs.com
Members: 52 service bureaus
President: Anthony L. Keenan

Historical Note
PTSA members are service bureaus which assist trucking companies in obtaining licensing and permits.

Professional Women in Construction (1980)

342 Madison Ave., Suite 451
New York, NY   10173
Tel: (212)687-0610   *Fax:* (212)490-1213
Members: 500 individuals
Staff: 2
Annual Budget: $100-250,000
V. President: Theresa Vigilante

Historical Note
Formerly (1982) the Ass'n of Business and Professional Women in Construction. Members are women who own their own companies or women and men in management positions in contruction and related fields. Monthly mailings reach 6,000 individuals. Membership: $150/year (individual), $500/year (company).

Publications:
Bulletin. m.
Newsletter. m.

Meetings/Conferences:
Annual Meetings: Monthly, in greater New York City area.

Professional Women Photographers (1975)

c/o Photgraphics Unlimited
17 West 17th St., #14
New York, NY   10011-5510
Tel: (212)726-8292

Members: 200 individuals
Annual Budget: under $10,000
President: Katherine Criss

Historical Note
Began in 1975 with the exhibition, "Breadth of Vision: Portfolios of Women Photographers" at the Fashion Institute of Technology. PWP proceeded with monthly meetings, newsletters and exhibitions. Incorporated in New York City. Has no paid staff. Membership: $35/year (New York City), $15/year (non-resident).

Publications:
PWP Newsletter. 3/year. adv.

Meetings/Conferences:
Monthly Meetings: New York, NY/1st Wednesday in the month

Professional Women Singers Ass'n *(1982)*
P.O. Box 884, Planetarium Station
New York, NY 10024
Tel: (212)969-0590   *Fax:* (212)255-4982
E-Mail: singerpwsa@aol.com
Members: 100 individuals
Annual Budget: under $10,000
President: Carol Flamm

Historical Note
PWSA serves as an information resource and referral network for professional women in opera, oratorio, musical theater, and related genres. Has no paid officers or full-time staff. Membership: $55/year (individual).

Professional Women's Appraisal Ass'n *(1986)*
1224 No. Nokomis N.E.
Alexandria, MN 56380
Tel: (320)763-7626   *Fax:* (320)763-9290
Members: 1,250 individuals
Staff: 6
Annual Budget: $100-250,000
Exec. Director: Deborah S. Johnson
Managing Director (Communications, Gov't, Meetings, Membership: Joan T. Powell

Historical Note
PWAA provides professional recognition to women involved in real estate valuation. Membership: $75/year (individual).

Publications:
Woman Appraiser Newsletter. m.

Meetings/Conferences:
Annual Meetings: in conjunction with the Nat'l Ass'n of Real Estate Appraisers

Professional Women's Bowlers Ass'n *(1981)*
7171 Cherryvale Blvd.
Rockford, IL 61112
Tel: (815)332-5756   *Fax:* (815)332-9636
E-Mail: pwbaoffice@pwba.com
Web Site: http://www.pwba.com
Members: 260 individuals
Staff: 8
Annual Budget: $1-2,000,000
President: John F. Falzone

Historical Note
LPBT members are women professional bowlers.

Publications:
LPBT Booster Club News. q.
LPBT Official Rules & Regulations. a.
LPBT Tour Guide a. adv. adv.

Meetings/Conferences:

Professors of Curriculum *(1971)*
Historical Note
Address unknown in 1996.

Profit Sharing/401(k) Council of America *(1947)*
10 South Riverside Plaza, Suite 1610
Chicago, IL 60606
Tel: (312)441-8550   *Fax:* (312)441-8559
E-Mail: psca@psca.org
Web Site: http://www.psca.org
Members: 1,200 companies
Staff: 6
Annual Budget: $500-1,000,000
President: David L. Wray

Historical Note
Formerly (1973) Council of Profit Sharing Industries. Members are companies with profit-sharing and 401(k) plans. Membership dues are based on size of company. PSCA represents its members' interests to federal policymakers and offers practical assistance with plan implementation, administration, and communications.

Publications:
Profit Sharing. m.
PSCA Executive Report. m.

Meetings/Conferences:
Annual Meetings: October
1999 – San Diego, CA

Project Management Institute *(1969)*
4 Campus Blvd,
Newtown Square, PA 19073-3299
Tel: (610)356-4600   *Fax:* (610)356-4647
E-Mail: pmihq@pmi.org
Web Site: www.pmi.org
Members: 40,000 individuals
Staff: 70
Annual Budget: $10-25,000,000
Exec. Director: Virgil Carter
Manager, Education: Michael Price
Manager, Membership: Phyllis Levine
Manager, Marketing: Sandra Ardis
Manager, Meetings and Conventions: Liz Ely
Manager, MIS: Lisa McCann

Manager, Research and Standards: Lew Gedansky
Interim Exec. Editor: Jeannette Cabanis

Historical Note
Dedicated to advancing the state-of-the-art in the profession of project management. Conducts a certification program for Project Management Professionals. Membership: $100/year (individual).

Publications:
PM network. m. adv.
PMI Today. m.
Project Management Journal. q. adv.

Meetings/Conferences:
Annual Meetings: Annual seminars and symposium
1999 – Philadelphia, PA/Oct. 10-16

PROMAX Internat'l *(1956)*
2029 Century Park East, Suite 555
Los Angeles, CA 90067-2906
Tel: (310)788-7600   *Fax:* (310)788-7616
Members: 2,000 companies
Staff: 13
Annual Budget: $2-5,000,000
President and C.E.O.: Jim Chabin
V. President, Communications: Scott Slaven
Director, Finance: Amy Koshkarian
Manager, Membership: Jill Masters
Senior V. President: Gregg B. Balko

Historical Note
Formerly (1993) the Broadcast Promotion and Marketing Executives. and (1984) the Broadcasters' Promotion Ass'n. PROMAX is the international ass'n of promotion and marketing professionals in the electronic media, dedicated to advancing the role and increasing the effectiveness of promotion and marketing within the industry, related industries and the academic community. Membership fees vary: $45-345/year.

Publications:
PROMAX Directory. a. adv.
PROMAX Image Magazine. 3/year. adv.
PROMO Fax. w. adv.

Meetings/Conferences:
Annual Meetings: June
1999 – San Francisco, CA/June 9-12
2000 – New Orleans, LA/June 14-17

Promotion Industry Council *(1940)*
1805 N. Mill St., Suite A
Naperville, IL 60563-1275
Tel: (630)369-3772   *Fax:* (630)369-3773
Members: 150 individuals
Annual Budget: $25-50,000
Business Manager: Karen Renk, CAE

Historical Note
Formerly Promotion Industry Club (1996). PIC members are manufacturers, distributors and users of promotion premiums. Organized to increase the understanding of the use of incentives and the process which creates premium promotions. Membership: $115/year (individual).

Publications:
Bulletin. m.
Membership Directory. a.
PIC of the News. q.

Meetings/Conferences:
Annual Meetings: November

Promotion Marketing Ass'n *(1911)*
257 Park Ave. South, 11th Floor
New York, NY 10010-7304
Tel: (212)420-1100   *Fax:* (212)533-7622
Members: 700 companies
Staff: 12
Annual Budget: $2-5,000,000
Exec. Director: Claire Rosenzweig, CAE
Dir., Memebership: Diane Feirman, CAE

Historical Note
Formerly (1998) Promotion Marketing Ass'n of America. Founded in 1911 as American Manufacturers Premiums Ass'n, it became Premium Advertising Ass'n of America in 1934 and Promotion Marketing Ass'n of America, Inc. (PMAA) in 1977. PMA represents the promotion marketing profession. PMAA's mission is to encourage the highest standards of excellence in promotion marketing. It represents member interests and promotes better understanding of the importance of promotion in the marketing mix. Membership: $1,300/year (organization).

Publications:
Legislative Bulletin. m.
Outlook. m.
Promotion Marketing Abstracts. q.

Meetings/Conferences:
Annual Meetings: March
1999 – New Orleans, LA(Sheraton)/March 23-25

Promotional Products Ass'n Internat'l *(1904)*
3125 Skyway Circle North
Irving, TX 75038-3541
Tel: (972)258-3090   *Fax:* (972)258-3006
E-Mail: SteveS@ppa.org
Web Site: http://www.ppa.org
Members: 6,000 companies
Staff: 58
Annual Budget: $5-10,000,000
President: G. Stephen Slagle, CAE
Director of Marketing Communications: Ray Finfer
V. President, Marketing Services: Lindsay Schieffelin, CAE
Manager, Advertising and Public Relations: Pamela Webb
Editor, Promotional Products Business: Tina Filipski
Manager, Government Relations: Laura Osborne
Director, Expositions and Convention: Paul Bellentone
Director of Education: Kim Novak-Dukes
V. President, Administration and Finance: Doug Heath
Director,Finance Affairs: Dennis Cormany

V. President, Program Services: Bren Clevenger-Ori
Director of Membership Services: John Mark Bonnot

Historical Note
Formed by a merger of the Specialty Advertising Nat'l Ass'n (1904) and the Specialty Advertising Guild Internat'l (1953) as the Specialty Advertising Ass'n. Became the Specialty Advertising Ass'n Internat'l in 1970 and assumed its present name in 1994. Represents the specialty advertising, premium, incentive and gift industry. Members are suppliers or distributors of imprinted promotional advertising products. Annual budget reported at $10 million. Membership: $313/year (minimum) for distributors; $641/year (minimum) for suppliers.

Publications:
Membership Directory. a. adv.
Promotional Products Business. m. adv.
Promotional Sense. q.

Meetings/Conferences:
Semi-Annual Meetings: Winter in Dallas and Summer
1999 – Dallas, TX

Propane Vehicle Council *(1994)*
1130 Connecticut Ave., N.W., Suite 700
Washington, DC 20036
Tel: (202)530-0479   *Fax:* (202)223-0479
E-Mail: information@propanegas.com
Web Site: http://www.propanegas.com
Exec. Director: Joseph L. Colaneri

Historical Note
A division of the Nat'l Propane Gas Ass'n, PVC represents equipment manufacturers, propane producers, and other companies interested in continuing development of propane-fueled vehicles. Monitors motor fuel-tax issues and other legislative developments of interest to its members.

Propeller Club of the U.S. *(1927)*
3927 Old Lee Highway, Suite 101A
Fairfax, VA 22030
Tel: (703)691-2777   *Fax:* (703)691-4173
Members: 57 local clubs
Staff: 4
Annual Budget: $250-500,000
Exec. V. President: J. Daniel Smith

Historical Note
Promotes and supports American water-borne commerce and the development of river, Great Lakes and harbor improvements. Founded in 1923 as The Propeller Club of New York, it became a multi-club national organization and assumed its present name in 1927.

Publications:
Proceedings of Am. Merchant Marine and.
The Propeller Club Quarterly. q.

Meetings/Conferences:
Annual Meetings: Fall
1999 – Houston, TX
2000 – Tampa, FL
2001 – Tacoma, WA

Property Casualty Conferences *(1930)*
P.O. Box 681098
3601 Vincennes Road
Indianapolis, IN 46268
Tel: (317)872-4061   *Fax:* (317)879-8408
Members: 152 companies
Staff: 1
Annual Budget: $100-250,000
Exec. V. President: Larry L. Forrester, CAE

Historical Note
Formerly (1977) Conference of Mutual Casualty Companies. Changed name to Conference of Casualty Insurance Companies and is now the Property Casualty Conferences. Members are insurance companies active in writing casualty coverages. CCIC is an education organization only: sponsors seven departmental and one management seminar each year and a "Claim Arbitration Program." Management and offices provided by the Nat'l Ass'n of Mutual Insurance Companies. Membership Fee: Based on premiums written.

Publications:
Directory.

Meetings/Conferences:
Annual Meetings: June

Property Loss Research Bureau *(1947)*
3025 Highland Parkway
Suite 800
Downers Grove, IL 60515-1291
Tel: (630)724-2201   *Fax:* (630)724-2260
E-Mail: whanson@plrb.org
Members: 560 insurance companies
Staff: 22
Annual Budget: $2-5,000,000
President: Wallace R. Hanson
Asst. V. President and Treasurer: Judith Bollman
V. President and General Counsel: Thomas W. Mallin

Historical Note
Founded as the Mutual Loss Research Bureau, it assumed its present name in 1972. Members are mutual and stock insurance companies. Membership: $220/yr. per million assessable premiums.

Publications:
Educational Program. m.
Law Reviews. m.
Newsletter. m.

Meetings/Conferences:
Annual Meetings: Spring/1,200
1999 – New Orleans, LA(New Orleans Hilton)/March 28-31

Property Owners Ass'n *(1949)*
1896 Morris Ave.
Union, NJ 07083-3508

Tel: (908)964-5010   *Fax:* (908)964-6526
E-Mail: poanj@worldnet.att.net
Members: 550 individuals
Staff: 2
Annual Budget: $50-100,000
Exec. Director: Maryanne S. Graham
Historical Note
Membership: $175/year (individual).
Publications:
POA News & Views. m. adv.

Protein Soc. *(1986)*
c/o FASEB
9650 Rockville Pike
Bethesda, MD   20814-3398
Tel: (301)571-0662   *Fax:* (301)571-0666
Toll Free: (800)992 - 6466
Web Site: http://www.faseb.org/protein
Members: 3,200 individuals
Contact: Robert W. Newburgh, Ph.D.
Historical Note
Members are scientists and research organizations interested in proteins. Affiliated with the Federation of American Socs. for Experimental Biology. Membership: $155/year (full); $50/year (student); $1,500/year (corporate).
Publications:
Membership Directory. a.
Newsletter. q.
Protein Science Journal. m. adv.
Meetings/Conferences:
1999 – Boston, MA(Convention Center)/July 24-28/1300

Protestant Church-Owned Publishers Ass'n *(1951)*
945 Jungermann Road
St. Peters, MO   63376-3095
Tel: (314)441-0880   *Fax:* (314)936-8785
Web Site: http://www.ltlb.com/pcpa
Members: 35 publishing houses
Staff: 2
Annual Budget: $50-100,000
Exec. Director: Alan Meyer
Historical Note
PCPA is a trade association of protestant church-owned publishing houses, incorporated in Pennsylvania. Membership: dues vary as a percentage of sales.
Publications:
PCPA Roundtable. q.
Meetings/Conferences:
Biennial Convention: Febuary-March, even yrs. Board
    Meeting: odd yrs.

Psi Omega *(1892)*
1040 Savannah Hwy.
Charleston, SC   29407
Tel: (803)556-0573
Members: 24,500 individuals
Staff: 3
Annual Budget: $100-250,000
Exec. Director: B. Thomas Kays
Historical Note
Professional dental fraternity. Organized at the Baltimore College of Dental Surgery in 1892. Affiliated with the Professional Fraternity Ass'n.
Publications:
The Frater of Psi Omega. 3/year.
Meetings/Conferences:
Annual Meetings: With American Dental Ass'n

Psychoanalytic Research Soc.
Historical Note
A section of the American Psychological Ass'n - Division of Psychoanalysis.

Psychology Soc. *(1960)*
100 Beekman St.
New York, NY   10038-1810
Tel: (212)285-1872
Members: 3,800 individuals
Staff: 4
Annual Budget: $250-500,000
Director: Pierre C. Haber, Ph.D.
Historical Note
Psychology as a science has three components: research, teaching and the application of these two components. The Society seeks the membership of practitioners who treat people, i.e. clinical psychologists exclusively. In turn, it seeks to promote the use of psychology in the treatment of human ills, social and political discord and other problems involving humanity. Membership: $200/year (individual).
Publications:
PS Quarterly. q. adv.
PS: It Is News. bi-m.
Meetings/Conferences:
Annual Meetings: Fall/400
1999 – Washington, DC

Psychometric Soc. *(1935)*
260 C Education Bldg.
1310 S. 6th St.
Champaign, IL   61820-6990
Tel: (217)244-3361   *Fax:* (217)244-7620
Members: 600 individuals
Staff: 2
Annual Budget: $50-100,000
Secretary: Terry A. Ackerman
Historical Note
Founded in Chicago in 1935 and incorporated in New Jersey in 1962. Promotes the use of quantitative models for psychological

phenomena and quantitative methodology in the social and behavioral sciences. Membership: $45/year (individual), $90/year (corporate).
Publications:
Psychometrika. q.
Meetings/Conferences:
Annual Meetings: Spring and Biennial European Meeting (Odd years)

Psychonomic Soc. *(1959)*
UTA Psychology
P.O. Box 19528
Arlington, TX   76019-0528
Tel: (817)272-2775   *Fax:* (817)272-2364
E-Mail: mellgren@uta.edu
Members: 2,500 individuals
Staff: 6
Annual Budget: $100-250,000
Secretary-Treasurer: Roger L. Mellgree
Historical Note
Members are psychologists conducting or supervising research. Membership: $55/year (individual).
Publications:
Animal Learning and Behavior. q. adv.
Behavior Research Methods, Instruments and Computers. bi-m. adv.
Bulletin of The Psychonomic Society. bi-m. adv.
Memory and Cognition. bi-m. adv.
Perception and Psychophysics. m. adv.
Psychobiology. q. adv.
Meetings/Conferences:
Annual Meetings: November/1,300

Public Affairs Council *(1954)*
2033 K St., N.W., Suite 700
Washington, DC   20006
Tel: (202)872-1790   *Fax:* (202)835-8343
Web Site: http://www.pac.org
Members: 400 corporate members
Staff: 17
Annual Budget: $2-5,000,000
President: Douglas G. Pinkham
Director of Communications/Public Relations: Wes Pedersen
Vice President: Peter B. Kennerdell
Director, Center for Public Affairs Management: Brian P. Hawkinson
Historical Note
Formed as the Effective Citizens Organization, it assumed its present name in 1965. The Council is a non-partisan organization of corporate public affairs officers. It serves its members through a clearinghouse of information on programs and problems, counseling, workshops and conferences, publications and job referral. Membership is by company. Affiliated with the Foundation for Public Affairs. Membership: $1,000-12,000/yr.
Publications:
IMPACT. m.
Meetings/Conferences:
Annual Meetings: October
1999 – Colorado Springs, CO(Broadmoor)/Oct. 13-15/75

Public Agency Risk Managers Ass'n *(1974)*
P.O. Box 6810
San Jose, CA   95150
Tel: (408)356-4627
Toll Free: (888)727 - 6290
E-Mail: bfrancis@parma.com
Web Site: http://www.parma.com
Members: 700 public and private agencies
Staff: 1
Annual Budget: $250-500,000
Secretary-Treasurer: Ben C. Francis
Historical Note
A forum for public agencies (cities, counties, universities, school districts, special districts) and associate members to discuss and exchange ideas for the improvement and functioning of risk management within governmental agencies.
Publications:
Parmafacts. bi-m.
Meetings/Conferences:
Annual Meetings: Winter
1999 – San Francisco, CA(Marriott)/Feb. 3-5
2000 – Palm Springs, CA(Wyndham)/Feb. 9-11
2001 – Monterey, CA(Doubletree)
2002 – San Diego, CA/Feb. 6-8

Public Broadcasting Management Ass'n *(1981)*
P.O. Box 50008
Columbia, SC   29250
Tel: (803)799-5517   *Fax:* (803)771-4831
Web Site: http://www.pbma.org
Members: 300 stations
Annual Budget: $100-250,000
Exec. Director: Chuck McConnell
Historical Note
Formerly (1997) Public Telecommunications Financial Management Ass'n, PBMA members are public broadcasting stations and others with an interest in financial management applications.
Publications:
Bottom Line. bi-m.
Meetings/Conferences:
1999 – Ft. Myers, FL(Santa Bell Harbor Resort & Spa)/June 1-4

Public Employees Roundtable *(1982)*
P.O. Box 44801
Washington, DC   20026-4801
Tel: (202)401-4344   *Fax:* (202)401-4433
E-Mail: permail@patriot.net

Web Site: http://www.patriot.net/users/permail
Members: 111 organizations & institutions
Staff: 4
Annual Budget: $250-500,000
Exec. Director: Nicholas Nolan
Historical Note
The Roundtable is composed of 35 associations, 30 government agencies, and 26 corporations representing 1,000,000 public employees. Its purposes are to: inform the American citizenry of the quality of life in government and the services they provide; develop a stronger espirit de corps among public service employees; and encourage interest in public service careers. Membership: $35/year (individual); $1000/year (government agencies).
Publications:
Unsung Heroes. q.
Meetings/Conferences:

Public Golf Management Ass'n *(1990)*
P.O. Box 385494
Bloomington, MN   55438-5494
Tel: (612)854-7272
E-Mail: p6ma@aol.com
Members: 200 individuals and organizations
Staff: 2
Exec. Director: Curtis M. Walker
Historical Note
PGMA is a professional and educational association for golf administrators and managers. Membership: $250/year (individual); $500/year (organization).
Meetings/Conferences:

Public Housing Authorities Directors Ass'n *(1979)*
511 Capitol Court, N.E., Suite 200
Washington, DC   20002-4937
Tel: (202)546-5445   *Fax:* (202)546-2280
E-Mail: avnews@worldweb.net
Web Site: http://www.phada.org
Members: 1,700 individuals
Staff: 8
Annual Budget: $500-1,000,000
Exec. Director: Timothy G. Kaiser
Meeting Planner: Tracy Peranich
Historical Note
Association of public housing agency executive directors. Membership: $60-2,280/year (based on agency size).
Publications:
Advocates. semi-m.
Legislative Update
PHADA Alert.
Meetings/Conferences:
Annual Meetings: May/June
1999 – Nashville, TN

Public Library Ass'n *(1944)*
50 East Huron St.
Chicago, IL   60611
Tel: (312)280-5752   *Fax:* (312)280-5029
Toll Free: (800)545 - 2433
Web Site: http://www.pla.org
Members: 7,800 individuals, 577 organizations
Staff: 8
Annual Budget: $500-1,000,000
Exec. Director: Greta Southard
Communications Manager: Kathleen M. Hughes
Historical Note
A division of the American Library Association, membership in which is a prerequisite. Membership: $50/year.
Publications:
Public Libraries. bi-m. adv.
Statistical Report of the Public Library Data Service. a.
Meetings/Conferences:
Semi-Annual Meetings: January, and June with American
    Library Ass'n
2000 – Charlotte, NC/March 28-Apr. 1

Public Radio News Directors *(1985)*
P.O. Box 8372
Grand Forks, ND   58202
Tel: (701)777-6505   *Fax:* (701)777-2339
E-Mail: cdiers@badlands.nodak.edu
Members: 125 individuals
Annual Budget: $10-25,000
Contact: Christine Paige Diers
Historical Note
Formerly (1994) Public Radio News Directors Ass'n. PRNDA provides a network for news directors; training for news personnel; a channel for the flow of information; and liaison with Nat'l Public Radio. Membership: $90-150/year, varies by size of news staff.
Publications:
PRNDI Newsletter. q.
Meetings/Conferences:
1999 – Boston, MA/July 15-17

Public Radio News Directors Ass'n
Historical Note
Became Public Radio News Directors Inc. in 1994.

Public Radio Program Directors Ass'n
517 Ocean Front Walk, Suite 10
Venice, CA   90291-2428
Tel: (310)664-1591
Members: 175 individuals
Staff: 1
Annual Budget: $100-250,000
Publications:
PRPD Newsletter. m.

Meetings/Conferences:
Annual Meetings: September

Public Relations Soc. of America *(1947)*
33 Irving Place, 3rd Floor
New York, NY   10003-2376
Tel: (212)995-2230   *Fax:* (212)995-0757
Web Site: http://www.prsa.org
Members: 18,000 individuals
Staff: 48
Annual Budget: $5-10,000,000
C.O.O.: Ray Gaulke
Public Relations Director: Richard George
Chief Staff Officer: Ellen Gerber, CAE
Director, Finance & Administration: Joseph P. Cussick, CPA

Historical Note
The major professional association of public relations practitioners in the U.S. Absorbed the American Public Relations Ass'n in 1961, the Nat'l Communication Council for Human Services in 1976, and the Academy of Hospital Public Relations in 1986. Has an annual budget of approximately $5.6 million. Membership: $175/year.

Publications:
Strategist. m. adv.
Tactics.

Meetings/Conferences:
Annual Meetings: Fall/1,500
1999 – Anaheim CA(Hilton)/Oct. 24-27

Public Risk Management Ass'n *(1978)*
1815 N. Ft. Myer Dr., Suite 1020
Arlington, VA   22209-1805
Tel: (703)528-7701   *Fax:* (703)528-7966
E-Mail: info@primacentral.org
Web Site: primacentral.org
Members: 2,800 individuals, 2,000 organizations
Staff: 16
Annual Budget: $1-2,000,000
Exec. Director: James F. Coyle
Dir., Communications: Barbara Oliver
Manager, Government Affairs: Senga Howat
Deputy Director: Melondee Newby
Chapter & Membership Coordinator: Christine Stollas

Historical Note
Formerly (1989) Public Risk and Insurance Management Ass'n. PRIMA promotes and encourages effective public risk management and risk management professionalism in the public sector. Members are local and state government entities, including intergovernmental risk pools. Member representatives include risk managers and other public servants who fulfill the risk management function including loss control, litigation and claims management, contract management, employee benefits, occupational safety and health insurance and risk financing. Membership: $205/year.

Publications:
Public Risk. m. adv.
Public Sector Risk Management.
Risk Watch. m.

Meetings/Conferences:
Annual Meetings: May/June
1999 – San Diego, CA
2000 – Charlotte, NC

Public Securities Ass'n *(1977)*
Historical Note
Became Bond Market Ass'n in 1997.

Public Telecommunications Financial Management Ass'n *(1981)*
Historical Note
Became Public Broadcasting Management Ass'n in 1997.

Public Works Historical Soc. *(1975)*
Historical Note
A division of American Public Works Ass'n, which provides administrative support.

Publishers Marketing Ass'n *(1983)*
627 Aviation Way
Manhattan Beach, CA   90266-7107
Tel: (310)372-2732   *Fax:* (310)374-3342
E-Mail: pmaonline@aol.com
Web Site: http://www.pma-online.org
Members: 3,000 publishers
Annual Budget: $1-2,000,000
Exec. Director: Jan Nathan

Historical Note
PMA is a non-profit trade association of independent publishers who cooperatively market their titles to the trade. Membership $80/year.

Publications:
PMA Catalogue. a.
PMA Newsletter. m. adv.

Meetings/Conferences:
Annual Meetings: May
1999 – Los Angeles, CA

Publishers' Publicity Ass'n *(1957)*
c/o Random House
201 E. 50th St.
New York, NY   10022
Tel: (212)572-2244   *Fax:* (212)572-4960
Members: 250 individuals
Annual Budget: $10-25,000
President: Mary Beth Roche

Historical Note
Founded as the Publishers' Adclub, it assumed its present name in 1963. Membership: $75-110/year.

Publications:
Newsletter. 10/yr.

Meetings/Conferences:
Monthly Meetings: except July and August

Pulp and Paper Safety Ass'n *(1942)*
103 Brentwood Drive
Rome, GA   30165
Tel: (706)234-1919   *Fax:* (706)295-7233
Members: 300 individuals
Staff: 1
Annual Budget: $50-100,000
Exec. Director: William E. Johns

Historical Note
Formerly (1992) Southern Pulp and Paper Safety Ass'n. PPSA members are safety and health advisers in the industry.

Publications:
PPSA Statistical Report. q.

Meetings/Conferences:
Annual Meetings: always April-May

Pulp, Paper and Paperboard Export Ass'n of the U.S. *(1952)*
2 South Point Trail, Cat Island
Beaufort, SC   29902
Tel: (803)525-0195
Members: 7 companies
Secretary-Treasurer: Thomas Costen

Historical Note
A Webb-Pomerene Act Ass'n; members are pulp and paper producers.

Pulverized Limestone Ass'n *(1954)*
Historical Note
Absorbed by the Nat'l Stone Ass'n in 1992. PLA is now a division of NSA.

Purebred Dairy Cattle Ass'n *(1940)*
c/o Holstein Foundation
P.O. Box 816
Brattleboro, VT   05302-0816
Tel: (802)254-4551   *Fax:* (802)254-8251
Members: 7 cattle breeders associations
Staff: 3
Annual Budget: $10-25,000
Program Specialist: Kelli Devino

Historical Note
Members are breeders of Ayrshire, Brown-Swiss, Guernsey, Holstein, Milking Shorthorn, Red and White and Jersey breed registry associations.

Meetings/Conferences:
Annual Meetings: February

Purebred Hanoverian Ass'n of America Breeders and Owners *(1983)*
P.O. Box 429
Rocky Hill, NJ   08553
Tel: (609)466-1383
Members: 300 individuals
Registrar: Barbara Dressler

Historical Note
Members are breeders and owners of purebred and halfbred Hanoverian horses. Maintains breed registry.

Publications:
Annual Report.
News of the Hanoverian Horse. q.

Pyrotechnic Signal Manufacturers Ass'n *(1973)*
28320 St. Michael's Road
Easton, MD   21601
Tel: (410)822-0318
Members: 3 companies
Staff: 2
Annual Budget: $10-25,000

Historical Note
Organization inactive in 1996.

Pyrotechnics Guild Internat'l *(1969)*
18021 Baseline Ave.
Jordan, MN   55352
Tel: (612)492-2061
Members: 1,700 individuals, 20 companies
Annual Budget: $50-100,000
Secretary-Treasurer: Ed Vanasek

Historical Note
PGII promotes the safe and sane display and use of pyrotechnics and encourages the display of pyrotechnics in conjunction with local and national events. Members are amateur and professional fireworks enthusiasts. Has no paid officers or full-time staff. Membership: $25/year.

Publications:
PGII Bulletin. 5/year. adv.

Meetings/Conferences:
Annual Meetings: August

Qualitative Research Consultants Ass'n *(1983)*
P.O. Box 2396
Gaithersburg, MD   20886-2396
Tel: (301)391-6644   *Fax:* (301)391-6281
Toll Free: (888)674 - 7722
E-Mail: qrca@qrca.org
Web Site: http://www.qrca.org
Members: 700 individuals
Annual Budget: $100-250,000
Exec. Director: Bo Palmer
President: Lynn Greenberg

Historical Note
Members are owners and employees of independent marketing and social research firms conducting qualitative research. Membership: $185/year (individual).

Publications:
Conference Proceedings. a.
Facilities and Services Directory. a.
Membership Roster. a.
QRCA Views. q.
Recommended Practices. a.

Meetings/Conferences:
1999 – Orlando, FL/Oct. 13-16

Quality and Productivity Management Ass'n *(1979)*
Historical Note
Address unknown in 1995.

Quality Bakers of America Cooperative *(1922)*
70 Riverdale Ave.
Greenwich, CT   06831
Tel: (203)531-7100   *Fax:* (203)531-1406
Members: 35 companies
Staff: 40
Annual Budget: $1-2,000,000
Exec. V. President: Ernie Stolzer

Historical Note
Members are independent wholesale bakeries and their suppliers.

Meetings/Conferences:
Annual Meetings: October

Quality Chekd Dairy Products Ass'n *(1944)*
Historical Note
Ceased non-profit operations in 1997.

Quarters Furniture Manufacturers Ass'n *(1995)*
Historical Note
Address unknown in 1998.

Race Horse Owners of America
Historical Note
Organization defunct in 1998.

Rack Manufacturers Institute *(1958)*
8720 Red Oak Blvd., Suite 201
Charlotte, NC   28217-3957
Tel: (704)676-1190   *Fax:* (704)676-1199
E-Mail: jnofsinger@mhia.org
Web Site: http://www.mhia.org
Members: 25 companies
Staff: 3
Annual Budget: $50-100,000
Managing Director: John B. Nofsinger

Historical Note
Makers of steel industrial storage racks.

Publications:
Product Directory. a.

Meetings/Conferences:
Semi-annual Meetings: Spring and Fall with Material
          Handling Institute
1999 – Charlotte, NC
1999 – Amelia Island, FL

Racking Horse Breeders Ass'n of America *(1971)*
67 Horse Center Road
Decatur, AL   35603
Tel: (256)353-7225   *Fax:* (256)353-7266
Members: 3,000 individuals
Staff: 10
Annual Budget: $500-1,000,000
Exec. Director: Dan R. Brown

Historical Note
Members are persons directly connected with Racking horses and the Racking horse industry. Membership: $25/year or $500 (lifetime).

Publications:
Racking Review. 19/year.

Meetings/Conferences:
Annual Meetings: Winter
1999 – Decatur, AL/Feb. 19-20

Racquetball Manufacturers Ass'n *(1984)*
Historical Note
Formerly independent, RMA is now a division of Sporting Goods Manufacturers Ass'n.

Radiant Panel Ass'n *(1994)*
P.O. Box 717
1440 W. 29th St., #100
Loveland, CO   80539-0717
Tel: (970)613-0100   *Fax:* (970)613-0098
Toll Free: (801)660 - 7187
E-Mail: misc@rpa-info.com
Web Site: http://www.rpa-info.com
Members: 620 companies
Staff: 2
Annual Budget: $250-500,000
Exec. Director: Larry Drake

Historical Note
RPA is a trade association of manufacturers, distributors, designers, dealers and installers of radiant panel heating and cooling systems and components. Membership: $100-$2,000/year (manufacturer); $500/year (distributor); $300/year (trade associate); $150/year (architect/engineer); $100/year (contractor).

Publications:
Membership Directory. bi-m.
Radiant Living Magazine. a. adv.
Radiant Panel Report. m.

Meetings/Conferences:
1999 – Chicago, IL(Holiday Inn O'Hare)/May 13-15

Radiation Research Soc. *(1952)*

820 Jury Blvd.
Oak Brook, IL   60523
Tel: (630)571-2881   *Fax:* (630)571-7837
Members: 2,025 individuals
Staff: 3
Exec. Secretary: Lise Swanson

Historical Note
Founded in 1952 and incorporated in the District of Columbia. A professional society of individuals studying radiation and its effects. Affiliated with the Internat'l Ass'n for Radiation Research. Membership: $90/year (members); $75/year (associate members); $15/year (student members); $1000/year (affiliate); $1000/year (supporting).

Publications:
Radiation Research Newsletter. 3/year. adv.
Radiation Research: An International Journal. m. adv.

Meetings/Conferences:
1999 – Dublin, Ireland/July 19-20

Radiation Therapy Oncology Group
1101 Market St., 14th Floor
Philadelphia, PA   19107
Tel: (215)574-3224
Admin. Director: Nancy W. Smith

Historical Note
RTOG is a cooperative research organization. Members are medical and research institutions. RTOG conducts clinical trials and compiles information on cancer treatment outcomes. An affiliate of American College of Radiology.

Radio Advertising Bureau (1951)
261 Madison Ave., 23rd Floor
New York, NY   10016-2303
Tel: (212)681-7200   *Fax:* (212)681-7223
Web Site: http://www.rab.com
Members: 5,000 individuals
Staff: 50
Annual Budget: $5-10,000,000
President & C.E.O.: Gary Fries
Exec. V. President, Marketing: Judy Carlough

Historical Note
Established originally as the Department of Radio Advertising of the National Association of Broadcasters, it became independent in 1951 as the Broadcast Advertising Bureau and assumed its present name in 1955. Members seek to increase national and local radio advertising, build the skills and professionalism of marketing personnel, and raise awareness of radio among advertising and business communities. Awards the CRMC (Certified Radio Marketing Consultant) designation. Has an annual budget of approximately $6.5 million.

Publications:
Instant Background , Vol. I and II.
Radio Co-op Directory. a.
Radio Marketing Guide and Fact Book for Advertisers. a.

Meetings/Conferences:
1999 – Atlanta, GA/Feb. 4-7
2000 – Denver, CO(Adam's Mark)/Feb. 3-6
2001 – Dallas, TX(Adam's Mark)/Feb. 1-4

Radio and Television Correspondents Ass'n (1939)
U.S. Capitol, Room S-325
Washington, DC   20510
Tel: (202)224-6421
Members: 2,400 individuals
Staff: 6
Annual Budget: $10-25,000
President: Jim Mills

Historical Note
Formerly (1949) Radio Correspondents Ass'n. Members are correspondents covering Congress. Its sole purpose is to oversee the work of the Senate and House press galleries. Has no paid staff; officers change annually. Membership: $15/year (individual).

Radio and Television Research Council (1941)
Historical Note
Address unknown in 1997.

Radio Control Hobby Trade Ass'n (1983)
560 E. Bonner Road
Wauconda, IL   60084-1104
Tel: (847)526-1222   *Fax:* (847)526-9987
E-Mail: rchta@lnd.com
Members: 150 companies
Staff: 3
Annual Budget: $500-1,000,000
Exec. Director: Kathleen Racine

Historical Note
Serving the radio-controlled and model hobby industries. RCHTA members include manufacturers, distributors and publishers involved in the industry. Membership: $100-600/year.

Publications:
Transmitter Newsletter. q.

Meetings/Conferences:
Annual Meetings: Fall/20,000
1999 – Rosemont, IL(Convention Center)

Radio Talk Show Hosts Ass'n (1989)
566 Commonwealth Ave., Suite 601
Boston, MA   02215
Tel: (617)437-9757   *Fax:* (617)437-0797
Toll Free: (888)562 - 2877
E-Mail: nartsh@priority1.net
Web Site: http://www.talkshowhosts.com
Members: 1000 individuals
Staff: 3
Annual Budget: $250-500,000
Exec. Director: Carol Nashe
Members Services: Keith Taylor

Historical Note
Formerly Nat'l Ass'n of Radio Talk Show Hosts. Members are radio hosts and other professionals involved in the production of radio talk shows. Membership: $25/year (regular); $50/year (associate); $299/year (company).

Publications:
Members Guide. a. adv.
Resource Directory. a.

Meetings/Conferences:

Radio-Television News Directors Ass'n (1946)
1000 Connecticut Ave., N.W., Suite 615
Washington, DC   20036-5302
Tel: (202)659-6510   *Fax:* (202)223-4007
E-Mail: rtnda@rtnda.org
Web Site: http://www.rtnda.org/rtnda/
Members: 3,600 individuals
Staff: 26
Annual Budget: $1-2,000,000
President: Barbara Cochran
Director, Communications: Noreen Welle
Director, Conventions and Meetings: Rick Osmanski
Director, Membership: Denise Smith
Managing Editor: Bryan Moffett
Director, Operations: Jim Trope
Assistant to the President: Edie Emery

Historical Note
Membership open to all broadcast journalists, suppliers and educators. Administers the Edward R. Murrow Awards, given in recognition of excellence in broadcast news in radio and television. Membership: $95-$145/year (individual).

Publications:
Assignment Desk Newsletter. q.
Job Bulletin. bi-w.
Legal Notes. m.
Radio Reporting Newsletter. q.
RTNDA Communicator. m. adv.
TV Production Newsletter. q.

Meetings/Conferences:
Annual Meetings: Fall
1999 – Charlotte, NC/Sept. 29-Oct. 2

Radiological Soc. of North America (1915)
2021 Spring Road, Suite 600
Oak Brook, IL   60523
Tel: (630)571-2670   *Fax:* (630)571-7837
Web Site: http://www.rsna.org
Members: 30,000 individuals
Staff: 90
Annual Budget: $10-25,000,000
Exec. Director: Delmar J. Stauffer
Director, Meetings and Conventions: Michael O'Connell
Asst. Exec. Director: Steve Drew
Asst. Exec. Director: Mark Watson
Director, Publications: Roberta E. Arnold
Assistant Exec. Director: Dana Davis

Historical Note
Founded as the Western Roentgen Society and assumed its present name in 1915. Members are individuals interested in the application of radiology to medicine. Has an annual budget of over $20 million. Membership: $215/year (individual).

Publications:
Cumulative Index of Radiologic Literature. a.
Directory of Members. a.
RadioGraphics. bi-m. adv.
Radiology. m. adv.
Scientific Assembly Program. a.

Meetings/Conferences:
Annual Meetings: usually Chicago, IL(McCormick Place)/November/55,000
1999 – /Nov. 28-Dec. 3

Radiology Business Management Ass'n (1968)
1550 South Coast Hwy., Suite 201
Laguna Beach, CA   92651
Toll Free: (888)224 - 7262
E-Mail: surch@rbma.org
Web Site: http://www.rbma.org
Members: 1,600 individuals
Staff: 2
Annual Budget: $500-1,000,000
Exec. Director: Sharon Urch

Historical Note
Formerly (1990) Radiologists Business Managers Ass'n. RBMA promotes the improvement of radiology practice management through legislative issues and business management. Membership: $275/year (individual); $450/year (corporation).

Publications:
Membership Directory.
RBMA Bulletin. m. adv.

Meetings/Conferences:
Annual Meetings: Semi-Annual Meetings
1999 – New Orleans. LA(The Fairmont)/May 8-11/500
1999 – San Diego, CA(Hyatt Regency)/Oct. 31-Nov. 3

Railroad Public Relations Ass'n (1952)
Historical Note
Organization defunct in 1997.

Railway Engineering-Maintenance Suppliers Ass'n (1965)
210 Little Falls St., Suite 100
Falls Church, VA   22046-4331
Tel: (703)241-8514   *Fax:* (703)241-8589
E-Mail: remsa@earthlink.net
Web Site: http://www.remsa.org
Members: 243 individuals
Staff: 2
Annual Budget: $250-500,000

Exec. Director: J.A. Meyerhoeffer
Historical Note
Merger (1965) of Nat'l Railway Appliance Ass'n (Est. 1894) and Ass'n of Track and Structures Suppliers (Est. 1914). Members are distributors and manufacturers of railway track machinery track supplies, and services. Membership: $600/year (organization), plus $650 initiation fee.

Publications:
Newsletter. q.

Meetings/Conferences:
1999 – Chicago, IL(Palmer House)

Railway Industrial Clearance Ass'n (1969)
c/o TGX Co., 101 N. Wacker Dr.
Chicago, IL   60606
Tel: (312)984-3770   *Fax:* (312)984-3781
E-Mail: wrthurow@ttxco.com
Web Site: http://www.rica.org
Members: 245 companies
Annual Budget: $10-25,000
Secretary-Treasurer: Bill Thurow

Historical Note
Members are railroads and shippers of dimensional loads (loads which require shipping clearance because they exceed railway size/weight standards). Membership: $25/year (individual).

Publications:
Newsletter. 3/year.

Meetings/Conferences:
1999 – Bloomingdale, IL(Indian Lake)/June 9-11

Railway Labor Executives Ass'n (1926)
10 G St., N.E., Suite 480
Washington, DC   20002-4213
Tel: (202)347-7936   *Fax:* (202)347-5237
Members: 14 unions
Annual Budget: $50-100,000

Historical Note
Composed of the chief executive officers of railway labor organizations. Affiliated with AFL-CIO.

Railway Progress Institute (1908)
700 N. Fairfax St.
Alexandria, VA   22314-2098
Tel: (703)836-2332   *Fax:* (703)548-0058
E-Mail: RPI@RPI.org
Members: 150 companies
Staff: 6
Annual Budget: $500-1,000,000
President: Robert A. Matthews

Historical Note
Formerly (1956) Railway Business Ass'n. The trade association of the railway equipment and supply industry. Membership: $1,050-20,000/year (company).

Publications:
Annual Report. a.
Railway Progress News. irreg.
Washington Report. irreg.

Meetings/Conferences:
Annual Meetings: Fall/1,000

Railway Supply Ass'n (1962)
29 W. 140 Butterfield Road, Suite 103-A
Warrenville, IL   60555
Tel: (630)393-0106   *Fax:* (630)393-0108
E-Mail: rsainc@earthlink.net
Members: 480 individuals
Staff: 2
Annual Budget: $250-500,000
Exec. Director: Howard Tonn

Historical Note
Merger of Allied Railway Supply Ass'n (1931) and Railway Electrical and Mechanical Supply Ass'n (1909). Principally coordinators of railway supply exhibitions. Membership: $400 initiation fee; $200/year (company).

Meetings/Conferences:
Annual Meetings: September, usually in Chicago, IL
1999 – Chicago, IL(Hilton)/Sept. 19-22

Railway Systems Suppliers, Inc. (1906)
9304 New LaGrange Road, Suite 200
Louisville, KY   40242
Tel: (502)327-7774   *Fax:* (502)327-0541
E-Mail: rssi@rssi.org
Web Site: http://www.rssi.org
Members: 240 companies
Staff: 2
Annual Budget: $250-500,000
Exec. Director, Secretary-Treasurer: Donald F. Remaley

Historical Note
Merger (1961) of the Railway Communications Suppliers Ass'n and Signal Appliance Ass'n. Formerly (1971) Railway Signal and Communications Suppliers Ass'n, and (1977) Railway Systems Suppliers Ass'n, Inc. RSSI is a trade ass'n serving the communication and signal segment of the rail transportation industry. It's primary effort each year is to organize and manage a trade show for its members to exhibit their products and services. Membership: $200-$600/year.

Publications:
International Railway Journal.
Progressive Railroading. adv. adv.
Railway Age. m. adv.
RSSI Info Letter. q.
RSSI Newsletter. bi-a.

Meetings/Conferences:
1999 – Baltimore, MD(Omni Hotel)/Aug. 29-Sept. 1

Railway Tie Ass'n (1919)
115 Commerce Dr., Suite C

Fayetteville, GA 30214
Tel: (770)460-5553 *Fax:* (770)460-5573
E-Mail: ties@sprynet.com
Members: 2,500 companies
Staff: 2
Annual Budget: $100-250,000
Exec. Director: Jim Gauntt

Historical Note
Formerly (1929) the Nat'l Ass'n of Railroad Tie Producers. Membership is comprised of crosstie producers, sawmill owners, chemical manufacturers, wood preservation companies railroad maintenance engineers, purchasing officials and others interesed in the manufacture and procurement of wood railroad ties. Membership: annual dues based on size and volume of production.

Publications:
Crossties Magazine. bi-m. adv.

Meetings/Conferences:
Annual Meetings: Fall
1999 – Tempe, AZ(Buttes)/Sept. 29-Oct. 1

Rapid Prototyping Ass'n of SME
One SME Drive
Dearborn, MI 48121-0930
Tel: (313)271-1500
Toll Free: (800)733 - 4763
Web Site: http://www.sme.org/rpa.html
Staff: 2
Association Manager: Kristen Dudash

Historical Note
Sponsored by the Soc. of Manufacturing Engineers.

Publications:
Rapid Prototyping Quarterly Newsletter. q.

Meetings/Conferences:
1999 – Rosemont, IL(Rosemont Convention Center)/April 20-22

Real Estate Aviation Chapter (1948)
5440 St. Charles Road
Berkeley, IL 60163-1287
Tel: (708)547-7100 *Fax:* (708)547-8000
Members: 125 individuals
Staff: 1
Annual Budget: under $10,000
Director: Warren J. Haeger

Historical Note
Formerly (1976) the Nat'l Real Estate Fliers Ass'n and (until 1978) the Real Estate Aviation Council. Main objective is to educate members and the public on the economic and social impact of aviation on cities, land values and uses and real estate ownership. A chapter of the Farm and Land Institute of the National Association of Realtors. Membership: $25/year (individual).

Publications:
Flight Lines. q.

Meetings/Conferences:
Annual Meetings: With the Nat'l Ass'n of Realtors

Real Estate Brokerage Managers Council (1968)
430 N. Michigan Ave., Suite 300
Chicago, IL 60611-4092
Tel: (312)321-4400 *Fax:* (312)329-8882
Web Site: http://www.crb.com
Members: 7,400 individuals
Staff: 12
Annual Budget: $2-5,000,000
Exec. V. President: Bonnie A. Cobean, CAE
Meetings Manager: Jan Aksztulewicz
Education Director: David Williams
Legal Director: Laurie Janik
Membership Services Director: Gwen Voelker

Historical Note
A division of the Realtors Nat'l Marketing Institute, MC are real estate firm owners and managers. Awards the designation Certified Real Estate Brokerage Manager (CRB). Membership: $150/year (individual).

Publications:
Issue and Trends Newsletter. q.
Real Estate Business Magazine. bi-w. adv.

Meetings/Conferences:
Annual Meetings: November, in conjunction with the Nat'l Ass'n of Realtors
1999 – Orlando, FL/November 10-14
2000 – San Francisco, CA/Nov. 8-12

Real Estate Buyers Agent Council
430 N. Michigan Ave.
Chicago, IL 60611
Tel: (312)329-8656 *Fax:* (312)329-6224
Toll Free: (800)648 - 6224
E-Mail: rebac@realtors.org
Web Site: http://www.rebac.org
Members: 22,000 individuals
Staff: 6
Director: David J. Martin, CAE

Historical Note
REBAC represents professional real estate agents who act as buyer's agents, as opposed to representing the seller of a property. Became an affiliate of Nat'l Ass'n of REALTORS in 1996. Membership: $110/year.

Publications:
Membership Directory. a. adv.
Newsletter. m.
Today's Buyer's Rep. m.

Meetings/Conferences:
Annual Meetings: unsually in conjunction with NAR

Real Estate Capital Resources Ass'n (1989)
1250 Connecticut Ave., N.W., Suite 700
Washington, DC 20036

Tel: (202)637-6481 *Fax:* (202)842-2869
Members: 40 companies
Staff: 3
Annual Budget: $100-250,000
Exec. Director: G. David Fensterheim

Historical Note
Formerly Real Estate Capital Recovery Ass'n (1994). RECRA represents firms with expertise in providing third party workout and capital recovery services in connection with distressed real estate and real estate related assets.

Meetings/Conferences:

Real Estate Educators Ass'n (1979)
740 Florida Central Pkwy., Suite 1020
Longwood, FL 32750-7652
Tel: (407)834-6688 *Fax:* (407)834-4747
E-Mail: reea@amni.net
Web Site: http://www.reea.org
Members: 1,400 individuals
Staff: 2
Annual Budget: $250-500,000
Exec. Director: Jone R. Sienkiewicz, CAE, CMP

Historical Note
Members are individuals involved in all types of real estate training and education. Membership: $80/yr. (individual), $150/yr. (organization/company).

Publications:
Proceedings. a.
REEA Journal. a. adv.
REEAction. m. adv.

Meetings/Conferences:
Annual Meetings: May
1999 – Pittsburgh, PA/June 3-5
2000 – Las Vegas, NV/June 3-5

Real Estate Information Providers Ass'n (1995)
1900 Arch St.
Philadelphia, PA 19103-1498
Tel: (215)564-3484 *Fax:* (215)963-9785
E-Mail: reipa@aol.com
Web Site: http://www.reipa.com
Members: 110 individuals
Staff: 2
Annual Budget: $100-250,000
Exec. Director: Maureen Brady

Historical Note
REIPA supports professional information providers in the real estate industry. Membership fee varies based on sales. $375-3,000/year.

Publications:
Newsletter. q.

Meetings/Conferences:

Real Estate Law Institute

Historical Note
Became (1995) Nat'l Soc. of Appraiser Specialists.

Real Estate Management Brokers Institute
Historical Note
An affiliate of the Nat'l Ass'n of Real Estate Brokers.

REALTORS Land Institute (1944)
430 N. Michigan Ave.
Chicago, IL 60611
Tel: (312)329-8440 *Fax:* (312)329-8633
Toll Free: (800)441 - 5263
Web Site: http://www.rliland.com
Members: 1,600 individuals
Staff: 3
Annual Budget: $250-500,000
Exec V. President: Belinda Carter

Historical Note
Formerly (1975) Nat'l Institute of Farm and Land Brokers and (1986) Farm and Land Institute, RLI is an affiliate of the Nat'l Ass'n of REALTORS. Members are those interested in the development and sale of all types of land. Offers the Accredited Land Consultant (ALC) designation. Membership: $185/year, plus chapter dues.

Publications:
Membership Roster. a.
Realtors Land Institute. m. adv.

Meetings/Conferences:
Triannual Meetings: Miami, FL/Nov. 8-14 and Anaheim, CA/Oct. 31-Nov. 6 and Atlanta, GA/Nov. 6-12
1999 – Atlanta, GA

Receptive Services Ass'n (1990)
236 Route 38 West, Suite 100
Moorestown, NJ 08057
Tel: (609)231-8500 *Fax:* (609)231-4664
Members: 320 individuals, 250 companies
Staff: 2
Annual Budget: $50-100,000
Exec. Director: Bill Pawlucy

Historical Note
Founded as Receptive Services Ass'n of New York and New Jersey in 1990, RSA became a national organization in 1995. Members are companies who provide tour and travel related services to groups visiting the U.S. from overseas. Membership: $350/year (full member), $300/year (associate), plus $100 initiation fee.

Publications:
RSAdvisor. q. adv.

Meetings/Conferences:

Recording Industry Ass'n of America (1952)
1330 Connecticut Ave., N.W., Suite 300
Washington, DC 20036
Tel: (202)775-0101 *Fax:* (202)775-7253
Members: 70 companies

Staff: 70
Annual Budget: $10-25,000,000
President and C.E.O.: Hilary B. Rosen
Senior V. President, Communications: Tim Sites
Senior V. President, Government Affairs: Jennifer L. Bendall
V. President, Government Affairs, State and Artist Relations: Joel E. Flatow
Senior V. President, Technology: David W. Stebbings
C.F.O.: Michael Williams
Senior Exec. V. President/General Counsel: Cary H. Sherman
Senior, V. President, Civil Litigation: Steven B. Fabrizio
V.P., Member Services: John H. Ganoe
Exec. V. President, Anti-Piracy: Steve D'Onofrio
Exec. V. President, International: Neil Turkewitz

Historical Note
Formerly (1970) Record Industry Ass'n of America. RIAA is the non-profit trade association representing the U.S. sound recording industry. RIAA member companies create, manufacture and market approximately 90% of all legitimate recordings produced and sold in the U.S. The principal goal of RIAA is to serve the common interests of recording companies and address their needs, worldwide, in the face of modern technology. A major concern is the unauthorized copying ("piracy") of recorded material and censorship issues. Has an annual budget of approximately $11 million.

Publications:
Fast Tracks. bi.

Recreation Vehicle Dealers Ass'n of North America (1968)
3930 University Drive, Suite 100
Fairfax, VA 22030-2515
Tel: (703)591-7130 *Fax:* (703)591-0734
Members: 1,400 companies
Staff: 9
Annual Budget: $1-2,000,000
President: Michael A. Molino, CAE
Director of Communications: Phil Ingrassia
State Affairs Manager: Holly James
Director of Education: Lee Elwell
Director of Administration: Ronnie Hepp
Director, Program Development and Marketing: Scott Myers
Editor & Media Manager: Frank Hurteau

Historical Note
Absorbed (1969) Recreational Dealer Ass'n; formerly (1970) Recreation Vehicle Dealers Institute, and (1976) the Recreational Vehicle Dealers of America, Inc. Absorbed Recreation Vehicle Rental Ass'n in 1982 and Recreation Vehicle After Market Ass'n in 1986.

Publications:
Legislative Reports. m.
RV Executive Today. m. adv.
Who's Who in RV Rentals. a. adv.

Meetings/Conferences:

Recreation Vehicle Industry Ass'n (1963)
1896 Preston White Drive
P.O.Box 2999
Reston, VA 20195
Tel: (703)620-6003 *Fax:* (703)620-5071
Members: 510 companies
Staff: 50
Annual Budget: $5-10,000,000
President: David J. Humphreys
V. President, Public Relations: Gary M. LaBalla
Director, Communications: Bill Baker
V. President, Government Affairs: Dianne Farrell
Dir., Govt. Affairs: Jay Landers
V. President, Meetings and Shows: Mary Huyta
V. President, Standards and Education: Bruce Hopkins
V. President, Administration: Robert M. Bryan, CAE
V. President and General Counsel: Craig A. Kirby

Historical Note
Established in 1963 as the Recreational Vehicle Institute, Inc. Merged in 1968 with Camping Trailer Manufacturers Ass'n and American Institute of Travel Trailer and Camper Manufacturers, Inc. The name was changed in 1975 to Recreation Vehicle Industry Ass'n. Members are manufacturers of motor homes, travel trailers, truck campers, folding camping trailers, and conversion vehicles, as well as suppliers of RV component parts. Has an annual budget of $6.8 million.

Publications:
Directory. a.
RV Financing. a.
RV Road Signs. q.
RVIA Marketing Report. m.
RVIA Today. m.
RVIA Update. q.
Year End Report. a.

Meetings/Conferences:
Annual Meetings: Spring
1999 – Hawaii/March 10-14

Recreation Vehicle Rental Ass'n (1982)
3930 University Drive, Suite 100
Fairfax, VA 22030-2515
Tel: (703)591-7130 *Fax:* (703)591-0734
Web Site: http://www.rvamerica.com/rvra
Members: 275 companies
Staff: 15
President: Michael A. Molino, CAE

Historical Note
A division of the Recreation Vehicle Dealers Ass'n of North America, which provides staff support and to which all members of RVRA belong.

Publications:
RVRA Rental. irreg.

Meetings/Conferences:
Annual Meetings: Winter, with Recreation Vehicle Dealers Ass'n of North America

Recreational Park Trailer Industry Ass'n (1993)

19 Perry St., Suite 204
Newnan, GA 30263-1918
Tel: (770)251-2672   *Fax:* (770)251-0025
E-Mail: rpt12@rvamerica.com
Web Site: http://www.rvamerica.com/rpt12
Members: 70 firms and organizations
Staff: 3
Annual Budget: $250-500,000
Exec. Director: William R. Garpow
Assistant to the Director: Laraine Ayers

Historical Note
Formerly a division of Recreation Vehicle Industry Ass'n; became an independent organization in 1993. RPTIA represents manufacturers, suppliers, and service firms producing park trailers. Other members include associations representing retailers, RV parks and resorts. RPTIA works to unite all segments of the industry so they may, in consort, have effective influence upon matters of public interest involving the betterment of the industry. Membership: $75-$10,000/year.

Publications:
RPTIA Newswatch. m.

Meetings/Conferences:

Recreational Vehicle Manufacturer's Clubs Ass'n (1973)

Newmar Kountry Klub
355 N. Delaware
Nappanee, IN 46550-0030
Tel: (219)773-7791   *Fax:* (219)773-5130
Toll Free: (877)639 - 5582
E-Mail: newmarklub@aol.com
Members: 24 organizations
Annual Budget: under $10,000
President: Dave Wilson

Historical Note
Members are managers/directors of manufacturer-sponsored travel clubs. Has no paid officers or full-time staff; officers change annually. Membership: $25/year.

Meetings/Conferences:
Annual Meetings: November, usually Louisville, KY(Executive West)

Recycled Paperboard Technical Ass'n (1953)

920 Davis Road, Suite 306
Elgin, IL 60123-1390
Tel: (847)622-2544   *Fax:* (847)622 2516
E-Mail: rpta@rpta.org
Members: 28 companies
Staff: 4
Annual Budget: $250-500,000
Exec. Director: Phillip W. Forsyth

Historical Note
Formerly (1991) the Boxboard Research and Development Ass'n. An association of U.S., Canadian and other foreign companies interested in cooperative research and development in technical and operational aspects of the recycled paperboard industry.

Meetings/Conferences:
Annual Meetings: Chicago, first week in May.

Red and White Dairy Cattle Ass'n (1964)

HC 1 Box 71B
Crystal Spring, PA 15536
Tel: (814)735-4221   *Fax:* (814)735-3473
Web Site: http://www.redandwhitecattle.com
Members: 1,400 individuals
Staff: 6
Annual Budget: $500-1,000,000
Exec. Secretary-Treasurer: Joan Carpenter

Historical Note
Members are owners and breeders of Red and White dairy cattle. Maintains breed registry.

Publications:
Red Bloodlines. m.

Meetings/Conferences:
Annual Meetings: Fall

Red Angus Ass'n of America (1954)

4201 North Interstate 35
Denton, TX 76207-3415
Tel: (940)387-3502   *Fax:* (940)383-4036
Web Site: http://www.redangus1.org
Members: 1,655 individuals
Staff: 14
Annual Budget: $1-2,000,000
Exec. Secretary: Robert Hough

Historical Note
Members are breeders and improvers of Red Angus Beef Cattle. Member of: Nat'l Pedigree Livestock Council; Nat'l Cattlemen's Ass'n; U.S. Beef Breeds Council; and Beef Improvement Federation. Membership: $50/year.

Publications:
American Red Angus. 10/yr. adv.

Meetings/Conferences:
Annual Meetings: Fall

Red Tag News Publications Ass'n (1971)

P.O. Box 429
Flossmoor, IL 60422-0429
Tel: (708)957-5525   *Fax:* (708)957-5546
Members: 57 publications
Staff: 3
Annual Budget: $50-100,000
General Manager: Rebecca Strupeck

Historical Note
RTNPA members are publications classified by the U.S. Postal Service as newspapers. Membership: based on circulation. Membership fee varies.

Publications:
Bulletin. irreg.
Newsletter.

Meetings/Conferences:
Annual Meetings: always in Washington, DC/September

Refractories Institute (1951)

650 Smithfield St., Suite 1160
Pittsburgh, PA 15222-3907
Tel: (412)281-6787   *Fax:* (412)281-6881
E-Mail: triassn@aol.com
Members: 100 companies
Staff: 4
Annual Budget: $500-1,000,000
Exec. Secretary: Florence R. Stony
President: Robert Wicrolius

Historical Note
Incorporated in 1951 as the national trade association for refractory manufacturers, suppliers of equipment and raw material, and installers. Refractories are heat-resistant materials that are used for lining high-temperature furnaces and reactors. Membership: $3,150-$29,400/year.

Publications:
Directory of the Refractories Industry. a. adv.
Refractories.
Refractory News. m.

Meetings/Conferences:
Annual Meetings: late Spring
1999 – Amelia Island, FL(Ritz-Carlton)/May 5-7/225
2000 – Ponte Vedia Beach, FL(Ponte Vedia Inn)/May 3-5/225
2001 – Napa, CA(Silverado Country Club)/June 13-15/225

Refractory Ceramic Fiber Coalition (1992)

1133 Connecticut Ave., N.W., Suite 1200
Washington, DC 20036
Tel: (202)775-2388   *Fax:* (202)833-8491
Members: 3 individuals
Staff: 1
Administrator: Hanne Alou

Historical Note
Formed by refractory ceramic fiber manufacturers after the dissolution of TIMA (Thermal Insulation Manufacturers Ass'n) in 1992.

Refractory Metals Ass'n (1970)

Historical Note
Producers of powders and products made from tungsten, molybdenum, tatalum and niobium. Formerly (1975) Refractory and Reactive Metals Ass'n. A constituent member of the Metal Powder Industries Federation.

Refrigerated Foods Ass'n (1980)

2971 Flowers Road South, Suite 266
Atlanta, GA 30341
Tel: (770)452-0660   *Fax:* (770)455-3879
E-Mail: RFASSN@aol.com
Members: 210 companies
Staff: 3
Annual Budget: $100-250,000
Exec. Director: Judy Stokes

Historical Note
Concerned with the manufacture and sale of refrigerated foods. Formerly (1991) Salud Manufacturers Ass'n. Membership: $400-1,500/year, based on gross sales (fullmember), $500/year (associate member).

Publications:
Chilled News Review.
Directory. a.
Technical Newsletter. q.

Meetings/Conferences:
Annual Meetings: January-March; Biennial Exhibition also held/odd years
1999 – Orlando, FL(Disney Contemporary)/Feb. 24-28/350

Refrigerating Engineers and Technicians Ass'n (1910)

401 N. Michigan Ave.
Chicago, IL 60611-4267
Tel: (312)527-6763   *Fax:* (312)245-1083
Members: 1,400 individuals and companies
Staff: 2
Annual Budget: $50-100,000
Exec. Director: Barbara Chalik

Historical Note
Formerly Nat'l Ass'n of Practical Refrigerating Engineers. Designers, installers, operators and maintainers of central refrigeration and air conditioning equipment. Membership: $60/year (individual); $300-750/year (company).

Publications:
RETA Breeze. q.
Technical Report. q. adv.

Meetings/Conferences:
Annual Meetings: November
1999 – Boise, ID

Refrigeration Service Engineers Soc. (1933)

1666 Rand Rd.
Des Plaines, IL 60016
Tel: (847)297-6464   *Fax:* (847)297-5038
Web Site: http://www.rses.org
Members: 40,000 individuals
Staff: 39
Annual Budget: $5-10,000,000
Exec. V. President: Joe Ziemba
Communications & Marketing Director: Thomas S. Catalano
Director, Conferences and Seminars: Kenneth Hajduk, CMP
Sr. Director, Education and Program Dev.: Dean Lewis, CM
Coordinator, Membership Services: Barbara Valasek

Historical Note
Membership: $51/year.

Publications:
RSES Journal.

Meetings/Conferences:
Annual Meetings: Fall

Regional Airline Ass'n (1968)

1200 19th St., N.W., Suite 300
Washington, DC 20036-2422
Tel: (202)857-1170   *Fax:* (202)429-5113
E-Mail: RAA@DC.SBA.COM
Web Site: http://www.RAA.org
Members: 410 companies and organizations
Staff: 4
Annual Budget: $500-1,000,000
President: Walt Coleman
V. President: Deborah McElroy

Historical Note
In 1968 the Ass'n of Commuter Airlines merged with the Nat'l Air Taxi Conference to form what became the Nat'l Air Transportation Conferences and, later, the Nat'l Air Transportation Ass'ns. In 1975 this group again became independent under the name Commuter Airline Ass'n of America until 1981 when it assumed its present name. Regional airlines provide short haul air transportation primarily connecting small and medium sized communities with larger cities and connecting hubs. Membership consists of more than 70 airlines, plus 350 associate members who provide goods and services.

Publications:
Annual Report of the RAA. a. adv.

Meetings/Conferences:
Semi-Annual Meetings: Spring and Fall
1999 – Phoenix, AZ/May 10-12

Regional and Distribution Carriers Conference (1943)

Historical Note
Merged with Distribution and LTL Carriers Ass'n in 1997.

Regional Orchestra Managers Ass'n

Historical Note
A sub-group of the American Symphony Orchestra League without dues structure or separate headquarters.

Regional Railroads of America (1987)

Historical Note
Merged with American Short Line Railroad Ass'n (1998).

Regional Science Ass'n, Internat'l (1954)

1 Observatory, Univ. of Illinois
901 S. Mathews
Urbana, IL 61801-3682
Tel: (217)333-8904   *Fax:* (217)333-3065
Members: 2,000 individuals
Staff: 2
Annual Budget: $100-250,000
Exec. Director: Kairin Donaghy

Historical Note
Formerly Regional Science Ass'n, became interntional in 1989. RSAI acts as an umbrella organization overseeing three major supraregional organizations in North America, Europe, and the Pacific. Members are professionals concerned with urban and regional planning, and with the study of those social, economic, political, and behavioral phenomena which have a spatial dimension. Membership: $60/year (individual); $40/year (students).

Publications:
Papers in Regional Science: Journal of the RSAI. q.

Meetings/Conferences:
Annual Meetings: November

Registered Mail Insurance Ass'n (1921)

100 William St.
New York, NY 10038
Tel: (212)425-1470   *Fax:* (212)425-2539
Toll Free: (800)969 - 7642
Members: 3 companies
Staff: 8
Annual Budget: $250-500,000
Manager: John Comean

Historical Note
A joint operation of insurance companies to provide insurance for shipments of currency, securities and other valuables. Formerly the Registered Mail Central Bureau.

Meetings/Conferences:
Annual Meetings: October

Registry of Interpreters for the Deaf (1964)

8630 Fenton St., Suite 324
Silver Spring, MD 20910
Tel: (301)608-0050   *Fax:* (301)608-0508
Members: 5,300 individuals, 57 affiliate chapters
Staff: 10
Annual Budget: $500-1,000,000
Association Administrator: Clay Nettles
Bookkeeper/Office Manager: Bill Shoemaker

Historical Note
Established to initiate, sponsor, promote and execute policies and activities that will further the profession of interpretation of American Sign Language and the transliteration of English. Membership: $100/year (certified); $70/year (associate); $25/year (student); $24/year (supporting).

Publications:
Views. m. adv.

Meetings/Conferences:
Biennial Meetings: odd years

Regular Common Carriers Conference

Historical Note
Became (1996) Distribution and LTL Carriers Ass'n.

Regulatory Affairs Professionals Soc. (1977)
12300 Twinbrook Pkwy., Suite 350
Rockville, MD 20852-1606
Tel: (301)770-2920   *Fax:* (301)770-2924
Toll Free: (800)963 - 7277
E-Mail: feedback@raps.org
Web Site: http://www.raps.org
Members: 7,000 individuals
Staff: 12
Annual Budget: $2-5,000,000
Exec. Director: Sherry Keramidas, Ph.D., CAE
Director, Communications: Heather Stewart
Director, Conventions & Meetings: Adena Bryant
Director, Education: Linda Temple
Director, Administration: Iris Rush
Director, Membership Services: Christopher Granger
Editor: Joan Bass
Manager, Information Technology: Brad Tuny

Historical Note
Members are regulatory affairs professionals, lawyers and consultants from drug, medical device, biologic and health care related industries who work with the Food and Drug Administration and other regulatory agencies. Membership: $170/year (new members).

Publications:
Membership Directory. a.
Regulatory Affairs Focus. m. adv.

Meetings/Conferences:
Annual Meetings: Fall in Washington, DC

Rehabilitation Engineering and Assistive Technology Soc. of North America (1979)
1700 N. Moore St., Suite 1540
Arlington, VA 22209-1903
Tel: (703)524-6686   *Fax:* (703)524-6630
E-Mail: natloffice@resna.org
Web Site: http://www.resna.org/resna/reshome.htm
Members: 1,900 individuals
Staff: 12
Annual Budget: $1-2,000,000
Exec. Director: James R. Geletka
Coordinator, Membership: Terry C. Reamer

Historical Note
Formerly (1995) RESNA, the Ass'n for the Advancement of Rehabilitation Technology. Established in Chicago, IL in 1979. Formerly (1986) Rehabilitation Engineering Soc. of North America. A professional organization of the rehabilitation technology community, the society brings together a diverse group of individuals whose credentials, activities and interests vary widely but who are all committed to designing, developing, evaluating and providing external and internal devices that will put the benefits of technology to work for disabled persons. A member society of the American Institute for Medical and Biological Engineering. Also known as the Ass'n for the Advancement of Rehabilitation Technology. Membership: $120/year (regular); $275-525/year (organization/company).

Publications:
Assistive Technology Journal. semi-a.
Proceedings of the RESNA Annual Conference. a.
RESNA News. bi-m.

Meetings/Conferences:
Annual Meetings: Summer/1,500
1999 – Long Beach, CA(Long Beach Convention Center)/June 25-29

Rehabilitation Nursing Foundation
Historical Note
The educational and research arm of the Association of Rehabilitation Nurses.

Rehabilitation Technology Ass'n (1982)
WV Research & Training Center
Barron Drive, P.O. Box 1004
Institute, WV 25112-1004
Tel: (304)766-2680   *Fax:* (304)766-2689
Toll Free: (800)624 - 8284
E-Mail: wvrrtc@rtc2.icdi.wvu.edu
Web Site: http://www.icdi.wvu.edu
Members: 4,000 individuals
Staff: 20
Annual Budget: $10-25,000
Contact: Ranjit K. Majumder
RTA Coordinator: Betty Tyler

Historical Note
Rehabilitation Professionals interested in the use of information technology.

Publications:
RTA Online. q. adv.

Meetings/Conferences:
1999 – Washington, DC/March 21-24

Reinforced Concrete Research Council (1948)
Texas A&M Univ.,
Dept. of Civil Engineering
College Station, TX 77843-3136
Tel: (409)845-3750   *Fax:* (409)845-6554
Members: 21 individuals
Annual Budget: $10-25,000
Secretary: Joseph Bracci

Historical Note
Affiliated with American Concrete Institute. Has no paid staff.

Publications:
RCRC Bulletins. irreg.

Meetings/Conferences:
1999 – Chicago, IL/March 14-19
1999 – Baltimore, MD/Oct. 31-Nov. 6
2000 – San Diego, CA/March 26-31
2000 – Toronto, ON, Canada/Oct. 15-20

Reinsurance Ass'n of America (1968)
1301 Pennsylvania Ave., N.W., Suite 900
Washington, DC 20004
Tel: (202)638-3690   *Fax:* (202)633-0936
E-Mail: nutter@reinsurance.org
Web Site: http://www.reinsurance.org
Members: 28 companies
Staff: 19
President: Franklin W. Nutter
V. President, Director Legislative Affairs: Bradley Kading, CPCU
Director, Federal Affairs Representative: Mary B. Zetwick
V. President, State Relations: Marsha A. Cohen
V. President and General Counsel: Debra J. Hall

Historical Note
Incorporated in the District of Columbia as the Nat'l Ass'n of Property and Casualty Reinsurers. Became the Reinsurance Ass'n of America in 1970.

Publications:
Loss Development Study.
Quarterly Report. q.
Reinsurance Underwriting Review. a.

Meetings/Conferences:
Annual Meetings: April
1999 – St. Helena, CA(Meadowood)/April 28-30

Reliability Soc.
Historical Note
A technical society of the Institute of Electrical and Electronics Engineers (IEEE). Membership in the Society, open only to IEEE members, includes a subscription to a technical periodical in the field published by IEEE. All administrative support is provided by IEEE.

Religion Newswriters Ass'n of U.S. and Canada (1949)
88 W. Plum St.
Westerville, OH 43081-2019
Tel: (614)891-9001   *Fax:* (614)891-9001
E-Mail: rnastuff@aol.com
Web Site: http://rna.org
Members: 250 individuals
Annual Budget: $25-50,000
Exec. Director: Debra Mason

Historical Note
A professional association of journalists covering religion for the secular press. Membership: $250/year (individual); $350/year (organization).

Publications:
Conference Program. a. adv.
RNA Extra. bi-m. adv.

Meetings/Conferences:
Annual Meetings: Spring or Summer
1999 – Orlando, FL/July 16-18

Religious Communication Ass'n (1973)
Weber State University
1605 University Circle
Ogden, UT 84408
Tel: (801)626-7455
E-Mail: bjohns@weber.edu
Members: 210 individuals, 2 institutions
Staff: 1
Annual Budget: under $10,000

Historical Note
Formerly (1998) Religious Speech Communication Ass'n, RCA is an academic society of individuals interested in the study of all aspects of public religious communication, RSCA members include teachers, students, clergy, broadcasters and other scholars and professionals. Until 1973 was the Religious Speech Division of the Speech Communication Ass'n. Membership: $20/year (individual); $50/year (institution).

Publications:
Homiletic. semi-a. adv.
Journal of Communication and Religion. semi-a. adv.
RCA Newsletter. 3/yr.

Meetings/Conferences:
Annual Meetings: With the Speech Communication Ass'n
1999 – Chicago, IL

Religious Conference Management Ass'n (1972)
One RCA Dome, Suite 120
Indianapolis, IN 46225
Tel: (317)632-1888   *Fax:* (317)632-7909
Members: 2,950 individuals
Staff: 5
Annual Budget: $250-500,000
Exec. Director and C.E.O.: DeWayne S. Woodring, D.D.
Director of Administration: Barbara Main
Director of Finance: Donna Woodring
Director of Advancement: Cindy Wheeler

Historical Note
Non-profit international organization of men and women who have responsibility for planning and/or managing meetings, seminars, conferences, conventions, assemblies, or other gatherings for religious organizations. Formerly (1982) the Religious Convention Managers Ass'n. Membership: $50/year (regular); $100/year (associate).

Publications:
RCMA Highlights. d. adv.
Religious Conference Manager. bi-m. adv.
Who's Who in Religious Conference Management. a. adv.

Meetings/Conferences:
Annual Meetings: January/1,160
1999 – Columbus, OH(Hyatt)/Feb. 2-5/1300
2000 – Dallas, TX(Adams Mark)/Feb. 1-4/1350

Religious Education Ass'n (1903)
Historical Note
Address unknown in 1998.

Religious Public Relations Council (1929)
475 Riverside Drive, Room 1948A
New York, NY 10115
Tel: (212)870-2985   *Fax:* (212)870-3578
Web Site: http://www.religioncommunicators.org
Members: 500 individuals
Staff: 1
Annual Budget: $50-100,000
President: Thomas May

Historical Note
RPRC membership is an interfaith association of individuals working in public relations or communications for any religious communion, organization or related agency. Formerly the Religious Publicity Council. Membership: $85/year.

Publications:
Membership Directory. a.
Public Relations Handbook for Religious Communicators.
RPRC Counselor. q.

Meetings/Conferences:
Annual Meetings: Spring
1999 – Arlington, VA/March 18-20
2000 – Chicago, IL/March 29-April 1

Religious Research Ass'n (1959)
Catholic University of America
Marist Hall, Room 108
Washington, DC 20064
Tel: (202)319-5447
Members: 550 individuals
Staff: 1
Annual Budget: $25-50,000
Business Manager: Lorraine D'Antonio

Historical Note
RRA is a professional society of individuals engaged in religious behavior research including social scientists, church researchers and planners, theologians, teachers, administrators, members of the clergy, editors and religious educators. Membership: $24/year (individual); $50/year (organization); $12/year (student).

Publications:
Review of Religious Research. q.

Meetings/Conferences:
Annual Meetings: Fall, in conjunction with Soc. for the Scientific Study of Religion

Religious Speech Communication Ass'n
Historical Note
Became (1998) Religious Communication Ass'n.

Remanufacturing Industries Council Internat'l (1995)
4401 Fair Lakes Court, Suite 210
Fairfax, VA 22033-3848
Tel: (703)968-2772   *Fax:* (703)968-2878
Members: 300 individuals, 11 trade associations
Staff: 2
Annual Budget: $10-25,000
Chairman: William C. Gager

Historical Note
RICI is a coalition of associations in the remanufacturing industry; members include the Electrical Apparatus Service Ass'n, Automotive Parts Rebuilders Ass'n, Internat'l Compressor Remanufacturers Ass'n, Office Furniture Dealers Alliance of the Business Products Industry Ass'n, United Laser Toner Recyclers Ass'n, Production Engine Remanufacturers Ass'n, Valve Remanufacturers Council, Automotive Engine Rebuilders Ass'n, and Professional Cartridge Remanufacturers Institute. Membership: $50/year (individual); $500/year (organization).

Publications:
RICI Newsletter. q.

Remedial Contractors Institute
Historical Note
A division of the Hazardous Waste Management Ass'n.

Remodeling Contractors Ass'n of America
Historical Note
Address unknown in 1996.

Renaissance Soc. of America (1954)
24 West 12th St.
New York, NY 10011
Tel: (212)998-3797   *Fax:* (212)995-4205
Web Site: http://www.r-s-a.org
Members: 3,400 individuals
Staff: 1
Annual Budget: $100-250,000
Exec. Director: John Monfasani
Membership: Laura Schwartz

Historical Note
A professional society of scholars of the Renaissance. Member of the American Council of Learned Societies. Affiliate of American Historical Association. Membership: $50/year (individual), $75/year (library).

Publications:
Renaissance News & Notes. semi-annual.
Renaissance Quarterly. q. adv.

Meetings/Conferences:
Annual Meetings: March
1999 – Los Angeles, CA/March 25-28
2000 – Florence, Italy

Renal Physicians Ass'n (1973)
4701 Randolph Rd.
Suite 102
Rockville, MD 20852-1808
Toll Free: (800)772 - 7525
Members: 1,825 individuals
Staff: 2
Annual Budget: $250-500,000

Exec. Director: Dale Singer

Historical Note
Members are physicians specializing in treatment of renal disease. Membership: $275/year.

Publications:
RPA News. 6/year.

Meetings/Conferences:
Annual Meetings: February
1999 – Washington, DC/March 6-9

Renewable Fuels Ass'n *(1981)*
One Massachusetts Ave., N.W., Suite 820
Washington, DC   20001-1431
Tel: (202)289-3835   *Fax:* (202)289-7519
E-Mail: etohfa@erols.com
Web Site: http://www.ethanolrfa.org
Members: 75 companies
Staff: 5
Annual Budget: $1-2,000,000
President: Eric Vaughn
Director of Communications: Mary Wertschnig
Legislative Director: Robert Dinneen
Office Manager: Jan Evered

Historical Note
Members are companies and individuals involved in the production and use of ethanol. Membership Fee: Based on capacity for producers.

Publications:
Changes in Gasoline.
Ethanol Report.

Meetings/Conferences:
Annual Meetings: No regularly scheduled meetings.

Renewable Natural Resources Foundation *(1972)*
5430 Grosvenor Lane
Bethesda, MD   20814-2193
Tel: (301)493-9101   *Fax:* (301)493-6148
E-Mail: rnrf@aol.com
Web Site: http://members.aol.com/rnrf
Members: 16 societies
Staff: 5
Annual Budget: $1-2,000,000
Exec. Director: Robert D. Day, J.D.
Director, Programs: Kristin L. Krapf, M.S.
Director, Administration and Finance: Chandru Krishna, M.B.A.

Historical Note
A consortium of professional and scientific societies whose members are concerned with the advancement of research, education, scientific practice and policy formulation for the conservation, replenishment and use of the earth's renewable natural resources. The member societies are: American Congress on Surveying and Mapping; American Fisheries Soc.; American Geophysical Union; American Meteorological Soc.; American Soc. for Photogrammetry and Remote Sensing; American Soc. of Agronomy; American Soc. of Civil Engineers; American Soc. of Landscape Architects; American Water Resources Ass'n; Ass'n of American Geographers; Humane Soc. of the U.S.; Soc. for Range Management; Soc. of Wood Science and Technology; Soil and Water Conservation Soc.; The Nature Conservancy; and The Wildlife Soc. Incorporated in the District of Columbia in January, 1972. Membership: $50/year (individual), $300/year (organization).

Publications:
Renewable Resources Journal. q.

Meetings/Conferences:
Annual Meetings: Autumn

Research and Development Associates for Military Food and Packaging Systems *(1946)*
16607 Blanco Rd., Suite 1506
San Antonio, TX   78232-1940
Tel: (210)493-8024   *Fax:* (210)493-8036
E-Mail: rdajff@flash.net
Members: 1,100 individuals
Staff: 3
Annual Budget: $250-500,000
Exec. Director: James F. Fagan

Historical Note
Founded as a forum for the interchange of technical data on food products, feeding systems, food and feeding equipment and food packaging between industry and professors of Food Science and Technology on one hand and the U.S. Armed Forces and Government on the other. Membership: $125/year (individual), $400/year (corporate).

Publications:
Activities Report. a.
Newsletter – "The Link". q.

Meetings/Conferences:
Semi-Annual Meetings: April and October/350-400
1999 – Galveston Island, TX(Galvex and Tremont Hotel)/April 19-21
1999 – Pittsburgh, PA(Westin)/Oct. 26-28
2000 – Tucson, AZ(National Resort)/June 5-7
2001 – Incline Village, NV(Hyatt Regency)/April 24-26

Research Ass'n of Minority Professors *(1976)*
Prairie View A&M University
Drawer 67
Prairie View, TX   77446
Tel: (409)857-3425   *Fax:* (409)857-2019
Toll Free: (800)434 - 5650
E-Mail: hfrank@ips.pvamu.edu
Annual Budget: $10-25,000
Exec. Director: Dr. Frank T. Hawkins

Historical Note
Membership: $45/year (individual); $150/year (organization/company).

Publications:
RAMP Journal. bi-a. adv.

Meetings/Conferences:
1999 – Houston, TX

Research Council on Structural Connections *(1946)*
Sargent & Lundy
55 E. Monroe St.
Chicago, IL   60603
Tel: (312)269-2424
Members: 45 individuals
Annual Budget: $10-25,000
Chairman: James M. Doyle

Historical Note
Researches the effects of stress on bolted and riveted joints for its member companies and institutions. Formerly (until 1980) known as the Research Council on Riveted and Bolted Structural Joints.

Meetings/Conferences:
1999 – Denver, CO/June 17-18/40

Research Soc. on Alcoholism *(1976)*
4314 Medical Pkwy., Suite 12
Austin, TX   78756
Tel: (512)454-0022   *Fax:* (512)454-0022
E-Mail: debbyrsa@bga.com
Web Site: http://www.rsa.am
Members: 1 individuals
Staff: 2
Annual Budget: $50-100,000
Director: Debra Sharp

Historical Note
RSA provides a forum for communication among scientists conducting research that may contribute to the prevention and treatment of alcoholism. RSA members are qualified scientists interested in alcohol research, including all biomedical sciences, clinical fields and psychosocial sciences. Membership: $125/year (individual).

Publications:
Alcoholism: Clinical & Experimental Research. 9 times/year.

Meetings/Conferences:
Annual Meetings: Montreal, Canada(Hilton)/June 23-28/1000
1999 – Santa Barbara, CA(Doubletree)/June 26-July 1/1000
2000 – Denver, CO(Marriott)/June 24-29/1000

Reserve Officers Ass'n of the U.S. *(1922)*
One Constitution Ave., N.E.
Washington, DC   20002-5655
Tel: (202)646-7727   *Fax:* (202)646-7762
Toll Free: (800)809 - 9448
Web Site: http://www.roa.org
Members: 90,000 individuals
Staff: 38
Annual Budget: $2-5,000,000
Exec. Director: Maj.Gen. Roger W. Sandler, USA(Ret.)
Comptroller: Christina Antonelos
Director, Membership Affairs: J.A. Barton Campbell

Historical Note
Membership is open to any regular, reserve or former officer of the Army, Navy, Air Force, Marine Corps, Coast Guard, Public Health Service, or Nat'l Oceanic and Atmospheric Administration. Membership: $40/year.

Publications:
ROA National Security Report. m.
The Officer. m. adv.

Meetings/Conferences:
Annual Meetings: Late June/1,200
1999 – Anaheim, CA(Marriott)/June 23-26

Residential Sales Council *(1977)*
430 N. Michigan Ave., Third Floor
Chicago, IL   60611-4092
Tel: (312)321-4400   *Fax:* (312)329-8882
Toll Free: (800)462 - 8841
Web Site: http://www.rscouncil.com
Members: 42,000 individuals
Staff: 28
Annual Budget: $5-10,000,000
Exec. V. President: Nina Cottrell
Dir., Communications: Mimi Levine
Meetings Manager: Octavia Toso
Director, Education: Joel Mendes
V.P., Operations: Carol Raabe
Director, Member Services: Mary Beth Ciukaj
Director of MIS: Keith Tristano

Historical Note
A council of the Realtors Nat'l Marketing Institute. Awards the Certified Residential Spectialist (CRS) designation. Membership: $70/year.

Publications:
CRS/CRB Directory of Members. a.
Insider. q.
Real Estate Business. q. adv.

Meetings/Conferences:
Annual Meetings: in conjunction with the Nat'l Ass'n of Realtors.
1999 – Orlando, FL(Stouffer)/Nov. 10-13

Residential Space Planners Internat'l *(1985)*
20 Ardmore Drive
Minneapolis, MN   55422
Toll Free: (800)548 - 0945
Exec. Director: Mary Knott

Historical Note
RSPI members are architects and interior designers specializing in planning residential interiors. Membership: $80/year.

Resilient Floor Covering Institute *(1929)*
966 Hungerford Drive, Suite 12-B
Rockville, MD   20850-1714
Tel: (301)340-8580   *Fax:* (301)340-7283
E-Mail: info@rfci.com

Web Site: http://www.rfci.com
Members: 19 companies
Staff: 3
Annual Budget: $500-1,000,000
Managing Director: Ed Stana

Historical Note
Formerly (1973) Asphalt and Vinyl Asbestos Tile Institute and (Jan. 1, 1976) the Resilient Tile Institute.

Meetings/Conferences:
Semi-annual Meetings: May/65 and October/65
1999 – Orlando, FL(Villas of Grand Cypress)/May 12-16
1999 – Pebble Beach, CA(Lodge)/Oct. 20-23

Resistance Welder Manufacturers Ass'n *(1935)*
1900 Arch St.
Philadelphia, PA   19103-1498
Tel: (215)564-3484   *Fax:* (215)963-9785
E-Mail: assnhqt@netaxs.com
Web Site: http://www.rwma.org
Members: 45 companies
Annual Budget: $100-250,000
Exec. Director: Charlene Mayfield
Director, Administrative: Kim Soldavin

Historical Note
Incorporated in Pennsylvania. RWMA strives to create widespread awareness and use of the various resistance welding processes and equipment; improve relations between individual manufacturers; foster higher ethical standards throughout the industry; develop industry standards to assist users of resistance welding equipment. Membership: sliding scale based on previous year's sales.

Publications:
Membership Directory.
Newsletter. q.

Meetings/Conferences:
1999 – Marco Island, FL(Hilton)/Oct. 20-23

RESNA

Historical Note
Became Rehabilitation Engineering and Assistive Technology Soc. of North America in 1995.

Resort and Commercial Recreation Ass'n *(1981)*
P.O. Box 1998
Tarpon Springs, FL   34688-1998
Tel: (813)939-8811
Members: 1,500 individuals, 300 companies
Staff: 1
Annual Budget: $50-100,000
Exec. Director: Frank Oliveto

Historical Note
RCRA seeks to provide appropriate services to professionals, educators and students in the commercial recreation field. RCRA also works to increase the profitability and efficiency of commercial enterprises. Membership: $90/year (individual), $195/year (company).

Publications:
Member Directory. a. adv.
RCRA Bulletin. 4/yr. adv.
Resort & Commercial Recreation Magazine. bi-m. adv.

Meetings/Conferences:
Annual Meetings: November
1999 – Orlando, FL

Respiratory Nursing Soc. *(1990)*
7794 Grow Drive
Pensacola, FL   32514
Tel: (850)474-8869   *Fax:* (850)484-8762
Toll Free: (888)330 - 4767
Members: 400 individuals
Staff: 6
Annual Budget: $100-250,000
Exec. Director: Belinda Puetz, Ph.D., RN
Member Services Representatives: Henrietta Elston
Member Services Representative: Anita Cormier

Historical Note
RNS is the professional association for nurses who care for clients with pulmonary dysfunction and who are interested in the promotion of pulmonary health. The Society was created to promote coordinated, comprehensive, high-level nursing care for these clients by fostering respiratory nurses' personal and professional development; providing educational opportunities through which nurses can enhance their knowledge and skills; and conducting, participating in, and disseminating research. Also serves as a formal network for communications in the field. Membership open to all registered professional nurses interested in respiratory nursing from a research, practice, and/or educational perspective. Associate membership available to persons other than registered nurses who are concerned with or engaged in the practice of respiratory care. Membership: $75/year (individual); $1,500/year (corporate).

Meetings/Conferences:
1999 – Chicago, IL/March 4-6

Retail Advertising and Marketing Ass'n Internat'l *(1952)*
333 N. Michigan Ave., Suite 3000
Chicago, IL   60601-4105
Tel: (312)251-7262   *Fax:* (312)251-7269
Web Site: http://www.ramarec.org
Members: 2,000 individuals
Staff: 6
Annual Budget: $500-1,000,000
President/C.E.O.: Douglas E. Raymond
Director of Finance: Amy Ahlgrim

Historical Note
Formerly (1991) the Retail Advertising Conference. International association of marketing and advertising executives. Membership: $95/year (company & individual); $665 (corporation).

Publications:
Excellence in Advertising/RAMA Membership Directory. a.

Meetings/Conferences:
Annual Meetings: Late Winter in Chicago, IL/1,100
1999 – Chicago, IL(Hyatt)/Feb 10-13

Retail Confectioners Internat'l *(1918)*
1807 Glenview Road, Suite 204
Glenview, IL 60025
Tel: (847)724-6120　　　　　*Fax:* (847)724-2719
Toll Free: (800)545 - 5381
Web Site: http://www.retconint.org
Members: 600 companies
Staff: 3
Annual Budget: $500-1,000,000
Exec. Director: Evans N. Billington

Historical Note
Founded in 1918 as Associated Retail Confectioners of the United States. In 1960 name was changed to Associated Retail Confectioners of North America to recognize members in Canada and Mexico. In 1969 changed to Retail Confectioners International to recognize membership in Europe, Australia and Japan.

Publications:
Kettletalk. m. adv.
RCI Convention Buyers Guide. a. adv.

Meetings/Conferences:
Annual Meetings: Summer/1,500
1999 – Columbus, GA/June 11-15

Retail Packaging Manufacturers Ass'n *(1989)*
P.O. Box 17656
Covington, KY 41017
Tel: (606)341-9623　　　　　*Fax:* (606)341-9624
Web Site: http://www.rpma.org
Members: 150 individuals, 100 associates
Staff: 2
Annual Budget: $500-1,000,000
Exec. Director: Vicki Miller

Historical Note
RPMA provides comprehensive educational and networking services and organizes an annual trade show to its members. Members of the association include manufactures, manufacturer representatives and distributors of retail packaging.

Meetings/Conferences:
Annual Meetings: Annual Meetings
1999 – Orlando, FL(Disney Contemporary)/1500
2000 – Las Vegas, NV(LV Hilton)
2001 – Miami Beach, FL(FountainBleau Hilton)

Retail Print Music Dealers Ass'n
4020 McEwen, Suite 105
Dallas, TX 75244-5019
Tel: (972)233-9107　　　　　*Fax:* (972)490-4219
E-Mail: office@printmusic.org
Web Site: http://www.printmusic.org
Members: 250 businesses
Staff: 5
Annual Budget: $25-50,000
Exec. Director: Madeleine Crouch

Historical Note
Membership: $150/year.

Publications:
RSMDA news. 6/year. adv.

Meetings/Conferences:
Annual Meetings: Spring
1999 – Las Vegas, NV
1999 – San Diego, CA
2000 – Atlanta, GA

Retail Stores Forum

Historical Note
A division of the Business Products Industry Ass'n.

Retail Tobacco Dealers of America *(1932)*
107 E. Baltimore St.
Baltimore, MD 21202
Tel: (410)547-6996　　　　　*Fax:* (410)727-7533
E-Mail: rtda@msn.com
Web Site: http://www.rtda.org
Members: 3,000 tobacco retailers
Annual Budget: $250-500,000
Exec. Director: Ira B. Fader, Jr.

Historical Note
Membership: $100/year (individual), $500/year (organization)

Publications:
Newsletter. m.
Smokeshop Magazine. bi-m. adv.
Tobacco Retailers' Almanac. a. adv.
Tobacconist Magazine. bi-m. adv.

Meetings/Conferences:
1999 – Las Vegas, NV(Hilton)/July 15-17/6000
2000 – San Antonio, TX(Marriott)/Aug. 2-5

Retail, Wholesale and Department Store Union *(1937)*
30 East 29th St., 4th Floor
New York, NY 10016
Tel: (212)684-5300　　　　　*Fax:* (212)779-2809
Members: 90,000 individuals
Staff: 40
Annual Budget: $5-10,000,000
President: Lenore Miller

Historical Note
Established in 1937 by dissidents from the Retail Clerks Internat'l Union and chartered by the Congress of Industrial Organizations as the United Retail Employees of America. Became the United Retail, Wholesale and Department Store Employees of America in 1940, a title that was later shortened to its present form. Absorbed the Distributive, Processing and Office Workers of America as well as

the Playthings, Jewelry and Novelty Workers Internat'l Union in 1954 and the Cigar Makers Internat'l Union of America in 1974.

Publications:
RWDSU Record. m.

Meetings/Conferences:
Quadrennial Meetings: Spring (1998)

Retailer's Bakery Ass'n *(1918)*
14239 Park Center Drive
Laurel, MD 20707
Tel: (301)725-2149　　　　　*Fax:* (301)725-2187
Members: 3,500 companies
Staff: 18
Annual Budget: $2-5,000,000
Exec. V. President: Peter M. Houstle
Director, Communications and Marketing: Diana Maness
Director, Conventions: Stew Taylor
General Counsel: Gerard P. Panaro
Director, Membership: Peggy M. Hoffman

Historical Note
Formerly (1994) Retail Bakers of America and (1996) Retailer's Bakery-Deli Ass'n. RBA produces workshops, conventions and training programs for the retail bakery-deli industry. RBA also provides political representation and promotes the bakery-deli profession. Membership: $85/year (single unit); $300/year (multi-unit); $150/year (suppliers).

Publications:
Insight. m.
Washington Bulletins. irreg.

Meetings/Conferences:
Annual Meetings: RBA Convention-Exhibition
1999 – Minneapolis, MN/April 24-26

Retired Officers Ass'n, The *(1929)*
201 N. Washington St.
Alexandria, VA 22314-2539
Tel: (703)549-2311　　　　　*Fax:* (703)838-8173
E-Mail: member@troa.org
Web Site: http://www.troa.org
Members: 400,000 individuals, 425 chapters
Staff: 87
Annual Budget: $10-25,000,000
President: Lt.Gen. Michael A. Nelson, USAF(Ret.)
Director, Public Relations: Marvin J. Harris
Director, Government Relations: Col. Paul Arcari, (Ret.)
Comptroller: Col. Glenn R. Zauber, (Ret.)
Secretary and General Counsel: Capt. Peter C. Wylie, (Ret.)
Director, contract Services and Marketing: Lt.Col. John Miller, (Ret.)
Director, Print & Electronic Publications: Warren Lacy

Historical Note
Composed of veteran and active members of the Army, Navy, Air Force, Marine Corps, Coast Guard, National Oceanic and Atmospheric Administration, and the Public Health Service, and widow(er)s of the above as auxilary members. Represents over two-thirds of the total retired officer community. Established in Los Angeles February 23, 1929 with 63 members to counsel and render assistance to its members in connection with their retired status. Moved to Washington in 1944 and expanded its purpose to include representing its members' rights and interests when service matters are considered by the Government. Now takes positions on a variety of personnel and healthcare issues. Has an annual budget of approximately $12 million. Membership: $20/year.

Publications:
The Retired Officer Magazine. m. adv.

Meetings/Conferences:
Annual Meetings: Fall
1999 – Jacksonville, FL/Oct. 21-23

Retirement Industry Trust Ass'n
4424 Montgomery Ave., Suite 102
Bethesda, MD 20814
Tel: (301)652-5066　　　　　*Fax:* (301)913-9146
Annual Budget: $10-25,000
Exec. Director: David S. O'Bryon, CAE

Rhetoric Soc. of America *(1968)*
Dept. of English, Univ. of Oklahoma
760 Van Fleet Oval
Norman, OK 73019
Tel: (405)325-4661　　　　　*Fax:* (405)325-7509
Members: 550 individuals
Staff: 1
Annual Budget: under $10,000
President: Kathleen Welch, Ph.D.

Historical Note
Teachers and students interested in promoting the development and dissemination of research and theory about the production and analysis of rhetorical discourse.

Publications:
Rhetoric Society Quarterly. q.

Meetings/Conferences:
Biennial Meetings: May (1996)

Rho Pi Phi *(1919)*

Historical Note
Declined to provide updated information for this edition.

Rice Millers' Ass'n *(1899)*
4301 N. Fairfax Dr., Suite 305
Arlington, VA 22203-1616
Tel: (703)351-8161　　　　　*Fax:* (703)351-8162
Members: 29 mills and cooperatives

Historical Note
The national trade association of the United States' rice milling industry, RMA is among the nation's oldest agricultural organizations. Membership includes both independent rice milling companies and farmer-owned cooperative rice milling firms which,

together, mill virtually all rice produced in the United States. RMA is a private, non-profit, non-stock organization and does not engage in rice trading. RMA is a charter member of the USA Rice Federation, which provides administrative support.

Meetings/Conferences:
Annual Meetings: June

Risk and Insurance Management Soc. *(1950)*
655 Third Ave.
New York, NY 10017
Tel: (212)286-9292　　　　　*Fax:* (212)986-9716
Web Site: http://www.RIMS.org
Members: 8,100 individuals, 4,400 organizations
Staff: 50
Annual Budget: $5-10,000,000
Exec. Director: Linda Lammel
Director, Communications: Stephanie Orango
Director of Conferences: Barbara Parker
Director, Finance and Administration: George M. Sauter, CAE
General Counsel: Paul S. Brown
Director of Professional Development: Amy Geffen, Ph. D.
Director, Membership and Chapter Services: Mary Roth

Historical Note
Founded as the Nat'l Insurance Buyers Ass'n, it became the American Soc. of Insurance Management in 1954 and assumed its present name in 1975. Membership consists of corporations, municipalities, universities and other entities who plan and purchase insurance or insurance services. Has an annual budget of approximately $8.4 million. Membership: $300/year (company).

Publications:
Rimscope. bi-w.
Risk Management. m. adv.

Meetings/Conferences:
Annual Meetings: Spring
1999 – Dallas, TX/Apr. 11-16

River Federation *(1980)*

Historical Note
Merged with the American River Management Soc. to form The River Management Soc. in 1996.

River Management Soc. *(1988)*
P.O. Box 9048
Missoula, MT 59807-9047
Tel: (406)549-0514　　　　　*Fax:* (406)542-6208
E-Mail: rms@igc.apc.org
Web Site: http://www.river-management.org
Members: 420 individuals, 40 companies and organizations
Staff: 1
Annual Budget: under $10,000
Program Director: Caroline Tan

Historical Note
The product of a merger of the American River Management Soc. and the River Federation in 1996. RMS serves as a forum for information on the appropriate use and management of river resources. Members are government agency employees, companies and organizations, and other private- and public-sector individuals concerned with holistic and ecosystem approaches to water quality, riparian health, and watershed management. Membership: $30/year (professional); $15/year (student); $50/year (organization); $20/year (associate).

Publications:
RMS News. q. adv.

Meetings/Conferences:
Biennial Meetings: Summer/300

RNA Soc. *(1993)*
9650 Rockville Pike
Bethesda, MD 20814-3998
Tel: (301)530-7120　　　　　*Fax:* (301)530-7049
E-Mail: rna@faseb.org
Web Site: http://www.pitt.edu/~na1/
Exec. Officer: Chris Greer

Historical Note
RNAS members are scientists engaged in research on ribonucleic acid. Membership: $137/year (individual); $68(student).

Publications:
Proceedings. a.
RNA Directory. a.
RNA Journal. bi-m.

Meetings/Conferences:

Roadmasters and Maintenance of Way Ass'n of America

Historical Note
Became American Railway Engineering and Maintenance of Way Ass'n in 1997.

Robert Morris Associates, the Ass'n of Lending and Credit Risk Professionals *(1914)*
One Liberty Place, Suite 2300
1650 Market St.
Philadelphia, PA 19103-7598
Tel: (215)446-4000　　　　　*Fax:* (215)446-4101
Web Site: http://www.mahq.org
Members: 17,500 individuals, 3,300 financial institutions
Staff: 41
Annual Budget: $10-25,000,000
President and C.E.O.: Allen W. Sanborn
Director, Regulatory Relations and Communications: Pam Martin
Director, Marketing: Paul Kushner
Administrative V. President: Ralph Hibbs
Meetings Manager: Kathy Phillips
Director, Professional Development: Ken Shipley
Dir., Lending/Finance Div.: James Nelson
Director, Chapters/Membership: Ned Miller
Director, Policy Division: Charles Huntington

Historical Note
Formerly (1994) Robert Morris Associates, the Nat'l Ass'n of Bank Loan and Credit Officers. Seeks to improve the principles and practice of commercial lending and credit functions, loan administration and asset management in commercial banks and other financial industires. Membership dues vary by asset size of institution. Has an annual budget of approximately $16 million.

Publications:
Annual Statement Studies. a.
Lending & Risk Management News.
The Journal of Lending and Credit Risk Management. m.

Meetings/Conferences:
Annual Meetings: Fall/800

Robotic Industries Ass'n

Historical Note
Became (1997) Automation Technologies Council; RIA now exists as a specialty division of ATC.

Robotics and Automation Soc. *(1989)*

Historical Note
A technical society of the Institute of Electrical and Electronics Engineers (IEEE). Membership in the Council is open only to IEEE members. All administrative support is provided by IEEE.

Robotics Internat'l of SME *(1980)*
P.O. Box 930
One SME Drive
Dearborn, MI   48121-0930
Tel: (313)271-1500   *Fax:* (313)271-2861
Web Site: http://www.sme.org/ri.html
Members: 3,500 individuals
Staff: 3
Association Manager: Sandra Marshall

Historical Note
A member association of the Soc. of Manufacturing Engineers. Members are scientists, engineers and managers involved in all phases of robotics research, design, application, installation, human factors, and education and training related to robots. Certification as CMfgE (Certified Manufacturing Engineer) or CMfgT (Certified Manufacturing Technologist) is offered through the Manufacturing Engineering Certification Institute of SME. Membership: $60/year (initiation fee $15).

Publications:
Bibliography of Robotic Technical Resources.
Directory of Robotic Research & Development Laboratories.
Robotics Research Transactions.
Robotics Today. q.
ROBOTS Annual Conference Proceedings. a.

Meetings/Conferences:
Annual Meetings: Spring

Rock Drill Bureau

Historical Note
A bureau of the Construction Industry Manufacturers Ass'n.

Rolf Institute *(1971)*
205 Canyon Blvd.
Boulder, CO   80302
Tel: (303)449-5903   *Fax:* (303)449-5978
Toll Free: (800)530 - 8875
E-Mail: roifinst@aol.com
Members: 800 individuals
Staff: 7
Annual Budget: $1-2,000,000
Exec. Director: Gary Wolfe
Director, Education: Liesel Orend
Membership Services Director: Karna Handy

Historical Note
Established and incorporated California, members are practioners of the technique of connective tissue manipulation developed by Dr. Ida P. Rolf. Street address is 205 Canyon Blvd., Boulder, CO. Membership: $450/year.

Publications:
Membership Directory. a.
Rolf Lines. a. adv.

Meetings/Conferences:
Annual Meetings: August

Roller Skating Ass'n Internat'l *(1937)*
6905 Corporate Drive
Indianapolis, IN   46278
Tel: (317)347-2626   *Fax:* (317)347-2636
Members: 2,500 individuals, 1,100 skating centers &
        manufacturers
Staff: 8
Annual Budget: $1-2,000,000
Exec. Director: Katherine M. McDonell, CAE
Director of Communications: Melissa Gibson
Director, Marketing: Randall Hoggard
Convention Planner: Anne Boley
Membership Coordinator: Dale Johnson
Database Manager: Roberta Waldman

Historical Note
Formerly (1991) Roller Skating Rink Operators Ass'n of America. RSA was originated by and exists for private businessmen and women engaged in the gainful enterprise of roller skating. Members either own or lease a roller skating facility. The RSA itself does not own or franchise any of the facilities enrolled in the ass'n. Affiliated organizations: Speed Coaches Ass'ns, Soc. of Roller Skating Teachers of America, Roller Hockey Coaches Ass'n, and the Roller Skating Manufacturers. Membership: $325/year (facility), $350/year (company).

Publications:
Roller Skating Business Magazine. bi-m. adv.
RSA Today Coaches' Edition Newsletter. m.
RSA Today Newsletter. bi-w.
RSM News Newsletter. bi-m. adv.

Meetings/Conferences:
Annual Meetings: May
1999 – Dallas, TX/May 9-13

Romance Writers of America *(1980)*
3707 FM 1960 Rd. W., #555
Houston, TX   77068-3526
Tel: (713)440-6885   *Fax:* (713)440-7510
E-Mail: info@rwanational.com
Web Site: http://www.rwanational.com
Members: 8,100 individuals, 150 chapters
Staff: 7
Annual Budget: $1-2,000,000
Exec. Director: Allison Kelley
Manager, Communication: Charis McEachern

Historical Note
Promotes excellence in the genre of romance fiction and provides networking opportunities to writers, published and unpublished, who are seriously pursuing a career in the romance fiction industry. Conducts workshops, sponsors national and regional conferences and awards accomplishments. Membership: $65/year.

Publications:
Romance Writers Report. m. adv.

Meetings/Conferences:
Annual Meetings: Summer/1,700
1999 – Chicago, IL(Sheraton)/July 28-Aug. 1
2000 – Washington, DC(Sheraton)/July 26-30
2001 – New Orleans, LA(Sheraton)
2002 – Denver, CO(Adams Mark)

Romanian Studies Ass'n of America *(1973)*
Dept. of English
Arizona State University
Tempe, AZ   85287-0302
Tel: (602)965-4658
Members: 55 individuals
Staff: 1
Annual Budget: under $10,000
Secretary: Prof. Ileana Orlich

Historical Note
RSAA's purpose is to foster and to advance Romanian studies on the American continent, particularly in the U.S.A. and Canada. An "allied" organization of the Modern Language Ass'n. Has no paid staff. Membership: $12/yr.

Publications:
RSAA Newsletter. semi-a.
Yearbook of Romanian Studies. a.

Meetings/Conferences:
Annual Meetings: December, with the Modern Language Ass'n

Romanian-American Chamber of Commerce
5530 Wisconsin Ave., Suite 1110
Chevy Chase, MD   20815-7003
Tel: (301)656-9022   *Fax:* (301)656-9008
Members: 150 businesses
Annual Budget: $50-100,000
Exec. Director: Jay McCrensky

Historical Note
Bilateral trade association dealing with Romania. Membership: $250/year (individual); $500/year (organization/company).

Publications:
RACC Newsletter. q. adv.

Romanian-United States Economic Council *(1974)*

Historical Note
Became (1997) Amerifcan Business Alliance for the Transition Economies of Eurasia.

Roof Coatings Manufacturers Ass'n *(1982)*
4041 Powder Mill Road, Suite 404
Calverton, MD   20705
Tel: (301)348-2003   *Fax:* (301)348-2020
E-Mail: sms1west@aol.com
Members: 64 companies
Staff: 8
Annual Budget: $100-250,000
Exec. V. President: Russell K. Snyder

Historical Note
RCMA represents the interests of manufacturers of cold applied roof coatings, cements, and waterproofing agents. Membership: annual dues vary by number of manufacturing plants and suppliers.

Publications:
Directory. a.
Government Issues Newsletter. q.
RCMA Report. q.
Technical Bulletins. irreg.

Meetings/Conferences:
Annual Meetings: January

Roof Consultants Institute *(1983)*
7424 Chapel Hill Road
Raleigh, NC   27607-5041
Tel: (919)859-0742   *Fax:* (919)859-1328
Toll Free: (800)828 - 1902
Members: 1,300 individuals
Staff: 7
Annual Budget: $1-2,000,000
Exec. Director: Francis A. Acquaviva

Historical Note
RCI members are professional roof consultants (those who derive 50% of their income from roof consulting) and industry members (individuals involved in contracting, sales or manufacturing). RCI provides educational programs for members. Membership: $280/year (professional); $320/year (industry).

Publications:
Interface Newsletter. 11/year. adv.
Internat'l Directory of Roofing Professionals. a. adv.

Meetings/Conferences:
Annual Meetings: Spring/700
1999 – Charlotte, NC/March 12-17

Roses Incorporated *(1936)*
P.O. Box 99
Haslett, MI   48840
Tel: (517)339-9544   *Fax:* (517)339-3760
E-Mail: jkrone@aol.com
Web Site: http://www.roseinc.com
Members: 300 individuals
Staff: 4
Exec. V. President: James C. Krone

Historical Note
Members produce greenhouse roses in the United States and Canada.

Publications:
Bulletin. m.

Meetings/Conferences:
1999 – Netherlands

Rough Terrain Forklifts Council

Historical Note
A council of the Equipment Manufacturers Institute.

Roundalab *(1977)*
4825-B Valley View Ave.
Yorba Linda, CA   92886-3645
Tel: (714)572-0480   *Fax:* (714)572-0931
Toll Free: (800)346 - 7522
E-Mail: roundalab@southland.net
Web Site: http://www.southland.net/roundalab/
Members: 1,400 individuals
Staff: 1
Annual Budget: $100-250,000
Exec. Secretary: Patricia Rardin

Historical Note
A professional internat'l society of individuals who teach round dancing at any phase. Membership: $70/Renewal Teaching Unit (internat'l); $60 (U.S.); $65 (Canada).

Publications:
Convention Proceedings and Directory. a.
Cueing Guidelines. a.
Journal. q.
Roundalab Manual. a.
Six Phase Standards of Round Dancing. a.

Meetings/Conferences:
Annual Meetings: June/200-250
1999   Indianapolis, IN

Roundtable for Women in Foodservice *(1983)*
1372 La Colina Dr.
Tustin, CA   92780
Tel: (714)838-2749   *Fax:* (714)838-2750
Toll Free: (800)898 - 2849
Web Site: http://www.rwf.org
Members: 750 individuals
Staff: 1
Annual Budget: $50-100,000
Exec. Director: Deborah Hicks

Historical Note
Established and incorporated in New York, the Roundtable serves as a central source of education, information, and local and national networking for all women in the food, beverage, and hospitality industry. Membership: $150/year (individual, including chapter dues).

Publications:
Pacesetter Journal. a. adv.
RWF Directory. a. adv.
RWF News. q. adv.

Meetings/Conferences:
Annual Meetings: Fall
1999 – Chicago, IL/May 23-24

Rubber and Plastics Industry Conference of the United Steelworkers of America *(1935)*
570 White Pond Dr.
Akron, OH   44320-1156
Tel: (412)562-6970   *Fax:* (412)562-6963
Web Site: http://www.uswa.org
Members: 90,000 individuals
Annual Budget: $10-25,000,000
Exec. V. President: John Sellers

Historical Note
Organized in Akron, Ohio September 12, 1935 as the United Rubber Workers of America and chartered as an industrial union the following year by the Congress of Industrial Organization. Became United Rubber, Cork, Linoleum and Plastic Workers of America in 1945; Merged with United Steelworkers of America and assumed its current name in 1995. Has an annual budget of approximately $12.5 million.

Meetings/Conferences:
Triennial Conference: (1996)

Rubber Manufacturers Ass'n *(1900)*
1400 K St., N.W., Suite 900
Washington, DC   20005
Tel: (202)682-4800   *Fax:* (202)682-4854
Web Site: http://www.rma.org
Members: 135 companies
Staff: 22
Annual Budget: $2-5,000,000
President: Donald B. Shea
V. President, Communications and Marketing: Kristen Udowitz
V. President, Technical and Standards Dept.: Steven Butcher
Treasurer and C.F.O.: Lisa I. Murphy
V. President, General Products Group: Kevin D. Ott
Director, Environmental Affairs: Tracey J. Norberg
V. President, Market Information Services: Steven Tesliki

Historical Note
Founded in 1900 as the New England Rubber Club. Incorporated in 1915 as the Rubber Club of America and became the Rubber Ass'n of America in 1917. Name changed to Rubber Manufacturers Ass'n in 1919. Members are manufacturers of rubber products of all types.

Publications:
Executive Update. m.

Meetings/Conferences:
Annual Meetings: 3rd Thursday in November
1999 – San Diego, CA/March 6-8

Rubber Pavements Ass'n *(1985)*
1801 S. Jentilly Ln., Suite A-2
Tempe, AZ   85281
Tel: (602)517-9944   *Fax:* (602)517-9959
E-Mail: donnac@rubberpavement.org
Web Site: http://www.rubberpavement.org
Members: 25 companies
Staff: 2
Annual Budget: $100-250,000
Exec. Director: Donna J. Carlson

Historical Note
Formerly (1993) the Asphalt Rubber Producers Group. RPA members are companies involved in the manufacture or application of asphalt-rubber or in the rubber recycling business. Membership: $500/year (producers/users); $550/year (associate).

Publications:
Rebounder Newsletter. q. adv.
RPA News. bi-m.

Meetings/Conferences:
Annual Meetings: February
1999 – Tempe, AZ/Feb. 3-4

Rubber Tired Backhoe Loader and Attachments Council
Historical Note
A council of the Equipment Manufacturers Institute.

Rubber Trade Ass'n of North America *(1914)*
220 Maple Ave.
P.O. Box 196
Rockville Center, NY   11571
Tel: (516)536-7228   *Fax:* (516)536-3771
Secretary: Fred B. Finley

Historical Note
RTA members are importers of natural rubber and exporters of synthetic rubber. Membership concentrated in the New York City area.

Meetings/Conferences:
Annual Meetings: always New York, NY/2nd Tuesday in December

Rural Sociological Soc. *(1937)*
Sociology Dept., Room 510, Arntzen Hall
Western Washington University
Bellingham, WA   98225-9081
Tel: (360)650-7571   *Fax:* (360)650-7295
E-Mail: ruralsoc@cc.wwu.edu
Web Site: http://www.missouri.edu/~rss/
Members: 1,020 individuals
Staff: 1
Annual Budget: $100-250,000
Treasurer: Rabel J. Burdge

Historical Note
Originally a section of the American Sociological Soc., the Rural Sociological Soc. became independent in 1937. Membership: dues based on salary.

Publications:
Rural Sociology. q.
The Rural Sociologist. q.

Meetings/Conferences:
Annual Meetings: August/500
1999 – Chicago, IL(Ambassador East)/435
2000 – Washington, DC(Mayflower
    Renaissance)/Aug. 17-20/500

Russian-American Chamber of Commerce
Historical Note
Address unknown in 1995.

Ruth Jackson Orthopaedic Soc. *(1983)*
6300 N. River Rd., Suite 727
Rosemont, IL   60018-4226
Tel: (847)698-1693   *Fax:* (847)823-0536
Members: 600 individuals
Staff: 3
Annual Budget: under $10,000
Society Manager: Priscilla Majewski

Historical Note
Formerly the Ruth Jackson Soc., the present name was assumed in 1990. Women engaged in the practice of orthopaedic surgery. All active members are certified by the American Board of Orthopaedic Surgery, belong to the American Academy of Orthopaedic Surgeons, or are in training programs leading to these two qualifications. Women orthopaedic surgeons in foreign countries are also members. Membership: $150/year (post-residents); $25/year (resident); $10/year (medical student).

Publications:
Membership List. a.
Ruth Jackson Soc. Newsletter.

Meetings/Conferences:
Annual Meetings: With the American Academy of Orthopaedic
    Surgeons. Mid-winter/100.
1999 – Anaheim, CA

Saddle, Harness, and Allied Trade Ass'n *(1993)*

---

347 Elk Road
Sylva, NC   28779
Tel: (704)586-6389   *Fax:* (704)586-8938
Members: 420 individuals
Staff: 2
Annual Budget: under $10,000
Exec. Director: Daniel S. Preston

Historical Note
SHATA represents professionals in the leather and nylon trade separate from the fashion industry. Serves as an information resource, providing technical information, networking, business expertise, and continuing education. Membership: $38/year.

Publications:
Harness Shop News. m. adv.
Official Leather Tradesman's Directory. a. adv.

Safe and Vault Technicians Ass'n *(1986)*
3003 Live Oak St.
Dallas, TX   75204
Tel: (214)827-7233
Members: 2,000 individuals
Staff: 3
Exec. Director: Charles W. Gibson, Jr., CAE
Editor: Amy Gallagher
Meetings Manager: Jessica Vasquez
Comptroller: Kathy Romo
Membership Manager: Brandon Durrett

Historical Note
SAVTA members are retail locksmiths. Associate membership is available for manufacturers, distributors and others with an interest in the industry. Membership: $161/year (individual); $500/year (company).

Publications:
Membership Directory. a.
Safe and Vault Technology Journal. m. adv.

Meetings/Conferences:
1999 – Las Vegas, NV(Riviera Hotel and Casino)/May 3-8
2000 – Birmingham, AL(Sheraton Birmingham)/May 1-6

SAFE Ass'n *(1957)*
107 Music City Circle, Suite 112
Nashville, TN   37214
Tel: (615)902-0056   *Fax:* (615)902-0077
E-Mail: SAFE@USIT.NET
Members: 950 individuals
Staff: 1
Annual Budget: $100-250,000
Business Administrator: Jeani Benton

Historical Note
Established as the Space and Flight Equipment Ass'n at Edwards Air Force Base in 1957 and moved to Los Angeles in 1960. Incorporated in California in 1964 as the Survival and Flight Equipment Ass'n and became the SAFE Ass'n in 1977. Promotes the science of survival and the development of air safety in all forms of transportation. Membership: $60/year (individual); $500/year (organization/company).

Publications:
SAFE Journal. q. adv.
Symposium Proceedings. a.

Meetings/Conferences:
Annual Meetings: December
1999 – Atlanta, GA(Atlanta Marriott)/Dec. 6-8/800
2000 – Reno, NV(Hilton)/Oct. 9-11
2001 – Nashville, TN(Opryland)/Sept. 17-19

Safety Equipment Distributors Ass'n *(1968)*
5024-R Campbell Blvd.
Baltimore, MD   21236
Tel: (410)931-8100   *Fax:* (410)931-8111
E-Mail: sking@unidial.com
Web Site: http://www.safetycentral.org
Members: 300 companies
Staff: 2
Annual Budget: $250-500,000
Exec. Director: Steven T. King, CAE

Historical Note
SEDA represents wholesaler-distributors of safety equipment and works to enhance and improve distribution through excellence in communications, training, education and services.

Publications:
Profit Report.
SEDA Catalog Program. irreg.
The SEDA Scene. bi-m.

Meetings/Conferences:
Annual Meetings: Summer
1999 – Palm Beach, FL(Ritz-Carlton)/May 16-19/350

Safety Equipment Manufacturers' Agents Ass'n *(1986)*
400 E. Randolph St., Suite 500-6
Chicago, IL   60601
Tel: (312)240-1104   *Fax:* (312)240-1005
E-Mail: semaa.org
Web Site: http://semaa.org
Members: 80 firms
Staff: 2
Annual Budget: $25-50,000
Exec. Director: Bill Weiner

Historical Note
Established in Scottsdale, AZ and incorporated in Cincinnati, OH. SEMAA members are manufacturers' agents or agencies that actively sell in the industrial safety equipment market. Members are not distributors or wholesalers in part or in whole. Others involved in the industrial safety industry are eligible for affiliate membership. Membership: $250/year, plus $50 initiation fee.

Publications:
Rep Rap Newsletter. 3/year. adv.
SEMAA Directory. a.

Meetings/Conferences:

Safety Glazing Cerification Council *(1971)*
P.O. Box 9
Henderson Harbor, NY   13651
Tel: (315)938-7444   *Fax:* (315)938-7453
E-Mail: jgkent@gisco.net
Web Site: http://www.sgcc.org
Members: 77 companies
Staff: 2
Annual Budget: $250-500,000
Administrative Manager: John G. Kent

Historical Note
SGCC members are manufacturers of safety glazing products and others concerned with the manufacture and application of safety glazing.

Publications:
SGCC Certified Products Directory. semi-a.

Meetings/Conferences:
1999 – Chicago, IL(Schiff, Hardin and Waite)/May 4-7/50
1999 – Tampa Bay, FL(Doubletree)/Oct. 26-29/50

Sailmakers' Institute *(1969)*
Historical Note
A division of the Industrial Fabrics Association International.

Sales and Marketing Executives Internat'l *(1935)*
5500 Interstate North Pkwy. NW
Suite 545
Atlanta, GA   30328-4662
Tel: (770)661-8500   *Fax:* (770)661-8512
Toll Free: (800)999-1414
E-Mail: smeihq@smei.org
Web Site: http://www.smei.org
Members: 12,000 individuals
Staff: 5
Annual Budget: $1-2,000,000
C.E.O.: Michael F. Price, CME

Historical Note
Established as Nat'l Federation of Sales Executives, it became Nat'l Sales Executives Internat'l in 1949 and assumed its present name in 1961. Members are most commonly professionals in the fields of sales and marketing management, market research management, sales training, distribution management and other senior executives in small and medium businesses. Offers many career development services including: Graduate School of Sales Management and Marketing (with Syracuse Univ.) and professional certification. Pi Sigma Epsilon(PSE), a professional fraternity, is an affiliate. Membership: $195/year.

Publications:
Leadership Directory. a.
Marketing Times. q. adv.

Meetings/Conferences:
Annual Meetings: Fall
1999 – Atlanta, GA(Marriott Marquis)
2000 – San Francisco, CA(Fairmont)

Sales Ass'n of the Chemical Industry *(1921)*
66 Morris Ave., Suite 2A
Springfield, NJ   07081
Tel: (973)379-1100   *Fax:* (973)379-6507
Members: 400 individuals
Staff: 1
Annual Budget: $50-100,000

Historical Note
Founded as the Salesmen's Ass'n of the American Chemical Industry by 96 charter members September 7, 1921 at the Chemists' Club, New York City. Membership is concentrated in New York, New Jersey and Connecticut. Incorporated 1944 in the State of New York. Membership: $90/year (active); $40/year (associate).

Publications:
SACI Slants. q.

Meetings/Conferences:
Annual Meetings: October

Sales Ass'n of the Paper Industry *(1919)*
P.O. Box 21926
Columbus, OH   43221
Tel: (614)326-3911   *Fax:* (614)326-3917
Members: 200 individuals
Staff: 1
Annual Budget: $50-100,000
President: James L. Hutchison

Historical Note
Formerly (1972) Salesmen's Ass'n of the Paper Industry. Formed in 1919, it opened its own office in New York in 1950. Membership: $95/year.

Publications:
Bulletin. m.

Meetings/Conferences:
Annual Meetings: New York, NY(Waldorf Astoria)/March

Salon Ass'n, The *(1995)*
11811 N. Tatum Blvd., Suite 1085
Phoenix, AZ   85028-1618
Tel: (602)996-0749   *Fax:* (602)404-8900
Toll Free: (800)211-4872
E-Mail: jill@bbsi.org
Web Site: http://www.salons.org
Members: 1,500 salons
Staff: 3
Annual Budget: $250-500,000
Managing Director: Jill Kohler

Historical Note
TSA members are owners of salons. TSA offers bankcard and insurance programs, information networking and opportunities for

---

continued professional business development. *Membership:*
$125/year.

Publications:
TSA News. bi-m.

Meetings/Conferences:
Annual Meetings: late January/location alternates between east
        coast(even years) and west coast(odd years)
1999 – Scottsdale, AZ
2000 – Orlando, FL

Salt Institute *(1914)*
700 N. Fairfax St., Suite 600
Alexandria, VA   22314-2040
Tel: (703)549-4648   *Fax:* (703)548-2194
E-Mail: info@saltinstitute.org
Web Site: http://www.saltinstitute.org
Members: 35 companies
Staff: 5
Annual Budget: $1-2,000,000
President: Richard L. Hanneman
Director, Public Policy: Andrew C. Briscoe, III
Technical Director: Bruce M. Bertram

Historical Note
Founded in 1914 as the Salt Producers Ass'n. Became the Salt
Institute in 1963. Supported by major salt producers worldwide.

Publications:
Salt and Highway Deicing. semi-a.
Salt and Trace Minerals. semi-a.

Meetings/Conferences:
1999 – Cancun, Mexico(Ritz-Carlton Cancun)/March 3-6

SAMA Group of Ass'ns *(1918)*
225 Reinekers Lane, Suite 625
Alexandria, VA   22314-2875
Tel: (703)836-1360   *Fax:* (703)836-6644
Members: 200 companies
Staff: 5
Annual Budget: $1-2,000,000
Exec. Director: Michael J. Duff

Historical Note
Formerly (1991) the Scientific Apparatus Makers Association, the
SAMA Group of Associations is a non-profit industry trade
association composed of three affiliated associations. The three are
the Analytical and Life Science Systems Ass'n; the Laboratory
Products Ass'n, and the Opto-Precision Instruments Ass'n. The
affiliated associations are composed of manufacturers, suppliers
and distributors of analytical instruments and life science systems
used for chemical and life science analysis,measurement, systems,
and laboratory products and supplies marketed worldwide to
industry, government, education and research organizations.

Meetings/Conferences:
Annual Meetings: None held.

Sanitary Supply Wholesalers Ass'n *(1981)*
P.O. Box 8008
Sylvania, OH   43560
Tel: (419)824-2056   *Fax:* (419)824-2499
E-Mail: sswa@ix.netcom.com
Members: 106 companies
Staff: 1
Annual Budget: $50-100,000
Exec. Director: Gretchen S. Carroll

Historical Note
Membership: $375/year.

Publications:
Membership Directory. a.
Wholesaler. q.

Meetings/Conferences:

Sanitation Suppliers and Contractors Institute *(1957)*
Historical Note
A component of the Environmental Management Association.

Santa Gertrudis Breeders Internat'l *(1951)*
P.O. Box 1257
Highway 141 West
Kingsville, TX   78364
Tel: (512)592-9357   *Fax:* (512)592-8572
Web Site: http://www.sgbi.org
Members: 2,000 individuals
Staff: 5
Annual Budget: $500-1,000,000
Assoc. Director: Robert Swize

Historical Note
Incorporated April 9, 1951 with 169 charter members to
standardize and certify those animals designated as "purebred"
and to establish rigorous controls for grading-up to purebred herds.
Member of the Nat'l Soc. of Livestock Record Ass'n. Membership:
$25/year (active).

Publications:
Directory. bien. adv.

Meetings/Conferences:
Annual Meetings: Spring
1999 – Houston, TX/Feb. 24-27

Satellite Broadcasting and Communications Ass'n *(1986)*
225 Reinekers Lane, Suite 600
Alexandria, VA   22314
Tel: (703)549-6990   *Fax:* (703)549-7640
Toll Free: (800)541 - 5981
Web Site: http://www.sbca.com
Members: 2,100 companies
Staff: 29
Annual Budget: $5-10,000,000
President: Charles C. Hewitt
V.P. Communications/Operations: Margaret J. Parone
Sr. V. President, Government Affairs: Andrew R. Paul

Director of Meetings and Conventions: Laurie Nappi

Historical Note
Formerly (1985) the Soc. for Private and Commercial Earth
Stations and (1986) Satellite Television Industry Ass'n. SBCA
Represents all segments of the satellite television industry, including
manufacturers, distributors, dealers, programmers, and satellite
service providers. SBCA provides data and representation on
legislative and regulatory actions affecting its members.
Membership: $70-$1,100/year (individual), corporate rate varies.

Publications:
Report from the President. w.
SBCA 2-day. semi-w.
SBCA Satellite Retail Report. bi-m.
Showguide. a. adv.

Meetings/Conferences:
Annual Meetings: Summer
1999 – Las Vegas, NV(Hilton)/July 19-21
2000 – Las Vegas, NV(Hilton)/July 19-21

SAVE Internat'l *(1959)*
60 Revere Drive, Suite 500
Northbrook, IL   60062
Tel: (847)480-1730   *Fax:* (847)480-9282
E-Mail: value@value-eng.com
Web Site: http://www.value-eng.com
Members: 1,300 individuals
Staff: 6
Annual Budget: $100-250,000
Exec. Director: John R. Waxman

Historical Note
Formerly Soc. of American Value Engineers (1998). Awards the
Certified Value Specialist (CVS) designation. Membership:
$125/year (individual); $1,000/year (organization).

Publications:
Interactions. m.
Value World. q. adv.

Meetings/Conferences:
1999 – San Antonio, TX(Hilton Palacio del Rio)/June 27-30

Savings and Community Bankers of America
Historical Note
Became America's Community Bankers in 1995.

SB Latex Council *(1988)*
1250 Connecticut Ave., NWn Suite 800
Washington, DC   20036
Tel: (202)637-9040   *Fax:* (202)637-9178
E-Mail: regnet@ricochet.net
Members: 5 manufacturers
Staff: 2
Annual Budget: $250-500,000
Exec. Director: Robert J. Fensterheim

Historical Note
Members are manufacturers of styrene/butadiene latex for carpet
manufacturing and paper coating. Membership: $20,000/year.

Scaffold Industry Ass'n *(1972)*
20335 Ventura Blvd., Suite 310
Woodland Hills, CA   91364-2444
Tel: (818)610-0320   *Fax:* (818)610-0323
Members: 925 companies
Staff: 7
Annual Budget: $1-2,000,000
Exec. V. President: Gary Larson

Historical Note
Formerly (1975) the Scaffold Contractors Ass'n. Membership:
$200-750/year (depending on type of company).

Publications:
Directory/Handbook. a. adv.
SIA Newsletter. m. adv.

Meetings/Conferences:
Annual Meetings: July

Scaffolding, Shoring and Forming Institute *(1960)*
1300 Sumner Ave.
Cleveland, OH   44115-2851
Tel: (216)241-7333   *Fax:* (216)241-0105
E-Mail: ssfi@taol.com
Web Site: http://www.taol.org/ssfi
Members: 15 companies
Staff: 2
Annual Budget: $25-50,000
Managing Director: John H. Addington

Historical Note
Formerly (1969) Steel Scaffolding and Shoring Institute and (1980)
Scaffolding and Shoring Institute. SSFI members are companies
manufacturing scaffolding, shoring and forming products.

Scale Manufacturers Ass'n *(1945)*
6724 Lone Oak Blvd.
Naples, FL   34109-6834
Tel: (941)514-3441   *Fax:* (941)514-3470
E-Mail: staff@scalemanufacturers.org
Web Site: www.scalemanufacturers.org
Members: 27 companies
Staff: 4
Annual Budget: $100-250,000
Exec. Director: Robert A. Reinfried

Historical Note
Manufacturers of general industrial scales, load cell weighing
devices, retail scales, and vehicle and livestock scales. Purpose is to
advance the science of weighing and force measuring, and the
engineering and manufacturing of instruments, apparatus,
equipment and facilities.

Publications:
Directory. a.
Weighlog. semi-a.

Meetings/Conferences:
Annual Meetings: April/60
1999 – Hilton Head, SC(Crowne Plaza)
2000 – Tucson, AZ(Sheraton El Conquistador)

Schiffli Lace and Embroidery Manufacturers Ass'n *(1937)*
596 Anderson Ave., Suite 203
Cliffside Park, NJ   07010-1831
Tel: (201)943-7757   *Fax:* (201)943-7793
Members: 210 companies
Staff: 2
Annual Budget: $100-250,000
Exec. Director: I. Leonard Seiler

Historical Note
Formerly Embroidery Manufacturers Bureau. Members are
manufacturers of machine made embroideries and laces
(concentrated principally in Northern New Jersey and New York
City). Membership: $125/year/machine.

Publications:
Embroidery Directory. a. adv.
Embroidery News. bi-m. adv.

Meetings/Conferences:
Annual Meetings: October-November

School and Community Safety Soc. of America *(1959)*
Historical Note
Formerly (1985) the American School and Community Safety
Ass'n, (1992) the Safety Soc.; SCSSA is an autonomous society
within the American Ass'n for Active Lifestyles and Fitness.
Members are school and community personnel with an interest in
and responsiblity for safety.

School and Home Office Products Ass'n *(1991)*
3131 Elbee Rd.
Dayton, OH   45439-1900
Tel: (937)297-2250   *Fax:* (937)297-2254
Toll Free: (800)854 - 7467
E-Mail: info@shopa.org
Web Site: http://www.shopa.org
Members: 1,400 organizations
Staff: 17
Annual Budget: $2-5,000,000
President: Steven L. Jacober
Director of Ass'n Development: Tammy Broskey-Lee
V. President: Lisa Feldman
Manager, Finance and Information Technologies: Daniel Jones
Manager of Member Services: Robin Miller

Historical Note
Formed to sponsor an annual trade show (SHOPA Show) and
conduct industry activities for the manufacturers, wholesalers,
distributors, service merchandisers, manufacturing reps and
retailers of school and home office products through mass retail
channels. Membership: $250/year (domestic); $350/year
(foreign).

Publications:
Membership Directory. a.
SHOPTALK. m.
Strategic Overview & Distribution Trends Report. a.

Meetings/Conferences:
1999 – New Orleans, LA/Nov. 17-20

School Management Study Group *(1969)*
P.O. Box 1865
Pocatello, ID   83205
Tel: (208)233-6822   *Fax:* (208)232-2928
E-Mail: agdavi@smsg.com
Members: 350 individuals
Staff: 5
Annual Budget: $100-250,000
Chief Operating Officer: E.E. ""Gene" Davis

Historical Note
School and college administrators interested in improving
educational institutions. Membership: $20/yr.

Meetings/Conferences:
Annual Meetings: In conjunction with the American Ass'n of
        School Administrators

School Science and Mathematics Ass'n *(1902)*
Bloomsburg University
Bloomsburg, PA   17815
Tel: (717)389-4915   *Fax:* (717)389-3615
Web Site: http://www.ssma.org
Members: 1000 individuals
Staff: 2
Annual Budget: $100-250,000
Exec. Secretary: Donald L. Pratt, Ph. D.

Historical Note
Incorporated in Illinois in 1902 as the Central Ass'n of Science and
Mathematics Teachers, Inc. Affiliated with the American Ass'n for
the Advancement of Science. Membership: $35/year (individual),
$58/year (institution), $41/year (foreign), $70/year (foreign
institution).

Publications:
School Science and Mathematics. 8/yr. adv.
SSMArrt Newsletter. q.

Meetings/Conferences:
Annual Meetings: Fall
1999 – Greensboro, NC(Four Seasons)/Sept. 30-Oct. 1

Science Fiction and Fantasy Writers of America *(1965)*
P.O. Box 171
Unity, ME   04988-0171
Tel: (207)861-8078   *Fax:* (207)861-8078
E-Mail: execdir@sfwa.org
Web Site: http://www.sfwa.org
Members: 1,428 individuals
Annual Budget: $50-100,000
Exec. Secretary: Sharon Lee

Historical Note
An organization of professional writers in the science fiction and fantasy field. Formerly (1992) Science Fiction Writers of America. Membership: $35(affiliate); $50(active/associate); $60 (institutional).

Publications:
Bulletin. q.
Directory of the SFWA. a.
SFWA Forum. bi-m.

Meetings/Conferences:
Annual Meetings: April
1999 – Pittsburg, PA(Marriott)/April 30-May 2/500
2000 – New York

Scientific Equipment and Furniture Ass'n *(1988)*
7 Wildbird Ln.
Hilton Head Island, SC 29926-2766
Tel: (843)689-6878   *Fax:* (843)689-9958
Web Site: http://www.sefalabfurn.com
Members: 47 companies
Staff: 1
Annual Budget: $50-100,000
Exec. Director: Joan R. Powers

Historical Note
SEFA represents designers and manufacturers of equipment and furniture for laboratories and other scientific installations. Provides standards for safe practice and planning. Membership fee varies, based on revenues.

Meetings/Conferences:
Semi-Annual Meetings: Spring and Fall
1999 – Oak Brook, IL(Oak Brook Hills Resort)/May 19-21/45
1999 – Rio Mar Beach, Puerto Rico(Westin Rio Mar)/50
2000 – Atlanta, GA(Wyndham Peachtree
    Center)/April 5-8/45
2000 – Savannah, GA(Westin Savannah)/Nov. 15-19/50

Scoliosis Research Soc. *(1966)*
6300 N. River Road, Suite 727
Rosemont, IL 60018-4226
Tel: (708)698-1627   *Fax:* (708)823-0536
Members: 670 individuals
Exec. Director: Tressa Goulding

Historical Note
SRS members are physicians with an interest in spinal deformities.

Meetings/Conferences:
Annual Meetings: Fall
1999 – San Diego, CA(Hyatt)/Sept. 22-25/950
2000 – Cairns(Cairns Convention Center)/Oct. 18-21/900

Scottish Blackface Sheep Breeders Ass'n *(1982)*
1699 HH Hwy.
Willow Springs, MO 65793
Tel: (417)962-5466
Members: 90 individuals, 65 companies
Annual Budget: under $10,000
Secretary: Richard J. Harward

Historical Note
Aids breeders in finding and perpetuating new blood lines. Membership fee: $10/year.

Publications:
Breed Specs.
Membership List.

Meetings/Conferences:
Biennial Meetings: Late Summer

Scrap Tire Management Council *(1990)*
1400 K St., N.W., Suite 900
Washington, DC 20005
Tel: (202)682-4880   *Fax:* (202)682-4854
E-Mail: john@rma.org
Web Site: www/rma.org/tires.html
Chairman: John Serumgard
Executive Director: Michael Blumenthal

Historical Note
STMC, an advocacy organization within the Rubber Manufacturers Association, was created to identify and promote environmentally and economically sound markets for scrap tires.

Screen Actors Guild *(1933)*
5757 Wilshire Blvd.
Hollywood, CA 90036-3600
Tel: (213)954-1600   *Fax:* (213)549-6603
Members: 90,000 individuals
Staff: 300
Annual Budget: $25-50,000,000
National Exec. Director: Kendall Orsatti
Nat'l Director, Communications: Katherine Moore
Nat'l Director, Administration: Clinta Dayton

Historical Note
Labor union affiliated with AFL-CIO. An autonomous branch union of Associated Actors and Artistes America representing actors in film, television, commercials, interactive multimedia

Publications:
Screen Actor Newsletter.

Meetings/Conferences:
1999 – University City, CA(Sheraton)

Screen Manufacturers Ass'n *(1955)*
2850 S. Ocean Blvd., Suite 114
Palm Beach, FL 33480-5535
Tel: (561)533-0991   *Fax:* (561)533-7466
E-Mail: FSCOTTFITZGERALD@compuserve.com
Members: 35 companies
Staff: 2
Annual Budget: $50-100,000
Exec. V. President: Frank S. Fitzgerald, CAE,DABFE,

Historical Note
Formerly (1957) Frame Screen Manufacturers Ass'n.

Publications:
Directory. a.
Screening Industry. q.

Meetings/Conferences:
1999 – Palm Beach, FL(Palm Beach Hilton)/May 2-4/30
2000 – Palm Beach, FL/April 27-29

Screen Printing Ass'n Internat'l
Historical Note
Became the Screenprinting and Graphic Imaging Ass'n Internat'l in January, 1995.

Screenprinting and Graphic Imaging Ass'n Internat'l *(1948)*
10015 Main St.
Fairfax, VA 22031-3489
Tel: (703)385-1335   *Fax:* (703)273-0456
Toll Free: (888)385 - 3588
E-Mail: sgia@sgia.org
Web Site: http://www.sgia.org
Members: 3,400 companies
Staff: 44
Annual Budget: $5-10,000,000
President: John M. Crawford, Jr., CAE,
Director, Communications: Bruce H. Joffe
Director, Technical Services: Johnny Shell
V.P., Governmental Affairs: Marcia Y. Kinter
V.P., Conventions/Conferences: Sylvia Hall
Exec. V. President: Michael Robertson
V. President, Finance: Carole E. Cook
V. President, Marketing: Sondra Fry Benoudiz
Director, Research: Dennis Hunt
V. President, Managerial Services: Alan Anderson

Historical Note
Formerly (1968) Screen Process Printing Association and (1994) the Screen Printing Ass'n Internat'l. Supports the Screen Printing Technical Foundation to conduct research, tests, studies and scientific examinations designed to provide information on screen printing, and to conduct indepth training workshops. Supports the Center for Digital Imaging. Embroidery, pad printing, and other related graphic processes are also supported by SGIA. Membership Fee: Sliding scale based on sales volume.

Publications:
Image Maker. q.
SGIA Journal. q.
The Tabloid. m.
Who's Who in SGIA. a.

Meetings/Conferences:
Annual Meetings: Fall/12,000-14,000
1999 – Las Vegas, NV(Convention Center)/Oct. 7-10
2000 – New Orleans, LA(Convention Center)/Nov. 1-4
2001 – Anaheim, CA(Convention Center)/Sept. 19-22
2002 – St. Louis, MO(Convention & Exposition
    Center)/Oct. 30-Nov. 2
2003 – Atlanta, GA(GA World Congress Center)/Oct. 15-18
2004 – Minneapolis, MN(Minneaplis Conv. Cntr.)/Oct. 7-10
2005 – New Orleans, LA/Sept. 28-Oct. 1

Scribes *(1953)*
Lefler Law Center, Univ. of Arkansas
Fayetteville, AR 72701-1201
Tel: (501)575-5604   *Fax:* (501)575-2053
Web Site: http://www.shepards.com/scribes.home.htm
Members: 900 individuals, 11 institutions
Staff: 2
Annual Budget: $10-25,000
Exec. Director: Glen-Peter Ahlers Sr.

Historical Note
Also known as the American Soc. of Writers on Legal Subjects. Members are judges, editors of legal publications, writers on legal topics, law professors and others with an interest in legal writing. Membership: $50/year (individual); $500/year (institution).

Publications:
Scribes Journal of Legal Writing. a.
Scrivener Newsletter. q.

Meetings/Conferences:
Annual Meetings: in conjunction with the ABA and the AALS.
1999 – Atlanta, GA

SCSI Trade Ass'n
404 Balboa St.
San Francisco, CA 94118
Tel: (415)750-8350   *Fax:* (415)751-4829
E-Mail: info@SCSITA.org
Web Site: http://www.SCSITA.org
Exec. Director: Michael T. LoBue

Scuba Retailers Ass'n *(1989)*
4 Florence St.
Somerville, MA 02143
Tel: (617)623-7722   *Fax:* (617)776-6890
E-Mail: SRA@Hotmail.com
Members: 500 stores
Staff: 3
Annual Budget: $10-25,000
Exec. Director: James Estabrook

Historical Note
Members are stores selling scuba and associated underwater equipment. Membership: $150/year (retail); $200/year (associate).

Publications:
Scuba Retailer Magazine. q. adv.
SRA News. q.

Meetings/Conferences:
Annual Meetings: January

Sculptors Guild *(1937)*
110 Greene St., Suite 603
New York, NY 10012

Tel: (212)431-5669   *Fax:* (212)431-5669
Web Site: http://www.sculptorsguild.org
Members: 123 individuals
Staff: 1
Annual Budget: $10-25,000
President: Steven Keltner

Historical Note
The Guild features work by member artists in exhibitions held in corporate and other public spaces throughout the year. Membership: $125-175/year.

Publications:
Guild Reporter. q. adv.

Meetings/Conferences:
Annual Meetings: always New York, NY/April-May
1999 – New York, NY(SoHo Building)

Seafarers' Internat'l Union of North America *(1938)*
5201 Auth Way
Camp Springs, MD 20746-4275
Tel: (301)899-0675   *Fax:* (301)899-7355
Members: 80,000 individuals
Staff: 125
Annual Budget: $2-5,000,000
President: Michael Sacco

Historical Note
Composed of 18 autonomous affiliated unions of seamen, fishermen, fish cannery workers, inland boatmen, transportation workers and industrial workers in the U.S., Canada, U.S. Virgin Islands and Puerto Rico. SIU was chartered by the American Federation of Labor October 14, 1938 as an outgrowth of the Sailor's Union of the Pacific.

Publications:
Seafarers Log. m.

Meetings/Conferences:
Quinquennial Meetings: (1997)

Sealant Engineering and Associated Lines *(1964)*
Historical Note
Address unknown in 1995.

Sealant, Waterproofing and Restoration Institute *(1976)*
2841 Main
Kansas City, MO 64108
Tel: (816)472-7974   *Fax:* (816)472-7765
E-Mail: swrionline.org
Members: 120 companies
Staff: 3
Annual Budget: $100-250,000
Exec. Director: Kenneth R. Bowman
Associate Director: Sheila R. Navis, CAE

Historical Note
Formerly the Sealant and Waterproofers Institute, the group adopted its present name in 1989. Regular members are sealant and waterproofing contractors; associate members are suppliers to the industry. Membership: $350/year (associates), $1,300/year (manufacturers), $650/year (contractors).

Publications:
The Applicator. q. adv.

Meetings/Conferences:
1999 – St. Petersburg, FL(Tradewinds)/Feb. 21-24/150

Sealed Insulating Glass Manufacturers Ass'n *(1963)*
401 N. Michigan Ave.
Chicago, IL 60611-4267
Tel: (312)644-6610   *Fax:* (312)321-6869
E-Mail: SIGMA@sba.com
Web Site: http://www.sigmaonline.org/sigma
Members: 130 companies
Staff: 2
Annual Budget: $250-500,000
Exec. Director: Christine Norris

Publications:
Directory. a.
SIGMA Newsletter. 3/year.
SIGMA-Gram. irreg.
Technical Bulletins.
Technical Manuals.

Meetings/Conferences:
Semi-Annual Meetings: Winter and Summer

Seaplane Pilots Ass'n *(1972)*
421 Aviation Way
Frederick, MD 21701-4756
Tel: (301)695-2083   *Fax:* (301)695-2375
Members: 6,600 individuals
Staff: 2
Annual Budget: $250-500,000
Exec. Director: Mike Volk

Historical Note
Established in Little Ferry, NJ as the U.S. Seaplane Pilots Ass'n. Seeks to protect right of access for seaplanes to waterways in the U.S. and Canada, to promote seaplane flying and to disseminate information to seaplane pilots. Membership: $36/year.

Publications:
SPA Water Landing Directory. bien. adv.
Water Flying. bi-m. adv.
Water Flying Annual a. adv. adv.

Meetings/Conferences:
Annual Meetings: Usually September (1st weekend after Labor Day), Greenville, ME

Secondary Materials and Recycled Textiles Ass'n *(1932)*
7910 Woodmont Ave., Suite 1212
Bethesda, MD 20814-3015
Tel: (301)656-1077   *Fax:* (301)656-1079
E-Mail: smartasn@erols.com

Web Site: http://smartasn.org
Members: 300 companies
Staff: 3
Annual Budget: $250-500,000
Exec. V. President: Bernard D. Brill

Historical Note
Founded as the Sanitary Institute of America, it became the Nat'l Ass'n of Wiping Cloth Manufacturers, (1977) the Internat'l Ass'n of Wiping Cloth Manufacturers, and (1993) Secondary Materials and Recycled Textiles Ass'n. SMART members are manufacturers and distributors of industrial wiping cloths, used clothing, mill ends, remnants, and recycled textiles. Membership: $1,100/year (company).

Publications:
SMART Membership & Buyers Guide. a. adv.

Meetings/Conferences:
1999 – Palm Beach, FL(Ritz-Carlton)/Jan. 17-20
2000 – Maui, HI(Four Seasons)January
2001 – Palm Beach, FL(Ritz Carlton)/Jan. 21-24

Section for Women in Public Administration *(1982)*
American Soc. for Public Administration
1120 G St., N.W., Suite 700
Washington, DC 20005
Tel: (202)393-7878   *Fax:* (202)638-4952
Members: 400 individuals
Annual Budget: under $10,000
Section Chair: Linda Lazer
Editor: Michelle St. Germain

Historical Note
Began as the Nat'l Committee for Women in Public Administration in 1971. Chartered as the Section for Women in Public Administration in July, 1982. Develops programs and projects which promote the full participation and recognition of women in all levels and areas of public service. The American Soc. for Public Administration provides administrative support for SWPA. Membership: $17/year (individual).

Publications:
Bridging the Gap. q. adv.

Meetings/Conferences:
Annual Meetings: Summer, in conjunction with the ASPA National Conference
1999 – Seattle, WA(Westin)/May 9-13
1999 – Orlando, FL(Omni Rosen)/Apr. 10-14

Securities Industry Ass'n *(1912)*
1401 I St., N.W., Suite 1000
Washington, DC 20005
Tel: (202)296-9410   *Fax:* (202)296-9775
Members: 700 firms
Staff: 100
Annual Budget: $10-25,000,000
President: Marc E. Lackritz
V.P., Corporate Communications: James D. Spellman
Senior V. President, Government Affairs: Steve Judge
Senior V. President and General Counsel: Stuart J. Kaswell

Historical Note
Merger in 1972 of the Ass'n of Stock Exchange Firms (1913) and the Investment Bankers Ass'n of America (1912). Investment bankers, brokers, dealers, mutual funds and others accounting for about 95% of the securities business in North America. Sponsors the Securities Industry Political Action Committee and the Securities Industry Foundation for Economic Education. Has an annual budget of approximately $19 million.

Publications:
Fixed Income Quarterly Report. q.
Human Resources Management Report. bi-m.
Operations Update. bi-m.
Securities Industries Trends. m.
SIA Capitol Chronicle. bi-m.
SIA Foreign Activity Report. q.
SIA Yearbook. a.

Meetings/Conferences:

Securities Transfer Ass'n *(1911)*
P.O. Box 5067
Hazlet, NJ 07730-5067
Tel: (732)888-6040   *Fax:* (732)888-2121
Web Site: http://www.stai.org
Members: 400 companies
Staff: 2
Annual Budget: $250-500,000
President: Robert Dietz

Historical Note
An association of representatives from banks and corporations in the U.S. and Canada who are involved in the issuance, transfer and registration of corporate securities or related duties. Membership: $500/year.

Publications:
Newsletter. q.
STA Rule Booklet. irreg.

Meetings/Conferences:
Annual Meetings: Fall/300-350
1999 – Naples, FL/Oct. 20-24

Security Hardware Distributors Ass'n *(1940)*
1900 Arch St.
Philadelphia, PA 19103-1498
Tel: (215)564-3484   *Fax:* (215)564-2175
Members: 170 manufacturers and distributors
Staff: 3
Annual Budget: $100-250,000
Exec. Director: Patricia A. Lilly

Historical Note
Formerly (1997) Nat'l Locksmith Suppliers Ass'n. Distributors and manufacturers of security hardware. Membership fee varies, based on sales volume.

Meetings/Conferences:
Annual Meetings: April/May

1999 – Phoenix, AZ

Security Industry Ass'n *(1969)*
635 Slaters Lane, Suite 110
Alexandria, VA 22314
Tel: (703)683-2075   *Fax:* (703)683-2469
Web Site: www.fiaonline.org
Members: 200 firms
Staff: 10
Annual Budget: $1-2,000,000
Exec. Director: Ronald F. Spiller
Dir., Communications: Richard Chace
Director, Technical and Education Services: Virginia Williams
Director, Membership: Moreen Beckman

Historical Note
A merger of the Security Equipment Manufacturers Ass'n and the Security Equipment Distributors Ass'n, both founded in 1969. Incorporated in Illinois in 1971; 1977 in California. Membership: sliding scale based on annual sales. Formerly Security Equipment Industry Ass'n (1988).

Publications:
Market Research Reports. 3/year.
Membership Directory. a. adv.
SIA News. m.

Meetings/Conferences:
1999 – New York, NY

Security Traders Ass'n *(1934)*
One World Trade Center, Suite 4511
New York, NY 10048
Tel: (212)524-0484   *Fax:* (212)321-3449
Members: 7,500 individuals
Staff: 5
Annual Budget: $1-2,000,000
President: John N. Tognino
Senior V. President/Counsel: Andrew N. Grass

Historical Note
Formerly (1988) Nat'l Security Traders Ass'n. Members are security traders and others involved in the securities industry. Members are located in the U.S., Canada and Western Europe. STA, composed of 35 affiliate organizations, maintains communications with self-regulatory organizations, local and national governments, and their agencies, and fosters cooperation among all segments of the worldwide securities industry. Membership: $50/year, plus local affiliate membership (individual).

Publications:
Newsletter. bi-m.
Pre-Convention Guide. a.
Traders Annual. a. adv.

Meetings/Conferences:
Annual Meetings: Fall/1,600

Seismological Soc. of America *(1906)*
201 Plaza Professional Building
El Cerrito, CA 94530
Tel: (510)525-5474   *Fax:* (510)525-7204
Web Site: http://www.seismosoc.org/ssa
Members: 1,900 individuals
Staff: 4
Annual Budget: $250-500,000
Exec. Director: Susan B. Newman

Historical Note
Established in San Francisco, CA in August 1906, and incorporated in California the same year. A member society of the American Geological Institute. Membership: $100/year (individual); $110/year (foreign); $270/year (company).

Publications:
Bulletin. bi-m.
Seismological Research Letters. bi-m.

Meetings/Conferences:
Annual Meetings: Spring
1999 – Seattle, WA/May 3-5
2000 – San Diego, CA/March 27-29

Self Insurance Institute of America *(1981)*
12241 Newport Ave., Suite 100
Santa Ana, CA 92705
Tel: (714)508-4920   *Fax:* (714)508-4904
Toll Free: (800)851 - 7789
E-Mail: webmaster@siia.org
Web Site: http://www.siia.org
Members: 1,500 companies
Staff: 15
Annual Budget: $2-5,000,000
C.E.O.: James A. Kinder
Communications: Kit Wilson
Public Affairs: Mike Ferguson
Meetings & Conventions: Judi Dokter
Exhibits/Advertising: Lisa Guilford
Finance and Administration: Mieka Scholten
Membership: Katie Miller

Historical Note
Established in Santa Ana, CA in 1981 in order to bring the three principal entities of the self-insurance industry - consumer employers, third party administrators and reinsurance companies - and other interested parties together for dialogue; incorporated in California. Members are companies involved or interested in self-funding risk for workers compensation insurance programs, employee benefit plans or property and casualty protection. Membership: $195/year (associate), $695/year (company).

Publications:
Hotline Legislative Report. irreg.
The Self Insurer Magazine. m. adv.
Who's Who Directory. a.

Meetings/Conferences:
Annual Meetings: October
1999 – Washington, DC(Hilton)/Oct. 12-16

Self Storage Ass'n *(1975)*

6506 Loisdale Rd., Suite 315
Springfield, VA 22150
Tel: (703)921-9123   *Fax:* (703)921-9105
Members: 1,600 companies
Staff: 7
Annual Budget: $1-2,000,000
Exec. Director: Michael Kidd
Director, Education: Martha M. Morrison
Director of Membership: Ginny Stengel

Historical Note
Formerly (1989) Self-Service Storage Ass'n. Self storage facility owners/operators and suppliers to the industry. Membership: $395/year (minimum).

Publications:
Newsletter. irreg.

Meetings/Conferences:
Semi-Annual Meetings: Spring and Fall
1999 – Chicago, IL/Apr. 14-17
1999 – Las Vegas, NV/Sept. 8-11

Semiconductor Equipment and Materials Internat'l *(1970)*
805 E. Middlefield Road
Mountain View, CA 94043-4080
Tel: (650)940-6911   *Fax:* (650)967-5375
Web Site: http://www.semi.org
Members: 150 individuals, 2,050 corporations
Staff: 126
Annual Budget: $25-50,000,000
President: Stanley T. Myers
V. President, Communications: Lisa Anderson
V. President, Expositions: Rick Heim
Chief Financial Officer: Al Drum

Historical Note
Formerly (1988) Semiconductor Equipment and Materials Institute. SEMI is an international trade association representing firms supplying equipment, materials and services to the semiconductor industry. Maintains regional offices in Brussels, Tokyo, Seoul, Moscow, Washington, D.C. and Singapore. Has an annual budget of approximately $45 million. Membership: $100/year (individual), $1,200-5,200/year (corporate); $250/year (business affiliate).

Publications:
Channel Magazine. 9/year. adv.
Forecast. a.
SEMI Membership Directory. bien.
SEMI Standards. a.

Meetings/Conferences:
Annual Meetings: Nine International Shows around the world

Semiconductor Industry Ass'n *(1977)*
181 Metro Drive, Suite 450
San Jose, CA 95110
Tel: (408)436-6600   *Fax:* (408)436-6646
Web Site: http://www.semichips.org
Members: 85 companies
Staff: 13
Annual Budget: $2-5,000,000
President: George Scalise
V. President, Internat'l Trade & Gov't Affairs: Daryl Hatano

Historical Note
Represents U.S. producers of all semiconductor products, such as discrete components, integrated circuits and microprocessors.

Publications:
SIA Status Report& Directory. a.

Meetings/Conferences:

Semiconductor Safety Ass'n *(1978)*
1313 Dolley Madison Blvd., Suite 402
McLean, VA 22101-3926
Tel: (703)790-1745   *Fax:* (703)790-2672
E-Mail: bburk@burkinc.com
Web Site: http://www.semiconductorsafety.org
Members: 1,200 individuals, 35 companies
Staff: 12
Annual Budget: $500-1,000,000
Exec. Director: Brett J. Burk

Historical Note
SSA members are individuals employed within the electronics and related high technology industries with an interest in environmental, health and safety issues. Corporate and associate membership categories are available Membership: $55/year (individual); $300-500/year (company).

Publications:
SSA Journal. q. adv.

Meetings/Conferences:
Annual Meetings: April
1999 – San Diego, CA
2000 – Washington, DC
2001 – New Orleans, LA

Semiotic Soc. of America *(1975)*
U of West Florida, Dept of Anthropology
11000 University Pkwy.
Pensacola, FL 32514
Tel: (904)474-2186   *Fax:* (904)474-3131
Members: 600 individuals and institutions
Exec. Director: Terry Prewitt

Historical Note
SSA members are academics and institutions with an interest in the function of signs and symbols. Membership: $35/year (individuals); $45/year (organizations).

Publications:
American Journal of Semiotics. semi-a. adv.

Meetings/Conferences:
Annual Meetings: October

Senior Army Reserve Commanders Ass'n *(1949)*
P.O. Box 11178

Blacksburg, VA   24062-1178
Tel: (301)229-1550
Members: 800 individuals
Staff: 3
Annual Budget: $100-250,000
Exec. Director: Brg.Gen. Lewis M. Helm, AUS(Ret.)
Historical Note
SARCA is a professional association of Army Reserve leadership formed to assure that the Army Reserve plays a major role in the defense of the United States. Membership: $125-175/year (active).
Publications:
Washington Update. m.
Meetings/Conferences:
1999 – Washington, DC(Washington Hilton)/Jan. 23-24

Senior Executives Ass'n *(1980)*
P.O. Box 44808
Washington, DC   20026
Tel: (202)927-7000
Web Site: http://www.seniorexecs.com
Members: 3,000 individuals
Staff: 8
Annual Budget: $500-1,000,000
President: Carol A. Bonosaro
Director, Communications: Daryl Richard
Dir., Member & Agency Liaison: Bert Subrin
Historical Note
Founded in 1980 as a tax-exempt, non-profit professional association representing career Federal executives. SEA is committed to effective and productive leadership in government; seeks to advance the professionalism and advocate the interests of member executives who manage the government's departments and agencies. Membership: $222/year.
Publications:
Action. m. adv.
Meetings/Conferences:
Annual Meetings: Summer in Washington, DC/300

SEPM - Soc. for Sedimentary Geology *(1926)*
1731 E. 71st St.
Tulsa, OK   74136-5108
Tel: (918)493-3361   *Fax:* (918)493-2093
Toll Free: (800)865 - 9765
E-Mail: ngeeslin@sepm.org
Web Site: http://www.sepm.org
Members: 4,919 individuals
Staff: 8
Annual Budget: $1-2,000,000
Exec. Director: Theresa L. Scott
Meetings Coordinator: Judy Tarpley
Member Services Associate: Emma Kelley
Manager, Publications/Marketing: Patricia Auberle
Historical Note
Formerly Soc. of Economic Paleontologists and Mineralogists, it assumed its present name in 1989. Originated in Fort Worth in 1926 and became an affiliated society of the American Ass'n of Petroleum Geologists in 1927. Later became a section, and in 1930 a technical division, of the AAPG. Membership: $70-115/year (individual).
Publications:
Journal of Sedimentary Research. bi-m. adv.
Membership Directory. bien. adv.
Newsletter. q. adv.
PALAIOS. bi-m.
Meetings/Conferences:
Semi-Annual Meetings: Annual with AAPG and Mid-Year
1999 – San Antonio, TX/April 11-14

Serial Storage Architecture Industry Ass'n *(1995)*
Department H65A/B-013
5600 Cottle Road
San Jose, CA   95193-0001
Tel: (408)256-3899   *Fax:* (408)256-0595
Members: 100 individuals
Staff: 1
Annual Budget: $100-250,000
Secretary: Claude Ricks
Historical Note
SSAIA members are computer industry firms with an interest in Serial Storage Architecture.
Publications:
Material distributed on web-site.
Meetings/Conferences:
Annual Meetings: Member meetings every two months.

Service Dealers Ass'n *(1986)*
P.O. Box 4315
Dallas, TX   75208
Tel: (214)946-5562   *Fax:* (214)946-1974
Toll Free: (888)293 - 5810
E-Mail: tsda@dallas.net
Web Site: www.dallas.net/ntsda
Members: 690 individuals
Staff: 2
Annual Budget: $100-250,000
Project Coordinator: Victor Medina
Historical Note
SDA represents dealers and distributors of power equipment. Membership: $95/year (individual); $250/year (company).
Publications:
Membership Directory. a. adv.
TSDA Newsletter. bi-m. adv.
Meetings/Conferences:

Service Employees Internat'l Union *(1921)*
1313 L St., N.W.
Washington, DC   20005
Tel: (202)898-3200   *Fax:* (202)898-3438

Web Site: http://www.seiu.org
Members: 1000,000,000 individuals
Staff: 325
Annual Budget: $50-100,000,000
Internat'l President: Andrew L. Stern
Director, Communications: Bill Pritchett
Director/Meetings & Travel: Sheila Edwards
Director/Education: Patricia Yeghissian
Secretary-Treasurer: Betty Bednarczyk
Historical Note
Chartered by the American Federation of Labor on April 23, 1921 as a union of custodial and building service employees, SEIU now represents building service workers, healthcare workers, public employees and office workers. Originally, the Building Service Employees Internat'l Union, it assumed its present name in 1968. Affiliated with AFL-CIO and CLC. Sponsors and supports the COPE Political Action Committee.
Publications:
SEIU Leadership News Update. m.
Union. q.
Meetings/Conferences:
Annual Meetings: Every 4 years (1996)

Service Industry Ass'n *(1998)*
494 Ansley Walk Terr., N.E.
Atlanta, GA   30309
Tel: (404)885-9908   *Fax:* (404)885-9909
E-Mail: cbetzner@servicenetwork.org
Web Site: http://www.servicenetwork.org
Members: 250 companies
Annual Budget: $100-250,000
Exec. Director: Claudia J. Betzner
Historical Note
SIA members are high tech service companies. Membership: $450-5,000 year (company).
Publications:
Membership List. a.
Network News Newsletter. q. adv.
Meetings/Conferences:
1999 – Newport Beach, CA(Four Seasons Hotel)/March 14-17/200

Service Specialists Ass'n *(1981)*
4015 Marks Road, Suite 2B
Medina, OH   44256
Tel: (330)725-7160   *Fax:* (330)722-5638
Toll Free: (800)763 - 5717
Members: 140 companies
Staff: 1
Annual Budget: $100-250,000
Exec. V. President: Cara R. Giebner
Historical Note
Formerly (1990) the Spring Service Ass'n and The Suspension Specialists Ass'n (1996). Members are persons, firms, or corporations who have operated a full line heavy duty repair service shop for at least one year with sufficient inventory to service market area, have rebuilding department capable of making all necessary repairs. Membership: $600/year.
Publications:
The Leaf Newsletter. m.
Meetings/Conferences:
Annual Meetings: October

Service Station Dealers of America and Allied Trades *(1947)*
9420 Annapolis Road, Suite 307
Lanham, MD   20706
Tel: (301)577-4956   *Fax:* (301)731-0039
Members: 60,000 individuals
Staff: 2
Annual Budget: $100-250,000
Exec. V. President: Roy Littlefield
Historical Note
Members are independent gasoline dealers who sell gasoline under the brand name of their supplier. Sponsors the SSDA Political Action Committee. Known as National Congress of Petroleum Retailers, Inc. until 1980.
Publications:
Legislative/Legal Update. irreg.
SSDA Newsletter. m.
Meetings/Conferences:

Service Technicians Soc.
Historical Note
A division of Soc. of Automotive Engineers, which provides administrative support.

Sewn Products Equipment Suppliers Ass'n *(1990)*
16 E. Rowan St., Suite 310
Raleigh, NC   27609
Tel: (919)881-0321   *Fax:* (919)881-0628
E-Mail: benton@cnewsgroup.com
Web Site: http://www.spesa.org
Members: 100 individuals, 80 companies
Staff: 8
Annual Budget: $100-250,000
Exec. V. President: Benton W. Gardner
Historical Note
Members are companies engaged in or connected with supplying equipment, including replacement parts and computer software, to the sewn products industry. Associate membership is available to non-qualifying individuals and corporations; affiliate membership is available to individuals and corporations organizing trade shows, trade press or allied trade associations. Membership: $850-5,000/year, based on U.S. gross revenues (regular); $750/year (associate or affiliate).
Publications:
Membership Directory.

Newsletter. bi-m.
Meetings/Conferences:

Shade Tobacco Growers Agricultural Ass'n *(1942)*
P.O. Box 480
Bloomfield, CT   06002
Tel: (860)522-1153
Members: 5 producers/processors
Staff: 2
Annual Budget: $25-50,000
President: Daniel Nunez
Historical Note
Growers and processors of shade-grown leaf tobacco for cigar wrappers.
Meetings/Conferences:
Annual Meetings: March

Sheet Metal and Air Conditioning Contractors' Nat'l Ass'n *(1943)*
4201 Lafayette Center Dr.,
Chantilly, VA   20153-1230
Tel: (703)803-2980   *Fax:* (703)803-3732
E-Mail: info@smacna.org
Web Site: http://www.smacna.org.
Members: 1,925 companies, 104 chapters
Staff: 38
Annual Budget: $5-10,000,000
Exec. V. President: John W. Sroka
Director of Communication: Rosalind Raymond
Director of Government Relations: Stanley Kolbe
Director of Meetings/Conventions: Mary Lou Taylor
Director, Administration: Ronald D. Lewis
Exec. Director, Member Services: Dennis Bradshaw
Director, Bus. Management and Membership: Kimberly Graver
Historical Note
Formerly (1956) Sheet Metal Contractors Nat'l Ass'n. Sponsors and supports the Sheet Metal and Air Conditioning Political Action Committee (SMAC PAC). Members are contractors in commercial and industrial heating, ventilating and air conditioning, architectural and industrial sheet metal, manufacturing, testing and balancing, and siding and decking. Has an annual budget of approximately $7.5 million.
Publications:
Annual Report. a.
Membership Directory. a.
SMACNews. m.
Meetings/Conferences:
Annual Meetings: Fall/2,500
1999 – Palm Desert, CA
2000 – Big Island, HI

Sheet Metal Workers' Internat'l Ass'n *(1888)*
1750 New York Ave., N.W.
6th Floor
Washington, DC   20006-5386
Tel: (202)783-5880   *Fax:* (202)662-0894
Members: 150,000 individuals
Staff: 125
Annual Budget: $5-10,000,000
President: Arthur Moore
Historical Note
Established in Toledo, Ohio on January 25, 1888 as the Tin, Sheet Iron and Cornice Workers' Internat'l Ass'n. Chartered by the American Federation of Labor in 1899. Became the Amalgamated Sheet Metal Workers' Internat'l Ass'n in 1897 and merged with the Sheet Metal Workers' Nat'l Alliance in 1903 to become the Amalgamated Sheet Metal Workers' Internat'l Alliance. Sponsors and supports the Sheet Metal Workers Internat'l Ass'n Political Action Committee.
Publications:
Focus on Funds. m.
Sheet Metal Workers' Journal. bi-m.
The Scene Today. bi-w.
Meetings/Conferences:
Annual Meetings: August/600

Shellfish Institute of North America *(1908)*
Historical Note
Became the Molluscan Shellfish Institute in 1997.

Shelving Manufacturers Ass'n
Historical Note
Became (1998) Storage Equipment Manufacturer's Ass'n.

Shipbuilders Council of America *(1920)*
901 N. Washington St., Suite 204
Alexandria, VA   22314-1535
Tel: (703)548-7447   *Fax:* (703)518-0276
Members: 30 companies
Staff: 5
Annual Budget: $500-1,000,000
Acting President: Lauren P. Howard
V. President: Robert O'Neill
Consultant: S.O. Nunn
Historical Note
Formerly Nat'l Council of American Shipbuilders. Absorbed Atlantic and Gulf Coasts Drydock Ass'n. Private shipbuilding and repair companies and related firms such as manufacturers of marine equipment and supplies, many of which do work for the federal government.
Publications:
Report. a.
Shipyard Chronicle. bi-m.
Meetings/Conferences:
Annual Meetings: Washington, in March.

Shipowners Claims Bureau *(1917)*
5 Hanover Sq., 20th Floor

New York, NY 10004
Tel: (212)269-2350   *Fax:* (212)825-1391
Toll Free: (800)730 - 2535
Web Site: http://www.american-club.com
Members: 31 companies
Staff: 30
President: Thomas J. McGowan
Historical Note
Members are claim managers and adjusters for shipping lines and protection and indemnity clubs.
Meetings/Conferences:
Annual Meetings: June

Shippers of Recycled Textiles (1988)
Historical Note
A division of Secondary Materials and Recycled Textiles Ass'n. which provides administrative support.

Shippers Oil Field Traffic Ass'n (1941)
Historical Note
Became Energy Traffic Ass'n in 1997.

Shock Soc. (1978)
1021 15th St., Suite 9
Augusta, GA 30901
Tel: (706)722-7511   *Fax:* (706)722-7515
E-Mail: maps@csra.net.com
Members: 700 individuals
Staff: 2
Annual Budget: $100-250,000
Exec. Director: Dr. Sherwood M. Reichard
Historical Note
Membership composed of individuals interested in extending basic and clinical knowledge of the nature and treatment of shock and trauma. Membership: $170/year (individual).
Publications:
Directory. a.
Shock. m. adv.
Meetings/Conferences:
Annual Meetings: June
1999 – Philadelphia, PA(Wyndham Franklin
        Plaza)/June 12-16
2000 – Snowbird, Ut(Snowbird Resort)/June 3-6

Shoe Service Institute of America (1905)
5024-R Campbell Blvd.
Baltimore, MD 21236-5974
Tel: (410)931-8100   *Fax:* (410)931-8111
E-Mail: lebovic@aol.com
Members: 160 companies
Annual Budget: $250-500,000
Exec. V. President: Fred C. Stringfellow
Membership Coordinator: Wendy Arthur
Editor, Shoe Service Magazine: Mitchell E. Lebovic, CAE
Historical Note
Formerly Nat'l Leather and Shoe Finders Ass'n, it assumed its present name in 1949. Members are wholesalers and suppliers of shoe repair, shoe care and related items to the shoe service industry. Membership Fee: $300-720/year, based on sales volume.
Publications:
Shoe Service Magazine. m. adv.
Meetings/Conferences:
Annual Meetings: July
1999 – Las Vegas, NV(Dessert Inn)/July 22-25/400

Showmen's League of America (1913)
300 West Randolph St.
Chicago, IL 60606-1705
Tel: (312)332-6236
Members: 1,650 individuals
Staff: 2
Annual Budget: $50-100,000
Exec. Secretary: Robert Drewke
Historical Note
A fraternal and benevolent organization of indoor and outdoor amusement operators and showmen. Membership: $25/year.
Publications:
Newsletter. 6/year.
Yearbook. a. adv.
Meetings/Conferences:
1999 – Las Vegas, NV/Nov. 29-Dec. 1

Shrimp Council
1901 N. Fort Myer Drive, Suite 700
Arlington, VA 22209
Tel: (703)524-8880   *Fax:* (703)524-4619
Exec. V. President: Dick Gutting, Jr.
Historical Note
A division of the Nat'l Fisheries Institute.

Sigma Delta Kappa (1914)
Historical Note
Address unknown in 1996.

Sigma Epsilon Delta Dental Fraternity (1901)
P.O. Box 278
Great Neck, NY 11022-0278
Tel: (516)482-0679
Staff: 1
Annual Budget: $25-50,000
Exec. Director: Mrs. Nathan Massoff
Historical Note
The oldest dental fraternity. Membership: $40/year (individual).
Publications:
Sedeltan Journal. a.

Meetings/Conferences:

Sigma Phi Delta (1924)
438 Smithfield St.
East Liverpool, OH 43920
Tel: (330)385-5287   *Fax:* (330)385-6185
Members: 7,500 individuals
Exec. Secretary: Robert J. Beals
Historical Note
A professional and social fraternity in engineering.
Publications:
Directory. a.
Sigma Phi Delta Castle. semi-a.
Star. 2/yr.
Meetings/Conferences:
1999 – Los Angeles, CA

Signal Processing Soc. (1948)
Historical Note
See IEEE Signal Processing Soc.

Silicones Environmental Health and Safety Council of North America (1971)
1767 Business Center Drive, Suite 302
Reston, VA 20190-5332
Tel: (703)438-3943   *Fax:* (703)438-3113
E-Mail: sehsc1@sehsc.com
Members: 10 companies
Annual Budget: $2-5,000,000
Exec. Director: William H. Smock
Operations Manager: Elizabeth D. Dombrowsky
Historical Note
Formerly (1993) Silicones Health Council. SEHSC is an organization of organosilicones manufacturers. The group was formed to coordinate programs dealing with health, environmental and safety issues of interest to the industry and to disseminate scientifically sound information regarding silicones.

Silver Institute (1971)
1112 16th St., N.W., Suite 240
Washington, DC 20036
Tel: (202)835-0185   *Fax:* (202)835-0155
E-Mail: info@silverinstitute.org
Web Site: http://www.silverinstitute.org
Members: 35 companies
Staff: 5
Annual Budget: $250-500,000
Exec. Director: Paul W. Bateman
Public Affairs Manager: Cristy Rosche
Manager, Meetings and Membership: Joan Rinaldi
Historical Note
Members, drawn from 14 foreign countries as well as the U.S., are companies which mine and refine silver, fabricators and manufacturers of products containing silver.
Publications:
Modern Silver Coinage. a.
Silver Institute News. bi-m.
Silver Mine Production - Worldwide. a.
World Silver Survey. a.
Meetings/Conferences:
1999 – Scottsdale, AZ/March 28-30

Silver Users Ass'n (1947)
1730 M St., N.W., Suite 911
Washington, DC 20036-4505
Tel: (202)785-3050   *Fax:* (202)659-5760
Toll Free: (800)245 - 6999
Members: 30 companies
Staff: 1
Annual Budget: $50-100,000
Exec. V. President & Secretary: Walter L. Frankland, Jr.
Historical Note
Founded in 1947 and incorporated in Washington, DC in April, 1971, the Silver Users Ass'n represents manufacturers and distributors of products in which silver is an essential element, such as photographic materials, medical and dental supplies, batteries and electronic and electrical equipment, silverware, mirrors, commemorative art and jewelry. SUA works for the recognition of silver as a commodity and the removal of governmental regulations which retard its free exchange in commerce both foreign and domestic. To help provide a stable trading climate in the metal, it monitors the silver market to insure that silver information available to the industry and public is accurate. Membership: annual dues vary according to silver usage and company share.
Publications:
U. S.
Meetings/Conferences:
Annual Meetings: Semi-Annual Meetings
1999 – Washington, DC(Army Navy Club)

Single Ply Roofing Institute (1982)
200 Reservoir St., Suite 309-A
Needham Heights, MA 02194
Tel: (781)444-0242   *Fax:* (781)444-6111
E-Mail: spri@spri.org
Web Site: http://www.spri.org
Members: 43 companies
Staff: 4
Annual Budget: $250-500,000
Managing Director: Linda King
Historical Note
Established in Illinois, SPRI is comprised of manufacturers and marketers of sheet-applied membrane roofing materials and supplies to the industry. Membership: $7,500/year (organization/company).
Publications:
A Professional's Guide to Specifications. a.
Sprinfo. q.

Meetings/Conferences:
Annual Meetings: January
1999 – Tucson, AZ(Omni National)
2000 – St. Peterburg, FL
2001 – Indian Wells, CA(Renaissance Esmeralda)

Singles Press Ass'n (1986)
P.O. Box 6243
Scottsdale, AZ 85261
Tel: (602)945-6746
Members: 32 companies
Annual Budget: under $10,000
Information Coordinator: Janet L. Jacobsen
Historical Note
SPA members are publishers of periodicals for singles. Membership: $75/year.
Publications:
SPA Newsletter. m.
Meetings/Conferences:
Semi-annual Meetings: May and November

Ski Industries of America (1954)
Historical Note
Became SnowSports Industries of America in 1997.

Sleep Disorders Dental Soc. (1990)
10592 Perry Hwy., Suite 220
Wexford, PA 15090-9244
Tel: (724)935-0836   *Fax:* (724)935-0383
Members: 500 individuals
Staff: 1
Annual Budget: $10-25,000
Exec. Director: Mary Beth Rogers
Historical Note
SDDS works to facilitate a coordinated synergistic approach with the medical community for research, treatment, education and professional development in the utilization of dental appliances as an integral part of overall therapy in the treatment of sleep disorders. Membership: $115/year, plus processing fee ($50) for new members.
Publications:
SDDS Newsletter. q.
Meetings/Conferences:
Annual Meetings: June

Sleep Research Soc. (1961)
Dept. of Neurology, Cleveland Clinic Fdn
9500 Euclid Ave., Desk S-83
Cleveland, OH 44195
Tel: (216)444-8275   *Fax:* (216)445-7471
E-Mail: mendelw@ccfadm.eeg.ccf.org
Members: 500 individuals
Staff: 1
Annual Budget: $25-50,000
President: Dr. Wallace B. Mendelson
Historical Note
Founded as Ass'n for the Psychophysiological Study of Sleep, it assumed its present name in 1983. SRS provides a forum for dialogue and cross-fertilization among sleep researchers. A constituent society of the Ass'n of Professional Sleep Socs. Membership: $145/year (individual).
Publications:
Membership Directory.
Newsletter. q.
Sleep. bi-m. adv.
Sleep Research. a.
Meetings/Conferences:
Annual Meetings: In conjunction with the Ass'n of Professional
        Sleep Socs.

Small Antique Restoration Ass'n (1987)
26491 Plotts Ave.
Worthington, MN 56187
Tel: (507)372-2717
Members: 500 individuals
Staff: 4
Annual Budget: $10-25,000
Exec. Director: LaVonne Lutterman
Historical Note
Formerly (1996) Internat'l Doll Restoration Artists Ass'n. Members are individuals specializing in the restoration of small antiques in the private sector. Purpose is chiefly educational; activities include educational workshops, seminars, and certification programs. Membership: $21/year.
Publications:
IDRAA Workshop. q. adv.
Meetings/Conferences:
Annual Meetings: Quarterly Board Meetings

Small Business Alliance on Communications (1991)
Historical Note
Address unknown in 1996.

Small Business Capital Ass'n
1030 15th St., N.W., Suite 870
Washington, DC 20005
Tel: (202)393-1780   *Fax:* (202)393-0336
Members: 40 individuals
Staff: 2
Director: Valerie Bergman Cooper

Small Business Council of America (1979)
4800 Hampden Lane, 7th Floor
Bethesda, MD 20814
Tel: (301)656-7603   *Fax:* (301)654-7354
Members: 700 business entities & individuals
Chair: Paula A. Calimafde

Small Business Exporters Ass'n

Historical Note
SBCA is a national organization exclusively representing the federal tax and employee benefit interests of small business. SBCA's primary goals are to prevent federal tax laws from becoming more burdensome on small businesses and their owners and to support legislation which creates needed economic incentives. Membership: $150/year (individual).

Publications:
News Flashes. irreg.
SBCA Alert. q.
SBCA Member and Congressional Directory. a.
Washington Audio Hotline. bi-m.

Meetings/Conferences:
Annual Meetings: always Washington, DC in May and Mid-Year Meeting

Small Business Exporters Ass'n (1990)
1350 Beverly Road, Suite 617
McLean, VA 22101-3924
Tel: (703)761-4140   *Fax:* (703)761-4151
E-Mail: eduggan126@aol.com
Web Site: http://www.sbea.org
President and C.E.O.: E. Martin Duggan

Historical Note
Members are exporters with fewer than 700 employees and servicers of the industry. Membership $250-500/year (corporate); $70-120/year (individual).

Publications:
SBEA This Week Fax Newsletter. w.

Small Business Legislative Council (1976)
Historical Note
Address unknown in 1998.

Small Hydro Soc. (1979)
Historical Note
Defunct in 1987.

Small Independent Record Manufacturers' Ass'n (1980)
Historical Note
Members are minority-owned record companies grossing less than $250,000 per year. Membership: $25-200/yr. Membership: $50/year (individual); $75/year (company).

Small Luxury Hotels (1985)
1716 Banks St.
Houston, TX 77098-5402
Tel: (713)522-9512   *Fax:* (713)524-7412
Toll Free: (800)525 - 4800
E-Mail: gracie@uetropolis.net
Web Site: http://www.slh.com
Members: 240 hotels
Staff: 3
Manager, Marketing & Communications: Gracie Hamilton-Canvar

Historical Note
Founded as Small Luxury Hotels and Resorts in 1985, the organization became Small Luxury Hotels of the World following a merger with Prestige Hotels. The present name was assumed in 1991. Members are independently owned and managed deluxe hotels with less than 200 rooms.

Publications:
Annual Membership Directory. a. adv.
Meetings & Incentives Guide. a.
SLH Update. q.

Small Motors and Motion Ass'n (1975)
P.O. Box 378
4 Hollis St.
Sherborn, MA 01770-0378
Tel: (508)655-4409   *Fax:* (508)651-3920
Members: 190 companies
Staff: 3
Annual Budget: $250-500,000
Exec. Director: Elizabeth Bevington-Chambers
Operations Director: W.H. Chambers

Historical Note
Users, suppliers, and original equipment manufacturers of fractional and sub-fractional horsepower motors. Formerly (1993) Small Motor Manufacturers' Ass'n.

Publications:
Membership Directory. a.
Motor Market Statistics. q.
Newsletter. q.
Operations Survey. a.
Wafe and Fringe Benefits Survey. a.

Meetings/Conferences:
Semi-annual Meetings: Spring and Fall
1999 – Asheville, NC(Grove Park Inn)/May 5-7

Small Publishers Ass'n of North America (1996)
P.O. Box 1306-EA
Buena Vista, CO 81211-1306
Tel: (719)395-4790   *Fax:* (719)395-8374
E-Mail: SPAN@SPANnet.org
Web Site: http://www.SPANnet.org
Staff: 1
Annual Budget: $100-250,000
Exec. Director: Marilyn Ross

Historical Note
SPAN members are small presses, self-publishers, authors and vendors offering products or services to the industry. Provides education and marketing opportunities to members, and discounts on freight, etc. Membership: $95/year (U.S.); $95/year (Canada).

Publications:
Membership Directory. a. adv.
SPAN Connection. m. adv.

Meetings/Conferences:
Annual Meetings: September
1999 – Denver, CO

Smart Card Industry Ass'n (1989)
191 Clarksville Road
Lawrenceville, NJ 08648
Tel: (609)799-5654   *Fax:* (609)799-7032
Toll Free: (800)848 - 7242
E-Mail: dcunningham@scia.com
Web Site: http://www.scia.org
Members: 84 companies
Staff: 6
Annual Budget: $100-250,000
President and C.E.O.: Daniel A. Cunningham
Ass'n Manager: Lynn M. Russo

Historical Note
SCIA represents manufacturers of electronic transaction systems. Associate members are resellers, card issuers, and other interested companies. Supersedes Associated Users of Smart Cardsystems and Technologies. Membership: $500-2,000/year.

Publications:
Smart Link. bi-m.

Meetings/Conferences:
Annual Meetings: February

Smelter Control Research Ass'n
Historical Note
Six copper, lead and zinc producers. Has no paid staff or permanent office. Administrative support, when needed, is provided by the American Bureau of Metal Statistics.

Smelter Environment Research Ass'n
Historical Note
Ten to fifteen copper, lead and zinc producers. Has no paid staff or permanent office. Intermittently becomes inactive. Administrative support, when needed, is provided by the American Bureau of Metal Statistics.

Smocking Arts Guild of America (1979)
1926 Waukegan Road, Suite #1
Glenview, IL 60025-1770
Tel: (847)657-6804   *Fax:* (847)657-6819
E-Mail: sagahg@tcag.com
Members: 3,200 individuals
Staff: 3
Annual Budget: $250-500,000
Exec. Director: Patricia Sistler
Director, Member Services: Janice Wangman

Historical Note
The purpose of SAGA is to preserve and foster the art of smocking and related needlework for future generations through education, communication, and quality workmanship. Membership: $28/year (domestic); $32/year (foreign & Canada).

Publications:
SAGA News. q.

Meetings/Conferences:
Annual Meetings: Fall

Smokeless Tobacco Council (1968)
1627 K St., N.W., Suite 700
Washington, DC 20006
Tel: (202)452-1252   *Fax:* (202)452-0118
Members: 5 companies
Staff: 10
Annual Budget: $5-10,000,000
President: Robert Maples
V. President, Administration: Mary V. Mock

Historical Note
Formerly (1971) Snuff Producers Council. Media source and information bureau for producers of snuff and chewing (smokeless) tobacco. STC has an annual budget of approximately $5.5 million.

Snack Food Ass'n (1937)
1711 King St., Suite 1
Alexandria, VA 22314-2720
Tel: (703)836-4500   *Fax:* (703)836-8262
Toll Free: (800)628 - 1334
E-Mail: SFA@SFA.ORG
Web Site: http://www.snax.com
Members: 800 companies
Staff: 16
Annual Budget: $2-5,000,000
President: James W. Shufelt
V.P., Communications: Ann Wilkes
Sr. V.P., Govt. Relations: James McCarthy
Dir., Meetings: Thomas Morano
Director, Administration: Elizabeth Wells
Controller: Bruce Monk
V.P., Mktg./Member Programs: Judith Barth
Membership Adminsitrator: Liz Tutwiller

Historical Note
Formerly (1976) the Potato Chip Institute Internat'l and (1985) the Potato Chip/Snack Food Ass'n. Represents manufacturers of snacks made from vegetables, grains, fruits, meats and nuts. Supports the Snack Political Action Committee (SnackPAC). Membership: annual dues vary, based on sales (company).

Publications:
Membership Buyer's Guide. a.
Snack World. m. adv.
Who's Who Membership Directory. a. adv.

Meetings/Conferences:
Annual Meetings: February-March
1999 – Atlanta, GA(World Congress Center)/March 6-9
2000 – Philadelphia, PA(Convention Center)/March 18-21

Snow Control Equipment Manufacturers Committee
Historical Note
An affiliate of the Nat'l Truck Equipment Council.

SnowSports Industries America (1954)
8377-B Greensboro Drive
McLean, VA 22102-3587
Tel: (703)556-9020   *Fax:* (703)821-8276
Web Site: http://www.snowlink.com
Members: 1,200 companies
Staff: 24
Annual Budget: $2-5,000,000
President: David J. Ingemie
Director, Public Relations and Communications: Mary Jo Tarallo
Director, Association Services and Government Affairs: Lisa Pierce
Director, Trade Show Operations: Debbie Brown DesRoches
Director, Education & Special Interests: Roger Lohr
Associate Director, Research: John Packer
Director, Operations & Finance: Guy L. Abernathey
Director, Marketing and Sales: Bill Travis
Publications and On-line Media Manager: Andrew Williams

Historical Note
Formerly (1997) Ski Industries of America. SIA is the national trade association of ski/snowboard and outdoor sports product manufacturers and distributors. Merged with the Nat'l Ski Areas Ass'n in 1989 to form the United Ski Industries Ass'n. In 1992 SIA again became an independent trade association upon the dissolution of USIA. Membership: dues based on sales volume.

Publications:
SIA Member Update. m.
SIA Retailer & Rep Advisor. q.
SIA Trade Show Directory. a.

Meetings/Conferences:
1999 – Las Vegas, NV/March 9-13

Soap and Detergent Ass'n (1926)
475 Park Avenue South
New York, NY 10016
Tel: (212)725-1262   *Fax:* (212)213-0685
Web Site: http://www.sdahq.org
Members: 140 companies
Staff: 20
Annual Budget: $2-5,000,000
President: Gerald R. Pslug, Ph.D.
Director of Communications: Janet Donohue
Public Affairs Director: Dennis C. Griesing
Coordinator, Conventions and Director Membership: Rose Api

Historical Note
Formerly Ass'n of American Soap & Glycerine Producers. Four divisions: Household; Industrial & Institutional; Technical & Materials; Glycerine & Oleochemical.

Publications:
SDA Newsletter. bi-w.

Meetings/Conferences:
Annual Meetings: Boca Raton in January
1999 – Boca Raton, FL/Feb. 3-7

Soc. for a Science of Clinical Psychology
Historical Note
A section of the American Psychological Ass'n - Clinical Psychology Division.

Soc. for Academic Emergency Medicine (1970)
901 N. Washington Ave.
Lansing, MI 48906
Tel: (517)485-5484   *Fax:* (517)485-0801
Web Site: http://www.saem.org
Members: 4,500 individuals
Staff: 5
Annual Budget: $1-2,000,000
Exec. Director: Mary Ann Schropp

Historical Note
Formerly (1977) the University Ass'n for Emergency Medicine. Merged with the Soc. of Teachers of Emergency Medicine in 1988. Dedicated to promoting research and education in emergency medicine. Membership open to physicians, nurses, allied health professionals, and those interested in academic emergency medicine. Membership: $60-295/year.

Publications:
Academic Emergency Medicine. m. adv.
SAEM Newsletter. m. adv.

Meetings/Conferences:
Annual Meetings: May
1999 – Boston, MA(Marriott)/May 20-23

Soc. for Adolescent Medicine (1968)
1916 N.W. Copper Oaks Circle
Blue Springs, MO 64015-8300
Tel: (816)224-8010   *Fax:* (816)224-8009
Web Site: http://cortex.uchc.edu/~sam/
Members: 1,300 individuals
Staff: 2
Administrative Director: Edie Moore

Historical Note
SAM members are professionals throughout the world who are involved in service, teaching, or research concerned with the health and well-being of adolescents including doctors, nurses, social workers, and psychologists. Membership: $150/year, doctoral level (individual); $105/year non-doctoral level (individual).

Publications:
Journal of Adolescent Health. m. adv.
SAM Newsletter. q.

Meetings/Conferences:
Annual Meetings: Spring
1999 – Los Angeles, CA(Century Plaza)/March 17-21
2000 – Arlington, VA(Marriott)

Soc. for Advancement of Management (1912)
Texas A&M University-Corpus Christi
Col of Business, 6300 Ocean Dr., FC111
Corpus Christi, TX 78412-5503
Tel: (512)994-6045   *Fax:* (512)994-2725

Members: 6,500 individuals
Staff: 2
Annual Budget: $100-250,000
Presdient & C.E.O.: Dr. Moustafa H. Abdelsamad
Director of Operations: Mervat M. Abdelsamad

Historical Note
A professional organization of management executives, it was formed by a merger of the Taylor Soc. and the Soc. of Industrial Engineers; Absorbed the Industrial Methods Soc. in 1946. Merged in 1973 with the American Management Ass'n, Inc. (1923), the American Foundation for Management Research, Inc. (1960), the Internat'l Management Ass'n, Inc., and the Presidents Ass'n, Inc. (1961), to form the American Management Ass'ns, of which it was a semi-autonomous division. SAM returned to independent status on July 1, 1983 and is no longer affiliated with American Management Ass'ns. Membership: $75/year (individual).

Publications:
Conference Program Book. a. adv.
Management in Practice. q.
SAM Advanced Management Journal. q.
SAM News Internat'l.

Meetings/Conferences:
1999 – Las Vegas, NV(Harra's Hotel)/March 28-30/500

Soc. for Ambulatory Care Professionals (1986)
One N. Franklin
Chicago, IL 60606
Tel: (312)422-3900   *Fax:* (312)422-4577
Web Site: http://www.sacp-net.org
Members: 1,250 individuals
Staff: 3
Annual Budget: $500-1,000,000
Exec. Director: Christopher Damon

Historical Note
Membership: $135/year (member); $250/year (consultant); $45/year (student).

Publications:
Ambulatory Outreach. q.
SACP Directory of Ambulatory Care Consultants. a.
SACP Membership Directory. a.
SACP News. 8/yr.

Meetings/Conferences:
Annual Meetings: Spring
1999 – Chicago, IL(Hyatt Regency)/April 28-30

Soc. for American Archaeology (1934)
900 2nd St., N.E., Suite 12
Washington, DC 20002-3557
Tel: (202)789-8200   *Fax:* (202)789-0284
E-Mail: headquarters@saa.org
Web Site: http://www.saa.org
Members: 6,500 individuals
Staff: 9
Annual Budget: $1-2,000,000
Exec. Director: Tobi A. Brimsek, CAE
Manager, Government Affairs and Counsel: Donald F. Craib
Mgr., Public Education: Dr. Dorothy Krass
Manager, Accounting Services: Leon Bathini
Manager, Membership & Marketing: Rick Peterson
Manager, Publications: Elizabeth Foxwell
Manager, Information Services: Jim Young

Historical Note
SAA is an international organization dedicated to the research, interpretation and protection of the archaeological heritage of the Americas. SAA members include student, avocational and professional archaeologists working in a variety of settings including government agencies, colleges and universities, museums and the private sector. Membership: $110/year (regular); $50/year (student); $57/year (retired); $34/year (associate).

Publications:
American Antiquity Journal. q. adv.
Latin American Antiquity Journal. q. adv.
SAA Bulletin. 5/year. adv.

Meetings/Conferences:
Annual Meetings: Spring
1999 – Chicago, IL/March 24-28
2000 – Philadelphia, PA/April 5-9

Soc. for American Baseball Research (1971)
812 Huron Rd. East #719
Cleveland, OH 44115
Tel: (216)575-0500   *Fax:* (216)575-0502
E-Mail: info@sabr.org
Members: 6,700 individuals
Staff: 3
Annual Budget: $250-500,000
Exec. Director: Morris Eckhouse

Historical Note
Membership: $50/year (individual), $300/year (organization/company).

Publications:
Baseball Research Journal. a.
SABR Membership Directory. semi-a. adv.
The National Pastime. a. adv.
The SABR Bulletin. 8-12/year. adv.

Meetings/Conferences:
1999 – Boca Raton, FL(Raddison Resort)/June 0-50

Soc. for Ancient Greek Philosophy (1953)
Binghamton Univ., Dept. of Philosophy
Binghamton, NY 13902-6000
Tel: (607)777-2886   *Fax:* (607)777-2734
E-Mail: apreus@bingvmb.cc.binghamton.edu
Web Site: http://www.philosophy.binghamton.edu
Members: 500 individuals
Annual Budget: under $10,000
Secretary-Treasurer: Anthony Preus

Historical Note
SAGP members are academics and others with an interest in classical philosophy. Membership: $10/year (individual).

Publications:
Newsletter. q. adv.

Meetings/Conferences:

Soc. for Anthropology in Community Colleges (1978)
Historical Note
A section of the American Anthropological Ass'n. Established to stimulate communication among anthropologists and teachers of anthropology in community colleges, colleges and pre-collegiate institutions.

Soc. for Applied Anthropology (1941)
P.O. Box 24083
Oklahoma City, OK 73124-0083
Tel: (405)843-5113   *Fax:* (405)843-8553
E-Mail: sfaa@telepath.com
Web Site: http://www.telepath.com/sfaa
Members: 2,500 individuals
Staff: 2
Annual Budget: $250-500,000
Exec. Director: J. Thomas May

Historical Note
Promotes the interdisciplinary scientific study of the principles controlling the relations of human beings to one another, and the wide application of those principles to practical problems. Membership: $42/year (individual); $60/year (institution).

Publications:
Human Organization. q.
Newsletter. q.
Practicing Anthropology. q.

Meetings/Conferences:
Annual Meetings: Spring
1999 – Tucson, AZ(Inn Suites)/April 20-25

Soc. for Applied Learning Technology (1972)
50 Culpeper St.
Warrenton, VA 20186
Tel: (540)347-0055   *Fax:* (540)349-3169
Toll Free: (800)457 - 6812
E-Mail: raymond_fox@salt.org
Web Site: http:www.salt.org
Members: 1,150 individuals
Staff: 2
Annual Budget: $250-500,000
President: Raymond G. Fox

Historical Note
Founded in Washington, DC in 1972. Members include industrial, military and academic managers involved in the design production or use of technology-based educational systems. Membership: $45/year.

Publications:
Journal of Educational Technology Systems. q.
Journal of Instruction Delivery Systems.
Journal of Interactive Instruction Development. q.
SALT Newsletter. q.

Meetings/Conferences:
Semi-Annual Meetings: February and August
1999 – Arlington, VA(Marriott)/July 7-9

Soc. for Applied Sociology (1978)
c/o Anne Arundel Community College
101 College Parkway
Arnold, MD 21012
Tel: (410)541-2369   *Fax:* (410)541-2239
E-Mail: ssteele@clark.net
Members: 425 individuals and companies
Staff: 1
Annual Budget: $25-50,000
Exec. Officer: Stephen Steele
Administrative Officer: Teri Kepner

Historical Note
The Society for Applied Sociology is an international organization for professionals involved in providing a forum for sociologists to apply their knowledge, enhancing understanding of knowledge and practice, and in increasing the practical use of research and training. Membership: $65/year (individual); $100/year (organization/company).

Publications:
Journal of Applied Sociology. a.
Social Insight: Knowledge at Work. a.
The Useful Sociologist Newsletter. 3/yr. adv.

Meetings/Conferences:
Annual Meetings: October

Soc. for Applied Spectroscopy (1958)
201-B Broadway St.
Frederick, MD 21701-6501
Tel: (301)694-8122   *Fax:* (301)694-6860
E-Mail: sasoffice@aol.com
Web Site: http://www.s-a-s.org
Members: 3,200 individuals
Staff: 2
Annual Budget: $500-1,000,000
Exec. Director: Bonnie Saylor

Historical Note
The Federation of Spectroscopic Societies was founded in Pittsburgh in March 1956. From this grew the Society for Applied Spectroscopy established in New York in November 1958 and incorporated in Pennsylvania in 1960. Affiliated with the Iron and Steel Chemists Association, the Fourier Transform Spectroscopy Group, the Coblentz Soc., and the Council for Infrared. Membership: $76/year (U.S. individual), $300-1,200/year (corporate sponsors), $117/year (foreign).

Publications:
Applied Spectroscopy. 12/year. adv.

Directory.
Newsletter. semi.

Meetings/Conferences:
Annual Meetings: Fall
1999 – Vancouver, BC, Canada

Soc. for Archaeological Studies (1977)
c/o Anthropology Dept.
Univ. of California
Riverside, CA 92521
Tel: (909)787-5524   *Fax:* (909)787-5409
E-Mail: RETaylor@UCRAC1.UCR.edu
Web Site: http://www.wisc.edu/anthropology/sas/sas.htm
Members: 600 individuals
Annual Budget: $10-25,000
General Secretary: R.E. Taylor

Historical Note
SAS was founded to provide for communication between scholars applying methods from the physical sciences to archaeological questions. Members are archaeological scientists working in business, academic, and government settings. Membership: $75/year.

Publications:
Advances in Archaeological and Museum Science.
Journal of Archaeological Science.
SAS Bulletin.

Soc. for Asian Music (1959)
Cornell Univ., Dept. of Music
Lincoln Hall
Ithaca, NY 14853
Tel: (607)255-5049   *Fax:* (607)254-2877
E-Mail: mfh2@cornell.edu
Web Site: http://asianmusic.skidmore.edu
Members: 500 individuals
Annual Budget: $10-25,000
Treasurer, Editor: Marty Hatch

Historical Note
SAM members are academics and others with an interest in the music of the middle and far east. Has no paid officers or full-time staff. Membership: $25/year (individual).

Publications:
Asian Music Journal. semi-a.

Soc. for Assisted Reproductive Technology (1987)
1209 Montgomery Hwy.
Birmingham, AL 35216-2809
Tel: (205)978-5000   *Fax:* (205)978-5005
E-Mail: joyce@asrm.org
Members: 344 institutions
Administrator: Joyce Zeitz

Historical Note
Members are practices facilities offering assisted reproductive procedures. Administrative support provided by the American Soc. of Reproductive Medicine. Membership:$25(individual); $800(organization).

Meetings/Conferences:
Annual Meetings: with the American Soc. for Reproductive Medicine.
1999 – Toronto, Canada
1999 – San Diego, CA/Sept. 25-29
2000 – San Diego, CA/Oct. 21-25
2001 – Orlando Fl/Oct. 20-24

Soc. for Behavioral Pediatrics
Historical Note
Became Soc. for Developmental and Behavioral Pediatrics in 1995.

Soc. for Bioethics Consultation (1985)
Historical Note
Organization defunct in 1997.

Soc. for Biomaterials (1974)
13355 10th Ave., N., #108
Minneapolis, MN 55441-5510
Tel: (612)543-0908   *Fax:* (612)545-0335
E-Mail: member@biomaterials.org
Web Site: http://www.biomaterials.org
Members: 1,900 individuals
Staff: 4
Exec. Director: Rosealee M. Lee

Historical Note
The Society for Biomaterials was incorporated as a non-profit organization in 1974. Serves to promote research, development, and education in the biomaterial sciences. Seeks to cooperate with scientific organizations, private industry, government agencies, and other interested parties, to establish the standards and test methods for biomaterials. Members are scientists, surgeons, dentists and others interested in the problems of developing replacements for living tissue. A member society of the American Institute for Medical and Biological Engineering. Membership: $180/year (individual).

Publications:
BioMaterials Forum. bi-m. adv.
Journal of Applied Biomaterials. q. adv.
Journal of Biomedical Materials Research. 16/year. adv.

Meetings/Conferences:
Annual Meetings: Spring
1999 – Providence, RI(Rhode Island Conven. Center)/April 28-May 2/1500
2000 – Kamuela, HI(Hilton Waholoa)/May 15-20/2000
2001 – St. Paul, MN(St. Paul Hotel/River Centre)

Soc. for Biomedical Equipment Technicians (1976)
c/o AAMI, 3330 Washington Blvd., Suite 400
Arlington, VA 22201-4598
Tel: (703)525-4890   *Fax:* (703)276-0793
Members: 1,100 individuals
Staff: 2
Annual Budget: under $10,000

Exec. Director: Michael J. Miller, J.D., CAE

Historical Note
Sponsored by the Ass'n for the Advancement of Medical Instrumentation to recognize biomedial equipment technicians as a specialty group. Sponsors a certification program (administered by AAMI) in which the designation "CBET" (Certified Biomedical Equipment Technician) is awarded. Membership: $65/year (individual).

Publications:
AAMI Membership Directory. a. adv.
AAMI News Newsletter. m. adv.
Biomedical Instrumentation & Technology. bi-m. adv.
Medical Device Research Report Newsletter. m. adv.

Meetings/Conferences:
Annual Meetings: Spring/2,500
1999 – Boston, MA/June 5-9
2000 – San Jose, CA/June 3-7

Soc. for Biomolecular Screening (1994)
36 Tamarack Ave., Suite 348
Danbury, CT   06811
Tel: (203)743-1336   *Fax:* (203)748-7557
E-Mail: c_giordano@prodigy.com
Web Site: http://www.SBSONLINE.ORG
Members: 1,080 individuals, 230 companies
Staff: 3
Annual Budget: $250-500,000
Exec. Director: Christine Giordano

Historical Note
Supports research and discovery in pharmaceutical biotechnology and the agrichemical industry that utilize chemical screening procedures. Membership: $125/year.

Publications:
Journal of Biomolecular Screening. q. adv.

Meetings/Conferences:
Annual Meetings: Fall
1999 – Edinburg, Scotland/Sept. 13-16
2000 – West Coast
2001 – West Coast

Soc. for Buddhist-Christian Studies
c/o Coun. of Soc. for Study of Religion
Valparaiso University
Valparaiso, IN   46383-6493
Tel: (219)464-6714   *Fax:* (219)464-6714
E-Mail: pam.gleason@valpo.edu
Web Site: www.cssr.org
Members: 500 individuals
Exec. Assistant: Pam Gleason

Historical Note
Members of the society provide an ongoing format and organization for those committed to study and practice of Buddhism and Christianity.

Publications:
Buddhist-Christian Studies Journal. a.
Newsletter. bi.

Meetings/Conferences:
1999 – Boston, MA

Soc. for Business Ethics (1979)
The American College
270 Bryn Mawr Ave.
Bryn Mawr, PA   19010-0219
Tel: (610)526-1387
E-Mail: RDuska@aol.com
Web Site: http://www.luc.edu/depts/business/sbe/index.htm
Members: 800 individuals
Staff: 1
Annual Budget: $25-50,000
Exec. Director: Ronald F. Duska

Historical Note
SBE members are academics and practitioners (such as ethics and compliance officers) and other interested in the field. Membership: $50/year (individual), $98/year (organization/company), $25/year (students and retirees).

Publications:
Business Ethics Quarterly. q.
SBE Newsletter. q.

Meetings/Conferences:
Annual Meetings: August, in conjunction with the Academy of Management
1999 – Chicago, IL(Knickerbocker Hotel)

Soc. for Cardiac Angiography and Interventions (1978)
4101 Lake Boone Trail
Suite 201
Raleigh, NC   27607-6518
Tel: (919)787-5181   *Fax:* (919)787-4916
Toll Free: (800)992 - 7224
Members: 1,200 individuals
Staff: 3
Annual Budget: $500-1,000,000
Exec. Director: Mary Alice Dilday

Historical Note
Membership: $175-335/year.

Publications:
Catheterization and Cardiovascular Diagnosis. m. adv.
News Highlights. 3/year.

Meetings/Conferences:
Annual Meetings: May
1999 – Montrey, CA(Hyatt Regency)/May 12-15
2000 – Charleston, SC(Charleston Place)/May 2-6

Soc. for Cardiovascular Magnetic Resonance
19 Mantua Road
Mount Royal, NJ   08061
Tel: (609)423-7222   *Fax:* (609)423-3420

Members: 230 individuals
Staff: 5
Annual Budget: $250-500,000
Exec. Director: Dale Zeigler

Historical Note
SCMR acts as an information resource for medical practitioners who are interested in applications of magnetic resonance in diagnosis of heart and circulatory conditions. Membership: $90/year (full member); $50/year (associate); $75/year (technologist).

Meetings/Conferences:
Semi-Annual Meetings: Spring and Fall

Soc. for Chaos Theory in Psychology and Life Sciences (1990)
Dept. of Psychology,
U. of Maryland-UMBC
Baltimore, MD   21250
Tel: (615)322-0600   *Fax:* (615)343-8449
E-Mail: keith.n.clayton@vanderbilt.edu
Web Site:
    http://www.vanderbilt.edu/ans/psychology/cogsci/chaos
Members: 300 individuals, 3 organizations
Annual Budget: under $10,000
Secretary: Mary Ann Metzger

Historical Note
An international forum. Membership: $60/year.

Publications:
Nonlinear Dynamics, Psychology & Life Sciences. q. adv.

Meetings/Conferences:
Annual Meetings: Summer

Soc. for Cinema Studies (1960)
English Department
University of Pittsburgh
Pittsburgh, PA   15213
Members: 1,200 individuals
Annual Budget: $25-50,000
Treasurer: Marcia Landy

Historical Note
An association of scholars and teachers devoted to the study of film, television and related media. SCS's main activity is scholarly interchange through its quarterly journal and annual conference. Membership: $45-50/year; $25/year (student).

Publications:
Cinema Journal. q. adv.

Meetings/Conferences:
Annual Meetings: Spring

Soc. for Clinical and Experimental Hypnosis (1949)
2201 Haeder Rd., Suite 1
Pullman, WA   99163-0619
Tel: (509)332-7555   *Fax:* (509)332-5907
E-Mail: sceh@pullman.com
Members: 900 individuals
Annual Budget: $100-250,000
Exec. Director: Cindy Scott

Historical Note
Founded June 12, 1949 and incorporated in New York in 1963. Affiliated with the American Ass'n for the Advancement of Science, the World Federation for Mental Health and the Internat'l Soc. of Hypnosis. Membership: $125/year.

Publications:
International Journal of Clinical and Experimental Hypnosis. q. adv.
SCEH Newsletter. q.

Meetings/Conferences:
Annual Meetings: Annually in November San Diego, CA/Nov.
1999 – New Orleans, LA(Doubletree)/Nov. 10-13

Soc. for Clinical Data Management (1994)
170 Township Line Road
Belle Mead, NJ   08502-4103
Tel: (908)359-0623   *Fax:* (908)359-7619
Members: 800 individuals
Annual Budget: $100-250,000
Exec. Director: Joanne J. Cole, CMP, CAE

Historical Note
Members are researchers and consultants involved in clinical trials results and data collection. Membership: $45/year.

Publications:
Databasics. q.

Meetings/Conferences:
1999 – San Diego, CA
1999 – Chicago, IL

Soc. for Clinical Trials (1978)
600 Wyndhurst Ave.
Baltimore, MD   21210-2425
Tel: (410)433-4722   *Fax:* (410)435-8631
E-Mail: sctbalt@aol.com
Members: 2,200 individuals
Staff: 1
Annual Budget: $50-100,000
Coordinator: Mary C. Burke

Historical Note
Incorporated in the State of Maryland. SCT members are involved in the controlled medical testing of procedures, drugs and other therapeutic agents. Membership: $72/year (individual); $40/year (student).

Publications:
Controlled Clinical Trials. bi-m. adv.

Meetings/Conferences:
Annual Meetings: Spring
1999 – Anaheim, CA(Marriott)/May 2-5/1000

Soc. for Clinical Vascular Surgery (1970)
13 Elm St.
Manchester, MA   01944
Tel: (978)526-8330   *Fax:* (978)526-4018
E-Mail: scvs@prri.com
Members: 860 individuals
Annual Budget: $100-250,000
Exec. Director: Kevin M. Cuff

Historical Note
Membership: $150/year.

Publications:
American Journal of Surgery. q. adv.

Meetings/Conferences:
Annual Meetings: March/450
1999 – Orlando, FL(Hilton Disney Village)/March 24-28/450
2000 – Rancho Mirage, CA(Westin Mission Hills)/March 15-18/450

Soc. for College and University Planning (1965)
4251 Plymouth Road, Suite D
Ann Arbor, MI   48105-2785
Tel: (734)998-7832   *Fax:* (734)998-6532
E-Mail: scup@umich.edu
Web Site: http://wwww.scup.org
Members: 4,200 individuals
Staff: 10
Annual Budget: $1-2,000,000
Exec. Director: Jolene Knapp
Director, Professional Development: Kathleen Benton
Director of Business Operations: Linda Halliburton
Director, Membership Services: Gundi Gaiser
Director, Print Publications: Sharon Marioka
Assistant Director, Electronic Communications: Terry Calhoun

Historical Note
SCUP is focused on promotion, advancement, and application of effective planning in higher education. Represents college and university administrators and faculty, corporate executives, and government officials involved in planning. Membership: $135/year (individual), $65/year (student/retired); $445-$605/year, based on enrollment (postsecondary institution); $665/year (nonuniversity organization).

Publications:
Membership Directory. a.
Planning for Higher Education. q.
SCUP News. q.

Meetings/Conferences:
Annual Meetings: July
1999 – Atlanta, GA(Marriott Marquis)/July 24-28/1000

Soc. for Community Research and Action
Historical Note
The Division of Community Psychology of the American Psychological Ass'n.

Soc. for Computer Applications in Radiology
1891 Preston White Drive
Reston, VA   20191
Tel: (703)716-7548   *Fax:* (703)648-9176
E-Mail: scar@acr.org
Web Site: http://www.scar.rad.washington.edu/
Annual Budget: $2-5,000,000
Exec. Director: Anna Marie Mason

Historical Note
SCAR members are physicians and other health care professionals with an interest in the application of computers in medical imaging and designers/manufacturers of equipment. Membership: $125/year (individual); $60/year (student); $1,500/year (industrial sponsor).

Publications:
Directory. a.
Journal of Digital Imaging. q.
SCAR News Newsletter. q.

Meetings/Conferences:
1999 – Houston, TX(Westin Galleria)/May 6-9
2000 – Philadelphia, PA(University of Pennsylvania)

Soc. for Computer Simulation (1952)
Box 17900
San Diego, CA   92177-1810
Tel: (619)277-3888   *Fax:* (619)277-3930
E-Mail: info@scs.org
Web Site: http://www.scs.org
Members: 1,900 individuals
Staff: 8
Annual Budget: $1-2,000,000
Exec. Director: William S. Gallagher
Marketing & Conference: Steve Branch

Historical Note
Founded in Oxnard, CA in 1952 as the Simulation Council and incorporated in California in 1957 as Simulation Councils, Inc. Became Soc. for Computer Simulation in 1973. A sponsoring society of the American Automatic Control Council. SCS is a multidisciplinary organization dedicated to advancing the use of computer simulation to solve real world problems. Membership: $75/year(individual); $500-10,000/year(company).

Publications:
Simulation. m. adv.
Simulation Series. q.
Transactions. q.

Meetings/Conferences:

Soc. for Conceptual and Content Analysis by Computer (1983)
Department of German and Russian
Bowling Green State University
Bowling Green, OH   43403-0219
Tel: (419)372-7397   *Fax:* (419)372-2571
Members: 260 individuals

Annual Budget: under $10,000
Secretary: Prof. Klaus M. Schmidt

Historical Note
Established in Raleigh, NC, SCCAC is a loosely organized group, composed of scholars from various disciplines interested and active in the field of conceptual and content analysis of texts by computer.

Publications:
Membership List. a.
Newsletter. a.

Meetings/Conferences:
Annual Meetings: Biennial. Usually meets with a group with related interests.

Soc. for Conservation Biology *(1985)*
Univ. of Washington, Box 351800
Seattle, WA   98195-1800
Tel: (206)616-4054   *Fax:* (206)543-3041
E-Mail: conbio@u.washington.edu
Web Site: http://conbio.rice.edu/scb/
Members: 5,000 individuals
Staff: 1
President: P. Dee Boersma
Exec. Coordinator: Alice Blandin

Historical Note
SCB is a profession society of biologists with an interest in the protection of biological diversity. It seeks to help develop the scientific and technical means for the protection, maintenance and restoration of life on this planet – its species, its ecological and evolutionary processes, and its particular and total environment. Membership: $75.00/year (USA individual); $47/year (USA student).

Publications:
Conservation Biology Journal. bi-m. adv.

Meetings/Conferences:
Annual Meetings: Summer
1999 – College Park, MD(Univ of Maryland)/June 17-20
2000 – University of Montana/June 9-12

Soc. for Consumer Psychology
Historical Note
A division of the American Psychological Ass'n.

Soc. for Cross-Cultural Research *(1965)*
Dept. of Psychology
Univ. of Wisconsin
La Crosse, WI   54601
Tel: (608)785-6884   *Fax:* (608)785-8443
E-Mail: harry_gardiner@uwlax.edu
Members: 200 individuals
Annual Budget: under $10,000
Secretary-Treasurer: Harry W. Gardiner

Historical Note
An interdisciplinary organization whose primary goal is to support and encourage comparative research which will aid in the establishment of scientifically derived generalizations about human behavior. Members come from a wide variety of social, behavioral and scientific professions. Has no paid staff. Membership fee: $50/year (individual).

Publications:
Cross-Cultural Research. q. adv.
SCCR Newsletter. 3/year. adv.

Meetings/Conferences:
Annual Meetings: February
1999 – Santa Fe, NM(La Fonda Hotel)

Soc. for Cryobiology *(1964)*
c/o FASEB
9650 Rockville Pike
Bethesda, MD   20814-3998
Tel: (301)530-7120   *Fax:* (301)530-7049
Members: 400 individuals
Annual Budget: $50-100,000
Secretary: Dr. Richard E. Lee

Historical Note
Organized March 20, 1964 and incorporated the same year in Maryland. Concerned with all aspects of low temperature biology and medicine including studies of freezing, freeze-drying, cryoprotective additives and their pharmacological actions, medical applications of reduced temperature, cryosurgery, hypothermia, perfusion of organs, hibernation, frost hardiness in plants, and all pertinent methodologies. Membership: $100/year, with subscription (individual); $40/year, without subscription (individual); $230/year (institutional); $715/year (organization).

Publications:
Cryobiology. bi-m. adv.
News Notes. q. adv.

Meetings/Conferences:
Annual Meetings: Summer in a university setting

Soc. for Cultural Anthropology *(1983)*
Historical Note
A section of the American Anthropological Ass'n. SCA is a broad, multidisciplinary organization of individuals interested in cultural, psychological, and social interrelations at all levels.

Soc. for Developmental and Behavioral Pediatrics *(1982)*
19 Station Lane
Philadelphia, PA   19118-2939
Tel: (215)248-9168   *Fax:* (215)248-1981
E-Mail: nmspota@aol.com
Members: 620 individuals
Staff: 1
Annual Budget: $100-250,000
Administrative Director: Noreen M. Spota

Historical Note
Formerly (1995) Soc. for Behavioral Pediatrics. Members are pediatricians, child psychologists and other professionals with an interest in developmental and behavioral pediatrics. Aim of SDBP is to improve the health care of infants, children, and adolescents by promoting research and teaching in developmental and behavioral pediatrics. Membership: $140/year (regular); $85/year (trainee & non-doctorate).

Publications:
Journal of Developmental and Behavioral Pediatrics. bi-m. adv.

Meetings/Conferences:
1999 – Seattle, WA(Cavanaugh's Fifth Avenue)/Sept. 23-27
2000 – Providence, RI(Providence Biltmore)/Sept. 21-25

Soc. for Developmental Biology *(1939)*
9650 Rockville Pike
Bethesda, MD   20814-3998
Tel: (301)571-0647   *Fax:* (301)571-5704
E-Mail: ichow@faseb.org
Web Site: http://www.sdb.bio.purdue.edu
Members: 2,000 individuals
Staff: 1
Annual Budget: $250-500,000
Exec. Officer: Ida Chow, Ph.D.

Historical Note
Formerly (1939-1965) the Soc.for the study of Development and Growth. Membership: $45/year.

Publications:
Developmental Biology. bi-w. adv.
SDB Directory. a.

Meetings/Conferences:
1999 – Charlottesville, VA(Univ. of Virginia)/June 13-18/800

Soc. for Disability Studies *(1986)*
Sch of Social Science, U of TX at Dallas
Box 830688
Richardson, TX   75083-0688
Tel: (972)883-4122   *Fax:* (972)883-2735
E-Mail: sdshq@utdallas.edu
Web Site: www.uipd.com/sds
Members: 350 individuals
Staff: 1
Annual Budget: $25-50,000
Exec. Officer: Richard Scotch

Historical Note
SDS is an international scientific and educational organization with a multidisciplinary membership composed of scholars in the social sciences and humanities who study the problems of disabled people in society. Membership: $30-60/year, based on income (individual).

Publications:
Disability Studies Quarterly. q.
Proceedings. a.

Meetings/Conferences:
Annual Meetings: June/200
1999 – Arlington, VA/June 17-20

Soc. for Ear, Nose and Throat Advances in Children *(1973)*
2160 S. First Ave., Bldg. 105, Rm. 1870
Maywood, IL   60163
Tel: (708)216-9637   *Fax:* (708)216-4834
Members: 300 individuals
Annual Budget: $25-50,000
Secretary-Treasurer: Andrew Hottaling, M.D.

Historical Note
SENTAC members are physicians and other health professionals with an interest in pediatric speech, hearing, and otorhinolaryngology. Has no paid officers or full-time staff.

Publications:
Directory and Meeting Abstracts. a.

Meetings/Conferences:
Annual Meetings: December

Soc. for Ecological Restoration *(1988)*
1207 Seminole Hwy.
Madison, WI   53711
Tel: (608)262-9547   *Fax:* (608)265-8557
E-Mail: ser@macc.wisc.edu
Web Site: http://www.ser.org
Members: 2,800 individuals
Staff: 3
Exec. Director: Don Falk, Ph.D.
Operations Coordinator: Laura Hoefs

Historical Note
Formerly Soc. for Ecological Restoration and Management. SER are academics, scientists, environmental consultants, government agencies and others with an interest in ecological restoration. Membership: $179/year (corporate); $99/year (individual); $220/year (library); $76/year (student).

Publications:
Restoration and Management Notes. semi-a.
Restoration Ecology Journal. q.
SER News Newsletter. q.

Meetings/Conferences:
1999 – San Francisco, CA/Sept. 23-25

Soc. for Economic Botany *(1959)*
New York Botanical Gardens
Bronx, NY   10458-5126
Tel: (718)817-8632   *Fax:* (718)220-6783
E-Mail: bboom@nybg.org
Web Site: http://www.econbot.org
Members: 1,200 individuals
Annual Budget: under $10,000
Secretary: Brian M. Boom, Ph.D.

Historical Note
Promotes research on the past, present and future uses of plants. Has no paid staff. Membership: $50/year (individual); $60/year (family); $30/year (student).

Publications:
Economic Botany. q.

Meetings/Conferences:
Annual Meetings: Summer
1999 – St. Louis, MO/Aug. 1-7

Soc. for Education and Research in Psychiatric Mental Health Nursing *(1983)*
7794 Grow Drive
Pensacola, FL   32514
Tel: (850)484-9024   *Fax:* (850)484-8762
Members: 400 individuals
Annual Budget: $25-50,000
Exec. Director: Belinda E. Puetz, Ph.D.

Historical Note
Provides support for nursing practitioners working in psychiatric and mental health capacities, and promotes advances in care related to the field. Membership: $100/year.

Publications:
Archives of Psychiatric Nursing. bi-m. adv.
News Series. bien. adv.

Meetings/Conferences:
1999 – Washington, DC

Soc. for Education in Anesthesia *(1984)*
P.O. Box 11086
Richmond, VA   23230-1086
Tel: (804)282-5427   *Fax:* (804)282-0090
E-Mail: sea@societyhq.com
Web Site: http://www.seahq.org
Members: 600 individuals
Staff: 4
Annual Budget: $25-50,000
Exec. Director: John A. Hinckley
Manager, Meetings/Conventions: Kevin Johns, CAE
Administrator: Joyie Stewart
Membership Coordinator: Daniel Gainyard

Historical Note
Formerly (1994) Soc. of Education in Anesthesia. SEA members are individuals within anesthesia departments responsible for direct involvement in teaching, administration and planning educational programs for residents and medical students. Membership: $100/year.

Publications:
Anesthesia Education. 3/yr.
Journal of Clinical Anesthesia.

Meetings/Conferences:
Semi-annual Meetings: Spring and October
1999 – Dallas TX/100
2000 – San Francisco, CA/100

Soc. for Environmental Geochemistry and Health *(1971)*
Dept. of Life Sciences/Univ. of Missouri
105B Schenck Hall
Rolla, MO   65401
Tel: (573)341-4831
Members: 400 individuals
Staff: 1
Annual Budget: under $10,000
Treasurer: Paula Lutz

Historical Note
SEGH was formed to promote a multi-disciplinary approach to research in fields of geochemistry and health, to facilitate and expand communication among scientists within these disciplines and advance knowledge in the area. Membership: $45/year.

Publications:
Environmental Geochemistry and Health. q.
Interface. q. adv.

Meetings/Conferences:
Annual Meetings: Summer-Fall

Soc. for Environmental Graphic Design *(1973)*
401 F St., N.W., Suite 333
Washington, DC   20001-2728
Tel: (202)638-5555   *Fax:* (202)638-0891
E-Mail: segdoffice@aol.com
Members: 1000 individuals, 120 companies
Staff: 3
Annual Budget: $10-25,000,000
Exec. Director: Leslie Gallery Dilworth
Managing Director: Elisabeth Banks
Conference and Events Manager: Nazie Dana

Historical Note
Formerly (1992) Soc. of Environmental Graphic Designers. SEGD members are individuals and corporations engaged in or affiliated with environmental graphic design including individuals from the fields of graphic design, architecture, interior and industrial design, education, research and sign manufacturing. Membership: $135-215/year (individual), $465/year (corporate).

Publications:
Dimension. semi-a.
Membership Directory. a.
Messages. q. adv.

Meetings/Conferences:
Annual Meetings: Spring
1999 – Cincinnati, OH/May 19-22

Soc. for Epidemiologic Research *(1967)*
c/o American Journal of Epidemiology
111 Market Place, Suite 840
Baltimore, MD   21202-6709
Tel: (410)223-1600   *Fax:* (410)223-1620
Members: 2,500 individuals
Staff: 1
Annual Budget: $50-100,000
Secretary-Treasurer: Joseph Lyon, M.D., M.P.
Subscription Manager: Sandy Adams

Historical Note
Established in Baltimore, MD. Membership: $125/year (domestic); $130/year (foreign); $75/year (domestic student); $80/year (foreign student).

Publications:
American Journal of Epidemiology. bi-m. adv.

Meetings/Conferences:
1999 – Baltimore, MD

Soc. for Ethnomusicology *(1956)*
Morrison Hall 005
Indiana University
Bloomington, IN   47405-2501
Tel: (812)855-6672   *Fax:* (812)855-6673
E-Mail: sem@indiana.edu
Web Site: http://www.indiana.edu/~ethmusic
Members: 2,200 individuals
Staff: 1
Annual Budget: $50-100,000
Office Coordinator: Lyn Pittman

Historical Note
Member American Council of Learned Societies. Has an international membership. The Society promotes the research, study, and performance of musics of all historical periods and cultural contexts. Membership: varies

Publications:
Ethnomusicology. q. adv.
Newsletter. q.

Meetings/Conferences:
Annual Meetings: Fall
1999 – Austin, TX/Nov. 18-21
2000 – Toronto, ON, Canada

Soc. for Excellence in Eyecare *(1989)*
P.O. Box 59935
Potomac, MD   20859
Tel: (301)881-5050   *Fax:* (301)881-2985
E-Mail: socex@aol.com
Members: 100 individuals
Staff: 3
Annual Budget: $100-250,000
Exec. Director: Charles Sonneborn

Historical Note
Membership: $1,000/year (individual).

Publications:
Viewpoints. q.

Meetings/Conferences:
Annual Meeting: Usually early March

Soc. for Experimental Biology and Medicine *(1903)*
162 West 56th St., Suite 203
New York, NY   10019
Tel: (212)541-7855   *Fax:* (212)541-7505
E-Mail: sebm@inch.com
Web Site: http://www.sebm.org
Members: 1,700 individuals
Staff: 2
Annual Budget: $250-500,000
Exec. Director: Felice O'Grady

Historical Note
Established February 25, 1903 to cultivate the experimental method of investigation in biology and medicine. Membership: $45/year (individual); $280/year (domestic organization).

Publications:
Proceedings of the SEBM. 11/year. adv.

Meetings/Conferences:
Annual Meetings: None held.

Soc. for Experimental Mechanics *(1943)*
7 School St.
Bethel, CT   06801-1405
Tel: (203)790-6373   *Fax:* (203)790-4472
E-Mail: sem@sem1.com
Web Site: http://www.sem.com
Members: 3,000 individuals
Staff: 10
Annual Budget: $500-1,000,000
Managing Director: Kristin L. MacDonald
Meetings Manager: Katherine Ramsay
Membership Services Manager: Michelle Skurat
Managing Editor: Patricia Brothers

Historical Note
Founded in 1943 and incorporated in Delaware in 1961. Formerly (1984) the Soc. for Experimental Stress Analysis. Promotes research in experimental mechanics. Membership: $57-134/year (individual); $450-750/year (organization/company).

Publications:
Experimental Mechanics. q.
Experimental Techniques. bi-m. adv.
Mechanics of Time Dependent Materials. q.

Meetings/Conferences:
Semi-annual Meetings: Spring and Fall/500
1999 – Orlando, FL(Hyatt Orlando)/Feb. 8-11/800
1999 – Cinncinati, OH(Omni Netherland)/June 7-9/500

Soc. for Foodservice Management *(1979)*
304 West Liberty St., Suite 201
Louisville, KY   40202
Tel: (502)583-3783   *Fax:* (502)589-3602
Members: 1,450 individuals
Staff: 4
Annual Budget: $250-500,000
Exec. V. President: Greg Jewell
Director, Education: Peg Plaut

Historical Note
Executives who are responsible for non-commercial food service, such as employee cafeterias, colleges and universities and healthcare facilities. Formed as the result of a merger between the

Ass'n for Food Service Management (established 1970) and the Nat'l Industrial Cafeteria Managers' Ass'n (established 1949) on July 1, 1979. Membership $180/year (active); $385/year (associate).

Publications:
Magazine. q.
Membership Roster. a.

Meetings/Conferences:
Annual Meetings: Fall
1999 – Philadelphia, PA(Marriott)

Soc. for Foodservice Systems *(1980)*
670 Transfer Road, Suite 21-A
St. Paul, MN   55114
Tel: (651)646-7077   *Fax:* (651)646-5984
E-Mail: osnyder@hi-tm.com
Web Site: http://www.hi-tm.com
Members: 25 individuals
Staff: 3
President: Oscar P. Snyder, Jr., Ph.D.

Historical Note
Members are professionals involved in all aspects of commercial and non-commercial foodservice systems. Membership: $60/year (individual), $525/year (corporation).

Publications:
Journal of Foodservice Systems. q. adv.

Meetings/Conferences:
Annual Meetings: Spring

Soc. for French Historical Studies *(1955)*
Department of History
University of Virginia
Charlottesville, VA   22903
Tel: (804)924-6386   *Fax:* (804)924-7891
E-Mail: lrb@virginia.edu
Members: 1,450 individuals
Staff: 1
Annual Budget: under $10,000
Exec. Director: Lenard Berlanstein

Historical Note
A professional society concerned with scholarly research and teaching on French History. Membership: $30/year (individual).

Publications:
French Historical Studies. q.

Meetings/Conferences:
Annual Meetings: Spring
1999 – Washington, DC/March 18-20

Soc. for General Music *(1982)*

Historical Note
A council of the Music Educators Nat'l Conference.

Soc. for German-American Studies *(1968)*
c/o Blegen Libray
P.O. Box 210113
Cincinnati, OH   45221
Tel: (513)556-1955   *Fax:* (513)556-2113
Members: 25,000 individuals
President: D. Don Heinrich Tolzmann

Historical Note
SGAS members are academics and others with an interest in German-American studies. Membership: $25/year (individual); $10/year (student).

Publications:
Newsletter of SGAS. q.
Yearbook of German-American Studies. a.

Meetings/Conferences:
1999 – New Ulm, NM

Soc. for Gynecologic Investigation *(1952)*
409 12th St., S.W.
Washington, DC   20024-2188
Tel: (202)863-2544   *Fax:* (202)863-0739
Members: 900 individuals
Staff: 2
Annual Budget: $500-1,000,000
Exec. Director: Ava Ann Tayman

Historical Note
Membership: $160/year (U.S.); $174/year (international).

Publications:
Journal of the SGI. bi-m.

Meetings/Conferences:
Annual Meetings: March
1999 – Atlanta, GA(Marriott)/March 10-13/1200
2000 – Chicago, IL(Sheraton)/March 22-25
2001 – Toronto, Canada(Sheraton Center)/March 14-17/1200
2002   Los Angeles, CA(Century City
        Plaza)/March 20-23/1200

Soc. for Health and Human Values *(1969)*
4700 W. Lake Ave.
Glenview, IL   60025-1468
Tel: (847)375-4700   *Fax:* (847)375-4777
Members: 950 individuals, 15 organizations
Staff: 3
Annual Budget: $100-250,000
Management Exec.: Mark Engle

Historical Note
A multidisciplinary organization (physicians, clergy, lawyers, educators, philosophers and nurses) involved in the promotion of the humanities disciplines in the curricula of health professional schools and in the presentation of programs dealing with human values, humanities and medical ethics. The Ass'n for Faculty in the Medical Humanities is a division of SHHV. Membership: $15-80/year (individual); $500/year (institutions).

Publications:
Medical Humanities Review. semi-a.

Of Value. q. adv.

Meetings/Conferences:
Annual Meetings: Fall

Soc. for Healthcare Consumer Advocacy *(1972)*
One North Franklin St.
Chicago, IL   60606
Tel: (312)422-3999   *Fax:* (312)422-4580
E-Mail: Vkizart1@aha.org
Members: 1000 individuals
Staff: 5
Annual Budget: $250-500,000
Director: Elanore Kirsch

Historical Note
Affiliated with the American Hospital Association. Formerly (1997) the Nat'l Soc. for Patient Representation and Consumer Affairs, (1988) the Nat'l Soc. of Patient Representatives, and (1981) the Soc. of Patient Representatives. Membership: $125/year.

Publications:
Healthcare Consumer Advocacy. bi-m.

Meetings/Conferences:
Annual Meetings: Fall
1999 – Toronto, PQ/Oct. 10-14

Soc. for Healthcare Epidemiology of America *(1980)*
19 Mantua Road
Mount Royal, NJ   08061
Tel: (609)423-0087   *Fax:* (609)423-3420
Web Site: http://www.medscape.com/affiliates/shea
Members: 1,400 individuals
Staff: 1
Exec. Director: Stephanie W. Dickinson

Historical Note
Formerly (1994) Soc. for Hospital Epidemiology of America. Purpose is to advance expertise and education in hospital epidemiology and quality assurance.

Publications:
Infection Control and Hospital Epidemiology. m.

Meetings/Conferences:
1999 – San Francisco, CA

Soc. for Healthcare Planning and Marketing *(1978)*

Historical Note
Merged with the American Soc. for Healthcare Marketing and Public Relations to form Soc. for Healthcare Strategy and Market Development in 1996.

Soc. for Healthcare Strategy and Market Development *(1996)*
One North Franklin
Chicago, IL   60606
Tel: (312)422-3888   *Fax:* (312)422-4579
Members: 5,000 individuals
Staff: 5
Annual Budget: $1-2,000,000
Exec. Director: Lauren A. Barnett
Product Manager: Liz Liwazer
Assoc. Director: Paula Szyper
Assoc. Director: Karen Thomas

Historical Note
Founded in 1996 as the result of a merger between Soc. for Healthcare Planning and Marketing (founded 1977) and American Soc. for Health Care Marketing and Public Relations (founded 1964). An affiliate of American Hospital Ass'n (same address), the Soc.'s membership include healthcare executives specializing in strategic planning, marketing, public relations, and other business and development functions. Membership: $185/year (individual).

Publications:
Career Opportunities Bulletin. bi-w.
Membership & Services Directory. a.
Newsletter. bi-m.

Meetings/Conferences:
Annual Meetings: Fall/800
1999 – Denver, CO(Adam's Mark)/Sept. 24-27

Soc. for Hematopathology *(1981)*
471 Porpoise Circle
Fripp Island, SC   29920-9795
Tel: (843)838-5564
Members: 500 individuals
Staff: 1
Exec. Assistant: Susan C. Berard

Historical Note
The society was created for the promotion and exchange of knowledge and the stimulation of clinical, morphologic, and functional investigation of the hematopoietic and lymphoreticular systems as its primary objectives.

Publications:
Newsletter.

Meetings/Conferences:
Annual Meetings: Annual/March
1999 – San Francisco, CA(San Francisco Hilton)
2000 – New Orleans, LA(Hilton)
2001 – Atlanta, GA(Marriott Marquis)
2002 – Chicago. IL(Sheraton Chicago)
2003 – Washington, DC(Marriott Wardman Park)

Soc. for Historians of American Foreign Relations *(1967)*
Department of History
Wright State University
Dayton, OH   45435
Tel: (937)775-2838   *Fax:* (937)775-3301
E-Mail: allan.spetter@wright.edu
Members: 1,800 individuals
Staff: 1
Annual Budget: $10-25,000
Exec. Secretary-Treasurer: Allan B. Spetter

Historical Note
Affiliated with the American Historical Ass'n and the Organization of American Historians. Promotes the study of diplomatic history in cooperation with the National Archives and other government agencies. Membership: $30/year (regular); $15/year (student).

Publications:
Diplomatic History. q. adv.
Newsletter. q. adv.
Roster and Research List. a.

Meetings/Conferences:
Annual Meetings: Summer
1999 – Princeton, NJ(Princeton Univ.)

Soc. for Historians of the Early American Republic *(1978)*
Department of History, 1358 Univ. Hall
Purdue University
West Lafayette, IN 47907-1358
Tel: (765)494-4135 *Fax:* (765)496-1755
E-Mail: jer@sla.purdue.edu
Web Site: www.sla.purdue.edu/jer/
Members: 1,500 individuals and organizations
Staff: 3
Annual Budget: $10-25,000
Exec. Director: John L. Larson
Editorial Assistant: Deborah Gray

Historical Note
SHEAR members are academic and others with an interest in American history in the period of the early republic. Membership: $15-30/year (individual); $40/year (organization).

Publications:
Journal of the Early Republic. q. adv.

Meetings/Conferences:
1999 – Lexington, KY(Transylvania College)

Soc. for Historians of the Gilded Age and Progressive Era *(1988)*
Hayes Presidential Center
Spiegel Grove
Fremont, OH 43420-2796
Tel: (419)332-2081 *Fax:* (419)332-4952
E-Mail: rdb9507@nwohio.com
Members: 250 individuals
Annual Budget: under $10,000
Secretary-Treasurer: Roger D. Bridges

Historical Note
SHGAPE members are academics and others with an interest in American history during the years 1865-1917. Membership: $10/year (individual); $5/year (student).

Publications:
Newsletter. semi-a.

Meetings/Conferences:
Annual Meetings: in conjunction with OAH annual meeting

Soc. for Historical Archaeology *(1967)*
P.O. Box 30446
Tucson, AZ 85751-0446
Tel: (520)886-8006 *Fax:* (520)886-0182
E-Mail: SHA@AZSTARNET.COM
Web Site: http://www.sha.org
Members: 1,950 individuals, 400 organizations
Annual Budget: $100-250,000
Secretary-Treasurer: Stephanie H. Rodeffer

Historical Note
Is concerned with the identification, excavation, interpretation and conservation of sites and materials and applies archaeological methods to the study of history. Has no paid officers or full-time staff. Membership: $75/year (individual), $105/year (organization).

Publications:
Historical Archaeology. q.
SHA Newsletter. q.
Special Publications. irreg.
Underwater Archaeology. a.

Meetings/Conferences:
Annual Meetings: Winter
1999 – Salt Lake City, UT(SLC Hilton)
2000 – Quebec City, PQ, Canada(Hilton)

Soc. for History Education *(1972)*
History Teacher, Cal. State University
1250 Bellflower Blvd.
Long Beach, CA 90840
Tel: (760)765-2205
Members: 2,000 individuals
Staff: 10
Annual Budget: $50-100,000
General Manager: Connie George

Historical Note
Formerly (1972) History Teachers Ass'n. Supports the improvement of history teaching at secondary and post-secondary levels. Membership: $27/year (individual); $33/year (institution); $18/year (student); $39/year (foreign institution).

Publications:
The History Teacher. q. adv.

Meetings/Conferences:
Annual Meetings: always Long Beach, CA(CA State Univ)/June

Soc. for History in the Federal Government *(1979)*
Box 14139, Benjamin Franklin Station
Washington, DC 20044
Tel: (301)530-7470 *Fax:* (301)530-7470
Web Site: http://shfg.org
Members: 500 individuals
Staff: 1
Annual Budget: under $10,000
Exec. Director: Maryellen Trautman

Historical Note
Promotes study and broad understanding of the history of the U.S. government. Professional society of historians, archivists, curators and others with an interest in the historical and archival activities of the U.S. government. Affiliated with the American Historical Ass'n. Membership: $22/year.

Publications:
Directory of Federal Historical Programs and Activities. irreg.
Roster. a.
The Federalist. q.

Meetings/Conferences:
Annual Meetings: Spring

Soc. for Human Ecology *(1981)*
College of the Atlantic
105 Eden St.
Bar Harbor, ME 04609
Tel: (207)288-5015 *Fax:* (207)288-4126
Members: 150 individuals
Annual Budget: under $10,000
Exec. Director: Melville P. Cote

Historical Note
SHE members are academics, scientists, health professionals and and others with an interest in studying the interrelationship of man's actions and his environment. Has no paid officers or full-time staff. Membership: $40/year (individual); $15/year (student).

Publications:
Convention Proceedings. 1/18 months. adv.
Human Ecology Review. semi-a. adv.
Internat'l Directory of Human Ecologists. irreg.

Meetings/Conferences:
1999 – Montreal, Canada(McGill University)/May 27-30

Soc. for Human Resource Management *(1948)*
1800 Duke St.
Alexandria, VA 22314-3499
Tel: (703)548-3440 *Fax:* (703)836-0367
E-Mail: shrm@shrm.org
Web Site: http://www.shrm.org
Members: 90,000 individuals
Staff: 150
Annual Budget: $25-50,000,000
President and C.E.O.: Michael R. Losey, SPHR, CAE
Director, Public Affairs: Kathron A. Compton
Senior V. President, Government and Public Affairs: Susan R. Meisinger, SPHR
Director, Government Affairs: Deanna Gelak
Director, Meetings and Conferences: Elizabeth W. Block
Director, Educational Programs: Barbara Sadek
V. President, Finance and Administration: Gerald F. Hay, CPA
V. President, Member/Chapter Services: Elizabeth S. Knight
V. President, Publications and New Media: John Adams, III
V.P., Professional & Product Development: David C. Forman

Historical Note
Formerly (1989) American Soc. for Personnel Administration. A professional society of human resource management professionals and others involved in human resources management. Institute for Internat'l Human Resources is a division of SHRM. The Human Resource Certification Institute is the certification arm of SHRM. The SHRM Foundation sponsors research and develops educational programs for its members. Has an annual budget of over $40 million. Membership: $160/year.

Publications:
HR Legal Report. q.
HR Magazine. m. adv.
HR News. m. adv.
Washington Insider. bi-w.
Workplace Visions. q.

Meetings/Conferences:
Annual Meetings: Spring/9,000
1999 – Atlanta, GA/June 27-30

Soc. for Humanistic Anthropology *(1974)*

Historical Note
A section of the American Anthropological Ass'n. Members are interested in the human meaning of anthropological inquiry and the anthropologist's commitment to experience and evaluation.

Soc. for Humanistic Judaism *(1969)*
28611 West Twelve Mile Road
Farmington Hills, MI 48334
Tel: (248)478-7610 *Fax:* (248)478-3159
E-Mail: info@shj.org
Members: 1,800 individuals
Staff: 4
Annual Budget: $100-250,000
Exec. Director: Bonnie Cousens

Historical Note
Creates, publishes and shares holiday and life cycle materials for secular humanistic Jews. Helps to organize communities of secular humanistic Jews. Membership: $50/year.

Publications:
Humanistic Judaism. 3/year.
Humanorah. 3/yea.

Meetings/Conferences:

Soc. for Imaging Science and Technology *(1947)*
7003 Kilworth Lane
Springfield, VA 22151
Tel: (703)642-9090 *Fax:* (703)642-9094
Toll Free: (800)478 - 5218
E-Mail: info@imaging.org
Web Site: http://www.imaging.org
Members: 2,500 individuals
Staff: 8
Annual Budget: $1-2,000,000
Exec. Director: Calva A. Leonard
Program Manager: Jennifer O'Brien
Program Manager: Pamela Forness

Historical Note
Originated in 1947 as the Soc. of Photographic Engineers. In 1957 merged with the Technical Division of the Photographic Soc. of America to form the Soc. of Photographic Scientists and Engineers. Became (1986) Soc. for Imaging Science and Technology. Incorporated in the District of Columbia in 1966. Members are persons who engage in imaging science or engineering or teachers of photography or imaging science. Membership: $70/year (domestic), $80/year (foreign), $750-5,000/year (organization).

Publications:
IS&T Reporter. q.
Journal of Electronic Imaging. q.
Journal of Imaging Science and Technology. bi-m. adv.

Meetings/Conferences:
1999 – Savannah, GA/April 25-28
1999 – Orlando, FL/Oct. 17-24
2000 – Portland, OR
2000 – Western USA

Soc. for In Vitro Biology *(1946)*
9315 Largo Drive West, Suite 255
Upper Marlboro, MD 20774-4755
Tel: (301)324-5054 *Fax:* (301)324-5057
Toll Free: (800)741 - 7476
E-Mail: sivb@sivb.org
Web Site: http://www.sivb.org
Members: 2,200 individuals
Staff: 5
Annual Budget: $500-1,000,000
Managing Director: Marietta W. Ellis
Meeting Coordinator: Tiffany McMillan
Membership Coordinator: Valerie Evans

Historical Note
Founded in 1946 as the Tissue Culture Commission, became the Tissue Culture Ass'n in 1950, and then the Soc. for In Vitro Biology in 1994. The society fosters exchange, publication and teaching of knowledge related to in vitro biology of cells, tissues and organs. Focuses on biological problems of significance to science and society. Membership: $100/year (individual), $400/year (company).

Publications:
In Vitro Cellular & Developmental Biology-Animal. 10/yr. adv.
In Vitro Cellular & Developmental Biology-Plant. q. adv.
In Vitro Report Newsletter. bi-m.
Meeting Program. a. adv.
Membeship Roster. a.

Meetings/Conferences:
Annual Meetings: June/1,000
1999 – New Orleans, LA(Radisson)/June 5-9
2000 – San Diego, CA(Town & Country)/June 8-15

Soc. for Industrial and Applied Mathematics *(1952)*
3600 University City Science Center
Philadelphia, PA 19104-2688
Tel: (215)382-9800 *Fax:* (215)386-7999
E-Mail: siam@siam.org
Web Site: http://www.siam.org
Members: 9,000 individuals, 21 corporations 343 academic
Staff: 56
Annual Budget: $5-10,000,000
Exec. Director: James M. Crowley
Conference Director: Coley Lyons
Director, Finance and Administration: A. Robert Bellace
Customer Service Manager: Marta K. Lafferty
Dir., Information Management Systems: James L. Goldman

Historical Note
Organized in Philadelphia in Nov., 1951 and incorporated in Delaware in April, 1952. Member of the American Ass'n for the Advancement of Science, the Conference Board of the Mathematical Sciences, the Council of Engineering and Scientific Society Executives, and the Council of Scientific Society Presidents and Joint Policy Board for Mathematics. SIAN was formed to further the application of mathmatics to industry and science, promote basic research in mathmatics leading to new methods and techniques useful to industry and science and to provide media for the exchange of information and ideas between mathmaticians and other technical as well as scientific personnel. Annual Budget: $5.6 million. Membership: $96/year (individual); $204-$3,520/year (academic); $3,300/year (corporate).

Publications:
SIAM Journal on Applied Mathematics. bi-m. adv.
SIAM Journal on Computing. bi-m. adv.
SIAM Journal on Control and Optimization. bi-m. adv.
SIAM Journal on Discrete Mathematics. q. adv.
SIAM Journal on Mathematical Analysis. bi-m. adv.
SIAM Journal on Matrix Analysis and Applications. q. adv.
SIAM Journal on Numerical Analysis. bi-m. adv.
SIAM Journal on Optimization. q. adv.
SIAM Journal on Scientific Computing. bi-m. adv.
SIAM News. 10/yr. adv.
SIAM Review. q. adv.
Theory of Probability and its Applications. q. adv.

Meetings/Conferences:
1999 – Atlanta, GA(Radisson Hotel)/May 12-15/800
2000 – Rio Grande, Puerto Rico(Westin Rio Beach Resort)/July 10-14/800
2001 – San Diego, CA(Town & Country Hotel)/July 9-13/800
2002 – Philadelphia, PA(Marriott)/1000

Soc. for Industrial and Organizational Psychology *(1946)*
P.O. Box 87
Bowling Green, OH 43402-0087
Tel: (419)353-0032 *Fax:* (419)352-2645
E-Mail: lhakel@siop.bgsu.edu
Web Site: http://siop.edu
Members: 5,500 individuals
Staff: 4
Annual Budget: $250-500,000
Office Manager: Lee Hakel

Historical Note

Affiliated with the American Psychological Ass'n and the American Psychological Soc., SIOP is concerned with the scientific application of psychology to all types of organizations providing goods or services, such as manufacturing concerns, commercial enterprises, labor unions, trade associations and public agencies. Members must be engaged in professional activites as demonstrated by research, teaching and practice related to the purpose of the society. Membership: $32/year (individual).

Publications:

TIP: The Industrial-Organizational Psychologist. q.

Meetings/Conferences:

Annual Meetings: Spring/2,000
1999 – Atlanta, GA(Marriott)/April 30-May 2
2000 – New Orleans, LA(Hyatt)/April 14-16
2001 – San Diego, CA(Sheraton)/April 25-29
2002 – Toronto, ON(Sheraton)/April 12-14

Soc. for Industrial Archeology *(1971)*

Dept. of Social Sciences
Michigan Technological University
Houghton, MI   49931
Tel: (906)487-2113   *Fax:* (906)487-2468
E-Mail: PEM-194@MTU.EDU
Members: 1,600 individuals
Annual Budget: $25-50,000
Editor: Patrick Martin

Historical Note

Founded to promote the study of the physical survivals of our technical and industrial past. Has no paid staff. Officers change biennially. Membership: $35/year (individual), $40/year (organization).

Publications:

IA. semi-a. adv.
SIA Newsletter. q.

Meetings/Conferences:

Annual Meetings: Spring
1999 – Savannah, GA/June 3-7

Soc. for Industrial Microbiology *(1949)*

3929 Old Lee Hwy., Suite 92-A
Fairfax, VA   22030-2421
Tel: (703)691-3357   *Fax:* (703)691-7991
E-Mail: info@simhq.org
Web Site: http://www.simhq.org
Members: 1,850 individuals
Staff: 3
Annual Budget: $50-100,000
Exec. Secretary: Ann Kulback

Historical Note

Founded in 1949 and incorporated in 1960. Promotes the advancement of the microbiological sciences especially as applied to industry. The Society is an Adherent Society member of the American Institute of Biological Sciences, Inc. Membership: $20/year (student), $75year (U.S.), $85/year (foreign), $350/year (corporate).

Publications:

Journal Industrial Microbiology. bi-m. adv.
SIM Focus. bi-m. adv.
SIM News. bi-m. adv.

Meetings/Conferences:

Annual Meetings: August
1999 – Arlington, VA(Gateway Marriott)/Aug. 1-6
2000 – San Diego, CA(Town & Country)

Soc. for Information Display *(1962)*

31 E. Julian St.
San Jose, CA   95112
Tel: (408)977-1013   *Fax:* (408)977-1531
E-Mail: office@sid.org
Web Site: http://www.sid.org
Members: 5,000 individuals
Staff: 3
Exec. Director: Dee Dumont
Exec. Assistant: Jenny Needham

Historical Note

Membership: $55/year (individual), $700/year (company).

Publications:

Digest of Technical Papers. a.
IDRC Conference Record. a.
Information Display Magazine. adv. adv.
Journal of the SID.
Seminar Lecture Notes. a.

Meetings/Conferences:

1999 – San Jose, CA/May 16-21
1999 – Berlin, Germany/Sept. 6-9

Soc. for Information Management *(1969)*

401 N. Michigan Ave.
Chicago, IL   60611-4267
Tel: (312)644-6610   *Fax:* (312)245-1081
Members: 2,700 individuals
Staff: 10
Annual Budget: $1-2,000,000
Assoc. Exec. Director: Steven A John

Historical Note

SIM was formed to enhance international recognition of information as a basic organizational resource and to promote the effective utilization and management of this resource towards the improvement of management performance. It attempts to enhance communications between IS executives and the senior executives responsible for management of the business enterprise. Formerly (until 1982) the Soc. for Management Information Systems. Membership: $250/year (corporate at-large), $125/year (academic at-large), $125/year (corporate chapter), $62.50/year (academic at-large).

Publications:

Conference Executive Summaries. semi-a.
Executive Brief. q.

MIS Quarterly Journal. q.
Network Newsletter. bi-m.

Meetings/Conferences:

Annual Meetings: Fall

Soc. for Integrative and Comparative Biology *(1890)*

401 N. Michigan Ave.
Chicago, IL   60611-4267
Tel: (312)527-6697   *Fax:* (312)245-1085
Toll Free: (800)955 - 1236
E-Mail: sicb@sba.com
Web Site: http://sicb.org
Members: 2,200 individuals
Staff: 4
Annual Budget: $500-1,000,000
Exec. Director: Laura Jungen

Historical Note

Formerly (1996) the American Soc. of Zoologists. The Eastern Branch of the American Soc. of Zoologists was founded in 1890 as the American Morphological Ass'n; the Central Branch developed from the Central Naturalists, founded in 1899; the two merged in 1901-3 and the American Soc. of Zoologists emerged from a joint meeting in Philadelphia in 1913. Incorporated in Illinois in 1964. Membership is open to individuals who are actively engaged in the field of zoology. Membership: $96/year (full member, with Ph.D.), $32/year (student).

Publications:

American Zoologist. bi-m. adv.
Newsletter. semi-a.

Meetings/Conferences:

Annual Meetings: usually January/800
1999 – Denver, CO(Adam's Mark)/Jan. 6-10

Soc. for Invertebrate Pathology *(1967)*

Historical Note

Address unknown in 1997.

Soc. for Investigative Dermatology *(1937)*

820 W. Superior Ave., Suite 340
Cleveland, OH   44113-1800
Tel: (216)579-9300   *Fax:* (216)579-9333
E-Mail: sid@sidnet.org
Web Site: http://www.sidnet.org
Members: 2,600 individuals
Staff: 4
Annual Budget: $250-500,000
Administrative Director: Angela Welsh

Historical Note

Founded and incorporated in New York, April 24, 1937. Membership: $135/year (individual); $1,200/year (organization).

Publications:

Journal of Investigative Dermatology. m. adv.

Meetings/Conferences:

Annual Meetings: Spring/1,000
1999 – Chicago, IL(Sheraton)/May 5-9

Soc. for Iranian Studies *(1967)*

Princeton Univ. Library
One Washington Road
Princeton, NJ   08544-2098
Tel: (609)258-1308   *Fax:* (609)258-0441
Web Site: http://www.iranian-studies.org
Members: 539 individuals, 232 institutions
Staff: 1
Annual Budget: $10-25,000
Exec. Secretary: Kambiz Eslami

Historical Note

Formerly (1969) Soc. for Iranian Cultural and Social Studies. Mmembership: $35/year (individual), $40/year institution.

Publications:

Iranian Studies. q.
SIS Newsletter. 3/yea.

Meetings/Conferences:

Annual Meetings: in conjunction with the MESA conference/Fall
1999 – Washington, DC
2000 – Washington, DC

Soc. for Italian Historical Studies *(1955)*

Department of History, Boston College
Chestnut Hill, MA   02167
Tel: (617)552-2267
Members: 350 individuals
Staff: 1
Annual Budget: under $10,000
Exec. Secretary: Alan J. Reinerman

Historical Note

Members are professors and students of Italian history. Encourages the study and teaching of Italian history; promotes research; and awards prizes. Membership: $5/year (individual); $25/year (organization).

Publications:

Newsletter. a.

Meetings/Conferences:

Annual Meetings: December, with the American Historical Ass'n

Soc. for Latin American Anthropology *(1969)*

Historical Note

A section of the American Anthropological Association. Founded as the Ad Hoc Group on Latin American Anthropology, it became the Latin American Anthropology Group in 1971 and assumed its present name in 1982. Members are professional anthropologists interested in Latin America.

Soc. for Leukocyte Biology *(1954)*

c/o FASEB
9650 Rockville Pike
Bethesda, MD   20814-3998
Tel: (301)571-5903   *Fax:* (301)571-5704

E-Mail: slb@faseb.org
Web Site: http://www.biosci.ohio-state.edu/ ~ slb
Members: 1,300 individuals
Staff: 2
Annual Budget: $250-500,000
Contact: Ida Chow, Ph.D.

Historical Note

Founded in 1954 and incorporated in 1965. Membership consists of those interested in phagocytic cells of the body, especially when concerned with host defense, immunity and cancer. Membership: $80/year (individual), $500/year (organization).

Publications:

SLB Newsletter. 3/year.
The Journal of Leukocyte Biology. m. adv.

Meetings/Conferences:

Annual Meetings: October (1996)
2000 – Boston, MA

Soc. for Life History Research *(1970)*

Historical Note

Reported inactive in 1997.

Soc. for Light Treatment and Biological Rhythms *(1988)*

842 Howard Ave.,
New Haven, CT   06519
Tel: (203)764-4326   *Fax:* (203)764-4324
E-Mail: sltbr@yale.edu
Web Site: www.websciences.org/sltbr
Members: 480 individuals
Staff: 15
Annual Budget: $25-50,000
Exec. Director: Stephanie Argraves

Historical Note

SLTBR fosters communication between scientists, clinicians, manufacturers, and others interested in the therapeutic use of lighting devices. Membership: $75/year (individual); $600/year (company).

Publications:

Light Treatment and Biological Rhythms. q.

Meetings/Conferences:

Soc. for Linguistic Anthropology *(1983)*

Historical Note

A section of the American Anthropological Ass'n. Established to advance the study of language in its social and cultural context.

Soc. for Luminescent Microscopy and Spectroscopy *(1988)*

c/o Univ. of Tennessee
Dept. of Geological Sciences
Knoxville, TN   37996-1410
Tel: (423)974-2366   *Fax:* (423)974-2368
E-Mail: kmisra@utk.edu
Web Site: http://zephyr.rice.edu/slms/slms.html
Members: 140 individuals
Annual Budget: under $10,000
Secretary/ Treasurer: Dr. Kula C. Misra

Historical Note

Established in Colorado. Members are geologists and physicists with an interest in research employing luminescent microscopy or spectroscopy. Membership: $10/year (individual); $5/year (student).

Publications:

Newsletter. semi-a. adv.

Soc. for Magnetic Resonance Imaging *(1982)*

Historical Note

Merged with the Soc. of Magnetic Resonance in Medicine to form the Soc. of Magnetic Resonance in 1994.

Soc. for Maintenance Reliability Professionals

401 N. Michigan Ave.
Chicago, IL   60611-4267
Tel: (312)321-5190   *Fax:* (312)527-6658
Toll Free: (800)950 - 7354
E-Mail: smrp@sba.com
Web Site: http://www.smrp.org
Members: 1,500 individuals
Staff: 4
Annual Budget: $250-500,000
Exec. Director: Larry Fleischman
Marketing and Communiciations Director: Christine Bennett
Membership Services Director: Dana Wulff

Historical Note

Membership:$125/year (individual); $1,000/year (organization).

Publications:

Annual Conference Proceedings. a.
SMRP Solutions. q.

Meetings/Conferences:

1999 – Denver, CO(Marriott)

Soc. for Marketing Professional Services *(1973)*

99 Canal Center Plaza, Suite 250
Alexandria, VA   22314-1588
Tel: (703)549-6117   *Fax:* (703)549-2498
E-Mail: info@smps.org
Web Site: http://www.smps.org
Members: 3,800 individuals
Staff: 8
Annual Budget: $1-2,000,000
Exec. Director: Bonnie L. Shelton, CAE
Manager, Marketing/Communications: Megan L. Eisel
Education Director: Stacey Ann P. Gardiner, CMP
Membership Director: Jane Patrick Casey
Membership Coordinator: Christine Mercado
Editor: Lisa S. Jenkins

Historical Note

Employees of architectural, engineering, planning, landscape architectural, interior design and construction management firms who are responsible for marketing their organizations' services. Membership: $225/year.

Publications:
SMPS Marketer. bi-m. adv.
The Forum. bi-m. adv.

Meetings/Conferences:
Annual Meetings: August
1999 – Portland, OR/August 11-14
2000 – Austin, TX
2001 – Orlando, FL

Soc. for Maternal Fetal Medicine *(1977)*
409 12th St., S.W.
Washington, DC   20024-2188
Tel: (202)863-2476   *Fax:* (202)554-1132
Members: 1,800 individuals
Exec. Director: Pat Stahr

Historical Note
Formerly Soc. of Perinatal Obstetricians (1998). SMFM members are physicians specializing in maternal-fetal medicine. Membership: $100/year (individual).

Publications:
Abstracts/Proceedings of Annual Meeting. a.
American Journal of Obstetrics and Gynecology. irreg.
Directory of Maternal-Fetal Fellowships. a.
SPO Newsletter. 2/year.

Meetings/Conferences:
Annual Meetings: late January-early February
1999 – San Francisco, CA(Hilton and
        Towers)/Jan. 18-23/1500
2000 – Miami Beach, FL(Fontainbleau Hilton)/Jan. 31-Feb.
        5/1500

Soc. for Mathematical Biology
P.O. Box 11283
Boulder, CO   80301
Tel: (303)665-8264
Web Site: http://www.smb.org
Contact: Dr. Torcom Chorbajian

Historical Note
Members are academics and others with an interest in the application of mathematics in biological research. Membership; $50/year (individual); $20/year (student).

Publications:
Bulletin of Mathematical Biology. irreg.

Meetings/Conferences:
1999 – Amsterdam, The Netherlands/June 29-July 3

Soc. for Medical Anthropology *(1968)*

Historical Note
A section of the American Anthropological Ass'n. Members are interested in the anthropological aspects of health, illness, health care and related topics.

Soc. for Medical Decision Making
Continuing Ed in the Health Professions
Geo. Washington Univ., 2300 K St., N.W.
Washington, DC   20037
Tel: (202)994-8929   *Fax:* (202)994-1791
Members: 1000 individuals
Staff: 3
Annual Budget: $100-250,000
Assoc. Administrative Director: Deborah Karpowicz

Historical Note
SMDM is an international society promoting the theory and practice of medical decision making through the application of analytical methods. Membership: $125/year (individual).

Publications:
Medical Decision Making. q. adv.

Meetings/Conferences:
Annual Meetings: Fall
1999 – Reno, NV/Oct. 2-5

Soc. for Medieval and Renaissance Philosophy *(1979)*
Dept. of Philosophy
Fairfield Univ.
Fairfield, CT   06430
Tel: (203)254-4000   *Fax:* (203)573-2096
Members: 525 individuals
President: Steve McGrade

Historical Note
SMRP members are academics with an interest in medieval or renaissance philosophy.

Publications:
Newsletter. semi-a.

Meetings/Conferences:
Annual Meetings: in conjunction with the American
        Philosophical Ass'n

Soc. for Menstrual Cycle Research *(1979)*
10559 North 104th Place
Scottsdale, AZ   85258
Tel: (602)451-9731
Members: 100 individuals
Annual Budget: under $10,000
Secretary-Treasurer: Mary Anna Friederich, M.D.

Historical Note
SMCR is an organization formed to meet the special needs of an interdisciplinary group of researchers, health care providers, students and others who share an interest in women's lives and health needs as these are related to the menstrual cycle. Membership is open to individuals who have demonstrated an interest in research on the menstrual cycle or related issues, and who support the purposes of the Society.

Publications:
Membership roster. a.
Newsletter. q.

Meetings/Conferences:
Biennial Meetings: (odd years)
1999 – Tucson, AZ

Soc. for Military History *(1938)*
910 Forbes Road
Carlisle, PA   17013
Tel: (717)249-5625   *Fax:* (717)249-5625
E-Mail: heriger@aol.com
Web Site: http://www.smh-jmh.org
Members: 1,980 individuals
Annual Budget: $50-100,000
Exec. Director: Charles R. Shrader, Ph.D.

Historical Note
SMH members are academics and others with an interest in the study of military history. Membership: $35/year (individual); $15/year (student).

Publications:
Directory of Members. bien.
Headquarters Gazette Newsletter. q.
Journal of Military History. q.

Meetings/Conferences:
Annual Meetings: April
1999 – State College, PA/April 15-18/400
2000 – Quantico, VA
2001 – Calgary, Canada

Soc. for Mining, Metallurgy, and Exploration *(1957)*
P.O. Box 625002
Littleton, CO   80162-5002
Tel: (303)973-9550   *Fax:* (303)973-3845
Toll Free: (800)763 - 3132
E-Mail: SMENET@aol.com
Web Site: http://smenet.org
Members: 17,000 individuals
Staff: 31
Annual Budget: $2-5,000,000
Exec. Director: Gary D. Howell
Manager, Publicity and Programming: Tara Davis
Manager, Meetings: Joette Cross
Education Assistant: Leslie Shivers
Director, Administrative Services: John J. Orologio
Membership Coordinator: Kristin Torres
Manager, Membership Services: Angela Giles
Publisher: Jeffrey Oates

Historical Note
Member of the American Institute of Mining, Metallurgical, and Petroleum Engineers (1871). Formerly the Soc. of Mining Engineers, the Society adopted its present name in 1989. Membership: $85/year.

Publications:
Minerals and Metallurgical Processing Journal. q. adv.
Mining Engineering. m. adv.
Mining Transactions, AIME. a.

Meetings/Conferences:
Annual Meetings: 6,000
1999 – Denver, CO/March 1-3
2000 – Salt Lake City, UT/Feb.28 28-March 1

Soc. for Natural Philosophy *(1963)*
Dept. of Math
University of Kentucky
Lexington, KY   40506-0027
Tel: (606)257-3849
Members: 300 individuals
Annual Budget: under $10,000
Secretary: Donald E. Carlson

Historical Note
Members are mathematicians, chemists, engineers, physicists, and other scientists interested in the foundations of mathematical sciences in nature. Membership: $15/yr. (individual).

Meetings/Conferences:
Annual Meetings: Usually in a university setting

Soc. for Neuroscience *(1969)*
11 Dupont Circle, N.W., Suite 500
Washington, DC   20036
Tel: (202)462-6688
E-Mail: info@sfn.org
Web Site: www.sfn.org
Members: 26,000 individuals
Staff: 45
Annual Budget: $5-10,000,000
Exec. Director: Nancy Beang
Communications/Mktg. Director: Judith Hittman
Govt./Public Affairs Manager: Kelli A. Mills
Annual Meeting Director: Julie Ziegler
Controller: Patricia Hershfeldt

Historical Note
Membership: $125/year (individual); $35/year (student); $2,500/year (company).

Publications:
Brain Briefings. q.
Brain Waves. q.
Journal of Neuroscience. m. adv.
Membership Directory. a.
Neuroscience Abstracts. a.
Neuroscience Newsletter. bi-m.
Neuroscience Training Programs in North America. trien.

Meetings/Conferences:
Annual Meetings: Fall/22,000
1999 – Miami Beach, FL(Convention Center)/Oct. 23-28
2000 – New Orleans, LA(Convention Center)/Nov. 4-9

Soc. for New Language Study *(1972)*
P.O. Box 100596

Denver, CO   80250-0596
Tel: (303)777-6115   *Fax:* (303)871-4432
Members: 15 individuals
Staff: 1
Annual Budget: under $10,000
Treasurer: Raymond P. Tripp, Jr.

Historical Note
To stimulate consideration, evaluation and cultivation of the study of language, literature and philosophy from new perspectives. Has no full-time staff; one part-time staff-member.

Publications:
In Gear Dargum. a.

Meetings/Conferences:
Annual Meetings: Fall, with the Rocky Mountain Modern
        Language Ass'n

Soc. for News Design *(1979)*
129 Dyer St.
Providence, RI   02903-3904
Tel: (401)276-2100   *Fax:* (401)276-2105
E-Mail: snd@snd.org
Web Site: http://www.snd.org
Members: 2,700 individuals
Staff: 2
Annual Budget: $500-1,000,000
Exec. Director: David B. Gray

Historical Note
Originally the Soc. of Newspaper Designers; became Soc. of Newspaper Design in 1981, and assumed its current name in 1998. Membership is international and open to anyone interested in newspaper design. Members include designers, graphics artists, editors, illustrators, photographers, art directors, paginators, advertising artists, students and faculty who design newspapers, magazines and Web pages. The Soc. of Newspaper Design Foundation is its educational arm. Membership: $95/yr; $65/year Small Newspapers; $45/year Students.

Publications:
Design. q. adv.
Membership Directory. a. adv.
SND Update Newsletter. m. adv.
The Best of Newspaper Design. a.

Meetings/Conferences:
Annual Meetings: Fall/800
1999 – Copenhagen, Denmark(Bella Center)/Sept. 9-11
2000 – Minneapolis, MN(Hilton)/Aug. 30-Sept. 2
2001 – Phoenix, AZ
2002 – Buenos Aires, Argentina

Soc. for Nutrition Education *(1967)*
7101 Wisconsin Ave., Suite 901
Bethesda, MD   20814-4805
Tel: (301)656-4938   *Fax:* (301)656-4958
Toll Free: (800)235 - 6690
E-Mail: info@sne.org
Web Site: http://pitt.ces.state.nc.us/sne
Members: 2,300 individuals
Staff: 3
Annual Budget: $500-1,000,000
Exec. Director: Allegra Tasaki
Director of Marketing & Meetings: Mary Meegan
Membership/Operations Coordinator: Santy Medina

Historical Note
Membership: $160/year.

Publications:
Abstracts.
Board Briefs. m.
Directory.
Journal of Nutrition Education. bi-m.
Proceedings.
SNE Communicator. q.
SNE Supplement.

Meetings/Conferences:
Annual Meetings: Summer/750
1999 – Baltimore, MD(Omni Inner Harbor Hotel)/July 24-28

Soc. for Obstetric Anesthesia and Perinatology *(1969)*
P.O. Box 11086
1910 Byrd Ave., Suite 100
Richmond, VA   23230-1086
Tel: (804)282-5051   *Fax:* (804)282-0090
E-Mail: soap@societyhq.com
Web Site: http://www.soap.org
Members: 1,200 individuals
Staff: 2
Annual Budget: $250-500,000
Exec. Secretary: Stewart A. Hinckley
Manager, Meetings and Conventions: Kevin Johns, CAE
Manager, Finance: David Vereen

Historical Note
The Society is a recognized subspecialty organization of the American Soc. of Anesthesiologists. SOAP was formed to provide a forum for the discussion of problems unique to the peripartum period, which includes the clinical practice of medicine, basic research, practical business and public health aspects of the field. Membership: $110/year.

Publications:
SOAP Newsletter. q.

Meetings/Conferences:
1999 – Denver, CO(Marriott)/May 19-22/400
2000 – Montreal, Canada(Queen Elizabeth)/May 29-June
        4/400
2001 – San Diego, CA/April 25-28

Soc. for Occlusal Studies *(1964)*

Historical Note
Organization defunct in 1998.

Soc. for Occupational and Environmental Health *(1972)*

6728 Old McLean Village Drive
McLean, VA   22101
Tel: (703)556-9222   *Fax:* (703)556-8729
E-Mail: soen@degnon.org
Web Site: http://www.soeh.org
Members: 300 individuals
Staff: 1
Annual Budget: $50-100,000
Exec. Director: Dan Denston

Historical Note
Founded at the New York Academy of Sciences on November 12, 1972. Incorporated in the District of Columbia. Members include physicians, hygienists, economists, laboratory scientists, academicians, labor and industry representatives, or anyone interested in occupational and/or environmental health. Serves as a forum for the presentation of scientific data and the exchange of information among members; sponsors conferences and meetings which address specific problem areas and policy questions. Officers are elected biennially; governing councillors triennially. Membership: $75/year (individual), $30/year (student).

Publications:
Archives of Environmental Health. bi-m.
SOEH Letter. q.

Meetings/Conferences:
Annual Meetings: Spring
2000 – Bethesda, MD/April 3-7

Soc. for Organic Petrology *(1984)*
c/o American Geological Institute
4220 King St.,
Alexandria, VA   22302-1502
Tel: (703)379-2480
E-Mail: barker@usgs.gov
Web Site: http://www.tsop.org/
Members: 250 individuals
Annual Budget: $10-25,000
President: Charles E. Barker, PhD.

Historical Note
TSOP are scientists and engineers with an interest in coal petrology, kerogen petrology, organic geochemistry, and related fields. Membership: $20/year (individual); $15/year (student).

Publications:
Journal of International Coal Geology. a. adv.
TSOP Annual Meeting Abstracts and Program. a. adv.
TSOP Newsletter. q.

Meetings/Conferences:
1999 – Salt Lake City, UT
2000 – Bloomington, IN
2001 – Banff, AB, Canada

Soc. for Pediatric Anesthesia
1910 Byrd Ave., Suite 100
P.O. Box 11086
Richmond, VA   23230-1086
Tel: (804)282-9780   *Fax:* (804)282-0090
E-Mail: spa@societyhq.com
Members: 2,000 individuals
Staff: 2
Annual Budget: $250-500,000
Exec. Director: John A. Hinckley
Meetings: Kevin Johns, CAE

Historical Note
The Society is a recognized subspecialty organization of the American Soc. of Anesthesiologists. Membership: $100/year.

Publications:
Anesthesia & Analgesia. m. adv.
Newsletter. semi-a.

Meetings/Conferences:
1999 – Las Vegas, NV(The Desert Inn)/Feb. 18-21/550
1999 – Dallas, TX/250
2000 – San Francisco, CA/250

Soc. for Pediatric Dermatology *(1976)*
5422 N. Bernard
Chicago, IL   60625
Tel: (773)583-9780   *Fax:* (773)583-9765
E-Mail: Patrici107@aol.com
Members: 500 individuals
Staff: 1
Annual Budget: $25-50,000
Administrator: Patricia L. Fraser

Historical Note
Members are physicians with an interest in pediatric dermatology. Membership: $150/year.

Publications:
Pediatric Dermatology. q. adv.
SPD Newsletter. q.

Meetings/Conferences:
1999 – Thompsonville, MIJuly /250
2000 – Ssanta Fe, NMJuly /250

Soc. for Pediatric Pathology *(1965)*
6728 Old McLean Village Dr.
McLean, VA   22101
Tel: (703)556-9222   *Fax:* (703)556-8729
E-Mail: socpedpath@degnon.org
Web Site: http://www.path.upmc.edu/spp
Members: 650 individuals
Staff: 2
Annual Budget: $100-250,000
Exec. Secretary: Johanna O'Toole

Historical Note
Promotes continuing education, training and standards for specialists in the field. Full members are pathologists and other physicians substantially involved in pathology as it relates to pediatric medicine. Membership: $200/year (full member), $100/year (junior member).

Publications:
Pediatric and Developmental Pathology. bi-m.

SPP Newsletter. 3/year.
Meetings/Conferences:
Semi-Annual Meetings: Spring and Fall
1999 – San Francisco, CA/Mar. 20-21/500

Soc. for Pediatric Psychology *(1968)*
Historical Note
Address unknown in 1996.

Soc. for Pediatric Radiology *(1958)*
802 Jorie Blvd.
Oak Brook, IL   60521
Tel: (630)571-2197   *Fax:* (630)571-7837
Members: 900 individuals
Staff: 2
Annual Budget: $250-500,000
Exec. Secretary: Jennifer K. Boylan

Historical Note
Members are pediatric radiologists interested in pediatric imaging. Membership: $278/year (individual).

Publications:
Membership Directory. a.
Pediatric Radiology. m.

Meetings/Conferences:
Annual Meetings: Spring/225

Soc. for Pediatric Research *(1926)*
3400 Research Forest Dr., Suite B7
The Woodlands, TX   77381
Tel: (281)419-0052   *Fax:* (281)419-0082
E-Mail: debbie @aps.spr.org
Web Site: http://aps.spr.org
Members: 2,026 individuals
Staff: 5
Annual Budget: $250-500,000
Exec. Director: Debbie Anagnostelis

Historical Note
Purpose is to provide a forum for pediatric researchers to present and receive information currently available in all fields of pediatric research. Membership: $175/year (active); $75/year (senior).

Publications:
Pediatric Research. m. adv.
Pediatric Research Program Issue. a. adv.

Meetings/Conferences:
Annual Meetings: Spring/4,000
1999 – San Francisco, CA(Moscone Convention
   Center)/April 30-May 3
2000 – Boston, MA(Convention Center)/May 12-16

Soc. for Pediatric Urology
Section of Urology, MC-4056
5841 S. Maryland Ave.
Chicago, IL   60637
Tel: (773)702-6150   *Fax:* (773)702-8702
E-Mail: wcromie@surgery.bsd.uchicago.edu
Web Site: http://www.spu.org
Members: 350 individuals
Staff: 1
Annual Budget: under $10,000
Secretary-Treasurer: William J. Cromie

Historical Note
An invitational professional society whose secretary changes every three years. Membership: $100/year (individual).

Publications:
Newsletter.
Society for Pediatric Urology. w.

Meetings/Conferences:
Annual Meetings: Immediately preceding those of the American Urological Ass'n

---

Soc. for Personality Assessment *(1938)*
6109 H Arlington Blvd
Falls Church, VA   22044
Tel: (703)534-4772   *Fax:* (703)534-6905
Members: 2,700 individuals
Staff: 2
Annual Budget: $250-500,000
Operations Manager: Manuela Schulze

Historical Note
Founded and incorporated in Newark, New Jersey in 1938 as the Rorschach Research Exchange. The name changed to: the Soc. for Projective Techniques; the Soc. for Projective Techniques and Personality Assessment; and, in 1971, the Soc. for Personality Assessment. Membership: $40/year (fellow/member/associate), $15/year (student).

Publications:
Journal of Personality Assessment. bi-m. adv.
SPA Exchange. semi-a.

Meetings/Conferences:
Annual Meetings: March

Soc. for Phenomenology and Existential Philosophy *(1962)*
Drawer 61 - Philosophy Dept.
Earlham College
Richmond, IN   47374
Tel: (765)983-1438   *Fax:* (765)983-1234
E-Mail: bowerma@earlham.edu
Members: 1,900 individuals
Secretary-Treasurer: Marya Bower

Historical Note
Membership: $35/year (individual); $10/year (student/retired).

Publications:
Annual Program. a. adv.
Selected Studies in Phenomenology & Existential Philosophy.
   a.

Meetings/Conferences:
Annual Meetings: October

Soc. for Philosophy and Technology *(1975)*
San Jose State University
Department of Philosophy
San Jose, CA   95192-0096
Tel: (408)924-4526
E-Mail: cook@parc.xerox.com
Web Site: http://www.spt.org
Members: 300 individuals
Secretary: Scott Noam Cook

Publications:
Newsletter. q.
Philosophy & Technology. a.

Meetings/Conferences:
Annual Meetings: in conjunction with the American
   Philosophical Ass'n
1999 – San Jose/Silicon Valley/Silicon 0-17

Soc. for Philosophy of Religion *(1940)*
Dept. of Philosophy, Univ. of Georgia
Athens, GA   30602
Tel: (404)542-2823
E-Mail: harrison@uga.cc.uga.edu
Members: 100 individuals
Staff: 1
Annual Budget: under $10,000
Secretary-Treasurer: Frank R. Harrison, III

Historical Note
Members are leading scholars in the philosophy of religion who must be nominated and voted upon. Membership is limited to 125. Sponsors the Southern Humanities Conference. Membership: $20/year.

Publications:
International Journal for Philosophy of Religion. bi-m.

Meetings/Conferences:
Annual Meetings: February-March

Soc. for Photographic Education *(1963)*
P.O. Box 2811
Daytona Beach, FL   32120-2811
Tel: (904)255-8131   *Fax:* (904)947-5497
E-Mail: SocPhotoEd@aol.com
Web Site: http://www.spenational.org
Members: 1,800 individuals
Staff: 1
Annual Budget: $100-250,000
Exec. Director: James J. Murphy

Historical Note
College and university teachers of photography, photographers, museum curators and students of photography. Membership: $55/year (professional/instructor); $35/year (student/retired).

Publications:
Exposure. 2/year. adv.
Membership Directory. a.
Newsletter. q.

Meetings/Conferences:
Annual Meetings: Spring
1999 – Tucson, AZ(Holiday Inn City Center)/March 11-14
2000 – Cincinnati, OH(Omni Netherland Plaza)/March 23-26

Soc. for Physical Regulation in Biology and Medicine *(1980)*
7519 Ridge Road
Frederick, MD   21702-3519
Tel: (301)663-1915   *Fax:* (301)371-8955
E-Mail: 75230.122@compuserve.com
Web Site: http://www.ec.hscsyr.edu/SPRBM
Members: 300 individuals
Staff: 1
Annual Budget: $10-25,000
Exec. Director: William G. Wisecup

Historical Note
Founded as Bioelectrical Repair and Growth Soc., assumed its current name in 1994. SPRBM members are persons conducting research relevant to electric or magnetic field effects on repair, growth, regeneration or other activity of living tissue and related fields including biologists, physical scientists, physicians, surgeons, engineers and members of industry. Membership: $75/year (individual).

Publications:
Transactions. a.

Meetings/Conferences:
Annual Meetings: October

Soc. for Psychological Anthropology *(1977)*
Historical Note
A section of the American Anthropological Ass'n. SPA is a broad, multidisciplinary organization of individuals interested in cultural, psychological and social interrelations at all levels.

Soc. for Psychophysiological Research *(1960)*
1010 Vermont Ave., N.W., Suite 1100
Washington, DC   20005
Tel: (202)783-2077   *Fax:* (202)783-2083
Web Site: www.sprweb.org
Members: 2,000 individuals
Staff: 16
Annual Budget: $25-50,000
Exec. Director: Alan G. Kraut

Historical Note
A multidisciplinary society of physicians, psychologists, and engineers. Administrative support provided by American Psychological Soc. (same address).

Publications:
Psychophysiology. bi-m.

Meetings/Conferences:
1999 – Spain/Oct. 6-10

Soc. for Public Health Education *(1950)*
1015 15th St., N.W., Suite 410
Washington, DC   20005-2605
Tel: (202)408-9804   *Fax:* (202)408-9815
E-Mail: info@sophe.org
Web Site: http://www.sophe.org
Members: 2,200 individuals, 18 chapters
Staff: 3
Annual Budget: $250-500,000
Exec. Director: Elaine Auld, MPH, CHES
Director of Professional Development: Eleanor Dixon-Terry

Historical Note
Formerly (1970) Soc. of Public Health Educators, Inc. Membership: $55/year (new member); $80/year (renewal); $40/year (student).

Publications:
Health Education & Behavior. bi-m.
News and Views. q.

Meetings/Conferences:
Semi-Annual Meetings: Fall, with American Public Health
    Ass'n & June
1999 – Chicago, IL

Soc. for Radiation Oncology Administrators *(1984)*
820 Jorie Blvd.
Oak Brook, IL   60523-2251
Tel: (630)571-9065   *Fax:* (630)571-7837
E-Mail: jendra@rsna.org
Web Site: http://www.sroa.org
Members: 500 individuals
Staff: 2
Annual Budget: $100-250,000
Exec. Secretary: Jeanne Jendra

Historical Note
Established in Philadelphia, SROA is concerned with the administration of the business and non-medical management aspects of radiation oncology. Membership: $175/year.

Publications:
Radiation Oncology New For Administrators Newsletter. q.
SROA Membership Directory. a.

Meetings/Conferences:
Annual Meetings: Fall/75
1999 – San Antonio, TX(Hyatt Regency)/Oct. 31-Nov. 3/450
2000 – Boston, MA(Boston Park Plaza)/Oct. 22-25/450
2001 – San Francisco, CA(The Fairmont)/Nov. 4-7/150
2002 – New Orleans, LA(Hotel Intercontinental)/Oct. 4-7/450

Soc. for Range Management *(1948)*
1839 York St.
Denver, CO   80206
Tel: (303)355-7070   *Fax:* (303)355-5059
E-Mail: srmden@ix.netcom.com
Web Site: http://www.srm.org
Members: 4,200 individuals
Staff: 6
Annual Budget: $250-500,000
Exec. V. President: J. Craig Whittekiend
Director of Administration: Ann Harris
Director of Accounting and Sales: Kirsten Tardy
Membership Services Manager: Matthew Wirt

Historical Note
Founded in Salt Lake City in January 1948 as the American Soc. of Range Management and incorporated in Wyoming in 1949. Became the Soc. for Range Management in 1971. Studies rangeland ecosystems and the principles of managing range resources. Membership: $55-$70/year (individual); $205/year (organization/company).

Publications:
Abstracts. a.
Journal of Range Management. bi-m. adv.
Rangelands. bi-m.
Trail Boss News. m.

Meetings/Conferences:
Annual Meetings: January-February/1,500
1999 – Omaha, NE(Holiday Inn)/Feb. 18-26/1300
2000 – Boise, ID

Soc. for Reformation Research *(1947)*
c/o Center for Reformation Research
6477 San Bonita Ave.
St. Louis, MO   63105
Tel: (314)727-6655
Members: 200 individuals
Annual Budget: under $10,000
President: James Tracy
Treasurer: William S. Maltby

Historical Note
Affiliated with the American Historical Ass'n and the American Society of Church History. Formerly (1985) the American Soc. for Reformation Research. Member of the Council on the Study of Religion. Membership: $10/year.

Publications:
Archive for Reformation History. a.

Meetings/Conferences:
Annual Meetings: With the American Historical Ass'n

Soc. for Reproductive Endocrinologists and Infertility *(1920)*
1209 Montgomery Hwy.
Birmingham, AL   35216-2809
Tel: (205)978-5000   *Fax:* (205)978-5005
E-Mail: pitman@asrm.org
Web Site: http://www.socrei.org
Members: 500 individuals
Administrator: Angelia Pitman

Historical Note
Formerly Soc. of Reproductive Endocrinologists (1998). Members are physicians, both in private practice and academia, who are certified by the American Board of Obstetrics and Gynecology as reproductive endocrinologists. Administrative support provided by the American Soc. for Reproductive Medicine.

Meetings/Conferences:
Annual Meetings: Annual meeting held with the American Soc.
    for Reproductive Medicine.

Soc. for Reproductive Surgeons *(1984)*
1209 Montgomery Hwy.
Birmingham, AL   35216-2809
Tel: (205)978-5000   *Fax:* (205)978-5005
E-Mail: joyce@asrm.org
Members: 500 individuals
Administrator: Joyce Zeitz

Historical Note
Members are doctors specializing in gynecologic and urologic surgery. Administrative support is provided by the American Soc. for Reproductive Medicine. Membership: $50/year (individual).

Meetings/Conferences:
Annual Meetings: Annual meeting held with the American Soc.
    for Reproductive Medicine.

Soc. for Research in Child Development *(1933)*
Center for Human Growth & Development
Univ. of Michigan 505 E. Huron St., #301
Ann Arbor, MI   48104-1522
Tel: (734)998-6578   *Fax:* (734)998-6569
E-Mail: jwhagen@umich.edu
Members: 5,000 individuals
Staff: 5
Annual Budget: $1-2,000,000
Exec. Officer: John W. Hagen
Administrator: Patricia Settimi
Membership Coordinator: Thelma Tucker

Historical Note
Founded in 1933 in the District of Columbia as an outgrowth of the Committee on Child Development of the Nat'l Research Council. The Committee, formed in 1925, was the successor to a subcommittee on Child Development under the Division of Anthropology and Psychology of the Nat'l Research Council which began in 1922. Incorporated in Illinois in 1950, in Indiana in 1956 and in Wisconsin in 1970. Affiliated with the American Ass'n for the Advancement of Science. Membership: $125/year.

Publications:
Abstracts. q.
Child Development. bi m. adv.
Child Development Abstracts and Bibliography. 3/year.
Monographs of the SRCD. 4-5/year.
Social Policy Reports. q.

Meetings/Conferences:
Biennial meetings: odd years in Spring
1999 – Albuquerque, NM(Convention Center)/April 15-18
2001 – Minneapolis, MN(Convention Center)/April 19-22

Soc. for Research in Music Education
Historical Note
A council of the Music Educators Nat'l Conference.

Soc. for Research on Adolescence *(1984)*
Loyola U.-Chicago, Dept. of Psychology
6525 N. Sheridan Road
Chicago, IL   60626
Tel: (773)508-3007   *Fax:* (773)508-8713
E-Mail: socresadol@luc.edu
Members: 900 individuals
Exec. Secretary: Maryse Richards

Historical Note
SRA is a dynamic, multidisciplinary, internat'l organization dedicated to understanding adolescence through research. Its members conduct theoretical studies, basic and applied research, and policy analyses to understand and enhance adolescent development. Membership: $100/year (individual); $50/year (student).

Publications:
Journal of Research on Adolescence. q.
Newsletter. bi-a.
SRA Directory of Members.

Meetings/Conferences:
Biennial Meetings: even years/Spring
2000 – Chicago, IL(Fairmont)

Soc. for Research on Nicotine and Tobacco *(1994)*
7611 Elmwood Ave., Suite 201
Middleton, WI   53562-3161
Tel: (608)836-3787
E-Mail: srnt1@aol.com
Web Site: http://www.srnt.org
Members: 425 individuals
Staff: 7
Annual Budget: $50-100,000
Exec. Director: Sarah E. Evans

Historical Note
Members are scientists and other researchers interested in societal, biobehavioral, and political aspects of tobacco and tobacco use. Membership: $80/year (full member/affiliate), $20/year (student).

Publications:
Nicotine and Tobacco Research. q. adv.
SRNT Newsletter. q. adv.

Meetings/Conferences:
Annual Meetings: Spring
1999 – San Diego, CA(Sheraton)/March 5-7/350

Soc. for Risk Analysis *(1982)*
1313 Dolly Madison Blvd., Suite 402
McLean, VA   22101-3926
Tel: (703)790-1745   *Fax:* (703)790-2672

E-Mail: srac@burkinc.com
Web Site: http://www.sra.org
Members: 2,090 individuals
Staff: 6
Annual Budget: $250-500,000
Exec. Secretary: Richard J. Burk, Jr.

Historical Note
Founded to study and understand on a scientific basis the risks posed by technological development. Membership: $95/year.

Publications:
Risk Analysis Journal. bi-m. adv.
Risk Newsletter. q. adv.

Meetings/Conferences:
Annual Meetings: Fall
1999 – Atlanta, GA/Dec. 5-8

Soc. for Romanian Studies *(1973)*
Dept. of History, Huntington College
Huntington, IN   46750
Tel: (219)359-4242   *Fax:* (219)356-9448
E-Mail: pmichelson@huntington.edu
Web Site: http://www.huntington.edu/srs
Members: 200 individuals
Annual Budget: under $10,000
Secretary: Paul Michelson

Historical Note
Has no paid officers or full-time staff. Membership: $15/year (full member); $10/year (student).

Publications:
SRS Newsletter. 3/year.

Meetings/Conferences:
1999 – St. Louis, MO

Soc. for Scholarly Publishing *(1978)*
10200 West 44th Ave., Suite 304
Wheat Ridge, CO   80033-2840
Tel: (303)422-3914   *Fax:* (303)422-8894
E-Mail: ssp@resourcecenter.com
Web Site: http://www.sspnet.org
Members: 800 individuals, 85 organizations
Staff: 2
Annual Budget: $100-250,000
Exec. Director: Francine Butler, Ph.D., CAE
Dir., Communications: Michael P. Thompson
Dir., Meetings: Kate Holland, CMP
Dir., Member Services: Suzanne Starr

Historical Note
Established on June 16, 1978, in Washington, DC. Members are individuals, publishing companies and professional societies involved in the production of scholarly books and periodicals. Membership: $60/year.

Publications:
Directory of Members. a.
SSP Bulletin. bi-m. adv.

Meetings/Conferences:
Annual Meetings: late Spring/450
1999 – Boston, MA/June 9-11

Soc. for Sedimentary Geology
Historical Note
See SEPM - Soc. for Sedimentary Geology.

Soc. for Service Professionals in Printing
433 E. Monroe Ave.
Alexandria, VA   22301-1645
Tel: (703)684-0044   *Fax:* (703)548-9137
E-Mail: ssppinfo@aol.com
Members: 1,500 individuals
Staff: 2
Annual Budget: $100-250,000
Director: Mike Matheny
V. President: Debbie Ayres

Historical Note
SSPP provides continuing education to customer service professionals in the printing industry. Membership: $220/year (individual); $230/year (company).

Publications:
Printing Service Specialist's Handbook. a.
Signature Service Newsletter. m. adv.

Soc. for Sex Therapy and Research *(1974)*
10751 Falls Rd., Suite 300
Fall Concourse
Lutherville, MD   21093
Tel: (410)583-2688   *Fax:* (410)583-2693
Members: 286 individuals
Annual Budget: $25-50,000
President: Peter Fagan, Ph.D.

Historical Note
Formerly the Eastern Ass'n of Sex Therapy, SSTAR is a professional society formed to enhance communication between clinicians and clinical investigators interested in the treatment of human sexual disorders. Membership is multidisciplinary with the criteria that members are actively involved in the treatment or clinical investigation of sexual disorders, possess superior clinical competence and high ethical standards. Membership: $75/year.

Publications:
Newsletter. q.

Meetings/Conferences:
Annual Meetings: Spring

Soc. for Slovene Studies *(1973)*
Dept. of Modern Lang. & Cultural Stds,
University of Alberta
Edmonton, AB   T6G 2-E6
Tel: (403)492-0789   *Fax:* (403)492-2906
E-Mail: tom.priestly@ualberta.ca.
Web Site: http://www.ualberta.ca/ ~ ljubljau/sss.html

Members: 350 individuals
Staff: 1
Annual Budget: under $10,000
President: Tom M.S. Priestly

Historical Note
An affiliate of American Ass'n for the Advancement of Slavic Studies and American Ass'n of Teachers of Slavic and East European Languages, SSS is a non-profit association of scholars dedicated to the research of Slovene culture. Its purpose is to promote the dissemination of scholarly information on Slovene studies through meetings, conferences, and the preparation of scholarly works for publication. Has no paid officers or full-time staff. Membership: $20/year (regular or sustaining), $5/year (students).

Publications:
Slovene Studies. semi-a. adv.

Meetings/Conferences:
Annual Meetings: September, with the American Ass'n for the
    Advancement of Slavic Studies
1999 – St. Louis, MO

Soc. for Social Studies of Science *(1975)*
Dept. of Sociology, 126 Stubbs Hall
Louisiana State University
Baton Rouge, LA 70803
Tel: (504)388-1645
Members: 550 individuals
Staff: 1
Annual Budget: $25-50,000
Secretary: Wesley Shrum

Historical Note
Affiliated with American Ass'n for the Advancement of Science. Also known as 4S. Membership: $30/year (individual), $15/year (student & developing country).

Publications:
Science, Technology & Human Values. q.
Technoscience Newsletter. bi-a.

Meetings/Conferences:

Soc. for Social Work Leadership in Health Care *(1965)*
One N. Franklin, 31st Floor
Chicago, IL 60606
Tel: (312)422-3777   *Fax:* (312)422-4580
Web Site: http://www.sswalhc.org
Members: 1,700 individuals
Staff: 5
Annual Budget: $250-500,000
Exec. Director: Richard Koepke
Manager, Education: Vanessa Kizart

Historical Note
Formerly (1993) the Society for Hospital Social Work Directors, and (1994) Social Work Administrators in Health Care and (1998)Society for Social Work Administrators in Health Care. Full membership is open to social workers with a BSW, MSW or doctoral degree in social work, employed in a heath care setting as an administrator, manager, supervisor, or leader. Membership is also open to health care professionals, consultants, educators, students, retirees, or other individuals with an interest or involvement in health care social work administration. The Society is affiliated with the American Hospital Ass'n.

Publications:
Continuum Journal. bi-m.
Social Work Administration (newsletter)/Career
    Opportunities. m.

Meetings/Conferences:
1999 – New York, NY(Marriott Marquis)/April 17-21

Soc. for Software Quality *(1984)*
P.O. Box 86958
San Diego, CA 92138-6958
Tel: (281)276-5577
E-Mail: ssq@ssq.org
Web Site: http://www.ssq.org
Members: 250 individuals
Annual Budget: $50-100,000
Secretary: Ralph Ambuehl

Historical Note
SSQ members are professionals interested in producing quality software. Membership: $30/year (individual).

Publications:
Journal. 11/year.

Meetings/Conferences:
1999 – Washington, DC

Soc. for Spanish and Portuguese Historical Studies *(1969)*
History Department, SSB 215
University of Arizona
Tucson, AZ 85721-0027
Tel: (520)621-5860   *Fax:* (520)621-2422
E-Mail: helen_nader@ns.arizona.edu
Members: 425 individuals
Staff: 1
Annual Budget: $10-25,000
General Secretary: Helen Nader

Historical Note
Founded to promote research in all aspects and epochs of Iberian historical studies. Membership: $20/year (individual), $23/year (organization).

Publications:
Bulletin of the SSPHS. 3/year. adv.

Meetings/Conferences:
Annual Meetings: Spring
1999 – San Diego, CA

Soc. for Surgery of the Alimentary Tract *(1960)*
6900 Grove Road
Thorofare, NJ 08086-9447

Tel: (609)251-0558   *Fax:* (609)848-5274
E-Mail: ssat@slackinc.com
Web Site: http://www.ssat.com
Members: 1,200 individuals
Staff: 1
Annual Budget: $500-1,000,000
Exec. Director: Clifford M. Brownstein
Manager, Membership: Diana Kipple

Historical Note
Formerly Ass'n of Colon Surgery. Membership: $150/year (individual).

Publications:
Journal of Gastrointestinal Surgey. q. adv.
SSAT Newsletter. q.

Meetings/Conferences:
Annual Meetings: May
1999 – Orlando, FL
2000 – San Diego, CA
2001 – Atlanta, GA

Soc. for Technical Communication *(1953)*
901 N. Stuart St., Suite 904
Arlington, VA 22203-1854
Tel: (703)522-4114   *Fax:* (703)522-2075
E-Mail: mbrship@stc-va.org
Web Site: www.stc-va.org
Members: 24,000 individuals
Staff: 12
Annual Budget: $2-5,000,000
Exec. Director and Counsel: William C. Stolgitis
Deputy Exec. Director: Peter R. Herbst

Historical Note
In 1953, two organizations interested in improving the practice of technical communication, the Soc. of Technical Writers and the Ass'n of Technical Writers and Editors, were founded simultaneously on the East Coast. These organizations merged in 1957 to form the Soc. of Technical Writers and Editors. This grew rapidly and, in 1960, merged with a Pacific Coast group, the Technical Publishing Soc., founded in 1954. This merger resulted in the Soc. of Technical Writers and Publishers. In 1971, the name was changed to Soc. for Technical Communication. Today, STC is the largest professional society in the world concerned primarily with all phases of technical communication. Incorporated in New York in 1958. Member of the Internat'l Council of Communication Societies. Membership: $95/year (individual).

Publications:
Conference Proceedings. a.
INTERCOM. m. adv.
Technical Communication. q. adv.

Meetings/Conferences:
Annual Meetings: Spring/Internat'l Technical Communication
    Conference/1,400
1999 – Cincinnati, OH/May 16-19
2000 – Orlando, FL/May 21-24
2001 – Chicago, IL/May 13-16
2002 – Nashville, TN/May 5-8
2003 – Dallas, TX/May 18-21

Soc. for Technological Advancement of Reporting
P.O. Box 150127
Altamonte Springs, FL 32715-0127
Tel: (407)774-7880   *Fax:* (407)774-6440
Staff: 2
Exec. Director: Tina Kautter

Soc. for Textual Scholarship *(1979)*
Ph.D. Program in English
CUNY Graduate Center, 33 W. 42nd St.
New York, NY 10036
Tel: (212)642-2227   *Fax:* (212)642-2205
Members: 600 individuals, 50 institutions
Staff: 1
Annual Budget: under $10,000
Exec. Director: David C. Greetham

Historical Note
STS was founded to overcome the disciplinary isolation of textual scholarship in various fields. It aims to discover common theories and procedures which could be of value to researchers in all areas of textual study. Membership: $15/year.

Publications:
Bulletin. irreg.
Newsletter. irreg.
TEXT. a.

Meetings/Conferences:
Annual Meetings: Biennial Meetings in April

Soc. for the Advancement of Behavior Analysis *(1980)*
Western Michigan Univ., 213 West Hall
1201 Oliver Street
Kalamazoo, MI 49008-5052
Tel: (616)387-8341   *Fax:* (616)387-8354
E-Mail: 76236.1312@compuserve.com
Web Site: http://www.wmich.edu/aba
Members: 400 donors
Staff: 3
Annual Budget: $10-25,000
Exec. Director: Maria E. Malott

Historical Note
Purpose is to provide instruction and training in behavior analysis and to disseminate information concerning it.

Meetings/Conferences:
Annual Meetings: None held.

Soc. for the Advancement of Economic Theory *(1990)*
330 Commerce Bldg. Univ. of Illinois
1206 S. 6th St.
Champaign, IL 61820
Tel: (217)333-0120   *Fax:* (217)244-6678
Members: 170 individuals

President: Nicholas Yannelis

Historical Note
SAET members are individuals with an interest in theoretical economics.

Publications:
Economic Theory Journal. q.

Meetings/Conferences:

Soc. for the Advancement of Education *(1939)*
99 W. Hawthorne Ave., Suite 518
Valley Stream, NY 11580-6101
Tel: (516)568-9191
Members: 1,900 individuals
Staff: 5
Annual Budget: $500-1,000,000
President: Stanley Lehrer

Historical Note
Membership: $29/year.

Publications:
USA Today Magazine. m. adv.

Meetings/Conferences:
1999 – Valley Stream, NY

Soc. for the Advancement of Food Service Research *(1958)*
P.O. Box 700
Ithaca, NY 14851
Tel: (607)257-6483   *Fax:* (607)257-1902
Members: 250 individuals
Staff: 4
Annual Budget: $10-25,000
Executive Director: Kristy Derovira
Membership and Marketing Coordinator: Amber Schlaht

Historical Note
SAFSR is the only national professional association devoted to the advancement of foodservice research and development. Membership: $100/year (individual); $25/year (student/retired).

Publications:
Annual Proceedings. a.
Newsletter. a.

Meetings/Conferences:
Annual Meetings: Spring
1999 – Chantilly, VA/March 26-29

Soc. for the Advancement of Material and Process Engineering *(1944)*
P.O. Box 2459
Covina, CA 91722-8459
Tel: (626)331-0616   *Fax:* (626)332-8929
Toll Free: (800)562 - 7360
E-Mail: SAMPEIBO@aol.com
Web Site: http://www.et.byu.edu/~sampe/
Members: 6,000 individuals
Staff: 12
Annual Budget: $1-2,000,000
Exec. Director: Daun White
Coordinator, Exhibits: Kadi Woolman

Historical Note
Founded in Hawthorne, CA as the Soc. of Aircraft Material and Process Engineers. Incorporated in California in 1960 as the Soc. of Aerospace Material and Process Engineers and assumed its present name in 1973. Membership: $63/year (professional/ associate), $15/year(student). Dues include subscription cost to the SAMPE Journal.

Publications:
SAMPE Journal. bi-m. adv.
SAMPE Journal of Advanced Materials. q.
Semi. Annual Proceedings.

Meetings/Conferences:
Semi-Annual Meetings: Spring and Fall
1999 – Long Beach, CA/May 24-27
2000 – Long Beach, CA(Long Beach Convention
    Center)/May 22-25/2000

Soc. for the Advancement of Scandinavian Study *(1911)*
Brigham Young Univ., 3003 JKHB
Provo, UT 84602
Tel: (801)378-5598   *Fax:* (801)378-4539
E-Mail: sass-subscriptions@email.byu.edu
Web Site: http://www.vbyu.edu/sasslink
Members: 800 individuals
Annual Budget: $25-50,000
Circulation Manager/Asst. Editor: Jason Francis

Historical Note
Scholars, teachers, and researchers in Scandinavian language, literature and culture. Regular membership: $50/year (individual), $60/year (organization).

Publications:
SASS News & Notes. semi-a.
Scandinavian Studies. q. adv.

Meetings/Conferences:
Annual Meetings: May
1999 – Seattle, WA/April 29-May 1

Soc. for the Advancement of Social Psychology *(1974)*
Department of Psychology
Mercer University
Macon, GA 31207-0001
Tel: (912)752-2972   *Fax:* (912)752-2956
E-Mail: dane_fc@mercer.edu
Members: 700 individuals
Annual Budget: under $10,000
Secretary: Francis C. Dane, Ph.D.

Historical Note
SASP is concerned with advancing social psychology as a profession, with deepening and broadening understanding of social

psychological phenomena, with improving communication among social psychologists, and with promoting effective, widespread dissemination and utilization of social psychological knowledge. Membership: $22/year (individual), $20/year (organization).

Publications:
Contemporary Social Psychology Newsletter. q.
Membership Directory. irreg.

Meetings/Conferences:
Annual Meetings: in conjunction with the American Psychological Ass'n

Soc. for the Advancement of Socio-Economics (1989)
P.O. Box 39008
Baltimore, MD 21212-6008
Tel: (410)435-6617   *Fax:* (410)377-7965
E-Mail: SASEORG@AOL.COM
Web Site: http://www.mpi-fg-koeln.mpg.de/sase99
Members: 900 individuals
Staff: 1
Annual Budget: $50-100,000
Executive Director: Mary Grossman

Historical Note
Academic disciplines represented in SASE includes economics, sociology, political science, psychology, anthropology, philosophy, history, law, and management. The membership of SASE includes business people and policy makers working in governmental and international organizations. Membership: $30/year (individual); $15/year (student).

Publications:
Journal of Social Economics. 4/year.
SASE News. 3/year. adv.
Series in Socio-Economics. a.

Meetings/Conferences:
1999 – Madison, WI/July 8-11

Soc. for the Advancement of Women's Health Research (1990)
1828 L St., N.W., Suite 625
Washington, DC 20036-5004
Tel: (202)223-8224   *Fax:* (202)833-3472
E-Mail: information@womens-health.org
Web Site: http://www.womens-health.org
Exec. Director: Phyllis M. Greenberger, MSW

Historical Note
SAWHR seeks to improve the health of women through research. Membership:$25/year.

Meetings/Conferences:
1999 – Hilton Head, SC/June 12-16

Soc. for the Anthropology in Consciousness (1980)
Historical Note
A section of the American Anthropological Ass'n. Established as a multidisciplinary organization designed to provide a forum for the study of consciousness for cross-cultural, experimental, experiential, and theoretical perspectives.

Soc. for the Anthropology of Europe (1986)
Historical Note
A section of the American Anthropological Ass'n.

Soc. for the Anthropology of North America
Historical Note
A section of the American Anthropological Ass'n.

Soc. for the Anthropology of Work
Historical Note
A section of the American Anthropological Ass'n. Provides a forum for discussing the study of work from a variety of perspectives, including those of achcheologists, linguists, and physical, cultural and practicing anthropologists.

Soc. for the Exploration of Psychotherapy Integration (1984)
134 Wooleys Lane
Great Neck, NY 11023
Tel: (516)877-4803   *Fax:* (516)877-4805
E-Mail: stricker@panther.adelphi.edu
Members: 750 individuals
Annual Budget: $10-25,000
Treasurer: George Stricker, Ph.D.
Education Coordinator: John C. Norcross, Ph.D.

Historical Note
SEPI is an interdisciplinary organization of professionals interested in approaches to psychotherapy that are not limited by a single orientation. Members are mental health professionals with an interest in integrating theories and techniques in psychotherapy. Membership: $40/year (individual); $20/year (student).

Publications:
Directory. a.
Journal of Psychotherapy Integration. q. adv.

Meetings/Conferences:
1999 – Miami, FL(Sheraton Four Points)/200

Soc. for the History of Discoveries (1960)
Northern Michigan University
1401 Presque Isle Aave.
Marquette, MI 49855-5352
Tel: (906)227-1229   *Fax:* (906)227-2229
E-Mail: rmagnagh@nmu.edu
Members: 300 individuals
Staff: 1
Annual Budget: under $10,000
Secretary-Treasurer: Russell Magnaghi

Historical Note
Affiliated with the American Historical Ass'n. Established as a result of the International Congress for the History of Discoveries, held in Lisbon in 1960. Membership: $30/year.

Publications:
Annual Report. a.
Newsletter. a.
Terrae Incognitae. a. adv.

Meetings/Conferences:
Annual Meetings: Fall
1999 – St. Louis, MI/Sept. 23-25

Soc. for the History of Technology (1958)
c/o Dept. History
Auburn University
Auburn, AL 36849-5259
Tel: (334)884-6645   *Fax:* (334)884-6673
Members: 2,000 individuals
Annual Budget: $10-25,000
Secretary: Lindy Biggs

Historical Note
Formed in Cleveland in 1958 and incorporated in Ohio in 1959. Affiliated with the American Ass'n for the Advancement of Science and the American Historical Ass'n. SHOT seeks to encourage the study of the development of technology and its relation with society and culture. U.S. Membership: $37/year (individual), $85/year (organization), $22/year (student).

Publications:
Newsletter. q. adv.
Technology and Culture. q. adv.

Meetings/Conferences:
1999 – Detroit
2000 – Munich, Germany

Soc. for the Philosophy of Sex and Love (1977)
Indiana University of Pennsylvania
Department of Philosophy and Religion
Indiana, PA 15705-1087
Tel: (724)357-2310   *Fax:* (724)357-4039
E-Mail: caraway@grove.iup.edu
Members: 60 individuals
Annual Budget: under $10,000
President: Carol Caraway, Ph.D.

Historical Note
Members are academics and others. Membership: $7/year (individual). Membership: $7/year (regular); $4/year (student); $14/year (foreign).

Publications:
SPSL Newsletter. a.

Meetings/Conferences:
Annual Meetings: in conjunction with the American Philosophical Ass'n

Soc. for the Preservation of Oral Health (1960)
155 Second St., SW
Winterhaven, FL 33880
Tel: (941)293-1807   *Fax:* (941)297-9077
Members: 75 individuals
Staff: 1
Annual Budget: $10-25,000
Secretary-Treasurer: Dr. Steven Hewett
President: Dr. Samuel F. Jirik

Historical Note
Members are those who have practiced for at least five years and who concentrate on or have a strong interest in preventive dentistry. Membership: $375/year.

Meetings/Conferences:
Annual Meetings: March

Soc. for the Psychological Study of Ethnic Minority Issues
Historical Note
A division of the American Psychological Ass'n.

Soc. for the Psychological Study of Lesbian and Gay Issues
Historical Note
A division of the American Psychological Ass'n.

Soc. for the Psychological Study of Men and Masculinity
Historical Note
A division of the American Psychological Ass'n.

Soc. for the Psychological Study of Social Issues (1936)
P.O. Box 1248
Ann Arbor, MI 48106-1248
Tel: (734)662-9130   *Fax:* (734)662-5607
E-Mail: spssi@spssi.org
Web Site: http://www.spssi.org
Members: 3,000 individuals
Staff: 2
Annual Budget: $250-500,000
Secretary-Treasurer: Geoffrey M. Maruyama

Historical Note
Seeks to bring behavioral and social science theory, empirical evidence and practice into focus on human problems. Members must be college students or professionals. A division (#9) of the American Psychological Ass'n. Membership: $10-75/year.

Publications:
Journal of Social Issues. q.
Newsletter.
Social Psychology. a.
SPSSI. Sponsored Volumes.

Meetings/Conferences:
Annual Meetings: Annual Council Meeting in August with American Psychological Ass'n; Mid-year Meeting in February-March

Soc. for the Scientific Study of Religion (1949)

1365 Stone Hall Sociology Dept.
Purdue University
West Lafayette, IN 47907-1365
Tel: (765)494-6286
E-Mail: sssr@sri.soc.purdue.edu
Members: 1,600 individuals, 1,300 libraries
Staff: 1
Annual Budget: $50-100,000
Business Manager: Anna T. Davidson

Historical Note
Founded at Harvard University in 1949 and incorporated the same year in Connecticut. Membership: $34/year (individual), $50-53/year (organization).

Publications:
Journal for the Scientific Study of Religion. q. adv.

Meetings/Conferences:
Annual Meetings: November/500

Soc. for the Scientific Study of Sexuality (1957)
P.O. Box 208
Mount Vernon, IA 52314-0208
Tel: (319)895-8407   *Fax:* (319)895-6203
E-Mail: TheSociety@worldnet.att.net
Web Site: http://www.ssc.wisc.edu/ssss
Members: 1000 individuals
Staff: 3
Annual Budget: $250-500,000
Exec. Director: Howard J. Ruppel, Jr., EdD,

Historical Note
An international professional association of researchers, clinicians educators, who share an interest and competency in the scientific pursuit of knowledge concerning sexuality. Membership: $110/year.

Publications:
Annual Review of Sex Research. a.
Journal of Sex Research. q. adv.
Membership Handbook. a.
SSSS Newsletter. q.

Meetings/Conferences:
Annual Meetings: November
1999 – St. Louis, MO(Hyatt at Union Station)/Nov. 3-7

Soc. for the Study of Amphibians and Reptiles (1958)
CT State Musuem of Natural History
University of Connecticut
Storrs, CT 06269-3023
Members: 2,100 individuals, 400 institutions
Staff: 12
Annual Budget: $100-250,000
Secretary: Ellen J. Censky

Historical Note
Formerly (1967) Ohio Herpetological Soc. Membership: $40/year (individual); $70/year (organization/company); $30/year (student).

Publications:
Herpetological Review. q. adv.
Journal of Herpetology. q.

Meetings/Conferences:
Annual Meetings: August University Park/Penn State University/June

Soc. for the Study of Evolution (1946)
P.O. Box 1897
Lawrence, KS 66044
Tel: (785)843-1221   *Fax:* (785)843-1274
Toll Free: (800)627 - 0629
E-Mail: kent@darwin.eeu.uconn.edu
Web Site: http://isul.la.asu.edu/evolution/
Members: 3,000 individuals
Staff: 1
Annual Budget: $250-500,000
Exec. V. President: Kent Holsinger

Historical Note
Founded in St. Louis on March 30, 1946 as an outgrowth of the Committee on Common Problems of Genetics, Paleontology and Systematics established in 1943 by the Nat'l Research Council. Absorbed the Society for the Study of Speciation. Promotes the study of organic evolution and the integration of the various fields of science concerned with evolution. Membership: $60-65/year (individual); $170-180/year (organization).

Publications:
Evolution. bi-m.

Meetings/Conferences:
Annual Meetings: June
1999 – Madison, WI/June 22-26

Soc. for the Study of Indigenous Languages of the Americas (1981)
P.O. Box 555
Arcata, CA 95518-0555
Tel: (707)826-4324   *Fax:* (707)677-1676
E-Mail: vkgolla@ucdavis.edu
Web Site: http://www.trc2.ucdavis.edu/ssila
Members: 850 individuals
Annual Budget: $10-25,000
Secretary-Treasurer\: Victor Golla

Historical Note
SSILA members are academics and others in the U.S. and Canada with an interest in the languages of the native peoples of North, Central and South America. Membership: $13/year (U.S.); $21/year (Canada).

Publications:
Directory. a.
SSILA Newsletter. q.

Meetings/Conferences:
Annual Meetings: alternately with Amer Anthropological Ass'n or Linguistic Soc. of Amer

Soc. for the Study of Male Psychology and Physiology *(1975)*
321 Iuka
Montpelier, OH 43543
Tel: (419)485-3602
Members: 180 individuals
Annual Budget: under $10,000
Exec. Officer: Jerry Bergman, Ph.D.

Historical Note
SSMPP members are psychiatrists, psychologists, sociologists and other professionals with an interest in the field.

Meetings/Conferences:
Annual Meetings: in conjunction with the American Psychological Ass'n

Soc. for the Study of Reproduction *(1967)*
1603 Monroe St.t.
Madison, WI 53711-2021
Tel: (608)256-2777 *Fax:* (608)256-4610
E-Mail: ssr@ssr.org
Web Site: ssr.htm@http://www.ssr.org
Members: 2,450 individuals
Staff: 1
Annual Budget: $500-1,000,000
Exec. Secretary: Judith Jansen
Meeting Manager and Membership Secretary: Melissa Clifton

Historical Note
Founded in 1967 at the University of Illinois, with roots that go back to the 1953 Biennial Symposia of Reproduction, SSR's members are researchers and clinicians representing many fields including physiology, immunology, molecular biology, genetic engineering, animal science, endocrinology and embryology. Membership: $112/year (U.S. individual); $130/year (overseas individual); $1,000/year (organization/company).

Publications:
Biology of Reproduction. m. adv.

Meetings/Conferences:
Annual Meetings: Summer/1,200
1999 - Pullman, WA(Washington State University)/July 31-Aug. 3
2000 - Madison, WI(Univ. of Wisconsin)/July 15-18

Soc. for the Study of Social Biology *(1926)*
c/o Dept. of Acct, Meinders Sch. of Bus.
Oklahoma City University
Oklahoma City, OK 73106
Tel: (405)521-5824
Members: 320 individuals
Annual Budget: under $10,000
Secretary-Treasurer: Jacci L. Rodgers

Historical Note
Founded, organized and incorporated in New York in January 1926 as the American Eugenics Soc., Inc.; assumed its present name in 1973. Promotes the study of the biological and sociocultural forces affecting the structure and composition of human populations. Membership: $25/year.

Publications:
Social Biology. q.

Meetings/Conferences:
Annual Meetings: December

Soc. for the Study of Social Problems *(1951)*
906 McClung Tower
University of Tennessee
Knoxville, TN 37996-0490
Tel: (423)974-3620 *Fax:* (423)974-7013
E-Mail: tomhood@utk.edu
Web Site: http://web.utk.edu/~sssp
Members: 1,820 individuals
Staff: 3
Annual Budget: $250-500,000
Exec. Officer: Thomas C. Hood, Ph.D.

Historical Note
The primary objective of the Society is to promote social science research and teaching in order to bring scholarly and practical attention to the social world and its problems. Incorporated in Indiana. Membership: $15-85/year, based on income (individual); $50/year (organization).

Publications:
Social Problems. 4/year. adv.
SSSP Newsletter. 3/year. adv.

Meetings/Conferences:
Annual Meetings: August/500
1999 - Chicago, IL(Swissotel)/Aug. 5-7
2000 - Washington, DC(Renaissance Mayflower)/Aug. 11-13
2001 - Anaheim, CA(Westcoast Anaheim)/Aug. 17-19

Soc. for the Study of Symbolic Interaction *(1975)*

Historical Note
Address unknown in 1996.

Soc. for the Teaching of Psychology

Historical Note
A division of the American Psychological Ass'n.

Soc. for Theriogenology *(1973)*
P.O. Box 2118
Hastings, NE 68902-2118
Tel: (402)463-0392 *Fax:* (402)463-5683
Members: 2,446 individuals
Annual Budget: $25-50,000
Exec. Director: Don Ellerbee

Historical Note
Formerly (1975) American Veterinary Soc. for the Study of Breeding Soundness. Members are veterinarians interested in animal reproduction. Membership: $65/year.

Publications:
Newsletter. bi-m.
Proceedings. a.

Meetings/Conferences:
Annual Meetings: Fall with the American College of Theriogenologists
1999 - Nashville, TN

Soc. for Urban Anthropology *(1979)*

Historical Note
A section of the American Anthropological Ass'n.

Soc. for Uroradiology *(1974)*
1891 Preston White Drive
Reston, VA 20191
Tel: (703)648-8900 *Fax:* (703)716-0418
E-Mail: bridgettel@acr.org
Members: 160 individuals
Exec. Secretary: Bridgette Bienacker

Historical Note
SUR members are clinical radiologists with an interest in the study of the normal and abnormal urinary tract with emphasis upon the integration of roentgenology, sonography, computed tomography, magnetic resonance imaging, interventional procedures and nuclear medicine.

Soc. for Values in Higher Education *(1923)*
c/o Portland State Univ.
633 S.W. Montgomery St.
Portland, OR 97201
Tel: (503)721-6520 *Fax:* (503)721-6523
E-Mail: svhe@unidial.com
Web Site: http://www-adm.pdx.edu/user/svhe/
Members: 1,350 individuals
Staff: 3
Annual Budget: $100-250,000
Exec. Director: Dr. Marvin Kaiser

Historical Note
Formerly (1962) Nat'l Council on Religion in Higher Education and (1976) Soc. for Religion in Higher Education. A network of persons in the academic world and the professions who have a special concern for the ethical and religious dimensions of their work. Membership: $75-125 (individual); $250-400/year (institution).

Publications:
SOUNDINGS. q. adv.
SVHE Newsletter. q. adv.

Meetings/Conferences:
Annual Meetings: August
2000 - Colorado Springs, CO(Colorado College)

Soc. for Vascular Medicine and Biology
13 Elm St.
Manchester, MA 01944-1314
Tel: (978)526-8330 *Fax:* (978)526-4018
Exec. Director: Kevin Cuff
Director, Membership: Julie Famico

Historical Note
Membership:$160 (individual).

Publications:
Vasecular Medicine. m. adv.

Meetings/Conferences:
1999 - Washington, DC(Sheraton)
2000 - Toronto, ON/June 9-14/300

Soc. for Vascular Nursing *(1982)*
7794 Grow Drive
Pensacola, FL 32514
Tel: (850)474-6963 *Fax:* (850)484-8762
Toll Free: (888)536 - 4786
Members: 800 individuals
Staff: 15
Annual Budget: $250-500,000
Exec. Director: Belinda E. Puetz, Ph.D.
Government Relations Specialist: Robert Rupp
Director of Convention Services: Henrietta Elston
Director of Education: Janice Ward
Publications Manager: Shay Stephens

Historical Note
Formerly (1992) the Soc. for Peripheral Vascular Nursing. Provides national educational programs, helps development of local programs, and supports research in this specialized field. Membership: $75/year (individual US and Canada), $95 (individual international).

Publications:
Journal of Vascular Nursing. q. adv.
SVN prn. bi-m. adv.

Meetings/Conferences:
Annual Meetings: June
1999 - Las Vegas, NV(Caesar's Palace)/June 10-12

Soc. for Vascular Surgery *(1945)*
13 Elm St.
Manchester, MA 01944
Tel: (978)526-8330 *Fax:* (978)526-4018
E-Mail: svs@prri.com
Web Site: www.vascsurg.org
Members: 625 individuals
Staff: 2
Exec. Director: William T. Maloney, CAE
Director, Meetings and Conventions: Terri Rojas

Historical Note
Organized in Hot Springs, VA on December 5, 1945 at a meeting of the Southern Surgical Ass'n. Membership: $100/year.

Publications:
Journal of Vascular Surgery. q. adv.

Meetings/Conferences:
Annual Meetings: June
1999 - Washington, DC(Sheraton Washington)/June 6-9/1300
2000 - Tornto, ON, Canada(Sheraton/Westin)/June 11-14/1500

Soc. for Vector Ecology *(1968)*
1966 Compton Ave.
Corona, CA 91719
Tel: (909)340-9792 *Fax:* (909)340-2515
Members: 850 individuals
Annual Budget: $25-50,000
Secretary-Treasurer: Major S. Dhillon

Historical Note
A vector ecologist studies the environmental interrelationships of arthropods and other animals of public health importance (eg mosquitoes) as a basis for developing improved prevention and control measures. Members work in Mosquito Abatement Districts, Health, Agricultural and Fish and Game Departments, universities, private industry, and the Armed Forces. Formerly (1988) Soc. of Vector Ecologists. Membership: $50/year.

Publications:
Journal of Vector Ecology. semi-a. adv.
Newsletter. q.

Meetings/Conferences:
Annual Meetings: October
1999 - Raleigh, NC

Soc. for Visual Anthropology *(1968)*

Historical Note
A section of the American Anthropological Ass'n.

Soc. for Women in Plastics *(1979)*
P.O. Box 325
Sterling Heights, MI 48311-0325
Tel: (248)443-1200 *Fax:* (248)443-0604
Members: 100 individuals
Annual Budget: under $10,000
President: Toni Strzalka

Historical Note
SWP promotes knowledge relating to the plastics industry, with particular reference to the female executive. Has no paid officers or full-time staff. Membership: $30/year (individual).

Publications:
SWP Dimensions Newsletter. m. adv.
SWP Membership Directory. a. adv.

Meetings/Conferences:
Monthly Meetings: September through May

Soc. of Accredited Marine Surveyors *(1986)*
4162 Oxford Ave.
Jacksonville, FL 32210
Tel: (904)384-1494 *Fax:* (904)388-3958
Toll Free: (800)344 - 9077
E-Mail: SAMSHQaol.com
Web Site: http://Marinesurvey.org
Members: 800 individuals
Staff: 2
Annual Budget: $100-250,000
President: Donald D. Warwer
Exec. Secretary: Mary Stahler

Historical Note
SAMS is committed to enhancing the profession of marine surveying, avoiding prejudice, conflict of interest, and maintaining professional independence. Incorporated in the State of Florida. Membership: $350/year (accredited marine surveyor).

Publications:
Membership Roster. a.
Subject to Survey Newsletter. q.

Meetings/Conferences:

Soc. of Actuaries *(1949)*
475 N. Martingale Road, Suite 800
Schaumburg, IL 60173-2226
Tel: (847)706-3500 *Fax:* (847)706-3599
Web Site: http://www.soa.org
Members: 16,800 individuals
Staff: 84
Annual Budget: $10-25,000,000
Exec. Director: John E. O'Connor, Jr.
Dir., Public Relations: Cecilia Green
Managing Dir., Membership Services & Marketing: Linda M. Delgadillo, CAE
Meetings Manager: Colleen Fiore
Managing Dir., Core Studies & Global Initiatives: Marta Holmberg
Managing Dir., Practice Area Education & Research: Jeffrey Allen
Director, Continuing Education: Barbara M. Choyke, CAE
Director of Modelling Education & Academic Relations: Warren Luckner
Director of Finance: William Kepraios
Director of Development and Research: Joe Abel
Dir., Information Services: Jim Weiss
Managing Dir., Operations: Kevin O'Brien

Historical Note
Merger of the American Institute of Actuaries (1909) and the Actuarial Soc. of America (1889). Has an annual budget of approximately $16 million. Membership: $325/year (fellows and any member of over 4 years duration); $165/year (associate members of less than 4 years).

Publications:
Monograph Series. irreg.
North American Actuarial Journal. q.
Record. 3/year.
The Actuary. 10/year.
The Future Actuary. 3/year.
Transactions Reports. a.
Yearbook. a.

Meetings/Conferences:
Annual Meetings: October/1,500
1999 - San Francisco, CA(Marriott)/Oct. 17-20

2000 – Chicago, IL(Sheraton & Towers)/Oct. 15-18
2001 – New Orleans, LA(Hilton Riverside)/Oct. 21-24
2002 – Boston, MA(Marriott & Westin)/Oct. 27-30
2003 – Orlando, FL(Walt Disney World Dolphin)/Oct. 26-29

Soc. of Air Force Clinical Surgeons
401 N. Michigan Ave.
Chicago, IL 60611-4267
Tel: (312)644-6610   *Fax:* (312)245-1084
E-Mail: safcs@sba.com
Members: 950 individuals
Annual Budget: $50-100,000
Exec. Director: Karen Carlson

Historical Note
The Society of Air Force Clinical Surgeons evolved from a strong movement on the part of practicing Air Force surgeons to foster excellence in surgical care. The Society blends the skills and knowledge of the medical profession with those of the military profession. The Society promotes excellence in surgery within the Air Force, serves as a forum for presentation of scientific papers, fosters esprite de corps, and promulgates military surgical objectives.

Meetings/Conferences:
1999 – Colorado Springs, CO(Broadmoor)

Soc. of Air Force Physicians *(1958)*
Historical Note
Address unknown in 1998.

Soc. of Allied Weight Engineers *(1939)*
5530 Aztec Dr.
La Mesa, CA 91942-2110
Tel: (619)465-1367   *Fax:* (619)465-2561
Members: 1000 individuals, 40 companies/libraries
Staff: 1
Annual Budget: $50-100,000
Exec. Director: Robert E. Johnston

Historical Note
Organized in Los Angeles in 1939 as the Soc. of Aeronautical Weight Engineers and incorporated in April 1941. The society is now international. Assumed its present name on January 1, 1973. The membership consists predominantly of engineers in aerospace, ground transportation, marine transport, and other industries concerned with mass properties or weight engineering. Membership: $30/year (individual); $300/year (company/library).

Publications:
Conference Papers. a.
Journal of Weight Engineering. 3/year. adv.
Publication & Technical Paper Index. trien.
Roster. a.
SAWE Newsletter. q. adv.

Meetings/Conferences:
Annual Meetings: Mid-May/175
1999 – San Jose, CA(Hyatt)/May 24-26
2000 – St. Louis, MO(Sheraton Westport)/June 5-7
2001 – Ft. Worth, TX

Soc. of American Archivists *(1936)*
527 S. Wells St., #5
Chicago, IL 60607-3922
Tel: (312)922-0140   *Fax:* (312)347-1452
Members: 3,500 individuals
Staff: 10
Annual Budget: $1-2,000,000
Exec. Director: Susan E. Fox
Director, Financial Operations: Carroll Dendler
Director, Publications: Theresa Brinati

Historical Note
A professional society of individuals and institutions interested in preservation and use of archives, manuscripts and current records as well as machine-readable records, sound recordings, pictures, films and maps. Membership: $40-170/year (individual, based on salary); $210/year (organization/company).

Publications:
American Archivist. semi-a.
SAA Newsletter. bi-m.

Meetings/Conferences:
Annual Meetings: Fall/1,200
1999 – Pittsburgh, PA(Hilton & Towers)/Aug. 23-29/1200
2000 – Denver, CO
2001 – Washington, DC
2002 – Birmingham, AL

Soc. of American Business Editors and Writers *(1963)*
120 Neff Hall, University of Missouri
School of Journalism
Columbia, MO 65211
Tel: (573)882-7862   *Fax:* (573)884-1372
E-Mail: carolyn.guniss@imail.jour.missouri.edu
Web Site: http://www.sabew.org
Members: 2,300 institutional and individuals
Staff: 2
Annual Budget: $50-100,000
Exec. Director: Carolyn Guniss

Historical Note
Founded in 1963 as an offspring of the professional journalist society, Sigma Delta Chi. The name was originally the Soc. of American Business Writers and was changed to the Soc. of American Business and Economic Writers in April, 1976. The present name became effective in May, 1986. Members are financial, business and economic news writers and editors for print and broadcast outlets. Membership: $40/year (individual); sliding scale for institutions.

Publications:
Business Journalist. bi-m. adv.
Membership Directory.

Meetings/Conferences:
Annual Meetings: April-May
1999 – Washington, DC(The Westin)/May 2-5

2000 – Atlanta, GA(Sheraton Colony)/April 30-May 3

Soc. of American Fight Directors *(1977)*
1513 Waunona Way
Madison, WI 53713-1708
Tel: (608)226-9540
E-Mail: chefprd@aol.com
Members: 700 individuals
Annual Budget: under $10,000
Secretary: Paul Denhardt

Historical Note
Members are stage fight choreographers, actors and other interested individuals. Certifies qualified performers and instructors on three levels: Actor/Combatant, Teacher, and Fight Master. Has no paid officers or full-time staff. Membership: $35/year (domestic); $40/year (foreign).

Publications:
Cutting Edge. bi-m.
Fight Master. 2/year. adv.

Soc. of American Florists *(1884)*
1601 Duke St.
Alexandria, VA 22314
Tel: (703)836-8700   *Fax:* (703)836-8705
Toll Free: (800)336 - 4743
Members: 18,000 individuals
Staff: 30
Annual Budget: $5-10,000,000
Exec. V. President and C.E.O.: Peter J. Moran
Director of Communications: Michael Baldwin
Senior Legislative Representative: Lin Schmale
Legislative Representative: Jeanne Little
Director, Meetings and Conventions: Nancy Lawler, CMP
Director, Finance: Leonard Bowers
Senior V. President: Drew N. Gruenburg
Dir., Member Services: Joaquin Erazo
Publisher & Editor: Kate Penn
Senior Editor: Kristin Young
Manager of Production: Cheryl Burke
Director, Research and Information: Ira T. Silvergleit
Dir., Operations: William Barnes
Dir., MIS: Steve Daigler
Dir., Consumer Marketing: Jennifer Sparks

Historical Note
Became SAF: The Center for Commercial Floriculture in 1983; resumed its original name in 1987. Sponsors the American Floral Marketing Council and the Society of American Florists Political Action Committee. Has an annual budget of approximately $7 million.

Publications:
Dateline: Washington. bi-w.
Floral Management Magazine. m. adv.
Week in Review. w.

Meetings/Conferences:
Annual Meetings: Fall
1999 – Tucson, AZ/Sept. 29-Oct. 2

Soc. of American Foresters *(1900)*
5400 Grosvenor Lane
Bethesda, MD 20814-2161
Tel: (301)897-8720   *Fax:* (301)897-3690
E-Mail: safweb@safnet.org
Web Site: http://www.safnet.org
Members: 19,000 individuals
Staff: 25
Annual Budget: $2-5,000,000
Exec. V. President: William H. Banzhaf, CAE
Director, Communications and Member Services: Lori Gardner
Director, Forest Policy: Larry W. Hill
Director, Meetings and Conventions: Diana Perl
Director, Science and Education: P. Gregory Smith
Director, Finance and Administration: Charles Jackson, II
Director, Meetings/Conventions: Diana Perl
Director, Publications: Rebecca Staebler

Historical Note
Founded by Gifford Pinchot and six other pioneer foresters. Scientific and educational association representing all segments of the forestry profession; including private and public practitioners, educators, researchers, technicians and students. It serves as the accreditation agency for professional forestry education in the U.S.

Publications:
Forest Science. bi-m.
Journal of Forestry. m. adv.
Northern Journal of Applied Forestry. q. adv.
Southern Journal of Applied Forestry. q. adv.
The Forestry Source. 10/year.
Western Journal of Applied Forestry. q. adv.

Meetings/Conferences:
Annual Meetings: Fall
1999 – Portland, OR/Sept. 11-15

Soc. of American Gastrointestinal Endoscopic Surgeons *(1980)*
2716 Ocean Park Blvd., Suite 3000
Santa Monica, CA 90405-5207
Tel: (310)314-2404   *Fax:* (310)314-2585
E-Mail: sagesmail@aol.com
Web Site: http://www.sages.org
Members: 3,500 individuals
Staff: 11
Annual Budget: $1-2,000,000
Exec. Director: Sallie Matthews

Historical Note
Members are surgeons performing gastrointestinal endoscopy and related minimal-access surgeries. SAGES promotes the concepts of and research in gastrointestinal endoscopy and encourages research. Membership: $200/year (individual); $650/year (organization/company).

Publications:
Scope Newsletter. q. adv.

Standards of Practice. irreg.
Surgical Endoscopy Journal. m. adv.

Meetings/Conferences:
Annual Meetings: Spring/3,000
1999 – San Antonio, TX(Convention Center)/March 24-27
2000 – Atlanta, GA(GA World Congress Center)/March 29-April 1

Soc. of American Graphic Artists *(1915)*
32 Union Square, Room 1214
New York, NY 10003
Tel: (212)260-5706
Members: 250 individuals
Annual Budget: $25-50,000
President: William Behnken

Historical Note
Founded (1915) as the Brooklyn Soc. of Etchers, it became the Soc. of American Graphic Artists in 1952 to include woodcut, lithography and other media. Any artist who has been selected twice for a SAGA exhibition in the last five years is eligible for invitation to membership. Membership enables artists to show their work in New York City through important exhibitions with substantial awards. Membership: $30/yr.

Publications:
Newsletter. q.
SAGA National Print Exhibition Catalogue. irreg.
Show Catalogues. irreg.

Soc. of American Historians *(1939)*
603 Fayerweather Hall, MC 2538
Columbia University
New York, NY 10027
Tel: (212)854-5943   *Fax:* (914)561-4017
E-Mail: es28@columbia.edu
Members: 350 individuals
Staff: 2
Annual Budget: $25-50,000
Secretary-Treasurer: Mark C. Carnes

Historical Note
Membership, by invitation, is composed of individuals who have written a scholarly historical work of literary distinction.

Meetings/Conferences:
Annual Meetings: Always in May in New York, NY

Soc. of American Historical Artists *(1980)*
146 Dartmouth Drive
Oyster Bay, NY 11801
Tel: (516)681-8820   *Fax:* (516)822-2253
Members: 18 individuals
Annual Budget: under $10,000
President: John Duillo

Historical Note
A group of artists interested in preserving and portraying historical truth through art. Membership is by invitation only. Membership: $100/year.

Meetings/Conferences:
Annual Meetings: October

Soc. of American Indian Dentists *(1990)*
P.O. Box 15107
Phoenix, AZ 85060-5107
Tel: (602)954-5160
Members: 40 individuals
Annual Budget: under $10,000
President: George Blue-Spruce, Jr., D.D.S

Historical Note
Organized to support the growing number of American Indians practicing dentistry and to promote dental health in the Indian community. American Indian heritage and traditional medicine. Has no paid officers or full-time staff. Membership: $50/year (individual); $100/year (organization).

Publications:
Membership Directory. a.

Meetings/Conferences:
Annual Meetings: July
1999 – Albuquerque, NM

Soc. of American Law Teachers *(1974)*
University of New Mexico, School of Law
1117 Stamford Dr., N.E.
Albuquerque, NM 87131-1431
Tel: (505)277-2113
Members: 750 individuals
Secretary/Treasurer: Scott Taylor

Historical Note
SALT members are law faculty.

Publications:
Equalizer Newsletter. q.

Soc. of American Magicians *(1902)*
P.O. Box 510260
St. Louis, MO 63151
Tel: (314)846-5659
E-Mail: SAMGOH@aol.com
Web Site: http://www.velectric.com/sam/
Members: 8,500 individuals
Staff: 2
Annual Budget: $100-250,000
President: Gary Hughes

Historical Note
Membership is open to professional and amateur magicians, manufacturers of magical apparatus, collectors, writers, and hobbyists. Membership: $35/year.

Publications:
M-U-M Magazine. m. adv.

Meetings/Conferences:
Annual Meetings: July

Soc. of American Military Engineers *(1920)*
607 Prince St.
P.O. Box 21289
Alexandria, VA 22314-3117
Tel: (703)549-3800 *Fax:* (703)684-0231
Members: 26,000 individuals, 3,100 corporations
Staff: 15
Annual Budget: $1-2,000,000
Exec. Director: V.Adm. A. Bruce Beran, USCG(Ret.)
Editor: Col. Gordon Bratz, USA(Ret)
Director, Operations & Support Services: Col. Natasha Rocheleau, P.E.
Controller: William Fey
Director of Membership: Capt. James Donahue, USCG(Ret.)

Historical Note
Founded January 1, 1920 and incorporated in the District of Columbia in 1924. SAME's primary mission is to encourage the free exchange of ideas among military and civilian engineers. Members are professional engineers, architects, planners, designers, other related professionals, and contractors, suppliers, and manufacturers of engineering and engineering-related products. Approximately 75% of members are employed in U.S. or foreign engineering firms in the private sector; the remainder are in government (primarily military) engineering positions. Membership: $36/year (individual), $120-700/year (corporate).

Publications:
Military Engineer News. bi-m.
The Military Engineer. bi-m. adv.

Meetings/Conferences:
Annual Meetings: Spring
1999 - Houston, TX/April 6-9
2000 - San Diego, CA/May 15-20
2001 - Nashville, TN

Soc. of American Registered Architects *(1956)*
303 South Broadway, Suite 322
Tarrytown, NY 10593
Tel: (914)631-3600 *Fax:* (914)631-1319
Web Site: http://www.sara-national.org/
Members: 400 individuals
Annual Budget: $100-250,000
President: Barry E. Milowitz
Program Administrator: Cathie Moscato

Historical Note
Established in Kansas City by Wilfred Gregson of Atlanta. Founded as a professional society that includes the participation of all architects regardless of their roles in the architectural community. SARA follows the Golden Rule and supports the concept of profitable professionalism for its members. Membership: $195/year (individual), $65/year (associate), $195/year (industry), $15/year (student).

Publications:
National Directory. a.
Sarascope. bi-m.

Meetings/Conferences:
Annual Meetings: Fall/150-200

Soc. of American Silversmiths *(1989)*
PO Box 704
Cephachet, RI 02814
Tel: (401)567-7800 *Fax:* (401)567-7801
E-Mail: sas@silversmithing.com
Web Site: http://www.silversmithing.com
Members: 275 individuals
Staff: 1
Annual Budget: under $10,000
Exec. Director: Jeffrey Herman

Historical Note
SAS is devited to the preservation and promotion of contemporary silversmithing. Its Artisan members are silversmiths, both practicing and retired, who have been juried into SAS based on their outstanding technical skill. SAS educates the public on silversmithing and demystifies techniques through its literature and national exhibits. SAS also assists students who have a strong interest in becoming silver craftsmen. Aids students with supplier discounts and workshops. All members have access to Society's technical and marketing expertise, Artisan archives, and referral service that commissions work from its Artisans. Membership fee: $45/year (artisan); $40/year (supporting); $45/year (foreign supporting); $20/year (student).

Publications:
American Silversmith. a.
SASnews. q.

Soc. of American Travel Writers *(1956)*
4101 Lake Boone Trail, Suite 201
Raleigh, NC 27607-7506
Tel: (919)787-5181 *Fax:* (919)787-4916
Members: 950 individuals
Staff: 1
Annual Budget: $100-250,000
Exec. Director: Cathy Karr

Historical Note
Organized as the American Ass'n of Travel Writers in Ellinor Village, FL during a convention of the Nat'l Ass'n of Travel Organizations. Assumed its present name in 1957 and was incorporated in the District of Columbia in 1958. Membership: $120/year and $240/year.

Publications:
Membership Directory. a.
The Travel Writer. 10/year.

Meetings/Conferences:
Annual Meetings: Fall

Soc. of American Value Engineers

Historical Note
Became (1998) SAVE Internat'l.

Soc. of Animal Artists *(1960)*
47 Fifth Ave.
New York, NY 10003
Tel: (212)741-2880
Members: 360 individuals
Exec. Director: Patricia Shanahan

Historical Note
SAA members are artists specializing in the portrayal of animals.

Publications:
Catalogue of Exhibition. a.
SAA Newsletter. q.

Meetings/Conferences:

Soc. of Architectural Historians *(1940)*
1365 N. Astor St.
Chicago, IL 60610-2144
Tel: (312)573-1365 *Fax:* (312)573-1141
E-Mail: info@sah.org
Web Site: http://www.sah.org
Members: 3,500 individuals
Staff: 6
Annual Budget: $250-500,000
Exec. Director: Pauline Saliga

Historical Note
Provides an international forum for those interested in architecture, encourages scholarly research in the field and promotes the preservation of significant architectural monuments. A member of the American Council of Learned Societies. Membership: $80/year (individual), $150/year (institutional).

Publications:
Journal. q. adv.
Newsletter. bi-m. adv.

Meetings/Conferences:
Annual Meetings: April
1999 - Houston, TX(Doubletree Allen Center)/April 14-18/500
2000 - Coral Gables, FL(Biltmore)/June 14-18/500
2001 - Toronto, Canada(The Royal York)/April 16-22

Soc. of Armenian Studies *(1974)*
4901 Evergreen Rd., Fairlane Apt. #1
Dearborn, MI 48128-1491
Tel: (313)593-5181 *Fax:* (313)593-5452
E-Mail: gottenbr@umich.edu
Web Site: http://www.umd.umich.edu/dept/armenian/sas
Members: 200 individuals
Annual Budget: under $10,000
President: Dennis R. Papazian, Ph.D.

Historical Note
Founded in 1974 by a group of scholars from the University of California, Columbia University and Harvard. An affiliate of the Middle East Studies Ass'n (Tucson, AZ), the American Historical Ass'n (Washington, DC), and the American Ass'n for the Advancement of Slavic Studies (Stanford, CA). SAS is dedicated to the development of Armenian Studies as an academic discipline. Has no paid officers or full-time staff. Membership fee: $40/year (individual), $15/year (student and retired), $75/year (organization/company), $50 (donors), $100 (patrons).

Publications:
Bibliography of Articles in Armenian Studies. a.
Journal of the SAS. a.
Newsletter. semi-a.
Roster of Members. a.

Meetings/Conferences:
Annual Meetings: in conjunction with MESA annual meeting

Soc. of Asian and Comparative Philosophy *(1968)*
University of Missouri, Philosophy Dept.
Columbia, MO 65211
Tel: (573)882-3065 *Fax:* (573)884-8949
E-Mail: gubtab@missouri.edu
Web Site: http://www.missouri.edu/~sacb/
Members: 200 individuals
Annual Budget: under $10,000
Exec. Officer: Bina Gupta

Historical Note
SACP members are academics and others with an interest in Asian philosophic systems. Membership: $20/year (individual).

Publications:
Forum Newsletter. semi-a.
Philosophy East & West Journal. q.
SACP Directory. quinq.

Soc. of Automotive Analysts *(1985)*
4700 W. Lake Ave.
Glenview, IL 60025-1485
Tel: (847)375-4722 *Fax:* (847)375-4777
E-Mail: info@autoanlyst.org
Web Site: http://www.autoanalyst.org
Members: 600 individuals
Staff: 2
Annual Budget: $100-250,000
Exec. V. President: Mark T. Engle

Historical Note
Members are analysts involved in the automotive industry through various fields: marketing, finance, advertising, production and public relations. Membership: $75/year (individual).

Publications:
AutoAnalyst. q.
Membership Directory. a.

Meetings/Conferences:
1999 - Detriot, MI/(Cobo Center)/250

Soc. of Automotive Engineers International *(1905)*
400 Commonwealth Drive
Warrendale, PA 15096-0001
Tel: (724)772-7168 *Fax:* (724)776-1830
E-Mail: sae@sae.org
Web Site: http://www.sae.org
Members: 80,000 individuals
Staff: 400
Annual Budget: $25-50,000,000
Exec. V. President and Secretary: Max E. Rumbaugh, Jr.
Manager, Meetings & Exhibits: David L. Amati, Ph.D.
Manager, Education Realtions Division: Robert S. Sechler
Director, Finance and Administration: Stanley C. Theobald
Legal and Marketing Administrator: Steve S. Daum
Manager, Membership and Customer Service: David M. Mitchell
Editor-in-Chief, Magazines Editorial/Production Division: Daniel J. Holt
Director, Publications Group: Antenor R. Williams
Exec. Director, Products and Services: Raymond A. Morris

Historical Note
Originated in 1905 as the Soc. of Automobile Engineers, became the Soc. of Automotive Engineers in 1916. SAE is a network of engineers, business executives, educators and students from more than 80 countries who come together to share information and exchange ideas for advancing the engineering of mobility systems. Advances all aspects of the design, construction and use of self-propelled mechanisms, prime movers, their components and related equipment. Service Technicians Soc. is a division of SAE. Has an annual budget of approximately $35 million. Membership: $75/year (individual).

Publications:
Aerospace Engineering. m. adv.
Automotive Engineering. m. adv.
Off Highway Engineering. q. adv.
SAE Transactions. a.
SAE Update. m. adv.
Truck Engineering. semi-a. adv.

Meetings/Conferences:
Annual Meetings: February in Detroit, MI(Cobo Hall)/50,000
1999 - /March 1-4

Soc. of Behavioral Medicine *(1978)*
7611 Elmwood Ave., Suite 201
Middleton, WI 53562-3161
Tel: (608)827-7267 *Fax:* (608)831-5122
E-Mail: sbm@thmahq.com
Web Site: http://www.sbmweb.org
Members: 3,000 individuals
Exec. Director: Traci Mayer

Historical Note
Members are primarily physicians, psychologists, nurses and health educators concerned with the interactions of health, illiness, and behavior. Membership: $90/year (associate); $105/year (full); $325/year (trainee/student), $5,000/year (organization/company).

Publications:
Annals of Behavioral Medicine. q. adv.
Behavioral Medicine Outlook. q. adv.
Directory. bien.
Proceedings. a.

Meetings/Conferences:
Annual Meetings: Spring/1,200-1,300
1999 - San Diego, CA(Sheraton Hotel and Marina)/March 3-6

Soc. of Biblical Literature *(1880)*
825 Houston Mill Rd., Suite 350
Atlanta, GA 30329
Tel: (404)727-3100 *Fax:* (404)727-3101
E-Mail: sblexec@emory.edu
Web Site: http://www.sbl-site.org
Members: 7,000 individuals and institutions
Staff: 6
Annual Budget: $2-5,000,000
Exec. Director: Kent Harold Richards

Historical Note
Formerly Soc. of Biblical Literature and Exegesis. A member of the American Council of Learned Societies and the Nat'l Humanities Alliance. Areas of focus include: technology and research and publications. Membership: $20-90/year.

Publications:
Journal of Biblical Literature. q. adv.
Multiple Monograph Series. irreg.
Openings; Job Opportunities for Scholars of Religion. bi-m.
Religious Studies News. q. adv.
Review of Biblical Literature. a. adv.
Semeia. q. adv.

Meetings/Conferences:
Annual Meetings: November/8,000
1999 - Helsinki/Lahti, Finland(University of Helsinki)/July 17-22
1999 - Boston, MA(Sheraton)/Nov. 20-23
2000 - Nashville, TN(Opryland Hotel)/Nov. 18-21
2001 - Denver, CO(Adams Mark Hotel)/Nov. 17-20
2002 - Toronto, ON, Canada/Nov. 23-27

Soc. of Biological Psychiatry *(1945)*
c/o Mayo Clinic Jacksonville
4500 San Pablo Road
Jacksonville, FL 32224
Tel: (904)953-2842 *Fax:* (904)953-7117
E-Mail: peterson.maggie@mayo.edu
Web Site: http://www.sobp.org
Members: 965 individuals
Staff: 1
Annual Budget: $50-100,000
Manager, Business Office: Maggie Peterson

Historical Note
Founded in San Francisco in 1945 and incorporated in California in 1949. SOBP members are psychiatrists and research scientists form related fields. SOBP promotes the study of the biological basis of human behavior. Membership: $150/year (individual).

Publications:
Biological Psychiatry. m. adv.

Meetings/Conferences:
Annual Meetings: Spring/500
1999 – Washington, DC(Mayflower Renaissance
Hotel)/May 12-16

Soc. of Broadcast Engineers (1963)
8445 Keystone Crossing, Suite 140
Indianapolis, IN 46240-2454
Tel: (317)253-1640 Fax: (317)253-0418
Web Site: http://www.sbe.org
Members: 5,400 individuals, 90 sustaining members
Staff: 5
Annual Budget: $250-500,000
Exec. Director: John L. Poray, CAE

Historical Note
Founded as the Institute of Broadcast Engineers. Membership
includes studio and transmitter operators, announcer technicians,
chief engineers of large and small television and radio stations and
others involved in broadcast engineering. Membership: $15/year
(student); $55/year (individual); $500/year (sustaining
membership).

Publications:
Engineering Conference Proceedings. a. adv.
Membership Directory. a. adv.
SBE Signal. q.

Meetings/Conferences:
Annual Meetings: Fall

Soc. of Cable Telecommunications Engineers (1969)
140 Philips Road
Exton, PA 19341-1318
Tel: (610)363-6888 Fax: (610)363-5898
Toll Free: (800)542 - 5040
E-Mail: info@scte.org
Web Site: http://www.scte.org
Members: 15,000 individuals, 250 companies
Staff: 30
Annual Budget: $2-5,000,000
President: William Riker
Sr. Production Editor: Howard Whitman
Director, National Conferences: Anna Riker
Director of Standards: Ted Woo, Ph.D.
Manager, Membership Services: Patricia Zelenka
Manager, Chapter Development: Steve Townsend
V. President, Technical Programs: Marvin Nelson

Historical Note
Formerly (1995) Soc. of Cable Television Engineers. Established to
promote the sharing of operational and technical knowledge in the
fields of cable television and broadband communications, SCTE
members are individuals and companies from all areas of the
telecommunications industry including engineers, technicians,
manufacturers, installers, construction personnel, system owners
and operations staff. SCTE is an ANSI-approved Standards
Development Organization for the cable telecommunications
industry. Membership: $40/year.

Publications:
Cable-Tec Expo Proceedings Manual. a.
Conference on Emerging Technologies Proceedings Manual.
a.
Interval. m. adv.
Membership Directory. a. adv.

Meetings/Conferences:
1999 – Dallas, TX/Jan. 19-21

Soc. of Cable Television Engineers
Historical Note
Became Soc. of Cable Telecommunications Engineers in 1995.

Soc. of Carbide and Tool Engineers (1947)
c/o ASM Internat'l, 9639 Kinsman Road
Materials Park, OH 44073-0002
Tel: (440)338-5151 Fax: (440)338-4634
Web Site: www.asm-intl.org
Members: 1,500 individuals
Annual Budget: $50-100,000
Dir., Membership: Tom Passek

Historical Note
Formerly (1976) the Soc. of Carbide Engineers. A division of ASM
Internat'l, which provides administrative support. Membership:
$62/year, plus $10 initiation fee.

Meetings/Conferences:
Meeting: every 18 months

Soc. of Cardiovascular and Interventional Radiology (1973)
10201 Lee Highway, Suite 500
Fairfax, VA 22030
Tel: (703)691-1805 Fax: (703)691-1855
E-Mail: info@scvir.org
Web Site: http://www.scvir.org
Members: 2,500 individuals, 29 companies and organizations
Staff: 19
Annual Budget: $2-5,000,000
Exec. Director: Paul Pomerantz, CAE
Director, Meetings: Mary Birnie
Director, Education: Toni Doolittle
Director, Financial Services: Les Briggs
Asst. Exec. Director: Tricia McClenny
Coordinator, Membership Services: Melissa Lynn McCoy
Director, Development: Joanne DiCesare

Historical Note
SCVIR is a non-profit, national scientific organization committed to
improving health and the quality of life through the practice of
cardiovascular and interventional radiology. The society promotes
education, research, quality of care and communication in the field.
Membership: $500/year (individual); $2,000/year (corporate).

Publications:
Journal of Vascular & Interventional Radiology. bi-m. adv.
SCVIR News. bi-m.

Meetings/Conferences:
Annual Meetings: Spring
1999 – Orlando, FL/March 20-25

Soc. of Cardiovascular Anesthesiologists (1978)
1910 Byrd Ave., Suite 100
P.O. Box 11086
Richmond, VA 23230-1086
Tel: (804)282-0084 Fax: (804)282-0090
E-Mail: sca@societyhq.com
Members: 6,400 individuals
Staff: 10
Annual Budget: $1-2,000,000
Exec. Secretary: John A. Hinckley
Director of Operations: Stewart A. Hinckley
Manager, Meetings: Kevin Johns, CAE

Historical Note
Membership: $150/yr. (individual).

Publications:
Anesthesia & Analgesia. m.
Monograph. a.
Newsletter. bi-m.

Meetings/Conferences:
Annual Meetings: Spring
1999 – Chicago, IL(Sheraton)/April 24-28/1000
2000 – Orlando, FL(Dolphin)/May 6-10

Soc. of Certified Credit Executives
Historical Note
The certification division of the Internat'l Credit Ass'n.

Soc. of Certified Insurance Counselors (1969)
P.O. Box 27027
Austin, TX 78755-1027
Tel: (512)345-7932 Fax: (512)343-2167
Members: 21,800 individuals
Staff: 70
President: Dr. William T. Hold, Ph.D.
Director of Marketing & Promotions: Lisa Joy DeAngelo

Historical Note
The Society is the largest professional education association for
insurance agents with a mandatory continuing education
requirement. Membership: $70/year.

Publications:
Resources. q.

Meetings/Conferences:
Annual Meetings: March

Soc. of Certified Kitchen and Bathroom Designers (1961)
687 Willow Grove St.
Hackettstown, NJ 07840
Tel: (908)852-0033 Fax: (908)852-1695
Web Site: http://www.nkba.org
Members: 2,459 individuals
Staff: 9
Annual Budget: $250-500,000
Dir., Societies: John S. Spitz, CKD, CBD,

Historical Note
Formerly (1990) Soc. of Certified Kitchen Designers. SCKBD is the
certifying arm of the Nat'l Kitchen and Bath Ass'n, which provides
administrative support. Awards the CKD (Certified Kitchen
Designer) and CBD (Certified Bath Designer) designations.
Membership: $150/year (individual employed by a member firm),
$300/yr. (individual employed by a non-member firm).

Meetings/Conferences:
Annual Meetings: In conjunction with the Nat'l Kitchen and
Bath Conference.
1999 – Orlando, FL

Soc. of Chairmen of Academic Radiology Oncology Programs (1966)
1891 Preston White Drive
Reston, VA 20191
Tel: (703)715-7588 Fax: (703)476-8167
E-Mail: vickic@acr.org
Members: 151 individuals
Administrator: Gregg F. Robinson

Historical Note
Formerly Soc. of Chairmen of Academic Radiology Departments.

Soc. of Chartered Property and Casualty Underwriters
Historical Note
Became (1995) Chartered Property and Casualty Underwriters Soc.

Soc. of Chemical Industry, American Section (1894)
Historical Note
Address unknown in 1997.

Soc. of Children's Book Writers and Illustrators (1968)
345 N. Maple, Suite 296
Beverly Hills, CA 90210
Tel: (310)859-9887 Fax: (310)859-4887
E-Mail: scbwi@juno.com
Web Site: http://www.scbwi.org
Members: 11,000 individuals
Staff: 3
Annual Budget: $500-1,000,000
Exec. Director: Lin Oliver

Historical Note
SCBWI acts as a network for the exchange of knowledge between
children's writers, illustrators, editors, publishers and agents.
Members include writers and illustrators of children's books,
magazine stories and articles; writers and producers of children's
television; children's book and magazine editors and publishers;
agents; children's librarians, teachers and educators; bookstore
owners and personnel. Membership: $50/year and $10 iniation fee.

Publications:
SCBWI Bulletin. bi-m.

Meetings/Conferences:
Annual Meetings: August
1999 – Los Angeles, CA(Century Plaza)
2000 – Los Angeles, CA(Century Plaza)

Soc. of Christian Ethics (1959)
DePaul Univ., Lewis Ctr. Room 1519
25 E. Jackson Blvd.
Chicago, IL 60614
Tel: (312)362-6631 Fax: (312)362-5026
E-Mail: chriseth@condor.depaul.edu
Members: 900 individuals
Staff: 1
Annual Budget: $50-100,000
Exec. Director: Dennis McCann

Historical Note
Formerly (1980) American Soc. of Christian Ethics. Promotes
scholarly work in the field of Christian ethics and in the relation of
Christian ethics to other traditions of ethics and to social,
economic, political and cultural problems. The Society also seeks to
encourage and improve the teaching of these fields in colleges,
universities, and theological schools and to provide a fellowship of
discourse and debate for those engaged professionally within these
general fields. Member of the Council of Societies for the Study of
Religion. Membership: $25-80/year.

Publications:
Annual of the Society of Christian Ethics. a.

Meetings/Conferences:
Annual Meetings: mid-January/400

Soc. of Christian Philosophers (1978)
Calvin College, Dept. of Philosophy
3201 Burton St., S.E.
Grand Rapids, MI 49546-4388
Tel: (616)957-6421 Fax: (616)957-8551
E-Mail: kclark@calvin.edu
Web Site: http://www.siu.edu/departments/cola/philos/SCP/
Members: 1,100 individuals
Annual Budget: $10-25,000
Secretary-Treasurer: Kelly James Clark

Historical Note
SCP members are professors, students and others with an interest in
the integration of Christianity and philosophy. Membership:
$40/year.

Publications:
Faith and Philosophy Journal. q.
Newsletter. q.

Soc. of Clinical and Medical Electrologists (1985)
132 Great Road, Suite 200
Stow, MA 01775-1189
Tel: (978)461-0313 Fax: (978)897-5442
Web Site: http://www.scmeweb.org
Members: 950 individuals
Staff: 3
Exec. Secretary: Lauren A. Hunte

Historical Note
Created by the merger of the Nat'l Electrolysis Organization and
the Electrolysis Soc. of America. Sponsors and supports the Nat'l
Commission for Electrologist Certification (same address).
Membership: $125/year (individual).

Publications:
Directory. a.
Perspectives Newsletter. q. adv.

Meetings/Conferences:
Annual Meetings: Summer
1999 – nashville, TN

Soc. of Collision Repair Specialists (1982)
131 N. Tustin Ave., Suite 210
P.O. Box 3765
Tustin, CA 92780
Tel: (714)835-3110 Fax: (714)835-3118
Members: 551 companies, 36 state affiliates
Staff: 4
Annual Budget: $25-50,000
Exec. Director: John Loftus

Historical Note
Organized in Schaumburg, IL September 26, 1982. Members are
owners and managers of auto collision repair shops, suppliers,
insurance and educational associates and suppliers in the U.S.,
Canada, Australia, and New Zealand. Distributes technical,
management, marketing and sales information; works to promote
professionalism within the collision repair industry; conducts
seminars and workshops on collision repair facility management
and selling and marketing collision repairs. Through its director
members and affiliate association, SCRS is comprised of 8,357
collision repairbusinesses and 58,577 specialized professionals
who work with customers and insurance associates to repair
collision-damaged vehicles. Membership: $300/year (individual),
$600/year, minimum (association).

Publications:
Collision Repair Specialists. m. adv.
Electronic Newsletter. m.
SCRS News. magazine.

Meetings/Conferences:
Annual Meetings: July-August/100

Soc. of Commercial Seed Technologists (1922)
2021 Coffey Rd., Rottman Hall 202
Columbus, OH 43210
Tel: (614)292-8242 Fax: (614)292-7162
Members: 250 individuals
Staff: 1
Annual Budget: $25-50,000
Secretary-Treasurer: Andy Evans

Historical Note
Formerly (1946) Ass'n of Commercial Seed Analysts of North America. Professionals involved in the testing and analysis of seeds, research on seed physiology, and seed production and handling based on the modern botanical and agricultural sciences. Membership: $100/year (Registered Seed Technologist); $100/year (research); $75/year (associate).

Meetings/Conferences:
Annual Meetings: June, with the Ass'n of Official Seed Analysts/250
1999 – Omaha, NE
2000 – Ames, IA

Soc. of Competitive Intelligence Professionals *(1986)*
1700 Diagonal Road, Suite 600
Alexandria, VA   22314-2866
Tel: (703)739-0696   *Fax:* (703)739-2524
E-Mail: info@scip.org
Web Site: http://www.scip.org
Members: 6,500 individuals
Staff: 19
Annual Budget: $2-5,000,000
Exec. Director: Guy D. Kolb
Media Coordinator/Exec. Editor: Stephen H. Miller
Manager, Communications: Charles R. Eaton
Manager, Conference: Sunita K. Dhawan
Manager, Administrative Membership: Anne Marie Hohman
Manager, International Operations: Simone Theiss

Historical Note
SCIP is a international non-profit organization providing education and networking opportunities for business professionals working in the field of competitive intelligence (CI). SCIP members have backgrounds in market research, government intelligence, or science and technology. SCIP members enable executives to make informed decisions that keep companies responsive, well-positioned, and profitable.

Publications:
Actionable Intelligence. m. adv.
Competitive Intelligence Review. q. adv.
SCIP Membership Directory (and Addendums). adv. adv.

Meetings/Conferences:
Annual Meetings: Spring
1999 – Montreal, Quebec, Canada
2000 – Atlanta, GA

Soc. of Composers *(1965)*
Historical Note
Address unknown in 1996.

Soc. of Computed Body Tomography and Magnetic Resonance *(1977)*
c/o Matrix Meetings
P.O. Box 1026
Rochester, MN   55903-1026
Tel: (507)288-5620   *Fax:* (507)288-0014
Web Site: http://www.scbtmr.org
Members: 74 individuals
Staff: 2
Annual Budget: $500-1,000,000
Exec. Director: Barbara McLeod, CMP

Historical Note
Primary goal of organization is to educate practicing radiologists in the use of body CT. Continuing medical education has remained the foremost goal for the Society, which has since changed its name to reflect its emphasis and activities in cross-sectional imaging, including magnetic resonance imaging. Membership in the Society is competitive, selecting only those physicians actively involved in academic practice and research dealing with Body Computed Tomography and Magnetic Resonance Imaging.

Meetings/Conferences:
1999 – New Orleans, LA/Apr. 12-16

Soc. of Consumer Affairs Professionals in Business *(1973)*
801 N. Fairfax St., Suite 404
Alexandria, VA   22314-1757
Tel: (703)519-3700   *Fax:* (703)549-4886
E-Mail: socap@aol.com
Web Site: http://www.socap.org
Members: 3,000 individuals
Staff: 8
Annual Budget: $1-2,000,000
Exec. Director: Louis Garcia, CAE
Director, Education and Publications: M. Lauren Basham

Historical Note
Individuals responsible for the management of consumer affairs or customer service in all types of businesses. Membership: $195/year (individual).

Publications:
Customer Relations Management. q. adv.
Membership Directory. a.
Update. m.

Meetings/Conferences:
Annual Meetings: Fall/600
1999 – Orlando, FL(Disney World Swan)

Soc. of Corporate Meeting Professionals *(1971)*
1819 Peachtree St., N.E., Suite 620
Atlanta, GA   30309
Tel: (404)355-9932   *Fax:* (404)351-3348
E-Mail: assnha@mindspring.com
Web Site: http://www.scmp.org
Members: 140 individuals
Staff: 3
Annual Budget: $100-250,000
Exec. Director: Michael Mazur

Historical Note
Formerly the Soc. of Company Meeting Planners. Assumed its present name in 1989. Corporate meeting planners and convention

service managers. Founded in Chicago in 1971, incorporated in Illinois. Membership: $250/year; $23/year (student).

Publications:
SCMP Directory. a. adv.
SCMP Newsletter. q.

Meetings/Conferences:
Semi-annual Meetings: Spring Education Conference and Fall Annual Meeting

Soc. of Cosmetic Chemists *(1945)*
120 Wall St., Suite 2400
New York, NY   10005-4068
Tel: (212)668-1500   *Fax:* (212)668-1504
E-Mail: societycoschem@worldnet.att.net
Web Site: http://www.scconline.org
Members: 3,600 individuals
Staff: 4
Annual Budget: $1-2,000,000
Senior Executive: Theresa Cesario
Manager, Production/Communications: William DeVita
Membership Coordinator: Helen McCarren

Historical Note
Founded in May 1945 and incorporated in Delaware in 1947. A member of the Internat'l Federation of Societies of Cosmetic Chemists. Membership: $100/year (individual).

Publications:
Journal of Cosmetic Science. bi-m. adv.

Meetings/Conferences:
Semi-annual Meetings: May/various locations and December/New York, NY
1999 – Chicago, IL(Hilton and Towers)/May 6-7
1999 – New York, NY(Hilton)/Dec. 9-10
2000 – Toronto, Ontario(Hilton)
2001 – New Orleans, LA

Soc. of Cost Estimating and Analysis *(1990)*
101 S. Whiting St., Suite 201
Alexandria, VA   22304
Tel: (703)751-8069   *Fax:* (703)461-7328
E-Mail: scea@erols.com
Web Site: http://www.erols.com/scea
Members: 1,500 individuals
Staff: 3
Annual Budget: $250-500,000
Exec. Director: LeRoy T. Baseman

Historical Note
Formed by a merger of the Nat'l Estimating Soc. (1966) and the Institute of Cost Analysis (1980) in 1990, SCEA members are professionals engaged primarily in the field of government contract estimating and pricing. Maintains a code of ethics to promote cooperation and good relations among members of the profession and to enhance the status of the profession. Provides certification program that supports technical and ethical standards through participation in regional workshops, involvement in professional programs, completion of accredited university courses, and successful completion of a certification examination. Membership: $55/year (individual).

Publications:
Journal of Cost Analysis. a.
The National Estimator. q. adv.

Meetings/Conferences:
Annual Meetings: June
1999 – San Antonio, TX(Hilton Palacio del Rio)/June 8-11/300
2000 – Los Angeles, CA

Soc. of Craft Designers *(1975)*
1100-H Brandywine Blvd.
P.O. Box 3388
Zanesville, OH   43702-3388
Tel: (740)452-4541   *Fax:* (740)452-2552
Members: 675 individuals, 150 companies
Staff: 2
Annual Budget: $50-100,000
Exec. Director: Marrijane Jones

Historical Note
Members are designers, manufacturers, and retailers of craft items, writers for the craft industry,and other related professionals. Membership: $100/year (individual); $200/year (company).

Publications:
Newsletter. bi-m.

Meetings/Conferences:
Annual Meetings: Summer/300
1999 – Long Beach, CA(Hyatt Regency)/Sept. 23-25

Soc. of Critical Care Medicine *(1970)*
8101 E. Kaiser Blvd., Suite 300
Anaheim, CA   92808-2259
Tel: (714)282-6000   *Fax:* (714)282-6050
E-Mail: steves@sccm.org
Web Site: http://www.sccm.org
Members: 9,100 individuals
Staff: 42
Annual Budget: $5-10,000,000
Exec. V. President and C.E.O.: Steven V. Seekins
Director, Editorial Affairs: Rene M. Arche
Manager, Public Affairs: Lisa K. Parks
Manager, Programs: Karen Tubowitz
Director, Education: Deborah Branch
C.O.O. and Director of Operations: Janice Jensen
Director of Member Services: Laurence E. Hines

Historical Note
Physicians, scientists, engineers, nurses and allied health personnel involved in critical care medicine, patient care, teaching or research. Founded the American College of Critical Care Medicine in 1988 to foster excellence in the practice of multidisciplinary critical care and to honor individuals whose endeavors and contributions demonstrate personal commitment to these goals. Has an annual budget of approximately $5.9 million. Membership: $40-280/year.

Publications:
Critical Care. a.
Critical Care Medicine. m. adv.
Forum. bi-m.
New Horizons. q. adv.

Meetings/Conferences:
1999 – San Francisco, CA

Soc. of Dance History Scholars *(1982)*
Department of Theatre Arts & Dance
106 Norris Hall, 172 Pillsbury Drive, SE
Minneapolis, MN   55455
Tel: (612)626-7211   *Fax:* (612)625-2849
Members: 425 individuals
Treasurer: Marge Maddux

Historical Note
Formerly (1983) Dance History Scholars. SDHS members are are academics and teachers in the field of dance. Membership: $55/year (individual); $30/year (student); $35/year (retired); $120/year (institutional).

Publications:
SDHS Newsletter. semi-a. adv.
SDHS Proceedings. a.
Studies in Dance History Monograph Series. semi-a.

Meetings/Conferences:
1999 – Albuquerque, NM(University of New Mexico)/June 11-13
2000 – Washington, DC/July 19-23

Soc. of Decorative Painters *(1972)*
393 N. McLean Blvd.
Wichita, KS   67203-5968
Tel: (316)269-9300   *Fax:* (316)269-9191
E-Mail: sdp@southwind.net
Web Site: http://www.decorativepainters.com
Members: 26,000 individuals
Staff: 15
Annual Budget: $1-2,000,000
Chief Team Administrator: Kay Blair
Editor: Cheryl Capps
Chapters Administrator: Doris Hawkey
Membership/Marketing/Web Coordinator: Teresa Veazey

Historical Note
Founded as Nat'l Soc. of Tole and Decorative Painters; assumed its current name in 1993. Seeks to raise and maintain a high quality decorative art standard, to stimulate interest in and appreciation for the art of decorative painting, and to act as an information source concerning activities in the field. There are over 200 chapters. Certification in the categories of stroke or still life painting are available for Certified Decorative Artists and in the fields of floral, still life and and stroke categories for Master Decorative Artists. Absorbed Soc. of Decorative Painters in 1993. Membership: $30/year.

Publications:
Business & Teacher Directory. a. adv.
Convention Special Catalogue. a. adv.
The Decorative Painter. bi-m. adv.

Meetings/Conferences:
1999 – Wichita, KS(Convention Center)/May 18-23

Soc. of Depreciation Professionals
5505 Connecticut Ave., N.W., Suite 280
Washington, DC   20015-2601
Tel: (202)362-0680   *Fax:* (202)966-2283
Annual Budget: $25-50,000
Exec. Director: Rod Daniel

Historical Note
Membership: $35/year.

Publications:
SDP Journal. a. adv.
SDP Newsletter. q.

Meetings/Conferences:

Soc. of Diagnostic Medical Sonographers *(1970)*
12770 Coit Road, Suite 708
Dallas, TX   75251-1319
Tel: (972)239-7367   *Fax:* (972)239-7378
E-Mail: sdms@sdms.org
Web Site: http://www.sdms.org
Members: 12,000 individuals
Staff: 12
Annual Budget: $1-2,000,000
Exec. Director: Gwen A. Grim
Meetings and Conventions Director: Suzann Oliver
Director, Marketing: George Junginger

Historical Note
Formerly (1981) the American Soc. of Ultrasound Technical Specialists. Individuals employing high frequency sound for medical diagnosis. Designed to provide members with continuing education, current information on standards, trends and opportunities in the field of diagnostic medical sonography. Membership: $80/year (individual); $500/year (organization/company).

Publications:
Journal of Dignostic Medical Sonography. bi-m.
SDMS News Wave. bi-m.

Meetings/Conferences:
Annual Meetings: Fall/800-1,000
1999 – Anaheim, CA(Marriott)/Oct. 7-10

Soc. of Economic Geologists *(1920)*
5808 S. Rapp St., Suite 209
Littleton, CO   80120-1942
Tel: (303)797-0332   *Fax:* (303)797-0417
E-Mail: socecongeol@csn.net
Web Site: http://www.mines.utah.edu/nwmgg/SEG.html
Members: 3,300 individuals
Staff: 5
Annual Budget: $250-500,000
Exec. Director: John A. Thoms

Historical Note
SEG advances the science of geology in relation to minerals exploration, mining and related industries. Membership includes geoscientists from 68 countries. Membership: $85/year; $42.50/year (students).

Publications:
Economic Geology. 8/year.
Reviews in Economic Geology. irreg.
SEG Field Trip Guide Books. 1-2/year.
SEG Membership Directory. bien. adv.
SEG Newsletter. q.
Special Publications Series. irreg.

Meetings/Conferences:
Semi-Annual Meetings: Fall with Geological Soc. of America/Spring with Soc. for Mining, Metallurgy, and Exploration

Soc. of Education in Anesthesia *(1984)*
Historical Note
Became Soc. for Education in Anesthesia.

Soc. of Engineering Science *(1963)*
Aerospace Engineering
University of Texas- Austin
Austin, TX   78712
Tel: (512)471-4212   *Fax:* (512)471-3788
E-Mail: mmear@max.ae.utexas.edu
Web Site: http://www.mech.nwu.edu/ses/
Members: 300 individuals
Annual Budget: under $10,000
Secretary: Mark Mear, Ph.D.

Historical Note
Multidisciplinary society of scientists and engineers concerned with research and communication between the fields of engineering and science. Membership: $25/year (individual).

Publications:
Abstracts of the Annual Meeting. a.
SES Newsletter. semi-a.

Meetings/Conferences:
Annual Meetings: November at a university and biennial int'l conferences (even years)

Soc. of Environmental Journalists *(1990)*
Box 27280
Philadelphia, PA   19118-0280
Tel: (215)836-9970   *Fax:* (215)836-9972
E-Mail: sejoffice@aol.com
Web Site: http://www.sej.org
Members: 1,130 individuals
Staff: 4
Annual Budget: $250-500,000
Exec. Director: Beth Parke

Historical Note
Vision is an informed society through excellence in environmental journalism. Members are journalists and educators united to enhance the quality, accuracy and visibility of reporting on environmental issues. Membership: $40/year (individual); $30/year (student).

Publications:
SEJournal. q.

Meetings/Conferences:
Annual Meetings: Fall/usually in a university setting
1999 – Los Angeles, CA/Sept. 16-19

Soc. of Environmental Toxicology and Chemistry *(1979)*
1010 North 12th Ave.
Pensacola, FL   32501-3367
Tel: (850)469-1500   *Fax:* (850)469-9778
E-Mail: setac@setac.org
Web Site: http://www.setac.org
Members: 4,000 individuals, 55 companies
Staff: 8
Annual Budget: $1-2,000,000
Exec. Director: Rodney Parrish

Historical Note
SETAC is a professional society established to promote the use of multidisciplinary approaches to solving problems of the impact of chemicals and technology on the environment. SETAC members are professionals in the fields of chemistry, toxicology, biology, ecology, atmospheric sciences, health sciences, earth,sciences, and environmental engineering. Membership: $90/year (individual), $2,000/year (sustaining member).

Publications:
Environmental Toxicology & Chemistry. m. adv.
SETAC News. bi-m. adv.

Meetings/Conferences:
1999 – Philadelphia, PA/Nov. 14-18

Soc. of Ethnobiology *(1978)*
Dept. of Anthropology, CB-1114
Washington Univ.
St. Louis, MO   63130-4899
Tel: (314)935-8588   *Fax:* (314)935-8535
E-Mail: gjfritz@artsci.wustl.edu
Members: 400 individuals and institutions
Annual Budget: $10-25,000
Secretary-Treasurer: Gayle J. Fritz, Ph.D.

Historical Note
Members are individuals and institutions with an interest the study of the interactions of plants and animals with and within the human cultural environment. Has no paid officers or full-time staff. Membership: $35/year (individual); $60/year (organization/company).

Publications:
Journal of Ethnobiology. semi-a. adv.

Meetings/Conferences:
Annual Meetings: Spring/200 Reno, NV(University of Neveda)

Soc. of Experimental Social Psychology *(1964)*
Historical Note
Organization defunct in 1995.

Soc. of Experimental Test Pilots *(1955)*
P.O. Box 986
Lancaster, CA   93584-0986
Tel: (805)942-9574   *Fax:* (805)940-0398
E-Mail: setp@netport.com
Web Site: http://www.netport.com/setp/
Members: 1,900 individuals
Staff: 5
Annual Budget: $100-250,000
Exec. Director: Paula S. Smith

Historical Note
Founded September 14, 1955 and incorporated in California in 1956. Sponsors the Soc. of Experimental Test Pilots Scholarship Foundation. Has an international membership comprising 29 countries. Membership: $96/year (member); $91/year (associate member).

Publications:
S. E.

Meetings/Conferences:
Annual Meetings: June in Europe and Fall in Los Angeles.
1999 – Beverly Hills, CA/Sept. 22-25

Soc. of Exploration Geophysicists *(1930)*
P.O. Box 702740
Tulsa, OK   74170-2740
Tel: (918)497-5500   *Fax:* (918)497-5557
Web Site: http://www.seg.org
Members: 15,000 individuals
Staff: 44
Annual Budget: $5-10,000,000
Exec. Director: Paul E. Hummel
Manager, Meetings and Expositions: Bob Lewis
Manager, Geoscience, Education and Members: Bob Wyckoff
Finance Director: Jack Ingram
Manager, Publications: Ted Bakamjian
Assoc. Exec. Dir., SEG Foundation: Phyllis Connor

Historical Note
Founded in Houston in 1930 and incorporated in Oklahoma. Has an annual budget of approximately $9 million. Membership: $70/year (individual), $1,450/year (company).

Publications:
Geophysics. bi-m. adv.
The Leading Edge of Exploration. m. adv.
Yearbook. a. adv.

Meetings/Conferences:
Annual Meetings: Fall
1999 – Houston, TX/Oct. 31-Nov. 5/10000
2001 – Calgary, AB, Canada/Aug. 6-11/9000
2001 – San Antonio, TX/Sept. 9-14/10000
2002 – Las Vegas, NV/Sept. 22-27/10000

Soc. of Eye Surgeons *(1969)*
7801 Norfolk Ave.
Bethesda, MD   20814
Tel: (301)986-1830   *Fax:* (301)986-1876
Staff: 2
Annual Budget: $2-5,000,000
Exec. Secretary: Larry Schwab, MD

Historical Note
An auxiliary of the Internat'l Eye Foundation, the purpose of SES is to assist programs dedicated to the restoration of sight/prevention of blindness. Promotes understanding of blindness. Membership: $50-200/year.

Publications:
Eye To Eye Newsletter. semi-a.

Soc. of Federal Labor Relations Professionals *(1972)*
P.O. Box 25112
Arlington, VA   22202
Tel: (703)685-4130   *Fax:* (703)685-1144
Members: 500 individuals
Staff: 1
Annual Budget: $10-25,000
Exec. Secretary: Francisco J. Martinez-Alvarez

Historical Note
Membership is open to representatives of unions and management and neutrals. Membership: $50/year (individual); $10/year (students).

Publications:
Occasional Papers. irreg.
SFLRP Reporter Newsletter. q. adv.

Meetings/Conferences:

Soc. of Federal Linguists *(1930)*
P.O. Box 7765
Washington, DC   20044
E-Mail: editor-sfl@federal-linguists.org
Web Site: http://federal-linguists.org
Members: 150 individuals
Staff: 1
Annual Budget: under $10,000
Newsletter Editor: Everett Larson

Historical Note
Formerly (1960) the Soc. of Federal Translators. Composed primarily of U.S. government employees whose occupations require the use of foreign-language skills. Federally employed translators, interpreters, librarians, teachers, etc., are eligible for full membership if they use foreign languages in 50% or more of their work. Professional linguists not employed by the U.S. Government and students pursuing courses of foreign language study may join as associate or student members. The primary objectives of the Society are to promote linguistic professionalism; to advance language knowledge and linguistic competency; to provide a forum for discussion of language problems and a means of disseminating language information; and to stimulate interest in linguistic activity through professional and social programs. All members are U.S. Citizens. Membership: $20/year (full member); $10/year (student).

Publications:
Membership Directory. a.
Newsletter. m.

Meetings/Conferences: *Annual Meetings:* Washington, DC/January

Soc. of Financial Examiners *(1973)*
4101 Lake Boone Trail, Suite 201
Raleigh, NC   27607-7506
Tel: (919)787-5181   *Fax:* (919)787-4916
Members: 1,800 individuals
Staff: 7
Annual Budget: $250-500,000
Exec. Director: Penney DePas, CAE

Historical Note
Membership: $65-100/year (individual).

Publications:
The Examiner. q.
The INSIGHT. m.

Meetings/Conferences:
Annual Meetings: July/500
1999 – Las Vegas, NV(Bally's)/July 26-31/600
2000 – San Diego, CA(Town & Country)/600

Soc. of Fire Protection Engineers *(1950)*
7315 Wisconsin Ave., Suite 1225W
Bethesda, MD   20814
Tel: (301)718-2910   *Fax:* (301)718-2242
E-Mail: sfpehqtrs@sfpe.org
Members: 4,150 individuals
Staff: 7
Annual Budget: $500-1,000,000
Exec. Director: Kathleen Almand, P.E.
Education Manager: Julie Maskas
Technical Director: Morgan Hurley

Historical Note
Founded October 31, 1950 as the professional section of the Nat'l Fire Protection Ass'n. Became independent of the NFPA on Feb. 10, 1971. Membership: $150/year.

Publications:
Journal of Fire Protection Engineering. q.
Proceedings. a.
Roster. a.
SFPE Bulletin. 6/yr.
Technology Reports. m.

Meetings/Conferences:
Annual Meetings: With Nat'l Fire Protection Ass'n in Spring.
1999 – Baltimore, MD/May 17-20/350

Soc. of Flavor Chemists *(1959)*
Historical Note
Address unknown in 1998.

Soc. of Flight Test Engineers *(1968)*
1007 West Ave. M-14, Suite F
Palmdale, CA   93551
Tel: (805)538-9715   *Fax:* (805)538-9715
E-Mail: sfte@hughes.net
Web Site: http://www.SFTE.org
Members: 975 individuals, 33 companies
Staff: 1
Annual Budget: $50-100,000
Exec. Director: Dianne Van Norman

Historical Note
Members are engineers whose principal professional interest is the flight testing of aircraft. Purpose of the Society is to improve communications in the fields of flight test operations, analysis, instrumentation and data systems. Membership: $48/year (individual), $900/year (company).

Publications:
Flight Test news. m.
International Symposium Proceedings. a.

Meetings/Conferences:
Annual Meetings: September/150
1999 – St. Louis, MO(Hyatt)/Aug. 16-20

Soc. of Forensic Toxicologists *(1970)*
P.O. Box 5543
Mesa, AZ   85211
Tel: (602)839-9106   *Fax:* (602)839-9106
Web Site: www.soft-tox.org
Members: 540 individuals
Annual Budget: $50-100,000
President: Joseph J. Sandy, Ph.D.

Historical Note
SOFT members are practicing forensic toxicologists and others with an interest in the analysis of tissue and bodily fluids for drugs and/or poisons and the interpretation of the information generated from such analyses in a judicial context. Membership: $50/year (full and associate); $15/year (student).

Publications:
Membership Directory. a.
Special Issue of the Journal of Analytical Toxicology. a. adv.
ToxTalk. q.

Meetings/Conferences:
Annual Meetings: October
1999 – San Juan, Puerto Rico
2000 – Milwaukee, WI
2001 – New Orleans, LA
2002 – Detroit, MI

Soc. of Former Special Agents of the Federal Bureau of Investigation *(1937)*
P.O. Box 1027
Quantico, VA   22134-1027

Tel: (703)640-6469   Fax: (703)640-6537
Members: 8,000 individuals
Staff: 2
Annual Budget: $250-500,000
Acting Managing Director: Becky S. Vance
Communications Director: Hillary Robinette

Historical Note
Founded and incorporated in New York in 1937. Created the Former Agents of the F.B.I. Foundation which assists needy members, deceased members' families, rehabilitation of the ill and education. Membership: $55/yr.

Publications:
Directory. a.
The Grapevine. m.

Meetings/Conferences:
1999 – Tarpon Springs, FL(Innesbrook)/1000

Soc. of Gastroenterology Nurses and Associates (1973)
401 N. Michigan Ave.
Chicago, IL 60611-4267
Tel: (312)321-5165   Fax: (312)321-5194
Toll Free: (800)245-7462
Members: 7,000 individuals
Staff: 6
Annual Budget: $1-2,000,000
Exec. Director: M. Eileen Widmer, CAE
Dir., Nursing Education: Kathleen Gugerty, MS,RNC

Historical Note
Formerly (1989) the Soc. of Gastrointestinal Assistants. Nurses and other allied health care individuals working in the fields of gastroenterology/endoscopy. Membership: $105/year (individual); $90/year (affiliate).

Publications:
Gastroenterology Nursing. q. adv.
SGNA News.

Meetings/Conferences:
Annual Meetings: Spring/1,500
1999 – Nashville, TN(Opryland Hotel)/May 15-19
2000 – Anaheim, CA(Anaheim Convention Center)/May 20-24

Soc. of Gastrointestinal Radiologists (1971)
4550 Post Oak Place, Suite 342
Houston, TX 77027
Tel: (713)965-0566   Fax: (713)960-0488
E-Mail: 74117.511@compuserve.com
Web Site: http://www.sgr.org
Members: 319 individuals
Exec. Director and Meeting Manager: Lynne K. Tiras, CMP

Historical Note
SGR members are radiologists with an interest in diseases of the gastrointestinal tract.

Meetings/Conferences:
1999 – Palm Beach, Fl(The Breakers)/March 21-26/400
2000 – Kauai, HI(Hyatt Regency)/500

Soc. of General Internal Medicine (1978)
2501 M St., N.W., Suite 575
Washington, DC 20037
Tel: (202)887-5150   Fax: (202)887-5405
Toll Free: (800)822-3060
E-Mail: KarlsonD@sgim.org
Web Site: http://www.sgim.org
Members: 2,800 individuals
Staff: 6
Annual Budget: $1-2,000,000
Exec. Director: David Karlson, Ph.D.
Membership Coordinator: Janice Clements

Historical Note
Members are health professionals interested in teaching and research related to general and primary care internal medicine. Membership: $185/year (full member), $85/year (associate).

Publications:
Journal of General Internal Medicine. m. adv.
SGIM Directory of General Internal Medicine Fellowship Programs. bien.
SGIM Forum Newsletter. m. adv.
SGIM PCIM Residency Programs Directory. bien.

Meetings/Conferences:
1999 – San Francisco, CA(Hyatt Regency)/April 29-May 1/1800
2000 – Boston, MA

Soc. of General Physiologists (1946)
P.O. Box 257
Woods Hole, MA 02543-0257
Tel: (508)540-6719   Fax: (508)540-0155
E-Mail: sgp@mbl.edi
Web Site: http://www.emory.edu/HEARTCELL/sgp.html
Members: 850 individuals
Staff: 2
Annual Budget: $10-25,000
Secretary: H. Criss Hartzell, M.D.

Historical Note
Founded in 1946 at the Marine Biological Laboratory, Woods Hole, and incorporated in Massachusetts in 1966. Affiliate of the American Ass'n for the Advancement of Science, Internat'l Union of Physiological Sciences, the Nat'l Research Council, Internat'l Union of Pure and Applied Biophysics, and the American Physiological Soc. Membership: $45/year.

Publications:
Journal of General Physiology. m.

Meetings/Conferences:
Annual Meetings: Woods Hole, MA(Marine Biological Lab.)/September/300
1999 – Woods Hole, MA

Soc. of Geriatric Ophthalmology (1975)
Historical Note
Address unknown in 1997.

Soc. of Glass and Ceramic Decorators (1963)
1627 K St., N.W., Suite 800
Washington, DC 20006-1702
Tel: (202)728-4132   Fax: (202)728-4133
E-Mail: sgcd@sgcd.org
Web Site: http://www.sgdc.org
Members: 750 individuals
Staff: 4
Annual Budget: $500-1,000,000
Exec. Director: Sandra Spence, CAE
Director of Communications: Andrew Bopp
Manager, Membership and Administration: Kimberly Williams

Historical Note
SGCD serves members, including retailers and suppliers, of commercial decorators of mugs, dinnerware, tile, glass packaging, auto window glass, and other glass and ceramic products. Formerly (1984) the Soc. of Glass Decorators. Membership: $250/year (individual); $1,000/year (company).

Publications:
Newsletter. adv. adv.
SGCD Directory. adv. adv.
SGCD Seminar Program.

Meetings/Conferences:
Annual Meetings: Fall
1999 – Pittsburgh, PA(Doubletree)/Sept. 26-29/750
2000 – San Diego, CA(San Diego Sheraton)/Sept. 10-13/700
2001 – Boca Raton, FL(Boca Raton Resort & Club)/Sept. 9-12/700

Soc. of Government Economists (1970)
1954-A Biltmore St., N.W.
Washington, DC 20009
Members: 500 individuals
President: Jules Lichtenstein
Manager, Business: Seth Bachman

Historical Note
Membership benefits economists employed in the public sector or who are interested in the economic aspects of government policies. Through membership, there are several opportunities to keep abreast of current economic and policy issues and to network with economists interested in the same areas. Membership: $30/year (individual); $150/year (organization/company).

Publications:
Membership Directory. bi-a.
Newsletter.
SGE Bulletin. m.

Meetings/Conferences:

Soc. of Government Meeting Planners
Historical Note
Became (1997) Soc. of Government Meeting Professionals.

Soc. of Government Meeting Professionals (1980)
6 Clouser Road
Mechanicsburg, PA 17055-6541
Tel: (717)795-7467   Fax: (717)795-7552
E-Mail: sgmp@epix.net
Members: 3,000 individuals
Staff: 3
Annual Budget: $500-1,000,000
Manager: Deborah A. Beamer

Historical Note
Formerly (1996) Soc. of Government Meeting Planners. Members are persons involved in planning government meetings and individuals who supply services to government planners. Membership: $75-250/year.

Publications:
Newsletter. m. adv.

Meetings/Conferences:
Annual Meetings: Spring-Summer
1999 – Ft. Lauderdale, FL
2000 – San Diego, CA

Soc. of Government Service Urologists (1952)
7027 Weathered Post
San Antonio, TX 78238
Tel: (210)681-0587   Fax: (210)680-7725
Members: 731 individuals
Staff: 2
Annual Budget: $100-250,000
Administrator: Preston Littrell

Historical Note
Membership: $50/year (individual); $800/year (organization).

Publications:
SGSU Newsletter. q.

Meetings/Conferences:
1999 – San Antonio, TX(Hilton Palacio del Rio)

Soc. of Graduate Surgeons (1949)
5820 Wilshire Blvd., Suite 500
Los Angeles, CA 90036
Tel: (213)937-5514   Fax: (213)937-0959
Members: 250 individuals
Annual Budget: $100-250,000
Exec. Director: C. James Dowden

Meetings/Conferences:
Annual Meetings: March, Los Angeles, CA(Sheraton Grande)/250

Soc. of Gynecologic Oncologists (1969)
401 N. Michigan Ave.
Chicago, IL 60611
Tel: (312)644-6610   Fax: (312)527-6640

E-Mail: sgo@sba.com
Members: 700 individuals
Staff: 6
Annual Budget: $500-1,000,000
Exec. Director: Irvin Bomberger

Historical Note
Formerly (1994) Soc. of Gynecological Oncologists. Founded in 1969 by a small group of doctors interested in advancing knowledge and raising standards of practice in gynecologic oncology within the disciplines of obstetrics and gynecology. Membership: $300/year + $60 journal subscription (individual).

Meetings/Conferences:
Annual Meetings: February-March

Soc. of Head and Neck Surgeons (1954)
Historical Note
Merged with American Head and Neck Surgery Soc. in 1998.

Soc. of Healthcare Executive Assistants
Historical Note
Organization defunct in 1998.

Soc. of Hispanic Professional Engineers (1974)
5400 E. Olympic Blvd.
Los Angeles, CA 90022
Tel: (323)725-3970   Fax: (323)725-0316
Web Site: http://www.shpe.org
Members: 7,000 individuals
Staff: 5
Office Manager: Lourdes Arce

Historical Note
Absorbed the Hispanic Soc. of Engineers in 1987. Membership: $45/year (individual); $500/year (organization/company).

Publications:
Hispanic Engineer. q.
Newsletter. q.

Meetings/Conferences:
Semi-Annual Meetings: February and June
1999 – Los Angeles, CA/Feb. 3-6

Soc. of Illustrators (1901)
128 East 63rd St.
New York, NY 10021-7303
Tel: (212)838-2560   Fax: (212)838-2561
Web Site: http://www.societyillustrators.com
Members: 900 individuals
Staff: 6
Annual Budget: $500-1,000,000
Director: Terrence Brown

Historical Note
A professional society of illustrators and art directors founded in New York in 1901 by ten of America's leading illustrators. Established a Hall of Fame in 1958 to recognize distinguished achievement in the field of illustration and a Museum of American Illustration in 1981. Most members come from the New York area. Membership: $448/year (resident artist); $272/year (non-resident); $1,500/year (corporate).

Publications:
Annual of American Illustration. a. adv.

Soc. of Incentive and Travel Executives (1973)
21 W. 38th St., 10th Floor
New York, NY 10018-5584
Tel: (212)575-0910   Fax: (212)575-1838
E-Mail: site1@ix.netcom.com
Web Site: http://www.site-intl.org
Members: 2,000 individuals
Staff: 8
Annual Budget: $1-2,000,000
Exec. V. President & C.E.O.: Robert Vitagliano
Director, Communications: Maureen P. Mangan
Director, Conferences & Meeting Services: Elizabeth Harvey
Director, Education: Gerry Couture
Asst. Managing Director: Maria Bachman
Manager, Membership: Trisha Walter

Historical Note
Formerly (1996) Soc. of Incentive Travel Executives. SITE is an individual membership society covering 70 countries. Members are: corporate users, airlines, Tourist Boards, cruise lines, destination management companies, consultants, hotels/resorts, travel agents, incentive travel houses and publications. Membership: $375/year.

Publications:
In-SITE Magazine. bi-m. adv.
Resource Directory. a. adv.

Meetings/Conferences:
Semi-Annual Meetings: Univ. of Incentive Travel/Summer and Internat'l Conference/Winter
1999 – /December 5-9

Soc. of Independent Gasoline Marketers of America (1958)
11911 Freedom Dr., Suite 590
Reston, VA 20190-5602
Tel: (703)709-7000   Fax: (703)709-7007
Members: 270 companies, 25 associates
Staff: 5
Annual Budget: $2-5,000,000
Exec. V. President: Kenneth A. Doyle, CAE
Director, Communications: Thomas L. Osborne, CAE
Meetings Manager: Heidi Prange
Education Specialist: Sheila Cavanaugh
Director, Administration: Larry Kaplan

Historical Note
Members are independent gasoline marketers. Sponsors and supports the SIGMA Political Action Committee. Absorbed the Southeast Independent Oil Marketers Ass'n in 1988. Membership: $600-9,000/year.

Publications:
Independent Gasoline Marketing. bi-m. adv.

Meetings/Conferences:
Semi-Annual Meetings: April and November (with American Petroleum Institute).

Soc. of Independent Professional Earth Scientists (1963)
4925 Greenville Ave., Suite 1106
Dallas, TX 75206-4008
Tel: (214)363-1780
E-Mail: sipes@sipes.org
Web Site: http://www.sipes.org
Members: 1,400 individuals
Staff: 2
Exec. Secretary: Diane M. Finstrom

Historical Note
Founded in Houston, TX and chartered as a professional and scientific scoiety in 1963, SIPES is a member society of the American Geological Institute and a cooperative association with the Independent Petroleum Association of America. Members are geologists, geophysicists, engineers and other earth scientists with at least twelve years professional experience who are independent or self-employed. Sponsors and supports the SIPES Foundation, a charitable and educational foundation, chartered in Texas in 1981. Membership: $75/year.

Publications:
Membership Directory. bien. adv.
Newsletter. q. adv.

Meetings/Conferences:
1999 – Wichita, KS
2000 – Denver, CO
2001 – Houston, TX

Soc. of Independent Show Organizers (1990)
P.O. Box 949
Framingham, MA 01701-0949
Tel: (508)270-2640   *Fax:* (508)270-2642
E-Mail: info@siso.org
Web Site: http://www.siso.org
Members: 177 companies
Staff: 2
Annual Budget: $100-250,000
Exec. Director: Stephen A. Schuldenfrei

Historical Note
Membership: $295-$1825/year (organization/company).

Publications:
News Now!.
SISO Update. m.
VIP Directory. a. adv.

Meetings/Conferences:

Soc. of Industrial and Office REALTORS (1941)
700 11th St., N.W., Suite 510
Washington, DC 20001-4511
Tel: (202)737-8787   *Fax:* (202)737-8797
Web Site: http://www.sior.com
Members: 1,900 individuals
Staff: 17
Annual Budget: $2-5,000,000
Exec. V. President: Nancy B. Bryant
Programs Director: Mark J. Crowley
Sr. Director, Membership: Pamela J. Hinton
Research and Publications Director: Linda Nasvaderani

Historical Note
A professional affiliate of the Nat'l Ass'n of Realtors, SIR was founded in Washington just prior to World War II at the instigation of the War Department to help locate specialized facilities suitable for the production of military equipment. Incorporated in the State of Illinois, active members are brokers, consultants and appraisers. Formerly (1986) Soc. of Industrial Realtors. Supports the REALTORS Political Action Committee (RPAC). Membership: $790/year (active members).

Publications:
Comparative Statistics of Industrial and Office Real Estate Markets.
Executive's Guide to Specialists in Office and Industrial Real Estate.
Professional Report of Industrial and Office Real Estate. q.

Meetings/Conferences:
1999 – Montreal, Quebec, Canada/Apr. 30-May 3
1999 – Orlando, FL(Hyatt regency Grand Cypress)/Nov. 6-8
2000 – Hilton Head, SC/May 4-7
2000 – San Francisco, CA(Fairmont)/Nov. 4-6

Soc. of Insurance Financial Management (1959)
P.O. Box 61, Bates Road Ext.
Hollowville, NY 12530-0061
Tel: (518)851-9780   *Fax:* (518)851-2521
Members: 968 individuals
Staff: 1
Annual Budget: $50-100,000
Administrative Services: Robert W. Bauer

Historical Note
Formerly (1994) Soc. of Insurance Accountants. Formed in 1959 by a merger of the Insurance Accountants Ass'n and the Ass'n of Casualty Accountants and Statisticians. Membership: $40/year (individual).

Meetings/Conferences:
1999 – Palm Beach, FL(The Breakers)/Sept. 26-29
2000 – Scottsdale, AZ(Scottsdale Princess)/Sept. 24-27

Soc. of Insurance Research (1970)
691 Cross Fire Road
Marietta, GA 30064-1394
Tel: (770)426-9270   *Fax:* (770)426-9298
Web Site: www.sirnet.org
Members: 450 individuals
Staff: 3

Annual Budget: $100-250,000
Exec. Director: Stanley M. Hopp

Historical Note
Founded under the sponsorship of the Griffith Foundation for Insurance Education, Ohio State University to provide a communication channel and a forum for the exchange of research ideas. Members are individuals actively engaged in some form of insurance research. Membership: $185/year (individual).

Publications:
Membership Directory. a.
Research Review. q. adv.
SIR Newsletter. bi-m.

Meetings/Conferences:
Annual Meetings: November
1999 – San Petersburg, FL(Tradewinds Resort)/Nov. 7-10/125

Soc. of Insurance Trainers and Educators (1953)
2120 Market St.
Suite 108
San Francisco, CA 94114
Tel: (415)621-2830   *Fax:* (415)621-0889
E-Mail: socinsedtr@aol.com
Web Site: http://www.connectyou.com/site.htm
Members: 800 individuals
Staff: 1
Annual Budget: $100-250,000
Exec. Director: Lois A. Markovich, CPCU, AIM

Historical Note
Formerly (1985) the Insurance Company Education Directors Soc. Membership composed of education and training personnel, personnel directors, and those responsible for the training function in insurance. Voting Membership: $90/year (designee); $60/year (associate); $25/year (retiree).

Publications:
In-Site. bi-m.
Training Journal. bi-a.

Meetings/Conferences:
Annual Meetings: June
1999 – San Diego, CA(Princess Hotel)/June 13-15
2000 – Nashville, TN/May 20-24

Soc. of Internat'l Business Fellows
191 Peachtree St., N.E., Suite 3220
Atlanta, GA 30303-1757
Tel: (404)525-7423   *Fax:* (404)525-5331
Web Site: www.sibf.org
Members: 480 individuals
Exec. Director: Kathryn Ratcliff Payne

Meetings/Conferences:

Soc. of Laparoendoscopic Surgeons (1990)
7330 S.W. 62nd Place, Suite 410
Miami, FL 33143-4825
Tel: (305)665-9959   *Fax:* (305)667-4123
Toll Free: (800)446 - 2659
E-Mail: Info@SLS.org
Web Site: http://www.sls.org and www.laparoscopy.org
Members: 5,951 individuals
Staff: 7
Annual Budget: $500-1,000,000
Chairman: Paul Alan Wetter, M.D.
Meeting Planner: Ileana Castillo
Operations Officer: Janis Chinnock
Coordinator, Membership Services: Flor Tilden
Director, Administration/Publications: Charlotte Donn

Historical Note
SLS members are surgeons from various specialties and other health professions who are interested in advancing their expertise in the diagnostic and therapeutic uses of laparoendoscopic techniques. Membership: $199/year (individual); $1,200/year (organziation/company)

Publications:
Conference Registration Booklet. semi-a.
Journal of the SLS. q.
SLS Report Newsletter. semi-.

Meetings/Conferences:
Annual Meetings: December/300
1999 – New York, NY(Sheraton)/Dec. 4-7

Soc. of Logistics Engineers (1966)
Historical Note
Became SOLE - The Internat'l Soc. of Logistics in 1996.

Soc. of Magnetic Resonance (1994)
Historical Note
Became Internat'l Soc. for Magnetic Resonance in Medicine (ISMRM) in 1996.

Soc. of Manufacturing Engineers (1932)
P.O. Box 930
One SME Drive
Dearborn, MI 48121-0930
Tel: (313)271-1500   *Fax:* (313)271-2861
Toll Free: (800)733 - 4763
Web Site: http://www.sme.org/
Members: 65,000 individuals, 275 chapters
Staff: 260
Annual Budget: $25-50,000,000
Exec. Director & General Manager: Philip Trimble
Director, Expositions: Nancy Berg
Director, Conferencing: John P. McEachran
Manager, Education: Mark Stratton
Director, Educations and Development: Robert E. King
Director, Finance and Administration: Robert Rochester
Director, Membership and Professional Interests: Michael Wright
Director, Publications: John R. Coleman
Director, Development: Helen Dorsey

Historical Note
Founded as the American Soc. of Tool Engineers, it became the American Soc. of Tool and Manufacturing Engineers in 1960 and the Soc. of Manufacturing Engineers in 1969. SME is a professional society dedicated to advancing scientific knowledge in the field of manufacturing and to applying its resources for researching, writing, publishing and disseminating information. Supports a number of associations and technical groups, including: Ass'n for Electronics Manufacturing, Ass'n for Finishing Processes, Composites Manufacturing Ass'n, Computer and Automated Systems Ass'n, Forming Technologies Ass'n, Machine Vision Ass'n, Machining Technology Ass'n, Networking and Communications in Manufacturing Group, North American Manufacturing Research Institution, Plastics Molders and Manufacturers Ass'n, Rapid Prototyping Ass'n, and Robotics Internat'l. Sponsors the Manufacturing Engineering Education Foundation and the Manufacturing Engineering Certification Institute, which grants the ""CMFgE" (Certified Manufacturing Engineer), ""CMFgT" (Certified Manufacturing Technologist), and CEI (Certified Enterprise Intergrator) designations. Membership: $60/year (individual), $200-500/year, varies by plant size (company).

Publications:
Composites in Manufacturing. q.
Electronics in Manufacturing. q. adv.
Finishing Line. q.
Forming & Fabricating. m. adv.
Intergrated Design & Manufacturing.
Machining Technology.
Manufacturing Engineering. m. adv.
Robotics Today. q.
Vision. q.

Meetings/Conferences:
Annual Meetings: May

Soc. of Marine Consultants (1982)
Historical Note
Address unknown in 1997.

Soc. of Marine Port Engineers (1946)
P.O. Box 466
Avenel, NJ 07001-2402
Tel: (908)381-7673   *Fax:* (908)381-2046
Members: 550 individuals
Staff: 1
Annual Budget: $50-100,000
Secretary: Benjamin A. Bailey

Historical Note
Membership: $75/year.

Publications:
The De-Air-Ator. q.

Meetings/Conferences:
Annual Meetings: May, in New York, NY

Soc. of Maritime Arbitrators (1963)
14 Wall St., Suite 8A-15
New York, NY 10005-2101
Tel: (212)587-0033   *Fax:* (212)587-6179
Members: 126 individuals
Staff: 1
Annual Budget: $50-100,000
President: Lucian C. Bulow

Historical Note
Members are drawn from such fields as surveying, engineering, finance, brokerage, stevedoring, construction, repairs, sales, insurance, and terminal and vessel operations; the bulk of the membership is in the New York area. SMA's purpose is to help settle disputes arising from contracts for all movements by water or involving shipbuilding and repair, and to maintain uniformity in U.S. maritime arbitration proceedings.

Publications:
The Arbitrator. q.

Meetings/Conferences:
1999 – Auckland, New Zealand/Mar. 1-5

Soc. of Medical Consultants to the Armed Forces (1946)
P.O. Box 2700
Kensington, MD 20891-2700
Tel: (301)295-3903   *Fax:* (202)726-3616
Members: 1,012 individuals
Staff: 1
Annual Budget: $10-25,000
Exec. Director: Anne Hufman

Historical Note
Organized by specialists who were consultants to the Armed Forces during World War II, SMCAF now includes individuals who have been consultants at any time to the Armed Services. Formerly Soc. of U.S. Medical Consultants in W.W. II.

Publications:
Newsletter. 3/year.
Roster. bien or trien.

Meetings/Conferences:
Annual Meetings: Fall, in Washington, DC

Soc. of Medical Jurisprudence (1883)
Historical Note
Address unknown in 1997.

Soc. of Medical-Dental Management Consultants (1968)
3646 E. Ray Road, Suite B16-45
Phoenix, AZ 85044
Tel: (602)759-5664   *Fax:* (602)759-3530
Toll Free: (800)826 - 2264
E-Mail: chuck@smdmc.org
Web Site: http://www.smdmc.org
Members: 65 individuals
Staff: 2

Annual Budget: $50-100,000
Exec. Secretary: Charles Wold

Historical Note
A professional society established in Kansas City, Missouri by 20 charter members in the spring of 1968. Membership: $435/year.

Publications:
Consultant's Newsletter. m. adv.
Membership Directory. a.
Newsletter. q. adv.

Meetings/Conferences:
1999 – Lake Tahoe, NV
1999 – San Juan, Puerto
2000 – Toronto, Canada
2000 – New Orleans, LA

Soc. of Mexican American Engineers and Scientists *(1974)*
P.O. Box 58923
Houston, TX   77258
Tel: (281)992-9639
E-Mail: RGGonzal@ems.jsc.nasa.gov
Web Site: http://www.tamu.edu/maes/
Members: 6,000 individuals, 20 professional & 60 univ. chaps.
Staff: 3
Annual Budget: $500-1,000,000
Chairman: Ralph Gonzalez
Conference Coordinator and Publiser/MAES National Magazine:
    Margaret G. Gonzales

Historical Note
MAES fosters cooperation among industrial, governmental, academic and professional communities to improve educational and employment opportunities for Mexican-Americans in engineering and science. Provides forums for technical presentations and runs educational assistance programs. Membership: $50/year (professional); $10/year (student); $500/year (organization/company).

Publications:
Annual MAES Symposium Proceedings and Career Fair. a.
    adv.
MAES National Magazine. q. adv.

Meetings/Conferences:
Annual Meetings: 1st Quarter

Soc. of Military Otolaryngologists - Head and Neck Surgeons *(1952)*
P.O. Box 923
Converse, TX   78109
Tel: (210)945-9006   *Fax:* (210)945-9024
E-Mail: spearce@worldnet.att.net
Members: 309 individuals
Staff: 1
Annual Budget: under $10,000
Administrative Secretary: Sue Pearce

Historical Note
Members are residents in training and otolaryngologists on active duty or who have served in the armed forces. Has no paid officers or full-time staff. Membership: $15/year (individual).

Meetings/Conferences:
Annual Meetings: In conjunction with the American Academy of
    Otolaryngology. Annually in September
1999 – New Orleans, LA
2000 – Washington, DC
2001 – Denver, CO
2002 – San Diego, CA

Soc. of Mineral Analysts *(1986)*
P.O. Box 5416
Elko, NV   89802
Tel: (702)753-5258   *Fax:* (702)778-8420
Members: 250 individuals
Annual Budget: $10-25,000
Secretary: Patrick Brown

Historical Note
SMA promotes cooperation in the minerals industry. Membership: $30 initiation, $20/year.

Publications:
Proceedings of Annual Conference. a. adv.

Meetings/Conferences:

Soc. of Motion Picture and Television Art Directors *(1937)*
11365 Ventura Blvd., Suite 315
Studio City, CA   91604-3148
Tel: (818)762-9995   *Fax:* (818)762-9997
E-Mail: adoffice@ni.net
Web Site: http://www.artdirectors.org
Members: 700 individuals
Staff: 5
Exec. Director: Scott Roth

Historical Note
A labor union formerly known (1960) as the Soc. of Motion Picture Art Directors. Affiliated with the Internat'l Alliance of Theatrical Stage Employees and Moving Picture Machine Operators of the U.S. and Canada, Local 876.

Publications:
Directory. a. adv.
Trace (newsletter). m.

Soc. of Motion Picture and Television Engineers *(1916)*
595 W. Hartsdale Ave.
White Plains, NY   10607
Tel: (914)761-1100   *Fax:* (914)761-3115
E-Mail: exec@smpte.org
Web Site: http://www.smpte.org
Members: 9,000 individuals
Staff: 21
Annual Budget: $2-5,000,000
Exec. Director: Frederick C. Motts

Historical Note
Founded in 1916 as the Soc. of Motion Picture Engineers. Incorporated in the District of Columbia. Became the Soc. of Motion Picture and Television Engineers in 1950. Membership: $80/year (active); $25/year (student).

Publications:
SMPTE Journal. m.

Meetings/Conferences:
1999 – New York, NY/Nov. 19-22

Soc. of Multivariate Experimental Psychology *(1960)*
Historical Note
Address unknown in 1996.

Soc. of Municipal Arborists *(1964)*
7000 Olive Blvd.
University City, MO   63130-2300
Tel: (314)862-1711
Web Site: http://www.urban-forestry.com
Members: 400 individuals
Staff: 1
Annual Budget: $10-25,000
Exec. Secretary: Norma Bonham

Historical Note
Full-time municipal arborists and companies representing products in the field. Membership: $40/year (individual); $100/year (company).

Publications:
City Trees. bi-m. adv.
Membership List. a.
Proceedings. a.

Meetings/Conferences:
Annual Meetings: Fall
1999 – Cincinnati, OH
2000 – Wichita, KS

Soc. of Nat'l Ass'n Publications *(1963)*
1650 Tysons Blvd., Suite 200
McLean, VA   22102
Tel: (703)506-3285   *Fax:* (703)506-3266
Members: 500 individuals
Staff: 3
Annual Budget: $250-500,000
Exec. Director: Laura Skoff

Historical Note
SNAP members are editors and publishers of association and professional society magazines. Associate members are suppliers of products and services to association publications. Affiliate members are publications whose primary publication is already a member of SNAP. Membership: $250-$695/year, based on net ad revenue (publication); $30/year (affiliate publication); $150-$450/year, based on gross revenues (associate).

Publications:
Association Publishing. magazine.
Membership Directory. a.
SnapFacts. newsletter.

Meetings/Conferences:
Annual Meetings: May in Washington, DC
1999 – Bethesda, MD(Bethesda Hyatt Regency)/June 7-9

Soc. of Naval Architects and Marine Engineers *(1893)*
601 Pavonia Ave., Suite 400
Jersey City, NJ   07306
Tel: (201)798-4800   *Fax:* (201)798-4975
Web Site: http://www.sname.org
Members: 11,000 individuals
Staff: 15
Annual Budget: $2-5,000,000
Exec. Director: Philip Kimball

Historical Note
Incorporated in New York April 28, 1893. Membership: $108/year (individual).

Publications:
Journal of Ship Production. q.
Journal of Ship Research. q.
Marine Technology/SNAME News. q. adv.
Transactions. a.

Meetings/Conferences:
Annual Meetings: Annual meetings in fall.
1999 – Baltimore, MD/Sept. 28-Oct. 2

Soc. of Nematologists *(1961)*
3012 Skyview Dr.,
Lakeland, FL   33801-7072
Web Site: see text
Members: 700 individuals
Annual Budget: $100-250,000

Historical Note
Members are individuals interested in nematodes, such as roundworms or threadworms. Member of the American Institute of Biological Sciences. Has no paid staff. Officers change annually in June. The Web site for the organization is http://iannwww.unl.edu/ianr/plntpath/nematode/son/sonhome.htm. Membership: $30/year (individual), $70/year (institutions/libraries).

Publications:
Annals of Applied Nematology. a.
Journal of Nematology. q.
Membership Directory. a.
Nematology Newsletter. q.

Meetings/Conferences:
Annual Meetings: Summer/300-400

Soc. of Neurological Surgeons *(1920)*
200 First St., S.W.
Rochester, MN   55905
Tel: (507)284-2254   *Fax:* (507)284-5206
Members: 200 individuals

Annual Budget: $10-25,000
Secretary: David Piepgras

Historical Note
The honorary society of neurological surgery. Has no paid officers or full-time staff.

Meetings/Conferences:
Annual Meetings: Spring/250
1999 – Colorado Springs, CO/May 16-18
2000 – Pasadena, CA/May 21-23

Soc. of Neurosurgical Anesthesia and Critical Care *(1973)*
1910 Byrd Ave., Suite 100
P.O. Box 11086
Richmond, VA   23230-1086
Tel: (804)673-9037   *Fax:* (804)282-0090
E-Mail: snacc@societyhq.com
Members: 500 individuals
Annual Budget: $50-100,000
Exec. Director: John A. Hinckley
Meeting/Conventions Manager: Kevin Johns, CMP

Historical Note
Formerly (1987) Soc. of Neurosurgical Anesthesia and Neurological Supportive Care. Members are board-certified anesthesiologists or surgeons. Provides clinical education programs and other services to members. Membership:(full member) $100/year; $219/year;(residency/emeritus) $25/year; w/JNA subscription $219/year; $144/year.

Publications:
Journal of Neurosurgical Anesthesiology. 4/year.
Selected References in Neurosurgical Anesthesia/Critical
    Care. bien.

Meetings/Conferences:
Annual Meetings: October, with the American Soc. of
    Anesthesiologists
1999 – Dallas, TX/200
2000 – San Francisco/200

Soc. of Newspaper Design
Historical Note
Became (1998) Soc. for News Design.

Soc. of North American Dog Trainers
Historical Note
Became (1995) American Dog Trainers Network.

Soc. of North American Goldsmiths *(1970)*
2275 Amigo Dr.
Missoula, MT   59808
Tel: (406)728-5248
Members: 5,500 individuals
Staff: 3
Annual Budget: $500-1,000,000
Exec. Administrator: Dana Singer

Historical Note
Concerned with the educational, scientific and aesthetic aspects of goldsmithing and metalsmithing. Membership: $55/year.

Publications:
Membership Directory. a.
Metalsmith. q. adv.
Newsletter. bi-m. adv.

Meetings/Conferences:
Annual Meetings: Spring/Summer

Soc. of Nuclear Medicine *(1954)*
1850 Samuel Morse Drive
Reston, VA   20190-5316
Tel: (703)708-9000   *Fax:* (703)708-9015
Web Site: http://www.snm.org
Members: 16,000 individuals
Staff: 34
Annual Budget: $5-10,000,000
Exec. Director: William Bertera
Director, Communications: John Childs
Director, Information Services: Mark Rogers
Dirctor, Marketing and Public Relations: Carolyn Pemberton
Director, Government Relation: David C. Nichols
Director, Meeting Services: Lauren Kramer-Whelan, CMP
Assoc. Director, Education: Marcia F. Ferg
Director, Financial and Administrative Services: Daniel J. Cassidy
Director, Membership Services: Lori Tremel Freeman
Administrator, Leadership Services: Ken K. Maynard
Deputy Exec. Director: Virginia M. Pappas, CAE
Director, Health Care Policy: Wendy J.M. Smith

Historical Note
SNM is a multi-disciplinary professional medical organization dedicated to the advancement of excellence in the education, research and clinical practice of nuclear medicine. Society membership consists of physicians, physicists, chemists, radiapharmacists, nuclear medicine technologists, and others interested in nuclear medicine and the use of radioactive isotopes in clinical practice, research and teaching. Promotes, presents and publishes research and information concerning the utilization of nuclear phenomena in the diagnosis and treatment of disease. Annual budget is approximately $7 million. Membership: $195/year (individual, full); $120/year (associate); $68/year (technologist); $145/year (affiliate).

Publications:
Journal of Nuclear Medicine m. adv. adv.
Journal of Nuclear Medicine Technology. q. adv.

Meetings/Conferences:
Semi-annual Meetings: June and midwinter
1999 – Los Angeles, CA/June 7-10

Soc. of Otorhinolaryngology and Head/Neck Nurses *(1976)*
116 Canal St., Suite A
New Smyrna Beach, FL   32168

Tel: (904)428-1695   *Fax:* (904)423-7566
Members: 1,200 individuals
Staff: 3
Exec. Director: Sandra Schwartz, RN
Historical Note
SOHN members are nurses specializing in ear, nose, throat, head
and neck.
Publications:
SOHN Journal. q. adv.
SOHN Update Newsletter. 5/yr. adv.
Meetings/Conferences:
1999 – New Orleans, LA/Sept. 25-29

Soc. of Park and Recreation Educators *(1966)*
c/o Nat'l Recreation & Park Ass'n
22377 Belmont Ridge Road
Ashburn, VA 20148
Tel: (703)858-0784   *Fax:* (703)858-0794
Toll Free: (800)626 - 6772
Web Site: http://www.uncwil.edu/spre
Members: 700 individuals
Staff: 1
Annual Budget: under $10,000
Exec. Secretary: Van F. Anderson
Historical Note
A branch of the Nat'l Recreation and Park Ass'n, which provides
administrative support.
Publications:
Leisure Research Symposium Abstracts. a.
SCHOLE Journal. a.
SPRE Newsletter. 3/year.
Meetings/Conferences:
Annual Meetings: Fall, with Nat'l Recreation and Park Ass'n
1999 – Nashville, TN

Soc. of Pediatric Nurses *(1990)*
2170 S. Parker Road, Suite 350
Denver, CO 80231-5711
Tel: (303)755-6304   *Fax:* (303)750-3212
Toll Free: (800)723 - 2902
E-Mail: pednurse.org
Members: 2,300 individuals
Staff: 3
Ass'n Coordinator: Gina R. Vargas
Historical Note
SPN members are nurses specializing in the nursing care of children
and families. Membership: $68/year.
Publications:
Journal of the Soc. of Pediatric Nurses. adv.
SPN News. q. adv.
Meetings/Conferences:
Annual Meetings: April
1999 – Houston, TX(Westin Galleria & Westin
     Oaks)/Apr. 25-28/1000
2000 – San Diego, CA(Sheraton)/Apr. 27-May 3/1000

Soc. of Pediatric Psychology
Historical Note
A section of the American Psychological Ass'n - Clinical
Psychology Division.

Soc. of Pelvic Surgeons *(1952)*
Division of Urology, Univ. of Kentucky
800 Rose St., MS 283
Lexington, KY 40536-0298
Tel: (606)323-6679   *Fax:* (606)323-1944
Members: 125 individuals
Annual Budget: under $10,000
Secretary-Treasurer: Dr. Randall G. Rowland, MD, PhD
Meetings/Conferences:
1999 – Banff, Canada/Sept. 15-19

Soc. of Personality and Social Psychology
Historical Note
A division of the American Psychological Ass'n.

Soc. of Petroleum Engineers *(1913)*
P.O. Box 833836
Richardson, TX 75083-3836
Tel: (972)952-9316   *Fax:* (972)952-9435
E-Mail: cladowski@spelink.spe.org
Web Site: http://www.spe.org
Members: 50,000 individuals
Staff: 90
Annual Budget: $10-25,000,000
Exec. Director: Dan K. Adamson
Public Relations Manager: Dave Cooney
Manager, Events: Lois Woods, CAE
Historical Note
Technical engineers, scientists and managers engaged in the
recovery of oil and gas related energy sources through wellbores. In
1913 a Standing Committee on Oil and Gas was established as part
of the American Institute of Mining and Metallurgical Engineers.
This became the Petroleum Division of the Institute in 1922, and
the Petroleum Branch in 1949. Petroleum was added to the Institute
name in 1955, and in 1957 the Soc. of Petroleum Engineers was
formed as one of three largely autonomous societies within the
AIME. In 1985, SPE incorporated separately from AIME. Street
address is 222 Palisades Creek Drive, Richardson, TX 75080. Has
an annual budget of over $12 million. Membership: $55/year.
Publications:
Journal of Petroleum Technology. m. adv.
SPE Drilling & Completion. q. adv.
SPE Journal. q. adv.
SPE Production & Facilities. q. adv.
SPE Reservoir Evaluation & Engineering. bi-m. adv.
Meetings/Conferences:
Annual Meetings: Fall

Soc. of Petroleum Evaluation Engineers *(1962)*
811 Dallas St., Suite 1416
Houston, TX 77002
Tel: (713)651-1639   *Fax:* (713)951-9659
E-Mail: spee@gnofin.org
Web Site: http://www.gnofin.org/spee
Members: 495 individuals
Staff: 1
Exec. Secretary: B.K. Starbuck-Buongiorno
Historical Note
SPEE members are engineers specializing in the evaluation of
petroleum and natural gas properties.
Meetings/Conferences:

Soc. of Philosophers in America *(1985)*
Westfield State College
Westfield, MA 01086
Tel: (413)572-5362   *Fax:* (413)562-3613
E-Mail: j-loughney@wsc.mass.edu
Members: 120 individuals
Annual Budget: under $10,000
Exec. Director: John A. Loughney
Historical Note
Dedicated to revitalizing the professional life of professors and
teachers of philosophy in the U.S.

Soc. of Photo-Technologists *(1959)*
Historical Note
Address unknown in 1995.

Soc. of Photographer and Artist Representatives
(1965)
60 East 42nd St., Suite 1166
New York, NY 10165-0006
Tel: (212)779-7464   *Fax:* (203)866-3321
Members: 108 individuals
Staff: 1
Annual Budget: $25-50,000
President: Harriet Kasak
Historical Note
SPAR members are professionals who represent artists,
photographers and stylists as well as hair and make-up artists.
Membership: $150/year (general), $100/year (national),
$100/year (associate).
Publications:
SPAR Directory. a.
SPAR Do-it-yourself Kit.
SPAR Newsletter. q. adv.

Soc. of Physician Assistants in Pediatrics
P.O. Box 6116
Hamden, CT 06517
Tel: (203)797-7940   *Fax:* (203)792-2173
E-Mail: PeKileen@aol.com
Members: 150 individuals
Staff: 1
President: JoAnna Mora
Historical Note
A specialty organization affiliated with the American Academy of
Physician Assistants interested in Pediatrics. Membership:
$30/year (individual).
Publications:
Newsletter. q.
Meetings/Conferences:
1999 – Atlanta, GA/May 29-June 3

Soc. of Physics Students *(1968)*
One Physics Ellipse
College Park, MD 20740-3843
Tel: (301)209-3009   *Fax:* (301)209-0839
Members: 7,500 individuals
Staff: 5
Annual Budget: $250-500,000
Acting Director: Bo Hammer
Historical Note
Formed through a merger of the Student Sections of the American
Institute of Physics and the physics honor society, Sigma Pi Sigma.
Affiliated with the American Institute of Physics, Inc. Membership:
$13/year.
Publications:
Journal of Undergraduate Research in Physics. semi-a.
Speakers, Tours & Films Book. a.
SPS Information Book. a.
SPS Newsletter. 5/yr.
Meetings/Conferences:
Annual Meetings: Fall

Soc. of Piping Engineers and Designers *(1980)*
One Main St., Suite N-717
Houston, TX 77002
Tel: (713)221-8224   *Fax:* (713)226-5230
E-Mail: ebher@dt.uh.edu
Web Site: http://web.wt.net/sped/
Members: 750 individuals, 50 companies
Staff: 2
Annual Budget: $250-500,000
Exec. Director & Treasurer: Stan Ebner
Historical Note
Members are piping professionals and technical experts interested in
staying abreast of the technological advances in the field of piping
and plant design. Membership: $35/year (individual); $300-
500/year (company); $20/year (student).
Publications:
Proceedings of the Annual Conference. a.
SPED Newsletter q. adv. adv.
Meetings/Conferences:
Annual Meetings: Annual in Houston, TX

Soc. of Plastics Engineers *(1942)*
14 Fairfield Dr.
Brookfield, CT 06804-0403
Tel: (203)775-0471   *Fax:* (203)775-8490
E-Mail: 4spemail@4spe.org
Web Site: www.4spe.org
Members: 35,000 individuals
Staff: 41
Annual Budget: $5-10,000,000
Exec. Director: Michael R. Cappelletti
Manager, Conference: Michelle O'Donnell
Managing Director, Education Svcs.: John J. Contessa
Managing Director, Finance/Administration: Lawrence E.
     McDowell
Managing Director, Member Services Department: Jeffrey A. Forger,
     CMP
Membership Programs and Services: Lisa M. Chirco
Director, Promotion Department: James P. Toner
Director, Field Svcs. and Development: Gail R. Bristol
Historical Note
Founded December 2, 1941 in Detroit as the Soc. of Plastics Sales
Engineers and incorporated in Michigan in 1942. Has an annual
budget of approximately $8.5 million. Membership: $84/year
(individuals).
Publications:
Journal of Applied Medical Polymers. semi-a.
Journal of Injection Molding Technology. q.
Journal of Vinyl & Additive Technology. q.
Plastics Engineering. m. adv.
Polymer Composites. bi-m.
Polymer Engineering and Science. m.
Meetings/Conferences:
Annual Meetings: Spring/5,000-6,000
1999 – New York, NY(NY Hilton)/May 2-6
2000 – Orlando, FL(Marriott Orlando & World
     Center)/May 7-11

Soc. of Professional Archeologists *(1976)*
Dept. of Anthropology
Florida State University
Tallahassee, FL 32306-2150
Tel: (850)644-8149   *Fax:* (850)644-4283
Members: 750 individuals
Staff: 1
Annual Budget: $25-50,000
Treasurer: Rochelle Marriman
Historical Note
Established to speak for professional archeologists and develop
professional standards in training, conduct and research.
Promulgates a Code of Ethics and certifies the qualifications of its
members. Membership fee varies, based on income.
Publications:
Directory of Professional Archeologists. a.
SOPAnews. m.
Meetings/Conferences:
Annual Meetings: With the Soc. for American Archaeology

Soc. of Professional Audio Recording Services *(1978)*
4300 10th Ave. N.
Lake Worth, FL 33461-2313
Tel: (561)641-6648   *Fax:* (561)642-8263
Toll Free: (800)771 - 7727
E-Mail: spars@spars.comm
Web Site: www.spars.com/spars/
Members: 350 companies
Staff: 5
Annual Budget: $100-250,000
Exec. Director: Shirley P. Kaye
Historical Note
Formerly (1987) the Soc. of Professional Audio Recording Studios.
Members are individuals, companies and studios connected with the
professional recording industry. Membership: $150-365/year
(individual), $1,250-2,500/year (manufacturer).
Publications:
Data Track Newsletter. q.
Meetings/Conferences:
Annual Meetings: Fall
1999 – New York, NY

Soc. of Professional Benefit Administrators *(1975)*
2 Wisconsin Circle, Suite 670
Chevy Chase, MD 20815-7003
Tel: (301)718-7722   *Fax:* (301)718-9440
Members: 425 companies
Staff: 6
Annual Budget: $1-2,000,000
President: Frederick D. Hunt, Jr.
V. President and Director, Federal Affairs: Anne c. Lennan
Director of Government Relations: Elizabeth Y. Leight
Director, Member Services: Kathryn Lafleur Strauss
Comptroller: Acacia G. Hunt
Historical Note
Third-party contract administration firms (TPAs), which administer
employee benefit plans for client employers and unions. Two-thirds
of all U.S. workers, retirees and dependents are covered by such
plans. SPBA is an active resource and reference for government
policy-shapers. Membership: $750-3,500/year. (based on size).
Publications:
List of State MEWA Requirements.
List of State TPA Statutes.
SPBA TPA Directory. a.
SPBA Update. w.
Meetings/Conferences:
Semi-annual Meetings: Spring in Washington, DC and
     Fall/350
1999 – Washington, DC(Capitol Hilton)
1999 – Columbus, OH(Adam's Mark)

Soc. of Professional Investigators (1956)

210 5th Ave., Suite 1102
New York, NY   10010-2102
Tel: (212)807-5658
Members: 500 individuals
Staff: 3
Annual Budget: $10-25,000
President: Dennis G. Lyons

Historical Note
SPI is dedicated to ethical principals in the field of private investigation. Membership, largely concentrated in the New York area, consists of individuals with at least five years of experience in investigation. Membership: $50/year (individual); $25/year (student).

Publications:
SPI Newsletter. 8/year. adv.

Meetings/Conferences:

Soc. of Professional Journalists (1909)

16 South Jackson, P.O. Box 77
Greencastle, IN   46135-0077
Tel: (765)653-3333   *Fax:* (765)653-4631
E-Mail: spj@link2000.net
Web Site: http://www.spj.org
Members: 13,500 individuals
Staff: 15
Annual Budget: $1-2,000,000
Exec. Director: Dennis Norris
Director, Education and Programs: Julie Grimes
Finance Director: Barbara Bryan
Membership Director: Lisa Mock

Historical Note
Founded at DePauw University in Greencastle, Indiana in 1909 as Sigma Delta Chi; became the Soc. of Professional Journalists, Sigma Delta Chi in 1972; assumed its present name in 1989. Membership is comprised of men and women in every field of journalism. Maintains over 300 local professional and campus chapters. Membership: $70/year (individual), $35/year (student/retired).

Publications:
Freedom of Information Report. a.
Internship Directory. a.
Membership Directory. a.
Quill. m. adv.

Meetings/Conferences:
Annual Meetings: October/1,200
1999 – Indianapolis, IN/Oct. 3-5
2000 – Columbus, OH/Oct. 5-7
2001 – Seattle, WA/Oct. 4-6

Soc. of Professional Well Log Analysts (1959)

8866 Gulf Fwy., Suite 320
Houston, TX   77017-6531
Tel: (713)947-8727   *Fax:* (713)947-7181
Web Site: http://www.spwla.org
Members: 3,700 individuals
Staff: 2
Annual Budget: $250-500,000
Exec. Director: Vicki J. King

Historical Note
Founded in Tulsa in January 1959 and incorporated in Oklahoma the same year. Promotes the evaluation of formations, through well logging techniques, in order to locate gas, oil and other minerals. Membership: $50/year.

Publications:
The Log Analyst. bi-m. adv.
Transactions. a.

Meetings/Conferences:
1999 – Oslo, Norway

Soc. of Professionals in Dispute Resolution (1972)

1527 New Hampsher Ave. N.W.
Washington, DC   20036
Tel: (202)667-9700   *Fax:* (202)783-7281
E-Mail: spidr@spidr.org
Web Site: http://www.spidr.org
Members: 3,600 individuals
Staff: 6
Annual Budget: $500-1,000,000
Exec. Director: Daniel Bowling
Associate Exec. Director/Programs Director: Janice Robertson
Director, Membership & Communications: Andre Owen

Historical Note
Members are specialists in labor, environment, family, community and other types of dispute resolution. Incorporated in the State of New York. Membership: $80-100/year.

Publications:
Membership Directory. a.
Proceedings. a.
SPIDR Newsletter. q.

Meetings/Conferences:
Annual Meetings: mid-October/600 Baltimore, MD(Omni)/Sept. 23-25

Soc. of Professors of Child and Adolescent Psychiatry (1969)

3615 Wisconsin Ave., N.W.
Washington, DC   20016-3007
Tel: (202)966-7300   *Fax:* (202)966-2891
Members: 160 individuals
Staff: 1
Annual Budget: $10-25,000
Administrative Assistant: Jean DeJarnette
Director, Conventions/Meetings: Charmaine Smiklo
Director, Finance and Administration: Robert Hendren,, P.O.

Historical Note
Formerly (1987) Soc. of Professors of Child Psychiatry. Membership: $100/year (individual).

Publications:
SPCAP Directory. a.
SPCAP Newsletter. semi-a.

Meetings/Conferences:

Soc. of Professors of Education (1902)

Dept. of Educational Leadership & FDTS
State U. of West Georgia, 1600 Maple St.
Carrollton, GA   30118-5160
Tel: (770)836-4439   *Fax:* (770)836-4646
Members: 400 individuals
Staff: 1
Annual Budget: under $10,000
Secretary-Treasurer: Dr. Robert C. Morris

Historical Note
Established as the Nat'l Soc. of College Teachers of Education, it assumed its present name in 1969. SPE is a professional and academic association open to all individuals engaged in teacher preparation or related activities. Membership: $25/year.

Publications:
DeGarmo Lectures. a.
SPE Monograph Series. a.
SPE Newsletter. irreg.

Meetings/Conferences:
Annual Meetings: April, in conjunction with the American Education Research Ass'n/100
1999 – Montreal, Canada/April 19-23

Soc. of Prospective Medicine (1972)

341 Ritter Road South South
Sewickley, PA   15143-9586
Tel: (412)749-1177
Web Site: http://www.spm.org
Members: 350 individuals
Staff: 3
Annual Budget: $50-100,000
Exec. Director: Janet J. Forester

Historical Note
Individuals interested in health care programs to extend life expectancy. Membership: $100/year (individual).

Publications:
An Ounce of Prevention. q.
Handbook of Health Risk Appraisals. bien.
Proceedings. a.

Meetings/Conferences:

Soc. of Protozoologists (1947)

151 Barrow Hall, Univ. of Georgia
Athens, GA   30602
Tel: (706)542-4080   *Fax:* (706)542-4271
Web Site: http://www.uga.edu/ ~ protozoa
Members: 1,100 individuals
Annual Budget: $100-250,000
Editor: Mark Farmer

Historical Note
Founded in 1947 as an international scientific society. An affiliate of the American Ass'n for the Advancement of Science and member of the World Federation of Parasitologists. Members are concerned with all aspects of the study of protozoa. Membership : $60/year.

Publications:
Journal of Eukaryotic Microbiology. bi-m.
Newsletter. 3/year.

Meetings/Conferences:
Annual Meetings: Summer

Soc. of Psychologists in Addictive Behaviors (1975)

Historical Note
Organization defunct in 1995; SPAB's programming functions have been largely superseded by the Division on Addictions of the American Psychological Ass'n.

Soc. of Publication Designers (1964)

60 East 42nd St., Suite 721
New York, NY   10165
Tel: (212)983-8585   *Fax:* (212)983-6043
Web Site: http://www.spd.org
Members: 800 individuals
Staff: 3
Annual Budget: $250-500,000
Exec. Director: Bride M. Whelan

Historical Note
A professional organization which includes primarily publication art directors, editors, designers, illustrators, photographers, printers and publishers. Serves the needs of the editorial designer and art director by sponsoring annual competitions, speakers evenings, exhibitions, conferences and other activities. Membership: $195/year (individual); $495/year (corporate).

Publications:
Grids. m.
Publication Design Annual. a. adv.

Meetings/Conferences:

Soc. of Quality Assurance (1980)

515 King St., Suite 420
Alexandria, VA   22314
Tel: (703)684-4050   *Fax:* (703)684-6048
Members: 1,200 individuals, 47 companies
Staff: 2
Annual Budget: $250-500,000
Exec. Director: Robin R. Smith
Director of Membership: Debbie Espinoza

Historical Note
Founded in 1980 as Quality Assurance Roundtable, became SQA in 1984. Members are professionals in the toxicological, pharmaceutical, biological, and chemical sciences responsible for quality assurance and standards maintenance in the laboratory and workplace. Membership: $90/year (active); $75/year (affiliate).

Publications:
QA Directory. a.
QA Newsletter. q.
Regulatory Review Bulletin. irreg.

Meetings/Conferences:
Annual Meetings: October/700-800
1999 – Chicago, IL(Palmer House Hilton)/Oct. 12-15/800
2000 – Montreal, CAN(The Quenn Elizabeth)/Oct. 10-13/800

Soc. of Quantitative Analysts (1989)

151 Herricks Road, Suite 1
Garden City Park, NY   11040-5200
Tel: (516)739-2510   *Fax:* (516)739-3803
Toll Free: (800)284 - 6228
Web Site: http://www.sqa.us.org
Members: 250 individuals
Staff: 1
Annual Budget: $10-25,000
Exec. Director: Harry A. Hansen

Historical Note
Originally established in 1972 as the Computer Applications Symposium of the New York Soc. of Security Analysts and in 1980 became the Investment Technology Ass'n. Adopted its present name upon incorporation in 1989. SQA is concerned with the application of new and innovative techniques for finance, with particular emphasis on the use of quantitative techniques in investment management. Membership: $150/year (individual).

Meetings/Conferences:
Annual Meetings: May
1999 – New York, NY

Soc. of Radiological Engineering (1968)

Historical Note
Defunct organization.

Soc. of Recreation Executives (1986)

P.O. Box 520
Gonzales, FL   32560-0520
Tel: (850)944-7992   *Fax:* (850)944-0081
E-Mail: NRVOCKWS@SPYDEE.NET
Web Site: rvadvice.com/nrvoc
Members: 3,462 individuals
Staff: 3
Annual Budget: $50-100,000
V. President and Director: David E. Dykes

Historical Note
Members are corporate executives, business owners and institutional professionals involved in the recreation, leisure and travel industries. Membership: $100/year (individual); $250/year (corporate).

Publications:
Recreation Executive Newsletter. bi-m. adv.
Who's Who in Recreation. a. adv.

Meetings/Conferences:
Annual Meetings: August/90
2000 – Dallas, TX
2001 – New Orleans, LA
2002 – Las Vegas, NV

Soc. of Reliability Engineers (1966)

Historical Note
SRE members are reliability, maintainability and component engineers.

Soc. of Research Administrators (1967)

1200 19th St., N.W., Suite 300
Washington, DC   20036-2422
Tel: (202)857-1141   *Fax:* (202)223-4579
E-Mail: sra@dc.sba.com
Web Site: http://www.sra.rams.com
Members: 2,800 individuals
Staff: 3
Annual Budget: $500-1,000,000
Exec. Director: Carolyn M. Freeland
Program Coordinator: Tamra Hackett
Membership Coordinator: Brian Russo

Historical Note
A professional association of individuals in industry, academia and government to improve the efficiency of research administration and the interface between the investigators and their administrative overseers. Membership: $120/year (individual).

Publications:
Membership Directory. a. adv.
Newsletter. bi-m.
SRA Journal. bi-m.

Meetings/Conferences:
Annual Meetings: Fall/1,300
1999 – Denver, CO(Adams Mark)/Oct. 16-20
2000 – St. Louis, MO(Adam's Mark)/Oct. 21-25
2001 – Vancouver, BC, Canada(Hyatt Regency)/Oct. 13-17

Soc. of Rheology (1929)

500 Sunnyside Blvd.
Woodbury, NY   11797-2999
Tel: (516)576-2403   *Fax:* (516)576-2223
E-Mail: jbennett@aip.org
Web Site: http://www.umecheme.maine.edu/sor
Members: 1,700 individuals
Annual Budget: $10-25,000
Secretary: Andrew Kraynik
Liaison: Janis Bennett

Historical Note
Chemists, physicists, biologists, chemical engineers, and others concerned with the theory and precise measurement of the flow of matter, and the response of materials to mechanical force. Has a permanent address at the American Institute of Physics, and is one of the five founding members of that organization. Membership: $40/year (regular), $25/year (student/retired).

Publications:
Journal of Rheology. bi-m.
Rheology Bulletin. semi-a.

Meetings/Conferences:
1999 – Madison, WI/Oct. 17-21

Soc. of Risk Management Consultants (1984)
300 Park Ave., 17th Floor
New York, NY   10022
Tel: (212)572-6246
Toll Free: (800)765 - 7762
Members: 150 individuals
Annual Budget: $10-25,000
Public Relations Chair: Charles Cox

Historical Note
Formed in 1984 by the consolidation of the Insurance Consultants Soc. and the Institute of Risk Management Consultants. Membership: $250/year.

Publications:
SRMC Journal. irreg.

Meetings/Conferences:
Semi-annual meetings: April, and October

Soc. of Roller Skating Teachers of America (1945)
6905 Corporate Dr.
Indianapolis, IN   46278-1927
Tel: (317)347-2626   *Fax:* (317)347-2636
Members: 650 individuals
Exec. Director: Katherine M. McDonell, CAE

Historical Note
Sponsored by Roller Skating Ass'n Internat'l.

Publications:
RSA Today-Coach's Edition. bi-m.

Meetings/Conferences:
Annual Meetings: held with the Nat'l Championship.
1999 – Lincoln, NE

Soc. of Satellite Professionals Internat'l (1983)
2225 Reinkers Lane
Alexandria, VA   22314
Tel: (703)549-8696   *Fax:* (703)549-9728
Web Site: http://www.sspi.org
Members: 1,100 individuals
Staff: 2
Annual Budget: $50-100,000
Exec. Director: La Rene C. Tondro

Historical Note
Formerly (1988) Soc. of Satellite Professionals. Members are individuals in the fields of business, education, entertainment, media, science and industry who share common interests in satellite technology. There are 35 corporate sponsors. Membership: $60/year (individual), $500-5,000/year (company).

Publications:
Membership Directory. a.
ORBITER. bi-m.
Update. bi-m.

Meetings/Conferences:
Semi-annual Meetings: Spring, and Fall with the Satellite Communications Users Conference

Soc. of School Librarians Internat'l (1985)
Historical Note
Address unknown in 1997.

Soc. of Scribes (1974)
P.O. Box 933
New York, NY   10150
Tel: (212)722-2344   *Fax:* (212)741-2787
Members: 700 individuals
Staff: 9
Contact: Mary Ann Wolfe

Historical Note
SOS members are calligraphers and others with an interest in book arts. Membership: 25/year (individual).

Publications:
NewSOS Newsletter. 3/yr. adv.

Meetings/Conferences:
Annual Meetings: always last Saturday in February

Soc. of Small Craft Designers (1949)
04294 Fontenoye St. East
Boyne City, MI   49712
Tel: (616)582-2924
Members: 250 individuals
Staff: 1
Annual Budget: under $10,000
President: William R. Mehaffey

Historical Note
Members are small craft designers concerned with the scientific design of yachts and small commercial vessels (up to 200 feet). Members are primarily naval architects. Membership: $20/year (individual).

Publications:
Log Newsletter. irreg.
Planimeter. a.

Soc. of Soft Drink Technologists (1953)
Historical Note
Became the Internat'l Soc. of Beverage Technologists in 1995.

Soc. of Stage Directors and Choreographers (1959)
1501 Broadway, Suite 1701
New York, NY   10036-5653
Tel: (212)391-1070   *Fax:* (212)302-6195
Toll Free: (800)541 - 5204
Web Site: http://www.ssdc.org
Members: 1,500 individuals

Staff: 10
Annual Budget: $500-1,000,000
Exec. Director: Barbara Hauptman

Historical Note
SSDC is an independent labor union representing directors and choreographers in American theatre as well as choreographers in film and television.

Publications:
Journal of SSDC. q.
SSDC Directory. bien.
SSDC Newsletter. bi-m.

Meetings/Conferences:
Semi-annual Conventions: May and November in New York and L.A.

Soc. of State Directors of Health, Physical Education and Recreation (1926)
1900 Association Drive
Reston, VA   20191
Tel: (703)476-3402   *Fax:* (703)476-9527
Members: 180 individuals
Staff: 1
Annual Budget: $25-50,000
Exec. Director: William H. Datema

Historical Note
An affiliate of American Alliance for Health, Physical Education, Recreation, and Dance, the Soc. seeks to promote and improve programs of health, physical education, recreation, athletics, dance and related subjects in elementary schools, secondary schools, colleges and universities, and teacher education programs in these disciplines. Has no paid officers or full-time staff. Membership: $35/year (full member), $25/year (associate).

Publications:
Directory. a.
Newsletter. q.

Meetings/Conferences:
Annual Meetings: Spring, with AAHPERD/100
1999 – Boston, MA/Apr. 3-4/150
2000 – Orlando, FL/Mar. 19-20/150
2001 – Cincinnati, OH/150
2002 – San Diego, CA/Apr. 14-15/150

Soc. of Surgical Oncology (1940)
85 W. Algonquin Road, Suite 550
Arlington Heights, IL   60005-4425
Tel: (847)427-1400   *Fax:* (847)427-9656
Members: 1,625 individuals
Staff: 4
Annual Budget: $1-2,000,000
Exec. Director: James R. Slawny
Associate Exec. Director: Rick Slawny
Financial Manager: Ramsey Swenson
Membership Director: Pat Sharpitas

Historical Note
Founded in 1940 as the James Ewing Soc. Became the Soc. of Surgical Oncology in 1975.

Publications:
Annals of Surgical Oncology. 8x/year. adv.

Meetings/Conferences:
Annual Meetings: March
1999 – Orlando, FL(Marriott World Center)/March 4-7/2000
2000 – New Orleans, LA(Hyatt)/March 16-19/2000
2001 – Washington, DC(Sheraton)/March 15-18/2000
2002 – Denver, CO(Adams Mark)
2003 – Los Angeles, CA(Century Plaza)

Soc. of Systematic Biologists (1948)
Dept. of Biology & Museum of Zoology
University of Michigan
Ann Arbor, MI   48109-1079
Tel: (313)647-2209   *Fax:* (313)763-4080
E-Mail: mindell@umich.edu
Web Site: http://www.utexas.edu/depts/syqtbiol/
Members: 1,500 individuals
Staff: 1
Annual Budget: under $10,000
Secretary: Dr. David Mindell

Historical Note
Formerly (1991) Soc. of Systematic Zoology. Founded in the District of Columbia in 1948. Affiliated with the American Ass'n for the Advancement of Science, the American Institute of Biological Sciences, the National Research Council and the American Soc. of Zoologists. Promotes zoological classification. Membership: $35/year (individual), $15/year (student), $60/year (organization).

Publications:
Systematic Biology. q.

Meetings/Conferences:
Annual Meetings: December, with the American Soc. of Zoologists

Soc. of Teachers of Family Medicine (1967)
P.O. Box 8729
8880 Ward Pkwy.
Kansas City, MO   64114
Tel: (816)333-9700   *Fax:* (816)333-3884
Members: 4,800 individuals
Staff: 15
Annual Budget: $2-5,000,000
Exec. Director: Roger A. Sherwood, CAE
Communications Director: Stacy H. Brungardt
Dep. Exec. Director: Marcia Neu, CAE
Coordinator, Membership: Mary Ruhl

Historical Note
Multidisciplinary society of health professionals concerned with family medicine education. Affiliated with the American Board of Family Practice, the American Academy of Family Physicians, and the American Academy of Family Physicians Foundation. Represents family medicine as an academic discipline on the

Council of Academic Societies of the Ass'n of American Medical Colleges.

Publications:
Family Medicine. m. adv.
STFM Messenger. bi-m. adv.

Meetings/Conferences:
Annual Meetings: Spring/950
1999 – Seattle, WA(Sheraton)/April 28-May 2/1200
2000 – Orlando, FL(Coronado Springs)/May 3-7/1200

Soc. of Telecommunications Consultants (1976)
13766 Center St., Suite 212
Carmel Valley, CA   93924
Tel: (831)659-0110   *Fax:* (831)659-0144
Toll Free: (800)782 - 7670
E-Mail: stchdq@stcconsultants.org
Web Site: www.stcconsultants.org
Members: 225 individuals, 90 companies
Staff: 3
Annual Budget: $250-500,000
Exec. Director: Susan Kuttner
General Counsel: Tom Crowe
Administration Manager: Rebecca Nast

Historical Note
Established to meet the need for a self-regulating body in the profession, STC members are telecommunications professionals who serve clients in business, industry and government. STC represents its members in regulatory, legislative and commercial affairs and maintains a vendor advisory council, comprised of companies offering telecommunications products and services, which supports consultant members with technical information and provides assistance in solving problems in the field. Membership: $375/year (individual); $850/year (vendor company).

Publications:
Speakers Bureau Directory. semi-a.
STC Consultant Directory. irreg.
STC Lines Newsletter. q.
Vendor Advisory Council Membership Directory. q.
Writers/Article Repository. semi-a.

Meetings/Conferences:
Semi-Annual Meetings: Spring and Fall/250
1999 – Vancouver, BC, Canada(Hyatt Regency)/April 28-May 2
1999 – Tampa, FL(Hyatt Regency)/Oct. 28-31

Soc. of the Plastics Industry (1937)
1801 K St., N.W., Suite 600-K
Washington, DC   20006-1301
Tel: (202)974-5200   *Fax:* (202)296-7005
Web Site: http://www.socplas.org
Members: 2,000 companies
Staff: 130
Annual Budget: $25-50,000,000
President: Larry L. Thomas
Director, Communications: Jennifer Dills
V. President, Government Affairs: Lewis R. Freeman, Jr.
V. President, Trade Shows: Jordan L. Morgenstern
V. President, Finance and Administration: John R. Maguire
V. President, Membership: Jeremy B. Taylor
Director, Information Services: Diana D. Wright

Historical Note
Absorbed (1998) Plastic Drum Institute. Promotes the application and use of plastics and is the principal representative of the plastics industry. Has an annual budget of approximately $35.9 million.

Publications:
Facts and Figures of the U. S.
Industrial Relations Newsletter. q.
Plastics NewsBriefs. m.
SPI Membership Directory and Buyers Guide. a.

Meetings/Conferences:
Annual Meetings: annual Plastics Conference & triennial National Plastics Exposition

Soc. of the Plastics Industry - EPS Division
Historical Note
Formerly a semi-autonomous division of Soc. of the Plastics Industry, the EPS Division was dissolved in 1995.

Soc. of the Plastics Industry - Polyurethane Division (1985)
1801 K St., N.W., Suite 600-K
Washington, DC   20006-1300
Tel: (202)974-5362
Web Site: polyurethane.org
Members: 46 companies
Staff: 5
Annual Budget: $2-5,000,000
Exec. Director: Fran Walker Lichtenberg
Coordinator, Confs./Meetings: Cindy Y. Kong

Historical Note
Founded as the Urethane Institute in 1959; assumed its present name in 1985. Members are polyurethane chemical producers; systems formulators; machinery manufacturers; manufacturers of polyurethane flexible and rigid foams, coatings, adhesives, sealants, elastomers, and molded polyurethane products; and manufacturers of rigid polyisocyanurate foams.

Publications:
Conference Proceedings.
Polyurethane News.
Technical, Marketing & Educational publications & audio visuals.

Meetings/Conferences:
Annual Meetings: Fall
1999 – Orlando, FL(The Dolphin)/Sept. 12-15

Soc. of Thoracic Radiology (1983)
P.O. Box 1925
Roswell, GA   30077
Tel: (770)641-9773

E-Mail: http://www.thoracicrad.org
Members: 200 individuals
Meeting Planner: Mary Ryals
Meetings/Conferences:

Soc. of Thoracic Surgeons *(1964)*
401 N. Michigan Ave.
Chicago, IL   60611-4267
Tel: (312)644-6610   *Fax:* (312)527-6635
Web Site: http://www.sts.org
Members: 4,000 individuals
Staff: 6
Annual Budget: $1-2,000,000
Exec. Director: Michael G. Thompson, Ph.D.
Historical Note
Membership: $300/year (individual).
Publications:
Annals of Thoracic Surgery. m. adv.
Meetings/Conferences:
Annual Meetings: mid-Winter/3000
1999 – San Antonio, TX(Convention Center)/Jan. 24-27
2000 – Ft. Lauderdale, FL(Convention Center)/Jan. 30-Feb. 2

Soc. of Toxicologic Pathologists *(1971)*
19 Mantua Road
Mount Royal, NJ   08061
Tel: (609)423-0087   *Fax:* (609)423-3420
Web Site: http://www.medscape.com/affiliates/stp
Members: 625 individuals
Annual Budget: $250-500,000
Exec. Director: Stephanie Dockinson
Historical Note
Originally the Society of Pharmalogical and Environmental Pathlolgists, incorporated in New Jersey in 1971; assumed its name in 1980. Aims of Society are to advance pathology as it pertains to changes elicited by pharmacological, chemical, and environmental agents, and to encourage communication and exchange of information in this field; to evaluate criteria and requirements applied to the interpretation of pathological changes produced by drugs, chemicals, and environmental agents; to encourage the training and recognition of pathologists in these fields; and to establish registries of pathologic entities in laboratory animals. Membership: $160/year (individual); $1,500/year (organization).
Publications:
Newsletter. q. adv.
Toxicologic Pathology. bi-m.
Meetings/Conferences:
1999 – San Francisco, CA

Soc. of Toxicology *(1961)*
1767 Business Center Drive, Suite 302
Reston, VA   22090-5332
Tel: (703)438-3115   *Fax:* (703)438-3113
E-Mail: sothq@toxicology.org
Web Site: http:\\www.toxicology.org
Members: 4,800 individuals
Staff: 10
Annual Budget: $2-5,000,000
Exec. Director: Shawn Douglas Lamb
CE/Public Communications: Deborah Hyman
Manager, Meetings/Exhibits: Clarissa Russell Wilson
Mgr., Annual Meeting Program: Nell Dillard
Director, Education: Dawn Caruso
Education Programs: Betty Eidemiller
Manager, Membership: Trish Strong
Historical Note
Founded and incorporated in the District of Columbia in 1961. Members are scientists concerned with the effects of chemicals on man and the environment. Membership: $141/year (individual); $2,000/year (organization).
Publications:
Communique. bi-m. adv.
Society of Toxicology Newsletter. bi-m. adv.
Toxicology and Applied Pharmacology. a. adv.
Meetings/Conferences:
Annual Meetings: late Winter/5,000
1999 – New Orleans, LA/March 14-18/5000

Soc. of Trauma Nurses
224 N. Des Plaines St., Suite 601
Chicago, IL   60661-1134
Tel: (312)993-0559   *Fax:* (312)993-0362
Toll Free: (888)786 - 5400
E-Mail: STRAUMA@aol. com
Web Site: http://www.straumanurse.org
Members: 600 individuals
Administrator: Joyce Griffin
Historical Note
Has no paid staff. Membership: $50/year (individual); $750/year (organization/company).
Publications:
Journal of Trauma Nursing. q. adv.
Meetings/Conferences:

Soc. of Travel Agents in Government *(1983)*
6935 Wisconsin Ave., Suite 200
Bethesda, MD   20815-6109
Tel: (301)654-8595   *Fax:* (301)654-6663
E-Mail: govtvlmkt@aol.com
Web Site: http://www.government-travel.org
Members: 470 organizations
Staff: 4
Annual Budget: $100-250,000
General Manager: Duncan G. Farrell, CMP
Historical Note
STAG was established for professional development of all organizations who provide travel services to government through mentoring and education; to promote professional standards for the

procurement and operation of government travel; and to otherwise advance the interest of travel managers. STAG members are ARC-appointed travel agents holding government travel contracts or servicing government contractors, suppliers and government or contractor travel managers. Membership: $195-450/year (by category).
Publications:
Accessibility of Fed. Gov't Travel Rates.
Membership Directory. q. adv.
STAG 101: Principles of Government Travel Management.
   semi-a. adv.
STAG Report Magazine. q. adv.
State & Provincial Travel Procurement Practices & Procedures.
   a. adv.
Meetings/Conferences:
Semi-Annual Meetings: February and September/450
1999 – Arlington, VA(Sheraton National)/Arlington, 0-12

Soc. of Travel and Tourism Educators
Historical Note
Became Internat'l Soc. of Travel and Tourism Educators in 1997.

Soc. of Tribologists and Lubrication Engineers *(1944)*
840 Busse Highway
Park Ridge, IL   60068-2376
Tel: (847)825-5536   *Fax:* (847)825-1456
E-Mail: STLE@interaccess.com
Web Site: http://www.stle.org
Members: 4,200 individuals, 200 companies
Staff: 10
Annual Budget: $1-2,000,000
Exec. Director: Edward P. Salek
Meetings Manager: Fay S. Bailiff
Historical Note
Formerly (1987) American Soc. of Lubrication Engineers. Founded to advance the science of lubrication (tribology). Provides technical information and support to the industry, academia, and government. Membership: $73/year (individual); $575/year (company).
Publications:
Lubrication Engineering. m. adv.
Tribology Transactions. q.
Meetings/Conferences:
Annual Meetings: Spring/1,500
1999 – Las Vegas, NV(Bally's)/May 23-27
2000 – Nashville, TN(Opryland)/May 7-12

Soc. of United States Air Force Flight Surgeons *(1960)*
Box 35387
Brooks AFB, TX   78235-5301
Tel: (210)536-2845   *Fax:* (210)536-1779
E-Mail: williamtarver@mirage.brooks.af.mil
Web Site: www.asma.orgs/soaffs
Members: 900 individuals
Annual Budget: under $10,000
Exec. Officer: William Tarver, M.D.
Historical Note
Affiliated with Aerospace Medical Ass'n. Membership: $15/year.
Publications:
Soc. of USAF Flight Surg.
Meetings/Conferences:
Annual Meetings: May/in conjunction with Aerospace Medical
   Ass'n.

Soc. of University Otolaryngologists *(1964)*
333 Longwood Ave., Suite 550
Boston, MA   02115
Tel: (617)732-7003
Members: 525 individuals
Staff: 1
Annual Budget: $10-25,000
Treasurer: Marvin Fried, M.D.
Historical Note
Members are ear, nose, throat, head and neck disorder specialists working at teaching hospitals or other academic settings. Has no paid officer or full-time staff. Membership: $60/year.

Soc. of University Surgeons *(1938)*
P.O. Box 16549
West Haven, CT   06516
Tel: (203)932-0541   *Fax:* (203)937-1669
Members: 1,400 individuals
Staff: 1
Annual Budget: $25-50,000
Secretary/President Elect: B. Mark Evers
Administrative Director: Mary E. Samokar
Historical Note
Membership: $150/year.
Publications:
Program Booklet. a.
Surgery. a. adv.
Meetings/Conferences:
Annual Meetings: February
1999 – New Orleans, LA
2000 – Toronto, ON, Canada
2001 – Chicago, IL
2002 – Honolulu, HI

Soc. of University Urologists *(1967)*
University of Nebraska Medical Center
600 S. 42nd St.
Omaha, NE   68198
Tel: (402)559-4292
Members: 492 individuals
Staff: 1
Annual Budget: under $10,000
Secretary-Treasurer: Robert Flanagan

Historical Note
Promotes high standards of urologic education and research. Membership: $70/year.
Publications:
Bulletin. 3/yea.
Roster. a.
Meetings/Conferences:
Annual Meetings: Fall, in conjunction with the American
   College of Surgeons/125

Soc. of Urologic Cryosurgeons *(1994)*
1950 Old Tustin Ave.
Santa Ana, CA   92705
Tel: (714)550-9155   *Fax:* (714)550-9234
Members: 100 individuals
Staff: 3
Annual Budget: $25-50,000
Exec. Director: Kathy DeSantis, CMP
Historical Note
Members are urologic surgeons interested in cryotherapy as a less-invasive alternative to traditional cancer therapies. Membership: $160/year.
Publications:
Cryogram. q. adv.
Meetings/Conferences:

Soc. of Urologic Nurses and Associates *(1972)*
East Holly Ave., P.O. Box 56
Pitman, NJ   08071-0056
Tel: (609)256-2335   *Fax:* (609)589-7463
E-Mail: SUNA@Mail.Ajj.com
Web Site: http://www.suna.inurse.com
Members: 2,000 individuals
Staff: 4
Annual Budget: $500-1,000,000
Exec. Director: Michael Cunningham
Historical Note
In 1970, the American Urological Ass'n organized a scientific program for urological allied health professionals. Interest was expressed throughout the United States, and local allied groups began top form. AUAA was incorporated as a non-profit organization in 1972. It's name was changed to Society of Urologic Nurses and Associates (SUNA) in 1995. SUNA unites urologic health care providers in promoting excellence in urologic education and professional standars for optimal care of the urologic patient. Membership: $60/year (individual); $1,500/year (company).
Publications:
Uro-Gram Newsletter. bi-m.
Urological Nursing Journal. q. adv.
Meetings/Conferences:
Annual Meetings: Spring/600
1999 – Dallas, TX(Hyatt Regency)/April 28-May 5/600

Soc. of Vacuum Coaters *(1957)*
71 Pinon Hill Place
Albuquerque, NM   87122-1914
Tel: (505)856-7188   *Fax:* (505)856-6716
E-Mail: svcinfo@svc.org
Web Site: http://www.svc.org
Members: 1000 individuals
Staff: 2
Annual Budget: $500-1,000,000
Exec. Director: Vivienne Harwood Mattox
Technical Director and News Bulletin Editor: Donald M. Mattox
Historical Note
Individuals concerned with the use and development of vacuum coatings for large and small scale applications. Membership: $70/year (domestic individual); $95/year (foreign individual); $1,000/year (company) 1st year; $500/year (company) thereafter.
Publications:
Conference Proceedings. a. adv.
SVC News Bulletin. 3/year. adv.
Meetings/Conferences:
1999 – Chicago, IL(Marriott Downtown)/April 17-22
2001 – Philadelphia, PA(Marriott)/April 20-26
2002 – Orlando, FL(Coronado Springs)/April 12-17

Soc. of Vascular Technology *(1977)*
4601 Presidents Drive, Suite 260
Lanham, MD   20706-4831
Tel: (301)459-7550   *Fax:* (301)459-5651
Toll Free: (800)788 - 8346
E-Mail: svtnet@msn.com
Web Site: http://www.svtnet.org
Members: 5,000 individuals
Staff: 6
Annual Budget: $500-1,000,000
Exec. Director: Suzanne Stone
Assoc. Director, Membership: Denise Silver
Historical Note
Founded and incorporated in Ohio. Formerly (1988) Soc. of Noninvasive Vascular Technology. Members perform diagnostic tests to determine the location of blockages in the body's circulatory system. Approximately 60% of SVT members are practicing noninvasive technologists or are involved in supervision and/or education in a clinical setting. Others include physicians, researchers, manufacturers and other health care providers. Serves as an education and information resource in matters pertaining to noninvasive vascular technology. Membership: $85/year (domestic); $105/year (foreign); $40/year (student); plus $10 initial application fee.
Publications:
Journal of Vascular Technology. q. adv.
Membership Directory. irreg.
Spectrum Newsletter. q. adv.
Meetings/Conferences:
Annual Meetings: August
1999 – Reno, NV(Hilton)/Aug. 29-Sept. 2
2000 – Orlando, FL(Hilton Disney Village)

2001 – Pittsburgh, PA(Hilton)

Soc. of Vertebrate Paleontology *(1941)*
401 N. Michigan Ave.
Chicago, IL 60611-4267
Tel: (312)321-3708 *Fax:* (312)245-1085
Web Site: http://www.eteweb.lscf.ucsb.edu/svp
Members: 1,700 individuals
Staff: 2
Annual Budget: $100-250,000
Exec. Director: Pam D'Argo

Historical Note
The Society of Vertebrate Patheontology was established Dec. 28, 1940. The object of the society is to advance the science of vertebrate paleontology, and to serve the common interests and facilitate the cooperation of all persons concerned with the history, evolution, comparative anatomy and taxonomy of vertebrate animals, as well as the field occurence, collection and study of fossil vertebrates and the stratigraphy of the beds in which they are found. Membership: $80/year (individual); $45/year (student).

Publications:
Bibliography of Fossil Vertebrates. a.
Journal of Vertebrate Palentology. q.
News Bulletin. 3/yr.

Meetings/Conferences:
Annual Meetings: October-November/900

Soc. of Woman Geographers *(1925)*
415 E. Captiol St., S.E.
Washington, DC 20003-3810
Tel: (202)546-9228 *Fax:* (202)546-5232
E-Mail: SWGHQ@aol.com
Members: 600 individuals
Staff: 1
Annual Budget: $50-100,000
President: Edith M. Ker
Office Administrator: Janet McGinn

Historical Note
Founded in New York City in 1925 and incorporated in the District of Columbia in 1937. Membership by invitation only. Officers change every three years in May. Publications distributed to members only. Membership: $40-60/year (individual).

Publications:
Bulletin. a.
Newsletter. q.

Meetings/Conferences:
Triennial Meetings: May (1999)
1999 – Florida

Soc. of Women Engineers *(1950)*
120 Wall St., 11th Floor
New York, NY 10005-3902
Tel: (212)509-9577 *Fax:* (212)509-0224
E-Mail: hq@swe.org
Web Site: http://www.swe.org
Members: 17,000 individuals
Staff: 8
Annual Budget: $5-10,000,000
Exec. Director(Interim): Gina Ryan, CAE
Editor: Anne Perusek
Convention Manager: Jeanne Elipani
Program Coordinator: Anette Sawer
Comptroller: Mohammed Sadique
Membership Supervisor: Estelle Zito

Historical Note
An educational service organization of engineering students and practicing engineers, both women and men. SWE was founded in 1949-50 when small groups of women engineers started meeting in New York, Boston, Philadelphia, and Washington. The society was incorporated in 1952. In 1976, membership was opened to men. Membership: $75/year (individual); $1,000/year (company); $15/year (student).

Publications:
SWE. bi-m. adv.

Meetings/Conferences:
Annual Meetings: June/2,300
1999 – Phoenix, AZ
2000 – Washington, DC
2002 – Detroit, MI
2003 – Birmingam, AL

Soc. of Wood Science and Technology *(1958)*
One Gifford Pinchot Dr.
Madison, WI 53705
Tel: (608)231-9347 *Fax:* (608)231-9592
E-Mail: vicki@ws13.fpl.fs.fed.hs
Web Site: http://www1.fpl.fs.fed.us/swst/
Members: 450 individuals
Staff: 2
Annual Budget: $100-250,000
Exec. Director: Vicki Herian

Historical Note
Founded in June 1958 as the American Soc. of Wood Engineering. Became the Soc. of Wood Science and Technology in 1961 and incorporated in Wisconsin in the same year. Membership: $50/year (individual); $110/year (organization).

Publications:
Wood and Fiber Science. q.

Meetings/Conferences:
Annual Meetings: Summer/100
1999 – Boise, ID/100
2000 – Lake Tahoe, NV

Soc. on Social Implications of Technology
Historical Note
A technical society of the Institute of Electrical and Electronics Engineers (IEEE). Membership includes a subscription to a technical periodical in the field published by IEEE. All administrative support provided by IEEE.

Soccer Industry Council of America *(1985)*
200 Castlewood Drive
North Palm Beach, FL 33408-5696
Tel: (561)840-1171 *Fax:* (561)840-1130
E-Mail: sbsgma@aol.com
Web Site: http://www.sportlink.com
Members: 110 individuals, 110 companies
Staff: 2
Annual Budget: $100-250,000
Exec. Director: J. Alden Briggs, Jr.
Director of Member Services: Paul Aleskovsky

Historical Note
SICA members are soccer goods manufacturers, distributors, representatives, sales agents, retailers and other soccer related businesses. SICA is a committee of the Sporting Goods Manufacturers Ass'n, which provides administrative support. Membership: $550-5,000/year (full member); $100/year (contributing).

Publications:
Community Soccer Center Planning Guide.
National Soccer Participation Survey. a.
Overview of the American Soccer Market. a.
Retail Soccer USA Directory a.
Soccer in the USA (statistical abstract). a.

Meetings/Conferences:
Semi-Annual Meetings: January and Sept. /125

Social Science History Ass'n *(1976)*
Inst. for Social Research
Univ. of Michigan
Ann Arbor, MI 48106
Tel: (313)936-1752 *Fax:* (313)764-8041
E-Mail: erik@icpsr.umich.edu
Members: 1,100 individuals, 450 libraries
Annual Budget: $50-100,000
Exec. Director: Erik W. Austin

Historical Note
SSHA members are historians and social scientists with an interest in interdisciplinary applications. Membership: $50/year (individual); $75/year (organization); $15/year (student).

Publications:
Social Science History Journal. q. adv.
SSHA Newsletter. semi-a. adv.

Meetings/Conferences:
1999 – Ft. Worth, TX(Worthington)/Nov. 11-14

Social Science Research Council *(1923)*
810 7th Ave., 31st Floor
New York, NY 10019-5818
Tel: (212)377-2700 *Fax:* (212)370-2727
E-Mail: lastname@ssrc.org
Web Site: http:ssrc.org
Members: 7 societies
Staff: 50
Annual Budget: $10-25,000,000
Interim President: Orville Gilbert Brim
Editor: Elsa Dixler
Exec. Program Director: Mary McDonnell
Chief Financial Officer: Kristine Dahlberg
Mgr., Computer Systems: Edward Lavelle

Historical Note
The SSRC is an independent, not-for-profit organization composed of social and behavioral scientists and humanists from all over the world. The Council advances the quality and usefulness of research in the social sciences. It encourages scholars in different disciplines to work together on topical, conceptual and methodical issues that can benefit from interdisciplinary and international collaboration. A central task of the Council is to be a resource for international scholarship. It does this thorugh international conferences and meetings, collaborative work, with institutional partners around the world and cross-regional structures for research and training.

Publications:
Annual report. a.
Items. q.

Meetings/Conferences:
Semi-Annual Meetings: June and December/New York, NY (SRCC Headquarters)

Societe des Professeurs Francais et Francophone d'Amerique *(1904)*
P.O. Box 6641, Yorkville Financial Stn.
New York, NY 10128
Tel: (212)751-3579 *Fax:* (212)996-2367
Members: 500 individuals
President: Gerard Roubichou

Historical Note
SPFA members are teachers of French and related subjects.

Publications:
Francographies - Bulletin de la SPFA. a.

Meetings/Conferences:
Annual Meetings: New York City/Annual/April

Society for Music Teacher Education

Society of Financial Service Professionals *(1928)*
270 South Bryn Mawr Avenue
Bryn Mawr, PA 19010
Tel: (610)526-2500 *Fax:* (610)527-4010
Web Site: http://www.financialpro.com
Members: 32,000 individuals
Staff: 50
Annual Budget: $5-10,000,000
Exec. V. President: John R. Driskill, CLU, ChFC
Manager, Meetings/Travel: Constance K. Bowen, CMP
V. President, Educational Services: Adelina G. Martorelli, JD,LLM,CLU
Finance and Administrative V. President: Joseph E. Frack, CPA
General Counsel: Anne M. Rigney, CLU, ChFC

V. President, Member Services: William J. Howell, CAE
Director, Membership Affairs: Marcia T. Seifert, CLU

Historical Note
Formerly (1998) American Soc. of CLU & ChFU and (1986) American Soc. of Chartered Life Underwriters. Members are insurance and financial service professionals who have earned the designation CLU (Chartered Life Underwriter) ChFC (Chartered Financial Consultant), REBC, RHU, CFP through The American College, Bryn Mawr, PA. Has an annual budget of approximately $9.0 million. Membership: $125/year (individual); $10,000/year (organization/company).

Publications:
Assets. bi-m. adv.
Journal of the American Society of CLU and ChFC. bi-m. adv.
Keeping Current. q.
Newsletters for Professional Interest Sections.
Query. m. adv.
Society Page. bi-m.

Meetings/Conferences:
Annual Meetings: October
1999 – Orlando, FL/Oct. 12-16/2500

Sociological Practice Ass'n *(1978)*
Anne Arundel Community College
Dept. of Soc. Sciences, 101 Coll. Pkwy.
Arnold, MD 21012-1895
Tel: (410)541-2835
E-Mail: REBEDEA@CLARK.NET
Members: 600 individuals
Annual Budget: under $10,000
Administrative Officer: Richard T. Bedea

Historical Note
Members include organizational developers, program planners, community organizers, sociotherapists, counselors, gerontologists, conflict interventionists, applied social science researchers, policy planners on all levels including international practice, and many others who practice, study, teach or do research by applying sociological knowledge for positive social change. Membership: $55/year (individual); $100/year (organization/company).

Publications:
Clinical Sociology Review. a.
Directory of Members. irreg.
Practicing Sociologist Newsletter. q. adv.
Sociological Practice. a.

Meetings/Conferences:
Annual Meetings: June/150

Software Management Ass'n *(1985)*
Historical Note
Formerly (1992) Software Maintenance Ass'n. Organization defunct in 1995.

Software Operations Ass'n *(1991)*
P.O. Box 338
Watertown, MA 02272-0338
Toll Free: (800)762 - 6285
Members: 650 individuals
Annual Budget: $50-100,000
Administrator: Gary Freeman

Historical Note
Membership: $100/year (individual); $1,000/year (company).

Publications:
Membership Directory. a.
Newsletter. q.

Meetings/Conferences:

Software Publishers Ass'n *(1984)*
1730 M St., N.W., Suite 700
Washington, DC 20036-4510
Tel: (202)452-1600 *Fax:* (202)223-8756
E-Mail: kwasch@spa.org
Web Site: http://www.spa.org
Members: 1,200 companies
Staff: 50
Annual Budget: $5-10,000,000
President: Kenneth A. Wasch
Director, Public Relations/Communications: Kathleen M. Rakestraw
V. President of Government Affairs: David Byer
Director, Conferences: Tina Hochberg
V. President, Finance/Administration: Thomas W. Meldrum, Jr.
Director, Litigation: Sandra A. Sellers
Manager, Membership Marketing: Kay Heiberg

Historical Note
Members are software developers and publishers. Services include: data collection program, software protection, contracts reference disk, conferences, and lobbying. Has an annual budget of approximately $9 million. Membership fee based on total organizational revenues.

Publications:
Membership Directory. a.
Upgrade. m. adv.

Meetings/Conferences:
1999 – Los Angeles, CA/March 6-9
1999 – Toronto, PQ/Sept. 15-18

Soil and Plant Analysis Council *(1970)*
1343 W. San Bernardino Road, #39
Covina, CA 91722-3424
E-Mail: apcouncil@aol.com
Members: 350 individuals
Staff: 1
Annual Budget: $10-25,000
Secretary-Treasurer: J. Benton Jones, Jr.

Historical Note
Formerly Council on Soil Testing and Plant Analysis(1994). Promotes uniform soil test and plant analysis methods, use, interpretation and terminology. Membership: $30/year.

Publications:
Soil-Plant Analyst. q.
Meetings/Conferences:

Soil and Water Conservation Soc. *(1945)*
7515 N.E. Ankeny Road
Ankeny, IA 50021-9764
Tel: (515)289-2331   *Fax:* (515)289-1227
E-Mail: swcs@netins.net
Web Site: http://www.swcs.org
Members: 11,000 individuals
Staff: 15
Annual Budget: $1-2,000,000
Exec. V. President: Craig Cox
Director, Publications: Sue Ballantine
Director, Professional Development: Charles Persinger
Marketing Director: Karen Howe

Historical Note
*Formerly (1987) the Soil Conservation Soc. of America.
Incorporated in the District of Columbia in 1949. Members are
researchers, consultants, and practitioners of soil and water
conservation, both in the public and private sectors. SWCS
promotes erosion control and water quality. Membership: $49/year
(individual), $250-750/year (organization/company).*

Publications:
Conservation Voices: Listening to the Land. bi-m. adv.
Journal of Soil and Water Conservation. q. adv.
SWCS Conservogram. 10/year. adv.
Meetings/Conferences:
Annual Meetings: Summer/1,200
1999 – Biloxi, MS(Grand Hotel)/Aug. 8-11

Soil Science Soc. of America *(1936)*
677 South Segoe Rd.
Madison, WI 53711
Tel: (608)273-8080   *Fax:* (608)273-2021
E-Mail: rbarnes@agronomy.org
Web Site: http://www.soils.org
Members: 6,500 individuals
Staff: 30
Annual Budget: $250-500,000
Exec. V. President: Robert F. Barnes

Historical Note
*Founded in 1936 and incorporated in Wisconsin in 1952. Shares
headquarters with the American Soc. of Agronomy and the Crop
Science Soc. of America. SSSA is dedicated to the advancement of
the discipline and practice of soil science and the dissemination of
information in the field especially in relation to crop production,
environmental quality, and wise land use. Membership: $64/year.*

Publications:
Agronomy News. m.
Journal of Environmental Quality. q.
Journal of Natural Resources/Life Sciences Education. semi-a.
Journal of Production Agriculture. q.
Soil Science Society of America Journal. bi-m.
Meetings/Conferences:
Annual Meetings: Fall, with ASA and CSSA
1999 – Salt Lake City, UT/Oct. 30-Nov. 4
2000 – Minneapolis, MN/Nov. 5-10

Solar Energy Industries Ass'n *(1974)*
122 C St., N.W., 4th Fl
Washington, DC 20001-2109
Tel: (202)383-2600   *Fax:* (202)383-2670
Members: 150 companies, 12 state chapters
Staff: 5
Annual Budget: $500-1,000,000
Exec. Director: Scott Sklar
Exec. Assistant: Linda Ladas
Deputy Director, Operations: Peter Lowenthal

Historical Note
*Membership consists of companies, universities and utilities
promoting the development of solar, thermal, and electric
technologies. Supports the Solar Energy Research and Education
Foundation.*

Publications:
SEIA Photovotaics Directory.
SEIA Solar Thermal Directory.
Solar Industry Journal.
Meetings/Conferences:
Annual Meetings: Winter
1999 – Kansas City, MO

Solar Rating and Certification Corp. *(1980)*
C/O FSEC
1679 Clearlake Rd.
Cocoa, FL 32922-5703
Tel: (407)638-1537   *Fax:* (407)638-1010
E-Mail: SRCC@FSEC.UCF.EDU
Web Site: http://www.solar-rating.edu
Members: 14 companies
Staff: 3
Annual Budget: $100-250,000
Technical Director: Jim Huggins

Historical Note
*The SRCC is a non-profit third party certification organization
whose primary purpose is the development and implementation of
certification programs for solar energy equipment including solar
collectors and solar water heating systems. In addition to its
certification programs, the corporation also administers a
laboratory accreditation program for independent test facilities
evaluating solar components, subsystems and systems. Program fee:
$500-2,000.*

Publications:
Dir. of SRCC Cert.
Meetings/Conferences:

SOLE - The Internat'l Soc. of Logistics *(1966)*
8100 Professional Place, Suite 211

Hyattsville, MD 20785-2225
Tel: (301)459-8446   *Fax:* (301)459-1522
E-Mail: solehq@erols.com
Web Site: http://www.sole.org
Members: 6,000 individuals
Staff: 5
Annual Budget: $1-2,000,000
Director, Administration: Babrbara King
Manager of Member Services: T. Nora Schwier

Historical Note
*Founded in 1966 as a non-profit international professional society
of individuals and corporate members to promote logistics
education and and technical activities. Membership: $75/year
(individuals).*

Publications:
Annals. a.
Directory. a.
Logistics Spectrum. bi-m. adv.
Meetings/Conferences:
Annual Meetings: August/750
1999 – Las Vegas, NV
2000 – Washington, DC

Solid Waste Ass'n of North America *(1961)*
1100 Wayne Aven. Suite 700
P.O. Box 7219
Silver Spring, MD 20907-7219
Tel: (301)585-2898   *Fax:* (301)589-7068
Web Site: www.swana.org
Exec. Director and C.E.O.: John H. Skinner, Ph.D.
Director, Marketing/Sales: Caroline E. Lacey
C.F.O.: Dawn M. Brown
Director, Member Services and Net. Admin.: Joe Brentzel

Historical Note
See under SWANA - Solid Waste Ass'n of North America.

Solid-State Circuits Soc.
Historical Note
*A technical society of the Institute of Electrical and Electronics
Engineers (IEEE). Membership, open only to IEEE members,
includes subscription to a technical periodical in the field published
by IEEE. All administrative support is provided by IEEE.*

Solution Mining Research Institute *(1958)*
3336 Lone Hill Lane
Encinitas, CA 92024
Tel: (619)759-7532   *Fax:* (619)759-7542
E-Mail: bdiamond@mcs.com
Web Site: http://www.solutionmining.org
Members: 70 organizations
Staff: 1
Annual Budget: $100-250,000
Exec. Director: H.W. Diamond

Historical Note
*SMRI members are companies interested in the production of salt
brine and solution mining of potash and soda ash, as well as
production of salt cavers, used for storage of oil, gas, chemicals,
compressed air, and waste. Sponsors research on behalf of the
industry, monitors regulatory developments, and disseminates
technical information to members and interested parties world-wide.
Membership: $4,000-6,000/year, depending on number of
different geographical operating sites (regular); $1,000-
2,500/year (associate).*

Meetings/Conferences:
1999 – Las Vegas, NV(Luxor Hotel)/April 11-15
2000 – The Hague, The Netherlands/May 7-11

Sommelier Soc. of America *(1954)*
P.O. Box 20080
New York, NY 10014-0708
Tel: (212)679-4190
Members: 500 individuals
Staff: 1
Annual Budget: $25-50,000
Administrative Manager: Barbara Petroske

Historical Note
*'Sommelier': French name for a wine steward. Members are wine
importers and merchants, restaurant owners, caterers and others.
Seeks to expand the knowledge and appreciation of fine wines and
liquors. Membership: $75/year (profit making) $100/year (non-
profit), $250-350/year (businesses or trade associations),
$25/year (students).*

Publications:
Le Sommelier Newsletter. bi-m.
Meetings/Conferences:
Annual Meetings: always New York, NY/April

Songwriters Guild of America *(1931)*
1500 Harbor Blvd.
Weehawken, NJ 07087-6732
Tel: (201)867-7603   *Fax:* (201)867-7535
E-Mail: songnews@AOL.COM
Web Site: http://www.songwriters.org
Members: 4,500 individuals
Staff: 20
Annual Budget: $250-500,000
Exec. Director: Lewis M. Bachman

Historical Note
*Formerly Songwriters Protective Ass'n and American Guild of
Authors and Composers. Provides agreements between songwriters,
composers and publishers. Maintains a Copyright Renewal Service,
Royalty Collection Service, Catalog Administration Plan,
songwriting workshops, collaboration service and legal activities.
Membership: $55-400 (individual).*

Publications:
National Newsletter. a. adv.
Regional Newsletter. q. adv.

Meetings/Conferences:

Sorptive Minerals Institute *(1970)*
818 Connecticut Ave., N.W., 2nd Floor
Washington, DC 20006
Tel: (202)289-2760   *Fax:* (202)289-1327
Members: 8 companies
Staff: 4
Annual Budget: $100-250,000
Exec. Director: Lee Coogan

Historical Note
*Members are companies mining, marketing and processing sorptive
minerals (clays and diatomaceous earths that can absorb 75-
125% of their weight in water). Membership is based on tonnage.*

Publications:
Memo. m.
Meetings/Conferences:
Semi-Annual Meetings: Spring and Fall

South Asian Journalists Ass'n *(1994)*
c/o Columbia Journalism School
2950 Broadway
New York, NY 10027
Tel: (212)854-5979   *Fax:* (212)854-7837
E-Mail: ss221@columbia.edu
Web Site: http://www.saja.org
Members: 350 individuals
Staff: 1
Annual Budget: under $10,000
Co-Founder: Sreenath Sreenivasan

Historical Note
*SAJA members are journalists of South Asian origin. Administers
the SAJA Journalism Awards, given to recognize coverage of the
region.*

Publications:
SAJA Directory.
SAJA-online Newsletter. irreg.
Meetings/Conferences:
Annual Dinner: early May

Southern Cypress Manufacturers Ass'n *(1905)*
400 Penn Center Blvd., Suite 530
Pittsburgh, PA 15235-5605
Tel: (412)829-0770   *Fax:* (412)829-0844
Members: 19 companies
Staff: 2
Annual Budget: $25-50,000
Exec. V. President: Susan Regan

Historical Note
*Administrative support for SCMA is provided by the Hardwood
Manufacturers Ass'n (same address).*

Meetings/Conferences:
Annual Meetings: March, with the Hardwood Manufacturers
     Ass'n

Southern Forest Products Ass'n *(1915)*
P.O. Box 641700
Kenner, LA 70064-1700
Tel: (504)443-4464   *Fax:* (504)443-6612
E-Mail: KLindberg@sfpa.org
Web Site: http://www.sfpa.org
Members: 256 companies
Staff: 27
Annual Budget: $2-5,000,000
President: Karl Lindberg
Manager, Communications Services: Dave Kellogg
V. President, Government Affairs: Digges Morgan
Director of Administration: Tami Kessler
Member Services: Carolyn Moynan
V. President, Marketing: Jeff Easterling

Historical Note
*Formerly (1970) Southern Pine Ass'n. Lumber manufacturers of
Southern pine. Member of the Forest Industries Council.
Membership: $1,750-350,000/yr. (company, based on shipment
size).*

Publications:
Annual Report. a.
Capital Communique. m.
Export Newsletter. m.
Federal Issue Communique. m.
Market News. q.
Newsletter. w.
Meetings/Conferences:
1999 – Amelia Island, FL(Amelia Island
     Plantation)/Sept. 25-28/250

Southern Transportation Logistics Ass'n *(1918)*
3426 N. Washington Blvd., Box 1240
Arlington, VA 22210
Tel: (703)525-4050   *Fax:* (703)525-4054
E-Mail: wpj@translaw.com
Members: 100 companies
Staff: 1
Annual Budget: $10-25,000
Exec. Director: William P. Jackson, Jr.

Historical Note
*Founded as the Southern Traffic League in 1918, became the
Southern Transportation League in 1985, assumed its current name
in 1994.*

Publications:
The STLA Light. w.
Meetings/Conferences:
Semi-Annual Meetings: Spring and Fall

Souvenirs and Novelties Trade Ass'n *(1962)*
7000 Terminal Square, Suite 210
Upper Darby, PA 19082
Tel: (610)734-2420   *Fax:* (610)734-2423

Members: 1,900 individuals
Staff: 14
Annual Budget: $500-1,000,000
President: Scott C. Borowsky

Historical Note
Membership: $30/year.

Publications:
Souvenirs, Gifts and Novelties Magazine. 7/year. adv.
Tourist Attractions and Parks. 7/year. adv.

Meetings/Conferences:
Annual Meetings: Winter/8,000
1999 – Orlando, FL(Orange County Convention
        Center)/Jan. 14-16
2000 – Orlando, FL(Orange County Convention
        Center)/Jan. 13-16

Soy Protein Council *(1971)*
1255 23rd St., N.W., Suite 850
Washington, DC   20037-1174
Tel: (202)467-6610   *Fax:* (202)833-3636
Members: 3 companies
Staff: 2
Annual Budget: $100-250,000
Exec. V. President: David Saunders

Historical Note
Members are processors and distributors of vegetable proteins and their products, for use and consumption in human food. Formerly (1982) the Food Protein Council.

Soyfoods Ass'n of North America *(1978)*
P.O. Box 234
Lafayette, CA   94549
Tel: (925)283-2991
Members: 50 companies
Staff: 1
Annual Budget: $50-100,000
Exec. Director: William Shurtleff

Historical Note
Sponsors a soyfoods information center and SoyaScan bibliographic database. Membership: $50-$2,000/year, based on sales volume.

Space Energy Ass'n *(1990)*
P.O. Box 1136
Clearwater, FL   33757-1136
Tel: (813)442-3923
E-Mail: http://www.websibizcom./sea.ne
Members: 250 individuals
Staff: 3
Annual Budget: under $10,000
Contact/Consultant: Donald A. Kelly
Editor/Publisher: Jim Kettner

Historical Note
Members are scientists and other professionals involved in study of advanced energy systems.

Publications:
SEA-Space Energy Journal. q.

Space Transportation Ass'n *(1990)*
2800 Shirlington Road, Suite 405
Arlington, VA   22206
Tel: (703)671-4116   *Fax:* (703)931-6432
Members: 20 organizations
Staff: 9
Annual Budget: $100-250,000
Exec. Director: Eric W. Stallmer

Historical Note
STA represents the interests of organizations which intend to develop, build, operate and use space transportation vehicles and systems in order to provide reliable, economical, safe and routine access to space for public and private entities.

Publications:
Journal of Practical Applications in Space. q. adv.
Space Energy & Transportation. q. adv.
SpaceTrans Newsletter. m.

Spain-U.S. Chamber of Commerce *(1959)*
350 Fifth Ave., Suite 2029
New York, NY   10118
Tel: (212)967-2170   *Fax:* (212)564-1415
E-Mail: spuscha@aol.com
Staff: 4
Annual Budget: $500-1,000,000
Exec. Director: Ana Diaz

Historical Note
Originated at a luncheon at the Biltmore Hotel February 9, 1959 and incorporated in New York April 2, 1959. Membership: $500/year (sustaining), $1,000/year (corporate), $200/year (in Spain) and $300/year(regular).

Publications:
The Business Link q. adv. adv.
Trade & Membership Directory. bien. adv.

Spanish-Barb Breeders Ass'n *(1972)*
P.O. Box 598
Anthony, FL   32617-0598
Tel: (352)622-5878
Members: 125 individuals
Annual Budget: under $10,000
Secretary: Marie Martineau

Historical Note
Members are owners and breeders of Spanish-Barb horses. Membership: $20/year (individual); $25/year (organization/company).

Publications:
Spanish-Barb Journal. semi-a.
Spanish-Barb Update. semi-a.

Meetings/Conferences:

Special Interest Group for Algorithm and Computation Theory
c/o Ass'n for Computing Machinery
1515 Broadway
New York, NY   10036
Tel: (212)869-7440   *Fax:* (212)302-5826
Web Site: http://www.acm.org
Members: 2,220 individuals
Annual Budget: $250-500,000
Program Director: Julie A. Goetz

Historical Note
Formerly (1992) Special Interest Group for Automata and Computability Theory. SIGACT is concerned with theoretical computer science, including analysis of algorithms. A semi-autonomous subsidiary of the Association for Computing Machinery. Membership: $18/year (ACM member); $18/year (non-ACM).

Publications:
ACM SIGACT News. q.
Proceedings. a.

Special Interest Group for Architecture of Computer Systems
c/o Ass'n for Computing Machinery
1515 Broadway
New York, NY   10036
Tel: (212)869-7440   *Fax:* (212)302-5826
E-Mail: burgos@acm.org
Web Site: http://www.acm.org/
Members: 3,600 individuals
Program Director: Lisette Burgos

Historical Note
SIGARCH is concerned with the constituents and arrangement of the physical resources of the computer system. A semi-autonomous subsidiary of the Association for Computing Machinery. Membership: $28/year (ACM member); $54/year (non-ACM).

Publications:
Computer Architecture News. 5/yr.
Proceedings of Annual Symposium on Computer Architecture. a.

Meetings/Conferences:
Annual Meetings: International Symposium on Computer Architecture/May

Special Interest Group for Biomedical Computing *(1967)*
c/o Ass'n for Computing Machinery
1515 Broadway
New York, NY   10036
Tel: (212)626-0613   *Fax:* (212)302-5826
Members: 620 individuals
Annual Budget: $25-50,000
Program Director: Heather Levell

Historical Note
SIGBIO, a semi-autonomous subsidiary of the Ass'n for Computing Machinery, facilitates the exchange of information concerning problem areas, computer routines, techniques, and activities between individuals and laboratories involved in biomedical research applications. Membership: $20/year (ACM members), $30/year (non-ACM).

Publications:
SIGBIO Newsletter. 2/year.

Meetings/Conferences:
Annual Meetings: With the Association for Computing Machinery

Special Interest Group for Computer Personnel Research *(1962)*
c/o Ass'n for Computing Machinery
1515 Broadway, 17th Floor
New York, NY   10036
Tel: (212)626-0607   *Fax:* (212)302-5826
E-Mail: rivkin@acm.org
Web Site: http://www.acm.org/sigcpr
Members: 250 individuals
Program Director: Alisa D. Rivkin

Historical Note
SIGCPR investigates the needs, interests and abilities of computer professionals, managers and end-users who work with information technology in their organizations. Members include computer professionals, educators, MIS managers and human resources specialists. A semi-autonomous subsidiary of the Association for Computing Machinery. Membership: $20/year (ACM member), $60/year (non-ACM); $8/year (student).

Publications:
Proceedings.
SIGCPR Newsletter. q.

Meetings/Conferences:
SIGCPR Conference: April
1999 – New Orleans, LA/Apr. 8-10

Special Interest Group for Computer Science
Historical Note
SIGCS is administered by Internat'l Soc. for Technology in Education (Eugene, OR) as a service to its members.

Special Interest Group for Computer Science Education *(1970)*
c/o Ass'n for Computing Machinery
1515 Broadway
New York, NY   10036
Tel: (212)626-0614   *Fax:* (212)302-5826
Members: 2,000 individuals
Annual Budget: $25-50,000
Program Director: Heather Levell

Historical Note
SIGCSE provides a forum for the problems common among college educators involved in computer science programs. A semi-autonomous subsidiary of the Association for Computing Machinery. Membership: $17/year (ACM member); $44/year (non-ACM).

Publications:
SIGCSE Bulletin. q.

Meetings/Conferences:
Annual Meetings: With the Ass'n for Computing Machinery
1999 – New Orleans, LA(Radisson)/March 24-28

Special Interest Group for Computer Uses in Education
c/o Ass'n for Computing Machinery
1515 Broadway
New York, NY   10036
Tel: (212)626-0614   *Fax:* (212)302-5826
Members: 500 individuals
Program Director: Heather Levell

Historical Note
SIGCUE is a semi-autonomous subsidiary of the Ass'n for Computing Machinery. Formerly Special Interest Group for Computer-assisted Instruction. SIGCUE is concerned with concepts, methods and policies that relate to the central issues of instructional computing. Membership: $19/year (ACM member); $56/year (non-ACM).

Publications:
SIGCUE Outlook Newsletter. q.

Meetings/Conferences:
Annual Meetings: With the Ass'n for Computing Machinery

Special Interest Group for Computer-Human Interaction *(1972)*
c/o Ass'n for Computing Machinery
1515 Broadway
New York, NY   10036
Tel: (212)626-0613   *Fax:* (212)302-5826
E-Mail: acmhelp@acm.org
Web Site: http://info.sigchi.acm.org/sigchi/
Members: 5,700 individuals
Staff: 2
Annual Budget: $2-5,000,000
Program Director: David Riederman, CAE

Historical Note
SIGCHI is a semi-autonomous subsidiary of the Ass'n for Computing Machinery. Formerly (1982) the Special Interest Group for Social and Behavioral Science Computing. SIGCHI is concerned with the study of the human-computer interaction process and with research and development efforts leading to the design and evaluation of user interfaces. Membership: $30/year (ACM member); $57/year (non-ACM).

Publications:
Proceedings. a.
SIGCHI Bulletin. q.

Meetings/Conferences:
1999 – Pittsburgh, PA(Convention Center)

Special Interest Group for Computers and Society *(1972)*
c/o Ass'n for Computing Machinery
1515 Broadway
New York, NY   10036
Tel: (212)626-0611   *Fax:* (212)302-5826
E-Mail: chair_sigcas@acm.org
Web Site: http://www.acm.org/sigcas
Members: 800 individuals
Staff: 1
Annual Budget: $10-25,000
Program Director: Heather Levell

Historical Note
SIGCAS was created by the Ass'n for Computing Machinery in 1969 and given permanent status in 1972. Concerned with the impact on society of computer enhancements to informational technology. Membership: $20/year (ACM member); $47/year (non-ACM).

Publications:
Computers and Society Newsletter. q.

Meetings/Conferences:
Annual Meetings: With the Association for Computing Machinery and the AFIPS Nat'l Computer Conference and Exposition.

Special Interest Group for Computers and the Physically Handicapped *(1970)*
c/o Ass'n for Computing Machinery
1515 Broadway
New York, NY   10036
Tel: (212)626-0607   *Fax:* (212)302-5826
E-Mail: rivkin@acm.org
Web Site: http://www.acm.org/sigcaph/
Members: 250 individuals
Staff: 2
Annual Budget: $10-25,000
Program Director: Alisa D. Rivkin

Historical Note
SIGCAPH is concerned with the professional interests of computing personnel with physical disabilities and the application of computing and information technology in solving relevant disability problems. SIGCAPH also strives to educate the public to support careers for the disabled. A program section of the Ass'n for Computing Machinery. Formerly (1978) the Special Interest Committee for Computers and the Physically Handicapped. Membership: $15/year (ACM member); $42/year (non-ACM); $6/year (student).

Publications:
Computers and the Physically Handicapped Newsletter. 3/year.

Meetings/Conferences:
Annual Meetings: ACM ComputerBased Assistive
    Technologies/May-Nov.(every 18 months)

Special Interest Group for Data Communication
(1970)
c/o Ass'n for Computing Machinery
1515 Broadway
New York, NY 10036
Tel: (212)626-0500   *Fax:* (212)302-5826
Members: 5,000 individuals
Annual Budget: $100-250,000
Assoc. Director: Patrick McCarren

Historical Note
SIGCOMM provides a forum for research and development in computer communications with a special focus on networks and network applications. A semi-autonomous subsidiary of the Association for Computing Machinery. Membership: $18/year (ACM member), $18/year (non-ACM).

Publications:
ACM/IEEE Transactions on Networking Journal.
Computer Communication Review. 5/yr.

Meetings/Conferences:
Annual Meetings: Summer
1999 – Boston, MA

Special Interest Group for Forth Programming Language *(1988)*
Historical Note
Defunct in 1995.

Special Interest Group for Information Retrieval
(1966)
c/o Ass'n for Computing Machinery
1515 Broadway
New York, NY 10036
Tel: (212)626-0607   *Fax:* (212)302-5826
E-Mail: rivkin@acm.org
Web Site: http://www.acm.org/sigir/
Members: 1,250 individuals
Annual Budget: $100-250,000
Program Director: Alisa D. Rivkin

Historical Note
SIGIR members work in all aspects of information storage, retrieval and dissemination including research strategies, output schemes and system evaluation. Of specall note is SIGIR's involvement with the Nat'l Science Foundation's initiative to form a Nat'l Electronic Science, Engineering, and Technology Library. A semi-autonomous subsidiary of the Association for Computing Machinery. Membership: $20/year (ACM member), $65/year (non-ACM); $10/year (student).

Publications:
IR-L Digest. Internet.
SIGIR Conference Proceedings. a.
SIGIR Forum. tri-a.

Meetings/Conferences:
Annual Meetings: July-August

Special Interest Group for Logo Educators
Historical Note
SIG/Logo is administered by Internat'l Soc. for Technology in Education (Eugene, OR) as a service to its members.

Special Interest Group for Management of Data
c/o Ass'n for Computing Machinery
1515 Broadway
New York, NY 10036
Tel: (212)626-0613   *Fax:* (212)302-5826
E-Mail: levell@acm.org
Web Site: http://www.acm.org/sigmod
Members: 2,500 individuals
Program Director: Heather Levell

Historical Note
SIGMOD is concerned with the development, management and evaluation of database technology. Formerly (1973) Special Interest Group for File Description and Translation. A semi-autonomous subsidiary of the Association for Computing Machinery. Membership: $20/year (ACM member); $23/year (non-ACM member).

Publications:
SIGMOD Record Newsletter. q.

Meetings/Conferences:
Annual Meetings: with Ass'n for Computing Machinery
1999 – Philadelphia, PA/May 31-June 3

Special Interest Group for Measurement and Evaluation *(1971)*
c/o Ass'n for Computing Machinery
1515 Broadway
New York, NY 10036
Tel: (212)626-0614   *Fax:* (212)302-5826
Members: 1,900 individuals
Annual Budget: $25-50,000
Program Director: Heather Levell

Historical Note
SIGMETRICS provides a forum for those interested in the measurement and evaluation of computer system performance. A semi-autonomous subsidiary of the Ass'n for Computing Machinery (ACM). Membership: $20/year (ACM member), $47/year (non-ACM).

Publications:
Performance Evaluation Review Newsletter. q.

Meetings/Conferences:
Semi-Annual Meetings: in May and with Ass'n for Computing
    Machinery.

Special Interest Group for Microprogramming and Microarchitecture *(1968)*
c/o Ass'n for Computing Machinery
1515 Broadway
New York, NY 10036
Tel: (212)869-7440   *Fax:* (212)302-5826
E-Mail: burgos@acm.org
Web Site: http://www.acm.org/
Members: 1,300 individuals
Program Director: Lisette Burgos

Historical Note
Formerly (1990) Special Interest Group for Microprogramming. SIGMICRO is a semi-autonomous subsidiary of the Ass'n for Computing Machinery. SIGMICRO is concerned with the implementation of control logic through the ordered storage of information; including logic design, operating systems design, finite state machinery theory, application system design and systems architecture. Membership: $21/year (ACM member), $35/year (non-ACM).

Publications:
SIGMICRO Newsletter/Proceedings. a.

Meetings/Conferences:
Annual MICRO Conference: Nov./Dec.

Special Interest Group for Simulation and Modeling *(1968)*
c/o Ass'n for Computing Machinery
1515 Broadway
New York, NY 10036
Tel: (212)869-7440   *Fax:* (212)302-5826
E-Mail: burgos@acm.org
Web Site: http://www.acm.org/
Members: 2,250 individuals
Annual Budget: $50-100,000
Program Director: Lisette Burgos

Historical Note
SIGSIM is a semi-autonomous subsidiary of the Ass'n for Computing Machinery. Members are interested in all aspects of modeling and simulation as performed in digital computers, including discrete, continuous and combined simulations. Membership: $22/year (ACM member), $44/year (non-ACM).

Publications:
Simulation Digest Newsletter. bi-a.

Meetings/Conferences:
Annual Meetings: With the Association for Computing
    Machinery
1999 – Phoenix, AZ/Dec. 5-8
1999 – Atlanta, GA(Hilton)/May 1-4

Special Interest Group for Symbolic and Algebraic Manipulation *(1967)*
c/o Ass'n for Computing Machinery
1515 Broadway
New York, NY 10036
Tel: (212)869-7440   *Fax:* (212)302-5826
Members: 860 individuals
Annual Budget: $50-100,000
Program Director: Julie A. Goetz

Historical Note
SIGSAM is a semi-autonomous subsidiary of the Ass'n for Computing Machinery. SIGSAM provides a forum for the discussion of the practical and theoretical aspects of the design, analysis and applications of algorithms, data structures, systems and languages for algebraic and symbolic mathematical computation. Membership: $23/year (ACM member); $44/year (non-ACM).

Publications:
SIGSAM Bulletin. q.

Meetings/Conferences:
Annual Meetings: With the Association for Computing
    Machinery (ISSAC Conference)

Special Interest Group for Teacher Educators
Historical Note
SIGTE is administered by Internat'l Soc. for Technology in Education (Eugene, OR) as a service to its members.

Special Interest Group for Technology Coordinators
Historical Note
SIGTC is administered by Internat'l Soc. for Technology in Education (Eugene, OR) as a service to its members.

Special Interest Group for Telecommunications
Historical Note
SIG/Tel is administered by Internat'l Soc. for Technology in Education (Eugene, OR) as a service to its members.

Special Interest Group for University and College Computing Services *(1962)*
c/o Ass'n for Computing Machinery
1515 Broadway
New York, NY 10036
Tel: (212)626-0607   *Fax:* (212)302-5826
E-Mail: rivkin@acm.org
Web Site: http://www.acm.org/siguccs/
Members: 550 individuals
Staff: 1
Annual Budget: $100-250,000
Program Director: Alisa D. Rivkin

Historical Note
SIGUCCS is a semi-autonomous subsidiary of the Ass'n for Computing Machinery. Formerly (1984) the Special Interest Group for University Computing Centers. SIGUCCS provides a forum and support services for those involved in supplying computing and other information technology services in higher education. Members include college and university computing service professionals, administrators, consultants, technical writers, and librarians.

Membership: $25/year (ACM member); $50/year (non-ACM);
$7/year (student).
Publications:
Proceedings. a.
SIGUCCS Newsletter. q.

Meetings/Conferences:
Annual Meetings: Services Managment Symposium/Spring &
    Users Services Conference/Nov.

Special Interest Group on Ada Programming Language
(1981)
c/o Ass'n for Computing Machinery
1515 Broadway
New York, NY 10036
Tel: (212)869-7440   *Fax:* (212)302-5826
E-Mail: levell@acm.org
Members: 1000 individuals
Annual Budget: $100-250,000
Program Director: Heather Levell

Historical Note
SIGAda is a semi-autonomous subsidiary of the Ass'n for Computing Machinery. SIGAda provides a forum on the scientific and technical aspects of the Ada language including its usage, environment, standardization and implementation. Membership: $20/year (ACM Member); $48/year (non-ACM Member); $200/year (organization/institution).

Publications:
ACM Ada Letters. bi-m.

Meetings/Conferences:
Annual Meetings: Winter
1999 – Redondo Beach, CA(Crown Plaza)/Oct. 16-21

Special Interest Group on APL Programming Language
(1970)
c/o Ass'n for Computing Machinery
1515 Broadway
New York, NY 10036
Tel: (212)869-7440   *Fax:* (212)302-5826
E-Mail: sigapl_bd@acm.org
Web Site: http://www.acm.org/sigapl/
Members: 820 individuals
Annual Budget: $25-50,000
Program Director: Julie A. Goetz

Historical Note
SIGAPL is a semi-autonomous subsidiary of the Ass'n for Computing Machinery. SIGAPL promotes the development and application of APL through the interchange of ideas and techniques. Membership: $30/year (ACM member), $60/year (non-ACM).

Publications:
APL Quote Quad. q.

Meetings/Conferences:
1999 – Scranton, PA/Aug. 10-14

Special Interest Group on Applied Computing
c/o Ass'n for Computing Machinery
1515 Broadway
New York, NY 10036
Tel: (212)626-0613   *Fax:* (212)302-5826
E-Mail: levell@acm.org
Members: 400 individuals
Program Director: Heather Levell

Historical Note
SIGAPP is a forum for the exchange of information on advanced and unique computing applications which involve the integration of such traditional computing disciplines as graphics, database, communication, software engineering, artificial intelligence, and office automation with emerging technologies like neural networks, logic and symbolic programming, expert systems, image information systems, parallel processing and object oriented programming. SIGAPP is a sem-autonomous subsidiary of the Ass'n for Computing Machinery. Membership: $15/year (ACM member); $37/year (non-ACM member).

Publications:
Applied Computing Review. semi-a.

Special Interest Group on Artificial Intelligence
c/o Ass'n for Computing Machinery
1515 Broadway
New York, NY 10036
Tel: (212)626-0607   *Fax:* (212)302-5826
E-Mail: rivkin@acm.org
Web Site: http://www.acm.org/sigart/
Members: 2,700 individuals
Annual Budget: $50-100,000
Program Director: Alisa D. Rivkin

Historical Note
Established in the mid-1960s, SIGART promotes meetings and discussions on artificial intelligence. Artificial intelligence seeks to understand and apply the principles and mechanisms underlying intelligent behavior. SIGART is a semi-autonomous subsidiary of the Ass'n for Computing Machinery. Membership: $15/year (ACM member); $42/year (non-ACM); $8/year (student).

Publications:
SIGART Bulletin. q.

Meetings/Conferences:
Annual Meetings: February, July, and November & Biennial
    Conference/January

Special Interest Group on Business Information Technology *(1961)*
Historical Note
Became the Special Interest Group on Management Information Systems in 1995.

Special Interest Group on Computer Graphics *(1968)*
c/o Ass'n for Computing Machinery
1515 Broadway
New York, NY 1003

Tel: (212)869-7440   *Fax:* (212)302-5826
Members: 7,000 individuals
Staff: 2
Annual Budget: $5-10,000,000
Assoc. Director: Patrick McCarren

Historical Note
A forum for the promotion and dissemination of current computer graphics research, technologies and applications. A semi-autonomous subsidiary of the Ass'n for Computing Machinery. Membership: $59/year (ACM member); $59/year (non-ACM).

Publications:
Computer Graphics. q. adv.
Proceedings. a.
SIGGRAPH Video Review (Video Tape). irreg.

Meetings/Conferences:
Annual Meetings: July-August/25,000
1999 – Los Angeles
2000 – New Orleans, LA

Special Interest Group on Computing at Community Colleges *(1994)*
c/o Ass'n for Computing Machinery
1515 Broadway
New York, NY   10036-5701
Tel: (212)869-7440   *Fax:* (212)944-1318
Members: 280 individuals
Annual Budget: under $10,000
Program Director: Julie A. Goetz

Historical Note
A semi-autonomous subsidiary of the Ass'n for Computing Machinery, SIG3C addresses the issues which affect computing at two-year colleges and promotes dialogue among those interested in computing at all colleges. Membership: $15/year (ACM member); $30/year (non-ACM).

Publications:
3C Online. q.

Special Interest Group on Design Automation *(1968)*
c/o Ass'n for Computing Machinery
1515 Broadway
New York, NY   10036
Tel: (212)869-7440   *Fax:* (212)302-5826
E-Mail: burgos@acm.org
Web Site: http://www.acm.org/
Members: 1,050 individuals
Annual Budget: $500-1,000,000
Program Director: Lisette Burgos

Historical Note
SIGDA is a semi-autonomous subsidiary of the Ass'n for Computing Machinery whose members are interested in theoretic, analytic and heuristic methods for performing and assisting design tasks and optimizing designs through the use of computer techniques, algorithms and programs. Awards travel grants and scholarships; provides University library support; and co-sponsors, with the IEEE/Computer Society and the IEEE/Circuit and Systems Society's Design Automation Technical Committee, the Design Automation Conference. Membership: $15/year (ACM member); $55/year (non-ACM).

Publications:
Conference Proceedings. a.
SIGDA Newsletter. semi-a.

Meetings/Conferences:
Semi-annual Meetings: June and November

Special Interest Group on Documentation *(1975)*
c/o Ass'n for Computing Machinery
1515 Broadway
New York, NY   10036
Tel: (212)869-7440   *Fax:* (212)302-5826
Members: 1000 individuals
Program Director: Julie A. Goetz

Historical Note
SIGDOC is a semi-autonomous subsidiary of the Ass'n for Computing Machinery. SIGDOC examines documents produced by systems analysts, programmers and project managers; reviews techniques applied in preparing user documents and reference material; and reports on hardware and software used to aid the documentation process. Membership: $19/year (ACM member); $45/year (non-ACM).

Publications:
Asterisk. q.
Journal of Computer Documentation. q.

Meetings/Conferences:
Annual Meetings: Fall
1999 – New Orleans, LA/Sept. 12-14

Special Interest Group on Hypertext/Hypermedia
c/o Ass'n for Computing Machinery
1515 Broadway
New York, NY   10036
Tel: (212)626-0607   *Fax:* (212)302-5826
Members: 700 individuals
Annual Budget: $100-250,000
Program Director: Alisa D. Rivkin

Historical Note
SIGLINK addresses the concerns of the multi-disciplinary fields of hypertext and hypermedia. It provides a forum for the promotion, dissemination, and exchange of ideas concerning hypertext research technologies, and applications among scientists, systems designers and end-users. SIGLINK is a semi-autonomous subsidiary of the Ass'n for Computing Machinery. Membership: $22/year (ACM member); $56/year (non-ACM); $12/year (student).

Publications:
SIGLINK Newsletter. 3/yr.

Meetings/Conferences:
Annual Meetings: USA/odd years & Europe/even years

Special Interest Group on Individual Computing Environments *(1975)*
Historical Note
SIGICE is primarily concerned with microprocessors and microcomputers. Formerly (1984) the Special Interest Group on Small Computing Systems and Applications and (1994) Special Interest Group on Small and Personal Computing Systems and Applications. A semi-autonomous subsidiary of the Ass'n for Computing Machinery. Membership: $17/year (ACM member); $38/year (non-ACM).

Special Interest Group on Management Information Systems *(1960)*
c/o Ass'n for Computing Machinery
1515 Broadway
New York, NY   10036
Tel: (212)626-0607   *Fax:* (212)302-5826
E-Mail: rivkin@acm.org
Web Site: http://www.acm.org/sigmis/
Members: 1,250 individuals
Annual Budget: $100-250,000
Program Director: Alisa D. Rivkin

Historical Note
Formerly (1993) the Special Interest Group on Business Data Processing and Management and (1995) Special Interest Group on Business Information Technology. SIGMIS is a semi-autonomous subsidiary of the Ass'n for Computing Machinery. Members are primarily interested in information systems and technologies for management and the management of these systems and technologies. Membership: $20/year (ACM member); $42/year (non-ACM member); $14/year (student).

Publications:
DataBase. q.

Meetings/Conferences:
Annual Meetings: With the National Computer Conference, and ACM Conference.

Special Interest Group on Mobility of Systems, Users, Data and Computing
c/o Ass'n for Computing Machinery
1515 Broadway
New York, NY   10036
Tel: (212)869-7440   *Fax:* (212)302-5826
E-Mail: bourgos@acm.org
Web Site: http://www.acm.org
Program Director: Lisette Burgos

Historical Note
SIGMOBILE, a semi-autonomous subsidiary of the Ass'n for Computing Machinery, is concerned with issues involving the mobility of systems, users, data and computing. Membership: $15/year (ACM member); $45/year (non-ACM).

Publications:
MC2R Newsletter. q.
Mobile Computing - MOBICOM.
Proceedings. a.

Meetings/Conferences:
Annual Meetings: November

Special Interest Group on Multimedia *(1994)*
c/o Ass'n for Computing Machinery
1515 Broadway
New York, NY   10036-5701
Tel: (212)626-0500   *Fax:* (212)302-5826
Assoc. Director: Patrick McCarren

Historical Note
A semi-autonomous subsidiary of the Ass'n for Computing Machinery, SIGMM provides a forum for researchers, engineers and practitioners in all aspects of multimedia computing, communications, storage and applications. Membership: $20/year (ACM member); $20/year (non-ACM).

Publications:
Multimedia Conference Proceedings. a.
SIG Multimedia Review. (e-mail).

Meetings/Conferences:
1999 – Orlando, FL/250

Special Interest Group on Numerical Mathematics *(1966)*
c/o Ass'n for Computing Machinery
1515 Broadway
New York, NY   10036
Tel: (212)869-7440   *Fax:* (212)302-5826
Members: 1,100 individuals
Program Director: Julie A. Goetz

Historical Note
SIGNUM is concerned with computational Mathematics. A semi-autonomous subsidiary of the Ass'n for Computing Machinery. Membership: $16/year (ACM member); $32/year (non-ACM).

Publications:
Numerical Mathematics Newsletter. q.

Meetings/Conferences:
Annual Meetings: With Ass'n for Computing Machinery

Special Interest Group on Office Information Systems
Historical Note
Became Special Interest Group on Supporting Group Work (SIGGROUP) in 1996.

Special Interest Group on Operating Systems
c/o Ass'n for Computing Machinery
1515 Broadway
New York, NY   10036
Tel: (212)626-0614   *Fax:* (212)302-5826
E-Mail: levell@acm.org
Members: 3,000 individuals
Annual Budget: $50-100,000
Program Director: Heather Levell

Historical Note
SIGOPS is a semi-autonomous subsidiary of the Ass'n for Computing Machinery. SIGOPS is concerned with computer operating systems and architecture for multiprogramming, multiprocessing, time-sharing, and networking; distributed computing systems resource management; evaluation and stimulation; reliability, integrity, and security of data; and communications among computing processes. Membership: $15/year (ACM members); $42/year (non-ACM).

Publications:
Operating Systems Review Newsletter. 5/yr.

Meetings/Conferences:
Biennial Meetings: (1995)
1999 – Kiawah Island, HI(Kiawah Resort)

Special Interest Group on Programming Languages *(1966)*
c/o Ass'n for Computing Machinery
1515 Broadway
New York, NY   10036
Tel: (212)869-7440   *Fax:* (212)869-0481
Members: 7,500 individuals
Staff: 2
Annual Budget: $2-5,000,000
Director: Donna Baglio

Historical Note
SIGPLAN is concerned with all aspects of programming languages and programming language processors.

Publications:
ACM SIGPLAN Notices. m.
Fortran Forum. 3/yr.

Meetings/Conferences:
Annual Meetings: June, ACM Conference on Programming Language Design
1999 – Atlanta, GA/May 1-4

Special Interest Group on Security, Audit, and Control *(1981)*
c/o Ass'n for Computing Machinery
1515 Broadway
New York, NY   10036
Tel: (212)626-0613   *Fax:* (212)302-5826
E-Mail: levell@acm.org
Members: 789 individuals
Annual Budget: $100-250,000
Program Director: Heather Levell

Historical Note
SIGSAC is a semi-autonomous subsidiary of the Ass'n for Computing Machinery. SIGSAC concerns include control of access to resources; verification of identity; risk analysis, testing and certification of applications; logging of transactions; data reduction; control of program development; and techniques and protocols for data encryption. Membership: $18/year (ACM member); $48/year (non-ACM).

Meetings/Conferences:
Annual Meetings: San Francisco, CA(Fairmont)/Nov. 2-5
2000 – Athens, Greece/Nov. 1-4

Special Interest Group on Software Engineering
c/o Ass'n for Computing Machinery
1515 Broadway
New York, NY   10036
Tel: (212)869-7440   *Fax:* (212)302-5826
Toll Free: (800)342 - 6626
Members: 6,000 individuals
Staff: 1
Annual Budget: $250-500,000
Program Director: Julie A. Goetz

Historical Note
SIGSOFT is a semi-autonomous subsidiary of the Ass'n for Computing Machinery. SIGSOFT is concerned with techniques and principles involved in the production of high quality software for practical application including solutions to problems inherent in program development, system design methodology, debugging, documentation, portability of programs, program validation and quality assurance. Membership: $23/year (ACM member); $47/year (non-ACM).

Publications:
Software Engineering Notes Newsletter. bi-m. adv.

Meetings/Conferences:

Special Interest Group on Supporting Group Work *(1980)*
c/o Ass'n for Computing Machinery
1515 Broadway
New York, NY   10036
Tel: (212)626-0607   *Fax:* (212)302-5826
E-Mail: rivkin@acm.org
Web Site: http://www.acm.org/siggroup/
Members: 1000 individuals
Annual Budget: $100-250,000
Program Director: Alisa D. Rivkin

Historical Note
Formerly (1997) Special Interest Group of Office Information Systems and (1986) Special Interest Group on Office Automation. SIGGROUP is a semi-autonomous subsidiary of the Ass'n for Computing Machinery. SIGGROUP is interested in topics related to computer-based systems that have a team or group impact in workplace settings. A strong emphasis of SIGGROUP is the integration of multiple computer-based tools and technologies and the impact on the human activities supported by those tools and technologies. Relevant issues include design, implementation, deployment, evaluation methodologies and impact that would arise when researching computer-based systems in a development environment. Membership: $24/year (ACM members); $46/year (non-ACM); $10/YEAR (student).

Publications:
Proceedings. a.
SIGGROUP Bulletin. 3/year.

Meetings/Conferences:
Annual Meetings: November

Special Interest Video Ass'n
Historical Note
Organization defunct in 1996.

Special Libraries Ass'n *(1909)*
1700 18th St., N.W.
Washington, DC 20009-2514
Tel: (202)234-4700 *Fax:* (202)265-9317
E-Mail: sla@sla.org
Web Site: http://www.sla.org
Members: 15,000 individuals
Staff: 39
Annual Budget: $5-10,000,000
Exec. Director: David R. Bender, Ph.D.
Director of Public Relations: Jennifer Stowe
Sr. Director, Publications/Public Affairs: Douglas Newcomb
Director, Government Relations: John H. Crosby, IV
Director, Conferences and Meetings: Stacey B. Malmgren
Sr. Director, Conferences/Prof. Development: James Mears
Asst. Exec. Director, Programs and Development: Robert Casey
Asst. Exec. Director: R. Frederick Casey, CAE
Asst. Exec. Director, Finance & Administration: Lynn K. Woodbury, CAE
Director, Development/Member Relations: Betsy Blume
Director, Membership Development: Christine Kennedy
Sr. Director, Computer Services/Technology: Maurice Harris
Manager, Internet Services: Shawn Oplinger

Historical Note
A member of the Council of Nat'l Library and Information Ass'ns, the Internat'l Federation of Library Ass'ns and Institutions. Incorporated in Rhode Island in 1928 and later in New York in 1959. Members are information professionals serving industry, business, research, education, news, trade and professional associations, and other institutions which use or produce specialized information. Membership: $105/year.

Publications:
Information Outlook.

Meetings/Conferences:
Annual Meetings: June/6,935
1999 – Minneapolis, MN/June 5-10
2000 – Philadelphia, PA/June 10-15
2001 – San Antonio, TX/June 9-14

Specialized Carriers and Rigging Ass'n *(1943)*
2750 Prosperity Ave., Suite 620
Fairfax, VA 22031-4312
Tel: (703)698-0291 *Fax:* (703)698-0297
E-Mail: info@scranet.org
Web Site: http://www.scranet.org
Members: 1000 individuals, 921 companies
Staff: 10
Annual Budget: $2-5,000,000
Exec. V. President: N. Eugene Brymer, APR, CAE
Senior V. President: William P. Rieck

Historical Note
Established as the Heavy Specialized Carriers Section-Local Cartage National Conference, it became the Heavy Specialized Carriers Conference in 1959 and assumed its present name in 1981. Affiliated with American Trucking Associations, members are carriers, crane and rigging operators and millwrights engaged in the transport of heavy goods. Membership: $570-2,715/year, varies by gross revenue (company); $440-1,560/year (allied industry).

Publications:
Lifting & Transportation Internat'l Magazine. 9/yr. adv.
News from SC&RA.
SC&RA Directory of Members and Equipment. a.
SC&RA Industrial Relations Bulletin.
SC&RA Newsletter.
SC&RA Safety Bulletin.

Meetings/Conferences:
Annual Meetings: Spring
1999 – Ft. Lauderdale, FL/April 16-20
2000 – San Francisco, CA/April 14-18

Specialty Coffee Ass'n of America *(1982)*
One World Trade Center, Suite 1200
Long Beach, CA 90831-1200
Tel: (310)624-4100 *Fax:* (310)624-4101
E-Mail: coffee@scaa.org
Web Site: http://www.scaa.org
Members: 2,250 companies
Staff: 6
Annual Budget: $2-5,000,000
Exec. Director: Ted Lingle
Director, Communication: Carla White
Administrative Director: Don Holly

Historical Note
Membership: $120-900/year (company).

Publications:
Membership Directory. a.
Specialty Coffee Chronicle. bi-m.

Meetings/Conferences:
1999 – Philadelphia, PA/April 30-May 3

Specialty Equipment Market Ass'n *(1963)*
1575 South Valley Vista Dr.
P.O. Box 4910
Diamond Bar, CA 91765-0910
Tel: (909)396-0289 *Fax:* (909)396-9569
Web Site: http://sema.org
Members: 3,300 companies
Staff: 50
Annual Budget: $2-5,000,000
President: Charles R. Blum, CAE
V. President, Communications: Sam Jackson

Historical Note
Formerly (1966) Speed Equipment Manufacturers Ass'n, and (1979) Specialty Equipment Manufacturers Ass'n. Composed of companies supplying performance motor vehicle parts and accessories. Sponsors and supports the SEMA Political Action Committee. Receives administrative support from the Coalition of Auotmotive Ass'n.

Publications:
SEMA News. m. adv.

Meetings/Conferences:
Annual Meetings: Fall in Las Vegas, NV(Convention Center)/25,000

Specialty Sleep Ass'n *(1987)*
236 Rt. 38 West, Suite 100
Moorestown, NJ 08057
Tel: (609)231-8500 *Fax:* (609)231-4664
Toll Free: (800)336 - 7322
E-Mail: llauer@ahint.com
Members: 200 companies
Staff: 5
Annual Budget: $250-500,000
Exec. Director: William D. Pawlucy

Historical Note
Formed from a merger of the Nat'l Waterbed Retailers Ass'n and the Waterbed Manufacturers Ass'n in 1994 as the Waterbed Council, assumed its current name in 1996. SSA is a national organization of manufacturers and retailers with a unified goal of serving the markets for specialty sleep services and related product lines.

Publications:
Bedroom Industry. bi-m. adv.

Meetings/Conferences:
Annual Meetings: March/1,000
1999 – Las Vegas, NV(Sands Convention Center)/March 15-18
2000 – Las Vegas, NV(Sands Convention Center)/March 8-10

Specialty Steel Industry of North America *(1962)*
c/o Collier, Shannon Rill & Scott
3050 K St., N.W., Suite 400
Washington, DC 20007
Tel: (202)342-8450 *Fax:* (202)338-5534
Members: 21 companies
Annual Budget: $500-1,000,000
Secretary and Counsel: David A. Hartquist

Historical Note
Formerly (1983) Tool and Stainless Steel Industry Committee and (1994) Specialty Steel Industry of the U.S. Has no paid officers or full-time staff; the above address is that of the law firm Collier Shannon, Rill and Scott.

Meetings/Conferences:
Quarterly Meetings: either Washington, DC or Pittsburgh, PA

Specialty Tobacco Council
8066 North Point Blvd., Suite 204
Winston-Salem, NC 27106
Tel: (336)759-0391 *Fax:* (336)759-0965
Members: 7 companies
Staff: 1
Annual Budget: $50-100,000
Exec. Director: Gabriel A. Avram

Historical Note
Represents manufacturers and importers of specialty tobacco products.

Publications:
Newsletter. m.

Meetings/Conferences:
Annual Meetings: none held.

Specialty Tool and Fastener Distributors Ass'n *(1976)*
P.O. Box 44
Elm Grove, WI 53122
Tel: (414)784-4774 *Fax:* (414)784-5059
Toll Free: (800)352 - 2981
E-Mail: STAFDA@execpc.com
Web Site: http://www.STAFDA.org
Members: 2,480 individuals
Staff: 3
Annual Budget: $2-5,000,000
Exec. Director: Morrie E. Halvorsen
Member Services Director: Georgia H. Foley

Historical Note
Members distribute or manufacture power tools, powder-actuated tools, anchors, diamond drilling equipment, fastening systems and related construction/industrial supplies. Membership: $350/year (company)

Publications:
Trade News. m.

Meetings/Conferences:
Annual Meetings: November

Specialty Vehicle Institute of America *(1983)*
2 Jenner St., Suite 150
Irvine, CA 92618-3806
Tel: (949)727-3727 *Fax:* (949)727-4216
Members: 5 companies
Staff: 40
Annual Budget: $2-5,000,000
V. President: Thomas Yager
V. President, Communications: Beverly St. Clair Baird
V. President, Administration: Carol Kington

Historical Note
A national, non-profit trade association representing manufacturers and distributors of all-terrain vehicles. SVIA's purpose is to foster and promote the safe and responsible use of specialty vehicles manufactured and/or distributed in the U.S.

Publications:
ATV RiderCourse Handbook.
Parents, Youngsters and ATVs.
Tips and Practice for the ATV Rider.

Meetings/Conferences:

Speech and Signal Processing Acoustics Soc.
Historical Note
A subsidiary of the Institute of Electrical and Electronics Engineers. Membership in the Society, open only to IEEE members, includes subscription to a technical periodical in the field published by IEEE. All administrative support is provided by IEEE.

Speech Communication Ass'n
Historical Note
Became the National Communication Ass'n in 1998.

Speed Coaches Ass'n *(1979)*
6905 Corporate Dr.
Indianapolis, IN 46278-1927
Tel: (317)347-2626 *Fax:* (317)347-2636
E-Mail: rsa@rollerskating.org
Web Site: http://www.rollerskating.org
Members: 100 individuals
Staff: 1
Annual Budget: under $10,000
Exec. Director: Katherine M. McDonell, CAE

Historical Note
A division of Roller Skating Ass'ns internat'l, which provides administrative support. Members are professional roller speed skating coaches, trainers and managers. Membership: $40/year.

Publications:
Membership Directory. a.
RSA Coaches Edition. bi.

Meetings/Conferences:
Annual Meetings: Held in conjunction with the Nat'l Roller Skating Championships

SPIE-Internat'l Soc. for Optical Engineering *(1955)*
1000 20th St.
P.O. Box 10
Bellingham, WA 98225
Tel: (360)676-3290 *Fax:* (360)647-1445
E-Mail: spie@spie.org
Web Site: http://www.spie.org
Members: 14,000 individuals, 320 companies
Staff: 115
Annual Budget: $10-25,000,000
Exec. Director: James Pearson, Ph.D.
Dir., Communications/Info. Services: Marybeth Manning
Dir., Exhibits: Sue Davis
Director, Technical Programs and Meetings: Marshall Weathersby
Director, Finance/Customer Service: Kurtis Roberts
Publication Director: Eric Pepper

Historical Note
Scientists, engineers and companies interested in technology and applications of optical, electro-optical, fiber-optic, laser, and photonic systems. Founded and incorporated in 1955 in California as the Soc. of Photographic Instrumentation Engineers, it later became the Soc. of Photo-Optical Instrumentation Engineers and assumed its present name in 1983. A member society of the American Institute for Medical and Biological Engineering and the American Ass'n of Engineering Socs., and an affiliate society of the American Institute of Physics. Has an annual budget of approximately $16 million. Membership: $95/year (individual); institutional dues based on annual sales volume.

Publications:
Journal of Biomedical Optics. q. adv.
Journal of Electronic Imaging. q. adv.
Optical Engineering. m. adv.
Optical Engineering Reports. m. adv.

Meetings/Conferences:
1999 – Denver, CO/July 25-30
2000 – San Diego, CA/July 30-Aug. 4

Spill Control Ass'n of America *(1973)*
400 Renaissance Center, Suite 1900
Detroit, MI 48243-1508
Tel: (313)259-9220 *Fax:* (313)259-8943
E-Mail: MSHAYE@CROSSWROCK.COM
Members: 125 individualsand corporations
Staff: 2
Annual Budget: $100-250,000
Exec. Director and Gen. Counsel: Marc K. Shaye

Historical Note
Established as the Oil Spill Control Ass'n of America, it assumed its present name in 1978. Members are companies and individuals concerned with cleaning up spills of oil and hazardous products and manufacturers of specialized products for spill control/clean–up and personnel protection. The above address is that of the law firm of Cross Wrock, P.C. Membership: $250/year (individual); $1000/year (company).

Publications:
Newsletter. q.
Spill Briefs. m. adv.

Meetings/Conferences:
1999 – Las Vegas, NV/Feb. 10-12

Spinal Stress Research Soc. *(1976)*
Historical Note
Also known as Precision Chiropractic Research Society.

Sponge and Chamois Institute *(1933)*
117 Wilmot Circle, Suite 2
Scarsdale, NY 10583-6721
Tel: (914)725-4646 *Fax:* (914)725-1183
Members: 9 companies
Staff: 2
Annual Budget: $25-50,000

Exec. Secretary: Jules Schwimmer

Historical Note
Members are dealers and suppliers of natural sponges and chamois leather.

Meetings/Conferences:
Annual Meetings: November

Sporting Arms and Ammunition Manufacturers' Institute *(1926)*
11 Mile Hill Road
Newtown, CT   06470-2359
Tel: (203)426-4358   *Fax:* (203)426-1087
Members: 21 companies
Staff: 2
Annual Budget: $500-1,000,000
President and C.E.O.: Robert T. Delfay

Historical Note
The trade association of major U.S. producers of sporting firearms, ammunition and smokeless propellants, SAAMI is active primarily in technical matters relating to voluntary industry standards and product safety.

Sporting Goods Agents Ass'n *(1934)*
Box 998
Morton Grove, IL   60053
Tel: (847)296-3670   *Fax:* (847)827-0196
Members: 1,400 individuals, 320 agencies
Staff: 2
Annual Budget: $500-1,000,000
Exec. Director: Lois E. Halinton

Historical Note
SGAA represents established independent manufacturers' agents in the sporting goods industry in the United States and Canada. Formerly (1977) Sporting Goods Representatives Ass'n. Membership: $150/year, plus $40/year (associate), plus $100 initiation fee for new applicants.

Publications:
Guide to the Business of Independent Sales Reps. (Q&A
     Brochure.
Lines Available Listing. m.
Manufacturers Guide to Sales Reps. (Q&A Brochure.
Membership Roster.
Newsletter. m.

Meetings/Conferences:

Sporting Goods Manufacturers Ass'n *(1906)*
200 Castlewood Drive
North Palm Beach, FL   33408-5696
Tel: (561)842-4100   *Fax:* (561)863-8984
Web Site: http://www.sportlink.com
Members: 2,500 companies, 150 associates
Staff: 36
Annual Budget: $5-10,000,000
President & Chief Exec. Officer: John D. Riddle
Director, Communications: Mike May
Director, Education: Maria Stefan
Comptroller & Chief Financial Officer: Robert Armstrong
Director, Member Services: Paul A. Aleskovsky

Historical Note
Established as the Athletic Goods Manufacturers Association, it assumed its present name in 1972. Supports the American Sports Education Institute, Athletic Institute, National Golf Foundation, Sports Apparel Products Council, Senior Games Development Council, Athletic Footwear Ass'n, and Coalition of Americans to Protect Sports (CAPS). The Racquetball Manufacturers Ass'n became a division of SGMA in 1992. Has an annual budget of approximately $9.1 million. Membership: sliding scale $440-$2640 (regular membership), $440/year (associate).

Publications:
Census Report. a.
SGMA Today. bi-m.

Meetings/Conferences:

Sports Card Ass'n
236 Route 38 West, Suite 100
Moorestown, NJ   08057
Tel: (609)231-8500   *Fax:* (609)231-4664
E-Mail: sea@ahint.com
Annual Budget: $250-500,000
President: William L. MacMillan, III, CAE
Exec. Director: Linda Lauer

Historical Note
Formerly (1997) Sports Card Manufacturers Ass'n.

Sports Card Manufracturers Ass'n
Historical Note
Became (1997) Sports Card Ass'n.

Sports Lawyers Ass'n *(1976)*
11250 Roger Bacon Drive, Suite 8
Reston, VA   20190
Tel: (703)437-4377   *Fax:* (703)435-4390
Members: 1000 individuals
Annual Budget: $100-250,000
Exec. Director: William M. Drohan, CAE
Dep. Exec. Director: Richard A. Guggloz

Historical Note
Members are attorney's specializing in sports law. Associate membership is available for professionals and entities having a legitimate interest in sports law. Other categories of membership available for educators and law students. Membership: $150/year (lawyer/regular); $300/year (associate); $50/year (educator); $25/year (law student); $75/year (libraries).

Publications:
Membership Directory. a.
Sports Lawyer. bi-m.
Sports Lawyers Journal. a.

Meetings/Conferences:
Annual Meetings: Spring
1999 – Washington, DC
2000 – San Francisco, CA

Sports Turf Contractors Ass'n *(1998)*
1375 Rolling Hills
Council Bluffs, IA   51503-8552
Tel: (712)366-2669   *Fax:* (712)366-9119
Annual Budget: $10-25,000
Exec. Director: Steven Trusty

Historical Note
STCA members are involved in the construction of sports and athletic fields for professional teams, colleges, universities, high schools, parks and recreation facilities.

Meetings/Conferences:
Annual Meetings: January
1999 – Mesa, AZ

Sports Turf Managers Ass'n *(1981)*
1375 Rolling Hills Loop
Council Bluffs, IA   51503
Tel: (712)366-2669   *Fax:* (712)366-9119
Toll Free: (800)323 - 3875
E-Mail: SportsTMgr@aol.com
Web Site: http://www.aip.com/stma
Members: 250 individuals
Staff: 4
Annual Budget: $250-500,000
Exec. Director: Steven Trusty

Historical Note
Members are involved in the construction and maintenance of sports turf areas at schools, parks, professional stadiums, race tracks, etc. Membership: $85/year (individual); $195/year (commercial affiliate); $20/year (student).

Publications:
Membership Directory. a. adv.
Sports Turf Manager. bi-m. adv.
Sports Turf Proceedings. a. adv.
sportsTurf Magazine. m. adv.

Meetings/Conferences:
Annual Meetings: December
1999 – Mesa, AZ(Sheraton Mesa)/Jan. 13-17
2000 – St. Louis, MO(Regal Riverfront)/Jan. 12-16/500

Sportsplex Operators and Developers of Ass'n *(1981)*
P.O. Box 24617, Westgate Station
Rochester, NY   14624-0617
Tel: (716)426-2215
E-Mail: sodasite@netacc.net
Web Site: http://gnv.fdt.net/~soda
Members: 276 sports facilities
Annual Budget: $500-1,000,000
Exec. Director: Don Aselin

Historical Note
Founded as Sportsplex Owners and Directors of America; assumed its current name in 1994. SODA was formed to meet the needs of the private concerns, public agencies, and other organizations that own or maintain sports complex facilities. Membership: $295/year (full member), $295/year (associate).

Publications:
SODAsite. bi-m. adv.

Meetings/Conferences:
Annual Meetings: January
1999 – Ft. Lauderdale, FL(Marriott North)

Sportswear Apparel Ass'n *(1933)*
450 Seventh Ave., Suite 1009
New York, NY   10123
Tel: (212)564-6161   *Fax:* (212)564-6166
Members: 150 companies
Staff: 2
Annual Budget: $100-250,000
Exec. Director: Sidney Reiff

Historical Note
Established as Infants and Children's Novelties Ass'n. Known as Infants, Children's and Sportswear Ass'n before assuming its present name.

Meetings/Conferences:
Annual Meetings: Spring in New York, NY with the Ladies
     Apparel Contractors Ass'n.

Spring Manufacturers Institute *(1933)*
2001 Midwest Road, Suite 106
Oak Brook, IL   60523-1335
Tel: (630)495-8588   *Fax:* (630)495-8595
Members: 335 companies
Staff: 6
Annual Budget: $1-2,000,000
Exec. V. President: Ken Boyce, CAE
Communications Manager: Rita Schauer
Regulations Compliance Manager: Jim Wood
Financial Administration Manager: Janice Mallo
Membership Services Manager: Jennifer Macklin

Historical Note
Founded as the Spring Manufacturers Ass'n, it assumed its present name in 1961.

Publications:
Springs Magazine. q. adv.

Meetings/Conferences:
Semi-Annual Meetings: Spring and Fall/300
1999 – Carlsbad, CA(LaCosta Resort)/Oct. 3-5/300
1999 – Acapulo, Mexico(Acapulco
     Princess)/March 21-23/300
2000 – Hawaii(Waikola Village)/Feb. 27-29/300
2000 – Whistler, BC, Canada(Chateau
     Whistler)/Sept. 10-12/300

Spring Research Institute *(1933)*

3034 N. Fleming Circle
Shelbyville, IN   46176
Tel: (317)398-3822
Members: 12 manufacturers 6 associates
Staff: 3
President: John Thompson

Historical Note
Members are manufacturers of leaf springs for the automotive aftermarket.

Meetings/Conferences:
Semi-annual Meetings: Spring and Fall

SSPC: the Soc. for Protective Coatings *(1950)*
40 24th St., 6th Floor
Pittsburgh, PA   15222-4656
Tel: (412)281-2331   *Fax:* (412)281-9993
E-Mail: members@sspc.org
Web Site: http://www.sspc.org
Members: 8,500 individuals, 685 organizations
Staff: 30
Annual Budget: $2-5,000,000
Exec. Director: Dr. Bernard R. Appleman

Historical Note
Founded as Steel Structures Painting Council; assumed its current name in 1997. Conducts research, develops standards, and disseminates information about surface preparation, application techniques, coatings, and related technology for protecting structural steel. Members include paint manufacturers, raw material suppliers, specifiers, applicators, government agencies, and a wide variety of end-users. Administers the Painting Contractor Certification Program. Membership: $85/year (individual); $600-5,000/year (organization).

Publications:
Compliance - Environmental Health & Safety News for SSPC.
     q.
Journal of Protective Coatings and Linings. m. adv.
Symposium Proceedings. a.

Meetings/Conferences:
Annual Meetings: Fall/3,400
1999 – Houston, TX(George R. Brown Center)/Nov. 14-18
2000 – Nashville, TN(Opryland)/Nov. 8-18
2001 – Atlanta, GA(World Congress Center)/Nov. 11-15

Stadium Managers Ass'n
19 Mantua Road
Mount Royal, NJ   08061
Tel: (609)423-7222   *Fax:* (609)423-3420
Members: 350 individuals
Annual Budget: $100-250,000
Exec. Director: Robert Talley
Manager, Meetings: Nick Montana

Historical Note
Membership: $50/year.

Publications:
SMA Score Board. 2/year.

Meetings/Conferences:
Annual Meetings: January/300

Stained Glass Ass'n of America *(1903)*
P.O. Box 22642
Kansas City, MO   64113
Tel: (816)333-6690   *Fax:* (816)361-9173
Toll Free: (800)888 - 7422
E-Mail: sgaofa@aol.com
Web Site: http://www.stainedglass.org
Members: 500 individuals
Staff: 3
Annual Budget: $250-500,000
Exec. Secretary: Kathy Murdock

Historical Note
Membership is composed of stained glass studios, artists, designers, craft suppliers and others actively engaged in the craft of stained glass. Officers change annually in June. Membership: $75/year (affiliate); $50/year (student affiliate); $350/year (company).

Publications:
Kaleidoscope. 3/year.
Stained Glass. q. adv.

Meetings/Conferences:
Annual Meetings: June
1999 – Jacksonville, FL

Standards Engineering Soc. *(1947)*
13340 S.W. 96th Ave.
Miami, FL   33176
Tel: (305)971-4798   *Fax:* (305)971-4799
E-Mail: hgziggy@worldnet.att.net
Web Site: http://www.ses-standards.org
Members: 400 individuals
Staff: 1
Annual Budget: $50-100,000
Exec. Director: Dr. H. Glenn Ziegenfuss

Historical Note
SES is professional membership society promoting the use of standards and enhancing the knowledge of standardization. Members are engineers, teachers, executives, scholars and others involved in the development and/or use of industry, government, national or international standards. Membership: $65/year (individual).

Publications:
Standards Engineering. bi-m. adv.

Meetings/Conferences:
Annual Meetings: Fall
1999 – Toronto, ON, Canada(Delta Chelsea)/100

State and Territorial Air Pollution Program Administrators *(1968)*
444 North Capitol St., N.W., Suite 307
Washington, DC   20001-1512

Tel: (202)624-7864   *Fax:* (202)624-7863
Web Site: www.4cleanair.org
Members: 55 state & territorial agencies
Staff: 6
Annual Budget: $100-250,000
Exec. Director: S. William Becker

Historical Note
Members are representatives from each state and territory. Shares headquarters and staff with the Ass'n of Local Air Pollution Control Officials.

Publications:
Washington Update. m.

Meetings/Conferences:
Semi-annual Meetings: Spring and Fall & Air Toxics Conf.
    Annually

State Debt Management Network
c/o NAST 2760 Research Park Drive
P.O. Box 11910
Lexington, KY   40578-1910
Tel: (606)244-8175   *Fax:* (606)244-8053
Annual Budget: $10-25,000
Chair: John Massey
Director: Pamela Taylor
Research and Publications Manager: Kathy Tyson

Historical Note
SDMN members are state officials concerned with the issuance or management of state debt. Affiliated with the Nat'l Ass'n of State Treasurers, serves as a professional organization for individuals responsible for the management of oversight of public debt at the state level. The purpose is to enhance debt management practices through training, development of educational materials, and data collection and dissemination. Membership: $200/year (individual) and $200/year (organization).

Meetings/Conferences:
1999 – Portland, OR

State Government Affairs Council *(1975)*
1255 23rd St., N.W., Suite 850
Washington, DC   20037-1174
Tel: (202)728-0500   *Fax:* (202)833-3636
Members: 125 companies
Annual Budget: $250-500,000
Exec. Director: Dinah D. McElfresh

Historical Note
Formed in October 1975 as an outgrowth of the Nat'l Soc. of State Legislators. Members are representatives of major U.S. companies and associations that participate in the state-level public policy process. Works with the Nat'l Conference of State Legislatures, the Council of State Governments, and various other national associations to improve state government and enhance cooperation between the business community and state government. Membership: $3,000/year.

Publications:
SGAC Annual Report. a.
SGAC News. bi-m.
SGAC Roster. a.

Meetings/Conferences:
Annual Meetings: In conjunction with Nat'l Conference of State
    Legislatures

State Guard Ass'n of the United States *(1985)*
P.O. Box 206
5087 Solomons Island Road
Lothian, MD   20711
Tel: (301)261-9099   *Fax:* (301)261-9099
Members: 2,600 individuals, 21 state defense forces
Staff: 3
Annual Budget: $25-50,000
Exec. Director: Col. Paul T. McHenry, Jr.

Historical Note
SGAUS is the association of State Guards (also known as state defense forces); members are active and retired members of state defense forces. Membership: $16/year (enlisted/NCO); $25/year (officers); $30/year (general officers).

Publications:
SGAUS Journal. q.

Meetings/Conferences:
Annual Meetings: October
1999 – Biloxi, MS(Broadwater)
2000 – Baltimore, MD(Marriott)/Oct. 12-15

State Higher Education Executive Officers *(1954)*
707 17th St., Suite 2700
Denver, CO   80202-3427
Tel: (303)299-3686   *Fax:* (303)296-8332
Staff: 5
Annual Budget: $500-1,000,000
Exec. Director: Dr. James R. Mingle
Exec. Assistant: Catherine Walker

Historical Note
Headquartered in Colorado, SHEEO members are the full-time chief executive officers serving statewide coordinating boards and governing boards of postsecondary education. Members include 49 states and the Commonwealth of Puerto Rico. Membership: $2,300-7,200/year.

Publications:
Directory of Professional Personnel. a.
Network News Newsletter. q.
State Higher Education Appropriations. a.

Meetings/Conferences:
Annual Meetings: Summer
1999 – Santa Fe, NM/July 24-27

State Medicaid Directors Ass'n

Historical Note
Became Nat'l Ass'n of Medicaid Directors in 1996.

State Risk and Insurance Management Ass'n
309 Administration Bldg.
400 W. King St., RM. 300
Carson City, NV   89703
Tel: (702)687-6721   *Fax:* (702)687-4235
Members: 50 individuals
Annual Budget: $50-100,000
President: David R. Thomas

Historical Note
STRIMA members are state government risk and insurance managers. Membership: $200/year (organization).

Meetings/Conferences:

States Organization for Boating Access
P.O. Box 25655
Washington, DC   20007
Tel: (202)721-1644   *Fax:* (202)721-1645
Members: 50 states and provinces
Staff: 1
Annual Budget: $500-1,000,000
Secretariat: Ron Stone

Historical Note
SOBA members are states and provinces. Advisory membership is open to federal agencies, local governments, and non-profit organizations. Associate membership is available for corporations. Membership: $445(state); $550 (corporate).

Publications:
Boating Access Quarterly Newsletter. q.
Recomm. Design Guidelines f.
SOBA Bibliography. a.

Meetings/Conferences:
Annual Meetings: Little Rock, AZ/125 Wilmington, NC/125

Station Representatives Ass'n *(1948)*
16 W. 77th St., Suite 9-E
New York, NY   10024-5126
Tel: (212)362-8868   *Fax:* (212)362-4999
Members: 9 organizations
Staff: 1
Annual Budget: $250-500,000
Managing Director: Jerome Feniger

Historical Note
Founded (1948) as the Nat'l Ass'n of Radio Station Representatives, Inc. Became Station Representatives Ass'n Inc., in 1952. Broadcast sales organizations, not affiliated with a national network, who sell non-network broadcast advertising.

Publications:
The Must Carry Rules.

Meetings/Conferences:
Annual Meetings: New York City

Stationery and Office Equipment Board of Trade

Historical Note
Became (1995) Business Products Credit Ass'n.

Statistical Paper Group *(1949)*

Historical Note
Organization defunct in 1997.

Statistical Process Control Soc. *(1987)*

Historical Note
Address unknown in 1996; presumed inactive or defunct.

Steel Deck Institute *(1936)*
P.O. Box 25
Fox River Grove, IL   60021-0025
Tel: (847)462-1930   *Fax:* (817)462-1940
Web Site: http://www.sdi.org
Members: 24 companies
Staff: 2
Annual Budget: $100-250,000
Managing Director: Steven A. Roehrig

Historical Note
Established as the Metal Roof Deck Technical Institute, it assumed its present name in 1939. A non-profit association of steel deck producers and associate members furnishing products allied to steel deck use in construction. SDI is a regulatory agency disseminating design standards to the industry.

Publications:
Composite Deck Design Handbook. a. adv.
Comprehensive Steel Deck Institute Binder. a. adv.
Diaphragm Design Manual. a. adv.
Manual of Construction with Steel Deck. adv. adv.
SDI Design Manual. a. adv.

Meetings/Conferences:
Annual Meetings: May
1999 – Naples, FL(LaPlaya Resort)/May 3-4/45

Steel Door Institute *(1954)*
30200 Detroit Road
Cleveland, OH   44145-1967
Tel: (440)899-0010   *Fax:* (440)892-1404
Web Site: http://www.steeldoor.org
Members: 9 companies
Staff: 2
Annual Budget: $50-100,000
Managing Director: J. Jeffery Wherry

Historical Note
Producers of all-metal frames and doors for commercial, industrial and residential construction.

Steel Erectors Ass'n of America *(1972)*

Historical Note
Address unknown in 1995.

Steel Founders' Soc. of America *(1902)*
Cast Metals Federation Bldg.

---

455 State St.
Des Plaines, IL   60016
Tel: (847)299-9160   *Fax:* (847)299-3105
E-Mail: monroe@scra.org
Web Site: http://www.sfsa.org
Members: 80 corporations
Staff: 6
Annual Budget: $500-1,000,000
Exec. V. President: Raymond W. Monroe
Exec. Assistant: Kathleen J. Reese

Historical Note
A technically oriented trade ass'n serving the steel casting industry. Absorbed the Alloy Casting Institute in 1970. Membership: No individual membership.

Publications:
Directory of Steel Foundries. bien.

Meetings/Conferences:
Annual Meetings: Fall
1999 – Asheville, NC(Grove Park)/Sept. 25-28
2000 – Monterey, CA(Monterey Plaza Hotel)/Sept. 23-27
2001 – Mackinac Island, MI(Grand Hotel)

Steel Joist Institute *(1928)*
3127 10th Ave. Ext. North
Myrtle Beach, SC   29577-6760
Tel: (803)626-1995   *Fax:* (803)626-5565
Members: 15 companies
Staff: 2
Managing Director: R. Donald Murphy

Historical Note
Composed of active manufacturers, the SJI cooperates with government and business agencies to establish steel joist standards.

Publications:
Catalogue of Specifications and Load Tables.
Technical Digests.

Meetings/Conferences:
Annual Meetings: May
1999 – Spring and Fall

Steel Manufacturers Ass'n *(1988)*
1730 Rhode Island Ave., N.W., Suite 907
Washington, DC   20036-3101
Tel: (202)296-1515   *Fax:* (202)296-2506
E-Mail: bechake@steelnet.org
Web Site: http://www.steelnet.org
Members: 61 steel companies
Staff: 5
Annual Budget: $500-1,000,000
President: James F. Collins

Historical Note
SMA is the largest steel trade group in North America. It is the primary ass'n for "minimills", companies engaged in electric arc furnace/continuous caster steel production as well as hot and cold rollers of steel mill products. A growing number of integrated steel producers are also members. There are 170 associate members who are providers of materials, equipment and services to the steel industry and 10 international steel company members.

Publications:
Annual Membership Directory. a. adv.
Steel Manufacturers Ass'n Newsletter. q.

Meetings/Conferences:
Annual Meetings: Spring
1999 – Washington, DC(Williard
    International)/April 25-29/200

Steel Plate Fabricators Ass'n *(1933)*
11315 Reed Hartman Hwy., Suite 104
Cincinnati, OH   45241-2488
Tel: (513)469-0500   *Fax:* (513)469-0599
Members: 120 companies
Staff: 3
Annual Budget: $500-1,000,000
Exec. Director: Joseph J. Hammoor

Historical Note
Membership: $750-7,000/year.

Publications:
Directory of SPFA Metal Plate Fabricators. a.
Steel Plate Update. q.

Meetings/Conferences:
Annual Meetings: Early Spring/250
1999 – La Costa, CA/March 27-30

Steel Recycling Institute *(1988)*
Foster Plaza 10, 680 Andersen Dr.
Pittsburgh, PA   15220-2700
Tel: (412)922-2772   *Fax:* (412)922-3213
Toll Free: (800)876 - 7274
E-Mail: sri@recycle-steel.org
Web Site: http://www.recycle-steel.org
Members: 60 companies
Staff: 30
Annual Budget: $2-5,000,000
President: William M. Heenan, Jr.
V. President, Public and Education Relations: Mary K. Norton
V. President, Marketing Communications: Brian A. Tedeschi
V. President, Government Affairs: Rebecca B. Linn
V. President, Operations: Gregory L. Crawford

Historical Note
Promotes steel recycling and works to forge a coalition of steelmakers, can manufacturers, beverage and food companies, legislators, government officials, solid waste managers, businesses, and consumer groups. Formerly (1993) Steel Can Recycling Institute. Membership: $5,000/year (associate), $500/year (supporting).

Publications:
The Recycling Magnet. q.

Meetings/Conferences:
Annual Meetings: Quarterly Meetings

Steel Service Center Institute *(1907)*

127 Public Sq., Suite 2400
Cleveland, OH   44114-1216
Tel: (216)694-3630   *Fax:* (216)694-3940
Web Site: http://www.ssci.org
Members: 410 companies
Staff: 22
Annual Budget: $5-10,000,000
President: Thomas Conley
V.P., Research/Information: Craig Schulz
V.P., Communications: Kurt T. Wiebe
V.P., Meetings/Conventions: Beverly A. Malcolm
V.P., Finance/Admin.: Bel S. Klockenga
Foundation V. President: James B. Collins
V.P., Membership: Mark William John

Historical Note
Formerly (1926) American Iron and Steel and Heavy Hardware Ass'n; (1932) American Steel and Heavy Hardware Ass'n; (1959) American Steel Warehouse Ass'n, Inc. Annual Budget: $6.2 million.

Publications:
Center Lines. m.
Government Action Report. m.

Meetings/Conferences:
Annual Meetings: May/1,000
1999 – Las Vegas, NV(Bellagio)/May 2-5
2000 – Vancouver, British
Columbia(Waterfront/PanPacific)/April 30-May 3
2001 – Palm Desert, CA(Marriott Desert Springs)/May 6-9

Steel Shipping Container Institute *(1944)*

1101 14th St., N.W., Suite 1020
Washington, DC   20005
Tel: (202)408-1900   *Fax:* (202)408-1972
Web Site: http://www.steelcontainers.com
Members: 57 companies
Staff: 2
Annual Budget: $500-1,000,000
Director, Technical and Regulatory Affairs: David L. Core

Historical Note
SSCI members are makers of steel drums, barrels and pails.

Publications:
Packaging Vision. q.
SSCI Newsletter. q.

Meetings/Conferences:
Semi-annual Meetings. Spring and Fall
1999 – Scottsdale, AZ(Radisson)/March 27-31
1999 – Orlando, FL(Disney Grand Floridian)/Sept. 26-Oct. 1

Steel Tank Institute *(1916)*

570 Oakwood Rd.
Lake Zurich, IL   60047-1559
Tel: (847)438-8265   *Fax:* (847)438-8766
E-Mail: ankiefer@interaccess.com
Web Site: http://www.steeltank.com
Members: 100 companies
Staff: 12
Annual Budget: $1-2,000,000
Exec. V. President: Wayne B. Geyer
Dir., Marketing: Wayne Stellmach
Dir., Member Services/Admin.: Anne Kiefer
Controller: Kevin Kroll
Director, Technical Affairs: Lorri Grainaw

Historical Note
Conducts research and develops underground and aboveground storage tank technologies and standards for the steel industry. Represents its members to Congress and the Executive Branch. Absorbed (1990) Ass'n for Composite Tanks.

Publications:
Annual Report.
Member Technology Guide. semi-a.
Membership Roster. a.
Tank Talk. m.

Meetings/Conferences:
Semi-Annual Meetings: January-February and August
1999 – Cayman Islands
1999 – Vancouver, Canada

Steel Tube Institute of North America *(1930)*

8500 Station St., Suite 270
Mentor, OH   44060
Members: 65 companies
Staff: 2
Annual Budget: $500-1,000,000
Exec. Director: Timothy Andrassy

Historical Note
Formerly (until 1960) the Formed Steel Tube Institute and (until August 1988) Welded Steel Tube Institute. Incorporated in Ohio in 1955. Members make steel tubes and pipes produced from carbon, stainless or alloy steel, for applications ranging from large structural tubing to small redrawn tubing. The Institute committees are: manufacturing/technical; standard pipe; structural tubing; mechanical tube; sprinkler/conduit; and supplier relations.

Meetings/Conferences:
Semi-annual Meetings: Spring and Fall Tucson, AZ(Westin La Pacoma)/March 19-21/150-175

Steel Window Institute *(1920)*

1300 Sumner Ave.
Cleveland, OH   44115-2851
Tel: (216)241-7333   *Fax:* (216)241-0105
E-Mail: swi@taol.com
Web Site: http://www.taol.com/swi
Members: 6 companies, 4 associates
Staff: 2
Exec. Director: John H. Addington

Historical Note
Formerly the Metal Window Institute, SWI members are United States manufacturers of windows made from hot-rolled, solid steel sections and such related products as castings, trim, mechanical operators, screens and moldings.

Publications:
The Specifiers Guide to Steel Windows.

Meetings/Conferences:
Annual Meetings: Fall

Sterling Silversmiths Guild of America *(1917)*

Historical Note
Defunct in 1995.

Stilbene Whitening Agents

Historical Note
An affiliate of the Synthetic Organic Chemicals Manufacturers Ass'n which provides administrative support.

Storage Equipment Manufacturer's Ass'n *(1972)*

8720 Red Oak Blvd., Suite 201
Charlotte, NC   28217-3957
Tel: (704)676-1190   *Fax:* (704)676-1199
E-Mail: jnofsinger@mhia.org
Web Site: http://www.mhia.org
Members: 16 individuals, 10 companies
Staff: 2
Annual Budget: $25-50,000
Managing Director: John B. Nofsinger

Historical Note
Formerly (1998) Shelving Manufacturers Ass'n. Industrial steel shelving is loaded by hand and generally stores materials that are small in size, with multiple parts stored on a given shelf separated by dividers, boxes and drawers. SMA, formed as an outgrowth of the Rack Manufacturers Institute, focuses specifically on the shelving industry.

Publications:
Membership Roster. irreg.

Meetings/Conferences:
Semi-Annual Meetings: Spring and Fall with Material
Handling Institute
1999 – Charlotte, NC
1999 – Amelia Island, FL

Strategic Leadership Forum *(1985)*

435 N. Michigan Ave., Suite 1717
Chicago, IL   60611-4067
Tel: (312)644-0829   *Fax:* (312)644-8557
Toll Free: (800)873 - 5995
E-Mail: 75677.1740@compuserve.com
Members: 5,000 individuals
Staff: 18
Annual Budget: $2-5,000,000
Exec. Director: Sharon Bennett

Historical Note
Formerly (1995) The Planning Forum. Result of a merger of the North American Soc. for Corporate Planning (1966) and the Planning Executives Institute (1951). Members are professionals and executives with strategic management responsibilities in the private or public sectors. Focuses on the integrating force for improving organizational performance and achieving global competitiveness. Membership: $140/year, plus chapter dues.

Publications:
Directory. a.
Network. bi-m.
Strategy & Leadership. bi-m. adv.

Meetings/Conferences:
Annual Meetings: Spring
1999 – Chicago, IL/April 18-20
2000 – Toronto, Canada

Structural Board Ass'n *(1976)*

45 Sheppard Ave. E., Suite 412
Toronto, ON   M2N 5-W9
Tel: (416)730-9090   *Fax:* (416)730-9013
E-Mail: osba@istar.ca
Web Site: http://www.osbgui.com
Members: 13 companies, 21 mills
Staff: 3
Annual Budget: $500-1,000,000
President and C.E.O/.: Mark Angelini

Historical Note
Formerly (1976) Canadian Waferboard Ass'n and (1982) The Waferboard Ass'n. SBA members are manufacturers and suppliers of structural panels, (oriented strandboard and waferboard). Maintains a U.S. office at 1133 Connecticut Ave., N.W., Washington, DC 20036.

Publications:
Newsletter. q.
OSB in Wood Frame Construction. bien.
Technical Bulletin. irreg.
Technical Forum Proceedings. semi-a.

Meetings/Conferences:
Semi-Annual Meetings: Spring and Fall
1999 – West Palm Beach, FL/Apr. 27-29
1999 – Halifax, Nova Scotia/Oct. 5-7

Structural Insulated Panel Ass'n *(1990)*

1511 K St., N.W., Suite 600
Washington, DC   20005
Tel: (202)347-7800   *Fax:* (202)393-5043
E-Mail: SIPADC@aol.com
Web Site: http://www.sips.org
Members: 130 companies and organizations
Annual Budget: $100-250,000
Exec. Director: Cynthia J. Gardstein
Director, Communications: Will Zachmann
Member Services and Outreach: Christian May

Historical Note
SIPA members are manufacturers of structural insulated panels. Supplier and associate memberships are available for suppliers, trade associations and other organizations with an interest in the industry. Membership:$300 (associate); $500 (fabricator/distributor); $1,700-$4,000 (supplier); $5,000 (manufacturer).

Publications:
SIPA Report.
Spotlight on SIPA Newsletter. q.
Update. m.

Meetings/Conferences:
Semi-Annual Meetings: Spring and Winter
1999 – Dallas, TX
1999 – Washington, DC

Structural Stability Research Council *(1944)*

Fritz Engineering Lab., Lehigh Univ.
13 East Packer Ave.
Bethlehem, PA   18015
Tel: (610)758-3522   *Fax:* (610)758-4522
Members: 400 individuals, 13 orgs, 15 sponsors, 70 firms
Staff: 2
Annual Budget: $100-250,000
Director: Dianna Walsh

Historical Note
An outgrowth of the American Society of Civil Engineers Committee on Design of Structural Members, The Column Research Council was established by the Engineering Foundation in 1944. In 1976, broadened scope of its interests led to the adoption of the present name. Members are individuals, organizations or firms concerned with the investigation of stability aspects of metal and composite structures. Membership: $40/year (individual); $175-500/year (firm); $300/year (organization); $500-750/year (company); $1,500/year (sponsor).

Publications:
Annual Report & Register. a.
Newsletter. semi-a.
Proceedings, Annual Technical Session. a.

Meetings/Conferences:
Annual Meetings: Fall

Stucco Manufacturers Ass'n *(1957)*

2402 Vista Nobleza
Newport Beach, CA   92660
Tel: (949)640-9902   *Fax:* (949)640-9991
E-Mail: rwelch@redshift.com
Members: 30 individuals, 30 companies
Staff: 1
Annual Budget: $10-25,000
Exec. Director: Norma Fox

Stuntmen's Ass'n of Motion Pictures *(1961)*

4810 Whitsett Ave.
Second Floor
North Hollywood, CA   91607
Tel: (818)766-4334   *Fax:* (818)766-5943
Members: 135 individuals
Staff: 1
Annual Budget: $50-100,000
Executive Secretary: George Fisher

Historical Note
Members are members of the Screen Actors Guild or the American Federation of Television and Radio Artists who perform stuntwork.

Stuntwomen's Ass'n of Motion Pictures *(1967)*

12457 Ventura Blvd., Suite 208
Studio City, CA   91604-2411
Tel: (818)762-0907   *Fax:* (818)762-9534
E-Mail: director@stuntwomen.com
Web Site: http://www.stuntwomen.com
Members: 33 individuals
Staff: 1
Annual Budget: $10-25,000
Office Manager: Kelly Besharaty

Historical Note
SWAMP is an organization representing professional stuntwomen who are also full members of the Screen Actors Guild and the American Federation of Television and Radio Artists. Applicants for membership must have been earning a living exclusively as a stuntperson for a minimum of five years.

Publications:
Creative Industry Handbook. a. adv.
Stuntplayers Directory. a. adv.
Women in Film. a. adv.

Meetings/Conferences:
Annual Meetings: Monthly Meetings

Styrene and Ethylbenzene Ass'n *(1985)*

Historical Note
Dissolved by its parent organization, Synthetic Organic Chemical Manufacturers Ass'n, in 1995.

Styrene/Butadiene Latex Manufacturers Council *(1988)*

Historical Note
Name changed to SB Latex Council in 1996.

Subcontractors Trade Ass'n *(1966)*

570 Seventh Ave., Suite 1100
New York, NY   10018
Tel: (212)398-6220   *Fax:* (212)398-6224
Members: 330 companies
Staff: 3
Annual Budget: $250-500,000
Exec. V. President: Warren O. Kogan

Historical Note
Members are specialty and supply companies in the construction industry. Membership fee: $695/year.

Publications:
Subcontractor News. m. adv.

Submersible Wastewater Pump Ass'n (1976)
1806 Johns Drive
Glenview, IL 60025-1657
Tel: (847)729-7972   *Fax:* (847)729-3670
Members: 30 companies
Staff: 2
Annual Budget: $50-100,000
Exec. Director: Charles Stolberg

Historical Note
Manufacturers of submersible wastewater pumps for municipal and industrial applications and their component parts and accessories manufactures. Membership: dues vary, based on sales volume (company).

Publications:
Annual Membership Directory. a.
Membership Roster and Product Reference Guide. a.

Meetings/Conferences:
Semi-annual Meetings: Fall and Spring
1999 – New Orleans, LA(InterContinental)/Oct. 9-10/50
2000 – Anaheim, CA/Oct. 14-15/50
2001 – Atlanta, GA/Oct. 13-17/50
2002 – Chicago, IL/Oct. 19-20/50

Substance Abuse Librarians and Information Specialists (1978)
P.O. Box 9513
Berkeley, CA 94709-0513
Tel: (510)642-5208   *Fax:* (510)642-7175
E-Mail: SALIS@ARG.ORG
Web Site: http://salis.org
Members: 150 individuals
Annual Budget: under $10,000
Contact: Andrea Mitchell

Historical Note
Serves as an international network for librarians and information professionals working with material on alcohol & drugs. SALIS is an affiliate of the Internat'l Council on Alcohol and Addictions. Membership: $40/year (associate); $30/year (institution); $75/year (full member).

Publications:
SALIS News. q.

Meetings/Conferences:
Annual Meetings: Fall
1999 – Bloomington, IN(Indiana University)/April 21-25/75
2000 – New York, NY
2001 – Anchorage, AK

Substance Abuse Program Administrators Ass'n
1550 S. Coast Hwy., Suite 201
Laguna Beach, CA 92651
Tel: (949)497-9007   *Fax:* (949)376-3456
Toll Free: (800)672 - 7229
Web Site: http://www.sapaa.com
Annual Budget: $250-500,000
Managing Director: Howard Adler

Historical Note
SAPAA members are individuals and companies which provide the majority of their services in the administration of workplace substance abuse prevention programs. Associate members are individuals or companies producing or manufacturing equipment or products related to drug testing services or drug testing laboratories. There is a special membership class for government entities. Membership: $500/year (regular); $275/year (auxillary); $400/year (associate); $125/year (government).

Publications:
A Matter of Substance Newsletter. q.

Meetings/Conferences:
Semi-annual Meetings: Spring and Fall
1999 – Long Beach, CA/May 19-22

Suburban Newspapers of America (1971)
401 N. Michigan Ave.
Chicago, IL 60611-4267
Tel: (312)644-6610   *Fax:* (312)527-6658
E-Mail: sna@sba.com
Web Site: http://www.suburban-news.org
Members: 110 companies, 2,000 newspapers
Staff: 2
Annual Budget: $250-500,000
Exec. Director: Larry M. Fleischman

Historical Note
Merger of Accredited Home Newspapers of America, the Suburban Press Foundation and the Suburban Section of the Nat'l Newspaper Ass'n. Membership: $320-2,850/year, based on size of circulation (regular); $460/year (associate).

Publications:
SNA Membership Directory. a. adv.
SubPub Newspaper. bi-m. adv.

Meetings/Conferences:
1999 – Palm Springs, CA(Marquis Resort)/Feb. 24-27/40
1999 – Chicago, IL(Knickerbocker)/Sept. 22-25/100

Successful Retirement Institute
Historical Note
An organization for people involved in retirement planning education who have no ties to any product or service.

Sugar Ass'n (1943)
1101 15th St., N.W., Suite 600
Washington, DC 20005
Tel: (202)785-1122   *Fax:* (202)785-5019
Members: 25 companies
Staff: 10
Annual Budget: $2-5,000,000
President/C.E.O.: Richard Keelor, Ph.D.
Director, Public Relations: Moira Saucer

V. President, Public Affairs: Sarah Barnett
V. President, Scientific Affairs: Charles W. Baker
V. President, Administration: Alica Overton

Historical Note
Members are processors and refiners of beet and cane sugar. Administers funds to promote research on sucrose and for public relations. Maintains a library of publications on the sugar industry.

Publications:
On Your Mark. q.

Sugar Industry Technologists (1941)
164 N. Hall Dr.
Sugar Land, TX 77478
Tel: (281)494-2046   *Fax:* (281)494-2304
Web Site: http://members.aol.com/sitorg/homepage.html
Members: 550 individuals
Staff: 2
Annual Budget: $50-100,000
Exec. Director: Leon A. Anhaiser

Historical Note
Technical and administrative personnel in the cane sugar refining industry. Membership: $30/year (individual), $450/year (company).

Publications:
Proceedings. a.

Meetings/Conferences:
Annual Meetings: May-June
1999 – Lisbon, Portugal

Sulfate of Potash Magnesia Export Ass'n (1982)
Historical Note
Organization defunct in 1997.

Sulphur Institute, The (1960)
1140 Connecticut Ave., N.W., Suite 612
Washington, DC 20036-4012
Tel: (202)331-9660   *Fax:* (202)293-2940
E-Mail: sulphur@sulphurinstitute.org
Members: 29 companies
Staff: 10
Annual Budget: $1-2,000,000
President: Robert J. Morris
Communications Coordinator: Gregory T. Brown
Director, Industrial Programs: Harold H. Weber
Dir., Ag. & Market Studies Programs: Donald L. Messick

Historical Note
The Sulphur Institute is an international, non-profit organization, representing the sulphur industy. The company's purpose is to promote and expand the use of sulphur in all forms throughout the world.

Publications:
Sulphur in Agriculture. bien. adv.

Meetings/Conferences:
2000 – Washington, DC

Summer and Casual Furniture Manufacturers Ass'n (1959)
P.O. Box HP-7
High Point, NC 27261
Tel: (336)884-5000   *Fax:* (336)884-5303
Members: 93 companies
Staff: 2
Annual Budget: $50-100,000
Exec. Director: Joseph Ziolkowski

Historical Note
Division of American Furniture Manufacturers Ass'n. Membership fee based on sales volume.

Meetings/Conferences:
Annual Meetings: Chicago, IL(Holiday Inn Merchandise
   Mart)/September

Sump and Sewage Pump Manufacturers Ass'n (1956)
P.O. Box 647
Northbrook, IL 60065-0647
Tel: (847)559-9233   *Fax:* (847)559-9235
Members: 30 companies
Staff: 2
Managing Director: Pamela W. Franzen

Historical Note
Formerly (1981) Sump Pump Manufacturers Ass'n.

Sunglass Ass'n of America (1970)
49 East Ave.
Norwalk, CT 06851-0493
Tel: (203)845-9015   *Fax:* (203)847-1304
E-Mail: info@sunglassassociation.com
Web Site: http://www.sunglassassociation.com/Events.htm
Members: 105 companies
Staff: 2
Exec. Director: Swea Nightingale

Historical Note
Members of the Association consist of firms actively engaged in the manufacture and/or importation and distribution of sunglasses, sunglass parts, components or materials.

Publications:
Newsletter. q.

Meetings/Conferences:
Annual Meetings: Fall
1999 – Sea Island, GA(Cloister)

Suntanning Ass'n for Education (1984)
P.O. Box 1181
913 Gulf Breeze Pkwy., Suite 22
Gulf Breeze, FL 32562-1181
Tel: (850)934-8460   *Fax:* (850)934-8335
E-Mail: sunassnedu@bellsouth.net
Members: 1,500 companies
Staff: 3

Annual Budget: $100-250,000
Senior Adviser for Development: Paul Germek

Historical Note
SAE is a non-profit trade association established to provide educational resources and legislative assistance to the indoor tanning industry. Membership: $90/year (salon); $250/year (distributor); $1,000/year (manufacturer).

Publications:
Chapter Newsletter. 8/yr.
Tanning Talk. q. adv.

Meetings/Conferences:

Superconductor Applications Ass'n (1987)
Historical Note
Organization defunct in 1997.

Supima Ass'n of America (1954)
4141 East Broadway Rd.
Phoenix, AZ 85040-8831
Tel: (602)437-1364   *Fax:* (602)437-0143
E-Mail: info@supimacotton.org
Web Site: http://www.supimacotton.org
Members: 3,000 individuals
Staff: 5
Annual Budget: $1-2,000,000
President: Jesse W. Curlee
Office Manager: Nancy Boyd
Exec. V. President: Matt Laughlin

Historical Note
Members are producers of Supima (extra-long staple) cotton. Most members are located in the Southwest. Sponsors and supports the Supima Political Action Committee (SuPac). Membership: $3/bale assessment.

Publications:
Supima News Newsletter. m.

Meetings/Conferences:

Suppliers of Advanced Composite Materials Ass'n (1984)
1600 Wilson Blvd., Suite 901
Arlington, VA 22209-2505
Tel: (703)841-1556   *Fax:* (703)841-1559
E-Mail: sacma@ibm.net
Members: 25 companies
Staff: 6
Annual Budget: $250-500,000
Exec. Director: William H. Werst, Jr.
Manager of Committee Affairs: Meredith Cawley
Manager of Government Affairs: Tamara Stretton
Manager of Membership Affairs: Jennifer Evanchik
Financial Director: Judith A. McCrovey
Manager Membership Affairs: Jennifer Evanchik

Historical Note
An international non-profit trade association of "Free World" manufacturers which produce materials used in construction of fiber-reinforced advanced composite finished products. Membership: based on sales volume (company), $1,000/year (associate); $500/yr. (affiliate).

Publications:
Materials Interface. m.

Meetings/Conferences:
Semi-annual Meetings: Spring and Fall

Supply Chain Council (1997)
303 Freeport Road
Pittsburgh, PA 15213-3131
Tel: (412)781-3255   *Fax:* (412)781-2871
Web Site: http://www.supply-chain.org
Members: 500 corporations
Exec. Director: William P. Hakanson, CAE

Historical Note
Membership: $1,750/year (company).

Surety Ass'n of America (1908)
1101 Cnnecticut Ave., NW.,Suite 800
Washington, DC 20036
Tel: (202)463-0600   *Fax:* (202)463-0606
E-Mail: information@surety.org
Web Site: http://www.surety.org
Members: 650 companies
Staff: 20
Annual Budget: $2-5,000,000
President: Lynn M. Schubert

Historical Note
Insurance companies underwriting fidelity, surety and forgery bonds. Absorbed the Towner Rating Bureau in 1947.

Meetings/Conferences:
Annual Meetings: New York, NY, second Thursday in May

Surface Design Ass'n (1976)
P.O. Box 20799
Oakland, CA 94620
Tel: (707)829-3110   *Fax:* (707)829-3285
Web Site: www.art.uidaho.edu/sda/
Members: 2,700 individuals, 300 businesses, schools, libraries
Staff: 3
Annual Budget: $25-50,000
Administrator: Joy Stocksdale

Historical Note
Membership consists of individuals involved in printing, designing and dyeing art fabrics, fibers and other materials. Incorporated in the State of Minnesota. Membership: $45/year (individual); $500/year (organization/company).

Publications:
SDA Newsletter. q.
Surface Design Journal. q. adv.

Meetings/Conferences:
Biennial Meetings: (1999)

Surface Finishing Industry Council
112-J Elden St.
Herndon, VA   20170
Tel: (703)709-1035   *Fax:* (703)709-1036
Annual Budget: $500-1,000,000
Exec. Officer: David Barrack
Historical Note
SFIC is comprized of three major trade associations representing the surface finishing industry.
Publications:
Guidance Manual to Environmental Compliance. a.
Surface Finishing Market Research Bureau Report. a.

Surface Mount Equipment Manufacturers Ass'n *(1987)*
1795 Lake Cook Road, Suite 205
Highland Park, IL   60035-4480
Tel: (847)831-1002   *Fax:* (847)831-1691
Members: 52 companies
Staff: 1
Annual Budget: $25-50,000
Exec. Director: Janet Schafer
Historical Note
SMEMA members are companies manufacturing equipment or producing software for surface mount board production (a process of placing and securing electrical components on printed circuit boards). SMEMA's objectives are to develop and promote standards for the interface and operation of equipment; to assure users that each machine in their production line will interface effectively and smoothly with others; to advance the technology, and to investigate areas where the association may act to the benefit of all its members. Membership: $900/year (company).
Publications:
Newsletter. q.
Meetings/Conferences:

Surface Mount Technology Ass'n *(1984)*
5200 Wilson Road, Suite 215
Edina, MN   55424-1338
Tel: (612)920-7682   *Fax:* (612)926-1819
E-Mail: smta@smta.org
Web Site: http://www.smta.org
Members: 3,200 individuals, 800 companies
Staff: 10
Annual Budget: $1-2,000,000
President: Greg Evans
Communications: David Gonnerman
Programs: Carla Wolf
Exec. Administrator: JoAnn Stromberg
Coordinator, Membership: Sid Sullivan
Historical Note
Membership: $60/year (individual), $395/year (company).
Publications:
Membership Directory. a. adv.
Newsletters. m.
Proceedings. a.
Technical Journal. q.
Meetings/Conferences:
1999 – San Jose, CA(Convention Center)/Sept. 12-16/5000

Surgical Infection Soc. *(1981)*
Toronto General Hospital
200 Elizabeth St., EN9-236
Toronto, ON   M5G 2-C4
Tel: (416)340-4988   *Fax:* (416)595-9486
Members: 450 individuals
Annual Budget: $25-50,000
President-Elect: Ori D. Rotstein, M.D.
Historical Note
Members are surgeons and other medical specialists with an interest in surgical infection.
Publications:
Program Book (for convention). a.
Meetings/Conferences:

Survival and Flight Equipment Ass'n *(1957)*
Historical Note
See the SAFE Ass'n.

Suspension Specialists Ass'n *(1981)*
Historical Note
Name changed to Service Specialists Ass'n in 1996.

SWANA - Solid Waste Ass'n of North America *(1961)*
1100 Wayne Ave., Suite 700
P.O. Box 7219
Silver Spring, MD   20907-7219
Tel: (301)585-2898   *Fax:* (301)589-7068
Web Site: http://www.swana.org
Members: 6,000 individuals, 1,500 companies
Staff: 25
Annual Budget: $2-5,000,000
Exec. Director: John H. Skinner, Ph.D.
Manager, Meetings: Michele Nebel Peake
C.O.O.: Lori Swain
Historical Note
Formerly the Governmental Refuse Collection and Disposal Ass'n (1990). SWANA members are government solid waste agency managers and their suppliers, vendors and consultants. Membership: $113/year (public); $273/year (private).
Publications:
Municipal Solid Waste News. m. adv.
Proceedings. a.
SWANA Newsletter.
Meetings/Conferences:
Annual Meetings: Summer
1999 – Reno, NV/Oct. 18-21
2000 – Cincinnati, OH/Oct. 23-25

2001 – Baltimore, MD/Oct. 15-18
2002 – Long Beach, CA/Oct. 28-31

Swedish-American Chamber of Commerce *(1906)*
599 Lexington Ave., 12th Floor
New York, NY   10022
Tel: (212)838-5530   *Fax:* (212)755-7953
Web Site: http://www.siccny.org
Members: 1,800 individuals
Staff: 10
Annual Budget: $500-1,000,000
President: Lars Christofferson
Historical Note
The purposes of SACC are to advance/foster and expand harmonious commerce and trade between Sweden and the US. Membership: $150/year (individual); $3,000/year (organization).
Publications:
Membership Directory. a. adv.
Newsletter. m. adv.
Subsidiary Listing. a. adv.
Meetings/Conferences:
Semi-Annual Meetings: Spring in New York, NY and Summer in Sweden
1999 – New York, NY

Sweet Potato Council of the United States *(1961)*
P.O. Box 14
McHenry, MD   21541-0014
Tel: (301)387-9537
Members: 2,500 individuals
Staff: 2
Annual Budget: $10-25,000
Exec. Secretary: Harold H. Hoecker
Publications:
Cooking with Sweet Potatoes.
Meetings/Conferences:
Annual Meetings: January
1999 – Lafayette, LA(Arcadian)

Sweetener Users Ass'n
3231 Valley Lane
Falls Church, VA   22044-1740
Tel: (703)532-2683
Members: 20 companies
Staff: 2
President: Thomas A. Hammer
Historical Note
Founded as Sugar Users Group, assumed its current name in 1987. Members are industrial users of sweeteners, and companies and organizations in the sweetener industry.
Meetings/Conferences:

Swimming Pool Chemical Manufacturers Ass'n
Historical Note
Address unknown in 1995.

Swimming Pool Trades and Contractors Ass'n *(1974)*
1804 W. Burbank Blvd.
Burbank, CA   91506-1315
Tel: (818)845-7565   *Fax:* (818)843-7423
Annual Budget: under $10,000
Exec. Director: Cathey J. Newell, CMP
Historical Note
Membership: $240/year (company).
Publications:
The Tradesman. m. adv.

Swimming Teachers of America *(1992)*
776 21st Ave. North
St. Petersburg, FL   33704-3348
Tel: (813)896-7946   *Fax:* (813)896-3933
E-Mail: STA@shamrockgroup.com
Members: 200 individuals
Staff: 1
Annual Budget: $25-50,000
Exec. Director: Stephen W. Graves
Historical Note
Membership: $45/year.
Publications:
Professional Swim Teacher. m. adv.
Meetings/Conferences:

Swimwear Industry Manufacturers Ass'n
Historical Note
A division of the American Apparel Manufacturers Ass'n.

Synagogue Council of America *(1926)*
Historical Note
Address unknown in 1997.

Synthetic Amorphous Silica and Silicates Industry Ass'n *(1982)*
c/o W.R. Grace Co.
10 E. Baltimore St.
Baltimore, MD   21202
Tel: (410)659-9058
Members: 12 companies
Annual Budget: under $10,000
V. Chairman: Julian Convey
Historical Note
A group of chemical manufacturers making synthetic amorphous silicas silicates. These substances are used in paints, varnishes, toothpaste, rubber, paper, etc. SASSI addresses technical, health and safety matters connected to these products. Has no paid officers or permanent staff. Membership: $100/year. Officers change biennially.

Publications:
None.

Synthetic Organic Chemical Manufacturers Ass'n *(1921)*
1850 M St., N.W., Suite 700
Washington, DC   20036
Tel: (202)721-4100   *Fax:* (202)296-8120
Web Site: http://www.socma.com
Members: 300 companies
Staff: 45
Annual Budget: $5-10,000,000
President: Edmund Fording
Manager, Communications: Ed Armstrong
V. President, Public Affairs: Robert J. Grasso
Senior Manager, Meetings & Membership: Diane McMahon
Director, Finance and Administration: Diane Dickson
Manager, Office Services: Jenne Glass
Director, Ass'n Management Center: Jack Murray
Director, Affiliate Associations: Richard E. Opatick
Historical Note
Represents membership on legislative, regulatory and international trade issues; implements commercial programs to provide members with new opportunities to increase their sales. SOCMA provides administrative, technical, scientific and regulatory support for its affiliates including: Acrylonitrile Group; Alkyl Amines Council; Biphenyl Work Group, Chlorobenzene Producers Ass'n; Commercial Development Ass'n; Dibasic Esters Group; Institute for Polyacrylate Absorbents; Petroleum Product Stewardship Council; Phosphonates Task Force; Stilbene Whitening Agents, Tetrahydrofuran Task Force, Thermal Fluids Council; Tributyl Phosphate Task Force; and United States Operating Committee of the Ecological and Toxicological Ass'n of the Dyestuffs Manufacturing Industry (ETAD). Has an annual budget of approximately $12 million.
Publications:
Commercial Guide. a. adv.
Executive Briefing. m.
SOCMA Membership Directory. a.
SOCMA Newsletter. bi-w.
Meetings/Conferences:
Semi-Annual Meeting: December, in New York City, and Spring.
1999 – Scottsdale, AZ(Hyatt Regency)/May 2-5

System Independent Data Format Ass'n
3335 N. Arlington Heights Road, Suite E
Arlington Heights, IL   60004
Tel: (847)577-7200   *Fax:* (847)577-7276
E-Mail: SIDF@SIDF.ORG
Web Site: SIDF.ORG
Members: 100 individuals
Administrator: C. Andrew Larsen, CAE
Historical Note
SIDFA members are companies providing computer back-up hardware and software. Primary purpose is to promote a single accepted standard for back-up tape drives. Membership: $1,500/year (corporate); $500/year (affiliate).
Publications:
SIDF Format Standard. irreg.

System Safety Soc. *(1964)*
P.O. Box 70
Unionville, VA   22567
Tel: (540)854-8630   *Fax:* (540)854-4561
E-Mail: syssafe@ns.gemlink.com
Web Site: http://www.system-safety.org
Members: 900 individuals, 20 companies
Staff: 1
Annual Budget: $25-50,000
Administrative Secretary: Cathy Carter
Historical Note
Formerly (1966) the Aerospace System Safety Society. Emphasis is on methodology, development and application for hazard identification, elimination and control, through system safety engineering and management in products, systems and services. Membership: $65/year (individual); $300/year (corporate).
Publications:
Conference Proceedings. bien.
Hazard Prevention Journal. q. adv.
Meetings/Conferences:
Annual Meetings: Odd Years

Systems Builders Ass'n *(1968)*
P.O. Box 117
28 Lowry Drive
West Milton, OH   45383-0117
Tel: (513)698-4127   *Fax:* (513)698-6153
Toll Free: (800)866 - 6722
E-Mail: chrislong@wesnet.com
Members: 400 companies
Staff: 10
Annual Budget: $250-500,000
Exec. V. President: Christopher S. Long
Historical Note
Formerly (1984) the Metal Building Dealers Ass'n.
Meetings/Conferences:
Annual Meetings: Winter

Systems, Man and Cybernetics Soc.
Historical Note
A technical society of the Institute of Electrical and Electronics Engineers (IEEE). Membership in the Society, open only to IEEE members, includes a subscription to a technical periodical in the field published by IEEE. All administrative support provided by IEEE.

TAC - Internat'l Telework Ass'n
204 E St., N.E.

Washington, DC 20002
Tel: (202)547-6157 *Fax:* (202)546-3289
E-Mail: tac4dc@aol.com
Web Site: http://telecommut.org
Members: 1000 individuals
Staff: 2
Exec. Director: Gail Martin

Historical Note
Founded as Telecommuting Advisory Council; assumed its current naame in 1996.

Meetings/Conferences:

Tackle and Shooting Sports Agents Ass'n *(1953)*
1033 N. Fairfax St., Suite 200
Alexandria, VA 22314-1540
Tel: (703)519-9691 *Fax:* (703)519-1872
Members: 350 individuals, 70 companies
Staff: 2
Annual Budget: $25-50,000
Managing Director: Andy Martin

Historical Note
Formerly (1976) Sporting Industries Representatives, (1977) Tackle Representatives Ass'n and (1985) Tackle Representatives Ass'n Internat'l. Assumed its present name in December 1986. Membership: $275/year.

Publications:
TSSA Report. q.

Meetings/Conferences:
Annual Meetings: July

Tag and Label Manufacturers Institute *(1933)*
40 Shuman Blvd., Suite 295
Naperville, IL 60563
Tel: (630)357-9222 *Fax:* (630)357-0192
Members: 301 companies
Staff: 5
Annual Budget: $500-1,000,000
Exec. Director: Frank Sablone
Meeting Planner: Karen Johnson
Director of Membership & Information Services: Sheri Laury
Secretary: Lesley Petroshus

Historical Note
Formally organized in Cleveland on June 15, 1933 as the Tag Manufacturers Institute. In 1962 the Bylaws were revised to include converters of pressure sensitive labels, and the present name was adopted. The supplier (Associates) division was formed in 1966 and now consists of suppliers of label base stocks, presses and auxiliary equipment, plates, dies, inks, adhesvies, tag and label papers. International members accepted in 1975. Membership: $850-3,600/year (company).

Publications:
Directory.
Glossary of Pressure Sensitive Terms. irreg.
Illuminator. bi-m.
LABELEXPO Proceedings. a.
North American Label Study. bi-a.
Products Guide. a.

Meetings/Conferences:
Annual Meetings: Fall/300 and Winter Converter Meeting

TAG Internat'l *(1963)*
17W662 Butterfield Rd., Suite 303
Oak Brook Terrace, IL 60181-4006
Tel: (630)916-0300 *Fax:* (630)916-0868
E-Mail: tag@pyrotechnics.com
Web Site: http://www.tagintl.org
Members: 56 firms
Staff: 4
Annual Budget: $250-500,000
Exec. Director: Nancy R. Honeycutt
Member Services Coordinator: Kathleen Caswell

Historical Note
Formerly (1994) American Group of Certified Public Accounting Firms. Seeks to maintain and enhance the ability of member firms to serve clients on a national and international basis and to increase public awareness of those objectives. Members are certified public accounting firms.

Publications:
Directory. a.
Newsletter. semi-a.

Meetings/Conferences:
1999 – Miguel, CA(Ritz Carlton)/Nov. 7-10

Tamworth Swine Ass'n *(1923)*
200 Centenary Road
Winchester, OH 45697
Tel: (937)695-0114
Members: 150 individuals
Staff: 1
Annual Budget: under $10,000
Secretary-Treasurer: Thomas Fenton, Jr.

Historical Note
Breeders and fanciers of Tamworth swine.

Publications:
Tamworth News. a.

Meetings/Conferences:
Annual Meetings: September
1999 – Washington Courthouse, OH

Tau Epsilon Rho Law Soc. *(1920)*
36 Kresson Road, Suite E
Cherry Hill, NJ 08034
Tel: (609)429-3901 *Fax:* (609)429-4846
Members: 7,500 individuals
Exec. Director: Alan M. Tepper

Historical Note
A professional law society of judges, lawyers and law students throughout the country. Membership: $65/year (individual).

Publications:
Chancellor's Newsletter. 3-4/year.
Membership Directory. bien.
Summons. 2-3/year.

Meetings/Conferences:

Tax Executives Institute *(1944)*
1200 G St., N.W., Suite 300
Washington, DC 20005-3814
Tel: (202)638-5601 *Fax:* (202)638-5607
E-Mail: mmurphy@tei.org
Members: 5,000 individuals
Staff: 12
Annual Budget: $2-5,000,000
Exec. Director: Michael Murphy
Director, Conference Planning: Deborah K. Gaffney
Director, Administration: Deborah C. Giesey
General Counsel/Director of Tax Affairs: Timothy McCarmally
Membership Coordinator: Rhonda Warren
Publications Coordinator: Kurt Larrick

Historical Note
A professional organization of corporate tax executives. Membership is open to corporate officers and employees charged with administering their company's tax affairs. Membership: $200/year, plus $200 initiation fee.

Publications:
The Tax Executive. bi-m. adv.

Meetings/Conferences:
Annual Meetings: Fall/800

Tea Ass'n of the United States of America *(1899)*
420 Lexington Ave., Suite 825
New York, NY 10170-0002
Tel: (212)986-9415 *Fax:* (212)697-8658
Members: 116 companies
Staff: 3
Annual Budget: $250-500,000
President: Joseph P. Simrany
Convention Manager: Sheila Kavanagh
Office Administrator: Jean Singer

Historical Note
Membership fee varies, based on revenue.

Publications:
Tea World. 2/year.

Meetings/Conferences:
Annual Meetings: October
1999 – Orlando, FL(Hyatt Grand Cypress)/Oct. 10-13

Tea Council of the U.S.A. *(1950)*
420 Lexington Ave., Suite 825
New York, NY 10170
Tel: (212)986-6998 *Fax:* (212)697-8658
Members: 40 companies, 6 governments
Staff: 3
Annual Budget: $1-2,000,000
President: Joseph P. Simrany
Convention and Meeting Manager: Sheila Kavanagh
Office Administrator: Jean Singer

Historical Note
Seeks to increase the consumption of hot and iced tea.

Publications:
Newsletter. bi-m.
Tea World. semi-a.

Meetings/Conferences:
Annual Meetings: with Tea Ass'n of the U.S.A.
1999 – Orlando, FL(Hyatt Grand Cypress)/Oct. 10-13

Teachers of English to Speakers of Other Languages *(1966)*
1600 Cameron St., Suite 300
Alexandria, VA 22314-2715
Tel: (703)836-0774 *Fax:* (703)836-6447
E-Mail: tesol@tesol.edu
Web Site: http://www.tesol.edu
Members: 17,000 individuals, 2,200 institutions
Staff: 26
Annual Budget: $2-5,000,000
Exec. Director: Charles S. Amorosino, Jr., CAE
Director of Communications & Marketing: Helen Kornblum
Director of Conventions/Expos: John Ellison Loth
Director of Education Programs: Louis Leto
Dep. Exec. Director: Terry O'Donnell
Director of Finance & Administration: Mimi Pollow
Director of Membership: Pamela C. Williams

Historical Note
Promotes instruction and research in the teaching of English to speakers of other languages while respecting individuals' language rights. Membership: $42.25/year.

Publications:
TESOL Journal. q. adv.
TESOL Matters. bi-m.
TESOL Membership Directory. bi-a. adv.
TESOL Placement Bulletin. bi-m. adv.
TESOL Quarterly. q. adv.

Meetings/Conferences:
Annual Meetings: March-April
1999 – New York, NY(New York Hilton and Towers)/March 9-13

Teaching-Family Ass'n *(1976)*
910 Charles St.
Fredericksburg, VA 22401
Tel: (540)370-4439 *Fax:* (540)370-0015
Web Site: http://www.teaching-family.org
Members: 400 individuals, 30 agencies
Staff: 2
Annual Budget: $100-250,000
Exec. Director: Peggy McElgunn

Historical Note
Members are individuals providing family services to children in group home, treatment foster care, and home-based service settings. Formerly (1992) the Nat'l Teaching-Family Ass'n. Membership: $30/year (individual); $3,000/year (agency).

Publications:
Directory of the Teaching-Family Association. a.
Standards of Ethical Conduct.
Teaching-Family Newsletter. q.

Meetings/Conferences:

TechLaw Group *(1986)*
7625 W. Hutchinson Ave.
Pittsburgh, PA 15218-1248
Tel: (412)244-0670 *Fax:* (412)244-9916
E-Mail: lawhel@aol.com
Web Site: http://www.techlaw.org
Members: 15 firms
Staff: 2
Annual Budget: $100-250,000
Exec. Director: Lawrence A. Heller, Ph.D.

Historical Note
TechLaw is an international network of law firms which serve the interests of businesses, institutions, and individuals involved with technology iundustries. Member firms comprise over 2,000 lawyers.

Publications:
TechLaw Update. 3-4/year.

Meetings/Conferences:
1999 – Seattle, WA(Four Seasons Hotel)
1999 – Cambridge, MA(Hyatt Regency)/Nov. 6-8/100

Technical Ass'n of the Graphic Arts *(1948)*
68 Lomb Memorial Dr.
Rochester, NY 14623-5604
Tel: (716)475-7470 *Fax:* (716)475-2250
E-Mail: tagaofc@aol.com
Members: 1,300 individuals
Staff: 2
Annual Budget: $100-250,000
Managing Director: Karen E. Lawrence

Historical Note
Organized to advance the science and technology of the graphic arts. Membership: $85/year (individual); $ 1,000/year (organization/company). Other membership categories available for organizations, students and retirees.

Publications:
TAGA Newsletter. 4/year.
TAGA Proceedings. a.

Meetings/Conferences:
Annual Meetings: Spring/250
1999 – Vancouver, British Columbia(Westin Bayshore)/May 2-5/250

Technical Ass'n of the Pulp and Paper Industry *(1915)*
P.O. Box 105113,15 Technology Park South
Atlanta, GA 30348-5113
Tel: (770)446-1400 *Fax:* (770)446-6947
Toll Free: (800)332 - 8686
E-Mail: wgross@tappi.org
Web Site: http://www.TAPPI.ORG
Members: 34,000 individuals
Staff: 100
Annual Budget: $10-25,000,000
Exec. Director and Chief Operating Officer: Wayne H. Gross
Group Director, Event Management: S.M. Blevins, CAE
Group Director, Education/Marketing: Carnie M. Wall, CAE
Group Director, Finance & Administration: Jeffrey J. Petro, CAE
Publisher: Matthew J. Culeman, CAE

Historical Note
Organized in 1915 as a section of the American Paper and Pulp Ass'n. The articles of organization were revised at the first annual meeting in 1916 and the name was changed to the Technical Ass'n of the Pulp and Paper Industry. Today, members include those professionals who work in the pulp, paper, packaging, converting, and nonwovens industries. Has an annual budget of approximately $17 million. Membership: $75/year (individual), $500/year (organization/company).

Publications:
TAPPI Journal. m. adv.

Meetings/Conferences:
Annual Meetings: Spring
1999 – Atlanta, GA(GA World Congress Center)/March 1-3

Technical Ceramics Manufacturers Ass'n *(1978)*
25 N. Broadway
Tarrytown, NY 10591-3201
Tel: (914)332-0040 *Fax:* (914)332-1541
Members: 12 companies
Staff: 2
Annual Budget: $25-50,000
Exec. Director: Richard C. Byrne

Historical Note
Established through a merger of the Steatite Manufacturers Ass'n (founded in 1956) and the Dry Process Ceramic Manufacturers Ass'n. Formerly (1988) the Dry Process Ceramic and Steatite Manufacturers Ass'n. Members are makers of ceramics and steatite used in the manufacturer of various electronic products.

Meetings/Conferences:
Annual Meetings: Spring

Technical Engineers Ass'n *(1933)*
4701 North 76th St.
Milwaukee, WI 53218
Tel: (414)443-0123
Members: 200 individuals
President: Richard Duernberger

Historical Note
Independent labor union.

Technology and Information Management Education Soc.

4500 Hugh Howell Road, Suite 340
Tucker, GA 30084
Tel: (770)270-9611   *Fax:* (770)270-0632
Web Site: http://www.insight/net.org
Staff: 2
Exec. Director: J.W. Holderfield, CAE
Meetings/Conferences:

Technology Education for Children Council (1965)

Historical Note
Address unknown in 1995.

Technology Student Ass'n (1978)

1914 Association Drive
Reston, VA 20191-1540
Tel: (703)860-9000   *Fax:* (703)758-4852
Members: 155,000 individuals
Staff: 8
Annual Budget: $250-500,000
Exec. Director: Rosanne White
Program Manager: Donna Andrews

Historical Note
Formerly (1988) American Industrial Arts Student Ass'n. Members are students enrolled in technology education classes. Through its national competitive program, TSA offers students a chance to make a technological contribution to society. Membership: $5/year (students); $10/year (professional/adult); $10/year (alumni).

Publications:
The Advisor Update. bi-m.
The School Scene. 3/yr.
TSA Curricular Resource Guide. a.

Meetings/Conferences:
Annual Meetings: Summer
1999 – Tulsa, OK/June 24-28

Technology Transfer Soc. (1975)

435 N. Michigan Ave., Suite 1717
Chicago, IL 60611-4067
Tel: (312)644-0828   *Fax:* (312)644-8557
E-Mail: 102234,166@compuserve.com
Members: 800 individuals
Staff: 2
Annual Budget: $100-250,000
Exec. Director: Bruce R. Becker

Historical Note
An international organization created to disseminate methods, knowledge and opportunities within the technology transfer community. Multidisciplinary membership is composed of professionals involved in the commercialization of technology. Membership: $85/year (individual); $600/year (corporate); $300/year (institutional and small businesses).

Publications:
Annual Meeting Proceedings. a. adv.
Directory. a.
Journal of Technology Transfer. q. adv.
Metrics Summit/Other Symposia Proceedigns. a. adv.
T'Squared Newsletter. 9-12/yr. adv.

Meetings/Conferences:
Annual Meetings: June-July

TeleCommunications Ass'n

Historical Note
Became (1996) Information Technology and Telecommunications Ass'n.

Telecommunications Industry Ass'n (1988)

2500 Wilson Blvd., Suite 300
Arlington, VA 22201-3834
Tel: (703)907-7700   *Fax:* (703)907-7727
Web Site: http://www.tiaonline.org
Members: 625 companies
Staff: 58
Annual Budget: $5-10,000,000
President: Matthew J. Flanigan
Dir., Communications: Sharon Grace
Dir., Membership and Marketing: Maryann Lesso
V.P., Government Affairs: Grant Seiffert
V.P., Trade Shows/Marketing: Hank Wieland
Director, Trade Shows/Conferences: Cathy E. Tavarozzo
V.P., Standards and Technology: Dan Bart
V.P., Finance and Administration: Matthew Kranz
Controller: Anna Amselle
Director, Membership/Marketing: Maryann C. Lesso
V.P., Mobile Communications/Network Equipt.: Eric J. Schimmel
Director, Technical and Regulatory Affairs: Roberta Breden

Historical Note
Formerly (1988) the United States Telecommunications Suppliers Ass'n. Originally a part of the United States Independent Telephone Ass'n with which it is affiliated. TIA is a trade group of manufacturers, suppliers and support service organizations of the telecommunications industry. Has an annual budget of approximately $7.0 million.

Publications:
Industry Beat News Bulletin (fax). w.
Industry Pulse Newsletter. m.

Meetings/Conferences:

Telecommunications Resellers Ass'n (1992)

1730 K St., N.W., Suite 1201
Washington, DC 20006-3868
Tel: (202)835-9898   *Fax:* (202)835-9893
E-Mail: tra@resellers.org
Web Site: http://www.tra.org
Members: 700 companies
Staff: 7
Annual Budget: $2-5,000,000

Exec. Director: Ernest B. Kelly, III
Director, Communications: Julie S. Hill
Mgr., Conference Services: Amy McCarthy
Manager, Member Services: Sue Palladino

Historical Note
Formed as the result of the merger of the Telecommunications Marketing Ass'n and the Interexchange Resellers Ass'n. TRA represents companies involved in the resale of enhanced telecommunications services. Membership: $1500/year (company).

Publications:
Infotrack. m.

Meetings/Conferences:
1999 – Pasadena, CA(Ritz Carlton-Huntington Hotel)/Jan. 26-28
1999 – San Diego, CA(Marriott)/May 10-13
1999 – Toronto, Canada(Westin)/July 26-28
1999 – Dallas, TX(Adams Mark)/Nov. 1-4

Telecommuting Advisory Council

Historical Note
Became (1996) TAC - Internat'l Telework Ass'n.

Teleprofessional Managers Ass'n (1982)

1821 University Ave. West Suite S-156
St. Paul, MN 55104-2804
Tel: (651)853-9849   *Fax:* (651)854-1402
Members: 222 individuals
Staff: 2
Annual Budget: $25-50,000
Managing Director: Kris Finger

Historical Note
Established and incorporated in Minnesota, TMA was founded to promote professional standards, provide information and education, provide a sense of community, and represent the interests of the telemarketing profession. Members are professionals who manage Inbound or Outbound, Business-to-Business or Business-to-Consumer telephone operations. TMA members have the opportunity to exchange information, ideas and experiences while gaining valuable contacts with other telemarketing professionals. Awards the CTR (Certified Telemarketing Representative) designation upon successful completion of course work and an examiniation. Membership: $95/year (individual); $295/year (corporate); $195/year (department); $35/year (student).

Publications:
Member Meeting Flyers. September-June.
TMA Directory. a. adv.
TMA Newsletter. bi-m. adv.

Meetings/Conferences:
Annual Meetings: October
1999 – Fall

Television Bureau of Advertising (1955)

850 Third Ave., 10th Floor
New York, NY 10022
Tel: (212)486-1111   *Fax:* (212)935-5631
Web Site: http://www.tvb.org
Members: 450 television stations
Staff: 25
Annual Budget: $5-10,000,000
President: Ave Butensky
President, Marketing Communications: Gary Belis
V President, Corporate Planning: Joseph Tirinato
V. President, Research: Harold Simpson
Manager, Corporate Planning: Janice Garjian

Historical Note
The Television Bureau of Advertising represents broadcast television stations to the advertising community. Its goal is to develop and increase advertiser dollars to U.S. Spot Television.

Meetings/Conferences:
1999 – Las Vegas, NV/Apr. 18-21(with Nat'l Ass'n of Broadcasters)

Television Critics Ass'n (1978)

Historical Note
Organization defunct in 1997.

Television Operators Caucus (1984)

600 New Hampshire Ave., N.W., 6th Floor
Washington, DC 20037
Tel: (202)944-5109   *Fax:* (202)944-1970
Coordinator: Mary Jo Manning

Historical Note
Caucus members are C.E.O.'s of television station groups.

Tennessee Walking Horse Breeders and Exhibitors Ass'n (1935)

Box 286
Lewisburg, TN 37091
Tel: (931)359-1574   *Fax:* (931)359-2539
Toll Free: (800)359 - 1574
E-Mail: twhbea@twhbea.com
Web Site: http://www.twhbea.com
Members: 20,000 individuals
Staff: 26
Annual Budget: $2-5,000,000
Exec. Director: Bob Cherry
Secretary/Treasurer: Sharon Brandon
Editor, Voice Magazine: P.J. Wamble

Historical Note
Members are owners and breeders of the Tennessee Walking horse. Formerly the Tennessee Walking Horse Breeders Ass'n of America (1974). Membership: $30/year.

Publications:
Breedjournal, Voice of the Tennessee Walking Horse. m. adv.

Meetings/Conferences:
Semi-annual Meetings: Lewisburg, TN/fourth Saturday in May and Nashville, TN/first Saturday in December

Tennis Industry Ass'n (1981)

200 Castlewood Drive
North Palm Beach, FL 33408
Tel: (561)848-1026   *Fax:* (561)863-8984
E-Mail: bptia@aol.com
Web Site: http://www.sportlink.com
Members: 130 companies
Staff: 6
Annual Budget: $2-5,000,000
President: Kurt Kamperman
Exec. Director: Brad Patterson

Historical Note
TIA was established in 1974 as the American Tennis Industry. In 1993 the name was changed to the Tennis Industry Association to better reflect the global interests of the membership. It is a non-profit association of approximately 130 companies and organizations that provide tennis equipment, apparel, footwear, services and information. Its primary objective is to encourage recreational tennis participation. Membership: $400-8,000, based on sales volume.

Publications:
Net Friends News. bi-m.

Meetings/Conferences:
Annual Meetings: Semi-Annual Meetings
1999 – Atlanta, GA(Georgia World Congress Center)/400

Teratology Soc. (1961)

1767 Business Center Drive, Suite 302
Reston, VA 20190-5332
Tel: (703)438-3101   *Fax:* (703)438-3113
Members: 750 individuals
Contact: Matt Rineer

Historical Note
Incorporated in the State of Ohio in 1961. The society is composed of professionals having a common interest in the research, prevention and treatment of birth defects.

Meetings/Conferences:

Tetrahydrofuran Task Force (1991)

1850 M St., N.W., Suite 700
Washington, DC 20036
Tel: (202)721-4160   *Fax:* (202)296-8120
E-Mail: THF@socma.com
Staff: 2
Annual Budget: $250-500,000
Exec. Director: Richard E. Opatick, CAE

Historical Note
An affiliate of the Synthetic Organic Chemical Manufacturers Ass'n.

Texas Longhorn Breeders Ass'n of America (1964)

2315 North Main St., Suite 402
Fort Worth, TX 76106
Tel: (817)625-6241   *Fax:* (817)625-1388
E-Mail: tlbaa@tlbaa.org
Web Site: http://www.tlbaa.org
Members: 4,600 individuals
Staff: 10
Annual Budget: $500-1,000,000
Exec. Director: Don L. King
Administrative Coordinator: SuzAnn Spindor

Historical Note
Founded in Lawton, OK to serve as the breed registry and to preserve the Texas Longhorn through promotion, education and research. Its members are breeders and fanciers of Texas Longhorn beef cattle. Member of the Nat'l Pedigree Livestock Council, Nat'l Cattlemen's Ass'n, and U.S. Beef Breeds Council. Membership: $50/year.

Publications:
Texas Longhorn Trails. m. adv.

Meetings/Conferences:
Annual Meetings: Fall

Texas Produce Export Ass'n (1980)

901 Business Park Dr., Suite 500
Mission, TX 78572
Tel: (956)581-8632   *Fax:* (956)581-3912
Members: 15 companies
Staff: 2
Annual Budget: $50-100,000
Exec. V. President: William E. Weeks

Historical Note
A Webb-Pomerene Act association. TPEA is the international exports marketing arm of the Texas Produce Ass'n (same address). Membership: $150/year (individual).

Text and Academic Authors Ass'n (1987)

University of South Florida
140 7th Ave. South
St. Petersburg, FL 33701
Tel: (727)553-1195   *Fax:* (727)553-3122
E-Mail: taa@bayflash.stpt.usf.edu
Web Site: http://www.winonanet.com/taa
Members: 700 individuals
Staff: 3
Annual Budget: $50-100,000
Program Assistant: Janet Tucker

Historical Note
Formerly (1993) Textbook Authors Ass'n. TAA members are creators of academic intellectual property at all levels. Primarily concerned with the improvement of performance and compensation. Membership: $60/year (full member); $30/year (first-year member); $15/year (student).

Publications:
The Academic Author. m. adv.

Meetings/Conferences:
1999 – Park City, UT(Shadow Ridge Resort)/June 24-25

Textile Bag and Packaging Ass'n *(1934)*
322 Davis Ave.
Dayton, OH   45401
Tel: (937)476-8272   *Fax:* (937)258-0029
Members: 175 companies
Staff: 1
Annual Budget: $50-100,000
Secretary: Susan Spiegel

Historical Note
Formerly (1968) Nat'l Burlap Bag Dealers Ass'n and (1984) Textile Bag Processors Ass'n; assumed its present name in 1985. Members are manufacturers and distributors of textile bags and packaging supplies. Membership: $400/year.

Publications:
Roster. bien. adv.
The Grab Bag. semi-a. adv.

Meetings/Conferences:
Annual Meetings: Semi Annual. Spring and Winter Winter
1999 – Amelia Island, FL
1999 – Washington, DC

Textile Bag Manufacturers Ass'n *(1925)*
P.O. Box 286
Harrison, OH   45030
Tel: (812)637-0445   *Fax:* (812)637-0445
E-Mail: Kingbag@one.net
Members: 40 companies
Staff: 2
Annual Budget: $10-25,000
Exec. V. President: Connie McCuan-Kirsch

Historical Note
TBMA members consist of makers of polypropylene bags, cotton bags, burlaps bags and a variety of sewn products. Membership:$200-400/year.

Meetings/Conferences:
1999 – Washington, DC(Ritz Carlton)/Oct. 13-16
2000 – Tucson, AZ(Sheraton El Conquistor)/March 11-18

Textile Care Allied Trades Ass'n *(1920)*
271 Rte. 46 West, Suite 203-D
Fairfield, NJ   07004
Tel: (973)244-1790   *Fax:* (973)244-4455
E-Mail: tcata@ix.netcom.com
Members: 300 companies
Staff: 2
Annual Budget: $250-500,000
Exec. Director: David Cotter

Historical Note
Absorbed the Nat'l Laundry Allied Trades Ass'n and the Laundry and Dry Cleaners Machinery Manufacturers Ass'n. Formerly (until 1982) the Laundry and Cleaners Allied Trades Ass'n. Members are manufacturers and distributors of commercial laundry and dry cleaning machinery, equipment and supplies.

Publications:
Allied Activities. q.

Meetings/Conferences:
1999 – Quebec City, Quebec(Chateau
     Frontenac)/Aug. 11-14/220
2000 – Ponte Vedre Beach, FL(Marriott
     Sawgrass)/May 2-7/220

Textile Converters Ass'n *(1958)*
575 Lexington Ave., 19th Floor
New York, NY   10022-6102
Tel: (212)754-3100   *Fax:* (212)371-2980
Members: 34 companies
Staff: 1
Annual Budget: $10-25,000
Exec. Director: Sidney Orenstein

Textile Distributors Ass'n *(1938)*
104 W. 40th St., 18th Floor
New York, NY   10018
Tel: (212)869-6300   *Fax:* (212)869-2346
Members: 160 companies
Staff: 4
Annual Budget: $250-500,000
Exec. Director: Bruce F. Roberts

Historical Note
Converters and distributors of fabrics selling primarily to apparel manufacturers and over-the-counter trade. Formerly Textile Distributors Institute and (1965) Textile Fabric Distributors Ass'n. Provides administrative support to the American Printed Fabrics Council, formed to promote printed fabrics.

Publications:
Newsletter. q.

Meetings/Conferences:
Annual Meetings: Spring, in the Poconos

Textile Fibers and By-Products Ass'n *(1931)*
P.O. Box 550326
Atlanta, GA   30355-2826
Tel: (404)262-2477   *Fax:* (404)261-0628
Web Site: http://www.tfbpa.org
Members: 166 individuals, 52 companies
Staff: 2
Annual Budget: $25-50,000
Exec. Secretary: John Coleman

Historical Note
Formerly (1966) Textile Waste Ass'n.

Publications:
General Communique. 16/year.

Meetings/Conferences:
Semi-Annual Meetings: Spring and Fall

Textile Information Users Council *(1969)*

Historical Note
TIUC declined to provide updated information for this edition.

Textile Laundry Council *(1962)*

Historical Note
Formerly Product Promotion Programs, Inc., TLC consists of a loosely organized group of individual diaper services which meet together periodically to exchange information on common problems. Membership: $1,200/year (company).

Textile Processors, Service Trades, Health Care, Professional and Technical Employees Internat'l Union *(1898)*
303 E. Wacker Drive, Suite 1109
Chicago, IL   60601
Tel: (312)946-0450   *Fax:* (312)946-0453
Members: 28,500 individuals
Staff: 6
Annual Budget: $250-500,000
General President: Frank A. Scalish

Historical Note
Organized in Troy, New York and chartered by the American Federation of Labor in 1900 as the Shirt, Waist and Laundry Workers Internat'l Union. Renamed the Laundry Workers Internat'l Union in 1909, it merged in 1956 with the Internat'l Ass'n of Cleaning and Dye House Workers to form the Laundry, Dry Cleaning and Dye House Workers' Internat'l Union; assumed its present name in 1980. Expelled for alleged corruption from the AFL-CIO in Dec., 1957, it entered into an affiliate agreement with the Internat'l Brotherhood of Teamsters in 1962 and ended the affiliate agreement in December 1994.

Publications:
The Reporter. a.

Meetings/Conferences:
Annual Meetings: Every 5 years in Spring

Textile Producers and Suppliers Ass'n
437 Madison Ave., 35th Floor
New York, NY   10022-7302
Tel: (212)907-7300   *Fax:* (212)754-0330
Members: 25 individuals
Annual Budget: $100-250,000
Counsel: Richard S. Taffet

Historical Note
TPSA was formed to address the problem of unauthorized copying of textile and decorative home furnishing designs in international markets.

Meetings/Conferences:
1999 – New York, NY

Textile Quality Control Ass'n *(1951)*
113 Hickory Leaf Ct.
Roxboro, NC   27573-5896
Members: 185 individuals
Staff: 1
Annual Budget: $10-25,000
Administrator: Renee W. Martin

Historical Note
Membership: $35/year.

Meetings/Conferences:
Semi-Annual Meetings: Spring/Charlotte, NC and Fall/various
     locations

Textile Rental Services Ass'n of America *(1913)*
P.O. Box 1283
1130 E. Beach. Blvd., Suite B
Hallandale, FL   33008-1283
Tel: (954)457-7555   *Fax:* (954)457-3890
Toll Free: (800)868 - 8772
Web Site: htyp://www.trsa.org
Members: 1,500 companies
Staff: 23
Annual Budget: $2-5,000,000
Exec. Director: John J. Contney, CAE
Manager, Marketing: Peter Corr
Manager, Adminstration and Meetings: Leslie Melvin, CMP, CAE
Manager, Production Operations: William Hoyt
Traffic Manager: Debra Dean
Manager, Membership and Strategic Management: Wayne Murphy
Exec. Editor: John Massey
Art Director: Candi Pillitteri
Advertising Manager: Steven Feldman

Historical Note
Members are textile rental service companies which provide uniform, linen and towel rental services to business and industry. Associate members are manufacturers, distributors and suppliers. Formerly (until 1979) known as the Linen Supply Ass'n of America. Sponsors and supports the Textile Rental Services Ass'n Political Action Committee.

Publications:
Roster and Buyers' Guide. a. adv.
Textile Rental. m. adv.
TRSA Confidential Facts.
TRSA Insider.

Meetings/Conferences:
Annual Meetings: Spring or Summer/350
1999 – Orlando, FL(Peabody Hotel)

Textured Yarn Ass'n of America *(1971)*
P.O. Box 66
Gastonia, NC   28053
Tel: (704)824-3522   *Fax:* (704)824-0630
Members: 300 individuals, 350 companies
Annual Budget: $100-250,000
Exec. Secretary: Jerry King

Historical Note
Members are individuals concerned with all aspects of production of man-made fibers. Membership: $60/year (individual).

Publications:
Newsletter. q.
Proceedings. semi-a.

Meetings/Conferences:
Semi-annual Meetings: February and July
1999 – Myrtle Beach, SC

Thai Chamber of Commerce, U.S.A. *(1991)*

Historical Note
Address unknown in 1997.

Theatre Education Ass'n *(1988)*
2343 Auburn Pkwy.
Cincinnati, OH   45219-2819
Tel: (513)421-3900   *Fax:* (513)421-7077
Members: 1000 individuals, 2,500 schools
Staff: 20
Annual Budget: $1-2,000,000
Exec. Director: Ronald L. Longstreth

Historical Note
The Theatre Education Ass'n is the professional component of the Educational Theatre Ass'n founded to advance quality theatre on the high school level. Membership: $65/year (adults); $16/year (students) plus school fee of $35.00.

Publications:
Dramatics Maagazine. 9/yr. adv.
Teaching Theatre. q.

Meetings/Conferences:
1999 – Chicago, IL(Holiday Inn Mart Plaza)July

Theatre Equipment Ass'n *(1971)*

Historical Note
Became the Internat'l Theatre Equipment Ass'n in 1996.

Theatre Library Ass'n *(1937)*
c/o Shubert Archive
149 W. 45th St.
New York, NY   10036
Tel: (212)944-3895   *Fax:* (212)944-4139
Members: 250 individuals, 250 institutions
Annual Budget: $10-25,000
Exec. Secretary: Maryann Chach

Historical Note
An affiliate of the American Library Ass'n and the Internat'l Federation for Theatre Research. Membership: $30/year (salaried individuals and institutions); $20/year (non-salaried individuals).

Publications:
Broadside. q.
Performing Arts Resources. a.

Meetings/Conferences:
Semi-Annual Meetings: Summer with ALA/100 and Fall with
     ASTR/200

Theatre Management Exchange

Historical Note
A focus group of the Ass'n for Theatre in Higher Education.

Therapeutic Communities of America *(1975)*
1611 Connecticut Ave., N.W., Suite 4-B
Washington, DC   20009
Tel: (202)296-3503   *Fax:* (202)518-5475
Members: 400 programs
Exec. Director: Linda R. Wolf Jones, DSW

Historical Note
TCA members are treatment and rehabilitation programs that emphasize wholistic, self-help intensive approaches to substance abuse.

Publications:
Legislative Update. irreg.
Newsletter. bi-m.
Proceedings.

Thermal Fluids Council

Historical Note
An affiliate of the Synthetic Organic Chemicals Manufacturers Ass'n which provides administrative support.

Thermoforming Institute

Historical Note
A division of Soc. of the Plastics Industry, which provides administrative support.

Theta Tau *(1904)*
655 Craig Rd., Suite 128
St. Louis, MO   63141-7168
Tel. (314)994-1904   *Fax:* (314)997-3234
Toll Free: (800)264 - 1904
E-Mail: Central@RTheTatau.org
Web Site: http://www.thetatau.org
Members: 27,500 individuals
Staff: 3
Annual Budget: $100-250,000
Exec. Director: Michael T. Abraham

Historical Note
A professional fraternity in engineering. Founded at the Univ. of Minnesota. Purpose of the fraternity is to develop and maintain a high standard of professional interest among its members, and to unite them in a strong bond of fraternal fellowship.

Publications:
Executive Council Bulletin. 6/yr.
Gear of Theta Tau. semi-a.
Membership Directory. quinq.

Meetings/Conferences:
Annual Meetings: mid-August

Thoroughbred Club of America *(1932)*
Box 8098

Lexington, KY 40533
Tel: (606)254-4282 *Fax:* (606)231-6131
Members: 1,500 individuals
Staff: 6
Annual Budget: $50-100,000
Director and Asst. Secretary-Treasurer: Cherie Little

Historical Note
Founded as the Thoroughbred Club in 1932; name was changed to its present form the following year. Although most members live in Kentucky, the membership represents all branches of the Thoroughbred industry and comes from all parts of the U.S., Europe and Canada.

Publications:
Membership Roster. a.

Thoroughbred Owners and Breeders Ass'n *(1961)*
P.O. Box 4367
Lexington, KY 40544
Tel: (606)276-2291 *Fax:* (606)276-2462
E-Mail: couto@lex.infi.net
Web Site: http://www.toba.org
Members: 3,160 individuals
Staff: 11
Annual Budget: $1-2,000,000
President: Drew J. Couto

Historical Note
Members include individual owners, breeders, trainers, jockeys, veterinarians, as well as twenty state breeders' organizations. TOBA strives to keep members informed of health regulations, research developments, and legislation affecting the industry and serves as a representative for U.S. breeders at annual international meetings. Membership: $225/year.

Publications:
Blood-Horse. w. adv.

Meetings/Conferences:
Annual Meetings: usually Saratoga Springs, NY/August

Thoroughbred Racing Ass'ns of North America *(1942)*
420 Fair Hill Drive, Suite 1
Elkton, MD 21921-2573
Tel: (410)392-9200 *Fax:* (410)398-1366
E-Mail: traoffice@dpnet.net
Members: 50 racing associations
Staff: 5
Annual Budget: $500-1,000,000
Exec. V. President: Christopher N. Scherf
Executive Assistant: Margie Pollard

Historical Note
Supports the Thoroughbred Racing Protective Bureau. Formerly (1977) the Thoroughbred Racing Ass'ns of the U.S., Inc.

Publications:
National Directory of Stakes Events. q. adv.
Newsletter. m.
TRA Directory & Record Book. a.

Meetings/Conferences:
Annual Meetings: February
1999 – Miami, FL

Tile Contractors' Ass'n of America *(1904)*
11501 Georgia Ave., Suite 203
Wheaton, MD 20902
Tel: (301)949-5995 *Fax:* (301)949-8373
Members: 150 companies
Staff: 2
Annual Budget: $100-250,000
Exec. Director: Helen Walsh

Historical Note
Sub-contractors engaged in installing ceramic tile. Formerly (1936) Tile and Mantle Contractors Ass'n of America.

Meetings/Conferences:
Annual Meetings: Fall

Tile Council of America *(1945)*
100 Clemson Research Blvd.
Anderson, SC 29625
Tel: (864)646-8453 *Fax:* (864)646-2821
E-Mail: tcalink@carol.net
Web Site: http://tileusa.com
Members: 84 companies
Staff: 7
Annual Budget: $1-2,000,000
Exec. Director: Robert E. Daniels

Historical Note
Manufacturers and suppliers of ceramic wall and floor tiles.

Publications:
Handbook for Ceramic Tile. a.

Meetings/Conferences:
Three Annual Meetings: Spring, Fall, and Winter

Tile, Marble, Terrazzo, Finishers, Shopworkers and Granite Cutters Internat'l Union *(1901)*
101 Constitution Ave., N.W., Room 321
Washington, DC 20001
Tel: (202)546-6206 *Fax:* (202)543-5724
Members: 9,000 individuals
Staff: 4
Annual Budget: $25-50,000
V. President: Douglas J. Baines

Historical Note
Organized in New York in 1901 and chartered by the American Federation of Labor in 1902 as the Internat'l Union of Marble Workers. Became the Internat'l Ass'n of Marble, Stone and Slate Polishers, Rubbers and Sawyers in 1917 and, after name changes resulting from changing jurisdictions too numerous to itemize, assumed its present name in 1980. Became a division of United Brotherhood of Carpenters and Joiners of America in 1989.

Meetings/Conferences:
Quinquennial Meetings: (1996)

Tillage Equipment Council
Historical Note
A council of the Equipment Manufacturers Institute.

Tilt-up Concrete Ass'n *(1986)*
P.O. Box 204
Mount Vernon, IA 52314-0204
Tel: (319)895-6911 *Fax:* (319)895-8830
E-Mail: esauter@tilt-up.org
Web Site: http://www.tilt-up.org
Members: 85 individuals, 300 companies
Staff: 3
Annual Budget: $100-250,000
Exec. Director: J. Edward Sauter
Business Manager: K.R. Steveley

Historical Note
Incorporated in Illinois, TCA represents builders, engineers and suppliers involved with tilt-up concrete construction. Membership: $150/year (individual); $250/year (firm); $450/year (contractor); $250 or 675/year (supplier).

Publications:
Tilt-Up Newsletter. q.

Meetings/Conferences:
Annual Meetings: January or February
1999 – Las Vegas, NV

Timber Frame Business Council *(1995)*
P.O. Box B1161
Hanover, NH 03755-5311
Exec. Director: Cynthia J. Gardstein

Historical Note
TFBC advances the business, communications and research interests of companies engaged in the timber framing industry.

Timber Framers Guild of North America *(1985)*
P.O. Box 1075
Bellingham, WA 98227
Tel: (360)733-4001 *Fax:* (360)733-4002
E-Mail: tfguild@telcomplus.net
Web Site: http://www.tfguild.org
Members: 1,100 individualscompanies
Staff: 1
Annual Budget: $100-250,000
Secretary: Sharon Grier

Historical Note
Guild members are individuals actively involved in designing and building timber frames; architects, designers and other building professionals; suppliers of tools and materials to the timber frame trade; owner-builders; timber frame owners and others with an interest in the craft. Membership: $60/year (individual).

Publications:
Scantlings Newsletter. 8/yr.
Timber Framing Journal. q.

Meetings/Conferences:

Timber Products Manufacturers *(1916)*
951 East Third Ave.
Spokane, WA 99202
Tel: (509)535-4646 *Fax:* (509)534-6106
E-Mail: tpm@tpmrs.com
Web Site: http://www.tpmrs.com
Members: 235 companies
Staff: 9
Annual Budget: $500-1,000,000
General Manager: Larry Carroll

Historical Note
Established as the Timber Products Manufacturers Ass'n, it assumed its present name in 1969. It was established to improve, promote and advance the Timber Industry; serves members throughout the Northwest and Intermountain area.

Publications:
Feature Member.
Frontline.
T. P.

Meetings/Conferences:
Annual Meetings: Summer
1999 – Coeur d'Alene, ID/June 23-25

Tire and Rim Ass'n *(1903)*
175 Montrose West Ave.
Copley, OH 44321
Tel: (216)666-8121 *Fax:* (216)666-8340
E-Mail: TireandRim@aol.com
Members: 110 companies
Staff: 2
Annual Budget: $250-500,000
Exec. V. President: J.F. Pacuit

Historical Note
The technical standardizing body for tire, rim and valve manufacturers.

Publications:
Engineering Design Information for Ground Vehicle Tires and Rims. q.
Year Book. a.

Meetings/Conferences:
Quarterly Meetings: various locations

Tire Ass'n of North America *(1921)*
11921 Freedom Dr., Suite 550
Reston, VA 20190-5608
Tel: (703)736-8082 *Fax:* (703)904-4339
Toll Free: (800)876 - 8372
E-Mail: dpoisson@gte.net
Web Site: http://www.tana.net
Members: 5,000 companies
Staff: 6
Annual Budget: $2-5,000,000
Exec. V. President: David E. Poisson

Director Finance/Admin.: Diane B. Case
Director, Technical Services: John Buettner

Historical Note
Formerly Nat'l Ass'n of Independent Tire Dealers. Absorbed the Tire Retreading Institute in 1978 and became Nat'l Tire Dealers and Retreaders Ass'n. Assumed its current name in 1997.

Publications:
CINTAS Unifax. w.
Tire Retailing Today. m. adv.

Meetings/Conferences:
Annual Meetings: Fall

Tire Industry Safety Council *(1969)*
1400 K St. N.W.
Washington, DC 20005
Tel: (202)783-1022 *Fax:* (202)783-3512
Web Site: www.tisc.org
Members: 11 companies
Staff: 1
Annual Budget: $100-250,000
Director: Kristen Udowitz

Historical Note
The Council's primary purpose is to disseminate information concerning tire care and safety to consumers. Affiliated with the Rubber Manufacturers Ass'n, the President of which is Chairman of the Council. Members are tire manufacturers.

Publications:
Motorist's Tire Care and Safety Guide. irreg.

Meetings/Conferences:
Annual Meetings: Not held

Tire Retread Information Bureau *(1974)*
900 Weldon Grove
Pacific Grove, CA 93950
Tel: (831)372-1917 *Fax:* (831)372-9210
Toll Free: (888)473 - 8732
E-Mail: retreads@aol.com
Web Site: http://www.retread.org
Members: 275 companies
Staff: 2
Annual Budget: $100-250,000
Managing Director: Harvey Brodsky

Historical Note
A non-profit organization which serves as the public relations arm of the retread industry. Gathers and disseminates information on retread passenger and truck tires to members and the general public. TRIB is not a lobbying organization. Receives logistical support from industry associations, suppliers, retreaders, and new tire manufacturers. Membership: $100/year (individual); $250/year (company).

Publications:
The Voice of Retreading. q.

Titanium Development Ass'n
Historical Note
Became (1995) Internat'l Titanium Ass'n.

Tobacco Ass'n of the U.S. *(1900)*
3716 National Drive, Suite 114
Raleigh, NC 27612
Tel: (919)782-5151 *Fax:* (919)781-0915
Members: 55 companies
Staff: 2
Annual Budget: $100-250,000
Exec. V. President: J.T. Bunn

Historical Note
Affiliated with Leaf Tobacco Exporters Ass'n.

Meetings/Conferences:
Annual Meetings: May, at the Greenbrier in White Sulphur Springs, WV/500.

Tobacco Associates *(1947)*
1725 K St., N.W., Suite 512
Washington, DC 20006
Tel: (202)828-9144 *Fax:* (202)828-9149
Members: 125,000 individuals
Staff: 6
Annual Budget: $1-2,000,000
President: Kirk Wayne

Historical Note
Promotes flue-cured tobacco.

Meetings/Conferences:
Annual Meetings: Raleigh, NC/early March
1999 – Raleigh, NC/500
2000 – Raleigh, NC/500
2001 – Raleigh, NC/500
2002 – Raleigh, NC/500

Tobacco Growers' Information Committee *(1958)*
Historical Note
Membership consists of tobacco growers' organizations and other leaf groups and not individual farmers. Represents the nation's tobacco growers on public policy issues, including creating better public understanding of economic contribution of tobacco, the smoking and health controversy, punitive legislation and taxation of tobacco.

Tobacco Industry Labor/Management Committee *(1984)*
10401 Connecticut Ave.
Kensington, MD 20895
Tel: (301)933-8600 *Fax:* (301)946-8452
Members: 6 organizations
Exec. Officer: Robert Curtis

Historical Note
Promotes cooperation between the tobacco industry and the labor unions that represent tobacco industry workers.

Tobacco Institute *(1958)*
1875 I St., N.W., Suite 800
Washington, DC 20006
Tel: (202)457-4800   *Fax:* (202)457-9350
Members: 10 companies
Staff: 60
President: Samuel D. Chilcote, Jr.
Senior V. President, Federal Relations: Scott Wilson
Senior V. President, Public Affairs: Walter Woodson
Sr. V.P., State Activities: Patrick Donoho
Sr. V.P., Finance/Administration: William A. Adams

Historical Note
Created in 1958 by a group of cigarette manufacturers to foster public understanding of the smoking and health controversy and to increase awareness of the historic role of tobacco and its place in the national economy. Sponsors and supports the Tobacco Institute Political Action Committee.

Publications:
Tax Burden on Tobacco. a.
Tobacco Industry Profile. a.

Meetings/Conferences:
Annual Meetings: New York City, in December

Tobacco Merchants Ass'n of the U.S. *(1915)*
P.O. Box 8019, 231 Clarksville Road
Princeton, NJ 08543-8019
Tel: (609)275-4900   *Fax:* (609)275-8379
Members: 150 companies
Staff: 14
Annual Budget: $1-2,000,000
President: Farrell Delman
Mgr., Marketing and Finance: Roberta Crosby
Director, Global Affairs: James F. Vari
V. President: Darryl Jayson

Historical Note
Founded in 1915, the Tobacco Merchants Ass'n was created to manage information of vital interest to the tobacco industry. The TMA continues to function as a trade association and remains dedicated to supplying fact-based information about the tobacco industry. The TMA's information is maintained through a computerized data base and is disseminated to a variety of interested groups, including the media. The TMA is supported by tobacco product manufacturers, industry suppliers, financial institutions, international leaf dealers, distributors and retailers all over the world. Membership fee dependent upon size and type of company.

Publications:
Cigarette Brands Directory. a.
Current Issues In Tobacco Economics. bi-a.
Executive Summary. w.
International Tobacco Guide.
Issues Monitor. q.
Leaf Bulletin. bi-w.
Legislative Bulletin. bi-w.
Special Reports. bi-m.
Tobacco Barometer (Smoking/Chewing/Snuff). q.
Tobacco Barometers. m.
Tobacco Tax Guide. q.
Tobacco Trade Barometers(Import/Export)(6 parts). m.
Tobacco USA.
Tobacco Weekly. w.
Trademark Report. m.
World Alert. w.

Meetings/Conferences:

Tobacconists' Ass'n of America *(1968)*
c/o Briar and Bean
Eastland Mall, Suite 121
Evansville, IN 47715
Tel: (812)479-8070   *Fax:* (812)479-5939
Members: 100 companies
Staff: 1
Annual Budget: under $10,000
Managing Director: Ted Clark

Historical Note
Members are quality retail tobacco dealers representing outlets throughout the U.S.

Publications:
TAA Catalog. a.

Meetings/Conferences:

Tooling Component Manufacturers Ass'n *(1958)*
5001 W. Florida Ave., Suite 779
Hemet, CA 92545
Tel: (909)766-7443
Members: 8 companies
Staff: 1
Annual Budget: under $10,000
Exec. Secretary: Ray Fuhrer

Historical Note
Founded as the Nat'l Institute of Jig and Fixture Component Manufacturers and incorporated in Michigan, it assumed its present name in 1981. Its members, most of whom are in the Midwest, are united primarily for the purpose oif coordinating and standardizing sizes. Has no paid staff.

Publications:
TCMA Newsletter. m.

Meetings/Conferences:
Semi-annual Meetings: February and October

Tortilla Industry Ass'n *(1990)*
8300 Douglas Ave., Suite 800
Dallas, TX 75225
Tel: (214)706-9193   *Fax:* (214)706-9194
E-Mail: TIA_TSC@msn.com
Web Site: http://www.Tortilla-info.com
Members: 154 companies
Staff: 2

Annual Budget: $500-1,000,000
Exec. Director: Irwin Steinberg

Historical Note
Members are manufacturers of tortillas. Affiliate members are industry suppliers. Membership: $500-2,000/year (depending on size or type).

Publications:
Tortilla Industry News. q. adv.

Meetings/Conferences:
Annual Meetings: September-October/800-1,000
1999 – Anaheim, CA(Disneyland Hotel)/Sept. 14-16

Tourist House Ass'n of America *(1975)*
R.D. 1, Box 12-A
Greentown, PA 18426
Tel: (717)676-3222   *Fax:* (717)676-3222
Toll Free: (888)888 - 4068
Web Site: http://bandb/999.com
Members: 950 individuals, 70 B&B reservation services
Staff: 2
Annual Budget: $10-25,000
Contact: Peggy Ackerman

Historical Note
Membership: $40/year.

Tourist Railway Ass'n *(1972)*
P.O. Box 1022
Madison, WI 53701-0010
Tel: (608)273-3470   *Fax:* (608)271-4339
Toll Free: (800)678 - 7246
Web Site: http://www.train.org
Members: 350 organizations
Staff: 1
Annual Budget: $25-50,000
Exec. Director: Steve Brist

Historical Note
TRAIN members are railway museums, tourist railroads, product suppliers, railroad publishers, private car owners, excursion operators, and other interested persons and organizations. Its goals are to establish a professional program of standards and safety within the industry; facilitate communication among members; and provide insurance programs and governmental representation. Membership: $175/year (initial membership); $125/year (renewal).

Publications:
Trainline. q. adv.

Meetings/Conferences:
Annual Meetings: Fall
1999 – Cass, WV/Nov. 3-7

Towing and Recovery Ass'n of America *(1979)*
2200 Mill Road
Alexandria, VA 22314-4686
Tel: (703)838-1897   *Fax:* (703)684-6720
E-Mail: towserver@aol.com
Members: 1,500 companies
Staff: 6
Annual Budget: $500-1,000,000
Exec. Director/ Dir. of Education: Harriet Cooley
Manager, Trade Show: Rosie Ogletree

Historical Note
Members are companies operating tow-trucks and automotive recovery equipment. Subsidiary organizations include Interstate Towing Ass'n, T.R.A.A. Education Foundation, and T.R.A.A. Political Action Committee. Membership: $200/year.

Publications:
Interstate Towing News. m.
TRAA Membership Directory/Buyers Guide. a.
TRAA Towing News. m.

Meetings/Conferences:
Annual Meetings: June
1999 – Las Vegas, NV/June 13-16

Towing Equipment Distributors Ass'n
Historical Note
Part of Towing and Recovery Ass'n of America.

Towing Equipment Manufacturers Ass'n
Historical Note
An affiliate of the Nat'l Truck Equipment Ass'n.

Toxicology Forum *(1975)*
1575 I St., N.W., Suite 325
Washington, DC 20005
Tel: (202)659-0030   *Fax:* (202)789-0905
E-Mail: toxforum@clark.net
Web Site: http://www.clark.net/pub/toxforum
Members: 127 Individuals
Staff: 2
Annual Budget: $100-250,000
President: Philippe Shubik

Historical Note
Forum members are individuals, corporations, universities, associations and government agencies with an interest in toxicology.

Publications:
European Meeting Proceedings. a.
Summer Meeting Proceedings. a.
Winter Meeting Proceedings. a.

Toy Manufacturers of America *(1916)*
1115 Broadway, Suite 400
New York, NY 10010-3303
Tel: (212)675-1141   *Fax:* (212)633-1429
Web Site: http://www.toy.tma.org
Members: 317 companies
Staff: 17
Annual Budget: $2-5,000,000

President: David A. Miller
Communications Director: Terri Bartlett
Finance Director: Ruth T. Fitzpatrick
Director, Finance: Ruth T. Fitzpatrick
Director, Standards & Regulatory Affairs: Joan Laurence

Historical Note
Formerly (1966) Toy Manufacturers of the U.S. Absorbed American Toy Export Ass'n in 1992. Commonly referred to as the Toy Association. Members are major American toy manufacturers and importers. Sponsors and produces the American International Toy Fair, the largest toy trade show in America.

Publications:
American Internat'l Toy Fair Directory. a.
Guide to Blind Children. a.
Toy Industry Fact Book. a.

Meetings/Conferences:
Annual Meetings: February in New York/Toy Center & Javits Convention Center/32,000

TPA/The Tube and Pipe Ass'n, Internat'l *(1983)*
833 Featherstone Road
Rockford, IL 61107-6302
Tel: (815)399-8700   *Fax:* (815)399-7279
E-Mail: info@fmametalfaborg
Web Site: http://www.fmametalfab.org
Members: 1000 individuals
President and C.E.O.: John P. Nandzik, CAE
Director of Membership: Sadra Stengel

Historical Note
Formed as Tube and Pipe Fabricators Ass'n by the merger of the Tube Fabricating Division of the Fabricators and Manufacturers Ass'n, Internation'l and the Internat'l Pipe Ass'n in 1990; merged with American Tube Ass'n and assumed its current name in 1996. TPA is an educational technology association serving the metal tube and pipe producing and fabricating industries. It is an affiliate association of FMA, which provides administrative support. TPA members are eligible for FMA member benefits. Membership: $25/year(student); $120/year (individuals); $425/year (company).

Publications:
Internat'l Tube & Pipe Services Directory. bien.
TPA Connections Newsletter. bi.
TPJ, The Tube & Pipe Journal. bi-m.

Meetings/Conferences:
Annual Meetings: October

TPF, The Tube and Pipe Fabricators Ass'n, Internat'l
Historical Note
Merged with American Tube Ass'n and became TPA, The Tube and Pipe Fabricators Ass'n, Internat'l in 1996.

Track Owners Ass'n *(1991)*
P.O. Box 354645
Palm Coast, FL 32135-4645
Tel: (904)446-3355   *Fax:* (904)446-4144
E-Mail: oldnslo@juno.com
Web Site: http://www.slotcar.org
Members: 300 individuals
Staff: 1
Annual Budget: $25-50,000
Editor and Treasurer: Ray Gardner

Historical Note
TOA members are owner/operators of commercial slot car racing tracks and suppliers of services and equipment. Membership: $60-120/year (operator); $100/year (manufacturer/distributor).

Publications:
TOA Newsletter. m. adv.

Meetings/Conferences:
1999 – Indianapolis, IN(Best Western Waterfront)/June 25-27

Trade Cable and Telecommunications Ass'n
P.O. Box 13518
Austin, TX 78711
Tel: (512)474-2082   *Fax:* (512)474-0966
Web Site: http://www.txcable.com
President: William D. Arnold

Meetings/Conferences:
1999 – San Antonio, TX(Convention Center)/Feb. 24-26

Trade Relations Council of the U.S. *(1885)*
Historical Note
Organization defunct in 1995.

Trade Show Bureau *(1977)*
Historical Note
Became the Center for Exhibition Industry Research in 1995.

Trade Show Exhibitors Ass'n *(1966)*
5501 Backlick Road, Suite 105
Springfield, VA 22151-3940
Tel: (703)941-3725   *Fax:* (703)941-8275
E-Mail: tsea@tsea.org
Web Site: http://www.tsea.org
Members: 2,200 companies
Staff: 10
Annual Budget: $2-5,000,000
President: Michael J. Bandy
Manager, Education and Conferences: Sharon Buckles
Director, Finance and Administration: Vivian Dee Bandy

Historical Note
Founded as the Nat'l Trade Show Exhibitors Ass'n; became Internat'l Exhibitors Ass'n in 1984, and assumed its present name in 1996. It awards the CME (Certified Manager of Exhibits) designation and is a member of the Center for Exhibition Industry Research. Members are companies using exhibits for marketing, advertising or public relations. Membership: $355/year (exhibit manager), $355/year (supplier).

Publications:
Annual Budget Guide. a.
IDEAS. m. adv.
Membership Directory. a.
Salary Survey. bien.
Meetings/Conferences:
1999 – Chicago, IL(Navy Pier)/July 19-22/4500

Trademark Soc. (1963)
P.O. Box 2631, Eads Station
Arlington, VA   22202
Tel: (703)308-9101
Members: 150 individuals
Annual Budget: under $10,000
President: Howard Friedman

Historical Note
Labor union of Patent Office Trademark examiners. Affiliated with the Nat'l Treasury Employees Union, Chapter 245. All members are attorneys. Has no paid officers or full-time staff; officers change annually.

Meetings/Conferences:
Annual Meetings: Not held.

Traffic Audit Bureau for Media Measurement (1933)
420 Lexington Ave., Room 2520
New York, NY   10170
Tel: (212)972-8075   *Fax:* (212)972-8928
Members: 425 companies
Staff: 6
Annual Budget: $1-2,000,000
President: Anna Fountas

Historical Note
Audits the circulation of the outdoor advertising media--the 8-sheet and 30-sheet poster medium, the shelter display medium, the painted bulletin medium and others; establishes the standards for the measurement of the circulation of the outdoor advertising media.

Publications:
Inside Out of Home. m.
Planning for Out-of-Home Media.
Summary of Audited Markets Book.

Meetings/Conferences:

Trailer Hitch Manufacturers' Ass'n (1967)
Historical Note
Organization ceased operations in 1995.

Training Directors' Forum (1905)
50 S. 9th St.
Minneapolis, MN   55402
Tel: (612)340-4912   *Fax:* (612)333-6526
Web Site: http://www.lakewoodpub.com
Members: 2,500 individuals
Staff: 5
Director: Marc Hequet

Publications:
Training Directors' Forum Newsletter. m.

Meetings/Conferences:
Annual Meetings: May
1999 – Phoenix, AZ/June 5-9

Training Media Ass'n (1978)
198 Thomas Johnson Drive, Suite 206
Frederick, MD   21702
Tel: (301)662-4268   *Fax:* (301)695-7627
E-Mail: RAGTMA@aol.com
Web Site: http://www.trainingmedia.org
Members: 95 individuals, 95 companies
Staff: 3
Annual Budget: $100-250,000
Exec. Director: Robert A. Gehrke

Historical Note
Formerly (1978) Training Media Distributors. Members are concerned with preventing unauthorized copying of training media, especially films, videotapes and printed media. Also promotes the use of film and video in training employees. Membership: $900-$3,000/year (company).

Publications:
Previews. q.

Meetings/Conferences:
Semi-Annual Meetings: February-Membership Meeting held in Atlanta, GA
1999 – Atlanta, GA(Convention Center)

Training Officers Conference
2000 L St., N.W., Suite 710
Washington, DC   20036
Tel: (202)973-8683   *Fax:* (202)331-0111
Annual Budget: $100-250,000
Administrator: Vernon Castle

Historical Note
Membership: $850/year.

Meetings/Conferences:
Annual Meetings: Spring
1999 – Hagerstown, MD/April 18-21

Trans-Atlantic American Flag Liner Operations (1985)
99 Wood Ave., Suite 308
Iselin, NJ   08830
Tel: (732)494-3114   *Fax:* (732)494-0591
Members: 3 companies
Annual Budget: $50-100,000
Chairman: David B. Letteney

Historical Note
Formerly (1985) Atlantic and Gulf American Flag Berth Operators. Major purpose is publication of ocean freight rates on movements of military goods. Has no paid officers or full-time staff.

Meetings/Conferences:
Annual Meetings: Not held

Transaction Processing Performance Council (1988)
c/o Shanley Public Relations
777 North 1st St., Suite 600
San Jose, CA   95112
Tel: (408)295-8894   *Fax:* (408)295-9768
Web Site: http://www.tpc.org
Members: 47 manufacturers
Staff: 1
Annual Budget: $250-500,000
C.O.O.: Kim Shanley

Historical Note
Members are computer manufacturers and individiuals with an interest in transaction processing.

Publications:
TPC Quarterly Report. q.

Transaction Switching and Transport Service Industry Forum (1994)
Historical Note
Address unknown in 1996.

Transplantation Soc. (Western Hemishpere) (1966)
SUNY at Stony Brook
Health Science Center, Dept. of Surgery
Stony Brook, NY   11794-8192
Tel: (516)444-2209   *Fax:* (516)444-3831
E-Mail: rapaport@surg.com.sunysb.edu
Members: 2,300 individuals
Staff: 2
Annual Budget: $250-500,000
Secretary: Felix Rapaport, Ph.D.

Historical Note
Formerly (1994) Transplantation Soc. (U.S. Section). An international society of scientists dealing with all aspects of transplantation of organs and tissues. Membership: $45/year.

Publications:
Transplantation. q. adv.
Transplantation Proceedings. 8/year. adv.

Meetings/Conferences:
Biennial meetings: Even years

Transport Workers Union of America (1934)
80 West End Ave.
New York, NY   10023
Tel: (212)873-6000   *Fax:* (212)721-1431
Web Site: http://www.twu.com
Members: 100,000 individuals
Staff: 60
Annual Budget: $5-10,000,000
Internat'l President: Sonny Hall
Director of Education: Robert Wechsler

Historical Note
Organized in April, 1934 in New York City as the Transport Workers Union. Chartered by the Congress of Industrial Organizations under its present title in 1937. Sponsors and supports the Transport Workers Union Political Contribution Committee.

Publications:
TWU Express. m.

Meetings/Conferences:
International Convention: Every four years in the Fall (1997)

Transportation . Communications Internat'l Union (1899)
3 Research Place
Rockville, MD   20850
Tel: (301)948-4910   *Fax:* (301)948-1369
Members: 120,000 individuals
Staff: 100
Annual Budget: $5-10,000,000
International President: Robert A. Scardelletti
Internat'l Secretary-Treasurer: F. Ferlin, Jr.
Exec. Director, Publications: Diane S. Curry

Historical Note
Established in Sedalia, Missouri December 31, 1899 as the Order of Railroad Clerks of America and chartered by the American Federation of Labor the following year. Became the Brotherhood of Railway and Steamship Clerks, Freight Handlers, Express and Station Employees in 1919 and then the Brotherhood of Railway, Airline, and Steamship Clerks, Freight Handlers, Express and Station Employees (BRAC)in 1967. Assumed its present name in 1987. In 1969 it absorbed the Transportation-Communication Employees Union, the Railway Patrolmen's International Union and the Federation of Business Machine Technicians and Engineers. In 1975 it merged with the United Transport Service Employees of America (founded in 1937), and in 1978 merged with the Brotherhood of Sleeping Car Porters (founded in 1925). Absorbed the American Railway and Airway Supervisors Association in 1980; in 1986, BRAC merged with Brotherhood Railway Carmen of the United States. In addition to bargaining and representation of its members, TCU provides mortgage and bankard programs, and other services to its members. Sponsors and supports the Responsible Citizens Political League.

Publications:
Interchange. 6/year.
Telling It Like It Is. 6/year.
The Winning Edge. q.

Meetings/Conferences:
Quadrennial Meetings: (1999)
1999 – Las Vegas, NV

Transportation Brokers Conference of America
Historical Note
A conference of Transportation Intermediaries Ass'n.

Transportation Claims and Prevention Council (1974)
Historical Note
Name changed to Transportation Consumer Protection Council in 1996.

Transportation Clubs Internat'l (1920)
7116 Stinson Ave., N.W., Suite B-315
Gig Harbor, WA   98335
Tel: (206)858-8627
Members: 10,000 individuals
Annual Budget: $50-100,000
Business Manager: Alice Warfield

Historical Note
Members are individuals in all phases of transportation, traffic management and physical distribution.

Meetings/Conferences:

Transportation Consumer Protection Council (1974)
120 Main St.
Huntington, NY   11743
Tel: (516)549-8984   *Fax:* (516)549-8962
E-Mail: tcpc@transportlaw.com
Web Site: http://www.transportlaw.com
Members: 550 companies
Staff: 5
Exec. Director: William J. Augello
Membership Secretary: Nancy O'Donnell

Historical Note
Formerly (1990) Shippers Nat'l Freight Claim Council and Transportation Claims and Prevention Council (1996). Name change was made in 1996 to indicate a broadened advocacy role on behalf of shippers/receivers. Founded as a non-profit membership association of U.S. and Canadian shippers, receivers, and carriers, TCPC is dedicated to the reduction of transit losses and the improvement of freight claim and freight charge payment procedures in domestic and international commerce. Membership: $395/year (regular); $345/year (associate).

Publications:
Directory of Members, Transportation Attorneys & Consultants. a.
Trans Digest. m. adv.

Meetings/Conferences:
Annual Meetings: March
1999 – Tucson, AZ(Sheraton El Conquistador)/May 23-26

Transportation Development Ass'n
22 N. Carroll St., Suite 102
Madison, WI   53703-2707
Tel: (608)230-7044
E-Mail: tda@itis.com
Members: 400 companies and municipalities
Staff: 1
Exec. Director: Philip Scherer

Transportation Institute (1968)
5201 Auth Way
Camp Springs, MD   20746
Tel: (301)423-3335   *Fax:* (301)423-0634
E-Mail: info@trans-inst.org
Web Site: http://www.trans-inst.org
Members: 140 companies
Staff: 15
Annual Budget: $2-5,000,000
President: James L. Henry
Director, Government Affairs: Gerard C. Snow

Historical Note
Members are U.S.-flag shipping, towing and dredging companies. Is concerned with maintaining the strength of U.S. water-borne commerce.

Transportation Intermediaries Ass'n (1978)
3601 Eisenhower Ave., Suite 110
Alexandria, VA   22304-6439
Tel: (703)329-1894   *Fax:* (703)329-1898
E-Mail: tray@tianet.org
Web Site: http://www.tianet.org
Members: 740 companies
Staff: 6
Annual Budget: $500-1,000,000
C.E.O.: Robert Voltmann
Communications and Policy Manager: Patrick Knight
Meetings and Marketing Manager: Michele Watson
Director of Finance and Administration: Rebecca J. Beverley
Manager of Member Services and Government Relations: Kelly Tray

Historical Note
Established as the Property Brokers Ass'n of America, it became the Transporation Brokers Conference of America in 1981 and assumed its present name in 1995. Members are companies working with truckers, carriers and shippers to arrange the transport of general freight. The Logistics Conference, the Intermodal Conference, the North American Conference of Freight Forwarders, the Perishable Agricultural and Foodstuff Conference, and the Transportation Brokers Conference of America are subsidiaries of TIA. Membership: $475-575/year.

Publications:
TIA Membership Directory & Handbook. a. adv.
TIA UPDATE. m. adv.

Meetings/Conferences:
Annual Meetings: Spring
1999 – San Diego, CA(Marriott/Marina)/Feb. 10-13
2000 – Disney World, FL(Corando Springs)/March 9-11

Transportation Lawyers Ass'n (1937)
P.O. Box 15122
Lenexa, KS   66285-5122
Tel: (913)541-9077   *Fax:* (913)541-0156
Members: 750 individuals
Staff: 3
Annual Budget: $100-250,000

Exec. Director: Michael Flamagan
Director of Meetings: Jennifer Kimzey

Historical Note
Founded in Louisville, KY as the Motor Carrier Lawyers Ass'n (MCLA), assumed its present name in 1983. Originally an international bar association for lawyers representing motor carriers before the Interstate Commerce Commission and Canadian regulatory agencies, membership is now open to attorneys representing any interstate, foreign or intrastate "transportation interest." Membership: $150/year (individual).

Publications:
Transportation Lawyer. bi-m.

Meetings/Conferences:
Annual Meetings: Spring
1999 – Victoria, BC, Canada(The Empress)/April 29-May 2
2000 – Hilton Head, SC(Hilton)/May 9-13/250

Transportation Loss Prevention and Security Council *(1937)*
2200 Mill Road
Alexandria, VA 22314-4677
Tel: (703)838-1864 *Fax:* (703)683-9752
E-Mail: tlpc@trucking.org
Web Site: http://www.truckline.com/tlpsc
Members: 400 individuals
Staff: 2
Annual Budget: $100-250,000
Exec. Director: Gail E. Toth
Manager, Government Relations, Meetings and Membership: Linda Simpson

Historical Note
An autonomous part of the American Trucking Ass'ns. Works to establish uniform standards of loss and damage claims, as well as ajudication of claims. TLP&SC members are claims and security professionals from motor carriers representing every segment of the industry. Allied membership is available for industry suppliers and associate membership for shipper/receivers. Membership: $160-450/year, varies by gross revenue (motor carrier); $300/year (supplier); $300/year (associate).

Publications:
Claim Ratio Survey. a.
Membership Directory. a. adv.
Security Report. q.
The Informer. m. adv.
TLP&SC Freight Claim Rule Book.

Meetings/Conferences:
Annual Meetings: June/200
1999 – Atlanta, GA(Crowne Plaza Ravenia)/April 11-13

Transportation Research Forum *(1961)*
11250-8 Roger Bacon Drive, Suite 8
Reston, VA 22190
Tel: (703)437-4377 *Fax:* (703)435-4390
Web Site: http://www.indiana.edu/~trf
Members: 550 individuals
Staff: 2
Annual Budget: $100-250,000
Exec. Director: Richard A. Guggolz

Historical Note
An independent organization of transportation professionals, TRF's purpose is to provide an impartial meeting ground for carriers, shippers, government officials, consultants, university researchers, suppliers, and others seeking an exchange of information related to both passenger and freight transportation. Membership: $60/year.

Publications:
Directory of Members.
Newsletter. 6/year.
Proceedings of Annual Meeting. a.
TRF Journal. 2/year.

Meetings/Conferences:
Annual Meetings: Fall
1999 – Washington, DC(Washington Marriott)/Sept. 30-Oct 2

Transportation Safety Equipment Institute *(1962)*
1225 New York Ave., N.W., 3rd Floor
Washington, DC 20005
Tel: (202)393-6362 *Fax:* (202)737-3742
E-Mail: lchristensen@mema.org
Members: 22 companies
Staff: 2
Annual Budget: $50-100,000
Exec. Director: Brian Duggan

Historical Note
Formerly (1986) the Truck Safety Equipment Institute. Manufacturers of lighting, mirrors and emergency-vehicle products, reflectors and other devices related to motor vehicle safety.

Publications:
TSEI Reports. irreg.

Meetings/Conferences:
Annual Meetings: October

Transporting Elevator and Grain Merchants Ass'n *(1918)*
1300 L St., N.W., Suite 925
Washington, DC 20005-4113
Tel: (202)842-0400 *Fax:* (202)789-7223
Members: 40 companies
Staff: 3
Annual Budget: $25-50,000
Secretary: Robert R. Petersen

Historical Note
Membership: $495-$1,950/year.

Meetings/Conferences:
Annual Meetings: May/50

Transworld Advertising Agency Network *(1936)*
1624 Bunting Lane

Sanibel, FL 33957
Tel: (941)472-0885 *Fax:* (941)472-0637
E-Mail: Taangary@aol.com
Members: 45 agencies
Staff: 2
Annual Budget: $250-500,000
President: Gary Lessner

Historical Note
Established as the Transamerica Advertising Agency Network, it assumed its present name in 1975. The association is an international group of medium-sized, cooperating, and independent advertising agencies. Membership: $2,500 (organization).

Publications:
Directory. a.
Newsletter. semi-a.
Transcript. semi-a.

Meetings/Conferences:
Semi-annual Meetings: Winter and Summer
1999 – Boca Raton, FL(Boca Raton Resort and Club)/Feb. 17-20
1999 – Boston, MA/Aug. 15-18
2000 – La Jolla, CA(Torrey Pines)/Feb. 2-5

Travel and Tourism Research Ass'n *(1970)*
P.O. Box 2133
Boise, ID 83701-2133
Tel: (208)853-2320 *Fax:* (208)853-2369
E-Mail: ttr@uswest.net
Web Site: http://www.ttra.com
Members: 850 firms, universities & agencies
Staff: 2
Annual Budget: $250-500,000
Exec. Director: Patty Morgan

Historical Note
Established as the Travel Research Ass'n as the result of a merger of the Eastern and Western Councils for Travel Research on January 1, 1970. The present name was adopted in 1980. Membership: $100/year (standard).

Publications:
Directory of Members. a.
Directory of Travel Research Suppliers. bi-a.
Journal of Travel Research. q. adv.
Proceedings of Annual Conference. semi-a.
TTRA Members Newsletter. q. adv.

Meetings/Conferences:
Annual Meetings: June/500
1999 – Halifax, Nova Scotia/June 20-23
2000 – Burbank, CA/June 11-14
2001 – Ft. Myers, FL/June 10-13

Travel Buyers Ass'n *(1996)*
Historical Note
Defunct in 1997.

Travel Industry Ass'n of America *(1941)*
1100 New York Ave., N.W., Suite 450
Washington, DC 20005-3934
Tel: (202)408-8422 *Fax:* (202)408-1255
Web Site: http://www.tia.org
Members: 2,500 organizations
Staff: 50
Annual Budget: $10-25,000,000
President & C.E.O.: William S. Norman
V.P., Public Relations: Dexter C. Koehl
Senior V. President, Marketing Programs: Ray Lutz
V. President, Government Affairs: Hallock Northcott
Sr. V. President, Finance & Administration: Frank O'Rourke
Senior V. President, Planning and Member Relations: Elyse G. Wander
V. President, Development and Membership Services: Robert C. McClure
Sr. V. President, Research: Suzanne Cook
V. President, Nat'l Councils Program: Patty Hubbard
Exec. Dir., Tourism Works for America: Dee Minic

Historical Note
The result of a merger of Discover America (founded in 1965) and the Nat'l Ass'n of Travel Organizations (founded in 1941). Members are organizations such as hotels, airlines, travel agencies, etc. interested in promoting increased travel to and within the United States. Formerly (1980) known as Discover America Travel Organizations. Nat'l Councils: Area and Regional Travel Organizations, State Travel Directors, Travel Attractions, and Urban Tourism Organizations. Has an annual budget of approximately $11 million.

Publications:
Contact USA. a.
News Line. m.

Meetings/Conferences:
Annual Meetings: Fall
1999 – Pittsburgh, PA/Oct. 20-23

Travel Journalists Guild *(1980)*
Box 10643
Chicago, IL 60610
Tel: (312)664-9279 *Fax:* (312)664-9279
Members: 75 individuals
Staff: 2
Annual Budget: $10-25,000
Exec. Secretary: Philip D. Hoffman
Office Manager: Eileen Hoffman

Historical Note
Established in Antigua, Guatemala in 1980, TJG members are freelance authors, photographers, artists, lecturers, fell makers, etc. specializing in travel with a minimum of three years experience. Membership: $150/year (individual), plus $250 initial fee.

Publications:
Travelwriter Marketletter. m.

Meetings/Conferences:
Annual Meetings: None held

Travel Professionals Ass'n *(1988)*
216 S. Bungalow Park Ave.
Tampa, FL 33609
Tel: (813)876-0286 *Fax:* (813)876-0286
Staff: 3
President: Claudine Dervaes

Publications:
TPA Membership Directory. a.
Travelspeak Newsletter. 4-6/yr. adv.

Travel Technology Ass'n *(1992)*
4521 Campus Dr.
Suite 340
Irvine, CA 92612
Tel: (949)574-8374 *Fax:* (949)574-8369
E-Mail: info@ten-io.com
Web Site: http://www.ten-io.com/tta
Members: 65 companies
Exec. Officer: Dayle de Raat

Historical Note
The Travel Technology Association exists to educate members and the industry regarding the use and benefits of travel technology as it contributes to the distribution of travel products. TTA accomplishes this mission by assisting other organizations to secure technology speakers, preparing education materials for publication in trade magazines and serving as the non-commercial source of information on travel technology.

Tread Rubber and Tire Repair Materials Manufacturers Group *(1978)*
c/o Bandag, Inc.
Bandag Center
Muscatine, IA 52761-5886
Tel: (319)262-1332 *Fax:* (319)262-1386
Members: 18 individuals, 9 companies
Annual Budget: $25-50,000
Secretary: Thomas Dvorchak

Historical Note
TRMG was established to foster the advancement of the retreading industry in the U.S. through cooperative efforts. Formerly (1992) the Tread Rubber Manufacturers Group. Membership: up to $6,000/year, based on size of company.

Meetings/Conferences:
Annual Meetings: Fall

Treasury Management Ass'n *(1979)*
7315 Wisconsin Ave., Suite 600 West
Bethesda, MD 20814-3211
Tel: (301)907-2862 *Fax:* (301)907-2864
E-Mail: tma@tma > net.org
Web Site: http://www.tma-net.org/treasury
Members: 11,000 individuals
Staff: 48
Annual Budget: $10-25,000,000
President/C.E.O.: James Kaitz
V.P., Communications and Marketing: Susan Bellinger
Director, Government Relations/Technical Standards: Frank P. Curran
Dir., Conferences/Education: Kati S. Schnell, CMP
Director, Executive Education: Nancy H. Aronson
Director of Research: Aaron J. Phillips, DBA, CCM
Dir., Publications and Creative: Ayo I. Mseka

Historical Note
Formerly Cash Management Practitioners Ass'n and Nat'l Corporate Cash Managment Ass'n, TMA assumed its present name in 1991. TMA is the principal organization of coprorate treasury executives. TMA supports the treasury management profession through continuing education, professional certification, publications, industry standards, government relations and research. Has an annual budget of approximately $7 million. Membership: $195/year (individual).

Publications:
Electronic Commerce Report. m.
Membership Directory & Guide to Treasury Services. a. adv.
Status Update of Current Issues. m.
TMA Journal. bi-m. adv.
TMA NEWS. m.

Meetings/Conferences:
Annual Meetings: Fall
1999 – Los Angeles, CA/Oct. 17-20
2000 – Philadelphia, PA/Nov. 12-15

Tree-Ring Soc. *(1934)*
University of Arizona
Laboratory of Tree-Ring Research
Tucson, AZ 85721-0058
Tel: (520)621-2320 *Fax:* (520)621-8229
Members: 310 individuals and institutions
Staff: 1
Annual Budget: under $10,000
Secretary: Jeffrey S. Dean, Ph.D.

Historical Note
Membership consists of those interested in dendrochronology, the science of determining dates by matching tree-rings for archaeological, hydrological or climatological purposes. Has no paid staff. Membership: $15/year.

Publications:
Tree-Ring Bulletin. a.

Meetings/Conferences:
Annual Meetings: not held

Trench Shoring and Shielding Ass'n
Historical Note
Defunct in 1997.

Tributyl Phosphate Task Force *(1987)*
1850 M St., N.W., Suite 700
Washington, DC 20036

Tel: (202)721-4156   *Fax:* (202)296-8120
Members: 4 companies
Staff: 1
Annual Budget: under $10,000
Technical Coordinator: Paula Podhasky

Historical Note
An affiliate of the Synthetic Organic Chemical Manufacturers Ass'n, which provides administrative support. Members are manufacturers and importers of tributyl phosphate.

Triological Soc.

Historical Note
Abbreviated name for the American Laryngological, Rhinological and Otological Society.

Truck and Heavy Equipment Claims Council

Historical Note
Became Nat'l Truck and Heavy Equipment Claims Council in 1995.

Truck Cap and Accessory Ass'n *(1989)*
6565 Loisdale Court, Suite 430
Springfield, VA 22150-1812
Tel: (703)922-7803   *Fax:* (703)922-7806
E-Mail: tcaa@trucksnstuff.com
Web Site: http://www.tcaa.net
Members: 925 companies
Staff: 4
Annual Budget: $500-1,000,000
Exec. Director: Michael R. Dwyer
Director, Meetings and Marketing: Kendra D. Moore
Director, Member Services: Robert E. Carnahan

Historical Note
Organized at a meeting in Omaha, Nebraska in 1989 by dealers, manufacturers and suppliers drawn from across the nation. Members include cap dealers, cap manufacturers, light truck accessory manufacturers and suppliers. TCAA was established to educate the public, develop industry standards for product quality and service, educate the membership, and provide national level representation. Formerly (1992) the Truck Cap Industry Ass'n. Membership: $125-1,500/year (organization/company).

Publications:
Annual Product Source Directory. a. adv.
TCAA News. m.

Meetings/Conferences:
Annual Meetings: Winter
1999 – Orlando, FL(Orange Cty. Convention Center)/Jan. 20-24/2500
2000 – Long Beach, CA(Long Beach Country Club)/Feb. 10-13/2500
2001 – Nashville, TN(Nashville Convention Center)/Feb. 15-18/2500

Truck Manufacturers Ass'n *(1995)*
1225 New York Ave., N.W., Suite 300
Washington, DC 20005
Tel: (202)638-7825   *Fax:* (202)737-3742
E-Mail: tma_dc@ix.netcom.com
Members: 7 companies
Staff: 1
Annual Budget: $250-500,000
Exec. Director: William A. Leasure, Jr.

Historical Note
TMA represents U.S. manufacturers of medium and heavy duty trucks.

Truck Mixer Manufacturers Bureau *(1945)*
900 Spring St.
Silver Spring, MD 20910
Tel: (301)587-1400   *Fax:* (301)585-4219
Members: 10 companies
Staff: 2
Annual Budget: $50-100,000
Exec. Secretary: Robert A. Garbini
Administrator: Nicole Maher

Historical Note
An affiliate of National Ready Mixed Concrete Ass'n. Purpose to develop standards and guidelines for equipment production.

Publications:
Truck Mixer & Agitator Standards. irreg.

Meetings/Conferences:
Annual Meetings: Always April in Phoenix, AZ

Truck Renting and Leasing Ass'n *(1978)*
1725 Duke St., Suite 600
Alexandria, VA 22314-3457
Tel: (703)299-9120   *Fax:* (703)299-9115
E-Mail: mpayne@trala.org
Web Site: http://www.trala.org
Members: 700 companies, 30,000 locations
Staff: 8
Annual Budget: $2-5,000,000
President and C.E.O.: J. Michael Payne
V.P., Govt. Relations: Steven Nousen
Meetings Manager: Leslie A. Hummel
V. President, Member Services: Mary S. Payne

Historical Note
Organized in 1978 to represent the U.S. truck renting and leasing industry. Full members are firms active in full-service truck leasing, dedicated contract carriage, commercial daily truck rental, and consumer truck rental. Membership now includes Canadian leasing firms as well as associate members from many industries, providing goods and services to truck lessors. Membership: range from $575-160,000 per year, based on sales volume.

Publications:
TRALA Legislative Report.
TRALA News Bulletin.
TRALA Vehicle. a. adv.
TRALA Weekly Wire (fax).

Meetings/Conferences:
Annual Meetings: Spring/550
1999 – Naples, FL(Registry Resort)/March 11-14
2000 – Rancho Mirage, CA(Mariott's Rancho Las Palmas Resort)/March 9-12

Truck Trailer Manufacturers Ass'n *(1941)*
1020 Princess St.
Alexandria, VA 22314-2289
Tel: (703)549-3010   *Fax:* (703)549-3014
Members: 200 companies
Staff: 6
Annual Budget: $500-1,000,000
President: Richard P. Bowling

Historical Note
Represents the manufacturers of truck trailers and intermodal containers; members are responsible for the manufacture of over 90% of the commercial trailers produced in the U.S.

Publications:
Membership Directory. a.
TTMA Bulletin. w.

Meetings/Conferences:
Annual Meetings: April-May/500
1999 – San Antonio, TX(Hyatt Hill Country)/April 23-26
2000 – Indian Wells, CA(Renaissance Esmeralda)/May 3-7/500
2001 – Orlando, FL(Hyatt Grand)/May 16-20/500

Truck Writers of North America *(1988)*
600 Reisterstown Road, Suite 404
Baltimore, MD 21208
Tel: (410)486-7430   *Fax:* (410)486-7478
Web Site: http://www.twna.org
Members: 240 individuals
President: David A. Kolman

Historical Note
Represents writers, editors, freelance journalists, and public relations and communications specialists producing information about trucks, trucking, and the trucking industry. Membership: $25/year (individual).

Publications:
TWNA Dispatch Newsletter. bi-m. adv.

Meetings/Conferences:
1999 – Louisville, KY/150
1999 – Las Vegas, NV/100

Truck-frame and Axle Repair Ass'n *(1966)*
3741 Enterprise Dr., S.W.
Rochester, MN 55902
Toll Free: (800)232 - 8272
Members: 61 companies, 41 associates
Staff: 1
Annual Budget: $50-100,000
Administrator: Wayne Reich

Historical Note
Founded in Louisville, KY by 13 frame and axle repair shops. Membership is open to all companies which have been in business for two years repairing heavy-duty trucks, tractors and trailers and straightening their frames, axles and housings, as well as aligning and balancing their wheels.

Publications:
TARA News & Topics. m.

Meetings/Conferences:
Semi-Annual Meetings: Spring and Fall
1999 – Nashville, TN(Opryland Hotel)/May 20-22
2000 – St. Louis, MO

Trucking Management

Historical Note
Became Motot Freight Carriers Ass'n in 1997.

Truckload Carriers Ass'n *(1938)*
2200 Mill Road
Alexandria, VA 22314-4627
Tel: (703)838-1950   *Fax:* (703)836-6610
E-Mail: tca@truckload.org
Web Site: http://www.truckload.org
Members: 650 carriers, 300 affiliates
Staff: 13
Annual Budget: $2-5,000,000
President: Lana R. Batts
Director, Communications: Kristie Kehoe
Manager, Meetings: Margaret Campione
Director, Conventions and Marketing: William Giroux, CMP
Director, Education and Training: Virginia DeRoze
Director of Operations: Cynthia Simpson
General Counsel: Robert Rothstein
Director, Membership and Development: Becky Shoemaker
Director, Membership and Marketing: Paula McElligott

Historical Note
The product of a merger in 1983 between the Common Carrier Conference-Irregular Route (founded in 1941) and the Contract Carrier Conference (founded in 1939). Formerly (1997) Interstate Truckload Carriers Conference and (1988) Interstate Carriers Conference. TCA serves as the national coordinating point, lobbying organization, and promotional arm for irregular-route common and contract truckload motor carriers. Affiliated with American Trucking Ass'ns. Membership: $250-$6,000/year, based on gross revenues (company).

Publications:
Careers in Trucking. a. adv.
Convention Magazine. semi-a. adv.
Membership Directory. a. adv.
Newsletter. bi-w.

Meetings/Conferences:
Annual Meetings: March
1999 – Las Vegas, NV(Bellagio)/March 14-18
2000 – Orlando, FL(Walt Disney)/March 19-23

Truss Plate Institute *(1961)*
583 D'Onofrio Dr., Suite 200
Madison, WI 53719
Tel: (608)833-5900   *Fax:* (608)833-4360
Members: 400 companies
Staff: 3
Annual Budget: $250-500,000
Managing Director: Charles B. Goehring

Historical Note
Trade association of truss plate manufacturers, allied suppliers and truss manufacturers. Incorporated in Florida. Membership: $300/year (professional); $100 and up/year (depending on type of company).

Publications:
TPI News. m.

Tube and Pipe Fabricators Ass'n, Internat'l *(1983)*

Historical Note
See TPF, The Tube and Pipe Fabricators Ass'n, Internat'l.

Tube Council of North America *(1957)*
72 Spring St., Room 208
New York, NY 10012-4019
Tel: (212)477-9007   *Fax:* (212)460-9028
E-Mail: tklein6398@aol.com
Members: 11 companies
Staff: 2
Annual Budget: $50-100,000
Exec. Secretary: Ted Klein

Historical Note
Established as the Collapsible Metal Tube Ass'n, it became the Metal Tube Packaging Council of North America in 1966 and assumed its present name in 1983. Membership fee varies, based on volume of production.

Publications:
Tube Topics. q.

Meetings/Conferences:
Semi-Annual Meetings: Spring and Fall

Tubular Exchanger Manufacturers Ass'n *(1939)*
25 N. Broadway
Tarrytown, NY 10591-3201
Tel: (914)332-0040   *Fax:* (914)332-1541
Members: 20 companies
Staff: 5
Annual Budget: $100-250,000
Secretary: Richard C. Byrne

Historical Note
Sets standards for the industry, known as TEMA Standards, which are sold to the chemical processing and petroleum refining industries.

Tubular Rivet and Machine Institute *(1937)*
25 N. Broadway
Tarrytown, NY 10591-3201
Tel: (914)332-0040   *Fax:* (914)332-1541
Members: 9 companies
Staff: 2
Annual Budget: $25-50,000
Secretary: Richard C. Byrne

Historical Note
Formerly Tubular and Split Rivet Council. The Institute's Technical Council has developed metric and inch engineering standards as well as safety standards for the use of rivet setting machines.

Publications:
Directory. irreg.

Tune-up Manufacturers Council *(1954)*
P.O. Box 13966
Research Triangle Pk, NC 27709
Tel: (919)549-4800   *Fax:* (919)549-4824
Members: 11 companies
Staff: 2
Annual Budget: $25-50,000
Exec. Director: Jim Lawrence

Historical Note
Founded as the Ignition Manufacturers Institute, it assumed its present name in 1981.

Meetings/Conferences:
Semi-Annual Meetings: Spring and Winter

Turf and Ornamental Communicators Ass'n *(1990)*
120 West Main, Suite 200
Box 156
New Prague, MN 56071
Tel: (612)758-6340   *Fax:* (612)758-5813
E-Mail: gard2@aol.com
Web Site: http://www.toca.org
Members: 120 individuals
Staff: 2
Exec. Director: Den Gardner

Historical Note
TOCA members are individuals and companies involved in communications in the turf and ornamentals industry. Membership: $90/year (individual); $150-210/year (organization/company).

Publications:
TOCA Talk. q.

Meetings/Conferences:
1999 – Orlando, FL(Grosvenor Resort at Walt Disney World)/May 1-3

Turfgrass Producers Internat'l *(1967)*
1855 Hicks Road, #A
Rolling Meadows, IL 60008
Tel: (847)705-9898   *Fax:* (847)705-8347
Toll Free: (800)405 - 8873
E-Mail: TURF-GRASS@MSN.COM
Web Site: http://turfgrassoc.org

Members: 1000 companies
Staff: 4
Annual Budget: $500-1,000,000

Historical Note
Formerly (1994) American Sod Producers Ass'n. TPI has continually advanced the trufgrass sod industry through the development of technical and marketing information, as well as supporting research in advancing the environmental benefits of high quality turfgrass. Membership: scale based on number of acres.

Publications:
TPI Business Management Newsletter. bi-m.
TPI Turf News. bi-m. adv.

Meetings/Conferences:
Semi-Annual Meetings: Winter and Summer/600-800

Turkish Studies Ass'n *(1971)*
Center for Middle Eastern Studies
Univ. of Chicago, 5828 S. University Ave
Chicago, IL   60637
Tel: (773)702-8297   *Fax:* (773)702-2587
Members: 500 individuals
Annual Budget: under $10,000
Secretary: Richard Chambers

Historical Note
TSA membership consists of academics, institutions and professional organizations with an interest in Turkish culture, history and language.

Publications:
Membership Roster. irreg.
TSA Bulletin. semi-a. adv.

Meetings/Conferences:
Annual Meetings: in conjunction with the Middle East Studies Ass'n of North America.

Turnaround Management Ass'n *(1988)*
541 N. Fairbanks Ct., Suite 1880
Chicago, IL   60611-3319
Tel: (312)822-9700   *Fax:* (312)857-7739
E-Mail: info@turnaround.org
Web Site: http://www.turnaround.org
Members: 3,100 individuals
Staff: 6
Annual Budget: $1-2,000,000
Exec. Director: Nancy H. Davis
Manager, Publications and Information: Jenny Dojuhty
Meetings & Education Coordinator: Laura Fialkoff
Administrator: Gabriela Sosa
Director, Member Services & Chapter Relations: Deborah Martin
Fund Development Coordinator: Joseph R. Karel

Historical Note
TMA members are financial advisers, operational consultants, crisis managers, corporate executives, attorneys, accountants, appraisers, commercial lenders, venture capitalists and other service providers who have an interest in the revitalization of financially distressed businesses and the representation of stakeholders in these entities. Associate membership is available for individuals in academia or government. TMA provides opportunities for professional development, networking, certification and reference/research services for its members. Membership: $295/year (1st corporate member), $195/year (additional member); $95/year (student/academic/government).

Publications:
Directory of Members & Services. a. adv.
Journal of Corporate Renewal. 10/yr. adv.

Meetings/Conferences:
Semi-annual Meetings: Spring and Fall
1999 – Miami, FL

Type Directors Club *(1947)*
60 East 42nd St., Suite 721
New York, NY   10165-0721
Tel: (212)983-6042   *Fax:* (212)983-6043
E-Mail: typeclub@aol.com
Members: 725 individuals, 8 companies
Staff: 1
Annual Budget: $100-250,000
Exec. Director: Carol Wahler

Historical Note
Members are professionals involved in typography. Membership is international. Membership: $125/year (individual); $400/year (corporate).

Publications:
Letterspace Newsletter. semi-a.
Typography Annual. a.

Typographers Internat'l Ass'n *(1920)*
Historical Note
Merged into the Internat'l Digital Imaging Ass'n in 1996.

U.S. African-American Chamber of Commerce *(1983)*
Historical Note
Address unknown in 1997.

U.S. Apple Ass'n *(1970)*
6707 Old Dominion Dr. Suite 320
McLean, VA   22101-4556
Tel: (703)442-8850   *Fax:* (703)790-0845
Toll Free: (800)781 - 4443
Members: 600 companies/24 state organizations
Staff: 8
Annual Budget: $1-2,000,000
President and C.E.O.: Kraig Naasz
Director, Communications: Julia Stewart Daly
Director, Industry Services: James R. Cranney, Jr.
Director, Finance/Admin.: Brenda Cordova

Historical Note
Formed by the merger of the Internat'l Apple Ass'n (1895) and the Nat'l Apple Institute (1935) as Internat'l Apple Institute; assumed its current name in 1996. Members are U.S. and foreign firms, other than retailers, which handle apples. Membership: $100-1,500/year (based on volume of apples grown, packed, processed, and/or sold annually).

Publications:
Apple News. bi-w.
Storage Reports. m.

Meetings/Conferences:
Annual Meetings: June

U.S. Feed Grains Council
Historical Note
Became U.S. Grains Council in 1998.

U.S. Grains Council *(1960)*
1400 K St., N.W., Suite 1200
Washington, DC   20005
Tel: (202)789-0789   *Fax:* (202)898-0522
E-Mail: grains@grains.org
Members: 110 producer groups & companies
Staff: 38
Annual Budget: $2-5,000,000
President and CEO: Kenneth Hobbie
Communications: Jennifer Morrill
Exec. Director: S. Richard Tolman
Exec. Director: Thomas N. Sleight
V. President: Richard W. Krajeck

Historical Note
Formerly (1998) U.S. Feed Grains Council. Founded by representatives of the agricultural community to promote the export of U.S. feed grain products (e.g., sorghum, barley, corn), USGC works under contract with the Foreign Agricultural Service of the U.S. Department of Agriculture to increase dollar sales abroad of U.S. feed grains. Membership: $3,000/year (producers) $6,000/year (agribusiness), $10,000/year (producer checkoff).

Publications:
Annual Report. a.
Focus Newsletter. m.
Meeting Program. semi-a.
Membership Directory. a.

Meetings/Conferences:
Semi-annual Meetings: Winter and Summer/300
1999 – Orlando, FL(Orlando Marriott)/Feb. 7-10
1999 – Boston, MA(Cambridge Marriott)/July 18-21
2000 – Monterey, CA/Feb. 6-9
2001 – Chicago, IL/July 16-19

U.S. Metric Ass'n *(1916)*
10245 Andasol Ave.
Northridge, CA   91325-1504
Tel: (818)363-5606   *Fax:* (818)368-7443
E-Mail: hillger@cira.ColoState.edu
Web Site: http://lamar.ColoState.edu/ ~ hillger/
Members: 2,000 individuals
Staff: 1
Annual Budget: $25-50,000
Exec. Director: Valerie Antoine

Historical Note
USMA is dedicated to the promotion of U.S. conversion to the use of the metric system as its only measurement system and assists the public in using the system correctly. Members are companies, government agencies, libraries, educators, industry personnel and other individuals with an interest in the metric system. Presents private sector information at government metric transition meetings and furnishes information on the modernized metric system Systeme International (SI). Membership: $30/year (individual); $150/year (corporate); $500/year (lifetime).

Publications:
Metric Today. bi-m. adv.

Meetings/Conferences:

U.S. Oil and Gas Ass'n *(1917)*
801 Pennsylvania Ave., N.W., Suite 840
Washington, DC   20004-2604
Tel: (202)638-4400
Members: 7,500 individuals
Staff: 4
Annual Budget: $500-1,000,000
President: Wayne Gibbens

Historical Note
Formerly Mid-Continent Oil and Gas Ass'n (1998).

Meetings/Conferences:

U.S. Rice Producers Group
Historical Note
A division of USA Rice Federation, which provides administrative support.

U.S.-ASEAN Business Council *(1983)*
1400 L St., N.W., Suite 375
Washington, DC   20005-3509
Tel: (202)289-1911   *Fax:* (202)289-0519
E-Mail: Mail@USasean.org
Web Site: http://us-asean.org
Members: 1 individuals, 600 companies
Staff: 16
Annual Budget: $2-5,000,000
President: Ernest Z. Bower

Historical Note
Formerly (1997) U.S.-ASEAN Council for Business and Technology, The Council strives to expand trade and investment ties between the U.S. and ASEAN (Ass'n of Southeast Asian Nations, including Brunei Darussalam, Indonesia, Malaysia, Philippines, Singapore Thailand and Vietnam) by implementing programs which assist companies to identify and compete for opportunities. The

Council also supports government policies that foster the expansion of commercial ties.

Publications:
U. S.

Meetings/Conferences:
Annual Meetings: always Washington, DC

U.S.-ASEAN Council for Business and Technology *(1983)*
Historical Note
Became the U.S.-ASEAN Business Council in 1997.

U.S.-Italy Chamber of Commerce *(1995)*
Historical Note
Address unknown in 1997.

U.S.-ROC (Taiwan) Business Council *(1976)*
1726 M St., N.W., Suite 601
Washington, DC   20036
Tel: (202)331-8966   *Fax:* (202)331-8985
E-Mail: Council@usa-roc.org
Web Site: http://www.usa-roc.org
Members: 300 organizations
Staff: 4
Annual Budget: $250-500,000
President: David N. Laux
Exec. V. President: Kenneth W. Allen

Historical Note
Council members are organizations with an interest in promoting economic ties between the two countries.

Publications:
Conference Report. a.
Membership List. a.
Progress Report. a.
Taiwan Business News. bi-m.
Taiwan Business Notes. q.

Meetings/Conferences:
1999 – San Antonio, TX/Nov. 18-19

U.S.-Russia Business Council *(1993)*
1701 Pennsylvania Ave., N.W., Suite 650
Washington, DC   20006
Tel: (202)739-9180   *Fax:* (202)659-5920
Web Site: http://www.usrbc.org
Members: 240 corporations
Staff: 12
Annual Budget: $1-2,000,000
President: Eugene K. Lawson
V. President, Gov't. Affairs: M. Kay Larcom
V. President, Membership & Policy Development: Z. Blake Marshall

Historical Note
Membership: $1,250-10,000/year (organization) according to annual sales.

Publications:
U. S.

Meetings/Conferences:
1999 – Atlanta, GA

U.S.A. Dry Pea and Lentil Council *(1949)*
5071 Highway 8 West
Moscow, ID   83843
Tel: (208)882-3023   *Fax:* (208)882-6406
E-Mail: Pulse@pea-lentil.com
Members: 1,350 individuals
Staff: 7
Annual Budget: $250-500,000
President and C.E.O.: Tim McGreevy

Historical Note
Merged with the American Dry Pea and Lentil Ass'n in 1994. USADPLC members are concerned with growing, warehousing, processing and merchandising peas and lentils.

Publications:
Newsletter. m.

Meetings/Conferences:

U.S.A. Poultry and Egg Export Council *(1984)*
2300 W. Park Place Blvd., Suite 100
Stone Mountain, GA   30087
Tel: (770)413-0006   *Fax:* (770)413-0007
E-Mail: info@usapeec.org
Web Site: http://www.usapeec.org
Members: 200 companies
Staff: 10
Annual Budget: $5-10,000,000
President: James H. Sumner
Director of Communications: Toby Moore
Exec. Assistant: Kay M. Phiel
Controller: Shep Tuller

Historical Note
Members are poultry and egg producers, processors, and traders interested in developing export markets. Membership: dues based on export volume. Has an annual budget of approximately $10 million.

Publications:
Monday Line. w.
U. S.

Meetings/Conferences:
Annual Meetings: Spring, usually 3rd week in June

U.S.A. Rice Council
Historical Note
A division of USA Rice Federation, which provides administrative support.

U.S.A. Rice Federation *(1994)*
4301 N. Fairfax Drive, Suite 305
Arlington, VA   22203-1627
Tel: (703)351-8161   *Fax:* (703)351-8162

Web Site: http://www.usarice.com
Members: 3 organizations
Staff: 40
Annual Budget: $5-10,000,000

Historical Note
Founded as The Rice Industry. Became the Rice Council for Market Development in 1960, and assumed its present name in 1990. The USA Rice Federation is an umbrella organization representing three associations: U.S. Rice Producers Group, Rice Millers Ass'n, and U.S.A. Rice Council. It supports the U.S.'s rice producers, millers, marketers and others in allied industries. Has an annual budget of approximately $5.6 million.

Publications:
Membership/Rice Industry Newsletter.
USA Rice Quarterly. q.

Meetings/Conferences:
1999 – New Orleans, LA/June 13-17

U.S.A. Toy Library Ass'n *(1984)*
2530 Crawford Ave., Suite 111
Evanston, IL 60201
Tel: (847)864-3330 *Fax:* (847)864-3331
E-Mail: FOLIOG@aol.com
Members: 200 individuals, 30 companies
Staff: 2
Annual Budget: $10-25,000
Exec. Director: Judith Q. Iacuzzi

Historical Note
Built on the idea that play and toys are an important part of a child's healthy growth and development; receives about ten inquiries per week from individuals interested in establishing a toy library or bettering an existing one. Membership: $55/year (basic), $165/year (organization).

Publications:
Child's Play Newsletter. q. adv.
Toy Library Directory. a.
Toy Library Operators Manual. a.

Meetings/Conferences:

UAN Solutions Export Ass'n
c/o Foley & Lardner
3000 K St., N.W., Suite 500
Washington, DC 20007-5109
Tel: (202)672-5378
Secretary: Howard W. Fogt, Jr.

Historical Note
A Webb-Pomerene Act registered export trade association.

UFCW Textile Council *(1901)*
1369 W. Andrew Johnson Hwy., Suite 200
Morristown, TN 37814-3728
Members: 20,000 individuals
Staff: 20
Annual Budget: $2-5,000,000
President: Ron Myslowka

Historical Note
Founded in Washington, DC on November 19, 1901 from the AFL-sponsored merger of Internat'l Union of Textile Workers (founded in 1890) and American Federation of Textile Operatives (founded in 1900); became an affiliate of United Food and Commercial Workers (Washington, DC) and assumed its current name in 1995.

Publications:
UFCW Action. q.

Meetings/Conferences:
Semi-annual Meetings: Memphis, TN in February and various locations in September.

Ukraine Working Group
Historical Note
Became (1997) American Business Alliance for the Transition Economies of Eurasia.

Ultrasonic Industry Ass'n *(1956)*
P.O. Box 1420
Cherry Hill, NJ 08034-0054
Tel: (609)424-8998 *Fax:* (609)424-9248
E-Mail: uia@howellmgt.com
Members: 106 companies
Staff: 1
Annual Budget: $50-100,000
Administrative Director: Cheryl Smithers

Historical Note
UIA members are united in changing the world of medicine and industry through ultrasonics by providing access to educators, researchers, engineers, users, products, and applications leading to the advancement of ultrasonic technology. Membership:$15/year (student); $85/year (individual); $60/year (foreign); $185/year (corporate); 575/year (sustaining).

Publications:
Membership Directory. a. adv.
Patent Review. bi.
Vibrations Newsletter. q. adv.

Meetings/Conferences:

Ultrasonics, Ferroelectrics and Frequency Control Soc.
Historical Note
A technical society of the Institute of Electrical and Electronics Engineers (IEEE). Membership in the Society, open only to IEEE members, includes a subscription to a technical periodical in the field published by IEEE. All administrative support is provided by IEEE.

UNDA-USA, Nat'l Catholic Ass'n for Broadcasters/Communicators *(1972)*
901 Irving Ave.
Dayton, OH 45409-2316
Tel: (513)229-2303 *Fax:* (513)229-2300
E-Mail: undausa1@aol.com

Members: 250 individuals
Staff: 3
Annual Budget: $100-250,000
Administrator, National Office: Sue West

Historical Note
UNDA is the Latin word for "wave". The Nat'l Catholic Ass'n for Communicators is the U.S. arm of UNDA, the international association of Catholic broadcasters. Absorbed the Catholic Broadcasters Ass'n (1948). Membership: $155/year (individual); $400/year (organization).

Publications:
UNDA-USA Newsletter. q.

Meetings/Conferences:
Annual Meetings: Fall
1999 – Las Vegas, NV
2000 – Baltimore, MD

Underground Equipment Council
Historical Note
A council of the Equipment Manufacturers Institute.

Undersea and Hyperbaric Medical Soc. *(1967)*
10531 Metropolitan Ave.
Kensington, MD 20895
Tel: (301)942-2980 *Fax:* (301)942-7806
E-Mail: uhms@uhms.org
Web Site: http://www.uhms.org
Members: 2,500 individuals
Staff: 8
Annual Budget: $500-1,000,000
Exec. Director: Leon J. Greenbaum, Jr., Ph.D.
Managing Editor: Ann Barker
Office Manager and Meetings Coordinator: Jane Dunne
Membership Secretary and Librarian: Kathy Davidson
Administrative Assistant: Denyse Spence

Historical Note
Formerly (1986) Undersea Medical Soc. Membership: $150/year (individual); $750/year (organization).

Publications:
Pressure. bi-m. adv.
Undersea & Hyperbaric Medicine. q.

Meetings/Conferences:
Annual Meetings: Summer
1999 – Boston, MA/June 26-30

Unfinished Furniture Ass'n *(1990)*
35 E. Wacker Dr., Suite 500
Chicago, IL 60601-2105
Tel: (312)782-5252 *Fax:* (312)236-1140
Members: 600 companies
Staff: 7
Annual Budget: $250-500,000
Exec. Director: JoAnne Webber

Historical Note
Membership: $100-500/year, based on sales (company).

Publications:
Unfinished Business News. bi-m. adv.

Meetings/Conferences:

Uni-Bell PVC Pipe Ass'n *(1971)*
2655 Villa Creek Drive, Suite 155
Dallas, TX 75234
Tel: (972)243-3902 *Fax:* (972)243-3907
Web Site: www.members.aol.com/unibell
Members: 40 companies
Staff: 3
Annual Budget: $500-1,000,000
Exec. Director: Robert Walker

Historical Note
A non-profit technical, educational and research oriented organization, association members are producers of gasketed PVC pipe used in buried water, sewer and irrigation lines.

Publications:
Uni-Bell PVC Pipe News. a.

Meetings/Conferences:
Annual Meetings: Spring

Unified Medical Group Ass'n
Historical Note
Merged with the American Group Practice Ass'n to form the American Medical Group Ass'n in 1996.

Uniform and Textile Service Ass'n *(1933)*
1300 North 17th St., Suite 750
Arlington, VA 22209-3801
Tel: (703)247-2600 *Fax:* (703)841-4750
Toll Free: (800)486 - 6745
Web Site: http://www.usta.com/whoweare.htm
Members: 900 companies
Staff: 15
Annual Budget: $2-5,000,000
President and C.E.O.: David F. Hobson
Dir., Communications/Editor: Kenneth E. Koepper
Dir., Govt./Public Affairs: Mary Anne Dolbearr
Dir., Environmental/Reg. Affairs: David Dunlap
Dir., Finance/Admin.: Deborah Hodges

Historical Note
Formerly (1993) the Institute of Industrial Launderers. Members are companies that rent reusable textile products (e.g., shop towels, uniforms), and provide laundering services to commercial and industrial customers.

Publications:
Industrial Launderer. m. adv.
This is the IIL. a. adv.

Meetings/Conferences:
Annual Meetings: Fall
1999 – Boston, MA(Westin)/Sept. 25-29

Uniform Boiler and Pressure Vessel Laws Soc. *(1915)*
308 N. Evergreen Rd., Suite 240
Louisville, KY 40243-1010
Tel: (502)244-6029 *Fax:* (502)244-6030
Members: 225 individuals, 90 member companies
Staff: 3
Annual Budget: $100-250,000
Exec. Director: Raymond P. Swanson

Historical Note
Formerly American Uniform Boiler Law Society. Established to promote uniformity in rules, laws and regulations for boiler and pressure vessel safety based on the requirements of the American Society of Mechanical Engineers Boiler and Pressure Vessel Code and other related American and Canadian national standards. Membership: $125/year, minimum.

Publications:
Data Sheet. a.
Synopsis of Boiler & Pressure Vessel Laws, Rules & Regulations. bien.

Meetings/Conferences:

Uniformed Services Academy of Family Physicians *(1973)*
Historical Note
Address unknown in 1997.

UniForum Ass'n *(1980)*
10440 Shaker Dr., Suite 203
Columbia, MD 21046-1292
Tel: (410)715-9500 *Fax:* (301)596-8803
Toll Free: (800)333 - 8649
E-Mail: membership@uniforum.org
Web Site: http://www.uniforum.org
Members: 5,000 individuals
President: Alan Fedder

Historical Note
Founded as Internat'l Ass'n of Open Systems; assumed its current name in 1997. UniForum members are computer hardware and software developers, vendors and users working in an open systems environment. Membership: $125/year.

Publications:
IT Soultions Index.
Journal of Open Computing. q.
Member Newsletter. m. adv.
Open Systems Product Directory. a. adv.

Meetings/Conferences:
1999 – San Jose, CA/Jan. 26-29

Union for Radical Political Economics *(1968)*
37 Howe Street
New Haven, CT 06511
Tel: (203)777-4605 *Fax:* (203)777-1625
E-Mail: urpe@labornet.org
Web Site: http://www.urpe.org
Members: 1,100 individuals
Staff: 2
Annual Budget: $100-250,000
Administrator: Germai Mehenie

Historical Note
An interdisciplinary association devoted to the study, development, and application of political economic analysis to social problems. A member of the Allied Social Science Ass'ns. Membership: $15/year ($30-55/year with subscription).

Publications:
Review of Radical Political Economics. q.
URPE Newsletter. q.

Meetings/Conferences:
Semi-annual Meetings: Summer Conference in August and with Allied Social Science Ass'ns in December

Union of American Hebrew Congregations *(1873)*
633 Third Ave.
New York, NY 10017-6778
Tel: (212)650-4000 *Fax:* (212)650-4159
E-Mail: UAHC@UAHC.ORG
Web Site: http://uahc.org
Members: 875 congregations
Staff: 240
Annual Budget: $10-25,000,000
President: Rabbi Eric H. Yoffie
Director of Communications: Emily Grotta
Director of Meetings: Robin Hirsh
Director of Program: Rabbi Daniel Freelander
Controller: Les Pitner
V. President: Rabbi Lennard Thal
Chief Administrative Officer: Monika Hamburger

Historical Note
UAHC is the parent body of Reform synagogues of the U.S. and Canada. It provides programs and services for every aspect of synagogue life such as worship, adult and child education, management, and religious action. Has a budget of approximately $14 million.

Publications:
Reform Judaism. q. adv.

Meetings/Conferences:
Biennial Meetings: Odd years/3,500-5,000
1999 – Boston, MA/Dec. 8-12

Union of American Physicians and Dentists *(1972)*
1330 Broadway, Suite 730
Oakland, CA 94612-2506
Tel: (510)839-0193 *Fax:* (510)763-8756
E-Mail: uapd@uapd.com
Members: 10,000 individuals
Staff: 16
Annual Budget: $1-2,000,000
Exec. Director: Gary Robinson

Historical Note
A labor union representing physicians and dentists in fourteen states who bargain with government entities, hospitals and employers. Membership: $420/year.

Publications:
UAPD Report. m.

Meetings/Conferences:

Union of Needletrades, Industrial and Textile Employees (1900)
1710 Broadway
New York, NY   10019
Tel: (212)265-7000   Fax: (212)265-3415
Web Site: http://www.uniteunion.org
Members: 200,000 individuals
Staff: 1000
Annual Budget: $5-10,000,000
President: Jay J. Mazur

Historical Note
Organized as Internat'l Ladies Garment Workers Union and chartered by the American Federation of Labor in 1900; absorbed Amalgamated Clothing and Textile Workers Union and assumed its current name in 1995.

Publications:
Justice. m.

Meetings/Conferences:
Triennial Meetings: (1998)

United Ass'n of Equipment Leasing (1975)
520 Third St., Suite 201
Oakland, CA   94607-3520
Tel: (510)444-9235   Fax: (510)444-1346
Staff: 5
Annual Budget: $1-2,000,000
Exec. V. President: Raymond Williams, Ph.D., CAE
Meeting Planner: Lavergne Malone
Director of Publications: Christine Delinsky

Historical Note
Founded as Western Ass'n of Equipment Lessors, became WAEL: a National Equipment Leasing Ass'n in 1993, and assumed its current name in 1995.

Publications:
Funding Source Profile Directory. a. adv.
Membership Directory. a. adv.

Meetings/Conferences:
Semi-Annual: May and Sept./Oct.

United Ass'n of Journeymen and Apprentices of the Plumbing and Pipe Fitting Industry of U.S. and Canada (1889)
901 Massachusetts Ave., N. W.
Washington, DC   20001
Tel: (202)628-5823   Fax: (202)628-5024
Web Site: http://www.ua.org
Members: 302,000 individuals
Staff: 150
Annual Budget: $5-10,000,000
General President: Martin J. Maddaloni

Historical Note
Organized in Washington, DC October 7, 1889 as the United Association of Journeymen, Plumbers, Gas Fitters, Steam Fitters and Steam Fitters Helpers of the United States and Canada. Affiliated with the American Federation of Labor in 1897 and adopted its present name in 1947. Has a budget of about $23 million. Sponsors and supports the U. A. Political Education Committee.

Publications:
General Officers Report. w.
U. A.

Meetings/Conferences:
Meetings: Every 5 years in Summer (1996)
2001 – Hollywood, FL

United Ass'n of Used Oil Services (1987)
318 Newman Road
Sebring, FL   33870-6702
Tel: (941)655-3880   Fax: (941)655-3713
Toll Free: (800)877 - 4356
Staff: 7
Annual Budget: $100-250,000
Exec. Director: Frank S. Bronstein

Historical Note
UAUOS was established to be an effective presence in dealing with regulations and to provide a network for those with an interest in the collection and proper disposition of used lubricating oils. Membership: $500/year (organization).

Publications:
Oil Drop Newsletter. m. adv.
Used Oil Report. q.
Used Oil Transporters Certification Manual.

Meetings/Conferences:
Quarterly Meetings: fall

United Better Dress Manufacturers Ass'n (1939)
110 West 40th St., 19th Floor
New York, NY   10018
Tel: (212)354-7042
Members: 100 companies
Staff: 2
Exec. Director: John Infantolino

Historical Note
Smaller manufacturers of quality dresses, mainly in the New York area. Major purpose is labor negotiating with the International Ladies Garment Workers Union.

United Braford Breeders (1969)
422 E. Main St., Suite 218
Nacogdoches, TX   75961-5214
Tel: (409)569-8200   Fax: (409)569-9556
E-Mail: ubb@brafords.org
Web Site: http://www.brafords.org
Members: 500 individuals
Staff: 4
Annual Budget: $100-250,000
Exec. Director: Rodney L. Roberson

Historical Note
Formerly (1994) Internat'l Braford Ass'n. Members are breeders of Braford cattle. Maintains breed registry. Membership: $50/year.

Publications:
Braford News. q. adv.

Meetings/Conferences:
1999 – Houston, TX/Feb. 23-24

United Brotherhood of Carpenters and Joiners of America (1881)
101 Constitution Ave., N.W., Room 432
Washington, DC   20001
Tel: (202)546-6206   Fax: (202)543-5724
Members: 550,000 individuals
Staff: 150
Annual Budget: $50-100,000,000
President: Douglas J. McCarron

Historical Note
Established August 8, 1881 in Chicago as the Brotherhood of Carpenters and Joiners. Merged in 1888 with the United Order of Carpenters to form the present organization. Absorbed the Wood, Wire and Metal Lathers International Union in 1979. Absorbed the Tile, Marble, Terrazzo, Finishers, Shopworkers & Granite Cutters Internat'l Union in 1988. A charter member of the American Federation of Labor, the Brotherhood today has an annual budget of approximately $66.5 million.

Publications:
The Carpenter. m. adv.

Meetings/Conferences:
Annual Meetings: Every 5 years (1996)

United Bus Owners of America (1971)
Historical Note
Became United Motorcoach Ass'n in 1995.

United Developers Council
Historical Note
An affiliate of the Nat'l Ass'n of Real Estate Brokers.

United Duroc Swine Registry (1936)
Historical Note
Registry merged with the Hampshire Swine Registry and the American Yorkshire Club in 1996 and is now under the title of Nat'l Swine Registry.

United Egg Ass'n (1982)
One Massachusetts Ave., N.W., Suite 800
Washington, DC   20001
Tel: (202)789-2499   Fax: (202)682-0775
Web Site: http://www.unitedegg.org
Members: 6 manufacturers
Staff: 4
President: Albert E. Pope
Director of Government Relations: Tom Montgomery

Historical Note
Trade association of manufacturers of egg products (liquid, dry and frozen) for use in further processed products.

Publications:
United Voices. bi-m.

Meetings/Conferences:
Annual Meetings: January

United Egg Producers (1968)
1303 Hightower Trail, Suite 200
Atlanta, GA   30350-2919
Tel: (770)587-5871   Fax: (770)587-0041
E-Mail: info@unitedegg.com
Web Site: http://www.unitedegg.org
Members: 360 individuals, 5 regional cooperatives
Staff: 6
Annual Budget: $500-1,000,000
President: Albert E. Pope

Historical Note
The largest federation of regional cooperatives in the egg industry. Maintains a Washington government liaison office. Sponsors the Egg Political Action Committee.

Publications:
United Voices. bi-w.

Meetings/Conferences:

United Electrical, Radio and Machine Workers of America (1936)
1 Gateway Center, Suite 1400
Pittsburgh, PA   15222
Tel: (412)471-8919   Fax: (412)471-8999
Web Site: http://www.ranknfile-ue.org
Members: 40,000 individuals
Staff: 90
Annual Budget: $2-5,000,000
President: John H. Hovis, Jr.
Publicity & Education Director: Carole Lambiase
Office Manager: Edward C. Huot

Historical Note
Established in Buffalo in March, 1936, and chartered by the Congress of Industrial Organizations the same year. Withheld per capita payments from the CIO in 1948 and later expelled. It is now an independent union.

Publications:
UE News. m.

Meetings/Conferences:
Annual Meetings: Fall

United Engineering Trustees (1904)
3 Park Ave., 27th Floor
New York, NY   10016-5902
Tel: (212)679-1645   Fax: (212)705-7441
Members: 7 engineering organizations
Staff: 20
Annual Budget: $5-10,000,000
Secretary & General Manager (C.E.O.): Jerome I. Fishel

Historical Note
Founded in New York, NY as the United Engineering Soc. Name changed in 1930 to Engineering Foundation, Inc., and again in 1931 to the present name. Constituent members include Founder (ASCE; AIME; ASME; IEEE; and AIChE) and Associate (IES; EI; WRC; MPC; ABET and SWE) Societies representing a collective membership of over 750,000. UET owns and operates the United Engineering Center; manages the Daniel Guggenheim and John Fritz Medal Boards of Award; and acts as fiscal agent for the Welding Research Council and the Metal Properties Council. UET maintains the Engineering Foundation which supports research projects and conducts interdisciplinay conferences, and the Engineering Societies Library, a free public engineering library. Has an annual budget of approximately $7.3 million.

Meetings/Conferences:
Annual Meetings: Fourth Thursday in January in New York, NY (by invitation only).

United Farm Workers of America (1962)
P.O. Box 62
Keene, CA   93531
Tel: (805)822-5571   Fax: (805)822-6103
Web Site: http://www.usw.org
Members: 26,000 individuals
Annual Budget: $2-5,000,000
President: Arturo S. Rodriguez
Secretary Treasurer: Dolores Huerta
Director of Finance: Liz Villarino

Historical Note
Organized in 1962 by Cesar E. Chavez as the Nat'l Farm Workers Ass'n. In 1966 the Nat'l Farm Workers Ass'n and the Agricultural Workers Organizing Committee merged to become the United Farm Workers of America affiliated with the AFL-CIO. Sponsors and supports the National United Farm Workers Volunteer Political Action Committee. Membership: 2% of what they earn while they work.

Meetings/Conferences:
Biennial meetings: even years

United Federation of Police Officers (1980)
540 N. State Rd.
Box 76
Briarcliff Manor, NY   10510-0076
Tel: (914)941-4103   Fax: (914)941-4472
Toll Free: (800)227 - 4291
Members: 1000 individuals
Staff: 2
Annual Budget: $500-1,000,000
President: Ralph M. Purdy

Historical Note
Promotes the welfare of its members, aids them in their need for mutual benefits, protection and improvement of their social and financial conditions. Membership: $.50/week.

Publications:
UFP News. 5/year. adv.

Meetings/Conferences:
Annual Meetings: September

United Fire Equipment Service Ass'n (1954)
P.O. Box 141
Lake Zurich, IL   60047
Tel: (847)438-2343
Members: 28 state associations
Treasurer: Jim Jarzembowski

Historical Note
UFESA members are state associations of companies selling and servicing fire extinguishers.

Publications:
Information Bulletin. irreg.

United Food and Commercial Workers Internat'l Union (1979)
1775 K St., N.W.
Washington, DC   20006
Tel: (202)223-3111   Fax: (202)466-1562
Web Site: http://www.ufcw.org
Members: 1,400,000 individuals
Annual Budget: $5-10,000,000
Internat'l President: Douglas H. Dority

Historical Note
Labor union affiliated with AFL/CIO and the Canadian Labour Congress. Formed by a merger of the Retail Clerks Internat'l Union (founded in 1888), the Amalgamated Meat Cutters and Butcher Workmen of North America (founded in 1897) in 1979. Absorbed Affiliated Barbers, Beauticians, and Allied Industries Internat'l Ass'n in 1980; United Retail Workers in 1981; Insurance Workers Internat'l Union in 1983; Canadian Brewery and Distillery Workers in 1986; Internat'l Union of Life Insurance Agents in 1992; United Garment Workers of America in 1994; Distillery, Wine and Allied Workers' Internat'l Union in 1996 and Internat'l Chemical Workers Union in 1997. The second largest union in the AFL-CIO. Represents workers in the retail, meat packing, food processing, hair care, insurance, health care, footwear and fur industry.

Publications:
UFCW Action. semi-m.

Meetings/Conferences:
Every 5 years: 1997 in July

United Fresh Fruit and Vegetable Ass'n *(1904)*
727 N. Washington St.
Alexandria, VA   22314
Tel: (703)836-3410   *Fax:* (703)836-7745
E-Mail: united@uffva.org
Members: 1,500 companies
Staff: 20
Annual Budget: $2-5,000,000
President and C.E.O.: Thomas E. Stenzel, CAE
V. President, Communications: Sarah Delea
V. President, Government Affairs: John J. Aguirre
Manager, Meetings: Erin E. McGee
V. President, Member Services and Marketing: Caren Schumacher

Historical Note
The United Fresh Fruit and Vegetable Association is an international trade association representing the fresh produce industry. Member firms supply the majority of fresh produce grown and sold in the United States, and include grower/shippers, brokers, truckers and other transportation specialists, wholesalers, foodservice distributors and operators, retailers and allied suppliers.

Publications:
United Today. q.

Meetings/Conferences:
Annual Meetings: February/8,000
1999 – San Diego, CA/Feb. 6-8

United Golfers' Ass'n *(1926)*
Historical Note
Address unknown in 1996.

United Infants and Childrens Wear Ass'n *(1933)*
1430 Broadway, Room 1603
New York, NY   10018-3308
Tel: (212)244-2953   *Fax:* (212)221-3540
Members: 4 companies
Staff: 1
Annual Budget: $100-250,000
President: Alex J. Glauberman

Historical Note
A member of the Federation of Apparel Manufacturers.

Meetings/Conferences:
Annual Meetings: Not held

United Knitwear Manufacturers League *(1938)*
500 Seventh Ave., 2nd Floor
New York, NY   10018
Tel: (212)819-1011
Members: 1 company
Staff: 2
Annual Budget: $25-50,000
General Counsel: Arnold R. Harris

Historical Note
Makers of knitted outergarments such as sweaters and swimming suits. Major purpose is the conduct of labor negotiations. Membership concentrated in the New York area.

United Laser Toner Recyclers Ass'n *(1991)*
Historical Note
Address unknown in 1998.

United Lightning Protection Ass'n *(1936)*
P.O. Box 22683
Lake Buena Vista, FL   32830-2683
Toll Free: (800)668 - 8572
Members: 95 individuals
Staff: 1
Annual Budget: $10-25,000
President: Guy C. Maxwell

Historical Note
ULPA members are manufacturers, distributors, field engineers and installers of lightning protection or supression equipment. Membership: $200/year (full member); $50/year (associate).

Publications:
More Static. q. adv.

Meetings/Conferences:
Annual Meetings: Spring
1999 – Longboat Key, FL(Holiday Inn)/Mar. 5-8

United Methodist Ass'n of Health and Welfare Ministries *(1940)*
601 West Riverview Ave.
Dayton, OH   45406-5543
Tel: (937)227-9494   *Fax:* (937)222-7364
Toll Free: (800)411 - 7364
E-Mail: uma@umassociation.org
Web Site: http://www.umassociation.org
Members: 75 individuals, 400 organizations
Staff: 5
Annual Budget: $500-1,000,000
President/C.E.O.: Dean W. Pulliam
Director, Communications: Teresa A. Trost
Director of Member Services: Misty A. Strawser

Historical Note
Organized in 1940 as the Nat'l Ass'n of Methodist Hospitals and Homes. Became the Nat'l Ass'n of Health and Welfare Ministries, United Methodist Church in 1969 and assumed its present name in 1983. Is now independent of The United Methodist Church. Acts as a network for the various long-term care, retirement, family and children's service and community organizations related to the UMC. Membership: $75/year (individual); $630-$4,275/year (institution, based on budget).

Publications:
UMA Journal. q. adv.

Meetings/Conferences:
Annual Meetings: Spring/500

1999 – Baltimore, MD/April 7-11
2000 – Dallas, TX/April 1-5

United Mine Workers of America Internat'l Union *(1890)*
900 15th St., N.W.
Washington, DC   20005
Tel: (202)842-7200   *Fax:* (202)842-7342
E-Mail: journal@umwa.com
Web Site: http://access.digex.net/~miner
Members: 130,000 individuals
Staff: 100
Annual Budget: $5-10,000,000
President: Cecil E. Roberts
Director, Communications: Doug Gibson

Historical Note
Formed January 25, 1890, in Columbus, Ohio, by the merger of the Knights of Labor and the National Progressive Union of Miners and Mine Laborers. Chartered as an industrial union by the American Federation of Labor, it left the AFL fo form the Congress of Industrial Organizations (CIO) in 1938. The union affiliated with the AFL-CIO in 1989. Has an annual budget of approximately $62.4 million. Sponsors and supports the Coal Miners Political Action Committee (COMPAC).

Publications:
UMW Journal. bi-m.

Meetings/Conferences:
Quadrennial Meetings: (1998)/2,000

United Motorcoach Ass'n *(1971)*
113 S. West St., 4th Floor
Alexandria, VA   22314
Tel: (703)838-2929   *Fax:* (703)838-2950
E-Mail: info@uma.org
Web Site: http://www.uma.org
Members: 1000 companies
Staff: 4
Annual Budget: $500-1,000,000
Exec. Director: Victor Parra
Director of Membership and Convention Services: Annette M. Ott

Historical Note
Formerly (1995) United Bus Owners of America. UMA serves the intercity bus industry, with particular emphasis on charter and tour transportation companies.

Publications:
Membership Directory. a.
The Docket. bi-m.

Meetings/Conferences:
1999 – Houston, TX/Jan. 21-26

United Nations Staff Union *(1946)*
United Nations, Room 525
New York, NY   10017
Tel: (212)963-7076   *Fax:* (212)963-3367
Members: 12,000 individuals
Staff: 3
Annual Budget: $1-2,000,000
President: Rosemarie Waters

Historical Note
Open to all staff of the United Nations Secretariat. Membership: monthly dues based on earnings.

Publications:
Staff Committee Bulletins (SCB's). irreg.
UN Staff Report. bi-m.
What's New. m.

Meetings/Conferences:
Annual Meetings: March

United Ostomy Ass'n *(1962)*
19772 MacArthur Blvd., Suite 200
Irvine, CA   92612-2405
Tel: (949)660-8624   *Fax:* (949)660-9262
Toll Free: (800)826 - 0826
E-Mail: uoa@deltanet.com
Web Site: www.uoa.org
Members: 34,000 individuals
Staff: 7
Annual Budget: $1-2,000,000
Exec. Director: Darlene A. Smith

Historical Note
Incorporated in New York, UOA is a not-for-profit mutual aid organization of individuals who have undergone ostomy surgery, their families, and members of the medical, enterostomal therapy and nursing professions. Membership: $15.50/year.

Publications:
Ostomy Quarterly. q. adv.

Meetings/Conferences:
Annual Meetings: August
1999 – Dallas, TX

United Paperworkers Internat'l Union *(1884)*
P.O. Box 1475
Nashville, TN   37202
Tel: (615)834-8590   *Fax:* (615)834-7741
Members: 245,000 individuals
Staff: 250
Annual Budget: $10-25,000,000
President: Boyd Young
Director, Communications: Keith Romig
Political Education Director: Rodney Green
Research/Education Director: Dennis Wenske
Internat'l Secretary-Treasurer: Jim Dunn
General Counsel: Lynn Agee

Historical Note
Merged with the Oil, Chemical, and Atomic Workers Int'l Union in 1999. The United Paperworkers of America (founded in 1944) and the International Brotherhood of Papermakers (founded in 1893) merged March 6, 1957 to form the United Papermakers and Paperworkers. This organization, in turn, merged on August 2,

1972 with the International Brotherhood of Pulp, Sulphite and Paper Mill Workers of the United States and Canada (founded in 1909), creating the United Paperworkers International Union as it exists today. Canadian members of UPIU formed a separate union in 1974. Merged with Internat'l Union, Allied Industrial Workers of America in 1993. Sponsors and supports the United Paperworkers International Union Political Education Program. Has an annual budget of approximately $24 million.

Publications:
The Paperworker. m.

Meetings/Conferences:
Semi-Annual Meetings: Winter and Summer

United Product Formulators and Distributors Ass'n *(1968)*
2034 Beaver Ruin Rd.
Norcross, GA   30071-3710
Members: 100 companies
Staff: 1
Annual Budget: $50-100,000
Exec. Director: Valera B. Jessee

Historical Note
Formerly (1988) United Pesticide Formulators and Distributors Ass'n. Members are firms which are directly involved in formulating and distributing products or equipment to the pest control industry. Seeks to upgrade the pest control industry by promoting cooperation between customer and supplier and cooperating with government authorities for proper liaison and communication. Membership: $300/year (company).

Publications:
Update. q.

Meetings/Conferences:
Annual Meetings: April

United Professional Horsemen's Ass'n *(1968)*
4059 Iron Works Pwy., Suite 4
Lexington, KY   40511
Tel: (606)231-5070   *Fax:* (606)255-2774
E-Mail: uphakgr@aol.com
Members: 1,300 individuals
Staff: 1
Annual Budget: $50-100,000
Exec. Secretary: Karen G. Richardson

Historical Note
Founded in 1968, so that professional trainers of American Saddlebreds, Morgan and Hackney ponies could have a united voice in the show horse industry. Membership: $50/year.

Publications:
UPHA Directory. bi-a. adv.
UPHAppenings. q.

Meetings/Conferences:
Annual Meetings: January/400-500
1999 – St. Louis, MO(Hyatt Regency)/Jan. 6-9/450
2000 – Nashville, TN(Opryland)/Jan. 5-8/450

United Rubber, Cork, Linoleum and Plastic Workers of America
Historical Note
Merged with United Steelworkers of America and became the Rubber and Plastics Industrial Conference of the U.S.W.A. in 1995.

United Scenic Artists *(1918)*
16 W. 61st St., 11th Floor
New York, NY   10023-7606
Tel: (212)581-0300   *Fax:* (212)977-2011
Members: 2,600 individuals
Staff: 12
Annual Budget: $1-2,000,000
National Business Manager: Paul G. Moore

Historical Note
Entertainment industry union. Members are highly skilled scenic artists, set designers, art directors, costume designers, lighting designers, and mural artists for Broadway, television, film, and commercial and regional theatre.

Publications:
Newsletter. m.

Meetings/Conferences:
Annual Meetings: New York, Chicago, Los Angeles and Miami

United Soybean Board *(1990)*
16305 Swingley Ridge Drive, Ste. 110
Chesterfield, MO   63017
Tel: (314)530-8955   *Fax:* (314)530-1560
Toll Free: (800)989 - 8721
E-Mail: info@talksoy.com
Web Site: http://www.talksoy.com
C.E.O: John Bechever
Exec. Director: James M. Palmer

Historical Note
Organized to manage the National Soybean Checkoff, USB provides scientific and technical information to member soybean farmers.

United States Advanced Ceramics Ass'n *(1985)*
1600 Wilson Blvd., Suite 901
Arlington, VA   22209
Tel: (703)812-8740   *Fax:* (703)812-8743
E-Mail: usaca@ibm.net
Members: 18 companies
Staff: 5
Exec. Director: William H. Werst
Mgr., Committee Affairs: Meredith Cawley
Manager, Government Affairs: Tamara Stretton
Manager, Membership Affairs: Jennifer Evanchik

Historical Note
USACA represents the advanced ceramics materials industry. Members include raw material suppliers, parts manufacturers and parts users with U.S. facilities.

United States Air Tour Ass'n (1995)
4041 PowderMill Road, Suite 201
Calverton, MD 20705
Tel: (301)931-8770   *Fax:* (703)683-6402
E-Mail: stevebassett@USATA.com
Web Site: http://www.usata.com
Members: 60 companies
Staff: 1
President: Steve Bassett

Historical Note
Formerly the Nat'l Air Access Council (1996). Represents air tour firms and individuals with interests in airspace rights, particularly in cases involving access to airspace over federally-controlled land.

Meetings/Conferences:

United States and Canadian Academy of Pathology (1906)
3643 Walton Way Extension
Augusta, GA 30909-6486
Tel: (706)733-7550   *Fax:* (706)733-8033
E-Mail: IAP@USCAP.USA.COM
Web Site: http://www.uscap.org
Members: 7,000 individuals
Staff: 5
Annual Budget: $1-2,000,000
Exec. Director: F. Stephen Vogel

Historical Note
Formerly Internat'l Ass'n of Medical Museums and (1987) Internat'l Academy of Pathology. USCAP seeks to advance Pathology teaching, practice and research. Seeks to provide its members with new information both at the investigative and applied practice levels and to reinforce and update their knowledge in their area of interest and expertise. Membership: $110/year (individual).

Publications:
Laboratory Investigation. m. adv.
Modern Pathology. m. adv.

Meetings/Conferences:
Annual Meetings: Febraury-March
1999 – San Francisco, CA(Hilton)/March 20-26
2000 – New Orleans, LA(Hilton)/March 25-31
2001 – Atlanta, GA(Marriott)/March 3-9
2002 – Chicago, IL(Sheraton)/February 23-March 1

United States Animal Health Ass'n (1896)
8100 Three Chopt Road, Suite 203
Richmond, VA 23229
Tel: (804)285-3210   *Fax:* (804)285-3367
E-Mail: ysaha@richmond.infi.net
Web Site: http://www.usaha.org
Members: 1,400 individuals, 17 organizations
Staff: 2
Annual Budget: $50-100,000
Administrative Secretary: Linda Ragland

Historical Note
Formed in 1896 as the Nat'l Ass'n of State Livestock Sanitary Boards to combat one disease affecting cattle, it became the United States Livestock Sanitary Ass'n in 1911 and assumed its present name in 1968. Absorbed the Nat'l Assembly of Chief Livestock Health Officials in 1973. Seeks to prevent, control and eliminate livestock diseases. Membership: $60/year (individual); $300/year (organization/company).

Publications:
Foreign Animal Disease Handbook. irreg.
Newsletter. q.
Proceedings. a.

Meetings/Conferences:
Annual Meetings: October/900
1999 – San Diego, CA(Town & Country Hotel)/Oct. 8-15
2000 – Birmingham, AL(Sheraton Civic Center)/Oct. 20-27/2000

United States Apple Export Council
6707 Old Dominion Dr., Suite 320
McLean, VA 22101-4503
Tel: (703)556-9300   *Fax:* (703)556-9301
Internat'l Marketing Director: Philip H. Kimball

United States Army Warrant Officers Ass'n (1974)
462 Herndon Pkwy., Suite 207
Herndon, VA 20170
Tel: (703)742-7727   *Fax:* (703)742-7728
Toll Free: (800)582 - 2967
E-Mail: usawoa@erols.com
Web Site: http://www.penfed.org/woa/home.htm
Members: 5,000 individuals
Staff: 4
Annual Budget: $250-500,000
Exec. Director: Raymond A. Bell
Manager, Financial: Herb Ruhdgren
Manager, Membership: Dave Welsh

Historical Note
USAWOA is a professional organization dedicated to the improvement of the Warrant Officer Corps through the dissemination of professional information. Membership is open to Army warrant officers regardless of component or status (active, reserve or retired). Membership: $24/year (retired warrant officers), $36/year (all others).

Publications:
Newsliner. m. adv.

Meetings/Conferences:
Annual Meetings: Always on military installation/Fall

United States Ass'n for Computational Mechanics (1988)
Langley Research Center, MS-201
11 West Taylor St. Building 1146

Hampton, VA 23681
Tel: (757)864-1978   *Fax:* (757)864-8089
Members: 500 individuals and institutions
Annual Budget: $50-100,000
President: Mark Shepard

Historical Note
Members are individuals and institutions concerned with computational mechanics. Membership: $25/year.

Publications:
Newsletter. bi-m.

Meetings/Conferences:
Biennial Meetings: (1997)
1999 – Boulder, CO(University of Colorado)/Aug. 4-6

United States Ass'n for Energy Economics (1992)
28790 Chagrin Blvd., Suite 350
Cleveland, OH 44122
Tel: (216)464-2785   *Fax:* (216)464-2768
E-Mail: iaee@iaee.org
Members: 1000 individuals, 10 companies
Staff: 2
Annual Budget: $25-50,000
Exec. Director: David L. Williams

Historical Note
An affiliate of the Internat'l Ass'n for Energy Economics (same address); USAEE members are automatically members of IAEE as well. USAEE provides a forum for the exchange of ideas, experience and issues among professionals interested in energy economics and to provide enhanced services to its membership. Members include economists, corporate planners, engineers, geologists, environmentalists, consultants, journalists, researchers from private industry/government and faculty from colleges and universities. Membership: $60/year (individual); $1,000/year (company).

Publications:
IAEE Newsletter. q. adv.
IAEE/USAEE Membership Directory. a. adv.
The Energy Journal. q. adv.
USAEE Dialogue. 3/yr. adv.

Meetings/Conferences:
1999 – Orlando, FL(Hilton)/Aug. 29-Sept. 1/350
2000 – Philadelphia, PA

United States Ass'n of Importers of Textiles and Apparel (1989)
13 East 16th St., Sixth Floor
New York, NY 10003-1114
Tel: (212)463-0089   *Fax:* (212)463-0583
Members: 175 companies
Staff: 3
Annual Budget: $250-500,000
Exec. Director: Laura E. Jones

Historical Note
USA-ITA, formed by nine founding company members in January 1989, represents members' interests to the government and within the industry. Membership: $1,000-15,000/year (corporate).

Publications:
Attn: Apparel Trade and Transportation Newsletter. m.
Customs Overview. m.
Electronic Bulletin Board for Textile & Apparel Information.
Intellectual Property Rights Review. bi-m.
USA-ITA Membership Directory. bien.

Meetings/Conferences:
Annual Meetings: Fall

United States Ass'n of Independent Gymnastic Clubs (1972)
235 Pinehurst Road
Wilmington, DE 19803
Tel: (302)656-3706
Members: 800 clubs
Staff: 2
Annual Budget: $50-100,000
Exec. Director: Edgar M. Knepper

Historical Note
Members are not-for-profit clubs.

Publications:
Club News. bi-m.

Meetings/Conferences:

United States Basketball Writers Ass'n (1956)
1000 St. Louis Union Station
St. Louis, MO 63103
Tel: (314)421-0339   *Fax:* (314)421-3505
Members: 1000 individuals
Staff: 1
Annual Budget: under $10,000
Exec. Director: Joe Mitch

Historical Note
Membership: $25/year.

Publications:
The Tip-Off. 7/year.

Meetings/Conferences:
Annual Meetings: In conjunction with finals of NCAA tournament

United States Beef Breeds Council (1952)
8288 Hascall St.
Omaha, NE 68124
Tel: (402)393-7200   *Fax:* (402)393-7203
Members: 22 associations
Annual Budget: $10-25,000
President: Dr. Roger E. Hunsley

Historical Note
Members are the chief executive officers of national purebred cattle organizations.

Meetings/Conferences:
1999 – Charlotte, NC/February 10-14/50

United States Beet Sugar Ass'n (1911)
1156 15th St., N.W., Suite 1019
Washington, DC 20005
Tel: (202)296-4820   *Fax:* (202)331-2065
Members: 8 companies
Staff: 4
Annual Budget: $500-1,000,000
President: Van Olsen
V. President: James Johnson

Historical Note
Established as the United States Beet Sugar Industry, it became the United States Sugar Manufacturers Ass'n in 1914 and assumed its present name in 1926. Sponsors the Beet Sugar Political Action Committee.

Publications:
American Beet Sugar Companies. a.

Meetings/Conferences:
Annual Meetings: February
1999 – Tucson, AZ

United States Bowling Instructors Ass'n (1984)
P.O. Box 564
Palatine, IL 60078
Tel: (847)359-0682   *Fax:* (847)550-0218
Members: 450 individuals
Annual Budget: under $10,000
Exec. Director: Thomas C. Kouros

United States Business and Industry Council (1933)
910 16th St., N.W. Suite 300
Washington, DC 20006
Tel: (202)628-2211   *Fax:* (202)628-3698
Toll Free: (800)767 - 2267
E-Mail: usbic@aol.com
Members: 1,500 companies
Staff: 7
Annual Budget: $500-1,000,000
President: Kevin L. Kearns

Historical Note
Formerly United States Business and Industrial Council (1998). Established as the Southern States Industrial Council, it became the United States Industrial Council in 1973 and assumed its present name in 1993. USBIC members come from family-owned and closely held domestic companies, representing their interests in trade, taxation and regulation.

Publications:
Bulletin. m.
Legislative Action Report. w.

Meetings/Conferences:
Annual Meetings: May/usually Washington, DC area

United States Business Council for Southeastern Europe (1974)
Historical Note
Address uunknown in 1997; superseded by American Business Alliance for the Transition Economies of Eurasia.

United States Cane Sugar Refiners' Ass'n (1936)
1730 Rhode Island Ave., N.W.
Washington, DC 20036
Tel: (202)331-1458   *Fax:* (202)785-5110
Members: 5 companies
Staff: 2
Annual Budget: $250-500,000
President: Nicholas Kominus

Historical Note
USCSRA represents sugar care refiners.

Meetings/Conferences:
Annual Meetings: Fall

United States Canola Ass'n (1989)
600 Pennsylvaia Ave., S.E., Suite 320
Washington, DC 20003-4316
Members: 50 producers and processors
Exec. Director: John Gordley

Historical Note
USCA members are producers and processors of canola and rapeseed. Membership: $25-50/year (individual); $500-2,500/year (organization/company).

United States Chamber of Shipping
Historical Note
Became Chamber of Shipping of America in 1998.

United States Cigarette Export Ass'n (1982)
Historical Note
Address unknown in 1997.

United States Committee on Irrigation and Drainage (1951)
1616 17th St., Suite 483
Denver, CO 80202
Tel: (303)628-5430   *Fax:* (303)628-5431
E-Mail: stephens@uscid.org
Web Site: http://www.uscid.org/ ~ uscid
Members: 500 individuals, 20 companies
Staff: 1
Annual Budget: $50-100,000
Exec. V. President: Larry D. Stephens

Historical Note
Incorporated in Colorado. Formerly (1967) United States Nat'l Committee, Internat'l Commission on Irrigation and Drainage and (1984) United States Committee on Irrigation, Drainage and Flood Control. USCID, a professional organization, is the U.S. national committee of the Internat'l Commission on Irrigation and Drainage. USCID provides a forum for multidisciplinary discussion of problems related to irrigation, drainage and flood control.

Membership: $50/year (individual); $95/year (library); $200/year (institution); $500/year (corporate).

Publications:
USCID Newsletter. q.

Meetings/Conferences:
Semi-Annual Meetings: Summer and Winter
1999 – San Louis Obispo, CA(Embassy Suites)/March 10-13
1999 – Phoenix, AZ(Holiday Inn)

United States Committee on Large Dams *(1928)*
1616 17th St., Suite 483
Denver, CO   80202
Tel: (303)628-5430   *Fax:* (303)628-5431
E-Mail: stephens@uscold.org
Web Site: www.uscold.org/ ~ uscold
Members: 1,150 individuals and companies
Staff: 1
Annual Budget: $50-100,000
Exec. Director: Larry D. Stephens

Historical Note
USCOLD members are individuals and organizations involved in the design, construction and maintenance of large dams. Membership: $60/year (individual), $450/year (organizaton).

Publications:
Membership Directory. a.
Newsletter. 3/year.
Proceedings of Annual Meetings. a.

Meetings/Conferences:
1999 – Atlanta, GA(Marriott North Central)/May 17-21

United States Conference of City Human Services Officials *(1980)*
1620 I St., N.W., 4th Floor
Washington, DC   20006
Tel: (202)293-7330   *Fax:* (202)293-2352
Members: 500 individuals
Staff: 2
Exec. Director: J. Thomas Cochran

Historical Note
Members are municipal employees responsible for human services issues.

United States Conference of Local Health Officers *(1960)*
Historical Note
Merged with the Nat'l Ass'n of County and City Health Officials in 1997.

United States Conference of Mayors *(1932)*
1620 I St., N.W., 4th Floor
Washington, DC   20006
Tel: (202)293-7330   *Fax:* (202)293-2352
Web Site: http://www.usmayors.org
Members: 1,050 individuals
Staff: 45
Annual Budget: $5-10,000,000
Exec. Director: J. Thomas Cochran
Director, Public Affairs: Michael W. Brown
Director, Meetings: Carol Edwards
Managing Director: Thomas McClimon
C.F.O.: Woodson Ward
General Counsel: John Daniel Reeves
Director, Member Services: Debra DeHaney

Historical Note
An organization of city governments. Membership limited to the 880 U.S. cities with more than 30,000 population. Affiliated with the United States Conference of Local Health Officers and the U.S. Conference of Human Services Officers. Has an annual budget of $7.6 million.

Publications:
AIDS Information Exchange. bi-m.
CORRE Newsletter. m.
Labor Management Relations Service. bi-m.
Local Health Officers News. bi-m.
Resolutions Adopted - Annual Conference of Mayors. a.
The Mayors of America's Principal Cities Directory. semi-a.
U. S. adv.

Meetings/Conferences:
Annual Meetings: June/950

United States Contract Tower Ass'n *(1995)*
Historical Note
A division of American Ass'n of Airport Executives, which provides administrative support.

United States Council for Internat'l Business *(1945)*
1212 Ave. of the Americas, 21st Fl
New York, NY   10036-1689
Tel: (212)354-4480   *Fax:* (212)575-0327
E-Mail: info@uscib.org
Web Site: http://www.uscib.org
Members: 300 companies and organizations
Staff: 45
Annual Budget: $5-10,000,000
President: Thomas Niles
Sr. V.P., Policy/Programs: Ronnie L. Goldberg
Sr. V.P., Admin./Development: Peter M. Robinson, CAE
V.P., Administration: Rasma Mednis
V.P., Environmental Affairs: Norine Kennedy
Electronic Commerce and General Counsel: Joseph H. Alhadeff

Historical Note
U.S. affiliate of the following international organizations having consultative status with intergovernmental agencies: the Internat'l Chamber of Commerce (ICC), the Internat'l Organization of Employers (IOE) and the Business and Industry Advisory Committee (BIAC) to the Organization for Economic Cooperation and Development (OECD). As the U.S. representative of each of these associations, the Council assures that their views are those endorsed by the American business community and endeavors to

similarly influence U.S. government policy. Also serves as the official issuing and guaranteeing authority for ATA Carnets (customs documents allowing temporary, duty-free import and export of goods destined for eventual export). Maintains a Washington, DC office. Has an annual budget of approximately $7 million.

Publications:
Annual Report. a.
Business & Environment Report.
Council Newsletter. bi-m.
East-West Legal Update. q.
Focus on Issues.
IGO Report. m.
International Labor Affairs Report.

Meetings/Conferences:
Annual Dinner: November-December

United States Council on Internat'l Banking
Historical Note
Became Internat'l Financial Services Ass'n in 1998.

United States Court Reporters Ass'n *(1946)*
5117 Primrose Circle
Wichita, KS   67219-2818
Tel: (316)832-0336   *Fax:* (316)832-0577
Toll Free: (800)628 - 2730
E-Mail: uscra@feist.com
Web Site: http://uscra.org
Exec. Director: Elizabeth A. Cauley-Fox

Historical Note
USCRA members are the official reporters in the United States District Courts. Membership: $150/year (regular); $50/year (associate); $75/year (job-share); $50/year (supporting); $35/year (student).

Publications:
Circuit Rider. q. adv.

Meetings/Conferences:
Annual Meetings: Columbus Day weekend, annually.

United States Cross Country Coaches Ass'n
Moby Arena - Track Office
Colorado State University
Fort Collins, CO   80523
Tel: (970)491-5434   *Fax:* (970)491-4343
Members: 295 individuals
Staff: 1
Annual Budget: under $10,000
Treasurer: Doug Max

Historical Note
Formerly Nat'l Collegiate Cross Country Coaches Ass'n. Membership: $225/year (individual).

Publications:
USCCCA Newsletter. a. adv.

Meetings/Conferences:
Annual Meetings: With Nat'l College Athletic Ass'n, in conjunction with the National Cross Country Meet.

United States Cutting Tool Institute *(1988)*
1300 Sumner Ave.
Cleveland, OH   44115-2851
Tel: (216)241-7333   *Fax:* (216)241-0105
E-Mail: uscti@taol.com
Web Site: http://www.taol.com/uscti
Members: 100 companies
Staff: 2
Annual Budget: $100-250,000
Secretary-Treasurer: Charles M. Stockinger

Historical Note
USCTI was formed in 1988 by the merger of the Metal Cutting Tool Institute and the Cutting Tool Manufacturers of America. USTCI represents more than two-thirds of the domestic cutting tool market.

United States Durum Growers Ass'n *(1957)*
824 Thompson St.
Bottineau, ND   58318
Tel: (701)228-3057
Web Site: http://www.durumgrowers.com
Members: 1000 individuals
Staff: 1
Annual Budget: $25-50,000
Exec. Secretary: Diane Scheflo

Historical Note
Until 1981 known as the Durum Growers Association of the United States.

Meetings/Conferences:
Annual Meetings: Minot, ND, 2nd week of Nov.

United States Dye Manufacturers Operating Committee of ETAD *(1982)*
1850 M Street, N.W. Suite 700
Washington, DC   20036
Tel: (202)721-4154   *Fax:* (202)296-8120
Members: 11 companies
Staff: 2
Annual Budget: $250-500,000
Exec. Director: Dr. C. Tucker Helmes

Historical Note
Formerly (1993) the United States Operating Committee of ETAD. The international association, ETAD (Ecological and Toxicological Ass'n of Dyes and Organic Manufacturers) was formed in 1974 to combine scientific and technical resources within companies in the dyestuffs industry to address ecotoxicological problems. In 1977 American companies formed the Dyes Environmental and Toxicology Organization (DETO); in 1982 most DETO members decided to join ETAD, and the two organizations were merged. The U.S. Committee of ETAD represents the interests of manufacturers of dyes with regard to environmental and health hazards in the manufacture, processing, shipment, use and disposal of their

products. Affiliated with the Synthetic Organic Chemical Manufacturers Ass'n, which provides administrative support.

Publications:
Annual Report. a.

Meetings/Conferences:

United States Egg Marketers *(1982)*
4500 Hugh Howell Road, Suite 270
Tucker, GA   30084
Members: 30 companies
Staff: 8
Annual Budget: $500-1,000,000
President: Jerry Faulkner
Director, Finance: Patrice Komisarow

Historical Note
A Webb-Pomerene Act association. USEM emphasis is on daily market activity and exporting. Established a cooperative buying program for packaging and supplies. Membership: $10,000/year (company).

Publications:
Egg Market Line. w.

Meetings/Conferences:
Annual Meetings: January

United States Energy Ass'n *(1930)*
1620 I St., N.W., Suite 1000
Washington, DC   20006
Tel: (202)331-0415   *Fax:* (202)331-0418
Members: 185 businesses and individuals
Staff: 30
Annual Budget: $5-10,000,000
Exec. Director: Barry K. Worthington
Director, Special Programs: Richard Williamson
Administration Manager: Eileen Murray

Historical Note
Supports the objectives of the World Energy Council and serves as the U.S. Member Committee. Has an annual budget of $6 million. Membership: $1,000/year (individual); $5,000/year (company).

Publications:
Annual Report. a.
Newsletter. q.
USEA Report. bi-m.
World Energy Council Journal. bien.

Meetings/Conferences:
Annual Meetings: May

United States Federation for Culture Collections *(1970)*
Roche Biological Systems
1145 Atlantic Ave.
Alameda, CA   94501
Tel: (510)814-2815
Members: 150 organizations and individuals
Staff: 1
Annual Budget: under $10,000
President: Jinna L. Keonig

Historical Note
Members are individuals and organizations concerned with maintaining culture collections and running taxonomic studies on micro-organisms. Has no paid staff. Leadership changes annually. Membership: $20/yr. (individual); $150/yr. (company).

Publications:
Advances in Culture Collections. irreg.
Perspectives in Culture Collections. irreg.
USFCC Newsletter. q. adv.

Meetings/Conferences:

United States Federation of Scholars and Scientists *(1938)*
c/o Physics Dept.
California State University
Fullerton, CA   92631
Tel: (714)278-3421   *Fax:* (714)278-5810
E-Mail: rdittmann@fullerton.edu
Members: 200 individuals
Staff: 2
Annual Budget: under $10,000
Nat'l Coordinator: Prof. Roger Dittmann

Historical Note
Formerly (1988) American Ass'n of Scientific Workers, the U.S. affiliate of the World Federation of Scientific Workers. Primarily concerned with the impact of science upon society, especially on a global/international scale. Also affiliated with the American Ass'n for the Advancement of Science Other affiliates include: Concerned Philosophers for Peace, Southern California Federation of Scientists, and the California Peace Academy. Membership: $25/year (individual), $2.50 per capita/year (organization).

Publications:
Concerned Scholar. bi-m.
Proceedings.
Scientific World. a.

Meetings/Conferences:
Annual Meetings: Held in conjunction with international conference.

United States Fencing Coaches Ass'n *(1941)*
P.O. Box 274
New York, NY   10159-0274
Tel: (212)532-2557
Members: 350 individuals
Annual Budget: under $10,000
Secretary: Richard Gradkowski

Historical Note
Established in 1941 as the Nat'l Fencing Coaches Ass'n of America, it assumed its present name in 1982. Member of the Nat'l Collegiate Athletic Ass'n and the Internat'l Academy of Arms. Affiliated with the U.S. Fencing Ass'n. Members are fencing teachers who conduct clinics and workshops to train fencing

instructors. The association accredits Fencing Masters in various grades. Membership: $25/year.

Publications:
Directory. a.
Swordmaster. q. adv.

Meetings/Conferences:
Annual Meetings: Summer
1999 – Charlotte, NC

United States Golf Ass'n *(1894)*
P.O. Box 708
Far Hills, NJ 07931-0708
Tel: (908)234-2300   *Fax:* (908)234-9687
Members: 750,000 individuals, 9,400 clubs and courses
Staff: 200
Annual Budget: $5-10,000,000
Exec. Director: David B. Fay

Historical Note
An association of member clubs and courses formed on December 22, 1894. Conducts the U.S. Open, Senior Open and Women's Open Championships, the Walker and Curtis Cup matches and ten national amateur championships. The governing body of golf in the United States. Has an annual budget of over $30 million. Street address is Liberty Corner Road, Far Hills, NJ. Membership: $100/year.

Publications:
Golf Journal. 10/year.
Green Section Record. bi-m.

Meetings/Conferences:
Annual Meetings: Winter
1999 – Clearwater, FL(Biltmore)

United States Harness Writers' Ass'n *(1947)*
Box Ten
Batavia, NY 14021
Tel: (716)343-5900   *Fax:* (716)344-1187
Members: 360 individuals
Staff: 1
Annual Budget: $25-50,000
Secretary: William F. Brown, Jr.

Historical Note
Members are members of the media who cover harness racing. Has no paid staff or permanent headquarters. Membership: $40/year.

Publications:
Newsletter. q.

Meetings/Conferences:
Annual Meetings: April
1999 – Orlando, FL(Caribe Royale)/Mar. 4-8/40

United States Hide, Skin and Leather Ass'n *(1980)*
1700 N. Moore St., Suite 1600
Arlington, VA 22209
Tel: (703)841-5485   *Fax:* (703)841-9656
Members: 125 companies
Staff: 2
Annual Budget: $100-250,000
President: Jerome J. Breiter, Ph.D.

Historical Note
Became a division of American Meat Institute in 1989. Formed Nov. 4, 1980 in Chicago by a merger of the American Ass'n of Hides, Skins and Leather Merchants (established 1918) and the Nat'l Hide Ass'n (established 1945). Membership: based on the volume of hides per week, averaged over one year.

Meetings/Conferences:
Annual Meetings: October/170

United States Hispanic Chamber of Commerce *(1979)*
1019 19th St., N.W., Suite 200
Washington, DC 20036-5105
Tel: (202)842-1212   *Fax:* (202)842-3221
Members: 1000,000 individuals
Staff: 15
Annual Budget: $1-2,000,000
V. President, Government Relations: Roxana Chahin
Senior V. President, Finance: Jorge Franchi

Historical Note
USHCC is a national trade association of local hispanic chambers of commerce, business associations and individuals advocating Hispanic domestic and international economic interests. Membership: $150/year (individual); $300/year (organization/company).

Publications:
Convention Magazine. a. adv.
Networking Newsletter. bi-m. adv.

Meetings/Conferences:
Annual Meetings: September
1999 – San Diego, CA
1999 – Seattle, WA
2000 – Washington, DC
2001 – Atlanta, GA

United States Industrial Fabrics Institute
Historical Note
A division of Industrial Fabrics Ass'n Internat'l.

United States Interactive and Microwave Television Ass'n *(1991)*

United States Junior Chamber of Commerce *(1920)*
P.O. Box 7
Tulsa, OK 74102-0007
Tel: (918)584-2481   *Fax:* (918)584-4422
Web Site: http://www.usjcees.org
Members: 107,000 individuals2600 chapters
Staff: 25
Annual Budget: $2-5,000,000
Exec. V. President: John K.S. Shiroma, CAE

Historical Note
Also known as the U.S. Jaycees, acts as a service training and advocacy organization for individuals between ages 21 and 39 providing leadership training through participation in community programs.

Publications:
Jaycees Magazine. q. adv.

Meetings/Conferences:
Annual Meetings: June
1999 – Niagra, NY/June 7-10

United States Lacrosse Coaches Ass'n
Historical Note
Became (1997) Lacrosse USA.

United States Lifesaving Ass'n *(1964)*
P.O. Box 366
Huntington Beach, CA 92648
Tel: (714)968-9360
Web Site: http://www.usla.org
Members: 6,000 individuals
Staff: 1
Annual Budget: $50-100,000
President: Bill Richardson

Historical Note
Founded as the Nat'l Surf Life Saving Ass'n of America, it assumed its present name in 1979. A professional and educational organization of open water lifeguards and rescue personnel, it supports the annual National Lifeguard Championships. Membership: $15/year.

Publications:
American Lifeguard. q. adv.

Meetings/Conferences:

United States Marine Safety Ass'n *(1987)*
1900 Arch St.
Philadelphia, PA 19103-1498
Tel: (215)564-3484   *Fax:* (215)963-9785
Members: 145 companies
Staff: 2
Annual Budget: $50-100,000
Exec. Director: Maureen Brady

Historical Note
Formerly U.S. Lifesaving Manufacturing Ass'n, USMSA was reorganized and incorporated in Philadelphia, PA in 1987. Members are manufacturers of and service organizations, including trainers, for all types of marine safety equipment. Promotes safety and survival for all who earn a living at sea and serves as a forum for the effective use of marine safety equipment. Membership: $100-800/year.

Publications:
Marine Safety Newsletter. q.
Membership Directory. a.

Meetings/Conferences:

United States Meat Export Federation *(1976)*
1050 17th St., Suite 2200
Denver, CO 80265
Tel: (303)623-6328   *Fax:* (303)623-0297
Web Site: http://www.usmef.org
Members: 150 organizations
Staff: 50
Annual Budget: $5-10,000,000
President & C.E.O.: Philip M. Seng
Director, Communications: K.T. Miller
V. President Administration and Operations: Janel Domurat

Historical Note
Trade association of livestock producers and feeders, packers, purveyors and exporters, agribusiness, agriservice interests, farm organizations, and other promotional groups united in their interest in developing international markets for U.S. beef, pork, and lamb. Has an annual budget of approximately $20 million. Membership: $6,000/year, incremental, (organization).

Publications:
Beef Letter. m.
Export Newsline. w.
Export Reports. irreg.
Exporter Directory. irreg.
MEF Action. irreg.
Pork Letter. m.

Meetings/Conferences:
Semi-annual Meetings: June and November

United States of America National Committee of the Internat'l Dairy Federation *(1980)*
c/o IDFA
1250 H Street, NW, Suite 900
Washington, DC 20005
Tel: (202)737-4332   *Fax:* (202)331-7820
Members: 57 companies
Staff: 2
Annual Budget: $100-250,000
National Secretary: Anne Divjak

Historical Note
Members are milk producers, dairy product maufacturers and suppliers, dairy scientists and educators, associations and other representatives of the U.S. dairy industry. IDF headquarters are in Brussels, Belgium. Membership: $150-750/year (individual); $1000-5,000/year (company).

Publications:
Annual Report.
Prodeedings of IDF Seminars and Meetings. 5/yr.
Technical Bulletins. 15-20/yr.
Technical Standards. 10-15/yr.

Meetings/Conferences:
Semi-Annual Meetings: Spring (Chicago, IL area) and Fall (abroad)

1999 – Athens, Greece
2000 – Dresden, Germany

United States Pan Asian American Chamber of Commerce *(1984)*
1329 18th St., N.W.
Washington, DC 20036
Tel: (202)296-5221   *Fax:* (202)296-5225
E-Mail: uspaacc@his.com
Web Site: http://www.uspaacc.org
Members: 1,800 individuals
Staff: 5
Annual Budget: $100-250,000
Exec. Director: James Epp
President: Susan Au Allen
Director, Corporate Development: Ray Torreon

Historical Note
USPAACC is a national non-profit organization representing Asian and non-Asian businesses and professionals. Its primary objective is to help members achieve their economic growth through a wide variety of educational and advocacy programs. Membership: $50/year (individual); $250-500/year (company).

Publications:
Business Tips. semi-a. adv.
Directory of Asian-American Organizations. a. adv.
East-West Report. q. adv.

Meetings/Conferences:

United States Parachute Ass'n *(1956)*
1440 Duke St.
Alexandria, VA 22314-0000
Tel: (703)836-3495   *Fax:* (703)836-2843
Toll Free: (800)371 - 8772
E-Mail: uspa@uspa.org
Web Site: http://www.uspa.org
Members: 33,000 individuals
Staff: 24
Annual Budget: $2-5,000,000
Exec. Director: Christopher J. Needels
Director, Communications: Dany Brooks
Director, Government Relations: Edward M. Scott
Dir., Safety & Training: Glenn Bangs
President: Sherry L. Schrimsher
Dir., Membership: Elaine Talbott
Director, Publications: Kevin Gibson

Historical Note
USPA members are individuals with an interest in skydiving, as well as drop groups and other organizations. Sponsors Instructor Rating Program to train and certify instructors, jumpmasters and examiners. Membership: $39.50/year (new member); $38.00/year (renewal).

Publications:
Parachutist Magazine. m.
Professional. q.

Meetings/Conferences:
Semi-Annual Meetings: Winter, usually in Alexandria, VA, and Summer

United States Pharmacopeia *(1820)*
12601 Twinbrook Parkway
Rockville, MD 20852-1790
Tel: (301)881-0666   *Fax:* (301)770-5193
Toll Free: (800)227 - 8772
E-Mail: exterrnal/affairs@usp.org
Web Site: http://www.usp.org
Members: 395 orgs., institutions & agencies
Staff: 230
Annual Budget: $25-50,000,000
Exec. V. President: Jerome A Halperin
V. President for External Affairs: Jacqueline L. Eng
Senior V. President and General Counsel: Joseph G. Valentino

Historical Note
Established January 1, 1820 as the result of a call by Dr. Lyman Spalding of New York for a convention to adopt a uniform national standards for drugs. Composed of representatives of medical and pharmaceutical organizations, colleges and the Federal Government. Establishes standards for drug quality and publishes information about the proper dispensing and use of drugs.

Publications:
Abstract of Proceedings. quinquennia.
Pharmacopeial Forum. bi-m.
The Standard. bi-m.
United States Pharmacopeia-National Formulary.
       continuously revise.
USP Dictionary of Drug Names. a.

Meetings/Conferences:
2000 – Washington, DC(J.W. Marriott)

United States Potters' Ass'n *(1875)*
Historical Note
Address unknown in 1996.

United States Professional Cycling Federation *(1968)*
Historical Note
Address unknown in 1995.

United States Professional Tennis Ass'n *(1927)*
One USPTA Centre
3535 Briarpark Dr.
Houston, TX 77042
Tel: (713)978-7782   *Fax:* (713)978-7780
Toll Free: (800)877 - 8248
E-Mail: uspta@uspta.org
Web Site: http://www.uspta.org
Members: 11,000 individuals
Staff: 25
Annual Budget: $5-10,000,000
C.E.O.: Tim Heckler

Historical Note
USPTA is the non-profit trade association for professional tennis teachers. It was created to raise the standards of tennis teaching as a profession and increase interest in and awareness of the sport. Membership: $193/year.

Publications:
Addvantage Magazine. m. adv.
Convention Commemorative Program. a. adv.
Directory. a. adv.

Meetings/Conferences:
Annual Meetings: September

United States Professional Tennis Registry (1976)
P.O. Box 4739
Hilton Head, SC   29938
Tel: (843)785-7244   Fax: (843)686-2033
Toll Free: (800)421 - 6289
E-Mail: usptr@InfoAve.Net
Web Site: http://www.usptr.org
Members: 10,400 individuals
Staff: 10
Annual Budget: $1-2,000,000
C.E.O./Exec. Director: Daniel Santorum

Historical Note
An international association of officially recognized, certified and registered tennis teaching professionals in 120 countries. Developed the Official Standard Method of instruction to certify tennis professionals. Membership: $120 (application fee/initial dues); $99/year (renewal, minimum).

Publications:
Convention Program. a. adv.
Membership Directory. a. adv.
Tennis Pro. bi-m. adv.

Meetings/Conferences:
Annual Meetings: Always Hilton Head, SC
1999 – /Feb. 17-20

United States Racquet Stringing Ass'n (1975)
337 South Cedros, Suite D
Solana Beach, CA   92075
Tel: (619)481-3545   Fax: (619)481-0624
E-Mail: USRSA@aol.com
Web Site: http://www.usrsa.com
Members: 7,500 tennis shops
Staff: 14
Annual Budget: $500-1,000,000
Exec. Director: Jill M. Fonte
Associate Director, Communications: Don Hightower
Editor: Crawford Lindsey
Director, Membership: Phyllis Zarro

Historical Note
USRSA provides information necessary for professional racquet stringing. Membership: $69/year.

Publications:
Racquet Tech Magazine.
Stringer's Digest. a. adv.

United States Shellac Importers Ass'n (1910)
Historical Note
Defunct in 1997.

United States Ski Coaches Ass'n (1977)
Box 100
Park City, UT   84060
Tel: (435)649-9090   Fax: (435)649-3613
E-Mail: tross@ussa.org
Web Site: http://www.usskiteam.com
Members: 4,200 individuals
Staff: 3
Annual Budget: $250-500,000
Exec. Officer: Tim Ross

Historical Note
Membership: $80/year.

Publications:
American Ski Coach. 5/year. adv.

Meetings/Conferences:
Annual Meetings: Spring with U.S. Skiing Ass'n and Level 2
   Nat'l Coaches Clinic School
1999 – Park City, UT/Sept. 14-19

United States Soccer Federation (1913)
1801-1811 S. Prairie Ave.
Chicago, IL   60616
Tel: (312)808-1300   Fax: (312)808-9566
Web Site: http://www.us-soccer.com
Members: 3,000,000 individuals, 106 affiliated associations
Staff: 100
Annual Budget: $10-25,000,000
President: Dr. Bob Contiguglia
Deputy Secy. General/Communications: Jim Trecker
Exec. V. President: John Motta
C.O.O.: Tom King
C.F.O.: Richard Matthys

Historical Note
A federation of amateur and youth soccer ass'ns, formerly United States Football Ass'n. U.S. Soccer is the governing body for the sport in the U.S. and manages nine national teams. Has an annual budget of approximately $8 million.

Publications:
Media Guide. a.
U. S.

Meetings/Conferences:
Annual Meetings: Summer

United States Sports Massage Federation (1989)
2156 Newport Blvd.
Costa Mesa, CA   92627
Tel: (949)642-0735   Fax: (949)642-1729

Members: 17 individuals
Staff: 2
President: M.K. Hungerford, Ph.D.

United States Taekwondo Union
One Olympic Plaza, Suite 405
Colorado Springs, CO   80909-5746
Tel: (719)578-4632   Fax: (719)578-4642
Web Site: http://www.ustu.org
Exec. Director: Robert K. Fujimura

United States Targhee Sheep Ass'n (1951)
P.O. Box 427
Chinook, MT   59523
Tel: (406)357-3337   Fax: (406)357-3744
Members: 270 individuals
Staff: 1
Annual Budget: $25-50,000
Secretary/Treasurer: Cheryl M. Schuldt

Historical Note
A member of the Nat'l Pedigreed Livestock Council. Membership: $25/life (individual).

Publications:
Directory. a. adv.
Targhee Talk.

Meetings/Conferences:
Annual Meetings: Summer
1999 – Sedelia, MO

United States Telephone Ass'n (1897)
1401 H St. N.W., Suite 600
Washington, DC   20005
Tel: (202)326-7300   Fax: (202)326-7333
Web Site: http://www.usta.org
Members: 1,200 telephone companies
Staff: 73
Annual Budget: $5-10,000,000
President and C.E.O.: Roy M. Neel
V.P., Communications: David Bolger
V.P., Government Relations: Tim McGivern
Director, Government Affairs: Bill Bates
Director, Conference and Meeting Management: JoAnn Bunge
Manager, Special Events: Kelly Brennan
Director, Exhibits: Ronald Schmiedekamp
V.P. and General Counsel: Larry Sarjeant
Director, Publications: Cheryl Sullivan

Historical Note
Formerly Independent Telephone Ass'n of America and Nat'l Independent Telephone, it took its present name in 1983. Originally formed to represent domestic non-Bell System companies in the telephone industry, USTA now accepts membership from companies previously affiliated with AT&T. Sponsors and supports the USTA Political Action Committee. Has an annual budget of approximately $12.4 million. Membership fee based on company size, measured by telephone access lines.

Publications:
Teletimes. 5/year.
USTA Weekly. w.

Meetings/Conferences:
Annual Meetings: October

United States Tennis Ass'n (1881)
2615 South King St. Suite 2A
Honolulu, HI   96826
Tel: (808)955-6696   Fax: (808)955-8363
E-Mail: beede@hawaii.usta.com
Web Site: http://www.usta.com
Members: 500,000 individuals
Staff: 150
Annual Budget: $5-10,000,000
Exec. Director: Mark A. Beede
Director of Communications: Page Crosland

Historical Note
An association of organizations and individuals interested in the promotion of tennis. Formerly (1975) United States Lawn Tennis Ass'n. Sponsors the U.S. teams for the Fed, Davis Cup, and Olympic competitions. Runs the U.S. Open Tennis Championships, held annually at Flushing, NY. Also runs the national championships for juniors, seniors and amateurs, as well as thousands of tournaments at the local level. Membership: $25/year (adult); $25-95/year (organization).

Publications:
Tennis USTA. m. adv.
Yearbook and Tennis Guide. a. adv.

Meetings/Conferences:
Annual Meetings: Spring

United States Tennis Court and Track Builders Ass'n (1965)
3525 Ellicott Mills Drive, Suite N
Ellicott City, MD   21043-4547
Tel: (410)418-4875   Fax: (410)418-4805
E-Mail: ustctba@association-hq.com
Web Site: http://www.ustctba.com
Members: 290 companies
Staff: 3
Annual Budget: $250-500,000
Exec. V. President: Carol T. Shaner, CAE

Historical Note
The only organization that represents tennis courts and track builders in the United States and Canada. Membership: $560/year (builders); $600/year (associates/affiliates); $290/year (professionals/ancillaries); $250/year (provisionals).

Publications:
Membership Directory. a.
Newsletter. q.

Meetings/Conferences:
Annual Meetings: November
1999 – St. Petersburg, FL

United States Tour Operators Ass'n (1972)
342 Madison Ave., Suite 1522
New York, NY   10173
Tel: (212)599-6599   Fax: (212)599-6744
E-Mail: ustoa@aol.com
Web Site: http://www.ustoa.com
Members: 61 individuals, 35 companies
Staff: 3
Annual Budget: $250-500,000
President: Robert E. Whitley

Historical Note
Organized in California but expanded to national membership in 1975. Members are wholesale tour operators.

Publications:
Membership Directory. a.
Newsletter. q.

Meetings/Conferences:
Annual Meetings: December

United States Trademark Ass'n (1878)
Historical Note
See Internat'l Trademark Ass'n.

United States Trotting Ass'n (1938)
750 Michigan Ave.
Columbus, OH   43215-1191
Tel: (614)224-2291   Fax: (614)224-4575
E-Mail: FJN@USTROTTING
Web Site: http://www.USTROTTING.COM
Members: 37,000 individuals, 375 tracks
Staff: 90
Annual Budget: $5-10,000,000
Exec. V. President: Fred J. Noe
Director, Publicity and Public Relations: John Pawlak
Director, Member Services: Bob Luehrman

Historical Note
USTA members include officials, breeders, owners, trainers and drivers of standardbred trotting horses. USTA licenses drivers/officials and maintains a registry of horses. Has an annual budget of approximately $7.8 million. Membership: $60/year (new members); $45/year (renewal).

Publications:
Hoof Beats. m. adv.
Membership List. a.
Sires & Dams Book. a.
Trotting & Pacing Guide. a.

Meetings/Conferences:
Annual Meetings: usually in Columbus, OH(Hyatt on Capitol
   Square)/March

United States Trout Farmers Ass'n (1952)
111 W. Washington St., Suite 1
Charles Town, WV   25414-1529
Tel: (304)728-2189   Fax: (304)728-2196
E-Mail: USTFA@intrepid.net
Members: 300 individuals
Staff: 1
Annual Budget: $50-100,000
Exec. Administrator: Mary Wiltshire

Historical Note
USTFA members are trout farmers, academics, equipment suppliers and others with an interest in raising trout commercially.

Publications:
Salmonid Magazine. q. adv.

Meetings/Conferences:
1999 – Tampa, FL/Jan. 27-30

United States Tuna Foundation (1977)
1101 17th St., N.W., Suite 609
Washington, DC   20036
Tel: (202)857-0610   Fax: (202)331-9686
Members: 4 companies and 50 boats
Staff: 5
Annual Budget: $250-500,000
Exec. Director: David G. Burney

Historical Note
Trade association representing the tuna industry.

Meetings/Conferences:

United States Wheat Associates (1980)
1620 I St., N.W., Suite 801
Washington, DC   20006-4005
Tel: (202)463-0999   Fax: (202)785-1052
Web Site: http://www.uswheat.org
Members: 18 state organizations
Staff: 20
Annual Budget: $5-10,000,000
President: Alan Tracy
Director, Communications: Lisa Jager

Historical Note
U.S. Wheat associates is the export market development organization representing the U.S. wheat industry. Market development activities include trade servicing, technical assistance, market analysis, and consumer promotion. Has an annual budget of approximately $10 million.

Publications:
U. S.

Meetings/Conferences:
Annual Meetings: January

United States Women's Track Coaches Ass'n (1967)
7263 Heartcrest Lane
Centerville, OH   45458
Tel: (937)439-4927   Fax: (937)439-4927
Members: 400 individuals
Annual Budget: under $10,000
President: Rita Somerlot

Historical Note
Has no paid officers or full-time staff. Membership: $10/year.
Publications:
Membership Directory. irreg.
Newsletter. q.
Meetings/Conferences:
Annual Meetings: late Nnovember
1999 – Los Angeles, CA/Dec. 29-Jan. 4

United States-Austrian Chamber of Commerce *(1949)*
165 W. 46th St., Suite 1112
New York, NY   10036
Tel: (212)819-0117
Members: 120 companies
Staff: 2
Annual Budget: $25-50,000
Exec. Director: Erika Borozan
Historical Note
Founded to promote trade between the United States and Austria through seminars and luncheon meetings. Membership: $200/year (individual); $450/year (organization/ company).
Publications:
Austrian Business. q. adv.
Meetings/Conferences:
Annual Meetings: New York, NY, last week in May

United States-China Business Council *(1973)*
1818 N St., N.W., Suite 200
Washington, DC   20036
Tel: (202)429-0340   *Fax:* (202)775-2476
E-Mail: info@uschina.org
Members: 290 companies
Staff: 19
Annual Budget: $2-5,000,000
President: Robert A. Kapp
Historical Note
Formerly (1988) Nat'l Council for U.S.-China Trade. Companies that invest or plan to invest in enterprises in the People's Republic of China.
Publications:
The China Business Review. bi-m. adv.
Meetings/Conferences:
Semi-Annual Meetings: January and June/usually in
   Washington, DC

United States-Cuba Business Council
5315 Lee Hwy.,
Arlington, VA   22207
Tel: (703)241-0038   *Fax:* (703)241-0548
E-Mail: uscubabiz@aol.com
Web Site: http://www.uscubabiz.org
Exec. Director: Paul L. Crespo
Historical Note
USCBC is a non-profit trade association of comprised of corporations which uphold principles of free enterprise, due process, contract sanctity and private property rights, as necessary conditions for U.S. commercial activity and economic development in Cuba. Membership: $10,000/year (organization).
Publications:
Executive Bulletin. bi-m.

United States-Mexico Chamber of Commerce *(1973)*
1300 Pennsylvania Ave. NW
Ronald Reagan Internat'l Trade Center
Washington, DC   20036
Tel: (202)296-5198   *Fax:* (202)728-0768
Toll Free: (888)876 - 2621
E-Mail: news-hq@usmcoc.org
Web Site: http://www.usmcoc.org/usmcoc/
Members: 1,500 companies
Staff: 5
Annual Budget: $500-1,000,000
President/C.E.O.: Al Zapanta
Director of Communications: Jeff Sparschott
Director of Environmental Affairs: Valerie Gray
Director of Education and Training: Dr. Ruth Martinez
Director of Business Development: Eric Rojo
Historical Note
Maintains offices in Los Angeles, Dallas, New York, Denver, Chicago, Detroit, Seattle, Mexico City, and Monterey. Membership: $200-5,000/year.
Publications:
Chamber News. q. adv.
Directory. a. adv.
Newsletter. m.
Special Reports. irreg.
Meetings/Conferences:
Monthly Meetings: in corresponding region for general
   members
1999 – Mexico City, Mexico/150
1999 – Washington, DC/500

United States-New Zealand Council *(1986)*
1801 F St., N.W.
Washington, DC   20006
Tel: (202)842-0772   *Fax:* (202)842-0749
E-Mail: usnzcounci@aol.com
Members: 400 individuals, 22 organizations
Staff: 2
Annual Budget: $100-250,000
Exec. Director: Hillary Troup
Historical Note
USNZC members are individuals and organizations with an interest in fostering good relations and improved economic ties between New Zealand and the United States. Membership: $100/year (individual); $1,000-$10,000/year (corporate).
Publications:
Across the Pacific. q.

New Zealand in the News. m.

United Steelworkers of America *(1942)*
Five Gateway Center
Pittsburgh, PA   15222
Tel: (412)562-2400
Members: 600,000 individuals
Staff: 900
Annual Budget: $5-10,000,000
President: George Becker
Historical Note
The United Steelworkers of America had its origin in the creation, in 1936, of the Steel Workers Organizing Committee created to unionize steelworkers for the CIO. The Amalgamated Ass'n of Iron, Steel and Tin Workers (founded in 1876) was incorporated in the effort. In 1942 the latter was dissolved and SWOC was transformed into the present organization. Merged in 1944 with Aluminum Workers of America (founded 1932); in 1967 with Internat'l Union of Mine, Mill and Smelter Workers (founded 1892); in 1970 with United Stone and Allied Products Workers of America (founded 1903); in 1972 with Internat'l Union of District 50, Allied and Technical Workers of the U.S. and Canada (founded 1936); in 1985 with Upholsters' Internat'l Union of North America (founded 1882); and in 1995 with United Rubber, Cork, Linoleum and Plastics Workers of America. Absorbed Aluminum, Brick and Glass Workers Internat'l union in 1997. Has a general strike and defense fund of about $145 million. Has an annual budget of approximately $240.3 million. Affiliated with AFL-CIO and the Canadian Labour Congress. Sponsors and supports the United Steelworkers of America Political Action Fund.
Publications:
Steelabor. m.
Meetings/Conferences:
Biennial Convention: Even years in Fall

United Synagogue of Conservative Judaism *(1913)*
155 Fifth Ave.
New York, NY   10010-6802
Tel: (212)533-7800   *Fax:* (212)353-9439
E-Mail: info@uscj.org
Web Site: http://www.uscj.org
Members: 800 congregations
Staff: 150
Annual Budget: $5-10,000,000
Exec. V. President: Rabbi Jerome M. Epstein
Director, Public Affairs: Lois Goldrich
Director of Special Projects: Sarrae Crane
Director, Conferences and Special Events: Dr. Mortoa Siegel
Historical Note
Conservative U.S. and Canadian congregations. Associated with the Federation of Jewish Men's Clubs, the Women's League for Conservative Judaism, the Jewish Theological Seminary of America and the Rabbinical Assembly. Has an annual budget of $14 million.
Publications:
Achshav. bi-m.
Dapim. irreg.
Kadima. 3/year.
News-in-Brief. m.
Program Bank. q.
United Synagogue Review. 2/year.
Yachad. q.
Your Child. 3/year.
Meetings/Conferences:
Biennial Meetings: odd years

United Textile Workers of America
Historical Note
Became (1995) UFCW Textile Council.

United Thoroughbred Trainers of America *(1956)*
P.O. Box 7065
Louisville, KY   40257-0065
Tel: (502)893-0025   *Fax:* (502)893-0026
Toll Free: (800)325 - 3487
E-Mail: uttainc@cariernet.insi.net
Members: 1,500 individuals
Staff: 7
Annual Budget: $500-1,000,000
Exec. Director: Sam Ramer
Historical Note
Established as the Nat'l Thoroughbred Trainers Guild, it assumed its present name in 1960. Members are licensed thoroughbred horse trainers united to elevate the standards of the professional trainer's vocation and to promote interest in the sport of thoroughbred racing. Membership: $100/year.
Publications:
The Backstretch. bi-m. adv.
Meetings/Conferences:
Annual Meetings: Annual

United Transportation Union *(1969)*
14600 Detroit Ave.
Cleveland, OH   44107-4250
Tel: (216)228-9400   *Fax:* (216)228-5755
Toll Free: (800)964 - 9464
Web Site: http://www.utu.org
Members: 82,000 individuals
Staff: 150
Annual Budget: $2-5,000,000
President: C.L. Little
Historical Note
Merger of Brotherhood of Locomotive Firemen and Enginemen (1873) Brotherhood of Railroad Trainmen (1883); Order of Railway Conductors and Brakemen (1868); Switchmen's Union of North America (1894). Absorbed (1972) Federated Council of the Internat'l Ass'n of Railway Employees and merged with Railroad Yardmasters of America in 1985. Sponsors and supports the Transportation Political Education League.

Publications:
UTU News. m.
Meetings/Conferences:
Quadriennial Meetings: (1999)

United Union of Roofers, Waterproofers and Allied Workers *(1919)*
1660 L St., N. W.
Washington, DC   20036
Tel: (202)463-7663   *Fax:* (202)463-6906
Web Site: http://www.unionroofers.com
Members: 24,000 individuals
Staff: 30
Annual Budget: $2-5,000,000
President: Earl Kruse
Historical Note
The result of a merger in Pittsburgh, Pennsylvania, September 8, 1919 of the International Slate and Tile Roofers Union of America (founded in 1902) and the International Brotherhood of Composition Roofers, Damp and Waterproof Workers of the United States and Canada (founded in 1905). Chartered by the American Federation of Labor in 1919. Known as the United Slate, Tile and Composition Roofers, Damp and Waterproof Workers Ass'n until 1978.
Publications:
adv. adv.
United Union of Roofers, Waterproofers and Allied Workers
   Journal. q.
Meetings/Conferences:
Quinquennial Meetings: Fall (1998)

United Weighers Ass'n
P.O.Box 1027
Floral Park, NY   11002
Tel: (516)352-2673   *Fax:* (516)352-3569
President/Business Agent: Michael Gorry
Historical Note
Members are weighers of raw material imported in to the United States by ship.

Universities Associated for Research and Education in Pathology *(1964)*
9650 Rockville Pike
Bethesda, MD   20814-3993
Tel: (301)571-1880   *Fax:* (301)571-1879
Members: 25 pathology departments
Exec. Officer: Frances A. Pitlick, Ph.D.
Meetings Coordinator: M.M. Nenere
Historical Note
UAREP members are college and university pathology departments.

Universities Council on Water Resources *(1962)*
4543 Faner Hall, Department of Geography
Southern Illinois Univ. at Carbondale
Carbondale, IL   62901-4526
Tel: (618)536-7571   *Fax:* (618)453-2671
E-Mail: ucowr@uwin.siu.edu
Web Site: http://www.uwin.siu.edu/ucowr
Members: 97 institutions; 6 foreign affil.
Staff: 2
Annual Budget: $50-100,000
Exec. Director: Duane Baumann, Ph.D.
Historical Note
Founded as the Universities Council on Hydrology in 1962; assumed its present name in 1964. A voluntary organization of universities engaged in education, research, public service, international activities, and legislative pursuits relevant to all aspects of water resources. Membership: $250/year (domestic institution), $75/year (foreign affiliate), $50/year (individual).
Publications:
Careers in Water Resources. irreg.
Course Listings in Water Resources. irreg.
Funding Opportunities in Water Resources Research. irreg.
Graduate Studies in Water Resources. irreg.
Proceedings of Annual Meetings. a.
Water Resources Update. q.
Meetings/Conferences:
1999 – Kailua-Kona, HI(The Royal Waikoloan)/June 28-July
   3

Universities Research Ass'n *(1965)*
1111 19th St., N.W., Suite 400
Washington, DC   20036
Tel: (202)293-1382   *Fax:* (202)293-5012
Members: 86 institutions
Staff: 8
Annual Budget: $5-10,000,000
President: Frederick H. Bernthal
V. President: Ezra Heitowit
C.F.O.: Gail Young
Exec. Secretary: Jean W. Boutchyard
Counsel: William Schmidt
Historical Note
URA is a consortium of universities whose purpose is to manage the Fermi National Laboratory in Chicago, IL. Has an annual budget of approximately $250 million. Initial membership cost $10,000; no annual dues.
Publications:
Annual Report of URA. a.
Meetings/Conferences:
January or February: always in Washington, DC

Universities Space Research Ass'n *(1969)*
American City Bldg., Suite 212
10227 Wincopin Circle
Columbia, MD   21044
Tel: (410)730-2656   *Fax:* (410)730-3496
Web Site: http://www.usra.edu
Members: 80 institutions

Staff: 18
Annual Budget: $250-500,000
Exec. Director: Dr. W.D. Cummings

Historical Note
A consortium of universities that manage research institutes and programs, primarily for NASA.

Publications:
Lunar and Planetary Information Bulletin. q.
USRA Newsletter. q.

Meetings/Conferences:
Annual Meetings: Washington, DC/March

University and College Designers Ass'n *(1971)*
122 S. Michigan Ave.
Suite 1776
Chicago, IL   60603-6107
Tel: (312)431-9395   *Fax:* (312)431-8697
E-Mail: info@ucda.com
Members: 800 individuals
Staff: 1
Exec. Director: Jennifer Salopek

Historical Note
Individuals involved in visual communication design for colleges and universities. Membership: $120/year (individual); $500/year (organization).

Publications:
Designer. q.
Home Page Newsletter. m.

Meetings/Conferences:
Annual Meetings: September-October
1999 – San Francisco, CA
2000 – Miami, FL

University and College Labor Education Ass'n *(1959)*
Institute of Indutrial Relations
Box 951478
Los Angeles, CA   90095-1478
Tel: (310)794-5981   *Fax:* (310)794-6410
E-Mail: kentwong@ucla.edu
Members: 300 individuals, 53 institutions
Director: Kent D. Wong

Historical Note
Members are institutions with labor education programs and individuals with an interest in labor education.

Publications:
Abstracts. a.
Labor Studies Forum. q.
Labor Studies Journal. q.
Membership Directory. a.
Research Resource Directory. a.

Meetings/Conferences:

University Aviation Ass'n *(1948)*
3410 Skyway Drive
Auburn, AL   36830-6444
Tel: (334)844-2434   *Fax:* (334)844-2432
Members: 450 individuals, 110 institutions, 65 companies
Staff: 4
Annual Budget: $250-500,000
Exec. Director: Gary W. Kiteley
Manager, Member Services: Charlotte Deweese

Historical Note
Members are individuals, institutions, and corporations concerned with aviation education at the university level. Membership: $45/year (individual); $200/year (organization/company).

Publications:
Collegiate Aviation Guide. 3/yr. adv.
Publications Directory. a. adv.
UAA Newsletter. bi-m. adv.
UAA Scholarship Directory. a.

Meetings/Conferences:
Annual Meetings: Fall

University Continuing Education Ass'n *(1915)*
One Dupont Circle, N.W., Suite 615
Washington, DC   20036-1168
Tel: (202)659-3130   *Fax:* (202)785-0374
E-Mail: postmaster@nucea.edu
Web Site: http://www.nucea.edu
Members: 2,000 individuals, 425 institutions
Staff: 10
Annual Budget: $500-1,000,000
Exec. Director: Dr. Kay Kohl
Dir., Info. Services: Joelle Brink
Dir., Govt. Relations: Phillip Robinson
Director of Conferences: Frances Glover
Director of Administration: John Hager
Director, Membership: Cyrus Homayounpour
Director, Publications: Susan Goewey Carey

Historical Note
Formerly (1980) known as the Nat'l University Extension Ass'n and (1996) Nat'l University Continuing Education Ass'n. Accredited colleges and universities with continuing higher education programs and professional staff.

Publications:
Continuing Education Recruiter. m. adv.
Continuing Higher Education Review (CHER) Journal. a.
Guide to Certificate Programs at American Colleges and Universities.
In Focus: A Newsletter of UCEA.
Independent Study Catalog. bien.
Innovations in Continuing Education. a.
Lifelong Learning Trends. bien.
Peterson's UCEA Guide to Distance Learning Programs. a.
UCEA Membership Directory. a.

Meetings/Conferences:
Annual Meetings: April/May
1999 – Washington, DC/April 9-13

2000 – San Diego, CA/April 14-18
2001 – Philadelphia, PA/April 4-7
2002 – Toronto, ON, Canada/April 17-20

University Council for Educational Administration *(1957)*
University of Missouri, Columbia
205 Hill Hall
Columbia, MO   65211
Tel: (573)884-8300   *Fax:* (573)884-8302
Web Site: http://www.ucea.org
Members: 54 universities
Staff: 6
Annual Budget: $250-500,000
Exec. Director: Patrick B. Forsyth

Historical Note
A private, non-profit corporation consisting of major universities of the United States and Canada. Established to improve the professional preparation of educational administrators. Proposed in 1954 and established at Columbia Univ. in 1957, the central office was moved to Ohio State and UCEA began operations with a full-time staff and 34 charter members in 1959. Membership: $2,000/yr.

Publications:
Educational Administration Quarterly. q.
UCEA Review. q.

Meetings/Conferences:
Annual Meetings: October
1999 – Minneapolis, MN/Oct. 25-27

University Film and Video Ass'n *(1947)*
Chapman University, School of Film & TV
333 North Glassell Ave.
Orange, CA   92866
Tel: (714)628-7244   *Fax:* (714)997-6700
E-Mail: UFVA@chapman.edu
Web Site: http://www.ufva.org
Members: 800 individuals
Administrative Contact: Bob Bassett

Historical Note
Members are instructors and film makers concerned with the production and study of film. Originally the University Film Producers Ass'n, it became the University Film Ass'n in 1968 and assumed its present name in 1982. Membership: $50/year (individual); $100/year (institution); $25/year (student); $250/year (sustaining member).

Publications:
Journal. q.
Membership Directory. a.
UFVA Digest. bi-m.

Meetings/Conferences:
Annual Meetings: August
1999 – /Aug. 4-7

University Photographers Ass'n of America *(1961)*
SUNY Brockport
350 New Campus Drive
Brockport, NY   14420-2931
Tel: (716)395-2133   *Fax:* (716)395-2723
E-Mail: jdusen@po.brockport.edu
Web Site: http://www.adm.uwaterloo.ca/infoupaa
Members: 250 individuals
Annual Budget: $10-25,000
President: Jim Dusen

Historical Note
Members are college and university photographers who are concerned with the application and practice of photography. Has no paid staff or permanent address; officers change annually. Membership: $25/year (individual); $100/year (organization).

Publications:
Contact Sheet Newsletter. 3-4/yr. adv.
University Photographer Magazine. a.

Meetings/Conferences:

University Risk Management and Insurance Ass'n *(1966)*
Two Wisconsin Circle
Suite 1040
Chevy Chase, MD   20815
Tel: (301)718-9711   *Fax:* (301)907-4830
Web Site: http://www.urmia.org
Members: 265 colleges/universities
Staff: 1
Annual Budget: $100-250,000
Program Administrator: Jeanne Bright

Historical Note
Members are colleges and universities with insurance or risk management offices.

Publications:
Newsletter. 5/year.

Meetings/Conferences:
Annual Meetings: September-October

University/Resident Theatre Ass'n *(1969)*
1560 Broadway, Suite 414
New York, NY   10036
Tel: (212)221-1130   *Fax:* (212)869-2752
E-Mail: U/RTA@aol.com
Web Site: http://www.urta.com
Members: 47 graduate schools and theaters
Staff: 3
Annual Budget: $500-1,000,000
Exec. Director: Scott L. Steele
Dir., Operations: Sara Falconer
Dir., Contact Services: Gina G. Cesari

Historical Note
U/RTA acts as a liaison between graduate educational training and professional theater in the U.S. Programs include the Nat'l Unified

Auditions, Contract Management Program, Master Auditions Programs and the U/RTA-Equity Contract, each of which help provide continuity between preprofessional and professional theater. Membership: $1,836/year (organization).

Publications:
U/RTA Dir. of Member Training. adv.
U/RTA Update Newsletter. 3/year. adv.

Meetings/Conferences:
Three Meetings Annually: Chicago, IL/February; New York, NY/February; Irvine, CA/January

Upholstered Furniture Action Council *(1975)*
Box 2436
High Point, NC   27261
Tel: (910)885-5065   *Fax:* (910)884-5303
Members: 6 associations
Staff: 2
Annual Budget: $100-250,000
Exec. Director: Joseph Ziolkowski

Historical Note
UFAC is an association of furniture manufacturers, retailers and suppliers organized to conduct research into more fire resistant upholstering methods and to encourage voluntary compliance throughout the industry.

Publications:
Directory of Materials Suppliers. a.
Honor Roll. a.
UFAC 95 Program Action Guide. a.

Meetings/Conferences:
Annual Meetings: Not held.

Urban Affairs Ass'n *(1969)*
University of Delaware
Newark, DE   19716
Tel: (302)831-1681
Web Site: http://www.udel.edu/uaa
Members: 550 individuals, 100 institutions
Staff: 2
Annual Budget: $100-250,000
Exec. Director: Mary Helen Callahan

Historical Note
Urban specialists from private or public universities who are involved in teaching, research or public service. Promotes more effective policies and procedures relating to the study of urban affairs and urbanization. Formerly (1981) Council of University Institutes for Urban Affairs. Membership: $45/year (individual); $275/year (institution).

Publications:
Journal of Urban Affairs. q.
Newsletter.
Urban Affairs. bi-m.

Meetings/Conferences:
Annual Meetings: Spring
1999 – Louisville, KY(Seelbach)/April 14-17
2000 – Los Angeles, CA(Omni)/May 3-6
2001 – Detroit, MI
2002 – Cleveland, OH

Urban and Regional Information Systems Ass'n *(1963)*
1460 Renaissance Drive, Suite 305
Park Ridge, IL   60068-1348
Tel: (847)824-6300   *Fax:* (847)824-6363
E-Mail: info@urisa.org
Web Site: http://www.urisa.org
Members: 3,600 individuals
Staff: 9
Annual Budget: $1-2,000,000
Exec. Director: David J. Martin, CAE
Director, Finance: Anna Mae Scolaro
Director, Marketing and Membership: Wendy Francis

Historical Note
URISA is the educational/professional association for users and providers of information systems and geographic information systems (GIS) in the public and private sector. Membership: $124/year.

Publications:
Conference Proceedings. a.
Journal of Urban and Regional Information Systems. semi-a.
URISA Marketplace. m. adv.
URISA News. 10/year. adv.

Meetings/Conferences:
Annual Meetings: Summer
1999 – Chicago, IL/Aug. 21-25
2000 – Orlando, Fl/Aug. 19-24
2001 – Long Beach, CA/Aug. 19-24

Urban Land Institute *(1936)*
1025 Thomas Jefferson St., N.W.
Suite 500-West
Washington, DC   20007-5201
Tel: (202)624-7000   *Fax:* (202)624-7140
Toll Free: (800)321 - 5011
Web Site: http://www.uli.org
Members: 14,200 individuals
Staff: 80
Annual Budget: $5-10,000,000
Exec. V. President: Richard M. Rosan
V. President, Marketing/Public Relations: Ann Oliveri
Public Rels. Coordinator: Terry Anne Hearne
V. President, Meetings: Cheryl Cummins
V. President, Public Policy and Practice: Rachelle Levitt
V. President, Finance: Mike Teresk
Director, MIS: Deborah A. Bennett

Historical Note
Conducts research in various fields of real estate including identifying and interpreting land use trends in relation to the changing needs of its users. Consists of developers, architects, public officials and others concerned with land planning and development. Official name is ULI - the Urban Land Institute. Has

an annual budget of approximately $13 million. Full Membership: $850/year (private-sector), $285/year (government official or academician). Associate Membership: $265/year (private sector), $165/year (public sector). Internat'l Membership: $330/year (individual), $185/year (public), $1,000/year (corporate), $65/year (student).

Publications:
Land Use Digest. m.
Project Reference File. q.
ULI in the Future. a.
Urban Land. m. adv.

Meetings/Conferences:
Semi-Annual Meetings: Fall and Spring
1999 – Los Angeles, CA(Beverly Hilton Hotel)/March 1-2

Urban Libraries Council *(1971)*
1603 Orrington Ave., Suite 1080
Evanston, IL   60201
Tel: (847)866-9999   *Fax:* (847)866-9989
Web Site: http://www.clpgh.org/ulc
Members: 120 libraries, 10 corporations
Staff: 4
Annual Budget: $1-2,000,000
President: Eleanor Jo Rodger

Historical Note
Formerly (1975) Urban Libraries Trustees Council. Members are public libraries of cities with a population above 50,000. Membership: $1,000-10,000/year.

Publications:
ULC Exchange. m.

Meetings/Conferences:
Annual Meetings: in conjunction with the American Libraries Ass'n.

Usability Professionals Ass'n *(1994)*
414 Plaza Dr., Suite 209
Westmont, IL   60559-5507
Tel: (630)655-0112   *Fax:* (630)655-0391
E-Mail: upadallas@aol.com
Web Site: http://www.upassoc.org
Members: 800 individuals
Annual Budget: $250-500,000
Exec. Director: Judy Keel

Historical Note
UPA is a professional organization established to aid in the creation of more usable products and services. Membership: $50/year (individual).

Publications:
Common Ground Newsletter. q. adv.

Meetings/Conferences:

Used Oil Management Ass'n *(1981)*
Patton Boggs LLP
2550 M St., N.W.
Washington, DC   20037-1350
Tel: (202)457-6420   *Fax:* (202)457-6315
Members: 5 companies
Contact: Mary Beth Bosco

Historical Note
Formerly the Waste Oil Heating Manufacturers Ass'n (1996). Members are manufacturers of heaters designed to burn used oil.

Meetings/Conferences:
Annual Meetings: November

Used Truck Ass'n *(1988)*
600 Reisterstown Road, Suite 404
Baltimore, MD   21208
Tel: (410)602-2470   *Fax:* (410)486-7478
Web Site: http://www.uta.org
Members: 90 companies
Exec. Director: David A. Kolman

Historical Note
Founded as Used Truck Sales Network; became Nat'l Used Truck Ass'n in 1994 and assumed its current name in 1995. UTA's mission is "To serve those companies, organizations and individuals involved in the used truck industry in support of their primary business activities, and to be a leader in promoting professionalism in the used truck industry." Membership: $25/year (individual); $350/year (company).

Publications:
UTA News. q. adv.

Meetings/Conferences:
Annual Meetings: June Maryland

USITT: Ass'n of Design, Production and Technology Professionals in the Performing Arts and Entertainment *(1960)*
6443 Ridings Road
Syracuse, NY   13206-1111
Tel: (315)463-6463   *Fax:* (315)463-6525
Toll Free: (800)938 - 7488
E-Mail: usittno@appmail.appliedtheory.com
Web Site: http://www.usitt.org
Members: 4,000 individuals, 500 organizations
Staff: 4
Annual Budget: $500-1,000,000
Marketing and Public Relations Manager: Mary Buffum

Historical Note
Formerly (1989) United States Institute for Theatre Technology. USITT promotes the advancement of knowledge and skills of its members. It does this through promoting innovation and creativity by sponsoring projects, programs, research and symposia and producing an annual conference and exposition. Membership: $80-125/year (individual), $125-800/year (organization/ company).

Publications:
Sightlines. 10/year. adv.
Theatre Design and Technology. q. adv.
USITT Membership Directory. a. adv.

Meetings/Conferences:
Annual Meetings: Spring
1999 – Toronto, Canada
2000 – Denver, CO

UTC - The Telecommunications Ass'n *(1948)*
1140 Connecticut Ave., N.W., Suite 1140
Washington, DC   20036-4001
Tel: (202)872-0030   *Fax:* (202)872-1331
Toll Free: (800)900 - 4882
Web Site: http://www.utc.org
Members: 1,500 companies
Staff: 20
Annual Budget: $1-2,000,000
General Counsel: Jeff Sheldon

Historical Note
Formerly (1994) the Utilities Telecommunications Council, UTC represents organizations using telecommunications in their operations before various federal and state legislative and regulatory agencies, particularly the FCC.

Publications:
UTC Reports On. m. adv.

Meetings/Conferences:
Annual Meetings: June/1,000

Utilities Telecommunications Council *(1948)*
Historical Note
Became UTC, The Telecommunications Ass'n in 1994.

Utility Arborist Ass'n *(1970)*
PO Box 3129
Champaign, IL   61826-3129
Tel: (217)355-9411   *Fax:* (217)355-9516
E-Mail: dvannice@isa-arbor.com
Web Site: www.ag.uiuc.edu/nisa-uaa
Members: 1,200 individuals
Exec. Director: Derek Vannice

Historical Note
UAA members are utility line clearance arborists and others involved in line clearance operations. Membership: $15/year (individual).

Publications:
Utility Arborist Membership Directory. a.
Utility Arborist Newsletter. q.

Meetings/Conferences:
Annual Meetings: always August

Utility Communicators Internat'l *(1922)*
5316 E. Kings Ave.
Scottsdale, AZ   85254
Tel: (602)971-1989   *Fax:* (602)971-2738
E-Mail: bjanke@compuserve.com
Members: 400 individuals
Staff: 1
Annual Budget: $50-100,000
Exec. Director: Bob Janke

Historical Note
Advertising, public relations and communications directors of public utilities, their agencies and trade allies. Formerly (1977) Public Utilities Advertising Ass'n, the association then became the Public Utilities Communicators Ass'n before adopting its present name in 1989. Membership: $350/year (individual); $550 (organization/company).

Publications:
Newsletter. bi-m.
UCI Communicator/Showcase. semi-a.

Meetings/Conferences:
Annual Meetings: June
1999 – San Antonio, TX(Palalio del Rio)/May 26-28/100
2000 – Scottsdale, AZ(Hyatt Regency Scottsdale)/June 16-19

Utility Workers Union of America *(1945)*
815 16th St., N.W.
Washington, DC   20006
Tel: (202)347-8105   *Fax:* (202)347-4872
Web Site: http://www.aflcio.org/uwua
Members: 50,000 individuals
Staff: 22
Annual Budget: $2-5,000,000
President: Donald E. Wightman
Editor/Assistant to the President: Sam Weinstein

Historical Note
Founded in 1945 through the merger of the Utility Workers Organizing Committee (which had been set up by the CIO in 1938) and the Brotherhood of Consolidated Edison Employees and chartered by the Congress of Industrial Organizations the same year. Affiliated with AFL-CIO. Sponsors and supports the Committee on Political Action as well as the Utility Workers Union of America Political Contributions Committee.

Publications:
Light. bi-m.

Meetings/Conferences:

Vacation Rental Managers Ass'n *(1985)*
P.O. Box 1202
Santa Cruz, CA   95061-1202
Tel: (408)458-3573   *Fax:* (408)458-3637
Toll Free: (800)871 - 8762
E-Mail: info@vrma.com
Web Site: http://www.vrma.com
Members: 325 companies
Staff: 2
Annual Budget: $100-250,000
Exec. Director: Michael Sarka

Historical Note
VRMA members are companies that manage short-term rental/vacation properties. Membership $300/year; $400/year (associate/supplier).

Publications:
Directory of Vacation Rentals, Townhouses, Villas and Condominiums.
VRMA Review. q. adv.

Meetings/Conferences:
Annual Meetings: September, October, or November Alternate East (odd numbered years) and West (even numbered years)
1999 – New Orleans, LA/Sept. 18-23

Vacuum Cleaner Manufacturers Ass'n *(1913)*
P.O. Box 2642ve.
North Canton, OH   44720-2851
Tel: (330)499-5998   *Fax:* (330)499-5292
Members: 20 companies
Staff: 1
Exec. V. President: Clifford J. Wood

Historical Note
Works to improve the business climate of the industry and protect it from unjust or unfair regulations and rules. Membership fee varies by dollar sales volume.

Meetings/Conferences:
Annual Meetings: Fall
1999 – Palm Beach, FL(Four Seasons)/Sept. 10-12

Vacuum Dealers Trade Ass'n *(1981)*
2724 2nd Ave.
Des Moines, IA   50313-4933
Tel: (515)282-9101   *Fax:* (515)282-4483
E-Mail: vdta.dsm@aol.com
Web Site: http://www.vdta.com
Members: 2,200 individuals
Staff: 9
Annual Budget: $250-500,000
President: Judy Patterson

Historical Note
Vacuum cleaner retailers, sewing machine retailers, manufacturers and distributors. Membership: $60/year (individual); $400/year (organization).

Publications:
VDTA Floor Care & Sewing Professional.
VDTA News. m.

Meetings/Conferences:
1999 – Las Vegas, NV

Valve Manufacturers Ass'n of America *(1938)*
1050 17th St., N.W., Suite 280
Washington, DC   20036-5503
Tel: (202)331-8105   *Fax:* (202)296-0378
Members: 130 companies
Staff: 9
Annual Budget: $1-2,000,000
President: William S. Sandler, CAE
V. President, Communications: Lisa Cherubini
V. President, International Trade/Government Relations: George K. Keliades
Meetings and Exhibits Manager: Ryda Ruth Cusack

Historical Note
Founded as the Valve Manufacturers Ass'n in 1938; added "of America" in 1985. Membership: $2,500-25,000/year (corporate).

Publications:
Valve Magazine. q. adv.
Valve Update. m.
Valve Variations. q.

Meetings/Conferences:
Annual Meetings: Fall
1999 – Boca Roton, FL
2000 – Maui, HI

Valve Repair Council *(1989)*
1050 17th St., N.W., Suite 280
Washington, DC   20036-5503
Tel: (202)331-0104   *Fax:* (202)296-0378
Members: 35 companies
Staff: 2
Annual Budget: $50-100,000
Exec. Director: William S. Sandler, CAE

Historical Note
Formerly (1994) Valve Remanufacturers Council. Affiliated with the Valve Manufacturers Ass'n of America, VRC promotes the OEM approach in valve and actuator repair. VRC membership is open to all VMA members who have either in-house service operations or out-of-plant service facilities, as well as their authorized independent facilities. Membership: $2,000/year (single location), $2,500/year (multiple locations).

Publications:
Membership Directory. a.
VRC Review. q.

Meetings/Conferences:
1999 – Houston, TX

Van Body Manufacturers Division
Historical Note
A division of the Nat'l Truck Equipment Ass'n.

Variable Electronic Components Institute *(1960)*
P.O. Box 1070
Vista, CA   92085-1070
Tel: (760)727-3011
E-Mail: vrci@aol.com
Web Site: http://www.newmarket-forum.com/asn/vrci/
Members: 35 companies
Staff: 2
Annual Budget: $25-50,000
Exec. Director: Stanley Kukawka

Historical Note
Formerly (1964) Precision Potentiometer Manufacturers Ass'n, and (1997) Variable Resistive Components Institute. Maintains and

publishes up-to-date information on potentiometer standards in various industrial applications. Membership: $1,250/year (organization), $750/year (supplier), $250/year (user).

Meetings/Conferences:
1999 – San Diego, CA/Apr. 18-20

Variable Resistive Components Institute

Historical Note
Became (1997) Variable Electronic Components Institute.

Vatel Club (1913)

Historical Note
Membership, concentrated in the New York area, consists of chefs. Vatel Club is primarily a social organization rather than a trade association.

Vehicle Maintenance Council

Historical Note
Organization inactive in 1998.

Vehicular Technology Soc.

Historical Note
A technical society of the Institute of Electrical and Electronics Engineers (IEEE). Membership in the Society, open only to IEEE members, includes a subscription to a technical periodical in the field published by IEEE. All administrative support is provided by IEEE.

Venezuelan American Ass'n of the U.S. (1936)
150 Nassau St.
Room 2015
New York, NY   10038
Tel: (212)233-7776   *Fax:* (212)233-7779
Members: 50 individuals, 90 companies
Staff: 3
Annual Budget: $25-50,000
Treasurer: Paul E. Calvet

Historical Note
Promotes the expansion of trade relations between the U.S. and Venezuela. Membership: $200/year (individual), $500/year (corporate) and $2,000/year(supporting).

Publications:
Venezuela News Bulletin. m.

Veterinary Cancer Soc. (1974)
825 White Spruce Blvd.
Rochester, NY   14623
Tel: (716)474-1260   *Fax:* (716)424-1335
Members: 600 individuals
Annual Budget: $10-25,000
Corr. Secretary: Robert Rosenthal, D.V.M.

Historical Note
Membership: $30/year (individual); $10/year (interns/students).

Publications:
Membership Directory. bien.
Proceedings of Annual Meeting. a.
Veterinary Cancer Society Newsletter. q.

Meetings/Conferences:
Annual Meetings: Fall

Veterinary Hospital Managers Ass'n (1981)
48 Howard St.
Albany, NY   12207
Tel: (518)433-8911   *Fax:* (518)463-8656
Web Site: http://www.uhma.com
Members: 1000 individuals
Staff: 4
Annual Budget: $100-250,000
Exec. Director: Christine Quinn

Historical Note
Formed to provide individuals who are actively involved in Veterinary Practice Management with a means of effective communication and interaction. Members include veterinarians, hospital administrators, practice managers and office managers. Membership: $95/year (individual).

Publications:
Practice Pulse Newsletter. bi-m.

Meetings/Conferences:
Annual Meetings: November
1999 – Tempe, AZ/Oct. 1-3

Veterinary Orthopedic Soc. (1972)
P.O. Box 313
Newmarket, NH   03857-0313
Tel: (603)659-8187   *Fax:* (603)659-7989
Members: 650 individuals
Annual Budget: under $10,000
Exec. Secretary: Mary Clark

Historical Note
VOS members are veterinarians with an interest in orthopedic surgery. Membership: $20/year (individual).

Publications:
Membership List. irreg.
VOS Newsletter. a.

Meetings/Conferences:
Annual Meetings: last week of February
1999 – Sun Valley, ID

Viatical Ass'n of America (1994)
1200 19th St., N.W., Suite 300
Washington, DC   20036
Tel: (202)429-5129   *Fax:* (202)429-5113
Toll Free: (800)842 - 9811
Members: 31 individuals
Staff: 2
Annual Budget: $100-250,000
Exec. Director: William E. Kelley, CAE

Historical Note
Members are companies who purchase life insurance policies from people with terminal illnesses. Works to establish reasonable regulation for the industry. Membership: $5,000/year.

Meetings/Conferences:

Vibrating Screen Manufacturers Ass'n (1959)

Historical Note
Organization defunct in 1995.

Vibration Institute (1972)
6262 S. Kingery Hwy, Suite 212
Willowbrook, IL   60514
Tel: (630)654-2254   *Fax:* (630)654-2271
E-Mail: vibinst@anet-chi.com
Web Site: http://www.vibinst.org
Members: 3,000 individuals
Staff: 6
Annual Budget: $250-500,000
Director: Ronald L. Eshleman, Ph.D.

Historical Note
Founded as the Vibration Foundation, it reorganized in 1973 under its present name. Members are companies and individuals concerned with measuring and analyzing machinery vibration. Membership: $50/year (US); $65/year (foreign); $500/year (corporate).

Publications:
Proceedings. a.
Vibrations Magazine. q. adv.

Meetings/Conferences:
Annual Meetings: June
1999 – Orlando, FL(Sheraton World Resort)/June 8-10
2000 – St. Louis, MO(Hyatt Regency)/June 20-22

Victorian Soc. in America (1966)
219 South 6th St.
Philadelphia, PA   19106
Tel: (215)627-4252   *Fax:* (215)627-7221
E-Mail: VicSoc@libertynet.org
Web Site: http://www.libertynet.org/~vicsoc
Members: 3,000 individuals
Staff: 1
Annual Budget: $100-250,000
Business Manager: Stacy Hampton
Membership: Nancy Golden

Historical Note
Members are historians, preservationists and others with an interest in the study of nineteenth century America. Membership: $40/year (individual), 350/year (museum house, libraries and university).

Publications:
Nineteenth Century. semi-a. adv.
Victorian. q. adv.

Meetings/Conferences:
1999 – St. Paul/Minneapolis, MN(St. Paul Hotel)/June 9-13
2000 – Philadelphia, PA(Doubletree)

Video Electronics Standards Ass'n (1989)
2150 North First St, Suite 440
San Jose, CA   95131-2020
Tel: (408)435-0333   *Fax:* (408)435-8225
E-Mail: pj@vesa.org
Web Site: http://www.vesa.org
Members: 350 companies
Staff: 10
Annual Budget: $500-1,000,000
Exec. Director: Bill Lempesis
Mktg. Development Manager: Cathy E. Egan

Historical Note
VESA was established in 1989 to set and support industry-wide interface standards designed for the PC environment. Vesa is committed to promoting and developing timely, relevant and open standards for the electronics industry, ensuring interoperability and encouraging innovation and market growth. As a leading organization and an internationally-recognized voice in the electronics industry, VESA is committed to developing and promoting standards for the display, system and interactive multimedia markets. Membership: $500/year (individual); corporate fee varies, based on annual revenues.

Publications:
Vesa Newsletter. 6/year.

Video Retailers Ass'n (1987)

Historical Note
Organization defunct in 1998.

Video Software Dealers Ass'n (1981)
16530 Ventura Blvd., Suite 400
Encino, CA   91436-4551
Tel: (818)385-1500   *Fax:* (818)385-0567
Web Site: http://www.vsda.org
Members: 3,600 companies
Staff: 28
Annual Budget: $5-10,000,000
President: Jeffrey P. Eves
V. President, Communications and Marketing: Cathy Scott
Senior V. President and General Counsel: Crossan R. Andersen
V. President, Finance and Administration: Richard Nissenbaum
Asst. V. President, Membership: Carrie Dieterich

Historical Note
Regular members are retailers and distributors of pre-recorded video products; associate members are manufacturers and suppliers of products to the industry. Has an annual budget of approximately $5.1 million. Membership fee varies with number of retail stores and volume, and depends upon type of membership (associate or regular).

Publications:
VSDA Voice. semi-m. adv.
VSDA Voice Supplement. semi-a. adv.

Meetings/Conferences:
Annual Meetings: July at the Convention Center in Las Vegas, NV

Vinegar Institute (1967)
5775 Peachtree-Dunwoody Rd., Suite 500-G
Atlanta, GA   30342-1558
Tel: (404)252-3663   *Fax:* (404)252-0774
E-Mail: vi@assnhq.com
Members: 42 companies
Staff: 5
Annual Budget: $100-250,000
Exec. Director: Pamela A. Chumley

Historical Note
Membership composed of makers and bottlers of vinegar, as well as suppliers to the industry. Membership: dues vary by sales (company).

Publications:
Basic Reference Manual.
Technically Speaking About Vinegar.

Meetings/Conferences:
Annual Meetings: February-March
1999 – Monterey, CA(Plaza)/March 7-10/100
2000 – Ft. Lauderdale, FL(The Registry)/March 3-8/125

Vinifera Wine Growers Ass'n (1973)
P.O. Box 10045
Alexandria, VA   22310
Tel: (703)922-7049   *Fax:* (703)922-0617
Members: 350 individuals
Staff: 1
Annual Budget: $25-50,000
Secretary and Editor: Anita Murchie
President: Gordon Murchie

Historical Note
Originally founded to support the growth of Vinifera variety wine grapes in the eastern U.S., VWGA now suports the whole spectrum of the U.S. wine industry. Disseminates information on the history and current developments in winemaking, and supports the production and marketing of quality wines. Membership: $25/year.

Publications:
Wine Exchange. q. adv.

Meetings/Conferences:
Annual Meetings: usually in conjunction with the Virginia Wine Festival/late August

Vinyl Acetate Toxicology Group (1995)
1250 Connecticut Ave., N.W., Suite 700
Washington, DC   20005
Tel: (202)637-9040   *Fax:* (202)637-9178
E-Mail: regnet@ricochet.net
Members: 4 individuals, 4 associate
Staff: 2
Annual Budget: $100-250,000
Exec. Director: Robert J. Fensterheim

Historical Note
VATG sponsors and monitors research to evaluate the health effects of vinyl acetate, and makes these evaluations available to the various regulatory agencies with an interest in health and safety. Membership: $50,000/year (full member); $3,000/year (associate).

Vinyl Institute (1982)
65 Madison Ave.
Morristown, NJ   07960-6078
Tel: (973)898-6699   *Fax:* (973)898-6633
Web Site: http://www.vinyl-info.org
Members: 32 companies
Staff: 4
Annual Budget: $2-5,000,000
Exec. Director: Robert H. Burnett

Historical Note
A division of the Soc. of the Plastics Industry, The Vinyl Institute is a trade association representing the leading U.S. manufacturers of vinyl, vinyl chloride monomer and vinyl additives and modifiers as well as film and sheet producers. The Institute's principal activities are education and advocacy, and include the sponsorship of extensive scientific research.

Meetings/Conferences:
Annual Meetings: May
1999 – Dallas, TX

Vinyl Siding Institute (1976)
1801 K St., N.W., Suite 600-K
Washington, DC   20006
Tel: (202)970-5200   *Fax:* (202)296-7005
Web Site: http://www.vinylsiding.org
Members: 250 individuals, 58 companies
Staff: 4
Annual Budget: $100-250,000
Exec. Director: Jery Huntley

Historical Note
A business unit of the Soc. of the Plastics Industry, VSI promotes the growth of the vinyl siding industry, acting as advocate and central communications resource for its membership, develops industry standards, work with code and regulatory bodies and provides a forum for the exchange of information on technology and issues important to the industry. Compiles statistics. Membership: cost varies in accordance with sales.

Meetings/Conferences:

Vinyl Window and Door Institute (1981)

Historical Note
Defunct in 1997.

Viola da Gamba Soc. of America (1962)
253 E. Delaware, #12F
Chicago, IL   60611
Tel: (312)654-9120

E-Mail: ejfish@mcs.net
Web Site: http://www.enteract.com/ ~ vdgsa
Members: 800 individuals
Staff: 1
President: Jack Ashworth

Historical Note
VdGSA members are professional musicians, music teachers and amateur players of the viola da gamba, a bass instrument related to the cello. Sponsors workshops, competitions, and other activities. Membership: $25/year (individual).

Publications:
Journal of the VdGSA. a.
Membership List. a.
VdGSA Newsletter. q. adv.

Meetings/Conferences:
Annual Meetings: late July-early August

Vision Council of America (1985)
1655 Fort Myer Drive, Lobby 200
Arlington, VA   22209-3108
Tel: (703)243-1508   Fax: (703)243-1537
Web Site: http://www.visionsite.org
Members: 470 companies
Staff: 8
Annual Budget: $5-10,000,000
Exec. V. President: Susan S. Burton, CAE
Director, Public Relations: William J. Wilson, CAE
Dir., Marketing: Diana Buttram

Historical Note
Formerly (1989) Vision Industry Council of America. Promotes eyecare and eyewear in the United States through public relations programs and trade shows.

Publications:
Focal Point. q.

Meetings/Conferences:
Annual Meetings: Spring

Visiting Nurse Ass'ns of America (1983)
11 Beacon St., Suite 910
Boston, MA   02108
Tel: (617)523-4042   Fax: (617)227-4843
Toll Free: (888)866 - 8773
Members: 211 organizations
Staff: 8
Annual Budget: $1-2,000,000
President & C.E.O.: Carolyn Markey
Government Affairs Coordinator: Kathy Thompson
V.President of Business Development: Pamela Sawyerane
Director of Finance: Patricia Bernard

Historical Note
Superseded the American Affiliation of Visiting Nurse Ass'ns and Services in 1986. Members are non-profit, community-based home and community health care providers. VNAA provides membership programs, educational events, business development, managed care marketing and contracting, communications, national imaging and group purchasing services for its members.

Publications:
All VNA's Directory. a.
VNA Membership Guide. a.

Meetings/Conferences:
Annual Meetings: Spring/500
1999 – Orlando, FL/Apr. 7-9

Visitor Studies Ass'n (1991)
c/o Center for Social Design
P.O. Box 1111
Jacksonville, AL   36265
Tel: (205)782-5640
Members: 390 individuals, 20 organizations
Annual Budget: $100-250,000
Treasurer: Arlene Benefield

Historical Note
Members are professionals at various institutions interested in studying audience experiences at museums, zoos, parks, etc. Promotes research in visitor participation and applications of such research to programming and policy. Membership: $50/year (individual); $100/year (supporting); $200/year (sustaining).

Publications:
Annual Proceedings. a. adv.
Membership Directory. a.

Meetings/Conferences:
Annual Meetings: Summer

Visually Impaired Data Processors Internat'l (1970)
c/o American Council of the Blind
1155 15th St., N.W., Suite 720
Washington, DC   20005
Tel: (202)467-5081   Fax: (202)467-5085
Toll Free: (800)424 - 8666
Web Site: http://www.acb.org
Members: 69 individuals
Annual Budget: under $10,000
Washington Representative: Oral O. Miller

Historical Note
VIDPI members are blind or visually impaired data processors. Membership:$20(individual); $25 (organization).

Publications:
Views. q.

Meetings/Conferences:
Annual Meetings: Los Angeles, CA(Westin)/July 3-9 Louisville, KY

Vocational Evaluation and Work Adjustment Ass'n (1967)
202 East Cheyenne Mountain Blvd, Suite N
Colorado Springs, CO   80906
Tel: (719)527-1800   Fax: (719)576-1818
E-Mail: 76101.3626@compuserve.com

Web Site: www.vewaa.org.
Members: 1,300 individuals
Annual Budget: $25-50,000
Home Office Liason: Geri Harrand

Historical Note
VEWAA is a professional division of the Nat'l Rehabilitation Ass'n, (Alexandria, VA), representing the interests of professionals in vocational evaluation. Membership: $35/year, plus NRA dues (individual).

Publications:
VEWAA Newsletter. q.
Vocational Evaluation and Work Adjustment Bulletin. q. adv.

Meetings/Conferences:

Vocational Industrial Clubs of America (1965)
Box 3000
Leesburg, VA   20177-3000
Tel: (703)777-8810   Fax: (703)777-8999
E-Mail: anyinfo@vica.org
Web Site: http://www.vica.org
Members: 250,000 individuals
Staff: 25
Annual Budget: $2-5,000,000
Exec. Director: Stephen Denby
College & Technical Programs: Thomas W. Holdsworth
Associate Exec. Director/Corprate Treasurer: Gary M. Diehl
Director, Administrative Services: Sylvia Merchant
Director, Career Education Programs: Michael H. Regauld
Director, Business and Industry Partnerships: Timothy W. Lawrence

Historical Note
Founded in 1965 as the national organization for students in trade, industrial, technical and health occupations programs. Members are students in high schools, area vocational schools and in community college training. Sponsors an annual National Leadership and Skills Conference. Membership: $7/year (student); $10/year (professional/associate).

Publications:
Connect: VICA Newsletter for College & Postsecondary
Instructors. 9/y.
Next: The college & Postsecondary Newsletter of VICA. q.
SHARP: Preparing for Leadership in the World of Work. semi-a.
VICA Professional. q.

Meetings/Conferences:
Annual Meetings: June
1999 – Kansas City, MO(Bartle Hall)/June 27-July 2
2000 – Kansas City, MO(Bartle Hall)/June 25-July 1/9000

Voice and Speech Trainer's Ass'n
Historical Note
A focus group of the Ass'n for Theatre in Higher Education.

Voluntary Protection Programs Participants Ass'n
7600-E Leesburg Pike, Suite 440
Falls Church, VA   22043-2004
Tel: (703)761-1146   Fax: (703)761-1148
Web Site: http://www.fiesta.com/vpppa
Exec. Director: Lee Anne Elliott, CAE
Communications Manager: Julie Phillips
Govt. Affairs Counsel: Mark Richter
Conference/Education Manager: Amy Hutto
Coordinator, Outreach and Education Programs: Nancy Lu
Membership/Development Manager: Amy Busby

Historical Note
Members are companies and sites which participate in voluntary protection programs coordinated by OSHA or the Dept. of Energy. Membership: $125-5,000/year.

Publications:
The Leader. q.

Meetings/Conferences:
Annual Meetings: Fall/1,900
1999 – Washington, DC(Hilton)/Sept. 14-17
2000 – Seattle, WA(Evergreen Conv. Center)/Aug. 28-31

WACRA - World Ass'n for Case Method Research & Application (1984)
23 Mackintosh Ave.
Needham, MA   02492-1218
Tel: (781)444-8982   Fax: (781)444-1548
Toll Free: (800)523 - 6468
E-Mail: wacra@msn.com
Web Site: http://www.agecon.uga.edu/ ~ wacra/wacra.htm
Members: 2,000 individuals, 100 organizations
President & Exec. Director: Dr. Hans E. Klein

Historical Note
WACRA members are professionals and academicians with an interest in the use of the case method and other interactive methods in teaching, training and planning. Membership: $65/yer (individual); $45/year (student); $350/year (organization).

Publications:
Case Method Research and Application. a.
Innovation Through Cooperation.
Interactive Teaching & Emerging Technologies.
Teaching & Interactive Methods.
The Art of Interactive Teaching.
WACRA NEWSletter. semi-a.

Meetings/Conferences:
Annual Meetings: June-July
1999 – Caceres, Spain
2000 – Budapest, Hungary
2001 – Lund, Sweden

WAEL: a National Equipment Leasing Ass'n
Historical Note
Became United Ass'n of Equipment Leasing in 1995.

Waiters Ass'n (1993)

Historical Note
Organization defunct in 1997.

Walking Horse Owners Ass'n of America (1975)
1535 W. Northfield Blvd., Suite 3A
Murfreesboro, TN   37129-1480
Tel: (615)890-9120   Fax: (615)890-2070
Members: 5,300 individuals
Staff: 5
Annual Budget: $100-250,000
Office Manager: Tommy Hall

Historical Note
Members own and exhibit Tennessee Walking horses. Sponsors the Internat'l Grand Championship Walking Horse Show held in Murfreesboro, TN. Membership: $35/yr.

Publications:
Voice of TWH. m.
Walking Horse Report. w.

Meetings/Conferences:
Annual Meetings: February
1999 – Murfreesboro, TN(Garden Plaza)/Feb. 19-20

Walking Horse Trainers Ass'n (1968)
P.O. Box 61
Shelbyville, TN   37162
Tel: (931)684-5866   Fax: (931)684-5895
Members: 700 individuals
Staff: 1
Annual Budget: $25-50,000
Exec. Secretary: Marcia M. Allison

Historical Note
Trainers of Tennessee Walking Horses. Works for unity in the horse industry and sponsors continuing research. Formerly Tennessee Walking Horse Trainers Ass'n. Membership: $50/year.

Publications:
From the Horse's Mouth. q.

Meetings/Conferences:
Annual Meetings: December
1999 – Nashville, TN

Wallcoverings Ass'n (1992)
401 N. Michigan Ave.
Chicago, IL   60611-4267
Tel: (312)644-6610   Fax: (312)527-6774
Members: 150 companies
Staff: 3
Annual Budget: $500-1,000,000
Exec. Director: Ron Pietrzak
Public Relations: Tina Gonsalves
Convention Manager: Sandy Reynolds

Historical Note
The product of a merger in 1992 of the Wallcovering Manufacturers Ass'n and the Wallcovering Distributors Ass'n in 1992. Membership: dues based on annual walcovering sales volume.

Meetings/Conferences:
1999 – Marco Island, FL(Marco Island
Marriott)/Jan. 24-27/400
2000 – Puerto Rico(Westin Rio Mar)/Jan. 23-26/400
2001 – Marco Island, FL(Marco Island
Marriott)/Jan. 21-24/400

Walnut Council (1970)
P.O. Box 5046
Zionsville, IN   46077-5046
Tel: (317)873-8780   Fax: (317)873-8788
E-Mail: FhvaAwmaWc@compuserve.com
Members: 960 individuals
Staff: 1
Annual Budget: $25-50,000
Director: Larry R. Frye

Historical Note
WC is an international association representing woodland owners, foresters, forest scientists and wood-producing industry representatives in over 45 states and seven foreign countries. Membership: $25/year (individual).

Publications:
Walnut Council Bulletin. q.

Meetings/Conferences:
1999 – Lexington, KY/Aug. 1-4
2000 – Michigan/July 30-Aug. 2
2001 – Wisconsin/Aug. 5-8
2002 – Maryland/Aug. 4-7

Warehouse Distributors Ass'n (1967)
104 S. Michigan, 15th Fl.
Chicago, IL   60603-1210
Tel: (312)553-0300   Fax: (312)201-0214
Members: 150 companies
Staff: 2
Annual Budget: $100-250,000
Exec. Director: James C. Stanley

Historical Note
Members are wholesale distributors of parts for manufactured housing and recreational vehicles. Membership: $605/year (suppliers and agents); $830/year (distributors)

Publications:
Communicator. m.
WDA Newsletter. q. adv.

Meetings/Conferences:
Annual Meetings: Fall

Warehousing Education and Research Council (1977)
1100 Jorie Blvd., Suite 170
Oak Brook, IL   60523-2243
Tel: (630)990-0001   Fax: (630)990-0256
Members: 3,400 individuals
Staff: 8

Annual Budget: $1-2,000,000
Exec. Director: Thomas E. Sharpe
Manager, Communications: Christine Massie
Director, Communications, Education and Research: Rita Coleman
Director, Conference and Chapter Relations: Jackie Mariani
Director, Operations: Steven Williams

Historical Note
A professional society for warehousing executives and managers designed to improve warehousing through education and research. Membership: $195/year.

Publications:
Membership Directory. a.
WERC Watch Report.
WERCSHEET. m.

Meetings/Conferences:
Annual Meetings: Spring
1999 – Orlando, FL(Marriott World Center)/April 18-21
2000 – San Antonio, TX(Marriott Rivercenter & Riverwalk)/April 30-May 3

Waste Equipment Technology Ass'n (1972)
4301 Connecticut Ave., N.W., Suite 300
Washington, DC 20008
Tel: (202)244-4700   *Fax:* (202)966-4824
Toll Free: (800)424 - 2869
E-Mail: jlegler@envasn.org
Web Site: http://www.envasns.org/wastec
Members: 272 individuals
Staff: 6
Annual Budget: $500-1,000,000
Exec. V. President: John A. Legler
Manager, Technical Programs: Nate Wall
Manager, Member Services: Kim Benz

Historical Note
A constituent group of Environmental Industry Ass'ns, WASTEC represents designers, manufacturers, distributors and consultants of technology and systems for the management of wastes and recycling. Membership: annual dues vary, based on revenue.

Publications:
ANSI Z245 Series Standards. irreg.
Directory of Member Products and Services. a.
Listing of WASTEC Rated Stationary Compactors. trien.
WASTEC Recommended Practices Series. irreg.
WASTEC's Equipment Technology News. m.

Meetings/Conferences:
Semi-annual Meetings: with the Environmental Industry Ass'ns
1999 – Jekyll Island, GA/March 5-0/75

Waste Oil Heating Manufacturers Ass'n (1981)
Historical Note
Name changed to Used Oil Management Ass'n in 1996.

Water and Sewer Distributors of America (1979)
1900 Arch St.
Philadelphia, PA 19103-1498
Tel: (215)564-3484   *Fax:* (215)564-2175
E-Mail: assnhqt@netaxs.com
Web Site: http://www.wasda.org
Members: 50 companies
Staff: 3
Annual Budget: $100-250,000
Exec. Director: Kenneth R. Hutton

Historical Note
Members are distributors of products to the contractor, municipal water and sewer markets. Membership: $300-5,000/year (company).

Publications:
Connections Newsletter. q.
Directory. a. adv.

Meetings/Conferences:
1999 – Miami Beach, FL(Wyndam Miami Beach)/Feb. 28-March 4/150
2000 – Cabo San Lucas, Mexico

Water and Wastewater Equipment Manufacturers Ass'n (1908)
Box 17402
Washington, DC 20041
Tel: (703)444-1777   *Fax:* (703)444-1779
E-Mail: wwema@erols.com
Web Site: http://www.wwea.com
Members: 80 individuals, 73 companies
Staff: 3
Annual Budget: $250-500,000
President: Dawn C. Kristof

Historical Note
Formerly Water and Sewage Works Manufacturers Ass'n. Membership: $950-13,350/year (company).

Publications:
WWEMA Washington Analysis. bi-m.

Meetings/Conferences:
Annual Meetings: November

Water and Wastewater Instrumentation Testing Ass'n of North America (ITA) (1984)
631 N. Stephanie St., Suite 279
Henderson, NV 89014
Tel: (702)568-1445   *Fax:* (702)568-1446
E-Mail: ita@instrument.org
Web Site: http://www.instrument.org
Members: 97 agencies
Staff: 2
Annual Budget: $100-250,000
Exec. Director: Tony M. Palmer
Technical Programs Director: Maureen C. Ross

Historical Note
Formerly (1988) Instrumentation Testing Service and (1993) Instrumentation Testing Ass'n. Established and incorporated in the District of Columbia, ITA members are public and private agencies utilizing instrumentation for the conduct or enhancement of water, wastewater and industrial waste. Associate membership is available for instrument manufacturers, consultants, and regulatory agencies responsible for the supervision of facilities which utilize instrumentation. Membership: $500-1,000/year.

Publications:
Flow Meter Designer Checklist. bi-m.
ITA Monthly News. m.
Test Evaluation Reports.

Meetings/Conferences:
1999 – New Orleans, LA/50
2000 – Anaheim, CA/50
2001 – Atlanta, GA/50
2002 – Chicago, IL/50

Water Environment Federation (1928)
601 Wythe St.
Alexandria, VA 22314-1994
Tel: (703)684-2400   *Fax:* (703)684-2492
Toll Free: (800)666 - 0206
E-Mail: webfeedback@wef.org
Web Site: http://www.wef.org
Members: 41,000 individuals
Staff: 125
Annual Budget: $10-25,000,000
Exec. Director: Quincalee Brown, Ph.D., CAE
Program Director, Public Information: Nancy L. Blatt
Dir., Government Affairs: Timothy S. Williams
Program Dir., Meetings and Operations: Rosemary Petruso
Deputy Exec. Director - Administrative: Timothy Ricker
Program Director, Financial Management: Mike Nutter
Director, Membership/Assn. Programs: Phyliss Eastman
Program Director, Membership Services: Susan O'Neill
Dir., Marketing/Member Development: Debra Sutton
Dep. Exec. Director, Technical: Albert C. Gray, CAE
Program Director: Berinda Ross
Dir., Technical & Educational Services: Eileen O'Neill
Dir., Expositions: Nanette Tucker
Dir., Technical Programs: Susan Merther
Dir., Technical Periodicals: Lisa Neal

Historical Note
The Water Environment Federartion is a not-for-profit technical and educational organization that was founded in 1928. Its mission is to preserve and enhance the global water environment. Federation members are water quality specialists from around the world, including environmental, civil and chemical engineers, biologists, chemists, government officials, treatment plant managers and operators, laboratory technicians, college professors, researchers, students and equipment manufacturers and distributors. Has an annual budget of approximately $17 million.

Publications:
Biosolids Technical Bulletin. bi-m.
Federation Highlights. m.
Industrial Wastewater. m. adv.
Operations Forum. m. adv.
Water Environment & Technology. m. adv.
Water Environment Laboratory Solutions.
Water Environment Regulation Watch.
Water Environment Research. m. adv.

Meetings/Conferences:
Annual Meetings: Fall/11,000
1999 – New Orleans, LA/Oct. 9-13
2000 – Anaheim, CA/Oct. 14-18

Water Equipment Wholesalers and Suppliers Ass'n (1960)
Historical Note
A division of the Nat'l Ground Water Ass'n.

Water Quality Ass'n (1974)
4151 Naperville Road
Lisle, IL 60532
Tel: (630)505-0160   *Fax:* (630)505-9637
Web Site: http://www.wqu.org
Members: 2,500 companies
Staff: 26
Annual Budget: $2-5,000,000
Exec. Director: Peter Censky
Director, Public Affairs: Carlyn Meyer
Director, Meetings and Conventions: Jeannine Collins, CMP
Director of Education: Dr. Judith A. Grove, CAE
Technical Director: Joe Harrison
Director, Membership: Margit Kronthaler

Historical Note
Merger of the Water Conditioning Ass'n Internat'l (1945) and the Water Conditioning Foundation (1948). A not-for-profit international trade association representing firms and individuals engaged in the design, manufacture, production, distribution, and sale of equipment, products, supplies and services for providing quality water for specific uses in residential, commercial, industrial and institutional establishments. Membership is voluntary. The Water Quality Research Council, formerly (1971) the Water Conditioning Research Council, is its research and educational arm. Sponsors and supports the AQUA Political Action Committee (AQUAPAC).

Publications:
WQA Newsletter. bi-m.

Meetings/Conferences:
Annual Meetings: March
1999 – Ft. Worth, TX(Tarrant County Covention Center)
2000 – Long Beach, CA(Long Beach Covention Center)

Water Quality Research Council (1950)
Historical Note
Educational and research arm of the Water Quality Ass'n. Formerly (1971) the Water Conditioning Research Council.

Water Resources Congress (1891)
Historical Note
Address unknown in 1996.

Water Sports Industry Ass'n (1977)
200 Castlewood Drive
North Palm Beach, FL 33408
Tel: (561)840-1185   *Fax:* (561)863-8984
Members: 170 companies
Staff: 2
Annual Budget: $100-250,000
Exec. Director: James Hotchkiss

Historical Note
Formerly known as Water Ski Industry Ass'n for 18 years, the Water Sports Industry Ass'n is an affiliate of the Sporting Goods Manufacturers Ass'n, which provides administrative support. Members are leading manufacturers, dealers and sales representatives of water sports. Works to promote the sport through activities such as International Novice Water Ski Tour sponsor (grassroots fun tournaments), national public relations programs promoting water sports and water recreation through print media, radio and television, publications, awards, market research and Census of Sales Reports. Incorporated in the State of Florida.

Publications:
WaterSki Business.

Meetings/Conferences:
Annual Meetings: September, at WaterSki/Wakeboard Expo

Water Systems Council (1932)
800 Roosevelt Road, Bldg. C, Suite 20
Glen Ellyn, IL 60137
Tel: (630)545-1762   *Fax:* (630)790-3095
Members: 61 companies
Staff: 2
Annual Budget: $250-500,000
Exec. Director: Richard W. Church

Historical Note
Formerly the Nat'l Ass'n of Domestic and Farm Pump Manufacturers, members are manufacturers and distributors of pumps, component products and accessories for private water systems (wells) for residential and agricultural applications. Membership: $350/year (distributors); manufacturers membership based on sales volume.

Publications:
Well Connected Newsletter. q.

Meetings/Conferences:
Semi-annual Meetings: Spring and Fall

Waterbed Council
Historical Note
Became (1996) Specialty Sleep Ass'n.

WaterJet Technology Ass'n
917 Locust St., Suite 1100
St. Louis, MO 63101-1413
Tel: (314)241-1445   *Fax:* (314)241-1449
E-Mail: wjta@primary.net
Web Site: http://www.wjta.org
Members: 650 individuals
Annual Budget: $50-100,000
Manager: Mark S. Birenbaum, Ph.D.

Historical Note
Created in 1983 by members of the water jetting industry acting in concert with university faculty and government officials to provide a means of service, communication, and education within the rapidly developing industry of water jet technology. Members include leading researchers, manufacturers, and users of water jet technology. Membership: $50/year (individual); $350/year (company).

Publications:
Jet News. bi-m. adv.
Proceedings of the American Water Jet Conference. bien.

Meetings/Conferences:
1999 – Houston, TX(J.W. Marriott)/Aug. 13-17/500

Waterproofing Contractors Ass'n (1971)
P.O. Box 10387
Raleigh, NC 27605
Tel: (919)834-1072   *Fax:* (919)821-3072
Members: 60 firms
Staff: 1
Annual Budget: $25-50,000
Exec. Director: Annette S. Boutwell

Historical Note
Founded as a regional association, WCA now provides representation and other benefits to member contractors around the country. Membership: $175/year (organization)

Publications:
Membership Directory. q.
Newsletter. m.

Meetings/Conferences:
Annual Meetings: September
1999 – Myrtle Beach, SC(Ocean Creek)/Sept. 9-12

Weather Modification Ass'n (1951)
P.O. Box 26926
Fresno, CA 93729-6926
Tel: (209)434-3486   *Fax:* (209)434-3486
E-Mail: wxmode@ix.netcom.com
Members: 200 individuals, 20 corporations
Staff: 1
Annual Budget: under $10,000
Exec. Secretary: Hilda Duckering

Historical Note
Formerly (1967) Weather Control Research Ass'n.

Publications:
Journal of Weather Modification. a.

Meetings/Conferences:

Web Host Guild (1998)
10001 N.W. 50th St., Suite 111
Sunrise, FL 33351
Tel: (954)572-7866
E-Mail: whg@whg.org
Web Site: http://www.whg.org
Members: 20 companies
President: Jonathan Caputo

Historical Note
WHG was founded to promote standards for internet service providers who host clients' information resources on the World Wide Web.

Web Offset Ass'n of Printing Industries of America (1952)
100 Daingerfield Road
Alexandria, VA 22314-2888
Tel: (703)519-8141   *Fax:* (703)519-7109
E-Mail: tbasore@printing.org
Web Site: http://www.printing.org
Staff: 4
Annual Budget: $500-1,000,000
Exec. Director: Thomas B. Basore
Programs & Publications Director: Beth Parrott

Historical Note
A special industry group of Printing Industries of America.

Publications:
Directory. a.
Market Outlook. a.
Product Catalog.

Meetings/Conferences:
Annual Meetings: May/1,800
1999 – Chicago, IL(Sheraton)/May 10-12

Web Sling and Tiedown Ass'n (1973)
710 E. Ogden Ave., Suite 600
Naperville, IL 60563
Tel: (630)369-2406   *Fax:* (630)369-2488
Members: 77 companies
Staff: 5
Annual Budget: $100-250,000
Exec. Director: Tim Seeden
Admin. Director: Tricia Burkyard

Historical Note
Manufacturers of web slings which are used as hoists in various industrial lifting operations and web tiedowns used in cargo control trucking operations. Formerly (1988) the Web Sling Ass'n. Membership: $500-2,200/year.

Publications:
Operating and Inspection Manual - Polyester Roundslings. trien.
Operating and Inspection Manual - Web Slings. trien.
Operating and Inspection Manual - Tiedowns. trien.
Recommended Standard Specification - Polyester Roundslings. trien.
Recommended Standard Specification - Tiedowns. trien.
Recommended Standard Specification - Web Slings. trien.
Uplifting News. 2/year. adv.

Meetings/Conferences:
1999 – Ft. Myers Beach, FL(Diamond Head Resort)/April 18-21/100
2000 – Maui, HI(Kapalua Bay)/March 26-30/100

WEB: Network of Benefit Professionals (1982)
P.O. Box 128
Brookfield, WI 53008-0128
Tel: (414)821-9080   *Fax:* (414)821-1275
E-Mail: web@execpc.com
Web Site: http://www.WEBENEFITS.org
Members: 2,400 individuals
Staff: 3
Annual Budget: $250-500,000
Exec. Director: Gabrielle Redfern

Historical Note
WEB members are benefits professionals including human resource managers, plan administrators, attorneys, consultants and actuaries. WEB provides education and networking opportunities. Membership: $125/year.

Publications:
JobBank. m.
Membership Directory. a.
WEB Network. 10/year.

Wedding and Event Videographers Ass'n Internat'l
8499 S. Tamiami Trail, Suite 208
Sarasota, FL 34238
Tel: (941)923-5334   *Fax:* (941)921-3836
E-Mail: info@weva.com
Web Site: http://www.weva.com
Chairman: Roy Chapman

Historical Note
WEVA members are professional wedding and event videographers.

Publications:
Wedding & Event Videography. bi-m. adv.

Wedding and Portrait Photographers Internat'l (1974)
P.O. Box 2003, 1312 Lincoln Blvd.
Santa Monica, CA 90406
Tel: (310)451-0090   *Fax:* (310)395-9058
Members: 3,500 individuals
Staff: 17
Annual Budget: $250-500,000
President: Steve Sheanin
Editor: Bill Hurter

Historical Note
Formerly Wedding Photographers of America and Wedding Photographers Internat'l, WPPI assumed its present name in 1995. Promotes high artistic and technical standards; serves as a forum for the exchange of knowledge and experience; and offers instruction in techniques, advertising, sales, promotion, marketing, public relations, accounting, management and tax planning. Membership: $75/year.

Publications:
Marketing and Technical Manual. q.
Rangefinder. m. adv.
WPPI Photography Monthly Newsletter. m.

Meetings/Conferences:
Annual Meetings: February-March

Wedding Photographers Internat'l (1974)
Historical Note
Became Wedding and Portrait Photographers Internat'l in 1995.

Weed Science Soc. of America (1953)
810 East 10th St.
Box 1897
Lawrence, KS 66044-8897
Tel: (785)843-1235   *Fax:* (785)843-1274
E-Mail: wssa@allenpress.com
Members: 2,300 individuals
Staff: 8
Annual Budget: $500-1,000,000
Exec. Secretary: David M. Wiley

Historical Note
Founded as the Weed Soc. of America, it absorbed the Ass'n of Regional Weed Control Conferences in 1956 and assumed its present name in 1963. Has members from the U.S., Mexico, overseas, and Canada. Membership: $75/year (individual); $139/year (organization/company).

Publications:
Weed Science. q.
Weed Technology. q. adv.

Meetings/Conferences:
Annual Meetings: February
1999 – San Diego, CA
2000 – Toronto, Ontario

Welding Research Council (1935)
3 Park Ave., 27th Floor
New York, NY 10016-5902
Tel: (212)705-7956   *Fax:* (212)591-7183
Web Site: http://www.forengineers.org/wrc
Members: 300 organizations
Staff: 4
Annual Budget: $2-5,000,000
Exec. Director: Martin Prager, Ph.D.

Historical Note
Established by the Engineering Foundation to conduct and coordinate welding research. Membership: $1,250/year (domestic); $1,320/year (international).

Publications:
Reports of Progress. bi-m.
Welding Research Abroad. 10/year.
Welding Research News. q.
Welding Research Supplement. m.
WRC Bulletin. 10/year.

Meetings/Conferences:
Annual Meetings: Not held

Wellness Councils of America (1985)
7101 Newport Ave., Suite 311
Omaha, NE 68152-2175
Tel: (402)572-3590   *Fax:* (402)572-3594
Web Site: http://www.welcoa.org
Members: 3,000 individuals, 28 wellness councils
Staff: 5
President: Dr. David M. Hunnicutt

Historical Note
WELCOA is dedicated to promoting healthier lifestyles for all Americans, especially through health promotion activities at the workplace. Membership: varies depending on local membership status.

Publications:
Work-Site Wellness Works. q.

Meetings/Conferences:
Annual Meetings: Fall

Welsh Black Cattle Ass'n (1975)
208 North Hymera East St.
Shelburn, IN 47879
Tel: (812)383-9233
Members: 75 individuals
Annual Budget: under $10,000
Secretary: Susan Case

Historical Note
Breeders and fanciers of Welsh black cattle. Membership: $25/year.

Publications:
Welsh Black World. a.

Meetings/Conferences:

Welsh Pony and Cob Soc. of America (1906)
P.O. Box 2977
Winchester, VA 22604
Tel: (540)667-6195
Toll Free: (540)667 - 3766
Web Site: http://www.scendtek.com/wpcsa
Members: 1,800 individuals
Staff: 4
Annual Budget: $100-250,000
Secretary: Lisa L. Landis

Historical Note
Founded as the Welsh Pony and Cob Soc. of America in Illinois in 1906; reinstituted after a period of inactivity in Indiana in 1946 as Welsh Pony Soc. of America; reassumed its original name in 1986. Membership: $30/yr. (individual); $40/yr. (organization/company).

Publications:
Member-Breeder Directory. a.
Nat'l Welsh Pony Yearbook. a. adv.
Welsh Pony Soc. Newsletter.
Welsh Pony Studbook. a.

Meetings/Conferences:
Annual Meetings: October/November
1999 – Baltimore, MD/Feb. 18-21

Western and English Manufacturers Ass'n (1963)
P.O.Box 468
451 E. 58th Avenue
Denver, CO 80216-1404
Tel: (303)295-2001   *Fax:* (303)295-6108
E-Mail: waema@netway.net
Web Site: http://waema.org
Members: 105 companies
Staff: 1
Annual Budget: $100-250,000
Exec. Director: Glenda Chipps

Historical Note
Manufacturers of Western and English style riding equipment and clothes. Until 1976 known as the Western and English Apparel and Equipment Manufacturers Ass'n.

Publications:
WAEMA Watch. q.

Meetings/Conferences:
Annual Meetings: Summer/250

Western Ass'n for Art Conservation (1975)
1272 N. Flores St.
Los Angeles, CA 90069-2904
Tel: (213)654-8748   *Fax:* (213)656-3220
E-Mail: cstavrou@ix.netcom.com
Web Site: http://palimpsest.stanford.edu/waac/
Members: 500 individuals
Annual Budget: $25-50,000
Secretary/Treasurer: Chris Stavroudis

Historical Note
WAAC members are art conservators, restorers and related professionals. Formerly (1977) Western Ass'n of Art Conservators. Membership: $25/year (individual), $30/year (U.S. organization/company).

Publications:
Membership Directory. a.
WAAC Newsletter. 3/yr.

Meetings/Conferences:
Annual Meetings: Fall
1999 – San Francisco, CA

Western Dredging Ass'n (1979)
P.O. Box 5797
Vancouver, WA 98668-5797
Tel: (360)750-0209   *Fax:* (360)750-1445
E-Mail: weda@juno.com
Members: 3,000 individuals, 35 companies
Annual Budget: $50-100,000
Exec. Director: Lawrence M. Patella

Historical Note
A non-profit organization encouraging growth and education in the fields of dredging, navigation and marine engineering. WEDA is a regional organization covering North, Central and South America and, in addition to the Central Dredging Association (CEDA) and the Eastern Dredging Association (EADA), constitutes the World Organization of Dredging Associations (WODA). World Dredging Conferences (WODCONs) with representatives from WEDA, CEDA, and EADA are held every three years in addition to the annual WEDA general meetings. Has no paid staff. Membership fee: $50/year (regular); $15/year (student); $250/year (organization).

Publications:
Directory. a.
Newsletter. q.
Proceedings of Technical Papers. a.

Meetings/Conferences:
Annual Meetings: May/150
1999 – Louisville, KY/May 16-18

Western Economic Ass'n Internat'l (1922)
7400 Center Ave., Suite 109
Huntington Beach, CA 92647-3039
Tel: (714)898-3222   *Fax:* (714)891-6715
E-Mail: info@weainternational.org
Web Site: http://www.weainternational.org
Members: 3,000 individuals, 40 organizations
Staff: 3
Annual Budget: $250-500,000
Exec. V. President: Eldon J. Dvorak

Historical Note
WEA is a non-profit educational organization which seeks to promote mutually beneficial exchange of ideas between economists in academia and those working in government and business. WEA strives to communicate economic knowledge outside the profession. Members are individuals, corporations, universities, and other organizations. Membership: $60/year.

Publications:
Conference Program. a. adv.
Contemporary Economic Policy. q. adv.
Economic Inquiry. q. adv.

Meetings/Conferences:
1999 – San Diego, CA(Sheraton Hotel and Marina)/July 6-10/1200
2000 – Sydney, Australia

2001 – Vancouver, BC, Canada/June 29-July 3/1200

Western Forest Industries Ass'n
Historical Note
Became (1995) Independent Forest Products Ass'n.

Western Hemisphere Ass'n of Meat Marketers *(1971)*
1700 N. Moore St. Suite 1600
Arlington, VA   22209
Tel: (703)841-3690   *Fax:* (703)841-9656
Members: 40 companies
Staff: 2
Annual Budget: $10-25,000
Exec. Secretary: Jerome J. Breiter, Ph.D.

Historical Note
Incorporated in the District of Columbia in 1972 as Canned and Cooked Meat Importers Ass'n; assumed its current name in 1995. A trade association whose members import meat from South American countries.

Meetings/Conferences:
Three Meetings Annually: January (New York, NY), May
   (Washington, DC) and October (Chicago, IL).

Western History Ass'n *(1961)*
University of New Mexico
1080 Mesa Vista Hall
Albuquerque, NM   87131-1181
Tel: (505)277-5234   *Fax:* (505)277-6023
E-Mail: wha@unm.edu
Web Site: http://www.unm.edu/~wha
Members: 1,900 individuals, 65 organizations
Staff: 2
Annual Budget: $250-500,000
Exec. Director: Paul Andrew Hutton

Historical Note
WHA members are academic historians and others with an interest in the history of the American West. Membership: $55/year (individual); $150/year (institution); $20/year (student).

Publications:
Montana, The Magazine of Western History. q.
Western Historical Quarterly Journal. q. adv.
WHA Newsletter. semi-a. adv.

Meetings/Conferences:
Annual Meetings: October
1999 – Portland, OR/Oct. 6-9

Western Literature Ass'n *(1966)*
Utah State University
English Department
Logan, UT   84322-3200
Tel: (801)797-1603   *Fax:* (801)797-4099
Members: 600 individuals
Staff: 3
Annual Budget: $25-50,000
Editor: Melody Graulich

Historical Note
WLA members are scholars and others with an interest in western regional literary genre. Membership: $30/year (individual).

Publications:
Western American Literature. q. adv.

Meetings/Conferences:

Western Music Ass'n *(1988)*
P.O. Box 35008
Tucson, AZ   85740-5008
Tel: (520)743-9794   *Fax:* (520)743-1165
E-Mail: wma@westernmusic.org
Web Site: http://www.westernmusic.org
Members: 850 individuals
Staff: 1
Annual Budget: $50-100,000
Exec. Director: Michelle Sundin

Historical Note
WMA is dedicated to preserving and advancing the history, literature and performance of western music. Members are western music afficionados and performers. Membership: $30-1000/year.

Publications:
Western Music Advocate. q.

Meetings/Conferences:
1999 – Tucson, AZ
2000 – Tucson, AZ

Western Railroad Ass'n *(1970)*
Historical Note
Organization defunct in 1995.

Western Range Ass'n *(1950)*
6060 Sunrise Vista Drive, Suite 2400
Citrus Heights, CA   95610-7057
Tel: (916)962-1500   *Fax:* (916)962-1626
Members: 240 individuals
Staff: 9
Annual Budget: $250-500,000
Exec. Director: Larry Garro

Historical Note
A group of western sheep producers united to expand the pool of shepherds from foreign and domestic labor sources.

Meetings/Conferences:
Annual Meetings: always June in Sparks, NV
1999 – Denver, CO/Jan. 8-9

Western Red Cedar Ass'n *(1898)*
P.O. Box 120786
New Brighton, MN   55112
Tel: (651)633-4334
Members: 6 companies
Staff: 1
Annual Budget: under $10,000

Secretary: Steven F. Kracht
Historical Note
Formerly (1993) the Western Red and Northern White Cedar Ass'n. Affiliated with the Western Wood Products Ass'n.

Publications:
Cedar Notes. 3/year.

Meetings/Conferences:
Annual Meetings: March

Western Red Cedar Lumber Ass'n *(1954)*
1200-555 Burrard St.
Vancouver, BC   V7X 1-S7
Tel: (604)684-0266   *Fax:* (604)687-4930
Web Site: http://www.WRCLA.org
Members: 18 companies
Staff: 2
Annual Budget: $1-2,000,000
Exec. Director: Arnie Nebelsick

Publications:
Buyer's Guide. a.
Cedar Scene. q.

Meetings/Conferences:
1999 – Kelowna, BC, Canada(Grand Okanagan)
2000 – British Columbia, Canada

Western Shoe Associates *(1942)*
1040 E. Wardlow Road
Long Beach, CA   90807
Tel: (562)427-5168   *Fax:* (562)427-2541
Members: 4,500 individuals
Staff: 8
Annual Budget: $5-10,000,000
Exec. Director: Chris Aiken

Historical Note
Organizes international buying markets. Represents the USA and 73 foreign countries. Membership: $20/year (regualr); $10/year (associate).

Publications:
Buyers Guide. q. adv.
Manufacturers-WSA Members Directory. bi-a. adv.
Show Guide. bi-a.
WSA Newsletter. q.
WSA Today. bi-a. adv.

Meetings/Conferences:
Quarterly Buying Markets: February and August

Western Shoe Retailers Ass'n *(1978)*
P.O. Box 4145
West Hills, CA   91308-4145
Tel: (818)340-6296   *Fax:* (818)340-6297
Members: 500 retailers
Staff: 1
President: Linda M. Hauss

Historical Note
WSRA represents shoe retailers nationwide. Membership: $95/year.

Publications:
Shoe Times Newsletter. bi-m.

Meetings/Conferences:
Annual Meetings: May/250

Western States Meat Ass'n
Historical Note
Became (1995) Nat'l Meat Ass'n.

Western Wood Products Ass'n *(1964)*
Yeon Building
522 SW Fifth Ave.
Portland, OR   97204-2122
Tel: (503)224-3930   *Fax:* (503)224-3934
E-Mail: info@wwpa.org
Web Site: http://www.wwpa.org
Members: 200 mills
Staff: 45
Annual Budget: $5-10,000,000
President: Walter M. Wirfs
Director of Communications: Robert Bernhardt

Historical Note
A consolidation in 1964 of the Western Pine Ass'n and the West Coast Lumbermen's Ass'n. Operates a lumber grade inspection bureau to ensure uniform grading standards, provides technical programs/support and business information programs. Has an annual budget of approximately $5 million. Membership: dues based on shipment volume (perMBf).

Publications:
Plumb Line. m.
Statistical Yearbook of the Western Lumber Industry.

Meetings/Conferences:

Western Writers of America *(1953)*
Historical Note
Address unknown in 1995.

Wheat Gluten Industry Council/Internat'l Wheat Gluten Ass'n *(1979)*
Historical Note
Address unknown in 1998.

Wheat Quality Council *(1938)*
PO Box 966
Pierre, SD   57501-0966
Tel: (605)224-5187   *Fax:* (605)224-0517
E-Mail: BhWQC@aol.com
Web Site: http://www.wheatqualitycouncil.org
Members: 225 organizations
Staff: 2
Annual Budget: $250-500,000

Exec. V. President: Ben Handcock
Historical Note
Established as the Kansas Wheat Improvemnt Association, it assumed its present name in 1980. A not-for-profit organization of Agri-Business groups that invest in continuing wheat quality improvement. Membership: $100-12,000/year.

Publications:
Wheat Briefs. irreg.

Meetings/Conferences:
Annual Meetings: Winter

White House Correspondents Ass'n *(1914)*
P.O. Box 77040
Washington, DC   20015
Tel: (202)737-2934   *Fax:* (202)783-0841
Members: 600 individuals
Staff: 1
Annual Budget: $100-250,000

Historical Note
Established in February, 1914. Newspaper, magazine, television and radio reporters of White House news. President changes annually in the spring.

Meetings/Conferences:
Annual Meetings: Washington, DC/Spring
1999 – San Diego, CA(Marriott & Marina)/April 5-10

White House News Photographers Ass'n *(1921)*
7119 Ben Franklin Station
Washington, DC   20044-7119
Tel: (202)785-5230   *Fax:* (202)333-7898
Web Site: http://www.whnpa.org
Members: 525 individuals
Staff: 11
Annual Budget: $250-500,000
President: Kevin T. Gilbert

Historical Note
Founded in June 1921 with 24 charter members, membership is limited to photojournalists who regularly cover the White House and Washington Metropolitan area for local and network TV and local and national newspapers and magazines. Annual events include a Photo Contest, professional seminars, worldwide Photo Exhibit, high school seminar, and an awards dinner honoring the President of the United States. Membership: $75/year (individual).

Publications:
Photo-Op. 4-6/yr. adv.
The White House News Photographer Awards Book. a. adv.

Meetings/Conferences:
Annual Meetings: Dinner in Washington, DC.

White Park Cattle Ass'n of America *(1975)*
419 N. Water St.
Madrid, IA   50156
Tel: (515)795-2013
Members: 527 individuals
Staff: 1
Annual Budget: $10-25,000
Office Secretary: Joyce Fisher

Historical Note
Breeders and fanciers of Park cattle.

Publications:
The Park Post. q.

Wholesale Beer Ass'n Executives of America *(1998)*
c/o Wholesale Beer & Wine Ass'n of Ohio
Suite 710
Columbus, OH   43215
Tel: (614)224-3500   *Fax:* (614)224-1348
Members: 42 individuals
Annual Budget: under $10,000
President: Timothy J. Bechtold

Historical Note
Formerly (1946) Nat'l Ass'n of State Beer Ass'n Secretaries, (1977) State Beer Ass'n of Executives of America. Members are executives of state beer distributor associations. Has no paid officers or full-time staff; officers change annually. Membership: $125/year (individual).

Publications:
Exectic Exhortations. bi-m.
WBAE Directory. a.

Meetings/Conferences:
Annual Meetings: Fall
1999 – Las Vegas, NV
2000 – New Orleans, LA

Wholesale Florists and Florist Suppliers of America *(1926)*
410 Pine St.
P.O. Box 639
Vienna, VA   22183
Tel: (703)242-7000   *Fax:* (703)319-1647
Members: 1,100 companies
Staff: 11
Annual Budget: $1-2,000,000
Exec. V. President and C.E.O.: Terry J. Burns
Director of Communications: William M. Brown
General Counsel: Timothy Waters
Deputy Exec. V.P.: Patricia A. Clinton

Historical Note
Until 1961 known as the Wholesale Commission Florists of America. Membership: $250-900/year (company).

Publications:
Membership Directory. a. adv.
The Link. 10/year. adv.

Meetings/Conferences:
Annual Meetings: March-April/800
1999 – Monterey, CA(DoubleTree)/April 7-10/400

Wholesale Nursery Growers of America *(1965)*
1250 I St., N.W., Suite 500
Washington, DC 20005
Tel: (202)789-2900   *Fax:* (202)789-1893
Members: 1,120 companies
Staff: 2
Annual Budget: $25-50,000
Exec. V. President: Robert J. Dolibois, CAE
Historical Note
WNGA is the grower division of the American Nursery and
Landscape Ass'n.
Publications:
The Grower. b-m.
Meetings/Conferences:
Semi-annual Meetings: January/Chicago and July with ANLA

Wholesale Stationers Ass'n *(1916)*
Historical Note
Merged with the Nat'l Ass'n of Wholesale Independent Distributors
to form the Office Products Wholesalers Ass'n in 1995.

Wholesale Variety Bakers Ass'n *(1964)*
215 Eva St.
St. Paul, MN 55107-1697
Tel: (651)224-5761
Members: 20 companies
President: Steve Baldinger
Historical Note
Has no paid officers or full-time staff.

Wild Bird Feeding Institute *(1984)*
2218 Crabtree Lane
Northbrook, IL 60062-3520
Tel: (847)272-0135
Members: 157 companies
Staff: 3
Annual Budget: $50-100,000
Exec. Director: Sue Wells
Manager, Information: Ralph Wells
Historical Note
Members are bird feeder manufacturing, seed packing, processing
companies and related brokers, distributors, retailers and suppliers.
Organized primarily to promote the sales of bird feeding products.
Publications:
WBFI Newsline. q.
Meetings/Conferences:
Semi-Annual Meetings: Summer and Fall

Wild Blueberry Ass'n of North America *(1981)*
59 Cottage St.
P.O. Box 180
Bar Harbor, ME 04609-0180
Tel: (207)288-2655   *Fax:* (207)288-2656
Toll Free: (800)223 - 9453
E-Mail: inquiries@wildblueberries.com
Web Site: http://www.wildblueberries.com
Members: 75 individuals, 15 companies
Staff: 3
Annual Budget: $1-2,000,000
Exec. Director: John M. Sauve
Historical Note
An international trade/promotion association of producers and
processors of wild blueberries from Maine and eastern Canada.
Membership fee varies, based on production.
Publications:
The Wild Times. q.
Meetings/Conferences:
Annual Meetings: Spring

Wilderness Education Ass'n *(1977)*
Dept. of Nat. Resources, Rec./Tourism
Colorado State University
Fort Collins, CO 80523
Members: 950 individuals
Staff: 3
Annual Budget: $25-50,000
Exec. Director: Jeff Liddle
Historical Note
WEA trains and certifies outdoor leaders. Membership: $15/year
(individual); $100/year (organization/company); $30/year
(student).
Publications:
Proceedings of the Annual National Conference. a. adv.
TABS (Trustees & Affiliates Briefing System). bi-m.
WEA Legend Newsletter. q. adv.
Meetings/Conferences:
Annual Meetings: February

Wilderness Medical Soc. *(1983)*
3595 East Fountain Blvd.
Suite A-1
Colorado Springs, CO 80910
Tel: (719)372-9255
E-Mail: wms@indy.net
Web Site: http://www.wms.org/wms
Members: 3,800 individuals
Staff: 3
Annual Budget: $250-500,000
Executive Director: David Van Der Wege
Historical Note
Members are physicians, allied health specialists and other qualified
individuals with an interest in wilderness medicine and the practice
of the health sciences in wilderness environments. Membership:
$90/year (individual).
Publications:
Wilderness and Environmental Medicine. q. adv.
Wilderness Medicine Letter. q. adv.

Meetings/Conferences:

Wildlife Disease Ass'n *(1951)*
810 E. 10th St.
Lawrence, KS 66044-0368
Tel: (785)843-1221   *Fax:* (785)843-1274
Web Site: www.upp.uet.uga.edu/wda/
Members: 1000 individuals
Staff: 1
Annual Budget: $25-50,000
Business Manager: Karen Hickey
Historical Note
Formed in March 1951 in Milwaukee at the North American
Wildlife Conference. Originally the Committee on Wildlife Diseases,
the name was changed to the Wildlife Disease Ass'n in 1952 and
the ass'n was incorporated in Illinois in 1964. Membership:
$55/year (individual); $95/year (organization).
Publications:
Journal of Wildlife Diseases. q.
Newsletter. q.
Meetings/Conferences:
Annual Meetings: August
1999 – Athens, GA/August 8-12

Wildlife Management Institute *(1911)*
1101 14th St., N.W., Suite 801
Washington, DC 20005
Tel: (202)371-1808   *Fax:* (202)408-5059
E-Mail: WMIHQ@AOL.COM
Members: 500 individuals
Staff: 14
Annual Budget: $1-2,000,000
President: Rollin D. Sparrowe
Secretary: Richard E. McCabe
V. President: Lonnie L. Williamson
Historical Note
The programs of the Institute have been in existence under various
names since 1911. Incorporated as WMI in New York in 1946.
Sponsors the annual North American Wildlife and Natural
Resources Conference. Membership: $35(individual);
variable(organization).
Publications:
Conference Transactions. a.
Outdoor News Bulletin. bi-w.
Meetings/Conferences:
Annual Meetings: Spring
1999 – San Francisco, CA(SF Airport Hyatt)/March 26-31
2000 – Chicago, IL(Hyatt Regency O'Hare)/March 25-29
2001 – Washington, DC(Omni Shoreham)/March 16-20
2002 – Dallas, TX(Hyatt Regency)/April 3-7/1000

Wildlife Soc., The *(1937)*
5410 Grosvenor Lane
Bethesda, MD 20814-2197
Tel: (301)897-9770   *Fax:* (301)530-2471
E-Mail: tws@wildlife.org
Web Site: http://www.wildlife.org/wildlife
Members: 9,700 individuals
Staff: 12
Annual Budget: $1-2,000,000
Exec. Director: Harry E. Hodgdon
Wildlife Policy Director: Thomas M. Franklin
Program Director: Sandra Staples-Bortner
Historical Note
Originated in the District of Columbia in 1936 during the North
American Wildlife Conference. Originally the Soc. of Wildlife
Specialists, it became The Wildlife Soc. in 1937 and was
incorporated in the District of Columbia in 1948. Member society
of the Renewable Natural Resources Foundation. Membership:
$40/year.
Publications:
Journal of Wildlife Management. q.
The Wildlifer. bi-m.
Wildlife Society Bulletin. q.
Meetings/Conferences:
Annual Meetings: September/October/1,500-2,200
1999 – Austin, TX(Convention Center)/Sept. 7-11/1500

Window Council *(1958)*
2850 S. Ocean Blvd., Suite 114
Palm Beach, FL 33480-5535
Tel: (561)533-0991   *Fax:* (561)533-7466
E-Mail: FSCOTTFITZGERALD@compuserve.com
Staff: 1
Annual Budget: under $10,000
President: Frank S. Fitzgerald CAE, DABFE, FAC
Historical Note
Organized to develop window safety programs for children.

Window Covering Safety Council
355 Lexington Ave., 17th Floor
New York, NY 10017-6603
Tel: (212)661-4261   *Fax:* (212)370-9047
Web Site: http://www.windowcoverings.com
Exec. Director: Peter S. Rush

Window Coverings Ass'n of America *(1987)*
2339 Meadow Park Court
Maryland Heights, MO 63043-1518
Toll Free: (888)298 - 9222
E-Mail: info@wcaa.org
Web Site: http://www.wcaa.org
Members: 625 companies
Staff: 1
Annual Budget: $100-250,000
Exec. Director: Mark Nortman
Historical Note
Members are window covering retailers. WCAA was established to
make available educational and motivational seminars, improve the

decorating industry and encourage a code of ethics for fair business
practices. Membership: $100/year (company).
Publications:
WCAA Cover Story Newsletter. q.
Meetings/Conferences:

Window Coverings Manufacturers Ass'n *(1985)*
355 Lexington Ave., 17th Floor
New York, NY 10017-6603
Tel: (212)661-4261   *Fax:* (212)370-9047
E-Mail: assocmgmt@aol.com
Members: 20 companies
Staff: 4
Annual Budget: $50-100,000
Exec. Director: Peter S. Rush
Program Director: Maria Ungaro
Historical Note
Originally the Venetian Blind Institute (1942); the Venetian Blind
Ass'n (1977); (1985) the United States Venetian Blind Ass'n;
(1995) American Window Coverings Manufacturers Ass'n.
Represents manufacturers of hard window coverings.
Publications:
American Nat'l Standard for Safety of Corded Window
    Products.
Meetings/Conferences:
Annual Meetings: Spring

Wine and Spirits Guild of America *(1947)*
30 West 39th Ave., Suite 106
San Mateo, CA 94403
Members: 40 companies, 500 stores
Staff: 1
Annual Budget: $25-50,000
Exec. Director: Priscilla Felton
Historical Note
Membership is limited to one member per market in the major
markets of non-control states in the U.S. Membership: $850/year
(stores).
Publications:
Checkout. m.
Meetings/Conferences:
Semi-annual Meetings: Spring and Fall

Wine and Spirits Shippers Ass'n *(1976)*
11800 Sunrise Valley Dr., Suite 332
Reston, VA 20191-5396
Tel: (703)860-2300   *Fax:* (703)860-2422
Toll Free: (800)368 - 3167
E-Mail: info@wssa.com
Members: 500 companies
Staff: 10
Annual Budget: $500-1,000,000
Managing Director: Geoffrey N. Giovanetti
Office Manager: Doug Mitchell
Traffic Manager: Deborah Harrigan
Historical Note
WSSA is a non-profit shippers association composed of importers
and exporters of beverages and allied products. The Association
negotiates for preferential ocean freight rates for members and
currently has contracts with 30 steamship lines. WSSA also
arranges for transportation and cargo insurance for products
shipped internationally. Membership: $100/year (company).
Publications:
WSSA Grapevine. q.
Meetings/Conferences:
Annual Meetings: In conjunction with the WSWA
1999 – New Orleans, LA

Wine and Spirits Wholesalers of America *(1943)*
805 15th St., N.W., Suite 430
Washington, DC 20005-2203
Tel: (202)371-9792   *Fax:* (202)789-2405
E-Mail: juanita.duggan@wswa.org
Web Site: http://www.wswa.org
Members: 550 establishments
Staff: 12
Annual Budget: $1-2,000,000
Exec. V. President & CEO: Juanita D. Duggan
V. President, Public Affairs and Communications: David Dickerson
Mgr., Convention Registration/Editor: Heidi Blakely
Senior V. President, Federal Government Relations: Harry Wiles
V. President, Federal Government Relations: Delanne Bernier
Senior V. President: Joseph C. Gegg
Historical Note
WSWA members handle 90% of all wine and spirits sold in free
market states. Sponsors and supports the Wine and Spirits
Wholesalers of America Political Action Committee. Membership:
$1,150-36,000/year (company).
Publications:
Blue Book-Industry Directory. a. adv.
Bulletin. irreg.
Positive Thinking. m.
Up Front. m.
Meetings/Conferences:
Annual Meetings: Spring/2,500
1999 – New Orleans, LA

Wine Institute *(1934)*
425 Market St., Suite 1000
San Francisco, CA 94105
Tel: (415)512-0151   *Fax:* (415)442-0742
Members: 450 companies
Staff: 40
Annual Budget: $5-10,000,000
President: John A. De Luca
Historical Note
Industry association for California wineries.

Publications:
Wine Institute News. m.
Meetings/Conferences:
Annual Meetings: San Francisco Bay Area, CA/June

Wire Ass'n Internat'l *(1930)*
1570 Boston Post Road, Box 578
Guilford, CT 06437-0578
Tel: (203)453-2777   *Fax:* (203)453-8384
Web Site: http://www.wirenet.org
Members: 4,600 individuals
Staff: 22
Annual Budget: $2-5,000,000
Exec. Director: Paul R. Casteran
Historical Note
Formerly (1977) the Wire Association Inc. Members are individuals involved in wire manufacturing, wire forming and fabricating and supplying the wire and cable industry. Membership: $75/year.
Publications:
Wire Journal International. m. adv.
Wire Journal International Reference Guide. a. adv.
Meetings/Conferences:
1999 – Atlanta, GA

Wire Fabricators Ass'n *(1976)*
710 E. Ogden Ave., Suite 600
Naperville, IL 60563-8614
Tel: (630)369-2406   *Fax:* (630)369-2488
E-Mail: rmhoban@b-online.com
Members: 52 companies
Staff: 5
Annual Budget: $10-25,000
Exec. Director: Roseanne M. Hoban
Historical Note
Members are manufacturers of items composed principally of low carbon steel wire. Membership: $300-500/year (company, based on number of employees).
Meetings/Conferences:
1999 – Marco Island, FL(Marco Island Hilton)/Mar. 3-6/50

Wire Industry Suppliers Ass'n *(1918)*
111 Park Place
Falls Church, VA 22046-4513
Tel: (703)538-1788   *Fax:* (703)241-5603
Members: 35 companies
Staff: 1
Annual Budget: $25-50,000
Exec. Director: Clay D. Tyeryar
Historical Note
Formerly (1987) Wire Machinery Builders Ass'n. Membership: $350-750/year (company)
Meetings/Conferences:
Annual Meetings: Spring

Wire Reinforcement Institute *(1930)*
301 E. Sandusky St.
P.O. Box 450
Findlay, OH 45839-0450
Tel: (419)425-9473   *Fax:* (419)425-5741
Members: 12 producing members; 12 associates
Staff: 1
Annual Budget: $100-250,000
Technical Director: Roy H. Reiterman, P.E.
Historical Note
Members produce welded wire fabric, wire reinforcement and wire products for the reinforcement of concrete and other construction materials according to the standards of the American Soc. for Testing and Materials.
Publications:
Best Sellers Publications Listing.
Membership Directory.
Meetings/Conferences:
Semi-Annual Meetings: Spring and Fall
1999 – Napa Valley, CA

Wire Rope Technical Board *(1959)*
Tel: (703)684-5570   *Fax:* (703)684-6048
Members: 8 companies
Staff: 2
Annual Budget: $50-100,000
Staff Exec.: Carole M. Rogin
Publications:
None.
Meetings/Conferences:
Annual Meetings: November

Wire Service Guild *(1958)*
1501 Broadway, Suite 708
New York, NY 10036
Tel: (212)869-9290   *Fax:* (212)840-0687
E-Mail: union@wsg.org
Web Site: http://www.wsg.org
Members: 1000 individuals
Staff: 3
Administrator: Kevin Keane
Historical Note
Labor union representing editorial and commercial department employees of two wire services, Associated Press and United Press Internat'l. An affiliate of the Newspaper Guild.
Publications:
WiReport Newsletter. m.
Meetings/Conferences:
1999 – New York, NY

Wirebound Box Manufacturers Ass'n *(1934)*
3263 Sprucewood Lane
Wilmette, IL 60091-1110

Tel: (847)251-5575   *Fax:* (847)251-5898
Members: 8 companies
Exec. V. President: Charles G. Whitchurch
Historical Note
Manufacturers of wirebound boxes and crates designed to ship meat, poultry, fruit and vegetables.
Publications:
Directory of the Wirebound Box Industry. bien.
Meetings/Conferences:
Semi-annual Meetings: Spring and Fall/75-100

Wireless Communications Ass'n Internat'l *(1987)*
1140 Connecticut Ave., N.W., Suite 810
Washington, DC 20036-4001
Tel: (202)452-7823   *Fax:* (202)452-0041
Web Site: http://www.wcai.com
Members: 235 companies
Staff: 10
Annual Budget: $1-2,000,000
President: Andrew T. Kreig
Manager, Communications: Ted Swiecichowski
Director, Events and Membership: Jenna Dahlgren
Director, Administration: Lauren L. Patrick
Dep. Director, Membership: Hillani Hawkins
System Manager: Angela Wagner
Historical Note
Absorbed MDS Industry Ass'n in 1986. Formerly (1987) the Microwave Communications Ass'n and Wireless Cable Ass'n Internat'l (1998). Became International in 1993. WCA represents the fixed wireless, broadband industry worldwide providing video, data and voice services. WCA's government affairs program represents member interest and promotes a competitive marketplace for the industry. Membership: $2,000/year (operator or manufacturer), $1,000/year (licensee or academic institution).
Publications:
LMDS Update. w.
U. S. adv.
WCA Spectrum. m.
Weekly Washington Fax Report.
Meetings/Conferences:
Annual Meetings: Summer
1999 – /July 12-14

Wireless Data Forum *(1993)*
1250 Connecticut Ave. N.W., Suite 800
Washington, DC 20036
Tel: (202)736-3663   *Fax:* (202)466-3413
E-Mail: info@wirelessdata.org
Members: 80 companies
Staff: 3
Annual Budget: $1-2,000,000
Historical Note
CDPD (Cellular Digital Packet Data) Forum is an industry association of cellular data end users, data service providers, equipment manufacturers, software developers, and information providers. Promotes the advancement of open cellular data technology and supports CDPD as an international standard for packet data transmission. Membership: $1,000-$90,000/year, varies by type of company and revenues (corporate).
Publications:
CDPD Forum News. q.
CDPD Report Card. q.
Meetings/Conferences:
Annual Meetings: usually with Cellular Telecommunications
        Industry Ass'n
1999 – New Orleans, LA/Feb. 8-10
1999 – Monterey, CA/May 3-5

Wireless Dealers Ass'n *(1987)*
9746 Tappenbeck Drive
Houston, TX 77055
Toll Free: (800)624 - 6918
E-Mail: bhut@accesscommnet
Web Site: http://www.wirelessindustry.com
Members: 2,500 locations
Staff: 20
Annual Budget: $500-1,000,000
President: Bob Hutchinson
Historical Note
Founded as Nat'l Ass'n of Cellular Agents; assumed its current name in 1996. Business association made up of cellular and wireless communications agents, dealers, resellers, carriers, manufacturers, distributors and importers. Membership: $395-$15,000/year (company).
Meetings/Conferences:
Annual Meetings: October/November

Wireless Information Networks Forum
1200 19th St., N.W., Suite 300
Washington, DC 20036-2422
Tel: (202)429-5138   *Fax:* (202)223-4579
Staff: 2
Annual Budget: $100-250,000
Exec. Director: Sharon Butalla
Historical Note
WINFORUM was establsihed as a result of the Federal Communications Commission's release of unlicensed wireless spectrum to ensure that the unlicensed spectrum could be used effectively for all products. Membership: Dues based on company's sales income.
Meetings/Conferences:
Annual Meetings: Spring

Wiring Harness Manufacturers Ass'n
3335 N. Arlington Heights Road, Suite E
Arlington Heights, IL 60004
Tel: (847)577-7200   *Fax:* (847)577-7276
Web Site: http://whma.org

Exec. Director: C. Andrew Larsen, CAE
Publications:
Wire Taps Newsletter. q.
Meetings/Conferences:
1999 – /May 16-18

WLUC-Women in Insurance and Financial Services *(1987)*
Blendonview Office Park
5008-45 Pine Creek Dr.
Westerville, OH 43081-4899
Tel: (614)882-6934   *Fax:* (614)895-3466
E-Mail: wluc@wluc.org
Web Site: http://www.wluc.org
Members: 1,200 individuals
Staff: 1
Annual Budget: $100-250,000
Exec. Director: Marlisa K. Bannister
Historical Note
Formerly (1987) the Women Life Underwriters Conference. Membership: $100/year (individual), $2,500-$25,000/year (company).
Publications:
WLUC News. m. adv.
WLUC Newsletter.
Meetings/Conferences:
Annual Meetings: September/150
1999 – Long Beach, CA(Queen Mary)/Oct. 15-17

Women Band Directors Nat'l Ass'n *(1969)*
345 Overlook Drive
West Lafayette, IN 47906-1210
Tel: (765)463-1738
Members: 355 individuals
Staff: 1
Annual Budget: under $10,000
Exec. Secretary: Gladys Stone Wright
Historical Note
WBNDA active members are women engaged in directing bands and all women who have been band directors but are not presently so engaged. Membership: $25/year (individual); $50/year (company).
Publications:
Band World Magazine. 5/yr. adv.
Newsletter. q.
WBDNA Directory. a.
Woman Conductor Journal. 3/year. adv.
Meetings/Conferences:

Women Chefs and Restaurateurs *(1993)*
304 W. Liberty St., Suite 201
Louisville, KY 40202-3011
Tel: (502)581-0300   *Fax:* (502)589-3602
E-Mail: wcr@hgtrs.com
Web Site: http://www.culinary.net
Members: 2,000 individuals
Staff: 2
Annual Budget: $250-500,000
Exec. Director: Frankie Whitman
Dir., Membership: Debbie Arnold
Historical Note
Founded as Internat'l Ass'n of Women Chefs and Restaurateurs; assumed its current name in 1997. WCR is a trade association for women employed in the restaurant industry. Its mission is to promote the advancement of women in the restaurant industry. Membership: $175/year (executive); $75/year (professional); $35/year (student); $250/year (small business); $1,500/year (coprorate).
Publications:
Entrez Newsletter. q.
Meetings/Conferences:
Annual Meetings: always New York, NY/Spring/300

Women Construction Owners and Executives, USA *(1983)*
4849 Connecticut Ave., N.W., Suite 702
Washington, DC 20008-5838
Toll Free: (800)788 - 3548
E-Mail: wcoeusa@aol.com
Web Site: http://www.wcoeusa.org
Members: 218 individuals
Staff: 1
Annual Budget: $50-100,000
Nat'l President: Patricia Magill
National Administrator: Linda J. Ferlaak
Historical Note
Members are women who seek to promote the role of women business enterprises in the construction industry. WCOE also seeks to provide resources for members to enhance their professional development, to create a legislative network to monitor and pursue legislation advantageous to the business community. Membership: $200-250/year, plus chapter dues.
Publications:
The Turning Point. m. adv.
Meetings/Conferences:
Semi-annual Meetings: Spring and Fall
1999 – Washington, DC(Hotel George)

Women Executives in Public Relations *(1946)*
P.O. Box 609
Westport, CT 06881
Tel: (203)226-4947   *Fax:* (203)226-9637
Web Site: http://www.wepr.org
Members: 125 individuals
Annual Budget: $25-50,000
Administrator: Frances D. Gallogly

Historical Note
WEPR members are women and men senior executives with an
interest in the professional advancement of women in the public
relations field. Membership: $150/year (individual).

Publications:
Network Newsletter. q.

Meetings/Conferences:
Monthly Meetings: September to June in New York City

Women Executives in State Government (1983)
1225 New York Ave., N.W., Suite 350
Washington, DC   20005
Tel: (202)628-9374   Fax: (202)628-9744
Web Site: http://www.wesg.org
Members: 280 individuals
Staff: 4
Annual Budget: $500-1,000,000
Exec. Director: Julienne Nelson
Director, Programs: Jane Moya
Membership Services: E. Dannyette Gadsden

Historical Note
Members are women serving in the statewide elected or cabinet-
level appointed positions in the executive branch of state
government. Membership: $150/year.

Publications:
Annual Report. a.
Newsletter. q.
WESG Membership Directory. a.

Meetings/Conferences:
Annual Meetings: July-September
1999 – Cleveland, OH/Sept. 12-14

Women in Advertising and Marketing (1980)
4200 Wisconsin Ave., N.W., Suite 106-238
Washington, DC   20016
Tel: (301)369-7400
Members: 100 individuals
Annual Budget: under $10,000
President: Linda Hagopian

Historical Note
Has no paid officers or full-time staff. Membership: $75/year
(individual).

Publications:
Membership Directory. a.
WAM News. bi-m. adv.

Meetings/Conferences:
Monthly Meetings: always Washington, DC metro area

Women in Aerospace (1984)
P.O. Box 16721
Alexandria, VA   22302
Tel: (202)547-9451   Fax: (202)546-4189
Web Site: http://www.enegialtd.com/wia/
Members: 300 individuals
Annual Budget: under $10,000
President: Elvia H. Thompson

Historical Note
WIA, a professional society providing a formal network for women
working in the aerospace field, is dedicated to expanding women's
opportunities for career advancement and increasing their visibility
as aerospace professionals. Members include journalists, industry
executives, government officials and congressional staff.
Membership: $35/year (individual); $500/year
(organization/company).

Publications:
WIA Newsletter. m. adv.

Women in Agribusiness
P.O. Box 986
Kearney, MO   64060-0986
Annual Budget: under $10,000
President: Dolores Hamelin

Historical Note
Has no paid staff. WIA was established to organize women in
agribusiness and to provide a forum on subjects concerning the
industry. Membership fee: $15/year (U.S.); $20/year (foreign).

Publications:
Women in Agribusiness Bulletin. q. adv.

Women in Aviation Internat'l
Morning Star Airport
3647 SR 503 South
West Alexandria, OH   45381-9354
Tel: (937)839-4647   Fax: (937)839-4645
Web Site: http://www.wiai.org
Members: 3,100 individuals
Staff: 3
Annual Budget: $500-1,000,000
President: Peggy Baty, Ph.D.

Historical Note
WAI members include pilots, air traffic controllers, airport
managers, engineers, flight attendants, and others with an internest
in encouraging women to seek professional opportunites in
aviation. Membership: $35/year (individual); $25/year (student);
$350/year (corporate).

Publications:
Annual Conference Program. a. adv.
Aviation for Women Magazine. bi-m. adv.

Meetings/Conferences:
Annual Meetings: March
1999 – Orlando, FL(Raddison Twin Towers)/Mar. 18-20/2400

Women in Cable and Telecommunications (1979)
230 W. Monroe St., Suite 730
Chicago, IL   60606-4702
Tel: (312)634-2330   Fax: (312)634-2345
Web Site: http://www.wict.org
Members: 4,000 individuals

Staff: 13
Annual Budget: $1-2,000,000
Exec. Director: Pamela V. Williams
Dir., Communications: Jim Flanigan
Director, Administration and Special Events: Tracy Mitchell
Director, Education: Christine Bollettino
Dir., Menber/Chapter Svcs.: Sarah Bilissis

Historical Note
Formerly (1994) Women in Cable. WICT's mission is to empower
women in the cable and telecommunications industry to attain their
professional, personal and economic goals, while influencing the
future of the industries it serves. The organization fulfills this
mission by empowering women through leadership, education and
advocacy. Membership is composed of 3,500 professionals in 22
chapters across the nation, including numerous satellite chapters.
These chapters address both national and industry issues and
concerns specific to their locales. Membership is open to all
individuals who are employed in a professional capacity in a facet
of the telecommunications industry or a closely related field.
Membership: $125/year; $200/year (executive); $50/year (entry).

Publications:
Insight Magazine. q.
Membership Directory. a.
The Source. bi-m.

Meetings/Conferences:
1999 – San Francisco, CA(Hilton)/May 3-6/350

Women in Cell Biology (1972)
Historical Note
A committee of American Soc. for Cell Biology, which provides
administrative support.

Women in Communications (1909)
Historical Note
Became Ass'n for Women in Communications in 1996.

Women in Defense
Historical Note
Merged with the American Defense Preparedness Ass'n in 1995.

Women in Design (1977)
3712 N Broadway
P.O. Box 319
Chicago, IL   60613
Tel: (312)409-9945   Fax: (773)871-0402
Annual Budget: $10-25,000
President: Janet Ocwieja

Historical Note
Women in Design is a nationally recognized not-for-profit
organization that focuses on the goals and interests of women in
the design profession. Members, predominantly located in the
greater Chicago area, are individuals engaged in the practice,
direction, instruction or production of graphic design and related
arts. Membership: $32/year (student, national), $65/year
(professional), $50/year (continuing).

Publications:
Design Directions. bi-m. adv.

Women in Endocrinology (1975)
Dept. of Cell Biology
One Baylor Plaza
Houston, TX   77030
E-Mail: ryankatht@pitt.edu
Web Site: http://www.women-in-endo.org
Secretary-Treasurer: Nancy Weigel, Ph.D.

Historical Note
Founded to help increase the visibility and participation by women
in the acitvities of the Endocrine Soc., and by extension the field of
endocrinology. Provides travel grants and other services to
members. Has no paid officers or full-time staff. Membership:
$30/year (professional); $15/year (resident/post-doctoral).

Publications:
Women in Endocrinology Newsletter. 3/year.

Meetings/Conferences:
Annual Meetings: June/200
1999 – San Diego, CA
2000 – Toronto, Ontario
2001 – Denver, CO

Women in Energy (1978)
P.O. Box 105252
Jefferson City, MO   65110-5252
Tel: (573)635-6448
Members: 200 individuals
Annual Budget: under $10,000
President: Lois Tully-Gerber

Historical Note
Members are persons employed in energy and related energy
businesses working in areas such as science, engineering, finance,
consumer education, communications, home economics, etc.
Membership: $50/year.

Publications:
Women in Energy Newsletter. q. adv.

Meetings/Conferences:
Annual Meetings: September

Women in Film (1973)
6464 Sunset Blvd., Suite 1080
Hollywood, CA   90028
Tel: (323)463-6040   Fax: (323)463-0963
E-Mail: reeleditor@wif.org
Members: 2,500 individuals
Staff: 5
Annual Budget: $250-500,000
Editor, Director of Communications: Mark Brown
Producer, Special Events: Bobbi Frank
Chief Financial Officer: Arnold Fram

Historical Note
WIF is a professional organization in the communications industry
with the commitment to recognize, develop and actively promote the
visions of women. General members of WIF must have a minimum
of three years of professional experience in the executive, guild or
craft areas of the industry. Membership: $100/year (individual).

Publications:
Calendar of Events. m.
Reel News Newsletter. bi-m. adv.
WIF Membership Directory. a. adv.

Meetings/Conferences:
Semi-Annual Meetings: June and September

Women in Film and Video (1979)
P.O. Box 19272
Washington, DC   20036
Tel: (202)333-1557   Fax: (202)463-0868
E-Mail: info@wifv.org
Web Site: http://www.wifv.org
Members: 15 affiliate chapters
Annual Budget: $100-250,000
Exec. Director: Marty Cavendish

Historical Note
WIFV members are women employed in film, television, video and
electronic multi-media production. Comprises an international
network of 40 chapters, representing over 10,000 individuals.
Membership: $75/year (professional); $125/year (senior);
$25/year (student).

Publications:
Film Festival Program Book. a. adv.
Gala Program Book. a. adv.
Membership Directory. a. adv.
Newsletter. m.

Women in Financial Development
250 W. 57th St., Suite 2301
New York, NY   10107
Tel: (212)265-7650   Fax: (212)265-4974
Members: 425 individuals
Annual Budget: $25-50,000
Association Manager: Anne Woodfield

Historical Note
WIFD is an informal association whose mission is to maintain a
supportive and collegial network through which women in the field
of development can assist in one another's professional growth.
Through monthly meetings, a mentoring program, a job bank, and
other activities, WIFD affords women the opportunity to augment
professional training and expand career opportunities. Members
must observe the highest professional and ethical standards and be
dedicated to the advancement of women in fundraising careers.

Publications:
Job Bank.
Newsletter. m.

Women in Government (1988)
2600 Virginia Ave., N.W., Suite 709
Washington, DC   20037-1905
Tel: (202)333-0825   Fax: (202)333-0875
Members: 1,200 individuals
Staff: 10
Annual Budget: $1-2,000,000
Exec. Director: Joy N. Newton

Historical Note
WIG members are women holding elected offices at the state and
national levels.

Publications:
Membership Directory. a.
Newsletter. q.

Women in Government Relations (1975)
1029 Vermont Ave., Suite 510
Washington, DC   20005-3527
Tel: (202)347-5432   Fax: (202)347-5434
E-Mail: wgr@earthlink.net
Members: 650 individuals
Staff: 2
Annual Budget: $250-500,000
Director: Maryann Leisher

Historical Note
An association of professionals in government relations dedicated to
the professional and educational development of women in the field
of government relations. Membership: $95 -175/year (individual).

Publications:
On The Record Newsletter. bi-m. adv.

Meetings/Conferences:
Annual Meetings: always Washington, DC in March or April
1999 – Washington, DC(Hyatt Regency)

Women in Health Administration
Historical Note
Address unknown in 1995.

Women in Internat'l Security (1987)
c/o Center for Int'l & Security Studies
Sch of Public Affairs, Univ of Maryland
College Park, MD   20742
Tel: (301)405-7612   Fax: (301)403-8107
E-Mail: wiis@puafmail.umd.edu
Members: 600 individuals
Staff: 3
Annual Budget: $250-500,000
Exec. Director: Margaret Knudson
Program Coordinator: Deirdre Smith
Membership Services Coordinator: Gisela Rots

Historical Note
WIIS is an international, nonpartisan network and educational
program dedicated to enhancing opportunities for women in the
fields of foreign and defense policy. Members are women and men
from academia, think tanks, the diplomatic corps, the intelligence

community, the media and private sector. They are involved in issues ranging from East-West arms control and arms transfers in the Third World to democratization in Latin America and the development of international trade blocs. Has a database of women in the field and organizes seminars and conferences highlighting women speakers on current issues. Membership: $20-300/year (individual); $200/year (non-profit institution).

Publications:
Directory of Fellowships in International Affairs.
Directory of Internships in Foreign and Defense Policy.
Jobs Hotline. bi-m.
WIIS Words. q.

Women in Management (1978)
30 N. Michigan, Suite 508
Chicago, IL   60602-3404
Tel: (312)263-3636
Members: 850 individuals
Staff: 3
Annual Budget: $50-100,000
Administrator: Betty Melton

Historical Note
Members are professionals in corporate, academic, not-for-profit, government, or entrepreneurial sectors of managment or are licensed, degreed professionals.

Publications:
Memorandum. q. adv.
National Directory. a. adv.

Meetings/Conferences:

Women in Mining Nat'l (1972)
1801 Broadway, Suite 760
Denver, CO   80202
Tel: (303)298-1535   *Fax:* (303)292-1734
Members: 600 individuals
Annual Budget: $10-25,000
Exec. Secretary: Minetta Miller

Historical Note
WIM is a nationwide organization composed of individuals employed by, associated with, or interested in the mining industry. Membership: $30/year (individual).

Publications:
WIM-Membership Directory. a.
Women in Mining - Nat'l Quarterly. q.

Meetings/Conferences:
Annual Meetings: April

Women in Municipal Government (1974)
c/o Nat'l League of Cities
1301 Pennsylvania Ave., N.W.
Washington, DC   20004
Tel: (202)626-3169   *Fax:* (202)626-3103
Members: 300 individuals
Staff: 2
Annual Budget: under $10,000
Manager: Mary France Gordon

Historical Note
Members are women holding elected or appointed municipal office. The organization serves as a leadership network for women and colleagues interested in women's issues and policy development. Membership: $35/year (individual), $55/year (organization).

Publications:
Constituency Report. q.

Meetings/Conferences:
Annual Meetings: December.
1999 – Los Angeles, CA(Convention Center)

Women in Packaging (1993)
4290 Bells Ferry Road, Suite 106-17
Kennesaw, GA   30144-1300
Tel: (770)924-3563   *Fax:* (770)928-1233
E-Mail: PackwM@aol.com
Web Site: http://www.napco.com/wp/index.html
Members: 800 individuals
Founding Exec. Director: JoAnn R. Hines

Historical Note
WP members are professionals employed at all levels in the packaging industry. Membership: $100/year (mentor); $80/year (individual); $35/year (student); $100-500/year, varies by annual sales and/or purchasing (corporate).

Publications:
Career Hotline. m.
Packaging Horizons Magazine. q.
Update Newsletter. bi-m.

Meetings/Conferences:

Women In Production (1977)
347 5th Ave., Suite 1406
New York, NY   10016
Tel: (212)481-7793   *Fax:* (212)481-7969
E-Mail: admin@wip.org
Web Site: http://www.wip.org
Members: 500 individuals
Annual Budget: $100-250,000
Exec. Director: Karen L. Koopman

Historical Note
Members are individuals involved in all phases of print and graphics production. Membership: $95/year (individual).

Publications:
WIP Roster. a.
Women in Production Calendar. m.

Meetings/Conferences:
1999 – New York, NY(Plaza)

Women in Sales Ass'n (1979)
P.O. Box M
8 Madison Ave.
Valhalla, NY   10595

Tel: (914)946-3802   *Fax:* (914)946-2674
Members: 100 individuals
Staff: 5
Annual Budget: under $10,000
Exec. Director: Marie T. Rossi, CAE

Historical Note
The Women in Sales Ass'n offers educational programs, seminars, and workshops through which members can develop professional skills and advance in their field. Membership: $75/year (individual).

Publications:
Membership Directory. irreg.
Sales Leader Newsletter. q.

Women in Scholarly Publishing (1979)
837 N. Woodstock St.
Philadelphia, PA   19130-1408
Tel: (215)235-9426   *Fax:* (215)235-9427
Members: 525 individuals
Annual Budget: under $10,000
President: Jean Sue Johnson-Libkind

Historical Note
WISP is a non-profit feminist organization devoted to the education and professional advancement of its members. Supports the principles and goals of equity for women on all levels and in all areas of scholarly publishing. Has no paid officers or full-time staff. Membership: $10-40/year.

Publications:
Membership Directory. a.
Newsletter. a.

Meetings/Conferences:
Annual Meetings: Held in conjunction with the Ass'n of American University Presses

Women in Technology Internat'l
4641 Burnet Ave.
Sherman Oaks, CA   91403
Tel: (818)990-6705   *Fax:* (818)906-3299
E-Mail: info@witi.org
Web Site: http://www.witi.org
Members: 6,000 individuals, 200 companies
Staff: 15
Annual Budget: $500-1,000,000
Exec. Director: Carolyn Leighton

Historical Note
WITI is a professional association of women working in private and public technology corporations. Seeks to support and expand the number of women working in managerial capacities in the technology industry. Sponsors several conferences and networking opportunities for its members. Membership: $125/year.

Publications:
WITI Magazine. 5/year.

Meetings/Conferences:
Annual Meetings: June

Women in the Fire Service (1983)
P.O. Box 5446
Madison, WI   53705
Tel: (608)233-4768   *Fax:* (608)233-4879
E-Mail: tfloren@wfsi.org
Members: 820 individuals, 250 organizations
Staff: 2
Annual Budget: $50-100,000
Exec. Director: Terese M. Floren

Historical Note
Formerly (1989) Women in Fire Suppression. WFS is a network of and for women firefighters and other fire service women. Membership: $40/year (individual), $50/year (company).

Publications:
Firework Newsletter. m.
WFS Quarterly Journal. q. adv.

Meetings/Conferences:
Annual Meetings: May
1999 – Los Angeles, CA(Omni Hotel)/500

Women of the Motion Picture Industry, Internat'l (1953)
Twentieth Century Fox
P.O. Box 900
Beverly Hills, CA   90213
Tel: (310)369-4083   *Fax:* (310)369-8903
Members: 600 individuals
Staff: 1
Annual Budget: $10-25,000
Contact: Lili Beaudin

Historical Note
A federation of 13 clubs throughout the United States and Canada. Membership: $35/year.

Meetings/Conferences:
Annual Meetings: September
1999 – Memphis, TN/Sept. 30-Oct. 2
2000 – Las Vegas, NV

Women's Basketball Coaches Ass'n (1981)
4646 Lawrenceville Hwy.
Lilburn, GA   30047-3620
Tel: (770)279-8027   *Fax:* (770)279-8473
Web Site: http://www.wbca.org
Members: 4,200 individuals
Staff: 14
Annual Budget: $1-2,000,000
CEO: Beth Bass
Director, Media/Public Relations: Sherilyn Fiveusch
Director, Events: Shannon Reynolds
Manager, Conventions: Ayanna E. Hines
Sr. Director, Marketing and Sales: Mara Keggi
Director, Membership: Cathy McGhee

Historical Note
WBCA members include coaches, athletic directors, officials and others with an interest in women's basketball. Membership: $75/year (individual); $150/year (organization/company).

Publications:
At the Buzzer. m.
Backboard Bulletin. bi-m.
Coaching Women's Basketball. bi-m. adv.
Fast Break Alert. q.

Meetings/Conferences:
Annual Meetings: March
1999 – San Jose, CA/March 24-28/2100
2000 – Philadelphia, PA
2001 – St. Louis, MO

Women's Caucus for Art (1972)
PO Box 1498
Canal Street Station
New York, NY   10013
Tel: (212)634-0007
E-Mail: info@nationalwca.com
Web Site: http://www.nationalwca.com
Members: 3,500 individuals
Staff: 1
Annual Budget: $50-100,000
Nat'l Administrator: Denise Mumm

Historical Note
WCA members are women artists and educators, art historians and critics, gallery and museum professionals and collectors. Membership: $30/year (individual); $75/year (organization).

Publications:
Honors Catalogue. a.
Member News. bi-an.

Meetings/Conferences:
Annual Meetings: February/300-800
1999 – Los Angeles, CA(Hyatt Regency)/Feb. 7-11

Women's Caucus for Political Science (1969)
Department of Political Science
Vassar College, Maildrop 455
Poughkeepsie, NY   12601
Tel: (914)437-5562
E-Mail: shanley@vassar.edu
Members: 900 individuals
President: Molly Shanley

Publications:
WCPS Membership Directory. bien.
WCPS Quarterly Newsletter. q. adv.

Meetings/Conferences:
Annual Meetings: in conjunction with the American Political Science Ass'n

Women's Caucus for the Modern Languages (1970)
Dept. of English
College of St. Catherine
St. Paul, MN   55105
Tel: (651)690-6559   *Fax:* (651)690-6024
E-Mail: ckfarr@stkate.edu
Members: 650 individuals
Annual Budget: under $10,000
President: Cecilia Konchar Farr

Historical Note
Women with a professional interest in the teaching and study of modern languages. Has no paid staff. Membership: $5-25/year, varies with salary (individual).

Publications:
Concerns. 3/yr.

Meetings/Conferences:
Annual Meetings: With the Modern Language Ass'n/Dec. 27-30

Women's Caucus: Religious Studies (1970)
Office of the Chaplain
Mills College
Oakland, CA   94613
Members: 800 individuals
Annual Budget: under $10,000
Co-convener: Dr. Linda A. Moody

Historical Note
The Caucus is an organization of and for women academically prepared to participate in the various professional fields of religious studies. Actively works to provide networking and mentoring opportunities for women involved in religious studies. Membership: $10-$50/year (individual); dues are not a requirement for membership.

Publications:
A registry of Women in Religious Studies. irreg.
Newsletter. semi-a.
Placement News and Notes. irreg.

Women's College Coalition (1972)
125 Michigan Ave., N.E., Suite 340
Washington, DC   20017
Tel: (202)234-0443   *Fax:* (202)234-0445
Web Site: http://www.womenscolleges.org
Members: 66 institutions
Staff: 3
Annual Budget: $100-250,000
President: Jadwiga S. Sebrechts

Historical Note
Founded in 1972 WCC is a national organization of women's two-year and four-year colleges, including both public and private, independent and church-related institutions. The Coalition's purpose is to communicate the contributions of both women's colleges and their graduates to their communities and the nation at large to initiate and support research dealing with women and higher education and through programming advocate for enhancing opportunities for women students.

Publications:
Publications List Available.

Meetings/Conferences:
Annual Meetings: Fall
1999 – Washington, DC

Women's Council of Realtors *(1938)*
430 N. Michigan Ave.
Chicago, IL   60611-4093
Tel: (312)329-8482   *Fax:* (312)329-3290
E-Mail: wcr@wcr.org
Web Site: http://www.wcr.org
Members: 12,000 individuals
Staff: 9
Annual Budget: $1-2,000,000
Exec. V. President: Samuel A. Wells, M.D., FACS

Historical Note
An educational group for women in real estate. Provides a referral network and referral, relocation training, leadership training, chapter programs on the local, state, and national levels. Membership: $71/year.

Publications:
Communique. 8/yr. adv.
Referral Roster. a. adv.

Meetings/Conferences:
Annual Meetings: November/with the Nat'l Ass'n of
        Realtors/1,000
1999 – Orlando, CA(Marriott)
2000 – San Francisco, CA(Hilton)

Women's Fisheries Network *(1983)*
2442 NW Market Street, Suite 243
Seattle, WA   98107
Tel: (206)789-1987   *Fax:* (206)789-1987
E-Mail: boomz@seanet.com
Web Site: http://web.mit.edu/seagrant/www/wfn.html
Members: 350 individuals
Staff: 1
Annual Budget: under $10,000
Administrator: Karen A. Hauger

Historical Note
The Women's Fisheries Network is a nat'l, nonprofit network of women and men dedicated to educating members and non-members alike about issues confronting the commercial fishing and seafood industry. Founded in 1983, WFN has grown to three chapters: Northwest, Northeast and Alaska. WFN opens doors for women in the seafood industry, helps foster understanding among participants of many industry related fields, and provides a forum for current fisheries issues. Membership is open to women and men interested in learning more about the fishing and seafood industries. Membership: $40/year (individual); $25/year (student); $100/year (associate).

Publications:
"Currents" NW Newsletter (NW and Alaska chapters). m.
        adv.
Membership Directory. a.
NE Chapter Newsletter. m. adv.

Meetings/Conferences:
Annual Meetings: Fall
1999 – Seattle, WA/100
2000 – Boston, MA/100

Women's Foodservice Forum *(1989)*
1250 Executive Place, Suite 501
Geneva, IL   60134-2482
Tel: (630)262-9992   *Fax:* (630)262-9994
Web Site: http://www.womensfoodserviceforum.com
Members: 1,180 individuals
Stuff: 6
Annual Budget: $1-2,000,000
Exec. Director: Mary O'Connor

Historical Note
WFF members are men and women executives in the Food Service & Hospitality industries. Membership: $195/year (individual); $110/year (educator).

Publications:
Newsletter. bi-m.
WFF Magazine. semi-a.

Meetings/Conferences:
1999 – Dallas, TX/March 21-24

Women's Independent Label Distribution Network *(1979)*
Historical Note
Organization defunct in 1995.

Women's Internat'l Network of Utility Professionals *(1925)*
P.O. Box 335
Whites Creek, TN   37189
Tel: (615)876-5444
E-Mail: winup@aol.com
Members: 350 individuals
Staff: 1
Annual Budget: $50-100,000
Exec. Director: Vickey Setters

Historical Note
Formerly (1998) Electrical Women's Round Table. Members are women in electric utilities or firms connected with the electrical industry who hold consumer-related positions in public relations, advertising, editing, and education. Formed in New York, NY with about 50 charter members. Incorporated in New York in 1927. Membership: $66/year, plus local chapter dues.

Publications:
Membership Directory. a.
Newsletter. q.

Meetings/Conferences:
Annual Meetings: Fall
1999 – Chattanooga, TN/Oct. 19-21

Women's Jewelry Ass'n *(1981)*
333-B Rte. 46 West, Suite B-201
Fairfield, NJ   07004
Tel: (973)575-7190   *Fax:* (973)575-1445
Members: 1000 individuals
Staff: 20
Annual Budget: $50-100,000
President: Phyllis Bergman

Historical Note
Members are women jewelry industry professionals. the association seeks to enhance the status of women, recognize the accomplishments of women and provide a network for women in the industry. Associate membership is available for men. Membership: $75/year (individual); $50/year (associate).

Publications:
Newsletter. 5/year.

Meetings/Conferences:
1999 – New York, NY

Women's Nat'l Book Ass'n *(1917)*
160 5th Ave., Room 604
New York, NY   10010
Tel: (212)675-7805   *Fax:* (212)989-7542
E-Mail: skpassoc@internetmci.com
Members: 1,200 individuals
Annual Budget: $10-25,000
President: Donna Paz

Historical Note
Founded in 1917 as an organization of women and men in all occupations allied to the book publishing industry. Members include publishers, authors, librarians, literary agents, editors, illustrators and booksellers. Has no paid staff. Membership: $15/year, minimum (individual); $200-$600/year (organization).

Publications:
Chapter Newsletters. m.
The Bookwoman. 3/year.

Women's Professional Rodeo Ass'n *(1948)*
1235 Lake Plaza Dr., Suite 134
Colorado Springs, CO   80906
Tel: (719)576-0900   *Fax:* (719)576-1386
Web Site: http://www.wpra.com
Members: 2,000 individuals
Staff: 4
Annual Budget: $250-500,000
Acting President: Carolynn Vietor
Secretary-Treasurer: Charlene Harris

Historical Note
WPRA was originally organized to replace trick riding in the rodeos. Modern purpose is to provide professional-level competitions and prize money for women athletes in the rodeo arena. Members are competitors in professional girl rodeos and in barrel races in rodeos sanctioned by the Rodeo Cowboys Ass'n. Formerly (1980) the Girls' Rodeo Ass'n and (1981) the Professional Women's Rodeo Ass'n. Membership: $250/year.

Publications:
Rule Book & Reference Guide. a.
Women's Pro Rodeo News. m. adv.

Meetings/Conferences:
Annual Meetings: December, in conjunction with the Nat'l
        Finals
1999 – Las Vegas, NV
2000 – Las Vegas, NV

Women's Tennis Ass'n
Historical Note
Became (1995) WTA Tour.

Women's Transportation Seminar *(1977)*
One Walnut St.
Boston, MA   02108-3616
Tel: (617)367-3273   *Fax:* (617)227-6783
E-Mail: wts@engineers.org
Web Site: http://www.wtsnational.org
Members: 3,000 individuals
Staff: 1
Annual Budget: $100-250,000
Administrative Manager: Joanne Durham

Historical Note
Members are male and female transportation professionals, and public and private users of transportation services. Founded in Washington, DC to enhance personal advancement and professional recognition for members. Membership: $60-95/year (individual); $1,000 (corporate membership).

Publications:
Local Chapter Newsletters. m.
WTS Nat'l Membership Directory. a.
WTS National Newsletter. bi-m.
WTS W/M/DBE Directory.

Meetings/Conferences:
Annual Meetings: May

Wood and Synthetic Flooring Institute *(1954)*
Historical Note
Merged into the Maple Flooring Manufacturers Ass'n in 1995.

Wood Component Manufacturers Ass'n *(1929)*
1000 Johnson Ferry Road, Suite A-130
Marietta, GA   30068
Tel: (770)565-6660
Web Site: http://www.woodcomponents.org
Members: 130 companies
Staff: 3
Annual Budget: $100-250,000

Exec. Director: Steven V. Lawser, CAE

Historical Note
Formerly (1984) Hardwood Dimension Manufacturers Ass'n and (1996) Nat'l Dimension Manufacturers Ass'n. Members are manufacturers of wood component products for the furniture and kitchen cabinet industries as well as other wood parts users.

Meetings/Conferences:
Annual Meetings: Spring/200
1999 – Savannah, GA(Hyatt Regency)/March 13-16/200
2000 – San Francisco, CA(Grand Hyatt)/April 8-11/200

Wood Machinery Manufacturers of America *(1899)*
1900 Arch St.
Philadelphia, PA   19103-1498
Tel: (215)564-3484   *Fax:* (215)963-9785
Toll Free: (800)289 - 9662
E-Mail: assnhqt@netaxs.com
Web Site: http://www.woodweb.com
Members: 204 companies
Staff: 6
Annual Budget: $250-500,000
Exec. V. President: Kenneth R. Hutton
Associate Director: Elizabeth B. Franks

Historical Note
Formerly (1983) the Woodworking Machinery Manfacturers of America. Membership: $550/year (company).

Publications:
Buyer's Guide and Directory. a.

Meetings/Conferences:
Annual Meetings: Spring/300
1999 – Maui, HI(Aston Wailea)/Apr. 14-18/400

Wood Moulding and Millwork Producers Ass'n *(1963)*
507 First St.
Woodland, CA   95695
Tel: (530)661-9591   *Fax:* (530)661-9586
Toll Free: (800)550 - 7889
E-Mail: bob@wmmpa.com
Web Site: http://wmmpa.com
Members: 110 companies
Staff: 3
Annual Budget: $500-1,000,000
Exec. V. President: Robert Weiglein

Historical Note
Established as the Western Wood Moulding Producers, it became the Western Wood Moulding and Millwork Producers in 1968 and assumed its present name in 1978. Membership: $195-1,100/mo., based on board footage production.

Publications:
Case 'n Base News. m.
Directory of Members, Products, & Services. a.

Meetings/Conferences:
Semi-annual Meetings: February and August
1999 – Monterey, CA(Hyatt Regency)/Feb. 9-14/120
2000 – Tucson, AZ(El Conquistador)/Feb. 18-22/120

Wood Products Manufacturers Ass'n *(1929)*
175 State Road East
Westminster, MA   01473-1208
Tel: (978)874-5445   *Fax:* (978)874-9946
Web Site: www.wpma.org
Members: 702 companies
Staff: 5
Exec. Director: Albert J. Bibeau

Historical Note
Formerly Wood Turners Service Bureau and Wood Turners and Shapers Ass'n (1978). Incorporated in Massachusetts in 1967, WPMA members represent all facets of the wood industry. Purpose is to promote friendly business relations by providing a forum through which information can be disseminated and shared among members Membership: $470-1,000/year, based on company size.

Publications:
Membership Directory. a. adv.
Newsletter. m.

Meetings/Conferences:
Semi-Annual Meetings: Spring and Fall
1999 – New Port, RI
1999 – Charleston, SC/April 28-May 2
2000 – Orlando, FL/March 15-19
2000 – Dixville Notch, NH/Sept. 20-24

Wood Tank Manufacturers Ass'n *(1982)*
Route 5
Renick, WV   24966
Tel: (304)497-3163   *Fax:* (304)497-2698
Members: 1,100 individuals, 10 companies
Staff: 6
Annual Budget: $50-100,000
President: Barry Glick

Historical Note
Formed to promote the manufacture and use of wooden hot tubs. Membership: $100-500/year.

Publications:
Newsletter. q.

Meetings/Conferences:

Wood Truss Council of America *(1983)*
One WTCA Center
6425 Normandy Lane
Madison, WI   53717
Tel: (608)274-4849   *Fax:* (608)274-3329
E-Mail: wtca@msn.com
Web Site: http://www.woodtruss.com
Members: 525 companies
Staff: 5
Annual Budget: $500-1,000,000
Exec. Director: Kirk Grundahl

Historical Note
Members formerly constituted the component manufacturers division of the Truss Plate Institute. Members are manufacturers and suppliers of wood trusses and related products. Membership: Dues vary based on sales volume (manufacturers); $400/year (associates), $100/year (professional members).

Publications:
WoodWords Newsletter. m. adv.

Meetings/Conferences:
Annual Meetings: Fall

Woodworking Machinery Distributors' Ass'n *(1959)*
Historical Note
Organization defunct in 1997.

Woodworking Machinery Importers Ass'n of America
Historical Note
Became (1997) Woodworking Machinery Industry Ass'n.

Woodworking Machinery Industry Ass'n *(1978)*
5024-R Campbell Blvd.
Baltimore, MD   21236-5974
Tel: (410)931-8100   *Fax:* (410)931-8111
E-Mail: wmiahq@aol.com
Members: 155 companies
Staff: 5
Annual Budget: $250-500,000
Exec. V. President: Calvin K. Clemons, CAE, CMP

Historical Note
Formerly (1997) Woodworking Machinery Importers Ass'n of America. WMIA members are chief executives of woodworking machinery distributing companies primarily concerned with the import of woodworking machinery. Membership: $600/year (company).

Publications:
Bulletin. q.
Directory. bien.

Meetings/Conferences:
Annual Meetings: Wailea, Maui, HI(Aston Wailea Resort)/April 14-18
2000 – Miami, FL(Loew's Miami Beach)/April 11-15/350
2001 – San Diego, CA(La Costa)

Wool Manufacturers Council *(1956)*
Historical Note
A council of the Northern Textile Ass'n.

Woolknit Associates *(1939)*
Historical Note
Address unknown in 1996.

Workgroup for Electronic Data Interchange *(1991)*
12020 Sunrise Valley Dr., Suite 100
Reston, VA   20191
Tel: (703)391-2716   *Fax:* (703)391-2759
E-Mail: WEBMASTER@WEDI.ORG
Members: 100 companies/individuals
Staff: 1
Annual Budget: $250-500,000
Exec. V. President: James A. Schuping, CAE

Historical Note
WEDI represents companies and organizations active in the healthcare industry. The Workgroup was created to help streamline the practice of healthcare administration by standardizing electronic communications and increasing members' knowledge of EDI (electronic data interchange) technology and electronic commerce. Membership: $300/year (individual); $1000-$5000/year (organization).

Meetings/Conferences:
1999 – San Antonio, TX(Hyatt Regency)

World Affairs Councils of America *(1964)*
1726 M St., N.W., Suite 800
Washington, DC   20036
Tel: (202)785-4703   *Fax:* (202)833-2369
E-Mail: NCWA@aol.com
Members: 84 organizations
Staff: 2
Annual Budget: $100-250,000
Exec. Director: Jerry W. Leach

Historical Note
Formerly (1982) Nat'l Council of Community World Affairs Organizations. Became Nat'l Council of World Affairs Organizations. Changed name to World Affairs Councils of America in 1997. NCWAO members are world affairs councils and similar organizations. Membership: $100-$900/year (organization).

Publications:
Directory of WCA. a.
Operations Papers. q.
Speakers Newsletter: May We Suggest. m.
Study Tour Reports. 3/yea.
World Affairs Newsletter. m.

Meetings/Conferences:
1999 – Washington, DC

World Airline Entertainment Ass'n
401 N. Michigan Ave.
Chicago, IL   60611-4267
Tel: (312)245-1034   *Fax:* (312)245-1080
E-Mail: waea@sba.com
Web Site: http://www.waea.org
Members: 330 companies
Staff: 9
Annual Budget: $1-2,000,000
Exec. Director: M. Bernadette Patton, CAE

Historical Note
WAEA members are companies involved in all aspects of the inflight entertainment and cabin management industry including airlines, equipment manufacturers, distributors and producers of short subject feature length films, audio and video program producers, advertising representatives and magazine publishers.

Publications:
Avion Magazine. q. adv.

Meetings/Conferences:
1999 – Salt Lake City, UT/Sept. 28-Oct. 1
2000 – Anaheim, CA/Sept. 19-22
2001 – Brisbane, Australia/Sept. 11-14

World Antique Dealers Ass'n *(1978)*
818 Marian Ave.
Mansfield, OH   44906
Tel: (419)756-4374   *Fax:* (419)756-4979
Members: 160 individuals
Staff: 1
Annual Budget: under $10,000
President: Don McLaughlin

Historical Note
Formerly (1995) Associated Antique Dealers of America. AADA members are antiques dealers who have been in business for at least 3 years. Membership: $100/year.

Publications:
Directory. a.
WADA Newsletter. m.

Meetings/Conferences:

World Aquaculture Soc. *(1970)*
143 J.M. Parker Coliseum
Louisiana State University
Baton Rouge, LA   70803
Tel: (504)388-3137   *Fax:* (504)388-3493
E-Mail: wasmas@aol.com
Web Site: http://www.was.org
Members: 2,400 individuals
Staff: 4
Annual Budget: $100-250,000
Dir., Home Office: Juliette L. Massey

Historical Note
Formerly (1986) the World Mariculture Soc. Members are individuals and companies interested in the cultivation of aquatic plants and animals for food purposes. Membership: $60/year (individual); $100/year (corporation); $40/year (student); $250/year (sustaining).

Publications:
Journal of the World Aquaculture Soc. q.
World Aquaculture Magazine. q.

Meetings/Conferences:
Annual Meetings: Spring
1999 – Snydey, Australia

World Ass'n for Infant Mental Health *(1992)*
Inst. for Children, Youth, and Families
Kellogg Center, Suite 27, MI State Univ.
East Lansing, MI   48824-1022
Tel: (517)432-3793   *Fax:* (517)432-3694
E-Mail: waimh@pilot.msu.edu
Web Site: http://www.msu.edu/user/waimh
Members: 1,700 individuals
Staff: 2
Annual Budget: $2-5,000,000
Exec. Director: Hiram E. Fitzgerald, Ph.D.

Historical Note
Formed (1992) by the merger of the World Ass'n for Infant Psychiatry and Allied Disciplines and the Internat'l Ass'n for Infant Mental Health. Members are child psychiatrists, child psychologists, nurses, social workers, and other professionals with an interest in mental development and disorders in children under 3 years of age and in families of small children. Membership: $55/year (individual), $40/year (student).

Publications:
Infant Mental Health Journal. q. adv.
Signal Newsletter. q.

Meetings/Conferences:
2000 – Montreal, PQ(Queen Elizabeth)/July 26-29/1500

World Ass'n of Alcohol Beverage Industries *(1944)*
1250 I St., N.W., Suite 900
Washington, DC   20005
Tel: (202)628-3544   *Fax:* (202)682-8832
Members: 26 chapters
Staff: 2
Annual Budget: $25-50,000
Headquarters Representative: Sue A. Silk
Administrator: Helen Gatewood Kenney

Historical Note
Formerly known as the Nat'l Women's Ass'n of Allied Beverage Industries. Administrative support provided by Distilled Spirits Council of the U.S. Membership: $35/year (individual); $25/year (company).

Publications:
Industry World. q.

Meetings/Conferences:
Annual Meetings: Summer/200
1999 – Louisville, KY/June 12-16

World Ass'n of Detectives *(1925)*
P.O. Box 441000-301
Denver, CO   80044
Tel: (303)368-7488   *Fax:* (303)671-6063
Toll Free: (800)962 - 0516
Web Site: http://www.wad.net
Members: 833 individuals
Staff: 2
Annual Budget: $100-250,000

Exec. Director: Robert Heales
Historical Note
Membership: $125/year.

Publications:
WAD News. m. adv.

Meetings/Conferences:
1999 – /Aug. 28-Sept. 2

World Ass'n of Document Examiners *(1973)*
111 N. Canal St.
Chicago, IL   60606
Tel: (312)930-9446   *Fax:* (312)930-5903
Members: 400 individuals
Staff: 6
Annual Budget: $100-250,000
Administrator: Kathleen Kusta

Historical Note
Document examiners organized to uphold high standards in the profession and to assist individual practitioners.

Publications:
WADE Exchange. m.
WADE Journal. q.

Meetings/Conferences:
Annual Meetings: Always Chicago in July
1999 – Chicago, IL(Drake Hotel)/Aug. 6-9

World Computer Graphics Ass'n *(1981)*
6121 Lincolnia Road, Suite 302
Alexandria, VA   22312-2707
Tel: (703)642-3050   *Fax:* (703)642-1663
Members: 13 companies
Staff: 7
Annual Budget: $500-1,000,000
President/Exec. Director: Caby C. Smith

Historical Note
Founded with the goal of promoting the growth and serving the needs of the global computer graphics community, through sponsoring annual exhibitions, conferences and seminars internationally.

Publications:
Association Update. semi-a.
Conference Proceedings. q.

World Council of Defense Investigators *(1994)*
P.O. Box 19431
Austin, TX   78760-9431
Tel: (512)370-4930   *Fax:* (512)442-9302
Staff: 1
Annual Budget: $25-50,000
Exec. Director: Lynzy Anne Wright

Historical Note
Members are licensed investigators who work as part of a defense team in civil or criminal court proceedings. Membership: $100/year (licensed or legal members); $125/year (associate).

Publications:
Foundation for Justice. m. adv.

Meetings/Conferences:
Annual Meetings: Winter
1999 – Las Vegas, NV
2000 – San Diego, CA

World Federation of Travel Writers *(1954)*
One Ballinswood Road
Atlantic Highlands, NJ   07716-1510
Tel: (732)291-2840   *Fax:* (732)291-9272
E-Mail: donbonhaus@aol.com
Members: 1,600 individuals
Annual Budget: under $10,000
Director, U.S.A.: Don Bonhaus

Historical Note
Formerly (1997) World Federation of Travel Writers and Journalists. The U.S. arm of the international organization, founded and located in Brussels, FIJET provides professional support to journalists and writers who specialize in travel and tourism.

Publications:
Vue Touristique. q.

Meetings/Conferences:
Annual Meetings: October-November

World Federation of Travel Writers and Journalists
Historical Note
Became (1997) World Federation of Travel Writers.

World Floor Covering Ass'n *(1960)*
2211 E. Howell Ave.
Anaheim, CA   92806-6009
Tel: (714)978-6440   *Fax:* (714)978-6066
Toll Free: (800)624 - 6880
E-Mail: wfca@wfca.org
Web Site: http://www.wfca.org
Members: 2,000 companies
Staff: 10
Annual Budget: $5-10,000,000
C.E.O.: D. Christopher Davis
Legislative Counsel: Sheldon London
Director of Finance and Administration: Cammie Weitzel
Director of Operations: Terry Hearne

Historical Note
WFCA is the largest advocacy association representing floor covering retailers and allied service providers. Product of a merger of the Western Floor Covering Ass'n and the American Floorcovering Ass'n in 1994. Membership: $225/year (regular); $800/year (associate).

Publications:
Directory. a.
Newsletter.

Meetings/Conferences:
1999 – Las Vegas, NV(Sands Expo Center)/Jan. 27-29
2000 – Las Vegas, NV(Sands Expo Center)/Jan. 26-28
2001 – Las Vegas, NV(Sands Expo Center)/Jan. 31-Feb. 2

World Future Soc. (1966)
7910 Woodmont Ave., Suite 450
Bethesda, MD　20814-3032
Tel: (301)656-8274　　　　　　*Fax:* (301)951-0394
Toll Free: (800)989 - 8274
E-Mail: wfsinfo@wfs.org
Web Site: http://wfs.org
Members: 30,000 individuals
Staff: 13
Annual Budget: $1-2,000,000
President: Edward S. Cornish
Director, Membership Department: Susan Echard
Historical Note
An association of scientists, educators, government officials and others interested in social and technological developments of the future. Membership: $35/year.
Publications:
Future Survey. m.
Futures Research Quarterly. q.
The Futurist. m. adv.
Meetings/Conferences:
1999 – Washington, DC(Washington Hilton)/July 29-Aug. 1
2000 – Houston, TX(West Galleria)/July 23-25

World Gold Council
444 Madison Ave.
New York, NY　10022
Tel: (212)317-3800　　　　　　*Fax:* (212)688-0410
Members: 25 individuals
Staff: 25
C.E.O.: Michael Barlerin

World History Ass'n (1982)
Department of History, Drexel University
Philadelphia, PA　19104
Tel: (215)895-2471　　　　　　*Fax:* (215)895-6614
E-Mail: rosenrl@post.drexel.edu
Web Site: http://www.hartford-hwp.com/wha/docs/about.html
Members: 1,400 individuals
Annual Budget: $10-25,000
Exec. Director: Richard L. Rosen
Historical Note
Members are teachers, academics and others with an interest in the teaching of and research in world and cross-cultural history. Membership: $30/year (individual); $15/year (student/retirees), $35/year (companies).
Publications:
Journal of World History. semi-a.
World History Bulletin. semi-a.
Meetings/Conferences:
Annual Meetings: in conjunction with AHA annual meeting
1999 – Victoria, British Columbia/June 24-27

World Internat'l Nail and Beauty Ass'n (1981)
1221 N. Lake View
Anaheim, CA　92807
Tel: (714)779-9883　　　　　　*Fax:* (714)779-9972
Members: 2,400 individuals
Staff: 2
Annual Budget: $250-500,000
President: Jim George
Historical Note
Formerly (1984) the Nat'l Ass'n of Nail Artists and (1987) the Nat'l Aesthetician and Nail Artist Ass'n. Members are manicurists, pedicurists and aestheticians as well as manufacturers and suppliers of beauty products. Membership: $40/year (individual).
Meetings/Conferences:
1999 – Anaheim, CA(Disneyland Hotel)
1999 – Anaheim, CA(Disneyland Hotel)June /6000
2000 – Anaheim, CA
2001 – Anaheim, CA

World Packaging Organisation (1968)
481 Carlisle Dr.
Herndon, VA　20170-4823
Tel: (703)318-5512　　　　　　*Fax:* (703)318-0310
Annual Budget: $50-100,000
General Secretary: William C. Pflaum
Historical Note
WPO was formed through inter-regional efforts in the packaging industry to facilitate global technology transfer and strengthen commercial links throughout the industry. Membership: $100/year (individual); $300-2,500/year (organization).
Publications:
World Packaging Directory. a. adv.
World Packaging News. bi-m. adv.
WorldStars Packaging Awards. a. adv.
Meetings/Conferences:

World Population Soc. (1973)
1050 17th St., N.W., Suite 1050
Washington, DC　20036
Tel: (202)898-1303　　　　　　*Fax:* (202)775-9694
Staff: 2
Annual Budget: $50-100,000
President: Philander P. Claxton
Historical Note
A multidisciplinary group supporting research on and communicating information about population and its impact on the quality of life, and promoting fulfillment of the World Population Plan of Action agreed to by 136 nations in Bucharest in 1974.
Meetings/Conferences:
Annual Meetings: Fall

World Pro Skiing-Racers Ass'n (1970)
Historical Note
Organization defunct in 1998.

World Research Foundation (1977)
P.O. Box 10187
Marina Del Rey, CA　90295
Tel: (310)827-0070　　　　　　*Fax:* (310)827-5010
E-Mail: lavern@wrf.org
Web Site: www.wrf.org
Members: 40,000 individuals
Staff: 6
Exec. Director: Steven Ross
Exec. Director: LaVerne Ross
Historical Note
Formerly known as the American Bio-Enviromental Association. Merged with the World Research Foundation in 1987 and adopted that name from Internat'l Bio-Environmental Foundation following that. Scientists concerned with the biological effects of atmospheric ions, electromagnetic fields, noise and artifical light.
Publications:
Bulletins. q.
World Research News.

World Sign Associates (1947)
8774 Yates Drive, Suite 120
Westminster, CO　80030
Tel: (303)427-7252　　　　　　*Fax:* (303)427-7090
Web Site: http://www.wsanetwork.org
Members: 175 companies
Staff: 3
Annual Budget: $250-500,000
Exec. V. President: Jerry L. Righthouse
Historical Note
WSA members are companies involved in the design, manufacture, installation and maintenance of electrical signs and suppliers to the industry. Membership: $780/year (company).
Publications:
Newsletter. q. adv.
Meetings/Conferences:
Annual Meetings: August-September/200

World Sports Medicine Ass'n of Registered Therapists (1993)
206 Marine Ave. Suite 5642
Newport Beach, CA　92662-5642
Tel: (626)574-1999　　　　　　*Fax:* (626)445-1943
Members: 4,500 individuals
Staff: 5
Annual Budget: $10-25,000
C.E.O.: Joe S. Borland, DO,RPT
Historical Note
Members are sports medicine therapists and personal fitness trainers. Awards the designations RSMT (Registered Sports Medicine Therapist) and RPFT (Registered Personal Fitness Trainer). Membership: $100/year.
Publications:
World SMART Newsletter. semi-a. adv.
Meetings/Conferences:
Annual Meetings: June

World Teleport Ass'n (1985)
One World Trade Center, Suite 8665
New York, NY　10048-0202
Tel: (212)432-2028　　　　　　*Fax:* (212)432-6356
E-Mail: 6174448@mcimail.com
Web Site: http://www.worldteleport.org
Members: 500 individuals, 106 companies
Staff: 4
Annual Budget: $250-500,000
Exec. Director: Robert Bell
Director, Global Marketing: Louis Zacharilla
Member Services Manager: Celia Hartmann
Historical Note
Mission is to promote the understanding, development and use of teleports as a means to achieve economic, political and social progress locally, regionally and worldwide. Membership: $3,000/year (organization/company).
Publications:
Business Development News. bi-m.
Membership Guide. bi-a. adv.
WTA Update. a. adv.
Meetings/Conferences:
1999 – New Orleans, LA

World War Two Studies Ass'n (1967)
Dept. of History, 208 Eisenhower Hall
Kansas State University
Manhattan, KS　66506-1002
Tel: (913)532-0374　　　　　　*Fax:* (913)532-7004
Web Site: http://h-net.msu.edu/~war/wwtsa/
Members: 350 individuals
Secretary-Treasurer and Editor: Mark Parillo
Historical Note
Members are academics and others with an interest in the study of the World War II period. Membership: $15/year (individual); $5/year (student).
Publications:
Newsletter. semi-a.
Meetings/Conferences:
Annual Meetings: in conjunction with AHA annual meeting

World Waterpark Ass'n (1980)
P.O. Box 14826
Lenexa, KS　66285-4826
Tel: (913)599-0300　　　　　　*Fax:* (913)599-0520
E-Mail: wwa@waterparks.com
Web Site: http://www.waterparks.com
Members: 900 parks; 450 suppliers
Staff: 5
Annual Budget: $500-1,000,000
Exec. Director: Al Turner
Director, Trade Show and Supplier Relations: Patty Miller
Director, Convention and Educational Program: Statia Leeds
Exec. V. President and C.O.O.: Dave Bruschi
Historical Note
Membership: $150-$775/year.
Publications:
Buyer's Guide. a. adv.
Developers Reference. a. adv.
News Drops Newsletter. 9/yr.
Splash. 9/yr. adv.
Meetings/Conferences:
Annual Meetings: Fall
1999 – Santa Clara, CA/Oct. 6-11

World Watusi Ass'n (1985)
PO Box 14
Crawford, NE　69339-0014
Tel: (308)665-3919　　　　　　*Fax:* (308)665-1931
Members: 300 individuals
Staff: 1
Annual Budget: $10-25,000
Registrar: Maureen Neidhardt
Historical Note
Members are owners, breeders and others interested in the Watusi cattle breed. Membership: $25/year.
Publications:
Rare Breeds Journal. bi-m. adv.
Watusi World. 6/yr. adv.
Meetings/Conferences:
Annual Meetings: September
1999 – Pueblo, CO

World Wide Pet Supply Ass'n (1951)
406 South 1st Ave.
Arcadia, CA　91006-3829
Tel: (626)447-2222　　　　　　*Fax:* (626)447-8350
E-Mail: info@wwpsa.com
Web Site: http://www.wwpsa.com
Members: 480 companies
Staff: 4
Annual Budget: $1-2,000,000
Exec. V. President: Douglas L. Poindexter
Historical Note
Formerly (1994) Western World Pet Supply Ass'n. WWPSA represents and promotes the interests of pet industry manufacturers, importers, product distributors, breeder/livestock distributors and manufactuers' representatives and retailers. Membership: $525/year (company).
Publications:
PET NEWS. q.
Meetings/Conferences:
Annual Trade Shows: July
1999 – Long Beach, CA(Convention Center)/July 9-11

World's Poultry Science Ass'n, U.S.A. Branch (1965)
USDA/ARS
Building 003, Room 208, BARC-W
Beltsville, MD　20705
Tel: (301)504-6421　　　　　　*Fax:* (301)504-6001
Members: 650 individuals
Staff: 1
Annual Budget: under $10,000
Secretary-Treasurer: Michael D. Ruff
Historical Note
U.S. members of the World's Poultry Science Association. Promotes U.S. participation in World's Poultry Congresses, held every 4 years. Membership: $20/year (individual); $48/year (organization); $10/year (student).
Publications:
World's Poultry Science Journal. 3/year.
Meetings/Conferences:
Annual Meetings: With Poultry Science Ass'n at Land Grant colleges.

Wound, Ostomy and Continence Nurses Soc. (1968)
1550 South Coast Hwy., Suite 201
Laguna Beach, CA　92651
Toll Free: (888)224 - 9626
E-Mail: Maria@wocn.org
Web Site: http://www.wocn.org
Members: 4,100 individuals, 105 industry members
Staff: 15
Annual Budget: $1-2,000,000
Exec. Director: Maria Garces
Meeting Planner: Neil Schwartz
Asst. Account Executive: Helen Tipton
Client Services Manager: Sheri Stoyanoff
Historical Note
Formerly (1992) Internat'l Ass'n for Enterostomal Therapy, WOCN is a professional, international nursing society representing WOC(ET) nurses and other nurse professionals who provide acute and rehabilitative care to people with select disorders of the gastrointestinal, genitourinary, and integumentary systems. Membership: $85-$90/year (individual), $600/year (industry).
Publications:
Guidelines for Management. irreg.
Journal of Wound, Ostomy and Continence Nursing. bi-m. adv.
Membership Directory. a.
WOCN News. q. adv.
Meetings/Conferences:
Annual Meetings: June

1999 – Minneapolis, MN(Convention
Center)/June 20-24/2400
2000 – Toronto, ON, Canada(Convention
Center)/June 3-9/2500

Woven Wire Products Ass'n (1942)

c/o Acorn Wire & Iron Works
4940 S. Kilbourn Ave.
Chicago, IL   60632-3011
Tel: (773)585-0600
Members: 25 companies
Staff: 1
Annual Budget: under $10,000
President: Bob Stitt

Historical Note
Promotes the use of wire mesh products.

Publications:
Newsletter. m.

Meetings/Conferences:
Semi-annual meetings: Spring and Fall

Writers Guild of America, East (1954)

555 West 57th St.
New York, NY   10019
Tel: (212)767-7800   *Fax:* (212)582-1909
Web Site: http://www.wgaeast.org
Members: 3,700 individuals
Staff: 21
Annual Budget: $2-5,000,000
Exec. Director: Mona Mangan

Historical Note
*Founded in New York City in 1954 as an independent labor union
representing writers in motion pictures, television and radio.
Affiliated with the Writers Guild of America, West.*

Publications:
On Writing. 3/yr.
Writers Guild East Newsletter. bi-m. adv.

Meetings/Conferences:
1999 – New York, NY(Warwick)/100

Writers Guild of America, west (1933)

7000 West 3rd St.
Los Angeles, CA   90048-4329
Tel: (323)951-4000   *Fax:* (323)782-4800
Web Site: http://www.wga.org
Members: 8,300 individuals
Staff: 96
Annual Budget: $2-5,000,000

Historical Note
*Founded in Los Angeles, CA in 1933 as an independent labor union
representing writers in the motion picture, broadcast, cable and new
technologies industries. Membership: 1.5% of income.*

Publications:
"Written By". 10/year. adv.

Meetings/Conferences:
Annual Meetings: Annual Membership Meeting in September in
Los Angeles, Awards Show in February, also in Los
Angeles

Writing Instrument Manufacturers Ass'n (1943)

236 Route 38 West, Suite 100
Moorestown, NJ   08057
Tel: (609)231-8500   *Fax:* (609)231-4664
E-Mail: wima@ahint.com
Members: 90 companies
Staff: 2
Annual Budget: $250-500,000
Exec. V. President: William L. MacMillan, III, CAE

Historical Note
*Founded as the Fountain Pen and Mechanical Pencil Manufacturers
Ass'n, it assumed its present name in 1963. Merged with Pencil
Makers Ass'n in 1994.*

Publications:
Manufacturers Directory. a. adv.

Meetings/Conferences:
Annual Meetings: Even years, Spring

Xi Psi Phi (1889)

1623 Washington Ave., Suite 300
Alton, IL   62002
Tel: (618)463-1889
Members: 20,000 individuals
Staff: 2
Supreme Secretary-Treasurer: Keith Dickey

Historical Note
*An international professional dental fraternity. Organized February
8, 1889 at the University of Michigan. Affiliated with the American
Dental Interfraternity Council.*

Publications:
Xi Psi Phi Quarterly. q. adv.

Publications:
Annual Meetings: Spring

Xplorer Internat'l (1981)

24238 Hawthorne Blvd.
Torrance, CA   90505-6505
Tel: (310)373-3633   *Fax:* (310)375-4240
Toll Free: (800)669 - 7567
E-Mail: info@xplor.org
Web Site: http://www.xplor.org
Members: 2,700 organizations
Staff: 45
Annual Budget: $2-5,000,000
President: Dr. Keith Davidson
Sr. Manager, Meetings and Conferences: Suzanne Davidson

Historical Note
*Formerly known as Electronic Document Systems Ass'n. Also
known as Xplorer Internat'l/Electronics Documents Systems Ass'n.
Provides programs, forums, and related services which enhance the
use of electronic document systems to achieve organizational goals.
Membership: $125/year (individual); $450/year
(organization/company).*

Publications:
Product and Services Directory. a. adv.
The Xplorer. m.
Xploration. semi-a.

Meetings/Conferences:
Annual Meetings: Spring.

Yacht Architects and Brokers Ass'n (1920)

105 Eastern Ave., Suite 104
Annapolis, MD   21403-3300
Tel: (410)263-1014   *Fax:* (410)263-1659
Members: 75 individuals, 196 companies
Staff: 6
Annual Budget: $50-100,000
Exec. Director: Joseph M. Thompson, Jr.
Director, Communications: Kristin B. Thompson
Director, Membership and Resources: Wendy Blumenthal

Historical Note
*YABA promotes the interests of professional yacht brokers through
its Code of Ethics, legislative and regulatory involvement, as well as
education and dissemination of pertinent information. Membership:
$250/year (corporate); $75/year (individual).*

Publications:
YABA Handbook. a. adv.
Yacht Brokerage News. q. adv.

Meetings/Conferences:
Annual Meetings: January
1999 – Hilton Head Island, SC(Westin Resort)/150

Yellow Pages Publishers Ass'n (1988)

3773 Cherry Creek North Dr., Suite 920
Denver, CO   80209
Tel: (303)333-9772   *Fax:* (303)320-6999
Web Site: http://www.yppa.org
Members: 400 companies
Staff: 40
Annual Budget: $10-25,000,000
President & C.E.O.: James C. Logan, Jr.

Historical Note
*Formed by a merger of the American Ass'n of Yellow Pages
Publishers and the Nat'l Yellow Pages Service Ass'n in 1988.
Members are companies publishing yellow pages and other
specialty directories. Suppliers to the industry are associate
members. The address above is for the YPPA executie offices;
production offices are located at 820 Kirts Blvd., Suite 100, Troy,
MI 48084. Has an annual budget of approximately $12 million.*

Publications:
Directory, Town & County Coverage. irreg.
Link Newsletter. 10/year. adv.
Rates & Data Publication.

Meetings/Conferences:
1999 – Denver, CO(Adams Mark Hotel)/Oct. 3-6
2000 – Boston, MA(Marriott Copley Plaza)/Oct. 1-4

Young Black Programming Coalition (1975)

P.O. Box 1051
Vicksburg, MS   39181-1051
Tel: (601)922-8395   *Fax:* (601)922-2856
Members: 1,500 individuals
Staff: 8
Annual Budget: $100-250,000
Nat'l Public Relations Manager: Robert Rosenthal

Historical Note
*Members are professionals in the music, radio, and communications
industries. YBPC represents all the major record labels and 96% of*

*black-programmed radio stations nationwide. Membership:
$120/year.*

Publications:
Programmer Newsletter. m.
Programming Radio. a. adv.
Who's Who in Black Music.

Meetings/Conferences:
1999 – New Orleans, LA(Hyatt)/2500

Young Entrepreneurs Organization (1987)

1321 Duke St., Suite 300
Alexandria, VA   22314
Tel: (703)519-6700   *Fax:* (703)519-1864
Web Site: http://www.yeo.org
Members: 1,500 individuals
Exec. Director: Brien Biondi

Historical Note
*YEO provides education and professional support to businesspeople
who are founders or controlling shareholders of their businesses.
Membership, by invitation only, is restricted to executives under the
age of 39 whose companies have gross annual sales of $1 million
or more.*

Meetings/Conferences:
Semi-Annual Meetings: Summer and Winter

Young Menswear Ass'n (1937)

1328 Broadway
New York, NY   10001
Tel: (212)594-6422   *Fax:* (212)594-6422
Members: 350 individuals
Staff: 1
Annual Budget: $100-250,000
Secretary/Treasurer: Theodore M. Kaufman

Historical Note
*Represents the textile and apparel industries. Scholarships and
financial funding to students interested in the industry promote
leadership and role models.*

Publications:
Newsletter. irreg.

Meetings/Conferences:
Annual Meetings: January/400

Young Presidents' Organization (1950)

451 S. Decker Dr.,
Irving, TX   75062-8102
Tel: (972)650-4600   *Fax:* (972)650-4777
Members: 8,500 individuals
Staff: 90
Annual Budget: $10-25,000,000
C.E.O.: Roger W. Johnson
Director, Finance/Administration: Kelly Parker

Historical Note
*Members are company presidents under age 50 whose companies
employ at least 50 individuals and have either US$7 million in
annual sales or US$140 million in total assets. Has an annual
budget of approximately $22 million.*

Publications:
YPO Worldwide. q.

Meetings/Conferences:
1999 – Hong Kong
1999 – San Francisco, CA
1999 – Rome, Italy
1999 – Hawaii
1999 – Dubai
2000 – Capetown, South Africa

Youth Symphony Orchestras

Historical Note
A division of the American Symphony Orchestra League.

Zonta Internat'l (1919)

557 W. Randolph
Chicago, IL   60661-2206
Tel: (312)930-5848   *Fax:* (312)930-0951
Members: 36,000 individuals, 1,200 clubs
Staff: 17
Annual Budget: $500-1,000,000
Exec. Director: Janet Halstead

Historical Note
*Classified service organization of executives in business and the
professions working to advance the status of women.*

Publications:
The Zontian. q.

Meetings/Conferences:
Biennial Meetings: June-July in even years
2000 – Honolulu, HI

Every active organization listed in NTPA has been indexed in one or more subject headings, which reflect the products or professions the organization in question represents. For example, the American Association of Nurse Anesthetists is listed under ANESTHESIOLOGY, MEDICINE, and NURSING.

ABRASIVES
Abrasive Grain Ass'n (7)
Abrasives Engineering Soc. (7)
Coated Abrasives Manufacturers' Institute (196)
Diamond Wheel Manufacturers Institute (222)
Grinding Wheel Institute (250)
Industrial Diamond Ass'n of America (262)
Masonry and Concrete Saw Manufacturers Institute (324)

ACCOUNTING
AACE Internat'l (7)
Academy of Accounting Historians (7)
Accountants for the Public Interest (10)
Accounting Firms Associated (10)
Affiliated Conference of Practicing Accountants Internat'l (13)
AGN Internat'l - North America (14)
American Accounting Ass'n (27)
American Ass'n for Budget and Program Analysis (29)
American Ass'n of Attorney-Certified Public Accountants (33)
American Ass'n of Hispanic Certified Public Accountants (37)
American Institute of Certified Public Accountants (76)
American Institute of Professional Bookkeepers (78)
American Soc. of Military Comptrollers (112)
American Soc. of Tax Professionals (116)
American Soc. of Women Accountants (117)
American Woman's Soc. of Certified Public Accountants (123)
Asian American Certified Public Accountants (128)
Ass'n for Accounting Administration (129)
Ass'n for Accounting Marketing (129)
Ass'n for Management Information in Financial Services (136)
Ass'n of Chartered Accountants in the United States (146)
Ass'n of College and University Auditors (147)
Ass'n of Government Accountants (152)
Ass'n of Information Technology Professionals (154)
Ass'n of Insolvency Accountants (154)
Benchmarking Network Ass'n (178)
Beta Alpha Psi (178)
BKR Internat'l (180)
Construction Financial Management Ass'n (206)
Construction Industry CPA/Consultants Ass'n (206)
Controllers Council (208)
Cost Management Group (210)
Council of Petroleum Accountants Socs. (215)
CPA Associates Internat'l (218)
CPA Auto Dealer Consultants Ass'n (218)
Financial Executives Institute (238)
FSC/DISC Tax Ass'n (244)
Government Finance Officers Ass'n of the United States and
　Canada (248)
Healthcare Financial Management Ass'n (252)
Hospitality Financial and Technology Professionals (256)
Information Systems Audit and Control Ass'n (264)
Institute for Certification of Tax Professionals (265)
Institute of Certified Financial Planners (266)
Institute of Certified Management Accountants (266)
Institute of Internal Auditors (267)
Institute of Management Accountants (268)
Insurance Accounting and Systems Ass'n (270)
Internat'l Affiliation of Independent Accounting Firms (272)
Internat'l Newspaper Financial Executives (298)
IS Financial Management Ass'n (313)
Law Firm Services Ass'n (318)
Nat'l Accounting and Finance Council (334)
Nat'l Ass'n of Black Accountants (344)
Nat'l Ass'n of Certified Valuation Analysts (346)
Nat'l Ass'n of Enrolled Agents (354)
Nat'l Ass'n of Enrolled Federal Tax Accountants (354)
Nat'l Ass'n of Local Government Auditors (362)
Nat'l Ass'n of Purchasing Management (368)
Nat'l Ass'n of Real Estate Companies (369)
Nat'l Ass'n of State Auditors, Comptrollers and
　Treasurers (374)
Nat'l Ass'n of State Boards of Accountancy (374)

Nat'l Conference of CPA Practitioners (390)
Nat'l CPA Health Care Advisors Ass'n (398)
Nat'l Litigation Support Services Ass'n (415)
Nat'l Soc. of Accountants (429)
Nat'l Soc. of Accountants for Cooperatives (429)
Nat'l Soc. of Insurance Premium Auditors (430)
Not-for-Profit Services Ass'n (446)
Polaris Internat'l (459)
Robert Morris Associates, the Ass'n of Lending and Credit
　Risk Professionals (476)
Soc. for Information Management (490)
Soc. of Cost Estimating and Analysis (500)
Soc. of Financial Examiners (501)
Soc. of Insurance Financial Management (503)
Strategic Leadership Forum (517)
TAG Internat'l (520)
Tax Executives Institute (520)
WACRA - World Ass'n for Case Method Research &
　Application (540)

ACOUSTICS
Acoustical Soc. of America (11)
Audio Engineering Soc. (172)
Electronic Forum on Sound Technology (228)
Nat'l Ass'n of Noise Control Officials (364)
Nat'l Council of Acoustical Consultants (393)

ACTORS see also THEATRE
Actors' Equity Ass'n (11)
American Guild of Variety Artists (71)
Associated Actors and Artistes of America (170)
Catholic Actors Guild of America (188)
Hebrew Actors Union (253)
Hispanic Organization of Latin Actors (254)
Italian Actors Union (313)
Screen Actors Guild (480)
Stuntwomen's Ass'n of Motion Pictures (517)

ACTUARIES
American Academy of Actuaries (20)
American Soc. of Pension Actuaries (114)
Casualty Actuarial Soc. (187)
Conference of Consulting Actuaries (204)
Soc. of Actuaries (496)
Soc. of Insurance Financial Management (503)

ADHESIVES
Adhesion Soc. (11)
Adhesive and Sealant Council (12)
Adhesives Manufacturers Ass'n (12)
Pressure Sensitive Tape Council (462)
Sealant, Waterproofing and Restoration Institute (480)

ADVERTISING INDUSTRY
Advertising and Marketing Internat'l Network (12)
Advertising Council (12)
Advertising Media Credit Executives Ass'n, Internat'l (12)
Advertising Photographers of America, Nat'l (12)
Advertising Research Foundation (12)
American Academy of Advertising (20)
American Advertising Federation (27)
American Ass'n for Public Opinion Research (31)
American Ass'n of Advertising Agencies (32)
American Council of Highway Advertisers (61)
Ass'n of Direct Marketing Agencies (149)
Ass'n of Directory Marketing (149)
Ass'n of Free Community Papers (152)
Ass'n of Independent Commercial Producers (153)
Ass'n of Nat'l Advertisers (158)
Ass'n of Promotion Marketing Agencies Worldwide (162)
Audit Bureau of Circulations (173)
Automotive Communications Council (174)
Bank Marketing Ass'n (176)

BPA Internat'l (181)
Business Marketing Ass'n (184)
Cabletelevision Advertising Bureau (185)
Direct Marketing Ass'n (223)
Eight Sheet Outdoor Advertising Ass'n (227)
Healthcare Marketing and Communications Council (253)
Inflatable Advertising Dealers Ass'n (263)
Insurance Marketing Communications Ass'n (270)
Intermarket Ass'n of Advertising Agencies (271)
Internat'l Advertising Ass'n (272)
Internat'l Communications Agency Network (286)
Internat'l Newspaper Marketing Ass'n (298)
Internat'l Sign Ass'n (302)
Internet Local Advertising and Commerce Ass'n (311)
League of Advertising Agencies (318)
Mail Advertising Service Ass'n Internat'l (322)
Media Credit Ass'n (326)
Mutual Advertising Agency Network (332)
Nat'l Ass'n for Promotional and Advertising Allowances (340)
Nat'l Ass'n of Publishers' Representatives (368)
Nat'l Potato Promotion Board (423)
Outdoor Advertising Ass'n of America (451)
Point-of-Purchase Advertising Institute (459)
PROMAX Internat'l (468)
Promotion Marketing Ass'n (468)
Promotional Products Ass'n Internat'l (468)
Publishers' Publicity Ass'n (470)
Radio Advertising Bureau (471)
Retail Advertising and Marketing Ass'n Internat'l (475)
Station Representatives Ass'n (516)
Television Bureau of Advertising (521)
Traffic Audit Bureau for Media Measurement (525)
Transworld Advertising Agency Network (526)
Utility Communicators Internat'l (538)
Women in Advertising and Marketing (546)

AEROSPACE
Aeronautical Navigator Ass'n (13)
Aerospace Department Chairmen's Ass'n (13)
Aerospace Electrical Soc. (13)
Aerospace Industries Ass'n of America (13)
Aerospace Medical Ass'n (13)
Air Traffic Control Ass'n (16)
Air Transport Ass'n of America (16)
Airports Council Internat'l/North America (17)
American Ass'n of Airport Executives (33)
American Astronautical Soc. (45)
American Institute of Aeronautics and Astronautics (76)
Ass'n for Unmanned Vehicle Systems Internat'l (140)
Cargo Airline Ass'n (187)
Council of Defense and Space Industry Ass'ns (213)
General Aviation Manufacturers Ass'n (246)
Institute of Navigation (268)
Internat'l Ass'n of Machinists and Aerospace Workers (280)
Internat'l Union, United Automobile, Aerospace and
　Agricultural Implement Workers of America (310)
Nat'l Aeronautic Ass'n (335)
Nat'l Air Carrier Ass'n (335)
Nat'l Air Traffic Controllers Ass'n (335)
Nat'l Ass'n of Air Traffic Specialists (343)
Nat'l Training Systems Ass'n (434)
Soc. for the Advancement of Material and Process
　Engineering (494)
Soc. of Allied Weight Engineers (497)
Soc. of Cost Estimating and Analysis (500)
Soc. of Flight Test Engineers (501)
Suppliers of Advanced Composite Materials Ass'n (518)
Women in Aerospace (546)

AESTHETICS
Aestheticians Internat'l Ass'n (13)
American Academy of Esthetic Dentistry (22)
American Soc. for Aesthetic Plastic Surgery (100)
American Soc. for Aesthetics (101)

American Soc. for Dental Aesthetics **(102)**

AGING
American Aging Ass'n **(27)**
American Ass'n for Geriatric Psychiatry **(30)**
American Ass'n of Homes and Services for the Aging **(37)**
American College of Health Care Administrators **(54)**
American Federation for Aging Research **(66)**
American Geriatrics Soc. **(71)**
American Seniors Housing Ass'n **(99)**
American Soc. on Aging **(117)**
Ass'n for Adult Development and Aging **(129)**
Ass'n for Gerontology in Higher Education **(134)**
Ass'n of Jewish Aging Services **(155)**
Assisted Living Federation of America **(170)**
Gerontological Soc. of America **(247)**
Nat'l Academy of Elder Law Attorneys **(334)**
Nat'l Ass'n for Senior Living Industries **(341)**
Nat'l Ass'n for the Support of Long-Term Care **(341)**
Nat'l Ass'n of Activity Professionals **(342)**
Nat'l Ass'n of Area Agencies on Aging **(343)**
Nat'l Ass'n of County Aging Programs **(350)**
Nat'l Ass'n of Nutrition and Aging Services Programs **(364)**
Nat'l Ass'n of Professional Geriatric Care Managers **(366)**
Nat'l Ass'n of Senior Companions Project Directors **(372)**
Nat'l Ass'n of State Units on Aging **(376)**
Nat'l Council on the Aging **(398)**
Nat'l Hospice Organization **(409)**
Nat'l Institute of Senior Centers **(412)**
Nat'l Institute on Community-based Long-term Care **(412)**
Pharmaceutical Care Management Ass'n **(456)**

AGRICULTURE
Ag Electronics Ass'n **(14)**
Agribusiness Council **(14)**
Agricultural and Industrial Manufacturers' Representatives Ass'n **(14)**
Agricultural Communicators in Education **(14)**
Agricultural History Soc. **(14)**
Agricultural Publishers Ass'n **(14)**
Agricultural Research Institute **(14)**
Agricultural Retailers Ass'n **(14)**
Agriculture Council of America **(15)**
Alfalfa Council **(17)**
Alpha Gamma Rho **(18)**
American Agricultural Economics Ass'n **(27)**
American Agricultural Editors Ass'n **(27)**
American Agricultural Law Ass'n **(27)**
American Agriculture Movement **(27)**
American Ass'n for Agricultural Education **(29)**
American Ass'n of Crop Insurers **(35)**
American Ass'n of Grain Inspection and Weighing Agencies **(37)**
American Crop Protection Ass'n **(62)**
American Farm Bureau Federation **(66)**
American Forage and Grassland Council **(69)**
American Herbalists Guild **(73)**
American Oat Ass'n **(87)**
American Peanut Research and Education Soc. **(90)**
American Polypay Sheep Ass'n **(93)**
American Seed Trade Ass'n **(99)**
American Sheep Industry Ass'n **(99)**
American Soc. for Plasticulture **(104)**
American Soc. of Agricultural Appraisers **(106)**
American Soc. of Agricultural Consultants **(106)**
American Soc. of Agricultural Engineers **(106)**
American Soc. of Agronomy **(106)**
American Soc. of Animal Science **(106)**
American Soc. of Farm Managers and Rural Appraisers **(109)**
American Sugar Alliance **(119)**
Animal Transportation Ass'n **(125)**
AOAC Internat'l **(125)**
Aquacultural Engineering Soc. **(126)**
Ass'n for Internat'l Agricultural and Extension Education **(135)**
Ass'n for Living History Farms and Agricultural Museums **(135)**
Ass'n of American Feed Control Officials **(142)**
Ass'n of American Plant Food Control Officials **(143)**
Ass'n of Internat'l Agriculture and Rural Development **(154)**
Ass'n of Official Seed Analysts **(158)**
Ass'n of Official Seed Certifying Agencies **(158)**
Braunvieh Ass'n of America **(181)**
Chemical Producers and Distributors Ass'n **(191)**
Construction and Agricultural Film Manufacturers Film Ass'n **(206)**
Council for Agricultural Science and Technology **(210)**
Cranberry Institute **(218)**
Crop Insurance Research Bureau **(219)**
Crop Science Soc. of America **(219)**
Epsilon Sigma Phi **(232)**
Farm Equipment Manufacturers Ass'n **(235)**
Farmers Educational and Co-operative Union of America **(235)**
Fertilizer Institute **(238)**
Fresh Produce and Floral Council **(244)**
Fresh Produce Ass'n of the Americas **(244)**
Futures Industry Ass'n **(245)**
Hop Growers of America **(256)**
Hydroponic Merchants Ass'n **(257)**
Hydroponic Soc. of America **(257)**
Internat'l Agricultural Aviation Foundation **(272)**
Internat'l Ass'n of Aquaculture Economics and Mangement **(275)**
Internat'l Herb Ass'n **(293)**
Internat'l Union, United Automobile, Aerospace and Agricultural Implement Workers of America **(310)**
Internat'l Weed Science Soc. **(311)**
Irrigation Ass'n **(313)**
Kamut Ass'n of North America **(315)**
Nat'l Agri-Marketing Ass'n **(335)**
Nat'l Agricultural Aviation Ass'n **(335)**
Nat'l Alliance of Independent Crop Consultants **(336)**
Nat'l Aquaculture Council **(337)**
Nat'l Ass'n of Agricultural Fair Agencies **(343)**
Nat'l Ass'n of Agricultural Journalists **(343)**
Nat'l Ass'n of Agriculture Employees **(343)**
Nat'l Ass'n of Colleges and Teachers of Agriculture **(348)**
Nat'l Ass'n of County Agricultural Agents **(350)**
Nat'l Ass'n of Extension 4-H Agents **(354)**
Nat'l Ass'n of FSA County Office Employees **(356)**
Nat'l Ass'n of State Departments of Agriculture **(374)**
Nat'l Ass'n of Wheat Growers **(380)**
Nat'l Block and Bridle Club **(383)**
Nat'l Cattlemen's Beef Ass'n **(386)**
Nat'l Cooperative Business Ass'n **(392)**
Nat'l Council for Agricultural Education **(393)**
Nat'l Council of Agricultural Employers **(394)**
Nat'l Council of Commercial Plant Breeders **(394)**
Nat'l Crop Insurance Services **(398)**
Nat'l Dairy Herd Improvement Ass'n **(399)**
Nat'l Extension Ass'n of Family and Consumer Sciences **(402)**
Nat'l Farmers Organization **(402)**
Nat'l FFA Organization **(404)**
Nat'l Grange **(407)**
Nat'l Grape Growers Cooperative **(407)**
Nat'l Hay Ass'n **(408)**
Nat'l Institute for Farm Safety **(411)**
Nat'l Land Improvement Contractors of America **(414)**
Nat'l Onion Ass'n **(419)**
Nat'l Plant Board **(422)**
Nat'l Postsecondary Agriculture Student Organization **(423)**
Nat'l Potato Council **(423)**
Nat'l Potato Promotion Board **(423)**
Nat'l Sunflower Ass'n **(432)**
Nat'l Vocational Agricultural Educators Ass'n **(435)**
New York Mercantile Exchange **(438)**
North American Agricultural Marketing Officials **(440)**
North American Maple Syrup Council **(443)**
Northeastern Weed Science Soc. **(446)**
Organic Crop Improvement Ass'n Internat'l **(449)**
Organic Growers and Buyers Ass'n **(449)**
Organic Trade Ass'n **(449)**
Organization of Professional Employees of the U.S. Department of Agriculture **(450)**
Potash and Phosphate Institute **(461)**
Shade Tobacco Growers Agricultural Ass'n **(482)**
Soc. for Biomolecular Screening **(486)**
Soc. of Commercial Seed Technologists **(499)**
Soil and Water Conservation Soc. **(510)**
Soil Science Soc. of America **(510)**
Sweet Potato Council of the United States **(519)**
Turf and Ornamental Communicators Ass'n **(527)**
Turfgrass Producers Internat'l **(527)**
U.S.A. Dry Pea and Lentil Council **(528)**
United Fresh Fruit and Vegetable Ass'n **(531)**
United States Apple Export Council **(532)**
United States Canola Ass'n **(532)**
United States Committee on Irrigation and Drainage **(532)**
United States Egg Marketers **(533)**
Weed Science Soc. of America **(542)**
Wheat Quality Council **(543)**
Wild Blueberry Ass'n of North America **(544)**
Women in Agribusiness **(546)**

AGRONOMY
American Heren Ass'n **(73)**
American Soc. of Agronomy **(106)**
Ass'n of Women Soil Scientists **(169)**
Crop Science Soc. of America **(219)**
Forest Farm and Community Tree Network **(242)**
Scottish Blackface Sheep Breeders Ass'n **(480)**
Soil and Plant Analysis Council **(509)**
Soil Science Soc. of America **(510)**
Weed Science Soc. of America **(542)**

AIR CONDITIONING
Air Conditioning Contractors of America **(15)**
Air Diffusion Council **(15)**
Air Distributing Institute **(15)**
Air Movement and Control Ass'n Internat'l **(16)**
Air-Conditioning and Refrigeration Institute **(16)**
Air-Conditioning and Refrigeration Wholesalers Ass'n Internat'l **(16)**
American Soc. of Heating, Refrigerating and Air-Conditioning Engineers **(110)**
Ass'n of Industry Manufacturers' Representatives **(154)**
Associated Air Balance Council **(170)**
Associated Specialty Contractors **(172)**
Cooling Tower Institute **(208)**
Internat'l Ass'n of Heat and Frost Insulators and Asbestos Workers **(279)**
Internat'l District Energy Ass'n **(289)**
Internat'l Ground Source Heat Pump Ass'n **(292)**
Internat'l Mobile Air Conditioning Ass'n **(297)**
Mechanical Service Contractors of America **(326)**
Mobile Air Conditioning Soc. Worldwide **(329)**
Nat'l Air Duct Cleaners Ass'n **(335)**
Nat'l Air Filtration Ass'n **(335)**
Nat'l Ass'n of Power Engineers **(365)**
Northamerican Heating, Refrigeration and Airconditioning Wholesalers Ass'n **(446)**
Plumbing-Heating-Cooling Contractors - Nat'l Ass'n **(459)**
Plumbing-Heating-Cooling Information Bureau **(459)**
Refrigerating Engineers and Technicians Ass'n **(473)**
Sheet Metal and Air Conditioning Contractors' Nat'l Ass'n **(482)**
Solar Energy Industries Ass'n **(510)**

AIR POLLUTION see also POLLUTION
Air and Waste Management Ass'n **(15)**
American Ass'n for Aerosol Research **(29)**
Ass'n of Local Air Pollution Control Officials **(156)**
Institute of Clean Air Companies **(266)**
Manufacturers of Emission Controls Ass'n **(323)**
Nat'l Air Duct Cleaners Ass'n **(335)**
Nat'l Council of the Paper Industry for Air and Stream Improvement **(397)**
Nat'l Spray Equipment Manufacturers Ass'n **(431)**
Professional Ass'n of Custom Clothiers **(464)**
State and Territorial Air Pollution Program Administrators **(515)**

AIRPLANES
Aeronautical Repair Station Ass'n **(13)**
Air Courier Conference of America **(15)**
Airborne Law Enforcement Ass'n **(16)**
Aircraft Electronics Ass'n **(16)**
Aircraft Locknut Manufacturers Ass'n **(16)**
Aircraft Owners and Pilots Ass'n **(16)**
Airline Suppliers Ass'n **(16)**
Aviation Distributors and Manufacturers Ass'n Internat'l **(175)**
Aviation Maintenance Foundation Internat'l **(176)**
Aviation Safety Institute **(176)**
General Aviation Manufacturers Ass'n **(246)**
Helicopter Ass'n Internat'l **(253)**
Internat'l Air Cargo Ass'n **(272)**
Light Aircraft Manufacturers Ass'n **(319)**
Nat'l Aircraft Finance Ass'n **(335)**
Nat'l Aircraft Resale Ass'n **(335)**
Organization of Black Airline Pilots **(450)**
Professional Aviation Maintenance Ass'n **(464)**
Seaplane Pilots Ass'n **(480)**
United States Parachute Ass'n **(534)**

AIRPORTS
Aeronautical Repair Station Ass'n **(13)**
Airport Consultants Council **(17)**
Airport Ground Transportation Ass'n **(17)**
Airports Council Internat'l/North America **(17)**
American Ass'n of Airport Executives **(33)**
Aviation Safety Institute **(176)**
Internat'l Ass'n of Airport Duty Free Stores **(275)**
Nat'l Air Traffic Controllers Ass'n **(335)**

ALLERGY
American Academy of Allergy, Asthma and Immunology **(20)**
American Academy of Otolaryngic Allergy **(24)**
American Ass'n of Certified Allergists **(34)**
American College of Allergy, Asthma and Immunology **(53)**
American In-vitro Allergy/Immunology Soc. **(75)**
Internat'l Ass'n of Allergology and Clinical Immunology **(275)**
Joint Council of Allergy, Asthma and Immunology **(315)**
Soc. for Investigative Dermatology **(490)**
Soc. for Leukocyte Biology **(490)**

ALUMINUM
Aluminum Ass'n **(19)**
Aluminum Extruders Council **(19)**
Aluminum Foil Container Manufacturers Ass'n **(19)**
American Architectural Manufacturers Ass'n **(29)**
Architectural Spray Coaters Ass'n **(127)**
Cookware Manufacturers Ass'n **(208)**
Nat'l Ass'n of Aluminum Distributors **(343)**
Non-Ferrous Founders' Soc. **(439)**
Tube Council of North America **(527)**

AMBULANCES
American Ambulance Ass'n **(28)**
Nat'l Ass'n of Emergency Medical Technicians **(353)**

ANATOMY
American Ass'n of Anatomists **(33)**
American Ass'n of Veterinary Anatomists **(44)**

ANESTHESIOLOGY
American Ass'n of Nurse Anesthetists **(39)**
American Dental Soc. of Anesthesiology **(64)**
American Osteopathic College of Anesthesiologists **(89)**
American Soc. for the Advancement of Anesthesia in Dentistry **(105)**
American Soc. of Anesthesiologists **(106)**
American Soc. of Peri-Anesthesia Nurses **(114)**
American Soc. of Regional Anesthesia **(115)**
Ass'n of University Anesthesiologists **(168)**
Internat'l Anesthesia Research Soc. **(273)**
Soc. for Education in Anesthesia **(487)**
Soc. for Obstetric Anesthesia and Perinatology **(491)**
Soc. for Pediatric Anesthesia **(492)**
Soc. of Cardiovascular Anesthesiologists **(499)**
Soc. of Neurosurgical Anesthesia and Critical Care **(504)**

ANTHROPOLOGY
African Studies Ass'n **(14)**
American Anthropological Ass'n **(28)**
American Ass'n of Physical Anthropologists **(41)**
American Ethnological Soc. **(66)**
American Folklore Soc. **(69)**
American Institute for Archaeological Research **(75)**
American Institute for Maghrib Studies **(76)**
American Quaternary Ass'n **(96)**
American Soc. for Ethnohistory **(102)**
Archaeological Institute of America **(126)**
Ass'n for Feminist Anthropology **(133)**
Ass'n for Political and Legal Anthropology **(136)**
Ass'n for Social Anthropology in Oceania **(137)**
Ass'n for the Study of Play **(139)**
Ass'n of Black Anthropologists **(144)**
Council for Museum Anthropology **(211)**
Council on Nutritional Anthropology **(217)**
Independent Scholars of Asia **(261)**
Internat'l Soc. for the Comparative Studies of Civilizations **(304)**
Nat'l Ass'n for the Practice of Anthropology **(341)**
Soc. for Anthropology in Community Colleges **(485)**
Soc. for Applied Anthropology **(485)**
Soc. for Cross-Cultural Research **(487)**
Soc. for Cultural Anthropology **(487)**
Soc. for Human Ecology **(489)**
Soc. for Humanistic Anthropology **(489)**
Soc. for Latin American Anthropology **(490)**
Soc. for Linguistic Anthropology **(490)**

554 National Trade and Professional Associations of the U.S. © 1999, Columbia Books, Inc.

AUDITORIUM MANAGERS Subject Index

American Soc. for Photogrammetry and Remote Sensing **(104)**
Ass'n for Educational Communications and Technology **(133)**
Ass'n for Recorded Sound Collections **(137)**
Ass'n of Biomedical Communications Directors **(144)**
Ass'n of Cinema and Video Laboratories **(146)**
Ass'n of Independent Video and Filmmakers **(154)**
Ass'n of Moving Image Archivists **(158)**
Audio Engineering Soc. **(172)**
Communications Media Management Ass'n **(200)**
Independent Professional Representatives Organization **(261)**
Interactive Audio Special Interest Group **(271)**
Internat'l Ass'n of Audio Visual Communicators **(276)**
Internat'l Communications Industries Ass'n **(286)**
Internat'l Documentary Ass'n **(289)**
Internat'l Quorum of Film and Video Producers **(301)**
Internat'l Recording Media Ass'n **(301)**
Internat'l Soc. for Performance Improvement **(304)**
Internat'l Soc. of Communication Specialists **(306)**
Internat'l Teleproduction Soc. **(308)**
MIDI Manufacturers Ass'n **(328)**
Nat'l Academy of Recording Arts and Sciences **(334)**
Nat'l Ass'n of Recording Merchandisers **(369)**
Nat'l Ass'n of Regional Media Centers **(369)**
Nat'l Ass'n of Self-Instructional Language Programs **(372)**
Nat'l Systems Contractors Ass'n **(433)**
Online Audiovisual Catalogers **(448)**
Professional Audio-Video Retailers Ass'n **(464)**
Recording Industry Ass'n of America **(472)**
Soc. for Cinema Studies **(486)**
Soc. of Professional Audio Recording Services **(505)**
Training Media Ass'n **(525)**
USITT: Ass'n of Design, Production and Technology Professionals in the Performing Arts and Entertainment **(538)**
Video Software Dealers Ass'n **(539)**

AUDITORIUM MANAGERS
Internat'l Ass'n of Assembly Managers **(276)**

AUTHORS see also PRESS, WRITERS
American Soc. of Composers, Authors and Publishers **(108)**
American Soc. of Journalists and Authors **(111)**
Ass'n of Authors' Representatives **(144)**
Authors Guild **(173)**
Authors League of America **(173)**
Children's Literature Ass'n **(192)**
Council of Literary Magazines and Presses **(214)**
Dramatists Guild **(224)**
Intellectual Property Owners Ass'n **(270)**
Internat'l Food, Wine and Travel Writers Ass'n **(291)**
Nat'l Alliance of Short Story Authors **(336)**
Nat'l Ass'n of Home and Workshop Writers **(358)**
Romance Writers of America **(477)**
Soc. of American Business Editors and Writers **(497)**
Songwriters Guild of America **(510)**
Text and Academic Authors Ass'n **(521)**

AUTOMOBILES see also MOTOR VEHICLES
Alliance of State Car and Truck Renting and Leasing Ass'ns **(18)**
American Internat'l Automobile Dealers Ass'n **(79)**
American Salvage Pool Ass'n **(99)**
Ass'n of Automotive Aftermarket Distributors **(144)**
Ass'n of Finance and Insurance Professionals **(151)**
Ass'n of Internat'l Automobile Manufacturers **(154)**
Autobody Representatives Council **(173)**
Automobile Dealers Ass'n **(174)**
Automotive Chemical Manufacturers Council **(174)**
Automotive Industry Action Group **(174)**
Automotive Maintenance and Repair Ass'n **(174)**
Automotive Presidents Council **(175)**
Automotive Public Relations Council **(175)**
Automotive Refrigeration Products Institute **(175)**
Automotive Service Ass'n **(175)**
Automotive Training Managers Council **(175)**
Automotive Wholesalers Ass'n Executives **(175)**
Collector Car Appraisers Internat'l **(197)**
Convenient Automotive Services Institute **(208)**
Driving School Ass'n of America **(224)**
Gasoline and Automotive Service Dealers Ass'n **(246)**
Heavy Duty Brake Manufacturers Council **(253)**
Inter-Industry Conference on Auto Collision Repair **(271)**
Internat'l Ass'n of Auto Theft Investigators **(276)**
Internat'l Manufacturers Representatives Ass'n **(296)**
Liability Insurance Research Bureau **(319)**
Limousine Industry Manufacturers Organization **(320)**
Nat'l Ass'n of Fleet Resale Dealers **(355)**
Nat'l Ass'n of Minority Automobile Dealers **(363)**
Nat'l Automobile Transporters Ass'n **(381)**
Nat'l Independent Automobile Dealers Ass'n **(410)**
Nat'l Limousine Ass'n **(415)**
Nat'l Mobility Equipment Dealers Ass'n **(417)**
Nat'l Motorsports Press Ass'n **(417)**
Nat'l Vehicle Leasing Ass'n **(435)**
Original Equipment Suppliers Association - MEMA **(450)**
Performance Warehouse Ass'n **(455)**
Soc. of Automotive Analysts **(498)**
Spring Research Institute **(515)**
Truck Manufacturers Ass'n **(527)**

AVIATION
Aerial Firefighting Industry Ass'n **(13)**
Aeronautical Navigator Ass'n **(13)**
Air and Expedited Motor Carriers Conference **(15)**
Air Force Ass'n **(15)**
Air Line Employees Ass'n, International **(15)**
Air Line Pilots Ass'n, Internat'l **(16)**
Air Traffic Control Ass'n **(16)**
Air Transport Ass'n of America **(16)**
Airline Industrial Relations Conference **(16)**
Airport Consultants Council **(17)**
American Helicopter Soc. **(73)**
American Soc. for Photogrammetry and Remote Sensing **(104)**
Army Aviation Ass'n of America **(127)**
Ass'n of Aviation Psychologists **(144)**
Ass'n of Flight Attendants **(151)**
Ass'n of Naval Aviation **(158)**
Aviation Distributors and Manufacturers Ass'n Internat'l **(175)**
Aviation Insurance Ass'n **(176)**
Aviation Maintenance Foundation Internat'l **(176)**
Aviation Safety Institute **(176)**
Aviation Technician Education Council **(176)**
Civil Aviation Medical Ass'n **(194)**
Flight Engineers' Internat'l Ass'n **(240)**
Flight Safety Foundation **(240)**
General Aviation Manufacturers Ass'n **(246)**
Helicopter Ass'n Internat'l **(253)**
Internat'l Agricultural Aviation Foundation **(272)**
Internat'l Aviation Women Ass'n **(283)**
Internat'l Council of Air Shows **(287)**
Internat'l Soc. of Air Safety Investigators **(305)**
Internat'l Soc. of Transport Aircraft Trading **(307)**
Nat'l Agricultural Aviation Ass'n **(335)**
Nat'l Air Carrier Ass'n **(335)**
Nat'l Air Traffic Controllers Ass'n **(335)**
Nat'l Air Transportation Ass'n **(335)**
Nat'l Ass'n of Air Communications Specialists **(343)**
Nat'l Ass'n of Flight Instructors **(355)**
Nat'l Ass'n of State Aviation Officials **(374)**
Nat'l Cargo Security Council **(385)**
Nat'l EMS Pilots Ass'n **(401)**
Organization of Flying Adjusters **(450)**
Professional Aeromedical Transport Ass'n **(464)**
Professional Aviation Maintenance Ass'n **(464)**
Real Estate Aviation Chapter **(472)**
Regional Airline Ass'n **(473)**
SAFE Ass'n **(478)**
Seaplane Pilots Ass'n **(480)**
Soc. of Experimental Test Pilots **(501)**
Soc. of Flight Test Engineers **(501)**
Transportation . Communications Internat'l Union **(525)**
Travel Industry Ass'n of America **(526)**
United States Air Tour Ass'n **(532)**
University Aviation Ass'n **(537)**
Women in Aviation Internat'l **(546)**
World Airline Entertainment Ass'n **(549)**

BACTERIOLOGY
American Soc. for Investigative Pathology **(103)**
American Soc. for Microbiology **(104)**
Soc. for In Vitro Biology **(489)**

BAGS see also BOXES, CONTAINERS
Retail Packaging Manufacturers Ass'n **(476)**
Textile Bag and Packaging Ass'n **(522)**
Textile Bag Manufacturers Ass'n **(522)**

BAKING
Allied Trades of the Baking Industry **(18)**
American Bakers Ass'n **(46)**
American Soc. of Baking **(107)**
Bakery, Confectionery and Tobacco Workers' Internat'l Union **(176)**
Baking Industry Sanitation Standards Committee **(176)**
BEMA - An Internat'l Ass'n Serving the Baking and Food Industries **(178)**
Biscuit and Cracker Manufacturers' Ass'n **(179)**
Cookie and Snack Bakers Ass'n **(208)**
Independent Bakers Ass'n **(259)**
Nat'l Ass'n of Flour Distributors **(355)**
Nat'l Frozen Pizza Institute **(406)**
Quality Bakers of America Cooperative **(470)**
Retailer's Bakery Ass'n **(476)**
Wholesale Variety Bakers Ass'n **(544)**

BANDS see also MUSIC
American Bandmasters Ass'n **(46)**
American Musicians Union **(86)**
American School Band Directors' Ass'n **(99)**
Ass'n of Concert Bands **(148)**
College Band Directors Nat'l Ass'n **(197)**
Nat'l Ass'n of Band Instrument Manufacturers **(344)**
Nat'l Ass'n of Professional Band Instrument Repair Technicians **(366)**
Nat'l Band Ass'n **(382)**
Nat'l Catholic Band Ass'n **(385)**

BANKING see also FINANCE, INVESTMENTS, SAVINGS & LOAN, SECURITIES INDUSTRY
American Ass'n of Bank Directors **(33)**
American Bankers Ass'n **(46)**
American Bankruptcy Institute **(46)**
American Finance Ass'n **(68)**
American Safe Deposit Ass'n **(98)**
Ass'n for Financial Technology **(133)**
Ass'n for Management Information in Financial Services **(136)**
Ass'n of Financial Services Holding Companies **(151)**
Ass'n of Independent Trust Companies **(154)**
Ass'n of Military Banks of America **(157)**
Bank Administration Institute **(176)**
Bank Marketing Ass'n **(176)**
Bankers Roundtable, The **(176)**
Bankers' Ass'n for Foreign Trade **(176)**
Community Banking Advisory Network **(201)**
Conference of State Bank Supervisors **(204)**
Consumer Bankers Ass'n **(207)**
Electronic Funds Transfer Ass'n **(228)**
Environmental Bankers Ass'n **(231)**
Financial Markets Ass'n **(239)**
Financial Stationers Ass'n **(239)**
Financial Women Internat'l **(239)**
Forex U.S.A.: the Financial Markets Ass'n **(243)**
Independent Bankers Ass'n of America **(260)**
Institute of Internat'l Bankers **(267)**
Internat'l Financial Services Ass'n **(291)**
Mastercard Internat'l **(324)**
Mortgage Bankers Ass'n of America **(330)**
Nat'l Ass'n for Check Safekeeping **(338)**
Nat'l Ass'n of Affordable Housing Lenders **(342)**
Nat'l Ass'n of Bankruptcy Trustees **(344)**
Nat'l Ass'n of Freight Payment Banks **(356)**
Nat'l Ass'n of Government Guaranteed Lenders **(357)**
Nat'l Ass'n of Mortgage Brokers **(363)**
Nat'l Ass'n of Professional Mortgage Women **(367)**
Nat'l Ass'n of Urban Bankers **(379)**
Nat'l Bankers Ass'n **(382)**
Nat'l Council for Uniform Interest Compensation **(393)**
Nat'l Home Equity Mortgage Ass'n **(409)**
Nat'l Independent Bank Equipment and Systems Ass'n **(410)**
Nat'l Marine Bankers Ass'n **(416)**
Nat'l Real Estate Forum **(424)**
Robert Morris Associates, the Ass'n of Lending and Credit Risk Professionals **(476)**
Securities Industry Ass'n **(481)**

BARBERS
American Beauty Ass'n **(47)**
Hair Internat'l **(250)**
Intercoiffure America **(271)**
Nat'l Cosmetology Ass'n **(392)**

BARRELS
Ass'n of Container Reconditioners **(148)**
Associated Cooperage Industries of America **(171)**
Steel Shipping Container Institute **(517)**

BASEBALL
American Baseball Coaches Ass'n **(46)**
American League of Professional Baseball Clubs **(81)**
Ass'n of Professional Ball Players of America **(160)**
Baseball Writers Ass'n of America **(177)**
Internat'l League of Professional Baseball Clubs **(296)**
Major League Baseball - Office of the Commissioner **(322)**
Major League Baseball Players Ass'n **(322)**
Major League Umpires Ass'n **(322)**
Nat'l Ass'n of Leagues, Umpires and Scorers **(361)**
Nat'l Ass'n of Professional Baseball Leagues **(366)**
Nat'l League of Professional Baseball Clubs **(415)**
Professional Baseball Athletic Trainers' Ass'n **(465)**
Soc. for American Baseball Research **(485)**

BASKETBALL
American Basketball League **(47)**
Continental Basketball Ass'n **(207)**
Internat'l Ass'n of Approved Basketball Officials **(275)**
Nat'l Ass'n of Basketball Coaches **(344)**
Nat'l Basketball Ass'n **(382)**
Nat'l Basketball Players Ass'n **(382)**
Nat'l Basketball Referees Ass'n **(382)**
Nat'l Basketball Trainers' Ass'n **(382)**
Professional Basketball Writers' Ass'n **(465)**
United States Basketball Writers Ass'n **(532)**
Women's Basketball Coaches Ass'n **(547)**

BATTERIES
American Ass'n for Fuel Cells **(30)**
Battery Council Internat'l **(177)**
Independent Battery Manufacturers Ass'n **(260)**
Portable Rechargeable Battery Ass'n **(460)**

BEARINGS
American Bearing Manufacturing Ass'n **(47)**
Bearing Specialist Ass'n **(177)**
Vibration Institute **(539)**

BEER
Beer Institute **(177)**
Home Wine and Beer Trade Ass'n **(256)**
Institute for Brewing Studies **(265)**
Master Brewers Ass'n of the Americas **(324)**
Nat'l Ass'n of Beverage Importers-Wine-Spirits-Beer **(344)**
Nat'l Beer Wholesalers Ass'n **(382)**
Wholesale Beer Ass'n Executives of America **(543)**

BEES
American Apitherapy Soc. **(28)**
American Beekeeping Federation **(47)**
Apiary Inspectors of America **(125)**

BELTS
Belt Ass'n **(178)**
Nat'l Industrial Belting Ass'n **(410)**

BETTER BUSINESS BUREAUS
Council of Better Business Bureaus **(212)**

BEVERAGE INDUSTRY
American Beverage Institute **(47)**
Beer Institute **(177)**
Beverage Network **(178)**
Distilled Spirits Council of the U.S. **(223)**
Flavor and Extract Manufacturers Ass'n of the United States **(240)**
Internat'l Beverage Dispensing Equipment Ass'n **(283)**
Internat'l Bottled Water Ass'n **(283)**
Internat'l Institute of Ammonia Refrigeration **(294)**
Internat'l Soc. of Beverage Technologists **(305)**
Nat'l Alcohol Beverage Control Ass'n **(335)**
Nat'l Ass'n of Bar and Tavern Owners **(344)**
Nat'l Ass'n of Beverage Importers-Wine-Spirits-Beer **(344)**
Nat'l Beverage Packaging Ass'n **(382)**
Nat'l Coffee Ass'n of the U.S.A. **(387)**
Nat'l Coffee Service Ass'n **(387)**
Nat'l Soft Drink Ass'n **(430)**
Nat'l United Affiliated Beverage Ass'n **(435)**
Specialty Coffee Ass'n of America **(514)**
Tea Ass'n of the United States of America **(520)**
Tea Council of the U.S.A. **(520)**

556 National Trade and Professional Associations of the U.S. © 1999, Columbia Books, Inc.

CAMPING

CANCER

CANS

CARDIOLOGY

CARPETS see also RUGS

CARWASH

CATHOLIC

CATS

CATTLE

CEMETERIES see also FUNERALS

CERAMICS see also CHINA

CHAINS

CHAMBER OF COMMERCE

Subject Index *CLUBS see also FRATERNAL ORGANIZATIONS*

American-Southern Africa Chamber of Trade and Industry **(124)**
American-Uzbekistan Chamber of Commerce **(124)**
Argentina-American Chamber of Commerce **(127)**
Ass'n of Applied Community Researchers **(143)**
Belgian American Chamber of Commerce in the United States **(178)**
Brazilian American Chamber of Commerce **(182)**
British-American Chamber of Commerce **(182)**
Chamber of Commerce of the Apparel Industry **(190)**
Chamber of Commerce of the United States of America **(190)**
Colombian American Ass'n **(198)**
Council of Better Business Bureaus **(212)**
Council of State Chambers of Commerce **(215)**
Danish-American Chamber of Commerce (USA) **(220)**
Ecuadorean American Ass'n **(226)**
European-American Business Council **(233)**
Finnish American Chamber of Commerce **(239)**
French-American Chamber of Commerce **(244)**
German American Chamber of Commerce **(247)**
Hellenic-American Chamber of Commerce **(253)**
Icelandic American Chamber of Commerce **(258)**
India-American Chamber of Commerce (N.Y.) **(262)**
Internat'l Downtown Ass'n **(289)**
Ireland Chamber of Commerce in the United States **(312)**
Italy-America Chamber of Commerce **(313)**
Latin Chamber of Commerce of U.S.A. **(317)**
Nat'l Ass'n for Membership Development **(340)**
Nat'l Black Chamber of Commerce **(383)**
Nat'l U.S.-Arab Chamber of Commerce **(435)**
Netherlands Chamber of Commerce in the United States **(438)**
North American-Chilean Chamber of Commerce **(446)**
Norwegian-American Chamber of Commerce **(446)**
Philippine-American Chamber of Commerce **(457)**
Portugal-United States Chamber of Commerce **(461)**
Romanian-American Chamber of Commerce **(477)**
Spain-U.S. Chamber of Commerce **(511)**
Swedish-American Chamber of Commerce **(519)**
United States Council for Internat'l Business **(533)**
United States Hispanic Chamber of Commerce **(534)**
United States Junior Chamber of Commerce **(534)**
United States-Austrian Chamber of Commerce **(536)**
United States-Mexico Chamber of Commerce **(536)**
United States-New Zealand Council **(536)**
Venezuelan American Ass'n of the U.S. **(539)**

CHAPLAINS
American Catholic Correctional Chaplains Ass'n **(50)**
Ass'n of Professional Chaplains **(160)**
Catholic Campus Ministry Ass'n **(188)**
Congress on Ministry in Specialized Settings **(205)**
JWB Jewish Chaplains Council **(315)**
Military Chaplains Ass'n of the U.S. **(328)**
Nat'l Ass'n of Catholic Chaplains **(346)**
Nat'l Catholic Conference of Airport Chaplains **(385)**

CHEMICALS & CHEMICAL INDUSTRY
Acrylonitrile Group **(11)**
Agricultural Retailers Ass'n **(14)**
Alkyl Amines Council **(17)**
Alliance for Responsible Atmospheric Policy **(17)**
Alpha Chi Sigma **(18)**
American Ass'n for Clinical Chemistry **(30)**
American Ass'n of Cereal Chemists **(34)**
American Ass'n of Textile Chemists and Colorists **(44)**
American Chemical Soc. **(51)**
American Coke and Coal Chemicals Institute **(52)**
American College of Toxicology **(58)**
American Crop Protection Ass'n **(62)**
American Fiber Manufacturers Ass'n **(68)**
American Hydrogen Ass'n **(74)**
American Industrial Health Council **(75)**
American Institute of Chemical Engineers **(77)**
American Institute of Chemists **(77)**
American Leather Chemists Ass'n **(81)**
American Methanol Institute **(84)**
American Oil Chemists' Soc. **(88)**
American Soc. for Biochemistry and Molecular Biology **(101)**
American Soc. for Mass Spectrometry **(104)**
American Soc. for Neurochemistry **(104)**
American Soc. of Brewing Chemists **(107)**
Aniline Ass'n **(124)**
AOAC Internat'l **(125)**
Aspirin Foundation of America **(129)**
Ass'n of Analytical Chemists **(143)**
Ass'n of Consulting Chemists and Chemical Engineers **(148)**
Ass'n of Defensive Spray Manufacturers **(149)**
Ass'n of Official Racing Chemists **(158)**
Automotive Chemical Manufacturers Council **(174)**
Basic Acrylic Monomer Manufacturers Ass'n **(177)**
Chemical Coaters Ass'n Internat'l **(191)**
Chemical Communications Ass'n **(191)**
Chemical Fabrics and Film Ass'n **(191)**
Chemical Industry Institute of Toxicology **(191)**
Chemical Management and Resources Ass'n **(191)**
Chemical Manufacturers Ass'n **(191)**
Chemical Producers and Distributors Ass'n **(191)**
Chemical Sources Ass'n **(191)**
Chemical Specialties Manufacturers Ass'n **(191)**
Chlorinated Paraffins Industry Ass'n **(192)**
Chlorine Chemistry Council **(192)**
Chlorine Institute **(193)**
Chlorobenzene Producers Ass'n **(193)**
Color Pigments Manufacturers Ass'n **(198)**
Combustion Institute **(198)**
Commercial Development Ass'n **(198)**
Council for Chemical Research **(211)**
Dibasic Esters Group **(222)**
Diethyl Ether Producers Ass'n **(222)**
Drug, Chemical and Allied Trades Ass'n **(225)**
Electrochemical Soc. **(228)**
Emulsion Polymers Council **(230)**
Ethylene Oxide Sterilization Ass'n **(233)**
Federation of Analytical Chemistry and Spectroscopy Societies **(236)**
Federation of Socs. for Coatings Technology **(237)**
Fertilizer Institute **(238)**
Fire Retardant Chemicals Ass'n **(240)**
Geochemical Soc. **(246)**
Halogenated Solvents Industry Alliance **(250)**
Halon Alternatives Research Corp. **(251)**
Histochemical Soc. **(254)**
Hydrogen Industry Council **(257)**
Independent Liquid Terminals Ass'n **(261)**
Industrial Chemical Research Ass'n **(262)**
Institute for Polyacrylate Absorbents **(265)**
Internat'l Cartridge Recycling Ass'n **(285)**
Internat'l Chemical Workers Union Council/UFCW **(285)**
Internat'l Glutamate Technical Committee **(292)**
Internat'l Ozone Ass'n-Pan American Group Branch **(299)**
Materials Marketing Associates **(325)**
Materials Technology Institute of the Chemical Process Industries **(325)**
Methacrylate Producers Ass'n **(327)**
Nat'l Aerosol Ass'n **(335)**
Nat'l Ass'n of Chemical Distributors **(347)**
Nat'l Ass'n of Chemical Recyclers **(347)**
Nat'l Ass'n of Gas Chlorinators **(356)**
Nat'l Pest Control Ass'n **(422)**
North American Catalysis Soc. **(441)**
Northeastern Weed Science Soc. **(446)**
Oil, Chemical and Atomic Workers Internat'l Union **(448)**
Oxygenated Fuels Ass'n **(452)**
Phosphate Chemicals Export Ass'n **(457)**
Photo Chemical Machining Institute **(457)**
Pine Chemicals Ass'n **(458)**
Polyisocyanurate Insulation Manufacturers Ass'n **(460)**
Polymer Particulate Inhalation Group **(460)**
Polyurethane Foam Ass'n **(460)**
Powder Coating Institute **(461)**
Process Equipment Manufacturers' Ass'n **(463)**
Professional Lawn Care Ass'n of America **(466)**
Sales Ass'n of the Chemical Industry **(478)**
SB Latex Council **(479)**
Silicones Environmental Health and Safety Council of North America **(483)**
Soc. for Environmental Geochemistry and Health **(487)**
Soc. of Cosmetic Chemists **(500)**
Soc. of Environmental Toxicology and Chemistry **(501)**
Soc. of Mineral Analysts **(504)**
Soc. of Toxicology **(508)**
Soil and Plant Analysis Council **(509)**
Solution Mining Research Institute **(510)**
Spill Control Ass'n of America **(514)**
Suppliers of Advanced Composite Materials Ass'n **(510)**
Synthetic Amorphous Silica and Silicates Industry Ass'n **(519)**
Synthetic Organic Chemical Manufacturers Ass'n **(519)**
Tetrahydrofuran Task Force **(521)**
Tributyl Phosphate Task Force **(526)**
Tubular Exchanger Manufacturers Ass'n **(527)**
United States Dye Manufacturers Operating Committee of ETAD **(533)**
Vinyl Acetate Toxicology Group **(539)**

CHILDREN
American Academy of Pediatric Dentistry **(25)**
American Ass'n of Children's Residential Centers **(34)**
American Ass'n of Early Childhood Educators **(36)**
American Professional Soc. on the Abuse of Children **(94)**
American Soc. of Pediatric Nephrology **(114)**
Ass'n for Child Psychoanalysis **(130)**
Ass'n for Childhood Education Internat'l **(131)**
Ass'n for the Care of Children's Health **(139)**
Ass'n of Administrators of the Interstate Compact on the Placement of Children **(141)**
Ass'n of Child and Adolescent Psychiatric Nurses **(146)**
Ass'n of Jewish Family and Children's Agencies **(155)**
Ass'n of Youth Museums **(170)**
Child Neurology Soc. **(192)**
Child Welfare League of America **(192)**
Children's Book Council **(192)**
Children's Literature Ass'n **(192)**
Childrenswear Marketing Ass'n **(192)**
Choristers Guild **(193)**
Council for Early Childhood Professional Recognition **(211)**
Council for Exceptional Children **(211)**
Foster Family-Based Treatment Ass'n **(243)**
Infant and Juvenile Manufacturers Ass'n **(263)**
Infants', Children's and Girls' Sportswear and Coat Ass'n **(263)**
Internat'l Academy for Child Brain Development **(272)**
Internat'l Nanny Ass'n **(298)**
Jewish Social Service Professionals Ass'n **(314)**
Nat'l Ass'n for Creative Children and Adults **(338)**
Nat'l Ass'n for Family Child Care **(339)**
Nat'l Ass'n for the Education of Young Children **(341)**
Nat'l Ass'n of Child Advocates **(347)**
Nat'l Ass'n of Child Care Professionals **(347)**
Nat'l Ass'n of Child Care Resource and Referral Agencies **(347)**
Nat'l Ass'n of Children's Hospitals and Related Institutions **(347)**
Nat'l Ass'n of Counsel for Children **(350)**
Nat'l Ass'n of Private Schools for Exceptional Children **(366)**
Nat'l Ass'n of Public Child Welfare Administrators **(367)**
Nat'l Ass'n of Student Assistance Professional **(377)**
Nat'l Child Care Ass'n **(386)**
Nat'l Child Transport Ass'n **(386)**
Nat'l Fellowship of Child Care Executives **(404)**
Nat'l Guardianship Ass'n **(408)**
Parenting Publications of America **(453)**
Soc. for Adolescent Medicine **(484)**
Soc. for Research in Child Development **(493)**
Soc. for Research on Adolescence **(493)**
Soc. of Children's Book Writers and Illustrators **(499)**
Teaching-Family Ass'n **(520)**
U.S.A. Toy Library Ass'n **(529)**
World Ass'n for Infant Mental Health **(549)**

CHINA see also CERAMICS
American Fine China Guild **(68)**
American Restaurant China Council **(98)**
Giftware Associates Interchange **(247)**
Nat'l Tabletop and Giftware Ass'n **(433)**

CHINESE
American Ass'n for Chinese Studies **(30)**
Ass'n for Asian Studies **(130)**
Chinese Language Teachers Ass'n **(192)**
Chinese-American Librarians Ass'n **(192)**
United States-China Business Council **(536)**

CHIROPRACTORS
American Chiropractic Ass'n **(51)**
American Chiropractic Registry of Radiologic Technologists **(51)**
American College of Chiropractic Orthopedists **(53)**
Ass'n of Chiropractic Colleges **(146)**
Congress of Chiropractic State Ass'ns **(205)**
Council on Chiropractic Education **(216)**
Council on Chiropractic Orthopedics **(216)**
Council on Chiropractic Physiological Therapeutics and Rehabilitation **(216)**
Council on Diagnostic Imaging to the A.C.A. **(216)**
Federation of Straight Chiropractors and Organizations **(238)**
Internat'l Chiropractors Ass'n **(285)**

CHOCOLATE
American Cocoa Research Institute **(52)**
Chocolate Manufacturers Ass'n of the U.S.A. **(193)**
Cocoa Merchants' Ass'n of America **(196)**
Nat'l Candy Brokers Ass'n **(385)**

CIRCULATION
Internat'l Newspaper Marketing Ass'n **(298)**

CLAY
American Ceramic Soc. **(51)**
Brick Industry Ass'n **(182)**
Clay Minerals Soc. **(194)**
Expanded Shale, Clay and Slate Institute **(234)**
Nat'l Clay Pipe Institute **(387)**
Nat'l Clay Pot Manufacturers Ass'n **(387)**
Refractories Institute **(473)**
Sorptive Minerals Institute **(510)**
Stucco Manufacturers Ass'n **(517)**
Tile Council of America **(523)**

CLEANERS
Appliance Parts Distributors Ass'n **(126)**
Ass'n of Specialists in Cleaning and Restoration Internat'l **(165)**
Building Service Contractors Ass'n Internat'l **(183)**
Cleaning Equipment Trade Ass'n **(194)**
Cleaning Management Institute **(194)**
Coin Laundry Ass'n **(196)**
Internat'l Drycleaners Congress **(289)**
Internat'l Fabricare Institute **(290)**
Internat'l Kitchen Exhaust Cleaning Ass'n **(295)**
Internat'l Maintenance Institute **(296)**
Internat'l Soc. of Cleaning Technicians **(306)**
Internat'l Window Cleaning Ass'n **(311)**
Laundry and Dry Cleaning Internat'l Union **(317)**
Multi-Housing Laundry Ass'n **(331)**
Nat'l Ass'n of Diaper Services **(352)**
Nat'l Ass'n of Institutional Linen Management **(360)**
Nat'l Chimney Sweep Guild **(386)**
Neighborhood Cleaners Ass'n-Internat'l **(438)**
Power Washers of North America **(461)**
Secondary Materials and Recycled Textiles Ass'n **(480)**
Soap and Detergent Ass'n **(484)**
Textile Care Allied Trades Ass'n **(522)**
Textile Processors, Service Trades, Health Care, Professional and Technical Employees Internat'l Union **(522)**
Textile Rental Services Ass'n of America **(522)**
Uniform and Textile Service Ass'n **(529)**
Vacuum Cleaner Manufacturers Ass'n **(538)**

CLUBS see also FRATERNAL ORGANIZATIONS
Alpha Chi Sigma **(18)**
Alpha Kappa Psi **(19)**
Alpha Omega Internat'l Dental Fraternity **(19)**
Alpha Zeta Omega **(19)**
American Community Cultural Center Ass'n **(59)**
American Dental Interfraternity Council **(64)**
Ass'n of College Honor Societies **(147)**
Ass'n of Faculty Clubs Internat'l **(150)**
Automotive Booster Clubs Internat'l **(174)**
Beta Alpha Psi **(178)**
Beta Phi Mu **(178)**
Business and Professional Women/USA **(184)**
Club Managers Ass'n of America **(195)**
College Fraternity Editors Ass'n **(197)**
Continental Dorset Club **(208)**
Delta Omicron Foundation, Inc. **(221)**
Delta Pi Epsilon **(221)**
Delta Sigma Delta **(221)**
Delta Sigma Pi **(221)**
Delta Theta Phi **(221)**
Distributive Education Clubs of America **(224)**
Fraternity Executives Ass'n **(244)**
Gamma Iota Sigma **(245)**
General Federation of Women's Clubs **(246)**
Girls Incorporated **(247)**
Internat'l Council for Computer Communication **(287)**
Internat'l Health, Racquet and Sportsclub Ass'n **(293)**
Internat'l League of Professional Baseball Clubs **(296)**
Internat'l Military Community Executives Ass'n **(297)**
Internat'l Pot and Kettle Club **(300)**
Iota Tau Tau **(312)**

National Trade and Professional Associations of the U.S. © 1999, Columbia Books, Inc. 559

COACHES

COAL

COLOR

COMMODITIES

COMMUNICATIONS

COMPOSERS

COMPTROLLERS

COMPUTERS see also DATA PROCESSING

CONCRETE

CONFECTIONERS

CONTAINERS see also BAGS, BOXES, CANS   Subject Index

Ass'n for Consumer Research **(131)**
Consumer Credit Insurance Ass'n **(207)**
Consumer Federation of America **(207)**
Electricity Consumers Resource Council **(228)**
Insurance Consumer Affairs Exchange **(270)**
Nat'l Ass'n of Consumer Advocates **(349)**
Nat'l Ass'n of Consumer Agency Administrators **(349)**
Nat'l Ass'n of State Utility Consumer Advocates **(376)**
Nat'l Consumers League **(392)**
Ombudsman Ass'n, The **(448)**
Soc. of Consumer Affairs Professionals in Business **(500)**

CONTAINERS see also BAGS, BOXES, CANS
Aluminum Foil Container Manufacturers Ass'n **(19)**
Ass'n of Container Reconditioners **(148)**
Ass'n of Independent Corrugated Converters **(153)**
Closure Manufacturers Ass'n **(195)**
Compressed Gas Ass'n **(202)**
Containerization and Intermodal Institute **(207)**
Fibre Box Ass'n **(238)**
Flexible Intermediate Bulk Container Ass'n **(240)**
Foodservice and Packaging Institute **(242)**
Glass Packaging Institute **(247)**
Internat'l Fibre Drum Institute **(291)**
Nat'l Ass'n of Container Distributors **(349)**
Nat'l Food Processors Ass'n **(405)**
Nat'l Wooden Pallet and Container Ass'n **(437)**
Paper Shipping Sack Manufacturers Ass'n **(453)**
Paperboard Packaging Council **(453)**
Plastic Shipping Container Institute **(459)**
Pressure Vessel Manufacturers Ass'n **(462)**
Research and Development Associates for Military Food and Packaging Systems **(475)**
Steel Shipping Container Institute **(517)**

CONTRACTORS
ADSC: The Internat'l Ass'n of Foundation Drilling **(12)**
Air Conditioning Contractors of America **(15)**
American Subcontractors Ass'n **(118)**
American Surety Ass'n **(119)**
Ass'n of Bituminous Contractors **(144)**
Ass'n of the Wall and Ceiling Industries-Internat'l **(167)**
Associated Builders and Contractors **(170)**
Associated General Contractors of America **(171)**
Associated Landscape Contractors of America **(171)**
Associated Specialty Contractors **(172)**
Building Service Contractors Ass'n Internat'l **(183)**
Ceilings and Interior Systems Construction Ass'n **(189)**
Certified Contractors NetWork **(190)**
Concrete Foundations Ass'n **(203)**
Concrete Modifications Contractors Ass'n **(203)**
Construction and Agricultural Film Manufacturers Film Ass'n **(206)**
Contract Services Ass'n of America **(208)**
Directional Crossing Contractors Ass'n **(223)**
Engineering Contractors' Ass'n **(230)**
Exposition Service Contractors Ass'n **(234)**
Floor Covering Installation Contractors Ass'n **(240)**
Greater Clothing Contractors Ass'n **(249)**
Gunite/Shotcrete Contractors Ass'n **(250)**
Highway Sign Support Ass'n **(254)**
Independent Electrical Contractors **(260)**
Independent Professional Painting Contractors Ass'n of America **(261)**
Instrument Contracting and Engineering Ass'n **(269)**
Insulation Contractors Ass'n of America **(270)**
Internat'l Ass'n of Cold Storage Contractors **(277)**
Internat'l Ass'n of Geophysical Contractors **(279)**
Internat'l Ass'n of Lighting Management Companies **(280)**
Internat'l Concrete Repair Institute **(286)**
Internat'l Council of Employers of Bricklayers and Allied Craftworkers **(287)**
Internat'l Institute for Lath and Plaster **(294)**
Ladies Apparel Contractors Ass'n **(316)**
Mason Contractors Ass'n of America **(324)**
Mechanical Contractors Ass'n of America **(326)**
Mechanical Service Contractors of America **(326)**
Nat'l Ass'n of Demolition Contractors **(352)**
Nat'l Ass'n of Minority Contractors **(363)**
Nat'l Ass'n of Miscellaneous, Ornamental and Architectural Products Contractors **(363)**
Nat'l Ass'n of Reinforcing Steel Contractors **(370)**
Nat'l Ass'n of Solar Contractors **(373)**
Nat'l Ass'n of Waterproofing Contractors **(380)**
Nat'l Certified Pipe Welding Bureau **(386)**
Nat'l Constructors Ass'n **(392)**
Nat'l Contract Management Ass'n **(392)**
Nat'l Council of Erectors, Fabricators and Riggers **(394)**
Nat'l Drilling Ass'n **(400)**
Nat'l Electrical Contractors Ass'n **(400)**
Nat'l Environmental Balancing Bureau **(401)**
Nat'l Insulation Ass'n **(412)**
Nat'l Land Improvement Contractors of America **(414)**
Nat'l Property Management Ass'n **(424)**
Nat'l Roof Deck Contractors Ass'n **(426)**
Nat'l Roofing Contractors Ass'n **(426)**
Nat'l School Transportation Ass'n **(427)**
Nat'l Tile Contractors Ass'n **(433)**
North American Soc. of Scaffold Professionals **(445)**
Painting and Decorating Contractors of America **(452)**
Pile Driving Contractors Ass'n **(458)**
Pipe Line Contractors Ass'n **(458)**
Plumbing-Heating-Cooling Contractors - Nat'l Ass'n **(459)**
Scaffold Industry Ass'n **(479)**
Sealant, Waterproofing and Restoration Institute **(480)**
Sheet Metal and Air Conditioning Contractors' Nat'l Ass'n **(482)**
Subcontractors Trade Ass'n **(517)**
Swimming Pool Trades and Contractors Ass'n **(519)**
Tile Contractors' Ass'n of America **(523)**
United Ass'n of Equipment Leasing **(530)**
Waterproofing Contractors Ass'n **(541)**

CONVENTIONS see also EXHIBITS
American Buyers of Meeting and Incentive Travel **(50)**
American Federation of Astrologers **(66)**
Ass'n for Convention Marketing Executives **(132)**
Ass'n for Convention Operations Management **(132)**
Ass'n of Collegiate Conference and Events Directors Internat'l **(148)**
Ass'n of Destination Management Executives **(149)**
Ass'n of Meeting Professionals **(157)**
Center for Exhibition Industry Research **(189)**
Connected Int'l Meeting Professionals Ass'n **(206)**
Convention Liaison Council **(208)**
Council of Protocol Executives **(215)**
Electronic Distribution Show Corporation **(228)**
Exposition Service Contractors Ass'n **(234)**
Foundation for Internat'l Meetings **(243)**
Insurance Conference Planners Ass'n **(270)**
Internat'l Ass'n for Modular Exhibitry **(274)**
Internat'l Ass'n of Assembly Managers **(276)**
Internat'l Ass'n of Conference Center Administrators **(277)**
Internat'l Ass'n of Conference Centers **(277)**
Internat'l Ass'n of Convention and Visitor Bureaus **(277)**
Internat'l Special Events Soc. **(307)**
Meeting Professionals Internat'l **(327)**
Nat'l Ass'n of Reunion Managers **(370)**
Nat'l Coalition of Black Meeting Planners **(387)**
North American Farm Show Council **(442)**
Professional Convention Management Ass'n **(465)**
Professional Show Managers Ass'n **(467)**
Religious Conference Management Ass'n **(474)**
Soc. of Corporate Meeting Professionals **(500)**
Soc. of Independent Show Organizers **(503)**

COOKING
American Culinary Federation **(63)**
Internat'l Ass'n of Culinary Professionals **(278)**
Internat'l Food Service Executives' Ass'n **(291)**
Nat'l Ass'n of Catering Executives **(346)**
Nat'l Barbecue Ass'n **(382)**
Women Chefs and Restaurateurs **(545)**

COOPERATIVES
ACL - Ass'n for Consortium Leadership **(11)**
Ass'n of Co-operative Educators **(147)**
Burley Tobacco Growers Cooperative Ass'n **(184)**
Cooperative Education Ass'n **(209)**
Farm Credit Council **(234)**
Farmers Educational and Co-operative Union of America **(235)**
Flue-Cured Tobacco Cooperative Stabilization Corporation **(240)**
Funeral and Memorial Socs. of America **(244)**
Interstate Producers Livestock Ass'n **(312)**
Nat'l Ass'n of Housing Cooperatives **(359)**
Nat'l Cooperative Business Ass'n **(392)**
Nat'l Council of Farmer Cooperatives **(394)**
Nat'l Farmers Organization **(402)**
Nat'l Rural Electric Cooperative Ass'n **(426)**
Nat'l Soc. of Accountants for Cooperatives **(429)**
Nat'l Telephone Cooperative Ass'n **(433)**
Profit Sharing/401 (k) Council of America **(468)**
Quality Bakers of America Cooperative **(470)**

COPPER
American Bureau of Metal Statistics **(49)**
American Copper Council **(60)**
Copper and Brass Fabricators Council **(209)**
Copper and Brass Servicenter Ass'n **(209)**
Copper Development Ass'n **(209)**
Internat'l Copper Ass'n **(287)**
Non-Ferrous Founders' Soc. **(439)**
Soc. of Mineral Analysts **(504)**

CORN
American Corn Millers Federation **(60)**
Corn Refiners Ass'n **(209)**
Home Baking Ass'n **(255)**
Nat'l Corn Growers Ass'n **(392)**
Nat'l Futures Ass'n **(406)**

CORRECTION see also LAW, POLICE, SECURITY
American Ass'n for Correctional Psychology **(30)**
American Ass'n of Mental Health Professionals in Corrections **(39)**
American Catholic Correctional Chaplains Ass'n **(50)**
American Correctional Ass'n **(60)**
American Correctional Food Service Ass'n **(60)**
American Correctional Health Services Ass'n **(60)**
American Criminal Justice Ass'n/Lambda Alpha Epsilon **(62)**
American Jail Ass'n **(79)**
American Jewish Correctional Chaplains Ass'n **(79)**
American Probation and Parole Ass'n **(94)**
American Soc. of Criminology **(109)**
Ass'n for Correctional Research and Information Management **(132)**
Ass'n of State Correctional Administrators **(166)**
Ass'n on Programs for Female Offenders **(170)**
Correctional Education Ass'n **(209)**
Correctional Industries Ass'n **(210)**
Correctional Service - U.S. Federation **(210)**
Internat'l Ass'n of Addictions and Offender Counselors **(275)**
Internat'l Ass'n of Correctional Officers **(278)**
Internat'l Community Corrections Ass'n **(286)**
Internat'l Conference of Police Chaplains **(287)**
Internat'l Juvenile Officers Ass'n **(295)**
Nat'l Ass'n of Juvenile Correctional Agencies **(361)**
Nat'l Council on Crime and Delinquency **(397)**
Nat'l Juvenile Detention Ass'n **(413)**
North American Ass'n of Wardens and Superintendents **(440)**
Osborne Ass'n **(451)**
United Federation of Police Officers **(530)**

COSMETICS & COSMETOLOGY
Aestheticians Internat'l Ass'n **(13)**
American Ass'n of Cosmetology Schools **(35)**
American Electrology Ass'n **(65)**
American Hair Loss Council **(71)**
American Health and Beauty Aids Institute **(72)**
American Soc. of Hair Restoration Surgery **(110)**
Ass'n of Cosmetologists and Hairdressers **(149)**
Beauty and Barber Supply Institute **(177)**
Cosmetic Executive Women **(210)**
Cosmetic, Toiletry and Fragrance Ass'n **(210)**
Drug, Chemical and Allied Trades Ass'n **(225)**
Foragers of America **(242)**
Fragrance Foundation **(243)**
Independent Cosmetic Manufacturers and Distributors **(260)**
Intercoiffure America **(271)**
Internat'l Aloe Science Council **(273)**
Internat'l Ass'n of Color Manufacturers **(277)**
Internat'l Ass'n of Trichologists **(283)**
Internat'l Electrology Educators **(289)**
Internat'l Guild of Professional Electrologists **(293)**
Internat'l Tanning Manufacturers Ass'n **(308)**
Nat'l Beauty Culturists' League **(382)**
Nat'l Cosmetology Ass'n **(392)**
Nat'l Interstate Council of State Boards of Cosmetology **(413)**
Regulatory Affairs Professionals Soc. **(474)**
Salon Ass'n, The **(478)**
Soc. of Clinical and Medical Electrologists **(499)**
Soc. of Cosmetic Chemists **(500)**
World Internat'l Nail and Beauty Ass'n **(550)**

COTTON
American Cotton Shippers Ass'n **(60)**
American Textile Manufacturers Institute **(119)**
Cotton Council Internat'l **(210)**
Cotton Warehouse Ass'n of America **(210)**
Industrial Fabrics Ass'n Internat'l **(262)**
Nat'l Cotton Batting Institute **(392)**
Nat'l Cotton Council of America **(392)**
Nat'l Cotton Ginners' Ass'n **(392)**
New York Board of Trade **(438)**
Supima Ass'n of America **(518)**

COTTONSEED
American Oil Chemists' Soc. **(88)**
Nat'l Cottonseed Products Ass'n **(393)**

COUNSEL
American Ass'n of Fund-Raising Counsel **(37)**
American College of Trust and Estate Counsel **(58)**
Federation of Insurance and Corporate Counsel **(237)**
Internat'l Ass'n of Marriage and Family Counselors **(281)**
Investment Counsel Ass'n of America **(312)**
North American Canon Law Soc. **(441)**

COUNSELING see also VOCATIONAL GUIDANCE
American Ass'n for Marriage and Family Therapy **(31)**
American Ass'n of Direct Human Service Personnel **(36)**
American Ass'n of Pastoral Counselors **(40)**
American Ass'n of Sex Educators, Counselors and Therapists **(42)**
American College Counseling Ass'n **(52)**
American Counseling Ass'n **(62)**
American Family Therapy Academy **(66)**
American Mental Health Counselors Ass'n **(84)**
American Rehabilitation Counseling Ass'n **(97)**
American School Counselor Ass'n **(99)**
Ass'n for Adult Development and Aging **(129)**
Ass'n for Assessment in Counseling **(130)**
Ass'n for Counselor Education and Supervision **(132)**
Ass'n for Counselors and Educators in Government **(132)**
Ass'n for Gay, Lesbian and Bisexual Issues in Counseling **(133)**
Ass'n for Humanistic Education and Development **(134)**
Ass'n for Multicultural Counseling and Development **(136)**
Ass'n for Specialists in Group Work **(137)**
Ass'n for Spiritual, Ethical and Religious Values in Counseling **(137)**
Ass'n for University and College Counseling Center Directors **(140)**
Internat'l Ass'n of Addictions and Offender Counselors **(275)**
Internat'l Ass'n of Counseling Services **(278)**
Internat'l Ass'n of Counselors and Therapists **(278)**
Nat'l Ass'n for College Admission Counseling **(338)**
Nat'l Ass'n of Alcoholism and Drug Abuse Counselors **(343)**
Nat'l Career Development Ass'n **(385)**
Nat'l Employment Counseling Ass'n **(401)**
Nat'l Rehabilitation Counseling Ass'n **(425)**

COUNTY
American Federation of State, County and Municipal Employees **(67)**
County Executives of America **(218)**
Internat'l Ass'n of Clerks, Recorders, Election Officials and Treasurers **(277)**
Nat'l Ass'n of Counties **(350)**
Nat'l Ass'n of County Administrators **(350)**
Nat'l Ass'n of County Aging Programs **(350)**
Nat'l Ass'n of County Agricultural Agents **(350)**
Nat'l Ass'n of County and City Health Officials **(350)**
Nat'l Ass'n of County Civil Attorneys **(350)**
Nat'l Ass'n of County Engineers **(350)**
Nat'l Ass'n of County Information Officers **(351)**
Nat'l Ass'n of County Intergovernmental Relations Officials **(351)**
Nat'l Ass'n of County Park and Recreation Officials **(351)**
Nat'l Ass'n of County Planners **(351)**
Nat'l Ass'n of County Recorders, Election Officials and Clerks **(351)**
Nat'l Ass'n of County Training and Employment Professionals **(351)**
Nat'l Ass'n of County Treasurers and Finance Officers **(351)**
Nat'l Ass'n of Hispanic County Officials **(358)**

562 National Trade and Professional Associations of the U.S. © 1999, Columbia Books, Inc.

Subject Index DENTISTRY

Nat'l Council of County Ass'n Executives **(394)**

CREDIT see also FINANCE
Advertising Media Credit Executives Ass'n, Internat'l **(12)**
Affordable Housing Tax Credit Coalition **(13)**
American Bankruptcy Institute **(46)**
American Collectors Ass'n **(52)**
American Finance Ass'n **(68)**
American Financial Services Ass'n **(68)**
American Recovery Ass'n **(97)**
Associated Credit Bureaus **(171)**
Broadcast Cable Credit Ass'n **(182)**
Coalition of Higher Education Assistance Organizations **(196)**
Commercial Finance Ass'n **(199)**
Consumer Bankers Ass'n **(207)**
Consumer Credit Insurance Ass'n **(207)**
Credit Professionals Internat'l **(218)**
Credit Research Foundation **(218)**
Credit Union Executives Soc. **(218)**
Credit Union Nat'l Ass'n **(218)**
Defense Credit Union Council **(220)**
Education Credit Union Council **(226)**
Electronic Transactions Ass'n **(228)**
Farm Credit Council **(234)**
FCIB-NACM Corp. **(235)**
Information Technologies Credit Union Ass'n **(264)**
Internat'l Ass'n of Financial Crimes Investigators **(279)**
Internat'l Credit Ass'n **(288)**
Internat'l Petroleum Credit Ass'n **(299)**
Mastercard Internat'l **(324)**
Media Credit Ass'n **(326)**
Motion Picture and Television Credit Ass'n **(330)**
Nat'l Ass'n of Consumer Credit Administrators **(349)**
Nat'l Ass'n of Credit Management **(351)**
Nat'l Ass'n of Credit Union Chairmen **(351)**
Nat'l Ass'n of Credit Union Service Organizations **(351)**
Nat'l Ass'n of Federal Credit Unions **(355)**
Nat'l Ass'n of Mortgage Brokers **(363)**
Nat'l Ass'n of State Credit Union Supervisors **(374)**
Nat'l Council of Postal Credit Unions **(395)**
Nat'l Credit Union Management Ass'n **(398)**
Nat'l Federation of Community Development Credit Unions **(403)**
Nat'l Foundation for Consumer Credit **(405)**
Robert Morris Associates, the Ass'n of Lending and Credit Risk Professionals **(476)**
Smart Card Industry Ass'n **(484)**

CRIMINOLOGY
Academy of Criminal Justice Sciences **(8)**
American Criminal Justice Ass'n/Lambda Alpha Epsilon **(62)**
American Polygraph Ass'n **(93)**
American Soc. of Criminology **(109)**
American Soc. of Questioned Document Examiners **(115)**
Ass'n of Certified Fraud Examiners **(146)**
Council of Internat'l Investigators **(214)**
Independent Ass'n of Questioned Document Examiners **(259)**
Internat'l Ass'n for Identification **(274)**
Internat'l Ass'n for the Study of Organized Crime **(275)**
Internat'l Soc. of Crime Prevention Practitioners **(306)**
Justice Research and Statistics Ass'n **(315)**
Nat'l Ass'n of Investigative Specialists **(360)**
Nat'l Criminal Justice Ass'n **(398)**
Soc. of Professional Investigators **(506)**

CRYOGENICS
American Ass'n of Tissue Banks **(44)**
Compressed Gas Ass'n **(202)**
Soc. for Cryobiology **(487)**
Soc. of Urologic Cryosurgeons **(508)**

CUSTOMS
Customs and Internat'l Trade Bar Ass'n **(219)**
Nat'l Customs Brokers and Forwarders Ass'n of America **(398)**
Nat'l Treasury Employees Union **(434)**

CYBERNETICS
Soc. for Computer Simulation **(486)**

CYTOLOGY
American Soc. for Cytotechnology **(102)**
American Soc. of Cytopathology **(109)**
Soc. for In Vitro Biology **(489)**

DAIRY INDUSTRY
American Butter Institute **(50)**
American Dairy Ass'n **(63)**
American Dairy Products Institute **(63)**
American Dairy Science Ass'n **(63)**
Certified Milk Producers Ass'n of America **(190)**
Cheese Importers Ass'n of America **(190)**
Dairy Management **(219)**
Dairy Soc. Internat'l **(220)**
Internat'l Ass'n of Food Industry Suppliers **(279)**
Internat'l Ass'n of Ice Cream Vendors **(280)**
Internat'l Dairy Foods Ass'n **(288)**
Internat'l Dairy-Deli-Bakery Ass'n **(288)**
Internat'l Ice Cream Ass'n **(294)**
Master Dairies **(324)**
Nat'l Ass'n of Barber Boards **(344)**
Nat'l Cheese Institute **(386)**
Nat'l Dairy Council **(398)**
Nat'l Dairy Herd Improvement Ass'n **(399)**
Nat'l Ice Cream and Yogurt Retailers Ass'n **(410)**
Nat'l Mastitis Council **(416)**
Nat'l Milk Producers Federation **(417)**
Nat'l Yogurt Ass'n **(437)**
New York Mercantile Exchange **(438)**
United States of America National Committee of the Internat'l Dairy Federation **(534)**

DANCE
American Alliance for Health, Physical Education, Recreation and Dance **(27)**
American Dance Guild **(63)**
American Dance Therapy Ass'n **(63)**
American Fitness Ass'n **(68)**
American Guild of Musical Artists **(71)**
Callerlab-Internat'l Ass'n of Square Dance Callers **(186)**
Congress on Research in Dance **(205)**
Council of Dance Administrators **(213)**
Dance Critics Ass'n **(220)**
Dance Educators of America **(220)**
Dance Masters of America **(220)**
Dance/USA **(220)**
Delta Psi Kappa **(221)**
IDEA, The Health and Fitness Source **(258)**
Nat'l Ass'n of Schools of Dance **(371)**
Nat'l Ballroom and Entertainment Ass'n **(382)**
Nat'l Dance Ass'n **(399)**
North American Folk Music and Dance Alliance **(442)**
Roundalab **(477)**
Soc. of Dance History Scholars **(500)**

DATA PROCESSING
AFSM Internat'l **(14)**
American Ass'n of Public Welfare Information Systems Management **(42)**
American Electronics Ass'n **(65)**
American Medical Informatics Ass'n **(84)**
American Payroll Ass'n **(90)**
American Soc. for Information Science **(103)**
Ass'n for Computational Linguistics **(131)**
Ass'n for Computers and the Humanities **(131)**
Ass'n for Computing Machinery **(131)**
Ass'n for Financial Technology **(133)**
Ass'n for Women in Computing **(140)**
Ass'n for Work Process Improvement **(141)**
Ass'n of Business Support Services Internat'l **(145)**
Ass'n of Information and Dissemination Centers **(154)**
Ass'n of Information Technology Professionals **(154)**
Ass'n of Management/Internat'l Ass'n of Management **(156)**
Ass'n of Public Data Users **(162)**
Ass'n of Rehabilitation Programs in Computer Technology **(163)**
Ass'n of Service and Computer Dealers Internat'l **(164)**
Ass'n of Small Research, Engineering and Technical Service Companies **(165)**
Automated Procedures for Engineering Consultants **(173)**
Black Data Processing Associates **(180)**
Business Software Alliance **(185)**
Classification Soc. of North America **(194)**
Commercial Internet Exchange Ass'n **(199)**
Computer and Automated Systems Ass'n of SME **(202)**
Computer and Communications Industry Ass'n **(202)**
Computer Assisted Language Instruction Consortium **(202)**
Computer Law Ass'n **(202)**
Computer Measurement Group **(202)**
Computer Press Ass'n **(202)**
Computer Security Institute **(203)**
Computer Use in Social Services Network **(203)**
Computerized Medical Imaging Soc. **(203)**
Computing Technology Industry Ass'n **(203)**
Consortium for Advanced Manufacturing Internat'l **(206)**
Council for Electronic Revenue Communication Advancement **(211)**
CUMREC Internat'l **(219)**
Data Administration Management Ass'n Internat'l **(220)**
Data Interchange Standards Ass'n **(220)**
EDUCAUSE **(227)**
EDUCAUSE **(226)**
Electronic Funds Transfer Ass'n **(228)**
Equipment Leasing Ass'n of America **(232)**
Federation of Government Information Processing Councils **(237)**
Geoscience Information Soc. **(247)**
Geospatial Information and Technology Ass'n **(247)**
Government Management Information Sciences **(248)**
IEEE Computer Soc. **(258)**
Independent Computer Consultants Ass'n **(260)**
Information Industry Ass'n **(263)**
Information Systems Audit and Control Ass'n **(264)**
Information Systems Consultants Ass'n **(264)**
Information Technology Ass'n of America **(264)**
Information Technology Industry Council **(264)**
Institute for Certification of Computing Professionals **(265)**
Instructional Systems Ass'n **(269)**
Internat'l Ass'n for Human Resource Information Management **(274)**
Internat'l Ass'n of Knowledge Engineers **(280)**
Internat'l Council for Computer Communication **(287)**
Internat'l Health Evaluation Ass'n **(293)**
Internat'l Information Management Congress **(294)**
Internat'l Interactive Communication Soc. **(295)**
Internat'l Recording Media Ass'n **(301)**
Internat'l Soc. for Technology in Education **(304)**
Internet Alliance **(311)**
IS Financial Management Ass'n **(313)**
IUA - The CA-IDMS Database and Applications User Ass'n **(313)**
MEMA Information Services Council **(327)**
MicroComputer Investors Ass'n **(328)**
NaSPA: the Network and System Professionals Ass'n **(333)**
Nat'l Ass'n of Computerized Tax Processors **(349)**
Nat'l Ass'n of Health Data Organizations **(357)**
Nat'l Ass'n of State Information Resource Executives **(375)**
Nat'l Federation of Abstracting and Information Services **(403)**
Nat'l Training Systems Ass'n **(434)**
Newspaper Systems Group **(439)**
North American Computer Service Ass'n **(441)**
North American Fuzzy Information Processing Soc. **(442)**
Online Audiovisual Catalogers **(448)**
Pattern Recognition Soc. **(454)**
Soc. for Applied Learning Technology **(485)**
Soc. for Conceptual and Content Analysis by Computer **(486)**
Soc. for Information Display **(490)**
Soc. for Information Management **(490)**
Software Publishers Ass'n **(509)**
Special Interest Group for Algorithm and Computation Theory **(511)**
Special Interest Group for Architecture of Computer Systems **(511)**
Special Interest Group for Biomedical Computing **(511)**
Special Interest Group for Computer Personnel Research **(511)**
Special Interest Group for Computer Science Education **(511)**
Special Interest Group for Computer Uses in Education **(511)**
Special Interest Group for Computer-Human Interaction **(511)**
Special Interest Group for Computers and Society **(511)**
Special Interest Group for Computers and the Physically Handicapped **(511)**
Special Interest Group for Data Communication **(512)**
Special Interest Group for Information Retrieval **(512)**
Special Interest Group for Management of Data **(512)**
Special Interest Group for Measurement and Evaluation **(512)**
Special Interest Group for Microprogramming and Microarchitecture **(512)**
Special Interest Group for Simulation and Modeling **(512)**
Special Interest Group for Symbolic and Algebraic Manipulation **(512)**
Special Interest Group for University and College Computing Services **(512)**
Special Interest Group on Ada Programming Language **(512)**
Special Interest Group on APL Programming Language **(512)**
Special Interest Group on Artificial Intelligence **(512)**
Special Interest Group on Computer Graphics **(512)**
Special Interest Group on Design Automation **(513)**
Special Interest Group on Documentation **(513)**
Special Interest Group on Management Information Systems **(513)**
Special Interest Group on Mobility of Systems, Users, Data and Computing **(513)**
Special Interest Group on Numerical Mathematics **(513)**
Special Interest Group on Operating Systems **(513)**
Special Interest Group on Programming Languages **(513)**
Special Interest Group on Security, Audit, and Control **(513)**
Special Interest Group on Software Engineering **(513)**
Special Interest Group on Supporting Group Work **(513)**
System Independent Data Format Ass'n **(519)**
Technology Transfer Soc. **(521)**
Urban and Regional Information Systems Ass'n **(537)**
Workgroup for Electronic Data Interchange **(549)**
World Computer Graphics Ass'n **(549)**
Xplorer Internat'l **(551)**

DEAF see also HEARING
Access Technology Ass'n **(10)**
ADARA **(11)**
Alexander Graham Bell Ass'n for the Deaf **(17)**
American Academy of Audiology **(20)**
American Ass'n of Eye and Ear Hospitals **(36)**
American Auditory Soc. **(46)**
American Neurotology Soc. **(87)**
American Speech-Language-Hearing Ass'n **(117)**
American Tinnitus Ass'n **(120)**
Ass'n of College Educators: Deaf and Hard of Hearing **(147)**
Conference of Educational Administrators of Schools and Programs for the Deaf **(204)**
Convention of American Instructors of the Deaf **(208)**
Council on Education of the Deaf **(216)**
Internat'l Hearing Soc. **(293)**
Internat'l Visual Literacy Ass'n **(310)**
Nat'l Hearing Conservation Ass'n **(408)**
Nat'l Student Speech Language Hearing Ass'n **(432)**
Registry of Interpreters for the Deaf **(473)**

DECORATORS
Laminating Materials Ass'n **(317)**
Residential Space Planners Internat'l **(475)**
Soc. of Glass and Ceramic Decorators **(502)**

DEHYDRATORS
American Alfalfa Processors Ass'n **(27)**

DENTISTRY
Academy for Implants and Transplants **(7)**
Academy of Dental Materials **(8)**
Academy of Dentistry for Persons with Disabilities **(8)**
Academy of Dentistry Internat'l **(8)**
Academy of General Dentistry **(8)**
Academy of Laser Dentistry **(8)**
Academy of Operative Dentistry **(9)**
Academy of Oral Dynamics **(9)**
Academy of Osseointegration **(9)**
Alpha Omega Internat'l Dental Fraternity **(19)**
American Academy of Cosmetic Dentistry **(21)**
American Academy of Dental Group Practice **(21)**
American Academy of Dental Practice Administration **(21)**
American Academy of Esthetic Dentistry **(22)**
American Academy of Fixed Prosthodontics **(22)**
American Academy of Gnathologic Orthopedics **(22)**
American Academy of Gold Foil Operators **(22)**
American Academy of Head, Neck and Facial Pain **(22)**
American Academy of Implant Dentistry **(22)**
American Academy of Implant Prosthodontics **(23)**
American Academy of Maxillofacial Prosthetics **(23)**
American Academy of Oral and Maxillofacial Pathology **(24)**
American Academy of Oral and Maxillofacial Radiology **(24)**
American Academy of Oral Medicine **(24)**
American Academy of Orofacial Pain **(24)**
American Academy of Orthotists and Prosthetists **(24)**
American Academy of Pediatric Dentistry **(25)**
American Academy of Periodontology **(25)**
American Academy of Physiologic Dentistry **(25)**
American Academy of the History of Dentistry **(26)**
American Ass'n for Dental Research **(30)**
American Ass'n for Functional Orthodontics **(30)**
American Ass'n of Dental Consultants **(35)**

National Trade and Professional Associations of the U.S. © 1999, Columbia Books, Inc. 563

Subject Index EDUCATION

American Ass'n of University Professors **(44)**
American Ass'n on Mental Retardation **(45)**
American Board of Medical Specialties **(47)**
American Bridge Teachers' Ass'n **(49)**
American Classical League **(52)**
American College Counseling Ass'n **(52)**
American College of Counselors **(53)**
American College of Musicians **(55)**
American College Personnel Ass'n **(58)**
American Collegiate Retailing Ass'n **(58)**
American Comparative Literature Ass'n **(59)**
American Conference of Academic Deans **(59)**
American Council of Learned Societies **(61)**
American Council of Nanny Schools **(61)**
American Council of Teachers of Russian **(61)**
American Council on Education **(61)**
American Council on Pharmaceutical Education **(62)**
American Council on Schools and Colleges **(62)**
American Council on the Teaching of Foreign Languages **(62)**
American Driver and Traffic Safety Education Ass'n **(65)**
American Education Finance Ass'n **(65)**
American Educational Research Ass'n **(65)**
American Educational Studies Ass'n **(65)**
American Federation of School Administrators **(67)**
American Federation of Teachers **(67)**
American Humor Studies Ass'n **(74)**
American Hungarian Educators Ass'n **(74)**
American Institute of Indian Studies **(77)**
American Legal Studies Ass'n **(81)**
American Management Ass'n Internat'l **(82)**
American Mathematical Ass'n of Two Year Colleges **(83)**
American Medical Rehabilitation Providers Ass'n **(84)**
American Montessori Soc. **(85)**
American Nature Study Soc. **(86)**
American Peanut Research and Education Soc. **(90)**
American Philosophical Ass'n **(91)**
American Rehabilitation Counseling Ass'n **(97)**
American School Counselor Ass'n **(99)**
American Schools Ass'n **(99)**
American Schools of Oriental Research **(99)**
American Soc. for Bioethics and Humanities **(101)**
American Soc. for Engineering Education **(102)**
American Soc. of Law Enforcement Trainers **(112)**
American String Teachers Ass'n **(118)**
American Technical Education Ass'n **(119)**
American Vocational Ass'n **(122)**
American Vocational Education Personnel Development Ass'n **(122)**
American Vocational Education Research Ass'n **(122)**
APPA: The Ass'n of Higher Education Facilities Officers **(126)**
Ass'n for Asian American Studies **(130)**
Ass'n for Biology Laboratory Education **(130)**
Ass'n for Borderlands Studies **(130)**
Ass'n for Business Simulation and Experiential Learning **(130)**
Ass'n for Canadian Studies in the United States **(130)**
Ass'n for Central Asian Studies **(130)**
Ass'n for Childhood Education Internat'l **(131)**
Ass'n for Clinical Pastoral Education **(131)**
Ass'n for College and University Religious Affairs **(131)**
Ass'n for Communication Administration **(131)**
Ass'n for Community Based Education **(131)**
Ass'n for Computers and the Humanities **(131)**
Ass'n for Continuing Higher Education **(131)**
Ass'n for Counselor Education and Supervision **(132)**
Ass'n for Counselors and Educators in Government **(132)**
Ass'n for Direct Instruction **(132)**
Ass'n for Documentary Editing **(132)**
Ass'n for Education and Rehabilitation of the Blind and Visually Impaired **(132)**
Ass'n for Education in Journalism and Mass Communication **(132)**
Ass'n for Educational Communications and Technology **(133)**
Ass'n for Experiential Education **(133)**
Ass'n for General and Liberal Studies **(133)**
Ass'n for Gerontology in Higher Education **(134)**
Ass'n for Graphic Arts Training **(134)**
Ass'n for Hospital Medical Education **(134)**
Ass'n for Humanistic Education and Development **(134)**
Ass'n for Informal Logic and Critical Thinking **(135)**
Ass'n for Information Media and Equipment **(135)**
Ass'n for Information Systems **(135)**
Ass'n for Institutional Research **(135)**
Ass'n for Integrative Studies **(135)**
Ass'n for Internat'l Agricultural and Extension Education **(135)**
Ass'n for Jewish Studies **(135)**
Ass'n for Library and Information Science Education **(135)**
Ass'n for Supervision and Curriculum Development **(138)**
Ass'n for Surgical Education **(138)**
Ass'n for Technology in Music Instruction **(138)**
Ass'n for the Advancement of Baltic Studies **(138)**
Ass'n for the Advancement of Internat'l Education **(138)**
Ass'n for the Education of Teachers in Science **(139)**
Ass'n for the Study of Higher Education **(139)**
Ass'n for the Study of Play **(139)**
Ass'n of Academic Chairmen of Plastic Surgery **(141)**
Ass'n of Advanced Rabbinical and Talmudic Schools **(141)**
Ass'n of American Colleges and Universities **(142)**
Ass'n of American Law Schools **(142)**
Ass'n of American Medical Colleges **(142)**
Ass'n of American Universities **(143)**
Ass'n of American Veterinary Medical Colleges **(143)**
Ass'n of Arts Administration Educators **(144)**
Ass'n of Astronomy Educators **(144)**
Ass'n of Biomedical Communications Directors **(144)**
Ass'n of Black Nursing Faculty in Higher Education **(145)**
Ass'n of Boarding Schools, The **(145)**
Ass'n of Catholic Colleges and Universities **(146)**
Ass'n of Chairmen of Departments of Mechanics **(146)**
Ass'n of Christian Schools Internat'l **(146)**
Ass'n of Co-operative Educators **(147)**
Ass'n of College Administration Professionals **(147)**
Ass'n of College and University Auditors **(147)**
Ass'n of College and University Housing Officers-Internat'l **(147)**
Ass'n of College and University Telecommunications Administrators **(147)**
Ass'n of College Unions-Internat'l **(147)**
Ass'n of Collegiate Business Schools and Programs **(148)**
Ass'n of Collegiate Schools of Architecture **(148)**
Ass'n of Collegiate Schools of Planning **(148)**
Ass'n of Commercial Diving Educators **(148)**
Ass'n of Community College Trustees **(148)**
Ass'n of Community Health Nursing Educators **(148)**
Ass'n of Departments of English **(149)**
Ass'n of Departments of Foreign Languages **(149)**
Ass'n of Educators in Private Practice **(150)**
Ass'n of Educators in Radiological Science **(150)**
Ass'n of Episcopal Colleges **(150)**
Ass'n of Governing Boards of Universities and Colleges **(152)**
Ass'n of Graduate Liberal Studies Programs **(152)**
Ass'n of Graduate Schools in Ass'n of American Universities **(152)**
Ass'n of Health Occupations Teacher Educators **(153)**
Ass'n of Independent Colleges of Art and Design **(153)**
Ass'n of Internat'l Agriculture and Rural Development **(154)**
Ass'n of Internat'l Education Administrators **(154)**
Ass'n of Jesuit Colleges and Universities **(155)**
Ass'n of Leadership Educators **(155)**
Ass'n of Lutheran College Faculties **(156)**
Ass'n of Lutheran Secondary Schools **(156)**
Ass'n of Management/Internat'l Ass'n of Management **(156)**
Ass'n of Mercy Colleges **(157)**
Ass'n of Military Colleges and Schools of the U.S. **(157)**
Ass'n of Minority Health Professions Schools **(157)**
Ass'n of Muslim Social Scientists **(158)**
Ass'n of Natural Resource Enforcement Trainers **(158)**
Ass'n of Naval R.O.T.C. Colleges and Universities **(158)**
Ass'n of Osteopathic Directors and Medical Educators **(159)**
Ass'n of Performing Arts Presenters **(160)**
Ass'n of Presbyterian Colleges and Universities **(160)**
Ass'n of Professional Schools of Internat'l Affairs **(161)**
Ass'n of Professors of Cardiology **(161)**
Ass'n of Professors of Medicine **(162)**
Ass'n of Professors of Mission **(162)**
Ass'n of Program Directors in Internal Medicine **(162)**
Ass'n of School Business Officials Internat'l **(164)**
Ass'n of Schools and Colleges of Optometry **(164)**
Ass'n of Schools of Allied Health Professions **(164)**
Ass'n of Schools of Journalism and Mass Communication **(164)**
Ass'n of Schools of Public Health **(164)**
Ass'n of Small Business Development Centers **(165)**
Ass'n of Southern Baptist Colleges and Schools **(165)**
Ass'n of Specialized and Professional Accreditors **(165)**
Ass'n of State Supervisors of Mathematics **(166)**
Ass'n of Supervisory and Administrative School Personnel **(166)**
Ass'n of Teacher Educators **(167)**
Ass'n of Teachers of Japanese **(167)**
Ass'n of Teachers of Latin American Studies **(167)**
Ass'n of Teachers of Maternal and Child Health **(167)**
Ass'n of Teachers of Preventive Medicine **(167)**
Ass'n of Teachers of Technical Writing **(167)**
Ass'n of Theological Schools in the United States and Canada **(168)**
Ass'n of University Architects **(168)**
Ass'n of University Professors of Ophthalmology **(168)**
Ass'n of University Programs in Health Administration **(168)**
Ass'n of University Programs in Occupational Health and Safety **(168)**
Ass'n of University Summer Sessions **(169)**
Ass'n of Vegetarian Dietitians and Nutrition Educators **(169)**
Ass'n on Higher Education and Disability **(170)**
Associated Collegiate Press, Nat'l Scholastic Press Ass'n **(171)**
Associated Schools of Construction **(172)**
Associated Writing Programs **(172)**
Augustinian Secondary Educational Ass'n **(173)**
Aviation Technician Education Council **(176)**
Bibliographical Soc. of America **(178)**
Brazilian Studies Ass'n **(182)**
Broadcast Education Ass'n **(182)**
Business Higher Education Forum **(184)**
Business Professionals of America **(185)**
Campus Safety Division of the Nat'l Safety Council **(186)**
Career College Ass'n **(186)**
Career Planning and Adult Development Network **(187)**
Catholic Fine Arts Soc. **(188)**
Chinese Language Teachers Ass'n **(192)**
Christian College Consortium **(193)**
Christian Schools Internat'l **(193)**
Classroom Publishers Ass'n **(194)**
Coalition for Christian Colleges and Universities **(195)**
Coalition of Higher Education Assistance Organizations **(196)**
College and University Personnel Ass'n **(197)**
College Art Ass'n **(197)**
College Band Directors Nat'l Ass'n **(197)**
College English Ass'n **(197)**
College Media Advisers **(197)**
College Music Soc. **(197)**
College Reading and Learning Ass'n **(198)**
College Theology Soc. **(198)**
Commission of Accredited Truck Driving Schools **(199)**
Commission on Accreditation of Allied Health Education Programs **(199)**
Community College Ass'n for Instruction and Technology **(201)**
Community College Business Officers **(201)**
Community College Journalism Ass'n **(201)**
Community Colleges Humanities Ass'n **(201)**
Comparative and Internat'l Education Soc. **(201)**
Computer Assisted Language Instruction Consortium **(202)**
Conference of Educational Administrators of Schools and Programs for the Deaf **(204)**
Conference on College Composition and Communication **(205)**
Conference on English Education **(205)**
Conference on English Leadership **(205)**
Conference on Jewish Social Studies **(205)**
Conflict Resolution Education Network **(205)**
Consortium for School Networking **(206)**
Consortium of College and University Media Centers **(206)**
Consortium of Social Science Ass'ns **(206)**
Convention of American Instructors of the Deaf **(208)**
Cooperative Education Ass'n **(209)**
Correctional Education Ass'n **(209)**
Council for Adult and Experiential Learning **(210)**
Council for Advancement and Support of Education **(210)**
Council for American Private Education **(210)**
Council for Art Education **(211)**
Council for Basic Education **(211)**
Council for Early Childhood Professional Recognition **(211)**
Council for Elementary Science Internat'l **(211)**
Council for Ethics in Economics **(211)**
Council for European Studies **(211)**
Council for Exceptional Children **(211)**
Council for Higher Education Accreditation **(211)**
Council for Jewish Education **(211)**
Council for Learning Disabilities **(211)**
Council for Spiritual and Ethical Education **(212)**
Council for the Advancement of Standards in Higher Education **(212)**
Council of 1890 College Presidents and Chancellors **(212)**
Council of Administrators of Special Education **(212)**
Council of Chief State School Officers **(213)**
Council of Colleges of Acupuncture and Oriental Medicine **(213)**
Council of Colleges of Arts and Sciences **(213)**
Council of Educational Facility Planners, Internat'l **(213)**
Council of Graduate Schools **(213)**
Council of Independent Colleges **(214)**
Council of the Great City Schools **(216)**
Council on Chiropractic Education **(216)**
Council on Education of the Deaf **(216)**
Council on Hotel, Restaurant and Institutional Education **(217)**
Council on Library-Media Technicians **(217)**
Council on Occupational Education **(217)**
Council on Social Work Education **(217)**
Council on Technology Teacher Education **(217)**
Creative Education Foundation **(218)**
Dance Educators of America **(220)**
Dance Masters of America **(220)**
Decision Sciences Institute **(220)**
Delta Pi Epsilon **(221)**
Delta Soc. **(221)**
Distance Education and Training Council **(223)**
Distributive Education Clubs of America **(224)**
EdPress--The Ass'n of Educational Publishers **(226)**
Education Law Ass'n **(226)**
Education Writers Ass'n **(226)**
Educational Dealers and Suppliers Ass'n Internat'l **(226)**
Educational Paperback Ass'n **(226)**
EDUCAUSE **(227)**
EDUCAUSE **(226)**
Engineering College Magazines Associated **(230)**
Evangelical Training Ass'n **(233)**
Family and Consumer Science Education Ass'n **(234)**
Federal Education Ass'n **(235)**
Federation of State Humanities Councils **(237)**
Foundation for Independent Higher Education **(243)**
Future Business Leaders of America-Phi Beta Lambda **(245)**
Future Homemakers of America **(245)**
Graduate Management Admission Council **(248)**
Hispanic Ass'n of Colleges and Universities **(254)**
History of Economics Soc. **(254)**
History of Education Soc. **(254)**
Independent Educational Consultants Ass'n **(260)**
Independent Research Libraries Ass'n **(261)**
Independent Scholars of Asia **(261)**
Indian Educators Federation **(262)**
Institute of Behavioral and Applied Management **(265)**
Institute of Financial Education **(267)**
Instructional Telecommunications Council **(269)**
Insulated Cable Engineers Ass'n **(270)**
Intercollegiate Broadcasting System **(271)**
Interior Design Educators Council **(271)**
Internat'l Ass'n for Computer Information Systems **(273)**
Internat'l Ass'n for Continuing Education and Training **(273)**
Internat'l Ass'n for Learning Laboratories **(274)**
Internat'l Ass'n of Campus Law Enforcement Administrators **(277)**
Internat'l Ass'n of Jazz Educators **(280)**
Internat'l Ass'n of Medical Science Educators **(281)**
Internat'l Ass'n of Pupil Personnel Workers **(282)**
Internat'l Ass'n of School Librarianship **(282)**
Internat'l Childbirth Education Ass'n **(285)**
Internat'l Council of Fine Arts Deans **(287)**
Internat'l Council of Regional School Accrediting Commissions **(288)**
Internat'l Council on Education for Teaching **(288)**
Internat'l Double Reed Soc. **(289)**
Internat'l Dyslexia Ass'n **(289)**
Internat'l Electrology Educators **(289)**
Internat'l Engineering Consortium **(290)**
Internat'l Graphic Arts Education Ass'n **(292)**
Internat'l Listening Ass'n **(296)**
Internat'l Piano Guild **(300)**
Internat'l Reading Ass'n **(301)**
Internat'l Soc. for Intercultural Education, Training and Research **(303)**
Internat'l Soc. for Performance Improvement **(304)**
Internat'l Soc. for Technology in Education **(304)**
Internat'l Soc. of Certified Employee Benefit Specialists **(305)**
Internat'l Soc. of Fire Service Instructors **(306)**
Internat'l Soc. of Travel and Tourism Educators **(307)**
Internat'l Technology Education Ass'n **(308)**
Internat'l Visual Literacy Ass'n **(310)**
Jean Piaget Soc./Soc. for the Study of Knowledge and Development **(313)**
Jesuit Secondary Education Ass'n **(313)**
Jewish Education Service of North America **(314)**
Jewish Educators Assembly **(314)**
Jewish Teachers Ass'n-Morim **(314)**
Journalism Education Ass'n **(315)**
Kappa Delta Epsilon **(315)**

National Trade and Professional Associations of the U.S. © 1999, Columbia Books, Inc. 565

ELECTRICITY & ELECTRONICS

North American Die Casting Ass'n (441)
North American Manufacturing Research Institution of SME (443)
North American Membrane Soc. (443)
Professional Engineers in Private Practice (465)
Professional Services Management Ass'n (467)
Railway Engineering-Maintenance Suppliers Ass'n (471)
Rapid Prototyping Ass'n of SME (472)
Refrigerating Engineers and Technicians Ass'n (473)
Refrigeration Service Engineers Soc. (473)
Rehabilitation Engineering and Assistive Technology Soc. of North America (474)
Reinforced Concrete Research Council (474)
Research Council on Structural Connections (475)
Robotics Internat'l of SME (477)
SAVE Internat'l (479)
Sigma Phi Delta (483)
Soc. for Experimental Mechanics (488)
Soc. for Imaging Science and Technology (489)
Soc. for Maintenance Reliability Professionals (490)
Soc. for Mining, Metallurgy, and Exploration (491)
Soc. for the Advancement of Material and Process Engineering (494)
Soc. for the History of Technology (495)
Soc. of Allied Weight Engineers (497)
Soc. of American Military Engineers (498)
Soc. of Automotive Engineers International (498)
Soc. of Broadcast Engineers (499)
Soc. of Cable Telecommunications Engineers (499)
Soc. of Carbide and Tool Engineers (499)
Soc. of Engineering Science (501)
Soc. of Fire Protection Engineers (501)
Soc. of Flight Test Engineers (501)
Soc. of Hispanic Professional Engineers (502)
Soc. of Independent Professional Earth Scientists (503)
Soc. of Manufacturing Engineers (503)
Soc. of Marine Port Engineers (503)
Soc. of Mexican American Engineers and Scientists (504)
Soc. of Motion Picture and Television Engineers (504)
Soc. of Naval Architects and Marine Engineers (504)
Soc. of Petroleum Engineers (505)
Soc. of Piping Engineers and Designers (505)
Soc. of Plastics Engineers (505)
Soc. of Rheology (506)
Soc. of Tribologists and Lubrication Engineers (508)
Soc. of Women Engineers (509)
SOLE - The Internat'l Soc. of Logistics (510)
Special Interest Group on Mobility of Systems, Users, Data and Computing (513)
SPIE-Internat'l Soc. for Optical Engineering (514)
Standards Engineering Soc. (515)
Structural Stability Research Council (517)
Surface Mount Technology Ass'n (519)
System Safety Soc. (519)
Technical Engineers Ass'n (520)
Theta Tau (522)
United Engineering Trustees (530)
Water Environment Federation (541)
Western Dredging Ass'n (542)

ENGINES
AERA - Engine Rebuilders Ass'n (12)
Ass'n of Marine Engine Manufacturers (156)
Contractors Pump Bureau (208)
Electrical Generating Systems Ass'n (227)
Engine Manufacturers Ass'n (230)
Engine Service Ass'n (230)
Filter Manufacturers Council (238)
Internat'l Gas Turbine Institute, ASME (292)
Nat'l Engine Parts Manufacturers Ass'n (401)
Small Motors and Motion Ass'n (484)

ENGLISH
American Comparative Literature Ass'n (59)
American Humor Studies Ass'n (74)
Ass'n for Communication Administration (131)
Ass'n for Documentary Editing (132)
Ass'n for Informal Logic and Critical Thinking (135)
Ass'n of Departments of English (149)
Ass'n of Literary Scholars and Critics (156)
College English Ass'n (197)
Conference on College Composition and Communication (205)
Conference on English Education (205)
Conference on English Leadership (205)
Internat'l Soc. for General Semantics (303)
Nat'l Conference on Research in Language and Literacy (391)
Nat'l Council of Teachers of English (396)
Nat'l Council of Writing Program Administrators (397)
Renaissance Soc. of America (474)
Rhetoric Soc. of America (476)
Soc. for New Language Study (491)
Teachers of English to Speakers of Other Languages (520)
Western Literature Ass'n (543)

ENTERTAINMENT
American Amusement Machine Ass'n (28)
American Disc Jockey Ass'n (64)
Amusement and Music Operators Ass'n (124)
Ass'n of Talent Agents (167)
Black Entertainment and Sports Lawyers Ass'n (180)
Clowns of America, Internat'l (195)
Comedy Writers and Performers Ass'n (198)
Entertainment Services and Technology Ass'n (231)
Interactive Digital Software Ass'n (271)
Internat'l Group of Agencies and Bureaus (293)
Nat'l Alliance for Musical Theatre (336)
Nat'l Ass'n for Campus Activities (338)
Nat'l Ass'n of Ticket Brokers (378)
Nat'l Ballroom and Entertainment Ass'n (382)
Nat'l Conference of Personal Managers (390)
North American Concert Promoters Ass'n (441)
Outdoor Amusement Business Ass'n (451)

Production Equipment Rental Ass'n (463)
Showmen's League of America (483)

ENTOMOLOGY
American Entomological Soc. (66)
American Phytopathological Soc. (92)
Ass'n of Applied Insect Ecologists (143)
Coleopterists Soc. (196)
Entomological Soc. of America (231)
Nat'l Ass'n for Interpretation (340)
Nat'l Pest Control Ass'n (422)
Soc. for Vector Ecology (496)

ENVIRONMENT
Acrylonitrile Group (11)
Air Conditioning Contractors of America (15)
American Ass'n for Aerosol Research (29)
American Council on Science and Health (62)
American Industrial Health Council (75)
American Institute of Hydrology (77)
American Soc. for Environmental History (102)
American Soc. for Surface Mining and Reclamation (105)
Aspirin Foundation of America (129)
Ass'n for the Environmental Health of Soils (139)
Ass'n of Environmental and Resource Economists (150)
Ass'n of Environmental Engineering Professors (150)
Ecotourism Soc. (225)
Environmental Assessment Ass'n (231)
Environmental Bankers Ass'n (231)
Environmental Business Ass'n, The (231)
Environmental Design Research Ass'n (231)
Environmental Information Ass'n (231)
Environmental Management Ass'n (232)
Environmental Mutagen Soc. (232)
Institute for Polyacrylate Absorbents (265)
Institute of Environmental Sciences and Technology (267)
Internat'l Ass'n of Aquaculture Economics and Mangement (275)
Internat'l Ass'n of Milk, Food and Environmental Sanitarians (281)
Internat'l Ass'n of Wildland Fire (283)
Internat'l Lead Zinc Research Organization (295)
Internat'l Soc. for Ecological Economics (303)
Internat'l Soc. for Ecological Modelling-North American Chapter (303)
Nat'l Ass'n for Environmental Management (339)
Nat'l Ass'n of Environmental Professionals (354)
Nat'l Ass'n of Noise Control Officials (364)
Nat'l Conference of Local Environmental Health Administrators (390)
Nat'l Environmental Balancing Bureau (401)
Nat'l Environmental Development Ass'n (401)
Nat'l Environmental Health Ass'n (401)
Nat'l Environmental Training Ass'n (401)
Nat'l Institutes for Water Resources (412)
Nat'l Registry of Environmental Professionals (424)
Nat'l Spray Equipment Manufacturers Ass'n (431)
North American Ass'n for Environmental Education (440)
Renewable Natural Resources Foundation (475)
Silicones Environmental Health and Safety Council of North America (483)
Soc. for Ecological Restoration (487)
Soc. for Environmental Geochemistry and Health (487)
Soc. for Human Ecology (489)
Soc. for Occupational and Environmental Health (491)
Soc. of Environmental Journalists (501)
Soc. of Environmental Toxicology and Chemistry (501)
Steel Recycling Institute (516)
Synthetic Organic Chemical Manufacturers Ass'n (519)
United States Dye Manufacturers Operating Committee of ETAD (533)
World Research Foundation (550)

EXAMINERS
American Soc. of Home Inspectors (111)
Internat'l Ass'n of Boards of Examiners in Optometry (276)
Nat'l Ass'n of Disability Examiners (353)
Nat'l Ass'n of Document Examiners (353)
Nat'l Conference of Bar Examiners (389)
Nat'l Council of Examiners for Engineering and Surveying (394)
World Ass'n of Document Examiners (549)

EXECUTIVES
Advertising Media Credit Executives Ass'n, Internat'l (12)
Aggregate and Concrete Executives (14)
American Ass'n of Airport Executives (33)
American Ass'n of Medical Soc. Executives (39)
American Buyers of Meeting and Incentive Travel (50)
American Chamber of Commerce Executives (51)
American College of Physician Executives (57)
American Soc. of Ass'n Executives (107)
American Soc. of Corporate Secretaries (109)
American Soc. of Internat'l Executives (111)
Ass'n of Executive Search Consultants (150)
Ass'n of Incentive Marketing (153)
Ass'n of Master of Business Administration Executives (157)
Automotive Presidents Council (175)
Automotive Trade Ass'n Executives (175)
Chief Executives Organization (191)
Congress of Chiropractic State Ass'ns (205)
Controllers Council (208)
Cosmetic Executive Women (210)
Council of Engineering and Scientific Soc. Executives (213)
Council of Insurance Company Executives (214)
Council of State Ass'n Presidents (215)
County Executives of America (218)
Credit Union Executives Soc. (218)
Executive Women Internat'l (233)
Financial Executives Institute (238)
Food Industry Ass'n Executives (241)
Fraternity Executives Ass'n (244)
Internat'l Ass'n of Golf Administrators (279)

Internat'l Ass'n of Optometric Executives (281)
Internat'l Builders Exchange Executives (284)
Internat'l Council of Library Ass'n Executives (288)
Internat'l Downtown Ass'n (289)
Internat'l Food Service Executives' Ass'n (291)
Internat'l Military Community Executives Ass'n (297)
Internat'l Soc. of Facilities Executives (306)
Internat'l Soc. of Hotel Ass'n Executives (306)
Internat'l Soc. of Restaurant Ass'n Executives (307)
Issues Management Ass'n (313)
Licensing Executives Soc. (319)
Nat'l Ass'n of Bar Executives (344)
Nat'l Ass'n of Catering Executives (346)
Nat'l Ass'n of Community Action Agencies (349)
Nat'l Ass'n of Corporate Real Estate Executives International (350)
Nat'l Ass'n of Corporate Treasurers (350)
Nat'l Ass'n of Credit Union Chairmen (351)
Nat'l Ass'n of Executive Secretaries and Administrative Assistants (354)
Nat'l Ass'n of Television Program Executives (378)
Nat'l Council of County Ass'n Executives (394)
Nat'l Council of Preservation Executives (395)
Nat'l Council of State Pharmacy Ass'n Executives (396)
Nat'l Soc. of Fund Raising Executives (429)
Newspaper Ass'n Managers (439)
Nursery Ass'n Executives of North America (447)
Police Executive Research Forum (459)
Professional Soc. for Sales and Marketing Training (467)
Railway Labor Executives Ass'n (471)
Sales and Marketing Executives Internat'l (478)
Senior Executives Ass'n (482)
Soc. of Incentive and Travel Executives (502)
Strategic Leadership Forum (517)
Tax Executives Institute (520)
Television Operators Caucus (521)
Zonta Internat'l (551)

EXHIBITS see also CONVENTIONS
American Academy of Equine Art (21)
American Ass'n of Owners and Breeders of Peruvian Paso Horses (40)
American Buyers of Meeting and Incentive Travel (50)
American Veterinary Exhibitors Ass'n (121)
Center for Exhibition Industry Research (189)
Convention Liaison Council (208)
Display Distributors Ass'n (223)
Exhibit Designers and Producers Ass'n (234)
Exposition Service Contractors Ass'n (234)
Healthcare Convention and Exhibitors Ass'n (252)
Internat'l Ass'n for Exposition Management (274)
Internat'l Ass'n of Assembly Managers (276)
Internat'l Ass'n of Fairs and Expositions (279)
Internat'l Festivals and Events Ass'n (291)
Internat'l Laser Display Ass'n (295)
Internat'l Special Events Soc. (307)
Meeting Professionals Internat'l (327)
Nat'l Ass'n of Agricultural Fair Agencies (343)
Nat'l Ass'n of Consumer Shows (349)
Nat'l Catholic Educational Exhibitors (385)
North American Farm Show Council (442)
Religious Conference Management Ass'n (474)
Soc. of Independent Show Organizers (503)
Sports Card Ass'n (515)
Trade Show Exhibitors Ass'n (524)
Visitor Studies Ass'n (540)

EXPLOSIVES
American Pyrotechnics Ass'n (96)
Institute of Makers of Explosives (268)
Internat'l Ass'n of Bomb Technicians and Investigators (276)
Munitions Carriers Conference (331)

EXPORTS
American Ass'n of Exporters and Importers (36)
American Hardwood Export Council (72)
American Soc. of Internat'l Executives (111)
Ass'n of Dark Leaf Tobacco Dealers and Exporters (149)
Ass'n of Foreign Trade Representatives (151)
Auto Internat'l Ass'n (173)
Burley and Dark Leaf Tobacco Ass'n (184)
California Dried Fruit Export Ass'n (185)
Coal Exporters Ass'n of the United States (195)
FCIB-NACM Corp. (235)
Independent Distributors Ass'n (260)
Leaf Tobacco Exporters Ass'n (318)
Minority Internat'l Network for Trade (329)
Nat'l Ass'n of Export Companies (354)
Nat'l Council of Music Importers and Exporters (395)
Nat'l Council on Internat'l Trade Development (397)
North American Export Grain Ass'n (442)
Northwest Fruit Exporters (446)
Organization of Women in Internat'l Trade (450)
Overseas Sales and Marketing Ass'n of America (452)
Small Business Exporters Ass'n (484)
Texas Produce Export Ass'n (521)
U.S. Grains Council (528)
United States Apple Export Council (532)
United States Meat Export Federation (534)

FARMS
American Farm Bureau Federation (66)
American Forage and Grassland Council (69)
Ass'n of Farmworker Opportunity Programs (151)
Equipment Manufacturers Institute (232)
Farm Credit Council (234)
Farm Equipment Manufacturers Ass'n (235)
Farm Equipment Wholesalers Ass'n (235)
Farmers Educational and Co-operative Union of America (235)
Herb Growing and Marketing Network (253)
Nat'l Ass'n of Agricultural Journalists (343)
Nat'l Ass'n of Farm Broadcasters (354)
Nat'l Council of Agricultural Employers (394)

Subject Index FOOD INDUSTRY

Nat'l Council of Farmer Cooperatives **(394)**
Nat'l Farmers Organization **(402)**
Nat'l FFA Organization **(404)**
Nat'l Food and Energy Council **(405)**
North American Equipment Dealers Ass'n **(442)**
REALTORS Land Institute **(472)**
United Farm Workers of America **(530)**

FASTENERS
Fastener Industry Coalition **(235)**
Gasket Fabricators Ass'n **(246)**
Industrial Fasteners Institute **(262)**
Internat'l Staple, Nail and Tool Ass'n **(307)**
Nat'l Fastener Distributors Ass'n **(402)**
Specialty Tool and Fastener Distributors Ass'n **(514)**
Tubular Rivet and Machine Institute **(527)**

FATS & OILS
American Oil Chemists' Soc. **(88)**
Drug, Chemical and Allied Trades Ass'n **(225)**
Independent Liquid Terminals Ass'n **(261)**
Institute of Shortening and Edible Oils **(269)**
Internat'l Castor Oil Ass'n **(285)**
Internat'l Oil Mill Superintendents Ass'n **(298)**
Nat'l Candle Ass'n **(385)**
Nat'l Cottonseed Products Ass'n **(393)**
Nat'l Institute of Oilseed Products **(412)**
Nat'l Oilseed Processors Ass'n **(419)**
Nat'l Renderers Ass'n **(425)**
Nat'l Sunflower Ass'n **(432)**

FEED & GRAIN
American Alfalfa Processors Ass'n **(27)**
American Corn Millers Federation **(60)**
American Feed Industry Ass'n **(67)**
Ass'n of American Feed Control Officials **(142)**
Ass'n of Operative Millers **(159)**
Distilled Spirits Council of the U.S. **(223)**
Distillers Grains Technology Council **(223)**
Grain Elevator and Processing Soc. **(249)**
Nat'l Corn Growers Ass'n **(392)**
Nat'l Grain and Feed Ass'n **(407)**
Nat'l Grain Trade Council **(407)**
U.S. Grains Council **(528)**
United States Durum Growers Ass'n **(533)**

FERTILIZERS
Agricultural Retailers Ass'n **(14)**
Ass'n of American Plant Food Control Officials **(143)**
Better Lawn and Turf Institute **(178)**
Fertilizer Institute **(238)**
Internat'l Union of Petroleum and Industrial Workers **(310)**
Potash and Phosphate Institute **(461)**

FILMS
Academy of Motion Picture Arts and Sciences **(9)**
Adult Video Ass'n **(12)**
Alliance of Black Entertainment Technicians **(18)**
Alliance of Motion Picture and Television Producers **(18)**
American Ass'n for Vocational Instructional Materials **(32)**
American Cinema Editors **(52)**
American Federation of Musicians of the United States and Canada **(67)**
American Federation of Television and Radio Artists **(67)**
American Film Marketing Ass'n **(68)**
American Soc. of Cinematographers **(107)**
Ass'n for Information Media and Equipment **(135)**
Ass'n of Cinema and Video Laboratories **(146)**
Ass'n of Film Commissioners Internat'l **(151)**
Ass'n of Independent Commercial Producers **(153)**
Ass'n of Independent Video and Filmmakers **(154)**
Ass'n of Moving Image Archivists **(158)**
Black Filmmaker Foundation **(180)**
Consortium of College and University Media Centers **(206)**
Directors Guild of America **(223)**
Historians Film Committee **(254)**
Independent Feature Project **(260)**
Internat'l Animated Film Soc. **(273)**
Internat'l Ass'n of Audio Visual Communicators **(276)**
Internat'l Motion Picture and Lecturers Ass'n **(297)**
Internat'l Quorum of Film and Video Producers **(301)**
Internat'l Theatre Equipment Ass'n **(308)**
Internat'l Ticketing Ass'n **(308)**
Motion Picture and Television Credit Ass'n **(330)**
Motion Picture Ass'n of America **(330)**
Nat'l Alliance for Media Arts and Culture **(335)**
Nat'l Ass'n of Theatre Owners **(378)**
Nat'l Ass'n of Video Distributors **(379)**
Nat'l Magazine, Book, and Film Carriers Conference **(415)**
Producer's Guild of America **(463)**
Professional Travelogue Sponsors **(467)**
Screen Actors Guild **(480)**
Soc. for Cinema Studies **(486)**
Soc. of Motion Picture and Television Art Directors **(504)**
Soc. of Motion Picture and Television Engineers **(504)**
Stuntmen's Ass'n of Motion Pictures **(517)**
Stuntwomen's Ass'n of Motion Pictures **(517)**
Training Media Ass'n **(525)**
United Scenic Artists **(531)**
University Film and Video Ass'n **(537)**
Wedding and Event Videographers Ass'n Internat'l **(542)**
Women in Film **(546)**
Women in Film and Video **(546)**
Women of the Motion Picture Industry, Internat'l **(547)**
Writers Guild of America, East **(551)**
Writers Guild of America, west **(551)**

FINANCE see also CREDIT
AACE Internat'l **(7)**
American Ass'n of Individual Investors **(38)**
American Association of Healthcare Administrative Management **(45)**
American Bankruptcy Institute **(46)**
American Cash Flow Ass'n **(50)**
American Education Finance Ass'n **(65)**
American Finance Ass'n **(68)**
American Financial Services Ass'n **(68)**
American Soc. of Military Comptrollers **(112)**
American Soc. of Payroll Management **(114)**
Ass'n for Management Information in Financial Services **(136)**
Ass'n of Commercial Finance Attorneys **(148)**
Ass'n of Finance and Insurance Professionals **(151)**
Ass'n of Government Accountants **(152)**
Ass'n of Local Housing Finance Agencies **(156)**
Bankers Roundtable, The **(176)**
Broadcast Cable Credit Ass'n **(182)**
Broadcast Cable Financial Management Ass'n **(182)**
Coalition of Publicly Traded Partnerships **(196)**
Commercial Finance Ass'n **(199)**
Community Development Venture Capital Ass'n **(201)**
Conference on Consumer Finance Law **(205)**
Corporate Facility Advisors **(209)**
Council of Development Finance Agencies **(213)**
Council of Infrastructure Financing Authorities **(214)**
Council of Institutional Investors **(214)**
Credit Research Foundation **(218)**
Credit Union Executives Soc. **(218)**
Credit Union Nat'l Ass'n **(218)**
Defense Credit Union Council **(220)**
Emerging Markets Traders Ass'n **(229)**
Financial Executives Institute **(238)**
Financial Institutions Insurance Ass'n **(239)**
Financial Management Ass'n **(239)**
Financial Managers Soc. **(239)**
Financial Markets Ass'n **(239)**
Financial Services Council **(239)**
Financial Services Technology Network **(239)**
Government Finance Officers Ass'n of the United States and Canada **(248)**
Healthcare Billing and Management Ass'n **(252)**
Healthcare Finance Study Group **(252)**
Home Improvement Lenders Ass'n **(255)**
Institute for Investment Management Consultants **(265)**
Institute for Responsible Housing Preservation **(265)**
Institute of Certified Financial Planners **(266)**
Institute of Financial Education **(267)**
Institute of Internat'l Finance **(267)**
Institute of Management Accountants **(268)**
Internat'l Ass'n for Financial Planning **(274)**
Internat'l Newspaper Financial Executives **(298)**
Internat'l Soc. of Financiers, Inc. **(306)**
Internat'l Swaps and Derivatives Ass'n **(308)**
Managed Futures Ass'n **(322)**
Municipal Finance Industry Ass'n **(331)**
Municipal Treasurers Ass'n of the United States and Canada **(331)**
Nat'l Accounting and Finance Council **(334)**
Nat'l Aircraft Finance Ass'n **(335)**
Nat'l Ass'n for Treasurers of Religious Institutes **(342)**
Nat'l Ass'n of Affordable Housing Lenders **(342)**
Nat'l Ass'n of Bankruptcy Trustees **(344)**
Nat'l Ass'n of Certified Valuation Analysts **(346)**
Nat'l Ass'n of Corporate Treasurers **(350)**
Nat'l Ass'n of County Treasurers and Finance Officers **(351)**
Nat'l Ass'n of Equipment Leasing Brokers **(354)**
Nat'l Ass'n of Federal Credit Unions **(355)**
Nat'l Ass'n of Independent Public Finance Advisors **(359)**
Nat'l Ass'n of Mortgage Brokers **(363)**
Nat'l Ass'n of Personal Financial Advisors **(365)**
Nat'l Ass'n of Purchasing Management **(368)**
Nat'l Ass'n of Settlement Purchasers **(372)**
Nat'l Ass'n of Small Business Investment Companies **(373)**
Nat'l Ass'n of State Budget Officers **(374)**
Nat'l Automated Clearing House Ass'n **(381)**
Nat'l Committee on Planned Giving **(388)**
Nat'l Community Capital Ass'n **(388)**
Nat'l Council of Health Facilities Finance Authorities **(395)**
Nat'l Defined Contribution Council **(399)**
Nat'l Federation of Municipal Analysts **(403)**
Nat'l Finance Adjusters **(404)**
Nat'l Institute of Pension Administrators **(412)**
Nat'l Investment Company Service Ass'n **(413)**
Nat'l Pawnbrokers Ass'n **(421)**
Nat'l Vehicle Leasing Ass'n **(435)**
Nat'l Venture Capital Ass'n **(435)**
Retirement Industry Trust Ass'n **(476)**
Robert Morris Associates, the Ass'n of Lending and Credit Risk Professionals **(476)**
Soc. for Information Management **(490)**
Soc. of Financial Examiners **(501)**
Soc. of Quantitative Analysts **(506)**
State Debt Management Network **(516)**
State Risk and Insurance Management Ass'n **(516)**
Tax Executives Institute **(520)**
Treasury Management Ass'n **(526)**
Women in Financial Development **(546)**

FIRE
Aerial Firefighting Industry Ass'n **(13)**
American Fire Sprinkler Ass'n **(68)**
American Pyrotechnics Ass'n **(96)**
Automatic Fire Alarm Ass'n **(173)**
Disaster Preparedness and Emergency Response Ass'n **(223)**
Fire Apparatus Manufacturers Ass'n **(239)**
Fire Equipment Manufacturers Suppliers Ass'n **(239)**
Fire Equipment Manufacturers' Ass'n **(239)**
Fire Marshals Ass'n of North America **(239)**
Fire Retardant Chemicals Ass'n **(240)**
Fire Suppression Systems Ass'n **(240)**
Internat'l Ass'n of Arson Investigators **(275)**
Internat'l Ass'n of Black Professional Fire Fighters **(276)**
Internat'l Ass'n of Fire Chiefs **(279)**
Internat'l Ass'n of Fire Fighters **(279)**
Internat'l Ass'n of Wildland Fire **(283)**
Internat'l Fire Photographers Ass'n **(291)**
Internat'l Firestop Council **(291)**
Internat'l Soc. of Fire Service Instructors **(306)**
Lighter Ass'n **(319)**
Nat'l Ass'n of Chiefs of Police **(347)**
Nat'l Ass'n of Fire Equipment Distributors **(355)**
Nat'l Ass'n of Fire Investigators **(355)**
Nat'l Ass'n of State Fire Marshals **(375)**
Nat'l Burglar and Fire Alarm Ass'n **(384)**
Nat'l Fire Protection Ass'n **(404)**
Nat'l Fire Sprinkler Ass'n **(404)**
Nat'l Volunteer Fire Council **(435)**
Pyrotechnic Signal Manufacturers Ass'n **(470)**
Soc. of Fire Protection Engineers **(501)**
United Fire Equipment Service Ass'n **(530)**
Women in the Fire Service **(547)**

FIREARMS
American Custom Gunmakers Guild **(63)**
Firearms Research and Indentification Ass'n **(240)**
Nat'l Ass'n of Federally Licensed Firearms Dealers **(355)**
Nat'l Ass'n of Sporting Goods Wholesalers **(373)**
Nat'l Reloading Manufacturers Ass'n **(425)**
Nat'l Rifle Ass'n of America **(426)**
Nat'l Shooting Sports Foundation **(428)**
Non-Powder Gun Products Ass'n **(439)**
North American Gamebird Ass'n **(442)**
Sporting Arms and Ammunition Manufacturers' Institute **(515)**
Sporting Goods Manufacturers Ass'n **(515)**

FISH AND FISHING
American Fisheries Soc. **(68)**
American Institute of Fishery Research Biologists **(77)**
American Littoral Soc. **(82)**
American Shrimp Processors Ass'n **(100)**
American Sport Fishing Ass'n **(118)**
American Tunaboat Ass'n **(121)**
American Zoo and Aquarium Ass'n **(124)**
Ass'n of Smoked Fish Processors **(165)**
At-sea Processors Ass'n **(172)**
Board of Trade of the Wholesale Seafood Merchants **(181)**
Catfish Farmers of America **(188)**
Internat'l Ass'n of Astacology **(276)**
Internat'l Ass'n of Fish and Wildlife Agencies **(279)**
Internat'l Institute of Fisheries Economics and Trade **(294)**
Meat Industry Suppliers Ass'n **(325)**
Molluscan Shellfish Institute **(330)**
Nat'l Blue Crab Industry Ass'n **(383)**
Nat'l Fisheries Institute **(404)**
Nat'l Ocean Industries Ass'n **(419)**
Nat'l Ornamental Goldfish Growers Ass'n **(420)**
Nat'l Party Boat Owners Alliance **(421)**
Nat'l Shellfisheries Ass'n **(427)**
Nat'l Shrimp Processors Ass'n **(428)**
Organization of Wildlife Planners **(450)**
Shrimp Council **(483)**
United States Trout Farmers Ass'n **(535)**
United States Tuna Foundation **(535)**
Women's Fisheries Network **(548)**

FLOORING
Ass'n of Specialists in Cleaning and Restoration Internat'l **(165)**
Carpet and Rug Institute **(187)**
Floor Covering Installation Contractors Ass'n **(240)**
Hardwood Plywood and Veneer Ass'n **(251)**
Maple Flooring Manufacturers Ass'n **(323)**
Marble Institute of America **(323)**
Nat'l Ass'n of Floor Covering Distributors **(355)**
Nat'l Oak Flooring Manufacturers Ass'n **(419)**
Nat'l Terrazzo and Mosaic Ass'n **(433)**
Nat'l Wood Flooring Ass'n **(436)**
Resilient Floor Covering Institute **(475)**
World Floor Covering Ass'n **(549)**

FOOD INDUSTRY
African-American Natural Foods Ass'n **(14)**
American Ass'n of Cereal Chemists **(34)**
American Beekeeping Federation **(47)**
American Dietetic Ass'n **(64)**
American Frozen Food Institute **(69)**
American Institute of Food Distribution **(77)**
American Meat Institute **(83)**
American Mushroom Institute **(86)**
American Peanut Council **(90)**
American Shrimp Processors Ass'n **(100)**
American Spice Trade Ass'n **(117)**
American Sugar Alliance **(119)**
American Sugar Cane League of the U.S.A. **(119)**
Apple Processors Ass'n **(126)**
Ass'n for the Study of Food and Society **(139)**
Ass'n of Farmworker Opportunity Programs **(151)**
Ass'n of Food and Drug Officials **(151)**
Ass'n of Food Industries **(151)**
Beet Sugar Development Foundation **(177)**
Biscuit and Cracker Distributors Ass'n **(179)**
Biscuit and Cracker Manufacturers' Ass'n **(179)**
Board of Trade of the City of New York **(180)**
Calorie Control Council **(186)**
Chemical Sources Ass'n **(191)**
Chilled Foods Ass'n **(192)**
Chinese American Food Soc. **(192)**
Corn Refiners Ass'n **(209)**
Environmental Management Ass'n **(232)**
Flavor and Extract Manufacturers Ass'n of the United States **(240)**
Food and Drug Law Institute **(241)**
Food Distribution Research Soc. **(241)**
Food Equipment Manufacturers Ass'n **(241)**
Food Industry Suppliers Ass'n **(241)**
Foodservice Equipment Distributors Ass'n **(242)**
Foodservice Group **(242)**
Fresh Produce and Floral Council **(244)**
Greek Food and Wine Institute **(249)**
Herb Growing and Marketing Network **(253)**

National Trade and Professional Associations of the U.S. © 1999, Columbia Books, Inc. 569

FOOD PROCESSORS

FOOD SERVICES

FOOTBALL

FOREIGN SERVICE

FOREIGN TRADE see also EXPORTS, IMPORTS, WEBB-POMERENE ACT

FORENSIC

FORESTRY

FOUNDATIONS

FOUNDRIES

FRANCHISES

FRATERNAL ORGANIZATIONS see also CLUBS

FREIGHT FORWARDERS

FRENCH

FRUIT

Subject Index *GOVERNMENT see also MILITARY*

Internat'l Dwarf Fruit Tree Ass'n **(289)**
Nat'l Ass'n of Fruits, Flavors and Syrups **(356)**
Nat'l Cherry Growers and Industries Foundation **(386)**
Nat'l Food Processors Ass'n **(405)**
Nat'l Juice Products Ass'n **(413)**
Nat'l Peach Council **(421)**
Nat'l Watermelon Ass'n **(436)**
North American Blueberry Council **(440)**
North American Strawberry Growers Ass'n **(445)**
Northwest Fruit Exporters **(446)**
Processed Apples Institute **(463)**
Soil and Plant Analysis Council **(509)**
U.S. Apple Ass'n **(528)**
United Fresh Fruit and Vegetable Ass'n **(531)**
United States Apple Export Council **(532)**
Wild Blueberry Ass'n of North America **(544)**

FUND-RAISING
American Ass'n of Fund-Raising Counsel **(37)**
Ass'n for Healthcare Philanthropy **(134)**
Ass'n of Fund Raisers and Direct Sellers **(152)**
Ass'n of Professional Researchers for Advancement **(161)**
Council for Advancement and Support of Education **(210)**
Foundation for Independent Higher Education **(243)**
Independent Sector **(261)**
Nat'l Ass'n of Athletic Development Directors **(343)**
Nat'l Ass'n of Independent Colleges and Universities **(359)**
Nat'l Catholic Development Conference **(385)**
Nat'l Soc. of Fund Raising Executives **(429)**
North American Ass'n of State and Provincial Lotteries **(440)**

FUNERALS see also CEMETERIES
Associated Funeral Directors, Internat'l **(171)**
Casket and Funeral Supply Ass'n of America **(187)**
Cremation Ass'n of North America **(219)**
Funeral and Memorial Socs. of America **(244)**
Internat'l Conference of Funeral Service Examining Boards **(287)**
Jewish Funeral Directors of America **(314)**
Monument Builders of North America **(330)**
Nat'l Concrete Burial Vault Ass'n **(389)**
Nat'l Funeral Directors and Morticians Ass'n **(406)**
Nat'l Funeral Directors Ass'n **(406)**
Nat'l Selected Morticians **(427)**
Preferred Funeral Directors Internat'l **(462)**

FURNITURE
American Furniture Manufacturers Ass'n **(69)**
American Innerspring Manufacturers **(75)**
American Soc. of Furniture Designers **(110)**
Ass'n of Bedding and Furniture Law Officials **(144)**
Ass'n of Progressive Rental Organizations **(162)**
Ass'n of Woodworking and Furnishings Suppliers **(170)**
Business and Institutional Furniture Manufacturers Ass'n Internat'l **(104)**
Casual Furniture Retailers **(187)**
Decorative Window Coverings Ass'n **(220)**
Futon Ass'n Internat'l **(245)**
Institute of Inspection Cleaning and Restoration **(267)**
Internat'l Furniture Rental Ass'n **(292)**
Internat'l Home Furnishings Marketing Ass'n **(293)**
Internat'l Interior Design Ass'n **(295)**
Internat'l Sleep Products Ass'n **(302)**
Internat'l Wholesale Furniture Ass'n **(311)**
Juvenile Products Manufacturers Ass'n **(315)**
Nat'l Ass'n of Office Furniture Dealers **(364)**
Nat'l Ass'n of Resale and Thrift Shops **(370)**
Nat'l Ass'n of Store Fixture Manufacturers **(377)**
Nat'l Cotton Batting Institute **(392)**
Nat'l Furniture Traffic Conference **(406)**
Nat'l Home Furnishings Ass'n **(409)**
Scientific Equipment and Furniture Ass'n **(480)**
Soc. of the Plastics Industry - Polyurethane Division **(507)**
Specialty Sleep Ass'n **(514)**
Summer and Casual Furniture Manufacturers Ass'n **(518)**
Unfinished Furniture Ass'n **(529)**
Upholstered Furniture Action Council **(537)**
Wood Component Manufacturers Ass'n **(548)**

FURS
American Karakul Sheep Registry **(80)**
American Legend Cooperative **(81)**
Fur Commission USA **(244)**
Fur Information Council of America **(244)**
Nat'l Trappers Ass'n **(434)**

GARAGES
Automotive Lift Institute **(174)**
Automotive Maintenance and Repair Ass'n **(174)**
Automotive Service Ass'n **(175)**
Convenient Automotive Services Institute **(208)**
Door and Access Systems Manufacturers' Ass'n, Internat'l **(224)**
Garage Door Council **(245)**
Internat'l Door Ass'n **(289)**
Nat'l Ass'n of Auto Trim and Restyling Shops **(344)**
Soc. of Collision Repair Specialists **(499)**

GARDENING
American Horticultural Soc. **(74)**
American Seed Trade Ass'n **(99)**
American Soc. of Consulting Arborists **(108)**
Better Lawn and Turf Institute **(178)**
Garden Centers of America **(245)**
Garden Writers Ass'n of America **(245)**
Internat'l Waterlily and Watergardening Soc. **(310)**
Lawn and Garden Dealers' Ass'n **(318)**
Lawn and Garden Marketing and Distribution Ass'n **(318)**
Nat'l Ass'n of Hose and Accessories Distributors **(358)**
Nat'l Bark and Soil Producers Ass'n **(382)**
Nat'l Council of State Garden Clubs **(396)**
North American Horticultural Supply Ass'n **(442)**
North American Plant Preservation Council **(443)**
Professional Grounds Management Soc. **(465)**
Professional Lawn Care Ass'n of America **(466)**

GAS
American Ass'n for Aerosol Research **(29)**
American Gas Ass'n **(70)**
American Public Gas Ass'n **(95)**
American Soc. of Gas Engineers **(110)**
Associated Gas Distributors **(171)**
Compressed Air and Gas Institute **(202)**
Compressed Gas Ass'n **(202)**
Distribution Contractors Ass'n **(224)**
Gas Appliance Manufacturers Ass'n **(245)**
Gas Processors Ass'n **(245)**
Gas Processors Suppliers Ass'n **(245)**
Gas Research Institute **(246)**
Gas Turbine Ass'n **(246)**
Institute of Gas Technology **(267)**
Interstate Natural Gas Ass'n of America **(311)**
Liaison Committee of Cooperating Oil and Gas Ass'ns **(319)**
Nat'l Ass'n of Royalty Owners **(370)**
Nat'l Energy Services Ass'n **(401)**
Nat'l Ocean Industries Ass'n **(419)**
Nat'l Propane Gas Ass'n **(423)**
Natural Gas Supply Ass'n **(437)**
Natural Gas Vehicle Coalition **(437)**
Pipe Line Contractors Ass'n **(458)**
Pressure Vessel Manufacturers Ass'n **(462)**
Propane Vehicle Council **(468)**
Soc. of Professional Well Log Analysts **(506)**
U.S. Oil and Gas Ass'n **(528)**

GASOLINE
American Truck Stop Operators Ass'n **(121)**
Gasoline and Automotive Service Dealers Ass'n **(246)**
Gasoline Pump Manufacturers Ass'n **(246)**
Renewable Fuels Ass'n **(475)**
Service Station Dealers of America and Allied Trades **(482)**
Soc. of Independent Gasoline Marketers of America **(502)**

GASTROENTEROLOGY
American College of Gastroenterology **(54)**
American Gastroenterological Ass'n **(70)**
American Lithotripsy Soc. **(81)**
American Motility Soc. **(85)**
American Soc. for Parenteral and Enteral Nutrition **(104)**
Gastroenterology Research Group **(246)**
North American Soc. for Pediatric Gastroenterology and Nutrition **(444)**
Soc. of American Gastrointestinal Endoscopic Surgeons **(497)**
Soc. of Gastroenterology Nurses and Associates **(502)**

GEARS
American Gear Manufacturers Ass'n **(70)**
Industrial Mathematics Soc. **(263)**

GENEALOGY
Nat'l Genealogical Soc. **(406)**

GENETICS
American Genetic Ass'n **(70)**
American Soc. of Human Genetics **(111)**
Behavior Genetics Ass'n **(177)**
Electrophoresis Soc. **(229)**
Environmental Mutagen Soc. **(232)**
Genetics Soc. of America **(246)**
Internat'l Embryo Transfer Soc. **(290)**
Nat'l Soc. of Genetic Counselors **(430)**
Nat'l Tay-Sachs and Allied Diseases Ass'n **(433)**
Soc. for the Study of Evolution **(495)**
Soc. for Theriogenology **(496)**

GEOGRAPHY
American Geographical Soc. **(70)**
American Institute of Bangladesh Studies **(76)**
American Institute of Indian Studies **(77)**
American Soc. of Geolinguistics **(110)**
Ass'n for Arid Lands Studies **(130)**
Ass'n of American Geographers **(142)**
Ass'n of Third World Studies **(168)**
Geospatial Information and Technology Ass'n **(247)**
Nat'l Council for Geographic Education **(393)**
Organization for Tropical Studies **(450)**
Soc. for the History of Discoveries **(495)**
Soc. of Woman Geographers **(509)**

GEOLOGY
American Ass'n of Petroleum Geologists **(40)**
American Ass'n of Stratigraphic Palynologists **(43)**
American Geological Institute **(70)**
American Geophysical Union **(70)**
American Institute of Professional Geologists **(78)**
American Rock Mechanics Ass'n **(98)**
ASFE: Professional Firms Practicing in the Geosciences **(128)**
Ass'n for Women Geoscientists **(140)**
Ass'n of American State Geologists **(143)**
Ass'n of Earth Science Editors **(150)**
Ass'n of Engineering Geologists **(150)**
Clay Minerals Soc. **(194)**
Computer Oriented Geological Soc. **(202)**
Earthquake Engineering Research Institute **(225)**
Geochemical Soc. **(246)**
Geological Soc. of America **(246)**
Geoscience Information Soc. **(247)**
History of Earth Sciences Soc. **(254)**
Internat'l Ass'n for Mathematical Geology **(274)**
Internat'l Ass'n of Hydrogeologists **(280)**
Nat'l Ass'n for Black Geologists and Geophysicists **(338)**
Nat'l Ass'n of Geoscience Teachers **(356)**
Nat'l Ass'n of State Boards of Geology **(374)**
Paleontological Soc. **(452)**
Seismological Soc. of America **(481)**
Soc. for Luminescent Microscopy and Spectroscopy **(490)**
Soc. for Mining, Metallurgy, and Exploration **(491)**
Soc. for Organic Petrology **(492)**
Soc. of Economic Geologists **(500)**
Soc. of Exploration Geophysicists **(501)**
Soc. of Independent Professional Earth Scientists **(503)**
Soc. of Professional Well Log Analysts **(506)**

GERMAN
American Ass'n of Teachers of German **(44)**
German American Chamber of Commerce **(247)**

GERONTOLOGY
American Aging Ass'n **(27)**
American Ass'n for Geriatric Psychiatry **(30)**
American Federation for Aging Research **(66)**
American Geriatrics Soc. **(71)**
American Soc. on Aging **(117)**
Ass'n for Adult Development and Aging **(129)**
Ass'n for Gerontology in Higher Education **(134)**
Council on Geriatric Cardiology **(217)**
Gerontological Soc. of America **(247)**
Internat'l Psychogeriatric Ass'n **(300)**
Nat'l Ass'n of Area Agencies on Aging **(343)**
Nat'l Certification Council for Activity Professionals **(386)**
Nat'l Council on the Aging **(398)**
Nat'l Gerontological Nursing Ass'n **(407)**

GLASS see also BOTTLES
American Ceramic Soc. **(51)**
American Flint Glass Workers Union **(68)**
American Scientific Glassblowers Soc. **(99)**
American Soc. of Scientific Glass Blowers **(116)**
Associated Glass and Pottery Manufacturers **(171)**
Giftware Associates Interchange **(247)**
Glass Art Soc. **(247)**
Glass Ass'n of North America **(247)**
Glass Packaging Institute **(247)**
Glass, Molders, Pottery, Plastics and Allied Workers International Union **(248)**
Glazing Industry Code Committee **(248)**
Laminators Safety Glass Ass'n **(317)**
Nat'l Ass'n of Container Distributors **(349)**
Nat'l Glass Ass'n **(407)**
Nat'l Industrial Sand Ass'n **(411)**
Nat'l Sunroom Ass'n **(432)**
Nat'l Tabletop and Giftware Ass'n **(433)**
North American Ass'n of Mirror Manufacturers **(440)**
Primary Glass Manufacturers Council **(462)**
Sealed Insulating Glass Manufacturers Ass'n **(480)**
Soc. of Glass and Ceramic Decorators **(502)**
Stained Glass Ass'n of America **(515)**

GLOVES
Internat'l Hand Protection Ass'n **(293)**
Nat'l Industrial Glove Distributors Ass'n **(411)**

GOATS
American Angora Goat Breeder's Ass'n **(28)**
American Ass'n of Small Ruminant Practitioners **(42)**
American Dairy Goat Ass'n **(63)**
American Goat Soc. **(71)**
Internat'l Nubian Breeders Ass'n **(298)**
Mohair Council of America **(330)**
Nat'l Pedigreed Livestock Council **(422)**

GOLD
Gold Institute **(248)**
Internat'l Precious Metals Institute **(300)**
Manufacturing Jewelers and Suppliers of America **(323)**
Soc. of Mineral Analysts **(504)**
Soc. of North American Goldsmiths **(504)**
World Gold Council **(550)**

GOLF
American Soc. of Golf Course Architects **(110)**
Ass'n of Golf Merchandisers **(152)**
Emerald Green Miniature Golf Ass'n **(229)**
Golf Coaches Ass'n of America **(248)**
Golf Course Builders Ass'n of America **(248)**
Golf Course Superintendents Ass'n of America **(248)**
Golf Range and Recreation Ass'n of America **(248)**
Golf Writers Ass'n of America **(248)**
Internat'l Ass'n of Amusement Parks and Attractions **(275)**
Internat'l Ass'n of Golf Administrators **(279)**
Ladies Professional Golf Ass'n **(316)**
Miniature Golf Ass'n of America/Miniature Golf Develoment of America **(329)**
Nat'l Ass'n of Golf Tournament Directors **(356)**
Nat'l Golf Car Manufacturers Ass'n **(407)**
Nat'l Golf Course Owners Ass'n **(407)**
Nat'l Golf Foundation **(407)**
PGA TOUR Tournaments Ass'n **(456)**
Professional Golfers Ass'n of America **(465)**
Professional Putters Ass'n **(466)**
Public Golf Management Ass'n **(469)**
United States Golf Ass'n **(534)**

GOVERNMENT see also MILITARY
Air Traffic Control Ass'n **(16)**
Airports Council Internat'l/North America **(17)**
American Ass'n for Budget and Program Analysis **(29)**
American Ass'n of Food Stamp Directors **(37)**
American Ass'n of Motor Vehicle Administrators **(39)**
American Ass'n of Police Polygraphists **(41)**
American Ass'n of Port Authorities **(41)**
American Ass'n of Public Health Dentistry **(42)**
American Ass'n of Public Welfare Attorneys **(42)**
American Ass'n of Public Welfare Information Systems Management **(42)**
American Ass'n of State Climatologists **(43)**
American Ass'n of State Highway and Transportation Officials **(43)**

National Trade and Professional Associations of the U.S. © 1999, Columbia Books, Inc. 571

Subject Index HEALTH CARE

North American Gaming Regulators Ass'n (442)
North American Securities Administrators Ass'n (444)
Nurses Organization of Veterans Affairs (447)
Organization of Professional Employees of the U.S. Department of Agriculture (450)
Organization of Wildlife Planners (450)
Patent and Trademark Office Soc. (454)
Political Products Manufacturers Ass'n (460)
Professional Managers Ass'n (466)
Public Agency Risk Managers Ass'n (469)
Public Employees Roundtable (469)
Public Housing Authorities Directors Ass'n (469)
Public Risk Management Ass'n (470)
Senior Executives Ass'n (482)
Soc. for History in the Federal Government (489)
Soc. of Cost Estimating and Analysis (500)
Soc. of Federal Labor Relations Professionals (501)
Soc. of Federal Linguists (501)
Soc. of Former Special Agents of the Federal Bureau of Investigation (501)
Soc. of Government Economists (502)
Soc. of Government Meeting Professionals (502)
Soc. of State Directors of Health, Physical Education and Recreation (507)
Soc. of Travel Agents in Government (508)
State and Territorial Air Pollution Program Administrators (515)
State Debt Management Network (516)
State Government Affairs Council (516)
State Higher Education Executive Officers (516)
State Risk and Insurance Management Ass'n (516)
States Organization for Boating Access (516)
SWANA - Solid Waste Ass'n of North America (519)
Trademark Soc. (525)
United States Animal Health Ass'n (532)
United States Conference of City Human Services Officials (533)
United States Conference of Mayors (533)
Urban and Regional Information Systems Ass'n (537)
Voluntary Protection Programs Participants Ass'n (540)
Women Executives in State Government (546)
Women in Government (546)
Women in Government Relations (546)
Women in Municipal Government (547)
World Affairs Councils of America (549)

GRAIN see also FEED & GRAIN
American Ass'n of Cereal Chemists (34)
American Ass'n of Grain Inspection and Weighing Agencies (37)
American Federation of Grain Millers Internat'l Union (67)
American Malting Barley Ass'n (82)
American Oat Ass'n (87)
Internat'l Wild Rice Ass'n (311)
Nat'l Futures Ass'n (406)
Nat'l Grain and Feed Ass'n (407)
Nat'l Grain Sorghum Producers (407)
Nat'l Grain Trade Council (407)
New York Mercantile Exchange (438)
North American Export Grain Ass'n (442)
Renewable Fuels Ass'n (475)
Transporting Elevator and Grain Merchants Ass'n (526)
U.S. Grains Council (528)
Wheat Quality Council (543)

GRAPHIC ARTS
American Academy of Equine Art (21)
American Center for Design (51)
American Institute of Graphic Arts (77)
Ass'n for Graphic Arts Training (134)
Ass'n of Professional Design Firms (161)
Business Forms Management Ass'n (184)
Graphic Artists Guild Nat'l (249)
Graphic Arts Employers of America (249)
Graphic Arts Marketing Information Service (249)
Graphic Arts Professionals (249)
Graphic Arts Sales Foundation (249)
Graphic Arts Technical Foundation (249)
Graphic Communications Internat'l Union (249)
Guild of Book Workers (250)
Guild of Natural Science Illustrators (250)
Internat'l Graphic Arts Education Ass'n (292)
Internat'l Publishing Management Ass'n (300)
Internat'l Thermographers Ass'n (308)
Nat'l Ass'n of Limited Edition Dealers (361)
Nat'l Ass'n of Printers and Lithographers (366)
Newspaper Features Council (439)
North American Graphic Arts Suppliers Ass'n (442)
NPES, the Ass'n for Suppliers of Printing and Publishing Technologies (446)
Printing Brokerage Buyers Ass'n (463)
Screenprinting and Graphic Imaging Ass'n Internat'l (480)
Soc. for Technical Communication (494)
Soc. of American Graphic Artists (497)
Special Interest Group on Computer Graphics (512)
Technical Ass'n of the Graphic Arts (520)
Type Directors Club (528)
World Computer Graphics Ass'n (549)

GROCERS
Ass'n of Coupon Professionals (149)
CIES, The Food Business Forum (193)
Food Distributors Internat'l (241)
Food Marketing Institute (241)
Fresh Produce Ass'n of the Americas (244)
Grocery Manufacturers of America (250)
Mexican-American Grocers Ass'n (327)
Nat'l Grocers Ass'n (407)

GYNECOLOGY
American Ass'n of Gynecological Laparoscopists (37)
American College of Obstetricians and Gynecologists (56)
American College of Osteopathic Obstetricians and Gynecologists (56)
American Soc. for Colposcopy and Cervical Pathology (101)
American Urogynecologic Soc. (121)
Ass'n of Maternal and Child Health Programs (157)
Ass'n of Professors of Gynecology and Obstetrics (161)
Ass'n of Women's Health, Obstetric and Neonatal Nurses (169)
Gynecologic Oncology Group (250)
Gynecologic Surgery Soc. (250)
Internat'l Childbirth Education Ass'n (285)
Nat'l Abortion Federation (333)
Nat'l Family Planning and Reproductive Health Ass'n (402)
Soc. for Gynecologic Investigation (488)
Soc. of Gynecologic Oncologists (502)

HANDICAPPED see also BLIND, DEAF
Access Technology Ass'n (10)
Ass'n on Higher Education and Disability (170)
Nat'l AMBUCS (336)
Nat'l Ass'n for Independent Living (339)
Soc. for Disability Studies (487)

HANDWRITING
American Ass'n of Handwriting Analysts (37)
American College of Forensic Examiners (54)
American Handwriting Analysis Foundation (71)
Internat'l Graphological Soc. (292)
Nat'l Ass'n of Document Examiners (353)
Nat'l Soc. for Graphology (428)

HARDWARE
American Hardware Manufacturers Ass'n (72)
American Rolling Door Institute (98)
Builders Hardware Manufacturers Ass'n (183)
Building Material Dealers Ass'n (183)
Door and Hardware Institute (224)
Garage Door Hardware Ass'n (245)
Internat'l Hardware Distributors Ass'n (293)
Nat'l Ass'n of Hose and Accessories Distributors (358)
Nat'l Marine Distributors Ass'n (416)
Nat'l Retail Hardware Ass'n (425)
Service Specialists Ass'n (482)
Tooling Component Manufacturers Ass'n (524)
Window Covering Safety Council (544)

HEALTH CARE
Academy of Clinical Laboratory Physicians and Scientists (8)
Academy of Dispensing Audiologists (8)
Academy of Managed Care Providers (9)
Accreditation Ass'n for Ambulatory Health Care (10)
Alliance for Healthcare Strategy and Marketing (17)
Alliance of Cardiovascular Professionals (18)
America's Blood Centers (19)
American Academy of Clinical Sexologists (21)
American Academy of Health Care Providers in the Addictive Disorders (22)
American Academy of Hospice and Palliative Medicine (22)
American Academy of Nurse Practitioners (23)
American Academy of Pain Management (24)
American Academy of Procedural Coders (25)
American Academy of Somnology (26)
American Ass'n for Active Lifestyles and Fitness (29)
American Ass'n for Continuity of Care (30)
American Ass'n for Health Education (31)
American Ass'n for Holistic Health (31)
American Ass'n for Medical Transcription (31)
American Ass'n of Eye and Ear Hospitals (36)
American Ass'n of Health Plans (37)
American Ass'n of Homes and Services for the Aging (37)
American Ass'n of Integrated Healthcare Delivery Systems (38)
American Ass'n of Spinal Cord Injury Nurses (42)
American Ass'n of Surgical Physician Assistants (43)
American Association of Healthcare Administrative Management (45)
American Baptist Homes and Hospitals Ass'n (46)
American Blood Resources Ass'n (47)
American Board of Quality Assurance and Utilization Review Physicians (48)
American Clinical Laboratory Ass'n (52)
American College Health Ass'n (52)
American College of Cardiovascular Administrators (53)
American College of Health Care Administrators (54)
American College of Healthcare Information Administrators (54)
American College of Managed Care Administrators (55)
American College of Medical Practice Executives (55)
American College of Physician Executives (57)
American Correctional Health Services Ass'n (60)
American Council on Science and Health (62)
American Federation of Home Health Agencies (67)
American Fitness Ass'n (68)
American Health Care Ass'n (72)
American Health Lawyers Ass'n (72)
American Health Planning Ass'n (72)
American Health Quality Ass'n (72)
American Herbal Products Ass'n (73)
American Holistic Medical Ass'n (73)
American Managed Behavioral Healthcare Ass'n (82)
American Massage Therapy Ass'n (83)
American Medical Directors Ass'n (83)
American Medical Group Ass'n (83)
American Medical Informatics Ass'n (84)
American Naprapathic Ass'n (86)
American Natural Hygiene Soc. (86)
American Obesity Ass'n (87)
American Oriental Bodywork Therapy Ass'n (88)
American Preventive Medical Ass'n (93)
American Psychiatric Nurses Ass'n (94)
American Registry of Medical Assistants (97)
American School Health Ass'n (99)
American Soc. for Bioethics and Humanities (101)
American Soc. of Addiction Medicine (106)
American Soc. of Cataract and Refractive Surgery (107)
American Subacute Care Ass'n (118)
American Therapeutic Ass'n (120)
American Trauma Soc. (121)
Animal Health Institute (125)
Ass'n for Death Education and Counseling (132)
Ass'n for Health Services Research (134)
Ass'n for Research in Otolaryngology (137)
Ass'n for Worksite Health Promotion (141)
Ass'n of Academic Health Centers (141)
Ass'n of Academic Health Sciences Library Directors (141)
Ass'n of Family Practice Residency Directors (151)
Ass'n of Health Occupations Teacher Educators (153)
Ass'n of Healthcare Internal Auditors (153)
Ass'n of Managed Healthcare Organizations (156)
Ass'n of Maternal and Child Health Programs (157)
Ass'n of Occupational and Environmental Clinics (158)
Ass'n of Occupational Health Professionals (in Healthcare) (158)
Ass'n of Oncology Social Work (159)
Ass'n of Pediatric Oncology Social Workers (160)
Ass'n of Public Health Laboratories (162)
Ass'n of Rheumatology Health Professionals (164)
Ass'n of SIDS and Infant Mortality Programs (165)
Ass'n of State and Territorial Directors of Health Promotion and Public Health (165)
Ass'n of State and Territorial Public Health Nutrition Directors (166)
Ass'n of Teachers of Maternal and Child Health (167)
Ass'n of University Environmental Health/Sciences Centers (168)
Assisted Living Federation of America (170)
Billings Ovulation Method Ass'n of the United States (179)
Catholic Health Ass'n of the United States (188)
Commission on Accreditation of Allied Health Education Programs (199)
Council of Colleges of Acupuncture and Oriental Medicine (213)
Drug and Alcohol Testing Industry Ass'n (225)
Global Health Council (248)
Health Care Resource Management Soc. (251)
Health Industry Business Communications Council (252)
Health Industry Group Purchasing Ass'n (252)
Health Industry Manufacturers Ass'n (252)
Health Industry Representatives Ass'n (252)
Health Insurance Ass'n of America (252)
Health Sciences Communications Ass'n (252)
Healthcare Billing and Management Ass'n (252)
Healthcare Compliance Packaging Council (252)
Healthcare Convention and Exhibitors Ass'n (252)
Healthcare Finance Study Group (252)
Healthcare Financial Management Ass'n (252)
Healthcare Forum, The (252)
Home Health Services and Staffing Ass'n (255)
Hospice Ass'n of America (256)
Hospital Presidents Ass'n (256)
Internat'l Academy for Child Brain Development (272)
Internat'l Academy of Behavioral Medicine, Counseling and Psychotherapy (272)
Internat'l Academy of Health Care Professionals (272)
Internat'l Ass'n Colon Hydro Therapy (273)
Internat'l Ass'n of Eating Disorders Professionals (278)
Internat'l Ass'n of Healthcare Central Service Material Management (279)
Internat'l College of Applied Kinesiology (286)
Internat'l Health Evaluation Ass'n (293)
Internat'l Institute for Bio-Energetic Analysis (294)
Internat'l Lactation Consultant Ass'n (295)
Internat'l Listening Ass'n (296)
Internat'l Phototherapy Ass'n (299)
Internat'l Soc. for Artificial Organs (303)
Internat'l Soc. for Prosthetics and Orthotics, United States Nat'l Member Soc. (304)
Jewish Social Service Professionals Ass'n (314)
Lipid Nurse Task Force (320)
Medical Records Institute (326)
Midwives Alliance of North America (328)
Nat'l Academies of Practice (333)
Nat'l Academy of Clinical Biochemistry (334)
Nat'l Alliance of State and Territorial AIDS Directors (336)
Nat'l Ass'n for Healthcare Quality (339)
Nat'l Ass'n for Home Care (339)
Nat'l Ass'n for Homecare (339)
Nat'l Ass'n for Medical Direction of Respiratory Care (340)
Nat'l Ass'n for Medical Equipment Services (340)
Nat'l Ass'n for Senior Living Industries (341)
Nat'l Ass'n for the Support of Long-Term Care (341)
Nat'l Ass'n Medical Staff Services (342)
Nat'l Ass'n of Addiction Treatment Providers (342)
Nat'l Ass'n of Air Nat'l Guard Health Technicians (343)
Nat'l Ass'n of Boards of Examiners of Long Term Care Administrators (345)
Nat'l Ass'n of Childbearing Centers (347)
Nat'l Ass'n of Community Health Centers (349)
Nat'l Ass'n of County and City Health Officials (350)
Nat'l Ass'n of County Health Facility Administrators (351)
Nat'l Ass'n of Health Data Organizations (357)
Nat'l Ass'n of Health Services Executives (357)
Nat'l Ass'n of Health Underwriters (357)
Nat'l Ass'n of Health Unit Coordinators (357)
Nat'l Ass'n of Healthcare Consultants (357)
Nat'l Ass'n of Hospital Hospitality Houses (358)
Nat'l Ass'n of Local Boards of Health (361)
Nat'l Ass'n of Managed Care Physicians (362)
Nat'l Ass'n of Medicaid Directors (362)
Nat'l Ass'n of Professional Geriatric Care Managers (366)
Nat'l Ass'n of Professionals in Women's Health (367)
Nat'l Ass'n of Public Hospitals and Health Systems (368)
Nat'l Ass'n of Rehabilitation Agencies (369)
Nat'l Ass'n of School Nurses (371)
Nat'l Ass'n of Social Workers (373)
Nat'l Ass'n of State Alcohol and Drug Abuse Directors (373)
Nat'l Ass'n of State Veterans Homes (376)

National Trade and Professional Associations of the U.S. © 1999, Columbia Books, Inc. 573

Nat'l Ass'n of Supervisors and Administrators of Health Occupations Education **(377)**
Nat'l Certification Council for Activity Professionals **(386)**
Nat'l Coalition of Hispanic Health and Human Services Organizations **(387)**
Nat'l Committee for Quality Assurance **(388)**
Nat'l Council for Prescription Drug Programs **(393)**
Nat'l Council of State Emergency Medical Services Training Coordinators **(396)**
Nat'l CPA Health Care Advisors Ass'n **(398)**
Nat'l Family Caregivers Ass'n **(402)**
Nat'l Health Care Anti-Fraud Ass'n **(408)**
Nat'l Health Council **(408)**
Nat'l Hospice Organization **(409)**
Nat'l Iridology Research Ass'n **(413)**
Nat'l Organization for Associate Degree Nursing **(419)**
Nat'l Organization for Competency Assurance **(419)**
Nat'l Organization of Nurse Practitioner Faculties **(420)**
Nat'l Perinatal Ass'n **(422)**
Nat'l Prison Hospice Ass'n **(423)**
Nat'l Register of Health Service Providers in Psychology **(424)**
Nat'l Soc. for Healthcare Foodservice Management **(429)**
Nat'l Soc. of Genetic Counselors **(430)**
Nat'l Spinal Cord Injury Ass'n **(431)**
Nat'l Stroke Ass'n **(432)**
Nat'l Subacute Care Ass'n **(432)**
Nat'l Tay-Sachs and Allied Diseases Ass'n **(433)**
Nat'l Wellness Ass'n **(436)**
Neurodevelopmental Treatment Ass'n **(438)**
Presbyterian Health, Education and Welfare Ass'n **(462)**
Professional Ass'n of Health Care Office Managers **(464)**
Regulatory Affairs Professionals Soc. **(474)**
Rolf Institute **(477)**
Soc. for Ambulatory Care Professionals **(485)**
Soc. for Computer Applications in Radiology **(486)**
Soc. for Health and Human Values **(488)**
Soc. for Medical Decision Making **(491)**
Soc. for Occupational and Environmental Health **(491)**
Soc. for Public Health Education **(493)**
Soc. of Professional Benefit Administrators **(505)**
Soc. of Prospective Medicine **(506)**
Soc. of State Directors of Health, Physical Education and Recreation **(507)**
Therapeutic Communities of America **(522)**
Visiting Nurse Ass'ns of America **(540)**
Wellness Councils of America **(542)**
Workgroup for Electronic Data Interchange **(549)**
World Research Foundation **(550)**

HEARING see also DEAF

Academy of Dispensing Audiologists **(8)**
Academy of Rehabilitative Audiology **(10)**
American Academy of Audiology **(20)**
American Academy of Otolaryngology-Head and Neck Surgery **(24)**
American Osteopathic Colleges of Ophthalmology and Otolaryngology, Head and Neck Surgery **(89)**
Ass'n of College Educators: Deaf and Hard of Hearing **(147)**
Hearing Industries Ass'n **(253)**
Nat'l Black Ass'n for Speech, Language and Hearing **(383)**

HEATING

Air Conditioning Contractors of America **(15)**
Air Movement and Control Ass'n Internat'l **(16)**
Air-Conditioning and Refrigeration Institute **(16)**
American Soc. of Heating, Refrigerating and Air-Conditioning Engineers **(110)**
American Solar Energy Soc. **(117)**
American Supply Ass'n **(119)**
Ass'n of Home Appliance Manufacturers **(153)**
Ass'n of Industry Manufacturers' Representatives **(154)**
Associated Air Balance Council **(170)**
Gas Appliance Manufacturers Ass'n **(245)**
Hearth Products Ass'n **(253)**
Heat Exchange Institute **(253)**
Hydronics Institute Division of GAMA **(257)**
Industrial Heating Equipment Ass'n **(263)**
Internat'l District Energy Ass'n **(289)**
Internat'l Ground Source Heat Pump Ass'n **(292)**
Masonry Heater Ass'n of North America **(324)**
Mechanical Service Contractors of America **(326)**
Nat'l Ass'n of Oil Heating Service Managers **(364)**
Nat'l Ass'n of Power Engineers **(365)**
Nat'l Electrical Contractors Ass'n **(400)**
Nat'l Electrical Manufacturers Ass'n **(400)**
Nat'l Kerosene Heater Ass'n **(414)**
Northamerican Heating, Refrigeration and Airconditioning Wholesalers Ass'n **(446)**
Passive Solar Industries Council **(454)**
Plumbing-Heating-Cooling Contractors - Nat'l Ass'n **(459)**
Plumbing-Heating-Cooling Information Bureau **(459)**
Radiant Panel Ass'n **(470)**
Solar Energy Industries Ass'n **(510)**
Used Oil Management Ass'n **(538)**

HELICOPTERS

American Helicopter Soc. **(73)**
Army Aviation Ass'n of America **(127)**
Ass'n of Air Medical Services **(141)**
Helicopter Ass'n Internat'l **(253)**

HERPETOLOGY

American Soc. of Ichthyologists and Herpetologists **(111)**
Herpetologists' League **(254)**
Soc. for the Study of Amphibians and Reptiles **(495)**

HISTORY

Academy of Accounting Historians **(7)**
Agricultural History Soc. **(14)**
American Academy of Research Historians of Medieval Spain **(26)**
American Academy of the History of Dentistry **(26)**
American Antiquarian Soc. **(28)**
American Ass'n for State and Local History **(32)**
American Ass'n for the History of Medicine **(32)**
American Ass'n for the History of Nursing **(32)**
American Catholic Historical Ass'n **(50)**
American College of Health Care Administrators **(54)**
American Conference for Irish Studies **(59)**
American Cultural Resources Ass'n **(63)**
American Folklore Soc. **(69)**
American Historical Ass'n **(73)**
American Institute for Conservation of Historic and Artistic Works **(75)**
American Institute for Patristic and Byzantine Studies **(76)**
American Institute of Bangladesh Studies **(76)**
American Institute of the History of Pharmacy **(78)**
American Italian Historical Ass'n **(79)**
American Jewish Historical Soc. **(80)**
American Journalism Historians Ass'n **(80)**
American Men's Studies Ass'n **(84)**
American Musicological Soc. **(86)**
American Numismatic Soc. **(87)**
American Oriental Soc. **(88)**
American Printing History Ass'n **(94)**
American Soc. for Environmental History **(102)**
American Soc. for Ethnohistory **(102)**
American Soc. for Legal History **(103)**
American Soc. of Church History **(107)**
American Soc. of Papyrologists **(114)**
American Studies Ass'n **(118)**
Archaeological Institute of America **(126)**
Archivists and Librarians in the History of the Health Sciences **(127)**
Ass'n for Asian Studies **(130)**
Ass'n for Documentary Editing **(132)**
Ass'n for Living History Farms and Agricultural Museums **(135)**
Ass'n for the Bibliography of History **(139)**
Ass'n for the Study of Afro-American Life and History **(139)**
Ass'n of Ancient Historians **(143)**
Ass'n of Caribbean Studies **(146)**
Business History Conference **(184)**
Cheiron: The Internat'l Soc. for the History of Behavioral and Social Sciences **(191)**
Committee on Lesbian and Gay History **(200)**
Conference for the Study of Political Thought **(204)**
Conference on Asian History **(205)**
Conference on Faith and History **(205)**
Coordinating Council for Women in History **(209)**
Costume Soc. of America **(210)**
Council for European Studies **(211)**
Economic History Ass'n **(225)**
Federation of State Humanities Councils **(237)**
Forest History Soc. **(242)**
Historians Film Committee **(254)**
Historians of American Communism **(254)**
History of Earth Sciences Soc. **(254)**
History of Economics Soc. **(254)**
History of Education Soc. **(254)**
History of Science Soc. **(254)**
Immigration and Ethnic History Soc. **(259)**
Independent Scholars of Asia **(261)**
Internat'l Psychohistorical Ass'n **(300)**
Latin American Studies Ass'n **(317)**
Medieval Academy of America **(326)**
Middle East Studies Ass'n of North America **(328)**
Modern Greek Studies Ass'n **(329)**
Nat'l Alliance of Preservation Commissions **(336)**
Nat'l Alliance of Statewide Preservation Organizations **(336)**
Nat'l Ass'n for Armenian Studies and Research **(337)**
Nat'l Ass'n for Ethnic Studies **(339)**
Nat'l Ass'n for Interpretation **(340)**
Nat'l Conference of State Historic Preservation Officers **(391)**
Nat'l Council on Public History **(397)**
Nat'l Genealogical Soc. **(406)**
North American Conference on British Studies **(441)**
North American Soc. for Sport History **(444)**
Oral History Ass'n **(449)**
Organization of American Historians **(450)**
Phi Alpha Theta **(456)**
Renaissance Soc. of America **(474)**
Romanian Studies Ass'n of America **(477)**
Soc. for Ancient Greek Philosophy **(485)**
Soc. for French Historical Studies **(488)**
Soc. for German-American Studies **(488)**
Soc. for Historians of American Foreign Relations **(488)**
Soc. for Historians of the Early American Republic **(489)**
Soc. for Historians of the Gilded Age and Progressive Era **(489)**
Soc. for Historical Archaeology **(489)**
Soc. for History Education **(489)**
Soc. for History in the Federal Government **(489)**
Soc. for Industrial Archeology **(490)**
Soc. for Italian Historical Studies **(490)**
Soc. for Military History **(491)**
Soc. for Reformation Research **(493)**
Soc. for Romanian Studies **(493)**
Soc. for Spanish and Portuguese Historical Studies **(494)**
Soc. for the History of Discoveries **(495)**
Soc. for the History of Technology **(495)**
Soc. of American Historians **(497)**
Soc. of American Historical Artists **(497)**
Soc. of Architectural Historians **(498)**
Soc. of Armenian Studies **(498)**
Social Science History Ass'n **(509)**
Social Science Research Council **(509)**
Turkish Studies Ass'n **(528)**
Victorian Soc. in America **(539)**
Western History Ass'n **(543)**
Western Music Ass'n **(543)**
World History Ass'n **(550)**
World War Two Studies Ass'n **(550)**

HOCKEY

American Hockey Coaches Ass'n **(73)**
American Hockey League **(73)**
Internat'l Hockey League **(293)**
Nat'l Hockey League **(409)**
Nat'l Hockey League Player's Ass'n **(409)**

HOME FURNISHINGS

American Craft Council **(62)**
American Lighting Ass'n **(81)**
Home Fashion Products Ass'n **(255)**
Home Furnishings Internat'l Ass'n **(255)**
Internat'l Furnishings and Design Ass'n **(292)**
Internat'l Furniture Rental Ass'n **(292)**
Internat'l Home Furnishings Representatives Ass'n **(293)**
Kitchen Cabinet Manufacturers Ass'n **(316)**
Nat'l Ass'n of Decorative Fabric Distributors **(352)**
Nat'l Ass'n of Floor Covering Distributors **(355)**
Nat'l Home Furnishings Ass'n **(409)**
Nat'l Kitchen and Bath Ass'n **(414)**
Paint and Decorating Retailers Ass'n **(452)**
Window Coverings Manufacturers Ass'n **(544)**

HONEY

American Beekeeping Federation **(47)**
Apiary Inspectors of America **(125)**
Nat'l Honey Packers and Dealers Ass'n **(409)**

HORSES

American Ass'n of Equine Practitioners **(36)**
American Ass'n of Owners and Breeders of Peruvian Paso Horses **(40)**
American Bashkir Curly Registry **(47)**
American Buckskin Registry Ass'n **(49)**
American Cream Draft Horse Ass'n **(62)**
American Crossbred Pony Registery **(63)**
American Donkey and Mule Soc. **(65)**
American Farriers Ass'n **(66)**
American Hackney Horse Soc. **(71)**
American Hanoverian Soc. **(71)**
American Horse Council **(74)**
American Horse Publications Ass'n **(74)**
American Horse Shows Ass'n **(74)**
American Miniature Horse Ass'n **(85)**
American Morgan Horse Ass'n **(85)**
American Mustang Ass'n **(86)**
American Paint Horse Ass'n **(90)**
American Paso Fino Horse Ass'n **(90)**
American Quarter Horse Ass'n **(96)**
American Saddlebred Horse Ass'n **(98)**
American Shetland Pony Club/American Miniature Horse Registry **(100)**
American Shire Horse Ass'n **(100)**
American Suffolk Horse Ass'n **(118)**
American Trakehner Ass'n **(120)**
American Warmblood Registry **(122)**
American Welara Pony Soc. **(122)**
American White/American Creme Horse Registry **(123)**
Appaloosa Horse Club **(126)**
Arabian Horse Registry of America, Inc. **(126)**
Ass'n for Equine Sports Medicine **(133)**
Ass'n of Official Racing Chemists **(158)**
Belgian Draft Horse Corp. of America **(178)**
CHA - Certified Horsemanship Ass'n **(190)**
Clydesdale Breeders of the United States **(195)**
Colorado Ranger Horse Ass'n **(198)**
Dude Ranchers' Ass'n **(225)**
Dutch Warmblood Ass'n **(225)**
Galiceno Horse Breeders Ass'n **(245)**
Harness Horsemen Internat'l **(251)**
Horsemen's Benevolent and Protective Ass'n **(256)**
Internat'l Arabian Horse Ass'n **(273)**
Internat'l Buckskin Horse Ass'n **(284)**
Internat'l Union of Journeymen Horseshoers of the United States and Canada **(310)**
Jockey Club **(314)**
Lipizzan Ass'n of North America **(320)**
Missouri Fox Trotting Horse Breed Ass'n **(329)**
Nat'l Cutting Horse Ass'n **(398)**
Nat'l Reining Horse Ass'n **(425)**
Nat'l Show Horse Registry **(428)**
Nat'l Spotted Saddle Horse Ass'n **(431)**
Nat'l Turf Writers Ass'n **(435)**
North American Morab Horse Ass'n/Registry **(443)**
North American Trakehner Ass'n **(445)**
Palomino Horse Ass'n **(453)**
Palomino Horse Breeders of America **(453)**
Paso Fino Horse Ass'n **(453)**
Percheron Horse Ass'n of America **(454)**
Peruvian Paso Horse Registry of North America **(455)**
Pinto Horse Ass'n of America **(458)**
Pony of the Americas Club **(460)**
Purebred Hanoverian Ass'n of America Breeders and Owners **(470)**
Racking Horse Breeders Ass'n of America **(470)**
Spanish-Barb Breeders Ass'n **(511)**
Tennessee Walking Horse Breeders and Exhibitors Ass'n **(521)**
Thoroughbred Club of America **(522)**
Thoroughbred Owners and Breeders Ass'n **(523)**
Thoroughbred Racing Ass'ns of North America **(523)**
United Professional Horsemen's Ass'n **(531)**
United States Harness Writers' Ass'n **(534)**
United Thoroughbred Trainers of America **(536)**
Walking Horse Owners Ass'n of America **(540)**
Walking Horse Trainers Ass'n **(540)**
Welsh Pony and Cob Soc. of America **(542)**
Women's Professional Rodeo Ass'n **(548)**

HORTICULTURE

All-America Rose Selections **(17)**
American Ass'n of Botanical Gardens and Arboreta **(33)**
American Herbalists Guild **(73)**
American Horticultural Soc. **(74)**
American Horticultural Therapy Ass'n **(74)**
American Institute of Floral Designers **(77)**
American Nursery and Landscape Ass'n **(87)**
American Pomological Soc. **(93)**

574 National Trade and Professional Associations of the U.S. © 1999, Columbia Books, Inc.

Consumer Credit Insurance Ass'n **(207)**
Council of Insurance Agents and Brokers **(214)**
Council of Insurance Company Executives **(214)**
Council on Employee Benefits **(216)**
Crop Insurance Research Bureau **(219)**
Employee Benefit Research Institute **(229)**
Federation of Insurance and Corporate Counsel **(237)**
Financial Institutions Insurance Ass'n **(239)**
Fraternal Field Managers Ass'n **(244)**
GAMA Internat'l **(245)**
Gamma Iota Sigma **(245)**
Health Insurance Ass'n of America **(252)**
Home Office Life Underwriters Ass'n **(256)**
Independent Automotive Damage Appraisers Ass'n **(259)**
Independent Insurance Agents of America **(261)**
Inland Marine Underwriters Ass'n **(264)**
Institute for Business and Home Safety **(265)**
Insurance Accounting and Systems Ass'n **(270)**
Insurance Conference Planners Ass'n **(270)**
Insurance Consumer Affairs Exchange **(270)**
Insurance Information Institute **(270)**
Insurance Institute for Highway Safety **(270)**
Insurance Loss Control Ass'n **(270)**
Insurance Marketing Communications Ass'n **(270)**
Inter-Industry Conference on Auto Collision Repair **(271)**
Intermediaries and Reinsurance Underwriters Ass'n **(272)**
Internat'l Ass'n for Financial Planning **(274)**
Internat'l Ass'n for Insurance Law - United States
    Chapter **(274)**
Internat'l Ass'n of Arson Investigators **(275)**
Internat'l Ass'n of Defense Counsel **(278)**
Internat'l Ass'n of Industrial Accident Boards and
    Commissions **(280)**
Internat'l Ass'n of Insurance Receivers **(280)**
Internat'l Claim Ass'n **(285)**
Internat'l Foundation of Employee Benefit Plans **(292)**
Internat'l Insurance Council **(295)**
Internat'l Insurance Soc. **(295)**
Intersure, Ltd. **(312)**
Liability Insurance Research Bureau **(319)**
Life Insurers Council **(319)**
Lightning Protection Institute **(319)**
LIMRA Internat'l **(320)**
LOMA **(321)**
Mass Marketing Insurance Institute **(324)**
Million Dollar Round Table **(328)**
Mortgage Insurance Companies of America **(330)**
Nat'l Ass'n of Bar-Related Title Insurers **(344)**
Nat'l Ass'n of Catastrophe Adjusters **(346)**
Nat'l Ass'n of Dental Plans **(352)**
Nat'l Ass'n of Disability Evaluating Professionals **(353)**
Nat'l Ass'n of Fire Investigators **(355)**
Nat'l Ass'n of Fraternal Insurance Counsellors **(356)**
Nat'l Ass'n of Health Underwriters **(357)**
Nat'l Ass'n of Independent Fee Appraisers **(359)**
Nat'l Ass'n of Independent Insurance Adjusters **(359)**
Nat'l Ass'n of Independent Insurance Auditors and
    Engineers **(359)**
Nat'l Ass'n of Independent Insurers **(359)**
Nat'l Ass'n of Independent Life Brokerage Agencies **(359)**
Nat'l Ass'n of Insurance Brokers **(360)**
Nat'l Ass'n of Insurance Commissioners **(360)**
Nat'l Ass'n of Insurance Women **(360)**
Nat'l Ass'n of Life Underwriters **(361)**
Nat'l Ass'n of Mutual Insurance Companies **(363)**
Nat'l Ass'n of Professional Insurance Agents **(367)**
Nat'l Ass'n of Professional Surplus Lines Offices **(367)**
Nat'l Ass'n of Public Insurance Adjusters **(368)**
Nat'l Ass'n of Surety Bond Producers **(377)**
Nat'l Cargo Bureau **(385)**
Nat'l Committee for Quality Assurance **(388)**
Nat'l Conference of Insurance Legislators **(390)**
Nat'l Council of Self-Insurers **(395)**
Nat'l Council on Compensation Insurance **(397)**
Nat'l Crop Insurance Services **(398)**
Nat'l Federation of Grange Mutual Insurance Companies **(403)**
Nat'l Fraternal Congress of America **(406)**
Nat'l Health Care Anti-Fraud Ass'n **(408)**
Nat'l Industrial Glove Distributors Ass'n **(411)**
Nat'l Insurance Ass'n **(412)**
Nat'l Insurance Crime Bureau **(412)**
Nat'l Organization of Life and Health Insurance Guaranty
    Ass'ns **(420)**
Nat'l Risk Retention Ass'n **(426)**
Nat'l Soc. of Insurance Premium Auditors **(430)**
Nat'l Structured Settlements Trade Ass'n **(432)**
Nat'l Truck and Heavy Equipment Claims Council **(434)**
Nat'l Viatical Ass'n **(435)**
Organization of Flying Adjusters **(450)**
Physician Insurers Ass'n of America **(458)**
Pollution Liability Insurance Ass'n **(460)**
Professional Insurance Communicators of America **(466)**
Professional Insurance Mass-Marketing Ass'n **(466)**
Professional Liability Underwriting Soc. **(466)**
Property Casualty Conferences **(468)**
Property Loss Research Bureau **(468)**
Public Agency Risk Managers Ass'n **(469)**
Public Risk Management Ass'n **(470)**
Registered Mail Insurance Ass'n **(473)**
Reinsurance Ass'n of America **(474)**
Risk and Insurance Management Soc. **(476)**
Self Insurance Institute of America **(481)**
Shipowners Claims Bureau **(482)**
Soc. for Risk Analysis **(493)**
Soc. of Actuaries **(496)**
Soc. of Certified Insurance Counselors **(499)**
Soc. of Insurance Financial Management **(503)**
Soc. of Insurance Research **(503)**
Soc. of Insurance Trainers and Educators **(503)**
Soc. of Professional Benefit Administrators **(505)**
Soc. of Risk Management Consultants **(507)**
Society of Financial Service Professionals **(509)**
State Risk and Insurance Management Ass'n **(516)**
Surety Ass'n of America **(518)**

Transportation Consumer Protection Council **(525)**
Transportation Loss Prevention and Security Council **(526)**
University Risk Management and Insurance Ass'n **(537)**
Viatical Ass'n of America **(539)**
WLUC-Women in Insurance and Financial Services **(545)**

INVENTORS
Affiliated Inventors Foundation **(13)**

INVESTMENTS see also FINANCE, SECURITIES INDUSTRY
American Ass'n of Individual Investors **(38)**
American Ass'n of Limited Partners **(38)**
Ass'n for Enterprise Opportunity **(133)**
Ass'n for Investment Management and Research **(135)**
Ass'n of Investment Management Sales Executives **(155)**
Colombian American Ass'n **(198)**
Council of Institutional Investors **(214)**
Ecuadorean American Ass'n **(226)**
Emerging Markets Traders Ass'n **(229)**
Fixed Income Analysts Soc. **(240)**
Forum for Investor Advice **(243)**
Independent Investors Protective League **(261)**
Institute for Investment Management Consultants **(265)**
Internat'l Ass'n for Financial Planning **(274)**
Investment Company Institute **(312)**
Investment Counsel Ass'n of America **(312)**
Investment Management Consultants Ass'n **(312)**
Investment Program Ass'n **(312)**
Investment Recovery Ass'n **(312)**
MicroComputer Investors Ass'n **(328)**
Nat'l Ass'n of Personal Financial Advisors **(365)**
Nat'l Ass'n of Real Estate Investment Managers **(369)**
Nat'l Ass'n of Real Estate Investment Trusts **(369)**
Nat'l Ass'n of Securities Dealers **(372)**
Nat'l Ass'n of Small Business Investment Companies **(373)**
Nat'l Council of Real Estate Investment Fiduciaries **(395)**
Nat'l Investor Relations Institute **(413)**
Nat'l Venture Capital Ass'n **(435)**
Organization for Internat'l Investment **(449)**
Pension Real Estate Ass'n **(454)**
Soc. of Quantitative Analysts **(506)**
Venezuelan American Ass'n of the U.S. **(539)**

IRON & STEEL INDUSTRY
American Foundrymen's Soc. **(69)**
American Institute for Internat'l Steel **(76)**
American Institute of Steel Construction **(78)**
American Iron and Steel Institute **(79)**
American Iron Ore Ass'n **(79)**
Ass'n of Container Reconditioners **(148)**
Ass'n of Iron and Steel Engineers **(155)**
Ass'n of Steel Distributors **(166)**
Bridge Grid Flooring Manufacturers Ass'n **(182)**
Cast Iron Soil Pipe Institute **(187)**
Cold Finished Steel Bar Institute **(196)**
Committee of Domestic Steel Wire Rope and Specialty Cable
    Manufacturers **(200)**
Concrete Reinforcing Steel Institute **(203)**
Cooling Tower Institute **(208)**
Ductile Iron Pipe Research Ass'n **(225)**
Ductile Iron Soc. **(225)**
Ferroalloys Ass'n **(238)**
Institute of Scrap Recycling Industries **(269)**
Institute of the Ironworking Industry **(269)**
Internat'l Ass'n of Bridge, Structural, Ornamental and
    Reinforcing Iron Workers **(276)**
Internat'l Brotherhood of Boilermakers, Iron Ship Builders,
    Blacksmiths, Forgers and Helpers **(284)**
Iron and Steel Soc. **(313)**
Nat'l Ass'n of Reinforcing Steel Contractors **(370)**
Nat'l Ass'n of Steel Pipe Distributors **(377)**
Nat'l Blacksmiths and Weldors Ass'n **(383)**
Nat'l Corrugated Steel Pipe Ass'n **(392)**
Nat'l Council of Erectors, Fabricators and Riggers **(394)**
Nat'l Erectors Ass'n **(402)**
Nat'l Institute of Steel Detailing **(412)**
Nat'l Slag Ass'n **(428)**
Rack Manufacturers Institute **(470)**
Scaffolding, Shoring and Forming Institute **(479)**
Specialty Steel Industry of North America **(514)**
SSPC: the Soc. for Protective Coatings **(515)**
Steel Deck Institute **(516)**
Steel Door Institute **(516)**
Steel Founders' Soc. of America **(516)**
Steel Joist Institute **(516)**
Steel Manufacturers Ass'n **(516)**
Steel Plate Fabricators Ass'n **(516)**
Steel Recycling Institute **(516)**
Steel Service Center Institute **(517)**
Steel Shipping Container Institute **(517)**
Steel Tank Institute **(517)**
Steel Tube Institute of North America **(517)**
Steel Window Institute **(517)**
Truss Plate Institute **(527)**
United Steelworkers of America **(536)**

ITALIAN
American Ass'n of Teachers of Italian **(44)**
Soc. for Italian Historical Studies **(490)**

JEWELRY & GEMS
Accredited Gemologists Ass'n **(10)**
American Gem and Mineral Suppliers Ass'n **(70)**
American Gem Soc. **(70)**
American Gem Trade Ass'n **(70)**
Brotherhood of Traveling Jewelers **(183)**
Costume Jewelry Salesmen's Ass'n **(210)**
Cultured Pearl Ass'n of America **(219)**
Diamond Council of America **(222)**
Diamond Manufacturers and Importers Ass'n of America **(222)**
Diamond Trade and Precious Stone Ass'n of America **(222)**
Fashion Jewelry Ass'n of America **(235)**

Gemological Institute of America **(246)**
Gift Ass'n of America **(247)**
Gold Institute **(248)**
Indian Arts and Crafts Ass'n **(262)**
Jewelers Board of Trade **(313)**
Jewelers of America **(314)**
Jewelers Shipping Ass'n **(314)**
Jewelers Vigilance Committee **(314)**
Jewelers' Security Alliance of the U.S. **(314)**
Jewelry Information Center **(314)**
Jewelry Manufacturers Ass'n **(314)**
Jewelry Manufacturers Guild **(314)**
Leading Jewelers Guild **(318)**
Manufacturing Jewelers and Suppliers of America **(323)**
Metal Findings Manufacturers Ass'n **(327)**
Nat'l Ass'n of Jewelry Appraisers **(361)**
Silver Users Ass'n **(483)**
Soc. of North American Goldsmiths **(504)**
Women's Jewelry Ass'n **(548)**

JEWISH
American Conference of Cantors **(59)**
American Jewish Correctional Chaplains Ass'n **(79)**
American Jewish Historical Soc. **(80)**
American Jewish Press Ass'n **(80)**
American Soc. of Sephardic Studies **(116)**
Ass'n for Jewish Studies **(135)**
Ass'n of Advanced Rabbinical and Talmudic Schools **(141)**
Ass'n of Jewish Aging Services **(155)**
Ass'n of Jewish Book Publishers **(155)**
Ass'n of Jewish Center Professionals **(155)**
Ass'n of Jewish Family and Children's Agencies **(155)**
Ass'n of Jewish Libraries **(155)**
Cantors Assembly **(186)**
Central Conference of American Rabbis **(189)**
Church and Synagogue Library Ass'n **(193)**
Council for Jewish Education **(211)**
Council of American Jewish Museums **(212)**
Council of Archives and Research Libraries in Jewish
    Studies **(212)**
Council of Jewish Federations **(214)**
Internat'l Ass'n of Jewish Vocational Services **(280)**
Internat'l Jewish Media Ass'n **(295)**
Jewish Book Council **(314)**
Jewish Community Centers Ass'n of North America **(314)**
Jewish Education Service of North America **(314)**
Jewish Educators Assembly **(314)**
Jewish Social Service Professionals Ass'n **(314)**
Jewish Teachers Ass'n-Morim **(314)**
JWB Jewish Chaplains Council **(315)**
Nat'l Ass'n of Hebrew Day School Administrators **(357)**
Nat'l Ass'n of Temple Administrators **(378)**
Nat'l Ass'n of Temple Educators **(378)**
Nat'l Conference of Yeshiva Principals **(391)**
Nat'l Soc. for Hebrew Day Schools **(429)**
Nat'l Tay-Sachs and Allied Diseases Ass'n **(433)**
Soc. for Humanistic Judaism **(489)**
Union of American Hebrew Congregations **(529)**
United Synagogue of Conservative Judaism **(536)**

JOURNALISM
Accrediting Council on Education in Journalism and Mass
    Communications **(11)**
American Journalism Historians Ass'n **(80)**
American Soc. of Journalists and Authors **(111)**
Asian American Journalists Ass'n **(128)**
Ass'n for Education in Journalism and Mass
    Communication **(132)**
Ass'n for Women in Communications **(140)**
Ass'n for Women Journalists **(141)**
Ass'n of Earth Science Editors **(150)**
Ass'n of Food Journalists **(151)**
Ass'n of Schools of Journalism and Mass Communication **(164)**
Associated Collegiate Press, Nat'l Scholastic Press Ass'n **(171)**
Boating Writers Internat'l **(181)**
Community College Journalism Ass'n **(201)**
Computer Press Ass'n **(202)**
Internat'l Jewish Media Ass'n **(295)**
Investigative Reporters and Editors **(312)**
Journalism Education Ass'n **(315)**
Nat'l Academy of Televisiion Journalists **(334)**
Nat'l Ass'n of Black Journalists **(345)**
Nat'l Ass'n of Hispanic Journalists **(358)**
Nat'l Lesbian and Gay Journalists Ass'n **(415)**
Professional Soccer Reporters Ass'n **(467)**
Soc. of Environmental Journalists **(501)**
Soc. of Professional Journalists **(506)**
South Asian Journalists Ass'n **(510)**
Travel Journalists Guild **(526)**
Truck Writers of North America **(527)**
White House Correspondents Ass'n **(543)**
World Federation of Travel Writers **(549)**

JUDGES
American Judges Ass'n **(80)**
American Judicature Soc. **(80)**
Ass'n of Administrative Law Judges **(141)**
Conference of Chief Justices **(204)**
Federal Administrative Law Judges Conference **(235)**
Judge Advocates Ass'n **(315)**
Nat'l Ass'n of Tribal Court Personnel **(379)**
Nat'l Ass'n of Women Judges **(380)**
Nat'l Conference of Bankruptcy Judges **(389)**
Nat'l Council of Juvenile and Family Court Judges **(395)**
Nat'l Gymnastics Judges Ass'n **(408)**
Nat'l Judges Ass'n **(413)**

LABOR UNIONS
Actors' Equity Ass'n **(11)**
Air Line Employees Ass'n, International **(15)**
Air Line Pilots Ass'n, Internat'l **(16)**
Amalgamated Transit Union **(19)**
American Ass'n of University Professors **(44)**

LABORATORIES

LACE

LADDERS

LANDSCAPING

LANGUAGE

LARYNGOLOGY

LAW

LEAD

LEATHER GOODS see also SHOES

LECTURES

LIBRARIES

LIGHTING

LINGERIE & UNDERWEAR

LINGUISTICS

LIQUOR

LIVESTOCK

Subject Index *MANUFACTURERS*

Ayrshire Breeders' Ass'n **(176)**
Barzona Breeders Ass'n of America **(177)**
Beefmaster Breeders United **(177)**
Braunvieh Ass'n of America **(181)**
Brown Swiss Cattle Breeders Ass'n of the U.S.A. **(183)**
Exotic Wildlife Ass'n **(234)**
Holstein Ass'n USA **(255)**
Internat'l Livestock Identification Ass'n **(296)**
Internat'l Livestock Theft Investigators Ass'n **(296)**
Internat'l Nubian Breeders Ass'n **(298)**
Interstate Producers Livestock Ass'n **(312)**
Livestock Conservation Institute **(320)**
Livestock Marketing Ass'n **(320)**
Livestock Publications Council **(320)**
Nat'l Ass'n of Animal Breeders **(343)**
Nat'l Block and Bridle Club **(383)**
Nat'l Cattlemen's Beef Ass'n **(386)**
Nat'l Congress of Animal Trainers and Breeders **(391)**
Nat'l Hereford Hog Record Ass'n **(409)**
Nat'l Lincoln Sheep Breeders Ass'n **(415)**
Nat'l Live Stock Producers Ass'n **(415)**
Nat'l Miniature Donkey Ass'n **(417)**
Nat'l Pedigreed Livestock Council **(422)**
Nat'l Suffolk Sheep Ass'n **(432)**
Nat'l Swine Improvement Federation **(433)**
North American Corriente Ass'n **(441)**
North American Deer Farmers Ass'n **(441)**
North American Elk Breeders Ass'n **(442)**
Poland China Record Ass'n **(459)**
Purebred Dairy Cattle Ass'n **(470)**
Santa Gertrudis Breeders Internat'l **(479)**
Soc. for Range Management **(493)**
White Park Cattle Ass'n of America **(543)**

LOCKS
Associated Locksmiths of America **(171)**
Internat'l Ass'n of Home Safety and Security Professionals **(280)**
Safe and Vault Technicians Ass'n **(478)**
Security Hardware Distributors Ass'n **(481)**

LUBRICANTS
Automotive Oil Change Ass'n **(175)**
Convenient Automotive Services Institute **(208)**
Independent Lubricant Manufacturers Ass'n **(261)**
Internat'l Castor Oil Ass'n **(285)**
Nat'l Lubricating Grease Institute **(415)**
Soc. of Tribologists and Lubrication Engineers **(508)**

MACHINE TOOL INDUSTRY
American Machine Tool Distributors Ass'n **(82)**
AMT - The Ass'n for Manufacturing Technology **(124)**
Cemented Carbide Producers Ass'n **(189)**
Equipment Service Ass'n **(232)**
Fluid Power Distributors Ass'n **(241)**
Fluid Power Soc. **(241)**
Hack and Band Saw Manufacturers Ass'n of America **(250)**
Hand Tools Institute **(251)**
Internat'l Ass'n of Tool Craftsmen **(282)**
Machine Knife Ass'n **(321)**
Machinery Dealers Nat'l Ass'n **(321)**
Machining Technology Ass'n of SME **(321)**
Nat'l Fluid Power Ass'n **(405)**
Nat'l Tooling and Machining Ass'n **(434)**
Power Tool Institute **(461)**
Soc. of Carbide and Tool Engineers **(499)**
Soc. of Manufacturing Engineers **(503)**
United States Cutting Tool Institute **(533)**

MACHINERY
Agricultural and Industrial Manufacturers' Representatives Ass'n **(14)**
American Gear Manufacturers Ass'n **(70)**
American Paper Machinery Ass'n **(90)**
American Supply and Machinery Manufacturers' Ass'n **(119)**
American Textile Machinery Ass'n **(119)**
Ass'n of Machinery and Equipment Appraisers **(156)**
Associated Equipment Distributors **(171)**
BEMA - An Internat'l Ass'n Serving the Baking and Food Industries **(178)**
Bituminous and Aggregate Equipment Bureau **(179)**
Cleaning Equipment Trade Ass'n **(194)**
Compressed Air and Gas Institute **(202)**
Construction Industry Manufacturers Ass'n **(206)**
Contractors Pump Bureau **(208)**
Conveyor Equipment Manufacturers Ass'n **(208)**
Crane Certification Ass'n of America **(218)**
Crane Manufacturers Ass'n of America **(218)**
Fabricators and Manufacturers Ass'n, Internat'l **(234)**
Farm Equipment Manufacturers Ass'n **(235)**
Farm Equipment Wholesalers Ass'n **(235)**
Fire Equipment Manufacturers' Ass'n **(239)**
Fluid Power Soc. **(241)**
Food Equipment Manufacturers Ass'n **(241)**
Food Processing Machinery and Supplies Ass'n **(242)**
Heat Exchange Institute **(253)**
Industrial Distribution Ass'n **(262)**
Internat'l Ass'n of Diecutting and Diemaking **(278)**
Internat'l Ass'n of Food Industry Suppliers **(279)**
Internat'l Ass'n of Machinists and Aerospace Workers **(280)**
Manufacturers Alliance **(322)**
Mechanical Power Transmission Ass'n **(326)**
Nat'l Emergency Equipment Dealers Ass'n **(401)**
Nat'l Fluid Power Ass'n **(405)**
Nat'l Troubleshooting Ass'n **(434)**
North American Equipment Dealers Ass'n **(442)**
Outdoor Power Equipment Aftermarket Ass'n **(451)**
Outdoor Power Equipment Distributors Ass'n **(451)**
Outdoor Power Equipment Institute **(451)**
Packaging Machinery Manufacturers Institute **(452)**
Power Transmission Distributors Ass'n **(461)**
Power-Motion Technology Representatives Ass'n **(462)**
Precision Machined Products Ass'n **(462)**
Service Dealers Ass'n **(482)**
Spring Manufacturers Institute **(515)**
Textile Care Allied Trades Ass'n **(522)**
Vibration Institute **(539)**
Wire Industry Suppliers Ass'n **(545)**
Wood Machinery Manufacturers of America **(548)**
Woodworking Machinery Industry Ass'n **(549)**

MAGIC
Internat'l Brotherhood of Magicians **(284)**
Magic Dealers Ass'n **(322)**
Soc. of American Magicians **(497)**

MAIL
Advertising Mail Marketing Ass'n **(12)**
Alliance of Nonprofit Mailers **(18)**
Ass'n of Paid Circulation Publications **(159)**
Direct Marketing Ass'n **(223)**
Direct Selling Ass'n **(223)**
Electronic Messaging Ass'n **(228)**
Mail Advertising Service Ass'n Internat'l **(322)**
Mail Order Ass'n of America **(322)**
Nat'l Mail Order Ass'n **(416)**
Nat'l Postal Mail Handlers Union **(423)**
Nat'l Star Route Mail Contractors Ass'n **(431)**
Nationwide Alternate Delivery Alliance **(437)**
Parcel Shippers Ass'n **(453)**
Pharmaceutical Care Management Ass'n **(456)**
Registered Mail Insurance Ass'n **(473)**

MAMMALOGY
American Soc. of Mammalogists **(112)**
American Soc. of Primatologists **(115)**

MANAGEMENT
Academy of Management **(9)**
AFSM Internat'l **(14)**
Alliance for Nonprofit Management **(17)**
American Academy of Ambulatory Care Nursing **(20)**
American Ass'n of Industrial Management **(38)**
American Ass'n of Managing General Agents **(38)**
American College of Healthcare Executives **(54)**
American Compensation Ass'n **(59)**
American Healthcare Radiology Administrators **(72)**
American Management Ass'n Internat'l **(82)**
American Soc. for Engineering Management **(102)**
American Soc. for Public Administration **(105)**
Analytical Laboratory Managers Ass'n **(124)**
APICS - The Educational Society for Resource Management **(125)**
APPA: The Ass'n of Higher Education Facilities Officers **(126)**
Ass'n Chief Executive Council **(129)**
Ass'n for Correctional Research and Information Management **(132)**
Ass'n for Data Center, Network and Enterprise Systems Management **(132)**
Ass'n for Information and Image Management International **(135)**
Ass'n for Public Policy Analysis and Management **(137)**
Ass'n for Volunteer Administration **(140)**
Ass'n of Information Technology Professionals **(154)**
Ass'n of Internal Management Consultants **(154)**
Ass'n of Management Analysts in State and Local Government **(156)**
Ass'n of Management Consulting Firms **(156)**
Ass'n of Productivity Specialists **(160)**
Ass'n of Professional Energy Managers **(161)**
Ass'n of Proposal Management Professionals **(162)**
Ass'n of Records Managers and Administrators **(163)**
Ass'n of Sales Administration Managers **(164)**
Ass'n of School Business Officials Internat'l **(164)**
Ass'n of University Related Research Parks **(169)**
Athletic Equipment Managers Ass'n **(172)**
Automotive Trade Ass'n Executives **(175)**
Building Owners and Managers Ass'n Internat'l **(183)**
Building Owners and Managers Institute Internat'l **(183)**
Business Forms Management Ass'n **(184)**
Center for Management Advisors **(189)**
Christian Management Ass'n **(193)**
CIM --The Business Owners Forum **(194)**
Clinical Laboratory Management Ass'n **(194)**
Club Managers Ass'n of America **(195)**
College Athletic Business Management Ass'n **(197)**
Communications Managers Ass'n **(200)**
Communications Media Management Ass'n **(200)**
Construction Financial Management Ass'n **(206)**
Construction Management Ass'n of America **(206)**
Cost Management Group **(210)**
Council of Logistics Management **(215)**
Decision Sciences Institute **(220)**
Employment Management Ass'n **(230)**
Environmental Industry Ass'ns **(231)**
Federal Managers Ass'n **(236)**
Financial Management Ass'n **(239)**
Fraternal Field Managers Ass'n **(244)**
Fulfillment Management Ass'n **(244)**
GAMA Internat'l **(245)**
Golf Course Superintendents Ass'n of America **(248)**
Groundwater Management Districts Ass'n **(250)**
Health Care Resource Management Soc. **(251)**
Healthcare Financial Management Ass'n **(252)**
Healthcare Information and Management Systems Soc. **(253)**
Hospitality Sales and Marketing Ass'n Internat'l **(256)**
Institute of Behavioral and Applied Management **(265)**
Institute of Certified Professional Managers **(266)**
Institute of Certified Records Managers **(266)**
Institute of Management Consultants **(268)**
Institute of Real Estate Management **(269)**
Internat'l Ass'n for Exposition Management **(274)**
Internat'l Ass'n of Ass'n Management Companies **(276)**
Internat'l Ass'n of Assembly Managers **(276)**
Internat'l Ass'n of Healthcare Central Service Material Management **(279)**
Internat'l City/County Management Ass'n **(285)**
Internat'l Council for Small Business **(287)**
Internat'l Customer Service Ass'n **(288)**
Internat'l Facility Management Ass'n **(290)**
Internat'l Management Council **(296)**
Internat'l Personnel Management Ass'n **(299)**
Internat'l Publishing Management Ass'n **(300)**
Internat'l Soc. for Performance Improvement **(304)**
Internat'l Soc. for Systems Sciences **(304)**
Internat'l Soc. for the Performing Arts **(304)**
Internat'l Soc. of Facilities Executives **(306)**
Internat'l Ticketing Ass'n **(308)**
LOMA **(321)**
Materials Handling and Management Soc. **(325)**
Medical Group Management Ass'n **(326)**
Mineral Economics and Management Soc. **(329)**
Nat'l Ass'n of Credit Management **(351)**
Nat'l Ass'n of Flood and Stormwater Management Agencies **(355)**
Nat'l Ass'n of Performing Arts Managers and Agents **(364)**
Nat'l Ass'n of Postal Supervisors **(365)**
Nat'l Ass'n of Professional Organizers **(367)**
Nat'l Ass'n of Purchasing Management **(368)**
Nat'l Ass'n of Resident Management Corporations **(370)**
Nat'l Ass'n of Scientific Materials Managers **(371)**
Nat'l Ass'n of Service Managers **(372)**
Nat'l Classification Management Soc. **(387)**
Nat'l Contract Management Ass'n **(392)**
Nat'l Council of Agricultural Employers **(394)**
Nat'l Council of Social Security Management Ass'ns **(396)**
Nat'l Credit Union Management Ass'n **(398)**
Nat'l Institute of Management Counsellors **(412)**
Nat'l Institute of Packaging, Handling and Logistics Engineers **(412)**
Nat'l Institute on Park and Grounds Management **(412)**
Nat'l Management Ass'n **(416)**
Nat'l Property Management Ass'n **(424)**
Nat'l Safety Management Soc. **(426)**
Newspaper Ass'n Managers **(439)**
Paper Industry Management Ass'n **(453)**
Product Development and Management Ass'n **(463)**
Professional Ass'n of Health Care Office Managers **(464)**
Professional Convention Management Ass'n **(465)**
Professional Managers Ass'n **(466)**
Professional Services Management Ass'n **(467)**
Project Management Institute **(468)**
Radiology Business Management Ass'n **(471)**
Religious Conference Management Ass'n **(474)**
School Management Study Group **(479)**
Section for Women in Public Administration **(481)**
Soc. for Advancement of Management **(484)**
Soc. for Foodservice Management **(488)**
Soc. for Information Management **(490)**
Soc. of Medical Dental Management Consultants **(503)**
Sports Turf Managers Ass'n **(515)**
State Risk and Insurance Management Ass'n **(516)**
Turnaround Management Ass'n **(528)**
University Council for Educational Administration **(537)**
Veterinary Hospital Managers Ass'n **(539)**
Women in Management **(547)**
Young Presidents' Organization **(551)**

MANUFACTURERS
Abrasive Grain Ass'n **(7)**
Adhesive and Sealant Council **(12)**
Adhesives Manufacturers Ass'n **(12)**
AERA - Engine Rebuilders Ass'n **(12)**
Aerospace Industries Ass'n of America **(13)**
Agricultural and Industrial Manufacturers' Representatives Ass'n **(14)**
Agricultural Retailers Ass'n **(14)**
AIM USA **(15)**
Air Brake Ass'n **(15)**
Air Diffusion Council **(15)**
Air Distributing Institute **(15)**
Air-Conditioning and Refrigeration Institute **(16)**
Aluminum Anodizers Council **(19)**
Aluminum Ass'n **(19)**
Aluminum Extruders Council **(19)**
Aluminum Foil Container Manufacturers Ass'n **(19)**
American Amusement Machine Ass'n **(28)**
American Apparel Manufacturers Ass'n **(28)**
American Architectural Manufacturers Ass'n **(29)**
American Ass'n of Automatic Door Manufacturers **(33)**
American Automobile Manufacturers Ass'n **(46)**
American Bearing Manufacturing Ass'n **(47)**
American Boiler Manufacturers Ass'n **(48)**
American Brush Manufacturers Ass'n **(49)**
American Chain Ass'n **(51)**
American Cloak and Suit Manufacturers Ass'n **(52)**
American Coke and Coal Chemicals Institute **(52)**
American Concrete Institute **(59)**
American Concrete Pavement Ass'n **(59)**
American Concrete Pipe Ass'n **(59)**
American Concrete Pressure Pipe Ass'n **(59)**
American Cutlery Manufacturers Ass'n **(63)**
American Dental Trade Ass'n **(64)**
American Electronics Ass'n **(65)**
American Electroplaters and Surface Finishers Soc. **(65)**
American Feed Industry Ass'n **(67)**
American Fence Ass'n **(67)**
American Fiber Manufacturers Ass'n **(68)**
American Fine China Guild **(68)**
American Fire Sprinkler Ass'n **(68)**
American Flock Ass'n **(68)**
American Foundrymen's Soc. **(69)**
American Furniture Manufacturers Ass'n **(69)**
American Galvanizers Ass'n **(70)**
American Gear Manufacturers Ass'n **(70)**
American Hardboard Ass'n **(72)**
American Hardware Manufacturers Ass'n **(72)**
American Herbal Products Ass'n **(73)**
American Incense Manufacturers Ass'n **(75)**

National Trade and Professional Associations of the U.S. © 1999, Columbia Books, Inc. 579

MAPS

MARKET RESEARCH

MARKETING

Distributive Education Clubs of America (224)
Electrical Generating Systems Ass'n (227)
Electronic Retailing Ass'n (228)
Field Services Marketing Ass'n (238)
Floral Marketing Ass'n (240)
Fulfillment Management Ass'n (244)
Glass Ass'n of North America (247)
Graphic Arts Marketing Information Service (249)
Incentive Federation (259)
Information Technology Resellers Ass'n (264)
Insurance Marketing Communications Ass'n (270)
Internat'l Soc. for Quality-of-Life Studies (304)
Interstate Producers Livestock Ass'n (312)
LIMRA Internat'l (320)
Livestock Marketing Ass'n (320)
Manufacturers' Agents Nat'l Ass'n (323)
Marketing Education Ass'n (324)
Marketing Research Ass'n (324)
Mass Marketing Insurance Institute (324)
Materials Marketing Associates (325)
Medical Marketing Ass'n (326)
Multi-Level Marketing Internat'l Ass'n (331)
Nat'l Account Management Ass'n (334)
Nat'l Agri-Marketing Ass'n (335)
Nat'l Ass'n for Campus Activities (338)
Nat'l Ass'n of Collegiate Marketing Administrators (348)
Nat'l Ass'n of Export Companies (354)
Nat'l Council of Exchangors (394)
Nat'l Law Firm Marketing Ass'n (414)
Nat'l Potato Promotion Board (423)
Nat'l Wool Marketing Corporation (437)
North American Agricultural Marketing Officials (440)
Package Design Council Int'l (452)
Petroleum Marketers Ass'n of America (456)
Photo Marketing Ass'n-Internat'l (457)
Private Label Manufacturers Ass'n (463)
Produce Marketing Ass'n (463)
Product Development and Management Ass'n (463)
Professional Insurance Mass-Marketing Ass'n (466)
Promotion Industry Council (468)
Promotion Marketing Ass'n (468)
Sales and Marketing Executives Internat'l (478)
Soc. for Marketing Professional Services (490)
Soc. of Independent Gasoline Marketers of America (502)
Specialty Equipment Market Ass'n (514)
Teleprofessional Managers Ass'n (521)
Trade Show Exhibitors Ass'n (524)
United States Egg Marketers (533)

MATERIAL HANDLING

AIM USA (15)
Ass'n of Professional Material Handling Consultants (161)
Automatic Guided Vehicle Systems (173)
Conveyor Equipment Manufacturers Ass'n (208)
Crane Manufacturers Ass'n of America (218)
Design-Build Manufacturers Ass'n (222)
Hazardous Materials Advisory Council (251)
Health Care Resource Management Soc. (251)
Hoist Manufacturers Institute (255)
Industrial Metal Containers Ass'n (263)
Industrial Truck Ass'n (263)
Institute of Caster Manufacturers (266)
Institute of Hazardous Materials Management (267)
Institutional and Service Textile Distributors Ass'n (269)
Loading Dock Equipment Manufacturers (320)
Material Handling Equipment Distributors Ass'n (325)
Material Handling Industry Ass'n (325)
Materials Handling and Management Soc. (325)
Monorail Manufacturers Ass'n (330)
Nat'l Industrial Belting Ass'n (410)
Nat'l Wooden Pallet and Container Ass'n (437)
Rack Manufacturers Institute (470)
Scale Manufacturers Ass'n (479)
Storage Equipment Manufacturer's Ass'n (517)
Web Sling and Tiedown Ass'n (542)

MATHEMATICS

American Academy of Actuaries (20)
American Mathematical Ass'n of Two Year Colleges (83)
American Mathematical Soc. (83)
American Statistical Ass'n (118)
Ass'n for Computing Machinery (131)
Ass'n for Symbolic Logic (138)
Ass'n for Women in Mathematics (140)
Ass'n of State Supervisors of Mathematics (166)
Casualty Actuarial Soc. (187)
Conference Board of the Mathematical Sciences (203)
Econometric Soc. (225)
Industrial Mathematics Soc. (263)
Institute for Operations Research and the Management Sciences (265)
Institute of Mathematical Statistics (268)
Internat'l Ass'n for Mathematical Geology (274)
Internat'l Biometric Soc. (283)
Internat'l Soc. for Ecological Modelling-North American Chapter (303)
Mathematical Ass'n of America (325)
Nat'l Council of Supervisors of Mathematics (396)
Nat'l Council of Teachers of Mathematics (396)
North American Fuzzy Information Processing Soc. (442)
Psychometric Soc. (469)
School Science and Mathematics Ass'n (479)
Soc. for Industrial and Applied Mathematics (489)
Soc. for Natural Philosophy (491)
Soc. of Actuaries (496)
Special Interest Group for Symbolic and Algebraic Manipulation (512)
Special Interest Group on Mobility of Systems, Users, Data and Computing (513)
Special Interest Group on Numerical Mathematics (513)
United States Ass'n for Computational Mechanics (532)

MEASUREMENT

American Nat'l Metric Council (86)
American Nat'l Standards Institute (86)
American Soc. for Precision Engineering (104)
Ass'n for Assessment in Counseling (130)
Benchmarking Network Ass'n (178)
Internat'l Function Point Users Group (292)
Mathematical Ass'n of America (325)
Measurement, Control and Automation Ass'n (325)
Nat'l Conference on Weights and Measures (391)
Nat'l Council of Teachers of Mathematics (396)
Tubular Rivet and Machine Institute (527)
U.S. Metric Ass'n (528)
United Weighers Ass'n (536)

MEAT

American Ass'n of Meat Processors (38)
American Importers and Exporters Meat Products Group (75)
American Meat Institute (83)
American Meat Science Ass'n (83)
American Nat'l CattleWomen (86)
Ass'n of Technical and Supervisory Professionals (167)
Beef Improvement Federation (177)
Meat Importers' Council of America (325)
Meat Industry Suppliers Ass'n (325)
Nat'l Food Processors Ass'n (405)
Nat'l Meat Ass'n (416)
Nat'l Meat Canners Ass'n (416)
Nat'l Pork Producers Council (423)
Nat'l Renderers Ass'n (425)
Nat'l Seasoning Manufacturers Ass'n (427)
New York Mercantile Exchange (438)
North American Meat Processors Ass'n (443)
United States Meat Export Federation (534)
Western Hemisphere Ass'n of Meat Marketers (543)

MEDICINE

Academy of Ambulatory Foot Surgery (7)
Academy of Aphasia (7)
Academy of Behavioral Medicine Research (7)
Academy of Clinical Laboratory Physicians and Scientists (8)
Academy of Medical-Surgical Nurses (9)
Academy of Psychosomatic Medicine (10)
Aerospace Medical Ass'n (13)
Airlines Medical Directors Ass'n (17)
Alliance for Continuing Medical Education (17)
Alliance of Cardiovascular Professionals (18)
Ambulatory Pediatric Ass'n (19)
America's Blood Centers (19)
American Academy for Cerebral Palsy and Developmental Medicine (20)
American Academy for Physician and Patient (20)
American Academy of Allergy, Asthma and Immunology (20)
American Academy of Clinical Neurophysiology (21)
American Academy of Clinical Sexologists (21)
American Academy of Cosmetic Surgery (21)
American Academy of Dermatology (21)
American Academy of Disability Evaluating Physicians (21)
American Academy of Emergency Medicine (21)
American Academy of Environmental Medicine (21)
American Academy of Facial Plastic and Reconstructive Surgery (22)
American Academy of Family Physicians (22)
American Academy of Gnathologic Orthopedics (22)
American Academy of Health Care Providers in the Addictive Disorders (22)
American Academy of Health Physics (22)
American Academy of Home Care Physicians (22)
American Academy of Hospice and Palliative Medicine (22)
American Academy of Implant Dentistry (22)
American Academy of Insurance Medicine (23)
American Academy of Medical Acupuncture (23)
American Academy of Medical Administrators (23)
American Academy of Neurological and Orthopaedic Surgeons (23)
American Academy of Neurological Surgery (23)
American Academy of Neurology (23)
American Academy of Ophthalmology (24)
American Academy of Oral and Maxillofacial Radiology (24)
American Academy of Oral Medicine (24)
American Academy of Orofacial Pain (24)
American Academy of Orthopaedic Surgeons (24)
American Academy of Orthotists and Prosthetists (24)
American Academy of Osteopathy (24)
American Academy of Otolaryngic Allergy (24)
American Academy of Otolaryngology-Head and Neck Surgery (24)
American Academy of Pain Medicine (25)
American Academy of Pediatrics (25)
American Academy of Physical Medicine and Rehabilitation (25)
American Academy of Physician Assistants (25)
American Academy of Podiatric Sports Medicine (25)
American Academy of Somnology (26)
American Academy of Thermology (26)
American Academy of Tropical Medicine (26)
American Academy of Wound Management (27)
American Acupuncture Ass'n (27)
American Aging Ass'n (27)
American Ambulance Ass'n (28)
American Ass'n for Accreditation of Ambulatory Surgery Facilities (29)
American Ass'n for Cancer Education (29)
American Ass'n for Cancer Research (30)
American Ass'n for Functional Orthodontics (30)
American Ass'n for Geriatric Psychiatry (30)
American Ass'n for Hand Surgery (31)
American Ass'n for Medical Transcription (31)
American Ass'n for Pediatric Ophthalmology and Strabismus (31)
American Ass'n for Respiratory Care (31)
American Ass'n for the History of Medicine (32)
American Ass'n for the Study of Headache (32)
American Ass'n for the Study of Liver Diseases (32)
American Ass'n for the Surgery of Trauma (32)
American Ass'n for Therapeutic Humor (32)
American Ass'n for Thoracic Surgery (32)
American Ass'n for Women Podiatrists (32)
American Ass'n of AIDS Executives (33)
American Ass'n of Ambulatory Surgery Centers (33)
American Ass'n of Anatomists (33)
American Ass'n of Bioanalysts (33)
American Ass'n of Blood Banks (33)
American Ass'n of Certified Allergists (34)
American Ass'n of Certified Orthoptists (34)
American Ass'n of Clinical Endocrinologists (34)
American Ass'n of Clinical Urologists (34)
American Ass'n of Colleges of Osteopathic Medicine (34)
American Ass'n of Colleges of Podiatric Medicine (35)
American Ass'n of Diabetes Educators (36)
American Ass'n of Electrodiagnostic Medicine (36)
American Ass'n of Gynecological Laparoscopists (37)
American Ass'n of Hip and Knee Surgeons (37)
American Ass'n of Immunologists (38)
American Ass'n of Medical Assistants (38)
American Ass'n of Medical Milk Commissions (39)
American Ass'n of Medical Soc. Executives (39)
American Ass'n of Naturopathic Physicians (39)
American Ass'n of Neurological Surgeons (39)
American Ass'n of Neuropathologists (39)
American Ass'n of Neuroscience Nurses (39)
American Ass'n of Nurse Anesthetists (39)
American Ass'n of Oral and Maxillofacial Surgeons (40)
American Ass'n of Oriental Medicine (40)
American Ass'n of Orthopaedic Medicine (40)
American Ass'n of Pathologists' Assistants (40)
American Ass'n of Physician Specialists (41)
American Ass'n of Physicists in Medicine (41)
American Ass'n of Plastic Surgeons (41)
American Ass'n of Public Health Physicians (42)
American Blood Resources Ass'n (47)
American Board of Medical Specialties (47)
American Board of Periodontology (48)
American Board of Quality Assurance and Utilization Review Physicians (48)
American Board of Sexology (48)
American Broncho-Esophagological Ass'n (49)
American Burn Ass'n (49)
American Cancer Soc. (50)
American Canine Sports Medicine Ass'n (50)
American Clinical and Climatological Ass'n (52)
American Clinical Neurophysiological Soc. (52)
American College for Advancement in Medicine (52)
American College of Addictions Treatment Administrators (52)
American College of Allergy, Asthma and Immunology (53)
American College of Angiology (53)
American College of Cardiology (53)
American College of Chest Physicians (53)
American College of Emergency Physicians (54)
American College of Epidemiology (54)
American College of Foot and Ankle Pediatrics (54)
American College of Foot and Ankle Surgeons (54)
American College of Gastroenterology (54)
American College of Internat'l Physicians (55)
American College of Legal Medicine (55)
American College of Managed Care Medicine (55)
American College of Medical Physics (55)
American College of Medical Quality (55)
American College of Medical Staff Development (55)
American College of Medical Toxicology (55)
American College of Medicine (55)
American College of Mohs Micrographic Surgery and Cutaneous Oncology (55)
American College of Neuropsychiatrists (55)
American College of Neuropsychopharmacology (55)
American College of Nuclear Medicine (56)
American College of Nuclear Physicians (56)
American College of Obstetricians and Gynecologists (56)
American College of Occupational and Environmental Medicine (56)
American College of Oral and Maxillofacial Surgeons (56)
American College of Osteopathic Emergency Physicians (56)
American College of Osteopathic Internists (56)
American College of Osteopathic Obstetricians and Gynecologists (56)
American College of Osteopathic Pain Management and Sclerotherapy (56)
American College of Osteopathic Pediatricians (56)
American College of Osteopathic Surgeons (56)
American College of Physician Executives (57)
American College of Physicians-American Soc. of Internal Medicine (57)
American College of Preventive Medicine (57)
American College of Radiology (57)
American College of Rheumatology (57)
American College of Sports Medicine (57)
American College of Surgeons (57)
American College of Veterinary Surgeons (58)
American Congress of Rehabilitation Medicine (59)
American Dental Soc. of Anesthesiology (64)
American Diabetes Ass'n (64)
American Epilepsy Soc. (66)
American Federation for Medical Research (66)
American Fracture Ass'n (69)
American Gastroenterological Ass'n (70)
American Geriatrics Soc. (71)
American Head and Neck Surgery Soc. (72)
American Health Care Ass'n (72)
American Health Information Management Ass'n (72)
American Health Quality Ass'n (72)
American Heart Ass'n (72)
American Hernia Soc. (73)
American Holistic Medical Ass'n (73)
American In-vitro Allergy/Immunology Soc. (75)
American Industrial Hygiene Ass'n (75)
American Institute of Biomedical Climatology (76)
American Institute of Homeopathy (77)

582 National Trade and Professional Associations of the U.S. © 1999, Columbia Books, Inc.

American Institute of Ultrasound in Medicine **(78)**
American Laryngological Ass'n **(80)**
American Laryngological, Rhinological and Otological Soc. **(81)**
American Lithotripsy Soc. **(81)**
American Lung Ass'n **(82)**
American Massage Therapy Ass'n **(83)**
American Medical Ass'n **(83)**
American Medical Electroencephalographic Ass'n **(83)**
American Medical Group Ass'n **(83)**
American Medical Informatics Ass'n **(84)**
American Medical Publishers' Ass'n **(84)**
American Medical Soc. for Sports Medicine **(84)**
American Medical Student Ass'n **(84)**
American Medical Technologists **(84)**
American Medical Women's Ass'n **(84)**
American Medical Writers Ass'n **(84)**
American Neurological Ass'n **(87)**
American Ophthalmological Soc. **(88)**
American Organization of Nurse Executives **(88)**
American Orthopaedic Ass'n **(88)**
American Orthopaedic Soc. for Sports Medicine **(88)**
American Orthotic and Prosthetic Ass'n **(89)**
American Osteopathic Academy for Sports Medicine **(89)**
American Osteopathic Academy of Addiction Medicine **(89)**
American Osteopathic Academy of Orthopedics **(89)**
American Osteopathic Ass'n **(89)**
American Osteopathic College of Anesthesiologists **(89)**
American Osteopathic College of Dermatology **(89)**
American Osteopathic College of Radiology **(89)**
American Osteopathic Healthcare Ass'n **(89)**
American Otological Soc. **(90)**
American Pain Soc. **(90)**
American Pancreatic Ass'n **(90)**
American Paraplegia Soc. **(90)**
American Pathology Foundation **(90)**
American Pediatric Soc. **(91)**
American Physiological Soc. **(92)**
American Podiatric Medical Ass'n **(93)**
American Psychiatric Ass'n **(94)**
American Psychopathological Ass'n **(95)**
American Psychosomatic Soc. **(95)**
American Radium Soc. **(97)**
American Registry of Diagnostic Medical Sonographers **(97)**
American Registry of Medical Assistants **(97)**
American Rhinologic Soc. **(98)**
American Roentgen Ray Soc. **(98)**
American School Health Ass'n **(99)**
American Sexually Transmitted Diseases Ass'n **(99)**
American Shoulder and Elbow Surgeons **(100)**
American Sleep Apnea Ass'n **(100)**
American Soc. for Aesthetic Plastic Surgery **(100)**
American Soc. for Apheresis **(101)**
American Soc. for Artificial Internal Organs **(101)**
American Soc. for Bone and Mineral Research **(101)**
American Soc. for Clinical Evoked Potentials **(101)**
American Soc. for Clinical Investigation **(101)**
American Soc. for Clinical Laboratory Science **(101)**
American Soc. for Clinical Pharmacology and Therapeutics **(101)**
American Soc. for Colposcopy and Cervical Pathology **(101)**
American Soc. for Gastrointestinal Endoscopy **(102)**
American Soc. for Histocompatability and Immunogenetics **(103)**
American Soc. for Investigative Pathology **(103)**
American Soc. for Laser Medicine and Surgery **(103)**
American Soc. for Mass Spectrometry **(104)**
American Soc. for Neurochemistry **(104)**
American Soc. for Pediatric Neurosurgery **(104)**
American Soc. for Photobiology **(104)**
American Soc. for Reconstructive Microsurgery **(105)**
American Soc. for Surgery of the Hand **(105)**
American Soc. for the Advancement of Anesthesia in Dentistry **(105)**
American Soc. for Therapeutic Radiology and Oncology **(105)**
American Soc. of Abdominal Surgeons **(106)**
American Soc. of Addiction Medicine **(106)**
American Soc. of Andrology **(106)**
American Soc. of Anesthesiologists **(106)**
American Soc. of Bariatric Physicians **(107)**
American Soc. of Breast Disease **(107)**
American Soc. of Clinical Oncology **(108)**
American Soc. of Clinical Pathologists **(108)**
American Soc. of Colon and Rectal Surgeons **(108)**
American Soc. of Contemporary Ophthalmology **(109)**
American Soc. of Cytopathology **(109)**
American Soc. of Electroneurodiagnostic Technologists **(109)**
American Soc. of Extra-Corporeal Technology **(109)**
American Soc. of Forensic Odontology **(110)**
American Soc. of General Surgeons **(110)**
American Soc. of Hand Therapists **(110)**
American Soc. of Hematology **(110)**
American Soc. of Human Genetics **(111)**
American Soc. of Hypertension **(111)**
American Soc. of Industrial Medicine **(111)**
American Soc. of Internal Medicine **(111)**
American Soc. of Law, Medicine and Ethics **(112)**
American Soc. of Maxillofacial Surgeons **(112)**
American Soc. of Nephrology **(113)**
American Soc. of Neuroimaging **(113)**
American Soc. of Neuroradiology **(113)**
American Soc. of Nuclear Cardiology **(113)**
American Soc. of Ophthalmic Administrators **(113)**
American Soc. of Orthopaedic Physician's Assistants **(113)**
American Soc. of Pain Management Nurses **(113)**
American Soc. of Parasitologists **(114)**
American Soc. of Pediatric Hematology/Oncology **(114)**
American Soc. of Pediatric Nephrology **(114)**
American Soc. of Plastic and Reconstructive Surgeons **(114)**
American Soc. of Podiatric Dermatology **(115)**
American Soc. of Preventive Oncology **(115)**
American Soc. of Psychoanalytic Physicians **(115)**
American Soc. of Psychopathology of Expression **(115)**
American Soc. of Radiologic Technologists **(115)**
American Soc. of Regional Anesthesia **(115)**
American Soc. of Transplant Physicians **(116)**
American Soc. of Tropical Medicine and Hygiene **(116)**
American Spinal Injury Ass'n **(118)**
American Sports Medicine Ass'n/Board of Certification **(118)**
American Subacute Care Ass'n **(118)**
American Surgical Ass'n **(119)**
American Telemedicine Ass'n **(119)**
American Thoracic Soc. **(120)**
American Thyroid Ass'n **(120)**
American Tinnitus Ass'n **(120)**
American Trauma Soc. **(121)**
American Urological Ass'n **(121)**
American Venous Forum **(121)**
American Veterinary Soc. of Animal Behavior **(122)**
Anxiety Disorders Ass'n of America **(125)**
Applied Research Ethics Nat'l Ass'n **(126)**
Ass'n for Academic Surgery **(129)**
Ass'n for Ambulatory Behavorial Healthcare **(129)**
Ass'n for Chemoreception Sciences **(130)**
Ass'n for Gerontology in Higher Education **(134)**
Ass'n for Hospital Medical Education **(134)**
Ass'n for Professionals in Infection Control and Epidemiology **(136)**
Ass'n for Psychoanalytic Medicine **(137)**
Ass'n for Research in Nervous and Mental Disease **(137)**
Ass'n for Research in Vision and Ophthalmology **(137)**
Ass'n for the Advancement of Automotive Medicine **(138)**
Ass'n for the Advancement of Medical Instrumentation **(138)**
Ass'n for the Advancement of Wound Care **(139)**
Ass'n for the Treatment of Sexual Abusers **(140)**
Ass'n of Academic Chairmen of Plastic Surgery **(141)**
Ass'n of Academic Physiatrists **(141)**
Ass'n of American Cancer Institutes **(142)**
Ass'n of American Medical Colleges **(142)**
Ass'n of American Physicians **(142)**
Ass'n of American Physicians and Surgeons **(142)**
Ass'n of Biomedical Communications Directors **(144)**
Ass'n of Bone and Joint Surgeons **(145)**
Ass'n of Children's Prosthetic-Orthotic Clinics **(146)**
Ass'n of Clinical Scientists **(147)**
Ass'n of Educators in Radiological Science **(150)**
Ass'n of Family Practice Residency Directors **(151)**
Ass'n of Freestanding Radiation Oncology Centers **(152)**
Ass'n of Genetic Technologists **(152)**
Ass'n of Medical Illustrators **(157)**
Ass'n of Medical School Pediatric Department Chairmen **(157)**
Ass'n of Military Surgeons of the U.S. **(157)**
Ass'n of Neurosurgical Physician Assistants **(158)**
Ass'n of Organ Procurement Organizations **(159)**
Ass'n of Osteopathic Directors and Medical Educators **(159)**
Ass'n of Osteopathic State Executive Directors **(159)**
Ass'n of Otolaryngology Administrators **(159)**
Ass'n of Pathology Chairs **(159)**
Ass'n of Pediatric Oncology Nurses **(159)**
Ass'n of Physician Assistant Programs **(160)**
Ass'n of Physician Assistants in Cardiovascular Surgery **(160)**
Ass'n of Plastic Surgery Assistants **(160)**
Ass'n of Polysomnographic Technologists **(160)**
Ass'n of Professors of Cardiology **(161)**
Ass'n of Professors of Gynecology and Obstetrics **(161)**
Ass'n of Professors of Medicine **(162)**
Ass'n of Program Directors in Internal Medicine **(162)**
Ass'n of Program Directors in Radiology **(162)**
Ass'n of Program Directors in Surgery **(162)**
Ass'n of Reproductive Health Professionals **(163)**
Ass'n of Rheumatology Health Professionals **(164)**
Ass'n of SIDS and Infant Mortality Programs **(165)**
Ass'n of Surgical Technologists **(166)**
Ass'n of Teachers of Preventive Medicine **(167)**
Ass'n of Telemedecine Service Providers **(167)**
Ass'n of Tongue Depressors **(168)**
Ass'n of University Anesthesiologists **(168)**
Ass'n of University Radiologists **(168)**
Ass'n of Vascular and Interventional Radiographers **(169)**
Ass'n of Women Surgeons **(169)**
Ass'n of Women's Health, Obstetric and Neonatal Nurses **(169)**
Associated Professional Sleep Socs. **(172)**
Behavior Genetics Ass'n **(177)**
BioCommunications Ass'n **(179)**
Biomedical Engineering Soc. **(179)**
Biomedical Marketing Ass'n **(179)**
Black Psychiatrists of America **(180)**
Case Management Soc. of America **(187)**
Catecholamine Club **(187)**
Certification Board for Urologic Nurses and Associates **(190)**
Cervical Spine Research Soc. **(190)**
Child Neurology Soc. **(192)**
Chinese American Medical Soc. **(192)**
Christian Medical and Dental Soc. **(193)**
Civil Aviation Medical Ass'n **(194)**
Clinical Immunology Soc. **(194)**
Clinical Ligand Assay Soc. **(195)**
Clinical Orthopaedic Soc. **(195)**
Clinical Soc. of Genito-Urinary Surgeons **(195)**
College of American Pathologists **(197)**
College of Osteopathic Healthcare Executives **(198)**
Computer-based Patient Record Institute **(203)**
Computerized Medical Imaging Soc. **(203)**
Congress of Lung Ass'n Staff **(205)**
Congress of Neurological Surgeons **(205)**
Conservative Orthopedics Internat'l Ass'n **(206)**
Council of Medical Specialty Socs. **(215)**
Council of Musculoskeletal Specialty Socs. **(215)**
Council of State and Territorial Epidemiologists **(215)**
Council on Diagnostic Imaging to the A.C.A. **(216)**
Council on Geriatric Cardiology **(217)**
Council on Resident Education in Obstetrics and Gynecology **(217)**
Cranial Academy **(218)**
Cystic Fibrosis Foundation **(219)**
Delta Soc. **(221)**
Drug and Alcohol Testing Industry Ass'n **(225)**
Drug Information Ass'n **(225)**
Emergency Medicine Residents' Ass'n **(229)**
Endocrine Fellows Foundation **(230)**
Endocrine Soc. **(230)**
Eye Bank Ass'n of America **(234)**
Federal Physicians Ass'n **(236)**
Federated Ambulatory Surgery Ass'n **(236)**
Federation of Spine Ass'ns **(237)**
Federation of State Medical Boards of the U. S. **(237)**
Foundation for Advances in Medicine and Science **(243)**
Gastroenterology Research Group **(246)**
Genetics Soc. of America **(246)**
Gerontological Soc. of America **(247)**
Gynecologic Oncology Group **(250)**
Gynecologic Surgery Soc. **(250)**
Harvey Soc. **(251)**
Health Industry Distributors Ass'n **(252)**
Health Physics Soc. **(252)**
Health Sciences Communications Ass'n **(252)**
Healthcare Convention and Exhibitors Ass'n **(252)**
Healthcare Leadership Council **(253)**
Histochemical Soc. **(254)**
Human Biology Ass'n **(257)**
Independent Medical Distributors Ass'n **(261)**
Infectious Diseases Soc. of America **(263)**
Internat'l Academy of Behavioral Medicine, Counseling and Psychotherapy **(272)**
Internat'l Academy of Oral Medicine and Toxicology **(272)**
Internat'l Academy of Podiatric Medicine **(272)**
Internat'l Anesthesia Research Soc. **(273)**
Internat'l Ass'n for Continuing Education and Training **(273)**
Internat'l Ass'n for the Study of Pain **(275)**
Internat'l Ass'n of Allergology and Clinical Immunology **(275)**
Internat'l Ass'n of Eating Disorders Professionals **(278)**
Internat'l Ass'n of Medical Science Educators **(281)**
Internat'l Ass'n of Pediatric Laboratory Medicine **(281)**
Internat'l Ass'n of Physicians and Health Care Professionals **(281)**
Internat'l Atherosclerosis Soc. **(283)**
Internat'l Childbirth Education Ass'n **(285)**
Internat'l College of Surgeons **(286)**
Internat'l Embryo Transfer Soc. **(290)**
Internat'l Health Evaluation Ass'n **(293)**
Internat'l League of Dermatological Socs. **(296)**
Internat'l Liver Transplantation Soc. **(296)**
Internat'l Oculoplastic Soc. **(298)**
Internat'l Pediatric Nephrology Ass'n **(299)**
Internat'l Plasma Products Industry Ass'n **(300)**
Internat'l Research Council of Neuromuscular Disorders **(301)**
Internat'l Skeletal Soc. **(302)**
Internat'l Soc. for Artificial Organs **(303)**
Internat'l Soc. for Cardiovascular Surgery - North American Chapter **(303)**
Internat'l Soc. for Environmental Toxicology and Cancer **(303)**
Internat'l Soc. for Experimental Hematology **(303)**
Internat'l Soc. for Heart and Lung Transplantation **(303)**
Internat'l Soc. for Infectious Diseases **(303)**
Internat'l Soc. for Magnetic Resonance in Medicine **(303)**
Internat'l Soc. for Peritoneal Dialysis **(304)**
Internat'l Soc. for Pharmacoeconomics and Outcomes Research **(304)**
Internat'l Soc. for Preventive Oncology **(304)**
Internat'l Soc. for the Study of Subtle Energies and Energy Medicine **(305)**
Internat'l Soc. for Traumatic Stress Studies **(305)**
Internat'l Soc. of Hepato-Biliary Pancreatic Radiology **(306)**
Internat'l Soc. of Orthopaedic Surgery - U.S. Chapter **(306)**
Internat'l Stress Management Ass'n **(307)**
Internat'l Trauma Anesthesia and Critical Care Soc. **(309)**
Internat'l Union of Industrial Service Transport Health Employees **(310)**
Intersocietal Commission for the Accreditation of Vascular Laboratories **(311)**
Iota Tau Sigma **(312)**
Islamic Medical Ass'n **(313)**
Joint Council of Allergy, Asthma and Immunology **(315)**
Lamaze International **(316)**
Latex Advisors Ass'n **(317)**
Long Term Acute Care Hospital Ass'n of America **(321)**
Medical Device Manufacturers Ass'n **(326)**
Medical Group Management Ass'n **(326)**
Medical Library Ass'n **(326)**
Medical Marketing Ass'n **(326)**
Medical Mycological Soc. of the Americas **(326)**
Medical Records Institute **(326)**
Medical-Dental-Hospital Business Associates **(326)**
Microcirculatory Soc. of America **(328)**
Midwives Alliance of North America **(328)**
Movement Disorder Soc. **(331)**
Musculoskeletal Tumor Soc. **(331)**
Nat'l Academy of Clinical Biochemistry **(334)**
Nat'l Academy of Neuropsychology **(334)**
Nat'l Ass'n For Ambulatory Care **(337)**
Nat'l Ass'n for Medical Direction of Respiratory Care **(340)**
Nat'l Ass'n for Medical Equipment Services **(340)**
Nat'l Ass'n for Proton Therapy **(340)**
Nat'l Ass'n Medical Staff Services **(342)**
Nat'l Ass'n of Apnea Professionals **(343)**
Nat'l Ass'n of Children's Hospitals and Related Institutions **(347)**
Nat'l Ass'n of Emergency Medical Technicians **(353)**
Nat'l Ass'n of EMS Physicians **(353)**
Nat'l Ass'n of Health Career Schools **(357)**
Nat'l Ass'n of Managed Care Physicians **(362)**
Nat'l Ass'n of Medical Examiners **(362)**
Nat'l Ass'n of Nephrology Technologists and Technicians **(364)**
Nat'l Ass'n of Orthopaedic Technologists **(364)**
Nat'l Ass'n of Physician Recruiters **(365)**
Nat'l Ass'n of Professional Geriatric Care Managers **(366)**
Nat'l Ass'n of State Emergency Medical Services Directors **(375)**
Nat'l Ass'n of VA Physicians and Dentists **(379)**

National Trade and Professional Associations of the U.S. © 1999, Columbia Books, Inc. 583

MENTAL HEALTH

MERCHANDISING

METAL WORKING

METALS

METEOROLOGY

MICROBIOLOGY

MICROFILMS

MICROSCOPES

MILITARY

Chorus America (193)
Church Music Publishers Ass'n (193)
Classical Music Broadcasters Ass'n (194)
College Band Directors Nat'l Ass'n (197)
College Music Soc. (197)
Conductors Guild (203)
Country Music Ass'n (217)
Country Radio Broadcasters (218)
Delta Omicron Foundation, Inc. (221)
Fellowship of United Methodists in Music and Worship Arts (238)
Gospel Music Ass'n (248)
Guild of American Luthiers (250)
Guitar and Accessories Marketing Ass'n (250)
Intercollegiate Men's Choruses, an Internat'l Ass'n of Male Choruses (271)
Internat'l Ass'n of Electronic Keyboard Manufacturers (278)
Internat'l Ass'n of Jazz Educators (280)
Internat'l Ass'n of Music Libraries, United States Branch (281)
Internat'l Bluegrass Music Ass'n (283)
Internat'l Business Music Ass'n (284)
Internat'l Clarinet Ass'n (285)
Internat'l Computer Music Ass'n (286)
Internat'l Conference of Symphony and Opera Musicians (287)
Internat'l Double Reed Soc. (289)
Internat'l Federation for Choral Music (290)
Internat'l Guild of Symphony, Opera and Ballet Musicians (293)
Internat'l Horn Soc. (294)
Internat'l Music Products Ass'n (298)
Internat'l Piano Guild (300)
Internat'l Soc. for the Performing Arts (304)
Internat'l Soc. of Bassists (305)
Internat'l Trombone Ass'n (309)
Keyboard Teachers Ass'n Internat'l (316)
Mu Phi Epsilon (331)
Music and Entertainment Industry Educators Ass'n (332)
Music Critics Ass'n of North America (332)
Music Distributors Ass'n (332)
Music Educators Nat'l Conference: The Nat'l Ass'n for Music Education (332)
Music Industry Conference (332)
Music Library Ass'n (332)
Music Publishers' Ass'n of the United States (332)
Music Teachers Nat'l Ass'n (332)
Nat'l Ass'n of Band Instrument Manufacturers (344)
Nat'l Ass'n of College Wind and Percussion Instructors (348)
Nat'l Ass'n of Music Education (363)
Nat'l Ass'n of Pastoral Musicians (364)
Nat'l Ass'n of Professional Band Instrument Repair Technicians (366)
Nat'l Ass'n of School Music Dealers (371)
Nat'l Ass'n of Schools of Music (371)
Nat'l Ass'n of State Supervisors of Music (376)
Nat'l Ballroom and Entertainment Ass'n (382)
Nat'l Band Ass'n (382)
Nat'l Catholic Band Ass'n (385)
Nat'l Council of Music Importers and Exporters (395)
Nat'l Federation Interscholastic Music Ass'n (402)
Nat'l Federation of Music Clubs (404)
Nat'l Flute Ass'n (405)
Nat'l Guild of Piano Teachers (408)
Nat'l Music Council (418)
Nat'l Music Publishers' Ass'n (418)
Nat'l Opera Ass'n (419)
North American Folk Music and Dance Alliance (442)
North American Saxophone Alliance (444)
Organization of American Kodaly Educators (450)
Percussive Arts Soc. (454)
Phi Mu Alpha - Sinfonia (457)
Piano Manufacturers Ass'n Internat'l (458)
Piano Technicians Guild (458)
Production Music Library Ass'n (464)
Retail Print Music Dealers Ass'n (476)
Soc. for Asian Music (485)
Soc. for Ethnomusicology (488)
Soc. of Professional Audio Recording Services (505)
Songwriters Guild of America (510)
Viola da Gamba Soc. of America (539)
Western Music Ass'n (543)
Women Band Directors Nat'l Ass'n (545)

NATURALISTS

Ass'n of Natural Resource Enforcement Trainers (158)
Guild of Natural Science Illustrators (250)
Nat'l Ass'n for Interpretation (340)

NECKWEAR

Neckwear Ass'n of America (438)

NEUROLOGY

Academy of Aphasia (7)
American Academy for Cerebral Palsy and Developmental Medicine (20)
American Academy of Neurological and Orthopaedic Surgeons (23)
American Academy of Neurological Surgery (23)
American Academy of Neurology (23)
American Ass'n for the Study of Headache (32)
American Ass'n of Electrodiagnostic Medicine (36)
American Ass'n of Neurological Surgeons (39)
American Ass'n of Neuropathologists (39)
American Ass'n of Neuroscience Nurses (39)
American Clinical Neurophysiological Soc. (52)
American College of Neuropsychopharmacology (55)
American Epilepsy Soc. (66)
American Medical Electroencephalographic Ass'n (83)
American Neurological Ass'n (87)
American Soc. for Neurochemistry (104)
American Soc. for Pediatric Neurosurgery (104)
American Soc. for Stereotactic and Functional Neurosurgery (105)
American Soc. of Electroneurodiagnostic Technologists (109)
American Soc. of Internal Medicine (111)
American Soc. of Neuroimaging (113)
American Soc. of Neuroradiology (113)
Ass'n for Research in Nervous and Mental Disease (137)
Child Neurology Soc. (192)
Congress of Neurological Surgeons (205)
Internat'l Neural Network Soc. (298)
Nat'l Multiple Sclerosis Soc. (418)
Nat'l Tay-Sachs and Allied Diseases Ass'n (433)
Neurosurgical Soc. of America (438)
Soc. for Neuroscience (491)
Soc. of Neurological Surgeons (504)
Soc. of Neurosurgical Anesthesia and Critical Care (504)

NEWSPAPERS

American Ass'n of Independent Newspaper Distributors (38)
American Ass'n of Sunday and Feature Editors (43)
American Court and Commercial Newspapers (62)
American Jewish Press Ass'n (80)
American Soc. of Newspaper Editors (113)
Ass'n of Alternative Newsweeklies (142)
Ass'n of Area Business Publications (144)
Ass'n of Food Journalists (151)
Associated Press Managing Editors (172)
Audit Bureau of Circulations (173)
Foreign Press Ass'n (242)
Graphic Communications Ass'n (249)
Independent Free Papers of America (260)
Inter American Press Ass'n (271)
Internat'l Newspaper Financial Executives (298)
Internat'l Newspaper Group (298)
Internat'l Newspaper Marketing Ass'n (298)
Internat'l Soc. of Weekly Newspaper Editors (307)
Investigative Reporters and Editors (312)
Media Human Resources Ass'n (326)
Nat'l Ass'n of Agricultural Journalists (343)
Nat'l Ass'n of Hispanic Publications (358)
Nat'l Ass'n of Minority Media Executives (363)
Nat'l Conference of Editorial Writers (390)
Nat'l Federation of Hispanic Owned Newspapers (403)
Nat'l Newspaper Ass'n (418)
Nat'l Newspaper Publishers Ass'n (418)
Nat'l Soc. of Newspaper Columnists (430)
Newspaper Ass'n Managers (439)
Newspaper Ass'n of America (439)
Newspaper Features Council (439)
Newspaper Guild (439)
Newspaper Systems Group (439)
Organization of News Ombudsmen (450)
Red Tag News Publications Ass'n (473)
Soc. for News Design (491)
Suburban Newspapers of America (518)
Wire Service Guild (545)

NONPROFIT

Alliance for Nonprofit Management (17)
Alliance of Nonprofit Mailers (18)
American Ass'n of AIDS Executives (33)
Internat'l Soc. for Third-Sector Research (305)
Nat'l Council of Nonprofit Ass'ns (395)
Not-for-Profit Services Ass'n (446)

NOTIONS

Ass'n of Crafts and Creative Industries (149)
Gift Ass'n of America (247)
Hobby Industry Ass'n of America (255)
Home Sewing Ass'n (256)
Soc. of Craft Designers (500)
Souvenirs and Novelties Trade Ass'n (510)

NUCLEAR ENERGY

American Ass'n of Physicists in Medicine (41)
American College of Nuclear Medicine (56)
American Nuclear Insurers (87)
American Nuclear Soc. (87)
Health Physics Soc. (252)
Institute of Nuclear Materials Management (268)
Institute of Nuclear Power Operations (268)
Internat'l Ass'n for Hydrogen Energy (274)
Nat'l Council on Radiation Protection and Measurements (398)
Nat'l Lead Burning Ass'n (414)
Nuclear Energy Institute (446)
Nuclear Information and Records Management Ass'n (447)
Nuclear Suppliers Ass'n (447)
Professional Reactor Operator Soc. (466)
Radiation Research Soc. (470)
Soc. of Nuclear Medicine (504)
Universities Research Ass'n (536)

NUMISMATICS

American Numismatic Soc. (87)
Industry Council for Tangible Assets (263)
Professional Currency Dealers Ass'n (465)
Professional Numismatists Guild (466)

NURSERIES

All-America Rose Selections (17)
American Nursery and Landscape Ass'n (87)
American Nursery and Landscape Ass'n - Landscape Division (87)
Horticultural Research Institute (256)
Nat'l Ass'n of Plant Patent Owners (365)
Nursery Ass'n Executives of North America (447)
Wholesale Nursery Growers of America (544)

NURSING

Academy of Medical-Surgical Nurses (9)
Alpha Tau Delta (19)
American Academy of Ambulatory Care Nursing (20)
American Academy of Nurse Practitioners (23)
American Academy of Nursing (23)
American Ass'n for the History of Nursing (32)
American Ass'n of Colleges of Nursing (34)
American Ass'n of Critical-Care Nurses (35)
American Ass'n of Diabetes Educators (36)
American Ass'n of Legal Nurse Consultants (38)
American Ass'n of Managed Care Nurses (38)
American Ass'n of Neuroscience Nurses (39)
American Ass'n of Nurse Anesthetists (39)
American Ass'n of Nurse Attorneys (39)
American Ass'n of Occupational Health Nurses (40)
American Ass'n of Office Nurses (40)
American Ass'n of Spinal Cord Injury Nurses (42)
American Assembly for Men in Nursing (45)
American Board of Nursing Specialties (48)
American College of Health Care Administrators (54)
American College of Nurse-Midwives (56)
American Holistic Nurses' Ass'n (73)
American Licensed Practical Nurses Ass'n (81)
American Nephrology Nurses Ass'n (86)
American Nurses Ass'n (87)
American Nurses in Business Ass'n (87)
American Organization of Nurse Executives (88)
American Psychiatric Nurses Ass'n (94)
American Radiological Nurses Ass'n (96)
American School Health Ass'n (99)
American Soc. of Ophthalmic Registered Nurses (113)
American Soc. of Pain Management Nurses (113)
American Soc. of Peri-Anesthesia Nurses (114)
American Soc. of Plastic and Reconstructive Surgical Nurses (115)
American Soc. of Podiatric Medical Assistants (115)
American Subacute Care Ass'n (118)
Ass'n of Black Nursing Faculty in Higher Education (145)
Ass'n of Camp Nurses (145)
Ass'n of Child and Adolescent Psychiatric Nurses (146)
Ass'n of Community Health Nursing Educators (148)
Ass'n of Nurses in AIDS Care (158)
Ass'n of Operating Room Nurses (159)
Ass'n of Pediatric Oncology Nurses (159)
Ass'n of Rehabilitation Nurses (163)
Ass'n of State and Territorial Directors of Nursing (166)
Ass'n of Women's Health, Obstetric and Neonatal Nurses (169)
Chi Eta Phi Sorority (191)
Dermatology Nurses Ass'n (221)
Developmental Disabilities Nurses Ass'n (222)
Drug and Alcohol Nursing Ass'n (225)
Emergency Nurses Ass'n (229)
Federation of Nurses and Health Professionals (237)
Home Healthcare Nurses Ass'n (255)
Hospice and Palliative Nurses Ass'n (256)
Internat'l Ass'n of Forensic Nurses (279)
Internat'l Soc. of Psychiatric Consultation Liaison Nurses (306)
Internat'l Transplant Nurses Soc. (309)
Intravenous Nurses Soc. (312)
Lipid Nurse Task Force (320)
Nat'l Alliance of Nurse Practitioners (336)
Nat'l Ass'n for Home Care (339)
Nat'l Ass'n for Practical Nurse Education and Service (340)
Nat'l Ass'n of Clinical Nurse Specialists (347)
Nat'l Ass'n of Directors of Nursing Administration in Long Term Care (352)
Nat'l Ass'n of Hispanic Nurses (358)
Nat'l Ass'n of Neonatal Nurses (363)
Nat'l Ass'n of Nurse Practitioners in Reproductive Health (364)
Nat'l Ass'n of Orthopaedic Nurses (364)
Nat'l Ass'n of Pediatric Nurse Associates and Practitioners (364)
Nat'l Ass'n of Physician Nurses (365)
Nat'l Ass'n of School Nurses (371)
Nat'l Black Nurses Ass'n (383)
Nat'l Consortium of Chemical Dependency Nurses (392)
Nat'l Council of State Boards of Nursing (396)
Nat'l Federation for Specialty Nursing Organizations (402)
Nat'l Federation of Licensed Practical Nurses (403)
Nat'l Flight Nurses Ass'n (405)
Nat'l Gerontological Nursing Ass'n (407)
Nat'l League for Nursing (414)
Nat'l Nurses Soc. on Addictions (418)
Nat'l Nursing Staff Development Organization (418)
Nat'l Organization for Associate Degree Nursing (419)
Nat'l Organization of Nurse Practitioner Faculties (420)
Nat'l Perinatal Ass'n (422)
Nat'l Rural Health Ass'n (426)
Nat'l Student Nurses Ass'n (432)
North American Nursing Diagnosis Ass'n (443)
Nurse Healers - Professional Associates Internat'l (447)
Nurses Organization of Veterans Affairs (447)
Nursing Touch and Massage Therapy Ass'n Internat'l (447)
Oncology Nursing Soc. (448)
Respiratory Nursing Soc. (475)
Soc. for Education and Research in Psychiatric Mental Health Nursing (487)
Soc. for Vascular Nursing (496)
Soc. of Gastroenterology Nurses and Associates (502)
Soc. of Otorhinolaryngology and Head/Neck Nurses (504)
Soc. of Pediatric Nurses (505)
Soc. of Trauma Nurses (508)
Soc. of Urologic Nurses and Associates (508)
Visiting Nurse Ass'ns of America (540)
Wound, Ostomy and Continence Nurses Soc. (550)

NUTRITION

American Academy of Pediatrics (25)
American Academy of Veterinary Nutrition (26)
American Ass'n of Nutritional Consultants (40)
American College of Nutrition (56)
American Council of Applied Clinical Nutrition (61)
American Council on Science and Health (62)
American Dietetic Ass'n (64)
American Soc. for Clinical Nutrition (101)
American Soc. for Nutritional Sciences (104)

586 National Trade and Professional Associations of the U.S. © 1999, Columbia Books, Inc.

American Soc. for Parenteral and Enteral Nutrition **(104)**
American Soc. of Animal Science **(106)**
Ass'n of State and Territorial Public Health Nutrition Directors **(166)**
Ass'n of Vegetarian Dietitians and Nutrition Educators **(169)**
Consultant Dietitians in Health Care Facilities **(207)**
Council for Responsible Nutrition **(212)**
Institute of Food Technologists **(267)**
Internat'l and American Ass'ns of Clinical Nutritionists **(273)**
Internat'l Formula Council **(292)**
Nat'l Ass'n of Nutrition and Aging Services Programs **(364)**
Nat'l Block and Bridle Club **(383)**
Nat'l Dairy Council **(398)**
Nat'l Nutritional Foods Ass'n **(419)**
Soc. for Nutrition Education **(491)**

NUTS
American Peanut Council **(90)**
American Peanut Research and Education Soc. **(90)**
American Peanut Shellers Ass'n **(91)**
Nat'l Pecan Shellers Ass'n **(421)**
Northern Nut Growers Ass'n **(446)**
Peanut and Tree Nut Processors Ass'n **(454)**
Walnut Council **(540)**

OBSTETRICS
American Academy of Thermology **(26)**
American College of Obstetricians and Gynecologists **(56)**
American College of Osteopathic Obstetricians and Gynecologists **(56)**
Ass'n of Maternal and Child Health Programs **(157)**
Ass'n of Professors of Gynecology and Obstetrics **(161)**
Ass'n of Women's Health, Obstetric and Neonatal Nurses **(169)**
Lamaze International **(316)**
Midwives Alliance of North America **(328)**
Nat'l Ass'n of Childbearing Centers **(347)**
Nat'l Family Planning and Reproductive Health Ass'n **(402)**
Nat'l Perinatal Ass'n **(422)**
Soc. for Obstetric Anesthesia and Perinatology **(491)**

OCEANOGRAPHY
American Meteorological Soc. **(84)**
American Soc. of Limnology and Oceanography **(112)**
Diving Equipment and Marketing Ass'n **(224)**
Estuarine Research Federation **(233)**
Institute of Diving **(266)**
Marine Technology Soc. **(324)**
Maritime Law Ass'n of the U.S. **(324)**
Nat'l Ass'n of Marine Surveyors **(362)**
Nat'l Marine Educators Ass'n **(416)**
Nat'l Ocean Industries Ass'n **(419)**
World Aquaculture Soc. **(549)**

OFFICE EQUIPMENT
Business and Institutional Furniture Manufacturers Ass'n Internat'l **(184)**
Business Products Credit Ass'n **(185)**
Business Products Industry Ass'n **(185)**
Business Technology Ass'n **(185)**
Independent Cash Register Dealers Ass'n **(260)**
Information Technology Industry Council **(264)**
ISDA - The Office Systems Cooperative **(313)**
Modular Building Institute **(330)**
Nat'l Ass'n of Office Furniture Dealers **(364)**
Nat'l Ass'n of State Catholic Conference Directors **(374)**
Nat'l Rep/Wholesaler Ass'n **(425)**
Office Furniture Distribution Ass'n **(447)**
Office Planners and Users Group **(447)**

OILS
Fragrance Materials Ass'n of the United States **(243)**
Nat'l Oil Recyclers Ass'n **(419)**
United Ass'n of Used Oil Services **(530)**

OPHTHALMOLOGY
Academy of Veterinary Allergy and Clinical Immunology **(10)**
American Academy of Ophthalmology **(24)**
American Ass'n for Pediatric Ophthalmology and Strabismus **(31)**
American Ass'n of Certified Orthoptists **(34)**
American College of Eye Surgeons **(54)**
American College of Veterinary Ophthalmologists **(58)**
American Ophthalmological Soc. **(88)**
American Osteopathic Colleges of Ophthalmology and Otolaryngology, Head and Neck Surgery **(89)**
American Soc. of Contemporary Ophthalmology **(109)**
American Soc. of Ophthalmic Plastic and Reconstructive Surgery **(113)**
American Soc. of Ophthalmic Registered Nurses **(113)**
American Soc. of Veterinary Ophthalmology **(117)**
Ass'n for Research in Vision and Ophthalmology **(137)**
Ass'n of University Professors of Ophthalmology **(168)**
Contact Lens Ass'n of Ophthalmologists **(207)**
Eye Bank Ass'n of America **(234)**
Internat'l Perimetric Soc. **(299)**
Internat'l Soc. of Refractive Surgery **(306)**
Kerato-Refractive Soc. **(315)**
Ophthalmic Photographers' Soc. **(448)**
Outpatient Ophthalmic Surgery Soc. **(451)**
Pharmacists in Ophthalmic Practice **(456)**
Soc. of Eye Surgeons **(501)**

OPTICAL
American Soc. for Precision Engineering **(104)**
American Soc. of Cataract and Refractive Surgery **(107)**
American Soc. of Ocularists **(113)**
Contact Lens Institute **(207)**
Contact Lens Manufacturers Ass'n **(207)**
Contact Lens Soc. of America **(207)**
Inter-Society Color Council **(271)**
Nat'l Academy of Opticianry **(334)**
Nat'l Ass'n of Manufacturing Opticians **(362)**
Nat'l Ass'n of Vision Professionals **(379)**
Optical Industry Ass'n: OMA **(448)**
Optical Laboratories Ass'n **(448)**
Optical Soc. of America **(449)**
Opticians Ass'n of America **(449)**
Opto-Precision Instruments Ass'n **(449)**
SPIE-Internat'l Soc. for Optical Engineering **(514)**
Vision Council of America **(540)**

OPTOMETRY
American Academy of Optometry **(24)**
American Optometric Ass'n **(88)**
American Optometric Student Ass'n **(88)**
Ass'n of Schools and Colleges of Optometry **(164)**
Ass'n of Vision Science Librarians **(169)**
College of Optometrists in Vision Development **(197)**
Contact Lens Manufacturers Ass'n **(207)**
Contact Lens Soc. of America **(207)**
Internat'l Academy of Sports Vision **(272)**
Internat'l Ass'n of Boards of Examiners in Optometry **(276)**
Internat'l Ass'n of Optometric Executives **(281)**
Nat'l Ass'n of Optometrists and Opticians **(364)**
Nat'l Optometric Ass'n **(419)**
Optometric Editors Ass'n **(449)**
Soc. for Excellence in Eyecare **(488)**

ORGANS
American Guild of Organists **(71)**
American Institute of Organbuilders **(78)**
Associated Pipe Organ Builders of America **(172)**
Internat'l Ass'n of Electronic Keyboard Manufacturers **(278)**

ORIENTAL
American Oriental Soc. **(88)**
American Schools of Oriental Research **(99)**
Ass'n for Asian Studies **(130)**
Oriental Rug Importers Ass'n of America **(450)**
Soc. of Asian and Comparative Philosophy **(498)**

ORTHODONTICS
American Academy of Gnathologic Orthopedics **(22)**
American Academy of Orthotists and Prosthetists **(24)**
American Ass'n of Orthodontists **(40)**
American Soc. for the Study of Orthodontics **(105)**
Internat'l Ass'n for Orthodontics **(275)**

ORTHOPEDICS
Academic Orthopaedic Soc. **(7)**
Academy of Osseointegration **(9)**
American Academy of Gnathologic Orthopedics **(22)**
American Academy of Neurological and Orthopaedic Surgeons **(23)**
American Academy of Orthopaedic Surgeons **(24)**
American Ass'n of Orthopaedic Medicine **(40)**
American Board of Podiatric Orthopedics and Primary Podiatric Medicine **(48)**
American College of Foot and Ankle Orthopedics and Medicine **(54)**
American College of Foot and Ankle Surgeons **(54)**
American Orthopaedic Ass'n **(88)**
American Orthopaedic Foot and Ankle Soc. **(88)**
American Orthopaedic Soc. for Sports Medicine **(88)**
American Osteopathic Academy of Orthopedics **(89)**
American Soc. for Surgery of the Hand **(105)**
American Spinal Injury Ass'n **(118)**
Arthroscopy Ass'n of North America **(128)**
Ass'n of Bone and Joint Surgeons **(145)**
Ass'n of Children's Prosthetic-Orthotic Clinics **(146)**
Clinical Orthopaedic Soc. **(195)**
Conservative Orthopedics Internat'l Ass'n **(206)**
Internat'l Soc. of Arthroscopy, Knee Surgery and Orthopaedic Sports Medicine **(305)**
Nat'l Ass'n of Orthopaedic Nurses **(364)**
Nat'l Ass'n of Orthopaedic Technologists **(364)**
Nat'l Student Osteopathic Medical Ass'n **(432)**
Orthopaedic Research Soc. **(451)**
Orthopaedic Section - American Physical Therapy Ass'n **(451)**
Orthopedic Surgical Manufacturers Ass'n **(451)**
Pediatric Orthopedic Soc. of North America **(454)**
Pedorthic Footwear Ass'n **(454)**
Ruth Jackson Orthopaedic Soc. **(478)**

OSTEOPATHY
American Academy of Osteopathy **(24)**
American Ass'n of Colleges of Osteopathic Medicine **(34)**
American College of Neuropsychiatrists **(55)**
American College of Osteopathic Emergency Physicians **(56)**
American College of Osteopathic Family Physicians **(56)**
American College of Osteopathic Internists **(56)**
American College of Osteopathic Obstetricians and Gynecologists **(56)**
American College of Osteopathic Pain Management and Sclerotherapy **(56)**
American College of Osteopathic Pediatricians **(56)**
American College of Osteopathic Surgeons **(56)**
American Osteopathic Academy for Sports Medicine **(89)**
American Osteopathic Academy of Orthopedics **(89)**
American Osteopathic Ass'n **(89)**
American Osteopathic College of Anesthesiologists **(89)**
American Osteopathic College of Dermatology **(89)**
American Osteopathic College of Occupational Preventive Medicine **(89)**
American Osteopathic College of Proctology **(89)**
American Osteopathic College of Radiology **(89)**
American Osteopathic College of Rehabilitation Medicine **(89)**
American Osteopathic Colleges of Ophthalmology and Otolaryngology, Head and Neck Surgery **(89)**
American Osteopathic Healthcare Ass'n **(89)**
Ass'n of Osteopathic Directors and Medical Educators **(159)**
Ass'n of Osteopathic State Executive Directors **(159)**
College of Osteopathic Healthcare Executives **(198)**
Cranial Academy **(218)**
Iota Tau Sigma **(312)**
Lambda Omicron Gamma Medical Society **(317)**

OXYGEN
Internat'l Ass'n for Oxygen Therapy **(275)**
Internat'l Oxygen Manufacturers Ass'n **(299)**
Internat'l Ozone Ass'n-Pan American Group Branch **(299)**
Oxygen Soc., The **(452)**

PACKAGING
Adhesives Manufacturers Ass'n **(12)**
Alliance of Foam Packaging Recyclers **(18)**
Aluminum Foil Container Manufacturers Ass'n **(19)**
American Family Therapy Academy **(66)**
American Flock Ass'n **(68)**
Aseptic Packaging Council **(128)**
Ass'n of Container Reconditioners **(148)**
Composite Can and Tube Institute **(201)**
Contract Packagers Ass'n **(208)**
Express Carriers Ass'n **(234)**
Fibre Box Ass'n **(238)**
Flexible Packaging Ass'n **(240)**
Foodservice and Packaging Institute **(242)**
Glass Packaging Institute **(247)**
Healthcare Compliance Packaging Council **(252)**
Institute of Packaging Professionals **(268)**
Internat'l Corrugated Packaging Foundation **(287)**
Internat'l Safe Transit Ass'n **(302)**
Label Packaging Suppliers Council **(316)**
Meat Industry Suppliers Ass'n **(325)**
Nat'l Beverage Packaging Ass'n **(382)**
Nat'l Institute of Packaging, Handling and Logistics Engineers **(412)**
Nat'l Paperbox Ass'n **(421)**
Package Design Council Int'l **(452)**
Packaging Machinery Manufacturers Institute **(452)**
Paper Shipping Sack Manufacturers Ass'n **(453)**
Paperboard Packaging Council **(453)**
Petroleum Packaging Council **(456)**
Polystyrene Packaging Council **(460)**
Produce Marketing Ass'n **(463)**
Recycled Paperboard Technical Ass'n **(473)**
Research and Development Associates for Military Food and Packaging Systems **(475)**
Retail Packaging Manufacturers Ass'n **(476)**
Tube Council of North America **(527)**
Wirebound Box Manufacturers Ass'n **(545)**
Women in Packaging **(547)**
World Packaging Organisation **(550)**

PAINT AND PAINTING
American Academy of Equine Art **(21)**
Architectural Spray Coaters Ass'n **(127)**
Chemical Coaters Ass'n Internat'l **(191)**
Federation of Socs. for Coatings Technology **(237)**
Finishing Contractors Ass'n **(239)**
Independent Professional Painting Contractors Ass'n of America **(261)**
Internat'l Brotherhood of Painters and Allied Trades **(284)**
Internat'l Cadmium Ass'n **(284)**
Nat'l Paint and Coatings Ass'n **(420)**
Nat'l Spray Equipment Manufacturers Ass'n **(431)**
Paint and Decorating Retailers Ass'n **(452)**
Paint, Body and Equipment Ass'n **(452)**
Painting and Decorating Contractors of America **(452)**
Powder Coating Institute **(461)**
SSPC: the Soc. for Protective Coatings **(515)**
Synthetic Amorphous Silica and Silicates Industry Ass'n **(519)**

PALEONTOLOGY
Paleontological Research Institution **(452)**
SEPM - Soc. for Sedimentary Geology **(482)**
Soc. of Vertebrate Paleontology **(509)**

PAPER INDUSTRY see also PULP
American Forest and Paper Ass'n **(69)**
American Paper Machinery Ass'n **(90)**
American Pulpwood Ass'n **(96)**
American Soc. of Papyrologists **(114)**
Ass'n for Engineering Graphics and Imaging Systems **(133)**
Ass'n of Independent Corrugated Converters **(153)**
Book Industry Study Group **(181)**
Foodservice and Packaging Institute **(242)**
INDA, Ass'n of the Nonwoven Fabrics Industry **(259)**
Institute of Paper Science and Technology **(268)**
Internat'l Corrugated Packaging Foundation **(287)**
Label Printing Industries of America **(316)**
Manufacturers Representatives of America **(323)**
Nat'l Council of the Paper Industry for Air and Stream Improvement **(397)**
Nat'l Paper Trade Ass'n **(421)**
Nat'l Paperbox Ass'n **(421)**
Paper and Plastic Representatives Management Council **(453)**
Paper Distribution Council **(453)**
Paper Industry Management Ass'n **(453)**
Paper Machine Clothing Council **(453)**
Paper Shipping Sack Manufacturers Ass'n **(453)**
Paperboard Packaging Council **(453)**
Pulp and Paper Safety Ass'n **(470)**
Sales Ass'n of the Paper Industry **(478)**
Sanitary Supply Wholesalers Ass'n **(479)**
Soc. of Scribes **(507)**
Technical Ass'n of the Pulp and Paper Industry **(520)**
United Paperworkers Internat'l Union **(531)**
Wallcoverings Ass'n **(540)**

PARASITOLOGY
American Ass'n of Veterinary Parasitologists **(45)**
American Soc. of Parasitologists **(114)**
Soc. of Nematologists **(504)**
Soc. of Protozoologists **(506)**

PARKING
Internat'l Parking Institute **(299)**

National Trade and Professional Associations of the U.S. © 1999, Columbia Books, Inc. 587

Nat'l Parking Ass'n **(421)**

PARKS
American Ass'n of Botanical Gardens and Arboreta **(33)**
American Land Rights Ass'n **(80)**
American Park and Recreation Soc. **(90)**
Ass'n of Partners for Public Lands **(159)**
Ecotourism Soc. **(225)**
Internat'l Ass'n of Amusement Parks and Attractions **(275)**
Nat'l Ass'n of County Park and Recreation Officials **(351)**
Nat'l Ass'n of Industrial and Office Properties **(360)**
Nat'l Ass'n of State Park Directors **(375)**
Nat'l Institute on Park and Grounds Management **(412)**
Nat'l Park Hospitality Ass'n **(421)**
Nat'l Parks and Conservation Ass'n **(421)**
Nat'l Recreation and Park Ass'n **(424)**
Nat'l Soc. for Park Resources **(429)**
Recreational Park Trailer Industry Ass'n **(473)**
Soc. of Municipal Arborists **(504)**
Soc. of Park and Recreation Educators **(505)**
Visitor Studies Ass'n **(540)**
World Waterpark Ass'n **(550)**

PATENTS
American Intellectual Property Law Ass'n **(79)**
Ass'n of University Technology Managers **(169)**
Intellectual Property Owners Ass'n **(270)**
Internat'l Intellectual Property Alliance **(295)**
Internat'l Intellectual Property Ass'n **(295)**
Licensing Executives Soc. **(319)**
Nat'l Ass'n of Plant Patent Owners **(365)**
Nat'l Council of Intellectual Property Law Ass'ns **(395)**
Patent and Trademark Office Soc. **(454)**
Patent Office Professional Ass'n **(454)**
Trademark Soc. **(525)**

PATHOLOGY
American Ass'n of Avian Pathologists **(33)**
American Ass'n of Pathologists' Assistants **(40)**
American College of Veterinary Pathologists **(58)**
American Pathology Foundation **(90)**
American Soc. for Investigative Pathology **(103)**
Ass'n for Molecular Pathology **(136)**
Ass'n of Pathology Chairs **(159)**
College of American Pathologists **(197)**
Intersociety Committee on Pathology Information **(311)**
Nat'l Soc. for Histotechnology **(429)**
Soc. of Toxicologic Pathologists **(508)**
United States and Canadian Academy of Pathology **(532)**
Universities Associated for Research and Education in Pathology **(536)**

PATTERNS
Home Sewing Ass'n **(256)**

PEDIATRICS
Ambulatory Pediatric Ass'n **(19)**
American Academy of Pediatrics **(25)**
American Ass'n for Pediatric Ophthalmology and Strabismus **(31)**
American College of Foot and Ankle Pediatrics **(54)**
American College of Osteopathic Pediatricians **(56)**
American Pediatric Soc. **(91)**
American Pediatric Surgical Ass'n **(91)**
American Soc. for Pediatric Neurosurgery **(104)**
American Soc. of Pediatric Hematology/Oncology **(114)**
American Soc. of Pediatric Nephrology **(114)**
Ass'n for the Care of Children's Health **(139)**
Ass'n of Children's Prosthetic-Orthotic Clinics **(146)**
Ass'n of Medical School Pediatric Department Chairmen **(157)**
Ass'n of Pediatric Oncology Nurses **(159)**
Ass'n of Pediatric Program Directors **(160)**
Internat'l Ass'n of Pediatric Laboratory Medicine **(281)**
Internat'l Pediatric Nephrology Ass'n **(299)**
Nat'l Ass'n for Families and Addiction Research and Education **(339)**
Nat'l Ass'n of Pediatric Nurse Associates and Practitioners **(364)**
North American Soc. for Pediatric Gastroenterology and Nutrition **(444)**
Pediatric Orthopedic Soc. of North America **(454)**
Soc. for Developmental and Behavioral Pediatrics **(487)**
Soc. for Pediatric Anesthesia **(492)**
Soc. for Pediatric Dermatology **(492)**
Soc. for Pediatric Radiology **(492)**
Soc. for Pediatric Research **(492)**
Soc. for Pediatric Urology **(492)**
Soc. of Pediatric Nurses **(505)**

PERSONNEL
American Ass'n for Employment in Education **(30)**
American Ass'n of School Personnel Administrators **(42)**
American College Personnel Ass'n **(58)**
American Council on Internat'l Personnel **(62)**
American Counseling Ass'n **(62)**
American Soc. for Healthcare Central Service Personnel **(102)**
American Soc. for Healthcare Human Resources Administration **(103)**
Ass'n for Humanistic Education and Development **(134)**
Ass'n for Multicultural Counseling and Development **(136)**
Ass'n for Specialists in Group Work **(137)**
Cement Employers Ass'n **(189)**
College and University Personnel Ass'n **(197)**
Employee Assistance Professionals Ass'n **(229)**
Employee Relocation Council **(229)**
Employment Management Ass'n **(230)**
Human Resource Planning Soc. **(257)**
Human Resources Research Organization **(257)**
Institute for Internat'l Human Resources **(265)**
Internat'l Ass'n for Human Resource Information Management **(274)**
Internat'l Ass'n of Corporate and Professional Recruitment **(277)**
Internat'l Ass'n of Correctional Training Personnel **(278)**
Internat'l Ass'n of Counseling Services **(278)**
Internat'l Ass'n of Personnel in Employment Security **(281)**
Internat'l Ass'n of Pupil Personnel Workers **(282)**
Internat'l Personnel Management Ass'n **(299)**
Jesuit Ass'n of Student Personnel Administrators **(313)**
Media Human Resources Ass'n **(326)**
Nat'l Ass'n for Law Placement **(340)**
Nat'l Ass'n of Church Personnel Administrators **(347)**
Nat'l Ass'n of Educational Office Professionals **(353)**
Nat'l Ass'n of Legal Search Consultants **(361)**
Nat'l Ass'n of Personnel Services **(365)**
Nat'l Ass'n of Professional Employer Organizations **(366)**
Nat'l Ass'n of State Personnel Executives **(376)**
Nat'l Ass'n of Student Personnel Administrators **(377)**
Nat'l Human Resources Ass'n **(409)**
Soc. for Human Resource Management **(489)**

PEST CONTROL
American Crop Protection Ass'n **(62)**
Ass'n of American Pesticide Control Officials **(142)**
Chemical Producers and Distributors Ass'n **(191)**
Nat'l Animal Control Ass'n **(336)**
Nat'l Animal Damage Control Ass'n **(337)**
Nat'l Pest Control Ass'n **(422)**
Northeastern Weed Science Soc. **(446)**
United Product Formulators and Distributors Ass'n **(531)**

PETROLEUM INDUSTRY
ADSC: The Internat'l Ass'n of Foundation Drilling **(12)**
American Ass'n of Petroleum Geologists **(40)**
American Ass'n of Professional Landmen **(41)**
American Independent Refiners Ass'n **(75)**
American Institute of Mining, Metallurgical, and Petroleum Engineers **(78)**
American Petroleum Institute **(91)**
American Soc. of Petroleum Operations Engineers **(114)**
Ass'n of Diving Contractors **(150)**
Ass'n of Energy Service Companies **(150)**
Ass'n of Oil Pipe Lines **(158)**
Ass'n of Petroleum Re-refiners **(160)**
Cathodic Protection Industry Ass'n **(188)**
Coordinating Research Council **(209)**
Council of Petroleum Accountants Socs. **(215)**
Energy Telecommunications and Electrical Ass'n **(230)**
Energy Traffic Ass'n **(230)**
Fiberglass Tank and Pipe Institute **(238)**
Independent Liquid Terminals Ass'n **(261)**
Independent Lubricant Manufacturers Ass'n **(261)**
Independent Petroleum Ass'n of America **(261)**
Independent Terminal Operators Ass'n **(262)**
Internat'l Ass'n of Drilling Contractors **(278)**
Internat'l Ass'n of Geophysical Contractors **(279)**
Internat'l Oil Scouts Ass'n **(299)**
Internat'l Petroleum Credit Ass'n **(299)**
Internat'l Slurry Surfacing Ass'n **(302)**
Internat'l Union of Petroleum and Industrial Workers **(310)**
Interstate Natural Gas Ass'n of America **(311)**
Interstate Oil and Gas Compact Commission **(312)**
Liaison Committee of Cooperating Oil and Gas Ass'ns **(319)**
Nat'l Ass'n of Chemical Recyclers **(347)**
Nat'l Ass'n of Division Order Analysts **(353)**
Nat'l Ass'n of Oil Heating Service Managers **(364)**
Nat'l Ass'n of Royalty Owners **(370)**
Nat'l Drilling Ass'n **(400)**
Nat'l Lubricating Grease Institute **(415)**
Nat'l Ocean Industries Ass'n **(419)**
Nat'l Petroleum Council **(422)**
Nat'l Petroleum Refiners Ass'n **(422)**
Nat'l Propane Gas Ass'n **(423)**
Nat'l Stripper Well Ass'n **(432)**
Natural Gas Supply Ass'n **(437)**
Oil, Chemical and Atomic Workers Internat'l Union **(448)**
Oxygenated Fuels Ass'n **(452)**
Petroleum Equipment Institute **(455)**
Petroleum Equipment Suppliers Ass'n **(455)**
Petroleum Industry Security Council **(455)**
Petroleum Marketers Ass'n of America **(456)**
Petroleum Packaging Council **(456)**
Petroleum Technology Transfer Council **(456)**
Service Station Dealers of America and Allied Trades **(482)**
Soc. of Exploration Geophysicists **(501)**
Soc. of Independent Gasoline Marketers of America **(502)**
Soc. of Petroleum Engineers **(505)**
Soc. of Professional Well Log Analysts **(506)**
Solution Mining Research Institute **(510)**
Spill Control Ass'n of America **(514)**
Tubular Exchanger Manufacturers Ass'n **(527)**
U.S. Oil and Gas Ass'n **(528)**

PETS see also SPECIFIC ANIMAL
Accredited Pet Cemetery Soc. **(10)**
American Animal Hospital Ass'n **(28)**
American Ass'n of Feline Practitioners **(37)**
American Boarding Kennels Ass'n **(48)**
American Grooming Shop Ass'n **(71)**
American Pet Boarding Ass'n **(91)**
American Pet Products Manufacturers Ass'n **(91)**
Independent Pet and Animal Transportation Ass'n Internat'l **(261)**
Internat'l Ass'n of Pet Cemeteries **(281)**
Internat'l Professional Groomers **(300)**
Nat'l Ass'n for Biomedical Research **(338)**
Nat'l Ass'n of Professional Pet Sitters **(367)**
Nat'l Dog Groomers Ass'n of America **(399)**
Nat'l Taxidermists Ass'n **(433)**
Pet Food Institute **(455)**
Pet Industry Distributors Ass'n **(455)**
Pet Industry Joint Advisory Council **(455)**
Pet Sitters Internat'l **(455)**
World Wide Pet Supply Ass'n **(550)**

PHARMACEUTICAL INDUSTRY see also DRUGS
Academy of Managed Care Pharmacy **(8)**
Alpha Zeta Omega **(19)**
American Ass'n of Colleges of Pharmacy **(35)**
American Ass'n of Pharmaceutical Scientists **(40)**
American Clinical Laboratory Ass'n **(52)**
American Council on Pharmaceutical Education **(62)**
American Pharmaceutical Ass'n **(91)**
American Soc. for Automation in Pharmacy **(101)**
Ass'n of Pharmaceutical Publishers **(160)**
Chain Drug Marketing Ass'n **(190)**
Controlled Release Soc. **(208)**
Generic Pharmaceutical Industry Ass'n **(246)**
Healthcare Compliance Packaging Council **(252)**
Healthcare Marketing and Communications Council **(253)**
Inter-Society Color Council **(271)**
Internat'l Academy of Compounding Pharmacists **(272)**
Internat'l Federation of Pharmaceutical Wholesalers **(290)**
Internat'l Pharmaceutical Excipients Council **(299)**
Internat'l Soc. for Pharmaceutical Engineering **(304)**
Kappa Psi Pharmaceutical Fraternity **(315)**
Nat'l Ass'n of Chain Drug Stores **(346)**
Nat'l Ass'n of Pharmaceutical Manufacturers **(365)**
Nat'l Community Pharmacists Ass'n **(388)**
Nat'l Council for Prescription Drug Programs **(393)**
Nat'l Council of State Pharmacy Ass'n Executives **(396)**
Nat'l Pharmaceutical Alliance **(422)**
Nat'l Pharmaceutical Ass'n **(422)**
Nat'l Pharmaceutical Council **(422)**
Nat'l Soc. of Pharmaceutical Sales Trainers **(430)**
Nat'l Wholesale Druggists' Ass'n **(436)**
Nonprescription Drug Manufacturers Ass'n **(440)**
Parenteral Drug Ass'n **(453)**
Pharmaceutical Care Management Ass'n **(456)**
Pharmaceutical Research and Manufacturers of America **(456)**
Regulatory Affairs Professionals Soc. **(474)**
Soc. for Biomolecular Screening **(486)**
Soc. for Clinical Data Management **(486)**

PHARMACOLOGY
Academy of Pharmaceutical Research and Science **(9)**
Academy of Pharmacy Practice and Management **(9)**
Academy of Students of Pharmacy **(10)**
American Academy of Clinical Toxicology **(21)**
American Academy of Veterinary and Comparative Toxicology **(26)**
American Academy of Veterinary Pharmacology and Therapeutics **(26)**
American Ass'n of Colleges of Pharmacy **(35)**
American College of Apothecaries **(53)**
American College of Clinical Pharmacology **(53)**
American College of Clinical Pharmacy **(53)**
American College of Neuropsychopharmacology **(55)**
American Council on Pharmaceutical Education **(62)**
American Institute of the History of Pharmacy **(78)**
American Soc. for Clinical Pharmacology and Therapeutics **(101)**
American Soc. for Pharmacology and Experimental Therapeutics **(104)**
American Soc. of Clinical Psychopharmacology **(108)**
American Soc. of Consultant Pharmacists **(108)**
American Soc. of Health-System Pharmacists **(110)**
American Soc. of Pharmacognosy **(114)**
Ass'n of Clinical Research Professionals **(147)**
Behavioral Pharmacology Soc. **(178)**
Biomedical Engineering Soc. **(179)**
Federation of American Socs. for Experimental Biology **(236)**
Internat'l Glutamate Technical Committee **(292)**
Internat'l Soc. for Pharmacoeconomics and Outcomes Research **(304)**
Lambda Kappa Sigma **(317)**
Nat'l Ass'n of Boards of Pharmacy **(345)**
Nat'l Catholic Pharmacists Guild of the United States **(386)**
Pharmacists in Ophthalmic Practice **(456)**
Phi Delta Chi **(456)**
United States Pharmacopeia **(534)**

PHILANTHROPY
Independent Sector **(261)**
Nat'l Network of Grantmakers **(418)**

PHILATELY
American Philatelic Soc. Writers Unit **(91)**
American Stamp Dealers' Ass'n **(118)**

PHILOLOGY
American Philological Ass'n **(91)**
American Soc. of Papyrologists **(114)**

PHILOSOPHY
American Ass'n of Philosophy Teachers **(40)**
American Catholic Philosophical Ass'n **(50)**
American Philosophical Ass'n **(91)**
American Philosophical Soc. **(91)**
American Soc. for Political and Legal Philosophy **(104)**
American Soc. for Value Inquiry **(106)**
Ass'n for Informal Logic and Critical Thinking **(135)**
Ass'n for Philosophy of the Unconscious **(136)**
Ass'n for Practical and Professional Ethics **(136)**
Ass'n for Symbolic Logic **(138)**
Ass'n of Muslim Social Scientists **(158)**
Ass'n of Philosophy Journal Editors **(160)**
Conference of Philosophical Societies **(204)**
Federation of State Humanities Councils **(237)**
Internat'l Ass'n for Philosophy of Law and Social Philosophy - American Section **(275)**
Jean Piaget Soc./Soc. for the Study of Knowledge and Development **(313)**
Metaphysical Soc. of America **(327)**
North American Soc. for Social Philosophy **(444)**
Philosophy of Education Soc. **(457)**
Philosophy of Science Ass'n **(457)**

588 National Trade and Professional Associations of the U.S. © 1999, Columbia Books, Inc.

Semiotic Soc. of America **(481)**
Soc. for Ancient Greek Philosophy **(485)**
Soc. for Business Ethics **(486)**
Soc. for Natural Philosophy **(491)**
Soc. for New Language Study **(491)**
Soc. for Phenomenology and Existential Philosophy **(492)**
Soc. for Philosophy and Technology **(492)**
Soc. for Philosophy of Religion **(492)**
Soc. for the Philosophy of Sex and Love **(495)**
Soc. of Asian and Comparative Philosophy **(498)**
Soc. of Christian Philosophers **(499)**
Soc. of Philosophers in America **(505)**

PHONOGRAPHS
American Soc. for Photogrammetry and Remote Sensing **(104)**
Amusement and Music Operators Ass'n **(124)**
Ass'n for Independent Music **(134)**
Music and Entertainment Industry Educators Ass'n **(332)**
Nat'l Academy of Recording Arts and Sciences **(334)**
Nat'l Ass'n of Recording Merchandisers **(369)**
Recording Industry Ass'n of America **(472)**

PHOTOGRAPHY
Advertising Photographers of America, Nat'l **(12)**
American Photographic Artisans Guild **(92)**
American Soc. for Photobiology **(104)**
American Soc. of Media Photographers **(112)**
American Soc. of Photographers **(114)**
American Soc. of Picture Professionals **(114)**
Antique and Amusement Photographers Internat'l **(125)**
Ass'n of Bridal Consultants **(145)**
Ass'n of Internat'l Photography Art Dealers **(155)**
Ass'n of Professional Color Imagers **(161)**
BioCommunications Ass'n **(179)**
Council on Fine Art Photography **(216)**
Evidence Photographers Internat'l Council **(233)**
Internat'l Fire Photographers Ass'n **(291)**
Internat'l Graphic Arts Education Ass'n **(292)**
Internat'l Reprographic Ass'n **(301)**
Nat'l Ass'n of Photo Equipment Technicians **(365)**
Nat'l Press Photographers Ass'n **(423)**
North American Nature Photography Ass'n **(443)**
Photo Chemical Machining Institute **(457)**
Photo Marketing Ass'n-Internat'l **(457)**
Photographic and Imaging Manufacturers Ass'n **(457)**
Photographic Manufacturers and Distributors Ass'n **(457)**
Picture Agency Council of America **(458)**
PrintImage Internat'l **(463)**
Professional Photographers of America **(466)**
Professional Travelogue Sponsors **(467)**
Professional Women Photographers **(467)**
Silver Users Ass'n **(483)**
Soc. for Imaging Science and Technology **(489)**
Soc. for Photographic Education **(492)**
Soc. of Photographer and Artist Representatives **(505)**
SPIE-Internat'l Soc. for Optical Engineering **(514)**
University Photographers Ass'n of America **(537)**
Wedding and Portrait Photographers Internat'l **(542)**
White House News Photographers Ass'n **(543)**

PHYSICAL EDUCATION
American Alliance for Health, Physical Education, Recreation and Dance **(27)**
Ass'n for the Advancement of Applied Sport Psychology **(138)**
Ass'n for Worksite Health Promotion **(141)**
Delta Psi Kappa **(221)**
IDEA, The Health and Fitness Source **(258)**
Internat'l Physical Fitness Ass'n **(299)**
Nat'l Ass'n for Girls and Women in Sport **(339)**
Nat'l Ass'n for Sport and Physical Education **(341)**
Phi Epsilon Kappa **(457)**
Soc. of State Directors of Health, Physical Education and Recreation **(507)**

PHYSICS
Acoustical Soc. of America **(11)**
American Academy of Thermology **(26)**
American Ass'n for Crystal Growth **(30)**
American Ass'n of Physicists in Medicine **(41)**
American Ass'n of Physics Teachers **(41)**
American Astronomical Soc. **(45)**
American College of Medical Physics **(55)**
American Crystallographic Ass'n **(63)**
American Geophysical Union **(70)**
American Institute of Physics **(78)**
American Nuclear Soc. **(87)**
American Physical Soc. **(92)**
American Soc. for Laser Medicine and Surgery **(103)**
American Solar Energy Soc. **(117)**
American Vacuum Soc. **(121)**
ASM Internat'l **(128)**
Biophysical Soc. **(179)**
Calorimetry Conference **(186)**
Combustion Institute **(198)**
Cryogenic Engineering Conference **(219)**
Fusion Power Associates **(244)**
Health Physics Soc. **(252)**
Internat'l Ass'n for Hydrogen Energy **(274)**
Microscopy Soc. of America **(328)**
Nat'l Soc. of Black Physicists **(429)**
Soc. for Applied Spectroscopy **(485)**
Soc. for Luminescent Microscopy and Spectroscopy **(490)**
Soc. of Physics Students **(505)**
Soc. of Rheology **(506)**

PHYSIOLOGY
American Ass'n for Aerosol Research **(29)**
American Clinical Neurophysiological Soc. **(52)**
American Medical Electroencephalographic Ass'n **(83)**
American Physiological Soc. **(92)**
American Soc. of Plant Physiologists **(114)**
Federation of American Socs. for Experimental Biology **(236)**
Internat'l Glutamate Technical Committee **(292)**
Microcirculatory Soc. of America **(328)**
Nat'l Ass'n for Medical Direction of Respiratory Care **(340)**
Optical Soc. of America **(449)**
Soc. of General Physiologists **(502)**

PHYTOPATHOLOGY
American Phytopathological Soc. **(92)**
Soc. of Nematologists **(504)**

PILOTS
Air Line Pilots Ass'n, Internat'l **(16)**
Aircraft Owners and Pilots Ass'n **(16)**
American Pilots' Ass'n **(92)**
Internat'l Ass'n of Natural Resource Pilots **(281)**
Internat'l Organization of Masters, Mates and Pilots **(299)**
Organization of Black Airline Pilots **(450)**
Soc. of Experimental Test Pilots **(501)**

PIPES
Air Distributing Institute **(15)**
American Concrete Pipe Ass'n **(59)**
American Concrete Pressure Pipe Ass'n **(59)**
American Pipe Fittings Ass'n **(92)**
Asbestos Cement Product Producers Ass'n **(128)**
Ass'n of Oil Pipe Lines **(158)**
Cast Iron Soil Pipe Institute **(187)**
Cathodic Protection Industry Ass'n **(188)**
Coal and Slurry Technology Ass'n **(195)**
Directional Crossing Contractors Ass'n **(223)**
Distribution Contractors Ass'n **(224)**
Ductile Iron Pipe Research Ass'n **(225)**
Expansion Joint Manufacturers Ass'n **(234)**
Fiberglass Tank and Pipe Institute **(238)**
Internat'l Slurry Surfacing Ass'n **(302)**
Nat'l Ass'n of Pipe Coating Applicators **(365)**
Nat'l Ass'n of Steel Pipe Distributors **(377)**
Nat'l Certified Pipe Welding Bureau **(386)**
Nat'l Clay Pipe Institute **(387)**
Nat'l Corrugated Steel Pipe Ass'n **(392)**
Pipe Fabrication Institute **(458)**
Pipe Line Contractors Ass'n **(458)**
Plastic Pipe and Fittings Ass'n **(459)**
Plastics Pipe Institute **(459)**
Soc. of Piping Engineers and Designers **(505)**
TPA/The Tube and Pipe Ass'n, Internat'l **(524)**
Uni-Bell PVC Pipe Ass'n **(529)**
United Ass'n of Journeymen and Apprentices of the Plumbing and Pipe Fitting Industry of U.S. and Canada **(530)**

PLANNING
American Economic Development Council **(65)**
American Health Planning Ass'n **(72)**
American Institute of Certified Planners **(76)**
American Planning Ass'n **(92)**
American Soc. of Consulting Planners **(108)**
Ass'n of Collegiate Schools of Planning **(148)**
Council for Urban Economic Development **(212)**
Council of Educational Facility Planners, Internat'l **(213)**
Council of Planning Librarians **(215)**
Disaster Recovery Institute Internat'l **(223)**
Forum for Health Care Planning **(243)**
Institute of Certified Financial Planners **(266)**
Insurance Conference Planners Ass'n **(270)**
Internat'l Ass'n for Financial Planning **(274)**
Internat'l Ass'n for Impact Assessment **(274)**
Internat'l Development Research Council **(288)**
Internat'l Soc. of Parametric Analysts **(306)**
Meeting Professionals Internat'l **(327)**
Nat'l Alliance of Preservation Commissions **(336)**
Nat'l Ass'n of County Planners **(351)**
Nat'l Ass'n of Development Organizations **(352)**
Nat'l Ass'n of Environmental Professionals **(354)**
Nat'l Ass'n of Housing and Redevelopment Officials **(358)**
Nat'l Ass'n of Recreation Resource Planners **(369)**
Nat'l Ass'n of Regional Councils **(369)**
Nat'l Ass'n of State Development Agencies **(374)**
Nat'l Criminal Justice Ass'n **(398)**
Nat'l Emergency Management Ass'n **(401)**
Nat'l Industrial Zoning Committee **(411)**
Nat'l Policy Ass'n **(423)**
Organization of Wildlife Planners **(450)**
Project Management Institute **(468)**
Regional Science Ass'n, Internat'l **(473)**
Soc. for College and University Planning **(486)**
Soc. of Competitive Intelligence Professionals **(500)**
Soc. of Government Meeting Professionals **(502)**
Strategic Leadership Forum **(517)**
Urban Land Institute **(537)**

PLASTICS INDUSTRY
Academy of Dental Materials **(8)**
Adhesive and Sealant Council **(12)**
Adhesives Manufacturers Ass'n **(12)**
Alliance of Foam Packaging Recyclers **(18)**
American Plastics Council **(92)**
American Soc. for Plasticulture **(104)**
American Soc. of Electroplated Plastics **(109)**
Ass'n of Rotational Molders **(164)**
Chemical Fabrics and Film Ass'n **(191)**
Closure Manufacturers Ass'n **(195)**
Composites Fabricators Ass'n **(201)**
Composites Institute **(202)**
Composites Manufacturing Ass'n of SME **(202)**
Diethyl Ether Producers Ass'n **(222)**
Film and Bag Federation **(238)**
Foil Stamping and Embossing Ass'n **(241)**
INDA, Ass'n of the Nonwoven Fabrics Industry **(259)**
Independent Sealing Distributors **(261)**
Internat'l Ass'n of Plastics Distributors **(281)**
Internat'l Card Manufacturers Ass'n **(285)**
Internat'l Cast Polymer Ass'n **(285)**
Internat'l Leather Goods, Plastics, Novelty, and Service Workers' Union **(296)**
Internat'l Soc. for Plastination **(304)**
Latex Advisors Ass'n **(317)**
Manufacturers Representatives of America **(323)**
Nat'l Ass'n for PET Container Resources **(340)**
Nat'l Plastercraft Ass'n **(422)**
Paper and Plastic Representatives Management Council **(453)**
Plastic and Metal Products Manufacturers Ass'n **(458)**
Plastic Shipping Container Institute **(459)**
Plastic Soft Materials Manufacturers Ass'n **(459)**
Plastics Pipe Institute **(459)**
Polymer Particulate Inhalation Group **(460)**
Polyurethane Manufacturers Ass'n **(460)**
Pressure Sensitive Tape Council **(462)**
Roof Coatings Manufacturers Ass'n **(477)**
Rubber and Plastics Industry Conference of the United Steelworkers of America **(477)**
Soc. for Women in Plastics **(496)**
Soc. of Plastics Engineers **(505)**
Soc. of the Plastics Industry **(507)**
Soc. of the Plastics Industry - Polyurethane Division **(507)**
Suppliers of Advanced Composite Materials Ass'n **(518)**
Vinyl Institute **(539)**
Vinyl Siding Institute **(539)**

PLUMBING
American Soc. of Plumbing Engineers **(115)**
American Soc. of Sanitary Engineering **(116)**
American Supply Ass'n **(119)**
Ass'n of Industry Manufacturers' Representatives **(154)**
Associated Specialty Contractors **(172)**
Cast Iron Soil Pipe Institute **(187)**
Internat'l Ass'n of Plumbing and Mechanical Officials **(282)**
Manufacturers Standardization Soc. of the Valve and Fittings Industry **(323)**
Nat'l Plumbing Bureau **(422)**
Plastic Pipe and Fittings Ass'n **(459)**
Plumbing and Drainage Institute **(459)**
Plumbing Manufacturers Institute **(459)**
Plumbing-Heating-Cooling Contractors - Nat'l Ass'n **(459)**
Plumbing-Heating-Cooling Information Bureau **(459)**
Porcelain Enamel Institute **(460)**
United Ass'n of Journeymen and Apprentices of the Plumbing and Pipe Fitting Industry of U.S. and Canada **(530)**
Valve Manufacturers Ass'n of America **(538)**

PLYWOOD
APA - The Engineered Wood Ass'n **(125)**
Hardwood Plywood and Veneer Ass'n **(251)**

PODIATRY
Academy of Ambulatory Foot Surgery **(7)**
American Academy of Podiatric Practice Management **(25)**
American Academy of Podiatric Sports Medicine **(25)**
American Ass'n for Women Podiatrists **(32)**
American Ass'n of Colleges of Podiatric Medicine **(35)**
American Ass'n of Hospital Podiatrists **(37)**
American Ass'n of Podiatric Physicians and Surgeons **(41)**
American Board of Podiatric Orthopedics and Primary Podiatric Medicine **(48)**
American College of Foot and Ankle Orthopedics and Medicine **(54)**
American College of Foot and Ankle Pediatrics **(54)**
American College of Foot and Ankle Surgeons **(54)**
American College of Podiatric Radiologists **(57)**
American Podiatric Circulatory Soc. **(93)**
American Podiatric Medical Ass'n **(93)**
American Podiatric Medical Students' Ass'n **(93)**
American Podiatric Medical Writers Ass'n **(93)**
American Soc. of Podiatric Dermatology **(115)**
American Soc. of Podiatric Executives **(115)**
American Soc. of Podiatric Medical Assistants **(115)**
American Soc. of Podiatric Medicine **(115)**
American Soc. of Podiatry Executives **(115)**
Federation of Podiatric Medical Boards **(237)**
Internat'l Academy of Podiatric Medicine **(272)**
Nat'l Podiatric Medical Ass'n **(422)**

POETRY
Nat'l Ass'n for Poetry Therapy **(340)**
Poetry Soc. of America **(459)**

POLICE
Airborne Law Enforcement Ass'n **(16)**
American Academy of Forensic Sciences **(22)**
American Ass'n of Motor Vehicle Administrators **(39)**
American Ass'n of Police Polygraphists **(41)**
American Criminal Justice Ass'n/Lambda Alpha Epsilon **(62)**
American Federation of Police and Concerned Citizens **(67)**
American Federation of Railroad Police **(67)**
American Jail Ass'n **(79)**
American Polygraph Ass'n **(93)**
American Soc. of Criminology **(109)**
American Soc. of Forensic Odontology **(110)**
American Soc. of Law Enforcement Trainers **(112)**
Ass'n of Former Agents of the U.S. Secret Service **(152)**
Ass'n of Public-Safety Communications Officials-Internat'l **(162)**
Central Station Alarm Ass'n **(189)**
Commission on Accreditation for Law Enforcement Agencies **(199)**
Evidence Photographers Internat'l Council **(233)**
Federal Bureau of Investigation Agents Ass'n **(235)**
Federal Law Enforcement Officers Ass'n **(236)**
Internat'l Ass'n for Identification **(274)**
Internat'l Ass'n of Arson Investigators **(275)**
Internat'l Ass'n of Auto Theft Investigators **(276)**
Internat'l Ass'n of Bomb Technicians and Investigators **(276)**
Internat'l Ass'n of Chiefs of Police **(277)**
Internat'l Ass'n of Correctional Officers **(278)**
Internat'l Ass'n of Financial Crimes Investigators **(279)**
Internat'l Ass'n of Law Enforcement Intelligence Analysts **(280)**
Internat'l Ass'n of Women Police **(283)**

National Trade and Professional Associations of the U.S. © 1999, Columbia Books, Inc. 589

POLITICAL SCIENCE
Subject Index

Internat'l Conference of Police Chaplains **(287)**
Internat'l Juvenile Officers Ass'n **(295)**
Internat'l Livestock Theft Investigators Ass'n **(296)**
Internat'l Municipal Lawyers Ass'n **(297)**
Internat'l Narcotic Enforcement Officers Ass'n **(298)**
Internat'l Security Officers, Police and Guards Union **(302)**
Internat'l Union of Police Ass'ns, AFL-CIO **(310)**
Nat'l Ass'n of Chiefs of Police **(347)**
Nat'l Ass'n of Police Equipment Distributors **(365)**
Nat'l Ass'n of Police Organizations **(365)**
Nat'l Ass'n of School Resource Officers **(371)**
Nat'l Black Police Ass'n **(383)**
Nat'l Child Support Enforcement Ass'n **(386)**
Nat'l Constables Ass'n **(392)**
Nat'l Fraternal Order of Police **(406)**
Nat'l Organization of Black Law Enforcement Executives **(420)**
Nat'l Police Officers Ass'n of America **(422)**
Nat'l Sheriffs' Ass'n **(427)**
North American Ass'n of Wardens and Superintendents **(440)**
Police Executive Research Forum **(459)**
Soc. of Former Special Agents of the Federal Bureau of Investigation **(501)**
United Federation of Police Officers **(530)**
World Ass'n of Detectives **(549)**

POLITICAL SCIENCE

Academy of Political Science **(9)**
American Academy of Political and Social Science **(25)**
American Ass'n of Political Consultants **(41)**
American Institute for Maghrib Studies **(76)**
American League of Lobbyists **(81)**
American Political Science Ass'n **(93)**
Ass'n for Public Policy Analysis and Management **(137)**
Conference for the Study of Political Thought **(204)**
Council for European Studies **(211)**
Internat'l Studies Ass'n **(307)**
Latin American Studies Ass'n **(317)**
Nat'l Ass'n of Business Political Action Committees **(346)**
Nat'l Conference of Black Political Scientists **(389)**
Social Science History Ass'n **(509)**
Union for Radical Political Economics **(529)**
Women's Caucus for Political Science **(547)**
World Future Soc. **(550)**

POLLUTION see also AIR POLLUTION

Acrylonitrile Group **(11)**
Air and Waste Management Ass'n **(15)**
American Academy of Environmental Engineers **(21)**
American Coal Ash Ass'n **(52)**
American Industrial Health Council **(75)**
Asbestos Information Ass'n/North America **(128)**
Aspirin Foundation of America **(129)**
Ass'n for Facilities Engineering **(133)**
Ass'n of American Pesticide Control Officials **(142)**
Ass'n of Boards of Certification **(145)**
Ass'n of Metropolitan Sewerage Agencies **(157)**
Ass'n of State and Interstate Water Pollution Control Administrators **(165)**
Environmental Industry Ass'ns **(231)**
Environmental Mutagen Soc. **(232)**
Federal Water Quality Ass'n **(236)**
Internat'l Desalination Ass'n **(288)**
Internat'l Soc. for Ecological Modelling-North American Chapter **(303)**
Nat'l Ass'n of Noise Control Officials **(364)**
Nat'l Ass'n of Sewer Service Companies **(372)**
Nat'l Council of the Paper Industry for Air and Stream Improvement **(397)**
Nat'l Institutes for Water Resources **(412)**
Process Equipment Manufacturers' Ass'n **(463)**
Soc. for Occupational and Environmental Health **(491)**
Water and Sewer Distributors of America **(541)**
Water Environment Federation **(541)**
Water Quality Ass'n **(541)**

POPULATION

American Public Health Ass'n **(95)**
American Soc. for Reproductive Medicine **(105)**
Ass'n for Population/Family Planning Libraries and Information Centers, Internat'l **(136)**
Ecological Soc. of America **(225)**
Population Ass'n of America **(460)**
Soc. for the Study of Social Biology **(496)**
World Population Soc. **(550)**

PORTUGUESE

American Ass'n of Teachers of Spanish and Portuguese **(44)**
Soc. for Spanish and Portuguese Historical Studies **(494)**

POST OFFICE

Advertising Mail Marketing Ass'n **(12)**
American Postal Workers Union **(93)**
Ass'n of Alternate Postal Systems **(142)**
Direct Marketing Ass'n **(223)**
Direct Selling Ass'n **(223)**
Mail Advertising Service Ass'n Internat'l **(322)**
Mail Order Ass'n of America **(322)**
Nat'l Alliance of Postal and Federal Employees **(336)**
Nat'l Ass'n of Letter Carriers **(361)**
Nat'l Ass'n of Postal Supervisors **(365)**
Nat'l Ass'n of Postmasters of the U.S. **(365)**
Nat'l Federation of Non-Profits **(404)**
Nat'l League of Postmasters of the U.S. **(414)**
Nat'l Rural Letter Carriers' Ass'n **(426)**
Nat'l Star Route Mail Contractors Ass'n **(431)**
Parcel Shippers Ass'n **(453)**
Registered Mail Insurance Ass'n **(473)**

POULTRY

American Ass'n of Avian Pathologists **(33)**
American Egg Board **(65)**
American Emu Ass'n **(66)**
American Feed Industry Ass'n **(67)**
American Genetic Ass'n **(70)**
American Ostrich Ass'n **(90)**
American Poultry Ass'n **(93)**
Meat Industry Suppliers Ass'n **(325)**
Nat'l Broiler Council **(384)**
Nat'l Goose Council **(407)**
Nat'l Poultry and Food Distributors Ass'n **(423)**
Nat'l Turkey Federation **(435)**
Poultry Science Ass'n **(461)**
U.S.A. Poultry and Egg Export Council **(528)**
United Egg Producers **(530)**
World's Poultry Science Ass'n, U.S.A. Branch **(550)**

POWDER METALLURGY

APMI Internat'l **(125)**
Metal Powder Industries Federation **(327)**

PREMIUMS

Ass'n of Incentive Marketing **(153)**
Incentive Manufacturers Representatives Ass'n **(259)**
Promotion Marketing Ass'n **(468)**

PRESS see also AUTHORS, WRITERS

American Agricultural Editors Ass'n **(27)**
American Ass'n of Dental Editors **(35)**
American Ass'n of Sunday and Feature Editors **(43)**
American Business Press **(50)**
American Jewish Press Ass'n **(80)**
American Soc. of Business Press Editors **(107)**
American Soc. of Magazine Editors **(112)**
American Soc. of Media Photographers **(112)**
American Soc. of Newspaper Editors **(113)**
Ass'n of American Editorial Cartoonists **(142)**
Ass'n of Philosophy Journal Editors **(160)**
Ass'n of Railway Communicators **(163)**
Associated Church Press **(171)**
Associated Collegiate Press, Nat'l Scholastic Press Ass'n **(171)**
Catholic Press Ass'n **(188)**
College Fraternity Editors Ass'n **(197)**
College Media Advisers **(197)**
Comics Magazine Ass'n of America **(198)**
Computer Press Ass'n **(202)**
Council of Literary Magazines and Presses **(214)**
Editorial Freelancers Ass'n **(226)**
EdPress--The Ass'n of Educational Publishers **(226)**
Evangelical Press Ass'n **(233)**
Foreign Press Ass'n **(242)**
Inter American Press Ass'n **(271)**
Internat'l Food, Wine and Travel Writers Ass'n **(291)**
Internat'l Labor Communications Ass'n **(295)**
Internat'l Motor Press Ass'n **(297)**
Internat'l Newspaper Financial Executives **(298)**
Internat'l Soc. of Weekly Newspaper Editors **(307)**
Investigative Reporters and Editors **(312)**
Media Human Resources Ass'n **(326)**
Music Critics Ass'n of North America **(332)**
Nat'l American Legion Press Ass'n **(336)**
Nat'l Ass'n of Agricultural Journalists **(343)**
Nat'l Ass'n of Government Communicators **(356)**
Nat'l Ass'n of Hispanic Publications **(358)**
Nat'l Ass'n of Real Estate Editors **(369)**
Nat'l Federation of Press Women **(404)**
Nat'l Motorsports Press Ass'n **(417)**
Nat'l Newspaper Ass'n **(418)**
Nat'l Newspaper Publishers Ass'n **(418)**
Nat'l Press Photographers Ass'n **(423)**
Newsletter Publishers Ass'n **(439)**
Newspaper Ass'n Managers **(439)**
Newspaper Features Council **(439)**
Newspaper Guild **(439)**
Overseas Press Club of America **(452)**
Professional Insurance Communicators of America **(466)**
Soc. for Technological Advancement of Reporting **(494)**
Soc. of Nat'l Ass'n Publications **(504)**
White House News Photographers Ass'n **(543)**
World Federation of Travel Writers **(549)**

PRINTING

Amalgamated Printers' Ass'n **(19)**
Ass'n of College and University Printers **(147)**
Binding Industries of America **(179)**
Business Forms Management Ass'n **(184)**
Calendar Marketing Ass'n **(185)**
Digital Distribution of Advertising for Publications **(222)**
Digital Printing and Imaging Ass'n **(222)**
Federation of Socs. for Coatings Technology **(237)**
Financial Stationers Ass'n **(239)**
Flexographic Technical Ass'n **(240)**
Foil Stamping and Embossing Ass'n **(241)**
Graphic Arts Employers of America **(249)**
Graphic Arts Marketing Information Service **(249)**
Graphic Communications Ass'n **(249)**
Graphic Communications Internat'l Union **(249)**
Gravure Ass'n of America **(249)**
IBFI, The Internat'l Ass'n for Document and Information Management Solutions **(257)**
Imaging Supplies Coalition for Internat'l Intellectual Property Protection **(259)**
Internat'l Allied Printing Trades Ass'n **(273)**
Internat'l Ass'n of Printing House Craftsmen **(282)**
Internat'l Digital Imaging Ass'n **(289)**
Internat'l Plate Printers', Die Stampers' and Engravers' Union of North America **(300)**
Internat'l Prepress Ass'n **(300)**
Internat'l Publishing Management Ass'n **(300)**
Internat'l Soc. of Copier Artists **(306)**
Internat'l Thermographers Ass'n **(308)**
Label Printing Industries of America **(316)**
Machine Printers and Engravers Ass'n of the United States **(321)**
Magazine Printers Section/Printing Industries of America **(321)**
Master Printers of America **(324)**
Nat'l Ass'n of Litho Clubs **(361)**
Nat'l Ass'n of Printers and Lithographers **(366)**
Nat'l Ass'n of Printing Ink Manufacturers **(366)**
Nat'l Metal Decorators Ass'n **(417)**
Nat'l State Publishing Ass'n **(431)**
Non-Heatset Web Section **(439)**
NPES, the Ass'n for Suppliers of Printing and Publishing Technologies **(446)**
PrintImage Internat'l **(463)**
Printing Brokerage Buyers Ass'n **(463)**
Printing Industries of America **(463)**
Screenprinting and Graphic Imaging Ass'n Internat'l **(480)**
Soc. for Service Professionals in Printing **(493)**
Soc. of Scribes **(507)**
Tag and Label Manufacturers Institute **(520)**
Web Offset Ass'n of Printing Industries of America **(542)**
Women In Production **(547)**

PROCTOLOGY

American Osteopathic College of Proctology **(89)**
American Soc. of Colon and Rectal Surgeons **(108)**

PSYCHOLOGY & PSYCHIATRY

Academy of Aphasia **(7)**
Academy of Organizational and Occupational Psychiatry **(9)**
American Academy of Addiction Psychiatry **(20)**
American Academy of Child and Adolescent Psychiatry **(20)**
American Academy of Clinical Psychiatrists **(21)**
American Academy of Forensic Psychology **(22)**
American Academy of Psychiatry and the Law **(25)**
American Academy of Psychoanalysis **(26)**
American Academy of Psychotherapists **(26)**
American Ass'n for Correctional Psychology **(30)**
American Ass'n for Geriatric Psychiatry **(30)**
American Ass'n for Marriage and Family Therapy **(31)**
American Ass'n of Children's Residential Centers **(34)**
American Ass'n of Community Psychiatrists **(35)**
American Ass'n of Directors of Psychiatric Residency Training **(36)**
American Ass'n of Mental Health Professionals in Corrections **(39)**
American Ass'n of Professional Hypnotherapists **(41)**
American Ass'n of Psychiatric Administrators **(42)**
American Ass'n of Psychiatric Technicians **(42)**
American Ass'n of Spinal Cord Injury Psychologists and Social Workers **(43)**
American Ass'n of Suicidology **(43)**
American Ass'n of University Affiliated Programs for Persons with Developmental Disabilities **(44)**
American Ass'n on Mental Retardation **(45)**
American Board of Professional Psychology **(48)**
American College of Forensic Psychiatry **(54)**
American College of Neuropsychiatrists **(55)**
American College of Neuropsychopharmacology **(55)**
American College of Psychiatrists **(57)**
American College of Psychoanalysts **(57)**
American Family Therapy Academy **(66)**
American Group Psychotherapy Ass'n **(71)**
American Mental Health Counselors Ass'n **(84)**
American Orthopsychiatric Ass'n **(89)**
American Pain Soc. **(90)**
American Psychiatric Ass'n **(94)**
American Psychiatric Nurses Ass'n **(94)**
American Psychoanalytic Ass'n **(94)**
American Psychological Ass'n **(94)**
American Psychological Ass'n - Division of Clinical Psychology **(95)**
American Psychological Ass'n - Division of Psychoanalysis **(95)**
American Psychological Ass'n - Division of Psychologists in Independent Practice **(95)**
American Psychological Ass'n - Division of Psychotherapy **(95)**
American Psychological Practitioners Ass'n **(95)**
American Psychological Soc. **(95)**
American Psychology-Law Soc. **(95)**
American Psychopathological Ass'n **(95)**
American Psychosomatic Soc. **(95)**
American Psychotherapy Ass'n **(95)**
American Sleep Disorders Ass'n **(100)**
American Soc. for Adolescent Psychiatry **(100)**
American Soc. of Addiction Medicine **(106)**
American Soc. of Clinical Psychopharmacology **(108)**
American Soc. of Electroneurodiagnostic Technologists **(109)**
American Soc. of Group Psychotherapy and Psychodrama **(110)**
American Soc. of Psychoanalytic Physicians **(115)**
American Soc. of Psychopathology of Expression **(115)**
American Soc. of Trial Consultants **(116)**
Ass'n for Advancement of Behavior Therapy **(129)**
Ass'n for Applied Psychoanalysis **(129)**
Ass'n for Applied Psychophysiology and Biofeedback **(129)**
Ass'n for Behavior Analysis **(130)**
Ass'n for Child Psychoanalysis **(130)**
Ass'n for Humanistic Psychology **(134)**
Ass'n for Psychoanalytic Medicine **(137)**
Ass'n for Psychological Type **(137)**
Ass'n for Research in Nervous and Mental Disease **(137)**
Ass'n for the Advancement of Applied Sport Psychology **(138)**
Ass'n for the Advancement of Psychoanalysis **(138)**
Ass'n for the Advancement of Psychology **(138)**
Ass'n for the Advancement of Psychotherapy **(138)**
Ass'n for the Care of Children's Health **(139)**
Ass'n for the Study of Dreams **(139)**
Ass'n for Transpersonal Psychology **(140)**
Ass'n for Women in Psychology **(140)**
Ass'n of Aviation Psychologists **(144)**
Ass'n of Black Psychologists **(145)**
Ass'n of Child and Adolescent Psychiatric Nurses **(146)**
Ass'n of Gay and Lesbian Psychiatrists **(152)**
Ass'n of Psychology Postdoctoral and Internship Centers **(162)**
Ass'n of State and Provincial Psychology Boards **(165)**
Ass'n of Traumatic Stress Specialists **(168)**
Behavioral Pharmacology Soc. **(178)**

590 National Trade and Professional Associations of the U.S. © 1999, Columbia Books, Inc.

REHABILITATION

RELIGION see also CATHOLIC, JEWISH

RENTALS

RESEARCH

RESTAURANTS Subject Index

Soc. for Pediatric Research **(492)**
Soc. for Research in Child Development **(493)**
Soc. for the Study of Male Psychology and Physiology **(496)**
Soc. of Armenian Studies **(498)**
Soc. of Insurance Research **(503)**
Soc. of Quality Assurance **(506)**
Soc. of Research Administrators **(506)**
Social Science Research Council **(509)**
Transportation Research Forum **(526)**
Travel and Tourism Research Ass'n **(526)**
Universities Council on Water Resources **(536)**
Universities Research Ass'n **(536)**
Universities Space Research Ass'n **(536)**
Welding Research Council **(542)**
Wheat Quality Council **(543)**

RESTAURANTS
American Culinary Federation **(63)**
American Dinner Theatre Institute **(64)**
American Truck Stop Operators Ass'n **(121)**
Broker Management Council **(182)**
Council of Hotel and Restaurant Trainers **(214)**
Council on Hotel, Restaurant and Institutional Education **(217)**
Hotel Employees and Restaurant Employees Internat'l Union **(256)**
Internat'l Food Service Executives' Ass'n **(291)**
Internat'l Soc. of Restaurant Ass'n Executives **(307)**
Mobile Industrial Caterers' Ass'n Internat'l **(329)**
Nat'l Ass'n of Black Hospitality Professionals **(344)**
Nat'l Council of Chain Restaurants **(394)**
Nat'l Licensed Beverage Ass'n **(415)**
Nat'l Restaurant Ass'n **(425)**
Women Chefs and Restaurateurs **(545)**

RETAILERS see also MERCHANDISING
American Ass'n of Franchisees and Dealers **(37)**
American Ass'n of Meat Processors **(38)**
American Booksellers Ass'n **(48)**
American Collegiate Retailing Ass'n **(58)**
Ass'n for Retail Technology Standards **(137)**
Ass'n of Booksellers for Children **(145)**
Ass'n of Coupon Professionals **(149)**
Ass'n of Retail Travel Agents **(163)**
Black Retail Action Group **(180)**
Building Material Dealers Ass'n **(183)**
Casual Furniture Retailers **(187)**
CBA **(188)**
CIES, The Food Business Forum **(193)**
Computing Technology Industry Ass'n **(203)**
Educational Dealers and Suppliers Ass'n Internat'l **(226)**
Food Marketing Institute **(241)**
Home Improvement Research Institute **(255)**
Internat'l Bowling Pro Shop and Instructors Ass'n **(283)**
Internat'l Council of Shopping Centers **(288)**
Internat'l Crystal Federation **(288)**
Internat'l Electronic Article Surveillance Manufacturers Ass'n **(289)**
Internat'l Map Trade Ass'n **(296)**
Internat'l Mass Retail Ass'n **(297)**
Internat'l Music Products Ass'n **(298)**
Jewelers of America **(314)**
Leading Jewelers Guild **(318)**
Marine Retailers Ass'n of America **(323)**
Nat'l Antique and Art Dealers Ass'n of America **(337)**
Nat'l Ass'n for Retail Merchandising Services **(341)**
Nat'l Ass'n of Catalog Showroom Merchandisers **(346)**
Nat'l Ass'n of College Stores **(348)**
Nat'l Ass'n of Convenience Stores **(349)**
Nat'l Ass'n of Office Furniture Dealers **(364)**
Nat'l Ass'n of Resale and Thrift Shops **(370)**
Nat'l Catalog Managers Ass'n **(385)**
Nat'l Community Pharmacists Ass'n **(388)**
Nat'l Grocers Ass'n **(407)**
Nat'l Home Furnishings Ass'n **(409)**
Nat'l Ice Cream and Yogurt Retailers Ass'n **(410)**
Nat'l Independent Flag Dealers Ass'n **(410)**
Nat'l Independent Textiles Retailers Organization **(410)**
Nat'l Luggage Dealers Ass'n **(415)**
Nat'l Retail Federation **(425)**
Nat'l Retail Hardware Ass'n **(425)**
Nat'l Retail Hobby Store Ass'n **(426)**
Nat'l Shoe Retailers Ass'n **(428)**
Nat'l Ski and Snowboard Retailers Ass'n **(428)**
Nat'l Sporting Goods Ass'n **(431)**
North American Retail Dealers Ass'n **(444)**
Oriental Rug Retailers of America **(450)**
Professional Ass'n of Comics Entertainment Retailers **(464)**
Professional Audio-Video Retailers Ass'n **(464)**
Professional Picture Framers Ass'n **(466)**
Professional Sales Ass'n **(467)**
Retail Advertising and Marketing Ass'n Internat'l **(475)**
Retail Confectioners Internat'l **(476)**
Retail Packaging Manufacturers Ass'n **(476)**
Retail Tobacco Dealers of America **(476)**
Retail, Wholesale and Department Store Union **(476)**
Retailer's Bakery Ass'n **(476)**
Scuba Retailers Ass'n **(480)**
Vacuum Dealers Trade Ass'n **(538)**
Wine and Spirits Guild of America **(544)**

RICE
Internat'l Wild Rice Ass'n **(311)**
Rice Millers' Ass'n **(476)**
U.S.A. Rice Federation **(528)**

ROADWAYS
American Ass'n of State Highway and Transportation Officials **(43)**
American Highway Users Alliance **(73)**
American Insurers Highway Safety Alliance **(79)**
American Road and Transportation Builders Ass'n **(98)**
Ass'n of Asphalt Paving Technologists **(144)**
Associated Equipment Distributors **(171)**
Internat'l Bridge, Tunnel and Turnpike Ass'n **(284)**
Internat'l Road Federation **(302)**
Nat'l Asphalt Pavement Ass'n **(337)**
Nat'l Ass'n of Women Highway Safety Leaders **(380)**

ROBOTICS
American Automatic Control Council **(46)**
American Soc. of Mechanical Engineers **(112)**
Ass'n for Unmanned Vehicle Systems Internat'l **(140)**
Automated Imaging Ass'n **(173)**
Automation Technologies Council **(174)**
Consortium for Advanced Manufacturing Internat'l **(206)**
Nat'l Ass'n of Relay Manufacturers **(370)**
Robotics Internat'l of SME **(477)**
Soc. of Manufacturing Engineers **(503)**

ROLLERSKATING
Roller Skating Ass'n Internat'l **(477)**
Soc. of Roller Skating Teachers of America **(507)**
Speed Coaches Ass'n **(514)**

ROOFING
Asphalt Roofing Manufacturers Ass'n **(129)**
Institute of Roofing and Waterproofing Consultants Internat'l **(269)**
Nat'l Roof Deck Contractors Ass'n **(426)**
Nat'l Roofing Contractors Ass'n **(426)**
Nat'l Tile Roofing Manufacturers Ass'n **(434)**
Perlite Institute **(455)**
Roof Coatings Manufacturers Ass'n **(477)**
Roof Consultants Institute **(477)**
Sealant, Waterproofing and Restoration Institute **(480)**
Single Ply Roofing Institute **(483)**
Steel Deck Institute **(516)**
United Union of Roofers, Waterproofers and Allied Workers **(536)**

RUBBER & RUBBER PRODUCTS
Carpet Cushion Council **(187)**
Fluid Sealing Ass'n **(241)**
Independent Sealing Distributors **(261)**
Internat'l Institute of Synthetic Rubber Producers **(295)**
Internat'l Tire and Rubber Ass'n **(309)**
Rubber and Plastics Industry Conference of the United Steelworkers of America **(477)**
Rubber Manufacturers Ass'n **(477)**
Rubber Trade Ass'n of North America **(478)**
Scrap Tire Management Council **(480)**
Soc. of the Plastics Industry **(507)**
Tire and Rim Ass'n **(523)**
Tire Ass'n of North America **(523)**
Tire Industry Safety Council **(523)**
Tire Retread Information Bureau **(523)**
Tread Rubber and Tire Repair Materials Manufacturers Group **(526)**

SAFETY
Alliance for Traffic Safety **(18)**
American Academy of Safety Education **(26)**
American Biological Safety Ass'n **(47)**
American Driver and Traffic Safety Education Ass'n **(65)**
American Highway Users Alliance **(73)**
American Insurers Highway Safety Alliance **(79)**
American Soc. for Testing and Materials **(105)**
American Soc. of Mechanical Engineers **(112)**
American Soc. of Safety Engineers **(116)**
American Traffic Safety Services Ass'n **(120)**
Ass'n for the Advancement of Automotive Medicine **(138)**
Ass'n of State Dam Safety Officials **(166)**
Automatic Fire Alarm Ass'n **(173)**
Automotive Occupant Protection Ass'n **(174)**
Automotive Occupant Restraints Council **(174)**
Aviation Safety Institute **(176)**
Board of Certified Safety Professionals **(180)**
Campus Safety Division of the Nat'l Safety Council **(186)**
Commercial Vehicle Safety Alliance **(199)**
Crane Certification Ass'n of America **(218)**
Disaster Preparedness and Emergency Response Ass'n **(223)**
Fire Suppression Systems Ass'n **(240)**
Flight Safety Foundation **(240)**
Forest Products Safety Conference **(242)**
Human Factors and Ergonomics Soc. **(257)**
Institute of Nuclear Materials Management **(268)**
Institute of Nuclear Power Operations **(268)**
Insurance Institute for Highway Safety **(270)**
Internat'l Ass'n of Dive Rescue Specialists **(278)**
Internat'l Ass'n of Electrical Inspectors **(278)**
Internat'l Ass'n of Home Safety and Security Professionals **(280)**
Internat'l Federation of Inspection Agencies - Americas Committee **(290)**
Internat'l Soc. of Air Safety Investigators **(305)**
ISEA-The Safety Equipment Ass'n **(313)**
Laminators Safety Glass Ass'n **(317)**
Lightning Protection Institute **(319)**
Maritime Fire and Safety Ass'n **(324)**
Mine Inspectors' Institute of America **(329)**
Motorcycle Safety Foundation **(331)**
Nat'l Ass'n of Elevator Safety Authorities Internat'l **(353)**
Nat'l Ass'n of Governors' Highway Safety Representatives **(357)**
Nat'l Ass'n of State Boating Law Administrators **(374)**
Nat'l Ass'n of Women Highway Safety Leaders **(380)**
Nat'l EMS Pilots Ass'n **(401)**
Nat'l Fire Protection Ass'n **(404)**
Nat'l Safety Council **(426)**
Nat'l Safety Management Soc. **(426)**
SAFE Ass'n **(478)**
Safety Equipment Distributors Ass'n **(478)**
Safety Equipment Manufacturers' Agents Ass'n **(478)**
System Safety Soc. **(519)**
Tire Industry Safety Council **(523)**
Transportation Safety Equipment Institute **(526)**
Uniform Boiler and Pressure Vessel Laws Soc. **(529)**
United States Lifesaving Ass'n **(534)**
United States Marine Safety Ass'n **(534)**
United States Parachute Ass'n **(534)**
Voluntary Protection Programs Participants Ass'n **(540)**
Window Council **(544)**

SALESMEN
Agricultural and Industrial Manufacturers' Representatives Ass'n **(14)**
Allied Trades of the Baking Industry **(18)**
Ass'n of Industry Manufacturers' Representatives **(154)**
Ass'n of Sales Administration Managers **(164)**
Automotive Booster Clubs Internat'l **(174)**
Bureau of Wholesale Sales Representatives **(184)**
Electrical Equipment Representatives Ass'n **(227)**
Electronics Representatives Ass'n **(229)**
Fabric Salesmen's Ass'n **(234)**
Foragers of America **(242)**
Graphic Arts Professionals **(249)**
Health Industry Representatives Ass'n **(252)**
Heavy Duty Representatives Ass'n **(253)**
Independent Professional Representatives Organization **(261)**
Internat'l Home Furnishings Representatives Ass'n **(293)**
Internat'l Pot and Kettle Club **(300)**
Luggage and Leather Goods Salesmen's Ass'n of America **(321)**
Manufacturers' Agents for Food Service Industry **(323)**
Manufacturers' Agents Nat'l Ass'n **(323)**
Materials Marketing Associates **(325)**
Multi-Level Marketing Internat'l Ass'n **(331)**
NAGMR Consumer Product Brokers **(333)**
Nat'l Ass'n of Business and Industrial Saleswomen **(346)**
Nat'l Ass'n of Flour Distributors **(355)**
Nat'l Ass'n of Health Underwriters **(357)**
Nat'l Ass'n of Independent Publishers Representatives **(359)**
Nat'l Confectionery Sales Ass'n of America **(389)**
Nat'l Electrical Manufacturers Representatives Ass'n **(400)**
Nat'l Field Selling Ass'n **(404)**
Nat'l Marine Representatives Ass'n **(416)**
Nat'l Shoe Travelers Ass'n **(428)**
Northamerican Industrial Representatives Ass'n **(446)**
Power-Motion Technology Representatives Ass'n **(462)**
Professional Sales Ass'n **(467)**
Professional Soc. for Sales and Marketing Training **(467)**
Radio Advertising Bureau **(471)**
Sales and Marketing Executives Internat'l **(478)**
Sales Ass'n of the Chemical Industry **(478)**
Sales Ass'n of the Paper Industry **(478)**
School and Home Office Products Ass'n **(479)**
Specialty Tool and Fastener Distributors Ass'n **(514)**
Sporting Goods Agents Ass'n **(515)**
Women in Sales Ass'n **(547)**

SALVAGE
American Salvage Pool Ass'n **(99)**
Ass'n of Diving Contractors **(150)**

SAND
Nat'l Aggregates Ass'n **(335)**
Nat'l Industrial Sand Ass'n **(411)**

SANITATION
American Academy of Sanitarians **(26)**
American Soc. of Sanitary Engineering **(116)**
Ass'n of Environmental Engineering Professors **(150)**
Ass'n of Metropolitan Sewerage Agencies **(157)**
Ass'n of State and Territorial Solid Waste Management Officials **(166)**
Baking Industry Sanitation Standards Committee **(176)**
Environmental Management Ass'n **(232)**
Internat'l Ass'n of Milk, Food and Environmental Sanitarians **(281)**
Internat'l Sanitary Supply Ass'n **(302)**
Nat'l Environmental Health Ass'n **(401)**
Portable Sanitation Ass'n Internat'l **(460)**
SWANA - Solid Waste Ass'n of North America **(519)**

SAVINGS & LOAN see also BANKING
America's Community Bankers **(20)**
American Council of State Savings Supervisors **(61)**
Ass'n of Financial Services Holding Companies **(151)**
Financial Managers Soc. **(239)**

SAWS
Concrete Sawing and Drilling Ass'n **(203)**
Hack and Band Saw Manufacturers Ass'n of America **(250)**
Portable Power Equipment Manufacturers Ass'n **(460)**

SCALES
Internat'l Soc. of Weighing and Measurement **(307)**
Scale Manufacturers Ass'n **(479)**

SCIENCE
American Academy of Arts and Sciences **(20)**
American Academy of Forensic Sciences **(22)**
American Ass'n for Artificial Intelligence **(29)**
American Ass'n for the Advancement of Science **(32)**
American Ass'n of Phonetic Sciences **(41)**
American Council on Science and Health **(62)**
American Dairy Science Ass'n **(63)**
American Filtration and Separations Soc. **(68)**
American Heartworm Soc. **(73)**
American Indian Science and Engineering Soc. **(75)**
American Institute of Biological Sciences **(76)**
American Meat Science Ass'n **(83)**
American Pain Soc. **(90)**
American Soc. for Clinical Laboratory Science **(101)**
American Soc. for Horticultural Science **(103)**
American Soc. of Animal Science **(106)**
Ass'n for Library and Information Science Education **(135)**
Ass'n for Molecular Pathology **(136)**
Ass'n for the Education of Teachers in Science **(139)**
Ass'n for Women Geoscientists **(140)**

594 National Trade and Professional Associations of the U.S. © 1999, Columbia Books, Inc.

Nat'l Tabletop and Giftware Ass'n **(433)**
Silver Institute **(483)**
Silver Users Ass'n **(483)**
Soc. of American Silversmiths **(498)**

SINGING

American Academy of Teachers of Singing **(26)**
American Choral Directors Ass'n **(51)**
Cantors Assembly **(186)**
Chorus America **(193)**
Nat'l Ass'n of Teachers of Singing **(378)**
Nat'l Opera Ass'n **(419)**
OPERA America **(448)**

SKIING

Cross Country Ski Areas Ass'n **(219)**
Nat'l Ski and Snowboard Retailers Ass'n **(428)**
Nat'l Ski Areas Ass'n **(428)**
Nat'l Ski Patrol System **(428)**
North American Snowsports Journalists Ass'n **(444)**
Professional Ski Instructors of America **(467)**
SnowSports Industries America **(484)**
United States Ski Coaches Ass'n **(535)**
Water Sports Industry Ass'n **(541)**

SLATE

Expanded Shale, Clay and Slate Institute **(234)**
Tile, Marble, Terrazzo, Finishers, Shopworkers and Granite Cutters Internat'l Union **(523)**

SLAVIC

American Ass'n for the Advancement of Slavic Studies **(32)**
American Council of Teachers of Russian **(61)**
Soc. for Romanian Studies **(493)**
Soc. for Slovene Studies **(493)**

SMALL BUSINESS

American Ass'n of Home-Based Businesses **(37)**
American Ass'n of Individual Investors **(38)**
Ass'n of Small Business Development Centers **(165)**
Future Business Leaders of America-Phi Beta Lambda **(245)**
Institute for Business Innovation **(265)**
Internat'l Ass'n of Airport Duty Free Stores **(275)**
Internat'l Council for Small Business **(287)**
Internat'l Reciprocal Trade Ass'n **(301)**
Knitting Guild of America **(316)**
Nat'l Ass'n for the Cottage Industry **(341)**
Nat'l Ass'n of Development Companies **(352)**
Nat'l Ass'n of Home Based Businesses **(358)**
Nat'l Ass'n of Investment Companies **(360)**
Nat'l Ass'n of Small Business Internat'l Trade Educators **(373)**
Nat'l Ass'n of Small Business Investment Companies **(373)**
Nat'l Business Incubation Ass'n **(384)**
Nat'l Federation of Independent Business **(403)**
Nat'l Small Business United **(428)**
Small Business Council of America **(483)**
Souvenirs and Novelties Trade Ass'n **(510)**

SOCCER

Nat'l Intercollegiate Soccer Officials Ass'n **(413)**
Nat'l Professional Soccer League **(423)**
Nat'l Soccer Coaches Ass'n of America **(430)**
Professional Soccer Reporters Ass'n **(467)**
Soccer Industry Council of America **(509)**
United States Soccer Federation **(535)**

SOCIAL WORKERS

Alliance for Children and Families **(17)**
Alliance of Information and Referral Systems **(18)**
American Ass'n of Spinal Cord Injury Psychologists and Social Workers **(43)**
American Ass'n of State Social Work Boards **(43)**
American Ass'n of Suicidology **(43)**
American Orthopsychiatric Ass'n **(89)**
Ass'n for Persons with Severe Handicaps, The **(136)**
Ass'n of Christian Therapists **(146)**
Ass'n of Family and Conciliation Courts **(150)**
Ass'n of Jewish Family and Children's Agencies **(155)**
Ass'n of Junior Leagues Internat'l **(155)**
Ass'n of Oncology Social Work **(159)**
Ass'n of Pediatric Oncology Social Workers **(160)**
Ass'n of Professional Directors of YMCAs in the United States **(161)**
Catholic Charities USA **(188)**
Clinical Social Work Federation **(195)**
Computer Use in Social Services Network **(203)**
Council on Social Work Education **(217)**
Internat'l Ass'n of Pupil Personnel Workers **(282)**
Internat'l Community Corrections Ass'n **(286)**
Jewish Social Service Professionals Ass'n **(314)**
Nat'l Ass'n for Community Mediation **(338)**
Nat'l Ass'n for Home Care **(339)**
Nat'l Ass'n for Rural Mental Health **(341)**
Nat'l Ass'n of Area Agencies on Aging **(343)**
Nat'l Ass'n of Black Social Workers **(345)**
Nat'l Ass'n of Community Action Agencies **(349)**
Nat'l Ass'n of Foster Grandparent Program Directors **(356)**
Nat'l Ass'n of Social Workers **(373)**
Nat'l Ass'n of Student Assistance Professional **(377)**
Nat'l Assembly of Nat'l Voluntary Health and Social Welfare Organizations **(381)**
Nat'l Network for Social Work Managers **(418)**
Nat'l Organization of Social Security Claimants' Representatives **(420)**
Nat'l Staff Development and Training Ass'n **(431)**
North American Ass'n of Christians in Social Work **(440)**
Soc. for Social Work Leadership in Health Care **(494)**
World Ass'n for Infant Mental Health **(549)**

SOCIOLOGY

African Studies Ass'n **(14)**
American Ass'n of Suicidology **(43)**
American Ass'n on Mental Retardation **(45)**
American Men's Studies Ass'n **(84)**
American Real Estate and Urban Economics Ass'n **(97)**
American Soc. of Geolinguistics **(110)**
American Sociological Ass'n **(117)**
Ass'n for Humanist Sociology **(134)**
Ass'n for the Sociology of Religion **(139)**
Ass'n of Black Sociologists **(145)**
Cheiron: The Internat'l Soc. for the History of Behavioral and Social Sciences **(191)**
Community Development Soc. **(201)**
Conflict Resolution Education Network **(205)**
Family Therapy Network **(234)**
Human Behavior and Evolution Soc. **(257)**
Internat'l Ass'n of Family Sociology **(279)**
Internat'l Soc. for Quality-of-Life Studies **(304)**
Internat'l Soc. for the Comparative Studies of Civilizations **(304)**
Internat'l Studies Ass'n **(307)**
Internat'l Transactional Analysis Ass'n **(309)**
Law and Society Ass'n **(318)**
Nat'l Ass'n of Neighborhoods **(363)**
Nat'l Council on Family Relations **(397)**
North American Soc. for the Sociology of Sport **(445)**
Population Ass'n of America **(460)**
Rural Sociological Soc. **(478)**
Soc. for Applied Sociology **(485)**
Soc. for Disability Studies **(487)**
Soc. for Social Studies of Science **(494)**
Soc. for the Advancement of Behavior Analysis **(494)**
Soc. for the Advancement of Socio-Economics **(495)**
Soc. for the Psychological Study of Social Issues **(495)**
Soc. for the Scientific Study of Religion **(495)**
Soc. for the Study of Social Problems **(496)**
Social Science History Ass'n **(509)**
Sociological Practice Ass'n **(509)**
Special Interest Group for Computer-Human Interaction **(511)**
World Population Soc. **(550)**

SOYBEANS

American Soybean Ass'n **(117)**
Nat'l Oilseed Processors Ass'n **(419)**
United Soybean Board **(531)**

SPANISH

American Ass'n of Teachers of Spanish and Portuguese **(44)**
Ass'n of Hispanic Arts **(153)**
Nat'l Ass'n of Hispanic County Officials **(358)**
Nat'l Coalition of Hispanic Health and Human Services Organizations **(387)**
Soc. for Spanish and Portuguese Historical Studies **(494)**

SPEAKERS

American Institute of Parliamentarians **(78)**
American Seminar Leaders Ass'n **(99)**
Internat'l Group of Agencies and Bureaus **(293)**
Internat'l Platform Ass'n **(300)**
Nat'l Ass'n of Parliamentarians **(364)**
Nat'l Speakers Ass'n **(431)**
Professional Speakers Network **(467)**

SPECTROSCOPY

American Soc. for Mass Spectrometry **(104)**
Federation of Analytical Chemistry and Spectroscopy Societies **(236)**
Soc. for Applied Spectroscopy **(485)**

SPEECH

Academy of Aphasia **(7)**
Alexander Graham Bell Ass'n for the Deaf **(17)**
American Cleft Palate-Craniofacial Ass'n **(52)**
American Forensic Ass'n **(69)**
American Neurotology Soc. **(87)**
American Speech-Language-Hearing Ass'n **(117)**
Ass'n for Communication Administration **(131)**
Conflict Resolution Education Network **(205)**
Internat'l Dyslexia Ass'n **(289)**
Nat'l Black Ass'n for Speech, Language and Hearing **(383)**
Nat'l Communication Ass'n **(388)**
Nat'l Federation Interscholastic Speech and Debate Ass'n **(402)**
Nat'l Student Speech Language Hearing Ass'n **(432)**
Religious Communication Ass'n **(474)**

SPELEOLOGY

Nat'l Caves Ass'n **(386)**
Nat'l Speleological Soc. **(431)**

SPORTING GOODS

Archery Manufacturers and Merchants Organization **(126)**
Ass'n of Surfing Professionals **(166)**
Awards and Recognition Ass'n **(176)**
Billiard and Bowling Institute of America **(178)**
Diving Equipment and Marketing Ass'n **(224)**
Internat'l Snowmobile Manufacturers Ass'n **(302)**
Internat'l Sport Show Producers Ass'n **(307)**
Nat'l Ass'n of Sporting Goods Wholesalers **(373)**
Nat'l Reloading Manufacturers Ass'n **(425)**
Nat'l Ski and Snowboard Retailers Ass'n **(428)**
Nat'l Sporting Goods Ass'n **(431)**
Nat'l Taxidermists Ass'n **(433)**
SnowSports Industries America **(484)**
Soccer Industry Council of America **(509)**
Sporting Arms and Ammunition Manufacturers' Institute **(515)**
Sporting Goods Agents Ass'n **(515)**
Sporting Goods Manufacturers Ass'n **(515)**
Sportswear Apparel Ass'n **(515)**
Tackle and Shooting Sports Agents Ass'n **(520)**
United States Racquet Stringing Ass'n **(535)**
Western and English Manufacturers Ass'n **(542)**

SPORTS see also SPECIFIC SPORT

Affiliated Boards of Officials **(13)**
American Academy of Podiatric Sports Medicine **(25)**
American Basketball League **(47)**
American Bridge Teachers' Ass'n **(49)**
American Canine Sports Medicine Ass'n **(50)**
American College of Sports Medicine **(57)**
American Orthopaedic Soc. for Sports Medicine **(88)**
American Osteopathic Academy for Sports Medicine **(89)**
American Soc. of Golf Course Architects **(110)**
American Sports Medicine Ass'n/Board of Certification **(118)**
American Volleyball Coaches Ass'n **(122)**
Archery Range and Retailers Organization **(127)**
Ass'n for the Advancement of Applied Sport Psychology **(138)**
Ass'n for the Study of Play **(139)**
Ass'n for Women in Sports Media **(141)**
Ass'n of Professional Directors of YMCAs in the United States **(161)**
Ass'n of Talent Agents **(167)**
Ass'n of Volleyball Professionals **(169)**
Athletic Equipment Managers Ass'n **(172)**
ATP Tour **(172)**
Billiard Congress of America **(178)**
Black Entertainment and Sports Lawyers Ass'n **(180)**
Bowling Proprietors Ass'n of America **(181)**
College Athletic Business Management Ass'n **(197)**
College Sports Information Directors of America **(198)**
Collegiate Commissioners Ass'n **(198)**
Football Writers Ass'n of America **(242)**
Game Manufacturers Ass'n **(245)**
Golf Coaches Ass'n of America **(248)**
Harness Tracks of America **(251)**
ICAAAA Coaches Ass'n **(257)**
Ice Skating Institute **(258)**
IDEA, The Health and Fitness Source **(258)**
Institute of Diving **(266)**
Internat'l Academy of Sports Vision **(272)**
Internat'l Ass'n of Golf Administrators **(279)**
Internat'l Ass'n of Sports Museums and Halls of Fame **(282)**
Internat'l Hockey League **(293)**
Internat'l Professional Rodeo Ass'n **(300)**
Internat'l Sport Show Producers Ass'n **(307)**
Ladies Professional Golf Ass'n **(316)**
Major League Umpires Ass'n **(322)**
Nat'l Aeronautic Ass'n **(335)**
Nat'l Alliance for Youth Sports **(336)**
Nat'l Ass'n for Girls and Women in Sport **(339)**
Nat'l Ass'n for Physical Education in Higher Education **(340)**
Nat'l Ass'n for Sport and Physical Education **(341)**
Nat'l Ass'n of Academic Advisors for Athletes **(342)**
Nat'l Ass'n of Athletic Development Directors **(343)**
Nat'l Ass'n of Collegiate Directors of Athletics **(348)**
Nat'l Ass'n of Collegiate Marketing Administrators **(348)**
Nat'l Ass'n of Golf Tournament Directors **(356)**
Nat'l Ass'n of Intercollegiate Athletics **(360)**
Nat'l Ass'n of Jai Alai Frontons **(360)**
Nat'l Ass'n of Leagues, Umpires and Scorers **(361)**
Nat'l Ass'n of Professional Baseball Leagues **(366)**
Nat'l Ass'n of Sports Officials **(373)**
Nat'l Athletic Trainers' Ass'n **(381)**
Nat'l Basketball Trainers' Ass'n **(382)**
Nat'l Christian College Athletic Ass'n **(387)**
Nat'l Collegiate Athletic Ass'n **(388)**
Nat'l Council of Athletic Training **(394)**
Nat'l Cutting Horse Ass'n **(398)**
Nat'l Federation Interscholastic Coaches Ass'n **(402)**
Nat'l Federation Interscholastic Officials Ass'n **(402)**
Nat'l Federation of State High School Ass'ns **(404)**
Nat'l Football League Players Ass'n **(405)**
Nat'l Golf Foundation **(407)**
Nat'l Gymnastics Judges Ass'n **(408)**
Nat'l High School Athletic Coaches Ass'n **(409)**
Nat'l Hockey League **(409)**
Nat'l Hockey League Player's Ass'n **(409)**
Nat'l Interscholastic Athletic Administrators Ass'n **(413)**
Nat'l Intramural-Recreational Sports Ass'n **(413)**
Nat'l Junior College Athletic Ass'n **(413)**
Nat'l Reining Horse Ass'n **(425)**
Nat'l Rifle Ass'n of America **(426)**
Nat'l Shooting Sports Foundation **(428)**
Nat'l Show Horse Registry **(428)**
Nat'l Soccer Coaches Ass'n of America **(430)**
Nat'l Sportscasters and Sportswriters Ass'n **(431)**
Nat'l Strength and Conditioning Ass'n **(432)**
North American Gamebird Ass'n **(442)**
North American Soc. for Sport History **(444)**
North American Soc. for Sport Management **(444)**
Professional Ass'n of Diving Instructors **(464)**
Professional Baseball Athletic Trainers' Ass'n **(465)**
Professional Bowlers Ass'n of America **(465)**
Professional Football Athletic Trainers Soc. **(465)**
Professional Golfers Ass'n of America **(465)**
Professional Hockey Writers' Ass'n **(466)**
Professional Putters Ass'n **(466)**
Professional Rodeo Cowboys Ass'n **(467)**
Professional Skaters Ass'n **(467)**
Professional Ski Instructors of America **(467)**
Professional Squash Ass'n **(467)**
Public Golf Management Ass'n **(469)**
Resort and Commercial Recreation Ass'n **(475)**
Roller Skating Ass'n Internat'l **(477)**
Soc. of Roller Skating Teachers of America **(507)**
Specialty Vehicle Institute of America **(514)**
Speed Coaches Ass'n **(514)**
Sports Card Ass'n **(515)**
Sports Lawyers Ass'n **(515)**
Sports Turf Managers Ass'n **(515)**
Sportsplex Operators and Developers of Ass'n **(515)**
Thoroughbred Owners and Breeders Ass'n **(523)**
United States Ass'n of Independent Gymnastic Clubs **(532)**
United States Fencing Coaches Ass'n **(533)**
United States Sports Massage Federation **(535)**
United States Taekwondo Union **(535)**
Women's Basketball Coaches Ass'n **(547)**

596 National Trade and Professional Associations of the U.S. © 1999, Columbia Books, Inc.

TENNIS
ATP Tour (172)
Corel WTA Tour (209)
Intercollegiate Tennis Ass'n (271)
Internat'l Health, Racquet and Sportsclub Ass'n (293)
Tennis Industry Ass'n (521)
United States Professional Tennis Ass'n (534)
United States Professional Tennis Registry (535)
United States Racquet Stringing Ass'n (535)
United States Tennis Ass'n (535)
United States Tennis Court and Track Builders Ass'n (535)

TESTING
ACIL (11)
American Ass'n for Laboratory Accreditation (31)
American Ass'n of Textile Chemists and Colorists (44)
American Soc. for Histocompatability and Immunogenetics (103)
American Soc. for Nondestructive Testing (104)
American Soc. for Quality (105)
American Soc. for Testing and Materials (105)
Ass'n for Assessment in Counseling (130)
Controlled Environment Testing Ass'n (208)
Internat'l Electrical Testing Ass'n (289)
Internat'l Test and Evaluation Ass'n (308)
Soc. for Clinical Trials (486)
Soc. of Experimental Test Pilots (501)
Soc. of Flight Test Engineers (501)

TEXTILES
American Ass'n of Textile Chemists and Colorists (44)
American Fiber Manufacturers Ass'n (68)
American Flock Ass'n (68)
American Reusable Textile Ass'n (98)
American Soc. of Knitting Technologists (111)
American Textile Machinery Ass'n (119)
American Textile Manufacturers Institute (119)
American Yarn Spinners Ass'n (124)
Ass'n of Knitted Fabrics Manufacturers (155)
Automotive Occupant Restraints Council (174)
Burlap and Jute Ass'n (184)
Carpet and Rug Institute (187)
Color Ass'n of the United States (198)
Cordage Institute (209)
Cotton Council Internat'l (210)
Fiber Soc. (238)
Handweavers Guild of America (251)
Home Fashion Products Ass'n (255)
INDA, Ass'n of the Nonwoven Fabrics Industry (259)
Industrial Fabrics Ass'n Internat'l (262)
Institutional and Service Textile Distributors Ass'n (269)
Internat'l Sleep Products Ass'n (302)
Internat'l Soc. of Industrial Fabric Manufacturers (306)
Internat'l Textile and Apparel Ass'n (308)
Knitted Textile Ass'n (316)
Knitting Guild of America (316)
Mohair Council of America (330)
Nat'l Ass'n of Decorative Fabric Distributors (352)
Nat'l Ass'n of Textile Supervisors (378)
Nat'l Council for Textile Education (393)
Nat'l Independent Textiles Retailers Organization (410)
Northern Textile Ass'n (446)
Pine Chemicals Ass'n (458)
Professional Knitwear Designers Guild (466)
Schiffli Lace and Embroidery Manufacturers Ass'n (479)
Surface Design Ass'n (518)
Textile Bag and Packaging Ass'n (522)
Textile Bag Manufacturers Ass'n (522)
Textile Care Allied Trades Ass'n (522)
Textile Converters Ass'n (522)
Textile Distributors Ass'n (522)
Textile Fibers and By-Products Ass'n (522)
Textile Producers and Suppliers Ass'n (522)
Textile Quality Control Ass'n (522)
Textile Rental Services Ass'n of America (522)
UFCW Textile Council (529)
United States Ass'n of Importers of Textiles and Apparel (532)
Young Menswear Ass'n (551)

THEATRE
American Alliance for Theatre and Education (27)
American Ass'n of Community Theatre (35)
American Dance Guild (63)
American Dinner Theatre Institute (64)
American Soc. for Theatre Research (105)
American Soc. of Group Psychotherapy and Psychodrama (110)
American Soc. of Theatre Consultants (116)
American Theatre Critics Ass'n (120)
Ass'n of Theatrical Press Agents and Managers (168)
Black Theatre Network (180)
Dramatists Guild (224)
Internat'l Museum Theater Alliance (298)
Internat'l Theatre Equipment Ass'n (308)
Internat'l Ticketing Ass'n (308)
League of American Theatres and Producers (318)
League of Historic American Theatres (318)
League of Resident Theatres (318)
Literary Managers and Dramaturgs of the Americas (320)
Nat'l Alliance for Musical Theatre (336)
Nat'l Ass'n for Drama Therapy (339)
Nat'l Ass'n of Schools of Theatre (371)
Nat'l Ass'n of Theatre Owners (378)
Nat'l Costumers Ass'n (392)
Nat'l Federation Interscholastic Speech and Debate Ass'n (402)
Nat'l Movement Theatre Ass'n (417)
Organization of Professional Acting Coaches and Teachers (450)
Soc. of American Fight Directors (497)
Soc. of Stage Directors and Choreographers (507)
Theatre Education Ass'n (522)
Theatre Library Ass'n (522)
United Scenic Artists (531)
University/Resident Theatre Ass'n (537)
USITT: Ass'n of Design, Production and Technology Professionals in the Performing Arts and Entertainment (538)

THERAPEUTICS
American Art Therapy Ass'n (29)
American Ass'n for Marriage and Family Therapy (31)
American Ass'n for Respiratory Care (31)
American Ass'n of Behavioral Therapists (33)
American Ass'n of Professional Hypnotherapists (41)
American Dance Therapy Ass'n (63)
American Family Therapy Academy (66)
American Group Psychotherapy Ass'n (71)
American Horticultural Therapy Ass'n (74)
American Kinesiotherapy Ass'n (80)
American Massage Therapy Ass'n (83)
American Music Therapy Ass'n (86)
American Occupational Therapy Ass'n (88)
American Oriental Bodywork Therapy Ass'n (88)
American Physical Therapy Ass'n (92)
American Physical Therapy Ass'n - Private Practice Section (92)
American Polarity Therapy Ass'n (93)
American Psychological Ass'n - Division of Psychotherapy (95)
American Soc. for Clinical Pharmacology and Therapeutics (101)
American Soc. for Pharmacology and Experimental Therapeutics (104)
American Soc. for Therapeutic Radiology and Oncology (105)
American Soc. of Group Psychotherapy and Psychodrama (110)
American Soc. of Hand Therapists (110)
American Therapeutic Ass'n (120)
American Therapeutic Recreation Ass'n (120)
Ass'n for Play Therapy (136)
Associated Bodywork and Massage Professionals (170)
Cancer Biotherapy Research Group (186)
Family Therapy Network (234)
Federation of American Socs. for Experimental Biology (236)
Federation of State Boards of Physical Therapy (237)
Floatation Tank Ass'n (240)
Internat'l REST Investigators Soc. (301)
Internat'l Sports Massage Federation (307)
Intravenous Nurses Soc. (312)
Nat'l Ass'n for Drama Therapy (339)
Nat'l Ass'n for Holistic Aromatherapy (339)
Nat'l Ass'n of Substance Abuse Trainers and Educators (377)
Nat'l Council for Therapeutic Recreation Certification (393)
Nat'l Remotivation Therapy Organization (425)
Nat'l Therapeutic Recreation Soc. (433)
North American Soc. of Teachers of the Alexander Technique (445)
Rehabilitation Technology Ass'n (474)
Soc. for Light Treatment and Biological Rhythms (490)
United States Sports Massage Federation (535)

TILES
Ceramic Tile Distributors Ass'n (189)
Ceramic Tile Institute of America (189)
Materials and Methods Standards Ass'n (325)
Nat'l Terrazzo and Mosaic Ass'n (433)
Nat'l Tile Contractors Ass'n (433)
Nat'l Tile Roofing Manufacturers Ass'n (434)
Resilient Floor Covering Institute (475)
Tile Contractors' Ass'n of America (523)
Tile Council of America (523)

TIMBER
Independent Forest Products Ass'n (260)
Nat'l Woodland Owners Ass'n (437)
Timber Products Manufacturers (523)
Western Red Cedar Ass'n (543)

TIN
American Tin Trade Ass'n (120)

TOBACCO INDUSTRY
Ass'n of Dark Leaf Tobacco Dealers and Exporters (149)
Bakery, Confectionery and Tobacco Workers' Internat'l Union (176)
Bright Belt Warehouse Ass'n (182)
Burley and Dark Leaf Tobacco Ass'n (184)
Burley Auction Warehouse Ass'n (184)
Burley Tobacco Growers Cooperative Ass'n (184)
Cigar Ass'n of America (194)
Council for Tobacco Research-U.S.A. (212)
Flue-Cured Tobacco Cooperative Stabilization Corporation (240)
Leaf Tobacco Exporters Ass'n (318)
Pipe Tobacco Council (458)
Retail Tobacco Dealers of America (476)
Shade Tobacco Growers Agricultural Ass'n (482)
Smokeless Tobacco Council (484)
Soc. for Research on Nicotine and Tobacco (493)
Specialty Tobacco Council (514)
Tobacco Ass'n of the U.S. (523)
Tobacco Associates (523)
Tobacco Industry Labor/Management Committee (523)
Tobacco Institute (524)
Tobacco Merchants Ass'n of the U.S. (524)
Tobacconists' Ass'n of America (524)

TOOLS
Equipment and Tool Institute (232)
Equipment Service Ass'n (232)
Hand Tools Institute (251)
Hydraulic Tool Manufacturers Ass'n (257)
Internat'l Ass'n of Tool Craftsmen (282)
Internat'l Saw and Knife Ass'n (302)
Internat'l Staple, Nail and Tool Ass'n (307)
Nat'l Tooling and Machining Ass'n (434)
North American Punch Manufacturers Ass'n (444)
Portable Power Equipment Manufacturers Ass'n (460)
Powder Actuated Tool Manufacturers Institute (461)
Power Tool Institute (461)
Specialty Steel Industry of North America (514)
Specialty Tool and Fastener Distributors Ass'n (514)
United States Cutting Tool Institute (533)

TOXICOLOGY
American Academy of Clinical Toxicology (21)
American Academy of Veterinary and Comparative Toxicology (26)
American College of Medical Toxicology (55)
American College of Toxicology (58)
Ass'n of American Pesticide Control Officials (142)
Internat'l Academy of Oral Medicine and Toxicology (272)
Internat'l Soc. for Environmental Toxicology and Cancer (303)
Soc. of Toxicology (508)
Toxicology Forum (524)

TOYS
American Specialty Toy Retailing Ass'n (117)
Ass'n for the Study of Play (139)
Cottage Industry Miniaturists Trade Ass'n (210)
Internat'l Union of Allied Novelty and Production Workers (309)
Kite Trade Ass'n Internat'l (316)
Miniatures Industry Ass'n of America (329)
Model Railroad Industry Ass'n (329)
Radio Control Hobby Trade Ass'n (471)
Small Antique Restoration Ass'n (483)
Toy Manufacturers of America (524)
U.S.A. Toy Library Ass'n (529)

TRACK AND FIELD
United States Tennis Court and Track Builders Ass'n (535)
United States Women's Track Coaches Ass'n (535)

TRADEMARKS
Ass'n of Collegiate Licensing Administrators (148)
Intellectual Property Owners Ass'n (270)
Internat'l Licensing Industry Merchandisers' Ass'n (296)
Internat'l Trademark Ass'n (309)
Licensing Executives Soc. (319)

TRAFFIC
Advanced Transit Ass'n (12)
Alliance for Traffic Safety (18)
American Soc. of Transportation and Logistics (116)
American Traffic Safety Services Ass'n (120)
Institute of Transportation Engineers (269)
Nat'l Ass'n of Traffic Accident Reconstructionists and Investigators (379)
Nat'l Industrial Transportation League (411)

TRAILERS
Manufactured Housing Institute (322)
Modular Building Institute (330)
Nat'l Trailer Dealers Ass'n (434)
Recreation Vehicle Industry Ass'n (472)
Recreational Park Trailer Industry Ass'n (473)
Truck Trailer Manufacturers Ass'n (527)

TRAINING
Academy of Security Educators and Trainers (10)
Accrediting Council for Continuing Education and Training (11)
American Council on Schools and Colleges (62)
American Dog Trainers Network (65)
American Soc. for Training and Development (106)
American Soc. of Law Enforcement Trainers (112)
American Technical Education Ass'n (119)
American Vocational Ass'n (122)
Ass'n for Information Media and Equipment (135)
Automotive Training Managers Council (175)
Driving School Ass'n of America (224)
Evangelical Training Ass'n (233)
Internat'l Ass'n of Correctional Training Personnel (278)
Internat'l Ass'n of Culinary Professionals (278)
Internat'l Soc. for Intercultural Education, Training and Research (303)
Internat'l Soc. for Performance Improvement (304)
Internat'l Soc. of Fire Service Instructors (306)
Nat'l Ass'n of Private Industry Councils (366)
Nat'l Ass'n of Workforce Development Professionals (381)
Nat'l Basketball Trainers' Ass'n (382)
Nat'l Business Incubation Ass'n (384)
Nat'l Environmental Training Ass'n (401)
Nat'l Training Systems Ass'n (434)
North American Transportation Management Institute (445)
Professional Baseball Athletic Trainers' Ass'n (465)
Professional Football Athletic Trainers Soc. (465)
Professional Soc. for Sales and Marketing Training (467)
Roundalab (477)
Soc. of Insurance Trainers and Educators (503)
Soc. of Roller Skating Teachers of America (507)
Special Interest Group for Computer Personnel Research (511)
Training Directors' Forum (525)
Training Media Ass'n (525)
Travel Professionals Ass'n (526)
United Professional Horsemen's Ass'n (531)
United States Fencing Coaches Ass'n (533)
United States Professional Tennis Registry (535)
United Thoroughbred Trainers of America (536)
Walking Horse Trainers Ass'n (540)
World Sports Medicine Ass'n of Registered Therapists (550)

TRANSLATORS
American Literary Translators Ass'n (81)
American Translators Ass'n (120)
Nat'l Ass'n of Judiciary Interpreters and Translators (361)
Soc. of Federal Linguists (501)

598 National Trade and Professional Associations of the U.S. © 1999, Columbia Books, Inc.

American College of Veterinary Internal Medicine (58)
American College of Veterinary Ophthalmologists (58)
American College of Veterinary Pathologists (58)
American College of Veterinary Radiology (58)
American College of Veterinary Surgeons (58)
American Embryo Transfer Ass'n (66)
American Heartworm Soc. (73)
American Holistic Veterinary Medical Ass'n (74)
American Soc. of Laboratory Animal Practitioners (111)
American Soc. of Veterinary Ophthalmology (117)
American Veterinary Dental Soc. (121)
American Veterinary Distributors Ass'n (121)
American Veterinary Exhibitors Ass'n (121)
American Veterinary Medical Ass'n (121)
American Veterinary Soc. of Animal Behavior (122)
Animal Health Institute (125)
Ass'n for Equine Sports Medicine (133)
Ass'n for Gnotobiotics (134)
Ass'n for Women Veterinarians (141)
Ass'n of American Veterinary Medical Colleges (143)
Conference of Research Workers in Animal Diseases (204)
Delta Soc. (221)
Internat'l Ass'n of Equine Dental Technicians (279)
Internat'l Embryo Transfer Soc. (290)
Nat'l Ass'n of Federal Veterinarians (355)
Nat'l Mastitis Council (416)
Nat'l Wildlife Rehabilitators Ass'n (436)
Omega Tau Sigma (448)
Soc. for Theriogenology (496)
United States Animal Health Ass'n (532)
Veterinary Cancer Soc. (539)
Veterinary Hospital Managers Ass'n (539)
Veterinary Orthopedic Soc. (539)
Wildlife Disease Ass'n (544)
Women in Agribusiness (546)

VITAMINS

Ass'n of Avian Veterinarians (144)
Council for Responsible Nutrition (212)

VOCATIONAL GUIDANCE

American Ass'n for Career Education (30)
American Ass'n for Employment in Education (30)
American Counseling Ass'n (62)
American Medical Rehabilitation Providers Ass'n (84)
American Rehabilitation Counseling Ass'n (97)
American Technical Education Ass'n (119)
American Vocational Ass'n (122)
American Vocational Education Personnel Development Ass'n (122)
American Vocational Education Research Ass'n (122)
Ass'n for Assessment in Counseling (130)
Ass'n for Counselors and Educators in Government (132)
Ass'n for Multicultural Counseling and Development (136)
Ass'n for Specialists in Group Work (137)
Ass'n for Spiritual, Ethical and Religious Values in Counseling (137)
Business Professionals of America (185)
Career Planning and Adult Development Network (187)
Commission on Certification of Work Adjustment and Vocational Evaluation Specialists (199)
Council of State Administrators of Vocational Rehabilitation (215)
Distributive Education Clubs of America (224)
Future Business Leaders of America-Phi Beta Lambda (245)
Future Homemakers of America (245)
Independent Educational Consultants Ass'n (260)
Internat'l Ass'n of Counseling Services (278)
Internat'l Ass'n of Jewish Vocational Services (280)
Nat'l Academic Advising Ass'n (333)
Nat'l Adult Vocational Education Ass'n (334)
Nat'l Ass'n for Trade and Industrial Education (342)
Nat'l Ass'n of Advisors for the Health Professions (342)
Nat'l Ass'n of Industrial and Technical Teacher Educators (360)
Nat'l Ass'n of Pupil Services Administrators (368)
Nat'l Ass'n of State Supervisors of Trade and Industrial Education (376)
Nat'l Career Development Ass'n (385)
Nat'l Conference of Diocesan Vocation Directors (390)
Nat'l FFA Organization (404)
Nat'l Postsecondary Agriculture Student Organization (423)
Nat'l Vocational Agricultural Educators Ass'n (435)
Technology Student Ass'n (521)
Vocational Evaluation and Work Adjustment Ass'n (540)
Vocational Industrial Clubs of America (540)

VOLUNTEER

American Soc. of Directors of Volunteer Services of the AHA (109)
Ass'n for Volunteer Administration (140)
Independent Sector (261)
Internat'l Soc. for Third-Sector Research (305)
Nat'l Ass'n of Foster Grandparent Program Directors (356)
Nat'l Ass'n of Retired Senior Volunteer Program Directors (370)
Nat'l Volunteer Fire Council (435)

WAREHOUSES

Affiliated Warehouse Companies (13)
American Chain of Warehouses (51)
Automotive Warehouse Distributors Ass'n (175)
Bright Belt Warehouse Ass'n (182)
Burley Auction Warehouse Ass'n (184)
Cotton Warehouse Ass'n of America (210)
Council of Logistics Management (215)
Design-Build Manufacturers Ass'n (222)
Engine Service Ass'n (230)
Internat'l Ass'n of Refrigerated Warehouses (282)
Internat'l Warehouse Logistics Ass'n (310)
Paint, Body and Equipment Ass'n (452)
Performance Warehouse Ass'n (455)
Self Storage Ass'n (481)
Warehouse Distributors Ass'n (540)
Warehousing Education and Research Council (540)

WASTE

Asphalt Recycling and Reclaiming Ass'n (129)
Ass'n of State and Territorial Solid Waste Management Officials (166)
Automotive Recyclers Ass'n (175)
Center for Waste Reduction Technologies (189)
Composting Council (202)
Environmental Business Ass'n, The (231)
Environmental Industry Ass'ns (231)
Environmental Management Ass'n (232)
Environmental Technology Council (232)
Ground Water Protection Council (250)
Integrated Waste Services Ass'n (270)
Internat'l Cartridge Recycling Ass'n (285)
Investment Recovery Ass'n (312)
Municipal Waste Management Ass'n (331)
Nat'l Ass'n of Sewer Service Companies (372)
Nat'l Ass'n of Waste Transporters (380)
Nat'l Onsite Wastewater Recycling Ass'n (419)
Nat'l Solid Waste Management Environmental (430)
Nat'l Solid Wastes Management Ass'n (431)
Plumbing and Drainage Institute (459)
Submersible Wastewater Pump Ass'n (518)
SWANA - Solid Waste Ass'n of North America (519)
Waste Equipment Technology Ass'n (541)
Water and Wastewater Equipment Manufacturers Ass'n (541)

WATCHES

American Watch Ass'n (122)
American Watchmakers-Clockmakers Institute (122)
Clock Manufacturers and Marketing Ass'n (195)
Jewelry Industry Distributors Ass'n (314)
Nat'l Time Equipment Ass'n (434)

WATER

American Desalting Ass'n (64)
American Filtration and Separations Soc. (68)
American Institute of Hydrology (77)
American Soc. of Irrigation Consultants (111)
American Soc. of Limnology and Oceanography (112)
American Water Resources Ass'n (122)
American Water Works Ass'n (122)
Ass'n of Boards of Certification (145)
Ass'n of Metropolitan Sewerage Agencies (157)
Ass'n of Metropolitan Water Agencies (157)
Ass'n of State and Interstate Water Pollution Control Administrators (165)
Ass'n of State Dam Safety Officials (166)
Ass'n of State Drinking Water Administrators (166)
Ass'n of Water Technologies (169)
Evaporative Cooling Institute (233)
Federal Water Quality Ass'n (236)
Ground Water Protection Council (250)
Groundwater Management Districts Ass'n (250)
Internat'l Bottled Water Ass'n (283)
Internat'l Desalination Ass'n (288)
Internat'l Ozone Ass'n-Pan American Group Branch (299)
Internat'l Water Resources Ass'n (310)
Interstate Council on Water Policy (311)
Irrigation Ass'n (313)
Nat'l Ass'n of Flood and Stormwater Management Agencies (355)
Nat'l Ass'n of Water Companies (380)
Nat'l Drilling Ass'n (400)
Nat'l Ground Water Ass'n (407)
Nat'l Hydropower Ass'n (410)
Nat'l Institutes for Water Resources (412)
Nat'l Marine Electronics Ass'n (416)
Nat'l Onsite Wastewater Recycling Ass'n (419)
Nat'l Rural Water Ass'n (426)
Nat'l Utility Contractors Ass'n (435)
Nat'l Water Resources Ass'n (435)
North American Lake Management Soc. (442)
Process Equipment Manufacturers' Ass'n (463)
River Management Soc. (476)
Soil and Water Conservation Soc. (510)
Sump and Sewage Pump Manufacturers Ass'n (518)
United States Committee on Irrigation and Drainage (532)
United States Committee on Large Dams (533)
Universities Council on Water Resources (536)
Water and Sewer Distributors of America (541)
Water and Wastewater Equipment Manufacturers Ass'n (541)
Water Environment Federation (541)
Water Quality Ass'n (541)
Water Sports Industry Ass'n (541)
Water Systems Council (541)
WaterJet Technology Ass'n (541)
World Waterpark Ass'n (550)

WATERPROOFERS

Asphalt Roofing Manufacturers Ass'n (129)
Institute of Roofing and Waterproofing Consultants Internat'l (269)
Sealant, Waterproofing and Restoration Institute (480)

WATERWAYS

American Waterways Operators (122)
Committee for Private Offshore Rescue and Towing (C-PORT) (200)
Dredging Contractors of America (224)
Estuarine Research Federation (233)
Independent Terminal Operators Ass'n (262)
Inland Rivers Ports and Terminals (264)
Lake Carriers' Ass'n (316)
Nat'l Shipyard Ass'n (428)
Nat'l Waterways Conference (436)
Professional Paddlesports Ass'n (466)
River Management Soc. (476)
Western Dredging Ass'n (542)

WEBB-POMERENE ACT

Afram Films (13)
American Cotton Shippers Ass'n (60)
American Natural Soda Ash Corporation (86)
American Poultry U.S.A. (93)
American Wood Chip Export Ass'n (123)
American-European Soda Ash Shipping Ass'n (124)
California Dried Fruit Export Ass'n (185)
Motion Picture Ass'n (330)
Northwest Fruit Exporters (446)
Phosphate Chemicals Export Ass'n (457)
Pulp, Paper and Paperboard Export Ass'n of the U.S. (470)
Texas Produce Export Ass'n (521)
UAN Solutions Export Ass'n (529)

WELFARE

American Ass'n of Food Stamp Directors (37)
American Ass'n of Public Welfare Attorneys (42)
American Ass'n of Public Welfare Information Systems Management (42)
American Public Human Services Ass'n (96)
Ass'n of Administrators of the Interstate Compact on the Placement of Children (141)
Ass'n of Jewish Family and Children's Agencies (155)
Ass'n of Private Pension and Welfare Plans (160)
Child Welfare League of America (192)
Nat'l Ass'n of Child Advocates (347)
Nat'l Ass'n of Community Action Agencies (349)
Nat'l Ass'n of Program Information and Performance Measurement (367)
Nat'l Ass'n of Public Child Welfare Administrators (367)
Nat'l Ass'n of State Retirement Administrators (376)
Nat'l Ass'n of WIC Directors (380)
Nat'l Conference of State Social Security Administrators (391)
Nat'l Council of Local Public Welfare Administrators (395)
Nat'l Council of State Human Service Administrators (396)
Nat'l Organization of Social Security Claimants' Representatives (420)
Presbyterian Health, Education and Welfare Ass'n (462)

WHEAT

Home Baking Ass'n (255)
Nat'l Ass'n of Wheat Growers (380)
Nat'l Futures Ass'n (406)
United States Durum Growers Ass'n (533)
United States Wheat Associates (535)
Wheat Quality Council (543)

WHOLESALERS

Air-Conditioning and Refrigeration Wholesalers Ass'n Internat'l (16)
American Ass'n of Meat Processors (38)
American Machine Tool Distributors Ass'n (82)
American Nursery and Landscape Ass'n (87)
American Supply Ass'n (119)
American Traffic Safety Services Ass'n (120)
American Wholesale Booksellers Ass'n (123)
American Wholesale Marketers Ass'n (123)
Appliance Parts Distributors Ass'n (126)
Ass'n for High Technology Distribution (134)
Ass'n of Food Industries (151)
Ass'n of Sales and Marketing Companies (164)
Ass'n of Steel Distributors (166)
Associated Equipment Distributors (171)
Automotive Service Industry Ass'n (175)
Automotive Wholesalers Ass'n Executives (175)
Aviation Distributors and Manufacturers Ass'n Internat'l (175)
Bearing Specialist Ass'n (177)
Beauty and Barber Supply Institute (177)
Bicycle Product Suppliers Ass'n (178)
Biscuit and Cracker Distributors Ass'n (179)
Biscuit and Cracker Manufacturers' Ass'n (179)
Board of Trade of the Wholesale Seafood Merchants (181)
Bureau of Wholesale Sales Representatives (184)
Business Products Industry Ass'n (185)
Copper and Brass Servicenter Ass'n (209)
Dental Dealers of America (221)
Display Distributors Ass'n (223)
Document Management Industries Ass'n (224)
Door and Hardware Institute (224)
Educational Dealers and Suppliers Ass'n Internat'l (226)
Electrical-Electronics Materials Distributors Ass'n (227)
Farm Equipment Wholesalers Ass'n (235)
Fluid Power Distributors Ass'n (241)
Food Distributors Internat'l (241)
Food Industry Suppliers Ass'n (241)
Food Marketing Institute (241)
Foodservice Equipment Distributors Ass'n (242)
General Merchandise Distributors Council (246)
Hardwood Distributors Ass'n (251)
Health Industry Distributors Ass'n (252)
Hobby Industry Ass'n of America (255)
Independent Laboratory Distributors Ass'n (261)
Independent Medical Distributors Ass'n (261)
Institutional and Service Textile Distributors Ass'n (269)
Internat'l Ass'n of Plastics Distributors (281)
Internat'l Communications Industries Ass'n (286)
Internat'l Federation of Pharmaceutical Wholesalers (290)
Internat'l Hardware Distributors Ass'n (293)
Internat'l Sanitary Supply Ass'n (302)
Internat'l Wholesale Furniture Ass'n (311)
Jewelry Industry Distributors Ass'n (314)
Lawn and Garden Marketing and Distribution Ass'n (318)
Machinery Dealers Nat'l Ass'n (321)
Material Handling Equipment Distributors Ass'n (325)
Monument Builders of North America (330)
Music Distributors Ass'n (332)
Nat'l Appliance Parts Suppliers Ass'n (337)
Nat'l Ass'n of Aluminum Distributors (343)
Nat'l Ass'n of Chemical Distributors (347)
Nat'l Ass'n of Container Distributors (349)
Nat'l Ass'n of Decorative Fabric Distributors (352)

600 National Trade and Professional Associations of the U.S. © 1999, Columbia Books, Inc.

Bowling Writers Ass'n of America (181)
Children's Literature Ass'n (192)
Construction Writers Ass'n (207)
Copywriter's Council of America (209)
Council of Literary Magazines and Presses (214)
Council of Writers Organizations (216)
Dance Critics Ass'n (220)
Dog Writers' Ass'n of America (224)
Editorial Freelancers Ass'n (226)
Education Writers Ass'n (226)
Football Writers Ass'n of America (242)
Freelance Editorial Ass'n (244)
Garden Writers Ass'n of America (245)
Golf Writers Ass'n of America (248)
Internat'l Black Writers Conference (283)
Internat'l Food, Wine and Travel Writers Ass'n (291)
Internat'l Motor Press Ass'n (297)
Internat'l Travel Writers and Editors Ass'n (309)
Internat'l Women's Writing Guild (311)
Mystery Writers of America (333)
Nat'l Ass'n of Hispanic Journalists (358)
Nat'l Ass'n of Science Writers (371)
Nat'l Book Critics Circle (384)
Nat'l Conference of Editorial Writers (390)
Nat'l Council of Writing Program Administrators (397)
Nat'l League of American Pen Women (414)
Nat'l Sportscasters and Sportswriters Ass'n (431)
Nat'l Turf Writers Ass'n (435)
Nat'l Writers Ass'n (437)

Nat'l Writers Union (437)
Nat'l Writing Centers Ass'n (437)
North American Snowsports Journalists Ass'n (444)
Outdoor Writers Ass'n of America (451)
Professional Ass'n of Resume Writers (464)
Professional Basketball Writers' Ass'n (465)
Professional Football Writers of America (465)
Professional Hockey Writers' Ass'n (466)
Religion Newswriters Ass'n of U.S. and Canada (474)
Romance Writers of America (477)
Science Fiction and Fantasy Writers of America (479)
Scribes (480)
Soc. for Technical Communication (494)
Soc. for Technological Advancement of Reporting (494)
Soc. of American Business Editors and Writers (497)
Soc. of American Travel Writers (498)
Soc. of Children's Book Writers and Illustrators (499)
South Asian Journalists Ass'n (510)
Travel Journalists Guild (526)
United States Basketball Writers Ass'n (532)
United States Harness Writers' Ass'n (534)
Writers Guild of America, East (551)
Writers Guild of America, west (551)

YARN

American Yarn Spinners Ass'n (124)
Internat'l Soc. of Industrial Fabric Manufacturers (306)
Nat'l Needlework Ass'n (418)
Textured Yarn Ass'n of America (522)

ZINC

American Bureau of Metal Statistics (49)
American Zinc Ass'n (124)
Independent Zinc Alloyers Ass'n (262)
Internat'l Lead Zinc Research Organization (295)
Non-Ferrous Metals Producers Committee (439)

ZOOLOGY

American Ass'n of Zoo Keepers (45)
American Ass'n of Zoo Veterinarians (45)
American Malacological Union (82)
American Soc. of Ichthyologists and Herpetologists (111)
American Soc. of Limnology and Oceanography (112)
American Zoo and Aquarium Ass'n (124)
Animal Behavior Soc. (124)
Ass'n of Systematics Collections (167)
Entomological Soc. of America (231)
Genetics Soc. of America (246)
Organization for Tropical Studies (450)
Paleontological Soc. (452)
Soc. for Integrative and Comparative Biology (490)
Soc. for the Study of Amphibians and Reptiles (495)
Soc. of Nematologists (504)
Soc. of Protozoologists (506)
Soc. of Systematic Biologists (507)

Geographic Index

All active organizations in NTPA can be found here under the city and state where they are headquartered.

ALABAMA

Auburn

American Ass'n of Veterinary Anatomists (44)
Associated Schools of Construction (172)
Soc. for the History of Technology (495)
University Aviation Ass'n (537)

Auburn University

Nat'l Academy of Arbitrators (333)

Birmingham

Alliance for Continuing Medical Education (17)
American Soc. for Automation in Pharmacy (101)
American Soc. for Reproductive Medicine (105)
Ass'n of Edison Illuminating Companies (150)
Congress of Neurological Surgeons (205)
Ductile Iron Pipe Research Ass'n (225)
Governmental Research Ass'n (248)
Kappa Delta Epsilon (315)
Professional Convention Management Ass'n (465)
Soc. for Assisted Reproductive Technology (485)
Soc. for Reproductive Endocrinologists and Infertility (493)
Soc. for Reproductive Surgeons (493)

Decatur

Racking Horse Breeders Ass'n of America (470)

Gulf Shores

Internat'l Ass'n of Travel Exhibitors (283)

Heflin

American Ass'n of University Administrators (44)

Huntsville

Metaphysical Soc. of America (327)
Nat'l Speleological Soc. (431)

Jacksonville

Visitor Studies Ass'n (540)

Madison

MicroStation Community (328)

Montgomery

Ass'n of Real Estate License Law Officials (163)
Ass'n of State and Provincial Psychology Boards (165)
Automotive Wholesalers Ass'n Executives (175)
Federation of Ass'ns of Regulatory Boards (237)
Nat'l Ass'n for Developmental Education (338)
Nat'l Weather Ass'n (436)

Mountain Brook

Aluminum Foil Container Manufacturers Ass'n (19)
Cookware Manufacturers Ass'n (208)

Northport

American Filtration and Separations Soc. (68)

Spanish Fort

Education Credit Union Council (226)

Tuscaloosa

Academy of Accounting Historians (7)
Academy of Ambulatory Foot Surgery (7)
American Comparative Literature Ass'n (59)
Nat'l Ass'n of Rehabilitation Instructors (369)

ALASKA

Juneau

Internat'l Horn Soc. (294)

ARIZONA

Chandler

IMAGE Soc. (259)

Flagstaff

American Holistic Nurses' Ass'n (73)

Glendale

American Salvage Pool Ass'n (99)

Lake Havasu City

Internat'l Facsimile Counsultative Council (290)

Mesa

American Hydrogen Ass'n (74)
Ass'n of Golf Merchandisers (152)
Nat'l Ass'n of Test Directors (378)
Soc. of Forensic Toxicologists (501)

Nogales

Fresh Produce Ass'n of the Americas (244)

Phoenix

American Academy of Dental Group Practice (21)
American Auditory Soc. (46)
American Indian Council of Architects and Engineers (75)
American Psychological Ass'n - Division of Psychoanalysis (95)
American Psychological Ass'n - Division of Psychologists in Independent Practice (95)
American Psychological Ass'n - Division of Psychotherapy (95)
American Soc. of Indexers (111)
Ass'n of Certified Professional Secretaries (146)
Ass'n of State and Territorial Dental Directors (165)
Beauty and Barber Supply Institute (177)
Communications Fraud Control Ass'n (200)
Continental Basketball Ass'n (207)
Dental Group Management Ass'n (221)
Health Industry Business Communications Council (252)
Institute for Investment Management Consultants (265)
Internat'l Ass'n of Career Management Professionals (277)
Nat'l Ass'n of Elevator Safety Authorities Internat'l (353)
Nat'l Ass'n of Solar Contractors (373)
Nat'l Council for Prescription Drug Programs (393)
Nat'l Environmental Training Ass'n (401)
Nat'l Extension Ass'n of Family and Consumer Sciences (402)
Nat'l Surgical Assistant Ass'n (432)
Post-Tensioning Institute (461)
Salon Ass'n, The (478)
Soc. of American Indian Dentists (497)
Soc. of Medical-Dental Management Consultants (503)
Supima Ass'n of America (518)

Prescott

Barzona Breeders Ass'n of America (177)

Scottsdale

American Compensation Ass'n (59)
Ass'n for Management Information in Financial Services (136)
Council of Educational Facility Planners, Internat'l (213)
Council on Chiropractic Education (216)
Game Manufacturers Ass'n (245)
Insurance Marketing Communications Ass'n (270)
Internat'l Federation of Women's Travel Organizations (291)
Singles Press Ass'n (483)
Soc. for Menstrual Cycle Research (491)
Utility Communicators Internat'l (529)

Tempe

American Alliance for Theatre and Education (27)
American Ass'n of Teachers of Italian (44)
American Federation of Astrologers (66)
Ass'n for Comparative Economic Studies (131)
Ass'n of College and University Printers (147)
Council of Colleges of Arts and Sciences (213)
Evangelical Christian Publishers Ass'n (233)
Nat'l Ass'n for Ethnic Studies (339)
Nat'l Ass'n of Purchasing Management (368)
Nat'l Speakers Ass'n (431)
Romanian Studies Ass'n of America (477)
Rubber Pavements Ass'n (478)

Tucson

American Ass'n of Teachers of Slavic and East European Languages (44)
American Soc. for Apheresis (101)
Ass'n of American Physicians and Surgeons (142)
Ass'n of Collegiate Schools of Planning (148)
Ass'n of Faculty Clubs Internat'l (150)
Harness Tracks of America (251)
Internat'l Ass'n of Severe Weather Specialists (282)
Internat'l Studies Ass'n (307)
Middle East Studies Ass'n of North America (328)
Nat'l Academy of Elder Law Attorneys (334)
Nat'l Ass'n of Professional Geriatric Care Managers (366)
Nat'l Ass'n of Self-Instructional Language Programs (372)
Nat'l Ass'n of State Park Directors (375)
Nat'l Dissemination Ass'n (399)
Nat'l Federation of Modern Language Teachers Ass'ns (403)
Nat'l Guardianship Ass'n (408)
Soc. for Historical Archaeology (489)
Soc. for Spanish and Portuguese Historical Studies (494)
Tree-Ring Soc. (526)
Western Music Ass'n (543)

Yuma

American Incense Manufacturers Ass'n (75)
Professional Aeromedical Transport Ass'n (464)

ARKANSAS

Arkadelphia

Nat'l Ass'n of Barber Boards (344)

Conway

American Academy of Research Historians of Medieval Spain (26)

Eureka Springs

Antique and Amusement Photographers Internat'l (125)

Fayetteville

American Agricultural Law Ass'n (27)
Nat'l Interstate Council of State Boards of Cosmetology (413)
Nat'l Verbatim Reporters Ass'n (435)

Scribes (480)

Gurdon

Internat'l Concatenated Order of Hoo-Hoo (286)

Huntsville

Internat'l Conference of Funeral Service Examining
Boards (287)

Litte Rock

Nat'l Ass'n of State Textbook Administrators (376)

Little Rock

Ass'n of Conservation Engineers (148)
Case Management Soc. of America (187)
Communications Supply Service Ass'n (200)
Delta Pi Epsilon (221)
Nat'l Ass'n of Rehabilitation Secretaries (370)
Nat'l Ass'n of State Radio Networks (376)
Nat'l Council on Student Development (398)

Morrilton

Forest Farm and Community Tree Network (242)

CALIFORNIA

Alameda

United States Federation for Culture Collections (533)

Aliso Viejo

American Ass'n of Critical-Care Nurses (35)

Anaheim

American Soc. of Gas Engineers (110)
Diving Equipment and Marketing Ass'n (224)
Mobile Industrial Caterers' Ass'n Internat'l (329)
Soc. of Critical Care Medicine (500)
World Floor Covering Ass'n (549)
World Internat'l Nail and Beauty Ass'n (550)

Arcadia

American Sports Medicine Ass'n/Board of Certification (118)
World Wide Pet Supply Ass'n (550)

Arcata

Soc. for the Study of Indigenous Languages of the
Americas (495)

Balboa Island

American College of Forensic Psychiatry (54)

Benicia

American College of Psychoanalysts (57)

Berkeley

American College of Psychiatrists (57)
Ass'n of Literary Scholars and Critics (156)
Independent Scholars of Asia (261)
Internat'l Coordinating Committee on Solid State Sensors and
Actuators Research (287)
Internat'l Soc. for Magnetic Resonance in Medicine (303)
Nat'l Ass'n for Chicana and Chicano Studies (338)
Substance Abuse Librarians and Information Specialists (518)

Beverly Hills

Academy of Motion Picture Arts and Sciences (9)
Adult Video Ass'n (12)
Advertising Photographers of America, Nat'l (12)
Ass'n of Moving Image Archivists (158)
Lepidoptera Research Foundation (319)
Producer's Guild of America (463)
Soc. of Children's Book Writers and Illustrators (499)
Women of the Motion Picture Industry, Internat'l (547)

Bodega Bay

American Academy of Fixed Prosthodontics (22)

Boulder Creek

Portable Computer and Communications Ass'n (460)

Buena Park

Crane Certification Ass'n of America (218)
Fresh Produce and Floral Council (244)

Burbank

American Auto Racing Writers and Broadcasters Ass'n (46)
Internat'l Animated Film Soc. (273)
Manuscript Soc. (323)
Motion Picture and Television Credit Ass'n (330)
Swimming Pool Trades and Contractors Ass'n (519)

Byron

American Soc. of Irrigation Consultants (111)

Campo

Nat'l Border Patrol Council (384)

Carlsbad

American Music Conference (86)

Gemological Institute of America (246)
Internat'l Music Products Ass'n (298)

Carmel

Ass'n of Biological Collections Appraisers (144)

Carmel Valley

Soc. of Telecommunications Consultants (507)

Carmichael

American Institute of Inspectors (77)

Chatsworth

Nat'l Notary Ass'n (418)

Chico

Futon Ass'n Internat'l (245)

Chino

Certified Milk Producers Ass'n of America (190)
Nat'l Home Equity Mortgage Ass'n (409)

Citrus Heights

Western Range Ass'n (543)

Claremont

Conference for the Study of Political Thought (204)
Internat'l Soc. of Political Psychology (306)

Concord

Internat'l Soc. for General Semantics (303)
Nat'l Ass'n of Stock Plan Professionals (377)

Corona

Fitness Trade Ass'n (240)
Soc. for Vector Ecology (496)

Corona del Mar

Coronado

Fur Commission USA (244)

Corte Madera

Ass'n of Winery Suppliers (169)
Financial Institutions Insurance Ass'n (239)

Costa Mesa

Educational Dealers and Suppliers Ass'n Internat'l (226)
Internat'l Sports Massage Federation (307)
United States Sports Massage Federation (535)

Covina

Soc. for the Advancement of Material and Process
Engineering (494)
Soil and Plant Analysis Council (509)

Culver City

Biomedical Engineering Soc. (179)
Ceramic Tile Institute of America (189)

Daly City

American Ass'n for Fuel Cells (30)

Davis

American Soc. for Enology and Viticulture (102)
American Warmblood Registry (122)
Geothermal Resources Council (247)

Del Mar

Information Technologies Credit Union Ass'n (264)
Nat'l Ass'n of Credit Union Chairmen (351)
Nat'l Council of Postal Credit Unions (395)

Diamond Bar

Christian Management Ass'n (193)
Specialty Equipment Market Ass'n (514)

Downey

Engineering Contractors' Ass'n (230)

El Centro

American College of Chiropractic Orthopedists (53)

El Cerrito

Hydroponic Soc. of America (257)
Seismological Soc. of America (481)

El Dorado Hills

North American Blueberry Council (440)

El Monte

Accordion Federation of North America (10)

El Segundo

Ass'n of Celebrity Personal Assistants (146)

El Sobrante

American Institute of Engineers (77)

Encinitas

Solution Mining Research Institute (510)

Encino

Alliance of Motion Picture and Television Producers (18)
American Soc. of Music Arrangers and Composers (113)
Motion Picture Ass'n (330)
Nat'l Ass'n for Research and Therapy of Homosexuality (341)
Video Software Dealers Ass'n (539)

Fairfax

Accredited Gemologists Ass'n (10)

Fallbrook

Professional Numismatists Guild (466)

Folsom

Alpha Tau Delta (19)

Fremont

Enterprise Computer Telephony Forum (231)
Internat'l Interactive Communication Soc. (295)

Fresno

Ass'n for Play Therapy (136)
Internat'l Bowling Pro Shop and Instructors Ass'n (283)
Internat'l Saw and Knife Ass'n (302)
Personalization and Identification Ass'n (455)
Weather Modification Ass'n (541)

Fullerton

American Endodontic Soc. (66)
United States Federation of Scholars and Scientists (533)

Garden Grove

Antique Appraisal Ass'n of America (125)
Ass'n of Professional Ball Players of America (160)

Gardena

Internat'l Right of Way Ass'n (301)

Glendale

American Council of Hypnotist Examiners (61)
Coordinating Council for Women in History (209)
Internat'l Motion Picture and Lecturers Ass'n (297)

Granada Hills

Phi Alpha Delta (456)

Grass Valley

Floatation Tank Ass'n (240)

Hayward

Institute of Mathematical Statistics (268)

Hemet

Tooling Component Manufacturers Ass'n (524)

Hermosa Beach

American Ass'n for Career Education (30)

Hollywood

Academy of Country Music (8)
American Harp Soc. (72)
American Soc. of Cinematographers (107)
Nat'l Black Public Relations Soc. (383)
Screen Actors Guild (480)
Women in Film (546)

Huntington Beach

Ass'n of Surfing Professionals (166)
Instructional Systems Ass'n (269)
Nat'l Basketball Referees Ass'n (382)
United States Lifesaving Ass'n (534)
Western Economic Ass'n Internat'l (542)

Idyllwild

Ass'n of Proposal Management Professionals (162)

Imperial Beach

Electrical Manufacturing and Coil Winding Ass'n (227)

Irvine

American College of Trial Lawyers (58)
American Osteopathic College of Occupational Preventive
Medicine (89)
Motorcycle Industry Council (330)
Motorcycle Safety Foundation (331)
Multi-Level Marketing Internat'l Ass'n (331)
Specialty Vehicle Institute of America (514)
Travel Technology Ass'n (526)
United Ostomy Ass'n (531)

Keene

United Farm Workers of America (530)

La Habra

Interactive Audio Special Interest Group (271)
MIDI Manufacturers Ass'n (328)

La Jolla

American Academy of Estate Planning Attorneys (22)
Ass'n of American Physicians (142)

La Mesa

Soc. of Allied Weight Engineers (497)

La Palma

Nat'l Ass'n of Minorities in Cable (363)

Lafayette

Soyfoods Ass'n of North America (511)

Laguna Beach

Ass'n of Freestanding Radiation Oncology Centers (152)
Institute for Applied Iridology (264)
Neurodevelopmental Treatment Ass'n (438)
Radiology Business Management Ass'n (471)
Substance Abuse Program Administrators Ass'n (518)
Wound, Ostomy and Continence Nurses Soc. (550)

Laguna Hills

American College for Advancement in Medicine (52)
Manufacturers' Agents Nat'l Ass'n (323)

Lakeside

Nat'l Council of Administrative Women in Education (394)

Lancaster

Independent Armored Car Operators Ass'n (259)
Soc. of Experimental Test Pilots (501)

Livermore

Concrete Modifications Contractors Ass'n (203)

Loma Linda

American Institute of Oral Biology (78)
Nat'l Ass'n of Seventh-Day Adventist Dentists (372)

Long Beach

Academy of Managed Care Providers (9)
American Fitness Ass'n (68)
Internat'l Food, Wine and Travel Writers Ass'n (291)
Internat'l Soc. of Restaurant Ass'n Executives (307)
Mu Phi Epsilon (331)
Soc. for History Education (489)
Specialty Coffee Ass'n of America (514)
Western Shoe Associates (543)

Los Alamitos

American Soc. for Aesthetic Plastic Surgery (100)

Los Angeles

African-American Library and Information Science Ass'n (14)
Alliance of Black Entertainment Technicians (18)
American Academy of Medical Acupuncture (23)
American Ass'n for the Surgery of Trauma (32)
American Ass'n of Medical Milk Commissions (39)
American College of Trust and Estate Counsel (58)
American Film Marketing Ass'n (68)
American Industrial Real Estate Ass'n (75)
American Pancreatic Ass'n (90)
Ass'n of Area Business Publications (144)
Ass'n of Black Women Entrepreneurs (145)
Ass'n of Catholic TV and Radio Syndicators (146)
Ass'n of Film Commissioners Internat'l (151)
Ass'n of Talent Agents (167)
Ass'n of Woodworking and Furnishings Suppliers (170)
Broadcast Designers' Ass'n (182)
City and Regional Magazine Ass'n (194)
Council on Governmental Ethics Law (217)
Directors Guild of America (223)
IEEE Industry Applications Soc. (258)
IEEE Instrumentation and Measurement Soc. (258)
IEEE Power Electronics Soc. (258)
Internat'l Documentary Ass'n (289)
Internat'l Institute for Lath and Plaster (294)
Jewelry Manufacturers Guild (314)
Latin Business Ass'n (317)
Leading Jewelers Guild (318)
Mexican-American Grocers Ass'n (327)
Nat'l Ass'n of Business Travel Agents (346)
Nat'l Ass'n of Composers, USA (349)
Nat'l Ass'n of Latino Elected and Appointed Officials (361)
Nat'l Ass'n of Real Estate Investment Managers (369)
Nat'l Federation of Hispanics in Communication (403)
Optical Video Disc Ass'n (449)
PROMAX Internat'l (468)
Soc. of Graduate Surgeons (502)
Soc. of Hispanic Professional Engineers (502)
University and College Labor Education Ass'n (537)
Western Ass'n for Art Conservation (542)
Writers Guild of America, west (551)

Los Olivos

Manhattan Beach

Audio Publishers Ass'n (173)

Marina Del Rey

Ass'n of Volleyball Professionals (169)
World Research Foundation (550)

Menlo Park

American Ass'n for Artificial Intelligence (29)
Asian American Manufacturers Ass'n (128)

Mill Valley

Forum for Health Care Planning (243)

Mission Viejo

American Ass'n of Attorney-Certified Public Accountants (33)
League for Innovation in the Community College (318)

Modesto

American Ass'n for Medical Transcription (31)

Monterey Park

Driving School Ass'n of America (224)

Moraga

College Theology Soc. (198)

Moreno Valley

Nat'l Patio Enclosure Ass'n (421)

Morro Bay

Nat'l Council of Exchangors (394)

Mountain View

Fibre Channel Ass'n (238)
Professional and Technical Consultants Ass'n (464)
Semiconductor Equipment and Materials Internat'l (481)

National City

Newport Beach

American Soc. of Dermatological Retailers (109)
Asian/Pacific American Librarians Ass'n (128)
Nat'l Bicycle Dealers Ass'n (382)
Nat'l Nutritional Foods Ass'n (419)
Stucco Manufacturers Ass'n (517)
World Sports Medicine Ass'n of Registered Therapists (550)

North Hollywood

American Teleservices Ass'n (119)
Internat'l Ass'n of Golf Administrators (279)
Nat'l Ass'n of Theatre Owners (378)
Stuntmen's Ass'n of Motion Pictures (517)

Northridge

U.S. Metric Ass'n (528)

Novato

California Redwood Ass'n (185)
Internat'l Ass'n of Financial Crimes Investigators (279)
Mining and Metallurgical Soc. of America (329)

Oakland

Black Psychiatrists of America (180)
Earthquake Engineering Research Institute (225)
Internet Local Advertising and Commerce Ass'n (311)
Nat'l Ass'n of Temple Administrators (378)
Nat'l Meat Ass'n (416)
Surface Design Ass'n (518)
Union of American Physicians and Dentists (529)
United Ass'n of Equipment Leasing (530)
Women's Caucus: Religious Studies (547)

Orange

Airforwarders Ass'n (16)
Ass'n for Data Center, Network and Enterprise Systems Management (132)
Ass'n of Professional Energy Managers (161)
Professional Speakers Network (467)
University Film and Video Ass'n (537)

Pacific Grove

Tire Retread Information Bureau (523)

Pacific Palisades

Nat'l Ass'n of Railroad Trial Counsel (368)

Pacifica

Laser and Electro-Optics Manufacturers' Ass'n (317)

Palm Desert

Independent Photo Imagers (261)

Palm Springs

Nat'l Ass'n of Credit Union Service Organizations (351)

Palmdale

American Soc. of Podiatric Dermatology (115)
Soc. of Flight Test Engineers (501)

Palo Alto

American Ass'n of Professional Hypnotherapists (41)
American Basketball League (47)
Electric Power Research Institute (227)

Paramount

Internat'l Union of Petroleum and Industrial Workers (310)

Pasadena

American Seminar Leaders Ass'n (99)
Christian Educators Ass'n Internat'l (193)
Internat'l Webmasters Ass'n (310)

Petaluma

Ass'n of Professional Bridge Players (160)
Nat'l Ass'n of Neonatal Nurses (363)

Placerville

Preferred Funeral Directors Internat'l (462)

Point Reyes

American Evaluation Ass'n (66)

Pomona

Institute for Certification of Tax Professionals (265)
North American Conference on British Studies (441)

Ramona

American Ass'n of Owners and Breeders of Peruvian Paso Horses (40)

Rancho Dominguez

College Athletic Business Management Ass'n (197)

Rancho Santa Fe

Internat'l Exchangors Ass'n (290)

Rancho Santa Margarito

Professional Ass'n of Diving Instructors (464)

Redding

American Buckskin Registry Ass'n (49)

Redondo Beach

Flight Engineers' Internat'l Ass'n (240)
Nat'l Council of Black Engineers and Scientists (394)

Riverside

Internat'l Organization of Citrus Virologists (299)
Internat'l Soc. of Chemical Ecology (306)
Soc. for Archaeological Studies (485)

Roland Heights

American Ass'n of Hispanic Certified Public Accountants (37)

Sacramento

American Ass'n of Mental Health Professionals in Corrections (39)
American Criminal Justice Ass'n/Lambda Alpha Epsilon (62)
American Desalting Ass'n (64)
American Down Ass'n (65)
Ass'n for Correctional Research and Information Management (132)
Ass'n of Applied Insect Ecologists (143)
California Dried Fruit Export Ass'n (185)
Coleopterists Soc. (196)
Internat'l Council of Library Ass'n Executives (288)
Nat'l Council of Investigation and Security Services (395)
Nat'l Postsecondary Agriculture Student Organization (423)
Organization of News Ombudsmen (450)

San Clemente

Photo Chemical Machining Institute (457)

San Diego

Academy of Scientific Hypnotherapy (10)
American Ass'n of Franchisees and Dealers (37)
American College of Veterinary Dermatology (58)
American Council on Exercise (62)
American Tunaboat Ass'n (121)
Ass'n for Borderlands Studies (130)
Ass'n of Ancient Historians (143)
Customer Relations Institute (219)
IDEA, The Health and Fitness Source (258)
Nat'l Ass'n for Year-Round Education (342)
Nat'l Bureau of Certified Consultants (384)
Nat'l Network of Grantmakers (418)
North American Council of Automotive Teachers (441)
Outpatient Ophthalmic Surgery Soc. (451)
Soc. for Computer Simulation (486)
Soc. for Software Quality (494)

San Dimas

Internat'l Institute of Municipal Clerks (294)

San Francisco

American Academy of Ophthalmology (24)
American Anaplastology Ass'n (28)
American Ass'n for Pediatric Ophthalmology and Strabismus (31)

American Dehydrated Onion and Garlic Ass'n (63)
American Ophthalmological Soc. (88)
American Sightseeing Internat'l (100)
American Soc. of Andrology (106)
American Soc. of Ocularists (113)
American Soc. of Ophthalmic Registered Nurses (113)
American Soc. on Aging (117)
Asian American Certified Public Accountants (128)
Asian American Journalists Ass'n (128)
Ass'n for Humanistic Psychology (134)
Ass'n for Women in Computing (140)
Ass'n of Aviation Psychologists (144)
Ass'n of Independent Colleges of Art and Design (153)
Ass'n of Professional Design Firms (161)
Ass'n of University Professors of Ophthalmology (168)
Computer Security Institute (203)
Display Distributors Ass'n (223)
Electric Vehicle Ass'n of the Americas (227)
Equity Asset Managers Ass'n, The (232)
Healthcare Forum, The (252)
Help Desk Institute (253)
I2O Special Interest Group (257)
Information Technology and Telecommunications Ass'n (264)
Institute of Intermodal Repairers (267)
Internat'l Ass'n of Business Communicators (276)
Internat'l Computer Music Ass'n (286)
Internat'l Longshoremen's and Warehousemen's Union (296)
Internat'l Skeletal Soc. (302)
Internat'l Transactional Analysis Ass'n (309)
IS Financial Management Ass'n (313)
Medical Marketing Ass'n (326)
Nat'l Alliance for Media Arts and Culture (335)
Nat'l Ass'n of Medical Minority Educators (362)
Nat'l Book Critics Circle (384)
Nat'l Council on Crime and Delinquency (397)
Nat'l Employment Lawyers Ass'n (401)
Nat'l Federation of Community Broadcasters (403)
Nat'l Vehicle Leasing Ass'n (435)
North American Soc. for Cardiac Imaging (444)
Oxygen Soc., The (452)
Professional Ass'n for Childhood Education (464)
SCSI Trade Ass'n (480)
Soc. of Insurance Trainers and Educators (503)
Wine Institute (544)

San Jose

American Handwriting Analysis Foundation (71)
Career Planning and Adult Development Network (187)
Electronic Design Automation Consortium (228)
Nat'l Ass'n for Physical Education in Higher Education (340)
Personal Computer Memory Card Internat'l Ass'n (455)
Public Agency Risk Managers Ass'n (469)
Semiconductor Industry Ass'n (481)
Serial Storage Architecture Industry Ass'n (482)
Soc. for Information Display (490)
Soc. for Philosophy and Technology (492)
Transaction Processing Performance Council (525)
Video Electronics Standards Ass'n (539)

San Juan Capistrano

Latex Advisors Ass'n (317)

San Leandro

Gunite/Shotcrete Contractors Ass'n (250)
Internat'l Union of Security Officers (310)

San Luis Obispo

Human Behavior and Evolution Soc. (257)

San Marcos

American Soc. of Primatologists (115)
Kamut Ass'n of North America (315)

San Mateo

ADARA (11)
Nat'l Ass'n of Real Estate Buyer Brokers (369)
Wine and Spirits Guild of America (544)

San Pedro

Nat'l Watercolor Soc. (436)

San Rafael

Institute of Political Campaign Consultants (268)

Santa Ana

Nat'l Ass'n of Graphic and Product Identification
    Manufacturers (357)
Optometric Editors Ass'n (449)
Self Insurance Institute of America (481)
Soc. of Urologic Cryosurgeons (508)

Santa Barbara

American Ass'n of Teachers of Esperanto (43)
American Luggage Dealers Ass'n (82)
Ass'n for Equine Sports Medicine (133)
Corporate Facility Advisors (209)
Internat'l Academy of Podiatric Medicine (272)
Professional Ass'n of Innkeepers Internat'l (464)

Santa Clara

American Electronics Ass'n (65)
Internat'l Disk Drive Equipment and Materials Ass'n (289)

Santa Clarita

Nat'l Flute Ass'n (405)

Santa Cruz

Phycological Soc. of America (457)
Vacation Rental Managers Ass'n (538)

Santa Fe Springs

American Ass'n of Gynecological Laparoscopists (37)

Santa Monica

American Gem and Mineral Suppliers Ass'n (70)
Ass'n of Managed Care Dentists (156)
Associated Surplus Dealers (172)
Human Factors and Ergonomics Soc. (257)
Nat'l Academy of Recording Arts and Sciences (334)
Nat'l Ass'n of Television Program Executives (378)
Soc. of American Gastrointestinal Endoscopic Surgeons (497)
Wedding and Portrait Photographers Internat'l (542)

Santa Rosa

Internat'l Soc. of Statistical Science (307)
Peruvian Paso Horse Registry of North America (455)

Santee

Nat'l Ass'n of Service Managers (372)

Sherman Oaks

Aerobics and Fitness Ass'n of America (13)
Production Equipment Rental Ass'n (463)
Women in Technology Internat'l (547)

Solana Beach

American Academy of Veterinary Dermatology (26)
United States Racquet Stringing Ass'n (535)

Solvang

American College of Foot and Ankle Orthopedics and
    Medicine (54)

Sonora

American Academy of Pain Management (24)

Spring Valley

Internat'l Ass'n of Audio Visual Communicators (276)

Stanford

Ass'n for Transpersonal Psychology (140)
Conference on Jewish Social Studies (205)

Stockton

ISDA - The Office Systems Cooperative (313)

Studio City

Organization of Professional Acting Coaches and
    Teachers (450)
Soc. of Motion Picture and Television Art Directors (504)
Stuntwomen's Ass'n of Motion Pictures (517)

Sun City

Armed Forces Broadcasters Ass'n (127)

Tarzana

American Hypnosis Ass'n (74)

Thousand Oaks

American Ass'n for Crystal Growth (30)
Community College Journalism Ass'n (201)
Nat'l Ass'n of REALTORS (369)

Torrance

American Board of Podiatric Orthopedics and Primary
    Podiatric Medicine (48)
Automotive Fleet and Leasing Ass'n (174)
Performance Warehouse Ass'n (455)
Xplorer Internat'l (551)

Trabuco Canyon

Nat'l Ass'n of Gas Chlorinators (356)
Nat'l Plasterers Council (422)

Tujunga

Ass'n of Railway Museums (163)

Turlock

American Ass'n of Veterinary Laboratory Diagnosticians (45)

Tustin

Roundtable for Women in Foodservice (477)
Soc. of Collision Repair Specialists (499)

Venice

Public Radio Program Directors Ass'n (469)

Ventura

Automatic Transmission Rebuilders Ass'n (173)

Villa Park

Aerospace Electrical Soc. (13)

Vista

Digital Distribution of Advertising for Publications (222)
Variable Electronic Components Institute (538)

Walnut

Firearms Research and Indentification Ass'n (240)
Internat'l Ass'n of Plumbing and Mechanical Officials (282)

Walnut Creek

American Ass'n of Independent Newspaper Distributors (38)
Infrared Data Ass'n (264)

West Hills

Internat'l Soc. of Introduction Services (306)
Western Shoe Retailers Ass'n (543)

West Hollywood

American Cinema Editors (52)

Westlake

American Soc. of Plumbing Engineers (115)

Whittier

Internat'l Conference of Building Officials (287)

Windsor

Marine Staff Officers (323)

Woodland

Alfalfa Council (17)
Internat'l Wild Rice Ass'n (311)
Wood Moulding and Millwork Producers Ass'n (548)

Woodland Hills

Internat'l Foundation for Telemetering (292)
North American Soc. of Scaffold Professionals (445)
Scaffold Industry Ass'n (479)

Yorba Linda

Ass'n of Business Support Services Internat'l (145)
Roundalab (477)

Yucaipa

American Construction Inspectors Ass'n (60)
American Mustang Ass'n (86)

Yucca Valley

American Welara Pony Soc. (122)

COLORADO

Arvada

American Institute of Professional Geologists (78)
Nat'l Translator Ass'n (434)

Aurora

AGN Internat'l - North America (14)
American Galvanizers Ass'n (70)
Associated Business Writers of America (171)
Farmers Educational and Co-operative Union of America (235)
Geospatial Information and Technology Ass'n (247)
Internat'l Arabian Horse Ass'n (273)
Nat'l Academy of Neuropsychology (334)
Nat'l Writers Ass'n (437)

Boulder

American Home Brewers Ass'n (74)
American Indian Science and Engineering Soc. (75)
American Journalism Historians Ass'n (80)
American Polarity Therapy Ass'n (93)
American Solar Energy Soc. (117)
Ass'n for Experiential Education (133)
Ass'n of Teachers of Japanese (167)
Clay Minerals Soc. (194)
EDUCAUSE (227)
Geological Soc. of America (246)
Institute for Brewing Studies (265)
Internat'l Information Management Congress (294)
Internat'l Titanium Ass'n (309)
Masonry Soc. (324)
Nat'l Conference of Standards Laboratories (391)
Nat'l Prison Hospice Ass'n (423)
Rolf Institute (477)
Soc. for Mathematical Biology (491)

Buena Vista

Small Publishers Ass'n of North America (484)

Castle Rock

Nat'l Ass'n of Business and Industrial Saleswomen (346)

Colorado Springs

Affiliated Boards of Officials (13)
Affiliated Inventors Foundation (13)
American Academy of Forensic Sciences (22)
American Ass'n of Orthopaedic Medicine (40)
American Boarding Kennels Ass'n (48)
American Grooming Shop Ass'n (71)
American Volleyball Coaches Ass'n (122)
Ass'n for the Advancement of Psychology (138)
Ass'n of Christian Schools Internat'l (146)

CBA (188)
Consultant Dietitians in Health Care Facilities (207)
General Merchandise Distributors Council (246)
Internat'l Academy of Behavioral Medicine, Counseling and Psychotherapy (272)
Nat'l Ass'n of Marine Services (362)
Nat'l Junior College Athletic Ass'n (413)
Nat'l Live Stock Producers Ass'n (415)
Nat'l Strength and Conditioning Ass'n (432)
North American Ass'n of Professors of Christian Education (440)
North American Professors of Christian Education (444)
Professional Rodeo Cowboys Ass'n (467)
United States Taekwondo Union (535)
Vocational Evaluation and Work Adjustment Ass'n (540)
Wilderness Medical Soc. (544)
Women's Professional Rodeo Ass'n (548)

Denver

Airlines Medical Directors Ass'n (17)
American Animal Hospital Ass'n (28)
American College of Veterinary Internal Medicine (58)
American Highland Cattle Ass'n (73)
American Horticultural Therapy Ass'n (74)
American Soc. of Agricultural Consultants (106)
American Soc. of Farm Managers and Rural Appraisers (109)
American Soc. of Sugar Beet Technologists (116)
American Water Works Ass'n (122)
Ass'n of American State Geologists (143)
Ass'n of Destination Management Executives (149)
Ass'n of Operating Room Nurses (159)
Ass'n of Pediatric Oncology Social Workers (160)
Ass'n of Physician Assistants in Cardiovascular Surgery (160)
Beet Sugar Development Foundation (177)
Disaster Preparedness and Emergency Response Ass'n (223)
Health Industry Representatives Ass'n (252)
Institute of Certified Financial Planners (266)
Internat'l BBSing and Electronic Communications Conference (283)
Internat'l Livestock Identification Ass'n (296)
Internat'l Livestock Theft Investigators Ass'n (296)
Internat'l Sport Show Producers Ass'n (307)
Investment Management Consultants Ass'n (312)
Museum Store Ass'n (332)
Nat'l Ass'n of Counsel for Children (350)
Nat'l Bison Ass'n (383)
Nat'l Conference of Local Environmental Health Administrators (390)
Nat'l Conference of State Legislatures (391)
Nat'l Council of State Emergency Medical Services Training Coordinators (396)
Nat'l Defined Contribution Council (399)
Nat'l Environmental Health Ass'n (401)
Nat'l Health Club Ass'n (408)
Nat'l Hearing Conservation Ass'n (408)
Nat'l Network of Estate Planning Attorneys (418)
Nat'l Potato Promotion Board (423)
Piedmontese Ass'n of the United States (458)
Soc. for New Language Study (491)
Soc. for Range Management (493)
Soc. of Pediatric Nurses (505)
State Higher Education Executive Officers (516)
United States Committee on Irrigation and Drainage (532)
United States Committee on Large Dams (533)
United States Meat Export Federation (534)
Western and English Manufacturers Ass'n (542)
Women in Mining Nat'l (547)
World Ass'n of Detectives (549)
Yellow Pages Publishers Ass'n (551)

Durango

Holistic Dental Ass'n (255)

Englewood

Adventure Travel Trade Ass'n (12)
American College of Medical Practice Executives (55)
American Institute of Timber Construction (78)
American Nat'l CattleWomen (86)
American Salers Ass'n (98)
American Sheep Industry Ass'n (99)
American Soc. of Bariatric Physicians (107)
Ass'n of Surgical Technologists (166)
Home Baking Ass'n (255)
Medical Group Management Ass'n (326)
Nat'l Cattlemen's Beef Ass'n (386)
Nat'l Potato Council (423)
Nat'l Stroke Ass'n (432)
North American Limousin Foundation (443)
North American South Devon Ass'n (445)

Evergreen

Associated Bodywork and Massage Professionals (170)

Fort Collins

Ass'n for University and College Counseling Center Directors (140)
Ass'n of Collegiate Conference and Events Directors Internat'l (148)
Conference of Research Workers in Animal Diseases (204)
Nat'l Ass'n for Interpretation (340)
Nat'l Block and Bridle Club (383)
Nat'l Rural Education Ass'n (426)
Organizational Behavior Teaching Soc. (450)
United States Cross Country Coaches Ass'n (533)
Wilderness Education Ass'n (544)

Golden

Computer Oriented Geological Soc. (202)
Internat'l Soc. for the Study of Subtle Energies and Energy Medicine (305)

Mountain Rescue Ass'n (331)
Nat'l Council of Supervisors of Mathematics (396)

Grand Junction

Nat'l Ass'n of Private, Nontraditional Schools and Colleges with Accrediting Commission for Higher Education (366)

Greeley

American Ass'n of Teachers of Spanish and Portuguese (44)
Nat'l Council for Marketing and Public Relations (393)
Nat'l Onion Ass'n (419)

Johnstown

Beef Friesian Soc. (177)

Lakewood

Nat'l Ski Areas Ass'n (428)
Nat'l Ski Patrol System (428)
Oil, Chemical and Atomic Workers Internat'l Union (448)
Paleontological Soc. (452)
Professional Ski Instructors of America (467)

LaPorte

Dude Ranchers' Ass'n (225)

Littleton

Nat'l Greenhouse Manufacturers Ass'n (407)
Soc. for Mining, Metallurgy, and Exploration (491)
Soc. of Economic Geologists (500)

Longmont

Keramos Fraternity (315)

Loveland

Radiant Panel Ass'n (470)

Monument

Internat'l Textile and Apparel Ass'n (308)

Morrison

Internat'l Electrical Testing Ass'n (289)

Newcastle

American Shire Horse Ass'n (100)

Niwot

American Psychological Ass'n - Division of Clinical Psychology (95)

Rollinsville

Internat'l Communications Agency Network (286)

Steamboat Springs

Internat'l Erosion Control Ass'n (290)

Westcliffe

Nat'l Judges Ass'n (413)

Westminster

American Gelbvieh Ass'n (70)
Arabian Horse Registry of America, Inc. (126)
World Sign Associates (550)

Wheat Ridge

Ass'n for Applied Psychophysiology and Biofeedback (129)
Convention Liaison Council (208)
Environmental and Engineering Geophysical Soc. (231)
Nat'l Quartz Producers Council (424)
North American Nature Photography Ass'n (443)
Soc. for Scholarly Publishing (493)

Windsor

Internat'l Ass'n of Dive Rescue Specialists (278)

CONNECTICUT

Avon

Nat'l Soc. of Pharmaceutical Sales Trainers (430)

Berlin

Nat'l Catalog Managers Ass'n (385)

Bethel

Soc. for Experimental Mechanics (488)

Bloomfield

American Academy of Psychiatry and the Law (25)
American Clinical Neurophysiological Soc. (52)
Professional Show Managers Ass'n (467)
Shade Tobacco Growers Agricultural Ass'n (482)

Botsford

North American Ass'n of Christians in Social Work (440)

Branford

Ass'n of Master of Business Administration Executives (157)

Brookfield

Soc. of Plastics Engineers (505)

Danbury

Soc. for Biomolecular Screening (486)

East Haven

Internat'l Ass'n of Tour Managers - North American Region (282)

East Windsor Hill

Internat'l Ass'n for Near Death Studies (274)

Easton

Internat'l Juvenile Officers Ass'n (295)

Fairfield

Ireland Chamber of Commerce in the United States (312)
Nat'l Council on Public Polls (397)
Soc. for Medieval and Renaissance Philosophy (491)

Farmington

American Ass'n of Directors of Psychiatric Residency Training (36)

Glastonbury

Nat'l Federation of Grange Mutual Insurance Companies (403)
Pension Real Estate Ass'n (454)

Greenwich

American Pet Products Manufacturers Ass'n (91)
Council on Geriatric Cardiology (217)
Newspaper Features Council (439)
Quality Bakers of America Cooperative (470)

Groton

American Academy of Veterinary Pharmacology and Therapeutics (26)
Nat'l Party Boat Owners Alliance (421)

Guilford

Wire Ass'n Internat'l (545)

Hamden

American Council for Southern Asian Art (61)
Soc. of Physician Assistants in Pediatrics (505)

Hartford

American Ass'n for Continuity of Care (30)
American Epilepsy Soc. (66)
Ass'n for Death Education and Counseling (132)
Ass'n of Collegiate Licensing Administrators (148)
Ass'n of State Supervisors of Mathematics (166)
Internat'l Ass'n of Campus Law Enforcement Administrators (277)
LIMRA Internat'l (320)

Jewett City

Health Sciences Communications Ass'n (252)

Lakeville

Nat'l Soc. of Compliance Professionals (429)

Mashantucket

Nat'l American Indian Court Judges Ass'n (336)

Middletown

Ass'n of State Correctional Administrators (166)

Monroe

Friction Materials Standards Institute (244)

New Canaan

Golf Range and Recreation Ass'n of America (248)

New Haven

Modern Greek Studies Ass'n (329)
Soc. for Light Treatment and Biological Rhythms (490)
Union for Radical Political Economics (529)

New Milford

Ass'n of Bridal Consultants (145)

Newington

American Radio Relay League (96)

Newtown

Nat'l Shooting Sports Foundation (428)
Sporting Arms and Ammunition Manufacturers' Institute (515)

Norwalk

Ass'n of University Technology Managers (169)
Nat'l Bed and Breakfast Ass'n (382)
Sunglass Ass'n of America (518)

Riverside

Carpet Cushion Council (187)

Internat'l Ass'n of Bridge, Structural, Ornamental and Reinforcing Iron Workers **(276)**
Internat'l Ass'n of Color Manufacturers **(277)**
Internat'l Ass'n of Convention and Visitor Bureaus **(277)**
Internat'l Ass'n of Fire Fighters **(279)**
Internat'l Ass'n of Fish and Wildlife Agencies **(279)**
Internat'l Ass'n of Heat and Frost Insulators and Asbestos Workers **(279)**
Internat'l Ass'n of Insurance Supervisors **(280)**
Internat'l Ass'n of Official Human Rights Agencies **(281)**
Internat'l Ass'n of Professional Security Consultants **(282)**
Internat'l Banana Ass'n **(283)**
Internat'l Biometric Soc. **(283)**
Internat'l Bridge, Tunnel and Turnpike Ass'n **(284)**
Internat'l Brotherhood of Electrical Workers **(284)**
Internat'l Brotherhood of Painters and Allied Trades **(284)**
Internat'l Brotherhood of Teamsters, AFL-CIO **(284)**
Internat'l City/County Management Ass'n **(285)**
Internat'l Claim Ass'n **(285)**
Internat'l Council for Computer Communication **(287)**
Internat'l Council of Cruise Lines **(287)**
Internat'l Council of Employers of Bricklayers and Allied Craftworkers **(287)**
Internat'l Crystal Federation **(288)**
Internat'l Dairy Foods Ass'n **(288)**
Internat'l District Energy Ass'n **(289)**
Internat'l Downtown Ass'n **(289)**
Internat'l Electronic Article Surveillance Manufacturers Ass'n **(289)**
Internat'l Fibre Drum Institute **(291)**
Internat'l Food Information Council **(291)**
Internat'l Franchise Ass'n **(292)**
Internat'l Furnishings and Design Ass'n **(292)**
Internat'l Glutamate Technical Committee **(292)**
Internat'l Hydrolized Protein Council **(294)**
Internat'l Ice Cream Ass'n **(294)**
Internat'l Institute of Ammonia Refrigeration **(294)**
Internat'l Insurance Council **(295)**
Internat'l Intellectual Property Alliance **(295)**
Internat'l Intellectual Property Ass'n **(295)**
Internat'l Labor Communications Ass'n **(295)**
Internat'l Mobile Telecommunications Ass'n **(297)**
Internat'l Municipal Lawyers Ass'n **(297)**
Internat'l Road Federation **(302)**
Internat'l Slurry Surfacing Ass'n **(302)**
Internat'l Soc. for Experimental Hematology **(303)**
Internat'l Soc. for Performance Improvement **(304)**
Internat'l Soc. for Peritoneal Dialysis **(304)**
Internat'l Trade Commission Trial Lawyers Ass'n **(309)**
Internat'l Union of Bricklayers and Allied Craftsmen **(309)**
Internat'l Union of Electronic, Electrical, Salaried Machine, and Furniture Workers **(309)**
Internat'l Union of Operating Engineers **(310)**
Internet Alliance **(311)**
Interstate Conference of Employment Security Agencies **(311)**
Interstate Council on Water Policy **(311)**
Interstate Natural Gas Ass'n of America **(311)**
Investment Company Institute **(312)**
Investment Counsel Ass'n of America **(312)**
Investment Program Ass'n **(312)**
Issues Management Ass'n **(313)**
Japan Automobile Manufacturers Ass'n **(313)**
Jesuit Secondary Education Ass'n **(313)**
Justice Research and Statistics Ass'n **(315)**
Laborers' Internat'l Union of North America **(316)**
Lamaze International **(316)**
Land Trust Alliance **(317)**
Latin American Management Ass'n **(317)**
Leather Industries of America **(318)**
Lighter Ass'n **(319)**
Linguistic Soc. of America **(320)**
Long Term Acute Care Hospital Ass'n of America **(321)**
Lutheran Educational Conference of North America **(321)**
Mail Order Ass'n of America **(322)**
Managed Futures Ass'n **(322)**
Manufactured Housing Ass'n for Regulatory Reform **(322)**
Manufacturers of Emission Controls Ass'n **(323)**
Marine Technology Soc. **(324)**
Maritime Fire and Safety Ass'n **(324)**
Mathematical Ass'n of America **(325)**
Medical Device Manufacturers Ass'n **(326)**
Messenger Courier Ass'n of the Americas **(327)**
Methacrylate Producers Ass'n **(327)**
Military Boot Manufacturers Ass'n **(328)**
Military Chaplains Ass'n of the U.S. **(328)**
Milk Industry Foundation **(328)**
Mineralogical Soc. of America **(329)**
Mortgage Bankers Ass'n of America **(330)**
Mortgage Insurance Companies of America **(330)**
Motion Picture Ass'n of America **(330)**
Motor Freight Carriers Ass'n **(330)**
Municipal Finance Industry Ass'n **(331)**
Municipal Treasurers Ass'n of the United States and Canada **(331)**
Municipal Waste Management Ass'n **(331)**
Museum Education Roundtable **(332)**
Museum Trustee Ass'n **(332)**
NAFSA: Ass'n of Internat'l Educators **(333)**
Nat'l Abortion Federation **(333)**
Nat'l Academy of Clinical Biochemistry **(334)**
Nat'l Academy of Engineering of the United States of America **(334)**
Nat'l Academy of Sciences **(334)**
Nat'l Adult Education Professional Development Consortium **(334)**
Nat'l Agricultural Aviation Ass'n **(335)**
Nat'l Air Carrier Ass'n **(335)**
Nat'l Air Duct Cleaners Ass'n **(335)**
Nat'l Air Filtration Ass'n **(335)**
Nat'l Air Traffic Controllers Ass'n **(335)**
Nat'l Alliance for Oral Health **(336)**
Nat'l Alliance of Black School Educators **(336)**
Nat'l Alliance of Nurse Practitioners **(336)**
Nat'l Alliance of Postal and Federal Employees **(336)**
Nat'l Alliance of State and Territorial AIDS Directors **(336)**
Nat'l American Indian Housing Council **(336)**
Nat'l Armored Car Ass'n **(337)**
Nat'l Artists Equity Ass'n **(337)**
Nat'l Ass'n for Bilingual Education **(338)**
Nat'l Ass'n for Biomedical Research **(338)**
Nat'l Ass'n for Community Mediation **(338)**
Nat'l Ass'n for County Community and Economic Development **(338)**
Nat'l Ass'n for Drama Therapy **(339)**
Nat'l Ass'n for Environmental Management **(339)**
Nat'l Ass'n for Home Care **(339)**
Nat'l Ass'n for Homecare **(339)**
Nat'l Ass'n for Law Placement **(340)**
Nat'l Ass'n for Public Health Statistics and Information Systems **(340)**
Nat'l Ass'n for State Community Service Programs **(341)**
Nat'l Ass'n for the Education of Young Children **(341)**
Nat'l Ass'n for the Self-Employed **(341)**
Nat'l Ass'n of Affordable Housing Lenders **(342)**
Nat'l Ass'n of Area Agencies on Aging **(343)**
Nat'l Ass'n of Artists' Organizations **(343)**
Nat'l Ass'n of Attorneys General **(343)**
Nat'l Ass'n of Beverage Importers-Wine-Spirits-Beer **(344)**
Nat'l Ass'n of Black County Officials **(344)**
Nat'l Ass'n of Black Procurement Professionals **(345)**
Nat'l Ass'n of Black Women Attorneys **(345)**
Nat'l Ass'n of Black-Owned Broadcasters **(345)**
Nat'l Ass'n of Blind Teachers **(345)**
Nat'l Ass'n of Boards of Education **(345)**
Nat'l Ass'n of Boards of Examiners of Long Term Care Administrators **(345)**
Nat'l Ass'n of Broadcast Employees and Technicians **(345)**
Nat'l Ass'n of Broadcasters **(345)**
Nat'l Ass'n of Business Economists **(346)**
Nat'l Ass'n of Chemical Recyclers **(347)**
Nat'l Ass'n of Child Advocates **(347)**
Nat'l Ass'n of Child Care Resource and Referral Agencies **(347)**
Nat'l Ass'n of College and University Attorneys **(347)**
Nat'l Ass'n of College and University Business Officers **(348)**
Nat'l Ass'n of Colored Women's Clubs **(349)**
Nat'l Ass'n of Community Action Agencies **(349)**
Nat'l Ass'n of Community Health Centers **(349)**
Nat'l Ass'n of Conservation Districts **(349)**
Nat'l Ass'n of Consumer Agency Administrators **(349)**
Nat'l Ass'n of Corporate Directors **(350)**
Nat'l Ass'n of Counties **(350)**
Nat'l Ass'n of County Administrators **(350)**
Nat'l Ass'n of County Aging Programs **(350)**
Nat'l Ass'n of County and City Health Officials **(350)**
Nat'l Ass'n of County Behavioral Health Directors **(350)**
Nat'l Ass'n of County Civil Attorneys **(350)**
Nat'l Ass'n of County Engineers **(350)**
Nat'l Ass'n of County Human Services Administrators **(351)**
Nat'l Ass'n of County Information Officers **(351)**
Nat'l Ass'n of County Information Technology Administrators **(351)**
Nat'l Ass'n of County Intergovernmental Relations Officials **(351)**
Nat'l Ass'n of County Park and Recreation Officials **(351)**
Nat'l Ass'n of County Planners **(351)**
Nat'l Ass'n of County Recorders, Election Officials and Clerks **(351)**
Nat'l Ass'n of County Surveyors **(351)**
Nat'l Ass'n of County Training and Employment Professionals **(351)**
Nat'l Ass'n of County Treasurers and Finance Officers **(351)**
Nat'l Ass'n of Criminal Defense Lawyers **(352)**
Nat'l Ass'n of Development Organizations **(352)**
Nat'l Ass'n of Developmental Disabilities Councils **(352)**
Nat'l Ass'n of Energy Service Companies **(354)**
Nat'l Ass'n of Federal Veterinarians **(355)**
Nat'l Ass'n of Federally Impacted Schools **(355)**
Nat'l Ass'n of Flood and Stormwater Management Agencies **(355)**
Nat'l Ass'n of Foreign-Trade Zones **(356)**
Nat'l Ass'n of Governmental Labor Officials **(357)**
Nat'l Ass'n of Governors' Highway Safety Representatives **(357)**
Nat'l Ass'n of Health Career Schools **(357)**
Nat'l Ass'n of Healthcare Access Management **(357)**
Nat'l Ass'n of Healthcare Consultants **(357)**
Nat'l Ass'n of Hispanic County Officials **(358)**
Nat'l Ass'n of Hispanic Journalists **(358)**
Nat'l Ass'n of Hispanic Nurses **(358)**
Nat'l Ass'n of Hispanic Publications **(358)**
Nat'l Ass'n of Home Builders of the U.S. **(358)**
Nat'l Ass'n of Housing and Redevelopment Officials **(358)**
Nat'l Ass'n of Independent Colleges and Universities **(359)**
Nat'l Ass'n of Independent Public Finance Advisors **(359)**
Nat'l Ass'n of Independent Schools **(360)**
Nat'l Ass'n of Installation Developers **(360)**
Nat'l Ass'n of Insurance Brokers **(360)**
Nat'l Ass'n of Investment Companies **(360)**
Nat'l Ass'n of Letter Carriers **(361)**
Nat'l Ass'n of Life Underwriters **(361)**
Nat'l Ass'n of Manufacturers **(362)**
Nat'l Ass'n of Margarine Manufacturers **(362)**
Nat'l Ass'n of Media Brokers **(362)**
Nat'l Ass'n of Medicaid Directors **(362)**
Nat'l Ass'n of Minority Automobile Dealers **(363)**
Nat'l Ass'n of Minority Contractors **(363)**
Nat'l Ass'n of Negro Business and Professional Women's Clubs **(363)**
Nat'l Ass'n of Neighborhoods **(363)**
Nat'l Ass'n of Nurse Practitioners in Reproductive Health **(364)**
Nat'l Ass'n of Pastoral Musicians **(364)**
Nat'l Ass'n of Plant Patent Owners **(365)**
Nat'l Ass'n of Police Organizations **(365)**
Nat'l Ass'n of Private Industry Councils **(366)**
Nat'l Ass'n of Private Schools for Exceptional Children **(366)**
Nat'l Ass'n of Professional Pet Sitters **(367)**
Nat'l Ass'n of Program Information and Performance Measurement **(367)**
Nat'l Ass'n of Protection and Advocacy Systems **(367)**
Nat'l Ass'n of Psychiatric Health Systems **(367)**
Nat'l Ass'n of Public Child Welfare Administrators **(367)**
Nat'l Ass'n of Public Hospitals and Health Systems **(368)**
Nat'l Ass'n of Real Estate Brokers **(368)**
Nat'l Ass'n of Real Estate Investment Trusts **(369)**
Nat'l Ass'n of Regional Councils **(369)**
Nat'l Ass'n of Regulatory Utility Commissioners **(369)**
Nat'l Ass'n of Resident Management Corporations **(370)**
Nat'l Ass'n of Schools of Public Affairs and Administration **(371)**
Nat'l Ass'n of Securities and Commercial Law Attorneys **(372)**
Nat'l Ass'n of Securities Dealers **(372)**
Nat'l Ass'n of Securities Professionals **(372)**
Nat'l Ass'n of Service and Conservation Corps **(372)**
Nat'l Ass'n of Settlement Purchasers **(372)**
Nat'l Ass'n of Small Business Investment Companies **(373)**
Nat'l Ass'n of Social Workers **(373)**
Nat'l Ass'n of State Alcohol and Drug Abuse Directors **(373)**
Nat'l Ass'n of State Budget Officers **(374)**
Nat'l Ass'n of State Departments of Agriculture **(374)**
Nat'l Ass'n of State Development Agencies **(374)**
Nat'l Ass'n of State Directors of Vocational-Technical Education **(375)**
Nat'l Ass'n of State Election Directors **(375)**
Nat'l Ass'n of State Foresters **(375)**
Nat'l Ass'n of State Units on Aging **(376)**
Nat'l Ass'n of State Universities and Land Grant Colleges **(376)**
Nat'l Ass'n of State Utility Consumer Advocates **(376)**
Nat'l Ass'n of Student Assistance Professional **(377)**
Nat'l Ass'n of Student Financial Aid Administrators **(377)**
Nat'l Ass'n of Student Personnel Administrators **(377)**
Nat'l Ass'n of Surety Bond Producers **(377)**
Nat'l Ass'n of Towns and Townships **(378)**
Nat'l Ass'n of Urban Bankers **(379)**
Nat'l Ass'n of Urban Critical Access Hospitals **(379)**
Nat'l Ass'n of Veterans Program Administrators **(379)**
Nat'l Ass'n of Vision Professionals **(379)**
Nat'l Ass'n of Water Companies **(380)**
Nat'l Ass'n of Waterfront Employers **(380)**
Nat'l Ass'n of Wheat Growers **(380)**
Nat'l Ass'n of Wholesaler-Distributors **(380)**
Nat'l Ass'n of WIC Directors **(380)**
Nat'l Ass'n of Women Judges **(380)**
Nat'l Ass'n of Workforce Development Professionals **(381)**
Nat'l Ass'n of Youth Clubs **(381)**
Nat'l Assembly of Nat'l Voluntary Health and Social Welfare Organizations **(381)**
Nat'l Assembly of State Arts Agencies **(381)**
Nat'l Bankers Ass'n **(382)**
Nat'l Bar Ass'n **(382)**
Nat'l Beauty Culturists' League **(382)**
Nat'l Bio-Energy Industries Ass'n **(383)**
Nat'l Black Ass'n for Speech, Language and Hearing **(383)**
Nat'l Black Caucus of Local Elected Officials **(383)**
Nat'l Black Caucus of State Legislators **(383)**
Nat'l Black Chamber of Commerce **(383)**
Nat'l Black Coalition of Federal Aviation Employees **(383)**
Nat'l Black Nurses Ass'n **(383)**
Nat'l Black Police Ass'n **(383)**
Nat'l Broadcast Ass'n for Community Affairs **(384)**
Nat'l Broiler Council **(384)**
Nat'l Building Granite Quarries Ass'n **(384)**
Nat'l Cable Television Ass'n **(384)**
Nat'l Candle Ass'n **(385)**
Nat'l Catholic Educational Ass'n **(385)**
Nat'l Cheese Institute **(386)**
Nat'l Child Support Enforcement Ass'n **(386)**
Nat'l Club Ass'n **(387)**
Nat'l Coalition for Advanced Manufacturing **(387)**
Nat'l Coalition of Hispanic Health and Human Services Organizations **(387)**
Nat'l Committee for Quality Assurance **(388)**
Nat'l Community Development Ass'n **(388)**
Nat'l Conference of Brewery and Soft Drink Workers - United States and Canada **(389)**
Nat'l Conference of Catechetical Leadership **(390)**
Nat'l Conference of Catholic Bishops/U.S. Catholic Conference **(390)**
Nat'l Conference of Firemen and Oilers **(390)**
Nat'l Conference of State Historic Preservation Officers **(391)**
Nat'l Conference on Public Employee Retirement Systems **(391)**
Nat'l Congress for Community Economic Development **(391)**
Nat'l Constructors Ass'n **(392)**
Nat'l Consumers League **(392)**
Nat'l Cooperative Business Ass'n **(392)**
Nat'l Corrugated Steel Pipe Ass'n **(392)**
Nat'l Council for Resource Development **(393)**
Nat'l Council for the Social Studies **(393)**
Nat'l Council of Agricultural Employers **(394)**
Nat'l Council of Architectural Registration Boards **(394)**
Nat'l Council of Catholic Women **(394)**
Nat'l Council of Chain Restaurants **(394)**
Nat'l Council of Commercial Plant Breeders **(394)**
Nat'l Council of Community Hospitals **(394)**
Nat'l Council of County Ass'n Executives **(394)**
Nat'l Council of Educational Opportunity Ass'ns **(394)**
Nat'l Council of Farmer Cooperatives **(394)**
Nat'l Council of Higher Education Loan Programs **(395)**
Nat'l Council of Intellectual Property Law Ass'ns **(395)**
Nat'l Council of Local Public Welfare Administrators **(395)**
Nat'l Council of Nonprofit Ass'ns **(395)**
Nat'l Council of State Agencies for the Blind **(396)**
Nat'l Council of State Directors of Community Junior Colleges **(396)**
Nat'l Council of State Education Ass'ns **(396)**
Nat'l Council of State Housing Agencies **(396)**
Nat'l Council of State Human Service Administrators **(396)**
Nat'l Council of State Tourism Directors **(396)**
Nat'l Council of University Research Administrators **(397)**
Nat'l Council on Internat'l Trade Development **(397)**
Nat'l Council on Measurement in Education **(397)**
Nat'l Council on the Aging **(398)**

610 National Trade and Professional Associations of the U.S. © 1999, Columbia Books, Inc.

FLORIDA

Altamonte Springs

Anthony

Atlantic Beach

Aventura

Boca Raton

Bonita Springs

Spring Hill

Nat'l Ass'n of State Agencies for Surplus Property **(373)**

St. Augustine

American Culinary Federation **(63)**
Conference of Educational Administrators of Schools and Programs for the Deaf **(204)**

St. Petersburg

Ass'n for Graphic Arts Training **(134)**
Club Pool Ass'n **(195)**
Nat'l Ass'n of Professional Baseball Leagues **(366)**
Nat'l Swim School Ass'n **(432)**
Professional Ass'n of Resume Writers **(464)**
Swimming Teachers of America **(519)**
Text and Academic Authors Ass'n **(521)**

Sunrise

Web Host Guild **(542)**

Surfside

American Ass'n of Family Businesses **(37)**

Tallahassee

American Ass'n of Business Valuation Specialists **(34)**
American Soc. of Notaries **(113)**
Ass'n for Chemoreception Sciences **(130)**
Ass'n for Institutional Research **(135)**
Beta Phi Mu **(178)**
Calorimetry Conference **(186)**
Internat'l Ass'n of Physicians and Health Care Professionals **(281)**
Nat'l Ass'n of Public Sector Equal Opportunity Officers **(368)**
Nat'l Ass'n of State Outdoor Recreation Liaison Officers **(375)**
Nat'l Ass'n of State Supervisors of Music **(376)**
Soc. of Professional Archeologists **(505)**

Tampa

Alpha Zeta Omega **(19)**
American Board of Quality Assurance and Utilization Review Physicians **(48)**
American College of Physician Executives **(57)**
American Council on Schools and Colleges **(62)**
American Natural Hygiene Soc. **(86)**
Ass'n of Battery Recyclers **(144)**
Construction Marketing Research Council **(207)**
Financial Management Ass'n **(239)**
Home Improvement Research Institute **(255)**
Internat'l Soc. for Pharmaceutical Engineering **(304)**
Jewelry Industry Distributors Ass'n **(314)**
Nat'l Ass'n of Reunion Managers **(370)**
Nat'l Ass'n of Underwater Instructors **(379)**
Nat'l Juice Products Ass'n **(413)**
Nat'l Mobility Equipment Dealers Ass'n **(417)**
Nat'l Perinatal Ass'n **(422)**
Packaged Ice Ass'n **(452)**
Travel Professionals Ass'n **(526)**

Tarpon Springs

Resort and Commercial Recreation Ass'n **(475)**

Treasure Island

Nat'l Hay Ass'n **(408)**

Valrico

Home Wine and Beer Trade Ass'n **(256)**

Vero Beach

American Ass'n of Police Polygraphists **(41)**
Health and Personal Care Distribution Conference **(251)**

West Palm Beach

Nat'l Alliance for Youth Sports **(336)**
Nat'l Ass'n of Corporate Real Estate Executives International **(350)**

Weston

Independent Professional Representatives Organization **(261)**

Winter Haven

Winter Park

American Soc. of Ophthalmic Plastic and Reconstructive Surgery **(113)**
Nat'l Ass'n of Minority Engineering Program Administrators **(363)**

Winterhaven

Soc. for the Preservation of Oral Health **(495)**

GEORGIA

Albany

American Peanut Shellers Ass'n **(91)**
Nat'l Ass'n of College Deans, Registrars, and Admissions Officers **(348)**
Nat'l Ass'n of Student Affairs Professionals **(377)**

Alpharetta

Nat'l Electronic Distributors Ass'n **(400)**

Americus

Ass'n of Third World Studies **(168)**

Athens

American Ass'n for Agricultural Education **(29)**
American Ass'n of Wildlife Veterinarians **(45)**
American Vocational Education Research Ass'n **(122)**
Ass'n of Information and Dissemination Centers **(154)**
Nat'l Alliance of Preservation Commissions **(336)**
Phi Delta Chi **(456)**
Soc. for Philosophy of Religion **(492)**
Soc. of Protozoologists **(506)**

Atlanta

American Academy of Religion **(26)**
American Apparel Producers Network **(28)**
American Ass'n of Occupational Health Nurses **(40)**
American Ass'n of Physician Specialists **(41)**
American Ass'n of Psychiatric Administrators **(42)**
American Cancer Soc. **(50)**
American College of Rheumatology **(57)**
American Educational Studies Ass'n **(65)**
American Sexually Transmitted Diseases Ass'n **(99)**
American Soc. of Heating, Refrigerating and Air-Conditioning Engineers **(110)**
American Soc. of Papyrologists **(114)**
Antenna Measurement Techniques Ass'n **(125)**
Ass'n for Convention Marketing Executives **(132)**
Ass'n for Convention Operations Management **(132)**
Ass'n for Dressings and Sauces. **(132)**
Ass'n for Information Systems **(135)**
Ass'n of Black Cardiologists **(145)**
Ass'n of Database Developers **(149)**
Ass'n of Energy Engineers **(150)**
Ass'n of Fund Raisers and Direct Sellers **(152)**
Ass'n of Medical Illustrators **(157)**
Ass'n of Rheumatology Health Professionals **(164)**
Behavioral Pharmacology Soc. **(178)**
BioCommunications Ass'n **(179)**
Bureau of Wholesale Sales Representatives **(184)**
Calorie Control Council **(186)**
Chilled Foods Ass'n **(192)**
College Language Ass'n **(197)**
Concord Grape Ass'n **(203)**
Construction Owners Ass'n of America **(207)**
Coordinating Research Council **(209)**
Council for Spiritual and Ethical Education **(212)**
Council of State and Territorial Epidemiologists **(215)**
Council on Occupational Education **(217)**
Decision Sciences Institute **(220)**
Exhibit Designers and Producers Ass'n **(234)**
Foodservice Group **(242)**
Healthcare Convention and Exhibitors Ass'n **(252)**
Home Office Life Underwriters Ass'n **(256)**
Industrial Distribution Ass'n **(262)**
Information Systems Consultants Ass'n **(264)**
Institute for Professionals in Taxation **(265)**
Institute of Nuclear Power Operations **(268)**
Institute of Paper Science and Technology **(268)**
Internat'l Ass'n for Financial Planning **(274)**
Internat'l Food Additives Council **(291)**
Internat'l Formula Council **(292)**
Internat'l Gas Turbine Institute, ASME **(292)**
Internat'l Jelly and Preserve Ass'n **(295)**
Internat'l Merger and Acquisition Professionals **(297)**
Legal Assistant Management Ass'n **(319)**
Life Insurers Council **(319)**
Lignin Institute **(319)**
LOMA **(321)**
Manufacturers' Agents for Food Service Industry **(323)**
Nat'l Ass'n of Auto Trim and Restyling Shops **(344)**
Nat'l Ass'n of Church and Institutional Financing Organizations **(347)**
Nat'l Ass'n of Church Food Service **(347)**
Nat'l Basketball Trainers' Ass'n **(382)**
Nat'l Conference of Black Mayors **(389)**
Nat'l Council of State Supervisors of Foreign Languages **(396)**
Nat'l Credit Union Management Ass'n **(398)**
Nat'l Golf Car Manufacturers Ass'n **(407)**
Nat'l Pecan Shellers Ass'n **(421)**
Nat'l Shrimp Processors Ass'n **(428)**
Nat'l Tutoring Ass'n **(435)**
Network of Ingredient Marketing Specialists **(438)**
Newspaper Systems Group **(439)**
Portable Rechargeable Battery Ass'n **(460)**
Processed Apples Institute **(463)**
Professional Baseball Athletic Trainers' Ass'n **(465)**
Professional Football Athletic Trainers Soc. **(465)**
Professional Photographers of America **(466)**
Refrigerated Foods Ass'n **(473)**
Sales and Marketing Executives Internat'l **(478)**
Service Industry Ass'n **(482)**
Soc. of Biblical Literature **(498)**
Soc. of Corporate Meeting Professionals **(500)**
Soc. of Internat'l Business Fellows **(503)**
Technical Ass'n of the Pulp and Paper Industry **(520)**
Textile Fibers and By-Products Ass'n **(522)**
United Egg Producers **(530)**
Vinegar Institute **(539)**

Auburn

Nat'l Council for Textile Education **(393)**

Augusta

American Soc. for Photobiology **(104)**
Shock Soc. **(483)**
United States and Canadian Academy of Pathology **(532)**

Brunswick

American Malacological Union **(82)**

Carrollton

Soc. of Professors of Education **(506)**

Columbus

Corporate Transfer Agents Ass'n **(209)**
Nat'l Ass'n of Black Hospitality Professionals **(344)**
North American Case Research Ass'n **(441)**

Conyers

American Commerce and Shipping Ass'n **(58)**
Nat'l Ass'n of Elevator Contractors **(353)**
Nat'l Child Care Ass'n **(386)**
Professional Trucking Services Ass'n **(467)**

Dalton

Carpet and Rug Institute **(187)**
Dalton Floor Covering Market Ass'n **(220)**
Floor Covering Installation Contractors Ass'n **(240)**

Decatur

American Soc. of Missiology **(112)**
Ass'n for Clinical Pastoral Education **(131)**
Nat'l American Legion Press Ass'n **(336)**
Nat'l Funeral Directors and Morticians Ass'n **(406)**
North American Serials Interest Group **(444)**

Duluth

Handweavers Guild of America **(251)**
Polaris Internat'l **(459)**

Fayetteville

Railway Tie Ass'n **(471)**

Flowery Branch

American Soc. of Certified Engineering Technicians **(107)**

Forest Park

Nat'l Ornamental and Miscellaneous Metals Ass'n **(420)**

Gainesville

Nat'l Poultry and Food Distributors Ass'n **(423)**

Jesup

American Beekeeping Federation **(47)**

Kennesaw

Government Management Information Sciences **(248)**
Women in Packaging **(547)**

Lilburn

Women's Basketball Coaches Ass'n **(547)**

Lula

American North Country Cheviot Sheep Ass'n **(87)**

Macon

Flexible Intermediate Bulk Container Ass'n **(240)**
Nat'l Ass'n of Baptist Professors of Religion **(344)**
Soc. for the Advancement of Social Psychology **(494)**

Marietta

Better Lawn and Turf Institute **(178)**
Internat'l Soc. of Communication Specialists **(306)**
North American Fuzzy Information Processing Soc. **(442)**
Professional Lawn Care Ass'n of America **(466)**
Soc. of Insurance Research **(503)**
Wood Component Manufacturers Ass'n **(548)**

Morrow

China Clay Producers Ass'n **(192)**
EIFS Industry Members Ass'n **(227)**
Internat'l Ass'n of Optometric Executives **(281)**

Morven

Nat'l Watermelon Ass'n **(436)**

Narcross

Associated Construction Publications **(171)**

Newnan

Recreational Park Trailer Industry Ass'n **(473)**

Norcross

American College of Medical Staff Development **(55)**
American Soc. of Professional Appraisers **(115)**
Institute of Industrial Engineers **(267)**
Internat'l Cartridge Recycling Ass'n **(285)**
Internat'l Development Research Council **(288)**
Nat'l Time Equipment Ass'n **(434)**
Pine Chemicals Ass'n **(458)**
Potash and Phosphate Institute **(461)**
United Product Formulators and Distributors Ass'n **(531)**

Rome

American Ass'n of Bovine Practitioners **(33)**
Pulp and Paper Safety Ass'n **(470)**

Roswell

American Academy of Implant Prosthodontics (23)
Soc. of Thoracic Radiology (507)

Savannah

Nat'l Federation of Housing Counselors (403)

Snellville

American Ass'n for Cancer Education (29)

Statesboro

American Collegiate Retailing Ass'n (58)

Stone Mountain

American Cultural Resources Ass'n (63)
American Fence Ass'n (67)
U.S.A. Poultry and Egg Export Council (528)

Tucker

Technology and Information Management Education
    Soc. (521)
United States Egg Marketers (533)

Valdosta

Professional and Organizational Development Network in
    Higher Education (464)

Waycross

American Ass'n of Certified Orthoptists (34)

Winder

Cast Stone Institute (187)
Internat'l Soc. of Weighing and Measurement (307)

Winterville

American Ass'n for Vocational Instructional Materials (32)

Woodstock

Associated Construction Distributors Internat'l (171)

HAWAII

Honolulu

Academy of Internat'l Business (8)
Ass'n for Social Anthropology in Oceania (137)
Internat'l Ass'n for Philosophy of Law and Social Philosophy -
    American Section (275)
Internat'l Ass'n of Aquaculture Economics and
    Mangement (275)
Internat'l Stress Management Ass'n (307)
Nat'l Ass'n of Apnea Professionals (343)
United States Tennis Ass'n (535)

Kihei

Multicultural Publishing and Education Council (331)

IDAHO

Boise

Nat'l Ass'n of Railroad Property Tax Representatives (368)
Nat'l Ass'n of State Veterans Homes (376)
Travel and Tourism Research Ass'n (526)

Moscow

Appaloosa Horse Club (126)
U.S.A. Dry Pea and Lentil Council (528)

Pocatello

School Management Study Group (479)

Priest River

Internat'l Ass'n for Oxygen Therapy (275)

Twin Falls

American Soc. of Agricultural Appraisers (106)

ILLINOIS

Alsip

Nat'l Ass'n of Independent Resurfacers (359)

Alton

Congress of Independent Unions (205)
Xi Psi Phi (551)

Argonne

Ass'n for Automated Reasoning (130)

Arlington Heights

Air Movement and Control Ass'n Internat'l (16)
American Academy of the History of Dentistry (26)
American Ass'n for Hand Surgery (31)
American Ass'n of Certified Allergists (34)
American College of Allergy, Asthma and Immunology (53)
American College of Occupational and Environmental
    Medicine (56)
American College of Osteopathic Family Physicians (56)
American Soc. for Reconstructive Microsurgery (105)
American Soc. of Colon and Rectal Surgeons (108)

American Soc. of Maxillofacial Surgeons (112)
American Soc. of Plastic and Reconstructive Surgeons (114)
Ass'n of Academic Chairmen of Plastic Surgery (141)
Ass'n of Plastic Surgery Assistants (160)
Lightning Protection Institute (319)
Microcirculatory Soc. of America (328)
Plastic Surgery Adminmstrative Ass'n (459)
Plastic Surgery Research Council (459)
Production Engine Remanufacturers Ass'n (463)
Soc. of Surgical Oncology (507)
System Independent Data Format Ass'n (519)
Wiring Harness Manufacturers Ass'n (545)

Aurora

American Purchasing Soc. (96)

Bannockburn

Phosphate Chemicals Export Ass'n (457)

Batavia

American Heartworm Soc. (73)
Cryogenic Engineering Conference (219)

Berkeley

Nat'l Retail Hobby Store Ass'n (426)
Real Estate Aviation Chapter (472)

Bloomington

American Fracture Ass'n (69)
American Rabbit Breeders Ass'n (96)
Nat'l Trappers Ass'n (434)

Bristol

Nat'l Lamb Feeders Ass'n (414)

Buffalo Grove

AERA - Engine Rebuilders Ass'n (12)
Ass'n of Pharmaceutical Publishers (160)
Automated Builders Consortium (173)
Conference of Consulting Actuaries (204)
Construction Writers Ass'n (207)
Nat'l Ass'n of Personal Financial Advisors (365)

Byron

Professional Reactor Operator Soc. (466)

Carbondale

American Ass'n of Teachers of French (44)
Internat'l Water Resources Ass'n (310)
Universities Council on Water Resources (536)

Champaign

American Oil Chemists' Soc. (88)
Ass'n of Environmental Engineering Professors (150)
Internat'l Soc. of Arboriculture (305)
Nat'l Ass'n of Advisors for the Health Professions (342)
Psychometric Soc. (469)
Soc. for the Advancement of Economic Theory (494)
Utility Arborist Ass'n (538)

Chicago

Academy of Dentistry for Persons with Disabilities (8)
Academy of General Dentistry (8)
Academy of Osseointegration (9)
Academy of Psychosomatic Medicine (10)
Adhesives Manufacturers Ass'n (12)
African-American Natural Foods Ass'n (14)
Ag Electronics Ass'n (14)
Air Diffusion Council (15)
Air Line Employees Ass'n, International (15)
All-America Rose Selections (17)
Alliance for Healthcare Strategy and Marketing (17)
American Academy of Cosmetic Surgery (21)
American Academy of Disability Evaluating Physicians (21)
American Academy of Esthetic Dentistry (22)
American Academy of Implant Dentistry (22)
American Academy of Matrimonial Lawyers (23)
American Academy of Pediatric Dentistry (25)
American Academy of Periodontology (25)
American Academy of Physical Medicine and
    Rehabilitation (25)
American Ass'n of Ambulatory Surgery Centers (33)
American Ass'n of Dental Examiners (36)
American Ass'n of Diabetes Educators (36)
American Ass'n of Endodontists (36)
American Ass'n of Hospital Dentists (37)
American Ass'n of Individual Investors (38)
American Ass'n of Law Libraries (38)
American Ass'n of Medical Assistants (38)
American Ass'n of Medical Soc. Executives (39)
American Ass'n of Neuroscience Nurses (39)
American Ass'n of Public Health Physicians (42)
American Ass'n of School Librarians (42)
American Ass'n of Women Dentists (45)
American Bar Ass'n (46)
American Beauty Ass'n (47)
American Burn Ass'n (49)
American Center for Design (51)
American College of Healthcare Executives (54)
American College of Osteopathic Emergency Physicians (56)
American College of Prosthodontists (57)
American College of Surgeons (57)
American Council on Pharmaceutical Education (62)
American Dairy Products Institute (63)
American Dental Ass'n (63)
American Dental Assistants Ass'n (64)

American Dental Hygienists' Ass'n (64)
American Dental Soc. of Anesthesiology (64)
American Dietetic Ass'n (64)
American Hair Loss Council (71)
American Health and Beauty Aids Institute (72)
American Health Information Management Ass'n (72)
American Hospital Ass'n (74)
American Institute of Indian Studies (77)
American Institute of Steel Construction (78)
American Judicature Soc. (80)
American Kinesiotherapy Ass'n (80)
American Ladder Institute (80)
American Library Ass'n (81)
American Library Trustee Ass'n (81)
American Marketing Ass'n (82)
American Medical Ass'n (83)
American Naprapathic Ass'n (86)
American Organization of Nurse Executives (88)
American Osteopathic Ass'n (89)
American Planning Ass'n (92)
American Prepaid Legal Services Institute (93)
American Professional Soc. on the Abuse of Children (94)
American Prosthodontic Soc. (94)
American Schools Ass'n (99)
American Soc. for Geriatric Dentistry (102)
American Soc. for Healthcare Central Service Personnel (102)
American Soc. for Healthcare Engineering (103)
American Soc. for Healthcare Environmental Services (103)
American Soc. for Healthcare Food Service
    Administrators (103)
American Soc. for Healthcare Human Resources
    Administration (103)
American Soc. for Healthcare Risk Management (103)
American Soc. of Baking (107)
American Soc. of Clinical Pathologists (108)
American Soc. of Consulting Planners (108)
American Soc. of Dentistry for Children (109)
American Soc. of Directors of Volunteer Services of the
    AHA (109)
American Soc. of Golf Course Architects (110)
American Soc. of Hair Restoration Surgery (110)
American Soc. of Hand Therapists (110)
American Soc. of Lipo-Suction Surgery (112)
American Soc. of Pediatric Nephrology (114)
American Soc. of Podiatry Executives (115)
American Spinal Injury Ass'n (118)
American Student Dental Ass'n (118)
American Supply Ass'n (119)
American Urogynecologic Soc. (121)
American Woman's Soc. of Certified Public Accountants (123)
Amusement and Music Operators Ass'n (124)
Appraisal Institute (126)
Ass'n for Enterprise Opportunity (133)
Ass'n for Healthcare Resource Materials and
    Management (134)
Ass'n for Library Collections and Technical Services (135)
Ass'n for Women Journalists (141)
Ass'n of Catholic Diocesan Archivists (146)
Ass'n of College and Research Libraries (147)
Ass'n of Coupon Professionals (149)
Ass'n of Free Community Papers (152)
Ass'n of Home Appliance Manufacturers (153)
Ass'n of Independent Trust Companies (154)
Ass'n of Industry Manufacturers' Representatives (154)
Ass'n of Interim Housing Providers (154)
Ass'n of Practical Theology (160)
Ass'n of Professional Landscape Designers (161)
Ass'n of Specialized and Cooperative Library Agencies (165)
Ass'n of Specialized and Professional Accreditors (165)
Ass'n of Steel Distributors (166)
Ass'n of University Programs in Occupational Health and
    Safety (168)
Awards and Recognition Ass'n (176)
Baking Industry Sanitation Standards Committee (176)
Bank Administration Institute (176)
Battery Council Internat'l (177)
BEMA - An Internat'l Ass'n Serving the Baking and Food
    Industries (178)
Binding Industries of America (179)
Biscuit and Cracker Distributors Ass'n (179)
Black Tie Bureau (180)
Blue Cross and Blue Shield Ass'n (180)
Brass and Bronze Ingot Manufacturers (181)
Business Marketing Ass'n (184)
Center for Management Advisors (189)
Classification Soc. of North America (194)
Clinical Orthopaedic Soc. (195)
Collectibles and Platemakers Guild (196)
Commercial Law League of America (199)
Commercial-Investment Real Estate Institute (199)
Commission on Accreditation of Allied Health Education
    Programs (199)
Committee of 200 (200)
Community Banking Advisory Network (201)
Construction and Agricultural Film Manufacturers Film
    Ass'n (206)
Construction Industry CPA/Consultants Ass'n (206)
Consumer Credit Insurance Ass'n (207)
Council for Adult and Experiential Learning (210)
Council of Planning Librarians (215)
Council of State Chambers of Commerce (215)
Counselors of Real Estate (217)
CPA Auto Dealer Consultants Ass'n (218)
CPA Manufacturing Services Ass'n (218)
Cremation Ass'n of North America (219)
Defense Research Institute (221)
Electronic Distribution Show Corporation (228)
Electronics Representatives Ass'n (229)
Employee Assistance Soc. of North America (229)
Endocrine Fellows Foundation (230)
Engine Manufacturers Ass'n (230)
Equipment Manufacturers Institute (232)
Federal Judges Ass'n (236)
Federation of Special Care Organizations (237)

Financial Managers Soc. **(239)**
Financial Services Technology Network **(239)**
First Amendment Lawyers Ass'n **(240)**
Food Equipment Manufacturers Ass'n **(241)**
Foodservice Equipment Distributors Ass'n **(242)**
Foundation for Independent Higher Education **(243)**
Gas Research Institute **(246)**
Government Finance Officers Ass'n of the United States and Canada **(248)**
Healthcare Information and Management Systems Soc. **(253)**
Hispanic Dental Ass'n **(254)**
Institute of Caster Manufacturers **(266)**
Institute of Certified Healthcare Business **(266)**
Institute of Financial Education **(267)**
Institute of Food Technologists **(267)**
Institute of Real Estate Management **(269)**
Institute of Roofing and Waterproofing Consultants Internat'l **(269)**
Internat'l Ass'n for Human Resource Information Management **(274)**
Internat'l Ass'n for the Study of Organized Crime **(275)**
Internat'l Ass'n of Assessing Officers **(276)**
Internat'l Ass'n of Defense Counsel **(278)**
Internat'l Ass'n of Healthcare Central Service Material Management **(279)**
Internat'l Ass'n of Lighting Designers **(280)**
Internat'l Ass'n of Physicians in AIDS Care **(281)**
Internat'l Ass'n of Women Police **(283)**
Internat'l Black Writers Conference **(283)**
Internat'l Carwash Ass'n **(285)**
Internat'l College of Surgeons **(286)**
Internat'l Customer Service Ass'n **(288)**
Internat'l Engineering Consortium **(290)**
Internat'l Federation for Choral Music **(290)**
Internat'l Foodservice Manufacturers Ass'n **(291)**
Internat'l Formalwear Ass'n **(291)**
Internat'l Graphoanalysis Soc. **(292)**
Internat'l Hardware Distributors Ass'n **(293)**
Internat'l Interior Design Ass'n **(295)**
Internat'l Reciprocal Trade Ass'n **(301)**
Internat'l Union of Allied Novelty and Production Workers **(309)**
Law Firm Services Ass'n **(318)**
Library Administration and Management Ass'n **(319)**
Library and Information Technology Ass'n **(319)**
Locomotive Maintenance Officers' Ass'n **(320)**
Magnet Distributors and Fabricators Ass'n **(322)**
Magnetic Materials Producers Ass'n **(322)**
Marine Retailers Ass'n of America **(323)**
Medical Library Ass'n **(326)**
Metal Construction Ass'n **(327)**
Metal Framing Manufacturers Ass'n **(327)**
Microscopy Soc. of America **(328)**
NAGMR Consumer Product Brokers **(333)**
Nat'l Account Management Ass'n **(334)**
Nat'l Ass'n for Families and Addiction Research and Education **(339)**
Nat'l Ass'n for the Cottage Industry **(341)**
Nat'l Ass'n of Architectural Metal Manufacturers **(343)**
Nat'l Ass'n of Bar Executives **(344)**
Nat'l Ass'n of Boat Manufacturers **(345)**
Nat'l Ass'n of Concessionaires **(349)**
Nat'l Ass'n of Diaconate Directors **(352)**
Nat'l Ass'n of Enrolled Federal Tax Accountants **(354)**
Nat'l Ass'n of Executive Recruiters **(354)**
Nat'l Ass'n of Fire Equipment Distributors **(355)**
Nat'l Ass'n of Floor Covering Distributors **(355)**
Nat'l Ass'n of Independent Insurance Adjusters **(359)**
Nat'l Ass'n of Marine Products and Services **(362)**
Nat'l Ass'n of Professionals in Women's Health **(367)**
Nat'l Ass'n of Residential Property Managers **(370)**
Nat'l Ass'n of Specialty Food and Confection Brokers **(373)**
Nat'l Ass'n of Sporting Goods Wholesalers **(373)**
Nat'l Ass'n of State Catholic Conference Directors **(374)**
Nat'l Ass'n of Ticket Brokers **(378)**
Nat'l Ass'n of Women Lawyers **(381)**
Nat'l Automatic Merchandising Ass'n **(381)**
Nat'l Black MBA Ass'n **(383)**
Nat'l Bulk Vendors Ass'n **(384)**
Nat'l Coil Coaters Ass'n **(388)**
Nat'l Conference of Bar Examiners **(389)**
Nat'l Conference of Bar Foundations **(389)**
Nat'l Conference of Bar Presidents **(389)**
Nat'l Conference of Commissioners on Uniform State Laws **(390)**
Nat'l Conference of Federal Trial Judges **(390)**
Nat'l Conference of Special Court Judges **(391)**
Nat'l Cosmetology Ass'n **(392)**
Nat'l Council of Real Estate Investment Fiduciaries **(395)**
Nat'l Council of State Boards of Nursing **(396)**
Nat'l CPA Health Care Advisors Ass'n **(398)**
Nat'l Electrical Engineering Department Heads Ass'n **(400)**
Nat'l Federation of Priests' Councils **(404)**
Nat'l Food Distributors Ass'n **(405)**
Nat'l Futures Ass'n **(406)**
Nat'l Institute of Pension Administrators **(412)**
Nat'l Law Firm Marketing Ass'n **(414)**
Nat'l Litigation Support Services Ass'n **(415)**
Nat'l Marine Bankers Ass'n **(416)**
Nat'l Marine Manufacturers Ass'n **(416)**
Nat'l Podiatric Medical Ass'n **(422)**
Nat'l Reading Conference **(424)**
Nat'l Roof Deck Contractors Ass'n **(426)**
Nat'l Soc. for the Study of Education **(429)**
Nat'l Student Osteopathic Medical Ass'n **(432)**
Natural Product Broker Ass'n **(437)**
North American Ass'n of Food Equipment Manufacturers **(440)**
North American Building Material Distribution Ass'n **(441)**
North American Professional Driver Education Ass'n **(443)**
North American Soc. of Adlerian Psychology **(445)**
Northamerican Industrial Representatives Ass'n **(446)**
Not-for-Profit Services Ass'n **(446)**
Open Applications Group **(448)**
Petroleum Packaging Council **(456)**
Plumbing-Heating-Cooling Information Bureau **(459)**
Popcorn Institute **(460)**
Power-Motion Technology Representatives Ass'n **(462)**
Precast/Prestressed Concrete Institute **(462)**
Preferred Hotels and Resorts Worldwide **(462)**
Pressure Sensitive Tape Council **(462)**
Pressure Vessel Manufacturers Ass'n **(462)**
PrintImage Internat'l **(463)**
Product Development and Management Ass'n **(463)**
Profit Sharing/401 (k) Council of America **(468)**
Public Library Ass'n **(469)**
Railway Industrial Clearance Ass'n **(471)**
Real Estate Brokerage Managers Council **(472)**
Real Estate Buyers Agent Council **(472)**
REALTORS Land Institute **(472)**
Refrigerating Engineers and Technicians Ass'n **(473)**
Research Council on Structural Connections **(475)**
Residential Sales Council **(475)**
Retail Advertising and Marketing Ass'n Internat'l **(475)**
Safety Equipment Manufacturers' Agents Ass'n **(478)**
Sealed Insulating Glass Manufacturers Ass'n **(480)**
Showmen's League of America **(483)**
Soc. for Ambulatory Care Professionals **(485)**
Soc. for Healthcare Consumer Advocacy **(488)**
Soc. for Healthcare Strategy and Market Development **(488)**
Soc. for Information Management **(490)**
Soc. for Integrative and Comparative Biology **(490)**
Soc. for Maintenance Reliability Professionals **(490)**
Soc. for Pediatric Dermatology **(492)**
Soc. for Pediatric Urology **(492)**
Soc. for Research on Adolescence **(493)**
Soc. for Social Work Leadership in Health Care **(494)**
Soc. of Air Force Clinical Surgeons **(497)**
Soc. of American Archivists **(497)**
Soc. of Architectural Historians **(498)**
Soc. of Christian Ethics **(499)**
Soc. of Gastroenterology Nurses and Associates **(502)**
Soc. of Gynecologic Oncologists **(502)**
Soc. of Thoracic Surgeons **(508)**
Soc. of Trauma Nurses **(508)**
Soc. of Vertebrate Paleontology **(509)**
Strategic Leadership Forum **(517)**
Suburban Newspapers of America **(518)**
Technology Transfer Soc. **(521)**
Textile Processors, Service Trades, Health Care, Professional and Technical Employees Internat'l Union **(522)**
Travel Journalists Guild **(526)**
Turkish Studies Ass'n **(528)**
Turnaround Management Ass'n **(528)**
Unfinished Furniture Ass'n **(529)**
United States Soccer Federation **(535)**
University and College Designers Ass'n **(537)**
Viola da Gamba Soc. of America **(539)**
Wallcoverings Ass'n **(540)**
Warehouse Distributors Ass'n **(540)**
Women in Cable and Telecommunications **(546)**
Women in Design **(546)**
Women in Management **(547)**
Women's Council of Realtors **(548)**
World Airline Entertainment Ass'n **(549)**
World Ass'n of Document Examiners **(549)**
Woven Wire Products Ass'n **(551)**
Zonta Internat'l **(551)**

Cicero
American Soc. of Podiatric Medical Assistants **(115)**

Country Club Hills
Building Officials and Code Administrators Internat'l **(183)**

Crystal Lake
Internat'l Ass'n of Diecutting and Diemaking **(278)**

Decatur
Nat'l Lincoln Sheep Breeders Ass'n **(415)**

Deerfield
Controlled Release Soc. **(208)**

DeKalb
Internat'l Ass'n of Family Sociology **(279)**

Des Plaines
American Foundrymen's Soc. **(69)**
American Osteopathic College of Rehabilitation Medicine **(89)**
American Soc. of Clinical Hypnosis **(108)**
American Soc. of Home Inspectors **(111)**
American Soc. of Safety Engineers **(116)**
Ass'n for the Advancement of Automotive Medicine **(138)**
Broadcast Cable Credit Ass'n **(182)**
Broadcast Cable Financial Management Ass'n **(182)**
Casting Industry Suppliers Ass'n **(187)**
Institute for Certification of Computing Professionals **(265)**
Institute of Gas Technology **(267)**
Monument Builders of North America **(330)**
MTM Ass'n for Standards and Research **(331)**
Nat'l Ass'n of Independent Insurers **(359)**
Nat'l Catholic Cemetery Conference **(385)**
Nat'l Wood Window and Door Ass'n **(437)**
Non-Ferrous Founders' Soc. **(439)**
Refrigeration Service Engineers Soc. **(473)**
Steel Founders' Soc. of America **(516)**

Downers Grove
Alliance of American Insurers **(18)**
American Insurers Highway Safety Alliance **(79)**
Coin Laundry Ass'n **(196)**
Islamic Medical Ass'n **(313)**
Liability Insurance Research Bureau **(319)**
Overseas Sales and Marketing Ass'n of America **(452)**
Pollution Liability Insurance Ass'n **(460)**
Property Loss Research Bureau **(468)**

Elgin
Internat'l Ass'n of Non-Vessel Operating Common Carriers **(281)**
Recycled Paperboard Technical Ass'n **(473)**

Elk Grove Village
American Academy of Pediatrics **(25)**
American Amusement Machine Ass'n **(28)**
Automotive Communications Council **(174)**
Automotive Service Industry Ass'n **(175)**
Internat'l Professional Groomers **(300)**

Evanston
Academy of Aphasia **(7)**
American Ass'n for Employment in Education **(30)**
American Automatic Control Council **(46)**
American Board of Medical Specialties **(47)**
American Massage Therapy Ass'n **(83)**
American Theological Library Ass'n **(120)**
Ass'n for College and University Religious Affairs **(131)**
Ass'n for Technology in Music Instruction **(138)**
Econometric Soc. **(225)**
North American Saxophone Alliance **(444)**
U.S.A. Toy Library Ass'n **(529)**
Urban Libraries Council **(538)**

Evergreen Park
Cottage Industry Miniaturists Trade Ass'n **(210)**

Flossmoor
Red Tag News Publications Ass'n **(473)**

Fox River Grove
Steel Deck Institute **(516)**

Frankfort
American Chain of Warehouses **(51)**
Internat'l Ass'n of Attorneys and Exec. in Corporate Real Estate **(276)**

Geneva
Women's Foodservice Forum **(548)**

Glen Ellyn
Bearing Specialist Ass'n **(177)**
Ceramic Tile Distributors Ass'n **(189)**
Design Professionals Ass'n **(222)**
Evangelical Church Library Ass'n **(233)**
Plastic Pipe and Fittings Ass'n **(459)**
Polyurethane Manufacturers Ass'n **(460)**
Water Systems Council **(541)**

Glencoe
American College of Veterinary Radiology **(58)**

Glenview
Academy of Veterinary Allergy and Clinical Immunology **(10)**
Alliance of Business Brokers and Intermediaries **(18)**
American Academy of Pain Medicine **(25)**
American Ass'n of Legal Nurse Consultants **(38)**
American Congress of Rehabilitation Medicine **(59)**
American Pain Soc. **(90)**
American Soc. for Bioethics and Humanities **(101)**
American Soc. of General Surgeons **(110)**
American Soc. of Pediatric Hematology/Oncology **(114)**
Ass'n for Corporate Growth **(132)**
Ass'n of Pediatric Oncology Nurses **(159)**
Ass'n of Rehabilitation Nurses **(163)**
Automotive Booster Clubs Internat'l **(174)**
Equipment and Tool Institute **(232)**
Freestanding Insert Council of North America **(244)**
Nat'l Ass'n for Healthcare Quality **(339)**
Nat'l Ass'n of Clinical Nurse Specialists **(347)**
Nat'l Ass'n of Fleet Resale Dealers **(355)**
Nat'l Interscholastic Swimming Coaches Ass'n **(413)**
Nat'l Luggage Dealers Ass'n **(415)**
Nat'l Registry of Environmental Professionals **(424)**
Retail Confectioners Internat'l **(476)**
Smocking Arts Guild of America **(484)**
Soc. for Health and Human Values **(488)**
Soc. of Automotive Analysts **(498)**
Submersible Wastewater Pump Ass'n **(518)**

Grayslake
Nat'l Congress of Animal Trainers and Breeders **(391)**

Harvard
American Shropshire Registry Ass'n **(100)**

Highland Park
Surface Mount Equipment Manufacturers Ass'n **(519)**

Hillside
Air Distributing Institute **(15)**

Hoffman Estates
Nat'l Ass'n of Fire Investigators **(355)**

National Trade and Professional Associations of the U.S. © 1999, Columbia Books, Inc. 615

Nat'l Soc. to Prevent Blindness/Prevent Blindness
America (430)
Plumbing Manufacturers Institute (459)
Soc. of Actuaries (496)

Schiller Park

American Board of Preventive Medicine (48)

Skokie

Accreditation Ass'n for Ambulatory Health Care (10)
American College of Medicine (55)
American Concrete Pavement Ass'n (59)
American Soc. of Contemporary Ophthalmology (109)
Beverage Network (178)
Casket and Funeral Supply Ass'n of America (187)
Portland Cement Ass'n (460)

Springfield

American Otological Soc. (90)
American Quaternary Ass'n (96)
Ass'n for Surgical Education (138)
Ass'n of Science Museum Directors (164)
Nat'l Ass'n of Special Needs State Administrators (373)
Nat'l Ass'n of State Land Reclamationists (375)
North American Ass'n of Educational Negotiators (440)

St. Charles

Ceilings and Interior Systems Construction Ass'n (189)
Dietary Managers Ass'n (222)
Pickle Packers Internat'l (458)

Stonington

American Oxford Sheep Ass'n (90)

Thornton

Nat'l Ass'n of Industrial and Technical Teacher
Educators (360)

Urbana

Ass'n for Symbolic Logic (138)
Ass'n of Internat'l Agriculture and Rural Development (154)
Conference on College Composition and
Communication (205)
Conference on English Education (205)
Conference on English Leadership (205)
Nat'l Council of Teachers of English (396)
Regional Science Ass'n, Internat'l (473)

Vernon Hills

Ass'n of Legal Administrators (155)
Material Handling Equipment Distributors Ass'n (325)

Warrenville

Railway Supply Ass'n (471)

Wauconda

Aluminum Anodizers Council (19)
Aluminum Extruders Council (19)
Radio Control Hobby Trade Ass'n (471)

Westchester

Healthcare Financial Management Ass'n (252)
Professional Currency Dealers Ass'n (465)

Westmont

Ass'n of Professional Researchers for Advancement (161)
Ass'n of Women Surgeons (169)
Internat'l Ass'n of Ass'n Management Companies (276)
Usability Professionals Ass'n (538)

Wheaton

Alliance of Claims Assistance Professionals (18)
Ass'n of Professors of Mission (162)
Communications Media Management Ass'n (200)
Evangelical Training Ass'n (233)
Nat'l Ass'n of Bond Lawyers (345)
Nat'l Ass'n of Evangelicals (354)

Wheeling

Ass'n for Manufacturing Excellence (136)
Internat'l Council on Education for Teaching (288)

Willowbrook

Vibration Institute (539)

Wilmette

Wirebound Box Manufacturers Ass'n (545)

Winnetka

Internat'l Ass'n of Corporate and Professional
Recruitment (277)
Internat'l Platform Ass'n (300)
Noah Worcester Dermatological Soc. (439)

INDIANA

Anderson

Lipizzan Ass'n of North America (320)

Bedford

Indiana Limestone Institute of America (262)

Bloomington

American Real Estate and Urban Economics Ass'n (97)
Animal Behavior Soc. (124)
Ass'n for Practical and Professional Ethics (136)
Ass'n of College Unions-Internat'l (147)
Ass'n of University Summer Sessions (169)
Aviation Insurance Ass'n (176)
Conference on Asian History (205)
Nat'l Orientation Directors Ass'n (420)
Nat'l Pan Hellenic Council (421)
Organization of American Historians (450)
Phi Delta Kappa (456)
Pi Lambda Theta (458)
Soc. for Ethnomusicology (488)

Carmel

Phi Delta Epsilon Medical Fraternity (456)

Clarks Hill

American Cheviot Sheep Soc. (51)

Elkhart

American Ass'n of Professional Sales Engineers (42)

Evansville

Phi Mu Alpha - Sinfonia (457)
Tobacconists' Ass'n of America (524)

Fort Wayne

Ass'n of Life Insurance Counsel (155)

Franklin

American Safe Deposit Ass'n (98)

Greencastle

Electronics Technicians Ass'n Internat'l (229)
Soc. of Professional Journalists (506)

Greenfield

American Ass'n of Veterinary Parasitologists (45)

Huntington

Soc. for Romanian Studies (493)

Indianapolis

Alpha Chi Sigma (18)
Alpha Kappa Psi (19)
American Academy of Osteopathy (24)
American College of Counselors (53)
American College of Sports Medicine (57)
Ass'n of Academic Physiatrists (141)
Ass'n of Biomedical Communications Directors (144)
Ass'n of Black Foundation Executives (145)
Ass'n of Fraternity Advisors (152)
Ass'n of Osteopathic State Executive Directors (159)
Biomedical Marketing Ass'n (179)
Commercial Food Equipment Service Ass'n (199)
Cranial Academy (218)
Custom Electronic Design and Installation Ass'n (219)
Delta Psi Kappa (221)
Fraternity Executives Ass'n (244)
Insurance Loss Control Ass'n (270)
Interior Design Educators Council (271)
Internat'l Furniture Rental Ass'n (292)
Internat'l Group of Agencies and Bureaus (293)
Internat'l Soc. of Hotel Ass'n Executives (306)
Internat'l Special Events Soc. (307)
Nat'l Alliance of Statewide Preservation Organizations (336)
Nat'l Appliance Service Ass'n (337)
Nat'l Ass'n for Community Leadership (338)
Nat'l Ass'n of Governors' Councils on Physical Fitness and
Sports (357)
Nat'l Ass'n of Mutual Insurance Companies (363)
Nat'l Chimney Sweep Guild (386)
Nat'l Committee on Planned Giving (388)
Nat'l Conference of Regulatory Utility Commission
Engineers (390)
Nat'l Council on Public History (397)
Nat'l Federation of Music Clubs (404)
Nat'l FFA Organization (404)
Nat'l Interfraternity Conference (413)
Nat'l Panhellenic Conference (421)
Nat'l Precast Concrete Ass'n (423)
Nat'l Retail Hardware Ass'n (425)
Phi Epsilon Kappa (457)
Phi Rho Sigma Medical Soc. (457)
Pony of the Americas Club (460)
Professional Fraternity Ass'n (465)
Professional Insurance Communicators of America (466)
Property Casualty Conferences (468)
Religious Conference Management Ass'n (474)
Roller Skating Ass'n Internat'l (477)
Soc. of Broadcast Engineers (499)
Soc. of Roller Skating Teachers of America (507)
Speed Coaches Ass'n (514)

Marion

Nat'l Christian College Athletic Ass'n (387)

Martinsville

American Camping Ass'n (50)

Michigan City

Air Brake Ass'n (15)

American Ass'n of Psychiatric Technicians (42)

Muncie

Ass'n for General and Liberal Studies (133)

Nappanee

Recreational Vehicle Manufacturer's Clubs Ass'n (473)

New Albany

Nat'l Ass'n of Pizza Operators (365)

Noblesville

American Academy of Gold Foil Operators (22)

Plainfield

Ass'n of Muslim Scientists and Engineers (158)
Montadale Sheep Breeders Ass'n (330)

Richmond

Soc. for Phenomenology and Existential Philosophy (492)

Shelburn

Welsh Black Cattle Ass'n (542)

Shelby

Internat'l Buckskin Horse Ass'n (284)

Shelbyville

Spring Research Institute (515)

South Bend

American Wholesale Booksellers Ass'n (123)
Nat'l Catholic Band Ass'n (385)

Speedway

Internat'l Soc. of Cleaning Technicians (306)

Terre Haute

Conference on Faith and History (205)
Independent Laboratory Distributors Ass'n (261)

Valparaiso

Council of Socs. for the Study of Religion (215)
Natural Colored Wool Growers Ass'n (437)
Soc. for Buddhist-Christian Studies (486)

Wabash

Belgian Draft Horse Corp. of America (178)

Warsau

American Ass'n of Nutritional Consultants (40)

West Lafayette

Aerospace Department Chairmen's Ass'n (13)
American Berkshire Ass'n (47)
American Landrace Ass'n (80)
Ass'n for Biology Laboratory Education (130)
Ass'n of American Feed Control Officials (142)
Kappa Delta Pi (315)
Nat'l Ass'n of Swine Records (377)
Nat'l Swine Registry (433)
Soc. for Historians of the Early American Republic (489)
Soc. for the Scientific Study of Religion (495)
Women Band Directors Nat'l Ass'n (545)

Zionsville

American Walnut Manufacturers Ass'n (122)
Walnut Council (540)

IOWA

Ames

American Agricultural Economics Ass'n (27)
American Soc. of Plant Taxonomists (114)
Ass'n of Boards of Certification (145)
Consortium of College and University Media Centers (206)
Council for Agricultural Science and Technology (210)
Nat'l Farmers Organization (402)

Ankeny

Soil and Water Conservation Soc. (510)

Burlington

American Custom Gunmakers Guild (63)

Carroll

American Soc. of Electroneurodiagnostic Technologists (109)

Cedar Rapids

Nat'l Systems Contractors Ass'n (433)

Centerville

American Soc. of Tax Professionals (116)

Charles City

American Cream Draft Horse Ass'n (62)

KANSAS (continued)

Coralville

Billiard Congress of America (178)

Council Bluffs

Sports Turf Contractors Ass'n (515)
Sports Turf Managers Ass'n (515)

Davenport

Council on Chiropractic Physiological Therapeutics and
Rehabilitation (216)

Decorah

Ass'n of Lutheran College Faculties (156)
Nat'l Ballroom and Entertainment Ass'n (382)

Des Moines

American Specialty Toy Retailing Ass'n (117)
Bedding Plants International (177)
Equipment Service Ass'n (232)
Internat'l Ass'n of Lighting Management Companies (280)
Internat'l Ass'n of Milk, Food and Environmental
Sanitarians (281)
Nat'l Ass'n for Family Child Care (339)
Nat'l Ass'n for Independent Living (339)
Nat'l Council of State Pharmacy Ass'n Executives (396)
Nat'l Pork Producers Council (423)
Vacuum Dealers Trade Ass'n (538)

Guttenberg

American School Band Directors' Ass'n (99)

Iowa City

American Soc. of Parasitologists (114)
Ass'n of Otolaryngology Administrators (159)
Clinical Soc. of Genito-Urinary Surgeons (195)
Electrophoresis Soc. (229)
Farm Equipment Wholesalers Ass'n (235)
Internat'l Perimetric Soc. (299)

Madrid

White Park Cattle Ass'n of America (543)

Milo

American Hampshire Sheep Ass'n (71)

Mount Vernon

Concrete Foundations Ass'n (203)
Soc. for the Scientific Study of Sexuality (495)
Tilt-up Concrete Ass'n (523)

Mt. Vernon

American Ass'n of Sex Educators, Counselors and
Therapists (42)

Muscatine

Tread Rubber and Tire Repair Materials Manufacturers
Group (526)

Perry

American Ass'n of Swine Practitioners (43)

Red Oak

Independent Ass'n of Questioned Document Examiners (259)

Sioux Center

Nat'l Ass'n of Regional Media Centers (369)

West Des Moines

KANSAS

Baldwin City

Ass'n for Informal Logic and Critical Thinking (135)

Colby

Groundwater Management Districts Ass'n (250)

Inman

Internat'l Nubian Breeders Ass'n (298)

Kansas City

Internat'l Brotherhood of Boilermakers, Iron Ship Builders,
Blacksmiths, Forgers and Helpers (284)
Nat'l Ass'n of Local Supervisors of Vocational Home
Economics (362)

Lawrence

Accrediting Council on Education in Journalism and Mass
Communications (11)
American Ass'n of Dental Consultants (35)
American Microscopical Soc. (85)
Ass'n of Field Ornithologists (151)
Catecholamine Club (187)
Economic History Ass'n (225)
Golf Course Superintendents Ass'n of America (248)
Internat'l Ass'n of Industrial Accident Boards and
Commissions (280)
Nat'l Frame Builders Ass'n (406)
Nat'l Network of Commercial Real Estate Women (418)
Print Council of America (462)

Soc. for the Study of Evolution (495)
Weed Science Soc. of America (542)
Wildlife Disease Ass'n (544)

Leawood

Ass'n of Operative Millers (159)
Council of Writers Organizations (216)
Internat'l Ass'n of Plastics Distributors (281)

Lenexa

American Ass'n of Code Enforcement (34)
American Soc. for Histocompatability and
Immunogenetics (103)
Ass'n of Genetic Technologists (152)
Ass'n of Polysomnographic Technologists (160)
Nat'l Ass'n of EMS Physicians (353)
Nat'l Cancer Registrar's Ass'n (385)
North American Transplant Coordinators Organization (445)
Transportation Lawyers Ass'n (525)
World Waterpark Ass'n (550)

Manhattan

Engineering College Magazines Associated (230)
Intercollegiate Men's Choruses, an Internat'l Ass'n of Male
Choruses (271)
Internat'l Ass'n of Jazz Educators (280)
Journalism Education Ass'n (315)
Nat'l Academic Advising Ass'n (333)
World War Two Studies Ass'n (550)

Mission

Agricultural and Industrial Manufacturers' Representatives
Ass'n (14)
Independent Medical Distributors Ass'n (261)
Internat'l Ass'n of Insurance Receivers (280)
Investment Recovery Ass'n (312)
Nat'l Soc. of Insurance Premium Auditors (430)
Nat'l Soccer Coaches Ass'n of America (430)
Professional Soccer Reporters Ass'n (467)

Newton

Midwives Alliance of North America (328)

Oskaloosa

American Ass'n of Industrial Veterinarians (38)

Overland Park

Agriculture Council of America (15)
American Alfalfa Processors Ass'n (27)
American Ass'n for Paralegal Education (31)
American Medical Soc. for Sports Medicine (84)
Ass'n of Collegiate Business Schools and Programs (148)
Auction Marketing Institute (172)
Autobody Representatives Council (173)
Commerical Real Estate Secondary Market and Securitization
Ass'n (199)
Council for Learning Disabilities (211)
Crop Insurance Research Bureau (219)
Internat'l Listening Ass'n (296)
Nat'l Ass'n of Basketball Coaches (344)
Nat'l Auctioneers Ass'n (381)
Nat'l Collegiate Athletic Ass'n (388)
Nat'l Crop Insurance Services (398)
Paint, Body and Equipment Ass'n (452)

Prairie Village

Allied Trades of the Baking Industry (18)
American Academy of Addiction Psychiatry (20)
Ass'n of Records Managers and Administrators (163)
Institute of Certified Records Managers (266)

Shawnee Mission

Internat'l Clarinet Ass'n (285)
Internat'l College of Applied Kinesiology (286)
Nat'l Agri-Marketing Ass'n (335)

Spring Hill

Ankole Watusi Internat'l Registry (125)

Topeka

American Ass'n of Zoo Keepers (45)
American Veterinary Exhibitors Ass'n (121)
Ass'n of State and Territorial Directors of Nursing (166)
Bath Enclosure Manufacturers Ass'n (177)
Glass Ass'n of North America (247)
Glazing Industry Code Committee (248)
Laminators Safety Glass Ass'n (317)
Nat'l Ass'n of Trailer Manufacturers (379)
Nat'l Soc. of Architectural Engineers (429)
Nat'l Sunroom Ass'n (432)
North American Ass'n of Mirror Manufacturers (440)
Primary Glass Manufacturers Council (462)

Walton

American Internat'l Marchigiana Soc. (79)

Wichita

Advertising and Marketing Internat'l Network (12)
Nat'l Ass'n of Educational Office Professionals (353)
Nat'l Ass'n of Leagues, Umpires and Scorers (361)
Soc. of Decorative Painters (500)
United States Court Reporters Ass'n (533)

KENTUCKY

Bowling Green

Livestock Conservation Institute (320)

Burlington

Nat'l Ass'n of Family and Community Education (354)

Butler

Professional Paddlesports Ass'n (466)

Covington

Retail Packaging Manufacturers Ass'n (476)

Frankfort

Conference of Radiation Control Program Directors (204)
Council of 1890 College Presidents and Chancellors (212)
Internat'l Ass'n of Personnel in Employment Security (281)
Nat'l Ass'n of Disability Examiners (353)
Nat'l Conference of State Social Security Administrators (391)

Glasgow

Commercial Travelers Ass'n (199)

Lexington

American Ass'n of Equine Practitioners (36)
American Farriers Ass'n (66)
American Hackney Horse Soc. (71)
American Hanoverian Soc. (71)
American Probation and Parole Ass'n (94)
American Saddlebred Horse Ass'n (98)
American Soc. for Surface Mining and Reclamation (105)
Asphalt Institute (128)
Ass'n of American Plant Food Control Officials (143)
Ass'n of Caribbean Studies (146)
Ass'n of College and University Telecommunications
Administrators (147)
Ass'n of Racing Commissioners Internat'l (162)
Ass'n of Retail Travel Agents (163)
Ass'n of State Dam Safety Officials (166)
Ass'n Retail Travel Agents (170)
Automotive Occupant Restraints Council (174)
Burley Auction Warehouse Ass'n (184)
Burley Tobacco Growers Cooperative Ass'n (184)
Chief Officers of State Library Agencies (192)
College Savings Plans Network (198)
Council of State Governments (216)
Council on Licensure, Enforcement and Regulation (217)
Imaging Supplies Coalition for Internat'l Intellectual Property
Protection (259)
Internat'l Spa and Fitness Ass'n (307)
Jockeys' Guild (315)
Nat'l Ass'n for Government Training and Development (339)
Nat'l Ass'n of Government Deferred Compensation
Administrators (356)
Nat'l Ass'n of Secretaries of State (372)
Nat'l Ass'n of State Auditors, Comptrollers and
Treasurers (374)
Nat'l Ass'n of State Boating Law Administrators (374)
Nat'l Ass'n of State Directors of Administration and General
Services (374)
Nat'l Ass'n of State Facilities Administrators (375)
Nat'l Ass'n of State Information Resource Executives (375)
Nat'l Ass'n of State Personnel Executives (376)
Nat'l Ass'n of State Purchasing Officials (376)
Nat'l Ass'n of State Telecommunications Directors (376)
Nat'l Ass'n of State Treasurers (376)
Nat'l Conference of Lieutenant Governors (390)
Nat'l Emergency Management Ass'n (401)
Nat'l Tour Ass'n (434)
North American Trakehner Ass'n (445)
Soc. for Natural Philosophy (491)
Soc. of Pelvic Surgeons (505)
State Debt Management Network (516)
Thoroughbred Club of America (522)
Thoroughbred Owners and Breeders Ass'n (523)
United Professional Horsemen's Ass'n (531)

Louisville

American Academy of Crisis Interveners (21)
American Ass'n of Philosophy Teachers (40)
Ass'n of Health Occupations Teacher Educators (153)
Ass'n of Presbyterian Colleges and Universities (160)
Associated Cooperage Industries of America (171)
Distillers Grains Technology Council (223)
Foodservice Consultants Soc. Internat'l (242)
Internat'l Ass'n of Culinary Professionals (278)
Internat'l Inflight Food Service Ass'n (294)
Internat'l Tire and Rubber Ass'n (309)
Nat'l Ass'n of Academic Advisors for Athletes (342)
Nat'l Police Officers Ass'n of America (422)
Nat'l Show Horse Registry (428)
Nat'l Turf Writers Ass'n (435)
Presbyterian Health, Education and Welfare Ass'n (462)
Railway Systems Suppliers, Inc. (471)
Soc. for Foodservice Management (488)
Uniform Boiler and Pressure Vessel Laws Soc. (529)
United Thoroughbred Trainers of America (536)
Women Chefs and Restaurateurs (545)

Middletown

American Institute of Commemorative Art (77)

Morehead

Nat'l Ass'n of African American Studies (342)
Nat'l Ass'n of Hispanic and Latino Studies (358)

Owensboro

Internat'l Bluegrass Music Ass'n (283)
Nat'l Ass'n of Video Distributors (379)

Richmond

Nat'l Ass'n of Institutional Linen Management (360)
Nat'l Juvenile Detention Ass'n (413)

Versailles

Nat'l Conference of State Fleet Administrators (391)

Whitesburg

Ass'n for Independent Music (134)

LOUISIANA

Baton Rouge

American Canine Sports Medicine Ass'n (50)
American College of Veterinary Ophthalmologists (58)
Food Distribution Research Soc. (241)
Nat'l Ass'n of Black Consulting Engineers (344)
Soc. for Social Studies of Science (494)
World Aquaculture Soc. (549)

Bunkie

Devon Cattle Ass'n (222)

Harahan

Offshore Marine Service Ass'n (447)

Kenner

American Guild of Hypnotherapists (71)
Southern Forest Products Ass'n (510)

Lafayette

Internat'l Ass'n of Astacology (276)
Internat'l Ass'n of Sports Museums and Halls of Fame (282)

Lake Charles

American Mosquito Control Ass'n (85)

Metairie

Contact Lens Ass'n of Ophthalmologists (207)

Monroe

American Council for Construction Education (61)

New Orleans

African American Travel and Tourism Ass'n (14)
American Recovery Ass'n (97)
American Shrimp Processors Ass'n (100)
Ass'n of Public Data Users (162)
Intercoiffure America (271)
Internat'l Fire Photographers Ass'n (291)
Mycological Soc. of America (332)
Nat'l Ass'n for Black Geologists and Geophysicists (338)
Nat'l Ass'n of Substance Abuse Trainers and Educators (377)
Nat'l Black American Paralegal Ass'n (383)

River Ridge

Black Coaches Ass'n (180)

Ruston

Ass'n for Social Economics (137)

Shreveport

American Rhinologic Soc. (98)
Nat'l Ass'n of Pipe Coating Applicators (365)

Slidell

Nat'l Taxidermists Ass'n (433)
Nursing Touch and Massage Therapy Ass'n Internat'l (447)

Thibodaux

American Sugar Cane League of the U.S.A. (119)

MAINE

Augusta

Bar Harbor

Soc. for Human Ecology (489)
Wild Blueberry Ass'n of North America (544)

Orono

Potato Ass'n of America (461)

Owls Head

Nursery Ass'n Executives of North America (447)

Scarborough

Nat'l Ass'n of School Nurses (371)

Unity

Science Fiction and Fantasy Writers of America (479)

York Harbor

Nat'l Remotivation Therapy Organization (425)

MARYLAND

Adelphia

Nat'l Ass'n of Black Journalists (345)

Annapolis

Airlines Electronic Engineering Committee (16)
American Academy of Environmental Engineers (21)
American Blood Resources Ass'n (47)
Apiary Inspectors of America (125)
Asphalt Emulsion Manufacturers Ass'n (128)
Asphalt Recycling and Reclaiming Ass'n (129)
Ass'n for Recorded Sound Collections (137)
Independent Sealing Distributors (261)
Internat'l Masonry Institute (297)
Internat'l Plasma Products Industry Ass'n (300)
Internat'l Regional Magazine Ass'n (301)
Nat'l Aerosol Ass'n (335)
Nat'l Ass'n of Hose and Accessories Distributors (358)
Nat'l Ass'n of Jewelry Appraisers (361)
Nat'l Ass'n of State Administrators and Supervisors of Private Schools (373)
Yacht Architects and Brokers Ass'n (551)

Annapolis Junction

Ass'n of Specialists in Cleaning and Restoration Internat'l (165)

Arnold

Ass'n for Women in Communications (140)
Building Owners and Managers Institute Internat'l (183)
Soc. for Applied Sociology (485)
Sociological Practice Ass'n (509)

Aspen Hill

American Dental Interfraternity Council (64)

Baltimore

Accountants for the Public Interest (10)
Alpha Omega Internat'l Dental Fraternity (19)
American Institute of Floral Designers (77)
American Urological Ass'n (121)
Ass'n for Persons with Severe Handicaps, The (136)
Ass'n for the Advancement of Wound Care (139)
Ass'n of Oncology Social Work (159)
Ass'n of SIDS and Infant Mortality Programs (165)
Ass'n of Small Research, Engineering and Technical Service Companies (165)
Black Broadcasters Alliance (180)
Correctional Industries Ass'n (210)
Electrical-Electronics Materials Distributors Ass'n (227)
Fire Suppression Systems Ass'n (240)
Industrial Union of Marine and Shipbuilding Workers of America (263)
Internat'l Alliance: An Ass'n of Executive and Professional Women, The (273)
Internat'l Ass'n of Special Investigation Units (282)
Internat'l Dyslexia Ass'n (289)
Internat'l Soc. for Plastination (304)
Internat'l Soc. for Third-Sector Research (305)
Internat'l Trauma Anesthesia and Critical Care Soc. (309)
Lacrosse USA (316)
League of Historic American Theatres (318)
Nat'l Ass'n of Sign Supply Distributors (373)
Nat'l Finance Adjusters (404)
Office Products Wholesalers Ass'n (447)
Pet Industry Distributors Ass'n (455)
Post Card Distributors Ass'n of North America (461)
Retail Tobacco Dealers of America (476)
Safety Equipment Distributors Ass'n (478)
Shoe Service Institute of America (483)
Soc. for Chaos Theory in Psychology and Life Sciences (486)
Soc. for Clinical Trials (486)
Soc. for Epidemiologic Research (487)
Soc. for the Advancement of Socio-Economics (495)
Synthetic Amorphous Silica and Silicates Industry Ass'n (519)
Truck Writers of North America (527)
Used Truck Ass'n (538)
Woodworking Machinery Industry Ass'n (549)

Bel Air

American Holistic Veterinary Medical Ass'n (74)

Beltsville

Ass'n of Official Seed Certifying Agencies (158)
Council for Near-Infrared Spectroscopy (212)
Council on Botanical and Horticultural Libraries (216)
World's Poultry Science Ass'n, U.S.A. Branch (550)

Berlin

Apparel Graphics Institute (126)

Bethesda

Adhesive and Sealant Council (12)
Agricultural Research Institute (14)
American Ass'n for Geriatric Psychiatry (30)
American Ass'n of Anatomists (33)
American Ass'n of Bank Directors (33)
American Ass'n of Blood Banks (33)
American Ass'n of Immunologists (38)
American Ass'n of Limited Partners (38)
American Board of Nursing Specialties (48)
American College of Cardiology (53)

American College of Medical Quality (55)
American College of Osteopathic Internists (56)
American College of Toxicology (58)
American College of Veterinary Surgeons (58)
American Congress on Surveying and Mapping (60)
American Fisheries Soc. (68)
American Gastroenterological Ass'n (70)
American Hungarian Educators Ass'n (74)
American In-vitro Allergy/Immunology Soc. (75)
American Medical Informatics Ass'n (84)
American Medical Writers Ass'n (84)
American Nat'l Metric Council (86)
American Occupational Therapy Ass'n (88)
American Physiological Soc. (92)
American Podiatric Medical Ass'n (93)
American Podiatric Medical Students' Ass'n (93)
American Soc. for Biochemistry and Molecular Biology (101)
American Soc. for Cell Biology (101)
American Soc. for Clinical Laboratory Science (101)
American Soc. for Clinical Nutrition (101)
American Soc. for Investigative Pathology (103)
American Soc. for Nutritional Sciences (104)
American Soc. for Pharmacology and Experimental Therapeutics (104)
American Soc. for Photogrammetry and Remote Sensing (104)
American Soc. of Health-System Pharmacists (110)
American Soc. of Human Genetics (111)
American Soc. of Nuclear Cardiology (113)
Ass'n for Molecular Pathology (136)
Ass'n for Research in Vision and Ophthalmology (137)
Ass'n of Biomolecular Resource Facilities (144)
Ass'n of Chiropractic Colleges (146)
Ass'n of Military Surgeons of the U.S. (157)
Ass'n of Pathology Chairs (159)
Ass'n of Professors of Cardiology (161)
Associated Specialty Contractors (172)
Automotive Parts and Accessories Ass'n (175)
Biophysical Soc. (179)
Center for Exhibition Industry Research (189)
Chief Executives Organization (191)
Commercial Vehicle Safety Alliance (199)
Composting Council (202)
Computer-based Patient Record Institute (203)
Contact Lens Manufacturers Ass'n (207)
Cystic Fibrosis Foundation (219)
Endocrine Soc. (230)
Environmental Information Ass'n (231)
Federation of American Socs. for Experimental Biology (236)
Forum for Investor Advice (243)
Genetics Soc. of America (246)
Healthcare Billing and Management Ass'n (252)
Internat'l Ass'n of Boards of Examiners in Optometry (276)
Internat'l Ass'n of Cold Storage Contractors (277)
Internat'l Ass'n of Refrigerated Warehouses (282)
Internat'l Hand Protection Ass'n (293)
Internat'l Health Evaluation Ass'n (293)
Internat'l Kitchen Exhaust Cleaning Ass'n (295)
Internat'l Pension and Employee Benefits Lawyers Ass'n (299)
Internat'l Truck Parts Ass'n (309)
Intersociety Committee on Pathology Information (311)
Medical-Dental-Hospital Business Associates (326)
Nat'l Ass'n for Proton Therapy (340)
Nat'l Ass'n for Senior Living Industries (341)
Nat'l Ass'n of Beverage Retailers (344)
Nat'l Ass'n of Hospital Hospitality Houses (358)
Nat'l Ass'n of School Psychologists (371)
Nat'l Ass'n of Veterans' Research and Education Foundations (379)
Nat'l Burglar and Fire Alarm Ass'n (384)
Nat'l Council on Radiation Protection and Measurements (398)
Nat'l Electrical Contractors Ass'n (400)
Nat'l Information Standards Organization (411)
Nat'l Soc. of Professional Surveyors (430)
Nat'l Subacute Care Ass'n (432)
North American Skull Base Soc. (444)
Parenteral Drug Ass'n (453)
Portable Power Equipment Manufacturers Ass'n (460)
Professional Insurance Mass-Marketing Ass'n (466)
Protein Soc. (469)
Renewable Natural Resources Foundation (475)
Retirement Industry Trust Ass'n (476)
RNA Soc. (476)
Secondary Materials and Recycled Textiles Ass'n (480)
Small Business Council of America (483)
Soc. for Cryobiology (487)
Soc. for Developmental Biology (487)
Soc. for Leukocyte Biology (490)
Soc. for Nutrition Education (491)
Soc. of American Foresters (497)
Soc. of Eye Surgeons (501)
Soc. of Fire Protection Engineers (501)
Soc. of Travel Agents in Government (508)
Treasury Management Ass'n (526)
Universities Associated for Research and Education in Pathology (536)
Wildlife Soc., The (544)
World Future Soc. (550)

Bowie

Nat'l Soc. for Histotechnology (429)

Buckeystown

American Genetic Ass'n (70)

Cabin John

Internat'l Hydrofoil Soc. (294)

Calverton

Asphalt Roofing Manufacturers Ass'n (129)
Nat'l Industrial Sand Ass'n (411)

Internat'l Federation of Professional and Technical
Engineers (291)
Laboratory Animal Management Ass'n (316)
Museum Computer Network (332)
Nat'l Aggregates Ass'n (335)
Nat'l Ass'n for Equal Opportunity in Higher Education (339)
Nat'l Ass'n for Practical Nurse Education and Service (340)
Nat'l Ass'n for Treasurers of Religious Institutes (342)
Nat'l Ass'n of Commissions for Women (349)
Nat'l Ass'n of Health Services Executives (357)
Nat'l Ass'n of State Aviation Officials (374)
Nat'l Ass'n of Women Business Owners (380)
Nat'l Board for Certified Clinical Hypnotherapists (383)
Nat'l Coalition of Black Meeting Planners (387)
Nat'l Foundation for Consumer Credit (405)
Nat'l Ready Mixed Concrete Ass'n (424)
Nat'l School Supply and Equipment Ass'n (427)
Nat'l Spinal Cord Injury Ass'n (431)
Population Ass'n of America (460)
Professional Handlers Ass'n (466)
Registry of Interpreters for the Deaf (473)
Solid Waste Ass'n of North America (510)
SWANA - Solid Waste Ass'n of North America (519)
Truck Mixer Manufacturers Bureau (527)

Solomons
Internat'l Soc. for Ecological Economics (303)

St. Leonard
Nat'l Shellfisheries Ass'n (427)

St. Michaels
Council of American Maritime Museums (212)

Takoma Park
Ass'n of Seventh-Day Adventist Librarians (165)

Temple Hills
Air Force Sergeants Ass'n (15)

Thurmont
Nat'l Ornamental Goldfish Growers Ass'n (420)

Timonium
Nat'l Metal Decorators Ass'n (417)

Towson
American Soc. of Trial Consultants (116)

Upper Marlboro
American Trauma Soc. (121)
Internat'l Ass'n of Machinists and Aerospace Workers (280)
Nat'l Ass'n of Women Highway Safety Leaders (380)
Soc. for In Vitro Biology (489)

West Bethesda
Council on Fine Art Photography (216)

Wheaton
American Soc. of Professional Estimators (115)
Nat'l Ass'n of Air Traffic Specialists (343)
Tile Contractors' Ass'n of America (523)

White Plains
Internat'l Beverage Dispensing Equipment Ass'n (283)

MASSACHUSETTS

Abington
Nat'l Shoe Travelers Ass'n (428)

Amherst
Ass'n for the Environmental Health of Soils (139)
Human Biology Ass'n (257)
Internat'l Institute of Forecasters (294)
Law and Society Ass'n (318)
Nat'l Institutes for Water Resources (412)

Bedford
Nat'l Ass'n of State Directors of Teacher Education and
Certification (375)

Belmont
Ethics Officer Ass'n (233)
Nat'l Ass'n for Armenian Studies and Research (337)

Boston
American Flock Ass'n (68)
American Legal Studies Ass'n (81)
American Meteorological Soc. (84)
American Schools of Oriental Research (99)
American Soc. of Law, Medicine and Ethics (112)
Applied Research Ethics Nat'l Ass'n (126)
Archaeological Institute of America (126)
Art and Creative Materials Institute (127)
Ass'n for Work Process Improvement (141)
Ass'n of Architectural Librarians (143)
Cashmere and Camel Hair Manufacturers Institute (187)
Council for Art Education (211)
Design Management Institute (222)
Family Firm Institute (234)
Institute for Business and Home Safety (265)

Internat'l Health, Racquet and Sportsclub Ass'n (293)
Internat'l Museum Theater Alliance (298)
Internat'l Security Management Ass'n (302)
Internat'l Soc. for Infectious Diseases (303)
Nat'l Ass'n of Consumer Advocates (349)
Nat'l Ass'n of Pupil Services Administrators (368)
Nat'l Ass'n of State Archaeologists (373)
North American Soc. for the Sociology of Sport (445)
Northern Textile Ass'n (446)
Radio Talk Show Hosts Ass'n (471)
Soc. of University Otolaryngologists (508)
Visiting Nurse Ass'ns of America (540)
Women's Transportation Seminar (548)

Brighton
Nat'l Tay-Sachs and Allied Diseases Ass'n (433)

Brookline
American Soc. of Psychopathology of Expression (115)
Institute on Religion in an Age of Science (269)

Burlington
American Academy of Arts and Sciences (20)
American Academy of Health Care Providers in the Addictive
Disorders (22)
American Ass'n for the Advancement of Slavic Studies (32)
American Ass'n of Variable Star Observers (44)
Freelance Editorial Ass'n (244)
Intravenous Nurses Soc. (312)
Jean Piaget Soc./Soc. for the Study of Knowledge and
Development (313)
Medieval Academy of America (326)

Canton
Music Library Ass'n (332)

Chelmsford
Advanced Transit Ass'n (12)

Chestnut Hill
Professional Squash Ass'n (467)
Soc. for Italian Historical Studies (490)

Chicopee
Nat'l Ass'n of Power Engineers (365)

Concord
Hospital Presidents Ass'n (256)
Nat'l Coalition of Girls Schools (387)

East Boston
Internat'l Union of Journeymen Horseshoers of the United
States and Canada (310)

East Bridgewater
Brotherhood of Shoe and Allied Craftsmen (183)

Framingham
Nat'l Ass'n of Rehabilitation Professionals in the Private
Sector (369)
Soc. of Independent Show Organizers (503)

Gardner
Nat'l Furniture Traffic Conference (406)

Gloucester
American Hockey Coaches Ass'n (73)
Associated Pipe Organ Builders of America (172)

Greenfield
Organic Trade Ass'n (449)

Groton
American Loudspeaker Manufacturers Ass'n (82)

Hingham
Cordage Institute (209)
Internat'l Marine Transit Ass'n (297)

Lexington
Academy of Family Mediators (8)

Lowell
Music and Entertainment Industry Educators Ass'n (332)

Ludlow
American Academy of Medical Hypnoanalysts (23)

Lynn
Jewish Funeral Directors of America (314)

Lynnfield
Fire Apparatus Manufacturers Ass'n (239)

Malden
American Finance Ass'n (68)

Manchester
American Ass'n for Thoracic Surgery (32)
American Pediatric Surgical Ass'n (91)
American Soc. for Gastrointestinal Endoscopy (102)
American Surgical Ass'n (119)
American Venous Forum (121)
Ass'n for Academic Surgery (129)
Internat'l Soc. for Cardiovascular Surgery - North American
Chapter (303)
Soc. for Clinical Vascular Surgery (486)
Soc. for Vascular Medicine and Biology (496)
Soc. for Vascular Surgery (496)

Medway
Nat'l Ass'n of Radio and Telecommunications Engineers (368)

Melrose
American Soc. of Abdominal Surgeons (106)

Mendon
American Poultry Ass'n (93)

Natick
North American Soc. of Pacing and Electrophysiology (445)

Needham
WACRA - World Ass'n for Case Method Research &
Application (540)

Needham Heights
Single Ply Roofing Institute (483)

Newtonville
Medical Records Institute (326)

North Andover
Affiliated Conference of Practicing Accountants Internat'l (13)

North Dartmouth
Nat'l Ass'n of Textile Supervisors (378)

Northampton
American Men's Studies Ass'n (84)

Peabody
Internat'l Soc. of Facilities Executives (306)

Petersham
Office Furniture Distribution Ass'n (447)

Pittsfield
Catholic Library Ass'n (188)

Plympton
American Cotswold Record Ass'n (60)

Quincy
Ass'n of Smoked Fish Processors (165)
Fire Marshals Ass'n of North America (239)
Nat'l Fire Protection Ass'n (404)

Rowley
Early Sites Research Soc. (225)

Salem
Newspaper Ass'n Managers (439)

Sherborn
PCPCI - The Transformer Ass'n (454)
Small Motors and Motion Ass'n (484)

Somerville
Scuba Retailers Ass'n (480)

South Easton
Plumbing and Drainage Institute (459)

South Yarmouth
Insulated Cable Engineers Ass'n (270)

Springfield
American Ass'n of Industrial Management (38)

Stow
Internat'l Electrology Educators (289)
Soc. of Clinical and Medical Electrologists (499)

Sudbury
American Healthcare Radiology Administrators (72)
Computer Event Marketing Ass'n (202)

Topsfield
Internat'l Desalination Ass'n (288)

Walpole
Federation of Insurance and Corporate Counsel (237)

Waltham

American Jewish Historical Soc. (80)
Ass'n for Jewish Studies (135)

Wareham

Cranberry Institute (218)

Watertown

Software Operations Ass'n (509)

Wellesley

Book Manufacturers Institute (181)
Institute of Certified Travel Agents (266)

Wellesley Hills

American Lithotripsy Soc. (81)
Nat'l Investment Company Service Ass'n (413)

West Springfield

American Hockey League (73)

Westfield

American Registry of Medical Assistants (97)
Soc. of Philosophers in America (505)

Westminster

Wood Products Manufacturers Ass'n (548)

Wilmington

Internat'l Ass'n for Modular Exhibitry (274)

Woburn

Nat'l Lead Burning Ass'n (414)

Woods Hole

Soc. of General Physiologists (502)

Worcester

American Antiquarian Soc. (28)
American Soc. for Political and Legal Philosophy (104)
Orthodox Theological Soc. in America (451)

Wrentham

Ass'n of Directory Publishers (149)

MICHIGAN

Adrian

Professional Travelogue Sponsors (467)

Allegan

American Beefalo World Registry (47)

Alpena

Lambda Kappa Sigma (317)

Ann Arbor

American Ass'n for Public Opinion Research (31)
American Oriental Soc. (88)
Ass'n for Asian Studies (130)
Athletic Equipment Managers Ass'n (172)
Automated Imaging Ass'n (173)
Automation Technologies Council (174)
Chinese-American Librarians Ass'n (192)
Cognitive Science Soc. (196)
Construction Industry Sales (206)
Internat'l Soc. of Barristers (305)
Nat'l Ass'n of Industrial Technology (360)
Nat'l Economic Ass'n (400)
Soc. for College and University Planning (486)
Soc. for Research in Child Development (493)
Soc. for the Psychological Study of Social Issues (495)
Soc. of Systematic Biologists (507)
Social Science History Ass'n (509)

Battle Creek

Children's Literature Ass'n (192)

Benton Harbor

Ass'n of Statisticians of American Religious Bodies (166)

Big Rapids

American Soc. of Pharmacognosy (114)

Bloomfield Hills

Internat'l Hockey League (293)

Boyne City

Soc. of Small Craft Designers (507)

Crystal Falls

Nat'l Ass'n of County Health Facility Administrators (351)

Dearborn

Ass'n for Electronics Manufacturing of SME (133)
Ass'n for Finishing Processes of SME (133)
Ass'n for Forming and Fabricating Technologies of SME (133)

Ass'n of Cosmetologists and Hairdressers (149)
Composites Manufacturing Ass'n of SME (202)
Computer and Automated Systems Ass'n of SME (202)
Conservative Orthopedics Internat'l Ass'n (206)
Industrial Chemical Research Ass'n (262)
Machine Vision Ass'n of SME (321)
Machining Technology Ass'n of SME (321)
North American Manufacturing Research Institution of
    SME (443)
Rapid Prototyping Ass'n of SME (472)
Robotics Internat'l of SME (477)
Soc. of Armenian Studies (498)
Soc. of Manufacturing Engineers (503)

Detroit

American Academy of Tropical Medicine (26)
Ass'n for Business Simulation and Experiential Learning (130)
Ass'n of Analytical Chemists (143)
Ass'n of Black Sociologists (145)
Internat'l Union, United Automobile, Aerospace and
    Agricultural Implement Workers of America (310)
Nat'l Ass'n for the Advancement of Black Americans in
    Vocational Education (341)
Nat'l Ass'n of Black Social Workers (345)
Nat'l Automobile Transporters Ass'n (381)
Spill Control Ass'n of America (514)

East Lansing

Ass'n of College Honor Societies (147)
Institute of Public Utilities (268)
Internat'l Safe Transit Ass'n (302)
Nat'l Ass'n of College and University Food Services (348)
Philosophy of Education Soc. (457)
World Ass'n for Infant Mental Health (549)

Farmington Hills

American College of Neuropsychiatrists (55)
American Concrete Institute (59)
American Soc. of Concrete Contractors (108)
Nat'l Truck Equipment Ass'n (434)
Soc. for Humanistic Judaism (489)

Flint

Ass'n of Women Soil Scientists (169)
Internat'l Physical Fitness Ass'n (299)

Gaylord

Ass'n of Alternate Postal Systems (142)

Grand Blanc

Nat'l Ass'n of Legal Investigators (361)

Grand Haven

Materials and Methods Standards Ass'n (325)

Grand Rapids

Business and Institutional Furniture Manufacturers Ass'n
    Internat'l (184)
Christian Schools Internat'l (193)
Nat'l Ass'n of Nutrition and Aging Services Programs (364)
Soc. of Christian Philosophers (499)

Harper Woods

Internat'l Soc. of Travel and Tourism Educators (307)

Haslett

Internat'l Snowmobile Manufacturers Ass'n (302)
Roses Incorporated (477)

Houghton

Mineral Economics and Management Soc. (329)
Soc. for Industrial Archeology (490)

Huntington Woods

Academy of Laser Dentistry (8)

Jackson

Ass'n of Professional Color Imagers (161)
Nat'l Ass'n of Photo Equipment Technicians (365)
Photo Marketing Ass'n-Internat'l (457)

Kalamazoo

American Chiropractic Registry of Radiologic
    Technologists (51)
Ass'n for Behavior Analysis (130)
Chinese Language Teachers Ass'n (192)
Internat'l Ass'n of Trichologists (283)
Internat'l Trumpet Guild (309)
Soc. for the Advancement of Behavior Analysis (494)

Lansing

American Academy of Industrial Hygiene (23)
American Board of Industrial Hygiene (47)
Cherry Marketing Institute (191)
Environmental Management Ass'n (232)
Nat'l Ass'n of Agricultural Fair Agencies (343)
Soc. for Academic Emergency Medicine (484)

Livonia

FTD Ass'n (244)
Internat'l Hearing Soc. (293)

Marquette

Soc. for the History of Discoveries (495)

Marshall

Independent Innkeepers Ass'n (260)

Mt. Pleasant

American Baseball Coaches Ass'n (46)

Novi

Chain Drug Marketing Ass'n (190)

Parma

American Ass'n of Direct Human Service Personnel (36)

Plainwell

Ass'n of Rehabilitation Programs in Computer
    Technology (163)

Pontiac

American College of Osteopathic Obstetricians and
    Gynecologists (56)
American Court and Commercial Newspapers (62)

Roseville

Industrial Mathematics Soc. (263)
Internat'l Union, United Plant Guard Workers of America (310)

Sault Ste. Marie

Ass'n for Politics and the Life Sciences (136)

Southfield

American Academy of Medical Administrators (23)
American Ass'n of Handwriting Analysts (37)
American College of Cardiovascular Administrators (53)
American College of Healthcare Information
    Administrators (54)
American College of Managed Care Administrators (55)
Automotive Industry Action Group (174)
Brotherhood of Maintenance of Way Employees (182)

St. Clair Shores

Nat'l Ass'n of Resale and Thrift Shops (370)

St. Joseph

American Soc. of Agricultural Engineers (106)

Sterling Heights

Soc. for Women in Plastics (496)

Troy

Original Equipment Suppliers Association - MEMA (450)
Professional Sales Ass'n (467)

University Center

American Council of Nanny Schools (61)

Wayne

Clinical Ligand Assay Soc. (195)

Ypsilanti

Ass'n of Teachers of Technical Writing (167)

Zeeland

Christian Labor Ass'n of the United States of America (193)

MINNESOTA

Alexandria

Ass'n of Construction Inspectors (148)
Internat'l Real Estate Institute (301)
Internat'l Travel Writers and Editors Ass'n (309)
Nat'l Ass'n of Real Estate Appraisers (368)
Nat'l Ass'n of Review Appraisers and Mortgage
    Underwriters (370)
Professional Women's Appraisal Ass'n (468)

Battle Lake

Epsilon Sigma Phi (232)

Bemidji

Ass'n of Camp Nurses (145)
Ornamental Concrete Producers Ass'n (451)

Bloomington

Ass'n of Professional Directors of YMCAs in the United
    States (161)
Internat'l League of Electrical Ass'ns (296)
Portable Sanitation Ass'n Internat'l (460)
Public Golf Management Ass'n (469)

Brooklyn Park

Organic Growers and Buyers Ass'n (449)

Duluth

Community Development Venture Capital Ass'n (201)
North American Canon Law Soc. (441)

Eagan

American Ass'n for Applied Linguistics (29)
Emerald Green Miniature Golf Ass'n (229)

Eden Prairie

American Railway Development Ass'n (97)

Edina

Internat'l Prepress Ass'n (300)
Library Binding Institute (319)
Surface Mount Technology Ass'n (519)

Jordan

Pyrotechnics Guild Internat'l (470)

Mendota Heights

Internat'l Ass'n for Identification (274)

Minneapolis

Academy of Rehabilitative Audiology (10)
American Ass'n of Neuropathologists (39)
American Collectors Ass'n (52)
American Correctional Food Service Ass'n (60)
American Federation of Grain Millers Internat'l Union (67)
American Neurological Ass'n (87)
American Oat Ass'n (87)
American Soc. of Neuroimaging (113)
American Underground-Construction Ass'n (121)
Archivists and Librarians in the History of the Health Sciences (127)
Ass'n of Booksellers for Children (145)
Associated Collegiate Press, Nat'l Scholastic Press Ass'n (171)
Captive Insurance Companies Ass'n (186)
Grain Elevator and Processing Soc. (249)
Internat'l Academy of Trial Lawyers (272)
Internat'l Ass'n of Printing House Craftsmen (282)
Internat'l Childbirth Education Ass'n (285)
Internat'l Petroleum Credit Ass'n (299)
Lutheran Church Library Ass'n (321)
Nat'l Ass'n For Ambulatory Care (337)
Nat'l Ass'n of Fund Raising Ticket Manufacturers (356)
Nat'l Ass'n of Home Inspectors (358)
Nat'l Ass'n of Independent Insurance Auditors and Engineers (359)
Nat'l Council on Family Relations (397)
Nat'l Dance-Exercise Instructor's Training Ass'n (399)
Nat'l Mail Order Ass'n (416)
Nat'l Marrow Donor Program (416)
Nat'l Movement Theatre Ass'n (417)
Nat'l Risk Retention Ass'n (426)
North American Soc. of Teachers of the Alexander Technique (445)
Outdoor Amusement Business Ass'n (451)
Professional Liability Underwriting Soc. (466)
Residential Space Planners Internat'l (475)
Soc. for Biomaterials (485)
Soc. of Dance History Scholars (500)
Training Directors' Forum (525)

Minnetonka

Internat'l Ceramic Ass'n (285)

Monticello

Internat'l Guards Union of America (293)

New Brighton

Western Red Cedar Ass'n (543)

New Prague

Turf and Ornamental Communicators Ass'n (527)

Northfield

Picture Agency Council of America (458)

Renville

North American Dairy Sheep Ass'n (441)

Rochester

American Ass'n of Electrodiagnostic Medicine (36)
American Clinical and Climatological Ass'n (52)
American Sleep Disorders Ass'n (100)
Associated Professional Sleep Socs. (172)
Callerlab-Internat'l Ass'n of Square Dance Callers (186)
Professional Skaters Ass'n (467)
Soc. of Computed Body Tomography and Magnetic Resonance (500)
Soc. of Neurological Surgeons (504)
Truck-frame and Axle Repair Ass'n (527)

Roseville

American Ass'n of Pathologists' Assistants (40)
Industrial Fabrics Ass'n Internat'l (262)

St. Cloud

Billings Ovulation Method Ass'n of the United States (179)
Nat'l Ass'n for Rural Mental Health (341)
Nat'l Wildlife Rehabilitators Ass'n (436)

St. Paul

American Academy of Neurology (23)
American Ass'n of Cereal Chemists (34)
American Institute of Hydrology (77)
American Phytopathological Soc. (92)

American Soc. of Brewing Chemists (107)
Ass'n for Women Geoscientists (140)
Ass'n of Asphalt Paving Technologists (144)
Ass'n of Co-operative Educators (147)
Child Neurology Soc. (192)
Cleaning Equipment Trade Ass'n (194)
Internat'l Ass'n for Learning Laboratories (274)
Internat'l Soc. for Molecular Plant Microbe Interactions (304)
Leafy Greens Council (318)
Marine Fabricators Ass'n (323)
Nat'l Ass'n of Farm Broadcasters (354)
Nat'l Ass'n of Waste Transporters (380)
Soc. for Foodservice Systems (488)
Teleprofessional Managers Ass'n (521)
Wholesale Variety Bakers Ass'n (544)
Women's Caucus for the Modern Languages (547)

Worthington

Small Antique Restoration Ass'n (483)

MISSISSIPPI

Belzoni

Catfish Institute (188)

Clarksdale

Ass'n for Information Media and Equipment (135)

Clinton

Nat'l Ass'n of Emergency Medical Technicians (353)

Hattiesburg

American Therapeutic Recreation Ass'n (120)
Nat'l State Publishing Ass'n (431)

Hollis Springs

Belted Galloway Soc. (178)

Indianola

Catfish Farmers of America (188)

Jackson

American Academy of Oral and Maxillofacial Radiology (24)
American Poultry U.S.A. (93)
Nat'l Ass'n of Activity Professionals (342)
Nat'l Tile Contractors Ass'n (433)

Ocean Springs

Nat'l Marine Educators Ass'n (416)

Vicksburg

Young Black Programming Coalition (551)

MISSOURI

Ava

Missouri Fox Trotting Horse Breed Ass'n (329)

Blue Springs

Soc. for Adolescent Medicine (484)

California

Ass'n of Paroling Authorities, Internat'l (159)

Chesterfield

Internat'l Soc. of Parametric Analysts (306)
United Soybean Board (531)

Columbia

American Academy of Forensic Psychology (22)
American Board of Professional Psychology (48)
American Council on Consumer Interests (61)
Ass'n for the Study of Higher Education (139)
Ass'n of University Interior Designers (168)
Investigative Reporters and Editors (312)
Nat'l Ass'n of Animal Breeders (343)
Nat'l Conference of Black Political Scientists (389)
Nat'l Food and Energy Council (405)
Nat'l Institute for Farm Safety (411)
Nat'l Suffolk Sheep Ass'n (432)
Soc. of American Business Editors and Writers (497)
Soc. of Asian and Comparative Philosophy (498)
University Council for Educational Administration (537)

Concordia

American Dexter Cattle Ass'n (64)

Ellisville

Nat'l Wood Flooring Ass'n (436)

Florissant

American Council of Applied Clinical Nutrition (61)

Grain Valley

Owner-Operator Independent Drivers Ass'n (452)

Independence

Aircraft Electronics Ass'n (16)
American Ass'n of Christian Schools (34)
American Osteopathic College of Anesthesiologists (89)

Nat'l Ass'n of Parliamentarians (364)
Parliamentary Associates (453)

Jackson

Nat'l Clay Pot Manufacturers Ass'n (387)

Jefferson City

Inland Rivers Ports and Terminals (264)
Women in Energy (546)

Kansas City

Alpha Gamma Rho (18)
American Academy of Family Physicians (22)
American Ass'n of Managing General Agents (38)
American Ass'n of Veterinary State Boards (45)
American Belgian Blue Breeders Ass'n (47)
American Blonde D'Aquitaine Ass'n (47)
American Business Women's Ass'n (50)
American College of Clinical Pharmacy (53)
American Hereford Ass'n (73)
American Internat'l Charolais Ass'n (79)
American Maine-Anjou Ass'n (82)
American Meat Science Ass'n (83)
American Public Works Ass'n (96)
American Tarentaise Ass'n (119)
American Veterinary Distributors Ass'n (121)
Ass'n for Accounting Marketing (129)
Ass'n for Psychological Type (137)
Ass'n of Diesel Specialists (149)
Ass'n of Family Practice Residency Directors (151)
Automotive Warehouse Distributors Ass'n (175)
Business Technology Ass'n (185)
Council of Fleet Specialists (213)
Diamond Council of America (222)
Electrical Equipment Representatives Ass'n (227)
Electronic Transactions Ass'n (228)
Hotel Motel Brokers of America (256)
Internat'l Ass'n of Administrative Professionals (275)
Internat'l Compressor Remanufacturers Ass'n (286)
Jesuit Ass'n of Student Personnel Administrators (313)
Livestock Marketing Ass'n (320)
Mass Marketing Insurance Institute (324)
Mutual Fund Education Alliance (332)
Nat'l Animal Control Ass'n (336)
Nat'l Ass'n of Forensic Economics (356)
Nat'l Ass'n of Insurance Commissioners (360)
Nat'l Ass'n of Professional Surplus Lines Offices (367)
Nat'l Barbecue Ass'n (382)
Nat'l Federation Interscholastic Coaches Ass'n (402)
Nat'l Federation Interscholastic Music Ass'n (402)
Nat'l Federation Interscholastic Officials Ass'n (402)
Nat'l Federation Interscholastic Speech and Debate Ass'n (402)
Nat'l Federation of Paralegal Ass'ns (404)
Nat'l Federation of State High School Ass'ns (404)
Nat'l Interscholastic Athletic Administrators Ass'n (413)
Nat'l Lubricating Grease Institute (415)
Nat'l Rural Health Ass'n (426)
North American Corriente Ass'n (441)
Philosophy of Science Ass'n (457)
Piano Technicians Guild (458)
Sealant, Waterproofing and Restoration Institute (480)
Soc. of Teachers of Family Medicine (507)
Stained Glass Ass'n of America (515)

Kearney

Women in Agribusiness (546)

Kirksville

American Osteopathic College of Dermatology (89)
Iota Tau Sigma (312)
Nat'l Ass'n of College Wind and Percussion Instructors (348)

Lee's Summit

Clowns of America, Internat'l (195)

Liberty

Internat'l Publishing Management Ass'n (300)

Manchester

Business Products Credit Ass'n (185)

Maryland Heights

Professional Football Writers of America (465)
Window Coverings Ass'n of America (544)

Milan

American Osteopathic College of Radiology (89)

Nixa

Independent Automotive Damage Appraisers Ass'n (259)
Ophthalmic Photographers' Soc. (448)

North Kansas City

American Brahmousin Council (49)
American Murray Grey Ass'n (86)
Braunvieh Breeders Internat'l (181)
Internat'l Union of Gospel Missions (310)

Platte City

American Chianina Ass'n (51)
North American Elk Breeders Ass'n (442)

Raymore

Golf Coaches Ass'n of America **(248)**

Rolla

American Soc. for Engineering Management **(102)**
Soc. for Environmental Geochemistry and Health **(487)**

Rollaton

Internat'l Soc. for the Comparative Studies of
    Civilizations **(304)**

Springfield

Internat'l Ass'n of Fairs and Expositions **(279)**
North American Ass'n of Wardens and Superintendents **(440)**

St. Ann

Decorative Window Coverings Ass'n **(220)**

St. Charles

Car Department Officers Ass'n **(186)**
Concrete Anchor Manufacturers Ass'n **(203)**
Nat'l Plastercraft Ass'n **(422)**
Powder Actuated Tool Manufacturers Institute **(461)**

St. Joseph

American Angus Ass'n **(28)**

St. Louis

AACSB - the Internat'l Ass'n for Management Education **(7)**
Agricultural Publishers Ass'n **(14)**
Agricultural Retailers Ass'n **(14)**
American Academy of Clinical Psychiatrists **(21)**
American Ass'n for Therapeutic Humor **(32)**
American Ass'n of Bioanalysts **(33)**
American Ass'n of Orthodontists **(40)**
American Optometric Ass'n **(88)**
American Optometric Student Ass'n **(88)**
American Soc. of Theatre Consultants **(116)**
American Soybean Ass'n **(117)**
Ass'n of Defensive Spray Manufacturers **(149)**
Catholic Health Ass'n of the United States **(188)**
College of Optometrists in Vision Development **(197)**
Consortium for Graduate Study and Management **(206)**
Credit Professionals Internat'l **(218)**
Disaster Recovery Institute Internat'l **(223)**
Electrical Apparatus Service Ass'n **(227)**
Farm Equipment Manufacturers Ass'n **(235)**
Independent Computer Consultants Ass'n **(260)**
Internat'l Ass'n of Arson Investigators **(275)**
Internat'l Ass'n of Conference Centers **(277)**
Internat'l Brotherhood of Magicians **(284)**
Internat'l Council for Small Business **(287)**
Internat'l Credit Ass'n **(288)**
Materials Technology Institute of the Chemical Process
    Industries **(325)**
Nat'l Ass'n for Holistic Aromatherapy **(339)**
Nat'l Ass'n of Diocesan Ecumenical Officers **(352)**
Nat'l Ass'n of Electrical Distributors **(353)**
Nat'l Ass'n of Independent Fee Appraisers **(359)**
Nat'l Ass'n of Medical Examiners **(362)**
Nat'l Ass'n of Retail Collection Attorneys **(370)**
Nat'l Ass'n of Temple Educators **(378)**
Nat'l Catholic Pharmacists Guild of the United States **(386)**
Nat'l Christmas Tree Ass'n **(387)**
Nat'l Corn Growers Ass'n **(392)**
Nat'l Council of State Garden Clubs **(396)**
Nat'l Federation of Nonpublic School State Accrediting
    Ass'ns **(404)**
Nat'l Troubleshooting Ass'n **(434)**
North American Equipment Dealers Ass'n **(442)**
Paint and Decorating Retailers Ass'n **(452)**
Pile Driving Contractors Ass'n **(458)**
Soc. for Reformation Research **(493)**
Soc. of American Magicians **(497)**
Soc. of Ethnobiology **(501)**
Theta Tau **(522)**
United States Basketball Writers Ass'n **(532)**
WaterJet Technology Ass'n **(541)**

St. Peters

Protestant Church-Owned Publishers Ass'n **(469)**

University City

Soc. of Municipal Arborists **(504)**

Warrensburg

Alliance for Traffic Safety **(18)**
American Academy of Safety Education **(26)**

Washington

Artist-Blacksmiths' Ass'n of North America **(128)**

Willow Springs

Scottish Blackface Sheep Breeders Ass'n **(480)**

MONTANA

Bozeman

American Simmental Ass'n **(100)**

Chinook

United States Targhee Sheep Ass'n **(535)**

Helena

Nat'l Council of Health Facilities Finance Authorities **(395)**

Missoula

American Galloway Breeders Ass'n **(69)**
College Music Soc. **(197)**
Nat'l Perishable Logistics Ass'n **(422)**
River Management Soc. **(476)**
Soc. of North American Goldsmiths **(504)**

Sidney

American Polypay Sheep Ass'n **(93)**

NEBRASKA

Arnold

Nat'l Blacksmiths and Weldors Ass'n **(383)**

Bellevue

Military Impacted Schools Ass'n **(328)**

Columbus

Nat'l Council for Occupational Education **(393)**

Crawford

World Watusi Ass'n **(550)**

Hastings

American College of Theriogenologists **(58)**
American Embryo Transfer Ass'n **(66)**
Amerifax Cattle Ass'n **(124)**
Soc. for Theriogenology **(496)**

Kearney

College Reading and Learning Ass'n **(198)**

Lincoln

American Psychology-Law Soc. **(95)**
Ass'n of Official Seed Analysts **(158)**
Braunvieh Ass'n of America **(181)**
Internat'l Ass'n of Correctional Officers **(278)**
Nat'l Ass'n of Housing Information Managers **(359)**
Nat'l Ass'n of Supervisors of Business Education **(377)**
Nat'l Gymnastics Judges Ass'n **(408)**
Nat'l Indian Counselors Ass'n **(410)**
Nat'l Plant Board **(422)**
North American Gaming Regulators Ass'n **(442)**
Office Systems Research Ass'n **(447)**
Omicron Kappa Upsilon **(448)**
Organic Crop Improvement Ass'n Internat'l **(449)**

Naper

American White/American Creme Horse Registry **(123)**

Omaha

American Laryngological, Rhinological and Otological
    Soc. **(81)**
American Shorthorn Ass'n **(100)**
Ass'n of Astronomy Educators **(144)**
Catholic Theological Soc. of America **(188)**
Internat'l Management Council **(296)**
Soc. of University Urologists **(508)**
United States Beef Breeds Council **(532)**
Wellness Councils of America **(542)**

NEVADA

Baker

Nat'l Ass'n of Home and Workshop Writers **(358)**

Carson City

Nat'l Ass'n of State Retirement Administrators **(376)**
State Risk and Insurance Management Ass'n **(516)**

Elko

Soc. of Mineral Analysts **(504)**

Henderson

Water and Wastewater Instrumentation Testing Ass'n of
    North America (ITA) **(541)**

Las Vegas

American Academy of Neurological and Orthopaedic
    Surgeons **(23)**
American Academy of Somnology **(26)**
American Gem Soc. **(70)**
American Soc. of TV Cameramen **(116)**
Casino and Theme Party Operators Ass'n **(187)**
Nat'l Insurance Ass'n **(412)**
Pierre Fauchard Academy **(458)**

Reno

Nat'l Ass'n of Golf Tournament Directors **(356)**
Nat'l Council of Juvenile and Family Court Judges **(395)**
Nat'l Juvenile Court Services Ass'n **(413)**
Nat'l Purchasing Institute **(424)**

NEW HAMPSHIRE

Amherst

Nat'l Arborist Ass'n **(337)**

Bow

Nat'l Ass'n of Juvenile Correctional Agencies **(361)**

Chester

American College of Laboratory Animal Medicine **(55)**

Concord

Nat'l Ass'n of State Charity Officials **(374)**

Dover

North American Ass'n of Summer Sessions **(440)**

Dunbarton

Christian College Consortium **(193)**

Gilford

Internat'l Ass'n of Law Enforcement Firearms Instructors **(280)**

Hanover

Ass'n of Ecosystem Research Centers **(150)**
Timber Frame Business Council **(523)**

Hillsboro

Internat'l Ass'n of Family Entertainment Centers **(279)**

Jaffrey

American Match Council **(83)**

Keene

Conference of Philosophical Societies **(204)**

Mt. Vernon

American Institute for Archaeological Research **(75)**

Nashua

American Community Cultural Center Ass'n **(59)**

New Durham

American Milking Devon Ass'n **(85)**

Newmarket

Veterinary Orthopedic Soc. **(539)**

Winchester

Cross Country Ski Areas Ass'n **(219)**

NEW JERSEY

Atlantic Highlands

World Federation of Travel Writers **(549)**

Avenel

Soc. of Marine Port Engineers **(503)**

Avon-by-the-Sea

Council of Hotel and Restaurant Trainers **(214)**

Belle Mead

Internat'l Digital Imaging Ass'n **(289)**
Soc. for Clinical Data Management **(486)**

Berkeley Heights

Hydronics Institute Division of GAMA **(257)**

Bernardsville

American Ass'n of Surgical Physician Assistants **(43)**
Ass'n of Neurosurgical Physician Assistants **(158)**

Bound Brook

American Soc. for the Advancement of Anesthesia in
    Dentistry **(105)**

Carlstadt

Green Olive Trade Ass'n **(249)**

Cedar Knolls

Power Sources Manufacturers Ass'n **(461)**

Cherry Hill

American Ass'n of Teachers of German **(44)**
Ass'n of Commercial Finance Attorneys **(148)**
Fluid Power Distributors Ass'n **(241)**
Nat'l Ass'n of Pediatric Nurse Associates and
    Practitioners **(364)**
Tau Epsilon Rho Law Soc. **(520)**
Ultrasonic Industry Ass'n **(529)**

Clifford Park

Embroidery Council of America **(229)**

Cliffside Park

Schiffli Lace and Embroidery Manufacturers Ass'n **(479)**

Clifton

Federation of Straight Chiropractors and Organizations **(238)**

Collingswood
Internat'l Nanny Ass'n (298)

Cranford
Nat'l Ass'n of Teachers' Agencies (378)

Dumont
American Musicians Union (86)

East Brunswick
Library Public Relations Council (319)

East Rutherford
Internat'l Silk Ass'n (302)

East Windsor
Drug, Chemical and Allied Trades Ass'n (225)

Edison
Nat'l Ass'n of Freight Payment Banks (356)

Elizabeth
American Importers and Exporters Meat Products Group (75)
Nat'l Florist Ass'n (405)

Elmwood Park
Hobby Industry Ass'n of America (255)

Englewood
Nat'l Guild of Community Schools of the Arts (408)
North American Indian Museums Ass'n (442)
Organization of Black Airline Pilots (450)

Englewood Cliffs
American Spice Trade Ass'n (117)
Deep Foundations Institute (220)

Fair Lawn
American Institute of Food Distribution (77)

Fairfield
Council of Communication Management (213)
Healthcare Marketing and Communications Council (253)
Textile Care Allied Trades Ass'n (522)
Women's Jewelry Ass'n (548)

Far Hills
United States Golf Ass'n (534)

Flanders
Computer Press Ass'n (202)

Flemington
Food Industry Ass'n Executives (241)

Ft. Lee
Ass'n of Managed Healthcare Organizations (156)
Nat'l Elevator Industry (400)

Gillette
Nat'l Ass'n of Used Fitness and Rehabilitation Equipment
   Dealers (379)

Glassboro
EdPress--The Ass'n of Educational Publishers (226)

Glen Rock
American Ass'n of Candy Technologists (34)

Hackettstown
Nat'l Kitchen and Bath Ass'n (414)
Soc. of Certified Kitchen and Bathroom Designers (499)

Hawthorne
Cathodic Protection Industry Ass'n (188)

Hazlet
Affiliated Warehouse Companies (13)
Securities Transfer Ass'n (481)

Highlands
American Littoral Soc. (82)

Hillsdale
Laminating Materials Ass'n (317)

Iselin
Academy of Veterinary Cardiology (10)
FCIB-NACM Corp. (235)
Nat'l Ass'n of Fleet Administrators (355)
Trans-Atlantic American Flag Liner Operations (525)

Jersey City
Soc. of Naval Architects and Marine Engineers (504)

Kearney
Community Colleges Humanities Ass'n (201)

Kendall Park
Ass'n of Jewish Family and Children's Agencies (155)
Jewish Social Service Professionals Ass'n (314)

Lakewood
American Ass'n of Stomatologists (43)

Lanoka Harbor
American Ass'n for the History of Nursing (32)

Laurence Harbor
Ass'n of Sales Administration Managers (164)

Lawrenceville
American Fine China Guild (68)
Internat'l Ass'n of Law Enforcement Intelligence
   Analysts (280)
Smart Card Industry Ass'n (484)

Livingston
Ass'n of Average Adjusters of the U.S. (144)

Mahwah
Foundation for Advances in Medicine and Science (243)

Manahawkin
American Bureau of Metal Statistics (49)
American Disc Jockey Ass'n (64)

Marlton
Nat'l Ass'n of Recording Merchandisers (369)

Matawan
Ass'n of Food Industries (151)
Nat'l Ass'n of Fruits, Flavors and Syrups (356)
Nat'l Honey Packers and Dealers Ass'n (409)

Middletown
Nat'l Ass'n of Sailing Instructors and Sailing Schools (370)

Midland Park
Nat'l Organization of Social Security Claimants'
   Representatives (420)

Millburn
Ass'n of Ship Brokers and Agents (U.S.A.) (165)

Montvale
American Ass'n of Office Nurses (40)
Controllers Council (208)
Cost Management Group (210)
Institute of Certified Management Accountants (266)
Institute of Management Accountants (268)

Montville
Nat'l Ass'n of Flour Distributors (355)

Moorestown
Childrenswear Marketing Ass'n (192)
Internat'l Hard Anodizing Ass'n (293)
Juvenile Products Manufacturers Ass'n (315)
Nat'l Ass'n of Chewing Gum Manufacturers (347)
Nat'l Ornament and Electric Lights Christmas Ass'n (420)
Receptive Services Ass'n (472)
Specialty Sleep Ass'n (514)
Sports Card Ass'n (515)
Writing Instrument Manufacturers Ass'n (551)

Morristown
Communications Managers Ass'n (200)
Financial Executives Institute (238)
Vinyl Institute (539)

Mount Arlington
Expediting Management Ass'n (234)

Mount Royal
American Academy of Orofacial Pain (24)
American Ass'n for the Study of Headache (32)
American College of Veterinary Pathologists (58)
Ass'n for Research in Otolaryngology (137)
Ass'n for the Care of Children's Health (139)
Internat'l Neural Network Soc. (298)
Movement Disorder Soc. (331)
Soc. for Cardiovascular Magnetic Resonance (486)
Soc. for Healthcare Epidemiology of America (488)
Soc. of Toxicologic Pathologists (508)
Stadium Managers Ass'n (515)

New Brunswick
African Studies Ass'n (14)
Ass'n for Computational Linguistics (131)

New Providence
Nat'l Council of Self-Insurers (395)

Newark
Community Colleges Humanities Ass'n (201)
Nat'l Catholic Conference of Airport Chaplains (385)

Newton
American Crossbred Pony Registry (63)

Norwood
Council of American Master Mariners (212)

Ocean Grove
Beta Beta Beta (178)

Oradell
Nat'l Prepared Food Ass'n (423)

Paramus
American Soc. for Value Inquiry (106)
Nat'l Ass'n of Printers and Lithographers (366)

Parsippany
Hydraulic Institute (257)

Pennington
Electrochemical Soc. (228)

Piscataway
Components, Packaging, and Manufacturing Technology
   Soc. (201)
IEEE Magnetics Soc. (258)
IEEE Power Engineering Soc. (258)
IEEE Signal Processing Soc. (259)
Institute of Electrical and Electronics Engineers (266)

Pitman
Academy of Medical-Surgical Nurses (9)
American Academy of Ambulatory Care Nursing (20)
American Nephrology Nurses Ass'n (86)
American Soc. of Plastic and Reconstructive Surgical
   Nurses (115)
Certification Board for Urologic Nurses and Associates (190)
Dermatology Nurses Ass'n (221)
Nat'l Ass'n of Orthopaedic Nurses (364)
Nat'l Federation for Specialty Nursing Organizations (402)
Soc. of Urologic Nurses and Associates (508)

Princeton
American Ass'n of Teachers of Turkic Languages (44)
American Soc. of Group Psychotherapy and
   Psychodrama (110)
APMI Internat'l (125)
Construction Financial Management Ass'n (206)
Intercollegiate Tennis Ass'n (271)
Internat'l Recording Media Ass'n (301)
Internat'l Soc. for Pharmacoeconomics and Outcomes
   Research (304)
Metal Powder Industries Federation (327)
Nat'l Ass'n of Document Examiners (353)
North American Electric Reliability Council (441)
Soc. for Iranian Studies (490)
Tobacco Merchants Ass'n of the U.S. (524)

Princeton Junction
American Soc. of Media Photographers (112)
Energy Efficient Lighting Ass'n (230)
Internat'l Card Manufacturers Ass'n (285)

Ramsey
Ass'n for Child Psychoanalysis (130)

Red Bank
American Apitherapy Soc. (28)
American Soc. of Church History (107)
Ass'n of Retail Marketing Services (163)
Incentive Federation (259)

Ridgewood
Internat'l Castor Oil Ass'n (285)

Robbinsville
Harness Horsemen Internat'l (251)

Rocky Hill
Purebred Hanoverian Ass'n of America Breeders and
   Owners (470)

Rutherford
CPA Associates Internat'l (218)
Nat'l Ass'n of Oil Heating Service Managers (364)

Secaucus
Chemical Sources Ass'n (191)
Oriental Rug Importers Ass'n of America (450)

Somerville
Intermediaries and Reinsurance Underwriters Ass'n (272)

South Orange
Organization Development Network (449)

Sparta
Lead Industries Ass'n (318)

Springfield
Converting Equipment Manufacturers Ass'n (208)
Nat'l Council of Acoustical Consultants (393)
Sales Ass'n of the Chemical Industry (478)

Teaneck
American Soc. of Wedding Professionals (117)
Ass'n of Tongue Depressors (168)
Chinese American Medical Soc. (192)
Foster Family-Based Treatment Ass'n (243)

Thorofare
American Motility Soc. (85)
American Soc. for Clinical Investigation (101)
American Soc. of Peri-Anesthesia Nurses (114)
American Soc. of Transplant Physicians (116)
Gastroenterology Research Group (246)
Gynecologic Surgery Soc. (250)
Internat'l Ass'n of Forensic Nurses (279)
Internat'l Liver Transplantation Soc. (296)
North American Soc. for Pediatric Gastroenterology and
    Nutrition (444)
Soc. for Surgery of the Alimentary Tract (494)

Trenton
Ass'n for Conservation Information (131)
Nat'l Ass'n of Noise Control Officials (364)
Nat'l Conference of State Liquor Administrators (391)

Tuckerton
American Mideast Business Associates (85)

Turnersville
Computer Measurement Group (202)

Union
Ass'n of Incentive Marketing (153)
Property Owners Ass'n (468)

Upper Montclair
Nat'l Music Council (418)

Upper Montclare
Internat'l Congress of Oral Implantologists (287)

Voorhees
American Oriental Bodywork Therapy Ass'n (88)

Waretown
Internat'l Institute of Connector and Interconnection
    Technology (294)

Wayne
Polyurethane Foam Ass'n (460)

Weehawken
Songwriters Guild of America (510)

West Caldwell
Containerization and Intermodal Institute (207)

West Deptford
Architectural Spray Coaters Ass'n (127)

West Orange
Professional Hockey Writers' Ass'n (466)

Westfield
Music Critics Ass'n of North America (332)

Whippany
Nat'l Exchange Carrier Ass'n (402)

Woodbridge
Nat'l Ass'n of Printing Ink Manufacturers (366)

Wyckoff
Internat'l Psychohistorical Ass'n (300)

NEW MEXICO

Albuquerque
American Ass'n of Feline Practitioners (37)
American Soc. for Pediatric Neurosurgery (104)
American Soc. of Radiologic Technologists (115)
Ass'n for Women Veterinarians (141)
Ass'n of Vacuum Equipment Manufacturers Internat'l (169)
Brazilian Studies Ass'n (182)
Communications Marketing Ass'n (200)
Council of Administrators of Special Education (212)
Indian Arts and Crafts Ass'n (262)
Nat'l Ass'n of Academies of Science (342)
Nat'l Ass'n of Freight Transportation Consultants (356)
Soc. of American Law Teachers (497)
Soc. of Vacuum Coaters (508)
Western History Ass'n (543)

Dulce
Nat'l Ass'n of Tribal Court Personnel (379)

Farmington
Indian Educators Federation (262)

Las Cruces
Evaporative Cooling Institute (233)

Roswell
Community College Ass'n for Instruction and Technology (201)

Santa Fe
American Soc. for Mass Spectrometry (104)
Analytical Laboratory Managers Ass'n (124)
Federation of Analytical Chemistry and Spectroscopy
    Societies (236)
Nat'l Coalition of Alternative Community Schools (387)

NEW YORK

Albany
Ass'n of Financial Guaranty Insurors (151)
Internat'l Ass'n of Milk Control Agencies (281)
Internat'l Narcotic Enforcement Officers Ass'n (298)
Nat'l Ass'n of Government Archives and Records
    Administrators (356)
Nat'l Conference of Insurance Legislators (390)
Nat'l Council of Legislators from Gaming States (395)
Veterinary Hospital Managers Ass'n (539)

Alfred
Committee on Lesbian and Gay History (200)

Armonk
Nat'l Electrical Manufacturers Representatives Ass'n (400)

Batavia
United States Harness Writers' Ass'n (534)

Bayside
Dance Masters of America (220)
Nat'l Conference of Personal Managers (390)

Bedford
Institute of Internat'l Container Lessors (267)

Berne
Ass'n of State Wetland Managers (166)

Binghamton
Soc. for Ancient Greek Philosophy (485)

Brewerton
Internat'l Ass'n of Conference Center Administrators (277)

Briarcliff Manor
Academy of Management (9)
United Federation of Police Officers (530)

Brockport
Congress on Research in Dance (205)
University Photographers Ass'n of America (537)

Bronx
American Ass'n for Correctional Psychology (30)
American Thyroid Ass'n (120)
Ass'n for the Advancement of Psychotherapy (138)
Internat'l Pediatric Nephrology Ass'n (299)
Internat'l Soc. for Adolescent Psychiatry (302)
Soc. for Economic Botany (487)

Brooklyn
American Ass'n of Hospital Podiatrists (37)
American Catholic Correctional Chaplains Ass'n (50)
American Podiatric Circulatory Soc. (93)
Comedy Writers and Performers Ass'n (198)
Gasoline and Automotive Service Dealers Ass'n (246)
Internat'l Security Officers, Police and Guards Union (302)
Internat'l Soc. of Copier Artists (306)
Italian Actors Union (313)
Knitwear Employers Ass'n (316)
Nat'l Ass'n of Hebrew Day School Administrators (357)
Nat'l Ass'n of Vertical Transportation Professionals (379)
Production Service Sales District Council (464)
Professional Ass'n of Comics Entertainment Retailers (464)

Buffalo
American Crystallographic Ass'n (63)
Ass'n for the Bibliography of History (139)
Ass'n of American Cancer Institutes (142)
Ass'n of Petroleum Re-refiners (160)
Collector Car Appraisers Internat'l (197)
Creative Education Foundation (218)
Giftware Associates Interchange (247)
Nat'l Ass'n for Industry-Education Cooperation (340)
Nat'l Ass'n of Independent Lighting Distributors (359)

Burdett
Ass'n of Vegetarian Dietitians and Nutrition Educators (169)

Chestnut Ridge
Production Music Library Ass'n (464)

Cicero
Nat'l Ass'n of Air Nat'l Guard Health Technicians (343)

Cohoes
Professional Service Ass'n (467)

Delmar
College of Diplomates of the American Board of
    Orthodontics (197)

Dix Hills
Internat'l Ass'n for Computer Systems Security (273)

East Hampton
Educational Paperback Ass'n (226)

East Northport
Federal Law Enforcement Officers Ass'n (236)

East Setauket
Nat'l Ass'n of Principals of Schools for Girls (366)

Elbridge
Internat'l Ass'n of Structural Movers (282)

Ellenburg Depot
Internat'l Ass'n of Pet Cemeteries (281)

Ely
American Bashkir Curly Registry (47)

Esperance
American Goat Soc. (71)

Farmingdale
Nat'l Metal Spinners Ass'n (417)

Floral Park
United Weighers Ass'n (536)

Flushing
American Acupuncture Ass'n (27)
Ass'n for the Study of Food and Society (139)
Ass'n of Teachers of Latin American Studies (167)
Jewish Educators Assembly (314)

Forest Hills
American Podiatric Medical Writers Ass'n (93)

Garden City
Nat'l Ass'n of Pharmaceutical Manufacturers (365)

Garden City Park
Fixed Income Analysts Soc. (240)
Soc. of Quantitative Analysts (506)

Geneva
Ass'n for Evolutionary Economics (133)

Glen Cove
American Stamp Dealers' Ass'n (118)

Great Neck
American College of Angiology (53)
Diamond Manufacturers and Importers Ass'n of America (222)
Nat'l Institute of Management Counsellors (412)
Nat'l Paper Trade Ass'n (421)
Paper Distribution Council (453)
Sigma Epsilon Delta Dental Fraternity (483)
Soc. for the Exploration of Psychotherapy Integration (495)

Greenlawn
Nat'l Ass'n of Science Writers (371)

Harrison
Composites Institute (202)
Photographic and Imaging Manufacturers Ass'n (457)

Hauppauge
Nat'l Ass'n of Educational Buyers (353)

Hempstead
Nat'l Catholic Development Conference (385)

Henderson Harbor
Safety Glazing Cerification Council (478)

Hollowville
Soc. of Insurance Financial Management (503)

Huntington
American Medical Publishers' Ass'n (84)

Independent Professional Painting Contractors Ass'n of America (261)
Transportation Consumer Protection Council (525)

Hyde Park

Internat'l Foodservice Editorial Council (291)

Ithaca

Ass'n for Asian American Studies (130)
Ass'n of Chairmen of Departments of Mechanics (146)
Ass'n for Women in Psychology (140)
Internat'l Ass'n of Music Libraries, United States Branch (281)
Paleontological Research Institution (452)
Soc. for Asian Music (485)
Soc. for the Advancement of Food Service Research (494)

Jackson Heights

American Ass'n of Spinal Cord Injury Nurses (42)
American Ass'n of Spinal Cord Injury Psychologists and Social Workers (43)
American Paraplegia Soc. (90)

Jamaica

Indian Dental Ass'n (USA) (262)
Nat'l Organization of Industrial Trade Unions (420)

Kerhonkson

Ass'n of Halfway House Alcoholism Programs of North America (153)

Kingston

American Institute for Patristic and Byzantine Studies (76)
NADD: Ass'n for Persons with Developmental Disabilities and Mental Health Needs (333)

Lake Grove

Baseball Writers Ass'n of America (177)

Lake Success

Nat'l Conference of CPA Practitioners (390)

Latham

American Assembly for Men in Nursing (45)
Cleaning Management Institute (194)

Lawrence

American Conference of Cantors (59)

Lewiston

Electrical Insulation Conference (227)

Liberty

Political Products Manufacturers Ass'n (460)

Lockport

North American Punch Manufacturers Ass'n (444)

Locust Valley

Nat'l Ass'n of Catalog Showroom Merchandisers (346)

Mamaroneck

American Jewish Correctional Chaplains Ass'n (79)

Manhasset

Catholic Book Publishers Ass'n (188)

Maspeth

American Federation of Railroad Police (67)

Melville

Internat'l Ass'n of Electronic Keyboard Manufacturers (278)

Middle Island

Copywriter's Council of America (209)

Millbrook

Nat'l Frozen Dessert and Fast Food Ass'n (406)

Mineola

American Accordionists Ass'n (27)

Mt. Vernon

American Risk and Insurance Ass'n (98)
Internat'l Ass'n for Insurance Law - United States Chapter (274)
Professional Tattoo Artists Guild (467)

Nesconset

Phlebology Soc. of America (457)

New City

Nat'l Council for Therapeutic Recreation Certification (393)

New Hartford

American College of Clinical Pharmacology (53)

New Rochelle

American Import Shippers Ass'n (75)
Federal Bureau of Investigation Agents Ass'n (235)

New Windsor

Intercollegiate Broadcasting System (271)

New York

Academy of Political Science (9)
Actors' Equity Ass'n (11)
Advertising Council (12)
Advertising Research Foundation (12)
Affiliated Dress Manufacturers (13)
Africa Travel Ass'n (13)
Allied Artists of America (18)
American Abstract Artists (20)
American Academy of Oral Medicine (24)
American Academy of Psychoanalysis (26)
American Academy of Teachers of Singing (26)
American Arbitration Ass'n (28)
American Artists Professional League (29)
American Ass'n for Chinese Studies (30)
American Ass'n of Advertising Agencies (32)
American Ass'n of Exporters and Importers (36)
American Ass'n of Fund-Raising Counsel (37)
American Boat Builders and Repairers Ass'n (48)
American Book Producers Ass'n (48)
American Bureau of Shipping and Affiliated Companies (49)
American Business Press (50)
American Cargo War Risk Reinsurance Exchange (50)
American Cloak and Suit Manufacturers Ass'n (52)
American College of Nutrition (56)
American Composers Alliance (59)
American Copper Council (60)
American Council of Learned Societies (61)
American Council on Internat'l Personnel (62)
American Council on Science and Health (62)
American Craft Council (62)
American Dance Guild (63)
American Diamond Industry Ass'n (64)
American Dog Trainers Network (65)
American Federation for Aging Research (66)
American Federation of Musicians of the United States and Canada (67)
American Federation of Television and Radio Artists (67)
American Federation of Violin and Bow Makers (67)
American Foreign Law Ass'n (69)
American Geographical Soc. (70)
American Geriatrics Soc. (71)
American Group Psychotherapy Ass'n (71)
American Guild of Musical Artists (71)
American Guild of Organists (71)
American Guild of Variety Artists (71)
American Horse Shows Ass'n (74)
American Indonesian Chamber of Commerce (75)
American Institute of Certified Public Accountants (76)
American Institute of Chemical Engineers (77)
American Institute of Graphic Arts (77)
American Institute of Marine Underwriters (77)
American Institute of Mining, Metallurgical, and Petroleum Engineers (78)
American Kennel Club (80)
American League of Professional Baseball Clubs (81)
American Lung Ass'n (82)
American Management Ass'n Internat'l (82)
American Maritime Ass'n (82)
American Montessori Soc. (85)
American Name Soc. (86)
American Nat'l Standards Institute (86)
American Numismatic Soc. (87)
American Orthopsychiatric Ass'n (89)
American Philological Ass'n (91)
American Printing History Ass'n (94)
American Psychoanalytic Ass'n (94)
American Skin Ass'n (100)
American Soc. for Dental Aesthetics (102)
American Soc. of Clinical Psychopharmacology (108)
American Soc. of Comparative Law (108)
American Soc. of Composers, Authors and Publishers (108)
American Soc. of Corporate Secretaries (109)
American Soc. of Geolinguistics (110)
American Soc. of Hypertension (111)
American Soc. of Industrial Medicine (111)
American Soc. of Journalists and Authors (111)
American Soc. of Knitting Technologists (111)
American Soc. of Magazine Editors (112)
American Soc. of Mechanical Engineers (112)
American Soc. of Music Copyists (113)
American Soc. of Payroll Management (114)
American Soc. of Roommate Services (116)
American Soc. of Sephardic Studies (116)
American Sportscasters Ass'n (118)
American Stock Exchange (118)
American Thoracic Soc. (120)
American Vacuum Soc. (121)
American-European Soda Ash Shipping Ass'n (124)
American-Israel Chamber of Commerce and Industry (124)
American-Southern Africa Chamber of Trade and Industry (124)
Antiquarian Booksellers Ass'n of America (125)
Appraisers Ass'n of America (126)
Argentina-American Chamber of Commerce (127)
Art and Antique Dealers League of America (127)
Art Dealers Ass'n of America (127)
Ass'n for Advancement of Behavior Therapy (129)
Ass'n for Computing Machinery (131)
Ass'n for Humanist Sociology (134)
Ass'n for Psychoanalytic Medicine (137)
Ass'n for Research in Nervous and Mental Disease (137)
Ass'n for the Advancement of Psychoanalysis (138)
Ass'n of Advanced Rabbinical and Talmudic Schools (141)
Ass'n of American University Presses (143)

Ass'n of Art Museum Directors (144)
Ass'n of Authors' Representatives (144)
Ass'n of Chartered Accountants in the United States (146)
Ass'n of Departments of English (149)
Ass'n of Departments of Foreign Languages (149)
Ass'n of Direct Marketing Agencies (149)
Ass'n of Episcopal Colleges (150)
Ass'n of Executive Search Consultants (150)
Ass'n of Foreign Trade Representatives (151)
Ass'n of Hispanic Arts (153)
Ass'n of Immigration Attorneys (153)
Ass'n of Independent Commercial Producers (153)
Ass'n of Independent Video and Filmmakers (154)
Ass'n of Internal Management Consultants (154)
Ass'n of Jewish Center Professionals (155)
Ass'n of Jewish Libraries (155)
Ass'n of Junior Leagues Internat'l (155)
Ass'n of Knitted Fabrics Manufacturers (155)
Ass'n of Management Consulting Firms (156)
Ass'n of Nat'l Advertisers (158)
Ass'n of Philosophy Journal Editors (160)
Ass'n of Productivity Specialists (160)
Ass'n of Publication Production Managers (162)
Ass'n of Rain Apparel Contractors (163)
Ass'n of Real Estate Women (163)
Ass'n of Theatrical Press Agents and Managers (168)
Ass'n of University Environmental Health/Sciences Centers (168)
Associated Actors and Artistes of America (170)
Associated Corset and Brassiere Manufacturers Ass'n (171)
Associated Press Managing Editors (172)
Audio Engineering Soc. (172)
Authors Guild (173)
Authors League of America (173)
Belgian American Chamber of Commerce in the United States (178)
Belt Ass'n (178)
Beta Alpha Psi (178)
Bibliographical Soc. of America (178)
BKR Internat'l (180)
Black Filmmaker Foundation (180)
Black Retail Action Group (180)
Black Women in Publishing (180)
Board of Trade of the City of New York (180)
Board of Trade of the Wholesale Seafood Merchants (181)
Bond Market Ass'n (181)
Book Industry Study Group (181)
BPA Internat'l (181)
Brazilian American Chamber of Commerce (182)
British-American Chamber of Commerce (182)
Brotherhood of Traveling Jewelers (183)
Builders Hardware Manufacturers Ass'n (183)
Cabletelevision Advertising Bureau (185)
Cantors Assembly (186)
Career Apparel Institute (186)
Cargo Reinsurance Ass'n (187)
Catholic Actors Guild of America (188)
Center for Waste Reduction Technologies (189)
Central Conference of American Rabbis (189)
Certified Ballast Manufacturers Ass'n (190)
Chamber Music America (190)
Chamber of Commerce of the Apparel Industry (190)
Cheese Importers Ass'n of America (190)
Chemical Communications Ass'n (191)
Children's Book Council (192)
Clothing Manufacturers Ass'n of the U.S.A. (195)
Cocoa Merchants' Ass'n of America (196)
College Art Ass'n (197)
Colombian American Ass'n (198)
Color Ass'n of the United States (198)
Comics Magazine Ass'n of America (198)
Commercial Finance Ass'n (199)
Consolidated Tape Ass'n (206)
Copper Development Ass'n (209)
Copyright Soc. of the U.S.A. (209)
Cosmetic Executive Women (210)
Council for European Studies (211)
Council for Jewish Education (211)
Council for Tobacco Research-U.S.A. (212)
Council of American Jewish Museums (212)
Council of Archives and Research Libraries in Jewish Studies (212)
Council of Fashion Designers of America (213)
Council of Jewish Federations (214)
Council of Literary Magazines and Presses (214)
Council of Protocol Executives (215)
Council of the Americas (216)
Cruise Lines Internat'l Ass'n (219)
Cultured Pearl Ass'n of America (219)
Customs and Internat'l Trade Bar Ass'n (219)
Danish-American Chamber of Commerce (USA) (220)
Diamond Trade and Precious Stone Ass'n of America (222)
Direct Marketing Ass'n (223)
Dramatists Guild (224)
Ecuadorean American Ass'n (226)
Editorial Freelancers Ass'n (226)
Electronic Forum on Sound Technology (228)
Emerging Markets Traders Ass'n (229)
Entertainment Services and Technology Ass'n (231)
Fabric Salesmen's Ass'n (234)
Fashion Accessories Shippers Ass'n (235)
Fashion Ass'n, The (235)
Fashion Group Internat'l (235)
Federation of Modern Painters and Sculptors (237)
Finnish American Chamber of Commerce (239)
Foragers of America (242)
Foreign Press Ass'n (242)
Forex U.S.A.: the Financial Markets Ass'n (243)
Fragrance Foundation (243)
French-American Chamber of Commerce (244)
Fulfillment Management Ass'n (247)
German American Chamber of Commerce (247)
Girls Incorporated (247)
Graphic Artists Guild Nat'l (249)

Penn Yan

North American Simulation and Gaming Ass'n (444)

Pomona

Nat'l Ass'n of Off-Track Betting (364)

Port Jefferson

Council for Marketing and Opinion Research (211)
Council of American Survey Research Organizations (212)

Port Washington

Nat'l Ass'n for Poetry Therapy (340)

Poughkeepsie

Institute of Noise Control Engineering (268)
Women's Caucus for Political Science (547)

Purchase

Mastercard Internat'l (324)

Purdys

Building Stone Institute (183)

Richmond Hill

Nat'l Ass'n of Ecumenical and Interreligious Staff (353)

Riverhead

Northeastern Weed Science Soc. (446)

Rochester

American Wine Soc. (123)
Ass'n of College Educators: Deaf and Hard of Hearing (147)
Ass'n of Naval R.O.T.C. Colleges and Universities (158)
Biological Stain Commission (179)
Council on Education of the Deaf (216)
Gravure Ass'n of America (249)
Sportsplex Operators and Developers of Ass'n (515)
Technical Ass'n of the Graphic Arts (520)
Veterinary Cancer Soc. (539)

Rockville Center

Catholic Fine Arts Soc. (188)
Rubber Trade Ass'n of North America (478)

Rome

Electrical Overstress/Electrostatic Discharge Ass'n (227)
Nat'l Miniature Donkey Ass'n (417)

Ronkonkoma

Catholic Press Ass'n (188)
Flexographic Technical Ass'n (240)

Roslyn Heights

Internat'l Academy of Health Care Professionals (272)

Rye

Internat'l Soc. for the Performing Arts (304)

Scarsdale

Sponge and Chamois Institute (514)

Skaneateles

Hard Fibers Ass'n (251)

Southampton

Elevator Industries Ass'n (229)

Sparta

Ass'n of Consulting Chemists and Chemical Engineers (148)

Staten Island

American Italian Historical Ass'n (79)
Perlite Institute (455)

Stony Brook

Transplantation Soc. (Western Hemishpere) (525)

Syracuse

USITT: Ass'n of Design, Production and Technology Professionals in the Performing Arts and Entertainment (538)

Tarrytown

American Booksellers Ass'n (48)
Expansion Joint Manufacturers Ass'n (234)
Hand Tools Institute (251)
Institute of Store Planners (269)
Internat'l Firestop Council (291)
Paper Shipping Sack Manufacturers Ass'n (453)
Soc. of American Registered Architects (498)
Technical Ceramics Manufacturers Ass'n (520)
Tubular Exchanger Manufacturers Ass'n (527)
Tubular Rivet and Machine Institute (527)

Valhalla

Women in Sales Ass'n (547)

Valley Stream

Soc. for the Advancement of Education (494)

West Rush

Accredited Pet Cemetery Soc. (10)

Westbury

Keyboard Teachers Ass'n Internat'l (316)

White Plains

American Soc. for Clinical Evoked Potentials (101)
FSC/DISC Tax Ass'n (244)
Soc. of Motion Picture and Television Engineers (504)

Woodbury

Acoustical Soc. of America (11)
Soc. of Rheology (506)

Wurstboroe

American Buyers of Meeting and Incentive Travel (50)

Yonkers

American Council on the Teaching of Foreign Languages (62)
American Institute of Stress (78)

NORTH CAROLINA

Asheville

Internat'l Soc. of Financiers, Inc. (306)

Cary

INDA, Ass'n of the Nonwoven Fabrics Industry (259)
Nat'l Pharmaceutical Ass'n (422)

Chapel Hill

American Cleft Palate-Craniofacial Ass'n (52)
Ass'n of Medical School Pediatric Department Chairmen (157)
Golf Course Builders Ass'n of America (248)

Charlotte

American Ass'n of Minority Businesses (39)
Ass'n of Mezzanine Manufacturers (157)
Ass'n of Professional Material Handling Consultants (161)
Automated Electrified Monorail Product Section - Material Handling Institute (173)
Automated Storage/Retrieval Systems (173)
Automatic Guided Vehicle Systems (173)
Crane Manufacturers Ass'n of America (218)
Hoist Manufacturers Institute (255)
Independent Cash Register Dealers Ass'n (260)
Industrial Metal Containers Ass'n (263)
Lift Manufacturers Product Section - Material Handling Institute (319)
Loading Dock Equipment Manufacturers (320)
Material Handling Industry Ass'n (325)
Materials Handling and Management Soc. (325)
Monorail Manufacturers Ass'n (330)
Nat'l Ass'n for PET Container Resources (340)
Nat'l Ass'n of Hosiery Manufacturers (358)
Order Selection, Staging and Storage Council (449)
Professional Construction Estimators Ass'n of America (465)
Rack Manufacturers Institute (470)
Storage Equipment Manufacturer's Ass'n (517)

Durham

American Ass'n of Physical Anthropologists (41)
American Soc. for Environmental History (102)
Automotive Cooling System Institute (174)
Automotive Public Relations Council (175)
Filter Manufacturers Council (238)
Forest History Soc. (242)
Heavy Duty Business Forum (253)
Insurance Accounting and Systems Ass'n (270)
Nat'l Ass'n of Blacks in Criminal Justice (345)
Nat'l Press Photographers Ass'n (423)
Organization for Tropical Studies (450)
Parapsychological Ass'n (453)

Fayetteville

Internat'l Oil Mill Superintendents Ass'n (298)
Professional Putters Ass'n (466)

Franklin

Internat'l Business Music Ass'n (284)

Garner

Nat'l Federation of Licensed Practical Nurses (403)

Gastonia

American Yarn Spinners Ass'n (124)
Textured Yarn Ass'n of America (522)

Greensboro

Food Industry Suppliers Ass'n (241)
Nat'l Ass'n of Computer Consultant Businesses (349)
Nat'l Soc. of Black Physicists (429)

Greenville

American Ass'n for the History of Medicine (32)
Ass'n for the Education of Teachers in Science (139)

High Point

American Furniture Manufacturers Ass'n (69)
American Soc. of Furniture Designers (110)
Appalachian Hardwood Manufacturers (126)
Internat'l Guild of Professional Electrologists (293)
Internat'l Home Furnishings Marketing Ass'n (293)
Internat'l Home Furnishings Representatives Ass'n (293)
Internat'l Wholesale Furniture Ass'n (311)
Nat'l AMBUCS (336)
Nat'l Home Furnishings Ass'n (409)
Summer and Casual Furniture Manufacturers Ass'n (518)
Upholstered Furniture Action Council (537)

Hillsborough

Organization of Teachers of Oral Diagnosis (450)

Huntersville

Nat'l Art Materials Trade Ass'n (337)

King

Pet Sitters Internat'l (455)

Lexington

New Bern

American Academy of Psychotherapists (26)
Nat'l Marine Electronics Ass'n (416)

Raleigh

American Soc. for Cytotechnology (102)
American Soc. for Precision Engineering (104)
American Soc. of Echocardiography (109)
Art Libraries Soc./North America (127)
Ass'n for Gnotobiotics (134)
Ass'n of American Editorial Cartoonists (142)
Ass'n of American Seed Control Officials (143)
Ass'n of Graduate Liberal Studies Programs (152)
Bright Belt Warehouse Ass'n (182)
Cable Tray Institute (185)
Flue-Cured Tobacco Cooperative Stabilization Corporation (240)
Internat'l Lactation Consultant Ass'n (295)
Leaf Tobacco Exporters Ass'n (318)
Multi-Housing Laundry Ass'n (331)
Nat'l Ass'n of Consumer Credit Administrators (349)
Nat'l Ass'n of State Directors of Migrant Education (274)
Nat'l Cartoonists Soc. (385)
Nat'l Council of Preservation Executives (395)
Nat'l Nurses Soc. on Addictions (418)
Nat'l Science Education Leadership Ass'n (427)
Nat'l Soc. for Experiential Education (428)
Nat'l Swine Improvement Federation (433)
North American Gamebird Ass'n (442)
Professional Records and Information Services Management Internat'l (467)
Professional Services Management Ass'n (467)
Roof Consultants Institute (477)
Sewn Products Equipment Suppliers Ass'n (482)
Soc. for Cardiac Angiography and Interventions (486)
Soc. of American Travel Writers (498)
Soc. of Financial Examiners (501)
Tobacco Ass'n of the U.S. (523)
Waterproofing Contractors Ass'n (541)

Research Triangle Pk

American Ass'n of Textile Chemists and Colorists (44)
Ass'n for Population/Family Planning Libraries and Information Centers, Internat'l (136)
Auto Internat'l Ass'n (173)
Automotive Market Research Council (174)
Brake Manufacturers Council (181)
Chemical Industry Institute of Toxicology (191)
Heavy Duty Brake Manufacturers Council (253)
Heavy Duty Manfacturers Ass'n (253)
Instrument Soc. of America (269)
Internat'l Lead Zinc Research Organization (295)
MEMA Information Services Council (327)
Motor and Equipment Manufacturers Ass'n (330)
Nat'l Ass'n of Orthopaedic Technologists (364)
Nat'l Council of the Paper Industry for Air and Stream Improvement (397)
Overseas Automotive Council, Internat'l Aftermarket Division - Motor and Equipment Manufacturers Ass'n (452)
Tune-up Manufacturers Council (527)

Roxboro

Textile Quality Control Ass'n (522)

Salisbury

Nat'l Sportscasters and Sportswriters Ass'n (431)

Skyland

Industrial Diamond Ass'n of America (262)

Spindale

American Dairy Goat Ass'n (63)

Sylva

Saddle, Harness, and Allied Trade Ass'n (478)

Thomasville

American Scientific Glassblowers Soc. (99)

Mentor

Steel Tube Institute of North America (517)

Montpelier

Soc. for the Study of Male Psychology and Physiology (496)

Newark

American Trakehner Ass'n (120)

North Bloomfield

Ass'n for Living History Farms and Agricultural Museums (135)

North Canton

Vacuum Cleaner Manufacturers Ass'n (538)

North Olmstead

Ductile Iron Soc. (225)

Norwalk

Internat'l Hot Rod Ass'n (294)

Oberlin

Ass'n of Specialty Cut Flower Growers (165)
Nat'l Ass'n of College Stores (348)

Oxford

Academy of Legal Studies in Business (8)
American Classical League (52)
Ass'n for Integrative Studies (135)
College Fraternity Editors Ass'n (197)
Delta Sigma Pi (221)
Internat'l Drycleaners Congress (289)
Nat'l Council of Writing Program Administrators (397)
Nat'l Staff Development Council (431)

Painesville

Internat'l Soc. for Artificial Organs (303)

Port Clinton

American Photographic Artisans Guild (92)
Car Care Council (186)
Nat'l Engine Parts Manufacturers Ass'n (401)

Reynoldsburg

American Guernsey Ass'n (71)
American Jersey Cattle Ass'n (79)

Rocky River

Delta Theta Phi (221)

Solon

Internat'l Compact Disc Interactive Ass'n (286)

Sylvania

American Osteopathic College of Proctology (89)
Sanitary Supply Wholesalers Ass'n (479)

Toledo

American Flint Glass Workers Union (68)
Cell Kinetics Soc. (189)
Internat'l REST Investigators Soc. (301)
Nat'l Writing Centers Ass'n (437)

Upper Sandusky

Columbia Sheep Breeders Ass'n of America (198)

West Alexandria

Women in Aviation Internat'l (546)

West Milton

American Rolling Door Institute (98)
Internat'l Door Ass'n (289)
Systems Builders Ass'n (519)

Westerville

American Ceramic Soc. (51)
American Motorcyclist Ass'n (85)
Ass'n for Financial Technology (133)
Internat'l Executive Housekeepers Ass'n (290)
Internat'l Function Point Users Group (292)
Nat'l Ground Water Ass'n (407)
Nat'l Institute of Ceramic Engineers (411)
Religion Newswriters Ass'n of U.S. and Canada (474)
WLUC-Women in Insurance and Financial Services (545)

Westlake

American Soc. of Sanitary Engineering (116)

Wilberforce

Ass'n of African American Museums (141)

Willoughby

Phi Beta (456)

Winchester

Tamworth Swine Ass'n (520)

Worthington

Aviation Safety Institute (176)
Delta Omicron Foundation, Inc. (221)
Nat'l Career Development Ass'n (385)
Nat'l Tractor Pullers Ass'n (434)

Youngstown

Internat'l Ass'n of Hygienic Physicians (280)

Zanesville

Art Glass Suppliers Ass'n Internat'l (127)
Ass'n of Crafts and Creative Industries (149)
Ceramic Manufacturers Ass'n (189)
Miniatures Industry Ass'n of America (329)
Nat'l Needlework Ass'n (418)
Soc. of Craft Designers (500)

OKLAHOMA

Ada

Nat'l Ass'n of Royalty Owners (370)

Ardmore

Nat'l Animal Damage Control Ass'n (337)

Cleveland

Historians Film Committee (254)

Duncan

Nat'l Rural Water Ass'n (426)

Edmond

Environmental Design Research Ass'n (231)

Lawton

American Choral Directors Ass'n (51)
Percussive Arts Soc. (454)

Madille

Gelbray Internat'l (246)

Miami

American Academy of Sanitarians (26)

Norman

American Bandmasters Ass'n (46)
Ass'n of College and University Museums and Galleries (147)
Rhetoric Soc. of America (476)

Oklahoma City

Civil Aviation Medical Ass'n (194)
Conference on Consumer Finance Law (205)
Ground Water Protection Council (250)
Internat'l Professional Rodeo Ass'n (300)
Interstate Oil and Gas Compact Commission (312)
Kappa Psi Pharmaceutical Fraternity (315)
Nat'l Ass'n of Pipe Fabricators (365)
Nat'l Reining Horse Ass'n (425)
Soc. for Applied Anthropology (485)
Soc. for the Study of Social Biology (496)

Shawnee

Motorist Information and Services Ass'n (331)

Stillwater

American Peanut Research and Education Soc. (90)
American Soc. of Veterinary Ophthalmology (117)
Internat'l Ass'n for Computer Information Systems (273)
Internat'l Ground Source Heat Pump Ass'n (292)
Nat'l Ass'n of Government Guaranteed Lenders (357)
Nat'l Ass'n of Vocational-Technical Education Communicators (380)

Stroud

Equipment Maintenance Council (232)

Tulsa

Airborne Law Enforcement Ass'n (16)
American Ass'n of Petroleum Geologists (40)
Gas Processors Ass'n (245)
Gas Processors Suppliers Ass'n (245)
Internat'l Manufacturers Representatives Ass'n (296)
Kappa Kappa Iota (315)
Lawn and Garden Dealers' Ass'n (318)
Nat'l Ass'n of Insurance Women (360)
Nat'l Ass'n of Intercollegiate Athletics (360)
Nat'l Ass'n of Legal Assistants (361)
Nat'l Ass'n of Legal Secretaries (361)
Palomino Horse Breeders of America (453)
Petroleum Equipment Institute (455)
SEPM - Soc. for Sedimentary Geology (482)
Soc. of Exploration Geophysicists (501)
United States Junior Chamber of Commerce (534)

Wagoner

American Breed Ass'n (49)

OREGON

Bandon

Nat'l Council on Education for the Ceramic Arts (397)

Beaverton

Ass'n for the Treatment of Sexual Abusers (140)
Independent Forest Products Ass'n (260)

Corvallis

American Ass'n of State Climatologists (43)
American Romney Breeders Ass'n (98)
Council on Forest Engineering (216)
Internat'l Institute of Fisheries Economics and Trade (294)
Internat'l Weed Science Soc. (311)
Nat'l Intramural-Recreational Sports Ass'n (413)

Crooked River Ranch

Professional Ass'n of Lumbermen - World Lumber Standards (464)

Eugene

Ass'n for Direct Instruction (132)
Developmental Disabilities Nurses Ass'n (222)
Forest Industries Telecommunications (242)
History of Education Soc. (254)
Institute of Certified Business Counselors (266)
Internat'l Soc. for Technology in Education (304)
Nat'l Consortium of Chemical Dependency Nurses (392)
Nat'l Student Employment Ass'n (432)
Nat'l Tile Roofing Manufacturers Ass'n (434)

Hood River

Nat'l Cherry Growers and Industries Foundation (386)

Lake Oswego

Nat'l Reloading Manufacturers Ass'n (425)

Medford

Ass'n of Insolvency Accountants (154)
Professional Ass'n of Custom Clothiers (464)

Portland

American Ass'n of Public Health Dentistry (42)
American Tinnitus Ass'n (120)
American Wood Chip Export Ass'n (123)
Ass'n for the Advancement of Baltic Studies (138)
Ass'n of Administrative Law Judges (141)
Ass'n of Telemedicine Service Providers (167)
Business Forms Management Ass'n (184)
Church and Synagogue Library Ass'n (193)
Foil Stamping and Embossing Ass'n (241)
Nat'l Ass'n of Consumer Shows (349)
Nat'l Ass'n of Professional Process Servers (367)
Nat'l Conference of Women's Bar Ass'ns (391)
Soc. for Values in Higher Education (496)
Western Wood Products Ass'n (543)

Rose Lodge

Kite Trade Ass'n Internat'l (316)

Roseburg

Forest Products Safety Conference (242)

Salem

Internat'l Guild of Candle Artisans (293)
Organization of Flying Adjusters (450)

Sutherlin

Dutch Warmblood Ass'n (225)

Tigard

Building Material Dealers Ass'n (183)

Wilsonville

Helicopter Loggers Ass'n (253)

PENNSYLVANIA

Allentown

Internat'l Periodical Distributors Ass'n (299)
Phi Alpha Theta (456)

Bethlehem

Cement Employers Ass'n (189)
Express Carriers Ass'n (234)
Gift Ass'n of America (247)
Nat'l Ass'n of Colleges and Employers (348)
Structural Stability Research Council (517)

Bloomsburg

Judge Advocates Ass'n (315)
School Science and Mathematics Ass'n (479)

Blue Bell

Federation of Socs. for Coatings Technology (237)

Broomall

Bryn Mawr

Soc. for Business Ethics (486)
Society of Financial Service Professionals (509)

Butler

Abrasives Engineering Soc. (7)

Carlisle
Nat'l Computer Security Ass'n (389)
Soc. for Military History (491)

Catasauqua
American Ass'n of Oriental Medicine (40)

Chambersburg
Dairy Soc. Internat'l (220)

Chester
Ass'n on Programs for Female Offenders (170)

Clark
Nat'l Dog Groomers Ass'n of America (399)

Coatesville
Dog Writers' Ass'n of America (224)

Conshohocken
American Soc. for Clinical Pharmacology and
    Therapeutics (101)

Coopersburg
Internat'l Council of Regional School Accrediting
    Commissions (288)

Crystal Spring
Red and White Dairy Cattle Ass'n (473)

Darlington
American Border Leicester Ass'n (49)

Dingmams Ferry
American Nature Study Soc. (86)

Dornside
Palomino Horse Ass'n (453)

Dover
American Soc. of Petroleum Operations Engineers (114)

Doylestown
Internat'l Plate Printers', Die Stampers' and Engravers' Union
    of North America (300)
Nat'l Ass'n of Demolition Contractors (352)

East Greenville
Mobile Air Conditioning Soc. Worldwide (329)
Nat'l Automotive Radiator Service Ass'n (381)

Elizabethtown
American Ass'n of Meat Processors (38)

Emlenton
Internat'l Soc. of Crime Prevention Practitioners (306)

Ephrata
American Academy of State Certified Appraisers (26)

Erie
Internat'l Ass'n of Home Safety and Security
    Professionals (280)

Exton
Engine Service Ass'n (230)
Soc. of Cable Telecommunications Engineers (499)

Fort Washington
Drug Information Ass'n (225)

Greensburg
Associated Glass and Pottery Manufacturers (171)

Greentown
Boating Writers Internat'l (181)
Tourist House Ass'n of America (524)

Harrisburg
American Academy of Clinical Toxicology (21)
American College of Medical Toxicology (55)
Ass'n of Bedding and Furniture Law Officials (144)
Aviation Technician Education Council (176)
Internat'l Academy of Sports Vision (272)
Nat'l Frozen Food Ass'n (406)

Honesdale
Evidence Photographers Internat'l Council (233)

Horsham
Council of Internat'l Investigators (214)

Hunker
Mine Inspectors' Institute of America (329)

Huntingdon
American Institute of Bangladesh Studies (76)

Indiana
American Driver and Traffic Safety Education Ass'n (65)
Nat'l Council for Geographic Education (393)
Soc. for the Philosophy of Sex and Love (495)

Jamison
Nat'l Ass'n of Traffic Accident Reconstructionists and
    Investigators (379)

Jeffersonville
Environmental Management Ass'n (232)

Kennett Square
American Ass'n of Avian Pathologists (33)
American Ass'n of Botanical Gardens and Arboreta (33)

Lancaster
Design-Build Manufacturers Ass'n (222)
Fire Retardant Chemicals Ass'n (240)

Landisville
American College of Nuclear Medicine (56)

Lemont
North American Soc. for Sport History (444)

Levittown
Nat'l Constables Ass'n (392)
Phi Lambda Kappa Medical Fraternity (457)

Lititz
American College of Addictions Treatment Administrators (52)
Nat'l Ass'n of Addiction Treatment Providers (342)

Lock Haven
American Soc. of Transportation and Logistics (116)

Malvern
American Institute for CPCU - Insurance Institute of
    America (75)
Chartered Property and Casualty Underwriters Soc. (190)

McDonald
Black Top and Nat'l Delaine-Merino Sheep Breeders
    Ass'n (180)

McKeesport
Nat'l Ass'n of Vocational Education Special Needs
    Personnel (379)

Mechanicsburg
Nat'l Ass'n of Local Government Auditors (362)
Soc. of Government Meeting Professionals (502)

Media
American Aging Ass'n (27)
American Ass'n of Zoo Veterinarians (45)
Glass, Molders, Pottery, Plastics and Allied Workers
    International Union (248)

Middleburg
Internat'l Dwarf Fruit Tree Ass'n (289)

Milford
Nat'l Church Goods Ass'n (387)

Moon Township
Ass'n of Directory Marketing (149)

Mount Pleasant
Bridge Grid Flooring Manufacturers Ass'n (182)

New Hope
American Academy of Environmental Medicine (21)

New Wilmington
Ass'n for the Advancement of Internat'l Education (138)

Newtown
American Institute of Biomedical Climatology (76)

Newtown Square
Project Management Institute (468)

North Wales
American Soc. of Marine Artists (112)

Palmyra
Hair Internat'l (250)

Perkiomenville
Nat'l Ass'n of Childbearing Centers (347)

Philadelphia
American Academy of Political and Social Science (25)
American Ass'n for Cancer Research (30)
American Brush Manufacturers Ass'n (49)
American College of Foot and Ankle Pediatrics (54)
American College of Physicians-American Soc. of Internal
    Medicine (57)
American Entomological Soc. (66)
American Law Institute (81)
American Musicological Soc. (86)
American Philosophical Soc. (91)
American Soc. of Internat'l Executives (111)
Ass'n for High Technology Distribution (134)
Ass'n of Child and Adolescent Psychiatric Nurses (146)
Ass'n of Gay and Lesbian Psychiatrists (152)
Ass'n of Management Analysts in State and Local
    Government (156)
Ass'n of Residents in Radiation Oncology (163)
Ass'n of Vision Science Librarians (169)
Atlantic Independent Union (172)
Aviation Distributors and Manufacturers Ass'n Internat'l (175)
Bicycle Product Suppliers Ass'n (178)
Dental Dealers of America (221)
Dental Manufacturers of America (221)
Gynecologic Oncology Group (250)
Independent Research Libraries Ass'n (261)
Inter-America Travel Agents Soc. (271)
Internat'l Ass'n of Business Forecasting (277)
Internat'l Ass'n of Ice Cream Vendors (280)
Internat'l Ass'n of Jewish Vocational Services (280)
Lawn and Garden Marketing and Distribution Ass'n (318)
Major League Umpires Ass'n (322)
Nat'l Ass'n of Aluminum Distributors (343)
Nat'l Ass'n of Catholic School Teachers (346)
Nat'l Ass'n of Container Distributors (349)
Nat'l Ass'n of Health Unit Coordinators (357)
Nat'l Community Capital Ass'n (388)
Nat'l Federation of Abstracting and Information Services (403)
Nat'l Federation of Independent Unions (403)
Nat'l Field Selling Ass'n (404)
Nat'l Industrial Glove Distributors Ass'n (411)
Nat'l Marine Distributors Ass'n (416)
Nat'l Refrigeration Contractors Ass'n (424)
Nat'l Technical Ass'n of Scientists (433)
Nat'l United Affiliated Beverage Ass'n (435)
Nat'l Welding Supply Ass'n (436)
Nat'l Wood Tank Institute (436)
North American Horticultural Supply Ass'n (442)
North American Nursing Diagnosis Ass'n (443)
Nurse Healers - Professional Associates Internat'l (447)
Office Planners and Users Group (447)
Outdoor Power Equipment Distributors Ass'n (451)
Pharmacists in Ophthalmic Practice (456)
Professional Soc. for Sales and Marketing Training (467)
Radiation Therapy Oncology Group (471)
Real Estate Information Providers Ass'n (472)
Resistance Welder Manufacturers Ass'n (475)
Robert Morris Associates, the Ass'n of Lending and Credit
    Risk Professionals (476)
Security Hardware Distributors Ass'n (481)
Soc. for Developmental and Behavioral Pediatrics (487)
Soc. for Industrial and Applied Mathematics (489)
Soc. of Environmental Journalists (501)
United States Marine Safety Ass'n (534)
Victorian Soc. in America (539)
Water and Sewer Distributors of America (541)
Women in Scholarly Publishing (547)
Wood Machinery Manufacturers of America (548)
World History Ass'n (550)

Pittsburgh
AIM USA (15)
Air and Waste Management Ass'n (15)
American College of Mental Health Administration (55)
American Head and Neck Surgery Soc. (72)
American Paso Fino Horse Ass'n (90)
Ass'n for Bridge Construction and Design (130)
Ass'n of Cinema and Video Laboratories (146)
Ass'n of Iron and Steel Engineers (155)
Ass'n of Theological Schools in the United States and
    Canada (168)
Combustion Institute (198)
Dance Critics Ass'n (220)
Hardwood Manufacturers Ass'n (251)
Hospice and Palliative Nurses Ass'n (256)
Hotel Electronic Distribution Network Ass'n (256)
Internat'l Ass'n of Career Consulting Firms (277)
Internat'l Transplant Nurses Soc. (309)
Latin American Studies Ass'n (317)
Laundry and Dry Cleaning Internat'l Union (317)
Model Railroad Industry Ass'n (329)
Nat'l Ass'n of Radio Reading Services (368)
Nat'l Federation of Municipal Analysts (403)
Oncology Nursing Soc. (448)
Refractories Institute (473)
Soc. for Cinema Studies (486)
Southern Cypress Manufacturers Ass'n (510)
SSPC: the Soc. for Protective Coatings (515)
Steel Recycling Institute (516)
Supply Chain Council (518)
TechLaw Group (520)
United Electrical, Radio and Machine Workers of
    America (530)
United Steelworkers of America (536)

Plymouth Meeting
ECRI (226)

Reading
Ass'n for Retail Technology Standards (137)

Richboro
American Tin Trade Ass'n (120)

Sewickley
Graphic Arts Technical Foundation (249)
Internat'l Graphic Arts Education Ass'n (292)
Soc. of Prospective Medicine (506)

Silver Spring
Herb Growing and Marketing Network (253)

Solebury
Nat'l Paralegal Ass'n (421)

Somerset
Nat'l Fellowship of Child Care Executives (404)

Springdale
Pipe Fabrication Institute (458)

State College
American Soc. for Plasticulture (104)
Outdoor Writers Ass'n of America (451)

Stroudsburg
Internat'l Ass'n of Women Ministers (283)

Susquehanna
Allied Stone Industries (18)

Towanda
Internat'l Soc. for Professional Hypnosis (304)

Union City
Internat'l Ass'n of Broadcast Monitors (276)

Uniontown
American Soc. of Highway Engineers (110)

University Park
Academy of Behavioral Medicine Research (7)
American Pomological Soc. (93)

Upper Darby
Souvenirs and Novelties Trade Ass'n (510)

Valley Forge
American Baptist Homes and Hospitals Ass'n (46)

Villanova
North American Soc. for Social Philosophy (444)

Wallingford
Nat'l Soc. of Genetic Counselors (430)

Wampum
Colorado Ranger Horse Ass'n (198)

Warrendale
Iron and Steel Soc. (313)
Materials Research Soc. (325)
Minerals, Metals and Materials Soc., The (329)
Soc. of Automotive Engineers International (498)

Wayne
Aircraft Locknut Manufacturers Ass'n (16)
Certified Contractors NetWork (190)
Clinical Laboratory Management Ass'n (194)
Copper and Brass Servicenter Ass'n (209)
Fluid Sealing Ass'n (241)
Gasket Fabricators Ass'n (246)
Nat'l Ass'n of Diaper Services (352)
Nat'l Ass'n of Equipment Leasing Brokers (354)
Nat'l Classification Management Soc. (387)
Nat'l Committee for Clinical Laboratory Standards (388)
Nat'l Slag Ass'n (428)
NCCLS (438)
Professional Apparel Ass'n (464)

West Chester
Conductors Guild (203)
Graphic Arts Sales Foundation (249)

West Conshohocken
American Soc. for Testing and Materials (105)
Internat'l Teleconferencing Ass'n (308)

Westchester
Nat'l Counter Intelligence Corps Ass'n (398)

Wexford
Biotech Medical Management Ass'n (179)
Sleep Disorders Dental Soc. (483)

Whitehall
Nat'l Soc. of Painters in Casein and Acrylic (430)

Wilkes-Barre
Institute of Behavioral and Applied Management (265)

Wyndmoor
Internat'l Academy for Child Brain Development (272)

Wynnewood
Lambda Omicron Gamma Medical Society (317)

York
Ass'n of Food and Drug Officials (151)
Nat'l Ass'n of Chain Manufacturers (346)

RHODE ISLAND

Cephachet
Soc. of American Silversmiths (498)

Cranston
Jewelers Shipping Ass'n (314)

East Providence
Machine Printers and Engravers Ass'n of the United States (321)

North Scituate
Continental Dorset Club (208)

Providence
American Mathematical Soc. (83)
American Soc. for Theatre Research (105)
Ass'n for Computers and the Humanities (131)
Costume Jewelry Salesmen's Ass'n (210)
Fashion Jewelry Ass'n of America (235)
Manufacturing Jewelers and Suppliers of America (323)
Metal Findings Manufacturers Ass'n (327)
Nat'l Ass'n of College Broadcasters (348)
Soc. for News Design (491)

Warwick
Jewelers Board of Trade (313)

SOUTH CAROLINA

Anderson
Tile Council of America (523)

Beaufort
Pulp, Paper and Paperboard Export Ass'n of the U.S. (470)

Charleston
American Soc. of Ichthyologists and Herpetologists (111)
Ass'n for Continuing Higher Education (131)
Psi Omega (469)

Clemson
Fiber Soc. (238)
Nat'l Council of Examiners for Engineering and Surveying (394)

Columbia
Academy of Dispensing Audiologists (8)
Ass'n for Education in Journalism and Mass Communication (132)
Ass'n of Schools of Journalism and Mass Communication (164)
CUMREC Internat'l (219)
Nat'l Ass'n for Campus Activities (338)
Nat'l Ass'n of Bankruptcy Trustees (344)
Nat'l Ass'n of Decorative Fabric Distributors (352)
Nat'l Ass'n of State Boards of Geology (374)
Nat'l Drilling Ass'n (400)
Nat'l Educational Telecommunications Ass'n (400)
Nat'l Peach Council (421)
Organization of Wildlife Planners (450)
Palmetto Baptist Medical Center (453)
Public Broadcasting Management Ass'n (469)

Darlington
Nat'l Motorsports Press Ass'n (417)

Fripp Island
Soc. for Hematopathology (488)

Ft. Mill
Ass'n of Industrial Metallizers, Coaters and Laminators (154)

Galizants Ferry
College Swimming Coaches Ass'n of America (198)

Hilton Head
United States Professional Tennis Registry (535)

Hilton Head Island
American Agents Ass'n (27)
Scientific Equipment and Furniture Ass'n (480)

Irmo
Ass'n of Traumatic Stress Specialists (168)

Lexington
Congress of Chiropractic State Ass'ns (205)
Nat'l Conference of Bankruptcy Judges (389)

Little River
Nat'l Conference of Diocesan Vocation Directors (390)

Monks Corner
Nat'l Ass'n of County Agricultural Agents (350)

Mt. Pleasant
Nat'l Golf Course Owners Ass'n (407)

Myrtle Beach
Steel Joist Institute (516)

Newberry
Internat'l Soc. of Industrial Fabric Manufacturers (306)

Ninety-Six
North American Flowerbulb Wholesalers Ass'n (442)

Rock Hill
College English Ass'n (197)

West Columbia
Nat'l Ass'n of State Controlled Substances Authorities (374)

SOUTH DAKOTA

Brookings
Beef Improvement Federation (177)
Internat'l Soc. of Weekly Newspaper Editors (307)
Nat'l Ass'n of University Fisheries and Wildlife Programs (379)

Flandreau
Nat'l Hereford Hog Record Ass'n (409)

Pierre
Nat'l Ass'n of State Directors of Veterans Affairs (375)
Wheat Quality Council (543)

Rapid City
Council for the Advancement of Standards in Higher Education (212)
Internat'l Builders Exchange Executives (284)

Sisseton
Nat'l Goose Council (407)

TENNESSEE

Brighton
Internat'l Ass'n of Personal Protection Agents (281)

Bristol
Christian Medical and Dental Soc. (193)

Bybee
Nat'l Institute of American Doll Artists (411)

Camden
Nat'l Marine Representatives Ass'n (416)

Chattanooga
American Polygraph Ass'n (93)
Cast Iron Soil Pipe Institute (187)

Cleveland
Cookie and Snack Bakers Ass'n (208)

Collierville
Nat'l Alliance of Independent Crop Consultants (336)
Nat'l Ass'n of Office Furniture Dealers (364)

Cookesville
American College of Internat'l Physicians (55)

Cordova
American Ass'n for Laboratory Animal Science (31)

Franklin
Cancer Biotherapy Research Group (186)
Nat'l Kerosene Heater Ass'n (414)

Germantown
American Soc. of Questioned Document Examiners (115)
Orthopedic Surgical Manufacturers Ass'n (451)

Jackson
American Academy of Ministry (23)

Knoxville
Airport Ground Transportation Ass'n (17)
America Outdoors (19)

American Academy of Podiatric Practice Management **(25)**
American Academy of Veterinary and Comparative
Toxicology **(26)**
Knitting Guild of America **(316)**
Soc. for Luminescent Microscopy and Spectroscopy **(490)**
Soc. for the Study of Social Problems **(496)**

Lewisburg

Tennessee Walking Horse Breeders and Exhibitors Ass'n **(521)**

Martin

History of Economics Soc. **(254)**

McMinnville

Nat'l Caves Ass'n **(386)**

Memphis

American College of Apothecaries **(53)**
American Cotton Shippers Ass'n **(60)**
American Innerspring Manufacturers **(75)**
American Mathematical Ass'n of Two Year Colleges **(83)**
Ass'n for the Advancement of Applied Sport Psychology **(138)**
Ass'n of Automotive Aftermarket Distributors **(144)**
College Media Advisers **(197)**
Franchise Consultants Internat'l Ass'n **(243)**
Internat'l Tanning Manufacturers Ass'n **(308)**
Nat'l Ass'n of Foster Grandparent Program Directors **(356)**
Nat'l Ass'n of Security Companies **(372)**
Nat'l Cotton Batting Institute **(392)**
Nat'l Cotton Council of America **(392)**
Nat'l Cotton Ginners' Ass'n **(392)**
Nat'l Cottonseed Products Ass'n **(393)**
Nat'l Hardwood Lumber Ass'n **(408)**
Nat'l Oak Flooring Manufacturers Ass'n **(419)**

Morristown

UFCW Textile Council **(529)**

Murfreesboro

Nat'l Spotted Saddle Horse Ass'n **(431)**
Walking Horse Owners Ass'n of America **(540)**

Nashville

American Ass'n for State and Local History **(32)**
American Ass'n of Small Ruminant Practitioners **(42)**
American Board of Veterinary Practitioners **(48)**
American Broncho-Esophagological Ass'n **(49)**
American College of Neuropsychopharmacology **(55)**
American Economic Ass'n **(65)**
American Laryngological Ass'n **(80)**
American Veterinary Dental Soc. **(121)**
Ass'n for the Development of Religious Information
Systems **(139)**
Ass'n of Southern Baptist Colleges and Schools **(165)**
Baptist Communicators Ass'n **(176)**
Church Music Publishers Ass'n **(193)**
Country Music Ass'n **(217)**
Country Radio Broadcasters **(218)**
Delta Nu Alpha Transportation Fraternity **(221)**
Engraved Stationery Manufacturers Ass'n **(231)**
Fellowship of United Methodists in Music and Worship
Arts **(238)**
Gospel Music Ass'n **(248)**
Internat'l Entertainment Buyers Ass'n **(290)**
Internat'l Quorum of Film and Video Producers **(301)**
Nat'l Ass'n of Schools and Colleges of the United Methodist
Church **(371)**
Nat'l Ass'n of State Boards of Accountancy **(374)**
Nat'l Ass'n of Teacher Educators for Family and Consumer
Sciences **(378)**
Nat'l Band Ass'n **(382)**
Nat'l Conference on Research in Language and Literacy **(391)**
Nat'l Fraternal Order of Police **(406)**
Nat'l Organization of Bar Counsel **(420)**
Porcelain Enamel Institute **(460)**
SAFE Ass'n **(478)**
United Paperworkers Internat'l Union **(531)**

Oak Ridge

Geochemical Soc. **(246)**

Savannah

American Theatre Critics Ass'n **(120)**

Shelbyville

Walking Horse Trainers Ass'n **(540)**

Springfield

Ass'n of Dark Leaf Tobacco Dealers and Exporters **(149)**

Whites Creek

Women's Internat'l Network of Utility Professionals **(548)**

TEXAS

Abernathy

Nat'l Grain Sorghum Producers **(407)**

Addison

Internat'l Soc. for Heart and Lung Transplantation **(303)**

Alvarado

American Miniature Horse Ass'n **(85)**

Amarillo

American Quarter Horse Ass'n **(96)**

Arlington

Bowling Proprietors Ass'n of America **(181)**
Broker Management Council **(182)**
Computer Use in Social Services Network **(203)**
Manufacturers Representatives of America **(323)**
Nat'l Conference of Executives of the Arc **(390)**
Nat'l Independent Automobile Dealers Ass'n **(410)**
Nat'l Institute of Steel Detailing **(412)**
Paper and Plastic Representatives Management Council **(453)**
Psychonomic Soc. **(469)**

Austin

Aggregate and Concrete Executives **(14)**
Amalgamated Printers' Ass'n **(19)**
American Academy of Nurse Practitioners **(23)**
American Agricultural Editors Ass'n **(27)**
American College of Musicians **(55)**
American Institute of Fishery Research Biologists **(77)**
American Jewish Press Ass'n **(80)**
Ass'n for Continuing Legal Education **(132)**
Ass'n of Certified Fraud Examiners **(146)**
Ass'n of Professional Model Makers **(161)**
Ass'n of Progressive Rental Organizations **(162)**
Associated Risk Managers Internat'l **(172)**
College Band Directors Nat'l Ass'n **(197)**
Council of State Ass'n Presidents **(215)**
Hospitality Financial and Technology Professionals **(256)**
Information Technology Training Ass'n **(264)**
Internat'l Communication Ass'n **(286)**
Internat'l Jewish Media Ass'n **(295)**
Internat'l Piano Guild **(300)**
Liaison Committee of Cooperating Oil and Gas Ass'ns **(319)**
Medical Mycological Soc. of the Americas **(326)**
Nat'l Ass'n for Promotional and Advertising Allowances **(340)**
Nat'l Ass'n of Investigative Specialists **(360)**
Nat'l Ass'n of Professional Organizers **(367)**
Nat'l Ass'n of Recreation Resource Planners **(369)**
Nat'l Council on Teacher Retirement **(398)**
Nat'l Guard Executive Directors Ass'n **(408)**
Nat'l Guild of Piano Teachers **(408)**
North American Membrane Soc. **(443)**
Research Soc. on Alcoholism **(475)**
Soc. of Certified Insurance Counselors **(499)**
Soc. of Engineering Science **(501)**
Trade Cable and Telecommunications Ass'n **(524)**
World Council of Defense Investigators **(549)**

Bedford

Ass'n of Finance and Insurance Professionals **(151)**
Automotive Service Ass'n **(175)**
Consortium for Advanced Manufacturing Internat'l **(206)**
Convention of American Instructors of the Deaf **(208)**

Belton

Nat'l Ass'n of Extension 4-H Agents **(354)**

Big Sandy

Independent Pet and Animal Transportation Ass'n
Internat'l **(261)**

Brooks AFB

Soc. of United States Air Force Flight Surgeons **(508)**

Burton

American Bralers Ass'n **(49)**

Cedar Hill

American Ass'n of Sunday and Feature Editors **(43)**

College Station

American Ass'n of Community Theatre **(35)**
Ass'n of Engineering Geologists **(150)**
Council for Elementary Science Internat'l **(211)**
Institute of Nautical Archaeology **(268)**
Reinforced Concrete Research Council **(474)**

Converse

Soc. of Military Otolaryngologists - Head and Neck
Surgeons **(504)**

Corpus Christi

Soc. for Advancement of Management **(484)**

Corsicana

Internat'l Visual Literacy Ass'n **(310)**

Dallas

Academic Language Therapy Ass'n **(7)**
Academy of Dental Materials **(8)**
ADSC: The Internat'l Ass'n of Foundation Drilling **(12)**
American Ass'n for Respiratory Care **(31)**
American Ass'n of Community Psychiatrists **(35)**
American College of Emergency Physicians **(54)**
American Emu Ass'n **(66)**
American Fire Sprinkler Ass'n **(68)**
American Gem Trade Ass'n **(70)**
American Heart Ass'n **(72)**
American Lighting Ass'n **(81)**
American Soc. for Adolescent Psychiatry **(100)**
American Soc. of Breast Disease **(107)**
American Therapeutic Ass'n **(120)**

Ass'n of Attorney-Mediators **(144)**
Ass'n of Energy Service Companies **(150)**
Ass'n of Independent Information Professionals **(153)**
Associated Locksmiths of America **(171)**
Automotive Oil Change Ass'n **(175)**
Collegiate Commissioners Ass'n **(198)**
Directional Crossing Contractors Ass'n **(223)**
Embroidery Trade Ass'n **(229)**
Exposition Service Contractors Ass'n **(234)**
Football Writers Ass'n of America **(242)**
Home Furnishings Internat'l Ass'n **(255)**
Ice Skating Institute **(258)**
Independent Distributors Ass'n **(260)**
Internat'l and American Ass'ns of Clinical Nutritionists **(273)**
Internat'l Ass'n for Exposition Management **(274)**
Internat'l Communications Ass'n **(286)**
Internat'l Graphological Soc. **(292)**
Internat'l Newspaper Marketing Ass'n **(298)**
Internat'l Soc. of Bassists **(305)**
Investment Casting Institute **(312)**
Kerato-Refractive Soc. **(315)**
Light Aircraft Manufacturers Ass'n **(319)**
Meeting Professionals Internat'l **(327)**
Nat'l Ass'n of Dental Plans **(352)**
Nat'l Ass'n of Division Order Analysts **(353)**
Nat'l Ass'n of Limited Edition Dealers **(361)**
Nat'l Ass'n of School Music Dealers **(371)**
Nat'l Ass'n of Small Business Internat'l Trade Educators **(373)**
Nat'l Athletic Trainers' Ass'n **(381)**
Nat'l Business Ass'n **(384)**
Nat'l Pawnbrokers Ass'n **(421)**
Nat'l Soc. of Hispanic MBAs **(430)**
Ombudsman Ass'n, The **(448)**
Piano Manufacturers Ass'n Internat'l **(458)**
Pipe Line Contractors Ass'n **(458)**
Professional Ass'n of Christian Educators **(464)**
Retail Print Music Dealers Ass'n **(476)**
Safe and Vault Technicians Ass'n **(478)**
Service Dealers Ass'n **(482)**
Soc. of Diagnostic Medical Sonographers **(500)**
Soc. of Independent Professional Earth Scientists **(503)**
Tortilla Industry Ass'n **(524)**
Uni-Bell PVC Pipe Ass'n **(529)**

Denison

Council of Petroleum Accountants Socs. **(215)**

Denton

American Donkey and Mule Soc. **(65)**
Internat'l Trombone Ass'n **(309)**
Red Angus Ass'n of America **(473)**

Dripping Springs

American Red Brangus Ass'n **(97)**

Euless

Federation of State Medical Boards of the U. S. **(237)**

Fort Worth

American Ass'n of Professional Landmen **(41)**
American Ostrich Ass'n **(90)**
American Paint Horse Ass'n **(90)**
Ass'n for Women in Sports Media **(141)**
Automotive Refrigeration Products Institute **(175)**
Internat'l Mobile Air Conditioning Ass'n **(297)**
Internat'l Soc. of Certified Electronics Technicians **(305)**
Livestock Publications Council **(320)**
Nat'l Ass'n of Church Business Administration **(347)**
Nat'l Ass'n of Women in Construction **(380)**
Nat'l Cutting Horse Ass'n **(398)**
Nat'l Electronic Service Dealers Ass'n **(400)**
Pinto Horse Ass'n of America **(458)**
Texas Longhorn Breeders Ass'n of America **(521)**

Fredonia

American Southdown Breeders Ass'n **(117)**

Gainesville

Energy Traffic Ass'n **(230)**

Galveston

American Soc. for Neurochemistry **(104)**
Internat'l Soc. for Chronobiology **(303)**

Garland

American Metal Detector Manufacturers Ass'n **(84)**
Choristers Guild **(193)**

Georgetown

American Forage and Grassland Council **(69)**

Godley

Galiceno Horse Breeders Ass'n **(245)**

Granbury

American Wood-Preservers' Ass'n **(123)**

Houston

American Ass'n of Stratigraphic Palynologists **(43)**
American Brahman Breeders Ass'n **(49)**
American Institute of Organbuilders **(78)**
American Neurotology Soc. **(87)**
American Nurses in Business Ass'n **(87)**
American Soc. for Stereotactic and Functional
Neurosurgery **(105)**

American Soc. of Laboratory Animal Practitioners (III)
Animal Transportation Ass'n (125)
Ass'n of Diving Contractors (150)
Ass'n of Lutheran Secondary Schools (156)
Ass'n of Visual Merchandise Representatives (169)
Automotive Body Parts Ass'n (174)
Benchmarking Network Ass'n (178)
Cooling Tower Institute (208)
Drilling Engineering Ass'n (224)
Fiberglass Tank and Pipe Institute (238)
Golf Writers Ass'n of America (248)
Industrial Foundation of America (263)
Internat'l Ass'n for Mathematical Geology (274)
Internat'l Ass'n of Clerks, Recorders, Election Officials and
      Treasurers (277)
Internat'l Ass'n of Drilling Contractors (278)
Internat'l Ass'n of Geophysical Contractors (279)
Internat'l Atherosclerosis Soc. (283)
Internat'l Facility Management Ass'n (290)
Internat'l Institute of Synthetic Rubber Producers (295)
Internat'l Maintenance Institute (296)
Internat'l Oil Scouts Ass'n (299)
NACE Internat'l (333)
Nat'l Ass'n of Steel Pipe Distributors (377)
Nat'l Energy Services Ass'n (401)
North American Soc. for Dialysis and Transplantation (444)
Petroleum Equipment Suppliers Ass'n (455)
Petroleum Industry Security Council (455)
Romance Writers of America (477)
Small Luxury Hotels (484)
Soc. of Gastrointestinal Radiologists (502)
Soc. of Mexican American Engineers and Scientists (504)
Soc. of Petroleum Evaluation Engineers (505)
Soc. of Piping Engineers and Designers (505)
Soc. of Professional Well Log Analysts (506)
United States Professional Tennis Ass'n (534)
Wireless Dealers Ass'n (545)
Women in Endocrinology (546)

Huntsville

Nat'l Ass'n of Colleges and Teachers of Agriculture (348)

Hurst

American Academy of Head, Neck and Facial Pain (22)
Nat'l Ass'n of Dog Obedience Instructors (353)

Ingram

Exotic Wildlife Ass'n (234)

Irving

American Concrete Pipe Ass'n (59)
Emergency Medicine Residents' Ass'n (229)
Internat'l Aloe Science Council (273)
Internat'l Ass'n of Assembly Managers (276)
Internat'l Television Ass'n (308)
Promotional Products Ass'n Internat'l (468)
Young Presidents' Organization (551)

Keller

Nat'l Soc. of Newspaper Columnists (430)

Kingsville

College Sports Information Directors of America (198)
Santa Gertrudis Breeders Internat'l (479)

Kingwood

Internat'l Soc. of Speakers, Authors and Consultants (307)

Ledbetter

American Suffolk Horse Ass'n (118)

Livingston

American Ass'n of Insurance Management Consultants (38)

Lubbock

Ass'n for Arid Lands Studies (130)
History of Earth Sciences Soc. (254)

Lufkin

Phi Chi Theta (456)

Mission

Texas Produce Export Ass'n (521)

Nacogdoches

United Braford Breeders (530)

North Richland Hills

Nat'l Ass'n of Catastrophe Adjusters (346)

Odessa

American College of Eye Surgeons (54)

Orange

Ass'n of Government Marketing Assistance Specialists (152)

Prairie View

Research Ass'n of Minority Professors (475)

Richardson

American Literary Translators Ass'n (81)
Council of Engineering and Scientific Soc. Executives (213)

Distribution Contractors Ass'n (224)
Internat'l Ass'n of Electrical Inspectors (278)
Nat'l Ass'n of Rail Shippers (368)
Soc. for Disability Studies (487)
Soc. of Petroleum Engineers (505)

Richmond

American Academy of Gnathologic Orthopedics (22)

Rocksprings

American Angora Goat Breeder's Ass'n (28)

Rockwall

Nat'l Ass'n of Manufacturing Opticians (362)

Sachse

Nat'l Rep/Wholesaler Ass'n (425)

San Angelo

American Rambouillet Sheep Breeders Ass'n (97)
Mohair Council of America (330)

San Antonio

Accredited Review Appraisers Council (II)
American College of Oral and Maxillofacial Surgeons (56)
American Payroll Ass'n (90)
American Soc. of Asset Managers (107)
Beefmaster Breeders United (177)
Hispanic Ass'n of Colleges and Universities (254)
Internat'l Ass'n Colon Hydro Therapy (273)
Internat'l Brangus Breeders Ass'n (284)
Nat'l Ass'n of Counselors (350)
Nat'l Ass'n of Master Appraisers (362)
Nat'l Ass'n of Property Inspectors (367)
Nat'l Soc. of Appraiser Specialists (429)
Nat'l Soc. of Environmental Consultants (429)
Neurosurgical Soc. of America (438)
Non Commissioned Officers Ass'n of the U.S.A. (439)
Parenting Publications of America (453)
Research and Development Associates for Military Food and
      Packaging Systems (475)
Soc. of Government Service Urologists (502)

San Marcos

Computer Assisted Language Instruction Consortium (202)
Internat'l Council of Psychologists (288)
Internat'l Soc. of Applied Intelligence (305)

Spring

Nat'l Ass'n of Private Enterprise (366)

Sugar Land

Internat'l Academy of Compounding Pharmacists (272)
Sugar Industry Technologists (518)

Sunnyvale

Aestheticians Internat'l Ass'n (13)

Sunray

American Agriculture Movement (27)

The Woodlands

American Pediatric Soc. (91)
Nat'l Stripper Well Ass'n (432)
Soc. for Pediatric Research (492)

Tomball

Energy Telecommunications and Electrical Ass'n (230)

Tyler

CHA - Certified Horsemanship Ass'n (190)

Waco

American Football Coaches Ass'n (69)
American Soc. of Limnology and Oceanography (112)
Oral History Ass'n (449)

UTAH

Logan

Nat'l Council on Rehabilitation Education (398)
Western Literature Ass'n (543)

Ogden

Religious Communication Ass'n (474)

Park City

United States Ski Coaches Ass'n (535)

Provo

American Ass'n of Presidents of Independent Colleges and
      Universities (41)
American Ass'n of Teachers of Arabic (43)
American Soc. of Mammalogists (112)
Ass'n for Consumer Research (131)
Council on Chiropractic Orthopedics (216)
Nat'l Ass'n for Humanities Education (339)
Soc. for the Advancement of Scandinavian Study (494)

Roosevelt

American Herbalists Guild (73)

Salt Lake City

Academy of Clinical Laboratory Physicians and Scientists (8)
American Academy of Procedural Coders (25)
Council of Dance Administrators (213)
Executive Women Internat'l (233)
Expanded Shale, Clay and Slate Institute (234)
Nat'l Ass'n of Certified Valuation Analysts (346)
Nat'l Ass'n of Senior Companions Project Directors (372)
Nat'l Flight Paramedics Ass'n (405)
North American Agricultural Marketing Officials (440)

VERMONT

Barre

Barre Granite Ass'n (177)

Brattleboro

Ayrshire Breeders' Ass'n (176)
Holstein Ass'n USA (255)
Purebred Dairy Cattle Ass'n (470)

Burlington

American Soc. of Forensic Odontology (110)

Hardwick

Ass'n of American Pesticide Control Officials (142)

Hinesburg

Funeral and Memorial Socs. of America (244)

Middlebury

Ass'n of Clinical Scientists (147)

North Bennington

Ecotourism Soc. (225)

Putney

Internat'l Soc. for Intercultural Education, Training and
      Research (303)

Randolph

Masonry Heater Ass'n of North America (324)

Shelburne

American Morgan Horse Ass'n (85)

St. Albans

North American Maple Syrup Council (443)

West Brattleboro

Nat'l Pedigreed Livestock Council (422)

Woodstock

Ass'n of Jewish Book Publishers (155)

VIRGINIA

Alexandria

Academy of Criminal Justice Sciences (8)
Academy of Managed Care Pharmacy (8)
Aeronautical Repair Station Ass'n (13)
Aerospace Medical Ass'n (13)
Agricultural Transportation Conference (15)
Air and Expedited Motor Carriers Conference (15)
Airport Consultants Council (17)
American Academy of Facial Plastic and Reconstructive
      Surgery (22)
American Academy of Orthotists and Prosthetists (24)
American Academy of Otolaryngology-Head and Neck
      Surgery (24)
American Academy of Physician Assistants (25)
American Academy of Physician Assistants in Occupational
      Medicine (25)
American Ass'n for Dental Research (30)
American Ass'n for the Study of Liver Diseases (32)
American Ass'n of Airport Executives (33)
American Ass'n of Colleges of Pharmacy (35)
American Ass'n of Cosmetology Schools (35)
American Ass'n of Family and Consumer Sciences (36)
American Ass'n of Pharmaceutical Scientists (40)
American Ass'n of Port Authorities (41)
American Bankruptcy Institute (46)
American Chamber of Commerce Executives (51)
American Coal Ash Ass'n (52)
American College Counseling Ass'n (52)
American College of Health Care Administrators (54)
American College of Osteopathic Surgeons (56)
American Counseling Ass'n (62)
American Dental Trade Ass'n (64)
American Diabetes Ass'n (64)
American Gear Manufacturers Ass'n (70)
American Geological Institute (70)
American Helicopter Soc. (73)
American Horticultural Soc. (74)
American Institute of Chemists (77)
American Institute of Homeopathy (77)
American Internat'l Automobile Dealers Ass'n (79)
American Internat'l Freight Ass'n (79)
American League of Lobbyists (81)
American Medical Group Ass'n (83)

Information Technology Ass'n of America (264)
Insurance Institute for Highway Safety (270)
Internat'l Chiropractors Ass'n (285)
Internat'l Federation of Inspection Agencies - Americas
   Committee (290)
Internat'l Mass Retail Ass'n (297)
Internat'l Pharmaceutical Excipients Council (299)
Internat'l Real Estate Federation - American Chapter (301)
ISEA-The Safety Equipment Ass'n (313)
Joint Electron Device Engineering Council (315)
Land Mobile Communications Council (317)
Manufactured Housing Institute (322)
Manufacturers Alliance (322)
Meat Importers' Council of America (325)
Molluscan Shellfish Institute (330)
MultiMedia Telecommunications Ass'n (331)
Nat'l Aeronautic Ass'n (335)
Nat'l Aquaculture Council (337)
Nat'l Ass'n of Alcoholism and Drug Abuse Counselors (343)
Nat'l Ass'n of Business Political Action Committees (346)
Nat'l Ass'n of Chemical Distributors (347)
Nat'l Ass'n of Federal Credit Unions (355)
Nat'l Ass'n of Federal Education Program Administrators (355)
Nat'l Ass'n of Health Underwriters (357)
Nat'l Ass'n of State Credit Union Supervisors (374)
Nat'l Blue Crab Industry Ass'n (383)
Nat'l Defense Industrial Ass'n (399)
Nat'l Erectors Ass'n (402)
Nat'l Federation of Press Women (404)
Nat'l Fisheries Institute (404)
Nat'l Genealogical Soc. (406)
Nat'l Hospice Organization (409)
Nat'l Industrial Transportation League (411)
Nat'l Lime Ass'n (415)
Nat'l Meat Canners Ass'n (416)
Nat'l Milk Producers Federation (417)
Nat'l Newspaper Ass'n (418)
Nat'l Pasta Ass'n (421)
Nat'l Rural Electric Cooperative Ass'n (426)
Nat'l Science Teachers Ass'n (427)
Nat'l Shipyard Ass'n (428)
Nat'l Training Systems Ass'n (434)
Nat'l Utility Contractors Ass'n (435)
Nat'l Venture Capital Ass'n (435)
Nat'l Water Resources Ass'n (435)
Nat'l Wooden Pallet and Container Ass'n (437)
Natural Gas Vehicle Coalition (437)
Newsletter Publishers Ass'n (439)
North American Soc. for Trenchless Technology (445)
Oxygenated Fuels Ass'n (452)
Packaging Machinery Manufacturers Institute (452)
Passenger Vessel Ass'n (454)
Patent and Trademark Office Soc. (454)
Patent Office Professional Ass'n (454)
Pellet Fuels Institute (454)
Petroleum Marketers Ass'n of America (456)
Pharmaceutical Care Management Ass'n (456)
Professional Services Council (467)
Public Risk Management Ass'n (470)
Rehabilitation Engineering and Assistive Technology Soc. of
   North America (474)
Rice Millers' Ass'n (476)
Shrimp Council (483)
Soc. for Biomedical Equipment Technicians (485)
Soc. for Technical Communication (494)
Soc. of Federal Labor Relations Professionals (501)
Southern Transportation Logistics Ass'n (510)
Space Transportation Ass'n (511)
Suppliers of Advanced Composite Materials Ass'n (518)
Telecommunications Industry Ass'n (521)
Trademark Soc. (525)
U.S.A. Rice Federation (528)
Uniform and Textile Service Ass'n (529)
United States Advanced Ceramics Ass'n (531)
United States Hide, Skin and Leather Ass'n (534)
United States-Cuba Business Council (536)
Vision Council of America (540)
Western Hemisphere Ass'n of Meat Marketers (543)

Ashburn

American Park and Recreation Soc. (90)
Nat'l Recreation and Park Ass'n (424)
Nat'l Soc. for Park Resources (429)
Nat'l Therapeutic Recreation Soc. (433)
Soc. of Park and Recreation Educators (505)

Berryville

Academy of Security Educators and Trainers (10)

Blacksburg

Adhesion Soc. (11)
American Academy of Mechanics (23)
Internat'l Soc. for Developmental Psychobiology (303)
Internat'l Soc. for Quality-of-Life Studies (304)
Senior Army Reserve Commanders Ass'n (481)

Burke

Council of Industrial Boiler Owners (214)

Catlett

Nat'l Ass'n of School Safety and Law Enforcement
   Officers (371)

Chantilly

Door and Hardware Institute (224)
Nat'l Ass'n for Search and Rescue (341)
Sheet Metal and Air Conditioning Contractors' Nat'l
   Ass'n (482)

Charlottesville

Ass'n for Investment Management and Research (135)
Evangelical Press Ass'n (233)
Modular Building Institute (330)
Soc. for French Historical Studies (488)

Chatham

American Vocational Education Personnel Development
   Ass'n (122)

Chesapeake

Nat'l Ass'n of Marine Surveyors (362)

Christiansburg

Nat'l Ass'n of Child Care Professionals (347)

Culpepper

American Ass'n of State Social Work Boards (43)

Dunn Loring

Nat'l Pest Control Ass'n (422)

Fairfax

American Ass'n of Healthcare Consultants (37)
American Ass'n of Pastoral Counselors (40)
American Bryological and Lichenological Soc. (49)
American College of Bankruptcy (53)
American Industrial Hygiene Ass'n (75)
American Public Communications Council (95)
American Public Gas Ass'n (95)
American Soc. of Cataract and Refractive Surgery (107)
American Soc. of Ophthalmic Administrators (113)
American Wood Preservers Institute (123)
Armed Forces Communications and Electronics Ass'n (127)
Armed Forces Marketing Council (127)
Assisted Living Federation of America (170)
Associated Writing Programs (172)
Automotive Parts Rebuilders Ass'n (175)
Automotive Recyclers Ass'n (175)
Building Service Contractors Ass'n Internat'l (183)
Cable Telecommunications Ass'n (185)
Commission on Accreditation for Law Enforcement
   Agencies (199)
Computer Law Ass'n (202)
Congress on Ministry in Specialized Settings (205)
Connected Int'l Meeting Professionals Ass'n (206)
Council of Landscape Architectural Registration Boards (214)
Digital Printing and Imaging Ass'n (222)
Federation of Government Information Processing
   Councils (237)
Independent Educational Consultants Ass'n (260)
Internat'l Ass'n of Fire Chiefs (279)
Internat'l Communications Industries Ass'n (286)
Internat'l Federation of Pharmaceutical Wholesalers (290)
Internat'l Soc. of Transport Aircraft Trading (307)
Internat'l Test and Evaluation Ass'n (308)
Irrigation Ass'n (313)
Munitions Carriers Conference (331)
Nat'l Ass'n of Miscellaneous, Ornamental and Architectural
   Products Contractors (363)
Nat'l Ass'n of Reinforcing Steel Contractors (370)
Nat'l Community Education Ass'n (388)
Nat'l Contact Lens Examiners (392)
Nat'l Council of Erectors, Fabricators and Riggers (394)
Nat'l Rifle Ass'n of America (426)
Optical Laboratories Ass'n (448)
Opticians Ass'n of America (449)
Painting and Decorating Contractors of America (452)
Propeller Club of the U.S. (468)
Recreation Vehicle Dealers Ass'n of North America (472)
Recreation Vehicle Rental Ass'n (472)
Remanufacturing Industries Council Internat'l (474)
Screenprinting and Graphic Imaging Ass'n Internat'l (480)
Soc. for Industrial Microbiology (490)
Soc. of Cardiovascular and Interventional Radiology (499)
Specialized Carriers and Rigging Ass'n (514)

Falls Church

Access Technology Ass'n (10)
Accrediting Bureau of Health Education Schools (11)
American Ass'n for Budget and Program Analysis (29)
American Ass'n of Early Childhood Educators (36)
American Health Planning Ass'n (72)
American Paper Machinery Ass'n (90)
American Pipe Fittings Ass'n (92)
American Textile Machinery Ass'n (119)
APICS - The Educational Society for Resource
   Management (125)
Ass'n for Healthcare Philanthropy (134)
Ass'n of Organ Procurement Organizations (159)
Ass'n of Part-Time Professionals (159)
Ass'n of Reporters of Judicial Decisions (163)
Ass'n of the Wall and Ceiling Industries-Internat'l (167)
Classroom Publishers Ass'n (194)
Council of American Building Officials (212)
Defense Fire Protection Ass'n (220)
Financial Markets Ass'n (239)
Food Distributors Internat'l (241)
Healthcare Compliance Packaging Council (252)
Internat'l Ass'n of Emergency Managers (278)
Limousine Industry Manufacturers Organization (320)
Meat Industry Suppliers Ass'n (325)
Nat'l Ass'n of Dental Assistants (352)
Nat'l Ass'n of Executive Secretaries and Administrative
   Assistants (354)
Nat'l Ass'n of Health Data Organizations (357)
Nat'l Ass'n of Physician Nurses (365)

Nat'l Ass'n of State Emergency Medical Services
   Directors (375)
Naval Enlisted Reserve Ass'n (437)
North American Natural Casing Ass'n (443)
Occupational Program Consultants Ass'n (447)
Optical Industry Ass'n: OMA (448)
Plumbing-Heating-Cooling Contractors - Nat'l Ass'n (459)
Process Equipment Manufacturers' Ass'n (463)
Railway Engineering-Maintenance Suppliers Ass'n (471)
Soc. for Personality Assessment (492)
Sweetener Users Ass'n (519)
Voluntary Protection Programs Participants Ass'n (540)
Wire Industry Suppliers Ass'n (545)

Fredericksburg

Alliance of Cardiovascular Professionals (18)
American Surety Ass'n (119)
American Traffic Safety Services Ass'n (120)
Ass'n for the Management of Organization Design (139)
Internat'l Parking Institute (299)
MicroComputer Investors Ass'n (328)
Nat'l Guild of Professional Paperhangers (408)
Teaching-Family Ass'n (520)

Glen Allen

American Ass'n of Integrated Healthcare Delivery
   Systems (38)
American Ass'n of Managed Care Nurses (38)
American College of Managed Care Medicine (55)
Nat'l Ass'n of Managed Care Physicians (362)

Gordonsville

Oriental Rug Retailers of America (450)

Great Falls

American Preventive Medical Ass'n (93)
Ass'n of Military Banks of America (157)
Industrial Designers Soc. of America (262)
Internat'l Cadmium Ass'n (284)

Hampton

United States Ass'n for Computational Mechanics (532)

Harrisonburg

Institute of Certified Professional Managers (266)

Hartfield

Internat'l Soc. of Beverage Technologists (305)

Herndon

Air Line Pilots Ass'n, Internat'l (16)
American Cutlery Manufacturers Ass'n (63)
American Soc. of Appraisers (106)
American Soc. of Electroplated Plastics (109)
American Soc. of Extra-Corporeal Technology (109)
American Water Resources Ass'n (122)
Ass'n of Major City Building Officials (156)
Ass'n of Muslim Social Scientists (158)
Associated Landscape Contractors of America (171)
Automotive Training Managers Council (175)
Commercial Internet Exchange Ass'n (199)
Contract Packagers Ass'n (208)
Electronic Funds Transfer Ass'n (228)
Fur Information Council of America (244)
Institute of Packaging Professionals (268)
Metal Finishing Suppliers Ass'n (327)
Nat'l Ass'n for Check Safekeeping (338)
Nat'l Ass'n of Hispanic Federal Executives (358)
Nat'l Ass'n of Industrial and Office Properties (360)
Nat'l Ass'n of Metal Finishers (363)
Nat'l Ass'n of Public Insurance Adjusters (368)
Nat'l Automated Clearing House Ass'n (381)
Nat'l Concrete Masonry Ass'n (389)
Nat'l Conference of States on Building Codes and
   Standards (391)
Nat'l Council for Uniform Interest Compensation (393)
Nat'l Institute of Governmental Purchasing (412)
Nat'l Organization of Life and Health Insurance Guaranty
   Ass'ns (420)
Package Design Council Int'l (452)
Surface Finishing Industry Council (519)
United States Army Warrant Officers Ass'n (532)
World Packaging Organisation (550)

Leesburg

American Roentgen Ray Soc. (98)
Internat'l Council of Air Shows (287)
Nat'l Ass'n for Trade and Industrial Education (342)
Nat'l Terrazzo and Mosaic Ass'n (433)
Professional Housing Management Ass'n (466)
Vocational Industrial Clubs of America (540)

Manassas

Academy of Oral Dynamics (9)
Garden Writers Ass'n of America (245)
Hydroponic Merchants Ass'n (257)
Internat'l Microwave Power Institute (297)
Nat'l Bark and Soil Producers Ass'n (382)
Nat'l Rehabilitation Counseling Ass'n (425)
Nat'l Religious Broadcasters (425)

Martinsville

Internat'l Window Film Ass'n (311)

McLean

Academy of Organizational and Occupational Psychiatry (9)

Monroe

Log House Builders Ass'n of North America (320)

Mount Vernon

Internat'l Agricultural Aviation Foundation (272)

Port Angeles

Internat'l Festivals and Events Ass'n (291)

Poulsbod

Nat'l Denturist Ass'n (399)

Pullman

American Ass'n of Veterinary Immunologists (45)
Ass'n of Internat'l Education Administrators (154)
Soc. for Clinical and Experimental Hypnosis (486)

Redmond

Aviation Maintenance Foundation Internat'l (176)

Renton

Delta Soc. (221)

Rice

American Karakul Sheep Registry (80)

Richland

Internat'l Soc. for Ecological Modelling-North American Chapter (303)

Seattle

Alliance of Information and Referral Systems (18)
American Ass'n of Naturopathic Physicians (39)
American Legend Cooperative (81)
American Orthopaedic Foot and Ankle Soc. (88)
Ass'n of Academic Health Sciences Library Directors (141)
Ass'n of Commercial Diving Educators (148)
Ass'n of University Anesthesiologists (168)
At-sea Processors Ass'n (172)
Glass Art Soc. (247)
Histochemical Soc. (254)
History of Science Soc. (254)
Internat'l Academy of Gnathology - American Section (272)
Internat'l Ass'n for the Study of Pain (275)
Internat'l Ass'n of School Librarianship (282)
Internat'l College of Cranio-Mandibular Orthopedics (286)
Internat'l Council on Systems Engineering (288)
Internat'l Guild of Symphony, Opera and Ballet Musicians (293)
Internat'l Plant Propagation Soc. (300)
Internat'l Soc. of Appraisers (305)
Middle East Librarians' Ass'n (328)
Nat'l Iridology Research Ass'n (413)
Nat'l Machine Embellishment Instructors and Artists (415)
Soc. for Conservation Biology (487)
Women's Fisheries Network (548)

Spokane

Buses Internat'l Ass'n (184)
Timber Products Manufacturers (523)

Sumas

Cedar Shake and Shingle Bureau (188)

Tacoma

APA - The Engineered Wood Ass'n (125)
Guild of American Luthiers (250)
Internat'l Pot and Kettle Club (300)
Nat'l Organization for Human Service Education (420)
Outpatient Intravenous Infusion Therapy Ass'n (451)

University Place

Magic Dealers Ass'n (322)

Vancouver

Institute of Inspection Cleaning and Restoration (267)
Nat'l Appliance Parts Suppliers Ass'n (337)
Western Dredging Ass'n (542)

Yakima

Hop Growers of America (256)
Northwest Fruit Exporters (446)

WEST VIRGINIA

Charles Town

United States Trout Farmers Ass'n (535)

Charleston

Nat'l Council of Coal Lessors (394)
North American Mycological Ass'n (443)

Institute

Rehabilitation Technology Ass'n (474)

Lewisburg

American Heren Ass'n (73)

Martinsburg

American College of Podiatric Radiologists (57)

Morgantown

AACE Internat'l (7)
Ass'n of Earth Science Editors (150)

Renick

North American Plant Preservation Council (443)
Wood Tank Manufacturers Ass'n (548)

Ripley

Nat'l Ass'n of FSA County Office Employees (356)

Shepherdstown

Aquacultural Engineering Soc. (126)

Wheeling

American Academy of Thermology (26)

WISCONSIN

Appleton

Fraternal Field Managers Ass'n (244)
Nat'l Ass'n of Tax Practitioners (377)
Nat'l Institute on Park and Grounds Management (412)

Beloit

American Milking Shorthorn Soc. (85)
Brown Swiss Cattle Breeders Ass'n of the U.S.A. (183)

Brookfield

Internat'l Foundation of Employee Benefit Plans (292)
Internat'l Soc. of Certified Employee Benefit Specialists (305)
Nat'l Funeral Directors Ass'n (406)
Nat'l Industrial Belting Ass'n (410)
WEB: Network of Benefit Professionals (542)

Delavan

American Cheese Soc. (51)

Dousman

Delta Sigma Delta (221)

Edgerton

ADED - the Ass'n for Driver Rehabilitation Specialists (11)

Elm Grove

American Medical Electroencephalographic Ass'n (83)
Nat'l Federation of Catholic Physicians' Guilds (403)
Specialty Tool and Fastener Distributors Ass'n (514)

Green Bay

Nat'l Ass'n of Computerized Tax Processors (349)

Greenbay

Nat'l Council of Social Security Management Ass'ns (396)

Greendale

Bowling (181)

Hilbert

North American Morab Horse Ass'n/Registry (443)

Hudson

American Academy of Clinical Neurophysiology (21)
Institute for Briquetting and Agglomeration (265)

Kenosha

Cheiron: The Internat'l Soc. for the History of Behavioral and Social Sciences (191)

La Crosse

Internat'l Community Corrections Ass'n (286)
Orthopaedic Section - American Physical Therapy Ass'n (451)
Soc. for Cross-Cultural Research (487)

Lake Geneva

Nat'l Clay Pipe Institute (387)

Lomira

Professional Knitwear Designers Guild (466)

Madison

American Academy of Cosmetic Dentistry (21)
American Institute of the History of Pharmacy (78)
American Soc. of Agronomy (106)
American Soc. of Preventive Oncology (115)
Ass'n for Central Asian Studies (130)
Ass'n of Family and Conciliation Courts (150)
Ass'n of State Floodplain Managers (166)
Credit Union Executives Soc. (218)
Credit Union Nat'l Ass'n (218)
Crop Science Soc. of America (219)
Forest Products Soc. (243)
Industrial Relations Research Ass'n (263)
Internat'l Dairy-Deli-Bakery Ass'n (288)
Nat'l Ass'n of Professors of Hebrew in American Institutions of Higher Learning (367)
Nat'l Ass'n of Scientific Materials Managers (371)
Nat'l Mastitis Council (416)
North American Lake Management Soc. (442)

Soc. for Ecological Restoration (487)
Soc. for the Study of Reproduction (496)
Soc. of American Fight Directors (497)
Soc. of Wood Science and Technology (509)
Soil Science Soc. of America (510)
Tourist Railway Ass'n (524)
Transportation Development Ass'n (525)
Truss Plate Institute (527)
Women in the Fire Service (547)
Wood Truss Council of America (548)

Menomonie

Academy of Operative Dentistry (9)

Middleton

American Ass'n of Cardiovascular and Pulmonary Rehabilitation (34)
American Osteopathic Academy for Sports Medicine (89)
Lipid Nurse Task Force (320)
Soc. for Research on Nicotine and Tobacco (493)
Soc. of Behavioral Medicine (498)

Milwaukee

Alliance for Children and Families (17)
American Academy of Allergy, Asthma and Immunology (20)
American Academy of Emergency Medicine (21)
American College of Forensic Examiners (54)
American College of Legal Medicine (55)
American Fern Soc. (68)
American Institute for Maghrib Studies (76)
American Malting Barley Ass'n (82)
American Psychotherapy Ass'n (95)
American Soc. for Aesthetics (101)
American Soc. for Ethnohistory (102)
American Soc. for Quality (105)
American Soc. for Quality Control (105)
American Soc. for Virology (106)
American Soc. of Scientific Glass Blowers (116)
Ass'n of Forensic Document Examiners (151)
Bituminous and Aggregate Equipment Bureau (179)
CIM --The Business Owners Forum (194)
Clinical Immunology Soc. (194)
Community Development Soc. (201)
Construction Industry Manufacturers Ass'n (206)
Contractors Pump Bureau (208)
Fluid Power Soc. (241)
Internat'l Ass'n of Allergology and Clinical Immunology (275)
Nat'l Ass'n of Catholic Chaplains (346)
Nat'l Ass'n of Credential Evaluation Services (351)
Nat'l Ass'n of Relay Manufacturers (370)
Nat'l Fluid Power Ass'n (405)
Nat'l Human Resources Ass'n (409)
Nine to Five, Nat'l Ass'n of Working Women (439)
North American Cartographic Information Soc. (441)
Technical Engineers Ass'n (520)

Newburg

Industrial Perforators Ass'n (263)

Oak Creek

Information Systems Security Ass'n (264)
NaSPA: the Network and System Professionals Ass'n (333)

Oconomowoc

Ass'n of Food Journalists (151)

Oregon

Archery Range and Retailers Organization (127)

Oshkosh

Nat'l Ass'n of Flight Instructors (355)

Plover

Nat'l Ass'n for Retail Merchandising Services (341)

Racine

Carwash Owner's and Supplier's Ass'n (187)
Hydraulic Tool Manufacturers Ass'n (257)
Internat'l Ass'n of Tool Craftsmen (282)
Nat'l Ass'n of Sports Officials (373)

River Falls

American Forensic Ass'n (69)

Sheboygan

Nat'l Ass'n of Fraternal Insurance Counsellors (356)

Stevens Point

Nat'l Wellness Ass'n (436)

Watertown

Ass'n of Educators in Private Practice (150)

Wausau

American Soc. for Laser Medicine and Surgery (103)

Wauwatosa

Bowling Writers Ass'n of America (181)
Master Brewers Ass'n of the Americas (324)

National Trade and Professional Associations of the U.S. © 1999, Columbia Books, Inc.

Budget Index

Every organization that has provided annual budget data will be found in one of the fourteen categories below, from Under $10,000 to Over $100 Million.

Over $100,000,000

Air Line Pilots Ass'n, Internat'l (16)
American Bureau of Shipping and Affiliated Companies (49)
American Cancer Soc. (50)
American Chemical Soc. (51)
American Diabetes Ass'n (64)
American Heart Ass'n (72)
American Institute of Certified Public Accountants (76)
American Medical Ass'n (03)
American Soc. of Composers, Authors and Publishers (108)
Blue Cross and Blue Shield Ass'n (180)
Electric Power Research Institute (227)
Gas Research Institute (246)
Institute of Electrical and Electronics Engineers (266)
Internat'l Ass'n of Machinists and Aerospace Workers (280)
Internat'l Union, United Automobile, Aerospace and
    Agricultural Implement Workers of America (310)
Mastercard Internat'l (324)
Nat'l Academy of Sciences (334)
Nat'l Ass'n of Securities Dealers (372)
Nat'l Collegiate Athletic Ass'n (388)
Nat'l Education Ass'n of the U.S. (400)
Nat'l Rifle Ass'n of America (426)
Nat'l Rural Electric Cooperative Ass'n (426)

$50-100,000,000

American Bankers Ass'n (46)
American Bar Ass'n (46)
American Dental Ass'n (63)
American Federation of Labor and Congress of Industrial
    Organizations (67)
American Federation of State, County and Municipal
    Employees (67)
American Federation of Teachers (67)
American Gas Ass'n (70)
American Hospital Ass'n (74)
American Institute of Physics (78)
American Petroleum Institute (91)
American Poultry U.S.A. (93)
American Psychological Ass'n (94)
American Quarter Horse Ass'n (96)
American Soc. of Mechanical Engineers (112)
ATP Tour (172)
Chamber of Commerce of the United States of America (190)
College of American Pathologists (197)
Communications Workers of America (200)
Edison Electric Institute (226)
Institute of Nuclear Power Operations (268)
Internat'l Brotherhood of Teamsters, AFL-CIO (284)
Laborers' Internat'l Union of North America (316)
Nat'l Ass'n of Letter Carriers (361)
Nat'l Ass'n of REALTORS (369)
Nat'l Council of the Churches of Christ in the U.S.A. (397)
Nat'l Council on Compensation Insurance (397)
Nat'l Federation of Independent Business (403)
Nat'l Fire Protection Ass'n (404)
Nat'l Marrow Donor Program (416)
Service Employees Internat'l Union (482)
United Brotherhood of Carpenters and Joiners of
    America (530)

$25-50,000,000

Air Transport Ass'n of America (16)
American Academy of Family Physicians (22)
American Academy of Pediatrics (25)
American Arbitration Ass'n (28)
American Ass'n of Motor Vehicle Administrators (39)
American Automobile Manufacturers Ass'n (46)
American College of Cardiology (53)
American College of Obstetricians and Gynecologists (56)
American College of Physicians-American Soc. of Internal
    Medicine (57)
American College of Surgeons (57)

American Council of Life Insurance (61)
American Forest and Paper Ass'n (69)
American Institute of Architects (76)
American Library Ass'n (81)
American Physical Soc. (92)
American Physical Therapy Ass'n (92)
American Plastics Council (92)
American Psychiatric Ass'n (94)
American Soc. for Microbiology (104)
American Soc. for Quality (105)
American Soc. of Civil Engineers (100)
American Soc. of Health-System Pharmacists (110)
American Soybean Ass'n (117)
American Trucking Ass'ns (121)
Ass'n for Computing Machinery (131)
Ass'n for Investment Management and Research (135)
Ass'n of American Medical Colleges (142)
Ass'n of American Railroads (143)
Chemical Manufacturers Ass'n (191)
Credit Union Nat'l Ass'n (218)
Electronic Industries Ass'n (228)
Food Marketing Institute (241)
Health Insurance Ass'n of America (252)
Hotel Employees and Restaurant Employees Internat'l
    Union (256)
IEEE Computer Soc. (258)
Institute of Gas Technology (267)
Internat'l Brotherhood of Boilermakers, Iron Ship Builders,
    Blacksmiths, Forgers and Helpers (284)
Internat'l Council of Shopping Centers (288)
Investment Company Institute (312)
Ladies Professional Golf Ass'n (316)
Mortgage Bankers Ass'n of America (330)
Nat'l Ass'n of Broadcasters (345)
Nat'l Ass'n of Chain Drug Stores (346)
Nat'l Ass'n of Home Builders of the U.S. (358)
Nat'l Ass'n of Insurance Commissioners (360)
Nat'l Cable Television Ass'n (384)
Nat'l Conference of Catholic Bishops/U.S. Catholic
    Conference (390)
Nat'l Council on the Aging (398)
Nat'l Futures Ass'n (406)
Nat'l Insurance Crime Bureau (412)
Nat'l Kidney Foundation (414)
Nat'l Multiple Sclerosis Soc. (418)
Nat'l Pork Producers Council (423)
Nat'l Safety Council (426)
Newspaper Ass'n of America (439)
Nuclear Energy Institute (446)
Portland Cement Ass'n (460)
Professional Ass'n of Diving Instructors (464)
Professional Rodeo Cowboys Ass'n (467)
Screen Actors Guild (480)
Semiconductor Equipment and Materials Internat'l (481)
Soc. for Human Resource Management (489)
Soc. of Automotive Engineers International (498)
Soc. of Manufacturing Engineers (503)
Soc. of the Plastics Industry (507)
United States Pharmacopeia (534)

$10-25,000,000

Academy of Motion Picture Arts and Sciences (9)
Actors' Equity Ass'n (11)
Air Force Ass'n (15)
America's Community Bankers (20)
American Academy of Allergy, Asthma and Immunology (20)
American Academy of Dermatology (21)
American Academy of Ophthalmology (24)
American Academy of Orthopaedic Surgeons (24)
American Ass'n for Cancer Research (30)
American Ass'n of Advertising Agencies (32)
American Ass'n of Critical-Care Nurses (35)
American Ass'n of Health Plans (37)
American Ass'n of Individual Investors (38)

American Ass'n of Neurological Surgeons (39)
American Ass'n of Orthodontists (40)
American Ass'n of Petroleum Geologists (40)
American College of Chest Physicians (53)
American College of Emergency Physicians (54)
American College of Healthcare Executives (54)
American College of Radiology (57)
American Compensation Ass'n (59)
American Council on Education (61)
American Dietetic Ass'n (64)
American Egg Board (65)
American Electronics Ass'n (65)
American Farm Bureau Federation (66)
American Gastroenterological Ass'n (70)
American Geophysical Union (70)
American Health Care Ass'n (72)
American Health Information Management Ass'n (72)
American Hotel and Motel Ass'n (74)
American Industrial Hygiene Ass'n (75)
American Institute of Aeronautics and Astronautics (76)
American Institute of Chemical Engineers (77)
American Insurance Ass'n (79)
American Kennel Club (80)
American Lung Ass'n (82)
American Mathematical Soc. (83)
American Nat'l Standards Institute (86)
American Nurses Ass'n (87)
American Occupational Therapy Ass'n (88)
American Optometric Ass'n (88)
American Payroll Ass'n (90)
American Pharmaceutical Ass'n (91)
American Physiological Soc. (92)
American Planning Ass'n (92)
American Postal Workers Union (93)
American Public Transit Ass'n (96)
American Soc. for Biochemistry and Molecular Biology (101)
American Soc. for Engineering Education (102)
American Soc. for Testing and Materials (105)
American Soc. of Anesthesiologists (106)
American Soc. of Ass'n Executives (107)
American Soc. of Clinical Pathologists (108)
American Soc. of Heating, Refrigerating and Air-Conditioning
    Engineers (110)
American Soc. of Travel Agents (116)
American Speech-Language-Hearing Ass'n (117)
American Urological Ass'n (121)
American Veterinary Medical Ass'n (121)
American Water Works Ass'n (122)
American Welding Soc. (123)
AMT - The Ass'n for Manufacturing Technology (124)
APA - The Engineered Wood Ass'n (125)
Appraisal Institute (126)
ASM Internat'l (128)
Ass'n for Information and Image Management
    International (135)
Ass'n for Supervision and Curriculum Development (138)
Ass'n of Christian Schools Internat'l (146)
Ass'n of Flight Attendants (151)
Ass'n of the United States Army (167)
Ass'n of Trial Lawyers of America (168)
Associated General Contractors of America (171)
Associated Surplus Dealers (172)
Audit Bureau of Circulations (173)
Automobile Dealers Ass'n (174)
Automotive Industry Action Group (174)
Bond Market Ass'n (181)
Building Officials and Code Administrators Internat'l (183)
Business Marketing Ass'n (184)
Catholic Health Ass'n of the United States (188)
Cellular Telecommunications Industry Ass'n (189)
Chemical Industry Institute of Toxicology (191)
Copper Development Ass'n (209)
Cosmetic, Toiletry and Fragrance Ass'n (210)
Cotton Council Internat'l (210)

$2-5,000,000

$500-1,000,000

$250-500,000

Internat'l Ass'n of Bomb Technicians and Investigators **(276)**
Internat'l Ass'n of Clothing Designers and Executives **(277)**
Internat'l Ass'n of Color Manufacturers **(277)**
Internat'l Ass'n of Diecutting and Diemaking **(278)**
Internat'l Ass'n of Eating Disorders Professionals **(278)**
Internat'l Ass'n of Family Entertainment Centers **(279)**
Internat'l Ass'n of Lighting Management Companies **(280)**
Internat'l Ass'n of Printing House Craftsmen **(282)**
Internat'l Ass'n of Tour Managers - North American Region **(282)**
Internat'l Bluegrass Music Ass'n **(283)**
Internat'l Cadmium Ass'n **(284)**
Internat'l Cartridge Recycling Ass'n **(285)**
Internat'l Childbirth Education Ass'n **(285)**
Internat'l Claim Ass'n **(285)**
Internat'l College of Applied Kinesiology **(286)**
Internat'l College of Dentists, U.S.A. Section **(286)**
Internat'l Communication Ass'n **(286)**
Internat'l Communications Agency Network **(286)**
Internat'l Communications Ass'n **(286)**
Internat'l Community Corrections Ass'n **(286)**
Internat'l Conference of Funeral Service Examining Boards **(287)**
Internat'l Conference of Symphony and Opera Musicians **(287)**
Internat'l Coordinating Committee on Solid State Sensors and Actuators Research **(287)**
Internat'l Council on Education for Teaching **(288)**
Internat'l Desalination Ass'n **(288)**
Internat'l Digital Imaging Ass'n **(289)**
Internat'l Documentary Ass'n **(289)**
Internat'l Electrical Testing Ass'n **(289)**
Internat'l Electronic Article Surveillance Manufacturers Ass'n **(289)**
Internat'l Exchangors Ass'n **(290)**
Internat'l Federation of Pharmaceutical Wholesalers **(290)**
Internat'l Food Service Executives' Ass'n **(291)**
Internat'l Formalwear Ass'n **(291)**
Internat'l Furnishings and Design Ass'n **(292)**
Internat'l Graphoanalysis Soc. **(292)**
Internat'l Hardware Distributors Ass'n **(293)**
Internat'l Home Furnishings Representatives Ass'n **(293)**
Internat'l Inflight Food Service Ass'n **(294)**
Internat'l Institute of Connector and Interconnection Technology **(294)**
Internat'l Institute of Forecasters **(294)**
Internat'l Interactive Communication Soc. **(295)**
Internat'l Lactation Consultant Ass'n **(295)**
Internat'l League of Dermatological Socs. **(296)**
Internat'l League of Professional Baseball Clubs **(296)**
Internat'l Marina Institute **(297)**
Internat'l Military Community Executives Ass'n **(297)**
Internat'l Mobile Air Conditioning Ass'n **(297)**
Internat'l Mobile Telecommunications Ass'n **(297)**
Internat'l Narcotic Enforcement Officers Ass'n **(298)**
Internat'l Natural Sausage Casing Ass'n **(298)**
Internat'l Oxygen Manufacturers Ass'n **(299)**
Internat'l Pediatric Nephrology Ass'n **(299)**
Internat'l Periodical Distributors Ass'n **(299)**
Internat'l Petroleum Credit Ass'n **(299)**
Internat'l Pharmaceutical Excipients Council **(299)**
Internat'l Platform Ass'n **(300)**
Internat'l Precious Metals Institute **(300)**
Internat'l Soc. for Intercultural Education, Training and Research **(303)**
Internat'l Soc. for Peritoneal Dialysis **(304)**
Internat'l Soc. for the Performing Arts **(304)**
Internat'l Soc. for the Study of Dissociation **(305)**
Internat'l Soc. for the Study of Subtle Energies and Energy Medicine **(305)**
Internat'l Soc. for Third-Sector Research **(305)**
Internat'l Soc. for Traumatic Stress Studies **(305)**
Internat'l Soc. of Weighing and Measurement **(307)**
Internat'l Studies Ass'n **(307)**
Internat'l Theatre Equipment Ass'n **(308)**
Internat'l Titanium Ass'n **(309)**
Internat'l Trumpet Guild **(309)**
Internat'l Union of Allied Novelty and Production Workers **(309)**
Internat'l Union of Security Officers **(310)**
Ireland Chamber of Commerce in the United States **(312)**
Jewish Funeral Directors of America **(314)**
Joint Council of Allergy, Asthma and Immunology **(315)**
Journalism Education Ass'n **(315)**
Knitted Textile Ass'n **(316)**
Lake Carriers' Ass'n **(316)**
Laundry and Dry Cleaning Internat'l Union **(317)**
Lawn and Garden Marketing and Distribution Ass'n **(318)**
Leather Apparel Ass'n **(318)**
Liability Insurance Research Bureau **(319)**
Library Administration and Management Ass'n **(319)**
Library and Information Technology Ass'n **(319)**
Linguistic Soc. of America **(320)**
Livestock Conservation Institute **(320)**
Machine Printers and Engravers Ass'n of the United States **(321)**
Machinery Dealers Nat'l Ass'n **(321)**
Manufactured Housing Ass'n for Regulatory Reform **(322)**
Manufacturers Standardization Soc. of the Valve and Fittings Industry **(323)**
Maple Flooring Manufacturers Ass'n **(323)**
Maritime Law Ass'n of the U.S. **(324)**
Marking Device Ass'n Internat'l **(324)**
Masonry Soc. **(324)**
Meals On Wheels Ass'n of America **(325)**
Measurement, Control and Automation Ass'n **(325)**
Meat Importers' Council of America **(325)**
Media Rating Council **(326)**
Medical Device Manufacturers Ass'n **(326)**
Medical Marketing Ass'n **(326)**
Medieval Academy of America **(326)**
Messenger Courier Ass'n of the Americas **(327)**
Metal Finishing Suppliers Ass'n **(327)**
Methacrylate Producers Ass'n **(327)**
Middle East Studies Ass'n of North America **(328)**
Modular Building Institute **(330)**
Multi-Level Marketing Internat'l Ass'n **(331)**
Municipal Treasurers Ass'n of the United States and Canada **(331)**
Museum Trustee Ass'n **(332)**
Music Library Ass'n **(332)**
NADD: Ass'n for Persons with Developmental Disabilities and Mental Health Needs **(333)**
Nat'l Affordable Housing Management Ass'n **(335)**
Nat'l Alliance of Independent Crop Consultants **(336)**
Nat'l Ass'n for Community Leadership **(338)**
Nat'l Ass'n for Environmental Management **(339)**
Nat'l Ass'n for Girls and Women in Sport **(339)**
Nat'l Ass'n for Industry-Education Cooperation **(340)**
Nat'l Ass'n for Membership Development **(340)**
Nat'l Ass'n for Practical Nurse Education and Service **(340)**
Nat'l Ass'n for Promotional and Advertising Allowances **(340)**
Nat'l Ass'n for the Advancement of Psychoanalysis **(341)**
Nat'l Ass'n of Activity Professionals **(342)**
Nat'l Ass'n of Addiction Treatment Providers **(342)**
Nat'l Ass'n of Advisors for the Health Professions **(342)**
Nat'l Ass'n of Affordable Housing Lenders **(342)**
Nat'l Ass'n of Architectural Metal Manufacturers **(343)**
Nat'l Ass'n of Beverage Importers-Wine-Spirits-Beer **(344)**
Nat'l Ass'n of Beverage Retailers **(344)**
Nat'l Ass'n of Business Economists **(346)**
Nat'l Ass'n of Business Political Action Committees **(346)**
Nat'l Ass'n of Catalog Showroom Merchandisers **(346)**
Nat'l Ass'n of Catering Executives **(346)**
Nat'l Ass'n of Chemical Recyclers **(347)**
Nat'l Ass'n of Chewing Gum Manufacturers **(347)**
Nat'l Ass'n of Child Care Professionals **(347)**
Nat'l Ass'n of Childbearing Centers **(347)**
Nat'l Ass'n of Church Business Administration **(347)**
Nat'l Ass'n of College Broadcasters **(348)**
Nat'l Ass'n of Corporate Treasurers **(350)**
Nat'l Ass'n of County Agricultural Agents **(350)**
Nat'l Ass'n of County Engineers **(350)**
Nat'l Ass'n of Cruise Oriented Agencies **(352)**
Nat'l Ass'n of Developmental Disabilities Councils **(352)**
Nat'l Ass'n of Disability Evaluating Professionals **(353)**
Nat'l Ass'n of Educational Office Professionals **(353)**
Nat'l Ass'n of Elevator Safety Authorities Internat'l **(353)**
Nat'l Ass'n of Emergency Medical Technicians **(353)**
Nat'l Ass'n of EMS Physicians **(353)**
Nat'l Ass'n of Energy Service Companies **(354)**
Nat'l Ass'n of Floor Covering Distributors **(355)**
Nat'l Ass'n of Golf Tournament Directors **(356)**
Nat'l Ass'n of Governors' Councils on Physical Fitness and Sports **(357)**
Nat'l Ass'n of Governors' Highway Safety Representatives **(357)**
Nat'l Ass'n of Health Data Organizations **(357)**
Nat'l Ass'n of Health Services Executives **(357)**
Nat'l Ass'n of Healthcare Access Management **(357)**
Nat'l Ass'n of Healthcare Consultants **(357)**
Nat'l Ass'n of Hispanic Publications **(358)**
Nat'l Ass'n of Housing Cooperatives **(359)**
Nat'l Ass'n of Installation Developers **(360)**
Nat'l Ass'n of Investment Companies **(360)**
Nat'l Ass'n of Leagues, Umpires and Scorers **(361)**
Nat'l Ass'n of Limited Edition Dealers **(361)**
Nat'l Ass'n of Local Boards of Health **(361)**
Nat'l Ass'n of Medicaid Directors **(362)**
Nat'l Ass'n of Minority Automobile Dealers **(363)**
Nat'l Ass'n of Minority Engineering Program Administrators **(363)**
Nat'l Ass'n of Neighborhoods **(363)**
Nat'l Ass'n of Nephrology Technologists and Technicians **(364)**
Nat'l Ass'n of Nutrition and Aging Services Programs **(364)**
Nat'l Ass'n of Parliamentarians **(364)**
Nat'l Ass'n of Physician Recruiters **(365)**
Nat'l Ass'n of Power Engineers **(365)**
Nat'l Ass'n of Private Industry Councils **(366)**
Nat'l Ass'n of Private Schools for Exceptional Children **(366)**
Nat'l Ass'n of Professional Mortgage Women **(367)**
Nat'l Ass'n of Professionals in Women's Health **(367)**
Nat'l Ass'n of Radio and Telecommunications Engineers **(368)**
Nat'l Ass'n of Railroad Trial Counsel **(368)**
Nat'l Ass'n of Real Estate Brokers **(368)**
Nat'l Ass'n of Real Estate Investment Managers **(369)**
Nat'l Ass'n of Resale and Thrift Shops **(370)**
Nat'l Ass'n of Resident Management Corporations **(370)**
Nat'l Ass'n of Schools of Art and Design **(371)**
Nat'l Ass'n of Secretaries of State **(372)**
Nat'l Ass'n of Service Managers **(372)**
Nat'l Ass'n of Sporting Goods Wholesalers **(373)**
Nat'l Ass'n of Sports Officials **(373)**
Nat'l Ass'n of State Aviation Officials **(374)**
Nat'l Ass'n of State Budget Officers **(374)**
Nat'l Ass'n of State Directors of Developmental Disability Services **(374)**
Nat'l Ass'n of State Directors of Migrant Education **(374)**
Nat'l Ass'n of State Directors of Teacher Education and Certification **(375)**
Nat'l Ass'n of State Directors of Vocational-Technical Education **(375)**
Nat'l Ass'n of State Radio Networks **(376)**
Nat'l Ass'n of State Telecommunications Directors **(376)**
Nat'l Ass'n of Teachers of Singing **(378)**
Nat'l Ass'n of Uniform Manufacturers and Distributors **(379)**
Nat'l Ass'n of VA Physicians and Dentists **(379)**
Nat'l Ass'n of Waterfront Employers **(380)**
Nat'l Ass'n of Women Business Owners **(380)**
Nat'l Ass'n of Women Judges **(380)**
Nat'l Ass'n of Workforce Development Professionals **(381)**
Nat'l Assembly of Nat'l Voluntary Health and Social Welfare Organizations **(381)**
Nat'l Automobile Transporters Ass'n **(381)**
Nat'l Bio-Energy Industries Ass'n **(383)**
Nat'l Black Nurses Ass'n **(383)**
Nat'l Bureau of Certified Consultants **(384)**
Nat'l Career Development Ass'n **(385)**
Nat'l Center for Homeopathy **(386)**
Nat'l Certification Council for Activity Professionals **(386)**
Nat'l Certified Pipe Welding Bureau **(386)**
Nat'l Cheese Institute **(386)**
Nat'l Child Care Ass'n **(386)**
Nat'l Chimney Sweep Guild **(386)**
Nat'l Christian College Athletic Ass'n **(387)**
Nat'l Christmas Tree Ass'n **(387)**
Nat'l Collegiate Honors Council **(388)**
Nat'l Conference of CPA Practitioners **(390)**
Nat'l Conference of Standards Laboratories **(391)**
Nat'l Conference of State Historic Preservation Officers **(391)**
Nat'l Conference of States on Building Codes and Standards **(391)**
Nat'l Conference on Public Employee Retirement Systems **(391)**
Nat'l Constructors Ass'n **(392)**
Nat'l Contact Lens Examiners **(392)**
Nat'l Council for Geographic Education **(393)**
Nat'l Council for Resource Development **(393)**
Nat'l Council of Agricultural Employers **(394)**
Nat'l Council of Chain Restaurants **(394)**
Nat'l Council of Nonprofit Ass'ns **(395)**
Nat'l Council of University Research Administrators **(397)**
Nat'l Council on Internat'l Trade Development **(397)**
Nat'l Council on Teacher Retirement **(398)**
Nat'l Credit Union Management Ass'n **(398)**
Nat'l Dairy Herd Improvement Ass'n **(399)**
Nat'l Dental Ass'n **(399)**
Nat'l Education Knowledge Industry Ass'n **(400)**
Nat'l Employee Services and Recreation Ass'n **(401)**
Nat'l Erectors Ass'n **(402)**
Nat'l Extension Ass'n of Family and Consumer Sciences **(402)**
Nat'l Eye Research Foundation **(402)**
Nat'l Fastener Distributors Ass'n **(402)**
Nat'l Federation of Abstracting and Information Services **(403)**
Nat'l Federation of Community Broadcasters **(403)**
Nat'l Federation of Licensed Practical Nurses **(403)**
Nat'l Federation of Non-Profits **(404)**
Nat'l Federation of Priests' Councils **(404)**
Nat'l Frame Builders Ass'n **(406)**
Nat'l Grain Sorghum Producers **(407)**
Nat'l Guild of Professional Paperhangers **(408)**
Nat'l Head Start Ass'n **(408)**
Nat'l Housing and Rehabilitation Ass'n **(409)**
Nat'l Hydrogen Ass'n **(410)**
Nat'l Institute for Architectural Education **(411)**
Nat'l Institute of Pension Administrators **(412)**
Nat'l Juice Products Ass'n **(413)**
Nat'l Kerosene Heater Ass'n **(414)**
Nat'l Lawyers Guild **(414)**
Nat'l Leased Housing Ass'n **(415)**
Nat'l Live Stock Producers Ass'n **(415)**
Nat'l Lubricating Grease Institute **(415)**
Nat'l Marine Electronics Ass'n **(416)**
Nat'l Metal Decorators Ass'n **(417)**
Nat'l Minority Business Council **(417)**
Nat'l Nursing Staff Development Organization **(418)**
Nat'l Oil Recyclers Ass'n **(419)**
Nat'l Onion Ass'n **(419)**
Nat'l Organization for Associate Degree Nursing **(419)**
Nat'l Organization for Competency Assurance **(419)**
Nat'l Organization of Industrial Trade Unions **(420)**
Nat'l Park Hospitality Ass'n **(421)**
Nat'l Perinatal Ass'n **(422)**
Nat'l Pharmaceutical Alliance **(422)**
Nat'l Phlebotomy Ass'n **(422)**
Nat'l Property Management Ass'n **(424)**
Nat'l Public Employer Labor Relations Ass'n **(424)**
Nat'l Reining Horse Ass'n **(425)**
Nat'l School Transportation Ass'n **(427)**
Nat'l Sculpture Soc. **(427)**
Nat'l Shipyard Ass'n **(428)**
Nat'l Soc. for Healthcare Foodservice Management **(429)**
Nat'l Soc. for Histotechnology **(429)**
Nat'l Soc. of Accountants for Cooperatives **(429)**
Nat'l Soc. of Genetic Counselors **(430)**
Nat'l Soc. of Pharmaceutical Sales Trainers **(430)**
Nat'l Solid Waste Management Environmental **(430)**
Nat'l Spinal Cord Injury Ass'n **(431)**
Nat'l Star Route Mail Contractors Ass'n **(431)**
Nat'l Subacute Care Ass'n **(432)**
Nat'l Sunflower Ass'n **(432)**
Nat'l Tank Truck Carriers **(433)**
Nat'l Tax Ass'n-Tax Institute of America **(433)**
Nat'l Tay-Sachs and Allied Diseases Ass'n **(433)**
Nat'l Terrazzo and Mosaic Ass'n **(433)**
Nat'l Tile Roofing Manufacturers Ass'n **(434)**
Nat'l Trappers Ass'n **(434)**
Nat'l Vehicle Leasing Ass'n **(435)**
Nat'l Volunteer Fire Council **(435)**
Nat'l Water Resources Ass'n **(435)**
Nat'l Watermelon Ass'n **(436)**
Nat'l Waterways Conference **(436)**
Nat'l Weather Service Employees Organization **(436)**
Nat'l Wellness Ass'n **(436)**
Nat'l Wheel and Rim Ass'n **(436)**
Nat'l Wireless Resellers Ass'n **(436)**
Nat'l Woodland Owners Ass'n **(437)**
Nat'l Yogurt Ass'n **(437)**
Naval Enlisted Reserve Ass'n **(437)**
NAWE: Advancing Women in Higher Education **(438)**
New Alternatives for Publishers, Retailers and Artists **(438)**
North American Blueberry Council **(440)**
North American Computer Service Ass'n **(441)**
North American Equipment Dealers Ass'n **(442)**
North American Skull Base Soc. **(444)**
North American Transportation Management Institute **(445)**
Northern Textile Ass'n **(446)**
Northwest Fruit Exporters **(446)**
Nurses Organization of Veterans Affairs **(447)**
Organization of Black Designers **(450)**
Oriental Rug Retailers of America **(450)**

National Trade and Professional Associations of the U.S. © 1999, Columbia Books, Inc. 651

Ornamental Concrete Producers Ass'n **(451)**
Orthopaedic Research Soc. **(451)**
Oxygen Soc., The **(452)**
Packaged Ice Ass'n **(452)**
Paleontological Research Institution **(452)**
Paleontological Soc. **(452)**
Paper Shipping Sack Manufacturers Ass'n **(453)**
Pediatric Orthopedic Soc. of North America **(454)**
Percussive Arts Soc. **(454)**
Performance Warehouse Ass'n **(455)**
Perlite Institute **(455)**
Pet Food Institute **(455)**
PGA TOUR Tournaments Ass'n **(456)**
Phi Mu Alpha - Sinfonia **(457)**
Photographic Manufacturers and Distributors Ass'n **(457)**
Phycological Soc. of America **(457)**
Pickle Packers Internat'l **(458)**
Picture Agency Council of America **(458)**
Pine Chemicals Ass'n **(458)**
Poetry Soc. of America **(459)**
Polyurethane Foam Ass'n **(460)**
Polyurethane Manufacturers Ass'n **(460)**
Pony of the Americas Club **(460)**
Popcorn Institute **(460)**
Porcelain Enamel Institute **(460)**
Portable Sanitation Ass'n Internat'l **(460)**
Power Washers of North America **(461)**
Pressure Sensitive Tape Council **(462)**
Primary Glass Manufacturers Council **(462)**
Production Engine Remanufacturers Ass'n **(463)**
Professional Ass'n of Resume Writers **(464)**
Professional Audio-Video Retailers Ass'n **(464)**
Professional Grounds Management Soc. **(465)**
Professional Numismatists Guild **(466)**
Professional Records and Information Services Management Internat'l **(467)**
Professional Services Management Ass'n **(467)**
Professional Soc. for Sales and Marketing Training **(467)**
Propeller Club of the U.S. **(468)**
Psychology Soc. **(469)**
Public Agency Risk Managers Ass'n **(469)**
Public Employees Roundtable **(469)**
Radiant Panel Ass'n **(470)**
Radio Talk Show Hosts Ass'n **(471)**
Railway Engineering-Maintenance Suppliers Ass'n **(471)**
Railway Supply Ass'n **(471)**
Railway Systems Suppliers, Inc. **(471)**
Real Estate Educators Ass'n **(472)**
REALTORS Land Institute **(472)**
Recreational Park Trailer Industry Ass'n **(473)**
Recycled Paperboard Technical Ass'n **(473)**
Registered Mail Insurance Ass'n **(473)**
Religious Conference Management Ass'n **(474)**
Renal Physicians Ass'n **(474)**
Research and Development Associates for Military Food and Packaging Systems **(475)**
Retail Tobacco Dealers of America **(476)**
Safety Equipment Distributors Ass'n **(478)**
Safety Glazing Cerification Council **(478)**
Salon Ass'n, The **(478)**
SB Latex Council **(479)**
Sealed Insulating Glass Manufacturers Ass'n **(480)**
Seaplane Pilots Ass'n **(480)**
Secondary Materials and Recycled Textiles Ass'n **(480)**
Securities Transfer Ass'n **(481)**
Seismological Soc. of America **(481)**
Shoe Service Institute of America **(483)**
Silver Institute **(483)**
Single Ply Roofing Institute **(483)**
Small Motors and Motion Ass'n **(484)**
Smocking Arts Guild of America **(484)**
Soc. for American Baseball Research **(485)**
Soc. for Applied Anthropology **(485)**
Soc. for Applied Learning Technology **(485)**
Soc. for Biomolecular Screening **(486)**
Soc. for Cardiovascular Magnetic Resonance **(486)**
Soc. for Developmental Biology **(487)**
Soc. for Experimental Biology and Medicine **(488)**
Soc. for Foodservice Management **(488)**
Soc. for Healthcare Consumer Advocacy **(488)**
Soc. for Industrial and Organizational Psychology **(489)**
Soc. for Investigative Dermatology **(490)**
Soc. for Leukocyte Biology **(490)**
Soc. for Maintenance Reliability Professionals **(490)**
Soc. for Obstetric Anesthesia and Perinatology **(491)**
Soc. for Pediatric Anesthesia **(492)**
Soc. for Pediatric Radiology **(492)**
Soc. for Pediatric Research **(492)**
Soc. for Personality Assessment **(492)**
Soc. for Public Health Education **(493)**
Soc. for Range Management **(493)**
Soc. for Risk Analysis **(493)**
Soc. for Social Work Leadership in Health Care **(494)**
Soc. for the Psychological Study of Social Issues **(495)**
Soc. for the Scientific Study of Sexuality **(495)**
Soc. for the Study of Evolution **(495)**
Soc. for the Study of Social Problems **(496)**
Soc. for Vascular Nursing **(496)**
Soc. of Architectural Historians **(498)**
Soc. of Broadcast Engineers **(499)**
Soc. of Certified Kitchen and Bathroom Designers **(499)**
Soc. of Cost Estimating and Analysis **(500)**
Soc. of Economic Geologists **(500)**
Soc. of Environmental Journalists **(501)**
Soc. of Financial Examiners **(501)**
Soc. of Former Special Agents of the Federal Bureau of Investigation **(501)**
Soc. of Nat'l Ass'n Publications **(504)**
Soc. of Physics Students **(505)**
Soc. of Piping Engineers and Designers **(505)**
Soc. of Professional Well Log Analysts **(506)**
Soc. of Publication Designers **(506)**
Soc. of Quality Assurance **(506)**
Soc. of Telecommunications Consultants **(507)**
Soc. of Toxicologic Pathologists **(508)**
Soil Science Soc. of America **(510)**
Songwriters Guild of America **(510)**
Special Interest Group for Algorithm and Computation Theory **(511)**
Special Interest Group on Software Engineering **(513)**
Specialty Sleep Ass'n **(514)**
Sports Card Ass'n **(515)**
Sports Turf Managers Ass'n **(515)**
Stained Glass Ass'n of America **(515)**
State Government Affairs Council **(516)**
Station Representatives Ass'n **(516)**
Subcontractors Trade Ass'n **(517)**
Substance Abuse Program Administrators Ass'n **(518)**
Suburban Newspapers of America **(518)**
Suppliers of Advanced Composite Materials Ass'n **(518)**
Systems Builders Ass'n **(519)**
TAG Internat'l **(520)**
Tea Ass'n of the United States of America **(520)**
Technology Student Ass'n **(521)**
Tetrahydrofuran Task Force **(521)**
Textile Care Allied Trades Ass'n **(522)**
Textile Distributors Ass'n **(522)**
Textile Processors, Service Trades, Health Care, Professional and Technical Employees Internat'l Union **(522)**
Tire and Rim Ass'n **(523)**
Transaction Processing Performance Council **(525)**
Transplantation Soc. (Western Hemishpere) **(525)**
Transworld Advertising Agency Network **(526)**
Travel and Tourism Research Ass'n **(526)**
Truck Manufacturers Ass'n **(527)**
Truss Plate Institute **(527)**
U.S.-ROC (Taiwan) Business Council **(528)**
U.S.A. Dry Pea and Lentil Council **(528)**
Unfinished Furniture Ass'n **(529)**
United States Army Warrant Officers Ass'n **(532)**
United States Ass'n of Importers of Textiles and Apparel **(532)**
United States Cane Sugar Refiners' Ass'n **(532)**
United States Dye Manufacturers Operating Committee of ETAD **(533)**
United States Ski Coaches Ass'n **(535)**
United States Tennis Court and Track Builders Ass'n **(535)**
United States Tour Operators Ass'n **(535)**
United States Tuna Foundation **(535)**
Universities Space Research Ass'n **(536)**
University Aviation Ass'n **(537)**
University Council for Educational Administration **(537)**
Usability Professionals Ass'n **(538)**
Vacuum Dealers Trade Ass'n **(538)**
Vibration Institute **(539)**
Water and Wastewater Equipment Manufacturers Ass'n **(541)**
Water Systems Council **(541)**
WEB: Network of Benefit Professionals **(542)**
Wedding and Portrait Photographers Internat'l **(542)**
Western Economic Ass'n Internat'l **(542)**
Western History Ass'n **(543)**
Western Range Ass'n **(543)**
Wheat Quality Council **(543)**
White House News Photographers Ass'n **(543)**
Wilderness Medical Soc. **(544)**
Women Chefs and Restaurateurs **(545)**
Women in Film **(546)**
Women in Government Relations **(546)**
Women in Internat'l Security **(546)**
Women's Professional Rodeo Ass'n **(548)**
Wood Machinery Manufacturers of America **(548)**
Woodworking Machinery Industry Ass'n **(549)**
Workgroup for Electronic Data Interchange **(549)**
World Internat'l Nail and Beauty Ass'n **(550)**
World Sign Associates **(550)**
World Teleport Ass'n **(550)**
Writing Instrument Manufacturers Ass'n **(551)**

$100-250,000

Academy of Dentistry Internat'l **(8)**
Academy of Internat'l Business **(8)**
Academy of Laser Dentistry **(8)**
Academy of Legal Studies in Business **(8)**
Academy of Marketing Science **(9)**
Academy of Medical-Surgical Nurses **(9)**
Academy of Operative Dentistry **(9)**
Academy of Pharmaceutical Research and Science **(9)**
Access Technology Ass'n **(10)**
Accountants for the Public Interest **(10)**
Accrediting Council on Education in Journalism and Mass Communications **(11)**
ADED - the Ass'n for Driver Rehabilitation Specialists **(11)**
Affordable Housing Tax Credit Coalition **(13)**
Agricultural and Industrial Manufacturers' Representatives Ass'n **(14)**
Agricultural Publishers Ass'n **(14)**
Agricultural Research Institute **(14)**
Agricultural Transportation Conference **(15)**
AIM USA **(15)**
Air and Expedited Motor Carriers Conference **(15)**
Airborne Law Enforcement Ass'n **(16)**
Airport Ground Transportation Ass'n **(17)**
Alfalfa Council **(17)**
Alliance for Nonprofit Management **(17)**
Alpha Chi Sigma **(18)**
Aluminum Anodizers Council **(19)**
American Academy of Ambulatory Care Nursing **(20)**
American Academy of Clinical Psychiatrists **(21)**
American Academy of Clinical Toxicology **(21)**
American Academy of Forensic Psychology **(22)**
American Academy of Industrial Hygiene **(23)**
American Academy of Neurological and Orthopaedic Surgeons **(23)**
American Academy of Nursing **(23)**
American Academy of Oral and Maxillofacial Pathology **(24)**
American Academy of Oral Medicine **(24)**
American Academy of Orofacial Pain **(24)**
American Academy of State Certified Appraisers **(26)**
American Academy of Tropical Medicine **(26)**
American Aging Ass'n **(27)**
American Alliance for Theatre and Education **(27)**
American Apitherapy Soc. **(28)**
American Apparel Producers Network **(28)**
American Ass'n for Accreditation of Ambulatory Surgery Facilities **(29)**
American Ass'n for Continuity of Care **(30)**
American Ass'n for Leisure and Recreation **(31)**
American Ass'n for Paralegal Education **(31)**
American Ass'n for Pediatric Ophthalmology and Strabismus **(31)**
American Ass'n for Public Opinion Research **(31)**
American Ass'n for Thoracic Surgery **(32)**
American Ass'n of Ambulatory Surgery Centers **(33)**
American Ass'n of Avian Pathologists **(33)**
American Ass'n of Community Theatre **(35)**
American Ass'n of Dental Consultants **(35)**
American Ass'n of Dental Examiners **(36)**
American Ass'n of Eye and Ear Hospitals **(36)**
American Ass'n of Industrial Management **(38)**
American Ass'n of Managed Care Nurses **(38)**
American Ass'n of Orthopaedic Medicine **(40)**
American Ass'n of Owners and Breeders of Peruvian Paso Horses **(40)**
American Ass'n of Plastic Surgeons **(41)**
American Ass'n of Political Consultants **(41)**
American Ass'n of Private Railroad Car Owners **(41)**
American Ass'n of Public Health Dentistry **(42)**
American Ass'n of Radon Scientists and Technologists **(42)**
American Ass'n of Veterinary Laboratory Diagnosticians **(45)**
American Ass'n of Women Dentists **(45)**
American Ass'n of Zoo Veterinarians **(45)**
American Assembly for Men in Nursing **(45)**
American Automatic Control Council **(46)**
American Beekeeping Federation **(47)**
American Berkshire Ass'n **(47)**
American Board of Sexology **(48)**
American Board of Veterinary Practitioners **(48)**
American Buyers of Meeting and Incentive Travel **(50)**
American Cargo War Risk Reinsurance Exchange **(50)**
American Chain of Warehouses **(51)**
American Cinema Editors **(52)**
American Clinical Neurophysiological Soc. **(52)**
American College of Angiology **(53)**
American College of Bankruptcy **(53)**
American College of Internat'l Physicians **(55)**
American College of Laboratory Animal Medicine **(55)**
American College of Mohs Micrographic Surgery and Cutaneous Oncology **(55)**
American College of Neuropsychopharmacology **(55)**
American College of Osteopathic Emergency Physicians **(56)**
American College of Radiation Oncology **(57)**
American College of Tax Counsel **(58)**
American College of Veterinary Ophthalmologists **(58)**
American Composers Alliance **(59)**
American Construction Inspectors Ass'n **(60)**
American Consultants League **(60)**
American Correctional Health Services Ass'n **(60)**
American Council for Construction Education **(61)**
American Council of Highway Advertisers **(61)**
American Council of Hypnotist Examiners **(61)**
American Council of State Savings Supervisors **(61)**
American Council on Consumer Interests **(61)**
American Council on Pharmaceutical Education **(62)**
American Dance Therapy Ass'n **(63)**
American Design Drafting Ass'n **(64)**
American Endodontic Soc. **(66)**
American Evaluation Ass'n **(66)**
American Federation of Home Health Agencies **(67)**
American Folklore Soc. **(69)**
American Hampshire Sheep Ass'n **(71)**
American Hardwood Export Council **(72)**
American Hernia Soc. **(73)**
American Highland Cattle Ass'n **(73)**
American Hockey Coaches Ass'n **(73)**
American Holistic Medical Ass'n **(73)**
American Holistic Veterinary Medical Ass'n **(74)**
American In-vitro Allergy/Immunology Soc. **(75)**
American Independent Refiners Ass'n **(75)**
American Indonesian Chamber of Commerce **(75)**
American Innerspring Manufacturers **(75)**
American Institute for Maghrib Studies **(76)**
American Institute of Chemists **(77)**
American Institute of Constructors **(77)**
American Institute of Hydrology **(77)**
American Institute of the History of Pharmacy **(78)**
American Ladder Institute **(80)**
American Landrace Ass'n **(80)**
American League of Lobbyists **(81)**
American Library Trustee Ass'n **(81)**
American Littoral Soc. **(82)**
American Maritime Ass'n **(82)**
American Medical Electroencephalographic Ass'n **(83)**
American Milking Shorthorn Soc. **(85)**
American Monument Ass'n **(85)**
American Musicological Soc. **(86)**
American Neurological Ass'n **(87)**
American Ornithologists' Union **(88)**
American Osteopathic College of Anesthesiologists **(89)**
American Osteopathic Colleges of Ophthalmology and Otolaryngology, Head and Neck Surgery **(89)**
American Pipe Fittings Ass'n **(92)**
American Polygraph Ass'n **(93)**
American Prosthodontic Soc. **(94)**
American Psychotherapy Ass'n **(95)**
American Radiological Nurses Ass'n **(96)**
American Radium Soc. **(97)**
American Real Estate Soc. **(97)**
American Risk and Insurance Ass'n **(98)**
American Safe Deposit Ass'n **(98)**
American Schools Ass'n **(99)**
American Scientific Glassblowers Soc. **(99)**
American Sleep Apnea Ass'n **(100)**

652 National Trade and Professional Associations of the U.S. © 1999, Columbia Books, Inc.

American Soc. for Aesthetics **(101)**
American Soc. for Engineering Management **(102)**
American Soc. for Reconstructive Microsurgery **(105)**
American Soc. for Surface Mining and Reclamation **(105)**
American Soc. of Access Professionals **(106)**
American Soc. of Agricultural Consultants **(106)**
American Soc. of Brewing Chemists **(107)**
American Soc. of Business Press Editors **(107)**
American Soc. of Consulting Arborists **(108)**
American Soc. of Contemporary Ophthalmology **(109)**
American Soc. of Group Psychotherapy and Psychodrama **(110)**
American Soc. of Ichthyologists and Herpetologists **(111)**
American Soc. of Mammalogists **(112)**
American Soc. of Maxillofacial Surgeons **(112)**
American Soc. of Ophthalmic Registered Nurses **(113)**
American Soc. of Pain Management Nurses **(113)**
American Soc. of Pharmacognosy **(114)**
American Soc. of Plant Taxonomists **(114)**
American Soc. of Preventive Oncology **(115)**
American Soc. of Professional Estimators **(115)**
American Soc. of Transportation and Logistics **(116)**
American Sportscasters Ass'n **(118)**
American Subacute Care Ass'n **(118)**
American Surety Ass'n **(119)**
American Telemedicine Ass'n **(119)**
American Trakehner Ass'n **(120)**
American Underground-Construction Ass'n **(121)**
American Veterinary Distributors Ass'n **(121)**
American Watch Ass'n **(122)**
American Wood-Preservers' Ass'n **(123)**
American Yarn Spinners Ass'n **(124)**
American-Israel Chamber of Commerce and Industry **(124)**
American-Uzbekistan Chamber of Commerce **(124)**
Appalachian Hardwood Manufacturers **(126)**
Apple Processors Ass'n **(126)**
Appliance Parts Distributors Ass'n **(126)**
Appraisers Ass'n of America **(126)**
Archery Manufacturers and Merchants Organization **(126)**
Argentina-American Chamber of Commerce **(127)**
Armed Forces Marketing Council **(127)**
Art Glass Suppliers Ass'n Internat'l **(127)**
Art Libraries Soc./North America **(127)**
Asphalt Recycling and Reclaiming Ass'n **(129)**
Ass'n for Academic Surgery **(129)**
Ass'n for Accounting Administration **(129)**
Ass'n for Accounting Marketing **(129)**
Ass'n for Behavior Analysis **(130)**
Ass'n for Canadian Studies in the United States **(130)**
Ass'n for Computational Linguistics **(131)**
Ass'n for Counselor Education and Supervision **(132)**
Ass'n for Death Education and Counseling **(132)**
Ass'n for Financial Technology **(133)**
Ass'n for Gerontology in Higher Education **(134)**
Ass'n for Hospital Medical Education **(134)**
Ass'n for Library and Information Science Education **(135)**
Ass'n for Molecular Pathology **(136)**
Ass'n for Practical and Professional Ethics **(136)**
Ass'n for Preservation Technology Internat'l **(136)**
Ass'n for Research in Otolaryngology **(137)**
Ass'n for Surgical Education **(138)**
Ass'n for the Advancement of Applied Sport Psychology **(138)**
Ass'n for the Advancement of Baltic Studies **(138)**
Ass'n for the Advancement of Psychotherapy **(138)**
Ass'n for the Study of Afro-American Life and History **(139)**
Ass'n for Transportation Law, Logistics and Policy **(140)**
Ass'n for Women in Development **(140)**
Ass'n of Advanced Rabbinical and Talmudic Schools **(141)**
Ass'n of African-American Women Business Owners **(141)**
Ass'n of Alternate Postal Systems **(142)**
Ass'n of American Cancer Institutes **(142)**
Ass'n of American Physicians and Surgeons **(142)**
Ass'n of Area Business Publications **(144)**
Ass'n of Art Museum Directors **(144)**
Ass'n of Asphalt Paving Technologists **(144)**
Ass'n of Battery Recyclers **(144)**
Ass'n of Bituminous Contractors **(144)**
Ass'n of Black Sociologists **(145)**
Ass'n of Business Support Services Internat'l **(145)**
Ass'n of Child and Adolescent Psychiatric Nurses **(146)**
Ass'n of Clinical Scientists **(147)**
Ass'n of Collegiate Schools of Planning **(148)**
Ass'n of Coupon Professionals **(149)**
Ass'n of Episcopal Colleges **(150)**
Ass'n of Food and Drug Officials **(151)**
Ass'n of Former Intelligence Officers **(152)**
Ass'n of Golf Merchandisers **(152)**
Ass'n of Image Consultants Internat'l **(153)**
Ass'n of Industry Manufacturers' Representatives **(154)**
Ass'n of Insolvency Accountants **(154)**
Ass'n of Insurance Compliance Professionals **(154)**
Ass'n of Internat'l Education Administrators **(154)**
Ass'n of Jesuit Colleges and Universities **(155)**
Ass'n of Literary Scholars and Critics **(156)**
Ass'n of Local Air Pollution Control Officials **(156)**
Ass'n of Meeting Professionals **(157)**
Ass'n of Official Seed Analysts **(158)**
Ass'n of Official Seed Certifying Agencies **(158)**
Ass'n of Otolaryngology Administrators **(159)**
Ass'n of Polysomnographic Technologists **(160)**
Ass'n of Professional Color Imagers **(161)**
Ass'n of Professional Schools of Internat'l Affairs **(161)**
Ass'n of Professors of Medicine **(162)**
Ass'n of Psychology Postdoctoral and Internship Centers **(162)**
Ass'n of Real Estate Women **(163)**
Ass'n of Service and Computer Dealers Internat'l **(164)**
Ass'n of Ship Brokers and Agents (U.S.A.) **(165)**
Ass'n of Specialized and Professional Accreditors **(165)**
Ass'n of State and Territorial Directors of Health Promotion and Public Health **(165)**
Ass'n of State and Territorial Public Health Nutrition Directors **(166)**
Ass'n of State Correctional Administrators **(166)**
Ass'n of State Floodplain Managers **(166)**
Ass'n of State Wetland Managers **(166)**
Ass'n of Systematics Collections **(167)**
Ass'n of Test Publishers **(167)**
Ass'n of University Technology Managers **(169)**
Ass'n of Women in the Metal Industries **(169)**
Associated Press Managing Editors **(172)**
Auto Internat'l Ass'n **(173)**
Automotive Occupant Restraints Council **(174)**
Automotive Trade Ass'n Executives **(175)**
Aviation Distributors and Manufacturers Ass'n Internat'l **(175)**
Aviation Safety Institute **(176)**
Ayrshire Breeders' Ass'n **(176)**
Belgian American Chamber of Commerce in the United States **(178)**
Bibliographical Soc. of America **(178)**
Biological Stain Commission **(179)**
Biomedical Engineering Soc. **(179)**
Biscuit and Cracker Distributors Ass'n **(179)**
Black Data Processing Associates **(180)**
Book Industry Study Group **(181)**
Brewers' Ass'n of America **(182)**
Bridge Grid Flooring Manufacturers Ass'n **(182)**
Bulk Carrier Conference **(184)**
Cable Tray Institute **(185)**
Campus Safety Division of the Nat'l Safety Council **(186)**
Cargo Airline Ass'n **(187)**
Cargo Reinsurance Ass'n **(187)**
Carpet Cushion Council **(187)**
Casual Furniture Retailers **(187)**
Catholic Campus Ministry Ass'n **(188)**
Catholic Library Ass'n **(188)**
Cement Employers Ass'n **(189)**
Certified Ballast Manufacturers Ass'n **(190)**
Certified Professional Insurance Agents Soc. **(190)**
Chain Link Fence Manufacturers Institute **(190)**
Chemical Coaters Ass'n Internat'l **(191)**
Chi Eta Phi Sorority **(191)**
Chief Petty Officers Ass'n **(192)**
Child Neurology Soc. **(192)**
Childrenswear Marketing Ass'n **(192)**
Chilled Foods Ass'n **(192)**
Chlorinated Paraffins Industry Ass'n **(192)**
Chlorobenzene Producers Ass'n **(193)**
Chocolate Manufacturers Ass'n of the U.S.A. **(193)**
City and Regional Magazine Ass'n **(194)**
Classification and Compensation Soc. **(194)**
Clinical Orthopaedic Soc. **(195)**
Clinical Social Work Federation **(195)**
Clothing Manufacturers Ass'n of the U.S.A. **(195)**
Clydesdale Breeders of the United States **(195)**
Coal and Slurry Technology Ass'n **(195)**
Coalition for Government Procurement **(196)**
Coalition of Labor Union Women **(196)**
Coalition of Publicly Traded Partnerships **(196)**
Cold Finished Steel Bar Institute **(196)**
College of Osteopathic Healthcare Executives **(198)**
College Swimming Coaches Ass'n of America **(198)**
Color Ass'n of the United States **(198)**
Commercial Development Ass'n **(198)**
Commercial Food Equipment Service Ass'n **(199)**
Computer Event Marketing Ass'n **(202)**
Concrete Foundations Ass'n **(203)**
Conductors Guild **(203)**
Conflict Resolution Education Network **(205)**
Congress of Lung Ass'n Staff **(205)**
Consortium of College and University Media Centers **(206)**
Consultant Dietitians in Health Care Facilities **(207)**
Contact Lens Manufacturers Ass'n **(207)**
Contact Lens Soc. of America **(207)**
Cookware Manufacturers Ass'n **(208)**
Copyright Soc. of the U.S.A. **(209)**
Corporate Facility Advisors **(209)**
Costume Soc. of America **(210)**
Cotton Warehouse Ass'n of America **(210)**
Council for American Private Education **(210)**
Council for Higher Education Accreditation **(211)**
Council for Learning Disabilities **(211)**
Council of Engineering and Scientific Soc. Executives **(213)**
Council of Professional Ass'ns on Federal Statistics **(215)**
Council of Socs. for the Study of Religion **(215)**
Council on Diagnostic Imaging to the A.C.A. **(216)**
County Executives of America **(218)**
Cranberry Institute **(218)**
Credit Professionals Internat'l **(218)**
Cryogenic Engineering Conference **(219)**
CUMREC Internat'l **(219)**
Custom Tailors and Designers Ass'n of America **(219)**
Delta Nu Alpha Transportation Fraternity **(221)**
Delta Pi Epsilon **(221)**
Delta Sigma Delta **(221)**
Delta Theta Phi **(221)**
Diamond Trade and Precious Stone Ass'n of America **(222)**
Dibasic Esters Group **(222)**
Door and Access Systems Manufacturers' Ass'n, Internat'l **(224)**
Driving School Ass'n of America **(224)**
Drug and Alcohol Testing Industry Ass'n **(225)**
Ductile Iron Soc. **(225)**
Dude Ranchers' Ass'n **(225)**
Econometric Soc. **(225)**
Economic History Ass'n **(225)**
Editorial Freelancers Ass'n **(226)**
Eight Sheet Outdoor Advertising Ass'n **(227)**
Electrical Equipment Representatives Ass'n **(227)**
Electrical Overstress/Electrostatic Discharge Ass'n **(227)**
Electromagnetic Energy Ass'n **(228)**
Embroidery Trade Ass'n **(229)**
Employee Assistance Soc. of North America **(229)**
Emulsion Polymers Council **(230)**
Environmental Design Research Ass'n **(231)**
Epsilon Sigma Phi **(232)**
Equipment Maintenance Council **(232)**
Estuarine Research Federation **(233)**
Ethylene Oxide Sterilization Ass'n **(233)**
EUCG **(233)**
Evangelical Press Ass'n **(233)**
Exotic Wildlife Ass'n **(234)**
Exposition Service Contractors Ass'n **(234)**
Farm Equipment Wholesalers Ass'n **(235)**
Federation of Analytical Chemistry and Spectroscopy Societies **(236)**
Federation of Behavioral, Psychological and Cognitive Sciences **(237)**
Federation of Straight Chiropractors and Organizations **(238)**
Fellowship of United Methodists in Music and Worship Arts **(238)**
Ferroalloys Ass'n **(238)**
Film and Bag Federation **(238)**
Filter Manufacturers Council **(238)**
Financial Markets Ass'n **(239)**
Financial Stationers Ass'n **(239)**
Fire Equipment Manufacturers' Ass'n **(239)**
Fire Suppression Systems Ass'n **(240)**
Floor Covering Installation Contractors Ass'n **(240)**
Food Industry Ass'n Executives **(241)**
Foodservice Equipment Distributors Ass'n **(242)**
Forum for Health Care Planning **(243)**
Franchise Consultants Internat'l Ass'n **(243)**
Fraternity Executives Ass'n **(244)**
Friction Materials Standards Institute **(244)**
Fur Commission USA **(244)**
Game Manufacturers Ass'n **(245)**
Garden Centers of America **(245)**
Gas Processors Suppliers Ass'n **(245)**
Gas Turbine Ass'n **(246)**
Gasket Fabricators Ass'n **(246)**
German American Business Ass'n **(247)**
Glass Art Soc. **(247)**
Golf Course Builders Ass'n of America **(248)**
Greater Clothing Contractors Ass'n **(249)**
Greek Food and Wine Institute **(249)**
Grinding Wheel Institute **(250)**
Guild of American Luthiers **(250)**
Gynecologic Surgery Soc. **(250)**
Halon Alternatives Research Corp. **(251)**
Health Industry Representatives Ass'n **(252)**
Health Sciences Communications Ass'n **(252)**
Healthcare Compliance Packaging Council **(252)**
Healthcare Finance Study Group **(252)**
Herb Growing and Marketing Network **(253)**
Hispanic Dental Ass'n **(254)**
Hispanic Nat'l Bar Ass'n **(254)**
Home Automation Ass'n **(255)**
Home Baking Ass'n **(255)**
Hop Growers of America **(256)**
Horsemen's Benevolent and Protective Ass'n **(256)**
Independent Armored Car Operators Ass'n **(259)**
Independent Automotive Damage Appraisers Ass'n **(259)**
Independent Distributors Ass'n **(260)**
Independent Laboratory Distributors Ass'n **(261)**
Independent Medical Distributors Ass'n **(261)**
Indian Educators Federation **(262)**
Industrial Ass'n of Juvenile Apparel Manufacturers **(262)**
Industrial Diamond Ass'n of America **(262)**
Industrial Heating Equipment Ass'n **(263)**
Industry Council for Tangible Assets **(263)**
Infants', Children's and Girls' Sportswear and Coat Ass'n **(263)**
Information Technologies Credit Union Ass'n **(264)**
Institute for Responsible Housing Preservation **(265)**
Institute of Diving **(266)**
Institute of Noise Control Engineering **(268)**
Institute of Shortening and Edible Oils **(269)**
Institute of Store Planners **(269)**
Instructional Telecommunications Council **(269)**
Insurance Marketing Communications Ass'n **(270)**
Inter-American Bar Ass'n **(271)**
Intercoiffure America **(271)**
Intercollegiate Broadcasting System **(271)**
Internat'l Academy of Oral Medicine and Toxicology **(272)**
Internat'l Academy of Sports Vision **(272)**
Internat'l Alliance: An Ass'n of Executive and Professional Women, The **(273)**
Internat'l Aloe Science Council **(273)**
Internat'l Ass'n Colon Hydro Therapy **(273)**
Internat'l Ass'n for Computer Systems Security **(273)**
Internat'l Ass'n for Continuing Education and Training **(273)**
Internat'l Ass'n for Hydrogen Energy **(274)**
Internat'l Ass'n for Modular Exhibitry **(274)**
Internat'l Ass'n of Black Professional Fire Fighters **(276)**
Internat'l Ass'n of Campus Law Enforcement Administrators **(277)**
Internat'l Ass'n of Corporate and Professional Recruitment **(277)**
Internat'l Ass'n of Emergency Managers **(278)**
Internat'l Ass'n of Financial Crimes Investigators **(279)**
Internat'l Ass'n of Forensic Nurses **(279)**
Internat'l Ass'n of Geophysical Contractors **(279)**
Internat'l Ass'n of Ice Cream Vendors **(280)**
Internat'l Ass'n of Jewish Vocational Services **(280)**
Internat'l Ass'n of Non-Vessel Operating Common Carriers **(281)**
Internat'l Ass'n of Official Human Rights Agencies **(281)**
Internat'l Ass'n of Structural Movers **(282)**
Internat'l Ass'n of Women Police **(283)**
Internat'l Atherosclerosis Soc. **(283)**
Internat'l Beverage Dispensing Equipment Ass'n **(283)**
Internat'l Brotherhood of Magicians **(284)**
Internat'l Buckskin Horse Ass'n **(284)**
Internat'l Business Brokers Ass'n **(284)**
Internat'l College of Surgeons **(286)**
Internat'l Compact Disc Interactive Ass'n **(286)**
Internat'l Concatenated Order of Hoo-Hoo **(286)**
Internat'l Conference of Police Chaplains **(287)**
Internat'l Corrugated Packaging Foundation **(287)**
Internat'l Council of Employers of Bricklayers and Allied Craftworkers **(287)**
Internat'l Dwarf Fruit Tree Ass'n **(289)**

National Trade and Professional Associations of the U.S. © 1999, Columbia Books, Inc. 653

$50-100,000

American Soc. of Professional Appraisers **(115)**
American Soc. of Sanitary Engineering **(116)**
American Soc. of Trial Consultants **(116)**
American Tarentaise Ass'n **(119)**
American Technical Education Ass'n **(119)**
Amusement Manufacturers and Suppliers Internat'l **(124)**
Animal Behavior Soc. **(124)**
Animal Transportation Ass'n **(125)**
Antenna Measurement Techniques Ass'n **(125)**
Archery Range and Retailers Organization **(127)**
Architectural Precast Ass'n **(127)**
Architectural Spray Coaters Ass'n **(127)**
Asbestos Cement Product Producers Ass'n **(128)**
Ass'n for Continuing Higher Education **(131)**
Ass'n for Convention Marketing Executives **(132)**
Ass'n for Equine Sports Medicine **(133)**
Ass'n for Evolutionary Economics **(133)**
Ass'n for Living History Farms and Agricultural Museums **(135)**
Ass'n for Specialists in Group Work **(137)**
Ass'n for the Advancement of Wound Care **(139)**
Ass'n for the Sociology of Religion **(139)**
Ass'n for the Study of Higher Education **(139)**
Ass'n for Tropical Biology **(140)**
Ass'n for Women Geoscientists **(140)**
Ass'n for Women in Mathematics **(140)**
Ass'n for Women in Psychology **(140)**
Ass'n of Academic Health Sciences Library Directors **(141)**
Ass'n of Administrative Law Judges **(141)**
Ass'n of Bone and Joint Surgeons **(145)**
Ass'n of Chartered Accountants in the United States **(146)**
Ass'n of Cinema and Video Laboratories **(146)**
Ass'n of Community Health Nursing Educators **(148)**
Ass'n of Departments of Foreign Languages **(149)**
Ass'n of Family Practice Residency Directors **(151)**
Ass'n of Food Journalists **(151)**
Ass'n of Independent Information Professionals **(153)**
Ass'n of Industrial Real Estate Brokers **(154)**
Ass'n of Internal Management Consultants **(154)**
Ass'n of Jewish Center Professionals **(155)**
Ass'n of Labor Relations Agencies **(155)**
Ass'n of Life Insurance Counsel **(155)**
Ass'n of Machinery and Equipment Appraisers **(156)**
Ass'n of Medical School Pediatric Department Chairmen **(157)**
Ass'n of Military Banks of America **(157)**
Ass'n of Moving Image Archivists **(158)**
Ass'n of Oncology Social Work **(159)**
Ass'n of Paroling Authorities, Internat'l **(159)**
Ass'n of Pathology Chairs **(159)**
Ass'n of Physician Assistant Programs **(160)**
Ass'n of Physician Assistants in Cardiovascular Surgery **(160)**
Ass'n of Presbyterian Colleges and Universities **(160)**
Ass'n of Professional Bridge Players **(160)**
Ass'n of Professional Design Firms **(161)**
Ass'n of Professional Model Makers **(161)**
Ass'n of Public Data Users **(162)**
Ass'n of Specialized and Cooperative Library Agencies **(165)**
Ass'n of State and Territorial Dental Directors **(165)**
Ass'n of Teachers of Latin American Studies **(167)**
Ass'n of Traumatic Stress Specialists **(168)**
Ass'n of Vacuum Equipment Manufacturers Internat'l **(169)**
Associated Actors and Artistes of America **(170)**
Associated Church Press **(171)**
Associated Construction Distributors Internat'l **(171)**
Associated Corset and Brassiere Manufacturers Ass'n **(171)**
Associated Funeral Directors, Internat'l **(171)**
Associated Schools of Construction **(172)**
Automotive Booster Clubs Internat'l **(174)**
Automotive Fleet and Leasing Ass'n **(174)**
Automotive Market Research Council **(174)**
Automotive Training Managers Council **(175)**
Aviation Technician Education Council **(176)**
Baking Industry Sanitation Standards Committee **(176)**
Bath Enclosure Manufacturers Ass'n **(177)**
Belt Ass'n **(178)**
Belted Galloway Soc. **(178)**
Beta Beta Beta **(178)**
Better Lawn and Turf Institute **(178)**
Bicycle Product Suppliers Ass'n **(178)**
Billiard and Bowling Institute of America **(178)**
Black Caucus of the American Library Ass'n **(180)**
Black Entertainment and Sports Lawyers Ass'n **(180)**
Black Retail Action Group **(180)**
Book Components Manufacturers Ass'n **(181)**
Brake Manufacturers Council **(181)**
Bright Belt Warehouse Ass'n **(182)**
Broker Management Council **(182)**
Brotherhood of Shoe and Allied Craftsmen **(183)**
Burley Auction Warehouse Ass'n **(184)**
Captive Insurance Companies Ass'n **(186)**
Career Planning and Adult Development Network **(187)**
Catholic Actors Guild of America **(188)**
Cemented Carbide Producers Ass'n **(189)**
Chefs de Cuisine Ass'n of America **(191)**
Chief Officers of State Library Agencies **(192)**
Chief Warrant and Warrant Officers Ass'n, United States Coast Guard **(192)**
Children's Literature Ass'n **(192)**
Christian College Consortium **(193)**
Classical Music Broadcasters Ass'n **(194)**
Classroom Publishers Ass'n **(194)**
Closed Circuit Television Manufacturers Ass'n **(195)**
Clowns of America, Internat'l **(195)**
Coalition of Higher Education Assistance Organizations **(196)**
Cognitive Science Soc. **(196)**
College Media Advisers **(197)**
College of Diplomates of the American Board of Orthodontics **(197)**
Collegiate Commissioners Ass'n **(198)**
Columbia Sheep Breeders Ass'n of America **(198)**
Comics Magazine Ass'n of America **(198)**
Commission on Certification of Work Adjustment and Vocational Evaluation Specialists **(199)**
Committee for Private Offshore Rescue and Towing (C-PORT) **(200)**
Communications Media Management Ass'n **(200)**
Community College Business Officers **(201)**
Community Development Soc. **(201)**
Computer Assisted Language Instruction Consortium **(202)**
Computer Law Ass'n **(202)**
Concrete Plant Manufacturers Bureau **(203)**
Conference of Educational Administrators of Schools and Programs for the Deaf **(204)**
Conference on English Leadership **(205)**
Congress of Chiropractic State Ass'ns **(205)**
Construction and Agricultural Film Manufacturers Film Ass'n **(206)**
Continental Dorset Club **(208)**
Contract Packagers Ass'n **(208)**
Convention of American Instructors of the Deaf **(208)**
Converting Equipment Manufacturers Ass'n **(208)**
Corporate Transfer Agents Ass'n **(209)**
Council of American Overseas Research Centers **(212)**
Council of Colleges of Acupuncture and Oriental Medicine **(213)**
Council of Communication Management **(213)**
Council of Defense and Space Industry Ass'ns **(213)**
Council on Chiropractic Orthopedics **(216)**
Cryogenic Soc. of America **(219)**
Cultured Pearl Ass'n of America **(219)**
Dalton Floor Covering Market Ass'n **(220)**
Dance Educators of America **(220)**
Danish-American Chamber of Commerce (USA) **(220)**
Digital Distribution of Advertising for Publications **(222)**
Display Distributors Ass'n **(223)**
Distillers Grains Technology Council **(223)**
Driver Employer Council of America **(224)**
Electrical-Electronics Materials Distributors Ass'n **(227)**
Engine Service Ass'n **(230)**
Engraved Stationery Manufacturers Ass'n **(231)**
Environmental Business Ass'n, The **(231)**
Environmental Management Ass'n **(232)**
Environmental Management Ass'n **(232)**
Equipment Service Ass'n **(232)**
Express Carriers Ass'n **(234)**
Fabric Salesmen's Ass'n **(234)**
Family and Consumer Science Education Ass'n **(234)**
Federation of Ass'ns of Regulatory Boards **(237)**
Federation of Materials Socs. **(237)**
Field Services Marketing Ass'n **(238)**
Fire Apparatus Manufacturers Ass'n **(239)**
Fire Equipment Manufacturers Suppliers Ass'n **(239)**
Fire Retardant Chemicals Ass'n **(240)**
Fixed Income Analysts Soc. **(240)**
Flexible Intermediate Bulk Container Ass'n **(240)**
Food Industry Suppliers Ass'n **(241)**
Foodservice Group **(242)**
Forestry Conservation Communications Ass'n **(243)**
Foundation for Internat'l Meetings **(243)**
Frozen Potato Products Institute **(244)**
Fulfillment Management Ass'n **(244)**
Funeral and Memorial Socs. of America **(244)**
Gift Ass'n of America **(247)**
Glazing Industry Code Committee **(248)**
Government Management Information Sciences **(248)**
Health Care Resource Management Soc. **(251)**
Heat Exchange Institute **(253)**
Heavy Duty Business Forum **(253)**
Helicopter Loggers Ass'n **(253)**
Herpetologists' League **(254)**
Hispanic Organization of Latin Actors **(254)**
Histochemical Soc. **(254)**
History of Education Soc. **(254)**
Home Fashion Products Ass'n **(255)**
Home Wine and Beer Trade Ass'n **(256)**
Hydroponic Merchants Ass'n **(257)**
Hydroponic Soc. of America **(257)**
Incentive Federation **(259)**
Independent Zinc Alloyers Ass'n **(262)**
Indiana Limestone Institute of America **(262)**
Industrial Perforators Ass'n **(263)**
Industry Coalition on Technology Transfer **(263)**
Inland Rivers Ports and Terminals **(264)**
Institute for Applied Iridology **(264)**
Institute for Briquetting and Agglomeration **(265)**
Institute of Caster Manufacturers **(266)**
Institute of Certified Records Managers **(266)**
Institute of Intermodal Repairers **(267)**
Institutional and Service Textile Distributors Ass'n **(269)**
Insulated Cable Engineers Ass'n **(270)**
Inter-Society Color Council **(271)**
Internat'l Ass'n for Impact Assessment **(274)**
Internat'l Ass'n for Insurance Law - United States Chapter **(274)**
Internat'l Ass'n for Mathematical Geology **(274)**
Internat'l Ass'n of Attorneys and Exec. in Corporate Real Estate **(276)**
Internat'l Ass'n of Auto Theft Investigators **(276)**
Internat'l Ass'n of Clerks, Recorders, Election Officials and Treasurers **(277)**
Internat'l Ass'n of Cold Storage Contractors **(277)**
Internat'l Ass'n of Conference Center Administrators **(277)**
Internat'l Ass'n of Counseling Services **(278)**
Internat'l Ass'n of Counselors and Therapists **(278)**
Internat'l Ass'n of Dive Rescue Specialists **(278)**
Internat'l Ass'n of Golf Administrators **(279)**
Internat'l Ass'n of Insurance Receivers **(280)**
Internat'l Ass'n of Marriage and Family Counselors **(281)**
Internat'l Ass'n of Pet Cemeteries **(281)**
Internat'l Ass'n of Physicians and Health Care Professionals **(281)**
Internat'l Ass'n of School Librarianship **(282)**
Internat'l Council for Computer Communication **(287)**
Internat'l Council for Small Business **(287)**
Internat'l Council of Fine Arts Deans **(287)**
Internat'l Council of Psychologists **(288)**
Internat'l Council of Regional School Accrediting Commissions **(288)**
Internat'l Double Reed Soc. **(289)**
Internat'l Drycleaners Congress **(289)**
Internat'l Family Recreation Ass'n **(290)**
Internat'l Federation of Women's Travel Organizations **(291)**
Internat'l Firestop Council **(291)**
Internat'l Group of Agencies and Bureaus **(293)**
Internat'l Health Evaluation Ass'n **(293)**
Internat'l Horn Soc. **(294)**
Internat'l Kitchen Exhaust Cleaning Ass'n **(295)**
Internat'l Listening Ass'n **(296)**
Internat'l Liver Transplantation Soc. **(296)**
Internat'l Motor Press Ass'n **(297)**
Internat'l Newspaper Group **(298)**
Internat'l Ozone Ass'n-Pan American Group Branch **(299)**
Internat'l Regional Magazine Ass'n **(301)**
Internat'l Security Officers, Police and Guards Union **(302)**
Internat'l Soc. for Adolescent Psychiatry **(302)**
Internat'l Soc. of Applied Intelligence **(305)**
Internat'l Soc. of Bassists **(305)**
Internat'l Soc. of Chemical Ecology **(306)**
Internat'l Soc. of Cleaning Technicians **(306)**
Internat'l Soc. of Financiers, Inc. **(306)**
Internat'l Soc. of Political Psychology **(306)**
Internat'l Tax Institute **(308)**
Internat'l Trombone Ass'n **(309)**
Internat'l Water Resources Ass'n **(310)**
Interstate Council on Water Policy **(311)**
Intersure, Ltd. **(312)**
Issues Management Ass'n **(313)**
Jewelry Industry Distributors Ass'n **(314)**
Kappa Delta Epsilon **(315)**
Laminating Materials Ass'n **(317)**
Laminators Safety Glass Ass'n **(317)**
League of Advertising Agencies **(318)**
Lignin Institute **(319)**
Limousine Industry Manufacturers Organization **(320)**
Lutheran Church Library Ass'n **(321)**
Lutheran Education Ass'n **(321)**
Manuscript Soc. **(323)**
Mass Marketing Insurance Institute **(324)**
Materials Handling and Management Soc. **(325)**
Materials Marketing Associates **(325)**
Metal Construction Ass'n **(327)**
Military Chaplains Ass'n of the U.S. **(328)**
Missouri Fox Trotting Horse Breed Ass'n **(329)**
Mobile Industrial Caterers' Ass'n Internat'l **(329)**
Molluscan Shellfish Institute **(330)**
Mountain Rescue Ass'n **(331)**
Municipal Waste Management Ass'n **(331)**
Munitions Carriers Conference **(331)**
Museum Computer Network **(332)**
Museum Education Roundtable **(332)**
Music Distributors Ass'n **(332)**
Mutual Advertising Agency Network **(332)**
Nat'l Academy of Clinical Biochemistry **(334)**
Nat'l Alliance of Preservation Commissions **(336)**
Nat'l Alliance of Short Story Authors **(336)**
Nat'l Ass'n for Check Safekeeping **(338)**
Nat'l Ass'n for Proton Therapy **(340)**
Nat'l Ass'n for Public Health Statistics and Information Systems **(340)**
Nat'l Ass'n of Academies of Science **(342)**
Nat'l Ass'n of Bankruptcy Trustees **(344)**
Nat'l Ass'n of Business and Industrial Saleswomen **(346)**
Nat'l Ass'n of Colored Women's Clubs **(349)**
Nat'l Ass'n of Consumer Shows **(349)**
Nat'l Ass'n of Container Distributors **(349)**
Nat'l Ass'n of County Recorders, Election Officials and Clerks **(351)**
Nat'l Ass'n of Crime Victim Compensation Boards **(351)**
Nat'l Ass'n of Dental Assistants **(352)**
Nat'l Ass'n of Disability Examiners **(353)**
Nat'l Ass'n of Division Order Analysts **(353)**
Nat'l Ass'n of Ecumenical and Interreligious Staff **(353)**
Nat'l Ass'n of Executive Secretaries and Administrative Assistants **(354)**
Nat'l Ass'n of Export Companies **(354)**
Nat'l Ass'n of Fire Investigators **(355)**
Nat'l Ass'n of Flour Distributors **(355)**
Nat'l Ass'n of Fruits, Flavors and Syrups **(356)**
Nat'l Ass'n of Geoscience Teachers **(356)**
Nat'l Ass'n of Government Archives and Records Administrators **(356)**
Nat'l Ass'n of Hispanic Federal Executives **(358)**
Nat'l Ass'n of Hispanic Nurses **(358)**
Nat'l Ass'n of Jewelry Appraisers **(361)**
Nat'l Ass'n of Legal Investigators **(361)**
Nat'l Ass'n of Litho Clubs **(361)**
Nat'l Ass'n of Marine Surveyors **(362)**
Nat'l Ass'n of Media Brokers **(362)**
Nat'l Ass'n of Medical Minority Educators **(362)**
Nat'l Ass'n of Property Inspectors **(367)**
Nat'l Ass'n of Public Insurance Adjusters **(368)**
Nat'l Ass'n of Rail Shippers **(368)**
Nat'l Ass'n of Real Estate Buyer Brokers **(369)**
Nat'l Ass'n of School Resource Officers **(371)**
Nat'l Ass'n of Schools and Colleges of the United Methodist Church **(371)**
Nat'l Ass'n of Schools of Dance **(371)**
Nat'l Ass'n of Small Business Internat'l Trade Educators **(373)**
Nat'l Ass'n of Solar Contractors **(373)**
Nat'l Ass'n of State Agencies for Surplus Property **(373)**
Nat'l Ass'n of State Directors of Administration and General Services **(374)**
Nat'l Ass'n of State Park Directors **(375)**
Nat'l Ass'n of State Personnel Executives **(376)**
Nat'l Ass'n of State Veterans Homes **(376)**
Nat'l Ass'n of Student Assistance Professional **(377)**
Nat'l Ass'n of Trailer Manufacturers **(379)**
Nat'l Ass'n of Waste Transporters **(380)**
Nat'l Band Ass'n **(382)**
Nat'l Basketball Trainers' Ass'n **(382)**
Nat'l Beverage Packaging Ass'n **(382)**
Nat'l Black Ass'n for Speech, Language and Hearing **(383)**
Nat'l Broadcast Ass'n for Community Affairs **(384)**

656 National Trade and Professional Associations of the U.S. © 1999, Columbia Books, Inc.

Ass'n for the Education of Teachers in Science **(139)**
Ass'n for the Study of Dreams **(139)**
Ass'n for Volunteer Administration **(140)**
Ass'n of American Editorial Cartoonists **(142)**
Ass'n of Applied Insect Ecologists **(143)**
Ass'n of Average Adjusters of the U.S. **(144)**
Ass'n of Celebrity Personal Assistants **(146)**
Ass'n of Children's Prosthetic-Orthotic Clinics **(146)**
Ass'n of Christian Librarians **(146)**
Ass'n of Concert Bands **(148)**
Ass'n of Consulting Chemists and Chemical Engineers **(148)**
Ass'n of Defense Trial Attorneys **(149)**
Ass'n of Direct Marketing Agencies **(149)**
Ass'n of Environmental and Resource Economists **(150)**
Ass'n of Environmental Engineering Professors **(150)**
Ass'n of Federal Communications Consulting Engineers **(151)**
Ass'n of Former Agents of the U.S. Secret Service **(152)**
Ass'n of Independent Trust Companies **(154)**
Ass'n of Jewish Libraries **(155)**
Ass'n of Management Analysts in State and Local Government **(156)**
Ass'n of Medical Diagnostic Manufacturers **(157)**
Ass'n of Military Colleges and Schools of the U.S. **(157)**
Ass'n of Muslim Scientists and Engineers **(158)**
Ass'n of Official Racing Chemists **(158)**
Ass'n of Osteopathic Directors and Medical Educators **(159)**
Ass'n of Part-Time Professionals **(159)**
Ass'n of Pediatric Oncology Social Workers **(160)**
Ass'n of Professors of Cardiology **(161)**
Ass'n of Southern Baptist Colleges and Schools **(165)**
Ass'n of Teachers of Japanese **(167)**
Ass'n of Third World Studies **(168)**
Ass'n of Tongue Depressors **(168)**
Ass'n of University Programs in Occupational Health and Safety **(168)**
Ass'n of University Radiologists **(168)**
Associated Specialty Contractors **(172)**
Automated Storage/Retrieval Systems **(173)**
Automatic Guided Vehicle Systems **(173)**
Automotive Chemical Manufacturers Council **(174)**
Automotive Cooling System Institute **(174)**
Barzona Breeders Ass'n of America **(177)**
Beef Improvement Federation **(177)**
Black Psychiatrists of America **(180)**
Board of Trade of the Wholesale Seafood Merchants **(181)**
Business Identity Council of America **(184)**
California Dried Fruit Export Ass'n **(185)**
Catholic Book Publishers Ass'n **(188)**
Chemical Sources Ass'n **(191)**
Chinese American Medical Soc. **(192)**
Chinese Language Teachers Ass'n **(192)**
Civil Aviation Medical Ass'n **(194)**
Clock Manufacturers and Marketing Ass'n **(195)**
Coal Exporters Ass'n of the United States **(195)**
Coleopterists Soc. **(196)**
Collectibles and Platemakers Guild **(196)**
Collector Car Appraisers Internat'l **(197)**
College Band Directors Nat'l Ass'n **(197)**
College English Ass'n **(197)**
College Reading and Learning Ass'n **(198)**
College Sports Information Directors of America **(198)**
College Theology Soc. **(198)**
Colombian American Ass'n **(198)**
Commercial Weather Services Ass'n **(199)**
Communications Marketing Ass'n **(200)**
Community Colleges Humanities Ass'n **(201)**
Comparative and Internat'l Education Soc. **(201)**
Concord Grape Ass'n **(203)**
Concrete Anchor Manufacturers Ass'n **(203)**
Concrete Modifications Contractors Ass'n **(203)**
Conference Board of the Mathematical Sciences **(203)**
Conference of Minority Public Administrators **(204)**
Conference of Research Workers in Animal Diseases **(204)**
Conference on Consumer Finance Law **(205)**
Congress on Research in Dance **(205)**
Contractors Pump Bureau **(208)**
Correctional Industries Ass'n **(210)**
Council for Art Education **(211)**
Council for Jewish Education **(211)**
Council of American Master Mariners **(212)**
Council of Hotel and Restaurant Trainers **(214)**
Council of Internat'l Investigators **(214)**
Council of Planning Librarians **(215)**
Council of State Ass'n Presidents **(215)**
Council on Education of the Deaf **(216)**
Council on Geriatric Cardiology **(217)**
Crane Manufacturers Ass'n of America **(218)**
Customs and Internat'l Trade Bar Ass'n **(219)**
Data Administration Management Ass'n Internat'l **(220)**
Decorative Window Coverings Ass'n **(220)**
Delta Omicron Foundation, Inc. **(221)**
Dental Dealers of America **(221)**
Diethyl Ether Producers Ass'n **(222)**
Disaster Preparedness and Emergency Response Ass'n **(223)**
Ecuadorean American Ass'n **(226)**
Energy Traffic Ass'n **(230)**
Federal Physicians Ass'n **(236)**
Finnish American Chamber of Commerce **(239)**
Fluid Controls Institute **(241)**
Food Distribution Research Soc. **(241)**
Food Equipment Manufacturers Ass'n **(241)**
Forest Products Safety Conference **(242)**
Freelance Editorial Ass'n **(244)**
Gamma Iota Sigma **(245)**
Gasoline Pump Manufacturers Ass'n **(246)**
Geochemical Soc. **(246)**
Guild of Natural Science Illustrators **(250)**
Guitar and Accessories Marketing Ass'n **(250)**
Harvey Soc. **(251)**
Heavy Duty Representatives Ass'n **(253)**
Hoist Manufacturers Institute **(255)**
Holistic Dental Ass'n **(255)**
Hospital Presidents Ass'n **(256)**
Human Biology Ass'n **(257)**
Icelandic American Chamber of Commerce **(258)**
Independent Computer Services Ass'n of America **(260)**
Independent Investors Protective League **(261)**
Independent Pet and Animal Transportation Ass'n Internat'l **(261)**
Independent Professional Representatives Organization **(261)**
Institute for Business Innovation **(265)**
Institute of Certified Business Counselors **(266)**
Institute of Roofing and Waterproofing Consultants Internat'l **(269)**
Institute on Religion in an Age of Science **(269)**
Instrument Contracting and Engineering Ass'n **(269)**
Intermarket Ass'n of Advertising Agencies **(271)**
Internat'l Academy of Behavioral Medicine, Counseling and Psychotherapy **(272)**
Internat'l Ass'n for Computer Information Systems **(273)**
Internat'l Ass'n of Addictions and Offender Counselors **(275)**
Internat'l Ass'n of Career Consulting Firms **(277)**
Internat'l Ass'n of Career Management Professionals **(277)**
Internat'l Ass'n of Correctional Officers **(278)**
Internat'l Ass'n of Law Enforcement Intelligence Analysts **(280)**
Internat'l Ass'n of Milk Control Agencies **(281)**
Internat'l Ass'n of Professional Security Consultants **(282)**
Internat'l Ass'n of Sports Museums and Halls of Fame **(282)**
Internat'l Black Writers Conference **(283)**
Internat'l Castor Oil Ass'n **(285)**
Internat'l Clarinet Ass'n **(285)**
Internat'l Entertainment Buyers Ass'n **(290)**
Internat'l Federation of Inspection Agencies - Americas Committee **(290)**
Internat'l Fibre Drum Institute **(291)**
Internat'l Graphic Arts Education Ass'n **(292)**
Internat'l Guild of Candle Artisans **(293)**
Internat'l Institute for Lath and Plaster **(294)**
Internat'l Laser Display Ass'n **(295)**
Internat'l Merger and Acquisition Professionals **(297)**
Internat'l Oil Mill Superintendents Ass'n **(298)**
Internat'l Perimetric Soc. **(299)**
Internat'l Planetarium Soc. **(300)**
Internat'l Pot and Kettle Club **(300)**
Internat'l Quorum of Film and Video Producers **(301)**
Internat'l Soc. for Cardiovascular Surgery - North American Chapter **(303)**
Internat'l Soc. for Professional Hypnosis **(304)**
Internat'l Soc. of Hotel Ass'n Executives **(306)**
Internat'l Soc. of Psychiatric Consultation Liaison Nurses **(306)**
Jewelry Manufacturers Ass'n **(314)**
Jewish Teachers Ass'n-Morim **(314)**
Judge Advocates Ass'n **(315)**
Kamut Ass'n of North America **(315)**
Lacrosse USA **(316)**
Leafy Greens Council **(318)**
Lightning Protection Institute **(319)**
Lipizzan Ass'n of North America **(320)**
Literary Managers and Dramaturgs of the Americas **(320)**
Locomotive Maintenance Officers' Ass'n **(320)**
Machine Vision Ass'n of SME **(321)**
Magazine Printers Section/Printing Industries of America **(321)**
Magnet Distributors and Fabricators Ass'n **(322)**
Magnetic Materials Producers Ass'n **(322)**
Maritime Fire and Safety Ass'n **(324)**
Masonry Heater Ass'n of North America **(324)**
Meat Industry Suppliers Ass'n **(325)**
Mechanical Power Transmission Ass'n **(326)**
Microcirculatory Soc. of America **(328)**
Mining and Metallurgical Soc. of America **(329)**
Model Railroad Industry Ass'n **(329)**
Modern Greek Studies Ass'n **(329)**
Motion Picture and Television Credit Ass'n **(330)**
Nat'l Ass'n for Creative Children and Adults **(338)**
Nat'l Ass'n for Drama Therapy **(339)**
Nat'l Ass'n for Government Training and Development **(339)**
Nat'l Ass'n for Physical Education in Higher Education **(340)**
Nat'l Ass'n for Rural Mental Health **(341)**
Nat'l Ass'n of African American Studies **(342)**
Nat'l Ass'n of Band Instrument Manufacturers **(344)**
Nat'l Ass'n of Bar-Related Title Insurers **(344)**
Nat'l Ass'n of Black Women Attorneys **(345)**
Nat'l Ass'n of Catastrophe Adjusters **(346)**
Nat'l Ass'n of Chain Manufacturers **(346)**
Nat'l Ass'n of Consumer Credit Administrators **(349)**
Nat'l Ass'n of Counselors **(350)**
Nat'l Ass'n of Forensic Economics **(356)**
Nat'l Ass'n of Governmental Labor Officials **(357)**
Nat'l Ass'n of Hispanic and Latino Studies **(358)**
Nat'l Ass'n of Independent Public Finance Advisors **(359)**
Nat'l Ass'n of Industrial and Technical Teacher Educators **(360)**
Nat'l Ass'n of Jai Alai Frontons **(360)**
Nat'l Ass'n of Judiciary Interpreters and Translators **(361)**
Nat'l Ass'n of Manufacturing Opticians **(362)**
Nat'l Ass'n of Performing Arts Managers and Agents **(364)**
Nat'l Ass'n of Publishers' Representatives **(368)**
Nat'l Ass'n of Railway Business Women **(368)**
Nat'l Ass'n of Recreation Resource Planners **(369)**
Nat'l Ass'n of Regional Media Centers **(369)**
Nat'l Ass'n of School Music Dealers **(371)**
Nat'l Ass'n of School Safety and Law Enforcement Officers **(371)**
Nat'l Ass'n of Scientific Materials Managers **(371)**
Nat'l Ass'n of Seventh-Day Adventist Dentists **(372)**
Nat'l Ass'n of State Outdoor Recreation Liaison Officers **(375)**
Nat'l Ass'n of Traffic Accident Reconstructionists and Investigators **(379)**
Nat'l Ass'n of University Fisheries and Wildlife Programs **(379)**
Nat'l Ass'n of Veterans Program Administrators **(379)**
Nat'l Ass'n of Vision Professionals **(379)**
Nat'l Ass'n of Vocational Education Special Needs Personnel **(379)**
Nat'l Ass'n of Waterproofing Contractors **(380)**
Nat'l Cargo Security Council **(385)**
Nat'l Catalog Managers Ass'n **(385)**
Nat'l Catholic Educational Exhibitors **(385)**
Nat'l Caves Ass'n **(386)**
Nat'l Child Transport Ass'n **(386)**
Nat'l Conference of Bar Foundations **(389)**
Nat'l Conference of Federal Trial Judges **(390)**
Nat'l Conference of Yeshiva Principals **(391)**
Nat'l Conference on Research in Language and Literacy **(391)**
Nat'l Council for Uniform Interest Compensation **(393)**
Nat'l Council of Commercial Plant Breeders **(394)**
Nat'l Council on Public History **(397)**
Nat'l Denturist Ass'n **(399)**
Nat'l Emergency Equipment Dealers Ass'n **(401)**
Nat'l Employment Counseling Ass'n **(401)**
Nat'l Federation of Independent Unions **(403)**
Nat'l Flight Paramedics Ass'n **(405)**
Nat'l Frozen Dessert and Fast Food Ass'n **(406)**
Nat'l Goose Council **(407)**
Nat'l Guard Executive Directors Ass'n **(408)**
Nat'l Gymnastics Judges Ass'n **(408)**
Nat'l Institute of American Doll Artists **(411)**
Nat'l Marine Bankers Ass'n **(416)**
Nat'l Marine Educators Ass'n **(416)**
Nat'l Music Council **(418)**
Nat'l Organization for Human Service Education **(420)**
Nat'l Organization of Bar Counsel **(420)**
Nat'l Pan Hellenic Council **(421)**
Nat'l Pedigreed Livestock Council **(422)**
Nat'l Prison Hospice Ass'n **(423)**
Nat'l Roadside Vegetation Management Ass'n **(426)**
Nat'l Safety Management Soc. **(426)**
Nat'l Science Education Leadership Ass'n **(427)**
Nat'l Soc. of Appraiser Specialists **(429)**
Nat'l Soc. of Architectural Engineers **(429)**
Nat'l Stripper Well Ass'n **(432)**
Newspaper Ass'n Managers **(439)**
Newspaper Features Council **(439)**
North American Farm Show Council **(442)**
North American Gamebird Ass'n **(442)**
North American Mycological Ass'n **(443)**
North American Plant Preservation Council **(443)**
North American Snowsports Journalists Ass'n **(444)**
North American Soc. for Sport History **(444)**
North American Trucking Industrial Relations Ass'n **(445)**
Northern Nut Growers Ass'n **(446)**
Nurse Healers - Professional Associates Internat'l **(447)**
Office Planners and Users Group **(447)**
Organization Development Institute **(449)**
Orthopedic Surgical Manufacturers Ass'n **(451)**
Paper and Plastic Representatives Management Council **(453)**
Philosophy of Education Soc. **(457)**
Pile Driving Contractors Ass'n **(458)**
Polymer Particulate Inhalation Group **(460)**
Professional Aeromedical Transport Ass'n **(464)**
Professional Currency Dealers Ass'n **(465)**
Professional Reactor Operator Soc. **(466)**
Promotion Industry Council **(468)**
Religion Newswriters Ass'n of U.S. and Canada **(474)**
Religious Research Ass'n **(474)**
Retail Print Music Dealers Ass'n **(476)**
Safety Equipment Manufacturers' Agents Ass'n **(478)**
Scaffolding, Shoring and Forming Institute **(479)**
Shade Tobacco Growers Agricultural Ass'n **(482)**
Sigma Epsilon Delta Dental Fraternity **(483)**
Sleep Research Soc. **(483)**
Soc. for Applied Sociology **(485)**
Soc. for Business Ethics **(486)**
Soc. for Cinema Studies **(486)**
Soc. for Disability Studies **(487)**
Soc. for Ear, Nose and Throat Advances in Children **(487)**
Soc. for Education and Research in Psychiatric Mental Health Nursing **(487)**
Soc. for Education in Anesthesia **(487)**
Soc. for Industrial Archeology **(490)**
Soc. for Light Treatment and Biological Rhythms **(490)**
Soc. for Pediatric Dermatology **(492)**
Soc. for Psychophysiological Research **(492)**
Soc. for Sex Therapy and Research **(493)**
Soc. for Social Studies of Science **(494)**
Soc. for the Advancement of Scandinavian Study **(494)**
Soc. for Theriogenology **(496)**
Soc. for Vector Ecology **(496)**
Soc. of American Graphic Artists **(497)**
Soc. of American Historians **(497)**
Soc. of Collision Repair Specialists **(499)**
Soc. of Commercial Seed Technologists **(499)**
Soc. of Depreciation Professionals **(500)**
Soc. of Photographer and Artist Representatives **(505)**
Soc. of Professional Archeologists **(505)**
Soc. of State Directors of Health, Physical Education and Recreation **(507)**
Soc. of University Surgeons **(508)**
Soc. of Urologic Cryosurgeons **(508)**
Sommelier Soc. of America **(510)**
Southern Cypress Manufacturers Ass'n **(510)**
Special Interest Group for Biomedical Computing **(511)**
Special Interest Group for Computer Science Education **(511)**
Special Interest Group for Measurement and Evaluation **(512)**
Special Interest Group on APL Programming Language **(512)**
Sponge and Chamois Institute **(514)**
State Guard Ass'n of the United States **(516)**
Storage Equipment Manufacturer's Ass'n **(517)**
Surface Design Ass'n **(518)**
Surface Mount Equipment Manufacturers Ass'n **(519)**
Surgical Infection Soc. **(519)**
Swimming Teachers of America **(519)**
System Safety Soc. **(519)**
Tackle and Shooting Sports Agents Ass'n **(520)**
Technical Ceramics Manufacturers Ass'n **(520)**
Teleprofessional Managers Ass'n **(521)**
Textile Fibers and By-Products Ass'n **(522)**
Tile, Marble, Terrazzo, Finishers, Shopworkers and Granite Cutters Internat'l Union **(523)**
Tourist Railway Ass'n **(524)**
Track Owners Ass'n **(524)**

658 National Trade and Professional Associations of the U.S. © 1999, Columbia Books, Inc.

$10-25,000

under $10,000

Executive Index

All Individuals appearing in the Association Index appear here, in alphabetical order.

Aandahl, Kevin
Nat'l Corn Growers Ass'n (392)

Aaron CAE, Larry E.
Internat'l Publishing Management Ass'n (300)

Abbe, George
Nat'l Shellfisheries Ass'n (427)

Abblett CPA, Thomas
American College of Internat'l Physicians (55)

Abbott, Barbara
American Soc. of Human Genetics (111)

Abbott, John T.
Nat'l Ass'n of Industrial and Office Properties (360)

Abboud, Jeffrey S.
Gas Turbine Ass'n (246)

Abdelsamad, Mervat M.
Soc. for Advancement of Management (484)

Abdelsamad, Dr. Moustafa H.
Soc. for Advancement of Management (484)

Abdullah, Dr. Samella
Ass'n of Black Psychologists (145)

Abel, Joe
Soc. of Actuaries (496)

Abel, Justine
Oxygen Soc., The (452)

Abel, Marilyn
Educational Paperback Ass'n (226)

Abenante, Paul C.
American Bakers Ass'n (46)

Aberg, Peter
Alliance of Information and Referral Systems (18)

Aberle, Denise R.
Soc. of Thoracic Radiology (507)

Abernathey, Guy L.
SnowSports Industries America (484)

Abernethy, Durant S.
Nat'l Foundation for Consumer Credit (405)

Able, Dr. Bill V.
American Internat'l Charolais Ass'n (79)

Able Jr., CAE, Edward H.
American Ass'n of Museums (39)

Abler, Dr. Ronald F.
Ass'n of American Geographers (142)

Abolt, Russell L.
Internat'l Sleep Products Ass'n (302)

Abraham, George
Institute of Certified Business Counselors (266)

Abraham, Mark
Ass'n of Publication Production Managers (162)

Abraham, Michael T.
Theta Tau (522)

Abraham, Rick
Ass'n of Sales and Marketing Companies (164)
Internat'l Foodservice Brokers Ass'n/Ass'n of Sales & Marketing Companies (291)

Abrams, George H.J.
North American Indian Museums Ass'n (442)

Abrate, Jayne
American Ass'n of Teachers of French (44)

Abu-Lughod, Deena
Nat'l Academy Museum and School Fine Arts (333)

Accardo, Leonard L.
Nat'l Ass'n of Legal Investigators (361)

Aceredo, Christina
American College of Legal Medicine (55)

Achilles, Charles
Institute of Real Estate Management (269)

Ackerman, Peggy
Tourist House Ass'n of America (524)

Ackerman, Terry A.
Psychometric Soc. (469)

Ackley, Sue
American Chiropractic Ass'n (51)

Acorn, Linda
Internat'l Cemetery and Funeral Ass'n (285)

Acott, Mike
Nat'l Asphalt Pavement Ass'n (337)

Acquard, Charles A.
Nat'l Ass'n of State Utility Consumer Advocates (376)

Acquaviva, Francis A.
Roof Consultants Institute (477)

Acunto, Carole H.
American Risk and Insurance Ass'n (98)

Acunto, Stephen C.
Internat'l Ass'n for Insurance Law - United States Chapter (274)

Adair, Katie
American Academy of Child and Adolescent Psychiatry (20)

Adair, Patricia
Institute of Scrap Recycling Industries (269)

Adams, Angelique
AOAC Internat'l (125)

Adams, Barry K.
Nat'l Council of Industrial Naval Air Stations (395)

Adams, Carol
Holstein Ass'n USA (255)

Adams, Charee L.
American Trakehner Ass'n (120)

Adams, Dr. Terri Y.
Nat'l Ass'n of Securities Professionals (372)

Adams, Elaine
American Vocational Ass'n (122)

Adams, Eva
Nat'l Ass'n of Managed Care Physicians (362)

Adams, Joan
Nat'l Student Employment Ass'n (432)

Adams III, John
Soc. for Human Resource Management (489)

Adams, Kenneth R.
Nat'l Ass'n for Medical Equipment Services (340)

Adams, Linda
Nat'l Child Support Enforcement Ass'n (386)

Adams, Patricia L.
Nat'l Pharmaceutical Council (422)

Adams, Ralph
Laborers' Internat'l Union of North America (316)

Adams, Sandy
Soc. for Epidemiologic Research (487)

Adams, Suzanne
Foreign Press Ass'n (242)

Adams, William A.
Tobacco Institute (524)

Adamson, Dan K.
Council of Engineering and Scientific Soc. Executives (213)
Soc. of Petroleum Engineers (505)

Adamson, J. Douglas
Bank Marketing Ass'n (176)

Adamson Ph.D., Richard H.
Nat'l Soft Drink Ass'n (430)

Addington, John H.
Pressure Washer Manufacturers Ass'n (462)
American Ass'n of Automatic Door Manufacturers (33)
Steel Window Institute (517)
Compressed Air and Gas Institute (202)
Fire Equipment Manufacturers' Ass'n (239)
Fluid Controls Institute (241)
Heat Exchange Institute (253)
Door and Access Systems Manufacturers' Ass'n, Internat'l (224)
Scaffolding, Shoring and Forming Institute (479)

Addison, Curtis A.
Nat'l Ass'n of Corporate Real Estate Executives International (350)

Addison, Natalie S.
Military Operations Research Soc. (328)

Adelizzi, Michael
Mason Contractors Ass'n of America (324)

Adelman D.O., Michael
American Osteopathic College of Proctology (89)

Adelman, Peter
Knitted Textile Ass'n (316)

Adkins, Darlene
Nat'l Consumers League (392)

Adkins, Dinah
Nat'l Business Incubation Ass'n (384)

Adkins, Shirlyn A.
American Ass'n of Electrodiagnostic Medicine (36)

Adler, Howard
Substance Abuse Program Administrators Ass'n (518)

Adlis, Debra
Nat'l Ass'n of Real Estate Investment Trusts (369)

Adsit, Laury L.
Nat'l Ass'n of Professional Geriatric Care Managers (366)
Nat'l Academy of Elder Law Attorneys (334)
Nat'l Guardianship Ass'n (408)

Aellos, Rathany
American Ass'n for Medical Transcription (31)

Aeschliman, Karin S.
Black Tie Bureau (180)
Internat'l Formalwear Ass'n (291)

Agar-Barwick, Timi
Ass'n of Physician Assistant Programs (160)

Agee, Lynn
United Paperworkers Internat'l Union (531)

Aguila, Tomas R.
American Therapeutic Ass'n (120)

Aguilar, Rossana
Jewelers of America (314)

Aguirre, John J.
United Fresh Fruit and Vegetable Ass'n (531)

Ahearn, Jennifer
American Ass'n of Colleges of Nursing (34)

Ahlers Sr., Glen-Peter
Scribes (480)

Ahlgrim, Amy
Retail Advertising and Marketing Ass'n Internat'l (475)

Ahmad, Mario
Nat'l Ass'n of Enrolled Agents (354)

Aho, Andrew
American Chiropractic Ass'n (51)

Aiken, Chris
Western Shoe Associates (543)

Aiken, Paul
Authors Guild (173)
Authors League of America (173)

Aiken D.C., Phil L.
Council on Chiropractic Orthopedics (216)

Aiken-O'Neill, Patricia
Eye Bank Ass'n of America (234)

Ainsworth, Susan L.
American College Health Ass'n (52)

Airth, Rachel
American Soc. of Women Accountants (117)

Aitken, Herve
North American Trucking Industrial Relations Ass'n (445)

Aitken, Michael P.
College and University Personnel Ass'n (197)

Aitken, Paul D.
American Ass'n on Mental Retardation (45)

Aizenberq, Stuart
Nat'l Automatic Merchandising Ass'n (381)

Akerman, Don B.
Nat'l Rep/Wholesaler Ass'n (425)

Akhter MD, MPH, Mohammad N.
American Public Health Ass'n (95)

Akin, Connie
Produce Marketing Ass'n (463)

Akins, Michael E.
Drilling Engineering Ass'n (224)

Akins, Zane
Nat'l Pedigreed Livestock Council (422)

Akst, Jason
Billiard Congress of America (178)

Akstens, Frank W.
Industrial Fasteners Institute (262)

Aksztulewicz, Jan
Real Estate Brokerage Managers Council (472)

Alampi, Richard
Converting Equipment Manufacturers Ass'n (208)

Alario, Robert
Offshore Marine Service Ass'n (447)

Albers, Donald J.
Mathematical Ass'n of America (325)

Albers D.V.M., John W.
American Animal Hospital Ass'n (28)

Albert, Holly
Arthroscopy Ass'n of North America (128)

Albert, Ida
American Guernsey Ass'n (71)

Albert, Sarah
General Federation of Women's Clubs (246)

Alberts, Dr. Bruce
Nat'l Academy of Sciences (334)

Albertson USMC (RET.), Col. Eileen M.
Judge Advocates Ass'n (315)

Albin, Clint
American Nursery and Landscape Ass'n (87)

Albizo APR, Joel
American Nursery and Landscape Ass'n (87)

Albrecht, Samuel
Nat'l Bison Ass'n (383)

Albritten, Arna
Nat'l Ass'n of College Deans, Registrars, and Admissions
Officers (348)

Alden CTC, Anita
Institute of Certified Travel Agents (266)

Alderson D.D.S., Larry M.
American Academy of Gnathologic Orthopedics (22)

Aldinger, Nancy M.
Nat'l Fisheries Institute (404)

Aldrete, Eddie
American Agricultural Editors Ass'n (27)

Aldridge, Blake
Livestock Conservation Institute (320)

Aleknavage, Debra
Ass'n of Medical Diagnostic Manufacturers (157)

Aleshire Ph.D., Rev. David O.
Ass'n of Theological Schools in the United States and
Canada (168)

Aleskovsky, Paul
Soccer Industry Council of America (509)

Aleskovsky, Paul A.
Sporting Goods Manufacturers Ass'n (515)

Alexander, Dr. Charles J.
Nat'l Ass'n of Medical Minority Educators (362)

Alexander, Diana
American Astronomical Soc. (45)

Alexander, Ed
Ass'n of Dark Leaf Tobacco Dealers and Exporters (149)

Alexander, Eugene
Nat'l Ass'n of Teachers' Agencies (378)

Alexander, Glen
Nat'l Ass'n of State Park Directors (375)

Alexander, Helena
NACE Internat'l (333)

Alexander, June G.
Immigration and Ethnic History Soc. (259)

Alexander CRNI, Mary
Intravenous Nurses Soc. (312)

Alfano M.D., Louis F.
American Soc. of Abdominal Surgeons (106)

Alfano, Peter
ATP Tour (172)

Alfaro, Manuel
Hispanic Organization of Latin Actors (254)

Alfaro, Teresa
American Soc. for Horticultural Science (103)

Alfaros, Carlos E.
Argentina-American Chamber of Commerce (127)

Alford, Brenda
Ass'n of African-American Women Business Owners (141)

Alford, Jimmie
American Ass'n of Fund-Raising Counsel (37)

Alhadeff, Joseph H.
United States Council for Internat'l Business (533)

Ali, Avis G.
Nat'l Council of Higher Education Loan Programs (395)

Ali Ph.D., Moonis
Internat'l Soc. of Applied Intelligence (305)

Alin, Michael
American Soc. of Interior Designers (111)

Allan, Berry
Internat'l Union of Electronic, Electrical, Salaried Machine,
and Furniture Workers (309)

Allan, Brian B.
Nat'l Automatic Merchandising Ass'n (381)

Allan CAE, ABC, Elizabeth J.
Internat'l Ass'n of Business Communicators (276)

Allbritten Ph.D., Drew W.
American Ass'n for Adult and Continuing Education (29)

Allbritten, Drew W.
Internat'l Ass'n for Continuing Education and Training (273)

Alleger, Robert B.
Internat'l Periodical Distributors Ass'n (299)

Allegretti, Thomas A.
American Waterways Operators (122)

Allen, Alexis
Aerospace Industries Ass'n of America (13)

Allen, Ann E.
American College of Obstetricians and Gynecologists (56)

Allen, C. Clifford
Ass'n of Reporters of Judicial Decisions (163)

Allen, Christopher E.
Financial Executives Institute (238)

Allen Ph.D, Dan J.
American Ass'n of Behavioral Therapists (33)

Allen, Dianne
Nat'l Retail Hardware Ass'n (425)

Allen, Donald R.
Nat'l Interscholastic Swimming Coaches Ass'n (413)

Allen, Geoff
Internat'l Institute of Forecasters (294)

Allen, H. Pamela
Coalition for Juvenile Justice (196)

Allen, James R.
Nat'l Ass'n of Securities Dealers (372)

Allen, Jeffrey
Soc. of Actuaries (496)

Allen, Judith A.
Institute for Investment Management Consultants (265)

Allen, Kenneth B.
Nat'l Newspaper Ass'n (418)

Allen, Kenneth W.
U.S.-ROC (Taiwan) Business Council (528)

Allen, Larry
Coalition for Government Procurement (196)

Allen, Larry W.
Industrial Designers Soc. of America (262)

Allen, Linda
American Physiological Soc. (92)

Allen, Marian K.
Handweavers Guild of America (251)

Allen, Paul
Country Radio Broadcasters (218)

Allen, Peter
Nat'l Council of Acoustical Consultants (393)

Allen USN (RET.), V.Adm. Richard C.
Ass'n of Naval Aviation (158)

Allen, Ronald A.
American Advertising Federation (27)

Allen, Sandy
American College of Nutrition (56)

Allen, Shirley Marcus
Child Welfare League of America (192)

Allen, Stephanie
Ass'n of Professional Design Firms (161)

Allen, Susan Au
United States Pan Asian American Chamber of
Commerce (534)

Allen, Wendy
American Gear Manufacturers Ass'n (70)

Alley, Richard L.
American Welding Soc. (123)

Allie M.D., Ben
American Academy of Tropical Medicine (26)

Allison, David C.
Cell Kinetics Soc. (189)

Allison, Frank
Automotive Refrigeration Products Institute (175)
Internat'l Mobile Air Conditioning Ass'n (297)

Allison, Marcia M.
Walking Horse Trainers Ass'n (540)

Allison, Richard
Internat'l Piano Guild (300)
American College of Musicians (55)
Nat'l Guild of Piano Teachers (408)

Allison, Richard G.
American Soc. for Nutritional Sciences (104)

Allmon, Dr. Warren D.
Paleontological Research Institution (452)

Alm, Carol
Internat'l Arabian Horse Ass'n (273)

Almand P.E., Kathleen
Soc. of Fire Protection Engineers (501)

Almanza, Ilse B.
American Soc. of Directors of Volunteer Services of the
AHA (109)

Almeida, Paul E.
Internat'l Federation of Professional and Technical
Engineers (291)

Almgren, Kenneth D.
Nat'l Ass'n of Broadcasters (345)

Alongi, Deene
American Urogynecologic Soc. (121)

Alonzo, R. Gregory
Professional Speakers Network (467)

Alou, Hanne
Refractory Ceramic Fiber Coalition (473)

Alp, Funda
American Pet Products Manufacturers Ass'n (91)

Alsmeyer, Dr. Richard
Nat'l Seasoning Manufacturers Ass'n (427)

Alt, Curt
Hardwood Plywood and Veneer Ass'n (251)

Alterman, Marsha
Affiliated Boards of Officials (13)

Alterman, Stephen A.
Cargo Airline Ass'n (187)

Altesman, Albert
Board of Trade of the Wholesale Seafood Merchants (181)

Althaus, David
Chemical Industry Institute of Toxicology (191)

Althouse, J. Kenneth
Ass'n for Information and Image Management
International (135)

Altman, Don
Ass'n of State and Territorial Dental Directors (165)

Altman, E.T. "Bill"
Hardwood Plywood and Veneer Ass'n (251)

Altman, Marilyn
Ass'n of Jewish Center Professionals (155)

Altmeyer, Thomas H.
Nat'l Mining Ass'n (417)

Altobelli, John A.
Internat'l Foundation of Employee Benefit Plans (292)

Altschul, Michael F.
Cellular Telecommunications Industry Ass'n (189)

Altvater, Ralph
Nat'l Ass'n of Educational Buyers (353)

Alvord, Ross
Nat'l Ass'n of Certified Valuation Analysts (346)

Amand, Dr. Wilbur
American Ass'n of Zoo Veterinarians (45)

Amatayakul, Margret
Computer-based Patient Record Institute (203)

Amati Ph.D., David L.
Soc. of Automotive Engineers International **(498)**

Ambach, Gordon M.
Council of Chief State School Officers **(213)**

Ambers CIC, CPSR, Kitty
Certified Professional Insurance Agents Soc. **(190)**

Ambrose, Darnell
American Soc. of Professional Estimators **(115)**

Ambrose, John
American Ass'n for Marriage and Family Therapy **(31)**

Ambrose, Kathleen
Chemical Manufacturers Ass'n **(191)**

Ambuehl, Ralph
Soc. for Software Quality **(494)**

Amde, Misrak
Ass'n of Applied Community Researchers **(143)**

Amenqual, Carolyn
American Soc. of Plastic and Reconstructive Surgeons **(114)**

Ament CAE, Ross
Incentive Manufacturers Representatives Ass'n **(259)**

Amerson, Amy
Internat'l Pension and Employee Benefits Lawyers Ass'n **(299)**

Ames Jr., John L.
Nat'l Ass'n of Tax Reducing Income Plans **(377)**

Ames, Steven
Community College Journalism Ass'n **(201)**

Ames, Terry
American Fisheries Soc. **(68)**

Amette, Pam
Motorcycle Industry Council **(330)**

Ammerman, Jay
American Bar Ass'n **(46)**

Amont, Deena
Golf Course Superintendents Ass'n of America **(248)**

Amorosino Jr., CAE, Charles S.
Teachers of English to Speakers of Other Languages **(520)**

Amos, Katherine
Ass'n of Theological Schools in the United States and Canada **(168)**

Ams, John G.
Interstate Natural Gas Ass'n of America **(311)**

Amselle, Anna
Telecommunications Industry Ass'n **(521)**

Amstutz, Daniel G.
North American Export Grain Ass'n **(442)**

Amundson, Jan S.
Nat'l Ass'n of Manufacturers **(362)**

Anagnostelis, Debbie
American Pediatric Soc. **(91)**
Soc. for Pediatric Research **(492)**

Anapolsky, Ellyce
Nat'l Conference of Commissioners on Uniform State Laws **(390)**

Anchors, Jerry K.
Nat'l Credit Union Management Ass'n **(398)**

Andelin, D.R.
Internat'l Foundation for Telemetering **(292)**

Andersen, Bob
Kamut Ass'n of North America **(315)**

Andersen, Crossan R.
Video Software Dealers Ass'n **(539)**

Andersen CAE, Gerald
Neckwear Ass'n of America **(438)**

Andersen, Kent
North American Limousin Foundation **(443)**

Anderson, A. Scott
Liaison Committee of Cooperating Oil and Gas Ass'ns **(319)**

Anderson, Alan
Screenprinting and Graphic Imaging Ass'n Internat'l **(480)**

Anderson, Bob
Nat'l Exchange Carrier Ass'n **(402)**

Anderson, Brenda
Internat'l Customer Service Ass'n **(288)**

Anderson, Christopher
Nat'l Conference of Catechetical Leadership **(390)**

Anderson, Curtis M.
Nat'l Ass'n of State Departments of Agriculture **(374)**

Anderson, Dale L.
Certified Claims Professional Accreditation Council **(190)**

Anderson Jr., Daniel S.
Nat'l Conference of Firemen and Oilers **(390)**

Anderson, Darrell D.
Nat'l Swine Registry **(433)**
American Landrace Ass'n **(80)**

Anderson, David B.
Internat'l Dairy Foods Ass'n **(288)**
Milk Industry Foundation **(328)**
Internat'l Ice Cream Ass'n **(294)**

Anderson, Debbe
American Polypay Sheep Ass'n **(93)**

Anderson, Ellie
Nat'l Ass'n of Minority Contractors **(363)**

Anderson, Frederick
American Rental Ass'n **(98)**

Anderson, Glen R.
Internat'l Hardware Distributors Ass'n **(293)**
Nat'l Coil Coaters Ass'n **(388)**
Pressure Sensitive Tape Council **(462)**

Anderson, Jeannette H.
American Peanut Council **(90)**

Anderson, Jim
Internat'l Hockey League **(293)**

Anderson, Joan
Nat'l Policy Ass'n **(423)**

Anderson, Joanne B.
American Academy of Actuaries **(20)**

Anderson, John A.
Electricity Consumers Resource Council **(228)**

Anderson, Judy
Optical Video Disc Ass'n **(449)**

Anderson, Katy
Nat'l Ass'n of Reunion Managers **(370)**

Anderson, Kevin
Nat'l Petroleum Refiners Ass'n **(422)**

Anderson, Kristen
American Vocational Ass'n **(122)**

Anderson, Lisa
Semiconductor Equipment and Materials Internat'l **(481)**

Anderson, Loretta
American Leather Chemists Ass'n **(81)**

Anderson, Lyndon
Lignite Energy Council **(320)**

Anderson, M. Kent
Internat'l Institute of Ammonia Refrigeration **(294)**

Anderson, Malina
Nat'l Ass'n of WIC Directors **(380)**

Anderson, Mark
American Soc. for Surgery of the Hand **(105)**

Anderson, Dr. Michael J.
Internat'l Federation for Choral Music **(290)**

Anderson, Mike
Asphalt Institute **(128)**

Anderson, Paul M.
Keramos Fraternity **(315)**

Anderson, Sharon
Nat'l League of Cities **(414)**

Anderson, Stacey E.
Design-Build Institute of America **(222)**

Anderson, Steve
Forest History Soc. **(242)**

Anderson, Steven C.
American Frozen Food Institute **(69)**
Internat'l Frozen Food Ass'n **(292)**

Anderson, Van
Nat'l Recreation and Park Ass'n **(424)**

Anderson, Van F.
Soc. of Park and Recreation Educators **(505)**

Anderson Jr., M.D., W. Banks
American Ophthalmological Soc. **(88)**

Anderson, Wanda
Nat'l Denturist Ass'n **(399)**

Anderson, William
American Film Marketing Ass'n **(68)**

Anderson, William C.
American Academy of Environmental Engineers **(21)**

Anderson, William R.
CBA **(188)**

Andersson, Theresa W.
Machinery Dealers Nat'l Ass'n **(321)**

Andis, Tammy G.
Nat'l Juice Products Ass'n **(413)**

Andosca, Kimberly
American Ass'n for Medical Transcription **(31)**

Andrassy, Timothy
Steel Tube Institute of North America **(517)**

Andrejeski, Mark
American College of Rheumatology **(57)**

Andres, Sue
Nat'l Burglar and Fire Alarm Ass'n **(384)**

Andresen, Randi V.
American Ass'n of Oral and Maxillofacial Surgeons **(40)**

Andrew, Suzanne
American Water Works Ass'n **(122)**

Andrews, David A.
American Hockey League **(73)**

Andrews, Donna
Technology Student Ass'n **(521)**

Andrews, Elizabeth W.
American Academy of Environmental Engineers **(21)**

Andrews, Holly
American Schools of Oriental Research **(99)**

Andrews, James D.
Nat'l Ass'n for the Education of Young Children **(341)**

Andrews, John
American Natural Soda Ash Corporation **(86)**

Andrews, Juanita
Petroleum Equipment Suppliers Ass'n **(455)**

Andrews Jr., Lewis D.
Glass Packaging Institute **(247)**

Andrews, Nancy
American Soc. of Tax Professionals **(116)**

Andringa, Robert C.
Coalition for Christian Colleges and Universities **(195)**

Angelini, Mark
Structural Board Ass'n **(517)**

Angelo, Julie
American Ass'n of Community Theatre **(35)**

Angerman CAE, Melissa
Nat'l Coffee Ass'n of the U.S.A. **(387)**

Angle, Casey
Intercollegiate Tennis Ass'n **(271)**

Angle, Joanne G.
Ass'n for Research in Vision and Ophthalmology **(137)**

Angove, R. Lawrence
Ass'n of Directory Publishers **(149)**

Anhaiser, Leon A.
Sugar Industry Technologists **(518)**

Anisfeld, Michael
Ass'n of Pharmaceutical Publishers **(160)**

Ankrapp Jr., Lyle N.
American College of Health Care Administrators **(54)**

Annotti, Joseph
Nat'l Ass'n of Independent Insurers **(359)**

Anson M.S. Ed., Joan J.
Ass'n of Schools and Colleges of Optometry **(164)**

Anson, Wilbur
Nat'l Conference of Standards Laboratories **(391)**

Anstrom, S. Decker
Nat'l Cable Television Ass'n **(384)**

Antall, Scott
Academy of Pharmaceutical Research and Science **(9)**

Anthony, Bob M.
American Poultry U.S.A. **(93)**

Anthony, Edwin R
Edison Electric Institute **(226)**

Anthony, Virginia Q.
American Academy of Child and Adolescent Psychiatry **(20)**

Anthony Ph.D., Calvin J.
Nat'l Community Pharmacists Ass'n **(388)**

Antil, M.C.
Cable and Telecommunications Ass'n for Marketing **(185)**

Antoine, Valerie
U.S. Metric Ass'n **(528)**

Antolick, Steven G.
Internat'l Ass'n of Airport Duty Free Stores **(275)**

Antonelos, Christina
Reserve Officers Ass'n of the U.S. **(475)**

Anwari, Shakila
Nat'l Court Reporters Ass'n **(398)**

Apgar, Barbara
Ass'n for Worksite Health Promotion **(141)**

Api, Rose
Soap and Detergent Ass'n **(484)**

Aplend, Richard
Council of State Chambers of Commerce **(215)**

Apodaca, Armando
Internat'l Right of Way Ass'n **(301)**

Appel, Bob
American Soc. of Consultant Pharmacists **(108)**

Appel, Mark
American Arbitration Ass'n **(28)**

Appel, Marsha
American Ass'n of Advertising Agencies **(32)**

Appelhans, Patricia
Nat'l Ass'n of Bond Lawyers **(345)**

Appelman, Lloyd P.
Aerospace Electrical Soc. **(13)**

Apple Ph.D., Martin A.
Council of Scientific Soc. Presidents **(215)**

Applebaum, Dr. Rhona
Nat'l Food Processors Ass'n **(405)**

Appleberry, James B.
American Ass'n of State Colleges and Universities **(43)**

Applegate, David
American Geological Institute **(70)**

Appleman, Dr. Bernard R.
SSPC: the Soc. for Protective Coatings **(515)**

Appy, Meredith K.
Nat'l Fire Protection Ass'n **(404)**

Arancia DPM, Louis J.
American Ass'n of Hospital Podiatrists **(37)**

Aravanis, Sara
Nat'l Ass'n of State Units on Aging **(376)**

Arbury, Sheila Brown
Ass'n of Occupational and Environmental Clinics (158)

Arcarese, Joseph
Food and Drug Law Institute (241)

Arcari (RET.), Col. Paul
Retired Officers Ass'n, The (476)

Arce, Lourdes
Soc. of Hispanic Professional Engineers (502)

Arche, Rene M.
Soc. of Critical Care Medicine (500)

Archer, Dean
Credit Union Nat'l Ass'n (218)

Archer, Jim
Northwest Fruit Exporters (446)

Archer, Mae
Knitting Guild of America (316)

Archer, Marlene
Nat'l Conference of Black Lawyers (389)

Archey, William T.
American Electronics Ass'n (65)

Archibald, Pat
Nat'l Business Ass'n (384)

Archibald-MacRae, Nancy
American Medical Ass'n (83)

Arcuri, Jeffrey V.
Ass'n for Information and Image Management
    International (135)

Arden, Janet
Polyurethane Manufacturers Ass'n (460)

Ardis, Mike
Nat'l Ass'n of Professional Surplus Lines Offices (367)

Ardis, Sandra
Project Management Institute (468)

Arendt, Lucie
Internat'l Dairy-Deli-Bakery Ass'n (288)

Arendt, Maggie
Ass'n of Golf Merchandisers (152)

Areno CAE, Patricia M.
Building Owners and Managers Ass'n Internat'l (183)

Arger, Marsha
Associated Equipment Distributors (171)

Argow, Keith A.
Nat'l Woodland Owners Ass'n (437)

Argraves, Stephanie
Soc. for Light Treatment and Biological Rhythms (490)

Argue, Dr. Dawn
Nat'l Ass'n of Evangelicals (354)

Arlandson, John
American Ass'n of Pathologists' Assistants (40)

Armacost, Patty
American Soc. of Cinematographers (107)

Armbruster, Debbie
American College of Nurse-Midwives (56)

Armitage, Ann M.
Ass'n of Public-Safety Communications Officials-
    Internat'l (162)

Armitage, Katie
Associated Bodywork and Massage Professionals (170)

Armstrong, Beverly
American Bar Ass'n (46)

Armstrong, Bob
Internat'l Institute of Ammonia Refrigeration (294)

Armstrong, Ed
Synthetic Organic Chemical Manufacturers Ass'n (519)

Armstrong CAE, Elizabeth B.
Internat'l Ass'n of Emergency Managers (278)
Nat'l Ass'n of State Emergency Medical Services
    Directors (375)
American Paper Machinery Ass'n (90)

Armstrong, Jack
Communications Marketing Ass'n (200)

Armstrong, Jan M.
Alliance of State Car and Truck Renting and Leasing
    Ass'ns (18)
American Car Rental Ass'n (50)

Armstrong, Robert
Sporting Goods Manufacturers Ass'n (515)

Armstrong, Robert G.
American Academy of Estate Planning Attorneys (22)

Arndt, Judy
American Cash Flow Ass'n (50)

Arneson, Janet
American College of Physicians-American Soc. of Internal
    Medicine (57)

Arnett, John E.
Copper and Brass Fabricators Council (209)

Arnett, Julie
Nat'l Ass'n of College Auxiliary Services (348)

Arnold, Daniel T.
Ass'n of Small Research, Engineering and Technical Service
    Companies (165)

Arnold, Debbie
Women Chefs and Restaurateurs (545)

Arnold, Jeff
North American Transportation Management Institute (445)

Arnold, Jon C.
Edison Electric Institute (226)

Arnold, Mary
Credit Union Executives Soc. (218)

Arnold, Philip A.
Golf Course Builders Ass'n of America (248)

Arnold, Roberta E.
Radiological Soc. of North America (471)

Arnold, William D.
Trade Cable and Telecommunications Ass'n (524)

Arnott, Ann
Institute of Real Estate Management (269)

Aronson, Nancy H.
Treasury Management Ass'n (526)

Arpino, Michael
Ass'n of Publication Production Managers (162)

Arredondo, Julian M.
Golf Course Superintendents Ass'n of America (248)

Arrindell, Deborah McNeal
Home Care Aide Ass'n of America (255)

Artemaks, Angelo
American Soc. of Neuroradiology (113)

Arthur, E. Vaughn
Hazardous Materials Advisory Council (251)

Arthur, Wendy
Shoe Service Institute of America (483)

Artman, Scott
Information Systems Audit and Control Ass'n (264)

Arzt, Leonard
Nat'l Ass'n for Proton Therapy (340)

Asbridge, Tom
American Agriculture Movement (27)

Asdal, Robert K.
Hydraulic Institute (257)

Aselin, Don
Sportsplex Operators and Developers of Ass'n (515)

Ash, Cindy
American Phytopathological Soc. (92)

Ashcraft, Sheila R.
American Court and Commercial Newspapers (62)

Asher, Frederick M.
American Institute of Indian Studies (77)

Asher, Kinda
American Volleyball Coaches Ass'n (122)

Ashford, Ellie
Nat'l School Boards Ass'n (427)

Ashley, Camilla
Counselors of Real Estate (217)

Ashley, Sydney
Gas Appliance Manufacturers Ass'n (245)

Ashton, Germaine
American Medical Women's Ass'n (84)

Ashworth, Jack
Viola da Gamba Soc. of America (539)

Asplen, Laure
Internat'l Union of Electronic, Electrical, Salaried Machine,
    and Furniture Workers (309)

Aspray, William
Computing Research Ass'n (203)

Assenzo Ph.D., Joseph R.
Drug Information Ass'n (225)

Astilla, Lissa M.
American Tort Reform Ass'n (120)

Astner, Janet L.
American Sociological Ass'n (117)

Astrene, Tom
Associated Equipment Distributors (171)

Atchison, Terry
American Chianina Ass'n (51)

Atchley, Kathy
American Oil Chemists' Soc. (88)

Aten, Carol
Nat'l Parks and Conservation Ass'n (421)

Atkins, Maria
American Academy of Facial Plastic and Reconstructive
    Surgery (22)

Atkinson, Sandi
American Football Coaches Ass'n (69)

Atnip, Jerry
Nat'l Fraternal Order of Police (406)

Attaway, Fritz
Motion Picture Ass'n of America (330)

Atwater, Frank G.
Nat'l Ass'n of Retired Federal Employees (370)

Atwood, Tyler
American Morgan Horse Ass'n (85)

Auberger, Craig
American Ass'n of Certified Appraisers (34)

Auberle, Patricia
SEPM - Soc. for Sedimentary Geology (482)

Aubin, Bonnie M.
Nat'l Organization for Competency Assurance (419)

Aubin, Stephen
Air Force Ass'n (15)

Aubrey, Annie
Internat'l Ass'n of Assessing Officers (276)

Audin DVM, Janis H.
American Veterinary Medical Ass'n (121)

Auerbach, James A.
Nat'l Policy Ass'n (423)

Augello, William J.
Transportation Consumer Protection Council (525)

Auins, Elizabeth
Nat'l Genealogical Soc. (406)

Auld MPH, CHES, Elaine
Soc. for Public Health Education (493)

Aulerich, Sylvia
Council on Forest Engineering (216)

Aunio, Anne
Finnish American Chamber of Commerce (239)

Auqustosky, Frank
Nat'l League of Postmasters of the U.S. (414)

Austin, Dale L.
Federation of State Medical Boards of the U. S. (237)

Austin, Erik W.
Social Science History Ass'n (509)

Austin, Gary
American Blind Lawyers Ass'n (47)

Austin, Ida
Associated Cooperage Industries of America (171)

Austin, Jerry L.
Flight Engineers' Internat'l Ass'n (240)

Autery, C. Reuben
Gas Appliance Manufacturers Ass'n (245)

Autry, Germaine M.
Nat'l Council of State Housing Agencies (396)

Auvenire, Christine
American Ass'n of Motor Vehicle Administrators (39)

Averick, Darlene
Nat'l Ass'n of Women Judges (380)

Averill, David
American Soc. of Forensic Odontology (110)

Avery, Andrew
Power Washers of North America (461)

Avram, Gabriel A.
Specialty Tobacco Council (514)

Awtrey, Jim
Professional Golfers Ass'n of America (465)

Ax Jr., Charles J.
Internat'l Dwarf Fruit Tree Ass'n (289)

Axisa, Lisa
Nat'l Ass'n of State Boards of Accountancy (374)

Ayers, Laraine
Recreational Park Trailer Industry Ass'n (473)

Ayers, Marty
Hospice and Palliative Nurses Ass'n (256)

Ayers, Rebecca
Nat'l Ski Patrol System (428)
Professional Ski Instructors of America (467)

Ayers, Tim
Cellular Telecommunications Industry Ass'n (189)

Ayotte CAE, James R.
Manufactured Housing Institute (322)

Ayres, Debbie
Soc. for Service Professionals in Printing (493)
Document Management Industries Ass'n (224)

Babb, Beverly
Nat'l Speakers Ass'n (431)

Babbitt, J. Randolph
Air Line Pilots Ass'n, Internat'l (16)

Babco, Eleanor L.
Commission on Professionals in Science and Technology (200)

Baber, Patti Jo
American League of Lobbyists (81)

Babigian, George R.
American Education Finance Ass'n (65)

Babione, William P.
American Agricultural Law Ass'n (27)

Babnis, Mariann
Nat'l Cable Television Ass'n (384)

Babyak, Gregory R.
Municipal Finance Industry Ass'n (331)

Bacak Jr., Walter W.
American Translators Ass'n (120)

Baccante, Richard
American Institute of Physics (78)

Baccari, Carmella
Data Interchange Standards Ass'n (220)

Bach APR, Dianne
American Gastroenterological Ass'n (70)

Bach, Greg
Nat'l Alliance for Youth Sports (336)

Bachenheimer, Cara C.
Health Industry Distributors Ass'n (252)

Bachman, Lewis M.
Songwriters Guild of America (510)

Bachman, Maria
Soc. of Incentive and Travel Executives (502)

Bachman, Seth
Soc. of Government Economists (502)

Bachner, John P.
ASFE: Professional Firms Practicing in the Geosciences (128)

Bachrach, Eve
Nonprescription Drug Manufacturers Ass'n (440)

Back, William W.
Internat'l Facility Management Ass'n (290)

Backer, Lisa K.
Internat'l Ass'n of Milk, Food and Environmental Sanitarians (281)

Bader, Bill
Internat'l Hot Rod Ass'n (294)

Badertscher, Nancy
Ass'n for Women in Communications (140)

Badger JD, CAE, Carole Z.
Nat'l Ass'n of Personal Financial Advisors (365)

Badillo, Kelly C.
Automotive Recyclers Ass'n (175)

Bae, Eric
Ass'n of Specialists in Cleaning and Restoration Internat'l (165)

Baebler, Paul
Contract Services Ass'n of America (208)

Baebler, Sharon
Credit Professionals Internat'l (218)

Baer, Edward F.
Newspaper Systems Group (439)

Baer, Edward J.
Nat'l Ass'n of Postmasters of the U.S. (365)

Baer, Stephanie J.
Nat'l Ass'n of Mortgage Brokers (363)

Baer, Wendy J.
IHPA - The Internat'l Wood Products Ass'n (259)

Baerg, Judith A.
Internat'l Academy of Podiatric Medicine (272)
American College of Foot and Ankle Orthopedics and Medicine (54)

Bagin, Richard
Nat'l School Public Relations Ass'n (427)

Baglini CPCU, CLU, Dr. Norman A.
American Institute for CPCU - Insurance Institute of America (75)

Baglio, Donna
Special Interest Group on Programming Languages (513)

Bagshaw, Suzanne
Organization for the Promotion and Advancement of Small Telecommunications Companies (449)

Bahin, Charlotte M.
America's Community Bankers (20)

Bahr, Morton
Communications Workers of America (200)

Baiardi, Kathy
French-American Chamber of Commerce (244)

Baie, Lyle F.
American Ass'n of Petroleum Geologists (40)

Baier, Kathy
Juvenile Products Manufacturers Ass'n (315)

Baile CAE, Robert Larry
Nat'l Ass'n of Mutual Insurance Companies (363)

Bailey, Benjamin A.
Soc. of Marine Port Engineers (503)

Bailey, Deborah
American Osteopathic Colleges of Ophthalmology and Otolaryngology, Head and Neck Surgery (89)

Bailey, K. Stephen
Nat'l Management Ass'n (416)

Bailey, Mary H.
Construction Specifications Institute (207)

Bailey, Pamela G.
Healthcare Leadership Council (253)

Bailey, Wilson P.
Iota Tau Sigma (312)

Bailiff, Fay S.
Soc. of Tribologists and Lubrication Engineers (508)

Baily, Richard
American College of Obstetricians and Gynecologists (56)

Baime, David
American Ass'n of Community Colleges (35)

Bainbridge, Ross C.
Nat'l Ass'n of Life Underwriters (361)

Baines, Douglas J.
Tile, Marble, Terrazzo, Finishers, Shopworkers and Granite Cutters Internat'l Union (523)

Bair OTR, FAOTA, Jeanette
American Occupational Therapy Ass'n (88)

Baird, Beverly St. Clair
Specialty Vehicle Institute of America (514)

Baird, Jeremy
American College Personnel Ass'n (58)

Baird, Robert W.
Independent Electrical Contractors (260)

Baith, Dana
Nat'l Agri-Marketing Ass'n (335)
Agriculture Council of America (15)

Bajardi, Stephen E.
Nat'l Hemophilia Foundation (409)

Bakamjian, Ted
Soc. of Exploration Geophysicists (501)

Baker, Angela
Forest Industries Telecommunications (242)

Baker, Bill
Recreation Vehicle Industry Ass'n (472)

Baker, Charles W.
Sugar Ass'n (518)

Baker, David
Plastic Shipping Container Institute (459)

Baker, David E.
Nat'l Institute for Farm Safety (411)

Baker, David H.
Lighter Ass'n (319)

Baker, Edwin W.
American Soc. of Appraisers (106)

Baker, Karen B.
Nat'l Science Teachers Ass'n (427)

Baker, Kathee
Nat'l Ass'n of Chemical Distributors (347)

Baker, Lynne
Oil, Chemical and Atomic Workers Internat'l Union (448)

Baker, Margery
Nat'l Institute for Dispute Resolution (411)

Baker MPH, Ned E.
Nat'l Ass'n of Local Boards of Health (361)

Baker, P. Jean
American Arbitration Ass'n (28)

Baker, Pam
North American Wholesale Lumber Ass'n (446)

Baker, Peter M.
Laser Institute of America (317)

Baker, Steve
Nat'l Ass'n of Intercollegiate Athletics (360)

Baker, Victoria J.
Nat'l Ass'n of Real Estate Investment Trusts (369)

Baker, William
Motion Picture Ass'n (330)

Bakke CAE, Kristin L.
Nat'l Ass'n for Community Leadership (338)

Balakgie, Carla
Nat'l Ass'n of College and University Business Officers (348)

Balasa JD,CAE, Donald A.
American Ass'n of Medical Assistants (38)

Balazs, Cecelia
Nat'l Kitchen and Bath Ass'n (414)

Baldinger, Steve
Wholesale Variety Bakers Ass'n (544)

Baldini, Pier Raimondo
American Ass'n of Teachers of Italian (44)

Baldwin, Barbara
American Soc. of Consulting Planners (108)

Baldwin, Elizabeth A.
Optical Soc. of America (449)

Baldwin, James G.
Soc. of Nematologists (504)

Baldwin, Jess
Nat'l Water Resources Ass'n (435)

Baldwin, Michael
Soc. of American Florists (497)

Baldwin, Paige
Comparative and Internat'l Education Soc. (201)

Baldwin, Richard
American Business Women's Ass'n (50)

Baldwin, Robert L.
American Academy of Safety Education (26)

Balek, William C.
Internat'l Sanitary Supply Ass'n (302)

Bales, Robert C.
Nat'l Computer Security Ass'n (389)

Balestrero, Gregory
Construction Specifications Institute (207)

Balice, Carmela
Internat'l Ass'n of Defense Counsel (278)

Balija, James J.
American Ass'n of Diabetes Educators (36)

Balin M.D., Arthur K.
American Aging Ass'n (27)

Balint, Annette
INDA, Ass'n of the Nonwoven Fabrics Industry (259)

Balk, Dr. Melvin
American College of Laboratory Animal Medicine (55)

Balko, Gregg B.
PROMAX Internat'l (468)

Ball, Andrea
Composite Can and Tube Institute (201)

Ball, Susan
College Art Ass'n (197)

Ball III, William L.
Nat'l Soft Drink Ass'n (430)

Ballance CAE, John B.
Materials Research Soc. (325)

Ballantine, Sue
Soil and Water Conservation Soc. (510)

Ballard, B. Joseph
Council for Exceptional Children (211)

Ballard, H. Lee
Internat'l Ass'n of Auto Theft Investigators (276)

Ballard, Paula
Ass'n for Professionals in Infection Control and Epidemiology (136)

Ballenger Ph.D., Charles
Nat'l Ass'n for Year-Round Education (342)

Ballentine, Jane
American Zoo and Aquarium Ass'n (124)

Ballinger, M. Pamela
American Soc. of Transplant Physicians (116)

Ballinger, Peggy
Internat'l Institute of Synthetic Rubber Producers (295)

Ballok, Ron
Nat'l Art Materials Trade Ass'n (337)

Ballon, Layla
Oncology Nursing Soc. (448)

Ballou Ph.D., Stephen W.
Ass'n of Boards of Certification (145)

Balmer, Thomas M.
Internat'l Ice Cream Ass'n (294)
Nat'l Cheese Institute (386)

Balmer, Tom
Nat'l Milk Producers Federation (417)

Balzan, Courtney
Accredited Gemologists Ass'n (10)

Balzer, Howard
Professional Football Writers of America (465)

Ban, Stephen D.
Gas Research Institute (246)

Bancou, Marielle
Color Ass'n of the United States (198)

Bandy, Michael J.
Trade Show Exhibitors Ass'n (524)

Bandy, Vivian Dee
Trade Show Exhibitors Ass'n (524)

Banes, Joan
American Soc. of Hypertension (111)

Bangs, Glenn
United States Parachute Ass'n (534)

Bankes, Joel
Nat'l Child Support Enforcement Ass'n (386)

Banks, Elisabeth
Soc. for Environmental Graphic Design (487)

Banks CAE, O. Gordon
American Industrial Hygiene Ass'n (75)

Bannister, James R.
Ass'n for Financial Technology (133)

Bannister, Marlisa K.
WLUC-Women in Insurance and Financial Services (545)

Bannister, Rick
Internat'l Function Point Users Group (292)

Bannon, Terri L.
Internat'l Foundation of Employee Benefit Plans (292)

Banowsky, Britton
Collegiate Commissioners Ass'n (198)

Bantham, Russel A.
Pharmaceutical Research and Manufacturers of America (456)

Banzhaf CAE, William H.
Soc. of American Foresters (497)

Baptista, Samuel J.
Financial Services Council (239)

Barach, Dr. Jeffery
Nat'l Food Processors Ass'n (405)

Baran, Leo J.
Diecasting Development Council (222)

Baranick, Anne Marie
Nat'l Ass'n of Chemical Distributors (347)

Baratelli, Rev. David J.
Nat'l Catholic Conference of Airport Chaplains (385)

Barbato, Olga
Italian Actors Union (313)

Barbee, Jean
Nat'l Soc. of Architectural Engineers (429)

Barber, Larry D.
American Federation of Grain Millers Internat'l Union (67)

Barber, Mary
Ecological Soc. of America (225)

Barber, Sharon
AACSB - the Internat'l Ass'n for Management Education (7)

Barber, Terri
Internat'l Brangus Breeders Ass'n (284)

Barbour, Charlene
Nat'l Federation of Licensed Practical Nurses (403)

Barclay AAE, Charles M.
American Ass'n of Airport Executives (33)

Barefoot, David B.
Ass'n of American Railroads (143)

Barefoot, Theresa H.
American North Country Cheviot Sheep Ass'n (87)

Barela, Karen
American Home Brewers Ass'n (74)

Barentine, Richard
Internat'l Home Furnishings Marketing Ass'n (293)

Barford, Mark A.
Appalachian Hardwood Manufacturers (126)

Baris, David H.
American Ass'n of Bank Directors (33)

Barker, Ann
Undersea and Hyperbaric Medical Soc. (529)

Barker PhD., Charles E.
Soc. for Organic Petrology (492)

Barker, Emmett
Equipment Manufacturers Institute (232)

Barker, Dr. Robert H.
American Fiber Manufacturers Ass'n (68)

Barker, Russell E.
American Academy of Insurance Medicine (23)
Peanut and Tree Nut Processors Ass'n (454)

Barker, Tim
Nat'l Council of Teachers of English (396)

Barlerin, Michael
World Gold Council (550)

Barna, Elisabeth
Motor Freight Carriers Ass'n (330)

Barna, Elisabeth A.
American Trucking Ass'ns (121)

Barnes, Bill
Nat'l League of Cities (414)

Barnes, Geraldine L.
NCCLS (438)

Barnes, Jack S.
Nat'l Finance Adjusters (404)

Barnes, Jerry G.
General Merchandise Distributors Council (246)

Barnes, Karie
Nat'l Ass'n for Senior Living Industries (341)

Barnes, Kathy
Professional Ass'n of Health Care Office Managers (464)

Barnes, Kimberly
American Ass'n of Clinical Urologists (34)

Barnes, Lisa
Investigative Reporters and Editors (312)

Barnes, Margi
Paint and Decorating Retailers Ass'n (452)

Barnes, Robert F.
Soil Science Soc. of America (510)
American Soc. of Agronomy (106)
Crop Science Soc. of America (219)

Barnes, Sharon W.
Nat'l Ass'n for Uniformed Services and Soc. of Military
Widows (342)

Barnes, Sheila
Appraisal Institute (126)

Barnes, Terrian
Internat'l Franchise Ass'n (292)

Barnes, William
Soc. of American Florists (497)

Barnett, Carol
American Veterinary Dental Soc. (121)

Barnett, Lauren A.
Soc. for Healthcare Strategy and Market Development (488)

Barnett, Paula
Independent Petroleum Ass'n of America (261)

Barnett, Sarah
Sugar Ass'n (518)

Barnett-Franks, Elizabeth
Bicycle Product Suppliers Ass'n (178)
Nat'l Refrigeration Contractors Ass'n (424)

Barnette, Diane
Nat'l Council of Juvenile and Family Court Judges (395)

Barney, George B.
Portland Cement Ass'n (460)

Barney, Joe
Nat'l Ass'n of Home Builders of the U.S. (358)

Barney, Phyllis
North American Folk Music and Dance Alliance (442)

Barnhardt, Dennis L.
Medical Group Management Ass'n (326)
American College of Medical Practice Executives (55)

Barnhart, Jeffrey E.
Energy Efficient Lighting Ass'n (230)
Internat'l Card Manufacturers Ass'n (285)

Barnhisel, Richard T.
American Soc. for Surface Mining and Reclamation (105)

Barnhurst, Kevin
Air Line Pilots Ass'n, Internat'l (16)

Baron, Carolyn
Institute of Internat'l Container Lessors (267)

Barondess, Linda Hiddemen
American Geriatrics Soc. (71)

Barone, Bruce
Fulfillment Management Ass'n (244)

Barone, Carole
EDUCAUSE (227)

Baroody, Michael E.
Nat'l Ass'n of Manufacturers (362)

Barr, Frankie Jean
Nat'l Ski Patrol System (428)

Barr, Karen
Investment Counsel Ass'n of America (312)

Barrack, David W.
American Cutlery Manufacturers Ass'n (63)
American Soc. of Electroplated Plastics (109)
Nat'l Ass'n of Metal Finishers (363)
Nat'l Ass'n of Public Insurance Adjusters (368)
Surface Finishing Industry Council (519)

Barratt, Michael E.
Automotive Parts and Accessories Ass'n (175)

Barreto, Julio
Nat'l Ass'n of Housing and Redevelopment Officials (358)

Barrett Jr., David C.
Nat'l Grain and Feed Ass'n (407)

Barrett, Gina
Internat'l Ass'n of Convention and Visitor Bureaus (277)

Barrett, Jerome A.
Associated Professional Sleep Socs. (172)
American Sleep Disorders Ass'n (100)

Barrett, Pamela
Healthcare Information and Management Systems Soc. (253)

Barrett, Stan
Nat'l Contract Management Ass'n (392)

Barrett, William O.
Ass'n of Independent Colleges of Art and Design (153)

Barrientos, June
American Institute of Oral Biology (78)

Barron, Deborah
Internat'l Interior Design Ass'n (295)

Barron, Margaret R.
Council on Library-Media Technicians (217)

Barron, Tracy
Internat'l Ass'n of Fire Chiefs (279)

Barros, Mary
Nat'l Ass'n of Service Providers in Private Rehabilitation (372)

Barry, Dave
Nat'l Private Truck Council (423)

Barry, John J.
Internat'l Brotherhood of Electrical Workers (284)

Barry, Marshall
Internat'l BBSing and Electronic Communications
Conference (283)

Barry, Patricia
Internat'l Financial Services Ass'n (291)

Barson, Daniel C.
American Internat'l Automobile Dealers Ass'n (79)

Barsook, Beverly
Museum Store Ass'n (332)

Barstow, Scott
American Counseling Ass'n (62)

Bart, Dan
Telecommunications Industry Ass'n (521)

Bartelmay, Janet L.
Ass'n of American Railroads (143)

Barth, Judith
Snack Food Ass'n (484)

Barthel, Frank
Ass'n of Administrators of the Interstate Compact on the
Placement of Children (141)

Bartholomew, Jean M.
Ass'n of Medical School Pediatric Department Chairmen (157)

Bartholomew, Joy A.
Estuarine Research Federation (233)

Bartholomew, Lori A.
Physician Insurers Ass'n of America (458)

Bartkovich, Diane
American Academy of Optometry (24)

Bartlett, John
Clear Channel Broadcasting Service (194)

Bartlett, Terri
Toy Manufacturers of America (524)

Bartling CHE, Ann
American College of Healthcare Executives (54)

Bartlow CAE, Gene S.
Painting and Decorating Contractors of America (452)

Barton, John M.
Contract Services Ass'n of America (208)

Baruth, Chris
North American Cartographic Information Soc. (441)

Baruth, Ed
American Water Works Ass'n (122)

Baruth, Monia Joda
American Water Works Ass'n (122)

Basa, Eniko Molnar
American Hungarian Educators Ass'n (74)

Basarich FLMI,ACS,A, Dr. Joel V.
LOMA (321)

Baseman, LeRoy T.
Soc. of Cost Estimating and Analysis (500)

Basham, M. Lauren
Soc. of Consumer Affairs Professionals in Business (500)

Basile, Jo-Anne R.
Cellular Telecommunications Industry Ass'n (189)

Basinger, Nancy
Ass'n for Management Information in Financial Services (136)

Basista CAE, Paul
Graphic Artists Guild Nat'l (249)

Basore, Thomas B.
Web Offset Ass'n of Printing Industries of America (542)
Non-Heatset Web Section (439)
Magazine Printers Section/Printing Industries of America (321)

Bass, Beth
Women's Basketball Coaches Ass'n (547)

Bass, Deborah
Community Ass'ns Institute (200)

Bass Ph.D., George F.
Institute of Nautical Archaeology (268)

Bass, Janet
Federation of Nurses and Health Professionals (237)

Bass, Joan
Regulatory Affairs Professionals Soc. (474)

Bassan, Ronny
American-Israel Chamber of Commerce and Industry (124)

Bassett, Bob
University Film and Video Ass'n (537)

Bassett, Steve
United States Air Tour Ass'n (532)

Bassi, Laurie J.
American Soc. for Training and Development (106)

Bassler, Mary B.
American Ass'n of Colleges of Pharmacy (35)

Bast, James L.
Council of Better Business Bureaus (212)

Bastarache, Gerald M.
Intelligent Transportation Soc. of America (270)

Basu, Ab
American Crop Protection Ass'n (62)

Basye, Katrina
Nat'l Ass'n of Railroad Property Tax Representatives (368)

Bateman, Paul W.
Gold Institute (248)
Silver Institute (483)

Bates, Alton
Nat'l Ass'n for Black Geologists and Geophysicists (338)

Bates, Bill
United States Telephone Ass'n (535)

Bates, Christopher
Motor and Equipment Manufacturers Ass'n (330)

Bates, Christopher M.
Automotive Presidents Council (175)

Bates, Gardner B.
Chlorine Institute (193)

Bates, Jeanna
Nat'l Ass'n of Hosiery Manufacturers (358)

Bates, Patty
Hydroponic Soc. of America (257)

Bathini, Leon
Soc. for American Archaeology (485)

Battaglia CAE, Richard D.
Internat'l Soc. for Performance Improvement (304)

Battle, A. Renee
Nat'l Head Start Ass'n (408)

Battles, Thomas B.
Precast/Prestressed Concrete Institute (462)

Batts, Lana R.
Truckload Carriers Ass'n (527)

Baty Ph.D., Peggy
Women in Aviation Internat'l (546)

Baudrau, Donna
American Physical Soc. (92)

Bauer, Anne Watson
Ass'n for Childhood Education Internat'l (131)

Bauer, Kate
Nat'l Ass'n of Childbearing Centers (347)

Bauer, Robert
Nat'l Honey Packers and Dealers Ass'n (409)
Nat'l Ass'n of Fruits, Flavors and Syrups (356)

Bauer, Robert W.
Soc. of Insurance Financial Management (503)

Bauerle, Robert J.
American Bureau of Shipping and Affiliated Companies (49)

Baugh, Jerry R.
Consumer Bankers Ass'n (207)

Baum, Mark
Ass'n of Sales and Marketing Companies (164)

Bauman, Christopher
American Soc. for Quality (105)

Baumann Ph.D., Duane
Universities Council on Water Resources (536)

Baumann, Greg
Nat'l Pest Control Ass'n (422)

Baumann, Henry L.
Nat'l Ass'n of Broadcasters (345)

Baumann, Lin
Internat'l Dyslexia Ass'n (289)

Baumruck, Scott A.
Paper Industry Management Ass'n (453)

Baumstark CAE, Laura M.
American Optometric Ass'n (88)

Baunton, R.L.
Internat'l Guild of Symphony, Opera and Ballet Musicians (293)

Bavaria, Susan
Internat'l Arabian Horse Ass'n (273)

Baxley, Sylvia
American Electroplaters and Surface Finishers Soc. (65)

Baxter, Craig
American Institute of Bangladesh Studies (76)

Baxter, James R.
Finishing Contractors Ass'n (239)

Baxter, Noreen
American Kennel Club (80)

Baxter, Shari
American Collectors Ass'n (52)

Bay CAE, Beth
Illuminating Engineering Soc. of North America (259)

Bayes, Ali
Internat'l Special Events Soc. (307)

Bayley, Susan
Nat'l Council of Teachers of Mathematics (396)

Bayne, Neil F.
Nat'l Academy of Television Journalists (334)

Beach, Jessica
Nat'l Ass'n of WIC Directors (380)

Beach, Mary
American Ass'n of Diabetes Educators (36)

Beakley, Josh
American Concrete Pipe Ass'n (59)

Beal, Danice
Ass'n of Professors of Gynecology and Obstetrics (161)

Beal, Jennifer
Nat'l Federation of Licensed Practical Nurses (403)

Beales, Char
Cable and Telecommunications Ass'n for Marketing (185)

Beales, Dana Lee
Cable and Telecommunications Ass'n for Marketing (185)

Beall Ph.D., Bret S.
Academy of Osseointegration (9)

Beall Ph.D., Robert
Cystic Fibrosis Foundation (219)

Beals, Alma
Nat'l Ass'n of Schools of Public Affairs and Administration (371)

Beals, Robert J.
Sigma Phi Delta (483)

Beam, Allen
Ass'n of Occupational Health Professionals (in Healthcare) (158)
Nat'l Organization for Associate Degree Nursing (419)

Beam, H. Allen
Ass'n of Nurses in AIDS Care (158)

Beam SPHR, CAE, Kenneth
American Ass'n of Motor Vehicle Administrators (39)

Beaman Jr., Charles
Palmetto Baptist Medical Center (453)

Beamer, Deborah A.
Nat'l Ass'n of Local Government Auditors (362)
Soc. of Government Meeting Professionals (502)

Beamer, Suzanne C.
Internat'l Sign Ass'n (302)

Bean, Mark
American Match Council (83)

Beang, Nancy
Soc. for Neuroscience (491)

Beard, Bob R.
Aggregate and Concrete Executives (14)

Beard, Jeffrey L.
Design-Build Institute of America (222)

Bearden, Georgia Anne
Internat'l Ass'n of Optometric Executives (281)

Bearn Ph.D., Alexander G.
American Philosophical Soc. (91)

Bears, Lisa
American Soc. of Law, Medicine and Ethics (112)

Bearse, Michael S.
Laborers' Internat'l Union of North America (316)

Beasley, Barbara
Nat'l Ass'n of Secondary School Principals (372)

Beasley, Edward
Ass'n for the Study of Afro-American Life and History (139)

Beasley CAE, Rita
Produce Marketing Ass'n (463)

Beaton, Agnes
Nat'l Ass'n of Women Highway Safety Leaders (380)

Beattie, Patricia M.
Nat'l Industries for the Blind (411)

Beattie, Steve
Associated Owners and Developers (171)

Beatty, Antonio T.
Commission on Accreditation for Law Enforcement Agencies (199)

Beatty, Barbara Fitzgerald
American Soc. of Ophthalmic Plastic and Reconstructive Surgery (113)

Beaty, Lisa
Institute of Navigation (268)

Beaty, Samantha
Internat'l Federation of Pharmaceutical Wholesalers (290)

Beauchamp, Darrell
Internat'l Visual Literacy Ass'n (310)

Beauchamp, L.G.
Internat'l Brotherhood of Boilermakers, Iron Ship Builders, Blacksmiths, Forgers and Helpers (284)

Beauchamp, Virginia K.
Nat'l Ass'n for the Self-Employed (341)

Beaudin, Lili
Women of the Motion Picture Industry, Internat'l (547)

Beaumont Jr., Guy D.
American College of Osteopathic Surgeons (56)

Beaumont CAE, Nancy Perkin
American Physical Therapy Ass'n (92)

Beazer, Vincent
Neighborhood Cleaners Ass'n-Internat'l (438)

Bechever, John
United Soybean Board (531)

Bechtel, Lee
American Soc. of Extra-Corporeal Technology (109)

Bechtel, Mary
Evangelical Church Library Ass'n (233)

Bechtold, Timothy J.
Wholesale Beer Ass'n Executives of America (543)

Beck, Allison
Internat'l Ass'n of Machinists and Aerospace Workers (280)

Beck, David
Internat'l Memorialization Supply Ass'n (297)

Beck, Deborah
Nurses Organization of Veterans Affairs (447)

Beck Ph.D., Edward
Nat'l Registry of Environmental Professionals (424)

Beck, J.Ann
American Medical Directors Ass'n (83)

Beck, Peter
American Ass'n of Law Libraries (38)

Beck, Randy
Internat'l Music Products Ass'n (298)

Becker, Bruce R.
Technology Transfer Soc. (521)

Becker, Christine
Nat'l League of Cities (414)

Becker, Darby
General Aviation Manufacturers Ass'n (246)

Becker, George
United Steelworkers of America (536)

Becker, Jeffrey G.
Beer Institute (177)

Becker, Julie
Nat'l Cosmetology Ass'n (392)

Becker, Katherine
Ass'n of Astronomy Educators (144)

Becker, Leslie
Guild of Natural Science Illustrators (250)

Becker, Mary Beth
Mystery Writers of America (333)

Becker, S. William
State and Territorial Air Pollution Program Administrators (515)
Ass'n of Local Air Pollution Control Officials (156)

Becker, Scott
Ass'n of Public Health Laboratories (162)

Becker-Doyle CAE, Eve
Nat'l Athletic Trainers' Ass'n (381)

Beckering, Dorothea
Nat'l Ass'n of Affordable Housing Lenders (342)

Beckerman, Joyce
Nat'l Honey Packers and Dealers Ass'n (409)

Becket, Jennifer
Agriculture Council of America (15)

Beckham, Tamera
Nat'l Ass'n of Extension 4-H Agents (354)

Beckman, Jennifer
Internat'l Soc. for Ecological Economics (303)

Beckman, Moreen
Security Industry Ass'n (481)

Beckner, William M.
Nat'l Council on Radiation Protection and Measurements (398)

Bedea, Richard T.
Sociological Practice Ass'n (509)

Bedell, Anthony
Independent Electrical Contractors (260)

Bedford, Frank
American Osteopathic Ass'n (89)

Beditz, Dr. Joseph
Nat'l Golf Foundation (407)

Bedlin, Howard
Nat'l Council on the Aging (398)

Bednarczyk, Betty
Service Employees Internat'l Union (482)

Bednarz, Marlene
American Ass'n for Public Opinion Research (31)

Bednash, Geraldine
American Ass'n of Colleges of Nursing (34)

Bedoya, Roberto
Nat'l Ass'n of Artists' Organizations (343)

Beeaf, Jeannie
American Psychological Ass'n - Division of Psychologists in Independent Practice (95)

Beecher, Crystal
American Academy of Pediatric Dentistry (25)

Beede, Mark A.
United States Tennis Ass'n (535)

Beedle, Ralph
Nuclear Energy Institute (446)

Beekwith, Betsy
American Ass'n for Geriatric Psychiatry (30)

Beene, Keith
Baptist Communicators Ass'n (176)

Beeton, Carrie
Nat'l Ass'n of Dental Laboratories (352)

Behl, Kathy
Nat'l Ass'n of Secondary School Principals (372)

Behme, D.F.
Nat'l Ass'n of Freight Transportation Consultants (356)

Behncke CMP, Laurie L.
American Ass'n of Neurological Surgeons (39)

Behnke, Carl D.
Edison Electric Institute (226)

Behnken, William
Soc. of American Graphic Artists (497)

Behrends, Dirk L.
Financial Managers Soc. (239)

Behrman, Rosemary
Internat'l Leather Goods, Plastics, Novelty, and Service Workers' Union (296)

Beidel, Dr. Deborah
American Psychopathological Ass'n (95)

Beilfuss, Rudolf
Polaris Internat'l (459)

Belden Ph.D., David L.
American Soc. of Mechanical Engineers (112)

Beless, Donald W.
Council on Social Work Education (217)

Beletz, Jamie
Internat'l Ass'n of Industrial Accident Boards and Commissions (280)

Belew, Joe
Consumer Bankers Ass'n (207)

Belfield, Doris A.
Nat'l Ass'n of Elementary School Principals (353)

Boillot CAE, James B.
Nat'l Agricultural Aviation Ass'n **(335)**

Bokat, Stephen A.
Chamber of Commerce of the United States of America **(190)**

Bolan, Jennifer
Ass'n of University Radiologists **(168)**

Boland, Mary C.
American Copper Council **(60)**
League of Advertising Agencies **(318)**

Bolen, Edward M.
General Aviation Manufacturers Ass'n **(246)**

Boley, Anne
Roller Skating Ass'n Internat'l **(477)**

Bolger, Christine
Nat'l Council of Athletic Training **(394)**

Bolger, David
United States Telephone Ass'n **(535)**

Boling, Jeanne H.
Case Management Soc. of America **(187)**

Bollettino, Christine
Women in Cable and Telecommunications **(546)**

Bolline, Tammy
Nat'l Auctioneers Ass'n **(381)**

Bollman, Judith
Property Loss Research Bureau **(468)**

Bollt, Anita S.
Soc. for the Advancement of Women's Health Research **(495)**

Bolman CAE, Thomas E.
Internat'l Ass'n of Conference Centers **(277)**

Bolton, Catherine
Internat'l Copper Ass'n **(287)**

Bolton, Eric
Oxygenated Fuels Ass'n **(452)**

Bolusky, Benjamin C.
American Nursery and Landscape Ass'n **(87)**

Bolzle, Nancy
Internat'l Brangus Breeders Ass'n **(284)**

Bomar, Susan
American Maine-Anjou Ass'n **(82)**

Bomberger, Dorothy
Optical Soc. of America **(449)**

Bomberger, Irvin
Soc. of Gynecologic Oncologists **(502)**
American Orthopaedic Soc. for Sports Medicine **(88)**

Bonacasa, Dino
Greater Clothing Contractors Ass'n **(249)**

Bonaparte, Sueli
Brazilian American Chamber of Commerce **(182)**

Bonbright, Jane
Nat'l Dance Ass'n **(399)**

Bonds, Roger G.
American College of Medical Staff Development **(55)**

Bone, David L.
Fellowship of United Methodists in Music and Worship Arts **(238)**

Boney, Maurice W.
Beef Friesian Soc. **(177)**

Bonfiglio, Lynn
American College of Rheumatology **(57)**

Bonham, Norma
Soc. of Municipal Arborists **(504)**

Bonhaus, Don
World Federation of Travel Writers **(549)**

Bonkowksi, John
Nat'l Ass'n of County Recorders, Election Officials and Clerks **(351)**

Bonn, Cecilia
Nat'l Academy Museum and School Fine Arts **(333)**

Bonner, T.J.
Nat'l Border Patrol Council **(384)**

Bonnot, John Mark
Promotional Products Ass'n Internat'l **(468)**

Bonoff, Steven
Internat'l Prepress Ass'n **(300)**

Bonosaro, Carol A.
Senior Executives Ass'n **(482)**

Booberg, Carl
American Thoracic Soc. **(120)**

Book, Lois
American Ass'n of Diabetes Educators **(36)**

Booker, Carl E.
Laborers' Internat'l Union of North America **(316)**

Boom Ph.D., Brian M.
Soc. for Economic Botany **(487)**

Boone, Daniel
Nat'l Wood Flooring Ass'n **(436)**

Boone, Tamea A.
Nat'l Ass'n for Uniformed Services and Soc. of Military Widows **(342)**

Boone, Xenia "Sonny"
Nat'l Newspaper Ass'n **(418)**

Boot, Neil
Nat'l Safety Council **(426)**

Bopp, Andrew
Soc. of Glass and Ceramic Decorators **(502)**

Borawski CAE, Paul
American Soc. for Quality **(105)**

Borchardt, Robert O.
American Ass'n of Health Plans **(37)**

Borchelt, Gregg
Brick Industry Ass'n **(182)**

Borchers, James A.
Concrete Anchor Manufacturers Ass'n **(203)**
Powder Actuated Tool Manufacturers Institute **(461)**

Borck, Noel C.
Nat'l Erectors Ass'n **(402)**

Borden, Enid A.
Meals On Wheels Ass'n of America **(325)**

Borden, Michael R.
Cable Tray Institute **(185)**

Borders, Brian T.
Ass'n of Publicly Traded Companies **(162)**
American Bearing Manufacturing Ass'n **(47)**

Bordui, Ronald J.
Paper Industry Management Ass'n **(453)**

Borelli, Kathy
Nat'l Ass'n of Veterans Program Administrators **(379)**

Borer, David
Ass'n of Flight Attendants **(151)**

Borger, Robert A.
Nat'l Wholesale Druggists' Ass'n **(436)**

Borich, Alexis
American College of Veterinary Dermatology **(58)**

Borkoski, I. Regina
Outdoor Power Equipment Aftermarket Ass'n **(451)**

Borkoski, Isabel Regina
Nurses Organization of Veterans Affairs **(447)**

Borland DO, RPT, Joe S.
American Sports Medicine Ass'n/Board of Certification **(118)**

Borland DO,RPT, Joe S.
World Sports Medicine Ass'n of Registered Therapists **(550)**

Born, Jamie
American Marketing Ass'n **(82)**

Bornstein Ph.D., Robert
Internat'l Neuropsychological Soc. **(298)**

Borowicz, Sharon
American Academy of Pediatrics **(25)**

Borowski CAE, Patricia A.
Nat'l Ass'n of Professional Insurance Agents **(367)**

Borowsky, Scott C.
Souvenirs and Novelties Trade Ass'n **(510)**

Borozan, Erika
United States-Austrian Chamber of Commerce **(536)**

Borrero CMT, Jennyfer M.
Pharmaceutical Care Management Ass'n **(456)**

Borron III, Paul G.
American Sugar Cane League of the U.S.A. **(119)**

Borschow CAE, Barbara S.
American School Food Service Ass'n **(99)**

Borut, Donald J.
Nat'l League of Cities **(414)**

Bory, Larry
Nat'l Soc. of Professional Engineers **(430)**

Borys, Stanley S.
Institute of Gas Technology **(267)**

Bosak, Kathy
Nat'l Ass'n of Counties **(350)**

Bosak, Roberta J.
American Academy of Pediatrics **(25)**

Bosco, Mary Beth
Used Oil Management Ass'n **(538)**

Bose, James
Internat'l Ground Source Heat Pump Ass'n **(292)**

Bose, Karen M.
Nat'l Ass'n of Urban Bankers **(379)**

Bosley, John
Nat'l Ass'n of Regional Councils **(369)**

Bosnak, Janine
Hydronics Institute Division of GAMA **(257)**

Bossert, Wayne
Groundwater Management Districts Ass'n **(250)**

Bossey, Robert D.
Internat'l Ass'n of Law Enforcement Firearms Instructors **(280)**

Bossman, David A.
American Feed Industry Ass'n **(67)**

Bostian, Larry
Nat'l Consumers League **(392)**

Bostley SSJ, Jean R.
Catholic Library Ass'n **(188)**

Bothwell, Stephanie
Ass'ns for Community Design **(170)**

Botkin, Linda
Asphalt Institute **(128)**

Boucher, Jennifer
Associated Builders and Contractors **(170)**

Bouchoux, Ann G.
Internat'l Food Information Council **(291)**

Boudjenah, Darla
Casting Industry Suppliers Ass'n **(187)**

Bouhan, Richard M.
Nat'l Ass'n of Professional Surplus Lines Offices **(367)**

Boulton, Lyndie McHenry
American Soc. for Enology and Viticulture **(102)**

Bourassa, Donna M.
American College Personnel Ass'n **(58)**

Bourdon, Cathleen
Ass'n of Specialized and Cooperative Library Agencies **(165)**

Bourdrez, Michiel M.
Nat'l Council of Architectural Registration Boards **(394)**

Bourgeois, Moira Coleman
Ass'n for Investment Management and Research **(135)**

Bourgholtzer, Tony
Foundation for Advances in Medicine and Science **(243)**

Bourseau, Sandy
American Soc. of Home Inspectors **(111)**

Bousquet, Carol
American Loudspeaker Manufacturers Ass'n **(82)**

Boutchyard, Jean W.
Universities Research Ass'n **(536)**

Boutwell, Annette S.
Waterproofing Contractors Ass'n **(541)**

Bowden, Henry W.
American Soc. of Church History **(107)**

Bowe, James J.
New York Board of Trade **(438)**
Board of Trade of the City of New York **(180)**

Bowen CMP, Constance K.
Society of Financial Service Professionals **(509)**

Bowen CHE, CAE, Deborah J.
American College of Healthcare Executives **(54)**

Bowen, Patsy
AGN Internat'l - North America **(14)**

Bower, Ernest Z.
U.S.-ASEAN Business Council **(528)**

Bower, Marya
Soc. for Phenomenology and Existential Philosophy **(492)**

Bower, Sharon
Internat'l Council for Small Business **(287)**

Bowers, Diane K.
Council for Marketing and Opinion Research **(211)**
Council of American Survey Research Organizations **(212)**

Bowers D.D.S., Gerald
American Board of Periodontology **(48)**

Bowers Ph.D., Jan
Family and Consumer Science Education Ass'n **(234)**

Bowers, John
Internat'l Longshoremen's Ass'n **(296)**

Bowers, Leonard
Soc. of American Florists **(497)**

Bowers, Michael
American Ass'n for Marriage and Family Therapy **(31)**

Bowlden, Taylor R.
American Highway Users Alliance **(73)**

Bowlen, William
American Collegiate Retailing Ass'n **(58)**

Bowles, Ruth
American Cheviot Sheep Soc. **(51)**

Bowles, Sandra
Handweavers Guild of America **(251)**

Bowling, Daniel
Soc. of Professionals in Dispute Resolution **(506)**

Bowling, Patricia N.
Nat'l Home Furnishings Ass'n **(409)**

Bowling, Richard P.
Truck Trailer Manufacturers Ass'n **(527)**

Bowman, Alison
Council of Insurance Agents and Brokers **(214)**

Bowman, Gloria
Counselors of Real Estate **(217)**

Bowman, Dr. Harry L.
Council on Occupational Education **(217)**

Bowman CAE, Jerry
Environmental and Engineering Geophysical Soc. **(231)**
North American Nature Photography Ass'n **(443)**

Bowman, Kellie
Ass'n of College and University Telecommunications Administrators **(147)**

Bowman, Kenneth R.
Mass Marketing Insurance Institute **(324)**
Electronic Transactions Ass'n **(228)**
Sealant, Waterproofing and Restoration Institute **(480)**

Bowman, Marjorie
Nat'l Ass'n of Personnel Services **(365)**

Bowman, Mary Jo
Diamond Council of America (222)
American Ass'n of Managing General Agents (38)
Bowman, P.
Brass and Bronze Ingot Manufacturers (181)
Bowman, Stan
American Soc. of Landscape Architects (111)
Bowman CFA, Thomas A.
Ass'n for Investment Management and Research (135)
Bowman Ph.D., Valcar
Nat'l Registry of Environmental Professionals (424)
Bowser, Judy
American Soc. of Preventive Oncology (115)
Bowser, Kathy
Professional Handlers Ass'n (466)
Boxall, James
Opticians Ass'n of America (449)
Boyce CAE, Ken
Spring Manufacturers Institute (515)
Boyd & I, Dennis W.
Federal Physicians Ass'n (236)
Boyd, Dennis W.
Nat'l Ass'n of Assistant United States Attorneys (343)
Boyd, Fran
Academy of Country Music (8)
Boyd, Franklin
Ass'n of Science-Technology Centers (164)
Boyd, Linda
American Zoo and Aquarium Ass'n (124)
Boyd, Nancy
Supima Ass'n of America (518)
Boyd Ph.D., Robert E.
Nat'l Ass'n of Pupil Services Administrators (368)
Boyd, Sheila
Nat'l Head Start Ass'n (408)
Boyer, Johanna
Nat'l Assembly of State Arts Agencies (381)
Boyer CAE, Kaye Kittle
Costume Soc. of America (210)
Boyer, Phil
Aircraft Owners and Pilots Ass'n (16)
Boyett, Jill
American Academy of Ophthalmology (24)
Boyko, Wally
Fitness Trade Ass'n (240)
Boylan, Jennifer K.
Ass'n of Program Directors in Radiology (162)
Soc. for Pediatric Radiology (492)
Boyle D.V.M., Dale D.
Nat'l Ass'n of Federal Veterinarians (355)
Boyle, Diane
Ass'n of Health Insurance Agents (153)
Boyle, J. Patrick
American Meat Institute (83)
Nat'l Meat Canners Ass'n (416)
Boyle, Joseph M.
Nat'l Ass'n of Federal Credit Unions (355)
Boyle, Terrence
Delta Phi Epsilon (221)
Boyler, Gary E.
Meeting Professionals Internat'l (327)
Boyles, Cindy
Internat'l Ass'n of Correctional Training Personnel (278)
Boyne, Gil
American Council of Hypnotist Examiners (61)
Boynton, Rex P.
North American Technician Excellence (445)
Bozarth, Marvin F.
Internat'l Tire and Rubber Ass'n (309)
Brabec, Todd
American Soc. of Composers, Authors and Publishers (108)
Brabson, Dr. Howard V.
Nat'l Ass'n of Black Social Workers (345)
Bracci, Joseph
Reinforced Concrete Research Council (474)
Bracken, Anne
American Corporate Counsel Ass'n (60)
Brackett, Douglas L.
American Furniture Manufacturers Ass'n (69)
Brackett, Teresa
Ass'n for Experiential Education (133)
Bracknell, Deborah J.
American Cash Flow Ass'n (50)
Brada, Josef C.
Ass'n for Comparative Economic Studies (131)
Braddom Ed.D., Carolyn L.
Ass'n of Academic Physiatrists (141)
Braden, Joseph
Nurse Healers – Professional Associates Internat'l (447)
North American Nursing Diagnosis Ass'n (443)
Ass'n of Child and Adolescent Psychiatric Nurses (146)
North American Nursing Diagnosis Ass'n (443)

Bradfield, John
Composite Panel Ass'n (201)
Bradle, Timothy
Nat'l Ass'n of Recreation Resource Planners (369)
Bradley, Beverly
American Professional Soc. on the Abuse of Children (94)
Bradley CSP, Janice Comer
ISEA-The Safety Equipment Ass'n (313)
Bradley, Jeanette
American Mold Builders Ass'n (85)
Bradley, Pam
Nat'l Ass'n of Public Hospitals and Health Systems (368)
Bradley, William
American Gear Manufacturers Ass'n (70)
Bradshaw, Beverly
General Federation of Women's Clubs (246)
Bradshaw, Christin
American Frozen Food Institute (69)
Bradshaw, Dennis
Sheet Metal and Air Conditioning Contractors' Nat'l Ass'n (482)
Bradshaw, Mary
MultiMedia Telecommunications Ass'n (331)
Bradstreet, Ken
Ass'n of Alternate Postal Systems (142)
Brady, David
Internat'l Facility Management Ass'n (290)
Brady, Dorothy
Internat'l Ass'n of Food Industry Suppliers (279)
Brady, Hailey
American Soc. for Eighteenth-Century Studies (102)
Brady, Maureen
Real Estate Information Providers Ass'n (472)
United States Marine Safety Ass'n (534)
Nat'l Ass'n of Container Distributors (349)
Brady, Phillip D.
American Automobile Manufacturers Ass'n (46)
Braen, Beth
Nat'l Ass'n of Television Program Executives (378)
Bragg, John H.
Nursery Ass'n Executives of North America (447)
Bragg, Marnelle
American Foundrymen's Soc. (69)
Bragg, Raymond F.
American Independent Refiners Ass'n (75)
Brahms, Thomas W.
Institute of Transportation Engineers (269)
Brahos, Sandra
American Ass'n of Hip and Knee Surgeons (37)
Bram, Jim
Nat'l Ass'n of Underwater Instructors (379)
Braman, Ed
Nat'l Conference on Public Employee Retirement Systems (391)
Bramante, Sylvia
Healthcare Leadership Council (253)
Bramlage MPH, MBA, Rusty
Chemical Industry Institute of Toxicology (191)
Branch, Deborah
Soc. of Critical Care Medicine (500)
Branch, Maurice
American Logistics Ass'n (82)
Branch, Steve
Soc. for Computer Simulation (486)
Brand, David
Institute of Certified Financial Planners (266)
Brand, Osa
Ass'n of American Geographers (142)
Brandanger, Dennis
Nat'l Ass'n of Independent Insurance Auditors and Engineers (359)
Brandel, Norma "Dusty"
American Auto Racing Writers and Broadcasters Ass'n (46)
Brandenberger, Joel
Nat'l Turkey Federation (435)
Brandenburg, Richard T.
Air Transport Ass'n of America (16)
Brandl, Philip J.
Nat'l Housewares Manufacturers Ass'n (409)
Brandon CPCU, AIM, Lawrence G.
American Institute for CPCU - Insurance Institute of America (75)
Brandon, Sharon
Tennessee Walking Horse Breeders and Exhibitors Ass'n (521)
Brandon, Tom
Nat'l Patio Enclosure Ass'n (421)
Brandt, Deborah K.
Nat'l Academy of Engineering of the United States of America (334)
Brandt, Susan
Hobby Industry Ass'n of America (255)

Brannen, Claire
American Consulting Engineers Council (60)
Brannery, Kevi
Nat'l Lawyers Guild (414)
Brannon, Sheryl
Council for Advancement and Support of Education (210)
Branslans, Jennifer
Internat'l Sign Ass'n (302)
Branson, Craig
American Soc. of Newspaper Editors (113)
Brant CAE, Jonathan J.
Nat'l Interfraternity Conference (413)
Branton, Fiona
Information Technology Industry Council (264)
Braslow, Susan A.
American Cotton Shippers Ass'n (60)
Brasse, Sally
American Hotel and Motel Ass'n (74)
Braswell, A.J.
Nat'l Ass'n of Church and Institutional Financing Organizations (347)
Braswell, Glenn E.
Flexible Packaging Ass'n (240)
Braswell, Robert
Maintenance Council of American Trucking Ass'ns (322)
Bratz USA (Ret), Col. Gordon
Soc. of American Military Engineers (498)
Brauer Ph.D., Roger L.
Board of Certified Safety Professionals (180)
Braun, Bill
Air and Waste Management Ass'n (15)
Braun, Warner
Chlorine Chemistry Council (192)
Brauner, Arthur B.
Forest Products Soc. (243)
Bravo, Ellen
Nine to Five, Nat'l Ass'n of Working Women (439)
Bray, Charles W.
Internat'l Ass'n of Food Industry Suppliers (279)
Bray CAE, Janet B.
Nat'l Ass'n of Enrolled Agents (354)
Bray, Sarah Hardesty
Council for Advancement and Support of Education (210)
Brazell ACA, Torryn P.
Internet Soc. (311)
Brazier, Marilyn
Nat'l Ass'n of School Psychologists (371)
Brebner, Nancy
Insurance Consumer Affairs Exchange (270)
Breck, Richard M.
Internat'l Microelectronics and Packaging Soc. (297)
Breckenridge, Gwynn
American Ass'n for Dental Research (30)
Breden CAE, CMP, Cathy
Internat'l Ass'n for Exposition Management (274)
Breden, Roberta
Telecommunications Industry Ass'n (521)
Breeden, Christine
American Ass'n of State Social Work Boards (43)
Breeden, Frank
Gospel Music Ass'n (248)
Breeden, Wanda
Ass'n for Graphic Arts Training (134)
Breiter, Jerome
American Meat Institute (83)
Breiter Ph.D., Jerome J.
United States Hide, Skin and Leather Ass'n (534)
Western Hemisphere Ass'n of Meat Marketers (543)
Brenen, Edward
American Legend Cooperative (81)
Brenkus, Christine
American Economic Development Council (65)
Brennan, Barry
Mail Advertising Service Ass'n Internat'l (322)
Brennan, Joseph P.
Bituminous Coal Operators Ass'n (179)
Brennan, Kelly
United States Telephone Ass'n (535)
Brennan, Michael
Dermatology Nurses Ass'n (221)
Brennan, Paul D.
Nat'l Board of Boiler and Pressure Vessel Inspectors (383)
Brenner, Edward T.
American Ass'n of Museums (39)
Brenner, Kyd D.
Corn Refiners Ass'n (209)
Brenner AIA, William
Nat'l Institute of Building Sciences (411)
Brentzel, Joe
Solid Waste Ass'n of North America (510)

Bresch, Joann
American College of Radiology **(57)**

Bresnahan DPM, Philip J.
American College of Foot and Ankle Pediatrics **(54)**

Bresnahan, Tom
Computer Oriented Geological Soc. **(202)**

Bresnan, Chris
Nat'l Recreation and Park Ass'n **(424)**
Nat'l Soc. for Park Resources **(429)**

Bretthauer, Don
Golf Course Superintendents Ass'n of America **(248)**

Brevik, Len
Independent Insurance Agents of America **(261)**

Brewer, Bill
American Quarter Horse Ass'n **(96)**

Brewer, John B.
American Moving and Storage Ass'n **(85)**

Brewer, Justina
Internat'l Fresh-cut Produce Ass'n **(292)**

Brewer, Lynn M.
American Bus Ass'n **(49)**

Brewer, Nancy A.
Nat'l Catholic Educational Ass'n **(385)**

Brewer, William E.
Ass'n for Quality and Participation **(137)**

Brickley, Susan
Internat'l Dyslexia Ass'n **(289)**

Bridel, Robert W.
American Gem Soc. **(70)**

Bridge, Debbie
American College of Emergency Physicians **(54)**

Bridgeforth, Chrystl L.
Coalition of Labor Union Women **(196)**

Bridges, Roger D.
Soc. for Historians of the Gilded Age and Progressive Era **(489)**

Bridgman, Elizabeth
Ass'n for the Advancement of Medical Instrumentation **(138)**

Brier, M. William
Edison Electric Institute **(226)**

Briese CAE, Garry L.
Internat'l Ass'n of Fire Chiefs **(279)**

Briese, CPA, Roni
Nat'l Ass'n for Search and Rescue **(341)**

Briggs Jr., J. Alden
Soccer Industry Council of America **(509)**

Briggs, Julie
Ass'n of Independent Corrugated Converters **(153)**

Briggs, Les
Soc. of Cardiovascular and Interventional Radiology **(499)**

Bright, Carrie
Associated Credit Bureaus **(171)**

Bright, Carrie D.
Footwear Distributors and Retailers of America **(242)**

Bright, Jeanne
University Risk Management and Insurance Ass'n **(537)**

Brill, Bernard D.
Secondary Materials and Recycled Textiles Ass'n **(480)**

Brill, Bonny
Investment Management Consultants Ass'n **(312)**

Brim, Orville Gilbert
Social Science Research Council **(509)**

Brimsek CAE, Tobi A.
Soc. for American Archaeology **(485)**

Brinati, Theresa
Soc. of American Archivists **(497)**

Brinegar, Pamela
Council on Licensure, Enforcement and Regulation **(217)**

Brinegar, Richard S.
Internat'l Webmasters Ass'n **(310)**

Brink, Cheryl
Nat'l Business Incubation Ass'n **(384)**

Brink, Joelle
University Continuing Education Ass'n **(537)**

Brink, John T.
American Gelbvieh Ass'n **(70)**

Brink, William S.
American Ass'n of Professional Hypnotherapists **(41)**

Brinkman, Charlie
Precision Metalforming Ass'n **(462)**

Brinkman, Jenny
Internat'l Ass'n of Dive Rescue Specialists **(278)**

Brintnall, Michael A.
Nat'l Ass'n of Schools of Public Affairs and Administration **(371)**

Briscoe III, Andrew C.
Salt Institute **(479)**

Brist, Steve
Tourist Railway Ass'n **(524)**

Bristol, Gail R.
Soc. of Plastics Engineers **(505)**

Bristol, Walter
American Heart Ass'n **(72)**

Brite, Susan
Child Welfare League of America **(192)**

Britt, Charles
Equipment Leasing Ass'n of America **(232)**

Britten, Karen
Nat'l Ass'n of State Telecommunications Directors **(376)**

Brizendine, Donald W.
American Occupational Therapy Ass'n **(88)**

Broaddus, James A.
Design-Build Institute of America **(222)**

Broadwell, William R.
Aerial Firefighting Industry Ass'n **(13)**

Brobeck, Stephen
Consumer Federation of America **(207)**

Broch, Javier
Nat'l League for Nursing **(414)**

Brock, Julie
Nat'l Ass'n of Rehabilitation Instructors **(369)**

Brock, Peggy A.
Embroidery Trade Ass'n **(229)**

Brock, Raymond W.
American Choral Directors Ass'n **(51)**

Broderick CAE, Angela
American Academy of Family Physicians **(22)**

Broderick, Bill
American Farm Bureau Federation **(66)**

Brodie, Bridget
American College of Medical Quality **(55)**

Brodman, James W.
American Academy of Research Historians of Medieval Spain **(26)**

Brodsky, Harvey
Tire Retread Information Bureau **(523)**

Brodsky, Leonard
Knitwear Employers Ass'n **(316)**

Brodsky, Marc H.
American Institute of Physics **(78)**

Broff, Nancy
Career College Ass'n **(186)**

Bronstein, Frank S.
United Ass'n of Used Oil Services **(530)**

Brook, David
Nat'l Council of Preservation Executives **(395)**

Brooker, Paul C.
Internat'l Union of Journeymen Horseshoers of the United States and Canada **(310)**

Brookhart, Sarah
American Psychological Soc. **(95)**

Brookhauser, Patrick
American Laryngological, Rhinological and Otological Soc. **(81)**

Brookman, Janet
American Hospital Ass'n **(74)**

Brookover, Pat
Plumbing-Heating-Cooling Contractors - Nat'l Ass'n **(459)**

Brooks, Alfredia
Nat'l Black Coalition of Federal Aviation Employees **(383)**

Brooks, C. Roger
College of American Pathologists **(197)**

Brooks, Dany
United States Parachute Ass'n **(534)**

Brooks Ph.D., Gene
American Choral Directors Ass'n **(51)**

Brooks, Heather
Nat'l Ass'n for Interpretation **(340)**

Brooks, James R.
Better Lawn and Turf Institute **(178)**

Brooks, Linda
American Soc. for Healthcare Human Resources Administration **(103)**

Broom, Lydell
Child Welfare League of America **(192)**

Broomfield, Terry K.
Instructional Systems Ass'n **(269)**

Brosche, Marcus
American Bralers Ass'n **(49)**

Brosche, Mark
American Bralers Ass'n **(49)**

Broskey-Lee, Tammy
School and Home Office Products Ass'n **(479)**

Brosky, Gene
Nat'l Ass'n of State Boards of Accountancy **(374)**

Brosnan, Michael
Nat'l Ass'n of Independent Schools **(360)**

Brothers, Patricia
Soc. for Experimental Mechanics **(488)**

Brotman CSWM, Judith
Nat'l Network for Social Work Managers **(418)**

Broughten, Deborah
Nat'l Institute of Senior Centers **(412)**

Brouha, Paul
American Fisheries Soc. **(68)**

Brouse, J. Robert
Nonprescription Drug Manufacturers Ass'n **(440)**

Brouwer, Eve
Campus Safety Division of the Nat'l Safety Council **(186)**

Brown, Alice
Nat'l Electronic Service Dealers Ass'n **(400)**
Internat'l Soc. of Certified Electronics Technicians **(305)**

Brown, Bob
Nat'l Ass'n of Home Builders of the U.S. **(358)**

Brown, Carol
Internat'l Ass'n of Women Ministers **(283)**

Brown, Carolyn F.
American Astronautical Soc. **(45)**

Brown, Carolyn W.
Future Homemakers of America **(245)**

Brown JD, Charles
American College of Internat'l Physicians **(55)**

Brown, Christopher
Nat'l Arborist Ass'n **(337)**

Brown, Cynthia
American Shipbuilding Ass'n **(100)**

Brown CAE, Dale E.
Internat'l Ass'n for Financial Planning **(274)**

Brown, Dan R.
Racking Horse Breeders Ass'n of America **(470)**

Brown, Darcee
American Soc. of Neuroradiology **(113)**

Brown, David L.
America Outdoors **(19)**

Brown, Dawn M.
Solid Waste Ass'n of North America **(510)**

Brown CAE, Dennis
Equipment Leasing Ass'n of America **(232)**

Brown, Dr. Diana R.
Ass'n of Black Sociologists **(145)**

Brown M.D., Douglas
American Orthopaedic Soc. for Sports Medicine **(88)**

Brown Jr., Earl B.
Nat'l Collegiate Honors Council **(388)**

Brown, Elsa P.
American College of Obstetricians and Gynecologists **(56)**

Brown, Frank
Nat'l Hockey League **(409)**

Brown, Fred
Nat'l Ass'n of Elementary School Principals **(353)**

Brown, George W.
Nat'l Aerosol Ass'n **(335)**

Brown, Grattan
Nat'l Hardwood Lumber Ass'n **(408)**

Brown, Gregory T.
Sulphur Institute, The **(518)**

Brown, J. Noah
Ass'n of Community College Trustees **(148)**

Brown, Jennifer
American Soc. of Music Copyists **(113)**

Brown, JoAnn
American Soc. of Landscape Architects **(111)**

Brown, Joell
Nat'l Intramural-Recreational Sports Ass'n **(413)**

Brown, John
American Federation of Railroad Police **(67)**

Brown, Joseph A.
American Nurses Ass'n **(87)**

Brown, Karen H.
Food Marketing Institute **(241)**

Brown, Laura L.
Nat'l Ass'n of Manufacturers **(362)**

Brown, Lisa
American Soc. of Ophthalmic Registered Nurses **(113)**

Brown, Lloyd W. "Bill"
Automotive Training Managers Council **(175)**

Brown, Margaret
Internat'l Psychogeriatric Ass'n **(300)**

Brown, Mark
Women in Film **(546)**

Brown, Martha S.
American Ass'n of Law Libraries **(38)**

Brown, Mary Ellen
Ass'n for Advancement of Behavior Therapy **(129)**

Brown, Melanie
Electronic Transactions Ass'n **(228)**

Brown, Michael W.
United States Conference of Mayors **(533)**

Brown, Mike
American Meat Institute **(83)**

Brown, Mildred E.
Montadale Sheep Breeders Ass'n **(330)**

Brown Ph.D., Murray
Nat'l Ass'n of Colleges and Teachers of Agriculture **(348)**

Brown, Nancy A.
American Soc. of Directors of Volunteer Services of the
AHA (109)

Brown, P. Hamilton
Ass'n of Former Agents of the U.S. Secret Service (152)

Brown, Patrick
Soc. of Mineral Analysts (504)

Brown, Paul S.
Risk and Insurance Management Soc. (476)

Brown Ph.D., CAE, Quincalee
Water Environment Federation (541)

Brown Jr., R. Franklin
Copper and Brass Servicenter Ass'n (209)

Brown, Regina
Nat'l Council on Education for the Ceramic Arts (397)

Brown, Richard
Nat'l Federation of Federal Employees (403)

Brown, Rick
Associated General Contractors of America (171)

Brown, Robin D.
America Outdoors (19)
American Ass'n of Cardiovascular and Pulmonary
Rehabilitation (34)

Brown, Scott
Associated Builders and Contractors (170)

Brown, Sheryl Marks
American Council on Exercise (62)

Brown, Steve
Internat'l Communications Ass'n (286)

Brown, Sue
American Academy of Ophthalmology (24)
American Ass'n for Pediatric Ophthalmology and
Strabismus (31)
American Soc. of Ophthalmic Registered Nurses (113)

Brown CMP, Suzy
Nat'l Ass'n of Temporary and Staffing Services (378)
Home Health Services and Staffing Ass'n (255)

Brown, Terrence
Soc. of Illustrators (502)

Brown, Tim
Nat'l Ass'n of Dental Plans (352)

Brown, Capt. Timothy A.
Internat'l Organization of Masters, Mates and Pilots (299)

Brown, Tracey
Nat'l Ass'n of Federal Credit Unions (355)

Brown LE,CPE, Trudy
Internat'l Guild of Professional Electrologists (293)

Brown Jr., William F.
United States Harness Writers' Ass'n (534)

Brown, William M.
Wholesale Florists and Florist Suppliers of America (543)

Brown Jr., Ph.D., William S.
American Ass'n of Phonetic Sciences (41)

Browne, Bill
Organization of Black Designers (450)

Browne Jr., Edmond R.
American Land Title Ass'n (80)

Browne, Frances Elizabeth
Nat'l Council of Examiners for Engineering and
Surveying (394)

Browne, Joe
Nat'l Football League (405)

Browne Ph.D., Ray B.
Popular Culture Ass'n (460)

Browne, Richard
Periodical and Book Ass'n of America (455)

Browne, Thomas
Internat'l Ass'n for Learning Laboratories (274)

Brownell, Gary G.
American Mathematical Soc. (83)

Browner, Donald
Community Transportation Ass'n of America (201)

Browning, Cathy
Opticians Ass'n of America (449)

Browning, Jane
Nat'l Ass'n of Social Workers (373)

Browning, Roger K.
American Pharmaceutical Ass'n (91)

Brownstein, Clifford M.
Soc. for Surgery of the Alimentary Tract (494)

Brubaker, Carol A.
Ass'n of Schools and Colleges of Optometry (164)

Bruce, Donna
Nat'l Committee for Quality Assurance (388)

Bruce, Gary M.
Internat'l Cartridge Recycling Ass'n (285)

Bruderle, Tom
Nat'l Ass'n of Health Underwriters (357)

Brueggeman, Robert
Professional Numismatists Guild (466)

Bruen, Jo
Nat'l Asphalt Pavement Ass'n (337)

Brugger, David J.
Ass'n of America's Public Television Stations (142)

Brummitt, Andria
American Medical Informatics Ass'n (84)

Brundick, Larry
Nat'l Marine Engineers Beneficial Ass'n (416)

Brune, Christine W.
American Horse Publications Ass'n (74)

Bruner, Ronald G.
Gas Processors Ass'n (245)

Brungardt, Stacy H.
Soc. of Teachers of Family Medicine (507)

Brunner CAE, Michael E.
Nat'l Telephone Cooperative Ass'n (433)

Bruns, Pamela
Nat'l Council of the Paper Industry for Air and Stream
Improvement (397)

Bruns, Ronald A.
American Soc. of Anesthesiologists (106)

Brunton, Melissa K.
Direct Selling Ass'n (223)

Bruschi, Dave
World Waterpark Ass'n (550)

Bruss, Joanne
Internat'l Soc. of Travel and Tourism Educators (307)

Brust CAE, Evelyn L.
Investment Management Consultants Ass'n (312)

Brutel, Moreen
Nat'l Abortion Federation (333)

Bryan, Barbara
Soc. of Professional Journalists (506)

Bryan, Jacalyn L.
Ass'n of State and Territorial Health Officials (166)

Bryan CAE, Robert M.
Recreation Vehicle Industry Ass'n (472)

Bryant, Adena
Regulatory Affairs Professionals Soc. (474)

Bryant Ed.D., CAE, Anne L.
Nat'l School Boards Ass'n (427)

Bryant, Jeff
Ground Water Protection Council (250)

Bryant, Kathy
Federated Ambulatory Surgery Ass'n (236)
American College of Obstetricians and Gynecologists (56)

Bryant, Nancy B.
Soc. of Industrial and Office REALTORS (503)

Bryant, Steven K.
Ass'n of Genetic Technologists (152)

Bryant Sr., M.D., Thomas E.
Aspirin Foundation of America (129)

Bryce, Robert
Investment Company Institute (312)

Brymer APR, CAE, N. Eugene
Specialized Carriers and Rigging Ass'n (514)

Bryson R.N., Randy
Nat'l Consortium of Chemical Dependency Nurses (392)
Developmental Disabilities Nurses Ass'n (222)

Buchanan, Regine
American Health Quality Ass'n (72)

Buche, E. Timothy
Motorcycle Safety Foundation (331)
Motorcycle Industry Council (330)

Bucher, Jeanie
NaSPA: the Network and System Professionals Ass'n (333)

Buchman, Barbara
American In-vitro Allergy/Immunology Soc. (75)

Buchs, Jerry
Nat'l Ass'n of College Stores (348)

Buck, Helen M.
Jewelers' Security Alliance of the U.S. (314)

Buckler, Robert
Fur Commission USA (244)

Buckles, Sharon
Trade Show Exhibitors Ass'n (524)

Buckley, Don
Nat'l Ice Cream and Yogurt Retailers Ass'n (410)

Buckley, Ellen R.
Nat'l Field Selling Ass'n (404)

Buckley Jr., CAE, George A.
Community Banking Advisory Network (201)
Nat'l Litigation Support Services Ass'n (415)
Not-for-Profit Services Ass'n (446)

Buckley Jr., George A.
Center for Management Advisors (189)

Buckley, Jean M.
Future Business Leaders of America-Phi Beta Lambda (245)

Buckley, JoAnn
Nat'l Lumber and Building Material Dealers Ass'n (415)

Buckley, John J.
Nat'l Paper Trade Ass'n (421)
Paper Distribution Council (453)

Buckley, Lorraine
Parliamentary Associates (453)

Buckley, Mary
American Art Therapy Ass'n (29)

Buckstead, John
Nat'l Ass'n of Community Action Agencies (349)

Buczak, Darlene J.
American College of Chest Physicians (53)

Buczkiewicz, Jeff
Mason Contractors Ass'n of America (324)

Budde, Norbert W.
American Osteopathic Ass'n (89)

Budetti, Maureen
Nat'l Ass'n of Independent Colleges and Universities (359)

Budig, Gene
American League of Professional Baseball Clubs (81)

Budlong, Karen
Nat'l Ass'n of Store Fixture Manufacturers (377)

Budway, Robert B.
Can Manufacturers Institute (186)

Budzinski, Joseph W.
Internat'l Cemetery and Funeral Ass'n (285)

Buettner, John
Tire Ass'n of North America (523)

Buffenbarger, R. Thomas
Internat'l Ass'n of Machinists and Aerospace Workers (280)

Buffington, Gary L.
Industrial Distribution Ass'n (262)

Buffum, Mary
USITT: Ass'n of Design, Production and Technology
Professionals in the Performing Arts and
Entertainment (538)

Buford, Phyllis Scott
Consortium for Graduate Study and Management (206)

Bukovskey, Lula B.
Nat'l Ass'n of Biology Teachers (344)

Bulcao, Douglas W.
American Textile Manufacturers Institute (119)

Bulger M.D., Roger J.
Ass'n of Academic Health Centers (141)

Bull, Nancy
Ass'n for Equine Sports Medicine (133)

Bullivant, John
Electrical Insulation Conference (227)

Bulow, Lucian C.
Soc. of Maritime Arbitrators (503)

Bumanis, Al
American Music Therapy Ass'n (86)

Bunch, Janis R.
Nat'l Auto Auction Ass'n (381)

Bunch, Michelle
North American Insulation Manufacturers Ass'n (442)

Bundy, Sam
Associated Surplus Dealers (172)

Bunge, JoAnn
United States Telephone Ass'n (535)

Bunn, J.T.
Tobacco Ass'n of the U.S. (523)
Leaf Tobacco Exporters Ass'n (318)

Buntin, Charlotte D.
Air Line Employees Ass'n, International (15)

Bunting, Stephen M.
American Soc. of Law Enforcement Trainers (112)

Buonaguro, Anthony
Nat'l Organization of Life and Health Insurance Guaranty
Ass'ns (420)

Buonora, David
Nat'l Council of State Directors of Community Junior
Colleges (396)

Burack, Jim
Police Executive Research Forum (459)

Burack, Martin
Internet Soc. (311)

Burandt, Gary
Internat'l Communications Agency Network (286)

Burbridge, Sandra
Healthcare Information and Management Systems Soc. (253)

Burch, Christine C.
Nat'l Ass'n of Public Hospitals and Health Systems (368)

Burch, David
Precision Machined Products Ass'n (462)

Burcham Jr., John B.
Nat'l Ass'n of Beverage Retailers (344)

Burd, Arlene
Nat'l Ass'n of Fleet Resale Dealers (355)

Burd, Gail
Ass'n for Chemoreception Sciences (130)

Burdett, Betty
Petroleum Industry Security Council (455)

Burdge, Rabel J.
Rural Sociological Soc. (478)

Cadena, Eugenia
Ass'n of Metropolitan Water Agencies (157)

Cady, John R.
Council of Food Processors Ass'n Executives (213)
Nat'l Food Processors Ass'n (405)

Caesar, Fred
Catholic Health Ass'n of the United States (188)

Caffarelli, Patrick
Nat'l Automatic Merchandising Ass'n (381)

Cafferty, Nancy
Nat'l Academy Museum and School Fine Arts (333)

Caffey, James
Institute of Scrap Recycling Industries (269)

Cafruny, Madalyn
American Public Power Ass'n (96)

Cahill, Irene
Nat'l Court Reporters Ass'n (398)

Cahill, Judith A.
Academy of Managed Care Pharmacy (8)

Cahill, Leslie
American Seed Trade Ass'n (99)

Cain, Dr. George D.
American Soc. of Parasitologists (114)

Cain, Herman
Nat'l Restaurant Ass'n (425)

Cain, Morrison
Internat'l Mass Retail Ass'n (297)

Cain, Patricia A.
American Jail Ass'n (79)

Caine Ph.D., Nancy
American Soc. of Primatologists (115)

Cairns, Richard
Bowling Proprietors Ass'n of America (181)

Calabrese, Katie
Career College Ass'n (186)

Calambokidis, Joan B.
Internat'l Masonry Institute (297)

Calderone, Jo Anne
Nat'l Chimney Sweep Guild (386)

Caldwell, Allen
Internat'l Ass'n of Fire Chiefs (279)

Caldwell, Barry H.
Pharmaceutical Research and Manufacturers of America (456)

Caldwell, Heather
Institute of Certified Financial Planners (266)

Caldwell, Susan M.
Information Systems Audit and Control Ass'n (264)

Calhoun, A. Cedric
Council for Advancement and Support of Education (210)

Calhoun, Terry
Soc. for College and University Planning (486)

Calimafde, Paula A.
Small Business Council of America (483)

Calkins, Barbara J.
Ass'n of Teachers of Preventive Medicine (167)

Call, Christine
Ass'n for Institutional Research (135)

Callahan, Amy
Information Technology Ass'n of America (264)

Callahan, Donna
Nat'l Ass'n of Independent Insurers (359)

Callahan, Edward J.
Mortgage Bankers Ass'n of America (330)

Callahan DPA, James F.
American Soc. of Addiction Medicine (106)

Callahan, Kathleen M.
NAGMR Consumer Product Brokers (333)

Callahan, Mary Helen
Urban Affairs Ass'n (537)

Callahan CCE, William Terence
Credit Research Foundation (218)

Callanan, Bob
American Soybean Ass'n (117)

Callery, T. Grant
Nat'l Ass'n of Securities Dealers (372)

Callis, Diane B.
Nat'l Ass'n of Personnel Services (365)

Calloway, Lee
American Quarter Horse Ass'n (96)

Calm, Kira
Nat'l Industrial Transportation League (411)

Calomino, Audrey J.
Nat'l Ass'n of Dental Laboratories (352)

Calore, Haidee
Nat'l Ass'n of Broadcasters (345)

Calvani, Terry
American Economic Ass'n (65)

Calverley, Mary Beth
American Massage Therapy Ass'n (83)

Calvert, Denise
American Congress on Surveying and Mapping (60)

Calvert, Mrs. E. Bruce
Independent Liquid Terminals Ass'n (261)

Calvert, Skipwith C.
American Psychological Ass'n (94)

Calvert, Timothy
American College of Sports Medicine (57)

Calvet, Linda
Ecuadorean American Ass'n (226)

Calvet, Paul E.
Venezuelan American Ass'n of the U.S. (539)
Colombian American Ass'n (198)

Calvo CAE, Roque J.
Electrochemical Soc. (228)

Camarillo, Martha
Nat'l Ass'n of Small Business Internat'l Trade Educators (373)

Camera CAE, Gaylen M.
American Industrial Health Council (75)

Cameron, Don
Nat'l Education Ass'n of the U.S. (400)

Camey, Brian
Catholic Health Ass'n of the United States (188)

Cammarata, Kenneth F.
Nat'l Employee Services and Recreation Ass'n (401)

Camp, Camille G.
Ass'n of State Correctional Administrators (166)

Camp, George M.
Ass'n of State Correctional Administrators (166)

Campbell CAE, Alan J.
Nat'l Wood Window and Door Ass'n (437)

Campbell, Amy E.
Ass'n of State and Provincial Psychology Boards (165)

Campbell, Candace
American Preventive Medical Ass'n (93)

Campbell Jr., Carroll A.
American Council of Life Insurance (61)

Campbell, Cathleen
Home Sewing Ass'n (256)

Campbell, Colin
Nat'l Hockey League (409)

Campbell, Dale F.
Community College Business Officers (201)

Campbell, Donald A.
Mutual Advertising Agency Network (332)

Campbell, Doug
Northern Nut Growers Ass'n (446)

Campbell, Duvonne
American Soc. of Radiologic Technologists (115)

Campbell, J.A. Barton
Reserve Officers Ass'n of the U.S. (475)

Campbell, Jeannie
Nat'l Council for Community Behavioral Healthcare (393)

Campbell, Rev. Dr. Joan Brown
Nat'l Council of the Churches of Christ in the U.S.A. (397)

Campbell CAE, Joan Carter
Home Sewing Ass'n (256)

Campbell, John
American Book Producers Ass'n (48)

Campbell, John C.
Ass'n for Asian Studies (130)

Campbell, Karen K.
American Criminal Justice Ass'n/Lambda Alpha Epsilon (62)

Campbell CMP, CAE, Linda
American Soc. of Pediatric Nephrology (114)

Campbell, Maureen E.
Financial Executives Institute (238)

Campbell, Renee
Internat'l Ass'n of Lighting Designers (280)

Campbell, Thomas J.
American Educational Research Ass'n (65)

Campiglia, Michael E.
Federal Bar Ass'n (235)

Campione, Margaret
Truckload Carriers Ass'n (527)

Campobenedetto Ph.D., E.J.
Institute of Clean Air Companies (266)

Canady-Foster, Debra
American Soc. of Heating, Refrigerating and Air-Conditioning Engineers (110)

Candler, Linda
Nat'l Fisheries Institute (404)

Canfield, Mare
Institute of Certified Financial Planners (266)

Canfield, Pat
Nat'l Soc. of Professional Surveyors (430)

Cann, Linda
American Diabetes Ass'n (64)

Cannata, Annet
Ass'n of Information Technology Professionals (154)

Cannon, Barbara
American Astronomical Soc. (45)

Cannon, Bruce
Internat'l Bridge, Tunnel and Turnpike Ass'n (284)

Cannon, Elizabeth
American Philological Ass'n (91)

Cannon, Fred
Nat'l Ass'n of Police Equipment Distributors (365)

Cannon Ph.D., Hugh M.
Ass'n for Business Simulation and Experiential Learning (130)

Cannon, John
Nat'l Academy of Television Arts and Sciences (334)

Cannon, Kathy A.
American Pediatric Soc. (91)

Cannon, Mary Ann
Ass'n of College Unions-Internat'l (147)

Cannon, Michael Q.
Council on Foundations (216)

Canon, Kate
Corporate Facility Advisors (209)

Cantrall, Richard
American Orthopaedic Foot and Ankle Soc. (88)

Cantrill, Richard
American Oil Chemists' Soc. (88)

Cantus, Charles H.
Professional Services Council (467)

Cantwell, SueEllan L.
Ass'n of Sales and Marketing Companies (164)

Canty, Henry L.
American Ass'n of Police Polygraphists (41)

Capas, Audra S.
Nat'l Realty Committee (424)

Capella, Elena
American Law Institute (81)

Capestany, Maria
American Soc. for Training and Development (106)

Caplow, Julie
Ass'n for the Study of Higher Education (139)

Capozzi, Sue
Internat'l Communications Industries Ass'n (286)

Capozzi, Susan U.
Internat'l Communications Industries Ass'n (286)

Cappelletti, Michael R.
Soc. of Plastics Engineers (505)

Capps, Cheryl
Soc. of Decorative Painters (500)

Capuco, Laura A.
Truck Renting and Leasing Ass'n (527)

Caputo, Jonathan
Web Host Guild (542)

Caradonna, William
Nat'l Iridology Research Ass'n (413)

Caraley, Demetrios
Academy of Political Science (9)

Caraway Ph.D., Carol
Soc. for the Philosophy of Sex and Love (495)

Caraway, Sherrie
American Ostrich Ass'n (90)

Carberry, Frank J.
Office Planners and Users Group (447)

Carbo, Geraldine M.
Internat'l Food Information Council (291)

Carbo, Rick
Nat'l Ass'n of RV Parks and Campgrounds (370)

Carbone, William J.
American Ass'n of Physician Specialists (41)

Carbott, Thomas A.
Automated Electrified Monorail Product Section - Material Handling Institute (173)
Lift Manufacturers Product Section - Material Handling Institute (319)

Card Jr., Andrew H.
American Automobile Manufacturers Ass'n (46)

Cardez, Anthony
Overseas Automotive Council, Internat'l Aftermarket Division - Motor and Equipment Manufacturers Ass'n (452)

Cardwell, Nancy
Internat'l Bluegrass Music Ass'n (283)

Care, Robert
IEEE Computer Soc. (258)

Carey, Bill
Computing Technology Industry Ass'n (203)

Carey, Catherine
Clinical Orthopaedic Soc. (195)

Carey, Dan
American Academy of Veterinary Nutrition (26)

Carey, Karen Clayton
Ass'n for Information and Image Management International (135)

Carey, Lisa
Nat'l Tour Ass'n (434)

Carey, Pat
American Academy of Otolaryngology-Head and Neck Surgery (24)

Carey, Steve
Nat'l Truck Equipment Ass'n (434)

Carillo, Carlos G.
Nat'l Federation of Hispanic Owned Newspapers (403)

Carl, Carlton
Ass'n of Trial Lawyers of America (168)

Carl, E.H.
Cellulose Insulation Manufacturers Ass'n (189)

Carley, Wayne W.
Nat'l Ass'n of Biology Teachers (344)

Carlough, Judy
Radio Advertising Bureau (471)

Carlson, Carol
Nat'l Ass'n of Agricultural Fair Agencies (343)

Carlson, Donald E.
Soc. for Natural Philosophy (491)

Carlson, Donna
Art Dealers Ass'n of America (127)

Carlson, Donna J.
Rubber Pavements Ass'n (478)

Carlson, Ginger Macchi
Congress on Research in Dance (205)

Carlson, John G.
Internat'l Stress Management Ass'n (307)

Carlson, Karen
Soc. of Air Force Clinical Surgeons (497)

Carlson, Lisa
Funeral and Memorial Socs. of America (244)

Carlson, Robert
Council of the Great City Schools (216)

Carman, Paul
Internat'l Information Management Congress (294)

Carmichael, Jean
Nat'l Ass'n of Home Builders of the U.S. (358)

Carnahan, Jennifer
Custom Electronic Design and Installation Ass'n (219)

Carnahan, Robert E.
Truck Cap and Accessory Ass'n (527)

Carnes, Mark C.
Soc. of American Historians (497)

Carnes, Mary
Armed Forces Broadcasters Ass'n (127)

Carnes, Woneta
American Construction Inspectors Ass'n (60)

Carnevale VMD, Richard A.
Animal Health Institute (125)

Carney, Burt
Ass'n of Christian Schools Internat'l (146)

Carney, James D.
Nat'l Truck Equipment Ass'n (434)

Carney, John
Motor and Equipment Manufacturers Ass'n (330)

Carney, John W.
Automotive Chemical Manufacturers Council (174)

Carney-Talley, Sandra
Aerospace Industries Ass'n of America (13)

Carothers, Donna J.
Hospice and Palliative Nurses Ass'n (256)

Carothers, Marcia
American Saddlebred Horse Ass'n (98)

Carow III, L. Jack
American Soc. of General Surgeons (110)

Carpenter, Edward K.
Cargo Reinsurance Ass'n (187)
American Cargo War Risk Reinsurance Exchange (50)

Carpenter, Ellen
Nat'l Cotton Council of America (392)

Carpenter CAE, Gary L.
American Ass'n of Equine Practitioners (36)

Carpenter, Isaac
American Dental Hygienists' Ass'n (64)

Carpenter, Jennifer
Ayrshire Breeders' Ass'n (176)

Carpenter, Joan
Red and White Dairy Cattle Ass'n (473)

Carpenter, Kathy
College Reading and Learning Ass'n (198)

Carpenter Jr., Orrin
American Academy of Ophthalmology (24)

Carpenter, W.D.
Nat'l Ass'n of State Agencies for Surplus Property (373)

Carper, Sherelle
Nat'l Ass'n of Negro Business and Professional Women's Clubs (363)

Carr, Eileen M.
Nat'l Hospice Organization (409)

Carr, Glen C.
American Rabbit Breeders Ass'n (96)

Carr, James
Nat'l Ass'n of Intercollegiate Athletics (360)

Carr CAE, Jennifer
Hospitality Financial and Technology Professionals (256)

Carr, John T.
Foundation for Independent Higher Education (243)

Carr-Smith, Kathleen
Council for Responsible Nutrition (212)

Carradine, Sam
Nat'l Organization of Minority Architects (420)

Carradine Jr., Samuel A.
Nat'l Ass'n of Minority Contractors (363)

Carre, Dan
Professional Convention Management Ass'n (465)

Carreiro, Betty
Nat'l Hydropower Ass'n (410)

Carreras, Lisa
Internat'l Ass'n of Attorneys and Exec. in Corporate Real Estate (276)

Carrico Ph.D., Christine K.
American Soc. for Pharmacology and Experimental Therapeutics (104)

Carrington, Georgianna
Nat'l Ass'n of Social Workers (373)

Carroll, Brain P.
Nat'l Ass'n of Criminal Defense Lawyers (352)

Carroll Jr., Charles T.
Nat'l Ass'n of Waterfront Employers (380)

Carroll, Gretchen S.
Sanitary Supply Wholesalers Ass'n (479)

Carroll, James
Nat'l Organization for Human Service Education (420)

Carroll, Larry
Timber Products Manufacturers (523)

Carroll, William F.
Portable Sanitation Ass'n Internat'l (460)

Carroll Jr., William J.
American Soc. for Training and Development (106)

Carroll Ph.D., William J.
American Reusable Textile Ass'n (98)

Carson, John R.
American Podiatric Medical Ass'n (93)

Cartee, Larry
Organization of Wildlife Planners (450)

Carter, Belinda
REALTORS Land Institute (472)

Carter, Cathy
System Safety Soc. (519)

Carter, Curtis L.
American Soc. for Aesthetics (101)

Carter, Dana A.
Nat'l Ass'n of State Directors of Administration and General Services (374)
Nat'l Ass'n of State Purchasing Officials (376)

Carter, Dr. Frances Tunnell
Kappa Delta Epsilon (315)

Carter, Gene R.
Ass'n for Supervision and Curriculum Development (138)

Carter, George M.
Laminating Materials Ass'n (317)

Carter, Gwendolyn M.
African American Travel and Tourism Ass'n (14)

Carter, Harriet
Document Management Industries Ass'n (224)

Carter, Joy
Livestock Conservation Institute (320)

Carter, Katherine French
Laboratory Products Ass'n (316)

Carter, Richard
American Law Institute (81)

Carter Ph.D., Robert N.
North American Case Research Ass'n (441)

Carter, Ron
Ass'n of Surgical Technologists (166)

Carter, Ryan S.
Lawn and Garden Dealers' Ass'n (318)

Carter, Steven D.
American Academy of Ophthalmology (24)

Carter, Virgil
Project Management Institute (468)

Cartwill, Matt
American Ass'n of Physical Anthropologists (41)

Cartwright, Patricia
Nat'l Recreation and Park Ass'n (424)

Carty, Beth
Nat'l Investor Relations Institute (413)

Caruso, Dawn
Soc. of Toxicology (508)

Caruso, George
Nat'l Affordable Housing Management Ass'n (335)

Caruthers, Bob
Ass'n of Surgical Technologists (166)

Carver, H. Jack
American Apparel Manufacturers Ass'n (28)

Carville OSF, Ann
Conference of Major Superiors of Men, U.S.A. (204)

Case, David R.
Environmental Technology Council (232)

Case, Diane B.
Tire Ass'n of North America (523)

Case, Glenna
American Academy of Neurology (23)

Case, Kathy
American College of Physicians-American Soc. of Internal Medicine (57)

Case Ed.D., Larry D.
Nat'l FFA Organization (404)

Case, Susan
Welsh Black Cattle Ass'n (542)

Casey, Dwight L.
Independent Electrical Contractors (260)

Casey, Eric
Mail Advertising Service Ass'n Internat'l (322)

Casey, Jane Patrick
Soc. for Marketing Professional Services (490)

Casey, Joanne
Intermodal Ass'n of North America (272)

Casey, Joseph G.
Nat'l Ass'n of Pediatric Nurse Associates and Practitioners (364)

Casey CAE, R. Frederick
Special Libraries Ass'n (514)

Casey, Robert
Special Libraries Ass'n (514)

Casey, Samuel B.
Christian Legal Soc. (193)

Casey, Victor
American Soc. of Law, Medicine and Ethics (112)

Casgar, Tina
Intermodal Ass'n of North America (272)

Cashen, Kathleen A.
Interstate Conference of Employment Security Agencies (311)

Caspers, Karen Dunn
American Dental Hygienists' Ass'n (64)

Cass, Peter
Preferred Hotels and Resorts Worldwide (462)

Casserly, Michael D.
Council of the Great City Schools (216)

Cassidy, Christine M.
American Academy of Actuaries (20)

Cassidy, Daniel J.
Soc. of Nuclear Medicine (504)

Cassidy, Kathleen M.
American Short Line and Regional Railroad Ass'n (100)

Cassidy, Lee M.
Nat'l Federation of Non-Profits (404)

Cassidy, Philip E.
Business Council (184)

Cassity, Pratt
Nat'l Alliance of Preservation Commissions (336)

Casso, Ann P.
Ass'n of Trial Lawyers of America (168)

Castaldo, John
Barre Granite Ass'n (177)

Casteran, Paul R.
Wire Ass'n Internat'l (545)

Castillo, C. Connie
American Sociological Ass'n (117)

Castillo, Ileana
Soc. of Laparoendoscopic Surgeons (503)

Castle, Vernon
Training Officers Conference (525)

Castles, Chrissy
American Resort Development Ass'n (98)

Castor, Harold
Industrial Chemical Research Ass'n (262)

Castor, Dr. Stephen R.
Conservative Orthopedics Internat'l Ass'n (206)

Caswell, Don
Internat'l Brotherhood of Boilermakers, Iron Ship Builders, Blacksmiths, Forgers and Helpers (284)

Caswell, Kathleen
TAG Internat'l (520)

Catalano, Thomas S.
Refrigeration Service Engineers Soc. (473)

Cataldo, Carol
Commission of Accredited Truck Driving Schools (199)

Cate, George M.
American Soc. of Extra-Corporeal Technology (109)

Cates, Mellony
Aestheticians Internat'l Ass'n (13)

Cathcart, D. Christopher
Nat'l Ass'n of Chemical Distributors (347)

Cathcart, Elisoe
Nat'l Council of State Boards of Nursing (396)

Cathcart CAE, Sherrie H.
American College of Rheumatology **(57)**

Cathey, Melody Curtiss
Internat'l Ass'n of Industrial Accident Boards and Commissions **(280)**

Catizone, Carmen A.
Nat'l Ass'n of Boards of Pharmacy **(345)**

Cato, Marcus
Nat'l Black MBA Ass'n **(383)**

Cattaneo, Joseph J.
Glass Packaging Institute **(247)**

Cauble CPA, Eric
Medical Group Management Ass'n **(326)**

Caudill, Debbie
Ass'n for Women in Communications **(140)**

Caudron, John Armand
Firearms Research and Indentification Ass'n **(240)**

Cauley-Fox, Elizabeth A.
United States Court Reporters Ass'n **(533)**

Caulk CRNA, Ronald F.
Internat'l Federation of Nurse Anesthetists **(290)**

Caulk CRNA, Susan Smith
American Ass'n of Nurse Anesthetists **(39)**

Causey, C. Dawn
America's Community Bankers **(20)**

Cavalli, Gary
American Basketball League **(47)**

Cavallo, Cindy F.
Milk Industry Foundation **(328)**
Internat'l Ice Cream Ass'n **(294)**

Cavanagh, Michael
Council for Electronic Revenue Communication Advancement **(211)**

Cavanaugh, Gloria
American Soc. on Aging **(117)**

Cavanaugh, Gordon
Council of Large Public Housing Authorities **(214)**

Cavanaugh, Sheila
Soc. of Independent Gasoline Marketers of America **(502)**

Cavarretta, Joseph
Electronic Retailing Ass'n **(228)**

Cave, Robert S.
American Public Gas Ass'n **(95)**

Cavell, Mark
Nat'l FFA Organization **(404)**

Cavender, Nadine
Ecological Soc. of America **(225)**

Cavendish, Marty
Women in Film and Video **(546)**

Cawley, Meredith
Suppliers of Advanced Composite Materials Ass'n **(518)**
United States Advanced Ceramics Ass'n **(531)**

Cebula, Andrew
Nat'l Air Transportation Ass'n **(335)**

Cebulash, Lisa
American Academy of Audiology **(20)**

Cecchetti, Elizabeth
OPERA America **(448)**

Cedola, Vince
Dental Group Management Ass'n **(221)**

Cella, Glenn
American Institute for Shippers Ass'ns **(76)**

Censky, Ellen J.
Soc. for the Study of Amphibians and Reptiles **(495)**

Censky, Peter
Water Quality Ass'n **(541)**

Censky, Steve
American Soybean Ass'n **(117)**

Centra, Cathy
Hearth Products Ass'n **(253)**

Cerane, Steve
Nat'l League for Nursing **(414)**

Cergol Jr., John J.
Nat'l Spa and Pool Institute **(431)**

Cerna, Ricardo G.
ADED - the Ass'n for Driver Rehabilitation Specialists **(11)**

Cernauskas, Michael R.
Institute of Food Technologists **(267)**

Cervarich, Margaret
Nat'l Asphalt Pavement Ass'n **(337)**

Cervenka CAE, CMP, Karen S.
American Student Dental Ass'n **(118)**

Cervero, Albert A.
Construction Industry Manufacturers Ass'n **(206)**

Cesari, Gina G.
University/Resident Theatre Ass'n **(537)**

Cesario, Theresa
Soc. of Cosmetic Chemists **(500)**

Chabin, Jim
PROMAX Internat'l **(468)**

Chace, Richard
Security Industry Ass'n **(481)**

Chach, Maryann
Theatre Library Ass'n **(522)**

Chadwick, Ann Collins
American Ass'n of Family and Consumer Sciences **(36)**

Chadwick, Lynn
Nat'l Federation of Community Broadcasters **(403)**

Chaffee, Anthony D.
Phi Delta Chi **(456)**

Chaffee, Clarence L.
Council of Landscape Architectural Registration Boards **(214)**

Chaffin, Diane
Nat'l Conference of State Legislatures **(391)**

Chafin, John F.
Internat'l Ass'n of Clerks, Recorders, Election Officials and Treasurers **(277)**

Chahin, Roxana
United States Hispanic Chamber of Commerce **(534)**

Chait, Andrew H.
Nat'l Antique and Art Dealers Ass'n of America **(337)**

Chalik, Barbara
Ass'n of Independent Trust Companies **(154)**
Refrigerating Engineers and Technicians Ass'n **(473)**

Chamberlain, Courtney
Center for Exhibition Industry Research **(189)**

Chamberlain CAE, Henry
Building Owners and Managers Ass'n Internat'l **(183)**

Chamberlin, Michael M.
Emerging Markets Traders Ass'n **(229)**

Chamberline, Richard
Nat'l Ass'n of College Stores **(348)**

Chambers, Letitia
Coalition of Publicly Traded Partnerships **(196)**

Chambers, Paul G.
American Mathematical Soc. **(83)**

Chambers, Richard
Turkish Studies Ass'n **(528)**

Chambers, Rose
Professional Ass'n of Health Care Office Managers **(464)**

Chambers, Susan K.
American Soc. of Plant Physiologists **(114)**

Chambers, WH.
PCPCI - The Transformer Ass'n **(454)**
Small Motors and Motion Ass'n **(484)**

Chambers, Walton
American Gaming Ass'n **(70)**

Chamblin, R. Anthony
Ass'n of Racing Commissioners Internat'l **(162)**

Chambliss, William H.
Internat'l Dairy Foods Ass'n **(288)**

Chamiec-Case, Rick
North American Ass'n of Christians in Social Work **(440)**

Chamness, Charles M.
Nat'l Ass'n of Mutual Insurance Companies **(363)**

Champagne, Richard D.
Hydrogen Industry Council **(257)**

Chan, Antony
American Academy of Pediatrics **(25)**

Chan, Susan D.
American Ass'n of Zoo Keepers **(45)**

Chana, Susan
Gypsum Ass'n **(250)**

Chanda, David
Ass'n for Conservation Information **(131)**

Chandler, Judy
Automotive Parts Rebuilders Ass'n **(175)**

Chandler, Karen
Ass'n of Arts Administration Educators **(144)**

Chandler, Linda
American Soc. of Ass'n Executives **(107)**

Chandler, Linda C.
Meeting Professionals Internat'l **(327)**

Chandler, Sylvia E.
Ass'n for the Advancement of Medical Instrumentation **(138)**

Chandler, William
Nat'l Parks and Conservation Ass'n **(421)**

Chanes, Barbara
Financial Executives Institute **(238)**

Chaney, G.P.Russ
Internat'l Ass'n of Plumbing and Mechanical Officials **(282)**

Chaney, W. Calvin
American College of Emergency Physicians **(54)**

Chang, Amy L.
American Soc. for Microbiology **(104)**

Chang, Eleanor
American Booksellers Ass'n **(48)**

Chanin, Robert
Nat'l Education Ass'n of the U.S. **(400)**

Chantos, Helen
Nat'l Housewares Manufacturers Ass'n **(409)**

Chantry, Chris
Nat'l Ass'n of Biology Teachers **(344)**

Chapin D.D.S., MS, Linda R.
Nat'l Wellness Ass'n **(436)**

Chapin, Rene
Internat'l Television Ass'n **(308)**

Chapman, Caron
Ass'n of Booksellers for Children **(145)**

Chapman, Kathryn
Petroleum Technology Transfer Council **(456)**

Chapman, Roy
Wedding and Event Videographers Ass'n Internat'l **(542)**

Chapman, Thomas B.
Aircraft Owners and Pilots Ass'n **(16)**

Chapot, Chip
American Soc. of Pension Actuaries **(114)**

Chappelear, Patsy
Nat'l Ass'n of Regional Councils **(369)**

Chappell, Cynthia T.
Industrial Telecommunications Ass'n **(263)**

Chappell, John
Land Trust Alliance **(317)**

Chappelle, Brian
Mortgage Bankers Ass'n of America **(330)**

Charles, Aubrey
Internat'l City/County Management Ass'n **(285)**

Charles, Jennifer
Internat'l Festivals and Events Ass'n **(291)**

Charles, Vivian Dandridge
Business and Professional Women/USA **(184)**

Charlson Ph.D., Elizabeth
ADARA **(11)**

Charlton, Knight
American Dental Soc. of Anesthesiology **(64)**

Charron, William J.
Nat'l Erectors Ass'n **(402)**

Chasar, Frank
Edison Welding Institute **(226)**

Chase, Alan W.
Ass'n of Public-Safety Communications Officials-Internat'l **(162)**

Chase, Joe
Nat'l Ass'n of Scientific Materials Managers **(371)**

Chase, Matthew
Nat'l Ass'n of Development Organizations **(352)**

Chase, Shelley Anne
Diving Equipment and Marketing Ass'n **(224)**

Chasen, Rebecca
American Institute of Biological Sciences **(76)**

Chasnoff, Ira J.
Nat'l Ass'n for Families and Addiction Research and Education **(339)**

Chastain Jr., Merritt B.
Nat'l Ass'n of Pipe Coating Applicators **(365)**

Chastian, Laura L.
Nat'l Organization of Bar Counsel **(420)**

Chattman, Ray
American Institute of Aeronautics and Astronautics **(76)**

Chattman CMP, Stacey
American Hotel and Motel Ass'n **(74)**

Chaudhry, Serena
Nat'l Ass'n of Professionals in Women's Health **(367)**

Chauvin, Lilyan
Organization of Professional Acting Coaches and Teachers **(450)**

Chauvin, William
American Shrimp Processors Ass'n **(100)**

Chavez, Linda
American Federation of Labor and Congress of Industrial Organizations **(67)**

Chavka, Daniel J.
Nat'l Dairy Council **(398)**
Dairy Management **(219)**

Chaw, Terisa E.
Nat'l Employment Lawyers Ass'n **(401)**

Cheaure, Alfred L.
American Kennel Club **(80)**

Checol, Assefa
Independent Electrical Contractors **(260)**

Chen, George
Ass'n of Jesuit Colleges and Universities **(155)**

Chene, Jill
American Geriatrics Soc. **(71)**

Chenevey, Cathy
American Institute of Aeronautics and Astronautics **(76)**

Cheney, Michelle
Nat'l Rural Health Ass'n **(426)**

Cheney, Rev. Peter G.
Nat'l Ass'n of Episcopal Schools **(354)**

Cherian, Dr. Joy
American Council for Trade in Services **(61)**

Cherico, Holly Thompson
Council of Better Business Bureaus **(212)**

Colglazier, E. William
Nat'l Academy of Sciences (334)

Colitz, Judy
Nat'l Housewares Manufacturers Ass'n (409)

Collado III, Emilio G.
American Watch Ass'n (122)

Collatz, Mark
Adhesive and Sealant Council (12)

Collet, Josh
Council of the Americas (216)

Collette, Robert
Nat'l Blue Crab Industry Ass'n (383)

Colley, Kathy
Forest Industries Telecommunications (242)

Colley, Lynda
American Ass'n of Trade and Industrial Instructors (44)

Collie III, H. Cris
Employee Relocation Council (229)

Collier, Bill
Intelligent Transportation Soc. of America (270)

Collier, Carmalita
BEMA - An Internat'l Ass'n Serving the Baking and Food Industries (178)

Collins, Al
Nat'l Ass'n of Metal Finishers (363)

Collins, Anita Bolen
Hobby Industry Ass'n of America (255)

Collins, Billie Jean
American Schools of Oriental Research (99)

Collins, James B.
Steel Service Center Institute (517)

Collins, James F.
Steel Manufacturers Ass'n (516)

Collins CMP, Jeannine
Water Quality Ass'n (541)

Collins, Jim
American Soc. of Composers, Authors and Publishers (108)

Collins, John H.
American Welara Pony Soc. (122)

Collins, John J.
American Trucking Ass'ns (121)

Collins, Kevin
American Ass'n of Crop Insurers (35)

Collins, Milton J.
Internat'l Concrete Repair Institute (286)

Collins, Mimi
Nat'l Ass'n of Colleges and Employers (348)

Collins, Patricia
Farm Equipment Wholesalers Ass'n (235)

Collins, Polly P.
Nat'l Soc. of Professional Engineers (430)

Collins D.M.D., MP, Robert J.
American Ass'n for Dental Research (30)

Collins, Susan
American Holistic Nurses' Ass'n (73)

Collishaw, Karen J.
American College of Cardiology (53)

Collom, Jonathan
Hazardous Materials Advisory Council (251)

Colomo, Diana
American Trauma Soc. (121)

Colopy, Michael
Healthcare Finance Study Group (252)

Colquhoun, Marcia
American Crystallographic Ass'n (63)

Colson, Ron
Internat'l Hot Rod Ass'n (294)

Colton, Barbara
Nat'l Ass'n of Performing Arts Managers and Agents (364)

Coltrane, Karen
American Waterways Operators (122)

Colvard, Jean
American Soc. of Clinical Oncology (108)

Colville, Mary
Nat'l Broiler Council (384)

Colvin, Joe F.
Nuclear Energy Institute (446)

Combes, Lee
Institute for Interconnecting and Packaging Electronic Circuits (265)

Combest, Hannes
Golf Course Superintendents Ass'n of America (248)

Combs, Ronda
Nat'l Ass'n of State Credit Union Supervisors (374)

Comean, John
Registered Mail Insurance Ass'n (473)

Comeau, Melissa
Ass'n for Work Process Improvement (141)

Comer, Amy L.
Nat'l Ass'n of Mortgage Brokers (363)

Comer, Edward H.
Edison Electric Institute (226)

Comi, Francine
American Thoracic Soc. (120)

Comley, Linda Jean
American Ass'n of Immunologists (38)

Comley, Tobin P.
Ass'n of American Colleges and Universities (142)

Comlish, Michael
American Counseling Ass'n (62)

Commings, Kathy
All-America Rose Selections (17)

Compton, Geordie
Deep Foundations Institute (220)

Compton, Kathron A.
Soc. for Human Resource Management (489)

Comstock, W. Stephen
American Soc. of Heating, Refrigerating and Air-Conditioning Engineers (110)

Conaty, Micheal J.
Ass'n of Performing Arts Presenters (160)

Concklin, Bert M.
Professional Services Council (467)

Conde, Alice
American College of Psychiatrists (57)

Condeelis, Mary
Bankers' Ass'n for Foreign Trade (176)

Condello, Katherine
Cellular Telecommunications Industry Ass'n (189)

Condon, Irene
Battery Council Internat'l (177)

Condon, Leonard W.
American Meat Institute (83)

Condon, Mark
American Seed Trade Ass'n (99)

Coneset, Phyllis
Institute of Real Estate Management (269)

Conkling Ph.D., John A.
American Pyrotechnics Ass'n (96)

Conley, Henry
Nat'l Cutting Horse Ass'n (398)

Conley, Joan C.
Nat'l Ass'n of Securities Dealers (372)

Conley, John
Nat'l Tank Truck Carriers (433)

Conley, Lola
Lawn and Garden Dealers' Ass'n (318)

Conley, Thomas
Steel Service Center Institute (517)

Conley, Tom
Ass'n for Manufacturing Excellence (136)

Connell CMP, CAE, Barbara A.
American Academy of Periodontology (25)

Connell, Frank W.
American Soc. of Anesthesiologists (106)

Connell, Karen
Internat'l Foodservice Brokers Ass'n/Ass'n of Sales & Marketing Companies (291)

Connelly, D. Barry
Associated Credit Bureaus (171)

Connelly, David
Open Applications Group (448)

Connelly, Elizabeth
Nat'l Petroleum Refiners Ass'n (422)

Connelly, Patricia
American Geriatrics Soc. (71)

Conner, Charles F.
Corn Refiners Ass'n (209)

Conner, Eamon
Internat'l Ass'n of Amusement Parks and Attractions (275)

Conner III, James J.
Motor and Equipment Manufacturers Ass'n (330)
Heavy Duty Manfacturers Ass'n (253)
Heavy Duty Business Forum (253)

Conner, Jim H.
American Yarn Spinners Ass'n (124)

Conner, Len
Internat'l Union of Gospel Missions (310)

Conner P.E., Terence D.
American Soc. of Highway Engineers (110)

Connolly, Dawn
Nat'l Shoe Retailers Ass'n (428)

Connolly, Jerome
American Physical Therapy Ass'n (92)

Connolly Ph.D., Peg
Nat'l Council for Therapeutic Recreation Certification (393)

Connor, Mary
Fluid Power Distributors Ass'n (241)

Connor, Patricia J.
Ass'n of Public Data Users (162)

Connor, Phyllis
Soc. of Exploration Geophysicists (501)

Connors, Jerry C.
Manufactured Housing Institute (322)

Connors, John P.
American Hotel and Motel Ass'n (74)

Connors Cates, Lorraine
Nat'l Ass'n of REALTORS (369)

Conover, Dave
American Farm Bureau Federation (66)

Conrad, Dr. Horst
American Otological Soc. (90)

Conrad, Shawn
Internat'l Sleep Products Ass'n (302)

Conroy, Julia
Oxygenated Fuels Ass'n (452)

Conroy CAE, Kathy
Nat'l Wooden Pallet and Container Ass'n (437)

Conroy M.D., Robert M.
Nat'l Ass'n of VA Physicians and Dentists (379)

Constantino Ph.D., James
Intelligent Transportation Soc. of America (270)

Conte, Vincent
AOAC Internat'l (125)

Contessa, John J.
Soc. of Plastics Engineers (505)

Conticelli, Peter
American Cloak and Suit Manufacturers Ass'n (52)

Contiguglia, Dr. Bob
United States Soccer Federation (535)

Contney CAE, John J.
Textile Rental Services Ass'n of America (522)

Converse, James D.
Instrument Soc. of America (269)

Convey, Julian
Synthetic Amorphous Silica and Silicates Industry Ass'n (519)

Conway, Bryan
American Geriatrics Soc. (71)

Coodermuth, Ann Louis
Ass'n for Research in Nervous and Mental Disease (137)

Coogan, Lee
Sorptive Minerals Institute (510)

Cook, Barbara H.
Nat'l Ornamental and Miscellaneous Metals Ass'n (420)

Cook, Billy D.
Institute for Professionals in Taxation (265)

Cook, Brian
Coalition of Service Industries (196)

Cook, Carole E.
Screenprinting and Graphic Imaging Ass'n Internat'l (480)
Digital Printing and Imaging Ass'n (222)

Cook, Charleen
Justice Research and Statistics Ass'n (315)

Cook, Christina E.
Nat'l Orientation Directors Ass'n (420)

Cook, Darren
Nat'l Ass'n of Insurance Commissioners (360)

Cook, Edwin
Conference of Minority Public Administrators (204)

Cook, Gloria
American Oil Chemists' Soc. (88)

Cook, Harry N.
Nat'l Waterways Conference (436)

Cook, Jackie
Ass'n for Forming and Fabricating Technologies of SME (133)
Ass'n for Finishing Processes of SME (133)

Cook, Joan
Internat'l Sanitary Supply Ass'n (302)

Cook, Kristina C.
Nat'l Paint and Coatings Ass'n (420)

Cook, Nancy K.
Pet Food Institute (455)

Cook, Peter L.
Nat'l Ass'n of Water Companies (380)

Cook, Roger
Catholic Health Ass'n of the United States (188)

Cook CMP, Sara Ann
American Soc. of Naval Engineers (113)

Cook, Scott Noam
Soc. for Philosophy and Technology (492)

Cook, Suzanne
Travel Industry Ass'n of America (526)

Cook, Tom
Nat'l Renderers Ass'n (425)

Cook, Victoria
North American Soc. of Pacing and Electrophysiology (445)

Cooke, Gwendolyn
Nat'l Ass'n of Secondary School Principals (372)

Cooke, Phillip S.
Internat'l Inflight Food Service Ass'n (294)
Foodservice Consultants Soc. Internat'l (242)

Cooke, Robert
Nat'l Council of Exchangors (394)

Cooke, Susan
Internat'l Bluegrass Music Ass'n (283)
Cooksey, Cyndi
Nat'l Institute of Governmental Purchasing (412)
Cooley, Harriet
Towing and Recovery Ass'n of America (524)
Cooley CEAP, Joni Reed
Employee Assistance Professionals Ass'n (229)
Cooney, Brian
Manufactured Housing Institute (322)
Cooney, Dave
Soc. of Petroleum Engineers (505)
Cooney, Nelson J.
Brick Industry Ass'n (182)
Cooper, Benjamin S.
Ass'n of Oil Pipe Lines (158)
Cooper, Benjamin Y.
Printing Industries of America (463)
Cooper, Jan
Nat'l Verbatim Reporters Ass'n (435)
Cooper, Michelle
Nat'l Ass'n of Dental Assistants (352)
Cooper, Monique
American Ass'n of Family and Consumer Sciences (36)
Cooper, Nancy
Nat'l Ass'n of Decorative Fabric Distributors (352)
Cooper, Robert W.
American Federation of Astrologers (66)
Cooper, Roger
American Gas Ass'n (70)
Cooper, Sara
Nat'l Consumers League (392)
Cooper, Terence
Nat'l Ass'n of Housing and Redevelopment Officials (358)
Cooper, Thomas
American Academy of Neurology (23)
Cooper, Valerie
Nat'l Viatical Ass'n (435)
Cooper, Yvonne
Nat'l Newspaper Publishers Ass'n (418)
Cooperman, Bruce
New York Board of Trade (438)
Cooperman, Richard M.
Independent Zinc Alloyers Ass'n (262)
Coorsh, Richard
Health Insurance Ass'n of America (252)
Copan, Jay
American Gas Ass'n (70)
Cope, James D.
Nonprescription Drug Manufacturers Ass'n (440)
Copeland, Daniel H.
Bridge Grid Flooring Manufacturers Ass'n (182)
Copeland, J. Joseph
Nat'l AMBUCS (336)
Copeland, Tamara Lucas
Nat'l Ass'n of Child Advocates (347)
Copess, Joyce Travis
Institute of Real Estate Management (269)
Copland, Ben
North American Elk Breeders Ass'n (442)
Coppola, Adrienne
Hobby Industry Ass'n of America (255)
Copsey, George F.
Aerospace Industries Ass'n of America (13)
Coral, Lenore
Internat'l Ass'n of Music Libraries, United States Branch (281)
Corbiere, Gail
Ass'n of Certified Professional Secretaries (146)
Corcoran, Diana
American Soc. of Sanitary Engineering (116)
Corcoran, Jim
Nat'l Confectioners Ass'n of the United States (389)
Corcoran, Kate E.
Medical Library Ass'n (326)
Corcoran, Kevin
Nat'l Ass'n of Health Underwriters (357)
Cordaro, John B.
Council for Responsible Nutrition (212)
Cordes, Anne M.
American Ass'n of Legal Nurse Consultants (38)
Ass'n of Rehabilitation Nurses (163)
Cordova, Brenda
U.S. Apple Ass'n (528)
Core, David L.
Steel Shipping Container Institute (517)
Corelitz, Dick
Carpet and Rug Institute (187)
Corkum, Lynda
North American Benthological Soc. (440)
Corliss, Carla
Mail Advertising Service Ass'n Internat'l (322)

Cormany, Dennis
Promotional Products Ass'n Internat'l (468)
Cormier, Anita
Respiratory Nursing Soc. (475)
Cornell, Elisabeth
Nat'l Account Management Ass'n (334)
Cornell, Faye M.
Internat'l Ass'n of Career Consulting Firms (277)
Corner, Richard M.
Internat'l Advertising Ass'n (272)
Corngold, Sally Marshall
Optometric Editors Ass'n (449)
Cornish, Edward S.
World Future Soc. (550)
Cornutt, Deborah
Internat'l Military Community Executives Ass'n (297)
Corr, Peter
Textile Rental Services Ass'n of America (522)
Corson, Harvey J.
Convention of American Instructors of the Deaf (208)
Cortina, Tom
Halon Alternatives Research Corp. (251)
Corwin, Michael
Nat'l Recreation and Park Ass'n (424)
Cosby NAFC, Bonnie E.
American Trucking Ass'ns (121)
Cosner, Sandy
Nat'l Chimney Sweep Guild (386)
Costa, Angela
Home Office Ass'n of America (255)
Costello, David A.
Nat'l Ass'n of State Boards of Accountancy (374)
Costello, Susan
Academy of Family Mediators (8)
Costen, Thomas
Pulp, Paper and Paperboard Export Ass'n of the U.S. (470)
Costopoulos, Nancy
American Marketing Ass'n (82)
Cote, Arthur E.
Nat'l Fire Protection Ass'n (404)
Cote, Melville P.
Soc. for Human Ecology (489)
Cote, Mari
Nat'l Conference of States on Building Codes and
Standards (391)
Cote-Schmader, Robyn
Brazilian Studies Ass'n (182)
Coticchio, Jean S.
Nat'l Ass'n of Catalog Showroom Merchandisers (346)
Cotter, David
Textile Care Allied Trades Ass'n (522)
Cottew, Bruce
Billiard Congress of America (178)
Cotton, Richard
American Council on Exercise (62)
Cotton, Todd M.
Nat'l Intramural-Recreational Sports Ass'n (413)
Cottone, Donna
Motion Picture and Television Credit Ass'n (330)
Cottrell, Nina
Residential Sales Council (475)
Coughlan CAE, William D.
Nat'l Ass'n for Medical Equipment Services (340)
Coughlin, Ed
Nat'l Milk Producers Federation (417)
Coughlin, Jeff
Ass'n of Professors of Medicine (162)
Coulter, Sally
Construction Owners Ass'n of America (207)
Councilor, James A.
Chemical Specialties Manufacturers Ass'n (191)
Countee, Thomas
Nat'l Spinal Cord Injury Ass'n (431)
Counter III, Nicholas
Alliance of Motion Picture and Television Producers (18)
Coursen, Dr. Cynthia L.
American Veterinary Medical Ass'n (121)
Coursey, Allan
Internat'l Graphological Soc. (292)
Courtney, Susan
Nat'l Ass'n of Boards of Examiners of Long Term Care
Administrators (345)
Courtney, Susan L.
American Consulting Engineers Council (60)
Cousens, Bonnie
Soc. for Humanistic Judaism (489)
Cousin, Kenya
COLA (196)
Coutellier, Connie
American Camping Ass'n (50)

Couto, Drew J.
Thoroughbred Owners and Breeders Ass'n (523)
Couts, Rodney J.
Nat'l Vehicle Leasing Ass'n (435)
Couture, Gerry
Soc. of Incentive and Travel Executives (502)
Couture, Maxine Lee
Food Equipment Manufacturers Ass'n (241)
North American Ass'n of Food Equipment
Manufacturers (440)
Couture, Susan
American College of Foot and Ankle Surgeons (54)
Covall, Mark J.
Nat'l Ass'n of Psychiatric Health Systems (367)
Cove, Bryan
Commercial Finance Ass'n (199)
Cover CAE, Eva
IBFI, The Internat'l Ass'n for Document and Information
Management Solutions (257)
Covert, Marty
Nat'l Renderers Ass'n (425)
Covey, Bill
Nat'l Ass'n of Photo Equipment Technicians (365)
Covey, William
Photo Marketing Ass'n-Internat'l (457)
Covington, Calvin
American Jersey Cattle Ass'n (79)
Cowan, Anne
Cable Telecommunications Ass'n (185)
Cowan CPA, Robert T.
American Ass'n of Neurological Surgeons (39)
Cowart, Vicki J.
Ass'n of American State Geologists (143)
Cowden, Richard
American Ass'n of Enterprise Zones (36)
Cowen, Pamela A.P.
Nat'l Ass'n of Private Schools for Exceptional Children (366)
Cowper D.D.S., Thomas
American Academy of Maxillofacial Prosthetics (23)
Cox, Angie
North American Elk Breeders Ass'n (442)
Cox CAE, Ann R.
American Ass'n of Occupational Health Nurses (40)
Cox, Charles
Soc. of Risk Management Consultants (507)
Cox, Craig
Soil and Water Conservation Soc. (510)
Cox, Joanne B.
American Frozen Food Institute (69)
Cox CAE, John B.
American Ass'n of Pharmaceutical Scientists (40)
Cox, Joseph J.
Chamber of Shipping of America (190)
Cox, Laquita
American Academy of Esthetic Dentistry (22)
Cox, Marguerite A.
Bankers Roundtable, The (176)
Cox, Philip H.
Internat'l Ass'n of Electrical Inspectors (278)
Cox, Robert L.
Internat'l Communication Ass'n (286)
Coyle, James F.
Public Risk Management Ass'n (470)
Coyne, James K.
Nat'l Air Transportation Ass'n (335)
Coyne Ph.D., Leslie J.
Ass'n of University Summer Sessions (169)
Cozzoli, Thomas
Design-Build Manufacturers Ass'n (222)
Crabb, Connie
Nat'l Funeral Directors Ass'n (406)
Crabtree, Nick
Internat'l Ass'n of Diecutting and Diemaking (278)
Craft, Edward M.
Battery Council Internat'l (177)
Craft, Lorie
Nat'l Perinatal Ass'n (422)
Craft, Loyce
Infectious Diseases Soc. of America (263)
Crahan, Therese
American Institute of Architects (76)
Craib, Donald F.
Soc. for American Archaeology (485)
Craig, Anita
AACSB - the Internat'l Ass'n for Management Education (7)
Craig, Elizabeth L.
Nat'l Prison Hospice Ass'n (423)
Craig, Rick
Owner-Operator Independent Drivers Ass'n (452)
Craigg, Dr. Gordon
American Soc. of Pharmacognosy (114)

Craigie, Mary
Employee Assistance Professionals Ass'n **(229)**

Crain, Greg
Nat'l Taxidermists Ass'n **(433)**

Craine, Kimber
Nat'l Assembly of State Arts Agencies **(381)**

Cram, Marcia
Financial Women Internat'l **(239)**

Cramer, Elizabeth
College of American Pathologists **(197)**

Cramer CAE, Pamela M.
College of American Pathologists **(197)**

Crampton, Lewis S.W.
American Medical Ass'n **(83)**

Crampton, Patricia
Cranial Academy **(218)**

Cran, Marsha
Cable and Telecommunications Ass'n for Marketing **(185)**

Crandall, Derrick A.
American Recreation Coalition **(97)**

Crane, Angus
North American Insulation Manufacturers Ass'n **(442)**

Crane, Lori
Internat'l Sanitary Supply Ass'n **(302)**

Crane, Sarrae
United Synagogue of Conservative Judaism **(536)**

Crane, Stacey L.
Municipal Treasurers Ass'n of the United States and Canada **(331)**

Crane, Steven C.
American Academy of Physician Assistants **(25)**

Cranford, Sharon H.
Nat'l Ass'n of Enrolled Agents **(354)**

Crank, Amy
American Counseling Ass'n **(62)**

Cranney Jr., James R.
U.S. Apple Ass'n **(528)**

Crassweller, Dr. Robert M.
American Pomological Soc. **(93)**

Crawford, Carol
Nat'l Conference of Black Mayors **(389)**

Crawford, Christopher L.
Nat'l Ass'n of Development Companies **(352)**

Crawford, Debra
Nat'l Ass'n of Resident Management Corporations **(370)**

Crawford, Diane C.
Nat'l Phlebotomy Ass'n **(422)**

Crawford, Gregory L.
Steel Recycling Institute **(516)**

Crawford Jr., CAE, John M.
Screenprinting and Graphic Imaging Ass'n Internat'l **(480)**

Creamer, Brian
Ass'n for Ambulatory Behavioral Healthcare **(129)**

Creamer, Jack
Automotive Warehouse Distributors Ass'n **(175)**

Crear, Pete
Credit Union Nat'l Ass'n **(218)**

Creeden, W.M.
Internat'l Brotherhood of Boilermakers, Iron Ship Builders, Blacksmiths, Forgers and Helpers **(284)**

Creighton, Richard C.
American Portland Cement Alliance **(93)**

Crerar, Ken
Council of Insurance Company Executives **(214)**

Crerar, Ken A.
Council of Insurance Agents and Brokers **(214)**

Creson, Emily
American Countertrade Ass'n **(62)**

Crespo, Paul L.
United States-Cuba Business Council **(536)**

Crews, MaryAnn S.
Nat'l Drilling Ass'n **(400)**
Nat'l Ass'n of Decorative Fabric Distributors **(352)**

Crisali, Karen
Guild of Book Workers **(250)**

Crisco CHR, Kelly R.
Internat'l Home Furnishings Representatives Ass'n **(293)**

Crispin, Rosalie A.
Cancer Biotherapy Research Group **(186)**

Criss, Katherine
Professional Women Photographers **(467)**

Crist, Jennifer
Nat'l Ass'n of Neonatal Nurses **(363)**

Crist, Katrina
American Soc. of Transplant Surgeons **(116)**

Cristan, Sue
Organic Growers and Buyers Ass'n **(449)**

Cristol, Richard E.
Ass'n for Dressings and Sauces. **(132)**
Nat'l Ass'n of Margarine Manufacturers **(362)**
Nat'l Institute of Oilseed Products **(412)**

Critchlow, Charles H.
American-European Soda Ash Shipping Ass'n **(124)**

Crittenden, Sherry
Outdoor Advertising Ass'n of America **(451)**

Croce, Ginger D.
American Bus Ass'n **(49)**

Crochett, Teressa
American Academy of Head, Neck and Facial Pain **(22)**

Crocker, Cary
Nat'l Agricultural Aviation Ass'n **(335)**

Crocker, Edwin L.
Ass'n of American Medical Colleges **(142)**

Cromartie, Eugene R.
Internat'l Ass'n of Chiefs of Police **(277)**

Crombie, Stephanie
Internat'l Ass'n for Human Resource Information Management **(274)**

Cromie, William J.
Soc. for Pediatric Urology **(492)**

Cronce, Richard
Holstein Ass'n USA **(255)**

Crone, Bebe C.
North American Ass'n of State and Provincial Lotteries **(440)**

Cronin, Carla H.
Institute of Internat'l Finance **(267)**

Cronin, Jim
Internat'l Radio and Television Soc. Foundation **(301)**

Cronin, John
Professional Ass'n of Diving Instructors **(464)**

Cronin, Kevin
Internat'l Ass'n of Insurance Supervisors **(280)**

Cronin, Michael
American Soc. of Naval Engineers **(113)**

Cronwall, James
Internat'l Ass'n of Defense Counsel **(278)**

Crook, Stephen
American Printing History Ass'n **(94)**

Cropper, Cabell C.
Nat'l Criminal Justice Ass'n **(398)**

Crosby, John
American Osteopathic Ass'n **(89)**

Crosby IV, John H.
Special Libraries Ass'n **(514)**

Crosby, Mark E.
Land Mobile Communications Council **(317)**
Industrial Telecommunications Ass'n **(263)**

Crosby, Mary
American Academy of Child and Adolescent Psychiatry **(20)**

Crosby, Miriam
American Peanut Shellers Ass'n **(91)**

Crosby, Roberta
Tobacco Merchants Ass'n of the U.S. **(524)**

Croser, M. Doreen
American Ass'n on Mental Retardation **(45)**

Crosland, Page
United States Tennis Ass'n **(535)**

Crosland, Philip
American Soc. of Composers, Authors and Publishers **(108)**

Croson, Matt
Packaging Machinery Manufacturers Institute **(452)**

Cross, Christopher T.
Council for Basic Education **(211)**

Cross, Joette
Soc. for Mining, Metallurgy, and Exploration **(491)**

Cross, S. Lorraine
Interstate Natural Gas Ass'n of America **(311)**

Cross, Susan
Nat'l Ass'n of Concessionaires **(349)**

Crossland, Carol
Nat'l Arborist Ass'n **(337)**

Crouch, Lori
Education Writers Ass'n **(226)**

Crouch, Madeleine
Academic Language Therapy Ass'n **(7)**
Internat'l Soc. of Bassists **(305)**
Retail Print Music Dealers Ass'n **(476)**
Nat'l Ass'n of School Music Dealers **(371)**

Crouch, Toni
American Soc. of Ass'n Executives **(107)**

Crouse, Dr. Barry
Institute of Paper Science and Technology **(268)**

Crouse, Cynthia C.
Internat'l Ass'n of Diecutting and Diemaking **(278)**

Crouse, Jeff
Nat'l Ass'n of Alcoholism and Drug Abuse Counselors **(343)**

Crouse, Rick
American Forests **(69)**

Crowe, Alan H.
Nat'l Ass'n of Professional Process Servers **(367)**

Crowe, Johnna
American Ambulance Ass'n **(28)**

Crowe, Tom
Soc. of Telecommunications Consultants **(507)**

Crowley, James M.
Soc. for Industrial and Applied Mathematics **(489)**

Crowley, Mark J.
Soc. of Industrial and Office REALTORS **(503)**

Crowson, Cathy
Nat'l Soc. of Hispanic MBAs **(430)**

Crowthor, Connie
Internat'l Air Cargo Ass'n **(272)**

Croy, Donna
Nat'l Ass'n of Alcoholism and Drug Abuse Counselors **(343)**

Croy, Richard S.
Internat'l Oxygen Manufacturers Ass'n **(299)**

Cruel, Doris J.
Nat'l Ass'n of State Boards of Education **(374)**

Crum Ph.D., John K.
American Chemical Soc. **(51)**

Crump CMP, CAE, John L.
Nat'l Bar Ass'n **(382)**

Crumpton CPA, Diana J.
Nat'l Ass'n of Hose and Accessories Distributors **(358)**

Crumpton, CPA, Diana J.
Independent Sealing Distributors **(261)**

Crutchfield, Sam S.
Phi Delta Phi **(457)**

Cryer MD, PhD, H. Gill
American Ass'n for the Surgery of Trauma **(32)**

Crystal D.D.S., David
American Soc. for the Advancement of Anesthesia in Dentistry **(105)**

Cudahy, James M.
Internat'l Communications Industries Ass'n **(286)**

Cudahy, John
Internat'l Council of Air Shows **(287)**

Cuervo, Asela M.
Nat'l Ass'n for Medical Equipment Services **(340)**

Cuff, Kevin M.
American Venous Forum **(121)**
Soc. for Clinical Vascular Surgery **(486)**
American Pediatric Surgical Ass'n **(91)**
Ass'n for Academic Surgery **(129)**
Soc. for Vascular Medicine and Biology **(496)**

Culburn, Barbara
Yacht Architects and Brokers Ass'n **(551)**

Culkin Jr., CGFM, Charles W.
Ass'n of Government Accountants **(152)**

Culkin CIC, CAE, Douglas S.
Nat'l Ass'n of Professional Insurance Agents **(367)**

Cullen, David
Nat'l Federation of Independent Business **(403)**

Cullen, Frank
Overseas Sales and Marketing Ass'n of America **(452)**

Culleton, Edward
Green Olive Trade Ass'n **(249)**

Cullinan, Christina M.
American Insurance Ass'n **(79)**

Culpepper, R. Lee
Nat'l Restaurant Ass'n **(425)**

Cultar, Kelly
Information Technology Ass'n of America **(264)**

Culver, Anne
Professional Aviation Maintenance Ass'n **(464)**

Culver, James
Internat'l Ass'n of Assessing Officers **(276)**

Culver, Dr. Virgil P.
Food Distribution Research Soc. **(241)**

Cumberland, William E.
Mortgage Bankers Ass'n of America **(330)**

Cumming, Charles S.
Nat'l Cargo Bureau **(385)**

Cummings, Kenneth C.
American College of Physician Executives **(57)**

Cummings, Dr. W.D.
Universities Space Research Ass'n **(536)**

Cummins, Cheryl
Urban Land Institute **(537)**

Cummins, Tracy L.
Nat'l Energy Services Ass'n **(401)**

Cummnins, Gloria
Hispanic Ass'n of Colleges and Universities **(254)**

Cunard, Manuel R.
Nat'l Ass'n of College Auxiliary Services **(348)**

Cuneo, Garrett F.
American Chiropractic Ass'n **(51)**

Cuneo Jr., John F.
Nat'l Congress of Animal Trainers and Breeders **(391)**

Cuneo, Kelley
American College of Managed Care Medicine **(55)**

Cunix, Nadine
American Ass'n of Diabetes Educators **(36)**

Cunningham, Daniel A.
Smart Card Industry Ass'n (484)

Cunningham, Gregory
Construction Specifications Institute (207)

Cunningham, Kelley
Nat'l Ass'n of College Broadcasters (348)

Cunningham, Krista
Internat'l Ass'n of Administrative Professionals (275)

Cunningham, Laurel
Nat'l Turkey Federation (435)

Cunningham, Linda H.
American Council of Life Insurance (61)

Cunningham, Mary
Internat'l Swaps and Derivatives Ass'n (308)

Cunningham, Michael
Soc. of Urologic Nurses and Associates (508)

Cunningham, Ray
Institute of Paper Science and Technology (268)

Cunzman, Cindy K.
American Ass'n of Electrodiagnostic Medicine (36)

Curlee, Jesse W.
Supima Ass'n of America (518)

Curran, Frank P.
Treasury Management Ass'n (526)

Curran, Sullivan D.
Fiberglass Tank and Pipe Institute (238)

Currey, Mary E.
Child Neurology Soc. (192)

Currie, Bobbie
American Institute of Building Design (76)

Currie S.J., Charles L.
Ass'n of Jesuit Colleges and Universities (155)

Curry, Diane S.
Transportation . Communications Internat'l Union (525)

Curry, John J.
American College of Radiology (57)

Curry, Serena R.
Ass'n of Academic Health Centers (141)

Curry, Sheila
Mass Marketing Insurance Institute (324)

Curtis, Bobbie
Materials Handling and Management Soc. (325)

Curtis, Douglas
American Traffic Safety Services Ass'n (120)

Curtis, Eugene C.
Ass'n of Professional Material Handling Consultants (161)

Curtis, Jody
Council on Foundations (216)

Curtis, Kerry L.
American Water Resources Ass'n (122)

Curtis, Laura
Plumbing-Heating-Cooling Contractors - Nat'l Ass'n (459)

Curtis, Millie
Intersure, Ltd. (312)

Curtis, Patrick
Child Welfare League of America (192)

Curtis, Robert
Tobacco Industry Labor/Management Committee (523)

Curto, Mary Ellen
Nat'l Family Caregivers Ass'n (402)

Cusack, Ryda Ruth
Valve Manufacturers Ass'n of America (538)

Cushman, Charles S.
American Land Rights Ass'n (80)

Cussick CPA, Joseph P.
Public Relations Soc. of America (470)

Cuthbertson, Bruce
Flexible Intermediate Bulk Container Ass'n (240)

Cutick, Lisa
Greek Food and Wine Institute (249)

Cutler J.D., Jay B.
American Psychiatric Ass'n (94)

Cutrona, Joseph F.H.
Nat'l Small Shipments Traffic Conference (428)

Cutting, Vickie B.
American Soc. for Eighteenth-Century Studies (102)

Cutts, Sandra
Ass'n of State and Territorial Health Officials (166)

Cyr, Lorraine
Nat'l Ass'n of Child Care Resource and Referral Agencies (347)

Cyros, Kreon L.
Internat'l Soc. of Facilities Executives (306)

Czaplewski Ph.D., Mary Jo
Nat'l Council on Family Relations (397)

Czarnecki, Mark T.
Benchmarking Network Ass'n (178)

D'Agostino, Maureen
Nat'l Ass'n of Pharmaceutical Manufacturers (365)

D'Agostino, Melissa
American Soc. of Clinical Psychopharmacology (108)

D'Ambrosi, Dean
Nat'l Ass'n of Printers and Lithographers (366)

D'Amelio, Patsy
Employee Benefit Research Institute (229)

D'Amore Ph.D., Michael
North American Catalysis Soc. (441)

D'Andrea, Susanne
Ass'n of Youth Museums (170)

D'Angelo, Cynthia
Nat'l Ass'n of College Stores (348)

D'Aniello, Charles A.
Ass'n for the Bibliography of History (139)

D'Antonio, Lorraine
Religious Research Ass'n (474)

D'Argo, Pam
Soc. of Vertebrate Paleontology (509)

D'Arms, John H.
American Council of Learned Societies (61)

D'Eramo, Paul N.
Internat'l Soc. for Pharmaceutical Engineering (304)

D'Onofrio, David
Nat'l Small Business United (428)

D'Onofrio, Steve
Recording Industry Ass'n of America (472)

D'Souza, Henry J.
Helicopter Ass'n Internat'l (253)

Dabrowski, Kari
American Ass'n of Ambulatory Surgery Centers (33)

Daggett Manner, Sharon
Nat'l Ass'n of Educational Office Professionals (353)

Dahan, Karla
Institute for Interconnecting and Packaging Electronic Circuits (265)

Dahl, Roger E.
Nat'l Public Employer Labor Relations Ass'n (424)

Dahlberg, Kristine
Social Science Research Council (509)

Dahlgren, Jenna
Wireless Communications Ass'n Internat'l (545)

Dahm, Ena
Council of Planning Librarians (215)

Dahne, Werner
CIES, The Food Business Forum (193)

Daigler, Steve
Soc. of American Florists (497)

Daignault, Thomas
Manufacturing Jewelers and Suppliers of America (323)

Dale, James R.
Metal Powder Industries Federation (327)

Dale, Mert
Internat'l Manufacturers Representatives Ass'n (296)

Daley CMP, Darline
American Water Works Ass'n (122)

Daley, Dema C.
Ass'n of Program Directors in Internal Medicine (162)

Daley, Gabriella M.
American Correctional Ass'n (60)

Dalheim, Mary
Council for Advancement and Support of Education (210)

Dallara, Charles H.
Institute of Internat'l Finance (267)

Dallas, Anita R.
Painting and Decorating Contractors of America (452)

Daly, H. Hope
American Mathematical Soc. (83)

Daly, Julia Stewart
U.S. Apple Ass'n (528)

Daly, Sharon
Catholic Charities USA (188)

Daly, William
Nat'l Hockey League (409)

Dalzell CLU, CAE, Bruce C.
LOMA (321)
Life Insurers Council (319)

Dalziel, Christine
Instructional Telecommunications Council (269)

Dalziel, Penny
Ass'n of University Technology Managers (169)

Daman, Bob
Nat'l Computer Security Ass'n (389)

Damazio, Kristen F.
Nat'l Potato Council (423)

Dambach, Charles F.
Museum Trustee Ass'n (332)

Dameron, Patricia S.
Nat'l Ass'n of Federal Credit Unions (355)

Damgard, John M.
Futures Industry Ass'n (245)

Dammrich, Thomas J.
Institute for Interconnecting and Packaging Electronic Circuits (265)

Damon, Christopher
Soc. for Ambulatory Care Professionals (485)

Damron, Terry
Emerald Green Miniature Golf Ass'n (229)

Damsky, Kenneth
Cabletelevision Advertising Bureau (185)

Dana, Kitty Hsu
American Public Health Ass'n (95)

Dana, Nazie
Soc. for Environmental Graphic Design (487)

Dane Ph.D., Francis C.
Soc. for the Advancement of Social Psychology (494)

Dangott, Donald E.
Nat'l Ass'n of Relay Manufacturers (370)

Daniel, Bryan
Nat'l Council for Agricultural Education (393)

Daniel, J. Todd
Nat'l Ornamental and Miscellaneous Metals Ass'n (420)

Daniel, Rod
Soc. of Depreciation Professionals (500)
Nat'l Ass'n for Drama Therapy (339)

Daniels, John Y.
American Ass'n of Textile Chemists and Colorists (44)

Daniels CSP, Larry
Nat'l Ass'n of College Stores (348)

Daniels CAE, Lisa
Ass'n for Accounting Marketing (129)
Ass'n for Psychological Type (137)

Daniels, Marcia C.
Precision Metalforming Ass'n (462)

Daniels, Margery Berg
Internat'l Soc. for Third-Sector Research (305)

Daniels, Robert E.
Tile Council of America (523)

Danielson, Crystal
Nat'l Panhellenic Conference (421)

Danker, Susan L.
Hobby Industry Ass'n of America (255)

Dankmeyer, Todd
Nat'l Community Pharmacists Ass'n (388)

Danner, Donald
Nat'l Federation of Independent Business (403)

Darakhan, Phetsamone
Nat'l Ass'n of Self-Instructional Language Programs (372)

Darazsdi, James
Nat'l Ass'n of Corporate Directors (350)

Darden, Charles F.
Internat'l Ass'n of Geophysical Contractors (279)

Darden, Michelle
Nat'l Black Chamber of Commerce (383)

Darmohraj, Andrew
American Pet Products Manufacturers Ass'n (91)

Darr, Carol
Interactive Digital Software Ass'n (271)

Darr, Linda
American Trucking Ass'ns (121)

Darrow, Alan
Nat'l Air Transportation Ass'n (335)

Darst, B.C.
Potash and Phosphate Institute (461)

Das, Man Singh
Internat'l Ass'n of Family Sociology (279)

Daschler, John P.
Internat'l Foodservice Manufacturers Ass'n (291)

Dassler, A. Fred
Internat'l Ass'n of Satellite Users and Suppliers (282)

Datema, William H.
Soc. of State Directors of Health, Physical Education and Recreation (507)

Dathorne Ph.D., O.R.
Ass'n of Caribbean Studies (146)

Daugherty, Carley
American White/American Creme Horse Registry (123)

Daughtry Ph.D., Lillian H.
American Vocational Education Personnel Development Ass'n (122)

Daulaire, Dr. Nils
Global Health Council (248)

Daulong, Renee
Ass'n of Independent Information Professionals (153)

Daum, Steve S.
Soc. of Automotive Engineers International (498)

Davenport, Cynthia A.
Ass'n of Specialized and Professional Accreditors (165)

Davey, Tara
Council of Hotel and Restaurant Trainers (214)

David, Dawny
Jewish Teachers Ass'n-Morim (314)

Davidge, Catherine
American Soc. of Addiction Medicine (106)

Davids, Susan
Nat'l Council of State Boards of Nursing (396)

Davidshofer, Charles
Ass'n for University and College Counseling Center Directors **(140)**

Davidson, Anna T.
Soc. for the Scientific Study of Religion **(495)**

Davidson Ph.D., Dan E.
American Council of Teachers of Russian **(61)**

Davidson, Daryl
Ass'n for Unmanned Vehicle Systems Internat'l **(140)**

Davidson Jr., Donald M.
Geological Soc. of America **(246)**

Davidson, Glenn K.
Computer and Communications Industry Ass'n **(202)**

Davidson, Jack W.
Cedar Shake and Shingle Bureau **(188)**

Davidson, Joel P.
Hospital Presidents Ass'n **(256)**

Davidson, June
American Seminar Leaders Ass'n **(99)**

Davidson, Kathy
Undersea and Hyperbaric Medical Soc. **(529)**

Davidson, Dr. Keith
Xplorer Internat'l **(551)**

Davidson, Richard J.
American Hospital Ass'n **(74)**

Davidson, Sandy
American Soc. for Industrial Security **(103)**

Davidson, Suzanne
Xplorer Internat'l **(551)**

Davie, Karen A.
Nat'l Hospice Organization **(409)**

Davies, Barbara
Internat'l Waterlily and Watergardening Soc. **(310)**

Davies, Garth H.
Internat'l Air Cargo Ass'n **(272)**

Davila, Antonio
Nat'l Ass'n of State Directors of Veterans Affairs **(375)**

Davis, Alan
Nat'l Ass'n for Campus Activities **(338)**

Davis, Anne McDonald
Associated Locksmiths of America **(171)**

Davis, Bill
American Anthropological Ass'n **(28)**

Davis, Bruce
Academy of Motion Picture Arts and Sciences **(9)**

Davis, Carol H.
Nat'l Ass'n of Bankruptcy Trustees **(344)**
Academy of Dispensing Audiologists **(8)**

Davis, D. Christopher
World Floor Covering Ass'n **(549)**

Davis, Dana
Radiological Soc. of North America **(471)**

Davis, Doreen
American Ass'n of Psychiatric Administrators **(42)**

Davis, Drew M.
Nat'l Soft Drink Ass'n **(430)**

Davis, E.E. ""Gene"
School Management Study Group **(479)**

Davis Ph.D., Edward L.
Distributive Education Clubs of America **(224)**

Davis, Elizabeth
APICS - The Educational Society for Resource Management **(125)**

Davis, Dr. Gary S.
North American Gamebird Ass'n **(442)**

Davis, Gerald E.
Mine Inspectors' Institute of America **(329)**

Davis, Harriet
American Soc. of Appraisers **(106)**

Davis, James E.
American Soc. of Civil Engineers **(108)**

Davis, Jim
Nat'l Ground Water Ass'n **(407)**

Davis, John
Nat'l Kidney Foundation **(414)**

Davis Ph.D., John M.
Internat'l Council of Psychologists **(288)**

Davis, Kathie
IDEA, The Health and Fitness Source **(258)**

Davis, Kim
American Soc. of Transplant Physicians **(116)**

Davis, Larry
Nat'l Ass'n of Leagues, Umpires and Scorers **(361)**

Davis, Lois
Nat'l Community Pharmacists Ass'n **(388)**

Davis, Lou Ann
Nat'l Independent Automobile Dealers Ass'n **(410)**

Davis, Lucille
Foodservice and Packaging Institute **(242)**

Davis, Maggie
Internat'l Radio and Television Soc. Foundation **(301)**

Davis, Matthew
Internat'l Soc. for Performance Improvement **(304)**

Davis, Michael G.
American Alliance for Health, Physical Education, Recreation and Dance **(27)**

Davis, Michael P.
American Malting Barley Ass'n **(82)**

Davis, Nancy H.
Turnaround Management Ass'n **(528)**

Davis, Pamela J.
Internat'l Cemetery and Funeral Ass'n **(285)**

Davis, Patrick A.
Food Marketing Institute **(241)**

Davis, Peter
IDEA, The Health and Fitness Source **(258)**

Davis, R. Richard
Congress of Independent Unions **(205)**

Davis M.D., Ramona
Black Psychiatrists of America **(180)**

Davis, Randall P.
Internat'l Ass'n of Amusement Parks and Attractions **(275)**

Davis, Richard
American Council for Southern Asian Art **(61)**

Davis, Robert
Internat'l Bridge, Tunnel and Turnpike Ass'n **(284)**
America's Community Bankers **(20)**

Davis, Robert E.
Air Movement and Control Ass'n Internat'l **(16)**

Davis, Steve
Ass'n of Database Developers **(149)**

Davis, Sue
SPIE-Internat'l Soc. for Optical Engineering **(514)**

Davis, Tara
Soc. for Mining, Metallurgy, and Exploration **(491)**

Davis, Terry
American Ass'n for State and Local History **(32)**

Davis, Tonya
Nat'l Ass'n of Resident Management Corporations **(370)**

Davis, W. Steven
American Academy of Podiatric Practice Management **(25)**

Davis, William
Nat'l Organization of Minority Architects **(420)**

Davison, Wendy
Nat'l Private Truck Council **(423)**

Davitian, Leigh
American Soc. of Consultant Pharmacists **(108)**

Davoran, Penny
Nat'l Truck Leasing System **(434)**

Dawkins, Diana
Nat'l Ass'n of Black Accountants **(344)**

Dawson, Kathleen
Ass'n of Small Business Development Centers **(165)**

Dawson, Rhett B.
Information Technology Industry Council **(264)**

Day, Charles
American Soc. of Civil Engineers **(108)**

Day, David
Internat'l Facsimile Counsultative Council **(290)**

Day Jr., Frederick J.
Industrial Telecommunications Ass'n **(263)**

Day J.D., Robert D.
Renewable Natural Resources Foundation **(475)**

Day, Stacey
American Institute of Ultrasound in Medicine **(78)**

Dayton, Clinta
Screen Actors Guild **(480)**

Dayton, Sandy
American Traffic Safety Services Ass'n **(120)**

Dayton, Treva
Nat'l Federation Interscholastic Music Ass'n **(402)**
Nat'l Federation Interscholastic Speech and Debate Ass'n **(402)**

de Beaufort, Arnold W.
Independent Sector **(261)**

de Campos, Betsy
Alliance of Foam Packaging Recyclers **(18)**

De Groot, Janice
Internat'l Health, Racquet and Sportsclub Ass'n **(293)**

De Groot, Simon
Business Products Industry Ass'n **(185)**

De Jong, Kersen J.
Netherlands Chamber of Commerce in the United States **(438)**

De KoKoker, Neil
Original Equipment Suppliers Association - MEMA **(450)**

de la Paz, Minnie
Council for Advancement and Support of Education **(210)**

De La Riva, Patricia
Inter-American Bar Ass'n **(271)**

De Laurier CAE, Dr. Frank G.
American Welding Soc. **(123)**

De Luca, John A.
Wine Institute **(544)**

de Martinez, Julie Warner
American Chiropractic Ass'n **(51)**

De Persig, Mary
Painting and Decorating Contractors of America **(452)**

de Peyster, Julie
Ass'n of Managed Healthcare Organizations **(156)**

de Raat, Dayle
Travel Technology Ass'n **(526)**

DeAcetis, Judy
American Soc. of Tropical Medicine and Hygiene **(116)**

Deal, Lee Ann
North American Soc. of Adlerian Psychology **(445)**

Deal, Martha P.
Machinery Dealers Nat'l Ass'n **(321)**

Deale CAE, Charles W.L.
Nat'l Concrete Masonry Ass'n **(389)**

Dean, Anne
Independent Laboratory Distributors Ass'n **(261)**

Dean, Carol A.
Building Service Contractors Ass'n Internat'l **(183)**

Dean, Debra
Textile Rental Services Ass'n of America **(522)**

Dean Ph.D., Jeffrey S.
Tree-Ring Soc. **(526)**

Dean Ph.D., Stephen O.
Fusion Power Associates **(244)**

Dean, Virginia
American Bankers Ass'n **(46)**

Deane, Deborah J.
Nat'l Ass'n of Master Appraisers **(362)**
Nat'l Ass'n of Property Inspectors **(367)**
Accredited Review Appraisers Council **(10)**
American Soc. of Asset Managers **(107)**

Deane, Gary T.
Nat'l Soc. of Appraiser Specialists **(429)**
Nat'l Soc. of Environmental Consultants **(429)**

Deane Ph.D., Marvin T.
Nat'l Ass'n of Property Inspectors **(367)**
Nat'l Ass'n of Master Appraisers **(362)**
Nat'l Ass'n of Counselors **(350)**

DeAngelis, Donna
American Ass'n of State Social Work Boards **(43)**

DeAngelis, Francesco
Italy-America Chamber of Commerce **(313)**

DeAngelo, Lisa Joy
Soc. of Certified Insurance Counselors **(499)**

DeAngelo, Raymond J.
Ass'n for Investment Management and Research **(135)**

Dearinger, Dr. David
Nat'l Academy Museum and School Fine Arts **(333)**

Dearstyne, Bruce W.
Nat'l Ass'n of Government Archives and Records Administrators **(356)**

Deatherage, Ann
Nat'l Institute of Governmental Purchasing **(412)**

Deatherage, Anne
Nat'l Institute of Governmental Purchasing **(412)**

Deaton, Reitzel
Nat'l Ass'n of Consumer Credit Administrators **(349)**

DeBoer, Jeffrey D.
Nat'l Realty Committee **(424)**

DeBolt CAE, Don J.
Internat'l Franchise Ass'n **(292)**

DeBow, Kay
Nat'l Black Chamber of Commerce **(383)**

DeBrunner, Charles L.
Nat'l Ass'n of Urban Critical Access Hospitals **(379)**

DeCaprio, Robert L.
Messenger Courier Ass'n of the Americas **(327)**

DeCelle, Arthur
Beer Institute **(177)**

deCerreno, Alison C.
New York Academy of Sciences **(438)**

DeCew, Prof. Judith
American Soc. for Political and Legal Philosophy **(104)**

DeCicco, Anne
Luggage and Leather Goods Manufacturers of America **(321)**

Decker, Carolyn Lee
American Ass'n of Colleges of Osteopathic Medicine **(34)**

Decker, Curtis R.
Nat'l Ass'n of Protection and Advocacy Systems **(367)**

Deckinger, Lance
Nat'l Ass'n of Leagues, Umpires and Scorers **(361)**

DeConcini, Barbara
American Academy of Religion **(26)**

Dee Ph.D., Norbert
Nat'l Petroleum Refiners Ass'n **(422)**

Deegan, John
Military Impacted Schools Ass'n **(328)**

Deeney, Kathy
Institute of Packaging Professionals **(268)**

Dees, Anne
American Industrial Hygiene Ass'n (75)

Defa, Rose
Executive Women Internat'l (233)

Deffner, Faithe
American Accordionists Ass'n (27)

deFilippis, Ellen R.
American Pharmaceutical Ass'n (91)

DeFiore Ph.D., Leonard
Nat'l Catholic Educational Ass'n (385)

DeFlorian, Terri A.
Orthopaedic Section - American Physical Therapy Ass'n (451)

DeForest CAE, Alice
American Academy of Periodontology (25)

Degen, Paula A.
Ass'n of Partners for Public Lands (159)

Degnon CAE, George K.
Internat'l Ass'n of Pediatric Laboratory Medicine (281)
Ass'n of Pediatric Program Directors (160)
Academy of Organizational and Occupational Psychiatry (9)
Ass'n of Christian Therapists (146)
American Academy for Physician and Patient (20)
American Psychosomatic Soc. (95)

Degnon, Laura
American Psychosomatic Soc. (95)

Degnon, Marge
Ambulatory Pediatric Ass'n (19)

DeGraaf, Rita K.
Conference of Consulting Actuaries (204)

DeHaemer, Michael J.
ASM Internat'l (128)

DeHaney, Debra
United States Conference of Mayors (533)

Deichler, William F.
Nat'l Ass'n of Professional Insurance Agents (367)

Deinhart, Gregg
American Coal Ash Ass'n (52)

DeJarnette, Jean
Soc. of Professors of Child and Adolescent Psychiatry (506)

Del Gandio, Frank
Internat'l Soc. of Air Safety Investigators (305)

Del Polito Ph.D., Gene A.
Advertising Mail Marketing Ass'n (12)

Del Valle, Casilda
Nat'l Minority Supplier Development Council (417)

Del Vecchio, Rick
Nat'l Precast Concrete Ass'n (423)

DeLancey, Patricia
Academy of Criminal Justice Sciences (8)

Delaney, Bill
Business Identity Council of America (184)

Delaney, Doug
Nat'l Ass'n of State Catholic Conference Directors (374)

Delaney, James
Nat'l Head Start Ass'n (408)

Delaney, Thomas J.
Professional Lawn Care Ass'n of America (466)

Delassandri, Ruth
Catholic Charities USA (188)

DeLay, William R.
American Academy of Family Physicians (22)

Delea, Sarah
United Fresh Fruit and Vegetable Ass'n (531)

Delfay, Robert T.
Sporting Arms and Ammunition Manufacturers' Institute (515)
Nat'l Shooting Sports Foundation (428)

Delfosse, Mary Jo
Nat'l Ass'n of Tax Practitioners (377)

Delgadillo CAE, Linda M.
Soc. of Actuaries (496)

Delgado Ph.D., Jane L.
Nat'l Coalition of Hispanic Health and Human Services Organizations (387)

Deligiorgis, Maria
American Resort Development Ass'n (98)

Delinsky, Christine
United Ass'n of Equipment Leasing (530)

Dellario, Bernie
American Soc. of Ophthalmic Administrators (113)
American Soc. of Cataract and Refractive Surgery (107)

Delman, Farrell
Tobacco Merchants Ass'n of the U.S. (524)

Delmontagne, Regis J.
NPES, the Ass'n for Suppliers of Printing and Publishing Technologies (446)

Delollis, Kathy M.
Precision Metalforming Ass'n (462)

DeLong, Karen G.
American Public Health Ass'n (95)

DeLosada, Denise
Ass'n of University Professors of Ophthalmology (168)

DeLuca, Fred R.
American Institute of Architects (76)

DeLucia, Michael
Nat'l Ass'n of State Charity Officials (374)

DeLucia, Robert J.
Airline Industrial Relations Conference (16)

DeMarchi, Mari Z.
American Academy of Nurse Practitioners (23)

DeMarco, Kathleen A.
Fluid Power Distributors Ass'n (241)

Demas, Terrance
League of Historic American Theatres (318)

DeMasters, Carol
Ass'n of Food Journalists (151)

DeMatteo, Lisa
Ass'n of Women's Health, Obstetric and Neonatal Nurses (169)

DeMichiel, Helen
Nat'l Alliance for Media Arts and Culture (335)

Dempsey, Cedric
Nat'l Collegiate Athletic Ass'n (388)

Dempsey, Donna
Film and Bag Federation (238)

Dempsey, Donna M.
Internat'l Institute for Bio-Energetic Analysis (294)

Dempsey Jr., CAE, Frederick G.
American Fence Ass'n (67)

Dempsey, Kathleen
American Psychiatric Ass'n (94)

Dempsey & I, Kathleen
Nat'l Ass'n of Corporate Real Estate Executives International (350)

Dempsey, Kathy
American Ass'n of Code Enforcement (34)

Dempster DNSC, Judith S.
American Academy of Nurse Practitioners (23)

Denby, Stephen
Vocational Industrial Clubs of America (540)

Dendler, Carroll
Soc. of American Archivists (497)

Deneau, Gerald
Internat'l Allied Printing Trades Ass'n (273)

Denet, Sharon
American Council on the Teaching of Foreign Languages (62)

Denhardt, Paul
Soc. of American Fight Directors (497)

Denil, Jennifer
Dietary Managers Ass'n (222)

Denison, Carlette
Petroleum Equipment Institute (455)

Denman, E.B. Anne
American Council of Railroad Women (61)

Denne, Eileen E.
American Ass'n of Port Authorities (41)

Dennett, Diana
American Ass'n of Health Plans (37)

Dennis, Bill
Nat'l Meat Canners Ass'n (416)

Dennis, Karen
Paso Fino Horse Ass'n (453)

Denny, Steve
American Heart Ass'n (72)

Denston, Dan
Soc. for Occupational and Environmental Health (491)

Denston, Sue
Process Equipment Manufacturers' Ass'n (463)

Denston, Susan
American Textile Machinery Ass'n (119)

Denston, Susan A.
North American Natural Casing Ass'n (443)

Dento, Jan
American Arts Alliance (29)

Denton, Dan
American Holistic Medical Ass'n (73)

Denton, Dani
Institute of Paper Science and Technology (268)

Denton, Neal
Alliance of Nonprofit Mailers (18)

DePas CAE, Penney
Soc. of Financial Examiners (501)

Depoy, Martin
Nat'l Ass'n of Real Estate Investment Trusts (369)

DePriest, Darryl L.
American Bar Ass'n (46)

DePriest, R.N., Carol
Cancer Biotherapy Research Group (186)

Derchang, Peter
Ass'n of Operating Room Nurses (159)

DeRevere, David W.
Internat'l Conference of Police Chaplains (287)

Derks, Paula
Aircraft Electronics Ass'n (16)

Dernell, Gerry
Nat'l Ass'n of Pizza Operators (365)

DeRocco, Emily S.
Interstate Conference of Employment Security Agencies (311)

DeRossi, Guy
Nat'l Industries for the Blind (411)

Derouin, Cherie
Independent Pet and Animal Transportation Ass'n Internat'l (261)

Derovira, Kristy
Soc. for the Advancement of Food Service Research (494)

DeRoze, Virginia
Truckload Carriers Ass'n (527)

Derrickson, John P.
Nat'l Welding Supply Ass'n (436)

Dervaes, Claudine
Travel Professionals Ass'n (526)

DeSantis CMP, Kathy
Soc. of Urologic Cryosurgeons (508)

DeSapio, Joseph C.
Nat'l Multiple Sclerosis Soc. (418)

DeSarno, Judith M.
Nat'l Family Planning and Reproductive Health Ass'n (402)

Desautels, Mark
Cellular Telecommunications Industry Ass'n (189)
Wireless Data Forum (545)

Desmarais CAE, Maurice A.
American Supply Ass'n (119)

DesRoches, Debbie Brown
SnowSports Industries America (484)

Detert, Karen
Aircraft Owners and Pilots Ass'n (16)

Detweiler, J. Roger
Internat'l Ass'n of Personnel in Employment Security (281)

Deutsch, JoEllen
Ass'n of Flight Attendants (151)

Deutsch-Layne, Erika
American Soc. for Precision Engineering (104)

DeVaul, Chuck
Owner Operators of America (452)

Develen, Carolyn
North American Menopause Soc. (443)

Devereux, Rick
Internat'l Health, Racquet and Sportsclub Ass'n (293)

Deville, Mark
Naval Reserve Ass'n (438)

Devine, Danny
Employee Benefit Research Institute (229)

Devine, James R.
Chain Drug Marketing Ass'n (190)

Devine, John R.
Internat'l Institute of Municipal Clerks (294)

Devine, Michele
American Soc. for Information Science (103)

Devino, Kelli
Purebred Dairy Cattle Ass'n (470)

DeVita, William
Soc. of Cosmetic Chemists (500)

DeVito Ph.D., Albert
Keyboard Teachers Ass'n Internat'l (316)

DeVito, David
Nat'l Council of Nonprofit Ass'ns (395)

DeVlieg, Julie
American Karakul Sheep Registry (80)

DeVore CAE, Ronald M.
American Ass'n of Attorney-Certified Public Accountants (33)

DeVroomen, Jack
North American Flowerbulb Wholesalers Ass'n (442)

Dew, Allen
Nat'l Press Photographers Ass'n (423)

DeWall, Marily
Nat'l Science Teachers Ass'n (427)

Deweese, Charlotte
University Aviation Ass'n (537)

DeWeese, Kathy
AACE Internat'l (7)

Dewey, Dennis
Nat'l Assembly of State Arts Agencies (381)

Dewhirst, Mary
Ass'n of America's Public Television Stations (142)

DeWilde, Moira
American Academy of Otolaryngology-Head and Neck Surgery (24)

Dewit, Jack
Internat'l Wild Rice Ass'n (311)

DeWyngaert, Brian
American Federation of Government Employees (67)

Dextor, Roger
Copywriter's Council of America (209)

Deyo, Lisa Carol
Nat'l Private Truck Council (423)

Dhawan, Sunita K.
Soc. of Competitive Intelligence Professionals (500)

Dheez, Ruth
American Soc. for Nondestructive Testing (104)

Dhillon, Major S.
Soc. for Vector Ecology (496)

Di Liberto, John G.
Nat'l Insurance Crime Bureau (412)

Di Polvere, Edward J.
Nat'l Ass'n of Noise Control Officials (364)

Diamond, H.W.
Solution Mining Research Institute (510)

Diaz, Ana
Spain-U.S. Chamber of Commerce (511)

Diaz, Lionel W.
Manufacturers' Agents Nat'l Ass'n (323)

Diaz-Kay, Angela
Nat'l Council of State Boards of Nursing (396)

Dibb, David W.
Potash and Phosphate Institute (461)

Dibbons, Donald B.
Precision Metalforming Ass'n (462)

DiBenedetto, Valerie
American Soc. for Industrial Security (103)

DiBitetto, Kate
Federal Managers Ass'n (236)

DiBlasi, Joan M.
Corporate Transfer Agents Ass'n (209)

DiBona, Charles J.
American Petroleum Institute (91)

DiCampli, Edward
Helicopter Ass'n Internat'l (253)

DiCarlo, Sam J.
Milk Industry Foundation (328)
Internat'l Ice Cream Ass'n (294)
Nat'l Cheese Institute (386)
Internat'l Dairy Foods Ass'n (288)

DiCasoli, Sebastian
Billiard and Bowling Institute of America (178)

DiCesare, Joanne
Soc. of Cardiovascular and Interventional Radiology (499)

Dickerman, Thomas
American Ass'n for Fuel Cells (30)

Dickerson, David
Wine and Spirits Wholesalers of America (544)

Dickerson, Kenneth R.
Parenteral Drug Ass'n (453)

Dickerson, Ruth A.
Nat'l Confectioners Ass'n of the United States (389)

Dickerson, Willard
American Booksellers Ass'n (48)

Dickerson-Jones, Terri
American Women in Radio and Television (123)

Dickey, Fern
Nat'l Ass'n of Printers and Lithographers (366)

Dickey, Keith
Xi Psi Phi (551)

Dickinson, Renee
Edison Welding Institute (226)

Dickinson, Stephanie W.
Soc. for Healthcare Epidemiology of America (488)

Dickson, Charles
Community Transportation Ass'n of America (201)

Dickson, Diane
Synthetic Organic Chemical Manufacturers Ass'n (519)

Dickson, Mary
Inter-Industry Conference on Auto Collision Repair (271)

Dickson, Mary P.
Nat'l Ass'n of Broadcasters (345)

DiCostanzo, Steven J.
Golf Range and Recreation Ass'n of America (248)

Dicus, Todd C.
American Academy of Family Physicians (22)

Didion, Catherine J.
Ass'n for Women in Science (140)

Diebold, Larry
Nat'l Council of State Education Ass'ns (396)

Dieck, Steven
Associated Pipe Organ Builders of America (172)

Diedrich, Marlene
Certification Board for Urologic Nurses and Associates (190)

Diegel, Rick
Internat'l Brotherhood of Electrical Workers (284)

Diehl, Gary M.
Vocational Industrial Clubs of America (540)

Diemer, David
American Shetland Pony Club/American Miniature Horse Registry (100)

DiEorio, Matt
Associated Equipment Distributors (171)

Dierks, Neil
Nat'l Pork Producers Council (423)

Diers, Christine Paige
Public Radio News Directors (469)

Dieterich, Carrie
Video Software Dealers Ass'n (539)

Dietz, Robert
Securities Transfer Ass'n (481)

DiFilippo, Francine
Independent Computer Services Ass'n of America (260)
Home Workers Ass'n (256)
Institute for Business Innovation (265)

Digby FOAA, David A.
Opticians Ass'n of America (449)

Diggs, David
Cellular Telecommunications Industry Ass'n (189)

DiGiovanni, Carvin
Nat'l Spa and Pool Institute (431)

Dijk, Gina van
Ass'n of Clinical Research Professionals (147)

Dilday, Mary Alice
Soc. for Cardiac Angiography and Interventions (486)

Dill, Kevin
American Soc. of Peri-Anesthesia Nurses (114)

Dillard, Nell
Soc. of Toxicology (508)

Dillenger, Steve
Latin American Management Ass'n (317)

Dillon, Bernie
Independent Petroleum Ass'n of America (261)

Dillon, Debra
Nat'l Family Planning and Reproductive Health Ass'n (402)

Dillon, Donald W.
Piano Manufacturers Ass'n Internat'l (458)

Dillon, Joseph E.
Council of Better Business Bureaus (212)

Dills, Jennifer
Soc. of the Plastics Industry (507)

Dilworth, Leslie Gallery
Soc. for Environmental Graphic Design (487)

Dimatteo, Katherine
Organic Trade Ass'n (449)

DiMichel, Linda
American Academy of Medical Administrators (23)

Dimperio, Al
American Salvage Pool Ass'n (99)

Dinegar, James
American Institute of Architects (76)

Dingess, Robert
American Traffic Safety Services Ass'n (120)

Dingley, David P.
Internat'l Castor Oil Ass'n (285)

Dinkel, Michele K.
American Soc. of Clinical Oncology (108)

Dinkins, Bobby
Professional Bowlers Ass'n of America (465)

Dinneen, Robert
Renewable Fuels Ass'n (475)

Dintrone, Patricia
Ass'n of Ancient Historians (143)

DiPrimo, Laura
Hydraulic Institute (257)

Dirkes, Robert
Preferred Hotels and Resorts Worldwide (462)

Dirks, Dale P.
Ass'n of Minority Health Professions Schools (157)

Dishaw, Nancy
Middle East Studies Ass'n of North America (328)

Dispensa, Paul
Liability Insurance Research Bureau (319)

Dittbrenner, Heather
Nat'l Ass'n for Home Care (339)

Dittmann, Prof. Roger
United States Federation of Scholars and Scientists (533)

Diven, Ann M.
Building Service Contractors Ass'n Internat'l (183)

DiVenere, Lucia
Nat'l Ass'n for Home Care (339)

Divjak, Anne
United States of America National Committee of the Internat'l Dairy Federation (534)

Dix CAE, Dennis C.
Outdoor Power Equipment Institute (451)

Dixler, Elsa
Social Science Research Council (509)

Dixon, Brent C.
Paper Shipping Sack Manufacturers Ass'n (453)

Dixon, Doris L.
Nat'l Collegiate Athletic Ass'n (388)

Dixon, Dorita M.
American Ass'n of Blacks in Energy (33)

Dixon, Liz
Flexible Packaging Ass'n (240)

Dixon, Robert
Ass'n for Direct Instruction (132)

Dixon, Valerie C.
Black Women in Publishing (180)

Dixon Ph.D., Walter R.
Catecholamine Club (187)

Dixon-Terry, Eleanor
Soc. for Public Health Education (493)

Dlugozima, Robert
Nat'l Ass'n of Professional Baseball Leagues (366)

Doak Ph.D., Gordon A.
Nat'l Ass'n of Animal Breeders (343)

Doan, James
American Conference for Irish Studies (59)

Doan, Violet S.
IEEE Computer Soc. (258)

Dobberman, Nancy L.
American Soc. of Travel Agents (116)

Dobbs CAE, Deborah S.
American Ass'n of Independent Newspaper Distributors (38)

Dobkin, Jon
Nat'l Ass'n of Television Program Executives (378)
Nat'l Ass'n of Television Program Executives (378)

Dobs, Darold
Bowling (181)

Dobson, E. Dan
Exposition Service Contractors Ass'n (234)

Dobson, Sharon
American Institute of Chemists (77)

Dock CAE, Yvonne D.H.
Automotive Parts and Accessories Ass'n (175)

Dockery, Marla
Ass'n of Clinical Research Professionals (147)

Dockery, Robert
Disaster Preparedness and Emergency Response Ass'n (223)

Dockinson, Stephanie
Soc. of Toxicologic Pathologists (508)

Dodd, Michael
American Soc. of Health-System Pharmacists (110)

Dodds, Cheryl
ACIL (11)

Dodds, Edward W.
Ass'n for the Development of Religious Information Systems (139)

Dodge, William R.
Nat'l Ass'n of Regional Councils (369)

Dodson, Paul E.
Internat'l Marina Institute (297)

Doerrer, Nancy G.
American Industrial Health Council (75)

Doeschot, Iola
Braunvieh Ass'n of America (181)

Doggett, J. Don
American Farm Bureau Federation (66)

Dohenhoff, Richard
American Soc. for Pharmacology and Experimental Therapeutics (104)

Doherty, Elizabeth M.
Direct Selling Ass'n (223)

Doherty CAE, Mark
Institute for Operations Research and the Management Sciences (265)

Doherty, Peter
Nat'l Ass'n of Mortgage Brokers (363)

Doi, David
Coalition for Juvenile Justice (196)

Dojuhty, Jenny
Turnaround Management Ass'n (528)

Doka, Janet
American Soc. of TV Cameramen (116)

Dokter, Judi
Nat'l Ass'n of Graphic and Product Identification Manufacturers (357)
Self Insurance Institute of America (481)

Dolan, Gregory A.
American Methanol Institute (84)

Dolan, Julie A.
American Advertising Federation (27)

Dolan PhD, FACHE, Thomas C.
American College of Healthcare Executives (54)

Dolbearr, Mary Anne
Uniform and Textile Service Ass'n (529)

Dolibois CAE, Robert J.
Wholesale Nursery Growers of America (544)
Garden Centers of America (245)
American Nursery and Landscape Ass'n (87)
Nat'l Ass'n of Plant Patent Owners (365)

Dolim, Barbara A.
Mechanical Service Contractors of America (326)

Dolim, Michael P.
Nat'l Environmental Balancing Bureau (401)

Dolling, Dave
Aerospace Department Chairmen's Ass'n (13)

Dollison, Carolyn
Internat'l Executive Housekeepers Ass'n (290)
Dolphin, Kathleen
Ass'n of Practical Theology (160)
Dombi, Bill
Nat'l Ass'n for Home Care (339)
Dombrowsky, Elizabeth D.
Silicones Environmental Health and Safety Council of North
America (483)
Domedion, George
Painting and Decorating Contractors of America (452)
Domenick, Julie
Investment Company Institute (312)
Domer, Paul
Maintenance Council of American Trucking Ass'ns (322)
Dominici de Maria O.P., Sr. Jean
Catholic Fine Arts Soc. (188)
Domnitz, Avin
American Booksellers Ass'n (48)
Domurat, Janel
United States Meat Export Federation (534)
Donadio, Brian J.
American College of Osteopathic Internists (56)
Donaghy, Kairin
Regional Science Ass'n, Internat'l (473)
Donahue USCG (RET.), Capt. James
Soc. of American Military Engineers (498)
Donahue, Marla
Paperboard Packaging Council (453)
Donahue, Mary Ellen
Nat'l Ass'n of Test Directors (378)
Donahue, Michael
American Ass'n of Advertising Agencies (32)
Donaldson FLMI, CLU, Thomas P.
LOMA (321)
Donegan Jr., Thomas J.
Cosmetic, Toiletry and Fragrance Ass'n (210)
Donica, John P.
Aviation Insurance Ass'n (176)
Donio, Jim
Nat'l Ass'n of Recording Merchandisers (369)
Donmez, Kadir
American Leather Chemists Ass'n (81)
Donn, Charlotte
Soc. of Laparoendoscopic Surgeons (503)
Donnally CPA, Bianca
American Public Power Ass'n (96)
Donnell, Christine
American Ass'n for Clinical Chemistry (30)
Donnell Jr., CAE, Harold E.
Academy of General Dentistry (8)
Donnelly, Brian J.
Nat'l Organization of Life and Health Insurance Guaranty
Ass'ns (420)
Donnelly CAE, Gary W.
Nat'l Lumber and Building Material Dealers Ass'n (415)
Donnelly, H. William
Institute of Certified Travel Agents (266)
Donnelly, Kyle
PrintImage Internat'l (463)
Donnelly, Maureen A.
Herpetologists' League (254)
Donnelly, Thomas F.
Nat'l Water Resources Ass'n (435)
Donnelly, Timothy
Poetry Soc. of America (459)
Donner, Martin
Internat'l Newspaper Group (298)
Donofrio, Carolyn
Floral Marketing Ass'n (240)
Donofrio, Dr. Joseph
Federation of Straight Chiropractors and Organizations (238)
Donoho, Patrick
Tobacco Institute (524)
Donohoe, Koula K.
Nat'l Ass'n of Surety Bond Producers (377)
Donohue Jr., CAE, Gerald
Professional Convention Management Ass'n (465)
Donohue, Janet
Soap and Detergent Ass'n (484)
Donohue, Thomas J.
Chamber of Commerce of the United States of America (190)
Donottue, Alison
Ass'n of Applied Community Researchers (143)
Donovan, Bob
American Hospital Ass'n (74)
Donovan, David L.
Ass'n of Local Television Stations (156)
Donovan, Kathi
Academy of General Dentistry (8)

Donovan, Maria K.
Ass'n of Government Accountants (152)
Donovan, William J.
Nat'l Ass'n of Federal Credit Unions (355)
Doodeman, Karen
Nat'l Ass'n of Store Fixture Manufacturers (377)
Dooley, Barbara A.
Commercial Internet Exchange Ass'n (199)
Dooley, Connie
Petroleum Equipment Institute (455)
Dooley, Edward
Air-Conditioning and Refrigeration Institute (16)
Doolittle, Susan
Nat'l Ass'n of Business Economists (346)
Doolittle, Toni
Soc. of Cardiovascular and Interventional Radiology (499)
Doran, Kelly
Chain Drug Marketing Ass'n (190)
Dority, Douglas H.
United Food and Commercial Workers Internat'l Union (530)
Dorman, Ann M.
Nat'l Council of State Housing Agencies (396)
Dornemann, Rudolph
American Schools of Oriental Research (99)
Dorr, Perle M.
Geothermal Energy Ass'n (247)
Dorsa, Robert
Nat'l Ass'n of Credit Union Service Organizations (351)
Dorsett, Charles
American Ass'n of Nurse Attorneys (39)
Dorsey, Helen
Soc. of Manufacturing Engineers (503)
Dorsey, Laura
Irrigation Ass'n (313)
Dorsey, Mark
Professional Ski Instructors of America (467)
Dorsey, Mike
Engineering College Magazines Associated (230)
Dorsey, Susan M.
Nat'l Council of Educational Opportunity Ass'ns (394)
Dorso, Sue
Nat'l Trailer Dealers Ass'n (434)
Dort, Terrie
Nat'l Council of Chain Restaurants (394)
Doss, Joseph K.
Nonprescription Drug Manufacturers Ass'n (440)
Dotchin, Susan
Nat'l Governors' Ass'n (407)
Dotolo Ph.D., Lawrence G.
ACL - Ass'n for Consortium Leadership (11)
Dotson, Earl
Nat'l Pork Producers Council (423)
Doty, Lisa
American Orthopaedic Soc. for Sports Medicine (88)
Doubek, Nancy
Information Systems Audit and Control Ass'n (264)
Doubet, Sherry
American Salers Ass'n (98)
Doucette, Roger
Construction Specifications Institute (207)
Dougherty, Jim
Air and Waste Management Ass'n (15)
Dougherty, John J.
Operative Plasterers' and Cement Masons' Internat'l Ass'n of
the United States and Canada (448)
Douglas, Fred
Laboratory Animal Management Ass'n (316)
Douglas, Merk
American Soc. of Interior Designers (111)
Douglas, Peggy A.
Outdoor Power Equipment Institute (451)
Douglas, William R.
American Ceramic Soc. (51)
Douglass, John W.
Aerospace Industries Ass'n of America (13)
Douthitt, Lois
American Gas Ass'n (70)
Doval, Alexis
College Theology Soc. (198)
Dove, Susan H.
Internat'l Mass Retail Ass'n (297)
Dove, Veronica M.
Automotive Recyclers Ass'n (175)
Dover CAE, Marge
Nat'l Ass'n of Legal Assistants (361)
Dow, Thomas A.
American Soc. for Precision Engineering (104)
Dowdell, William C.
Flexographic Technical Ass'n (240)
Dowden, C. James
American Academy of Medical Acupuncture (23)

Soc. of Graduate Surgeons (502)
Ass'n of Area Business Publications (144)
City and Regional Magazine Ass'n (194)
Downes, Kathy
Global Health Council (248)
Downes, Laura M.
Microcirculatory Soc. of America (328)
Downey, J. Thomas
Casualty Actuarial Soc. (187)
Downey, Morgan
American Obesity Ass'n (87)
Downey, Myrna
Hardwood Plywood and Veneer Ass'n (251)
Downham, Max C.
Internat'l College of Surgeons (286)
Downing, Dan
ECRI (226)
Downing, Jere
Cranberry Institute (218)
Downs, Maureen E.
American Ass'n of Pharmaceutical Scientists (40)
Downs, Thomas M.
Nat'l Ass'n of Home Builders of the U.S. (358)
Doyle, Amy
Ass'n of Nurses in AIDS Care (158)
Doyle, Elizabeth
Meals On Wheels Ass'n of America (325)
Doyle OSU, Ellen
Nat'l Ass'n of Church Personnel Administrators (347)
Doyle, Frank M.
Nat'l Restaurant Ass'n (425)
Doyle, J. Andrew
Nat'l Paint and Coatings Ass'n (420)
Doyle, James M.
Research Council on Structural Connections (475)
Doyle CAE, Kenneth A.
Soc. of Independent Gasoline Marketers of America (502)
Doyle, Stephen P.
Central Station Alarm Ass'n (189)
Doyle, Thomas B.
Nat'l Sporting Goods Ass'n (431)
Nat'l Ski and Snowboard Retailers Ass'n (428)
Doyle-Kimball, Mary
Nat'l Ass'n of Real Estate Editors (369)
Doyon, Mark W.
Nat'l Wholesale Druggists' Ass'n (436)
Dozier, Amy S.
Nat'l Apartment Ass'n (337)
Draba Ph.D., Robert E.
American Ass'n of Neurological Surgeons (39)
Drain, David L.
Foodservice Consultants Soc. Internat'l (242)
Drake, Larry
Radiant Panel Ass'n (470)
Drake, Lisa C.
American Ass'n for Laboratory Accreditation (31)
Drake, O. Burtch
American Ass'n of Advertising Agencies (32)
Drake, Steven
Agricultural Publishers Ass'n (14)
Drake CAE, Thomas G.
Nat'l Sporting Goods Ass'n (431)
Dresia, David R.
American Soc. of Civil Engineers (108)
Dressendorfer, John H.
American Forest and Paper Ass'n (69)
Dresser, Tim
American Collectors Ass'n (52)
Dressler, Barbara
Purebred Hanoverian Ass'n of America Breeders and
Owners (470)
Dressler CPMBG,HCFC, Barry M.
Environmental Management Ass'n (232)
Dressler, Kellie
Justice Research and Statistics Ass'n (315)
Dressler D.D.S., Ronald M.
Internat'l Academy of Oral Medicine and Toxicology (272)
Drever, Jane
Forum for Health Care Planning (243)
Drevna, Charles
Oxygenated Fuels Ass'n (452)
Drew, Steve
Radiological Soc. of North America (471)
Drewke, Robert
Showmen's League of America (483)
Drewsen, Allen
Internat'l Trademark Ass'n (309)
Dreyer, Johnny
Gas Processors Ass'n (245)
Dreyman, Edgar W.
Cathodic Protection Industry Ass'n (188)

Driggs, Kathi
Club Managers Ass'n of America **(195)**

Drinan, James M.
American Ass'n of Orthodontists **(40)**

Driscoll, Daniel A.
Nat'l Futures Ass'n **(406)**

Driscoll, Dick
Business and Institutional Furniture Manufacturers Ass'n
   Internat'l **(184)**

Driscoll, Edward J.
Nat'l Air Carrier Ass'n **(335)**

Driscoll, Rev. Joseph
Nat'l Ass'n of Catholic Chaplains **(346)**

Drisdell, Tammy
Architectural Precast Ass'n **(127)**

Driskill CLU, ChFC, John R.
Society of Financial Service Professionals **(509)**

Driver, Jamie
OPERA America **(448)**

Drohan CAE, William M.
American Academy of Hospice and Palliative Medicine **(22)**
Nat'l Renal Administrators Ass'n **(425)**
Sports Lawyers Ass'n **(515)**

Drollinger, Darrin
Ag Electronics Ass'n **(14)**

Drown, Peter
Internat'l Ass'n of Pet Cemeteries **(281)**

Droz, Fred
Neurodevelopmental Treatment Ass'n **(438)**
Ass'n of Freestanding Radiation Oncology Centers **(152)**

Druart, Therese-Anne
American Catholic Philosophical Ass'n **(50)**

Druhan, Christine V.
Ass'n of Machinery and Equipment Appraisers **(156)**

Drum, Al
Semiconductor Equipment and Materials Internat'l **(481)**

Drum, Margaret A.
Nat'l Music Publishers' Ass'n **(418)**

Drummer, Robert
Nat'l Technical Services Ass'n **(433)**

Drumming, Patricia F.
Black Data Processing Associates **(180)**

Dubenitz, Elizabeth B.
American Academy of Equine Art **(21)**

Ducat, Howard S.
American Soc. of Appraisers **(106)**

Ducate, Douglas
Center for Exhibition Industry Research **(189)**

Duckering, Hilda
Weather Modification Ass'n **(541)**

Dudash, Kristen
Rapid Prototyping Ass'n of SME **(472)**
Machining Technology Ass'n of SME **(321)**
North American Manufacturing Research Institution of
   SME **(443)**

Dudley, Penny
Financial Women Internat'l **(239)**

Dudley, Stephanie D.
Population Ass'n of America **(460)**

Duduit, Michael
American Academy of Ministry **(23)**

Dueitt, Dala
American Brahman Breeders Ass'n **(49)**

Dueppen, Muri
AOAC Internat'l **(125)**

Duerksen, Roger L.
Preferred Funeral Directors Internat'l **(462)**

Duernberger, Richard
Technical Engineers Ass'n **(520)**

Duerr, Douglas
Nat'l Ass'n of State Credit Union Supervisors **(374)**

Duff, Daniel
American Public Transit Ass'n **(96)**

Duff, Michael J.
Analytical and Life Science Sytems Ass'n **(124)**
SAMA Group of Ass'ns **(479)**

Dufficy, Thomas J.
Photographic and Imaging Manufacturers Ass'n **(457)**

Duffy, John J.
American Concrete Pipe Ass'n **(59)**

Duffy, Kevin R.
Ass'n of Public-Safety Communications Officials-
   Internat'l **(162)**

Duffy, Stephen
American Academy of Facial Plastic and Reconstructive
   Surgery **(22)**

Duffy, William R.
Imaging Supplies Coalition for Internat'l Intellectual Property
   Protection **(259)**

Duffy, William T.
Nat'l School Supply and Equipment Ass'n **(427)**

Dugan USAF (RET.), Gen. Michael J.
Nat'l Multiple Sclerosis Soc. **(418)**

Dugard, Paul
Halogenated Solvents Industry Alliance **(250)**

Duggan, Brian
Transportation Safety Equipment Institute **(526)**

Duggan, E. Martin
Small Business Exporters Ass'n **(484)**

Duggan, Juanita D.
Wine and Spirits Wholesalers of America **(544)**

Duillo, John
Soc. of American Historical Artists **(497)**

Duke, Rose
Nat'l Soc. of Hispanic MBAs **(430)**

Dulmaine, Brian
Internat'l Sleep Products Ass'n **(302)**

Dumaresq Ph.D., R.
Aviation Technician Education Council **(176)**

Dumont, Dee
Soc. for Information Display **(490)**

Dumper, Brenda
Evangelical Training Ass'n **(233)**

Dunagan, Daryl
Nat'l Conference of State Social Security Administrators **(391)**

Dunay, Jeanne M.
Nat'l Ass'n for Campus Activities **(338)**

Dunbar, Michael
American Camping Ass'n **(50)**

Duncan, Bonnie N.
Nat'l Electrical Contractors Ass'n **(400)**

Duncan, Daniel C.
Information Industry Ass'n **(263)**

Duncan, Ellen
Institute for Operations Research and the Management
   Sciences **(265)**

Duncan, Harley
Federation of Tax Administrators **(228)**

Duncan, Jack
Nat'l Council of State Agencies for the Blind **(396)**

Duncan, Jack G.
Council of State Administrators of Vocational
   Rehabilitation **(215)**

Duncan, Lena
Nat'l American Indian Housing Council **(336)**

Duncan, Mallory B.
Nat'l Retail Federation **(425)**

Duncan, Michael P.
Nat'l Ass'n of Independent Insurers **(359)**

Duncan, Roberta
Nat'l Ass'n of Independent Life Brokerage Agencies **(359)**

Duncan, Susan J.
Investment Company Institute **(312)**

Duncan, Wilbur
Nat'l Alliance of Postal and Federal Employees **(336)**

Duncan, Will
Coalition of Black Trade Unionists **(196)**

Duncan, William
Japan Automobile Manufacturers Ass'n **(313)**

Duncavage M.D., James
American Broncho-Esophagological Ass'n **(49)**

Dungy, Gwendolyn Jordan
Nat'l Ass'n of Student Personnel Administrators **(377)**

Dunham, Don
Binding Industries of America **(179)**

Dunham, Karen
Nat'l Ass'n of the Remodeling Industry **(378)**

Dunham, Susan
Construction Financial Management Ass'n **(206)**

Dunkel, Dr. Alexander
Nat'l Ass'n of Self-Instructional Language Programs **(372)**

Dunkelman, Susan
Council of Communication Management **(213)**

Dunkless, Debra
Nat'l Tay-Sachs and Allied Diseases Ass'n **(433)**

Dunkley, Mac
Bright Belt Warehouse Ass'n **(182)**

Dunlap, David
Uniform and Textile Service Ass'n **(529)**

Dunlap, Earl
Nat'l Juvenile Detention Ass'n **(413)**

Dunlap, Ellen S.
American Antiquarian Soc. **(28)**

Dunlavey CMP, Barbara
Nat'l Ass'n of Health Underwriters **(357)**

Dunleavy, Jennifer
Direct Selling Ass'n **(223)**

Dunn, Donna F.
American Agricultural Economics Ass'n **(27)**

Dunn, Jim
United Paperworkers Internat'l Union **(531)**

Dunn, Patrice M.
Digital Distribution of Advertising for Publications **(222)**

Dunn, Warren
Nat'l Rural Electric Cooperative Ass'n **(426)**

Dunne, James
Institute of Gas Technology **(267)**

Dunne, Jane
Undersea and Hyperbaric Medical Soc. **(529)**

Dunne, Joanne
American Medical Rehabilitation Providers Ass'n **(84)**

Dunne, Joanne E.
Institute of Management Consultants **(268)**

Dunnick, Kim
Internat'l Trumpet Guild **(309)**

Dunnington, Richard H.
Gravure Ass'n of America **(249)**

Duprat, Melissa
Ass'n of Trial Lawyers of America **(168)**

Dupree, Daniel E.
American Council for Construction Education **(61)**

Duran Ed.D., Grace Z.
Council for Exceptional Children **(211)**

Durani, Ajay
Advertising Research Foundation **(12)**

Durant M.D., John R.
American Soc. of Clinical Oncology **(108)**

Durgam, Kathy
Graphic Communications Internat'l Union **(249)**

Durgin, Gloria
Nat'l Ass'n of School Nurses **(371)**

Durham, Emma Lee B.
Internat'l Development Research Council **(288)**

Durham, Joanne
Women's Transportation Seminar **(548)**

Durham, Judith B.
Architectural Woodwork Institute **(127)**

Durham, Leon
Nat'l Ass'n of Housing and Redevelopment Officials **(358)**

Durham, Michelle
Center for Management Advisors **(189)**
CPA Auto Dealer Consultants Ass'n **(218)**
Construction Industry CPA/Consultants Ass'n **(206)**
Law Firm Services Ass'n **(318)**
CPA Manufacturing Services Ass'n **(218)**
Not-for-Profit Services Ass'n **(446)**
Community Banking Advisory Network **(201)**
Nat'l CPA Health Care Advisors Ass'n **(398)**

Durheim, Harold
Business Technology Ass'n **(185)**

Durkin, Helen A.
Internat'l Health, Racquet and Sportsclub Ass'n **(293)**

Durnell, Gerry
Nat'l Ass'n of Pizza Operators **(365)**

Durocher, Cort
American Institute of Aeronautics and Astronautics **(76)**

Duros, Sally
American Economic Development Council **(65)**

DuRoss, Gregory
American Machine Tool Distributors Ass'n **(82)**

Durrett, Brandon
Safe and Vault Technicians Ass'n **(478)**
Associated Locksmiths of America **(171)**

Dusen, Jim
University Photographers Ass'n of America **(537)**

Duska, Ronald F.
Soc. for Business Ethics **(486)**

Dussor, William
Internat'l Health, Racquet and Sportsclub Ass'n **(293)**

Dutra, Geri
American Classical League **(52)**

Duty, Kimberly
Nat'l Multi Housing Council **(417)**

Duval, Jeanne-Marie
NAFSA: Ass'n of Internat'l Educators **(333)**

Duvall, Henry
Council of the Great City Schools **(216)**

Duvall, Suzanne B.
Food Marketing Institute **(241)**

Duxbury, Dean
Institute of Food Technologists **(267)**

Dvorak, Eldon J.
Western Economic Ass'n Internat'l **(542)**

Dvorak, Thomas
American Ass'n of Occupational Health Nurses **(40)**

Dvorchak, Lisa
AIM USA **(15)**

Dvorchak, Thomas
Tread Rubber and Tire Repair Materials Manufacturers
   Group **(526)**

Dwyer, John W.
Lignite Energy Council **(320)**

Dwyer, Michael R.
Truck Cap and Accessory Ass'n **(527)**

Dwyer, Rita
Ass'n for the Study of Dreams **(139)**

Elews, Michael W.
Foundation for Independent Higher Education (243)

Elgin, Dr. James
Ass'n of Official Seed Certifying Agencies (158)

Elias, Vanessa
Executive Women Internat'l (233)

Elipani, Jeanne
Soc. of Women Engineers (509)

Elkins, Angie
American Music Therapy Ass'n (86)

Ellacott, Meg
Helicopter Ass'n Internat'l (253)

Ellashek CAE, Daniel E.
Precision Metalforming Ass'n (462)

Ellenberg, Ivy
American Institute of Food Distribution (77)

Ellerbee, Don
American Embryo Transfer Ass'n (66)
American College of Theriogenologists (58)
Soc. for Theriogenology (496)

Ellerbrock, Mary
Ass'n of College and University Housing Officers-Internat'l (147)

Ellingsworth, William
Nat'l Ass'n of Home Builders of the U.S. (358)

Elliot, Joanne P.
Nat'l Ass'n of Bar-Related Title Insurers (344)

Elliot, Steven C.
Nat'l Ass'n of Mutual Insurance Companies (363)

Elliot, Troy
American Ass'n of State Social Work Boards (43)

Elliott, Amy
Casual Furniture Retailers (187)
Ass'n of Industrial Real Estate Brokers (154)

Elliott CAE, Lee Anne
Voluntary Protection Programs Participants Ass'n (540)

Elliott, M. Diane
American Ass'n of Private Railroad Car Owners (41)

Elliott, Sean
Nat'l Ass'n of Flight Instructors (355)

Elliott, Susan K.
Nat'l Ass'n of Limited Edition Dealers (361)

Elliott Ph.D., T. Michael
IEEE Computer Soc. (258)

Ellis, Kim
Professional Construction Estimators Ass'n of America (465)

Ellis, Marietta W.
Soc. for In Vitro Biology (489)

Ellis, R. Anthony
Ass'n of College Unions-Internat'l (147)

Ellis, Dr. Robert P.
Conference of Research Workers In Animal Diseases (204)

Ellis, Ursula
Nat'l Community Education Ass'n (388)

Ellis, Wanda
Dalton Floor Covering Market Ass'n (220)

Ellsworth, Deborah D.
American Health Care Ass'n (72)

Ellsworth, DeWelle F. "Skip"
Log House Builders Ass'n of North America (320)

Ellzy, Tiffany
Fashion Ass'n, The (235)

Elman, Carolyn Bufton
American Business Women's Ass'n (50)

Elman, Janet Rice
Ass'n of Youth Museums (170)

Elmendorf, Edward M.
American Ass'n of State Colleges and Universities (43)

Elmendorf, Friedrich M.
Consumer Bankers Ass'n (207)

Elsea, Bud
Internat'l Ass'n for Financial Planning (274)

Elsner, Christina M.
Design-Build Institute of America (222)

Elston, Henrietta
Soc. for Vascular Nursing (496)
Home Healthcare Nurses Ass'n (255)
American Soc. of Pain Management Nurses (113)
Respiratory Nursing Soc. (475)

Elum, F. Joseph
Internat'l Business Music Ass'n (284)

Elwell, Lee
Recreation Vehicle Dealers Ass'n of North America (472)

Elwood, Thomas W.
Ass'n of Schools of Allied Health Professions (164)

Ely, Liz
Project Management Institute (468)

Ely, Meredith
Nat'l Ass'n of Concessionaires (349)

Ely, Sarah
American Wood Preservers Institute (123)

Embody, Mary Barnes
Nat'l Club Ass'n (387)

Emely Ph.D.,CMP, Charles
American Railway Engineering and Maintenance of Way Ass'n (97)

Emely CAE, Mary Ann
Federation of Government Information Processing Councils (237)

Emerson, Jan
Healthcare Forum, The (252)

Emery, Amy
American Soc. of Pension Actuaries (114)

Emery, Barbara
Academy of General Dentistry (8)

Emery, Edie
Radio-Television News Directors Ass'n (471)

Emery, Priscilla
Ass'n for Information and Image Management International (135)

Emig, Michael
Internat'l Brotherhood of Electrical Workers (284)

Emmert Jr., John C.
American Arbitration Ass'n (28)

Emmett, Edward M.
Nat'l Industrial Transportation League (411)

Emnett, Julie
American Academy of Neurology (23)

Ence, Ronald C.
Independent Bankers Ass'n of America (260)

Endicott, Sheila
American Osteopathic Academy for Sports Medicine (89)

Endrich, Phyllis
Nat'l Shoe Retailers Ass'n (428)

Endthoff, Gene
Nat'l Fire Sprinkler Ass'n (404)

Eng, Anne
Internat'l Trademark Ass'n (309)

Eng, Jacqueline L.
United States Pharmacopeia (534)

Engebretson, Gary D.
Contract Services Ass'n of America (200)

Engel, Ralph
Chemical Specialties Manufacturers Ass'n (191)

Engelbreit, Ronald
American College of Foot and Ankle Surgeons (54)

Engelhardt, Christin
American Sleep Apnea Ass'n (100)

Engels, Ann Lawrence
American Apparel Manufacturers Ass'n (28)

Engh, Fred C.
Nat'l Alliance for Youth Sports (336)

Engh, John
Nat'l Alliance for Youth Sports (336)

England, Lan C.
American Academy of Procedural Coders (25)

England, Norm
Portable Rechargeable Battery Ass'n (460)

Engle CMP, CAE, Jeffrey W.
American Academy of Pain Medicine (25)

Engle, Mark
Soc. for Health and Human Values (488)

Engle, Mark T.
Freestanding Insert Council of North America (244)
Soc. of Automotive Analysts (498)
Nat'l Ass'n of Fleet Resale Dealers (355)

Englehart, Amy
Internat'l Road Federation (302)

English, Clea
American Ass'n for Geriatric Psychiatry (30)

English, Glenn L.
Nat'l Rural Electric Cooperative Ass'n (426)

English, Helen
Passive Solar Industries Council (454)

Englund, Cathy
Ass'n of Family Practice Residency Directors (151)

Englund, Thomas H.
Christian College Consortium (193)

Engquist, Chris
Laborers' Internat'l Union of North America (316)

Ensinger, Robert
Internat'l Ass'n of Convention and Visitor Bureaus (277)

Ensley, Cindy G.
Nat'l Marine Electronics Ass'n (416)

Entin, Fredric
American Hospital Ass'n (74)

Epp, James
United States Pan Asian American Chamber of Commerce (534)

Epperson CAE, Gary L.
Alpha Kappa Psi (19)

Epps, Julie
Ass'n of Rheumatology Health Professionals (164)

Epstein, Rabbi Jerome M.
United Synagogue of Conservative Judaism (536)

Epstein, Mark H.
Nat'l Ass'n of Health Data Organizations (357)

Epstein, Rikki
Nat'l Therapeutic Recreation Soc. (433)

Eramian, Daniel G.
Biotechnology Industry Organization (179)

Erazo, Joaquin
Soc. of American Florists (497)

Erbe, Gary
Allied Artists of America (18)

Erceg, Linda Ebner
Ass'n of Camp Nurses (145)

Erickson, Eric B.
American Ass'n of Electrodiagnostic Medicine (36)

Erickson, Irene
Inter-Industry Conference on Auto Collision Repair (271)

Erickson, L. Eileen
Nat'l Council of Teachers of Mathematics (396)

Erman, Elizabeth
American Spice Trade Ass'n (117)

Ernst, Don
Ass'n for Supervision and Curriculum Development (138)

Ernst, Mary Fran
Nat'l Ass'n of Medical Examiners (362)

Eruin, Ellen
Business Technology Ass'n (185)

Ervin Ph.D., Gerard L.
American Ass'n of Teachers of Slavic and East European Languages (44)
Nat'l Federation of Modern Language Teachers Ass'ns (403)

Escamilla, Marie
Building Material Dealers Ass'n (183)

Esher, Cynthia A.
Measurement, Control and Automation Ass'n (325)

Eshleman Ph.D., Ronald L.
Vibration Institute (539)

Eskridge, Robert L.
American Chamber of Commerce Executives (51)

Eslami, Kambiz
Soc. for Iranian Studies (490)

Esparza, Alma
Federally Employed Women (236)

Espenshade, Scott
Independent Petroleum Ass'n of America (261)

Espinoza, Debbie
Soc. of Quality Assurance (506)

Espiritu, Yen Le
Ass'n for Asian American Studies (130)

Esposito, Dawn
American Italian Historical Ass'n (79)

Esposito, Donna
Nat'l Ass'n of Cruise Oriented Agencies (352)

Esposito, Tess
Ass'n of Maternal and Child Health Programs (157)

Esser, Jeffrey L.
Government Finance Officers Ass'n of the United States and Canada (248)

Estabrook, James
Scuba Retailers Ass'n (480)

Estes, Deborah M.
American Gas Ass'n (70)

Estes M.D., J. Worth
American Ass'n for the History of Medicine (32)

Estes, James
Nat'l Apartment Ass'n (337)

Estes, Nancy
Independent Distributors Ass'n (260)

Estes, Rich A.
Internat'l Union of Police Ass'ns, AFL-CIO (310)

Esthus, Kenneth P.
Hospitality Sales and Marketing Ass'n Internat'l (256)

Estover, Janet
American Medical Rehabilitation Providers Ass'n (84)

Estrada, Ramon A.
Commission on Certification of Work Adjustment and Vocational Evaluation Specialists (199)

Estreicher, Samuel
Institute of Judicial Administration (267)

Estridge, Barbara
American Feed Industry Ass'n (67)

Ethier CAE, Donald
American Industrial Hygiene Ass'n (75)

Ethridge, Winifred E.
Nat'l Frozen Food Ass'n (406)

Etkin CAE, Steven A.
Ass'n of the Wall and Ceiling Industries-Internat'l (167)

Eubanks Ed.D., RRT, David H.
American College of Chest Physicians (53)

Euler, Diane R.
Flexographic Technical Ass'n (240)

Fischer, Kurt W.
Jean Piaget Soc./Soc. for the Study of Knowledge and Development (313)

Fischer, Leslie
Nat'l Ass'n for Membership Development (340)

Fischer, Nellie M.
American Pewter Guild (91)

Fischer, Robert
Computer Assisted Language Instruction Consortium (202)

Fischetti, Carlotta
Nat'l Ass'n of Biology Teachers (344)

Fischetti, Thomas D.
Accrediting Commission for Career Schools and Colleges of Technology (11)

Fischione, Deborah A.
North American Securities Administrators Ass'n (444)

Fise, Thomas F.
Ass'n of Program Directors in Surgery (162)
American College of Gastroenterology (54)

Fish, Carleton
American Collectors Ass'n (52)

Fishburn, Ellen
Ass'n of Railway Museums (163)

Fishel, Jerome I.
United Engineering Trustees (530)

Fisher, Beth
American Institute of the History of Pharmacy (78)

Fisher, Colleen M.
Council for Affordable and Rural Housing (210)

Fisher, Cynthia
Internat'l Ass'n of Convention and Visitor Bureaus (277)

Fisher Ph.D., CAE, Donald W.
American Medical Group Ass'n (83)

Fisher, Elaine L.
Dietary Managers Ass'n (222)

Fisher, George
Stuntmen's Ass'n of Motion Pictures (517)

Fisher, Janis
American Mustang Ass'n (86)

Fisher, Joyce
White Park Cattle Ass'n of America (543)

Fisher, Linda
Laborers' Internat'l Union of North America (316)

Fisher, Lisa K.
American Soc. of Notaries (113)

Fisher, Maria De Leon
Internat'l Radio and Television Soc. Foundation (301)

Fisher, Michael
Nat'l Ass'n of Consumer Shows (349)

Fisher, Ron
Defense Fire Protection Ass'n (220)

Fisher, William E.
Internat'l Fabricare Institute (290)

Fisher, William P.
American Hotel and Motel Ass'n (74)

Fishman, Betty
Institute of Hazardous Materials Management (267)

Fishman, Rabbi Joshua
Nat'l Soc. for Hebrew Day Schools (429)

Fishman, Marilyn
Endocrine Fellows Foundation (230)

Fisk, Carol Fraser
American Academy of Audiology (20)

Fiste, William R.
Commercial Vehicle Safety Alliance (199)

Fitch, Laura Macary
Employee Relocation Council (229)

Fitch-Swanson, Susan
American Business Women's Ass'n (50)

Fitzgerald, Amy K.
Internat'l Titanium Ass'n (309)

Fitzgerald Ph.D., Hiram E.
World Ass'n for Infant Mental Health (549)

Fitzgerald, Jay
Ass'n of Information Technology Professionals (154)

Fitzgerald, Judy
Nat'l Insurance Crime Bureau (412)

Fitzgerald, Marilyn H.
American Academy of Physician Assistants (25)

Fitzgerald, Sally
Internat'l Ass'n of Defense Counsel (278)

Fitzgerald CAE, DABFE, FACHE, Frank S.
Screen Manufacturers Ass'n (480)
Window Council (544)

Fitzgerald Johnson, Mildred
Nat'l Technical Ass'n of Scientists (433)

Fitzgerald, Jr. CPA, James M.
Ass'n of Information Technology Professionals (154)

Fitzpatrick, James
American Agents Ass'n (27)

Fitzpatrick, John J.
Ass'n of American Railroads (143)

Fitzpatrick, Ruth T.
Air Force Ass'n (15)

Fitzsimmons, Carolyn
Ass'n of Progressive Rental Organizations (162)

Fitzsimmons III, Frank
Nat'l Ass'n of County Agricultural Agents (350)

Fitzsimmons, Ron
Nat'l Coalition of Abortion Providers (387)

FitzSimons, Charles B.
Producer's Guild of America (463)

Fiveusch, Sherilyn
Women's Basketball Coaches Ass'n (547)

Flaherty, Richard G.
American Ass'n for Clinical Chemistry (30)

Flaherty, Roberta D.
Nat'l Academic Advising Ass'n (333)

Flamagan, Michael
Transportation Lawyers Ass'n (525)

Flamm, Carol
Professional Women Singers Ass'n (468)

Flanagan, Anne
Nat'l Ass'n of Insurance Brokers (360)

Flanagan, Michael P.
American Soc. for Histocompatability and Immunogenetics (103)

Flanagan, Newman
Nat'l District Attorneys Ass'n (399)

Flanagan, Robert
Soc. of University Urologists (508)

Flanagan, Sarah A.
Nat'l Ass'n of Independent Colleges and Universities (359)

Flangas, Amanda
Nat'l Ass'n of Golf Tournament Directors (356)

Flanigan, Jim
Women in Cable and Telecommunications (546)

Flanigan, Matthew J.
Telecommunications Industry Ass'n (521)

Flanner, Tim
Nat'l Federation Interscholastic Coaches Ass'n (402)
Nat'l Federation Interscholastic Officials Ass'n (402)

Flannery, Suzanne
Nat'l Shoe Travelers Ass'n (428)

Flannery III, William J.
Nat'l Ass'n of Manufacturing Opticians (362)

Flater, Morris E.
American Helicopter Soc. (73)

Flatow, Joel E.
Recording Industry Ass'n of America (472)

Fleck, Maylu
American Ass'n of Orthopaedic Medicine (40)

Fleckenstein CAE, Jim
Nat'l Soc. of Fund Raising Executives (429)

Fleharty, Rosemary
American Dexter Cattle Ass'n (64)

Fleischman, Catherine
Ass'n for Professionals in Infection Control and Epidemiology (136)

Fleischman, Larry
Soc. for Maintenance Reliability Professionals (490)

Fleischman, Larry M.
Suburban Newspapers of America (518)

Fleischmann, Mary Walker
Counselors of Real Estate (217)

Fleiss M.D., Paul
American Ass'n of Medical Milk Commissions (39)

Fleming, Anne
Insurance Institute for Highway Safety (270)

Fleming, Edie
Chemical Manufacturers Ass'n (191)

Fleming, Holly
American Waterways Operators (122)

Fleming, Mac A.
Brotherhood of Maintenance of Way Employees (182)

Fleming, Mary
American Statistical Ass'n (118)

Fleming CAE, Michael J.
Equipment Leasing Ass'n of America (232)

Fleming, Richard H.
Child Welfare League of America (192)

Fleming, Robert
Internat'l Soc. of Fire Service Instructors (306)

Fleming, Russell P.
Nat'l Fire Sprinkler Ass'n (404)

Fletcher, J.M.
Power Sources Manufacturers Ass'n (461)

Fletcher, Jeff
Nat'l League of Cities (414)

Fletcher, Nancy J.
Outdoor Advertising Ass'n of America (451)

Fletcher D.S.W., Robert
NADD: Ass'n for Persons with Developmental Disabilities and Mental Health Needs (333)

Flikeld, Jack
American Academy of Child and Adolescent Psychiatry (20)

Flint, Jerry
Internat'l Motor Press Ass'n (297)

Floden, Robert
Philosophy of Education Soc. (457)

Floor M.D., MPH, Marianne K.
Internat'l Health Evaluation Ass'n (293)

Floor, Ronald L.
American Textile Manufacturers Institute (119)

Floren, Terese M.
Women in the Fire Service (547)

Flores Ph.D., Antonio R.
Hispanic Ass'n of Colleges and Universities (254)

Flores, Edward
Internat'l Ass'n for Healthcare Security and Safety (274)

Flores, Melissa
American Ass'n for Medical Transcription (31)

Flores, Ray
Natural Product Broker Ass'n (437)

Florine, Bruce
Nat'l Golf Foundation (407)

Flory CAE, Dona
American Academy of Family Physicians (22)

Flower, Nancy
Compressed Gas Ass'n (202)

Flower, Ruth
American Ass'n of University Professors (44)

Flowers, Tracye
Optical Soc. of America (449)

Fluegel, Pat
Kappa Kappa Iota (315)

Flynn, Ms. Daryl
Laser Institute of America (317)

Flynn, Deirdre
Popcorn Institute (460)
Ass'n of Free Community Papers (152)

Flynn, Dennis J.
Nat'l Council of Architectural Registration Boards (394)

Flynn, Gerri
Mu Phi Epsilon (331)

Flynn, James F.
CPA Associates Internat'l (218)

Flynn, Janet
Chlorine Chemistry Council (192)

Flynn, Kevin
American Congress on Surveying and Mapping (60)

Flynn Ph.D., Patrice
Independent Sector (261)

Fochs, Patricia
North American Morab Horse Ass'n/Registry (443)

Fogarty, Cele
American Soc. for Bone and Mineral Research (101)
American Soc. of Nephrology (113)

Fogel CAE, Jerry
American Ass'n of Managing General Agents (38)
Diamond Council of America (222)

Fogleman, Ken
Internat'l Transactional Analysis Ass'n (309)

Fogt Jr., Howard W.
UAN Solutions Export Ass'n (529)

Fogus, Lowell
Ass'n of Farmworker Opportunity Programs (151)

Foley, David L.
American Ass'n of Equine Practitioners (36)

Foley, Georgia H.
Specialty Tool and Fastener Distributors Ass'n (514)

Foley, Linda
Newspaper Guild (439)

Foley, Martin E.
Nat'l Motor Freight Traffic Ass'n (417)

Foley, Roselle
American Boiler Manufacturers Ass'n (48)

Folkerts, Brian B.
Nat'l Food Processors Ass'n (405)

Folkerts, Yvonne A.
Aluminum Ass'n (19)

Fonkelstein, Libby
American Jewish Historical Soc. (80)

Fonte, Jill M.
United States Racquet Stringing Ass'n (535)

Fontes, Brian
Cellular Telecommunications Industry Ass'n (189)

Forbes, Gordon
Ass'n of Theatrical Press Agents and Managers (168)

Forbes, Roy
Nat'l Education Knowledge Industry Ass'n (400)

Forbes Ph.D., FLM, Stephen
LOMA (321)

Forbis, CMT, Pat
American Ass'n for Medical Transcription (31)

Force, Marie S.
Ass'n of Government Accountants (152)

Ford, Dorie
Advertising Photographers of America, Nat'l (12)

Ford, Gina
Internat'l Academy of Compounding Pharmacists (272)

Ford, Michael Q.
Nat'l Nutritional Foods Ass'n (419)

Ford, William C.
Nat'l Stone Ass'n (431)

Ford, William J.
Nat'l Truck Leasing System (434)

Forde, Kevin M.
Federal Judges Ass'n (236)

Fording, Edmund
Synthetic Organic Chemical Manufacturers Ass'n (519)

Fore Jr., Troy H.
American Beekeeping Federation (47)

Foreman, Julie R.
Healthcare Information and Management Systems Soc. (253)

Forester, Janet J.
Soc. of Prospective Medicine (506)

Forgarty, Cele
Internat'l Institute of Ammonia Refrigeration (294)

Forger CMP, Jeffrey A.
Soc. of Plastics Engineers (505)

Forkenbrock, John B.
Nat'l Ass'n of Federally Impacted Schools (355)

Forman, David C.
Soc. for Human Resource Management (489)

Forness, King
Nat'l Ass'n of Independent Public Finance Advisors (359)

Forness, Pamela
Soc. for Imaging Science and Technology (489)

Forrest, Dr. Gary
Internat'l Academy of Behavioral Medicine, Counseling and Psychotherapy (272)

Forrest, Wayne
American Indonesian Chamber of Commerce (75)

Forrester CAE, Larry L.
Property Casualty Conferences (468)
Nat'l Ass'n of Mutual Insurance Companies (363)

Forsen, Harold K.
Nat'l Academy of Engineering of the United States of America (334)

Forst, Chris
American Soc. of Interior Designers (111)

Forst, Paul
Nat'l Head Start Ass'n (408)

Forsyth, Patrick B.
University Council for Educational Administration (537)

Forsyth, Phillip W.
Recycled Paperboard Technical Ass'n (473)

Forte, Patrick A.
Ass'n of Financial Services Holding Companies (151)

Forte CPL, Robin
American Ass'n of Professional Landmen (41)

Fortier, Ian
Congress of Lung Ass'n Staff (205)

Fortin, Adnew
Contract Services Ass'n of America (208)

Fortman, Fred
American Soc. of Safety Engineers (116)

Fortney, Mary Martha
Nat'l Ass'n of State Credit Union Supervisors (374)

Foss, Dorothy
Nat'l Conference of Diocesan Vocation Directors (390)

Foss CAE, Jody
Ass'n of Operating Room Nurses (159)

Foss, Robin
Aerobics and Fitness Ass'n of America (13)

Foss, Vanessa O.
American Soc. for Information Science (103)

Foster, Allison
Ass'n of Schools of Public Health (164)

Foster, Cheri
American Guernsey Ass'n (71)

Foster, Dawn O'Day
Internat'l Soc. of Transport Aircraft Trading (307)

Foster, G.P.
Cordage Institute (209)

Foster, James
Airforwarders Ass'n (16)

Foster CMP, Maurice
Nat'l Bar Ass'n (382)

Foster, Nancy E.
American Crop Protection Ass'n (62)

Foster, Robert
Evaporative Cooling Institute (233)

Foster, Steve
Nat'l Ass'n for Search and Rescue (341)

Foster, Susan A.
Animal Behavior Soc. (124)

Foti, Margaret
American Ass'n for Cancer Research (30)

Fountas, Anna
Traffic Audit Bureau for Media Measurement (525)

Fournier, Catherine
American Supply Ass'n (119)

Fowler, Donna
American Federation of Teachers (67)

Fowler, James
Institute of Scrap Recycling Industries (269)

Fowler Ph.D., Raymond D.
American Psychological Ass'n (94)

Fowler, Ruth Bennett
Ass'n of Energy Engineers (150)

Fowler Ph.D., Stewart H.
Devon Cattle Ass'n (222)

Fox, Barbara Ramey
North American Deer Farmers Ass'n (441)

Fox, E.K. (Chic)
Automotive Lift Institute (174)

Fox, Frank X.
Professional Ass'n of Resume Writers (464)

Fox, Gary C.
Medical Group Management Ass'n (326)

Fox, James
Internat'l Ass'n of Amusement Parks and Attractions (275)

Fox CAE, Joan S.
Nat'l Ass'n of Educational Buyers (353)

Fox, Karen
American Academy of Pediatric Dentistry (25)

Fox, Kenneth M.
Institute of Scrap Recycling Industries (269)

Fox, Lisa J.
Ass'n of Nurses in AIDS Care (158)

Fox, Norma
Stucco Manufacturers Ass'n (517)

Fox, Rachel
Nat'l Ass'n of Women in Construction (380)

Fox, Raymond G.
Soc. for Applied Learning Technology (485)

Fox, Susan E.
Soc. of American Archivists (497)

Fox, William
Nat'l Safety Council (426)

Foxen CAE, CDT, Jan
Ceilings and Interior Systems Construction Ass'n (189)

Foxwell, Elizabeth
American Ass'n of Colleges for Teacher Education (34)
Soc. for American Archaeology (485)

Foy, Chris
Internat'l Hockey League (293)

Frack CPA, Joseph E.
Society of Financial Service Professionals (509)

Frado, Chris
Cross Country Ski Areas Ass'n (219)

Fram, Arnold
Women in Film (546)

Frame, Kathy
Nat'l Ass'n of Biology Teachers (344)

France Jr., William C.
Nat'l Ass'n for Stock Car Auto Racing (341)

Franchi, Jorge
United States Hispanic Chamber of Commerce (534)

Francis, Ben C.
Public Agency Risk Managers Ass'n (469)

Francis, Carl
Nat'l Football League Players Ass'n (405)

Francis, Delores
Ass'n of Biomolecular Resource Facilities (144)

Francis, Fara
American Ass'n of Colleges of Nursing (34)

Francis, Jason
Soc. for the Advancement of Scandinavian Study (494)

Francis, John
Nat'l Ass'n of Home Inspectors (358)

Francis, Stephen J.
Ass'n of Real Estate License Law Officials (163)

Francis, Wendy
Urban and Regional Information Systems Ass'n (537)

Francisco Jr., George G.
Nat'l Conference of Firemen and Oilers (390)

Francois, Francis B.
American Ass'n of State Highway and Transportation Officials (43)

Frank, Barry
Nat'l Golf Foundation (407)

Frank, Bobbi
Women in Film (546)

Frank, Jean Harris
LOMA (321)

Frank Ph.D., Martin
American Physiological Soc. (92)

Frank, Paul
American Federation of Musicians of the United States and Canada (67)

Frank, Sharon
Institute for Certification of Computing Professionals (265)

Frankel, Lee
Fresh Produce Ass'n of the Americas (244)

Frankenberg Ph.D., Julian M.
Nat'l Ass'n of Advisors for the Health Professions (342)

Frankland Jr., Walter L.
Paper Machine Clothing Council (453)
Silver Users Ass'n (483)

Franklin, Ed
Nat'l Council on Student Development (398)

Franklin Jr., CAE, Joe T.
American Gear Manufacturers Ass'n (70)

Franklin Ph.D., Phyllis
Modern Language Ass'n of America (329)

Franklin, Ruth W.
Council of Defense and Space Industry Ass'ns (213)

Franklin, Thomas M.
Wildlife Soc., The (544)

Franks, Elizabeth B.
Wood Machinery Manufacturers of America (548)

Frantz, David
Paper Machine Clothing Council (453)

Franz, Jerry
American Diabetes Ass'n (64)

Franz Ph.D., Judy R.
American Physical Soc. (92)

Franzel, Robert H.
Air Transport Ass'n of America (16)

Franzen, Pamela W.
Sump and Sewage Pump Manufacturers Ass'n (518)
Nat'l Onsite Wastewater Recycling Ass'n (419)

Franzon, Nancy
Orthopaedic Trauma Ass'n (451)
Academic Orthopaedic Soc. (7)

Fraser, Craig
Police Executive Research Forum (459)

Fraser, Patricia L.
Soc. for Pediatric Dermatology (492)

Frawley, Kathleen A.
American Health Information Management Ass'n (72)

Frazier, Kendal
Nat'l Cattlemen's Beef Ass'n (386)

Frazier, Steven
Nat'l Ass'n of Criminal Defense Lawyers (352)

Frazier-Lindsey, Lorna A.
Ass'n for Education and Rehabilitation of the Blind and Visually Impaired (132)

Frederick, Charles D.
Ass'n of Rotational Molders (164)

Frederick, Fred
Internat'l Ass'n of Administrative Professionals (275)

Frederickson, Maureen
Delta Soc. (221)

Frederickson, Michael L.
Nat'l Lesbian and Gay Journalists Ass'n (415)

Fredrickson Ph.D., Scott
Music and Entertainment Industry Educators Ass'n (332)

Free, Bill
American Corporate Counsel Ass'n (60)

Freedenberg, Sam
Machinery Dealers Nat'l Ass'n (321)

Freedman CAE, Adina Rae
Ass'n of Avian Veterinarians (144)

Freedman, Alan
American Center for Design (51)

Freedman, Marc D.
Painting and Decorating Contractors of America (452)

Freedman, Mike
American Academy of Wound Management (27)
American Subacute Care Ass'n (118)

Freel CMP, Barbara A.
American Public Health Ass'n (95)

Freeland, Carolyn M.
Soc. of Research Administrators (506)

Freeland, Lois J.
Ass'n for Educational Communications and Technology (133)

Freelander, Rabbi Daniel
Union of American Hebrew Congregations (529)

Freeman, Andrea
Land Trust Alliance (317)

Freeman, Anita
Internat'l Hot Rod Ass'n (294)

Freeman, Gary
Software Operations Ass'n (509)

Freeman, Julie A.
Professional Picture Framers Ass'n **(466)**

Freeman Jr., Lewis R.
Soc. of the Plastics Industry **(507)**

Freeman, Lori Tremel
Soc. of Nuclear Medicine **(504)**

Freeman, Michael V.
Healthcare Leadership Council **(253)**

Fregin, Nancy J.
American Soc. of Artists **(107)**

Freihaut, Carol
American Optometric Student Ass'n **(88)**

Freihofer, Stan
Nat'l Ass'n of Agriculture Employees **(343)**

Freitag, Sandria B.
American Historical Ass'n **(73)**

French, Michael
American Holistic Nurses' Ass'n **(73)**

Frendak, Diane
Ass'n of Science-Technology Centers **(164)**

Frendak, Diane K.
Internat'l Soc. for Intercultural Education, Training and Research **(303)**

Frentz, Peter W.
Institute of Transportation Engineers **(269)**

Frerichs, Stephen
American Ass'n of Crop Insurers **(35)**

Frett, Deborah L.
American Hospital Ass'n **(74)**

Freundt, Dorothy
Lutheran Education Ass'n **(321)**

Frey, Charles H.
Construction Industry Manufacturers Ass'n **(206)**

Frey, Jane
American Ass'n of Meat Processors **(38)**

Frey, Ruth
Foundation for Independent Higher Education **(243)**

Freyer, Thom D.
Healthcare Financial Management Ass'n **(252)**

Freyn, Liz
Ass'n for Worksite Health Promotion **(141)**

Frick, G. William
American Petroleum Institute **(91)**

Fricke, Karen
Ass'n for Asian Studies **(130)**

Fricke, Stuart
American Indian Council of Architects and Engineers **(75)**

Friday, Sandra V.
Music Industry Conference **(332)**

Fridrich, Kimberly
Investment Counsel Ass'n of America **(312)**

Frie, Cary
Internat'l Dairy Foods Ass'n **(288)**

Fried, Lisa
American Medical Technologists **(84)**

Fried M.D., Marvin
Soc. of University Otolaryngologists **(508)**

Fried, Phillip P.
Chemical Communications Ass'n **(191)**

Friederich M.D., Mary Anna
Soc. for Menstrual Cycle Research **(491)**

Friedman, Barbara
American Urological Ass'n **(121)**

Friedman, Harold B.
Nat'l Ass'n of Freight Payment Banks **(356)**

Friedman, Howard
Trademark Soc. **(525)**

Friedman, Marsha
Nat'l Wholesale Druggists' Ass'n **(436)**

Friedman, Miles
Nat'l Ass'n of State Development Agencies **(374)**

Friedman, Paula G.
Federal Communications Bar Ass'n **(235)**

Friedman, Peter
Maritime Fire and Safety Ass'n **(324)**

Friedmann, Gay
Interstate Natural Gas Ass'n of America **(311)**

Friend, Patricia A.
Ass'n of Flight Attendants **(151)**

Fries, Gary
Radio Advertising Bureau **(471)**

Fries, James L.
American Veterinary Distributors Ass'n **(121)**
American Veterinary Exhibitors Ass'n **(121)**

Frimpong, Kwame
Nat'l Order of Women Legislators/Nat'l Foundation for Women Legislators **(419)**

Frink, Diane
Nat'l Ass'n of Student Affairs Professionals **(377)**

Frisby Jr., H. Russell
Competitive Telecommunications Ass'n **(201)**

Frischkorn Jr., CAE, Allen R.
American Film Marketing Ass'n **(68)**

Fristensky, Jean
Professional Ass'n of Custom Clothiers **(464)**

Fritts, Edward O.
Nat'l Ass'n of Broadcasters **(345)**

Fritz, Betsy
American Fisheries Soc. **(68)**

Fritz Ph.D., Gayle J.
Soc. of Ethnobiology **(501)**

Fritz, Joni
American Network of Community Options and Resources **(87)**

Fritzlen, Susan
Ass'n of Government Accountants **(152)**

Froeschl, Carol
Soc. for the Advancement of Economic Theory **(494)**

Frohlich, William H.
Nat'l Paper Trade Ass'n **(421)**

Frohmader, Kellie
American Soc. for Engineering Management **(102)**

Froilan, Kathy
Ass'n of College and University Housing Officers-Internat'l **(147)**

Frolicher, Jean S.
Nat'l Council of Higher Education Loan Programs **(395)**

Fromet, Avery H.
Nat'l Ass'n of Waterproofing Contractors **(380)**

Frost, James Ed
Livestock Marketing Ass'n **(320)**

Fry, Edmund M.
Parenteral Drug Ass'n **(453)**

Fry, Gordon
Aluminum Ass'n **(19)**

Fry, Richard N.
Academy of Managed Care Pharmacy **(8)**

Fry, Sonya K.
Overseas Press Club of America **(452)**

Frydman, Hank
Diamond Trade and Precious Stone Ass'n of America **(222)**

Frye, Larry R.
American Walnut Manufacturers Ass'n **(122)**
Walnut Council **(540)**

Frye, Mary
Home Furnishings Internat'l Ass'n **(255)**

Fryer, Michael A.
Nat'l Bareboat Charter Ass'n **(382)**

Fryshman Ph.D., Bernard
Ass'n of Advanced Rabbinical and Talmudic Schools **(141)**

Fuchs, Caroline Hearn
Mathematical Ass'n of America **(325)**

Fuhrer, Ray
Tooling Component Manufacturers Ass'n **(524)**

Fujimura, Robert K.
United States Taekwondo Union **(535)**

Fulcher, Robert A.
American Pharmaceutical Ass'n **(91)**

Fulkerson, Jerry
Design-Build Manufacturers Ass'n **(222)**

Full, Sharon
Nat'l Ass'n of Special Needs State Administrators **(373)**

Fullagar, Paul R.
American Roentgen Ray Soc. **(98)**

Fuller, Mary
American Ass'n for Functional Orthodontics **(30)**

Fuller, Mary P.
Foil Stamping and Embossing Ass'n **(241)**

Fuller, Patricia
North American Spine Soc. **(445)**

Fullerton, Madeline
Central Station Alarm Ass'n **(189)**

Fullilove, Morag
Internat'l Ass'n of Lighting Designers **(280)**

Fullmer, Paul
All-America Rose Selections **(17)**
American Soc. of Golf Course Architects **(110)**

Fulton, Kenneth R.
Nat'l Academy of Sciences **(334)**

Funesti, Charles
Car Department Officers Ass'n **(186)**

Funk, Carla J.
Medical Library Ass'n **(326)**

Funk, Pat
Ass'n of Retail Travel Agents **(163)**

Funk, Rev. Virgil C.
Nat'l Ass'n of Pastoral Musicians **(364)**

Furlow, Brenda
Credit Union Nat'l Ass'n **(218)**

Furmanski, William
Nat'l Foundation for Consumer Credit **(405)**

Furness, Roger K.
Audio Engineering Soc. **(172)**

Fursland, Richard
British-American Chamber of Commerce **(182)**

Fusco, Gregory
Council for Higher Education Accreditation **(211)**

Fuscus, David A.
Air Transport Ass'n of America **(16)**

Futoran D.C., Robin
American College of Chiropractic Orthopedists **(53)**

Futral, Gary
Engineering Contractors' Ass'n **(230)**

Futrell, Catherine
American Soc. for Healthcare Human Resources Administration **(103)**

Futterer, Bobbi & Jim
Dude Ranchers' Ass'n **(225)**

Gabay, Jeannette
Laser Institute of America **(317)**

Gable, Mark
Federal Managers Ass'n **(236)**

Gable, CAE, Ty E.
Nat'l Precast Concrete Ass'n **(423)**

Gabriel, Jeff
Agricultural Retailers Ass'n **(14)**

Gabriel, Rob
Nat'l Mental Health Ass'n **(416)**

Gabrielle, Dianne
American Academy of Psychoanalysis **(26)**
Ass'n for the Advancement of Psychotherapy **(138)**

Gaddy, Catherine D.
Commission on Professionals in Science and Technology **(200)**

Gaddy CAE, Dale
Council on Hotel, Restaurant and Institutional Education **(217)**

Gadsden, E. Dannyette
Women Executives in State Government **(546)**

Gady, Cynthia
Optical Soc. of America **(449)**

Gaffney, Deborah K.
Tax Executives Institute **(520)**

Gaffney, Nancy A.
Council of Graduate Schools **(213)**

Gaffney, Theresa A.
American Nurses Ass'n **(87)**

Gage Jr., Norman H.
Nat'l Time Equipment Ass'n **(434)**

Gager, Russ
North American Retail Dealers Ass'n **(444)**

Gager, William C.
Remanufacturing Industries Council Internat'l **(474)**
Automotive Parts Rebuilders Ass'n **(175)**

Gagliardo, Michael
Municipal Waste Management Ass'n **(331)**

Gahr, Pam
Nat'l Property Management Ass'n **(424)**

Gaigulis, Janis
Ass'n for the Advancement of Baltic Studies **(138)**

Gaillard, John
American Institute of Architects **(76)**

Gaine, John G.
Managed Futures Ass'n **(322)**

Gainyard, Daniel
Soc. for Education in Anesthesia **(487)**
American Soc. of Regional Anesthesia **(115)**

Gaiser, Gundi
Soc. for College and University Planning **(486)**

Gaither, Anne
American Electroplaters and Surface Finishers Soc. **(65)**

Gaivar, Carlos
Nat'l Federation of Hispanics in Communication **(403)**

Galanis, Gary
Brewers' Ass'n of America **(182)**

Galbraith, Suellen
American Network of Community Options and Resources **(87)**

Galbreath, Judy
Air Force Ass'n **(15)**

Gale, David B.
North American Ass'n of State and Provincial Lotteries **(440)**

Gale Ph.D., George D.
Philosophy of Science Ass'n **(457)**

Gale, Michael
American Apparel Manufacturers Ass'n **(28)**

Gale, Robert A.
Nat'l Aggregates Ass'n **(335)**

Gallagher, Amy
Safe and Vault Technicians Ass'n **(478)**

Gallagher, G. James
American Urological Ass'n **(121)**

Gallagher, Helen
Nat'l Committee for Clinical Laboratory Standards **(388)**
NCCLS **(438)**

Gallagher, Jane
American Ass'n of Petroleum Geologists **(40)**
Catholic Charities USA **(188)**

Gecowets, George A.
Council of Logistics Management (215)
Gedance, Suzanne
Nat'l Soc. to Prevent Blindness/Prevent Blindness
America (430)
Gedansky, Lew
Project Management Institute (468)
Gede, Leigh Anne
Interior Design Educators Council (271)
Geer, Ira
American Meteorological Soc. (84)
Geerdes, Richard M.
Nat'l Automatic Merchandising Ass'n (381)
Geerken, Andrew
Nat'l Ass'n of Basketball Coaches (344)
Geffen Ph. D., Amy
Risk and Insurance Management Soc. (476)
Gegg, Joseph C.
Wine and Spirits Wholesalers of America (544)
Gehrisch, Michael
American Hotel and Motel Ass'n (74)
Gehrke, Robert A.
Training Media Ass'n (525)
Geiger, N.J.
Ass'n for Communication Administration (131)
Geisler, A. Richard
Ass'n of Bedding and Furniture Law Officials (144)
Geiss, Valerie
American Kennel Club (80)
Gelak, Deanna
Soc. for Human Resource Management (489)
Gelardi, Robert C.
Healthcare Convention and Exhibitors Ass'n (252)
Internat'l Formula Council (292)
Geldof, Dick
Child Welfare League of America (192)
Geleerd, Zoie
Ass'n for Worksite Health Promotion (141)
Geletka, James R.
Rehabilitation Engineering and Assistive Technology Soc. of
North America (474)
Gellert, George
American Importers and Exporters Meat Products Group (75)
Gelsinger, Roger D.
Ass'n of Operative Millers (159)
Gelvin, Ron
American Dairy Goat Ass'n (63)
Gemelke, Jennifer
Associated Professional Sleep Socs. (172)
Gemmell CAE, Michael K.
Ass'n of Schools of Public Health (164)
Genant, Dr. Harry
Internat'l Skeletal Soc. (302)
Gennardo, Ann
Internat'l Ticketing Ass'n (308)
Gennaro, Mary M.
Nat'l Ass'n of Developmental Disabilities Councils (352)
Genovese, Tammy
Country Music Ass'n (217)
Gent, Michehl R.
North American Electric Reliability Council (441)
Gentes, Bill
Paper Industry Management Ass'n (453)
Gentile Ph.D., Anthony L.
American Ass'n for Crystal Growth (30)
Gentille, John
Nat'l Plumbing Bureau (422)
Gentille, John R.
Mechanical Contractors Ass'n of America (326)
Gentles, Karen
Nat'l Wood Flooring Ass'n (436)
George, Connie
Soc. for History Education (489)
George, Jim
World Internat'l Nail and Beauty Ass'n (550)
George, Richard
Public Relations Soc. of America (470)
George, Rosemary
Nat'l Ass'n of Federal Credit Unions (355)
George, Teresa
Country Music Ass'n (217)
Gephart, Chris
American Urogynecologic Soc. (121)
Gephart, William
American Academy of Teachers of Singing (26)
Gerace, Karen M.
Nat'l Committee for Clinical Laboratory Standards (388)
Gerardi, Pamela
American Council of Teachers of Russian (61)
Gerbakher, Nina
Fashion Ass'n, The (235)

Gerber CAE, Ellen
Public Relations Soc. of America (470)
Gerber, Phyllis
Columbia Sheep Breeders Ass'n of America (198)
Gerber, Stuart
American Ass'n of Exporters and Importers (36)
Gerberich, Mark
Professional Bowlers Ass'n of America (465)
Gerdano, Samuel J.
American Bankruptcy Institute (46)
Gerkin, Daniel R.
Nat'l Mining Ass'n (417)
Gerlach, Lawrence A.
Nat'l Ass'n of Real Estate Companies (369)
German, Jacquilyn
Ass'n of Black Cardiologists (145)
Germek, Paul
Suntanning Ass'n for Education (518)
Germroth, David
Household Goods Forwarders Ass'n of America (257)
Gershen, Ronald I.
Internat'l Soc. of Financiers, Inc. (306)
Gershenow, Rochelle P.
Council on Social Work Education (217)
Gerst, Leesa
Nat'l Coalition for Advanced Manufacturing (387)
Gerstenberger, Peter
Nat'l Arborist Ass'n (337)
Gertel, Susan D.
Ass'n for Institutional Research (135)
Gertzog CAE, Matthew
Nat'l Ass'n of Life Underwriters (361)
Gervasi, Rosetta
American Dental Hygienists' Ass'n (64)
Gerwin, Mary Berry
American Gastroenterological Ass'n (70)
Gessner, David M.
American Podiatric Medical Ass'n (93)
Gettings, Robert M.
Nat'l Ass'n of State Directors of Developmental Disability
Services (374)
Gettys, Angela
Cancer Biotherapy Research Group (186)
Geyer, Wayne B.
Steel Tank Institute (517)
Ghikas, Mary
American Library Ass'n (81)
Ghorbani, Danny D.
Manufactured Housing Ass'n for Regulatory Reform (322)
Giampietro, Wayne
First Amendment Lawyers Ass'n (240)
Giancola P.E., Anthony R.
Nat'l Ass'n of County Engineers (350)
Giannakos, Carrie
Nat'l Appliance Service Ass'n (337)
Giardina, Susan P.
Fur Information Council of America (244)
Gibb, Dr. Jim
Nat'l Cattlemen's Beef Ass'n (386)
Gibbens, Wayne
U.S. Oil and Gas Ass'n (528)
Gibbons, James
Nat'l Industries for the Blind (411)
Gibbons, Jerry
American Ass'n of Advertising Agencies (32)
Gibbs Ph.D., Thomas W.
Materials Technology Institute of the Chemical Process
Industries (325)
Gibson Jr., CAE, Charles W.
Safe and Vault Technicians Ass'n (478)
Associated Locksmiths of America (171)
Gibson, Claudia G.
Nat'l Ass'n of Community Health Centers (349)
Gibson, Doug
United Mine Workers of America Internat'l Union (531)
Gibson, Kevin
United States Parachute Ass'n (534)
Gibson, Larry
Nat'l Grocers Ass'n (407)
Gibson, Leslie
American Ass'n of Cereal Chemists (34)
American Soc. of Brewing Chemists (107)
Gibson, Mark
Aircraft Electronics Ass'n (16)
Gibson, Melissa
Roller Skating Ass'n Internat'l (477)
Giddings, Paul
American Internat'l Automobile Dealers Ass'n (79)
Giebel, Greg
Laborers' Internat'l Union of North America (316)
Giebner, Cara R.
Service Specialists Ass'n (482)

Heavy Duty Representatives Ass'n (253)
Giese, Theodore L.
Abrasives Engineering Soc. (7)
Giesey, Deborah C.
Tax Executives Institute (520)
Giesler, Scott D.
Precision Machined Products Ass'n (462)
Gilanshah, Ellie
Nat'l Industrial Transportation League (411)
Gilbert, Don
Nat'l Retail Federation (425)
Gilbert, Janelle
Artist-Blacksmiths' Ass'n of North America (128)
Gilbert, Kevin T.
White House News Photographers Ass'n (543)
Gilbert, Robert A.
Hospitality Sales and Marketing Ass'n Internat'l (256)
Gilbertson-Smock, Katherine
North American Trakehner Ass'n (445)
Gilcrest, Marlynn
American Miniature Horse Ass'n (85)
Gildee, Tisha
Internat'l Executive Housekeepers Ass'n (290)
Gildenberg M.D., Philip L.
American Soc. for Stereotactic and Functional
Neurosurgery (105)
Giles, Angela
Soc. for Mining, Metallurgy, and Exploration (491)
Giles, Chris
Galiceno Horse Breeders Ass'n (245)
Gilkenson, Beth
American Bankruptcy Institute (46)
Gilkey, Sharada
Ass'n for Professionals in Infection Control and
Epidemiology (136)
Gill, Brian W.
Printing Industries of America (463)
Master Printers of America (324)
Gill, John
Ass'n of Certified Fraud Examiners (146)
American Ass'n for Clinical Chemistry (30)
Gill, Lori L.
Plastic Pipe and Fittings Ass'n (459)
Gill, Samuel H.
American Trucking Ass'ns (121)
Gillan, John T.
Professional Grounds Management Soc. (465)
Gillespie, Ann
American Ass'n of Homes and Services for the Aging (37)
Gillespie, Mike
Plastic Pipe and Fittings Ass'n (459)
Gillespie, Rory
Bowling Writers Ass'n of America (181)
Gillette, Dr. Robert L.
American Canine Sports Medicine Ass'n (50)
Gilligan CAE, Daniel
Petroleum Marketers Ass'n of America (456)
Gilman, Kate
Nat'l Realty Committee (424)
Gilmore, Anna
American Nurses Ass'n (87)
Gilmore, James L.
At-sea Processors Ass'n (172)
Gilmore, Louise J.
American Guild of Musical Artists (71)
Gilpin, Jan
Professional Golfers Ass'n of America (465)
Gilroy, David
IDEA, The Health and Fitness Source (258)
Gilson Ph.D., Erika H.
American Ass'n of Teachers of Turkic Languages (44)
Gilson, Susan
Nat'l Ass'n of Flood and Stormwater Management
Agencies (355)
Interstate Council on Water Policy (311)
Gimbell, Duane
Alliance of Information and Referral Systems (18)
Gioffre, Patrick
Nat'l Rural Electric Cooperative Ass'n (426)
Giordano, Christine
Soc. for Biomolecular Screening (486)
Giordano, Elizabeth
Hispanic Nat'l Bar Ass'n (254)
Giordano, Sam P.
American Ass'n for Respiratory Care (31)
Giovanetti, Geoffrey N.
Wine and Spirits Shippers Ass'n (544)
Giovanni, John
Jockeys' Guild (315)
Girardo, Gunilla
Industrial Designers Soc. of America (262)

Girdner, Milt
Footwear Industries of America (242)

Girolami, Celeste
American Marketing Ass'n (82)

Girolami, Les
American Marketing Ass'n (82)

Girompini, Jack
American Morgan Horse Ass'n (85)

Giroux, Angela
Ass'n of Local Television Stations (156)

Giroux CMP, William
Truckload Carriers Ass'n (527)

Gisin, Jennifer L.
Nat'l Ass'n for Medical Equipment Services (340)

Gitelman, Leslie
American Corporate Counsel Ass'n (60)

Giuffrida, Michael J.
Nat'l Soc. for Healthcare Foodservice Management (429)

Giustino, Maryanne
American Dietetic Ass'n (64)

Givens, Holly
Organic Trade Ass'n (449)

Givler, Peter J.
Ass'n of American University Presses (143)

Glade, Brian J.
Institute for Internat'l Human Resources (265)

Gladics, Frank M.
Independent Forest Products Ass'n (260)

Gladner, Neal
Nat'l Ass'n of State Radio Networks (376)

Gladstone, Debbe
General Federation of Women's Clubs (246)

Gladstone, Vic S.
American Speech-Language-Hearing Ass'n (117)

Glas, Bradley J.
Nat'l Party Boat Owners Alliance (421)

Glascock, David G.
North American Computer Service Ass'n (441)

Glascock, John L.
American Real Estate and Urban Economics Ass'n (97)

Glasgow, Lisa A.
American College of Osteopathic Surgeons (56)

Glasper, Mark
American Ceramic Soc. (51)

Glass, Dick
Electronics Technicians Ass'n Internat'l (229)

Glass, Jason
Medical Records Institute (326)

Glass, Jenne
Synthetic Organic Chemical Manufacturers Ass'n (519)

Glass, Kristy
American Foundrymen's Soc. (69)

Glass, Maureen
American College of Healthcare Executives (54)

Glass, Thomas
Electronics Technicians Ass'n Internat'l (229)

Glasser, Walter A.
American Soc. of Heating, Refrigerating and Air-Conditioning
   Engineers (110)

Glauberman, Alex J.
United Infants and Childrens Wear Ass'n (531)
Associated Corset and Brassiere Manufacturers Ass'n (171)
Industrial Ass'n of Juvenile Apparel Manufacturers (262)
Intimate Apparel Manufacturers Ass'n (312)

Glaze D.V.M., Mary Belle
American College of Veterinary Ophthalmologists (58)

Glazner, Steve
APPA: The Ass'n of Higher Education Facilities Officers (126)

Gleason, Barbara
Ass'n for Supervision and Curriculum Development (138)

Gleason Jr., John P.
Portland Cement Ass'n (460)

Gleason, Kathryn
Nat'l Pharmaceutical Council (422)

Gleason, Pam
Soc. for Buddhist-Christian Studies (486)

Glen, Alixe R.
Pharmaceutical Research and Manufacturers of America (456)

Glenn, Dr. James
Council for Tobacco Research-U.S.A. (212)

Glenn, Michael
Nat'l Religious Broadcasters (425)

Glenn, Robert E.
Nat'l Industrial Sand Ass'n (411)

Glenwick Ph.D., David
American Ass'n for Correctional Psychology (30)

Glezin, Misha
Jewelers of America (314)

Glick, Barry
North American Plant Preservation Council (443)
Wood Tank Manufacturers Ass'n (548)

Glickman, Todd
American Meteorological Soc. (84)

Glisson, Jo Anne
American Clinical Laboratory Ass'n (52)

Gloe, Donna
Dermatology Nurses Ass'n (221)

Gloninger, Marian H.
Nat'l Federation of Abstracting and Information Services (403)

Glover, Frances
University Continuing Education Ass'n (537)

Glover Ph.D., Robert W.
Nat'l Ass'n of State Mental Health Program Directors (375)

Glover, Thomas D.
Christian Schools Internat'l (193)

Gobel, Roger
American Foreign Law Ass'n (69)

Gober, Nancy C.
Nat'l Ass'n of Surety Bond Producers (377)

Godard, Montrice
Conference of State Bank Supervisors (204)

Goddard, Carol A.
Ass'n of Physician Assistants in Cardiovascular Surgery (160)

Goddard, Stephen
Print Council of America (462)

Godfrey, Gary L.
Independent Free Papers of America (260)

Godfrey Ph.D., Paul Joseph
Nat'l Institutes for Water Resources (412)

Godley USNR, Captain John
Naval Reserve Ass'n (438)

Godsman, James G.
Cruise Lines Internat'l Ass'n (219)

Godwin, Jean C.
American Ass'n of Port Authorities (41)

Goebel, Christopher
Nat'l Ass'n of Chemical Recyclers (347)

Goebeler, Fred
CUMREC Internat'l (219)

Goecks, Donald
Emerging Markets Traders Ass'n (229)

Goehring, Charles B.
Truss Plate Institute (527)

Goertz, Dr. Christine
American Chiropractic Ass'n (51)

Goessel CAE, Arthur D.
Internat'l Affiliation of Independent Accounting Firms (272)

Goetz, Christopher
Internat'l Federation of Pharmaceutical Wholesalers (290)

Goetz, Julie A.
Special Interest Group on Computing at Community
   Colleges (513)
Special Interest Group for Algorithm and Computation
   Theory (511)
Special Interest Group for Symbolic and Algebraic
   Manipulation (512)
Special Interest Group on Documentation (513)
Special Interest Group on APL Programming Language (512)
Special Interest Group on Numerical Mathematics (513)
Special Interest Group on Software Engineering (513)

Goetz, Steven
Health Care Resource Management Soc. (251)

Goetz, Tom
Associated Construction Distributors Internat'l (171)

Goetz, William
Internat'l Federation of Pharmaceutical Wholesalers (290)

Goetze, Marian E.
Internat'l Alliance: An Ass'n of Executive and Professional
   Women, The (273)

Goewey Carey, Susan
University Continuing Education Ass'n (537)

Goff Ph.D., Linda
Phycological Soc. of America (457)

Goff, Mary
Nat'l Ass'n of Railroad Trial Counsel (368)

Goff, Dr. Will
American Ass'n of Veterinary Immunologists (45)

Goggins CPCM, CAE, James W.
Nat'l Contract Management Ass'n (392)

Gold, Heather
Ass'n of Local Telecommunications Services (156)

Gold, Jody
American Medical Soc. for Sports Medicine (84)

Gold, Nancy
Endocrine Soc. (230)

Goldberg, Barbara
American Speech-Language-Hearing Ass'n (117)

Goldberg, Bert J.
Ass'n of Jewish Family and Children's Agencies (155)

Goldberg, Casey
American Academy of Audiology (20)

Goldberg M.D., David A.
American Ass'n of Directors of Psychiatric Residency
   Training (36)

Goldberg Ph.D., Michael I.
American Soc. for Microbiology (104)

Goldberg, Peter
Alliance for Children and Families (17)

Goldberg, Robert C.
Business Technology Ass'n (185)

Goldberg, Robert J.
Nat'l Health Council (408)

Goldberg, Robert L.
Nat'l Investment Company Service Ass'n (413)

Goldberg, Ronnie L.
United States Council for Internat'l Business (533)

Goldberg, Sharon T.
Pediatric Orthopedic Soc. of North America (454)

Golden, James
Energy Efficient Building Ass'n (230)

Golden, Nancy
Victorian Soc. in America (539)

Golden, Peggy L.
Nat'l Ass'n of Women Lawyers (381)

Golden, William
FTD Ass'n (244)

Goldfarb, Bob
American Composers Alliance (59)

Goldfarb, Ron
IEEE Magnetics Soc. (258)

Goldhaber, Richard F.
Nat'l Metal Spinners Ass'n (417)

Goldhammer Ph.D., Alan
Biotechnology Industry Organization (179)

Golding, Lloyd L.
American Truck Stop Operators Ass'n (121)

Goldman, James L.
Soc. for Industrial and Applied Mathematics (489)

Goldman, Marlene
Internat'l Information Management Congress (294)

Goldman, Patricia
American Ass'n of Colleges for Teacher Education (34)

Goldman, Seth
Internat'l Soc. for Experimental Hematology (303)

Goldman Ph.D., Solomon
Council for Jewish Education (211)

Goldrich, Lois
United Synagogue of Conservative Judaism (536)

Goldring, Katherine T.
New York Academy of Sciences (438)

Goldsborough, Margaret
Nat'l Ass'n of Independent Schools (360)

Goldsmith Ph.D., Barbara
Nat'l Academy of Clinical Biochemistry (334)

Goldsmith, Barry
Nat'l Ass'n of Securities Dealers (372)

Goldstein, Gary
Nat'l Coffee Ass'n of the U.S.A. (387)

Goldstein CMP, FACS, Jerome
American Academy of Otolaryngology-Head and Neck
   Surgery (24)

Goldstein, Robert
Internat'l Soc. for Magnetic Resonance in Medicine (303)

Goldstein, Dr. Stanley
American Podiatric Circulatory Soc. (93)

Goldstein, Steven
Insurance Information Institute (270)

Golisch, Jennifer
Internat'l Fresh-cut Produce Ass'n (292)

Golla, Victor
Soc. for the Study of Indigenous Languages of the
   Americas (495)

Golodner, Linda F.
Nat'l Consumers League (392)

Golub, Judith
American Immigration Lawyers Ass'n (74)

Gomberg, Irene
American Council on Education (61)

Gomez, Dr. Manuel
American Industrial Hygiene Ass'n (75)

Gondles Jr., James A.
American Correctional Ass'n (60)

Gonnerman, David
Surface Mount Technology Ass'n (519)

Gonsalves, Tina
Wallcoverings Ass'n (540)

Gonzales, Anita
Petroleum Marketers Ass'n of America (456)

Gonzales, Jesse
American Academy of Nurse Practitioners (23)

Gonzales, Margaret G.
Soc. of Mexican American Engineers and Scientists (504)

Gonzales, Mary
Nat'l Spinal Cord Injury Ass'n (431)

Gonzalez, Imelda
Nat'l Ass'n for Treasurers of Religious Institutes (342)

Gonzalez, Ralph
Soc. of Mexican American Engineers and Scientists (504)

Gonzalez, Rene
Hispanic Ass'n of Colleges and Universities (254)

Gonzalez-Cerda, Alejandra
Nat'l Alliance of Short Story Authors (336)

Good, Carl
Nat'l Roofing Contractors Ass'n (426)

Good, Lisa S.
Nat'l Federation of Municipal Analysts (403)

Good, Shelly
Nat'l Utility Contractors Ass'n (435)

Good CAE, William A.
Nat'l Roofing Contractors Ass'n (426)

Goodenow, Robert W.
Nat'l Hockey League Player's Ass'n (409)

Goodhope, Randy
American Resort Development Ass'n (98)

Goodman, Alan
Jewish Social Service Professionals Ass'n (314)

Goodman, Don
Ass'n for Humanist Sociology (134)

Goodman, G. Thomas
Nat'l Ass'n of Counties (350)
Nat'l Ass'n of County Information Officers (351)

Goodman, Gennie
League for Innovation in the Community College (318)

Goodman, Jane
Ass'n of Flight Attendants (151)

Goodman Jr., John L.
Nat'l Multi Housing Council (417)

Goodman, Michael E.
American Soc. of Corporate Secretaries (109)

Goodmiller, Brian D.
Precast/Prestressed Concrete Institute (462)

Goodrich, Kristina
Industrial Designers Soc. of America (262)

Goodridge, Cindy
Electrocoat Ass'n (228)

Goodridge, Patricia
American Marketing Ass'n (82)

Goodspeed, David M.
Nat'l Council for Prescription Drug Programs (393)

Goodwin, Barbara
Lutheran Education Ass'n (321)

Goodwin, Becky
American Guernsey Ass'n (71)

Goodwin Jr., D.V.M, Bradford S.
American Soc. of Laboratory Animal Practitioners (111)

Goodwin, Frank
Internat'l Lead Zinc Research Organization (295)

Goodwin II, James
Ass'n of Clinical Research Professionals (147)

Goodwin, Jennifer
Nat'l Ass'n of Industrial and Office Properties (360)

Goodwin, Joan
Institute on Religion in an Age of Science (269)

Goodwin, Michael
Office and Professional Employees Internat'l Union (447)

Goodwin, Rod
American Academy of Estate Planning Attorneys (22)

Goodwin, William
Institute of Internat'l Bankers (267)

Goodwine, Joan
Ductile Iron Pipe Research Ass'n (225)

Goodyear, Al
North American Council of Automotive Teachers (441)

Goolsby, Larry
Nat'l Ass'n of Program Information and Performance Measurement (367)
American Ass'n of Food Stamp Directors (37)

Goon, Julie
American Ass'n of Health Plans (37)

Gordan D.V.M., John
Omega Tau Sigma (448)

Gordley, John
United States Canola Ass'n (532)

Gordon, David
Associated Equipment Distributors (171)

Gordon, Gloria
Internat'l Ass'n of Business Communicators (276)

Gordon, Herbert D.
Ass'n of Directory Marketing (149)

Gordon, Jim
Nat'l Ass'n of Chiefs of Police (347)

Gordon Ph.D., Julie
Econometric Soc. (225)

Gordon, Mary France
Hispanic Elected Local Officials (254)
Nat'l Black Caucus of Local Elected Officials (383)

Women in Municipal Government (547)

Gordon Ph.D., Michael
Nat'l Pan Hellenic Council (421)

Gordon, Randall C.
Nat'l Grain and Feed Ass'n (407)

Gordon, Sandra R.
American Academy of Dermatology (21)

Gordon, Shannon
Ass'n for Educational Communications and Technology (133)

Gordon, Timothy W.
American Psychiatric Nurses Ass'n (94)

Gordon, William R.
American Library Ass'n (81)

Gore, Dorothy
CBA (188)

Gore Peters, Shannon
Institute of Transportation Engineers (269)

Goree, Sonja D.
American Ass'n of Colleges for Teacher Education (34)

Gorelick, Richard
Graphic Arts Sales Foundation (249)

Gorham, Millicent
Nat'l Black Nurses Ass'n (383)

Gorin, David
Nat'l Ass'n of RV Parks and Campgrounds (370)

Gorin CAE, Susan
Nat'l Ass'n of School Psychologists (371)

Gorman, Bridget
Club Managers Ass'n of America (195)

Gorman, John A.
Internat'l Organization of Masters, Mates and Pilots (299)

Gorman, Judith
Institute of Electrical and Electronics Engineers (266)

Gorman, Mary
Nat'l Ass'n of Children's Hospitals and Related Institutions (347)

Gorman CAE, R. Mickey
Nat'l Paperbox Ass'n (421)

Gorn, Kimberly
Nat'l Air Duct Cleaners Ass'n (335)

Gorry, Michael
United Weighers Ass'n (536)

Gorsegner, Betty
Ass'n for Information Media and Equipment (135)

Gorski CAE, Thomas A.
American Academy of Orthotists and Prosthetists (24)

Gorson, Craig
American Ass'n of Family Businesses (37)

Gortenburg, Gary
Nat'l Ass'n of County Training and Employment Professionals (351)

Gorup CAE, Jerry
Internat'l Furniture Rental Ass'n (292)

Gorup CAE, Sharon R.
Ass'n of Interim Housing Providers (154)

Gorzelnik, Eugene F.
North American Electric Reliability Council (441)

Goss, Edward
Arthroscopy Ass'n of North America (128)

Goss, Kenneth A.
Air Force Ass'n (15)

Goswami Ph.D., Bhuvenesh C.
Fiber Soc. (238)

Gottlieb, Martin S.
American Institute of Engineers (77)

Gottschall, Kate
American Council of Teachers of Russian (61)

Gottwald, Rich
Plastics Pipe Institute (459)

Gould, Alissa
Graphic Arts Technical Foundation (249)

Gould, Rebecca M.
Business Software Alliance (185)

Goulding, Tressa
Scoliosis Research Soc. (480)

Govindan M.D., Srini
American Academy of Thermology (26)

Goyer, Anne
Chemical Coaters Ass'n Internat'l (191)

Goyette, Diane
Nat'l Wholesale Druggists' Ass'n (436)

Grabau, Thomas
Council for Advancement and Support of Education (210)

Graber, Norman
Nat'l Labor Relations Board Professional Ass'n (414)

Grabowski, Gene
Grocery Manufacturers of America (250)

Grace, Sharon
Telecommunications Industry Ass'n (521)

Grad, Robert
Institute for Applied Iridology (264)

Graddy, Julia
Agricultural Communicators in Education (14)

Gradison Jr., Bill
Health Insurance Ass'n of America (252)

Gradkowski, Richard
United States Fencing Coaches Ass'n (533)

Grady, Clarissa L.
Nat'l Ass'n of Blacks in Criminal Justice (345)

Grady, Kathryn
American Soc. of Orthopaedic Physician's Assistants (113)
Internat'l Soc. of Arthroscopy, Knee Surgery and Orthopaedic Sports Medicine (305)

Grady, Tim
American Psychological Practitioners Ass'n (95)

Graetzer, Kurt S.
Internat'l Dairy Foods Ass'n (288)

Graf Ph.D., David
Professional and Organizational Development Network in Higher Education (464)

Graff, Brian
American Soc. of Pension Actuaries (114)

Graff, John R.
Internat'l Ass'n of Amusement Parks and Attractions (275)

Graff Ph.D., Karl
Edison Welding Institute (226)

Gragg, Bill
Internat'l Tire and Rubber Ass'n (309)

Graham, Alex
Ass'n of School Business Officials Internat'l (164)

Graham, Daniel
Internat'l Foundation of Employee Benefit Plans (292)

Graham, Daniel W.
Internat'l Soc. of Certified Employee Benefit Specialists (305)

Graham, Dennis
Institute of Financial Education (267)

Graham, Elaine Z.
Nat'l Restaurant Ass'n (425)

Graham, John
Nat'l Ass'n of Electrical Distributors (353)

Graham IV, John H.
American Diabetes Ass'n (64)

Graham, Lauren J.
Investment Company Institute (312)

Graham, Lawrence T.
American Cocoa Research Institute (52)
Chocolate Manufacturers Ass'n of the U.S.A. (193)
Nat'l Confectioners Ass'n of the United States (389)

Graham, Mark
Nat'l Roofing Contractors Ass'n (426)

Graham, Mary
Nat'l Mental Health Ass'n (416)

Graham, Maryanne S.
Property Owners Ass'n (468)

Graham M.D., Michael
Nat'l Ass'n of Medical Examiners (362)

Graham M.D., CAE, Robert
American Academy of Family Physicians (22)

Graham Poole, Kathleen
American Soc. for Colposcopy and Cervical Pathology (101)

Grainaw, Lorri
Steel Tank Institute (517)

Gramp, Gary
Hardwood Plywood and Veneer Ass'n (251)

Granados, Ruth
Nat'l Ass'n for College Admission Counseling (338)

Granath CMP, Kay V.
Ass'n of Rehabilitation Nurses (163)

Grande M.D., MPH, Christopher M.
Internat'l Trauma Anesthesia and Critical Care Soc. (309)

Grande Brady, Linda
Ass'n of Teachers of Preventive Medicine (167)

Grandel, Beth
American Lighting Ass'n (81)

Grandstaff, Herald
Graphic Communications Internat'l Union (249)

Granger, Christopher
Regulatory Affairs Professionals Soc. (474)

Granger, Robin
Cleaning Management Institute (194)

Grant, Carl N.
Chamber of Commerce of the United States of America (190)

Grant, Caryl S.
American College of Osteopathic Surgeons (56)

Grant, Daniel
North American Building Material Distribution Ass'n (441)

Grant, Kevin
Institute of Roofing and Waterproofing Consultants Internat'l (269)

Grant, Mary Ann
Internat'l Institute of Ammonia Refrigeration (294)

Grant, Susan
Nat'l Consumers League (392)

Grass, Andrew N.
Security Traders Ass'n (481)

Grasser, John
Nat'l Mining Ass'n (417)

Grassman, Paul
Institute of Food Technologists (267)

Grasso, Mary Ann
Nat'l Ass'n of Theatre Owners (378)

Grasso, Richard A.
New York Stock Exchange (438)

Grasso, Robert J.
Synthetic Organic Chemical Manufacturers Ass'n (519)

Grau, John M.
Nat'l Electrical Contractors Ass'n (400)

Grauberger, Janice
American Sheep Industry Ass'n (99)

Graulich, Melody
Western Literature Ass'n (543)

Gravatt, Nancy
American Iron and Steel Institute (79)

Graveline, Denise
American Chemical Soc. (51)

Gravelle, Norm
Ass'n for Institutional Research (135)

Graver, Kimberly
Sheet Metal and Air Conditioning Contractors' Nat'l Ass'n (482)

Graves, David R.
Nat'l Council of Farmer Cooperatives (394)

Graves, Laurie
American Healthcare Radiology Administrators (72)

Graves, Stephen W.
Nat'l Swim School Ass'n (432)
Swimming Teachers of America (519)

Graves, Steve
Club Pool Ass'n (195)

Graves, Victoria
Federation of Socs. for Coatings Technology (237)

Gray CAE, Albert C.
Water Environment Federation (541)

Gray, Bonnie
Internat'l Right of Way Ass'n (301)

Gray, Cary
Nat'l Spa and Pool Institute (431)

Gray, Charles D.
Nat'l Ass'n of Regulatory Utility Commissioners (369)

Gray, David B.
Soc. for News Design (491)

Gray, Deborah
Soc. for Historians of the Early American Republic (489)

Gray, Fred A.
Industrial Diamond Ass'n of America (262)

Gray, G. Stephen
Automatic Transmission Rebuilders Ass'n (173)

Gray, Geoffrey P.
Ass'n of Financial Services Holding Companies (151)

Gray, Gerald
American Forests (69)

Gray, John
Food Distributors Internat'l (241)

Gray, Margie
Institute of Public Utilities (268)

Gray, Nancy R.
American Chemical Soc. (51)

Gray, Neil
Internat'l Bridge, Tunnel and Turnpike Ass'n (284)

Gray, Peggy
American Soc. for Clinical Investigation (101)

Gray, Philip H.
Ass'n of American Pesticide Control Officials (142)

Gray Jr., Robin B.
Nat'l Electronic Distributors Ass'n (400)

Gray CAE, Sandra Trice
Independent Sector (261)

Gray, Sky
Ass'n for Experiential Education (133)

Gray, Thomas
American Wind Energy Ass'n (123)

Gray, Valerie
United States-Mexico Chamber of Commerce (536)

Grayson, Helen D.
American Restaurant China Council (98)

Grayson, Mark
Pharmaceutical Research and Manufacturers of America (456)

Graziano Ph.D., Joseph
Ass'n of University Environmental Health/Sciences Centers (168)

Grear, Sandra
College of American Pathologists (197)

Greeley Esq., Donald
American Fiber Manufacturers Ass'n (68)

Greeley Jr., CAE, Paul J.
American Chamber of Commerce Executives (51)

Green, Annette
Fragrance Foundation (243)

Green, Cecilia
Soc. of Actuaries (496)

Green, Jeff
Country Music Ass'n (217)

Green, Joseph S.
Ass'n of State and Territorial Health Officials (166)

Green, Judy L.
Family Firm Institute (234)

Green, Kimberly A.
Nat'l Ass'n of State Directors of Vocational-Technical Education (375)

Green, Maggie
American Institute of Constructors (77)

Green CFC, CPSS, Marj
Document Management Industries Ass'n (224)

Green, Marjorie
Earthquake Engineering Research Institute (225)

Green, Paul
Information Technology Ass'n of America (264)

Green, Paulette
American Finance Ass'n (68)

Green, Peggy
American Soc. of Radiologic Technologists (115)

Green, Rich
Edison Welding Institute (226)

Green, Rodney
United Paperworkers Internat'l Union (531)

Green D.V.M., Ronnie
Nat'l Block and Bridle Club (383)

Green, Stacey
American Immigration Lawyers Ass'n (74)

Green-Sappington, Harriet
Ass'n of University Interior Designers (168)

Greenaway, Douglas A.
Nat'l Ass'n of WIC Directors (380)

Greenbaum Jr., Ph.D., Leon J.
Undersea and Hyperbaric Medical Soc. (529)

Greenberg, Lynn
Qualitative Research Consultants Ass'n (470)

Greenberg M.P.P., Pamela
American Managed Behavioral Healthcare Ass'n (82)

Greenberg, Maj. Gen. Paul
Nat'l Defense Industrial Ass'n (399)

Greenberg, Robert
American Gastroenterological Ass'n (70)

Greenberger MSW, Phyllis M.
Soc. for the Advancement of Women's Health Research (495)

Greene, Jack
American Correctional Ass'n (60)

Greene, Joe L.
American Federation of School Administrators (67)

Greene SPHR, Keith J.
Media Human Resources Ass'n (326)

Greene, Michael
Nat'l Academy of Recording Arts and Sciences (334)

Greene, Richard
Laser Institute of America (317)

Greene, Sarah M.
Nat'l Head Start Ass'n (408)

Greene Smith, Julie
Electric Power Supply Ass'n (227)

Greenfield, Jennifer
Nat'l Institute of Governmental Purchasing (412)

Greenland, Donald R.
American Chain of Warehouses (51)

Greenleaf, Ted
Nat'l Ass'n of Elementary School Principals (353)

Greenlee Ph.D., Jason M.
Internat'l Ass'n of Wildland Fire (283)

Greenly, Ray M.
American Soc. of Travel Agents (116)

Greenslit, John F.
Bedding Plants International (177)

Greenstone, S.M.
Phi Delta Epsilon Medical Fraternity (456)

Greenwald, Michael
American Law Institute (81)

Greenway CMP, Julia
Futures Industry Ass'n (245)

Greenwood, Karen E.
American Medical Informatics Ass'n (84)

Greer, Chris
RNA Soc. (476)

Greer, Jean
Customer Relations Institute (219)

Greer, Tami
Ass'n of Official Seed Analysts (158)

Greer, William
Food Marketing Institute (241)

Greetham, David C.
Soc. for Textual Scholarship (494)

Grefe, Richard
American Institute of Graphic Arts (77)

Gregoire, John
Credit Union Nat'l Ass'n (218)

Gregory, Cathy
Nat'l Hardwood Lumber Ass'n (408)

Gregory, Janice M.
ERISA Industry Committee (232)

Gregory, Janis
Pedorthic Footwear Ass'n (454)

Gregory, Mariann B.
Nat'l Ass'n of Floor Covering Distributors (355)

Gregory, Dr. Richard O.
American Soc. for Laser Medicine and Surgery (103)

Grehan, Arthur
American Innerspring Manufacturers (75)

Greifer M.D., Ira
Internat'l Pediatric Nephrology Ass'n (299)

Grell Ed.D., Lewis A.
Ass'n for the Advancement of Internat'l Education (138)

Grenham, Ginny
Healthcare Leadership Council (253)

Grieb, Gina
Nat'l Ass'n of School Psychologists (371)

Grier, Sharon
Timber Framers Guild of North America (523)

Grieshaber, Mel
Internat'l Ass'n of Correctional Officers (278)

Griesing, Dennis C.
Soap and Detergent Ass'n (484)

Griffee, Ellen
Ass'n of Science-Technology Centers (164)

Griffenhagen, George
American Philatelic Soc. Writers Unit (91)

Griffin, Daniel E.
Motor and Equipment Manufacturers Ass'n (330)

Griffin, Daniell
Nat'l Soc. of Accountants (429)

Griffin Jr., CAE, Edwin L.
Meeting Professionals Internat'l (327)

Griffin, Joyce
Soc. of Trauma Nurses (508)

Griffin, Kim G.
Nat'l Tour Ass'n (434)

Griffin, Marian Long
Amusement and Music Operators Ass'n (124)

Griffin, Michael G.
County Executives of America (218)

Griffin, Shelley
Archaeological Institute of America (126)

Griffin, Susan
Nat'l Council for the Social Studies (393)

Griffin, Toni
American Arbitration Ass'n (28)

Griffith, Carl
Nat'l Safety Management Soc. (426)

Griffith, Carlsen
Nat'l League of Cities (414)

Griffith, David
Nat'l Ass'n of State Boards of Education (374)

Griffith, Don
American Compensation Ass'n (59)

Griffith, Joan
Nat'l Paperbox Ass'n (421)

Griffith, Prescott F.
American Dinner Theatre Institute (64)

Griffith, Ralph E.
Nat'l Ass'n of School Safety and Law Enforcement Officers (371)

Griffiths, L. Gene
Marking Device Ass'n Internat'l (324)

Griggs, Gregory K.
Filter Manufacturers Council (238)

Griggs, Harris B.
Engraved Stationery Manufacturers Ass'n (231)

Griggs, Karen C.
Nat'l Aircraft Finance Ass'n (335)

Grigsby, Lucy
College Language Ass'n (197)

Grikmanis, Tina
American Dental Assistants Ass'n (64)

Grilliot D.C., James R.
Internat'l Research Council of Neuromuscular Disorders (301)

Grim, Gwen A.
Soc. of Diagnostic Medical Sonographers (500)

Grimes, Joe
Nat'l Paint and Coatings Ass'n (420)

Grimes, Julie
Soc. of Professional Journalists (506)

Grimes, Rick
Academy of Medical-Surgical Nurses (9)
American Nephrology Nurses Ass'n (86)

Grimes, Susan
American Academy of Optometry (24)

Grimm, Jane
American Soc. of Pension Actuaries (114)

Grimm, Rick
Nat'l Institute of Governmental Purchasing (412)

Grisamore, Judith S.
American Ass'n for Laboratory Animal Science (31)

Grisham, R.B.
Nat'l Independent Automobile Dealers Ass'n (410)

Grisso, Cindy
Independent Petroleum Ass'n of America (261)

Grissom, Joe
Pinto Horse Ass'n of America (458)

Gristci, Joseph A.
Motor and Equipment Manufacturers Ass'n (330)

Grizzell, Adrienne
Nat'l Ass'n of Institutional Linen Management (360)

Groat, Vicki
American Planning Ass'n (92)

Grodensky, Sara Jeen
Luggage and Leather Goods Salesmen's Ass'n of America (321)

Groeneveld CAE, Susan J.
Commercial-Investment Real Estate Institute (199)

Gross, Brenda
American Electroplaters and Surface Finishers Soc. (65)

Gross, David
American Soc. of Knitting Technologists (111)

Gross, Debbie
Council of Large Public Housing Authorities (214)

Gross, Gail
Nat'l Ass'n of Elementary School Principals (353)

Gross, Wayne H.
Technical Ass'n of the Pulp and Paper Industry (520)

Grossberg Ph.D., Sydney
American Soc. for Virology (106)

Grossgart, Chris
Internat'l Ass'n of Business Communicators (276)

Grossman, Donna
Nat'l Ass'n of County and City Health Officials (350)

Grossman, Lawrence
Council on Superconductivity (217)

Grossman, Mary
Soc. for the Advancement of Socio-Economics (495)

Grossman Quinn CPA, Lynn
APICS - The Educational Society for Resource Management (125)

Groth, Donald
Nat'l Ass'n of Off-Track Betting (364)

Grotta, Emily
Union of American Hebrew Congregations (529)

Groundwater, John
Passenger Vessel Ass'n (454)

Grove, Henry S.
Internat'l Teleconferencing Ass'n (308)

Grove CAE, Dr. Judith A.
Water Quality Ass'n (541)

Grove Jr., Richard E.
Internat'l Swaps and Derivatives Ass'n (308)

Grover, Christopher
California Redwood Ass'n (185)

Groves, Betty J.
Clydesdale Breeders of the United States (195)

Grubb, Kathryn K.
Advertising Research Foundation (12)

Gruber, Barbara
Parapsychological Ass'n (453)

Grucza, Margaret R.
Industrial Research Institute (263)

Gruenburg, Drew N.
Soc. of American Florists (497)

Grumbacher, Jacqueline W.
Mortgage Bankers Ass'n of America (330)

Grundahl, Kirk
Wood Truss Council of America (548)

Grunewald, Benjamin J.
Ground Water Protection Council (250)

Grunig, Andy
Nat'l School Public Relations Ass'n (427)

Gschwend MA, MBA, Rebecca R.
Council of Medical Specialty Socs. (215)

Guarino, Carol
Nat'l Council of Juvenile and Family Court Judges (395)

Guder, Darrell
American Soc. of Missiology (112)

Gudinas, Dave
Internat'l Ass'n of Fire Chiefs (279)

Guenther, Kenneth A.
Independent Bankers Ass'n of America (260)

Guerin, Doreen
Toy Manufacturers of America (524)

Guernsey, Nellie E.
American Institute of Mining, Metallurgical, and Petroleum Engineers (78)

Gugerty MS,RNC, Kathleen
Soc. of Gastroenterology Nurses and Associates (502)

Guggloz, Richard A.
Sports Lawyers Ass'n (515)

Guggolz, Richard A.
Transportation Research Forum (526)
Nat'l Ass'n of Rehabilitation Agencies (369)
Fire Equipment Manufacturers Suppliers Ass'n (239)

Guhl, Tracey
American Public Communications Council (95)

Guice, Mary
Ass'n of Automotive Aftermarket Distributors (144)

Guida, Al
Nat'l Mental Health Ass'n (416)

Guilford, Lisa
Self Insurance Institute of America (481)

Guinn, Jim
American Soybean Ass'n (117)

Guldin, Robert
American Foreign Service Ass'n (69)

Gumaru, Wilfredo
American Compensation Ass'n (59)

Gummer, George
Gamma Iota Sigma (245)

Gump Jr., Richard A.
Directional Crossing Contractors Ass'n (223)

Guniss, Carolyn
Soc. of American Business Editors and Writers (497)

Gunn, Gil
Ass'n of Automotive Aftermarket Distributors (144)

Gunster, Doug
Nat'l Ass'n of WIC Directors (380)

Gunstream, Robby D.
College Music Soc. (197)

Gunzburg Ph.D., Frank
Nat'l Board for Certified Clinical Hypnotherapists (383)

Gupta, Bina
Soc. of Asian and Comparative Philosophy (498)

Gupta Ph.D., Sushil K.
Production and Operations Management Soc. (463)

Gural, Barbara
Cable and Telecommunications Ass'n for Marketing (185)

Gurthet, H. Louis
American Institute of Steel Construction (78)

Gusdorf, Lori
Nat'l Soc. of Fund Raising Executives (429)

Gusky, David
Nat'l Wireless Resellers Ass'n (436)

Gustafson, Deborah S.
Council for Art Education (211)
Art and Creative Materials Institute (127)

Gustafson, Elyse R.
Institute of Mathematical Statistics (268)

Gustafson, Jack
Nat'l Ass'n of State Alcohol and Drug Abuse Directors (373)

Gustavson Ph.D., E. Brandt
Nat'l Religious Broadcasters (425)

Gustavson, Mary Agnes
Leather Industries of America (318)

Guthrie, Marty
Nat'l Ass'n of Student Financial Aid Administrators (377)

Guthrie, Nancy M.
Ass'n of Legal Administrators (155)

Guthrie, Robert W.
Non Commissioned Officers Ass'n of the U.S.A. (439)

Gutstein, Martin
Fuel Cell Institute (244)

Gutt CAE, Phillip A.
American Soc. for Apheresis (101)
Ass'n of Faculty Clubs Internat'l (150)

Gutting Jr., Dick
Shrimp Council (483)

Gutting Jr., Richard E.
Nat'l Fisheries Institute (404)

Guy, Laura
Ass'n of Automotive Aftermarket Distributors (144)

Guy, IV, John H.
Nat'l Petroleum Council (422)

Guzman, David
Nat'l Ass'n of Veterans Program Administrators (379)

Guzman, Vivianna
American Management Ass'n Internat'l (82)

Gwin Jr., George B.
American Innerspring Manufacturers (75)

Gyomory, Barbara
American Ass'n of Pastoral Counselors (40)

Haack, Susan
American Health Information Management Ass'n (72)

Haas, Frank
America's Community Bankers (20)

Haas, Richard
Associated Builders and Contractors (170)

Haase, Ken
Nat'l Futures Ass'n (406)

Haber Ph.D., Bernard
American Soc. for Neurochemistry (104)

Haber, Joram Graf
American Soc. for Value Inquiry (106)

Haber Ph.D., Pierre C.
Psychology Soc. (469)

Haber, Sherry J.
Nat'l Wholesale Druggists' Ass'n (436)

Haberman, Louise Dratler
Nat'l Ass'n of State Boards of Accountancy (374)

Habingreither, William
American College of Physicians-American Soc. of Internal Medicine (57)

Hacke, Kevin R.
Ass'n for Worksite Health Promotion (141)
Maple Flooring Manufacturers Ass'n (323)

Hacker CAE, Steven G.
Internat'l Ass'n for Exposition Management (274)

Hackett CHE, CAE, Karen L.
American College of Healthcare Executives (54)

Hackett, Susan
American Corporate Counsel Ass'n (60)

Hackett, Tamra
Soc. of Research Administrators (506)

Hackney, Ellen
Nat'l Retail Hardware Ass'n (425)

Haddad Ph.D., Abraham H.
American Automatic Control Council (46)

Hadden, Eddie R.
Organization of Black Airline Pilots (450)

Hadeed, Sam
Ass'n of Metropolitan Sewerage Agencies (157)

Haden, Mabel Dole
Nat'l Ass'n of Black Women Attorneys (345)

Haders, Donna
Diamond Wheel Manufacturers Institute (222)

Hadley Jr., Joseph E.
Ethylene Oxide Sterilization Ass'n (233)
Aniline Ass'n (124)

Hadley, Kay S.
Fashion Group Internat'l (235)

Hadley M.D., Mark
Congress of Neurological Surgeons (205)

Hadley, Sherry W.
Airborne Law Enforcement Ass'n (16)

Hadley, William T.
Insurance Marketing Communications Ass'n (270)

Haeger, Warren J.
Real Estate Aviation Chapter (472)

Haenszel, Rhonda
Nat'l Sporting Goods Ass'n (431)

Haerle, William R.
American Electronics Ass'n (65)

Haftl, Emily
Nat'l School Supply and Equipment Ass'n (427)

Hagaman, Karen
Professional Ski Instructors of America (467)

Hagan, Lawrence F.
Internat'l Concrete Repair Institute (286)

Hagee CAE, Charles G.
Nat'l Ass'n of Corporate Treasurers (350)

Hageman, Charles H.
Forging Industry Ass'n (243)

Hagen, John W.
Soc. for Research in Child Development (493)

Hagen, Sandy
Gas Research Institute (246)

Hager, John
University Continuing Education Ass'n (537)

Haggerty, Michael
American Ass'n of AIDS Executives (33)

Hagin, Leslie J.
Nat'l Ass'n of Criminal Defense Lawyers (352)

Hagler, Chuck
Nat'l Ass'n of Professional Band Instrument Repair Technicians (366)

Hagopian, Linda
Women in Advertising and Marketing (546)

Hagy, Keith
Internat'l Soc. of Air Safety Investigators (305)

Hahn, Bruce
Computing Technology Industry Ass'n (203)
Hahn, Curt
Internat'l Quorum of Film and Video Producers (301)
Hahn FACHE, Cynthia
American College of Healthcare Executives (54)
Hahn, Hannelore
Internat'l Women's Writing Guild (311)
Hahn, Patricia A.
Airports Council Internat'l/North America (17)
Hahn, Russell H.
American Soc. of Agricultural Engineers (106)
Hailey CAE, Tammy
Nat'l Ass'n of Legal Secretaries (361)
Haines, Donna
Nat'l School Boards Ass'n (427)
Haines, Hunter
Collectibles and Platemakers Guild (196)
Haines, Thomas
Aircraft Owners and Pilots Ass'n (16)
Hairston, Torrey E.
Independent Electrical Contractors (260)
Hairston, Valerie
Nat'l Affordable Housing Management Ass'n (335)
Hajduk CMP, Kenneth
Refrigeration Service Engineers Soc. (473)
Hajek, Brian K.
American Nuclear Soc. (87)
Hakanson CAE, William P.
Hotel Electronic Distribution Network Ass'n (256)
Supply Chain Council (518)
Hakel, Lee
Soc. for Industrial and Organizational Psychology (489)
Halamandaris, Bill
Nat'l Ass'n for Homecare (339)
Halamandaris, Val J.
Nat'l Ass'n for Home Care (339)
Halbert, Roger
Nat'l Grange (407)
Halbun, Bernie
Alliance for Continuing Medical Education (17)
Hale, Cathy
American Ass'n for Continuity of Care (30)
Hale, Gene
Internat'l Aloe Science Council (273)
Hale, Mark
Automotive Service Ass'n (175)
Hale M.D., Ralph W.
American College of Obstetricians and Gynecologists (56)
Hale, Thomas M.
American Boat and Yacht Council (40)
Hale, William
Internat'l Ass'n of Official Human Rights Agencies (281)
Haledjian, Gregory V.
American Public Communications Council (95)
Haley, Nancy
American Intellectual Property Law Ass'n (79)
Haley, Stephanie
Nat'l Ass'n of Real Estate Brokers (368)
Halford, Karen
Barzona Breeders Ass'n of America (177)
Halicki, Tom
Nat'l Ass'n of Towns and Townships (378)
Halinton, Lois E.
Sporting Goods Agents Ass'n (515)
Hall, Debra J.
Reinsurance Ass'n of America (474)
Hall, Fletcher R.
Agricultural Transportation Conference (15)
Hall, Gary E.
Nat'l Ass'n of Independent Fee Appraisers (359)
Hall, Jan
Internat'l Communications Ass'n (286)
Hall, Janet
AACSB - the Internat'l Ass'n for Management Education (7)
Hall, Jason Y.
American Ass'n of Museums (39)
Hall, John
American Wood-Preservers' Ass'n (123)
Hall, John V.
Ductile Iron Soc. (225)
Hall Ph.D., Judy E.
Nat'l Register of Health Service Providers in Psychology (424)
Hall, Larry B.
Motorist Information and Services Ass'n (331)
Hall, Marti
Nat'l Florist Ass'n (405)
Hall, Nancy
North American Fuzzy Information Processing Soc. (442)
Ass'n for Child Psychoanalysis (130)

Hall, Raymond J.
Electronics Representatives Ass'n (229)
Hall, Reggie R.
Newspaper Ass'n of America (439)
Hall III, Robert P.
Nat'l Retail Federation (425)
Hall, Rosemary
Ass'n of Diesel Specialists (149)
Automotive Warehouse Distributors Ass'n (175)
Hall, Sarah M.
American Soc. of Criminology (109)
Hall, Sonny
Transport Workers Union of America (525)
Hall, Sylvia
Screenprinting and Graphic Imaging Ass'n Internat'l (480)
Digital Printing and Imaging Ass'n (222)
Hall, Terry W.
Nat'l Community Pharmacists Ass'n (388)
Hall USN (RET.), R.Adm. Thomas
Naval Reserve Ass'n (438)
Hall, Tommy
Walking Horse Owners Ass'n of America (540)
Hall, Wayne W.
Nat'l Ass'n of State Telecommunications Directors (376)
Hall, William C.
Perlite Institute (455)
Hall Jamieson, Kathleen
American Academy of Political and Social Science (25)
Hallagan, John B.
Internat'l Ass'n of Color Manufacturers (277)
Hallberg, Evelyne A.
Academy of Psychosomatic Medicine (10)
Halle, Titi
Nat'l Antique and Art Dealers Ass'n of America (337)
Hallett, Carol B.
Air Transport Ass'n of America (16)
Hallgren, Dr. Richard E.
American Meteorological Soc. (84)
Halliburton, Linda
Soc. for College and University Planning (486)
Halligan, Karen
American Petroleum Institute (91)
Hallisay, Paul L.
Air Line Pilots Ass'n, Internat'l (16)
Halliwill, John M.
Internat'l Ass'n of Plumbing and Mechanical Officials (282)
Hallman, Linda D.
American Horticultural Soc. (74)
Hallongren, Brett
Internat'l Graphoanalysis Soc. (292)
Halpenny, Elizabeth
Ecotourism Soc. (225)
Halper, Shela
Nat'l Mental Health Ass'n (416)
Halperin, Fredric
Nat'l Ass'n of Real Estate Investment Managers (369)
Halperin, Jerome A
United States Pharmacopeia (534)
Halprin, Eleanor G.
Phi Lambda Kappa Medical Fraternity (457)
Halstead, Janet
Zonta Internat'l (551)
Halverson, Craig
Photo Marketing Ass'n-Internat'l (457)
Halvorsen, Jerald V.
Interstate Natural Gas Ass'n of America (311)
Halvorsen, Morrie E.
Specialty Tool and Fastener Distributors Ass'n (514)
Hamburger, Ed
Ass'n of American Railroads (143)
Hamburger, Monika
Union of American Hebrew Congregations (529)
Hamburger, Ron
Appraisal Institute (126)
Hamburger, Sylvan
Nat'l Ass'n of Boat Manufacturers (345)
Hamby-Nye, Zhi Marie
Nat'l Military Intelligence Ass'n (417)
Operations Security Professionals Soc. (448)
Hamel Ph.D., Dr. Willem A.
Ass'n of Management/Internat'l Ass'n of Management (156)
Hamelin, Dolores
Women in Agribusiness (546)
Hames, Jim
Golf Coaches Ass'n of America (248)
Hames, Richard
American Academy of Neurology (23)
Hamidullah, Matthew
Nat'l Ass'n of Blacks in Criminal Justice (345)
Hamilton, Alan M.
North American Punch Manufacturers Ass'n (444)

Hamilton, Carol M.
American Ass'n for Artificial Intelligence (29)
Hamilton, Irwin Y.
Black Top and Nat'l Delaine-Merino Sheep Breeders Ass'n (180)
Hamilton Ph.D., J. Ogden
Pi Lambda Theta (458)
Hamilton, Jenifer
American Soc. of Hematology (110)
Hamilton, Mary
American Soc. for Public Administration (105)
Hamilton, Rae Mark
Nat'l Electrical Manufacturers Ass'n (400)
Hamilton, Shannon
American Roentgen Ray Soc. (98)
Hamilton, W. Mark
American Mental Health Counselors Ass'n (84)
Hamilton, Winthrop W.
American Dietetic Ass'n (64)
Hamilton-Canvar, Gracie
Small Luxury Hotels (484)
Hamlen, Albert R.
Brotherhood of Shoe and Allied Craftsmen (183)
Hamlin CAE, Deborah M.
Internat'l Ass'n of Plastics Distributors (281)
Hamlin, Tina
Independent Petroleum Ass'n of America (261)
Hamm, Michael S.
Nat'l Ass'n for Public Health Statistics and Information Systems (340)
Hamm, Rita
Internat'l Ass'n for Impact Assessment (274)
Hammer, Bo
American Institute of Physics (78)
Soc. of Physics Students (505)
Hammer, John H.
Nat'l Humanities Alliance (410)
Hammer, Thomas A.
Sweetener Users Ass'n (519)
Hammerberg, Tom
Automatic Fire Alarm Ass'n (173)
Hammond, John
Nat'l Retail Hardware Ass'n (425)
Hammond, Mark N.
Nat'l Soft Drink Ass'n (430)
Hammond, Mike
Latex Advisors Ass'n (317)
Hammond, Steve
Laborers' Internat'l Union of North America (316)
Hammonds, Barbara
American Soc. of Health-System Pharmacists (110)
Hammonds, Timothy
Food Marketing Institute (241)
Hammoor, Joseph J.
Steel Plate Fabricators Ass'n (516)
Hampel, William
Credit Union Nat'l Ass'n (218)
Hampshire, Frank
Automotive Market Research Council (174)
Hampton, Beth T.
Personal Communications Industry Ass'n (455)
Hampton, Ronald E.
Nat'l Black Police Ass'n (383)
Hampton, Stacy
Victorian Soc. in America (539)
Hamre, Julie
Nat'l Ass'n for Law Placement (340)
Hanagan, Nancy E.
Nat'l Wholesale Druggists' Ass'n (436)
Hanback, Brandi B.
Nat'l Ass'n of Foreign-Trade Zones (356)
Hancock, Charles C.
American Soc. for Biochemistry and Molecular Biology (101)
Hancock Ph.D., CAE, Don
Internat'l Ass'n of Assembly Managers (276)
Hancock, John
Construction Industry Sales (206)
Hancock, Nancy S.
American Ass'n of Philosophy Teachers (40)
Handcock, Ben
Wheat Quality Council (543)
Handcock, Chris
Design Management Institute (222)
Handley, Dr. Gene
American College of Occupational and Environmental Medicine (56)
Handman, Jill
Internat'l Fabricare Institute (290)
Handy, Karna
Rolf Institute (477)
Hane, Carrie
Ass'n of Foreign Investors in Real Estate (151)

Haney, Carol
Nat'l Ass'n of Basketball Coaches (344)

Haney, James A.
Nat'l Ass'n of Basketball Coaches (344)

Haney, Karen S.
Nat'l Council of Higher Education Loan Programs (395)

Haney, Regina
Nat'l Ass'n of Boards of Education (345)

Hangley, Lu
Nat'l Federation of Paralegal Ass'ns (404)

Hankin Ph.D., Robert A.
Health Industry Business Communications Council (252)
American Academy of Dental Group Practice (21)

Hanle, John
American Bar Ass'n (46)

Hanley, Edward T.
Hotel Employees and Restaurant Employees Internat'l
Union (256)

Hanley, Frank
Internat'l Union of Operating Engineers (310)

Hanley CAE, William H.
Illuminating Engineering Soc. of North America (259)

Hanly, Peter N.
Air Movement and Control Ass'n Internat'l (16)

Hanna, Betty
Internat'l Ass'n of Healthcare Central Service Material
Management (279)

Hanna, Dennis L.
American School Band Directors' Ass'n (99)

Hanna, Pally
Accredited Pet Cemetery Soc. (10)

Hannah, Gary L.
Business Professionals of America (185)

Hanneman, Richard L.
Salt Institute (479)

Hanner, Connie
Master Brewers Ass'n of the Americas (324)

Hanni Jr., CAE, M. John
American Soc. of Dermatology (109)

Hannon, Cecelia
Nat'l Ass'n of Criminal Defense Lawyers (352)

Hannum, Jane
Nuclear Information and Records Management Ass'n (447)

Hansell Jr., William H.
Internat'l City/County Management Ass'n (285)

Hansen, B.J.
Adventure Travel Trade Ass'n (12)

Hansen, Carole J.
Institute of Real Estate Management (269)

Hansen, Christine
Interstate Oil and Gas Compact Commission (312)

Hansen, Ed
American Ass'n of Zoo Keepers (45)

Hansen, Harry A.
Fixed Income Analysts Soc. (240)
Soc. of Quantitative Analysts (506)

Hansen, Jay
American Bus Ass'n (49)
Nat'l Asphalt Pavement Ass'n (337)

Hansen, Linda
American Ass'n of Radon Scientists and Technologists (42)

Hansen, Michael D.
Nat'l Candy Brokers Ass'n (385)

Hanson, Jacy
American Diabetes Ass'n (64)

Hanson, Leslie
Internat'l Soc. of Orthopaedic Surgery - U.S. Chapter (306)

Hanson CAE, Mark
BEMA - An Internat'l Ass'n Serving the Baking and Food
Industries (178)

Hanson, Wallace R.
Liability Insurance Research Bureau (319)
Property Loss Research Bureau (468)

Hanus, Chrystine
American Ass'n of Neurological Surgeons (39)

Hanye, Robert
Nat'l Industries for the Blind (411)

Hanzlick, David K.
Piano Technicians Guild (458)

Haracznak, Steve
Nat'l Ass'n for Medical Equipment Services (340)
American Ambulance Ass'n (28)

Harbit, Doug
Nat'l Institute for Dispute Resolution (411)

Hardardt, Kevin
American Gas Ass'n (70)

Harden CAE, Robert E.
Nat'l Funeral Directors Ass'n (406)

Hardiman, Nancy Reeves
American Soc. of Farm Managers and Rural Appraisers (109)

Hardin, Charles M.
Conference of Radiation Control Program Directors (204)

Harding, Juliet
Nat'l Ass'n of Retired Federal Employees (370)

Hardwick, Jane P.
Leather Industries of America (318)

Hardy, Derrick
Nat'l Terrazzo and Mosaic Ass'n (433)

Hardy, George D.
Nat'l Terrazzo and Mosaic Ass'n (433)

Hardy, Lanny
American College of Occupational and Environmental
Medicine (56)

Hardy, Margaret J.
Pharmaceutical Care Management Ass'n (456)

Hardy, Michael
Internat'l Soc. for the Performing Arts (304)

Hardy, Pat
Professional Ass'n of Innkeepers Internat'l (464)

Hardy, Shaun
Geoscience Information Soc. (247)

Hare, Daniel
Composite Panel Ass'n (201)

Hare, Linda
Internat'l Laser Display Ass'n (295)

Hargbol, Dana
Internat'l Communications Industries Ass'n (286)

Harke, Jerry R.
American Soc. of Interior Designers (111)

Harker, Roy
Ass'n of Gay and Lesbian Psychiatrists (152)

Harkins, Richard W.
Lake Carriers' Ass'n (316)

Harlan, Mimi
Internat'l Soc. of Weighing and Measurement (307)

Harland CPA, CAE, Richard
American College of Healthcare Executives (54)

Harless, Carol M.
Nat'l Academy of Engineering of the United States of
America (334)

Harley, William G.
Nat'l Utility Contractors Ass'n (435)

Harmon, Jack
American Academy of Otolaryngology-Head and Neck
Surgery (24)

Harmon MPH, Linda L.
Lamaze International (316)

Harnage, Bobby L.
American Federation of Government Employees (67)

Harness, Charles
Nat'l Pork Producers Council (423)

Harnett, Craig
Nat'l Hockey League (409)

Harney, Penny
American Electroplaters and Surface Finishers Soc. (65)

Harootunian, Brett
Board of Trade of the City of New York (180)

Harper, Margareth C.
Conference of Minority Transportation Officials (204)

Harper, R.L.
Internat'l Communications Ass'n (286)

Harper Jr., William T.
Nat'l Energy Services Ass'n (401)

Harpham, Joan
Institute of Environmental Sciences and Technology (267)

Harr, Joseph
Ass'n for Professionals in Infection Control and
Epidemiology (136)

Harr, Lucy
Credit Union Nat'l Ass'n (218)

Harrand, Geri
Vocational Evaluation and Work Adjustment Ass'n (540)

Harrell, Alvin C.
Conference on Consumer Finance Law (205)

Harrell, Dr. Edward
Ass'n for Gnotobiotics (134)

Harrigan, Deborah
Wine and Spirits Shippers Ass'n (544)

Harriman, Rob
Nat'l Ass'n of Consumer Shows (349)

Harrington CAE, Ed A.
Captive Insurance Companies Ass'n (186)

Harrington, Judith A.
Nat'l Risk Retention Ass'n (426)

Harrington, Lynn
Nat'l Utility Contractors Ass'n (435)

Harrington, Pat
American Bridge Teachers' Ass'n (49)

Harrington CAE, Wesley E.
American Lithotripsy Soc. (81)

Harris, Adam
Affiliated Dress Manufacturers (13)

Harris, Ann
Soc. for Range Management (493)

Harris, Arnold R.
United Knitwear Manufacturers League (531)
Ass'n of Rain Apparel Contractors (163)

Harris, Benjamin
Cheiron: The Internat'l Soc. for the History of Behavioral and
Social Sciences (191)

Harris, Byron J.
Nat'l Alliance of State and Territorial AIDS Directors (336)

Harris, C. Coleman
Nat'l FFA Organization (404)

Harris, Charlene
Women's Professional Rodeo Ass'n (548)

Harris, Christopher
Council on Foundations (216)

Harris, Claudia
Plumbing-Heating-Cooling Contractors - Nat'l Ass'n (459)

Harris FAIA, David A.
Nat'l Institute of Building Sciences (411)

Harris CAE, Don A.
Bowling Proprietors Ass'n of America (181)

Harris, Fran
American Ass'n of Plastic Surgeons (41)

Harris II, Herbert E.
Committee of Domestic Steel Wire Rope and Specialty Cable
Manufacturers (200)
Committee of American Axle Producers (200)

Harris, J.G.
Nat'l Academy of Neuropsychology (334)

Harris M.Ed., James L.
Civil Aviation Medical Ass'n (194)

Harris, Dr. Jim
Medical Mycological Soc. of the Americas (326)

Harris, Marvin J.
Retired Officers Ass'n, The (476)

Harris, Maurice
Special Libraries Ass'n (514)

Harris, Nadine
Internat'l Fabricare Institute (290)

Harris, Nicole
Nat'l Glass Ass'n (407)

Harris, Patricia R.
Nat'l Information Standards Organization (411)

Harris, Rick
Internat'l Communications Industries Ass'n (286)

Harris, Robert E.
Nat'l Marine Manufacturers Ass'n (416)

Harris, Robert J.
Industrial Fasteners Institute (262)

Harris, Ronald K.
American Academy of Gold Foil Operators (22)

Harris, Ryan
Independent Insurance Agents of America (261)

Harris, Teri
Golf Course Superintendents Ass'n of America (248)

Harris, Trish W.
Institute of Internal Auditors (267)

Harris, Walter S.
Nuclear Energy Institute (446)

Harris, Wendy
Ass'n of Program Directors in Internal Medicine (162)

Harris, Dr. William G.
Ass'n of Test Publishers (167)

Harris Jr., William R.
Army Aviation Ass'n of America (127)

Harrison III, Frank R.
Soc. for Philosophy of Religion (492)

Harrison, James D.
Internat'l Chiropractors Ass'n (285)

Harrison, Joe
Water Quality Ass'n (541)

Harrison, Joseph M.
American Moving and Storage Ass'n (85)

Harrison, Kim
Automotive Maintenance and Repair Ass'n (174)

Harrison, Kristin
Associated Builders and Contractors (170)

Harrison, Sarah
American Institute of Inspectors (77)

Harrison CAE, Sheilah J.
American Financial Services Ass'n (68)

Harrison, Thomas
Building Owners and Managers Ass'n Internat'l (183)

Harrison, W. Joan
American Electroplaters and Surface Finishers Soc. (65)

Harrison, Wallace S.
Nat'l Electronic Service Dealers Ass'n (400)

Harrold, Mary Jo
Ass'n of Plastic Surgery Assistants (160)
American Ass'n for Hand Surgery (31)

Harrold, Rita
Illuminating Engineering Soc. of North America (259)

Harsh, John F.
Internat'l Ass'n of Hydrogeologists (280)

Harsha, Barbara L.
Nat'l Ass'n of Governors' Highway Safety Representatives (357)

Hart, Chrissy
Internat'l Ass'n of Chiefs of Police (277)

Hart, Elena
Fashion Ass'n, The (235)

Hart, Elizabeth Kirby
Nat'l Club Ass'n (387)

Hart, Lonnie
Nat'l Potato Promotion Board (423)

Hart, Norma
Nat'l Bankers Ass'n (382)

Hart, Velma
American Ass'n for the Study of Liver Diseases (32)

Hartford, Holly
Internat'l Inflight Food Service Ass'n (294)

Hartl, Col. Gabriel A.
Air Traffic Control Ass'n (16)

Hartle, Terry W.
American Council on Education (61)

Hartley, Gregg
Athletic Footwear Ass'n (172)

Hartley, Steve
American Diabetes Ass'n (64)

Hartman CAE, Charles H.
American College Health Ass'n (52)

Hartman, Larry
American Ass'n of Cereal Chemists (34)
American Phytopathological Soc. (92)

Hartman, Stanley I.
American Institute of Professional Bookkeepers (78)

Hartmann, Celia
World Teleport Ass'n (550)

Hartnett, Elizabeth A.
Electronic Industries Ass'n (228)

Hartquist, David A.
Specialty Steel Industry of North America (514)

Hartranft, Scott
Nat'l Committee for Quality Assurance (388)

Hartsell, H.E.
American Board of Quality Assurance and Utilization Review Physicians (48)

Hartshorn, Gary S.
Organization for Tropical Studies (450)

Hartwell, Rob
American Health Care Ass'n (72)

Hartwick, Ken
Police Executive Research Forum (459)

Hartwig Ph.D., Robert
Insurance Information Institute (270)

Hartzell M.D., H. Criss
Soc. of General Physiologists (502)

Harvey, Brett
Graphic Artists Guild Nat'l (249)

Harvey, Christine
Nat'l Insurance Crime Bureau (412)

Harvey, Elizabeth
Soc. of Incentive and Travel Executives (502)

Harvey, Glenn F.
Instrument Soc. of America (269)

Harvey, Glynis
American Institute of Ultrasound in Medicine (78)

Harvey, Karen
Ass'n for Professionals in Infection Control and Epidemiology (136)

Harvey, Marsha
Nat'l Board of Boiler and Pressure Vessel Inspectors (383)

Harvey Ph.D., Neil
Internat'l Academy for Child Brain Development (272)

Harvison, Clifford J.
Nat'l Tank Truck Carriers (433)

Harward, Richard J.
Scottish Blackface Sheep Breeders Ass'n (480)

Harwood Ph.D., Frederic
Ass'n of Clinical Research Professionals (147)

Harwood, Sandra
Infectious Diseases Soc. of America (263)

Harwood Mattox, Vivienne
Soc. of Vacuum Coaters (508)
Ass'n of Vacuum Equipment Manufacturers Internat'l (169)

Haselbuch, Jewetta
Industrial Fasteners Institute (262)

Haselby, Kate Miller
Helicopter Ass'n Internat'l (253)

Haske, Melanie
Information Technology Resellers Ass'n (264)

Haskell, Phyllis
Council of Dance Administrators (213)

Hasselmo Ph.D., Nils
Ass'n of American Universities (143)
Ass'n of Graduate Schools in Ass'n of American Universities (152)

Hasser Jr., CAE, Clayton
American Academy of Family Physicians (22)

Hassinger, Catherine
American Academy of Orthotists and Prosthetists (24)

Hastie, William J.
Institute of Nuclear Power Operations (268)

Hastings SPHR, Rebecca R.
Employment Management Ass'n (230)

Hasty FLMI, ACS, Jeffrey L.
LOMA (321)

Hatano, Daryl
Semiconductor Industry Ass'n (481)

Hatch, Henry L.
Internat'l Prepress Ass'n (300)

Hatch, Marty
Soc. for Asian Music (485)

Hatch Smith, Laura
Gravure Ass'n of America (249)

Hatchell, Steven J.
Professional Rodeo Cowboys Ass'n (467)

Hatcher, Dr. Donald L.
Ass'n for Informal Logic and Critical Thinking (135)

Hatem, Mary Beth
Ass'n for the Advancement of Medical Instrumentation (138)

Hatfield, Kevin
Internat'l Conference of Funeral Service Examining Boards (287)

Hatfield, Dr. Thomas A.
Nat'l Art Education Ass'n (337)

Hatfield Goldman, Jan
Employee Relocation Council (229)

Hatherill, William
Federation of State Boards of Physical Therapy (237)

Hattenhauer, Lori H.
American Ass'n of Electrodiagnostic Medicine (36)

Hauck, Robert J.P.
American Political Science Ass'n (93)

Hauck, Sheldon
Internat'l Intellectual Property Ass'n (295)

Haugen, Barbara
Nat'l Ass'n of Insurance Brokers (360)

Hauger, Karen A.
Women's Fisheries Network (548)

Haugh, LeRoy J.
Aerospace Industries Ass'n of America (13)

Haught, Evelyn L.
Institute of Scrap Recycling Industries (269)

Hauptman, Barbara
Soc. of Stage Directors and Choreographers (507)

Hauser, Joanne
American Institute of Aeronautics and Astronautics (76)

Hauser, Melanie
Golf Writers Ass'n of America (248)

Hausman, William J.
Business History Conference (184)

Hauss, Linda M.
Western Shoe Retailers Ass'n (543)

Havlina, Ed
Ass'n of Analytical Chemists (143)

Hawbecker, Mary
Nat'l Ass'n of Community Health Centers (349)

Hawes, Jean
Outdoor Power Equipment Institute (451)

Hawkey, Doris
Soc. of Decorative Painters (500)

Hawkins, Alissa
American Library Trustee Ass'n (81)

Hawkins, Brian L.
EDUCAUSE (226)

Hawkins, C. Joyce
American Academy of Clinical Psychiatrists (21)

Hawkins Jr., Daniel R.
Nat'l Ass'n of Community Health Centers (349)

Hawkins, Dr. Frank T.
Research Ass'n of Minority Professors (475)

Hawkins, Hillani
Wireless Communications Ass'n Internat'l (545)

Hawkins, Janet
Nat'l Sheriffs' Ass'n (427)

Hawkins, Joleen A.
American Council on Internat'l Personnel (62)

Hawkins, Judy
Broadcast Education Ass'n (182)

Hawkinson, Brian P.
Public Affairs Council (469)

Hawks, John
Ass'n Retail Travel Agents (170)

Hawks APR, John K.
Ass'n of Retail Travel Agents (163)

Haws, Sue
Internat'l Bowling Pro Shop and Instructors Ass'n (283)

Hay, Catherine
Ass'n of Academic Chairmen of Plastic Surgery (141)
American Ass'n for Hand Surgery (31)

Hay, Cathy
Plastic Surgery Admininstrative Ass'n (459)
American Soc. for Reconstructive Microsurgery (105)

Hay CPA, Gerald F.
Soc. for Human Resource Management (489)

Haycock, Dr. Ken
Internat'l Ass'n of School Librarianship (282)

Hayden, Bonnie
Nat'l Ass'n of Water Companies (380)

Hayden, Dorothy L.
American Institute for Archaeological Research (75)

Hayden, Mike
American Sport Fishing Ass'n (118)

Hayden, Pamela M.
North American Spine Soc. (445)

Hayden, Robert
Electric Vehicle Ass'n of the Americas (227)

Hayenga, Rolland
American Farm Bureau Federation (66)

Hayes, Allison
North American Wholesale Lumber Ass'n (446)

Hayes, Anna K.
Federation of State Boards of Physical Therapy (237)

Hayes, Carnie
Council of Chief State School Officers (213)

Hayes, Darrell
Air Force Ass'n (15)

Hayes Jr., Hubert H.
Nat'l Ass'n of Vertical Transportation Professionals (379)

Hayes, Margaret
Fashion Group Internat'l (235)

Hayes, Pamela
Ass'n of Collegiate Licensing Administrators (148)

Hayes, Sheila
Outdoor Advertising Ass'n of America (451)

Hayholo, Sally
Nat'l Business Incubation Ass'n (384)

Hayley, Nancy C.
American Soc. for Reproductive Medicine (105)

Haynes, Gail C.
Pension Real Estate Ass'n (454)

Haynes, James P.
Commercial Travelers Ass'n (199)

Haynes, Janet L.
American College of Legal Medicine (55)

Hays, Dan
Internat'l Bluegrass Music Ass'n (283)

Hays, Molly
British-American Chamber of Commerce (182)

Hazard Jr., Geoffrey C.
American Law Institute (81)

Hazelett, Brent
Automotive Cooling System Institute (174)

Hazeltine, Derek
Professional Liability Underwriting Soc. (466)

Hazen, Paul
Nat'l Cooperative Business Ass'n (392)

Hazle, Jeff
Nat'l Petroleum Refiners Ass'n (422)

Heaberlin, Sandra
Lipizzan Ass'n of North America (320)

Head, Terry
Household Goods Forwarders Ass'n of America (257)

Heales, Robert
World Ass'n of Detectives (549)

Healy, James
Northamerican Heating, Refrigeration and Airconditioning Wholesalers Ass'n (446)

Healy CAE, John J.
Nat'l Wooden Pallet and Container Ass'n (437)

Hearne, Terry
World Floor Covering Ass'n (549)

Hearne, Terry Anne
Urban Land Institute (537)

Heath, Becky
Assisted Living Federation of America (170)

Heath, Donald M.
Internet Soc. (311)

Heath, Doug
Promotional Products Ass'n Internat'l (468)

Heath, Geri
Institute of Environmental Sciences and Technology (267)

Heath, Janel
American Ass'n for Medical Transcription (31)

Heberlein, John R.
Gas Appliance Manufacturers Ass'n **(245)**

Hecht Ed.D., Kathryn
American Academy of Ophthalmology **(24)**

Heck, Kim
Golf Course Superintendents Ass'n of America **(248)**

Heck, Maelo
Consultant Dietitians in Health Care Facilities **(207)**

Heckeler, David
Inter-Industry Conference on Auto Collision Repair **(271)**

Hecker CAE, Lawrence S.
Automotive Maintenance and Repair Ass'n **(174)**

Heckler, Tim
United States Professional Tennis Ass'n **(534)**

Heckman, Amy Marcenaro
American Ass'n of Political Consultants **(41)**

Hedeman, Jody
Nat'l Ass'n of Police Organizations **(365)**

Hedges, Mike
Fabricators and Manufacturers Ass'n, Internat'l **(234)**

Hedland, Kathleen L.
Council of Logistics Management **(215)**

Hedlund, James B.
Ass'n of Local Television Stations **(156)**

Hedrick, Janet
American Foreign Service Ass'n **(69)**

Hedrick, Lisa V.
American Kinesiotherapy Ass'n **(80)**

Hedrick, Shelly
American Soc. of Cataract and Refractive Surgery **(107)**

Heenan Jr., William M.
Steel Recycling Institute **(516)**

Hefferan, Richard P.
Alliance of American Insurers **(18)**

Heffner, John
Associated General Contractors of America **(171)**

Hegyi, Albert P.
Ass'n of Master of Business Administration Executives **(157)**

Heiberg, Kay
Software Publishers Ass'n **(509)**

Heidrich, Greg
American Insurers Highway Safety Alliance **(79)**

Heidrich, Gregory W.
Alliance of American Insurers **(18)**

Heier, Rev. Vincent A.
Nat'l Ass'n of Diocesan Ecumenical Officers **(352)**

Heilstedt P.E., Paul K.
Building Officials and Code Administrators Internat'l **(183)**

Heim, Rick
Semiconductor Equipment and Materials Internat'l **(481)**

Heimpl, Carol
American Ass'n of Physics Teachers **(41)**

Hein, Debra
Nat'l Ass'n of Fleet Resale Dealers **(355)**

Hein, Matthew
Beer Institute **(177)**

Heinemeier, Dan C.
Electronic Industries Ass'n **(228)**

Heinlen, Sharon
Ass'n for Experiential Education **(133)**

Heinrich, Dr. Janet
American Academy of Nursing **(23)**

Heinze Ph.D., Ruth-Inge
Independent Scholars of Asia **(261)**

Heitowit, Ezra
Universities Research Ass'n **(536)**

Held, David
Environmental Assessment Ass'n **(231)**

Helein, Ruth
Nat'l Surgical Assistant Ass'n **(432)**
American Psychological Ass'n - Division of Psychoanalysis **(95)**
Nat'l Extension Ass'n of Family and Consumer Sciences **(402)**

Helfand, Sacha
Food Processing Machinery and Supplies Ass'n **(242)**

Helfrich, Janet
Clock Manufacturers and Marketing Ass'n **(195)**

Hellem, Steve
Nat'l Environmental Development Ass'n **(401)**

Heller, Christian
AACE Internat'l **(7)**

Heller Ph.D., Lawrence A.
TechLaw Group **(520)**
American College of Mental Health Administration **(55)**

Hellerstein, Alice
American Physiological Soc. **(92)**

Hellmke, Anne
Nat'l Wellness Ass'n **(436)**

Hellner, Richard T.
Nat'l Soc. to Prevent Blindness/Prevent Blindness America **(430)**

Hellwig, Dr. Monika
Ass'n of Catholic Colleges and Universities **(146)**

Helm, Carla M.
Commercial Food Equipment Service Ass'n **(199)**

Helm AUS (RET.), Brg.Gen. Lewis M.
Senior Army Reserve Commanders Ass'n **(481)**

Helmer, Abigail E.
Internat'l Special Events Soc. **(307)**

Helmes, Dr. C. Tucker
United States Dye Manufacturers Operating Committee of ETAD **(533)**

Helmlinger, Constance S.
American Nurses Ass'n **(87)**

Helms, Jeff
American Down Ass'n **(65)**

Helmsing, Pam
Pile Driving Contractors Ass'n **(458)**

Helmuth, Joy
Internat'l Ass'n of Broadcast Monitors **(276)**

Helson, Cynthia M.
Nat'l Employee Services and Recreation Ass'n **(401)**

Helton, Jonathan
North American Saxophone Alliance **(444)**

Helwig, H. Kurt
Electronic Funds Transfer Ass'n **(228)**

Hembree, Trina
Nat'l Emergency Management Ass'n **(401)**

Hemming, Kathleen
Healthcare Compliance Packaging Council **(252)**

Hemminger, Bob
American Agriculture Movement **(27)**

Hemphill, John
North American Soc. for Trenchless Technology **(445)**

Henault, David
AFSM Internat'l **(14)**

Hench, John B.
American Antiquarian Soc. **(28)**

Hendel, Patricia T.
Nat'l Ass'n of Commissions for Women **(349)**

Henderson, Brenda
American Institute of Architects **(76)**

Henderson, Cheryl
American Red Brangus Ass'n **(97)**

Henderson, Gwen
American Registry of Diagnostic Medical Sonographers **(97)**

Henderson, Harold
Nat'l Football League **(405)**

Henderson, James
Music Library Ass'n **(332)**

Henderson Ph.D., Janet L.
Ass'n for Internat'l Agricultural and Extension Education **(135)**

Henderson CPA, John B.
American Medical Rehabilitation Providers Ass'n **(84)**

Henderson, Kathy
Nat'l Turkey Federation **(435)**

Henderson, Kevin
Nat'l Ass'n of Basketball Coaches **(344)**

Henderson, Linda
Nat'l Ass'n of College and University Attorneys **(347)**

Henderson, Pat
American Oat Ass'n **(87)**

Henderson, Russell L.
Nat'l Genealogical Soc. **(406)**

Henderson Jr., CAE, Thomas H.
Ass'n of Trial Lawyers of America **(168)**

Hendren, P.O., Robert
Soc. of Professors of Child and Adolescent Psychiatry **(506)**

Hendricks, Kathryn L.
Grain Elevator and Processing Soc. **(249)**

Hendrickson, Judy
Nat'l Ass'n of State Administrators and Supervisors of Private Schools **(373)**

Hendrickson, Ronald M.
Internat'l Chiropractors Ass'n **(285)**

Hendrickson, Shari
Council of State Governments **(216)**

Hendrix, Jason
Nat'l Alliance of State and Territorial AIDS Directors **(336)**

Hendrix, M. Kathleen
American Land Title Ass'n **(80)**

Heney, Daniel
Maple Flooring Manufacturers Ass'n **(323)**

Hengstler, Gary
American Bar Ass'n **(46)**

Henn, Barbara
American Soc. of Interior Designers **(111)**

Hennage Ph.D., David W.
American Nurses Ass'n **(87)**

Hennessy, Mary
Industrial Fabrics Ass'n Internat'l **(262)**

Henrich, Rev. Steven
Conference of Major Superiors of Men, U.S.A. **(204)**

Henrichs CAE, Ronald A.
American Academy of Physical Medicine and Rehabilitation **(25)**

Henriksen, Missy
Composites Fabricators Ass'n **(201)**

Henriquez, Santa
American College of Nutrition **(56)**

Henry CAE, Howard C.
Incentive Federation **(259)**

Henry, James L.
Transportation Institute **(525)**

Henry, James Robert
Internat'l and American Ass'ns of Clinical Nutritionists **(273)**

Henry, Kevin
Nat'l Ass'n of Intercollegiate Athletics **(360)**

Henry, Michele M.
Internat'l Ass'n of Chiefs of Police **(277)**

Henry, Mina K.
Fashion Ass'n, The **(235)**

Henry, Thomas W.
Paleontological Soc. **(452)**

Henry CCN, Winna
Internat'l and American Ass'ns of Clinical Nutritionists **(273)**

Hensel, George R.
Driving School Ass'n of America **(224)**

Hensing, David J.
American Ass'n of State Highway and Transportation Officials **(43)**

Hensley, Paul
American Health Care Ass'n **(72)**

Henson, John
Internat'l Facility Management Ass'n **(290)**

Hentschel, Richard
Pickle Packers Internat'l **(458)**

Hepner, Robert P.
Associated Builders and Contractors **(170)**

Hepp, Betty
Investment Management Consultants Ass'n **(312)**

Hepp, Ronnie
Recreation Vehicle Dealers Ass'n of North America **(472)**

Heppenheimer, Susan
American Soc. of Master Dental Technologists **(112)**

Heppes CAE, Jerry
Door and Hardware Institute **(224)**

Hequet, Marc
Training Directors' Forum **(525)**

Herbert, Charlotte W.
Associated Builders and Contractors **(170)**

Herbert, Victor J.
Air Line Employees Ass'n, International **(15)**

Herbst, Peter R.
Soc. for Technical Communication **(494)**

Herbst, Richard A.
Nat'l Ass'n of Sailing Instructors and Sailing Schools **(370)**

Herbster, Carl
American Ass'n of Christian Schools **(34)**

Hercey, Connie
Ass'n of Psychology Postdoctoral and Internship Centers **(162)**

Herd, Michael
Nat'l Automated Clearing House Ass'n **(381)**

Herho, Lauren
Committee of 200 **(200)**

Herian, Vicki
Soc. of Wood Science and Technology **(509)**

Herman, Andrea
Internat'l Sleep Products Ass'n **(302)**

Herman, Betsy
American Podiatric Medical Students' Ass'n **(93)**

Herman, Guy
Museum Computer Network **(332)**

Herman, Jeffrey
Soc. of American Silversmiths **(498)**

Herman, Jonathan
Nat'l Guild of Community Schools of the Arts **(408)**

Herman, Roberta
American Water Works Ass'n **(122)**

Herman-Betzen, Marsha
Ass'n of College Unions-Internat'l **(147)**

Hermanek, Bill
Associated Equipment Distributors **(171)**

Hermann, Karen
Construction Management Ass'n of America **(206)**

Hermann CAE, Peter R.
Ass'n of Records Managers and Administrators **(163)**

Hermanson Chennault, Ann
Nat'l Ass'n of Women Artists **(380)**

Hermit, Bruce
Ass'n of Independent Corrugated Converters **(153)**

Hernandez, Bertha
Ass'n for Borderlands Studies (130)

Hernandez, John R.
American Ass'n of Hispanic Certified Public Accountants (37)

Hernandez, Turney J.
Nat'l Roadside Vegetation Management Ass'n (426)

Herndon, Michael
Internat'l Ass'n for Financial Planning (274)

Heros, Dr. Roberto
American Academy of Neurological Surgery (23)

Herrera, George
United States Hispanic Chamber of Commerce (534)

Herrera, Maricel M.
Ass'n for Molecular Pathology (136)

Herrett, Richard
Agricultural Research Institute (14)

Herrick, John
American Electronics Ass'n (65)

Herrick, Julie
Internat'l Ass'n of Assembly Managers (276)

Herrick II, CAE, Raymond W.
Foodservice Equipment Distributors Ass'n (242)

Herrin, Carl A.
American Council of Teachers of Russian (61)

Herring, Sandra
Nat'l Soc. of Accountants (429)

Herring, Sandy
Nat'l Soc. of Accountants (429)

Herring, W.E.
Nat'l Engine Parts Manufacturers Ass'n (401)

Herrington, Caryl
American Academy of Facial Plastic and Reconstructive Surgery (22)

Herrington, Christie
Home Healthcare Nurses Ass'n (255)

Herron, Dr. Daniel J.
Academy of Legal Studies in Business (8)

Herschel, Mike
Internat'l Wholesale Furniture Ass'n (311)

Herschlag, Jack
Nat'l Ass'n of Men's Sportswear Buyers (363)

Herselius, Nancy
American Agricultural Economics Ass'n (27)

Hershfeldt, Patricia
Soc. for Neuroscience (491)

Hershman, Jerome
Guitar and Accessories Marketing Ass'n (250)
Music Distributors Ass'n (332)
Nat'l Ass'n of Band Instrument Manufacturers (344)
Nat'l Council of Music Importers and Exporters (395)

Hertfelder, Eric
Nat'l Conference of State Historic Preservation Officers (391)

Herto, Joan T.
American Soc. for Horticultural Science (103)

Hertz, Eric
Fashion Ass'n, The (235)

Hertzberg, Randi
Nat'l Concrete Masonry Ass'n (389)

Herzau, Irene
Ass'n for the Advancement of Automotive Medicine (138)

Herzog, John
Air Conditioning Contractors of America (15)

Herzog, Michael
American Medical Electroencephalographic Ass'n (83)
Nat'l Federation of Catholic Physicians' Guilds (403)

Hess, Catherine A.
Ass'n of Maternal and Child Health Programs (157)

Hessel, Carolyn
Jewish Book Council (314)

Hession, Missy
Nat'l Ass'n of Professionals in Women's Health (367)

Hessler, Clare
Institute of Scrap Recycling Industries (269)

Hessman, Norinne
American Soc. of Consultant Pharmacists (108)

Hester, Julie
Internat'l Festivals and Events Ass'n (291)

Heuser, Patricia E.
American Soc. for Plasticulture (104)

Heusser Ed.D., H. Earl
Nat'l Ass'n of Private, Nontraditional Schools and Colleges with Accrediting Commission for Higher Education (366)

Heusser Psy.D., Irene Dolly
Nat'l Ass'n of Private, Nontraditional Schools and Colleges with Accrediting Commission for Higher Education (366)

Hewett, Dr. Steven
Soc. for the Preservation of Oral Health (495)

Hewitt, Charles C.
Satellite Broadcasting and Communications Ass'n (479)

Heylin, G. Brockwel
American Ass'n of Colleges of Nursing (34)

Heyman, Annette H.
American Registry of Medical Assistants (97)

Hiatt, Richard S.
Nat'l Food and Energy Council (405)

Hibbs, Ralph
Robert Morris Associates, the Ass'n of Lending and Credit Risk Professionals (476)

Hichcock, Chuck
Nat'l Lubricating Grease Institute (415)

Hickerson, Debbie
Nat'l Ass'n of Women Business Owners (380)

Hickey, Barbra C.
Nat'l Soc. of Accountants for Cooperatives (429)

Hickey Jr., James J.
American Horse Council (74)

Hickey, Karen
Wildlife Disease Ass'n (544)

Hickey, Matt
Foodservice Consultants Soc. Internat'l (242)
Internat'l Inflight Food Service Ass'n (294)

Hickman, Charles
AACSB - the Internat'l Ass'n for Management Education (7)

Hickman, Tiana
Composites Fabricators Ass'n (201)

Hicks, Ann
Nat'l Ass'n of Independent Schools (360)

Hicks, Barbara
Optical Soc. of America (449)

Hicks, Dr. Clayton
Nat'l Optometric Ass'n (419)

Hicks, Deborah
Roundtable for Women in Foodservice (477)

Hicks, June
American Council on the Teaching of Foreign Languages (62)

Hicks Jr., Raymond M.
Ass'n of Average Adjusters of the U.S. (144)

Hicks, Shelley L.
American Academy of Physician Assistants (25)

Hicks, Shelly
Nat'l Hardwood Lumber Ass'n (408)

Hiebert, Roz
Nat'l Ass'n of State Universities and Land Grant Colleges (376)

Hiernu, C. Penny
Internat'l Soc. for the Study of Subtle Energies and Energy Medicine (305)

Hieronymus, Clara
American Theatre Critics Ass'n (120)

Higby, Dr. Gregory J.
American Institute of the History of Pharmacy (78)

Higgens, Barbara C.
Plumbing Manufacturers Institute (459)

Higginbotham, Charles
Internat'l Ass'n of Chiefs of Police (277)

Higgins, Billy K.
American Ass'n of State Highway and Transportation Officials (43)

Higgins, Terrence S.
Nat'l Petroleum Refiners Ass'n (422)

Higgs, Olevia
Internat'l Ceramic Ass'n (285)

High, Karen
Nat'l Ass'n of Government Guaranteed Lenders (357)

High, Nancy
American Furniture Manufacturers Ass'n (69)

Highfill, William N.
ISDA - The Office Systems Cooperative (313)

Hightower, Don
United States Racquet Stringing Ass'n (535)

Hilbert, James A.
Automotive Parts and Accessories Ass'n (175)

Hilke, Sharon
Nat'l Council of Investigation and Security Services (395)

Hill, Beverly
Ass'n of Biomedical Communications Directors (144)

Hill, Carol C.
Ass'n of Directory Publishers (149)

Hill, Cece
Internat'l Ass'n of Correctional Officers (278)

Hill, Debbie
Nat'l Ass'n of Professional Surplus Lines Offices (367)

Hill, Edwin D.
Internat'l Brotherhood of Electrical Workers (284)

Hill, George
Internat'l Festivals and Events Ass'n (291)

Hill, Gregory
Ass'n of American Railroads (143)

Hill, Julie S.
Telecommunications Resellers Ass'n (521)

Hill, Karen
American Gas Ass'n (70)

Hill, Larry W.
Soc. of American Foresters (497)

Hill, Lee H.
American Waterways Operators (122)

Hill, Linda
Medical-Dental-Hospital Business Associates (326)

Hill, Liz
Paperboard Packaging Council (453)

Hill Jr., Norbert S.
American Indian Science and Engineering Soc. (75)

Hill, Paula Glick
Jewelry Manufacturers Guild (314)

Hill, Richard B.
American Soc. for Information Science (103)

Hill, Robert L.
American Ass'n of Blacks in Energy (33)

Hill, Sanford J.
Healthcare Billing and Management Ass'n (252)
Internat'l Hand Protection Ass'n (293)
Nat'l Subacute Care Ass'n (432)
Medical-Dental-Hospital Business Associates (326)

Hill, Sean
Internat'l Ass'n for the Study of Organized Crime (275)

Hill, Terry
Internat'l Franchise Ass'n (292)

Hill, Thomas S.
American Ass'n of Professional Sales Engineers (42)

Hilla, Elizabeth B.
Health Industry Distributors Ass'n (252)

Hilleary, Daniel J.
Internat'l Ass'n of Food Industry Suppliers (279)

Hillegas, Katherine
American Soc. for Parenteral and Enteral Nutrition (104)

Hiller, Arlene J.
Optical Laboratories Ass'n (448)

Hillman, Bill
Nat'l Utility Contractors Ass'n (435)

Hilt, Sue
American College of Sports Medicine (57)

Hilvers, Anthony
Institute for Interconnecting and Packaging Electronic Circuits (265)

Himelfarb, Laurence
Nat'l Restaurant Ass'n (425)

Himmelfarb CAE, Phyllis R.
Optical Laboratories Ass'n (448)

Hinchman, Joan
Nat'l Soc. of Compliance Professionals (429)

Hincilley CMP, Stewart
American Soc. of Regional Anesthesia (115)

Hinckley, John A.
Soc. for Pediatric Anesthesia (492)
Soc. of Neurosurgical Anesthesia and Critical Care (504)
Soc. for Education in Anesthesia (487)
American Soc. of Regional Anesthesia (115)
Soc. of Cardiovascular Anesthesiologists (499)

Hinckley, June
Nat'l Ass'n of State Supervisors of Music (376)

Hinckley, Stewart A.
Soc. of Cardiovascular Anesthesiologists (499)
Soc. for Obstetric Anesthesia and Perinatology (491)

Hindle, Mary Kay
American Crop Protection Ass'n (62)

Hineman, Bruce
Nat'l Council on Teacher Retirement (398)

Hines, Ayanna E.
Women's Basketball Coaches Ass'n (547)

Hines, JoAnn R.
Women in Packaging (547)

Hines, Laurence E.
Soc. of Critical Care Medicine (500)

Hines, Linda L.
Ass'n of Military Surgeons of the U.S. (157)

Hines, Steve
American College of Prosthodontists (57)

Hines, Walter J.
Board of Trade of the City of New York (180)

Hing, Sokhan
American Soc. for Photogrammetry and Remote Sensing (104)

Hinko, Marsha
American College of Foot and Ankle Surgeons (54)

Hinko, Susan
Internat'l Swaps and Derivatives Ass'n (308)

Hinton, Pamela J.
Soc. of Industrial and Office REALTORS (503)

Hinton, Robert M.
American Road and Transportation Builders Ass'n (98)

Hinton Jr., Thomas D.
Customer Relations Institute (219)

Hinton, Wilbur H. "Skip"
Nat'l Educational Telecommunications Ass'n (400)

Hipp, Janet
Electronics Representatives Ass'n (229)

Hirschfeld, Audrey
Board of Trade of the City of New York (180)

Hirschhorn, Eric L.
Industry Coalition on Technology Transfer (263)

Hirschmann, David T.
Ass'n of American Chamber of Commerce in Latin
America (142)

Hirsh, Robin
Union of American Hebrew Congregations (529)

Hirshfeld, Dr. Marvin
American Soc. of Internat'l Executives (III)

Hirt, James
Nat'l Ass'n of Mortgage Brokers (363)

Hirt, Paula A.
American Ass'n on Mental Retardation (45)

Hiser, Kimberly
Botanical Soc. of America (181)

Hitchcock, Jaime E.
Nat'l Council for the Social Studies (393)

Hittman, Judith
Soc. for Neuroscience (491)

Hitz, C. Breck
Laser and Electro-Optics Manufacturers' Ass'n (317)

Hixon, Thomas E.
Nat'l Electrical Manufacturers Ass'n (400)
Nonprescription Drug Manufacturers Ass'n (440)

Hoagland, Larry
Communications Supply Service Ass'n (200)

Hoagland, Michael P.
American Forest and Paper Ass'n (69)

Hoard, Cheryl
Nat'l Ass'n for Holistic Aromatherapy (339)

Hoback, Gina
Nat'l Ass'n of Wheat Growers (380)

Hoban, Roseanne M.
Wire Fabricators Ass'n (545)

Hobart, Robert E.
American Medical Ass'n (83)

Hobbie, Kenneth
U.S. Grains Council (528)

Hobbie, Richard A.
Interstate Conference of Employment Security Agencies (311)

Hobson, David F.
Uniform and Textile Service Ass'n (529)

Hobson, Joseph
Asphalt Roofing Manufacturers Ass'n (129)

Hoch, Susan C.
Internet Alliance (311)

Hochberg, Tina
Software Publishers Ass'n (509)

Hochheim, Hanne
Danish-American Chamber of Commerce (USA) (220)

Hochman, Norman
American Soc. of Health-System Pharmacists (110)

Hochstadt, Adrian
American Soc. of Plastic and Reconstructive Surgeons (114)

Hock, Cindy
American Medical Directors Ass'n (83)

Hocker, Jean
Land Trust Alliance (317)

Hockman, Lawson L.
Environmental Industry Ass'ns (231)

Hodgdon, Harry E.
Wildlife Soc., The (544)

Hodges, Christy
Home Furnishings Internat'l Ass'n (255)

Hodges, Deborah
Uniform and Textile Service Ass'n (529)

Hodges, James H.
American Meat Institute (83)

Hodges, Mary
Ass'n of Records Managers and Administrators (163)

Hodges, Rick
Aircraft Owners and Pilots Ass'n (16)

Hodges, Ron
Internat'l Food, Wine and Travel Writers Ass'n (291)

Hodgins, Uve
Professional Aviation Maintenance Ass'n (464)

Hodgkinson, Virginia
Independent Sector (261)

Hodgson, Joni
Nat'l Ass'n of Manufacturers (362)

Hodos, Dorothy W.
American Handwriting Analysis Foundation (71)

Hoecker, Harold H.
Sweet Potato Council of the United States (519)

Hoefs, Laura
Soc. for Ecological Restoration (487)

Hoehn-Zimmerman, Jean
Cosmetic Executive Women (210)

Hoel CMP, Annette
American Academy of Family Physicians (22)

Hoellering, Michael F.
American Arbitration Ass'n (28)

Hoemann, Howard H.
Internat'l Credit Ass'n (288)

Hoeppner, Christine K.
American College of Veterinary Internal Medicine (58)

Hoerle, Heather
Nat'l Ass'n of Independent Schools (360)

Hoffbuhr, Jack
American Water Works Ass'n (122)

Hoffman, Donna M.
Advertising Mail Marketing Ass'n (12)

Hoffman, Eileen
Travel Journalists Guild (526)

Hoffman, Eric
American Philosophical Ass'n (91)

Hoffman, J. Stuart
Nat'l Rural Health Ass'n (426)

Hoffman, Kathleen
American Ass'n of State Social Work Boards (43)

Hoffman, Peggy M.
Retailer's Bakery Ass'n (476)

Hoffman, Philip D.
Travel Journalists Guild (526)

Hoffman, William R.
Nat'l Ass'n of Golf Tournament Directors (356)

Hoffmann, Heinz K.
Independent Professional Painting Contractors Ass'n of
America (261)

Hofford, Merry
Nat'l Council of Juvenile and Family Court Judges (395)

Hoffpauir, Elvis Lynn
Mobile Air Conditioning Soc. Worldwide (329)

Hoffstein, Yale
Nat'l Ass'n of Recording Merchandisers (369)

Hofman, Steven
American Ass'n of School Librarians (42)

Hofmann Jr., USMCR, Col. George
Marine Corps Reserve Officers Ass'n (323)

Hogan, Jana
Medical Records Institute (326)

Hogan Ph.D., M. Michelle
American Ass'n of Immunologists (38)

Hogan, Mark
Nat'l Concrete Masonry Ass'n (389)

Hogan, Thomas
Ass'n of Information and Dissemination Centers (154)

Hoggard CAE, Kerry B.
American Health Lawyers Ass'n (72)

Hoggard, Randall
Roller Skating Ass'n Internat'l (477)

Hoggarth, Robert L.
Personal Communications Industry Ass'n (455)

Hohimer, Colette
Ass'n of Bone and Joint Surgeons (145)
Orthopaedic Research Soc. (451)

Hohman, Anne Marie
Soc. of Competitive Intelligence Professionals (500)

Hoiland CAE, Joel
Nat'l Ass'n of Electrical Distributors (353)

Hoke, Tara
American Soc. of Extra-Corporeal Technology (109)

Holbrook, Carole
Nat'l Intramural-Recreational Sports Ass'n (413)

Holbrook, W. Paul
American Ceramic Soc. (51)
Nat'l Institute of Ceramic Engineers (411)

Holbrow, Alice
Lipid Nurse Task Force (320)

Holbus, Ed
Carwash Owner's and Supplier's Ass'n (187)

Holcomb, Howard E.
Council of Independent Colleges (214)

Hold Ph.D., Dr. William T.
Soc. of Certified Insurance Counselors (499)

Holder, Debra A.
Associated Landscape Contractors of America (171)

Holderfield CAE, J.W.
Technology and Information Management Education
Soc. (521)

Holdsworth, Thomas W.
Vocational Industrial Clubs of America (540)

Holhouser III, Jesse A.
Professional Golfers Ass'n of America (465)

Holladay CPA, Fred
Nat'l Federation of Independent Business (403)

Holland, Dorothy
American Ass'n of Teachers of Esperanto (43)

Holland CMP, Kate
Soc. for Scholarly Publishing (493)
Ass'n for Applied Psychophysiology and Biofeedback (129)
North American Nature Photography Ass'n (443)

Holleman, Linda
Nat'l Network of Commercial Real Estate Women (418)

Hollenbeck, Sonya
Earthquake Engineering Research Institute (225)

Holley Jr., William H.
Nat'l Academy of Arbitrators (333)

Holleyman II, Robert W.
Business Software Alliance (185)

Holliday, Peggy W.
Nat'l Science Education Leadership Ass'n (427)

Hollins, Cheryl J.
American Highway Users Alliance (73)

Hollis, Barbara
Endocrine Soc. (230)

Hollis, David
Holstein Ass'n USA (255)

Hollis, Nicholas E.
Agribusiness Council (14)

Holloway, Anne
American Wood Preservers Institute (123)

Holloway, George T.
Nat'l Catholic Development Conference (385)

Holly, Don
Specialty Coffee Ass'n of America (514)

Holm, Robin
Internat'l Hearing Soc. (293)

Holman, Earl Rodney
Black Retail Action Group (180)

Holman Jr., Francis W.
Manufacturers Alliance (322)

Holman, James E.
Nat'l Blacksmiths and Weldors Ass'n (383)

Holman, Jan
Instrument Soc. of America (269)

Holman, Pamela
Product Development and Management Ass'n (463)

Holmberg, John B.
Nat'l Ass'n of Radio and Telecommunications Engineers (368)

Holmberg, Marta
Soc. of Actuaries (496)

Holmberg, Selby
Nat'l Ass'n of Independent Schools (360)

Holmer, Alan F.
Pharmaceutical Research and Manufacturers of America (456)

Holmes, Bonnie J.
Nat'l Wood Flooring Ass'n (436)

Holmes, Constance D.
Nat'l Mining Ass'n (417)

Holmes, Hollis
Ass'n of American University Presses (143)

Holmes, Hyla
Ass'n for Worksite Health Promotion (141)

Holmes, June T.
Nat'l Ass'n of Independent Insurers (359)

Holmes, Madelyn
Council for Basic Education (211)

Holmes, Maggie
Nat'l Head Start Ass'n (408)

Holmes, Paul G.
Internat'l Compact Disc Interactive Ass'n (286)

Holmes, Richard P.
Nat'l U.S.-Arab Chamber of Commerce (435)

Holmgren, Cathy
Accreditation Ass'n for Ambulatory Health Care (10)

Holsinger, Kent
Soc. for the Study of Evolution (495)

Holstrom, Holly
American Psychological Ass'n (94)

Holt, Brad
Document Management Industries Ass'n (224)

Holt, Daniel J.
Soc. of Automotive Engineers International (498)

Holt, Donna M.
North American Securities Administrators Ass'n (444)

Holt, Eda
American Rehabilitation Counseling Ass'n (97)

Holt, Katrina
Ass'n of Teachers of Maternal and Child Health (167)

Holt, Lawrence J.
Nat'l Council of Self-Insurers (395)

Holt, Patricia
Nat'l Book Critics Circle (384)

Holt, Robert C.
Associated Equipment Distributors (171)

Holt, Tim
Nat'l School Supply and Equipment Ass'n (427)

Holton, Ann
American Academy of Facial Plastic and Reconstructive
Surgery (22)

Holtz, Jane L.
Farm Equipment Wholesalers Ass'n (235)

Holtzman, Nancy
Ass'n of Corporate Travel Executives (149)

Holub, Marsha
American Planning Ass'n (92)

Holub, Steven
Internat'l Council of Shopping Centers (288)

Holzman M.D., Gerald
American College of Obstetricians and Gynecologists (56)

Homayounpour, Cyrus
University Continuing Education Ass'n (537)

Homiak, Diane
American Council of State Savings Supervisors (61)

Hon, Teresa
Nat'l Federation Interscholastic Music Ass'n (402)

Honaman, John
Nat'l Soc. of Hispanic MBAs (430)

Hone, Karen A.
Health Industry Representatives Ass'n (252)

Honeycutt, Michael
Air Conditioning Contractors of America (15)

Honeycutt, Nancy R.
TAG Internat'l (520)

Honor USA (RET.), Lt.Gen. Edward
Nat'l Defense Transportation Ass'n (399)

Honor, Kim
Nat'l Congress for Community Economic Development (391)

Hood, Rita J.
AGN Internat'l - North America (14)

Hood Ph.D., Thomas C.
Soc. for the Study of Social Problems (496)

Hook, Virginia M.
Field Services Marketing Ass'n (238)

Hoort, Daniel
American Massage Therapy Ass'n (83)

Hooten, George W.
Nat'l American Legion Press Ass'n (336)

Hoover, Jerry
Nat'l Council of Health Facilities Finance Authorities (395)

Hoover Ed.D., Stephanie
American Occupational Therapy Ass'n (88)

Hope, Amy
American Ass'n of Cereal Chemists (34)

Hope, Samuel
Nat'l Ass'n of Schools of Dance (371)
Nat'l Ass'n of Schools of Art and Design (371)
Nat'l Ass'n of Schools of Music (371)
Nat'l Ass'n of Schools of Theatre (371)

Hopkins, Bruce
Recreation Vehicle Industry Ass'n (472)

Hopkins, Celwyn E.
Independent Battery Manufacturers Ass'n (260)

Hopkins, Debra
Continental Dorset Club (208)

Hopkins, Gerri
Ass'n of Retail Marketing Services (163)
Ass'n of Incentive Marketing (153)

Hopkins, Mary Jane
Ass'n of Catholic TV and Radio Syndicators (146)

Hopkins, Russell G.
Beverage Network (178)

Hopkinson, Karen
Insurance Conference Planners Ass'n (270)

Hopp, Stanley M.
Soc. of Insurance Research (503)

Hoppe, Glenn W.
Professional Reactor Operator Soc. (466)

Hopper Ph.D., David L.
American Academy of Somnology (26)

Hopper, J. Alexander
Professional Photographers of America (466)

Horak, Abby
Ass'n of State and Territorial Directors of Nursing (166)

Horeff, Eric
American Forest and Paper Ass'n (69)

Horel, Paul L.
Crop Insurance Research Bureau (219)

Horelick, Andrew L.
Aircraft Owners and Pilots Ass'n (16)

Horgsberg, Yvette
Nat'l Pawnbrokers Ass'n (421)

Hori-Ankrom, Beverly
Jewelers of America (314)

Horkheimer, Dwight
Internat'l Ass'n of Fire Fighters (279)

Horn, Betty B.
Label Packaging Suppliers Council (316)

Horn, Eric Z.
Beauty and Barber Supply Institute (177)

Horn, Lucille Dinon
American Anthropological Ass'n (28)

Hornberger, Patrick
Internat'l Regional Magazine Ass'n (301)

Horne, Scott
Institute of Scrap Recycling Industries (269)

Horne, Steven
American Herbalists Guild (73)

Horne, Tom
Nat'l Pawnbrokers Ass'n (421)

Horner, Michael J.
Nat'l Ass'n of Water Companies (380)

Hornung, Susan
Alliance for Children and Families (17)

Horovitz, Pamela
Nat'l Ass'n of Recording Merchandisers (369)

Horowitz, Doron
American Ass'n of Language Specialists (38)

Horshok, Randall P.
Business Products Industry Ass'n (185)

Horsley DPM, Dr. Neil
Nat'l Podiatric Medical Ass'n (422)

Horst-Martz, Jenny Anne
American Ass'n for Cancer Research (30)

Horton, Gaye
Nat'l Conference of State Fleet Administrators (391)

Horton, Tommy
Cotton Council Internat'l (210)
Nat'l Cotton Batting Institute (392)

Horton, Trey
American Ass'n of Physician Specialists (41)

Horvath, R. Skip
Interstate Natural Gas Ass'n of America (311)

Hosinski, Theresa
American Ass'n of University Affiliated Programs for Persons with Developmental Disabilities (44)

Hoskins, Cathy
Council of Biology Editors (213)

Hoskins Jr., Dr. H. Dunbar
American Academy of Ophthalmology (24)

Hoskins, Howard
American Optometric Ass'n (88)

Hoskins, Terry
Nat'l Contract Management Ass'n (392)

Hosler, Daryl
American Soc. of Gas Engineers (110)

Hostetler, Kathleen
Oil, Chemical and Atomic Workers Internat'l Union (448)

Hotchkiss, James
Water Sports Industry Ass'n (541)

Hoting, Hilarie
Grocery Manufacturers of America (250)

Hottaling M.D., Andrew
Soc. for Ear, Nose and Throat Advances in Children (487)

Hou, Paul
Nat'l Electrical Manufacturers Ass'n (400)

Houck Talbott, Tammy
Nat'l Rural Health Ass'n (426)

Hough, Douglas R.
Institute of Diving (266)

Hough, Harry E.
American Purchasing Soc. (96)

Hough, James A.
Nat'l Petroleum Council (422)

Hough, Robert
Red Angus Ass'n of America (473)

Houghland Jr., CAE, Paul
Nat'l Hardwood Lumber Ass'n (408)

Houghton, Kendall
Committee on State Taxation (200)

Houliston, Michael L.
American Soc. of Extra-Corporeal Technology (109)

Houstle, Peter M.
Retailer's Bakery Ass'n (476)

Houston, Betsy
Federation of Materials Socs. (237)

Houston, Brant
Investigative Reporters and Editors (312)

Houston, Elisabeth G.
Internat'l Interior Design Ass'n (295)

Houston CAE, James J.
Industrial Heating Equipment Ass'n (263)

Houston, Paul D.
American Ass'n of School Administrators (42)

Hovanky, Thoai
Nat'l Ass'n of Independent Schools (360)

Hovis Jr., John H.
United Electrical, Radio and Machine Workers of America (530)

Howard, Angelina S.
Nuclear Energy Institute (446)

Howard, Ann B.
American Federation of Home Health Agencies (67)

Howard, Bruce
Nat'l Federation of State High School Ass'ns (404)

Howard, Jane
American Academy of Physician Assistants (25)

Howard, Jerry
Nat'l Ass'n of Home Builders of the U.S. (358)

Howard, Julie
Nat'l Ass'n of Mortgage Brokers (363)

Howard, Keith
Nat'l Tour Ass'n (434)

Howard, Kimberly
Ass'n of Specialists in Cleaning and Restoration Internat'l (165)

Howard, Laura
Nat'l Ass'n of Wholesaler-Distributors (380)

Howard, Lauren P.
Shipbuilders Council of America (482)

Howard, Rachel H.
American Design Drafting Ass'n (64)

Howard Juzkiw, Laurel
Nat'l Ass'n Medical Staff Services (342)

Howarth, Rob
American Zoo and Aquarium Ass'n (124)

Howat, Senga
Public Risk Management Ass'n (470)

Howe, Allan T.
Nat'l Park Hospitality Ass'n (421)

Howe, Allynn L.
Nat'l Lumber and Building Material Dealers Ass'n (415)

Howe M.D., Ph.D., Craig W.S.
Nat'l Marrow Donor Program (416)

Howe, Karen
Soil and Water Conservation Soc. (510)

Howe, Matthew
American Ass'n for Applied Linguistics (29)

Howe, William H.
Ass'n of Bituminous Contractors (144)

Howell, Christopher E.
Precision Metalforming Ass'n (462)

Howell, Gary D.
Soc. for Mining, Metallurgy, and Exploration (491)

Howell, Jack
IEEE Communications Soc. (258)

Howell, Jerry
Painting and Decorating Contractors of America (452)

Howell, Jim
Internat'l Soc. of Crime Prevention Practitioners (306)

Howell, Sandy
American Rental Ass'n (98)

Howell, Sarah
Council on Geriatric Cardiology (217)

Howell CAE, William J.
Society of Financial Service Professionals (509)

Howery, Carla
American Sociological Ass'n (117)

Howie, Allan M.
Industrial Metal Containers Ass'n (263)
Loading Dock Equipment Manufacturers (320)

Howland, John
American Goat Soc. (71)

Howlett Jr., CMA, Clifford T.
Chlorine Chemistry Council (192)

Howley, John
Philippine-American Chamber of Commerce (457)

Hoye, Donna
American Concrete Pipe Ass'n (59)

Hoyt, Steven
American Soc. for Nondestructive Testing (104)

Hoyt, William
Textile Rental Services Ass'n of America (522)

Hryhorczuk M.D., Daniel
Ass'n of University Programs in Occupational Health and Safety (168)

Hsi, Dr. David
Nat'l Ass'n of Academies of Science (342)

Huard, Paul
Nat'l Ass'n of Manufacturers (362)

Huband, Dr. Frank L.
American Soc. for Engineering Education (102)

Hubbard, Patty
Travel Industry Ass'n of America (526)

Hubbard, Patty H.
Nat'l Council of State Tourism Directors (396)

Hubbs, Dr. Clark
American Institute of Fishery Research Biologists (77)

Huber CAE, Janet C.
Crane Certification Ass'n of America (218)

Huber, R. James
Nat'l Ass'n of Chain Drug Stores (346)

Huberman, Mark A.
Internat'l Ass'n of Hygienic Physicians (280)

Huddleston, Porter
Business Forms Management Ass'n (184)

Hudson, J. William
Internat'l Ass'n of Refrigerated Warehouses **(282)**
Internat'l Ass'n of Cold Storage Contractors **(277)**

Hudson, Peggy Renken
American Portland Cement Alliance **(93)**

Hudson, Sojn
Ass'n for Women in Computing **(140)**

Huegle, Crystal
Lamaze International **(316)**

Huer, Greg
Architectural Woodwork Institute **(127)**

Huerta, Dolores
United Farm Workers of America **(530)**

Huff, Charles
Internat'l Ass'n of Milk Control Agencies **(281)**

Huff-Ritts, Joanne
Belted Galloway Soc. **(178)**

Hufferd, Donna
Industrial Distribution Ass'n **(262)**

Huffhines, Craig
American Hereford Ass'n **(73)**

Huffman Jr., Dr. D.C.
American College of Apothecaries **(53)**

Huffman, Robert
Ass'n of Edison Illuminating Companies **(150)**

Hufman, Anne
Soc. of Medical Consultants to the Armed Forces **(503)**

Huger, Missy
American Film Marketing Ass'n **(68)**

Huget, Laurie
Cryogenic Soc. of America **(219)**

Huggins, Banner
Multi-Housing Laundry Ass'n **(331)**

Huggins, Grant
Nat'l Animal Damage Control Ass'n **(337)**

Huggins, Jim
Solar Rating and Certification Corp. **(510)**

Huggins P.E., Roland
American Fire Sprinkler Ass'n **(68)**

Hughes, Catherine
Internat'l Museum Theater Alliance **(298)**

Hughes, Delia A.
Nat'l Ass'n of Women in Construction **(380)**

Hughes, Dyanne
American Soc. for Engineering Education **(102)**

Hughes, Gail D.
Ass'n of Paroling Authorities, Internat'l **(159)**

Hughes, Gary
Soc. of American Magicians **(497)**

Hughes, Geraldine
Nat'l Ski Areas Ass'n **(428)**

Hughes, John P.
Electricity Consumers Resource Council **(228)**

Hughes, Joy Kennedy
Chocolate Manufacturers Ass'n of the U.S.A. **(193)**

Hughes, Kathleen M.
Public Library Ass'n **(469)**

Hughes, Linda
Ass'n for the Study of Play **(139)**

Hughes, Melanie K.
Nat'l Greenhouse Manufacturers Ass'n **(407)**

Hughes, Mike
Nat'l Golf Course Owners Ass'n **(407)**

Hughes, Nancy
American Academy of Physician Assistants **(25)**

Hughes, Sister Patrice
Nat'l Catholic Educational Ass'n **(385)**

Hughes Ph.D., Ruth A.
Internat'l Ass'n of Psychosocial Rehabilitation Services **(282)**

Hughes, Sandra Lynn
Internat'l Magnesium Ass'n **(296)**

Hughes CAE, Sharon M.
Nat'l Council of Agricultural Employers **(394)**

Hughes, CMT, Peggy
American Ass'n for Medical Transcription **(31)**

Huheey, Cynthia A.
American Resort Development Ass'n **(98)**

Huizenga, Walter E.
American Internat'l Automobile Dealers Ass'n **(79)**

Hulin, Tracy Lee
Nat'l Ass'n of College and University Food Services **(348)**

Hull, Donna M.
American Soc. of Agricultural Engineers **(106)**

Hull, Patricia
Nat'l Ass'n of Professional Mortgage Women **(367)**

Hull, Warren R.
American Paso Fino Horse Ass'n **(90)**

Hullander, Jerry L.
Carpet and Rug Institute **(187)**

Hultquist, Nancy
Nat'l Shoe Retailers Ass'n **(428)**

Hume, Susan
Catholic Health Ass'n of the United States **(188)**

Hume-Pratuch, Jeffery E.
Nat'l Ass'n of Independent Colleges and Universities **(359)**

Humes, Paul
Nat'l Ground Water Ass'n **(407)**

Humes, Suzanne M.
New Alternatives for Publishers, Retailers and Artists **(438)**

Humfeld, Terry
Produce Marketing Ass'n **(463)**

Humm, Marilyn
Nat'l Register of Health Service Providers in Psychology **(424)**

Hummel, Leslie A.
Truck Renting and Leasing Ass'n **(527)**

Hummel, Paul E.
Soc. of Exploration Geophysicists **(501)**

Hummel, Peggy
Building Service Contractors Ass'n Internat'l **(183)**

Humphrey, Judith
Music Educators Nat'l Conference: The Nat'l Ass'n for Music Education **(332)**
Music Industry Conference **(332)**

Humphrey, Lucretia S.
Materials Technology Institute of the Chemical Process Industries **(325)**

Humphrey, Tricia
American Soc. of Transportation and Logistics **(116)**

Humphreys, David J.
Recreation Vehicle Industry Ass'n **(472)**

Humphries, Xantippe
Land Trust Alliance **(317)**

Hunderman, Harry
Ass'n for Preservation Technology Internat'l **(136)**

Huner, Jay
Internat'l Ass'n of Astacology **(276)**

Huneycutt, Kimberly
Internat'l Home Furnishings Representatives Ass'n **(293)**

Hung, Dr. David P.J.
American Acupuncture Ass'n **(27)**

Hungerford Ph.D., M.K.
United States Sports Massage Federation **(535)**
Internat'l Sports Massage Federation **(307)**

Hunkler, Chris
Professional Golfers Ass'n of America **(465)**

Hunn, Bruce D.
American Soc. of Heating, Refrigerating and Air-Conditioning Engineers **(110)**

Hunnam, Joan
Ass'n of Container Reconditioners **(148)**

Hunnicutt, Dr. David M.
Wellness Councils of America **(542)**

Hunsicker, Dr. Ronald J.
Nat'l Ass'n of Addiction Treatment Providers **(342)**

Hunsicker, Ronald J.
American College of Addictions Treatment Administrators **(52)**

Hunsley, Dr. Roger E.
American Shorthorn Ass'n **(100)**
United States Beef Breeds Council **(532)**

Hunt Jr., A. Lee
Internat'l Ass'n of Drilling Contractors **(278)**

Hunt, Acacia G.
Soc. of Professional Benefit Administrators **(505)**

Hunt, Chris
Intravenous Nurses Soc. **(312)**

Hunt, Dennis
Screenprinting and Graphic Imaging Ass'n Internat'l **(480)**

Hunt, Elizabeth K.
Diethyl Ether Producers Ass'n **(222)**
Polymer Particulate Inhalation Group **(460)**
Basic Acrylic Monomer Manufacturers Ass'n **(177)**
Methacrylate Producers Ass'n **(327)**

Hunt Jr., Frederick D.
Soc. of Professional Benefit Administrators **(505)**

Hunt, Jayne E.
Consumer Bankers Ass'n **(207)**

Hunt, Keith
Ass'n for Consumer Research **(131)**

Hunt, Nancy
American Academy of Psychotherapists **(26)**

Hunt, Scott
Endocrine Soc. **(230)**

Hunte, Lauren A.
Soc. of Clinical and Medical Electrologists **(499)**
Internat'l Electrology Educators **(289)**

Hunter, Bruce
American Ass'n of School Administrators **(42)**

Hunter, Erica
Internat'l Digital Imaging Ass'n **(289)**

Hunter, G. William
Nat'l Basketball Players Ass'n **(382)**

Hunter, Gary
Continental Basketball Ass'n **(207)**

Hunter, Jody
Internat'l Chiropractors Ass'n **(285)**

Hunter, John T.
Ass'n of Civilian Technicians **(147)**

Hunter, Rachel
Internat'l Ass'n for Continuing Education and Training **(273)**

Huntington, Charles
Robert Morris Associates, the Ass'n of Lending and Credit Risk Professionals **(476)**

Huntley, Jery
Vinyl Siding Institute **(539)**

Huot, Edward C.
United Electrical, Radio and Machine Workers of America **(530)**

Hurd, Frank
Chlorine Chemistry Council **(192)**

Hurlburt, Alice
Nat'l Turkey Federation **(435)**

Hurlburt, Carol J.
NPES, the Ass'n for Suppliers of Printing and Publishing Technologies **(446)**

Hurlbut, Millie
Ass'n of the United States Army **(167)**

Hurley, Beverly
Council of Writers Organizations **(216)**

Hurley, Gerald C.
Nat'l Industrial Sand Ass'n **(411)**

Hurley CAE, Loyce
Energy Telecommunications and Electrical Ass'n **(230)**

Hurley, Morgan
Soc. of Fire Protection Engineers **(501)**

Hurley, William F.
Nat'l Automatic Merchandising Ass'n **(381)**

Hurlocker, Michael
Coalition for Juvenile Justice **(196)**

Hurst, Floyd
Missouri Fox Trotting Horse Breed Ass'n **(329)**

Hurt, Frank
Bakery, Confectionery and Tobacco Workers' Internat'l Union **(176)**

Hurt, Stacy
Institute of Internal Auditors **(267)**

Hurteau, Frank
Recreation Vehicle Dealers Ass'n of North America **(472)**

Hurter, Bill
Wedding and Portrait Photographers Internat'l **(542)**

Hurwitz Ph.D., CAE, Mark W.
American Institute of Architects **(76)**

Huschka, Judy
Nat'l Human Resources Ass'n **(409)**

Huske RPh, Cindy Porter
American Soc. of Consultant Pharmacists **(108)**

Hussey, Michael F.
American Resort Development Ass'n **(98)**

Huston NPA, CTRS, Ann D.
American Therapeutic Recreation Ass'n **(120)**

Huston, Melissa
American Soc. of Hematology **(110)**

Hutcherson, Carolyn
Nat'l Council of State Boards of Nursing **(396)**

Hutchins, Alan
Intelligent Transportation Soc. of America **(270)**

Hutchins, Betsy
American Donkey and Mule Soc. **(65)**

Hutchins PhD, Michael
American Zoo and Aquarium Ass'n **(124)**

Hutchinson, Bob
Wireless Dealers Ass'n **(545)**

Hutchinson Jr., Philip A.
Ass'n of Internat'l Automobile Manufacturers **(154)**

Hutchinson, Sean
Appraisal Institute **(126)**

Hutchinson, Suzanne C.
Mortgage Insurance Companies of America **(330)**

Hutchison, James L.
Sales Ass'n of the Paper Industry **(478)**

Hutchison, Karen
Portable Power Equipment Manufacturers Ass'n **(460)**

Hutchison, Kay B.
Industrial Relations Research Ass'n **(263)**

Hutner, Anita J.
Nat'l Defined Contribution Council **(399)**

Hutter, Lindsay
Nat'l Ass'n of Convenience Stores **(349)**

Hutto, Amy
Voluntary Protection Programs Participants Ass'n **(540)**

Hutton, Kenneth R.
Wood Machinery Manufacturers of America **(548)**
Water and Sewer Distributors of America **(541)**
American Brush Manufacturers Ass'n **(49)**

Hutton, Paul Andrew
Western History Ass'n **(543)**

Hutton, Sandra S.
Internat'l Textile and Apparel Ass'n (308)

Hutton, Terrence
Case Management Soc. of America (187)

Huynh, Thuan
American Ass'n of School Administrators (42)

Huyta, Mary
Recreation Vehicle Industry Ass'n (472)

Hyacinth, Susan
Professional Ass'n of Comics Entertainment Retailers (464)

Hyatt, Richard
Internat'l Ass'n of Fire Fighters (279)

Hyde, Barbara
American Soc. for Microbiology (104)

Hyers, Suzanne
Ass'n of American Colleges and Universities (142)
American Conference of Academic Deans (59)

Hyman, Alexander
Nat'l Ass'n of School Psychologists (371)

Hyman, Deborah
Soc. of Toxicology (508)

Hyps, Brian M.
American Soc. of Plant Physiologists (114)

Iacuzzi, Judith Q.
U.S.A. Toy Library Ass'n (529)

Iarossi, Frank J.
American Bureau of Shipping and Affiliated Companies (49)

Iatrides, John O.
Modern Greek Studies Ass'n (329)

Iber, Rick
American Academy of Allergy, Asthma and Immunology (20)
Internat'l Ass'n of Allergology and Clinical Immunology (275)

Ibrahim, Tod
Ass'n of Professors of Medicine (162)

Iciek, James E.
Nat'l Academy of Opticianry (334)

Ignagni, Karen M.
American Ass'n of Health Plans (37)

Ihara, Randal H.
Edison Electric Institute (226)

Ihrig, Elizabeth
Archivists and Librarians in the History of the Health Sciences (127)

Ikenberry, Stanley O.
American Council on Education (61)

Ilbaugh, Sandy
Nat'l Conference of Regulatory Utility Commission Engineers (390)

Illig, Linda
American Soc. for Microbiology (104)

Imbergamo, William G.
Nat'l Ass'n of State Foresters (375)

Imig, David G.
American Ass'n of Colleges for Teacher Education (34)

Imus, Scot
NATSO, Representing America's Travel Plaza and Truckstops (437)

Infantolino, John
United Better Dress Manufacturers Ass'n (530)

Ing, George
Nat'l Cherry Growers and Industries Foundation (386)

Ing, Muriel
Nat'l Cherry Growers and Industries Foundation (386)

Ingemie, David J.
SnowSports Industries America (484)

Inger, Arleen
Ass'n for Quality and Participation (137)

Ingle, Gary
Music Teachers Nat'l Ass'n (332)

Ingley, Gwyn Smith
Correctional Industries Ass'n (210)

Ingley, Stephen J.
American Jail Ass'n (79)

Ingraham, Margaret B.
Nat'l Ass'n of VA Physicians and Dentists (379)

Ingraham, Peggy
Meals On Wheels Ass'n of America (325)

Ingram MSN, CANP, Ann K.
Nat'l Alliance of Nurse Practitioners (336)

Ingram, Charles
Nat'l Ass'n of State Departments of Agriculture (374)

Ingram, Chris
American Soc. of Interior Designers (111)

Ingram, Jack
Soc. of Exploration Geophysicists (501)

Ingram, Richard T.
Ass'n of Governing Boards of Universities and Colleges (152)

Ingrassia, Gloria
Fashion Group Internat'l (235)

Ingrassia, Phil
Recreation Vehicle Dealers Ass'n of North America (472)

Inlow, Allen R.
Plumbing-Heating-Cooling Contractors - Nat'l Ass'n (459)

Inomata, Yoshio
Nat'l Music Publishers' Ass'n (418)

Intorre, Ben
American Musicians Union (86)

Ireland, Elaine C.
American Academy of Ophthalmology (24)

Ireland CAE, Evelyn F.
Nat'l Ass'n of Dental Plans (352)

Ireland, Michael
American Traffic Safety Services Ass'n (120)

Ireton, Frank Watt
Nat'l Earth Science Teachers Ass'n (400)

Irish, James R.
American Rental Ass'n (98)

Irish, Maureen E.P.
Institute of Certified Financial Planners (266)

Irons, Peggy
Nat'l Constables Ass'n (392)

Irvine, M. Susie
American Financial Services Ass'n (68)

Irwin, Joan M.
Internat'l Reading Ass'n (301)

Irwin, Judy
Business Higher Education Forum (184)

Isaac, Connie D.
Ass'n for the Treatment of Sexual Abusers (140)

Isaacs, Ann Fabe
Nat'l Ass'n for Creative Children and Adults (338)

Isaacs Ph.D., Harold
Ass'n of Third World Studies (168)

Isaacs, Michael L.
Nat'l Prepared Food Ass'n (423)

Isaacs, Stanley
American Buyers of Meeting and Incentive Travel (50)

Isaak, Ruth
Nat'l Sunflower Ass'n (432)

Isackson, Gloria
Nat'l Ass'n of Home Inspectors (358)

Isbell, Elizabeth A.
Council of Landscape Architectural Registration Boards (214)

Isenhour, Cynthia S.
Nat'l Ass'n of Real Estate Companies (369)

Isham, Tracy Himmel
American Hardwood Export Council (72)

Iskander, Sylvia
Children's Literature Ass'n (192)

Ison, Jennie
Autobody Representatives Council (173)

Israel, Lillian
Ass'n for Computing Machinery (131)

Issing, David
Internat'l Ass'n of Psychosocial Rehabilitation Services (282)

Istok, Margit H.
Internat'l Ozone Ass'n-Pan American Group Branch (299)

Italia, Nancy
League for Innovation in the Community College (318)

Iversen, Ellen
Organization for the Promotion and Advancement of Small Telecommunications Companies (449)

Iverson, Maynard
American Ass'n for Agricultural Education (29)

Ives, Alden A.
Nat'l Federation of Grange Mutual Insurance Companies (403)

Ivey, David L.
Internat'l Parking Institute (299)

Ivory, Glo
Nat'l Ass'n of Negro Business and Professional Women's Clubs (363)

Ivory, Shanda T.
Nat'l Ass'n for College Admission Counseling (338)

Ivy, Lloyd M.
American Fire Sprinkler Ass'n (68)

Izzo, Michael
Harness Horsemen Internat'l (251)

Jaafar, Carol
Nat'l Rehabilitation Ass'n (425)

Jachnicki, Robert
Nat'l Insurance Crime Bureau (412)

Jackier, Barbara
American College of Emergency Physicians (54)

Jackman, Kenneth W.
China Clay Producers Ass'n (192)

Jackman Ph.D., Wm. Jay
Nat'l Vocational Agricultural Educators Ass'n (435)

Jacks, Marina
American Bar Ass'n (46)

Jackson, Angie
Ass'n of American Geographers (142)

Jackson II, Charles
Soc. of American Foresters (497)

Jackson, Cherrell
American Soc. for Healthcare Risk Management (103)

Jackson, Debra B.
Halogenated Solvents Industry Alliance (250)

Jackson, Elizabeth
Internat'l Downtown Ass'n (289)

Jackson, Eugene
Internat'l Ass'n of Assessing Officers (276)

Jackson, H. Bernie
Nat'l Ass'n of Real Estate Brokers (368)

Jackson, Katharine
American Horse Shows Ass'n (74)

Jackson, Kim E.
Internat'l Parking Institute (299)

Jackson, Larry R.
American Federation of Grain Millers Internat'l Union (67)

Jackson, Liz
Associated Luxury Hotels (171)

Jackson Ph.D., Marcia J.
American College of Cardiology (53)

Jackson, Megan
Nat'l Family Planning and Reproductive Health Ass'n (402)

Jackson, Dr. Michael J.
Federation of American Socs. for Experimental Biology (236)

Jackson, Patricia
Council for Advancement and Support of Education (210)

Jackson, Richard J.
American Hotel and Motel Ass'n (74)

Jackson, Robin
Internat'l Corrugated Packaging Foundation (287)

Jackson, Rubin
Independent Bankers Ass'n of America (260)

Jackson, Sam
Specialty Equipment Market Ass'n (514)

Jackson, Suzanne
Equipment Leasing Ass'n of America (232)

Jackson Jr., William P.
Southern Transportation Logistics Ass'n (510)

Jackson Fiegener, Janice
Nat'l Ass'n of Area Agencies on Aging (343)

Jaco, John L.
Internat'l Ass'n of Marriage and Family Counselors (281)
Ass'n for Multicultural Counseling and Development (136)

Jacober, Steven L.
School and Home Office Products Ass'n (479)

Jacobs, David
Eight Sheet Outdoor Advertising Ass'n (227)

Jacobs, Gabriella
Ass'n for Facilities Engineering (133)

Jacobs, Graziella
Business Products Industry Ass'n (185)

Jacobs, Jerald
American Institute of Architects (76)

Jacobs, Jerald A.
American Soc. of Ass'n Executives (107)

Jacobs, Michelle
American Frozen Food Institute (69)

Jacobs, Steven
Computer and Communications Industry Ass'n (202)

Jacobs, Timothy A.
Futon Ass'n Internat'l (245)

Jacobs-Welch, Laura
American Cheese Soc. (51)

Jacobsen, Janet L.
Singles Press Ass'n (483)

Jacobson, Carolyn
Bakery, Confectionery and Tobacco Workers' Internat'l Union (176)

Jacobson, Cynthia
Ass'n of Federal Communications Consulting Engineers (151)

Jacobson, Eric
American Lighting Ass'n (81)

Jacobson, Jackie
Forest Industries Telecommunications (242)

Jacobson, Jeri
American Evaluation Ass'n (66)

Jacobson, Lawrence A.
Nat'l Ass'n for Search and Rescue (341)

Jacobson, Mike
Professional Reactor Operator Soc. (466)

Jacobson, Robert
Ass'n of Productivity Specialists (160)

Jacobson, JD, Larry
Nat'l Ass'n for Search and Rescue (341)

Jacoby, Karen S.
Nat'l Court Reporters Ass'n (398)

Jacoby, Laurian
American Soc. for Clinical Evoked Potentials (101)

Jacuk, Darlene
Cedar Shake and Shingle Bureau (188)

Jaeger, Stefan
Nat'l Soc. of Professional Engineers (430)

Jaffe, Alan S.
League of American Theatres and Producers (318)

Jaffe, Caroline
Nat'l Student Nurses Ass'n (432)

Jaffe, Eileen
Home Office Ass'n of America (255)

Jaffe, Lloyd
American Diamond Industry Ass'n (64)

Jaffe, Shirley
Nat'l Ass'n of Convenience Stores (349)

Jaffeson AICP, ACA, Richard C.
Nat'l Certification Commission (386)

Jager, Lisa
United States Wheat Associates (535)

Jain, Vijay
Hispanic Ass'n of Colleges and Universities (254)

Jakab M.D., Irene
American Soc. of Psychopathology of Expression (115)

Jakuowski, Daria
Nat'l Affordable Housing Management Ass'n (335)

James, Angela Moore
American Group Psychotherapy Ass'n (71)

James, Connie
Nat'l Air Transportation Ass'n (335)

James, Cynthia
Internat'l Facility Management Ass'n (290)

James, Dr. Floyd
Nat'l Soc. of Black Physicists (429)

James, Gary
Nat'l Ass'n of Convenience Stores (349)

James, Holly
Recreation Vehicle Dealers Ass'n of North America (472)

James CAE, Philip J.
Nat'l Glass Ass'n (407)

Jameson, Mary Joy
American Forest and Paper Ass'n (69)

Jameson, Steve
Institute of Internal Auditors (267)

Jamison, Dixie
Nat'l Alcohol Beverage Control Ass'n (335)

Jamison, Jeff
Nat'l United Affiliated Beverage Ass'n (435)

Janik, Laurene K.
Nat'l Ass'n of REALTORS (369)

Janik, Laurie
Real Estate Brokerage Managers Council (472)

Janis, Lenore
Professional Women in Construction (467)

Janke, Bob
Utility Communicators Internat'l (538)

Janke, Delmar
Council for Elementary Science Internat'l (211)

Janko, Julia A.
American Soc. for Bone and Mineral Research (101)

Jannetti, Anthony J.
Nat'l Ass'n of Orthopaedic Nurses (364)

Jannetti, Kristine
American Nephrology Nurses Ass'n (86)

Janny, June
America's Community Bankers (20)

Janofsky, Bonnie
American Soc. of Music Arrangers and Composers (113)

Janowiak, Robert M.
Nat'l Electrical Engineering Department Heads Ass'n (400)
Internat'l Engineering Consortium (290)

Janowitz, Barbara
League of American Theatres and Producers (318)

Jansen, Judith
Soc. for the Study of Reproduction (496)

Janssen, Nancy
Food Processing Machinery and Supplies Ass'n (242)

Janz, Milli
American Community Cultural Center Ass'n (59)

Janzen, Judith M.
Church and Synagogue Library Ass'n (193)

Jarboe, Bob
American Medical Rehabilitation Providers Ass'n (84)

Jared, Karen
American Shoulder and Elbow Surgeons (100)

Jarman Jr., Rufus E.
Customs and Internat'l Trade Bar Ass'n (219)

Jarr, Paul W.
American Dental Ass'n (63)

Jarrett, Dr. James A.
American Ass'n of Bovine Practitioners (33)

Jarvie, Robert
American Supply Ass'n (119)

Jarvis, Steve
American Pulpwood Ass'n (96)

Jarzembowski, Jim
United Fire Equipment Service Ass'n (530)

Jasinowski, Jerry J.
Nat'l Ass'n of Manufacturers (362)

Jask CAE, Roger
Air Conditioning Contractors of America (15)

Jastram, Elaine
American College of Emergency Physicians (54)

Jawgiel, Mary J.
Academy of General Dentistry (8)

Jaworski, Desiree
Nat'l Ass'n for College Admission Counseling (338)

Jaynes, Betty
Women's Basketball Coaches Ass'n (547)

Jayson, Darryl
Tobacco Merchants Ass'n of the U.S. (524)

Jean Johnson, Emma
Nat'l Housing and Rehabilitation Ass'n (409)

Jeffers, Elvina T.
American Ass'n of Electrodiagnostic Medicine (36)

Jellison, James V.
Parcel Shippers Ass'n (453)

Jendra, Jeanne
Soc. for Radiation Oncology Administrators (493)

Jengeleski, Cindy
Internat'l Bottled Water Ass'n (283)

Jenkins, Althea H.
Ass'n of College and Research Libraries (147)

Jenkins, Clara
Council of State and Territorial Epidemiologists (215)

Jenkins, James T.
Ass'n of Chairmen of Departments of Mechanics (146)

Jenkins, Judy P.
Military Boot Manufacturers Ass'n (328)

Jenkins, Lisa S.
Soc. for Marketing Professional Services (490)
APICS - The Educational Society for Resource
   Management (125)

Jenkins, Michael L.
Internat'l Warehouse Logistics Ass'n (310)

Jenkins CMP, Ozzie
Nat'l Coalition of Black Meeting Planners (387)
Nat'l Ass'n of Health Services Executives (357)

Jenkinson, William
American Academy of Ophthalmology (24)

Jennett M.D., Ph.D, Cary
Nat'l Committee for Quality Assurance (388)

Jennings, Carolynn
Dance/USA (220)

Jennings, Gary
American Southdown Breeders Ass'n (117)

Jennings, James M.
Nat'l Industrial Zoning Committee (411)

Jennings, Joan J.
Nat'l Environmental Training Ass'n (401)

Jennings, Patricia T.
American Moving and Storage Ass'n (85)

Jennings, Robert
Evidence Photographers Internat'l Council (233)

Jennings, Teresa
Direct Selling Ass'n (223)

Jenny, Louis J.
Nat'l Ass'n of Water Companies (380)

Jensen, Eleanor
Federation of American Scientists (236)

Jensen, James E.
Nat'l Academy of Sciences (334)

Jensen, Janice
Soc. of Critical Care Medicine (500)

Jensen, Jim
Institute of Medicine (268)

Jensen O.S.B., Joseph
Catholic Biblical Ass'n of America (188)

Jensen, Mr. Lynn
American Medical Ass'n (83)

Jensen, Neil A.
American Guernsey Ass'n (71)

Jensen, Shirley
Nat'l Ass'n for Year-Round Education (342)

Jenson CAE, Jon E.
Precision Metalforming Ass'n (462)

Jenulsen, Christi
Council for Responsible Nutrition (212)

Jerman, Terry
Broadcast Cable Credit Ass'n (182)

Jernigan, Dr. Ann D.
American Academy of Veterinary Pharmacology and
   Therapeutics (26)

Jernigan, Bryan
Nat'l Pest Control Ass'n (422)

Jeschke, Katherine R.
Nat'l Ass'n of Credit Management (351)

Jessee, Valera B.
United Product Formulators and Distributors Ass'n (531)

Jessen, Joanne K.
American Speech-Language-Hearing Ass'n (117)

Jessup, Bonnie
Coalition of Service Industries (196)
Intelligent Transportation Soc. of America (270)

Jessup, Donald R.
Design-Build Institute of America (222)

Jester, Jennifer
American Arbitration Ass'n (28)

Jester, Stephanie
American Ass'n for Marriage and Family Therapy (31)

Jett, Richard S.
Nat'l Ass'n of Bar and Tavern Owners (344)

Jetton, Laura
Nat'l Athletic Trainers' Ass'n (381)

Jewell, Greg
Soc. for Foodservice Management (488)

Jewell-Kelly, Starla
Nat'l Community Education Ass'n (388)

Jimenez, Leticia
Internat'l Ass'n of Allergology and Clinical Immunology (275)

Jirik, Dr. Samuel F.
Soc. for the Preservation of Oral Health (495)

Jobes, Christine
Nat'l Retail Federation (425)

Joekel, Dr. Ron
Phi Delta Kappa (456)

Joelson, Mark R.
Gasoline Pump Manufacturers Ass'n (246)

Joffe, Bruce H.
Screenprinting and Graphic Imaging Ass'n Internat'l (480)
Digital Printing and Imaging Ass'n (222)

Joffe, Joan
Nat'l Home Equity Mortgage Ass'n (409)

Johansen, Bruce
Nat'l Ass'n of Television Program Executives (378)

Johanssen, Pamela
Ass'n of Professors of Gynecology and Obstetrics (161)

John, Jan
Omicron Kappa Upsilon (448)

John, Mark William
Steel Service Center Institute (517)

John, Meride
American Health Information Management Ass'n (72)

John, Dr. Robert
American-Southern Africa Chamber of Trade and
   Industry (124)

John, Steven A
Soc. for Information Management (490)

Johns, Becky
Religious Communication Ass'n (474)

Johns CAE, CMP, Kevin
American Soc. of Regional Anesthesia (115)

Johns CMP, Kevin
Soc. of Neurosurgical Anesthesia and Critical Care (504)

Johns CAE, Kevin
Soc. for Education in Anesthesia (487)
Soc. for Pediatric Anesthesia (492)
Soc. for Obstetric Anesthesia and Perinatology (491)
Soc. of Cardiovascular Anesthesiologists (499)

Johns, Robert
Nat'l Dental Ass'n (399)

Johns, William E.
Pulp and Paper Safety Ass'n (470)

Johnson, Allen F.
Nat'l Oilseed Processors Ass'n (419)

Johnson, Amber T.
Nat'l Ass'n of Mortgage Brokers (363)

Johnson, Anna
American Ass'n of Medical Assistants (38)

Johnson, Carl T.
Compressed Gas Ass'n (202)

Johnson, Cathy
American Gear Manufacturers Ass'n (70)

Johnson, Dale
Roller Skating Ass'n Internat'l (477)

Johnson, Dr. David H.
Federation of Behavioral, Psychological and Cognitive
   Sciences (237)

Johnson, Deborah S.
Professional Women's Appraisal Ass'n (468)

Johnson, Diane E.
Livestock Publications Council (320)

Johnson, Dudley
Nat'l Ass'n of Bar and Tavern Owners (344)

Johnson CAE, E.G. (John)
Internat'l Sign Ass'n (302)

Johnson, Elizabeth F.
American College of Osteopathic Surgeons (56)

Johnson, Emily M.
American Wire Producers Ass'n (123)

Johnson CMP, Eric
Meeting Professionals Internat'l (327)

Johnson, Fred
Credit Union Executives Soc. (218)

Johnson, Frederick T.
Infants', Children's and Girls' Sportswear and Coat
Ass'n (263)

Johnson, Dr. Gary R.
Ass'n for Politics and the Life Sciences (136)

Johnson, Geraldine
Nat'l Ass'n of Teacher Educators for Family and Consumer
Sciences (378)

Johnson, Glendale V.
Nat'l Ass'n of Area Agencies on Aging (343)

Johnson, Glenn W.
American Soc. of Anesthesiologists (106)

Johnson, Gloria
Internat'l Union of Electronic, Electrical, Salaried Machine,
and Furniture Workers (309)

Johnson, Haley
American College of Nuclear Physicians (56)

Johnson, Harold W.
American Ass'n of Family and Consumer Sciences (36)

Johnson, Holly LaCroix
Nat'l Ass'n of Purchasing Management (368)

Johnson, James
United States Beet Sugar Ass'n (532)

Johnson, Jean
American College of Nurse Practitioners (56)

Johnson, Jerrold
Alfalfa Council (17)

Johnson CMP, Jessica
American Academy of Actuaries (20)

Johnson, Jill
Internat'l Cast Polymer Ass'n (285)

Johnson, Jim
Nat'l Ass'n of Home Builders of the U.S. (358)

Johnson, Joel L.
Aerospace Industries Ass'n of America (13)

Johnson, John M.
Nat'l Ass'n of State Boating Law Administrators (374)

Johnson M.D., Jonas T.
American Head and Neck Surgery Soc. (72)

Johnson, Karen
Tag and Label Manufacturers Institute (520)

Johnson CAE, Kathryn E.
Healthcare Forum, The (252)

Johnson, Kathy
Organization of Black Designers (450)

Johnson, Kathy A.
Nat'l Ass'n of Minorities in Cable (363)

Johnson, Kelly
Nat'l Ass'n for Year-Round Education (342)
American Payroll Ass'n (90)

Johnson, Larry
Assisted Living Federation of America (170)

Johnson, Laura
American Medical Group Ass'n (83)

Johnson, Mark
Internat'l Conference of Building Officials (287)

Johnson, Marlene M.
NAFSA: Ass'n of Internat'l Educators (333)

Johnson, Mary A.
Internat'l Cast Polymer Ass'n (285)

Johnson, Mary Frances
Nat'l Juvenile Detention Ass'n (413)

Johnson, Mildred
Internat'l Pot and Kettle Club (300)

Johnson, Patricia J.
Internat'l Graphological Soc. (292)

Johnson, Penelope
Council of Musculoskeletal Specialty Socs. (215)

Johnson, Peter C.
Plastic Surgery Research Council (459)

Johnson CAE, Peter K.
Metal Powder Industries Federation (327)

Johnson, R. Craig
Internat'l Congress of Oral Implantologists (287)

Johnson, R.A.
Brotherhood Railway Carmen/TCU (183)

Johnson, Rebecca
Nat'l Order of Women Legislators/Nat'l Foundation for
Women Legislators (419)

Johnson, Robert
Log House Builders Ass'n of North America (320)

Johnson, Robert A.
Nat'l Ass'n of Surety Bond Producers (377)

Johnson, Robert G.
Environmental Assessment Ass'n (231)
Ass'n of Construction Inspectors (148)
Internat'l Real Estate Institute (301)
Internat'l Travel Writers and Editors Ass'n (309)
Nat'l Ass'n of Review Appraisers and Mortgage
Underwriters (370)

Johnson, Robert K.
Nat'l Rural Water Ass'n (426)
American Soc. of Ichthyologists and Herpetologists (111)

Johnson, Robert R.
Nat'l Council of Writing Program Administrators (397)

Johnson, Robert W.
Outdoor Amusement Business Ass'n (451)

Johnson, Roger W.
Young Presidents' Organization (551)

Johnson, Sara
Internat'l Ass'n of Chiefs of Police (277)

Johnson, Seth
American Guernsey Ass'n (71)
Home Health Services and Staffing Ass'n (255)

Johnson, Shelly
American Ass'n of Neuroscience Nurses (39)

Johnson, Stephen V.
Nat'l Plant Board (422)

Johnson, Steven D.
American Hardware Manufacturers Ass'n (72)

Johnson, Susan B.
Gemological Institute of America (246)

Johnson CAE, Tanya Howe
Nat'l Committee on Planned Giving (388)

Johnson Jr., Thomas
American College of Nuclear Medicine (56)

Johnson, Thomas P.
Bank Administration Institute (176)

Johnson, Tom
Nat'l Directory Publishing Ass'n (399)

Johnson, Troy
Environmental Assessment Ass'n (231)

Johnson, Vic
NAFSA: Ass'n of Internat'l Educators (333)

Johnson, Vicki
Master Dairies (324)

Johnson, Wilma
American Ass'n of Nutritional Consultants (40)

Johnson III M.D., F.A., Joseph E.
American College of Physicians-American Soc. of Internal
Medicine (57)

Johnson-Libkind, Jean Sue
Women in Scholarly Publishing (547)

Johnston, David A.
Design-Build Institute of America (222)
Defense Fire Protection Ass'n (220)

Johnston, James J.
Owner-Operator Independent Drivers Ass'n (452)

Johnston, Kelly D.
Nat'l Food Processors Ass'n (405)

Johnston, Paul
Internat'l Soc. for General Semantics (303)

Johnston, Robert A.
American Academy of Physician Assistants (25)

Johnston, Robert E.
Soc. of Allied Weight Engineers (497)

Johnston Wilson, Lorna
Federal Energy Bar Ass'n (235)

Johnstone, Kevin
Internat'l Music Products Ass'n (298)

Joiner, Steven K.
Nat'l Ass'n of Federal Credit Unions (355)

Jolliff, James V.
Nat'l Ass'n of Jewelry Appraisers (361)

Jones, Alan
MEMA Information Services Council (327)

Jones, Alan F.
Motor and Equipment Manufacturers Ass'n (330)

Jones, Allison
Nat'l Alliance of Independent Crop Consultants (336)

Jones, Arnita A.
Organization of American Historians (450)

Jones, Barbara
Nat'l Grange (407)

Jones, Belva
Nat'l Institute of Oilseed Products (412)

Jones, Beverlee
Ass'n of Health Insurance Agents (153)

Jones, Bruce H.
Commercial Finance Ass'n (199)

Jones, Charles H.
American Foundrymen's Soc. (69)

Jones, Charles W.
Internat'l Brotherhood of Boilermakers, Iron Ship Builders,
Blacksmiths, Forgers and Helpers (284)

Jones, Charlotte
Internat'l Trademark Ass'n (309)

Jones, Christina
Central Station Alarm Ass'n (189)

Jones Ph.D., Claudia
Ass'n of Caribbean Studies (146)

Jones, Daniel
School and Home Office Products Ass'n (479)

Jones, David C.
American Iron and Steel Institute (79)

Jones, Dawn
Pedorthic Footwear Ass'n (454)

Jones, Denise
NAFSA: Ass'n of Internat'l Educators (333)

Jones, Denise M.
American Soc. of Anesthesiologists (106)

Jones, Dennis W.
Alliance for Traffic Safety (18)

Jones, Dolores C.
Nat'l Ass'n of Pediatric Nurse Associates and
Practitioners (364)

Jones, Donald R.
American College of Chest Physicians (53)

Jones, E. Dale
Ass'n for Transportation Law, Logistics and Policy (140)

Jones, Ed
Nat'l Ass'n of Wholesaler-Distributors (380)

Jones, Elizabeth F. (Penny)
American Institute for Conservation of Historic and Artistic
Works (75)

Jones, Georgi
American Buckskin Registry Ass'n (49)

Jones, Geri Duncan
American Health and Beauty Aids Institute (72)

Jones Jr., J. Benton
Soil and Plant Analysis Council (509)

Jones, Jennifer
Composites Fabricators Ass'n (201)

Jones, Jo Ann
Ass'n for Quality and Participation (137)

Jones, Joan M.
Internat'l Mobile Air Conditioning Ass'n (297)

Jones, Laura E.
United States Ass'n of Importers of Textiles and Apparel (532)

Jones, Laura Fleming
Ass'n for Healthcare Philanthropy (134)

Jones, Lee
Nat'l Ass'n of Retired Federal Employees (370)

Jones, Louisa E.
Internat'l Ass'n for the Study of Pain (275)

Jones, Lynn A.
Nat'l Cottonseed Products Ass'n (393)

Jones, Marion L.
American Luggage Dealers Ass'n (82)

Jones, Marrijane
Soc. of Craft Designers (500)
Ass'n of Crafts and Creative Industries (149)

Jones, Michael
American Optometric Ass'n (88)

Jones, Michael A.
Nat'l Juvenile Detention Ass'n (413)

Jones CMP, Michele M.
Nat'l Insulation Ass'n (412)

Jones, Michelle L.
Biotech Medical Management Ass'n (179)

Jones, Nori
Nat'l Mining Ass'n (417)

Jones, Paul R.
Alpha Chi Sigma (18)

Jones, Penni
Independent Cosmetic Manufacturers and Distributors (260)

Jones, Penny
American Ass'n for Clinical Chemistry (30)

Jones, Phil
Land Trust Alliance (317)

Jones, Randy
Nat'l Council of Farmer Cooperatives (394)

Jones, Rich
Nat'l Conference of State Legislatures (391)

Jones, Richard
Internat'l Air Cargo Ass'n (272)

Jones, Richard M.
American Institute of Physics (78)

Jones, Stella
Food Industry Suppliers Ass'n (241)

Jones, Steve
Academy of Managed Care Pharmacy (8)

Jones, Thomas A.
Internat'l Ass'n for Mathematical Geology (274)

Jones, Tom
Nat'l School Public Relations Ass'n (427)

Jonkers, Roy K.
Ass'n of Former Intelligence Officers (152)

Jordan, Bryan
Nat'l Ass'n of Bar Executives (344)

Jordan, Janet
Congress of Chiropractic State Ass'ns (205)

Jordan, Jason
Ass'n of University Related Research Parks (169)

Jordan, Jim
FTD Ass'n (244)

Jordan CRNA, PhD, Lorraine M.
American Ass'n of Nurse Anesthetists (39)

Jordan Ed.D., Mary R.
Internat'l Electrical Testing Ass'n (289)

Jordan, Robert T.
Nat'l Ass'n of Pizza Operators (365)

Jordan, Tim
Internet Alliance (311)

Jores, Ann
American Seed Trade Ass'n (99)

Jorgensen, Cheryl
Nat'l Ass'n of Consumer Shows (349)

Jorgenson, Chris
Nat'l Nutritional Foods Ass'n (419)

Jorgenson, Mary E.
Food Distributors Internat'l (241)

Jorkasky, James F.
Health Industry Manufacturers Ass'n (252)

Jorpeland, Marshall S.
Nat'l Court Reporters Ass'n (398)

Joseph, Jeff
Consumer Electronics Manufacturers Ass'n (207)

Joseph III, Thomas
Nat'l Ass'n of County Behavioral Health Directors (350)

Joseph-Biddle, Jacqui
Nat'l Council of Teachers of English (396)

Josephson, Philip
Alpha Gamma Rho (18)

Josey, Wayne
Nat'l Black MBA Ass'n (383)

Jost, Rosemary
Decorative Window Coverings Ass'n (220)

Joyce, John T.
Internat'l Union of Bricklayers and Allied Craftsmen (309)

Joyce, Larry
American Heart Ass'n (72)

Joyce, Sherman
American Tort Reform Ass'n (120)

Joycedt, Theresa
Nat'l Chimney Sweep Guild (386)

Joyner, Nelson T.
Federation of Internat'l Trade Ass'ns (237)

Juchno, Wayne H.
Nat'l Automotive Radiator Service Ass'n (381)

Judd, Michelle
Internat'l Technology Education Ass'n (308)

Judd, Robert
American Musicological Soc. (86)

Judd, William
Nat'l Ass'n of Power Engineers (365)

Judge, Steve
Securities Industry Ass'n (481)

Judson CMP, Bennett
Nat'l Roofing Contractors Ass'n (426)

Jukarovich, Jennifer M.
Coalition for Christian Colleges and Universities (195)

Julia, Thomas A.
Composite Panel Ass'n (201)

Junclans, Joyce
American Public Works Ass'n (96)

Jundt, Valerie
Nat'l Ass'n of Unclaimed Property Administrators (379)

Junemann, Gregory J.
Internat'l Federation of Professional and Technical Engineers (291)

Jungen, Laura
Soc. for Integrative and Comparative Biology (490)

Junginger, George
Soc. of Diagnostic Medical Sonographers (500)

Jurigian, Sandra L.
Nat'l Ass'n for Armenian Studies and Research (337)

Jurow, Susan
College and University Personnel Ass'n (197)

Just, Mary
Internat'l Foundation of Employee Benefit Plans (292)

Just CAE, CMP, William H.
Ass'n for Convention Operations Management (132)
Ass'n for Convention Marketing Executives (132)
Ass'n of Medical Illustrators (157)
BioCommunications Ass'n (179)

Justice, Dave
American Soc. of Radiologic Technologists (115)

Justice, Diane
Nat'l Ass'n of State Units on Aging (376)

Justin, Albert J.
Nat'l Board of Boiler and Pressure Vessel Inspectors (383)

Jutz, Patricia
American Academy of Child and Adolescent Psychiatry (20)

Jweied, Reema
Nat'l U.S.-Arab Chamber of Commerce (435)

Kabay Ph.D., Dr. Michel E.
Nat'l Computer Security Ass'n (389)

Kabir, Dr. Abdulfazal M.F.
Asian/Pacific American Librarians Ass'n (128)

Kachelski, Barbara
Credit Union Executives Soc. (218)

Kading CPCU, Bradley
Reinsurance Ass'n of America (474)

Kadrich, Lee
Automotive Parts and Accessories Ass'n (175)

Kaempffer, Catherine
Nat'l Ass'n of Real Estate Investment Trusts (369)

Kagan, Eveu
American College of Toxicology (58)

Kagarice, Dr. Vern
Internat'l Trombone Ass'n (309)

Kahan, Marlene
American Soc. of Magazine Editors (112)

Kahl, Steve
Billiard Congress of America (178)

Kahn Ph.D., Richard
American Diabetes Ass'n (64)

Kaiser, Dr. Marvin
Soc. for Values in Higher Education (496)

Kaiser, Timothy G.
Public Housing Authorities Directors Ass'n (469)

Kaitz, James
Treasury Management Ass'n (526)

Kalafuf, Richard
Nat'l Soc. of Accountants (429)

Kalaski, Robert J.
Internat'l Ass'n of Machinists and Aerospace Workers (280)

Kalavitrinos, John
American Consulting Engineers Council (60)

Kalert, Jane
American Ass'n of Gynecological Laparoscopists (37)

Kalish, Brad
Ass'n of Managed Healthcare Organizations (156)

Kalish, Susan
Hearth Products Ass'n (253)

Kaller, Kim
Ass'n on Higher Education and Disability (170)

Kaller, Richard
Certified Contractors NetWork (190)

Kallmiris, Paul
Nat'l Ass'n of Installation Developers (360)

Kallsen CAE, Patricia G.
American Ass'n of Homes and Services for the Aging (37)

Kaloi, Laura
American Health Quality Ass'n (72)

Kalteis, Natasha
General Federation of Women's Clubs (246)

Kamen, Fern M.
Nat'l Ass'n of Temple Administrators (378)

Kamin Ph.D., Deborah Y.
American Soc. of Clinical Oncology (108)

Kammer S.J., Fred
Catholic Charities USA (188)

Kamperman, Kurt
Tennis Industry Ass'n (521)

Kampert Jr., Keith
American Academy of Pediatrics (25)

Kanaby, Robert F.
Nat'l Federation of State High School Ass'ns (404)

Kanagy, David
Iron and Steel Soc. (313)

Kane, Annette
Nat'l Council of Catholic Women (394)

Kane, John E.
Nuclear Energy Institute (446)

Kane, John W.
Engine Service Ass'n (230)

Kanicki, David
American Foundrymen's Soc. (69)

Kaniewski, Daniel J.
Laborers' Internat'l Union of North America (316)

Kann, Marian
Nat'l Contract Management Ass'n (392)

Kaplan, Ann
American Ass'n of Fund-Raising Counsel (37)

Kaplan DDS, Gegory
Ass'n of Managed Care Dentists (156)

Kaplan, Joe
Professional Tattoo Artists Guild (467)

Kaplan, Larry
Soc. of Independent Gasoline Marketers of America (502)

Kaplan CAE, Linda P.
Nat'l Ass'n of Alcoholism and Drug Abuse Counselors (343)

Kaplan, Marcia
Internat'l Teleconferencing Ass'n (308)

Kaplan, Marianne G.
American Spinal Injury Ass'n (118)

Kaplan, Nancy
American Soc. on Aging (117)

Kaplan, Robert A.
Clothing Manufacturers Ass'n of the U.S.A. (195)

Kaplan, Rochelle
Nat'l Ass'n of Colleges and Employers (348)

Kapp, Robert A.
United States-China Business Council (536)

Kappas, George
American Hypnosis Ass'n (74)

Kappeler, Joyce
Mortgage Bankers Ass'n of America (330)

Kappeler, Sue
Nat'l Management Ass'n (416)

Karabetsos, Jennifer
Internat'l Reprographic Ass'n (301)

Karasu M.D., T. Byram
Ass'n for the Advancement of Psychotherapy (138)

Karcher, David A.
American Soc. of Cataract and Refractive Surgery (107)

Kardy C.A.E., Walter M.
Instrument Contracting and Engineering Ass'n (269)

Kardy CAE, Walter M.
Internat'l Council of Employers of Bricklayers and Allied Craftworkers (287)

Karel, Joseph R.
Turnaround Management Ass'n (528)

Karl, Donna
American Academy of Pediatrics (25)

Karlson Ph.D., David
Soc. of General Internal Medicine (502)

Karmazin, Sharon
Library Public Relations Council (319)

Karmol, David L.
Nat'l Spa and Pool Institute (431)

Karovic, Jackie
Distributive Education Clubs of America (224)

Karpat, Kemal H.
Ass'n for Central Asian Studies (130)

Karpel, Richard
Ass'n of Alternative Newsweeklies (142)

Karpick, Suzanne
Nat'l Ass'n of Real Estate Investment Trusts (369)

Karpinski, Babara
American Speech-Language-Hearing Ass'n (117)

Karpowicz, Deborah
Soc. for Medical Decision Making (491)

Karr, Cathy
Soc. of American Travel Writers (498)

Karr, Christy
American Ass'n of Industrial Management (38)

Karr, Norman
Internat'l Ass'n of Clothing Designers and Executives (277)

Karwoski, Marlene
Nat'l Head Start Ass'n (408)

Kasabian, Robert J.
Internat'l Newspaper Financial Executives (298)

Kasak, Harriet
Soc. of Photographer and Artist Representatives (505)

Kasdan, Lilli
Leather Apparel Ass'n (318)

Kaser, Richard
Nat'l Federation of Abstracting and Information Services (403)

Kasold, Allison
Ass'n of Public-Safety Communications Officials-Internat'l (162)

Kasperian, Seta
Motion Picture and Television Credit Ass'n (330)

Kass, Fritz
Intercollegiate Broadcasting System (271)

Kassalen MBA, Beth A.
Internat'l Transplant Nurses Soc. (309)

Kassouf, Kass
Nonprescription Drug Manufacturers Ass'n (440)

Kaswell, Stuart J.
Securities Industry Ass'n (481)

Katanick, Sandy
Intersocietal Commission for the Accreditation of Vascular Laboratories (311)

Katchen, Dr. Aaron L.
Ass'n for Jewish Studies (135)

Katchur, Kathleen
Nat'l Ass'n of Colleges and Employers (348)

Kates, Donna
American Alliance for Health, Physical Education, Recreation and Dance (27)

Katterman, William
Internat'l Silk Ass'n (302)

Katz, Frances
Institute of Food Technologists (267)

Katz, Jonathan
Nat'l Assembly of State Arts Agencies (381)

Katz, Marc
Nat'l Ass'n of Convenience Stores (349)

Katz, Richard
EDUCAUSE (227)

Katz, Dr. William D.
Ass'n for Applied Psychoanalysis (129)

Katzenberger, Amy
American College of Sports Medicine (57)

Katzman, Michael
Independent Business Alliance (260)

Kauderer, Dr. Corinne
American Ass'n for Women Podiatrists (32)

Kaufman, Amy
Council of Colleges of Acupuncture and Oriental Medicine (213)

Kaufman CMP, Debra E.
Professional Insurance Mass-Marketing Ass'n (466)

Kaufman, Larry
Magazine Publishers of America (321)

Kaufman, Theodore M.
Young Menswear Ass'n (551)

Kaufman-Purcell Ph.D., Susan
Council of the Americas (216)

Kauka, Sharon
Nat'l Ass'n of Local Supervisors of Vocational Home Economics (362)

Kautter, Tina
Soc. for Technological Advancement of Reporting (494)

Kautter CAE, Willard S.
Nat'l Ass'n of Physician Recruiters (365)
Nat'l Ass'n of Legal Search Consultants (361)

Kavanagh, Sheila
Tea Council of the U.S.A. (520)
Tea Ass'n of the United States of America (520)

Kavanaugh, E. Edward
Cosmetic, Toiletry and Fragrance Ass'n (210)

Kavanaugh, Kevin
American Diabetes Ass'n (64)

Kavanaugh, Larry
American Iron and Steel Institute (79)

Kavanaugh, Marty
Professional Golfers Ass'n of America (465)

Kay, Ian
American Foundrymen's Soc. (69)

Kay, S. Wayne
Health Industry Distributors Ass'n (252)

Kay, Sally
Nat'l Ass'n of Hosiery Manufacturers (358)

Kaye, Kerri
Alpha Tau Delta (19)

Kaye, Ron
American Academy of Orthopaedic Surgeons (24)

Kaye, Shirley P.
Soc. of Professional Audio Recording Services (505)

Kaylor, Debbie
Nat'l Cattlemen's Beef Ass'n (386)

Kays, B. Thomas
Psi Omega (469)

Kayser, John
Geospatial Information and Technology Ass'n (247)

Kean, Richard I.
Business Marketing Ass'n (184)

Keane, Kevin
Wire Service Guild (545)

Keane, Kevin P.
Internat'l Ass'n of Printing House Craftsmen (282)

Kearns, Kevin L.
United States Business and Industry Council (532)

Kearns, Robert
Ass'n of College and University Housing Officers-Internat'l (147)

Keating, Fiona
NCCLS (438)

Keating, Patricia H.
Air Distributing Institute (15)

Keating, Rev. Ted
Conference of Major Superiors of Men, U.S.A. (204)

Keating, Ted
Nat'l Ass'n of Postal Supervisors (365)

Keating, Will
Nat'l Ass'n of State Retirement Administrators (376)

Keaton, John C.
IEEE Computer Soc. (258)

Keebler, Barbara
Nat'l Catholic Educational Ass'n (385)

Keefe, Marilyn
Nat'l Family Planning and Reproductive Health Ass'n (402)

Keefe, Patrick M.
Nat'l Ass'n of Federal Credit Unions (355)

Keefer, J. Michael
Ass'n of Life Insurance Counsel (155)

Keefhaver, Joseph G.
Nat'l Auctioneers Ass'n (381)

Keel, Judith K.
Internat'l Ass'n of Ass'n Management Companies (276)
Ass'n of Professional Researchers for Advancement (161)
Ass'n of Women Surgeons (169)

Keel, Judy
Usability Professionals Ass'n (538)

Keelan, Laura
American Wind Energy Ass'n (123)

Keeley, George
Nat'l Engine Parts Manufacturers Ass'n (401)

Keeling CAE, J. Michael
ESOP Ass'n (232)

Keelor Ph.D., Richard
Sugar Ass'n (518)

Keen, Howard
Internat'l Ass'n of Business Forecasting (277)

Keen, Mary Lou
American Gem Trade Ass'n (70)

Keenan, Anthony L.
American Commerce and Shipping Ass'n (58)
Professional Trucking Services Ass'n (467)

Keenan CAE, Barbara A.
Community Ass'ns Institute (200)

Keenan Ed.D., Derek
Ass'n of Christian Schools Internat'l (146)

Keenan, Mary
American Nuclear Soc. (87)

Keene, Kerry
Interstate Council on Water Policy (311)

Keene, Steve
Disaster Preparedness and Emergency Response Ass'n (223)

Keeney, Keith C.
Calorie Control Council (186)

Keeney, Tyler
Mail Advertising Service Ass'n Internat'l (322)

Keenum, John M.
American Antiquarian Soc. (28)

Keepnews, David
American Nurses Ass'n (87)

Keese, Bill
Ass'n of Progressive Rental Organizations (162)

Keesee, Susan
American Ass'n of Textile Chemists and Colorists (44)

Keeter, Phil
Marine Retailers Ass'n of America (323)

Keferl, Dr. Eugene
American Malacological Union (82)

Keggi, Mara
Women's Basketball Coaches Ass'n (547)

Kehler, Betty
American Soc. of Transplant Physicians (116)

Kehoe, Kristie
Truckload Carriers Ass'n (527)

Keid, Robert
Institute of Certified Professional Managers (266)

Keilitz, Dave
American Baseball Coaches Ass'n (46)

Keisek, Laurie
Polystyrene Packaging Council (460)

Keith, Kendell W.
Nat'l Grain and Feed Ass'n (407)

Keithley, Carter E.
Hearth Products Ass'n (253)

Keitt, Rosalind
American Psychiatric Ass'n (94)

Kelderman, Jake
Automobile Dealers Ass'n (174)

Keliades, George K.
Valve Manufacturers Ass'n of America (538)

Kellar, Elizabeth
Internat'l City/County Management Ass'n (285)

Kelleher, Debra W.
Internat'l Special Events Soc. (307)

Kelleher, William D.
Nat'l Stone Ass'n (431)

Keller, Billilynne
Custom Electronic Design and Installation Ass'n (219)

Keller, Glenn F.
Engine Manufacturers Ass'n (230)

Keller, Joyce C.
American Ass'n of Dental Schools (36)

Keller, Michael
Commercial Finance Ass'n (199)

Keller, Robin
Business Technology Ass'n (185)

Kelley, Allison
Romance Writers of America (477)

Kelley, Carolyn
Nat'l Technical Services Ass'n (433)

Kelley, Casey
North American Limousin Foundation (443)

Kelley, Emma
SEPM - Soc. for Sedimentary Geology (482)

Kelley, Jean
Pony of the Americas Club (460)

Kelley, M.E.
American Dairy Science Ass'n (63)

Kelley CAE, William E.
Nat'l Ass'n of Settlement Purchasers (372)
Viatical Ass'n of America (539)

Kellner, John R.
Gynecologic Oncology Group (250)

Kellner, Stephen S.
Chemical Specialties Manufacturers Ass'n (191)

Kellogg, Dave
Southern Forest Products Ass'n (510)

Kellough, David L.
Air-Conditioning and Refrigeration Wholesalers Ass'n Internat'l (16)
Electrical Generating Systems Ass'n (227)

Kelly, Anne Marie
IEEE Computer Soc. (258)

Kelly, Camille
Business Products Industry Ass'n (185)

Kelly, Candi
Council for Agricultural Science and Technology (210)

Kelly, Charles L.
American Ass'n of Minority Businesses (39)

Kelly, Christine B.
Chlorine Institute (193)

Kelly, Colleen R.
American Zoo and Aquarium Ass'n (124)

Kelly, Donald A.
Space Energy Ass'n (511)

Kelly, Elizabeth A.
Nat'l Marine Distributors Ass'n (416)

Kelly III, Ernest B.
Telecommunications Resellers Ass'n (521)

Kelly CEM, Harry J.
Expediting Management Ass'n (234)

Kelly, Jennifer A.
American Waterways Operators (122)

Kelly, John J.
Electronic Industries Ass'n (228)

Kelly, Joseph
Nat'l Alliance of State and Territorial AIDS Directors (336)

Kelly, Marsha
Fur Commission USA (244)

Kelly, Maureen
American Professional Soc. on the Abuse of Children (94)

Kelly, Michael
Ass'n of Philosophy Journal Editors (160)

Kelly, Mike
Nat'l Cutting Horse Ass'n (398)

Kelly, Sharon
American Paper Machinery Ass'n (90)
Internat'l Ass'n of Emergency Managers (278)

Kelly, Thomas H.
LIMRA Internat'l (320)

Keltner, Steven
Sculptors Guild (480)

Kemery Ph.D., William E.
Academy of Scientific Hypnotherapy (10)

Kemeyer, Jim Leut
ESOP Ass'n (232)

Kemp, Frank B.
American Institute of Certified Public Accountants (76)

Kemp, Steven C.
Nat'l Legal Aid and Defender Ass'n (415)

Kemper, Coletta I.
Council of Insurance Agents and Brokers (214)

Kempner, Jonathan L.
Nat'l Multi Housing Council (417)

Kendal, Christine
American Soc. of Hand Therapists (110)

Kendall, Miriam
Nat'l Sheriffs' Ass'n (427)

Kender, Dorothy
Building Stone Institute (183)

Kendrick, Barbara
American College of Cardiology (53)

Kendrick, Julie
Institute of Environmental Sciences and Technology (267)

Kennaugh, Scott
Nat'l Ass'n of Personnel Services (365)

Kennedy, Christine
Special Libraries Ass'n (514)

Kennedy, Dennis J.
Distribution Contractors Ass'n (224)

Kennedy CSP, George
Nat'l Utility Contractors Ass'n (435)

Kennedy, Gerald O.
American Zoo and Aquarium Ass'n (124)

Kennedy, Jacqueline
American Psychological Soc. (95)

Kennedy, Janice
American Medical Informatics Ass'n (84)

Kennedy, Jill
American Public Power Ass'n (96)

Kennedy, John
Nat'l Safety Council (426)

Kennedy, John J.
Jewelers' Security Alliance of the U.S. (314)

Kennedy, Judith A.
Nat'l Ass'n of Affordable Housing Lenders (342)

Kennedy, Kimberly
Architectural Woodwork Institute (127)

Kennedy, Michael E.
Associated General Contractors of America (171)

Kennedy, Norine
United States Council for Internat'l Business (533)

Kennedy, Patrick
Nat'l Ass'n of Fire Investigators (355)

Kennedy, Robert
Ass'n for the Advancement of Psychotherapy (138)

Kennedy, Sandra
Nat'l Retail Federation (425)

Kennedy, Steven
NAFSA: Ass'n of Internat'l Educators (333)

Kennedy, Thomas
Ass'n of State and Territorial Solid Waste Management Officials (166)

Kennedy, Thomas J.
Ass'n of State and Territorial Solid Waste Management Officials (166)

Kennelly, Kathleen
Ass'n for Health Services Research (134)

Kennerdell, Peter B.
Public Affairs Council (469)

Kennett, Earle
Nat'l Institute of Building Sciences (411)

Kenney, Dennis
Police Executive Research Forum (459)

Kenney, Helen Gatewood
World Ass'n of Alcohol Beverage Industries (549)

Kenney, Jeffrey F.
Nat'l Council of Architectural Registration Boards (394)

Kenney, Lynn
American Academy of Otolaryngology-Head and Neck Surgery (24)

Kennison, Sasha D.
Internat'l Alliance for Women in Music (273)

Kenny, Thomas
Nat'l Ass'n of State Boards of Accountancy (374)

Kent, Cindy S.
Ass'n for Investment Management and Research (135)

Kent, David L.
Amalgamated Printers' Ass'n (19)

Kent, John G.
Safety Glazing Cerification Council (478)

Kent, Lorna D.
American Soc. for Microbiology (104)

Kent, Nicholas R.
North American Wholesale Lumber Ass'n (446)

Kent, Norma
American Ass'n of Community Colleges (35)

Kenty, John M.
Forestry Conservation Communications Ass'n (243)

Kenworthy, Gary
Carpet and Rug Institute (187)

Kenyon, Lowell Anson
Council on Fine Art Photography (216)

Kenyon, Stephanie
American Soc. of Travel Agents (116)
Fur Information Council of America (244)

Keohane, Patrick
North American Ass'n of Wardens and Superintendents (440)

Keonig, Jinna L.
United States Federation for Culture Collections (533)

Kepner, Linda
American Ass'n of Clinical Endocrinologists (34)

Kepner, Susan
Ass'n for Surgical Education (138)

Kepner, Teri
Soc. for Applied Sociology (485)

Kepraios, William
Soc. of Actuaries (496)

Ker, Edith M.
Soc. of Woman Geographers (509)

Keramidas Ph.D., CAE, Sherry
Regulatory Affairs Professionals Soc. (474)

Kerby, Zane
American Academy of Audiology (20)

Kerchner, Steven
Manufacturers Alliance (322)

Kerkhoven, Paul
Natural Gas Vehicle Coalition (437)

Kerley, Michael L.
Nat'l Ass'n of Life Underwriters (361)

Kerley, Robert
American Microscopical Soc. (85)

Kerman, Candace
Institute for Responsible Housing Preservation (265)

Kerman, Candace M.
Affordable Housing Tax Credit Coalition (13)

Kern, CoraLee Smith
Nat'l Ass'n for the Cottage Industry (341)

Kern, Thomas E.
American Consulting Engineers Council (60)

Kerns, La Mar C.
Nat'l Costumers Ass'n (392)

Kerr, David C.G.
Nat'l Juice Products Ass'n (413)

Kerr, John W.
Atlantic Independent Union (172)

Kerr, Dr. Larry
American Academy of Veterinary and Comparative Toxicology (26)

Kerr, Sandra
Nat'l Committee on Planned Giving (388)

Kerr, Stephen R.
Holstein Ass'n USA (255)

Kerrick, Sharon
American Nuclear Soc. (87)

Kerrigan, Deanna J.
American Ass'n for State and Local History (32)

Kershow, Michael R.
Internat'l Crystal Federation (288)

Kersteter CAE, Margaret S.
American Collectors Ass'n (52)

Kerwood, Lewis O.
Nat'l Real Estate Forum (424)

Keshishian, Elsa
Nat'l Order of Women Legislators/Nat'l Foundation for Women Legislators (419)

Kessler, Dr. A.D.
Internat'l Exchangors Ass'n (290)

Kessler, Christy L.
American Soc. for Healthcare Risk Management (103)

Kessler, Tami
Southern Forest Products Ass'n (510)

Ketchum, Richard G.
Nat'l Ass'n of Securities Dealers (372)

Kettering, Carolyn K.
American Soc. of Heating, Refrigerating and Air-Conditioning Engineers (110)

Kettner, Jim
Space Energy Ass'n (511)

Kevlin, Dean
American Institute of Chemical Engineers (77)

Key, Robert
Ass'n of Energy Service Companies (150)

Key, Sheri
Internet Alliance (311)

Keyes DDS, Dr. Alan C.
American Prosthodontic Soc. (94)

Keyes, Elizabeth
American Pharmaceutical Ass'n (91)

Keyser, Angela R.
American Ass'n of Physicists in Medicine (41)

Kezer, Kevin
Nat'l Ass'n of Wheat Growers (380)

Khan, Muggedar
Ass'n of Muslim Social Scientists (158)

Khan, Sarah
Black Filmmaker Foundation (180)

Khanna, Davinder S.
Nat'l Parks and Conservation Ass'n (421)

Khanna, Rajiv
India-American Chamber of Commerce (N.Y.) (262)

Khoury, Dr. Bernard V.
American Ass'n of Physics Teachers (41)

Khoury, Maria Elena
American Ass'n of Physics Teachers (41)

Kianka, Kim
Nat'l Ass'n for Medical Equipment Services (340)

Kibbee, Larry E.
Alliance of American Insurers (18)

Kidd, Michael
Self Storage Ass'n (481)

Kidd, Tricia
Art Glass Suppliers Ass'n Internat'l (127)

Kidder, Russell
Fire Retardant Chemicals Ass'n (240)

Kiefer, Anne
Steel Tank Institute (517)

Kieffer, Beverly
Health Industry Business Communications Council (252)

Kieffer, Donald
Nat'l Hay Ass'n (408)

Kieffer, Suzanne
Hospice Ass'n of America (256)

Kiener, Robert C.
Precision Machined Products Ass'n (462)

Kienitz PHR, Trish
Credit Union Executives Soc. (218)

Kienzle, Anne R.
American Academy of Otolaryngology-Head and Neck Surgery (24)

Kiernan, Patrick
Grocery Manufacturers of America (250)

Kiernan, Tom
Nat'l Parks and Conservation Ass'n (421)

Kiffel, Martin
Catholic Actors Guild of America (188)

Kight, Kimberly
Mail Advertising Service Ass'n Internat'l (322)

Kilczewski, Charles
American Podiatric Medical Ass'n (93)

Kilduff, Bonnie
Packaging Machinery Manufacturers Institute (452)

Kilfeather, Stephanie
Ass'n of American Railroads (143)

Kilgannon, Leslie
Assisted Living Federation of America (170)

Kilgore, Peter G.
Nat'l Restaurant Ass'n (425)

Kilgore, Suzanne
Custom Tailors and Designers Ass'n of America (219)

Kilian, Ann M.
Aircraft Owners and Pilots Ass'n (16)

Kilian, Joseph H.
Art and Antique Dealers League of America (127)

Killian, George E.
Nat'l Junior College Athletic Ass'n (413)

Killian, Randall
Nat'l Ass'n of Managed Care Physicians (362)

Killian, Richard J.
Internat'l Institute of Synthetic Rubber Producers (295)

Killy, Jude
Nat'l Ass'n of Collegiate Directors of Athletics (348)

Kilmer, Chris
NACE Internat'l (333)

Kilpatrick, Judy A.
Data Interchange Standards Ass'n (220)

Kim, Andrew K.
Nat'l Eye Research Foundation (402)

Kim, Dr. Christopher
American Apitherapy Soc. (28)

Kimball, Donna
American College of Radiology (57)

Kimball, John
Newspaper Ass'n of America (439)

Kimball, Philip
Soc. of Naval Architects and Marine Engineers (504)

Kimball, Philip H.
United States Apple Export Council (532)
Nat'l Dry Bean Council (400)

Kimble CMP, Viveca
Nat'l Ass'n of College Stores (348)

Kimmel, Brian
Nat'l Ass'n of Convenience Stores (349)

Kimmell, Thomas
Irrigation Ass'n (313)

Kimzey, Jennifer
Transportation Lawyers Ass'n (525)

Kinard, D.H.
Nat'l Cottonseed Products Ass'n (393)

Kincaide CAE, Gail G.
Ass'n of Women's Health, Obstetric and Neonatal Nurses (169)

Kinder, James A.
Nat'l Ass'n of Graphic and Product Identification Manufacturers (357)
Self Insurance Institute of America (481)

Kindinger, Paul E.
Agricultural Retailers Ass'n (14)

King, Babrbara
SOLE - The Internat'l Soc. of Logistics (510)

King, Benny
Internat'l Ass'n of Arson Investigators (275)

King, Catharine
American Bus Ass'n (49)

King, Char
Nat'l Ass'n of Business and Industrial Saleswomen (346)

King, Don L.
Texas Longhorn Breeders Ass'n of America (521)

King Ph.D., Dr. T
Internat'l Soc. for Ecological Modelling-North American Chapter (303)

King, Eileen N.
Outdoor Writers Ass'n of America (451)

King, Gene P.
American Ass'n of Veterinary Clinicians (45)

King, George W.K.
American Institute of Biomedical Climatology (76)

King, Jack
Nat'l Ass'n of Criminal Defense Lawyers (352)

King Ph.D., James A.
Internat'l Ass'n of Personal Protection Agents (281)

King, Janis
Internat'l Soc. for Ecological Economics (303)

King, Jerry
Textured Yarn Ass'n of America (522)

King, Josephine
Nat'l Insurance Ass'n (412)

King, Kay
Ass'n of Professional Schools of Internat'l Affairs (161)

King, Laura B.
Ass'n of Part-Time Professionals (159)

King, Laurel
Academy of Internat'l Business (8)

King, Leslie
Ladies Professional Golf Ass'n (316)

King, Linda
Single Ply Roofing Institute (483)

King, Lyn D.
North American Ass'n of Educational Negotiators (440)

King, Marilou M.
American Health Lawyers Ass'n (72)

King, Martin
Nat'l Rural Electric Cooperative Ass'n (426)

King, Pat
Handweavers Guild of America (251)

King, Peter B.
American Public Works Ass'n (96)

King, Robert E.
Soc. of Manufacturing Engineers (503)

King, Dr. Robert L.
American Academy of Advertising (20)

King, Roland
Nat'l Ass'n of Independent Colleges and Universities (359)

King, Rosalyn
American Public Human Services Ass'n (96)

King, Rosilyn
American Ass'n of Public Welfare Attorneys (42)

King, Rosslyn
American Ass'n of Public Welfare Information Systems Management (42)

King, Sheril
Ass'n of Children's Prosthetic-Orthotic Clinics (146)

King, Sheril B.
American Academy for Cerebral Palsy and Developmental Medicine (20)

King CAE, Steven T.
Post Card Distributors Ass'n of North America (461)
Pet Industry Distributors Ass'n (455)
Safety Equipment Distributors Ass'n (478)

King, Susan
ADSC: The Internat'l Ass'n of Foundation Drilling (12)

King, Tom
United States Soccer Federation (535)

King, Vicki J.
Soc. of Professional Well Log Analysts (506)

King, William P.
American Ass'n of Colleges of Osteopathic Medicine (34)

Kinghorn Jr., Edward J.
Ferroalloys Ass'n (238)

Kingman, Gay
Nat'l Indian Gaming Ass'n (410)

Kingsley, Daniel T.
Nat'l Venture Capital Ass'n (435)

Kingston, Janet
Internat'l Microelectronics and Packaging Soc. (297)

Kington, Carol
Motorcycle Industry Council (330)
Specialty Vehicle Institute of America (514)

Motorcycle Safety Foundation (331)

Kink, Annette
Nat'l Ass'n of Educational Buyers (353)

Kinkdale, Carol
Internat'l Bottled Water Ass'n (283)

Kinnaird, Jula J.
Nat'l Pasta Ass'n (421)

Kinsella, Brian J.
Nat'l Ass'n of Mortgage Brokers (363)

Kinter, Marci
Digital Printing and Imaging Ass'n (222)

Kinter, Marcia Y.
Screenprinting and Graphic Imaging Ass'n Internat'l (480)

Kinziger, Peter
Internat'l Community Corrections Ass'n (286)

Kinzler, Ben
Diamond Manufacturers and Importers Ass'n of America (222)

Kipnis, Ken
Internat'l Ass'n for Philosophy of Law and Social Philosophy - American Section (275)

Kipple, Diana
Soc. for Surgery of the Alimentary Tract (494)

Kirby, Craig A.
Recreation Vehicle Industry Ass'n (472)

Kirby, George W.
Nat'l Catholic Educational Ass'n (385)

Kirby, Liby
Flight Safety Foundation (240)

Kirchbaum, John
American Burn Ass'n (49)

Kircher, Karen
Ass'n of Incentive Marketing (153)

Kirchhoff, Richard W.
Nat'l Ass'n of State Departments of Agriculture (374)

Kirchner, Paul G.
American Pilots' Ass'n (92)

Kirk, Carl
Maintenance Council of American Trucking Ass'ns (322)

Kirk CAE, Ken
Ass'n of Metropolitan Sewerage Agencies (157)

Kirk, Michael K.
American Intellectual Property Law Ass'n (79)

Kirk, Nancye
Institute of Real Estate Management (269)

Kirk, Sharon
Nat'l Petroleum Refiners Ass'n (422)

Kirkland, Carol
Ass'n of Community Cancer Centers (148)

Kirkland, Katherine H.
Ass'n of Occupational and Environmental Clinics (158)

Kirkman, Patricia
Nat'l Ass'n of Hosiery Manufacturers (358)

Kirkpatrick, Charles
Nat'l Ass'n of Barber Boards (344)

Kirsch, Elanore
Soc. for Healthcare Consumer Advocacy (488)

Kirsch, Gesa
Conference on English Education (205)

Kirsch, Peter
American Soc. of Landscape Architects (111)

Kisha, Mike
Nat'l Religious Broadcasters (425)

Kistucentz, Steve
American Portland Cement Alliance (93)

Kitchen Jr., Emmett B. "Jay"
Personal Communications Industry Ass'n (455)

Kitchin, Rosemarie
Motor and Equipment Manufacturers Ass'n (330)
Automotive Public Relations Council (175)

Kiteley, Gary W.
University Aviation Ass'n (537)

Kitlass, Donna
CIM --The Business Owners Forum (194)

Kitterman Jr., Richard F.
Commission on Accreditation for Law Enforcement Agencies (199)

Kittner, Craig
Nat'l Artists Equity Ass'n (337)

Kittredge, Frank D.
Nat'l Foreign Trade Council (405)

Kitty, Margie
Nat'l Ass'n of Pastoral Musicians (364)

Kizart, Vanessa
Soc. for Social Work Leadership in Health Care (494)

Kizer, Maria
American School Health Ass'n (99)

Kjellstrom, Page
Council of Protocol Executives (215)

Kjera AA, CLA, Aron J.
North American Canon Law Soc. (441)

Klaeser CAE, M. Kathleen
Ass'n of Pediatric Oncology Nurses (159)

Klamfoth, Roger L.
Appaloosa Horse Club (126)

Klamke, Stephan E.
EIFS Industry Members Ass'n (227)

Klasko, H. Ronald
American Immigration Lawyers Ass'n (74)

Klawans, Arthur H.
Nat'l Food Distributors Ass'n (405)

Kleckner, Dean R.
American Farm Bureau Federation (66)

Kleffner, Martin
Nat'l Ass'n of Area Agencies on Aging (343)

Kleffner, Veronica
Internat'l Municipal Lawyers Ass'n (297)

Klein, Allen
North American Soc. for the Sociology of Sport (445)

Klein, Barry
Children's Book Council (192)

Klein, Gary
Electronic Industries Ass'n (228)

Klein, Gary S.
Consumer Electronics Manufacturers Ass'n (207)

Klein, Dr. Hans E.
WACRA - World Ass'n for Case Method Research & Application (540)

Klein, James A.
Ass'n of Private Pension and Welfare Plans (160)

Klein, Janice
Nat'l Soc. for Graphology (428)

Klein, Josephine
Federal Law Enforcement Officers Ass'n (236)

Klein CAAC, Ron
Nat'l Board for Certified Clinical Hypnotherapists (383)

Klein, Susan E.
American Arbitration Ass'n (28)

Klein, Susan Humphreys
Internat'l Soc. for Pharmaceutical Engineering (304)

Klein, Ted
Tube Council of North America (527)

Kleinc, Douglas M
Entomological Soc. of America (231)

Kleine, Karen
Nat'l School Public Relations Ass'n (427)

Kleingartner, Larry
Nat'l Sunflower Ass'n (432)

Kleinstiver, Louis
Nat'l Truck Equipment Ass'n (434)

Klich, Maren
Mycological Soc. of America (332)

Klim, Edward J.
Internat'l Snowmobile Manufacturers Ass'n (302)

Klimisch, Dr. Richard
American Automobile Manufacturers Ass'n (46)

Klindworth, Christine
Nat'l Ass'n of Advisors for the Health Professions (342)

Kline, Amy E.
Mobile Air Conditioning Soc. Worldwide (329)

Kline, Beth
American Institute for Conservation of Historic and Artistic Works (75)

Klinger, Raymond W.
Nat'l Ornamental Goldfish Growers Ass'n (420)

Klipstein, Richard
Nat'l Organization of Life and Health Insurance Guaranty Ass'ns (420)

Klo, Alex
American Ass'n of Oriental Medicine (40)

Klockenga, Bel S.
Steel Service Center Institute (517)

Kloempken, Leanna D.
Lutheran Church Library Ass'n (321)

Kloese, Barbara
Natural Colored Wool Growers Ass'n (437)

Kloostra, David
Nat'l Suffolk Sheep Ass'n (432)

Klopfer, Jerry
Community College Ass'n for Instruction and Technology (201)

Klos CMP, Denise
Gravure Ass'n of America (249)

Klose, Christopher
American Crop Protection Ass'n (62)

Klose, Helen
American Institute of Hydrology (77)

Klose, Lisa
Institute for Operations Research and the Management Sciences (265)

Kloss RRA, Linda L.
American Health Information Management Ass'n (72)

Klug, Kevin
Ass'n of American Geographers (142)

Knapp Ph.D., Deirdre
Human Resources Research Organization (257)

Knapp, Jolene
Soc. for College and University Planning (486)
Knapp Ph.D., Richard M.
Ass'n of American Medical Colleges (142)
Knarr CMP, Jean
Cosmetic, Toiletry and Fragrance Ass'n (210)
Knebel, John A.
Nat'l Ass'n of Broadcasters (345)
Kneeland, Bruce
Nat'l Wholesale Druggists' Ass'n (436)
Kneiss, John
Oxygenated Fuels Ass'n (452)
Knell, Margaret
Inter-Industry Conference on Auto Collision Repair (271)
Knell, Steve
American Sport Fishing Ass'n (118)
Knepp, Melissa
Committee of 200 (200)
Knepper, Edgar M.
United States Ass'n of Independent Gymnastic Clubs (532)
Knezovich, Jeffrey P.
American Soc. of Lipo-Suction Surgery (112)
American Academy of Cosmetic Surgery (21)
Knight, Brian D.
Nat'l Ass'n of State Credit Union Supervisors (374)
Knight Ph.D., Carol
Nat'l Confectioners Ass'n of the United States (389)
Knight, Carol
Nat'l Council of the Paper Industry for Air and Stream
    Improvement (397)
Knight, Elizabeth S.
Soc. for Human Resource Management (489)
Knight, Frances
Nat'l Ass'n of Limited Edition Dealers (361)
Knight, James T.
Nat'l Frame Builders Ass'n (406)
Knight MSW, Mark A.
Ass'n for Ambulatory Behavorial Healthcare (129)
Knight, Maureen
Coin Laundry Ass'n (196)
Knight, Patrick
American Internat'l Freight Ass'n (79)
Transportation Intermediaries Ass'n (525)
Knight, Robert F.
Nat'l Ass'n of Private Industry Councils (366)
Knight, William V.
American Institute of Professional Geologists (78)
Kniseley, Sina
American Ass'n of Physics Teachers (41)
Knoblauch, Mark
American Library Ass'n (81)
Knopp, Gregory
Automobile Dealers Ass'n (174)
Knotek, George
Nat'l Mail Order Ass'n (416)
Knott, Mary
Residential Space Planners Internat'l (475)
Knott, Vicki
Belgian Draft Horse Corp. of America (178)
Knowdell, Richard L.
Career Planning and Adult Development Network (187)
Knowles, Janet K.
American Fire Sprinkler Ass'n (68)
Knowles, Shirley
Nat'l Ass'n of Federal Credit Unions (355)
Knowles, Dr. W. Douglas
ASM Internat'l (128)
Knowlton, Ginger
Ass'n of Authors' Representatives (144)
Knowlton, Thomas E.
Pollution Liability Insurance Ass'n (460)
Knudsen, Martie
American Internat'l Marchigiana Soc. (79)
Knudson, Margaret
Women in Internat'l Security (546)
Knutsen, Arvid
Nat'l Opera Ass'n (419)
Knutson, Donna
Council of State and Territorial Epidemiologists (215)
Knutson, Monika
American Ass'n for Medical Transcription (31)
Kobel, Mike
Internat'l Ass'n of Plumbing and Mechanical Officials (282)
Kobetz, Dr. Richard W.
Academy of Security Educators and Trainers (10)
Kobos, Carolyn
American Payroll Ass'n (90)
Koch, Christopher P.
African Studies Ass'n (14)
Koch, Julia Bowers
Produce Marketing Ass'n (463)

Kocher, David
Nat'l Council on Compensation Insurance (397)
Kockenmeister, William H.
Gas Research Institute (246)
Koebnick, Vicki
Minerals, Metals and Materials Soc., The (329)
Koehl, Dexter C.
Travel Industry Ass'n of America (526)
Koehler, Wade
Foodservice Consultants Soc. Internat'l (242)
Koepke, Richard
Internat'l Soc. for the Study of Dissociation (305)
Soc. for Social Work Leadership in Health Care (494)
Koepper, Kenneth E.
Uniform and Textile Service Ass'n (529)
Koerner, Janet
American Specialty Toy Retailing Ass'n (117)
Koerner, Thomas F.
Nat'l Ass'n of Secondary School Principals (372)
Koetke, Richard
Internat'l Soc. for Analytical Cytology (303)
Kogan, Warren O.
Subcontractors Trade Ass'n (517)
Kogler, Kathleen
American Phytopathological Soc. (92)
Kohl, Dr. Kay
University Continuing Education Ass'n (537)
Kohler, Jill
Beauty and Barber Supply Institute (177)
Salon Ass'n, The (478)
Kohles, Judy
CBA (188)
Kohn, Peter
New York Academy of Sciences (438)
Kohut, Carleen
Personal Communications Industry Ass'n (455)
Kokes, Marvin
Nat'l Cattlemen's Beef Ass'n (386)
Kolanowski, Ron
Nat'l Ass'n for Home Care (339)
Kolar CAE, Mary Jane
Nat'l Cargo Security Council (385)
Kolb, Guy D.
Soc. of Competitive Intelligence Professionals (500)
Kolbe, Sherry L.
Nat'l Ass'n of Private Schools for Exceptional Children (366)
Kolbe, Stanley
Sheet Metal and Air Conditioning Contractors' Nat'l
    Ass'n (482)
Kolber, Warren
Ass'n of Operating Room Nurses (159)
Koleda, Michael
Energy Frontiers Internat'l (230)
Kolehmainen, Jan W.
American Academy of Neurology (23)
Kolling, Linda W.
Polyurethane Manufacturers Ass'n (460)
Kolman, David A.
Used Truck Ass'n (538)
Truck Writers of North America (527)
Kolodziej, Richard R.
Natural Gas Vehicle Coalition (437)
Koloski, Judith Ann
Nat'l Adult Education Professional Development
    Consortium (334)
Kominus, Nicholas
United States Cane Sugar Refiners' Ass'n (532)
Komisarow, Patrice
United States Egg Marketers (533)
Komon, Maria P.
American Foundrymen's Soc. (69)
Konarski III, John
Internat'l Council of Shopping Centers (288)
Koneo, Jon
Nat'l Ass'n of Securities and Commercial Law Attorneys (372)
Kong Ph.D., J.D., B. Waine
Ass'n of Black Cardiologists (145)
Kong, Cindy Y.
Soc. of the Plastics Industry - Polyurethane Division (507)
Konnor, Delbert D.
Pharmaceutical Care Management Ass'n (456)
Koonan, Karen Jo
Nat'l Lawyers Guild (414)
Koons, Lucy
Nat'l Air Transportation Ass'n (335)
Koontz, Michele Smith
Soc. for the Study of Social Problems (496)
Koopman, Karen L.
Women in Production (547)
Kopcinski, Ray
Million Dollar Round Table (328)

Kopernick, James
Internat'l Plate Printers', Die Stampers' and Engravers' Union
    of North America (300)
Koppenol, Mike
Christian Labor Ass'n of the United States of America (193)
Kopperud, Steven L.
American Feed Industry Ass'n (67)
Kopperud, Dr. William
American Academy of Physiologic Dentistry (25)
Koranda, Donald J.
Nat'l Aeronautic Ass'n (335)
Korb, Thomas
Ass'n for Advanced Life Underwriting (129)
Korbel, Kimberly A.
American Wire Producers Ass'n (123)
Korczak CAE, Edward S.
Nat'l Wood Flooring Ass'n (436)
Kornblau, William S.
ASM Internat'l (128)
Kornblum, Helen
Teachers of English to Speakers of Other Languages (520)
Korner, Dr. Tom
Nat'l Ass'n of Secondary School Principals (372)
Kornfeld, Marilyn
Nat'l Customs Brokers and Forwarders Ass'n of America (398)
Korolevich, Ysabel S.
Aluminum Ass'n (19)
Korolishi, Jennifer
Internat'l Dairy Foods Ass'n (288)
Koros, William J.
North American Membrane Soc. (443)
Korotky, Kenneth
Nat'l Conference of Catholic Bishops/U.S. Catholic
    Conference (390)
Korson II, Philip J.
Cherry Marketing Institute (191)
Korson, Teri
Distribution Contractors Ass'n (224)
Korte, Charles
Ass'n of Graduate Liberal Studies Programs (152)
Korzun, Cynthia
Forging Industry Ass'n (243)
Koshkarian, Amy
PROMAX Internat'l (468)
Kosiba, Janet
American Ass'n of Diabetes Educators (36)
Kosior, Laurel
Colorado Ranger Horse Ass'n (198)
Koski-Grafer, Susan
Financial Executives Institute (238)
Koslowe, Rabbi Irving
American Jewish Correctional Chaplains Ass'n (79)
Koss, Elaine
College Art Ass'n (197)
Kost, Kathryn
Iron and Steel Soc. (313)
Kost, Richard S.
Aviation Maintenance Foundation Internat'l (176)
Kostecki Ph.D., Paul T.
Ass'n for the Environmental Health of Soils (139)
Koszyn, Jayme
Literary Managers and Dramaturgs of the Americas (320)
Kotula, Corinta N.C.
Newspaper Features Council (439)
Kouneski, Anthony M.
American Public Transit Ass'n (96)
Kouris, John
Defense Research Institute (221)
Kouros, Thomas C.
United States Bowling Instructors Ass'n (532)
Kourouma, Michelle D.
Nat'l Conference of Black Mayors (389)
Kovakefsky, Frank
Nat'l Federation of State High School Ass'ns (404)
Kovaleski, Frank
Nat'l Interscholastic Athletic Administrators Ass'n (413)
Kovary, Robin
American Dog Trainers Network (65)
Kovins, Mike
Internat'l Ass'n of Electronic Keyboard Manufacturers (278)
Kowalczyk, Mercy
IEEE Signal Processing Soc. (259)
Kowalski, Michael J.
American Water Resources Ass'n (122)
Kowitz, Aletha A.
American Academy of the History of Dentistry (26)
Kozack, Jerome J.
Internat'l Ice Cream Ass'n (294)
Kozak, Jerome J.
Nat'l Cheese Institute (386)
American Butter Institute (50)
Nat'l Milk Producers Federation (417)

Kozal, Dr. Richard A.
Pierre Fauchard Academy **(458)**
Koziol, Patricia S.
Hobby Industry Ass'n of America **(255)**
Kozlowski Ph.D., Lynn T.
Academy of Behavioral Medicine Research **(7)**
Kozol, Patrick
Million Dollar Round Table **(328)**
Kracht, Steven F.
Western Red Cedar Ass'n **(543)**
Krack CAE, James J.
American Boarding Kennels Ass'n **(48)**
Kraemer, Mike
North American Equipment Dealers Ass'n **(442)**
Kraich, Jeni
Nat'l Wooden Pallet and Container Ass'n **(437)**
Kraich, Norbert
Ass'n of Investment Management Sales Executives **(155)**
Krajeck, Richard W.
U.S. Grains Council **(528)**
Kral, Kenneth H.
Internat'l Tax Institute **(308)**
Kralicek CAE, Robert H.
Hotel Motel Brokers of America **(256)**
Krall, Janet
Precision Metalforming Ass'n **(462)**
Kramer Ph.D., Cathy E.
Ass'n for Quality and Participation **(137)**
Kramer, Eileen
Internat'l Teleproduction Soc. **(308)**
Freelance Editorial Ass'n **(244)**
Kramer, Dr. Elizabeth
Jesuit Ass'n of Student Personnel Administrators **(313)**
Kramer, Maria
Indian Arts and Crafts Ass'n **(262)**
Kramer, Mitchell
Power-Motion Technology Representatives Ass'n **(462)**
Kramer, Terry
American Bar Ass'n **(46)**
Kramer, Walter M.
American Institute of Marine Underwriters **(77)**
Kramer, William C.
Portland Cement Ass'n **(460)**
Kramer-Whelan CMP, Lauren
Soc. of Nuclear Medicine **(504)**
Kranowitz, Alan
Nat'l Ass'n of Wholesaler-Distributors **(380)**
Kranz, Matthew
Telecommunications Industry Ass'n **(521)**
Kranz, Sally
General Federation of Women's Clubs **(246)**
Krapf M.S., Kristin L.
Renewable Natural Resources Foundation **(475)**
Krapp, Christian
American Nuclear Soc. **(87)**
Krasner MS, RN, CE, Diane
Ass'n for the Advancement of Wound Care **(139)**
Krass, Dr. Dorothy
Soc. for American Archaeology **(485)**
Kraus CLU, ChFC, Arthur D.
Nat'l Ass'n of Life Underwriters **(361)**
Kraus, Lawrence B.
Chamber of Commerce of the United States of America **(190)**
Kraus, Maribeth T.
Modern Language Ass'n of America **(329)**
Krause, Barbara K.
North American Soc. of Pacing and Electrophysiology **(445)**
Krause, Dennis
Internat'l Interior Design Ass'n **(295)**
Krause, Jane
American Soc. of Ophthalmic Administrators **(113)**
Krause CMP, Jane
American Soc. of Cataract and Refractive Surgery **(107)**
Kraushaar, Kevin
Nonprescription Drug Manufacturers Ass'n **(440)**
Krauskopf, Sharma J.
American Ass'n of Direct Human Service Personnel **(36)**
Kraut, Alan G.
American Psychological Soc. **(95)**
Soc. for Psychophysiological Research **(492)**
Krawiec, Virginia
American Ass'n for Cancer Education **(29)**
Krawisz, Robert
American Soc. for Quality **(105)**
Kraynik, Andrew
Soc. of Rheology **(506)**
Kreblein, Karla
American Massage Therapy Ass'n **(83)**
Krebs, Frederick J.
American Corporate Counsel Ass'n **(60)**

Krediet, R.
Internat'l Soc. for Peritoneal Dialysis **(304)**
Kreer, Irene Overman
Petroleum Packaging Council **(456)**
Krehbiel, Ken
American Academy of Actuaries **(20)**
Kreig, Andrew T.
Wireless Communications Ass'n Internat'l **(545)**
Kreimer, Stephen H.
Professional Bail Agents of the United States **(465)**
Krejci, David
Grain Elevator and Processing Soc. **(249)**
Kremer, CeCe
Plumbing Manufacturers Institute **(459)**
Krentz, Shirley A.
American Soc. for Quality **(105)**
Krese, Christopher P.
American Frozen Food Institute **(69)**
Kress, John
Ass'n of University Programs in Health Administration **(168)**
Krial, Traci
Council of Insurance Agents and Brokers **(214)**
Kriegel CAE, Robin
American Ass'n of Medical Soc. Executives **(39)**
Krieger, Elaine B.
Healthcare Financial Management Ass'n **(252)**
Krisberg, Dr. Barry
Nat'l Council on Crime and Delinquency **(397)**
Kriser, Jill A.
Independent Insurance Agents of America **(261)**
Krisher, Richard
Nat'l Automotive Radiator Service Ass'n **(381)**
Krishna M.B.A., Chandru
Renewable Natural Resources Foundation **(475)**
Krissoff, Michael R.
Asphalt Emulsion Manufacturers Ass'n **(128)**
Asphalt Recycling and Reclaiming Ass'n **(129)**
Krist, Bill
American Electronics Ass'n **(65)**
Kristof, Dawn C.
Water and Wastewater Equipment Manufacturers Ass'n **(541)**
Kroger, Dr. J. Stephen
COLA **(196)**
Kroh, Lerrene
Nat'l Sunflower Ass'n **(432)**
Krohn, Jeri
American Academy of Cosmetic Dentistry **(21)**
Kroll, Kevin
Steel Tank Institute **(517)**
Krolman, Walter
ICAAAA Coaches Ass'n **(257)**
Krone, James C.
Roses Incorporated **(477)**
Kronthaler, Margit
Water Quality Ass'n **(541)**
Krosnick, David L.
Nat'l Soc. of Professional Engineers **(430)**
Krouse, Ronald
American Federation of Teachers **(67)**
Krueger, Keith
Consortium for School Networking **(206)**
Krueger, Roy P.
American Naprapathic Ass'n **(86)**
Kruger, Kevin
Nat'l Ass'n of Student Personnel Administrators **(377)**
Kruger, Robert M.
Business Software Alliance **(185)**
Kruidenier, William P.
Internat'l Soc. of Arboriculture **(305)**
Krull, Donald M.
Air Line Employees Ass'n, International **(15)**
Krump, Betty
American Technical Education Ass'n **(119)**
Kruse, Becky
American Soc. of Radiologic Technologists **(115)**
Kruse USN (RET.), Capt. Dennis K.
American Soc. of Naval Engineers **(113)**
Kruse, Earl
United Union of Roofers, Waterproofers and Allied Workers **(536)**
Kruse, Teresa M.
Nat'l Lincoln Sheep Breeders Ass'n **(415)**
Kruskol, Ron
Ass'n of Rehabilitation Nurses **(163)**
Krut, Stephen F.
American Ass'n of Meat Processors **(38)**
Krzyminski, James S.
Nat'l Council of Farmer Cooperatives **(394)**
Ku, Charlotte
American Soc. of Internat'l Law **(111)**

Kube, Thomas A.
Accrediting Commission for Career Schools and Colleges of Technology **(11)**
Council of Educational Facility Planners, Internat'l **(213)**
Kubesh Ph.D., RN, Donna
Ass'n of Lutheran College Faculties **(156)**
Kubicek, Kari
American Sleep Disorders Ass'n **(100)**
Kubis, Dianne
American College of Allergy, Asthma and Immunology **(53)**
Kubis, Dianne K.
American Soc. of Colon and Rectal Surgeons **(108)**
Kuchnicki, Richard P.
Council of American Building Officials **(212)**
Kucinski, Lorraine
Building Owners and Managers Institute Internat'l **(183)**
Kudo, Irma S.
American Ass'n of Endodontists **(36)**
Kudravi, Kathy
Ass'n for Women in Sports Media **(141)**
Kuehl, Peggy
American College of Clinical Pharmacy **(53)**
Kueter Jr., Dean
Nat'l Sheriffs' Ass'n **(427)**
Kuffner, Libby
Nat'l Ass'n of School Psychologists **(371)**
Kugler, Ellen Finkelstein
Nat'l Ass'n of Urban Critical Access Hospitals **(379)**
Kugler, Phil
Federation of Nurses and Health Professionals **(237)**
Kuhach, Sandra
American Soc. of Hypertension **(111)**
Kuhlman, Stacey
Printing Industries of America **(463)**
Kuhn, Kathryn
Nat'l Community Pharmacists Ass'n **(388)**
Kuhn, Peter
American Soc. of Plastic and Reconstructive Surgeons **(114)**
Kuhn CAE, Thomas R.
Edison Electric Institute **(226)**
Kuk, Thomas J.
American Soc. of Baking **(107)**
Kukawka, Stanley
Variable Electronic Components Institute **(538)**
Kukolich, Vernette A.
Nat'l Beer Wholesalers Ass'n **(382)**
Kulawiak, Carolyn M.
Nat'l Electronic Distributors Ass'n **(400)**
Kulback, Ann
Soc. for Industrial Microbiology **(490)**
Kulcincki, Gerald L.
Fusion Power Associates **(244)**
Kummerfeld, Donald D.
Magazine Publishers of America **(321)**
Kun, Paula
Nat'l Ass'n for Sport and Physical Education **(341)**
Kundu, Jay
North American Transportation Management Institute **(445)**
Kunkle, JJ
American Trauma Soc. **(121)**
Kupec, C.J.
Council of Growing Companies **(214)**
Kupferman Ph.D., Michael
American Soc. of Civil Engineers **(108)**
Kurk, Jessica
Jewish Education Service of North America **(314)**
Kurkian, Scott
Professional Photographers of America **(466)**
Kurpiel, Judy
Internat'l Professional Groomers **(300)**
Kurtis, Dean
Nat'l Housewares Manufacturers Ass'n **(409)**
Kurtz, Betsy
Independent Insurance Agents of America **(261)**
Kurtz, Diane
Nat'l Community Education Ass'n **(388)**
Kurtz, John
Internat'l Staple, Nail and Tool Ass'n **(307)**
Kurtz, Karl
Nat'l Conference of State Legislatures **(391)**
Kurtzig, Barbara
Nat'l Ass'n of Health Data Organizations **(357)**
Kurzeja, Richard E.
Internat'l Buckskin Horse Ass'n **(284)**
Kushner CAE, CMP, David L.
Ass'n of Osteopathic Directors and Medical Educators **(159)**
American Osteopathic Academy of Addiction Medicine **(89)**
American College of Osteopathic Pediatricians **(56)**
American Osteopathic Healthcare Ass'n **(89)**
Kushner, Paul
Robert Morris Associates, the Ass'n of Lending and Credit Risk Professionals **(476)**

Kusler, Jon A.
Ass'n of State Wetland Managers (166)
Kusta, Kathleen
Internat'l Graphoanalysis Soc. (292)
World Ass'n of Document Examiners (549)
Kutska, Helen
Nat'l Petroleum Refiners Ass'n (422)
Kuttner, Susan
Soc. of Telecommunications Consultants (507)
Kuyper, Mark
CBA (188)
Kwart, Michael
Insulation Contractors Ass'n of America (270)
Kwitowski, Marlene
Council of Large Public Housing Authorities (214)
Kyles CMP, Sandra
Nat'l Hospice Organization (409)
Kysilko, David
Nat'l Ass'n of State Boards of Education (374)
L'Born, Micheal
Aeronautical Repair Station Ass'n (13)
L'Heureux Jr., Rev. N.J.
Nat'l Ass'n of Ecumenical and Interreligious Staff (353)
La Casse, Janet
College Athletic Business Management Ass'n (197)
La Porta, Carol
LOMA (321)
La Sala, James
Amalgamated Transit Union (19)
Laabs, Jonathan
Lutheran Education Ass'n (321)
Laatsch, Shawn
Internat'l Planetarium Soc. (300)
LaBalla, Gary M.
Recreation Vehicle Industry Ass'n (472)
LaBatt, Faye
American Ass'n of Cereal Chemists (34)
Labatt, Faye
American Phytopathological Soc. (92)
LaBella, Jeanne
American Public Power Ass'n (96)
LaBranche CAE, Gary A.
American Soc. of Ass'n Executives (107)
LaCava, Patricia K.
Nat'l Alcohol Beverage Control Ass'n (335)
Lacey, Caroline E.
Solid Waste Ass'n of North America (510)
LaChance, Christine
American Ass'n for Budget and Program Analysis (29)
LaChappelle, Sue
Ass'n of Directory Publishers (149)
Lackritz, Marc E.
Securities Industry Ass'n (481)
LaCorte, Jean
Nat'l Ass'n of Flour Distributors (355)
LaCour, Nat
American Federation of Teachers (67)
Lacy, Warren
Retired Officers Ass'n, The (476)
Lacy, Warren S.
American College of Clinical Pharmacy (53)
Ladas, Linda
Solar Energy Industries Ass'n (510)
LaDuca, Kendra
American Ass'n for Higher Education (31)
Lafferty, Marta K.
Soc. for Industrial and Applied Mathematics (489)
Laffey, Martharose
Nat'l Council for the Social Studies (393)
Lafleur, David
Internat'l Swaps and Derivatives Ass'n (308)
LaFortune, Gray
Ceramic Tile Institute of America (189)
LaFourest, Judith
Nat'l League of American Pen Women (414)
LaGasse, Alfred B.
Internat'l Taxicab and Livery Ass'n (308)
LaGasse CAE, Robert C.
Garden Writers Ass'n of America (245)
Internat'l Microwave Power Institute (297)
Nat'l Bark and Soil Producers Ass'n (382)
LaGasse, Robert C.
Hydroponic Merchants Ass'n (257)
Lagershausen, Jack L.
Ass'n of Professional Landscape Designers (161)
Air Diffusion Council (15)
Institute of Caster Manufacturers (266)
Lagios M.D., Michael D.
American Soc. of Breast Disease (107)
Laidlaw Jr., William K.
AACSB - the Internat'l Ass'n for Management Education (7)

Laing, Roland L.
Institute of Internal Auditors (267)
Lake, Kerry L.
Adhesive and Sealant Council (12)
Lakin, David N.
American Highway Users Alliance (73)
Laliberte, Mark
Energy Efficient Building Ass'n (230)
Lally, Sue
Coin Laundry Ass'n (196)
LaMar, Doris
Music Critics Ass'n of North America (332)
LaMar, Kathleen A.
Dental Dealers of America (221)
Dental Manufacturers of America (221)
LaMarre, Mary Anne
Photo Marketing Ass'n-Internat'l (457)
Lamb, Ellen C.
Conference of State Bank Supervisors (204)
Lamb, Shawn Douglas
Soc. of Toxicology (508)
Lamb, Steve
Nat'l Committee for Quality Assurance (388)
Lambe, Maureen
Nat'l Apartment Ass'n (337)
Lambert, David F.
Nat'l Ass'n of Chain Drug Stores (346)
Lambert, Diane
Internat'l Credit Ass'n (288)
Lambert, Kristen
Ass'n for Worksite Health Promotion (141)
Lambert, Michael P.
Distance Education and Training Council (223)
Lambert, Mike
Ass'n of Automotive Aftermarket Distributors (144)
Lambert, Theresa N.
Nat'l Ass'n of State Units on Aging (376)
Lambiase, Carole
United Electrical, Radio and Machine Workers of America (530)
Lamm, Thomas
Information Systems Audit and Control Ass'n (264)
Lammel, Linda
Risk and Insurance Management Soc. (476)
Lamoglia, Jan
American College of Health Care Administrators (54)
LaMotta, Connie F.
Direct Marketing Ass'n (223)
Lampe, Betsy
Nat'l Ass'n of Independent Publishers (359)
Lancaster, Jill
Ass'n of Collegiate Conference and Events Directors Internat'l (148)
Lanctot, Suzanne
Nat'l Environmental Training Ass'n (401)
Land, Dina Moses
American Frozen Food Institute (69)
Land, Karen
Nat'l Certification Council for Activity Professionals (386)
Landers, Jay
Recreation Vehicle Industry Ass'n (472)
Landers, Roger
Professional Ass'n of Health Care Office Managers (464)
Landers, Valerie
Illuminating Engineering Soc. of North America (259)
Landes, Julie
Council for Advancement and Support of Education (210)
Landis, Dede
American Sleep Disorders Ass'n (100)
Landis, Lisa L.
Welsh Pony and Cob Soc. of America (542)
Landis, Robert D.
Nat'l Ass'n of Industrial and Office Properties (360)
Landrum, Ney C.
Nat'l Ass'n of State Outdoor Recreation Liaison Officers (375)
Landy, Marcia
Soc. for Cinema Studies (486)
Landy, Rosalie
Internat'l Soc. for Adolescent Psychiatry (302)
Lane, Bob
Ass'n of College and University Printers (147)
Lane, Carol Ann
Lake Carriers' Ass'n (316)
American Iron Ore Ass'n (79)
Lane, Carol M.
Nat'l Ass'n of Principals of Schools for Girls (366)
Lane, Mary
American Oil Chemists' Soc. (88)
Lane, Mary Ellen
Council of American Overseas Research Centers (212)
Lane, Scott
American Internat'l Automobile Dealers Ass'n (79)

Lang, Scott
Nat'l Automated Clearing House Ass'n (381)
Lange, Douglas
Council for the Advancement of Standards in Higher Education (212)
Langendorfer, William
Disaster Recovery Institute Internat'l (223)
Langer, Betsy
Ass'n of Maternal and Child Health Programs (157)
Langer, Janine M.
Precision Metalforming Ass'n (462)
Langlais, John
Industrial Fabrics Ass'n Internat'l (262)
Langley, Steven
Nat'l Food Processors Ass'n (405)
Langley, Vivian
American Volleyball Coaches Ass'n (122)
Langstraat, Laura A.
Nat'l Crop Insurance Services (398)
Lanier, Ivan
Nat'l Black Caucus of State Legislators (383)
Lanier, Robin
Internat'l Mass Retail Ass'n (297)
Lanke, Eric
American Academy of Emergency Medicine (21)
Lansner, Petra
Aerobics and Fitness Ass'n of America (13)
Lantos, John
American Soc. of Law, Medicine and Ethics (112)
LaPierre, Steve
American Chiropractic Ass'n (51)
LaPierre Jr., Wayne R.
Nat'l Rifle Ass'n of America (426)
LaPious Ph.D., Jules B.
Council of Graduate Schools (213)
Laport, Margaret
Biscuit and Cracker Distributors Ass'n (179)
Lapp, Rabbi David
JWB Jewish Chaplains Council (315)
Lappen, Mark
Internat'l Sign Ass'n (302)
Lapsansky, Mary Ellen
Fragrance Foundation (243)
Laramie, Roland
American Soc. of Photographers (114)
Larcom, M. Kay
U.S.-Russia Business Council (528)
Large, Anne
Ass'n of Professors of Gynecology and Obstetrics (161)
Largent, Christina
American Academy of Physician Assistants in Occupational Medicine (25)
Larger, Christine
Nat'l Ass'n of College and University Business Officers (348)
Larimer, Gail Pierce
Antique and Amusement Photographers Internat'l (125)
Larimer, Jane
Nat'l Automated Clearing House Ass'n (381)
Larkin, J. Stephen
Aluminum Ass'n (19)
Larkin, John
American Soc. for Public Administration (105)
Larkin, Larry
Nat'l Federation of Independent Business (403)
Larking-Coste, Denise
CIES, The Food Business Forum (193)
Larmett, Kathleen M.
Nat'l Council of University Research Administrators (397)
Larocca, Eve C.
American Heartworm Soc. (73)
LaRoche, John A.
Infrared Data Ass'n (264)
Larrick, Kurt
Tax Executives Institute (520)
Larsen CAE, C. Andrew
Wiring Harness Manufacturers Ass'n (545)
System Independent Data Format Ass'n (519)
Lightning Protection Institute (319)
Larsen, Christopher D.
American Resort Development Ass'n (98)
Larsen, Dana B.
Internat'l Studies Ass'n (307)
Larsen, David
American College of Chest Physicians (53)
Larson, Charles F.
Industrial Research Institute (263)
Larson, Everett
Soc. of Federal Linguists (501)
Larson, Gary
Scaffold Industry Ass'n (479)
Larson, Gary W.
North American Soc. of Scaffold Professionals (445)

Larson, John L.
Soc. for Historians of the Early American Republic **(489)**

Larson Sr., Larry
Organization of Flying Adjusters **(450)**

Larson, Larry A.
Ass'n of State Floodplain Managers **(166)**

Larson II, Loren R.
Ass'n of Consulting Foresters of America **(148)**

Larson, Marcia R.
Interstate Conference of Employment Security Agencies **(311)**

Larson, Robert
Independent Ass'n of Questioned Document Examiners **(259)**

Larson, Susan
Industrial Fabrics Ass'n Internat'l **(262)**

Lary, Dinah
Ass'n of Celebrity Personal Assistants **(146)**

Lascoutx, Elizabeth
Council of Better Business Bureaus **(212)**

Lasday, Lori Serbin
Nat'l Ass'n of Temple Educators **(378)**

Lash, Fred
Nat'l Defense Industrial Ass'n **(399)**

Laskey, Linda
American Water Works Ass'n **(122)**

Lasser, Dr. Alan
Noah Worcester Dermatological Soc. **(439)**

Lathrop, Lori
American Soc. of Indexers **(111)**

Latin, Gary A.
American Bureau of Shipping and Affiliated Companies **(49)**

Latin-Kasper, Steve
Nat'l Fluid Power Ass'n **(405)**

Latta, Carol J.
Decision Sciences Institute **(220)**

Latta, Karen
American Quarter Horse Ass'n **(96)**

Lattimer, Dick
Archery Manufacturers and Merchants Organization **(126)**

Lau, Regina
Asian American Manufacturers Ass'n **(128)**

Lauber M.D., Jeffrey
American Soc. of Dermatological Retailers **(109)**

Lauck, Larry
American Lighting Ass'n **(81)**

Lauer, Linda
Sports Card Ass'n **(515)**
Childrenswear Marketing Ass'n **(192)**

Lauer, Peter
American Medical Ass'n **(83)**

Laufer, Lucille J.
Oriental Rug Importers Ass'n of America **(450)**

Laughlin, Donald D.
Internat'l Ass'n of Plumbing and Mechanical Officials **(282)**

Laughlin, Janice
Employee Assistance Professionals Ass'n **(229)**

Laughlin, Matt
Supima Ass'n of America **(518)**

Laughton, David W.
Nat'l Conference of Brewery and Soft Drink Workers - United States and Canada **(389)**

Laun, Skip
Miniature Golf Ass'n of America/Miniature Golf Development of America **(329)**

Launchbaugh, Cynthia
Ass'n of Records Managers and Administrators **(163)**

Laurence, David
Ass'n of Departments of English **(149)**

Laurence, Joan
Toy Manufacturers of America **(524)**

Laurenson, Mark T.
Building Owners and Managers Institute Internat'l **(183)**

Lauria, Greta
Ass'n of Statisticians of American Religious Bodies **(166)**

Laurie, Joyce A.
Automotive Oil Change Ass'n **(175)**

Laury, Sheri
Tag and Label Manufacturers Institute **(520)**

Laushman, Judy M.
Ass'n of Specialty Cut Flower Growers **(165)**

Lauth, Rosemary S.
American Ass'n of State Colleges and Universities **(43)**

Laux, David N.
U.S.-ROC (Taiwan) Business Council **(528)**

LaValley CAE, Alison L.
Nat'l Roofing Contractors Ass'n **(426)**

Lavarello, Curtis
Nat'l Ass'n of School Resource Officers **(371)**

Lavella, Andrew
Minerals, Metals and Materials Soc., The **(329)**

Lavelle, Edward
Social Science Research Council **(509)**

LaVelle, Jillian R.
Internat'l Ass'n of Counselors and Therapists **(278)**

Laven, Frances J.
Academy of Rehabilitative Audiology **(10)**

Lavery, Michael J.
Audit Bureau of Circulations **(173)**

Lavin, J. Kevin
Nat'l Weather Ass'n **(436)**

Lavine, Eileen M.
Intersociety Committee on Pathology Information **(311)**

Lavvis, Jeffrey
American Craft Council **(62)**

Lavway, David R.
Nat'l Potato Council **(423)**

Lawler CMP, Nancy
Soc. of American Florists **(497)**

Lawless, Sherri
Nat'l Ass'n of Certified Valuation Analysts **(346)**

Lawlor, Anita Horne
Internat'l Health, Racquet and Sportsclub Ass'n **(293)**

Lawner, Kathleen H.
American Law Institute **(81)**

Lawrence, Brian D.
American Soc. of Wedding Professionals **(117)**

Lawrence, Irene
Nat'l Soc. for Graphology **(428)**

Lawrence, Jim
Brake Manufacturers Council **(181)**
Tune-up Manufacturers Council **(527)**
Heavy Duty Brake Manufacturers Council **(253)**

Lawrence CMP, Joanne T.
Nat'l Ass'n of Life Underwriters **(361)**

Lawrence, Karen E.
Technical Ass'n of the Graphic Arts **(520)**

Lawrence, Marilyn E.
Internat'l Municipal Signal Ass'n **(298)**

Lawrence, Paul E.
Nat'l Criminal Justice Ass'n **(398)**

Lawrence, Timothy W.
Vocational Industrial Clubs of America **(540)**

Lawrey, James D.
American Bryological and Lichenological Soc. **(49)**

Laws, Toni F.
Newspaper Ass'n of America **(439)**

Lawser CAE, Steven V.
Wood Component Manufacturers Ass'n **(548)**

Lawson Sr., Dennis
Ass'n of Academic Physiatrists **(141)**

Lawson, Eugene K.
U.S.-Russia Business Council **(528)**

Lawson, Justin
Gospel Music Ass'n **(248)**

Lawson, Lynn
Ass'n of Academic Physiatrists **(141)**
Nat'l Council of Coal Lessors **(394)**

Lawson, Dr. Michael S.
Professional Ass'n of Christian Educators **(464)**

Lawson, Quentin
Nat'l Alliance of Black School Educators **(336)**

Lawson, Richard C.
American Insurance Ass'n **(79)**

Lawson USAF (RET.), Gen. Richard L.
Nat'l Mining Ass'n **(417)**

Lawson, Rodger S.
Alliance of American Insurers **(18)**
American Insurers Highway Safety Alliance **(79)**

Lawton, Henry
Internat'l Psychohistorical Ass'n **(300)**

Laxton, Christopher E.
Ass'n for Professionals in Infection Control and Epidemiology **(136)**

Laycock, Gilbert N.
Friction Materials Standards Institute **(244)**

Layton, Mary J.
Child Welfare League of America **(192)**

Layton, Sarah
American Public Works Ass'n **(96)**

Layton, Stephen P.
Nat'l Stripper Well Ass'n **(432)**

Lazaro, Vincent
Hispanic Ass'n of Colleges and Universities **(254)**

Lazarus, Jennie C.
Pine Chemicals Ass'n **(458)**

Lazer, Linda
Section for Women in Public Administration **(481)**

Lazier CMP, Carol L.
American Soc. of Plastic and Reconstructive Surgeons **(114)**

Lazzari, Cindy
American Ass'n for Therapeutic Humor **(32)**

Lazzari CAE, Margaret L.
Air and Waste Management Ass'n **(15)**

Le Gates, Charlotte
Natural Gas Supply Ass'n **(437)**

Lea, Daniel
Cellulose Insulation Manufacturers Ass'n **(189)**
Nat'l Independent Flag Dealers Ass'n **(410)**

Leab, Daniel
Historians of American Communism **(254)**

Leach, Debra A.
Nat'l Licensed Beverage Ass'n **(415)**

Leach, Jerry W.
World Affairs Councils of America **(549)**

Leahy, Betteanne
Hearth Products Ass'n **(253)**

Leahy, P. Patrick
Internat'l Ass'n of Hydrogeologists **(280)**

Leahy, Robert D.
Nat'l Ass'n of Securities Dealers **(372)**

Leary, Lou Ann
American Nephrology Nurses Ass'n **(86)**

Leasure, Mark
Infectious Diseases Soc. of America **(263)**

Leasure Jr., William A.
Truck Manufacturers Ass'n **(527)**

Leatherman, Sandra E.
APMI Internat'l **(125)**

Leatzow, Jim
Design Professionals Ass'n **(222)**

Leavens, Donald
Nat'l Electrical Manufacturers Ass'n **(400)**

Leaver, Judy
Nat'l Mental Health Ass'n **(416)**

Lebby, Kathryn
Ass'n for Play Therapy **(136)**

Lebeau, Alysa
Polyisocyanurate Insulation Manufacturers Ass'n **(460)**

LeBoeuf, Kerley
Nat'l Ass'n of Convenience Stores **(349)**

Lebovic CAE, Mitchell E.
Shoe Service Institute of America **(483)**

Lebowski, Bob R.
Nat'l Community Pharmacists Ass'n **(388)**

Lechner, Wendy
Printing Industries of America **(463)**

LeClerg, Robert E.
Nat'l Safety Management Soc. **(426)**

Ledenican, Cathy
Precision Metalforming Ass'n **(462)**

Lederer CAE, Gerard Lavery
Building Owners and Managers Ass'n Internat'l **(183)**

Lederer Jr., Robert F
Nat'l Pest Control Ass'n **(422)**

Lederman, Dr. David A.
American Ass'n of Stomatologists **(43)**

Lederman, Stephanie
American Federation for Aging Research **(66)**

Ledley, Dr. Robert S.
Computerized Medical Imaging Soc. **(203)**
Pattern Recognition Soc. **(454)**

Ledoux, Amy
Electronic Retailing Ass'n **(228)**

LeDuff, Charsie
Nat'l Black American Paralegal Ass'n **(383)**

Lee, April C.T.
Ass'n for Maximum Service Television **(136)**

Lee D.Ch.E., Bernard S.
Institute of Gas Technology **(267)**

Lee, Charles
Council for Advancement and Support of Education **(210)**

Lee, David C.
Nat'l Truck Equipment Ass'n **(434)**

Lee, Debbie
Internat'l Disk Drive Equipment and Materials Ass'n **(289)**

Lee, Eileen
Nat'l Multi Housing Council **(417)**

Lee, Dr. Grayce
American Guild of Hypnotherapists **(71)**

Lee, Ilka
American Soc. for Precision Engineering **(104)**

Lee, Judith
Nat'l Ass'n of Insurance Commissioners **(360)**

Lee, Dr. Richard E.
Soc. for Cryobiology **(487)**

Lee, Richard W.
Internat'l Soc. of Weekly Newspaper Editors **(307)**

Lee, Rosealee M.
Soc. for Biomaterials **(485)**

Lee, Sander
Conference of Philosophical Societies **(204)**

Lee, Sharon
Science Fiction and Fantasy Writers of America **(479)**

Lee, T.S.
Instrument Soc. of America (269)

Lee III, Dr. William F.
Internat'l Ass'n of Jazz Educators (280)

Leeds, Robert X.
American Pet Boarding Ass'n (91)

Leeds, Statia
World Waterpark Ass'n (550)

Leedy, Lynda M.
American Academy of Physical Medicine and
Rehabilitation (25)

Leete, Dr. Jeanette H.
Ass'n for Women Geoscientists (140)

Lefcourt APR, Hal
Nat'l Constables Ass'n (392)

Lefebvre, Stephen M.
Nat'l Art Materials Trade Ass'n (337)

Lefever CAE, David P.
Nat'l Ass'n of Fleet Administrators (355)

Leffel, William
American Ass'n of Cooperative/Mutual Insurance Socs. (35)

Leffler, Albert L.
Material Handling Industry Ass'n (325)

Leftwich, Bruce
Career College Ass'n (186)

Leftwich, Gail
Federation of State Humanities Councils (237)

Leftwood, Annie
Nat'l Ass'n of Wheat Growers (380)

Legacy, Leora
American Ass'n of Clinical Endocrinologists (34)

Legard, Ted
ADSC: The Internat'l Ass'n of Foundation Drilling (12)

Legaspi, Angie
American Concrete Institute (59)

Legg, Julie
Ass'n of Sales and Marketing Companies (164)

Legler, John A.
Waste Equipment Technology Ass'n (541)

Legon, Richard D.
Ass'n of Governing Boards of Universities and Colleges (152)

LeGrand, Charles H.
Institute of Internal Auditors (267)

Lehfeldt, William W.
Diplomatic and Consular Officers, Retired (223)

Lehman, Sherri K.
Corn Refiners Ass'n (209)

Lehmann, Ronald
Emergency Nurses Ass'n (229)

Lehner, Darcy
Ass'n of College and University Housing Officers-
Internat'l (147)

Lehnerd, Lori P.
Nat'l Ass'n of State Aviation Officials (374)

LeHouillier, Brian
American Soc. for Quality (105)

Lehr, Scott
Internat'l Franchise Ass'n (292)

Lehrer, Stanley
Soc. for the Advancement of Education (494)

Lehrman, Margie
Ass'n of Trial Lawyers of America (168)

Leibow, Sherman D.
North American Wholesale Lumber Ass'n (446)

Leibundgut, Peter
Ass'n of Commercial Finance Attorneys (148)

Leiby, Vanessa M.
Ass'n of State Drinking Water Administrators (166)

Leidlein, Bob
Photo Marketing Ass'n-Internat'l (457)

Leidy, Dr. Lynette E.
Human Biology Ass'n (257)

Leight, Elizabeth Y.
Soc. of Professional Benefit Administrators (505)

Leighton, Carolyn
Women in Technology Internat'l (547)

Leighton, Maureen
Child Welfare League of America (192)

Leighty, Carol
Nat'l Council of Administrative Women in Education (394)

Leiken, Samuel
Council for Adult and Experiential Learning (210)

Leiser, Serena E.
American Ass'n of Orthodontists (40)

Leisher, Maryann
Women in Government Relations (546)

Leishman, Marguerite
Nat'l Ass'n of Elementary School Principals (353)

Leitsch, Pat
Ass'n of Health Occupations Teacher Educators (153)

Leland, W. Ted
Air-Conditioning and Refrigeration Institute (16)

Lema, Joseph E.
Nat'l Mining Ass'n (417)

Lemaire, Pam
Internat'l Public Relations Ass'n - United States Chapter (300)

LeMaster, Lynn H.
Edison Electric Institute (226)

Lemieux, Russell A.
Ass'n of Fund Raisers and Direct Sellers (152)
Nat'l Pecan Shellers Ass'n (421)

Lemily, Capt. John T.
Council of American Master Mariners (212)

Lemire, Carol
American College of Toxicology (58)

Lemke, George W.
Casket and Funeral Supply Ass'n of America (187)

Lemke, Randal
Internat'l Communications Industries Ass'n (286)

Lemoine, Ronnie
Nat'l Council for Prescription Drug Programs (393)

Lemon, Benjie
North American Limousin Foundation (443)

Lemon, George L.
American Heren Ass'n (73)

Lemon, Sharon
Hotel Motel Brokers of America (256)

Lempert, Robin
American Wholesale Marketers Ass'n (123)

Lempesis, Bill
Video Electronics Standards Ass'n (539)

Lence-Talley, Elena
Internat'l Clarinet Ass'n (285)

Leneway, Dr. Robert
Ass'n of Rehabilitation Programs in Computer
Technology (163)

Lenke, Greg
Nat'l Truck and Heavy Equipment Claims Council (434)

Lennan, Anne c.
Soc. of Professional Benefit Administrators (505)

Lennes Jr., John
Alliance of American Insurers (18)

Lennon, James Michael
American Natural Hygiene Soc. (86)

Lentz, Carolyn
Electronics Technicians Ass'n Internat'l (229)

Lenz, Edward A.
Nat'l Ass'n of Temporary and Staffing Services (378)

Lenz, Gretchen
Electronic Industries Ass'n (228)

Leon, Pete
American Ass'n of Engineering Societies (36)

Leonard, Calva A.
Soc. for Imaging Science and Technology (489)

Leonard, Jeff
Petroleum Technology Transfer Council (456)

Leonard, John
American Swimming Coaches Ass'n (119)

Leonard, Nancy H.
Fraternity Executives Ass'n (244)

Leondedis, Angie
American Soc. of Women Accountants (117)

Leong CMP, Lawrence
North American Skull Base Soc. (444)

Leopold, Bea
Nat'l Soc. of Genetic Counselors (430)

Leous, Suzanne
American College of Preventive Medicine (57)

Lepisto CTC, Robert W.
Institute of Certified Travel Agents (266)

Leppellere, Terrence A.
Building Officials and Code Administrators Internat'l (183)

Lepper, Bernard J.
Career Apparel Institute (186)
Nat'l Ass'n of Uniform Manufacturers and Distributors (379)

Lereah, David
Mortgage Bankers Ass'n of America (330)

Lerner Ph.D., Jeffrey
ECRI (226)

Lerner, Ruby
Ass'n of Independent Video and Filmmakers (154)

LeRoux, Jacques
CIES, The Food Business Forum (193)

Leshan, Tim
American Soc. for Cell Biology (101)

Lesser PhD, CAE, Philip
Microscopy Soc. of America (328)

Lessing, Katherine B.
Ass'n of Earth Science Editors (150)

Lessner, Gary
Transworld Advertising Agency Network (526)

Lesso, Maryann
Telecommunications Industry Ass'n (521)

Lesso, Maryann C.
Telecommunications Industry Ass'n (521)

Letarte, Marie
Nat'l Ass'n of Printers and Lithographers (366)

Letchworth, Joan
Hearth Products Ass'n (253)

Leto, Louis
Teachers of English to Speakers of Other Languages (520)

Letsinger, Martha H.
Internat'l Brotherhood of Electrical Workers (284)

Letteney, David B.
Trans-Atlantic American Flag Liner Operations (525)

Lettieri, Trish
American Physical Soc. (92)

LeVan, William H.
Cast Iron Soil Pipe Institute (187)

Levell, Heather
Special Interest Group for Biomedical Computing (511)
Special Interest Group for Computer Science Education (511)
Special Interest Group for Computer Uses in Education (511)
Special Interest Group for Computers and Society (511)
Special Interest Group for Management of Data (512)
Special Interest Group for Measurement and Evaluation (512)
Special Interest Group on Operating Systems (513)
Special Interest Group on Security, Audit, and Control (513)
Special Interest Group on Ada Programming Language (512)
Special Interest Group on Applied Computing (512)

Lever, Alvin
American College of Chest Physicians (53)

Levin, Barbara
Forum for Investor Advice (243)

Levin, Daniel J.
Ass'n of Governing Boards of Universities and Colleges (152)

Levin, Jodi S.
Internat'l Licensing Industry Merchandisers' Ass'n (296)

Levin, Mark
Chain Link Fence Manufacturers Institute (190)

Levin, Mike
Exhibit Designers and Producers Ass'n (234)

Levine, Andrea
Council of Better Business Bureaus (212)

Levine, Bruce
Independent Lubricant Manufacturers Ass'n (261)

Levine, Felice J.
American Sociological Ass'n (117)

Levine, Mimi
Residential Sales Council (475)

Levine, Phyllis
Project Management Institute (468)

Levine, Rachel
American Philological Ass'n (91)

Levine, Robert J.
Independent Business Alliance (260)

Levinson MD, Richard
American Public Health Ass'n (95)

Levitt, Rachelle
Urban Land Institute (537)

Levrio PhD, Jay
American Podiatric Medical Ass'n (93)

Levy, David
Institute of Industrial Engineers (267)

Levy, Lisa
American Teleservices Ass'n (119)

Levy, Michael
Polystyrene Packaging Council (460)

Levy, Richard A.
Nat'l Pharmaceutical Council (422)

Lew, Margaret A.
Footwear Distributors and Retailers of America (242)

Lewicki CAE, Jane C.
Information Technology Industry Council (264)

Lewin, Brian
Internat'l Recording Media Ass'n (301)

Lewinsky, John
American Foundrymen's Soc. (69)

Lewis, Betty Jean
Nat'l Ass'n of Water Companies (380)

Lewis, Bob
Soc. of Exploration Geophysicists (501)

Lewis Ph.D.,CPCU, Christine L.
American Institute for CPCU - Insurance Institute of
America (75)

Lewis, David
Financial Executives Institute (238)

Lewis C.A.E., David
American Board of Nursing Specialties (48)

Lewis CM, Dean
Refrigeration Service Engineers Soc. (473)

Lewis CAE, Dina
American Chamber of Commerce Executives (51)

Lewis, Don
American Ass'n of Advertising Agencies (32)

Lewis, Faith
Footwear Distributors and Retailers of America (242)

Lewis, Flint H.
American Chemical Soc. (51)

Lewis, Floyd
Nat'l Ass'n of Social Workers (373)

Lewis, Frederick L.
Nat'l Training Systems Ass'n (434)

Lewis, Howard
Nat'l Ass'n of Manufacturers (362)

Lewis, Janet
Nat'l FFA Organization (404)

Lewis, Jennifer A.
Internat'l Furnishings and Design Ass'n (292)

Lewis, John
Billiard Congress of America (178)

Lewis, Linda
American Ass'n of Motor Vehicle Administrators (39)

Lewis, Lucinda
Internat'l Conference of Symphony and Opera
Musicians (287)

Lewis, Mark
Computer and Communications Industry Ass'n (202)

Lewis, Melissa
Nat'l Council for Agricultural Education (393)

Lewis, Michael J.
American Institute of Aeronautics and Astronautics (76)

Lewis, Pete
Institute of Electrical and Electronics Engineers (266)

Lewis CAE, Richard
American Pulpwood Ass'n (96)

Lewis, Rita
Internat'l Downtown Ass'n (289)

Lewis, Robert
Chief Warrant and Warrant Officers Ass'n, United States
Coast Guard (192)

Lewis, Robert J.
Nat'l Ass'n of Water Companies (380)

Lewis, Ronald D.
Sheet Metal and Air Conditioning Contractors' Nat'l
Ass'n (482)

Lewis, Rudolph
Nat'l Ass'n of Home Based Businesses (358)

Lewis, Sharon
Council of the Great City Schools (216)

Lewis, Stephen
American Water Works Ass'n (122)

Lewis, Sylvia
American Planning Ass'n (92)

Lewis, Zev
American Ass'n for Geriatric Psychiatry (30)

Ley, Kathleen
Nat'l Ass'n of Academic Advisors for Athletes (342)

Li, Christina
Ass'n of Managed Healthcare Organizations (156)

Li, Peter
Nat'l Catholic Educational Exhibitors (385)

Liable, Myron
Outdoor Advertising Ass'n of America (451)

Liakos, James C.
American Physiological Soc. (92)

Libby, Dave
Industrial Union of Marine and Shipbuilding Workers of
America (263)

Liberatore, Roz
Nat'l Constables Ass'n (392)

Licata, Lisa
Nat'l Alliance for Youth Sports (336)

Licata, Michael J
Internat'l Foodservice Manufacturers Ass'n (291)

Lichtenberg, Fran Walker
Soc. of the Plastics Industry - Polyurethane Division (507)

Lichtenberger, Mark
North American Hyperthermia Soc. (442)

Lichtenstein, Jules
Soc. of Government Economists (502)

Lichtenstein, Michael
Ass'n for Computing Machinery (131)

Lickliter, Robert
Internat'l Soc. for Developmental Psychobiology (303)

Liddicoat, Lorie
Internat'l Arabian Horse Ass'n (273)

Liddle, Jeff
Wilderness Education Ass'n (544)

Lieberman, Janet
Nat'l Council for the Social Studies (393)

Liebman, Dan
Nat'l Turf Writers Ass'n (435)

Liebman, Nina
Nat'l Ass'n of Export Companies (354)

Liebscher, Sheryl
Internat'l Soc. for Magnetic Resonance in Medicine (303)

Liederman, David S.
Child Welfare League of America (192)

Lief, Brett E.
Nat'l Council of Higher Education Loan Programs (395)

Lief, Dr. Thomas
Nat'l Ass'n of Substance Abuse Trainers and Educators (377)

Liesemer, Ronald N.
American Plastics Council (92)

Ligda, Stephen
American Ass'n of Law Libraries (38)

Liggett, Martha L.
American Soc. of Hematology (110)

Lightfield, Amy
Ass'n for Healthcare Philanthropy (134)

Liimatta, Michael
Internat'l Union of Gospel Missions (310)

Liller, Kathleen
Casualty Actuarial Soc. (187)

Lilly, Patricia A.
Ass'n for High Technology Distribution (134)
Aviation Distributors and Manufacturers Ass'n Internat'l (175)
Security Hardware Distributors Ass'n (481)

Lilygren, Sara
American Meat Institute (83)

Lim, Marc
Golf Course Superintendents Ass'n of America (248)

Linander, Sherry
American Clinical and Climatological Ass'n (52)

Lincoln, Catherine R.
American Academy of Otolaryngology-Head and Neck
Surgery (24)

Lincoln, Sharon
Non-Powder Gun Products Ass'n (439)

Lindberg, Karl
Southern Forest Products Ass'n (510)

Linde, Rob
Nat'l Ski Areas Ass'n (428)

Lindeman CMP, Kent A.
Oxygen Soc., The (452)

Linden, Bob
American Ass'n of Advertising Agencies (32)

Lindenberg, Robin
Brown Swiss Cattle Breeders Ass'n of the U.S.A. (183)

Linder, Carol Ann
Edison Electric Institute (226)

Linder, Ronald G.
American Ass'n of Colleges of Pharmacy (35)

Lindley, Scott
Nat'l Ass'n for College Admission Counseling (338)

Lindmark, Christine
Ass'n of Operating Room Nurses (159)

Lindner, Eileen W.
Nat'l Council of the Churches of Christ in the U.S.A. (397)

Lindner, Kathy
Direct Selling Ass'n (223)

Lindner CAE, Randy L.
Nat'l Ass'n of Boards of Examiners of Long Term Care
Administrators (345)

Lindsay, Lisa
Nat'l Ass'n of Emergency Medical Technicians (353)

Lindsay, M. Drennan
American Public Communications Council (95)

Lindsey, Crawford
United States Racquet Stringing Ass'n (535)

Lindsey, Elaine
Hotel Motel Brokers of America (256)

Lindsey, Elise
Nat'l Ass'n of Dental Laboratories (352)

Lindsey CMP, Elise J.
Associated Landscape Contractors of America (171)

Lindsey, Vernetta
Nat'l Ass'n of Workforce Development Professionals (381)

Line, Carol
American Ass'n of Botanical Gardens and Arboreta (33)

Lingle, Ted
Specialty Coffee Ass'n of America (514)

Linial C.A.E., George T.
Clinical Laboratory Management Ass'n (194)

Linkin, Larry R.
Internat'l Music Products Ass'n (298)

Linkous, Jonathan
American Telemedicine Ass'n (119)

Linkous, Rick
American Soc. of Radiologic Technologists (115)

Linn, Mary
Nat'l Ass'n of Rehabilitation Secretaries (370)

Linn, Rebecca B.
Steel Recycling Institute (516)

Linney Jr., Thomas J.
Council of Graduate Schools (213)

Linton, Steven J.
Internat'l Ass'n of Dive Rescue Specialists (278)

Liodice, Robert D.
Ass'n of Nat'l Advertisers (158)

Lioeanjai, Rene
Nat'l Marine Engineers Beneficial Ass'n (416)

Lipetzky, Thomas
American Soc. of Farm Managers and Rural Appraisers (109)

Lipetzky, Thomas E.
American Soc. of Agricultural Consultants (106)

Lipsen, Linda
Ass'n of Trial Lawyers of America (168)

Lipsey, Jerry
American Simmental Ass'n (100)

Lipton, Karen Shoos
American Ass'n of Blood Banks (33)

Lis, Craig
Promotion Marketing Ass'n (468)

Lisa Panjada, Dede
Nat'l Cancer Registrar's Ass'n (385)

Lisack Jr., CAE, John
American Congress on Surveying and Mapping (60)
American Soc. of Plant Physiologists (114)

Lisk, Edward
Nat'l Band Ass'n (382)

Liskar, Jeff
Appraisal Institute (126)

Liskey, John F.
Outdoor Power Equipment Institute (451)

Liss, Walter E.
Institute of Internal Auditors (267)

List, Barry
Institute for Operations Research and the Management
Sciences (265)

Lister, Ruth
American Camping Ass'n (50)

Litch, Scott
Nat'l Alliance for Oral Health (336)

Litke, Scot
ADSC: The Internat'l Ass'n of Foundation Drilling (12)

Litman, Gary
American Business Alliance for the Transition Economies of
Eurasia (49)

Litsinger, Beverly A.
Accountants for the Public Interest (10)

Little, Dr. Bruce
American Veterinary Medical Ass'n (121)

Little, C.L.
United Transportation Union (536)

Little, Cherie
Thoroughbred Club of America (522)

Little, Diana F.
Professional Services Council (467)

Little, Dianne
Institute of Certified Professional Managers (266)

Little, Elsa M.
Council for Basic Education (211)

Little, Jeanne
Soc. of American Florists (497)

Little, Nancy
Nat'l Academy Museum and School Fine Arts (333)

Little, Ruthann
Juvenile Products Manufacturers Ass'n (315)

Little, Thomas
Nat'l Council of Farmer Cooperatives (394)

Little, Traci
American Congress on Surveying and Mapping (60)

Littlefield, Cyndy
Ass'n of Jesuit Colleges and Universities (155)

Littlefield, Roy
Service Station Dealers of America and Allied Trades (482)

Littleton, Jeff
NACE Internat'l (333)

Littleway, Lorna
Black Theatre Network (180)

Littrell, Preston
Soc. of Government Service Urologists (502)

Liu, Donald
American Bureau of Shipping and Affiliated Companies (49)

Lively Jr., H. Randolph
American Financial Services Ass'n (68)

Livesay, Bob
Nat'l Tour Ass'n (434)

Livingston, David William
American Heart Ass'n (72)

Liwazer, Liz
Soc. for Healthcare Strategy and Market Development (488)

Llewelyn, Cerise
Expanded Shale, Clay and Slate Institute (234)

Lloyd, Anna K.
Committee of 200 (200)

Malcolm, Beverly A.
Steel Service Center Institute (517)

Maldonado, Dr. Carlos S.
Nat'l Ass'n for Chicana and Chicano Studies (338)

Maldonado, Kristyanne
American Physical Therapy Ass'n (92)

Male CAE, Jane
Nat'l Soc. of Insurance Premium Auditors (430)
Investment Recovery Ass'n (312)

Males, Eric
Nat'l Lime Ass'n (415)

Malhame, David R.
Nat'l Church Goods Ass'n (387)

Maline, Karen F.
Justice Research and Statistics Ass'n (315)

Maling Jr., G.C.
Institute of Noise Control Engineering (268)

Mallardi, Vincent
Printing Brokerage Buyers Ass'n (463)

Mallernee II, Rollin E.
Nat'l Basketball Trainers' Ass'n (382)
Professional Baseball Athletic Trainers' Ass'n (465)
Professional Football Athletic Trainers Soc. (465)

Mallia, Robert A.
Internat'l Council of Shopping Centers (288)

Mallick M.D., Khursheed
Islamic Medical Ass'n (313)

Mallin, Thomas W.
Property Loss Research Bureau (468)

Mallis, Fern
Council of Fashion Designers of America (213)

Mallo, Janice
Spring Manufacturers Institute (515)

Mallon, Francis J.
American Physical Therapy Ass'n (92)

Mallonee, Lynne
American Mobile Telecommunications Ass'n (85)

Mallory CAE, James L.
Non-Ferrous Founders' Soc. (439)

Mallory-Smith, Dr. Carol
Internat'l Weed Science Soc. (311)

Malloy, Cheryl Patton
Mortgage Bankers Ass'n of America (330)

Malloy, Cyril I.
American Concrete Pipe Ass'n (59)

Malmgren, Kurt
Pharmaceutical Research and Manufacturers of America (456)

Malmgren, Stacey B.
Special Libraries Ass'n (514)

Malone, Deena
Ass'n of Theological Schools in the United States and Canada (168)

Malone, Karen
Edison Welding Institute (226)

Malone, Lavergne
United Ass'n of Equipment Leasing (530)

Malone, Robert J.
History of Science Soc. (254)

Malone, William A.
Internat'l Guards Union of America (293)

Maloney, Lawrence G.
Ass'n of Iron and Steel Engineers (155)

Maloney, Lisa B.
American Bakers Ass'n (46)

Maloney, Sally A.
Equipment Leasing Ass'n of America (232)

Maloney, Shirley A.
Nat'l Ass'n of Industrial and Office Properties (360)

Maloney, Vicki
Nat'l Soc. of Newspaper Columnists (430)

Maloney C.A.E., William T.
American Soc. for Gastrointestinal Endoscopy (102)

Maloney CAE, William T.
Internat'l Soc. for Cardiovascular Surgery - North American Chapter (303)
American Surgical Ass'n (119)
Soc. for Vascular Surgery (496)

Malott, Maria E.
Soc. for the Advancement of Behavior Analysis (494)
Ass'n for Behavior Analysis (130)

Maltby, William S.
Soc. for Reformation Research (493)

Maluso, Diane
Ass'n for Women in Psychology (140)

Malveaux, Antoinette
Nat'l Black MBA Ass'n (383)

Mamel, Perla C.
American Financial Services Ass'n (68)

Mamone, John
American Ass'n of Motor Vehicle Administrators (39)

Man D.V.M., Dr. Curt J.
Ass'n of American Veterinary Medical Colleges (143)

Manak, Pat
Nat'l Ass'n of Collegiate Directors of Athletics (348)
Nat'l Ass'n of Athletic Development Directors (343)

Manasse, Dr. Henri R.
American Soc. of Health-System Pharmacists (110)

Mance, Katherine
Nat'l Retail Federation (425)

Mancini Jr., Frank W.
Internat'l Security Officers, Police and Guards Union (302)

Mancini, John F.
Ass'n for Information and Image Management International (135)

Mancino Ed.D., RN, Diane J.
Nat'l Student Nurses Ass'n (432)

Mancuso, Dawn
Ass'n of Air Medical Services (141)

Mancuso CAE, Dawn
Nat'l EMS Pilots Ass'n (401)

Mandelbaum, Mark
Ass'n for Computing Machinery (131)

Mandesich, Stephanie
Internat'l Documentary Ass'n (289)

Mandlawitz, Myrna
Nat'l Ass'n of State Directors of Special Education (375)

Manes, Stone
Nat'l Clay Pot Manufacturers Ass'n (387)

Maness, Diana
Retailer's Bakery Ass'n (476)

Mangan, Lynne
American Soc. for Healthcare Risk Management (103)

Mangan, Maureen P.
Soc. of Incentive and Travel Executives (502)

Mangan, Mona
Writers Guild of America, East (551)

Manger-Hague, Kay
American Dietetic Ass'n (64)

Mangiameli, John
Disaster Recovery Institute Internat'l (223)

Mangione, Peter T.
Footwear Distributors and Retailers of America (242)

Maniscalco, Msgr. Francis W.
Nat'l Conference of Catholic Bishops/U.S. Catholic Conference (390)

Mankin, Marian
Ass'n for Health Services Research (134)

Manley CFE,DHFSA, Edward H.
Internat'l Food Service Executives' Ass'n (291)

Mann, Mark
Jewelers of America (314)

Mann, Robert
Dance Masters of America (220)

Mann Ph.D., Sheilah
American Political Science Ass'n (93)

Mann CAE, Wendy
APICS - The Educational Society for Resource Management (125)

Mannarelli, Agnes
European-American Business Council (233)

Mannen, Ted R.
Health Industry Manufacturers Ass'n (252)

Mannillo, Paula
Ass'n for Enterprise Opportunity (133)

Manning, Gail B.
Nat'l Conference of Lieutenant Governors (390)

Manning, Mary Jo
Television Operators Caucus (521)

Manning, Marybeth
SPIE-Internat'l Soc. for Optical Engineering (514)

Manoly Ph.D., Brena
American Occupational Therapy Ass'n (88)

Manoogian, Antran
Internat'l Animated Film Soc. (273)

Manser, Virginia A.
Cooling Tower Institute (208)

Mansfield, Rebecca A.
American Osteopathic College of Dermatology (89)

Manspeaker, Barbara
American Ass'n of Zoo Keepers (45)

Mansur, Bernadette
Nat'l Hockey League (409)

Manteria, Bill
Nat'l Retail Federation (425)

Mantler, Francis
Nat'l Council of State Garden Clubs (396)

Manuel, Cleo
Nat'l Consumers League (392)

Maple, Howard
American Institute of Organbuilders (78)

Maples, Robert
Smokeless Tobacco Council (484)

Mara, Sherri
American Academy of Appellate Lawyers (20)

Mara, Sherri A.
American Soc. of Nephrology (113)

Maraney, John V. "Skip"
Nat'l Star Route Mail Contractors Ass'n (431)

Marano, Rocco
Nat'l Ass'n of Student Activity Advisors (377)

Marans, Jerrold
Sheet Metal and Air Conditioning Contractors' Nat'l Ass'n (482)

Marcello Jr., C.J.
Paso Fino Horse Ass'n (453)

Marchesano, Michael
BPA Internat'l (181)

Marchese, Anthony J.
Internat'l Foodservice Manufacturers Ass'n (291)

Marchi, Richard
Airports Council Internat'l/North America (17)

Marchibroda, Janet
Nat'l Committee for Quality Assurance (388)

Marcuccio, Phyllis
Nat'l Science Teachers Ass'n (427)

Marcum, Larry
Nat'l Environmental Health Ass'n (401)

Marcus, Lynne G.
American College of Chest Physicians (53)

Marcus, Shel
American Equilibration Soc. (66)

Marden, Judith C.
Financial Women Internat'l (239)

Maresch, Wayne
Nat'l Land Improvement Contractors of America (414)

Margaritis, John
Independent Armored Car Operators Ass'n (259)

Margine, Bruce
Internat'l Development Research Council (288)

Margold, William
Adult Video Ass'n (12)

Margolis, Kari
Nat'l Movement Theatre Ass'n (417)

Margosian, Rich
Composite Panel Ass'n (201)

Margula, George
Nat'l Restaurant Ass'n (425)

Mariani, Jackie
Warehousing Education and Research Council (540)

Mariano, Joseph N.
Direct Selling Ass'n (223)

Marigliano, Peter J.
Nat'l Organization of Life and Health Insurance Guaranty Ass'ns (420)

Marin, Diana
Hispanic Ass'n of Colleges and Universities (254)

Marincola, Elizabeth
American Soc. for Cell Biology (101)

Marincola, John
American Philological Ass'n (91)

Marinko, William s.
American Soc. of Anesthesiologists (106)

Marino, John
Nat'l Ass'n of Broadcasters (345)

Marino Esq., Paul
Nat'l Ass'n of School Resource Officers (371)

Marioka, Sharon
Soc. for College and University Planning (486)

Marion, James
Nat'l Counter Intelligence Corps Ass'n (398)

Marion, Joseph
North-American Ass'n of Telecommunications Dealers (446)
Ass'n of Service and Computer Dealers Internat'l (164)

Mark, Grace Ann
Ass'n for Corporate Growth (132)

Mark, Rachael
Emerging Markets Traders Ass'n (229)

Markels, Gail
Interactive Digital Software Ass'n (271)

Marker, Sam
American Breed Ass'n (49)

Marker Ph.D., Victoria A.
Academy of Dental Materials (8)

Markey, Carolyn
Visiting Nurse Ass'ns of America (540)

Markham JD, CPCU, James J.
American Institute for CPCU - Insurance Institute of America (75)

Markham, Scott
Magic Dealers Ass'n (322)

Markovich CPCU, AIM, Lois A.
Soc. of Insurance Trainers and Educators (503)

Markowitz, Morry B.
Ass'n of Internat'l Automobile Manufacturers (154)

Marks CPCU, AIM, James R.
Chartered Property and Casualty Underwriters Soc. (190)

Marks, Michael T.
College Band Directors Nat'l Ass'n (197)

Markwart, Luther A.
American Sugarbeet Growers Ass'n (119)

Markwood, Sandra
Nat'l Ass'n of Counties (350)

Markwood, Sandra Reinsel
Nat'l Ass'n of County Aging Programs (350)

Markwood, Tim
American Ass'n of Immunologists (38)

Marlette, C. Alan
Automotive Trade Ass'n Executives (175)

Marlin, Nancy
Concord Grape Ass'n (203)
Internat'l Jelly and Preserve Ass'n (295)
Nat'l Pecan Shellers Ass'n (421)
Processed Apples Institute (463)

Marlowe P.E., Walter
Nat'l Soc. of Professional Engineers (430)

Marmen, Rosemary
Interstate Oil and Gas Compact Commission (312)

Marois, Beverly J.
Masonry Heater Ass'n of North America (324)

Maroulis-Cronmiller, Alexandra
Independent Bankers Ass'n of America (260)

Marquart CAE, James F.
Manufacturing Jewelers and Suppliers of America (323)

Marredeth, Meg
Information Systems Security Ass'n (264)

Marriman, Rochelle
Soc. of Professional Archeologists (505)

Marrinan, James T.
Long Term Acute Care Hospital Ass'n of America (321)

Marschner, Richard
Classical Music Broadcasters Ass'n (194)

Marshall, Allan
Children's Book Council (192)

Marshall, Brian
North American Free Trade Ass'n (442)

Marshall, Charles A.
American Ass'n for Employment in Education (30)

Marshall, Danielle
Case Management Soc. of America (187)

Marshall, Georgette
American Ass'n of Fund-Raising Counsel (37)

Marshall, Janis C.
Contact Lens Manufacturers Ass'n (207)

Marshall, Judy
American Soc. of Heating, Refrigerating and Air-Conditioning Engineers (110)

Marshall, Sandra
Robotics Internat'l of SME (477)
Machine Vision Ass'n of SME (321)
Ass'n for Electronics Manufacturing of SME (133)
Computer and Automated Systems Ass'n of SME (202)

Marshall, Stephanie
Nat'l Health Council (408)
American Council on Education (61)

Marshall, Z. Blake
U.S.-Russia Business Council (528)

Marsico, Dale
Community Transportation Ass'n of America (201)

Marsten, Steve
Nat'l Ass'n of Certified Valuation Analysts (346)

Martell, Peter
Ice Skating Institute (258)

Martens, Jack
Automotive Occupant Protection Ass'n (174)

Martens, Pamela
Arthroscopy Ass'n of North America (128)

Martens M.D., R.
American Institute of Homeopathy (77)

Martenson, Jeanne
Nat'l Machine Embellishment Instructors and Artists (415)

Martin Ph.D., A. Dallas
Nat'l Ass'n of Student Financial Aid Administrators (377)

Martin, Andy
Tackle and Shooting Sports Agents Ass'n (520)

Martin, Barbara K.
Building Systems Councils of the Nat'l Ass'n of Home Builders (183)

Martin, Bill
Ass'n of Sales Administration Managers (164)

Martin, Brett
Nat'l Ass'n of the Remodeling Industry (378)

Martin, Carmel
Marketing Education Ass'n (324)

Martin Jr., CAE, Charles L.
American Physical Therapy Ass'n (92)

Martin, Daivd
North American Soc. for Trenchless Technology (445)

Martin CAE, David J.
Urban and Regional Information Systems Ass'n (537)

Real Estate Buyers Agent Council (472)

Martin, Deborah
Turnaround Management Ass'n (528)
Internat'l Merger and Acquisition Professionals (297)

Martin, Dick
Naval Reserve Ass'n (438)

Martin, Dr. Elaine
American Comparative Literature Ass'n (59)

Martin, Gail
TAC - Internat'l Telework Ass'n (519)

Martin, Gregory P.
Poultry Science Ass'n (461)

Martin, James L.
Nat'l Governors' Ass'n (407)

Martin, Jody
Lacrosse USA (316)

Martin, Kim L.
Portland Cement Ass'n (460)

Martin, Larry
American Apparel Manufacturers Ass'n (28)

Martin, Dr. Laurie
American Veterinary Soc. of Animal Behavior (122)

Martin, Laurie
Electric Power Supply Ass'n (227)

Martin, Leland
Investment Casting Institute (312)

Martin, Pam
Robert Morris Associates, the Ass'n of Lending and Credit Risk Professionals (476)

Martin, Pamela C.
Nat'l Computer Security Ass'n (389)

Martin, Patricia
Internat'l Sleep Products Ass'n (302)

Martin, Patrick
Soc. for Industrial Archeology (490)

Martin, Renee
Nat'l Ass'n of Document Examiners (353)

Martin, Renee W.
Textile Quality Control Ass'n (522)

Martin, Roy E.
Nat'l Fisheries Institute (404)
Nat'l Aquaculture Council (337)
Molluscan Shellfish Institute (330)

Martin, Sandra
American Ass'n of Clinical Endocrinologists (34)

Martin, Sandra L.
Nat'l Ass'n of College Stores (348)

Martin, Steve
Helicopter Loggers Ass'n (253)

Martin Bradley, Pat
Ass'n for Independent Music (134)

Martine, Brian
Metaphysical Soc. of America (327)

Martineau, Marie
Spanish-Barb Breeders Ass'n (511)

Martinec, Daniel A.
Airlines Electronic Engineering Committee (16)

Martinez, Anne R.
American Podiatric Medical Ass'n (93)

Martinez, Antonio C.
Ass'n of Immigration Attorneys (153)

Martinez, Debbie
Internat'l Ass'n of Plumbing and Mechanical Officials (282)

Martinez, Jenny
Nat'l Student Speech Language Hearing Ass'n (432)

Martinez, Martha
Earthquake Engineering Research Institute (225)

Martinez, Dr. Ruth
United States-Mexico Chamber of Commerce (536)

Martinez-Alvarez, Francisco J.
Soc. of Federal Labor Relations Professionals (501)

Martino, Frank D.
Internat'l Chemical Workers Union Council/UFCW (285)

Martorelli JD,LLM,CLU, Adelina G.
Society of Financial Service Professionals (509)

Martori, Joseph J.
American Soc. for Healthcare Engineering (103)

Martucci Jr., James C.
American Ass'n of Advertising Agencies (32)

Martz, Dave
Air-Conditioning and Refrigeration Institute (16)

Maruyama, Geoffrey M.
Soc. for the Psychological Study of Social Issues (495)

Marvel, Dr. Kevin B.
American Astronomical Soc. (45)

Masenior, Michael
Nat'l Metal Decorators Ass'n (417)

Mask CMP, Laurie J.
Internat'l Soc. for Pharmaceutical Engineering (304)

Maskas, Julie
Soc. of Fire Protection Engineers (501)

Maslow CMP, Connie
American Soc. of Bariatric Physicians (107)

Mason, Ann
Chlorine Chemistry Council (192)

Mason, Anna Marie
Soc. for Computer Applications in Radiology (486)

Mason, Cathy
American Academy of Physical Medicine and Rehabilitation (25)

Mason, Charleta
American Ass'n for Women Radiologists (32)

Mason, Cordelia
American Academy of Head, Neck and Facial Pain (22)

Mason, Debra
Religion Newswriters Ass'n of U.S. and Canada (474)

Mason, Michael D.
American Maritime Congress (82)

Mason, Rita
American Federation of Government Employees (67)

Mason, Robert
Nat'l Insurance Crime Bureau (412)

Massare, John S.
Contact Lens Ass'n of Ophthalmologists (207)

Massey, John
State Debt Management Network (516)
Textile Rental Services Ass'n of America (522)

Massey, Juliette L.
World Aquaculture Soc. (549)

Massiah, Michael
Conference of Minority Public Administrators (204)

Massie, Carl Edward
Professional Ass'n of Lumbermen - World Lumber Standards (464)

Massie, Christine
Warehousing Education and Research Council (540)

Massoff, Mrs. Nathan
Sigma Epsilon Delta Dental Fraternity (483)

Masters, Jill
PROMAX Internat'l (468)

Mata, Grace
Geothermal Resources Council (217)

Materna, Robert
Internat'l Development Research Council (288)

Matheny, Cheryl-Lynn
American Soc. for Nondestructive Testing (104)

Matheny, Mike
Soc. for Service Professionals in Printing (493)

Mathers, Kathleen O'Hara
Fertilizer Institute (238)

Mathews, Alexander S.
Animal Health Institute (125)

Mathis, Monica
Internat'l Teleproduction Soc. (308)

Mathis, Sharon
American Nurses in Business Ass'n (87)

Mathisen, William R.
Nat'l Soc. of Accountants (429)

Mathson, Jim
Intravenous Nurses Soc. (312)

Maticic, Marilyn A.
Ass'n for Advanced Life Underwriting (129)

Matlaga, Terry
Nat'l Ass'n of Housing and Redevelopment Officials (358)

Matlins, Stuart M.
Ass'n of Jewish Book Publishers (155)

Matlon Ph.D., Ronald J.
American Soc. of Trial Consultants (116)

Matsoukas, James
American Institute for CPCU - Insurance Institute of America (75)

Matsumae, Satomi
American Ass'n of Collegiate Registrars and Admissions Officers (35)

Mattei, Dr. Janet A.
American Ass'n of Variable Star Observers (44)

Matter, John
Nat'l Ballroom and Entertainment Ass'n (382)

Matternas, John J.
American Academy of State Certified Appraisers (26)

Matterson, Elizabeth V.
College of Diplomates of the American Board of Orthodontics (197)

Mattheis, Ann
Foodservice and Packaging Institute (242)

Matthews, Audrey
Conference of Minority Public Administrators (204)

Matthews, Cheryl
Nat'l Paint and Coatings Ass'n (420)

Matthews, I. Clayton
Marine Technology Soc. (324)

Matthews, Kelly M.
Alliance for Community Media (17)

Matthews, Robert A.
American Railway Car Institute (97)
Railway Progress Institute (471)
Matthews, Sallie
Soc. of American Gastrointestinal Endoscopic Surgeons (497)
Matthews, Stuart
Flight Safety Foundation (240)
Matthews, Suzette
Air Traffic Control Ass'n (16)
Matthys, Richard
United States Soccer Federation (535)
Mattingly, Joseph M.
Gas Appliance Manufacturers Ass'n (245)
Mattocks CAE, Ron
American Academy of Ophthalmology (24)
Mattoni, Rudolf H.T.
Lepidoptera Research Foundation (319)
Mattox, Donald M.
Soc. of Vacuum Coaters (508)
Matulionis MSPH, Rose Marie
Ass'n of State and Territorial Directors of Health Promotion
    and Public Health (165)
Matus, Dennis
American Soc. of Addiction Medicine (106)
Matyas PhD, Marsha Lakes
American Physiological Soc. (92)
Matz, Mark V.
Commercial Law League of America (199)
Matz, Marshall
American School Food Service Ass'n (99)
Mau, Rennie
Multicultural Publishing and Education Council (331)
Maurer, Dr. Edward
American Chiropractic Registry of Radiologic
    Technologists (51)
Mauro, Bob
Nat'l Hydrogen Ass'n (410)
Maury, Marilynn
American Institute of Biological Sciences (76)
Mavros, Robert
American Ceramic Soc. (51)
Mawby, Michael
American Diabetes Ass'n (64)
Max, Doug
United States Cross Country Coaches Ass'n (533)
Maxfield, Brenda
Personal Communications Industry Ass'n (455)
Maxfield, Elizabeth
Cellular Telecommunications Industry Ass'n (189)
Maxwell, Guy C.
United Lightning Protection Ass'n (531)
Maxwell, John
American Compensation Ass'n (59)
American Ass'n of Motor Vehicle Administrators (39)
Maxwell, Kathy
American Ass'n of Museums (39)
Maxwell, Robert J.
Nat'l Ass'n of Beverage Importers-Wine Spirits-Beer (344)
May, Christian
Structural Insulated Panel Ass'n (517)
May, Craig
American Medical Ass'n (83)
May, J. Thomas
Soc. for Applied Anthropology (485)
May, James C.
Nat'l Ass'n of Broadcasters (345)
May, Katherine
NAFSA: Ass'n of Internat'l Educators (333)
May, Lois B.
Ass'n of College and University Auditors (147)
May CAE, Lynn
American Psychiatric Ass'n (94)
May, Lynn
American Soc. of Radiologic Technologists (115)
May, Margaret
Ass'n of Community Cancer Centers (148)
May, Mike
Sporting Goods Manufacturers Ass'n (515)
May, Simeon
Nat'l Ass'n of Church Business Administration (347)
May, Thomas
Religious Public Relations Council (474)
May III, Virgil Robert
Nat'l Ass'n of Disability Evaluating Professionals (353)
May, William E.
American Cotton Shippers Ass'n (60)
Mayadas, Azim L.
Nat'l Guild of Community Schools of the Arts (408)
Mayadas, Lolita
Nat'l Guild of Community Schools of the Arts (408)
Mayberry, Peter G.
INDA, Ass'n of the Nonwoven Fabrics Industry (259)

Healthcare Compliance Packaging Council (252)
Maye, Daniel D.
Internat'l Ass'n of Culinary Professionals (278)
Mayer, Joseph L.
Copper and Brass Fabricators Council (209)
Mayer, Traci
Soc. of Behavioral Medicine (498)
Mayers, Paul
Internat'l Soc. of Air Safety Investigators (305)
Mayes, Cheryll
Iron and Steel Soc. (313)
Mayfield, Charlene
Internat'l Ass'n of Ice Cream Vendors (280)
Professional Soc. for Sales and Marketing Training (467)
Resistance Welder Manufacturers Ass'n (475)
Mayfield, Jane
Assisted Living Federation of America (170)
Mayfield, Karin
Nat'l Home Furnishings Ass'n (409)
Mayfield CMP, Karin
Nat'l Home Furnishings Ass'n (409)
Mayfield, Michelle
American Ass'n of Petroleum Geologists (40)
Maynard, Ken K.
Soc. of Nuclear Medicine (504)
Mayrides, Maurice
American Soc. of Hematology (110)
Mays, John
Nat'l Animal Control Ass'n (336)
Mazur, Jay J.
Union of Needletrades, Industrial and Textile Employees (530)
Mazur, Michael
Soc. of Corporate Meeting Professionals (500)
Mazur Jr., Michael J.
Legal Assistant Management Ass'n (319)
Mazza, Lorraine
Internat'l Council of Shopping Centers (288)
Mazza, Sergio
American Nat'l Standards Institute (86)
Mazzella, Sheree
Nat'l Welding Supply Ass'n (436)
McAbee, Linda
Fertilizer Institute (238)
McAdoo, Doug
American Soc. of Consultant Pharmacists (108)
McAlister, Roy E.
American Hydrogen Ass'n (74)
McAlister-Kizzier, Donna
Office Systems Research Ass'n (447)
McAllister, Douglas B.
Internat'l Sleep Products Ass'n (302)
McAllister CMP, Mindy
Door and Hardware Institute (224)
McAndrews, Lawrence A.
Nat'l Ass'n of Children's Hospitals and Related
    Institutions (347)
McArthur Jr., J. William
Committee on State Taxation (200)
McAuliffe, Jack
American Symphony Orchestra League (119)
McBride, Deborah L.
American Dietetic Ass'n (64)
McBride III, James
Affiliated Warehouse Companies (13)
McBride, John J.
Livestock Marketing Ass'n (320)
McBride, Kirsten
Council for Learning Disabilities (211)
McBride CAE, Maurice H.
Nat'l Petroleum Refiners Ass'n (422)
McBride, Dr. Neal
Nat'l Network of Estate Planning Attorneys (418)
McCabe, John
Nat'l Conference of Commissioners on Uniform State
    Laws (390)
McCabe, John J.
Ass'n of Foreign Trade Representatives (151)
McCabe, Richard E.
Wildlife Management Institute (544)
McCabe, T.J.
Nat'l Ass'n for Home Care (339)
McCachran, Andrew
Ass'n of Schools of Public Health (164)
McCaffrey, Barbara
Fashion Jewelry Ass'n of America (235)
McCain, Kerry F.
MicroStation Community (328)
McCall, James F.
American Soc. of Military Comptrollers (112)
McCallen CAE, Janet G.
Internat'l Ass'n for Financial Planning (274)

McCalley, Barbara
Ophthalmic Photographers' Soc. (448)
McCammon, Bob
Internat'l Hockey League (293)
McCann, Daisy S.
Clinical Ligand Assay Soc. (195)
McCann, Dennis
Soc. of Christian Ethics (499)
McCann RN, Kathleen
Nat'l Ass'n of Psychiatric Health Systems (367)
McCann, Lisa
Project Management Institute (468)
McCann, Nancey Kaplan
American Soc. for Cataract and Refractive Surgery (107)
McCann, Nancy
American Soc. of Ophthalmic Administrators (113)
McCarmally, Timothy
Tax Executives Institute (520)
McCarren, Helen
Soc. of Cosmetic Chemists (500)
McCarren, Patrick
Electronic Forum on Sound Technology (228)
Special Interest Group on Multimedia (513)
Special Interest Group on Computer Graphics (512)
Special Interest Group for Data Communication (512)
McCarron, Douglas J.
United Brotherhood of Carpenters and Joiners of
    America (530)
McCart, Jan
Ass'n of Rheumatology Health Professionals (164)
McCarter, Katherine
Ecological Soc. of America (225)
McCarthy, Amy
Telecommunications Resellers Ass'n (521)
McCarthy, Anne M.
Organizational Behavior Teaching Soc. (450)
McCarthy, Brian
Ass'n for Engineering Graphics and Imaging Systems (133)
McCarthy, Brian A.
Internat'l Reprographic Ass'n (301)
McCarthy DPM, Ph.D., Daniel J.
American Soc. of Podiatric Dermatology (115)
McCarthy, Elsie
Nat'l Minority Business Council (417)
McCarthy, Frank E.
Automobile Dealers Ass'n (174)
McCarthy, James
Snack Food Ass'n (484)
McCarthy CAE, John
Internat'l Health, Racquet and Sportsclub Ass'n (293)
McCarthy, Dr. John
American Crop Protection Ass'n (62)
McCarthy CMP, Margaret L.
American Ass'n of Museums (39)
McCarthy, Tom
Internat'l Soc. of Air Safety Investigators (305)
McCarty, Cathy
Community Ass'ns Institute (200)
McCarty, Debra
American Soc. for Aesthetic Plastic Surgery (100)
McCashion, Linda
Nat'l Potato Promotion Board (423)
McCaskill, Elmer
American Professional Soc. on the Abuse of Children (94)
McCauley, Diana
American Institute of Chemical Engineers (77)
McCauley, Gail
Building Service Contractors Ass'n Internat'l (183)
McCawley, Gail R.
Building Service Contractors Ass'n Internat'l (183)
McClain, Elisabeth
Nat'l League of Cities (414)
McClellan, Mary Beth
Internat'l Federation of Women's Travel Organizations (291)
McClellan DVM, Roger O.
Chemical Industry Institute of Toxicology (191)
McClendon, Brent
Hardwood Plywood and Veneer Ass'n (251)
McClendon, Carol
Nat'l Institute on Community-based Long-term Care (412)
McClenny, Tricia
Soc. of Cardiovascular and Interventional Radiology (499)
McClimon, Thomas
United States Conference of Mayors (533)
McCloskey, David
Nat'l Marine Representatives Ass'n (416)
McClure CAE, Ann
Internat'l Gas Turbine Institute, ASME (292)
McClure, David P.
Ass'n of On-Line Professionals (159)
McClure, Robert C.
Travel Industry Ass'n of America (526)

McColl, Bill
Nat'l Ass'n of Alcoholism and Drug Abuse Counselors (343)

McConihe, Michael
American Pharmaceutical Ass'n (91)

McConkey, Max
Nat'l Dissemination Ass'n (399)

McConnell, Ann
General Merchandise Distributors Council (246)

McConnell, Barbara
Food Industry Ass'n Executives (241)

McConnell, Chuck
Public Broadcasting Management Ass'n (469)

McConnell, David
Nat'l Stone Ass'n (431)

McConnell, David T.
General Merchandise Distributors Council (246)

McConnell, Dr. Doug
Ass'n of Professors of Mission (162)

McConnell, Sally N.
Nat'l Ass'n of Elementary School Principals (353)

McConville, Eugene P.
Internat'l Union, United Plant Guard Workers of America (310)

McCool, Betsy
Master Dairies (324)

McCormack, Adele C.
American Soc. of Pension Actuaries (114)

McCormack, Howard
Maritime Law Ass'n of the U.S. (324)

McCormack, Jim
Emergency Nurses Ass'n (229)

McCormick, Amy
Ass'n of Reproductive Health Professionals (163)

McCormick, Connie
Nat'l Ass'n of Student Financial Aid Administrators (377)

McCormick, Duncan
Nat'l Wool Marketing Corporation (437)

McCormick, Jenni
American Cinema Editors (52)

McCormick, Mary Jo
Piedmontese Ass'n of the United States (458)

McCowen, Dr. Thomas A.
Ass'n of Internat'l Agriculture and Rural Development (154)

McCoy, Gary
IDEA, The Health and Fitness Source (258)

McCoy, Gary D.
Automotive Service Industry Ass'n (175)

McCoy, Melissa Lynn
Soc. of Cardiovascular and Interventional Radiology (499)

McCoy, Wendy M.
American Romney Breeders Ass'n (98)

McCracken, Terri
Ladies Professional Golf Ass'n (316)

McCracken, Todd O.
Nat'l Small Business United (428)

McCraken, Brenna
Nat'l Stroke Ass'n (432)

McCray, Harvey L.
Ass'n of Operative Millers (159)

McCray, Kevin
Nat'l Ground Water Ass'n (407)

McCrea, Edward J.
North American Ass'n for Environmental Education (440)

McCrensky, Jay
Romanian-American Chamber of Commerce (477)

McCrossan, Richard J.
Nat'l Fire Protection Ass'n (404)

McCrovey, Judith A.
Suppliers of Advanced Composite Materials Ass'n (518)

McCuan-Kirsch, Connie
Textile Bag Manufacturers Ass'n (522)

McCue, Lisa
Grocery Manufacturers of America (250)

McCullough, Brian
North American Soc. of Teachers of the Alexander Technique (445)

McCullough, Gordon
American Heart Ass'n (72)

McCullough, Lynn
Internat'l Card Manufacturers Ass'n (285)

McCullough, Philip N.
Institute of Nuclear Power Operations (268)

McCullough, Randy
Federation of State Medical Boards of the U. S. (237)

McCurdy CAE, David
Electronic Industries Ass'n (228)

McCusker, Andrew
Nat'l Ass'n of Environmental Professionals (354)

McCutchan, Lee I.
American Soc. of Professional Appraisers (115)

McDaniel, Barbara
Nat'l Training Systems Ass'n (434)

McDaniel, James A.
Nat'l Catholic Educational Ass'n (385)

McDaniel, Wayne
Internat'l Road Federation (302)

McDavid, Wendy
Internat'l Dairy Foods Ass'n (288)

McDermott CAE, John S.
Electrical Equipment Representatives Ass'n (227)

McDermott, Marianne
American College of Construction Lawyers (53)
Nat'l Ass'n of Professional Pet Sitters (367)
American College of Tax Counsel (58)
Greeting Card Ass'n (250)
Nat'l Candle Ass'n (385)

McDermott, Mary
Personal Communications Industry Ass'n (455)

McDermott, Terrence M.
Nat'l Ass'n of REALTORS (369)

McDonald, Sr. Dale
Nat'l Catholic Educational Ass'n (385)

McDonald, Gordon
Dairy Management (219)

McDonald, John
Indian Educators Federation (262)

McDonald, Mary
American Ornithologists' Union (88)

McDonald, Pamela K.
Professional Convention Management Ass'n (465)

McDonald, Sandran
American Academy of Physical Medicine and Rehabilitation (25)

McDonald M.D., F.A., Walter J.
American College of Physicians-American Soc. of Internal Medicine (57)

McDonell CAE, Katherine M.
Soc. of Roller Skating Teachers of America (507)
Speed Coaches Ass'n (514)
Roller Skating Ass'n Internat'l (477)

McDonnell, Mary
Social Science Research Council (509)

McDonough, Doug
American Dental Assistants Ass'n (64)

McDowell, Ella
Nat'l Ass'n of WIC Directors (380)

McDowell, Lawrence E.
Soc. of Plastics Engineers (505)

McDowell, Micahel
Council for Advancement and Support of Education (210)

McEachern, Charis
Romance Writers of America (477)

McEachran, John P.
Soc. of Manufacturing Engineers (503)

McElfresh, Dinah D.
State Government Affairs Council (516)
Electromagnetic Energy Ass'n (228)

McElgunn, Peggy
Ass'n for the Management of Organization Design (139)
Nat'l Guild of Professional Paperhangers (408)
Teaching-Family Ass'n (520)
American Surety Ass'n (119)
Alliance of Cardiovascular Professionals (18)

McElhaney, Sandra
Nat'l Mental Health Ass'n (416)

McElligott, Paula
Truckload Carriers Ass'n (527)

McElroy, Deborah
Regional Airline Ass'n (473)

McElroy, Edward
American Federation of Teachers (67)

McElroy, Suzanne
American Entomological Soc. (66)

McElvain, Linda
Internat'l and American Ass'ns of Clinical Nutritionists (273)

McElveen, Mary
Chamber of Commerce of the United States of America (190)

McEntee, Christine W.
American College of Cardiology (53)

McEntee, Elliott C.
Nat'l Ass'n for Check Safekeeping (338)
Nat'l Automated Clearing House Ass'n (381)

McEntee, Gerald W.
American Federation of State, County and Municipal Employees (67)

McEvoy, John T.
Nat'l Council of State Housing Agencies (396)

McEvoy, Mike
Internat'l Hockey League (293)

McEwen, Darryl D.
Machinery Dealers Nat'l Ass'n (321)

McEwen, Jane W.
Packaged Ice Ass'n (452)

McFadden, Lisa
American Ass'n of Immunologists (38)

McFarland, Debbie A.
Aircraft Electronics Ass'n (16)

McFarland, Mike
Nat'l Soccer Coaches Ass'n of America (430)
Professional Soccer Reporters Ass'n (467)

McFarland, Stanley J.
Nat'l Ass'n of Federal Education Program Administrators (355)

McFarland, Steven T.
Christian Legal Soc. (193)

McGarry, Dennis
Document Management Industries Ass'n (224)

McGarry, James A.
Business Products Industry Ass'n (185)

McGeachey, Mary
Magazine Publishers of America (321)

McGee, Erin E.
United Fresh Fruit and Vegetable Ass'n (531)

McGee, Fred L.
Architectural Precast Ass'n (127)

McGee, Gerald J.
Internat'l Copper Ass'n (287)

McGee, James M.
Nat'l Alliance of Postal and Federal Employees (336)

McGee, Thomas
Inter-Industry Conference on Auto Collision Repair (271)

McGeein, Mary M.
Nat'l Council of Community Hospitals (394)

McGencey, Stephanie
Nat'l Ass'n of State Alcohol and Drug Abuse Directors (373)

McGettigan, Timothy
Nat'l Council for the Social Studies (393)

McGhee, Cathy
Women's Basketball Coaches Ass'n (547)

McGill, Jennifer
Ass'n of Schools of Journalism and Mass Communication (164)
Ass'n for Education in Journalism and Mass Communication (132)

McGill, Kathleen
Investment Program Ass'n (312)

McGill, Kristin
American Dental Hygienists' Ass'n (64)

McGillicuddy, Linda K.
American Ass'n for the Study of Headache (32)

McGillivray, Stephen
American Soc. of Travel Agents (116)

McGinly Ph.D.,CAE, William C.
Ass'n for Healthcare Philanthropy (134)

McGinn, Janet
Soc. of Woman Geographers (509)

McGinty, Frank M.
Industrial Fabrics Ass'n Internat'l (262)

McGinty M.D., John B.
Arthroscopy Ass'n of North America (128)

McGivern, Tim
United States Telephone Ass'n (535)

McGlinchey, Carol J.
North American Soc. of Pacing and Electrophysiology (445)

McGovern, Owen P.
Catholic Press Ass'n (188)

McGowan, J.C.
Hydroponic Merchants Ass'n (257)

McGowan, Thomas J.
Shipowners Claims Bureau (482)

McGrade, Steve
Soc. for Medieval and Renaissance Philosophy (491)

McGrady, Bill
Nat'l Ass'n of State Directors of Migrant Education (374)

McGrane, Mary
Internat'l Trademark Ass'n (309)

McGrath, Charles
Interlocking Concrete Pavement Institute (271)

McGrath CAE, Charles A.
Home Automation Ass'n (255)
Internat'l Biometric Soc. (283)

McGrath CAE, JD, Eileen
American Medical Women's Ass'n (84)

McGrath, Raymond J.
Beer Institute (177)

McGrath, Richard
Augustinian Secondary Educational Ass'n (173)

McGraw, James L.
Internat'l Institute of Synthetic Rubber Producers (295)

McGraw, Michael
Chemical Manufacturers Ass'n (191)

McGree, Sean
Hop Growers of America (256)

McGreery, Lisa
Conference of State Bank Supervisors (204)

McGreevey Jr., John D.
Nat'l Field Selling Ass'n (404)
Nat'l Industrial Glove Distributors Ass'n (411)
Lawn and Garden Marketing and Distribution Ass'n (318)

McGreevy, Tim
U.S.A. Dry Pea and Lentil Council (528)

McGuckin, Tim
Internat'l Bridge, Tunnel and Turnpike Ass'n (284)

McGuinness Jr., Richard J.
American Cancer Soc. (50)

McGuire, Bara
Corel WTA Tour (209)

McGuire, Gerard J.
Post-Tensioning Institute (461)

McGuire, Joseph
Ass'n of Home Appliance Manufacturers (153)

McGuire, Marilyn
New Alternatives for Publishers, Retailers and Artists (438)

McGuire, Mavis
Nat'l Ass'n of Pediatric Nurse Associates and Practitioners (364)

McGuire, Paul
American Soc. of Plumbing Engineers (115)
Nat'l Beer Wholesalers Ass'n (382)

McGuirk, Dennis P.
Nat'l Fluid Power Ass'n (405)

McGurgan, Diane
Nat'l Ass'n of Science Writers (371)

McHardy, Louis W.
Nat'l Council of Juvenile and Family Court Judges (395)

McHenry Jr., Col. Paul T.
State Guard Ass'n of the United States (516)

McHenry Jr., Wendell
Ass'n of Military Banks of America (157)

McHugh, James
American Psychological Ass'n (94)

McHugh Sanner, Brigid
American Heart Ass'n (72)

McIlveen, Edward E.
Insulated Cable Engineers Ass'n (270)

McInerney USAF (RET.), Maj.Gen. Jim
Nat'l Defense Industrial Ass'n (399)

McInerney, Marianne
Nat'l Business Travel Ass'n (384)

McIntire, Paul
American Soc. for Nondestructive Testing (104)

McIntosh, Bruce D.
Portland Cement Ass'n (460)

McIntosh, Ken
Carpet and Rug Institute (187)

McIntyre, Jean
American Academy of Otolaryngology-Head and Neck Surgery (24)

McIntyre, Maria A.
Council of Logistics Management (215)

McIrath, Thomas
American Physical Soc. (92)

Mcluer, James
Nat'l Organization of Black Law Enforcement Executives (420)

McIver, Krystyna
AOAC Internat'l (125)

McKay, Charles
American Psychological Ass'n (94)

McKay USMC (RET.), Brg.Gen. Gerald
Nat'l Defense Industrial Ass'n (399)

McKay, Michael W.
American Craft Council (62)

McKeagney, Robert
Child Welfare League of America (192)

McKean, James
American Federation of Violin and Bow Makers (67)

McKee, David
American Traffic Safety Services Ass'n (120)

McKee, Thomas D.
Ass'n of American Publishers (143)

McKeever III, Joseph F.
Committee of Annuity Insurers (200)

McKendree, John D.
Internat'l Council for Computer Communication (287)

McKenzie CFO, Gary
Nat'l Pest Control Ass'n (422)

McKenzie, Steve
American Health Information Management Ass'n (72)

McKenzie, Sue
Nat'l Ass'n of State Textbook Administrators (376)

McKew, Robert E.
American Financial Services Ass'n (68)

McKim, Patrick
Human Behavior and Evolution Soc. (257)

McKinney, Danny
Burley Tobacco Growers Cooperative Ass'n (184)

McKinney, John
American Academy of Ophthalmology (24)

McKinney, Lily
Internat'l Reprographic Ass'n (301)

McKinnis, Marilyn
Helicopter Ass'n Internat'l (253)

McKinnon, Rhonda
Nat'l Ass'n of Orthopaedic Technologists (364)

McKinnon, Russell
Nat'l Rural Electric Cooperative Ass'n (426)

McKinnon, Susanne
Nat'l Business Incubation Ass'n (384)

McKnight, John
Ass'n of Marine Engine Manufacturers (156)

McKnight, Patti
Internet Alliance (311)

McKuen, Rod
American Guild of Variety Artists (71)

McLane Ph. D., Betsy
Internat'l Documentary Ass'n (289)

McLaren, Bruce
Community College Ass'n for Instruction and Technology (201)

McLaughlan, Laura
Musculoskeletal Tumor Soc. (331)

McLaughlin, David R.
American Land Title Ass'n (80)

McLaughlin, Don
World Antique Dealers Ass'n (549)

McLaughlin, Piper
Chief Officers of State Library Agencies (192)

McLean, Caroline
Commercial Development Ass'n (198)

McLean, Ephraim R.
Ass'n for Information Systems (135)

McLellan, Bruce
Nat'l Tax Lien Ass'n (433)

McLellan, Sharon K.
Ass'n of Official Racing Chemists (158)

McLennan, Kenneth
Manufacturers Alliance (322)

McLeod CMP, Barbara
Soc. of Computed Body Tomography and Magnetic Resonance (500)

McLeod, Michael R.
American Ass'n of Crop Insurers (35)

McLin, Joyce A.
American Safe Deposit Ass'n (98)

McLin, Sharon
American Shire Horse Ass'n (100)

McIlmoil, L.N.
Metal Treating Institute (327)

McMahon, Diane
Synthetic Organic Chemical Manufacturers Ass'n (519)

McMahon, Donna R.
Professional Photographers of America (466)

McMahon, John J.
Institute of the Ironworking Industry (269)

McMahon, Shaine
Nat'l Air Duct Cleaners Ass'n (335)

McMannus, Sheila
American Ass'n of Airport Executives (33)

McManus, Carolyn
Nat'l Home Furnishings Ass'n (409)

McMillan, Barry G.
AACE Internat'l (7)

McMillan, Kurt C.
Contract Services Ass'n of America (208)

McMillan, Leigh
Lamaze International (316)

McMillan, Dr. R. Bruce
Ass'n of Science Museum Directors (164)

McMillan, Tiffany
Soc. for In Vitro Biology (489)

McMillen, Jenna Lee
Nat'l Soc. of Hispanic MBAs (430)

McMillen, Ronald E.
American Psychiatric Ass'n (94)

McMonagle, Amy C.
Building Owners and Managers Institute Internat'l (183)

McMullen, Ann
American Soc. for Ethnohistory (102)

McMullen, Hollis
Nat'l Ass'n of State Alcohol and Drug Abuse Directors (373)

McMullen, Tim
Associated Locksmiths of America (171)

McNally, Michael
Nat'l Air Traffic Controllers Ass'n (335)

McNally CAE, Ronald F.
Nat'l Beverage Packaging Ass'n (382)

McNally, Steve
Composites Fabricators Ass'n (201)
Internat'l Cast Polymer Ass'n (285)

McNamara, Captain James J.
Nat'l Cargo Bureau (385)

McNamara, Jody
Ass'n for Healthcare Philanthropy (134)

McNamara, K. Brian
Internat'l Sign Ass'n (302)

McNamee, Nikki
American Council of Life Insurance (61)

McNaughton CAE, Jack D.
Precision Machined Products Ass'n (462)

McNeal, Heidi
Internat'l Ass'n of Food Industry Suppliers (279)

McNeal, Joan
American Apparel Manufacturers Ass'n (28)

McNeil, Catherine Masterson
Internat'l Health, Racquet and Sportsclub Ass'n (293)

McNeil, Jean
Professional Insurance Mass-Marketing Ass'n (466)

McNeirney, Frank
Central Station Alarm Ass'n (189)

McNevin CAE, Anthony J.
American Ass'n of Colleges of Podiatric Medicine (35)

McNulty, Diane
New York Academy of Sciences (438)

McNulty, Kevin
Internat'l Warehouse Logistics Ass'n (310)

McPherson, Vilma
Internat'l Radio and Television Soc. Foundation (301)

McQuade, Brian
Laborers' Internat'l Union of North America (316)

McQuade, Michael E.
American Electronics Ass'n (65)

McQuaid, J. Dennis
American Dehydrated Onion and Garlic Ass'n (63)

McQuaid, John A.
Nat'l Private Truck Council (423)

McQuire, Paul
Independent Bankers Ass'n of America (260)

McSpadden, Floyd F.
Civil Aviation Medical Ass'n (194)

McSpadden, Steve
Nat'l Ass'n of Police Organizations (365)

McSweeney, Beth
American Podiatric Medical Ass'n (93)

McTighe, Joseph W.
Council for American Private Education (210)

McVay, Robert
Nat'l Rural Health Ass'n (426)

McWhorter, Kristin
Nat'l Poultry and Food Distributors Ass'n (423)

McWilliams, Brian
Internat'l Longshoremen's and Warehousemen's Union (296)

McWilliams, Kathryn
Nat'l Oil Recyclers Ass'n (419)

Meacham, J.D.
American Soc. for Healthcare Central Service Personnel (102)

Mead, Chris
Council for Urban Economic Development (212)

Mead, Kenway
Institute of Inspection Cleaning and Restoration (267)

Meade, Elizabeth W.
Helicopter Ass'n Internat'l (253)

Meade, Robert E.
American Arbitration Ass'n (28)

Meadows CPA, Thomas W.
American Optometric Ass'n (88)

Mean, Ravi
Soc. of Collision Repair Specialists (499)

Means CAE, Kathy
Produce Marketing Ass'n (463)

Means, Kathy
Healthcare Leadership Council (253)

Mear Ph.D., Mark
Soc. of Engineering Science (501)

Mears, James
Special Libraries Ass'n (514)

Meckley, Kaye
Entomological Soc. of America (231)

Medaris, Bruce
Ass'n for Facilities Engineering (133)

Medert, Kurt
American Gear Manufacturers Ass'n (70)

Medick CPA, Susan
Automotive Parts and Accessories Ass'n (175)

Medina, Adelita M.
Ass'n of Hispanic Arts (153)

Medina, Frank
American Anthropological Ass'n (28)

Medina, Santy
Soc. for Nutrition Education (491)

Medina, Victor
Service Dealers Ass'n (482)

Medley, Larry
Ass'n of Clinical Research Professionals (147)

Medlin CAE, E. Lander
APPA: The Ass'n of Higher Education Facilities Officers (126)

Medlin, E. Lander
Ass'n of Higher Education Facilities Officers (153)

Medlock CPP, Jim
American Payroll Ass'n (90)

Mednis, Rasma
United States Council for Internat'l Business (533)

Meegan, Jo
Evangelical Christian Publishers Ass'n (233)

Meegan, Mary
Soc. for Nutrition Education (491)

Meehan APR, Joan
American Nurses Ass'n (87)

Meehan, Shana
Ass'n of Performing Arts Presenters (160)

Meehan CAE, Sharon A.
American Ass'n for the Study of Liver Diseases (32)

Meenan, John M.
Air Transport Ass'n of America (16)

Meents, Peg
American Pinzgauer Ass'n (92)

Meersman, Peter
Internat'l Soc. of Restaurant Ass'n Executives (307)

Meeter, Glenn
Ass'n of Christian Schools Internat'l (146)

Megahan, Darlene
Nat'l Ass'n of Manufacturers (362)

Megenney Ph.D., William
Ass'n of Caribbean Studies (146)

Megivern, Kathleen
Commission on Accreditation of Allied Health Education Programs (199)

Mehaffey, William R.
Soc. of Small Craft Designers (507)

Mehenie, Germai
Union for Radical Political Economics (529)

Mehren, David F.
Nat'l Ass'n of Independent Insurance Adjusters (359)

Meijer, Jon
Internat'l Fabricare Institute (290)

Meima, Steve
Gypsum Ass'n (250)

Meimann, Jim
Nat'l Pork Producers Council (423)

Meinsler, Lucille
American Ass'n of Directors of Psychiatric Residency Training (36)

Meirose S.J., Carl E.
Jesuit Secondary Education Ass'n (313)

Meisinger SPHR, Susan R.
Soc. for Human Resource Management (489)

Meisnere, Robert
Organization for the Promotion and Advancement of Small Telecommunications Companies (449)

Meister, Frederick A.
Distilled Spirits Council of the U.S. (223)

Meister, Mark J.
Archaeological Institute of America (126)

Meksher, Andrea
Ass'n of Applied Community Researchers (143)

Melancon, Barry C.
American Institute of Certified Public Accountants (76)

Melancon, Charles
American Sugar Cane League of the U.S.A. (119)

Melancon, Nita
Nat'l Community Capital Ass'n (388)

Melby, Nancy
American Wood Preservers Institute (123)

Meldrum Jr., Thomas W.
Software Publishers Ass'n (509)

Mele, Chris
Nat'l Ass'n of Regulatory Utility Commissioners (369)

Melendez, Dr. Sara E.
Independent Sector (261)

Meliloo, Paul
Marketing Research Ass'n (324)

Mell, Kandi
Juvenile Products Manufacturers Ass'n (315)

Mellgree, Roger L.
Psychonomic Soc. (469)

Melnicove, Susan A.
American Soc. for Industrial Security (103)

Melnykovich Ph.D., George O.
Food Processing Machinery and Supplies Ass'n (242)

Meloche, Lynn
Door and Hardware Institute (224)

Meloon, Jeannine
American Soc. for Clinical Laboratory Science (101)

Melton, Betty
Women in Management (547)

Melton-Bitterman, Cynthia
Nat'l Leased Housing Ass'n (415)

Meltzer, Donna Ledder
American Ass'n of University Affiliated Programs for Persons with Developmental Disabilities (44)

Meltzer, Robert L.
American Soc. for Testing and Materials (105)

Melvin CMP, CAE, Leslie
Textile Rental Services Ass'n of America (522)

MeNamara, Amb. Thomas E.
Council of the Americas (216)

Mendelson, Haim
Federation of Modern Painters and Sculptors (237)

Mendelson, Dr. Wallace B.
Sleep Research Soc. (483)

Mendes, David
American Subcontractors Ass'n (118)

Mendes, Joel
Residential Sales Council (475)

Mendez, C. Paul
Nat'l Ass'n of Workforce Development Professionals (381)

Mendez, Sonya
Ass'n of Internal Management Consultants (154)

Mendicino Jr., Joseph A.
American Law Institute (81)

Mengel, Gordon
Nat'l Council for Agricultural Education (393)

Menitoff, Rabbi Paul J.
Central Conference of American Rabbis (189)

Menn III, Henry W.
Generic Pharmaceutical Industry Ass'n (246)

Mennis, Jack
American Ass'n of Advertising Agencies (32)

Mennite, Mary Anne
American Ass'n for Cancer Research (30)

Mentzer, Kenneth D.
North American Insulation Manufacturers Ass'n (447)

Menyes, Tom
Professional Bowlers Ass'n of America (465)

Menzer, Mark
Air-Conditioning and Refrigeration Institute (16)

Mercado, Christine
Soc. for Marketing Professional Services (490)

Mercer, Lee W.
Nat'l Ass'n of Small Business Investment Companies (373)

Merchant, Sylvia
Vocational Industrial Clubs of America (540)

Mercill, Alan
Internat'l Pharmaceutical Excipients Council (299)

Meredith, George
Ass'n of Retail Marketing Services (163)

Meredith, Joseph
Internat'l Brotherhood of Boilermakers, Iron Ship Builders, Blacksmiths, Forgers and Helpers (284)

Meredith, Suzan
Ass'n for Health Services Research (134)

Mericsko, John
Ass'n of Science-Technology Centers (164)
Nat'l Soc. of Accountants (429)

Merifield, Cynthia E.
Motion Picture Ass'n of America (330)

Meritt, Mark
American Ass'n of Health Plans (37)

Meriwether, Lanie
Ass'n of Child and Adolescent Psychiatric Nurses (146)

Merkel, Jeanean D.
Conference of Major Superiors of Men, U.S.A. (204)

Merkel, Susan
Ass'n of On-Line Professionals (159)

Merker CAE, James F.
American Soc. of Bariatric Physicians (107)

Merlis, Edward A.
Air Transport Ass'n of America (16)

Merrell, Halley A.
American Chemical Soc. (51)

Merrifield, Dave
Fastener Industry Coalition (235)
Nat'l Fastener Distributors Ass'n (402)

Merrill, Greg
Chlorine Chemistry Council (192)

Merrill, Nancy
Ass'n of Theological Schools in the United States and Canada (168)

Merrill, Shirlene
Nat'l Ass'n of Home Inspectors (358)

Merriman, Klein S.
Nat'l Ass'n of Store Fixture Manufacturers (377)

Merriman, Tim
Nat'l Ass'n for Interpretation (340)

Merritt, Becca
Independent Forest Products Ass'n (260)

Merritt USA (RET.), Gen. Jack N.
Ass'n of the United States Army (167)

Mertens, Sally
Nat'l Ass'n of Corporate Real Estate Executives International (350)

Mertes, Kate
American Soc. of Indexers (111)

Merther, Susan
Water Environment Federation (541)

Mertz, Jonathan
American Academy of Optometry (24)

Merwin III, George W.
Automotive Service Ass'n (175)

Mesirow, Robert
Cellular Telecommunications Industry Ass'n (189)

Messervey, John E.
Nat'l Family Business Council (402)

Messick, Donald L.
Sulphur Institute, The (518)

Messner, Howard M.
American Consulting Engineers Council (60)

Messner, Murray
Nat'l Truck Leasing System (434)

Metcalf, Allan
American Dialect Soc. (64)

Metcalf, Kathy J.
Chamber of Shipping of America (190)

Metcalf, Mary Kay
Internat'l Card Manufacturers Ass'n (285)

Metcalf, Peter F.
Hard Fibers Ass'n (251)

Metcalfe, Sandy
American Soc. of Addiction Medicine (106)

Metha, Rachna
Ass'n of Sales and Marketing Companies (164)

Metz, Carol Lally
Internat'l Foodservice Editorial Council (291)

Metz, Sheldon
Nat'l Nutritional Foods Ass'n (419)

Metzen, Anita
American Council on Consumer Interests (61)

Metzger, Kristen
Internat'l Ass'n of Aquatic and Marine Science Libraries and Information Centers (275)

Metzger, Mary Ann
Soc. for Chaos Theory in Psychology and Life Sciences (486)

Metzger, Raphael
Nat'l Coalition of Hispanic Health and Human Services Organizations (387)

Metzger, Tim
Equipment Manufacturers Institute (232)

Meushaw, Anthony J.
Internat'l Soc. of Beverage Technologists (305)

Mevis, Howard
American Academy of Orthopaedic Surgeons (24)

Mewshaw, Elizabeth
American Soc. for Industrial Security (103)

Meyer, Adele R.
Nat'l Ass'n of Resale and Thrift Shops (370)

Meyer, Al
Internat'l Ass'n of Conference Center Administrators (277)

Meyer, Alan
Protestant Church-Owned Publishers Ass'n (469)

Meyer, Amy M.
Nat'l Council of State Housing Agencies (396)

Meyer, Brian
American Soc. of Health-System Pharmacists (110)

Meyer, Carlyn
Water Quality Ass'n (541)

Meyer, Douglas
Internat'l Union of Electronic, Electrical, Salaried Machine, and Furniture Workers (309)

Meyer, Ellen
American Public Health Ass'n (95)

Meyer CAE, CLU, Jill
Million Dollar Round Table (328)

Meyer, John M.
Brown Swiss Cattle Breeders Ass'n of the U.S.A. (183)

Meyer, Kathryn
Investment Management Consultants Ass'n (312)

Meyer, Kimberly A.
Meeting Professionals Internat'l (327)

Meyer, Linn
American College of Surgeons (57)

Meyer, M. Barry
Aluminum Ass'n (19)

Meyer, Michelle
Nat'l Ass'n of Professional Employer Organizations (366)

Meyer LUTCF, CAE, Paul D.
American Soc. of Ass'n Executives (107)

Meyer, Susan M.
American Ass'n of Colleges of Pharmacy (35)

Meyer, Tamzen
Organization of American Historians (450)

Meyerhoeffer, J.A.
Railway Engineering-Maintenance Suppliers Ass'n (471)

Meyerholz, John P.
Internat'l Insurance Soc. (295)

Meyers, Mary
American College of Foot and Ankle Surgeons (54)

Meyers, N. Marshall
Pet Industry Joint Advisory Council (455)

Meyers, Sherry
Nat'l Ass'n of Healthcare Access Management (357)

Mezibov, Dan
American Ass'n of Colleges of Nursing (34)

Mica, Daniel A.
Credit Union Nat'l Ass'n (218)

Miceer, Katie
Nat'l Ass'n of Graphic and Product Identification
    Manufacturers (357)

Michael, Janetta
Peruvian Paso Horse Registry of North America (455)

Michael, Marlene
American Soc. for Bone and Mineral Research (101)

Michaels, Bonnie J.
American Boat and Yacht Council (48)

Michalik, John J.
Ass'n of Legal Administrators (155)

Michalski, Richard P.
Internat'l Ass'n of Machinists and Aerospace Workers (280)

Michel, Harriet R.
Nat'l Minority Supplier Development Council (417)

Michell, Lisa
Lambda Omicron Gamma Medical Society (317)

Michelson, Paul
Soc. for Romanian Studies (493)

Michioku, Sandra
Asian American Journalists Ass'n (128)

Michnich Dr.P.H., Marie E.
American College of Cardiology (53)

Mickel, Chris
Internat'l Fire Photographers Ass'n (291)

Mickey, Larry
American Ass'n of Orthodontists (40)

Mickle, Linda
Internat'l Map Trade Ass'n (296)

Middaugh, Alan R.
Nat'l Potato Council (423)

Middlebrooks, Sally
Ass'n of Science-Technology Centers (164)

Middleton, Fred
Nat'l Cotton Council of America (392)

Midford, Debbie
Marketing Research Ass'n (324)

Midgley, Donald B.
Car Care Council (186)

Mieacham, J.D.
American Ass'n of Neuroscience Nurses (39)

Mighetto, Lisa
American Soc. for Environmental History (102)

Migliore, Sally
Nat'l Soc. for Experiential Education (428)

Mignini Jr., CAE, Paul J.
Credit Research Foundation (218)
Nat'l Ass'n of Credit Management (351)

Mihalik, Lisa
American College Personnel Ass'n (58)

Mihelich, Kathleen
Building Officials and Code Administrators Internat'l (183)

Mikes, Richard
Calendar Marketing Ass'n (185)

Milan, Dennis
Nat'l Systems Contractors Ass'n (433)

Milan, Noel
Nat'l Governors' Ass'n (407)

Milanese, Robert S.
Nat'l Ass'n of Pharmaceutical Manufacturers (365)

Milbergs, Egils
Nat'l Coalition for Advanced Manufacturing (387)

Milburn, Susan
Independent Educational Consultants Ass'n (260)

Mildon, Marie
Nat'l Council of Juvenile and Family Court Judges (395)

Miles, Barbro
American Family Therapy Academy (66)

Miles, Carol
American Booksellers Ass'n (48)

Miles, Janet L.
Nat'l Ass'n of Federal Credit Unions (355)

Miles, Ken
Professional Ass'n for Childhood Education (464)

Miles, Mark
ATP Tour (172)

Miles, Raymond C.
Institute of Business Appraisers (266)

Miles, Esq., Michele G.
Institute of Business Appraisers (266)

Milkey, Dr. Robert W.
American Astronomical Soc. (45)

Milks, Linda
Healthcare Forum, The (252)

Millar, Heather
Nat'l Ass'n of Managed Care Physicians (362)

Millar, Jocelyn G.
Internat'l Soc. of Chemical Ecology (306)

Millar, William W.
American Public Transit Ass'n (96)

Miller, Andrew
American Counseling Ass'n (62)

Miller, Bradley
Business and Institutional Furniture Manufacturers Ass'n
    Internat'l (184)

Miller, Brent
Nat'l Ass'n for Home Care (339)

Miller, Brent V.
American Medical Group Ass'n (83)

Miller, Carlean
American Ass'n of Health Plans (37)

Miller, Carol
Material Handling Industry Ass'n (325)
Global Health Council (248)

Miller, Carole
Pedorthic Footwear Ass'n (454)

Miller, Charla
AACE Internat'l (7)

Miller, Christine
Magazine Publishers of America (321)

Miller, Christopher A.
Hardwood Distributors Ass'n (251)

Miller, Cordie
Internat'l Soc. for Magnetic Resonance in Medicine (303)

Miller, Darell D.
Black Entertainment and Sports Lawyers Ass'n (180)

Miller, Darlene
Automotive Industry Action Group (174)

Miller, David A.
Toy Manufacturers of America (524)

Miller, David P.
American Wood Chip Export Ass'n (123)

Miller, Diane
American Thyroid Ass'n (120)

Miller, Ed
American College of Forensic Psychiatry (54)

Miller, Edward L.
Asphalt Institute (128)

Miller, Eleanor C.
Nat'l Rural Electric Cooperative Ass'n (426)

Miller, Elizabeth
Nat'l Ass'n of State Information Resource Executives (375)

Miller, Ellen
Employee Assistance Professionals Ass'n (229)

Miller, Fred
Home Improvement Research Institute (255)

Miller, Gary
Hydraulic Institute (257)

Miller, George D.
Nat'l Fire Protection Ass'n (404)

Miller, Harris
Information Technology Ass'n of America (264)

Miller, Heather
American College of Medical Toxicology (55)
American Academy of Clinical Toxicology (21)

Miller, Hydi
Professional Managers Ass'n (466)

Miller, Jeffrey M.
Communications Workers of America (200)

Miller, Jeffrey T.
Lead Industries Ass'n (318)

Miller, Jennifer
Nat'l Welding Supply Ass'n (436)

Miller, Jim
Nat'l Ass'n of Wheat Growers (380)
Nat'l Concrete Masonry Ass'n (389)

Miller (RET.), Lt.Col. John
Retired Officers Ass'n, The (476)

Miller Ph.D., DVM, John G.
Ass'n for Assessment and Accreditation of Laboratory Animal
    Care Internat'l (130)

Miller, Joseph J.
North American Mycological Ass'n (443)

Miller, Joyce
American Soc. for Histocompatability and
    Immunogenetics (103)

Miller, Judy
Entomological Soc. of America (231)
American Academy of Audiology (20)

Miller, Juliet
Nat'l Career Development Ass'n (385)

Miller, K.T.
United States Meat Export Federation (534)

Miller, Karen
Nat'l Hydrogen Ass'n (410)

Miller, Katie
Self Insurance Institute of America (481)

Miller, Kenneth E.
Office Furniture Distribution Ass'n (447)

Miller, Kenneth W.
American Ass'n of Colleges of Pharmacy (35)

Miller, Lance R.
Internat'l Shooting Coaches Ass'n (302)

Miller, Lenne
Endocrine Soc. (230)

Miller, Lenore
Retail, Wholesale and Department Store Union (476)

Miller, Lewis
Internat'l Ass'n of Fairs and Expositions (279)

Miller, Linda M.
American Booksellers Ass'n (48)

Miller, Lois
Luggage and Leather Goods Manufacturers of America (321)

Miller CAE, M. Lance
Metal Treating Institute (327)

Miller, Margaret A.
American Ass'n for Higher Education (31)

Miller, Matt
Ass'n of Independent Commercial Producers (153)

Miller, Meghan P.
Nat'l Account Management Ass'n (334)

Miller CAE, Michael J.
Ass'n for the Advancement of Medical Instrumentation (138)

Miller J.D., CAE, Michael J.
Soc. for Biomedical Equipment Technicians (485)

Miller, Minetta
Women in Mining Nat'l (547)

Miller, Ned
Robert Morris Associates, the Ass'n of Lending and Credit
    Risk Professionals (476)

Miller, Nina
Intercollegiate Tennis Ass'n (271)

Miller, Oral O.
Visually Impaired Data Processors Internat'l (540)

Miller, Patty
World Waterpark Ass'n (550)

Miller, Paul
Nat'l Dairy Herd Improvement Ass'n (399)

Miller, Peggy
American Ass'n of Industrial Veterinarians (38)

Miller, R. Michael
American Academy of Family Physicians (22)

Miller, Richard F.
American Institute of Certified Public Accountants (76)

Miller, Rob
Nat'l Christian College Athletic Ass'n (387)

Miller, Robert
Nat'l Ass'n of Tribal Court Personnel (379)

Miller, Robert R.
Motor and Equipment Manufacturers Ass'n (330)

Miller, Robin
School and Home Office Products Ass'n (479)

Miller, Ron
Ass'n of Surgical Technologists (166)

Miller, Scott
Nat'l Paperbox Ass'n (421)

Miller O.D., Stephen C.
College of Optometrists in Vision Development (197)

Miller MPH, Stephen H.
American Board of Medical Specialties (47)

Miller, Stephen H.
Soc. of Competitive Intelligence Professionals (500)

Miller, Toni
Consortium for School Networking (206)

Miller, Vicki
Retail Packaging Manufacturers Ass'n (476)

Miller, W. Kirk
North American Export Grain Ass'n (442)

Miller, Whitney
American College of Managed Care Medicine (55)
Nat'l Ass'n of Managed Care Physicians (362)

Milliken, Christine T.
Nat'l Ass'n of Attorneys General (343)

Milling, Marcus E.
American Geological Institute (70)

Mills, Amy L.
Agricultural Retailers Ass'n (14)

Mills, Jean Dougherty
Biotechnology Industry Organization (179)

Mills, Jim
Radio and Television Correspondents Ass'n (471)

Mills, Kelli A.
Soc. for Neuroscience (491)

Mills, Kelly
American Medical Women's Ass'n (84)

Mills, Kimberly A.
Adhesion Soc. (11)

Mills, Patricia
American Wind Energy Ass'n (123)

Mills, Penny S.
American College of Cardiology (53)

Mills, Susan
Nat'l Restaurant Ass'n (425)

Mills, T.J.
Ass'n of Management/Internat'l Ass'n of Management (156)

Mills, Tom
Ass'n of Management Analysts in State and Local Government (156)

Mills, Vicki
American Ass'n for the Advancement of Slavic Studies (32)

Millson, Jay
American Ass'n of Clinical Endocrinologists (34)

Milne, Ann L.
Ass'n of Family and Conciliation Courts (150)

Milne, Peggy
Accordion Federation of North America (10)

Milne, Thomas
Nat'l Ass'n of County and City Health Officials (350)

Milner CMP, Dawn
Nat'l Speakers Ass'n (431)

Milner, Maryann
Computer Measurement Group (202)

Milner CAE, Neil
Conference of State Bank Supervisors (204)

Milosh, Eugene J.
American Ass'n of Exporters and Importers (36)

Milowitz, Barry E.
Soc. of American Registered Architects (498)

Milroy, Mark C.
Nat'l Ass'n for College Admission Counseling (338)

Mindel, Aaron
Council of Development Finance Agencies (213)

Mindell, Dr. David
Soc. of Systematic Biologists (507)

Miner, Aniya
American Butter Institute (50)

Minett, Jeff
American Ass'n of Museums (39)

Mingle, Dr. James R.
State Higher Education Executive Officers (516)

Minic, Dee
Travel Industry Ass'n of America (526)

Minieri, Michael
Nat'l Ass'n of State Fire Marshals (375)

Minigiello, Louis P.
Nat'l Ass'n of Oil Heating Service Managers (364)

Mininger, Wayne
Nat'l Onion Ass'n (419)

Minnich, Mary
American Soc. of Newspaper Editors (113)

Mintz, Suzanne
Nat'l Family Caregivers Ass'n (402)

Mirand, Dr. Edwin A.
Ass'n of American Cancer Institutes (142)

Miranda, Peter M.
American Wire Cloth Institute (123)

Mirick USAF,MSC (R, Col. Steven C.
Ass'n of Military Surgeons of the U.S. (157)

Mirin M.D., Steven M.
American Psychiatric Ass'n (94)

Mirmelstein, Ross F.
Nat'l Sheriffs' Ass'n (427)

Misra, Dr. Kula C.
Soc. for Luminescent Microscopy and Spectroscopy (490)

Mitch, Joe
United States Basketball Writers Ass'n (532)

Mitchel, Lynn
Nat'l Ass'n of Government Communicators (356)

Mitchell, Andrea
Substance Abuse Librarians and Information Specialists (518)

Mitchell, Ann
Nat'l Council of Nonprofit Ass'ns (395)

Mitchell, Beverly
American Dietetic Ass'n (64)

Mitchell, Carol L.
Nat'l Potato Council (423)

Mitchell, David M.
Soc. of Automotive Engineers International (498)

Mitchell, Denise
College Art Ass'n (197)

Mitchell, Doug
Wine and Spirits Shippers Ass'n (544)

Mitchell, Peter
Internat'l Union of Electronic, Electrical, Salaried Machine, and Furniture Workers (309)

Mitchell, Rick
Internat'l Information Management Congress (294)

Mitchell, Dr. Robert B.
Delta Pi Epsilon (221)

Mitchell, Tracy
Women in Cable and Telecommunications (546)

Mitchem Ph.D., Arnold
Nat'l Council of Educational Opportunity Ass'ns (394)

Mitler, Milton E.
Chamber of Commerce of the United States of America (190)

Mitstifer, Dorothy I.
Ass'n of College Honor Societies (147)

Mittler, Kathy H.
Parenting Publications of America (453)

Mitz, Carl
Internat'l Ass'n of Equine Dental Technicians (279)

Miyamoto, Pat K.
American Psychological Ass'n (94)

Mizer, Susan
American Business Women's Ass'n (50)

Mobley, Randy
Internat'l League of Professional Baseball Clubs (296)

Mochnal, George
Forging Industry Ass'n (243)

Mock Jr., Joseph V.
American Bankers Ass'n (46)

Mock, Linda
American Soc. of Clinical Oncology (108)

Mock, Lisa
Soc. of Professional Journalists (506)

Mock, Mary V.
Smokeless Tobacco Council (484)

Moczynski, Gerald
Ass'n of Air Medical Services (141)

Modecki CAE, Carl A.
Nat'l Ass'n of Insurance Brokers (360)

Modesette, Deborah
Federation of State Medical Boards of the U. S. (237)

Modrick, James E.
Nat'l Art Education Ass'n (337)

Moeller Jr., G. Martin
Ass'n of Collegiate Schools of Architecture (148)

Moen, Melanie
American Film Marketing Ass'n (68)

Moen, Ronald S.
American Ass'n of Orthodontists (40)

Moeser, Erica
Nat'l Conference of Bar Examiners (389)

Moffat, George
American Soc. of Ass'n Executives (107)

Moffat, Henry M.
Nat'l Ass'n of Railroad Trial Counsel (368)

Moffatt, Dave
Nat'l Ass'n of College Stores (348)

Moffett, Bryan
Radio-Television News Directors Ass'n (471)

Mogan, Karen
American Meat Institute (83)

Mogle, Phillip
Professional Convention Management Ass'n (465)

Mohan, Barry
American Meteorological Soc. (84)

Mohling, Wendell
Nat'l Science Teachers Ass'n (427)

Mohnacs, J. Jack
Architectural Spray Coaters Ass'n (127)

Mohrman-Gillis, Marilyn
Ass'n of America's Public Television Stations (142)

Moir, Brian
Internat'l Communications Ass'n (286)

Mol, Hendrick D.
Associated Schools of Construction (172)

Molaro, Michael
Construction Financial Management Ass'n (206)

Molchan, Andrew
Nat'l Ass'n of Federally Licensed Firearms Dealers (355)

Molick, Christine
Nat'l Conference of Bankruptcy Judges (389)

Molina, Ariana R.
Precision Metalforming Ass'n (462)

Molino, John M.
Ass'n of the United States Army (167)

Molino CAE, Michael A.
Recreation Vehicle Dealers Ass'n of North America (472)
Recreation Vehicle Rental Ass'n (472)

Moll, Gary
American Forests (69)

Mollison, Char
Independent Sector (261)

Mollo, Barbara G.
Government Finance Officers Ass'n of the United States and Canada (248)

Molnar, Terry
Fragrance Foundation (243)

Molony, David
American Ass'n of Oriental Medicine (40)

Molotsky, Iris
American Ass'n of University Professors (44)

Molpus, C. Manly
Grocery Manufacturers of America (250)

Molumby, Jeanne
Internat'l Cast Polymer Ass'n (285)

Molyneaux, Keri
Internat'l Soc. of Refractive Surgery (306)

Mona CAE, Stephen F.
Golf Course Superintendents Ass'n of America (248)

Monaghan, Eileen P.
Ass'n of Bridal Consultants (145)

Monaghan, Gerard J.
Ass'n of Bridal Consultants (145)

Monahan, Frank
Nat'l Conference of Catholic Bishops/U.S. Catholic Conference (390)

Monahan CAE, Thomas A.
Ass'n of Healthcare Internal Auditors (153)
Nat'l Concrete Burial Vault Ass'n (389)

Monday, Thomas G.
Nat'l Ass'n of Convenience Stores (349)

Monello, Midge
Nat'l Ass'n of Housing and Redevelopment Officials (358)

Moneymaker, Carol
Accrediting Bureau of Health Education Schools (11)

Monfasani, John
Renaissance Soc. of America (474)

Monin, Clarence V.
Brotherhood of Locomotive Engineers (182)

Monk, Bruce
Snack Food Ass'n (484)

Monk, Carl C.
Ass'n of American Law Schools (142)

Monk, Randall
Composting Council (202)

Monroe, Eric G.
IMAGE Soc. (259)

Monroe, Michael E.
Internat'l Brotherhood of Painters and Allied Trades (284)

Monroe, Patricia E.
Construction Industry Manufacturers Ass'n (206)

Monroe, Raymond W.
Steel Founders' Soc. of America (516)

Montagnolo, Anthony
ECRI (226)

Montague, Patti
American School Food Service Ass'n (99)

Montalvo, Delia
Ass'n of Hispanic Arts (153)

Montana, Nick
Stadium Managers Ass'n (515)

Montelieu, Ana
American Ass'n on Mental Retardation (45)

Montesa, Noel E.
Ass'n of School Business Officials Internat'l (164)

Montgomery, Dean
American Health Planning Ass'n (72)

Montgomery, Nevin B.
Nat'l Frozen Food Ass'n (406)

Montgomery, Terry
Ass'n for Psychoanalytic Medicine (137)

Montgomery, Tom
United Egg Ass'n (530)

Monti, Sita
Construction Marketing Research Council (207)

Montoya CAE, James D.
Internat'l Group of Agencies and Bureaus (293)

Montoya, Ken
Nat'l Air Traffic Controllers Ass'n (335)

Montplaisir, Ronald J.
Nat'l Troubleshooting Ass'n (434)

Montwieler, William J.
Industrial Truck Ass'n (263)

Moody Jr., James E.
American College of Rheumatology (57)

Moody, Karen
Nat'l Ass'n for Campus Activities (338)

Moody, Dr. Linda A.
Women's Caucus: Religious Studies **(547)**

Moody, Michelle
American Soc. of Hematology **(110)**

Mook, Dean T.
American Academy of Mechanics **(23)**

Moon, Elizabeth Chisman
American Subcontractors Ass'n **(118)**

Mooney, James E.
Inland Marine Underwriters Ass'n **(264)**

Mooney, Nancy
American Public Power Ass'n **(96)**

Mooneyham, G. Scott
Internat'l Lead Zinc Research Organization **(295)**

Moore, Albert W.
AMT - The Ass'n for Manufacturing Technology **(124)**

Moore, Alice M.
Automotive Service Industry Ass'n **(175)**

Moore, Andrew
Nat'l Ass'n of Service and Conservation Corps **(372)**

Moore, Arthur
Sheet Metal Workers' Internat'l Ass'n **(482)**

Moore, Carlos F.J.
American Textile Manufacturers Institute **(119)**

Moore, Chuck
Ass'n of Natural Resource Enforcement Trainers **(158)**

Moore, Deborah
Council of Educational Facility Planners, Internat'l **(213)**

Moore, Detlef B.
American Ass'n of Dental Editors **(35)**
Internat'l Ass'n for Orthodontics **(275)**

Moore, Donna
Insurance Loss Control Ass'n **(270)**

Moore, Edie
Soc. for Adolescent Medicine **(484)**

Moore, Emily
American Psychological Soc. **(95)**

Moore, Heath D.
Professional Lawn Care Ass'n of America **(466)**

Moore, Hugh
Bond Market Ass'n **(181)**

Moore, J.Ashton
Dutch Warmblood Ass'n **(225)**

Moore, John R.
Organic Crop Improvement Ass'n Internat'l **(449)**

Moore, John R. &
Nat'l Police Officers Ass'n of America **(422)**

Moore, Jon
Professional Housing Management Ass'n **(466)**

Moore, Karyn
Ass'n for Experiential Education **(133)**

Moore, Katherine
Screen Actors Guild **(480)**

Moore, Kendra D.
Truck Cap and Accessory Ass'n **(527)**

Moore, Linda L.
Internat'l Council of Fine Arts Deans **(287)**

Moore, Lois A.
Pipe Fabrication Institute **(458)**

Moore, Lynn S.
American Ceramic Soc. **(51)**

Moore, M. Melissa
American Soc. of Agricultural Engineers **(106)**

Moore, Michael
American Rental Ass'n **(98)**

Moore, Mike
Nat'l Ass'n of Professional Baseball Leagues **(366)**

Moore, Patricia
Internat'l Soc. of Introduction Services **(306)**

Moore, Paul G.
United Scenic Artists **(531)**

Moore R.N., Pearl
Oncology Nursing Soc. **(448)**

Moore, Reggie
Nat'l Environmental Health Ass'n **(401)**

Moore, Robert M.
Internat'l Banana Ass'n **(283)**

Moore, Ryan J.
Non-Ferrous Founders' Soc. **(439)**

Moore CAE, Scott J.
Internat'l Gas Turbine Institute, ASME **(292)**

Moore, Sherley
American College of Preventive Medicine **(57)**

Moore, Shirley
Alliance of Black Entertainment Technicians **(18)**

Moore, Steve
Auto Internat'l Ass'n **(173)**

Moore, Sue C.
Independent Innkeepers Ass'n **(260)**

Moore, Susan P.
American Plastics Council **(92)**

Moore, Taryn
American Soc. of Travel Agents **(116)**

Moore, Toby
U.S.A. Poultry and Egg Export Council **(528)**

Moore, Tom
Nat'l Ski Areas Ass'n **(428)**

Moore, W. Henson
American Forest and Paper Ass'n **(69)**

Moore, Wanda L.
Council on Social Work Education **(217)**

Moorefield, Bari
Nat'l Ass'n of Professional Employer Organizations **(366)**

Moorehead, Tracey A.
Ass'n of Home Appliance Manufacturers **(153)**

Mooring, John E.
Nat'l Ass'n of Housing Information Managers **(359)**

Mora, JoAnna
Soc. of Physician Assistants in Pediatrics **(505)**

Morahg, Gilead
Nat'l Ass'n of Professors of Hebrew in American Institutions
of Higher Learning **(367)**

Morales, Joyce
Ass'n of Battery Recyclers **(144)**

Morales, Loren
Academy of Political Science **(9)**

Moran, John A.
American Waterways Operators **(122)**

Moran, Medina S.
Nat'l Waterways Conference **(436)**

Moran, Patti J.
Pet Sitters Internat'l **(455)**

Moran, Peter J.
Soc. of American Florists **(497)**

Moran, William
Health and Personal Care Distribution Conference **(251)**

Morano, Linda
American Mental Health Counselors Ass'n **(84)**

Morano, Thomas
Snack Food Ass'n **(484)**

Morasky, Frank
Plumbing-Heating-Cooling Information Bureau **(459)**

Mordente, Giacomo
Nat'l Ass'n of Veterans Program Administrators **(379)**

Mordente, Jack
Nat'l Ass'n of Veterans Program Administrators **(379)**

Moreland, T. Michael
Geological Soc. of America **(246)**

Morelli, Genevieve
Competitive Telecommunications Ass'n **(201)**

Moreschi, Jill
Ass'n of Major City Building Officials **(156)**

Moret, Phyllis
American Soc. of Consultant Pharmacists **(108)**

Morga, Celeste
Internat'l Narcotic Enforcement Officers Ass'n **(298)**

Morgan, Denise
Nat'l Ass'n of RV Parks and Campgrounds **(370)**

Morgan, Digges
Southern Forest Products Ass'n **(510)**

Morgan, E. Joyce
Nat'l Mining Ass'n **(417)**

Morgan, Harold E.
Internat'l Taxicab and Livery Ass'n **(308)**

Morgan, J. Ben
Nat'l Cottonseed Products Ass'n **(393)**

Morgan CAE, Jeffrey D.
Nat'l Ass'n of Professional Insurance Agents **(367)**

Morgan, Karen
Outpatient Ophthalmic Surgery Soc. **(451)**

Morgan, Madelaine
American Academy of Facial Plastic and Reconstructive
Surgery **(22)**

Morgan, Patty
Travel and Tourism Research Ass'n **(526)**

Morgan, Richard
Nat'l Asphalt Pavement Ass'n **(337)**
American Flint Glass Workers Union **(68)**

Morgan CAE, Robert S.
Council of Growing Companies **(214)**

Morgenstern, Jordan L.
Soc. of the Plastics Industry **(507)**

Morin, Don
American Academy of Periodontology **(25)**

Morin, Nancy
American Ass'n of Botanical Gardens and Arboreta **(33)**

Morin, William G.
Coalition for Intelligent Manufacturing Systems **(196)**

Moring, Frederick
Associated Gas Distributors **(171)**

Moritz, Rhonda
Nat'l Kitchen and Bath Ass'n **(414)**

Morje, Morton
American Soc. of TV Cameramen **(116)**

Morley Jr., James E.
Nat'l Ass'n of College and University Business Officers **(348)**

Morman, Deborah
Ass'n for Women in Science **(140)**

Morrill, Jennifer
U.S. Grains Council **(528)**

Morris, Cheryl
Internat'l Soc. of Applied Intelligence **(305)**

Morris, Cyndi
Nat'l Catholic Educational Exhibitors **(385)**

Morris, Deborah W.
Nat'l Concrete Masonry Ass'n **(389)**

Morris, Dolores
Industrial Perforators Ass'n **(263)**

Morris, James P.
Phi Mu Alpha - Sinfonia **(457)**

Morris, Jay
Nat'l Ass'n of Life Underwriters **(361)**

Morris, Jerry
Federation of Nurses and Health Professionals **(237)**

Morris, Joseph B.
Nat'l Ass'n of Healthcare Consultants **(357)**
Air Courier Conference of America **(15)**
Nat'l Corrugated Steel Pipe Ass'n **(392)**

Morris D.O., J.D., Morton
American Osteopathic Academy of Orthopedics **(89)**

Morris, Raymond A.
Soc. of Automotive Engineers International **(498)**

Morris, Dr. Robert C.
Soc. of Professors of Education **(506)**

Morris, Robert J.
Sulphur Institute, The **(518)**

Morris, Sheila
American Resort Development Ass'n **(98)**

Morris, V.B.
American Agriculture Movement **(27)**

Morrison Ph.D., CAE, Barbara
Nat'l Ass'n of Neonatal Nurses **(363)**

Morrison CAE, Barbara L.
American Industrial Hygiene Ass'n **(75)**

Morrison, Greg
American Soc. of Radiologic Technologists **(115)**

Morrison, Jeffrey Michael
American Herbal Products Ass'n **(73)**

Morrison, K.C.
Nat'l Conference of Black Political Scientists **(389)**

Morrison, Laurin B.
American Ass'n of Bank Directors **(33)**

Morrison, Martha M.
Self Storage Ass'n **(481)**

Morrison, Marvin
Internat'l Council of Shopping Centers **(288)**

Morrison, Robert B.
American Music Conference **(86)**

Morrison, Seth
Cable and Telecommunications Ass'n for Marketing **(185)**

Morrison, Victoria
Gemological Institute of America **(246)**

Morrison, William
Meat Importers' Council of America **(325)**

Morrissette, Michael
Hazardous Materials Advisory Council **(251)**

Morrissette, Peggy
Manufacturers Alliance **(322)**

Morrow, Hugh
Internat'l Cadmium Ass'n **(284)**

Morse, Cristina
Internat'l Masonry Institute **(297)**

Morse M.D., Stephen
American Sexually Transmitted Diseases Ass'n **(99)**

Mortensen, Frank
Magazine Publishers of America **(321)**

Mortenson, Lee E.
Ass'n of Community Cancer Centers **(148)**

Mortimor, Sandy
Internat'l Motion Picture and Lecturers Ass'n **(297)**

Morton, Judith B.
American Sleep Disorders Ass'n **(100)**

Morton, Lisa
American Symphony Orchestra League **(119)**

Morton, Tex
Independent Professional Representatives Organization **(261)**

Morze, Frank
Cottage Industry Miniaturists Trade Ass'n **(210)**

Mosca, Bob
American Soc. for Automation in Pharmacy **(101)**

Moscato, Cathie
Soc. of American Registered Architects **(498)**

Mosedale, Roberta
Nat'l Soc. for Histotechnology (429)

Mosedale, Susan E.
Internat'l Ass'n of Amusement Parks and Attractions (275)

Moser Jr., A. N. "Bubby"
Nat'l Sheriffs' Ass'n (427)

Moser, Constance L.
Nat'l Cooperative Business Ass'n (392)

Moser, Greg
Credit Union Nat'l Ass'n (218)

Moser CNA, Kenneth
APICS - The Educational Society for Resource
  Management (125)

Moses, Ginnah
American Highland Cattle Ass'n (73)

Moses, Kim
Envelope Manufacturers Ass'n (231)

Moses, Max G.
Commercial Law League of America (199)

Moses, Thomas J.
Holstein Ass'n USA (255)

Moses, Tim
American Soc. of Neuroradiology (113)

Mosgkowicz, Joe
Internat'l Mass Retail Ass'n (297)

Mosher, Russell N.
American Boiler Manufacturers Ass'n (48)

Mosier, Dr. Kathy
Ass'n of Aviation Psychologists (144)

Moskal, Patt L.
American Ass'n of Endodontists (36)

Mosley, Kimberly
American College of Healthcare Executives (54)

Moss, Debra A.
Internat'l Franchise Ass'n (292)

Moss, Doug
Internat'l Hockey League (293)

Moss C.P.A., Hazel
Nat'l Coalition of Hispanic Health and Human Services
  Organizations (387)

Moss, Robert E.
American Automobile Manufacturers Ass'n (46)

Mosser, Dan
Associated Builders and Contractors (170)

Mossner, Dabielle
Lutheran Educational Conference of North America (321)

Motelet, Cie
Nat'l Industrial Belting Ass'n (410)

Motley, John
Nat'l Retail Federation (425)

Motta, John
United States Soccer Federation (535)

Mottl, John
American Soc. for Nondestructive Testing (104)

Motts, Frederick C.
Soc. of Motion Picture and Television Engineers (504)

Mouchka, Carol F.
Internat'l Ass'n of Milk, Food and Environmental
  Sanitarians (281)

Moulton, Benjamin
American Soc. of Law, Medicine and Ethics (112)

Moulton, Meg
Nat'l Coalition of Girls Schools (387)

Mount, Margaret J.
Flavor and Extract Manufacturers Ass'n of the United
  States (240)

Mount, Melinda
Intelligent Transportation Soc. of America (270)

Mountford, Mardi K.
Internat'l Formula Council (292)

Mountjoy, E. Leo
Nat'l Ass'n of Rail Shippers (368)

Mouro, Florence
American Nature Study Soc. (86)

Moursund, David
Internat'l Soc. for Technology in Education (304)

Moustis, Linda
American Soc. for Healthcare Risk Management (103)

Mowe, Jeanne
American Ass'n of Tissue Banks (44)

Mowery, Jenifer
Nat'l Guardianship Ass'n (408)
Nat'l Ass'n of Professional Geriatric Care Managers (366)

Moya, Jane
Women Executives in State Government (546)

Moyer III, C.T. "Skip"
American Boat and Yacht Council (48)

Moyer, Sally M.
Library Binding Institute (319)

Moynan, Carolyn
Southern Forest Products Ass'n (510)

Mozier, Richard
American Counseling Ass'n (62)

Mseka, Ayo I.
Treasury Management Ass'n (526)

MsSwegin, Catharine
Nat'l Ass'n of Store Fixture Manufacturers (377)

Much, Morrie
Nat'l Bulk Vendors Ass'n (384)

Muchow, David J.
American Gas Ass'n (70)

Mucklow, Rosemary M.
Nat'l Meat Ass'n (416)

Muehlbauer, Eric J.
North American Spine Soc. (445)
American Patient Ass'n (90)

Muehlberg, Robert J.
American Soc. of Questioned Document Examiners (115)

Muellebauer, Charles
Nat'l Building Granite Quarries Ass'n (384)

Mueller, Camille
Nat'l Speleological Soc. (431)

Mueller, Robert
American Soc. of Business Press Editors (107)

Mueller-Farber, Trysh
American Rental Ass'n (98)

Mugan, Daniel J.
Ass'n of Teachers of Latin American Studies (167)

Mugo, Janice
Internat'l and American Ass'ns of Clinical Nutritionists (273)

Muha, Denise
Nat'l Leased Housing Ass'n (415)

Muia, Connie
Internat'l Soc. for Pharmaceutical Engineering (304)

Muir, Patricia
Federal Librarians Roundtable (236)

Muir, Richard
American Soc. for Bioethics and Humanities (101)

Muir, Dr. Richard G.
American Pain Soc. (90)

Mujica, Amanda
Ethics Officer Ass'n (233)

Mulckhuyse, Marlies
American Chamber of Commerce Executives (51)

Muler, Stephanie
Nat'l Abortion Federation (333)

Mulholland, Jill P.
Automotive Occupant Restraints Council (174)

Mull, L. Diane
Ass'n of Farmworker Opportunity Programs (151)

Mullaly, Cynthia
Pedorthic Footwear Ass'n (454)

Mullane-Corvi, Sheryl
Medieval Academy of America (326)

Mullen, Dan
AIM USA (15)

Mullendore, Bob
American Galloway Breeders Ass'n (69)

Muller, Karen
Library Administration and Management Ass'n (319)
Ass'n for Library Collections and Technical Services (135)

Muller, Kathleen L.
Nat'l Ass'n of Broadcasters (345)

Muller, Richard
Internat'l Coordinating Committee on Solid State Sensors and
  Actuators Research (287)

Mulligan, Clark
Powder Coating Institute (461)

Mulligan, George M.
American Insurance Ass'n (79)

Mulligan Jr., William
Nat'l Ass'n of Produce Market Managers (366)

Mullin, Joan
Nat'l Writing Centers Ass'n (437)

Mullin, Tracy
Nat'l Retail Federation (425)

Mullins, Hugh
Medical-Dental-Hospital Business Associates (326)

Mullins, Larry
Music Industry Conference (332)
Music Educators Nat'l Conference: The Nat'l Ass'n for Music
  Education (332)

Mullins, Lawrence W.
Independent Electrical Contractors (260)

Mumm, Denise
Women's Caucus for Art (547)

Munari CAE, Donna
Door and Hardware Institute (224)

Muncy C.A.E., Steve A.
American Fire Sprinkler Ass'n (68)

Mundell, George
Intermodal Ass'n of North America (272)

Mundell, Jacqueline
Library and Information Technology Ass'n (319)

Mundy, Sandra
Airport Ground Transportation Ass'n (17)

Munk, William
American Soc. for Nondestructive Testing (104)

Munley, Katie
Commercial Law League of America (199)

Munoz Sr., Carlos A.
American Insurance Ass'n (79)

Munoz, Julio E.
Inter American Press Ass'n (271)

Munson, Barbara
Nat'l Caves Ass'n (386)

Munstermann, Gary
Precast/Prestressed Concrete Institute (462)

Munter, Holly J.
Home Fashion Products Ass'n (255)

Munter-Koenig, Holly J.
Nat'l Independent Textiles Retailers Organization (410)
Comics Magazine Ass'n of America (198)

Muravchik, Sally
American Federation of Teachers (67)

Murawski, D.H.
American Veterinary Medical Ass'n (121)

Murchie, Anita
Vinifera Wine Growers Ass'n (539)

Murchie, Gordon
Vinifera Wine Growers Ass'n (539)

Murdock, Danielle
Nat'l Ass'n for Variable Annuities (342)

Murdock, Kathy
Stained Glass Ass'n of America (515)

Murha, Annette
Infectious Diseases Soc. of America (263)

Murmo, Jonathan
Emerging Markets Traders Ass'n (229)

Murphey, Carmen
Bowling Proprietors Ass'n of America (181)

Murphy, Carole
American Academy of Orthopaedic Surgeons (24)

Murphy, Christopher
Chemical Management and Resources Ass'n (191)

Murphy, Christopher M.
Ass'n of Meeting Professionals (157)
Internat'l Claim Ass'n (285)

Murphy, Connor
Ass'n of Chartered Accountants in the United States (146)

Murphy, Dana
Ass'n of American Medical Colleges (142)

Murphy CAE, Dana
Internat'l Ass'n for Exposition Management (274)

Murphy, Deborah
American Ass'n of Medical Assistants (38)

Murphy, Edward P.
Nat'l Music Publishers' Ass'n (418)

Murphy, James A.
Latex Advisors Ass'n (317)

Murphy, James J.
Soc. for Photographic Education (492)

Murphy, Jean
Internat'l Tire and Rubber Ass'n (309)

Murphy, Jeanne
Nat'l Council of Catholic Women (394)

Murphy, John C.
Ass'n of Local Housing Finance Agencies (156)
Nat'l Ass'n for County Community and Economic
  Development (338)

Murphy, Kevin J.
Manufacturers Alliance (322)

Murphy, Kristin
Christian Legal Soc. (193)

Murphy, Lisa I.
Rubber Manufacturers Ass'n (477)

Murphy, Michael
Tax Executives Institute (520)

Murphy, Nancy
Internat'l Taxicab and Livery Ass'n (308)

Murphy, R. Donald
Steel Joist Institute (516)

Murphy, Wayne
Textile Rental Services Ass'n of America (522)

Murray, Candy
Institute of Internal Auditors (267)

Murray, Donald
Nat'l Ass'n of County Civil Attorneys (350)

Murray, Donna
Organization of Women in Internat'l Trade (450)

Murray, Eileen
United States Energy Ass'n (533)

Murray, Jack
Synthetic Organic Chemical Manufacturers Ass'n (519)

Commercial Development Ass'n (198)

Murray, James
American Council on Education (61)

Murray CAE, John F.
Acrylonitrile Group (11)

Murray, Marrilyn
Nat'l Luggage Dealers Ass'n (415)

Murray, Michael A.
American Medical Ass'n (83)

Murray USAF, Maj.Gen. Richard D.
Nat'l Ass'n for Uniformed Services and Soc. of Military Widows (342)

Murray, Suzanne
Nat'l Genealogical Soc. (406)

Murtaugh, Pat
Nat'l Ass'n of Fleet Administrators (355)

Musacchio, Robert A.
American Medical Ass'n (83)

Muse, Tonya
Envelope Manufacturers Ass'n (231)

Musick, Virgil O.
Energy Traffic Ass'n (230)

Mustafa, Zulma
Ass'n for Enterprise Opportunity (133)

Mustain, Chris
European-American Business Council (233)

Mutnansky, Jodi
Beta Alpha Psi (178)

Mutter, Reginald
Bulk Carrier Conference (184)

Myara, Norma
Motion Picture and Television Credit Ass'n (330)

Myers, Bill
Nat'l Ass'n of Electrical Distributors (353)

Myers, Charles S.
Leather Industries of America (318)

Myers, Daniel N.
Nat'l Propane Gas Ass'n (423)

Myers CAE, Elissa Matulis
Electronic Retailing Ass'n (228)

Myers, Gary D.
Fertilizer Institute (238)

Myers, Melanie
American Traffic Safety Services Ass'n (120)

Myers, Molly M.
Nat'l Venture Capital Ass'n (435)

Myers, Robert
IEEE Industry Applications Soc. (258)
IEEE Power Electronics Soc. (258)
IEEE Instrumentation and Measurement Soc. (258)
Internat'l Ass'n of Golf Administrators (279)

Myers III, Roland H.
Nat'l Ass'n of Federal Credit Unions (355)

Myers, Scott
Recreation Vehicle Dealers Ass'n of North America (472)

Myers, Stanley T.
Semiconductor Equipment and Materials Internat'l (481)

Myers, Tina
APPA: The Ass'n of Higher Education Facilities Officers (126)

Myers, Vickie Rideout
American Sugar Alliance (119)

Myers, Victoria R.
American Gas Ass'n (70)

Myers, William
Data Interchange Standards Ass'n (220)

Mykwest, Beverly
Nat'l Ass'n of Regional Councils (369)

Mylonas, Elli
Ass'n for Computers and the Humanities (131)

Myren, Sarah
American Sleep Disorders Ass'n (100)

Myslowka, Ron
UFCW Textile Council (529)

Myzk, Leigh
American Roentgen Ray Soc. (98)

Naake, Larry E.
Nat'l Ass'n of Counties (350)

Naasz, Kraig
U.S. Apple Ass'n (528)

Naber, Thomas
Nat'l Electrical Contractors Ass'n (400)

Nabors, Clyde W.
Internat'l Soc. of Certified Electronics Technicians (305)
Nat'l Electronic Service Dealers Ass'n (400)

Nabors, Lyn O'Brien
Calorie Control Council (186)

Nader, Helen
Soc. for Spanish and Portuguese Historical Studies (494)

Nadler, Molly
American Ass'n of Dental Examiners (36)

Naegele, Ray
Medical Library Ass'n (326)

Nagel, Ed
Nat'l Coalition of Alternative Community Schools (387)

Nagel, Fern
Internat'l Builders Exchange Executives (284)

Nagel, James L.
American Soybean Ass'n (117)

Nagelberg, Al
American Academy of Orthopaedic Surgeons (24)

Nagle, Kurt J.
American Ass'n of Port Authorities (41)

Nagy, Edward C.
Academy of Radiology Research (10)

Nagy, Joanne
Nat'l Ass'n of Graduate Admissions Professionals (357)

Nahin, Linda
Nuclear Energy Institute (446)

Nail, Michael
Nat'l Ass'n of Housing and Redevelopment Officials (358)

Naimark, Richard
American Arbitration Ass'n (28)

Nakas, Vida
Nat'l Ass'n of Housing and Redevelopment Officials (358)

Nakashian, Peter
American Academy of Environmental Medicine (21)

Nakayama, Jodi-Ann
American Soc. of Ophthalmic Registered Nurses (113)

Nakoneczny, Laura A.
Precision Metalforming Ass'n (462)

Nalin M.D., Howard
American College of Podiatric Radiologists (57)

Namini ACS, R.Afsoon
Nat'l Ass'n of Life Underwriters (361)

Nandzik CAE, John P.
TPA/The Tube and Pipe Ass'n, Internat'l (524)
Fabricators and Manufacturers Ass'n, Internat'l (234)

Napier, Jeffrey W.
Nat'l Marine Manufacturers Ass'n (416)

Naples-Nye, Suzanne
Council of Independent Colleges (214)

Napolitano, Lisa
Nat'l Account Management Ass'n (334)

Nappi, Laurie
Satellite Broadcasting and Communications Ass'n (479)

Nappi CAE, Ralph J.
American Machine Tool Distributors Ass'n (82)

Nardi, Mary Beth
Ass'n of Educators in Radiological Science (150)

Nardone, Angel E.
American Wine Soc. (123)

Narug, Scott
American Oil Chemists' Soc. (88)

Nary, Gordon
Internat'l Ass'n of Physicians in AIDS Care (281)

Nasca Ph.D., Philip
American College of Epidemiology (54)

Nash, Audrey
Museum Education Roundtable (332)

Nash, Janet K.
American Iron and Steel Institute (79)

Nash, Jennifer
Maintenance Council of American Trucking Ass'ns (322)

Nash, Pamela
American Ass'n for Clinical Chemistry (30)

Nashe, Carol
Radio Talk Show Hosts Ass'n (471)

Nast, Rebecca
Soc. of Telecommunications Consultants (507)

Nasvaderani, Linda
Soc. of Industrial and Office REALTORS (503)

Nathan, Bruce
Associated Press Managing Editors (172)

Nathan, Jan
Audio Publishers Ass'n (173)
Publishers Marketing Ass'n (470)

Nation, Kimber
American Orthotic and Prosthetic Ass'n (89)

Nation, Larry M.
American Ass'n of Petroleum Geologists (40)

Nauman, Art
Organization of News Ombudsmen (450)

Navis CAE, Sheila R.
Sealant, Waterproofing and Restoration Institute (480)
Electronic Transactions Ass'n (228)

Naylor, Brooke
Nat'l Apartment Ass'n (337)

Naylor, Randy
Nat'l Council of the Churches of Christ in the U.S.A. (397)

Neaderland, Louise
Internat'l Soc. of Copier Artists (306)

Neagle, Patrick
Institute of Industrial Engineers (267)

Neal CHE, CAE, Arthur D.
American College of Healthcare Executives (54)

Neal, Lisa
Water Environment Federation (541)

Neary, Pat
Nat'l Air Transportation Ass'n (335)

Nebelsick, Arnie
Western Red Cedar Lumber Ass'n (543)

Needels, Christopher J.
United States Parachute Ass'n (534)

Needham, Jenny
Soc. for Information Display (490)

Needle, Jerome
Internat'l Ass'n of Chiefs of Police (277)

Neel, Roy M.
United States Telephone Ass'n (535)

Neely, Susan
Ass'n of American Medical Colleges (142)

Neer, Michael R.
Personalization and Identification Ass'n (455)

Neff, Dennis C.
Internat'l Hard Anondizing Ass'n (293)

Neff, Michael W.
American Soc. for Horticultural Science (103)

Negens, Jack
American Soybean Ass'n (117)

Nehls, Brad
American Soc. of Home Inspectors (111)

Nehra, DeAnne
Council on Resident Education in Obstetrics and Gynecology (217)

Neibauer, Larry
Automatic Fire Alarm Ass'n (173)

Neibergall, Nora
Nat'l Ass'n of Purchasing Management (368)

Neiburgs M.D., Herbert E.
Internat'l Soc. for Preventive Oncology (304)

Neider, Barbara S.
ESOP Ass'n (232)

Neidhardt, Maureen
World Watusi Ass'n (550)

Neigh, Janet
Nat'l Ass'n for Home Care (339)

Neigus, David
Internat'l Brotherhood of Teamsters, AFL-CIO (284)

Neiman, Carol
American Counseling Ass'n (62)

Neiman, Jennifer
Americans for the Arts (124)

Nekvasil, Glen
Lake Carriers' Ass'n (316)

Nelken, Annabella B.
Nat'l Psychological Ass'n for Psychoanalysis (424)

Nelligan, William D.
American Soc. of Nuclear Cardiology (113)

Nellis, Adell T.
Lawn and Garden Dealers' Ass'n (318)

Nellis, Robert
Chemical Industry Institute of Toxicology (191)

Neloon, Jeannine
American Ass'n for Geriatric Psychiatry (30)

Nelson, Angie
Aquatic Exercise Ass'n (126)

Nelson, Bill
American Vintners Ass'n (122)

Nelson, Catherine
Bank Marketing Ass'n (176)

Nelson, Cheryl
IDEA, The Health and Fitness Source (258)

Nelson, David G.
Air Line Employees Ass'n, International (15)

Nelson, Donna
Intelligent Transportation Soc. of America (270)

Nelson, Douglas T.
American Crop Protection Ass'n (62)

Nelson, E. Colette
American Subcontractors Ass'n (118)

Nelson, James
Robert Morris Associates, the Ass'n of Lending and Credit Risk Professionals (476)

Nelson, Jane
OPERA America (448)

Nelson, Julie
Internat'l Ass'n for Exposition Management (274)

Nelson, Julienne
Women Executives in State Government (546)

Nelson, Kristy
Gospel Music Ass'n (248)

Nelson, Marvin
Soc. of Cable Telecommunications Engineers (499)

Nelson, Maura
American Hotel and Motel Ass'n (74)

Nelson USAF (RET.), Lt.Gen. Michael A.
Retired Officers Ass'n, The (476)

Nelson, Michael U.
North American Ass'n of Summer Sessions (440)

Nelson, Mo
Nat'l Council of Supervisors of Mathematics (396)

Nelson, Dr. Paul
Neurosurgical Soc. of America (438)

Nelson Jr., Richard Y.
Nat'l Ass'n of Housing and Redevelopment Officials (358)

Nelson, Robert F.
Nat'l Coffee Ass'n of the U.S.A. (387)

Nelson, Ron
Latex Advisors Ass'n (317)

Nelson CMP, Steven C.
American Ass'n of Cereal Chemists (34)

Nelson, Steven C.
Internat'l Soc. for Molecular Plant Microbe Interactions (304)
American Phytopathological Soc. (92)
American Soc. of Brewing Chemists (107)

Nelson, Susan J.
American Soc. of Transplant Physicians (116)
American Soc. for Clinical Investigation (101)

Nelson, Susan R.
American Underground-Construction Ass'n (121)

Nelson, Theron
American Real Estate Soc. (97)

Nelson, Dr. Wanda J.
Nat'l Beauty Culturists' League (382)

Nelson, William
Ass'n of Co-operative Educators (147)

Nelson, William B.
Nat'l Automated Clearing House Ass'n (381)

Nenere, M.M.
Universities Associated for Research and Education in Pathology (536)

Nesbit, Dr. Sam
Organization of Teachers of Oral Diagnosis (450)

Nesbitt, Fred
Internat'l Ass'n of Fire Fighters (279)

Ness, Lisa
Institute of Scrap Recycling Industries (269)

Netherton, James D.
Internat'l Ground Source Heat Pump Ass'n (292)

Nettles, Clay
Registry of Interpreters for the Deaf (473)

Nettles, Dr. Victor F.
American Ass'n of Wildlife Veterinarians (45)

Nettleton, Joyce
Institute of Food Technologists (267)

Neu CAE, Marcia
Soc. of Teachers of Family Medicine (507)

Neubauer, Nancy F.
Ass'n of America's Public Television Stations (142)

Neuberger EdD, JD, Carmen Guevara
American College Personnel Ass'n (58)

Neuman, Holly
Nat'l Auctioneers Ass'n (381)

Neuman, Mary Ann
Ass'n of Cosmetologists and Hairdressers (149)

Neuman, Nicole
Internat'l Bridge, Tunnel and Turnpike Ass'n (284)

Neumann, E. John
Edison Electric Institute (226)

Neuvelt, Carol Singer
Nat'l Ass'n for Environmental Management (339)

Nevins, Cathy
American Ambulance Ass'n (28)

Newborn, Tangie
American Medical Women's Ass'n (84)

Newburgh Ph.D., Robert W.
Protein Soc. (469)

Newby, Melondee
Public Risk Management Ass'n (470)

Newcomb, Douglas
Special Libraries Ass'n (514)

Newell CMP, Cathey J.
Swimming Pool Trades and Contractors Ass'n (519)

Newell, William H.
Ass'n for Integrative Studies (135)

Newell Winchester, Selina
Council for Basic Education (211)

Newlin, Joseph T.
Nat'l Rural Education Ass'n (426)

Newman, Edward
American Soc. for Cell Biology (101)

Newman, Jacqueline M.
Ass'n for the Study of Food and Society (139)

Newman, Jeffrey
American Oil Chemists' Soc. (88)

Newman, Karen
Ceilings and Interior Systems Construction Ass'n (189)

Newman, Lisa
Ass'n for Population/Family Planning Libraries and Information Centers, Internat'l (136)

Newman, Mark
Illuminating Engineering Soc. of North America (259)

Newman, Susan
Gas Research Institute (246)
Internat'l Real Estate Federation - American Chapter (301)

Newman, Susan B.
Seismological Soc. of America (481)

Newman, William A.
Automobile Dealers Ass'n (174)

Newmaster, Carol
Air Traffic Control Ass'n (16)

Newton, Dean
Animal Transportation Ass'n (125)

Newton, Harvey
Nat'l Strength and Conditioning Ass'n (432)

Newton, Joy N.
Women in Government (546)

Newville, Todd
Internat'l Professional Rodeo Ass'n (300)

Newweiler, David
Nat'l Burglar and Fire Alarm Ass'n (384)

Nezin, Rochelle A.
Paperboard Packaging Council (453)

Nguyen, H.T.
Federal Education Ass'n (235)

Nicholas, Bob
Internat'l Brotherhood of Teamsters, AFL-CIO (284)

Nichols, Barbara C.
Internat'l League of Dermatological Socs. (296)

Nichols, David C.
Soc. of Nuclear Medicine (504)

Nichols, Jack L.
American Academy of Physical Medicine and Rehabilitation (25)

Nichols, Marshall W.
Nat'l Petroleum Council (422)

Nichols, Martin
American Council of Teachers of Russian (61)

Nichols, Nancy
Nat'l Ass'n for Interpretation (340)

Nichols, Rodney W.
New York Academy of Sciences (438)

Nichols CCP, Wallace J.
American Compensation Ass'n (59)

Nicholson, Fred
Internat'l Ass'n of Lighting Management Companies (280)

Nicholson, Richard S.
American Ass'n for the Advancement of Science (32)

Nickel-Snowiss, Sharon
Conference for the Study of Political Thought (204)

Nickerson, Christine
American Academy of Actuaries (20)

Nickl, Bud
Independent Automotive Damage Appraisers Ass'n (259)

Nicklas, Rev.Dr. Anthony
Orthodox Theological Soc. in America (451)

Nicolato, Michelle
Cost Management Group (210)
Controllers Council (208)

Nicolosi Ph.D., Joseph
Nat'l Ass'n for Research and Therapy of Homosexuality (341)

Niebrzydowski, Richard
Automotive Service Industry Ass'n (175)
Automotive Communications Council (174)

Niebuhr, Mary
Linguistic Soc. of America (320)

Nielsen, Barbara
American Federation of Musicians of the United States and Canada (67)

Nielsen, Edward
Internat'l Ass'n of Convention and Visitor Bureaus (277)

Nielsen, Louisa A.
Broadcast Education Ass'n (182)

Nieman, Donald G.
American Soc. for Legal History (103)

Niemicc, Edward W.
American Institute of Certified Public Accountants (76)

Niepoth, Curt
Institute of Certified Financial Planners (266)

Niespodziewanski, Felix
American College of Surgeons (57)

Niett, Sarah
Nat'l Ass'n of Parliamentarians (364)

Nieves, Josephine
Nat'l Ass'n of Social Workers (373)

Nightingale, Swea
Sunglass Ass'n of America (518)

Nikkel, Donna K.
Arthroscopy Ass'n of North America (128)

Niles, Marianne C.
Nat'l Ass'n of Investment Companies (360)

Niles, Thomas
United States Council for Internat'l Business (533)

Nilsen, Michael
Nat'l Soc. of Fund Raising Executives (429)

Nimick, John
Professional Squash Ass'n (467)

Nipper, James J.
American Public Power Ass'n (96)

Nirpourfard, Darush
Nat'l Certified Pipe Welding Bureau (386)

Nissalke, Alan
American Logistics Ass'n (82)

Nissenbaum, Beverly
American Academy of Otolaryngology-Head and Neck Surgery (24)

Nissenbaum, Richard
Video Software Dealers Ass'n (539)

Nitschke, John
Bank Administration Institute (176)

Nivasabut, Sawanee
Consortium for School Networking (206)

Nobel, Dr. Joel J.
ECRI (226)

Noble, David
Nat'l Ass'n of Radio Reading Services (368)

Noe, Fred J.
United States Trotting Ass'n (535)

Noe, Lorie
American Board of Professional Psychology (48)

Noel, Dr. Rodney
Ass'n of American Feed Control Officials (142)

Nofsinger, John
Material Handling Industry Ass'n (325)

Nofsinger, John B.
Order Selection, Staging and Storage Council (449)
Ass'n of Mezzanine Manufacturers (157)
Rack Manufacturers Institute (470)
Storage Equipment Manufacturer's Ass'n (517)

Nokes, Mary
Nat'l Mental Health Ass'n (416)

Nolan, Ellin
Coalition of Higher Education Assistance Organizations (196)

Nolan, Helen
Antique Appraisal Ass'n of America (125)

Nolan, Jean
American Federation of State, County and Municipal Employees (67)

Nolan, Nicholas
Public Employees Roundtable (469)

Nolan, Pat
General Federation of Women's Clubs (246)

Nolan, Susan F.
Nat'l Conference of Insurance Legislators (390)

Nolan, Walker F.
Edison Electric Institute (226)

Noland, Al
Meeting Professionals Internat'l (327)

Noland, Tom
Ass'n for Applied Psychophysiology and Biofeedback (129)

Nombalais, Barbara
At-sea Processors Ass'n (172)

Nona, Daniel A.
American Council on Pharmaceutical Education (62)

Noone CAE, Stephen J.
American Academy of Osteopathy (24)

Norberg, Tracey J.
Rubber Manufacturers Ass'n (477)

Norcross Ph.D., John C.
Soc. for the Exploration of Psychotherapy Integration (495)

Nord, Dr. G. Daryl
Internat'l Ass'n for Computer Information Systems (273)

Nordone, Lynne
Cabletelevision Advertising Bureau (185)

Nordstedt, Cheryl K.
American Soc. for Dermatologic Surgery (102)

Nordstrom, Jane L.
Nat'l Ass'n of RV Parks and Campgrounds (370)

Nordtvedt, Judith
American College of Allergy, Asthma and Immunology (53)

Norfleet, Patricia
American Academy of Periodontology (25)

Norfleet Brown, Katrina
Ass'n of Maternal and Child Health Programs (157)

Norfolk, Laura
Drug and Alcohol Testing Industry Ass'n (225)
Nat'l Ass'n of Charterboat Operators (346)
Commercial Weather Services Ass'n (199)
Committee for Private Offshore Rescue and Towing (C-PORT) (200)

Norlin, Dennis
American Theological Library Ass'n (120)
Norman, Dawn
IDEA, The Health and Fitness Source (258)
Norman, Mark R.
Institute of Transportation Engineers (269)
Norman, William S.
Travel Industry Ass'n of America (526)
Norman-McNaney, Rosalie
American Baptist Homes and Hospitals Ass'n (46)
Normand, William J.
Nat'l Electrical Contractors Ass'n (400)
Normandy, Joseph
Nat'l Ass'n of Independent Life Brokerage Agencies (359)
Norris, Christine
Adhesives Manufacturers Ass'n (12)
Sealed Insulating Glass Manufacturers Ass'n (480)
Norris, Dennis
Soc. of Professional Journalists (506)
Norris, Natalie
American Ass'n for State and Local History (32)
North, Mark C.
Institute of Intermodal Repairers (267)
Northcott, Hallock
Travel Industry Ass'n of America (526)
Northcutt, Ben
Internat'l Erosion Control Ass'n (290)
Northrop, Clyde
Nationwide Alternate Delivery Alliance (437)
Northrup, Judith A.
American Soc. of Plastic and Reconstructive Surgeons (114)
Northrup, Stephen J.
Medical Device Manufacturers Ass'n (326)
Northup, G. Lawrence
Convenient Automotive Services Institute (208)
Nortman, Mark
Window Coverings Ass'n of America (544)
Norton, James J.
Graphic Communications Internat'l Union (249)
Norton, Karin L.
Industrial Telecommunications Ass'n (263)
Norton, Lawrence
American Crop Protection Ass'n (62)
Norton, Mary K.
Steel Recycling Institute (516)
Norton, Rick
Nat'l Golf Foundation (407)
Norvay PsyD, Zoltan
Ass'n for the Advancement of Psychoanalysis (138)
Nosal, Judi
North American Building Material Distribution Ass'n (441)
Nose M.D., PhD, Yukihiko
Internat'l Soc. for Artificial Organs (303)
Nousen, Steven
Truck Renting and Leasing Ass'n (527)
Novak CPM, Paul
Nat'l Ass'n of Purchasing Management (368)
Novak, Robert J.
Materials Research Soc. (325)
Novak-Dukes, Kim
Promotional Products Ass'n Internat'l (468)
Novick, Amy R.
American Immigration Lawyers Ass'n (74)
Novy, Richard W.
California Dried Fruit Export Ass'n (185)
Nowak, John L.
Construction Industry Manufacturers Ass'n (206)
Nowicki EdD, RN, CAE, Cynthia
American Academy of Ambulatory Care Nursing (20)
Nat'l Federation for Specialty Nursing Organizations (402)
Nat'l Ass'n of Orthopaedic Nurses (364)
Dermatology Nurses Ass'n (221)
Nowicki APR, Susan A.
American Ass'n of Neurological Surgeons (39)
Nowling, Lee Ann
Internat'l Sanitary Supply Ass'n (302)
Noxon, Woody
Consortium for Advanced Manufacturing Internat'l (206)
Nuckols, Murray
Game Manufacturers Ass'n (245)
Nudel, Martha
Land Trust Alliance (317)
Nuesch, Fred
College Sports Information Directors of America (198)
Nuessle, Virginia D.
American Ass'n of Homes and Services for the Aging (37)
Nuhn, Peter
Nat'l Weather Service Employees Organization (436)
Nuland, Esq., Chris L.
American Ass'n of Clinical Endocrinologists (34)
Null, Kathy
Marketing Research Ass'n (324)

Nunez, Daniel
Shade Tobacco Growers Agricultural Ass'n (482)
Nunn, S.O.
Shipbuilders Council of America (482)
Nunn, Susan
Nat'l Investor Relations Institute (413)
Nunnery, Ronald L.
American Meat Institute (83)
Nurko, Michael
Production Music Library Ass'n (464)
Nus Ph.D., Jeff
Golf Course Superintendents Ass'n of America (248)
Nuss, Channing
Nat'l Ass'n of Mortgage Brokers (363)
Nussbaum, Esther
Ass'n of Jewish Libraries (155)
Nussman, Mike
American Sport Fishing Ass'n (118)
Nuttall, Anne
American Internat'l Automobile Dealers Ass'n (79)
Nutter, Franklin W.
Reinsurance Ass'n of America (474)
Nutter, Mike
Water Environment Federation (541)
Nuzum, Janet A.
Milk Industry Foundation (328)
Internat'l Ice Cream Ass'n (294)
Internat'l Dairy Foods Ass'n (288)
Nat'l Cheese Institute (386)
Nuzzaco, Mark J.
NPES, the Ass'n for Suppliers of Printing and Publishing Technologies (446)
Nygren, Eric
Government Finance Officers Ass'n of the United States and Canada (248)
Nyhart, George V.
American College of Osteopathic Family Physicians (56)
O' Brien, Joseph A.
Golf Course Superintendents Ass'n of America (248)
O'Banion, Terry
League for Innovation in the Community College (318)
O'Block Ph.D., Robert L.
American College of Forensic Examiners (54)
O'Boyle, Edward J.
Ass'n for Social Economics (137)
O'Brien, Carol
American Ass'n of Oral and Maxillofacial Surgeons (40)
O'Brien, Jackie
Cervical Spine Research Soc. (190)
Federation of Spine Ass'ns (237)
O'Brien, Jennifer
Soc. for Imaging Science and Technology (489)
O'Brien, John
American Soc. of Plastic and Reconstructive Surgeons (114)
O'Brien Ph.D., John
Ass'n of Ecosystem Research Centers (150)
O'Brien, Karen M.
North American Securities Administrators Ass'n (444)
O'Brien, Kevin
Soc. of Actuaries (496)
O'Brien, Lynn
Internat'l Masonry Institute (297)
O'Brien, Marlene
Precision Metalforming Ass'n (462)
O'Brien, Mary
Laundry and Dry Cleaning Internat'l Union (317)
O'Brien, Nancy
American Vocational Ass'n (122)
O'Brien, Pat
Nat'l Forest Recreation Ass'n (405)
O'Brien, Patrick A.
Concrete Sawing and Drilling Ass'n (203)
O'Brien, Robert F.
Nat'l Catholic Band Ass'n (385)
O'Bryant, Kay
Nat'l Ass'n of Insurance Women (360)
O'Bryon, David
Composting Council (202)
O'Bryon CAE, David S.
American Ass'n of Limited Partners (38)
Retirement Industry Trust Ass'n (476)
Ass'n of Chiropractic Colleges (146)
O'Carroll, Dr. M. Kevin
American Academy of Oral and Maxillofacial Radiology (24)
O'Connal, Joe
Communications Marketing Ass'n (200)
O'Connell, Adeline C.
Nat'l Ass'n for Medical Direction of Respiratory Care (340)
O'Connell, Caroline
American Ass'n for Geriatric Psychiatry (30)
O'Connell, Edward L.
American Ass'n of Port Authorities (41)

O'Connell, Jack
Baseball Writers Ass'n of America (177)
O'Connell, Michael
Radiological Soc. of North America (471)
O'Conner, Allen
Internat'l Ass'n of Career Management Professionals (277)
O'Connor, Brigid
Institute of Certified Financial Planners (266)
O'Connor, Jane
BPA Internat'l (181)
O'Connor, John
Soc. of Actuaries (496)
O'Connor Jr., John E.
Soc. of Actuaries (496)
O'Connor, Judith
Council on Foundations (216)
O'Connor, Kathleen N.
Nat'l Rural Letter Carriers' Ass'n (426)
O'Connor, Kevin
Ass'n for Play Therapy (136)
O'Connor, Mark J.
Minerals, Metals and Materials Soc., The (329)
O'Connor, Mary
Women's Foodservice Forum (548)
Nat'l Ass'n of College and University Food Services (348)
O'Connor, Mary Ellen
American Institute of Physics (78)
O'Connor, Mary Kay
Internat'l Dairy-Deli-Bakery Ass'n (288)
O'Day, Paul T.
American Fiber Manufacturers Ass'n (68)
O'Dea, Mary G.
Internat'l Ass'n of Food Industry Suppliers (279)
O'Dell CEM, Barbara
Nat'l Parking Ass'n (421)
O'Donnell, Celia
Council of Literary Magazines and Presses (214)
O'Donnell, Jean
American College of Physicians American Soc. of Internal Medicine (57)
O'Donnell, Kathleen
Internat'l Ticketing Ass'n (308)
O'Donnell, Kerry
Internat'l Ticketing Ass'n (308)
O'Donnell CIH, Lynn
American Academy of Industrial Hygiene (23)
American Board of Industrial Hygiene (47)
O'Donnell, M.A.
American Osteopathic Healthcare Ass'n (89)
O'Donnell, Michelle
Soc. of Plastics Engineers (505)
O'Donnell, Nancy
Transportation Consumer Protection Council (525)
O'Donnell, Rosemary
Nat'l Ass'n of School Psychologists (371)
O'Donnell, Terry
Teachers of English to Speakers of Other Languages (520)
O'Donnell, Tina
American Soc. for Nondestructive Testing (104)
O'Donovan Ph.D., Thomas R.
American College of Managed Care Administrators (55)
American Academy of Medical Administrators (23)
American College of Cardiovascular Administrators (53)
American College of Healthcare Information Administrators (54)
O'Grady, Felice
Soc. for Experimental Biology and Medicine (488)
O'Grady Ph.D., Richard T.
American Institute of Biological Sciences (76)
O'Hagan Ph.D., Malcolm E.
Nat'l Electrical Manufacturers Ass'n (400)
O'Hallaron, Jim
Nat'l Ass'n of Electrical Distributors (353)
O'Hara, Geoff
Nat'l Ass'n of Chemical Distributors (347)
O'Hara, Linda N.
Ass'n for Work Process Improvement (141)
O'Hare, Andrew
American Portland Cement Alliance (93)
O'Hare, Margaret F.
Nat'l Ass'n of Social Workers (373)
O'Kane, Margaret
Nat'l Committee for Quality Assurance (388)
O'Keefe STD,D.Hum., F. Richard
American Council on Schools and Colleges (62)
O'Keefe, Robert T.
Nat'l Sash and Door Jobbers Ass'n (426)
O'Keefe, William F.
American Petroleum Institute (91)
O'Kelley, Patric
Edison Electric Institute (226)

Osorio, Ana M.
Portugal-United States Chamber of Commerce (461)

Ossanna, Dean D.
Internat'l Foundation of Employee Benefit Plans (292)

Ossoff M.D., Dr. Robert H.
American Laryngological Ass'n (80)

Ostenweis Ph.D., Marian
Ass'n of Academic Health Centers (141)

Oster, Susan
Nat'l Flight Nurses Ass'n (405)
American Woman's Soc. of Certified Public Accountants (123)

Ostergaard, Daniel J.
American Academy of Family Physicians (22)

Ostrach, Simon
Nat'l Academy of Engineering of the United States of America (334)

Ostrander, Susan A.
Nat'l Ass'n of Corporate Directors (350)

Ostrow, Joseph W.
Cabletelevision Advertising Bureau (185)

Ostrum, Gus
American Soc. of Plastic and Reconstructive Surgical Nurses (115)
American Nephrology Nurses Ass'n (86)

Otero, Dr. Raymond
Nat'l Ass'n of Institutional Linen Management (360)

Ott, Annette M.
United Motorcoach Ass'n (531)

Ott, Kevin D.
Rubber Manufacturers Ass'n (477)

Ott, Tina
Internat'l Personnel Management Ass'n (299)

Ottaway CAE, CMP, David G.
North American Equipment Dealers Ass'n (442)

Otte, Nicole R.
Ecotourism Soc. (225)

Otto Sr., George M.
Nat'l Roof Deck Contractors Ass'n (426)

Ouchida, Grace
Internat'l Documentary Ass'n (289)

Oulouhojian, Simon A.
Mobile Air Conditioning Soc. Worldwide (329)

Outlaw, Judith M.
Nat'l Ski Patrol System (428)

Outlaw, William
American Diabetes Ass'n (64)

Over, Stephen M.
Nat'l Ski Patrol System (428)
Professional Ski Instructors of America (467)

Overaker, Dian
Nat'l Ass'n of Leagues, Umpires and Scorers (361)

Overbey, Mary Margaret
American Anthropological Ass'n (28)

Overbey, Peggy
American Anthropological Ass'n (28)

Overkamp, Sunshine Janda
Council on Foundations (216)

Overly, Mike
Aviation Safety Institute (176)

Overstreet, Liz
Internat'l Ass'n of Food Industry Suppliers (279)

Overton, Alica
Sugar Ass'n (518)

Overton, Jack
American Ass'n of Franchisees and Dealers (37)

Owen, Andre
Soc. of Professionals in Dispute Resolution (506)

Owen, Judy
American Soc. of Naval Engineers (113)

Owen Jr., Stephen F.
Classroom Publishers Ass'n (194)

Owens, Alexandra
American Soc. of Journalists and Authors (111)

Owens, Barbara
Nat'l Committee on Planned Giving (388)

Owens, David K.
Edison Electric Institute (226)

Owens, Doug
American Salvage Pool Ass'n (99)

Owens, Jim
Indiana Limestone Institute of America (262)

Owens, Joe
Manufactured Housing Institute (322)

Owens Jr., Joseph H.
Council of State Administrators of Vocational Rehabilitation (215)

Owens, Luvie M.
Internat'l Platform Ass'n (300)

Owens, Patricia
American College Health Ass'n (52)

Owings, Alison B.
American Ass'n of Homes and Services for the Aging (37)

Owings, Julie A.
COLA (196)

Oxley, Barbi
Ass'n of Diesel Specialists (149)

Ozburn, Grant
American Short Line and Regional Railroad Ass'n (100)

Ozlu, Nina
Americans for the Arts (124)

Pabst, Kathy
Inland Rivers Ports and Terminals (264)

Pace, Jill H.
American College of Real Estate Lawyers (57)

Pace, Robert S.
American-Uzbekistan Chamber of Commerce (124)

Pacenta, Rosemary
Air Force Ass'n (15)

Pachavis, Robert H.
Materials Research Soc. (325)

Packard, Michael
Minerals, Metals and Materials Soc., The (329)

Packer, John
SnowSports Industries America (484)

Pacuit, J.F.
Tire and Rim Ass'n (523)

Padden, A.
American Railway Engineering and Maintenance of Way Ass'n (97)

Padden USAF (RET.), Maj.Gen. Tim
Armed Forces Communications and Electronics Ass'n (127)

Paduano, Maria
Ass'n for Work Process Improvement (141)

Page, Deborah
Nat'l Ass'n of Basketball Coaches (344)

Page, John A.
Healthcare Information and Management Systems Soc. (253)

Page, Pat
American Music Conference (86)

Page, Rodney
Nat'l Council of the Churches of Christ in the U.S.A. (397)

Pagliaro, Anthony P.
ACIL (11)

Pagonis, George G.
Offshore Valve Ass'n (447)

Pailet JD, Janet L.
American Ass'n for Geriatric Psychiatry (30)

Painder, Margaret
American Emu Ass'n (66)

Paine CMP, Elizabeth
Federation of State Humanities Councils (237)

Paine, Glen
Internat'l Organization of Masters, Mates and Pilots (299)

Palatiello, John M.
Management Ass'n for Private Photogrammetric Surveyors (322)

Palatka CAE, Andrew
Business Forms Management Ass'n (184)

Palazzolo, Enid
Nat'l Ass'n of Metal Finishers (363)

Palladino, Sue
Telecommunications Resellers Ass'n (521)

Palladino, Vincent
Nat'l Ass'n of Postal Supervisors (365)

Pallasch CAE, Brian T.
American Subcontractors Ass'n (118)

Palleschi, Nancy
Personal Communications Industry Ass'n (455)

Palm, Barry J.
PGA TOUR Tournaments Ass'n (456)

Palm, Debra L.
Internat'l Interactive Communication Soc. (295)

Palmai, Fred
Anxiety Disorders Ass'n of America (125)

Palmer, Bo
Qualitative Research Consultants Ass'n (470)

Palmer, James M.
United Soybean Board (531)

Palmer, Jeff
Powder Coating Institute (461)

Palmer, Michael E.
Internat'l Development Research Council (288)

Palmer RN MS MNM, Pat
Ass'n of Operating Room Nurses (159)

Palmer, Sara
Middle East Studies Ass'n of North America (328)

Palmer, Tony M.
Water and Wastewater Instrumentation Testing Ass'n of North America (ITA) (541)

Palmer Jr., William D.
Masonry Soc. (324)

Palo, Nicholas
American Board of Professional Psychology (48)
American Academy of Forensic Psychology (22)

Palys CAE, Beth W.
Conference on the Safe Transportation of Hazardous Articles (205)
American Soc. of Consulting Arborists (108)
Nat'l Conference on Weights and Measures (391)

Pan, Percy S.
American Ass'n for Laboratory Accreditation (31)

Panagopoulos Ph.D., Jennifer
Internat'l Ass'n of Defense Counsel (278)

Panaro, Gerard P.
Retailer's Bakery Ass'n (476)

Pancratz, Christopher N.
Health Industry Distributors Ass'n (252)

Pang Ph.D., David
American Ass'n of Pharmaceutical Scientists (40)

Pangburn, Wendy S.
Chief Executives Organization (191)

Panjada, Deidre Gish
North American Transplant Coordinators Organization (445)

Pannone, Barbara
Copyright Soc. of the U.S.A. (209)

Pantos, George
Nat'l Ass'n of Graphic and Product Identification Manufacturers (357)

Pantuso, Peter J.
American Bus Ass'n (49)

Papa, Charles A.
Nat'l Multi Housing Council (417)

Papazian Ph.D., Dennis R.
Soc. of Armenian Studies (498)

Papilion, Andrea
Nat'l Contract Management Ass'n (392)

Papke, Brenda K.
American Academy of Forensic Sciences (22)

Papp, Sharon
American Foreign Service Ass'n (69)

Pappas CAE, Virginia M.
Soc. of Nuclear Medicine (504)

Paque CAE, Michel J.
Ground Water Protection Council (250)

Paradise, Connie
Nat'l Ass'n of Professional Insurance Agents (367)

Parcells, Brad
Manufacturers' Agents for Food Service Industry (323)

Parent, Neil
Nat'l Conference of Catechetical Leadership (390)

Parent, Roger H.
American Ass'n of Law Libraries (38)

Parham, Shannon
Ass'n of American Editorial Cartoonists (142)
Nat'l Cartoonists Soc. (385)

Parillo, Mark
World War Two Studies Ass'n (550)

Paris, Mary
Nat'l Soc. of Professional Engineers (430)

Parise, Becky
Nat'l Ass'n of Collegiate Directors of Athletics (348)

Parise, Brigette
Nat'l Ass'n of Television Program Executives (378)

Parisi, Michele E.
American Bankruptcy Institute (46)

Park, Judy
Nat'l Ass'n of Retired Federal Employees (370)

Parke, Beth
Soc. of Environmental Journalists (501)

Parker, Barbara
Risk and Insurance Management Soc. (476)

Parker, Bruce J.
Environmental Industry Ass'ns (231)

Parker, Cary
Nat'l Ass'n of Computerized Tax Processors (349)

Parker, David
Nat'l Home Furnishings Ass'n (409)

Parker CAE, David N.
American Gas Ass'n (70)

Parker, Erich
Aseptic Packaging Council (128)

Parker, Kelly
Young Presidents' Organization (551)

Parker CAE, Kerry G.
Medical Marketing Ass'n (326)

Parker, Laura
Ass'n of Surgical Technologists (166)

Parker, Randy
North American Agricultural Marketing Officials (440)

Parker, Stephen D.
Accrediting Council for Independent Colleges and Schools (11)

Parker, Suzanne
Internat'l Institute of Connector and Interconnection Technology (294)

Parker Ph.D., Sydney
American College of Chest Physicians (53)

Parkerson, Robert W.
Nat'l Crop Insurance Services **(398)**

Parkhurst, Kim
Nat'l Ass'n of Graphic and Product Identification Manufacturers **(357)**

Parkin, Scott L.
American Ass'n of Homes and Services for the Aging **(37)**

Parkinson, Dorothy
Institute of Diving **(266)**

Parkinson, Susan
America's Blood Centers **(19)**

Parks, Lisa K.
Soc. of Critical Care Medicine **(500)**

Parks-Davies, Bonnie
American Soc. of Indexers **(III)**

Parlette CAE, Carol Holland
American Soc. of Andrology **(106)**

Parmelee, Ken
Nat'l Rural Letter Carriers' Ass'n **(426)**

Parone, Jim
American Animal Hospital Ass'n **(28)**

Parone, Margaret J.
Satellite Broadcasting and Communications Ass'n **(479)**

Parra, Victor
United Motorcoach Ass'n **(531)**

Parramore Ed.D., CAE, Katherine
Nat'l Business Travel Ass'n **(384)**

Parris Ph.D., George
American Wood Preservers Institute **(123)**

Parrish, Craig
Cookie and Snack Bakers Ass'n **(208)**

Parrish, Pamela
Electronic Design Automation Consortium **(228)**

Parrish, Patty
Nat'l Needlework Ass'n **(418)**

Parrish, Robin
Internat'l Ass'n of Administrative Professionals **(275)**

Parrish, Rodney
Soc. of Environmental Toxicology and Chemistry **(501)**

Parrott, Beth
Web Offset Ass'n of Printing Industries of America **(542)**

Parrott, Betti
Non-Heatset Web Section **(439)**

Parry, Leo S.
Industrial Mathematics Soc. **(263)**

Parsons, Paul L.
Nat'l Ass'n of College and University Attorneys **(347)**

Parsons, Peggy
NACE Internat'l **(333)**

Parsons, Steve
Ass'n of Mental Health Librarians **(157)**

Partridge USA (Ret), Col. Charles
Nat'l Ass'n for Uniformed Services and Soc. of Military Widows **(342)**

Partridge, Lee
Nat'l Ass'n of Medicaid Directors **(362)**

Paschal, Jeanette D.
Nat'l Ass'n of Small Business Investment Companies **(373)**

Paschall, Joyce
Automatic Meter Reading Ass'n **(173)**
American Soc. of Tropical Medicine and Hygiene **(116)**

Paschen, Elise
Poetry Soc. of America **(459)**

Pashby, Michael
Magazine Publishers of America **(321)**

Passarelli, G. Domenic
Internat'l Ass'n of Tour Managers - North American Region **(282)**

Passek, Thomas S.
ASM Internat'l **(128)**

Passek, Tom
Soc. of Carbide and Tool Engineers **(499)**

Passiment EdM, Elissa
American Soc. for Clinical Laboratory Science **(101)**

Passons, Donna
Ass'n for Continuing Legal Education **(132)**

Pastor, Mark
Internat'l Juvenile Officers Ass'n **(295)**

Pataky, Judith
Nat'l Ass'n of College Stores **(348)**

Pateas, Joanne
Hellenic-American Chamber of Commerce **(253)**

Patek, Frank
Phi Alpha Delta **(456)**

Patella, Lawrence M.
Western Dredging Ass'n **(542)**

Paterkiewicz CAE, Robert J.
American Soc. of Home Inspectors **(III)**

Patierno, Louise
American Council on the Teaching of Foreign Languages **(62)**

Paton Ph.D., Garth
North American Soc. for Sport Management **(444)**

Patrick, Lauren L.
Wireless Communications Ass'n Internat'l **(545)**

Patrina Jr., Michael J.
Cosmetic, Toiletry and Fragrance Ass'n **(210)**

Patt, Raymond M.
Ass'n of Retail Marketing Services **(163)**

Patterson, Brad
Tennis Industry Ass'n **(521)**

Patterson, Judy
Vacuum Dealers Trade Ass'n **(538)**

Patterson, Judy Layne
American Gaming Ass'n **(70)**

Patterson, Mary Ann
American Horticultural Soc. **(74)**

Pattie, Kenton
Ass'n Chief Executive Council **(129)**
Nat'l Emergency Equipment Dealers Ass'n **(401)**
Nat'l Ass'n of Police Equipment Distributors **(365)**

Patton, Bernadette
Internat'l Ass'n for Human Resource Information Management **(274)**

Patton, Charlene
Home Baking Ass'n **(255)**

Patton CAE, M. Bernadette
World Airline Entertainment Ass'n **(549)**

Patton, Paula A.
Nat'l Ass'n for Law Placement **(340)**

Patton-Pace, Denise
Automobile Dealers Ass'n **(174)**

Patty, Birgit
American Ass'n of Textile Chemists and Colorists **(44)**

Patzer, Greg
Monument Builders of North America **(330)**

Paul, Andrew R.
Satellite Broadcasting and Communications Ass'n **(479)**

Paul, Deborah
Business Professionals of America **(185)**

Paul, Gene
Nat'l Farmers Organization **(402)**

Paul, Joel M.
Federal Administrative Law Judges Conference **(235)**

Paul, John
American Heart Ass'n **(72)**

Paul, Kenneth M.
Institute of Real Estate Management **(269)**

Paul, Mike
Nat'l Ass'n of Swine Records **(377)**

Paul, Nancy E.
Internat'l Cemetery and Funeral Ass'n **(285)**

Paul, Sandra K.
Book Industry Study Group **(181)**

Pavlik, Donald
Internat'l Military Community Executives Ass'n **(297)**

Pavlik, John M.
Academy of Motion Picture Arts and Sciences **(9)**

Pawlak, John
United States Trotting Ass'n **(535)**

Pawlucy, William D.
Receptive Services Ass'n **(472)**
Nat'l Ornament and Electric Lights Christmas Ass'n **(420)**
Specialty Sleep Ass'n **(514)**

Paxos, Steve
Nat'l Professional Soccer League **(423)**

Paxton CAE, James E.
Medical Group Management Ass'n **(326)**

Paymer, Lyn
Nat'l Ass'n of Gas Chlorinators **(356)**
Nat'l Plasterers Council **(422)**

Payne Jr., CFA, George
Ass'n for Investment Management and Research **(135)**

Payne, J. Michael
Truck Renting and Leasing Ass'n **(527)**

Payne, John R.
Audit Bureau of Circulations **(173)**

Payne, Jon
American Nuclear Soc. **(87)**

Payne, Kathryn Ratcliff
Soc. of Internat'l Business Fellows **(503)**

Payne, Mary S.
Truck Renting and Leasing Ass'n **(527)**

Payne, Michael L.
American Soc. of Hematology **(110)**
Internat'l Ass'n of Airport Duty Free Stores **(275)**

Payne, Priscilla
Institute of Certified Management Accountants **(266)**

Payne, Robert M.
Copper Development Ass'n **(209)**

Paz, Donna
Women's Nat'l Book Ass'n **(548)**

Peacock, Glenn L.
Internat'l Hearing Soc. **(293)**

Peake, Michele Nebel
SWANA - Solid Waste Ass'n of North America **(519)**

Peaks, Kimberly
Computing Research Ass'n **(203)**

Pearce, Jo Dorcas
Financial Markets Ass'n **(239)**

Pearce, Lisa
Executive Suite Ass'n **(233)**

Pearce, Sue
Soc. of Military Otolaryngologists - Head and Neck Surgeons **(504)**

Pearl, Marc A.
Information Technology Ass'n of America **(264)**

Pearson, Ed
Ass'n of Automotive Aftermarket Distributors **(144)**

Pearson Ph.D., James
SPIE-Internat'l Soc. for Optical Engineering **(514)**

Pearson, John
Christian Management Ass'n **(193)**

Pearson, Ken
American Soc. for Testing and Materials **(105)**

Pearson, Kymberle
Internat'l Entertainment Buyers Ass'n **(290)**

Pearson, Steve
Nat'l Ass'n of Farm Broadcasters **(354)**

Pearson Ed.D., Thomas
American Academy of Dermatology **(21)**

Pebley, Mary
American Business Women's Ass'n **(50)**

Pechilio, Sue
Ass'n for Advanced Life Underwriting **(129)**

Pecilunas, Rita Rubidge
Nat'l Propane Gas Ass'n **(423)**

Peck, Ernie
Council of Colleges of Arts and Sciences **(213)**

Peck, Joe
Consumer Electronics Manufacturers Ass'n **(207)**

Peck, Judith A.
Nat'l Wooden Pallet and Container Ass'n **(437)**

Peck, Norm
American Council on Exercise **(62)**

Peck, Rebecca
Independent Educational Consultants Ass'n **(260)**

Peck, Robert S.
Ass'n of Trial Lawyers of America **(168)**

Peck, Stanley B.
American Dental Hygienists' Ass'n **(64)**

Peckinpaugh, Martha
Nat'l Oil Recyclers Ass'n **(419)**

Pecoulas, Margo
American Academy of Periodontology **(25)**

Pedelty, M. Fran
American Soc. of Electroneurodiagnostic Technologists **(109)**

Pedersen, Wes
Public Affairs Council **(469)**

Pederson Ph.D., Jon E.
Ass'n for the Education of Teachers in Science **(139)**

Pedicone CPA, Francis J.
American Institute for CPCU - Insurance Institute of America **(75)**

Peebles, Robert
Nat'l Show Horse Registry **(428)**

Peeler, Alexandra
Catholic Charities USA **(188)**

Pees, James W.
American Academy of Sanitarians **(26)**

Peirick, Edward
Credit Union Executives Soc. **(218)**

Pelham, Peter
Ass'n of Boarding Schools, The **(145)**

Pellegrini, Ann M.
Commercial-Investment Real Estate Institute **(199)**

Pelletier, Stephen G.
Council of Independent Colleges **(214)**

Pelrine, Jack
Medical Records Institute **(326)**

Pelton, Vicky L.
American College of Veterinary Internal Medicine **(58)**

Pemberton, Carolyn
Soc. of Nuclear Medicine **(504)**

Pemberton, Phyllis
Nat'l Flute Ass'n **(405)**

Pembroke Callihan, Le'ann
American Ass'n of Professional Landmen **(41)**

Pence, Paige
Ass'n of American Veterinary Medical Colleges **(143)**

Pence, Randall
Nat'l Concrete Masonry Ass'n **(389)**

Pencil, Sarah
American Neurotology Soc. **(87)**

Pendleton, Andrea
Optical Soc. of America **(449)**
American Ass'n of Anatomists **(33)**

Pendola, Paul
American Urogynecologic Soc. **(121)**

Penhale, Laurel
American Advertising Federation **(27)**

Penn, Dave
American Public Power Ass'n **(96)**

Penn, Deborah
American Public Power Ass'n **(96)**

Penn, Kate
Soc. of American Florists **(497)**

Penna, Dick
Aluminum Extruders Council **(19)**

Penna Pharm.D., Richard P.
American Ass'n of Colleges of Pharmacy **(35)**

Pennacchio, April L.
Internat'l Digital Imaging Ass'n **(289)**

Penney Ph.D., David P.
Biological Stain Commission **(179)**

Pennington, Martha
Nat'l Ornamental and Miscellaneous Metals Ass'n **(420)**

Peno, Thomas
American Nat'l Metric Council **(86)**

Penoyer, Melanie
American Car Rental Ass'n **(50)**

Pentimonti, Gene
American Trucking Ass'ns **(121)**

Peoples, Deborah
American College Health Ass'n **(52)**

Peplow, Gary M.
Ass'n of Defense Trial Attorneys **(149)**

Pepper, Eric
SPIE-Internat'l Soc. for Optical Engineering **(514)**

Pepper, Vincent
Nat'l Ass'n of Media Brokers **(362)**

Peranich, Tracy
Public Housing Authorities Directors Ass'n **(469)**

Perdue, David
Nat'l Federation of Independent Business **(403)**

Perdue, Jeffery
Nat'l Ass'n of College Auxiliary Services **(348)**

Perdue, Susan
Ass'n for Documentary Editing **(132)**

Perez, Sandra M.
Ass'n of Hispanic Arts **(153)**

Perez, Dr. Hely M.
Black Theatre Network **(180)**

Perham, Charlotte
Plumbing-Heating-Cooling Contractors - Nat'l Ass'n **(459)**

Perkins, Linda D.
Nat'l Ass'n for Court Management **(338)**

Perl, Diana
Soc. of American Foresters **(497)**

Perleman M.D., Robert
American Academy of Pediatrics **(25)**

Perlin, Jeremy
American Prepaid Legal Services Institute **(93)**

Perlman, Jeffrey
American Advertising Federation **(27)**

Perlman, Victor
American Soc. of Media Photographers **(112)**

Perner, Fred
Ass'n of Operating Room Nurses **(159)**

Perone, Marie
Nat'l Student Osteopathic Medical Ass'n **(432)**

Perrell, Beverly S.
American Soc. of Professional Estimators **(115)**

Perri, Pamela A.
Nat'l Ass'n of Fund Raising Ticket Manufacturers **(356)**

Perriguey, Charles D.
Airborne Law Enforcement Ass'n **(16)**

Perrin, Barbara
Brotherhood of Traveling Jewelers **(183)**

Perrin, Cidette
Nat'l Ass'n of Psychiatric Health Systems **(367)**

Perrin CAE, Joan
American Psychological Ass'n **(94)**

Perrin, Nancy
American College of Health Care Administrators **(54)**

Perry, Clyde
Internat'l Soc. of Parametric Analysts **(306)**

Perry, Kimberly A.
Nat'l Postsecondary Agriculture Student Organization **(423)**

Perry, Lee
Floatation Tank Ass'n **(240)**

Perry, Nancy
American School Counselor Ass'n **(99)**

Perry CAE, Sharon
American Soc. of Echocardiography **(109)**

Perry, Susan E.
Internat'l Sleep Products Ass'n **(302)**

Perry, William
Internat'l Union of Industrial Service Transport Health Employees **(310)**

Persechino, Tom
American Quarter Horse Ass'n **(96)**

Persinger, Charles
Soil and Water Conservation Soc. **(510)**

Persinger, Del
Pharmaceutical Research and Manufacturers of America **(456)**

Persinger, Gary S.
Nat'l Pharmaceutical Council **(422)**

Person, Virginia
Nat'l Ass'n of State Alcohol and Drug Abuse Directors **(373)**

Perusek, Anne
Soc. of Women Engineers **(509)**

Pesce CAE, Irene K.
Nat'l Catholic Cemetery Conference **(385)**

Pesci, Janine
Building Owners and Managers Ass'n Internat'l **(183)**

Pesta, Michael
Aerobics and Fitness Ass'n of America **(13)**

Peterman, Tara A.
Ass'n of Clinical Research Professionals **(147)**

Peters, Eugene
Electric Power Supply Ass'n **(227)**

Peters, Helen
Insurance Conference Planners Ass'n **(270)**

Peters, Kathleen C.
American Law Institute **(81)**

Peters, Louis H.
Polyurethane Foam Ass'n **(460)**

Peters CAE, Terry L.
Nat'l Ass'n of Dental Laboratories **(352)**
Nat'l Coffee Service Ass'n **(387)**

Peters, Vickie
American Heart Ass'n **(72)**

Petersen, John W.
Hydraulic Tool Manufacturers Ass'n **(257)**

Petersen, Pat
Nat'l Flight Paramedics Ass'n **(405)**

Petersen, Robert R.
Transporting Elevator and Grain Merchants Ass'n **(526)**
Nat'l Grain Trade Council **(407)**

Peterson, Betsy
Marketing Research Ass'n **(324)**

Peterson CAE, C. Curtis
American Fiberboard Ass'n **(68)**
American Hardboard Ass'n **(72)**

Peterson, Faye
American Correctional Ass'n **(60)**

Peterson, Gary
American Polarity Therapy Ass'n **(93)**

Peterson, Glenn
Nat'l League for Nursing **(414)**

Peterson, Julie
Coalition for Christian Colleges and Universities **(195)**

Peterson, Karen
Fragrance Foundation **(243)**

Peterson, Lynn
American Psychological Ass'n - Division of Clinical Psychology **(95)**

Peterson, Maggie
Soc. of Biological Psychiatry **(498)**

Peterson, Marilyn B.
Internat'l Ass'n of Law Enforcement Intelligence Analysts **(280)**

Peterson, Maya
American Soc. of Farm Managers and Rural Appraisers **(109)**

Peterson, R. Max
Internat'l Ass'n of Fish and Wildlife Agencies **(279)**

Peterson, Richard N.
American Academy of Orthopaedic Surgeons **(24)**

Peterson, Rick
Soc. for American Archaeology **(485)**

Peterson, Teresa
Percussive Arts Soc. **(454)**

Peterson, William
Ass'n of Presbyterian Colleges and Universities **(160)**

Petherick, Glenn
Nat'l Housing and Rehabilitation Ass'n **(409)**

Petit, Michael
Child Welfare League of America **(192)**

Petko, Mike
Community College Business Officers **(201)**

Petricca CPE, Teresa E.
American Electrology Ass'n **(65)**

Petrick, Camille
American Orthopaedic Soc. for Sports Medicine **(88)**

Petrillo, Scott
American Gem and Mineral Suppliers Ass'n **(70)**

Petro CAE, Jeffrey J.
Technical Ass'n of the Pulp and Paper Industry **(520)**

Petronio, Alan
Ass'n of Local Television Stations **(156)**

Petroshus, Lesley
Tag and Label Manufacturers Institute **(520)**

Petroske, Barbara
Sommelier Soc. of America **(510)**

Petrovic CAE, Nikolaj M.
American Dental Trade Ass'n **(64)**

Petrucelli, Elaine
Ass'n for the Advancement of Automotive Medicine **(138)**

Petruso, Rosemary
Water Environment Federation **(541)**

Petry Ph.D., Edward
Ethics Officer Ass'n **(233)**

Petta, Ralph A.
Equipment Leasing Ass'n of America **(232)**

Pettersen, Alicia
Customer Relations Institute **(219)**

Petterson, Paul
Nat'l Ass'n of Criminal Defense Lawyers **(352)**

Pettit, Daille G.
American Hotel and Motel Ass'n **(74)**

Pettit, Dawn
Cooperative Education Ass'n **(209)**

Petty, Susan
American Medical Directors Ass'n **(83)**

Peyton, James A.
Photographic and Imaging Manufacturers Ass'n **(457)**

Pfaff, Rick
American Institute of Food Distribution **(77)**

Pfahl, Michael
Nat'l Alliance for Youth Sports **(336)**

Pfeffer RN, Linda D.
Aerobics and Fitness Ass'n of America **(13)**

Pfeiffer Ph.D., Stephen M.
Ass'n for the Advancement of Psychology **(138)**

Pferchy, Susan
Nat'l Glass Ass'n **(407)**

Pfister, Steve
Nat'l Retail Federation **(425)**

Pflaum, William C.
World Packaging Organisation **(550)**
Contract Packagers Ass'n **(208)**
Package Design Council Int'l **(452)**
Institute of Packaging Professionals **(268)**

Phalen, Tonda
American Horticultural Soc. **(74)**

Pham, Kim
American Consulting Engineers Council **(60)**

Phaneuf, Joseph
Nat'l Council of Examiners for Engineering and Surveying **(394)**

Phaneuf, Sarah
Construction Specifications Institute **(207)**

Phelleps, Moya
Coal Exporters Ass'n of the United States **(195)**

Phelps, David
American Institute for Internat'l Steel **(76)**

Phelps, Laura
American Mushroom Institute **(86)**

Phelps, Laura L.
American Ass'n of Crop Insurers **(35)**

Phelus, Dean
American Ass'n of Museums **(39)**

Phiel, Kay M.
U.S.A. Poultry and Egg Export Council **(528)**

Philbin (RET.), Maj.Gen. Edward J.
Nat'l Guard Ass'n of the U.S. **(408)**

Philibin, Tamara
American Chamber of Commerce Executives **(51)**

Phillips DBA, CCM, Aaron L.
Treasury Management Ass'n **(526)**

Phillips, Bill
Internat'l Ass'n of Home Safety and Security Professionals **(280)**

Phillips Ph.D., Carol B.
Council for Early Childhood Professional Recognition **(211)**

Phillips Jr., David K.
Mortgage Bankers Ass'n of America **(330)**

Phillips, Hank
Nat'l Tour Ass'n **(434)**

Phillips, John
Nat'l Ass'n of Life Underwriters **(361)**

Phillips, John J.
Machine Printers and Engravers Ass'n of the United States **(321)**

Phillips M.D., Jordan M.
American Ass'n of Gynecological Laparoscopists **(37)**

Phillips, Jose
Forest Products Safety Conference **(242)**

Phillips, Julie
Voluntary Protection Programs Participants Ass'n (540)

Phillips, Karen
Ass'n of American Railroads (143)

Phillips, Kathy
Robert Morris Associates, the Ass'n of Lending and Credit Risk Professionals (476)

Phillips, Larisa K.
Appraisal Institute (126)

Phillips, Marilyn
American Ostrich Ass'n (90)

Phillips, Michael D.
Nat'l Ass'n for Humanities Education (339)

Phillips, Pamela
American Chiropractic Ass'n (51)

Phillips, Richard G.
Major League Umpires Ass'n (322)

Phillips MD, Ph.D., Robert T.M.
American Psychiatric Ass'n (94)

Phillips, Ron
Fertilizer Institute (238)

Phillips, Susan
Internat'l Labor Communications Ass'n (295)

Piatt, Helen J.
Parcel Shippers Ass'n (453)

Pichon, Sharon R.
American Ass'n of Pharmaceutical Scientists (40)

Picillo, Sara
Ass'n of Performing Arts Presenters (160)

Pickard, Elizabeth
Ass'n of Performing Arts Presenters (160)

Pickard, Geoffrey L.
American Institute of Certified Public Accountants (76)

Pickel, Robert G.
Internat'l Swaps and Derivatives Ass'n (308)

Pickett, Jenny
Nat'l Agri-Marketing Ass'n (335)

Pickett, Julie
American Osteopathic College of Rehabilitation Medicine (89)

Pickett, Peggy J.
American Ass'n of Textile Chemists and Colorists (44)

Pickett, W.D.
Brotherhood of Railroad Signalmen (183)

Piepgras, David
Soc. of Neurological Surgeons (504)

Pier, Gwen
Nat'l Sculpture Soc. (427)

Pierard, R.V.
Conference on Faith and History (205)

Pierce, Carol
Nat'l Federation of Press Women (404)

Pierce, Cathy
Internat'l Development Research Council (288)

Pierce, Darlene
American Ass'n of School Administrators (42)

Pierce, David
American Ass'n of Community Colleges (35)

Pierce, James F.
Professional Engineers in Private Practice (465)

Pierce, Janice L.
Nat'l Ass'n of College Stores (348)

Pierce, John L.
Ass'n of Iron and Steel Engineers (155)

Pierce, Lawrence D.
Armed Forces Communications and Electronics Ass'n (127)

Pierce, Lisa
SnowSports Industries America (484)

Pierpoint, Paul
Chemical Specialties Manufacturers Ass'n (191)

Pierson, Donna
Home Sewing Ass'n (256)

Pierson, Pamela
Institute of Food Technologists (267)

Pietrangelo Ph.D., Renee
GAMA Internat'l (245)

Pietrzak, Ron
Wallcoverings Ass'n (540)
Ass'n of Steel Distributors (166)

Pietrzak, Ronald
American Ladder Institute (80)

Pifel, Bruce A.
Nat'l Officers Ass'n (419)

Pifer, Tippi
Nat'l Reading Conference (424)

Pigg, Bob J.
Asbestos Information Ass'n/North America (128)
Asbestos Cement Product Producers Ass'n (128)

Piggott, William
Dairy Management (219)

Pignotti, Dennis
American Soc. of Naval Engineers (113)

Pike, Mary L.
Nat'l Ass'n of Housing and Redevelopment Officials (358)

Pike, Wally
Nat'l Ass'n of Air Traffic Specialists (343)

Pilger, Phyllis
Nat'l Ass'n of Professional Organizers (367)

Pillitteri, Candi
Textile Rental Services Ass'n of America (522)

Pillsworth, Betty Ann
Commercial Finance Ass'n (199)

Pimpinella, Lisa
Electrical Overstress/Electrostatic Discharge Ass'n (227)

Pincon, Deborah
Information Systems Audit and Control Ass'n (264)

Pincus, Arthur
Nat'l Hockey League (409)

Pincus, Harold A.
American Psychiatric Ass'n (94)

Pincus, Shirley
Inter-Industry Conference on Auto Collision Repair (271)

Pinder, Joan
Internat'l Disk Drive Equipment and Materials Ass'n (289)

Pinderhughes, Robert
Nat'l Marrow Donor Program (416)

Pines, Patricia L.
American Meat Institute (83)

Pinkham, Douglas G.
Public Affairs Council (469)

Pinnock, Sharon
American Federation of Government Employees (67)

Pinsky, Mark
Nat'l Community Capital Ass'n (388)

Pinson, Kelly
Asphalt Institute (128)

Pintarelli, Chester
Nat'l Ass'n of County Health Facility Administrators (351)

Pinto, John E.
Nat'l Ass'n of Securities Dealers (372)

Pinzon, Beverly
Human Resource Planning Soc. (237)

Piper, Morley
Newspaper Ass'n Managers (439)

Pipers D.V.M., Frank
Academy of Veterinary Cardiology (10)

Pipkin, Ronald M.
Law and Society Ass'n (318)

Pisani, Donald
American Soc. for Environmental History (102)

Pisano, Susan
American Ass'n of Health Plans (37)

Pistona, George
Coin Laundry Ass'n (196)

Pitkin, William
Nat'l Insulation Ass'n (412)

Pitlick Ph.D., Frances A.
Universities Associated for Research and Education in Pathology (536)
Ass'n for Molecular Pathology (136)
American Soc. for Investigative Pathology (103)
Ass'n of Pathology Chairs (159)

Pitman, Angelia
Soc. for Reproductive Endocrinologists and Infertility (493)

Pitner, Les
Union of American Hebrew Congregations (529)

Pitt, Stephen R.
Automobile Dealers Ass'n (174)

Pittenger, Michele Marini
Luggage and Leather Goods Manufacturers of America (321)

Pittler, Brenda
Institute for Professionals in Taxation (265)

Pittman, Lyn
Soc. for Ethnomusicology (488)

Pitzer, Rob
Internat'l Bridge, Tunnel and Turnpike Ass'n (284)

Pizzigati, Karabelle
Child Welfare League of America (192)

Place STD, Rev. Michael D.
Catholic Health Ass'n of the United States (188)

Placek, Tom
Automotive Maintenance and Repair Ass'n (174)

Plain, John F.
Ass'n of Applied Insect Ecologists (143)

Plamondon, Ron
Assisted Living Federation of America (170)

Plank, Rebecca D.
Nat'l Mobility Equipment Dealers Ass'n (417)

Planner, Kate
Nat'l Academy of Arbitrators (333)

Plasker, Jim
American Soc. for Photogrammetry and Remote Sensing (104)

Platt, Judith
Ass'n of American Publishers (143)

Platt, Roger
Nat'l Realty Committee (424)

Plaut, Peg
Soc. for Foodservice Management (488)

Plavin, David Z.
Airports Council Internat'l/North America (17)

Plawin, Paul
American Vocational Ass'n (122)

Playford, Thomas C.
IBFI, The Internat'l Ass'n for Document and Information Management Solutions (257)

Pleasants, Tammy
Nat'l Ass'n of Childbearing Centers (347)

Plescia, Anthony
Institute of Management Accountants (268)

Plishker, R. Alan
Internat'l Test and Evaluation Ass'n (308)

Plona, Katie
Equipment Leasing Ass'n of America (232)

Plotkin, Martha
Police Executive Research Forum (459)

Plott CAE, Curtis E.
American Soc. for Training and Development (106)

Plowden, Carrie
Anxiety Disorders Ass'n of America (125)

Plummer Ph.D., Stuart
Ass'n for Clinical Pastoral Education (131)

Pluto, Pat
Internat'l Communications Industries Ass'n (286)

Pochelski, Louise A.
Council of Logistics Management (215)

Pocknall Ph.D., David T.
American Ass'n of Stratigraphic Palynologists (43)

Podhasky, Paula
Tributyl Phosphate Task Force (526)

Podos M.D., Steven
Ass'n of University Professors of Ophthalmology (168)

Poe, Michelle
Ass'n for Quality and Participation (137)

Pogrund, Sherman
Nat'l Ass'n of the Remodeling Industry (370)

Pohlman, Jeff
Automotive Oil Change Ass'n (175)

Pohlman, Lori B.
Nat'l Frozen Food Ass'n (406)

Pohlmann, Susan
Internat'l Security Management Ass'n (302)

Poindexter, Douglas L.
World Wide Pet Supply Ass'n (550)

Poisson, David E.
Tire Ass'n of North America (523)
Information Technology Resellers Ass'n (264)

Polachek, Jason
Nat'l Ass'n of Dental Laboratories (352)

Polhemus, Craig
American Accounting Ass'n (27)

Polhill, Paige
American Soc. for Engineering Education (102)

Polich, Gerald
Intercollegiate Men's Choruses, an Internat'l Ass'n of Male Choruses (271)

Polich, Joe
Production Engine Remanufacturers Ass'n (463)

Polk, Maria
American Sightseeing Internat'l (100)

Pollack, Anne S.
American Medallic Sculpture Ass'n (83)

Pollack, Bry
American Ass'n for Higher Education (31)

Pollard, Alfred
Bankers Roundtable, The (176)

Pollard, Barbara
Nat'l Academy Museum and School Fine Arts (333)

Pollard, Doris
Nat'l Staff Development and Training Ass'n (431)

Pollard, Margie
Thoroughbred Racing Ass'ns of North America (523)

Polley IV, James D.
Nat'l District Attorneys Ass'n (399)

Pollich, Lisa
American Ass'n of Spinal Cord Injury Nurses (42)

Pollock, Wendy
Ass'n of Science-Technology Centers (164)

Pollow, Mimi
Teachers of English to Speakers of Other Languages (520)

Polly, Kris D.
Nat'l Water Resources Ass'n (435)

Polovy, Carolyn
Nat'l Ass'n of Social Workers (373)

Polsinelli D.O., Jerry
American College of Osteopathic Obstetricians and Gynecologists (56)

Polski, Joseph P.
Internat'l Ass'n for Identification (274)
Polvinale, Bonnie
American Physical Therapy Ass'n (92)
Pomerantz CAE, Paul
Soc. of Cardiovascular and Interventional Radiology (499)
Pond, Debra
Ass'n of State Floodplain Managers (166)
Pondel, Ron
Locomotive Maintenance Officers' Ass'n (320)
Ponder Ph.D., Henry
Nat'l Ass'n for Equal Opportunity in Higher Education (339)
Pooler, Susanne J.
Nat'l Ass'n of Government Employees (356)
Pooley, June
American College of Veterinary Internal Medicine (58)
Pope, Albert E.
United Egg Producers (530)
United Egg Ass'n (530)
Pope, Don
Nat'l Institute of Steel Detailing (412)
Pope, Jack E.
Physician Insurers Ass'n of America (458)
Popham, James J.
Ass'n of Local Television Stations (156)
Popkin, Karol J.
American Public Transit Ass'n (96)
Poplin, Heidi
Internat'l Ass'n of Diecutting and Diemaking (278)
Popovich, Lori
Ass'n of Celebrity Personal Assistants (146)
Popp, Janet
Ass'n of Rotational Molders (164)
Poray CAE, John L.
Soc. of Broadcast Engineers (499)
Porinchak, Laura
Ass'n of the Wall and Ceiling Industries-Internat'l (167)
Porr, Susannah F.
Nat'l Ass'n of Steel Pipe Distributors (377)
Portantiere, Diane
Insurance Information Institute (270)
Porte, Phillip
Nat'l Ass'n for Medical Direction of Respiratory Care (340)
Porteous, Cindy
Nat'l Ass'n of Governors' Councils on Physical Fitness and Sports (357)
Porter, Cynthia S.
American Soc. of Pediatric Hematology/Oncology (114)
Porter, Fatima
American Academy of Facial Plastic and Reconstructive Surgery (22)
Porter, Faye
Counselors of Real Estate (217)
Portmann, Marcel
Internat'l Franchise Ass'n (292)
Porzio, Steve
American Statistical Ass'n (118)
Posner, Katherine B.
Internat'l Aviation Women Ass'n (283)
Posner, Marc
Nat'l Ass'n for Campus Activities (338)
Posselt, Jo Ellyn
Academy of General Dentistry (8)
Possick, Rabbi A. Moshe
Nat'l Conference of Yeshiva Principals (391)
Potter, Carol
Professional Ass'n of Health Care Office Managers (464)
Potter, Chuck
American Animal Hospital Ass'n (28)
Potter, James G.
American College of Radiology (57)
Potter, Kathryn
American Hotel and Motel Ass'n (74)
Potter, Kelly
Chemical Producers and Distributors Ass'n (191)
Potter, Mary
American Soc. for Nondestructive Testing (104)
Potter, William A.
Automotive Service Industry Ass'n (175)
Poulos, David
Nat'l Grain and Feed Ass'n (407)
Pound, William T.
Nat'l Conference of State Legislatures (391)
Povich, Harris
OPERA America (448)
Powell, Beth
American Mental Health Counselors Ass'n (84)
Powell, Caletha M.
African American Travel and Tourism Ass'n (14)
Powell, Diane
American Medical Technologists (84)

Powell, Dianne
Ice Skating Institute (258)
Powell, Earl N.
Design Management Institute (222)
Powell, Elaine S.
Insurance Accounting and Systems Ass'n (270)
Powell, Gregg
Nat'l Head Start Ass'n (408)
Powell, Harvey J.
Materials and Methods Standards Ass'n (325)
Powell, Joan
Environmental Assessment Ass'n (231)
Nat'l Ass'n of Real Estate Appraisers (368)
Powell, Joan T.
Professional Women's Appraisal Ass'n (468)
Powell, John T.
American Peanut Shellers Ass'n (91)
Powell, Lynn S.
Physician Insurers Ass'n of America (458)
Powell, Mark
Forest Farm and Community Tree Network (242)
Powell, Staccato
Nat'l Council of the Churches of Christ in the U.S.A. (397)
Powell, Thomas
American Meat Science Ass'n (83)
Powers CAE, Celeste
Electrical-Electronics Materials Distributors Ass'n (227)
Nat'l Ass'n of Sign Supply Distributors (373)
Powers, Celeste
Fire Suppression Systems Ass'n (240)
Powers, Dr. James
Biological Stain Commission (179)
Powers, Joan R.
Scientific Equipment and Furniture Ass'n (480)
Powers, Kate
Nat'l Ski Areas Ass'n (428)
Prager Ph.D., Martin
Welding Research Council (542)
Materials Properties Council (325)
Prahl, Alan S.
Nat'l Ass'n of Tax Practitioners (377)
Prairie, Pamela
Institute of Public Utilities (268)
Pramstaller CFC,CAE, Michael E.
Document Management Industries Ass'n (224)
Prange, Heidi
Soc. of Independent Gasoline Marketers of America (502)
Prass, Paul F.
Fluid Power Soc. (241)
Prast CAE, LLIF, John J.
Million Dollar Round Table (328)
Prather, Ashley
Art Libraries Soc./North America (127)
Prats CAE, Lisa M.
Building Owners and Managers Ass'n Internat'l (183)
Pratt, Andy
Mineralogical Soc. of America (329)
Pratt, Cynthia
American Consulting Engineers Council (60)
Pratt Ph. D., Donald L.
School Science and Mathematics Ass'n (479)
Pratt, James
American Forensic Ass'n (69)
Pratt, Stuart
Associated Credit Bureaus (171)
Prazmark, Julie
American Trucking Ass'ns (121)
Precourt CAE, Ronald D.
Nat'l Telephone Cooperative Ass'n (433)
Prendergast, James W.
Graphic Arts Professionals (249)
Ass'n of Direct Marketing Agencies (149)
Nat'l Ass'n of Publishers' Representatives (368)
Prenovost, Gary
Professional Ass'n of Diving Instructors (464)
Prentice, Kim
Flavor and Extract Manufacturers Ass'n of the United States (240)
Pressman CAE, Florence
Jewish Funeral Directors of America (314)
Prest, Arthur
Cellular Telecommunications Industry Ass'n (189)
Preston, Daniel S.
Saddle, Harness, and Allied Trade Ass'n (478)
Preston, Lisa M.
American Soc. for Horticultural Science (103)
Preston, Robin R.
American School Food Service Ass'n (99)
Pretanik, Stephen
Nat'l Broiler Council (384)
Preus, Anthony
Soc. for Ancient Greek Philosophy (485)

Preuss, Charles Anthony
Insurance Institute for Highway Safety (270)
Preuss, Del R.
Ornamental Concrete Producers Ass'n (451)
Prevatte, Virginia
Nat'l Ass'n of Hosiery Manufacturers (358)
Prewitt, Terry
Semiotic Soc. of America (481)
Prey D.D.S., John H.
Delta Sigma Delta (221)
Price, Gary W.
American College of Radiology (57)
Price, Jeff
Nat'l Ass'n of Disability Examiners (353)
Price, Jennifer
American Academy of Estate Planning Attorneys (22)
Price, Jenny
Internat'l Parking Institute (299)
Price, Jim
Ass'n of Conservation Engineers (148)
Price, Kevin
American Supply Ass'n (119)
Price, Lari
Internat'l Technology Education Ass'n (308)
Price, Larry
Bank Marketing Ass'n (176)
Price, Michael
Project Management Institute (468)
Price CME, Michael F.
Sales and Marketing Executives Internat'l (478)
Price, Pamella
Ass'n of Schools of Journalism and Mass Communication (164)
Price CAE, Randall
Ass'n of Occupational Health Professionals (in Healthcare) (158)
Price CAE, Randall C.
Ass'n of Nurses in AIDS Care (158)
Nat'l Organization for Associate Degree Nursing (419)
Environmental Mutagen Soc. (232)
Price, Thomas J.
American Ass'n of Engineering Societies (36)
Prickett, Stacy
Dance Critics Ass'n (220)
Priddy, Dana
American Public Works Ass'n (96)
Priester, Rosalyn Averette
American Dental Hygienists' Ass'n (64)
Priestly, Tom M.S.
Soc. for Slovene Studies (493)
Prillaman, Hunter
Nat'l Lime Ass'n (415)
Prince, Paul M.
Nat'l Sporting Goods Ass'n (431)
Prindiville, Sheila M.
Nat'l Solid Wastes Management Ass'n (431)
Prink, Harold
Healthcare Financial Management Ass'n (252)
Prisak, Sandy
American Jail Ass'n (79)
Pritchett, Bill
Service Employees Internat'l Union (482)
Pritz, Brenda
Data Interchange Standards Ass'n (220)
Procsal Ph.D., Dana
College of American Pathologists (197)
Proctor CMP, Karen A.
American Ass'n of Advertising Agencies (32)
Proctor Ph.D., Kurt A.
Nat'l Ass'n of Chain Drug Stores (346)
Proctor Jr., Stuart E.
Nat'l Turkey Federation (435)
Prokop, John
Independent Liquid Terminals Ass'n (261)
Proost, Jay
American Soc. of Agricultural Appraisers (106)
Proscia, Michael
Internat'l Alliance of Theatrical Stage Employees and Moving Picture Technicians of the U.S. and Canada (273)
Prosser, David
American Concrete Pressure Pipe Ass'n (59)
Prosser, Norville
American Sport Fishing Ass'n (118)
Prosser, Paige
Nat'l Pawnbrokers Ass'n (421)
Proteau, Gregory
Nat'l Marine Bankers Ass'n (416)
Protzel, Janet
Internat'l Credit Ass'n (288)
Proven, Donn R.
Automotive Booster Clubs Internat'l (174)
Equipment and Tool Institute (232)

Prue, Penny L.
American Health Care Ass'n (72)

Prueser, Bill
Nat'l Fluid Power Ass'n (405)

Pruitt, Christine P.
American Chemical Soc. (51)

Prusik, Gregory C.
Nat'l Futures Ass'n (406)

Pruteanu, Laura
Alliance for Nonprofit Management (17)

Pruter, Walter F.
Internat'l Institute for Lath and Plaster (294)

Przybyszeski, Victoria
American Soc. of Dermatopathology (109)

Psidsikas, Thomas
American Soc. of Law, Medicine and Ethics (112)

Pslug Ph.D., Gerald R.
Soap and Detergent Ass'n (484)

Puente, Celso
Air Conditioning Contractors of America (15)

Puetz Ph.D., RN, Belinda E.
Respiratory Nursing Soc. (475)
Nat'l Gerontological Nursing Ass'n (407)
American Soc. of Pain Management Nurses (113)
American Ass'n of Nurse Attorneys (39)
Ass'n of Community Health Nursing Educators (148)
Home Healthcare Nurses Ass'n (255)
Internat'l Soc. of Psychiatric Consultation Liaison
    Nurses (306)
Soc. for Education and Research in Psychiatric Mental Health
    Nursing (487)
Nat'l Nursing Staff Development Organization (418)
Soc. for Vascular Nursing (496)

Pugh, William W.
Nat'l Motor Freight Traffic Ass'n (417)

Pugliese, Erica
Construction Financial Management Ass'n (206)

Pugliese, Lola
NCCLS (438)

Pullen, Rick
Nat'l Ass'n of Insurance Brokers (360)

Pulley, William
Internat'l Drycleaners Congress (289)

Pulliam, Dean W.
United Methodist Ass'n of Health and Welfare Ministries (531)

Pulliam, Mel
American Football Coaches Ass'n (69)

Pung, Roy S.
Ass'n of Professional Color Imagers (161)
Photo Marketing Ass'n-Internat'l (457)

Puntney, Linda S.
Journalism Education Ass'n (315)

Purcell, Bernardine
Nat'l Ass'n of Electrical Distributors (353)

Purcell, Donald E.
Portable Power Equipment Manufacturers Ass'n (460)

Purcell, Gerard W.
Nat'l Conference of Personal Managers (390)

Purcell CMP, Tracy
Nat'l Ass'n of the Remodeling Industry (378)

Purdun, Candace
Nat'l Contact Lens Examiners (392)

Purdy, Ralph M.
United Federation of Police Officers (530)

Purdy M.D., Robert
American Academy of Podiatric Practice Management (25)

Purr, Ann
LOMA (321)

Purser, Craig
Nat'l Beer Wholesalers Ass'n (382)

Purvin Jr., Robert L.
American Ass'n of Franchisees and Dealers (37)

Pusey, Leigh Ann
American Insurance Ass'n (79)

Putala, Christopher
Cellular Telecommunications Industry Ass'n (189)

Putens, Kim C.
Nat'l Ass'n of State Departments of Agriculture (374)

Puthuff, Ed
Professional Sales Ass'n (467)

Putman, Lewayne
Nat'l Athletic Trainers' Ass'n (381)

Putnam, Rob
Internat'l Lead Zinc Research Organization (295)

Putnam, Roger
Non Commissioned Officers Ass'n of the U.S.A. (439)

Pye, Debbie
American Ass'n of Owners and Breeders of Peruvian Paso
    Horses (40)

Pyeatt, Dale M.
Nat'l Guard Executive Directors Ass'n (408)

Pyle, Nicholas A.
Nat'l Grape Growers Cooperative (407)

Pyle, Robert N.
Independent Bakers Ass'n (259)

Pyles, Cindy
Internat'l Publishing Management Ass'n (300)

Pyzik, Dr. Lawrence
Council on Diagnostic Imaging to the A.C.A. (216)

Quackenbush, David J.
American Institute of Aeronautics and Astronautics (76)

Quackenbush, Margery
Nat'l Ass'n for the Advancement of Psychoanalysis (341)

Qualey, Sondra
Air Conditioning Contractors of America (15)

Quarles, Diane
Nat'l Council of Examiners for Engineering and
    Surveying (394)

Quarles, Susan D.
American Immigration Lawyers Ass'n (74)

Queen, Carolyn
Computer and Communications Industry Ass'n (202)

Queen, Pam
Internat'l Professional Rodeo Ass'n (300)

Quest, Judith
Clowns of America, Internat'l (195)

Quick, Bryce
American Nursery and Landscape Ass'n (87)

Quigley, Elizabeth
Alexander Graham Bell Ass'n for the Deaf (17)

Quincey, Pam
Internat'l Ass'n of Personnel in Employment Security (281)

Quinlan, Liz W.
Ass'n of Junior Leagues Internat'l (155)

Quinlan, Patricia F.
Produce Marketing Ass'n (463)

Quinlan, Terence A.
IS Financial Management Ass'n (313)

Quinley, John
College and University Personnel Ass'n (197)

Quinn, Charles
Nat'l Ass'n of Black Accountants (344)

Quinn, Christine
Veterinary Hospital Managers Ass'n (539)

Quinn Jr., Harold P.
Nat'l Mining Ass'n (417)

Quinn, Pamela
American School Health Ass'n (99)

Quinn, Sheila
American Ass'n of Naturopathic Physicians (39)

Quinn, Susan McAllister
American College of Physician Executives (57)

Quinn, Warren
American Nursery and Landscape Ass'n - Landscape
    Division (87)

Quinn, Warren A.
American Nursery and Landscape Ass'n (87)

Quinn, William H.
Nat'l Postal Mail Handlers Union (423)

Quint, Paula
Children's Book Council (192)

Quirk Ph.D., Daniel A.
Nat'l Ass'n of State Units on Aging (376)

Quirk, John
Amerifax Cattle Ass'n (124)

Raabe, Carol
Residential Sales Council (475)

Rabatin, Joanne
Grain Elevator and Processing Soc. (249)

Rabel PhD, FLMI, William H.
LOMA (321)

Raber, Roger
America's Community Bankers (20)

Raboud, Diane
Internat'l Ticketing Ass'n (308)

Rachlin, Joan
Applied Research Ethics Nat'l Ass'n (126)

Rachlin, Joe
American Institute of Fishery Research Biologists (77)

Racicot, Linda
Dairy Management (219)

Racine, Kathleen
Radio Control Hobby Trade Ass'n (471)

Rackstraw, Kevin
American Wind Energy Ass'n (123)

Raczynski, Donna L.
Nat'l Ass'n for College Admission Counseling (338)

Raddock, Steve
Cabletelevision Advertising Bureau (185)

Rademacher, John J.
American Farm Bureau Federation (66)

Rader, Jack S.
Financial Management Ass'n (239)

Rae, Linda S.
Institute of Internat'l Container Lessors (267)

Raevis, Thomas
Ass'n of Government Accountants (152)

Rafey, Joy
Nat'l Council for Resource Development (393)

Raffel CAE, Louis B.
American Egg Board (65)

Ragland, Linda
United States Animal Health Ass'n (532)

Raguse, Tom
Ass'n of Visual Merchandise Representatives (169)

Rahrig, Philip G.
American Galvanizers Ass'n (70)

Raiman, Gail A.
American Textile Manufacturers Institute (119)

Rainey, Terence J.
Internat'l Teleproduction Soc. (308)

Rainger, Ronald
History of Earth Sciences Soc. (254)

Rains Jr., Alan T.
Future Homemakers of America (245)

Rajsky, Greg
Aluminum Extruders Council (19)

Rakestraw, Kathleen M.
Software Publishers Ass'n (509)

Rakowski, Veronica
Master Brewers Ass'n of the Americas (324)

Raley, Gordon A.
Nat'l Assembly of Nat'l Voluntary Health and Social Welfare
    Organizations (381)

Ralls D.D.S., Stephen A.
American College of Dentists (54)

Ralls, Steve
American Horse Council (74)

Ramer, Sam
United Thoroughbred Trainers of America (536)

Ramin, Robert
American Zoo and Aquarium Ass'n (124)

Ramirez MD, Bernardo
Ass'n of University Programs in Health Administration (168)

Ramirez, Bruce A.
Council for Exceptional Children (211)

Ramirez, Jack F.
Nat'l Ass'n of Independent Insurers (359)

Ramirez, Kelly
Mobile Industrial Caterers' Ass'n Internat'l (329)

Ramminger, Scott
American Wood Preservers Institute (123)

Rampersad, Mia
Nat'l Housewares Manufacturers Ass'n (409)

Ramsay, Katherine
Soc. for Experimental Mechanics (488)

Ramsay, Kay
Nat'l Committee on Planned Giving (388)

Ramsborg CRNA,Ph.D., Glen C.
American Ass'n of Nurse Anesthetists (39)

Ramsey, John
Ass'n of Public-Safety Communications Officials-
    Internat'l (162)

Ramsey, Kimberly H.
Internat'l Frozen Food Ass'n (292)

Ramsey, Lynn
Jewelry Information Center (314)

Ranck, Medea
Ass'n of Higher Education Facilities Officers (153)

Randall, Michele G.
Bibliographical Soc. of America (178)

Randall JD, Richard
Nat'l Network of Estate Planning Attorneys (418)

Randall, Susan
American Milking Devon Ass'n (85)

Randazzo, Catherine A.
Composites Institute (202)

Randle, Jackie
Nat'l Ass'n of Government Guaranteed Lenders (357)

Randolph, Larry
American Soc. for Training and Development (106)

Rangnath, Molly
Internat'l Chiropractors Ass'n (285)

Rankin, James H.
Glass, Molders, Pottery, Plastics and Allied Workers
    International Union (248)

Rankin, Matt
Council of Landscape Architectural Registration Boards (214)

Rankin, Paul W.
Ass'n of Container Reconditioners (148)

Ransome, Whitney
Nat'l Coalition of Girls Schools (387)

Rao, Piersandro
Italy-America Chamber of Commerce (313)

Rao, Robert J.
Production Service Sales District Council **(464)**

Rapalus, Patrice
Computer Security Institute **(203)**

Rapaport Ph.D., Felix
Transplantation Soc. (Western Hemisphere) **(525)**

Rapone, Debra
Packaging Machinery Manufacturers Institute **(452)**

Rapoport, David
Anxiety Disorders Ass'n of America **(125)**

Rapp, Barbara Ellen
American College of Radiology **(57)**

Rardin, Patricia
Roundalab **(477)**

Rasmussen, Dwight
Nat'l Ass'n of Senior Companions Project Directors **(372)**

Rasmussen, Priscilla
Ass'n for Computational Linguistics **(131)**

Rasor, Robert
American Motorcyclist Ass'n **(85)**

Rasplica Rodd, Laurel
Ass'n of Teachers of Japanese **(167)**

Rassan, Ghassan
Optical Soc. of America **(449)**

Rastatter, Edward
Nat'l Industrial Transportation League **(411)**

Ratcliff, Deborah
Floor Covering Installation Contractors Ass'n **(240)**

Ratcliff-Daffron, Sandra
American Judicature Soc. **(80)**

Ratcliffe, Dolores
Ass'n of Black Women Entrepreneurs **(145)**

Rathbone, Susan G.
Biotechnology Industry Organization **(179)**

Rathbun, Jill
American Soc. of Nephrology **(113)**

Rather, Beth
Nat'l Assembly of State Arts Agencies **(381)**

Ratley, James D.
Ass'n of Certified Fraud Examiners **(146)**

Rauch, Carolyn
Interactive Digital Software Ass'n **(271)**

Rauglas, Dirk
MTM Ass'n for Standards and Research **(331)**

Rauner, Brenda
American Physiological Soc. **(92)**

Raut, Shirley Armitage
Music Teachers Nat'l Ass'n **(332)**

Rauzino-Heller, Rosemarie
Physician Insurers Ass'n of America **(458)**

Rawson, W. Randall
American Boiler Manufacturers Ass'n **(48)**

Ray, Charles G.
Nat'l Council for Community Behavioral Healthcare **(393)**

Ray, Larry E.
Nat'l Ass'n for Community Mediation **(338)**

Ray, Mitzi
Offshore Marine Service Ass'n **(447)**

Ray M.D., Oakley
American College of Neuropsychopharmacology **(55)**

Ray, Ron
Inter-Industry Conference on Auto Collision Repair **(271)**

Rayburn, Wendell
American Ass'n of State Colleges and Universities **(43)**

Rayman M.D., Russell B.
Aerospace Medical Ass'n **(13)**

Raymond, Douglas E.
Retail Advertising and Marketing Ass'n Internat'l **(475)**

Raymond, Rosalind
Sheet Metal and Air Conditioning Contractors' Nat'l Ass'n **(482)**

Raynes CAE, Jeffry W.
APICS - The Educational Society for Resource Management **(125)**

Raynes, Linda J.
Electrical Apparatus Service Ass'n **(227)**

Read, Mary Margaret
American Suffolk Horse Ass'n **(118)**

Read, Robin
Nat'l Order of Women Legislators/Nat'l Foundation for Women Legislators **(419)**

Reading, Reid
Latin American Studies Ass'n **(317)**

Reagan, Michael
Business and Institutional Furniture Manufacturers Ass'n Internat'l **(184)**

Reale, Richard A.
Nat'l Catholic Development Conference **(385)**

Reamer, Terry C.
Rehabilitation Engineering and Assistive Technology Soc. of North America **(474)**

Reams, J. Lorraine
Ass'n of Universities for Research in Astronomy **(168)**

Reams, Renee
Calorimetry Conference **(186)**

Reamy, Karen
American Soc. for Industrial Security **(103)**

Reardon, Martha A.
Internat'l Marine Transit Ass'n **(297)**

Reardon, Sarah
Electronic Messaging Ass'n **(228)**

Reardon, Susan
American Foreign Service Ass'n **(69)**

Reardon, Thomas
Business and Institutional Furniture Manufacturers Ass'n Internat'l **(184)**

Reaves, Randolph P.
Federation of Ass'ns of Regulatory Boards **(237)**

Reaves JD, Randolph P.
Ass'n of State and Provincial Psychology Boards **(165)**

Reber M.D., Howard A.
American Pancreatic Ass'n **(90)**

Rebuck, Steven D.
Palomino Horse Ass'n **(453)**

Reck, Barbara
American Public Health Ass'n **(95)**

Reckstraw, Lisa
ESOP Ass'n **(232)**

Rector, John
Nat'l Community Pharmacists Ass'n **(388)**

Redden, Marlene
Nat'l Frozen Food Ass'n **(406)**

Redding, Whitney
Assisted Living Federation of America **(170)**

Reddy, Leo
Nat'l Coalition for Advanced Manufacturing **(387)**

Redfern, Gabrielle
WEB: Network of Benefit Professionals **(542)**

Redmon, Patricia
Council of Large Public Housing Authorities **(214)**

Redmond, John
Professional Picture Framers Ass'n **(466)**

Redstone, Virginia D.
Ass'n of Ship Brokers and Agents (U.S.A.) **(165)**

Reece, Joan
Leading Jewelers Guild **(318)**

Reed, Ann
ASFE: Professional Firms Practicing in the Geosciences **(128)**

Reed, Doris A.
Ass'n of Supervisory and Administrative School Personnel **(166)**

Reed, Elsie
Nat'l Ass'n of Fashion and Accessory Designers **(355)**

Reed, John W.
Internat'l Soc. of Barristers **(305)**

Reed, Lydia Middleton
Ass'n of University Programs in Health Administration **(168)**

Reed Ed.D., CNA, Marie A.
Nat'l Soc. of Fund Raising Executives **(429)**

Reed, Sandy
Hispanic Dental Ass'n **(254)**

Reed, Sloane
American College of Managed Care Medicine **(55)**
American Ass'n of Managed Care Nurses **(38)**

Reed, Thomas M.
American School Health Ass'n **(99)**

Rees Jr., Clifford H.
Air-Conditioning and Refrigeration Institute **(16)**

Reese, Bud
Council of Fleet Specialists **(213)**

Reese, Doug
Christian Labor Ass'n of the United States of America **(193)**

Reese, Gregory L.
Black Caucus of the American Library Ass'n **(180)**

Reese, Kathleen J.
Steel Founders' Soc. of America **(516)**

Reets, Joel
Internat'l Soc. of Cleaning Technicians **(306)**

Reeve, Hazel
Limousine Industry Manufacturers Organization **(320)**

Reeve, Wendy Sue
American Welding Soc. **(123)**

Reeves, Jim
American Brahman Breeders Ass'n **(49)**
Council for Near-Infrared Spectroscopy **(212)**

Reeves, John Daniel
United States Conference of Mayors **(533)**

Reeves, Patricia
CPA Associates Internat'l **(218)**

Reeves, Robert M.
Institute of Shortening and Edible Oils **(269)**

Reeves, Sandy
Knitting Guild of America **(316)**

Reeves, Shelly
Nat'l Ass'n of Women in Construction **(380)**

Regan, Susan
Southern Cypress Manufacturers Ass'n **(510)**
Hardwood Manufacturers Ass'n **(251)**

Regauld, Michael H.
Vocational Industrial Clubs of America **(540)**

Regehr, Barbara
Internat'l Nubian Breeders Ass'n **(298)**

Reggio, Gail
Eye Bank Ass'n of America **(234)**

Regiani D.D.S., David W.
Internat'l Academy of Oral Medicine and Toxicology **(272)**

Regitsky, Andrew
Competitive Telecommunications Ass'n **(201)**

Rehage, Kenneth J.
Nat'l Soc. for the Study of Education **(429)**

Rehr, David K.
Nat'l Beer Wholesalers Ass'n **(382)**

Reich Ph.D., Gloria E.
American Tinnitus Ass'n **(120)**

Reich, Jill
American Psychological Ass'n **(94)**

Reich, Leah R.
Electric Vehicle Ass'n of the Americas **(227)**

Reich, Nancy
Nat'l Health Council **(408)**

Reich, Wayne
Truck-frame and Axle Repair Ass'n **(527)**

Reichard Ph.D., Sherwood M.
American Soc. for Photobiology **(104)**

Reichard, Dr. Sherwood M.
Shock Soc. **(483)**

Reichbart, Susan
College and University Personnel Ass'n **(197)**

Reichelt-Pepper, Christine
Nat'l Funeral Directors Ass'n **(406)**

Reichenberg CAE, Neil E.
Internat'l Personnel Management Ass'n **(299)**

Reichertz, John J.
Clinical Immunology Soc. **(194)**

Reid II, C.J.
American Ass'n of School Administrators **(42)**

Reid, Donna Chowning
American Soc. of Appraisers **(106)**

Reid Ph.D., George W.
Council of 1890 College Presidents and Chancellors **(212)**

Reid, Karen A.
Employee Relocation Council **(229)**

Reid CAE, Kenneth D.
American Water Resources Ass'n **(122)**

Reid, Paul S.
Mortgage Bankers Ass'n of America **(330)**

Reid, Robert J.
Nat'l Housing Conference **(409)**

Reiff, Sidney
Sportswear Apparel Ass'n **(515)**
Ladies Apparel Contractors Ass'n **(316)**

Reilly, Deborah Sykes
Nat'l Ass'n of Independent Colleges and Universities **(359)**

Reilly, Eliza
American Conference of Academic Deans **(59)**

Reilly, James
American Blood Resources Ass'n **(47)**

Reilly, John
Automotive Parts and Accessories Ass'n **(175)**

Reilly, Mary
Council of Better Business Bureaus **(212)**

Reilly, Matthew B.
American Short Line and Regional Railroad Ass'n **(100)**

Reilly CAE, Richard M.
American Arbitration Ass'n **(28)**

Reilly, Robert W.
Internat'l Plasma Products Industry Ass'n **(300)**

Reilly, Sheila
Interstate Council on Water Policy **(311)**

Reilly, Tammy
Ass'n of Independent Corrugated Converters **(153)**

Reily, Barbara
Nat'l Customs Brokers and Forwarders Ass'n of America **(398)**

Reimer, Chris
Nat'l Ground Water Ass'n **(407)**

Reindhart, Don
American Vocational Ass'n **(122)**

Reinemer, Michael
Nat'l Council on the Aging **(398)**

Reiner D.D.S., Abraham
American Academy of Oral Medicine **(24)**

Reinerman, Alan J.
Soc. for Italian Historical Studies **(490)**

Rigel, Vicki
American Cotswold Record Ass'n **(60)**

Riggins, Lowry
Internat'l Double Reed Soc. **(289)**

Riggs, David
Nat'l Ass'n of State Veterans Homes **(376)**

Righthouse, Jerry L.
World Sign Associates **(550)**

Rigney CLU, ChFC, Anne M.
Society of Financial Service Professionals **(509)**

Riker, Anna
Soc. of Cable Telecommunications Engineers **(499)**

Riker, William
Soc. of Cable Telecommunications Engineers **(499)**

Riley, Adrienne
American Resort Development Ass'n **(98)**

Riley, Donald J. "Skip"
Nat'l Ass'n of Marine Surveyors **(362)**

Riley, John
Institute for Interconnecting and Packaging Electronic Circuits **(265)**

Riley, Michael
Bank Marketing Ass'n **(176)**

Rimel, Robert A.
Nat'l Plumbing Bureau **(422)**

Rimmer, Walter
American Soc. of Petroleum Operations Engineers **(114)**

Rinaldi, Dr. Bob
American Ass'n of Oral and Maxillofacial Surgeons **(40)**

Rinaldi, Joan
Silver Institute **(483)**

Rineer, Matt
Teratology Soc. **(521)**

Ringo, Lori
Nat'l Ass'n of Catastrophe Adjusters **(346)**

Rinker, Martha L.
American Orthotic and Prosthetic Ass'n **(89)**

Riordan, John T.
Internat'l Council of Shopping Centers **(288)**

Riotto, Charles
Internat'l Licensing Industry Merchandisers' Ass'n **(296)**

Ripin, Barrett
American Physical Soc. **(92)**

Rippen, Harrison W.
Nat'l Wood Tank Institute **(436)**

Rippentrop CAE, Gary D.
American Collectors Ass'n **(52)**

Rish EFTA, Seymour A.
Nat'l Ass'n of Enrolled Federal Tax Accountants **(354)**

Risinger, Beth B.
Internat'l Executive Housekeepers Ass'n **(290)**

Risley, Jeff
Plastic Pipe and Fittings Ass'n **(459)**

Risotto, Steven P.
Halogenated Solvents Industry Alliance **(250)**

Ritchey, David
Architectural Woodwork Institute **(127)**

Ritchie, Joan D.
American Ass'n for Cancer Research **(30)**

Ritchie, Mary R.
Industrial Distribution Ass'n **(262)**

Rittenberg, Karen
American Judicature Soc. **(80)**

Ritter, John
Ass'n of Commercial Diving Educators **(148)**

Ritter, Sandra
Internat'l Ass'n of Addictions and Offender Counselors **(275)**

Ritts, Jim
Ladies Professional Golf Ass'n **(316)**

Ritz Ph.D., John M.
Council on Technology Teacher Education **(217)**

Riva, Valentin
American Concrete Pavement Ass'n **(59)**

Rival, Audra
Internat'l Liver Transplantation Soc. **(296)**
Gynecologic Surgery Soc. **(250)**

Rivard, Karen
Ass'n for the Advancement of Psychology **(138)**

Rivera, Carlos
Nat'l Student Nurses Ass'n **(432)**

Rivera, Connie
American Dietetic Ass'n **(64)**

Rivera, Rafael
Nat'l Soc. of Hispanic MBAs **(430)**

Rivero, Jerry
American Ass'n of Clinical Endocrinologists **(34)**

Rivkin, Alisa D.
Special Interest Group for Computer Personnel Research **(511)**
Special Interest Group for Computers and the Physically Handicapped **(511)**
Special Interest Group for Information Retrieval **(512)**

Special Interest Group for University and College Computing Services **(512)**
Special Interest Group on Artificial Intelligence **(512)**
Special Interest Group on Management Information Systems **(513)**
Special Interest Group on Supporting Group Work **(513)**
Special Interest Group on Hypertext/Hypermedia **(513)**

Rizner, Glenn
Helicopter Ass'n Internat'l **(253)**

Riznikove, Allyn
American Photographic Artisans Guild **(92)**

Rizzo, Liliana
Chartered Property and Casualty Underwriters Soc. **(190)**

Rizzuto, Anthony
American Conference of Governmental Industrial Hygienists **(59)**

Roach, Doris
Hospitality Financial and Technology Professionals **(256)**

Roach, Virginia
Nat'l Ass'n of State Boards of Education **(374)**

Robbins, Chad
Advertising Mail Marketing Ass'n **(12)**

Robbins, Chad W.
Advertising Mail Marketing Ass'n **(12)**

Robbins, Mark
Community Ass'ns Institute **(200)**

Roberson, Dee
Home Wine and Beer Trade Ass'n **(256)**

Roberson, Rodney L.
United Braford Breeders **(530)**

Roberts, Amy
American Council of Highway Advertisers **(61)**

Roberts, Bruce F.
Textile Distributors Ass'n **(522)**

Roberts, Carol
Nat'l Ass'n for Government Training and Development **(339)**
Nat'l Ass'n of Government Deferred Compensation Administrators **(356)**

Roberts, Cassandra
Nat'l Council for the Social Studies **(393)**

Roberts, Cecil E.
United Mine Workers of America Internat'l Union **(531)**

Roberts, Chilton
Council of State Ass'n Presidents **(215)**

Roberts, Craig
Intelligent Transportation Soc. of America **(270)**

Roberts, Dave
Nat'l Frozen Dessert and Fast Food Ass'n **(406)**

Roberts, Diana T.
Aircraft Owners and Pilots Ass'n **(16)**

Roberts, Ed
American Paint Horse Ass'n **(90)**

Roberts, Glenn
Flavor and Extract Manufacturers Ass'n of the United States **(240)**

Roberts, Jennifer
Internat'l Mass Retail Ass'n **(297)**

Roberts, Julie
ADSC: The Internat'l Ass'n of Foundation Drilling **(12)**

Roberts, Karen L.
American Desalting Ass'n **(64)**

Roberts, Ken
Automotive Service Ass'n **(175)**

Roberts, Kurtis
SPIE-Internat'l Soc. for Optical Engineering **(514)**

Roberts CAE, Larry W.
AIM USA **(15)**

Roberts, Margaret Jenkins
Ass'n of the Wall and Ceiling Industries-Internat'l **(167)**

Roberts, Mark C.
Mineral Economics and Management Soc. **(329)**

Roberts, R.T.
Potash and Phosphate Institute **(461)**

Roberts, Richard R.
American Council of Highway Advertisers **(61)**

Roberts, Susan
American Roentgen Ray Soc. **(98)**

Roberts, Susan
Internat'l Ass'n of Corporate and Professional Recruitment **(277)**

Roberts, Virginia
Nat'l Industrial Transportation League **(411)**

Robertson, Charles
Nat'l Indian Gaming Ass'n **(410)**

Robertson, D. Mark
American College of Sports Medicine **(57)**

Robertson, Dan E.
Printing Industries of America **(463)**

Robertson, David N.
Ass'n of Finance and Insurance Professionals **(151)**

Robertson, Janice
Soc. of Professionals in Dispute Resolution **(506)**

Robertson, Jennifer
Nat'l Parks and Conservation Ass'n **(421)**

Robertson, Joan
American College of Nurse-Midwives **(56)**

Robertson, Maria
American School Food Service Ass'n **(99)**

Robertson, Michael
Screenprinting and Graphic Imaging Ass'n Internat'l **(480)**

Robertson, Ric
Academy of Motion Picture Arts and Sciences **(9)**

Robeson, Kathleen
Financial Women Internat'l **(239)**

Robeson, Robert E.
Aerospace Industries Ass'n of America **(13)**

Robey, Kate
Ass'n for Experiential Education **(133)**

Robey, Sheri Rene
Information Industry Ass'n **(263)**

Robinett, Pam
Nat'l Marrow Donor Program **(416)**

Robinette, Hillary
Soc. of Former Special Agents of the Federal Bureau of Investigation **(501)**

Robinson Ph.D., Allen
American Driver and Traffic Safety Education Ass'n **(65)**

Robinson, Anna
American Alliance for Health, Physical Education, Recreation and Dance **(27)**

Robinson, Dale
Ass'n for Public Policy Analysis and Management **(137)**

Robinson, Dorothy
Eye Bank Ass'n of America **(234)**

Robinson, Gary
Ass'n for Information and Image Management International **(135)**
Aluminum Extruders Council **(19)**
Union of American Physicians and Dentists **(529)**

Robinson, Gregg
American Soc. for Therapeutic Radiology and Oncology **(105)**

Robinson, Gregg F.
Soc. of Chairmen of Academic Radiology Oncology Programs **(499)**

Robinson CAE, J. Lawrence
Color Pigments Manufacturers Ass'n **(198)**

Robinson, John F.
Nat'l Minority Business Council **(417)**

Robinson, Joyce B.
American Postal Workers Union **(93)**

Robinson, Judith
Nat'l Ass'n of School Nurses **(371)**

Robinson, Kenneth
American Psychiatric Ass'n **(94)**

Robinson, Lynne
American Gastroenterological Ass'n **(70)**

Robinson, Melinda
Institute for Interconnecting and Packaging Electronic Circuits **(265)**

Robinson, Nancy J.
Livestock Marketing Ass'n **(320)**

Robinson, Pamela E.
Nat'l Conference of Bar Presidents **(389)**

Robinson, Peter
Minority Internat'l Network for Trade **(329)**

Robinson CAE, Peter M.
United States Council for Internat'l Business **(533)**

Robinson, Phillip
University Continuing Education Ass'n **(537)**

Robinson, Rachel R.
Nat'l Conference of Commissioners on Uniform State Laws **(390)**

Robinson, Rob
Armed Forces Communications and Electronics Ass'n **(127)**

Robinson, Roxanne M.
American Ass'n for Laboratory Accreditation **(31)**

Robinson, Sullivan
Congress of Nat'l Black Churches **(205)**

Robinson, William L.
Nat'l Ass'n of Marine Services **(362)**

Robiso, Eileen
Ass'n of Industry Manufacturers' Representatives **(154)**
American Supply Ass'n **(119)**

Roch, Thierry G.
American Hotel and Motel Ass'n **(74)**

Rocha, David
Jewelers of America **(314)**

Roche, James
EDUCAUSE **(227)**

Roche, Mary Beth
Publishers' Publicity Ass'n **(470)**

Rocheleau P.E., Col. Natasha
Soc. of American Military Engineers **(498)**

Rochell, Judy
American College of Physician Executives **(57)**

Rochester, Robert
Soc. of Manufacturing Engineers (503)

Rochman, Julie
Insurance Institute for Highway Safety (270)

Rock M.D., Robert C.
American Soc. of Clinical Pathologists (108)

Rocker, Regina
Board of Trade of the City of New York (180)

Rockwell, Shelley
American Judges Ass'n (80)
Conference of State Court Adminstrators (204)
Nat'l Conference of Appellate Court Clerks (389)

Rockwell, Susan L.
Nat'l Ass'n for Ethnic Studies (339)

Roddy-Burns, Lisa M.
American Public Communications Council (95)

Rodeffer, Stephanie H.
Soc. for Historical Archaeology (489)

Rodenberg, Harriet
Delta Psi Kappa (221)
Phi Rho Sigma Medical Soc. (457)
Professional Fraternity Ass'n (465)

Rodenstein, Morris
Nat'l Ass'n of Child Advocates (347)

Rodger, Eleanor Jo
Urban Libraries Council (538)

Rodgers, Alexis L.
American Board of Medical Specialties (47)

Rodgers Jr., Clifton E.
Nat'l Realty Committee (424)

Rodgers, Jacci L.
Soc. for the Study of Social Biology (496)

Rodgers, Jonathan
American Oriental Soc. (88)

Rodgers, Michael F.
American Ass'n of Homes and Services for the Aging (37)

Rodgers, Paul
American Sheep Industry Ass'n (99)

Rodi, Catherine
American Recovery Ass'n (97)

Rodman, Beverly
Internat'l Jewish Media Ass'n (295)
American Jewish Press Ass'n (80)

Rodman, Bob
Nat'l Soc. of Pharmaceutical Sales Trainers (430)

Rodman, Stanley A.
Automotive Body Parts Ass'n (174)

Rodrigues, Gloria
Internat'l Disk Drive Equipment and Materials Ass'n (289)

Rodriguez, Arturo S.
United Farm Workers of America (530)

Rodriguez, Tom Blackburn
Nat'l Ass'n of Community Action Agencies (349)

Roe, David W.
Communications Media Management Ass'n (200)

Roeder, Henry J.
Nat'l Business Travel Ass'n (384)

Roeding, Russell
American Ass'n of Homes and Services for the Aging (37)

Roehrig, Steven A.
Steel Deck Institute (516)

Roenigk, William P.
Nat'l Broiler Council (384)

Roesen, Mark D.
American Ass'n of Colleges of Pharmacy (35)

Roesslein, Corrie
Institute of Environmental Sciences and Technology (267)

Rogala CAE, Joan
Lambda Kappa Sigma (317)

Rogala, Kathy
American Ass'n of School Librarians (42)

Rogan, Elizabeth
Optical Soc. of America (449)

Roger, Doris
American Holistic Nurses' Ass'n (73)

Rogers, Beth
Nat'l Ass'n of Personnel Services (365)

Rogers, Carol S.
AACE Internat'l (7)

Rogers, Christine
Ass'n for Quality and Participation (137)

Rogers, Heather
Internat'l Soc. for Prosthetics and Orthotics, United States
 Nat'l Member Soc. (304)

Rogers, Iris
American Ass'n of Motor Vehicle Administrators (39)

Rogers, Jill
Personal Communications Industry Ass'n (455)

Rogers, Joseph E.L.
Center for Waste Reduction Technologies (189)

Rogers, Mark
Soc. of Nuclear Medicine (504)

Rogers, Mary Beth
Sleep Disorders Dental Soc. (483)

Rogers, Maureen
Herb Growing and Marketing Network (253)

Rogers, Rich
Nat'l Athletic Trainers' Ass'n (381)

Rogers, Richard
American Academy of Health Care Providers in the Addictive
 Disorders (22)

Rogers, Sharon
Ass'n for Library and Information Science Education (135)

Rogers, Singe
Midwives Alliance of North America (328)

Rogers, Suzanne
Endocrine Soc. (230)

Rogers, Todd P.
Casualty Actuarial Soc. (187)

Rogin, Carole M.
Wire Rope Technical Board (545)
Hearing Industries Ass'n (253)

Rogoway, David L.
APA - The Engineered Wood Ass'n (125)

Rogstad Ph.D., Barry K.
American Business Conference (50)

Rohde, Diann
Nat'l Multiple Sclerosis Soc. (418)

Rohn, David W.
Ass'ns Council of the Nat'l Ass'n of Manufacturers (170)

Rohr, Betty
Ass'n of Vascular and Interventional Radiographers (169)
Ass'n of Educators in Radiological Science (150)
American Radiological Nurses Ass'n (96)

Rohrbacker, Jihane K.
Nat'l Guardianship Ass'n (408)
Nat'l Ass'n of Professional Geriatric Care Managers (366)

Rohrs, Dawn B.
Beta Beta Beta (178)

Roistacher, C.N.
Internat'l Organization of Citrus Virologists (299)

Rojas, Terri
Soc. for Vascular Surgery (496)

Rojo, Eric
United States-Mexico Chamber of Commerce (536)

Roland, Anne V.
Interstate Natural Gas Ass'n of America (311)

Roland, Becky
Nat'l Environmental Health Ass'n (401)

Rolfs, Bernadette
Indian Educators Federation (262)

Rollins, Billie
Council of Chief State School Officers (213)

Rollins, JoAnn
Nat'l Business Incubation Ass'n (384)

Rollins, Peter C.
Historians Film Committee (254)

Rolnicki, Tom E.
Associated Collegiate Press, Nat'l Scholastic Press Ass'n (171)

Roloff, Donald
Nat'l Ass'n of State Supervisors of Trade and Industrial
 Education (376)

Roman, David M.
Internat'l Right of Way Ass'n (301)

Romanick, Sara J.
Nat'l Ass'n of Federal Credit Unions (355)

Romero, Gladys
Nat'l Apartment Ass'n (337)

Romig, Candace
Ass'n of Operating Room Nurses (159)

Romig, Keith
United Paperworkers Internat'l Union (531)

Rommel, Floyd
Nat'l Ass'n of Elevator Safety Authorities Internat'l (353)

Romo, Kathy
Safe and Vault Technicians Ass'n (478)
Associated Locksmiths of America (171)

Ronan, Charlotte P.
American Ass'n of Veterinary State Boards (45)

Ronay, J. Christopher
Institute of Makers of Explosives (268)

Roncketti, Nancy E.
Internat'l Ass'n of Counseling Services (278)

Roney, Jack
American Sugar Alliance (119)

Ronk, Theresa
Council of Growing Companies (214)

Rood, Anne
Nat'l Ass'n of School Psychologists (371)

Rood, David
Nat'l Ass'n of College Auxiliary Services (348)

Rooks, Alan
Paper Industry Management Ass'n (453)

Rooney, Denise C.
Ass'n of Food and Drug Officials (151)

Rooney, Francis P.
Biscuit and Cracker Manufacturers' Ass'n (179)

Roorbach, Douglas
Envelope Manufacturers Ass'n (231)

Roos, Joe
Associated Church Press (171)

Root, Laurie
Nat'l Ass'n of Industrial and Office Properties (360)

Roper, Catherine K.
Health Industry Distributors Ass'n (252)

Roper CAE, Ray W.
Printing Industries of America (463)

Rorrie Jr., Ph.D., Colin C.
American College of Emergency Physicians (54)

Rosado, Edwin
Nat'l Ass'n of Counties (350)

Rosalba, Kampman
Biophysical Soc. (179)

Rosales, Henry
Geospatial Information and Technology Ass'n (247)

Rosan, Richard M.
Urban Land Institute (537)

Rosanova, Amy
Home Improvement Research Institute (255)

Rosch M.D., Paul J.
American Institute of Stress (78)

Rosche, Cristy
Silver Institute (483)

Roschwalb, Jerold
Nat'l Ass'n of State Universities and Land Grant Colleges (376)

Roscoe, Wilma
Nat'l Ass'n for Equal Opportunity in Higher Education (339)

Rose, Bill
Help Desk Institute (253)

Rose, John N.
Organization for the Promotion and Advancement of Small
 Telecommunications Companies (449)

Rose, Judy
Law and Society Ass'n (318)

Rose, Kay
Nat'l Ass'n of Dental Plans (352)

Rose, Lu N.
American Forests (69)

Rose, Stephen L.
Council of Better Business Bureaus (212)

Rose, Wendi
Allied Trades of the Baking Industry (18)

Roseman, M. Judith
Controlled Release Soc. (208)

Rosen, Hilary B.
Recording Industry Ass'n of America (472)

Rosen, Myra
Private Label Manufacturers Ass'n (463)

Rosen, Richard L.
World History Ass'n (550)

Rosen M.D., Stanford
Academy of Ambulatory Foot Surgery (7)

Rosenberg, Linda
American Pulpwood Ass'n (96)

Rosenberg CAE, Raymond H.
Internat'l Right of Way Ass'n (301)

Rosenberg, Robert
Nat'l Pest Control Ass'n (422)

Rosenberg, Samuel H.
Nat'l Ass'n of Retired Federal Employees (370)

Rosenblatt, Daniel N.
Internat'l Ass'n of Chiefs of Police (277)

Rosenblatt, Sherrie
Nat'l Turkey Federation (435)

Rosenbloom, Alan G.
American Ass'n of Homes and Services for the Aging (37)

Rosenbloom, Sandra
Ass'n of Collegiate Schools of Planning (148)

Rosenbluh Ph.D., Edward S.
American Academy of Crisis Interveners (21)

Rosenblum, Jay
American Soc. of Industrial Medicine (111)

Rosenburg, Judi
Flexible Packaging Ass'n (240)

Rosencrance CMP, Debra
American Academy of Ophthalmology (24)

Rosenker, Heather Beldon
Professional Services Council (467)

Rosenker, Mark V.
Electronic Industries Ass'n (228)

Rosenthal, Bruce G.
Nat'l Ass'n of Women Business Owners (380)

Rosenthal, Clifford N.
Nat'l Federation of Community Development Credit Unions (403)

Rosenthal, Gwenn E.
ESOP Ass'n (232)

Rosenthal D.V.M., Robert
Veterinary Cancer Soc. (539)

Rosenthal, Robert
Young Black Programming Coalition (551)

Rosenzweig CAE, Claire
Promotion Marketing Ass'n (468)

Rosier, Ronald C.
Conference Board of the Mathematical Sciences (203)

Rosignol, Denise
Phlebology Soc. of America (457)

Ross, Berinda
Water Environment Federation (541)

Ross, Corrina A.
Military Operations Research Soc. (328)

Ross, David
Political Products Manufacturers Ass'n (460)

Ross CAE, Debra Lynn
American Soc. of Women Accountants (117)

Ross, Denise C.
Ass'n of Business Support Services Internat'l (145)

Ross, Diane
Nat'l Dairy Herd Improvement Ass'n (399)

Ross, Diedre Irwin
American Library Ass'n (81)

Ross, Douglas
Evangelical Christian Publishers Ass'n (233)

Ross, Jan
Anxiety Disorders Ass'n of America (125)

Ross, Jenetta
Nat'l Ass'n of Concessionaires (349)

Ross, John
Appraisal Institute (126)

Ross, Kristin
Custom Electronic Design and Installation Ass'n (219)

Ross, LaVerne
World Research Foundation (550)

Ross, Linda
Concrete Reinforcing Steel Institute (203)

Ross, Lisa
Nat'l Council of Higher Education Loan Programs (395)

Ross, Louis A.
Nat'l Ass'n for Campus Activities (338)

Ross, Marilyn
Small Publishers Ass'n of North America (484)

Ross, Maureen C.
Water and Wastewater Instrumentation Testing Ass'n of North America (ITA) (541)

Ross CAE, Robert H.
FSC/DISC Tax Ass'n (244)

Ross, Sandy
Evangelical Christian Publishers Ass'n (233)

Ross, Sherry L.
Professional Hockey Writers' Ass'n (466)

Ross, Steven
World Research Foundation (550)

Ross, Tim
United States Ski Coaches Ass'n (535)

Rossell, Kathleen
Emergency Nurses Ass'n (229)

Rossi CAE, Marie T.
Women in Sales Ass'n (547)

Rossi, Paul R.
American Bankers Ass'n (46)

Rossiter, Andrea M.
American College of Medical Practice Executives (55)

Rossiter, David
American Water Works Ass'n (122)

Rossman D.V.M., Richard
Academy of Veterinary Allergy and Clinical Immunology (10)

Rosso, Cynthia
Nat'l Council of Teachers of Mathematics (396)

Rossow, Tammy
Nat'l Marine Manufacturers Ass'n (416)
Nat'l Ass'n of Marine Products and Services (362)

Rosum, Holly
Nat'l Ass'n of Recording Merchandisers (369)

Roszkowski P.E., Edward L.
Construction Industry Manufacturers Ass'n (206)

Roszkowski, P.E., Edward L.
Bituminous and Aggregate Equipment Bureau (179)

Rotchford, Jennifer
Ass'n for Health Services Research (134)

Roth, Charles
Catholic Book Publishers Ass'n (188)

Roth, Daniel J.
Nat'l Futures Ass'n (406)

Roth, Jay
Directors Guild of America (223)

Roth, Mark
American Federation of Government Employees (67)

Roth, Mary
Risk and Insurance Management Soc. (476)

Roth, Scott
Soc. of Motion Picture and Television Art Directors (504)

Rothaermel, Diane
Forging Industry Ass'n (243)

Rothbart, Cheryl
American Soc. of Consultant Pharmacists (108)

Rothberg, Jay L.
American Institute of Certified Public Accountants (76)

Rothenberger, Dolores J.
Internat'l Ass'n of Defense Counsel (278)

Rothkin, Michael H.
Council of the Americas (216)

Rothman, Hal
American Soc. for Environmental History (102)

Rothman-Marshall Ph.D., Gail
Council on Education of the Deaf (216)

Rothstein, Audrey R.
College and University Personnel Ass'n (197)

Rothstein, Robert
Truckload Carriers Ass'n (527)

Roton, Frances
American Ass'n of Community Psychiatrists (35)

Rots, Gisela
Women in Internat'l Security (546)

Rotstein M.D., Ori D.
Surgical Infection Soc. (519)

Rottman, Sylvia A.
Ass'n of Destination Management Executives (149)

Roubichou, Gerard
Societe des Professeurs Francais et Francophone d'Amerique (509)

Rounsavill, Brian E.
Electrochemical Soc. (228)

Rouse, Geri
American Seminar Leaders Ass'n (99)

Rousseau, Gordon
Internat'l Fibre Drum Institute (291)

Rouzie, Patricia
Nat'l Beer Wholesalers Ass'n (382)

Rovston, Heather
Nat'l Sheriffs' Ass'n (427)

Row, Constance
Nat'l Academies of Practice (333)

Rowan, George "Rip"
Armed Forces Marketing Council (127)

Rowan, Matthew J.
Health Industry Distributors Ass'n (252)

Rowan, Patricia
Hospice and Palliative Nurses Ass'n (256)

Rowe, Amanda W.
Internat'l Soc. for Heart and Lung Transplantation (303)

Rowe, Constance F.
American Academy of Home Care Physicians (22)

Rowe, Deborah
Nat'l Conference on Research in Language and Literacy (391)

Rowe, Robert
Independent Bankers Ass'n of America (260)

Rowe, Stuart
American Milking Shorthorn Soc. (85)

Rowe, Sylvia B.
Internat'l Food Information Council (291)

Rowell, Deborah
Petroleum Technology Transfer Council (456)

Rowland, Ellis E.
Internat'l Council of Shopping Centers (288)

Rowland MD, PhD, Dr. Randall G.
Soc. of Pelvic Surgeons (505)

Rowley, George
American Occupational Therapy Ass'n (88)

Rowley, Jack
Health Industry Group Purchasing Ass'n (252)

Rowley, Karen L.
Institute of Nuclear Power Operations (268)

Rowley, Ronald F.
Photo Marketing Ass'n-Internat'l (457)

Rowson, Janet E.
Nat'l Ass'n of Real Estate Investment Trusts (369)

Roxbury, Jane
Ass'n of Performing Arts Presenters (160)

Roy, P. Norman
Financial Executives Institute (238)

Royal, Valerie
Ass'n of Science-Technology Centers (164)

Royce, Jeri
American Symphony Orchestra League (119)

Royer, Kyle
Coalition for Christian Colleges and Universities (195)

Rozak, Frank
Nat'l Ass'n of Optometrists and Opticians (364)

Rozell, Denise
Ass'n for Education and Rehabilitation of the Blind and Visually Impaired (132)

Rozelle, Roger
Flight Safety Foundation (240)

Rozynski, Edward M.
Health Industry Manufacturers Ass'n (252)

Ruane CAE, T. Peter
American Road and Transportation Builders Ass'n (98)

Ruark, Eugene
Council of Logistics Management (215)

Rubel, David
American Book Producers Ass'n (48)

Rubel, Joseph
Internat'l Ass'n of Amusement Parks and Attractions (275)

Ruben, Jeffrey M.
American Ass'n for Cancer Research (30)

Rubin, Burton J.
American Soc. of Travel Agents (116)

Rubin Ph.D., Elaine R.
Ass'n of Academic Health Centers (141)

Rubin, Jane T.
AACSB - the Internat'l Ass'n for Management Education (7)

Rubin, Marcia
American School Health Ass'n (99)

Rubin Ph.D., Norma H.
Internat'l Soc. for Chronobiology (303)

Rubin, Roger
Nat'l Soc. for Graphology (428)

Rubino, Victor J.
Practising Law Institute (462)

Rubinstein, Lori
Entertainment Services and Technology Ass'n (231)

Rubsamen, Chris
American Boiler Manufacturers Ass'n (48)

Rucci, Denise M.
Beauty and Barber Supply Institute (177)

Ruck, Lee
Nat'l Ass'n of Telecommunications Officers and Advisers (378)

Ruckman, Cynthia E.
Nat'l Ass'n of College Stores (348)

Rudansky, Jill
American Medical Publishers' Ass'n (84)

Rudd M.D., Gene
Christian Medical and Dental Soc. (193)

Rudder, Catherine E.
American Political Science Ass'n (93)

Ruden, Ashby P.
American Nursery and Landscape Ass'n (87)
Horticultural Research Institute (256)

Ruden, Paul
American Soc. of Travel Agents (116)

Rudisill Ph.D., Alvin E.
Nat'l Ass'n of Industrial Technology (360)

Rudolph, Joan
American Ass'n of Candy Technologists (34)

Ruehle, Melanie
American Spa and Health Resort Ass'n (117)

Ruff, Eric
Nat'l Restaurant Ass'n (425)

Ruff, Michael D.
World's Poultry Science Ass'n, U.S.A. Branch (550)

Ruffing, Mimi
American Academy of Cosmetic Surgery (21)

Rugens, Steve
American Epilepsy Soc. (66)

Rugh, Tim
Internat'l Cast Polymer Ass'n (285)

Rugoff, Lynn
Ass'n of Attorney-Mediators (144)

Ruhdgren, Herb
United States Army Warrant Officers Ass'n (532)

Ruhl, Mary
Soc. of Teachers of Family Medicine (507)

Ruiz, Adolph
Nat'l Ass'n of Postal Supervisors (365)

Ruiz, Hermes
Internat'l Union of Allied Novelty and Production Workers (309)

Ruiz, Jessica
Fresh Produce Ass'n of the Americas (244)

Ruksznis, Elizabeth
American Psychological Soc. (95)

Ruland, Susan E.
Internat'l Dairy Foods Ass'n (288)
Milk Industry Foundation (328)
Internat'l Ice Cream Ass'n (294)
Nat'l Cheese Institute (386)

Sanchez, Ricardo D.
Internat'l Ass'n for Financial Planning **(274)**

SandBakken, John
Nat'l Sunflower Ass'n **(432)**

Sanders, Barbara
Nat'l Ass'n of Emergency Medical Technicians **(353)**

Sanders Ph.D., David
Nat'l Music Council **(418)**

Sanders, Gary
Ass'n of Health Insurance Agents **(153)**

Sanders, James
Associated Risk Managers Internat'l **(172)**

Sanders Jr., M.D., Joe M.
American Academy of Pediatrics **(25)**

Sandherr, Stephen E.
Associated General Contractors of America **(171)**

Sandler, Charles E.
American Petroleum Institute **(91)**

Sandler Ph.D., Dale
American College of Epidemiology **(54)**

Sandler, Neil W.
Nat'l Institute of Building Sciences **(411)**

Sandler USA (RET.), Maj.Gen. Roger W.
Reserve Officers Ass'n of the U.S. **(475)**

Sandler CAE, William S.
Valve Manufacturers Ass'n of America **(538)**
Valve Repair Council **(538)**

Sandoro, James T.
Collector Car Appraisers Internat'l **(197)**

Sandretti, Richard
American Soc. for Quality **(105)**

Sands, Merrill
Independent Investors Protective League **(261)**

Sandstedt Ph.D., Lynn A.
American Ass'n of Teachers of Spanish and Portuguese **(44)**

Sandusky, Vincent R.
American Public Communications Council **(95)**

Sandy Ph.D., Joseph J.
Soc. of Forensic Toxicologists **(501)**

Sanford CAE, Donn W.
Aluminum Anodizers Council **(19)**
Aluminum Extruders Council **(19)**

Sanford MC, USN (RET.), RADM Frederic G.
Ass'n of Military Surgeons of the U.S. **(157)**

Sanford, Joyce
Aluminum Extruders Council **(19)**

Sanford, Sandra
Ass'n of Clinical Research Professionals **(147)**

Sanford, Sarah J.
American Ass'n of Critical-Care Nurses **(35)**

Sanford, Tom
Porcelain Enamel Institute **(460)**

Sanini, David
Internat'l Biometric Soc. **(283)**

Sankey, C. Patrick
American Road and Transportation Builders Ass'n **(98)**

Sanner, Ed
Internat'l Soc. of Communication Specialists **(306)**

Sansolo, Michael
Food Marketing Institute **(241)**

Sansone CAE, David C.
Precision Metalforming Ass'n **(462)**

Sansone, Torry
American College of Radiation Oncology **(57)**

Sansone, Torry Mark
American Soc. of Head and Neck Radiology **(110)**

Santa Anna, Gloria
Nine to Five, Nat'l Ass'n of Working Women **(439)**

Santalla, Anne P.
American Industrial Health Council **(75)**

Santamour, Rhonda
American Payroll Ass'n **(90)**

Santi, Pat
Dog Writers' Ass'n of America **(224)**

Santiago, Luz M.
American Soc. of Ophthalmic Administrators **(113)**

Santini, David L.
Internat'l Soc. for Intercultural Education, Training and Research **(303)**

Santomauro, Michael
American Soc. of Roommate Services **(116)**

Santore, Richard A.
Associated Funeral Directors, Internat'l **(171)**

Santoro, Carlo
Italy-America Chamber of Commerce **(313)**

Santorum, Daniel
United States Professional Tennis Registry **(535)**

Santos, Phyllis
Council of State Governments **(216)**

Sanz, Marilina
Nat'l Ass'n of Hispanic County Officials **(358)**
Nat'l Ass'n of County Human Services Administrators **(351)**

Saolati, Elizabeth
American Soc. for Aesthetic Plastic Surgery **(100)**

Sapienza, Charles D.
Nat'l Conference of State Liquor Administrators **(391)**

Sapin, Barbara
American Nurses Ass'n **(87)**

Saporta, Vicki
Nat'l Abortion Federation **(333)**

Sapp, Charles L.
American Dairy Science Ass'n **(63)**
Internat'l Embryo Transfer Soc. **(290)**

Sarasin, Leslie G.
Internat'l Frozen Food Ass'n **(292)**
Nat'l Yogurt Ass'n **(437)**
American Frozen Food Institute **(69)**

Sarasin, Ronald A.
Nat'l Beer Wholesalers Ass'n **(382)**

Sares, Tim
American Registry of Diagnostic Medical Sonographers **(97)**

Saris, Andrea
American Ass'n of School Administrators **(42)**

Sarjeant, Larry
United States Telephone Ass'n **(535)**

Sarka, Michael
Vacation Rental Managers Ass'n **(538)**

Sarkissian, Nellie
Nat'l Court Reporters Ass'n **(398)**

Sarni, Shirley
Nat'l District Attorneys Ass'n **(399)**

Sarrge, Lisa
American Academy of Facial Plastic and Reconstructive Surgery **(22)**

Sarsen Jr., John J.
Ass'n of Nat'l Advertisers **(158)**

Sarsfield, Wanda M.
American Soc. of Irrigation Consultants **(111)**

Sasavage, Nancy
American Ass'n for Clinical Chemistry **(30)**

Sasso, John A.
Nat'l Community Development Ass'n **(388)**

Satkowski CCE, Leonard J.
FCIB-NACM Corp. **(235)**

Satten, Dede
Equity Asset Managers Ass'n, The **(232)**

Satterfield, Gary T.
Financial Stationers Ass'n **(239)**

Satterlee USAF (RET.), Maj. Francis N.
Internat'l Ass'n of Natural Resource Pilots **(281)**

Sattler, Dale
Nat'l Rehabilitation Administration Ass'n **(425)**

Saucer, Moira
Sugar Ass'n **(518)**

Saunders, Charolette
Nat'l Ass'n of FSA County Office Employees **(356)**

Saunders, David
Soy Protein Council **(511)**
American Coke and Coal Chemicals Institute **(52)**

Saunders III, John E.
Nat'l Forum for Black Public Administrators **(405)**

Saunders, Laurie
Associated Landscape Contractors of America **(171)**

Sauter CAE, George M.
Risk and Insurance Management Soc. **(476)**

Sauter, J. Edward
Tilt-up Concrete Ass'n **(523)**
Concrete Foundations Ass'n **(203)**

Sauve, John M.
Wild Blueberry Ass'n of North America **(544)**

Savage, Bruce A.
Manufactured Housing Institute **(322)**

Savage, Cindy
Distribution Contractors Ass'n **(224)**

Savage, Kris
American Border Leicester Ass'n **(49)**

Savage, Roberta (Robbi)
Ass'n of State and Interstate Water Pollution Control Administrators **(165)**

Savarese, Joseph B.
American Stamp Dealers' Ass'n **(118)**

Savary, Paul
NATSO, Representing America's Travel Plaza and Truckstops **(437)**

Savin, Scott
Horsemen's Benevolent and Protective Ass'n **(256)**

Savino, Alice J.
Cleaning Management Institute **(194)**

Savino, Sandra
Ass'n of Sales and Marketing Companies **(164)**

Savoy, Dianne
Nat'l Telephone Cooperative Ass'n **(433)**

Savoy Thaxton, Sharon
American Astronomical Soc. **(45)**

Sawer, Anette
Soc. of Women Engineers **(509)**

Sawyer, Amy Jo
Accordionists and Teachers Guild Internat'l **(10)**

Sawyer, Richard D.
Healthcare Marketing and Communications Council **(253)**

Sawyer, Ron
Professional Service Ass'n **(467)**

Sawyer, Steven
Fire Marshals Ass'n of North America **(239)**

Sawyerane, Pamela
Visiting Nurse Ass'ns of America **(540)**

Saxon, Ross
Ass'n of Diving Contractors **(150)**

Saye, Sandy
Internat'l Soc. of Industrial Fabric Manufacturers **(306)**

Sayers, Constance
Food and Drug Law Institute **(241)**

Sayers, Maria J.
Nat'l Housing Conference **(409)**

Saylor, Bonnie
Soc. for Applied Spectroscopy **(485)**

Sazima D.D.S., Henry J.
Academy of Dentistry Internat'l **(8)**

Scalco, Mary
Internat'l Fabricare Institute **(290)**

Scalet Ph.D., Charles G.
Nat'l Ass'n of University Fisheries and Wildlife Programs **(379)**

Scalise, George
Semiconductor Industry Ass'n **(481)**

Scalish, Frank A.
Textile Processors, Service Trades, Health Care, Professional and Technical Employees Internat'l Union **(522)**

Scanlan, Joanne
Council on Foundations **(216)**

Scanlan, Mark
Independent Bankers Ass'n of America **(260)**

Scanlin, Marge
American Camping Ass'n **(50)**

Scanlon, Colleen
American Nurses Ass'n **(87)**

Scannell, Gerard F.
Nat'l Safety Council **(426)**

Scaramastro, Thomas R.
Chief Petty Officers Ass'n **(192)**

Scarbro, Maxine
General Federation of Women's Clubs **(246)**

Scarbrough, Don R.
Nat'l Spray Equipment Manufacturers Ass'n **(431)**

Scardelletti, Robert A.
Transportation . Communications Internat'l Union **(525)**

Scarino, Richard F.
Organization for the Promotion and Advancement of Small Telecommunications Companies **(449)**

Scarth, Jonathan
Delta Waterfowl Foundation **(221)**

Scebold, C. Edward
American Council on the Teaching of Foreign Languages **(62)**

Schacher M.D., Ronald A.
Kerato-Refractive Soc. **(315)**

Schadle, Lauren
Institute of Certified Financial Planners **(266)**

Schaefer, Mickey
American Academy of Family Physicians **(22)**

Schafer, Heather
Nat'l Volunteer Fire Council **(435)**

Schafer, Janet
Surface Mount Equipment Manufacturers Ass'n **(519)**

Schaffer, Gail
Business and Professional Women/USA **(184)**

Schaffer, Rita
Biomedical Engineering Soc. **(179)**

Schapiro, Mary L.
Nat'l Ass'n of Securities Dealers **(372)**

Scharpf, Norman W.
Graphic Communications Ass'n **(249)**

Schaszheck, Dick
American College of Occupational and Environmental Medicine **(56)**

Schatzman, Margit A.
Nat'l Ass'n of Credential Evaluation Services **(351)**

Schauer, Rita
Spring Manufacturers Institute **(515)**

Schauseil CMP, Robin
Nat'l Ass'n of Credit Management **(351)**

Scheck, Cathy L.
Endocrine Soc. **(230)**

Schedler, Michael F.
Nat'l Ass'n for PET Container Resources **(340)**

Schedler CAE, Thomas R.
American Soc. of Podiatric Executives **(115)**
American College of Foot and Ankle Surgeons **(54)**

Schulz, Joseph A.
American Soc. of Agricultural Engineers **(106)**

Schulz, Monika
Ass'n for Healthcare Philanthropy **(134)**

Schulz, Paul
Food Distributors Internat'l **(241)**

Schulz, Vickie Braxton
North American Graphic Arts Suppliers Ass'n **(442)**

Schulze, Manuela
Soc. for Personality Assessment **(492)**

Schumacher, Caren
United Fresh Fruit and Vegetable Ass'n **(531)**

Schumann Ph.D., Nancy
Phi Beta **(456)**

Schuping CAE, James A.
Workgroup for Electronic Data Interchange **(549)**

Schurrmans Ph.D., Franck
Credit Union Executives Soc. **(218)**

Schust, Sunny Mays
American Ass'n of State Highway and Transportation
    Officials **(43)**

Schuster, Deryl
Nat'l Ass'n of Government Guaranteed Lenders **(357)**

Schuster, Kerianne
Ass'n of Automotive Aftermarket Distributors **(144)**

Schuster, Neil D.
Internat'l Bridge, Tunnel and Turnpike Ass'n **(284)**

Schut, Karen
Contact Lens Institute **(207)**

Schute, Diane
Chemical Producers and Distributors Ass'n **(191)**

Schutz, Carol A.
Gerontological Soc. of America **(247)**

Schwab MD, Larry
Soc. of Eye Surgeons **(501)**

Schwab, William M.
Construction Financial Management Ass'n **(206)**

Schwallie-Giddis Ph.D., Patricia
American Vocational Ass'n **(122)**

Schwartz, Alec M.
American Prepaid Legal Services Institute **(93)**

Schwartz, Arthur
American Real Estate Soc. **(97)**

Schwartz, Arthur D.
Nat'l Soc. of Professional Engineers **(430)**

Schwartz, Bonnie
Nat'l Ass'n of Sports Officials **(373)**

Schwartz, Dick
Institute of Electrical and Electronics Engineers **(266)**

Schwartz, Jessica
Nat'l Ass'n of Graphic and Product Identification
    Manufacturers **(357)**

Schwartz, Karl D.
Internat'l Organization of Masters, Mates and Pilots **(299)**

Schwartz, Kathleen A.
American Rental Ass'n **(98)**

Schwartz, Kimberly
Ass'n for Work Process Improvement **(141)**

Schwartz, Laura
Renaissance Soc. of America **(474)**

Schwartz, Louis O.
American Sportscasters Ass'n **(118)**

Schwartz, Maureen M.
BKR Internat'l **(180)**

Schwartz, Neil
Wound, Ostomy and Continence Nurses Soc. **(550)**

Schwartz, Peter
Nat'l Ass'n of Ticket Brokers **(378)**
Nat'l Ass'n of Fire Equipment Distributors **(355)**

Schwartz, Rita C.
Nat'l Ass'n of Catholic School Teachers **(346)**

Schwartz, Robert T.
Industrial Designers Soc. of America **(262)**

Schwartz RN, Sandra
Soc. of Otorhinolaryngology and Head/Neck Nurses **(504)**

Schwartz, Stanley M.
American Ass'n of Homes and Services for the Aging **(37)**

Schwartz, Thomas K.
American Soc. of Sugar Beet Technologists **(116)**
Beet Sugar Development Foundation **(177)**

Schwartzentrover, Kathy
Nat'l Truck Equipment Ass'n **(434)**

Schwarz, C.J.
American Ass'n for Higher Education **(31)**

Schwarz, Dr. Eli
American Ass'n for Dental Research **(30)**

Schwarze, Robert C.
Ass'n of Sales and Marketing Companies **(164)**

Schwarzmueller, Gary
Ass'n of College and University Housing Officers-
    Internat'l **(147)**

Schweitzer, Lisa T.
Nat'l Telephone Cooperative Ass'n **(433)**

Schweitzer, Michele L.
Airline Suppliers Ass'n **(16)**

Schwenger, Brian
Nat'l Ass'n of Specialty Food and Confection Brokers **(373)**

Schwid, Bonnie L.
Ass'n of Forensic Document Examiners **(151)**

Schwier, T. Nora
SOLE - The Internat'l Soc. of Logistics **(510)**

Schwimmer, Jules
Sponge and Chamois Institute **(514)**

Schwitz, James R.
Nat'l Air Traffic Controllers Ass'n **(335)**

Sciotto, Angela
Nat'l Ass'n of Equipment Leasing Brokers **(354)**

Sciotto, Nancy J.
Nat'l Electrical Manufacturers Representatives Ass'n **(400)**

Sclove Ph.D., Stanley L.
Classification Soc. of North America **(194)**

Scofield, Julie M.
Nat'l Alliance of State and Territorial AIDS Directors **(336)**

Scolaro, Anna Mae
Urban and Regional Information Systems Ass'n **(537)**

Scollo, Janet
Internat'l Ass'n for Near Death Studies **(274)**

Scoma, Allene M.
Nat'l Shrimp Processors Ass'n **(428)**

Scorca, Marc A.
OPERA America **(448)**

Scotch, Richard
Soc. for Disability Studies **(487)**

Scott, Alexander R.
Minerals, Metals and Materials Soc., The **(329)**

Scott, Barbara A.
Institute of Nuclear Materials Management **(268)**

Scott, Carol
Automatic Meter Reading Ass'n **(173)**

Scott, Cathy
Video Software Dealers Ass'n **(539)**

Scott, Cindy
Soc. for Clinical and Experimental Hypnosis **(486)**

Scott, David
Nat'l Ass'n of State Election Directors **(375)**
Nat'l Ass'n of Governmental Labor Officials **(357)**

Scott, Dena
Nat'l Ass'n of Government Guaranteed Lenders **(357)**

Scott, Deven L.
North American Meat Processors Ass'n **(443)**

Scott, Donald A.
Associated General Contractors of America **(171)**

Scott, Edward M.
United States Parachute Ass'n **(534)**

Scott, John A.
American Academy of Medical Hypnoanalysts **(23)**

Scott, Kimberly
Ass'n of Paid Circulation Publications **(159)**

Scott, Malvise A.
Nat'l Ass'n of Community Health Centers **(349)**

Scott, Minerva
American Mobile Telecommunications Ass'n **(85)**

Scott, Nancy
American Bashkir Curly Registry **(47)**

Scott, Pat
Ass'n of College and University Telecommunications
    Administrators **(147)**

Scott CAE, CMP, Randall W.
Nat'l Ass'n of the Remodeling Industry **(378)**

Scott, Sherry
Ass'n of Professional Communication Consultants **(161)**

Scott, Sherry L.
Nat'l Juvenile Detention Ass'n **(413)**

Scott, Theresa L.
SEPM - Soc. for Sedimentary Geology **(482)**

Scott Jr., Dr. William W.
ASM Internat'l **(128)**

Scott-Pinkney, Pamela
American Historical Ass'n **(73)**

Scotti, Marie J.
Internat'l Advertising Ass'n **(272)**

Scoville, Thomas W.
American Maritime Congress **(82)**

Scrabeck CMP, DeAnn L.
Nat'l Funeral Directors Ass'n **(406)**

Scrivner, Pete
Nat'l Defense Industrial Ass'n **(399)**

Scruggs, Sandy
Christian Management Ass'n **(193)**

Scully, John
Automotive Service Ass'n **(175)**

Scully, Robert T.
Nat'l Ass'n of Police Organizations **(365)**

Scully, Thomas A.
Federation of American Health Systems **(236)**

Seaberg, Lori
North American Building Material Distribution Ass'n **(441)**
Ass'n of Steel Distributors **(166)**

Seago, Jane
Information Systems Audit and Control Ass'n **(264)**

Seal, Lucy
Printing Industries of America **(463)**

Seal, Marilyn
Geospatial Information and Technology Ass'n **(247)**

Seal, Shirley
Nat'l Fluid Power Ass'n **(405)**

Seaman Ph.D., Janet
American Ass'n for Active Lifestyles and Fitness **(29)**

Seamon CAE, Harold P.
Nat'l School Boards Ass'n **(427)**

Sears, Albert B.
Nat'l Fire Protection Ass'n **(404)**

Seatter, Donald E.
Nat'l Council of Social Security Management Ass'ns **(396)**

Seavey, Jennifer
Future Business Leaders of America-Phi Beta Lambda **(245)**

Seay, Sharon L.
Nat'l Funeral Directors and Morticians Ass'n **(406)**

Sebastian, Cathy
Internat'l Herb Ass'n **(293)**

Sebrechts, Jadwiga S.
Women's College Coalition **(547)**

Sechler, Robert S.
Soc. of Automotive Engineers International **(498)**

Seckman, David R.
American Health Care Ass'n **(72)**

Seddelmeyer, David
Nat'l Labor Relations Board Professional Ass'n **(414)**

Seeden, Tim
Casual Furniture Retailers **(187)**
Web Sling and Tiedown Ass'n **(542)**

Seefeldt, Jerry
NaSPA: the Network and System Professionals Ass'n **(333)**

Seeger, Alicia
Nat'l Ass'n for Poetry Therapy **(340)**

Seeger, Arline
Nat'l Lime Ass'n **(415)**

Seekins, Steven V.
Soc. of Critical Care Medicine **(500)**

Seem, Sam H.
Ass'n of Iron and Steel Engineers **(155)**

Seemann, Rose
Geospatial Information and Technology Ass'n **(247)**

Seeno, Terry
Coleopterists Soc. **(196)**

Seetoo, Amy
Chinese-American Librarians Ass'n **(192)**

Seffrin Ph.D., John R.
American Cancer Soc. **(50)**

Segal, Carol
American Ass'n for Geriatric Psychiatry **(30)**

Segal, Ruth L.
Outdoor Advertising Ass'n of America **(451)**

Segall, J. Peter
Health Insurance Ass'n of America **(252)**

Seghers, Louise Gates
Nat'l Ass'n of Temporary and Staffing Services **(378)**

Seho, Karen
Nat'l Bio-Energy Industries Ass'n **(383)**

Seibert, H. Richard
Nat'l Ass'n of Manufacturers **(362)**

Seidel, Chris
Nat'l Roofing Contractors Ass'n **(426)**

Seiders, Dave
Nat'l Ass'n of Home Builders of the U.S. **(358)**

Seidl, Larry
Congress on Ministry in Specialized Settings **(205)**

Seidman, Karen R.
Council of Insurance Agents and Brokers **(214)**

Seidman, Nadine
American Academy of Periodontology **(25)**

Seifert, Colleen
Cognitive Science Soc. **(196)**

Seifert CLU, Marcia T.
Society of Financial Service Professionals **(509)**

Seiffert, Grant
Telecommunications Industry Ass'n **(521)**

Seigfried, John
American Economic Ass'n **(65)**

Seigfried, Mary Lou
Future Homemakers of America **(245)**

Seiler, I. Leonard
Embroidery Council of America (229)
Schiffli Lace and Embroidery Manufacturers Ass'n (479)

Seim M.D., M.P., Hal
American Soc. of Bariatric Physicians (107)

Seitz, Kimberly
Hazardous Materials Advisory Council (251)

Seitz, William
Neighborhood Cleaners Ass'n-Internat'l (438)

Seiver, Kate
Internat'l Downtown Ass'n (289)

Selby, Anne
Nat'l Football League Players Ass'n (405)

Selehdar, Karima
American Corporate Counsel Ass'n (60)

Selender, Robert W.
Mastercard Internat'l (324)

Self, Sue
Nat'l Ass'n of Child Care Professionals (347)

Selig, Bud
Major League Baseball - Office of the Commissioner (322)

Sell, Arden
Nat'l Asphalt Pavement Ass'n (337)

Sell, James
Jewelers Shipping Ass'n (314)

Sellers CAE, Barney
American Soc. for Parenteral and Enteral Nutrition (104)

Sellers, John
Rubber and Plastics Industry Conference of the United
    Steelworkers of America (477)

Sellers, Sandra A.
Software Publishers Ass'n (509)

Sells, William H.
Environmental Industry Ass'ns (231)

Selman, Catherine R.
Nat'l Ass'n of Activity Professionals (342)

Selvitelli, Marc
American Soc. of Landscape Architects (111)

Selz, Kathleen
Nat'l Ass'n of Service and Conservation Corps (372)

Semer CAE, Jeri A.
Ass'n of College and University Telecommunications
    Administrators (147)

Semioli PE, William J.
American Concrete Institute (59)

Semo, Joseph
Nat'l Employee Benefits Institute (401)

Sendish Peters, Edna
Internat'l Beverage Dispensing Equipment Ass'n (283)

Senecaut, Susie
Affiliated Boards of Officials (13)

Senesac, Andy
Northeastern Weed Science Soc. (446)

Senese, Daniel J.
Institute of Electrical and Electronics Engineers (266)

Seng, Philip M.
United States Meat Export Federation (534)

Senior, Charles
American College of Physicians-American Soc. of Internal
    Medicine (57)

Senko, Margaret A.
Music Educators Nat'l Conference: The Nat'l Ass'n for Music
    Education (332)

Senn, Rob
Nat'l Academy of Recording Arts and Sciences (334)

Sennett, John J.
Federal Bureau of Investigation Agents Ass'n (235)

Sennewald, Kelly A.
Council of Independent Colleges (214)

Sensenick, Chris
Design-Build Manufacturers Ass'n (222)

Sepin, Lawrence H.
American Dental Assistants Ass'n (64)

Serchak, Bridget Ann
Internat'l Council of Cruise Lines (287)

Serels Ph.D., M. Mitchell
American Soc. of Sephardic Studies (116)

Serena, Thomas J.
American Gastroenterological Ass'n (70)

Serepca, Mark
Paperboard Packaging Council (453)

Serfass, Jeffrey A.
Nat'l Hydrogen Ass'n (410)

Serfling, Steven
Institute of Food Technologists (267)

Serkin, Stuart D.
Coal and Slurry Technology Ass'n (195)

Serrano, Ligia
Nat'l Coalition of Hispanic Health and Human Services
    Organizations (387)

Serumgard, John
Scrap Tire Management Council (480)

Sessions, Kathy
Miniature Golf Ass'n of America/Miniature Golf Develoment
    of America (329)

Setters, Vickey
Women's Internat'l Network of Utility Professionals (548)

Settimi, Patricia
Soc. for Research in Child Development (493)

Settlemire, Mary Ann
American Ass'n of Community Colleges (35)

Severen, Scott
Light Aircraft Manufacturers Ass'n (319)

Sevilla, Susan D.
Internat'l Transactional Analysis Ass'n (309)

Seville, Dorothy
American College Personnel Ass'n (58)

Sewell, Beth A.
Internat'l Special Events Soc. (307)

Seymour, Christopher R.
American Ass'n of Clinical Endocrinologists (34)

Seymour, Cynthia
Child Welfare League of America (192)

Seymour, Dianne
Internat'l Sport Show Producers Ass'n (307)

Seymour, Magda Lynn
American Federation of Government Employees (67)

Sforza, Wayne V.
American Ass'n of State Colleges and Universities (43)

Sgueo, James M.
Nat'l Alcohol Beverage Control Ass'n (335)

Shaefer Ph.D., Jodi
Ass'n of SIDS and Infant Mortality Programs (165)

Shaevel, Evelyn
Medical Library Ass'n (326)

Shafe Ed. D., Marie C.
Internat'l Ass'n of Eating Disorders Professionals (278)

Shafer, Rita
American Academy of Periodontology (25)

Shaffer, Jane
Ass'n of Information Technology Professionals (154)

Shaffer, Joan
American College of Angiology (53)

Shaffer D.D.S., Richard G.
Internat'l College of Dentists, U.S.A. Section (286)

Shaffer, Scott E.
Internat'l Cemetery and Funeral Ass'n (285)

Shafroth, Frank
Nat'l League of Cities (414)

Shaginaw, George
Cellular Telecommunications Industry Ass'n (189)

Shah, Mahendra
American Soc. for Public Administration (105)

Shaikh Ph.D., Rashid
New York Academy of Sciences (438)

Shakarun, Micheal
Nat'l Accounting and Finance Council (334)

Shalhoub, Robyn K.
Internat'l Mobile Telecommunications Ass'n (297)

Shambarger, Peter
Ass'n for Recorded Sound Collections (137)

Shanahan, Patricia
Soc. of Animal Artists (498)

Shanahan CAE, Thomas
Nat'l Roofing Contractors Ass'n (426)

Shane, Curt
Internat'l Ass'n for Identification (274)

Shane, Francis J.
Nat'l Genealogical Soc. (406)

Shane, Larry I.
Federation of Podiatric Medical Boards (237)
American Academy of Podiatric Sports Medicine (25)

Shaner CAE, Carol T.
United States Tennis Court and Track Builders Ass'n (535)

Shaner CAE, Thomas C.
American Institute of Floral Designers (77)

Shang Ph.D., Yung C.
Internat'l Ass'n of Aquaculture Economics and
    Mangement (275)

Shank, Richard
Nat'l Council for Occupational Education (393)

Shankel CAE, Gerald M.
NACE Internat'l (333)

Shankle, Kim
American Soc. for Microbiology (104)

Shanklin, Patty C.
American Angora Goat Breeder's Ass'n (28)

Shanley, Claire
American Soc. of Access Professionals (106)
Internat'l Ass'n of Professional Security Consultants (282)

Shanley, Kim
Transaction Processing Performance Council (525)

Shanley, Molly
Women's Caucus for Political Science (547)

Shanne, Marianna
Internat'l Soc. of Refractive Surgery (306)

Shannon, Daryl
Nat'l Precast Concrete Ass'n (423)

Shannon, James E.
Nat'l Fire Protection Ass'n (404)

Shapiro, Abraham B.
Cantors Assembly (186)

Shapiro, Gary J.
Consumer Electronics Manufacturers Ass'n (207)

Shapiro, Mary Jo
American Bus Ass'n (49)

Sharbaugh, John M.
American Institute of Certified Public Accountants (76)

Shark CAE, Alan R.
Internat'l Mobile Telecommunications Ass'n (297)
American Mobile Telecommunications Ass'n (85)

Sharkey III, Andrew G.
American Iron and Steel Institute (79)

Sharma, Sabeena
Composites Fabricators Ass'n (201)

Sharoff, Brian
Private Label Manufacturers Ass'n (463)

Sharp, Debra
Research Soc. on Alcoholism (475)

Sharp, Norman F.
Pipe Tobacco Council (458)
Cigar Ass'n of America (194)

Sharpe, Thomas E.
Warehousing Education and Research Council (540)

Sharpitas, Pat
Soc. of Surgical Oncology (507)

Sharpless, Rebecca
Oral History Ass'n (449)

Sharpless, Stacey
Biscuit and Cracker Manufacturers' Ass'n (179)

Shaud USAF (RET.), Gen. John A.
Air Force Ass'n (15)

Shaumyan, Galina
American Ass'n for the Advancement of Slavic Studies (32)

Shavalay, Peter
American College of Radiology (57)

Shaw, Amy
Nat'l Ass'n of Dental Plans (352)

Shaw, Carol
Mathematical Ass'n of America (325)

Shaw, Connie
Data Interchange Standards Ass'n (220)

Shaw AAP, Deborah
Nat'l Automated Clearing House Ass'n (381)

Shaw, Diane
Clinical Ligand Assay Soc. (195)

Shaw, Douglas
Nat'l Management Ass'n (416)

Shaw Ph.D., Edward A.
American College for Advancement in Medicine (52)

Shaw, H.V. Skip
Nat'l Frozen Food Ass'n (406)

Shaw, John S.
Digital Printing and Imaging Ass'n (222)

Shaw, Patrick
American Ass'n of University Professors (44)

Shaw, Richard
American Seminar Leaders Ass'n (99)

Shaw, Robert
Nat'l Music Publishers' Ass'n (418)

Shaw, Susanne
Accrediting Council on Education in Journalism and Mass
    Communications (11)

Shaw, Wayne
Academy of Homiletics (8)

Shay, Matt
Internat'l Franchise Ass'n (292)

Shay, Russell
Land Trust Alliance (317)

Shaye, Marc K.
Spill Control Ass'n of America (514)

Shayka, David
Nat'l Council of Teachers of Mathematics (396)

Shea, Donald B.
Rubber Manufacturers Ass'n (477)

Shea, Ernest C.
Nat'l Ass'n of Conservation Districts (349)

Shea, Gerald P.
Internat'l Road Federation (302)

Sheahan, Virginia
Cheese Importers Ass'n of America (190)

Sheanin, Steve
Wedding and Portrait Photographers Internat'l (542)

Shears, Todd T.
Ass'n for Educational Communications and Technology (133)

Sheehan, Denise
Nat'l Glass Ass'n **(407)**

Sheehan, Kathleen
Nat'l Ass'n of State Alcohol and Drug Abuse Directors **(373)**
Internat'l Technology Education Ass'n **(308)**

Sheehan, Lourdes
Nat'l Catholic Educational Ass'n **(385)**

Sheehy, Carol
Nat'l Speakers Ass'n **(431)**

Sheehy, Therese
American Soc. of Clinical Hypnosis **(108)**

Sheer, Vickie
Dance Educators of America **(220)**

Sheets, Brenda S.
American College of Eye Surgeons **(54)**

Sheets, Susan L.
Nat'l Aircraft Resale Ass'n **(335)**

Sheffield, Constance
Intermodal Ass'n of North America **(272)**

Shehan, Jennifer B.
Nat'l Ass'n of Community Health Centers **(349)**

Sheilds, Wayne C.
Ass'n of Reproductive Health Professionals **(163)**

Shein, Henry
Institute of Electrical and Electronics Engineers **(266)**

Shelburne, Frances
Independent Insurance Agents of America **(261)**

Sheldon, Jeff
UTC - The Telecommunications Ass'n **(538)**

Sheldon, Jim
Nat'l Soccer Coaches Ass'n of America **(430)**

Sheldrick Ph.D., Reg
American Guild of Hypnotherapists **(71)**

Shelk, John
American Gaming Ass'n **(70)**

Shell, Johnny
Screenprinting and Graphic Imaging Ass'n Internat'l **(480)**

Shelley, Barry J.
American Radio Relay League **(96)**

Shelton CAE, Bonnie L.
Soc. for Marketing Professional Services **(490)**

Shelton, Jeff
Professional and Technical Consultants Ass'n **(464)**

Shelton, Joy
American Council of Nanny Schools **(61)**

Shelton, Susan Browne
Nat'l Ass'n of College and University Attorneys **(347)**

Sheneberger, Ted
American Compensation Ass'n **(59)**

Shepard, Mark
United States Ass'n for Computational Mechanics **(532)**

Shepard, Dr. R.S.
Holistic Dental Ass'n **(255)**

Shepherd, Donna M.
Nat'l Ass'n of Chiefs of Police **(347)**
American Federation of Police and Concerned Citizens **(67)**

Sheppard, Craig
Ass'n of Industrial Metallizers, Coaters and Laminators **(154)**

Sheppard, Jeffrey
Nat'l Ass'n of Student Financial Aid Administrators **(377)**

Sheppard, Mike
American Urological Ass'n **(121)**

Sher, Debra
American Soc. of Ass'n Executives **(107)**

Sherer, Scott P.
NaSPA: the Network and System Professionals Ass'n **(333)**

Sheridan, Cindy
Bank Marketing Ass'n **(176)**

Sheridan, John J.
Nat'l Ass'n of Juvenile Correctional Agencies **(361)**

Sheridan, Judy
Ass'n for Living History Farms and Agricultural Museums **(135)**

Sheridan, Mary S.
Nat'l Ass'n of Apnea Professionals **(343)**

Sheridan, Michael M.
American College of Emergency Physicians **(54)**

Sheridan, Rosemary
American Public Transit Ass'n **(96)**

Sherlock, Norman R.
Nat'l Business Travel Ass'n **(384)**

Sherman, Betsy D.
Internat'l City/County Management Ass'n **(285)**

Sherman, Cary H.
Recording Industry Ass'n of America **(472)**

Sherrerd CFA, Katrina F.
Ass'n for Investment Management and Research **(135)**

Sherrier, Julie Stephens
Ass'n of Progressive Rental Organizations **(162)**

Sherry, Karen
American Soc. of Composers, Authors and Publishers **(108)**

Sherwin, David
Associated Writing Programs **(172)**

Sherwood, Jennifer
Chorus America **(193)**

Sherwood, Larry
American Solar Energy Soc. **(117)**

Sherwood CAE, Roger A.
Soc. of Teachers of Family Medicine **(507)**

Sherwood, Susan
American Plastics Council **(92)**

Shewan Ph.D., Cynthia M.
American Physical Therapy Ass'n **(92)**

Shibles, Judge Jill
Nat'l American Indian Court Judges Ass'n **(336)**

Shields, Debby
North American Soc. for Trenchless Technology **(445)**

Shields, Robert
NACE Internat'l **(333)**

Shields, Tina
Aluminum Extruders Council **(19)**

Shields, William.
American College of Radiology **(57)**

Shiffert CAE, John A.
Aircraft Locknut Manufacturers Ass'n **(16)**
Nat'l Ass'n of Diaper Services **(352)**

Shiffert, Sarah
Internat'l Personnel Management Ass'n **(299)**

Shifflett, Michael
American Vocational Ass'n **(122)**

Shifflette, Kimberly
Mason Contractors Ass'n of America **(324)**

Shiflett, Laura W.
Nat'l Governors' Ass'n **(407)**

Shils Ph.D., Edward B.
Dental Dealers of America **(221)**
Dental Manufacturers of America **(221)**

Shim, Sherrod
Nat'l Air Traffic Controllers Ass'n **(335)**

Shimpi, Arun
Nat'l Industries for the Blind **(411)**

Shine M.D., Kenneth I.
Institute of Medicine **(268)**

Shinko, Patricia
Food Marketing Institute **(241)**

Shipiro, Micheal
Council for Higher Education Accreditation **(211)**

Shipley, Ken
Robert Morris Associates, the Ass'n of Lending and Credit Risk Professionals **(476)**

Shipp, Brad
Nat'l Burglar and Fire Alarm Ass'n **(384)**

Shipp, Daniel K.
ISEA-The Safety Equipment Ass'n **(313)**

Shippy, Kevin
Professional Bowlers Ass'n of America **(465)**

Shire, Bernard F.
American Ass'n of Meat Processors **(38)**

Shirey, Ruth I.
Nat'l Council for Geographic Education **(393)**

Shirley, Jane
Nat'l Ass'n of Rehabilitation Instructors **(369)**

Shirley, Teresa M.
Nat'l Ass'n of Elevator Contractors **(353)**

Shirling, Kathy
Nat'l Ass'n of School Resource Officers **(371)**

Shiroma CAE, John K.S.
United States Junior Chamber of Commerce **(534)**

Shiva, Jean
Internat'l Test and Evaluation Ass'n **(308)**

Shively, Robert
Golf Course Superintendents Ass'n of America **(248)**

Shivers, Leslie
Soc. for Mining, Metallurgy, and Exploration **(491)**

Shoemaker, Barbara N.
Cold Finished Steel Bar Institute **(196)**

Shoemaker, Becky
Truckload Carriers Ass'n **(527)**

Shoemaker, Bill
Registry of Interpreters for the Deaf **(473)**

Shoemaker, Janet
American Soc. for Microbiology **(104)**

Shoemaker, Tina
Nat'l Marine Educators Ass'n **(416)**

Shoesmith, Shannon
Corn Refiners Ass'n **(209)**

Sholar Ph.D., J. Ronald
American Peanut Research and Education Soc. **(90)**

Shomers, Suzanne
Door and Hardware Institute **(224)**

Shonerd, Jon S.
Building Service Contractors Ass'n Internat'l **(183)**

Shor, Nancy G.
Nat'l Organization of Social Security Claimants' Representatives **(420)**

Shore, Barbara
Ass'n of Film Commissioners Internat'l **(151)**

Shorr, Scott
Nat'l Ass'n of Veterans Program Administrators **(379)**

Short, Thomas
Internat'l Alliance of Theatrical Stage Employees and Moving Picture Technicians of the U.S. and Canada **(273)**

Shotkin, Andrea
North American Ass'n for Environmental Education **(440)**

Shoun, Gary
Internat'l Livestock Theft Investigators Ass'n **(296)**

Shrader Ph.D., Charles R.
Soc. for Military History **(491)**

Shriner-Cahn, David
Jewish Education Service of North America **(314)**

Shriver, Ann L.
Internat'l Institute of Fisheries Economics and Trade **(294)**

Shropshire, Cheryl
American Hackney Horse Soc. **(71)**

Shrum, Wesley
Soc. for Social Studies of Science **(494)**

Shubik, Philippe
Toxicology Forum **(524)**

Shuck, J. Vincent
American Academy of Implant Dentistry **(22)**

Shuey, Phillip N.
Internat'l Ass'n of Audio Visual Communicators **(276)**

Shufelt, James W.
Snack Food Ass'n **(484)**

Shuld, Marcy
Nat'l Insurance Crime Bureau **(412)**

Shulman, Brian B.
Nat'l Student Speech Language Hearing Ass'n **(432)**

Shulman, Carole K.
Professional Skaters Ass'n **(467)**

Shultz, Paul
Nat'l Telephone Cooperative Ass'n **(433)**

Shumate, Ron
Ass'n of Railway Communicators **(163)**

Shuping CAE, Frances
Air Conditioning Contractors of America **(15)**

Shurtleff, William
Soyfoods Ass'n of North America **(511)**

Shute, Lynda
Electronics Technicians Ass'n Internat'l **(229)**

Shute, Richard H.
Photo Chemical Machining Institute **(457)**

Shuter, Dale
Internat'l Ass'n of Administrative Professionals **(275)**

Shvyrkov, Vladislav V.
Internat'l Soc. of Statistical Science **(307)**

Shwidock, Carolyn
American Ass'n of Healthcare Consultants **(37)**

Shyposh, Philip C.
Ass'n of Nat'l Advertisers **(158)**

Sibert, Bonnie
Nat'l Ass'n of Supervisors of Business Education **(377)**

Sibert, Steve
Grocery Manufacturers of America **(250)**

Sibley, Elizabeth A.
Emergency Medicine Residents' Ass'n **(229)**

Sickles, Mark D.
Dredging Contractors of America **(224)**

Siddon, Arthur
Forum for Investor Advice **(243)**

Sides, Angela
Nat'l Ass'n of County Surveyors **(351)**

Sidlow, Terry
College of American Pathologists **(197)**

Sidor, John
Council of State Community Development Agencies **(215)**

Sidwell, Kathleen
Internat'l Institute of Ammonia Refrigeration **(294)**

Sieben, Steve
American Academy of Periodontology **(25)**

Siegal, Nancy L.
Ass'n of Academic Health Centers **(141)**

Siegel, Esther
Nat'l Ass'n of Housing Cooperatives **(359)**

Siegel, Gail A.
Nat'l Ass'n of Resale and Thrift Shops **(370)**

Siegel MSW, Gale
American Orthopsychiatric Ass'n **(89)**

Siegel, Dr. Mortoa
United Synagogue of Conservative Judaism **(536)**

Siegel, Phillip
Nat'l Organization of Industrial Trade Unions **(420)**

Siegel, Stanley
Aerospace Industries Ass'n of America (13)

Siegl, Simon
American Vintners Ass'n (122)

Sienkiewicz CAE, CMP, Jone R.
Real Estate Educators Ass'n (472)
Ass'n of Insurance Compliance Professionals (154)
Employee Involvement Ass'n (229)
Ass'n for Volunteer Administration (140)

Sigel, Robert F.
Automotive Service Industry Ass'n (175)

Sigler Ph.D., Andrea
Connected Int'l Meeting Professionals Ass'n (206)

Sigmon CAE, Joyce
American Academy of Implant Dentistry (22)

Sikkila, Dorothy A.
Nat'l Ass'n of Collegiate Directors of Athletics (348)

Sikora, Edward J.
Nat'l Clay Pipe Institute (387)

Silbermann CAE, Bryan E.
Produce Marketing Ass'n (463)

Silcox, Clark R.
Nat'l Electrical Manufacturers Ass'n (400)

Silk, Sue A.
World Ass'n of Alcohol Beverage Industries (549)

Silos, Beth
Power Transmission Distributors Ass'n (461)

Silva-Reyes, Eliana
American Soc. for Aesthetic Plastic Surgery (100)

Silvanik, Bob
Council of State Governments (216)

Silver, Denise
Soc. of Vascular Technology (508)

Silver, Howard J.
Consortium of Social Science Ass'ns (206)

Silver, Martha
Organization for the Promotion and Advancement of Small Telecommunications Companies (449)

Silvergleit, Ira T.
Soc. of American Florists (497)

Silverio, Craig
Packaging Machinery Manufacturers Institute (452)

Silverman CAE, SPHR, Dale K.
Ass'n of Woodworking and Furnishings Suppliers (170)

Silverman, Hope
Professional Apparel Ass'n (464)

Silverman, Paul K.
Jewelers' Security Alliance of the U.S. (314)

Silverman, Richard S.
Internat'l Hydrolized Protein Council (294)

Simek, James
Professional Currency Dealers Ass'n (465)

Simmering, Jeff
Council of the Great City Schools (216)

Simmonds, Dr. Warren L.
American Soc. of Podiatric Medicine (115)

Simmons DVM, Donald G.
American Veterinary Medical Ass'n (121)

Simmons, Karen
Alliance for Nonprofit Management (17)

Simmons, Mike
Log House Builders Ass'n of North America (320)

Simmons, Pope
Nat'l Council for Community Behavioral Healthcare (393)

Simmons, Rhonda
American Soc. for Clinical Investigation (101)
North American Soc. for Pediatric Gastroenterology and Nutrition (444)

Simmons, Thomas S.
Investment Company Institute (312)

Simmons, Vicki
Internat'l Ass'n for Exposition Management (274)

Simms, Cheryl
African-American Natural Foods Ass'n (14)

Simon, Brona
Nat'l Ass'n of State Archaeologists (373)

Simon, Lisa
Nat'l Tour Ass'n (434)

Simon, Richard
Family Therapy Network (234)

Simonds, Lisa
Nat'l Ass'n of Women in Construction (380)

Simone, Anthony
Nat'l Subacute Care Ass'n (432)

Simonse, Dr. Arnold
Nat'l Ass'n of Vision Professionals (379)

Simonski, Robert E.
Council of Industrial Boiler Owners (214)

Simonton, Gail M.
Nat'l Ass'n of Security Companies (372)

Simpson, Brian
American Bureau of Metal Statistics (49)

Simpson, Cynthia
Truckload Carriers Ass'n (527)

Simpson, Harold
Television Bureau of Advertising (521)

Simpson, Linda
Transportation Loss Prevention and Security Council (526)

Simpson, Mary Ann
American Alliance for Health, Physical Education, Recreation and Dance (27)

Simpson, Michael
Nat'l Council for the Social Studies (393)

Simpson, Sheila
Nat'l Ass'n of Hosiery Manufacturers (358)

Simpson, Ted
Construction Management Ass'n of America (206)

Simrany, Joseph P.
Tea Ass'n of the United States of America (520)
Tea Council of the U.S.A. (520)

Sims, Craig
Farm Equipment Manufacturers Ass'n (235)

Sims, Helena
Nat'l Automated Clearing House Ass'n (381)

Sinanoglou, Ioannis
Council for European Studies (211)

Sinclair, Bertie
Nat'l Ass'n of Secretaries of State (372)

Sinex, Debbie
American Ass'n of Meat Processors (38)

Singer Ph.D., Allen M.
American Ass'n of Colleges of Osteopathic Medicine (34)

Singer CMP, Ann E.
American School Food Service Ass'n (99)

Singer, Barbara
Footwear Industries of America (242)

Singer, Dale
Renal Physicians Ass'n (474)

Singer, Dana
Soc. of North American Goldsmiths (504)

Singer, Franz
Hair Internat'l (250)

Singer, Janet
Environmental Design Research Ass'n (231)

Singer, Jean
Tea Council of the U.S.A. (520)
Tea Ass'n of the United States of America (520)

Singer, Terry
Nat'l Ass'n of Energy Service Companies (354)

Singerling CCM,CEC, James B.
Club Managers Ass'n of America (195)

Singla D.D.S., Raj
Indian Dental Ass'n (USA) (262)

Singleton, Barbara
Community Transportation Ass'n of America (201)

Sink, Vaughn
Advertising and Marketing Internat'l Network (12)

Sinkford D.D.S., Ph, Jeanne C.
American Ass'n of Dental Schools (36)

Sinkle, Jefferey
Nat'l Ass'n of Installation Developers (360)

Sirgy, M. Joseph
Internat'l Soc. for Quality-of-Life Studies (304)

Sirois, R.J.
Commercial-Investment Real Estate Institute (199)

Sirovatka, Kristen
Nat'l Conference on Public Employee Retirement Systems (391)

Sisco, August L.
Magnet Distributors and Fabricators Ass'n (322)
Magnetic Materials Producers Ass'n (322)
Nat'l Ass'n of Architectural Metal Manufacturers (343)
Pressure Vessel Manufacturers Ass'n (462)

Sistler, Patricia
Smocking Arts Guild of America (484)

Sisto, Gary
American Institute of Graphic Arts (77)

Sites, Tim
Recording Industry Ass'n of America (472)

Siu, Jenny
Asian American Certified Public Accountants (128)

Sivia, Karen
American Camping Ass'n (50)

Siviter, Kathleen
Advertising Mail Marketing Ass'n (12)

Sizemore, Christina
Nat'l Pharmaceutical Alliance (422)

Sjoberg, Judith
American Soc. for Mass Spectrometry (104)
Analytical Laboratory Managers Ass'n (124)
Federation of Analytical Chemistry and Spectroscopy Societies (236)

Sjolander CAE, Carole
Internat'l Ass'n of Family Entertainment Centers (279)

Skaggs, Bruce
Delta Dental Plans Ass'n (221)

Skelton, Barbara
Interstate Oil and Gas Compact Commission (312)

Skiados, Don P.
Air Line Pilots Ass'n, Internat'l (16)

Skibbie USAF (RET.), Lt.Gen. Lawrence F.
Nat'l Defense Industrial Ass'n (399)

Skiles, James H.
Grocery Manufacturers of America (250)

Skillman, Barbara
American School Food Service Ass'n (99)

Skinner, Bruce
Internat'l Festivals and Events Ass'n (291)

Skinner Ph.D., John H.
Solid Waste Ass'n of North America (510)
SWANA - Solid Waste Ass'n of North America (519)

Skinner, Peter
American Soc. of Media Photographers (112)

Skiver, LaJuan
CHA - Certified Horsemanship Ass'n (190)

Skjervem, Harley
Credit Union Nat'l Ass'n (218)

Skjothaldg, Jolene K.
Timber Products Manufacturers (523)

Sklar, Scott
Solar Energy Industries Ass'n (510)
Nat'l Bio-Energy Industries Ass'n (383)

Sklarow, Mark H.
Independent Educational Consultants Ass'n (260)

Skoff, Laura
Soc. of Nat'l Ass'n Publications (504)

Skomra, Cheri
Composites Manufacturing Ass'n of SME (202)
Ass'n for Forming and Fabricating Technologies of SME (133)
Ass'n for Finishing Processes of SME (133)

Skopp, Lori
New York Academy of Sciences (438)

Skurat, Michelle
Soc. for Experimental Mechanics (488)

Slaby, Patty
Nat'l Ass'n of Blind Teachers (345)

Slack, Glenn N.
Livestock Conservation Institute (320)

Slagle CAE, G. Stephen
Promotional Products Ass'n Internat'l (468)

Slate II, William K.
American Arbitration Ass'n (28)

Slater, Charels E.
Concrete Reinforcing Steel Institute (203)

Slater, Dennis J.
Construction Industry Manufacturers Ass'n (206)

Slaven, Scott
PROMAX Internat'l (468)

Slavik, Julie
Council for Basic Education (211)

Slavin, Jennifer
Nat'l Ass'n of State Credit Union Supervisors (374)

Slaw Ph.D., Kenneth M.
American Academy of Pediatrics (25)

Slawny, James R.
Soc. of Surgical Oncology (507)
American College of Allergy, Asthma and Immunology (53)
American Soc. of Colon and Rectal Surgeons (108)

Slawny, Rick
Soc. of Surgical Oncology (507)
American Ass'n of Certified Allergists (34)

Sleeper, Steve
Beauty and Barber Supply Institute (177)

Sleigh, Stephen R.
Internat'l Ass'n of Machinists and Aerospace Workers (280)

Sleight, Thomas N.
U.S. Grains Council (528)

Sloan CAE, Holly
Ass'n of Junior Leagues Internat'l (155)

Sloan CMM, Suzanne B.
American Boat Builders and Repairers Ass'n (48)

Sloane, David
American Humor Studies Ass'n (74)

Sloper, Tamara
American Registry of Diagnostic Medical Sonographers (97)

Slothower, Douglas W.
Nat'l Potato Promotion Board (423)

Sloyan, Peggy
Academy of Osseointegration (9)

Smariga, Rob
American Anthropological Ass'n (28)

Smarr, Lawrence
Physician Insurers Ass'n of America (458)

Smeage, Dennis E.
American Association of Healthcare Administrative Management (45)
Ass'n for Hospital Medical Education (134)

Smeallie, Peter
American Rock Mechanics Ass'n (98)

Smerko, Robert G.
Chlorine Institute (193)

Smigel D.D.S., Irwin
American Soc. for Dental Aesthetics (102)

Smiklo, Charmaine
Soc. of Professors of Child and Adolescent Psychiatry (506)

Smilley, Patricia
American Camping Ass'n (50)

Smiroldo, Diane
Business Software Alliance (185)

Smith, Andre
Internat'l Oculoplastic Soc. (298)

Smith, Barbara
Ass'n for Healthcare Philanthropy (134)

Smith, Bea Pace
Nat'l Ass'n for Equal Opportunity in Higher Education (339)

Smith Ph.D., Becky J.
American Ass'n for Health Education (31)

Smith, Caby C.
World Computer Graphics Ass'n (549)

Smith, Cate K.
Delta Theta Phi (221)

Smith, Catherine
American Desalting Ass'n (64)

Smith Ph.D., Clarence T.
American Council of Applied Clinical Nutrition (61)

Smith CAE, Cynthia Kelly
Golf Course Superintendents Ass'n of America (248)

Smith, Dale
Internat'l Ass'n of Fire Chiefs (279)

Smith, Daniel
American Forests (69)

Smith, Darlene A.
United Ostomy Ass'n (531)

Smith, Darrell
Internat'l Window Film Ass'n (311)

Smith, Dave
Forest Industries Telecommunications (242)

Smith Ph.D., David C.
Council for Ethics in Economics (211)

Smith &, David R.
Manuscript Soc. (323)

Smith, David W.
American Soc. of Corporate Secretaries (109)

Smith, Deborah
Bankers' Ass'n for Foreign Trade (176)

Smith CMP, Deborah K.
EDUCAUSE (227)

Smith, Deirdre
Women in Internat'l Security (546)

Smith, Denise
Radio-Television News Directors Ass'n (471)

Smith, Dereka
Nat'l Genealogical Soc. (406)

Smith CMC, Dudley C.
Ass'n of Management Consulting Firms (156)

Smith, Eileen
Ass'n for the Advancement of Medical Instrumentation (138)

Smith, Eleanor
Ass'n of College and University Telecommunications
   Administrators (147)

Smith, Elizabeth M.
American Federation of Teachers (67)

Smith, Eric H.
Internat'l Intellectual Property Alliance (295)

Smith, Estela
Geothermal Resources Council (247)

Smith, Eve
OPERA America (448)

Smith, Gary S.
Livestock Marketing Ass'n (320)

Smith Jr., George W.
American Ass'n for Vocational Instructional Materials (32)

Smith, Georgette
American Soc. for Therapeutic Radiology and Oncology (105)

Smith M.D., Greg
Academy of Operative Dentistry (9)

Smith, Greg
Internat'l Franchise Ass'n (292)

Smith Ph.D., H. Duane
American Soc. of Mammalogists (112)

Smith Jr., I. Barton
Apiary Inspectors of America (125)

Smith, J. Daniel
Propeller Club of the U.S. (468)

Smith, J. Sharpe
Industrial Telecommunications Ass'n (263)

Smith, J. Thomas
Nat'l Kerosene Heater Ass'n (414)

Smith, J.P.
American Soc. of Bariatric Physicians (107)

Smith, Jacqueline
Foragers of America (242)

Smith, James N.
Council of Infrastructure Financing Authorities (214)

Smith, Jamie
Broadcast Cable Financial Management Ass'n (182)

Smith, Jeffrey
Drug and Alcohol Testing Industry Ass'n (225)

Smith, Jeffrey C.
Committee for Private Offshore Rescue and Towing (C-
   PORT) (200)
Commercial Weather Services Ass'n (199)
Nat'l Ass'n of Charterboat Operators (346)
Institute of Clean Air Companies (266)

Smith Jr., Jesse M.
American Morgan Horse Ass'n (85)

Smith, Joyce E.
Nat'l Ass'n for College Admission Counseling (338)

Smith CMP, Judy M.
Modular Building Institute (330)

Smith, Julie
Business and Professional Women/USA (184)

Smith, Karen
Internat'l Personnel Management Ass'n (299)

Smith, Katherine
APPA: The Ass'n of Higher Education Facilities Officers (126)

Smith, Katherine J.
Ass'n of Higher Education Facilities Officers (153)

Smith, Kathleen A.
American School Counselor Ass'n (99)

Smith, Kathleen M.
American Forest and Paper Ass'n (69)

Smith, Kathryn J.
American Ass'n of Electrodiagnostic Medicine (36)

Smith, Kevin
Government Finance Officers Ass'n of the United States and
   Canada (248)

Smith, Kim
American Helicopter Soc. (73)

Smith, Laura
Nat'l Ocean Industries Ass'n (419)

Smith, Leslie
American Collectors Ass'n (52)

Smith MSN,RN,CNN, Linda J.
American Nephrology Nurses Ass'n (86)

Smith, Lisa Keller
Nat'l Council of Farmer Cooperatives (394)

Smith CPS, Lynette M.
Ass'n of Business Support Services Internat'l (145)

Smith, Lynn
Nat'l Soc. of Fund Raising Executives (429)

Smith, Marilyn Dix
Internat'l Soc. for Pharmacoeconomics and Outcomes
   Research (304)

Smith Ph.D., Marilyn M.
Nat'l Ass'n for the Education of Young Children (341)

Smith, Matthew
America's Community Bankers (20)

Smith, Michael J.
American Geological Institute (70)

Smith, Michelle
Mutual Fund Education Alliance (332)

Smith, Nancy W.
Radiation Therapy Oncology Group (471)

Smith, P. Gregory
Soc. of American Foresters (497)

Smith, Pamela A.
American Osteopathic College of Radiology (89)

Smith, Paula S.
Soc. of Experimental Test Pilots (501)

Smith, Peg L.
American Camping Ass'n (50)

Smith, Peggy
Nat'l Ass'n of Computer Consultant Businesses (349)

Smith R.N., M.B., Petrina M.
American Soc. of Cytopathology (109)

Smith, Polly
Employee Relocation Council (229)

Smith, Rick
American Ass'n of Health Plans (37)

Smith, Robin R.
Soc. of Quality Assurance (506)

Smith, Roger
Compressed Gas Ass'n (202)

Smith, Ron
FTD Ass'n (244)

Smith, Ronald A.
North American Soc. for Sport History (444)

Smith, Ronald E.
American Ass'n of Cosmetology Schools (35)

Smith, Rudolph C.
Nat'l Ass'n of Black Social Workers (345)

Smith, Ruth N.
Nat'l Ass'n of State Universities and Land Grant Colleges (376)

Smith, Samuel
OPERA America (448)

Smith, Shandee J.
Nat'l Ass'n of Insurance Women (360)

Smith, Sherman
Internat'l Ass'n of Business Communicators (276)

Smith, Sid
Nat'l Ass'n of Hosiery Manufacturers (358)

Smith, Stacey
American Business Women's Ass'n (50)

Smith, Steven M.
Internat'l Ass'n of Conference Centers (277)

Smith, Steven R.
Nat'l Rural Letter Carriers' Ass'n (426)

Smith, Susan
Chocolate Manufacturers Ass'n of the U.S.A. (193)

Smith, Susan M.
Ass'n of Information Technology Professionals (154)

Smith, Susan Snyder
Nat'l Confectioners Ass'n of the United States (389)
American Cocoa Research Institute (52)

Smith CAE, Ted M.
American Collectors Ass'n (52)

Smith, Thomas M.
American Speech-Language-Hearing Ass'n (117)

Smith, Thomas W.
Nat'l Retail Hardware Ass'n (425)

Smith, Vaughan A.
American Ass'n of Healthcare Consultants (37)

Smith CMP, Vicki Glass
Nat'l Ass'n of Development Organizations (352)

Smith, Wayne J.
NGV Producers Ass'n (439)
Nat'l Limousine Ass'n (415)

Smith, Wayne M.
Non Commissioned Officers Ass'n of the U.S.A. (439)

Smith, Wendy J.M.
Soc. of Nuclear Medicine (504)

Smith Jr, William C.
Industrial Foundation of America (263)

Smith, William E.
Popcorn Institute (460)

Smith, Ph.D., Rosemarie
Nat'l Ass'n of Certified Valuation Analysts (346)

Smitherman, Dr. Ken
Ass'n of Christian Schools Internat'l (146)

Smithers, Cheryl
Fluid Power Distributors Ass'n (241)
Ultrasonic Industry Ass'n (529)

Smock, William H.
Silicones Environmental Health and Safety Council of North
   America (483)

Smoczynski, Mary Ellen
Footwear Distributors and Retailers of America (242)

Smolders, Jan
Internat'l Copper Ass'n (287)

Smolskis, Joseph
Nat'l Council of Farmer Cooperatives (394)

Smoot, Oliver R.
Information Technology Industry Council (264)

Smucker, Bob
Independent Sector (261)

Smyth, Theresa
College Art Ass'n (197)

Smythe, Alison
Internat'l Swaps and Derivatives Ass'n (308)

Smythe, Nancy
American Cleft Palate-Craniofacial Ass'n (52)

Smythe, William K.
NPES, the Ass'n for Suppliers of Printing and Publishing
   Technologies (446)

Snachez, Ozi
American Ass'n of Clinical Endocrinologists (34)

Snapp, David
Broadcast Designers' Ass'n (182)

Sneed, Helen
Nat'l Alliance for Musical Theatre (336)

Sneed, Robert
Nat'l Ass'n of Independent Fee Appraisers (359)

Sneeringer, Thomas M.
American Iron and Steel Institute (79)

Snell, Ronald
Nat'l Conference of State Legislatures (391)

Snelson, Kathy
American Desalting Ass'n (64)

Snider, Olive L.
Internat'l Compressor Remanufacturers Ass'n (286)

Snow, Gerard C.
Transportation Institute (525)

Snyder, Bill
Automation Forum (174)

Snyder, Dr. Daniel E.
American Ass'n of Veterinary Parasitologists (45)

Snyder, Karol B.
American Geophysical Union (70)

Snyder Jr., Ph.D., Oscar P.
Soc. for Foodservice Systems (488)

Snyder CAE, Richard D.
Asphalt Roofing Manufacturers Ass'n (129)

Snyder, Russell K.
Roof Coatings Manufacturers Ass'n (477)

Snyder, Shelly R.
General Aviation Manufacturers Ass'n (246)

Snyder, Stephen F.
Nat'l Ass'n of Jai Alai Frontons (360)

Snyder, Stephen P.
Book Manufacturers Institute (181)

Snyder, Wallace S.
American Advertising Federation (27)

So, Frank
American Institute of Certified Planners (76)
American Planning Ass'n (92)

Sodano, Salvatore F.
Nat'l Ass'n of Securities Dealers (372)

Sohl, Bruce
Illuminating Engineering Soc. of North America (259)

Sokolek, Beverly M.
Nat'l Ass'n of Mutual Insurance Companies (363)

Sokolowski, Ron
Health Sciences Communications Ass'n (252)

Solarz, Barry
American Iron and Steel Institute (79)

Soldavin, Kim
Resistance Welder Manufacturers Ass'n (475)
Internat'l Ass'n of Ice Cream Vendors (280)
Professional Soc. for Sales and Marketing Training (467)

Soldier, Helen Long
Nat'l Indian Counselors Ass'n (410)

Solomon J.D., Ronni
ECRI (226)

Solomon, Stephen
Nat'l Hockey League (409)

Soloway, Rose Ann G.
American Ass'n of Poison Control Centers (41)

Soltz, Barry E.
AERA - Engine Rebuilders Ass'n (12)

Sombrotto, Vincent R.
Nat'l Ass'n of Letter Carriers (361)

Somerlot, Rita
United States Women's Track Coaches Ass'n (535)

Somers Jr., Fred L.
Nat'l Golf Car Manufacturers Ass'n (407)

Somers, Frederick P.
American Occupational Therapy Ass'n (88)

Somerville, Nancy
American Institute of Architects (76)

Somerville, Robert D.
American Bureau of Shipping and Affiliated Companies (49)

Somes-Schloesser, Jayne
Nat'l Multi Housing Council (417)

Sommer, Ken
American Soc. of Ass'n Executives (107)

Sommer, Richard
American Soc. for Cell Biology (101)

Sommer, Wayne
Internat'l City/County Management Ass'n (285)

Sommermeyer, David
Ass'n of Lutheran Secondary Schools (156)

Sommers, Dave
Non Commissioned Officers Ass'n of the U.S.A. (439)

Sommers, Wendy
Ass'n of Professional Model Makers (161)

Sondag, Michael
American Ass'n for Laboratory Animal Science (31)

Song, Kathleen
Nat'l Ass'n of Public Hospitals and Health Systems (368)

Sonke, Sarah
American Bed and Breakfast Ass'n (47)

Sonneborn, Charles
Soc. for Excellence in Eyecare (488)

Sophos, Mary
Grocery Manufacturers of America (250)

Sorensen, Alexis
Internat'l Festivals and Events Ass'n (291)

Sorensen, Mitch
Professional Show Managers Ass'n (467)

Sorenson, Lisa
Automotive Warehouse Distributors Ass'n (175)

Soriano, Adela
Latin Business Ass'n (317)

Sorley, Dr. Lewis
Ass'n of Military Colleges and Schools of the U.S. (157)

Sorrell, Kimberley B.
North American Trucking Industrial Relations Ass'n (445)

Sorrell, Susan
Ass'n of State Dam Safety Officials (166)

Sosa, Gabriela
Turnaround Management Ass'n (528)

Sotack, Noelle C.
Nat'l Business Education Ass'n (384)

Sottosanti, Vincent
Ass'n of Promotion Marketing Agencies Worldwide (162)

Soule, Jeff
American Planning Ass'n (92)

Sousa, Barbara
Marketing Research Ass'n (324)

Souters, Ron
Health Insurance Ass'n of America (252)

Southard, Greta
Public Library Ass'n (469)

Southerland Smith, Sharon
Internat'l Ass'n of Fire Chiefs (279)

Souza, Caryn
Community Transportation Ass'n of America (201)

Souza, Jennifer
American Health Care Ass'n (72)

Sowards, Gregory
Drug, Chemical and Allied Trades Ass'n (225)

Sowers, Becky
Country Music Ass'n (217)

Spada, Abbe
Nat'l Air Duct Cleaners Ass'n (335)

Spader, Richard L.
American Angus Ass'n (28)

Spaeth, Jim
Advertising Research Foundation (12)

Spague, Jackie
Ass'n for Hospital Medical Education (134)

Spahr CAE, Frederick T.
American Speech-Language-Hearing Ass'n (117)

Spangler, Kathy J.
American Park and Recreation Soc. (90)

Spangler, Larry
Nat'l Kitchen and Bath Ass'n (414)

Spangler, Peggy
Nat'l Cooperative Business Ass'n (392)

Spano, Michael A.
Beauty and Barber Supply Institute (177)

Spanos, Nicole R.J.
American Soc. of TV Cameramen (116)

Spar, Edward J.
Council of Professional Ass'ns on Federal Statistics (215)

Sparacino CAE, Katherine
Nat'l Vehicle Leasing Ass'n (435)

Sparkf, Stacy
Internat'l Physical Fitness Ass'n (299)

Sparks Ph.D., Dennis
Nat'l Staff Development Council (431)

Sparks, Jennifer
Soc. of American Florists (497)

Sparks, John
American Symphony Orchestra League (119)

Sparrough, Michael E.
Internat'l Union of Bricklayers and Allied Craftsmen (309)

Sparrowe, Rollin D.
Wildlife Management Institute (544)

Sparschott, Jeff
United States-Mexico Chamber of Commerce (536)

Spaulding, Karen
American Institute of Professional Geologists (78)

Spaulding, Kenneth B.
Internat'l Hydrofoil Soc. (294)

Spaulding, Romeo O.
Internat'l Ass'n of Black Professional Fire Fighters (276)

Spawn, James A.
American Murray Grey Ass'n (86)
American Tarentaise Ass'n (119)
American Blonde D'Aquitaine Ass'n (47)
North American Corriente Ass'n (441)
American Belgian Blue Breeders Ass'n (47)
American Brahmousin Council (49)

Spear, M. A.
Nat'l Propane Gas Ass'n (423)

Spear, Susan
Nat'l Propane Gas Ass'n (423)

Spears, Ruth
Nat'l Ass'n of Railway Business Women (368)

Spears, Sandra
Healthcare Information and Management Systems Soc. (253)

Speath, Mike
Nat'l Ass'n of Printers and Lithographers (366)

Specht, Phyllis
Costume Soc. of America (210)

Speckhardt, Lisa
Internat'l Soc. for Ecological Economics (303)

Speer Ph.D., J. Alexander
Mineralogical Soc. of America (329)

Speer, Kathie
American Booksellers Ass'n (48)

Speer ACS, Ken
LOMA (321)

Speer, Wilbur
Nat'l Ass'n of Retired Federal Employees (370)

Spehar, Ann E.
EUCG (233)

Spehar CAE, Ann E.
American Academy of Oral and Maxillofacial Pathology (24)
Calendar Marketing Ass'n (185)
Barbecue Industry Ass'n (177)

Speight, Emily
Marine Technology Soc. (324)

Speiser, Abraham A.
Ass'n of Junior Leagues Internat'l (155)

Spellane, C. James
Internat'l Brotherhood of Electrical Workers (284)

Spellman, James D.
Securities Industry Ass'n (481)

Spellman, Nancy W.
American Institute for CPCU - Insurance Institute of America (75)

Spence, Denyse
Undersea and Hyperbaric Medical Soc. (529)

Spence CAE, Sandra
Soc. of Glass and Ceramic Decorators (502)

Spence, Tara
Nat'l Soft Drink Ass'n (430)

Spencer, Anthony
American Council on Exercise (62)

Spencer Jr., Jeff
Nat'l Ass'n for Bilingual Education (338)

Spencer, Jody
Ceramic Manufacturers Ass'n (189)
Miniatures Industry Ass'n of America (329)

Spencer, John S.
American Bureau of Shipping and Affiliated Companies (49)

Spencer, Todd
Owner-Operator Independent Drivers Ass'n (452)

Spencer, William B.
Associated Builders and Contractors (170)

Spengler, Anne
American Soc. of Heating, Refrigerating and Air-Conditioning Engineers (110)

Sperger, Marlys
American Massage Therapy Ass'n (83)

Speros, Kelley
American Institute of Ultrasound in Medicine (78)

Spetter, Allan B.
Soc. for Historians of American Foreign Relations (488)

Spiegel, Susan
Textile Bag and Packaging Ass'n (522)
Burlap and Jute Ass'n (184)
Jute Carpet Backing Council (315)

Spielberger, Marcia
Nat'l Council of State Supervisors of Foreign Languages (396)

Spielberger, Ronald E.
College Media Advisers (197)

Spilhaus Jr., Ph.D., Athelstan F.
American Geophysical Union (70)

Spilhaus, Karl H.
Cashmere and Camel Hair Manufacturers Institute (187)
Northern Textile Ass'n (446)

Spillane, Megan
Internat'l Soc. for Performance Improvement (304)

Spillane, Michael J.
Federation of Diocesan Liturgical Commissions (237)

Spiller, Ronald F.
Security Industry Ass'n (481)

Spina Ph.D., CAE, Joseph H.
Nat'l Ass'n of College and University Food Services (348)

Spindler, Dean
Nat'l Ass'n of State Land Reclamationists (375)

Spindler, Michelle
American Ass'n of Pathologists' Assistants (40)

Spindler, Robert P.
Nat'l Council of Postal Credit Unions (395)

Spindor, SuzAnn
Texas Longhorn Breeders Ass'n of America (521)

Spira CAE, Patricia G.
Internat'l Ticketing Ass'n (308)

Spitz CKD, CBD,N, John S.
Nat'l Kitchen and Bath Ass'n (414)

Spitz CKD, CBD, John S.
Soc. of Certified Kitchen and Bathroom Designers **(499)**

Splete Ph.D., Allen P.
Council of Independent Colleges **(214)**

Spolyar, Robert
Nat'l Ass'n of Mutual Insurance Companies **(363)**

Spong, Ruth
American Ass'n of Physics Teachers **(41)**

Spoores, Craig
Nat'l Trappers Ass'n **(434)**

Spota, Noreen M.
Soc. for Developmental and Behavioral Pediatrics **(487)**

Spradlin, Sarah
American Soc. for Public Administration **(105)**

Spragens, Ann W.
Alliance of American Insurers **(18)**

Spragens, Lori
Ass'n of State Dam Safety Officials **(166)**

Sprague, Daniel M.
Council of State Governments **(216)**

Sprague, Stephen R.
American Federation of Musicians of the United States and Canada **(67)**

Spring, Michelle P.
Nat'l Food Processors Ass'n **(405)**

Springer, Jack M.
Metal Framing Manufacturers Ass'n **(327)**
Internat'l Formalwear Ass'n **(291)**
Cremation Ass'n of North America **(219)**
NAGMR Consumer Product Brokers **(333)**

Springer, Kay
Employee Assistance Professionals Ass'n **(229)**

Springirth, Sue
Nat'l FFA Organization **(404)**

Sproul, Pamela D.
American Soc. for Cytotechnology **(102)**

Sproull, Barbara
Nat'l Ass'n of Private Enterprise **(366)**

Sprung, Lowri
Nat'l Watercolor Soc. **(436)**

Spurdle, Cindy
Nat'l Ass'n of Equipment Leasing Brokers **(354)**

Spurlock, Michelle
American Academy of Facial Plastic and Reconstructive Surgery **(22)**

Squiers, Laura
Nat'l Ass'n of Private Enterprise **(366)**

Sreenivasan, Sreenath
South Asian Journalists Ass'n **(510)**

Sroka, John W.
Sheet Metal and Air Conditioning Contractors' Nat'l Ass'n **(482)**

St. Aubin, Barbara
Paint, Body and Equipment Ass'n **(452)**

St. Clair, Byron
Nat'l Translator Ass'n **(434)**

St. Germain, Mary
Middle East Librarians' Ass'n **(328)**

St. Germain, Michelle
Section for Women in Public Administration **(481)**

St. John CAE, William S.
Dietary Managers Ass'n **(222)**

Staab Ph.D., Wayne J.
American Auditory Soc. **(46)**

Stabler, Jim
Nat'l Ass'n of County Intergovernmental Relations Officials **(351)**

Stachura, Celine
Brass and Bronze Ingot Manufacturers **(181)**

Stack, E. Gifford
Nat'l Soft Drink Ass'n **(430)**

Stack, John W.
American Hardware Manufacturers Ass'n **(72)**

Stack, Michael J.
American Soc. for Industrial Security **(103)**

Stackpole CAE, Kerry C.
Electronic Messaging Ass'n **(228)**

Staebler, Rebecca
Soc. of American Foresters **(497)**

Staehle, Beth
Entomological Soc. of America **(231)**

Staff, Charlie
Distillers Grains Technology Council **(223)**

Staffan, Brenda
American Ambulance Ass'n **(28)**

Staffanou, Dr. Robert S.
American Academy of Fixed Prosthodontics **(22)**

Staffieri Pitsilos, Lenore
Gift Ass'n of America **(247)**

Stafford, James L.
Nat'l Ass'n of Royalty Owners **(370)**

Stafford, Michael
Ass'n for Health Services Research **(134)**

Stafford, Sandra R.
Nat'l Ass'n of Royalty Owners **(370)**

Stager, Elizabeth
OPERA America **(448)**

Stagg, William
Nat'l FFA Organization **(404)**

Stahl, Hans
Jockey Club **(314)**

Stahl, Howard M
American Conference of Cantors **(59)**

Stahl Ph.D., William
Histochemical Soc. **(254)**

Stahler, Mary
Soc. of Accredited Marine Surveyors **(496)**

Stahr, Pat
Soc. for Maternal Fetal Medicine **(491)**

Stahr, Steve
Million Dollar Round Table **(328)**

Staiger, Jeffrey
Ass'n of Literary Scholars and Critics **(156)**

Stalknecht, Paul T.
American Trucking Ass'ns **(121)**

Staller, Bernie
Nat'l FFA Organization **(404)**

Stallings, Margaret
North American Soc. for Pediatric Gastroenterology and Nutrition **(444)**

Stallmer, Eric W.
Space Transportation Ass'n **(511)**

Stallworth, Shauna D.
Organization of Black Designers **(450)**

Stambone, Deneen
American Corporate Counsel Ass'n **(60)**

Stamos, Marian D.
Ass'n of Home Appliance Manufacturers **(153)**

Stana, Ed
Resilient Floor Covering Institute **(475)**

Stanek, Kathy
Nat'l Ass'n of Tax Practitioners **(377)**

Stanfield, Shirley
Ass'n of Insolvency Accountants **(154)**

Stanford, Celenda A.
Nat'l Council of Agricultural Employers **(394)**

Stanhope, Victoria
Nat'l Ass'n of School Psychologists **(371)**

Staniec R.Ph., Daniel J.
Nat'l Council for Prescription Drug Programs **(393)**

Stanislaw Ph.D., Charles
Nat'l Swine Improvement Federation **(433)**

Stanke, Catherine
Institute of Management Accountants **(268)**

Stanley, James C.
Warehouse Distributors Ass'n **(540)**
Metal Construction Ass'n **(327)**
Construction and Agricultural Film Manufacturers Film Ass'n **(206)**

Stanley, Lynda
Federal Facilities Council **(236)**

Stanley, R. Brent
Americans for the Arts **(124)**

Stanonik, Frank A.
Gas Appliance Manufacturers Ass'n **(245)**

Stanton, Robert G.
American Soc. for Aesthetic Plastic Surgery **(100)**

Stapelberg, Graham
Ass'n of Surfing Professionals **(166)**

Staples, Maurice
Chorus America **(193)**

Staples-Bortner, Sandra
Wildlife Soc., The **(544)**

Star, Melissa
Internat'l Trademark Ass'n **(309)**

Starbuck-Buongiorno, B.K.
Soc. of Petroleum Evaluation Engineers **(505)**

Starke, M.D., Rod
American Heart Ass'n **(72)**

Starkey, Jane
America's Blood Centers **(19)**

Starkweather, Kendall N.
Internat'l Technology Education Ass'n **(308)**

Starr, Jan
American Dental Hygienists' Ass'n **(64)**

Starr, Suzanne
Soc. for Scholarly Publishing **(493)**

Staska, Amy
Nat'l Roofing Contractors Ass'n **(426)**

Stasko, Steve
Air and Waste Management Ass'n **(15)**

Statler, Stuart
Nat'l Ass'n of Criminal Defense Lawyers **(352)**

Staub, Shalom
American Folklore Soc. **(69)**

Staub, Steve
American Architectural Manufacturers Ass'n **(29)**

Stauffer, Delmar J.
Radiological Soc. of North America **(471)**

Stautzenbach, Tom
Academy of Osseointegration **(9)**

Stavneak, Jim
Nat'l Pork Producers Council **(423)**

Stavroudis, Chris
Western Ass'n for Art Conservation **(542)**

Steadman, Ann
Council of Insurance Agents and Brokers **(214)**

Stebbings, David W.
Recording Industry Ass'n of America **(472)**

Stech, Judy
Institute of Industrial Engineers **(267)**

Stech, Teri
Pediatric Orthopedic Soc. of North America **(454)**

Steel, Suzanne
Nat'l Ass'n of Agricultural Journalists **(343)**

Steele, Colin
Institute of Certified Professional Managers **(266)**

Steele, Cynthia
American Professional Soc. on the Abuse of Children **(94)**

Steele, Robert
American Soc. of Naval Engineers **(113)**

Steele, Scott L.
University/Resident Theatre Ass'n **(537)**

Steele, Stephen
Soc. for Applied Sociology **(485)**

Steensland, Mollie
Lawn and Garden Dealers' Ass'n **(318)**

Stefan, Maria
Sporting Goods Manufacturers Ass'n **(515)**

Stegen, P.J.
Fibre Channel Ass'n **(238)**

Steich, Thomas J.
American Occupational Therapy Ass'n **(88)**

Steighner, Dan
Minerals, Metals and Materials Soc., The **(329)**

Stein, Becky
American Academy of Addiction Psychiatry **(20)**

Stein, Dean K.
Chamber Music America **(190)**

Stein, Norman R.
Internat'l Soc. for Infectious Diseases **(303)**

Stein, Robert
American Bar Ass'n **(46)**

Stein CAE, Robert G.
Healthcare Forum, The **(252)**

Steinbach, John W.
Internat'l Foundation of Employee Benefit Plans **(292)**

Steinbach, Sheldon
American Council on Education **(61)**

Steinberg, Irwin
Tortilla Industry Ass'n **(524)**

Steinbrecher, Hank
United States Soccer Federation **(535)**

Steiner, Alan
Ass'n of America's Public Television Stations **(142)**

Steiner, Bruce A.
American Iron and Steel Institute **(79)**

Steiner, Peter J.
American Concrete Institute **(59)**
American Soc. of Concrete Contractors **(108)**

Steiner, Tmelia
Internat'l Food Information Council **(291)**

Steinhardt, David J.
North American Graphic Arts Suppliers Ass'n **(442)**
PrintImage Internat'l **(463)**

Steinkamp, Roger
North American Dairy Sheep Ass'n **(441)**

Steinke, Marilyn
Internat'l Special Events Soc. **(307)**

Steinkuller, William P.
Automotive Recyclers Ass'n **(175)**

Steinwachs, Barbara
North American Simulation and Gaming Ass'n **(444)**

Steitman, Roger
Independent Photo Imagers **(261)**

Steketee, Drew
Aircraft Owners and Pilots Ass'n **(16)**

Stellar, Charles
American Ass'n of Health Plans **(37)**

Stellitano, Faith
Nat'l Ass'n of Veterans Program Administrators **(379)**

Stellmach, Wayne
Steel Tank Institute **(517)**

Stellwagen, Nancy
Electrophoresis Soc. (229)

Stember, Lee Ann C.
Nat'l Council for Prescription Drug Programs (393)

Stemper CMP, Linda
Credit Union Executives Soc. (218)

Stempson, Brenda
Nat'l Glass Ass'n (407)

Stener, Sylvar
Nat'l Music Publishers' Ass'n (418)

Stengel, Ginny
Self Storage Ass'n (481)

Stengel, Nancy
Internat'l Microelectronics and Packaging Soc. (297)

Stengel, Sadra
TPA/The Tube and Pipe Ass'n, Internat'l (524)

Stensvold, Beverly
American Sleep Disorders Ass'n (100)

Stenzel, Denise
Nat'l Tour Ass'n (434)

Stenzel CAE, Thomas E.
United Fresh Fruit and Vegetable Ass'n (531)

Stepanovich Ph.D., Pamela Hopkins
Institute of Behavioral and Applied Management (265)

Stephens, Ben
Internat'l Warehouse Logistics Ass'n (310)

Stephens, Jacqueline
Internat'l Fabricare Institute (290)

Stephens, Jim
Agricultural Retailers Ass'n (14)

Stephens Ph.D., John F.
American Studies Ass'n (118)

Stephens, K.W.
Internat'l Family Recreation Ass'n (290)

Stephens, Larry D.
United States Committee on Irrigation and Drainage (532)
United States Committee on Large Dams (533)

Stephens, Shay
Nat'l Nursing Staff Development Organization (418)
Home Healthcare Nurses Ass'n (255)
Soc. for Vascular Nursing (496)
American Soc. of Pain Management Nurses (113)

Stephens, Sherry A.
Petroleum Equipment Suppliers Ass'n (455)

Stephens Jackson, Ann
Internat'l Atherosclerosis Soc. (283)

Stepp, Derek
Ass'n for Gerontology in Higher Education (134)

Steranka, Joe
Professional Golfers Ass'n of America (465)

Sterba, Jodeen M.
Internat'l Management Council (296)

Sterdivant, Tifanni
American Professional Soc. on the Abuse of Children (94)

Sterler, Lewis
Private Label Manufacturers Ass'n (463)

Sterling, Kim
Institute for Interconnecting and Packaging Electronic Circuits (265)

Sterling, Lesley
Equipment Leasing Ass'n of America (232)

Stern, Andrew L.
Service Employees Internat'l Union (482)

Stern, David
Nat'l Basketball Ass'n (382)

Stern, Larry D.
Commercial Vehicle Safety Alliance (199)

Stern, Liz
American Ass'n of Exporters and Importers (36)

Stern, Robert M.
Council on Governmental Ethics Law (217)

Stern, Ronald J.
Patent Office Professional Ass'n (454)

Sternfels, Urvan R.
Nat'l Petroleum Refiners Ass'n (422)

Stertzer, David
Ass'n for Advanced Life Underwriting (129)

Stetson, Wayne
Nat'l Ass'n of Home Builders of the U.S. (358)

Steurer, Stephen J.
Correctional Education Ass'n (209)

Steve, Jaime
American Wind Energy Ass'n (123)

Steveley, K.R.
Tilt-up Concrete Ass'n (523)

Stevens, Caroline
American Diabetes Ass'n (64)

Stevens M.D., David
Christian Medical and Dental Soc. (193)

Stevens, Joann
Ass'n of American Colleges and Universities (142)

Stevens, Maryanne
Catholic Theological Soc. of America (188)

Stevens, Meg Nagle
Licensing Executives Soc. (319)

Stevens, Michelle
Adhesive and Sealant Council (12)

Stevens Ph.D., Timothy S.
Ass'n for College and University Religious Affairs (131)

Stevenson, Bill
Internat'l Ass'n of Amusement Parks and Attractions (275)

Stevenson, Ian
Nat'l Minority Business Council (417)

Stevenson, Phoebe
American Sociological Ass'n (117)

Stevenson, Sharon
Nat'l Center for Homeopathy (386)

Stevenson, Terry
Ass'n of Industrial Real Estate Brokers (154)

Steward Ph.D., Colette
Clinical Laboratory Management Ass'n (194)

Steward, Lisa
Nuclear Energy Institute (446)

Stewart Ph.D., Bess B.
Ass'n of Black Nursing Faculty in Higher Education (145)

Stewart, Cathy
Nat'l Mental Health Ass'n (416)

Stewart, Dee
Nat'l Ass'n of Neonatal Nurses (363)

Stewart, Don
Nat'l Executive Service Corps (402)

Stewart, Ernest W.
Paint and Decorating Retailers Ass'n (452)

Stewart, Gordon C.
Insurance Information Institute (270)

Stewart, Heather
Regulatory Affairs Professionals Soc. (474)

Stewart, Rev. Imagene B.
African American Women's Clergy Ass'n (14)

Stewart, Isabel C.
Girls Incorporated (247)

Stewart Ph.D., NA, Jack
Nat'l Soc. of Mural Painters (430)

Stewart, Joyie
Soc. for Education in Anesthesia (487)

Stewart, Julie
American Gas Ass'n (70)

Stewart, Julie
Produce Marketing Ass'n (463)

Stewart, Robert
Nat'l Organization of Black Law Enforcement Executives (420)

Stewart, Robert B.
Nat'l Ocean Industries Ass'n (419)

Stewart, Robert G.
Ass'n of Diesel Specialists (149)

Stewart, Scott
Nat'l Live Stock Producers Ass'n (415)

Stewart, Sharon
American Bus Ass'n (49)

Stewart, Terri
Biotechnology Industry Organization (179)

Stewart, Thomas
Nat'l Rehabilitation Ass'n (425)

Stewart-Tavares, LaShonda
America's Blood Centers (19)

Stickle Ph.D., Warren E.
Chemical Producers and Distributors Ass'n (191)

Stidinger, Stephen H.
American Ass'n on Mental Retardation (45)

Stiklestad, Lynn
Archery Range and Retailers Organization (127)

Stiles, Janet
American Soc. for Bone and Mineral Research (101)

Stiles, Nancy
American Soc. of Marine Artists (112)

Still, Bob
Nat'l Ass'n of Sports Officials (373)

Still, Linda
Nat'l Ass'n of Recording Merchandisers (369)

Still Ph.D., Steven M.
Perennial Plant Ass'n (454)

Stillings Ph.D., Bruce R.
Chocolate Manufacturers Ass'n of the U.S.A. (193)
American Cocoa Research Institute (52)

Stilwill, Suzanne
Nat'l Appliance Parts Suppliers Ass'n (337)

Stine, Linda
Fresh Produce and Floral Council (244)

Stinger, Joseph A.
Internat'l Brotherhood of Boilermakers, Iron Ship Builders, Blacksmiths, Forgers and Helpers (284)

Stinnett, Lee
American Soc. of Newspaper Editors (113)

Stinson, Patrick B.
Nat'l Employee Services and Recreation Ass'n (401)

Stinton CAE, Dale Alexander
Nat'l Ass'n of REALTORS (369)

Stinziano Ph.D., Mike
Alliance of American Insurers (18)

Stirpe, David
Alliance for Responsible Atmospheric Policy (17)

Stitt, Bob
Woven Wire Products Ass'n (551)

Stitt-Gohdes, Dr. Wanda
American Vocational Education Research Ass'n (122)

Stluka, Thomas H.
American Academy of Dermatology (21)

Stock CAE, Arlene
Nat'l Ass'n of Judiciary Interpreters and Translators (361)

Stocker, Frederick T.
Manufacturers Alliance (322)

Stockinger, Charles M.
United States Cutting Tool Institute (533)
American Supply and Machinery Manufacturers' Ass'n (119)
Chemical Fabrics and Film Ass'n (191)
Hack and Band Saw Manufacturers Ass'n of America (250)
Metal Building Manufacturers Ass'n (327)
Power Tool Institute (461)

Stockman, Brian
Nat'l Corn Growers Ass'n (392)

Stockschlaeder, Ann
Ass'n of Former OSI Special Agents (152)

Stocksdale, Joy
Surface Design Ass'n (518)

Stohlton, John B.
American Ass'n of Presidents of Independent Colleges and Universities (41)

Stoiber, Susanne
Institute of Medicine (268)

Stoike, Donald A.
Lutheran Educational Conference of North America (321)

Stokes, Gail
Ass'n of Flight Attendants (151)

Stokes, Janet
Nat'l Ass'n of Health Underwriters (357)

Stokes, Judy
Refrigerated Foods Ass'n (473)

Stokes, Sharon McIntosh
Nat'l Ass'n of Child Advocates (347)

Stokes, Suzanne
Business and Professional Women/USA (184)

Stokesbury, Becky
Business Professionals of America (185)

Stoklosa, Raymond J.
Nat'l Ass'n of Real Estate Buyer Brokers (369)

Stolberg, Charles
Submersible Wastewater Pump Ass'n (518)

Stolgitis, William C.
Soc. for Technical Communication (494)

Stoll, Karl
Nat'l Religious Broadcasters (425)

Stollas, Christine
Public Risk Management Ass'n (470)

Stolzer, Ernie
Quality Bakers of America Cooperative (470)

Stone, Cheryl
Nat'l Ass'n of Government Guaranteed Lenders (357)

Stone, Denise
Irrigation Ass'n (313)

Stone, Jeremy J.
Federation of American Scientists (236)

Stone, Marcia
Nat'l Ass'n of State Facilities Administrators (375)
Nat'l Ass'n of State Personnel Executives (376)

Stone, Patricia
Nat'l Fellowship of Child Care Executives (404)

Stone, Ron
States Organization for Boating Access (516)

Stone, Suzanne
Ass'n for the Advancement of Medical Instrumentation (138)
Soc. of Vascular Technology (508)

Stone, Svetlana
New York Academy of Sciences (438)

Stoneburner, Connie
Nat'l Needlework Ass'n (418)

Stonehill, Charles F.
Alliance of American Insurers (18)

Stoner, Dennis
Nat'l Ass'n of Educational Buyers (353)

Stony, Florence R.
Refractories Institute (473)

Stooke, James G.
Ass'n of Professional Directors of YMCAs in the United States (161)

Stoops, John A.
Internat'l Council of Regional School Accrediting
Commissions (288)

Stopka D.D.S., Janet
Internat'l Academy of Oral Medicine and Toxicology (272)

Stopka, JoAnn
Alliance of American Insurers (18)

Storrs M.D., Bruce
American Soc. for Pediatric Neurosurgery (104)

Story, Deborah
Business and Professional Women/USA (184)

Stotts, Michael L.
Nat'l Remotivation Therapy Organization (425)

Stoupa CPA, Steve
Nat'l Ass'n of Health Underwriters (357)

Stove, Patty
American College of Emergency Physicians (54)

Stowe, Eric L.
American Chamber of Commerce Executives (51)

Stowe, Jennifer
Special Libraries Ass'n (514)

Stoy, Carol
American Mathematical Ass'n of Two Year Colleges (83)

Stoyanoff, Sheri
Wound, Ostomy and Continence Nurses Soc. (550)

Strachan CAE, David E.
American Wholesale Marketers Ass'n (123)

Strackbein, William C.
Laboratory Products Ass'n (316)
Opto-Precision Instruments Ass'n (449)

Strahm, Kenneth A.
Institute of Nuclear Power Operations (268)

Strain, Cara
Internat'l Livestock Theft Investigators Ass'n (296)
Internat'l Livestock Identification Ass'n (296)

Stramberg, Ruth
Ass'n of Service and Computer Dealers Internat'l (164)
North-American Ass'n of Telecommunications Dealers (446)

Strang, Lynne
American Financial Services Ass'n (68)

Strang, Terry
Internat'l Oil Scouts Ass'n (299)

Strange, Allen
Internat'l Computer Music Ass'n (286)

Strano CAE, Richard A.
American Ass'n for Aerosol Research (29)
American Conference of Governmental Industrial
Hygienists (59)

Strasma, E.J.
Interstate Producers Livestock Ass'n (312)

Strasma, Norman
Internat'l Map Trade Ass'n (296)

Strass, Elaine
American Soc. of Human Genetics (111)
Genetics Soc. of America (246)

Stratigos, Nicholas G.
Iron and Steel Soc. (313)

Stratman SM, Bernard F.
Nat'l Federation of Priests' Councils (404)

Stratton, Judy
American Ass'n of Sunday and Feature Editors (43)

Stratton, Mark
Soc. of Manufacturing Engineers (503)

Straub, Fred E.
American Economic Development Council (65)

Straub Ph.D., CAE, Sylvia A.
Employee Assistance Professionals Ass'n (229)

Strauss, Frank
Council of Jewish Federations (214)

Strauss, Kathryn Lafleur
Soc. of Professional Benefit Administrators (505)

Strawser, Misty A.
United Methodist Ass'n of Health and Welfare Ministries (531)

Streck, Ronald J.
Nat'l Wholesale Druggists' Ass'n (436)

Streeper, Michael
Jewelry Industry Distributors Ass'n (314)

Strell, Bruce
Alpha Zeta Omega (19)

Stretton, Tamara
Suppliers of Advanced Composite Materials Ass'n (518)
United States Advanced Ceramics Ass'n (531)

Stricker Ph.D., George
Soc. for the Exploration of Psychotherapy Integration (495)

Strickland, Darchelle
Nat'l Dental Hygienists' Ass'n (399)

Strickland, Herschel
Government Management Information Sciences (248)

Strickland, Nancy
Nat'l Ass'n of Steel Pipe Distributors (377)

Strickland, Sue
American Apparel Producers Network (28)

Stringfellow, Fred C.
Shoe Service Institute of America (483)

Stripling, Charlotte
American Filtration and Separations Soc. (68)

Strittmatter, Philip
Nat'l Ass'n of Professional Educators (366)

Strom, David J.
Federation of Nurses and Health Professionals (237)
American Federation of Teachers (67)

Stromberg, JoAnn
Surface Mount Technology Ass'n (519)

Stromberg, Roger
Conference of State Bank Supervisors (204)

Strong, Pamela A.
Ass'n of Legal Administrators (155)

Strong, Trish
Soc. of Toxicology (508)

Strother, Lynn
Human Factors and Ergonomics Soc. (257)

Strother, Michael E.
Power and Communication Contractors Ass'n (461)

Strother, Sandy
Nat'l Ass'n of Development Organizations (352)

Stroud, Elaine
American Institute of the History of Pharmacy (78)

Stroud, Troy F.
Ductile Iron Pipe Research Ass'n (225)

Stroufe, Gerald E.
American Educational Research Ass'n (65)

Stroup Jr., USA (R, Lt.Gen. Theodore G.
Ass'n of the United States Army (167)

Strunk, William
Aestheticians Internat'l Ass'n (13)

Strupeck, Rebecca
Red Tag News Publications Ass'n (473)

Strupp, Werner
American Podiatric Medical Ass'n (93)

Stryjewski, Stacy
Nat'l Ass'n of Telecommunications Officers and Advisers (378)

Strzaika, Toni
Soc. for Women in Plastics (496)

Stuart, Beverly
American Culinary Federation (63)

Stuart, Karen
Ass'n of Talent Agents (167)

Stuart, Mark
Nat'l Industrial Council - Employer Ass'n Group (410)

Stuchell, Judy
Nat'l Institute of Certified Moving Consultants (412)

Stuck, Earl
Child Welfare League of America (192)

Stucker M.D., FACS, Fred J.
American Rhinologic Soc. (98)

Stuckey, Richard E.
Council for Agricultural Science and Technology (210)

Stultz, Mark
Electric Power Supply Ass'n (227)

Stultz, Mark E.
American Gas Ass'n (70)

Stump, Maj.Gen. E. Gordon
Adjutants General Ass'n of the United States (12)

Stunson, Charles
American Federation of Teachers (67)

Stuntz, Franki K.
Nat'l Ocean Industries Ass'n (419)

Sturdevant, Kenton E.
Forest Industries Telecommunications (242)

Sturm, John F.
Newspaper Ass'n of America (439)

Stutz, Ward
American Quarter Horse Ass'n (96)

Stygar Jr., Edward J.
American Ass'n for Accreditation of Ambulatory Surgery
Facilities (29)
American Art Therapy Ass'n (29)
American Pathology Foundation (90)
American Biological Safety Ass'n (47)

Styles, Bonnie
American Quaternary Ass'n (96)

Suabert, Mike
American Concrete Pipe Ass'n (59)

Subick, Bill
Nat'l Council of Teachers of English (396)

Subrin, Bert
Senior Executives Ass'n (482)

Sucevic, Slavka
American Soc. of Dentistry for Children (109)

Suddath, Ed
Ass'n on Higher Education and Disability (170)

Sudy, Mitch
American Council on Exercise (62)

Sufka, Kenneth M.
Controlled Environment Testing Ass'n (208)
Associated Air Balance Council (170)
Nat'l Air Duct Cleaners Ass'n (335)
Nat'l Air Filtration Ass'n (335)
Ass'n for Commuter Transportation (131)

Sugg, Ike
Exotic Wildlife Ass'n (234)

Suiter, Marilyn J.
American Geological Institute (70)

Sukert, Shelly
Internat'l Festivals and Events Ass'n (291)

Suki M.D., Wadi
North American Soc. for Dialysis and Transplantation (444)

Sulen, Frank
Nat'l Ass'n of College Stores (348)

Sullivan, Cheryl
United States Telephone Ass'n (535)

Sullivan, Christopher
Offshore Marine Service Ass'n (447)

Sullivan, Eugene
Council for Exceptional Children (211)

Sullivan, Holly
Nat'l Ass'n of School Psychologists (371)

Sullivan, Isabel F.
Automotive Recyclers Ass'n (175)

Sullivan, James
Water Environment Federation (541)

Sullivan, Jerry
American Ass'n of Collegiate Registrars and Admissions
Officers (35)

Sullivan, Judy
Nat'l Ass'n of Housing Cooperatives (359)

Sullivan, Larry
Nat'l Ass'n of School Psychologists (371)

Sullivan, Marcia Zucker
Consumer Bankers Ass'n (207)

Sullivan, Marilyn J.
American Soc. of Health-System Pharmacists (110)

Sullivan, Patrick
Computer Ethics Institute (202)

Sullivan, Richard D.
Nat'l Fire Sprinkler Ass'n (404)

Sullivan CAE, Richard J.
Ass'n of Food Industries (151)
Nat'l Honey Packers and Dealers Ass'n (409)

Sullivan, Shelley
Biscuit and Cracker Manufacturers' Ass'n (179)

Sullivan, Sid
Surface Mount Technology Ass'n (519)

Sullivan, Stephen K.
American Architectural Manufacturers Ass'n (29)

Sullivan, Terry
American Seed Trade Ass'n (99)

Sultan, Sally
Academy of Marketing Science (9)

Sulzbach, Charles
Nat'l Ass'n of Traffic Accident Reconstructionists and
Investigators (379)

Summerfelt Ph.D., Steven T.
Aquacultural Engineering Soc. (126)

Summers, Angela
Ass'n of Community College Trustees (148)

Summers, Darlene
American Rental Ass'n (98)

Summers Ph.D., F. William
Beta Phi Mu (178)

Summers, Joyce
Internat'l Teleproduction Soc. (308)

Summers, William C.
Professional Insurance Mass-Marketing Ass'n (466)

Sumner, David
American Radio Relay League (96)

Sumner, James H.
U.S.A. Poultry and Egg Export Council (528)

Sumner, Kimberly P.
Nat'l Ass'n of Convenience Stores (349)

Sun, Benny
Metal Powder Industries Federation (327)

Sun, Qingshun
Chinese Language Teachers Ass'n (192)

Sunderman Jr., M.D., F. William
Ass'n of Clinical Scientists (147)

Sundin, Michelle
Western Music Ass'n (543)

Sunseri, Albert
Ass'n for Healthcare Resource Materials and
Management (134)

Sunshine, Robert
Internat'l Theatre Equipment Ass'n (308)

Sunter, Bill
Gravure Ass'n of America (249)

Suplizio, Paul E.
Internat'l Reciprocal Trade Ass'n **(301)**

Surace, Ronald
American Industrial Real Estate Ass'n **(75)**

Surdi, Jana
Institute of Medicine **(268)**

Suriani, Annette
American Orthotic and Prosthetic Ass'n **(89)**

Surks M.D., Martin I.
American Thyroid Ass'n **(120)**

Surprenant, Nancy
Nat'l Ass'n of Independent Resurfacers **(359)**

Susano, Maria T.
Nat'l Account Management Ass'n **(334)**

Susko, Christie J.
American Physical Therapy Ass'n **(92)**

Susser, Peter A.
Driver Employer Council of America **(224)**

Sussman, Sandra L.
Nat'l Ass'n of Stock Plan Professionals **(377)**

Sutlitt, Patrick
Nat'l Ass'n of Veterans Program Administrators **(379)**

Sutter, Julie
Ass'n of Polysomnographic Technologists **(160)**

Sutton, Debra
Water Environment Federation **(541)**

Sutton, Karen
Nat'l Ass'n of Seventh-Day Adventist Dentists **(372)**

Sutton, Mark
Gas Processors Ass'n **(245)**
Gas Processors Suppliers Ass'n **(245)**

Svedman, Katherine J.
American Soc. for Healthcare Environmental Services **(103)**

Svinicki CAE, Jane A.
American Soc. of Scientific Glass Blowers **(116)**

Svwalski, Micahel B.
LOMA **(321)**

Swafford, Steven W.
American Subcontractors Ass'n **(118)**

Swaim, Sue
Nat'l Middle School Ass'n **(417)**

Swain, Lori
SWANA - Solid Waste Ass'n of North America **(519)**

Swamidoss, Ponnuswamy
American Public Health Ass'n **(95)**

Swan, James
Accountants for the Public Interest **(10)**

Swank, Debbie J.
American Electroplaters and Surface Finishers Soc. **(65)**

Swann, Judy
Patent and Trademark Office Soc. **(454)**

Swanson, David L.
Edison Electric Institute **(226)**

Swanson, Judith
American Collectors Ass'n **(52)**

Swanson, Lise
North American Hyperthermia Soc. **(442)**
Radiation Research Soc. **(470)**

Swanson, Raymond P.
Uniform Boiler and Pressure Vessel Laws Soc. **(529)**

Swanson, Richard
Institute of Management Accountants **(268)**

Swanson, Roger
American Ass'n of Collegiate Registrars and Admissions Officers **(35)**

Swanson, Sylvia
Internat'l Bottled Water Ass'n **(283)**

Sward Ph.D., Marcia P.
Mathematical Ass'n of America **(325)**

Swarm, Geraldine
Nat'l Ass'n of Postmasters of the U.S. **(365)**

Swarts, Robert F.
American Logistics Ass'n **(82)**

Swatos, William H.
Ass'n for the Sociology of Religion **(139)**

Swatski, Susan
Nat'l Shipyard Ass'n **(428)**

Sweeney, John J.
American Federation of Labor and Congress of Industrial Organizations **(67)**

Sweeney, Les
Associated Bodywork and Massage Professionals **(170)**

Sweeney, Stephanie
Ass'n of Theological Schools in the United States and Canada **(168)**

Sweetman, Bonnie
Baking Industry Sanitation Standards Committee **(176)**

Swenson, Diane K.
American Tort Reform Ass'n **(120)**

Swenson, Kurt
Nat'l Building Granite Quarries Ass'n **(384)**

Swenson, Leland H.
Farmers Educational and Co-operative Union of America **(235)**

Swenson, Ramsey
Soc. of Surgical Oncology **(507)**
American Soc. of Colon and Rectal Surgeons **(108)**

Swiacki, Eve C.
American College of Physicians-American Soc. of Internal Medicine **(57)**

Swiecichowski, Ted
Wireless Communications Ass'n Internat'l **(545)**

Swiecicki, Bruce J.
Nat'l Propane Gas Ass'n **(423)**

Swift, Clint
Institute for Interconnecting and Packaging Electronic Circuits **(265)**

Swigart, Anne H.
American Institute for CPCU - Insurance Institute of America **(75)**

Swinburn CAE, John
Internat'l Ass'n for Exposition Management **(274)**

Swindle, Geri
Federation of American Socs. for Experimental Biology **(236)**

Swinehart, Sam
Nat'l Ass'n of State Boards of Geology **(374)**

Swinford, Yolanda
American Probation and Parole Ass'n **(94)**

Swisher, Randall S.
American Wind Energy Ass'n **(123)**

Swize, Robert
Santa Gertrudis Breeders Internat'l **(479)**

Syence, Sherry
Petroleum Marketers Ass'n of America **(456)**

Sylstra, Susan L.
Internat'l Ass'n of Financial Crimes Investigators **(279)**

Synovitz, Bob
American School Health Ass'n **(99)**

Syron, Richard S.
American Stock Exchange **(118)**

Syverson, Peter D.
Council of Graduate Schools **(213)**

Szpak, Carole
Nat'l Ass'n of Psychiatric Health Systems **(367)**

Szwalek, Jennifer
Internat'l Card Manufacturers Ass'n **(285)**

Szyper, Paula
Soc. for Healthcare Strategy and Market Development **(488)**

Tabat, Lou
Nat'l Constables Ass'n **(392)**

Tabor CAE, Janis L.
Council for Chemical Research **(211)**

Tabor, Ralph
Nat'l Ass'n of County Treasurers and Finance Officers **(351)**

Tabora, Carlos
American Soc. of Home Inspectors **(111)**

Taffet, Richard S.
Textile Producers and Suppliers Ass'n **(522)**

Tagliabue, Paul
Nat'l Football League **(405)**

Taglienti, Laura
Nat'l Football League Players Ass'n **(405)**

Tahirkheli, Sharon N.
American Geological Institute **(70)**

Takacs, Catherine
Communications Managers Ass'n **(200)**

Talbot, John
Nat'l Precast Concrete Ass'n **(423)**

Talbott, Elaine
United States Parachute Ass'n **(534)**

Taliaferro, Michael
Nat'l Directory Publishing Ass'n **(399)**

Talisman, Bobbi Brown
American Osteopathic Healthcare Ass'n **(89)**

Talkin, Pamela
Ass'n of Labor Relations Agencies **(155)**

Tallaksen, Inger M.
Norwegian-American Chamber of Commerce **(446)**

Talley, C. Richard
American Soc. of Health-System Pharmacists **(110)**

Talley, Gregg H.
Movement Disorder Soc. **(331)**

Talley, Robert
Ass'n for the Care of Children's Health **(139)**
Stadium Managers Ass'n **(515)**

Tan, Caroline
River Management Soc. **(476)**

Tan, Lillian
Internat'l Transactional Analysis Ass'n **(309)**

Tank, Alan
Nat'l Pork Producers Council **(423)**

Tannahill, Sharon K.
Nat'l Classification Management Soc. **(387)**

Tannenbaum, Gail
Nat'l Council of Farmer Cooperatives **(394)**

Tanner, Brenda
Nat'l League of Postmasters of the U.S. **(414)**

Tansey, Susan
Internat'l Sanitary Supply Ass'n **(302)**

Tantum, Anne
American Ass'n of Meat Processors **(38)**

Tanzi, Vito A.
Nat'l Bureau of Certified Consultants **(384)**

Tapia, Tony
Ass'n of Performing Arts Presenters **(160)**

Tarallo, Mary Jo
SnowSports Industries America **(484)**

Tarantino, Teresa
Nat'l Confectionery Sales Ass'n of America **(389)**

Tarbert, Jeffrey
American Public Power Ass'n **(96)**

Tardy, Kirsten
Soc. for Range Management **(493)**

Tarnove, Lorraine
American Medical Directors Ass'n **(83)**

Tarpley, Judy
SEPM - Soc. for Sedimentary Geology **(482)**

Tarver, Joe A.
Nat'l Tile Contractors Ass'n **(433)**

Tarver M.D., William
Soc. of United States Air Force Flight Surgeons **(508)**

Tasaki, Allegra
Soc. for Nutrition Education **(491)**

Tasini, Jonathan
Nat'l Writers Union **(437)**

Tassey, Jeffrey A.
American Financial Services Ass'n **(68)**

Tate, Cassandra
American Ass'n of Collegiate Registrars and Admissions Officers **(35)**

Tate, June
Catfish Institute **(188)**

Tate, Lisa M.
Nat'l Ass'n of Children's Hospitals and Related Institutions **(347)**

Tate, Margaret
Ass'n of State and Territorial Public Health Nutrition Directors **(166)**

Tate, Pamela
Council for Adult and Experiential Learning **(210)**

Tate, Thomas N.
Aerospace Industries Ass'n of America **(13)**

Tate-Taylor, Tonja
American Wood Preservers Institute **(123)**

Tatum, Angie
American Public Works Ass'n **(96)**

Tavarozzo, Cathy E.
Telecommunications Industry Ass'n **(521)**

Tavenner, Mary T.
American Automotive Leasing Ass'n **(46)**

Tayloe, Brian D.
Nat'l Council for Prescription Drug Programs **(393)**

Taylor, Amy
Drug and Alcohol Testing Industry Ass'n **(225)**
Nat'l Ass'n of Charterboat Operators **(346)**
Committee for Private Offshore Rescue and Towing (C-PORT) **(200)**
Commercial Weather Services Ass'n **(199)**

Taylor, Beth
Museum Store Ass'n **(332)**

Taylor, Christy M.
American Alliance for Theatre and Education **(27)**

Taylor, Chuck
Occupational Program Consultants Ass'n **(447)**

Taylor, Cindy
Ass'n for Facilities Engineering **(133)**

Taylor, Dan
Internat'l Financial Services Ass'n **(291)**

Taylor, Denise
Nat'l Ass'n of Negro Business and Professional Women's Clubs **(363)**

Taylor, Donald
American Concrete Pumping Ass'n **(59)**

Taylor, Gary J.
Internat'l Ass'n of Fish and Wildlife Agencies **(279)**

Taylor, George H.
American Ass'n of State Climatologists **(43)**

Taylor, Glenn E.
American Institute of Chemical Engineers **(77)**

Taylor, Gregg
American Nuclear Soc. **(87)**

Taylor, Harold D.
Nat'l Judges Ass'n **(413)**

Taylor, Ingrid
Joint Electron Device Engineering Council **(315)**

Taylor, Jannie G.
American Ass'n of Colleges for Teacher Education (34)

Taylor, Jeremy B.
Soc. of the Plastics Industry (507)

Taylor, Joan
American Academy of Audiology (20)

Taylor Sr., John S.
Nat'l Venture Capital Ass'n (435)

Taylor, Karen Lewis
Forging Industry Ass'n (243)

Taylor, Keith
Radio Talk Show Hosts Ass'n (471)

Taylor, Libby
Chocolate Manufacturers Ass'n of the U.S.A. (193)

Taylor, Lonnie
Chamber of Commerce of the United States of America (190)

Taylor, Marilyn
Ass'n for Women in Communications (140)

Taylor, Mary Lou
Sheet Metal and Air Conditioning Contractors' Nat'l Ass'n (482)

Taylor, Michael R.
Nat'l Ass'n of Demolition Contractors (352)

Taylor, Nancy
Internat'l Ass'n of Lighting Management Companies (280)

Taylor, Pamela
College Savings Plans Network (198)
State Debt Management Network (516)
Nat'l Ass'n of State Treasurers (376)

Taylor, Peter
Nat'l Ass'n of Federal Credit Unions (355)

Taylor, Phillipa P.
Council on Foundations (216)

Taylor, Phyllis M.
Nonprescription Drug Manufacturers Ass'n (440)

Taylor, R.E.
Soc. for Archaeological Studies (485)

Taylor, Ray
Ass'n of Community College Trustees (148)

Taylor, Scott
Soc. of American Law Teachers (497)

Taylor, Stew
Retailer's Bakery Ass'n (476)

Taylor, W. Carl
American Fern Soc. (68)

Tayman, Ava Ann
Soc. for Gynecologic Investigation (488)

Tayman, W.
American Railway Engineering and Maintenance of Way Ass'n (97)

Tays, Sarah
Nat'l Ass'n of Division Order Analysts (353)

Teaff, Grant
American Football Coaches Ass'n (69)

Teague, Merlyn
Ass'n for Facilities Engineering (133)

Teasley, Mary Elizabeth
Nat'l Education Ass'n of the U.S. (400)

Tedeschi, Brian A.
Steel Recycling Institute (516)

Tedesco, Philip B.
Nat'l Ass'n for Interpretation (340)

Teich, Scottie
Nat'l District Attorneys Ass'n (399)

Teicher, Oren
American Booksellers Ass'n (48)

Teisler CAE, David
Ass'n for Advancement of Behavior Therapy (129)

Teister, Mary
Broadcast Cable Financial Management Ass'n (182)

Teitler, Robert
Institute of Hazardous Materials Management (267)

Teksten, Nancy
Nat'l Onion Ass'n (419)

Telego, D.J.
Environmental Bankers Ass'n (231)

Tellmann, Ron
Nat'l Committee on Planned Giving (388)

Temple, Linda
Regulatory Affairs Professionals Soc. (474)

Temple, Marsha
Institute of Certified Financial Planners (266)

Temple, Thomas
Nat'l Council of State Pharmacy Ass'n Executives (396)

Tendler, Elaine
Nat'l Ass'n of Waterfront Employers (380)

Tendler, Paul M.
American Licensed Practical Nurses Ass'n (81)

Tennyson VMD, Arthur V.
American Veterinary Medical Ass'n (121)

Teplansky, Robert
Nat'l Ass'n of Rehabilitation Professionals in the Private Sector (369)

Tepper, Alan M.
Tau Epsilon Rho Law Soc. (520)

Tepper APR, Donald
Building Service Contractors Ass'n Internat'l (183)

Teresk, Mike
Urban Land Institute (537)

Terhaar, Allen
Cotton Council Internat'l (210)

Terpack, Sue
Combustion Institute (198)

Terrana, Maryann
Nat'l Ass'n of College and University Business Officers (348)

Terranova, John J.
American Ass'n of Orthodontists (40)

Terrell, Daphne
Infrared Data Ass'n (264)

Terrell, Joseph
American Sugar Alliance (119)

Terrell, Mable J.
Internat'l Black Writers Conference (283)

Terrone, Dominick
American Institute of Constructors (77)

Terry, D.L.
Ass'n of American Plant Food Control Officials (143)

Teschke, Debbie
Nat'l Housewares Manufacturers Ass'n (409)

Teske, David
Ass'n of College Unions-Internat'l (147)

Teslik, Sarah A.B.
Council of Institutional Investors (214)

Tesliki, Steven
Rubber Manufacturers Ass'n (477)

Tessier CAE, Claudia
American Ass'n for Medical Transcription (31)

Tessier, Richard
American Logistics Ass'n (82)

Tessler Ph.D., Mark
American Institute for Maghrib Studies (76)

Test, Gretchen
Nat'l Ass'n of Public Child Welfare Administrators (367)

Teter, Harry
American Trauma Soc. (121)

Tetschner, Stacy
Nat'l Speakers Ass'n (431)

Tetzlaff FLMI, David A.
Nat'l Fraternal Congress of America (406)

Teuscher, Carol A.
American Soc. of Dentistry for Children (109)

Teutsch, William J.
Ass'n of Surgical Technologists (166)

Thackston, Chris
American Bankruptcy Institute (46)

Thakrar, Neela
Ass'n of Steel Distributors (166)

Thal, Rabbi Lennard
Union of American Hebrew Congregations (529)

Thane, Julie S.
North American Horticultural Supply Ass'n (442)
Nat'l Ass'n of Aluminum Distributors (343)
Outdoor Power Equipment Distributors Ass'n (451)

Tharp, David W.
Internat'l Ass'n of Milk, Food and Environmental Sanitarians (281)

Tharpe Ed.D., Don I.
Ass'n of School Business Officials Internat'l (164)

Thaw, Deborah M.
Nat'l Notary Ass'n (418)

Thaxton, Jim
Professional Paddlesports Ass'n (466)

Thayer, Bennie L.
Nat'l Ass'n for the Self-Employed (341)

Thayer, Robert
Industrial Union of Marine and Shipbuilding Workers of America (263)

Thayer, Susan C.
Ass'n of Professors of Cardiology (161)

Theilacker, Jay
Cryogenic Engineering Conference (219)

Theismann, Britt D.
Internat'l Institute of Synthetic Rubber Producers (295)

Theiss, Simone
Soc. of Competitive Intelligence Professionals (500)

Theobald, Stanley C.
Soc. of Automotive Engineers International (498)

Theodore, Eustace D.
Council for Advancement and Support of Education (210)

Thevenot, Laura Ison
Federation of American Health Systems (236)

Thibault, Eloise
Academy of Students of Pharmacy (10)

Thiebert-Knobloch, Karen
Nat'l Retail Federation (425)

Thiel, Christopher
APICS - The Educational Society for Resource Management (125)

Thierry, Patricia
American Health Information Management Ass'n (72)

Thies, Kim
Internat'l Microwave Power Institute (297)

Thiessen, Terry
North American Lake Management Soc. (442)

Thigpen, Jonathan
Evangelical Training Ass'n (233)

Thigpen, Yvonne E.
Evangelical Training Ass'n (233)

Thomas CAE, Adria L.
Nat'l School Boards Ass'n (427)

Thomas, Allen
Nat'l Ass'n of Sewer Service Companies (372)

Thomas, Beth A.
Internat'l Concatenated Order of Hoo-Hoo (286)

Thomas, Bob
Nat'l Concrete Masonry Ass'n (389)

Thomas, Brenda
Nat'l Ass'n of Minority Engineering Program Administrators (363)

Thomas, David
Endocrine Soc. (230)

Thomas, David R.
State Risk and Insurance Management Ass'n (516)

Thomas, Donald E.
American Cancer Soc. (50)

Thomas, Greg
American Academy of Physician Assistants (25)

Thomas, Greg
Ass'n of Cinema and Video Laboratories (146)

Thomas, James A.
American Soc. for Testing and Materials (105)

Thomas, Jeff
American Simmental Ass'n (100)

Thomas, Jennifer
Ass'n for Professionals in Infection Control and Epidemiology (136)

Thomas, Jennifer L.
American Ass'n for Holistic Health (31)

Thomas, Jim
Laborers' Internat'l Union of North America (316)

Thomas, John H.
Independent Sector (261)

Thomas, Judith A.
American Soc. of Nephrology (113)

Thomas, Karen
Soc. for Healthcare Strategy and Market Development (488)

Thomas, Larry L.
Soc. of the Plastics Industry (507)

Thomas, Linda
Nat'l Wholesale Druggists' Ass'n (436)

Thomas, Ralph D.
Nat'l Ass'n of Investigative Specialists (360)

Thomas, Richard
Nat'l Soc. of Professional Engineers (430)

Thomas CIC, Roger E.
American Ass'n of Insurance Management Consultants (38)

Thomas, Sandra I.
Emergency Nurses Ass'n (229)

Thomas, Stan
American Lighting Ass'n (81)

Thomas, Susan
Audit Bureau of Circulations (173)

Thomas, Thomas L.
American Financial Services Ass'n (68)

Thomas, Valerie
Ass'n of Trial Lawyers of America (168)

Thomas, William C.
Optical Industry Ass'n: OMA (448)

Thomas-Buckle, Suzann
American Legal Studies Ass'n (81)

Thomashower, James
American Guild of Organists (71)

Thomason, Jo
Council of Administrators of Special Education (212)

Thompson, Barbara J.
Nat'l Council of State Housing Agencies (396)

Thompson CAE, Carole
Air Line Pilots Ass'n, Internat'l (16)
Nat'l Ass'n for Family Child Care (339)
Equipment Service Ass'n (232)

Thompson, Cynthia
Employee Relocation Council (229)
Academy of Aphasia (7)

Thompson, Daniel R.
Fragrance Materials Ass'n of the United States (243)
Chemical Sources Ass'n (191)
Flavor and Extract Manufacturers Ass'n of the United States (240)

Thompson, Dorothy
Printing Industries of America (463)

Thompson, Doug
Carpet and Rug Institute (187)

Thompson Jr., Douglas H.
Accounting Firms Associated (10)

Thompson, Duane
Institute of Certified Financial Planners (266)

Thompson, Elvia H.
Women in Aerospace (546)

Thompson, Frances
Nat'l Grain Sorghum Producers (407)

Thompson, Hugh
Ass'n of College and Research Libraries (147)

Thompson, J. Michael
Nat'l Electrical Contractors Ass'n (400)

Thompson, John
Spring Research Institute (515)

Thompson Jr., Joseph M.
Independent Sealing Distributors (261)
Nat'l Ass'n of Hose and Accessories Distributors (358)
Yacht Architects and Brokers Ass'n (551)

Thompson, Kaistin B.
Yacht Architects and Brokers Ass'n (551)

Thompson, Kathy
Visiting Nurse Ass'ns of America (540)

Thompson, Kelly
Nat'l Child Support Enforcement Ass'n (386)

Thompson, Kristin B.
Independent Sealing Distributors (261)
Nat'l Ass'n of Hose and Accessories Distributors (358)

Thompson, Lisa
Computing Research Ass'n (203)

Thompson Jr., Louis M.
Nat'l Investor Relations Institute (413)

Thompson, Marion
Cleaning Management Institute (194)

Thompson, Maureen
Environmental Mutagen Soc. (232)
Ass'n of Occupational Health Professionals (in Healthcare) (158)
Nat'l Organization for Associate Degree Nursing (419)

Thompson Ph.D., Michael G.
Soc. of Thoracic Surgeons (508)

Thompson, Michael P.
Soc. for Scholarly Publishing (493)
Ass'n for Applied Psychophysiology and Biofeedback (129)
North American Nature Photography Ass'n (443)

Thompson, Otis N.
Organization of Professional Employees of the U.S. Department of Agriculture (450)

Thompson, Patrick
New York Mercantile Exchange (438)

Thompson, Reece
Investment Company Institute (312)

Thompson, Sally
American Consulting Engineers Council (60)

Thompson, Trudy
America's Blood Centers (19)

Thompson, Esq., Lonna
Ass'n of America's Public Television Stations (142)

Thoms, John A.
Soc. of Economic Geologists (500)

Thomson, Kristi
American Ass'n of Feline Practitioners (37)

Thomson, W. Campbell
Federation of American Health Systems (236)

Thoren, Don
Nat'l Restaurant Ass'n (425)

Thorman, Judith
Nat'l Soft Drink Ass'n (430)

Thormodsgard, Jay
Nat'l Foundation for Consumer Credit (405)

Thorn, Amy Z.
Design-Build Manufacturers Ass'n (222)

Thornburg, Rick
Flexible Packaging Ass'n (240)

Thorne, Judy Hare
College Fraternity Editors Ass'n (197)

Thorner CAE, John A.
Air and Waste Management Ass'n (15)

Thorner, John A.
Optical Soc. of America (449)

Thornton, Donna K.
Nat'l Ass'n of Child Care Professionals (347)

Thornton, Olen
Manufacturers Standardization Soc. of the Valve and Fittings Industry (323)

Thornton, Terry
American Chemical Soc. (51)

Thorpe Ph.D., John A.
Nat'l Council of Teachers of Mathematics (396)

Thorsby, Mark O.
Internat'l Carwash Ass'n (285)

Threndyle, Steve
North American Snowsports Journalists Ass'n (444)

Throckmorton, Kelly
American Land Title Ass'n (80)

Thronton, J. Scott
American Teleservices Ass'n (119)

Throssell, Carole
Food Marketing Institute (241)

Thrune, Elaine M.
Nat'l Wildlife Rehabilitators Ass'n (436)

Thulean, Don
American Symphony Orchestra League (119)

Thumann, Albert
Ass'n of Energy Engineers (150)

Thurm, Gil
Independent Petroleum Ass'n of America (261)

Thurman, Charles E.
Electrical Manufacturing and Coil Winding Ass'n (227)

Thurmond, Jeffrey
Nat'l Soc. of Accountants (429)

Thurow, Bill
Railway Industrial Clearance Ass'n (471)

Thurston Ph.D., Richard E.
American Bandmasters Ass'n (46)

Tice, Alan
Outpatient Intravenous Infusion Therapy Ass'n (451)

Tice, R. Dean
Nat'l Recreation and Park Ass'n (424)

Tickman, Marsha S.
Components, Packaging, and Manufacturing Technology Soc. (201)

Tidwoll, Ritchie
Ass'n of Traumatic Stress Specialists (168)

Tiede, Patricia
Industrial Research Institute (263)

Tiekert D.V.M., Carvel G.
American Holistic Veterinary Medical Ass'n (74)

Tielborg, J. Patrick
Pipe Line Contractors Ass'n (458)

Tiemann, Jane
Internat'l Soc. for Magnetic Resonance in Medicine (303)

Tilden, Flor
Soc. of Laparoendoscopic Surgeons (503)

Till, Alice E.
Generic Pharmaceutical Industry Ass'n (246)

Tiller, Michael
Compressed Gas Ass'n (202)

Tiller N.D., William T.
Internat'l Ass'n Colon Hydro Therapy (273)

Tillett, G. Douglas
Nat'l Ass'n of Life Underwriters (361)

Tilley, Karen
Ass'n of Pediatric Oncology Social Workers (160)

Tilley, Kimberly A.
American Soc. for Photogrammetry and Remote Sensing (104)

Tilley, Linda
Nat'l Athletic Trainers' Ass'n (381)

Tillman, Wallace F.
Nat'l Rural Electric Cooperative Ass'n (426)

Tilton, Richard W.
General Merchandise Distributors Council (246)

Timmel, Barbare
North American Lake Management Soc. (442)

Timmer, Gloria
Nat'l Ass'n of State Budget Officers (374)

Timmons, Deborah
Ass'n for Professionals in Infection Control and Epidemiology (136)
American Soc. for Parenteral and Enteral Nutrition (104)

Tindall, Barry
Nat'l Recreation and Park Ass'n (424)

Tingley, Staci
Nat'l Committee on Planned Giving (388)

Tinkleman, Alan
American Podiatric Medical Ass'n (93)

Tinklepaugh, William C.
Master Dairies (324)

Tinsley, James H.
Casualty Actuarial Soc. (187)

Tippett, Peter S.
Nat'l Computer Security Ass'n (389)

Tippins, Jean W.
Nat'l Futures Ass'n (406)

Tipton, Constance E.
Milk Industry Foundation (328)
Internat'l Ice Cream Ass'n (294)

Nat'l Cheese Institute (386)
Internat'l Dairy Foods Ass'n (288)

Tipton, E. Linwood
Internat'l Dairy Foods Ass'n (288)
Internat'l Ice Cream Ass'n (294)
Milk Industry Foundation (328)
Nat'l Cheese Institute (386)

Tipton, Helen
Wound, Ostomy and Continence Nurses Soc. (550)

Tipton Jr., M.D., William W.
American Academy of Orthopaedic Surgeons (24)

Tiras CMP, Lynne K.
Soc. of Gastrointestinal Radiologists (502)

Tirinato, Joseph
Television Bureau of Advertising (521)

Tirrell, Peter B.
Ass'n of College and University Museums and Galleries (147)

Tissier, Suzannne
AFSM Internat'l (14)

Tita, Nancy
Nat'l Ass'n of Hispanic Journalists (358)

Tite, Janet
Nat'l Ass'n of Professional Geriatric Care Managers (366)
Nat'l Guardianship Ass'n (408)

Tittsworth, David
Investment Counsel Ass'n of America (312)

Titus, C. Richard
Kitchen Cabinet Manufacturers Ass'n (316)

Titus, Janet
Kitchen Cabinet Manufacturers Ass'n (316)

Tjornechoj, Dan
American Academy of Clinical Neurophysiology (21)

Tobar, Andres
Nat'l Ass'n of Hispanic Publications (358)

Tobias, Joyce
Nat'l Catalog Managers Ass'n (385)

Tobias, Karen
Nat'l Management Ass'n (416)

Tobias, Robert M.
Nat'l Treasury Employees Union (124)

Tobin, Carol B.
American Industrial Hygiene Ass'n (75)

Tobin, John
Design Management Institute (222)

Tobin JD, Mitchell H.
American Ass'n of Nurse Anesthetists (39)

Tobin, Patricia L.
Nat'l Black Public Relations Soc. (383)

Tobin Ph.D., William J.
American Ass'n of Early Childhood Educators (36)
Access Technology Ass'n (10)

Toblin, Jane
Nat'l Child Support Enforcement Ass'n (386)

Todd, Brian
American Institute of Food Distribution (77)

Todd, David C.
Mail Order Ass'n of America (322)

Todd, Pete
Nat'l Stroke Ass'n (432)

Todd, Richard
Ass'n of Records Managers and Administrators (163)

Tode, Donna
Internat'l Sanitary Supply Ass'n (302)

Tognino, John N.
Security Traders Ass'n (481)

Tolbert, Terry
Nat'l Federation of Housing Counselors (403)

Tollerton, Kathy
American Soc. for Engineering Education (102)

Tollett Ph.D., Eileen
American Literary Translators Ass'n (81)

Tolley, William R.
American Concrete Institute (59)

Tollison Jr., Alfred C.
Institute of Nuclear Power Operations (268)

Tolliver, Nancey Jo
Nat'l Private Truck Council (423)

Tolman Ph.D., Jon M.
Brazilian Studies Ass'n (182)

Tolman, S. Richard
U.S. Grains Council (528)

Tolzmann, D. Don Heinrich
Soc. for German-American Studies (488)

Tompkins, Cathy
Ass'n for Gerontology in Higher Education (134)

Tompkuis, Jill
Internat'l Sign Ass'n (302)

Tondro, La Rene C.
Soc. of Satellite Professionals Internat'l (507)

Toner, James P.
Soc. of Plastics Engineers (505)

Toner, M. James
Nat'l Council of Juvenile and Family Court Judges **(395)**

Tonks, Heather
Nat'l Child Support Enforcement Ass'n **(386)**

Tonn, Howard
Railway Supply Ass'n **(471)**

Tony, Bill
Air and Waste Management Ass'n **(15)**

Tony, William
American Soc. for Quality **(105)**

Toohey CAE, Michael
Ass'n of Records Managers and Administrators **(163)**

Toohey, Michael
Electrical Apparatus Service Ass'n **(227)**

Toohey Jr., William D.
American Road and Transportation Builders Ass'n **(98)**

Tooker M.D., FACP, John
American College of Physicians-American Soc. of Internal Medicine **(57)**

Toothaker DDS, MPH, James W.
American Ass'n of Public Health Dentistry **(42)**

Tornbom, Catherine
Professional and Technical Consultants Ass'n **(464)**

Torreon, Ray
United States Pan Asian American Chamber of Commerce **(534)**

Torres, Alicia
American Institute of Physics **(78)**

Torres, Jose
American Orthotic and Prosthetic Ass'n **(89)**

Torres, Kristin
Soc. for Mining, Metallurgy, and Exploration **(491)**

Torrey, Michael
Internat'l Dairy Foods Ass'n **(288)**

Tosello, Carey
Bowling Proprietors Ass'n of America **(181)**

Tosi, Gloria Cataneo
American Maritime Congress **(82)**

Tosini, Paula A.
Futures Industry Ass'n **(245)**

Toso, Octavia
Residential Sales Council **(475)**

Toth, Gail E.
Transportation Loss Prevention and Security Council **(526)**

Toth, Lorli
American Ass'n for the Study of Liver Diseases **(32)**

Totten, Larry
Gunite/Shotcrete Contractors Ass'n **(250)**

Tougaw, Amy
Institute of Certified Financial Planners **(266)**

Tower, Anne
Nat'l Religious Broadcasters **(425)**

Towery, Dorann
American Feed Industry Ass'n **(67)**

Towle, John M.
Performance Warehouse Ass'n **(455)**

Towle, William H.
Nat'l Perishable Logistics Ass'n **(422)**

Towns, Pamela R.
Nat'l Institute of Building Sciences **(411)**

Townsend, Anne
Nat'l Academy Museum and School Fine Arts **(333)**

Townsend, Hallie
American Soc. of Regional Anesthesia **(115)**

Townsend, Linda
Ass'n of Consulting Chemists and Chemical Engineers **(148)**

Townsend, Margaret W.
American Osteopathic Healthcare Ass'n **(89)**

Townsend, Robert
American Historical Ass'n **(73)**

Townsend, Steve
Soc. of Cable Telecommunications Engineers **(499)**

Towse, Yvonne
American Vacuum Soc. **(121)**

Tozer, E. Christine
American Bar Ass'n **(46)**

Tracy, Alan
United States Wheat Associates **(535)**

Tracy, Ann
Practising Law Institute **(462)**

Tracy, James
Soc. for Reformation Research **(493)**

Traficano, Sherryl
American College of Mohs Micrographic Surgery and Cutaneous Oncology **(55)**

Trapp, Stephanie
Ass'n of Women in the Metal Industries **(169)**

Trauger, Tracy
Nat'l Ass'n of Health Unit Coordinators **(357)**

Trautman, Maryellen
Soc. for History in the Federal Government **(489)**

Travis, Bill
SnowSports Industries America **(484)**

Travis, R.
Nuclear Suppliers Ass'n **(447)**

Traw, Jon S.
Internat'l Conference of Building Officials **(287)**

Traxler, Sallie
Nat'l Business Incubation Ass'n **(384)**

Tray, Kelly
Transportation Intermediaries Ass'n **(525)**

Traylor Jr., Dr. Idris R.
Ass'n for Arid Lands Studies **(130)**

Treadway, Don
American Quarter Horse Ass'n **(96)**

Treanor, Mr. John Joseph
Ass'n of Catholic Diocesan Archivists **(146)**

Trecker, Jim
United States Soccer Federation **(535)**

Treichel, Janet M.
Nat'l Business Education Ass'n **(384)**

Tremper, Charles Robert
American Ass'n of Homes and Services for the Aging **(37)**

Tresnowski, Bernard
Blue Cross and Blue Shield Ass'n **(180)**

Trey, Liza
American Land Title Ass'n **(80)**

Tribble, Jayne A.
Allied Stone Industries **(18)**

Trice, Eleanor
Internat'l Personnel Management Ass'n **(299)**

Trimarchi, Laurie
Cocoa Merchants' Ass'n of America **(196)**

Trimble, Philip
Soc. of Manufacturing Engineers **(503)**

Trimble, Tod
College Music Soc. **(197)**

Tringali, Diana
Nat'l Ass'n of Metal Finishers **(363)**

Tringall, Diana L.
Metal Finishing Suppliers Ass'n **(327)**

Tripp Jr., Raymond P.
Soc. for New Language Study **(491)**

Trippler, Aaron
American Industrial Hygiene Ass'n **(75)**

Trisco, Rev. Robert
American Catholic Historical Ass'n **(50)**

Tristano, Keith
Residential Sales Council **(475)**

Trocchio, Carole M.
Ombudsman Ass'n, The **(448)**

Trofi Jr., Salvatore
American Ass'n of Physicists in Medicine **(41)**

Trombino CAE, C. James
Metal Powder Industries Federation **(327)**

Trometter, Robert
Chartered Property and Casualty Underwriters Soc. **(190)**

Trope, Jim
Radio-Television News Directors Ass'n **(471)**

Trost, Teresa A.
United Methodist Ass'n of Health and Welfare Ministries **(531)**

Trouly, Karen
Nat'l Potato Promotion Board **(423)**

Troup, Hillary
United States-New Zealand Council **(536)**

Trout, Leslie A.
Phi Chi Theta **(456)**

Trowbridge, James W.
Council of the Americas **(216)**

Troy, Janet E.
New York Board of Trade **(438)**
Board of Trade of the City of New York **(180)**

Troy, Patricia H.
Ass'n for Women in Communications **(140)**

Troyer, Laura
Nat'l Electronic Service Dealers Ass'n **(400)**

Trsar, Terence
Information Systems Audit and Control Ass'n **(264)**

Trudell, Darlene
American Academy of Medical Administrators **(23)**

Truemper, David G.
Council of Socs. for the Study of Religion **(215)**

Trueschel, Jack
Nat'l Tutoring Ass'n **(435)**

Truitt, Dr. Gordon E.
Nat'l Ass'n of Pastoral Musicians **(364)**

Trujillo, Rachelle
Nat'l Stroke Ass'n **(432)**

Trull, Frankie L.
Nat'l Ass'n for Biomedical Research **(338)**

Trumble, Jeanne
American Academy of Addiction Psychiatry **(20)**

Trumbo Ph.D., Richard B.
Aerospace Medical Ass'n **(13)**

Trumbull, David
American Flock Ass'n **(68)**

Trumka, Richard L.
American Federation of Labor and Congress of Industrial Organizations **(67)**

Truncale CAE, Joseph P.
Nat'l Ass'n of Printers and Lithographers **(366)**

Trupp, Barbara
Pickle Packers Internat'l **(458)**

Trust, David
Professional Photographers of America **(466)**

Trusty, Steven
Sports Turf Contractors Ass'n **(515)**
Sports Turf Managers Ass'n **(515)**

Truswell, Hallie
Internat'l College of Cranio-Mandibular Orthopedics **(286)**

Tsirpanlis, Dr. Constantine N.
American Institute for Patristic and Byzantine Studies **(76)**

Tsujimoto, Jackie
Christian Management Ass'n **(193)**

Tubbesing, Susan
Earthquake Engineering Research Institute **(225)**

Tubowitz, Karen
Soc. of Critical Care Medicine **(500)**

Tucci, Amy
American Public Human Services Ass'n **(96)**

Tucker, Dana
American Forage and Grassland Council **(69)**

Tucker, Douglas K.
American Gem Trade Ass'n **(70)**

Tucker, Herta
Ass'n of TeleServices Internat'l **(167)**

Tucker, Janet
Text and Academic Authors Ass'n **(521)**

Tucker CAE, Karen S.
American College of Health Care Administrators **(54)**

Tucker, Louise
Internat'l Mobile Telecommunications Ass'n **(297)**

Tucker, Mark A.
Internat'l Festivals and Events Ass'n **(291)**

Tucker CAE, Nancy
Produce Marketing Ass'n **(463)**

Tucker, Nanette
Water Environment Federation **(541)**

Tucker, Thelma
Soc. for Research in Child Development **(493)**

Tudryn, Joyce M.
Internat'l Radio and Television Soc. Foundation **(301)**

Tuff, Suzanne
Internat'l Ass'n of Administrative Professionals **(275)**

Tuggle, Nora
American Soc. of Radiologic Technologists **(115)**

Tulipane, Barbara
NATSO, Representing America's Travel Plaza and Truckstops **(437)**

Tuller, Shep
U.S.A. Poultry and Egg Export Council **(528)**

Tulloch, Thomas C.
North American Ass'n of State and Provincial Lotteries **(440)**

Tully, Brian
Food Marketing Institute **(241)**

Tully-Gerber, Lois
Women in Energy **(546)**

Tuncer, Deniz
Nat'l Ass'n of Housing Cooperatives **(359)**

Tune, Sharon K.
American Historical Ass'n **(73)**

Tunis, Harry
Nat'l Council of Teachers of Mathematics **(396)**

Tunstall Jr., Graydon A.
Phi Alpha Theta **(456)**

Tuny, Brad
Regulatory Affairs Professionals Soc. **(474)**

Turf, Ellen
Nat'l Ass'n of Personal Financial Advisors **(365)**

Turkewitz, Neil
Recording Industry Ass'n of America **(472)**

Turner, Al
World Waterpark Ass'n **(550)**

Turner, Archie
Nat'l Academy of Sciences **(334)**

Turner, Edward C.
Building Owners and Managers Ass'n Internat'l **(183)**

Turner, Garry
American Nurses Ass'n **(87)**

Turner, George D.
American Nuclear Insurers **(87)**

Turner III, James M.
American Wholesale Marketers Ass'n **(123)**

Turner, Jane L.
American Forest and Paper Ass'n (69)

Turner, Jerry
Munitions Carriers Conference (331)

Turner, Julie A.
Plumbing-Heating-Cooling Contractors - Nat'l Ass'n (459)

Turner, Larry
Internat'l Institute of Synthetic Rubber Producers (295)

Turner, Mikoel
Nat'l Ass'n of Black Hospitality Professionals (344)

Turner, Rebecca
Animal Transportation Ass'n (125)

Turner, Shannon
Ass'n of State and Territorial Health Officials (166)

Turner, Susan B.
American Ass'n of Medical Soc. Executives (39)

Turner-Lowe, Susan
Nat'l Academy of Sciences (334)

Turpen, Forrest L.
Christian Educators Ass'n Internat'l (193)

Turpin, Jim
American Correctional Ass'n (60)

Turriff, Tod
Nat'l Soc. to Prevent Blindness/Prevent Blindness
America (430)

Turschmann, Lynne M.
Interstate Natural Gas Ass'n of America (311)

Tuthill, Maria
Calendar Marketing Ass'n (185)

Tutka, Richard
Electrical Apparatus Service Ass'n (227)

Tutt, George L.
American Soc. of Ass'n Executives (107)

Tuttle CAE, Marvin W.
Institute of Certified Financial Planners (266)

Tutwiler, Margaret
Cellular Telecommunications Industry Ass'n (109)

Tutwiller, Liz
Snack Food Ass'n (484)

Tuxill, Carl
Internat'l Ass'n of Structural Movers (282)

Tvaroh, Deborah
American Ass'n of Clinical Urologists (34)

Twarog, Daniel
North American Die Casting Ass'n (441)

Twillman, Mary M.
Ass'n for Educational Communications and Technology (133)

Twitmyer, Robert W.
Nat'l Slag Ass'n (428)

Twombly, Elizabeth
Nat'l Investment Company Service Ass'n (413)

Tyckoson Jr., E. Gilbert
American Railway Development Ass'n (97)

Tyeryar, Barbara B.
Limousine Industry Manufacturers Organization (320)

Tyeryar CAE, Clay D.
American Paper Machinery Ass'n (90)
Limousine Industry Manufacturers Organization (320)
North American Natural Casing Ass'n (443)
Internat'l Ass'n of Emergency Managers (278)
Wire Industry Suppliers Ass'n (545)
American Textile Machinery Ass'n (119)
American Pipe Fittings Ass'n (92)
Meat Industry Suppliers Ass'n (325)

Tyle, Craig S.
Investment Company Institute (312)

Tyle, Mark
American Massage Therapy Ass'n (83)

Tyler, Betty
Rehabilitation Technology Ass'n (474)

Tyler CAE, Judy
Nat'l Student Nurses Ass'n (432)

Tyler, LuAnne O.
Independent Petroleum Ass'n of America (261)

Tyler, Patricia
Nat'l Ass'n of Health Underwriters (357)

Tynan, Brandon
Marine Staff Officers (323)

Tyree, Joan
Ass'n of Rheumatology Health Professionals (164)

Tyree, Ketti
Hardwood Plywood and Veneer Ass'n (251)

Tyrell, Tamara
Nat'l Beer Wholesalers Ass'n (382)

Tyson, Karen
Ass'n for Advanced Life Underwriting (129)

Tyson, Kathy
College Savings Plans Network (198)
State Debt Management Network (516)

Tyson, Samuel
American Coal Ash Ass'n (52)

Tzamaras, George
American Podiatric Medical Ass'n (93)

Uchic, David J.
Internat'l Fabricare Institute (290)

Uddin, Syed Mansoor
Islamic Medical Ass'n (313)

Udowitz, Kristen
Rubber Manufacturers Ass'n (477)
Tire Industry Safety Council (523)

Udvardy, Steven P.
North American Die Casting Ass'n (441)

Uebel, Kathleen
American Academy of Dental Practice Administration (21)

Ufholz, Philip J.
Building Service Contractors Ass'n Internat'l (183)

Ugai, Susan
North American Gaming Regulators Ass'n (442)

Ugeux, George
Belgian American Chamber of Commerce in the United
States (178)

Ugoretz, Mark J.
ERISA Industry Committee (232)

Uhl, Robert C.
ASM Internat'l (128)

Uhlick, Lawrence R.
Institute of Internat'l Bankers (267)

Ullman, Eloise
Industry Council for Tangible Assets (263)

Ullrich, Melinda S.
Nat'l Federation of Music Clubs (404)

Ulmer, Mike
Nat'l Ass'n of Mutual Insurance Companies (363)

Ulrich, Robert
Internat'l Union of Security Officers (310)

Ulrich R.Ph., Susan
American College of Clinical Pharmacology (53)

Underhill, Christine
Nat'l Ass'n for Variable Annuities (342)

Underhill Jr., Henry W.
Internat'l Municipal Lawyers Ass'n (297)

Underwood, Julie
Nat'l School Boards Ass'n (427)

Underwood, Terry Kay
Internat'l College of Applied Kinesiology (286)

Ungaro, Maria
Window Coverings Manufacturers Ass'n (544)
Builders Hardware Manufacturers Ass'n (183)
Nat'l Tabletop and Giftware Ass'n (433)
Certified Ballast Manufacturers Ass'n (190)

Unger, Peter S.
American Ass'n for Laboratory Accreditation (31)

Ungerer, Richard A.
Organization Development Network (449)

Unscapher, Mark
Information Technology Ass'n of America (264)

Unus, Iqbal
Ass'n of Muslim Scientists and Engineers (158)

Upchurch, Doug
Information Technology Training Ass'n (264)

Upshaw, Gene
Nat'l Football League Players Ass'n (405)

Upton, Richard D.
American Lighting Ass'n (81)

Urban Ph.D., Wayne
American Educational Studies Ass'n (65)

Urbanowicz, Nancy
Academy of Management (9)

Urbanski, Diane
Financial Managers Soc. (239)

Urbanski, Verna
Online Audiovisual Catalogers (448)

Urch, Sharon
Radiology Business Management Ass'n (471)

Urmston, Dean
American Seed Trade Ass'n (99)
Nat'l Council of Commercial Plant Breeders (394)

Usovicz, Elizabeth
Ass'n of Records Managers and Administrators (163)

Ussery, Joanne
Inter-America Travel Agents Soc. (271)

Utian M.D., Ph.D, Wulf H.
North American Menopause Soc. (443)

Vaccaro, Jack A.
Institute of Management Accountants (268)

Vaccaro, Nick
Internat'l Inflight Food Service Ass'n (294)

Vadas, David
Aerospace Industries Ass'n of America (13)

Vadell, Jan I.
American Group Psychotherapy Ass'n (71)

Vaden-Williams, Sheila
Nat'l Ass'n of Minority Automobile Dealers (363)

Vagley, Robert E.
American Insurance Ass'n (79)

Vaillancourt, David
FTD Ass'n (244)

Valachovic D.M.D., Richard W.
American Ass'n of Dental Schools (36)

Valas, Elly S.
Appliance Parts Distributors Ass'n (126)
North American Retail Dealers Ass'n (444)

Valasek, Barbara
Refrigeration Service Engineers Soc. (473)

Vale, Norman
Internat'l Advertising Ass'n (272)

Valecruz, Teresita T.
Council of the Great City Schools (216)

Valente Ph.D., CAE, Carmine M.
American Institute of Ultrasound in Medicine (78)

Valenti, Jack J.
Motion Picture Ass'n (330)
Motion Picture Ass'n of America (330)

Valentic CMP, Lynne
Nat'l Ass'n of Credit Management (351)

Valentine, H. Jeffrey
Nat'l Paralegal Ass'n (421)

Valentine, Tony
American Disc Jockey Ass'n (64)

Valentino, Joseph G.
United States Pharmacopeia (534)

Valeri, Gina
American Pet Products Manufacturers Ass'n (91)

Valerio, Marcie
Automatic Meter Reading Ass'n (173)

Valin, Marjorie
American Advertising Federation (27)
Flexible Packaging Ass'n (240)

Valino, Karyn
Color Ass'n of the United States (198)

Vallarta, Ludita H.
Industrial Research Institute (263)

Valliant, John R.
Council of American Maritime Museums (212)

Van Amburg, Kent
Nat'l Magazine, Book, and Film Carriers Conference (415)

Van Beuren, Victor
American Geological Institute (70)

Van Buren, Michael
Hearth Products Ass'n (253)
Pellet Fuels Institute (454)

Van Coverden, Thomas
Nat'l Ass'n of Community Health Centers (349)

Van Daniker, Relmond P.
Nat'l Ass'n of State Auditors, Comptrollers and
Treasurers (374)

Van Den Berghe, Randall
Case Management Soc. of America (187)

Van der Weert, Susan
Internat'l Lactation Consultant Ass'n (295)
Professional Services Management Ass'n (467)

Van Dongen, Dirk
Nat'l Ass'n of Wholesaler-Distributors (380)

Van Doren-Blake CAE, Patricia
American Academy of Neurology (23)

Van Heuven, G.J.
North American Free Trade Ass'n (442)

Van Hook, Robert T.
American Orthotic and Prosthetic Ass'n (89)

Van Horn, Charles
Internat'l Recording Media Ass'n (301)

Van Horne Ph.D., John C.
Independent Research Libraries Ass'n (261)

Van Kleeck, Bruce
Nat'l Retail Federation (425)

Van Norman, Dianne
Soc. of Flight Test Engineers (501)

van Rein, Feikje
Internat'l Trademark Ass'n (309)

Van Vlack, Charles W.
Chemical Manufacturers Ass'n (191)

Van Vort, Marjorie
America's Community Bankers (20)

Van Wert, I. Gregg
Nat'l Ass'n of Printers and Lithographers (366)

Van Wieren, Robert
Christian Schools Internat'l (193)

Van Winter, Shannon M.
Internat'l Window Cleaning Ass'n (311)

van Zanten, Anneke
Home Sewing Ass'n (256)

Vanasek, Ed
Pyrotechnics Guild Internat'l (470)

VanBremen Ph.D.,CAE, Lee
College of American Pathologists (197)

Vance, Becky S.
Soc. of Former Special Agents of the Federal Bureau of Investigation (501)

Vanchel CPA, James E.
Nat'l Ass'n of Credit Management (351)

VanDe Hei, Diane
Ass'n of Metropolitan Water Agencies (157)

Vandel, Robert
Flight Safety Foundation (240)

Vander Ark, Daniel R.
Christian Schools Internat'l (193)

Vanderbilt, Marjorie
American Nurses Ass'n (87)

Vanderpoge, James
American Board of Preventive Medicine (48)

Vanderstel, David G.
Nat'l Council on Public History (397)

Vandervoet, Kathleen
Fresh Produce Ass'n of the Americas (244)

VanderZalm, Jeannine
Nat'l Council of Examiners for Engineering and Surveying (394)

Vandeyar, David J.
Nat'l Fire Sprinkler Ass'n (404)

Vandiver, F. Hal
Crane Manufacturers Ass'n of America (218)
Hoist Manufacturers Institute (255)
Monorail Manufacturers Ass'n (330)

VanDorn, Bonnie
Ass'n of Science-Technology Centers (164)

VanGelderen, Ronald E.
Carpet and Rug Institute (187)

Vanim, Marci Y.
Professional Insurance Mass-Marketing Ass'n (466)

VanLangdeghem, Karen
Ass'n of Maternal and Child Health Programs (157)

Vann, Carole
Ass'n of Old Crows (158)

Vannice, Derek
Utility Arborist Ass'n (538)

VanVeen, Kristin
Ass'n of Energy Service Companies (150)

Varchione, Bob
Nat'l Ass'n of Collegiate Marketing Administrators (348)

Vargas, Arturo
Nat'l Ass'n of Latino Elected and Appointed Officials (361)

Vargas, Cheryl
American Ass'n of School Librarians (42)

Vargas, Gina R.
Soc. of Pediatric Nurses (505)

Vari, James F.
Tobacco Merchants Ass'n of the U.S. (524)

Varieur, Adrienne
Forum for Investor Advice (243)

Varjonack, John
Oil, Chemical and Atomic Workers Internat'l Union (448)

Varrone, Angelo
Nat'l Ass'n of Auto Trim and Restyling Shops (344)

Vars Ph.D., Gordon F.
Nat'l Ass'n for Core Curriculum (338)

Vartan, Dot
Ass'n of Rehabilitation Nurses (163)

Vary, George F.
American Zinc Ass'n (124)

Vasquez, Jessica
Safe and Vault Technicians Ass'n (478)
Associated Locksmiths of America (171)

Vassiliades, John
Coin Laundry Ass'n (196)

Vassilikos, Margaret
Newspaper Ass'n of America (439)

Vastine Jr., J. Robert
Coalition of Service Industries (196)

Vaughan, Michelle
Nat'l Rehabilitation Ass'n (425)

Vaughan, Patricia M.
Nat'l Soft Drink Ass'n (430)

Vaughn, Eric
Renewable Fuels Ass'n (475)

Vaughn, John C.
Ass'n of Graduate Schools in Ass'n of American Universities (152)
Ass'n of American Universities (143)

Vaughn, Rosco
Nat'l Council for Agricultural Education (393)

Veal, Steve
Nat'l Soccer Coaches Ass'n of America (430)

Veale, Paula A.
Advertising Council (12)

Veazey, Teresa
Soc. of Decorative Painters (500)

Vecchione, Bob
Nat'l Ass'n of Athletic Development Directors (343)
Nat'l Ass'n of Collegiate Directors of Athletics (348)

Veech, Barbara
Nat'l League of Postmasters of the U.S. (414)

Veeck, Lisa
Internat'l Sanitary Supply Ass'n (302)

Veerappan, V.
Ass'n of American Geographers (142)

Vehrs, Kristin L.
American Zoo and Aquarium Ass'n (124)

Venator, John A.
Computing Technology Industry Ass'n (203)

Vencl, Nada
Ass'n of Concert Bands (148)

Venit, Mark L.
Apparel Graphics Institute (126)

Venker, Ted
Petroleum Equipment Suppliers Ass'n (455)

Venter, Bob
Portable Computer and Communications Ass'n (460)

Ventrell, Marvin R.
Nat'l Ass'n of Counsel for Children (350)

Ver Eecke, W.
Ass'n for Philosophy of the Unconscious (136)

Ver Straeten, Robert J.
Council for Agricultural Science and Technology (210)

Verberg, Kelly
Nat'l Ass'n of Temporary and Staffing Services (378)
Home Health Services and Staffing Ass'n (255)

Verdeyen, Robert J.
American Correctional Ass'n (60)

Verdisco, Robert J.
Internat'l Mass Retail Ass'n (297)

Vereen, David
American Soc. of Regional Anesthesia (115)
Soc. for Obstetric Anesthesia and Perinatology (491)

Verkler, Robert C.
Institute for Certification of Tax Professionals (265)

Vernon, Steve
Nat'l Ass'n of Metal Finishers (363)

Vertino, Sheila K.
Nat'l Ass'n of Industrial and Office Properties (360)

Veshosky, Leigh
Personal Communications Industry Ass'n (455)

Vessels Ph.D., William A.
Nat'l Ass'n of Teachers of Singing (378)

Vessely Ed.D., Jeffery
Phi Epsilon Kappa (457)

Veziroglu Ph.D., T. Nejat
Internat'l Ass'n for Hydrogen Energy (274)

Viall, J. Thomas
Internat'l Dyslexia Ass'n (289)

Vicek, Thomas
Nat'l Council of State Boards of Nursing (396)

Vich, Miles A.
Ass'n for Transpersonal Psychology (140)

Vickerman, John C.
Book Components Manufacturers Ass'n (181)
American Academy of Otolaryngology-Head and Neck Surgery (24)
Ass'n of Business Products Manufacturers (145)

Vickers, Mary Susan
Interstate Conference of Employment Security Agencies (311)

Vickery, Allison
American Ass'n of Children's Residential Centers (34)

Vickery, Roger P.
Nat'l Ass'n for Promotional and Advertising Allowances (340)

Vickroy, John
Nat'l Ass'n of Veterans Program Administrators (379)

Victoria, Anthony
Nat'l Antique and Art Dealers Ass'n of America (337)

Viehland, Doug
American Hotel and Motel Ass'n (74)

Vietor, Carolynn
Women's Professional Rodeo Ass'n (548)

Vigilante, Theresa
Professional Women in Construction (467)

Villarino, Liz
United Farm Workers of America (530)

Villarruel RN, Ph.D., Antonia M.
Nat'l Ass'n of Hispanic Nurses (358)

Villata, Mark
North American Blueberry Council (440)

Villforth, John C.
Food and Drug Law Institute (241)

Vincent CAE, Donald A.
Automation Technologies Council (174)

Vincent, Keith J.
Internat'l Ass'n for Exposition Management (274)

Vinci, Yasmina S.
Nat'l Ass'n of Child Care Resource and Referral Agencies (347)

Vines, Terry
Nat'l Parks and Conservation Ass'n (421)

Viniello, John A.
Nat'l Fire Sprinkler Ass'n (404)

Viola, Thomas
Manufacturing Jewelers and Suppliers of America (323)

Viscidio D.D.S., Anthony J.
Academy for Implants and Transplants (7)

Visconti, Charles G.
Internat'l Cargo Gear Bureau (285)

Viscovich, Melissa A.
Nat'l Ass'n of Professional Employer Organizations (366)

Vitagliano, Robert
Soc. of Incentive and Travel Executives (502)

Vittoria, Andy
Ass'n of Old Crows (158)

Vivas, Sandra L.
American Volleyball Coaches Ass'n (122)

Vlahos, Len
American Booksellers Ass'n (48)

Vnuk, Antoinette
Construction Industry Manufacturers Ass'n (206)

Voegtlin, Gene
Internat'l Ass'n of Chiefs of Police (277)

Voelker, Gwen
Real Estate Brokerage Managers Council (472)

Vogel, F. Stephen
United States and Canadian Academy of Pathology (532)

Vogel, Heidi
Internat'l Horn Soc. (294)

Vogel DVM, Lyle
American Veterinary Medical Ass'n (121)

Vogelsinger P.E., Bruce
Nat'l Institute of Building Sciences (411)

Vogt, Gerry
American College of Trust and Estate Counsel (58)

Vohs CAE, Maggie
Kite Trade Ass'n Internat'l (316)

Voigt, Marilyn
Ass'n of Environmental and Resource Economists (150)

Volgy, Thomas J.
Internat'l Studies Ass'n (307)

Volk, Kim E.
Delta Dental Plans Ass'n (221)

Volk, Mike
Seaplane Pilots Ass'n (480)

Volkmer, Jane
Internat'l and American Ass'ns of Clinical Nutritionists (273)

Volpe, Angelo
Nat'l Wheel and Rim Ass'n (436)

Volpe-Viles, Maria
American Corporate Counsel Ass'n (60)

Voltman, Robert A.
American Internat'l Freight Ass'n (79)

Voltmann, Robert
Transportation Intermediaries Ass'n (525)

vom Eigen, Ann
American Land Title Ass'n (80)

Voois, Judy A.
Conductors Guild (203)

Vorbach, Joseph E.
American Bureau of Shipping and Affiliated Companies (49)

Vorbeck, Regina
Modern Language Ass'n of America (329)

Votaw, Ty M.
Ladies Professional Golf Ass'n (316)

Votta-Ali, Kim
Ass'n for Work Process Improvement (141)

Vowell CAE, John
APICS - The Educational Society for Resource Management (125)

Voyiaziakas, Barbara
Nat'l Ass'n for Medical Equipment Services (340)

Vrac, James
Internat'l Ass'n of Boards of Examiners in Optometry (276)

Vranas, Chris P.
American Soc. of Travel Agents (116)

Vroom, Jay J.
American Crop Protection Ass'n (62)

Vuilleevmier Jr., George
Nat'l Ass'n of Chiefs of Police (347)

Wachowicz, Mark
Audit Bureau of Circulations (173)

Wachs, Edward
Aviation Safety Institute (176)

Wachter, Adam
Nat'l Newspaper Ass'n (418)

Wachter, Donna
Ass'n of Professors of Gynecology and Obstetrics (161)

Wachtler, Janice
American College of Osteopathic Emergency Physicians (56)

Waddles, Omer E.
Career College Ass'n (186)

Wade, Liane
Antiquarian Booksellers Ass'n of America (125)

Wade, Lisa
American Physical Therapy Ass'n - Private Practice Section (92)

Wade, Mylea
Nat'l Ass'n for Search and Rescue (341)

Wade, Ronn
Internat'l Soc. for Plastination (304)

Wade, Stewart H.
American Bureau of Shipping and Affiliated Companies (49)

Wade, William
Nat'l Directory Publishing Ass'n (399)

Waegemann, C. Peter
Medical Records Institute (326)

Wages, Robert E.
Oil, Chemical and Atomic Workers Internat'l Union (448)

Waggoner, Debra
American Electronics Ass'n (65)

Wagner, Angela
Wireless Communications Ass'n Internat'l (545)

Wagner, Carol
Exercise-Safety Ass'n (233)

Wagner, Cheryl
American Soc. of Landscape Architects (111)

Wagner, Donna
Car Care Council (186)

Wagner, Louis
American Fiberboard Ass'n (68)

Wagner, Robert
Education Law Ass'n (226)

Wagner, Steve
Outdoor Writers Ass'n of America (451)

Wahler, Carol
Type Directors Club (520)

Wahlquist, Richard
Nat'l Ass'n of Temporary and Staffing Services (378)

Wainwright, Sherrilyn
Ass'n for Women Veterinarians (141)

Wakefield, Henrianne
Nat'l Kitchen and Bath Ass'n (414)
American Ass'n of Collegiate Registrars and Admissions Officers (35)

Wakelyn, Jo Ann
Nat'l Ass'n of Supervisors and Administrators of Health Occupations Education (377)

Walberg, Ronald
North American Equipment Dealers Ass'n (442)

Walbrol, Werner
German American Chamber of Commerce (247)

Walch, Margaret
Color Ass'n of the United States (198)

Wald, Anne S.
Ass'n for the Advancement of Medical Instrumentation (138)

Wald, Matt
Nat'l Burglar and Fire Alarm Ass'n (384)

Walden, Cindy
Meeting Professionals Internat'l (327)

Walden, Diane
Nat'l Family Caregivers Ass'n (402)

Walden, Guy
MultiMedia Telecommunications Ass'n (331)

Walden, Shauna
Nat'l Family Planning and Reproductive Health Ass'n (402)

Waldman, Roberta
Roller Skating Ass'n Internat'l (477)

Waldorf, Barbara
Business Marketing Ass'n (184)

Waldron, Dillan
Human Resource Planning Soc. (257)

Waldron, Paul W.
Physician Insurers Ass'n of America (458)

Waldvogel, Grace
American Soc. of Civil Engineers (108)

Waldvogel, Karen
Federal Water Quality Ass'n (236)

Walk, Ann
Business Systems Ass'n (185)
Nat'l Independent Bank Equipment and Systems Ass'n (410)

Walker, Allen
Nat'l Shipyard Ass'n (428)

Walker, Bonnie
Nat'l Council of Supervisors of Mathematics (396)

Walker, Catherine
State Higher Education Executive Officers (516)

Walker, Charles
Nat'l Peach Council (421)

Walker, Chris
American Desalting Ass'n (64)

Walker, Curtis M.
Public Golf Management Ass'n (469)

Walker CAE, Dee Ann
American Board of Veterinary Practitioners (48)
Delta Nu Alpha Transportation Fraternity (221)
American Ass'n of Small Ruminant Practitioners (42)

Walker, Donald L.
Ass'n of Trial Lawyers of America (168)

Walker Jr., E. James
Nat'l Elevator Industry (400)

Walker, Jerry A.
Gypsum Ass'n (250)

Walker, Julie A.
American Ass'n of School Librarians (42)

Walker, Kiki
British-American Chamber of Commerce (182)

Walker, Leigh
Computer Event Marketing Ass'n (202)

Walker, Lisa
Nat'l Ass'n of Biology Teachers (344)

Walker, Lisa J.
Education Writers Ass'n (226)

Walker, Lynne
Internat'l Spa and Fitness Ass'n (307)

Walker, Mary
Nat'l Federation of Black Women Business Owners (403)

Walker Ph.D., Paul D.
Council on Chiropractic Education (216)

Walker, Richard
Ass'n of Field Ornithologists (151)

Walker, Robert
Uni-Bell PVC Pipe Ass'n (529)

Walker, T.J.
Professional Rodeo Cowboys Ass'n (467)

Walker, Wendy
American Ass'n for the Advancement of Slavic Studies (32)

Wall CAE, Carnie M.
Technical Ass'n of the Pulp and Paper Industry (520)

Wall, Dobby
American Physical Therapy Ass'n (92)

Wall, Jack
Nat'l Spotted Swine Record (431)
Poland China Record Ass'n (459)
Chester White Swine Record Ass'n (191)

Wall CAE, Martin A.
Ass'n of Schools and Colleges of Optometry (164)

Wall M.D., Michael
Internat'l Perimetric Soc. (299)

Wall, Nate
Waste Equipment Technology Ass'n (541)

Wallace, Al
American Soc. of Composers, Authors and Publishers (108)

Wallace, Brian
Coin Laundry Ass'n (196)

Wallace, Cynthia
North American Concert Promoters Ass'n (441)

Wallace Jr., Donald L.
Cotton Warehouse Ass'n of America (210)

Wallace, Doris J.
Automated Procedures for Engineering Consultants (173)

Wallace, Judy
Institute of Certified Financial Planners (266)

Wallace, Mary
American Public Health Ass'n (95)

Wallach M.D., Stanley
American College of Nutrition (56)

Wallbeoff Jr., James
Nat'l Ass'n for Trade and Industrial Education (342)

Wallenborn, Linda
American College of Prosthodontists (57)

Waller, Brian
Nat'l Ass'n of Health Underwriters (357)

Waller Ph.D., Ray A.
American Statistical Ass'n (118)

Waller Jr., Robert
Nat'l Ass'n of Chewing Gum Manufacturers (347)
Childrenswear Marketing Ass'n (192)
Juvenile Products Manufacturers Ass'n (315)

Waller, William
Ass'n for Evolutionary Economics (133)

Wallich, Lynn
Nat'l Middle School Ass'n (417)

Walls CMP, David
Ass'n of Community Cancer Centers (148)

Walsh, Carol
GAMA Internat'l (245)

Walsh, Dianna
Structural Stability Research Council (517)

Walsh, Elizabeth
Beta Alpha Psi (178)

Walsh, Helen
Tile Contractors' Ass'n of America (523)

Walsh, Lydia
Nat'l Ass'n of Industrial and Technical Teacher Educators (360)

Walsh, Mary-Lacey
Medical Device Manufacturers Ass'n (326)

Walsh, Patricia
American Wholesale Booksellers Ass'n (123)

Walsh, Pete
Closed Circuit Television Manufacturers Ass'n (195)

Walsh, Richard
Point-of-Purchase Advertising Institute (459)

Walsh Ph.D., William K.
Nat'l Council for Textile Education (393)

Walter, Daniel
Associated Specialty Contractors (172)

Walter, Daniel G.
Nat'l Electrical Contractors Ass'n (400)

Walter, Diane
Financial Managers Soc. (239)

Walter, Trisha
Soc. of Incentive and Travel Executives (502)

Walters, Barbara
Nat'l Institute on Park and Grounds Management (412)

Walters, Frank
Manufactured Housing Institute (322)

Walters, James K.
American Petroleum Institute (91)

Walters, Michael E.
American Veterinary Medical Ass'n (121)

Walters, Sean
Internat'l Ass'n for Financial Planning (274)

Walvoord, Allison
Nat'l Ass'n of Residential Property Managers (370)

Walz, Renee
Lignite Energy Council (320)

Wamble, P.J.
Tennessee Walking Horse Breeders and Exhibitors Ass'n (521)

Wampler, Pauline
American Psychological Ass'n - Division of Psychotherapy (95)

Wamsley, Herbert
Air Force Sergeants Ass'n (15)

Wamsley, Herbert C.
Nat'l Council of Intellectual Property Law Ass'ns (395)
Air Force Sergeants Ass'n (15)
Intellectual Property Owners Ass'n (270)

Wanca, Margaret A.
Parenteral Drug Ass'n (453)

Wander, Elyse G.
Travel Industry Ass'n of America (526)

Wandersman, Suzanne S.
American Psychological Ass'n (94)

Wang, Charles
Greater Blouse, Skirt and Undergarment Ass'n (249)

Wang M.D., H.H.
Chinese American Medical Soc. (192)

Wang, Ted
Chemical Producers and Distributors Ass'n (191)

Wangman CAE, Carl A.
Alliance of Business Brokers and Intermediaries (18)
EPS Molders Ass'n (232)
Ass'n for Corporate Growth (132)

Wangman, Janice
Smocking Arts Guild of America (484)

Wangman, Janice H.
Ass'n for Corporate Growth (132)

Wannamaker, Bill
Helicopter Ass'n Internat'l (253)

Warburton, Albert E.
American Water Works Ass'n (122)

Warchot, Louis P.
Ass'n of American Railroads (143)

Ward, Arleen
American Oil Chemists' Soc. (88)

Ward, Jane Robinson
Nat'l Council of Nonprofit Ass'ns (395)

Ward, Janice
Nat'l Nursing Staff Development Organization (418)
Soc. for Vascular Nursing (496)
American Soc. of Pain Management Nurses (113)
American Ass'n of Nurse Attorneys (39)
Home Healthcare Nurses Ass'n (255)

Ward, Joann
Institute for Certification of Computing Professionals (265)

Ward CAE, Michael F.
Biomedical Marketing Ass'n (179)

Ward, Neil A.
American Pulpwood Ass'n (96)

Ward, Randall H.
Automotive Wholesalers Ass'n Executives (175)

Ward Ph.D., Richard E.
Material Handling Industry Ass'n (325)
Automated Storage/Retrieval Systems (173)

Automatic Guided Vehicle Systems (173)

Ward, Robert
Nat'l Honey Packers and Dealers Ass'n (409)

Ward, Sandy
Nat'l Athletic Trainers' Ass'n (381)

Ward, Woodson
United States Conference of Mayors (533)

Ward-Callan, Mary
Institute of Electrical and Electronics Engineers (266)

Wardell, Jay H.
Nat'l Cattlemen's Beef Ass'n (386)

Warden, Sean
Professional Ass'n of Health Care Office Managers (464)

Ware, Richard
American Trucking Ass'ns (121)

Ware, Sylvia A.
American Chemical Soc. (51)

Ware, Viveca
Independent Bankers Ass'n of America (260)

Warfield, Alice
Transportation Clubs Internat'l (525)

Warkentin, Jeane
Nat'l Small Business United (428)

Warlick, LaVerne
Nat'l Restaurant Ass'n (425)

Warner, Ann Iona
American Institute of Parliamentarians (78)

Warner CAE, Betty A.
Academy of General Dentistry (8)

Warner, John G.
Ass'n of Winery Suppliers (169)

Warner, Richard D.
Graphic Arts Technical Foundation (249)

Warner, Stephen M.
Industrial Fabrics Ass'n Internat'l (262)

Warren, Allen
Educational Dealers and Suppliers Ass'n Internat'l (226)

Warren, David L.
Nat'l Ass'n of Independent Colleges and Universities (359)

Warren, Elizabeth
American Academy of Forensic Sciences (22)

Warren III, Hugh
Catfish Farmers of America (188)

Warren, James
Ass'n of American Seed Control Officials (143)

Warren, James M.
Laborers' Internat'l Union of North America (316)

Warren, Judy M.
Graphic Arts Sales Foundation (249)

Warren, Mason
Laborers' Internat'l Union of North America (316)

Warren, Rhonda
Tax Executives Institute (520)

Warren, Robert P.
Air Transport Ass'n of America (16)

Warren, Willard
Nat'l Institute of Management Counsellors (412)

Warskow, Kay
Ass'n of Rehabilitation Nurses (163)

Warwer, Donald D.
Soc. of Accredited Marine Surveyors (496)

Warye, Kathy
Ass'n for the Advancement of Medical Instrumentation (138)

Wasch, Kenneth A.
Software Publishers Ass'n (509)

Washington Ph.D., Ethel O.
Nat'l Ass'n for the Advancement of Black Americans in Vocational Education (341)

Washington, Jeff
American Correctional Ass'n (60)

Wasieleski, Carol
Cleaning Equipment Trade Ass'n (194)

Wasow, Molly
American Ass'n of Fund-Raising Counsel (37)

Wassekman, Lisa
Appraisal Institute (126)

Wasser, Daniel
Internat'l Ticketing Ass'n (308)

Wasserman, Margery
Nat'l Ass'n of Personal Financial Advisors (365)

Wasson, Steve
American Paint Horse Ass'n (90)

Watchinski, Robert I.
American Academy of Family Physicians (22)

Waterman, Eric S.
Nat'l Erectors Ass'n (402)

Waterman, Ron
Nat'l Ass'n of Consumer Advocates (349)

Waters, Alexis B.
American Physical Therapy Ass'n (92)

Waters, Eva M.
Ass'n of Racing Commissioners Internat'l (162)

Waters, John
American Culinary Federation (63)

Waters, Ron
Ass'n of Progressive Rental Organizations (162)

Waters, Rosemarie
United Nations Staff Union (531)

Waters, Susan
American Angus Ass'n (28)

Waters, Timothy
Wholesale Florists and Florist Suppliers of America (543)

Watkins, Jane
Nat'l Ass'n of Foster Grandparent Program Directors (356)

Watkins, Ruth
Fusion Power Associates (244)

Watson Ph.D., Allan
American Ass'n of University Administrators (44)

Watson, Beth E.
Nat'l Organization of Life and Health Insurance Guaranty Ass'ns (420)

Watson, Betty Ann
Professional Picture Framers Ass'n (466)

Watson, Charles
Ass'n of State Supervisors of Mathematics (166)

Watson, Charlotte
American Soc. for Engineering Education (102)

Watson, Diane Alicia
Ass'n of State Floodplain Managers (166)

Watson, Mark
Radiological Soc. of North America (471)

Watson, Michele
Transportation Intermediaries Ass'n (525)

Watters, Melinda A.
Hearing Industries Ass'n (253)

Watters CAE, Thomas A.
Internat'l Ass'n of Administrative Professionals (275)

Watts, Adrienne
Nat'l School Supply and Equipment Ass'n (427)

Watts, George B.
Nat'l Broiler Council (384)

Watts Jr., Robert C.
Diving Equipment and Marketing Ass'n (224)

Waugh, Jan M.
Ass'n of Legal Administrators (155)

Waxman M.D., F.A., Herbert S.
American College of Physicians-American Soc. of Internal Medicine (57)

Waxman, John R.
Nat'l Ass'n of Catering Executives (346)
SAVE Internat'l (479)

Way, James A.
Nat'l Aeronautic Ass'n (335)

Way, Jeff
Antenna Measurement Techniques Ass'n (125)

Way, Sheila
ACIL (11)

Wayne, Karen A.
Assisted Living Federation of America (170)

Wayne, Kirk
Tobacco Associates (523)

Weatherford, Catherine J.
Nat'l Ass'n of Insurance Commissioners (360)

Weatherhead, John
Associated Construction Publications (171)

Weathersby, George B.
American Management Ass'n Internat'l (82)

Weathersby, Marshall
SPIE-Internat'l Soc. for Optical Engineering (514)

Weathington, Kerry
Nat'l Automated Clearing House Ass'n (381)

Weaver CMP, Brenda L.
American Geophysical Union (70)

Weaver, Carolyn
American Soc. of Indexers (111)

Weaver CAE, David A.
Mail Advertising Service Ass'n Internat'l (322)

Weaver, Jack
American Institute of Chemical Engineers (77)

Weaver, John
Institute of Scrap Recycling Industries (269)
Plumbing-Heating-Cooling Contractors - Nat'l Ass'n (459)

Weaver, Rodney
Ass'n of Refrigerant Desuperheater Manufacturers (163)

Weaver Barnes, Lori
American Internat'l Automobile Dealers Ass'n (79)

Webb, C. Edwin
American Ass'n of Colleges of Pharmacy (35)

Webb, Connie
North American Trucking Industrial Relations Ass'n (445)

Webb, Frances
Federal Managers Ass'n (236)

Webb, Gayle
Ass'n of Fraternity Advisors (152)

Webb, James R.
American Real Estate Soc. (97)

Webb, Jim
Ladies Professional Golf Ass'n (316)

Webb, N. Douglas
Nat'l Conference of State Legislatures (391)

Webb, Pamela
Promotional Products Ass'n Internat'l (468)

Webb Jr., William H.
Nat'l Sporting Goods Ass'n (431)

Webber, David S.
American Bearing Manufacturing Ass'n (47)

Webber, Deborah
Nat'l Ass'n of Purchasing Management (368)

Webber, Frederick L.
Chemical Manufacturers Ass'n (191)

Webber, JoAnne
Unfinished Furniture Ass'n (529)

Weber, Daniel E.
Institute of Food Technologists (267)

Weber, Harold H.
Sulphur Institute, The (518)

Weber, Jeff D.
American Welding Soc. (123)

Weber, Karen
Professional Lawn Care Ass'n of America (466)

Weber, Larry
Nat'l Council of State Emergency Medical Services Training Coordinators (396)

Weber, William
Farm Credit Council (234)

Webster, Ann Marie
Ass'n of Residents in Radiation Oncology (163)

Webster, Duane
Ass'n of Research Libraries (163)

Webster, Hugh
Packaging Machinery Manufacturers Institute (452)

Webster, Irena L.
Ass'n for the Study of Afro-American Life and History (139)

Webster, Lorraine B.
Education Credit Union Council (226)

Webster, Peter
Ass'n for Technology in Music Instruction (138)

Webster, R. Tim
American Soc. of Consultant Pharmacists (108)

Webster, Robin
Ass'n of Nat'l Advertisers (158)

Wechsler, Robert
Transport Workers Union of America (525)

Wechsler, Steven A.
Nat'l Ass'n of Real Estate Investment Trusts (369)

Wecker, Richard A.
LIMRA Internat'l (320)

Weed, Fran
Ass'n of Women's Health, Obstetric and Neonatal Nurses (169)

Weekley, Mary E.
American Gas Ass'n (70)

Weeks, Karen
Plumbing-Heating-Cooling Contractors - Nat'l Ass'n (459)

Weeks, William E.
Texas Produce Export Ass'n (521)

Weerts, Richard
Nat'l Ass'n of College Wind and Percussion Instructors (348)

Wege, David Van Der
Wilderness Medical Soc. (544)

Weggel, Ralph W.
Institute for Briquetting and Agglomeration (265)

Wegner, Marilou
American Internat'l Charolais Ass'n (79)

Wegrzyn, Susanne R.
Nat'l Club Ass'n (387)

Wehking, Chris
American Hardware Manufacturers Ass'n (72)

Wehrli CAE, CEM, Fredrick M.
Internat'l Television Ass'n (308)

Wehrman, Christine
Nat'l Corn Growers Ass'n (392)

Wei, Zhong
Nat'l Ass'n of College and University Business Officers (348)

Weickert, Brent
Nat'l Nutritional Foods Ass'n (419)

Weidler, Joyce
American Skin Ass'n (100)

Weidner, K. David
American Ass'n of School Administrators (42)

Weigel Ph.D., Nancy
Women in Endocrinology (546)

Weiglein, Robert
Wood Moulding and Millwork Producers Ass'n (548)

Weigold, George W.
Dairy Soc. Internat'l (220)

Weil Ph.D., FAC, Peter
American College of Healthcare Executives (54)

Weiland, J.J.
Nat'l Grain Trade Council (407)

Weiler Ph.D., C. Susan
American Soc. of Limnology and Oceanography (112)

Weiler, Greg
American Soc. for Quality (105)

Weiler, Hildegard A.
American Orthopaedic Ass'n (88)

Weilinich, Tom
American College of Emergency Physicians (54)

Weinberg CAE, Myrl
Nat'l Health Council (408)

Weinberg, Richard A.
Nat'l League of Postmasters of the U.S. (414)

Weinberg, Wendy
Nat'l Ass'n of Consumer Agency Administrators (349)

Weindruch, Larry
Nat'l Sporting Goods Ass'n (431)

Weiner, Bennett
Council of Better Business Bureaus (212)

Weiner, Bill
Safety Equipment Manufacturers' Agents Ass'n (478)

Weiner Ph.D., Kathryn A.
American Academy of Pain Management (24)

Weiner, Melanie
American Psychological Soc. (95)

Weiner Ph.D., Richard S.
American Academy of Pain Management (24)

Weiner, William
Northamerican Industrial Representatives Ass'n (446)

Weinraub, Ellen
Nat'l Investment Company Service Ass'n (413)

Weinrich, Yancy
American Gem Soc. (70)

Weinstein, Celia
Industrial Designers Soc. of America (262)

Weinstein, Richard
Media Rating Council (326)

Weinstein, Sam
Utility Workers Union of America (538)

Weintraub, Harry
League of Resident Theatres (318)

Weir, Margaret M.
ASM Internat'l (128)

Weirs, Christopher
American Soc. of Addiction Medicine (106)

Weisbecker, Clement A.
Pharmacists in Ophthalmic Practice (456)

Weiser, Judy
Internat'l Phototherapy Ass'n (299)

Weiser, Wendy J.
American Ass'n of Clinical Urologists (34)

Weisgrau, Richard
American Soc. of Media Photographers (112)

Weisman, Avril
Nat'l Ass'n of Community Action Agencies (349)

Weismiller, Toby
Nat'l Ass'n of Social Workers (373)

Weiss CAE, Dr. Armand B.
Internat'l Ass'n of Medical Science Educators (281)

Weiss, Cliff
Nat'l Ass'n of Enrolled Agents (354)

Weiss, Elaine
American Bar Ass'n (46)

Weiss, Jim
Soc. of Actuaries (496)

Weiss, Joan C.
Justice Research and Statistics Ass'n (315)

Weiss, Karl E.
Nat'l Lead Burning Ass'n (414)

Weiss, Lisa
American Health Quality Ass'n (72)

Weiss, Nancy
Ass'n for Persons with Severe Handicaps, The (136)

Weiss M.D., M.B., Ronald L.
Academy of Clinical Laboratory Physicians and Scientists (8)

Weiss, Steve
Council for Advancement and Support of Education (210)

Weiss, Suzanne M.
American Ass'n of Homes and Services for the Aging (37)

Weiss, Thomas
Economic History Ass'n (225)

Weissmann, Patricia
American Ass'n of Railroad Superintendents (42)

Weitkunat, Janet
Nat'l Fluid Power Ass'n (405)

Weitzel, Cammie
World Floor Covering Ass'n (549)

Weitzerfield, JoAnn
Ass'n for Manufacturing Excellence (136)

Welburn, Brenda
Nat'l Ass'n of State Boards of Education (374)

Welch CAM, Arthur S.
Ass'n of the United States Army (167)

Welch, Brenda
Art and Creative Materials Institute (127)

Welch, Dawn
American Sleep Disorders Ass'n (100)

Welch, Gordon
Club Managers Ass'n of America (195)

Welch, Julie
American Subcontractors Ass'n (118)

Welch Ph.D., Kathleen
Rhetoric Soc. of America (476)

Welch, Stephen J.
American College of Chest Physicians (53)

Welch, Teresa Foster
Nat'l Athletic Trainers' Ass'n (381)

Welch, Deacon Thomas
Nat'l Ass'n of Diaconate Directors (352)

Welcome, Jerry
Packaging Machinery Manufacturers Institute (452)

Welen, Bettianne
American Soc. of Interior Designers (111)

Wellamn, Nancy
American Watchmakers-Clockmakers Institute (122)

Welle, Noreen
Radio-Television News Directors Ass'n (471)

Weller Jr., Paul S.
Apple Processors Ass'n (126)
American Ass'n of Grain Inspection and Weighing Agencies (37)
Canadian-American Business Council (186)

Welles, Elizabeth
Ass'n of Departments of Foreign Languages (149)

Welling, Kathleen
Music Educators Nat'l Conference: The Nat'l Ass'n for Music Education (332)

Wells, Byron
American Soc. for Eighteenth-Century Studies (102)

Wells, Carolyn S.
Nat'l Barbecue Ass'n (382)

Wells, Elizabeth
Snack Food Ass'n (484)

Wells, Maggie
Nat'l Soc. of Compliance Professionals (429)

Wells, Ralph
Wild Bird Feeding Institute (544)

Wells M.D., FACS, Samuel A.
Women's Council of Realtors (548)

Wells, Sue
Wild Bird Feeding Institute (544)

Wells, Todd
Nat'l Ass'n of Criminal Defense Lawyers (352)

Welsh, Angela
Soc. for Investigative Dermatology (490)

Welsh, Dave
United States Army Warrant Officers Ass'n (532)

Welsh, Joyce
Nat'l Council on the Aging (398)

Welsh, Margaret A.
Nat'l Ass'n of Regulatory Utility Commissioners (369)

Wemstrom, Rosemary
North American Retail Dealers Ass'n (444)

Wenderski, Susan L.
Nat'l Sporting Goods Ass'n (431)

Wenger, Luke
Medieval Academy of America (326)

Wenhold, Dave
Nat'l Court Reporters Ass'n (398)

Wenmark, William H.
Nat'l Ass'n For Ambulatory Care (337)

Wenning, Thomas F.
Nat'l Grocers Ass'n (407)

Wenninger, Shannon
American Academy of Periodontology (25)

Wenske, Dennis
United Paperworkers Internat'l Union (531)

Wente, Karen
Laser Institute of America (317)

Wentworth, Eric
Council for Advancement and Support of Education (210)

Wentz, Marilyn
Farmers Educational and Co-operative Union of America (235)

Wentz, Roger
American Traffic Safety Services Ass'n (120)

Werdy, Arthur L.
Internat'l Air Cargo Ass'n (272)

Werner, Aviva
Emerging Markets Traders Ass'n (229)

Werner, Jeffrey
European-American Business Council (233)

Werner, Kathryn E.
Nat'l Organization of Nurse Practitioner Faculties (420)

Werner, Kelly L.
American Farriers Ass'n (66)

Wernette DVM, Karen M.
American Veterinary Medical Ass'n (121)

Wernick, David
Council of the Americas (216)

Werst Jr., William H.
Suppliers of Advanced Composite Materials Ass'n (518)
United States Advanced Ceramics Ass'n (531)

Werts D.D.S., Ramon
American Endodontic Soc. (66)

Wertschnig, Mary
Renewable Fuels Ass'n (475)

Wertz, Sheila
Automated Builders Consortium (173)
Construction Writers Ass'n (207)

Weskock, Carlese
American Business Press (50)

Wesley, Morgan N.
Nat'l Eye Research Foundation (402)

Wesloh, Karen
American Correctional Food Service Ass'n (60)

Wesolowski, David J.
Geochemical Soc. (246)

Wessel, Robert A.
Gypsum Ass'n (250)

West, Barbara F.
Nat'l Ass'n of Veterans' Research and Education Foundations (379)

West, Brenda
American Soc. of Agricultural Engineers (106)

West, Debra
American Soc. of Farm Managers and Rural Appraisers (109)

West, Donna D.
Nat'l Spotted Saddle Horse Ass'n (431)

West, Elizabeth
American Land Rights Ass'n (80)

West, Ford B.
Fertilizer Institute (238)

West, Jake
Internat'l Ass'n of Bridge, Structural, Ornamental and Reinforcing Iron Workers (276)

West, Lean M.
Congress of Nat'l Black Churches (205)

West, Lorraine J.
American Academy of Matrimonial Lawyers (23)

West, Sue
UNDA-USA, Nat'l Catholic Ass'n for Broadcasters/Communicators (529)

Wester O.P., Carol
Nat'l Ass'n for Treasurers of Religious Institutes (342)

Wester, Shirley
American Academy of Otolaryngology-Head and Neck Surgery (24)

Westerhold, William F.
Nat'l Ass'n of Chain Manufacturers (346)

Western, Ann W.
American Forest and Paper Ass'n (69)

Western, Linda
Nat'l Fluid Power Ass'n (405)

Westlake, James H.
American Truck Dealers (121)

Westra, Kathy
Nat'l Parks and Conservation Ass'n (421)

Wetchey, Kirk
Internat'l Saw and Knife Ass'n (302)

Wetter M.D., Paul Alan
Soc. of Laparoendoscopic Surgeons (503)

Wexler, Chuck
Police Executive Research Forum (459)

Whalen, Claire
Nat'l Ass'n of Independent Schools (360)

Whalen, Kay
American Academy of Emergency Medicine (21)

Whaler, Victoria
Material Handling Industry Ass'n (325)

Whaley, James
Nat'l Ass'n of State Units on Aging (376)

Wharff, Agatha
Ass'n for Healthcare Resource Materials and Management (134)

Wharton, Dennis
Nat'l Ass'n of Broadcasters (345)

Wharton, Donald E.
Internat'l Ass'n of Machinists and Aerospace Workers (280)

Wheatly, Carolyn R.
Nat'l Investor Relations Institute (413)

Wheaton, Thomas R.
American Cultural Resources Ass'n (63)

Wheeler, Cindy
Religious Conference Management Ass'n (474)

Wheeler, Dawn
Ass'n for Women in Mathematics (140)

Wheeler, Enily T.
Nat'l Ass'n of Chain Drug Stores (346)

Wheeler Ph.D., Gerald F.
Nat'l Science Teachers Ass'n (427)

Wheeler, James
Nat'l Council on Internat'l Trade Development (397)

Wheeler, Leslie G.
Pellet Fuels Institute (454)

Wheeler, M. Cass
American Heart Ass'n (72)

Wheeler, Richard M.
Elevator Industries Ass'n (229)

Wheeler, Terry
Conflict Resolution Education Network (205)

Wheeler, Thomas E.
Cellular Telecommunications Industry Ass'n (189)

Whelan, Bride M.
Soc. of Publication Designers (506)

Whelan Sc.D., MPH, Elizabeth M.
American Council on Science and Health (62)

Whelan Ph.D., Jim
Ass'n for the Advancement of Applied Sport Psychology (138)

Whelan, June M.
Nat'l Petroleum Refiners Ass'n (422)

Whelan, Wayne L.
Ass'n for Continuing Higher Education (131)

Whelchel, Sandy
Associated Business Writers of America (171)
Nat'l Writers Ass'n (437)

Wherry, J. Jeffery
Steel Door Institute (516)
Abrasive Grain Ass'n (7)
Cemented Carbide Producers Ass'n (189)
Diamond Wheel Manufacturers Institute (222)
Grinding Wheel Institute (250)
Insulated Steel Door Institute (270)
Machine Knife Ass'n (321)
Coated Abrasives Manufacturers' Institute (196)

Whidden, Glenn
Business Espionage Controls and Countermeasures Ass'n (184)

Whisler, Donna
American Ass'n of School Administrators (42)

Whitaker, Gail
American Pharmaceutical Ass'n (91)

Whitchurch, Charles G.
Wirebound Box Manufacturers Ass'n (545)

White, Amy
Committee of 200 (200)

White, Arthur L.
Nat'l Ass'n for Research in Science Teaching (341)

White, Carla
Specialty Coffee Ass'n of America (514)

White, Carol
Advertising Research Foundation (12)

White, Chester
Nat'l Organization of Black Law Enforcement Executives (420)

White, Daun
Soc. for the Advancement of Material and Process Engineering (494)

White, David. E.
Military Chaplains Ass'n of the U.S. (328)

White, Donald G.
APMI Internat'l (125)
Metal Powder Industries Federation (327)

White, E. Patrick
American Ass'n of Immunologists (38)

White, Eldon
Agriculture Council of America (15)
Nat'l Agri-Marketing Ass'n (335)

White, George
Nat'l Electrical Contractors Ass'n (400)
Callerlab-Internat'l Ass'n of Square Dance Callers (186)

White CPCU, AIM, George A.
American Institute for CPCU - Insurance Institute of America (75)

White DBA, Jack W.
American Psychiatric Ass'n (94)

White, Janet
American Institute of Architects (76)

White, Jennifer
Corn Refiners Ass'n (209)

White, Jerry L.
Internat'l Ass'n of Conference Centers (277)

White, John
Ass'n for Computing Machinery (131)

White Jr., John W.
North American Clinical Dermatological Soc. (441)

White, Karen
Nat'l Ass'n of Real Estate Investment Trusts (369)

White, Kay
Nat'l Ass'n of Family and Community Education (354)

White, Lynn
Nat'l Child Care Ass'n (386)

White, Margita E.
Ass'n for Maximum Service Television (136)

White CMP, Martha
American Ass'n of Physician Specialists (41)

White, Rebecca
Emergency Nurses Ass'n (229)

White, Rosanne
Technology Student Ass'n (521)

White, Roy
General Merchandise Distributors Council (246)

White, Sam
Home Office Life Underwriters Ass'n (256)

White, Steven
Delta Dental Plans Ass'n (221)

White, Tim
Nat'l Ski Areas Ass'n (428)

White, Tom
MIDI Manufacturers Ass'n (328)
Interactive Audio Special Interest Group (271)

White-Martin, Deborah
Nat'l Ass'n of State Units on Aging (376)

Whitehead, Alfred K.
Internat'l Ass'n of Fire Fighters (279)

Whitehead, James R.
American College of Sports Medicine (57)

Whitehead, William C.
Plumbing and Drainage Institute (459)

Whitehouse, Susan
Ass'n for Research in Otolaryngology (137)
American College of Veterinary Pathologists (58)

Whiteley, Grice
Airport Consultants Council (17)

Whiteside D.D.S., Daniel
Ass'n of Organ Procurement Organizations (159)

Whiting, Fred
American Occupational Therapy Ass'n (88)

Whiting, Jason
Nat'l Food Processors Ass'n (405)

Whiting, Richard M.
Bankers Roundtable, The (176)

Whitley, Robert E.
United States Tour Operators Ass'n (535)

Whitman, Clint
Metal Findings Manufacturers Ass'n (327)

Whitman, Frankie
Women Chefs and Restaurateurs (545)

Whitman, Howard
Soc. of Cable Telecommunications Engineers (499)

Whitmarsh, Don
Nat'l Ass'n of Regional Media Centers (369)

Whitmire, Ronald
Independent Petroleum Ass'n of America (261)

Whitsett, Louise
Institute of Internal Auditors (267)

Whittall, James
Early Sites Research Soc. (225)

Whittekiend, J. Craig
Soc. for Range Management (493)

Whittingbill, James B.
American Trucking Ass'ns (121)

Whittlesey, Karen L.
American Theological Library Ass'n (120)

Whoelre, Bill
Nat'l Ass'n of Community Action Agencies (349)

Whyte CAE, Bonnie
Employers Council on Flexible Compensation (230)

Wible, Mildred A.
Associated Glass and Pottery Manufacturers (171)

Wible, Robert C.
Nat'l Conference of States on Building Codes and Standards (391)

Wicklund, Carl
American Probation and Parole Ass'n (94)

Wickwire Ph.D., Pat Nellor
American Ass'n for Career Education (30)

Wicrolius, Robert
Refractories Institute (473)

Widmayer, Kate
Nat'l Electrical Contractors Ass'n (400)

Widmer, Janet M.
Congress of Lung Ass'n Staff (205)

Widmer CAE, M. Eileen
Soc. of Gastroenterology Nurses and Associates (502)

Wiebe, Kurt T.
Steel Service Center Institute (517)

Wiedemer, Kathleen
Nat'l Mental Health Ass'n (416)

Wieder, Lori
Ass'n for Assessment and Accreditation of Laboratory Animal Care Internat'l (130)

Wieland, Hank
Telecommunications Industry Ass'n (521)

Wiener, Robin K.
Institute of Scrap Recycling Industries (269)

Wiener, Victor
Appraisers Ass'n of America (126)

Wientzen, H. Robert
Direct Marketing Ass'n (223)

Wierzynski, Barbara
Futures Industry Ass'n (245)

Wiese, Arthur E.F.
American Petroleum Institute (91)

Wiesenmaier, Hubert
American Import Shippers Ass'n (75)

Wieting, Mark
American Academy of Orthopaedic Surgeons (24)

Wigfall, Cynthia
Composite Can and Tube Institute (201)

Wiggins, M. Eugene
Nat'l Black Ass'n for Speech, Language and Hearing (383)

Wigginton, Carol
Knitting Guild of America (316)

Wigglesworth, Ms. Terry
Oxygenated Fuels Ass'n (452)

Wight, Scott
Microbeam Analysis Soc. (328)

Wightman, Donald E.
Utility Workers Union of America (538)

Wigington, Robert R.
Airports Council Internat'l/North America (17)

Wignes, Glenys
Organization of American Kodaly Educators (450)

Wikson, Galen
American String Teachers Ass'n (118)

Wilbank, Judy
American College of Osteopathic Pain Management and Sclerotherapy (56)

Wilcox Ph.D., Earl
College English Ass'n (197)

Wilcox, Roger
Indian Arts and Crafts Ass'n (262)

Wilcox, Shirley
Nat'l Genealogical Soc. (406)

Wilder, James D.
Northamerican Heating, Refrigeration and Airconditioning Wholesalers Ass'n (446)

Wildgrube, Dianne
American Ass'n of State Social Work Boards (43)

Wilding, Holly
Nat'l Organization of Life and Health Insurance Guaranty Ass'ns (420)

Wilds, Donna
Infectious Diseases Soc. of America (263)

Wiles, Harry
Wine and Spirits Wholesalers of America (544)

Wiles, Richard I.
Military Operations Research Soc. (328)

Wiley, David M.
Weed Science Soc. of America (542)

Wilhelm, Lawrence
American Hotel and Motel Ass'n (74)

Wilk, Robert J.
Internat'l Ass'n for Computer Systems Security (273)

Wilke, Carol
Medical Group Management Ass'n (326)
American College of Medical Practice Executives (55)

Wilkerson, Betty
Nat'l Ass'n of Black Procurement Professionals (345)

Wilkerson, Linda
American Soc. of Neuroimaging (113)
American Neurological Ass'n (87)
Internat'l Academy of Trial Lawyers (272)

Wilkerson, Ronald
Nat'l Ass'n of Vocational-Technical Education Communicators (380)

Wilkerson, Sunny
Agricultural Retailers Ass'n (14)

Wilkes, Ann
Snack Food Ass'n (484)

Wilkes, Shelburn
American Hernia Soc. (73)

Wilkinson, Anthony R.
Nat'l Ass'n of Government Guaranteed Lenders (357)

Wilkinson, Earl
Internat'l Newspaper Marketing Ass'n **(298)**

Wilkinson, Rev. John H.
American Catholic Correctional Chaplains Ass'n **(50)**

Wilkoff, Leslie
Nat'l Ass'n of Service and Conservation Corps **(372)**

Willard, Greg
Nat'l Basketball Referees Ass'n **(382)**

Willard, Tim
Nat'l Food Processors Ass'n **(405)**

Willard, Zane
Mohair Council of America **(330)**

Willburn, Jerry
Internat'l Brotherhood of Boilermakers, Iron Ship Builders, Blacksmiths, Forgers and Helpers **(284)**

Willer, Barbara A.
Nat'l Ass'n for the Education of Young Children **(341)**

Willett, Ralph
Associated General Contractors of America **(171)**

Willging Ph.D., Paul R.
American Health Care Ass'n **(72)**

Williams Ph.D., Allan F.
Insurance Institute for Highway Safety **(270)**

Williams, Andrew
SnowSports Industries America **(484)**

Williams, Angela
Business Technology Ass'n **(185)**

Williams, Antenor R.
Soc. of Automotive Engineers International **(498)**

Williams, Beth M.
Ass'n of Otolaryngology Administrators **(159)**

Williams, Beverley
American Ass'n of Home-Based Businesses **(37)**

Williams, Brenda A.
Conference of Chief Justices **(204)**

Williams, Carol A.
Aluminum Ass'n **(19)**

Williams, Carole
Nat'l Mail Order Ass'n **(416)**

Williams Ph.D., Cathlene
Nat'l Soc. of Fund Raising Executives **(429)**

Williams, David
Real Estate Brokerage Managers Council **(472)**

Williams, David L.
Conference of Business Economists **(204)**
United States Ass'n for Energy Economics **(532)**

Williams, Deanne
American College of Nurse-Midwives **(56)**

Williams, Dennis
American Soc. for Environmental History **(102)**

Williams Ph.D., Dennis E.
North American Ass'n of Professors of Christian Education **(440)**

Williams, Dr. Dennis E.
North American Professors of Christian Education **(444)**

Williams, Donna M.
Nat'l Rural Health Ass'n **(426)**

Williams, Fred
Ass'n of Schools of Journalism and Mass Communication **(164)**

Williams, Harding de C.
Ass'n of Financial Services Holding Companies **(151)**

Williams Ph.D., Jack
MicroComputer Investors Ass'n **(328)**

Williams, Jacqueline
Nat'l Ass'n of School Psychologists **(371)**

Williams Jr., James W.
Governmental Research Ass'n **(248)**

Williams, Janelle
Nat'l Ass'n of EMS Physicians **(353)**

Williams, Jeanne
Nat'l Shoe Retailers Ass'n **(428)**

Williams, Jeannie
American Concrete Pipe Ass'n **(59)**

Williams, Jennifer
Passenger Vessel Ass'n **(454)**

Williams, Karen
Nat'l Pharmaceutical Council **(422)**

Williams, Karen
Professional Ass'n of Health Care Office Managers **(464)**

Williams, Kevin M.
Distribution and LTL Carriers Ass'n **(224)**

Williams, Kimberly
Soc. of Glass and Ceramic Decorators **(502)**

Williams, Linda M.
American Ass'n of Pharmaceutical Scientists **(40)**

Williams, Lynn
Internat'l Soc. for Magnetic Resonance in Medicine **(303)**

Williams, Mele
Nat'l Ass'n of Industrial and Office Properties **(360)**

Williams, Michael
Recording Industry Ass'n of America **(472)**

Williams, Nancy J.
AGN Internat'l - North America **(14)**

Williams, Pamela
Nat'l Institute of Building Sciences **(411)**

Williams, Pamela C.
Teachers of English to Speakers of Other Languages **(520)**

Williams, Pamela V.
Women in Cable and Telecommunications **(546)**

Williams, Patricia E.
American Ass'n of Museums **(39)**

Williams Ph.D., CAE, Raymond
United Ass'n of Equipment Leasing **(530)**

Williams, Richard
Nat'l Ass'n of Industrial and Office Properties **(360)**

Williams M.D., Richard D.
Clinical Soc. of Genito-Urinary Surgeons **(195)**

Williams, Roger J.
Accrediting Council for Continuing Education and Training **(11)**

Williams, Ronald L.
American Pharmaceutical Ass'n **(91)**

Williams, Ronnie
Internat'l Professional Rodeo Ass'n **(300)**

Williams, Sandra
Business Products Industry Ass'n **(185)**

Williams, Sarah
Ass'n of Naval R.O.T.C. Colleges and Universities **(158)**

Williams, Steven
Warehousing Education and Research Council **(540)**

Williams, Terry
Pattern, Model and Plastic Toolbuilders Ass'n **(454)**

Williams, Timothy S.
Water Environment Federation **(541)**

Williams, Tracy
Education Writers Ass'n **(226)**

Williams, Virginia
Security Industry Ass'n **(481)**

Williams, Vivienne
American Public Transit Ass'n **(96)**

Williams III, M.D., W.C.
American College of Managed Care Medicine **(55)**
American Ass'n of Integrated Healthcare Delivery Systems **(38)**

Williams III, USAF (RET.), Col. Walker M.
Reserve Officers Ass'n of the U.S. **(475)**

Williams, Wendi A.
Commission on Accreditation of Allied Health Education Programs **(199)**

Williams II, Wlliam Clyde
Nat'l Ass'n of Managed Care Physicians **(362)**

Williamson, Cheryle
Express Carriers Ass'n **(234)**

Williamson, Darla J.
Closure Manufacturers Ass'n **(195)**

Williamson M.N., RNC, Geraldine C.
American Ass'n of Occupational Health Nurses **(40)**

Williamson, Jeffrey
American Medical Informatics Ass'n **(84)**

Williamson, Kent
Nat'l Council of Teachers of English **(396)**

Williamson, Lonnie L.
Wildlife Management Institute **(544)**

Williamson, Richard
United States Energy Ass'n **(533)**

Williamson, Sandy
Nat'l Soccer Coaches Ass'n of America **(430)**

Willis, Thomas R.
Nat'l Council for Community Behavioral Healthcare **(393)**

Willox, Marsha
Internat'l Ass'n of Assembly Managers **(276)**

Willox Jr., Norman A.
Council of Internat'l Investigators **(214)**

Wills, Jean
American Oil Chemists' Soc. **(88)**

Willson, Peters D.
Nat'l Ass'n of Children's Hospitals and Related Institutions **(347)**

Willson, Ron
Photo Marketing Ass'n-Internat'l **(457)**

Wilmeth, Don B.
American Soc. for Theatre Research **(105)**

Wilmouth, Robert K.
Nat'l Futures Ass'n **(406)**

Wilsey, Michelle F.
Institute of Public Utilities **(268)**

Wilson, A. Bruce
American Economic Development Council **(65)**

Wilson, Alton R.
Nat'l Ass'n of Textile Supervisors **(378)**

Wilson, Anna
Ass'n for Biology Laboratory Education **(130)**

Wilson, Anne
Nat'l Volunteer Fire Council **(435)**

Wilson, Bascombe J.
Disaster Preparedness and Emergency Response Ass'n **(223)**

Wilson, Bruce A.
Physician Insurers Ass'n of America **(458)**

Wilson, Carol
Healthcare Convention and Exhibitors Ass'n **(252)**

Wilson, Carolyn
Nat'l Asphalt Pavement Ass'n **(337)**

Wilson, Charles J.
Industrial Fasteners Institute **(262)**

Wilson, Chris
Dramatists Guild **(224)**

Wilson, Chuck
Nat'l Systems Contractors Ass'n **(433)**

Wilson, Dave
Recreational Vehicle Manufacturer's Clubs Ass'n **(473)**

Wilson, David
Graduate Management Admission Council **(248)**

Wilson, Denny
Burley Auction Warehouse Ass'n **(184)**

Wilson, Edmond
Professional Travelogue Sponsors **(467)**

Wilson, Erica
American College Health Ass'n **(52)**

Wilson, Prof. George M.
Conference on Asian History **(205)**

Wilson, J.D.
Internat'l Ass'n of Assembly Managers **(276)**

Wilson, Jeff
PrintImage Internat'l **(463)**

Wilson, Jennifer Joy
Nat'l Stone Ass'n **(431)**

Wilson, John
American Academy of Physical Medicine and Rehabilitation **(25)**

Wilson, John S.
Information Technology Industry Council **(264)**

Wilson, Kit
Self Insurance Institute of America **(481)**

Wilson, Lorraine
Nat'l Education Ass'n of the U.S. **(400)**

Wilson Ph.D., Lucy
Ass'n of Caribbean Studies **(146)**

Wilson, Lynn
Ass'n of Consulting Foresters of America **(148)**

Wilson, Michael
Automotive Recyclers Ass'n **(175)**

Wilson, Phyllis
Internat'l Hearing Soc. **(293)**

Wilson, Richard F.
Nat'l Ass'n of Baptist Professors of Religion **(344)**

Wilson, Ronald
Evangelical Press Ass'n **(233)**

Wilson, Scott
Tobacco Institute **(524)**

Wilson, Terrance
Ass'n for Information and Image Management International **(135)**

Wilson, Tim
Irrigation Ass'n **(313)**

Wilson, Walter
Internat'l Municipal Lawyers Ass'n **(297)**

Wilson CAE, William J.
Vision Council of America **(540)**

Wilt, Glenn E.
Internat'l Ass'n of Bomb Technicians and Investigators **(276)**

Wilton, Frank S.
Label Printing Industries of America **(316)**
Internat'l Thermographers Ass'n **(308)**

Wiltraut, Douglas
Nat'l Soc. of Painters in Casein and Acrylic **(430)**

Wiltshire, Mary
United States Trout Farmers Ass'n **(535)**

Winans, Charles A.
Nat'l Ass'n of Concessionaires **(349)**

Winchester, Nancy
American Soc. of Plant Physiologists **(114)**

Winckler, Susan C.
American Pharmaceutical Ass'n **(91)**

Windbigler, Jeanine
Executive Suite Ass'n **(233)**

Windhorst, Carla
Alliance for Healthcare Strategy and Marketing **(17)**

Windsor, Robert
American Soc. for Nondestructive Testing **(104)**

Winer, Janet
American College of Nurse-Midwives **(56)**

Winer, Mary L.
American Economic Ass'n **(65)**

Winkelmann, John Paul
Nat'l Catholic Pharmacists Guild of the United States **(386)**

Winkleman, Al
Nat'l Federation of Nonpublic School State Accrediting Ass'ns (404)

Winkler, Klaus
Internat'l Communications Industries Ass'n (286)

Winkler, Lisa
Enterprise Computer Telephony Forum (231)

Winkler, Pamela
American Academy of Orthopaedic Surgeons (24)

Winn M.D., James R.
Federation of State Medical Boards of the U. S. (237)

Winn, Micahel
Hearth Products Ass'n (253)

Winnie, Beverly
Ass'n of Asphalt Paving Technologists (144)

Winston, James
Nat'l Ass'n of Black-Owned Broadcasters (345)

Winter, Cynthia
Nat'l Council on Family Relations (397)

Winter, Debrise A.
Cotton Council Internat'l (210)

Winter, Elaine M.
Council of Logistics Management (215)

Winter, Gaia
Nat'l Notary Ass'n (418)

Winters, Jim
American Council on Exercise (62)

Winton, David L.
Ass'n of Proposal Management Professionals (162)

Wire, Lorett
American Desalting Ass'n (64)

Wirfs, Walter M.
Western Wood Products Ass'n (543)

Wirt, Linda
American Ass'n of Professional Landmen (41)

Wirt, Matthew
Soc. for Range Management (493)

Wirtz, Ted
INDA, Ass'n of the Nonwoven Fabrics Industry (259)

Wise, Susan L.
Nat'l Council of Architectural Registration Boards (394)

Wisecup, William G.
Soc. for Physical Regulation in Biology and Medicine (492)
Bioelectromagnetics Soc. (179)

Wisel, Lee Marie
Ass'n of Seventh-Day Adventist Librarians (165)

Wisniewski, Joseph
Chartered Property and Casualty Underwriters Soc. (190)

Wisocki, Marcia
Internat'l Ass'n for Exposition Management (274)

Wisor, Julie
Ass'n for Childhood Education Internat'l (131)

Withers, Barbara
Nat'l Ass'n of Institutional Linen Management (360)

Witherspoon, Marjorie J.
Nat'l Ass'n for State Community Service Programs (341)

Witmeyer, Kathy
Agricultural Retailers Ass'n (14)

Witsken, John
Institute of Electrical and Electronics Engineers (266)

Witt, Lou
Nat'l Ass'n of County Park and Recreation Officials (351)
Nat'l Ass'n of County Planners (351)

Witt, Ted
American Electroplaters and Surface Finishers Soc. (65)

Witter, David
Ass'n of American Medical Colleges (142)

Witting, Sharon
Ass'n of Youth Museums (170)

Wittrock, Cindy
American Soc. of Home Inspectors (111)

Wnubel, Stephanie
Nat'l Ass'n of Educational Buyers (353)

Wohlbruck, Aliceann
Nat'l Ass'n of Development Organizations (352)

Wojdyla, Karen
Nat'l Hearing Conservation Ass'n (408)

Wold, Charles
Soc. of Medical-Dental Management Consultants (503)

Wolf, Carla
Surface Mount Technology Ass'n (519)

Wolf, Jonathan
American Film Marketing Ass'n (68)

Wolf, Linda
American Public Human Services Ass'n (96)

Wolf CAE, Lisa
Air Conditioning Contractors of America (15)

Wolf, Marty
Casino and Theme Party Operators Ass'n (187)

Wolf, Shelley
Institute of Hazardous Materials Management (267)

Wolf Jones DSW, Linda R.
Therapeutic Communities of America (522)

Wolfe, Connie Benton
Nat'l Ass'n of Nutrition and Aging Services Programs (364)

Wolfe CAE, Frank I.
Hospitality Financial and Technology Professionals (256)

Wolfe, Gary
Rolf Institute (477)

Wolfe, Jaclyn
Nat'l Solid Waste Management Environmental (430)

Wolfe, Mark
Nat'l Energy Assistance Directors Ass'n (401)

Wolfe, Mary Ann
Soc. of Scribes (507)

Wolfe, Michael P.
Kappa Delta Pi (315)

Wolfe, Sheemon
Internat'l Ass'n of Audio Visual Communicators (276)

Wolferman, Eric
Newspaper Ass'n of America (439)

Wolff, Roger
Nat'l Ass'n of Independent Fee Appraisers (359)

Wolfsohn, Venlo J.
Internat'l Truck Parts Ass'n (309)

Wolfson, Stanley
American Soc. of Plumbing Engineers (115)

Wollman, Michael
Nat'l Dance-Exercise Instructor's Training Ass'n (399)

Wolseley, Paul V.
Ass'n of Technical and Supervisory Professionals (167)

Wolyn, Michael A.
Bureau of Wholesale Sales Representatives (184)

Womack, James
American Genetic Ass'n (70)

Womack, Vicki
Nat'l Ass'n of Housing Cooperatives (359)

Won, Candy
American Psychological Ass'n (94)

Wong, Cindy
Internat'l Ticketing Ass'n (308)

Wong, Elaine
American Geriatrics Soc. (71)

Wong CMP, Erica
North American Transportation Management Institute (445)

Wong, Kent D.
University and College Labor Education Ass'n (537)

Woo Ph.D., Savio
Harvey Soc. (251)

Woo Ph.D., Ted
Soc. of Cable Telecommunications Engineers (499)

Woocher Ph.D., Jonathan
Jewish Education Service of North America (314)

Wood, Ann C.
Auction Marketing Institute (172)

Wood USAF (RET.), Lt.Gen. C. Norman
Armed Forces Communications and Electronics Ass'n (127)

Wood, Clifford J.
Vacuum Cleaner Manufacturers Ass'n (538)

Wood, Doris
Multi-Level Marketing Internat'l Ass'n (331)

Wood D.O., Ph.D, Douglas L.
American Ass'n of Colleges of Osteopathic Medicine (34)

Wood, Janet
Nat'l Electronic Distributors Ass'n (400)

Wood, Jim
Spring Manufacturers Institute (515)

Wood, Joel
Council of Insurance Agents and Brokers (214)

Wood, Megan Epler
Ecotourism Soc. (225)

Wood, Melissa
Ass'n of Coupon Professionals (149)

Wood, Tom J.
Internat'l Agricultural Aviation Foundation (272)

Wood-Holmes, Carolyn
Ass'n of Old Crows (158)

Woodard, Tom
Nat'l Antique and Art Dealers Ass'n of America (337)

Woodbury, David
American Wire Producers Ass'n (123)

Woodbury, David E.
Hearing Industries Ass'n (253)

Woodbury CAE, Lynn K.
Special Libraries Ass'n (514)

Wooden, Ruth A.
Advertising Council (12)

Woodfield, Ann L.
Ass'n of Real Estate Women (163)

Woodfield, Anne
Women in Financial Development (546)

Woodmansee, Shannon
American Gem Trade Ass'n (70)

Woodring D.D., DeWayne S.
Religious Conference Management Ass'n (474)

Woodring, Donna
Religious Conference Management Ass'n (474)

Woodruff Ph.D., C. Roy
American Ass'n of Pastoral Counselors (40)

Woods, Alex
Black Coaches Ass'n (180)

Woods, Barbara
Nat'l Ass'n of State Administrators for Family and Consumer Sciences (373)

Woods, Karen
Hospice Ass'n of America (256)

Woods CAE, Lois
Soc. of Petroleum Engineers (505)

Woods, Steve
Nat'l Federation of Independent Business (403)

Woodson, Walter
Tobacco Institute (524)

Woodward CAE, Judith C.
American College of Epidemiology (54)

Woodward, Michael
American Ass'n of Physicists in Medicine (41)

Woodward, Patricia
American Soc. for Public Administration (105)

Woodward, Peggie
Nat'l Utility Contractors Ass'n (435)

Woodward, Ralph
Nat'l Ass'n of Independent Publishers Representatives (359)

Woodward, Risa
American Ass'n for State and Local History (32)

Woodward, Susan
Nat'l Council of State Boards of Nursing (396)

Woolard, Renee
Internat'l Ass'n of Financial Crimes Investigators (279)

Woolard, Sandra
American Resort Development Ass'n (98)

Wooldridge, John G.
Health Industry Distributors Ass'n (252)

Wooley, Masdeleine
Internat'l Union of Gospel Missions (310)

Wooley Ph.D., CHE, Susan
American School Health Ass'n (99)

Woolley, Edward A.
Institute of Internat'l Container Lessors (267)

Woolley, Jack
Food Marketing Institute (241)

Woolley, Mary Ellen
American Advertising Federation (27)

Woolman, Kadi
Soc. for the Advancement of Material and Process Engineering (494)

Woolner, Ray
Professional Managers Ass'n (466)

Worcester, Caryn
Nat'l Ass'n of Service Managers (372)

Worcester, Dana
Ass'n of Container Reconditioners (148)

Word, John H.
Nat'l Ass'n for Practical Nurse Education and Service (340)

Worden, Vicki L.
Nat'l Lumber and Building Material Dealers Ass'n (415)

Workman, James
Graphic Arts Technical Foundation (249)
American Ass'n of Airport Executives (33)
Internat'l Graphic Arts Education Ass'n (292)

Workman, Mark E.
Nat'l Council of Teachers of Mathematics (396)

Workosky, Cynthia S.
Nat'l Science Teachers Ass'n (427)

Worley, Jill C.
American Ass'n for Laboratory Animal Science (31)

Worrall, Linda
Oncology Nursing Soc. (448)

Worth, Barbara C.
Council of Educational Facility Planners, Internat'l (213)

Worthington, Barry K.
United States Energy Ass'n (533)

Worthington, Esther
Credit Professionals Internat'l (218)

Worthington, Patrice
Mobile Air Conditioning Soc. Worldwide (329)

Worthington, Richard M.
Nat'l Ass'n of Litho Clubs (361)

Wos Ph.D., Lawrence
Ass'n for Automated Reasoning (130)

Woschitz, Frank
Nat'l Football League Players Ass'n (405)

Wott, John A.
Internat'l Plant Propagation Soc. (300)

Wray, David L.
Profit Sharing/401 (k) Council of America (468)

Wren, James E.
American Ass'n for Vocational Instructional Materials (32)

Wright, Christina
American Beekeeping Federation (47)

Wright, Diana D.
Soc. of the Plastics Industry (507)

Wright, Gladys Stone
Women Band Directors Nat'l Ass'n (545)

Wright, Gwen A.
Ass'n of Records Managers and Administrators (163)

Wright, J. Warren
Giftware Associates Interchange (247)

Wright, James R.
Nat'l Academy of Sciences (334)

Wright, Janet E.H.
Professional Insurance Communicators of America (466)

Wright, Janice
American Soc. of Psychoanalytic Physicians (115)

Wright, Joann
Nat'l Ass'n of Chemical Recyclers (347)

Wright, Karen
Financial Management Ass'n (239)

Wright, Kate
American Ass'n of Handwriting Analysts (37)

Wright, Lynzy Anne
World Council of Defense Investigators (549)

Wright, Marilyn
Ass'n for Information and Image Management International (135)

Wright, Mark
Nat'l Ass'n of Boards of Examiners of Long Term Care Administrators (345)
Automotive Maintenance and Repair Ass'n (174)

Wright, Michael
Soc. of Manufacturing Engineers (503)

Wright, Paul R.
American Medical Student Ass'n (84)

Wright, Rosa
Nat'l Small Business United (428)

Wright, Ted
Nat'l Ass'n of Pipe Fabricators (365)

Wright, W. Robert
Medical Group Management Ass'n (326)

Wristen, Paula A.
Construction Financial Management Ass'n (206)

Wu, Pamela White
Internat'l Soc. of Certified Employee Benefit Specialists (305)

Wukitsch, Michael R.
Business Technology Ass'n (185)

Wulf Ph.D., William A.
Nat'l Academy of Engineering of the United States of America (334)

Wulff, Dana
Soc. for Maintenance Reliability Professionals (490)

Wulff, Eleanor
Internat'l Guild of Candle Artisans (293)

Wyatt Jr., Thomas D.
Nat'l Ass'n of State Controlled Substances Authorities (374)

Wyatt Jr., Wilson W.
American Academy of Actuaries (20)

Wyckoff, Bob
Soc. of Exploration Geophysicists (501)

Wylie (RET.), Capt. Peter C.
Retired Officers Ass'n, The (476)

Wyllie, H. Gordon
Nat'l Ass'n of Corporate Real Estate Executives International (350)

Wyman, Howard
Nat'l Lamb Feeders Ass'n (414)

Wynn, Suzanne
Internat'l Disk Drive Equipment and Materials Ass'n (289)

Wynne, Carol
Fur Information Council of America (244)

Wysocki, Patricia
Newsletter Publishers Ass'n (439)

Wysocki, Susan
Nat'l Ass'n of Nurse Practitioners in Reproductive Health (364)

Wyss, Dianne
Nat'l Indian Gaming Ass'n (410)

Yacker, Jeffrey
BPA Internat'l (181)

Yacker, Marc
Electricity Consumers Resource Council (228)

Yaeger, Pamela
Internat'l Advertising Ass'n (272)

Yager, Milan P.
Nat'l Ass'n of Professional Employer Organizations (366)

Yager, Thomas
Specialty Vehicle Institute of America (514)
Motorcycle Safety Foundation (331)

Yamada Ph.D., Ken
Nat'l Ass'n of Schools and Colleges of the United Methodist Church (371)

Yamada, Teri
Internat'l Turfgrass Soc. (309)

Yannelis, Nicholas
Soc. for the Advancement of Economic Theory (494)

Yardley, Richard
American Apparel Manufacturers Ass'n (28)

Yates, Becky
American Ass'n of Orthodontists (40)

Yates, Cathy
Nat'l District Attorneys Ass'n (399)

Yates, Jeffrey M.
Independent Insurance Agents of America (261)

Ybarra, Tanis
United Farm Workers of America (530)

Yeager, Barbara
Nat'l Committee on Planned Giving (388)

Yeager, Don M.
Gelbray Internat'l (246)

Yeager, Kurt
Electric Power Research Institute (227)

Yeast, Cindy
American Chiropractic Ass'n (51)

Yeaton, Dr. George
American Crossbred Pony Registery (63)

Yeghissian, Patricia
Service Employees Internat'l Union (482)

Yelich, Chris
Ass'n of Educators in Private Practice (150)

Yelverton, P. Whitney
Fertilizer Institute (238)

Yeni, Leo
American Artists Professional League (29)

Yeninas, Barbara Spector
Containerization and Intermodal Institute (207)

Yeo CPA, BBA, William E.
American Ass'n of Nurse Anesthetists (39)

Yep, Richard
Ass'n for Adult Development and Aging (129)
Ass'n for Gay, Lesbian and Bisexual Issues in Counseling (133)
Ass'n for Counselors and Educators in Government (132)
American College Counseling Ass'n (52)
American Counseling Ass'n (62)
Ass'n for Counselor Education and Supervision (132)
Ass'n for Humanistic Education and Development (134)
Ass'n for Assessment in Counseling (130)
Ass'n for Spiritual, Ethical and Religious Values in Counseling (137)
Ass'n for Specialists in Group Work (137)
Nat'l Employment Counseling Ass'n (401)

Yerkovich, Sally
Council for Museum Anthropology (211)

Yeske Ph.D., Ronald
Nat'l Council of the Paper Industry for Air and Stream Improvement (397)

Yingling, Edward L.
American Bankers Ass'n (46)

Yingst, Richard A.
Financial Managers Soc. (239)

Yoch, Norene M.
Health Insurance Ass'n of America (252)

Yoder Ph.D., Robert L.
Academy of Parish Clergy (9)

Yoder, Susan
American College of Sports Medicine (57)

Yodice, John S.
Aircraft Owners and Pilots Ass'n (16)

Yoffie, Rabbi Eric H.
Union of American Hebrew Congregations (529)

Yohnke, Dale
Internat'l League of Electrical Ass'ns (296)

Yokage, Stephen P.
Internat'l Union, United Automobile, Aerospace and Agricultural Implement Workers of America (310)

Yolles, Kathy
Coin Laundry Ass'n (196)

York, Brian
American Health Quality Ass'n (72)

York, Bruce A.
American Federation of Television and Radio Artists (67)

York, Jim
Nat'l Private Truck Council (423)

York, Nan
Nat'l Ass'n of Retired Senior Volunteer Program Directors (370)

Yoskowitz, Jay
Council of Jewish Federations (214)

Yost, Sandra L.
American Academy of Disability Evaluating Physicians (21)

Youmers, Richard
Manufacturing Jewelers and Suppliers of America (323)

Young, Amy
Chorus America (193)

Young, Bob
Nat'l Professional Soccer League (423)

Young, Boyd
United Paperworkers Internat'l Union (531)

Young, Charlene E.
American Water Resources Ass'n (122)

Young, Dr. Donald
American Ass'n of Health Plans (37)

Young, Donald A.
Internat'l Facility Management Ass'n (290)

Young, Frank R.
American Chemical Soc. (51)

Young, Gail
Universities Research Ass'n (536)

Young, Gay A.
Oriental Rug Retailers of America (450)

Young, Jim
Soc. for American Archaeology (485)

Young Ph.D., Judith C.
Nat'l Ass'n for Sport and Physical Education (341)

Young, Judith Schaeffer
Ass'n of Vision Science Librarians (169)

Young, Kristen
Internat'l Communications Industries Ass'n (286)

Young, Kristin
Soc. of American Florists (497)

Young, Lauren
Home Health Services and Staffing Ass'n (255)

Young, Mac
American Ostrich Ass'n (90)

Young, Mark
ATP Tour (172)

Young, Mary K.
Distilled Spirits Council of the U.S. (223)

Young, Meredith L.
Internat'l Safe Transit Ass'n (302)

Young Sr., Michael
Precision Metalforming Ass'n (462)

Young, Rachel
Mason Contractors Ass'n of America (324)

Young, Richard A.
Nat'l Registry of Environmental Professionals (424)

Young, Robert A.
American College of Trial Lawyers (58)

Young, S.
Nat'l Ass'n of Physician Nurses (365)

Young, Steve G.
American Federation of Musicians of the United States and Canada (67)

Young, Steven
Ass'n of Independent Corrugated Converters (153)

Young, Susan
Nat'l Ass'n of Executive Secretaries and Administrative Assistants (354)

Young-Horvath, Viola
Federation of Organizations for Professional Women (237)

Youngblood, James
American Heart Ass'n (72)

Younger, Benjamin
American Soc. for Reproductive Medicine (105)

Younger, Loretta
Nat'l Women's Studies Ass'n (436)

Younger, Melanie
American Urological Ass'n (121)

Younghans, Greg
Nat'l Electronic Distributors Ass'n (400)

Yount, Jean
Professional Records and Information Services Management Internat'l (467)

Yurek, Steven R.
Nat'l Ass'n of Secondary School Principals (372)

Yurish, Ellen
Children's Book Council (192)

Yusif CAE, I.F.
American Mideast Business Associates (85)

Yuska, Charles D.
Packaging Machinery Manufacturers Institute (452)

Zachar, Mary Evelyn
Nat'l Nurses Soc. on Addictions (418)

Zachariadis, Christofer
Ass'n for Community Based Education (131)

Zacharilla, Louis
World Teleport Ass'n (550)

Zachmann, Will
Structural Insulated Panel Ass'n (517)

Zack, Stephen
Nat'l Conference of Bar Presidents (389)

Zack-Olson, Laurie
Internat'l Ass'n of Non-Vessel Operating Common Carriers (281)

Zackery, Dale
Internat'l Documentary Ass'n (289)

Zahran, Zena J.
Fashion Ass'n, The (235)

Zak CAE, Noel
American Soc. of Home Inspectors (III)

Zakariasen, Kenneth L.
American Academy of Cosmetic Dentistry (21)

Zaken, Lisa
Institute of Industrial Engineers (267)

Zambello, Carlos
Internat'l Wild Rice Ass'n (311)

Zamudio, Arlene
American Ass'n of Individual Investors (38)

Zando, Kate
Adhesive and Sealant Council (12)

Zanghi, Linda
Nat'l Ass'n of Independent Lighting Distributors (359)

Zangl, Diane
Professional Knitwear Designers Guild (466)

Zaniello, James
OsteoArthritis Research Soc. Internat'l (451)

Zannes, Maria
Integrated Waste Services Ass'n (270)

Zapanta, Al
United States-Mexico Chamber of Commerce (536)

Zapata, Jaime
Nat'l Ass'n for Bilingual Education (338)

Zapata, Nannette
American Welding Soc. (123)

Zapp D.D.S., John S.
American Dental Ass'n (63)

Zappala, Fern
American Soc. of Health-System Pharmacists (110)

Zappone, Toni
American Soc. of Ocularists (113)
American Anaplastology Ass'n (28)

Zarb, Frank G.
Nat'l Ass'n of Securities Dealers (372)

Zarin MD, Deborah
American Psychiatric Ass'n (94)

Zarrillo, Michael
Nat'l Ass'n of Used Fitness and Rehabilitation Equipment Dealers (379)

Zarro, Phyllis
United States Racquet Stringing Ass'n (535)

Zaterman, Sunia
Council of Large Public Housing Authorities (214)

Zatorski, Michele
Computer Press Ass'n (202)

Zauber (RET.), Col. Glenn R.
Retired Officers Ass'n, The (476)

Zaucha, Thomas K.
Nat'l Grocers Ass'n (407)

Zawacki, Andrew
Poetry Soc. of America (459)

Zedalis, Stella
American Soc. of Colon and Rectal Surgeons (108)

Zedd, Sherri
American Iron and Steel Institute (79)

Zehnle, A. Dennis
Nat'l Network of Estate Planning Attorneys (418)

Zeigler, Dale
Soc. for Cardiovascular Magnetic Resonance (486)
American Academy of Orofacial Pain (24)

Zeigler, Dale B.
Internat'l Neural Network Soc. (298)

Zeigler, John R.
Nat'l Council of Black Engineers and Scientists (394)

Zeisel, Steven I.
Consumer Bankers Ass'n (207)

Zeitz, Joyce
Soc. for Assisted Reproductive Technology (485)

Soc. for Reproductive Surgeons (493)

Zelasko, Nancy
Nat'l Ass'n for Bilingual Education (338)

Zelenka, Patricia
Soc. of Cable Telecommunications Engineers (499)

Zelenski, Sheila
American Soc. for Quality (105)

Zellmer M.P.H., William
American Soc. of Health-System Pharmacists (110)

Zeltzer, Jeffrey L.
Nat'l Home Equity Mortgage Ass'n (409)

Zeltzer, Jennifer
Nat'l Home Equity Mortgage Ass'n (409)

Zeman, Jody
Ass'n of Operating Room Nurses (159)

Zengel CAE, Alan E.
Coordinating Research Council (209)

Zenor, Stanley D.
Ass'n for Educational Communications and Technology (133)

Zepp, Alan
Nat'l Cooperative Business Ass'n (392)

Zepp, James
Justice Research and Statistics Ass'n (315)

Zerla, Aimee F.
American Ceramic Soc. (51)

Zetwick, Mary B.
Reinsurance Ass'n of America (474)

Ziaya, Sarah Jane
Nat'l Ass'n of Metal Finishers (363)

Zick, Bernard Hale
Internat'l Soc. of Speakers, Authors and Consultants (307)

Zidock Jr., Alex
Boating Writers Internat'l (181)

Ziebart, Geoff
Nat'l Ass'n of Business Political Action Committees (346)

Ziebell, Elizabeth A.
American Cream Draft Horse Ass'n (62)

Ziegenfuss, Dr. H. Glenn
Standards Engineering Soc. (515)

Ziegler CPCU, Cynthia R.
Chartered Property and Casualty Underwriters Soc. (190)

Ziegler, Julie
Soc. for Neuroscience (491)

Ziegler, Mary Beth
Ass'n of Flight Attendants (151)

Ziegler, Robert F.
Federation of Socs. for Coatings Technology (237)

Ziegler, Ronald L.
Nat'l Ass'n of Chain Drug Stores (346)

Ziegler, Sharon
American Conference of Governmental Industrial Hygienists (59)

Zielke, Mark D.
American Soc. of Agricultural Engineers (106)

Ziemba, Joe
Refrigeration Service Engineers Soc. (473)

Ziembinski, Wanda
Ass'n of Publication Production Managers (162)

Ziemer, Teresa
Forest Industries Telecommunications (242)

Zierman, Susan A.
Nat'l Ass'n of Developmental Disabilities Councils (352)

Ziff D.D.S., Michael F.
Internat'l Academy of Oral Medicine and Toxicology (272)

Ziffren, Lester
North American-Chilean Chamber of Commerce (446)

Zigo, Cynthia L.
American Ass'n of Exporters and Importers (36)

Zil M.D., J.D., J.S.
American Ass'n of Mental Health Professionals in Corrections (39)

Zimmer CAE, John R.
Internat'l Ass'n of Assembly Managers (276)

Zimmer-Loew, Helene
American Ass'n of Teachers of German (44)

Zimmerman, Arnold
Nat'l Ass'n of Executive Recruiters (354)

Zimmerman, Bill
Ass'n for Experiential Education (133)

Zimmerman, Carole
American Public Health Ass'n (95)

Zimmerman, William T.
American Medical Ass'n (83)

Zinner, David
Ass'n for Professionals in Infection Control and Epidemiology (136)

Ziolkowski, Joseph
Summer and Casual Furniture Manufacturers Ass'n (518)
Upholstered Furniture Action Council (537)

Zipperstein, Steven J.
Conference on Jewish Social Studies (205)

Zippin, Lawrence M.
Ass'n of Jewish Aging Services (155)

Zipser, Andrew
Newspaper Guild (439)

Zito, Estelle
Soc. of Women Engineers (509)

Zito, Lorraine
Nat'l Ass'n of Social Workers (373)

Zito, Robert T.
New York Stock Exchange (438)

Zitowski, Marcia
Healthcare Information and Management Systems Soc. (253)

Zitowsky, Marcia
Academy of General Dentistry (8)

Zizis, Margaret
NaSPA: the Network and System Professionals Ass'n (333)

Zlatnik, Barbara
NACE Internat'l (333)

Zolezzi, Julius
American Tunaboat Ass'n (121)

Zoll, David F.
Chemical Manufacturers Ass'n (191)

Zollar, Carolyn
American Medical Rehabilitation Providers Ass'n (84)

Zoller, Dorthy E.
Internat'l Psychogeriatric Ass'n (300)

Zorman, Kathie D.
General Merchandise Distributors Council (246)

Zotz, Karen
Ass'n of Leadership Educators (155)

Zschock, Charles W.
German American Business Ass'n (247)

Zuby, David S.
Insurance Institute for Highway Safety (270)

Zuckerman, David
American Occupational Therapy Ass'n (88)

Zuckerman, Mark
American Ass'n of Franchisees and Dealers (37)

Zulu, Itibari
African-American Library and Information Science Ass'n (14)

Zuraski, Theresa
Ass'n for the Advancement of Medical Instrumentation (138)

Zurek, John
Professional Golfers Ass'n of America (465)

Zweck, Robert
American Soc. of TV Cameramen (116)

Zych, David
American Podiatric Medical Ass'n (93)

Zyniewicz, Matthew
Ass'n of Theological Schools in the United States and Canada (168)

Acronym Index

All the organizations that have supplied an acronym are listed here in alphabetical order by acronym.

AOHA American Osteopathic Healthcare Ass'n **(89)**
AOHP Ass'n of Occupational Health Professionals (in Healthcare) **(158)**
AoM Academy of Management **(9)**
Ass'n of Management **(156)**
Ass'n of Operative Millers **(159)**
AoM/IAoM Ass'n of Management/Internat'l Ass'n of Management **(156)**
AONE American Organization of Nurse Executives **(88)**
AOOP Academy of Organizational and Occupational Psychiatry **(9)**
AOP Ass'n of On-Line Professionals **(159)**
AOPA Aircraft Owners and Pilots Ass'n **(16)**
American Orthotic and Prosthetic Ass'n **(89)**
Automotive Occupant Protection Ass'n **(174)**
AOPL Ass'n of Oil Pipe Lines **(158)**
AOPO Ass'n of Organ Procurement Organizations **(159)**
AORC Ass'n of Official Racing Chemists **(158)**
Automotive Occupant Restraints Council **(174)**
AORN Ass'n of Operating Room Nurses **(159)**
AOS Academic Orthopaedic Soc. **(7)**
American Ophthalmological Soc. **(88)**
American Oriental Soc. **(88)**
American Otological Soc. **(90)**
AOSA American Optometric Student Ass'n **(88)**
American Oxford Sheep Ass'n **(90)**
Ass'n of Official Seed Analysts **(158)**
AOSC Ass'n of Oilwell Servicing Contractors **(158)**
AOSCA Ass'n of Official Seed Certifying Agencies **(158)**
AOSED Ass'n of Osteopathic State Executive Directors **(159)**
AOSSM American Orthopaedic Soc. for Sports Medicine **(88)**
AOSW Ass'n of Oncology Social Work **(159)**
AOTA American Occupational Therapy Ass'n **(88)**
AOU American Ornithologists' Union **(88)**
AP-LS American Psychology-Law Soc. **(95)**
APA Agricultural Publishers Ass'n **(14)**
Amalgamated Printers' Ass'n **(19)**
Ambulatory Pediatric Ass'n **(19)**
American Pancreatic Ass'n **(90)**
American Patient Ass'n **(90)**
American Payroll Ass'n **(90)**
American Philological Ass'n **(91)**
American Philosophical Ass'n **(91)**
American Pilots' Ass'n **(92)**
American Pinzgauer Ass'n **(92)**
American Planning Ass'n **(92)**
American Polygraph Ass'n **(93)**
American Poultry Ass'n **(93)**
American Psychiatric Ass'n **(94)**
American Psychological Ass'n **(94)**
American Psychotherapy Ass'n **(95)**
American Pulpwood Ass'n **(96)**
American Pyrotechnics Ass'n **(96)**
APA - The Engineered Wood Ass'n **(125)**
Apple Processors Ass'n **(126)**
Architectural Precast Ass'n **(127)**
Audio Publishers Ass'n **(173)**
APA-DP American Psychological Ass'n - Division of Psychotherapy **(95)**
APA/CP American Psychological Ass'n - Division of Clinical Psychology **(95)**
APAA Automotive Parts and Accessories Ass'n **(175)**
APACVS Ass'n of Physician Assistants in Cardiovascular Surgery **(160)**
APAG American Photographic Artisans Guild **(92)**
APAI Ass'n of Paroling Authorities, Internat'l **(159)**
APALA Asian/Pacific American Librarians Ass'n **(128)**
APAN Advertising Photographers of America, Nat'l **(12)**
APAP Ass'n of Physician Assistant Programs **(160)**
APBA American Pet Boarding Ass'n **(91)**
APBP Ass'n of Professional Bridge Players **(160)**
APBPA Ass'n of Professional Ball Players of America **(160)**
APC Academy of Parish Clergy **(9)**
American Peanut Council **(90)**
American Plastics Council **(92)**
Aseptic Packaging Council **(128)**
Ass'n of Pathology Chairs **(159)**
Ass'n of Professional Chaplains **(160)**
Ass'n of Professional Chaplains **(160)**
Ass'n of Professors of Cardiology **(161)**
APCA American Portland Cement Alliance **(93)**
APCC American Public Communications Council **(95)**
Ass'n of Professional Communication Consultants **(161)**
APCI Ass'n of Professional Color Imagers **(161)**
APCO Internat'l Ass'n of Public-Safety Communications Officials-Internat'l **(162)**
APCP Ass'n of Paid Circulation Publications **(159)**
APCS Accredited Pet Cemetery Soc. **(10)**
American Podiatric Circulatory Soc. **(93)**
APCU Ass'n of Presbyterian Colleges and Universities **(160)**
APCUG Ass'n of Personal Computer User Groups **(160)**
APD Ass'n of Professional Directors of YMCAs in the United States **(161)**
APDA Appliance Parts Distributors Ass'n **(126)**
APDF Ass'n of Professional Design Firms **(161)**
APDIM Ass'n of Program Directors in Internal Medicine **(162)**
APDR Ass'n of Program Directors in Radiology **(162)**
APDS Ass'n of Program Directors in Surgery **(162)**
APDU Ass'n of Public Data Users **(162)**
APEC Automated Procedures for Engineering Consultants **(173)**
APEM Ass'n of Professional Energy Managers **(161)**
APF American Pathology Foundation **(90)**
APFA American Pipe Fittings Ass'n **(92)**
APFHA American Paso Fino Horse Ass'n **(90)**
APFO Ass'n on Programs for Female Offenders **(170)**
APFPL Ass'n of Partners for Public Lands **(159)**
APG American Pewter Guild **(91)**
APGA American Public Gas Ass'n **(95)**
APGO Ass'n of Professors of Gynecology and Obstetrics **(161)**
APHA American Paint Horse Ass'n **(90)**
American Pharmaceutical Ass'n **(91)**
American Printing History Ass'n **(94)**
American Public Health Ass'n **(95)**
APhA-APPM Academy of Pharmacy Practice and Management **(9)**
APhA-ASP Academy of Students of Pharmacy **(10)**
ApHC Appaloosa Horse Club **(126)**
APHL Ass'n of Public Health Laboratories **(162)**
APHSA American Public Human Services Ass'n **(96)**
API Accountants for the Public Interest **(10)**
American Petroleum Institute **(91)**
American Prepaid Legal Services Institute **(93)**
APIC Ass'n for Professionals in Infection Control and Epidemiology **(136)**
APICS APICS - The Educational Society for Resource Management **(125)**
APJE Ass'n of Philosophy Journal Editors **(160)**
APLD Ass'n of Professional Landscape Designers **(161)**
APLIC Ass'n for Population/Family Planning Libraries and Information Centers, Internat'l **(136)**
APLS Ass'n for Politics and the Life Sciences **(136)**
APM Academy of Psychosomatic Medicine **(10)**
Ass'n for Psychoanalytic Medicine **(137)**
Ass'n of Professors of Medicine **(162)**
Ass'n of Professors of Mission **(162)**
APMA American Paper Machinery Ass'n **(90)**
American Podiatric Medical Ass'n **(93)**
American Preventive Medical Ass'n **(93)**
APMA Worldwide Ass'n of Promotion Marketing Agencies Worldwide **(162)**
APME Associated Press Managing Editors **(172)**
APMHC Ass'n of Professional Material Handling Consultants **(161)**
APMI-I APMI Internat'l **(125)**
APMP Ass'n of Proposal Management Professionals **(162)**
APMSA American Podiatric Medical Students' Ass'n **(93)**
APMWA American Podiatric Medical Writers Ass'n **(93)**
APNA American Psychiatric Nurses Ass'n **(94)**
APOBA Associated Pipe Organ Builders of America **(172)**
APON Ass'n of Pediatric Oncology Nurses **(159)**
APOSW Ass'n of Pediatric Oncology Social Workers **(160)**
APPA American Probation and Parole Ass'n **(94)**
American Psychological Practitioners Ass'n **(95)**
American Psychopathological Ass'n **(95)**
American Public Power Ass'n **(96)**
APPA: The Ass'n of Higher Education Facilities Officers **(126)**
Ass'n of Higher Education Facilities Officers **(153)**
APPAM Ass'n for Public Policy Analysis and Management **(137)**
APPD Ass'n of Pediatric Program Directors **(160)**
APPE Ass'n for Practical and Professional Ethics **(136)**
APPIC Ass'n of Psychology Postdoctoral and Internship Centers **(162)**
APPM American Peanut Product Manufacturers **(90)**
Ass'n of Publication Production Managers **(162)**
APPMA American Pet Products Manufacturers Ass'n **(91)**
APPWP Ass'n of Private Pension and Welfare Plans **(160)**
APR Ass'n of Petroleum Re-refiners **(160)**
APRA Ass'n of Professional Researchers for Advancement **(161)**
Automotive Parts Rebuilders Ass'n **(175)**
APRC Automotive Public Relations Council **(175)**
APRES American Peanut Research and Education Soc. **(90)**
APRO Ass'n of Progressive Rental Organizations **(162)**
APRS Academy of Pharmaceutical Research and Science **(9)**
American Park and Recreation Soc. **(90)**
APS Academy of Political Science **(9)**
American Pain Soc. **(90)**
American Paraplegia Soc. **(90)**
American Pediatric Soc. **(91)**
American Philosophical Soc. **(91)**
American Physical Soc. **(92)**
American Physiological Soc. **(92)**
American Phytopathological Soc. **(92)**
American Pomological Soc. **(93)**
American Prosthodontic Soc. **(94)**
American Psychological Soc. **(95)**
American Psychosomatic Soc. **(95)**
American Purchasing Soc. **(96)**
Ass'n of Productivity Specialists **(160)**
APSA American Peanut Shellers Ass'n **(91)**
American Pediatric Surgical Ass'n **(91)**
American Political Science Ass'n **(93)**
American Polypay Sheep Ass'n **(93)**
Ass'n of Plastic Surgery Assistants **(160)**
APsaA American Psychoanalytic Ass'n **(94)**
APSAC American Professional Soc. on the Abuse of Children **(94)**
APSIA Ass'n of Professional Schools of Internat'l Affairs **(161)**
APSS Associated Professional Sleep Socs. **(172)**
APSWU American Philatelic Soc. Writers Unit **(91)**
APT Ass'n for Play Therapy **(136)**
Ass'n for Psychological Type **(137)**
Ass'n of Polysomnographic Technologists **(160)**
Ass'n of Practical Theology **(160)**
APT Int'l Ass'n for Preservation Technology Internat'l **(136)**
APTA American Physical Therapy Ass'n **(92)**
American Polarity Therapy Ass'n **(93)**
American Public Transit Ass'n **(96)**
APTC Ass'n of Publicly Traded Companies **(162)**
APTP Ass'n of Part-Time Professionals **(159)**
APTS Ass'n of America's Public Television Stations **(142)**
APU Ass'n for Philosophy of the Unconscious **(136)**
APUSA American Poultry U.S.A. **(93)**
APWA American Public Works Ass'n **(96)**
APWU American Postal Workers Union **(93)**
AQHA American Quarter Horse Ass'n **(96)**
AQP Ass'n for Quality and Participation **(137)**
ARA Academy of Rehabilitative Audiology **(10)**
Agricultural Retailers Ass'n **(14)**
American Recovery Ass'n **(97)**
American Rental Ass'n **(98)**
American Retreaders' Ass'n **(98)**
Automotive Recyclers Ass'n **(175)**
Awards and Recognition Ass'n **(176)**
ARAC Accredited Review Appraisers Council **(11)**
Ass'n of Rain Apparel Contractors **(163)**
ARAF Polaris Internat'l **(459)**
ARBA American Rabbit Breeders Ass'n **(96)**
American Red Brangus Ass'n **(97)**
American Romney Breeders Ass'n **(98)**
ARC American Recreation Coalition **(97)**
Ass'n of Railway Communicators **(163)**
ARCA American Rehabilitation Counseling Ass'n **(97)**
ARCC American Restaurant China Council **(98)**
ARCI American Railway Car Institute **(97)**
Ass'n of Racing Commissioners Internat'l **(162)**
ARDA American Railway Development Ass'n **(97)**
American Resort Development Ass'n **(98)**
ARDI American Rolling Door Institute **(98)**
ARDM Ass'n of Refrigerant Desuperheater Manufacturers **(163)**
ARDMS American Registry of Diagnostic Medical Sonographers **(97)**
ARELLO Ass'n of Real Estate License Law Officials **(163)**
AREMA American Railway Engineering and Maintenance of Way Ass'n **(97)**
ARENA Applied Research Ethics Nat'l Ass'n **(126)**
ARES American Real Estate Soc. **(97)**
AREUEA American Real Estate and Urban Economics Ass'n **(97)**
AREW Ass'n of Real Estate Women **(163)**
ARF Advertising Research Foundation **(12)**
ARHP Ass'n of Reproductive Health Professionals **(163)**
Ass'n of Rheumatology Health Professionals **(164)**
ARI Agricultural Research Institute **(14)**
Air-Conditioning and Refrigeration Institute **(16)**
ARIA American Risk and Insurance Ass'n **(98)**
ARJD Ass'n of Reporters of Judicial Decisions **(163)**
ARL Ass'n of Research Libraries **(163)**
ARLIS/NA Art Libraries Soc./North America **(127)**
ARM Ass'n of Railway Museums **(163)**
Ass'n of Rotational Molders **(164)**
ARMA American Registry of Medical Assistants **(97)**
American Rock Mechanics Ass'n **(98)**
Asphalt Roofing Manufacturers Ass'n **(129)**
ARMA Int'l Ass'n of Records Managers and Administrators **(163)**
ARMI Associated Risk Managers Internat'l **(172)**
ARMS Ass'n of Retail Marketing Services **(163)**
ARN Ass'n of Rehabilitation Nurses **(163)**
ARNA American Radiological Nurses Ass'n **(96)**
ARNMD Ass'n for Research in Nervous and Mental Disease **(137)**
ARO Ass'n for Research in Otolaryngology **(137)**
ARPCT Ass'n of Rehabilitation Programs in Computer Technology **(163)**
ARPI Automotive Refrigeration Products Institute **(175)**
ARR Academy of Radiology Research **(10)**
ARRA Asphalt Recycling and Reclaiming Ass'n **(129)**
ARRL American Radio Relay League **(96)**
ARRO Archery Range and Retailers Organization **(127)**
Ass'n of Residents in Radiation Oncology **(163)**
ARRS American Roentgen Ray Soc. **(98)**
ARS American Radium Soc. **(97)**
American Rhinologic Soc. **(98)**
ARSA Aeronautical Repair Station Ass'n **(13)**
ARSBA American Rambouillet Sheep Breeders Ass'n **(97)**
ARSC Ass'n for Recorded Sound Collections **(137)**
ARTA American Reusable Textile Ass'n **(98)**
Ass'n of Retail Travel Agents **(163)**
ARTBA American Road and Transportation Builders Ass'n **(98)**
ARTS Ass'n for Retail Technology Standards **(137)**
ARVC Nat'l Ass'n of RV Parks and Campgrounds **(370)**
ARVO Ass'n for Research in Vision and Ophthalmology **(137)**
ARW Air-Conditioning and Refrigeration Wholesalers Ass'n Internat'l **(16)**
AS Adhesion Soc. **(11)**
AS/RS Automated Storage/Retrieval Systems **(173)**
ASA Acoustical Soc. of America **(11)**
African Studies Ass'n **(14)**
Airline Suppliers Ass'n **(16)**
American Salers Ass'n **(98)**
American Schools Ass'n **(99)**
American Shipbuilding Ass'n **(100)**
American Shorthorn Ass'n **(100)**

National Trade and Professional Associations of the U.S. © 1999, Columbia Books, Inc. 785

American Simmental Ass'n (100)
American Skin Ass'n (100)
American Soc. for Aesthetics (101)
American Soc. of Agronomy (106)
American Soc. of Anesthesiologists (106)
American Soc. of Appraisers (106)
American Soc. of Artists (107)
American Soc. on Aging (117)
American Sociological Ass'n (117)
American Soybean Ass'n (117)
American Sportscasters Ass'n (118)
American Statistical Ass'n (118)
American Studies Ass'n (118)
American Subcontractors Ass'n (118)
American Sugar Alliance (119)
American Supply Ass'n (119)
American Surety Ass'n (119)
American Surgical Ass'n (119)
Automotive Service Ass'n (175)
ASAA American Sleep Apnea Ass'n (100)
American Soc. of Agricultural Appraisers (106)
ASAAD American Soc. for the Advancement of Anesthesia in Dentistry (105)
ASAC American Soc. of Agricultural Consultants (106)
ASACTI American-Southern Africa Chamber of Trade and Industry (124)
ASAE American Soc. of Agricultural Engineers (106)
American Soc. of Ass'n Executives (107)
ASAHP Ass'n of Schools of Allied Health Professions (164)
ASAIO American Soc. for Artificial Internal Organs (101)
ASALH Ass'n for the Study of Afro-American Life and History (139)
ASAM American Soc. of Addiction Medicine (106)
American Soc. of Asset Managers (107)
Ass'n of Sales Administration Managers (164)
ASAO Ass'n for Social Anthropology in Oceania (137)
ASAP American Soc. for Adolescent Psychiatry (100)
American Soc. for Automation in Pharmacy (101)
American Soc. of Access Professionals (106)
ASAPS American Soc. for Aesthetic Plastic Surgery (100)
ASARB Ass'n of Statisticians of American Religious Bodies (166)
ASAS American Soc. of Abdominal Surgeons (106)
American Soc. of Animal Science (106)
ASASP Ass'n of Supervisory and Administrative School Personnel (166)
ASBA American Southdown Breeders Ass'n (117)
Ass'n of Ship Brokers and Agents (U.S.A.) (165)
ASBC American Soc. of Brewing Chemists (107)
ASBCS Ass'n of Southern Baptist Colleges and Schools (165)
ASBD American Soc. of Breast Disease (107)
ASBDA American School Band Directors' Ass'n (99)
ASBDC Ass'n of Small Business Development Centers (165)
ASBE American Soc. of Baking (107)
ASBH American Soc. for Bioethics and Humanities (101)
ASBMB American Soc. for Biochemistry and Molecular Biology (101)
ASBMR American Soc. for Bone and Mineral Research (101)
ASBO Ass'n of School Business Officials Internat'l (164)
ASBP American Soc. of Bariatric Physicians (107)
ASBPE American Soc. of Business Press Editors (107)
ASC Adhesive and Sealant Council (12)
American Soc. of Cinematographers (107)
American Soc. of Criminology (109)
American Soc. of Cytopathology (109)
Ass'n of Systematics Collections (167)
Associated Schools of Construction (172)
Associated Specialty Contractors (172)
ASCA American School Counselor Ass'n (99)
American Soc. of Consulting Arborists (108)
American Subacute Care Ass'n (118)
American Swimming Coaches Ass'n (119)
Architectural Spray Coaters Ass'n (127)
Ass'n of State Correctional Administrators (166)
ASCAP American Soc. of Composers, Authors and Publishers (108)
ASCB American Soc. for Cell Biology (101)
ASCC American Soc. of Concrete Contractors (108)
ASCCP American Soc. for Colposcopy and Cervical Pathology (101)
ASCD Ass'n for Supervision and Curriculum Development (138)
ASCDI Ass'n of Service and Computer Dealers Internat'l (164)
ASCE American Soc. of Civil Engineers (108)
ASCEP American Soc. for Clinical Evoked Potentials (101)
ASCET American Soc. of Certified Engineering Technicians (107)
ASCFG Ass'n of Specialty Cut Flower Growers (165)
ASCH American Soc. of Church History (107)
American Soc. of Clinical Hypnosis (108)
ASCI American Soc. for Clinical Investigation (101)
ASCL American Soc. of Comparative Law (108)
American Sugar Cane League of the U.S.A. (119)
ASCLA Ass'n of Specialized and Cooperative Library Agencies (165)
ASCLS American Soc. for Clinical Laboratory Science (101)
ASCN American Soc. for Clinical Nutrition (101)
ASCO American Soc. of Clinical Oncology (108)
American Soc. of Contemporary Ophthalmology (109)
Ass'n of Schools and Colleges of Optometry (164)
ASCP American Soc. of Clinical Pathologists (108)
American Soc. of Clinical Psychopharmacology (108)
American Soc. of Consultant Pharmacists (108)
American Soc. of Consulting Planners (108)
ASCPT American Soc. for Clinical Pharmacology and Therapeutics (101)
ASCRI Ass'n of Specialists in Cleaning and Restoration Internat'l (165)
ASCRS American Soc. of Cataract and Refractive Surgery (107)
American Soc. of Colon and Rectal Surgeons (108)
ASCS American Soc. of Corporate Secretaries (109)
ASCT American Soc. for Cytotechnology (102)
ASD American Soc. of Dermatology (109)
Ass'n for the Study of Dreams (139)
Ass'n of Steel Distributors (166)
Associated Surplus Dealers (172)
ASDA American Sleep Disorders Ass'n (100)
American Soc. for Dental Aesthetics (102)
American Stamp Dealers' Ass'n (118)
American Student Dental Ass'n (118)
ASDAL Ass'n of Seventh-Day Adventist Librarians (165)
ASDC American Soc. of Dentistry for Children (109)
ASDP American Soc. of Dermatopathology (109)
ASDR American Soc. of Dermatological Retailers (109)
ASDS American Soc. for Dermatologic Surgery (102)
ASDSO Ass'n of State Dam Safety Officials (166)
ASDVS American Soc. of Directors of Volunteer Services of the AHA (109)
ASDWA Ass'n of State Drinking Water Administrators (166)
ASE American Soc. for Ethnohistory (102)
American Soc. of Echocardiography (109)
American Stock Exchange (118)
Ass'n for Social Economics (137)
Ass'n for Surgical Education (138)
ASEA Augustinian Secondary Educational Ass'n (173)
ASECS American Soc. for Eighteenth-Century Studies (102)
ASEE American Soc. for Engineering Education (102)
ASEH American Soc. for Environmental History (102)
ASEM American Soc. for Engineering Management (102)
ASEP American Soc. of Electroplated Plastics (109)
ASERVIC Ass'n for Spiritual, Ethical and Religious Values in Counseling (137)
ASES American Shoulder and Elbow Surgeons (100)
American Solar Energy Soc. (117)
ASET Academy of Security Educators and Trainers (10)
American Soc. of Electroneurodiagnostic Technologists (109)
ASEV American Soc. for Enology and Viticulture (102)
ASFA American Soc. for Apheresis (101)
American Sport Fishing Ass'n (118)
ASFD American Soc. of Furniture Designers (110)
ASFE ASFE: Professional Firms Practicing in the Geosciences (128)
ASFMRA American Soc. of Farm Managers and Rural Appraisers (109)
ASFO American Soc. of Forensic Odontology (110)
ASFP Ass'n of Smoked Fish Processors (165)
ASFPM Ass'n of State Floodplain Managers (166)
ASFS Ass'n for the Study of Food and Society (139)
ASFSA American School Food Service Ass'n (99)
ASG American Soc. of Geolinguistics (110)
ASGA American Sugarbeet Growers Ass'n (119)
ASGCA American Soc. of Golf Course Architects (110)
ASGD American Soc. for Geriatric Dentistry (102)
ASGE American Soc. for Gastrointestinal Endoscopy (102)
American Soc. of Gas Engineers (110)
ASGPP American Soc. of Group Psychotherapy and Psychodrama (110)
ASGS American Scientific Glassblowers Soc. (99)
American Soc. of General Surgeons (110)
ASGW Ass'n for Specialists in Group Work (137)
ASH Academy of Scientific Hypnotherapy (10)
American Soc. of Hematology (110)
American Soc. of Hypertension (111)
ASHA American Saddlebred Horse Ass'n (98)
American School Health Ass'n (99)
American Seniors Housing Ass'n (99)
American Shire Horse Ass'n (100)
American Speech-Language-Hearing Ass'n (117)
American Suffolk Horse Ass'n (118)
ASHCSP American Soc. for Healthcare Central Service Personnel (102)
ASHE American Soc. for Healthcare Engineering (103)
American Soc. of Highway Engineers (110)
Ass'n for the Study of Higher Education (139)
ASHES American Soc. for Healthcare Environmental Services (103)
ASHFSA American Soc. for Healthcare Food Service Administrators (103)
ASHG American Soc. of Human Genetics (111)
ASHHRA American Soc. for Healthcare Human Resources Administration (103)
ASHI American Soc. for Histocompatability and Immunogenetics (103)
American Soc. of Home Inspectors (111)
ASHNR American Soc. of Head and Neck Radiology (110)
ASHP American Soc. of Health-System Pharmacists (110)
ASHRA American Spa and Health Resort Ass'n (117)
ASHRAE American Soc. of Heating, Refrigerating and Air-Conditioning Engineers (110)
ASHRM American Soc. for Healthcare Risk Management (103)
ASHS American Soc. for Horticultural Science (103)
ASHT American Soc. of Hand Therapists (110)
ASI Allied Stone Industries (18)
American Sheep Industry Ass'n (99)
American Sightseeing Internat'l (100)
American Soc. of Indexers (111)
Aviation Safety Institute (176)
ASIA American Spinal Injury Ass'n (118)
Automotive Service Industry Ass'n (175)
ASIC American Soc. of Irrigation Consultants (111)
ASID American Soc. of Interior Designers (111)
ASIDIC Ass'n of Information and Dissemination Centers (154)
ASIE American Soc. of Internat'l Executives (111)
ASIFA Internat'l Animated Film Soc. (273)
ASIH American Soc. of Ichthyologists and Herpetologists (111)
ASIL American Soc. of Internat'l Law (111)
ASIM American Soc. of Industrial Medicine (111)
ASIMP Ass'n of SIDS and Infant Mortality Programs (165)
ASIP American Soc. for Investigative Pathology (103)
ASIS American Soc. for Industrial Security (103)
American Soc. for Information Science (103)
ASIWPCA Ass'n of State and Interstate Water Pollution Control Administrators (165)
ASJA American Soc. of Journalists and Authors (111)
ASJMC Ass'n of Schools of Journalism and Mass Communication (164)
ASKT American Soc. of Knitting Technologists (111)
ASL Ass'n for Symbolic Logic (138)
ASLA American Seminar Leaders Ass'n (99)
American Soc. of Landscape Architects (111)
ASLAP American Soc. of Laboratory Animal Practitioners (111)
ASLET American Soc. of Law Enforcement Trainers (112)
ASLH American Soc. for Legal History (103)
ASLME American Soc. of Law, Medicine and Ethics (112)
ASLMS American Soc. for Laser Medicine and Surgery (103)
ASLO American Soc. of Limnology and Oceanography (112)
ASLRA American Short Line and Regional Railroad Ass'n (100)
ASLSS American Soc. of Lipo-Suction Surgery (112)
ASM American Soc. for Microbiology (104)
American Soc. of Mammalogists (112)
American Soc. of Missiology (112)
ASMA Aerospace Medical Ass'n (13)
American Soc. of Marine Artists (112)
American Sports Medicine Ass'n/Board of Certification (118)
ASMAC American Soc. of Music Arrangers and Composers (113)
ASMC American Soc. of Military Comptrollers (112)
American Soc. of Music Copyists (113)
Ass'n of Sales and Marketing Companies (164)
ASMD Ass'n of Science Museum Directors (164)
ASMDT American Soc. of Master Dental Technologists (112)
ASME American Soc. of Magazine Editors (112)
American Soc. of Mechanical Engineers (112)
ASMEIGTI Internat'l Gas Turbine Institute, ASME (292)
ASMMA American Supply and Machinery Manufacturers' Ass'n (119)
ASMP American Soc. of Media Photographers (112)
ASMS American Soc. for Mass Spectrometry (104)
American Soc. of Maxillofacial Surgeons (112)
ASN American Soc. for Neurochemistry (104)
American Soc. of Nephrology (113)
American Soc. of Neuroimaging (113)
American Soc. of Notaries (113)
ASNC American Soc. of Nuclear Cardiology (113)
ASNE American Soc. of Naval Engineers (113)
American Soc. of Newspaper Editors (113)
ASNR American Soc. of Neuroradiology (113)
ASNS American Soc. for Nutritional Sciences (104)
ASNT American Soc. for Nondestructive Testing (104)
ASO American Soc. of Ocularists (113)
ASOA American Soc. of Ophthalmic Administrators (113)
ASOL American Symphony Orchestra League (119)
ASOPA American Soc. of Orthopaedic Physician's Assistants (113)
ASOPRS American Soc. of Ophthalmic Plastic and Reconstructive Surgery (113)
ASOR American Schools of Oriental Research (99)
ASORN American Soc. of Ophthalmic Registered Nurses (113)
ASOSS American Soc. of Sephardic Studies (116)
ASP American Soc. for Photobiology (104)
American Soc. for Plasticulture (104)
American Soc. of Papyrologists (114)
American Soc. of Parasitologists (114)
American Soc. of Pharmacognosy (114)
American Soc. of Photographers (114)
American Soc. of Primatologists (115)
Ass'n of Surfing Professionals (166)
ASPA American Salvage Pool Ass'n (99)
American Shrimp Processors Ass'n (100)
American Soc. for Public Administration (105)
American Soc. of Pension Actuaries (114)
American Soc. of Professional Appraisers (115)
Ass'n of Specialized and Professional Accreditors (165)
At-sea Processors Ass'n (172)
ASPAN American Soc. of Peri-Anesthesia Nurses (114)
ASPC/AMHR American Shetland Pony Club/American Miniature Horse Registry (100)
ASPD American Soc. of Podiatric Dermatology (115)
ASPE American Soc. for Precision Engineering (104)
American Soc. of Plumbing Engineers (115)
American Soc. of Podiatry Executives (115)
American Soc. of Professional Estimators (115)

786 National Trade and Professional Associations of the U.S. © 1999, Columbia Books, Inc.

CerMA Ceramic Manufacturers Ass'n (189)
CES Consumer Electronics Soc. (207)
Council for European Studies (211)
CESI Council for Elementary Science Internat'l (211)
CESSE Council of Engineering and Scientific Soc. Executives (213)
CETA Cleaning Equipment Trade Ass'n (194)
Controlled Environment Testing Ass'n (208)
CETGI CISA Export Trade Group, Inc. (194)
CEW Cosmetic Executive Women (210)
CFA Catfish Farmers of America (188)
Chilled Foods Ass'n (192)
Commercial Finance Ass'n (199)
Composites Fabricators Ass'n (201)
Concrete Foundations Ass'n (203)
Consumer Federation of America (207)
CFAP Council on Fine Art Photography (216)
CFAS Catholic Fine Arts Soc. (188)
CFCA Communications Fraud Control Ass'n (200)
CFDA Council of Fashion Designers of America (213)
CFEA College Fraternity Editors Ass'n (197)
CFESA Commercial Food Equipment Service Ass'n (199)
CFF Cystic Fibrosis Foundation (219)
CFFA Chemical Fabrics and Film Ass'n (191)
CFH Conference on Faith and History (205)
Soc. for Hematopathology (488)
CFMA Construction Financial Management Ass'n (206)
CFPAE Council of Food Processors Ass'n Executives (213)
CFR Casual Furniture Retailers (187)
CFS Council of Fleet Specialists (213)
CFSA Casket and Funeral Supply Ass'n of America (187)
CFSBI Cold Finished Steel Bar Institute (196)
CFSEB Internat'l Conference of Funeral Service Examining Boards (287)
CG Choristers Guild (193)
Conductors Guild (203)
CGA Compressed Gas Ass'n (202)
Concord Grape Ass'n (203)
CGC Council of Growing Companies (214)
Council on Geriatric Cardiology (217)
CGCS Council of the Great City Schools (216)
CGP Coalition for Government Procurement (196)
CGS Council of Graduate Schools (213)
CGSM Consortium for Graduate Study and Management (206)
CHA CHA - Certified Horsemanship Ass'n (190)
CHA-US Catholic Health Ass'n of the United States (188)
CHART Council of Hotel and Restaurant Trainers (214)
CHEA Council for Higher Education Accreditation (211)
ChLA Children's Literature Ass'n (192)
CHRIE Council on Hotel, Restaurant and Institutional Education (217)
CI Catfish Institute (188)
Chlorine Institute (193)
Combustion Institute (198)
Composites Institute (202)
Cordage Institute (209)
Cranberry Institute (218)
CIA Correctional Industries Ass'n (210)
CIAA Cheese Importers Ass'n of America (190)
CIAB Council of Insurance Agents and Brokers (214)
CIBO Council of Industrial Boiler Owners (214)
CIC Council of Independent Colleges (214)
CICA Captive Insurance Companies Ass'n (186)
CICE Council of Insurance Company Executives (214)
CICPAC Construction Industry CPA/Consultants Ass'n (206)
CIES CIES, The Food Business Forum (193)
Comparative and Internat'l Education Soc. (201)
CIFA Council of Infrastructure Financing Authorities (214)
CII Containerization and Intermodal Institute (207)
Council of Institutional Investors (214)
Council of Internat'l Investigators (214)
CIIT Chemical Industry Institute of Toxicology (191)
CIM CIM --The Business Owners Forum (194)
CIMA Cellulose Insulation Manufacturers Ass'n (189)
Construction Industry Manufacturers Ass'n (206)
CIMPA Connected Int'l Meeting Professionals Ass'n (206)
CIMS Coalition for Intelligent Manufacturing Systems (196)
CIMTA Cottage Industry Miniaturists Trade Ass'n (210)
CIRB Crop Insurance Research Bureau (219)
CIREI Commercial-Investment Real Estate Institute (199)
CIS Clinical Immunology Soc. (194)
Construction Industry Sales (206)
CISA Casting Industry Suppliers Ass'n (187)
CISCA Ceilings and Interior Systems Construction Ass'n (189)
CISPI Cast Iron Soil Pipe Institute (187)
CITBA Customs and Internat'l Trade Bar Ass'n (219)
CIU Congress of Independent Unions (205)
CIX Commercial Internet Exchange Ass'n (199)
CJE Council for Jewish Education (211)
CJF Council of Jewish Federations (214)
CJJ Coalition for Juvenile Justice (196)
CJSA Costume Jewelry Salesmen's Ass'n (210)
CJSS Conference on Jewish Social Studies (205)
CKRC Cement Kiln Recycling Coalition (189)
CKS Cell Kinetics Soc. (189)
CLA Catholic Library Ass'n (188)
Coin Laundry Ass'n (196)
College Language Ass'n (197)
Computer Law Ass'n (202)
CLA-USA Christian Labor Ass'n of the United States of America (193)
CLAO Contact Lens Ass'n of Ophthalmologists (207)
CLARB Council of Landscape Architectural Registration Boards (214)
CLAS Clinical Ligand Assay Soc. (195)
Congress of Lung Ass'n Staff (205)
CLC Convention Liaison Council (208)
CLD Council for Learning Disabilities (211)
CLEAR Council on Licensure, Enforcement and Regulation (217)
CLFMI Chain Link Fence Manufacturers Institute (190)
CLGH Committee on Lesbian and Gay History (200)
CLI Contact Lens Institute (207)
CLIA Cruise Lines Internat'l Ass'n (219)
CLLA Commercial Law League of America (199)
CLM Council of Logistics Management (215)
CLMA Clinical Laboratory Management Ass'n (194)
Contact Lens Manufacturers Ass'n (207)
CLMP Council of Literary Magazines and Presses (214)
CLPHA Council of Large Public Housing Authorities (214)
CLRA Information Technology Resellers Ass'n (264)
CLS Christian Legal Soc. (193)
CLSA Canon Law Soc. of America (186)
Contact Lens Soc. of America (207)
CLTA Chinese Language Teachers Ass'n (192)
CLUW Coalition of Labor Union Women (196)
CMA Calendar Marketing Ass'n (185)
Center for Management Advisors (189)
Chamber Music America (190)
Chemical Manufacturers Ass'n (191)
Childrenswear Marketing Ass'n (192)
Chocolate Manufacturers Ass'n of the U.S.A. (193)
Christian Management Ass'n (193)
Closure Manufacturers Ass'n (195)
College Media Advisers (197)
Communications Managers Ass'n (200)
Communications Marketing Ass'n (200)
Cookware Manufacturers Ass'n (208)
Council for Museum Anthropology (211)
Country Music Ass'n (217)
CMA-USA Clothing Manufacturers Ass'n of the U.S.A. (195)
CMA/SME Composites Manufacturing Ass'n of SME (202)
CMAA Club Managers Ass'n of America (195)
Cocoa Merchants' Ass'n of America (196)
Comics Magazine Ass'n of America (198)
Construction Management Ass'n of America (206)
Crane Manufacturers Ass'n of America (218)
CMBA Classical Music Broadcasters Ass'n (194)
CMCA Concrete Modifications Contractors Ass'n (203)
CMDS Christian Medical and Dental Soc. (193)
CMG Color Marketing Group (198)
Computer Measurement Group (202)
Cost Management Group (210)
CMI Can Manufacturers Institute (186)
Cherry Marketing Institute (191)
Cleaning Management Institute (194)
CMIS Computerized Medical Imaging Soc. (203)
CMMA Clock Manufacturers and Marketing Ass'n (195)
Communications Media Management Ass'n (200)
CMOR Council for Marketing and Opinion Research (211)
CMPA Church Music Publishers Ass'n (193)
CMPAA Certified Milk Producers Ass'n of America (190)
CMRA Chemical Management and Resources Ass'n (191)
CMRC Construction Marketing Research Council (207)
CMS Clay Minerals Soc. (194)
College Music Soc. (197)
CMSA Case Management Soc. of America (187)
CMSM Conference of Major Superiors of Men, U.S.A. (204)
CMSS Council of Medical Specialty Socs. (215)
CNBC Congress of Nat'l Black Churches (205)
CNIRS Council for Near-Infrared Spectroscopy (212)
CNNT Council of Nephrology Nurses and Technicians (215)
CNS Child Neurology Soc. (192)
Congress of Neurological Surgeons (205)
CNSW Council of Nephrology Social Workers (215)
COA Commissioned Officers Ass'n of the United States Public Health Service (200)
Council of the Americas (216)
COAA Construction Owners Ass'n of America (207)
COAI Clowns of America, Internat'l (195)
CODA Council of Dance Administrators (213)
CODSIA Council of Defense and Space Industry Ass'ns (213)
COE Council on Occupational Education (217)
COF Council on Foundations (216)
COFE Council on Forest Engineering (216)
COGEL Council on Governmental Ethics Law (217)
COGS Computer Oriented Geological Soc. (202)
COHE College of Osteopathic Healthcare Executives (198)
COHEAO Coalition of Higher Education Assistance Organizations (196)
COIA Conservative Orthopedics Internat'l Ass'n (206)
COLA COLA (196)
COLT Council on Library-Media Technicians (217)
COMISS Congress on Ministry in Specialized Settings (205)
COMPA Conference of Minority Public Administrators (204)
COMPTEL Competitive Telecommunications Ass'n (201)
CompTIA Computing Technology Industry Ass'n (203)
COMSOC IEEE Communications Soc. (258)
COMSS Council of Musculoskeletal Specialty Socs. (215)
COMTO Conference of Minority Transportation Officials (204)
COPAFS Council of Professional Ass'ns on Federal Statistics (215)
COPAS Council of Petroleum Accountants Socs. (215)
COPE American Soc. of Podiatric Executives (115)
Council of Protocol Executives (215)
COPS Conference of Philosophical Societies (204)
CORD Congress on Research in Dance (205)
CORFAC Int'l Corporate Facility Advisors (209)
CORPA Commission on Recognition of Postsecondary Accreditation (200)
COS Clinical Orthopaedic Soc. (195)
COSA Carwash Owner's and Supplier's Ass'n (187)
COSCA Conference of State Court Adminstrators (204)
COSCDA Council of State Community Development Agencies (215)
CoSIDA College Sports Information Directors of America (198)
COSLA Chief Officers of State Library Agencies (192)
CoSN Consortium for School Networking (206)
COSSA Consortium of Social Science Ass'ns (206)
COSSMHO Nat'l Coalition of Hispanic Health and Human Services Organizations (387)
COST Committee on State Taxation (200)
COSTHA Conference on the Safe Transportation of Hazardous Articles (205)
COVD College of Optometrists in Vision Development (197)
CPA Catholic Press Ass'n (188)
Chlorobenzene Producers Ass'n (193)
Classroom Publishers Ass'n (194)
Club Pool Ass'n (195)
Composite Panel Ass'n (201)
Computer Press Ass'n (202)
Contract Packagers Ass'n (208)
CPAA Cultured Pearl Ass'n of America (219)
CPAAI CPA Associates Internat'l (218)
CPADN Career Planning and Adult Development Network (187)
CPB Contractors Pump Bureau (208)
CPCU Chartered Property and Casualty Underwriters Soc. (190)
CPDA Chemical Producers and Distributors Ass'n (191)
CPG Collectibles and Platemakers Guild (196)
CPI Credit Professionals Internat'l (218)
CPIA Cathodic Protection Industry Ass'n (188)
Certified Professional Insurance Agents Soc. (190)
Chlorinated Paraffins Industry Ass'n (192)
CPL Council of Planning Librarians (215)
CPMA Color Pigments Manufacturers Ass'n (198)
CPMB Concrete Plant Manufacturers Bureau (203)
CPMTS Components, Packaging, and Manufacturing Technology Soc. (201)
CPOA Chief Petty Officers Ass'n (192)
CPRI Computer-based Patient Record Institute (203)
CPST Commission on Professionals in Science and Technology (200)
CPTP Coalition of Publicly Traded Partnerships (196)
CRA California Redwood Ass'n (185)
Cargo Reinsurance Ass'n (187)
Computing Research Ass'n (203)
Corn Refiners Ass'n (209)
CRB Country Radio Broadcasters (218)
CRC Coordinating Research Council (209)
CRCPD Conference of Radiation Control Program Directors (204)
CRE Counselors of Real Estate (217)
CREnet Conflict Resolution Education Network (205)
CREOG Council on Resident Education in Obstetrics and Gynecology (217)
CRESMSA Commerical Real Estate Secondary Market and Securitization Ass'n (199)
CRF Credit Research Foundation (218)
CRHA Colorado Ranger Horse Ass'n (198)
CRI Carpet and Rug Institute (187)
Customer Relations Institute (219)
CRLA College Reading and Learning Ass'n (198)
CRMA City and Regional Magazine Ass'n (194)
Commercial Refrigerator Manufacturers Ass'n (199)
CRN Council for Responsible Nutrition (212)
Council on Renal Nutrition (217)
CRS Controlled Release Soc. (208)
CRSI Concrete Reinforcing Steel Institute (203)
CRWAD Conference of Research Workers in Animal Diseases (204)
CSA Chamber of Shipping of America (190)
Chemical Sources Ass'n (191)
Contract Services Ass'n of America (208)
Costume Soc. of America (210)
Cryogenic Soc. of America (219)
CSAA Central Station Alarm Ass'n (189)
CSAP Council of State Ass'n Presidents (215)
CSAVR Council of State Administrators of Vocational Rehabilitation (215)
CSBA Columbia Sheep Breeders Ass'n of America (198)
Cookie and Snack Bakers Ass'n (208)
CSBS Conference of State Bank Supervisors (204)
CSC Council on Superconductivity (217)
Internat'l Soc. for the Comparative Studies of Civilizations (304)
CSCAA College Swimming Coaches Ass'n of America (198)
CSCC Council of State Chambers of Commerce (215)
CSDA Concrete Sawing and Drilling Ass'n (203)
CSEE Council for Spiritual and Ethical Education (212)
CSG Council of State Governments (216)

National Trade and Professional Associations of the U.S. © 1999, Columbia Books, Inc. 789

CSGUS Clinical Soc. of Genito-Urinary Surgeons (195)
CSHEMA Campus Safety Division of the Nat'l Safety Council (186)
CSI Cast Stone Institute (187)
Christian Schools Internat'l (193)
Coalition of Service Industries (196)
Computer Security Institute (203)
Construction Specifications Institute (207)
CSLA Church and Synagogue Library Ass'n (193)
CSMA Chemical Specialties Manufacturers Ass'n (191)
CSNA Classification Soc. of North America (194)
CSPN College Savings Plans Network (198)
CSPT Conference for the Study of Political Thought (204)
CSRS Cervical Spine Research Soc. (190)
CSS Cognitive Science Soc. (196)
Control Systems Soc. (208)
CSSA Communications Supply Service Ass'n (200)
Crop Science Soc. of America (219)
CSSB Cedar Shake and Shingle Bureau (188)
CSSP Council of Scientific Soc. Presidents (215)
CSSR Council of Socs. for the Study of Religion (215)
CSTA Coal and Slurry Technology Ass'n (195)
CSTE Council of State and Territorial Epidemiologists (215)
CSUSA Copyright Soc. of the U.S.A. (209)
CSWE Council on Social Work Education (217)
CSWF Clinical Social Work Federation (195)
CTA Commercial Travelers Ass'n (199)
Consolidated Tape Ass'n (206)
Corporate Transfer Agents Ass'n (209)
CTAA Community Transportation Ass'n of America (201)
CTDA Ceramic Tile Distributors Ass'n (189)
Custom Tailors and Designers Ass'n of America (219)
CTFA Cosmetic, Toiletry and Fragrance Ass'n (210)
CTI Cable Tray Institute (185)
Cooling Tower Institute (208)
CTIA Cellular Telecommunications Industry Ass'n (189)
CTIOA Ceramic Tile Institute of America (189)
CTPOA Casino and Theme Party Operators Ass'n (187)
CTR-USA Council for Tobacco Research-U.S.A. (212)
CTS College Theology Soc. (198)
CTSA Catholic Theological Soc. of America (188)
CTTE Council on Technology Teacher Education (217)
CUED Council for Urban Economic Development (212)
CUES Credit Union Executives Soc. (218)
CUNA Credit Union Nat'l Ass'n (218)
CUPA College and University Personnel Ass'n (197)
CUSSN Computer Use in Social Services Network (203)
CUTWA UFCW Textile Council (529)
CVSA Commercial Vehicle Safety Alliance (199)
CWA Comedy Writers and Performers Ass'n (198)
Communications Workers of America (200)
Construction Writers Ass'n (207)
CWAA Cotton Warehouse Ass'n of America (210)
CWLA Child Welfare League of America (192)
CWO Council of Writers Organizations (216)
CWOA Chief Warrant and Warrant Officers Ass'n, United States Coast Guard (192)
CWRT Center for Waste Reduction Technologies (189)
CWSA Commercial Weather Services Ass'n (199)
CWSRA Chester White Swine Record Ass'n (191)
DACC Danish-American Chamber of Commerce (USA) (220)
DACOR Diplomatic and Consular Officers, Retired (223)
DAMA Data Administration Management Ass'n Internat'l (220)
DASMAI Door and Access Systems Manufacturers' Ass'n, Internat'l (224)
DATIA Drug and Alcohol Testing Industry Ass'n (225)
DBE Dibasic Esters Group (222)
DBIA Design-Build Institute of America (222)
DBM Design-Build Manufacturers Ass'n (222)
DCA Dance Critics Ass'n (220)
Devon Cattle Ass'n (222)
Diamond Council of America (222)
Distribution Contractors Ass'n (224)
Dredging Contractors of America (224)
DCAT Drug, Chemical and Allied Trades Ass'n (225)
DCCA Directional Crossing Contractors Ass'n (223)
DCUC Defense Credit Union Council (220)
DDA Dental Dealers of America (221)
Display Distributors Ass'n (223)
DDAP Digital Distribution of Advertising for Publications (222)
DDC Diecasting Development Council (222)
DDNA Developmental Disabilities Nurses Ass'n (222)
DDPA Delta Dental Plans Ass'n (221)
DEA Dance Educators of America (220)
Drilling Engineering Ass'n (224)
DECA Distributive Education Clubs of America (224)
Driver Employer Council of America (224)
DEMA Diving Equipment and Marketing Ass'n (224)
DEPA Diethyl Ether Producers Ass'n (222)
DERA Disaster Preparedness and Emergency Response Ass'n (223)
DETC Distance Education and Training Council (223)
DFCMA Dalton Floor Covering Market Ass'n (220)
DFI Deep Foundations Institute (220)
DFPA Defense Fire Protection Ass'n (220)
DG Dramatists Guild (224)
DGA Directors Guild of America (223)
DGMA Dental Group Management Ass'n (221)
DGTC Distillers Grains Technology Council (223)
DHI Door and Hardware Institute (224)
DIA Drug Information Ass'n (225)
DIPRA Ductile Iron Pipe Research Ass'n (225)
DIS Ductile Iron Soc. (225)
DISA Data Interchange Standards Ass'n (220)
DISCUS Distilled Spirits Council of the U.S. (223)
DLCA Distribution and LTL Carriers Ass'n (224)
DMA Dance Masters of America (220)
Dental Manufacturers of America (221)
Dietary Managers Ass'n (222)
Direct Marketing Ass'n (223)
DMI Dairy Management (219)
Design Management Institute (222)
DMIA Diamond Manufacturers and Importers Ass'n of America (222)
Document Management Industries Ass'n (224)
DNA Dermatology Nurses Ass'n (221)
DO Delta Omicron Foundation, Inc. (221)
DPA Design Professionals Ass'n (222)
DPE Delta Pi Epsilon (221)
DPI Digital Printing and Imaging Ass'n (222)
DRA Dude Ranchers' Ass'n (225)
DRI Defense Research Institute (221)
Disaster Recovery Institute Internat'l (223)
DSA Direct Selling Ass'n (223)
DSAA Driving School Ass'n of America (224)
DSD Delta Sigma Delta (221)
DSI Dairy Soc. Internat'l (220)
Decision Sciences Institute (220)
DSP Delta Sigma Pi (221)
DTAA Diamond Trade and Precious Stone Ass'n of America (222)
DTP Delta Theta Phi (221)
DWAA Dog Writers' Ass'n of America (224)
DWCA Decorative Window Coverings Ass'n (220)
DWF Delta Waterfowl Foundation (221)
DWMI Diamond Wheel Manufacturers Institute (222)
EA Electrocoat Ass'n (228)
EAA Ecuadorean American Ass'n (226)
Environmental Assessment Ass'n (231)
EABC European-American Business Council (233)
EANGUS Enlisted Ass'n of Nat'l Guard of the United States (231)
EAPA Employee Assistance Professionals Ass'n (229)
EASA Electrical Apparatus Service Ass'n (227)
EASNA Employee Assistance Soc. of North America (229)
EBA Environmental Bankers Ass'n (231)
EBAA Eye Bank Ass'n of America (234)
EBRI Employee Benefit Research Institute (229)
ECA Embroidery Council of America (229)
Engineering Contractors' Ass'n (230)
Express Carriers Ass'n (234)
ECFC Employers Council on Flexible Compensation (230)
ECI Evaporative Cooling Institute (233)
ECLA Evangelical Church Library Ass'n (233)
ECMA Engineering College Magazines Associated (230)
ECPA Evangelical Christian Publishers Ass'n (233)
ECRI ECRI (226)
ECS Electrochemical Soc. (228)
ECTF Enterprise Computer Telephony Forum (231)
ECUC Education Credit Union Council (226)
EDAC Electronic Design Automation Consortium (228)
EDPA Exhibit Designers and Producers Ass'n (234)
EDPRESS EdPress--The Ass'n of Educational Publishers (226)
EDRA Environmental Design Research Ass'n (231)
EDS Electronic Distribution Show Corporation (228)
EDSA Xplorer Internat'l (551)
EDSA Int'l Educational Dealers and Suppliers Ass'n Internat'l (226)
EDUCAUSE EDUCAUSE (226)
EEA Electromagnetic Energy Ass'n (228)
EEBA Energy Efficient Building Ass'n (230)
EEGS Environmental and Engineering Geophysical Soc. (231)
EEI Edison Electric Institute (226)
EELA Energy Efficient Lighting Ass'n (230)
EEMDA Electrical-Electronics Materials Distributors Ass'n (227)
EERA Electrical Equipment Representatives Ass'n (227)
EERI Earthquake Engineering Research Institute (225)
EFA Editorial Freelancers Ass'n (226)
EFF Endocrine Fellows Foundation (230)
EFI Energy Frontiers Internat'l (230)
EFTA Electronic Funds Transfer Ass'n (228)
EGMGA Emerald Green Miniature Golf Ass'n (229)
EGSA Electrical Generating Systems Ass'n (227)
EHA Economic History Ass'n (225)
EIA Electronic Industries Ass'n (228)
Elevator Industries Ass'n (229)
Employee Involvement Ass'n (229)
Environmental Industry Ass'ns (231)
Environmental Information Ass'n (231)
EIC Electrical Insulation Conference (227)
EIMA EIFS Industry Members Ass'n (227)
EJMA Expansion Joint Manufacturers Ass'n (234)
ELA Education Law Ass'n (226)
Equipment Leasing Ass'n of America (232)
ELCON Electricity Consumers Resource Council (228)
EM/SME Ass'n for Electronics Manufacturing of SME (133)
EMA Electronic Messaging Ass'n (228)
Employment Management Ass'n (230)
Engine Manufacturers Ass'n (230)
Envelope Manufacturers Ass'n (231)
Environmental Management Ass'n (232)
Environmental Management Ass'n (232)
Expediting Management Ass'n (234)
EMC Equipment Maintenance Council (232)
EMCWA Electrical Manufacturing and Coil Winding Ass'n (227)
EMI Equipment Manufacturers Institute (232)
EMRA Emergency Medicine Residents' Ass'n (229)
EMS Environmental Mutagen Soc. (232)
EMTA Emerging Markets Traders Ass'n (229)
ENA Emergency Nurses Ass'n (229)
ENTELEC Energy Telecommunications and Electrical Ass'n (230)
EOA Ethics Officer Ass'n (233)
EOS/ESD Electrical Overstress/Electrostatic Discharge Ass'n (227)
EOSA Ethylene Oxide Sterilization Ass'n (233)
EPA Educational Paperback Ass'n (226)
Evangelical Press Ass'n (233)
EPC Emulsion Polymers Council (230)
EPIC Evidence Photographers Internat'l Council (233)
EPRI Electric Power Research Institute (227)
EPSA Electric Power Supply Ass'n (227)
EPSMA EPS Molders Ass'n (232)
ERA Electronic Retailing Ass'n (228)
Electronics Representatives Ass'n (229)
ERC Employee Relocation Council (229)
ERF Estuarine Research Federation (233)
ERIC ERISA Industry Committee (232)
ES Econometric Soc. (225)
Electrophoresis Soc. (229)
Endocrine Soc. (230)
ESA Ecological Soc. of America (225)
Engine Service Ass'n (230)
Entomological Soc. of America (231)
Equipment Service Ass'n (232)
Executive Suite Ass'n (233)
Exercise-Safety Ass'n (233)
ESCA Exposition Service Contractors Ass'n (234)
ESCSI Expanded Shale, Clay and Slate Institute (234)
ESMA Engraved Stationery Manufacturers Ass'n (231)
ESOAA Eight Sheet Outdoor Advertising Ass'n (227)
ESP Epsilon Sigma Phi (232)
ESRS Early Sites Research Soc. (225)
ESTA Entertainment Services and Technology Ass'n (231)
ETA Electronic Transactions Ass'n (228)
Electronics Technicians Ass'n Internat'l (229)
Embroidery Trade Ass'n (229)
Energy Traffic Ass'n (230)
Evangelical Training Ass'n (233)
ETC Environmental Technology Council (232)
ETI Equipment and Tool Institute (232)
EUCG Electric Utility Cost Group (227)
EUCG (233)
EVAA Electric Vehicle Ass'n of the Americas (227)
EWA Education Writers Ass'n (226)
Exotic Wildlife Ass'n (234)
EWI Edison Welding Institute (226)
Executive Women Internat'l (233)
FA Foragers of America (242)
FACC Finnish American Chamber of Commerce (239)
French-American Chamber of Commerce (244)
FACSS Federation of Analytical Chemistry and Spectroscopy Societies (236)
FAHS Federation of American Health Systems (236)
FAI Futon Ass'n Internat'l (245)
FALA First Amendment Lawyers Ass'n (240)
FALJC Federal Administrative Law Judges Conference (235)
FAMA Fire Apparatus Manufacturers Ass'n (239)
FAMS Foundation for Advances in Medicine and Science (243)
FAMSA Funeral and Memorial Socs. of America (244)
FARB Federation of Ass'ns of Regulatory Boards (237)
FAS Federation of American Scientists (236)
FASA Fashion Accessories Shippers Ass'n (235)
Federated Ambulatory Surgery Ass'n (236)
FASEB Federation of American Socs. for Experimental Biology (236)
FBA Federal Bar Ass'n (235)
Fibre Box Ass'n (238)
FBF Film and Bag Federation (238)
FBIAA Federal Bureau of Investigation Agents Ass'n (235)
FBLA-PBL Future Business Leaders of America-Phi Beta Lambda (245)
FBPCS Federation of Behavioral, Psychological and Cognitive Sciences (237)
FCA Fibre Channel Ass'n (238)
FCBA Federal Communications Bar Ass'n (235)
FCC Farm Credit Council (234)
FCCA Forestry Conservation Communications Ass'n (243)
FCE Nat'l Ass'n of Family and Community Education (354)
FCI Fluid Controls Institute (241)
Fuel Cell Institute (244)
FCIA Franchise Consultants Internat'l Ass'n (243)
FCICA Floor Covering Installation Contractors Ass'n (240)
FCSEA Family and Consumer Science Education Ass'n (234)
FCSI Foodservice Consultants Soc. Internat'l (242)

790 National Trade and Professional Associations of the U.S. © 1999, Columbia Books, Inc.

FCTCSC Flue-Cured Tobacco Cooperative Stabilization Corporation (240)
FCUSA Fur Commission USA (244)
FDLI Food and Drug Law Institute (241)
FDRA Footwear Distributors and Retailers of America (242)
FDRS Food Distribution Research Soc. (241)
FDTA FSC/DISC Tax Ass'n (244)
FEA Federal Education Ass'n (235)
Fraternity Executives Ass'n (244)
FEBA Federal Energy Bar Ass'n (235)
FECUA Farmers Educational and Co-operative Union of America (235)
FEDA Foodservice Equipment Distributors Ass'n (242)
FEI Financial Executives Institute (238)
FEIA Flight Engineers' Internat'l Ass'n (240)
FEMA Farm Equipment Manufacturers Ass'n (235)
Fire Equipment Manufacturers' Ass'n (239)
Flavor and Extract Manufacturers Ass'n of the United States (240)
Food Equipment Manufacturers Ass'n (241)
FEMSA Fire Equipment Manufacturers Suppliers Ass'n (239)
FEW Federally Employed Women (236)
FEWA Farm Equipment Wholesalers Ass'n (235)
FF Fragrance Foundation (243)
FFA Nat'l FFA Organization (404)
FFC Federal Facilities Council (236)
FFCT Forest Farm and Community Tree Network (242)
FFI Family Firm Institute (234)
FFMA Fraternal Field Managers Ass'n (244)
FFTA Foster Family-Based Treatment Ass'n (243)
FGI Fashion Group Internat'l (235)
FGIPC Federation of Government Information Processing Councils (237)
FHA/HERO Future Homemakers of America (245)
FHCP Forum for Health Care Planning (243)
FHS Forest History Soc. (242)
FIA Footwear Industries of America (242)
Forging Industry Ass'n (243)
Forum for Investor Advice (243)
Futures Industry Ass'n (245)
FIABCI-USA Internat'l Real Estate Federation - American Chapter (301)
FIAE Food Industry Ass'n Executives (241)
FIASI Fixed Income Analysts Soc. (240)
FIBCA Flexible Intermediate Bulk Container Ass'n (240)
FICA Fur Information Council of America (244)
FICC Federation of Insurance and Corporate Counsel (237)
FICNA Freestanding Insert Council of North America (244)
FIHE Foundation for Independent Higher Education (243)
FIIA Financial Institutions Insurance Ass'n (239)
FIJET World Federation of Travel Writers (549)
FIM Foundation for Internat'l Meetings (243)
FISA Food Industry Suppliers Ass'n (241)
FIT Forest Industries Telecommunications (242)
FITA Federation of Internat'l Trade Ass'ns (237)
FJAA Fashion Jewelry Ass'n of America (235)
FLEOA Federal Law Enforcement Officers Ass'n (236)
FLRT Federal Librarians Roundtable (236)
FMA Fabricators and Manufacturers Ass'n, Internat'l (234)
Federal Managers Ass'n (236)
Financial Management Ass'n (239)
Financial Markets Ass'n (239)
Floral Marketing Ass'n (240)
Fragrance Materials Ass'n of the United States (243)
Fulfillment Management Ass'n (244)
FMANA Fire Marshals Ass'n of North America (239)
FMC Filter Manufacturers Council (238)
FMI Food Marketing Institute (241)
FMPS Federation of Modern Painters and Sculptors (237)
FMS Federation of Materials Socs. (237)
Financial Managers Soc. (239)
FMSI Friction Materials Standards Institute (244)
FNHP Federation of Nurses and Health Professionals (237)
FOPW Federation of Organizations for Professional Women (237)
FOSA Federation of Spine Ass'ns (237)
FPA Federal Physicians Ass'n (236)
Flexible Packaging Ass'n (240)
Foreign Press Ass'n (242)
Fusion Power Associates (244)
FPAA Fresh Produce Ass'n of the Americas (244)
FPDA Fluid Power Distributors Ass'n (241)
FPFC Fresh Produce and Floral Council (244)
FPI Foodservice and Packaging Institute (242)
FPM&SA Food Processing Machinery and Supplies Ass'n (242)
FPPI Frozen Potato Products Institute (244)
FPRMR Foundation for Pavement Rehabilitation and Maintenance Research (243)
FPS Fluid Power Soc. (241)
Forest Products Soc. (243)
FPSC Forest Products Safety Conference (242)
FRIA Firearms Research and Indentification Ass'n (240)
FS Fiber Soc. (238)
FSA Alliance for Children and Families (17)
Fabric Salesmen's Ass'n (234)
Financial Stationers Ass'n (239)
Fluid Sealing Ass'n (241)
FSC Financial Services Council (239)
FSCO Federation of Straight Chiropractors and Organizations (238)
FSCT Federation of Socs. for Coatings Technology (237)
FSEA Foil Stamping and Embossing Ass'n (241)

FSF Flight Safety Foundation (240)
FSG Foodservice Group (242)
FSHC Federation of State Humanities Councils (237)
FSMA Field Services Marketing Ass'n (238)
FSMB Federation of State Medical Boards of the U. S. (237)
FSSA Fire Suppression Systems Ass'n (240)
FSTN Financial Services Technology Network (239)
FTA Federation of Tax Administrators (238)
Fitness Trade Ass'n (240)
Flexographic Technical Ass'n (240)
Floatation Tank Ass'n (240)
FTDA FTD Ass'n (244)
FTN Family Therapy Network (234)
FTPI Fiberglass Tank and Pipe Institute (238)
FUMMWA Fellowship of United Methodists in Music and Worship Arts (238)
FWAA Football Writers Ass'n of America (242)
FWC Fourdrinier Wire Council (243)
FWI Financial Women Internat'l (239)
FWQA Federal Water Quality Ass'n (236)
G/SCA Gunite/Shotcrete Contractors Ass'n (250)
GA Gypsum Ass'n (250)
GAA Gift Ass'n of America (247)
Gravure Ass'n of America (249)
GABA German American Business Ass'n (247)
GACC German American Chamber of Commerce (247)
GAGN Graphic Artists Guild Nat'l (249)
GAIN Giftware Associates Interchange (247)
GAL Guild of American Luthiers (250)
GAMA Game Manufacturers Ass'n (245)
Gas Appliance Manufacturers Ass'n (245)
General Aviation Manufacturers Ass'n (246)
Guitar and Accessories Marketing Ass'n (250)
GAMA Internat'l GAMA Internat'l (245)
GAMIS Graphic Arts Marketing Information Service (249)
GANA Glass Ass'n of North America (247)
GAP Graphic Arts Professionals (249)
GAS Glass Art Soc. (247)
GASDA Gasoline and Automotive Service Dealers Ass'n (246)
GASF Graphic Arts Sales Foundation (249)
GATF Graphic Arts Technical Foundation (249)
GBSUA Greater Blouse, Skirt and Undergarment Ass'n (249)
GBW Guild of Book Workers (250)
GCA Garden Centers of America (245)
Graphic Communications Ass'n (249)
Greeting Card Ass'n (250)
GCAA Golf Coaches Ass'n of America (248)
GCBAA Golf Course Builders Ass'n of America (248)
GCCA Greater Clothing Contractors Ass'n (249)
GCIU Graphic Communications Internat'l Union (249)
GCM Nat'l Ass'n of Professional Geriatric Care Managers (366)
GCSAA Golf Course Superintendents Ass'n of America (248)
GEA Geothermal Energy Ass'n (247)
GEAPS Grain Elevator and Processing Soc. (249)
GFA Gasket Fabricators Ass'n (246)
GFOA Government Finance Officers Ass'n of the United States and Canada (248)
GFWC General Federation of Women's Clubs (246)
GFWI Greek Food and Wine Institute (249)
GHBA Galiceno Horse Breeders Ass'n (245)
GHC Global Health Council (248)
GI Gelbray Internat'l (246)
Gold Institute (248)
GIA Gemological Institute of America (246)
GICC Glazing Industry Code Committee (248)
GIS Gamma Iota Sigma (245)
Geoscience Information Soc. (247)
GITA Geospatial Information and Technology Ass'n (247)
GMA Gospel Music Ass'n (248)
Grocery Manufacturers of America (250)
GMAC Graduate Management Admission Council (248)
GMDA Groundwater Management Districts Ass'n (250)
GMDC General Merchandise Distributors Council (246)
GMIS Government Management Information Sciences (248)
GMP Glass, Molders, Pottery, Plastics and Allied Workers International Union (248)
GNSI Guild of Natural Science Illustrators (250)
GOG Gynecologic Oncology Group (250)
GOTA Green Olive Trade Ass'n (249)
GPA Gas Processors Ass'n (245)
GPI Glass Packaging Institute (247)
GPIA Generic Pharmaceutical Industry Ass'n (246)
GPMA Gasoline Pump Manufacturers Ass'n (246)
GPSA Gas Processors Suppliers Ass'n (245)
GRA Governmental Research Ass'n (248)
GRAA Golf Range and Recreation Ass'n of America (248)
GRC Geothermal Resources Council (247)
GRG Gastroenterology Research Group (246)
GRI Gas Research Institute (246)
GS Geochemical Soc. (246)
GSA Genetics Soc. of America (246)
Geological Soc. of America (246)
Gerontological Soc. of America (247)
GSS Gynecologic Surgery Soc. (250)
GTA Gas Turbine Ass'n (246)
GTC Gasification Technologies Council (246)
GWAA Garden Writers Ass'n of America (245)
Golf Writers Ass'n of America (248)

GWI Grinding Wheel Institute (250)
GWPC Ground Water Protection Council (250)
H&PCDC Health and Personal Care Distribution Conference (251)
HAA Home Automation Ass'n (255)
Hospice Ass'n of America (256)
HACC Hellenic-American Chamber of Commerce (253)
HACU Hispanic Ass'n of Colleges and Universities (254)
HAI Helicopter Ass'n Internat'l (252)
HARC Halon Alternatives Research Corp. (251)
HAU Hebrew Actors Union (253)
HBA Home Baking Ass'n (255)
Human Biology Ass'n (257)
HBES Human Behavior and Evolution Soc. (257)
HBMA Healthcare Billing and Management Ass'n (252)
HBPA Horsemen's Benevolent and Protective Ass'n (256)
HBSMAA Hack and Band Saw Manufacturers Ass'n of America (250)
HCAA Nat'l CPA Health Care Advisors Ass'n (398)
HCAAA Home Care Aide Ass'n of America (255)
HCEA Healthcare Convention and Exhibitors Ass'n (252)
HCPC Healthcare Compliance Packaging Council (252)
HCRMS Health Care Resource Management Soc. (251)
HCS Histochemical Soc. (254)
HDA Hardwood Distributors Ass'n (251)
Hispanic Dental Ass'n (254)
Holistic Dental Ass'n (255)
HDBF Heavy Duty Business Forum (253)
HDBMC Heavy Duty Brake Manufacturers Council (253)
HDMA Heavy Duty Manfacturers Ass'n (253)
HDRA Heavy Duty Representatives Ass'n (253)
HEDNA Hotel Electronic Distribution Network Ass'n (256)
HEI Heat Exchange Institute (253)
HELO Hispanic Elected Local Officials (254)
HEREIU Hotel Employees and Restaurant Employees Internat'l Union (253)
HERS Home Energy Rating Systems Council (255)
HES History of Economics Soc. (254)
History of Education Soc. (254)
HeSCA Health Sciences Communications Ass'n (252)
HESS History of Earth Sciences Soc. (254)
HFA Hard Fibers Ass'n (251)
HFC Historians Film Committee (254)
HFES Human Factors and Ergonomics Soc. (257)
HFIA Home Furnishings Internat'l Ass'n (255)
HFM Nat'l Soc. for Healthcare Foodservice Management (429)
HFMA Healthcare Financial Management Ass'n (252)
HFPA Home Fashion Products Ass'n (255)
HFSG Healthcare Finance Study Group (252)
HFTP Hospitality Financial and Technology Professionals (256)
HGA Handweavers Guild of America (251)
Hop Growers of America (256)
HGMN Herb Growing and Marketing Network (253)
HHGFAA Household Goods Forwarders Ass'n of America (257)
HHI Harness Horsemen Internat'l (251)
HHNA Home Healthcare Nurses Ass'n (255)
HHSSA Home Health Services and Staffing Ass'n (255)
HI Hair Internat'l (250)
Hydraulic Institute (257)
Hydronics Institute Division of GAMA (257)
HIA Hearing Industries Ass'n (253)
Hobby Industry Ass'n of America (255)
HIAA Health Insurance Ass'n of America (252)
HIB Headwear Information Bureau (251)
HIBCC Health Industry Business Communications Council (252)
HIDA Health Industry Distributors Ass'n (252)
HIGPA Health Industry Group Purchasing Ass'n (252)
HILA Home Improvement Lenders Ass'n (255)
HIMA Health Industry Manufacturers Ass'n (252)
HIMSS Healthcare Information and Management Systems Soc. (253)
HIRA Health Industry Representatives Ass'n (252)
HIRI Home Improvement Research Institute (255)
HL Herpetologists' League (254)
HLA Helicopter Loggers Ass'n (253)
HLC Healthcare Leadership Council (253)
HMA Hardwood Manufacturers Ass'n (251)
Hydroponic Merchants Ass'n (257)
HMAC Hazardous Materials Advisory Council (251)
HMBA Hotel Motel Brokers of America (256)
HMC Council Healthcare Marketing and Communications Council (252)
HMI Hoist Manufacturers Institute (255)
HNBA Hispanic Nat'l Bar Ass'n (254)
HOAA Home Office Ass'n of America (255)
HOAC Historians of American Communism (254)
HOLA Hispanic Organization of Latin Actors (254)
HOLUA Home Office Life Underwriters Ass'n (256)
HPA Hearth Products Ass'n (253)
Hospital Presidents Ass'n (256)
HPNA Hospice and Palliative Nurses Ass'n (256)
HPS Health Physics Soc. (252)
HPVA Hardwood Plywood and Veneer Ass'n (251)
HRI Horticultural Research Institute (256)
HRPS Human Resource Planning Soc. (257)
HS Harvey Soc. (251)
HSA Home Sewing Ass'n (256)

Hydroponic Soc. of America (257)
HSGT High Speed Ground Transportation Ass'n (254)
HSMAI Hospitality Sales and Marketing Ass'n Internat'l (256)
HSR Hampshire Swine Registry (251)
HSS History of Science Soc. (254)
HTA Harness Tracks of America (251)
HTI Hand Tools Institute (251)
HTMA Hydraulic Tool Manufacturers Ass'n (257)
HWA Home Workers Ass'n (256)
HWBTA Home Wine and Beer Trade Ass'n (256)
HWMA Nat'l Solid Waste Management Environmental (430)
I&MS/IEEE IEEE Instrumentation and Measurement Soc. (258)
I-CAR Inter-Industry Conference on Auto Collision Repair (271)
I-PRO Independent Professional Representatives Organization (261)
I2O SIG I2O Special Interest Group (257)
IA Intercoiffure America (271)
Internet Alliance (311)
Irrigation Ass'n (313)
IA-SIG Interactive Audio Special Interest Group (271)
IAA Institute for Alternative Agriculture (264)
Internat'l Advertising Ass'n (272)
Internat'l Ass'n of Astacology (276)
IAAA Intermarket Ass'n of Advertising Agencies (271)
Internat'l American Albino Ass'n (273)
IAABO Internat'l Ass'n of Approved Basketball Officials (275)
IAACI Internat'l Ass'n of Allergology and Clinical Immunology (275)
IAACN Internat'l and American Ass'ns of Clinical Nutritionists (273)
IAADFS Internat'l Ass'n of Airport Duty Free Stores (275)
IAAEM Internat'l Ass'n of Aquaculture Economics and Mangement (275)
IAAF Internat'l Agricultural Aviation Foundation (272)
IAAI Internat'l Ass'n of Arson Investigators (275)
IAAM Internat'l Ass'n of Assembly Managers (276)
IAAMC Internat'l Ass'n of Ass'n Management Companies (276)
IAAO Internat'l Ass'n of Assessing Officers (276)
IAAOC Internat'l Ass'n of Addictions and Offender Counselors (275)
IAAPA Internat'l Ass'n of Amusement Parks and Attractions (275)
IAATI Internat'l Ass'n of Auto Theft Investigators (276)
IAAVC Internat'l Ass'n of Audio Visual Communicators (276)
IAB Internat'l Ass'n of Boards of Examiners in Optometry (276)
IABA Inter-American Bar Ass'n (271)
IABC Internat'l Ass'n of Business Communicators (276)
IABF Internat'l Ass'n of Business Forecasting (277)
IABM Internat'l Ass'n of Broadcast Monitors (276)
IABMCP Internat'l Academy of Behavioral Medicine, Counseling and Psychotherapy (272)
IABPFF Internat'l Ass'n of Black Professional Fire Fighters (276)
IABSORIW Internat'l Ass'n of Bridge, Structural, Ornamental and Reinforcing Iron Workers (276)
IABTI Internat'l Ass'n of Bomb Technicians and Investigators (276)
IACA Indian Arts and Crafts Ass'n (262)
IACBD Internat'l Academy for Child Brain Development (272)
IACC Icelandic American Chamber of Commerce (258)
India-American Chamber of Commerce (N.Y.) (262)
Internat'l Ass'n of Conference Centers (277)
Italy-America Chamber of Commerce (313)
IACCA Internat'l Ass'n of Conference Center Administrators (277)
IACCF Internat'l Ass'n of Career Consulting Firms (277)
IACDE Internat'l Ass'n of Clothing Designers and Executives (277)
IACET Internat'l Ass'n for Continuing Education and Training (273)
IACHT Internat'l Ass'n Colon Hydro Therapy (273)
IACIS Internat'l Ass'n for Computer Information Systems (273)
IACLEA Internat'l Ass'n of Campus Law Enforcement Administrators (277)
IACM Internat'l Ass'n of Color Manufacturers (277)
IACMP Internat'l Ass'n of Career Management Professionals (277)
IACO Internat'l Ass'n of Correctional Officers (278)
IACOA Independent Armored Car Operators Ass'n (259)
IACP Internat'l Academy of Compounding Pharmacists (272)
Internat'l Ass'n of Chiefs of Police (277)
Internat'l Ass'n of Culinary Professionals (278)
IACPR Internat'l Ass'n of Corporate and Professional Recruitment (277)
Internat'l Ass'n of Corporate and Professional Resources (277)
IACREOT Internat'l Ass'n of Clerks, Recorders, Election Officials and Treasurers (277)
IACS Internat'l Ass'n of Counseling Services (278)
IACSC Internat'l Ass'n of Cold Storage Contractors (277)
IACSS Internat'l Ass'n for Computer Systems Security (273)
IACT Internat'l Ass'n of Counselors and Therapists (278)
IACTP Internat'l Ass'n of Correctional Training Personnel (278)
IACVB Internat'l Ass'n of Convention and Visitor Bureaus (277)
IADA Independent Automotive Damage Appraisers Ass'n (259)
Inflatable Advertising Dealers Ass'n (263)
IADC Internat'l Ass'n of Defense Counsel (278)
Internat'l Ass'n of Drilling Contractors (278)
IADD Internat'l Ass'n of Diecutting and Diemaking (278)
IADR Internat'l Ass'n for Dental Research (274)
IADRS Internat'l Ass'n of Dive Rescue Specialists (278)
IAEDP Internat'l Ass'n of Eating Disorders Professionals (278)
IAEDT Internat'l Ass'n of Equine Dental Technicians (279)
IAEI Internat'l Ass'n of Electrical Inspectors (278)
IAEKM Internat'l Ass'n of Electronic Keyboard Manufacturers (278)
IAEM Internat'l Ass'n for Exposition Management (274)
Internat'l Ass'n of Emergency Managers (278)
IAFC Internat'l Ass'n of Fire Chiefs (279)
IAFCI Internat'l Ass'n of Financial Crimes Investigators (279)
IAFE Internat'l Ass'n of Fairs and Expositions (279)
IAFEC Internat'l Ass'n of Family Entertainment Centers (279)
IAFF Internat'l Ass'n of Fire Fighters (279)
IAFIS Internat'l Ass'n of Food Industry Suppliers (279)
IAFN Internat'l Ass'n of Forensic Nurses (279)
IAFP Internat'l Ass'n for Financial Planning (274)
IAFS Internat'l Ass'n of Family Sociology (279)
IAFWA Internat'l Ass'n of Fish and Wildlife Agencies (279)
IAG Internat'l Academy of Gnathology - American Section (272)
IAGA Internat'l Ass'n of Golf Administrators (279)
IAGC Internat'l Ass'n of Geophysical Contractors (279)
IAH Internat'l Ass'n of Hydrogeologists (280)
IAHA Internat'l Arabian Horse Ass'n (273)
IAHCP Internat'l Academy of Health Care Professionals (272)
IAHCSMM Internat'l Ass'n of Healthcare Central Service Material Management (279)
IAHE Internat'l Ass'n for Hydrogen Energy (274)
IAHFIAW Internat'l Ass'n of Heat and Frost Insulators and Asbestos Workers (279)
IAHP Internat'l Ass'n of Hygienic Physicians (280)
IAHSS Internat'l Ass'n for Healthcare Security and Safety (274)
IAHSSP Internat'l Ass'n of Home Safety and Security Professionals (280)
IAI Internat'l Affiliation of Independent Accounting Firms (272)
Internat'l Ass'n for Identification (274)
IAIA Internat'l Ass'n for Impact Assessment (274)
IAIABC Internat'l Ass'n of Industrial Accident Boards and Commissions (280)
IAICV Internat'l Ass'n of Ice Cream Vendors (280)
IAIR Internat'l Ass'n of Insurance Receivers (280)
IAIS Internat'l Ass'n of Insurance Supervisors (280)
IAJAM Industrial Ass'n of Juvenile Apparel Manufacturers (262)
IAJE Internat'l Ass'n of Jazz Educators (280)
IAJVS Internat'l Ass'n of Jewish Vocational Services (280)
IAKE Internat'l Ass'n of Knowledge Engineers (280)
IALD Internat'l Ass'n of Lighting Designers (280)
IALEFI Internat'l Ass'n of Law Enforcement Firearms Instructors (280)
IALEIA Internat'l Ass'n of Law Enforcement Intelligence Analysts (280)
IALL Internat'l Ass'n for Learning Laboratories (274)
IAMA Intimate Apparel Manufacturers Ass'n (312)
IAMAW Internat'l Ass'n of Machinists and Aerospace Workers (280)
IAMC Institute of Ass'n Management Companies (265)
IAMCA Internat'l Ass'n of Milk Control Agencies (281)
IAME Internat'l Ass'n for Modular Exhibitry (274)
IAMFC Internat'l Ass'n of Marriage and Family Counselors (281)
IAMFES Internat'l Ass'n of Milk, Food and Environmental Sanitarians (281)
IAMG Internat'l Ass'n for Mathematical Geology (274)
IAML-US Internat'l Ass'n of Music Libraries, United States Branch (281)
IAMSLIC Internat'l Ass'n of Aquatic and Marine Science Libraries and Information Centers (275)
IANA Intermodal Ass'n of North America (272)
IANDS Internat'l Ass'n for Near Death Studies (274)
IANRP Internat'l Ass'n of Natural Resource Pilots (281)
IANVOCC Internat'l Ass'n of Non-Vessel Operating Common Carriers (281)
IAO Internat'l Ass'n for Orthodontics (275)
IAOE Internat'l Ass'n of Optometric Executives (281)
IAOHRA Internat'l Ass'n of Official Human Rights Agencies (281)
IAOMT Internat'l Academy of Oral Medicine and Toxicology (272)
IAOT Internat'l Ass'n for Oxygen Therapy (275)
IAPA/SIP Inter American Press Ass'n (271)
IAPAC Internat'l Ass'n of Physicians in AIDS Care (281)
IAPC Internat'l Ass'n of Pet Cemeteries (281)
IAPD Internat'l Ass'n of Plastics Distributors (281)
IAPES Internat'l Ass'n of Personnel in Employment Security (281)
IAPHC Internat'l Ass'n of Printing House Craftsmen (282)
IAPLM Internat'l Ass'n of Pediatric Laboratory Medicine (281)
IAPM Internat'l Academy of Podiatric Medicine (272)
IAPMO Internat'l Ass'n of Plumbing and Mechanical Officials (282)
IAPPA Internat'l Ass'n of Personal Protection Agents (281)
IAPPW Internat'l Ass'n of Pupil Personnel Workers (282)
IAPSC Internat'l Ass'n of Professional Security Consultants (282)
IAPSRS Internat'l Ass'n of Psychosocial Rehabilitation Services (282)
IAPTA Internat'l Allied Printing Trades Ass'n (273)
IAQDE Independent Ass'n of Questioned Document Examiners (259)
IARS Internat'l Anesthesia Research Soc. (273)
IARW Internat'l Ass'n of Refrigerated Warehouses (282)
IAS Internat'l Atherosclerosis Soc. (283)
IASA Insurance Accounting and Systems Ass'n (270)
IASC Internat'l Aloe Science Council (273)
IASL Internat'l Ass'n of School Librarianship (282)
IASM Internat'l Ass'n of Structural Movers (282)
IASMHF Internat'l Ass'n of Sports Museums and Halls of Fame (282)
IASOC Internat'l Ass'n for the Study of Organized Crime (275)
IASP Internat'l Ass'n for the Study of Pain (275)
IASUS Internat'l Ass'n of Satellite Users and Suppliers (282)
IASWS Internat'l Ass'n of Severe Weather Specialists (282)
IAT Internat'l Ass'n of Trichologists (283)
IATC Internat'l Ass'n of Tool Craftsmen (282)
IATE Internat'l Ass'n of Travel Exhibitors (283)
IATL Internat'l Academy of Trial Lawyers (272)
IATM Internat'l Ass'n of Tour Managers - North American Region (282)
IATSE Internat'l Alliance of Theatrical Stage Employees and Moving Picture Technicians of the U.S. and Canada (273)
IAU Italian Actors Union (313)
IAWA Internat'l Aviation Women Ass'n (283)
IAWF Internat'l Ass'n of Wildland Fire (283)
IAWM Internat'l Alliance for Women in Music (273)
Internat'l Ass'n of Women Ministers (283)
IAWP Internat'l Ass'n of Women Police (283)
IBA Independent Bakers Ass'n (259)
Independent Business Alliance (260)
Institute for Briquetting and Agglomeration (265)
Institute of Business Appraisers (266)
Internat'l Banana Ass'n (283)
IBAA Independent Bankers Ass'n of America (260)
IBAM Institute of Behavioral and Applied Management (265)
IBB Internat'l Brotherhood of Boilermakers, Iron Ship Builders, Blacksmiths, Forgers and Helpers (284)
IBBA Internat'l Brangus Breeders Ass'n (284)
Internat'l Business Brokers Ass'n (284)
IBDEA Internat'l Beverage Dispensing Equipment Ass'n (283)
IBECC Internat'l BBSing and Electronic Communications Conference (283)
IBEE Internat'l Builders Exchange Executives (284)
IBEW Internat'l Brotherhood of Electrical Workers (284)
IBFI IBFI, The Internat'l Ass'n for Document and Information Management Solutions (257)
IBHA Internat'l Buckskin Horse Ass'n (284)
IBHS Institute for Business and Home Safety (265)
IBI Institute for Business Innovation (265)
IBM Internat'l Brotherhood of Magicians (284)
IBMA Independent Battery Manufacturers Ass'n (260)
Internat'l Bluegrass Music Ass'n (283)
Internat'l Business Music Ass'n (284)
IBPAT Internat'l Brotherhood of Painters and Allied Trades (284)
IBPSA Internat'l Bowling Pro Shop and Instructors Ass'n (283)
IBS Institute for Brewing Studies (265)
Intercollegiate Broadcasting System (271)
Internat'l Biometric Soc. (283)
IBT Internat'l Brotherhood of Teamsters, AFL-CIO (284)
IBTTA Internat'l Bridge, Tunnel and Turnpike Ass'n (284)
IBWA Internat'l Bottled Water Ass'n (283)
IBWC Internat'l Black Writers Conference (283)
IC4A ICAAAA Coaches Ass'n (257)
ICA Internat'l Carwash Ass'n (285)
Internat'l Ceramic Ass'n (285)
Internat'l Chiropractors Ass'n (285)
Internat'l Claim Ass'n (285)
Internat'l Clarinet Ass'n (285)
Internat'l Communication Ass'n (286)
Internat'l Communications Ass'n (286)
Internat'l Copper Ass'n (287)
Internat'l Credit Ass'n (288)
ICAA Insulation Contractors Ass'n of America (270)
Investment Counsel Ass'n of America (312)
ICAC Institute of Clean Air Companies (266)
ICAE Insurance Consumer Affairs Exchange (270)
ICAK Internat'l College of Applied Kinesiology (286)
ICAN Internat'l Communications Agency Network (286)
ICAS Internat'l Council of Air Shows (287)
ICAVL Intersocietal Commission for the Accreditation of Vascular Laboratories (311)
ICBC Institute of Certified Business Counselors (266)
ICBO Internat'l Conference of Building Officials (287)

792 National Trade and Professional Associations of the U.S. © 1999, Columbia Books, Inc.

NATOA Nat'l Ass'n of Telecommunications Officers and Advisers (378)
NATP Nat'l Ass'n of Tax Practitioners (377)
NATPE Nat'l Ass'n of Television Program Executives (378)
NATRI Nat'l Ass'n for Treasurers of Religious Institutes (342)
NATRIP Nat'l Ass'n of Tax Reducing Income Plans (377)
NATS Nat'l Ass'n of Teachers of Singing (378)
Nat'l Ass'n of Textile Supervisors (378)
NATSO NATSO, Representing America's Travel Plaza and Truckstops (437)
NATSS Nat'l Ass'n of Temporary and Staffing Services (378)
NAUB Nat'l Ass'n of Urban Bankers (379)
NAUFRED Nat'l Ass'n of Used Fitness and Rehabilitation Equipment Dealers (379)
NAUFWP Nat'l Ass'n of University Fisheries and Wildlife Programs (379)
NAUI Nat'l Ass'n of Underwater Instructors (379)
NAUMD Nat'l Ass'n of Uniform Manufacturers and Distributors (379)
NAUPA Nat'l Ass'n of Unclaimed Property Administrators (379)
NAUS/SMW Nat'l Ass'n for Uniformed Services and Soc. of Military Widows (342)
NAVAPD Nat'l Ass'n of VA Physicians and Dentists (379)
NAVD Nat'l Ass'n of Video Distributors (379)
NAVEA Nat'l Adult Vocational Education Ass'n (334)
NAVESNP Nat'l Ass'n of Vocational Education Special Needs Personnel (379)
NAVP Nat'l Ass'n of Vision Professionals (379)
NAVPA Nat'l Ass'n of Veterans Program Administrators (379)
NAVREF Nat'l Ass'n of Veterans' Research and Education Foundations (379)
NAVTEC Nat'l Ass'n of Vocational-Technical Education Communicators (380)
NAVTP Nat'l Ass'n of Vertical Transportation Professionals (379)
NAW Nat'l Ass'n of Wholesaler-Distributors (380)
NAWA Nat'l Ass'n of Women Artists (380)
NAWBO Nat'l Ass'n of Women Business Owners (380)
NAWC Nat'l Ass'n of Water Companies (380)
Nat'l Ass'n of Waterproofing Contractors (380)
NAWD Nat'l Ass'n of WIC Directors (380)
NAWDP Nat'l Ass'n of Workforce Development Professionals (381)
NAWE Nat'l Ass'n for Women in Education (342)
Nat'l Ass'n of Waterfront Employers (380)
NAWG Nat'l Ass'n of Wheat Growers (380)
NAWGA/IFDA Food Distributors Internat'l (241)
NAWHSL Nat'l Ass'n of Women Highway Safety Leaders (380)
NAWIC Nat'l Ass'n of Women in Construction (380)
NAWJ Nat'l Ass'n of Women Judges (380)
NAWL Nat'l Ass'n of Women Lawyers (381)
NAWLA North American Wholesale Lumber Ass'n (446)
NAWT Nat'l Ass'n of Waste Transporters (380)
NAYC Nat'l Ass'n of Youth Clubs (381)
NAYRE Nat'l Ass'n for Year-Round Education (342)
NAYS Nat'l Alliance for Youth Sports (336)
NBA Nat'l Band Ass'n (382)
Nat'l Bankers Ass'n (382)
Nat'l Bar Ass'n (382)
Nat'l Basketball Ass'n (382)
Nat'l Bison Ass'n (383)
Nat'l Business Ass'n (384)
NBACA Nat'l Broadcast Ass'n for Community Affairs (384)
NBAPA Nat'l Black American Paralegal Ass'n (383)
NBASLH Nat'l Black Ass'n for Speech, Language and Hearing (383)
NBBA Nat'l Bed and Breakfast Ass'n (382)
NBBC Nat'l Block and Bridle Club (383)
NBBI Nat'l Board of Boiler and Pressure Vessel Inspectors (383)
NBBQA Nat'l Barbecue Ass'n (382)
NBC Nat'l Broiler Council (384)
NBCA Nat'l Bareboat Charter Ass'n (382)
NBCC Nat'l Black Chamber of Commerce (383)
Nat'l Book Critics Circle (384)
Nat'l Bureau of Certified Consultants (384)
NBCCH Nat'l Board for Certified Clinical Hypnotherapists (383)
NBCFAE Nat'l Black Coalition of Federal Aviation Employees (383)
NBCIA Nat'l Blue Crab Industry Ass'n (383)
NBCL Nat'l Beauty Culturists' League (382)
NBCLEO Nat'l Black Caucus of Local Elected Officials (383)
NBCSL Nat'l Black Caucus of State Legislators (383)
NBDA Nat'l Bicycle Dealers Ass'n (382)
NBEA Nat'l Ballroom and Entertainment Ass'n (382)
Nat'l Business Education Ass'n (384)
NBFA Nat'l Business Forms Ass'n (384)
NBFAA Nat'l Burglar and Fire Alarm Ass'n (384)
NBGQA Nat'l Building Granite Quarries Ass'n (384)
NBIA Nat'l Bio-Energy Industries Ass'n (383)
Nat'l Business Incubation Ass'n (384)
NBMBAA Nat'l Black MBA Ass'n (383)
NBMDA North American Building Material Distribution Ass'n (441)
NBNA Nat'l Black Nurses Ass'n (383)
NBPA Nat'l Basketball Players Ass'n (382)
Nat'l Beverage Packaging Ass'n (382)
Nat'l Black Police Ass'n (383)
NBPC Nat'l Border Patrol Council (384)
NBPRS Nat'l Black Public Relations Soc. (383)
NBRA Nat'l Basketball Referees Ass'n (382)
NBSPA Nat'l Bark and Soil Producers Ass'n (382)
NBTA Nat'l Basketball Trainers' Ass'n (382)
Nat'l Business Travel Ass'n (384)
NBVA Nat'l Bulk Vendors Ass'n (384)
NBWA Nat'l Beer Wholesalers Ass'n (382)
Nat'l Blacksmiths and Weldors Ass'n (383)
NCA Nat'l Candle Ass'n (385)
Nat'l Caves Ass'n (386)
Nat'l Club Ass'n (387)
Nat'l Coffee Ass'n of the U.S.A. (387)
Nat'l Communications Ass'n (388)
Nat'l Confectioners Ass'n of the United States (389)
Nat'l Constables Ass'n (392)
Nat'l Constructors Ass'n (392)
Nat'l Cosmetology Ass'n (392)
Nat'l Costumers Ass'n (392)
NCA-I Neighborhood Cleaners Ass'n-Internat'l (438)
NCAA Nat'l Collegiate Athletic Ass'n (388)
NCAC Nat'l Council of Acoustical Consultants (393)
NCACC Nat'l Conference of Appellate Court Clerks (389)
NCACS Nat'l Coalition of Alternative Community Schools (387)
NCAE Nat'l Council for Agricultural Education (393)
Nat'l Council of Agricultural Employers (394)
NCAP Nat'l Coalition of Abortion Providers (387)
NCARB Nat'l Council of Architectural Registration Boards (394)
NCASI Nat'l Council of the Paper Industry for Air and Stream Improvement (397)
NCAT Nat'l Council of Athletic Training (394)
NCATB Nat'l Congress of Animal Trainers and Breeders (391)
NCAWE Nat'l Council of Administrative Women in Education (394)
NCB Nat'l Cargo Bureau (385)
NCBA Nat'l Candy Brokers Ass'n (385)
Nat'l Catholic Band Ass'n (385)
Nat'l Cattlemen's Beef Ass'n (386)
Nat'l Cooperative Business Ass'n (392)
NCBE Nat'l Conference of Bar Examiners (389)
NCBES Nat'l Council of Black Engineers and Scientists (394)
NCBF Nat'l Conference of Bar Foundations (389)
NCBFAA Nat'l Customs Brokers and Forwarders Ass'n of America (398)
NCBI Nat'l Cotton Batting Institute (392)
NCBJ Nat'l Conference of Bankruptcy Judges (389)
NCBL Nat'l Conference of Black Lawyers (389)
NCBM Nat'l Conference of Black Mayors (389)
NCBMP Nat'l Coalition of Black Meeting Planners (387)
NCBP Nat'l Conference of Bar Presidents (389)
NCBVA Nat'l Concrete Burial Vault Ass'n (389)
NCC Nat'l Certification Commission (386)
Nat'l Cotton Council of America (392)
Nat'l Council of the Churches of Christ in the U.S.A. (397)
NCCA Nat'l Child Care Ass'n (386)
Nat'l Coil Coaters Ass'n (388)
Nat'l Community Capital Ass'n (388)
NCCAA Nat'l Christian College Athletic Ass'n (387)
NCCAC Nat'l Catholic Conference of Airport Chaplains (385)
NCCAE Nat'l Council of County Ass'n Executives (394)
NCCAP Nat'l Certification Council for Activity Professionals (386)
NCCB-USCC Nat'l Conference of Catholic Bishops/U.S. Catholic Conference (390)
NCCBH Nat'l Council for Community Behavioral Healthcare (393)
NCCC Nat'l Catholic Cemetery Conference (385)
NCCD Nat'l Council on Crime and Delinquency (397)
NCCDN Nat'l Consortium of Chemical Dependency Nurses (392)
NCCED Nat'l Congress for Community Economic Development (391)
NCCH Nat'l Council of Community Hospitals (394)
NCCI Nat'l Council on Compensation Insurance (397)
NCCL Nat'l Conference of Catechetical Leadership (390)
Nat'l Council of Coal Lessors (394)
NCCLS Nat'l Committee for Clinical Laboratory Standards (388)
NCCLS (438)
NCCPAP Nat'l Conference of CPA Practitioners (390)
NCCPB Nat'l Council of Commercial Plant Breeders (394)
NCCR Nat'l Council of Chain Restaurants (394)
NCCUSL Nat'l Conference of Commissioners on Uniform State Laws (390)
NCCW Nat'l Council of Catholic Women (394)
NCDA Nat'l Career Development Ass'n (385)
Nat'l Community Development Ass'n (388)
NCDC Nat'l Catholic Development Conference (385)
NCDRE Nat'l Conference of Directors of Religious Education (390)
NCDVD Nat'l Conference of Diocesan Vocation Directors (390)
NCE Nat'l Council of Exchangors (394)
NCEA Nat'l Catholic Educational Ass'n (385)
Nat'l Community Education Ass'n (388)
NCEarc Nat'l Conference of Executives of the Arc (390)
NCECA Nat'l Council on Education for the Ceramic Arts (397)
NCEE Nat'l Catholic Educational Exhibitors (385)
NCEES Nat'l Council of Examiners for Engineering and Surveying (394)
NCEFR Nat'l Council of Erectors, Fabricators and Riggers (394)
NCEOA Nat'l Council of Educational Opportunity Ass'ns (394)
NCEW Nat'l Conference of Editorial Writers (390)
NCFC Nat'l Council of Farmer Cooperatives (394)
NCFO Nat'l Conference of Firemen and Oilers (390)
NCFR Nat'l Council on Family Relations (397)
NCFTJ Nat'l Conference of Federal Trial Judges (390)
NCGA Nat'l Church Goods Ass'n (387)
Nat'l Corn Growers Ass'n (392)
Nat'l Cotton Ginners' Ass'n (392)
NCGE Nat'l Council for Geographic Education (393)
NCGIF Nat'l Cherry Growers and Industries Foundation (386)
NCGS Nat'l Coalition of Girls Schools (387)
NCH Nat'l Center for Homeopathy (386)
NCHA Nat'l Cutting Horse Ass'n (398)
NCHC Nat'l Collegiate Honors Council (388)
NCHELP Nat'l Council of Higher Education Loan Programs (395)
NCHFFA Nat'l Council of Health Facilities Finance Authorities (395)
NCI Nat'l Cheese Institute (386)
NCICA Nat'l Counter Intelligence Corps Ass'n (398)
NCINAS Nat'l Council of Industrial Naval Air Stations (395)
NCIPLA Nat'l Council of Intellectual Property Law Ass'ns (395)
NCIS Nat'l Crop Insurance Services (398)
NCISS Nat'l Council of Investigation and Security Services (395)
NCITD Nat'l Council on Internat'l Trade Development (397)
NCJA Nat'l Criminal Justice Ass'n (398)
NCJFCJ Nat'l Council of Juvenile and Family Court Judges (395)
NCL Nat'l Consumers League (392)
NCLE Nat'l Contact Lens Examiners (392)
NCLEHA Nat'l Conference of Local Environmental Health Administrators (390)
NCLG Nat'l Conference of Lieutenant Governors (390)
NCLGS Nat'l Council of Legislators from Gaming States (395)
NCLPWA Nat'l Council of Local Public Welfare Administrators (395)
NCMA Nat'l Catalog Managers Ass'n (385)
Nat'l Concrete Masonry Ass'n (389)
Nat'l Contract Management Ass'n (392)
NCME Nat'l Council on Measurement in Education (397)
NCMIE Nat'l Council of Music Importers and Exporters (395)
NCMPR Nat'l Council for Marketing and Public Relations (393)
NCMS Nat'l Classification Management Soc. (387)
NCNA Nat'l Council of Nonprofit Ass'ns (395)
NCOA Nat'l Council on the Aging (398)
Non Commissioned Officers Ass'n of the U.S.A. (439)
NCOBPS Nat'l Conference of Black Political Scientists (389)
NCOE Nat'l Council for Occupational Education (393)
NCOIL Nat'l Conference of Insurance Legislators (390)
NCOPE Nat'l Council of Preservation Executives (395)
NCPA Nat'l Community Pharmacists Ass'n (388)
Nat'l Cottonseed Products Ass'n (393)
NCPCU Nat'l Council of Postal Credit Unions (395)
NCPDP Nat'l Council for Prescription Drug Programs (393)
NCPERS Nat'l Conference on Public Employee Retirement Systems (391)
NCPG Nat'l Catholic Pharmacists Guild of the United States (386)
Nat'l Committee on Planned Giving (388)
NCPH Nat'l Council on Public History (397)
NCPI Nat'l Clay Pipe Institute (387)
NCPM Nat'l Conference of Personal Managers (390)
NCPMA Nat'l Clay Pot Manufacturers Ass'n (387)
NCPP Nat'l Council on Public Polls (397)
NCPWB Nat'l Certified Pipe Welding Bureau (386)
NCQA Nat'l Committee for Quality Assurance (388)
NCRA Nat'l Cancer Registrar's Ass'n (385)
Nat'l Center on Rural Aging (386)
Nat'l Court Reporters Ass'n (398)
NCRD Nat'l Council for Resource Development (393)
NCRE Nat'l Conference on Research in English (391)
Nat'l Council on Rehabilitation Education (398)
NCREIF Nat'l Council of Real Estate Investment Fiduciaries (395)
NCRLL Nat'l Conference on Research in Language and Literacy (391)
NCRP Nat'l Council on Radiation Protection and Measurements (398)
NCRUCE Nat'l Conference of Regulatory Utility Commission Engineers (390)
NCS Nat'l Cartoonists Soc. (385)
NCSA Nat'l Coffee Service Ass'n (387)
Nat'l Computer Security Ass'n (389)
NCSAA Nat'l Confectionery Sales Ass'n of America (389)
NCSAB Nat'l Council of State Agencies for the Blind (396)
NCSBCS Nat'l Conference of States on Building Codes and Standards (391)
NCSBN Nat'l Council of State Boards of Nursing (396)
NCSC Nat'l Cargo Security Council (385)
NCSCJ Nat'l Conference of Special Court Judges (391)
NCSD Nat'l Council on Student Development (398)
NCSDCJC Nat'l Council of State Directors of Community Junior Colleges (396)
NCSEA Nat'l Child Support Enforcement Ass'n (386)

National Trade and Professional Associations of the U.S. © 1999, Columbia Books, Inc. 799

NKHA Nat'l Kerosene Heater Ass'n **(414)**
NKSA Nat'l Knitwear and Sportswear Ass'n **(414)**
NL Nat'l League of Professional Baseball Clubs **(415)**
NLA Nat'l Lime Ass'n **(415)**
Nat'l Limousine Ass'n **(415)**
NLADA Nat'l Legal Aid and Defender Ass'n **(415)**
NLAPW Nat'l League of American Pen Women **(414)**
NLBA Nat'l Lead Burning Ass'n **(414)**
Nat'l Licensed Beverage Ass'n **(415)**
NLBMDA Nat'l Lumber and Building Material Dealers Ass'n **(415)**
NLC Nat'l League of Cities **(414)**
NLDA Nat'l Luggage Dealers Ass'n **(415)**
NLFA Nat'l Lamb Feeders Ass'n **(414)**
NLG Nat'l Lawyers Guild **(414)**
NLGI Nat'l Lubricating Grease Institute **(415)**
NLGJA Nat'l Lesbian and Gay Journalists Ass'n **(415)**
NLGLA Nat'l Lesbian and Gay Lawyers Ass'n **(415)**
NLHA Nat'l Leased Housing Ass'n **(415)**
NLICA Nat'l Land Improvement Contractors of America **(414)**
NLN Nat'l League for Nursing **(414)**
NLPM Nat'l League of Postmasters of the U.S. **(414)**
NLRBPA Nat'l Labor Relations Board Professional Ass'n **(414)**
NLSBA Nat'l Lincoln Sheep Breeders Ass'n **(415)**
NLSPA Nat'l Live Stock Producers Ass'n **(415)**
NLSSA Nat'l Litigation Support Services Ass'n **(415)**
NMA Nat'l Management Ass'n **(416)**
Nat'l Meat Ass'n **(416)**
Nat'l Medical Ass'n **(416)**
Nat'l Mining Ass'n **(417)**
NMBA Nat'l Marine Bankers Ass'n **(416)**
NMBC Nat'l Minority Business Council **(417)**
NMBFC Nat'l Magazine, Book, and Film Carriers Conference **(415)**
NMC Nat'l Mastitis Council **(416)**
Nat'l Music Council **(418)**
NMCA Nat'l Meat Canners Ass'n **(416)**
NMDA Nat'l Marine Distributors Ass'n **(416)**
Nat'l Metal Decorators Ass'n **(417)**
Nat'l Miniature Donkey Ass'n **(417)**
NMDP Nat'l Marrow Donor Program **(416)**
NMEA Nat'l Marine Educators Ass'n **(416)**
Nat'l Marine Electronics Ass'n **(416)**
NMEBA Nat'l Marine Engineers Beneficial Ass'n **(416)**
NMEDA Nat'l Mobility Equipment Dealers Ass'n **(417)**
NMEIA Nat'l Machine Embellishment Instructors and Artists **(415)**
NMFC Nat'l Magazine and Film Carriers **(415)**
NMFTA Nat'l Motor Freight Traffic Ass'n **(417)**
NMHA Nat'l Mental Health Ass'n **(416)**
NMHC Nat'l Multi Housing Council **(417)**
NMIA Nat'l Military Intelligence Ass'n **(417)**
NMMA Nat'l Marine Manufacturers Ass'n **(416)**
NMOA Nat'l Mail Order Ass'n **(416)**
NMPA Nat'l Motorsports Press Ass'n **(417)**
Nat'l Music Publishers' Ass'n **(418)**
NMPF Nat'l Milk Producers Federation **(417)**
NMRA Nat'l Marine Representatives Ass'n **(416)**
NMSA Nat'l Metal Spinners Ass'n **(417)**
Nat'l Middle School Ass'n **(417)**
NMSDC Nat'l Minority Supplier Development Council **(417)**
NMSS Nat'l Multiple Sclerosis Soc. **(418)**
NMTA Nat'l Movement Theatre Ass'n **(417)**
NNA Nat'l Newspaper Ass'n **(418)**
Nat'l Notary Ass'n **(418)**
NNCREW Nat'l Network of Commercial Real Estate Women **(418)**
NNFA Nat'l Nutritional Foods Ass'n **(419)**
NNG Nat'l Network of Grantmakers **(418)**
NNGA Northern Nut Growers Ass'n **(446)**
NNPA Nat'l Newspaper Publishers Ass'n **(418)**
NNSA Nat'l Nurses Soc. on Addictions **(418)**
NNSDO Nat'l Nursing Staff Development Organization **(418)**
NNSWM Nat'l Network for Social Work Managers **(418)**
NOA Nat'l Officers Ass'n **(419)**
Nat'l Onion Ass'n **(419)**
Nat'l Opera Ass'n **(419)**
Nat'l Optometric Ass'n **(419)**
NOBC Nat'l Organization of Bar Counsel **(420)**
NOBCO Nat'l Organization of Black County Officials **(420)**
NOBLE Nat'l Organization of Black Law Enforcement Executives **(420)**
NOCA Nat'l Organization for Competency Assurance **(419)**
NODA Nat'l Orientation Directors Ass'n **(420)**
NOEL Nat'l Ornament and Electric Lights Christmas Ass'n **(420)**
NOFMA Nat'l Oak Flooring Manufacturers Ass'n **(419)**
NOGGA Nat'l Ornamental Goldfish Growers Ass'n **(420)**
NOHSE Nat'l Organization for Human Service Education **(420)**
NOIA Nat'l Ocean Industries Ass'n **(419)**
NOITU Nat'l Organization of Industrial Trade Unions **(420)**
NOLHGA Nat'l Organization of Life and Health Insurance Guaranty Ass'ns **(420)**
NOLSW Nat'l Organization of Legal Services Workers **(420)**
NOMA Nat'l Organization of Minority Architects **(420)**
NOMMA Nat'l Ornamental and Miscellaneous Metals Ass'n **(420)**
NONPF Nat'l Organization of Nurse Practitioner Faculties **(420)**
NOPA Nat'l Oilseed Processors Ass'n **(419)**
NORA Nat'l Oil Recyclers Ass'n **(419)**
NOSSCR Nat'l Organization of Social Security Claimants' Representatives **(420)**
NOVA Nurses Organization of Veterans Affairs **(447)**
NOWL/NFWL Nat'l Order of Women Legislators/Nat'l Foundation for Women Legislators **(419)**
NOWRA Nat'l Onsite Wastewater Recycling Ass'n **(419)**
NPA Nat'l Paperbox Ass'n **(421)**
Nat'l Paralegal Ass'n **(421)**
Nat'l Parking Ass'n **(421)**
Nat'l Pasta Ass'n **(421)**
Nat'l Pawnbrokers Ass'n **(421)**
Nat'l Perinatal Ass'n **(422)**
Nat'l Pharmaceutical Alliance **(422)**
Nat'l Phlebotomy Ass'n **(422)**
Nat'l Policy Ass'n **(423)**
Newsletter Publishers Ass'n **(439)**
NPAP Nat'l Psychological Ass'n for Psychoanalysis **(424)**
NPB Nat'l Plant Board **(422)**
Nat'l Plumbing Bureau **(422)**
NPBA Natural Product Broker Ass'n **(437)**
NPBOA Nat'l Party Boat Owners Alliance **(421)**
NPC Nat'l Panhellenic Conference **(421)**
Nat'l Peach Council **(421)**
Nat'l Petroleum Council **(422)**
Nat'l Pharmaceutical Council **(422)**
Nat'l Plasterers Council **(422)**
Nat'l Potato Council **(423)**
NPCA Nat'l Paint and Coatings Ass'n **(420)**
Nat'l Parks and Conservation Ass'n **(421)**
Nat'l Pest Control Ass'n **(422)**
Nat'l Precast Concrete Ass'n **(423)**
NPCD Nat'l Ass'n for Parish Coordinators and Directors of Religious Education **(340)**
Nat'l Ass'n of Parish Coordinators/Directors of Religious Education **(364)**
NPEA Nat'l Patio Enclosure Ass'n **(421)**
NPELRA Nat'l Public Employer Labor Relations Ass'n **(424)**
NPES NPES, the Ass'n for Suppliers of Printing and Publishing Technologies **(446)**
NPFA Nat'l Prepared Food Ass'n **(423)**
NPFDA Nat'l Poultry and Food Distributors Ass'n **(423)**
NPGA Nat'l Propane Gas Ass'n **(423)**
NPGPA Non-Powder Gun Products Ass'n **(439)**
NPHA Nat'l Park Hospitality Ass'n **(421)**
Nat'l Pharmaceutical Ass'n **(422)**
Nat'l Prison Hospice Ass'n **(423)**
NPHC Nat'l Pan Hellenic Council **(421)**
NPI Nat'l Purchasing Institute **(424)**
NPLA Nat'l Perishable Logistics Ass'n **(422)**
NPLC Nat'l Pedigreed Livestock Council **(422)**
NPM Nat'l Ass'n of Pastoral Musicians **(364)**
NPMA Nat'l Podiatric Medical Ass'n **(422)**
Nat'l Property Management Ass'n **(424)**
NPMHU Nat'l Postal Mail Handlers Union **(423)**
NPOAA Nat'l Police Officers Ass'n of America **(422)**
NPPA Nat'l Press Photographers Ass'n **(423)**
NPPB Nat'l Potato Promotion Board **(423)**
NPPC Nat'l Pork Producers Council **(423)**
NPRA Nat'l Petroleum Refiners Ass'n **(422)**
NPSA Nat'l Pecan Shellers Ass'n **(421)**
NPSL Nat'l Professional Soccer League **(423)**
NPTA Nat'l Paper Trade Ass'n **(421)**
NPTC Nat'l Private Truck Council **(423)**
NQPC Nat'l Quartz Producers Council **(424)**
NR/WA Nat'l Rep/Wholesaler Ass'n **(425)**
NRA Nat'l Rehabilitation Ass'n **(425)**
Nat'l Renderers Ass'n **(425)**
Nat'l Restaurant Ass'n **(425)**
Nat'l Rifle Ass'n of America **(426)**
Naval Reserve Ass'n **(438)**
NRAA Nat'l Rehabilitation Administration Ass'n **(425)**
Nat'l Renal Administrators Ass'n **(425)**
NRB Nat'l Religious Broadcasters **(425)**
NRC Nat'l Railroad Construction and Maintenance Ass'n **(424)**
Nat'l Reading Conference **(424)**
Nat'l Realty Committee **(424)**
NRCA Nat'l Refrigeration Contractors Ass'n **(424)**
Nat'l Rehabilitation Counseling Ass'n **(425)**
Nat'l Roofing Contractors Ass'n **(426)**
NRDCA Nat'l Roof Deck Contractors Ass'n **(426)**
NREA Nat'l Rural Education Ass'n **(426)**
NRECA Nat'l Rural Electric Cooperative Ass'n **(426)**
NREP Nat'l Registry of Environmental Professionals **(424)**
NRF Nat'l Retail Federation **(425)**
NRHA Nat'l Reining Horse Ass'n **(425)**
Nat'l Retail Hardware Ass'n **(425)**
Nat'l Rural Health Ass'n **(426)**
NRHSA Nat'l Retail Hobby Store Ass'n **(426)**
NRHSPP Nat'l Register of Health Service Providers in Psychology **(424)**
NRLCA Nat'l Rural Letter Carriers' Ass'n **(426)**
NRMA Nat'l Reloading Manufacturers Ass'n **(425)**
NRMCA Nat'l Ready Mixed Concrete Ass'n **(424)**
NRPA Nat'l Recreation and Park Ass'n **(424)**
NRRA Nat'l Risk Retention Ass'n **(426)**
NRTO Nat'l Remotivation Therapy Organization **(425)**
NRVMA Nat'l Roadside Vegetation Management Ass'n **(426)**
NRWA Nat'l Rural Water Ass'n **(426)**
NSA Nat'l Shellfisheries Ass'n **(427)**
Nat'l Sheriffs' Ass'n **(427)**
Nat'l Shipyard Ass'n **(428)**
Nat'l Slag Ass'n **(428)**
Nat'l Soc. of Accountants **(429)**
Nat'l Speakers Ass'n **(431)**
Nat'l Stone Ass'n **(431)**
Nat'l Stroke Ass'n **(432)**
Nat'l Sunflower Ass'n **(432)**
Nat'l Sunroom Ass'n **(432)**
Neurosurgical Soc. of America **(438)**
Not-for-Profit Services Ass'n **(446)**
Nuclear Suppliers Ass'n **(447)**
NSAA Nat'l Ski Areas Ass'n **(428)**
Nat'l Surgical Assistant Ass'n **(432)**
NSAC Nat'l Soc. of Accountants for Cooperatives **(429)**
NSAE Nat'l Soc. of Architectural Engineers **(429)**
NSAS Nat'l Soc. of Appraiser Specialists **(429)**
NSBA Nat'l School Boards Ass'n **(427)**
Nat'l Sugar Brokers Ass'n **(432)**
NSBP Nat'l Soc. of Black Physicists **(429)**
NSBU Nat'l Small Business United **(428)**
NSC Nat'l Safety Council **(426)**
NSCA Nat'l Strength and Conditioning Ass'n **(432)**
Nat'l Systems Contractors Ass'n **(433)**
NSCAA Nat'l Soccer Coaches Ass'n of America **(430)**
NSCIA Nat'l Spinal Cord Injury Ass'n **(431)**
NSCP Nat'l Soc. of Compliance Professionals **(429)**
NSDA Nat'l Soft Drink Ass'n **(430)**
NSDC Nat'l Staff Development Council **(431)**
NSDJA Nat'l Sash and Door Jobbers Ass'n **(426)**
NSDTA Nat'l Staff Development and Training Ass'n **(431)**
NSEC Nat'l Soc. of Environmental Consultants **(429)**
NSEE Nat'l Soc. for Experiential Education **(428)**
NSEMA Nat'l Spray Equipment Manufacturers Ass'n **(431)**
NSFRE Nat'l Soc. of Fund Raising Executives **(429)**
NSG Nat'l Soc. for Graphology **(428)**
Newspaper Systems Group **(439)**
NSGA Nat'l Sporting Goods Ass'n **(431)**
NSGC Nat'l Soc. of Genetic Counselors **(430)**
NSH Nat'l Soc. for Histotechnology **(429)**
NSHDS Nat'l Soc. for Hebrew Day Schools **(429)**
NSHMBA Nat'l Soc. of Hispanic MBAs **(430)**
NSHR Nat'l Show Horse Registry **(428)**
NSIF Nat'l Swine Improvement Federation **(433)**
NSIPA Nat'l Soc. of Insurance Premium Auditors **(430)**
NSLEA Nat'l Science Education Leadership Ass'n **(427)**
NSM Nat'l Selected Morticians **(427)**
NSMA Nat'l Seasoning Manufacturers Ass'n **(427)**
NSMP Nat'l Soc. of Mural Painters **(430)**
NSMPA Nat'l Screw Machine Products Ass'n **(427)**
NSMS Nat'l Safety Management Soc. **(426)**
NSNA Nat'l Student Nurses Ass'n **(432)**
NSNC Nat'l Soc. of Newspaper Columnists **(430)**
NSP Nat'l Ski Patrol System **(428)**
NSPA Nat'l Shrimp Processors Ass'n **(428)**
Nat'l State Publishing Ass'n **(431)**
NSPB/PBA Nat'l Soc. to Prevent Blindness/Prevent Blindness America **(430)**
NSPCA Nat'l Soc. of Painters in Casein and Acrylic **(430)**
NSPE Nat'l Soc. of Professional Engineers **(430)**
NSPI Nat'l Spa and Pool Institute **(431)**
NSPR Nat'l Soc. for Park Resources **(429)**
NSPRA Nat'l School Public Relations Ass'n **(427)**
NSPS Nat'l Soc. of Professional Surveyors **(430)**
NSPST Nat'l Soc. of Pharmaceutical Sales Trainers **(430)**
NSR Nat'l Swine Registry **(433)**
NSRA Nat'l Shoe Retailers Ass'n **(428)**
NSREA Nat'l Soc. of Real Estate Appraisers **(430)**
NSREF Nat'l Real Estate Forum **(424)**
NSRMCA Nat'l Star Route Mail Contractors Ass'n **(431)**
NSS Nat'l Sculpture Soc. **(427)**
Nat'l Speleological Soc. **(431)**
NSSA Nat'l Sportscasters and Sportswriters Ass'n **(431)**
Nat'l Suffolk Sheep Ass'n **(432)**
Nat'l Swim School Ass'n **(432)**
NSSE Nat'l Soc. for the Study of Education **(429)**
NSSEA Nat'l School Supply and Equipment Ass'n **(427)**
NSSF Nat'l Shooting Sports Foundation **(428)**
NSSHA Nat'l Spotted Saddle Horse Ass'n **(431)**
NSSLHA Nat'l Student Speech Language Hearing Ass'n **(432)**
NSSR Nat'l Spotted Swine Record **(431)**
NSSRA Nat'l Ski and Snowboard Retailers Ass'n **(428)**
NSSTA Nat'l Structured Settlements Trade Ass'n **(432)**
NSTA Nat'l School Transportation Ass'n **(427)**
Nat'l Science Teachers Ass'n **(427)**
Nat'l Shoe Travelers Ass'n **(428)**
NSWA Nat'l Stripper Well Ass'n **(432)**
NSWMA Nat'l Solid Wastes Management Ass'n **(431)**
NTA Nat'l Tax Ass'n-Tax Institute of America **(433)**
Nat'l Taxidermists Ass'n **(433)**
Nat'l Tour Ass'n **(434)**
Nat'l Translator Ass'n **(434)**
Nat'l Trappers Ass'n **(434)**
Nat'l Troubleshooting Ass'n **(434)**
Nat'l Tutoring Ass'n **(435)**
Northern Textile Ass'n **(446)**
NTCA Nat'l Telephone Cooperative Ass'n **(433)**
Nat'l Tile Contractors Ass'n **(433)**
NTDA Nat'l Trailer Dealers Ass'n **(434)**
NTEA Nat'l Time Equipment Ass'n **(434)**
Nat'l Truck Equipment Ass'n **(434)**
NTEU Nat'l Treasury Employees Union **(434)**
NTF Nat'l Turkey Federation **(435)**

National Trade and Professional Associations of the U.S. © 1999, Columbia Books, Inc. 801

NTGA Nat'l Tabletop and Giftware Ass'n (433)
NTHECC Nat'l Truck and Heavy Equipment Claims Council (434)
NTLA Nat'l Tax Lien Ass'n (433)
NTLS Nat'l Truck Leasing System (434)
NTMA Nat'l Terrazzo and Mosaic Ass'n (433)
Nat'l Tooling and Machining Ass'n (434)
NTMTAI Nursing Touch and Massage Therapy Ass'n Internat'l (447)
NTPA Nat'l Tractor Pullers Ass'n (434)
NTRMA Nat'l Tile Roofing Manufacturers Ass'n (434)
NTRS Nat'l Therapeutic Recreation Soc. (433)
NTSA Nat'l Technical Services Ass'n (433)
Nat'l Training Systems Ass'n (434)
NTSAD Nat'l Tay-Sachs and Allied Diseases Ass'n (433)
NTTC Nat'l Tank Truck Carriers (433)
NTWA Nat'l Turf Writers Ass'n (435)
NUABA Nat'l United Affiliated Beverage Ass'n (435)
NUCA Nat'l Utility Contractors Ass'n (435)
NUSACC Nat'l U.S.-Arab Chamber of Commerce (435)
NVA Nat'l Viatical Ass'n (435)
NVATA Nat'l Vocational Agricultural Educators Ass'n (435)
NVCA Nat'l Venture Capital Ass'n (435)
NVFC Nat'l Volunteer Fire Council (435)
NVLA Nat'l Vehicle Leasing Ass'n (435)
NVOILA Nat'l Voluntary Organizations for Independent Living for the Aging (435)
NVRA Nat'l Verbatim Reporters Ass'n (435)
NWA Nat'l Watermelon Ass'n (436)
Nat'l Weather Ass'n (436)
Nat'l Wellness Ass'n (436)
Nat'l Writers Ass'n (437)
NWC Nat'l Waterways Conference (436)
NWCA Nat'l Writing Centers Ass'n (437)
NWDA Nat'l Wholesale Druggists' Ass'n (436)
NWDS Noah Worcester Dermatological Soc. (439)
NWEAF Nat'l Women's Economic Alliance Foundation (436)
NWFA Nat'l Wood Flooring Ass'n (436)
NWMC Nat'l Wool Marketing Corporation (437)
NWOA Nat'l Woodland Owners Ass'n (437)
NWPCA Nat'l Wooden Pallet and Container Ass'n (437)
NWRA Nat'l Water Resources Ass'n (435)
Nat'l Wheel and Rim Ass'n (436)
Nat'l Wildlife Rehabilitators Ass'n (436)
Nat'l Wireless Resellers Ass'n (436)
NWS Nat'l Watercolor Soc. (436)
Non-Heatset Web Section (439)
NWSA Nat'l Welding Supply Ass'n (436)
Nat'l Women's Studies Ass'n (436)
NWSEO Nat'l Weather Service Employees Organization (436)
NWTI Nat'l Wood Tank Institute (436)
NWU Nat'l Writers Union (437)
NWWDA Nat'l Wood Window and Door Ass'n (437)
NYA Nat'l Yogurt Ass'n (437)
NYAS New York Academy of Sciences (438)
NYCE New York Board of Trade (438)
NYMEX New York Mercantile Exchange (438)
NYSE New York Stock Exchange (438)
O.D. Institute Organization Development Institute (449)
O.O.A. Owner Operators of America (452)
OA Osborne Ass'n (451)
OAA Opticians Ass'n of America (449)
OAAA Outdoor Advertising Ass'n of America (451)
OABA Outdoor Amusement Business Ass'n (451)
OAC Overseas Automotive Council (451)
OAC/MEMA Overseas Automotive Council, Internat'l Aftermarket Division - Motor and Equipment Manufacturers Ass'n (452)
OAGI Open Applications Group (448)
OAH Organization of American Historians (450)
OAKE Organization of American Kodaly Educators (450)
OARSI OsteoArthritis Research Soc. Internat'l (451)
OBAP Organization of Black Airline Pilots (450)
OBD Organization of Black Designers (450)
OBTS Organizational Behavior Teaching Soc. (450)
OCAW Oil, Chemical and Atomic Workers Internat'l Union (448)
OCIA Organic Crop Improvement Ass'n Internat'l (449)
OCPA Ornamental Concrete Producers Ass'n (451)
ODN Organization Development Network (449)
OEA Optometric Editors Ass'n (449)
Overseas Education Ass'n (452)
OFA Organization of Flying Adjusters (450)
Oxygenated Fuels Ass'n (452)
OFDA Office Furniture Distribution Ass'n (447)
OFII Organization for Internat'l Investment (449)
OGBA Organic Growers and Buyers Ass'n (449)
OHA Oral History Ass'n (449)
OKU Omicron Kappa Upsilon (448)
OLA Optical Laboratories Ass'n (448)
OLAC Online Audiovisual Catalogers (448)
OMA Optical Industry Ass'n: OMA (448)
OMSA Offshore Marine Service Ass'n (447)
ONO Organization of News Ombudsmen (450)
ONS Oncology Nursing Soc. (448)
OOIDA Owner-Operator Independent Drivers Ass'n (452)
OOSS Outpatient Ophthalmic Surgery Soc. (451)
OPACT Organization of Professional Acting Coaches and Teachers (450)
OPASTCO Organization for the Promotion and Advancement of Small Telecommunications Companies (449)
OPC Overseas Press Club of America (452)
OPCA Occupational Program Consultants Ass'n (447)
OPCMIA Operative Plasterers' and Cement Masons' Internat'l Ass'n of the United States and Canada (448)
OPEAA Outdoor Power Equipment Aftermarket Ass'n (451)
OPEDA Organization of Professional Employees of the U.S. Department of Agriculture (450)
Outdoor Power Equipment Distributors Ass'n (451)
OPEI Outdoor Power Equipment Institute (451)
OPEIU Office and Professional Employees Internat'l Union (447)
OPIA Opto-Precision Instruments Ass'n (449)
OPIVITA Outpatient Intravenous Infusion Therapy Ass'n (451)
OPS Operations Security Professionals Soc. (448)
Ophthalmic Photographers' Soc. (448)
OPUG Office Planners and Users Group (447)
OPWA Office Products Wholesalers Ass'n (447)
ORIA Oriental Rug Importers Ass'n of America (450)
ORRA Oriental Rug Retailers of America (450)
ORS Orthopaedic Research Soc. (451)
ORTHO American Orthopsychiatric Ass'n (89)
OSA Optical Soc. of America (449)
OSMA Orthopedic Surgical Manufacturers Ass'n (451)
Overseas Sales and Marketing Ass'n of America (452)
OSRA Office Systems Research Ass'n (447)
OSSSC Order Selection, Staging and Storage Council (449)
OTA Organic Trade Ass'n (449)
Orthopaedic Trauma Ass'n (451)
OTOD Organization of Teachers of Oral Diagnosis (450)
OTS Omega Tau Sigma (448)
Organization for Tropical Studies (450)
OTSA Orthodox Theological Soc. in America (451)
OVA Offshore Valve Ass'n (447)
OVDA Optical Video Disc Ass'n (449)
OWAA Outdoor Writers Ass'n of America (451)
OWIT Organization of Women in Internat'l Trade (450)
OWP Organization of Wildlife Planners (450)
PA Parapsychological Ass'n (453)
Parliamentary Associates (453)
PAA Population Ass'n of America (460)
Potato Ass'n of America (461)
Professional Apparel Ass'n (464)
PAC Public Affairs Council (469)
PACA Picture Agency Council of America (458)
PACC Professional Ass'n of Custom Clothiers (464)
PACE Professional Ass'n for Childhood Education (464)
Professional Ass'n of Christian Educators (464)
PACER Professional Ass'n of Comics Entertainment Retailers (464)
PAD Phi Alpha Delta (456)
PADA Private Art Dealers Ass'n (463)
PADI Professional Ass'n of Diving Instructors (464)
PAHCOM Professional Ass'n of Health Care Office Managers (464)
PAI Processed Apples Institute (463)
PAII Professional Ass'n of Innkeepers Internat'l (464)
PAL Professional Ass'n of Lumbermen - World Lumber Standards (464)
PAMA Professional Aviation Maintenance Ass'n (464)
PARA Professional Audio-Video Retailers Ass'n (464)
PARMA Public Agency Risk Managers Ass'n (469)
PARW Professional Ass'n of Resume Writers (464)
PAS Nat'l Postsecondary Agriculture Student Organization (423)
Percussive Arts Soc. (454)
PASS Professional Airways Systems Specialists (464)
PATA Professional Aeromedical Transport Ass'n (464)
PATCA Professional and Technical Consultants Ass'n (464)
PATMI Powder Actuated Tool Manufacturers Institute (461)
PAUS Piedmontese Ass'n of the United States (458)
PBA Professional Bowlers Ass'n of America (465)
PBAA Periodical and Book Ass'n of America (455)
PBATS Professional Baseball Athletic Trainers' Ass'n (465)
PBBA Printing Brokerage Buyers Ass'n (463)
PBEA Paint, Body and Equipment Ass'n (452)
PBMA Public Broadcasting Management Ass'n (469)
PBNPA Peanut and Tree Nut Processors Ass'n (454)
PBUS Professional Ball Agents of the United States (465)
PBWA Professional Basketball Writers' Ass'n (465)
PCA Nat'l Plastercraft Ass'n (422)
Pine Chemicals Ass'n (458)
Popular Culture Ass'n (460)
Portland Cement Ass'n (460)
Print Council of America (462)
PCCA Portable Computer and Communications Ass'n (460)
Power and Communication Contractors Ass'n (461)
PCDA Professional Currency Dealers Ass'n (465)
PCDANA Post Card Distributors Ass'n of North America (461)
PCEA Professional Construction Estimators Ass'n of America (465)
PCI Powder Coating Institute (461)
Precast/Prestressed Concrete Institute (462)
PCIA Personal Communications Industry Ass'n (455)
PCMA Pharmaceutical Care Management Ass'n (456)
Professional Convention Management Ass'n (465)
PCMCIA Personal Computer Memory Card Internat'l Ass'n (455)
PCMI Photo Chemical Machining Institute (457)
PCPA Protestant Church-Owned Publishers Ass'n (469)
PCPCI PCPCI - The Transformer Ass'n (454)
PCRA Poland China Record Ass'n (459)
PCUS Propeller Club of the U.S. (468)
PDA Parenteral Drug Ass'n (453)
PDC Package Design Council Int'l (452)
Paper Distribution Council (453)
PDCA Painting and Decorating Contractors of America (452)
Pile Driving Contractors Ass'n (458)
Purebred Dairy Cattle Ass'n (470)
PDI Plumbing and Drainage Institute (459)
PDK Phi Delta Kappa (456)
PDMA Product Development and Management Ass'n (463)
PDP Phi Delta Phi (457)
PDRA Paint and Decorating Retailers Ass'n (452)
PEI Petroleum Equipment Institute (455)
Porcelain Enamel Institute (460)
PELS Power Electronics Soc. (461)
PEMA Process Equipment Manufacturers' Ass'n (463)
PEPP Professional Engineers in Private Practice (465)
PER Public Employees Roundtable (469)
PERA Production Engine Remanufacturers Ass'n (463)
Production Equipment Rental Ass'n (463)
PERF Police Executive Research Forum (459)
PES Philosophy of Education Soc. (457)
Power Engineering Soc. (461)
PESA Petroleum Equipment Suppliers Ass'n (455)
PFA Pedorthic Footwear Ass'n (454)
Pierre Fauchard Academy (458)
Polyurethane Foam Ass'n (460)
Professional Fraternity Ass'n (465)
PFATS Professional Football Athletic Trainers Soc. (465)
PFDI Preferred Funeral Directors Internat'l (462)
PFHA Paso Fino Horse Ass'n (453)
PFI Pellet Fuels Institute (454)
Pet Food Institute (455)
Pipe Fabrication Institute (458)
PFWA Professional Football Writers of America (465)
PGA Producer's Guild of America (463)
Professional Golfers Ass'n of America (465)
PGI Pyrotechnics Guild Internat'l (470)
PGMA Public Golf Management Ass'n (469)
PGMC Primary Glass Manufacturers Council (462)
PGMS Professional Grounds Management Soc. (465)
PHA Palomino Horse Ass'n (453)
Percheron Horse Ass'n of America (454)
Professional Handlers Ass'n (466)
PHAABO Purebred Hanoverian Ass'n of America Breeders and Owners (470)
PHADA Public Housing Authorities Directors Ass'n (469)
PHBA Palomino Horse Breeders of America (453)
PHCC-NA Plumbing-Heating-Cooling Contractors - Nat'l Ass'n (459)
PHCIB Plumbing-Heating-Cooling Information Bureau (459)
PHEWA Presbyterian Health, Education and Welfare Ass'n (462)
Phi Dex Phi Delta Chi (456)
PhiDe Phi Delta Epsilon Medical Fraternity (456)
PHILAMCHAM Philippine-American Chamber of Commerce (457)
PHMA Professional Housing Management Ass'n (466)
PHOSCHEM Phosphate Chemicals Export Ass'n (457)
PhRMA Pharmaceutical Research and Manufacturers of America (456)
PHRW Preferred Hotels and Resorts Worldwide (462)
PHWA Professional Hockey Writers' Ass'n (466)
PI Perlite Institute (455)
Popcorn Institute (460)
PrintImage Internat'l (463)
PIA Nat'l Ass'n of Professional Insurance Agents (367)
Packaged Ice Ass'n (452)
Personalization and Identification Ass'n (455)
Printing Industries of America (463)
PIAA Physician Insurers Ass'n of America (458)
PIC Promotion Industry Council (468)
PICA Professional Insurance Communicators of America (466)
PICE Printing Industry Credit Executives (463)
PIDA Pet Industry Distributors Ass'n (455)
PIJAC Pet Industry Joint Advisory Council (455)
PIMA Paper Industry Management Ass'n (453)
Photographic and Imaging Manufacturers Ass'n (457)
Polyisocyanurate Insulation Manufacturers Ass'n (460)
Professional Insurance Mass-Marketing Ass'n (466)
PIOP Pharmacists in Ophthalmic Practice (456)
PISC Petroleum Industry Security Council (455)
PKDG Professional Knitwear Designers Guild (466)
PLA Public Library Ass'n (469)
PLCA Pipe Line Contractors Ass'n (458)
PLCAA Professional Lawn Care Ass'n of America (466)
PLI Practising Law Institute (462)
PLMA Private Label Manufacturers Ass'n (463)
PLRB Property Loss Research Bureau (468)
PLT Pi Lambda Theta (458)
PLUS Professional Liability Underwriting Soc. (466)
PMA Polyurethane Manufacturers Ass'n (460)
Precision Metalforming Ass'n (462)
Produce Marketing Ass'n (463)
Professional Managers Ass'n (466)
Promotion Marketing Ass'n (468)

802 National Trade and Professional Associations of the U.S. © 1999, Columbia Books, Inc.

Surgical Infection Soc. (519)
SISO Soc. of Independent Show Organizers (503)
SIT Sugar Industry Technologists (518)
SITE Soc. of Incentive and Travel Executives (502)
Soc. of Insurance Trainers and Educators (503)
SIU Seafarers' Internat'l Union of North America (480)
SIVB Soc. for In Vitro Biology (489)
SJI Steel Joist Institute (516)
SLA Showmen's League of America (483)
Special Libraries Ass'n (514)
Sports Lawyers Ass'n (515)
SLAA Soc. for Latin American Anthropology (490)
SLB Soc. for Leukocyte Biology (490)
SLEMA Schiffli Lace and Embroidery Manufacturers Ass'n (479)
SLF Strategic Leadership Forum (517)
SLMS Soc. for Luminescent Microscopy and Spectroscopy (490)
SLS Soc. of Laparoendoscopic Surgeons (503)
SLTBR Soc. for Light Treatment and Biological Rhythms (490)
SMA Scale Manufacturers Ass'n (479)
Screen Manufacturers Ass'n (480)
Soc. for Medical Anthropology (491)
Soc. of Maritime Arbitrators (503)
Soc. of Mineral Analysts (504)
Soc. of Municipal Arborists (504)
Stadium Managers Ass'n (515)
Steel Manufacturers Ass'n (516)
Storage Equipment Manufacturer's Ass'n (517)
Stucco Manufacturers Ass'n (517)
SMACNA Sheet Metal and Air Conditioning Contractors' Nat'l Ass'n (482)
SMART Secondary Materials and Recycled Textiles Ass'n (480)
SMB Soc. for Mathematical Biology (491)
SMCAF Soc. of Medical Consultants to the Armed Forces (503)
SMCR Soc. for Menstrual Cycle Research (491)
SMD Soc. of Medical-Dental Management Consultants (503)
SMDM Soc. for Medical Decision Making (491)
SME Soc. for Mining, Metallurgy, and Exploration (491)
Soc. of Manufacturing Engineers (503)
SMEI Sales and Marketing Executives Internat'l (478)
SMEMA Surface Mount Equipment Manufacturers Ass'n (519)
SMFM Soc. for Maternal Fetal Medicine (491)
SMH Soc. for Military History (491)
SMI Sorptive Minerals Institute (510)
Spring Manufacturers Institute (515)
SMMA Small Motors and Motion Ass'n (484)
SMPE Soc. of Marine Port Engineers (503)
SMPS Soc. for Marketing Professional Services (490)
SMPTAD Soc. of Motion Picture and Television Art Directors (504)
SMPTE Soc. of Motion Picture and Television Engineers (504)
SMR Soc. of Magnetic Resonance (503)
SMRI Solution Mining Research Institute (510)
SMRP Soc. for Maintenance Reliability Professionals (490)
Soc. for Medieval and Renaissance Philosophy (491)
SMSG School Management Study Group (479)
SMT Professional Soc. for Sales and Marketing Training (467)
SMTA Surface Mount Technology Ass'n (519)
SMWIA Sheet Metal Workers' Internat'l Ass'n (482)
SNA Suburban Newspapers of America (518)
SNACC Soc. of Neurosurgical Anesthesia and Critical Care (504)
SNAG Soc. of North American Goldsmiths (504)
SNAME Soc. of Naval Architects and Marine Engineers (504)
SNAP Soc. of Nat'l Ass'n Publications (504)
SND Soc. for News Design (491)
SNE Soc. for Nutrition Education (491)
SNLS Soc. for New Language Study (491)
SNM Soc. of Nuclear Medicine (504)
SNP Soc. for Natural Philosophy (491)
SNS Soc. of Neurological Surgeons (504)
SOA Soc. of Actuaries (496)
Software Operations Ass'n (509)
SOAP Soc. for Obstetric Anesthesia and Perinatology (491)
SOBA States Organization for Boating Access (516)
SOBP Soc. of Biological Psychiatry (498)
SOCAP Soc. of Consumer Affairs Professionals in Business (500)
SOCISAFFS Soc. of United States Air Force Flight Surgeons (508)
SOCMA Synthetic Organic Chemical Manufacturers Ass'n (519)
SODA Sportsplex Operators and Developers of Ass'n (515)
SOEH Soc. for Occupational and Environmental Health (491)
SOFE Soc. of Financial Examiners (501)
SOFT Soc. of Forensic Toxicologists (501)
SOHN Soc. of Otorhinolaryngology and Head/Neck Nurses (504)
SOLE SOLE - The Internat'l Soc. of Logistics (510)
SOMA Nat'l Student Osteopathic Medical Ass'n (432)
SON Soc. of Nematologists (504)
SOP Soc. for Organic Petrology (492)
Soc. of Protozoologists (506)
SOPA Soc. of Professional Archeologists (505)
SOPHE Soc. for Public Health Education (493)
SOPHIA Soc. of Philosophers in America (505)
SOS Soc. of Scribes (507)
SOT Soc. of Toxicology (508)
SOVE Soc. for Vector Ecology (496)
SPA Seaplane Pilots Ass'n (480)
Singles Press Ass'n (483)
Soc. for Pediatric Anesthesia (492)
Soc. for Personality Assessment (492)
Soc. for Psychological Anthropology (492)
Sociological Practice Ass'n (509)
Software Publishers Ass'n (509)
SPAC Soil and Plant Analysis Council (509)
SPAN Small Publishers Ass'n of North America (484)
SPAP Soc. of Physician Assistants in Pediatrics (505)
SPAR Soc. of Photographer and Artist Representatives (505)
SPARS Soc. of Professional Audio Recording Services (505)
SPBA Soc. of Professional Benefit Administrators (505)
SPC Soy Protein Council (511)
Sweet Potato Council of the United States (519)
SPCAP Soc. of Professors of Child and Adolescent Psychiatry (506)
SPD Soc. for Pediatric Dermatology (492)
Soc. of Publication Designers (506)
SPE Soc. for Photographic Education (492)
Soc. of Petroleum Engineers (505)
Soc. of Plastics Engineers (505)
Soc. of Professors of Education (506)
SPED Soc. of Piping Engineers and Designers (505)
SPEE Soc. of Petroleum Evaluation Engineers (505)
SPEP Soc. for Phenomenology and Existential Philosophy (492)
SPESA Sewn Products Equipment Suppliers Ass'n (482)
SPFA Steel Plate Fabricators Ass'n (516)
SPFFA Societe des Professeurs Francais et Francophone d'Amerique (509)
SPI Soc. of Professional Investigators (506)
Soc. of the Plastics Industry (507)
Soc. of the Plastics Industry - Polyurethane Division (507)
SPIDR Soc. of Professionals in Dispute Resolution (506)
SPIE SPIE-Internat'l Soc. for Optical Engineering (514)
SPJ Soc. of Professional Journalists (506)
SPM Soc. of Prospective Medicine (506)
SPN Soc. of Pediatric Nurses (505)
SPOH Soc. for the Preservation of Oral Health (495)
SPP Soc. for Pediatric Pathology (492)
SPR Soc. for Pediatric Radiology (492)
Soc. for Pediatric Research (492)
Soc. for Philosophy of Religion (492)
Soc. for Psychophysiological Research (492)
SPRBM Soc. for Physical Regulation in Biology and Medicine (492)
SPRE Soc. of Park and Recreation Educators (505)
SPRI Single Ply Roofing Institute (483)
SPS IEEE Signal Processing Soc. (259)
Soc. of Pelvic Surgeons (505)
Soc. of Physics Students (505)
SPSL Soc. for the Philosophy of Sex and Love (495)
SPSSI Soc. for the Psychological Study of Social Issues (495)
SPT Soc. for Philosophy and Technology (492)
SPTCA Swimming Pool Trades and Contractors Ass'n (519)
SPU Soc. for Pediatric Urology (492)
SPWLA Soc. of Professional Well Log Analysts (506)
SQA Soc. of Quality Assurance (506)
Soc. of Quantitative Analysts (506)
SR Soc. of Rheology (506)
SRA Scuba Retailers Ass'n (480)
Soc. for Research on Adolescence (493)
Soc. for Risk Analysis (493)
Soc. of Research Administrators (506)
Station Representatives Ass'n (516)
SRCC Solar Rating and Certification Corp. (510)
SRCD Soc. for Research in Child Development (493)
SRE Soc. of Recreation Executives (506)
SREI Soc. for Reproductive Endocrinologists and Infertility (493)
SRI Spring Research Institute (515)
Steel Recycling Institute (516)
SRM Soc. for Range Management (493)
SRMC Soc. of Risk Management Consultants (507)
SRNT Soc. for Research on Nicotine and Tobacco (493)
SROA Soc. for Radiation Oncology Administrators (493)
SRR Soc. for Reformation Research (493)
SRS Scoliosis Research Soc. (480)
Sleep Research Soc. (483)
Soc. for Reproductive Surgeons (493)
Soc. for Romanian Studies (493)
SRSTA Soc. of Roller Skating Teachers of America (507)
SS Shock Soc. (483)
SSA Seismological Soc. of America (481)
Self Storage Ass'n (481)
Semiconductor Safety Ass'n (481)
Semiotic Soc. of America (481)
Service Specialists Ass'n (482)
Sommelier Soc. of America (510)
Specialty Sleep Ass'n (514)
Suspension Specialists Ass'n (519)
SSAIA Serial Storage Architecture Industry Ass'n (482)
SSAR Soc. for the Study of Amphibians and Reptiles (495)
SSAT Soc. for Surgery of the Alimentary Tract (494)
SSB Soc. of Systematic Biologists (507)
SSCD Soc. of Small Craft Designers (507)
SSCI Steel Service Center Institute (517)
Steel Shipping Container Institute (517)
SSDA-AT Service Station Dealers of America and Allied Trades (482)
SSDC Soc. of Stage Directors and Choreographers (507)
SSDHPER Soc. of State Directors of Health, Physical Education and Recreation (507)
SSE Soc. for the Study of Evolution (495)
SSFI Scaffolding, Shoring and Forming Institute (479)
SSHA Social Science History Ass'n (509)
SSIA Shoe Service Institute of America (483)
SSILA Soc. for the Study of Indigenous Languages of the Americas (495)
SSINA Specialty Steel Industry of North America (514)
SSMA School Science and Mathematics Ass'n (479)
SSMPP Soc. for the Study of Male Psychology and Physiology (496)
SSO Soc. of Surgical Oncology (507)
SSP Soc. for Scholarly Publishing (493)
SSPC SSPC: the Soc. for Protective Coatings (515)
SSPHS Soc. for Spanish and Portuguese Historical Studies (494)
SSPI Soc. of Satellite Professionals Internat'l (507)
SSPMA Sump and Sewage Pump Manufacturers Ass'n (518)
SSPP Soc. for Service Professionals in Printing (493)
SSQ Soc. for Software Quality (494)
SSR Soc. for the Study of Reproduction (496)
SSRC Social Science Research Council (509)
Structural Stability Research Council (517)
SSS Soc. for Slovene Studies (493)
System Safety Soc. (519)
SSSA Soil Science Soc. of America (510)
SSSB Soc. for the Study of Social Biology (496)
SSSP Soc. for the Study of Social Problems (496)
SSSR Soc. for the Scientific Study of Religion (495)
SSSS Soc. for Social Studies of Science (494)
Soc. for the Scientific Study of Sexuality (495)
SSTAR Soc. for Sex Therapy and Research (493)
SSWA Sanitary Supply Wholesalers Ass'n (479)
SSWLHC Soc. for Social Work Leadership in Health Care (494)
ST Soc. for Theriogenology (496)
STA Securities Transfer Ass'n (481)
Security Traders Ass'n (481)
Space Transportation Ass'n (511)
Subcontractors Trade Ass'n (517)
Swimming Teachers of America (519)
STAFDA Specialty Tool and Fastener Distributors Ass'n (514)
STAG Soc. of Travel Agents in Government (508)
STAPPA State and Territorial Air Pollution Program Administrators (515)
STAR Soc. for Technological Advancement of Reporting (494)
STATENETS Radio Nat'l Ass'n of State Radio Networks (376)
STC Smokeless Tobacco Council (484)
Soc. for Technical Communication (494)
Soc. of Telecommunications Consultants (507)
Specialty Tobacco Council (514)
STCA Sports Turf Contractors Ass'n (515)
STFM Soc. of Teachers of Family Medicine (507)
STGAA Shade Tobacco Growers Agricultural Ass'n (482)
STI Steel Tank Institute (517)
Steel Tube Institute of North America (517)
STLA Southern Transportation Logistics Ass'n (510)
STLE Soc. of Tribologists and Lubrication Engineers (508)
STMA Sports Turf Managers Ass'n (515)
STMC Scrap Tire Management Council (480)
STN Soc. of Trauma Nurses (508)
STP Soc. of Toxicologic Pathologists (508)
STR Soc. of Thoracic Radiology (507)
STRIMA State Risk and Insurance Management Ass'n (516)
STS Soc. for Textual Scholarship (494)
Soc. of Thoracic Surgeons (508)
SUA Silver Users Ass'n (483)
Sweetener Users Ass'n (519)
SUC Soc. of Urologic Cryosurgeons (508)
SUNA Soc. of Urologic Nurses and Associates (508)
SUO Soc. of University Otolaryngologists (508)
SUR Soc. for Uroradiology (496)
SUS Soc. of University Surgeons (508)
SUU Soc. of University Urologists (508)
SVC Soc. of Vacuum Coaters (508)
SVHE Soc. for Values in Higher Education (496)
SVIA Specialty Vehicle Institute of America (514)
SVMB Soc. for Vascular Medicine and Biology (496)
SVN Soc. for Vascular Nursing (496)
SVP Soc. of Vertebrate Paleontology (509)
SVS Soc. for Vascular Surgery (496)
SVT Soc. of Vascular Technology (508)
SWAMP Stuntwomen's Ass'n of Motion Pictures (517)
SWANA SWANA - Solid Waste Ass'n of North America (519)
SWANA/GRCDA Solid Waste Ass'n of North America (510)
SWCS Soil and Water Conservation Soc. (510)
SWE Soc. of Women Engineers (509)
SWG Soc. of Woman Geographers (509)
SWI Steel Window Institute (517)
SWP Soc. for Women in Plastics (496)
SWPA Section for Women in Public Administration (481)
Submersible Wastewater Pump Ass'n (518)
SWRI Sealant, Waterproofing and Restoration Institute (480)

National Trade and Professional Associations of the U.S. © 1999, Columbia Books, Inc. 805

SWST Soc. of Wood Science and Technology **(509)**
T2S Technology Transfer Soc. **(521)**
TA Tea Ass'n of the United States of America **(520)**
Tobacco Associates **(523)**
TAA Text and Academic Authors Ass'n **(521)**
Tobacconists' Ass'n of America **(524)**
TAAFLO Trans-Atlantic American Flag Liner Operations **(525)**
TAALS American Ass'n of Language Specialists **(38)**
TAAN Transworld Advertising Agency Network **(526)**
TAB Traffic Audit Bureau for Media Measurement **(525)**
TABS Ass'n of Boarding Schools, The **(145)**
TAC TAC - Internat'l Telework Ass'n **(519)**
TAG Ass'n for the Gifted, The **(139)**
TAG Internat'l **(520)**
TAGA Technical Ass'n of the Graphic Arts **(520)**
TANA Tire Ass'n of North America **(523)**
TAPPI Technical Ass'n of the Pulp and Paper Industry **(520)**
TARA Truck-frame and Axle Repair Ass'n **(527)**
TASDA American Safe Deposit Ass'n **(98)**
TASH Ass'n for Persons with Severe Handicaps, The **(136)**
TASP Ass'n for the Study of Play **(139)**
TAUS Tobacco Ass'n of the U.S. **(523)**
TAWPI Ass'n for Work Process Improvement **(141)**
TBMA Bond Market Ass'n **(181)**
Textile Bag Manufacturers Ass'n **(522)**
TBNA Benchmarking Network Ass'n **(178)**
TBP Tributyl Phosphate Task Force **(526)**
TBPA Textile Bag and Packaging Ass'n **(522)**
TBR Bankers Roundtable, The **(176)**
TC Tea Council of the U.S.A. **(520)**
TCA Information Technology and Telecommunications Ass'n **(264)**
Textile Converters Ass'n **(522)**
Therapeutic Communities of America **(522)**
Thoroughbred Club of America **(522)**
Tile Council of America **(523)**
Tilt-up Concrete Ass'n **(523)**
Truckload Carriers Ass'n **(527)**
TCAA Tile Contractors' Ass'n of America **(523)**
Truck Cap and Accessory Ass'n **(527)**
TCATA Textile Care Allied Trades Ass'n **(522)**
TCI Transportation Clubs Internat'l **(525)**
TCMA Tooling Component Manufacturers Ass'n **(524)**
TCNA Tube Council of North America **(527)**
TCPC Transportation Consumer Protection Council **(525)**
TCU Transportation . Communications Internat'l Union **(525)**
TDA Textile Distributors Ass'n **(522)**
Transportation Development Ass'n **(525)**
TDC Type Directors Club **(528)**
TEA Technical Engineers Ass'n **(520)**
Theatre Education Ass'n **(522)**
TEAM A Equity Asset Managers Ass'n, The **(232)**
TEBA Environmental Business Ass'n, The **(231)**
TECMA Technical Ceramics Manufacturers Ass'n **(520)**
TEGMA Transporting Elevator and Grain Merchants Ass'n **(526)**
TEI Tax Executives Institute **(520)**
TEMA Towing Equipment Manufacturers Ass'n **(524)**
Tubular Exchanger Manufacturers Ass'n **(527)**
TER Tau Epsilon Rho Law Soc. **(520)**
TES Ecotourism Soc. **(225)**
TESOL Teachers of English to Speakers of Other Languages **(520)**
TF Toxicology Forum **(524)**
TFA Fashion Ass'n, The **(235)**
Ferroalloys Ass'n **(238)**
Teaching-Family Ass'n **(520)**
TFBC Timber Frame Business Council **(523)**
TFBPA Textile Fibers and By-Products Ass'n **(522)**
TFGNA Timber Framers Guild of North America **(523)**
TFI Fertilizer Institute **(238)**
THAA Tourist House Ass'n of America **(524)**
THECC Nat'l Dissemination Ass'n **(399)**
THF Healthcare Forum, The **(252)**
Tetrahydrofuran Task Force **(521)**
TI Tobacco Institute **(524)**
Transportation Institute **(525)**
TIA Internat'l Alliance: An Ass'n of Executive and Professional Women, The **(273)**
Telecommunications Industry Ass'n **(521)**
Tennis Industry Ass'n **(521)**
Tortilla Industry Ass'n **(524)**
Transportation Intermediaries Ass'n **(525)**
Travel Industry Ass'n of America **(526)**
TIACA Internat'l Air Cargo Ass'n **(272)**
TILMC Tobacco Industry Labor/Management Committee **(523)**
TISC Tire Industry Safety Council **(523)**
TJC Jockey Club **(314)**
TJG Travel Journalists Guild **(526)**
TKGA Knitting Guild of America **(316)**
TLA Theatre Library Ass'n **(522)**
Transportation Lawyers Ass'n **(525)**
TLBAA Texas Longhorn Breeders Ass'n of America **(521)**
TLMI Tag and Label Manufacturers Institute **(520)**
TLP&SC Transportation Loss Prevention and Security Council **(526)**
TMA Teleprofessional Managers Ass'n **(521)**
Tobacco Merchants Ass'n of the U.S. **(524)**
Toy Manufacturers of America **(524)**
Training Media Ass'n **(525)**
Treasury Management Ass'n **(526)**
Truck Manufacturers Ass'n **(527)**
Turnaround Management Ass'n **(528)**
TMC Maintenance Council of American Trucking Ass'ns **(322)**
MicroStation Community **(328)**
Tune-up Manufacturers Council **(527)**
TMMB Truck Mixer Manufacturers Bureau **(527)**
TMS Masonry Soc. **(324)**
Minerals, Metals and Materials Soc., The **(329)**
TMTFSGCIU Tile, Marble, Terrazzo, Finishers, Shopworkers and Granite Cutters Internat'l Union **(523)**
TNG Newspaper Guild **(439)**
TNNA Nat'l Needlework Ass'n **(418)**
TOA Ombudsman Ass'n, The **(448)**
Track Owners Ass'n **(524)**
TOBA Thoroughbred Owners and Breeders Ass'n **(523)**
TOC Television Operators Caucus **(521)**
TOCA Turf and Ornamental Communicators Ass'n **(527)**
TOS Oceanography Soc. **(447)**
Oxygen Soc., The **(452)**
TPA TPA/The Tube and Pipe Ass'n, Internat'l **(524)**
Travel Professionals Ass'n **(526)**
TPC Transaction Processing Performance Council **(525)**
TPEA Texas Produce Export Ass'n **(521)**
TPI Truss Plate Institute **(527)**
Turfgrass Producers Internat'l **(527)**
TPM Timber Products Manufacturers **(523)**
TPSA Textile Producers and Suppliers Ass'n **(522)**
TPSTHCP&TEIU Textile Processors, Service Trades, Health Care, Professional and Technical Employees Internat'l Union **(522)**
TQCA Textile Quality Control Ass'n **(522)**
TRA Telecommunications Resellers Ass'n **(521)**
Thoroughbred Racing Ass'ns of North America **(523)**
Tire and Rim Ass'n **(523)**
TRAA Towing and Recovery Ass'n of America **(524)**
TRAIN Tourist Railway Ass'n **(524)**
TRALA Truck Renting and Leasing Ass'n **(527)**
TRF Transportation Research Forum **(526)**
TRI Refractories Institute **(473)**
TRIB Tire Retread Information Bureau **(523)**
TriBeta Beta Beta Beta **(178)**
TRMG Tread Rubber and Tire Repair Materials Manufacturers Group **(526)**
TRMI Tubular Rivet and Machine Institute **(527)**
TROA Retired Officers Ass'n, The **(476)**
TRS Tree-Ring Soc. **(526)**
TRSA Textile Rental Services Ass'n of America **(522)**
TS Trademark Soc. **(525)**
Transplantation Soc. (Western Hemishpere) **(525)**
TSA Salon Ass'n, The **(478)**
Tamworth Swine Ass'n **(520)**
Technology Student Ass'n **(521)**
Turkish Studies Ass'n **(528)**
TSDA Service Dealers Ass'n **(482)**
TSEA Trade Show Exhibitors Ass'n **(524)**
TSEI Transportation Safety Equipment Institute **(526)**
TSI Sulphur Institute, The **(518)**
TSSA Tackle and Shooting Sports Agents Ass'n **(520)**
TTA Travel Technology Ass'n **(526)**
TTMA Truck Trailer Manufacturers Ass'n **(527)**
TTRA Travel and Tourism Research Ass'n **(526)**
TVB Television Bureau of Advertising **(521)**
TWHBEA Tennessee Walking Horse Breeders and Exhibitors Ass'n **(521)**
TWNA Truck Writers of North America **(527)**
TWS Wildlife Soc., The **(544)**
TWU Transport Workers Union of America **(525)**
TYAA Textured Yarn Ass'n of America **(522)**
U/RTA University/Resident Theatre Ass'n **(537)**
UA United Ass'n of Journeymen and Apprentices of the Plumbing and Pipe Fitting Industry of U.S. and Canada **(530)**
UAA University Aviation Ass'n **(537)**
Urban Affairs Ass'n **(537)**
Utility Arborist Ass'n **(538)**
UAEL United Ass'n of Equipment Leasing **(530)**
UAHC Union of American Hebrew Congregations **(529)**
UAPD Union of American Physicians and Dentists **(529)**
UAREP Universities Associated for Research and Education in Pathology **(536)**
UAUOS United Ass'n of Used Oil Services **(530)**
UAW Internat'l Union, United Automobile, Aerospace and Agricultural Implement Workers of America **(310)**
UBB United Braford Breeders **(530)**
UBC United Brotherhood of Carpenters and Joiners of America **(530)**
UBDMA United Better Dress Manufacturers Ass'n **(530)**
UBPVLS Uniform Boiler and Pressure Vessel Laws Soc. **(529)**
UCDA University and College Designers Ass'n **(537)**
UCEA University Continuing Education Ass'n **(537)**
University Council for Educational Administration **(537)**
UCI Utility Communicators Internat'l **(538)**
UCLEA University and College Labor Education Ass'n **(537)**
UCOWR Universities Council on Water Resources **(536)**
UDC United Developers Council **(530)**
UDSR United Duroc Swine Registry **(530)**
UE United Electrical, Radio and Machine Workers of America **(530)**
UEA United Egg Ass'n **(530)**
UEP United Egg Producers **(530)**
UET United Engineering Trustees **(530)**
UFA Unfinished Furniture Ass'n **(529)**
UFAC Upholstered Furniture Action Council **(537)**
UFCW United Food and Commercial Workers Internat'l Union **(530)**
UFESA United Fire Equipment Service Ass'n **(530)**
UFFVA United Fresh Fruit and Vegetable Ass'n **(531)**
UFP United Federation of Police Officers **(530)**
UFVA University Film and Video Ass'n **(537)**
UFW United Farm Workers of America **(530)**
UHMS Undersea and Hyperbaric Medical Soc. **(529)**
UIA Ultrasonic Industry Ass'n **(529)**
UICWA United Infants and Childrens Wear Ass'n **(531)**
UKML United Knitwear Manufacturers League **(531)**
ULC Urban Libraries Council **(538)**
ULI Urban Land Institute **(537)**
ULPA United Lightning Protection Ass'n **(531)**
UMA United Methodist Ass'n of Health and Welfare Ministries **(531)**
United Motorcoach Ass'n **(531)**
UMWA United Mine Workers of America Internat'l Union **(531)**
UNDA-USA UNDA-USA, Nat'l Catholic Ass'n for Broadcasters/Communicators **(529)**
UNIFORUM UniForum Ass'n **(529)**
UNITE Union of Needletrades, Industrial and Textile Employees **(530)**
UNSU United Nations Staff Union **(531)**
UOA United Ostomy Ass'n **(531)**
UOMA Used Oil Management Ass'n **(538)**
UPA Usability Professionals Ass'n **(538)**
UPAA University Photographers Ass'n of America **(537)**
UPFD United Product Formulators and Distributors Ass'n **(531)**
UPHA United Professional Horsemen's Ass'n **(531)**
UPIU United Paperworkers Internat'l Union **(531)**
URA Universities Research Ass'n **(536)**
URISA Urban and Regional Information Systems Ass'n **(537)**
URMIA University Risk Management and Insurance Ass'n **(537)**
URPE Union for Radical Political Economics **(529)**
US Soccer United States Soccer Federation **(535)**
US-RBC U.S.-Russia Business Council **(528)**
USA United Scenic Artists **(531)**
USA-ITA United States Ass'n of Importers of Textiles and Apparel **(532)**
USA-ROC U.S.-ROC (Taiwan) Business Council **(528)**
USA-TLA U.S.A. Toy Library Ass'n **(529)**
USAA U.S. Apple Ass'n **(528)**
USABC U.S.-ASEAN Business Council **(528)**
USACA United States Advanced Ceramics Ass'n **(531)**
USACM United States Ass'n for Computational Mechanics **(532)**
USADPLC U.S.A. Dry Pea and Lentil Council **(528)**
USAEC United States Apple Export Council **(532)**
USAEE United States Ass'n for Energy Economics **(532)**
USAHA United States Animal Health Ass'n **(532)**
USAIGC United States Ass'n of Independent Gymnastic Clubs **(532)**
USAPEEC U.S.A. Poultry and Egg Export Council **(528)**
USATA United States Air Tour Ass'n **(532)**
USAWOA United States Army Warrant Officers Ass'n **(532)**
USB United Soybean Board **(531)**
USBBC United States Beef Breeds Council **(532)**
USBIA United States Bowling Instructors Ass'n **(532)**
USBIC United States Business and Industry Council **(532)**
USBSA United States Beet Sugar Ass'n **(532)**
USBWA United States Basketball Writers Ass'n **(532)**
USCA United States Canola Ass'n **(532)**
USCAP United States and Canadian Academy of Pathology **(532)**
USCBC United States-China Business Council **(536)**
United States-Cuba Business Council **(536)**
USCCCA United States Cross Country Coaches Ass'n **(533)**
USCCHSO United States Conference of City Human Services Officials **(533)**
USCIB United States Council for Internat'l Business **(533)**
USCID United States Committee on Irrigation and Drainage **(532)**
USCJ United Synagogue of Conservative Judaism **(536)**
USCM United States Conference of Mayors **(533)**
USCOLD United States Committee on Large Dams **(533)**
USCRA United States Court Reporters Ass'n **(533)**
USCSRA United States Cane Sugar Refiners' Ass'n **(532)**
USCTI United States Cutting Tool Institute **(533)**
USDGA United States Durum Growers Ass'n **(533)**
USEA United States Energy Ass'n **(533)**
USEM United States Egg Marketers **(533)**
USFCA United States Fencing Coaches Ass'n **(533)**
USFCC United States Federation for Culture Collections **(533)**
USFSS United States Federation of Scholars and Scientists **(533)**
USGA United States Golf Ass'n **(534)**
USGC U.S. Grains Council **(528)**
USHCC United States Hispanic Chamber of Commerce **(534)**
USHSLA United States Hide, Skin and Leather Ass'n **(534)**
USHWA United States Harness Writers' Ass'n **(534)**
USJCC United States Junior Chamber of Commerce **(534)**

806 National Trade and Professional Associations of the U.S. © 1999, Columbia Books, Inc.

Association Management Firms Index

Listed here are over 400 firms providing administrative and management services to associations on a contract basis. In addition to contact information and the names and titles of firm principals, a list of clients managed on a full-time basis by the firm is included, when available.

ABLE MANAGEMENT SOLUTIONS, INC.

5310 E. Main St., Suite 104
Columbus, OH 43213-2598
Tel: (614)868-1144 *Fax:* (614)868-1177

Sammi Soutar, *President*

Central Ohio Retail Grocers
Ohio Bed and Breakfast Ass'n

ACCENT ON MANAGEMENT

173. High St., Suite 200
Columbus, OH 43215-3458
Tel: (614)221-1900 *Fax:* (614)221-1989

David W. Field, *President*

AIA Ohio
Chartered Life Underwriters and Financial Consultants - Columbus Chapter
Nat'l Ass'n of Industrial and Office Parks - Central Ohio Chapter
Ohio Ass'n of Civil Trial Attorneys
Ohio Ass'n of Life Underwriters
Ohio Ass'n of Rehabilitation Facilities
Ohio Ass'n of Textile Services
Ohio Auctioneers Ass'n
Ohio Cleaners Ass'n
Ohio Concrete Masonry Ass'n
Ohio Government Finance Officers Ass'n
Ohio Petroleum Retailers and Repair Ass'n
Ohio Propane Gas Ass'n
Ohio School Food Service Ass'n
Ohio State Ass'n of Nurse Anesthetists

ACCESS GROUP, INC.

35 E. Wacker Dr., Suite 500
Chicago, IL 60601-2102
Tel: (312)782-5252 *Fax:* (312)236-1140

Ralph J. Bloch, *President*

Ass'n of Coupon Professionals
Awards and Recognition Ass'n
Comprehensive Information Management for Schools User Support Ass'n (CIMS-USA)
Nat'l Ass'n of Residential Property Managers
Unfinished Furniture Ass'n

ACCURATE IMAGE MARKETING

212 S. Henry St.
Alexandria, VA 22314-3522
Tel: (703)549-9500 *Fax:* (703)549-9074

Walter E. Galanty Jr., *President*

Fore Others Foundation
Minority Golf Ass'n of America
Nat'l Ass'n Tournament for Suppliers
The Golfe

ADLER DROZ, INC.

1550 S. Coast Hwy., Suite 201
Laguna Beach, CA 92651
Tel: (714)497-9007 *Fax:* (714)376-3456

Fred Droz, *President*

Ass'n of Freestanding Radiation Oncology Centers
Neurodevelopmental Treatment Ass'n
Radiology Business Management Ass'n
Substance Abuse Program Administrators Ass'n
Wound Healing Soc.

Wound, Ostomy and Continence Nurses Soc.
Wound, Ostomy, and Continence Nurses Soc. Certification Board

ADMINISTRATIVE MANAGEMENT SERVICES, INC.

28790 Chagrin Blvd., Suite 350
Cleveland, OH 44122-4630
Tel: (216)464-2137 *Fax:* (216)464-0397

David L. Williams, *President*

Conference of Business Economists
Internat'l Ass'n for Energy Economics
Quarter Midgets of America
United States Ass'n for Energy Economics

ADMINISTRATIVE OFFICE

2545 Ridgeway Drive, Suite B
National City, CA 91950-7733
Tel: (619)267-2236 *Fax:* (619)472-5857

Charles A. Pratt CAE, *President*

San Diego Dry Cleaners Ass'n
San Diego Soc. of Ass'n Executives

ADMINISTRATIVE SYSTEMS, INC.

414 Plaza Drive, Suite 209
Westmont, IL 60559-9000
Tel: (630)655-0112 *Fax:* (630)655-0391

Judith K. Keel, *Owner and President*

Angelman Syndrome Foundation
Ass'n of Philanthropic Counsel
Ass'n of Professional Researchers for Advancement
Ass'n of Professional Researchers for Advancement Foundation
Ass'n of Women Surgeons
Ass'n of Women Surgeons Foundation
Chicago Council on Planned Giving
Internat'l Ass'n of Ass'n Management Companies
Nat'l Soc. of Fund Raising Executives - Chicago Chapter

THE ADMINISTRATORS, INC.

867 Sussex Blvd.
Broomall, PA 19008-0080

Stephen Markowitz, *President and Chief Exec. Officer*
Della Harris-Smith, *V. President*
Dnne Gualtieri, *Director, Financial Systems*

Business New York Ass'n
Continuing Education and Travel Soc.
Marple-Newtown Div./SBADU

ADVANCED MANAGEMENT CONCEPTS

136 S. Keowee St.
Dayton, OH 45402
Tel: (937)222-1024 *Fax:* (937)222-5794

Daniel Lea, *C.E.O.*
Kimberly A. Fantaci, *V. President*

Ass'n for Accounting Administration
Cellulose Insulation Manufacturers Ass'n
Central States Insulation and Abatement Contractors Ass'n
Inflatable Advertising Dealers Ass'n
Materials Marketing Associates
Miami Valley NARI
Nat'l Associated CPA Firms
Nat'l Independent Flag Dealers Ass'n
Ohio Valley NARI

Strategic Leadership Forum - Dayton Chapter

ADVANCEMENT PLANNING GROUP

1156 Dublin Road, Suite 105
Columbus, OH 43215
Tel: (614)486-3923 *Fax:* (614)486-5845

Margaret H. Vild, *President*

Columbus Academy of Osteopathic Medicine
Columbus Osteopathic Foundation
Ohio Campground Owners Ass'n

AGRI WASHINGTON

1629 K St., N.W., Suite 1100
Washington, DC 20006
Tel: (202)785-6710 *Fax:* (202)331-4212

Paul S. Weller Jr., *President*

American Ass'n of Grain Inspection and Weighing Agencies
Apple Processors Ass'n
Canadian-American Business Council
Maryland Dairy Industry Ass'n
Washington Caucus

ALAMPI & ASSOCIATES MANAGEMENT CORP.

66 Morris Ave., #2-A
Springfield, NJ 07081-1450
Tel: (201)379-1100 *Fax:* (201)379-6507

Richard Alampi, *President*

Atlantic Coast Veterinary Foundation
Converting Equipment Manufacturers Ass'n
Golf Course Superintendents Ass'n of New Jersey
Inland Marine Underwriters Ass'n
Irrigation Ass'n of New Jersey
Metropolitan New York Paint and Coatings Ass'n
New Jersey Health Underwriters Ass'n
New Jersey Lumber Dealers Ass'n
New Jersey Veterinary Foundation
New Jersey Veterinary Medical Ass'n
New York Soc. for Coatings Technology
Sales Ass'n of the Chemical Industry

ALEXANDER AND ASSOCIATES

780 Riverside Drive., Suite 9-A
New York, NY 10032-7418
Tel: (212)234-4470 *Fax:* (212)964-1557

Steven M. Wolfe CAE, *Managing Partner*

Space Frontier Soc. of New York

THE ALEXANDRIA GROUP

526 King St., Suite 423
Alexandria, VA 22314-3143
Tel: (703)706-9580 *Fax:* (703)706-9583

Mary Jane Kolar CAE, *Principal*
M. Lynn Mitchel, *Principal*

American Water Works Ass'n - Chesapeake Section
Nat'l Ass'n of Government Communicators
Nat'l Ass'n of Government Communicators Foundation
Nat'l Cargo Research and Education Foundation
Nat'l Cargo Security Council

PETER ALLEN, INC.

66 Morris Ave., Suite 1-A
Springfield, NJ 07081
Tel: (201)564-5859 *Fax:* (201)564-7480

Peter Allen CAE, *President*

Nat'l Council of Acoustical Consultants

ALTERNATIVE MANAGEMENT

3068 E. Sunset Rd., Suite 5
Las Vegas, NV 89120
Tel: (702)798-5156   *Fax:* (702)798-8653

Katrina Ekedahl, *Owner*

American Consultng Engineers Council of Nevada
Nat'l Ass'n of Industrial and Office Properties - Southern
    Nevada Chapter
Nevada Apartment Ass'n
Nevada Ass'n of Land Surveyors
Nevada Professional Facility Managers Ass'n
Soc. for Marketing Professional Services-Las Vegas Chapter
Southern Nevada CCIM Chapter
Western Pension and Benefits Conference-Las Vegas Chapter

AMERICAN HEALTHCARE CONSULTANTS

1472 Kennedy Causeway, Suite 109
North Bay Village, FL 33141
Tel: (305)864-0021   *Fax:* (305)868-0905

Mike Freedman, *Exec. Officer*

American Academy of Wound Management
American Subacute Care Ass'n

AMERICAN TRADE AND PROFESSIONAL ASSOCIATION MANAGEMENT

P.O. Box 59811
Potomac, MD 20859-9811
Tel: (301)365-2521   *Fax:* (301)365-7705

Russell E. Barker, *President*

American Academy of Insurance Medicine
Peanut and Tree Nut Processors Ass'n

AMS PROFESSIONAL SERVICES

1250 Long Beach Ave., Suite 328
Los Angeles, CA 90021
Tel: (213)624-2225   *Fax:* (213)624-2229

Lorraine P. Auerbach, *President and C.E.O.*
Carole A. Lambert CAE, *V.P., Professional Services*

California Ass'n of Health Plans
California Nursing Students Ass'n
Case Management Soc. of America - Southern California
    Chapter

ANDERSON MANAGEMENT SERVICES, INC.

1111 Lincoln Mall, Suite 308
Lincoln, NE 68508-2882
Tel: (402)476-1528   *Fax:* (402)476-1259

Robert L. Anderson, *President*

American Soc. of Interior Designers - Nebraska/Iowa Chapter
Automotive Recycling Industry of Nebraska
Nebraska Fertilizer and Ag-Chemical Institute
Nebraska Hotel and Motel Ass'n
Nebraska State Pest Control Ass'n

APPLIED MEASUREMENT PROFESSIONALS (AMP)

8310 Nieman Road
Lenexa, KS 66214-1598
Tel: (913)541-0400   *Fax:* (913)541-0156

Steven K. Bryant MBA, *President*
William D. Hogan, *V.P., Marketing & Business Products*
Deidre Gish Panjada MBA, *Dir., Management Services*
Janelle R. Williams, *Mgr., Operations*
Cheri D. Jones, *Mgr., Meeting Services*

Academy of Breastfeeding Medicine
American Board of Histocompatability and Immunogenetics
American Board of Transplant Coordinators
American Soc. for Histocompatability and Immunogenetics
Ass'n of Genetic Technologists
Ass'n of Polysomnographic Technologists
Board for Orthotist Certification
Board of Nephrology Examiners Nursing and Technology
Board of Registered Polysomnographic Technologists
Nat'l Ass'n of EMS Physicians
Nat'l Board for Certification of Registrars
Nat'l Cancer Registrar's Ass'n
Nat'l Certification Agency for Medical Laboratory Personnel
North American Transplant Coordinators Organization
Oak Park Homes Ass'n
Transportation Lawyers Ass'n

APT, INC.

P.O. Box 2264
2900 E. Broadway
Bismarck, ND 58502-2264
Tel: (701)224-1815   *Fax:* (701)224-9824

Thomas C. Tupa, *President*

Ass'n of Former Public Employees
Bismarck/Mandan Apartment Ass'n
Independent North Dakota State Employees Ass'n
North Dakota Apartment Ass'n
North Dakota Ass'n of Home Care
North Dakota Ass'n of Life Underwriters
North Dakota Board of Social Work Examiners

North Dakota Retired Teachers Ass'n

the ARDEL group

13355 Tenth Ave. North, Suite 108
Minneapolis, MN 55441-5510
Tel: (612)545-1919   *Fax:* (612)545-0335

Rosealee M. Lee CICM, CEP, *President*
Judith Bourdeau, *V. President*

Academy of Surgical Research
Soc. for Biomaterials
Surfaces in Biomaterials Foundation

ARDMORE MANAGEMENT GROUP

2500 E. Main St., Suite 100
Columbus, OH 43209-2483
Tel: (614)235-5001   *Fax:* (614)235-0880

Daniel H. Dozer CAE, *President*

ASSOCIATED MANAGEMENT SERVICES

444 East Algonquin Ave.
Arlington Heights, IL 60005-4654
Tel: (847)228-8375   *Fax:* (847)228-6509

Laura M. Downes CAE, *Dir., Management Services*

American Ass'n for Hand Surgery
American Soc. for Reconstructive Microsurgery
American Soc. of Maxillofacial Surgeons
Ass'n of Academic Chairmen of Plastic Surgery
Ass'n of Plastic Surgery Assistants
Microcirculatory Soc. of America
Plastic Surgery Admininstrative Ass'n

ASSOCIATED SERVICES

P.O. Box 1184
Irmo, SC 29063
Tel: (803)772-5354   *Fax:* (803)798-0670

Kelly Smith, *Exec. Director*

Independent Banks of South Carolina
Mining Ass'n of South Carolina
South Carolina Ass'n of Special Purpose Districts
South Carolina Dairy Ass'n

ASSOCIATES SAFETY MANAGEMENT

145 W. 45th St., Suite 800
New York, NY 10036
Tel: (212)398-5700   *Fax:* (212)398-7818

Sheldon M. Edelman, *Executive Director*

Belt Ass'n
Plastic and Metal Products Manufacturers Ass'n
Plastic Soft Materials Manufacturers Ass'n
Pleaters, Stitchers and Embroiderers Ass'n

ASSOCIATION ADMINISTRATIVE MANAGEMENT SERVICES, INC.

P.O. Box 140046
Austin, TX 78714-0046
Tel: (512)452-4571   *Fax:* (512)452-5255

Chilton Roberts, *President and C.E.O.*
Cheryl Wiles, *Exec. V. President*

Austin Ass'n of Remodeling Contractors
Council of State Ass'n Presidents
Soc. of Infectious Diseases Pharmacists
Southwest Paper and Sanitary Supply Ass'n
Texas Ass'n of Acupuncturists
Texas Ass'n of Pawnbrokers
Texas Concrete Pipe Ass'n
Texas Rural Health Ass'n
Texas Soc. of Health-System Pharmacists

THE ASSOCIATION ADVANTAGE

P.O. Box 81362
Wellesley, MA 02481-0004
Tel: (781)239-3262   *Fax:* (781)239-3259

Sherri L. Oken CAE, *Principal*

American Academy of Anesthesiologist Assistants
Connecticut Academy of Physicians Assistants
Internat'l Facility Management Ass'n - Boston Area Chapter

ASSOCIATION AND GOVERNMENT RELATIONS MANAGEMENT

4900-B South 31st St.
Arlington, VA 22206
Tel: (703)820-7400   *Fax:* (703)931-4520

Thomas Fise, *President*
Ernest Bomar, *V. President*

American College of Gastroenterology
Ass'n of Program Directors in Surgery
Soc. of Head and Neck Surgeons
Southeastern Soc. of Plastic and Reconstructive Surgeons

ASSOCIATION AND SOCIETY MANAGEMENT

9 Escalle Lane
Larkspur, CA 94939-1217
Tel: (415)924-7441   *Fax:* (415)974-7463

Robert M. Crum CAE, *President*

Mining and Metallurgical Soc. of America

ASSOCIATION AND SOCIETY MANAGEMENT INTERNATIONAL, INC.

111 Park Place
Falls Church, VA 22046-4513
Tel: (703)533-0251   *Fax:* (703)241-5603

Harry W. Buzzerd Jr., CAE, *President*
Elizabeth B. Armstrong CAE, *V. President*

American Paper Machinery Ass'n
American Pipe Fittings Ass'n
American Textile Machinery Ass'n
Capital Equipment Export Council
Internat'l Ass'n of Emergency Managers
Internat'l Facility Management Ass'n
Limousine Industry Manufacturers Organization
Meat Industry Suppliers Ass'n
Nat'l Ass'n of State Emergency Medical Services Directors
North American Natural Casing Ass'n
Process Equipment Manufacturers' Ass'n
Product Liability Prevention and Defense Group
Sewn Products Equipment Suppliers Ass'n
Wire Industry Suppliers Ass'n

ASSOCIATION AND SOCIETY MANAGEMENT, INC.

1033 La Posada Drive, Suite 220
Austin, TX 78752-3880
Tel: (512)454-8626   *Fax:* (512)454-3036

Don R. McCullough CAE, *President*

Career Colleges and Schools of Texas
Dental Laboratory Ass'n of Texas
Licensed Vocational Nurses Ass'n of Texas
Mechanical Contractors Ass'n of Texas
Nat'l Ass'n of Professional Organizers
Texas Affiliation of Affordable Housing Providers
Texas Ass'n for Marriage and Family Therapy
Texas Ass'n of Addiction Professionals
Texas Ass'n of Agricultural Consultants
Texas Ass'n of Health Underwriters
Texas Ass'n of Mortgage Brokers
Texas Ass'n of Nurse Anesthetists
Texas Ass'n of Property Tax Professionals
Texas Ass'n of Storage Tank Professionals
Texas Auctioneers Ass'n
Texas Corrections Ass'n
Texas Cowboy Alumni Ass'n
Texas Dietetic Ass'n
Texas Independent Insurance Adjusters Ass'n
Texas Professional Benefit Administrators Ass'n
Texas Soc. for Medical Staff Services

THE ASSOCIATION COMPANY

P.O. Box 644
Millersville, MD 21108
Tel: (410)987-4847   *Fax:* (410)987-5442

John C. Vickerman CMP, *President*

Ass'n of Business Products Manufacturers
Book Components Manufacturers Ass'n
Neurofibromatosis, Inc.

ASSOCIATION DEVELOPMENT GROUP, INC.

1767 Business Center Dr., Suite 302
Reston, VA 20190-5332
Tel: (703)438-3101   *Fax:* (703)438-3113

Denny R. Harris, *President*

Institute of Real Estate Management - Chapter Eight
Silicones Environmental Health and Safety Council of North
    America
Small Office/Home Office Ass'n
Soc. of Toxicology
Teratology Soc.
Toxicology Education Foundation

ASSOCIATION EXCHANGE

P.O. Box 1519
Winter Haven, FL 33882-1519
Tel: (941)293-5710   *Fax:* (941)299-5154

David Boozer, *President*

Florida Aquaculture Ass'n
Florida Ground Water Ass'n
Florida Tropical Fish Farms Ass'n

ASSOCIATION EXECUTIVE SERVICES

22 Cartright St.
Wellesley, MA 02482
Tel: (781)235-2900   *Fax:* (781)237-8745

Judith Weil, *President*

Northeast Human Resources Ass'n

ASSOCIATION EXECUTIVES, LLC

6610 Hwy. 100, #203
P.O. Box 50452
Nashville, TN 37205
Tel: (615)353-9200   *Fax:* (615)353-9499

Elliott McNiel, *Exec. Officer*

ASSOCIATION EXPOSITIONS & SERVICES

383 Main Avenue
Norwalk, CT 06852-6059
Tel: (203)840-5404   *Fax:* (203)840-9404

Margaret Pederson, *Senior V. President*

ASSOCIATION HEADQUARTERS OF CALIFORNIA

One Capitol Mall, Suite 320
Sacramento, CA 95814
Tel: (916)658-0250   *Fax:* (916)658-0252

Skip Daum, *President*

California Ambulatory Surgery Ass'n
California Aviation Business Ass'n
California Recreation Vehicle Dealers Ass'n
Community Ass'ns Institute/California Legislative Action
    Committee
Construction Industry Legislative Council

ASSOCIATION HEADQUARTERS, INC.

236 Rte. 38 West, Suite 100
Moorestown, NJ 08057-3276
Tel: (609)231-8500   *Fax:* (609)231-4664

1919 Pennsylvania Ave., N.W., Suite 800
Washington, DC 20006
Tel: (202)887-1434   *Fax:* (202)466-2198

William L. MacMillan CAE, *President*
William Waller, *Exec. V. President*
Bruce McLellan, *V. President*

Childrenswear Marketing Ass'n
Juvenile Products Manufacturers Ass'n
Nat'l Ass'n of Chewing Gum Manufacturers
Nat'l Ornament and Electric Lights Christmas Ass'n
Nat'l Tax Lien Ass'n
Office Products Dealers Alliance
Receptive Services Ass'n
Specialty Sleep Ass'n
Sports Card Ass'n
Writing Instrument Manufacturers Ass'n

ASSOCIATION ISSUES AND MANAGEMENT

2111 Wilson Blvd., Suite 700
Arlington, VA 22201
Tel: (703)875-8650   *Fax:* (703)351-9750

980 Ninth St., 16th Floor
Sacramento, CA 95814

Marshall Cohen, *President*

Aseptic Packaging Council

ASSOCIATION MANAGEMENT & LEGISLATIVE SERVICES

P.O. Box 6296
Harrisburg, PA 17112
Tel: (717)545-2755

John J. Burton, *President*

Pennsylvania State Brewers Ass'n

ASSOCIATION MANAGEMENT AND CONSULTING RESOURCES

200 Wheeler Road, Suite 700
Burlington, MA 01803-5500
Tel: (617)272-7737   *Fax:* (617)272-5447

William E. Boutwell, *President*

Connecticut Car Wash Ass'n
Massachusetts Auto Body Ass'n
Massachusetts Independent Auto Dealers Ass'n
New England Car Wash Ass'n
New England Independent Auto Dealers Ass'n
New England Promotional Products Ass'n
Northeast Regional Car Wash Convention

ASSOCIATION MANAGEMENT BUREAU

1650 Tysons Blvd., Suite 200
McLean, VA 22102-3915
Tel: (703)506-3260   *Fax:* (703)506-3266

Thomas C. Gibson, *President*
Laura D. Skoff, *V.P., Client Operations*

American Women in Radio and Television
Emergency Department Practice Management Ass'n
Foundation of American Women in Radio and Television
Nat'l Ass'n of Telecommunications Officers and Advisers
Soc. of Nat'l Ass'n Publications
Women Inc.

ASSOCIATION MANAGEMENT CENTER

4700 W. Lake Ave.
Glenview, IL 60025-1485
Tel: (847)375-4700   *Fax:* (847)375-4777

900 2nd St., N.E., Suite 109
Washington, DC 20002
Tel: (202)289-4703   *Fax:* (202)898-0188

Mark T. Engle, *V. President*
Diana Waterman, *Principal, Washington Office*

American Academy of Pain Medicine
American Ass'n of Legal Nurse Consultants

American Board of Pain Medicine
American Board of Vocational Experts
American Congress of Rehabilitation Medicine
American Pain Soc.
American Soc. for Bioethics and Humanities
American Soc. of Pediatric Hematology/Oncology
Ass'n of Pediatric Oncology Nurses
Ass'n of Rehabilitation Nurses
Certification Board for Infection Control and Epidemiology
Certification Corporation of Pediatric Oncology Nurses
Chicago Advertising Federation
Freestanding Insert Council of North America
Healthcare Quality Educational Foundation
Midwest Nursing Research Soc.
Nat'l Ass'n for Healthcare Quality
Nat'l Ass'n of Clinical Nurse Specialists
Nat'l Ass'n of Fleet Resale Dealers
Rehabilitation Nursing Certification Board
Rehabilitation Nursing Foundation
Soc. for Health and Human Values
Soc. of Automotive Analysts

ASSOCIATION MANAGEMENT GROUP INTERNATIONAL, INC.

355 Lexington Ave., 17th Floor
New York, NY 10017-6603
Tel: (212)661-4261   *Fax:* (212)370-9047

4041 Powder Mill Road, Suite 404
Calverton, MD 20705-3106
Tel: (301)328-2001   *Fax:* (301)348-2020

Peter Rush, *C.E.O.*
Holly Munter Koenig, *V. President*
Russell Snyder, *V. President*

Asphalt Roofing Manufacturers Ass'n
Builders Hardware Manufacturers Ass'n
Certified Ballast Manufacturers Ass'n
Comics Magazine Ass'n of America
Cool Roof Ratings Council
Film and Bag Federation
Home Fashion Products Ass'n
Internat'l Interior Design Ass'n - New York Chapter
Nat'l Ass'n of Legal Search Consultants
Nat'l Coalition of Petroleum Dry Cleaners
Nat'l Independent Textiles Retailers Organization
Nat'l Tabletop and Giftware Ass'n
New York Women in Communications
Roof Coatings Manufacturers Ass'n
Window Covering Safety Council
Window Coverings Manufacturers Ass'n

ASSOCIATION MANAGEMENT GROUP, INC.

8201 Greensboro Drive, Suite 300
McLean, VA 22102
Tel: (703)610-9000   *Fax:* (703)610-9005

Charles D. Rumbarger CAE, *President*
J. Bruce Wardle, *Exec. V. President*

American Academy of Audiology
Ass'n of Hispanic Advertising Agencies
Ass'n of Water Technologies
Consulting Engineers Council of Metropolitan Washington
Internat'l Cast Polymer Ass'n
Nat'l Ass'n of Dental Laboratories
Nat'l Ass'n of Independent Life Brokerage Agencies
Nat'l Ass'n of Mortgage Brokers
Nat'l Board Certification for Dental Technicians
Nat'l Certification Board for Therapeutic Massage &
    Bodywork
Nat'l Hispanic Corporate Council
Nat'l Hispanic Corporate Council
North American Technician Excellence
Smart Card Forum

ASSOCIATION MANAGEMENT NETWORK, INC.

740 Florida Central Pkwy., Suite 1020
Longwood, FL 32750
Tel: (407)834-6688   *Fax:* (407)834-4747

Jone R. Sienkiewicz CAE, CMP, *President/C.E.O.*

Ass'n for Volunteer Administration
Ass'n of Insurance Compliance Professionals
Employee Involvement Ass'n
Heavy Construction Contractors Ass'n
Real Estate Educators Ass'n
Sidney R. Johnston Memorial Trust

ASSOCIATION MANAGEMENT PLUS

P.O. Box 6322
Helena, MT 59604
Tel: (406)442-5490   *Fax:* (406)442-8018

Stuart H. Doggett, *Owner*

Montana Inn-Keepers
Montana Land Title Ass'n
Montana Manufactured Housing and Recreational Vehicle
    Ass'n
Montana Veterinary Medical Ass'n

ASSOCIATION MANAGEMENT RESOURCES

3300 Washtenaw Ave., Suite 225
Ann Arbor, MI 48104
Tel: (313)973-7100

Richard A. Correll, *President*

Andover Working Group
CHIME Foundation

College of Healthcare Information Management Executives
Health Level Seven
Michigan Ass'n of Professional Court Reporters
Michigan Occupational Therapy Ass'n
Michigan School Food Service Ass'n
Microsoft Healthcare Users Group
Nat'l Ass'n of Industrial Technology
Professional Speakers Ass'n of Michigan

ASSOCIATION MANAGEMENT RESOURCES INTERNATIONAL

121 Cayuga St.
Seneca Falls, NY 13148-1117
Tel: (315)568-0082

Edward D. Shanken CAE, *President*

Ass'n of Ghana Industries
Federation of Ass'ns of Ghanaian Exporters
Ghana Soc. of Ass'n Executives
Internat'l Center for Professional Development
Internat'l Executive Service Corps
One Source Publishing
Philanthropic Development Group
Seneca Valley Chamber of Commerce
USAID

ASSOCIATION MANAGEMENT RESOURCES, INC.

167 W. Main St., Suite 600
Lexington, KY 40507-1324
Tel: (606)231-1875   *Fax:* (606)231-1928

John A. Ruffin, *President*

Chief Officers of State Library Agencies
Nat'l Ass'n for Government Training and Development
Nat'l Ass'n of Government Deferred Compensation
    Administrators
Nat'l Ass'n of State Directors of Administration and General
    Services
Nat'l Ass'n of State Information Resource Executives
Nat'l Ass'n of State Purchasing Officials

ASSOCIATION MANAGEMENT SERVICES

4500 Shannon Lakes Plaza, Suite 108
Tallahassee, FL 32308
Tel: (850)906-9314   *Fax:* (850)906-9315

Bennett W. Napier, *President*

Florida Life Care Residents Ass'n
Florida Rental Ass'n

ASSOCIATION MANAGEMENT SERVICES

116 Main St.
P.O. Box 738
Medway, MA 02053
Tel: (508)533-1444   *Fax:* (508)533-4180

Bradley L. Sell, *Principal*

Credit Research, Inc.
JCA of New York
New England Wholesalers Ass'n
New York State Plumbing and Heating Wholesalers
Plumbing and Heating Wholesalers Employers Ass'n
Plumbing and Heating Wholesalers Group Insurance Trust
Unity of Boston

ASSOCIATION MANAGEMENT SERVICES

323 Geary St., Suite 319
San Francisco, CA 94102
Tel: (415)398-7848   *Fax:* (415)398-7983

Blanche Berger, *President*

American Soc. of Travel Agents - Northern California Chapter
Foreign Travel Club of San Francisco
Pacific Area Travel Ass'n - Northern California Chapter

ASSOCIATION MANAGEMENT SERVICES

207 Shelby St., P.O. Box 1183
Frankfort, KY 40602
Tel: (502)875-5858   *Fax:* (502)875-7536

D. Ray Gillespie, *President*

Kentucky Beverage Industry Recycling Program
Kentucky Hotel and Motel Ass'n
Kentucky Self-Insurers Ass'n
Kentucky Soft Drink Ass'n
Outdoor Advertising Ass'n of Kentucky

ASSOCIATION MANAGEMENT SERVICES COMPANY

1116 24th St.
Sacramento, CA 95816
Tel: (916)448-5655   *Fax:* (916)448-1329

William P. Conway Jr., *President*

California Autobody Ass'n
California Mortuary Alliance
Interment Ass'n of California
Western Cemetery Alliance

ASSOCIATION MANAGEMENT SERVICES, INC.

33 S. Catalina Ave., Suite 202
Pasadena, CA 91106-2426
Tel: (626)449-4356   *Fax:* (626)564-8540

Pamela Hemann CAE, *President*

Alzheimer's Ass'n Biennial Conference
Building Industry Ass'n of Southern California - LA County
    East Chapter
Leadership California
Pasadena Child Health Foundation
Southern California Soc. of Ass'n Executives

ASSOCIATION MANAGEMENT SERVICES, INC. (AMS)

4510 West 89th St., Suite 100
Prairie Village, KS 66207-2282
Tel: (913)341-0765   *Fax:* (913)341-3625

Wendi Rose, *Director, Client Services*

Allied Trades of the Baking Industry
American Board of Environmental Medicine
American Water Works Ass'n - Kansas Section

ASSOCIATION MANAGEMENT SOLUTIONS, L.L.C

230 W. Monroe St., Suite 2930
Chicago, IL 60606-2788
Tel: (312)263-4260   *Fax:* (312)263-0923

Patricia A. Kelps, *Owner*
Richard C. Dole

Chicago Software Ass'n
Communications Systems Contractors Ass'n
CrimeStoppers
Cyborg Users Ass'n
Executives Guild, Ltd.
Women in Direct Marketing Internat'l - Chicago Chapter

ASSOCIATION MANAGEMENT SPECIALISTS

5049 The Woods Resort
Hedgesville, WV 25427-5049
Tel: (304)754-6184

Elizabeth A. Dunleavy, *President*

Mid-Atlantic Glass Ass'n
Potomac Highlands Golf and Travel Soc.
Women Executive Golf Organization

ASSOCIATION MANAGEMENT SYSTEMS

P.O. Box 15215
Hattiesburg, MS 39404-5215
Tel: (601)264-3442

F. Lamar Evans, *C.E.O.*

American Soc. of Landscape Architects - Mississippi Chapter
American Therapeutic Recreation Ass'n
Bent Creek Homeowners Ass'n
Hattiesburg Home Builders Ass'n
Mississippi Contract Poultry Growers Ass'n
Mississippi Recreation and Parks Ass'n
Nat'l State Publishing Ass'n

ASSOCIATION MANAGEMENT SYSTEMS

710 E. Ogden Ave., Suite 600
Naperville, IL 60563-8603
Tel: (630)369-2406   *Fax:* (630)369-2488

Michael D. Hansen, *President*

American Academy of Oral and Maxillofacial Pathology
Ass'n of Industrial Real Estate Brokers
Barbecue Industry Ass'n
Calendar Marketing Ass'n
Casual Furniture Retailers
Chicago Building Congress
Chicagoland Ass'n of Savings Institutions
Clock Manufacturers and Marketing Ass'n
EUCG
ICMOA Political Action Committee
Illinois CCIM Chapter
Illinois Coin Machine Operators Ass'n
Illinois Electronic Security Ass'n
Illinois Video Lottery Committee
Metropolitan Ambulance Ass'n
Nat'l Candy Brokers Ass'n
Nat'l Spa and Pool Institute - Midwest Chapter
Nat'l Spa and Pool Institute - Region V
Network Professionals Ass'n
Web Sling and Tiedown Ass'n
Wire Fabricators Ass'n

ASSOCIATION MANAGEMENT, INC.

3225 Candelaria Road, N.E.
Albuquerque, NM 87107
Tel: (505)888-0752   *Fax:* (505)884-0668

David M. McCoy, *President*

American Fire Sprinkler Ass'n - New Mexico Chapter
New Mexico Ready Mix Concrete and Aggregates Ass'n
New Mexico Sheet Metal Contractors Ass'n
Rio Grande Underground Contractors Ass'n

ASSOCIATION MANAGERS

P.O. Box 370
Bath, MI 48808-0370
Tel: (517)641-6554   *Fax:* (517)641-4402

Jon Hayes, *President*

Independent Accountants Ass'n of Michigan

ASSOCIATION MANAGERS, INC.

3900 E. Timrod
Tucson, AZ 85711-4170
Tel: (520)881-1788   *Fax:* (520)322-6778

Phillip A. Gutt CAE, *President*

American Soc. for Apheresis
Ass'n of Faculty Clubs Internat'l
South Central Ass'n of Blood Banks

ASSOCIATION MAX

1424 N. High Point Road, Suite 201
P.O. Box 620830
Middleton, WI 53562-0830
Tel: (608)836-3851   *Fax:* (608)836-3890

Maxine D. O'Brien, *Owner*

Badger State Car Wash Ass'n
Central Sign Council
Central States Car Wash Ass'n
Nat'l Air/Vac Ass'n
Wisconsin Amusement and Music Operators
Wisconsin Ass'n for Children with Behavior Disorders
Wisconsin Auctioneers Ass'n
Wisconsin Liquid Waste Carriers Ass'n
Wisconsin Sign Ass'n

ASSOCIATION PARTNERS INC.

209 10th Ave. South, Suite 506
Nashville, TN 37203
Tel: (615)254-1233   *Fax:* (615)254-1186

Connie C. Wallace CAE, *President*
Kimberly A. Settle, *V. President*

AIA Tennessee
Tennessee Ass'n of Health Maintenance Organizations
Tennessee Ass'n of Roofing Contractors
Tennessee Ass'n of Wine and Spirits Retailers
Tennessee Leadership
Tennessee Psychiatric Ass'n
Tennessee Public Transportation Ass'n

ASSOCIATION PROFESSIONAL MANAGEMENT SERVICES

532 42nd St.
Des Moines, IA 50312
Tel: (515)277-4821   *Fax:* (515)277-5604

Beverly V. Thomas, *President*

Iowa Hearing Aid Soc.
Iowa Public Transit Ass'n
Opticians Ass'n of Iowa
UNICON

ASSOCIATION PROFESSIONALS

1005 Bullard Court, Suite 104
Raleigh, NC 27615-6802
Tel: (919)878-3125   *Fax:* (919)878-3021

Wendy Scott, *President*

American Ass'n for Marriage and Family Therapy - North
    Carolina Chapter
American Soc. of Interior Designers - North Carolina/South
    Carolina Chapter
Opera Company of North Carolina

ASSOCIATION PROFESSIONALS OF THE SOUTH

1050 E. Piedmont Road, Suite E-302
Marietta, GA 30062-4744
Tel: (770)973-9797   *Fax:* (770)565-9670

imo K. Todd, *Consultant*

Alliance of American Agents
Professional Insurance Agents of Alabama
Savoyards Musical Theatre

ASSOCIATION RESOURCE CENTER, INC.

347 Main St.
Placerville, CA 95667-9925
Tel: (530)295-2000   *Fax:* (530)295-2009

Roger L. Duerksen, *President and C.E.O.*

California Funeral Directors' Ass'n
California Soc. of Ass'n Executives
Funeral Directors Service Corp.
Preferred Funeral Directors Internat'l

ASSOCIATION RESOURCES, INC.

638 Prospect Ave.
Hartford, CT 06105-4250
Tel: (860)586-7523   *Fax:* (860)586-7550

Peter J. Berry CAE, *President*
M. Suzanne C. Berry CAE, *Exec. V. President*

American Ass'n for Continuity of Care
American Epilepsy Soc.
Ass'n for Death Education and Counseling
Ass'n of Collegiate Licensing Administrators
Ass'n of Connecticut Career Schools
Connecticut Ass'n of Optometrists
Connecticut Law Enforcement Foundation
Connecticut Medical Group Management Ass'n
Connecticut Podiatric Medical Ass'n
Connecticut Police Chiefs Ass'n
Connecticut Women in Healthcare
Internat'l Ass'n of Campus Law Enforcement Administrators
Nat'l Board for Certification in Continuity of Care
New England Soc. of Healthcare Communicators

ASSOCIATION RESOURCES, INC.

3522 Habersham at Northlake
Tucker, GA 30084
Tel: (770)939-9882   *Fax:* (770)939-9883

Frank R. Rizzo, *President*

Southern Telemessaging Ass'n
Southern Wholesalers Ass'n

ASSOCIATION SERVICES

8 Shackleford Plaza, Suite 208
Little Rock, AR 72211
Tel: (501)221-1477   *Fax:* (501)225-6691

Bob Blount, *President*

Arkansas Veterinary Medical Ass'n
Rural Rental Housing Ass'n of Arkansas

ASSOCIATION SERVICES

30575 Trabuco Canyon Road, Suite 105
Trabuco Canyon, CA 92678
Tel: (714)459-8735   *Fax:* (714)858-9607

Lyn Paymer, *Principal*

Guy Muto Memorial Scholarship Fund
Nat'l Ass'n of Gas Chlorinators
Nat'l Plasterers Council

ASSOCIATION SERVICES CORP.

2945 S.W. Wanamaker Dr., Suite A
Topeka, KS 66614-5321
Tel: (785)271-0208   *Fax:* (785)271-0166

William J. Birch, *President*

Bath Enclosure Manufacturers Ass'n
Glass Ass'n of North America
Glass Week
Glazing Industry Code Committee
Laminators Safety Glass Ass'n
Nat'l Ass'n of Mirror Manufacturers
Nat'l Ass'n of Trailer Manufacturers
Nat'l Sunroom Ass'n
North American Ass'n of Mirror Manufacturers
Primary Glass Manufacturers Council

ASSOCIATION SERVICES GROUP

301 S. Broome St., Suite 203
P.O. Box 2945
LaGrange, GA 30241-2945
Tel: (706)845-9085   *Fax:* (706)883-8215

Charles T. Hall Jr., *President*

Georgia Commercial Flower Growers
Georgia Fruit and Vegetable Growers Ass'n
Georgia Sanitary Suppliers Ass'n
Southeast Greenhouse Conference and Trade Show
Southeast Soc. of American Foresters
Troup Clean and Beautiful

ASSOCIATION SERVICES GROUP

595 South 14th St.
Boise, ID 83702
Tel: (208)344-0781   *Fax:* (208)336-2901

Wendy J. Tippetts, *Owner*

Idaho Insurance Council
Independent Insurance Agents of Idaho
Surplus Line Ass'n of Idaho

ASSOCIATION SERVICES GROUP INC.

P.O. Box 1515
Milwaukee, WI 53201
Tel: (414)475-7022

Alan J. Carlson, *President*

Wisconsin Ass'n of Outpatient Mental Health Facilities
Wisconsin Network Administrators Group

ASSOCIATION SERVICES INTERNATIONAL, LTD.

5800 Foxridge Dr., Suite 115
Mission, KS 66202-2333
Tel: (913)262-4510   *Fax:* (913)262-0174

Frank A. Bistrom CAE, *President*
Betchie S. Bistrom CAE, *Senior V. President*
Jane Male CAE, *V. President*

Agricultural and Industrial Manufacturers' Representatives
    Ass'n
American Coaster Enthusiasts
Independent Medical Distributors Ass'n
Internat'l Ass'n of Insurance Receivers
Investment Recovery Ass'n
Nat'l Soc. of Insurance Premium Auditors
Power-Motion Technology Representatives Ass'n

ASSOCIATION SERVICES OF MICHIGAN

209 Seymour Ave., Suite 2
Lansing, MI 48933-1159
Tel: (517)372-8270   Fax: (517)372-1731

Brian P. Lovellette CAE, President

Michigan Ass'n of Ambulance Services
Michigan Ass'n of Emergency Medical Technicians

ASSOCIATION SERVICES, INC.

P.O. Box 2524
Fargo, ND 58108
Tel: (701)293-6822   Fax: (701)293-6824

Robert L. Lamp, Exec. V. President

Automobile Dealers Ass'n of North Dakota
North Dakota Implement Dealers Ass'n

ASSOCIATIONS INTERNATIONAL, INC.

6878 Fleetwood Road, Suite D
McLean, VA 22101-3618
Tel: (703)442-8780   Fax: (703)448-6914

Dr. Armand B. Weiss CAE, President

Children's Fund
Data Administration Management Ass'n - Nat'l Capital
   Region
Internat'l Ass'n of Medical Science Educators
Potomac Pedalers Touring Club
University of Pennsylvania Alumni Club of Washington
Washington Management and Business Ass'n
Wharton School Club of Washington
World Future Soc. - Washington Metro Area Chapter

ASSOCIATIONS PLUS

8 Madison Ave., P.O. Box M
Valhalla, NY 10595
Tel: (914)946-3802   Fax: (914)946-2674

Marie Rossi CAE, President

New York State Ass'n for Superintendents of School Buildings
   and Grounds
Women in Sales Ass'n

ASSOCIATIONS PLUS INC.

P.O. Box 11035
Columbia, SC 29211-1035
Tel: (803)252-7128   Fax: (803)252-7799

Leigh M. Burns, President and Owner

South Carolina Aviation Ass'n
South Carolina Child Care Ass'n
South Carolina Heat Pump Ass'n
South Carolina Tire Dealers and Retreaders Ass'n

ATTACHE INTERNATIONAL

1912 Clay St.
North Kansas City, MO 64116
Tel: (816)421-1991

James A. Spawn, Exec. Officer

American Belgian Blue Breeders Ass'n
American Blonde D'Aquitaine Ass'n
American Brahmousin Council
American Murray Grey Ass'n
American Tarentaise Ass'n
Braunvieh Breeders Internat'l
North American Corriente Ass'n
United States Beef Breeds Council

BACHNER COMMUNICATIONS, INC.

8811 Colesville Road, Suite G-106
Silver Spring, MD 20910
Tel: (301)589-9121   Fax: (301)589-2017

John P. Bachner, President
Lorie Meier, V. President

ASFE: Professional Firms Practicing in the Geosciences
Metropolitan Washington Heat Pump Ass'n
Professional Liability Agents Network

BILL BAER ASSOCIATION MANAGEMENT, INC.

3600 Raymond St.
Reading, PA 19605
Tel: (610)921-3070   Fax: (610)921-3075

William C. Baer, C.E.O.

Ambulance Ass'n of Pennsylvania
Easter Seal Soc. of Pennsylvania
Finnegan Foundation
Pennsylvania Ass'n of Nurse Anesthetists
Pennsylvania Dental Hygienists Ass'n

BAI, INC.

9891 Broken Land Pkwy., Suite 300
Columbia, MD 21046
Tel: (301)596-2584   Fax: (301)596-2594

Mark Levin CAE, President

Chain Link Fence Manufacturers Institute

BANNISTER & ASSOCIATES, INC.

Blendonview Office Park
5008-01 Pine Creek Drive
Westerville, OH 43081-4899
Tel: (614)895-1355   Fax: (614)895-3466

James R. Bannister CEM, Chairman and C.E.O.
Marlisa K. Bannister, President
Richard C. Bannister, V. President

Ass'n for Financial Technology
HUG Internat'l
Internat'l Function Point Users Group
Ohio Dietetic Ass'n
WLUC-Women in Insurance and Financial Services

BARBEE & ASSOCIATES

700 S.W. Jackson, Suite 702
Topeka, KS 66603-3758
Tel: (785)233-0555   Fax: (785)357-6629

George P. Barbee CAE, President

Kansas Ass'n of Financial Services
Kansas Consulting Engineers
Kansas Lodging Ass'n
Kansas Self-Insurers Ass'n
Travel Industry Ass'n of Kansas

BARRACK ASSOCIATION MANAGEMENT

112-J Elden St.
Herndon, VA 20170
Tel: (703)709-1035   Fax: (703)709-1036

David Barrack, President
Diana Tringali, Senior Account Exec.

American Cutlery Manufacturers Ass'n
American Soc. of Electroplated Plastics
Metal Finishing Suppliers Ass'n
Nat'l Ass'n of Metal Finishers
Nat'l Ass'n of Public Insurance Adjusters
Surface Finishing Industry Council

THE BASINGER GROUP

7950 E. La Junta Road
Scottsdale, AZ 85255-2798
Tel: (602)515-2420   Fax: (602)515-2101

Nancy Basinger, President

Ass'n for Management Information in Financial Services

THE BAYFIELD GROUP

49 East Ave.
Norwalk, CT 06851-4903
Tel: (203)854-9015   Fax: (203)847-1304

Penny Dalziel, President
Swea Nightingale CAE, V. President

Ass'n of University Technology Managers
Connecticut Soc. of Ass'n Executives
Sunglass Ass'n of America
Women in Communications - Fairfield Chapter

BB MANAGEMENT

3741 E. Rollins, Suite 1
Catalina, AZ 85739
Tel: (520)825-6621   Fax: (520)825-3704

Rebecca Bobb, Exec. Secretary-Director

Sheriff's Posse - Tucson
Western Music Ass'n

BEAMER & ASSOCIATES, INC.

6 Clouser Road
Mechanicsburg, PA 17055-6541
Tel: (717)795-7474   Fax: (717)795-7473

Deborah A. Beamer, President

Nat'l Ass'n of Local Government Auditors
Pennsylvania Organization of Nurse Leaders
Pennsylvania Propane Gas Ass'n
Soc. of Government Meeting Professionals

WILLIAM BELL ASSOCIATES

P.O. Box 725
Augusta, ME 04330
Tel: (207)622-4443   Fax: (207)623-3748

William A. Bell, President

Maine Ass'n of Conservation Districts
Maine Veterinary Medical Ass'n
New England Brown Egg Council
New England Grain and Feed Council
New England Poultry Ass'n

WILLIAM S. BERGMAN ASSOCIATES

1726 M St., N.W., Suite 1101
Washington, DC 20036-4502
Tel: (202)452-1520   Fax: (202)833-1577

William S. Bergman CAE, President
Deborah I. Beck, V. Preisdent

Consumers for World Trade
North American Ass'n of State and Provincial Lotteries
NOVA Foundation
Nurses Organization of Veterans Affairs
Outdoor Power Equipment Aftermarket Ass'n

BESS MANAGEMENT SERVICES

7208 Forestburg Dr.
Arlington, TX 76001
Tel: (817)561-7272   Fax: (817)561-7275

William R. Bess, President

Broker Management Council
Internat'l Ass'n for Financial Planning - Dallas/Ft. Worth
   Chapter
Manufacturers Representatives of America
Paper and Plastic Representatives Management Council

BETSY HOUSTON

1899 L St., N.W., Suite 500
Washington, DC 20036
Tel: (202)296-9282   Fax: (202)833-3014

Betsy Houston, Principal

Federation of Materials Socs.

BIRENBAUM AND ASSOCIATES

917 Locust St., Suite 1100
St. Louis, MO 63101-1413
Tel: (314)241-1445   Fax: (314)241-1449

Dr. Mark Birenbaum, President

American Ass'n of Bioanalysts
American Board of Bioanalysis
Ass'n of Defensive Spray Manufacturers
Dry Cleaners Exchange
WaterJet Technology Ass'n

SHIRLEY BISHOP, INC.

2033 6th Ave., Suite 804
Seattle, WA 98121-2526
Tel: (206)441-6020   Fax: (206)441-8262

Shirley Bishop, President

Ass'n of Academic Health Sciences Library Directors
Ass'n of University Anesthesiologists
Greater Seattle Business Ass'n
Internat'l Council on Systems Engineering
Northwest Development Officers Ass'n
Pacific Northwest Writers Conference
Soc. for Information Management - Seattle Area Chapter
Washington Speech and Hearing Ass'n
Washington State Soc. of Anesthesiologists

THE BISTI GROUP, INC.

1301 S.W. Topeka Blvd., Suite 101
Topeka, KS 66612
Tel: (785)234-3240   Fax: (785)357-1025

William J. Stinchcomb, President
Craig E. Collins, V. President

Kansas Alcoholism and Drug Addiction Counselors Ass'n

S.J. BLAIR ASSOCIATION MANAGEMENT

P.O. Box 70027
Shawnee Mission, KS 66207
Tel: (913)661-0084   Fax: (913)661-9939

Sharon J. Blair, Executive Director

Iowa Jewelers Ass'n
Kansas Jewelers Ass'n
Missouri Jewelers and Watchmakers Ass'n
Nebraska and South Dakota Jewelers Ass'n
Oklahoma Jewelers Ass'n

BOTZEK ASSOCIATES

26 Exchange St. East, Suite 120
St. Paul, MN 55101-2264
Tel: (651)293-9295   Fax: (651)293-0373

Gary Botzek, Principal
Luci Botzek, Principal

Minnesota Ass'n of County Officers
Minnesota Concrete and Masonry Contractors Ass'n
Minnesota Fish and Wildlife Legislative Alliance

BRENDEN & ASSOCIATES, INC.

6767 Forest Hill Ave., Suite 220
Richmond, VA 23225
Tel: (804)272-9004   Fax: (804)272-9006

Brenda Ferguson CMP, CAE, President

Architectural Woodwork Institute - Virginia Chapter
Nat'l Ass'n of Women Business Owners - Richmond Chapter
Recreational Vehicle Dealers Ass'n of Virginia
Virginia Ass'n of Nurse Anesthetists
Virginia Community Colleges Ass'n
Virginia Floorcovering Ass'n

G.W. BROWN AND ASSOCIATES

787 Windgate Dr.
Annapolis, MD 21401
Tel: (410)349-8614   Fax: (410)349-8616

George W. Brown, *President*

Nat'l Aerosol Ass'n

R. FRANKLIN BROWN, JR., INC.

994 Old Eagle School Road, Suite 1019
Wayne, PA   19087-1802
Tel: (610)971-4850   *Fax:* (610)971-4859

R. Franklin Brown Jr., *President*

Copper and Brass Servicenter Ass'n

BURK AND ASSOCIATES, INCORPORATED

1313 Dolley Madison Blvd., Suite 402
McLean, VA   22101-3926
Tel: (703)790-1745   *Fax:* (703)790-2672

Richard J. Burk Jr., *President*
Brett J. Burk, *V. President*

American Academy of Health Physics
American Ass'n of Radon Scientists and Technologists
Health Physics Soc.
Semiconductor Safety Ass'n
Soc. for Risk Analysis

BURNISON CHASNOFF ASSOCIATION MANAGEMENT

122 S. Michigan Ave., Suite 1776
Chicago, IL   60603-6107
Tel: (312)541-1272   *Fax:* (312)541-1271

Judith C. Burnison, *President and C.E.O.*

Illinois Ass'n for the Education of Young Children
Nat'l Ass'n for Families and Addiction Research and
    Education
Nat'l Coalition for Campus Children's Centers
Nat'l Reading Conference
Near North Ass'n of Condominium Presidents
University and College Designers Ass'n

BURROUGHS ASSETS MANAGEMENT GROUP

The Courtyard Office Complex
107 Kilmayne Drive, Suite C
Cary, NC   27511
Tel: (919)469-5858   *Fax:* (919)469-5870

Terence V. Burroughs, *President*

Nat'l Pharmaceutical Ass'n

CAG MANAGEMENT COMPANY, INC.

104 S. Michigan Ave., Suite 1500
Chicago, IL   60603
Tel: (312)201-0101   *Fax:* (312)201-0214

George M. Otto Sr., *Chairman*
George M. Otto Jr., *President*

Air Diffusion Council
Ass'n of Professional Landscape Designers
Chicago Book Clinic
Construction and Agricultural Film Manufacturers Film Ass'n
Consumer Financial Education Foundation
Corporate Relocation Council
Illinois Turfgrass Foundation
Institute of Caster Manufacturers
Lambda Alpha Internat'l
Land Economics Foundation of Lambda Alpha
Metal Construction Ass'n
Nat'l Roof Deck Contractors Ass'n
Warehouse Distributors Ass'n

CANNON COCHRAN MANAGEMENT SERVICES, INC.

2 E. Main St., Towne Centre Bldg.
Danville, IL   61832
Tel: (217)446-1089   *Fax:* (217)443-0927

1420 Kensington Road, Suite 202
Oak Brook, IL   60521
Tel: (630)571-2920   *Fax:* (630)571-0110

133 S. 11th St., Suite 430
St. Louis, MO   63102
Tel: (314)231-4094   *Fax:* (314)231-7041

2301 Burlington, Suite 230
North Kansas City, MO   64116
Tel: (816)472-7720   *Fax:* (816)472-7721

1025 Ashworth Road, Suite 400
West Des Moines, IA   50265
Tel: (515)223-9022   *Fax:* (515)223-9387

Bryan G. Thomas, *President/C.E.O.*
Penny Solski, *Branch Manager, Oak Brook*
Pat Steward, *V.P./Regional Operations Manager*

CAPITOL ADVOCACY SERVICES GROUP, LLC

3303 W. Saginaw, Suite B-3
Lansing, MI   48917
Tel: (517)321-1886   *Fax:* (517)321-2988

Donnelly K. Eurich CAE, *President*

CAPITOL HILL MANAGEMENT SERVICES, INC.

48 Howard St.
Albany, NY   12207
Tel: (518)463-8644   *Fax:* (518)463-8656

Fred G. Field, *President*

Academy of Certified Archivists
Albany Executives Ass'n
Capitol Region Human Resource Ass'n
Helderberg Workshop
Nat'l Ass'n of Government Archives and Records
    Administrators
New York State Ass'n of Renewal and Housing Officials
New York State Coalition of Nurse Practitioners
New York State Cosmetology Ass'n
New York State Dietetic Ass'n
New York State Glass Ass'n
New York State Occupational Therapy Ass'n
New York State Soc. of Opticians
New York State Speech Language Hearing Ass'n
Northeast New York Professional Golfers Ass'n
Veterinary Hospital Managers Ass'n

CARUSO ASSOCIATES INC., ASSOCIATION MANGEMENT SERVICES

7853 Arapahoe Court, Suite 2100
Englewood, CO   80112
Tel: (303)694-4728   *Fax:* (303)694-4869

Ellen Caruso, *President*
Fred Caruso CAE, *C.E.O.*

American Physical Therapy Ass'n - Colorado Chapter
Colorado Funeral Directors Ass'n
Colorado Funeral Service Board
Home Care Ass'n of Colorado
Internat'l Llama Ass'n
Occupational Therapy Ass'n of Colorado
Wood Organization of Denver

CAVANAGH ASSOCIATES

1800 Diagonal Road, Suite 600
Alexandria, VA   22314
Tel: (703)684-3147   *Fax:* (703)684-0128

Michael Cavanagh, *Principal*

Council for Electronic Revenue Communication Advancement

CENTER FOR ASSOCIATION GROWTH

1926 Waukegan Road, Suite #1
Glenview, IL   60025-1770
Tel: (847)657-6700   *Fax:* (847)657-6819

Carl A. Wangman CAE, *Chairman*
David L. Stumph CAE, *President*

Alliance of Business Brokers and Intermediaries
American Production and Inventory Control Soc. (Chicago
    Chapter)
Ass'n for Corporate Growth
Ass'n for Corporate Growth - New York Chapter
Commission on Accreditation of Ambulance Services
Illinois Dietetic Ass'n
Smocking Arts Guild of America

CEO PARTNERS

5445 N. Sheridan Road, Suite 1001
Chicago, IL   60640
Tel: (773)784-3649   *Fax:* (773)784-3894

910 West End Ave., Suite 1-D
New York, NY   10025
Tel: (212)978-9553   *Fax:* (212)865-8291

Gina Ryan MSW, CAE, *President*
Elizabeth Vasquez, *Office Manager*
Stanley Matek, *V. President*

THE CHARLES GROUP

333 B Route 46 West, Suite B-201
Fairfield, NJ   07004
Tel: (973)575-1444   *Fax:* (973)575-1445

Carol Davis-Grossman, *Managing Partner*

Council of Communication Management
Healthcare Business Women's Ass'n
Healthcare Marketing and Communications Council
Public Relations Soc. of America - New York and New Jersey
    Chapters
Women's Jewelry Ass'n

F.D. CHEW & ASSOCIATES

190 Duke of Glouster St.
Annapolis, MD   21401
Tel: (410)269-0134   *Fax:* (410)263-4228

Fred D. Chew Jr., *President*

Maryland State Child Care Ass'n

THE CHRISTOPHER GROUP

725 Farmers Lane, Suite 5
Santa Rosa, CA   95405
Tel: (707)544-9639   *Fax:* (707)575-8620

Linda E. Christopher CAE, *President & C.E.O.*

California Coalition of Nurse Practitioners
Commercial Real Estate Women - San Francisco Chapter

CLARION MANAGEMENT RESOURCES, INC.

515 King St., Suite 420
Alexandria, VA   22314-3103
Tel: (703)684-5570   *Fax:* (703)684-6048

Carole M. Rogin, *President*

Alliance of Work/Life Professionals
American Wire Producers Ass'n
Ass'n of Women in the Metal Industries
Friends of NIDCD
Hearing Industries Ass'n
Soc. of Quality Assurance
Wire Rope Technical Board

CLEAN LISTS ASSOCIATES

122 East 42nd St., 17th Floor
New York, NY   10168
Tel: (212)551-1013   *Fax:* (212)551-1107

Tamara Beck, *Owner/Partner*

Beta Gamma Sigma Alumni of New York
Internat'l Ass'n of Corporate Real Estate Executives - New
    York Chapter

CLEMONS & ASSOCIATES, INC.

5024-R Campbell Blvd.
Baltimore, MD   21236-5974
Tel: (410)931-8100   *Fax:* (410)931-8111

Calvin K. Clemons CAE, *President*
Steven T. King CAE, *Exec. V. President*

Electrical-Electronics Materials Distributors Ass'n
Fire Suppression Systems Ass'n
Flexographic Prepress Platemakers Ass'n
Internat'l Ass'n of Special Investigation Units
Nat'l Ass'n of Sign Supply Distributors
Office Products Wholesalers Ass'n
Pet Industry Distributors Ass'n
Post Card Distributors Ass'n of North America
Safety Equipment Distributors Ass'n
Shoe Service Institute of America
Woodworking Machinery Industry Ass'n

RICHARD H. CLOUGH CO.

76 S. State St.
Concord, NH   03301-3520
Tel: (603)228-1231   *Fax:* (603)228-2118

Richard H. Clough CAE, *Owner*

American College of Cardiology - Northern New England Tri-
    State Chapter
American Soc. of Home Inspectors - New England Chapter
Granite State Designers and Installers Ass'n
New Hampshire Ass'n of Life Underwriters
New Hampshire Manufactured Home Ass'n
New Hampshire School Transportation Ass'n
Vermont School Transportation Ass'n
Vermont/New Hampshire Direct Marketing Group

CM SERVICES

800 Roosevelt Road, Suite C-20
Glen Ellyn, IL   60137-5839
Tel: (630)858-7337   *Fax:* (630)790-3095

1825 I St., N.W., Suite 400
Washington, DC   20006
Tel: (202)429-5252   *Fax:* (205)411

Richard W. Church, *President*
Jerilyn J. Church CAE, *V. President*
Richard W. Church II, *Managing Director*
Jeff Risley, *Managing Director, Washington*

Bearing Specialist Ass'n
Ceramic Tile Distributors Ass'n
Plastic Pipe and Fittings Ass'n
Polyurethane Manufacturers Ass'n
Water Systems Council

COMPREHENSIVE ASSOCIATION CONSULTANTS

P.O. Box 2604
Fairfax, VA   22031-2604
Tel: (703)690-2100   *Fax:* (703)690-8129

Charles H. Emely Ph.D., CAE, *President/C.E.O.*
Mary Ann Emely CAE, *V. President*

Federation of Government Information Processing Councils
Nat'l Economists Club
Nat'l Economists Club Education Foundation
Univ. of Connecticut Alumni Ass'n - Washington, DC Chapter
Washington Foundation for Psychiatry

CONFERENCE AND MANAGEMENT SPECIALISTS

6740 E. Hampden Ave., Suite 306
Denver, CO   80224
Tel: (303)756-5120   *Fax:* (303)756-5699

Karen A. Hone, *Executive Director*

Colorado Ass'n of Mortgage Brokers
Community Ass'ns Institute - Rocky Mountain Chapter
Health Industry Representatives Ass'n
Rocky Mountain Chapter - Electronics Representatives Ass'n

COURTESY ASSOCIATES

2000 L St., N.W., Suite 710
Washington, DC   20036
Tel: (202)331-2000   *Fax:* (202)331-0111

Louise Lynch, *C.E.O.*
Sheila Stampfli, *President*

Commercial Real Estate Women - Washington DC Chapter
Training Officers Conference
Washington Space Business Roundtable

CREATIVE MARKETING ALLIANCE, INC.

P.O. Box 727
Princeton Junction, NJ 08550
Tel: (609)799-6000   *Fax: (609)799-7032*

Jeffery E. Barnhart, *President*

Energy Efficient Lighting Ass'n
Internat'l Card Manufacturers Ass'n
Smart Card Industry Ass'n

CROW-SEGAL MANAGEMENT COMPANY

1133 W. Morse Blvd., Suite 201
Winter Park, FL 32789
Tel: (407)647-8839   *Fax: (407)629-2502*

Pat Crow-Segal CAE, *President*

American Soc. of Ophthalmic Plastic and Reconstructive
    Surgery
Florida Apartment Ass'n
Florida Auto Dismantlers and Recyclers Ass'n
Florida Library Ass'n
Florida Motorcoach Ass'n
Florida Soc. of Facial Plastic and Reconstructive Surgery
Florida Soc. of Ophthalmology
Florida Soc. of Otolaryngology-Head and Neck Surgery
Florida Urological Soc.
MISER Users Group
Mortgage Bankers Ass'n of Florida
Nat'l Ass'n of Minority Engineering Program Administrators

RICHARD S. CROY & COMPANY

14701 Detroit Ave., Suite 385
Cleveland, OH 44107-4109
Tel: (216)228-2166   *Fax: (216)228-5810*

Richard S. Croy, *President*

American Marketing Ass'n - Cleveland Chapter
Internat'l Oxygen Manufacturers Ass'n

CRYAN ASSOCIATES

P.O. Box 910
Sudbury, MA 01776-0910
Tel: (978)443-6911   *Fax: (978)443-0197*

Teresa V. Cryan, *Partner*

AHRA Education Foundation
American Healthcare Radiology Administrators
New England Institute of Restoration and Cleaning
New England Veterinary Medical Ass'n

CUTTING EDGE RESOURCES, INC.

6441 Enterprise Lane, Suite 102-A
Madison, WI 53719
Tel: (608)277-7663   *Fax: (608)277-7685*

David B. Glomp CAE, *President*

Ass'n of Wisconsin Cleaning Contractors
Wisconsin Ass'n of Health Underwriters

DANIELS ASSOCIATION MANAGEMENT SERVICES

1260 New Britain Ave.
West Hartford, CT 06110
Tel: (860)561-3250   *Fax: (860)561-2473*

Catherine B. Dangona, *Exec. Director*

Limousine Operators of Connecticut
Northeast Bottled Water Ass'n

DAVIS/REPLOGLE & ASSOCIATES

5820 Wilshire Blvd., Suite 500
Los Angeles, CA 90036-4594
Tel: (213)937-5514   *Fax: (213)937-0959*

C. James Dowden, *President*

GEORGE K. DEGNON ASSOCIATES, INC.

6728 Old McLean Village Drive
McLean, VA 22101
Tel: (703)556-9222   *Fax: (703)556-8729*

George K. Degnon CAE, *President*
Marge Degnon, *V. President*

Academy of Organizational and Occupational Psychiatry
Ambulatory Pediatric Ass'n
American Academy for Physician and Patient
American Holistic Medical Ass'n
American Holistic Medical Foundation
American Psychosomatic Soc.
Ass'n of Christian Therapists
Ass'n of Pediatric Program Directors
Internat'l Ass'n of Pediatric Laboratory Medicine
Multinational Working Teams on Functional Gastrointestinal
    Disorders
Soc. for Occupational and Environmental Health
Soc. for Pediatric Pathology

DEMPSEY MANAGEMENT SERVICES, INC.

5300 Memorial Drive, Suite 116
Stone Mountain, GA 30083
Tel: (404)297-9200   *Fax: (404)299-8927*

Frederick G. Dempsey Jr., CAE, *President*

DIFILIPPO BUSINESS SERVICES

7235 Saddle Creek Circle
Sarasota, FL 34241
Tel: (941)925-1909

Francine DiFilippo, *President*

Home Workers Ass'n
Independent Computer Services Ass'n of America
Institute for Business Innovation
T.Q.M. Network

DON DILLON ASSOCIATES

4020 McEwen, Suite 105
Dallas, TX 75244-5019
Tel: (972)233-9107   *Fax: (972)490-4219*

Donald W. Dillon, *President*

Academic Language Therapy Ass'n
American College of Cardiology - Texas Chapter
American Marketing Ass'n-Dallas/Fort Worth Chapter
Commercial Real Estate Women
CREW Classic
D/FW Direct Marketing Ass'n
Dallas/Ft. Worth Soc. of Ass'n Executives
Internat'l Soc. of Bassists
Internat'l Trade Ass'n - D/FW Chapter
Meeting Professionals Internat'l - D/FW Chapter
Nat'l Ass'n of School Music Dealers
Nat'l Piano Foundation
North Texas Speakers Ass'n
Piano Manufacturers Ass'n Internat'l
Retail Print Music Dealers Ass'n
Texas Art Education Ass'n
Transportation Club of Dallas

DIRECT CONNECTION INC.

2218 Crabtree
Northbrook, IL 60062-3520
Tel: (847)498-5550

Sue Wells, *President*

Nat'l Bird Feeding Soc.
Wild Bird Feeding Institute

DIVERSIFIED CONSULTANTS

P.O. Box 36972
Birmingham, AL 35236
Tel: (205)985-9488   *Fax: (205)737-1006*

Bob Mosca, *President*

Alabama Ass'n of Temporary and Staffing Services
Alabama Pawnbrokers Ass'n
Alabama Veterans Memorial Foundation
American Ass'n of Physicians
American Soc. for Automation in Pharmacy
Southern Dental Ass'n

DIVERSIFIED CONSULTANTS, INC.

6405 Metcalf, Suite 503
Shawnee Mission, KS 66202-3929
Tel: (913)384-2345   *Fax: (913)384-5112*

Terry Kay Underwood, *President*

DIVERSIFIED MANAGEMENT SERVICES, INC.

1225 Crater Lake Ave., Suite 116
Medford, OR 97504
Tel: (541)773-2515   *Fax: (541)770-7041*

Jean Fristensky, *President*

Professional Ass'n of Custom Clothiers

DIVERSIFIED MANAGEMENT SERVICES, INC.

206 6th Ave., Suite 900 Midland Bldg.
Des Moines, IA 50309-4018
Tel: (515)282-8192   *Fax: (515)282-9117*

Richard L. Goodson Jr., *C.E.O.*

American Specialty Toy Retailing Ass'n
Appraisal Institute - Iowa Chapter
Bedding Plants Internat'l
Equipment Service Ass'n
Iowa Alliance for Fair Competition
Iowa Greenhouse Growers Ass'n
Iowa Medical Group Management Ass'n
Iowa Podiatric Medical Soc.
Iowa Talented and Gifted
Iowa's Community Bankers
Mobile Equipment and Crane Ass'n
Morris Scholarship Fund, Inc.
Nat'l Ass'n for Family Child Care
Plumbing-Heating-Cooling Contractors of Iowa

DMD MANAGEMENT SERVICES, INC.

825 E. Golf Road, Suite 1141
Arlington Heights, IL 60005-5200
Tel: (847)228-9299   *Fax: (847)228-9322*

Debra Weidner, *President*

DOLCI MANAGEMENT SERVICES, INC.

322 8th Ave., Suite 1400
New York, NY 10001-8001
Tel: (212)206-8301   *Fax: (212)645-1147*

Joel A. Dolci CAE, *President*
Kathleen A. Dolci, *Principal*

Contact Group, The
New York Soc. of Ass'n Executives
New York State Soc. of Physicians Assistants
Tri-State Acura Dealers Ass'n

DRAKE AND COMPANY

P.O. Box 410260
1000 Executive Pkwy., Suite 220
St. Louis, MO 63141-0260
Tel: (314)576-7960   *Fax: (314)576-7989*

Steven Drake, *President*

Agricultural Publishers Ass'n
Alpha Zeta Foundation
Alpha Zeta Fraternity
Call Center Network Group
Farm Publications Reports
Foundation E.A.R.T.H.
Nat'l Christmas Tree Ass'n
Pile Driving Contractors Ass'n

DROHAN MANAGEMENT GROUP

11250 Roger Bacon Dr., Suite 8
Reston, VA 22090-5202
Tel: (703)437-4377   *Fax: (703)435-4390*

William M. Drohan CAE, *President*

American Academy of Hospice and Palliative Medicine
Ass'n of Nurses in AIDS Care
Ass'n of Occupational Health Professionals (in Healthcare)
Council of Biology Editors
Eastern North American Region of the Biometric Soc.
Environmental Mutagen Soc.
Fire Equipment Manufacturers Suppliers Ass'n
Fire Equipment Manufacturers Suppliers Ass'n
HIV/AIDS Nursing Certification Board
Internat'l Business Brokers Ass'n
Nat'l Ass'n of Corporate Treasurers
Nat'l Ass'n of Rehabilitation Agencies
Nat'l Organization for Associate Degree Nursing
Nat'l Renal Administrators Ass'n
Sports Lawyers Ass'n
Transportation Research Forum

DYNAMIC MANAGEMENT SERVICES, INC.

551 5th Ave., Suite 3025
New York, NY 10176
Tel: (212)687-4010   *Fax: (212)687-4016*

Arlene Stock CAE, *President*

Contingency Planning Exchange
Nat'l Ass'n of Judiciary Interpreters and Translators
New York State Court Reporters Ass'n
Real Estate Lenders Ass'n

DYNAMIC RESOURCES, INC.

8345 University Blvd., Suite F-1
Des Moines, IA 50325-1168
Tel: (515)225-2323   *Fax: (515)225-6363*

Alda Post Helvey, *President*

Accountants Ass'n of Iowa
Iowa Convention and Visitor Bureau Ass'n
Iowa Court Reporters Ass'n
Iowa Dietetic Ass'n
Iowa Nursing Home Social Workers Ass'n
Iowa Occupational Therapy Ass'n
Iowa Speech-Language-Hearing Ass'n

EASTER ASSOCIATES

630 Country Green Lane
Charlottesville, VA 22902-6478
Tel: (804)977-3716   *Fax: (804)979-2439*

Peter Easter CAE, *President*

Car and Truck Renting and Leasing Ass'n of Virginia
Virginia Ass'n of Broadcasters
Virginia Ass'n of Marine Industries
Virginia Automotive Recyclers Ass'n
Virginia Ready-Mixed Concrete Ass'n

EBBEN MARKETING, INC.

2720 Springville Dr.
P.O. Box 936
Plover, WI 54467
Tel: (715)342-1960   *Fax: (715)342-1943*

Gary J. Ebben, *Principal*

Nat'l Ass'n for Retail Merchandising Services

THE ENGINEERING CENTER

One Walnut St.
Boston, MA 02108-3616
Tel: (617)227-5551   *Fax: (617)227-6783*

Abbie R. Goodman, *Exec. Director*

American Consulting Engineers Council of Massachusetts
Boston Soc. of Civil Engineers
Massachusetts Ass'n of Land Surveyors and Civil Engineers
Women's Transportation Seminar

BARRY R. EPSTEIN ASSOCIATES, INC.

11922 Waterwood Dr.
Boca Raton, FL   33428-1026
Tel: (561)750-0000   *Fax:* (561)447-0001

Suite 315, Atrium Financial Center
1515 N. Federal Hwy.
Boca Raton, FL   33432-1953
Tel: (561)447-0000   *Fax:* (561)447-0001

Barry R. Epstein APR, CCE, *President*

Derail the Bullet Train
Together Against Gangs

J. EDGAR EUBANKS AND ASSOCIATES, INC.

3008 Millwood Ave.
Columbia, SC   29205
Tel: (803)252-5646   *Fax:* (803)765-0860

MaryAnn S. Crews, *President*

Academy of Dispensing Audiologists
Flying Scot Sailing Ass'n
Nat'l Ass'n of Bankruptcy Trustees
Nat'l Ass'n of Decorative Fabric Distributors
Nat'l Drilling Ass'n
Reprographic Dealers Ass'n
South Carolina Ass'n of Convenience Stores
South Carolina Defense Trial Attorneys
South Carolina Orthopaedic Ass'n
South Carolina Speech-Language-Hearing Ass'n

EWALD CONSULTING GROUP

26 E. Exchange St., Suite 507
St. Paul, MN   55101-2264
Tel: (612)290-6260   *Fax:* (612)290-2266

Douglas R. Ewald CAE, *President*
David C. Ewald CAE, *V. President*

American College of Cardiology - Minnesota Chapter
Automotive Recyclers of Minnesota
Economic Development Ass'n of Minnesota
Metalcasters of Minnesota
Minnesota Council of Child Caring Agencies
Minnesota Fabricare Institute
Minnesota Forestry Ass'n
Minnesota Glass Ass'n
Minnesota Internet Services Trade Ass'n
Minnesota Legislative Soc.
Minnesota Magazine Publishers Ass'n
Minnesota Sign Ass'n
Minnesota Water Well Ass'n
United Concrete and Masonry Contractors Ass'n

KATHLEEN EWING & ASSOCIATES

1609 Connecticut Ave., N.W., Suite 200
Washington, DC   20009
Tel: (202)986-0105   *Fax:* (202)986-0448

Kathleen Ewing, *President*

Art Dealers Ass'n of Greater Washington
Ass'n of Internat'l Photography Art Dealers
Institutional and Service Textile Distributors Ass'n

EXECUTIVE ADMINISTRATION, INC.

85 W. Algonquin Road, Suite 550
Arlington Heights, IL   60005-4425
Tel: (847)427-9600   *Fax:* (847)427-1294

James R. Slawny, *President*

American Ass'n of Certified Allergists
American College of Allergy, Asthma and Immunology
American Soc. for Blood and Marrow Transplantation
American Soc. of Colon and Rectal Surgeons
Illinois Soc. of Allergy, Asthma and Immunology
Research Foundation of the American Soc. of Colon and
     Rectal Surgeons
Soc. of Surgical Oncology

EXECUTIVE ASSOCIATION MANAGEMENT, INC.

823 Congress Ave., Suite 1300
Austin, TX   78701
Tel: (512)479-0425   *Fax:* (512)495-9031

Michael T. Marks, *President*

Austin Auto Show
Austin Automobile Dealers Ass'n
Building Officials Ass'n of Texas
College Band Directors Nat'l Ass'n
Metro Houston Ford Dealers Advertising Committee
Mid South Associates
Nat'l Ass'n of Professional Employer Organizations - Texas
     Chapter
Painting and Decorating Contractors of America - Texas
     Council
South Texas Ford Dealers Advertising Fund
South Texas Lincoln Mercury Dealers Advertising Fund
Southwest Alliance of Hearing Care Providers
Southwestern Ice Ass'n
Texas Alliance of Recreational Organizations
Texas Ass'n of Real Estate Inspectors
Texas Automotive Dismantlers and Recyclers Ass'n

Texas Burglar and Fire Alarm Ass'n
Texas Club Ass'n
Texas Lyceum Ass'n
Texas Motorcycle Dealers Ass'n
Texas Water Quality Ass'n

EXECUTIVE DIRECTOR, INC.

611 E. Wells St.
Milwaukee, WI   53202-3892
Tel: (414)276-6445   *Fax:* (414)276-3349

35 E. Wacker Dr., Suite 500
Chicago, IL   60601
Tel: (312)782-5252   *Fax:* (312)236-1140

Rick Iber, *President*
Kay Whalen, *V. President*
David Baumann, *Managing Partner*

Academy of Assisted Reproductive Technology Professionals
American Academy of Allergy, Asthma and Immunology
American Academy of Emergency Medicine
American College of Forensic Examiners
American College of Legal Medicine
Clinical Immunology Soc.
Collegium Internationale Allergologicum
Council for Accreditation in Occupational Hearing
     Conservation
Emissions Marketing Ass'n
Internat'l Ass'n of Allergology and Clinical Immunology
Professional Systems Network
TransPacific Allergy & Immunology Soc.

EXECUTIVE MANAGEMENT ASSOCIATES

1804 W. Burbank Blvd.
Burbank, CA   91506-1315
Tel: (818)843-5660   *Fax:* (818)843-7423

Larry Newell, *Partner*
Janine Newell, *Partner*

Ass'n of Educational Therapists
Harvard Radcliff Club of Southern California
Internat'l Ass'n of Financial Planners - Los Angeles Chapter
Los Angeles Business Travel Ass'n
Los Angeles County Chiropractic Ass'n
Nat'l Ass'n of Women Business Owners - Los Angeles
     Chapter
Risk and Insurance Management Soc. - Los Angeles Chapter
Soc. of Logistics Engineers - District 9
Southern California Mediation Ass'n
Swimming Pool Trades and Contractors Ass'n
Treasury Ass'n of Southern California
Western Pension and Benefits Conference - Los Angeles
     Chapter

EXECUTIVE MANAGMENT SERVICES, INC.

P.O. Box 13089
Tallahassee, FL   32317
Tel: (904)878-3134   *Fax:* (904)878-1291

Robert S. Rhinehart, *President*

American Ass'n of Business Valuation Specialists
American Ass'n of Processors
Amusement and Music Owners Ass'n of Florida
Coalition of Tax and Accountants of Florida
Elephant Marketing Services, Inc.
Internat'l Ass'n of Physicians and Health Care Professionals

EXECUTIVES CONSULTANTS, INC.

10210 Leatherleaf Court
Manassas, VA   20111-4245
Tel: (703)257-1512   *Fax:* (703)257-0213

Robert C. LaGasse, *President*

Garden Writers Ass'n of America
Hydroponic Merchants Ass'n
Internat'l Microwave Power Institute
Nat'l Bark and Soil Producers Ass'n

NORMAN FERACHI AND ASSOCIATES

603 Europe St.
Baton Rouge, LA   70802
Tel: (225)387-3261   *Fax:* (225)387-3262

Norman C. Ferachi, *Principal*

Ass'n of Louisiana Lobbyists
Louisiana Ass'n of Chiefs of Police
Louisiana Ass'n of Criminal Defense Lawyers
Louisiana Ass'n of Plumbing-Heating-Cooling Contractors
Louisiana Soc. of Ass'n Executives
Louisiana Soft Drink Ass'n

FERNLEY AND FERNLEY, INC.

1900 Arch St.
Philadelphia, PA   19103-1498
Tel: (215)564-3484   *Fax:* (215)564-2175

G.A. Taylor Fernley, *President & C.E.O.*
Suzanne C. Pine, *Exec. V. President*

American Brush Manufacturers Ass'n
Ass'n for High Technology Distribution
Aviation Distributors and Manufacturers Ass'n Internat'l
Bicycle Product Suppliers Ass'n
Internat'l Ass'n of Ice Cream Vendors
Lawn and Garden Marketing and Distribution Ass'n
Nat'l Ass'n of Aluminum Distributors
Nat'l Ass'n of Container Distributors
Nat'l Field Selling Ass'n

Nat'l Industrial Glove Distributors Ass'n
Nat'l Refrigeration Contractors Ass'n
Nat'l Welding Supply Ass'n
North American Horticultural Supply Ass'n
Outdoor Power Equipment Distributors Ass'n
Professional Soc. for Sales and Marketing Training
Real Estate Information Providers Ass'n
Resistance Welder Manufacturers Ass'n
Security Hardware Distributors Ass'n
United States Marine Safety Ass'n
Water and Sewer Distributors of America
Wood Machinery Manufacturers of America

FITZGERALD MANAGEMENT CORP.

2850 S. Ocean Blvd., Suite 114
Palm Beach, FL   33480-5535
Tel: (561)533-0991   *Fax:* (561)533-7466

Frank S. Fitzgerald CAE, *President*
Kathryn R. Fitzgerald, *Exec. V. President*

Highway Sign Support Ass'n
House Sitters Ass'n
Screen Manufacturers Ass'n
Window Council

FLYNN MANAGEMENT ASSOCIATES

731 Hebron Ave.
Glastonbury, CT   06033-2457
Tel: (860)633-4464   *Fax:* (860)657-8241

Simon A. Flynn, *President*

American College of Cardiology - Connecticut Chapter
Connecticut Lodging Ass'n
Connecticut Metalworking Network
Connecticut Restaurant Ass'n
Connecticut Tooling and Machining Ass'n

FRANKLIN/THOMAS ASSOCIATION MANAGEMENT

3525 Ellicott Mills Dr., Suite N
Ellicott City, MD   21043-4547
Tel: (410)418-4800   *Fax:* (410)418-4805

Carol T. Shaner CAE, *President*

American College of Cardiology - Maryland Chapter
Baltimore Estate Planning Council
Certifying Board for Gastroenterology Nurses and Associates
Council of Administrative and Supervisory Employees
Joint Review Committee for Education in Cardiovascular
     Technology
Maryland Independent Automobile Dealers Ass'n
Maryland Soc. of Health System Pharmacists
Maryland Soc. of Professional Engineers
United States Tennis Court and Track Builders Ass'n

MARTIN FROMM & ASSOCIATES, INC.

9140 Ward Parkway
Kansas City, MO   64114-3306
Tel: (816)444-3500   *Fax:* (814)444-0330

Jerry Fogel CAE, *President and C.E.O.*

American Ass'n of Managing General Agents
American Ass'n of Managing General Agents University
     Foundation
American Meat Science Ass'n
American Sewing Guild
Ass'n for Accounting Marketing
Ass'n for Psychological Type
Ass'n of Diesel Specialists
Autobody Representatives Council
Automotive Warehouse Distributors Ass'n
Automotive Warehouse Distributors Ass'n University
     Foundation
Diamond Council of America
Hand Therapy Certification Commission
Helzberg Entreprenneurial Mentoring Program
Hotel and Motel Ass'n of Greater Kansas City
Internat'l Trade Club of Greater Kansas City
Meeting Professionals Internat'l - Kansas City Chapter
Mental Health in Corrections Consortium

FSA GROUP

304 W. Liberty St., Suite 201
Louisville, KY   40202-3068
Tel: (502)583-3783   *Fax:* (502)589-3602

Phillip S. Cooke, *President*

Foodservice Consultants Soc. Internat'l
Internat'l Ass'n of Culinary Professionals
Internat'l Inflight Food Service Ass'n
Soc. for Foodservice Management
Women Chefs and Restaurateurs

G & T ENTERPRISES, INC.

P.O. Box 1053
Skyland, NC   28776
Tel: (704)684-1987   *Fax:* (704)684-7372

Fred A. Gray, *President*
Julie B. Gray, *V. President*

Industrial Diamond Ass'n of America

G.M.O., INC.

P.O. Box 2118
Hastings, NE   68902-2118
Tel: (402)463-5691   *Fax:* (402)463-5683

Don Ellerbee, *President*

American College of Theriogenologists
American Embryo Transfer Ass'n
Nebraska Funeral Directors Ass'n
Nebraska Turfgrass Foundation
Nebraska Veterinary Medical Ass'n
Soc. for Theriogenology

GATEKEEPER MANAGEMENT SERVICES

20335 Ventura Blvd., Suite 310
Woodland Hills, CA 91364-2599
Tel: (818)610-0320   *Fax:* (818)610-0323

Gary W. Larson, *Exec. V. President*

North American Soc. of Scaffold Professionals
Scaffold Industry Ass'n
SIA Educational Foundation

GERBER & ASSOCIATES, INC.

1400 K St., Suite 301
Sacramento, CA 95814
Tel: (916)446-4656   *Fax:* (916)446-4318

Edward R. Gerber, *C.E.O.*

California Transit Ass'n
California Transit Insurance Pool
Solid Waste Ass'n of North America - California Chapter

GIUFFRIDA ASSOCIATES

204 E St., N.E.
Washington, DC 20002
Tel: (202)547-6340   *Fax:* (202)547-6348

Michael Giuffrida, *President*

Nat'l Soc. for Healthcare Foodservice Management
TAC - Internat'l Telework Ass'n

ED GLASSGOW & ASSOCIATES

P.O. Box 1580
Rapid City, SD 57709-1580
Tel: (605)343-6917   *Fax:* (605)342-2053

Ed Glassgow CAE, *President*

South Dakota Propane Gas Ass'n

GOLDEN MANAGEMENT

6404 Wilshire Blvd., Suite 1111
Los Angeles, CA 90048
Tel: (213)655-1951   *Fax:* (213)655-8627

Carol Golden, *President*

Advertising Club of Los Angeles
Advertising Industry Emergency Fund
Los Angeles Creative Club
Magazine Representatives Ass'n of Southern California
Minority Advertising Training Program
Western States Advertising Agencies Ass'n

DANIEL GOLDSTEIN AND ASSOCIATES

582 New Loudon Road
Latham, NY 12110
Tel: (518)785-0721   *Fax:* (518)785-3579

Daniel A. Goldstein, *President*

GREAT ASSOCIATIONS

P.O. Box 545
Los Olivos, CA 93441
Tel: (805)693-9137   *Fax:* (805)693-9758

Judith A. Baerg, *President*

American College of Foot and Ankle Orthopedics and
   Medicine
Internat'l Academy of Podiatric Medicine

GREAT WESTERN ASSOCIATION MANAGEMENT, INC.

9101 E. Kenyon Ave., Suite 3000
Denver, CO 80237
Tel: (303)770-2220   *Fax:* (303)770-1812

Albert E. Brust, *President*

Ass'n of Professional Investment Consultants
Colorado Payphone Ass'n
Colorado State Managers Ass'n
Colorado TeleServ
Nat'l Defined Contribution Council
Nat'l Hearing Conservation Ass'n
Pacific Insurance and Surety Conference
Rocky Mountain Regional Turfgrass Ass'n
Rocky Mountain Turfgrass Research Foundation

GROOME MARKETING ASSOCIATES

36 Taylor Road
Princeton, NJ 08540
Tel: (908)329-6706

James J. Groome CMP, CAE, *President*

GROUP CONCEPTS, INC.

1240 N. Jefferson, Suite G
Anaheim, CA 92807
Tel: (714)632-6800   *Fax:* (714)632-5405

Kelly William Ramirez, *President*

California Associated Truckers
California Furniture Manufacturers Ass'n
California Locksmiths Ass'n
Industrial Caterers Ass'n
Mobile Industrial Caterers' Ass'n Internat'l

GROUP IV ASSOCIATION MANAGEMENT

3300 Bass Lake Road, Suite 120
Minneapolis, MN 55429
Tel: (612)566-6098   *Fax:* (612)566-5780

JoAnn Hiebel, *President*

Internat'l Facilities Management Ass'n - Minnesota Chapter
Minnesota Outdoor Heritage Ass'n
Minnesota Precision Manufacturing Ass'n

GROUP MANAGEMENT SERVICES

P.O. Box 11628
Montgomery, AL 36111-0628
Tel: (334)260-7970   *Fax:* (334)272-7128

Larry A. Vinson CAE, *Principal*

Alabama Council of Ass'n Executives
Alabama Dietetic Ass'n
Solid Waste Ass'n of North America - Alabama Chapter
Southern Community Bankers

GROUP MANAGEMENT, INC.

10 N. Norton, Suite 120
Tucson, AZ 85719
Tel: (520)622-6229   *Fax:* (520)622-6246

Brent L. Davis, *President*

American Institute of Architects - Southern Arizona Chapter
Cornerstone Building Foundation

GROUP MANAGMENT RESOURCES

132 Great Road, Suite 200
Stow, MA 01775
Tel: (978)897-9808   *Fax:* (978)897-5442

Lauren A. Hunte, *President*

Ass'n for the Calligraphic Arts
Internat'l Electrology Educators
Massachusetts Soc. of Radiologic Technolgists
Nat'l Commission for Electrologist Certification
Soc. of Clinical and Medical Electrologists

THE GUILD ASSOCIATES, INC.

100 Boylston St., Suite 1050
Boston, MA 02116-4610
Tel: (617)426-6400   *Fax:* (617)426-6639

Richard S. Guild CAE, *President*
Deborah M. Fanning CAE, *V. President*

Art and Creative Materials Institute
Coin Machine Industries Ass'n of Massachusetts
Council for Art Education
Massachusetts Ass'n of Staffing Services
Massachusetts Gaming Ass'n
Massachusetts Vending Ass'n
New England Marine Trade Ass'n
North East Ass'n of Telemessaging
Tascom Users Group

HAB ASSOCIATES, INC.

645 N. Michigan Ave., Suite 900
Chicago, IL 60611
Tel: (312)951-0106   *Fax:* (312)932-3201

Betty Burns, *President*

Center for Certification Preparation and Review
Nat'l Certification Corp. for the Obstetric, Gynecologic, and
   Neonatal Nursing Specialties

HAKANSON AND COMPANY, INC.

303 Freeport Road
Pittsburgh, PA 15215-3131
Tel: (412)781-3255   *Fax:* (412)781-2871

5301 Shilshole Ave., N.W., Suite 340
Seattle, WA 98107
Tel: (206)783-5010   *Fax:* (206)783-4992

William P. Hakanson CAE, *C.E.O.*
Scott Palmer, *President*
Julie Schaffer, *Principal, Seattle Ofc.*

Hotel Electronic Distribution Network Ass'n
MESA Internat'l
Model Railroad Industry Ass'n
Supply Chain Council

HANGLEY MANAGEMENT SERVICES, INC.

P.O. Box 33108
Kansas City, MO 64114-0108
Tel: (816)941-4000   *Fax:* (816)941-2725

Lu Hangley, *Managing Director*

Nat'l Federation of Paralegal Ass'ns

HARRY HANSEN MANAGEMENT, INC.

151 Herricks Road, Suite 1
Garden City Park, NY 11040
Tel: (516)739-2510   *Fax:* (516)739-3803

Harry A. Hansen, *President*

American Soc. of Hypertension
Capital Markets Credit Analysts Soc.
Fixed Income Analysts Soc.
Soc. of Quantitative Analysts

the HARRINGTON co.

4248 Park Glen Road
Minneapolis, MN 55416-4758
Tel: (612)927-9220   *Fax:* (612)929-1318

Ed A. Harrington CAE, *President*

Air Conditioning Contractors of America - Minnesota Chapter
Aircraft Builders Council
American Correctional Food Service Ass'n
Captive Insurance Companies Ass'n
Coalition of Alternative Risk Funding Mechanisms
Community Ass'ns Institute - Minnesota Chapter
Dr. Anthony Downs Annual Real Estate Outlook
Hearing Aide of Minnesota
Midwest Direct Marketing Ass'n
Minnesota Construction Management Ass'n
Minnesota Public Health Ass'n
Minnesota Real Estate Services Ass'n
Minnesota Shopping Center Ass'n
Nat'l Ass'n of Home Inspectors
Nat'l Ass'n of Industrial and Office Properties - Minnesota
   Chapter
Nat'l Ass'n of Investment Professionals
Nat'l Ass'n of Women Business Owners - Minnesota Chapter
Nat'l Risk Retention Ass'n
Northland Heat Pump Ass'n
Professional Liability Underwriting Soc.
Public Entity Risk Institute
Registered Professional Liability Underwriters
Starkey Hearing Foundation
World Captive Forum

HARRINGTON MANAGEMENT, INC.

70 Walnut St.
Wellesley Hills, MA 02481-2175
Tel: (781)239-8215   *Fax:* (781)239-7553

Wesley E. Harrington CAE, *President*

American Ass'n of Healthcare Management
American Hepato-Pancreato-Biliary Ass'n
American Lithotripsy Soc.
Boston Healthcare Internat'l
Disease Management Ass'n of America

HARRIS MANAGEMENT GROUP, INC.

335 Beard St.
Tallahassee, FL 32303-6227
Tel: (850)222-6000   *Fax:* (850)681-2890

Robert C. Harris CAE, *President*
Mark A. Miller CMP, *V. President, Meetings and Conventions*

Automatic Merchandising Ass'n of Florida
Florida Ass'n of Speech-Language Pathologists and
   Audiologists
Florida Dental Hygiene Ass'n
Florida Motorcycle Dealers Ass'n
Florida Movers and Warehousemen's Ass'n
Florida Occupational Therapy Ass'n
Florida Skin Cancer Foundation
Florida Soc. of Anesthesiologists
Florida Soc. of Dermatologists
Florida Soc. of OB-GYN
Professional Opticians of Florida

HAUCK AND ASSOCIATES, INC.

1255 23rd St., N.W., Suite 850
Washington, DC 20037-1125
Tel: (202)452-8100   *Fax:* (202)833-3636

Sheldon J. Hauck, *President*
Chris Murphy, *V. President*

Air Courier Conference of America
American Coke and Coal Chemicals Institute
American Oilseed Coaltion
Ass'n of Meeting Professionals
Electromagnetic Energy Ass'n
Intellectual Property Owners Ass'n
Internat'l Ass'n of Seed Crushers
Internat'l Claim Ass'n
Internat'l Intellectual Property Ass'n
Nat'l Ass'n of Healthcare Consultants
Nat'l Corrugated Steel Pipe Ass'n
Nat'l Council of Intellectual Property Law Ass'ns
Nat'l Health Care Anti-Fraud Ass'n
Nat'l Oilseed Processors Ass'n
Soy Protein Council
State Government Affairs Council

LAWRENCE A. HELLER ASSOCIATES

7625 W. Hutchinson Ave.
Pittsburgh, PA 15218-1248
Tel: (412)244-0670   *Fax:* (412)244-9916

Lawrence A. Heller Ph.D., *President*

American College of Mental Health Administration
Healthcare Management Ass'n
TechLaw Group

RICHARD HESS AND ASSOCIATES

601 I-44 Service Road, Suite C
Oklahoma City, OK 73154-0508
Tel: (405)879-0027   *Fax:* (405)879-0304

4200 N. Lindsay
Oklahoma City, OK 73105
Tel: (405)424-1775

Richard L. Hess CAE, *President*

Metro Area Development Corporation
Nat'l Ass'n of Sonic Drive-In Franchisees
Natural Resources Education Foundation
Oklahoma Ass'n of Defense Counsel
Oklahoma Ass'n of Regional Councils
Oklahoma L-P Gas Research, Marketing and Safety
   Commission
Oklahoma Propane Gas Ass'n
Oklahoma Psychological Ass'n
Oklahoma Soc. of Ass'n Executives
Oklahomans for Energy and Jobs

HESSER GROUP, INC.

4510 West 89th St., Suite 101
Prairie Village, KS 66207-2282
Tel: (913)341-1155   *Fax:* (913)341-3625

J.M. Hesser, *President*

HILLIARD ASSOCIATION MANAGEMENT, INC.

P.O. Box 6524
Raleigh, NC 27628
Tel: (919)787-5859   *Fax:* (919)783-9563

William N. Hilliard, *President*

American College of Physicians-North Carolina Chapter
North Carolina Soc. of Anesthesiologists
North Carolina Soc. of Internal Medicine

HOLLAND-PARLETTE ASSOCIATES, INC

74 New Montgomery St., Suite 230
San Francisco, CA 94105-3411
Tel: (415)764-4822   *Fax:* (415)764-4915

Carol H. Parlette CAE, *Principal*
Kerry Parker CAE, *Principal*

American Soc. of Andrology
American Soc. of Civil Engineers - San Francisco Section
Carpet Fabricare Institute
Executive Council Western Conference of Association
   Executives
Information Technology and Telecommunications Ass'n
INQ - Your Thinking Profile
Marketing Ass'n of California
Medical Marketing Ass'n
Northern California Meeting Professionals Internat'l
Northern California Soc. of Ass'n Executives
Oxygen Soc., The
Professional Ass'n for Childhood Education
Structural Engineers Ass'n of Northern California
TeleCommunications Ass'n
Western Occupational and Environmental Medical Ass'n
Women's Forum West

HOST COMMUNICATIONS

546 E. Main St.
Lexington, KY 40508

Lynne Walker, *Principal*

Internat'l Spa and Fitness Ass'n

HOWELL MANAGEMENT COMPANY

P.O. Box 1420
Cherry Hill, NJ 08034-0054
Tel: (609)424-8998   *Fax:* (609)424-9248

Mary Connor, *President*

Fluid Power Distributors Ass'n
New Jersey Pest Control Ass'n
Philadelphia Suburban Gas Ass'n
Ultrasonic Industry Ass'n

HQ SERVICES

5775-G Peachtree-Dunwoody Road
Suite 500 G
Atlanta, GA 30342-1507
Tel: (404)252-3663   *Fax:* (404)252-0774

Robert C. Gelardi, *President & C.E.O.*
Richard C. Cristol, *Exec. V. President, Washington*

Ass'n of Fund Raisers and Direct Sellers
Board on Certification for Corporate Real Estate
Exhibit Designers and Producers Ass'n
Georgia Financial Services Ass'n
Lignin Institute
Messenger Courier Ass'n of the Americas

HUGHES MANAGEMENT SERVICES

214 S. Pearl St.
Natchez, MS 39120-3421
Tel: (601)446-5110   *Fax:* (601)446-7113

Casey Ann Hughes Ph.D., *President*

HUNT MANAGEMENT SYSTEMS

2 Wisconsin Circle, Suite 670
Chevy Chase, MD 20815-7003
Tel: (301)718-7722   *Fax:* (301)718-9440

Frederick D. Hunt Jr., *President*

Soc. of Professional Benefit Administrators

INDUSTRIAL ASSOCIATION MANAGEMENT, INC.

1901 N. Ft. Myer Dr.
Arlington, VA 22209-1706
Tel: (703)525-2514   *Fax:* (703)525-2515

James J. Houston CAE, *President*

Industrial Heating Equipment Ass'n

INFOMARKETING, INC.

P.O. Box 3159
Durham, NC 27715-3159
Tel: (919)383-0044   *Fax:* (919)383-0035

Stevie Hughes, *President and C.E.O.*

Ad Club of the Triangle
Ass'n for Corporate Growth - Triangle Chapter
Atlantic Coast Exposition
Carolina/Virginia Dairy Products Ass'n
Dixie Flyers Ass'n
North Carolina Amusement Machine Ass'n
North Carolina Vending Ass'n
South Carolina Automatic Merchandising Ass'n
Southeastern Refreshment Ass'n
Southern Ass'n of Dairy Food Manufacturers
Virginia Automatic Merchandising Ass'n

INFORM, INC.

P.O. Box 1708
Hickory, NC 28603
Tel: (704)322-7766   *Fax:* (704)322-4868

Paul F. Fogleman, *Exec. Director*

Carolina Foodservice Suppliers Ass'n
Carolina Hosiery Ass'n

INNOVATIVE ASSOCIATION SERVICES, INC.

P.O. Box 130220
Birmingham, AL 35213
Tel: (205)802-7551   *Fax:* (205)802-7553

Byron W. McCain CAE, *President*

Alabama Ass'n of Health Plans
Alabama Marine and Recreation Ass'n
Birmingham Hospitality Ass'n
Southeastern Regional Ass'n of Physical Plant Administrators
Speech and Hearing Ass'n of Alabama

INTEGRATED CAPITOL STRATEGIES

Ruggles Bldg. III, Suite I
553 Rte. 3-A
Bow, NH 03304
Tel: (603)226-4400   *Fax:* (603)226-4406

Clark T. Corson, *President*

Atlantic Procurement Affiliates
Compaq Services, Inc.
Jefson, Inc.
New Hampshire Troopers Ass'n
New Hampshire Wholesale Beverage Ass'n

INTEGRATED SOLUTIONS AND SERVICES, INC.

P.O. Box 515
Somers, NY 10589
Tel: (914)276-2910   *Fax:* (914)276-2816

John H. Powers, *President*

INTER-ASSOCIATES INC.

1600 Wilson Blvd., Suite 901
Arlington, VA 22209-2505
Tel: (703)812-9433   *Fax:* (703)812-8743

William H. Werst Jr., *President*

Suppliers of Advanced Composite Materials Ass'n
United States Advanced Ceramics Ass'n

INTERACTIVE MANAGEMENT

3867 Tennyson St.
Denver, CO 80212-2107
Tel: (303)433-4446   *Fax:* (303)458-0002

Roberta Bourn, *President*
Gary Leeper, *V. President and C.E.O.*

Colorado Ass'n of Distributors
Professional Engineers of Colorado
Rocky Mountain Fabricare Ass'n

INTERNATIONAL ASSOCIATION MANAGERS

1224 N. Nokomis, N.E.
Alexandria, MN 56308
Tel: (320)763-5190   *Fax:* (320)763-9290

Robert G. Johnson, *Executive Director*

Ass'n of Construction Inspectors
Environmental Assessment Ass'n
Housing Inspection Foundation
Internat'l Real Estate Institute
Internat'l Travel Writers and Editors Ass'n
Nat'l Ass'n of Real Estate Appraisers
Nat'l Ass'n of Review Appraisers and Mortgage Underwriters
Professional Women's Appraisal Ass'n

INTERNATIONAL MEETINGS, INC.

4424 Montgomery Ave., Suite 201
Bethesda, MD 20814
Tel: (301)654-6499   *Fax:* (301)654-3739

Suzette Gomolisky, *President*

Internat'l Pension and Employee Benefits Lawyers Ass'n
Nat'l Soc. of Fund Raising Executives - Greater Washington,
   DC Area Chapter

JAFIC ASSOCIATION MANAGEMENT, INC.

P.O. Box 180458
Casselberry, FL 32718-0458
Tel: (407)260-1313   *Fax:* (407)260-5732

Janice Ficarrotto, *President*

Air Conditioning Contractors Ass'n - Central Florida
Air Conditioning Contractors Ass'n Apprenticeship Program
American Soc. of CLU and ChFC - Central Florida Chapter
Central Florida Plumbing, Heating, and Cooling Contractors
   Ass'n
Florida Air Conditioning Contractors Ass'n
Florida Ass'n of Electrical Contractors
Florida Ass'n of Electrical Contractors - Central Florida
Florida Ass'n of Electrical Contractors Apprenticeship
   Program

ANTHONY J. JANNETTI, INC.

East Holly Ave., Box 56
Pitman, NJ 08071-0056
Tel: (609)256-2300   *Fax:* (609)589-7463

Anthony J. Jannetti, *President*

Academy of Medical-Surgical Nurses
American Academy of Ambulatory Care Nursing
American Nephrology Nurses Ass'n
American Soc. of Plastic and Reconstructive Surgical Nurses
Certification Board for Urologic Nurses and Associates
Dermatology Nurses Ass'n
NAON Foundation
Nat'l Ass'n of Orthopaedic Nurses
Nat'l Federation for Specialty Nursing Organizations
Nephrology Nursing Certification Board
Orthopaedic Nurses Certification Board
Plastic Surgical Nursing Certification Board
Soc. of Urologic Nurses and Associates

JN EXECUTIVE MANAGEMENT

1651 East 4th St., Suite 244
Santa Ana, CA 92701
Tel: (714)835-6209   *Fax:* (714)835-7742

Jo Nichols, *Executive Director*

American Soc. of Civil Engineers-Los Angeles Section
Nat'l Soc. of Fund Raising Executives - Orange County
Orange Coast Estate Planning Council
Orange County Ass'n of Health Underwriters
Orange County Chapter - Internat'l Ass'n for Financial
   Planners
Orange County Life Underwriters Ass'n
Planned Giving Roundtable of Orange County
Southern California Financial Planning Conference

JONES McADEN AND ASSOCIATES

P.O. Box 11937
Columbia, SC 29211-1937
Tel: (803)771-4271   *Fax:* (803)771-4272

Joe S. Jones III, *Owner*

American College of Cardiology - South Carolina Chapter
American Physical Therapy Ass'n - South Carolina Chapter
Consulting Engineers of South Carolina
South Carolina Economic Developers Ass'n
South Carolina Soc. of Ass'n Executives
South Carolina Soc. of Professional Engineers

JTL & ASSOCIATES, INC.

6057 Arlington Expressway
P.O. Box 8826
Jacksonville, FL 32239
Tel: (904)724-3003   *Fax:* (904)725-9993

John T. Lowe, *President*

Jacksonville Marine Ass'n

KARE ASSOCIATION MANAGEMENT SERVICES

2170 S. Parker Road, Suite 263
Denver, CO 80231
Tel: (303)750-9764   *Fax:* (303)750-0085

Karen M. Renshaw CAE, *President*

Colorado Human Resource Ass'n
Colorado Solar Energy Industries Ass'n
Colorado Speakers Ass'n
Colorado Technical Recruiters Network
Rocky Mountain Region Professional Products Ass'n

KAUTTER MANAGEMENT GROUP, INC.

P.O. Box 150127
Altamonte Springs, FL   32715-0127
Tel: (407)774-7880   *Fax:* (407)774-6440

Willard S. Kautter CAE, *President*

Downtown Athletic Club of Orlando
Downtown Athletic Club of Orlando Foundation
Florida Academy of Physicians Assistants
Florida Ass'n of Nurse Anesthetists
Florida Ass'n of Self Insurance
Florida Ass'n of Special Districts
Florida CCIM Chapter
Florida Court Reporters Ass'n
Florida Legal Assistants Ass'n
Florida Lipid Ass'n
Florida Magazine Ass'n
Florida Vacation Rental Managers Ass'n
Institute of Real Estate Management - Central Florida
Legal Image Network Communications
Michael J. Reid Memorial Scholarship Fund
NAPR Services, Inc.
Nat'l Ass'n of Industrial and Office Properties - Central Florida
Nat'l Ass'n of Physician Recruiters
Soc. for Technological Advancement of Reporting
Space Coast Apartment Ass'n
U.S. Optimist Dinghy Ass'n

THE KELLEN COMPANY

5775 Peachtree-Dunwoody Road
Suite 500-G
Atlanta, GA   30342-1507
Tel: (404)252-3663   *Fax:* (404)252-0774

1101 15th St., N.W., Suite 202
Washington, DC   20005-5002
Tel: (202)785-3232   *Fax:* (202)223-9741

Robert C. Gelardi, *President & C.E.O.*
Richard E. Cristol, *Exec. V President*

Ass'n for Dressings and Sauces
Calorie Control Council
Chilled Foods Ass'n
Concord Grape Ass'n
Food Update
Healthcare Convention and Exhibitors Ass'n
Internat'l Food Additives Council
Internat'l Formula Council
Internat'l Glutamate Technical Committee
Internat'l Jelly and Preserve Ass'n
Nat'l Ass'n of Margarine Manufacturers
Nat'l Institute of Oilseed Products
Nat'l Pecan Shellers Ass'n
Processed Apples Institute
Vinegar Institute

THE KELLOUGH GROUP

1650 S. Dixie Hwy., 5th Floor
Boca Raton, FL   33432
Tel: (561)395-7557   *Fax:* (561)395-8557

David L. Kellough, *President*

ACCA Gold Coast
Air-Conditioning and Refrigeration Wholesalers Ass'n Internat'l
ARW Research and Educational Foundation
Electrical Generating Systems Ass'n

KEENEY CORPORATION, INC.

118 North 8th St.
Richmond, VA   23219-2306
Tel: (804)643-0312   *Fax:* (804)643-0311

Bruce B. Keeney Sr., *President*

Ass'n of Independent Funeral Homes of Virginia
Virginia Ass'n of Convenience Stores
Virginia Automotiove Repair Ass'n
Virginia Gasoline Marketers Council
Virginia Optometric Ass'n

KIMBALL & ASSOCIATES

6707 Old Dominion Dr., Suite 315
McLean, VA   22101-4503
Tel: (703)556-9300   *Fax:* (703)556-9301

Philip Kimball, *President*

Nat'l Ass'n of the Remodeling Industry - Metropolitan
     Washington Chapter
Nat'l Dry Bean Council
United States Apple Export Council

KINDER AND ASSOCIATES, INC.

P.O. Box 15466
Santa Ana, CA   92735
Tel: (714)508-4900   *Fax:* (714)261-2594

2000 K St., N.W., Suite 401
Washington, DC   20006
Tel: (202)463-8162   *Fax:* (202)463-8155

James A. Kinder, *Chairman of the Board*
George J. Pantos, *Managing Partner, Washington*

American Motorsports Public Affairs Council
ERISA Compliance Institute
Nat'l Ass'n of Graphic and Product Identification
     Manufacturers
Public Communicators of Los Angeles
Self Insurance Educational Foundation
Self Insurance Institute of America
Self Insurers Publishing Corporation

KING & ASSOCIATES, INC.

1024 Dublin Road
Columbus, OH   43215-1167
Tel: (614)488-0617   *Fax:* (614)488-0352

Gene P. King, *President*

American Ass'n of Veterinary Clinicians
Franklin County Trial Lawyers Ass'n
Ohio Court Reporters Ass'n
Opticians Ass'n of Ohio
Professional Photographers of Ohio

KLEIN & SAKS, INC.

1026 16th St., N.W., Suite 101
Washington, DC   20036
Tel: (202)835-0952   *Fax:* (202)835-0155

John H. Lutley, *Chairman*

American Zinc Ass'n
Gold Institute
Silver Institute

KNIGHT ENTERPRISES LTD

4840 West 15th St., Suite 1000
Lawrence, KS   66049
Tel: (785)843-5511   *Fax:* (785)843-7555

James T. Knight, *President*

Building Component Manufacturers Conference
Kansas Ass'n of Life Underwriters
Kansas Internat'l
Kansas Vocational Ass'n
Midwest Roofing Contractors Ass'n
Nat'l Frame Builders Ass'n

KRISSOFF & ASSOCIATES, INC.

3 Church Circle, Suite 250
Annapolis, MD   21401-1933
Tel: (410)267-0023   *Fax:* (410)267-7546

Michael R. Krissoff, *President*

Asphalt Emulsion Manufacturers Ass'n
Asphalt Recycling and Reclaiming Ass'n

LANGLEY GROUP INC.

7920 Ward Pkwy., Suite 208
Kansas City, MO   64114
Tel: (816)444-1220   *Fax:* (816)363-0027

100 N. Broadway, Mezzanine Level
Aberdeen, WA   98520
Tel: (360)533-7895   *Fax:* (360)538-7208

Charles G. Langley, *President*

City of Norfolk, Virginia Convention and Visitors Bureau
Missouri Public Transit Ass'n
Tourism Grays Harbor

LARIMER ASSOCIATION & SPECIAL EVENTS RESOURCES

5 Spring St.
P.O. Box 150
Eureka Springs, AR   72632-0150
Tel: (501)253-8226   *Fax:* (501)253-8225

Gail Larimer, *Principal*

Antique and Amusement Photographers Internat'l

C.A. LARSEN AND ASSOCIATES

3335 N. Arlington Heights Road, Suite E
Arlington Heights, IL   60004
Tel: (847)577-7200   *Fax:* (847)577-7276

C. Andrew Larsen CAE, CCM, *President*

Lightning Protection Institute
System Independent Data Format Ass'n
Wiring Harness Manufacturers Ass'n

LEGISLATIVE AND ASSOCIATION MANAGEMENT

P.O. Box 50025
Austin, TX   78763
Tel: (512)345-8299   *Fax:* (512)346-9905

Charles H. Huff CAE, *President*

LEGISLATIVE INFORMATION SERVICES OF HAWAII

677 Ala Moana Blvd., Suite 815
Honolulu, HI   96813-5416
Tel: (808)533-6750   *Fax:* (808)599-2606

Richard C. Botti CAE, *President*

Autobody and Paint Ass'n of Hawaii
Hawaii Automotive Repair and Retail Gasoline Dealers Ass'n
Hawaii Fashion Industry Ass'n
Hawaii Food and Beverage Ass'n
Hawaii Food Industry Ass'n
Hawaii Publishers Ass'n
Retail Liquor Dealers Ass'n of Hawaii

LEONG AND ASSOCIATES

4815 Rugby Ave., Suite 203
Bethesda, MD   20814-3033
Tel: (301)654-3967   *Fax:* (301)718-8692

Lawrence H. Leong CMP, *President*

North American Skull Base Soc.

LESTER MANAGEMENT SERVICES

P.O. Box 15322
Long Beach, CA   90815-0322
Tel: (562)425-1721   *Fax:* (562)425-0199

Vickie Lester, *President*

Los Angeles Fastener Ass'n
Southern California Decorating Products Ass'n
Western Ass'n of Fastener Distributors

LIVENGOOD SOARDS AND ASSOCIATES, INC.

115 W. Washington St., Suite 1165 South
Indianapolis, IN   46204-3407
Tel: (317)673-4200   *Fax:* (317)673-4210

John Livengood, *President*
Bill Soards, *V President*

Indiana Ass'n of Beverage Retailers
Indiana Hotel and Motel Ass'n
Restaurant and Hospitality Ass'n of Indiana

LOBUE & COMPANY

404 Balboa St.
San Francisco, CA   94118
Tel: (415)750-8350   *Fax:* (415)751-4829

Michael LoBue, *President*

California Group of Accounting Firms
HomeRF Working Group
I2O Special Interest Group
Key Recovery Alliance
SCSI Trade Ass'n

LONG & ASSOCIATES, INC.

28 Lowry Drive
P.O. Box 117
West Milton, OH   45383-0117
Tel: (513)698-4188   *Fax:* (513)698-6153

Roe Long, *C.E.O.*
Christopher S. Long, *Exec. V. President*

American Rolling Door Institute
Institute of Door Dealers Accreditation
Internat'l Door Ass'n
Systems Builders Ass'n

LOVELESS MANAGEMENT & LEGISLATIVE SERVICES, INC.

P.O. Box 43668
Jacksonville, FL   32203-3668
Tel: (904)641-2733   *Fax:* (904)396-9928

Gary W. Loveless CAE, *President*

Community Resource Institute
Florida Enterprise Zone Coalition
Jacksonville Wrecker Ass'n
TECHNET Internat'l - Atlantic Coast Chapter

'M COMPANIES

3942 N. Upland St.
Arlington, VA   22207-4642
Tel: (703)533-9539   *Fax:* (703)533-1612

Milton M. Bush JD, CAE, *Principal*

Independent Ass'n of Accredited Registrars
Industrial Computing Soc.
Internat'l Federation of Inspection Agencies - Americas
     Committee

MACKIN AND COMPANY

122 S. Swan St.
Albany, NY   12210--175
Tel: (518)449-4698   *Fax:* (518)432-5651

Robert E. Mackin, *Principal*

Ass'n of Financial Guaranty Insurors
Nat'l Conference of Insurance Legislators
Nat'l Council of Legislators from Gaming States

MAINE ASS'N MANAGEMENT SERVICES

RFD #7, Box 1940
Augusta, ME   04330
Tel: (207)623-7521

Richard W. Billings Ph.D., *Exec. Director*

Informed Notaries of Maine

MANAGEMENT ALTERNATIVES, INC.

11 Tamarac Ave.
New City, NY 10956-6304
Tel: (914)639-1166   Fax: (914)639-1168

Leslie A. Davis, *President*

Illinois Soc. of Oral and Maxillofacial Surgeons

MANAGEMENT CONCEPTS, INC.

1418 Aversboro Road
Garner, NC 27529-4547
Tel: (919)779-5709   Fax: (919)779-5642

Charlene B. Barbour, *President*

Duke University Medical Center Nurse Anesthetists Alumni
  Ass'n
Nat'l Federation of Licensed Practical Nurses
North Carolina Acupuncture Licensing Board
North Carolina Ass'n of Nurse Anesthetists
North Carolina Ass'n of Teacher Assistants
North Carolina Ass'n on Aging
North Carolina Board of Dietetics and Nutrition
North Carolina Campground Owners Ass'n
North Carolina Soc. of Accountants
North Carolina Soc. of Oral and Maxillofacial Surgeons
North Carolina Soc. of Radiologic Technologists

MANAGEMENT EXCELLENCE, INC.

11 W. Monument Ave., Suite 510
P.O. Box 2307
Dayton, OH 45401-2307
Tel: (937)586-3700   Fax: (937)586-3699

F.W. Rickenbach CAE, *President*

American College of Surgeons - Ohio Chapter
BARCO Graphics Users Ass'n
Body Shop Owners Ass'n
GMV Emergency Medical Services Council
Nat'l Ass'n of Nephrology Technologists and Technicians
Nat'l Nephrology Technology Certification Board
Ohio Committee on Trauma
Ohio Users Ass'n
Sonitrol Nat'l Dealers Ass'n

MANAGEMENT OPTIONS, INC.

107 S. West St., Suite 110
Alexandria, VA 22314-2891
Tel: (703)486-8722   Fax: (703)486-8724

Thomas C. Osina CAE, *President and C.E.O.*
Lee Smith CAE, *V.P., Administration and Finance*

Mid-Atlantic Propane Gas Ass'n
Virginia Propane Gas Ass'n
West Virginia Propane Gas Ass'n

MANAGEMENT PLUS

415 W. Golf Road, Suite 43
Arlington Heights, IL 60005-3923
Tel: (847)439-0492   Fax: (847)439-7294

Joe Polich, *President*

Production Engine Remanufacturers Ass'n

MANAGEMENT PLUS, INC.

71 Pinon Hill Place, N.E.
Albuquerque, NM 87122-1914
Tel: (505)856-6810   Fax: (505)856-6716

Vivienne Harwood Mattox, *Exec. Officer*

Ass'n of Vacuum Equipment Manufacturers Internat'l
Soc. of Vacuum Coaters

MANAGEMENT PLUS, LTD.

1604 N. Country Club Road
Tucson, AZ 85716
Tel: (520)325-1055   Fax: (520)325-7925

Laury L. Adsit, *President*
Deborah J. Barnett, *V. President*

Arizona Soc. of Health System Pharmacists
Building Owners and Managers of Greater Tucson
Nat'l Academy of Elder Law Attorneys
Nat'l Ass'n of Professional Geriatric Care Managers
Nat'l Elder Law Foundation
Nat'l Guardianship Ass'n
Nat'l Guardianship Foundation
Nat'l Spa and Pool Institute - Regional Chapter
Southern Arizona Veterinary Medical Ass'n

MANAGEMENT SERVICES

P.O. Box 579
Moorestown, NJ 08057
Tel: (609)234-0330   Fax: (609)727-9504

Dennis C. Neff, *President*
June P. Neff, *V. President*

Delaware Valley Planned Giving Council
Greater Philadelphia Area Meeting Planners Internat'l
Hospitality Sales and Marketing Ass'n - Greater Philadelphia
  Chapter
Internat'l Hard Anondizing Ass'n
Philadelphia Area Chapter - Internat'l Ass'n for Financial
  Planning
Philadelphia Ass'n of Metal Finishers
Philadelphia Business Executives
Philadelphia Estate Planning Council
Wise Foods Distributors Ass'n

MANAGEMENT SERVICES

P.O. Box 3050
Cheyenne, WY 82003
Tel: (307)637-7575   Fax: (307)634-0804

Dan J. Lex CAE, *President*

Northern Rockies Optometric Conference
Quality Health Care Foundation of Wyoming
Wyoming Optometric Ass'n

MANAGEMENT SERVICES TO ASSOCIATIONS

8421 Frost Way
Annandale, VA 22003
Tel: (703)280-4622   Fax: (703)280-0942

Kenton Pattie, *President*

Ass'n Chief Executive Council
Nat'l Ass'n of Police Equipment Distributors
Nat'l Center for Fair Competition
Nat'l Emergency Equipment Dealers Ass'n
Public Safety Coalition

MANAGEMENT SOLUTION FOR ASSOCIATIONS

234 Fifth Ave., Suite 403
New York, NY 10001
Tel: (212)481-3038   Fax: (212)481-3071

Rosemarie Sharpe, *President*

MANAGEMENT SOLUTIONS PLUS, INC.

15245 Shady Grove Road, Suite 130
Rockville, MD 20850
Tel: (301)258-9210   Fax: (301)990-9771

Beth W. Palys CAE, *President*

American Academy of Appellate Lawyers
American Soc. of Consulting Arborists
Council of Tree and Landscape Appraisers
Eastern Regional Nurserymen's Ass'n
Landscape Contractors Ass'n of Maryland, District of
  Columbia and Virginia
Nat'l Conference on Weights and Measures
Public Relations Soc. of America - Maryland Chapter

MARION ASSOCIATES

1045 E. Atlantic Ave., Suite 206
Delray Beach, FL 33483
Tel: (561)266-9016   Fax: (561)266-9017

P.O. Box 100
Ho-Ho-Kus, NJ 07423
Tel: (201)445-4223   Fax: (201)445-3181

Joseph Marion, *President*
Ruth Stramberg, *Manager, New Jersey Office*

Ass'n of Service and Computer Dealers Internat'l
Florida Internet Service Providers Ass'n
North-American Ass'n of Telecommunications Dealers

MARKETSHARE, INC.

5530 Wisconsin Ave., Suite 1110
Bethesda, MD 20815
Tel: (301)656-9011   Fax: (301)656-9008

Jay McCrensky, *President*

American Ass'n for Affirmative Action
American Ass'n for Chinese Companies
Ass'n for Competitive Internat'l Telecommunications
Ass'n for Internet Marketing
Employment Legal Issue Forum
End Users of Derivatives Ass'n
Internat'l Private Energy Ass'n
Moldovan-American Chamber of Commerce
Romanian-American Chamber of Commerce
S-Corporation Ass'n
World Poker Alliance

MARSHALL AND COMPANY ASSOCIATION MANAGEMENT

7702 Leesburg Pike, Suite 400
Tysons Corner, VA 22043-2612
Tel: (703)442-0759   Fax: (703)821-3694

Sherryl Marshall, *President*

Advertising Club of Metropolitan Washington
Direct Marketing Ass'n of Washington
Meeting Planners Internat'l - Potomac Chapter
Professional Convention Management Ass'n - Washington DC
  Chapter
Washington Ass'n - Financial Management Roundtable

MATTERSON ASSOCIATES, INC.

427 Kenwood Ave.
Delmar, NY 12054-1805
Tel: (518)439-0981   Fax: (518)439-0980

Elizabeth V. Matterson, *V. President*

College of Diplomates of the American Board of Orthodontics
Northeastern Soc. of Orthodontists

THE MATTISON COMPANY

430 N. Park Ave., Suite 210
Indianapolis, IN 46202-3677
Tel: (317)685-8433   Fax: (317)684-9457

Gary A. Price, *President*

Indiana Academy of Family Physicians Foundation
Indiana Construction Roundtable
Indiana Subcontractors Ass'n
Indiana Water Pollution Control Ass'n
Metro Indianapolis Coalition for Construction Safety

McBRIDE & ASSOCIATES, INC.

201 North 8th St., Suite 400
Lincoln, NE 68508-1347
Tel: (402)476-3852   Fax: (402)476-6547

David S. McBride, *President*

Ass'n of Official Seed Analysts
Nat'l Ass'n of Social Workers - Nebraska Chapter
Nebraska Arborists Ass'n
Nebraska Blue Flame Gas Ass'n
Nebraska Optometric Ass'n
Nebraska Soc. of Health-System Pharmacists
Nebraska State Ass'n of Life Underwriters
Nebraska Statewide Independent Living Council
North Central States Optometric Council

MCCULLOCH AND ASSOCIATES, INC.

584 Bellerive Drive, Suite 3-D
Annapolis, MD 21401
Tel: (410)974-4472   Fax: (410)757-3809

Mary Jo McCulloch, *President*

Air Conditioning Contractors of America, Central Maryland
  Chapter
Alcohol Beverage Commission of Prince George's County
Capitol Region USA
Maryland Ass'n of Private Career Schools
Maryland Hotel and Motel Ass'n
Maryland Recyclers Coalition
Maryland Tourism Council
Nat'l Spa and Pool Institute - Chesapeake Chapter

McKELLAR, INC

2985 River Road South
P.O. Box 2167
Salem, OR 97308-2167
Tel: (503)581-7245   Fax: (503)585-9684

Robert H. McKellar, *President*

Oregon Forest Products Transportation Ass'n

MCLEAN GROUP

1242 Colonial Road
McLean, VA 22101
Tel: (703)748-2678   Fax: (703)748-2679

Robert S. Bolan Ph.D., CAE, *Principal*

Citizens for Public Research and Education Funding
Health Care Quality Alliance

McRAE & COMPANY, INC.

1401 Maclay Commerce Dr.
P.O. Box 12187
Tallahassee, FL 32317-2187
Tel: (904)906-0099   Fax: (904)906-0077

Herbert W. McRae CAE, *President*

Independent Insurance Agents of Tallahassee

MEDICAL ASSOCIATION MANAGEMENT COMPANY

1950 Old Tustin Ave.
Santa Ana, CA 92705
Tel: (714)550-9155   Fax: (714)550-9234

Frank DeSantis CAE, *President*
Kathy DeSantis CMP, *V. President*

American College of Physician Inventors
American Urological Ass'n - Western Section
California Urological Ass'n
Inland Empire Urological Soc.
Orange County Renaissance Foundation
Soc. of Urologic Cryosurgeons

MEDICAL EDUCATION COLLABORATIVE

1800 Jackson St., Suite 200
Golden, CO 80401
Tel: (303)278-1900   Fax: (303)278-1985

462 30th St.
San Francsico, CA 94131
Tel: (415)643-3470   Fax: (415)643-3471

Charles Spickert MPH, *President & C.E.O.*
Mark Madsen, *Director, San Francisco Office*

MELBY CAMERON AND HULL

23607 Hwy. 99, Suite 2-C
P.O. Box 2016
Edmonds, WA 98020-9516
Tel: (206)774-7479 *Fax:* (206)771-9588

Lynn L. Melby CAE, *C.E.O.*
Donna J. Cameron CAE, *President*
Patricia A. Hull, *V. President*

AIDS Services and Prevention Coalition
Home Care Ass'n of Washington
Independent Insurance Agents and Brokers of King County
Nat'l Ass'n of Industrial and Office Properties - Washington
  State Chapter
Nat'l Ass'n of Professional Mortgage Women
Nat'l Ass'n of Purchasing Management - Western
  Washington
Northwest Florists' Ass'n
Northwest Hearth Products Ass'n
Washington Medical Case Management Ass'n
Washington State Federation of Clubs
Washington State Psychological Ass'n

MEREDITH AND HOPKINS, INC.

244 Broad St.
Red Bank, NJ 07701-2315
Tel: (732)842-5070 *Fax:* (732)219-1938

Gerri Hopkins, *President*
George Meredith, *Partner*

Ass'n of Incentive Marketing
Ass'n of Retail Marketing Services
Premium Marketing Club of New York
Radio Club of America

MERIDETH ASSOCIATION MANAGEMENT

4725 E. Sunrise Dr., Suite 139
Tucson, AZ 85718
Tel: (520)299-6787 *Fax:* (520)299-6431

Jeanie Merideth, *Owner*

Chefs Ass'n of Southern Arizona
Greater Tucson Ass'n of Life Underwriters
Inventors Ass'n of Arizona
Southern Arizona Inn-Keepers Ass'n

THE MERIDIAN GROUP

P.O. Box 160
Del Mar, CA 92014
Tel: (619)792-3883 *Fax:* (619)792-3884

Katherine Clark, *Partner*

Information Technologies Credit Union Ass'n
Nat'l Ass'n of Credit Union Chairmen
Nat'l Ass'n of Credit Union Supervisory and Auditing
  Committees
Nat'l Council of Postal Credit Unions
Western Ass'n of Technology Credit Unions

THE MESSERSMITH GROUP

1730 I St., Suite 240
Sacramento, CA 95814-3017
Tel: (916)443-9023 *Fax:* (916)443-8065

Dr. Lloyd E. Messersmith, *President*

Building Owners and Managers Ass'n of Sacramento
California Ass'n of Mortgage Brokers
California Cleaners Ass'n
California Council of Western Ass'n of Convention and
  Visitors Bureaus
California Travel Industry Ass'n
Sacramento Hotel Ass'n
Taxicab Paratransit Ass'n of California
Western Ass'n of Convention and Visitors Bureaus

MINETTA A. MILLER MULTIPLE MANAGEMENT

1801 Broadway, Suite 760
Denver, CO 80202
Tel: (303)298-1700 *Fax:* (303)861-2895

Minetta A. Miller, *Owner*

Air Force Academy Quarterback Club of Denver
Professional Secretaries Internat'l - Denver Chapter
Rocky Mountain Petroleum Pioneers
Women in Mining Nat'l
Women in Mining Nat'l - Denver Chapter

MILLIRON AND ASSOCIATES

200 N. Third St., Suite 1500
Harrisburg, PA 17101
Tel: (717)232-5322 *Fax:* (717)232-1544

John P. Milliron, *Principal*
Ken Brandt, *Acct. Executive*

Bowling Proprietors Ass'n of Pennsylvania
Pennsylvania Amusement and Music Machine Ass'n
Pennsylvania State Council of Farm Organizations

MISSISSIPPI ASSOCIATION MANAGERS

812 N. President St.
Jackson, MS 39202-2560
Tel: (601)354-2049 *Fax:* (601)352-4384

Kathy C. Jackson CAE, *President*

American Institute of Architects - Mississippi
Louisiana Mississippi Drycleaners & Laundry Ass'n
Mississippi Architectural Foundation
Mississippi Psychological Ass'n
Mississippi Soc. of Ass'n Executives
Mississippi State Board of Psychological Examiners
Mississippi Tourism Promotion Ass'n
Mississippi-Louisiana Brick Manufacturers Ass'n

MMA MANAGEMENT SERVICES

60 Temple Pl.
Boston, MA 02111
Tel: (617)426-6060 *Fax:* (617)695-1314

111 Winners Circle
P.O. Box 12250
Albany, NY 12212-2250
Tel: (518)458-1026 *Fax:* (518)458-7811

Brent Wilkes, *President*
Kevin Hume, *Exec. V. President*

Public Employee Risk Management Ass'n

MONTOYA MANAGEMENT INC.

6845 Parkdale Place, Suite A
Indianapolis, IN 46254
Tel: (317)297-5875 *Fax:* (317)387-3387

James D. Montoya CAE, *President*

Central Indiana Chapter - American Soc. for Training and
  Development
Electronics Representatives Ass'n - Indiana/Kentucky Chpter
Internat'l Group of Agencies and Bureaus
Nat'l Center for Creativity

MULTISERVICE MANAGEMENT COMPANY

994 Old Eagle School Road, Suite 1019
Wayne, PA 19087-1802
Tel: (610)971-4850 *Fax:* (610)971-4859

Robert H. Ecker, *President and C.E.O.*

Aircraft Locknut Manufacturers Ass'n
American Soc. of Heating, Refrigeration, and Air Conditioning
  Engineers - Philadelphia Area
Fluid Sealing Ass'n
Gasket Fabricators Ass'n
Nat'l Ass'n of Diaper Services
Nat'l Classification Management Soc.
Professional Apparel Ass'n

MYERS/SMITH, INC.

3685 Motor Ave., Suite 240
Los Angeles, CA 90034-5750
Tel: (310)287-1826 *Fax:* (310)287-1851

Robert Myers, *President*
Leslee C. Myers, *V. President*

Autotestcon
Electronics Representatives Ass'n
IEEE Industry Applications Soc.
IEEE Instrumentation and Measurement Soc.
IEEE Instrumentation and Measurement Technology
  Conference
IEEE Power Electronics Soc.
Nat'l Electronic Distributors Ass'n

NEER COMMUNICATIONS CO.

5342 N. Reese Ave.
Fresno, CA 93722
Tel: (209)276-8494 *Fax:* (209)276-8496

Michael R. Neer, *President*

Personalization and Identification Ass'n

NET, INC.

8000 Towers Crescent Dr., Suite 1350
Vienna, VA 22182
Tel: (703)760-7874 *Fax:* (703)641-0185

Katherine M. Nickell, *President and C.E.O.*

NIKE ASSOCIATION MANAGEMENT, INC.

P.O. Box 647
Northbrook, IL 60065-0647
Tel: (847)559-9233

Pamela W. Franzen, *President*

Associated Fur Industries of Chicagoland
Nat'l Onsite Wastewater Recycling Ass'n
Sump and Sewage Pump Manufacturers Ass'n

NONPROFIT MANAGEMENT ASSOCIATES INCORPORATED

1555 Connecticut Ave., N.W., Suite 200
Washington, DC 20036
Tel: (202)462-9600 *Fax:* (202)462-9043

Keith R. Krueger CAE, *Exec. Director*

Aspirin Foundation of America
Associates of the Nat'l Agricultural Library
Choo San Goh Foundation
Consortium for School Networking
Friends of the Libraries of the Blind and Physically
  Handicapped

Friends of the Nat'l Library of Medicine

NORBERG & ASSOCIATES

P.O. Box 2296
Littleton, CO 80161-2296
Tel: (303)791-4482

Carl O. Norberg CAE, *President*

Colorado-Wyoming Hospitality Sales and Marketing Ass'n
Multi-Cultural Events Committee

O'BRYON AND COMPANY

4424 Montgomery Ave., Suite 102
Bethesda, MD 20814
Tel: (301)652-5066 *Fax:* (301)913-9146

6707 Old Dominion Dr., Suite 315
McLean, VA 22101

David S. O'Bryon CAE, *President*

American Ass'n of Limited Partners
Ass'n of Chiropractic Colleges
Composting Council
Composting Council Research and Education Foundation
Retirement Industry Trust Ass'n

O'DONNELL ASSOCIATES, INC.

364 Parsippany Road, Suitre 9-B
Parsippany, NJ 07054
Tel: (973)887-4889 *Fax:* (973)887-8145

Jeanne O'Donnell, *President*

New Jersey Ass'n of Temporary Services
Outplacement Internat'l

OEI - AN ASSOCIATION MANAGEMENT COMPANY

1711 West County Road B, Suite 300-North
Roseville, MN 55113-4036
Tel: (651)635-0206 *Fax:* (651)635-0307

John Arlandson, *President*

OFFINGER MANAGEMENT COMPANY

1100-H Brandywine Blvd.
P.O. Box 2188
Zanesville, OH 43702-2188
Tel: (614)452-4541 *Fax:* (614)452-2552

Walter E. Offinger, *President*
Sarel Offinger, *Exec. V. President*

Art Glass Suppliers Ass'n Internat'l
Ass'n of Crafts and Creative Industries
Ceramic Manufacturers Ass'n
Miniatures Industry Ass'n of America
Nat'l Needlework Ass'n
Ohio Turfgrass Ass'n
Soc. of Craft Designers

OLSON MANAGEMENT GROUP

4101 Lake Boone Trail, Suite 201
Raleigh, NC 27607-7506
Tel: (919)787-5181 *Fax:* (919)787-4916

Ralph Marlett, *Interim Director*

American College of Cardiology - North Carolina Chapter
American Holistic Medical Foundation
American Soc. for Cytotechnology
American Soc. of Echocardiography
Art Libraries Soc./North America
Ass'n of American Editorial Cartoonists
Cable Tray Institute
Conference Travel Ltd.
Florida Multi-Housing Laundry Ass'n
Internat'l Lactation Consultant Ass'n
Internat'l Soc. for Adult Congenital Cardiac Disease
Mid-Atlantic Newspaper Advertising and Marketing
  Executives
Multi-Housing Laundry Ass'n
Nat'l Cartoonists Soc.
Nat'l Nurses Soc. on Addictions
North Carolina Ass'n of Mortgage Brokers
North Carolina College of Emergency Physicians
North Carolina Land Title Ass'n
North Carolina Press Ass'n
North Carolina Press Services
North Carolina Travel and Tourism Coalition
North Carolina Utility Contractors Ass'n
Soc. for Cardiac Angiography and Interventions
Soc. of American Travel Writers
Soc. of Financial Examiners
Soc. of Healthcare Executive Assistants
Southern Innkeepers Ass'n
Tourism Education Foundation of North Carolina
Travel Council of North Carolina
Triangle Area Hotel-Motel Ass'n

ORGANIZATION ADMINISTRATORS, INC.

P.O. Box 7130
Deerfield, IL 60015-7130
Tel: (847)317-0033 *Fax:* (847)317-0036

Dorothy J. Collins, *President*

Illinois Development Council
Robert Morris Associates - Chicago Chapter
Sales and Marketing Executives - Chicago

ORGANIZATION MANAGEMENT

2971 Flowers Road South, Suite 266
Atlanta, GA 30341
Tel: (770)452-0660   *Fax:* (770)455-3879

Judy Stokes, *President*

Refrigerated Foods Ass'n

ORGANIZATION MANAGEMENT SERVICES OF WEST VIRGINIA

P.O. Box 1335
Charleston, WV 25325-1335
Tel: (304)342-4441   *Fax:* (304)345-0308

Floyd M. Sayre Jr., CAE, *President*

West Virginia Public Accountants Ass'n
West Virginia Tire Dealers Ass'n

ORGANIZATION MANAGEMENT, INC.

P.O. Box 896
Olympia, WA 98507
Tel: (360)943-8155   *Fax:* (360)586-5538

Jerry Crabill, *President*

Corvette and High Performance Soc.
Volunteer Leadership Institute
Washington Ass'n of Building Officials

ORGANIZATION MANAGEMENT, INC.

P.O. Box 56
Montgomery, AL 36101-0056
Tel: (334)263-3407   *Fax:* (334)263-3426

Tina Turner CAE, *President*

Alabama Aggregates Ass'n
Alabama Auctioneers Ass'n
Alabama Funeral Directors Ass'n
Alabama Hospitality Ass'n
Alabama Vending Ass'n
Vending Machine Ass'n of the Gulf South

ORGANIZATION SERVICES GROUP, INC.

222 S. Meramec, Suite 303
St. Louis, MO 63105-3514
Tel: (314)863-6232   *Fax:* (314)863-6457

Tonya J. Ferguson, *President*

American Ass'n for Therapeutic Humor
American College of Cardiology - Missouri Chapter
Missouri Women's Forum
St. Louis Area Hotel Ass'n
St. Louis Soc. of Ass'n Executives

ORGANIZATIONAL SERVICES, INC.

P.O. Box 6
Kearney, NJ 07032
Tel: (201)998-5153

Marianne H. Carney, *President*

Building Owners and Managers Ass'n - New Jersey Chapter
Building Owners and Managers Ass'n of Westchester County
Middle Atlantic Conference of Building Owners and Managers
New Jersey Advertising Club

PAI MANAGEMENT CORPORATION

4340 East West Hwy., Suite 401
Bethesda, MD 20814-4408
Tel: (301)656-4224   *Fax:* (301)656-0989

Norman E. Wallis Ph.D., *President*

American Board of Nursing Specialties
American Nat'l Metric Council
CMP Board (Convention Liaison Council)
Internat'l Council for Caring Communities
Nat'l Ass'n for Senior Living Industries
Soc. for Mucosal Immunology

THE PARKER ORGANIZATION

P.O. Box 33116
Indialantic, FL 32903
Tel: (407)722-1251   *Fax:* (407)722-9931

E.K. Fox, *President*

Automotive Lift Institute

PENCOR MAZUR LTD.

111 E. Wacker Dr., Suite 990
Chicago, IL 60601
Tel: (312)729-9900   *Fax:* (312)729-9800

Joel Shiffrin, *Chairman*
Mark D. Mazur, *President*
John Corcoran, *V. President*
George A. Buckley Jr., CAE, *V.P. and Director, Ass'n Operations*
Dan Shiffrin, *V.P. and Editorial Director*
Ruth Ann Southgate, *Asst. Director, Ass'n Operations*
Michelle Durham, *Director, Communications*

Alliance of Technology Professionals
Center for Management Advisors
Community Banking Advisory Network
Construction Industry CPA/Consultants Ass'n
CPA Auto Dealer Consultants Ass'n
CPA Manufacturing Services Ass'n

Law Firm Services Ass'n
Nat'l CPA Health Care Advisors Ass'n
Nat'l Litigation Support Services Ass'n
Not-for-Profit Services Ass'n

WILLIAM C. PFLAUM COMPANY

481 Carlisle Drive
Herndon, VA 20170-4823
Tel: (703)318-8966   *Fax:* (703)814-4961

William C. Pflaum, *President*
Erin Edwards, *Manager, Fin./Administration*

Contract Packagers Ass'n
Institute of Packaging Professionals
Packaging Education Forum
World Packaging Organisation

PERIPHERAL SERVICES, INC.

183 E. Main St., Suite 1200
P.O. Box 631 (ZIP Code 14603-0631)
Rochester, NY 14604-1617
Tel: (716)797-0705   *Fax:* (716)797-0708

Nancy C. Carleton CAE, *President*

Diversified Marketing Group
Genesee Land Trust
Nat'l Soc. of Fund Raising Executives - Genesee Valley Chapter
Rochester Advertising Federation
Rochester Chapter - CPCU
Upstate New York Chapter - IAFP

PHYLLIS PERRON & ASSOCIATES, INC.

451 Florida St., North Tower Suite 1400
Baton Rouge, LA 70801
Tel: (504)344-0620   *Fax:* (504)344-1132

Phyllis Perron, *President*

Louisiana Insurers' Conference
Louisiana Life and Health Insurance Guaranty Ass'n
Louisiana United Businesses Ass'n

JOE PHILLIPS

9910 W. Layton Ave.
Greenfield, WI 53228
Tel: (414)529-4702   *Fax:* (414)529-4722

Joe Phillips, *Executive Director*

Fair Aid Coalition
Illinois Sign Ass'n
Independent Heating Contractors Ass'n
Wisconsin Ass'n of Textile Services
Wisconsin Fabricare Institute
Wisconsin Landscape Federation
Wisconsin Nursery Ass'n

PHOENIX PROFESSIONAL PARTNERSHIPS, INC.

401 E. Jefferson St., Suite 205
Rockville, MD 20850-2617
Tel: (301)251-9133   *Fax:* (301)279-6749

Judith Costine Woodward CAE, *President*

American College of Epidemiology
Internat'l Ass'n of Business Communicators - Washington, DC Chapter
Soc. of Behavioral Medicine
Washington EdPress

PJ ASSOCIATES, INC.

19564 Club House Road
Montgomery Village, MD 20886-3002
Tel: (301)670-6734   *Fax:* (301)670-6735

E. Dale Jones, *President*

Ass'n for Transportation Law, Logistics and Policy

J.W. PRENDERGAST & ASSOCIATES

P.O. Box 3139, Grand Central Stn.
New York, NY 10163-3139
Tel: (212)644-8085   *Fax:* (212)644-0296

James W. Prendergast, *Principal*

Ass'n of Direct Marketing Agencies
Graphic Arts Professionals
Mail Advertising Service Ass'n of New York
Nat'l Ass'n of Publishers' Representatives

PRICE MANAGEMENT CORP.

815 Quarrier St., Suite 215
Charleston, WV 25301
Tel: (304)345-4710   *Fax:* (304)346-6416

Roger K. Price, *President*

West Virginia Funeral Directors Ass'n
West Virginia Optometric Ass'n

PROFESSIONAL ADMINISTRATIVE SERVICES

6729-A Fairview Road
Charlotte, NC 28210
Tel: (704)442-1535   *Fax:* (704)442-1563

Janice M. Stevens, *President*

American Soc. for Training and Development - Charlotte Chapter
American Soc. of Chartered Life Underwriters - Charlotte Chapter
Charlotte Estate Planning Council
Nat'l Ass'n of Health Underwriters - Charlotte Ass'n
Nat'l Ass'n of Life Underwriters - Charlotte Ass'n
Women Business Owners of Charlotte
Women Executives of Charlotte

PROFESSIONAL ASSOCIATION & SOCIETY MANAGEMENT

34615 Road E
Oconomowoc, WI 53066-2543
Tel: (414)567-2160

Robert J. Finnegan CAE, *President*

PROFESSIONAL ASSOCIATION MANAGEMENT SERVICES, INC.

3504 Tilbury Ct.
Springfield, IL 62704-2500
Tel: (217)528-5230   *Fax:* (217)241-4683

Michael R. Lane, *President*

Automotive Service Professionals of Illinois
Coalition for Collision Repair Equality
Illinois Land Title Ass'n
Illinois Self Storage Ass'n
Illinois State Ambulance Ass'n

PROFESSIONAL ASSOCIATION MANAGEMENT, INC.

4500 Hugh Howell Road, Suite 340
Tucker, GA 30084
Tel: (770)270-1511   *Fax:* (770)270-0632

J.W. Holderfield CAE, *President*

American College of Cardiology - Georgia Chapter
DeKalb Medical Soc.
Georgia Academy of General Dentistry
Georgia Soc. of Oral and Maxillofacial Surgeons
Northern District Dental Soc.
Southeastern Soc. of Oral and Maxillofacial Surgeons
Technology and Information Management Education Soc.

PROFESSIONAL MANAGEMENT ASSOCIATES, L.L.C.

170 Township Line Road
Belle Mead, NJ 08502-4103
Tel: (908)359-1184   *Fax:* (908)359-7619

Joanne Cole CAE, CMP, *Managing Member*

Internat'l Digital Imaging Ass'n
New Jersey Ass'n of School Psychologists
New Jersey Dietetic Ass'n
New Jersey Municipal Management Ass'n
New Jersey Soc. of Ass'n Executives
New Jersey Speech-Language-Hearing Ass'n
Organization of Nurse Executives - New Jersey
Registered Municipal Accountants Ass'n
Soc. for Clinical Data Management

PROFESSIONAL MEETINGS AND ASSOCIATION SERVICES

5050 N. 19th Ave., Suite 408
Phoenix, AZ 85015
Tel: (602)249-2212   *Fax:* (602)249-2789

Patricia W. Herrington, *Owner*

Airzona Millwright Employers Ass'n
Arizona Coalition for Tomorrow

PROFESSIONAL ORGANIZATION MANAGEMENT, INC.

1105 Main St.
P.O. Box 99
Blue Springs, MO 64013-0099
Tel: (816)229-1666

Lois Lauer Wolfe CAE, *President*

American Marketing Ass'n - Kansas City
Chartered Property Casualty Underwriters
Kansas City Claim Ass'n
Mid-America Congress on Aging

PROFESSIONAL RELATIONS AND RESEARCH INSTITUTE, INC.

13 Elm St.
Manchester, MA 01944-1314
Tel: (978)526-8330   *Fax:* (978)526-4018

William T. Maloney, *President*

American Ass'n for Thoracic Surgery
American College of Surgeons - Massachusetts Chapter
American Pediatric Surgical Ass'n
American Soc. for Gastrointestinal Endoscopy
American Surgical Ass'n
American Urological Ass'n - Mid-Atlantic Section
American Urological Ass'n - New England Section
American Urological Ass'n - Northeastern Section
American Venous Forum
Ass'n for Academic Surgery
Collegium Internationale Chirurgiae Digestivae
Internat'l Soc. for Cardiovascular Surgery
Internat'l Soc. for Cardiovascular Surgery - North American Chapter

Midwestern Vascular Surgical Soc.
New England Surgical Soc.
Soc. for Clinical Vascular Surgery
Soc. for Vascular Medicine and Biology
Soc. for Vascular Surgery
Southern Ass'n for Vascular Surgery
Western Thoracic Surgical Ass'n

PROFESSIONAL-ASSOCIATION MANAGERS & CONSULTANTS

P.O. Box 1761
Rockville, MD   20849-1761
Tel: (301)963-1967

William H. Wymer RPE, CAE, *Executive Manager*

PROGRAM MANAGEMENT GROUP, INC.

P.O. Box 669
Annapolis, MD   21404-0669
Tel: (410)268-2011   Fax: (410)263-2298

James P. Reilly, *President*

American Blood Resources Ass'n
European Ass'n of the Plasma Products Industry
Internat'l Plasma Products Industry Ass'n

PUBLIC AFFAIRS CONSULTING ASSOCIATION MANAGEMENT, INC.

1175 S. Main St.
Cheshire, CT   06410
Tel: (203)272-9955   Fax: (203)271-1279

Carroll J. Hughes, *C.E.O.*

Connecticut Ambulance Ass'n
Connecticut Ass'n of Metal Finishers
Connecticut Bus Ass'n
Connecticut Catholic Hospital Council
Connecticut Package Stores Ass'n
Connecticut State Ass'n of Life Underwriters

PUBLIC OFFICE SERVICES

204 E. High St.
Jefferson City, MO   65101
Tel: (573)636-7521   Fax: (573)636-5783

Patricia S. Riner Amick, *President*

AIA Missouri
Missouri Economic Development Council
Missouri Travel Council

PUBLIC STRATEGIES/IMPACT L.L.C.

196 W. State St.
Trenton, NJ   08608-1105
Tel: (609)393-7799   Fax: (609)393-9891

Joseph A. Simonetta CAE, *Partner*

AIA New Jersey
American Soc. of Landscape Architects - New Jersey Chapter
Highlands Alliance
New Jersey Hotel-Motel Ass'n
New Jersey Soc. of Municipal Engineers
New Jersey Soc. of Professional Engineers
New Jersey Soc. of Professional Engineers Educational Foundation
New Jersey Travel Industry Ass'n
Opticians Ass'n of New Jersey

PUETZ & ASSOCIATES

7794 Grow Dr.
Pensacola, FL   32514
Tel: (850)484-9987   Fax: (850)484-8762

Belinda E. Puetz, *C.E.O.*

American Soc. of Pain Management Nurses
Ass'n of Community Health Nursing Educators
Home Healthcare Nurses Ass'n
Internat'l Soc. of Psychiatric Consultation Liaison Nurses
Nat'l Gerontological Nursing Ass'n
Nat'l Nursing Staff Development Organization
Respiratory Nursing Soc.
Soc. for Education and Research in Psychiatric Mental Health Nursing
Soc. for Vascular Nursing
Soc. of Gastroenterology Nurses and Associates Foundation for Education and Research
Southern Nursing Research Soc.
Vascular Nursing Certification Board

ROBERT N. PYLE & ASSOCIATES

1223 Potomac St., N.W.
Washington, DC   20007-3212
Tel: (202)333-8190   Fax: (202)337-3809

Robert N. Pyle, *Chairman*
Nicholas A. Pyle, *President*
Alexis Hersh, *V. President*

Independent Bakers Ass'n
Nat'l Grape Growers Cooperative

RAMCO/REESE ASSOCIATION MANAGEMENT COMPANY

P.O. Box 1144
Highland Park, IL   60035
Tel: (847)433-1335   Fax: (847)433-3769

Gerald H. Reese CAE, *President*

CASMI Educational Foundation
Chicago Ass'n of Spring Manufacturers

RAMSEY MANAGEMENT GROUP

2101 Libbie Ave.
Richmond, VA   23230-2621
Tel: (804)288-3065   Fax: (804)285-3093

Robert M. Ramsey CAE, *President*

Virginia Campground Ass'n
Virginia Hospitality and Travel Ass'n

RAYBOURN GROUP INTERNATIONAL, INC.

9202 N. Meridian St., Suite 200
Indianapolis, IN   46260
Tel: (317)571-5600   Fax: (317)571-5604

One E. Wacker Dr., Suite 3600
Chicago, IL   60614
Tel: (312)923-8500   Fax: (312)923-8509

7101 Wisconsin Ave., Suite 901
Bethesda, MD   20814
Tel: (301)656-4950

Sharon R. Gorup CAE, *President*
Peter Schwartz, *Manager*

Ass'n of Interim Housing Providers
Custom Electronic Design and Installation Ass'n
Indiana Cast Metals Ass'n
Indiana Soc. of Ass'n Executives
Interior Design Educators Council
Internat'l Furniture Rental Ass'n
Internat'l Special Events Soc.
Nat'l Ass'n of Ticket Brokers
Northern Indiana Apartment Council

THE REBEDEAU GROUP

7000 W. Southwest Hwy.
Chicago Ridge, IL   60415
Tel: (708)361-6000   Fax: (708)361-6166

Mary Beth Rebedeau, *President*

Breeders and Trainers Exposition Conference
Lexington Equestrian Gift Show
Religious Audio/Video/Computer Equipment/Security Conference
The Wedding Show

REINFRIED AND ASSOCIATES, INC.

6724 Lone Oak Blvd.
Naples, FL   34109
Tel: (941)514-3441   Fax: (941)514-3470

Robert A. Reinfried, *President*

American Chain Ass'n
Conveyor Equipment Manufacturers Ass'n
Mechanical Power Transmission Ass'n
Scale Manufacturers Ass'n

RENAISSANCE ASSOCIATION MANAGEMENT

1566 Kenzie Ct., Suite 1001
Suwanee, GA   30024
Tel: (770)418-0226   Fax: (770)418-0291

Greg Martin, *President*

Georgia Shorthand Reporters Ass'n
Southern Ass'n of Wholesale Distributors

RESOURCE CENTER FOR ASSOCIATIONS LIMITED

10200 West 44th Ave., Suite 304
Wheat Ridge, CO   80033-2840
Tel: (303)422-2615   Fax: (303)422-8894

Francine Butler Ph.D., CAE, *President*
R.G. Bowman CAE, *Exec. V. President*

Ass'n for Applied Psychophysiology and Biofeedback
Biofeedback Certification Institute of America
Colorado Treasury Management Ass'n
Convention Liaison Council
Environmental and Engineering Geophysical Soc.
North American Nature Photography Ass'n
Soc. for Light Treatment and Biological Rhythms
Soc. for Scholarly Publishing

RESOURCE MANAGEMENT PLUS

1211 Locust St.
Philadelphia, PA   19107-5409

Joseph Braden, *President*
Margo Neal, *V. President & Publisher*
Tracy Trauger, *Ass'n Services Director*

Alliance of Psychiatric and Mental Health Nurses
American Pain Foundation
Ass'n of Child and Adolescent Psychiatric Nurses
Certification Board of Nat'l Ass'n of Health Unit Coordinators
Health Care Compliance Ass'n
Health Care Education Ass'n
NANDA Foundation
Nat'l Ass'n of Health Unit Coordinators
North American Nursing Diagnosis Ass'n
Nurse Healers - Professional Associates Internat'l

RESOURCES FOR GROUP MANAGEMENT, INC.

1030 15th St., N.W., Suite 870
Washington, DC   20005
Tel: (202)393-1780   Fax: (202)393-0336

Marianne McDermott, *President*
Valerie Bergman-Cooper, *Sr. Accout Manager*

American College of Construction Lawyers
American College of Tax Counsel
American Tax Policy Institute
Greeting Card Ass'n
Home Infusion Therapy Franchise Owners Ass'n
Nat'l Ass'n of Professional Pet Sitters
Nat'l Candle Ass'n
Nat'l Viatical Ass'n
Romanian-American Foundation for Mutual Cooperation
Small Business Capital Ass'n

K.W. REYNOLDS & ASSOCIATES

P.O. Box 76533
Atlanta, GA   30358
Tel: (770)977-1476   Fax: (770)973-6662

Kenneth W. Reynolds, *President*

Foodservice Group
Network of Ingredient Marketing Specialists
Southern Bakers Ass'n

RIGHT DIRECTIONS CONSULTING

2001 Midwest Road, Suite 106
Oak Brook, IL   60521-1335
Tel: (630)495-8597   Fax: (630)495-8595

Ken Boyce, *President*

Spring Manufacturers Institute

ROBINSON ASSOCIATION MANAGEMENT SERVICES

2990 Bethesda Place, Suite 601-C
Winston-Salem, NC   27103-3314
Tel: (910)760-1235   Fax: (910)760-2491

James T. Robinson, *President*

21st Judicial District Bar
DoctorsCare, Inc.
Forsyth County Bar Ass'n
Forsyth Medicine/Business Coalition
Forsyth-Stokes-Davie County Medical Soc
Tel-Med of Forsyth County

ROBSTAN GROUP, INC.

2841 Main
Kansas City, MO   64108-3315
Tel: (816)472-8870   Fax: (816)472-7765

Kenneth R. Bowman, *President*

Electronic Transactions Ass'n
Human Resource Management Ass'n - Kansas City Chapter
Internat'l Midas Dealers Ass'n
Mass Marketing Insurance Institute
Sealant, Waterproofing and Restoration Institute

ROCKY MOUNTAIN MANAGEMENT SERVICES

P.O. Box 4553
Missoula, MT   59806-4553
Tel: (406)721-7334   Fax: (406)721-7016

Robin L. Childers, *Principal*

Montana Chapter of the American Physical Therapy Ass'n
Montana Nursery and Landscape Ass'n
Rehabilitation Ass'n of Montana
Section on Health Policy, Legislation, and Regulation of the American Physical Therapy Ass'n

ROGERS ENTERPRISES

13577 Grain Lane
San Diego, CA   92129-2581
Tel: (619)484-1681

Frederick J. Rogers, *President*

Energy Products and Services Ass'n

PHILLIP ROLLINS AND ASSOCIATES

1323 Columbus Ave., Suite 301
San Francisco, CA   94133
Tel: (415)441-0804   Fax: (415)441-5683

Phillip Rollins, *President*

California Ass'n of Orthodontists
Pacific Coast Soc. of Orthodontists

RUGGLES SERVICE CORP.

1910 Byrd Ave., Suite 100
P.O. Box 11086
Richmond, VA   23230-1086
Tel: (804)282-0062   Fax: (804)282-0090

John A. Hinckley, *President*
Stewart A. Hinckley CMP, *V. President*

American Soc. of Regional Anesthesia
New England Pain Ass'n
Soc. for Education in Anesthesia
Soc. for Obstetric Anesthesia and Perinatology
Soc. for Pediatric Anesthesia

Soc. of Cardiovascular Anesthesiologists
Soc. of Neurosurgical Anesthesia and Critical Care
Virginia Soc. of Anesthesiologists

S & S MANAGEMENT SERVICES

One Regency Drive
P.O. Box 30
Bloomfield, CT   06002-0030
Tel: (860)243-3977   *Fax: (860)286-0787*

Arthur N. Schuman, *President*

American Academy of Psychiatry and the Law
American Clinical Neurophysiological Soc.
Associated Sheet Metal/Roofing Contractors - Connecticut
    Chapter
Committee of Concerned Psychiatrists
Connecticut Academy of Family Physicians
Connecticut Ass'n of Personnel Consultants
Connecticut Bar and Cafe Council
Connecticut Council - Painting and Decorating Contractors
Connecticut Psychiatric Soc.
Connecticut Roofing Contractors Ass'n
Core Content Review of Family Medicine (Internat'l)
Eastern Connecticut Physician Delivery Services
Family Medicine Political Action Committee
Mason Contractors Ass'n of Connecticut
Middlesex County Medical Ass'n
New London County Medical Ass'n
Printing Industry Ass'n of Connecticut and Western
    Massachusetts
Professional Show Managers Ass'n
Tolland County Medical Ass'n
Waterbury Medical Ass'n
Windham County Medical Ass'n

SAINTSING MANAGEMENT SERVICES

P.O. Box 1642
Lexington, NC   27293
Tel: (910)956-2952   *Fax: (910)956-1647*

Kay K. Saintsing, *C.E.O.*

Davidson County Medical Soc.
Mental Health in Davidson County
North Carolina Ass'n of Festivals and Events

THE SANFORD ORGANIZATION, INC.

1000 N. Rand Road, Suite 214
Wauconda, IL   60084-3102
Tel: (847)526-2010   *Fax: (847)526-3993*

Donn W. Sanford CAE, *President*

Aluminum Anodizers Council
Aluminum Extruders Council
Mid-America Horticulture Trade Show

SCHLOSSER MANAGEMENT COMPANY

P.O. Box 310
Caledonia, OH   43314-0310
Tel: (419)845-2023   *Fax: (419)845-2026*

Dan L. Schlosser, *President*

Central Wholesalers Ass'n
Michigan Ass'n of Distributors
Ohio Water Well Ass'n

THE SCHNEIDER GROUP, INC.

5400 Bosque Blvd., Suite 680
Waco, TX   76710
Tel: (254)776-3550   *Fax: (254)776-3767*

3624 Stone Creek Lane South
Ft. Worth, TX   76137
Tel: (817)232-3834   *Fax: (817)232-8353*

Helen Schneider Lemay, *President*
Lester Lemay, *V. President*

American Soc. of Limnology and Oceanography

SERVICES FOR ORGANIZATION RENEWAL

P.O. Box 2502
San Rafael, CA   94912-4155
Tel: (415)485-1463   *Fax: (415)460-1921*

Don L. Organ CAE, *President*

Institute of Political Campaign Consultants
Supporters of Quality Healthcare

LARRY SHANE COMMUNICATIONS

1729 Glastonberry Road
Potomac, MD   20854
Tel: (301)424-1000   *Fax: (301)424-1002*

Larry I. Shane, *President*

American Academy of Podiatric Sports Medicine
District of Columbia Podiatric Medical Ass'n
Federation of Podiatric Medical Boards

THE JOSEPH E. SHANER COMPANY

720 Light St.
Baltimore, MD   21230-3826
Tel: (410)752-3318   *Fax: (410)752-8295*

Thomas C. Shaner CAE, APR, *President*

American Institute of Floral Designers
Baltimore City Dental Soc.

Baltimore General Agents and Managers Ass'n
Baltimore Life Underwriters Ass'n
Baltimore Life Underwriters Charitable Foundation
Building Owners and Managers of Greater Baltimore
Chesapeake Human Resources Ass'n
Maryland Ass'n of Mortgage Brokers
Maryland Chiropractic Ass'n
Maryland Improvement Contractors Ass'n
Maryland Optometric Ass'n
Maryland State Ass'n of Life Underwriters
Nat'l Ass'n of Industrial and Office Parks - Maryland/D.C.
    Chapter

THE SHERWOOD GROUP, INC.

60 Revere Drive, Suite 500
Northbrook, IL   60062-1577
Tel: (847)480-9080   *Fax: (847)480-9282*

John R. Waxman, *President*
Gregory L. Schultz, *V. President*
Liz Freyn, *V.P., Meeting Services*

Ass'n of Mental Health Administrators

SHORE MANAGEMENT SERVICES

7060 Hollywood Blvd., Suite 614
Los Angeles, CA   90028-6931
Tel: (323)461-5770

Barbara Shore, *Principal*

American Soc. of Travel Agents - Southern California Chapter
Ass'n of Film Commissioners Internat'l
Public Relations Soc. of America - Los Angeles Area Chapter
Women in Business - Los Angeles Chapter

SIERRA DELTA INTERNATIONAL MANAGEMENT

5777 W. Century Blvd., Suite 503
Los Angeles, CA   90045-5675
Tel: (310)417-3929   *Fax: (310)417-8078*

Raymond P. Delrich, *C.E.O.*

Harbor Ass'n of Industry and Commerce
Los Angeles Soc. of Internal Medicine
Maritime Coalition for Clean Air
Nat'l Ass'n of Industrial and Office Parks - Los Angeles
    Chapter

SIMONELLI & ASSOCIATES

1011 St. Andrews Drive, Suite 1
El Dorado Hills, CA   95762
Tel: (916)933-3061   *Fax: (916)933-3072*

Frederick J. Simonelli Ph.D., *President*
Dorothy Simonelli, *Administrative Director*
James F. Simonelli, *Dir., Client Services*

California Cast Metals Ass'n
California Foundry History Institute
Metalcasting Stormwater Monitoring Group
Nat'l Ass'n of Fire Equipment Distributors
Soc. for Nutrition Education

SMALL ASSOCIATION MANAGEMENT OF GEORGIA

6282 Indian Field
Atlanta, GA   30092-1372
Tel: (770)300-9891   *Fax: (770)300-9815*

Carole R. Teja CAE, CMP, *Principal*

Georgia Antique Dealers Ass'n
Southeast Food Service Council

SMITH BUCKLIN & ASSOCIATES

401 N. Michigan Ave.
Chicago, IL   60611-4267
Tel: (312)644-6610   *Fax: (312)321-6869*

1200 19th St., N.W., Suite 300
Washington, DC   20036-2401
Tel: (202)857-1100   *Fax: (202)223-4579*

Duane H. Ekedahl, *Chairman*
J. Dollard Carey, *President*

Academy of Osseointegration
Adhesives Manufacturers Ass'n
Alliance of the American Dental Ass'n
America's SAP Users Group
American Academy of Cosmetic Surgery
American Ass'n for Adult and Continuing Education
American Ass'n of Ambulatory Surgery Centers
American Ass'n of Healthcare Administration Management
American Bearing Manufacturing Ass'n
American Beauty Ass'n
American Federation for Medical Research
American Hair Loss Council
American Health and Beauty Aids Institute
American Ladder Institute
American Orthopaedic Soc. for Sports Medicine
American Psychiatric Nurses Ass'n
American Soc. for Bone and Mineral Research
American Soc. of Hair Restoration Surgery
American Soc. of Hand Therapists
American Soc. of Hematology
American Soc. of Lipo-Suction Surgery
American Soc. of Nephrology
American Software Users Group
American Urogynecologic Soc.
American Woman's Soc. of Certified Public Accountants
Amusement and Music Operators Ass'n
Ass'n for Governmental Leasing and Finance

Ass'n for Unmanned Vehicle Systems Internat'l
Ass'n of Career Management Consulting Firms Internat'l
Ass'n of Free Community Papers
Ass'n of Independent Trust Companies
Ass'n of Local Housing Finance Agencies
Ass'n of Publicly Traded Companies
Ass'n of Steel Distributors
Ass'n of TeleServices Internat'l
Battery Council Internat'l
BEMA - An Internat'l Ass'n Serving the Baking and Food
    Industries
Biscuit and Cracker Distributors Ass'n
Black Tie Bureau
CA-PRMS Internat'l User Group
CATIA Operators Exchange
Central Ass'n of OB-GYN
Chicago Cosmetologists Ass'n
Chicago Estate Planning Council
Clinical Orthopaedic Soc.
Commercial Refrigerator Manufacturers Ass'n
COMMON - An IBM Computer Users Group
CONNECT: User Group for Texas Instruments Software
Cosmetic Surgery Information Service
Council of Development Finance Agencies
Cremation Ass'n of North America
Endocrine Fellows Foundation
Engine Manufacturers Ass'n
Financial Institutions Marketing Ass'n
Financial Serivces Technology Consortium
Financial Stationers Ass'n
Food Equipment Manufacturers Ass'n
Foundation for Pavement Rehabilitation and Maintenance
    Research
GUIDE Internat'l Corporation
Gynecologic Cancer Foundation
Illinois Cosmetology Ass'n
Infinium Usernet
Information Users Ass'n
Institute of Roofing and Waterproofing Consultants Internat'l
Internat'l Ass'n for Continuing Education and Training
Internat'l Ass'n for Human Resource Information
    Management
Internat'l Ass'n of Airport Duty Free Stores
Internat'l Carwash Ass'n
Internat'l Customer Service Ass'n
Internat'l DB2 Users Group
Internat'l District Energy Ass'n
Internat'l Formalwear Ass'n
Internat'l Forum, The
Internat'l Furnishings and Design Ass'n
Internat'l Hardware Distributors Ass'n
Internat'l Institute of Ammonia Refrigeration
Internat'l Oracle Users Group - Americas
Internat'l Slurry Surfacing Ass'n
Internat'l Soc. for Clinical Densitometry
Internat'l Soc. for Experimental Hematology
Internat'l Tandem Users Group
IUA-CA/IDMS Database and Applications User Assn
Lamaze Internat'l, Inc.
Lamaze International
Legal Marketing Ass'n
Managed Funds Ass'n
Metal Framing Manufacturers Ass'n
Midwest Beauty Show
Midwest Healthcare Marketing Ass'n
Museum Trustee Ass'n
NAGMR Consumer Product Brokers
Nat'l Amtelco Equipment Owners
Nat'l Ass'n for County Community and Economic
    Development
Nat'l Ass'n of Affordable Housing Lenders
Nat'l Ass'n of Floor Covering Distributors
Nat'l Ass'n of Healthcare Access Management
Nat'l Ass'n of Settlement Purchasers
Nat'l Ass'n of Special Market Agents
Nat'l Broadcast Ass'n for Community Affairs
Nat'l Coil Coaters Ass'n
Nat'l Education Knowledge Industry Ass'n
Nat'l Education Knowledge Industry Ass'n
Nat'l Food Distributors Ass'n
Nat'l Food Service Security Council
Nat'l Institute of Pension Administrators
Nat'l Organization for Competency Assurance
Nat'l ROLM Users Group
North American Ass'n of Food Equipment Manufacturers
North American Building Material Distribution Ass'n
Open Applications Group
Osseointegration Foundation
OsteoArthritis Research Soc. Internat'l
Parents Without Partners
Pet Food Institute
Popcorn Institute
Pressure Sensitive Tape Council
Product Development and Management Ass'n
Professional Detail Ass'n
Proud Lady Beauty Show
Refrigerating Engineers and Technicians Ass'n
Regional Airline Ass'n
Sealed Insulating Glass Manufacturers Ass'n
SHARE
Soc. for Information Management
Soc. for Integrative and Comparative Biology
Soc. for Maintenance Reliability Professionals
Soc. of Gastroenterology Nurses and Associates
Soc. of Gynecologic Oncologists
Soc. of Thoracic Surgeons
Soc. of Vertebrate Paleontology
Southern Cemetery Ass'n
Southern Thoracic Surgical Ass'n
Southwestern Surgical Congress
Space Station Associates
Special Interest Group on Computer Graphics
Startel Nat'l Users Group
Suburban Newspapers of America

Symbol Technologies
Thoracic Surgery Foundation for Research and Education
TSW Internat'l
United States Corporate Athletics Ass'n
Viatical Ass'n of America
Voyager Expanded Learning, Inc.
Wallcoverings Ass'n
Wireless Information Networks Forum
World Airline Entertainment Ass'n

THE WAYNE SMITH CO., INC.

901 N. Pitt St., Suite 220
Alexandria, VA 22314-1536
Tel: (703)838-2933　　　　　Fax: (703)838-2936

Wayne J. Smith, *President*

Financial Management Roundtable
Nat'l Limousine Ass'n
NGV Producers Ass'n
United Motorcoach Ass'n

SOCIAL ENGINEERING ASSOCIATES

343 S. Dearborn, Suite 304
Chicago, IL 60604
Tel: (312)939-4987　　　　　Fax: (312)939-7590

940 1/2 Second Ave.
Springfield, IL 62704
Tel: (217)522-6066

Richard Lockhart, *President*
Gael Mennecke, *V. President*

Ass'n of Condominium, Townhouse, and Homeowners' Ass'ns
Illinois Council of Voluntary Health Agencies
Illinois Soft Drink Ass'n

SOUTHEASTERN MANAGEMENT SERVICES

P.O. Box 95564
Atlanta, GA 30347
Tel: (404)329-1600　　　　　Fax: (404)325-1898

Thomas G. Cook, *President*

SOUTHERN ASSOCIATION SERVICES

1239 2nd St.
P.O. Box 801
Macon, GA 31202
Tel: (912)743-8612　　　　　Fax: (912)743-8278

Joe W. Andrews Jr., *President*

Alabama Lenders Ass'n
Georgia Ass'n of Sales Professionals
Georgia Dairy Products Ass'n
Georgia Equity Lenders Ass'n
Georgia Industrial Loan Ass'n
Mortgage Bankers Ass'n of Georgia

SPECIALTY CONTRACTORS MANAGEMENT, INC.

P.O. Box 42558, Northwest Station
Washington, DC 20015-0558
Tel: (301)933-7430

Walter M. Kardy, *President*
Betsy Kardy, *Secretary-Treasurer*

Instrument Contracting and Engineering Ass'n
Instrument Technicians Labor-Management Cooperation
　　Fund
Internat'l Council of Employers of Bricklayers and Allied
　　Craftworkers

SPECIALTY SOCIETY SERVICES

6300 N. River Road, Suite 727
Rosemont, IL 60018-4226
Tel: (847)823-7186　　　　　Fax: (847)823-0536

Dr. William Tipton, *Exec. V. President*
Karen Jared, *Exec. Officer*

Academic Orthopaedic Soc.
American Academy for Cerebral Palsy and Developmental
　　Medicine
American Ass'n of Hip and Knee Surgeons
American Shoulder and Elbow Surgeons
American Soc. of Orthopaedic Physician's Assistants
Ass'n of Bone and Joint Surgeons
Ass'n of Children's Prosthetic-Orthotic Clinics
Bones Soc.
BONES Soc.
Cervical Spine Research Soc.
Clinical Orthopaedics and Related Research Journal.
Council of Musculoskeletal Specialty Socs.
Federation of Spine Ass'ns
Internat'l Soc. of Arthroscopy, Knee Surgery and Orthopaedic
　　Sports Medicine
Knee Soc.
Musculoskeletal Tumor Soc.
Orthopaedic Research Soc.
Orthopaedic Trauma Ass'n
Pediatric Orthopedic Soc. of North America
Ruth Jackson Orthopaedic Soc.
Scoliosis Research Soc.

SPECTRUM MANAGEMENT, INC.

P.O. Box 7010
Silver Spring, MD 20907
Tel: (301)588-9077　　　　　Fax: (301)588-9076

Glenn L. Northup, *President*

Convenient Automotive Services Institute

GAYLE STEWART ENTERPRISES

195 South C St., Suite 250
Tustin, CA 92780-3666
Tel: (714)832-1113　　　　　Fax: (714)669-9341

Gayle Stewart CAE, *President*

American Soc. for Training and Development - Orange County
　　Chapter
Executives Ass'n of Orange County
Home Builders Council of the BIA
Institute of Real Estate Management - Orange County Chapter
Nat'l Spa and Pool Institute - Orange County Chapter
Painting and Decorating Contractors of America - Golden
　　State Council
Painting and Decorating Contractors of America - Southern
　　California Chapter
Sales and Marketing Council of the BIA
Seniors Housing Council of the BIA
Southern California Ass'n of Civil Engineers and Land
　　Surveyors

STYGAR ASSOCIATES, INC.

1202 Allanson Road
Mundelein, IL 60060-3808
Tel: (847)566-4566　　　　　Fax: (847)566-4580

Edward J. Stygar Jr., *President*

American Art Therapy Ass'n
American Ass'n for Accreditation of Ambulatory Surgery
　　Facilities
American Biological Safety Ass'n
American Pathology Foundation

SUFKA AND ASSOCIATES

1518 K St., N.W., Suite 503
Washington, DC 20005-1203
Tel: (202)737-0202　　　　　Fax: (202)638-4833

Kenneth M. Sufka, *President*

American Soc. of Architectural Perspectivists
Ass'n for Commuter Transportation
Associated Air Balance Council
Controlled Environment Testing Ass'n
Nat'l Air Duct Cleaners Ass'n
Nat'l Air Filtration Ass'n

SVINICKI ASSOCIATION SERVICES

1123 N. Water St.
Milwaukee, WI 53202
Tel: (414)276-8788　　　　　Fax: (414)276-7704

Jane A. Svinicki CAE, *President*

American College of Cardiology - Wisconsin Chapter
American Soc. of Scientific Glass Blowers
American Water Works Ass'n - Wisconsin Section
Ass'n of Manpower Franchise Owners
Community Development Soc.
Milwaukee Chapter Chartered Life Underwriters
Wisconsin Ass'n of Residential Facilities
Wisconsin Concrete Masonry Ass'n
Wisconsin Direct Marketing Ass'n
Wisconsin Soc. of Ass'n Executives
Wisconsin Soc. of Internal Medicine

TAC, INC.

444 N. Larchmont Blvd., Suite 107
Los Angeles, CA 90004
Tel: (213)463-8836　　　　　Fax: (213)463-6345

Veronica Urias, *President*

Advertising Production Ass'n of Los Angeles
Broadway Rosecrans Industrial and Commercial Ass'n
Rancho Dominguez Industrial Ass'n

TAI/EXPOGROUP

867 Sussex Blvd.
Broomall, PA 19008-0800
Tel: (610)604-4500　　　　　Fax: (610)604-4922

Stephen E. Markowitz, *President & C.E.O.*
Charles Sagerman, *Exec. V. President and C.F.O.*

Philadelphia Ass'n of Retail Druggists
Small Business Ass'n of Delaware Valley

STAN TAIT & ASSOCIATES

2952 Wellington Circle
Tallahassee, FL 32308
Tel: (850)906-9220　　　　　Fax: (850)906-9228

David L. Tait, *President*

Economic Club of Florida
Florida Shore and Beach Preservation Ass'n
Nat'l Conference on Beach Preservation Technology
Nat'l Hurricane Conference

TALLEY AND ASSOCIATES, INC.

500 N. State College Blvd., Suite 1020
Orange, CA 92868-1604
Tel: (714)935-1999　　　　　Fax: (714)935-1145

30442 Via Cantabria
San Juan Capistrano, CA 92675
Tel: (714)489-1113　　　　　Fax: (714)489-9200

Vickie Talley, *President*

Cypress Economic Development Council
Manufactured Housing Educational Trust of Orange,
　　Riverside, and San Bernardino Counties
Nat'l Ass'n of Office and Industrial Properties - Orange
　　County Chapter

TALLEY MANAGEMENT GROUP, INC.

19 Mantua Road
Mt. Royal, NJ 08061
Tel: (609)845-7220　　　　　Fax: (609)853-0411

1825 I St., N.W., Suite 400
Washington, DC 20006
Tel: (202)429-2710　　　　　Fax: (202)429-9574

Robert K. Talley, *President*
Gregg Talley, *V. President*

American Academy of Orofacial Pain
American Ass'n for the Study of Headache
American College of Veterinary Pathologists
American Council for Headache Education
American Soc. for Experimental Neurotherapeutics
Ass'n for Research in Otolaryngology
Ass'n for the Care of Children's Health
Internat'l Neural Network Soc.
Movement Disorder Soc.
Soc. for Cardiovascular Magnetic Resonance
Soc. for Healthcare Epidemiology of America
Soc. of Toxicologic Pathologists
Stadium Managers Ass'n

TASC, INC.

1420 16th St., N.W.
Washington, DC 20036-2218
Tel: (202)328-7460　　　　　Fax: (202)332-2301

Randy Dyer CAE, *President*

Conservation Council
Early Childhood Education Institute
Internat'l Electronic Article Surveillance Manufacturers Ass'n
Nat'l Structured Settlements Trade Ass'n
NSSTA Political Action Committee
Potomac Valley Orthopedic Ass'n

TEAM MANAGEMENT -- A DIVISION OF SLACK, INC.

6900 Grove Road
Thorofare, NJ 08086-9447
Tel: (609)848-1000　　　　　Fax: (609)848-5274

2000 L St., N.W., Suite 200
Washington, DC 20036
Tel: (202)416-1647　　　　　Fax: (202)833-3843

Peter Slack, *President*
Clifford M. Brownstein, *V. President and C.O.O.*

American Motility Soc.
American Soc. for Clinical Investigation
American Soc. of Anesthesia Technicians and Technologists
American Soc. of Peri-Anesthesia Nurses
American Soc. of Transplant Physicians
American Soc. of Transplant Surgeons
CenterSpan
Gastroenterology Research Group
Gynecologic Surgery Soc.
Inpact Americas
Internat'l Ass'n of Forensic Nurses
Internat'l Liver Transplantation Soc.
Internat'l Soc. for Pharmacoepidemiology
North American Soc. for Pediatric Gastroenterology and
　　Nutrition
Pan-Pacific Surgical Ass'n
Soc. for Surgery of the Alimentary Tract

TECHNICAL ENTERPRISES FOR ASSOCIATION MANAGEMENT

10 W. Kimball St.
Winder, GA 30680-2535
Tel: (770)868-5300　　　　　Fax: (770)868-5301

Mimi Harlan, *President*

Cast Stone Institute
Internat'l Soc. of Weighing and Measurement

TECHNICAL ENTERPRISES, INC.

7044 S. 13th St.,
Oak Creek, WI 53154-1429
Tel: (414)768-8000　　　　　Fax: (414)768-8001

Scott P. Sherer, *President*

Ass'n of Contingency Planners
Information Soc.
Institute for Certification of Computing Professionals
NaSPA Education Foundation
NaSPA: the Network and System Professionals Ass'n

TH MGMT, INC.

4425 Randolph Road, Suite 304
Charlotte, NC 28211
Tel: (704)365-3622　　　　　Fax: (704)365-3678

Theresa Salmen CMP, *Principal*

Construction Financial Management Ass'n - Charlotte
   Chapter
Metrolina Business Council
NAIOP - Charlotte Chapter
NCACPA (North Carolina Ass'n of Certified Public
   Accountants) - Charlotte Chapter
North Carolina Medical Group Managers
North Carolina World Trade Ass'n

THOMAS ASSOCIATES, INC.

1300 Sumner Ave.
Cleveland, OH 44115-2851
Tel: (216)241-7333   *Fax:* (216)241-0105

Charles M. Stockinger, *President*
John H. Addington, *Exec. V. President*

American Ass'n of Automatic Door Manufacturers
American Supply and Machinery Manufacturers' Ass'n
Ass'n of Ingersoll-Rand Distributors
Building Systems Industry Forum
Chemical Fabrics and Film Ass'n
Compressed Air and Gas Institute
Door and Access Systems Manufacturers' Ass'n, Internat'l
Fire Equipment Manufacturers' Ass'n
Fluid Controls Institute
Hack and Band Saw Manufacturers Ass'n of America
Heat Exchange Institute
Metal Building Manufacturers Ass'n
Metal Roofing Systems Ass'n
Power Tool Institute
Pressure Washer Manufacturers Ass'n
Scaffolding, Shoring and Forming Institute
Steel Window Institute
United States Cutting Tool Institute

THOMAS MILLER ASSOCIATES

7611 Elmwood Ave., Suite 201
Middleton, WI 53562-3161
Tel: (608)831-3611   *Fax:* (608)831-5122

Thomas Miller, *C.E.O.*
Jane C. Shepard CMP, *President*

American Ass'n of Cardiovascular and Pulmonary
   Rehabilitation
American Osteopathic Academy for Sports Medicine
Lipid Nurse Task Force
Soc. for Research on Nicotine and Tobacco

THOMPSON MANAGEMENT ASSOCIATES

105 Eastern Ave., Suite 104
Annapolis, MD 21403-3300
Tel: (410)263-1014   *Fax:* (410)263-1659

Joseph M. Thompson Jr., *President*

Independent Sealing Distributors
Nat'l Ass'n of Hose and Accessories Distributors
University of Industrial Distribution
Yacht Architects and Brokers Ass'n

TLC - THE LEGISLATIVE CENTER, INC.

677 Ala Moana Blvd., Suite 815
Honolulu, HI 96813-5416
Tel: (808)537-4308   *Fax:* (808)533-2739

Tim Lyons CAE, *President*

Hawaii Business League
Hawaii Flooring Ass'n
Hawaii Pest Control Ass'n
Hawaii Roofing Contractors Ass'n
Pacific Insulation Contractors Ass'n
Subcontractors Ass'n of Hawaii

TOTAL ASSOCIATION MANAGEMENT SERVICES, INC.

1819 Peachtree St., N.E., Suite 620
Atlanta, GA 30309-1849
Tel: (404)355-2400   *Fax:* (404)351-3348

William H. Just CAE, CMP, *President*

Ass'n for Convention Marketing Executives
Ass'n for Convention Operations Management
Ass'n of Medical Illustrators
BioCommunications Ass'n
Legal Assistant Management Ass'n
Soc. of Corporate Meeting Professionals

TRADE ASSOCIATION MANAGEMENT

P.O. Box 360329
Decatur, GA 30036
Tel: (404)288-8473   *Fax:* (404)288-8531

Ski Bashinski, *President*

Georgia Coroners Ass'n
Greater Atlanta Fabricare Ass'n
Southeast Sign Ass'n
Southern States Sign Council
Surveying and Mapping Soc. of Georgia

TRADE ASSOCIATION MANAGEMENT, INC.

25 N. Broadway
Tarrytown, NY 10591-3201
Tel: (914)332-0040   *Fax:* (914)332-1541

Richard C. Byrne, *President*

Die Set Manufacturers Service Bureau
Expansion Joint Manufacturers Ass'n
Hand Tools Institute
Institute of Store Planners
Internat'l Firestop Council
New York Ass'n of Mortgage Brokers
Technical Ceramics Manufacturers Ass'n
Tubular Exchanger Manufacturers Ass'n
Tubular Rivet and Machine Institute

TRICORP MANAGEMENT

910 Charles St.
Fredericksburg, VA 22401
Tel: (540)370-0012   *Fax:* (540)370-0015

Peggy McElgunn, *Exec. V. President*

JOHN L. TWEED AND ASSOCIATES

19 8th Ave.
Seaside Park, NJ 08752-1811
Tel: (732)854-9137   *Fax:* (732)854-9146

John L. Tweed, *President*

Ass'n of Residential Care Homes of New Jersey
Coalition for Responsible Day Care
Critical Care Carriers Coalition
Livery Operators Coalition of Essex and Hudson Counties
Medical Transportation Ass'n of New Jersey
Northeast Limousine and Transporters Ass'n

UPDATE MANAGEMENT, INC.

147 S.E. 102nd
Portland, OR 97216-2703
Tel: (503)253-9385   *Fax:* (503)253-9172

Michael A. Fisher CAE, *President*

Carpet Cleaners Institute of the Northwest
Cemetery Ass'n of Oregon
Nat'l Ass'n of Consumer Shows
Nat'l Ass'n of Purchasing Management - Oregon
Oregon Ass'n for Home Care
Oregon Ass'n of Defense Counsel
Oregon Landscape Contractors Ass'n
Oregon Nurses Ass'n - District One
Oregon Psychological Ass'n
Oregon Soc. of Ass'n Executives
Pacific Northwest Precast Concrete Ass'n
Pacific Northwest Steel Fabricators Ass'n

VANNATTA PUBLIC RELATIONS & ASSOCIATION MANAGEMENT

P.O. Box 135
565 Union St., N.E., Suite 104
Salem, OR 97308-0135
Tel: (503)585-8254   *Fax:* (503)585-8547

G. Harvey Gail, *President*
Mary L. VanNatta-Gail, *Exec. Director*

Appraisal Institute - Greater Oregon Chapter
Oregon Chimney Sweeps Ass'n
Oregon Hearth Products Ass'n
Oregon Highway Users Alliance

VK ASSOCIATION MANAGEMENT

2915 Kerner Blvd., Suite A
P.O. Box 151403
San Rafael, CA 94915-1403
Tel: (415)459-2235   *Fax:* (415)459-6298

Cres Van Keulen CAE, *Principal*

American Camping Ass'n - Northern California Section
Ass'n of Housing Management Agents - No. California and
   Nevada
California Landscape Contractors Ass'n - North Coast
   Chapter
ESOP Ass'n - California/Western States Chapter
Internat'l Ass'n for Financial Planning - North Bay Chapter
Western Pension and Benefits Conference - San Francisco
   Chapter

W/L ASSOCIATES, LTD.

7519 Ridge Road
Frederick, MD 21702-3519
Tel: (301)663-1915   *Fax:* (301)371-8955

William G. Wisecup, *President and C.E.O.*

Bioelectromagnetics Soc.
First Australasian Conference on Bioelectromagnetics
Second World Congress for Electricity and Magnetism in
   Biology and Medicine
Soc. for Physical Regulation in Biology and Medicine

WALKER MANAGEMENT GROUP, INC.

530 Church St., Suite 700
Nashville, TN 37219-2321
Tel: (615)254-3687   *Fax:* (615)254-7047

Dee Ann Walker CAE, *President*

American Ass'n of Small Ruminant Practitioners
American Board of Veterinary Practitioners
American College of Cardiology - Tennessee Chapter
American Veterinary Dental Soc.
Delta Nu Alpha Transportation Fraternity

Tennessee Ass'n of Audiologists and Speech Language
   Pathologists
Tennessee Consumer Finance Ass'n
Tennessee Occupational Therapy Ass'n
Tennessee Osteopathic Medical Ass'n
Tennessee Veterinary Medical Ass'n

DON WALLACE ASSOCIATES

1156 15th St., N.W., Suite 1103
Washington, DC 20005
Tel: (202)331-4331   *Fax:* (202)331-4330

Donald L. Wallace Jr., *President*

Cotton Warehouse Ass'n of America

WALTER AND ASSOCIATES

9001 Hickman Road, Suite 220
Des Moines, IA 50332
Tel: (515)278-8700   *Fax:* (515)278-0245

Craig D. Walter, *President*

Iowa Bed and Breakfast Guild
Iowa Blue Flame Gas Ass'n
Iowa Lodging Ass'n
Iowa One Call

WANNER ASSOCIATES

908 North 2nd St.
Harrisburg, PA 17102-3119
Tel: (717)236-2050   *Fax:* (717)236-2046

John D. Wanner CAE, *President*

American Soc. of Landscape Architects -
   Pennsylvania/Delaware Chapter
Chiropractic Fellowship of Pennsylvania
General Contractors Ass'n of Pennsylvania
Lawn Care Ass'n of Pennsylvania
Pennsylvania Ass'n of Convention and Visitors Bureaus
Pennsylvania Economic Development Ass'n
Pennsylvania Federation of Fraternal and Social
   Organizations
Pennsylvania Flower Growers Ass'n
Pennsylvania Planning Ass'n
Pennsylvania Soc. of Professional Engineers
Pupil Transportation Ass'n of Pennsylvania
Sheet Metal and Air Conditioning Contractors Ass'n of
   Pennsylvania

THE WARD MANAGEMENT GROUP, INC.

10293 N. Meridian St., Suite 175
Indianapolis, IN 46290-1073
Tel: (317)816-1619   *Fax:* (317)816-1633

Michael F. Ward CAE, *President*

Biomedical Marketing Ass'n
D.A.R.E Indiana
Indiana Ass'n of Chiefs of Police
Indiana Retail Scuba Dealers Ass'n
Midwest Retail Scuba Dealers Ass'n

WASHINGTON POLICY ASSOCIATES, INC.

1600 Duke St., Suite 220
Alexandria, VA 22314
Tel: (703)519-1715   *Fax:* (703)519-1807

Jeffrey C. Smith, *President*

Commercial Weather Services Ass'n
Committee for Private Offshore Rescue and Towing (C-PORT)
Drug and Alcohol Testing Industry Ass'n
Drug and Alcohol Testing Industry Ass'n
Maritime Consortium
Nat'l Ass'n of Charterboat Operators

WATSON AND ASSOCIATES

13102 Laurinda Way
Santa Ana, CA 92705-1821
Tel: (714)744-6789   *Fax:* (714)771-4463

Lita L. Watson, *President*

American College of Cardiology - California Chapter
American Soc. of General Surgeons - California Chapter

M. WEGENER AND ASSOCIATES

P.O. Box 4250
Sunland, CA 91041-4250
Tel: (818)951-2842   *Fax:* (818)353-5876

Monika Wegener, *Owner*

Information Systems Agreement
Los Angeles Customs Brokers and Freight Fowarders Ass'n
Los Angeles-Pusan Sister City
Los Angeles-Vancouver Sister City Ass'n
Propeller Club - Los Angeles/Long Beach

WESTENBERGER MANAGEMENT, INC.

201 Indian Hills Court
Marietta, GA 30068
Tel: (770)977-3918   *Fax:* (770)977-5567

John Westenberger CAE, *President*

Alabama Ass'n of RV Parks and Campgrounds
Georgia Ass'n of RV Parks and Campgrounds
Georgia Recreation Coalition
Tennessee Ass'n of RV Parks and Campgrounds
Tennessee Recreation Coalition

WHERRY ASSOCIATES

30200 Detroit Road
Cleveland, OH 44145-1967
Tel: (440)899-0010   *Fax:* (440)892-1404

J. Jeffrey Wherry, *President*

Abrasive Grain Ass'n
Cemented Carbide Producers Ass'n
Coated Abrasives Manufacturers' Institute
Diamond Wheel Manufacturers Institute
Grinding Wheel Institute
Insulated Steel Door Institute
Machine Knife Ass'n
Nat'l Tooling and Machining Ass'n - Cleveland Chapter
Steel Door Institute

WHITCHURCH MANAGEMENT CORPORATION

3263 Sprucewood Lane
Wilmette, IL 60091-1110
Tel: (847)251-5575   *Fax:* (847)251-5898

Charles G. Whitchurch, *President*

Internat'l Net Set
Wirebound Box Manufacturers Ass'n

WILKES MANAGEMENT ASSOCIATES

P.O. Box 536544
Orlando, FL 32853-6544
Tel: (407)898-1695   *Fax:* (407)894-2312

1811 Wycliff Dr.
Orlando, FL 32803
Tel: (407)896-3308

Shelburn M. Wilkes, *President*

American Hernia Soc.
Florida Healthcare Engineering Ass'n
Florida Soc. of Neurology

Florida Soc. of Pathologists
Florida Surgical Soc.

STEVEN WINTER ASSOCIATES, INC.

1511 K St., N.W., Suite 600
Washington, DC 20005
Tel: (202)628-6100   *Fax:* (202)393-5043

50 Washington St.,
Norwalk, CT 06854
Tel: (203)857-0200   *Fax:* (203)852-0741

Helen English, *Principal*
Steven Winter, *President*

Ass'n for Safe and Accessible Products
Home Energy Rating Systems Council
Passive Solar Industries Council
Structural Insulated Panel Ass'n

WOODFIELD MANAGEMENT RESOURCES, LLC

250 W. 57th St., Suite 2301-2302
New York, NY 10107
Tel: (212)957-4430   *Fax:* (212)265-4974

Ann L. Woodfield, *President*

Ass'n of Real Estate Women
Columbia Business School Alumni Club of New York
Internat'l Ass'n for Financial Planning - New York Chapter
Nat'l Soc. of Fund Raising Executives - Greater New York
    Chapter
Planned Giving Group of Greater New York
Soc. for Human Resource Management - New York Metro
    Chapter
Women in Financial Development

WILSON W. WRIGHT

217 S. Adams St.
Tallahassee, FL 32301-1708
Tel: (850)224-5169   *Fax:* (850)224-1033

Wilson W. Wright, *Exec. Officer*

Chris Craft Antique Boat Club
Florida Tobacco and Candy Ass'n

ZAPPONE AND SMITH

493 8th Ave.
San Francisco, CA 94118
Tel: (415)221-4022   *Fax:* (415)221-0755

Toni Zappone, *Partner*
Margaret Smith, *Partner*

American Anaplastology Ass'n
American Soc. of Ocularists
Chartered Property and Casualty Underwriters - Golden Gate
    Chapter
Executives Ass'n of San Francisco
San Francisco Soc. of Illustrators

BEVERLY ZIEGLER & ASSOCIATES

200 N. Mariposa Ave.
Los Angeles, CA 90004
Tel: (213)389-1037   *Fax:* (213)383-6505

Beverly Ziegler, *Executive Officer/Owner*

Apartment Ass'n of Greater Los Angeles
Apartment Ass'n of San Fernando Valley/Ventura
Beverly Hills Gun Club and Rifle Range
Botach Management
Calibre Collision Centers
California Electric Sign Ass'n
Epicentre Restaurant
Jeskor Research
Kawada Company of America/Kawada Hotel
Los Angeles Water and Power Ass'n
Mar-Scott Properties
Sign Users Council of California